RUSSIA
48

SWEDEN
18

FINLAND
18

EST. 53
LAT. 53
LITH. 53
BELARUS 52
POLAND
47

UKRAINE
52

ROM.
45

YUGO.
45

GREECE
45

TURKEY
62

CYPRUS
62

SYR.
62

IRAQ
66

KUWAIT 58

IRAN
66

AFGHAN.
68

PAKISTAN
68

KAZAKHSTAN
48

UZBEKISTAN
48

TURKMENISTAN
48

KYRGYZSTAN
48

TAJIKISTAN
48

MONGOLIA
77

CHINA
77

N. KOREA
80

S. KOREA
80

JAPAN
81

NEPAL
68

BH.

INDIA
68

BANG.
68

BURMA
72

LAOS

THAILAND
72

CAMB.
72

VIETNAM
72

HONG KONG
78

TAIWAN
77

PHILIPPINES
82

GUAM
86

PACIFIC OCEAN
Page 87

LIBYA
110

EGYPT
110

SAUDI
ARABIA
58

BAH.
QATAR
58

U.A.E.
58

OMAN
58

YEMEN
58

CHAD
110

SUDAN
110

DJIB.
110

ETHIOPIA
110

C. AFR. REF.
110

UGANDA
114

KENYA
114

SOMALIA
115

SRI
LANKA
68

ASIA
Page 54

SEYCHELLES
119

MALAYSIA
72

BRUNEI

SING
72

INDONESIA
85

PAPUA
NEW
GUINEA
84

SOLOMON IS.
86

SAMOA
86

VANUATU
87

FIJI
86

NEW
CALEDONIA
86

CONGO
114

ZAIRE
114

RWA.
BUR.
114

TANZANIA
114

MAL.
114

ANGOLA
114

ZAMBIA
114

MOZAMBIQUE
119

MADAGASCAR
119

MAURITIUS
119

REUNION
119

NAMIBIA
118

BOTSWANA
119

ZIMBABWE
119

SWAZILAND 119

SOUTH
AFRICA
119

LESOTHO
119

WESTERN
AUSTRALIA
92

NORTHERN
TERRITORY
93

SOUTH
AUSTRALIA
94

QUEENSLAND
95

NEW SOUTH WALES
96

VICTORIA
96

TASMANIA
99

NEW
ZEALAND
100

AUSTRALIA
Page 88

NORWAY
18

SWEDEN
18

FINLAND
18

UNITED KINGDOM
10

SCOTLAND
15

IRELAND 17

ENGLAND
13

WALES

DENMARK 21

RUSSIA
48

ESTONIA
53

LATVIA
53

LITHUANIA
53

BELARUS
52

GERMANY
22

POLAND
47

UKRAINE
52

BELG.
LUX.

FRANCE

SWITZ. 39

CZECH
41

AUST.
41

HUN. 41

MOLDOVA 52

27

28

AND.

MON.

ITALY

ROMANIA
45

YUGOSLAVIA
45

BULGARIA
45

GEORGIA
52

ARMENIA 52

AZERBAIJAN
52

34

ALB.
45

GREECE
45

TURKEY
62

PORTUGAL
32

SPAIN
33

MEDITERRANEAN
36

MALTA
34

CYPRUS
62

SYRIA
62

IRAN
66

TUNISIA
106

LEBANON 62

ISRAEL
65

IRAQ
66

MOROCCO
106

ALGERIA
106

LIBYA
110

EGYPT
110

JORDAN
65

SAUDI ARABIA 58

THE VOLUME LIBRARY

A Modern, Authoritative Reference for Home and School Use

Clear and Complete · Colorfully Illustrated · Totally Indexed

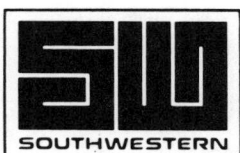

THE SOUTHWESTERN COMPANY

Nashville, Tennessee

THE VOLUME LIBRARY

INCLUDING A MAJOR WORLD ATLAS AND COMPREHENSIVE INDEX FROM THE WORLD RENOWNED PUBLISHER, HAMMOND INCORPORATED.

Hammond Publications Advisory Board

Contents

Introduction to the World Atlas

The current edition of the Hammond World Atlas features an outstanding new section devoted to THE PHYSICAL WORLD — a series of terrain maps of land forms and ocean floors. These physical maps were originally produced as sculptured terrain models, thus simulating the earth's surface in a highly realistic manner. The three-dimensional effect is both instructive and pleasing to the eye.

As in previous editions, the atlas is organized to make the retrieval of information as simple and quick as possible. The guiding principle in organizing the atlas material has been to present separate subjects on *separate* maps. In this way, each individual map topic is shown with the greatest degree of clarity, unencumbered with extraneous information that is best revealed on separate maps. Of equal importance from the standpoint of good atlas design is the treatment of all current information on a given country or state as a single atlas unit. Thus, the basic reference map of an area is accompanied on adjacent pages by all supplementary information pertaining to that area. For example, the detailed index for a given map always appears on the same page as, or on the pages immediately following, the reference map. This same map index provides population data for the many cities, towns and villages shown on the map. Highlight information on the area, i.e., the total population and area, the capital, the highest point, is listed in the summary fact listings accompanying each unit. An adjacent locator map relates the subject area to the larger world beyond. A three-dimensional picture of the area is exhibited by means of the accompanying full-color topographic map. A separate economic map defines the vital agricultural, industrial and mineral resources of the area. In the case of the foreign maps, the flag of each independent nation appears on the appropriate page. Finally, certain country units contain special subject maps dealing with the history, climate, demography and vegetation of the area.

An important feature of the atlas is the addition of ZIP codes to the index entries for each of the legion of communities shown on the state maps. With the exception of the U.S. Postal Service directories of limited availability, the ZIP code listings herein are the most extensive published.

The back of the book contains a second type of index. This is a multi-paged "A-to-Z" index of all the world's places that appear on the maps. The use of this map index is essential when the name of a place is known but its country, state, or province is unknown.

Of course, the maps have been thoroughly updated. These revisions echo the new nations, shifting boundaries and the fluid internal divisions of many countries. New communities generated by the opening up of resources in the developing nations are also noted. Up-to-date geographical information, both foreign and domestic, is received daily by the atlas editors. A worldwide correspondence and thorough research brings to the atlas user the latest geographical and demographic information obtainable.

In closing it may be said that the atlas has truly been designed for contemporary use. Just as the information presented on the following pages is as current and up to date as the editors and cartographers could issue it, so the design and organization has been as well planned as possible to create a work useful to present generations.

President
HAMMOND INCORPORATED

Introduction to the Maps and Indexes

The following notes have been added to aid the reader in making the best use of this atlas. Though the reader may be familiar with maps and map indexes, the publisher believes that a quick review of the material below will add to his enjoyment of this reference work.

Arrangement—*The Plan of the Atlas.* The atlas has been designed with maximum convenience for the user as its objective. Part I of the atlas is devoted to the physical world—terrain maps of land forms and the sea floor. Part II features thematic maps and diagrams on a wide variety of subjects such as climate, languages and energy. Part III contains the general political reference maps, area by area. All geographically related information pertaining to a country or region appears on adjacent pages, eliminating the task of searching throughout the entire volume for data on a given area. Thus, the reader will find, conveniently assembled, political, topographic, economic and special maps of a political area or region, accompanied by detailed map indexes, statistical data, and illustrations of the national flags of the area.

The sequence of country units in this American-designed atlas is international in arrangement. Units on the world as a whole are followed by a section on the polar regions which, in turn, is followed by pages devoted to Europe and its countries. Every continent map is accompanied by special population distribution, climatic and vegetation maps of that continent. Following the maps of the European continent and its countries, the geographic sequence plan proceeds as follows: Asia, the Pacific and Australia, Africa, South America, North America, and ends with detailed coverage on the United States.

Political Maps—*The Primary Reference Tool.* The most detailed maps in each country unit are the *political maps.* It is our feeling that the reader is likely to refer to these maps more often than to any other in the book when confronted by such questions as—Where? How big? What is it near? Answering these common queries is the function of the political maps. Each political map stresses *political* phenomena—countries, internal political divisions, boundaries, cities and towns. The major political unit or units, shown on the map, are banded in distinctive colors for easy identification and delineation. First-order political subdivisions (states, provinces, counties on the state maps) are shown, scale permitting.

The reader is advised to make use of the *legend* appearing under the title on each political map. Map *symbols,* the special "language" of maps, are explained in the legend. Each variety of dot, circle, star or interrupted line has a special meaning which should be clearly understood by the user so that he may interpret the map data correctly.

Each country has been portrayed at a *scale* commensurate with its political, areal, economic or tourist importance. In certain cases, a whole map unit may be devoted to a single nation if that nation is considered to be of prime interest to most atlas users. In other cases, several nations will be shown on a single map if, as separate entities, they are of lesser relative importance. Areas of dense settlement and important significance within a country have been enlarged and portrayed in inset maps inserted on the margins of the main map. The scale of each map is indicated as a fractional representation (1:1,000,000). The reader is advised to refer to the linear or "bar" scale appearing on each map or map inset in order to determine the distance between points.

The *projection* system used for each map is noted near the title of the map. Map projections are the special graphic systems used by cartographers to render the curved three-dimensional surface of the globe on a flat surface. Optimum map projections determined by the attributes of the area have been used by the publishers for each map in the atlas.

A word here as to the choice of place names on the maps. Throughout the atlas names appear, with a few exceptions, in their local official spellings. However, conventional Anglicized spellings are used for major geographical divisions and for towns and topographic features for which English forms exist; i.e., "Spain" instead of "España" or "Munich" instead of "München." Names of this type are normally followed by the local official spelling in parentheses. As an aid to the user the indexes are cross-referenced for all current and most former spellings of such names.

Names of cities and towns in the United States follow the forms listed in the *Post Office Directory* of the United States Postal Service. Domestic physical names follow the decisions of the Board on Geographic Names, U.S. De-

partment of the Interior, and of various state geographic name boards.

It is the belief of the publishers that the boundaries shown in a general reference atlas should reflect current geographic and political realities. This policy has been followed consistently in the atlas. The presentation of *de facto* boundaries in cases of territorial dispute between various nations does not imply the political endorsement of such boundaries by the publisher, but simply the honest representation of boundaries as they exist at the time of the printing of the atlas maps.

Indexes—*Pinpointing a Location.* Each political map is accompanied by a comprehensive index of the place names appearing on the map. If you are unfamiliar with the location of a particular geographical place and wish to find its position within the confines of the subject area of the map, consult the map index as your first step. The name of the feature sought will be found in its proper alphabetical sequence with a key reference letter-number combination corresponding to its location on the map. After noting the key reference letter-number combination for the place name, turn to the map. The place name will be found within the square formed by the two lines of latitude and the two lines of longitude which enclose the coordinates—i.e., the marginal letters and numbers. The diagram below illustrates the system of indexing.

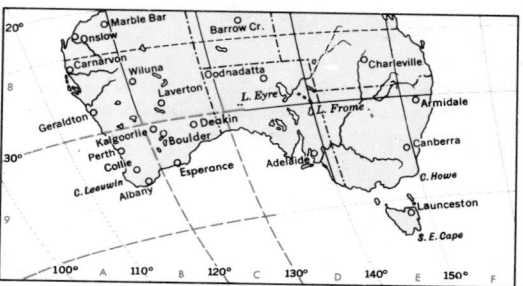

In the case of maps consisting entirely of insets, the place name is found near the intersection point of the imaginary lines connecting the coordinates at right angles. See below.

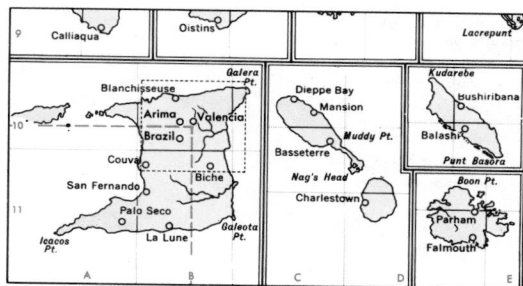

Where space on the map has not permitted giving the complete form of the place name, the complete form is shown in the index. Where a place is known by more than one name or by various spellings of the same name, the different forms have been included in the index. Physical features are listed under their proper names and not according to their generic terms; that is to say, Rio Negro will be found under Negro and not under Rio Negro. On the other hand, Rio Grande will be found under Rio Grande. Accompanying most index entries for cities and towns, and for other political units, are *population figures* for the particular entries. The large number of population figures in the atlas makes this work one of the most comprehensive statistical sources available to the public today. The population figures have been taken from the latest official censuses and estimates of the various nations. Dates and sources for the population figures are listed in the Gazetteer-Index of the World following this section.

Population and area figures for countries and major political units are listed in bold type *fact lists* on the margins of the indexes. In addition, the capital, largest city, highest point, monetary unit, principal languages and the prevailing religions of the country concerned are also listed. The Gazetteer-Index of the World on the following pages provides a quick reference index for countries and other important areas. Though population and area figures for each major unit are also found in the map section, the Gazetteer-Index provides a conveniently arranged statistical comparison contained in five pages. As mentioned, dates and sources of the population figures appearing in the country indexes are also listed in this section.

All index entries for cities and towns in the indexes accompanying individual state maps for the United States are preceded by a five-digit postal ZIP code number applying to the community. A dagger (†) designates those places that do not possess a post office. The ZIP code number listed in such cases refers to that of the nearest post office. An asterisk (*) marks those larger cities which are divided into multiple ZIP code areas. Using the single ZIP code number listed in such cases will direct your letter to the proper city with dispatch. However, if the precise ZIP code number of the address within the city is needed, it is suggested that the reader refer to the latest National ZIP Code Directory at his local post office. This detailed guide lists every street in a multiple ZIP code city with the proper ZIP code for the street.

Relief Maps. Accompanying each political map is a relief map of the area. The purpose of the relief map is to illustrate the surface configuration (TOPOGRAPHY) of the region. A shading technique in color simulates the relative ruggedness of the terrain—plains, plateaus, valleys, hills and mountains. Graded colors, ranging from greens for lowlands, yellows for intermediate evaluations to brown in the highlands, indicate the height above sea level of each part of the land. A vertical scale at the margin of the map shows the approximate height in meters and feet represented by each color.

Economic Maps—Agriculture, Industry and Resources. One of the most interesting features that will be found in each country unit is the economic map. From this map one can determine the basic activities of a nation as expressed through its economy. A perusal of the map yields a full understanding of the area's economic geography and natural resources.

The agricultural economy is manifested in two ways: color bands and commodity names. The color bands express broad categories of *dominant land use*, such as cereal belts, forest lands, livestock range lands or nonagricultural wastes. The red commodity names, on the other hand, pinpoint the areas of production of *specific* crops, i.e., wheat, cotton, sugar beets, etc.

Major mineral occurrences are denoted by standard letter symbols appearing in blue. The relative size of the letter symbols signifies the relative importance of the deposit.

The manufacturing sector of the economy is presented by means of diagonal line patterns expressing the various *industrial* areas of consequence within a country.

The fishing industry is represented by names of commercial fish species appearing offshore in blue letters. Major waterpower sites are designated by blue symbols.

The publishers have tried to make this work the most comprehensive and useful atlas available, and it is hoped that it will prove a valuable reference work. Any constructive suggestions from the reader will be welcomed.

Sources and Acknowledgements

A multitude of sources goes into the making of a large-scale reference work such as this. To list them all would take many pages and would consume space better devoted to the maps and reference materials themselves. However, certain general sources were very useful in preparing this work and are listed below.

STATISTICAL OFFICE OF THE UNITED NATIONS.
Demographic Yearbook. New York. Issued annually.

STATISTICAL OFFICE OF THE UNITED NATIONS.
Statistical Yearbook. New York. Issued annually.

THE GEOGRAPHER, U.S. DEPARTMENT OF STATE.
International Boundary Study papers. Washington. Various dates.

THE GEOGRAPHER, U.S. DEPARTMENT OF STATE.
Geographic Notes. Washington. Various dates.

UNITED STATES BOARD ON GEOGRAPHIC NAMES.
Decisions on Geographic Names in the United States. Washington. Various dates.

UNITED STATES BOARD ON GEOGRAPHIC NAMES.
Official Standard Names Gazetteers. Washington. Various dates.

CANADIAN PERMANENT COMMITTEE ON GEOGRAPHICAL NAMES.
Gazetteer of Canada series. Ottawa. Various dates.

UNITED STATES POSTAL SERVICE.
National Five Digit ZIP Code and Post Office Directory. Washington. Issued annually.

UNITED STATES POSTAL SERVICE.
Postal Bulletin. Washington. Issued weekly.

UNITED STATES DEPARTMENT OF THE INTERIOR. BUREAU OF MINES.
Minerals Yearbook. 4 vols. Washington. Various dates.

UNITED STATES GEOLOGICAL SURVEY.
Elevations and distances in the United States. Reston, Va. 1980.

CARTACTUAL.
Cartactual—Topical Map Service. Budapest. Issues bi-monthly.

AMERICAN GEOGRAPHICAL SOCIETY.
Focus. New York. Issued ten times a year.

THE AMERICAN UNIVERSITY.
Foreign Area Studies. Washington. Various dates.

CENTRAL INTELLIGENCE AGENCY.
General reference maps. Washington. Various dates.

A sample list of sources used for specific countries follows:

Afghanistan
CENTRAL STATISTICS OFFICE.
Preliminary Results of the First Afghan Population Census 1979. Kabul.

Albania
DREJTORIA E STATISTIKES.
1979 Census. Tiranë.

Argentina
INSTITUTO NACIONAL DE ESTADISTICA Y CENSOS.
Censo Nacional de Población y Vivienda 1980. Buenos Aires.

Australia
AUSTRALIAN BUREAU OF STATISTICS.
Census of Population and Housing 1981. Canberra.

Brazil
FUNDACAO INSTITUTO BRASILEIRO DE GEOGRAFIA E ESTATISTICA.
IX Recenseamento Geral do Brasil 1980. Rio de Janeiro.

Canada
STATISTICS CANADA.
1981 Census of Canada. Ottawa.

Cuba
COMITE ESTATAL DE ESTADISTICAS.
Censo de Población y Viviendas 1981. Havana.

Hungary
HUNGARIAN CENTRAL STATISTICAL OFFICE.
1980 Census. Budapest.

Indonesia
BIRO PUSAT STATISTIK.
Sensus Penduduk 1980. Jakarta.

Kuwait
CENTRAL OFFICE OF STATISTICS.
1980 Census. Al Kuwait.

New Zealand
DEPARTMENT OF STATISTICS.
New Zealand Census of Population and Dwellings 1981. Wellington.

Panama
DIRECCION DE ESTADISTICA Y CENSO.
Censos Nacionales de 1980. Panamá.

Papua New Guinea
BUREAU OF STATISTICS.
National Population Census 1980. Port Moresby.

Philippines
NATIONAL CENSUS AND STATISTICS OFFICE.
1980 Census of Population. Manila.

Saint Lucia
CENSUS OFFICE.
1980 Population Census. Castries.

Singapore.
DEPARTMENT OF STATISTICS.
Census of Population 1980. Singapore.

Russia
CENTRAL STATISTICAL ADMINISTRATION.
1989 Census. Moscow.

United States
BUREAU OF THE CENSUS.
1990 Census of Population. Washington.

Vanuatu
CENSUS OFFICE.
1979 Population Census. Port Vila.

Zambia
CENTRAL STATISTICAL OFFICE.
1980 Census of Population and Housing. Lusaka.

Gazetteer-Index of the World

This alphabetical list of continents, countries, states, possessions and other major geographical areas provides a quick reference to their area in square miles and square kilometers, population, capital or chief town, map page number and an alpha-numeric index reference. The index reference indicates the square on the respective page in which the name may be found. The population figures used in each case are the latest reliable figures obtainable. The government listings are based primarily on the nomenclature contained in the World Factbook published by the CIA of the United States Government. Those governments currently unsettled or in transition are indicated with a † symbol.

Country	Area Square Miles	Square Kilometers	Population	Capital or Chief Town	Page and Index Ref.	Government or Ownership
*Afghanistan	250,775	649,507	15,814,000	Kabul	68/A 2	authoritarian
Africa	11,707,000	30,321,130	648,000,000	....	102/....	
Alabama, U.S.	51,705	133,916	4,062,608	Montgomery	195/....	state of the U.S.
Alaska, U.S.	591,004	1,530,700	551,947	Juneau	196/....	state of the U.S.
*Albania	11,100	28,749	3,199,000	Tiranë	45/E 5	communist†
Alberta, Canada	255,285	661,185	2,365,825	Edmonton	182/....	province of Canada
*Algeria	919,591	2,381,740	22,971,000	Algiers	106/D 3	republic
American Samoa	77	199	32,297	Pago Pago	87/J 7; 86/....	unincorporated, unorganized territory of the U.S.
Andorra	188	487	50,000	Andorra la Vella	33/G 1	co-prinicipality (France and Spain)
*Angola	481,351	1,246,700	9,747,000	Luanda	114/C 6	Marxist people's republic
Anguilla, U.K.	35	91	6,519	The Valley	156/F 3	dependent territory of the U.K.
Antarctica	5,500,000	14,245,000	....	....	5/....	
*Antigua and Barbuda	171	443	76,000	St. John's	161/E11; 156/G 3	parliamentary democracy
*Argentina	1,072,070	2,776,661	31,929,000	Buenos Aires	143/....	republic
Arizona, U.S.	114,000	295,260	3,677,985	Phoenix	198/....	state of the U.S.
Arkansas, U.S.	53,187	137,754	2,362,239	Little Rock	202/....	state of the U.S.
Armenia	11,506	29,800	3,283,000	Yerevan	52/F 6	republic
Aruba, Netherlands	75	193	66,790	Oranjestad	161/E 9	autonomous member of the Netherlands realm
Ascension Island, St. Helena	34	88	719	Georgetown	102/A 5	part of St. Helena
Ashmore & Cartier Islands, Australia	61	159	....	(Canberra, Austr.)	88/C 2	territory of Australia
Asia	17,128,500	44,362,815	3,176,000,000	....	54/....	
*Australia	2,966,136	7,682,300	15,602,156	Canberra	88/....	federal parliamentary state
Australian Capital Territory	927	2,400	221,609	Canberra	96/E 4	territory of Australia
*Austria	32,375	83,851	7,635,000	Vienna	40/B 3	federal republic
Azerbaijan	33,436	86,600	7,029,000	Baku	52/G 6	republic
Azores, Portugal	902	2,335	275,900	Ponta Delgada	32/....	autonomous region of Portugal
*Bahamas	5,382	13,939	253,000	Nassau	156/C 1	independent commmonwealth
*Bahrain	240	622	489,000	Manama	58/F 4	traditional monarchy
Baker Island, U.S.	1	2	.6	....	87/J 5	unincorporated territory of the U.S.
Balearic Islands, Spain	1,936	5,014	655,909	Palma	33/H 3	autonomous community of Spain
*Bangladesh	55,126	142,776	106,507,000	Dhaka	68/G 4	republic
*Barbados	166	430	256,000	Bridgetown	161/B 8	parliamentary democracy
*Belarus	80,154	207,600	10,200,000	Minsk	52/C 4	republic
*Belgium	11,781	30,513	9,883,000	Brussels	27/E 7	constitutional monarchy
*Belize	8,867	22,966	180,000	Belmopan	154/C 2	parliamentary
*Benin	43,483	112,620	4,591,000	Porto-Novo	106/E 6	democratic reform†
Bermuda, U.K.	21	54	67,761	Hamilton	156/H 3	dependent territory of the U.K.
*Bhutan	18,147	47,000	1,483,000	Thimphu	68/G 3	monarchy
*Bolivia	424,163	1,098,582	7,193,000	La Paz; Sucre	136/.....	republic
Bonaire, Neth. Antilles	112	291	8,087	Kralendijk	161/E 9	part of Netherland Antilles
Bophuthatswana, South Africa	15,570	40,326	1,200,000	Mmabatho	119/D 5	self-governing black African "homeland"
*Botswana	224,764	582,139	1,256,000	Gaborone	119/C 4	parliamentary republic
Bouvet Island, Norway	22	57	....	....	5/D 1	territory of Norway
*Brazil	3,284,426	8,506,663	150,368,000	Brasília	132/.....	federal republic
British Columbia, Canada	366,253	948,596	2,883,367	Victoria	184/....	province of Canada
British Indian Ocean Terr., U.K.	29	75	2,000	(London, U.K.)	54/L10	dependent territory of the U.K.
British Virgin Islands	59	153	11,006	Road Town	157/H 1	dependent territory of the U.K.
Brunei	2,226	5,765	249,000	Bandar Seri Begawan	85/E 4	constitutional sultanate
*Bulgaria	42,823	110,912	8,981,000	Sofia	45/F 4	democratic reform†
*Burkina Faso	105,869	274,200	9,001,000	Ouagadougou	106/D 6	military
*Burma (Myanmar)	261,789	678,034	38,541,000	Rangoon	72/B 2	military
*Burundi	10,747	27,835	5,302,000	Bujumbura	114/E 4	republic
California, U.S.	158,706	411,049	29,839,250	Sacramento	204/.....	state of the U.S.
*Cambodia (Kampuchea)	69,898	181,036	8,055,000	Phnom Penh	72/E 4	in dispute
*Cameroon	183,568	475,441	11,540,000	Yaoundé	114/B 2	one-party republic
*Canada	3,851,787	9,976,139	25,309,331	Ottawa	162/.....	confederation with parliamentary democracy
Canary Islands, Spain	2,808	7,273	1,367,646	Las Palmas; Santa Cruz	32/B 4	autonomous community of Spain
Cape Province, South Africa	261,705	677,816	5,543,506	Cape Town	118/C 6	province of South Africa
*Cape Verde	1,557	4,033	347,000	Praia	106/B 8	republic
Cayman Islands, U.K.	100	259	18,000	Georgetown	156/B 3	dependent territory of the U.K.
Celebes, Indonesia	72,986	189,034	7,732,383	Ujung Pandang	85/G 6	part of Indonesia
*Central African Republic	242,000	626,780	2,740,000	Bangui	114/C 2	republic
Central America	197,480	511,475	28,296,000	....	154/.....	
*Chad	495,752	1,283,998	5,538,000	N'Djamena	111/C 4	republic
Channel Islands, U.K.	75	194	133,000	St. Helier; St. Peter Port	13/E 8	part of the United Kingdom
*Chile	292,257	756,946	12,961,000	Santiago	138/.....	republic
*China, People's Rep. of	3,691,000	9,559,690	1,133,682,501	Beijing	77/.....	communist party-led state
China, Republic of (Taiwan)	13,971	36,185	20,204,880	Taipei	77/K 7	one-party presidential regime
Christmas Island, Australia	52	135	3,184	Flying Fish Cove	54/M184	territory of Australia
Ciskei, S. Africa	2,988	7,740	635,631	Bisho	119/D 6	self-governing black African "homeland"
Clipperton Island, France	2	5.2	....	....	146/H 8	possession of France
Cocos (Keeling) Islands, Australia	5.4	14	555	West Island	54/N11	territory of Australia

*Member of the United Nations

II

Gazetteer-Index of the World

Country	Area Square Miles	Area Square Kilometers	Population	Capital or Chief Town	Page and Index Ref.	Government or Ownership
*Colombia	439,513	1,138,339	30,241,000	Bogotá	126/.....	republic
Colorado, U.S.	104,091	269,596	3,307,912	Denver	208/.....	state of the U.S.
*Comoros	719	1,862	484,000	Moroni	119/G 2	republic
*Congo	132,046	342,000	1,843,000	Brazzaville	114/B 4	people's republic
Connecticut, U.S.	5,018	12,997	3,295,669	Hartford	210/.....	state of the U.S.
Cook Islands, New Zealand	91	236	17,695	Avarua	87/K 7	self-governing in free association with New Zealand
Coral Sea Islands, Australia	8.5	22	....	....	88/J 3	territory of Australia
Corsica, France	3,352	8,682	289,842	Ajaccio; Bastia	28/B 6	part of France
*Costa Rica	19,575	50,700	2,959,000	San José	154/E 5	democratic republic
Côte d'Ivoire, see Ivory Coast						
*Cuba	44,206	114,494	10,617,000	Havana	158/.....	communist state
Curaçao, Neth. Antilles	178	462	145,430	Willemstad	161/G 7	part of Netherlands Antilles
*Cyprus	3,473	8,995	699,000	Nicosia	62/E 5	republic
*Czechoslovakia	49,373	127,876	15,679,000	Prague	41/C 2	republic
Delaware, U.S.	2,044	5,294	668,696	Dover	245/R 3	state of the U.S.
*Denmark	16,629	43,069	5,135,000	Copenhagen	21/.....	constitutional monarchy
District of Columbia, U.S.	69	179	609,909	Washington	244/F 5	district of the United States
*Djibouti	8,880	23,000	456,000	Djibouti	111/H 5	republic
*Dominica	290	751	81,000	Roseau	161/E 7	parliamentary democracy
*Dominican Republic	18,704	48,443	6,867,000	Santo Domingo	158/D 6	republic
*Ecuador	109,483	283,561	10,490,000	Quito	128/C 3	republic
*Egypt	386,659	1,001,447	53,080,000	Cairo	110/E 2	republic
*El Salvador	8,260	21,393	5,207,000	San Salvador	154/C 4	republic
England, U.K.	50,516	130,836	46,220,955	London	13/.....	part of the United Kingdom
*Equatorial Guinea	10,831	28,052	341,000	Malabo	114/A 3	republic
*Estonia	17,413	45,100	1,573,000	Tallinn	53/.....	republic
*Ethiopia	471,776	1,221,900	50,774,000	Addis Ababa	110/G 5	communist†
Europe	4,057,000	10,507,630	689,000,000	....	7/.....	
Falkland Islands & Dependencies, U.K.	6,198	16,053	1,813	Stanley	120/E 8; 143/D 7	dependent territory of the U.K.
Faroe Islands, Denmark	540	1,399	41,969	Tórshavn	21/B 2	self-governing overseas administrative division of Denmark
*Fiji	7,055	18,272	727,000	Suva	87/H 8; 86/.....	republic
*Finland	130,128	337,032	4,973,000	Helsinki	18/O 6	republic
Florida, U.S.	58,664	151,940	13,003,362	Tallahassee	212/.....	state of the U.S.
*France	210,038	543,998	56,160,000	Paris	28/.....	republic
French Guiana	35,135	91,000	90,000	Cayenne	131/E 3	overseas department of France
French Polynesia	1,544	4,000	137,382	Papeete	87/L 8	overseas territory of France
*Gabon	103,346	267,666	1,206,000	Libreville	114/B 4	republic
*Gambia	4,127	10,689	688,000	Banjul	106/A 6	republic
Gaza Strip	139	360	400,000	Gaza	65/A 4	occupied by Israel
Georgia	26,911	69,700	5,449,000	Tbilisi	52/F 6	republic
Georgia, U.S.	58,910	152,577	6,508,419	Atlanta	217/.....	state of the U.S.
*Germany	137,753	356,780	78,890,000	Berlin	22/.....	republic
*Ghana	92,099	238,536	13,391,000	Accra	106/D 7	military
Gibraltar, U.K.	2.28	5.91	31,000	Gibraltar	33/D 4	dependent territory of the U.K.
*Great Britain & Northern Ireland (United Kingdom)	94,399	244,493	57,236,000	London	10/.....	see United Kingdom
*Greece	50,944	131,945	9,983,000	Athens	45/F 6	presidential parliamentary republic
Greenland, Denmark	840,000	2,175,600	49,773	Nuuk (Godthåb)	4/B12	self-governing overseas administrative division of Denmark
*Grenada	133	344	103,103	St. George's	161/D 9; 156/G 4	parliamentary democracy
Guadeloupe & Dependencies, France	687	1,779	328,400	Basse-Terre	161/A 5; 156/F 4	overseas department of France
Guam, U.S.	209	541	105,979	Agaña	87/E 4; 86/.....	organized, unincorporated territory of the U.S.
*Guatemala	42,042	108,889	9,197,000	Guatemala	154/B 3	republic
*Guinea	94,925	245,856	6,706,000	Conakry	106/B 6	republic
*Guinea-Bissau	13,948	36,125	943,000	Bissau	106/A 6	republic
*Guyana	83,000	214,970	1,024,000	Georgetown	131/B 3	republic
*Haiti	10,694	27,697	5,609,000	Port-au-Prince	158/C 5	republic
Hawaii, U.S.	6,471	16,760	1,115,274	Honolulu	218/.....	state of the U.S.
Heard & McDonald Islands, Australia	113	293	....	....	2/N 8	territory of Australia
Holland, see Netherlands						
*Honduras	43,277	112,087	4,951,000	Tegucigalpa	154/D 3	republic
Hong Kong, U.K.	403	1,044	5,761,000	Victoria	77/H 7; 78/.....	colony of the U.K.
Howland Island, U.S.	1	2.6	....	....	87/J 5	unincorporated territory of the U.S.
*Hungary	35,919	93,030	10,553,000	Budapest	41/D 3	republic
*Iceland	39,768	103,000	250,000	Reykjavík	21/B 1	republic
Idaho, U.S.	83,564	216,431	1,011,986	Boise	220/.....	state of the U.S.
Illinois, U.S.	56,345	145,934	11,466,682	Springfield	222/.....	state of the U.S.
*India	1,269,339	3,287,588	843,930,861	New Delhi	68/D 4	federal republic
Indiana, U.S.	36,185	93,719	5,564,228	Indianapolis	227/.....	state of the U.S.
*Indonesia	788,430	2,042,034	179,136,000	Jakarta	85/D 7	republic
Iowa, U.S.	56,275	145,752	2,787,424	Des Moines	229/.....	state of the U.S.
*Iran	636,293	1,648,000	55,208,000	Tehran	66/F 4	theocratic republic
*Iraq	172,476	446,713	16,335,000	Baghdad	66/C 4	republic
*Ireland	27,136	70,282	3,540,643	Dublin	17/.....	republic

Gazetteer-Index of the World

Country	Square Miles	Area Square Kilometers	Population	Capital or Chief Town	Page and Index Ref.	Government or Ownership
Ireland, Northern, U.K.	5,452	14,121	1,543,000	Belfast	17/F 2	part of the United Kingdom
Isle of Man, U.K.	227	588	64,000	Douglas	13/C 3	part of the United Kingdom
*Israel	7,847	20,324	4,625,000	Jerusalem	65/B 4	republic
*Italy	116,303	301,225	57,574,000	Rome	34/.....	republic
*Ivory Coast (Côte d'Ivoire)	124,504	322,465	9,300,000	Yamoussoukro	106/C 7	republic
*Jamaica	4,411	11,424	2,392,000	Kingston	158/.....	parliamentary democracy
Jan Mayen, Norway	144	373	....	....	6/D 1	territory of Norway
*Japan	145,730	377,441	123,116,000	Tokyo	81/.....	constitutional monarchy
Jarvis Island, U.S.	1	2.6	....	....	87/K 6	unincorporated territory of the U.S.
Java, Indonesia	48,842	126,500	73,712,411	Jakarta	85/J 2	part of Indonesia
Johnston Atoll, U.S.	.91	2.4	327	....	87/K 4	unincorporated territory of the U.S.
*Jordan	35,000	90,650	2,779,000	Amman	65/D 3	constitutional monarchy
*Kampuchea (Cambodia)	69,898	181,036	5,200,000	Phnom Penh	72/E 4	in dispute
Kansas, U.S.	82,277	213,097	2,485,600	Topeka	232/.....	state of the U.S.
Kazakhstan	1,048,300	2,715,100	16,538,000	Alma-Ata	48/G 5	republic
Kentucky, U.S.	40,409	104,659	3,698,969	Frankfort	237/.....	state of the U.S.
*Kenya	224,960	582,646	24,872,000	Nairobi	115/G 3	republic
Kermadec Islands, New Zealand	13	33	5	....	87/J 9	part of New Zealand
Kingman Reef, U.S.	0.1	0.26	....	....	87/K 5	unincorporated territory of the U.S.
Kiribati	291	754	64,000	Bairiki	87/J 6	republic
*Korea, North	46,540	120,539	22,419,000	P'yŏngyang	80/D 3	communist
*Korea, South	38,175	98,873	42,793,000	Seoul	80/D 5	republic
*Kuwait	6,532	16,918	2,048,000	Al Kuwait	58/E 4	constitutional monarchy
Kyrgyzstan	76,641	198,500	4,291,000	Bishkek	48/H 5	republic
*Laos	91,428	236,800	3,721,000	Vientiane	72/D 3	communist
*Latvia	24,595	63,700	2,681,000	Riga	53/.....	republic
*Lebanon	4,015	10,399	2,897,000	Beirut	62/F 6	republic
*Lesotho	11,720	30,355	1,700,000	Maseru	119/D 5	military†
*Liberia	43,000	111,370	2,508,000	Monrovia	106/C 7	republic
*Libya	679,358	1,759,537	3,773,000	Tripoli	110/B 2	socialist people's (masses) state
*Liechtenstein	61	158	28,000	Vaduz	39/J 2	hereditary constitutional monarchy
*Lithuania	25,174	65,200	3,690,000	Vilnius	53/.....	republic
Louisiana, U.S.	47,752	123,678	4,238,216	Baton Rouge	238/.....	state of the U.S.
*Luxembourg	999	2,587	378,000	Luxembourg	27/J 9	constitutional monarchy
Macau, Portugal	6	16	448,000	Macau	77/H 7	overseas territory of Portugal
*Madagascar	226,657	587,041	9,985,000	Antananarivo	119/H 3	republic
Madeira Islands, Portugal	307	796	262,800	Funchal	32/A 2	autonomous region of Portugal
Maine, U.S.	33,265	86,156	1,233,223	Augusta	243/.....	state of the U.S.
*Malawi	45,747	118,485	8,022,000	Lilongwe	114/F 6	one-party state
Malaya, Malaysia	50,806	131,588	11,138,227	Kuala Lumpur	72/D 6	part of Malaysia
*Malaysia	128,308	332,318	17,377,000	Kuala Lumpur	72/D 6; 85/E 4	federated parliamentary democracy
*Maldives	115	298	206,000	Male	54/L 9	republic
*Mali	464,873	1,204,021	7,960,000	Bamako	106/C 6	republic
*Malta	122	316	353,000	Valletta	34/E 7	parliamentary democracy
Manitoba, Canada	250,999	650,087	1,063,016	Winnipeg	179/.....	province of Canada
Marquesas Islands, French Polynesia	492	1,274	5,419	Atuona	87/N 6	part of French Polynesia
*Marshall Islands	70	181	30,873	Majuro	87/G 4	constitutional; free association with the U.S.
Martinique, France	425	1,101	328,566	Fort-de-France	161/D 5	overseas department of France
Maryland, U.S.	10,460	27,091	4,798,622	Annapolis	245/.....	state of the U.S.
Massachusetts, U.S.	8,284	21,456	6,029,051	Boston	249/.....	state of the U.S.
*Mauritania	419,229	1,085,803	1,970,000	Nouakchott	106/B 5	military republic
*Mauritius	790	2,046	1,068,000	Port Louis	119/G 5	parliamentary democracy
Mayotte, France	144	373	47,300	Dzaoudzi	119/G 2	territorial collectivity of France
*Mexico	761,601	1,972,546	86,154,000	Mexico City	150/.....	federal republic
Michigan, U.S.	58,527	151,585	9,328,784	Lansing	250/.....	state of the U.S.
*Micronesia, Federated States of	....	....	73,160	Kolonia	87/E 5	constitutional; free association with the U.S.
Midway Islands, U.S.	1.9	4.9	453	....	87/J 3	unincorporated territory of the U.S.
Minnesota, U.S.	84,402	218,601	4,387,029	St. Paul	255/.....	state of the U.S.
Mississippi, U.S.	47,689	123,515	2,586,443	Jackson	256/.....	state of the U.S.
Missouri, U.S.	69,697	180,515	5,137,804	Jefferson City	261/.....	state of the U.S.
Moldova	13,012	33,700	4,341,000	Kishinev	52/C 5	republic
Monaco	368 acres	149 hectares	27,063	....	28/G 6	constitutional monarchy
*Mongolia	606,163	1,569,962	2,070,000	Ulaanbaatar	77/E 2	socialist†
Montana, U.S.	147,046	380,849	803,655	Helena	262/.....	state of the U.S.
Montserrat, U.K.	40	104	12,073	Plymouth	157/G 3	dependent territory of the U.K.
*Morocco	172,414	446,550	24,522,000	Rabat	106/C 2	constitutional monarchy
*Mozambique	303,769	786,762	15,326,000	Maputo	119/E 4	people's republic
Myanmar, see Burma						
*Namibia	317,827	823,172	1,818,000	Windhoek	118/B 3	republic
Natal, South Africa	33,578	86,967	5,722,215	Pietermaritzburg	119/E 5	province of South Africa
Nauru	7	.720	9,000	Yaren (district)	87/G 6	republic
Navassa Island, U.S.	2	5	....	....	156/C 3	unincorporated territory of the U.S.
Nebraska, U.S.	77,355	200,349	1,584,617	Lincoln	264/.....	state of the U.S.
*Nepal	54,663	141,577	18,442,000	Kathmandu	68/E 3	constitutional monarchy
*Netherlands	15,892	41,160	14,906,000	The Hague; Amsterdam	27/F 5	constitutional monarchy
Netherlands Antilles	390	1,010	246,000	Willemstad	156/C 4	autonomous member of the Netherlands realm
Nevada, U.S.	110,561	286,353	1,206,152	Carson City	266/.....	state of the U.S.
New Brunswick, Canada	28,354	73,437	709,442	Fredericton	170/.....	province of Canada
New Caledonia & Dependencies, France	7,335	18,998	133,233	Nouméa	87/G 8	overseas territory of France

Gazetteer-Index of the World

Country	Area Square Miles	Area Square Kilometers	Population	Capital or Chief Town	Page and Index Ref.	Government or Ownership
Newfoundland, Canada	156,184	404,517	568,349	St. John's	166/.....	province of Canada
New Hampshire, U.S.	9,279	24,033	1,113,915	Concord	268/.....	state of the U.S.
New Jersey, U.S.	7,787	20,168	7,748,634	Trenton	273/.....	state of the U.S.
New Mexico, U.S.	121,593	314,926	1,521,779	Santa Fe	274/.....	state of the U.S.
New South Wales, Australia	309,498	801,600	5,401,881	Sydney	96/B 2	state of Australia
New York, U.S.	49,108	127,190	18,044,505	Albany	276/.....	state of the U.S.
*New Zealand	103,736	268,676	3,389,000	Wellington	100/.....	parliamentary democracy
*Nicaragua	45,698	118,358	3,384,000	Managua	154/D 4	republic
*Niger	489,189	1,267,000	7,250,000	Niamey	106/F 5	republic
*Nigeria	357,000	924,630	104,957,000	Lagos	106/F 6	military
Niue, New Zealand	100	259	3,578	Alofi	87/K 7	self-governing territory in free association with New Zealand
Norfolk Island, Australia	13.4	34.6	2,175	Kingston	88/L 5	territory of Australia
North America	9,363,000	24,250,170	427,000,000	....	146/.....	
North Carolina, U.S.	52,669	136,413	6,657,630	Raleigh	281/.....	state of the U.S.
North Dakota, U.S.	70,702	183,118	641,364	Bismarck	282/.....	state of the U.S.
Northern Ireland, U.K.	5,452	14,121	1,543,000	Belfast	17/F 2	part of the United Kingdom
Northern Marianas, U.S.	184	477	16,780	Capitol Hill	87/E 4	commonwealth associated with the U.S.
Northern Territory, Australia	519,768	1,346,200	154,848	Darwin	93/.....	territory of Australia
*North Korea	46,540	120,539	17,914,000	P'yŏngyang	80/D 3	communist state
Northwest Territories, Canada	1,304,896	3,379,683	52,238	Yellowknife	187/G 3	territory of Canada
*Norway	125,053	323,887	4,242,000	Oslo	18/F 7	constitutional monarchy
Nova Scotia, Canada	21,425	55,491	873,176	Halifax	168/.....	province of Canada
Oceania	3,292,000	8,526,280	23,000,000	....	87/.....	
Ohio, U.S.	41,330	107,045	10,887,325	Columbus	284/.....	state of the U.S.
Oklahoma, U.S.	69,956	181,186	3,157,604	Oklahoma City	288/.....	state of the U.S.
*Oman	120,000	310,800	2,000,000	Muscat	58/G 6	absolute monarchy
Ontario, Canada	412,580	1,068,582	9,101,694	Toronto	175,177/	province of Canada
Orange Free State, South Africa	49,866	129,153	1,833,216	Bloemfontein	119/D 5	province of South Africa
Oregon, U.S.	97,073	251,419	2,853,733	Salem	291/.....	state of the U.S.
Orkney Islands, Scotland	376	974	17,675	Kirkwall	15/E 1	part of the United Kingdom
*Pakistan	310,403	803,944	112,050,000	Islamabad	68/B 3	parliamentary democracy
Palau	188	487	12,116	Koror	86/D 5	U.N. trusteeship administered by the U.S.
Palmyra Atoll, U.S.	3.85	1			87/K 5	unincorporated territory of the U.S.
*Panama	29,761	77,082	2,418,000	Panamá	154/G 6	centralized republic
*Papua New Guinea	183,540	475,369	3,593,000	Port Moresby	85/B 7; 87/E 6	parliamentary democracy
Paracel Islands, China	....	....	....	....	85/E 2	occupied by China; claimed by Taiwan and Vietnam
*Paraguay	157,047	406,752	4,157,000	Asunción	144/.....	republic
Pennsylvania, U.S.	45,308	117,348	11,924,710	Harrisburg	294/.....	state of the U.S.
*Peru	496,222	1,285,215	22,332,000	Lima	128/.....	republic
*Philippines	115,707	299,681	60,097,000	Manila	82/.....	republic
Pitcairn Islands, U.K.	18	47	54	Adamstown	87/O 8	dependent territory of the U.K.
*Poland	120,725	312,678	37,931,000	Warsaw	47/.....	democratic
*Portugal	35,549	92,072	10,467,000	Lisbon	32/B 3	republic
Prince Edward Island, Canada	2,184	5,657	126,646	Charlottetown	168/E 2	province of Canada
Puerto Rico, U.S.	3,515	9,104	3,522,037	San Juan	161/.....	commonwealth associated with the U.S.
*Qatar	4,247	11,000	422,000	Doha	58/F 4	traditional monarchy
Québec, Canada	594,857	1,540,680	6,532,461	Québec	172,174/	province of Canada
Queensland, Austraila	666,872	1,727,200	2,587,315	Brisbane	95/.....	state of Australia
Réunion, France	969	2,510	570,000	St-Denis	119/F 5	overseas department of France
Rhode Island, U.S.	1,212	3,139	1,005,984	Providence	249/H 5	state of the U.S.
*Romania	91,699	237,500	23,249,000	Bucharest	45/F 3	democratic reform†
*Russia	6,592,812	17,075,400	147,386,000	Moscow	48/D 4	republic
*Rwanda	10,169	26,337	6,274,000	Kigali	114/E 4	republic
Sabah, Malaysia	29,300	75,887	1,002,608	Kota Kinabalu	85/F 4	state of Malaysia
Saint Helena & Dependencies, U.K.	162	420	5,147	Jamestown	102/B 6	dependent territory of the U.K.
*Saint Kitts and Nevis	104	269	44,404	Basseterre	156/F 3; 161/C11	constitutional monarchy
*Saint Lucia	238	616	148,000	Castries	161/G 6	parliamentary democracy
Saint Pierre & Miquelon, France	93.5	242	6,034	Saint-Pierre	166/C 4	territorial collectivity of France
*Saint Vincent & the Grenadines	150	388	124,000	Kingstown	161/A 8; 157/G 4	constitutional monarchy
Sakhalin, Russia	29,500	76,405	655,000	Yuzhno-Sakhalinsk	48/P 4	part of Russia
San Marino	23.4	60.6	23,000	San Marino	34/D 3	republic
*São Tomé and Príncipe	372	963	116,000	São Tomé	106/F 8	republic
Sarawak, Malaysia	48,202	124,843	1,294,753	Kuching	85/E 5	state of Malaysia
Sardinia, Italy	9,301	24,090	1,450,483	Cagliari	34/B 4	region of Italy
Saskatchewan, Canada	251,699	651,900	1,009,613	Regina	181/.....	province of Canada
*Saudi Arabia	829,995	2,149,687	14,435,000	Riyadh	58/D 4	monarchy
Scotland, U.K.	30,414	78,772	5,117,146	Edinburgh	15/.....	part of the United Kingdom
*Senegal	75,954	196,720	7,113,000	Dakar	106/A 5	republic
*Seychelles	145	375	67,000	Victoria	119/H 5	republic
Shetland Islands, Scotland	552	1,430	18,494	Lerwick	15/G 2	part of the United Kingdom
Siam, see Thailand						
Sicily, Italy	9,926	25,708	4,628,918	Palermo	34/D 6	region of Italy
*Sierra Leone	27,925	72,325	4,047,000	Freetown	106/B 7	one-party presidential republic
*Singapore	226	585	2,704,000	Singapore	72/F 6	republic
Society Islands, French Polynesia	677	1,753	117,703	Papeete	87/L 7	part of French Polynesia
*Solomon Islands	11,500	29,785	299,000	Honiara	87/G 6; 86/.....	parliamentary democracy

Gazetteer-Index of the World

Country	Area Square Miles	Square Kilometers	Population	Capital or Chief Town	Page and Index Ref.	Government or Ownership
*Somalia	246,200	637,658	7,339,000	Mogadishu	115/H 3	republic
*South Africa	455,318	1,179,274	34,492,000	Cape Town; Pretoria	118/C 5	republic
South America	6,875,000	17,806,250	297,000,000	....	120/.....	
South Australia, Australia	379,922	984,000	1,345,945	Adelaide	94/.....	state of Australia
South Carolina, U.S.	31,113	80,583	3,505,707	Columbia	296/.....	state of the U.S.
South Dakota, U.S.	77,116	199,730	699,999	Pierre	298/.....	state of the U.S.
*South Korea	38,175	98,873	37,448,836	Seoul	80/D 5	republic
*Spain	194,881	504,742	39,328,000	Madrid	33/.....	parliamentary monarchy
Spratly Islands	....	....	....	....	85/E 4	in dispute; claims by China, Malaysia, Philippines, Taiwan, Vietnam
*Sri Lanka	25,332	65,610	16,806,000	Colombo	68/E 7	republic
*Sudan	967,494	2,505,809	24,485,000	Khartoum	110/E 4	military
Sumatra, Indonesia	164,000	424,760	19,360,400	Medan	84/B 5	see Indonesia
*Suriname	55,144	142,823	400,000	Paramaribo	131/C 3	republic
Svalbard, Norway	23,957	62,049	3,431	Longyearbyen	18/C 2	territory of Norway
*Swaziland	6,705	17,366	681,000	Mbabane	119/E 5	monarchy
*Sweden	173,665	449,792	8,541,000	Stockholm	18/J 8	constitutional monarchy
Switzerland	15,943	41,292	6,647,000	Bern	39/.....	federal republic
*Syria	71,498	185,180	11,719,000	Damascus	62/G 5	military republic
Tahiti, French Polynesia	402	1,041	95,604	Papeete	87/L 7	see French Polynesia
Taiwan	13,971	36,185	16,609,961	Taipei	77/K 7	one-party presidential regime
Tajikistan	55,251	143,100	5,112,000	Dushanbe	48/G 6	republic
*Tanzania	363,708	942,003	24,802,000	Dar es Salaam	114/F 5	republic
Tasmania, Australia	26,178	67,800	436,353	Hobart	99/.....	state of Australia
Tennessee, U.S.	42,144	109,153	4,896,641	Nashville	237/.....	state of the U.S.
Texas, U.S.	266,807	691,030	17,059,805	Austin	303/.....	state of the U.S.
*Thailand	198,455	513,998	55,448,000	Bangkok	72/D 3	constitutional monarchy
Tibet, China	463,320	1,200,000	1,790,000	Lhasa	76/C 5	part of China
*Togo	21,622	56,000	3,296,000	Lomé	106/E 7	republic
Tokelau, New Zealand	3.9	10	1,575	Fakaofo	87/J 6	territory of New Zealand
*Tonga	270	699	95,000	Nuku'alofa	87/J 8	constitutional monarchy
Transkei, South Africa	16,910	43,797	2,000,000	Umtata	119/D 6	self-governing black African "homeland"
Transvaal, South Africa	109,621	283,918	10,673,033	Pretoria	119/D 4	province of South Africa
*Trinidad and Tobago	1,980	5,128	1,212,000	Port-of-Spain	157/G 5; 161/A10	parliamentary democracy
Tristan da Cunha, St. Helena	38	98	251	Edinburgh	2/J 7	see St. Helena
Tuamotu Archipelago, French Polynesia	341	883	9,052	Apataki	87/M 7	see French Polynesia
*Tunisia	63,378	164,149	7,465,000	Tunis	106/F 1	republic
*Turkey	300,946	779,450	56,741,000	Ankara	62/D 3	republican parliamentary democracy
Turkmenistan	188,455	488,100	3,534,000	Ashkhabad	48/F 6	republic
Turks and Caicos Islands, U.K.	166	430	7,436	Cockburn Town, Grand Turk	156/D 2	dependent territory of the U.K.
Tuvalu	9.78	25.33	9,000	Fongafale, Funafuti	87/H 6	democracy
*Uganda	91,076	235,887	17,804,000	Kampala	114/F 3	republic
*Ukraine	233,089	603,700	51,704,000	Kiev	52/D 5	republic
*United Arab Emirates	32,278	83,600	1,206,000	Abu Dhabi	58/F 5	federation of sheikdoms
*United Kingdom	94,399	244,493	57,236,000	London	10/.....	constitutional monarchy
*United States	3,623,420	9,384,658	249,632,692	Washington	188/.....	federal republic
*Uruguay	72,172	186,925	3,077,000	Montevideo	145/.....	republic
Utah, U.S.	84,899	219,888	1,727,784	Salt Lake City	304/.....	state of the U.S.
Uzbekistan	173,591	449,600	19,906,000	Tashkent	48/G 5	republic
*Vanuatu	5,700	14,763	155,000	Vila	87/G 7	republic
Vatican City	108.7 acres 44 hectares		1,000	....	34/B 6	sacerdotal (priest-related) monarchy
Venda, South Africa	2,510	6,501	450,000	Thohoyandou	119/E 4	self-governing black African "homeland"
*Venezuela	352,143	912,050	19,246,000	Caracas	124/.....	republic
Vermont, U.S.	9,614	24,900	564,964	Montpelier	268/.....	state of the U.S.
Victoria, Australia	87,876	227,600	4,019,478	Melbourne	96/B 5	state of Australia
*Vietnam	128,405	332,569	64,412,000	Hanoi	72/E 3	communist state
Virginia, U.S.	40,767	105,587	6,216,568	Richmond	307/.....	state of the U.S.
Virgin Islands, British	59	153	11,006	Road Town	157/H 1	dependent territory of the U.K.
Virgin Islands, U.S.	132	342	96,569	Charlotte Amalie	161/A 4	organized, unincorporated territory of the U.S.
Wake Island, U.S.	2.5	6.5	302	Wake Islet	87/G 4	unincorporated territory of the U.S.
Wales, U.K.	8,017	20,764	2,790,462	Cardiff	13/D 5	part of the United Kingdom
Wallis and Futuna, France	106	275	9,192	Mata Utu	87/J 7	overseas territory of France
Washington, U.S.	68,139	176,480	4,887,941	Olympia	310/.....	state of the U.S.
West Bank	2,100	5,439	c. 800,000	....	65/C 3	occupied by Israel
Western Australia, Australia	975,096	2,525,500	1,406,929	Perth	92/.....	state of Australia
Western Sahara	102,703	266,000	174,000	....	106/B 3	occupied by Morocco
Western Samoa	1,133	2,934	163,000	Apia	87/J 7	constitutional monarchy
West Virginia, U.S.	24,231	62,758	1,801,625	Charleston	312/.....	state of the U.S.
Wisconsin, U.S.	56,153	145,436	4,906,745	Madison	317/.....	state of the U.S.
World	(land) 57,970,000	150,142,300	5,292,000,000	....	1,2/.....	
Wyoming, U.S.	97,809	253,325	455,975	Cheyenne	319/.....	state of the U.S.
*Yemen	188,321	487,752	10,183,000	San'a	58/D 7	republic
*Yugoslavia	98,766	255,804	23,798,000	Belgrade	45/C 3	socialist federal republic
Yukon Territory, Canada	207,075	536,324	23,504	Whitehorse	186/E 3	territory of Canada
*Zaire	905,063	2,344,113	34,491,000	Kinshasa	114/D 4	republic
*Zambia	290,586	752,618	8,073,000	Lusaka	114/E 7	one-party state
*Zimbabwe	150,803	390,580	9,122,000	Harare	119/D 3	parliamentary democracy

Glossary of Abbreviations

A

A.A.F. — Army Air Field
Acad. — Academy
A.C.T. — Australian Capital Territory
adm. — administration; administrative
A.F.B. — Air Force Base
Afgh., Afghan. — Afghanistan
Afr. — Africa
Ala. — Alabama
Alb. — Albania
Alg. — Algeria
Alta. — Alberta
Amer. — American
Amer. Samoa — American Samoa
And. — Andorra
Ant., Antarc. — Antarctica
Ant. & Bar. — Antigua and Barbuda
Ar. — Arabia
arch. — archipelago
Arg. — Argentina
Ariz. — Arizona
Ark. — Arkansas
Arm. — Armenia
Aust. — Austria
Aust. Cap. Terr. — Australian Capital Territory
Austr., Austral. — Australian, Australia
aut. — autonomous
Aut. Obl. — Autonomous Oblast
Aut. Rep. — Autonomous Republic
Azer. — Azerbaijan

B

B. — Bay
Bah. — Bahamas
Barb. — Barbados
Battlef. — Battlefield
Bch. — Beach
Bel. — Belarus
Belg. — Belgium
Berm. — Bermuda
Bol. — Bolivia
Bots. — Botswana
Br. — Branch
Br. — British
Braz. — Brazil
Br. Col. — British Columbia
Br. Ind. Oc. Terr. — British Indian Ocean Territory
Bulg. — Bulgaria

C

C. — Cape
Calif. — California
Can. — Canada
can. — canal
cap. — capital
Cent. Afr. Rep. — Central African Republic
Cent. Amer. — Central America
C.G. Sta. — Coast Guard Station
C.H. — Court House
chan. — channel
Chan. Is. — Channel Islands
Chem. Ctr. — Chemical Center
co. — county
Col. — Colombia
Colo. — Colorado
comm. — commissary
Conn. — Connecticut
cont. — continent
cord. — cordillera (mountain range)
C. Rica — Costa Rica
C.S. — County Seat
C. Verde — Cape Verde
Czech. — Czechoslovakia

D

D.C. — District of Columbia
Del. — Delaware
Dem. — Democratic
Den. — Denmark
depr. — depression
dept. — department
des. — desert
dist., dist's — district, districts
div. — division
Dom. Rep. — Dominican Republic

E

E. — East
Ec., Ecua. — Ecuador
elec. div. — electoral division
El Salv. — El Salvador
Eng. — England

Equat. Guinea, Eq. Guin. — Equatorial Guinea
escarp. — escarpment
est. — estuary
Est. — Estonia
Eth. — Ethiopia

F

Falk. Is. — Falkland Islands
Fin. — Finland
Fk., Fks. — Fork, Forks
Fla. — Florida
for. — forest
Fr. — France, French
Fr. Gui. — French Guiana
Fr. Poly. — French Polynesia
Ft. — Fort

G

G. — Gulf
Ga. — Georgia (state)
Game Res. — Game Reserve
Geo. — Georgia (nation)
Ger. — Germany
geys. — geyser
Gibr. — Gibraltar
glac. — glacier
gov. — governorate
Gr. — Group
Greenl. — Greenland
Gren. — Grenada
Gt. Brit. — Great Britain
Guad. — Guadeloupe
Guat. — Guatemala
Guinea-Biss. — Guinea-Bissau
Guy. — Guyana

H

har., harb., hbr. — harbor
hd. — head
highl. — highland, highlands
Hist. — Historic, Historical
Hond. — Honduras
Hts. — Heights
Hung. — Hungary

I

I., isl. — island, isle
I.C. — independent city
Ice., Icel. — Iceland
Ida. — Idaho
Ill. — Illinois
Ind. — Indiana
ind. city — independent city
Indon. — Indonesia
Ind. Res. — Indian Reservation
int. div. — internal division
inten. — intendency
Int'l — International
Ire. — Ireland
Is., isls. — islands
Isr. — Israel
isth. — isthmus
Iv. Coast — Ivory Coast

J

Jam. — Jamaica
Jct. — Junction

K

Kans. — Kansas
Kaz., Kazakh. — Kazakhstan
Ky. — Kentucky
Kyr. — Kyrgyzstan

L

L. — Lake, Loch, Lough
La. — Louisiana
Lab. — Laboratory
lag. — lagoon
Lat. — Latvia
ld. — land
Leb. — Lebanon
Les. — Lesotho
Liecht. — Liechtenstein
Lith. — Lithuania
Lux. — Luxembourg

M

Mad., Madag. — Madagascar
Man. — Manitoba
Mart. — Martinique
Mass. — Massachusetts
Maur. — Mauritania
Md. — Maryland
met. area — metropolitan area

Mex. — Mexico
Mich. — Michigan
Minn. — Minnesota
Miss. — Mississippi
Mo. — Missouri
Mold. — Moldova
Mon. — Monument
Mong. — Mongolia
Mont. — Montana
Mor. — Morocco
Moz., Mozamb. — Mozambique
mt. — mount
mtn. — mountain

N

N., No. — North
N. Amer. — North America
Nam., Namib. — Namibia
N.A.S. — Naval Air Station
Nat'l — National
Nat'l Cem. — National Cemetery
Nat'l Mem. Park — National Memorial Park
Nat'l Mil. Park — National Military Park
Nat'l Pkwy. — National Parkway
Nav. Base — Naval Base
Nav. Sta. — Naval Station
N.B., N. Br. — New Brunswick
N.C. — North Carolina
N. Dak. — North Dakota
Nebr. — Nebraska
Neth. — Netherlands
Neth. Ant. — Netherlands Antilles
Nev. — Nevada
New Bruns. — New Brunswick
New Cal., New Caled. — New Caledonia
Newf. — Newfoundland
New Hebr. — New Hebrides
N.H. — New Hampshire
Nic. — Nicaragua
N. Ire. — Northern Ireland
N.J. — New Jersey
N. Mex. — New Mexico
Nor. — Norway, Norwegian
North. — Northern
North. Terr., No. Terr. — Northern Territory (Australia)
N.S. — Nova Scotia
N.S.W., N.S. Wales — New South Wales
N.W.T., N.W. Terrs. — Northwest Territories (Canada)
N.Y. — New York
N.Z., N. Zealand — New Zealand

O

Obl. — Oblast
O.F.S. — Orange Free State
Okla. — Oklahoma
Okr. — Okrug
Ont. — Ontario
Ord. Depot — Ordnance Depot
Oreg. — Oregon

P

Pa. — Pennsylvania
Pak. — Pakistan
Pan. — Panama
Papua N.G. — Papua New Guinea
Par. — Paraguay
par. — parish
passg. — passage
P.E.I. — Prince Edward Island
pen. — peninsula
Phil., Phil. Is. — Philippines
Pk. — Park
pk. — peak
plat. — plateau
P.N.G. — Papua New Guinea
Pol. — Poland
Port. — Portugal, Portuguese
Pr. Edward I. — Prince Edward Island
pref. — prefecture
P. Rico — Puerto Rico
prom. — promontory
prov. — province, provincial
pt. — point

Q

Que. — Québec
Queens. — Queensland

R

R. — River

ra. — range
Rec., Recr. — Recreation, Recreational
reg. — region
Rep. — Republic
res. — reservoir
Res. — Reservation, Reserve
R.I. — Rhode Island
riv. — river
Rom. — Romania

S

S. — South
sa. — sierra, serra
S. Afr., S. Africa — South Africa
salt dep. — salt deposit
salt des. — salt desert
S. Amer. — South America
São T. & Pr. — São Tomé and Príncipe
Sask. — Saskatchewan
Saudi Ar. — Saudi Arabia
S. Aust., S. Austral. — South Australia
S.C. — South Carolina
Scot. — Scotland
Sd. — Sound
S. Dak. — South Dakota
Sen. — Senegal
Seych. — Seychelles
Sing. — Singapore
S. Leone — Sierra Leone
S. Marino — San Marino
Sol. Is. — Solomon Islands
Sp. — Spanish
Spr., Sprs. — Spring, Springs
St., Ste. — Saint, Sainte
Sta. — Station
St. P.& M. — Saint Pierre and Miquelon
St. Vin. & Grens. — St. Vincent & The Grenadines
str., strs. — strait, straits
Sur. — Suriname
Swaz. — Swaziland
Switz. — Switzerland

T

Taj. — Tajikistan
Tanz. — Tanzania
Tas. — Tasmania
Tenn. — Tennessee
terr., terrs. — territory, territories
Tex. — Texas
Thai. — Thailand
trad. — traditional
Trin. & Tob. — Trinidad and Tobago
Tun. — Tunisia
Turk. — Turkmenistan
twp. — township

U

U.A.E. — United Arab Emirates
U.K. — United Kingdom
Ukr. — Ukraine
urb. area — urban area
Urug. — Uruguay
U.S. — United States
Uzb. — Uzbekistan

V

Va. — Virginia
Ven., Venez. — Venezuela
V.I. (U.K.) — Virgin Islands (U.K.)
V.I. (U.S.) — Virgin Islands (U.S.)
Vic. — Victoria
Viet. — Vietnam
Vill. — Village
vol. — volcano
Vt. — Vermont

W

W. — West, Western
Wash. — Washington
W. Aust., W. Austral. — Western Australia
W. Indies — West Indies
Wis. — Wisconsin
W. Samoa — Western Samoa
W. Va. — West Virginia
Wyo. — Wyoming

Y

Yugo. — Yugoslavia
Yukon — Yukon Territory

Z

Zim. — Zimbabwe

Index to Terrain Maps
on pages X through XXXII

This index contains only names of land and ocean physical features. Names of towns, internal divisions and countries are not included. The entry name is followed by a letter-number combination which refers to the area on the map in which the name will be found. The number following the map reference for the entry refers, not to the page on which the entry will be found, but to the map plate number.

Index Continued

HAMMOND®
THE PHYSICAL WORLD
Terrain Maps of Land Forms and Ocean Floors

CONTENTS

RELIEF MODELS BY ERNST G. HOFMANN, ASSISTED BY RAFAEL MARTINEZ

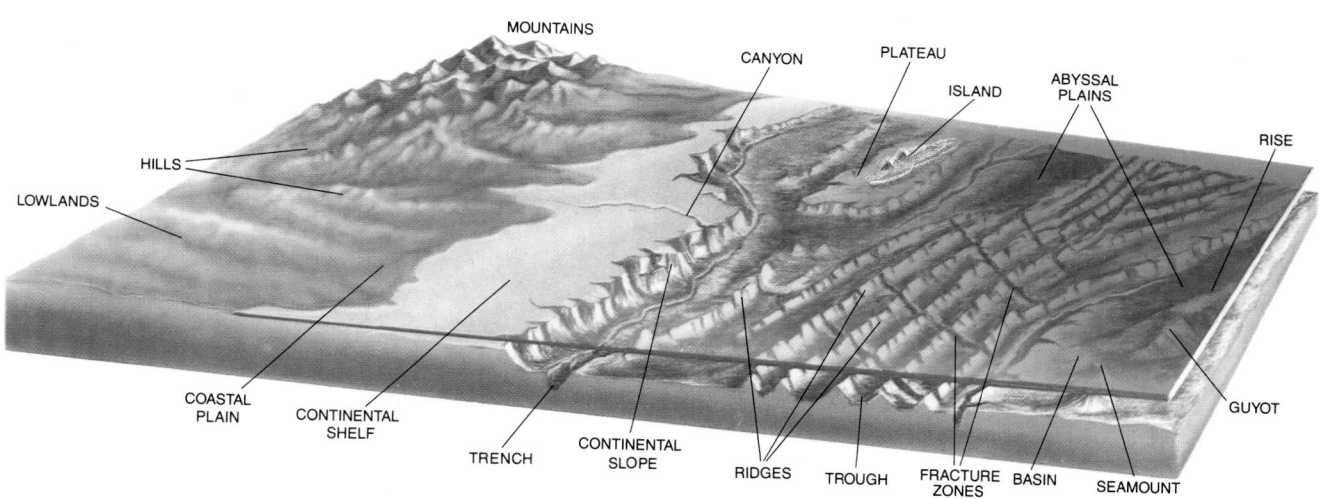

The oblique view diagram above is designed to provide a detailed view of the ocean floor as if seen through the depth of the sea. Graduating blue tones are used to contrast ocean floor depths: from light blue to represent shallow continental shelves to dark blues in the greater depths. Land relief is shown in conventional hypsometric tints.

In this dramatic collection of topographic maps of continents, oceans and major regions of the world, Hammond introduces a revolutionary new technique in cartography.

While most maps depicting terrain are created from painted artwork that is then photographed, Hammond now premiers the use of a remarkable sculptured model mapping technique created by one of our master cartographers.

The process begins with the sculpting of large scale three-dimensional models. Once physical details have been etched on the models and refinements completed, relief work is checked for accurate elevation based on a vertical scale exaggerated for visual effect.

Finished models are airbrushed and painted, then photographed using a single northwesterly light source to achieve a striking three-dimensional effect. The result is the dynamic presentation of mountain ranges and peaks on land, and canyons, trenches and seamounts on the ocean floor. Never before have maps conveyed such rich beauty while providing a realistic representation of the world as we know it.

ARCTIC OCEAN

QUEEN ELIZABETH
ISLANDS

CANADA
BASIN

Ellesmere I.

GREENLAND

Green...

Devon I.

Baffin

Beaufort Sea

Banks I.

Baffin
Island

Bay

Arctic Circle

Wrangel I.

Chukchi
Sea

Victoria
I.

LABRADOR
BASIN

IRMINGER BASIN

Denmark

Iceland

ICELAND BASIN

Norway

Yukon

Great Bear
L.

Great
Britain

Bering Sea

Mt. McKinley

Mackenzie

Great Slave
L.

Hudson
Bay

CHARLIE GIBBS
FRACTURE ZONE

Ireland

ALEUTIAN
BASIN

Gulf of Alaska

ROCKY

NORTH

Peace

Newfoundland

ALEUTIAN ISLANDS

AMERICA

Great
Lakes

C. Race

ALEUTIAN TRENCH

MENDOCINO FRACTURE ZONE

C. Mendocino

Mountains

Great
Plains

Missouri

Ohio

Appalachian Mts.

ATLANTIC

HAWAIIAN

Colorado

Mississippi

C. Hatteras

ISLANDS

RIDGE

Lower

Rio
Grande

Gulf of
Mexico

WEST

S
E
A

Tropic of Cancer

California

Cuba

MOLOKAI FRACTURE ZONE

Caribbean
Sea

INDIES

C. Verde

CENTRAL

PACIFIC

GUATEMALA
BASIN

Orinoco

A

PACIFIC

CLIPPERTON FRACTURE ZONE

BASIN

Equator

Negro

Amazon

ROMANCHE FRACTURE ZONE

Andes

Madeira

C. de São Roque

BRAZIL

PERU

PERU-CHILE TRENCH

SOUTH

São Francisco

BASIN

FERU
BASIN

AMERICA

Parana

OCEAN

NAZCA RIDGE

TONGA
TRENCH

Tropic of Capricorn

CHILE
BASIN

Cerro
Aconcagua

Paraná

KERMADEC
TRENCH

SOUTHWEST

EAST

Mountains

ARGENTINE

PACIFIC

BASIN

BASIN

Falkland Is.

PACIFIC

Tierra del Fuego

SOUTH
SANDWICH
TRENCH

C. Horn

ANTARCTIC

Drake Passage

RIDGE

Antarctic
Peninsula

WEDDELL

AMUNDSEN ABYSSAL PLAIN

ABYSSAL PLAIN

Antarctic Circle

Bellingshausen
Sea

W e d d e l l

S e a

ANTARCTICA

0 500 1000 1500 2000 2500 3000 MILES at Equator

0 500 1000 1500 2000 2500 3000 KILOMETERS at Equator

LEGEND FOR TERRAIN MAPS

International Boundaries	—··—	Mountain Peaks ▲
State and Provincial Boundaries	—·—·	National Capitals ⊛
Other Boundaries	- - - -	Other Capitals ⊙
Boundaries Along Rivers	⌒⌒	Canals

World | Plate 1

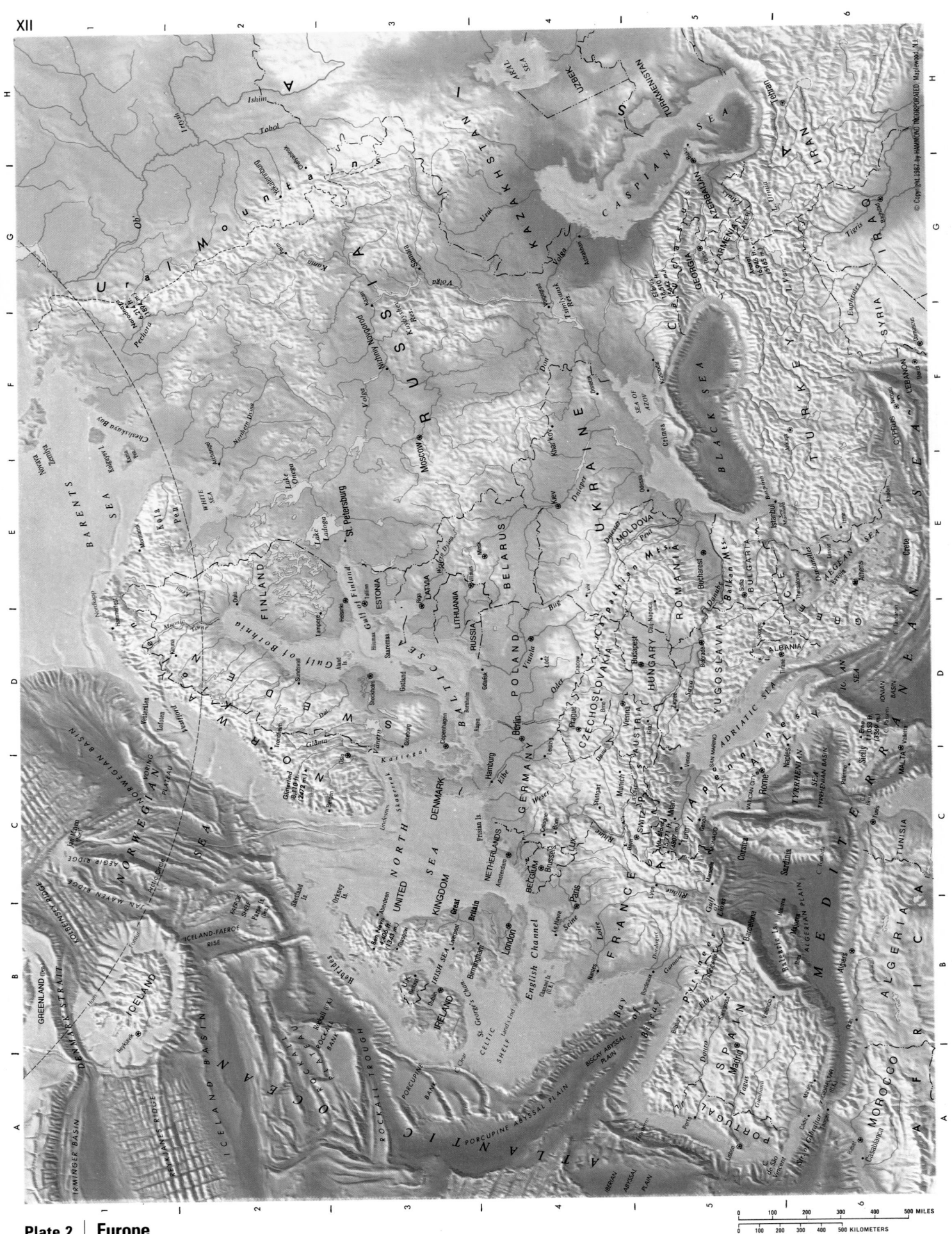

Plate 2 | **Europe**

0 100 200 300 400 500 MILES

0 100 200 300 400 500 KILOMETERS

Western Europe | **Plate 3**

© Copyright 1987 by HAMMOND INCORPORATED, Maplewood, N.J.

0 100 200 300 400 500 MILES

0 100 200 300 400 500 KILOMETERS

GREENLAND (Den.)
ICELAND
ATLANTIC OCEAN
ROCKALL TROUGH
NORWEGIAN SEA
NORWEGIAN BASIN
VORING PLATEAU
IRELAND
UNITED KINGDOM
London
NORTH SEA
English Chan.
Bay of Biscay
PORTUGAL
SPAIN
Paris
FRANCE
GERMANY
Berlin
POLAND
NORWAY
SWEDEN
FINLAND
BALTIC SEA
ESTONIA
LATVIA
LITHUANIA
BELARUS
UKRAINE
MOLDOVA
ROMANIA
Danube
YUGOSLAVIA
HUNGARY
GREECE
Rome
MEDITERRANEAN SEA
BLACK SEA
CYPRUS
LEBANON
ISRAEL
Cairo
EGYPT
SYRIA
JORDAN
IRAQ
TURKEY
Caucasus
CASPIAN SEA
Tehran
IRAN
Zagros Mountains
Euphrates
Tigris
KUWAIT
Persian Gulf
BAHRAIN
QATAR
UAE
SAUDI ARABIA
Riyadh
Rub' al Khali
Gulf of Oman
Muscat
OMAN
YEMEN
Gulf of Aden
SOMALIA
ETHIOPIA
AFRICA
RED SEA
SUDAN
BARENTS SEA
Nordkapp
Svalbard (Nor.)
Franz Josef Ld.
Novaya Zemlya
KARA SEA
Severnaya Zemlya
LAPTEV SEA
New Siberian Is.
EAST SIBERIAN SEA
ARCTIC OCEAN
LOMONOSOV RIDGE
MAKAROV BASIN
MENDELEYEV RIDGE
AMUNDSEN BASIN
NANSEN BASIN
LINCOLN SEA
CANADA BASIN
BEAUFORT SEA
Pt. Barrow
Alaska
UNITED STATES
Kodiak I.
Alaska Pen.
Bering Str.
C. Dezhnev
BERING SEA
ALEUTIAN BASIN
BOWERS RIDGE
Kolyma Ra.
Kolyma
Kamchatka Peninsula
SEA OF OKHOTSK
Sakhalin
KURIL BASIN
Hokkaido
Honshu
Tokyo
Nagoya
Osaka
Kyushu
JAPAN BASIN
SEA OF JAPAN
JAPAN TRENCH
PACIFIC OCEAN
RUSSIA
Moscow
Volga
Ural Mountains
Ob'
Yenisey
Norilsk
Siberia
Yakutsk
Lena
Vilyuy
Aldan
Amur
Angara
Lake Baykal
Irkutsk
Yablonovyy Ra.
Yekaterinburg
Chelyabinsk
Tobol
Omsk
Irtysh
Novosibirsk
Krasnoyarsk
Khabarovsk
Vladivostok
KAZAKHSTAN
ARAL SEA
Karaganda
L. Balkhash
Altai Mts.
UZBEKISTAN
TURKMENISTAN
Ashkhabad
Tashkent
Alma-Ata
KYRGYZSTAN
Tien Shan
Urumqi
MONGOLIA
Ulaanbaatar
Gobi
Great Khingan Ra.
Harbin
Shenyang
N. KOREA
S. KOREA
Seoul
Beijing
Tianjin
Dalian
YELLOW SEA
Taiyuan
Huang
Lanzhou
Xi'an
Tarim
Taklimakan
Kunlun
Tibet
CHINA
Nanjing
Shanghai
EAST CHINA SEA
Wuhan
Chengdu
Chongqing
Chang
Xi
Guangzhou
HONG KONG (U.K.)
Taipei
Taiwan
RYUKYU TRENCH
Tropic of Cancer
Hindu Kush
K2 (Godwin Austen) 28,250 ft. (8611 m)
AFGHANISTAN
Kabul
Islamabad
Helmand
PAKISTAN
Lahore
Indus
Karachi
Delhi
New Delhi
Himalaya
NEPAL
Mt. Everest 29,028 ft. (8848 m)
BHUTAN
Brahmaputra
Kanpur
Ganges
Jumna
INDIA
Ahmadabad
Narbada
Bombay
Godavari
Hyderabad
Kistna
Western Ghats
Bangalore
Madras
Calcutta
BANGLADESH
Dhaka
C. Comorin
SRI LANKA (CEYLON)
Colombo
Dondra Head
MALDIVES
BAY OF BENGAL
GANGES CONE
BURMA
Rangoon
Salween
Irrawaddy
Mekong
Hanoi
Hainan
THAILAND
Bangkok
CAMBODIA
VIETNAM
Ho Chi Minh City
Gulf of Thailand
Andaman Is.
ANDAMAN SEA
ANDAMAN BASIN
Nicobar Is.
SOUTH CHINA SEA
SOUTH CHINA BASIN
Luzon
Manila
PHILIPPINES
PHILIPPINE SEA
PHILIPPINE BASIN
PHILIPPINE TRENCH
Palawan
SULU SEA
SULU BASIN
Mindanao
CELEBES SEA
Celebes
MALAYSIA
Kuala Lumpur
SINGAPORE
SUNDA SHELF
BRUNEI
Borneo
Sumatra
INDONESIA
JAVA SEA
Jakarta
Java
Surabaya
FLORES SEA
BANDA SEA
SAVU BASIN
TIMOR TROUGH
Timor
TIMOR SEA
LOMBOK BASIN
Sunda Islands
JAVA TRENCH
SUNDA TRENCH
New Guinea
KYUSHU-PALAU RIDGE
PARECE VELA BASIN
PALAU TRENCH
ARABIAN SEA
ARABIAN BASIN
INDUS CONE
OWEN FRACTURE ZONE
CARLSBERG RIDGE
SOMALI BASIN
SEYCHELLES
MASCARENE PLATEAU
MASCARENE BASIN
MASCARENE PLAIN
MADAGASCAR
MAURITIUS
Tropic of Capricorn
CHAGOS-LACCADIVE RIDGE
CENTRAL INDIAN RIDGE
CEYLON PLAIN
Equator
MID-INDIAN OCEAN BASIN
BRITISH INDIAN OCEAN TERR.
CHAGOS TRENCH
INDIAN OCEAN
NINETY EAST RIDGE
COCOS BASIN
INVESTIGATOR RIDGE
NORTH AUSTRALIA BASIN
EXMOUTH PLATEAU
Great Sandy Desert
AUSTRALIA
0 300 600 900 1200 1500 MILES
0 300 600 900 1200 1500 KILOMETERS

Plate 4 | **Asia**

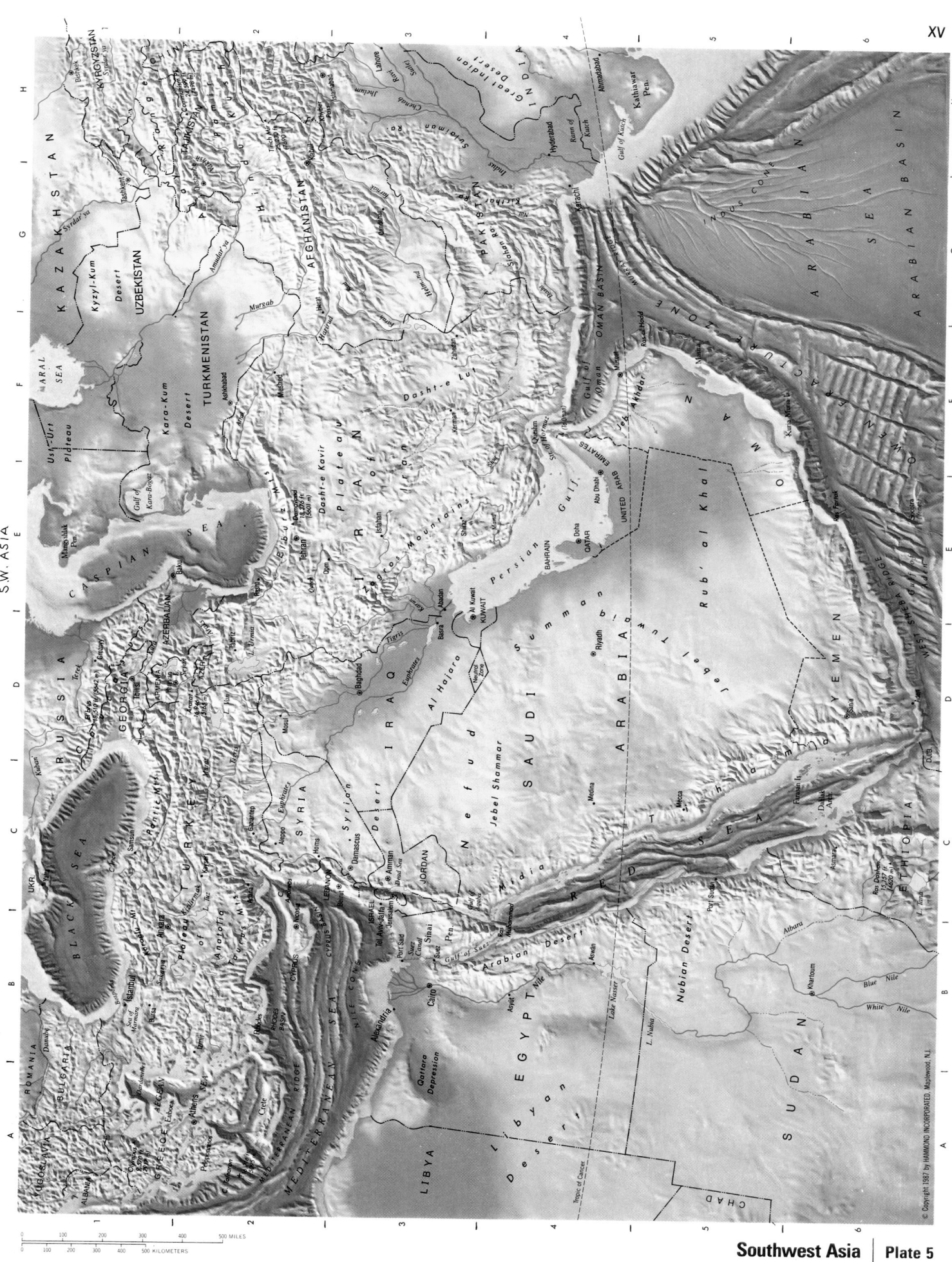

S.W. ASIA

KYRGYZSTAN
KAZAKHSTAN
UZBEKISTAN
TURKMENISTAN
AFGHANISTAN
PAKISTAN
INDIA

Great Indian Desert

Ahmadabad
Kathiawar Pen.
Gulf of Kutch
Rann of Kutch
Hyderabad
Karachi

ARABIAN BASIN

ARABIAN SEA

OWEN FRACTURE ZONE

INDUS CONE

OMAN BASIN

MURRAY RIDGE

Gulf of Oman

OMAN

Ras al Hadd
Masirah
Kuria Muria Is.

Socotra (Yemen)

Jeb. Akhdar
Ra's al Khaymah
Abu Dhabi
UNITED ARAB EMIRATES
Str. of Hormuz
Qeshm
Bandar Abbas

QATAR
Doha
BAHRAIN
Persian Gulf

Rub' al Khali

Summan
Jafurah
Tuwaiq

SAUDI ARABIA

Riyadh

Jebel Shammar
Nefud
Medina
Mecca

RED SEA

Midian

Farasan Is.
Dahlak Arch.
Massawa

ETHIOPIA
Ras Dashen
15,157 ft.
(4620 m)

SUDAN
Khartoum
Blue Nile
White Nile
Atbara
Port Sudan
Nubian Desert

EGYPT
Lake Nasser
L. Nubia
Aswan
Asyut
Nile
Cairo
Alexandria
Qattara Depression

Arabian Desert
Libyan Desert
Tropic of Cancer
CHAD
LIBYA

Suez Canal
Port Said
Suez
Gulf of Suez
Sinai Pen.
Ras Muhammad
Gulf of Aqaba

ISRAEL
Tel Aviv-Jaffa
Jerusalem
Dead Sea
JORDAN
Amman
LEBANON
Beirut
Damascus
Homs
Aleppo
Gaziantep
SYRIA
Euphrates
Syrian Desert
Al Hajara
Neutral Zone
IRAQ
Baghdad
Mosul
Tigris
Euphrates
Basra
Abadan
KUWAIT
Al Kuwait

CYPRUS
Nicosia
CYPRUS BASIN
MEDITERRANEAN SEA
Crete
Rhodes
RHODES BASIN
AEGEAN SEA
GREECE
Athens
ALBANIA
YUGOSLAVIA
BULGARIA
ROMANIA
Danube

BLACK SEA
Istanbul
Sea of Marmara
Bursa
Izmir
Ankara
TURKEY
Plateau of Anatolia
Taurus Mts.
Kizil Irmak
Samsun
Pontic Mts.

RUSSIA
Kuban
Terek
Elbrus
18,510 ft.
(5642 m)
GEORGIA
Tbilisi
ARMENIA
Yerevan
Ararat
16,945 ft.
(5165 m)
AZERBAIJAN
Baku
L. Urmia
L. Van
Van

CASPIAN SEA
Mangyshlak Pen.
Ust'-Urt Plateau
Gulf of Kara-Bogaz

ARAL SEA
Syrdar'ya
Tashkent
Kyzyl-Kum Desert
Kara-Kum Desert
Ashkhabad
Murgab
Mashhad
Ariat

IRAN
Elburz Mts.
Damavand
18,376 ft.
(5601 m)
Tehran
Dasht-e Kavir
Dasht-e Lut
Plateau of Iran
Isfahan
Qom
Zagros Mountains
Shiraz
Kerman
Zahedan

Hindu Kush
Kabul
Kandahar
Herat
Helmand
Lahore
Jhelum
Sutlej
Indus
Quetta
Sulaiman Range
Pamir
Karakoram
Khyber Pass
KASHMIR
CHINA

© Copyright 1987 by HAMMOND INCORPORATED, Maplewood, N.J.

0   100   200   300   400   500 MILES
0 100 200 300 400 500 KILOMETERS

Southwest Asia | Plate 5

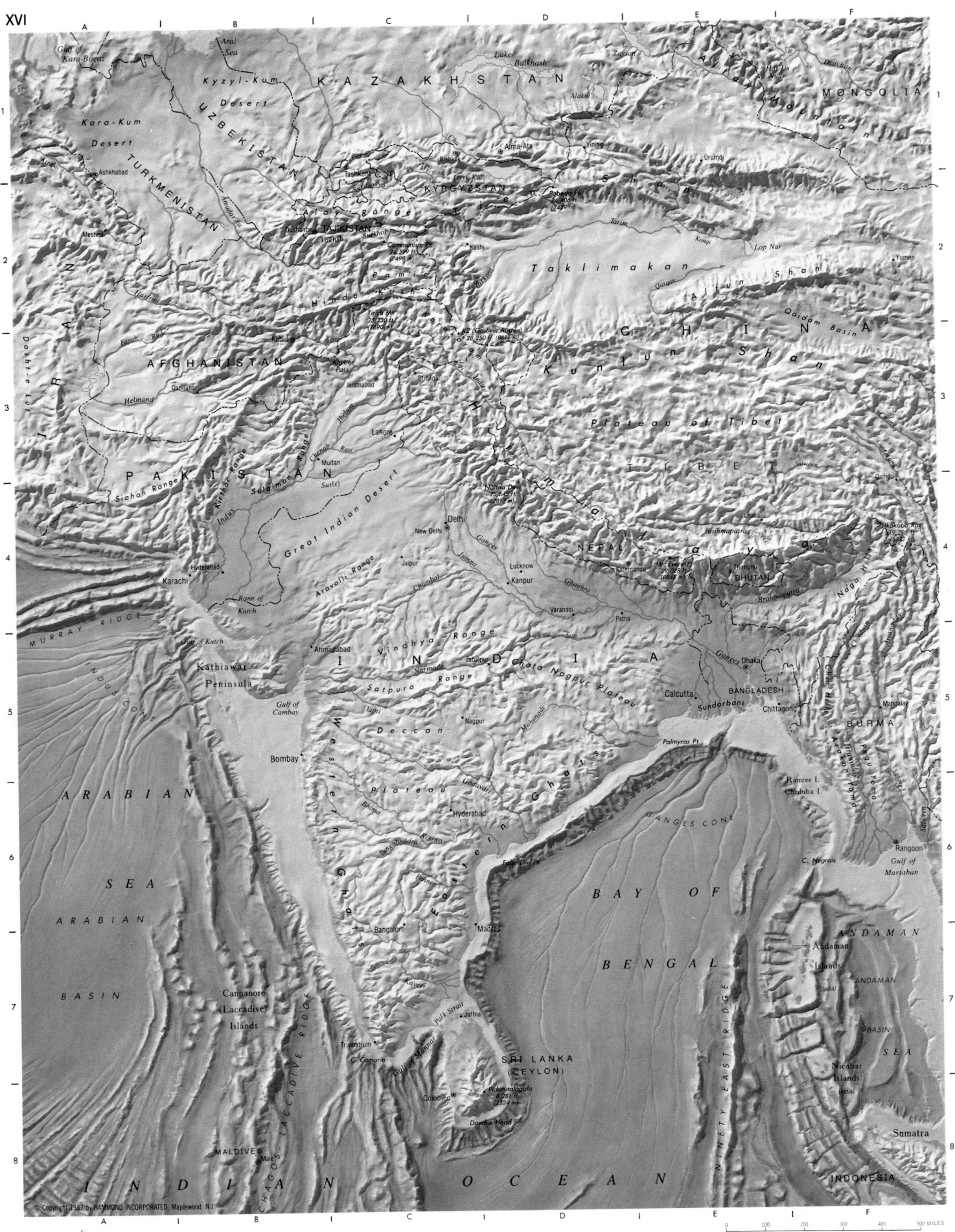
A
B
C
D
E
F
1
2
3
4
5
6
7
8
Gulf of Kara-Bogaz
Aral Sea
Kyzyl-Kum Desert
KAZAKHSTAN
Lake Balkhash
Zaysan
Alakol
Ili
MONGOLIA
Altay Mountains
Kara-Kum Desert
UZBEKISTAN
TURKMENISTAN
Ashkhabad
Atrek
Amudar'ya
Chu
Bishkek
Alma-Ata
Yining
Ürümqi
Tashkent
Syrdar'ya
Issyk-Kul
KYRGYZSTAN
Tien Shan
Pobeda Pk.
24,406 ft.
(7439 m)
Alai Range
Dushanbe
TAJIKISTAN
Vakhsh
Surkhob
Communism Pk.
24,599 ft.
(7498 m)
Kashi
Tarim
Konqi
Lop Nur
Yumen
Meshed
IRAN
Pamir
Taklimakan
Qarqan
Altun Shan
Harirud
Hindu Kush
Tirich Mir
25,230 ft.
(7690 m)
Karakoram
K2 (Godwin Austen)
28,250 ft. (8611 m)
Qaidam Basin
CHINA
Farah Rud
Kabul
Dasht-e Lut
AFGHANISTAN
Khyber Pass
Islamabad
Srinagar
Indus
Kunlun Shan
Qandahar
Helmand
Jhelum
Lahore
Plateau of Tibet
Chenab
Ravi
Multan
Kirthar Range
Sulaiman Range
PAKISTAN
Sutlej
Siahan Range
TIBET
Salween
Mekong
Chang
Qamdo
Nanda Devi
25,645 ft.
(7817 m)
Himalaya
Delhi
New Delhi
Lhasa
Brahmaputra
Namcha Barwa
Hkakabo Razi
19,296 ft.
(5881 m)
Great Indian Desert
Ganges
Jumna
NEPAL
Mt. Everest
29,028 ft.
(8848 m)
Kathmandu
Thimphu
BHUTAN
Hyderabad
Karachi
Jaipur
Lucknow
Kanpur
Ghaghara
Aravalli Range
Chambal
Naga Hills
Rann of Kutch
Varanasi
Patna
Brahmaputra
MURRAY RIDGE
Son
Chindwin
Irrawaddy
Gulf of Kutch
Ahmadabad
Vindhya Range
INDIA
Jabalpur
Narmada
Chota Nagpur Plateau
Ganges
Dhaka
Kathiawar Peninsula
INDUS CONE
Satpura Range
Chin Hills
Calcutta
BANGLADESH
Gulf of Cambay
Tapti
Nagpur
Mahanadi
Sundarbans
Chittagong
Mandalay
Deccan
BURMA
Western Ghats
Palmyras Pt.
Bombay
Eastern Ghats
Arakan Yoma
Pegu Yoma
Sittang
ARABIAN
Plateau
Godavari
Ramree I.
Cheduba I.
Bhima
Hyderabad
GANGES CONE
Tungabhadra
Kistna
Salween
Rangoon
False Divi Pt.
C. Negrais
Gulf of Martaban
SEA
BAY OF
Penner
ARABIAN
Bangalore
Madras
ANDAMAN
Andaman Islands
(India)
BENGAL
ANDAMAN
BASIN
Kaveri
Cannanore
(Laccadive)
Islands
Palk Strait
Jaffna
LACCADIVE RIDGE
BASIN
SEA
Trivandrum
C. Comorin
Gulf of Mannar
SRI LANKA
(CEYLON)
Nicobar Islands
(India)
Colombo
Pidurutalagala
8,281 ft.
(2524 m)
NINETY EAST RIDGE
Dondra Head
Sumatra
MALDIVES
Male
CHAGOS
INDIAN OCEAN
INDONESIA
0 100 200 300 400 500 MILES
0 100 200 300 400 500 KILOMETERS

Plate 6 | **Southern Asia**

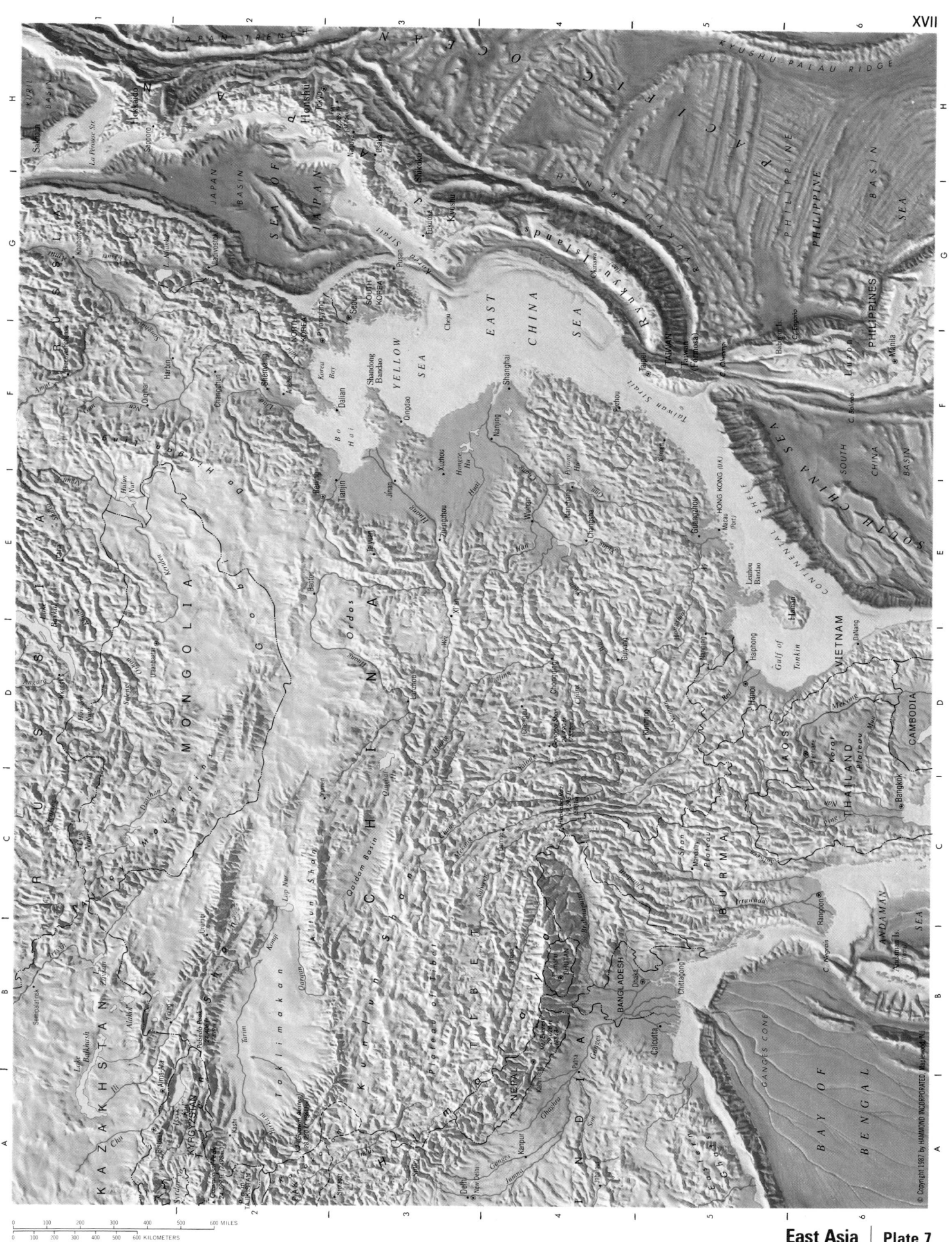

East Asia | **Plate 7**

0   100   200   300   400   500   600 MILES
0   100   200   300   400   500   600 KILOMETERS

Plate 8 | Southeast Asia

0 100 200 300 400 500 600 MILES

0 100 200 300 400 500 600 KILOMETERS

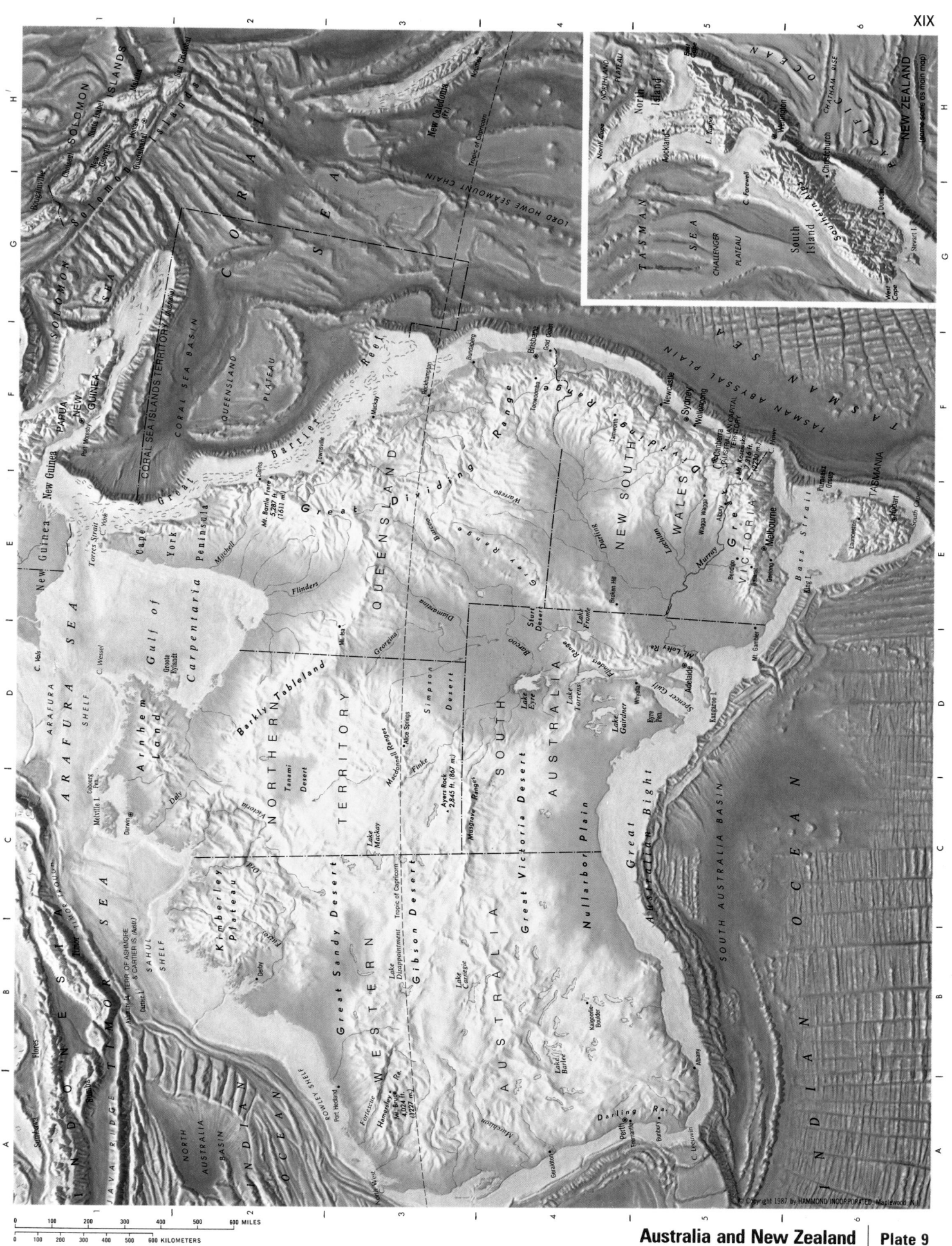

XIX

NEW ZEALAND
(same scale as main map)

Australia and New Zealand | Plate 9

© Copyright 1987 by HAMMOND INCORPORATED, Maplewood, N.J.

0 100 200 300 400 500 600 MILES

0 100 200 300 400 500 600 KILOMETERS

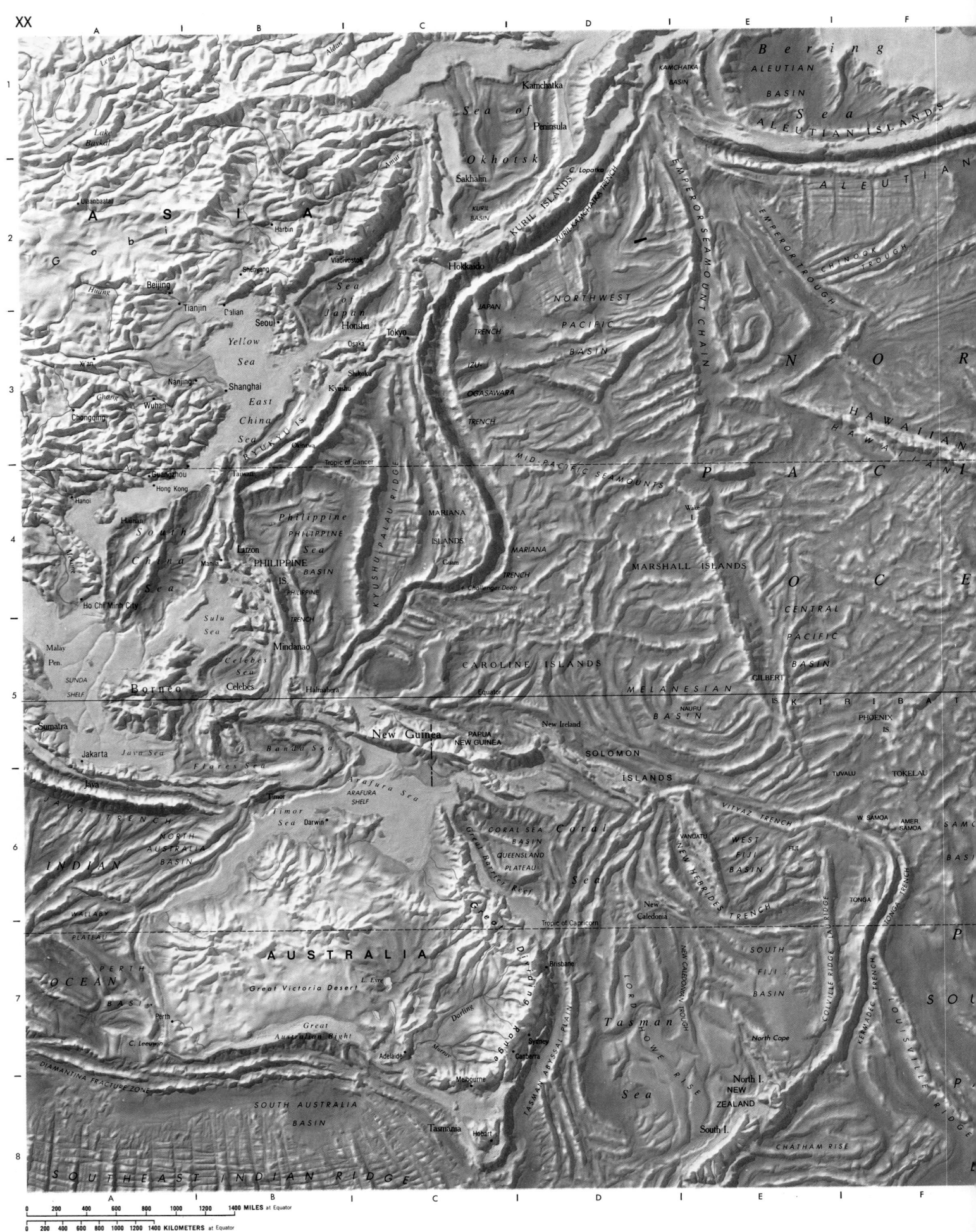

A I B I C I D I E I E I F I F

1

Lena

Aldan

Sea of

Kamchatka

Bering

ALEUTIAN

KAMCHATKA

BASIN

Okhotsk

Peninsula

KAMCHATKA

BASIN

Sea

ALEUTIAN ISLANDS

2

Lake Baykal

Amur

C. Lopatka

ALEUTIAN

EMPEROR SEAMOUNT CHAIN

CHINOOK TROUGH

EMPEROR TROUGH

A S I A

Sakhalin

KURIL
BASIN

KURIL ISLANDS

KURIL-KAMCHATKA TRENCH

Ulaanbaatar

Harbin

Hokkaido

JAPAN

NORTHWEST

N

O

R

G O B i

Shenyang

Vladivostok

Sea of Japan

TRENCH

PACIFIC

Beijing

IZU

BASIN

Huang

Tianjin

Dalian

Honshu

Tokyo

Seoul

Osaka

OGASAWARA

HAWAIIAN

3

Xi'an

Shanghai

Shikoku

TRENCH

HAWAIIAN

Nanjing

Kyushu

Wuhan

East

Chongqing

China

RYUKYU IS

MID-PACIFIC SEAMOUNTS

P

A

C

I

Guangzhou

Okinawa

Taiwan

Tropic of Cancer

Sea

Hanoi

Hong Kong

Philippine

KYUSHU PALAU RIDGE

Wake

4

Hainan

PHILIPPINE

MARIANA

South

Sea

ISLANDS

MARIANA

MARSHALL ISLANDS

O

C

E

China

Luzon

BASIN

Guam

TRENCH

PHILIPPINE

Manila

PHILIPPINE

CENTRAL

Sea

IS

Challenger Deep

PACIFIC

Ho Chi Minh City

PHILIPPINE

BASIN

MEKONG

Sulu

TRENCH

Sea

Mindanao

Malay
Pen.

*Celebes
Sea*

CAROLINE ISLANDS

GILBERT

5

SUNDA
SHELF

Borneo

Celebes

Halmahera

Equator

MELANESIAN

IS

K I R I B A T

PHOENIX
IS

Sumatra

NAURU

BASIN

Jakarta

Java Sea

Banda Sea

New Guinea

PAPUA
NEW GUINEA

New Ireland

Java

Flores Sea

SOLOMON

TUVALU

TOKELAU

JAVA TRENCH

Timor

Arafura Sea

ISLANDS

VITYAZ TRENCH

W SAMOA

AMER.
SAMOA

SAMO

6

NORTH
AUSTRALIA
BASIN

*Timor
Sea*

Darwin

ARAFURA
SHELF

CORAL SEA
BASIN

Coral

VANUATU

WEST
FIJI
BASIN

FIJI

BASI

INDIAN

QUEENSLAND
PLATEAU

Sea

NEW HEBRIDES TRENCH

TONGA

WALLABY

Great Barrier Reef

New
Caledonia

SOUTH
FIJI
BASIN

PLATEAU

Tropic of Capricorn

NEW CALEDONIA

TONGA TRENCH

OCEAN

A U S T R A L I A

Brisbane

LORD HOWE RISE

COLVILLE RIDGE

KERMADEC TRENCH

SOU

PERTH

L. Eyre

Dividing Range

7

BASIN

Great Victoria Desert

Darling

Tasman

North Cape

LOUISVILLE RIDGE

Perth

*Great
Australian Bight*

Sydney

Canberra

TASMAN ABYSSAL PLAIN

C. Leeuwin

Murray

Adelaide

Sea

North I.
NEW
ZEALAND

DIAMANTINA FRACTURE ZONE

Melbourne

South I.

SOUTH AUSTRALIA
BASIN

Tasmania

Hobart

CHATHAM RISE

8

S O U T H E A S T   I N D I A N   R I D G E

A I B I C I D I E I F

0   200   400   600   800   1000   1200   1400 **MILES** at Equator

0   200   400   600   800   1000   1200   1400 **KILOMETERS** at Equator

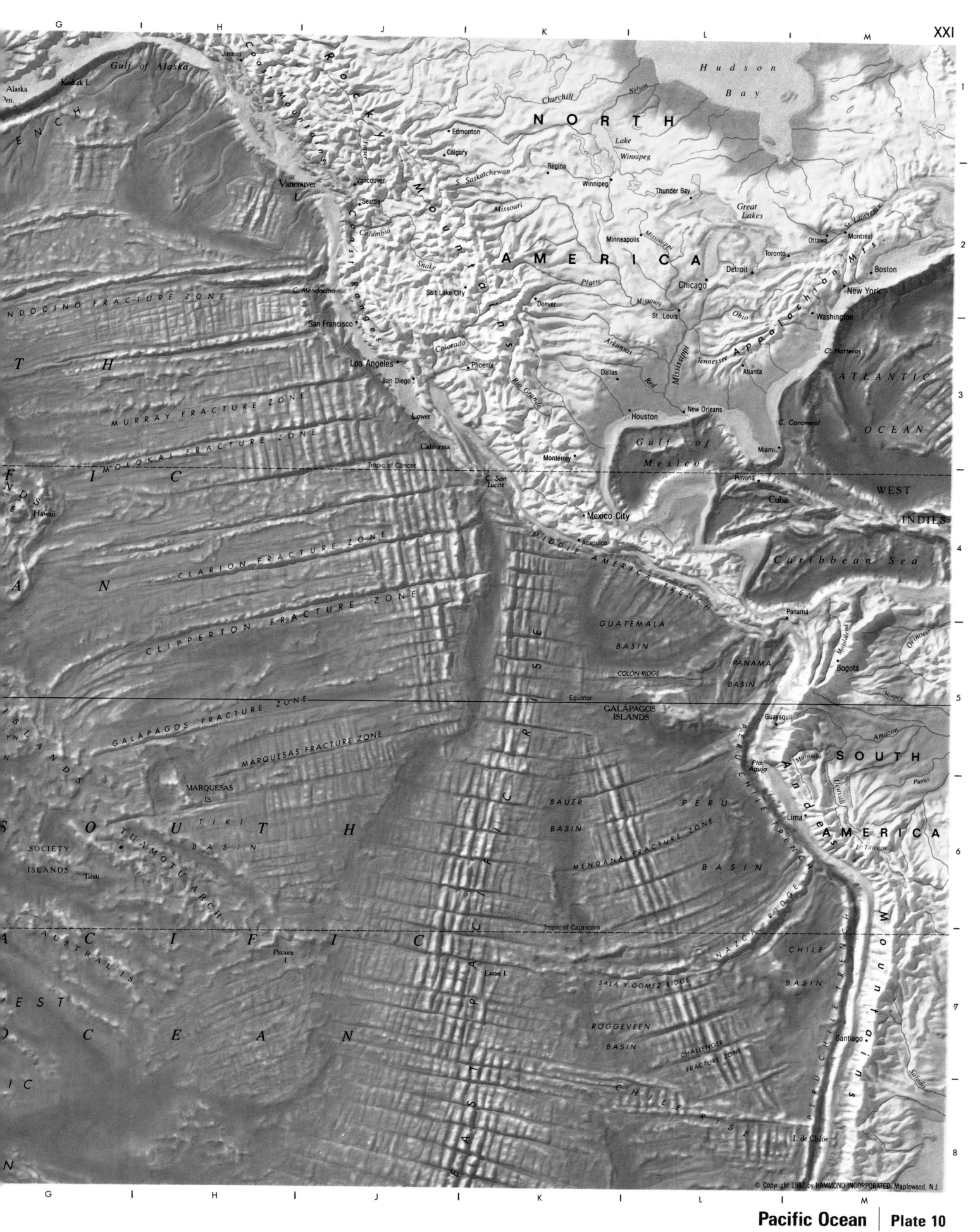

G   H   I   H   J   K   I   L   I   M   1

Gulf of Alaska

Kodiak I.   Juneau   Coast Mountains   R O C K Y

Alaska Pen.

FRENCH

Vancouver I.   Vancouver   Fraser   Mountains

Seattle   Columbia   Coast Ranges

Snake

NDOCINO FRACTURE ZONE   C. Mendocino   Salt Lake City

San Francisco   Colorado

T   H   MURRAY FRACTURE ZONE   Los Angeles   Phoenix

MOLOKAI FRACTURE ZONE   San Diego

I   Lower   Tropic of Cancer

FDS   California   C. San Lucas

Hawaii   CLARION FRACTURE ZONE   Mexico City

A   N   Acapulco

A   CLIPPERTON FRACTURE ZONE   MIDDLE AMERICA TRENCH

GUATEMALA   BASIN

COLÓN RIDGE

Equator   GALÁPAGOS FRACTURE ZONE   GALÁPAGOS ISLANDS

ISLANDS   MARQUESAS FRACTURE ZONE

MARQUESAS IS.   BAUER   PERU

S   O   U   T   H   TIKI   BASIN   BASIN

SOCIETY   TUAMOTU ARCH   BASIN   MENDAÑA FRACTURE ZONE   BASIN

ISLANDS   Tahiti

A   C   I   F   I   C   Tropic of Capricorn

AUSTRALIS   SALA Y GOMEZ RIDGE   CHILE

EST   Pitcairn I.   Easter I.   BASIN

ROGGEVEEN

OCEAN   E   A   N   BASIN   CHALLENGER

FRACTURE ZONE

IC   CHILE RISE

N

NORTH

Edmonton

Calgary   Lake Winnipeg

Regina   Winnipeg   Thunder Bay

S. Saskatchewan

Missouri   Minneapolis   Mississippi

AMERICA   Platte   Chicago   Detroit   Toronto

Denver   Missouri   St. Louis

St. Louis   Ohio

Arkansas   Tennessee   Atlanta

Dallas   Red   Mississippi

Rio Grande   Houston   New Orleans

Monterrey   Gulf of   Mexico

Havana

Cuba

Caribbean   Sea

Panamá

PANAMA   Bogotá

BASIN

Guayaquil

Pta.   SOUTH

Aguja   Marañón

Lima   AMERICA

L. Titicaca

Santiago

I. de Chiloé

Churchill   Nelson   Hudson   Bay

Lake Winnipeg

Great   Lakes   St. Lawrence

Ottawa   Montréal

Toronto   Appalachian Mts.   Boston

New York

Washington

C. Hatteras

ATLANTIC

OCEAN

WEST

INDIES

Orinoco

Vaupés

Amazon

Ucayali   Purus

Andes   Mountains

WALCH   RIDGE

PERU-CHILE TRENCH

A   n   d   e   s   M   o   u   n   t   a   i   n   s

Salado

© Copyright 1987 by HAMMOND INCORPORATED, Maplewood, N.J.

G   H   I   H   J   K   I   L   I   M

Pacific Ocean | **Plate 10**

A
B
C
D
E
F
1
2
3
4
5
6
7
8
IRELAND
UNITED KINGDOM
NETH.
Berlin
GER.
POLAND
BELARUS
RUSSIA
CELTIC SHELF
BELG.
Paris
WEST GERMANY
CZECH.
UKRAINE
KAZAKHSTAN
MID-ATLANTIC RIDGE
ATLANTIC
BISCAY ABYSSAL PLAIN
Bay of Biscay
FRANCE
SW.
AUST.
HUNGARY
ROMANIA
Dnieper
Don
Volga
Ural
ARAL SEA
CASPIAN SEA
Caucasus
BLACK SEA
AZORES-BISCAY RISE
OCEAN
Alps
Danube
YUGOSLAVIA
BULGARIA
Istanbul
TURKM.
Madrid
PORTUGAL
SPAIN
Corsica
Sardinia
Rome
ITALY
ADRIATIC SEA
ALB.
GREECE
AEGEAN SEA
TURKEY
Balearic Is.
MEDITERRANEAN SEA
Algiers
Annaba
Sicily
Crete
CYPRUS
SYRIA
Tigris
Tehran
IRAN
Str. of Gibraltar
Tangier
Oran
Tunis
MALTA
TUNISIA
Sfax
LEBANON
IRAQ
ASIA
MADEIRA ABYSSAL PLAIN
Madeira (Port.)
Rabat
Casablanca
MOROCCO
Atlas Mountains
Jeb. Toubkal 13,665 ft. (4165 m.)
Tripoli
Benghazi
Gulf of Sidra
Alexandria
ISRAEL
Port Said
Suez Canal
Sinai Pen.
JORDAN
Euphrates
KUWAIT
Canary Is. (Sp.)
Las Palmas
Wadi Dra
Laayoune
SAHARIAN SEAMOUNTS
ALGERIA
LIBYA
Libyan Desert
Cairo
EGYPT
Asyût
Nile
SAUDI
Persian Gulf
QATAR
WESTERN SAHARA
Tanezrouft
Ahaggar
Aswân
Tropic of Cancer
U.A.E.
ARABIA
Sahara
Tamanrasset
Tibesti
Lake Nasser
RED SEA
Rub' al Khali
MAURITANIA
CAPE VERDE PLATEAU
Nouakchott
L. Nubia
Nubian Desert
Port Sudan
YEMEN ARAB REP.
PEOP. DEM. REP. YEMEN
MALI
Timbuktu
Niger
NIGER
Bodélé Depression
Senegal
Dakar
SENEGAL
GAMBIA
Banjul
CHAD
L. Chad
Khartoum
SUDAN
El Fasher
El Obeid
Blue Nile
White Nile
Asmara
Ras Dashen 15,157 ft. (4620 m.)
DJIBOUTI
Gulf of Aden
Ras Aser
Bissau
GUINEA-BISSAU
Bamako
BURKINA FASO
Niamey
Ouagadougou
Kano
N'Djamena
Ethiopian Highlands
Addis Ababa
ETHIOPIA
GUINEA
Conakry
Freetown
SIERRA LEONE
GHANA
TOGO
BENIN
NIGERIA
IVORY COAST
Bouaké
L. Volta
Porto Novo
Ibadan
Lagos
Benue
Sarh
Sudd
SIERRA LEONE RISE
Monrovia
LIBERIA
Yamoussoukro
Kumasi
Accra
Lomé
CENTRAL AFRICAN REPUBLIC
CAMEROON
Wabi Shebelle
SOMALIA
SIERRA LEONE BASIN
Abidjan
Malabo
Bioko
Cameroon 13,350 ft. (4069 m.)
Yaoundé
Bangui
Ubangi
Bomu
Uele
Juba
L. Turkana
GUINEA BASIN
Gulf of Guinea
EQUAT. GUINEA
SÃO TOMÉ E PRINCIPE
Congo
L. Mobutu Sese Seko
UGANDA
KENYA
Kisangani
Margherita 16,795 ft. (5119 m.)
Kampala
Kenya 17,058 ft. (5199 m.)
Mogadishu
Equator
Libreville
Stanley Falls
ROMANCHE FRACTURE ZONE
GABON
Mbandaka
L. Victoria
Nairobi
SOMALI BASIN
C. Lopez
Annobon (Equat. Guinea)
ZAIRE
RWANDA
Kigali
BURUNDI
Bukavu
Bujumbura
Kilimanjaro 19,340 ft. (5895 m.)
Mombasa
Lualaba
Brazzaville
Kinshasa
Tanga
CABINDA (Angola)
TANZANIA
Zanzibar
CONGO CANYON
Kananga
Lake Tanganyika
Dar es Salaam
AMIRANTE TRENCH
ASCENSION FRACTURE ZONE
Ascension (St. Helena)
Kasai
Katanga
Lake Mweru
Luanda
Malange
Lubumbashi
Ruvuma
C. Delgado
ATLANTIC
ANGOLA
ANGOLA
COMOROS
Kitwe
MALAWI
Lake Nyasa
Huambo
ANGOLA ABYSSAL PLAIN
ZAMBIA
Lilongwe
Zomba
Zambezi
Lusaka
Cunene
Cubango
Nampula
MADAGASCAR
Lake Kariba
Livingstone
Victoria Falls
Harare
Mozambique Channel
ST. HELENA FRACTURE ZONE
St. Helena (U.K.)
BASIN
C. Fria
Etosha Pan
ZIMBABWE
MOZAMBIQUE
Toamasina
Antananarivo
Beira
Makgadikgadi Salt Pan
Bulawayo
NAMIBIA
Windhoek
BOTSWANA
Namib Desert
Kalahari Desert
Limpopo
MASCARENE PLAIN
OCEAN
Tropic of Capricorn
Walvis Bay (S. Afr.)
(SOUTH-WEST AFRICA)
Gaborone
Pretoria
Maputo
Mbabane
SWAZILAND
WALVIS RIDGE
Johannesburg
Vaal
C. Vohimena
MADAGASCAR BASIN
RIO GRANDE FRACTURE ZONE
NAMIBIA ABYSSAL PLAIN
CONTINENTAL SHELF
Orange
SOUTH AFRICA
LESOTHO
Maseru
Drakensberg
Durban
MOZAMBIQUE PLATEAU
MOZAMBIQUE BASIN
MADAGASCAR RIDGE
Great Karoo
East London
Cape Town
C. of Good Hope
CAPE BASIN
C. Agulhas
Port Elizabeth
INDIAN OCEAN
SOUTHWEST INDIAN RIDGE
Tristan da Cunha (St. Helena)
TRISTAN DA CUNHA FRACTURE ZONE
AGULHAS RIDGE
AGULHAS PLATEAU
MID-ATLANTIC RIDGE
© Copyright 1987 by HAMMOND INCORPORATED, Maplewood, N.J.
0
200
400
600
800
1000 MILES
0
200
400
600
800
1000 KILOMETERS

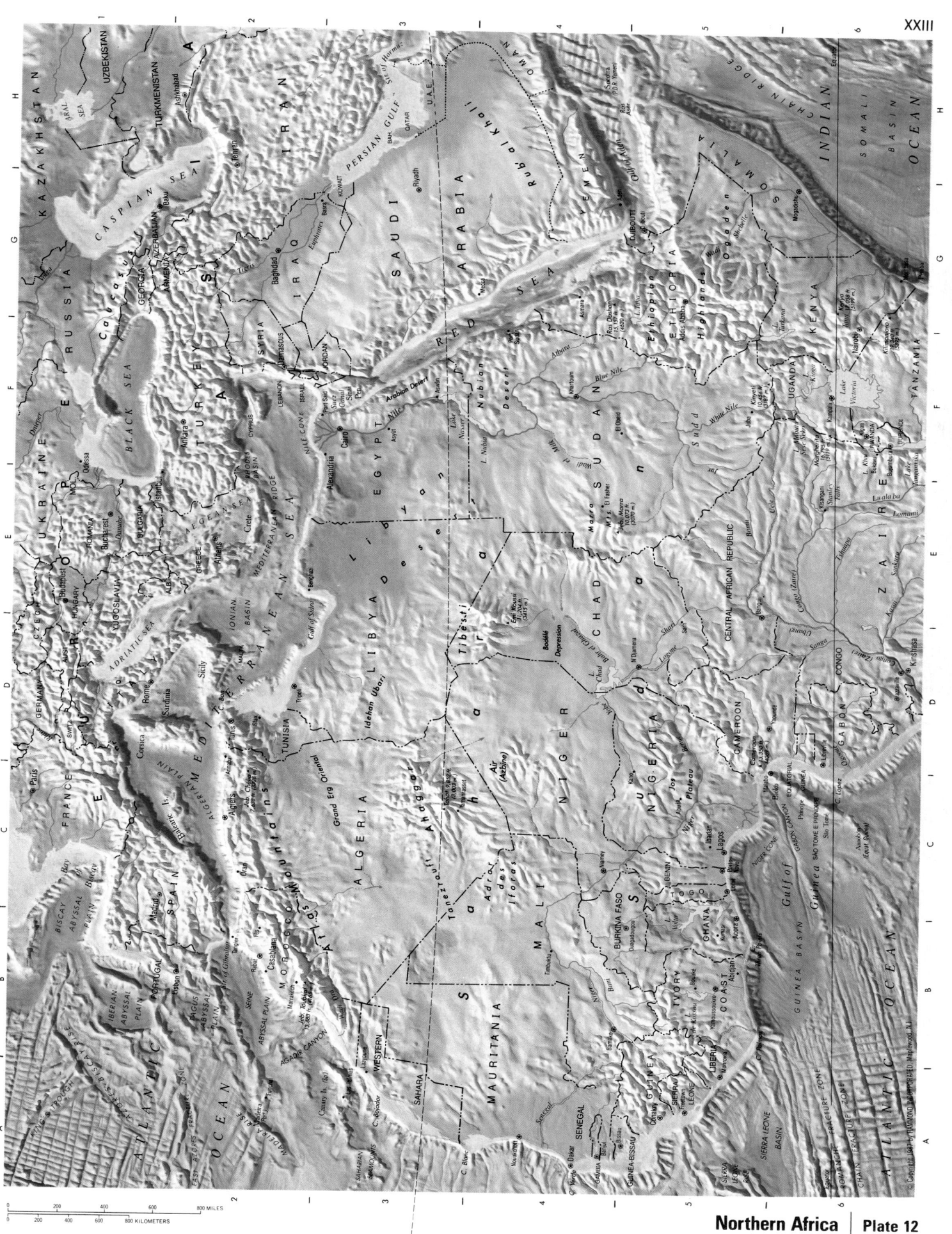

Northern Africa | Plate 12

0   200   400   600   800 MILES
0   200   400   600   800 KILOMETERS

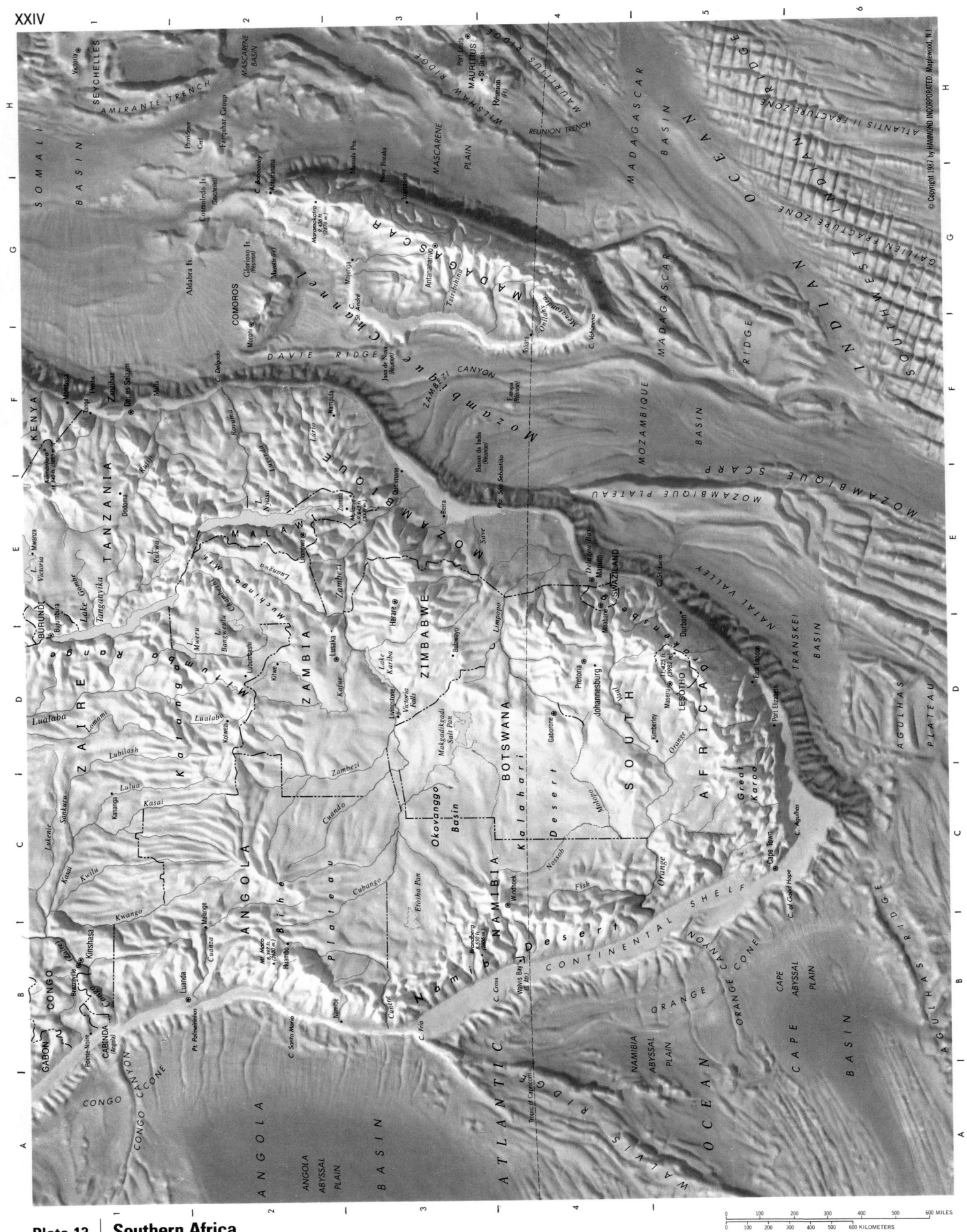

Plate 13 | **Southern Africa**

0 100 200 300 400 500 600 MILES
0 100 200 300 400 500 600 KILOMETERS

South America | Plate 14

200   400   600   800 MILES

200   400   600   800 KILOMETERS

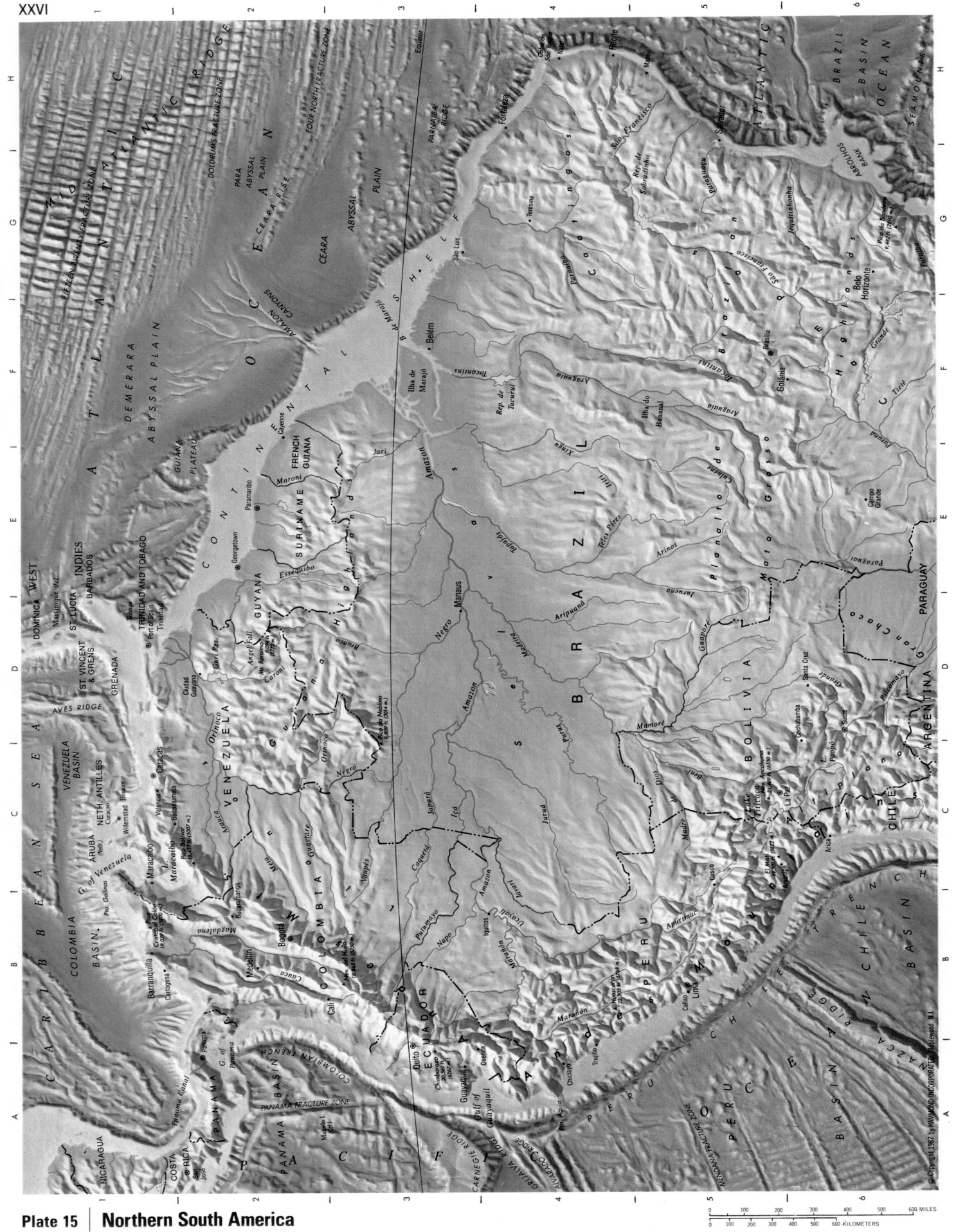

Plate 15 | **Northern South America**

0   100   200   300   400   500   600 MILES
0   100   200   300   400   500   600 KILOMETERS

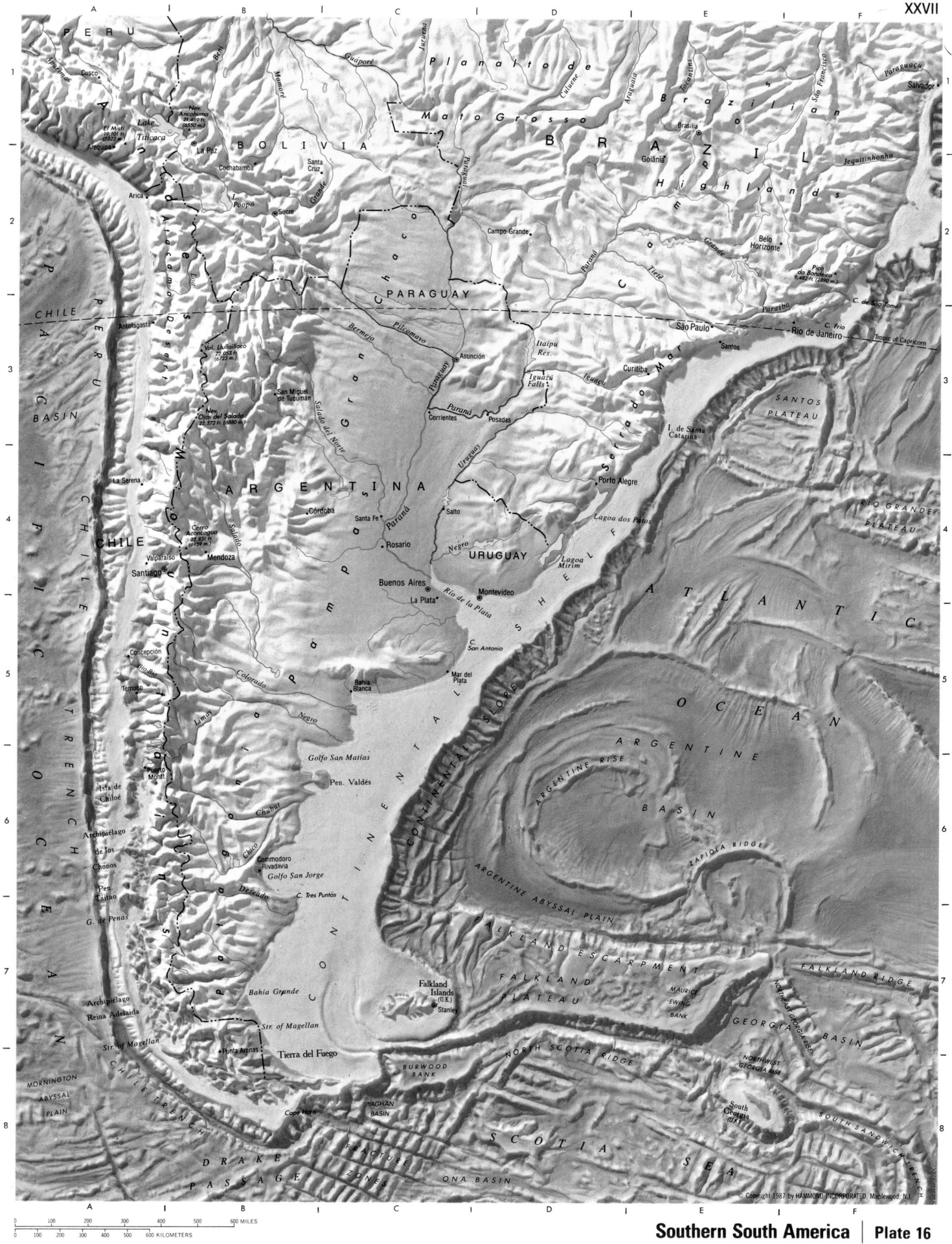

A | B | C | D | E | F

1

PERU

Cusco

El Misti
19,101 ft.
(5822 m.)

Nev. Ancohuma
21,489 ft.
(6550 m.)

Arequipa

Lake
Titicaca

La Paz

BOLIVIA

Cochabamba

Santa
Cruz

Arica

L. Poopó

Sucre

Antofagasta

Vol. Llullaillaco
22,058 ft.
(6723 m.)

Nev. del Salado
22,572 ft. (5880 m.)

San Miguel
de Tucumán

La Serena

Cerro Aconcagua
22,831 ft.
(6959 m.)

CHILE

Valparaíso

Mendoza

Santiago

Concepción

Río Bío

Temuco

Isla de
Chiloé

Archipiélago
de los
Chonos

Pen.
Taitao

G. de Penas

Archipiélago
Reina Adelaida

Str. of Magellan

Punta Arenas

MORNINGTON
ABYSSAL
PLAIN

Cape Horn

DRAKE
PASSAGE

FRACTURE
ZONES

ONA BASIN

YAGHAN
BASIN

BURWOOD
BANK

Tierra del Fuego

SCOTIA SEA

NORTH SCOTIA RIDGE

Bahía Grande

C. Tres Puntas

Deseado

Golfo San Jorge

Commodoro
Rivadavia

Chico

Chubut

Pen. Valdés

Golfo San Matías

Limay

Negro

Colorado

Bahía
Blanca

Mar del
Plata

Buenos Aires

La Plata

C.
San Antonio

Río de la Plata

Montevideo

URUGUAY

Lagoa
Mirim

Lagoa dos Patos

Negro

Salto

Rosario

Santa Fe

Córdoba

Paraná

Salado del Norte

Salado

ARGENTINA

Corrientes

Paraná

Posadas

Uruguay

Porto Alegre

Paraná

Asunción

PARAGUAY

Pilcomayo

Bermejo

Gran Chaco

Grande

Pampa

Paraguay

Iguazú
Falls

Iguaçu

Itaipú
Res.

Curitiba

I. de Santa
Catarina

São Paulo

Santos

Rio de Janeiro

Tropic of Capricorn

C. Frio

C. de São Tomé

Paraíba

Pico
da Bandeira
9,482 ft. (2890 m.)

Belo
Horizonte

Campo Grande

Mato Grosso

Planalto de

Guaporé

Mamoré

Beni

Apurímac

Pacaguaçu

Salvador

São Francisco

Jequitinhonha

BRAZIL

Brazilian

Highlands

Brasília

Goiânia

Grande

Tietê

Araguaia

Tocantins

Culuene

Jurueña

Serra do Mar

SANTOS
PLATEAU

RIO GRANDE
PLATEAU

ATLANTIC

OCEAN

ARGENTINE RISE

ARGENTINE

BASIN

ZAPIOLA RIDGE

ARGENTINE ABYSSAL PLAIN

CONTINENTAL SLOPE

CONTINENTAL SHELF

FALKLAND ESCARPMENT

FALKLAND
PLATEAU

Falkland
Islands
(U.K.)

Stanley

MAURICE
EWING
BANK

FALKLAND RIDGE

GEORGIA RISE

NORTHEAST GEORGIA BASIN

NORTHWEST
GEORGIA RISE

South
Georgia
(U.K.)

SOUTH SANDWICH TRENCH

SOUTH ATLANTIC
PARU
CHILE

PERU-CHILE TRENCH

PACIFIC OCEAN

PERU BASIN

Puerto
Montt

0 100 200 300 400 500 600 MILES

0 100 200 300 400 500 600 KILOMETERS

© Copyright 1987 by HAMMOND INCORPORATED, Maplewood, N.J.

Southern South America | Plate 16

© Copyright 1987 by HAMMOND INCORPORATED, Maplewood, N.J.

Plate 17 | **North America**

MILES					
0	200	400	600	800	1000 MILES
0	200	400	600	800	1000 KILOMETERS

ARCTIC OCEAN
GREENLAND
(Denmark)
ICELAND
Reykjavík
DENMARK STRAIT
IRMINGER BASIN
REYKJANES
LABRADOR SEA
LABRADOR BASIN
DAVIS STRAIT
BAFFIN BAY
Baffin Island
Arctic Circle
QUEEN ELIZABETH ISLANDS
Ellesmere Island
Axel Heiberg I.
Devon I.
Bylot I.
Brodeur Pen.
Gulf of Boothia
Somerset I.
Boothia Pen.
Bathurst I.
Ellef Ringnes I.
N. Mag. Pole
Pr. of Wales I.
M'Clintock Chan.
Parry Channel
Melville I.
Prince Patrick I.
Victoria Island
Cambridge Bay
Banks Island
Amundsen Gulf
CANADA BASIN
BEAUFORT SEA
BEAUFORT SHELF
NORTHWIND RIDGE
Pt. Barrow
CHUKCHI SEA
Bering Strait
RUSSIA
Nome
Brooks Range
UNITED STATES
ALASKA
Alaska Range
Fairbanks
Anchorage
Tanana
Yukon
Gulf of Alaska
Alexander Archipelago
Queen Charlotte Is.
Prince Rupert
Vancouver I.
Vancouver
Victoria
Seattle
Portland
CASCADIA BASIN
PACIFIC OCEAN
Coast Mts.
Coast Ranges
C. Mendocino
YUKON TERRITORY
BRITISH COLUMBIA
Dawson
Whitehorse
Juneau
Williston L.
Prince George
Fraser
Kelowna
Columbia
Rocky Mountains
Inuvik
Mackenzie
Great Bear Lake
Great Slave Lake
Yellowknife
Coppermine
Liard
Ft. Nelson
Peace
Athabasca
L. Athabasca
ALBERTA
NORTHWEST TERRITORIES
SASKATCHEWAN
MANITOBA
Edmonton
Calgary
Lethbridge
Swift Current
Saskatoon
Prince Albert
Regina
Brandon
Winnipeg
L. Winnipeg
L. Manitoba
L. of the Woods
Reindeer L.
So. Indian L.
Nelson
Churchill
Back
Dubawnt
Kazan
Rankin Inlet
Laurentian Plateau
HUDSON BAY
Coats I.
Southampton I.
Mansel I.
Belcher Is.
James Bay
Akimiski I.
Foxe Basin
Foxe Pen.
Melville Pen.
Pt. Charles I.
Hudson Strait
Frobisher Bay
Cumberland Sd.
Cumberland Pen.
Ungava Peninsula
Ungava Bay
C. Chidley
Labrador
NEWFOUNDLAND
Goose Bay
Smallwood Res.
Churchill
Caniapiscau
La Grande
Rupert
L. Mistassini
L. St-Jean
Peribonca
QUÉBEC
ONTARIO
Rouyn
Timmins
Sudbury
Sault Ste. Marie
Thunder Bay
Lake Superior
Lake Huron
Lake Michigan
L. Erie
L. Ontario
Georgian Bay
L. Nipigon
Albany
Abitibi
Severn
Toronto
Hamilton
Niagara Falls
Detroit
Windsor
Cleveland
Pittsburgh
Chicago
Milwaukee
Minneapolis
Mississippi
Missouri
Yellowstone
Red
Snake
Great Salt Lake
UNITED STATES
Ottawa
Montréal
Québec
St. Lawrence
Hudson
New York
Philadelphia
Boston
C. Cod
Bay of Fundy
Saint John
Fredericton
NEW BR.
Gaspé Pen.
Sept-Îles
Île d'Anticosti
Gulf of St. Lawrence
P.E.I.
Charlottetown
Halifax
NOVA SCOTIA
C. Sable
Sable I.
Cape Breton I.
Newfoundland
St. John's
C. Race
GRAND BANKS OF NEWFOUNDLAND
CONTINENTAL SHELF
ATLANTIC OCEAN
Nuuk
C. Farewell
0 100 200 300 400 500 600 MILES
0 100 200 300 400 500 600 KILOMETERS
© Copyright 1987 by HAMMOND INCORPORATED, Maplewood, N.J.

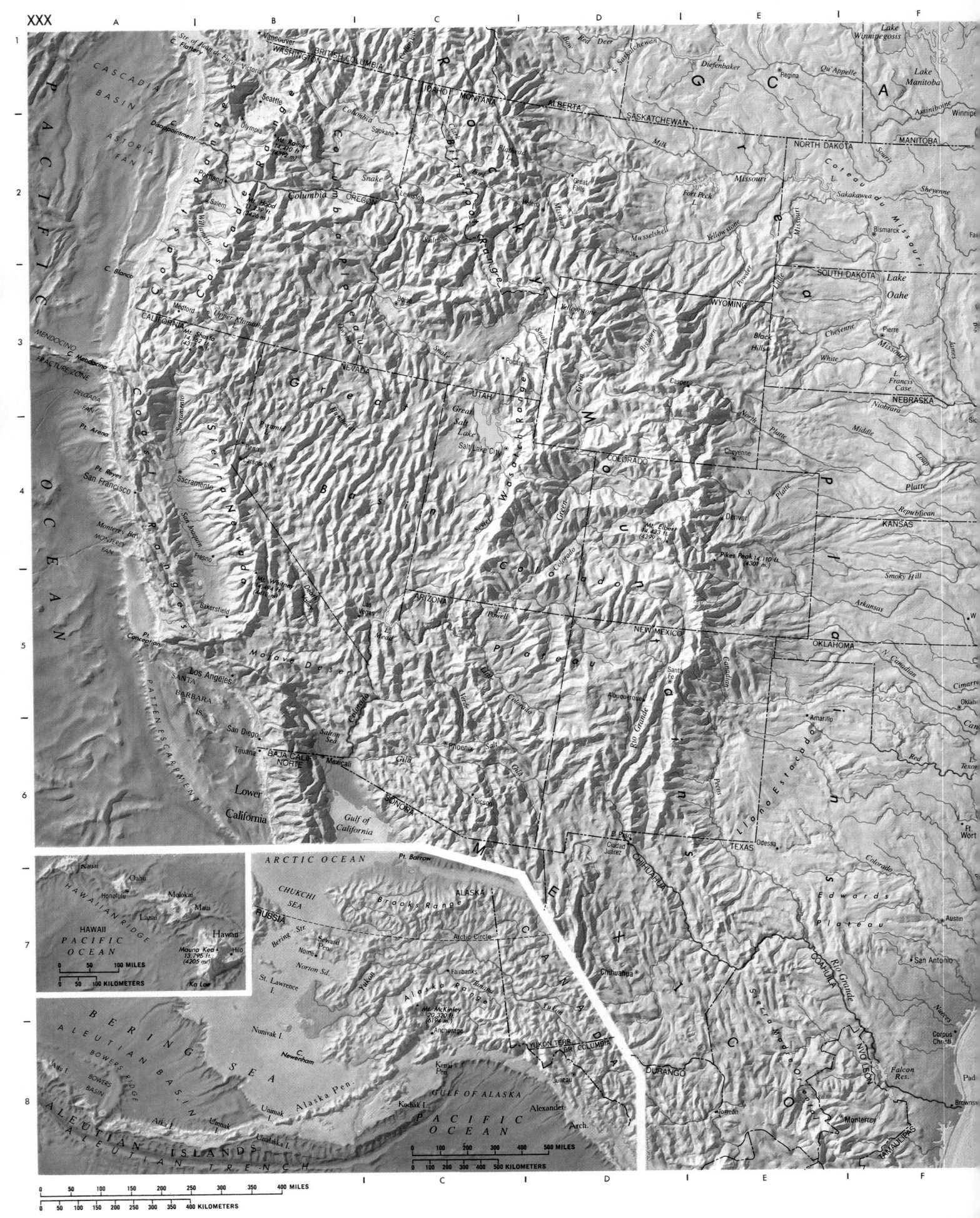
PACIFIC OCEAN
CASCADIA BASIN
ASTORIA FAN
Str. of Juan de Fuca
C. Flattery
Victoria
Vancouver
BRITISH COLUMBIA
WASHINGTON
Seattle
Olympia
C. Disappointment
Mt. Rainier 14,410 ft. (4392 m.)
Portland
Salem
Mt. Hood 11,239 ft. (3426 m.)
Willamette
Columbia
Snake
Spokane
Lewiston
OREGON
Columbia Plateau
Cascade Range
Coast Ranges
C. Blanco
Medford
Upper Klamath L.
CALIFORNIA
Mt. Shasta 14,162 ft. (4317 m.)
MENDOCINO FRACTURE ZONE
C. Mendocino
DELGADA FAN
Pt. Arena
Sacramento
Sierra Nevada
Pyramid L.
Reno
Carson City
Pt. Reyes
San Francisco
Monterey Bay
MONTEREY FAN
San Joaquin
Fresno
Mt. Whitney 14,494 ft. (4418 m.)
Death Valley
Bakersfield
Pt. Conception
Los Angeles
SANTA BARBARA IS.
PATTEN ESCARPMENT
San Diego
Tijuana
BAJA CALIF. NORTE
Mexicali
Salton Sea
Mojave Desert
Lower California
Gulf of California
SONORA
Las Vegas
L. Mead
NEVADA
Great Basin
Humboldt
UTAH
Great Salt Lake
Salt Lake City
Wasatch Range
Sevier
IDAHO
MONTANA
Clark Fork
Flathead L.
Bitterroot Range
Salmon
Boise
Snake
Owyhee
Pocatello
Rocky Mountains
Great Falls
Helena
Missouri
Musselshell
Yellowstone
Billings
Fort Peck L.
Milk
ALBERTA
SASKATCHEWAN
Bow
Red Deer
S. Saskatchewan
L. Diefenbaker
Regina
Qu'Appelle
Lake Winnipegosis
Lake Manitoba
Assiniboine
Winnipeg
MANITOBA
NORTH DAKOTA
Souris
Coteau du Missouri
L. Sakakawea
Sheyenne
Bismarck
SOUTH DAKOTA
Lake Oahe
Little Missouri
Powder
WYOMING
Yellowstone L.
Bighorn
Green
Casper
Black Hills
Cheyenne
Pierre
Missouri
White
James
L. Francis Case
NEBRASKA
Niobrara
North Platte
Middle Loup
Platte
Cheyenne
COLORADO
Denver
S. Platte
Republican
KANSAS
Mt. Elbert 14,433 ft. (4399 m.)
Pikes Peak 14,110 ft. (4301 m.)
Smoky Hill
Arkansas
Colorado Plateau
Colorado
Powell
ARIZONA
Little Colorado
Verde
Phoenix
Salt
Gila
Tucson
NEW MEXICO
Santa Fe
Albuquerque
Rio Grande
Canadian
Pecos
OKLAHOMA
N. Canadian
Cimarron
Oklahoma
Amarillo
Llano Estacado
Red
Great Plains
El Paso
Ciudad Juárez
TEXAS
Odessa
Ft. Worth
Colorado
Edwards Plateau
Austin
San Antonio
Nueces
Corpus Christi
Falcon Res.
Brownsville
CHIHUAHUA
Chihuahua
COAHUILA
Rio Grande
NUEVO LEON
Monterrey
TAMAULIPAS
Sierra Madre Oriental
DURANGO
Torreón
MEXICO
Kauai
Oahu
Honolulu
Molokai
Maui
Lanai
HAWAIIAN RIDGE
HAWAII
PACIFIC OCEAN
Hawaii
Hilo
Mauna Kea 13,796 ft. (4205 m.)
Ka Lae
0 50 100 MILES
0 50 100 KILOMETERS
ARCTIC OCEAN
Pt. Barrow
CHUKCHI SEA
Brooks Range
ALASKA
RUSSIA
Bering Str.
Seward Pen.
Nome
Arctic Circle
Norton Sd.
St. Lawrence I.
Yukon
Fairbanks
Tanana
Alaska Range
Mt. McKinley 20,320 ft. (6194 m.)
Anchorage
Nunivak I.
C. Newenham
CANADA
YUKON TERR.
BR. COLUMBIA
Juneau
Kenai Pen.
BERING SEA
ALEUTIAN BASIN
BOWERS RIDGE
BOWERS BASIN
Attu I.
Alaska Pen.
Unimak I.
Umnak I.
Atka I.
Unalaska I.
Kodiak I.
GULF OF ALASKA
Alexander Arch.
PACIFIC OCEAN
ALEUTIAN ISLANDS
ALEUTIAN TRENCH
0 100 200 300 400 500 MILES
0 100 200 300 400 500 KILOMETERS
0 50 100 150 200 250 300 350 400 MILES
0 50 100 150 200 250 300 350 400 KILOMETERS

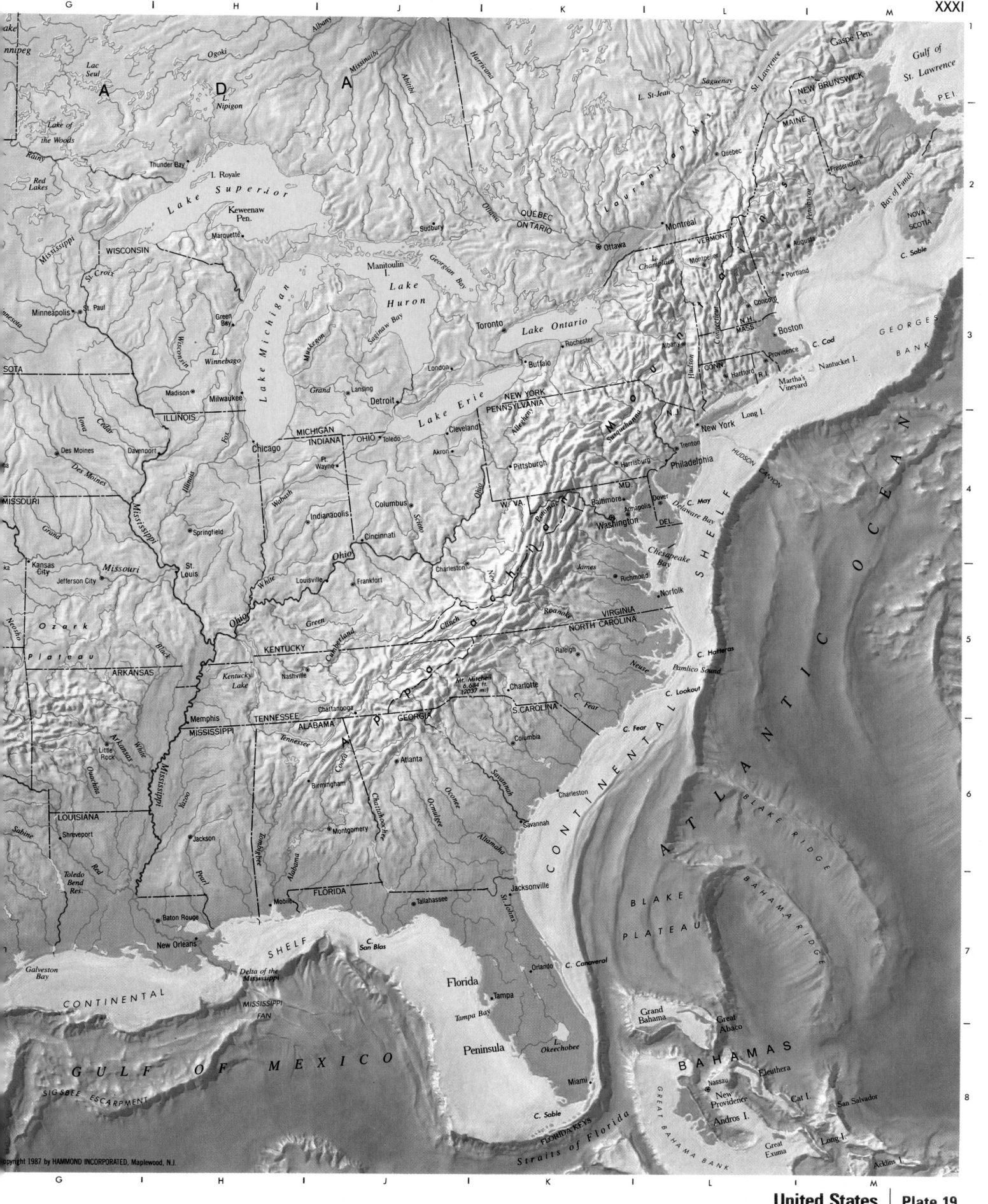
G
H
J
K
L
M
C A N A D A
Lac Seul
Ogoki
Albany
Missinaibi
Abitibi
Harricana
L. Nipigon
Lake of the Woods
Rainy
Red Lakes
Thunder Bay
I. Royale
Lake Superior
Keweenaw Pen.
Marquette
Mississippi
WISCONSIN
St. Croix
Minneapolis
St. Paul
Green Bay
Wisconsin
L. Winnebago
Madison
Milwaukee
Lake Michigan
Manitoulin I.
Lake Huron
Georgian Bay
Saginaw Bay
Muskegon
Grand
Lansing
Detroit
London
Sudbury
Ottawa
QUÉBEC
ONTARIO
Ottawa
Montréal
Québec
L. St-Jean
Saguenay
St. Lawrence
Laurentian Mts.
Gaspé Pen.
Gulf of St. Lawrence
NEW BRUNSWICK
P.E.I.
MAINE
Fredericton
Penobscot
Augusta
Bay of Fundy
NOVA SCOTIA
C. Sable
Portland
VERMONT
L. Champlain
Montpelier
Concord
N.H.
MASS.
Boston
C. Cod
GEORGES BANK
Providence
R.I.
CONN.
Hartford
Nantucket I.
Martha's Vineyard
Albany
Hudson
Connecticut
Toronto
Lake Ontario
Rochester
Buffalo
Lake Erie
NEW YORK
PENNSYLVANIA
N.J.
New York
Long I.
Allegheny
Susquehanna
Trenton
Philadelphia
Harrisburg
HUDSON CANYON
Pittsburgh
Cleveland
Akron
MICHIGAN
INDIANA
OHIO
Toledo
Ft. Wayne
Chicago
ILLINOIS
SOTA
Iowa
Cedar
Des Moines
Davenport
Fox
Illinois
Wabash
MISSOURI
Columbus
Scioto
Ohio
Indianapolis
Springfield
Cincinnati
Grand
Kansas City
Jefferson City
Missouri
St. Louis
Ohio
White
Louisville
Frankfort
Charleston
New
W. VA.
MD.
Baltimore
Annapolis
Dover
DEL.
Washington
Potomac
C. May
Delaware Bay
Chesapeake Bay
James
Richmond
Norfolk
SHELF
Neosho
Ozark
Plateau
Black
Green
Clinch
Roanoke
VIRGINIA
NORTH CAROLINA
KENTUCKY
ARKANSAS
Cumberland
Kentucky Lake
Nashville
Raleigh
C. Hatteras
Neuse
Pamlico Sound
C. Lookout
Mt. Mitchell 6,684 ft. (2037 m.)
Charlotte
Appalachian Mountains
Memphis
TENNESSEE
Chattanooga
GEORGIA
S.CAROLINA
C. Fear
MISSISSIPPI
ALABAMA
Tennessee
Columbia
C. Fear
Arkansas
Little Rock
White
Ouachita
Mississippi
Yazoo
Coosa
Atlanta
Birmingham
Chattahoochee
Ocmulgee
Oconee
Savannah
Charleston
Savannah
LOUISIANA
Sabine
Shreveport
Jackson
Montgomery
Tombigbee
Alabama
Altamaha
CONTINENTAL
ATLANTIC OCEAN
BLAKE RIDGE
Toledo Bend Res.
Red
Pearl
FLORIDA
Jacksonville
St. Johns
Tallahassee
Mobile
BAHAMA RIDGE
BLAKE PLATEAU
Baton Rouge
New Orleans
SHELF
C. San Blas
Orlando
C. Canaveral
Galveston Bay
Delta of the Mississippi
Florida
Tampa
Tampa Bay
CONTINENTAL
MISSISSIPPI FAN
Grand Bahama
Great Abaco
Peninsula
L. Okeechobee
BAHAMAS
GULF OF MEXICO
Miami
Eleuthera
Nassau
New Providence
Cat I.
San Salvador
SIGSBEE ESCARPMENT
Andros I.
GREAT BAHAMA BANK
C. Sable
FLORIDA KEYS
Straits of Florida
Great Exuma
Long I.
Acklins I.
opyright 1987 by HAMMOND INCORPORATED, Maplewood, N.J.
1
2
3
4
5
6
7
8

ATLANTIC OCEAN
PACIFIC OCEAN
Gulf of Mexico
CARIBBEAN SEA
UNITED STATES
MEXICO
MIDDLE AMERICA
GREATER ANTILLES
LESSER ANTILLES
West Indies
BAHAMAS
CUBA
Hispaniola
VENEZUELA
COLOMBIA
BRAZIL
GUYANA
PANAMA
COSTA RICA
NICARAGUA
HONDURAS
EL SALVADOR
GUATEMALA
BELIZE
HAITI
DOMINICAN REPUBLIC
JAMAICA
PUERTO RICO (U.S.)
HATTERAS ABYSSAL PLAIN
NARES ABYSSAL PLAIN
BLAKE RIDGE
BAHAMA RIDGE
BLAKE PLATEAU
BERMUDA RISE
CONTINENTAL SHELF
SIGSBEE DEEP
SIGSBEE ESCARPMENT
MISSISSIPPI FAN
CAMPECHE BANK
YUCATAN BASIN
CAYMAN TRENCH
NICARAGUA RISE
COLOMBIA BASIN
BEATA RIDGE
VENEZUELA BASIN
MUERTOS TROUGH
PUERTO RICO TRENCH
AVES RIDGE
MIDDLE AMERICA TRENCH
GUATEMALA BASIN
PANAMA BASIN
COCOS RIDGE
COLON RIDGE
TEHUANTEPEC FRACTURE ZONE
OROZCO FRACTURE ZONE
DELFIN BASIN
Gulf of California
Lower California
Sierra Madre Oriental
Sierra Madre Occidental
Sierra Madre del Sur
Appalachian Mountains
Florida Peninsula
Yucatán Pen.
Bay of Campeche
Isthmus of Tehuantepec
Gulf of Panama
Guiana Highlands
Tropic of Cancer
Washington
Richmond
Norfolk
Charleston
Savannah
Jacksonville
Miami
Tampa
Atlanta
Nashville
Memphis
St. Louis
Cincinnati
Louisville
Mobile
New Orleans
Houston
Dallas
Ft. Worth
San Antonio
Corpus Christi
Oklahoma City
Tulsa
Wichita
Albuquerque
El Paso
Phoenix
Tucson
San Diego
Tijuana
Ciudad Juárez
Chihuahua
Monterrey
Nuevo Laredo
Tampico
Veracruz
Mexico City
Puebla
Guadalajara
Acapulco
Mazatlán
Culiacán
Mérida
Campeche
Havana
Nassau
Kingston
Port-au-Prince
Santo Domingo
San Juan
Caracas
Maracaibo
Barranquilla
Cartagena
Medellín
Bogotá
Panamá
Colón
San José
Managua
Tegucigalpa
San Salvador
Guatemala
Belmopan
Port of Spain
Mississippi
Missouri
Arkansas
Red
Rio Grande
Pecos
Colorado
Gila
Ohio
Orinoco
Magdalena
Meta
Lake Okeechobee
Lake Maracaibo
Lake Nicaragua
0 100 200 300 400 500 600 MILES
0 100 200 300 400 500 600 KILOMETERS
© Copyright 1987 by HAMMOND INCORPORATED, Maplewood, N.J.

This map has been prepared with the North Pole as the mathematical center. From it, distances to any part of the world may be measured. On Mercator's map of the world, the polar regions are so scattered that their relatively small area and availability for flight routes are disregarded. Today, with airplanes following great circle courses, often within the Arctic Circle, polar projection maps are indispensable to the people of this air-minded age.

Map of The World Polar Projection

SCALES ON MERIDIANS

MILES
0   500   1000 1500 2000

KILOMETERS
0   500 1000 1500 2000

Azimuthal Equidistant Projection
Tangent at North Pole

The World

BRIESEMEISTER ELLIPTICAL
EQUAL-AREA PROJECTION

Capitals of Countries .... ⊛
Other Capitals .... ⊛
International Boundaries ..... – – –

TIME ZONES

STANDARD
TIME
ZONES

Areas using half
hour deviations.

Areas not using
zone system.

NOTE: Standard time zones in the U.S.S.R. are
always advanced one hour.

World 3

LAND AREA 57,970,000 sq. mi.
(150,142,300 sq. km.)
WATER AREA 139,781,000 sq. mi.
(362,032,790 sq. km.)
TOTAL SURFACE AREA 197,751,000 sq.mi.
(512,175,090 sq. km.)
POPULATION 5,292,000,000

Antarctica
AZIMUTHAL EQUIDISTANT PROJECTION

© Copyright HAMMOND INCORPORATED, Maplewood, N.J.

4 Arctic Ocean

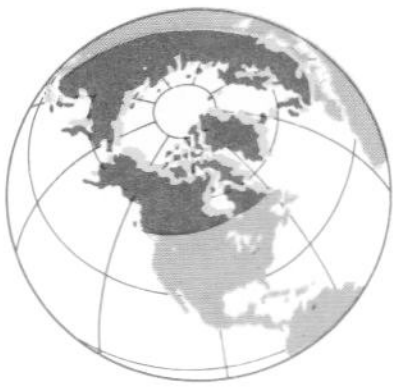

Arctic Ice

Bering Sea · Nome · Ambarchik
UNITED STATES · ALASKA · CANADA · RUSSIA
Barrow · Beaufort Sea · East Siberian Sea
Approximate Limit of Pack Ice in September
CANADA · ARCTIC · NORTH POLE · OCEAN · Laptev Sea · Nordvik
Kara Sea
Baffin Bay · Thule Air Base
GREENLAND · Qeqertarsuaq
Approximate Limit of Pack Ice in March · Barents Sea · Murmansk · Archangel
ATLANTIC OCEAN · ICELAND · Norwegian Sea · FINLAND · RUSSIA
NORWAY · SWEDEN
© C.S. Hammond & Co.

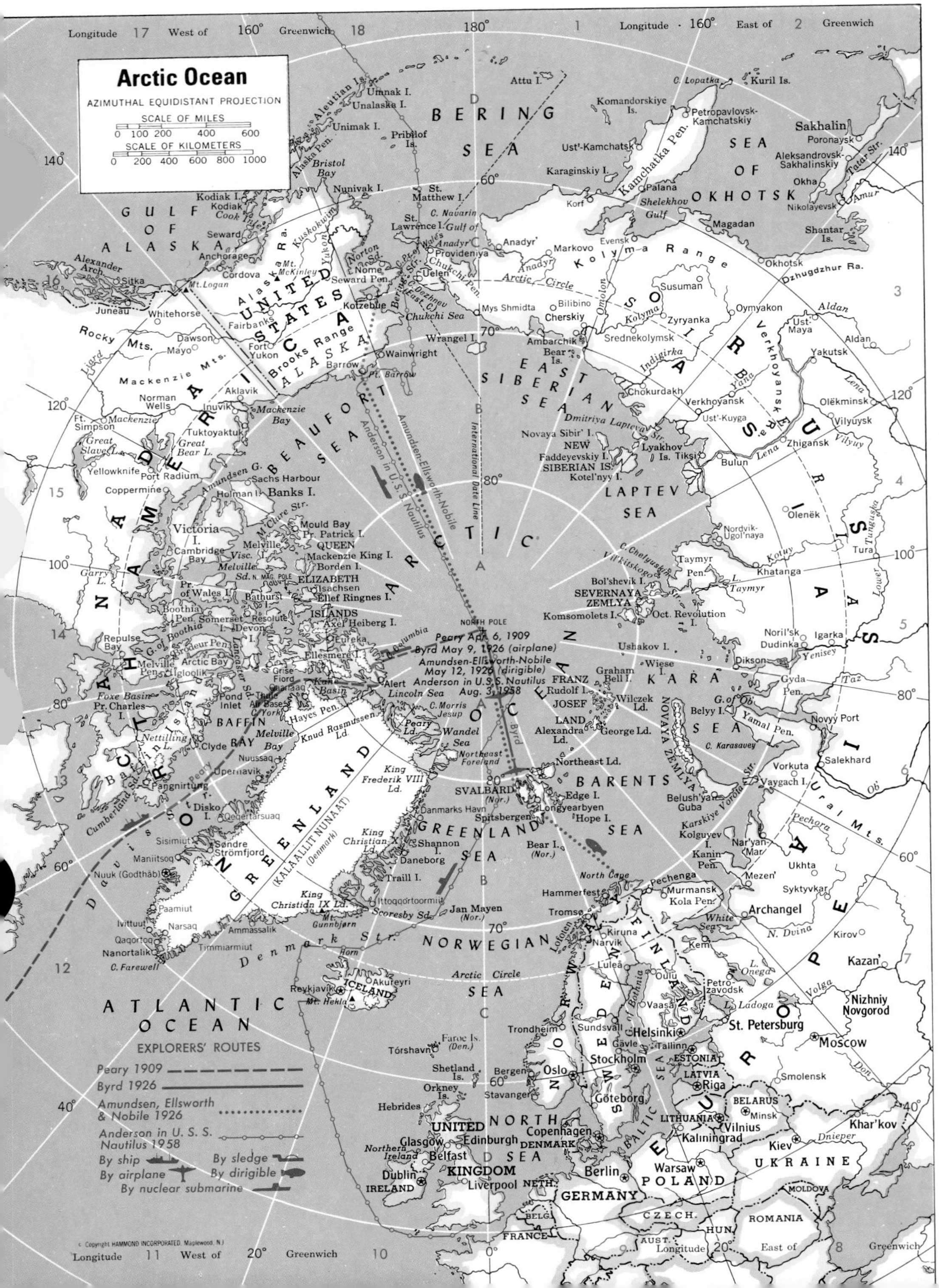

Arctic Ocean

AZIMUTHAL EQUIDISTANT PROJECTION

SCALE OF MILES
0 100 200 400 600

SCALE OF KILOMETERS
0 200 400 600 800 1000

EXPLORERS' ROUTES

Peary 1909
Byrd 1926
Amundsen, Ellsworth & Nobile 1926
Anderson in U.S.S. Nautilus 1958

By ship · By sledge
By airplane · By dirigible
By nuclear submarine

Copyright HAMMOND INCORPORATED, Maplewood, N.J.

Antarctica
AZIMUTHAL EQUIDISTANT PROJECTION
SCALE OF MILES
0 200 400 600 800
KILOMETERS
0 200 400 600 800 1000
© Copyright HAMMOND INCORPORATED, Maplewood, N.J.

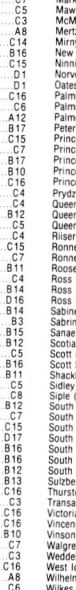
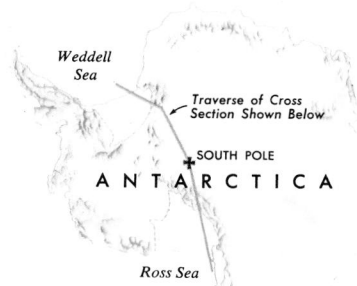

Traverse of Cross Section Shown Below
Weddell Sea
Ross Sea
+SOUTH POLE
ANTARCTICA

Index

Name	Ref	Name	Ref
Adare (cape)	B9	Larsen Ice Shelf	C16
Adelaide (isl.)	C15	Lazarev Station	C1
Adélie Coast (reg.)	C7	Levick (mt.)	B8
Alexander (isl.)	B15	Lister (mt.)	B8
American Highland	B4	Little America	B10
Amery Ice Shelf	C4	Luitpold Coast (reg.)	B17
Amundsen (bay)	C3	Lützow-Holm (bay)	C3
Amundsen (sea)	B13	Mackenzie (bay)	C4
Amundsen-Scott Station	A14	Mac-Robertson Land (reg.)	B4
Antarctic (pen.)	C15	Marguerite	C15
Balleny (isls.)	C9	Marie Byrd Land (reg.)	B13
Banzare Coast (reg.)	C7	Markham (mt.)	A8
Barr Smith (mt.)	C5	Mawson	C4
Batterbee (cape)	C3	McMurdo (sound)	B9
Beardmore (glac.)	A8	Mertz Glacier Tongue	C8
Bellingshausen (sea)	C14	Mirny	C5
Berkner (isl.)	B16	New Schwabenland (reg.)	B1
Biscoe (isls.)	C15	Ninnis Glacier Tongue	C8
Bouvet (isl.)	D1	Norvegia (cape)	B18
Bouvetøya (Bouvet) (isl.)	D1	Oates Coast (reg.)	B8
Bransfield (str.)	C16	Palmer (arch.)	C15
Budd Coast (reg.)	C6	Palmer Land (reg.)	B15
Byrd Station	A12	Palmer Station	C15
Caird Coast (reg.)	B17	Peter I (isl.)	B14
Charcot (isl.)	C15	Prince Edward (isls.)	E2
Clarie Coast (reg.)	C7	Prince Olav Coast (reg.)	C3
Coats Land (reg.)	B17	Princess Astrid Coast (reg.)	B1
Colbeck (cape)	B10	Princess Martha Coast (reg.)	B18
Coronation (isl.)	C16	Princess Ragnhild Coast (reg.)	B2
Daly (cape)	C4	Prydz (bay)	C4
Darnley (cape)	C4	Queen Mary Coast (reg.)	C5
Dart (cape)	B12	Queen Maud (mts.)	A12
Davis (sea)	C5	Queen Maud Land (reg.)	B1
Davis Station	C4	Riiser-Larsen (pen.)	C2
Drake (passage)	C15	Ronne Entrance (inlet)	B15
Dumont d'Urville Station	C7	Ronne Ice Shelf	B15
Edward VII (pen.)	B11	Roosevelt (isl.)	A10
Edward VIII (bay)	C4	Ross (isl.)	B9
Eights Coast (reg.)	B14	Ross (sea)	B10
Elephant (isl.)	D16	Ross Ice Shelf	A10
Ellsworth Land (reg.)	B14	Sabine (mt.)	B9
Enderby Land (reg.)	B3	Sabrina Coast (reg.)	C6
English Coast (reg.)	B15	Sanae Station	B18
Executive Committee (range)	B12	Scotia (sea)	C16
Farr (bay)	C5	Scott (isl.)	C10
Filchner Ice Shelf	B16	Scott Station	B9
Ford Ranges (mts.)	B11	Shackleton Ice Shelf	C5
Gaussberg (mt.)	C5	Sidley (mt.)	B12
George V Coast (reg.)	C8	Siple (mt.)	B12
Getz Ice Shelf	B12	South Georgia (isl.)	D17
Goodenough (cape)	C7	South Magnetic Pole	C8
Graham Land (reg.)	C15	South Orkney (isls.)	C16
Grytviken	D17	South Polar (plat.)	A1
Hearst (isl.)	B16	South Pole	A4
Hilton (inlet)	B16	South Sandwich (isls.)	D17
Hobbs Coast (reg.)	B12	South Shetland (isls.)	C15
Hollick-Kenyon (plat.)	B13	Sulzberger (bay)	B11
Hope (bay)	C16	Thurston (isl.)	B14
Indian Ocean	C3	Transantarctic (mts.)	B17
James Ross (isl.)	C16	Victoria Land (reg.)	B8
Joinville (isl.)	C16	Vincennes (bay)	C6
Kainan (bay)	B10	Vinson Massif (mt.)	B14
Keltie (cape)	C7	Walgreen Coast (reg.)	B13
Kemp Coast (reg.)	C3	Weddell (sea)	C16
King George (isl.)	C16	West Ice Shelf	C5
Kirkpatrick (mt.)	A8	Wilhelm II Coast (reg.)	C5
Knox Coast (reg.)	C6	Wilkes Land (reg.)	B7

Explorers' Routes
Palmer 1820
Amundsen 1910-12
Scott 1910-13
Byrd 1928-30
Fuchs 1957-58
By ship   By sledge   By airplane
By snow tractor

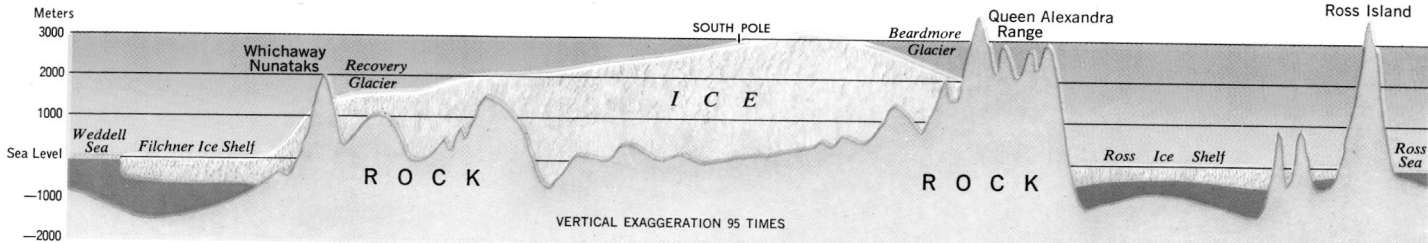

Antarctic Cross Section: Weddell Sea to Ross Sea

Meters
3000
2000
1000
Sea Level
−1000
−2000

Whichaway Nunataks   Recovery Glacier   SOUTH POLE   Beardmore Glacier   Queen Alexandra Range   Ross Island

Weddell Sea   Filchner Ice Shelf   I C E   Ross Ice Shelf   Ross Sea

R O C K   R O C K

VERTICAL EXAGGERATION 95 TIMES

Information Based on American Geographical Society's "Antarctic Map Folio Series"

Europe

POLYCONIC PROJECTION

SCALE OF MILES

0   100   200   300   400

KILOMETERS

0   100   200   300   400

Capitals of Countries ....⊛
Other Capitals ....⊛
International Boundaries ....—·—·—
Internal Boundaries ....—··—··—
Canals ....++++++

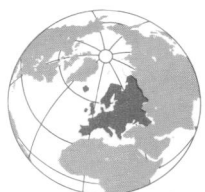

AREA 4,057,000 sq. mi.
(10,507,630 sq. km.)
POPULATION 689,000,000
LARGEST CITY Paris
HIGHEST POINT El'brus 18,510 ft.
(5,642 m.)
LOWEST POINT Caspian Sea -92 ft.
(-28 m.)

Population Distribution

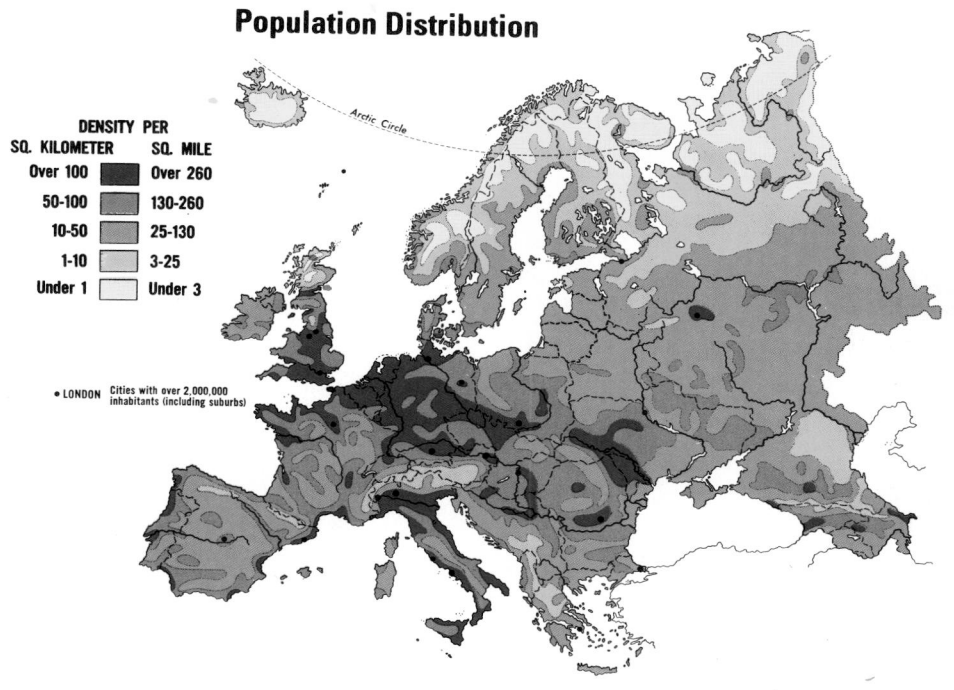

DENSITY PER

SQ. KILOMETER	SQ. MILE
Over 100	Over 260
50-100	130-260
10-50	25-130
1-10	3-25
Under 1	Under 3

• LONDON Cities with over 2,000,000 inhabitants (including suburbs)

Vegetation

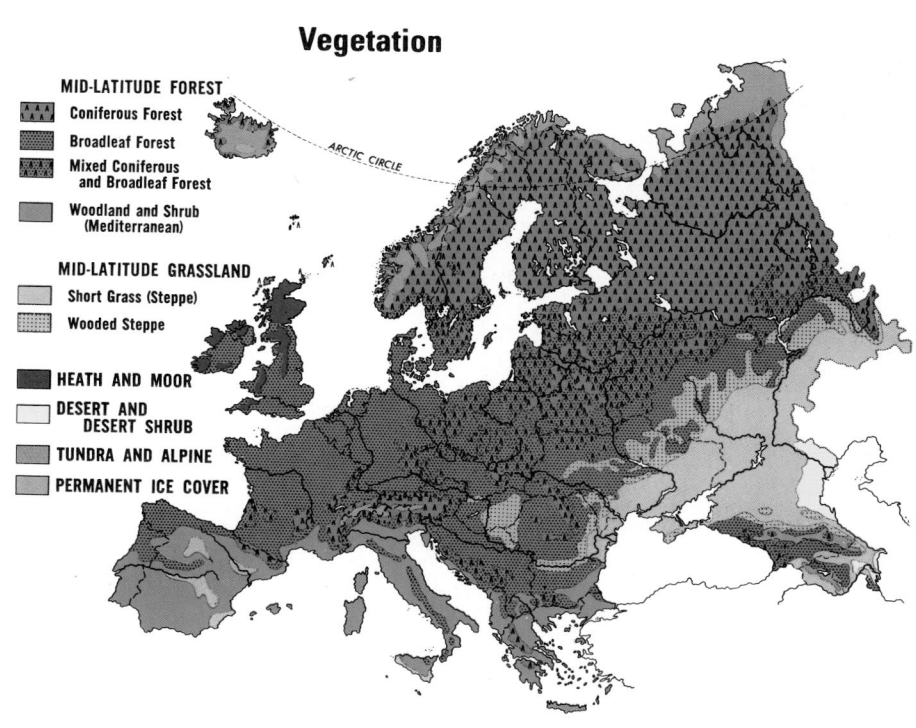

MID-LATITUDE FOREST

Coniferous Forest

Broadleaf Forest

Mixed Coniferous and Broadleaf Forest

Woodland and Shrub (Mediterranean)

MID-LATITUDE GRASSLAND

Short Grass (Steppe)

Wooded Steppe

HEATH AND MOOR

DESERT AND DESERT SHRUB

TUNDRA AND ALPINE

PERMANENT ICE COVER

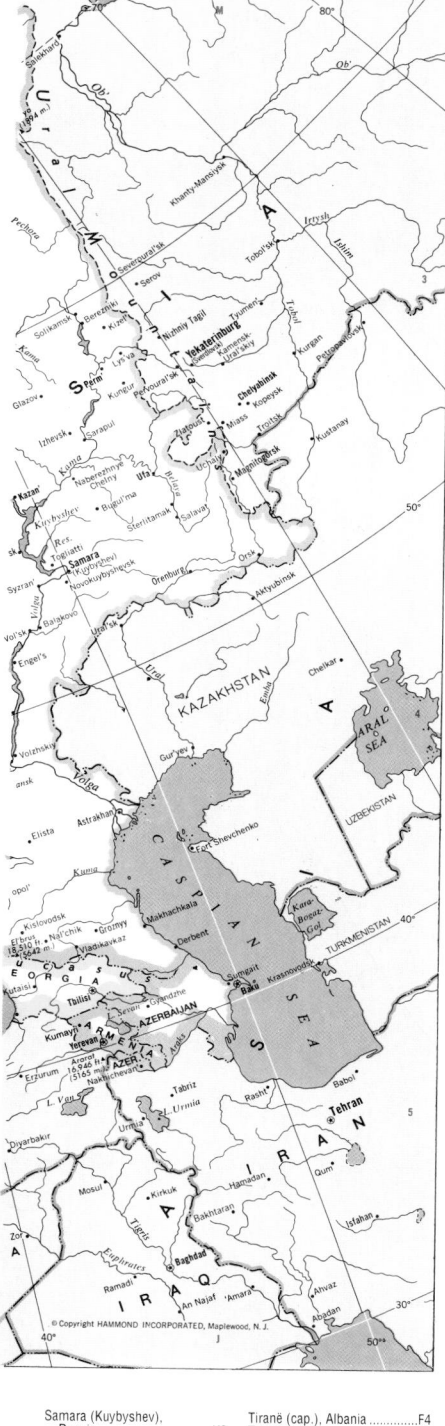

© Copyright HAMMOND INCORPORATED, Maplewood, N.J.

NORWEGIAN

SEA

BARENTS
SEA

Arctic Circle

ICELAND
Reykjavik

Hornur
Fontur

Kolguyev I.

Pechora

Faroe Is.
(Den.)

Shetland
Is.

FINLAND

Oulu

WHITE
SEA

Archangel

Northern Dvina

Hebrides

Orkney
Is.

Moray Firth

Hardangerfjord

Bergen

Tampere

Lake
Ladoga

St. Petersburg

Volga

Nizhniy
Novgorod

NORTH

SEA

Skagerrak

Gulf of Bothnia

Sundsvall

Stockholm

Gotland

Helsinki

Tallinn

ESTONIA

Gulf of Finland

Moscow

UNITED

KINGDOM

Aberdeen

Glasgow

Göteborg

Copenhagen

Riga

LATVIA

Dublin

DENMARK

BALTIC SEA

Bornholm

LITHUANIA

Vilnius

Minsk

IRELAND

IRISH SEA

Great

Liverpool

Britain

Birmingham

C. Clear

St. George's Chan.

London

Land's End

NETHERLANDS

Amsterdam

Hamburg

Elbe

Rügen

Gdansk

RUSSIA

BELARUS

ATLANTIC

English Channel

Channel Is.
(U.K.)

BELGIUM

Brussels

GERMANY

Berlin

POLAND

Lodz

Vistula

Oder

Bug

Kiev

Kharkov

Don

OCEAN

Le Havre

LUX.

Leipzig

Prague

Cracow

Lviv

UKRAINE

Seine

Paris

Dnieper

Bay of

Nantes

Loire

FRANCE

Stuttgart

CZECHOSLOVAK

Brno

Moldova

Odesa

Biscay

Bordeaux

Dordogne

Lyon

Munich

AUSTRIA

Vienna

Budapest

Cluj-Napoca

HUNGARY

ROMANIA

SEA OF
AZOV

Crimea

Krasnodar

Finisterre

SWITZ.

Venice

Zagreb

YUGOSLAVIA

Belgrade

Danube

Bucharest

BLACK SEA

Porto

Garonne

Pyrenees

MONACO

Genoa

SAN MARINO

Balkan Mt.

Douro

SPAIN

Madrid

Barcelona

Corsica

VATICAN CITY

Rome

ADRIATIC SEA

Sofia

BULGARIA

Istanbul

Bosporus

PORTUGAL

Lisbon

Tagus

Balearic Is.

Minorca

Sardinia

Naples

Tirana

Skopje

Macedonia

Thessaloniki

TURKEY

Guadiana

Valencia

Ibiza

Majorca

TYRRHENIAN

SEA

IONIAN
SEA

Lesvos

Cádiz

C. Teulada

Palermo

MEDITER

Str. of Gibraltar

Tangier

GIBRALTAR
(U.K.)

Algiers

Oran

Constantine

Sicily

Etna
10,053 ft.
(3,269 m.)

C. Passero

Rhodes

CYPRUS

Nicosia

LEBANON

Beirut

SY

Rabat

Casablanca

MOROCCO

ALGERIA

TUNISIA

Tunis

MALTA

Valletta

Crete

Damascus

Longitude West of Greenwich 0° Longitude East of Greenwich 10°

Vegetation/Relief

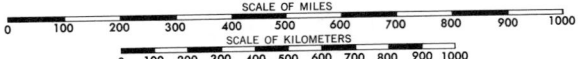

SCALE OF MILES
0   100   200   300   400   500   600   700   800   900   1000

SCALE OF KILOMETERS
0   100 200 300 400 500 600 700 800 900 1000

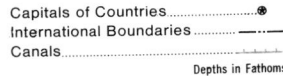

Capitals of Countries........................⊛
International Boundaries............─·─·─
Canals...

Depths in Fathoms

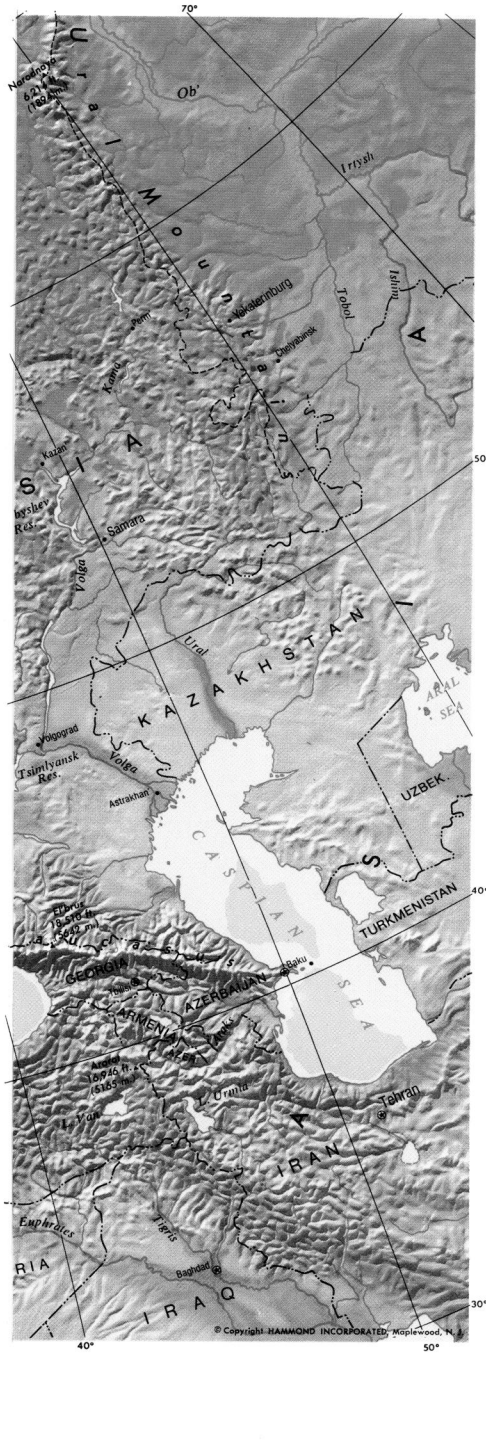

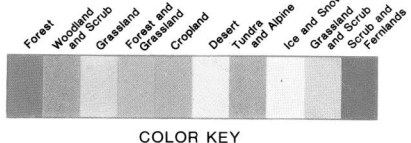

COLOR KEY

Forest | Woodland and Scrub | Grassland | Forest and Grassland | Cropland | Desert | Tundra and Alpine | Ice and Snow | Grassland and Scrub | Scrub and Farmlands

Rainfall

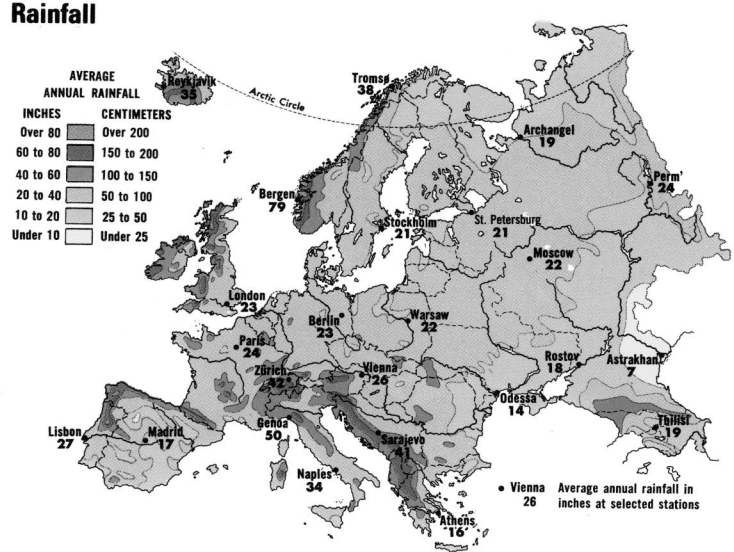

AVERAGE ANNUAL RAINFALL

INCHES	CENTIMETERS
Over 80	Over 200
60 to 80	150 to 200
40 to 60	100 to 150
20 to 40	50 to 100
10 to 20	25 to 50
Under 10	Under 25

Reykjavik 35 · Tromsø 38 · Archangel 19 · Perm' 24 · Bergen 79 · Stockholm 21 · St. Petersburg 21 · Moscow 22 · London 23 · Berlin 23 · Warsaw 22 · Rostov 18 · Astrakhan 7 · Paris 24 · Zürich 32 · Vienna 26 · Odessa 14 · Tbilisi 19 · Lisbon 27 · Madrid 17 · Genoa 50 · Sarajevo 41 · Naples 34 · Athens 16

Vienna 26 — Average annual rainfall in inches at selected stations

Average January Temperature

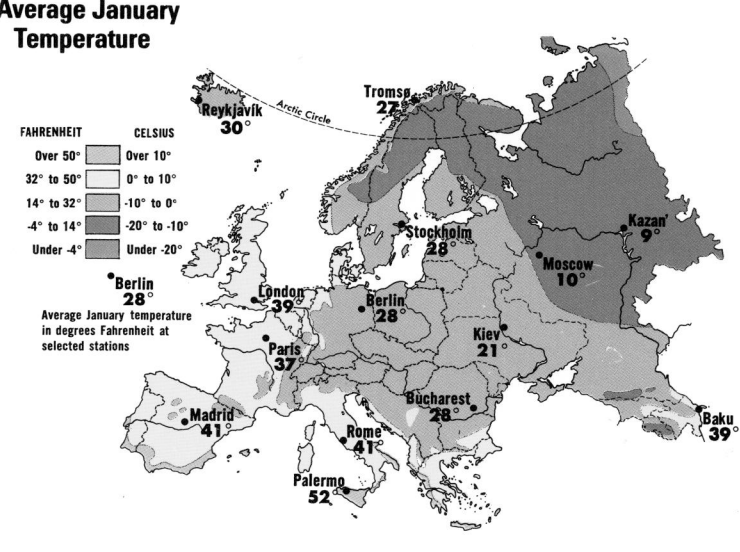

FAHRENHEIT	CELSIUS
Over 50°	Over 10°
32° to 50°	0° to 10°
14° to 32°	-10° to 0°
-4° to 14°	-20° to -10°
Under -4°	Under -20°

Reykjavik 30° · Tromsø 27° · Stockholm 28° · Kazan' 9° · Moscow 10° · Berlin 28° · London 39° · Berlin 28° · Kiev 21° · Paris 37° · Bucharest 28° · Baku 39° · Madrid 41° · Rome 41° · Palermo 52°

Average January temperature in degrees Fahrenheit at selected stations

Average July Temperature

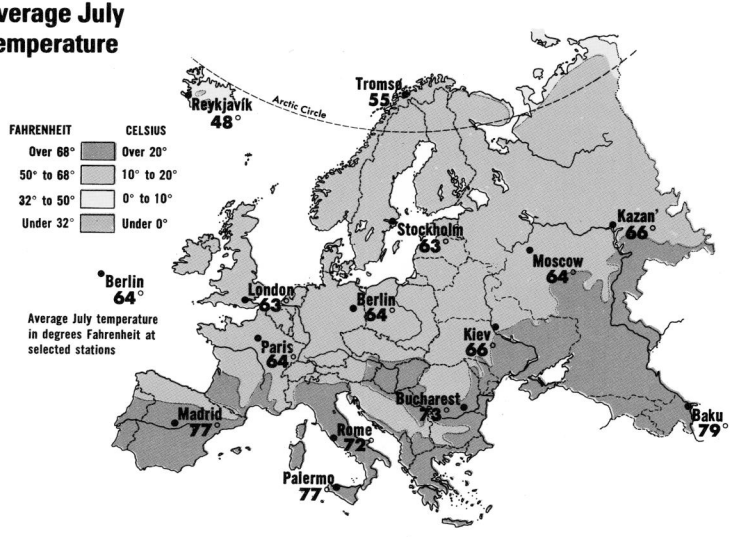

FAHRENHEIT	CELSIUS
Over 68°	Over 20°
50° to 68°	10° to 20°
32° to 50°	0° to 10°
Under 32°	Under 0°

Reykjavik 48° · Tromsø 55° · Stockholm 63° · Kazan' 66° · Moscow 64° · Berlin 64° · London 63° · Berlin 64° · Kiev 66° · Paris 64° · Bucharest 73° · Baku 79° · Madrid 77° · Rome 72° · Palermo 77°

Average July temperature in degrees Fahrenheit at selected stations

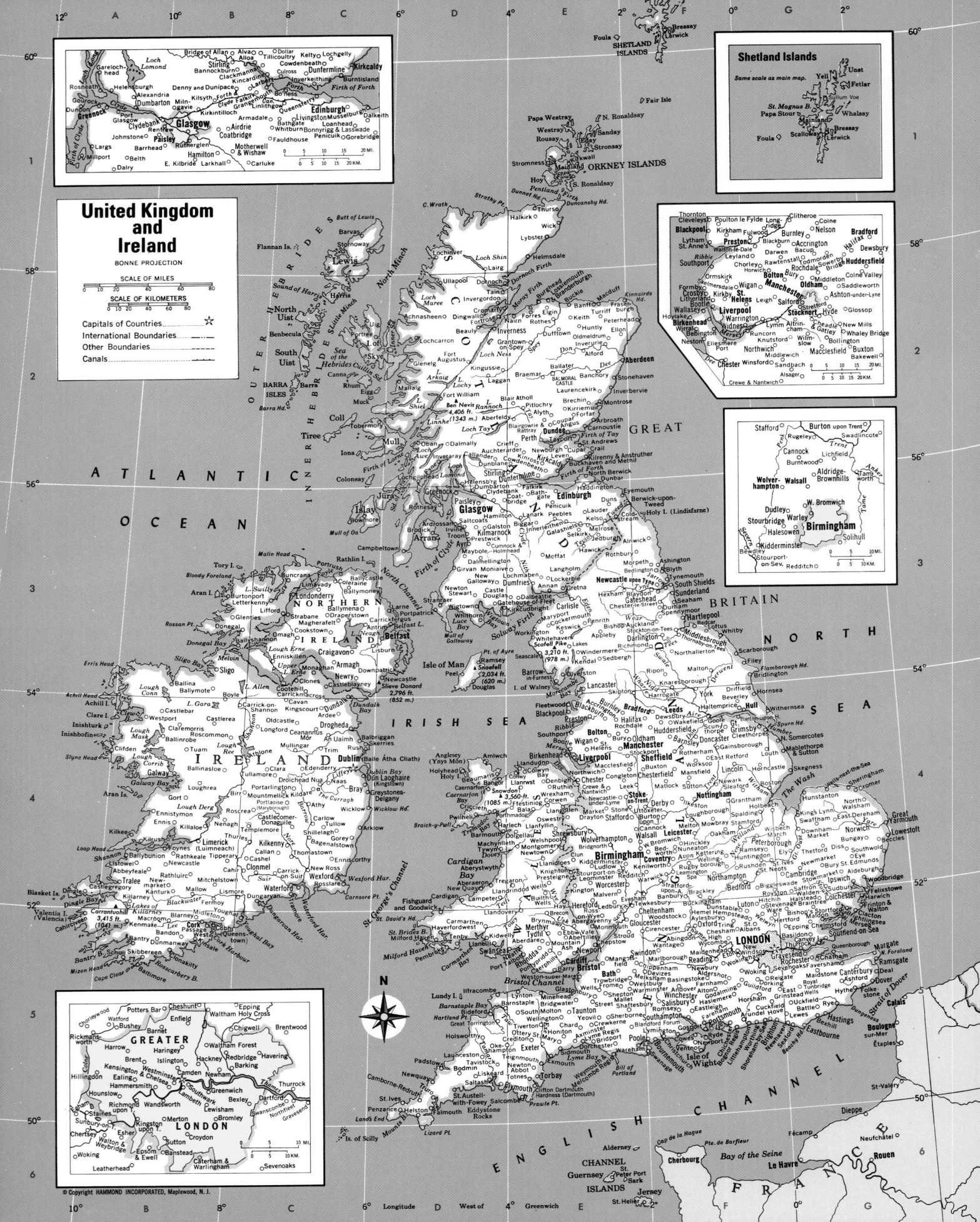

United Kingdom and Ireland

BONNE PROJECTION

SCALE OF MILES

SCALE OF KILOMETERS

Capitals of Countries........★
International Boundaries......—·—·—
Other Boundaries.............———
Canals

Shetland Islands

Same scale as main map.

© Copyright HAMMOND INCORPORATED, Maplewood, N.J.

UNITED KINGDOM

AREA 94,399 sq. mi. (244,493 sq. km.)
POPULATION 57,236,000
CAPITAL London
LARGEST CITY London
HIGHEST POINT Ben Nevis 4,406 ft. (1,343 m.)
MONETARY UNIT pound sterling
MAJOR LANGUAGES English, Gaelic, Welsh
MAJOR RELIGIONS Protestantism, Roman Catholicism

IRELAND

AREA 27,136 sq. mi. (70,282 sq. km.)
POPULATION 3,540,643
CAPITAL Dublin
LARGEST CITY Dublin
HIGHEST POINT Carrantuohill 3,415 ft. (1,041 m.)
MONETARY UNIT Irish pound
MAJOR LANGUAGES English, Gaelic (Irish)
MAJOR RELIGION Roman Catholicism

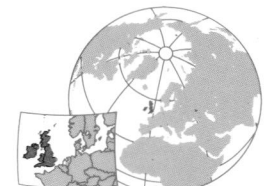

ENGLAND
(map on page 13)

COUNTIES

Avon 900,947	E6
Bedfordshire 502,164	G5
Berkshire 670,859	F6
Buckinghamshire 562,221	G6
Cambridgeshire 569,893	G5
Cheshire 921,623	E4
Cleveland 565,845	F3
Cornwall 418,631	C7
Cumbria 471,696	D3
Derbyshire 901,831	F5
Devon 930,112	D7
Dorset 578,993	E7
Durham 598,881	F3
East Sussex 641,016	H7
Essex 1,416,890	H6
Gloucestershire 493,166	E6
Hampshire 1,442,598	F6
Hereford and Worcester 624,393	E5
Hertfordshire 950,760	G6
Humberside 843,282	G4
Isle of Wight 114,879	F7
Isles of Scilly	A7
Kent 1,448,393	H6
Lancashire 1,362,801	E4
Leicestershire 835,647	F5
Lincolnshire 542,944	G4
London 6,608,598	H8
Manchester 2,575,407	H2

Merseyside 1,503,120	G2
Norfolk 685,232	H5
North Yorkshire 653,456	F3
Northamptonshire 524,967	G5
Northumberland 295,451	E2
Nottinghamshire 976,748	F4
Oxfordshire 507,230	F6
Shropshire 370,355	E5
Somerset 417,457	E6
South Yorkshire 1,292,029	F4
Staffordshire 1,005,641	E5
Suffolk 590,133	H5
Surrey 992,489	G6
Tyne and Wear 1,135,492	H3
Warwickshire 469,801	F5
West Midlands 2,628,419	F5
West Sussex 650,124	G7
West Yorkshire 2,021,707	J1
Wiltshire 512,635	E6
Yorkshire, North 653,456	F3
Yorkshire, South 1,292,029	F4
Yorkshire, West 2,021,707	J1

CITIES and TOWNS

Abingdon 29,130	F6
Accrington 36,459	H1
Adwickle Street 10,293	K2
Aldershot 53,665	G8
Aldridge 17,549	E5
Alfreton 21,284	F4
Alsager 12,944	E4
Alton 14,163	G6
Altrincham 39,528	H2

Amersham○ 21,326	G7
Andover 30,632	F6
Arnold 37,721	F4
Ashford 45,198	H6
Ashington 27,786	F2
Ashton-under-Lyne 43,605	H2
Aylesbury 51,999	G6
Aylesford 21,017	J8
Bacup 14,082	H1
Banbury 37,463	F5
Banstead 35,360	H8
Barking 149,132	H8
Barnet 289,277	H7
Barnoldswick 10,125	H1
Barnsley 76,783	J2
Barnstaple 24,490	D6
Barrow-in-Furness 50,174	D3
Basildon 94,800	J8
Basingstoke 73,027	F6
Bath 84,283	E6
Batley 45,582	J1
Beaconsfield 13,397	G8
Bebington 62,618	G2
Beccles 10,677	J5
Bedford 75,632	G5
Bedlington 15,074	F2
Bedworth 29,192	F5
Beeston and Stapleford 64,785	F5
Benfleet 50,783	J8
Bentley with Arksey 34,273	F4
Berkhamsted 16,874	G7
Berwick-upon-Tweed 12,772	F2
Beverley 19,368	G4

Bexhill 34,625	H7
Bexley 213,215	H8
Bicester 15,946	F6
Biddulph 16,697	H2
Bideford 13,826	C6
Biggleswade 10,905	G5
Birkenhead 99,075	G2
Birmingham 1,013,995	F5
Bishop Auckland 23,560	E3
Bishop's Stortford 22,535	H6
Blackburn 109,564	H1
Blackpool 146,297	G1
Blaydon 16,719	H3
Blyth 35,101	F2
Bodmin 11,992	C7
Bognor Regis 50,323	G7
Boldon 11,639	J3
Bolsover 11,497	J2
Bolton 143,960	H1
Bootle 70,860	G2
Boston 33,908	G5
Bournemouth 142,829	F7
Bracknell 52,257	G8
Bradford 293,336	J1
Braintree 30,975	H6
Brent 251,238	H8
Brentwood 51,212	J8
Bridgnorth 10,332	E5
Bridgwater 30,782	E6
Bridlington 28,426	G3
Bridport 10,615	E7
Brighouse 32,597	J1
Brighton 134,581	G7
Bristol 413,861	E6

Broadstairs 21,551	J6
Bromley 280,525	H8
Bromsgrove 24,576	E5
Brownhills 18,200	E5
Buckingham 6,439	G6
Burgess Hill 23,577	G7
Burnham-on-Sea 17,022	D6
Burnley 76,365	H1
Burntwood 28,938	F5
Burton upon Trent 59,040	F5
Bury 61,785	H2
Bury Saint Edmunds 30,563	H5
Bushey 15,759	H7
Buxton 19,502	J2
Calne 10,235	E6
Camborne-Redruth 34,262	B7
Cambridge 87,111	G5
Camden 161,098	H8
Cannock 54,503	E5
Canterbury 34,546	H6
Canvey Island 35,243	J8
Carlisle 72,206	D3
Carlton 46,053	F5
Carterton 10,876	F6
Caterham and Warlingham 30,331	H8
Charlton Kings 10,786	F6
Chatham 65,835	J8
Cheadle 10,470	E5
Cheadle and Gatley 59,478	H2
Chelmsford 91,109	J7
Cheltenham 87,188	E6
Chertsey 10,195	G8
Chesham 20,883	G7
Cheshunt 49,616	H7
Chester 80,154	G2
Chester-le-Street 34,776	J3
Chesterfield 73,352	J2
Chichester 26,050	G7
Chippenham 21,325	E6
Chorley 33,465	G2
Christchurch 32,854	F7
Cirencester 13,491	E6
Clacton 39,618	J6
Clay Cross 22,635	J2
Cleethorpes 33,238	H4
Clevedon 17,875	D6
Clitheroe 13,671	H1
Coalville 28,831	F5
Colchester 87,476	H6
Colne 19,094	H1
Congleton 23,482	H2
Consett 22,409	H3
Corby 48,704	G5
Corsham 11,259	E6
Coventry 318,718	F5
Cowes 16,134	F7
Cranleigh 10,334	G6
Crawley 80,113	G6
Crewe 59,097	E4
Crosby 54,103	G2
Crowborough 17,008	H6
Croydon 298,794	H8
Darlington 85,519	F3
Dartford 62,032	J8
Darton 13,743	J2
Darwen 30,883	H1
Daventry 16,096	F5
Deal 26,311	J6
Dearne 13,391	K2
Denton 37,784	H2
Derby 218,026	F5
Devizes 12,430	F6
Dewsbury 49,612	J1
Didcot○ 15,147	F6
Doncaster 74,727	F4
Dorchester 13,734	E7
Dorking 14,602	G8
Dover 33,461	J6
Droitwich 18,025	E5
Dronfield 22,641	J2
Dudley 186,513	E5
Dunstable 48,436	G6
Durham 38,105	J3
Ealing 278,677	H8
East Dereham 11,798	H5
East Grinstead 22,382	G6
East Retford 19,308	G4
Eastbourne 86,715	H7
Eastleigh 58,585	F7
Egham 21,810	G8
Ellesmere Port 65,829	G2

Enfield 257,154	H7
Epping 10,148	H7
Epsom and Ewell 65,830	G8
Esher 46,688	H8
Eston○ 37,694	F3
Eton	G8
Evesham 15,069	F5
Exeter 88,235	D7
Exmouth 28,037	D7
Fareham 55,563	F7
Farnborough 48,063	G8
Farnham 34,541	G8
Farnworth 25,591	H2
Faversham 15,914	H6
Felixstowe 24,207	J6
Felling 36,377	J3
Fleet 27,406	G8
Fleetwood 27,899	D4
Folkestone 42,949	J6
Formby 26,852	G2
Frinton and Walton 12,689	J6
Frome 19,678	E6
Gainsborough 20,326	G4
Gateshead 91,421	J3
Gillingham 92,531	J8
Glastonbury 6,751	E6
Glossop 29,923	J2
Gloucester 106,526	E6
Godalming 18,758	G8
Golborne 20,633	G2
Goole 19,394	G4
Gosport 69,664	F7
Grantham 30,700	G5
Gravesend 53,450	J8
Great Grimsby 91,532	G4
Great Harwood 10,968	H1
Great Malvern (Malvern) 30,153	E5
Great Yarmouth 54,777	J5
Greenwich 211,013	H8
Guildford 61,509	G8
Guisborough 19,242	F3
Hackney 179,529	H8

Hailsham 16,367	H7
Hale 16,362	H2
Halesowen 57,533	E5
Halifax 76,675	J1
Hammersmith 144,616	H8
Haringey 202,650	H8
Harlow 79,150	H7
Harrogate 63,637	J1
Harrow 195,292	G8
Hartlepool 91,749	F3
Harwich 17,245	J6
Haslemere 10,544	G8
Haslingden 14,347	H1
Hastings 74,979	H7
Hatfield 33,174	H7
Havant 50,098	G7
Haverhill 16,970	H5
Havering 238,335	J8
Haxby 11,415	F3
Hazel Grove and Bramhall 40,819	H2
Heanor 21,863	F4
Hebburn 20,098	J3
Hemel Hempstead 80,110	G7
Henley-on-Thames 10,910	G8
Hereford 48,277	E5
Hertford 21,350	H7
Hetton 14,529	J3
Heywood 29,639	H2
High Wycombe 69,575	G8
Hillingdon 226,659	G8
Hinckley 35,510	F5
Hitchin 33,480	G6
Hoddesdon 37,960	H7
Holmfirth 21,138	J2
Horley 17,700	H8
Horsham 38,356	G6
Horwich 16,758	G2
Houghton-le-Spring 35,337	J3
Hounslow 198,938	G8
Hove 66,591	G7
Hoylake 24,815	G2
Hoyland Nether 15,845	J2
Hucknall 27,463	F4

(continued on following page)

UNITED KINGDOM

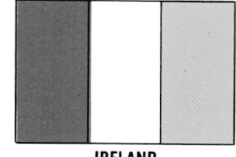

IRELAND

ENGLAND
50,516 sq. mi. (130,836 sq. km.)
46,220,955
London
London
Scafell Pike
3,210 ft. (978 m.)

WALES
8,017 sq. mi. (20,764 sq. km.)
2,749,640
Cardiff
Cardiff
Snowdon 3,560 ft. (1,085 m.)

SCOTLAND
30,414 sq. mi. (78,772 sq. km.)
5,130,735
Edinburgh
Glasgow
Ben Nevis 4,406 ft. (1,343 m.)

NORTHERN IRELAND
5,452 sq. mi. (14,121 sq. km.)
1,543,000
Belfast
Belfast
Slieve Donard
2,796 ft. (852 m.)

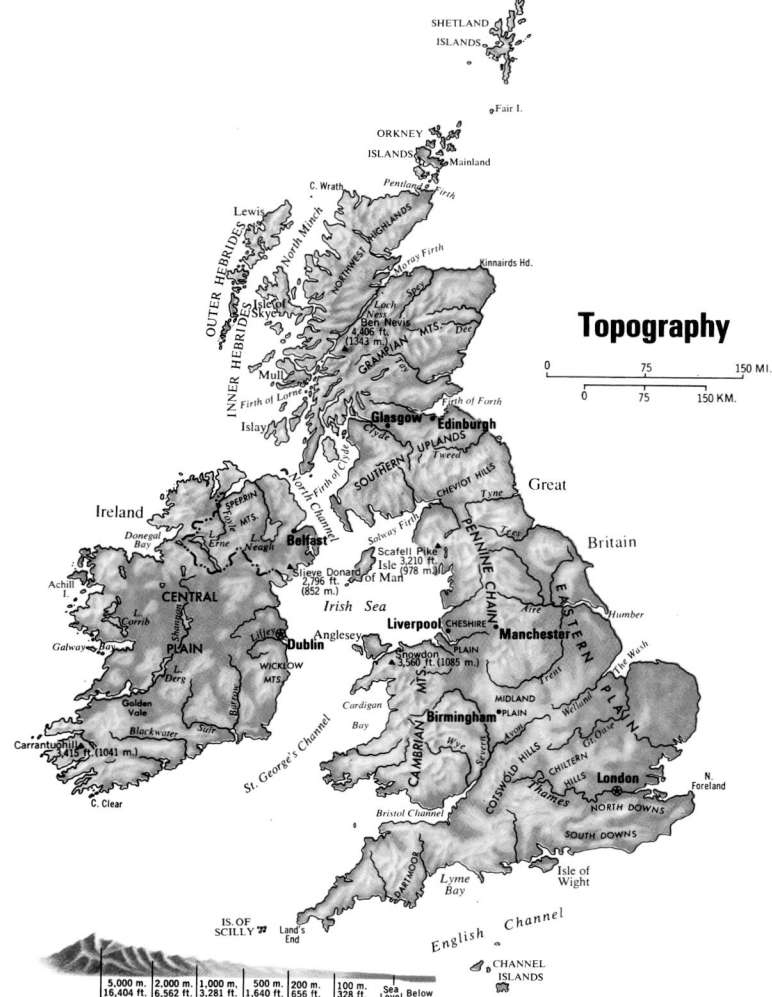

Topography

0 75 150 MI.
0 75 150 KM.

SHETLAND ISLANDS

Fair I.

ORKNEY ISLANDS

Mainland

C. Wrath

Pentland Firth

Lewis

OUTER HEBRIDES

North Minch

NORTHWEST HIGHLANDS

Moray Firth

Kinnairds Hd.

Isle of Skye

Loch Ness

Ben Nevis 4,406 ft. (1343 m.)

GRAMPIAN MTS.

Spey

Dee

INNER HEBRIDES

Mull

Firth of Lorne

Islay

Firth of Clyde

Glasgow

Edinburgh

SOUTHERN UPLANDS

Firth of Forth

Tweed

CHEVIOT HILLS

Tyne

Great

SPERRIN MTS.

Belfast

North Channel

Solway Firth

Slieve Donard 2,796 ft. (852 m.)

Scafell Pike 3,210 ft. (978 m.)

Isle of Man

Britain

Ireland

Donegal Bay

Lough Erne

Lough Neagh

Irish Sea

PENNINE CHAIN

EASTERN PLAIN

Humber

Achill I.

CENTRAL PLAIN

Shannon

Liffey

Dublin

Liverpool

CHESHIRE

Manchester

Aire

Galway Bay

Corrib

WICKLOW MTS.

Anglesey

Snowdon 3,560 ft. (1085 m.)

CAMBRIAN MTS.

MIDLAND PLAIN

Trent

The Wash

Welland

Golden Vale

Blackwater

Slee

Cardigan Bay

Birmingham

COTSWOLD HILLS

CHILTERN HILLS

Ouse

Carrantuohill 3,415 ft. (1041 m.)

C. Clear

St. George's Channel

Severn

Bristol Channel

Avon

London

N. Foreland

NORTH DOWNS

Thames

DARTMOOR

EXMOOR

SOUTH DOWNS

Isle of Wight

IS. OF SCILLY

Land's End

Lyme Bay

English Channel

CHANNEL ISLANDS

5,000 m. 16,404 ft. | 2,000 m. 6,562 ft. | 1,000 m. 3,281 ft. | 500 m. 1,640 ft. | 200 m. 656 ft. | 100 m. 328 ft. | Sea Level | Below

12 United Kingdom and Ireland
(continued)

Huddersfield 147,825 J2
Hugh Town⊙ A8
Hull 322,144 G4
Huntingdon 14,395 G5
Huyton-with-Roby 62,011 G2
Hyde 30,461 H2
Hythe 13,118 H6
Ilkeston 34,683 F5
Immingham⊙ 11,480 G4
Ipswich 129,661 J5
Islington 157,522 H8
Jarrow 31,345 J3
Kempston 15,454 G5
Kendal 23,710 E3
Kenilworth 18,782 F5
Kensington and Chelsea 125,892 G8
Kettering 44,758 G5
Kidderminster 50,385 E5
Kidsgrove 27,999 E4
King's Lynn 37,323 H5
Kingston upon Thames 130,829 H8
Kingswood 54,736 E6
Kirkby 52,825 G2
Knaresborough 12,910 F4
Knutsford 13,628 H2
Lambeth 244,143 H8
Lancaster 43,902 E3
Leamington Spa 56,552 F5
Leatherhead 42,399 G8
Leeds 451,841 J1
Leek 18,495 H2
Leicester 324,394 F5
Leigh 42,627 H2
Letchworth 31,146 G6
Lewes 14,499 H7
Lewisham 230,488 H8
Leyland 36,694 G1
Lichfield 25,408 F5
Lincoln 79,980 G4
Litherland 21,989 G2
Littlehampton 46,028 G7
Liverpool 538,809 G2
London (cap.) 7,566,620 H8
Long Eaton 42,285 F5
Longbenton 36,780 J3
Loughborough 44,895 F5
Louth 13,019 H4
Lowestoft 59,430 J5
Luton 163,209 G6
Lymington 11,614 F7
Lymm 10,036 H2
Lytham Saint Anne's 39,559 G1
Macclesfield 47,525 H2
Maidenhead 59,809 G8
Maidstone 86,067 J8
Maldon 14,638 H6
Malvern 30,153 E5
Manchester 448,604 H2
Mangotsfield 28,664 E6
Mansfield 71,325 K2
Mansfield Woodhouse 17,564 F4
March 14,155 H5
Margate 53,137 J6
Market Harborough 15,852 G5
Marlow 18,584 G8
Matlock 13,706 J2
Melksham 13,248 E6
Melton Mowbray 23,379 G5
Merton 165,102 H8
Middlesbrough 158,516 F3
Middleton 51,373 H2
Milton Keynes 93,305 G5
Morpeth 14,301 F2
Nantwich 11,867 E4
Nelson 30,449 H1
Neston 14,902 G2
New Romney 6,559 J7
Newark 33,143 G4
Newbury 31,488 F6
Newcastle upon Tyne 199,064 H3
Newcastle-under-Lyme 73,208 E4
Newham 209,128 H8
Newhaven 10,697 H7
Newmarket 15,861 H5
Newport, Isle of Wight 19,758 F7
Newport, Shropshire 10,339 E5
Newport Pagnell 10,733 G5
Newquay 13,905 B7
Newton Abbot 20,567 D7
Newton-le-Willows 19,466 H2
Northallerton 13,566 F3
Northampton 154,172 F5
Northfleet 21,400 J8
Northwich 32,664 H2
Norton-Radstock 17,668 E6
Norwich 169,814 J5
Nottingham 273,300 F5
Nuneaton 60,337 F5
Oadby 18,331 F5
Oldham 107,095 H2
Ormskirk 22,308 G2
Oswaldtwistle 11,188 H1
Oswestry 13,200 E5
Oxford 113,847 F6
Padiham 13,856 H1
Penrith 12,086 E3
Penzance 18,501 B7
Peterborough 113,404 G5
Peterlee⊙ 31,405 J3
Petersfield 10,078 F6
Plymouth 238,583 C7
Ponteland 10,215 H3
Poole 122,815 E7
Portishead 13,684 E6
Portslade 17,831 G7
Portsmouth 174,218 F7
Potters Bar 22,610 H7
Poulton-le-Fylde 18,477 G1
Preston 166,675 G1
Prestwich 31,854 H2
Prudhoe 11,140 H3
Radcliffe 27,664 H2
Ramsbottom 16,334 H2
Ramsgate 36,678 J6
Rawtenstall 21,247 H1
Rayleigh 28,574 J8
Reading 194,727 G8
Redbridge 226,977 H8
Redcar⊙ 35,373 F3
Redditch 61,639 E5
Reigate 48,241 H8
Richmond upon Thames 157,304 H8
Rickmansworth 15,960 G8
Ringwood 10,941 F7
Ripley 17,548 F4
Ripon 13,036 F3
Rochdale 97,292 H2
Rochester 23,840 J8
Romney (New Romney) 6,559 J7
Romsey 14,818 F6
Rotherham 122,374 K2
Royal Leamington Spa 56,552 F5
Royal Tunbridge Wells 57,699 H6
Royston 12,904 G5
Rugby 59,039 F5
Rugeley 23,751 E5
Runcorn 63,995 G2
Rushden 22,394 G5
Ryde 19,384 F7
Ryton 15,138 H3
Saffron Walden 11,879 H5
Saint Albans 76,709 H7
Saint Austell 20,267 C7
Saint Helens 114,397 G2
Saint Ives, Cambridgeshire 13,431 G5
Saint Ives, Cornwall 9,439 B7
Saint Neots 12,468 G5
Sale 57,872 H2
Salford 96,525 H2
Salisbury 36,890 F6
Saltash 12,486 C7
Sandbach 13,734 H2
Sandhurst 13,539 G8
Sandown-Shanklin 15,252 F7
Scarborough 36,665 G3
Scunthorpe 79,043 G4
Seaford 16,367 H7
Seaham 21,807 J3
Selby 12,224 F4
Sevenoaks 24,493 J8
Sheffield 470,685 J2
Shepshed 10,479 F5
Shildon 11,583 F3
Shoreham 20,562 G7
Shrewsbury 57,731 E5
Sidmouth 10,808 D7
Sittingbourne 35,893 H6
Skegness 12,645 H4
Skelmersdale 42,611 G2
Skipton 13,009 H1
Slough 106,341 G8
Solihull 93,940 F5
South Shields 86,488 J3
Southampton 211,321 F7
Southend-on-Sea 155,720 H6
Southport 88,596 G1
Southwark 209,735 H8
Southwick 11,364 G7
Sowerby Bridge 11,280 H1
Spalding 18,182 G5
Spennymoor 18,563 F3
Stafford 60,915 E5
Staines 51,949 G8
Stamford 16,127 G5
Standish 11,504 G2
Stanley 20,058 H3
Staveley 24,457 K2
Stevenage 74,757 G6
Stockport 135,489 H2
Stocksbridge 13,394 J2
Stockton-on-Tees 86,699 F3
Stoke-on-Trent 272,446 E4
Stone 12,119 E5
Stourbridge 55,136 E5
Stourport-on-Severn 17,880 E5
Stowmarket 10,913 J5
Stratford-upon-Avon 20,941 F5
Stretford 47,522 H2
Stroud 37,791 E6
Sudbury 17,723 H5
Sunbury 28,240 G8
Sunderland 195,064 J3
Sutton 165,323 H8
Sutton in Ashfield 39,536 K2
Swadlincote 33,667 F5
Swindon 127,348 F6
Tadley 13,668 F6
Tamworth 63,260 F5
Taunton 47,793 D6
Teignmouth 11,995 D7
Telford⊙ 28,645 E5
Tewkesbury 9,454 E6
Thatcham 14,940 F6
Thetford 19,529 H5
Thornaby⊙ 26,319 F3
Thornbury 11,948 E6
Thorne⊙ 16,662 F4
Thornton Cleveleys 26,697 G1
Tiverton 14,745 D7
Todmorden 11,936 H1
Tonbridge 34,407 H8
Torbay 93,995 D7
Tower Hamlets 139,996 H8
Tring 10,610 G7
Trowbridge 27,299 E6
Truro 17,852 B7
Tynemouth 17,877 J3
Uckfield 10,749 H7
Ulverston 11,976 D3
Urmston 43,706 H2
Uttoxeter 10,008 E5
Wakefield 74,764 J2
Wallasey 62,465 G2
Wallsend 44,542 J3
Walsall 177,923 E5
Waltham Forest 214,595 H8
Waltham Holy Cross 16,498 H7
Walton and Weybridge 50,031 G8
Wandsworth 252,240 H8
Ware 15,344 H7
Warminster 14,826 E6
Warrington 81,366 G2
Warsop 10,294 F4
Warwick 21,701 F5
Washington 48,856 J3
Waterloo 57,296 G7
Watford 109,503 H7
Wellingborough 38,598 G5
Wellington 8,980 D7
Welwyn 40,665 H7
West Bridgford 27,463 F5
West Bromwich 153,725 F5
Westminster 163,892 H8
Weston-super-Mare 60,821 D6
Weymouth 38,384 E7
Whickham 17,882 J3
Whitby 12,982 G3
Whitehaven 27,512 D3
Whitley Bay 36,040 J3
Widnes 55,973 G2
Wigan 88,725 G2
Wigston 32,373 F5
Wilmslow 28,827 H2
Wilton 4,002 F6
Wimborne Minster 14,193 E7
Winchester 34,127 F6
Windermere 6,835 E3
Windsor 30,832 G8
Winsford 26,548 G2
Wisbech 22,932 H5
Witham 21,875 H6
Witney 14,215 F6
Woking 92,667 G8
Wokingham 30,344 G8
Wolverhampton 263,501 E5
Wombwell 17,143 K2
Worcester 75,466 E5
Workington 25,978 D3
Worksop 34,551 F4
Worsbrough 10,821 J2
Worthing 90,687 G7
Yateley⊙ 14,121 G8
Yeovil 36,114 E7
York 123,126 F4

OTHER FEATURES

Aire (riv.) F4
Avon (riv.) F5
Barnstaple (bay) C6
Beachy (head) H7
Blackwater (riv.) H6
Bristol (chan.) C6
Cheviot (hills) E2
Chiltern (hills) G6
Cleveland (hills) F3
Colne (riv.) G8
Cotswold (hills) E6
Cross Fell (mt.) E3
Cumbrian (mts.) D3
Dart (riv.) D7
Dartmoor National Park C7
Dee (riv.) D4
Derwent (riv.) G3
Derwent (riv.) H3
Don (riv.) F4
Dove (riv.) J2
Dover (strait) J7
Dungeness (prom.) J7
Eddyston (rocks) C7
Eden (riv.) E3
English (chan.) D8
Esk (riv.) D2
Exe (riv.) D7
Exmoor National Park D6
Fens, The (reg.) G5
Flamborough (head) G3
Foulness Island (pen.) J6
Great Ouse (riv.) H5
Hartland (pt.) C6
Holderness (pen.) G4
Holy (isl.) F2
Humber (riv.) G4
Irish (sea) B4
Kennet (riv.) F6
Lake District National Park D3
Land's End (prom.) B7
Lea (riv.) G6
Lincoln Wolds (hills) G4
Lindisfarne (Holy) (isl.) F2
Lizard (pt.) B8
Lundy (isl.) C6
Lyme (bay) D7
Medway (riv.) H6
Mendip (hills) E6
Mersey (riv.) G2
Morecambe (bay) D3
Mounts (bay) B7
Naze, The (prom.) J6
Nene (riv.) H5
New (for.) F6
North (sea) J4
North Downs (hills) G6
North Foreland (prom.) J6
Northumberland National Park E2
North York Moors National Park G3
Ouse (riv.) G6
Ouse (riv.) G4
Peak District National Park F4
Peak, The (mt.) J2
Pennine Chain (range) E3
Portland, Bill of (pt.) E7
Purbeck, Isle of (pen.) F7
Ribble (riv.) E4
Saint Bees (head) D3
Saint Mary's (isl.) A8
Scafell Pike (mt.) D3
Scilly (isls.) A7
Severn (riv.) E6
Sheppey (isl.) J6
Sherwood (for.) F4
Solent (chan.) F7
Solway (firth) D3
South Downs (hills) G7
South Foreland (prom.) J6
Spithead (chan.) F7
Stonehenge (ruin) F6
Stour (riv.) H6
Stour (riv.) E7
Stour (riv.) J6
Swale (riv.) F3
Tees (riv.) F3
Thames (riv.) H6
Tintagel (head) C7
Trent (riv.) G4
Tweed (riv.) E2
Tyne (riv.) F3
Ure (riv.) F3
Walney, Isle of (isl.) D3
Wash, The (bay) H5
Weald, The (reg.) H6
Wear (riv.) F3
Welland (riv.) G5
Wey (riv.) G6
Wharfe (riv.) E3
Wight (isl.) 114,879 F7
Wirral (pen.) G2
Wolds, The (hills) G4
Wye (riv.) D5
Yare (riv.) J5
Yorkshire Dales National Park E3

CHANNEL ISLANDS

CITIES and TOWNS

Saint Helier (cap.), Jersey⊙ 27,549 E8
Saint Peter Port (cap.), Guernsey⊙ 16,085 E8
Saint Sampson's⊙ 7,475 E8

OTHER FEATURES

Alderney (isl.) 2,130 E8
Guernsey (isl.) 55,421 E8
Herm (isl.) 59 E8
Jersey (isl.) 82,809 E8
Sark (isl.) 560 E8

ISLE of MAN

CITIES and TOWNS

Castletown 2,788 C3
Douglas (cap.) 19,897 C3
Laxey 1,242 C3
Onchan 6,395 C3
Peel 3,295 C3
Port Erin 2,356 C3
Port Saint Mary 1,525 C3
Ramsey 5,372 C3

OTHER FEATURES

Ayre (pt.) C3
Calf of Man (isl.) C3
Langness (prom.) C3
Snaefell (mt.) C3

WALES

COUNTIES

Clwyd 385,581 D4
Dyfed 323,040 C6
Gwent 436,500 D6
Gwynedd 222,291 C4
Mid Glamorgan 533,770 D6
Powys 108,121 D5
South Glamorgan 376,718 A7
West Glamorgan 363,619 D6

CITIES and TOWNS

Abercarn 16,811 B6
Aberdare 31,617 A6
Abergavenny 13,880 B6
Abergele 12,264 D4
Abertillery and Brynmawr 28,239 B6
Aberystwyth 10,290 C5
Ammanford 10,735 C6
Bangor 12,244 C4
Barry 44,443 B7
Bethesda 3,558 D4
Brecknock (Brecon) 7,166 D6
Bridgend 31,008 A7
Brynmawr and Abertillery 28,239 B6
Buckley 16,693 G2
Caernarfon 9,271 C4
Caerphilly 28,681 B6
Caldicot 12,310 E6
Cardiff (cap.) 262,313 B7
Cardigan 3,815 C5
Carmarthen 13,860 C6
Chepstow 9,039 E6
Colwyn Bay 27,002 D4
Connah's Quay 14,785 G2
Cwmbran 44,592 B6
Denbigh 7,710 D4
Ebbw Vale 21,048 B6
Ffestiniog 4,507 D5
Flint 11,411 G2
Gelligaer 16,812 A6
Gwersyllt 13,374 E4
Harlech⊙ 1,292 C5
Haverfordwest 13,572 B6
Hawarden⊙ 22,361 G2
Holyhead 12,569 C4
Holywell 11,101 G2
Llandeilo 1,598 C6
Llandovery 1,676 D5
Llandrindod Wells 4,232 D5
Llandudno 13,202 D4
Llanelli 45,336 C6
Llanfairfechan 3,173 D4
Llangollen 2,546 D5
Llanidloes 2,392 D5
Llantrisant⊙ 8,317 A7
Llantwit Major 13,375 A7
Maesteg 21,821 D6
Menai Bridge 2,942 C4
Merthyr Tydfil 38,893 A6
Milford Haven 13,883 B6
Mold 8,487 G2
Monmouth 7,379 E6
Montgomery D5
Mountain Ash 23,520 A6
Narberth C6
Neath 48,687 D6
Nefyn⊙ 2,086 C5
Newport 115,896 B6
Newtown 8,906 D5
Neyland 3,095 B6
Ogmore 7,092 A6
Pembroke 8,235 C6
Penarth 22,467 B7
Pontypool 36,064 B6
Pontypridd 29,465 A6
Port Talbot 40,078 D6
Porthcawl 15,162 D6
Prestatyn 16,246 D4
Pwllheli 3,978 C5
Rhondda 70,980 A6
Rhosllanerchrugog 11,080 D4
Rhyl 23,130 D4
Risca 16,627 B6
Ruthin 4,417 D4
Saint David's⊙ 1,428 B6
Swansea 172,433 C6
Tenby 5,226 C6
Tredegar 16,188 B6
Welshpool 4,869 D5
Wrexham 39,929 E4
Ystradgynlais 10,406 D6

OTHER FEATURES

Anglesey (isl.) C4
Bardsey (isl.) C5
Brecon Beacons National Park D6
Bristol (chan.) C6
Caldy (isl.) C6
Cambrian (mts.) D5
Cardigan (bay) C5
Carmarthen (bay) C6
Conwy (bay) C4
Dee (riv.) D4
Gower (pen.) C6
Great Ormes (head) C4
Holy (isl.) C4
Irish (sea) B4
Lleyn (pen.) C5
Menai (strait) C4
Milford Haven (inlet) B6
Pembrokeshire Coast National Park C6
Radnor (for.) D5
Saint Brides (bay) B6
Saint George's (chan.) B5
Severn (riv.) E6
Snowdon (mt.) C4
Snowdonia National Park D4
Taff (riv.) B7
Teifi (riv.) C5
Towy (riv.) D6
Tremadoc (prom.) C5
Usk (riv.) B6
Wye (riv.) D5
Ynys Môn (Anglesey) (isl.) C4

⊙ Population of parish.

SCOTLAND

(map on page 15)

REGIONS

Borders 99,784 E5
Central 273,391 D4
Dumfries and Galloway 145,139 E5
Fife 327,362 E4
Grampian 471,942 F3
Highland 200,150 D3
Lothian 738,372 E5
Orkney (islands area) 19,056 E1
Shetland (islands area) 27,277 F2
Strathclyde 2,404,532 C4
Tayside 391,846 E4
Western Isles (islands area) 31,884 A3

CITIES and TOWNS

Aberchirder 1,021 F3
Aberdeen 190,465 F3
Aberfeldy 1,613 E4
Aberfoyle 793 D4
Abernethy 776 E4
Aboyne 1,529 F3
Achiltibuie⊙ 1,564 C3
Achnasheen⊙ 1,078 C3
Airdrie 45,747 C2
Alexandria 26,329 A1
Alford 764 F3
Alloa 26,428 C1
Alness 6,289 D3
Altnaharra⊙ 1,227 D2
Alva 4,874 C1
Alyth 2,289 E4
Annan 8,314 E6
Annbank Station 3,223 D5
Arbroath 24,119 F4
Ardrishaig 1,325 C4
Ardrossan 11,421 D5
Armadale 9,527 C2
Auchinleck 4,463 D5
Auchterarder 2,904 E4
Auchtermuchty 1,646 E4
Aviemore 1,224 E3
Ayr 49,522 D5
Baillieston 7,671 B2
Balerno 3,576 D2
Balfron 1,127 B1
Ballantrae 262 C5
Ballater 1,218 F3
Ballingry 7,021 D1
Balloch 1,484 B1
Banchory 4,890 F3
Banff 3,938 F3
Bankhead 1,492 F3
Bannockburn 5,889 C1
Barrhead 18,418 B2
Bathgate 14,477 C2
Bearsden 27,183 B2
Beauly 1,148 D3
Beith 5,742 D5
Bellsbank 2,482 D5
Bellshill 39,676 C2
Berriedale⊙ 1,927 E2
Bieldside 1,137 F3
Biggar 1,938 E5
Bishopbriggs 23,501 B2
Bishopton 5,283 B2
Blackburn 5,785 C2
Blair Atholl 437 E4
Blairgowrie and Rattray 7,184 E4
Blantyre 19,948 B2
Bo'ness 14,641 C1
Boddam 1,367 G3
Bonhill 4,385 B1
Bonnybridge 5,701 C1
Bonnyrigg and Lasswade 14,399 D2
Brechin 7,692 F4
Bridge of Allan 4,694 C1
Bridge of Don 4,086 F3
Bridge of Weir 4,724 A2
Brightons 3,106 C1
Brora 1,736 E2
Broxburn 12,032 D1
Buckhaven and Methil 18,265 F4
Buckie 7,839 E3
Bucksburn 6,567 F3
Burghead 1,380 E3
Burntisland 5,865 D1
Callander 2,520 D4
Cambuslang 14,607 B2
Campbeltown 6,098 C5
Caol 3,719 C4
Cardenden 5,898 D1
Carluke 11,674 E5
Carnoustie 9,225 F4
Carnwath 1,374 E5
Carron 2,626 C1
Castle Douglas 3,521 E6
Catrine 2,790 D5
Cawdor 111 E3
Chirnside 1,263 F5
Chryston 11,067 C2
Clackmannan 3,258 C1
Clarkston 8,404 B2
Clydebank 51,854 B2
Coalburn 1,241 E5
Coatbridge 50,957 C2
Cockenzie and Port Seton 3,760 D1
Coldstream 1,645 F5
Comrie 1,477 E4
Cononbridge 2 187 D3
Corpach 1,296 C4
Coupar Angus 2,186 E4
Cove and Kilcreggan 1,220 A1
Cove Bay 2,840 F3
Cowdenbeath 12,272 D1
Cowie 2,513 C1
Crail 1,181 F4
Creetown 769 D6
Crieff 5,477 E4
Crimond 1,002 G3
Cromarty 492 E3
Cruden Bay 1,453 G3
Cullen 1,414 F3
Culross 504 C1
Cults 3,336 F3
Cumbernauld 47,901 C1
Cumnock and Holmhead 9,650 D5
Cupar 6,637 E4
Currie 6,764 D2
Dailly 1,098 D5
Dalbeattie 3,917 E6
Dalkeith 11,255 D2
Dalmellington 1,425 D5
Dalry 5,856 D5
Dalrymple 1,237 D5
Darvel 3,461 D5
Denny and Dunipace 23,158 C1
Dervaig⊙ 1,081 B4
Dingwall 4,842 D3
Dollar 2,486 E4
Dornoch 880 D3
Douglas 1,727 E5
Doune 1,046 D4
Drongan 3,129 D5
Dufftown 1,643 E3
Dumbarton 23,430 B1
Dumfries 32,100 E5
Dunbar 6,035 F4
Dunblane 6,855 E4
Dundee 174,345 F4
Dundonald 2,669 D5
Dunfermline 52,227 D1
Dunoon 9,369 A2
Duns 2,253 F5
Duntocher 3,532 B2
Dyce 7,039 F3
Eaglesham 3,166 D5
Earlston 1,610 F5
East Calder 5,112 D2
East Kilbride 70,676 B2
East Linton 1,206 F5
Eastriggs 1,845 E5
East Wemyss 1,782 D1
Edinburgh (cap.) 420,169 D1
Elderslie 5,204 B2
Elgin 18,908 E3
Ellon 6,319 F3
Errol 762 E4
Eyemouth 3,398 F5
Fairlie 1,326 D5
Falkirk 36,880 C1
Falkland 998 E4
Fallin 2,663 C1
Fauldhouse 5,036 C2
Findhorn 664 E3
Findochty 1,019 E3
Fochabers 1,483 E3
Forfar 12,770 F4
Forres 8,354 E3
Forth 2,890 C2
Fortrose 1,332 D3
Fort William 11,061 C4
Fraserburgh 12,512 G3
Gairloch 125 C3
Galashiels 12,244 F5
Galston 5,311 D5
Garelochhead 2,072 A1
Gatehouse-of-Fleet 835 D6
Giffnock 33,634 B2
Girvan 7,795 D5
Glamis 190 F4
Glasgow 765,030 B2
Glenbarr⊙ 691 C5
Glencoe 195 C4
Glenelg⊙ 1,468 C3
Glenrothes 32,971 E4
Golspie 1,491 E3
Gorebridge 6,036 D2
Gourock 11,203 A1
Grangemouth 21,599 C1
Grantown-on-Spey 2,034 E3
Greenock 59,016 A2
Gretna 2,811 E5
Gullane 2,232 F4
Haddington 8,139 F5
Halkirk 679 E2
Hamilton 51,718 C2
Harthill 4,161 C2
Hawick 16,364 F5
Heathhall 1,365 E5
Helensburgh 16,621 A1
Helmsdale 727 E2
Hillside 1,233 F4
Hillswick⊙ 696 G2
Hopeman 1,398 E3
Huntly 3,952 F3
Hurlford 4,294 D5
Inchnadamph⊙ 833 D2
Innerleithen 2,468 E5
Insch 1,256 F3
Inveraray 473 C4
Inverbervie 1,799 F4
Invercassley⊙ 1,067 D3
Invergordon 4,067 D3
Invergowrie 1,389 E4
Inverie⊙ 1,468 C3
Inverkeithing 5,770 D1
Inverness 40,010 D3
Inverurie 7,680 F3
Irvine 32,968 D5
Jedburgh 4,069 F5
John O'Groats 195 E2
Johnstone 42,669 B2
Keith 4,407 F3
Kelso 5,648 F5
Kelty 5,623 D1
Kemnay 3,034 F3
Kilbarchan 2,669 A2
Kilbirnie 8,710 A2
Kilchoan⊙ 764 B4
Kildonan⊙ 1,105 E2
Killearn 1,771 B1
Kilmacolm 3,676 A2
Kilmarnock 52,083 D5
Kilmaurs 2,738 D5
Kilrenny and Anstruther 2,951 F4
Kilsyth 10,538 B1
Kilwinning 16,266 D5
Kinbrace⊙ 1,105 E2
Kincardine 3,166 C1
Kinghorn 2,698 D1
Kingussie 1,229 D3
Kinlochewe⊙ 1,794 C3
Kinlochleven 1,047 D4
Kinloss 2,813 E3
Kinross 3,496 E4
Kintore 1,644 F3
Kirkcaldy 46,522 D1
Kirkconnel 2,656 E5
Kirkcudbright 3,427 E6
Kirkintilloch 33,148 B2
Kirkmuirhill 3,624 E5
Kirkwall 5,995 E2
Kirriemuir 5,326 E4
Kyle of Lochalsh 687 C3
Kylestrome⊙ 745 D2
Ladybank 1,355 E4
Lairg 572 D2
Lanark 9,806 E5
Langholm 2,615 E5
Larbert 4,922 C1
Largs 9,905 A2
Larkhall 16,216 E5
Lauder 639 F5
Laurencekirk 1,329 F4
Lennoxtown 4,829 B1
Lerwick 7,561 G2
Leslie 3,551 E4
Lesmahagow 3,408 E5
Letham 804 F4
Leuchars 2,244 F4
Leven 8,624 F4
Lhanbryde 1,811 E3
Limekilns 1,444 D1
Linlithgow 9,582 C1
Linwood 10,510 B2
Livingston 38,954 C2
Loanhead 6,159 D2
Lochailort⊙ 673 C4
Locharbriggs 4,230 E5
Lochgelly 7,334 D1
Lochgilphead 2,461 C4
Lochinver 283 C2
Lochmaben 1,713 E5
Lochore 2,994 D1
Lochwinnoch 2,273 A2
Lockerbie 3,561 E5

(continued)

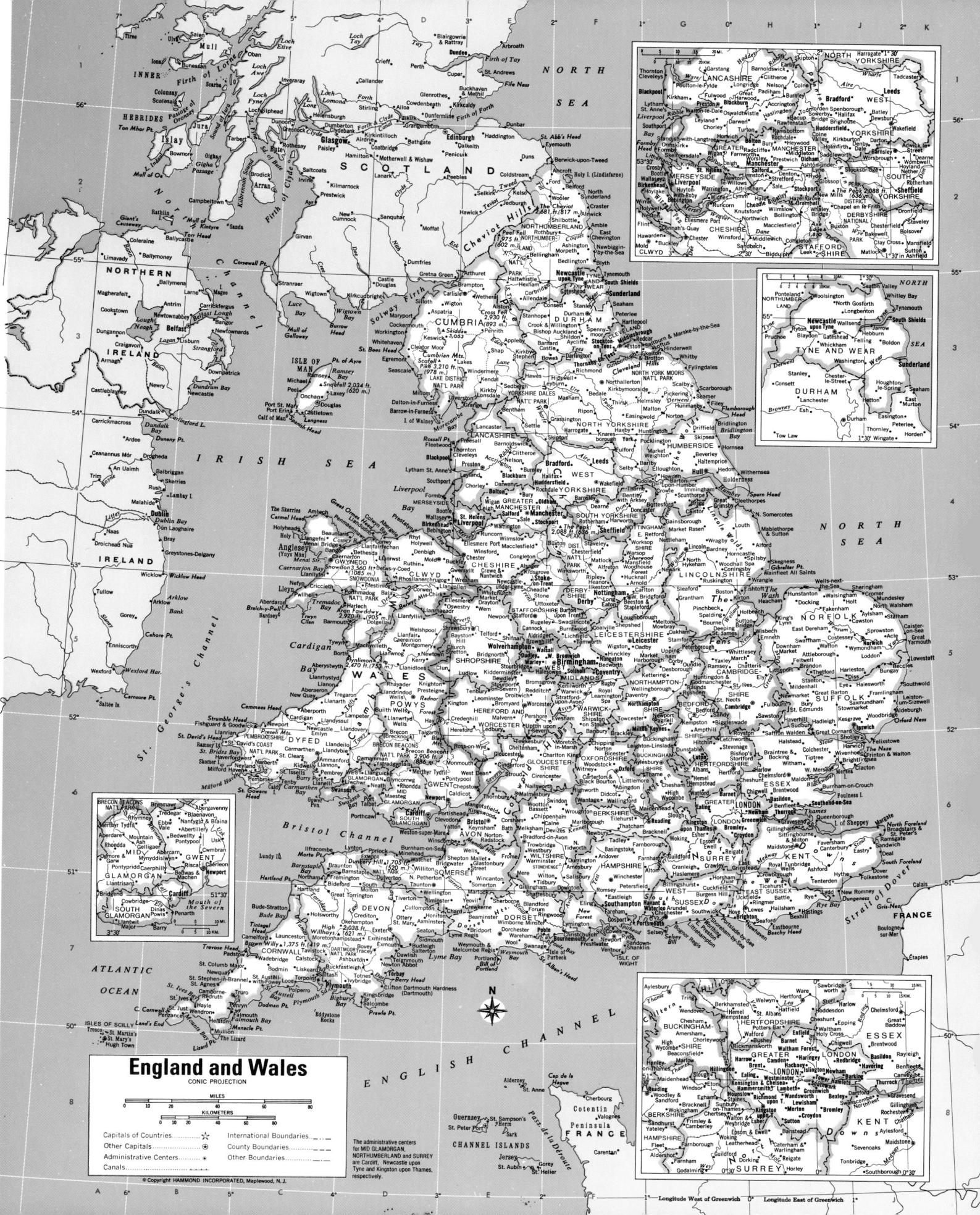

England and Wales

CONIC PROJECTION

MILES

0   10   20   40   60   80

KILOMETERS

Capitals of Countries .... ☆
Other Capitals .... ⊛
Administrative Centers .... ✴
Canals .... ⎯⎯⎯

International Boundaries .... ⎯⎯⎯
County Boundaries .... ⎯⎯⎯
Other Boundaries .... ⎯⎯⎯

The administrative centers
for MID GLAMORGAN,
NORTHUMBERLAND and SURREY
are Cardiff, Newcastle upon
Tyne and Kingston upon Thames,
respectively.

© Copyright HAMMOND INCORPORATED, Maplewood, N.J.

Lossiemouth and Branderburgh 6,847 .... E3
Macduff 3,887 .... F3
Mallaig 903 .... C4
Markinch 2,078 .... E4
Mauchline 3,663 .... D5
Maud 634 .... F3
Maybole 4,798 .... D5
Mayfield 1,333 .... D2
Melrose 2,345 .... F5
Melvaig⊙ 1,794 .... C3
Millport 1,472 .... A2
Milnathort 1,118 .... E4
Milngavie 12,067 .... B1
Mintlaw 2,299 .... F3
Moffat 2,051 .... E5
Monifieth 7,100 .... F4
Montrose 12,325 .... F4
Motherwell 30,676 .... C2
Muir of Ord 1,714 .... D3
Muirkirk 2,356 .... E5
Musselburgh 19,081 .... D2
Nairn 7,705 .... E3
Neilston 4,678 .... B2
Newarthill 7,003 .... C2
Newburgh 2,002 .... E4
Newcastleton 903 .... F5
New Cumnock 4,484 .... D5
New Galloway 337 .... D5
Newmains 6,847 .... C2
Newmilns and Greenholm 3,339 .... D5
New Pitsligo 1,125 .... F3
Newport-on-Tay 3,652 .... F4
New Scone 4,173 .... E4
Newtongrange 4,555 .... D2
Newton Mearns 15,543 .... B2
Newton Stewart 3,246 .... D6
Newtown Saint Boswells 1,095 .... F5
North Berwick 5,162 .... F4
Oakley 4,157 .... C1
Oban 8,111 .... C4
Old Kilpatrick 3,256 .... B2
Oldmeldrum 1,356 .... F3
Paisley 84,954 .... B2
Patna 2,490 .... D5
Peebles 6,692 .... E5
Penicuik 17,607 .... D2
Perth 43,010 .... E4
Peterculter 3,226 .... F3
Peterhead 17,085 .... G3
Pitlochry 12,621 .... E4
Pitmedden 1,103 .... F3
Pittenweem 1,544 .... F4
Poolewe⊙ 1,794 .... C3
Port Appin⊙ 2,172 .... C4
Port Askaig⊙ 1,795 .... B5
Port Bannatyne 1,414 .... A2
Port Ellen 1,020 .... B5
Port Glasgow 22,580 .... A2
Portknockie 1,239 .... F3
Portree 1,505 .... B3
Portsoy 1,784 .... F3
Prestonpans 7,621 .... D1
Prestwick 13,599 .... D5
Queensferry 7,540 .... D1
Renfrew 21,458 .... B2
Renton 3,443 .... A1
Rhu 1,540 .... A1
Rigside 1,066 .... E5
Rosehearty 1,243 .... F3
Rosneath 1,439 .... A1
Rothes 1,425 .... E3
Rothesay 5,455 .... A2
Rutherglen 24,091 .... B2
Saint Andrews 11,369 .... F4
Saint Monance 1,244 .... F4
Saline 1,192 .... C1
Saltcoats 12,834 .... D5
Sandbank 1,435 .... A1
Sanquhar 2,082 .... D5
Sauchie 6,082 .... C1
Selkirk 5,437 .... F5
Shotts 9,427 .... C2
Skelmorlie 1,689 .... A2
Slamannan 1,578 .... C2
Stanley 1,170 .... E4
Stenhousemuir 19,771 .... C1
Stevenston 11,337 .... D5
Stewarton 6,330 .... D5
Stirling 38,842 .... C1
Stonehaven 7,922 .... F4
Stonehouse 5,308 .... D5
Stornoway 8,638 .... B2
Stranraer 10,873 .... C6
Strathaven 6,152 .... D5
Stromeferry⊙ 1,724 .... C3
Stromness 1,832 .... E2
Sullam Voe G2
Tain 3,486 .... D3
Tarbert 1,403 .... C5
Tarbolton 2,012 .... D5
Tayport 3,029 .... F4
Thornhill, Central 443 .... D4
Thornhill, Dumfries and Galloway 1,473 .... E5
Thurso 8,896 .... E2
Tillicoultry 6,161 .... C1
Tobermory 652 .... B4
Tolob⊙ 2,033 .... G2
Tranent 8,079 .... F5
Troon 14,233 .... D5
Tullibody 6,082 .... C1
Turriff 3,683 .... F3
Tweedsmuir⊙ 105 .... E5
Tyndrum⊙ 1,153 .... D4
Uddingston 10,678 .... B2
Uig, Highland 103 .... B3
Uig, Western Isles⊙ 1,948 .... A2
Ullapool 1,146 .... C3
Uphall 3,035 .... C1
Viewpark 15,343 .... C2
Walkerburn 842 .... F5
Wemyss Bay 1,322 .... A2
West Calder 2,281 .... C2
West Kilbride 4,241 .... D5
West Linton 705 .... D2
Whitburn 12,610 .... C2
Whitehills 875 .... F3
Whithorn 990 .... D6
Wick 7,900 .... E2
Wigtown 1,015 .... D6
Winchburgh 2,398 .... D1
Wishaw 37,783 .... C2

OTHER FEATURES

A'Chralaig (mt.) C3
Annan (riv.) E5
Appin (dist.) 2,006 .... C4
Ardgour (dist.) 315 .... C4
Ardnamurchan (pt.) B4
Ardnamurchan (pen.) 764 .... B4
Argyll (dist.) 4,940 .... C4
Arisaig (sound) C4
Arkaig, Loch (lake) C4
Arran (isl.) 3,564 .... C5
Askival (mt.) B4
Assynt (dist.) 833 .... C2
Athol (dist.) 1,082 .... D4
Atlantic Ocean B2
Awe, Loch (lake) C4
Ayr (riv.) D5
Badenoch (dist.) 2,717 .... D4
Baleshare (isl.) 64 .... A3
Balmoral Castle (site) E3
Barra (head) A4
Barra (isl.) 1,005 .... A4
Barra Isles (isls.) 1,092 .... A4
Beauly (riv.) D3
Beinn a Ghlo (mt.) E4
Beinn Bheigeir (mt.) B5
Beinn Dearg (mt.) D3
Beinn Dhorain (mt.) E2
Beinn Eighe (mt.) C3
Ben Alder (mt.) D4
Ben Barvas (mt.) B2
Benbecula (isl.) 1,355 .... A3
Ben Cruachan (mt.) C4
Ben Hope (mt.) D2
Ben Kilbreck (mt.) D2
Ben Lawers (mt.) D4
Ben Lomond (mt.) D4
Ben Macdhui (mt.) E3
Ben Mhor (mt.) A3
Ben More (mt.) D4
Ben More Assynt (mt.) D2
Ben Nevis (mt.) D4
Bernera (isl.) 276 .... B2
Berneray (isl.) 131 .... A3
Berneray (isl.) 6 .... A4
Bidean nam Bian (mt.) D4
Black Isle (pen.) 7,209 .... D3
Blackwater (res.) D4
Bracadale, Loch (inlet) B3
Braemar (dist.) 7,624 .... E3
Bran (riv.) D3
Breadalbane (dist.) 3,649 .... D4
Bressay (isl.) 248 .... G2
Broad (bay) B2
Broad Law (mt.) E5
Broom, Loch (inlet) C3
Brough Ness (prom.) F2
Buchan (dist.) 40,089 .... F3
Buchan Ness (prom.) G3
Burray (isl.) 209 .... F2
Burrow (head) D6
Bute (isl.) 8,423 .... C5
Butt of Lewis (prom.) B2
Cairn Gorm (mt.) E3
Cairngorm (mts.) E3
Cairnsmore (mt.) D5
Caledonian (canal) D3
Canna (isl.) 22 .... B3
Carn Eige (mt.) C3
Carrick (dist.) 21,425 .... D5
Carron (riv.) C1
Cheviot (hills) F5
Cheviot, The (mt.) F5
Clisham (mt.) B3
Clyde (firth) D5
Clyde (riv.) D5
Coll (isl.) 144 .... B4
Colonsay (isl.) 137 .... B4
Corserine (mt.) D5
Corsewall (pt.) C5
Cowal (dist.) 15,548 .... C4
Cromarty (firth) D3
Cuillin (hills) B3
Cuillin (sound) B3
Dee (riv.) F3
Dennis (head) F1
Deveron (riv.) F3
Don (riv.) F3
Doon (riv.) D5
Dornoch (firth) D3
Duirinish (dist.) 1,085 .... B3
Duncansby (head) F2
Dunnet (head) E2
Dunnet (bay) E2
Earn (riv.) E4
Earn, Loch (lake) D4
East Loch Tarbert (inlet) B3
Eday (isl.) 179 .... F1
Eddrachillis (bay) C2
Eigg (isl.) 69 .... B4
Eishort, Loch (inlet) B3
Enard (bay) C2
Eriboll, Loch (inlet) D2
Ericht, Loch (lake) D4
Eriskay (isl.) 219 .... A3
Erisort, Loch (inlet) B2
Esk (riv.) F5
Etive, Loch (inlet) C4
Ewe, Loch (inlet) C3
Eye (pen.) 850 .... B2
Eynhallow (sound) E1
Eynort, Loch (inlet) A3
Fair Isle (isl.) 65 .... F3
Fannich, Loch (lake) D3
Fetlar (isl.) 88 .... G2
Fife Ness (prom.) F4
Findhorn (riv.) E3
Fionn Loch (lake) C3
Flannan (isls.) 3 .... A2
Fleet, Loch (inlet) D3
Formartine (dist.) 10,768 .... F3
Forth (firth) F4
Forth (riv.) B1
Forth and Clyde (canal) B2
Foula (isl.) 33 .... F2
Fyne, Loch (inlet) C5
Gairloch, Loch (inlet) C3
Gallan (head) A2
Galloway (dist.) 54,972 .... D5
Galloway, Mull of (prom.) D6
Garioch (dist.) 6,863 .... F3
Garry, Loch (lake) D3
Gigha (isl.) 174 .... C5
Glen More (dist.) 55,035 .... D3
Goat Fell (mt.) C5
Grampian (mts.) D4
Great Cumbrae (isl.) 1,296 .... A2
Green Lowther (mt.) E5
Greenstone (pt.) C3
Gruinard (bay) C3
Harris (dist.) 2,175 .... B3
Heads of Ayr (cape) D5
Hebrides (sea) B3
Hebrides, Inner (isls.) 14,881 .... B4
Hebrides, Outer (isls.) 29,615 .... A3
Helmsdale (riv.) E2
Herma Ness (prom.) G2
Hope, Loch (lake) D2
Hourn, Loch (inlet) C3
Hoy (isl.) 419 .... E2
Indaal, Loch (inlet) B5
Inner (sound) C3
Inner Hebrides (isls.) 14,881 .... B4
Iona (isl.) 145 .... B4
Islay (isl.) 3,816 .... B5
Jura (isl.) 210 .... C5
Katrine, Loch (lake) D4
Kerrera (isl.) 27 .... C4
Kilbrannan (sound) C5
Kinnairds (head) G3
Kintyre (pen.) 10,077 .... C5
Kintyre, Mull of (prom.) C5
Knapdale (dist.) 4,082 .... C5
Kyle of Tongue (inlet) D2
Ladder (hills) E3
Lammermuir (hills) F5
Langavat (lake) B2
Laxford, Loch (inlet) C2
Lennox (hills) B1
Leven (lake) E4
Leven, Loch (inlet) D4
Lewis (dist.) 20,047 .... B2
Lewis, Butt of (prom.) B2
Liddel Water (riv.) F5
Linnhe, Loch (inlet) C4
Lismore (isl.) 166 .... C4
Little Minch (sound) B3
Lochaber (dist.) 13,813 .... D4
Lochnagar (mt.) E4
Lochy, Loch (lake) D3
Lomond, Loch (lake) D4
Long, Loch (inlet) D4
Lorne (dist.) 12,162 .... C4
Lorne (firth) C4
Loyal, Loch (lake) D2
Loyne, Loch (lake) C3
Luce (bay) D6
Luing (isl.) 151 .... C4
Machers, The (pen.) 6,192 .... D6
Maddy, Loch (inlet) A3
Mainland (isl.) 12,747 .... E1
Mainland (isl.) 12,944 .... G2
Mar (dist.) 23,931 .... F3
Maree, Loch (lake) C3
May, Isle of (isl.) 10 .... F4
Merrick (mt.) D5
Minginish (dist.) 772 .... B3
Mingulay (isl.) A4
Moidart (dist.) 155 .... C4
Monach (isls.) A3
Monadhliath (mts.) D3
Monar, Loch (lake) C3
Moorfoot (hills) E5
Morar, Loch (lake) C4
Moray (firth) E3
Morven (mt.) E2
Morven (dist.) 398 .... C4
Muck (isl.) 24 .... B4
Muckle Flugga (isl.) 3 .... G2
Mull (isl.) 2,024 .... C4
Mull (head) F2
Mullardoch, Loch (lake) C3
Mull of Galloway (prom.) D6
Mull of Kintyre (prom.) C5
Mull of Oa (prom.) B5
Nairn (riv.) D3
Naver (riv.) D2
Ness (riv.) D3
Ness, Loch (lake) D3
Nevis, Loch (inlet) C3
Nith (riv.) E5
North (chan.) C5
North (sea) G4
North (sound) F1
North Esk (riv.) F4
North Minch (sound) B3
North Ronaldsay (isl.) 134 .... F1
North Uist (isl.) 1,469 .... A3
Noss (head) F2
Noup (head) E1
Oa, Mull of (prom.) B5
Ochil (hills) E4
Oich (riv.) D3
Oich, Loch (lake) D3
Orkney (isls.) 17,675 .... F1
Oronsay (isl.) 2 .... B4
Outer Hebrides (isls.) 29,615 .... A3
Oykel (riv.) D3
Pabbay (isl.) 4 .... A3
Papa Stour (isl.) 24 .... F2
Papa Westray (isl.) 106 .... F1
Paps of Jura (mt.) C5
Park (dist.) 210 .... B2
Peel Fell (mt.) F5
Pentland (firth) E2
Pentland (hills) D2
Quoich, Loch (lake) C3
Raasay (isl.) 163 .... C3
Rannoch (dist.) 1,177 .... D4
Rannoch, Loch (lake) D4
Renish (pt.) B3
Resort, Loch (inlet) A2
Rhinns (pt.) B5
Rhinns, The (pen.) 8,295 .... C6
Rhum (sound) B4
Riddon, Loch (inlet) C5
Roag, Loch (inlet) B2
Rona (isl.) 3 .... B3
Ronay (isl.) A3
Rora (head) E2
Ross of Mull (pen.) 585 .... B4
Rousay (isl.) 181 .... E1
Rudha Hunish (cape) B3
Rum (sound) B4
Rum (isl.) 40 .... B3
Ryan, Loch (inlet) C5
Saint Abbs (head) F5
Saint Kilda (isl.) 65 .... A2
Saint Magnus (bay) F2
Sanday (isl.) 592 .... F1
Sandray (isl.) A4
Scalpay (isl.) 483 .... B3
Scalpay (isl.) 5 .... C3
Scapa Flow (chan.) E2
Scarba (isl.) C4
Scarp (isl.) 12 .... A2
Scridain, Loch (inlet) B4
Seaforth, Loch (inlet) B3
Seil (isl.) 326 .... C4
Sgurr Alasdair (mt.) B3
Sgurr Mor (mt.) C3
Sgurr na Ciche (mt.) C3
Sgurr na Lapaich (mt.) C3
Shapinsay (isl.) 346 .... F1
Shetland (isls.) 18,494 .... G2
Shiant (isls.) B3
Shiel, Loch (lake) C4
Shin, Loch (lake) D2
Sidlaw (hills) E4
Sinclair's (bay) E2
Skye, Isle of (isl.) 7,183 .... B3
Sleat (dist.) 449 .... C3
Sleat (pt.) B4
Sleat (sound) C3
Small Isles (isls.) 171 .... B4
Snizort, Loch (inlet) B3
Soay (isl.) 5 .... B3
Solway (firth) E6
South Esk (riv.) F4
South Ronaldsay (isl.) 776 .... F2
South Uist (isl.) 2,281 .... A3
Spean (riv.) D4
Spey (riv.) E3
Staffa (isl.) B4
Start (pt.) F1
Stoer (pt.) C2
Storr, The (mt.) B3
Strathbogie (dist.) 7,959 .... F3
Strathmore (valley) E4
Strathspey (dist.) 6,668 .... E3
Striven Loch (inlet) A2
Stroma (isl.) 8 .... E2
Stronsay (isl.) 436 .... F1
Sumburgh (head) G2
Summer Isles (isls.) C2
Sunart Loch (inlet) C4
Taransay (isl.) 5 .... A3
Tarbat Ness (prom.) E3
Tarbert, East Loch (inlet) B3
Tarbert, Loch (inlet) B5
Tarbert, West Loch (inlet) A3
Tarbert, West Loch (inlet) C5
Tay (firth) F4
Tay (riv.) E4
Tay, Loch (lake) D4
Teith (riv.) D4
Teviot (riv.) F5
Thurso (riv.) E2
Tiree (isl.) 875 .... B4
Tiumpan (head) B2
Toe (head) A3
Tolsta (head) B2
Tor Ness (prom.) E2
Torridon, Loch (inlet) C3
Trossachs, The (valley) D4
Trotternish (dist.) 1,948 .... B3
Troup (head) F3
Tummel (lake) E4
Tweed (riv.) F5
Tyne (riv.) F5
Ulva (isl.) 23 .... B4
Unst (isl.) 1,124 .... G2
Vaternish (pt.) B3
Vaternish (dist.) 162 .... B3
Vatersay (isl.) 77 .... A4
Watten, Loch (lake) E2
West Loch Tarbert (inlet) C5
West Loch Tarbert (inlet) A3
Westray (isl.) 735 .... E1
Whalsay (isl.) 870 .... G2
White Coomb (mt.) E5
Wiay (isl.) A3
Wigtown (bay) D6
Wrath (cape) C2
Yarrow (riv.) E5
Yell (isl.) 1,143 .... G2
Yell (sound) G2

⊙ Population of parish.

Agriculture, Industry and Resources

DOMINANT LAND USE

- Cereals (chiefly oats, barley)
- Truck Farming, Horticulture
- Dairy, Mixed Farming
- Livestock, Mixed Farming
- Pasture Livestock

MAJOR MINERAL OCCURRENCES

Ba	Barite	Na	Salt
C	Coal	O	Petroleum
F	Fluorspar	Pb	Lead
Fe	Iron Ore	Pe	Peat
G	Natural Gas	Sn	Tin
K	Potash	Zn	Zinc
Ka	Kaolin (china clay)		

Water Power

Major Industrial Areas

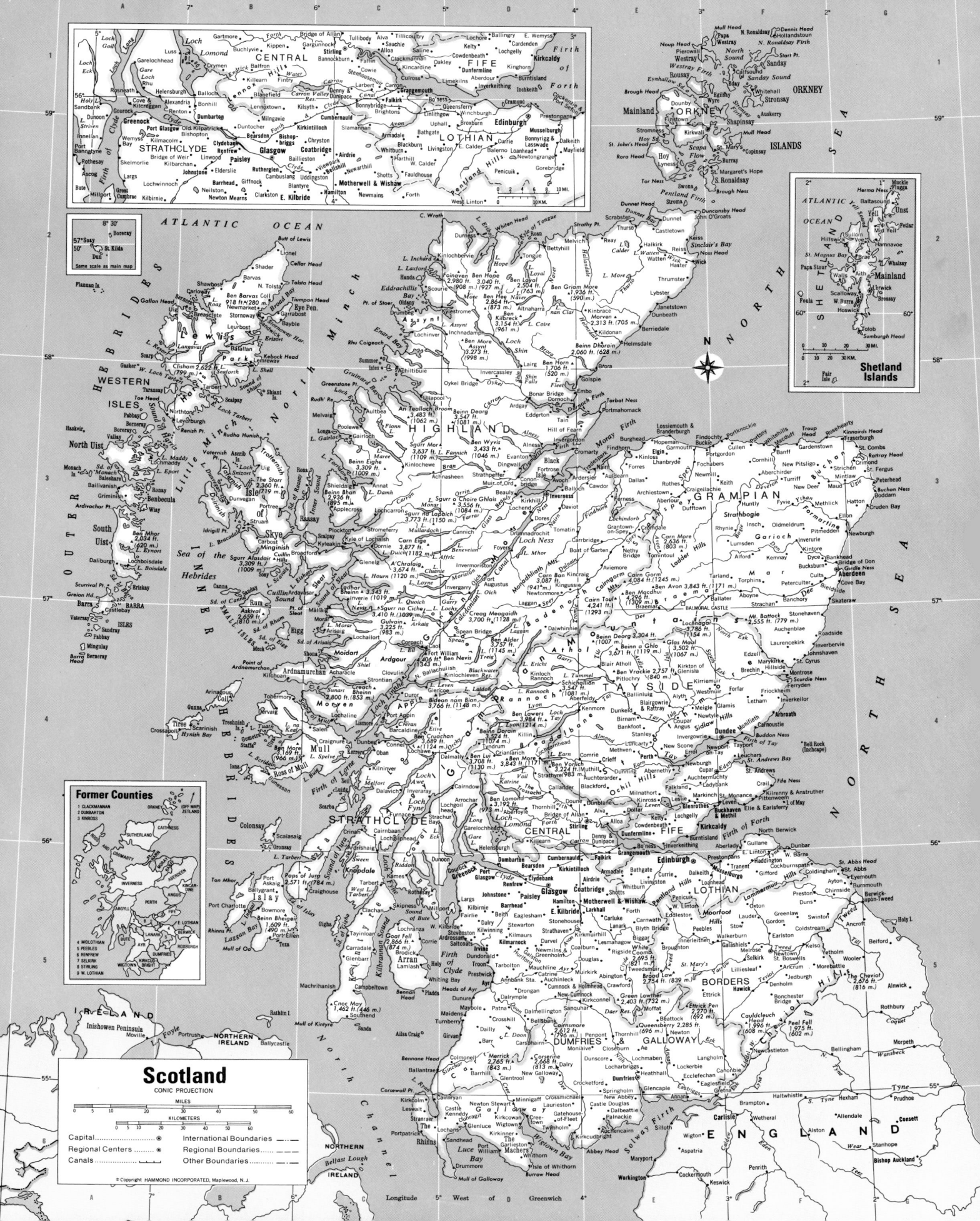

Scotland

CONIC PROJECTION

MILES

KILOMETERS

Capital.................................⊛   International Boundaries ___ ___
Regional Centers...............⊛   Regional Boundaries ....
Canals..................................   Other Boundaries ___ ___

© Copyright HAMMOND INCORPORATED, Maplewood, N.J.

Former Counties

1 CLACKMANNAN
2 DUNBARTON
3 KINROSS
4 MIDLOTHIAN
5 PEEBLES
6 RENFREW
7 SELKIRK
8 STIRLING
9 W. LOTHIAN

Shetland Islands

ATLANTIC OCEAN

Same scale as main map

16 United Kingdom and Ireland

(continued)

IRELAND

COUNTIES

Carlow 40,988 ....H6
Cavan 53,965 ....G4
Clare 91,344 ....D6
Cork 412,735 ....D7
Donegal 129,664 ....F2
Dublin 1,021,449 ....J5
Galway 178,552 ....D5
Kerry 124,159 ....B7
Kildare 116,247 ....H5
Kilkenny 73,186 ....G6
Laois 53,284 ....G6
Leitrim 27,035 ....E3
Leix (Laois) 53,284 ....G6
Limerick 164,569 ....D7
Longford 31,496 ....F4
Louth 91,810 ....J4
Mayo 115,184 ....C4
Meath 103,881 ....H4
Monaghan 52,379 ....H3
Offaly 59,835 ....F5
Roscommon 54,592 ....E4
Sligo 56,046 ....D3
Tipperary 136,619 ....F6
Waterford 91,151 ....F7
Westmeath 63,379 ....G5
Wexford 102,552 ....H7
Wicklow 94,542 ....J6

CITIES and TOWNS

Abbeyfeale 1,483 ....C7
Abbeyleix 1,468 ....G6
Adare 792 ....D6
Aghada-Farsid-Rostellan 818 ..E8
An Uaimh 3,660 ....H4
Ardee 3,253 ....H4
Ardfinnan 827 ....F7
Ardmore 343 ....F8
Arklow 8,388 ....J6
Ashford 782 ....J5
Askeaton 951 ....D6
Athboy 1,055 ....H4
Athenry 1,642 ....D5
Athlone 8,815 ....F5
Athy 4,734 ....H6
Aughrim 756 ....J6
Avoca 490 ....J6
Bagenalstown (Muinebeag) 2,653 ....H6
Baile Atha Cliath (Dublin) (cap.) 502,749 ....K5
Bailieborough 1,645 ....G4
Balbriggan 5,680 ....J4
Ballaghaderreen 1,366 ....E4
Ballina, Mayo 6,714 ....C3
Ballina, Tipperary 507 ....E6
Ballinamore 810 ....F3
Ballinasloe 6,125 ....E5
Ballincollig-Carrigrohane 7,231 ....D8
Ballineen 592 ....D8
Ballinrobe 1,270 ....C4
Ballybofey-Stranorlar 2,964 ....F2
Ballybunion 1,452 ....B7
Ballycastle 219 ....C3
Ballyconnell 466 ....F3
Ballygar 472 ....E4
Ballygeary 891 ....J7
Ballyhaunis 1,338 ....D4
Ballyheigue 660 ....B7
Ballyjamesduff 842 ....G4
Ballylanders 343 ....E7
Ballylongford 523 ....B6
Ballymahon 859 ....F4
Ballymore Eustace 575 ....J5
Ballymote 1,064 ....D3
Ballyragget 833 ....G6
Ballyshannon 2,573 ....E3
Baltinglass 1,089 ....H6
Banagher 1,465 ....F5
Bandon 1,943 ....D8
Bantry 2,811 ....C8
Belmullet 1,033 ....B3
Belturbet 1,228 ....G3
Bennettsbridge 601 ....G6
Birr 3,417 ....F5
Blanchardstown H5
Blarney 1,952 ....D8
Blessington 1,322 ....J5
Borrisokane 837 ....E6
Borrisoleigh 624 ....E6
Boyle 1,859 ....E4
Bray 24,686 ....K5
Bri Chualann (Bray) 24,686 ....K5
Bruff 819 ....D7
Bunbeg-Derrybeg 1,469 ....E1
Bunclody-Carrickduff 1,423 ....H6
Buncrana 3,106 ....G1
Bundoran 1,535 ....E3
Buttevant 1,133 ....D7
Cahir 2,118 ....F7
Cahirciveen 1,310 ....A8
Callan 1,266 ....G7
Cappamore 765 ....E6
Cappoquin 920 ....F7
Carlingford 635 ....J3
Carlow 11,509 ....H6
Carndonagh 1,600 ....G1
Carnew 723 ....H6
Carrickmacross 1,815 ....H4
Carrick-on-Shannon 1,984 ....F4
Carrick-on-Suir 5,353 ....F7
Carrigaline 5,893 ....E8
Carrigtwohill 1,272 ....E8
Cashel 2,458 ....F7
Castlebar 6,349 ....C4
Castlebellingham 848 ....J4
Castleblayney 2,157 ....H3
Castlebridge 655 ....J7
Castlecomer-Donaguile 1,490 ....G6
Castledermot 792 ....H6
Castlefin 694 ....F2
Castleisland 2,281 ....B7
Castlemartyr 585 ....E8
Castlepollard 803 ....G4
Castlerea 1,840 ....D4
Castletown 303 ....F6
Castletownbere 905 ....B8
Castletownroche 474 ....D7
Cavan 3,381 ....G3
Ceanannus Mór 2,413 ....G4
Celbridge 7,135 ....H5
Charlestown-Bellahy 754 ....D4
Charleville (Rathluirc) 2,814 ....D7
Clara 2,736 ....F5
Claremorris 1,992 ....C4
Clifden 896 ....B5
Cloghan 496 ....F5
Clogh-Chatsworth 319 ....G6
Clogheen 502 ....F7
Clogherhead 765 ....J4
Clonakilty 2,567 ....D8
Clones 2,280 ....G3
Clonfert E5
Clonmel 11,759 ....F7
Cloughjordan 499 ....E6
Cloyne 721 ....E8
Cóbh 6,369 ....E8
Coill Dubh 772 ....H5
Collooney 705 ....E3
Convoy 891 ....F2
Coolgreany 352 ....J6
Cootehill 1,487 ....G3
Cork 133,271 ....E8
Corofin 391 ....C6
Courtown Harbour 317 ....J6
Creeslough 340 ....F1
Croom 1,024 ....D6
Crosshaven 1,362 ....E8
Crossmolina 1,250 ....C3
Daingean 659 ....G5
Delvin 309 ....G4
Dingle 1,253 ....A7
Donabate 599 ....J5
Donegal 2,242 ....F2
Doneraile 846 ....D7
Dooagh-Keel 650 ....A4
Doon 308 ....E6
Drimoleague 381 ....C8
Drogheda 24,086 ....J4
Droichead Nua 5,983 ....H5
Dromahair 353 ....E3
Drumconrath 334 ....H4
Drumshanbo 622 ....E3
Dublin (cap.) 502,749 ....K5
Duleek 1,679 ....J4
Duncannon 388 ....H7
Dundalk 26,669 ....H3
Dunfanaghy 314 ....F1
Dungarvan 6,849 ....F7
Dungloe 940 ....E2
Dún Laoghaire 54,715 ....K5
Dunkineely 442 ....E2
Dunlavin 734 ....H5
Dunleer 1,184 ....J4
Dunmanway 1,382 ....C8
Dunmore 445 ....D4
Dunmore East 1,041 ....G7
Dunshaughlin 878 ....H5
Durrow 707 ....G6
Edenderry 3,539 ....G5
Elphin 513 ....E4
Emyvale 464 ....G3
Ennis 5,917 ....D6
Enniscorthy 4,483 ....J7
Enniskerry 1,229 ....J5
Ennistymon 1,039 ....C6
Eyrecourt 351 ....E5
Fahan 367 ....G1
Falcarragh 996 ....E1
Fenit 401 ....B7
Ferbane 1,374 ....F5
Fermoy 2,872 ....E7
Ferns 811 ....J6
Fethard 982 ....F7
Foxford 1,033 ....C4
Foynes 707 ....C6
Frankford (Kilcormac) 1,118 ....F5
Freshford 700 ....G6
Galbally 248 ....E7
Galway 47,104 ....C5
Geashill 339 ....G5
Glanworth 379 ....E7
Glenamaddy 369 ....D4
Glenties 914 ....E2
Glin 569 ....C6
Golden 295 ....F7
Gorey 2,445 ....J6
Gormanston 870 ....J4
Gort 1,021 ....D5
Gowran 517 ....G6
Graiguenamanagh-Tinnahinch 1,485 ....H6
Granard 1,338 ....F4
Greencastle 584 ....H1
Greystones 8,455 ....K5
Hacketstown 710 ....H6
Headford 675 ....C5
Holycross 274 ....F6
Hospital 751 ....E7
Inniscrone 633 ....C3
Johnstown 408 ....G6
Kanturk 1,870 ....D7
Keel-Dooagh 650 ....A4
Kells (Ceanannus Mór) 2,413 ....G4
Kenmare 1,130 ....B8
Kilbeggan 603 ....G5
Kilcar 345 ....D2
Kilcock 1,414 ....H5
Kilcoole 2,335 ....K5
Kilcormac 1,118 ....F5
Kilcullen 1,693 ....H5
Kildare 4,268 ....H5
Kildysart 347 ....C6
Kilfinane 788 ....D7
Kilkee 1,448 ....B6
Kilkenny 8,969 ....G6
Killala 674 ....C3
Killaloe 1,033 ....D6
Killarney 7,837 ....C7
Killenaule 717 ....F6
Killeshandra 455 ....F3
Killorglin 1,304 ....B7
Killucan-Rathwire 353 ....G4
Killybegs 1,632 ....E2
Kilmacrennan 412 ....F1
Kilmacthomas 648 ....G7
Kilmallock 1,424 ....D7
Kilmihill 338 ....C6
Kilmore Quay 458 ....H7
Kilnaleck 321 ....G4
Kilronan 282 ....B5
Kilrush 2,961 ....C6
Kiltimagh 982 ....C4
Kilworth 411 ....E7
Kingscourt 1,242 ....H4
Kingstown (Dún Laoghaire) 54,715 ....K5
Kinnegad 433 ....G5
Kinnitty 261 ....F5
Kinsale 1,811 ....D8
Kinvara 425 ....D5
Knightstown 204 ....A8
Knock 332 ....D4
Knocklong 273 ....D7
Lahinch 511 ....C6
Lanesborough-Ballyleague 1,058 ....E4
Laytown-Bettystown-Mornington 3,321 ....J4
Leighlinbridge 540 ....H6
Leitrim F3
Leixlip 11,938 ....H5
Letterkenny 6,691 ....F2
Lifford 1,478 ....F2
Limerick 56,279 ....D6
Lisdoonvarna 648 ....C5
Lismore 703 ....F7
Listowel 3,494 ....C7
Littleton 566 ....F6
Longford 6,457 ....F4
Loughrea 3,360 ....E5
Louisburgh 209 ....B4
Louth 435 ....J4
Lucan 12,259 ....J5
Luimneach (Limerick) 56,279 ..D6
Lusk 1,831 ....J4
Macroom 2,449 ....C8
Malahide 9,940 ....J5
Mallow 6,488 ....D7
Manorhamilton 1,031 ....E3
Maryborough (Portlaoise) 3,773 ....G5
Maynooth 4,768 ....H5
Meathas Truim 806 ....G4
Midleton 3,111 ....E8
Milford 981 ....F1
Millstreet 1,330 ....D7
Milltown 347 ....A7
Miltownmalbay 719 ....C6
Mitchelstown 3,210 ....E7
Moate 1,659 ....F5
Mohill 930 ....F4
Monaghan 6,075 ....G3
Monasterevan 2,143 ....H5
Moneygall 346 ....F6
Mooncoin 868 ....G7
Mount Bellew 519 ....D5
Mountcharles 480 ....E2
Mountmellick 2,789 ....G5
Mountrath 1,402 ....F5
Moville 1,331 ....G1
Moycullen 366 ....C5
Muinebeag 2,653 ....H6
Mullagh 462 ....H4
Mullinahone 385 ....F7
Mullinavat 355 ....G7
Mullingar 8,077 ....G4
Naas 10,017 ....H5
Navan (An Uaimh) 3,660 ....H4
Nenagh 5,483 ....E6
Newbliss 293 ....G3
Newbridge (Droichead Nua) 5,983 ....H5
Newcastle 3,370 ....C7
Newmarket 1,022 ....C7
Newmarket-on-Fergus 1,678 ..D6
Newport, Mayo 492 ....C4
Newport, Tipperary 857 ....E6
New Ross 5,343 ....H7
Newtown Forbes 393 ....F4
Newtownmountkennedy 2,183 ....J5
Newtownsandes 357 ....C6
O'Briensbridge-Montpelier 385 ....D6
Oldcastle 869 ....G4
Oola 451 ....E6
Oranmore 1,064 ....D5
Oughterard 682 ....C5
Passage East 563 ....G7
Passage West 3,511 ....E8
Patrickswell 905 ....D6
Piltown 691 ....G7
Portarlington 3,295 ....G5
Portlaoise 3,773 ....G5
Portlaw 1,260 ....G7
Portmarnock 9,055 ....J5
Portumna 1,062 ....E5
Queenstown (Cóbh) 6,369 ....E8
Ramelton 989 ....F1
Raphoe 1,027 ....F2
Rathangan 1,270 ....G5
Rathcoole 2,991 ....J5
Rathdowney 1,095 ....F6
Rathdrum 1,307 ....J6
Rathkeale 1,815 ....D7
Rathluirc 2,814 ....D7
Rathmore 548 ....J5
Rathmullen 554 ....F1
Rathnew 1,389 ....J6
Rathvilly 512 ....H6
Ratoath 551 ....J5
Riverstown 1,416 ....E8
Roscommon 1,363 ....E4
Roscrea 4,378 ....F6
Rosscarbery 425 ....C8
Rosses Point 598 ....D3
Rosslare 704 ....J7
Rosslare Harbour (Ballygeary) 891 ....J7
Roundwood 371 ....J5
Rush 4,513 ....J4
Saint Johnston 468 ....F2
Scarriff 847 ....E6
Schull 509 ....B8
Shanagolden 402 ....C6
Shannon 8,005 ....D6
Shannon Bridge 310 ....F5
Shercock 406 ....G4
Shillelagh 334 ....J6
Shinrone 479 ....F5
Sixmilebridge 1,182 ....D6
Skerries 6,864 ....J4
Skibbereen 1,999 ....C8
Slane 689 ....H4
Sligo 17,259 ....E3
Sneem 309 ....B8
Stepaside 748 ....J5
Stradbally, Laois 1,046 ....G5
Stradbally, Waterford 255 ....F7
Strokestown 620 ....E4
Swinford 1,197 ....C4
Swords 15,312 ....J5
Taghmon 607 ....H7
Tallow 867 ....F7
Tarbert 683 ....C6
Templemore 2,258 ....F6
Templetuohy 242 ....F6
Termonfeckin 741 ....J4
Thomastown 1,465 ....G7
Thurles 7,049 ....F6
Timoleague 330 ....D8
Tinahely 594 ....H6
Tipperary 5,033 ....E7
Toomevara 428 ....E6
Tralee 17,109 ....B7
Tramore 5,999 ....G7
Trim 1,967 ....H4
Tuam 4,109 ....D4
Tubbercurry 1,250 ....D3
Tulla 403 ....D6
Tullamore 8,484 ....G5
Tullow 2,324 ....H6
Tyrrellspass 328 ....G5
Urlingford 676 ....F6
Virginia 699 ....G4
Waterford 39,529 ....G7
Waterville-Spunkane 475 ....A8
Westport 3,456 ....C4
Wexford 10,336 ....H7
Wicklow 5,304 ....K6
Woodford 242 ....E5
Youghal 5,706 ....F8

OTHER FEATURES

Achill (head) A4
Achill (isl.) A4
Allen (lake) E3
Allen, Bog of (marsh) H5
Annalee (riv.) G3
Aran (isls.) B5
Aran (isl.) D2
Arrow (lake) E3
Ballinskelligs (bay) A8
Ballyhoura (hills) E7
Ballyteige (bay) H7
Bandon (riv.) D8
Bantry (bay) B8
Barrow (riv.) H7
Baurtregaum (mt.) A7
Bear (isl.) B8
Ben Dash (hill) C6
Bertraghboy (bay) A5
Black (head) C5
Blacksod (bay) A3
Blackstairs (mt.) H6
Blackwater (riv.) H4
Blackwater (riv.) D7
Blasket (isls.) A7
Bloody Foreland (prom.) E1
Blue Stack (mts.) E2
Boderg (lake) E4
Boggeragh (mts.) D7
Bolus (head) A8
Boyne (riv.) J4
Brandon (bay) A7
Brandon (head) A7
Brandon (mt.) A7
Bray (head) A8
Bride (riv.) E7
Broad Haven (harb.) B3
Brosna (riv.) F5
Bull, The (isl.) A8
Caha (mts.) B8
Cahore (pt.) J6
Cark (mt.) F2
Carlingford (inlet) J3
Carnsore (pt.) J7
Carra (lake) C4
Carrantuohill (mt.) B7
Carrowmore (lake) B3
Clare (isls.) A4
Clare (riv.) D5
Clear (cape) B9
Clear (isl.) C9
Clew (bay) B4
Clonakilty (bay) D8
Comeragh (mts.) F7
Conn (lake) C3
Connacht (prov.) 431,409 ....C4
Connemara (dist.) B5
Cork (harb.) E8
Corrib (lake) C5
Croagh Patrick (mt.) C4
Cuilcagh (mt.) F3
Cullin (lake) C4
Curragh, The (plain) H5
Dash, Ben (hill) C6
Dee (riv.) H4
Deel (riv.) C3
Deel (riv.) C7
Deel (riv.) G4
Deele (riv.) F2
Derg (lake) F2
Derg (lake) E6
Derravaragh (lake) G4
Derryveagh (mts.) E2
Devilsbit (mt.) E6
Dingle (bay) A7
Donegal (bay) D3
Donegal (pt.) B6
Doulus (head) A8
Downpatrick (head) C3
Drum (hills) F7
Dublin (bay) J5
Dunany (pt.) J4
Dundalk (bay) J4
Dungarvan (harb.) G7
Dunkellin (riv.) D5
Dunmanus (bay) B8
Dursey (isl.) A8
Eask (lake) E2
Ennell (lake) G5
Erne (riv.) E3
Errigal (mt.) E1
Erris (head) A3
Fanad (head) F1
Fastnet Rock (isl.) B9
Feale (riv.) C7
Feeagh (lake) B4
Fergus (riv.) D6
Finn (riv.) F2
Finn (riv.) G3
Foul (sound) B5
Foyle (inlet) G1
Foyle (riv.) G2
Galley (head) D9
Galtee (mts.) E7
Galtymore (mt.) E7
Galway (bay) C5
Gara (lake) D4
Garadice (lake) F3
Gill (lake) E3
Gola (isl.) E1
Golden Vale (plain) E7
Gorumna (isl.) B5
Gowna (lake) G4
Grand (canal) G5
Great Blasket (isl.) A7
Gregory's (sound) B5
Gweebarra (bay) D2
Hags (head) B6
Hook (head) H7
Horn (head) E1
Iar Connacht (dist.) C5
Inishbofin (isl.) A4
Inisheer (isl.) B5
Inishmaan (isl.) C5
Inishmore (isl.) B5
Inishmurray (isl.) D3
Inishowen (head) H1
Inishowen (pen.) G1
Inishshark (isl.) A4
Inishtrahull (isl.) G1
Inishtrahull (sound) G1
Inishturk (isls.) A4
Inny (riv.) F4
Ireland's Eye (isl.) K5
Irish (sea) K4
Joyce's Country (dist.) B4
Keeper (hill) E6
Kenmare (riv.) A8
Kerry (head) A7
Key (lake) E3
Kilkieran (bay) B5
Killala (bay) C3
Killary (harb.) A4
Kinsale (harb.) E8
Kinsale, Old Head of (head) E8
Kippure (mt.) J5
Knockanefune (mt.) C7
Knockboy (mt.) B8
Knockmealdown (mts.) F7
Lambay (hill) K4
Laune (riv.) B7
Leane (lake) G4
Lee (riv.) D8
Leinster (mt.) H6
Leinster (prov.) 1,852,649 ....G5
Lettermullan (isl.) B5
Liffey (riv.) H5
Liscannor (bay) B6
Loop (head) A6
Loughros More (bay) D2
Lugnaquillia (mt.) J5
Lung (riv.) D4
Macgillicuddy's Reeks (mts.) ..B7
Macnean (lake) F3
Maigue (riv.) D6
Malin (head) F1
Mangerton (mt.) C8
Mask (lake) C4
Maumakeogh (mt.) C3
Maumturk (mts.) B5
Melvin (lake) E3
Mine (head) F8
Mizen (head) B9
Mizen (head) K6
Moher (cliff) B6
Monavullagh (mts.) F7
Moy (riv.) C3
Mullaghareirk (mts.) C7
Mulroy (bay) F1
Munster (prov.) 1,020,577 ....D7
Mutton (isl.) B6
Mweelrea (mt.) B4
Nagles (mts.) E7
Nephin (mt.) C3
Nephin Beg (mt.) B3
Nore (riv.) G7
North (sound) B5
North Inishkea (isl.) A3
Oughter (lake) G3
Ovoca (riv.) J6
Owenmore (riv.) B3
Owenmore (riv.) D3
Paps, The (mt.) C7
Partry (mts.) C4
Pollaphuca (res.) J5
Puffin (isl.) A8
Punchestown H5
Ramor (lake) G4
Rathlin O'Birne (isl.) C2
Ree (lake) F5
Rinn (lake) F4
Roaringwater (bay) B9
Rosscarbery (bay) D9
Rosskeeragh (pt.) D3
Royal (canal) G4
Saint Finan's (bay) A8
Saint George's (chan.) K7
Saint John's (pt.) D2
Saltee (isls.) H7
Scarriff (isl.) A8
Seven Hogs, The (isls.) A7
Shannon (riv.) E6
Shannon, Mouth of the (delta) B6
Sheeffry (hills) B4
Sheelin (lake) G4
Sheep Haven (harb.) F1
Sheeps (head) B8
Shehy (mts.) C8
Sherkin (isl.) C9
Silvermine (mts.) E6
Slaney (riv.) H7
Slieve Anierin (mt.) F3
Slieve Aughty (mts.) D5
Slieve Bernagh (mt.) D6
Slieve Bloom (mts.) F5
Slieve Callan (mt.) C6
Slieve Car (mt.) B3
Slieve Elva (mt.) C5
Slieve Gamph (Ox) (mts.) D3
Slievefelim (mts.) E6
Slievenaman (mt.) F7
Sligo (bay) D3
Slyne (head) A5
Smerwick (harb.) A7
South (sound) C5
Stacks (mts.) B7
Suck (riv.) E5
Sugarloaf (mt.) B8
Suir (riv.) G7
Swilly (inlet) F1
Tara (hill) H4
Toe (head) C9
Tory (isl.) E1
Tory (sound) E1
Tralee (bay) B7
Tramore (bay) G7
Truskmore (mt.) E3
Twelve Pins (mt.) B4
Ulster (part) (prov.) 236,008 ..G2
Valencia (Valentia) (isl.) A8
Valentia (isl.) A8
Waterford (harb.) G7
Wexford (harb.) J7
Wexford (bay) J7
Wicklow (mts.) J6
Youghal (bay) F8

NORTHERN IRELAND

DISTRICTS

Antrim 44,384 ....J2
Ards 57,626 ....K2
Armagh 47,618 ....H3
Ballymena 54,426 ....J2
Ballymoney 22,873 ....J1
Banbridge 29,885 ....J3
Belfast 295,223 ....J2
Carrickfergus 28,458 ....K2
Castlereagh 60,757 ....K2
Coleraine 46,272 ....H1
Cookstown 26,624 ....H2
Craigavon 71,202 ....J3
Down 52,869 ....K3
Dungannon 41,073 ....H3
Fermanagh 51,008 ....F3
Larne 28,929 ....K2
Limavady 26,270 ....H1
Lisburn 82,091 ....J2
Londonderry 83,384 ....G2
Magherafelt 30,825 ....H2
Mourne (Newry and Mourne) 72,243 ....J3
Moyle 14,252 ....J1
Newtownabbey 71,631 ....J2
North Down 65,849 ....K2
Omagh 41,159 ....G2
Strabane 35,028 ....G2

CITIES and TOWNS

Annalong 1,823 ....K3
Antrim 22,342 ....J2
Armagh 12,700 ....H3
Augher 1,874 ....G3
Aughnacloy 1,659 ....H3
Ballycarry 1,652 ....K2
Ballycastle 3,284 ....J1
Ballyclare 6,159 ....J2
Ballygawley 2,099 ....G3
Ballymena 28,166 ....J2
Ballymoney 5,679 ....J1
Ballynahinch 3,721 ....J3
Banbridge 9,650 ....J3
Bangor 46,585 ....K2
Belfast (cap.) 295,223 ....J2
Bellaghy 1,854 ....H2
Belleek and Boa 2,469 ....E3
Beragh 2,028 ....G2
Bessbrook 2,756 ....J3
Brookeborough 2,250 ....G3
Broughshane 1,503 ....J2
Bushmills 1,381 ....J1
Caledon 1,633 ....H3
Carnlough 1,462 ....K2
Carrickfergus 17,633 ....K2
Carrowdore 3,019 ....K2
Carryduff 2,666 ....K2
Castledawson 1,460 ....H2
Castlederg 1,730 ....F2
Castlewellan 2,105 ....K3
Claudy 2,516 ....G2
Clogher 1,792 ....G3
Cloughmills 1,558 ....J2
Coalisland 3,324 ....H2
Coleraine 15,967 ....H1
Comber 7,600 ....K2
Cookstown 7,649 ....H2
Craigavon 10,195 ....J3
Crumlin 1,708 ....J2
Cullybackey 2,098 ....J2
Derrygonnelly 2,627 ....F3
Donaghadee 3,874 ....K2
Downpatrick 8,245 ....K3
Dromore, Banbridge 3,089 ....J3
Dromore, Omagh 2,286 ....G3
Drumquin 1,865 ....F2
Dundrum 2,295 ....K3
Dungannon 8,295 ....H3
Dungiven 2,249 ....H2
Dunloy 1,593 ....J1
Dunnamanagh 2,191 ....G2
Ederney, Kesh and Lark 2,607 ....F2
Enniskillen 10,429 ....F3
Feeny 1,402 ....H2
Fintona 1,353 ....G3
Fivemiletown 1,758 ....G3
Garvagh 2,222 ....H2
Gilford 1,512 ....J3
Glenarm 1,533 ....J2
Glenavy 2,402 ....J2
Glynn 1,689 ....K2
Gortin 1,877 ....G2
Greenisland 5,103 ....K2
Grey Abbey 2,945 ....K2
Groomsport 3,870 ....K2
Holywood 9,462 ....K2
Irvinestown 1,827 ....F3
Keady 2,561 ....H3
Kells 2,564 ....J2
Kesh, Ederney and Lark 2,607 ....F3
Kilkeel 6,036 ....K3
Killough 3,104 ....K3
Killyclogher 5,557 ....G2
Killyleagh 2,094 ....K3
Kilrea 1,320 ....H2
Lambeg J2
Larne 18,224 ....K2
Limavady 8,015 ....H1
Lisbellaw 2,395 ....K2
Lisburn 40,391 ....J2
Lisnaskea 1,568 ....G3
Londonderry (Derry) 62,692 ....G2
Loughbrickland 2,244 ....J3
Lurgan 20,991 ....J3
Macosquin 2,267 ....H1
Maghera 1,953 ....H2
Magherafelt 5,044 ....H2
Millisle 1,373 ....K2
Moy 2,163 ....H3
Newcastle 6,246 ....J3
Newry 19,426 ....J3
Newtownabbey 56,149 ....K2
Newtownards 20,531 ....K2
Newtownbutler 2,632 ....G3
Newtownhamilton 1,654 ....H3
Newtownstewart 1,425 ....G2
Omagh 14,627 ....G2
Pomeroy 1,638 ....H2
Portadown 21,333 ....H3
Portaferry 2,148 ....K3
Portglenone 2,017 ....H2
Portrush 5,114 ....H1
Portstewart 5,312 ....H1
Randalstown 3,591 ....J2
Rathfriland 2,243 ....J3
Richhill 1,728 ....H3
Rostrevor 1,852 ....J3
Sion Mills 1,771 ....G2
Sixmilecross 1,613 ....G2
Stewartstown 1,554 ....H2
Strabane 9,413 ....G2
Strangford 2,062 ....K3
Strathfoyle 2,050 ....G1
Tandragee 2,224 ....J3
Tempo 2,149 ....G3
Trillick 2,017 ....G3
Warrenpoint 4,798 ....J3
Whitehead 3,546 ....K2

OTHER FEATURES

Arney (riv.) F3
Bann (riv.) H2
Beg (lake) J2
Belfast (inlet) K2
Blackwater (riv.) H3
Bush (riv.) H1
Copeland (isl.) K2
Derg (riv.) F2
Divis (mt.) J2
Dundrum (bay) K3
Erne, Lough (lake) F3
Fair (head) J1
Foyle (riv.) G2
Foyle (inlet) G1
Garron (pt.) K1
Giant's Causeway H1
Lagan (riv.) K2
Larne (inlet) K2
Macnean (lake) F3
Magee, Island (pen.) K2
Main (riv.) J2
Mourne (riv.) G2
Mourne (mts.) J3
Neagh (lake) J2
North (chan.) K1
Owenkillew (riv.) G2
Rathlin (sound) J1
Rathlin (isl.) J1
Red (bay) K1
Roe (riv.) H1
Saint John's (pt.) K3
Slieve Beagh (mt.) G3
Slieve Donard (mt.) K3
Sperrin (mts.) G2
Strangford (inlet) K3
Trostan (mt.) J1
Ulster (part) (prov.) G2
Upper Lough Erne (lake) F3

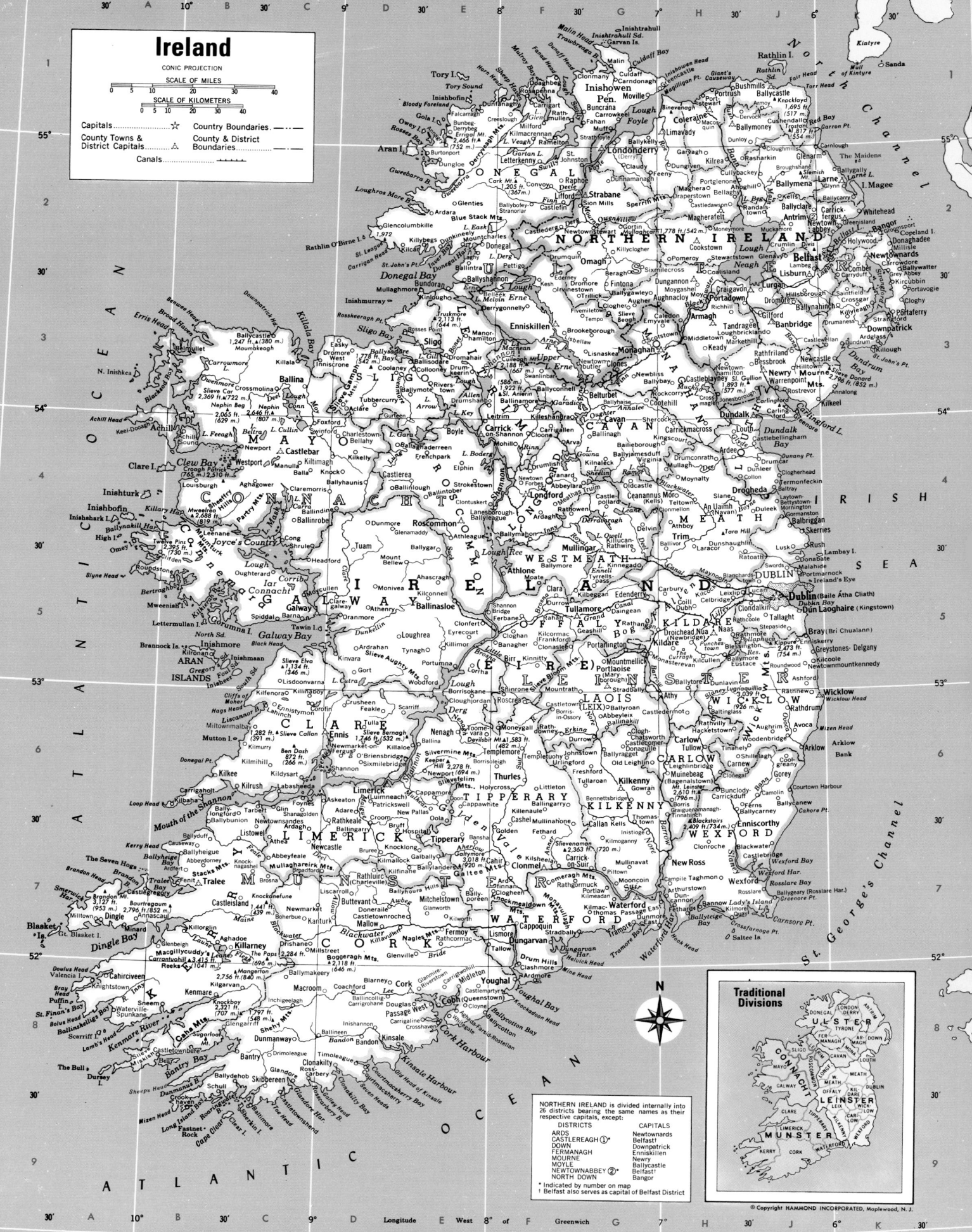

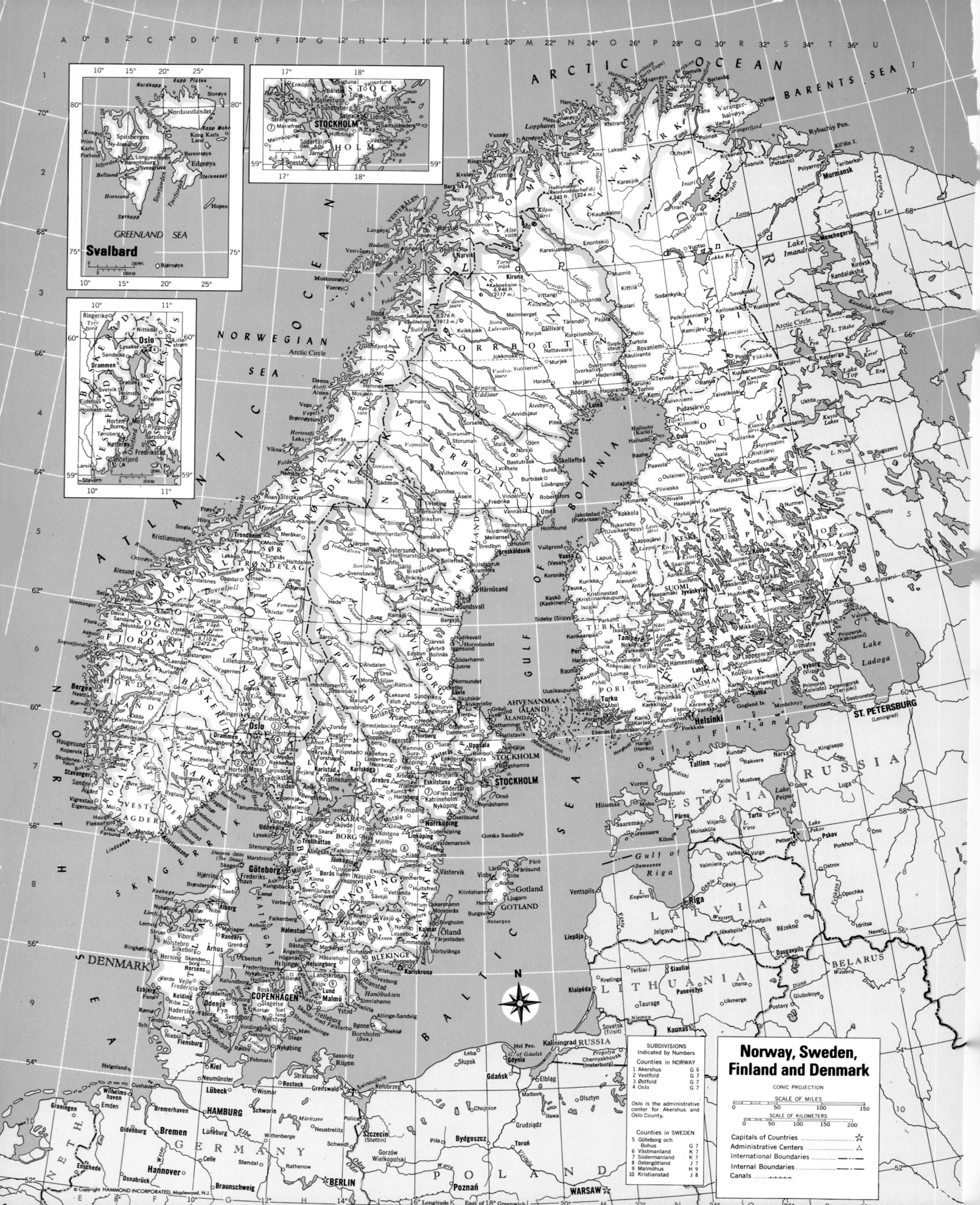

Svalbard

SCALE
0   100 MI.
0   100 KM.

STOCKHOLM

Oslo

Norway, Sweden, Finland and Denmark

CONIC PROJECTION

SCALE OF MILES
0   150

SCALE OF KILOMETERS
0   200

SUBDIVISIONS
Indicated by Numbers

Counties in NORWAY
1 Akershus .... G 6
2 Vestfold .... G 7
3 Østfold .... G 7
4 Oslo

Oslo is the administrative
center for Akershus and
Oslo County.

Counties in SWEDEN
5 Göteborg och
  Bohus .... G 7
6 Västmanland .... K 7
7 Södermanland .... K 7
8 Östergötland .... K 7
9 Malmöhus .... H 9
10 Kristianstad .... J 8

Capitals of Countries .... ☆
Administrative Centers .... △
International Boundaries .... —·—·—
Internal Boundaries .... ——
Canals .... ┼┼┼┼

© Copyright HAMMOND INCORPORATED, Maplewood, N.J.

AREA 125,053 sq. mi.
(323,887 sq. km.)
POPULATION 4,242,000
CAPITAL Oslo
LARGEST CITY Oslo
HIGHEST POINT Glittertinden
8,110 ft. (2,472 m.)
MONETARY UNIT krone
MAJOR LANGUAGE Norwegian
MAJOR RELIGION Protestantism

AREA 173,665 sq. mi.
(449,792 sq. km.)
POPULATION 8,541,000
CAPITAL Stockholm
LARGEST CITY Stockholm
HIGHEST POINT Kebnekaise 6,946 ft.
(2,117 m.)
MONETARY UNIT krona
MAJOR LANGUAGE Swedish
MAJOR RELIGION Protestantism

AREA 130,128 sq. mi.
(337,032 sq. km.)
POPULATION 4,973,000
CAPITAL Helsinki
LARGEST CITY Helsinki
HIGHEST POINT Haltiatunturi
4,343 ft. (1,324 m.)
MONETARY UNIT markka
MAJOR LANGUAGES Finnish, Swedish
MAJOR RELIGION Protestantism

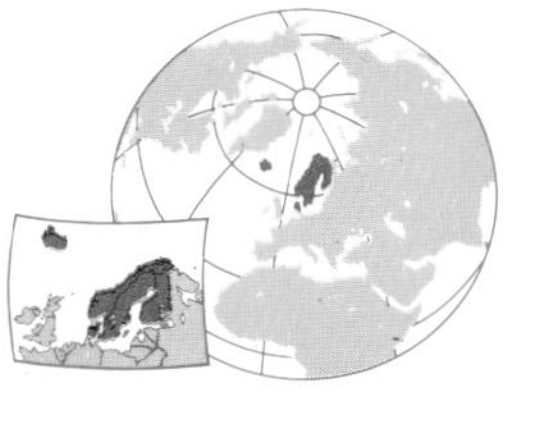

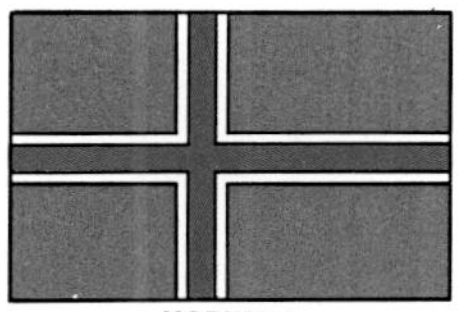

NORWAY

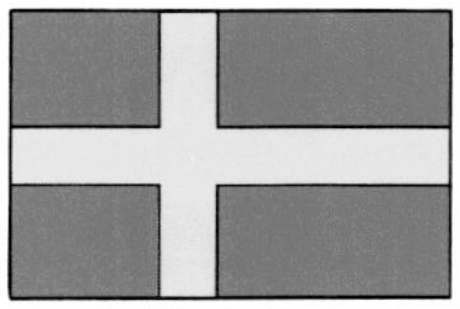

SWEDEN

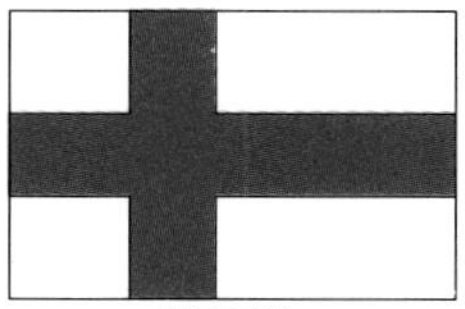

FINLAND

FINLAND

PROVINCES

Ahvenanmaa 23,591	L6
Åland (Ahvenanmaa) 23,591	L6
Häme 677,750	O6
Keski-Suomi 247,693	O5
Kuopio 256,036	P5
Kymi 340,665	O6
Lappi 200,943	P3
Mikkeli 239,029	P6
Oulu 432,141	P4
Pohjois-Karjala 177,567	Q5
Turku ja Pori 713,050	N6
Uusimaa 1,187,851	O6
Vaasa 444,348	N5

CITIES and TOWNS

Abo (Turku) 161,398	N6
Alavus 10,701	N5

Äänekoski 11,447	O5
Anjalamkoski 19,703	P6
Borga 19,513	O6
Espoo 156,778	O6
Forssa 20,074	N6
Haapajärvi 8,454	O5
Hämeenlinna 42,382	O6
Hamina 10,313	P6
Hangö 12,071	N7
Hanko (Hangö) 12,071	N7
Harjavalta 8,955	N6
Heinola 16,112	P6
Helsinki (cap.) 485,795	O6
Hyvinkää 38,742	O6
Iisalmi 23,612	P5
Ikaalinen 8,184	N6
Imatra 35,085	Q6
Jakobstad 20,458	N5
Jämsä 12,498	O6
Järvenpää 27,220	O6
Joensuu 46,850	R5
Jyväskylä 65,282	O5

Kajaani 36,020	P4
Kankaanpää 13,652	M6
Karis (Karjaa)	N6
Karkkila 8,355	N6
Kauniainen 7,746	O6
Kemi 26,421	O4
Kemijärvi 12,762	P3
Kerava 26,207	O6
Kokemäki 9,741	N6
Kokkola 34,489	N5
Kotka 58,956	P6
Kouvola 31,829	P6
Kristiinankaupunki	
(Kristinestad) 9,081	N5
Kristinestad 9,081	N5
Kuopio 78,124	Q5
Kurikka 11,512	N6
Kuusankoski 22,089	P6
Lahti 94,447	O6
Lappeenranta 54,102	P6
Lapua 14,644	N5
Lieksa 18,588	R5

Loimaa 7,053	N6
Lovisa 8,697	P6
Maarianhamina	
(Mariehamn) 9,829	M7
Mänttä 8,092	O6
Mariehamn 9,829	M7
Mikkeli 31,636	P6
Naantali 10,246	N6
Nokia 24,325	N6
Nurmes 11,419	Q5
Nykarleby 7,768	N5
Oulainen 8,225	O4
Oulu 97,297	O4
Outokumpu 9,678	Q5
Parainen 11,618	M6
Parkano 8,692	N6
Pieksämäki 14,372	P5
Pietarsaari	
(Jakobstad) 20,458	N5
Pori 78,376	M6
Pudasjärvi 11,453	P4
Raahe 18,932	O4

Raisio 19,671	M6
Rauma 30,921	M6
Riihimäki 24,366	O6
Rovaniemi 32,782	O3
Salo 20,495	N6
Savonlinna 28,667	Q6
Seinäjoki 26,257	N5
Suonenjoki 8,981	P5
Tampere 169,026	N6
Toijala 8,046	N6
Tornio 22,328	O4
Turku 161,398	N6
Utsjoki 1,548	P2
Uusikaarlepyy	
(Nykarleby) 7,768	N5
Uusikaupunki 14,026	M6
Vaasa 54,333	M5
Valkeakoski 22,582	N6
Vammala 16,024	N6
Vantaa 143,844	O6
Varkaus 24,856	Q5
Vasa (Vaasa) 54,333	M5
Virrat 9,391	N5
Ylivieska 12,559	O4

OTHER FEATURES

Åland (isls.)	L6
Baltic (sea)	K9
Bothnia (gulf)	M5
Finland (gulf)	P7
Hailuoto (isl.)	O4
Haltiatunturi (mt.)	M2
Haukivesi (lake)	Q5
Iijoki (riv.)	O4
Inari (lake)	P2
Ivalojoki (riv.)	P2
Kallavesi (lake)	P5
Karlö (Hailuoto) (isl.)	O4
Keitele (lake)	O5
Kemijärvi (lake)	Q3
Kemijoki (riv.)	O3
Lapland (reg.)	O2
Lappajärvi (lake)	O5
Lapuanjoki (riv.)	N5
Lokka (reg.)	Q3
Muojärvi (lake)	R4
Muonio (riv.)	M2
Näsijärvi (lake)	O6
Orihvesi (lake)	P4
Oulujärvi (lake)	O4
Oulujoki (riv.)	O3
Ounasjoki (riv.)	O3
Päijänne (lake)	O6
Pielinen (lake)	Q5
Porkkala (pen.)	O7
Puruvesi (lake)	Q6
Saimaa (lake)	Q6
Tana (riv.)	P2
Tornionjoki (riv.)	O3
Ylikitka (lake)	Q3

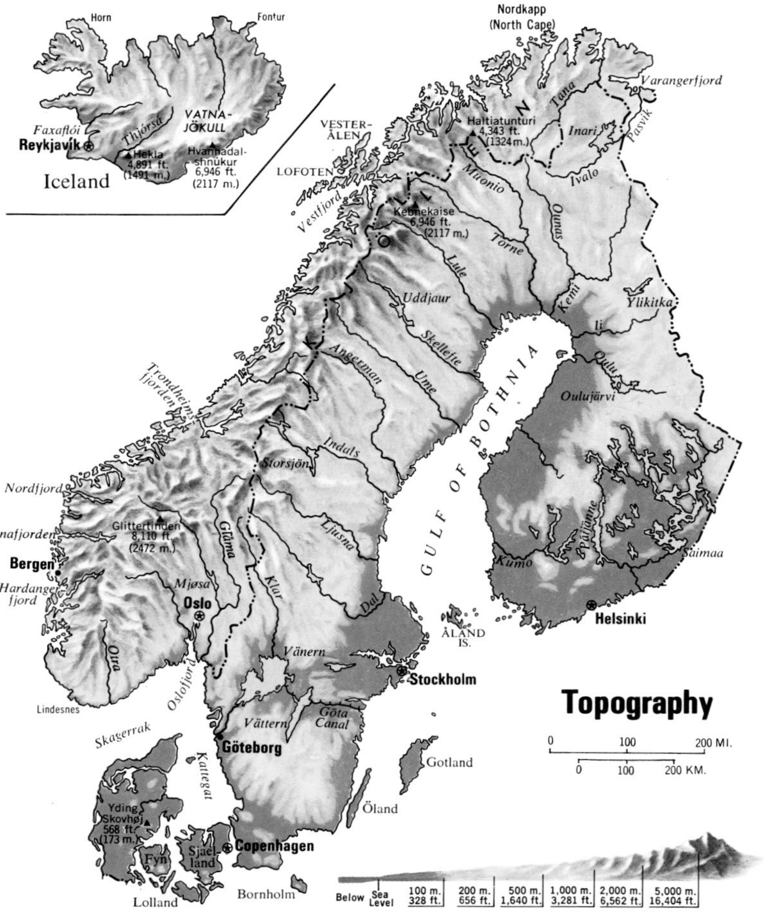

NORWAY

COUNTIES

Akershus 399,797	G6
Aust-Agder 95,475	E7
Buskerud 221,384	F6
Finnmark 74,690	O2
Hedmark 186,305	G6
Hordaland 402,343	E6
Møre og Romsdal 237,489	E5
Nordland 241,048	J3
Nord-Trøndelag 126,648	H4
Oppland 181,620	F6
Oslo (city) 449,220	D3
Østfold 235,813	G7
Rogaland 326,611	D7
Sogn og Fjordane 105,466	E6
Sør-Trøndelag 247,354	G5
Telemark 162,595	F7
Troms 146,595	L2
Vest-Agder 141,284	E7
Vestfold 192,934	G7

CITIES and TOWNS

Ålesund 40,868	D5
Ålgård 2,322	D7

Alta 5,582	N2
Åndalsnes 2,574	F5
Årdalstangen 2,360	F6
Arendal 11,701	F7
Årnes 2,267	G6
Askim 8,413	E4
Bamble† 7,031	F7
Bergen 213,434	D6
Bodø 31,077	J3
Borge† 3,294	H2
Brate 2,107	G7
Brønnøysund 3,130	G4
Drammen 50,777	C4
Drøbak 4,538	D4
Eidsvoll 2,906	D4
Eigersund 11,379	D7
Elverum 7,391	G6
Farsund 8,908	E7
Flekkefjord 8,750	D7
Flora 8,822	D6
Fredrikstad 29,024	D4
Gjøvik 25,963	G6
Grimstad 13,091	F7
Halden 27,087	G7
Hamar 16,418	G6
Hammerfest 7,610	N1
Harstad 21,125	K2
Hauge 2,079	E7
Haugesund 27,386	D7
Holmestrand 8,246	C4
Honningsvåg 3,780	O1
Horten 13,746	D4
Kirkenes 4,466	Q2
Kongsberg 19,854	F7
Kongsvinger 16,146	H6
Kopervik 4,221	D7
Kornsjø† 6,079	G7
Kragerø 5,249	F7
Kristiansand 59,488	F8
Kristiansund 18,847	E5
Kvinnherad† 2,898	E6
Larvik 9,097	C4
Lenvik† 11,098	L2
Levanger 5,066	G5
Lillehammer 21,248	F6
Lillesand 3,028	F7
Lillestrøm† 11,550	E3
Lodingen 1,840	J2
Longyearbyen	D2
Lysaker† 81,612	D3
Mandal 11,579	E7
Meråker† 2,907	G5
Mo 21,033	J3
Molde 20,334	E5
Mosjøen 9,341	H4
Moss 25,786	D4
Mysen 3,760	G7
Namsos 11,452	G4
Narvik 19,582	K2
Nesttun† 11,519	D6
Nittedal† 8,889	D3
Notodden 12,970	F7
Nøtterøy 11,944	D4
Odda 7,401	E6
Oppdal 2,173	F5
Orkanger 3,685	F5
Oslo (cap.) 462,732	D3
Oslo* 645,413	D3
Porsgrunn 31,709	G7
Rakkestad 2,392	G7
Ringerike 30,156	C3
Risør 6,560	F7
Rjukan 5,334	F7
Røros 3,041	G5
Saetermoen 2,114	L2
Sandefjord 33,350	C4
Sandnes 33,934	D7
Sandvika† 34,337	C3
Sarpsborg 12,889	D4
Seljef 3,386	D5
Ski 9,081	D4
Skien 47,105	F7
Skudeneshavn 2,206	D7
Stavanger 86,639	D7
Stavern 2,604	D4
Steinkjer 20,553	G4
Stor-Elvdal† 2,993	G6
Sunndalsøra 5,114	F5
Svelvik 2,256	D4
Svolvær 3,942	J2

Tana 1,893	Q1
Tønsberg 9,964	D4
Tromsø 43,830	L2
Trondheim 134,910	F5
Tvedestrand 1,689	F7
Ullensvang† 2,326	E6
Vadsø 6,019	Q1
Vanylven 1,966	E5
Vardø 3,875	R1
Vik 1,019	E6
Volda 3,511	E5
Voss 5,944	E6

OTHER FEATURES

Andøya (isl.)	J2
Barentsøya (isl.)	D2
Bjørnøya (isl.)	D3
Boknafjord (fjord)	D7
Dovrefjell (hills)	F5
Edgeøya (isl.)	E2
Femundsjø (lake)	G5
Folda (fjord)	G4
Folda (fjord)	J3
Frohavet (bay)	F5
Frøya (isl.)	F5
Glittertinden (mt.)	F6
Greenland (sea)	C3
Hadselfjorden (fjord)	J2
Haltiatunturi (mt.)	M2
Hardangerfjord (fjord)	D7
Hardangervidda (plat.)	E6
Hinlopenstreten (strait)	C1
Hinnøya (isl.)	K2
Hitra (isl.)	F5
Hortensfjord (fjord)	G4
Isfjorden (fjord)	C2
Kjølen (mts.)	K3
Kvaenangen (fjord)	N2
Kvaløy (isl.)	K2
Kvaløya (isl.)	O1
Laksefjorden (fjord)	P1
Langøya (isl.)	J2
Lapland (isl.)	K2
Lindesnes (cape)	E8
Lofoten (isls.)	H2
Lopphavet (bay)	M1
Magerøya (isl.)	P1
Moskenesøya (isl.)	H3
Namsen (riv.)	H4
Nordaustlandet (isl.)	D1
Nordfjord (fjord)	E6
Nordkapp (pt.)	C1
North Cape	
(Nordkapp) (cape)	P1
Norwegian (sea)	F3
Ofotfjorden (fjord)	K2
Oslofjord (fjord)	D4
Otra (riv.)	E7
Pasvikelv (riv.)	Q2
Porsangen (fjord)	O1
Prins Karls Forland (isl.)	B2
Rana (riv.)	H3
Rauma (riv.)	F5
Ringvassøy (isl.)	L2
Romsdalsfjorden (fjord)	E5
Saltfjorden (fjord)	J3
Seiland (isl.)	N1
Senja (isl.)	K2
Skagerrak (strait)	F8
Sognafjorden (fjord)	D6
Sørkapp (pt.)	C2
Sørøya (isl.)	N1
Spitsbergen (isl.)	C2
Steinneset (cape)	E2
Storfjorden (fjord)	D2
Sulitjelma (mt.)	J3
Svalbard (isls.)	C3
Tana (riv.)	P1
Tanafjord (fjord)	Q1
Trondheimsfjorden (fjord)	G5
Tyrifjord (lake)	C3
Vannøy (isl.)	L1
Varangerfjord (fjord)	Q2
Varangerhalvøya (pen.)	Q1
Vegafjorden (fjord)	G4
Vesterålen (isls.)	J2
Vestfjord (fjord)	H3
Vestvågøya (isl.)	H3
Vikna (isls.)	G4

(continued on following page)

Topography map labels

Horn, Fontur, Nordkapp (North Cape), Varangerfjord, Faxaflói, VATNA-JÖKULL, Þórsá, VESTER-ÁLEN, Haltiatunturi 4,343 ft. (1324 m.), Inari, Tana, Tana, Pasvik, Reykjavík, Hekla 4,891 ft. (1491 m.), Hvannadalshnúkur 6,946 ft. (2117 m.), LOFOTEN, Iceland, Vestfjord, Kebnekaise 6,946 ft. (2117 m.), Muonio, Ivalo, Hitra, Ounas, Kemi, Uddjaur, Torne, Ylikitka, Lapland (reg.), Trondheimsfjorden, Angerman, Ume, Skellefte, Lule, Kemi, Ii, Oulu, Oulujärvi, Nordfjord, Sognafjorden, Glittertinden 8,110 ft. (2472 m.), Storsjön, Indals, Ljusna, Klar, Dal, Glåma, Oulu, Kumo, Pyhä, Päijänne, Saimaa, GULF OF BOTHNIA, Bergen, Hardanger fjord, Mjøsa, Oslo, Otra, Orkla, Lindesnes, Skagerrak, Vänern, Vättern, Göta Canal, Helsinki, ÅLAND IS., Stockholm, Göteborg, Gotland, Kattegat, Öland, Yding Skovhøj 568 ft. (173 m.), Fyn, Sjaelland, Copenhagen, Lolland, Bornholm

Topography

0	100	200 MI.
0	100	200 KM.

Below Sea Level	100 m. 328 ft.	200 m. 656 ft.	500 m. 1,640 ft.	1,000 m. 3,281 ft.	2,000 m. 6,562 ft.	5,000 m. 16,404 ft.

SWEDEN

COUNTIES

Älvsborg 433,417 ....H7
Blekinge 149,544 ....J8
Gävleborg 287,004 ....K6
Göteborg och Bohus
  729,629 ....G7
Gotland 56,383 ....L8
Halland 247,417 ....H8
Jämtland 134,116 ....J5
Jönköping 304,021 ....H8
Kalmar 237,781 ....K8
Kopparberg 284,407 ....J6
Kristianstad 283,818 ....J8
Kronoberg 175,427 ....J8
Malmöhus 763,349 ....H9
Norrbotten 261,536 ....L3
Örebro 270,031 ....J7
Östergötland 396,919 ....J7
Skaraborg 272,126 ....H7
Södermanland 251,423 ....J7
Stockholm 1,617,038 ....L7
Uppsala 260,476 ....K7
Värmland 280,694 ....H7
Västerbotten 247,521 ....L4
Västernorrland 259,964 ......K5
Västmanland 254,847 ....K7

CITIES and TOWNS

Åhus 6,125 ....J9
Ålingsås 32,402 ....H7
Almhult 15,645 ....J8
Älvkarleby 9,175 ....K6
Alvesta 19,579 ....J8
Älvsbyn 9,373 ....M4
Ängelholm 32,998 ....H8
Åmål 13,130 ....H7
Ånge 12,653 ....J5
Arboga 14,457 ....J7
Åre 9,787 ....H5
Arjäng 10,050 ....H7
Arvika 26,668 ....H7
Askim 17,609 ....G8
Atvidaberg 12,677 ....K7
Avesta 24,671 ....J6
Båstad 12,862 ....H8
Bengtsfors 11,836 ....H7
Boden 29,160 ....M4
Bollnäs 27,724 ....K6
Borås 100,795 ....H8
Borgholm 11,170 ....K8
Borlänge 46,343 ....J6
Danderyd 28,525 ....H1

Eksjö 17,857 ....J8
Emmaboda 10,694 ....J8
Enköping 33,700 ....G1
Eskilstuna 88,850 ....K7
Eslöv 27,097 ....H9
Fagersta 13,744 ....J6
Falkenberg 36,536 ....H8
Falköping 31,532 ....H7
Falun 52,448 ....J6
Filipstad 13,481 ....J7
Finspång 23,378 ....J7
Flen 17,016 ....K7
Forshaga 11,739 ....H7
Frösö 10,274 ....J5
Gällivare 22,717 ....M3
Gävle 87,747 ....K6
Göteborg 430,763 ....G8
Hagfors 16,346 ....H6
Hällefors 9,402 ....J7
Hallsberg 16,405 ....J7
Hallstahammar 16,637 ....K7
Halmstad 78,607 ....H8
Haparanda 10,159 ....N4
Härnösand 27,248 ....L5
Hässleholm 48,658 ....H8
Hedemora 16,644 ....K6
Helsingborg 107,443 ....H8
Hjo 8,952 ....J7
Hofors 12,204 ....K6
Höganäs 10,866 ....H8
Huddinge 71,921 ....H1
Hudiksvall 37,603 ....K6
Jönköping 109,890 ....H8
Kalix 19,160 ....N4
Kalmar 55,129 ....K8
Karlshamn 31,377 ....J8
Karlskoga 34,316 ....J7
Karlskrona 58,634 ....J8
Karlstad 75,412 ....H7
Katrineholm 32,254 ....K7
Kinna 13,676 ....H8
Kiruna 26,312 ....L3
Köping 26,253 ....J7
Kramfors 24,607 ....K5
Kristianstad 70,491 ....J9
Kristinehamn 26,006 ....J7
Kumla 17,884 ....J7
Kungälv 32,549 ....G8
Kungsbacka 52,027 ....G8
Laholm 21,881 ....H8
Landskrona 35,393 ....H9
Leksand 14,115 ....J6
Lessebo 8,769 ....J8
Lidingö 38,819 ....H1
Lidköping 35,168 ....H7
Lindesberg 24,415 ....J7

Linköping 119,167 ....K7
Ljungby 27,176 ....J8
Ljusdal 21,026 ....J6
Ludvika 29,283 ....J6
Luleå 67,443 ....N4
Lund 85,150 ....H9
Lycksele 14,020 ....L4
Malmberget 10,239 ....M3
Malmö 231,575 ....H9
Malung 11,611 ....H6
Mariestad 24,508 ....H7
Markaryd 11,044 ....H8
Märsta 17,066 ....K7
Mellerud 10,455 ....H7
Mjölby 25,952 ....J7
Mölndal 47,248 ....H8
Mönsterås 12,911 ....K8
Mörbylanga 13,029 ....K8
Motala 41,502 ....J7
Nacka 61,931 ....H1
Nässjö 30,623 ....J8
Nora 10,200 ....J7
Norrköping 119,370 ....K7
Norrtälje 43,741 ....L7
Nybro 20,706 ....J8
Nyköping 64,739 ....K7
Nynäshamn 21,395 ....L7
Olofström 14,883 ....J8
Örebro 119,824 ....J7
Örnsköldsvik 58,967 ....L5
Oskarshamn 27,217 ....K8
Östersund 57,281 ....J5
Oxelösund 12,923 ....K7
Piteå 39,079 ....M4
Rättvik 11,048 ....J6
Ronneby 28,868 ....J8
Säffle 17,935 ....H7
Sala 21,381 ....K7
Sandviken 39,740 ....K6
Säter 11,490 ....J6
Sävsjö 11,730 ....J8
Sigtuna 30,182 ....H1
Simrishamn 19,709 ....J9
Skara 18,402 ....H7
Skellefteå 74,127 ....M4
Skövde 46,712 ....H7
Smedjebacken 13,183 ....J6
Söderhamn 29,606 ....K6
Söderköping 12,838 ....K7
Södertälje 80,660 ....G1
Sollefteå 25,114 ....K5
Sollentuna 50,242 ....G1
Solna 50,964 ....H1
Sölvesborg 15,782 ....J9

Stenungsund 17,792 ....G7
Stockholm (cap.) 669,485 ...G1
Strängnäs 25,841 ....K7
Strömstad 10,457 ....G7
Strömsund 16,164 ....J4
Sundbyberg 31,095 ....G1
Sundsvall 92,983 ....K5
Sunne 13,245 ....H7
Surahammar 11,287 ....J7
Svenljunga 11,004 ....H8
Täby 56,339 ....H1
Tibro 11,044 ....J7
Tidaholm 13,048 ....J7
Tierp 19,620 ....K6
Timrå 18,392 ....K5
Tomelilla 12,241 ....J9
Torsby 15,030 ....H6
Tranås 17,675 ....J7
Trelleborg 34,846 ....H9
Trollhättan 50,296 ....H7
Uddevalla 46,489 ....G7
Ulricehamn 22,405 ....H8
Umeå 88,726 ....M5
Uppsala 161,820 ....K7
Vaggeryd 12,185 ....J8
Vallentuna 20,823 ....H1
Vänersborg 36,151 ....G7
Vara 16,787 ....H7
Varberg 47,566 ....G8
Värnamo 31,040 ....J8
Västeras 117,717 ....K7
Västerhaninge 14,125 ....H1
Västervik 39,522 ....K8
Växjö 68,499 ....J8
Vetlanda 27,833 ....J8
Vimmerby 15,688 ....J8
Visby 19,886 ....L8
Ystad 24,484 ....H9

OTHER FEATURES

Ångermanälven (riv.) K5
Baltic (sea) K9
Bothnia (gulf) N4
Dalälven (riv.) K6
Göta (canal) J7
Göta (riv.) J7
Gotland (isl.) L8
Hanöbukten (bay) J9
Hjälmaren (lake) J7
Hornslandet (pen.) L6
Indalsälven (riv.) H5
Kalixälv (riv.) N3
Kallsjö (lake) H5
Kalmarsund (sound) K8
Kattegat (strait) G8

Kebnekaise (mt.) L3
Klarälv (riv.) H6
Kölen (mts.) K3
Lapland (reg.) M2
Ljungan (riv.) K5
Ljusnan (riv.) H5
Luleälv (riv.) M4
Mälaren (lake) G1
Muonioälven (riv.) M2
Öland (isl.) K8
Öresund (sound) H9
Österdalälven (riv.) H6
Piteälv (riv.) M4
Siljan (lake) J6
Skagerrak (strait) F8
Skellefteälv (riv.) L4
Stora Lulevatten (lake) L3
Storsjön (lake) J5
Torneälv (riv.) M3
Torneträsk (lake) L2
Uddjaur (lake) L4
Umeälv (riv.) L4
Vänern (lake) H7
Västerdalälven (riv.) H6
Vättern (lake) J7

* City and suburbs.
† Population of commune.
† Population of parish.

DENMARK

COUNTIES

Århus 575,540 ....D5
Bornholm 47,499 ....F9
Copenhagen
  (commune) 493,771 ....F6
Faroe Islands 41,969 ....B2
Frederiksberg
  (commune) 88,167 ....F6
Frederiksborg 329,992 ....E5
Fyn 453,626 ....D7
København (Copenhagen)
  (commune) 493,771 ....F6
København 624,684 ....F6
Nordjylland 482,501 ....D4
Ribe 213,503 ....B7
Ringkøbing 263,519 ....B5
Roskilde 203,246 ....E6
Sønderjylland 250,872 ....C7
Storstrøm 260,160 ....E7
Vejle 326,559 ....C6
Vestsjaelland 278,592 ....E6
Viborg 231,758 ....C4

CITIES and TOWNS

Åbenrå 15,341 ....C7
Åbybro 4,229 ....C3
Ålborg-Nørresundby 114,302 .C3
Ålestrup 2,288 ....C4
Århus 181,830 ....D5
Ars 5,972 ....C4
Asnaes 2,361 ....E6
Assens, Fyn 5,736 ....D7
Augustenborg 3,114 ....D8
Auning 2,293 ....D5
Avlum 2,719 ....B5
Ballerup 48,697 ....F6
Birkerød 13,513 ....F6
Bjerringbro 6,033 ....C5
Bogense 3,057 ....D6
Braedstrup 2,912 ....C6
Bramming 5,857 ....B7
Brande 5,693 ....C6
Broager 2,890 ....C8
Brønderslev 10,748 ....C3
Brørup 3,846 ....C7
Brovst 2,589 ....C3
Copenhagen
  (cap.) 1,381,882 ....F6
Dronninglund 2,715 ....D3
Ebeltoft 3,763 ....D5
Esbjerg 70,220 ....B7
Fåborg 6,795 ....D7
Fakse 3,350 ....F7
Fakse Ladeplads 2,111 ......F7
Farsø 2,954 ....C4
Farum 16,664 ....F6
Fjerritslev 2,780 ....C3
Fredensborg 17,667 ....F6
Fredericia 29,350 ....C6
Frederiksberg 88,167 ....F6
Frederikshavn 24,938 ....D3
Frederikssund 13,584 ....E6
Frederiksvaerk 11,559 ....E6
Gentofte 66,782 ....F6
Gilleleje 3,976 ....F5
Give 3,522 ....C6
Glamsbjerg 2,853 ....D7
Glostrup 19,645 ....F6
Gørlev 2,113 ....E6
Graested 2,735 ....F5
Gram 2,462 ....C7
Gråsten 3,441 ....C8
Grenå 13,638 ....D5
Grindsted 8,742 ....B6
Haderslev 19,374 ....C7
Hadsten 5,563 ....C5
Hadsund 4,257 ....C4
Hammel 4,828 ....C5
Hammerum 2,984 ....C5
Hanstholm 2,490 ....B3
Hårby 2,240 ....D7
Haslev 9,146 ....E7
Havdrup 3,374 ....F6
Hedensted 3,397 ....C6
Hellebaek 4,123 ....F5
Helsinge 5,813 ....F6

Helsingør 44,068 ....F6
Herning 29,522 ....B5
Hillerød 25,441 ....F6
Hinnerup 4,517 ....C5
Hirtshals 6,865 ....C2
Hjallerup 2,769 ....C3
Hjørring 23,697 ....C3
Hobro 8,889 ....C4
Holbaek 19,485 ....E6
Holstebro 28,270 ....B5
Høng 3,430 ....E7
Hornslet 3,296 ....D5
Horsens 46,855 ....C6
Hørsholm 21,572 ....F6
Hørve 2,055 ....E6
Hundested 5,443 ....E6
Hurup 2,747 ....B4
Hvide Sande 3,100 ....A6
Ikast 11,716 ....C5
Juelsminde 2,609 ....D6
Jyderup 3,441 ....E6
Kalundborg 15,413 ....D6
Karup 2,133 ....C5
Kastrup 10,550 ....F6
Kerteminde 4,984 ....D7
Kjellerup 3,848 ....C5
København (Copenhagen)
  (cap.) 1,381,882 ....F6
Køge 25,683 ....F7
Kolding 41,374 ....C7
Korsør 15,281 ....E7
Langå 2,498 ....C5
Lemvig 7,303 ....B4
Løgstør 4,160 ....C4
Løgumkloster 2,840 ....B7
Løsning 3,234 ....C6
Lunderskov 2,083 ....C7
Lyngby 51,703 ....F6
Malling 2,451 ....D5
Maribo 5,490 ....E8
Marstal 2,702 ....D8
Middelfart 12,064 ....C6
Naestved 38,455 ....E7
Nakskov 16,218 ....E8
Nekso 3,783 ....F9
Nibe 3,139 ....C4
Nordborg 8,403 ....C7
Nordby, Ribe 2,419 ....B7
Nørre Aby 2,541 ....C7
Nørre Alslev 2,024 ....E8
Nyborg 15,466 ....D7
Nykøbing, Storstrøm 19,038 .F8
Nykøbing,
  Vestsjaelland 5,062 ....E6
Nykøbing, Viborg 9,503 .....B4
Odder 8,198 ....D6
Odense 136,646 ....D7
Ølgod 3,470 ....B6
Otterup 3,976 ....D7
Padborg 4,332 ....C8
Pandrup 2,257 ....C3
Praestø 3,110 ....F7
Randers 56,672 ....C5
Ribe 7,646 ....B7

Agriculture, Industry and Resources

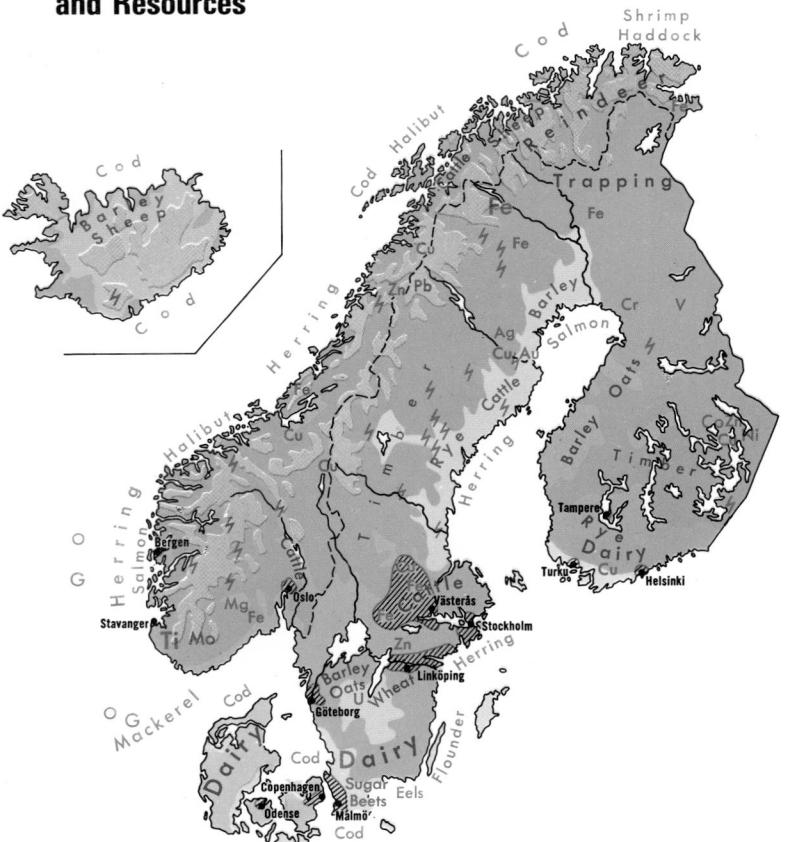

DOMINANT LAND USE

Cash Cereals, Dairy

Dairy, Cattle, Hogs

Dairy, General Farming

General Farming (chiefly cereals)

Nomadic Sheep Herding

Forests, Limited Mixed Farming

Nonagricultural Land

MAJOR MINERAL OCCURRENCES

Ag Silver   Ni Nickel

Au Gold   O Petroleum

Co Cobalt   Pb Lead

Cr Chromium   Ti Titanium

Cu Copper   U Uranium

Fe Iron Ore   V Vanadium

Mg Magnesium   Zn Zinc

Mo Molybdenum

 Water Power

Major Industrial Areas

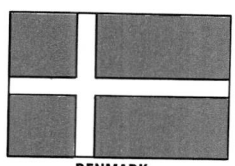

DENMARK

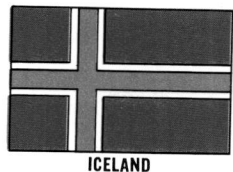

ICELAND

DENMARK
AREA 16,629 sq. mi. (43,069 sq. km.)
POPULATION 5,135,000
CAPITAL Copenhagen
LARGEST CITY Copenhagen
HIGHEST POINT Yding Skovhøj
568 ft. (173 m.)
MONETARY UNIT krone
MAJOR LANGUAGE Danish
MAJOR RELIGION Protestantism

ICELAND
AREA 39,768 sq. mi. (103,000 sq. km.)
POPULATION 250,000
CAPITAL Reykjavík
LARGEST CITY Reykjavík
HIGHEST POINT Hvannadalshnúkur
6,952 ft. (2,119 m.)
MONETARY UNIT króna
MAJOR LANGUAGE Icelandic
MAJOR RELIGION Protestantism

Denmark and Iceland

CONIC PROJECTION

SCALE OF MILES
SCALE OF KILOMETERS

Capitals of Countries................☆
Capitals of Counties (amter).....△
International Boundaries............
Internal Boundaries..................

Denmark is divided into fourteen Counties plus
Copenhagen and Frederiksberg communes.

© Copyright HAMMOND INCORPORATED, Maplewood, N.J.

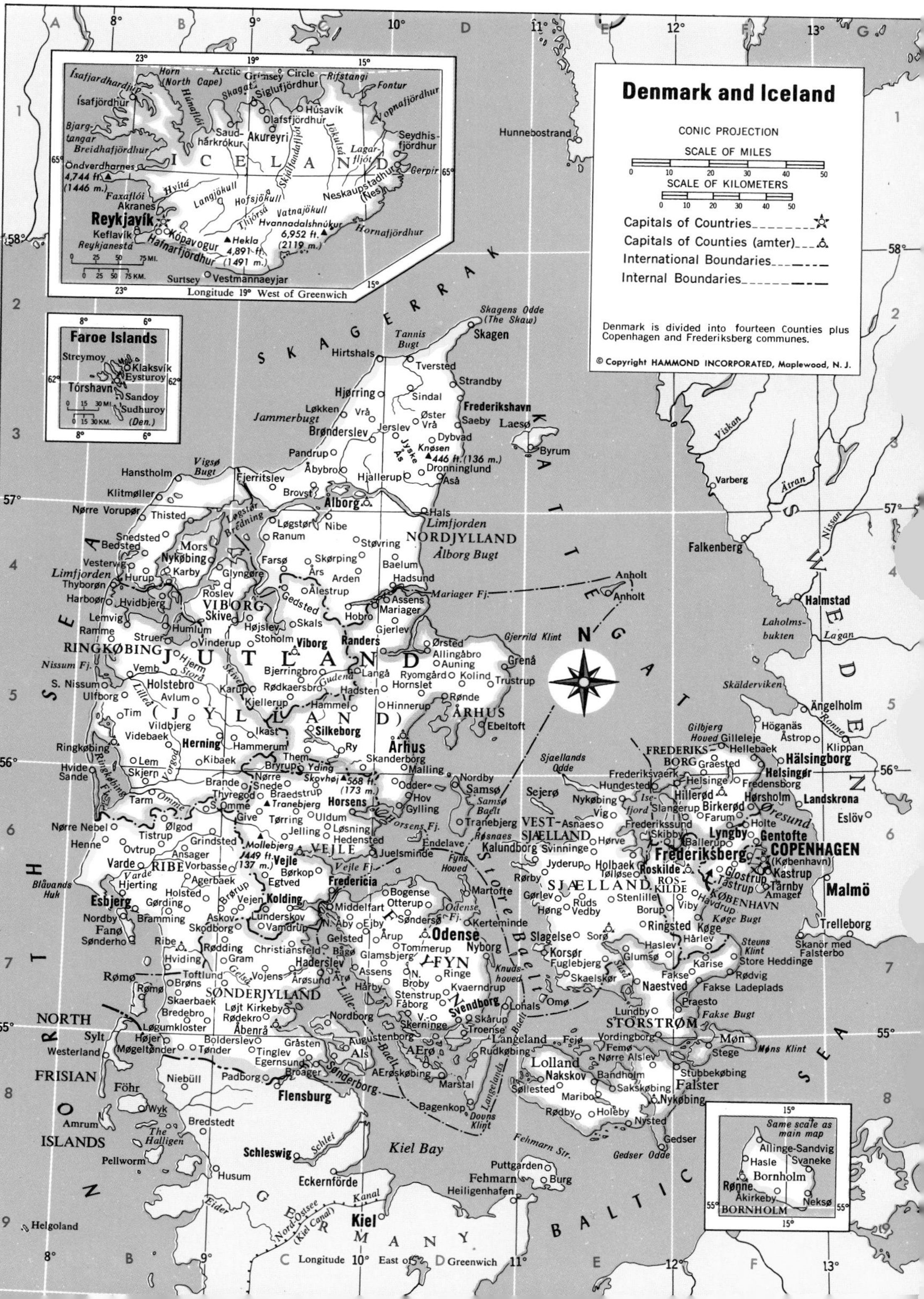

Germany

CONIC PROJECTION
SCALE OF MILES
SCALE OF KILOMETERS

Capitals of Countries .... ☆
State Capitals .... ⊙
International Boundaries ....
State Boundaries ....
Canals ....

© Copyright HAMMOND INCORPORATED, Maplewood, N.J.

AREA 137,753 sq. mi. (356,780 sq. km.)
POPULATION 78,890,000
CAPITAL Berlin
LARGEST CITY Berlin
HIGHEST POINT Zugspitze 9,718 ft. (2,962 m.)
MONETARY UNIT Deutsche mark
MAJOR LANGUAGE German
MAJOR RELIGIONS Protestantism, Roman Catholicism

GERMANY

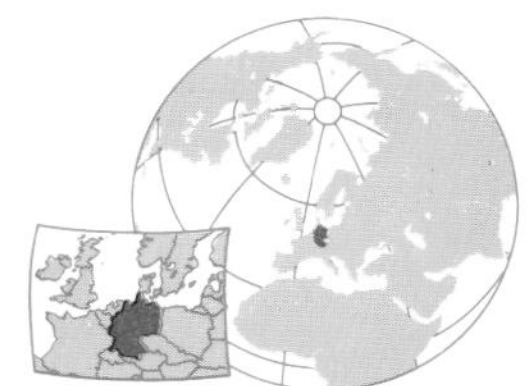

Topography

0 50 100 MI.
0 50 100 KM.

Below Sea Level | 100 m. 328 ft. | 200 m. 656 ft. | 500 m. 1,640 ft. | 1,000 m. 3,281 ft. | 2,000 m. 6,562 ft. | 5,000 m. 16,404 ft.

GERMANY

STATES

Baden-Württemberg 9,432,709 ..... C4
Bavaria 11,049,263 ..... D4
Berlin 3,304,561 ..... E4
Brandenberg* E2
Bremen 661,992 ..... C2
Hamburg 1,603,070 ..... D2
Hesse 5,568,892 ..... C3
Lower Saxony 7,184,943 ..... C2
Mecklenburg-Western Pomerania* E2
North Rhine-Westphalia 16,874,059 ..... B3
Rhineland-Palatinate 3,653,155 ..... B4
Saarland 1,054,142 ..... B4
Saxony* E3
Saxony-Anhalt* D3
Schleswig-Holstein 2,564,565 ..... C1
Thuringia* D3

*East German States 15,611,488 ..... D-E 2-3

CITIES and TOWNS

Aachen 233,255 ..... B3
Aalen 62,812 ..... D4
Ahaus 30,180 ..... B2
Ahlen 52,836 ..... B3
Ahrensburg 27,174 ..... D2
Alfeld 21,986 ..... C2
Alsdorf 46,328 ..... B3
Alsfeld 16,686 ..... C3
Altena 23,301 ..... B3
Altenburg 53,602 ..... E3
Amberg 42,246 ..... D4
Andernach 27,171 ..... B3
Anklam 19,946 ..... E2
Annaberg-Buchholz 26,002 ..... E3
Ansbach 36,912 ..... D4
Apolda 28,230 ..... D3
Arnsberg 73,912 ..... C3
Arnstadt 30,207 ..... D3
Aschaffenburg 62,048 ..... C4
Aschersleben 34,166 ..... D3
Aue 27,935 ..... E3
Auerbach 22,324 ..... E3
Augsburg 247,731 ..... D4
Aurich 36,063 ..... B2
Backnang 30,583 ..... C4
Bad Berleburg 20,080 ..... C3
Bad Driburg 16,698 ..... C3
Bad Dürkheim 16,670 ..... C4
Baden-Baden 50,761 ..... C4
Bad Harzburg 23,079 ..... D3
Bad Hersfeld 28,214 ..... C3
Bad Homburg vor der Höhe 51,035 ..... C3
Bad Honnef 21,812 ..... B3
Bad Kissingen 20,237 ..... D3
Bad Kreuznach 39,400 ..... B4
Bad Langensalza 17,027 ..... D3
Bad Mergentheim 19,801 ..... C4
Bad Münstereifel 15,232 ..... B3
Bad Nauheim 27,561 ..... C3
Bad Neuenahr-Ahrweiler 24,610 ..... B3
Bad Oldesloe 20,473 ..... D2
Bad Pyrmont 20,437 ..... C3
Bad Reichenhall 16,365 ..... E5
Bad Salzuflen 50,875 ..... C2
Bad Salzungen 21,387 ..... C3
Bad Schwartau 19,960 ..... D2
Bad Vilbel 24,567 ..... C3
Bad Zwischenahn 23,348 ..... B2
Balingen 30,615 ..... C4
Bamberg 69,809 ..... D4
Barsinghausen 37,792 ..... C2
Bautzen 52,354 ..... F3
Bayreuth 70,933 ..... D4
Bensheim 34,241 ..... C4
Berchtesgaden 7,644 ..... E5
Bergen 16,713 ..... E1
Bergisch Gladbach 101,983 ..... B3
Berleburg (Bad Berleburg) 20,080 ..... C3
Berlin (cap.) 3,304,561 ..... E4
Bernau bei Berlin 19,919 ..... E2
Bernburg 40,834 ..... D3
Biberach an der Riss 28,319 ..... C4
Bielefeld 311,946 ..... C2
Bietigheim-Bissingen 37,573 ..... C4
Bingen 23,141 ..... B4
Bitburg 10,758 ..... B4
Bitterfeld 20,869 ..... E3
Blankenburg am Harz 19,279 ..... D3
Böblingen 43,400 ..... C4
Bocholt 67,565 ..... B3
Bochum 389,087 ..... B3
Bonn 282,190 ..... B3
Borghorst 17,238 ..... B2
Borken 34,710 ..... B3
Borna 24,397 ..... E3
Bornheim 34,536 ..... B3
Bottrop 116,363 ..... B3
Brake 16,069 ..... C2
Bramsche 24,653 ..... B2
Brandenburg 94,755 ..... E2
Braunschweig 253,794 ..... D2
Bremen 535,058 ..... C2
Bremerhaven 126,934 ..... C2
Bremervörde 17,629 ..... C2
Bretten 23,894 ..... C4
Brilon 24,341 ..... C3
Bruchsal 36,831 ..... C4
Brühl 40,710 ..... B3
Buchholz in der Nordheide 30,523 ..... C2
Bückeburg 19,758 ..... C2
Büdingen 17,013 ..... C3
Bühl 23,470 ..... C4
Bünde 39,103 ..... C2
Büren 17,720 ..... C3
Burg bei Magdeburg 28,359 ..... D2
Burghausen 16,761 ..... E4
Burgsteinfurt 31,367 ..... B2
Butzbach 21,095 ..... C3
Buxtehude 31,132 ..... C2
Castrop-Rauxel 77,660 ..... B3
Celle 71,050 ..... D2
Cham 16,641 ..... E4
Chemnitz 313,799 ..... E3
Clausthal-Zellerfeld 16,069 ..... D3
Cloppenburg 22,536 ..... B2
Coburg 43,233 ..... D3
Coesfeld 31,979 ..... B3
Cologne 937,482 ..... B3
Coswig 27,590 ..... E3
Cottbus 126,592 ..... F3
Crailsheim 26,678 ..... D4
Crimmitschau 24,440 ..... E3
Cuxhaven 55,249 ..... C2
Dachau 34,183 ..... D4
Darmstadt 136,067 ..... C4
Deggendorf 28,680 ..... E4
Delitzsch 27,636 ..... E3
Delmenhorst 72,901 ..... C2
Demmin 16,992 ..... E2
Dessau 103,538 ..... E3
Detmold 66,809 ..... C3
Dillenburg 23,672 ..... C3
Dillingen 21,358 ..... B4
Döbeln 27,706 ..... E3
Donaueschingen 18,296 ..... C5
Donauwörth 17,420 ..... D4
Dorsten 75,518 ..... B3
Dortmund 587,328 ..... B3
Dresden 519,810 ..... E3
Duderstadt 22,265 ..... D3
Duisburg 527,447 ..... B3
Dülmen 39,344 ..... B3
Düren 83,120 ..... B3
Düsseldorf 569,641 ..... B3
Eberswalde-Finow 54,566 ..... E2
Eckernförde 22,197 ..... C1
Ehingen 22,580 ..... C4
Eilenburg 21,931 ..... E3
Einbeck 25,813 ..... C3
Eisenach 49,534 ..... D3
Eisenhüttenstadt 51,729 ..... F2
Eisleben 26,484 ..... D3
Ellwangen 21,857 ..... D4
Elmshorn 42,784 ..... C2
Emden 49,803 ..... B2
Emmendingen 22,959 ..... B4
Emmerich 27,906 ..... B3
Emsdetten 31,063 ..... B2
Erfurt 217,134 ..... D3
Erkelenz 36,525 ..... B3
Erlangen 100,583 ..... D4
Eschwege 21,527 ..... C3
Eschweiler 53,516 ..... B3
Espelkamp 23,868 ..... C2
Essen 620,594 ..... B3
Esslingen am Neckar 90,537 ..... C4
Ettlingen 37,269 ..... C4
Euskirchen 47,756 ..... B3
Eutin 16,567 ..... D1
Falkensee 23,024 ..... E3
Fellbach 39,612 ..... C4
Finsterwalde 23,857 ..... E3
Flensburg 85,830 ..... C1
Forchheim 28,784 ..... D4
Forst 26,501 ..... F3
Frankenberg-Eder 16,283 ..... C3
Frankenthal 45,408 ..... C4
Frankfurt am Main 625,258 ..... C3
Frankfurt an der Oder 86,441 ..... F2
Frechen 42,516 ..... B3
Freiberg 50,415 ..... E3
Freiburg im Breisgau 183,979 ..... B5
Freising 35,201 ..... D4
Freital 43,092 ..... E3
Freudenstadt 21,355 ..... C4
Friedberg 24,279 ..... C3
Friedrichshafen 52,295 ..... C5
Fulda 54,320 ..... C3
Fürstenfeldbruck 30,313 ..... D4
Fürstenwalde 35,282 ..... F2
Fürth 98,832 ..... D4
Füssen 13,173 ..... D5
Gaggenau 28,182 ..... C4
Garbsen 59,225 ..... C2
Garmisch-Partenkirchen 25,908 ..... D5
Geesthacht 25,054 ..... D2
Geislingen an der Steige 26,176 ..... C4
Geldern 28,465 ..... B3
Gelnhausen 18,866 ..... C3
Gelsenkirchen 287,255 ..... B3
Genthin 17,347 ..... E2
Georgsmarienhütte 30,880 ..... B2
Gera 132,319 ..... E3
Geretsried 21,081 ..... D5
Gifhorn 35,697 ..... D2
Glauchau 28,309 ..... E3
Goch 29,592 ..... B3
Göppingen 52,873 ..... C4
Görlitz 78,856 ..... F3
Goslar 45,614 ..... D3
Gotha 57,423 ..... D3
Göttingen 118,073 ..... D3
Greifswald 67,298 ..... E1
Greiz 34,858 ..... E3
Greven 29,671 ..... B2
Grevenbroich 59,204 ..... B3
Griesheim 20,531 ..... C4
Grimma 17,812 ..... E3
Gronau 39,397 ..... B2
Guben 34,665 ..... F3
Gummersbach 49,017 ..... B3
Günzburg 18,303 ..... D4
Güstrow 38,971 ..... E2
Gütersloh 83,407 ..... C3
Haar 16,553 ..... D4
Hagen 210,640 ..... B3
Halberstadt 47,017 ..... D3
Haldensleben 20,369 ..... D2
Halle 236,148 ..... D3
Halle-Neustadt 93,477 ..... D3
Haltern 33,093 ..... B3
Hamburg 1,603,070 ..... D2
Hameln 57,642 ..... C2
Hamm 173,611 ..... B3
Hanau 84,300 ..... C3
Hannover 498,495 ..... C2
Hassloch 18,646 ..... C4
Heide 19,909 ..... C1
Heidelberg 131,429 ..... C4
Heidenau 19,133 ..... E3
Heidenheim an der Brenz 48,497 ..... D4
Heilbronn 112,279 ..... C4
Helmstedt 26,554 ..... D2
Hennef 30,516 ..... B3
Hennigsdorf bei Berlin 26,574 ..... E3
Herborn 20,409 ..... C3
Herford 61,700 ..... C2
Herne 174,664 ..... B3
Hettstedt 21,861 ..... D3
Hildesheim 103,512 ..... D2
Hof 50,938 ..... D3
Holzminden 20,877 ..... C3
Homburg 41,888 ..... B4
Höxter 31,925 ..... C3
Hoyerswerda 69,113 ..... F3
Hückelhoven 33,841 ..... B3
Hürth 49,094 ..... B3
Husum 20,649 ..... C1
Ibbenbüren 43,424 ..... B2
Idar-Oberstein 33,227 ..... B4
Ilmenau 29,338 ..... D3
Ingolstadt 97,702 ..... D4
Iserlohn 93,337 ..... B3
Itzehoe 32,342 ..... C2
Jena 107,610 ..... D3
Jülich 30,496 ..... B3
Kaiserslautern 96,990 ..... B4
Kamenz 18,323 ..... F3
Karlsruhe 265,100 ..... C4
Kassel 189,156 ..... C3
Kaufbeuren 39,192 ..... D5
Kehl 28,902 ..... B4
Kempten 60,052 ..... D5
Kevelaer 22,633 ..... B3
Kiel 240,675 ..... D1
Kirchheim unter Teck 34,534 ..... C4
Kitzingen 19,085 ..... C4
Koblenz 107,286 ..... B3
Köln (Cologne) 937,482 ..... B3
Königs Wusterhausen 19,085 ..... E2
Königswinter 34,136 ..... B3
Konstanz 72,862 ..... C5
Köpenick 118,059 ..... F4
Korbach 21,406 ..... C3
Kornwestheim 28,519 ..... C4
Köthen 34,617 ..... E3
Krefeld 235,423 ..... B3
Kreuztal 29,716 ..... C3
Kronach 18,246 ..... D3
Kulmbach 27,116 ..... D3
Lage 32,612 ..... C3
Lahnstein 17,972 ..... B3
Lahr 33,369 ..... B4
Lampertheim 30,263 ..... C4
Landau in der Pfalz 36,297 ..... C4
Landsberg am Lech 19,808 ..... D4
Landshut 57,194 ..... E4
Langen 31,206 ..... C4
Langenhagen 46,298 ..... C2
Lauchhammer 24,391 ..... E3
Lauenburg an der Elbe 10,786 ..... D2
Lauf an der Pegnitz 22,593 ..... D4
Leer 31,292 ..... B2
Lehrte 39,600 ..... D2
Leipzig 550,641 ..... E3
Lemgo 38,351 ..... C2
Lengerich 20,235 ..... B2
Leverkusen 157,358 ..... B3
Lichtenberg 95,426 ..... F4
Lichtenfels 20,252 ..... D3
Limburg an der Lahn 29,196 ..... C3
Limbach-Oberfrohna 22,059 ..... E3
Lindau 23,699 ..... C5
Lingen 47,837 ..... B2
Lippstadt 60,396 ..... C3
Löbau 18,492 ..... F3
Löhne 36,882 ..... C2
Lörrach 41,087 ..... B5
Lübbenau 20,815 ..... F3
Lübeck 210,681 ..... D2
Luckenwalde 26,761 ..... E2
Lüdenscheid 76,118 ..... B3
Ludwigsburg 79,342 ..... C4
Ludwigshafen am Rhein 158,478 ..... C4
Lüneburg 60,053 ..... D2
Lünen 85,584 ..... B3
Magdeburg 288,975 ..... D2
Mainz 174,828 ..... C4
Mannheim 300,468 ..... C4
Marburg 70,905 ..... C3
Markkleeberg 19,240 ..... E3
Marktredwitz 18,605 ..... E4
Marl 89,601 ..... B3
Mayen 18,427 ..... B3
Mechernich 21,986 ..... B3
Meerane 21,879 ..... E3
Meiningen 25,823 ..... D3
Meissen 37,757 ..... E3
Melle 40,490 ..... C2
Memmingen 37,942 ..... D5
Meppen 29,900 ..... B2
Merseburg 46,188 ..... D3
Merzig 29,312 ..... B4
Meschede 30,853 ..... C3
Metzingen 19,895 ..... C4
Minden 75,169 ..... C2
Mittenwald 7,998 ..... D5
Mittweida 18,469 ..... E3
Mönchengladbach 252,910 ..... B3
Mosbach 23,897 ..... C4
Mülhausen 43,046 ..... D3
Mülheim an der Ruhr 175,454 ..... B3
München (Munich) 1,211,617 ..... D4
Münden 24,794 ..... C3
Munich 1,211,617 ..... D4
Münster 248,919 ..... B3
Nagold 20,405 ..... C4
Naumburg 32,100 ..... D3
Neckarsulm 21,765 ..... C4
Neubrandenburg 87,235 ..... E2
Neuburg an der Donau 24,502 ..... D4
Neu-Isenburg 34,896 ..... C3
Neumarkt in der Oberpfalz 33,603 ..... D4
Neumünster 79,574 ..... C1
Neunkirchen 50,784 ..... B4
Neuruppin 26,934 ..... E2
Neuss 143,976 ..... B3
Neustadt an der Weinstrasse 50,453 ..... B4
Neustadt bei Coburg 16,211 ..... D3
Neustrelitz 27,300 ..... E2
Neu-Ulm 45,116 ..... D4
Neuwied 60,665 ..... B3
Nienburg 29,545 ..... C2
Norden 23,655 ..... B2
Nordenham 28,393 ..... C2
Norderstedt 66,747 ..... D2
Nordhausen 47,681 ..... D3
Nordhorn 48,556 ..... B2
Nördlingen 18,278 ..... D4
Northeim 30,349 ..... C3
Nuremberg 480,078 ..... D4
Nürnberg (Nuremberg) 480,078 ..... D4
Nürtingen 36,807 ..... C4
Oberammergau 4,980 ..... D5
Oberhausen 221,017 ..... B3
Oberursel 39,105 ..... C3
Offenbach am Main 112,450 ..... C3
Offenburg 51,730 ..... B4
Oldenburg 140,785 ..... C2
Oranienburg 28,667 ..... E2
Oschatz 19,100 ..... E3
Oschersleben 16,976 ..... D2
Osnabrück 154,594 ..... C2
Osterholz-Scharmbeck 24,205 ..... C2
Osterode am Harz 26,631 ..... D3
Paderborn 114,148 ..... C3
Pankow 62,847 ..... F3
Papenburg 29,237 ..... B2
Parchim 23,454 ..... D2
Passau 49,137 ..... E4
Peenemünde E1
Peine 45,522 ..... D2
Pfaffenhofen an der Ilm 18,335 ..... D4
Pforzheim 108,887 ..... C4
Pinneberg 36,583 ..... C2
Pirmasens 47,102 ..... B4
Pirna 46,991 ..... E3
Plauen 77,514 ..... E3
Plettenberg 28,113 ..... C3
Pössneck 17,895 ..... D3
Potsdam 141,231 ..... E2
Prenzlau 23,642 ..... E2
Quedlinburg 29,168 ..... D3
Radeberg 15,702 ..... E3
Radebeul 33,757 ..... E3
Radolfzell 25,712 ..... C5
Rastatt 40,909 ..... C4
Rastede 18,191 ..... C2
Rathenow 31,302 ..... E2
Ratingen 89,880 ..... B3
Ravensburg 44,146 ..... C5
Recklinghausen 121,666 ..... B3
Regensburg 119,078 ..... E4

(continued on following page)

Germany Before World War I 1871-1914

Germany Between Wars 1919-1937

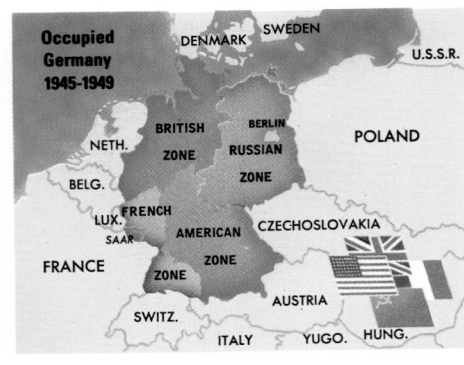

Occupied Germany 1945-1949

Reichenbach 24,749 ....E3	Schwalmstadt 17,371 ....C3	Telgte 16,834 ....B3
Remagen 14,375 ....B3	Schwandorf im Bayern 25,874 ...E4	Tempelhof F4
Remscheid 120,979 ....B3	Schwedt 51,753 ....F2	Thale 16,605 ....D3
Rendsburg 30,752 ....C1	Schweinfurt 52,818 ....D3	Torgau 22,749 ....D3
Reutlingen 100,400 ....C4	Schwelm 29,564 ....B3	Traunstein 17,145 ....E5
Rheda-Wiedenbrück 36,990 ..C3	Schwetzingen 18,029 ....C4	Treuchtlingen 12,314 ....D4
Rheine 69,324 ....B2	Seesen 21,604 ....D3	Triberg im Schwarzwald 5,697 ...C4
Rheinfelden 27,711 ....B5	Selb 19,275 ....E3	Trier 95,692 ....B4
Ribnitz-Damgarten 17,512 ....E1	Senftenberg 32,428 ....F3	Troisdorf 62,011 ....B3
Riesa 49,108 ....E3	Siegburg 34,402 ....B3	Tübingen 76,046 ....C4
Rietberg 23,058 ....C3	Siegen 106,160 ....C3	Tuttlingen 31,752 ....C5
Rinteln 26,120 ....C2	Sigmaringen 15,270 ....C4	Übach-Palenberg 23,005 .....B3
Rosenheim 54,304 ....D5	Sindelfingen 57,524 ....C4	Überlingen 18,043 ....C5
Rostock 249,349 ....E1	Singen 42,605 ....C5	Ueckermünde 12,304 ....F1
Rotenburg 18,392 ....C2	Soest 40,775 ....C3	Uelzen 34,891 ....D2
Roth bei Nürnberg 20,288 ...D4	Solingen 160,824 ....B3	Uetersen 17,218 ....C2
Rothenburg ob der Tauber 11,071 ...D4	Soltau 19,115 ....C2	Ulm 106,508 ....C4
Rottenburg am Neckar 33,907 ...C4	Sömmerda 23,398 ....D3	Varel 23,718 ....C2
Rottweil 23,080 ....C4	Sondershausen 24,178 ....D3	Vechta 22,759 ....C2
Rudolstadt 32,264 ....D3	Sonneberg 28,512 ....D3	Verden 23,770 ....C2
Rüsselsheim 58,426 ....C4	Sonthofen 20,037 ....D5	Viersen 76,163 ....B3
Saalfeld 33,453 ....D3	Spandau E3	Villingen-Schwenningen 76,258 ...C4
Saarbrücken 188,467 ....B4	Speyer 45,089 ....C4	Völklingen 42,916 ....B4
Saarlouis 37,662 ....B4	Spremberg 24,815 ....F3	Waldheim 10,316 ....E3
Salzgitter 111,674 ....D2	Springe 29,209 ....C2	Waldkirch 18,893 ....B4
Salzwedel 23,163 ....D2	Stade 41,223 ....C2	Waldkraiburg 23,177 ....E4
Sangerhausen 33,604 ....D3	Stadthagen 22,218 ....C2	Waldshut-Tiengen 21,372 ....C5
Sankt Ingbert 40,527 ....B4	Starnberg 19,845 ....D4	Walsrode 22,232 ....C2
Sankt Wendel 26,649 ....B4	Stassfurt 27,372 ....D3	Waltershausen 14,127 ....D3
Saulgau 14,864 ....C5	Stendal 47,880 ....D2	Wangen im Allgäu 23,822 ....C5
Schleswig 26,648 ....C1	Stolberg 56,182 ....B3	Warburg 21,802 ....C3
Schmalkalden 17,409 ....D3	Stralsund 75,857 ....E1	Waren 24,318 ....E2
Schneeberg 22,105 ....E3	Straubing 40,612 ....E4	Warendorf 33,891 ....B3
Schönebeck 45,155 ....D2	Strausberg 27,527 ....F2	Wedel 30,158 ....C2
Schramberg 18,208 ....C4	Stuttgart 562,658 ....C4	Weida 10,602 ....D3
Schwabach 34,217 ....D4	Suhl 55,295 ....D3	Weiden in der Oberpfalz 41,539 ...D4
Schwäbisch Gmünd 57,861 ...C4	Sulzbach 19,753 ....B4	
Schwäbisch Hall 31,375 .....C4	Sulzbach-Rosenberg 18,134 ..D4	

Weilheim im Oberbayern 17,602 ...D5	**OTHER FEATURES**	
Weimar 63,910 ....D3		
Weingarten 21,522 ....C5	Aller (riv.) C2	Havel (riv.) E2
Traunstein 17,145 ....E5	Allgäu (reg.) D5	Hegau (reg.) C5
Weinheim 41,876 ....C4	Altmark (reg.) D2	Helgoland (bay) C1
Weissenburg im Bayern 17,318 ...D4	Ammersee (lake) D4	Helgoland (isl.) B1
Weissenfels 38,763 ....D3	Amrum (isl.) C1	Hunsrück (mts.) B4
Weissensee 31,858 ....F3	Arkona (cape) E1	Iller (riv.) D4
Weisswasser 36,472 ....F3	Baltic (sea) E1	Ilmenau (riv.) D2
Werdau 19,451 ....D3	Bavarian (forest) E4	Inn (riv.) E4
Wernigerode 36,499 ....D3	Bavarian Alps (range) D5	Isar (riv.) E4
Wertheim 20,457 ....C4	Bayerischer Wald Nat'l Park ...E4	Jade (bay) C2
Wesel 57,986 ....B3	Black (forest) C4	Juist (isl.) B2
Westerstede 18,184 ....B2	Black Elster (riv.) E3	Kaiserstuhl (mt.) B4
Wiehl 21,897 ....B3	Bodensee (Constance) (lake) ...C5	Kiel (bay) D1
Wiesbaden 254,209 ....B3	Bohemian (forest) E4	Kiel (Nord-Ostsee) (canal) ...C1
Wiesmoor 10,827 ....B2	Borkum (isl.) B2	Königssee (lake) E5
Wilhelmshaven 89,892 ......B2	Breisgau (reg.) B5	Lahn (riv.) C3
Winsen 26,139 ....D2	Brocken (mt.) D3	Langeoog (isl.) D4
Wismar 58,066 ....D2	Chiemsee (lake) E5	Lech (riv.) D4
Witten 103,637 ....B3	Constance (lake) C5	Leine (riv.) C2
Wittenberg 53,670 ....E3	Danube (riv.) C4	Lippe (riv.) C3
Wittenberge 30,389 ....D2	Donau (Danube) (riv.) C4	Lüneburger Heide (dist.) ...D2
Wolfen 43,606 ....E3	East Friesland (reg.) B2	Lusatia (reg.) F3
Wolfenbüttel 50,960 ....D2	Eder (riv.) C3	Main (riv.) C4
Wolfsburg 125,831 ....D2	Elbe (riv.) D2	Mecklenburg (bay) D1
Worms 74,809 ....C4	Elde (riv.) D2	Mosel (riv.) B4
Wunstorf 37,115 ....C2	Ems (riv.) B2	Mulde (riv.) E3
Wuppertal 371,283 ....B3	Erzgebirge (mts.) E3	Müritzsee (lake) E2
Würzburg 125,589 ....C4	Fehmarn (isl.) D1	Naab (riv.) E4
Wurzen 19,330 ....E3	Feldberg (mt.) C5	Neckar (riv.) C4
Xanten 16,097 ....B3	Fichtelberg (mt.) E3	Neisse (riv.) F3
Zeitz 42,985 ....E3	Fichtelgebirge (range) E3	Norderney (isl.) B2
Zerbst 18,717 ....E3	Föhr (isl.) C1	Nord-Ostsee (canal) C1
Zeulenroda 14,409 ....D3	Franconian Jura (range) D4	Nordstrand (isl.) C1
Zirndorf 21,608 ....D4	Frisian, East (isls.) B2	North (sea) B2
Zittau 39,305 ....F3	Frisian, North (isls.) B1	North Friesland (reg.) C1
Zweibrücken 33,377 ....B4	Fulda (riv.) C3	Oder (riv.) F2
Zwickau 120,923 ....E3	Grosser Arber (mt.) E4	Oder-Haff (lag.) F2
	Harz (mts.) D3	Our (riv.) B3
		Peene (riv.) E2

Pellworm (isl.) C1	
Plauersee (lake) E2	
Pomeranian (bay) F1	
Regnitz (riv.) D4	
Rhine (riv.) B3	
Rhön (mts.) D3	
Rügen (isl.) E1	
Ruhr (riv.) B3	
Saale (riv.) D3	
Saar (riv.) B4	
Salzach (riv.) E5	
Sauer (riv.) B4	
Sauerland (reg.) B3	
Schwarzwald (Black) (forest) ...B4	
Schwerinersee (lake) D2	
Spessart (range) C4	
Spiekeroog (isl.) B2	
Spree (riv.) F3	
Spreewald (forest) F3	
Starnberger (lake) D5	
Swabian Jura (range) C4	
Sylt (isl.) C1	
Taunus (range) C3	
Tegernsee (lake) D5	
Teutoburger Wald (forest) ...C2	
Thüringer Wald (forest) D3	
Unstrut (riv.) D3	
Usedom (isl.) F1	
Vechte (riv.) B2	
Vogelsberg (mts.) C3	
Walchensee (lake) D5	
Wasserkuppe (mt.) C3	
Watzmann (mt.) E5	
Werra (riv.) C3	
Weser (riv.) C2	
Westerwald (forest) B3	
White Elster (riv.) E3	
Würmsee (Starnbergersee) (lake) ...D5	
Zugspitze (mt.) D5	

Agriculture, Industry and Resources

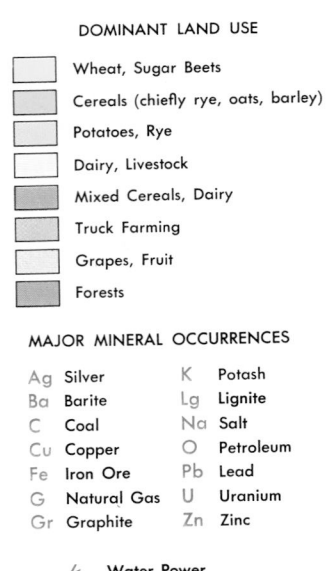

DOMINANT LAND USE

- Wheat, Sugar Beets
- Cereals (chiefly rye, oats, barley)
- Potatoes, Rye
- Dairy, Livestock
- Mixed Cereals, Dairy
- Truck Farming
- Grapes, Fruit
- Forests

MAJOR MINERAL OCCURRENCES

Ag	Silver	K	Potash
Ba	Barite	Lg	Lignite
C	Coal	Na	Salt
Cu	Copper	O	Petroleum
Fe	Iron Ore	Pb	Lead
G	Natural Gas	U	Uranium
Gr	Graphite	Zn	Zinc

⚡ Water Power
▨ Major Industrial Areas

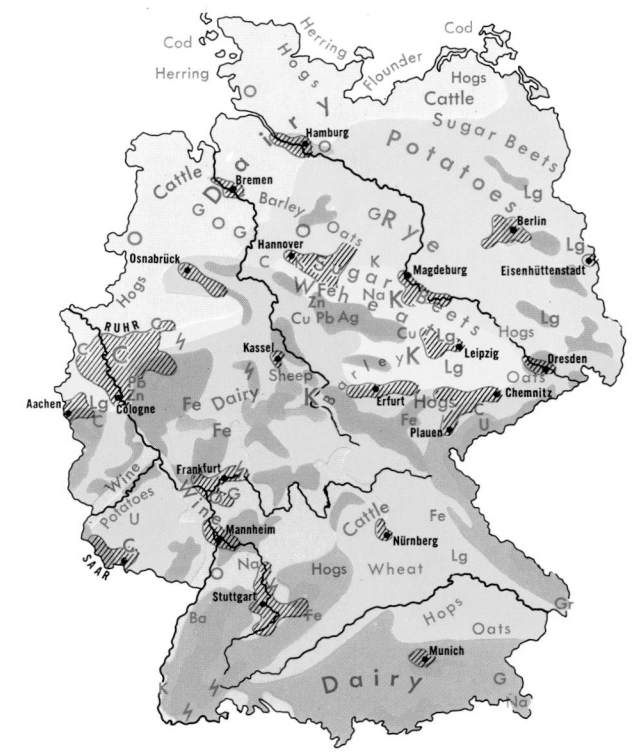

AREA 15,892 sq. mi. (41,160 sq. km.)
POPULATION 14,906,000
CAPITALS The Hague, Amsterdam
LARGEST CITY Amsterdam
HIGHEST POINT Vaalserberg 1,056 ft. (322 m.)
MONETARY UNIT guilder (florin)
MAJOR LANGUAGE Dutch
MAJOR RELIGIONS Protestantism, Roman Catholicism

AREA 11,781 sq. mi. (30,513 sq. km.)
POPULATION 9,883,000
CAPITAL Brussels
LARGEST CITY Brussels (greater)
HIGHEST POINT Botrange 2,277 ft. (694 m.)
MONETARY UNIT Belgian franc
MAJOR LANGUAGES French (Walloon), Flemish
MAJOR RELIGION Roman Catholicism

AREA 999 sq. mi. (2,587 sq. km.)
POPULATION 378,000
CAPITAL Luxembourg
LARGEST CITY Luxembourg
HIGHEST POINT Ardennes Plateau 1,825 ft. (556 m.)
MONETARY UNIT Luxembourg franc
MAJOR LANGUAGES Luxembourgeois (Letzeburgisch), French, German
MAJOR RELIGION Roman Catholicism

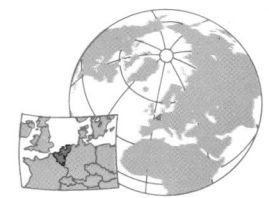

NETHERLANDS

BELGIUM

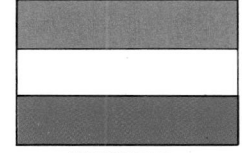

LUXEMBOURG

BELGIUM

PROVINCES

Antwerp 1,569,876 ....F6
Brabant 2,221,222 ....F7
East Flanders 1,331,192 ....D7
Hainaut 1,301,477 ....D7
Liège 999,413 ....H7
Limburg 716,888 ....G7
Luxembourg 221,926 ....G9
Namur 407,400 ....F8
West Flanders 1,079,253 ....B7

CITIES and TOWNS

Aalst 78,938 ....D7
Aalter 15,554 ....C6
Aarlen (Arlon) 22,279 ....H9
Aarschot 25,168 ....F7
Alken 9,563 ....H7
Amay 12,725 ....G8
Andenne 22,341 ....G8
Anderlecht 94,764 ....B9

Anderlues 11,700 ....E8
Ans 26,016 ....H7
Antoing 7,970 ....C7
Antwerp 185,897 ....E6
Antwerp* 918,144 ....E6
Antwerpen (Antwerp) 185,897 .....E6
Ardooie 9,458 ....C7
Arendonk 10,561 ....G6
Arlon 22,279 ....H9
Asse 26,425 ....E7
Assenede 13,353 ....D6
Bocholt 10,142 ....H6
Borgerhout 43,521 ....E6
Borgworm (Waremme) 11,907 ....G7
Bourg-Léopold (Leopoldsburg) 9,593 ...G6
Boussu 21,558 ....D8
Braine-l'Alleud 30,028 ....E7
Braine-le-Comte 16,475 ....D7
Brecht 16,391 ....F6
Bredene 10,538 ....B6
Bree 13,345 ....H6

Beloeil 13,553 ....D7
Berchem 45,423 ....F6
Berchem-Sainte-Agathe 18,719 .....B9
Bergen (Mons) 94,417 ....D8
Beringen 34,254 ....G6
Bertrix 7,244 ....G9
Beveren 40,857 ....E6
Bilzen 25,683 ....G7
Binche 33,651 ....E8
Blankenberge 14,832 ....C6
Bocholt 10,142 ....H6
Boom 14,827 ....E6
Borgerhout 43,521 ....E6
Auderghem 30,435 ....C9
Aywaille 8,194 ....H8
Baerle-Hertog 2,111 ....F6
Balen 18,162 ....G6
Bastenaken (Bastogne) 11,386 .....H9
Bastogne 11,386 ....H9
Beauraing 7,641 ....F8
Beernem 13,526 ....C6

Bruges 118,020 ....C6
Brugge (Bruges) 118,020 ....C6
Brussels (cap.)* 997,293 ....C9
Bruxelles (Brussels) (cap.)* 997,293 ...C9
Charleroi 222,343 ....E8
Charleroi* 443,832 ....E8
Châtelet 38,506 ....E8
Chimay 9,273 ....E8
Ciney 13,330 ....G8
Comines 18,034 ....B7
Courcelles 29,757 ....E8
Courtrai (Kortrijk) 75,917 ....C7
Couvin 12,909 ....F8
Damme 9,881 ....C6
De Haan 8,655 ....C6
Deinze 24,871 ....C7
Denderleeuw 16,497 ....E7
Dendermonde 22,119 ....E6
De Panne 9,507 ....B6
Dessel 8,573 ....G6
Destelbergen 15,741 ....D6
Deurne 77,635 ....F6
Diest 20,491 ....F7

Diksmuide 15,347 ....B6
Dilbeek 35,050 ....B9
Dilsen 15,910 ....H6
Dinant 12,105 ....G8
Dison 14,225 ....H7
Dixmude (Diksmuide) 15,347 ....B6
Doornik (Tournai) 67,906 ....C7
Dour 17,737 ....D8
Duffel 14,684 ....F6
Durbuy 7,729 ....H8
Ecaussinnes 9,739 ....E7
Edingen (Enghien) 10,095 ....D7
Eeklo 19,637 ....D6
Éghezée 10,683 ....F7
Eigenbrakel (Braine-l'Alleud) 30,028 ...E7
Ekeren 30,520 ....E6
Enghien 10,095 ....D7
Erquelinnes 10,029 ....E8
Esneux 11,559 ....H7
Essen 12,505 ....F6
Estampuis 9,601 ....C7
Etterbeek 44,218 ....B9
Eupen 16,847 ....J7

Evere 30,520 ....C9
Evergem 28,974 ....D6
Farciennes 12,205 ....E8
Flémalle 28,217 ....G7
Fleurus 22,574 ....E8
Florennes 10,537 ....F8
Forest 50,607 ....B9
Fosses-La-Ville 7,678 ....F8
Frameries 21,470 ....D8
Frasnes-lez Anvaing 10,751 ....D7
Furnes (Veurne) 11,253 ....B6
Ganshoren 21,445 ....B9
Geel 31,463 ....F6
Geldenaken (Jodoigne) 8,983 ......F7
Gembloux-sur-Orneau 17,636 ....F7
Genk 61,502 ....H7
Gent (Ghent) 239,256 ....D6
Geraardsbergen 17,533 ....D7
Gerpinnes 10,808 ....F8
Ghent 239,256 ....D6
Ghent* 485,565 ....D6
Gistel 9,531 ....B6
Grammont (Geraardsbergen) 17,533 ...D7
Grez-Doiceau 8,795 ....F7
Grimbergen 32,038 ....F7
Haacht 11,285 ....E7
Hal (Halle) 15,293 ....E7
Halen 7,865 ....G7
Halle 15,293 ....E7
Hamme 22,790 ....E6
Hamont-Achel 11,939 ....H6
Hannuit (Hannut) 11,527 ....G7
Hannut 11,527 ....G7
Harelbeke 25,214 ....C7
Hasselt 64,613 ....G7
Heist-op-den-Berg 34,617 ....F6
Hensies 6,806 ....D8
Herentals 23,797 ....F6
Herselt 11,340 ....F6
Herstal 38,592 ....H7
Herve 14,276 ....H7
Heuvelland 8,540 ....B7
Hoboken 34,563 ....E6
Hoei (Huy) 17,331 ....G8
Hoeselt 8,497 ....G7
Hoogstraten 14,368 ....F6
Huy 17,331 ....G8
Ichtegem 12,259 ....B6
Ieper 34,425 ....B7
Izegem 26,410 ....C7
Ingelmunster 10,434 ....C7
Ixelles 75,723 ....C9
Izegem 26,410 ....C7
Jabbeke 10,629 ....C6
Jemappes 18,632 ....D8
Jemeppe-sur-Sambre 17,120 ....F8
Jette 40,109 ....B9
Jodoigne 8,983 ....F7
Kalmthout 14,960 ....F6
Kapellen 14,536 ....F6
Kasterlee 14,612 ....F6
Kinrooi 10,138 ....H6
Knokke-Heist 28,868 ....C6
Koekelare 7,606 ....B6
Koekelberg 16,643 ....B9
Koksijde 13,679 ....B6
Kontich 17,878 ....E6
Kortemark 12,580 ....C6
Kortrijk 75,917 ....C7
Kraainem 11,780 ....C9
La Louvière 77,326 ....E8
Lanaken 20,272 ....H7
Landen 14,081 ....G7
Langemark-Poelkapelle 7,097 ......B7
Lasne 10,919 ....F7
Lede 17,249 ....D7
Lens 3,726 ....D8
Leopoldsburg 9,593 ....G6
Le Roeulx 7,754 ....E8
Lessen (Lessines) 16,553 ....D7
Lessines 16,553 ....D7
Leuven 85,076 ....F7
Leuze-en-Hainaut 12,863 ....D7
Libramont-Chevigny 7,859 ....G9
Lichtervelde 7,459 ....C6
Liedekerke 11,609 ....E7
Liège 214,119 ....H7
Liège* 605,123 ....H7

Lier 31,261 ....F6
Lierre (Lier) 31,261 ....F6
Limburg 5,350 ....J7
Limburg (Limbourg) 5,350 ....J7
Linter 6,568 ....G7
Lochristi 16,125 ....D6
Lokeren 33,369 ....D6
Lommel 25,412 ....G6
Louvain (Leuven) 85,076 ....F7
Luik (Liège) 214,119 ....H7
Lummen 11,793 ....G7
Maaseik 20,056 ....H6
Maasmechelen 33,618 ....H7
Machelen 11,273 ....C9
Maldegem 42,694 ....C6
Malines (Mechelen) 77,269 ....F6
Malmédy 10,036 ....J8
Marche-en-Famenne 14,115 ....G8
Mechelen 77,269 ....F6
Meerhout 8,613 ....G6
Meise 15,170 ....E7
Menen 33,542 ....C7
Menin (Menen) 33,542 ....C7
Merchtem 12,972 ....E7
Merelbeke 19,773 ....D7
Merksem 41,600 ....E6
Merksplas 6,136 ....F6
Mettet 9,958 ....F8
Meulebeke 10,471 ....C7
Middelkerke 14,168 ....B6
Moeskroen (Mouscron) 54,590 ......C7
Mol 29,798 ....G6
Molenbeek-Saint-Jean 70,850 ......B9
Mons 94,417 ....D8
Montigny-le-Tilleul 9,726 ....E8
Moorslede 10,974 ....C7
Mortsel 26,746 ....E6
Mouscron 54,590 ....C7
Namen (Namur) 102,321 ....F8
Namur 102,321 ....F8
Nazareth 9,248 ....D7
Neerpelt 12,779 ....G6
Neufchâteau 6,039 ....G9
Nevele 10,471 ....D6
Nieuport (Nieuwpoort) 8,195 ......B6
Nieuwpoort 8,195 ....B6
Nijvel (Nivelles) 21,580 ....E7
Ninove 33,393 ....E7
Nivelles 21,580 ....E7
Oostende (Ostend) 68,915 ....B6
Oostkamp 19,747 ....C6
Opwijk 11,451 ....E7
Ostend 68,915 ....B6
Oudenaarde 26,615 ....D7
Oudenburg 8,138 ....B6
Oud-Turnhout 10,733 ....F6
Oupeye 22,453 ....H7
Overijse 21,428 ....F7
Peer 12,099 ....G6
Péruwelz 16,664 ....D8
Philippeville 6,916 ....E8
Poelkapelle-Langemark 7,097 ......B7
Pont-à-Celles 15,444 ....E8
Poperinge 19,886 ....B7
Profondeville 8,724 ....F8
Putte 14,017 ....F6
Quaregnon 20,071 ....D8
Quévy 7,391 ....D8
Quiévrain 6,945 ....D8
Raeren 8,046 ....J7
Ravels 10,328 ....G6
Rebecq 8,891 ....E7
Renaix (Ronse) 25,056 ....D7
Retie 8,359 ....G6
Rochefort 4,357 ....G8
Roeselare 51,984 ....C7
Ronse (Renaix) 25,056 ....D7
Roulers (Roeselare) 51,984 ....C7
Saint-Gilles 46,076 ....B9
Saint-Josse-ten-Noode 20,381 .....C9
Saint-Nicolas 25,755 ....G7
Saint-Trond (Sint-Truiden) 36,374 ...G7
Saint-Vith (Sankt Vith) 8,434 ....J8

(continued on following page)

Agriculture, Industry and Resources

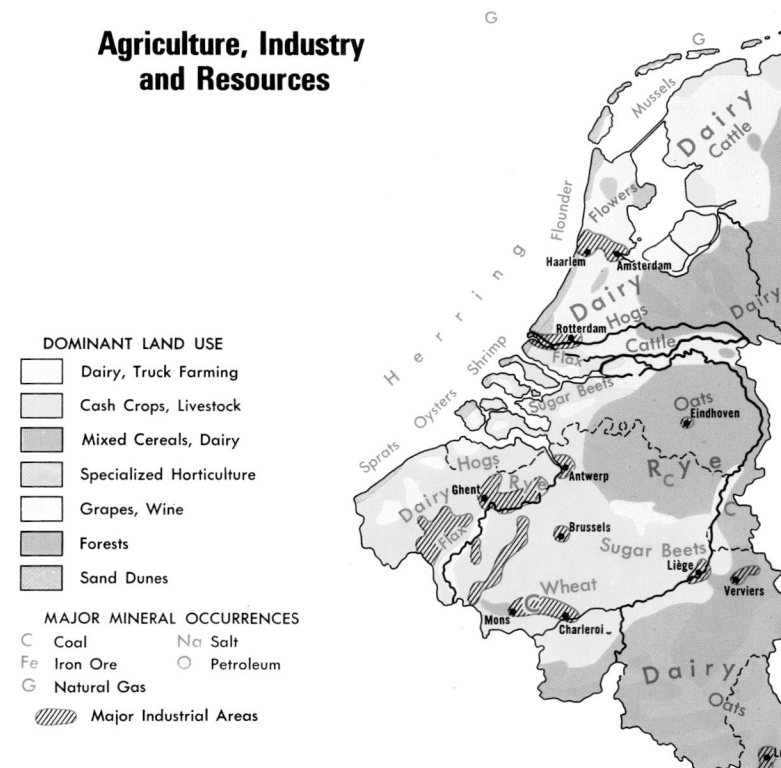

DOMINANT LAND USE

- Dairy, Truck Farming
- Cash Crops, Livestock
- Mixed Cereals, Dairy
- Specialized Horticulture
- Grapes, Wine
- Forests
- Sand Dunes

MAJOR MINERAL OCCURRENCES

- C Coal
- Fe Iron Ore
- G Natural Gas
- Na Salt
- O Petroleum

▨ Major Industrial Areas

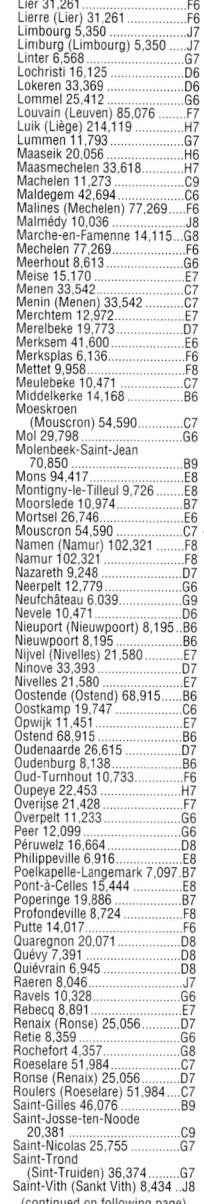

26 Netherlands, Belgium and Luxembourg

(continued)

Sankt Vith 8,434 .... J8
Schaerbeek 106,754 .... C9
Schoten 31,128 .... F6
Seraing 64,543 .... G7
's-Gravenbrakel
(Braine-le-Comte) 16,475 .... D7
Sint-Laureins 6,620 .... D6
Sint-Niklaas 67,992 .... E6
Sint-Pieters-Leeuw 27,968 .... B9
Sint-Truiden 36,374 .... G7
Soignies 23,352 .... D7
Spa 9,619 .... H8
Sprimont 9,660 .... H8
Staden 11,135 .... B7
Steenokkerzeel 9,638 .... C9
Stekene 14,125 .... E6
Tamise (Temse) 23,525 .... E6
Temse 23,525 .... E6
Termonde
(Dendermonde) 22,119 .... E6
Tessenderlo 13,800 .... G6
Theux 9,167 .... H8
Thuin 13,757 .... E8
Tielt 19,103 .... C7
Tielt-Winge 8,237 .... F7
Tienen 32,620 .... F7
Tirlemont 32,620 .... F7
Tongeren 29,603 .... G7
Tongres (Tongeren) 29,603 .... G7
Torhout 17,165 .... C6
Tournai 67,906 .... C7
Tubeke (Tubize) 19,827 .... E7
Tubize 19,827 .... E7
Turnhout 37,453 .... F6
Uccle 76,004 .... B9
Ukkel (Uccle) 76,004 .... B9
Verviers 55,371 .... H7
Veurne 11,253 .... B6
Vielsalm 6,731 .... H8
Vilvoorde 33,264 .... F7
Vilvorde (Vilvoorde) 33,264 .... F7
Viroinval 5,589 .... F8
Virton 10,490 .... H9
Visé 16,469 .... H7
Vorst (Forest) 50,607 .... B9
Waarschoot 7,574 .... D6
Wachtebeke 6,951 .... D6
Waimes (Weismes) 5,713 .... J8
Walcourt 14,866 .... F8
Waregem 32,810 .... C7
Waremme 11,907 .... G7
Waterloo 24,755 .... E7
Watermael-Boitsfort 24,880 .... C9
Watermael-Bosvoorde
(Watermael-Boitsfort)
24,880 .... C9
Waver (Wavre) 25,153 .... F7
Wavre 25,153 .... F7
Wemmel 13,547 .... B9
Wervik 18,086 .... B7
Westerlo 19,459 .... F6
Wetteren 23,460 .... D7
Wezembeek-Oppem 12,006 .... D9
Wezet (Visé) 16,469 .... H7
Willebroek 22,265 .... E6
Wilrijk 42,328 .... E6
Wingene 12,188 .... C6
Woluwe-Saint-Lambert
48,801 .... C9
Woluwe-Saint-Pierre 40,686 .... C9
Ypres (Ieper) 34,425 .... B7
Yvoir 6,527 .... F8
Zaventem 25,393 .... C9
Zedelgem 19,198 .... C6
Zele 19,631 .... E6
Zelzate 12,934 .... D6
Zemst 17,167 .... E7
Zinnik (Soignies) 23,352 .... D7
Zonhoven 15,965 .... G6
Zottegem 25,109 .... D7

OTHER FEATURES

Albert (canal) F6
Ardennes (forest) F9
Botrange (mt.) J8
Dender (riv.) D7
Deûle (riv.) B7
Dyle (riv.) F7
Hohe Venn (plat.) H8
Lys (riv.) B7
Mark (riv.) F6
Meuse (riv.) F8
Nethe (riv.) F6
North (sea) D4
Ourthe (riv.) G8
Rupel (riv.) F7
Sambre (riv.) D8
Schelde (Scheldt) (riv.) C7
Scheldt (riv.) C7
Semois (riv.) G9
Senne (riv.) E7
Vaalserberg (mt.) J7
Vesdre (riv.) H7
Yser (riv.) B7

LUXEMBOURG

CITIES and TOWNS

Bascharage 4,870 .... H9
Diekirch† 5,470 .... J9
Differdange 15,940 .... H9
Dudelange† 14,070 .... J1
Echternach† 4,290 .... J9
Esch-sur-Alzette† 23,800 .... H9
Ettelbruck† 6,600 .... J9
Grevenmacher† 2,940 .... J9
Hesperange 9,470 .... J9
Luxembourg (cap.) 75,540 .... J9
Mamer 6,090 .... H9
Mersch 5,560 .... J9
Mertert 3,000 .... J9
Pétange 11,800 .... H9
Remich 2,430 .... J9
Troisvierges 1,890 .... J9
Vianden† 1,510 .... J9
Wasserbillig 2,097 .... J9
Wiltz 3,850 .... H9

OTHER FEATURES

Alzette (riv.) J9
Clerf (riv.) J8
Mosel (riv.) J9
Our (riv.) J9
Sauer (riv.) J9

NETHERLANDS

PROVINCES

Drenthe 439,066 .... K3
Flevoland 202,678 .... G4
Friesland 599,190 .... H2
Gelderland 1,794,678 .... H4
Groningen 555,200 .... K2
Limburg 1,099,622 .... H6
North Brabant 2,172,604 .... F5
North Holland 2,365,160 .... F3
Overijssel 1,014,949 .... J4
South Holland 3,200,408 .... E5
Utrecht 1,004,632 .... G4
Zeeland 355,585 .... D6

CITIES and TOWNS

Aalsmeer 21,984 .... F4
Aalten 18,202 .... K5
Alkmaar 88,571 .... F3
Almelo 62,008 .... K4
Almere 63,785 .... G4
Alphen aan de Rijn 59,586 .... F4
Amersfoort 96,072 .... G4
Amstelveen 69,505 .... B5
Amsterdam (cap.) 694,680 .... B4
Apeldoorn 147,270 .... H4
Appingedam 12,668 .... K2
Arnhem 128,946 .... H4
Assen 49,398 .... K3
Asten 14,965 .... H6
Axel 12,219 .... D6
Baarn 24,897 .... G4
Barneveld 41,649 .... H4
Beilen 14,057 .... K3
Bemmel 15,842 .... H5
Bergen 14,075 .... F3
Bergen op Zoom 46,842 .... E5
Berkel 15,690 .... F5
Beverwijk 35,126 .... F4
Bloemendaal 8,977 .... E4
Bodegraven 17,720 .... F4
Bolsward 9,799 .... H2
Borculo 10,057 .... J4
Borger 12,730 .... K3
Borne 21,261 .... K4
Boskoop 14,524 .... F4
Boxmeer 14,363 .... H5
Boxtel 24,951 .... G5
Breda 121,362 .... F5
Brielle 14,973 .... E5
Brummen 20,802 .... J4
Brunssum 29,799 .... J7
Bussum 31,988 .... G4
Capelle 57,423 .... F5
Castricum 22,433 .... F3
Coevorden 14,344 .... K3
Culemborg 21,116 .... G5
De Bilt 31,729 .... G4
Delft 88,135 .... E4
Delfzijl 23,472 .... K2
Denekamp 12,206 .... L4
Den Helder 62,094 .... F3
Deurne 29,308 .... H6
Deventer 66,398 .... J4
Didam 16,036 .... J5
Diemen 18,083 .... C5
Dinxperlo 8,133 .... K5
Dirksland 7,341 .... E5
Doesburg 10,578 .... J4
Doetinchem 41,260 .... J5
Dongen 21,124 .... F5
Doorn 10,419 .... G4
Dordrecht 108,519 .... F5
Driebergen 18,294 .... G4
Dronten 24,281 .... H3
Druten 14,630 .... H5
Echt 16,927 .... H6
Edam-Volendam 24,572 .... G4
Ede 92,293 .... H4
Egmond aan Zee 11,163 .... E3
Eindhoven 190,736 .... G6
Elst 17,654 .... H5
Emmen 92,422 .... K3
Enkhuizen 15,939 .... G3
Enschede 145,223 .... K4
Epe 33,872 .... H4
Ermelo 25,644 .... H4
Etten-Leur 32,010 .... F5
Flushing 44,022 .... C6
Geertruidenberg 6,645 .... F5
Geldermalsen 22,017 .... G5
Geldrop 25,817 .... H6
Geleen 33,756 .... H7
Gemert 17,613 .... H5
Gendringen 20,186 .... J5
Genemuiden 7,545 .... H3
Gennep 16,264 .... H5
Giessendam 16,722 .... F5
Gilze 22,577 .... F5
Goes 31,815 .... D6
Goirle 18,852 .... G5
Goor 11,804 .... K4
Gorinchem 28,222 .... G5
Gouda 63,232 .... F4
Gramsbergen 6,080 .... K3
Grave 10,447 .... H5
Groenlo 8,895 .... K4
Groesbeek 18,221 .... H5
Groningen 167,788 .... K2
Haaksbergen 22 690 .... K4
Haarlem 149,198 .... F4
Haarlemmermeer
(Hoofddorp) 93,427 .... F4
Hague, The (cap.) 443,845 .... E4
Hardenberg 32,065 .... J3
Harderwijk 34,600 .... H4
Hardinxveld-Giessendam
16,722 .... G5
Harlingen 15,727 .... G2
Hasselt 6,871 .... J3
Hattem 11,571 .... H4
Heemskerk 32,910 .... F3
Heemstede 26,308 .... F4
Heerde 18,171 .... H4
Heerenveen 37,700 .... H3
Heerhugowaard 35,522 .... F3
Heerlen 94,149 .... J7
Heesch 11,309 .... G5
Heiloo 20,467 .... F3
Hellendoorn 34,287 .... J4
Hellevoetsluis 34,276 .... E5
Helmond 66,791 .... H6
Hengelo 76,175 .... J4
's Hertogenbosch 90,584 .... G5
Heusden 5,761 .... G5
Hillegom 20,001 .... E4
Hilvarenbeek 9,975 .... G6
Hilversum 84,983 .... G4
Hoek van Holland
(Hook of Holland) D4
Hoofddorp
(Haarlemmermeer) 93,427 .... F4
Hoogeveen 45,601 .... J3
Hoogezand-Sappemeer
34,618 .... K2
Hook of Holland D4
Hoorn 56,474 .... G3
Horst 17,614 .... H6
Huissen 15,544 .... H5
Huizen 20,501 .... G4
Hulst 18,575 .... E6
IJsselstein 19,516 .... F4
Kampen 32,769 .... H3
Katwijk aan Zee 39,441 .... E4
Kerkrade 52,994 .... J7
Kesteren 9,389 .... G5
Krimpen aan den IJssel
27,638 .... F5
Landsmeer 9,121 .... C4
Laren 11,643 .... G4
Leek 17,743 .... J2
Leerdam 19,015 .... G5
Leeuwarden 85,296 .... H2
Leiden 109,254 .... E4
Lelystad 58,125 .... H3
Lisse 20,826 .... F4
Lith 6,115 .... G5
Lochem 18,295 .... J4
Loon op Zand 21,372 .... G5
Losser 22,526 .... L4
Maarssen 37,629 .... F4
Maasbree 11,752 .... H6
Maassluis 33,155 .... E5
Maastricht 116,380 .... H7
Margraten 13,365 .... H7
Medemblik 6,876 .... G3
Meerssen 20,462 .... H7
Meppel 23,492 .... J3
Middelburg 39,462 .... C6
Middelharnis 15,480 .... E5
Millingen aan den Rijn 5,287 .... J5
Monnickendam 9,953 .... C4
Montfoort 12,397 .... G4
Muiden 6,772 .... G4
Muntendam 5,022 .... K2
Naaldwijk 27,683 .... E4
Naarden 16,101 .... G4
Neede 10,982 .... K4
Nieuwegein 58,316 .... G4
Nieuwkoop 10,723 .... F4
Nijkerk 25,613 .... H4
Nijmegen 145,405 .... H5
Noordwijk 24,996 .... E4
Norg 6,595 .... J2
Nunspeet 24,573 .... H4
Odoorn 12,225 .... K3
Oisterwijk 18,177 .... G5
Oldenzaal 29,680 .... K4
Olst 9,039 .... J4
Ommen 17,957 .... J3
Oostburg 18,145 .... C6
Oosterhout 48,157 .... F5
Oostzaan 7,292 .... C4
Oss 50,987 .... H5
Oud-Beijerland 20,385 .... E5
Oude-Pekela 8,028 .... K2
Oudenbosch 12,576 .... E5
Oudewater 9,410 .... F4
Purmerend 56,233 .... F4
Putten 20,898 .... H4
Raalte 26,883 .... J4
Renkum 33,841 .... H5
Reusel 7,813 .... G6
Rheden 46,088 .... J4
Rhenen 16,613 .... H5
Ridderkerk 46,163 .... F5
Rijnsburg 13,412 .... F4
Rijssen 23,927 .... J4
Rijswijk 48,189 .... E4
Roden 18,331 .... J2
Roermond 38,486 .... J6
Roosendaal 59,237 .... F5
Rotterdam 576,232 .... E5
Ruurlo 7,418 .... J4
Sappemeer-Hoogezand
34,618 .... K2
Schagen 16,759 .... F3
Schiedam 69,438 .... E5
Schijndel 21,397 .... G5
Schoonebeek 7,740 .... K3
Schoonhoven 11,231 .... F5
's Gravendeel 8,424 .... E5
's Gravenhage (The Hague)
(cap.) 443,845 .... E4
's Gravenzande 18,453 .... E4
Simpelveld 11,882 .... J7
Sittard 44,894 .... H6
Sliedrecht 22,833 .... F5
Slochteren 13,958 .... K2
Sloten H3
Sluis 2,882 .... C6
Smilde 9,212 .... K3
Sneek 29,408 .... H2
Soest 41,598 .... G4
Stadskanaal 33,047 .... L3
Staphorst 13,580 .... J3
Staveren G3
Steenbergen 13,826 .... E5
Steenwijk 20,907 .... J3
Stiens H2
Tegelen 18,991 .... J6
Ter Apel L3
Termunten 4,378 .... K2
Terneuzen 35,043 .... D6
The Hague (cap.) 443,845 .... E4
Tholen 19,019 .... E5
Tiel 31,394 .... G5
Tilburg 155,110 .... G5
Twello J4
Uden 35,057 .... H5
Uithoorn 22,205 .... F4
Uithuizen K2
Ulrum 3,657 .... J2
Urk 12,728 .... H3
Utrecht 230,634 .... G4
Vaals 10,639 .... H7
Valkenswaard 29,811 .... H6
Veendam 28,234 .... K2
Veenendaal 47,258 .... G4
Veere 4,836 .... D5
Veghel 25,701 .... H5
Veldhoven 38,644 .... G6
Velsen 57,608 .... F4
Venlo 63,607 .... J6
Venraij 34,172 .... H6
Vianen 18,704 .... G5
Vlaardingen 74,480 .... E5
Vlagtwedde 16,181 .... L3
Vlijmen 15,655 .... G5
Vlissingen (Flushing) 44,022 .... C6
Volendam-Edam 24,572 .... G4
Voorburg 40,455 .... E4
Voorst 23,678 .... J4
Vorden 8,282 .... J4
Vriezenveen 18,601 .... K4
Vught 23,718 .... G5
Waalre 15,126 .... G6
Waalwijk 28,674 .... F5
Wageningen 32,370 .... H5
Warmenhuizen 4,765 .... F3
Weert 40,068 .... H6
Weesp 18,362 .... C5
Westkapelle 2,666 .... C5
Wierden 22,200 .... K4
Wijhe 7,155 .... J4
Wijk bij Duurstede 15,401 .... G5
Willemstad 3,357 .... F5
Winschoten 19,680 .... L2
Winsum 6,583 .... K2
Winterswijk 28,024 .... K5
Woensdrecht 10,077 .... E6
Woerden 34,166 .... F4
Wolvega J3
Workum G3
Zaandam (Zaanstad) 129,653 .... B4
Zaltbommel 9,534 .... G5
Zandvoort 15,428 .... E4
Zeewolde 5,930 .... G4
Zeist 59,431 .... G4
Zevenaar 26,848 .... J5
Zevenbergen 15,562 .... E5
Zierikzee 9,804 .... D5
Zundert 13,385 .... F6
Zutphen 31,144 .... J4
Zwartsluis 4,465 .... H3
Zwijndrecht 41,357 .... E5
Zwolle 92,517 .... J3

OTHER FEATURES

Alkmaardermeer (lake) F3
Ameland (isl.) H2
Beulaker Wijde (lake) H3
Borndiep (chan.) H2
De Fluessen (lake) G3
De Honte (bay) D6
De Peel (reg.) H6
De Twente (reg.) K4
De Zaan (riv.) B4
Dollard (bay) L2
Dommel (riv.) H6
Duiveland (isl.) D5
Eems (riv.) K2
Eijerlandsche Gat (strait) F2
Flevoland Polders G4
Frisian, West (isls.) G2
Goeree (isl.) D5
Grevelingen (strait) E5
Griend (isl.) G2
Groninger Wad (sound) J2
Groote IJ Polder B4
Haarlemmermeer Polder B5
Haringvliet (strait) E5
Het IJ (est.) C4
Hoek van Holland (cape) D5
Houtrak Polder A4
Hunse (riv.) K3
IJmeer (bay) C4
IJssel (riv.) J4
IJsselmeer (lake) G3
Lauwers (chan.) J1
Lauwers Zee (bay) J2
Lek (riv.) F5
Lower Rhine (riv.) H5
Maas (riv.) G5
Marken (isl.) G4
Markerwaard Polder G3
Marsdiep (chan.) F3
North (sea) E3
North Beveland (isl.) D5
North East Polder H3
North Holland (canal) C4
North Sea (canal) F4
Old Rhine (riv.) E4
Oostzaan Polder B4
Orange (canal) K3
Overflakkee (isl.) E5
Rhine (riv.) J5
Roer (riv.) J6
Scheldt, Eastern (est.) D5
Scheldt, Western
(De Honte) (bay) D6
Schiermonnikoog (isl.) J1
Schouwen (isl.) D5
Slotermeer (lake) H3
Sneekermeer (lake) H2
South Beveland (isl.) D6
Terschelling (isl.) G2
Texel (isl.) F2
Tjeukemeer (lake) H3
Vaalserberg (mt.) J7
Vecht (riv.) F4
Vechte (riv.) J3
Veersche Meer (lake) D5
Veluwe (reg.) H4
Vlieland (isl.) F2
Vliestroom (strait) G2
Voorne (isl.) D5
Waal (riv.) G5
Waddenzee (sound) G2
Walcheren (isl.) C5
West Frisian (isls.) F2
Wester Eems (chan.) K1
Western Scheldt
(De Honte) (bay) D6
Wieringermeer Polder G3
Wilhelmina (canal) G6
Willems (canal) G5

* City and suburbs.
† Population of urban area.

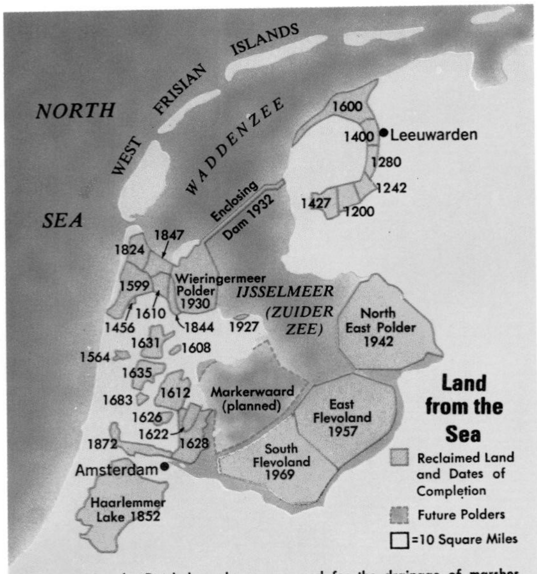

NORTH
SEA
WEST FRISIAN ISLANDS
WADDENZEE
Enclosing Dam 1932
Leeuwarden
1600
1400
1280
1242
1427
1200
1847
1824
1599
1610
1456
1844
1927
1631
1608
1564
1635
1612
1683
1626
1622
1628
1872
Wieringermeer Polder 1930
IJSSELMEER (ZUIDER ZEE)
North East Polder 1942
Markerwaard (planned)
East Flevoland 1957
South Flevoland 1969
Amsterdam
Haarlemmer Lake 1852
Land from the Sea
Reclaimed Land and Dates of Completion
Future Polders
=10 Square Miles

For centuries the Dutch have been renowned for the drainage of marshes and the construction of polders, i.e., arable land reclaimed from the sea. Future projects will convert much of the present IJsselmeer to agricultural land.

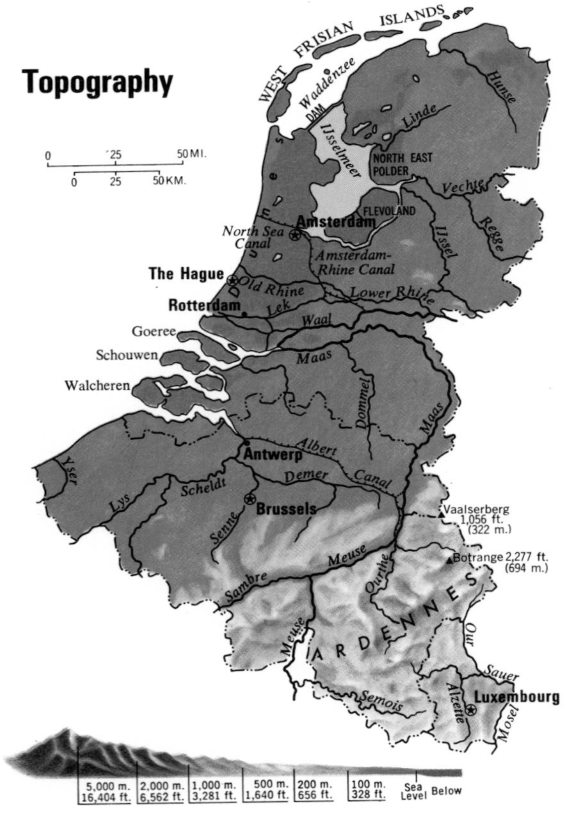

Topography
0 25 50 MI.
0 25 50 KM.
WEST FRISIAN ISLANDS
Waddenzee
DAM
IJsselmeer
NORTH EAST POLDER
FLEVOLAND
Linde
Hunse
Vechte
Regge
IJssel
North Sea Canal
Amsterdam
Amsterdam-Rhine Canal
The Hague
Old Rhine
Rotterdam
Lek
Lower Rhine
Waal
Goeree
Schouwen
Walcheren
Maas
Dommel
Antwerp
Albert
Canal
Scheldt
Demer
Lys
Yser
Brussels
Senne
Vaalserberg 1,056 ft. (322 m.)
Botrange 2,277 ft. (694 m.)
Meuse
Sambre
Ourthe
ARDENNES
Our
Sauer
Semois
Alzette
Luxembourg
Mosel
5,000 m. 16,404 ft.
2,000 m. 6,562 ft.
1,000 m. 3,281 ft.
500 m. 1,640 ft.
200 m. 656 ft.
100 m. 328 ft.
Sea Level
Below

Netherlands, Belgium and Luxembourg

CONIC PROJECTION

SCALE OF MILES

0 5 10   20   30   40

SCALE OF KILOMETRES

0 5 10   20   30   40   50

Capitals of Countries .... ☆
Provincial Capitals .... △
International Boundaries .... — ·· —
Provincial Boundaries .... — · —
Canals ....

© Copyright HAMMOND INCORPORATED, Maplewood, N.J.

AMSTERDAM

BRUSSELS

© Copyright HAMMOND INCORPORATED, Maplewood, N.J.

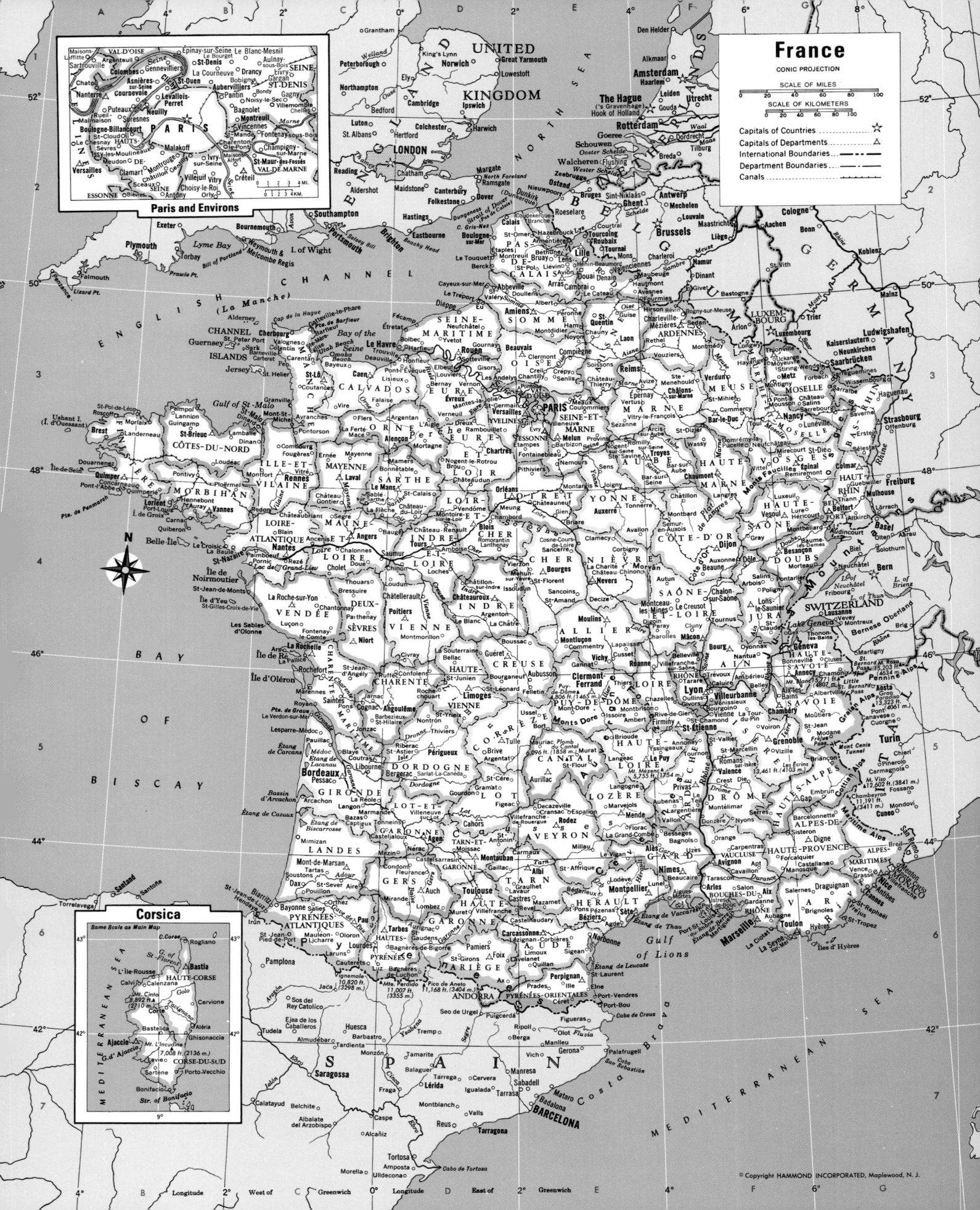

France

Paris and Environs

Corsica
Same Scale as Main Map

France
CONIC PROJECTION
SCALE OF MILES
SCALE OF KILOMETERS

Capitals of Countries .... ☆
Capitals of Departments .... △
International Boundaries .... ·—·—·
Department Boundaries .... ·····
Canals .... ———

© Copyright HAMMOND INCORPORATED, Maplewood, N.J.

DEPARTMENTS

Ain 418,516 F 4
Aisne 533,970 E 3
Allier 369,580 E 4
Alpes-de-Haute-Provence 119,068 G 5
Alpes-Maritimes 881,198 G 6
Ardèche 267,970 F 5
Ardennes 302,338 F 3
Ariège 135,725 D 6
Aube 289,300 E 3
Aude 280,686 E 6
Aveyron 278,654 E 5
Bas-Rhin 915,676 G 3
Belfort 131,999 G 4
Bouches-du-Rhône 1,724,199 F 6
Calvados 589,559 C 3
Cantal 162,838 E 5
Charente 340,770 D 5
Charente-Maritime 513,220 C 5
Cher 320,174 E 4
Corrèze 241,448 D 5
Corse du Sud 108,604 B 6
Côte-d'Or 473,548 F 4
Côtes-du-Nord 538,869 B 3
Creuse 139,968 D 4
Deux-Sèvres 342,812 C 4
Dordogne 377,356 D 5
Doubs 477,163 G 4
Drôme 389,781 F 5
Essonne 988,000 E 3
Eure 462,323 D 3
Eure-et-Loir 362,813 D 3
Finistère 828,364 A 3
Gard 530,478 F 6
Gers 174,154 D 6
Gironde 1,127,546 C 5
Haute-Corse 131,574 B 6
Haute-Garonne 824,501 D 6
Haute-Loire 205,895 E 5
Haute-Marne 210,670 F 3
Hautes-Alpes 105,070 G 5
Haute-Saône 231,962 G 4
Haute-Savoie 494,505 G 5
Hautes-Pyrénées 227,922 D 6
Haute-Vienne 355,737 D 5
Haut-Rhin 650,372 G 4
Hauts-de-Seine 1,387,039 A 2
Hérault 706,499 E 6
Ille-et-Vilaine 749,764 C 3
Indre 243,191 D 4
Indre-et-Loire 506,097 D 4
Isère 936,771 F 5
Jura 242,925 F 4
Landes 297,424 C 5
Loire 739,521 F 5
Loire-Atlantique 995,498 C 4
Loiret 535,669 E 4
Loir-et-Cher 296,220 D 4
Lot 154,533 D 5
Lot-et-Garonne 298,522 D 5
Lozère 74,294 E 5
Maine-et-Loire 675,321 C 4
Manche 465,948 C 3
Marne 543,627 F 3
Mayenne 271,784 C 3
Meurthe-et-Moselle 716,846 G 3
Meuse 200,101 F 3
Morbihan 590,889 B 4
Moselle 1,007,189 G 3
Nièvre 239,635 E 4
Nord 2,520,526 E 2
Oise 661,781 E 3
Orne 295,472 C 3
Paris 2,188,918 B 2
Pas-de-Calais 1,412,413 E 2
Puy-de-Dôme 594,365 E 5
Pyrénées-Atlantiques 555,696 C 6
Pyrénées-Orientales 334,557 E 6
Rhône 1,445,208 F 5
Saône-et-Loire 571,852 F 4
Sarthe 504,768 D 3
Savoie 323,675 G 5
Seine-et-Marne 887,112 E 3
Seine-Maritime 1,324,301 D 3
Seine-Saint-Denis 1,324,301 C 1
Somme 544,570 E 3
Tarn 339,345 E 6
Tarn-et-Garonne 190,485 D 5
Val-de-Marne 1,193,655 C 1
Val-d'Oise 920,598 E 3
Var 708,331 G 6
Vaucluse 427,343 F 6
Vendée 483,027 C 4
Vienne 371,428 D 4
Vosges 395,769 G 3
Yonne 311,019 E 4
Yvelines 1,196,111 D 3

CITIES and TOWNS

Aigues-Mortes 4,106 F 6
Aix-en-Provence 100,221 F 6
Aix-les-Bains 22,331 G 5
Ajaccio 48,324 B 7
Alençon 30,952 D 3
Amboise 10,823 D 4
Amiens 130,302 E 3
Angers 135,293 C 4
Angoulême 45,495 D 5
Annecy 49,753 G 5
Antibes 62,427 G 6
Argenteuil 94,826 A 1
Arles 37,554 F 6
Armentières 22,849 E 2
Arras 41,376 E 2
Asnières-sur-Seine 71,058 A 1
Aubervilliers 67,684 B 1
Aubusson 5,326 E 4
Aulnay-sous-Bois 75,543 B 1
Aurignac 772 D 6
Avignon 75,178 F 6
Ax-les-Thermes 1,283 D 6
Bagnolet 32,556 B 2
Barbizon 478 E 3
Barcelonnette 2,674 G 5
Barfleur 617 C 3
Bastia 43,502 B 6
Bayeux 14,568 C 3
Bayonne 40,088 C 6
Beaucaire 10,622 F 6
Beaune 19,110 F 4
Beauvais 51,542 E 3
Belfort 51,034 G 4
Bergerac 24,604 D 5
Besançon 112,023 G 4
Bessèges 4,352 F 5
Béziers 74,114 E 6
Biarritz 26,579 C 6
Blois 46,925 D 4
Bobigny 42,630 B 1
Bonifacio 1,727 B 7
Bordeaux 201,965 C 5
Boulogne-Billancourt 102,582 A 2
Boulogne-sur-Mer 47,482 D 2
Bourg-en-Bresse 37,582 F 4
Bourges 74,622 E 4
Brest 154,110 A 3
Brignoles 8,529 G 6
Brive-la-Gaillarde 50,898 D 5
Bruay-en-Artois 22,502 E 2
Caen 112,332 C 3
Calais 76,206 D 2
Caluire-et-Cuire 41,864 F 5
Cambrai 35,070 E 2
Cannes 71,888 G 6
Carcassonne 38,379 E 6
Castres 39,216 E 6
Châlons-sur-Marne 49,941 F 3

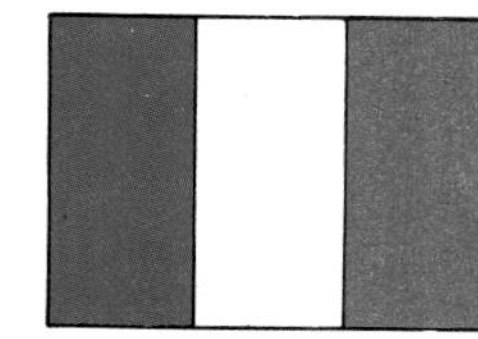

AREA 210,038 sq. mi. (543,998 sq. km.)
POPULATION 56,160,000
CAPITAL Paris
LARGEST CITY Paris
HIGHEST POINT Mont Blanc 15,771 ft. (4,807 m.)
MONETARY UNIT franc
MAJOR LANGUAGE French
MAJOR RELIGION Roman Catholicism

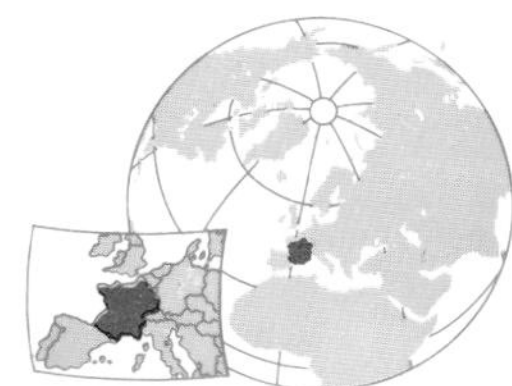

Topography

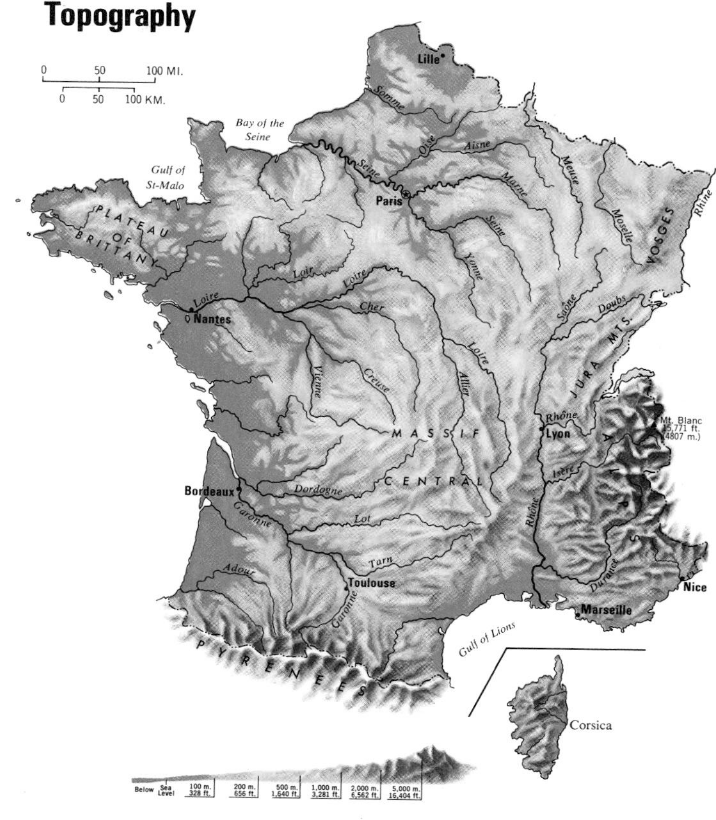

Historic Provinces

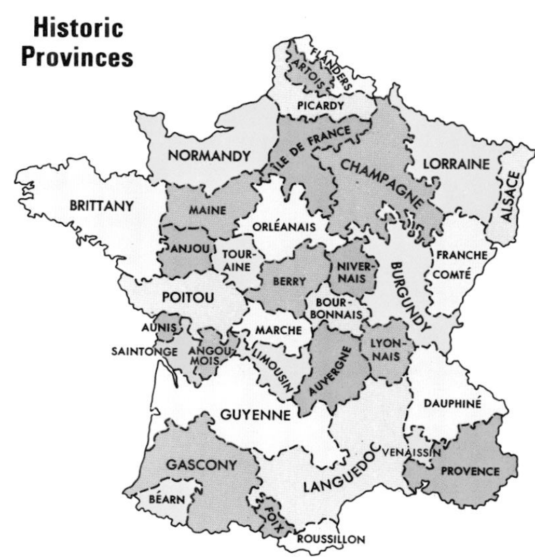

A resident of the city of Caen thinks of himself as a Norman rather than as a citizen of the modern department of Calvados. In spite of the passing of nearly two centuries, the historic provinces which existed before 1790 command the local patriotism of most Frenchmen.

Chalon-sur-Saône 53,893 F 4
Chambéry 49,465 F 5
Chambord 159 D 4
Chamonix-Mont-Blanc 7,406 G 5
Champigny-sur-Marne 76,039 C 2
Chantilly 10,065 E 3
Charleville-Mézières 7,814 F 3
Chartres 36,706 D 3
Châteaudun 15,905 D 3
Châteauneuf-sur-Loire 5,630 E 4
Châteauroux 51,744 D 4
Château-Thierry 14,427 E 3
Chatou 28,435 A 1
Cherbourg 28,324 C 3
Chinon 6,030 D 4
Choisy-le-Roi 35,443 B 2
Cholet 51,620 C 4
Clamart 48,210 A 2
Clermont-Ferrand 145,901 E 5
Clichy 46,830 B 1
Cluny 4,133 F 4
Cognac 20,247 C 5
Colmar 61,560 G 3
Colombes 78,485 A 1
Compiègne 39,909 E 3
Courbevoie 59,821 A 1
Creil 34,332 E 3
Créteil 71,559 B 2
Deauville 4,682 C 3
Dieppe 35,659 D 3
Digne 12,540 G 5
Dijon 139,188 F 4
Dinard 9,562 B 3
Domrémy-la-Pucelle 162 F 3
Douai 41,576 E 2
Drancy 60,122 B 1
Dunkirk 71,756 E 2
Ernée 5,253 C 3
Évreux 45,215 D 3
Falaise 8,424 C 3
Fécamp 21,212 D 3
Foix 9,212 D 6
Fontainebleau 14,687 E 3
Fontenay-sous-Bois 52,397 C 2
Gex 4,776 G 4
Grasse 24,257 G 6
Grenoble 156,437 F 5
Guise 6,179 E 3
Harfleur 9,470 D 3
Hazebrouck 19,266 E 2
Hendaye 10,492 C 6
Héricourt 9,239 G 4
Honfleur 8,125 D 3
Issy-les-Moulineaux 45,702 A 2
Istres 21,286 F 6
Ivry-sur-Seine 55,682 B 2
La Baule-Escoublac 13,151 B 4
La Courneuve 33,525 B 1
Langres 9,718 F 4
Lapalisse 3,173 E 4
La Rochelle 74,728 C 4
La Roche-sur-Yon 42,026 C 4
Laval 53,582 C 3
Le Bourget 11,020 B 1
Le Creusot 32,013 F 4
Le Havre 198,700 C 3
Le Mans 145,976 C 3
Le Puy 22,806 F 5
Le Tréport 6,330 D 2
Levallois-Perret 53,485 B 1
Lille 167,791 E 2
Limoges 137,809 D 5
Lisieux 24,454 D 3
Lorient 62,207 B 4
Lourdes 17,252 C 6
Lunéville 21,200 G 3
Lyon 410,455 F 5
Mâcon 36,517 F 4
Maisons-Alfort 51,041 B 2
Maisons-Laffitte 22,565 A 1
Mantes-la-Jolie 43,551 D 3
Marmande 14,264 C 5
Marseille 868,435 F 6
Maubeuge 35,424 F 2
Mayenne 12,156 C 3
Meaux 44,386 E 3
Melun 34,379 E 3
Mende 10,520 E 5
Menton 22,234 G 6
Metz 113,236 G 3
Meudon 29,356 A 2
Montauban 36,122 D 5
Montbéliard 31,174 G 4
Montceau-les-Mines 26,877 F 4
Mont-de-Marsan 25,896 C 6
Mont-Dore 2,091 E 5
Montfort 4,029 C 3
Montluçon 49,737 E 4
Montmédy 1,880 F 3
Montpellier 190,423 E 6
Montreuil 96,441 B 2
Mont-Saint-Michel 65 C 3
Mulhouse 111,742 G 4
Nancy 95,654 G 3
Nanterre 88,567 A 1
Nantes 237,789 C 4
Narbonne 38,222 E 6
Nemours 11,624 E 3
Neufchâtel-en-Bray 5,452 D 3
Neuilly-sur-Seine 64,093 A 1
Nice 331,165 G 6
Nîmes 120,515 F 6
Niort 56,256 C 4
Nogent-le-Rotrou 11,963 D 3
Noisy-le-Sec 36,821 B 1
Nontron 3,407 D 5
Noyon 13,949 E 3
Nyons 5,219 F 5
Orléans 81,615 D 3
Orly 23,729 B 2
Oyonnax 22,516 F 4
Paris (cap.) 2,165,892 B 2
Paris *10,073,059 B 2
Pau 82,186 C 6
Périgueux 32,632 D 5
Perpignan 107,812 E 6
Pessac 49,019 C 5
Poitiers 76,793 D 4
Pontoise 27,885 E 3
Port-Vendres 4,871 E 6
Privas 9,253 F 5
Quimper 52,335 A 4
Rambouillet 21,136 D 3
Redon 9,071 C 4
Reims 176,419 E 3
Rennes 190,861 C 3
Roanne 48,574 E 4
Rochefort 25,392 C 4
Roubaix 101,488 E 2
Rouen 100,696 D 3
Rueil-Malmaison 63,310 A 2
Saint-Brieuc 48,259 B 3
Saint-Cloud 28,561 A 2
Saint-Denis 90,686 B 1
Saint-Dizier 34,074 F 3
Sainte-Mère-Église 1,205 C 3
Saint-Étienne 193,938 F 5
Saint-Germain-en-Laye 36,585 D 3
Saint-Jean-d'Angély 8,268 C 4

(continued on following page)

Wine Regions

CHAMPAGNE
ALSACE
CALVADOS
(distilled from cider)
Caen
Reims
Colmar
Chablis
BURGUNDY
Côte-d'Or
LOIRE VALLEY
POUILLY
SANCERRE
Angers
Tours
Anjou
Touraine
QUINCY
REUILLY
Beaune
JURA
COGNAC
Mâconnais
Mâcon
Beau-
jolais
Cognac
Médoc
BORDEAUX
Bordeaux
Bergerac
CÔTES DE DURAS
Graves
Sauternes
GAILLAC
LANGUEDOC
CÔTES
DU
RHÔNE
Valence
Avignon
ARMAGNAC
Auch
PROVENCE
JURANÇON
Pau
LIMOUX
ROUSSILLON
Béziers
Toulon

Climate, soil and variety of grape planted determine the quality of wine. Long, hot and fairly dry summers with cool, humid nights constitute an ideal climate. The nature of the soil is such a determining influence that identical grapes planted in Bordeaux, Burgundy and Champagne, will yield wines of widely different types.

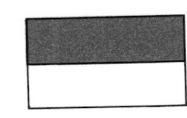

MONACO

368 acres
(149 hectares)
27,063

Agriculture, Industry and Resources

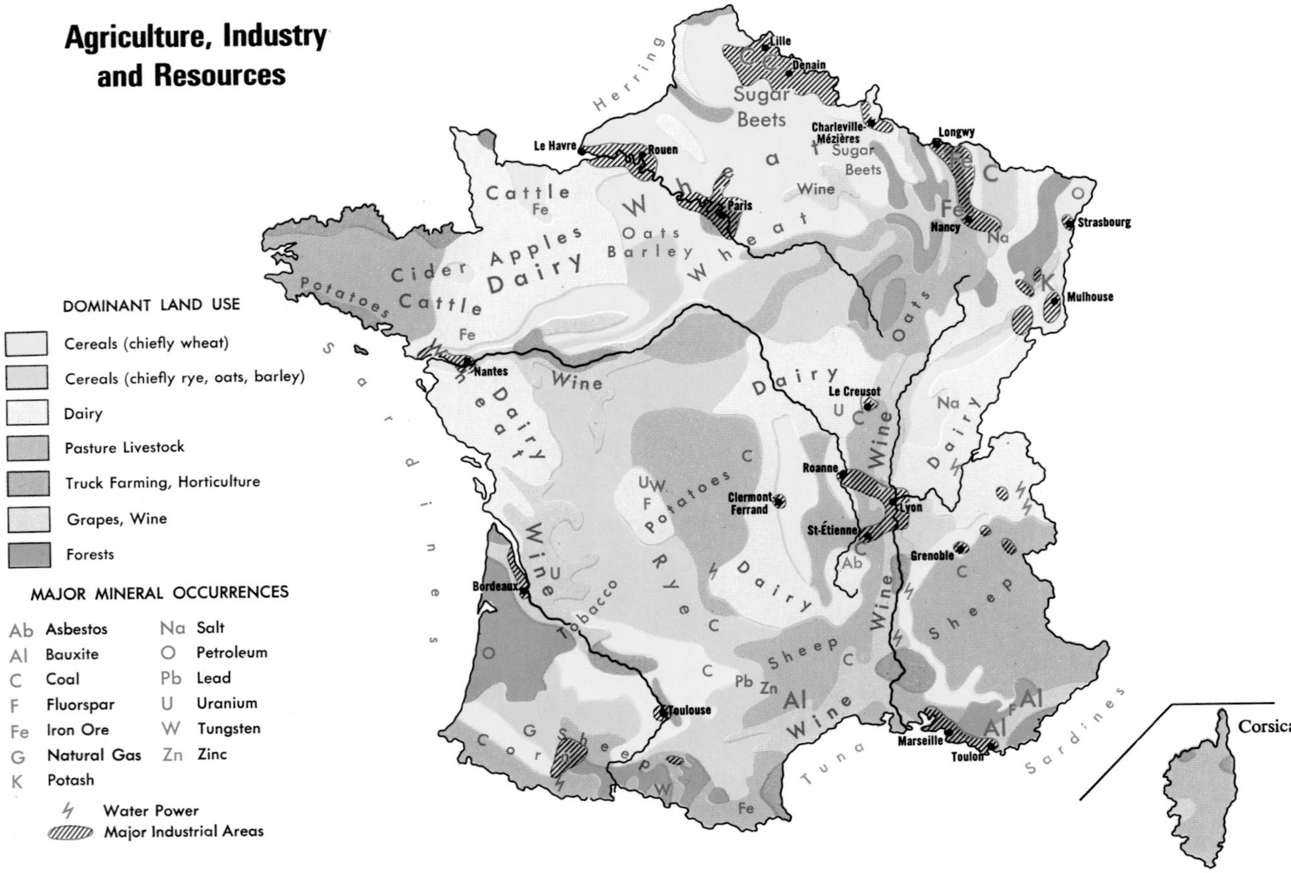

DOMINANT LAND USE

- Cereals (chiefly wheat)
- Cereals (chiefly rye, oats, barley)
- Dairy
- Pasture Livestock
- Truck Farming, Horticulture
- Grapes, Wine
- Forests

MAJOR MINERAL OCCURRENCES

Ab	Asbestos	Na	Salt
Al	Bauxite	O	Petroleum
C	Coal	Pb	Lead
F	Fluorspar	U	Uranium
Fe	Iron Ore	W	Tungsten
G	Natural Gas	Zn	Zinc
K	Potash		

⚡ Water Power
▨ Major Industrial Areas

Lille
Denain
Sugar Beets
Charleville-Mézières
Longwy
Le Havre
Rouen
Sugar Beets
Wine
Paris
Nancy
Strasbourg
Herring
Cattle
Fe
Cider Apples
Dairy
Cattle
Oats
Barley
Wheat
Potatoes
Fe
Wine
Na
Mulhouse
Nantes
Wine
Dairy
Dairy
Le Creusot
Oats
Dairy
Potatoes
Clermont Ferrand
Roanne
Lyon
Na
St-Étienne
Grenoble
Ab
Bordeaux
Wine
Rye
Dairy
Sheep
Tobacco
Sheep
Wine
Pb
Zn
Al
Wine
Toulouse
Marseille
Toulon
Al
Fe
Tuna
Sardines
Corsica

ANDORRA

SPAIN

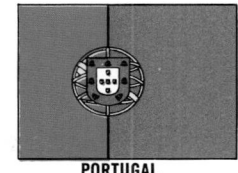
PORTUGAL

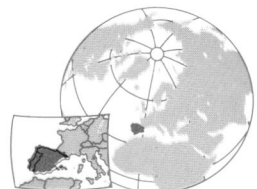

SPAIN

REGIONS

Andalusia 6,440,985	D4
Aragón 1,196,952	F2
Asturias 1,129,556	C1
Balearic Islands 655,909	H3
Basque Country 2,141,809	E1
Canary Islands 1,367,646	F4
Cantabria 513,115	D1
Castile and León 2,583,137	D2
Castile-La Mancha 1,648,584	E3
Catalonia 5,956,414	G2
Estremadura 1,064,968	C3
Galicia 2,811,912	B1
La Rioja 254,349	E1
Madrid 4,686,895	E2
Murcia 955,487	F4
Navarre 509,002	F1
Valencia 3,646,778	F3

PROVINCES

Álava 257,850	E1
Albacete 339,373	E3
Alicante 1,149,181	F3
Almería 410,831	E4
Ávila 183,586	D2
Badajoz 643,519	C3
Baleares 655,509	H3
Barcelona 4,623,204	G2
Burgos 363,523	E1
Cáceres 421,449	C3
Cádiz 988,388	D4
Castellón 431,893	G2
Ciudad Real 475,129	D3
Córdoba 720,823	D3
Cuenca 215,975	E2
Girona (Gerona) 467,000	H1
Granada 758,618	E4
Guadalajara 143,473	E2
Guipúzcoa 694,681	E1
Huelva 418,584	C4
Huesca 214,907	F1
Jaén 639,821	E4
La Coruña 1,093,121	B1
Las Palmas 708,762	C4
León 523,607	C1
Lleida (Lérida) 353,160	G2
Logroño 254,349	E1
Lugo 405,365	C1
Madrid 4,686,895	E2
Málaga 1,025,609	D4
Murcia 955,487	F4
Navarra 509,002	F1
Orense 430,159	C1
Oviedo 1,129,556	C1
Palencia 188,479	D1
Pontevedra 883,267	B1
Salamanca 364,305	C2
Santa Cruz de Tenerife 658,847	B5
Santander 513,115	D1
Segovia 149,361	D2
Sevilla 1,478,311	D4
Soria 100,719	E2
Tarragona 513,050	G2
Teruel 153,457	F2
Toledo 474,634	D3
Valencia 2,065,704	F3
Valladolid 481,786	D2
Vizcaya 1,189,278	E1
Zamora 227,771	D2
Zaragoza 828,588	F2

CITIES and TOWNS

Adra 10,851	E4
Aguilar 12,893	D4
Aguilas 15,525	F4
Albacete 82,607	F3
Alburquerque 7,530	C3
Alcalá de Guadaira 28,781	D4
Alcalá de Henares 59,783	E2
Alcalá de los Gazules 5,262	D4
Alcalá la Real 9,849	E4
Alcanar 5,961	G2
Alcañiz 10,229	F2
Alcantarilla 19,895	F4
Alcaudete 8,557	E4
Alcázar de San Juan 24,620	E3
Alcira 30,493	F3
Alcora 6,711	F2
Alcoy 61,371	F3
Alfaro 8,766	F1
Algeciras 74,754	D4
Algemesí 21,158	F3
Alhama de Granada 6,148	E4
Alhama de Murcia 9,274	F4
Alicante 177,918	F3
Almadén 10,713	D3
Almagro 9,066	E3
Almansa 16,965	F3
Almendralejo 21,929	C3
Almería 104,008	E4
Almodóvar del Campo 7,310	D3
Almonte del Río 9,960	C4
Almuñécar 7,812	E4
Alora 8,209	D4
Altea 7,262	G3
Amposta 11,767	G2
Andorra 6,485	F2
Andújar 25,962	D3
Antequera 28,039	D4
Aracena 5,390	C4
Aranda de Duero 18,183	E2
Aranjuez 28,559	E2
Archena 7,118	F3
Archidona 6,084	D4
Arcos de la Frontera 16,217	D4
Arenys de Mar 8,325	H2
Arganda 11,876	G4
Arnedo 9,809	E1
Arrecife 21,310	G4
Arroyo de la Luz 8,130	C3
Arucas 9,095	G4
Aspe 13,229	F3

Astorga 11,794	C1
Ávila de los Caballeros 30,958	D2
Avilés 67,186	C1
Ayamonte 9,897	C4
Azpeitia 7,835	E1
Azuaga 10,719	D3
Badajoz 80,793	C3
Badalona 162,888	H2
Baena 16,496	D4
Baeza 12,607	E4
Bailén 13,207	E3
Balaguer 11,676	G2
Banyoles 9,807	H1
Baracaldo 108,757	E1
Barbastro 13,243	F1
Barcarrota 5,012	C3
Barcelona 1,741,144	J1
Barcelona‡ 2,000,000	H2
Baza 14,290	E4
Béjar 16,804	D2
Benavente 11,779	D2
Benicarló 12,831	G2
Berga 11,163	G1
Berja 7,081	E4
Bermeo 16,714	E1
Betanzos 7,283	B1
Bilbao 393,179	E1
Bilbao‡ 450,000	E1
Binéfar 6,821	G2

Blanes 15,810	H2
Bujalance 8,236	D4
Bullas 8,131	F3
Burgos 118,366	E1
Burriana 21,298	F3
Cabeza del Buey 8,704	D3
Cabra 16,177	D4
Cáceres 53,108	C3
Cádiz 135,743	C4
Calahorra 16,315	E1
Calasparra 7,238	F3
Calatayud 16,524	F2
Calella 9,696	H2
Callosa de Ensarriá 5,701	G3
Calzada de Calatrava 5,751	C3
Campanario 7,722	D3
Campillos 7,014	D4
Campo de Criptana 12,604	E3
Candás 5,517	D1
Candeleda 5,153	D2
Cangas de Narcea 4,826	C1
Caniles 5,099	E4
Caravaca de le Cruz 10,411	F3
Carballo 5,542	B1
Carcagente 18,223	F3
Carmona 22,832	D4
Cartagena 52,312	F4
Caspe 8,766	F2
Castellón de la Plana 79,773	G2
Castro del Río 10,087	D4

Castro-Urdiales 8,369	E1
Castuera 8,060	D3
Caudete 7,332	F3
Cazalla de la Sierra 5,382	D4
Cazorla 6,938	E4
Cehegín 9,661	F3
Cervera 5,693	G2
Ceuta 65,264	D5
Chiclana de la Frontera 22,986	C4
Cieza 22,929	F3
Ciudad Real 39,931	D3
Ciudad-Rodrigo 11,694	C2
Cocentaina 8,375	F3
Coín 14,190	D4
Colmenar Viejo 12,886	E2
Constantina 10,227	D4
Consuegra 10,026	E3
Córdoba 216,049	D4
Corella 8,083	F1
Coria 8,083	C3
Coria del Río 18,085	C4
Corral de Almaguer 8,006	E3
Crevillente 15,749	F3
Cuéllar 6,118	D2
Cuenca 33,980	E2
Cullera 15,128	F3
Daimiel 17,710	E3
Denia 14,514	G3
Don Benito 21,351	C3

Dos Hermanas 36,921	D4
Durango 20,403	E1
Écija 27,295	D4
Eibar 36,729	E1
Ejea de los Caballeros 9,766	F1
El Arahal 14,703	D4
Elche 101,271	F3
Elda 41,404	F3
El Ferrol 75,464	B1
Elizondo 2,516	F1
El Puerto de Santa María 36,451	C4
El Vendrell 7,951	G2
Espejo 5,925	D4
Estella 10,371	E1
Estepa 9,376	D4
Estepona 18,560	D4
Felanitx 9,100	H3
Figueres 22,087	H1
Fraga 9,665	G2
Fregenal de la Sierra 6,826	C3
Fuengirola 20,597	D4
Fuente de Cantos 5,967	C3
Gandía 30,702	F3
Gerona (Girona) 37,095	H1
Getafe 68,680	G4
Gijón 159,806	D1
Girona 37,095	H2
Granada 185,799	E4
Granollers 30,066	H2

Guadalajara 30,924	E2
Guadix 15,311	E4
Guareña 7,706	C3
Guernica y Luno 12,046	E1
Haro 8,393	E1
Hellin 15,934	F3
Herencia 8,212	E3
Hinojosa del Duque 9,873	D3
Hospitalet 241,978	H1
Huelma 5,260	E4
Huelva 96,689	C4
Huercal-Overa 5,158	F4
Huesca 33,076	F1
Huéscar 6,384	E4
Ibiza 16,943	G3
Igualada 27,941	G2
Inca 16,930	H3
Irún 38,014	F1
Iscar 5,192	D2
Isla Cristina 11,402	C4
Jaca 9,375	F1
Jaén 71,145	E4
Jaraíz de la Vera 6,379	C2
Játiva 20,934	F3
Jávea 6,228	G3
Jerez de la Frontera 112,411	C4
Jerez de los Caballeros 8,607	C3
Jijona 8,117	F3
Jódar 11,973	E4
Jumilla 16,407	F3
La Bañeza 8,480	D1
La Bisbal 6,374	H2
La Carolina 13,138	E3
La Coruña 184,372	B1
La Línea de la Concepción 51,021	D4
La Orotava 8,246	F5
La Palma del Condado 9,256	C4
La Puebla 9,923	H3
La Puebla de Montalbán 6,629	D3
La Rambla 6,525	D4
La Unión 9,998	F4
Laredo 9,114	E1
La Roda 11,544	E3
La Seu d'Urgell 6,604	G1
La Solana 13,894	E3
Las Palmas de Gran Canaria 260,368	G5
Las Pedroñeras 5,846	E3
Lebrija 15,081	C4
Leganés 57,537	G4
León 99,702	D1
Lérida (Lleida) 73,148	G2
Linares 45,330	E3
Liria 11,323	F3
Lleida 73,148	G2
Llerena 5,728	C3

Llodio 15,587	E1
Lluchmayor 9,630	H3
Logroño 83,117	E1
Loja 11,549	D4
Lora del Río 15,741	D4
Lorca 25,208	F4
Los Santos de Maimona 7,899	C3
Los Yébenes 5,477	D3
Lucena 21,527	D4
Lugo 53,504	C1
Madrid (cap.) 3,146,071	G4
Madrid‡ 3,500,000	F4
Madridejos 9,948	E3
Madroñera 5,397	C3
Mahón 17,802	J3
Málaga 334,988	D4
Malpartida de Cáceres 5,054	C3
Manacor 20,266	H3
Mancha Real 7,547	E4
Manlleu 13,169	H1
Manresa 52,526	G2
Manzanares 15,024	E3
Marbella 19,648	D4
Marchena 16,227	D4
Marin 10,948	B1
Martos 16,395	E4
Mataró 73,129	H2
Medina del Campo 16,345	D2
Medina-Sidonia 7,523	D4
Mérida 36,916	C3
Miajadas 8,042	C3
Mieres 22,790	D1
Miranda de Ebro 29,355	E1
Moguer 7,629	C4
Mollerusa 6,685	G2
Monesterio 5,923	C3
Monforte 14,002	C1
Monóvar 9,071	F3
Montehermoso 5,952	C2
Montijo 11,931	C3
Montilla 18,670	D4
Montoro 9,295	D3
Monzón 14,089	G2
Mora 10,523	E3
Moratalla 5,101	E3
Morón de la Frontera 25,662	C4
Mota del Cuervo 5,130	E3
Motril 25,121	E4
Mula 9,168	F3
Munera 5,003	E3
Murcia 102,242	F4
Navalmoral de la Mata 9,650	D3
Nerja 7,413	E4
Nerva 10,830	C4
Novelda 16,867	F3
Nules 9,027	F3
Ocaña 5,603	E3

(continued on following page)

SPAIN

AREA 194,881 sq. mi. (504,742 sq. km.)
POPULATION 39,328,000
CAPITAL Madrid
LARGEST CITY Madrid
HIGHEST POINT Pico de Teide 12,172 ft. (3,710 m.) (Canary Is.); Mulhacén 11,411 ft. (3,478 m.) (mainland)
MONETARY UNIT peseta
MAJOR LANGUAGES Spanish, Catalan, Basque, Galician, Valencian
MAJOR RELIGION Roman Catholicism

ANDORRA

AREA 188 sq. mi. (487 sq. km.)
POPULATION 50,000
CAPITAL Andorra la Vella
MONETARY UNITS French franc, Spanish peseta
MAJOR LANGUAGE Catalan
MAJOR RELIGION Roman Catholicism

PORTUGAL

AREA 35,549 sq. mi. (92,072 sq. km.)
POPULATION 10,467,000
CAPITAL Lisbon
LARGEST CITY Lisbon
HIGHEST POINT Malhão da Estrela 6,532 ft. (1,991 m.)
MONETARY UNIT escudo
MAJOR LANGUAGE Portuguese
MAJOR RELIGION Roman Catholicism

GIBRALTAR

AREA 2.28 sq. mi. (5.91 sq. km.)
POPULATION 31,000
CAPITAL Gibraltar
MONETARY UNIT pound sterling
MAJOR LANGUAGES English, Spanish
MAJOR RELIGION Roman Catholicism

Agriculture, Industry and Resources

DOMINANT LAND USE

- Cereals (chiefly wheat)
- Livestock (chiefly sheep, goats)
- Mixed Cereals, Livestock
- Olives, Fruit
- Grapes, Fruit, Nuts, Mixed Cereals
- Forests
- Nonagricultural Land

MAJOR MINERAL OCCURRENCES

Ag	Silver	Na	Salt
C	Coal	O	Petroleum
Cu	Copper	Pb	Lead
Fe	Iron Ore	Py	Pyrites
G	Natural Gas	Sb	Antimony
Hg	Mercury	Sn	Tin
K	Potash	U	Uranium
Lg	Lignite	W	Tungsten
Mg	Magnesium	Zn	Zinc

Water Power

Major Industrial Areas

(continued on following page)

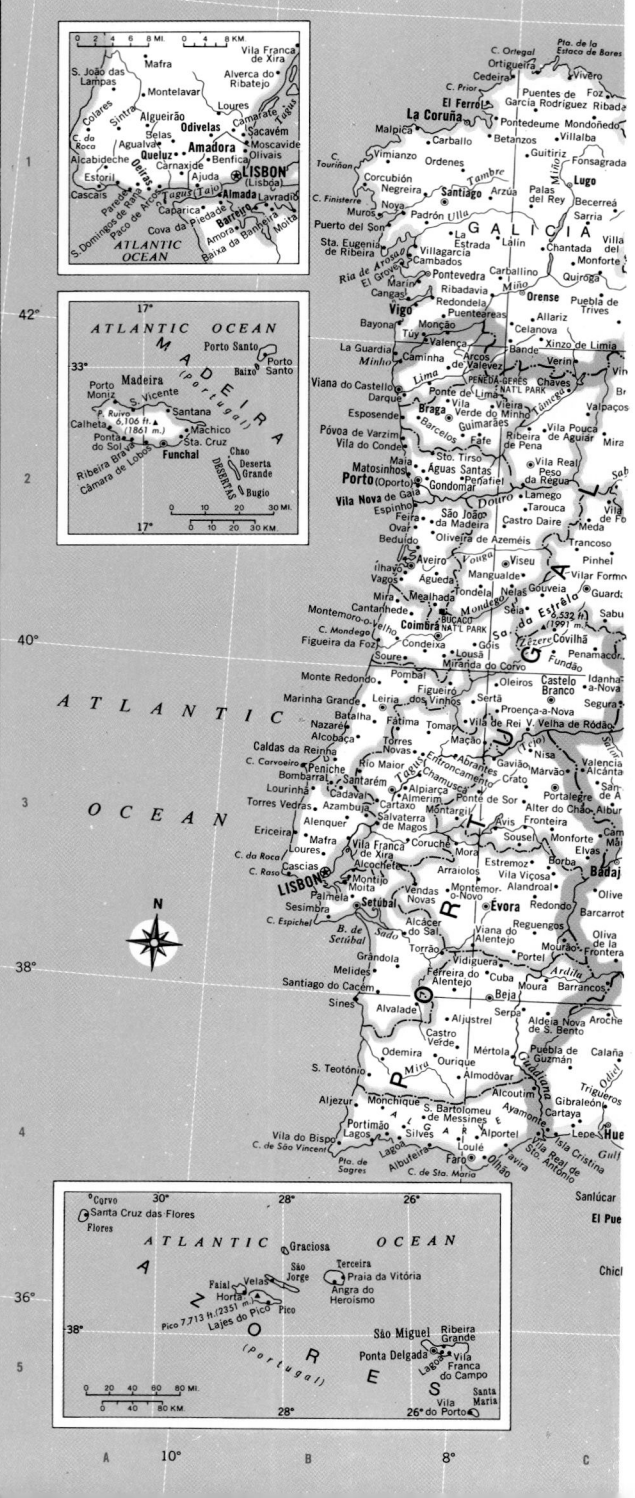

Topography

0   50   100 MI.

0   50   100 KM.

Below Sea Level	100 m. 328 ft.	200 m. 656 ft.	500 m. 1,640 ft.	1,000 m. 3,281 ft.	2,000 m. 6,562 ft.	5,000 m. 16,404 ft.

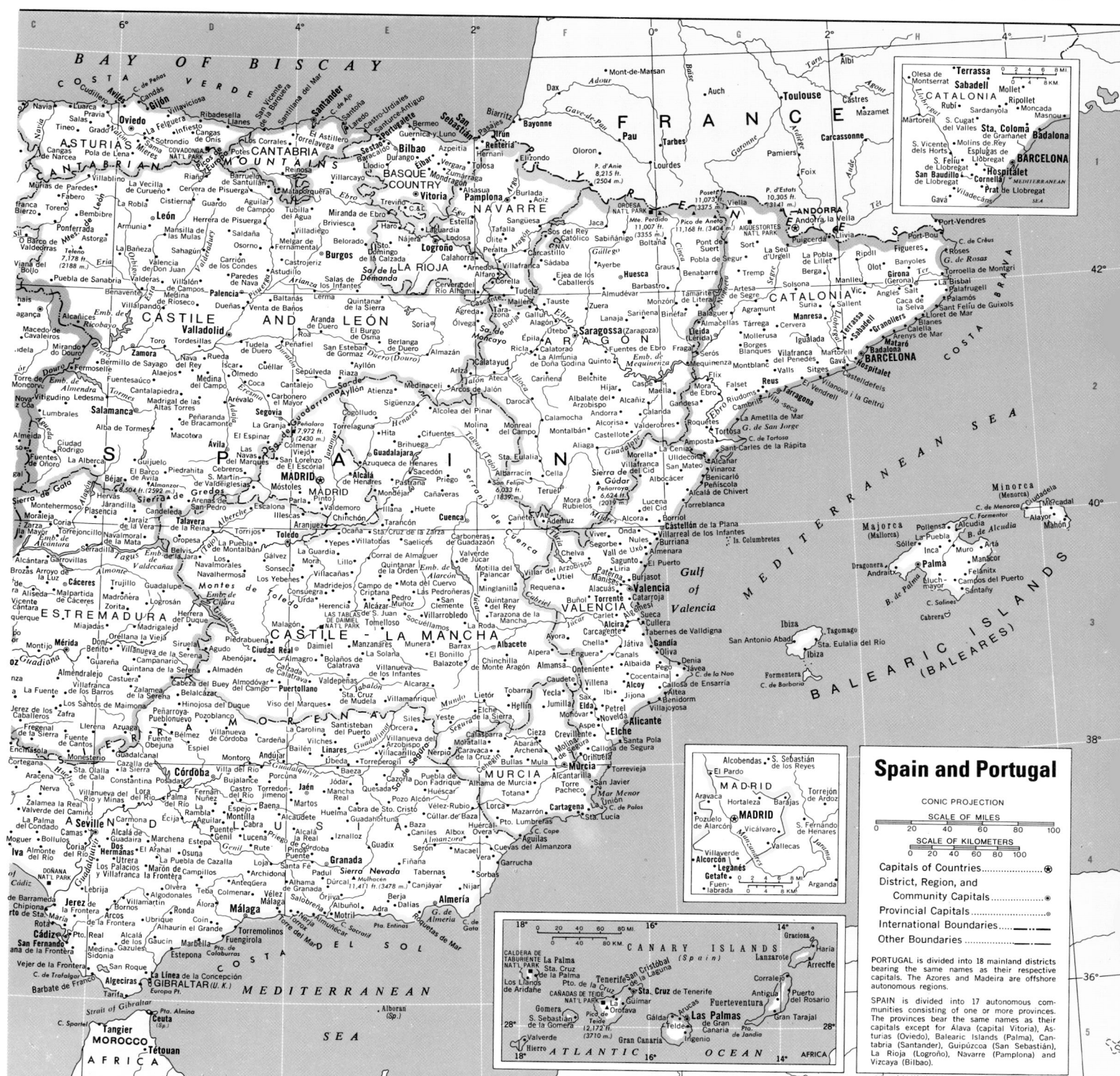

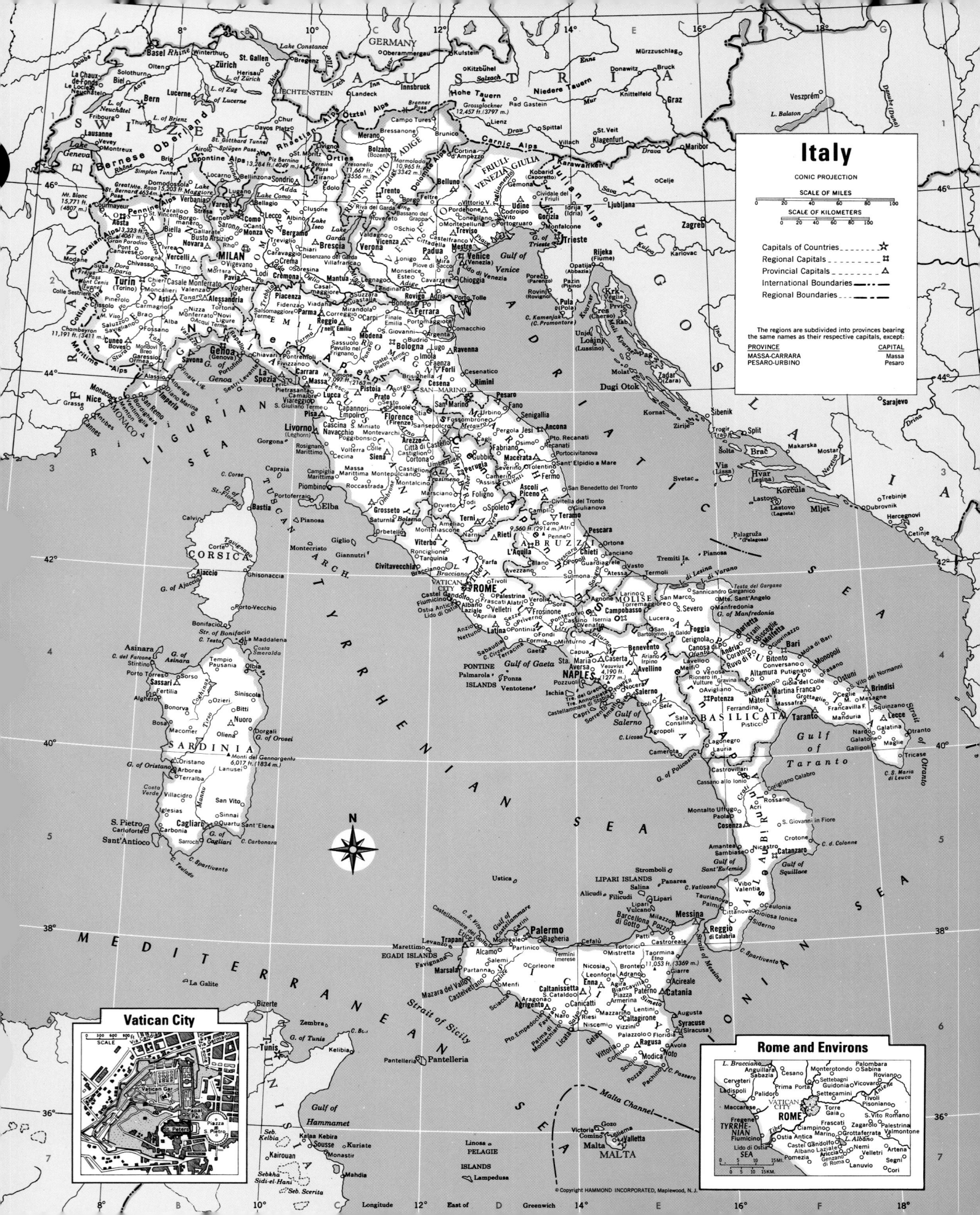
Italy
CONIC PROJECTION
SCALE OF MILES
0 20 40 60 80 100
SCALE OF KILOMETERS
0 20 40 60 80 100
Capitals of Countries
Regional Capitals
Provincial Capitals
International Boundaries
Regional Boundaries
The regions are subdivided into provinces bearing the same names as their respective capitals, except:
PROVINCE CAPITAL
MASSA-CARRARA Massa
PESARO-URBINO Pesaro
Vatican City
Rome and Environs
SWITZERLAND
AUSTRIA
GERMANY
FRANCE
YUGOSLAVIA
TUNISIA
CORSICA
SARDINIA
MALTA
LIGURIAN SEA
TYRRHENIAN SEA
ADRIATIC SEA
IONIAN SEA
MEDITERRANEAN SEA
Gulf of Taranto
Strait of Sicily
Malta Channel
ROME
MILAN
NAPLES
Longitude East of Greenwich
© Copyright HAMMOND INCORPORATED, Maplewood, N. J.

VATICAN CITY

AREA 108.7 acres (44 hectares)
POPULATION 1,000

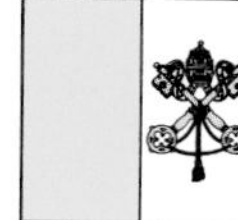

SAN MARINO

AREA 23.4 sq. mi. (60.6 sq. km.)
POPULATION 23,000

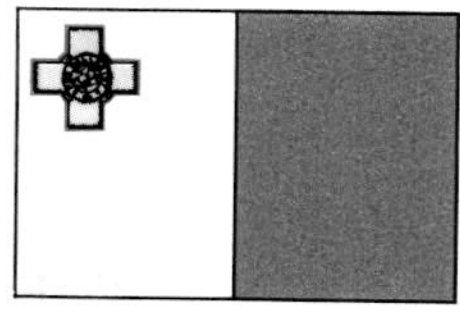

MALTA

AREA 122 sq. mi. (316 sq. km.)
POPULATION 353,000
CAPITAL Valletta
LARGEST CITY Sliema
HIGHEST POINT 787 ft. (240 m.)
MONETARY UNIT Maltese lira
MAJOR LANGUAGES Maltese, English
MAJOR RELIGION Roman Catholicism

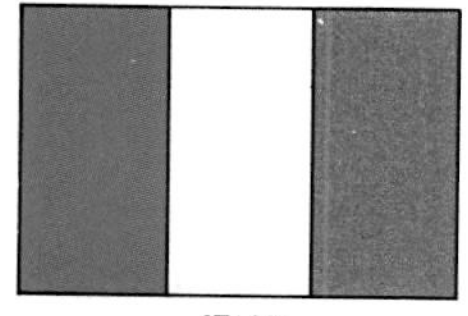

ITALY

AREA 116,303 sq. mi. (301,225 sq. km.)
POPULATION 57,574,000
CAPITAL Rome
LARGEST CITY Rome
HIGHEST POINT Dufourspitze (Mte. Rosa) 15,203 ft. (4,634 m.)
MONETARY UNIT lira
MAJOR LANGUAGE Italian
MAJOR RELIGION Roman Catholicism

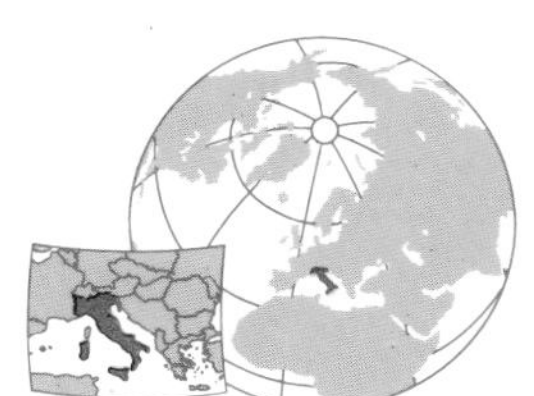

ITALY

REGIONS

Abruzzi 1,217,791 .... D3
Aosta 112,353 .... A2
Apulia (Puglia) 3,871,617 .... F4
Basilicata 610,186 .... F4
Calabria 2,061,182 .... F5
Campania 5,463,134 .... E4
Emilia-Romagna 3,957,513 .... C2
Friuli-Venezia Giulia 1,233,984 .... D1
Latium (Lazio) 5,001,684 .... D3
Liguria 1,807,893 .... B2
Lombardy 8,891,652 .... B2
Marche 1,412,404 .... D3
Molise 328,371 .... E4
Piedmont 4,479,031 .... A2
Sardinia 1,594,175 .... B4
Sicily 4,906,878 .... D6
Trentino-Alto Adige 873,413 .... C1
Tuscany 3,581,051 .... C3
Umbria 807,552 .... D3
Veneto 4,345,047 .... C2

PROVINCES

Agrigento 466,495 .... D6
Alessandria 466,102 .... B2
Ancona 433,417 .... D3
Arezzo 313,157 .... C3
Ascoli Piceno 352,567 .... D3
Asti 215,382 .... B2
Avellino 434,021 .... E4
Bari 1,464,627 .... F4
Belluno 220,335 .... D1
Benevento 289,143 .... E4
Bergamo 896,117 .... B2
Bologna 930,284 .... C2
Bolzano-Bozen 430,568 .... C1
Brescia 1,017,093 .... C2
Brindisi 391,064 .... G4
Cagliari 730,473 .... B5
Caltanissetta 285,829 .... D6
Campobasso 235,847 .... E4
Caserta 755,628 .... E4
Catania 1,005,577 .... E6
Catanzaro 744,834 .... F5
Chieti 370,534 .... E3
Como 755,979 .... B2
Cosenza 743,255 .... F5
Cremona 332,236 .... B2
Cuneo 548,452 .... A2
Enna 190,939 .... E6
Ferrara 381,118 .... C2
Florence 1,202,013 .... C3
Foggia 681,595 .... E4
Forlì 599,420 .... D2
Frosinone 460,395 .... D4
Genoa 1,045,109 .... B2
Gorizia 144,726 .... D2
Grosseto 220,905 .... C3
Imperia 223,738 .... B3
Isernia 92,524 .... E4
L'Aquila 291,742 .... D3
La Spezia 241,371 .... B2
Latina 434,086 .... D4
Lecce 762,017 .... G4
Livorno (Leghorn) 346,657 .... C3
Lucca 385,876 .... C3
Macerata 292,932 .... D3
Mantua 377,158 .... C2
Massa-Carrara 203,530 .... C2
Matera 203,570 .... F4
Messina 669,323 .... E5
Milan 4,018,108 .... B2
Modena 596,025 .... C2
Naples 2,970,563 .... E4
Novara 507,367 .... B2
Nuoro 274,817 .... B4
Padua 809,667 .... C2
Palermo 1,198,575 .... D5
Parma 400,192 .... C2
Pavia 512,895 .... B2
Perugia 580,988 .... D3
Pesaro e Urbino 333,488 .... D3
Pescara 286,240 .... E3
Piacenza 278,424 .... B2
Pisa 388,800 .... C3
Pistoia 264,995 .... C3
Pordenone 275,888 .... D2
Potenza 406,616 .... E4
Ragusa 274,583 .... E6
Ravenna 358,654 .... D2
Reggio di Calabria 573,093 .... E5
Reggio nell'Emilia 413,396 .... C2
Rieti 142,794 .... D3
Rome 3,695,961 .... F6
Rovigo 253,508 .... C2
Salerno 1,013,779 .... E4
Sassari 433,842 .... B4
Savona 297,675 .... B2
Siena 255,118 .... C3
Sondrio 174,009 .... B1
Syracuse 394,692 .... E6
Taranto 572,314 .... F4
Teramo 269,275 .... D3
Terni 807,552 .... D3
Trapani 420,865 .... D5
Trento 442,845 .... C1
Treviso 720,580 .... D2
Trieste 283,641 .... D2
Turin 2,345,771 .... A2
Udine 529,729 .... D1
Varese 788,057 .... B2
Venice 838,794 .... D2
Vercelli 395,957 .... B2
Verona 775,745 .... C2
Vicenza 726,418 .... C2
Viterbo 268,448 .... C3

CITIES and TOWNS

Acireale 46,711 .... E6
Acqui Terme 20,951 .... B2
Adrano 32,865 .... E6
Agrigento 38,681 .... D6
Alba 25,853 .... B2
Albano Laziale 27,796 .... F7
Alcamo 41,626 .... D6
Alessandria 79,552 .... B2
Alghero 32,519 .... B4
Altamura 50,539 .... F4
Amalfi 4,423 .... E4
Ancona 97,118 .... D3
Andria 84,070 .... F4
Anzio 25,932 .... D4
Aosta 36,649 .... A2
Aprilia 31,604 .... D4
Arezzo 74,477 .... C3
Ascoli Piceno 44,411 .... D3
Assisi 4,683 .... D3
Asti 65,483 .... B2
Augusta 37,162 .... E6
Avellino 50,894 .... E4
Aversa 55,788 .... E4
Avezzano 30,227 .... D3
Avola 30,360 .... E6
Bagheria 39,869 .... D5
Barcellona Pozzo di Gotto 33,404 .... E5
Bari 369,444 .... F4
Barletta 82,290 .... F4
Bassano del Grappa 33,724 .... C2
Belluno 28,468 .... D1
Benevento 51,831 .... E4
Bergamo 121,389 .... B2
Biancavilla 20,047 .... E6
Biella 52,587 .... B2
Bisceglie 46,209 .... F4
Bitonto 46,538 .... F4
Bologna 454,897 .... C2
Bolzano (Bolzen) 103,241 .... C1
Borgomanero 18,701 .... B2
Bra 21,304 .... A2
Brescia 202,539 .... C2
Brindisi 84,887 .... G4
Bronte 17,477 .... E6
Busto Arsizio 79,321 .... B2
Cagliari 219,423 .... B5
Caltagirone 32,860 .... E6
Caltanissetta 57,704 .... D6
Camaiore 24,284 .... C3
Campobasso 41,687 .... E4
Canicattì 31,726 .... D6
Canosa di Puglia 30,555 .... E4
Cantù 35,644 .... B2
Capannori 39,717 .... C3
Carbonia 25,140 .... B5
Carmagnola 19,581 .... A2
Carpi 49,370 .... C2
Carrara 61,709 .... C2
Casale Monferrato 37,157 .... B2
Cascina-Navacchio 32,570 .... C3
Caserta 59,185 .... E4
Cassino 22,406 .... D4
Castel Gandolfo 6,176 .... F7
Castelfranco Veneto 20,196 .... D2
Castellammare di Stabia 70,507 .... E4
Castelvetrano 29,503 .... D6
Castrovillari 18,648 .... F5
Catania 379,754 .... E6
Catanzaro 96,930 .... F5
Cava de'Tirreni 47,007 .... E4
Cecina 22,264 .... C3
Ceglie Messapico 17,915 .... F4
Cerignola 48,105 .... E4
Cesena 72,145 .... D2
Cesenatico 15,634 .... D2
Chiavari 29,171 .... B2
Chieri 28,296 .... A2
Chieti 49,267 .... E3
Chioggia 46,728 .... D2
Chivasso 22,230 .... A2
Ciampino 31,981 .... F7
Città di Castello 21,492 .... C3
Civitavecchia 46,465 .... C3
Comiso 25,469 .... E6
Como 94,167 .... B2
Conegliano 32,406 .... D2
Conversano 18,518 .... F4
Corato 41,078 .... F4
Cosenza 101,144 .... F5
Crema 33,901 .... B2
Cremona 74,341 .... B2
Crotone 51,204 .... F5
Cuneo 47,836 .... A2
Desenzano del Garda 17,296 .... C2
Domodossola 19,825 .... A1
Eboli 24,152 .... E4
Empoli 34,066 .... C3
Enna 26,760 .... E6
Fabriano 21,155 .... D3
Faenza 40,635 .... D2
Fano 42,440 .... D3
Fasano 22,918 .... F4
Favara 30,031 .... D6
Fermo 17,603 .... D3
Ferrara 117,590 .... C2
Fidenza 19,482 .... B2
Fiesole 3,711 .... C3
Firenze (Florence) 442,721 .... C3
Fiumicino 21,167 .... F7
Florence 442,721 .... C3
Floridia 17,790 .... E6
Foggia 150,480 .... E4
Foligno 41,696 .... D3
Fondi 19,580 .... D4
Forlì 91,366 .... D2
Formia 29,147 .... D4
Fossano 17,116 .... A2
Francavilla Fontana 31,371 .... F4
Frascati 18,356 .... F7
Frosinone 42,626 .... D4
Gaeta 23,190 .... D4
Galatina 22,611 .... G4
Gallarate 47,259 .... B2
Gela 74,077 .... E6
Genoa 755,389 .... B2
Genova (Genoa) 787,011 .... B2
Giarre 23,377 .... E6
Gioia del Colle 23,868 .... F4
Giovinazzo 18,832 .... F4
Giulianova 20,189 .... E3
Gorizia 40,679 .... D2
Gravina in Puglia 35,891 .... F4
Grosseto 55,569 .... C3
Grottaglie 27,140 .... F4
Iglesias 26,313 .... B5
Imola 47,365 .... C2
Imperia 39,151 .... B3
Isernia 16,919 .... E4
Ivrea 26,446 .... B2
Jesi 37,075 .... D3
L'Aquila 40,467 .... D3
La Spezia 110,632 .... B2
Lanciano 25,828 .... E3
Latina 64,529 .... D4
Lecce 80,127 .... G4
Lecco 51,160 .... B2
Leghorn (Livorno) 171,811 .... C3
Legnago 23,232 .... C2
Lentini 30,950 .... E6
Leonforte 15,745 .... E6
Licata 40,309 .... D6
Lido di Ostia 85,043 .... F7
Lido di Venezia 20,863 .... D2
Livorno 171,811 .... C3
Lodi 41,338 .... B2
Lucca 84,836 .... C3
Lucera 31,252 .... E4
Lugo 21,593 .... D2
Macerata 34,409 .... D3
Manduria 28,112 .... F4
Manfredonia 52,162 .... F4
Mantua 52,477 .... C2
Marino 30,261 .... F7
Marsala 76,843 .... D6
Martina Franca 34,911 .... F4
Massa 60,810 .... C2
Massafra 26,172 .... F4
Matera 48,226 .... F4
Mazara del Vallo 42,320 .... D6
Merano 31,854 .... C1
Mesagne 29,770 .... G4
Messina 240,121 .... E5
Mestre 197,952 .... D2
Milan 1,601,797 .... B2
Milazzo 29,868 .... E5
Minturno 15,795 .... D4
Mira Taglio 26,031 .... D2
Modena 164,529 .... C2
Modica 34,488 .... E6
Mola di Bari 25,744 .... F4
Molfetta 64,738 .... F4
Moncalieri 59,344 .... A2
Monfalcone 29,960 .... D2
Monopoli 33,928 .... F4
Monreale 18,168 .... D5
Monte Sant'Angelo 16,491 .... F4
Montebelluna 19,708 .... D2
Monterotondo 25,383 .... F6
Montevarchi 17,110 .... C3
Monza 122,541 .... B2
Naples 1,210,365 .... E4
Nardò 27,384 .... F4
Nettuno 27,929 .... D4
Nicastro-Sambiase 49,325 .... F5
Niscemi 25,677 .... E6
Nocera Inferiore 43,879 .... E4
Noto 20,609 .... E6
Novara 94,477 .... B2
Novi Ligure 28,756 .... B2
Nuoro 35,491 .... B4
Olbia 26,702 .... B4
Oristano 23,938 .... B5
Orvieto 7,509 .... D3
Ostia Antica 3,939 .... F7
Ostuni 27,948 .... F4
Otranto 4,334 .... G4
Pachino 20,631 .... E6
Padua 228,333 .... C2
Palermo 698,481 .... D5
Palma di Montechiaro 23,918 .... D6
Palmi 16,394 .... E5
Pantelleria 3,454 .... C6
Parma 160,374 .... C2
Partinico 27,479 .... D6
Paternò 42,916 .... E6
Pavia 82,629 .... B2
Perugia 103,542 .... D3
Pesaro 78,550 .... D3
Pescara 131,016 .... E3
Piacenza 103,584 .... B2
Piazza Armerina 20,119 .... E6
Pietrasanta 20,404 .... B3
Pinerolo 33,176 .... A2
Piombino 35,312 .... C3
Pisa 95,015 .... C3
Pistoia 78,105 .... C3
Poggibonsi 22,644 .... C3
Pomezia 19,453 .... F7
Pordenone 51,270 .... D2
Porto Empedocle 16,126 .... D6
Porto Torres 20,233 .... B4
Portocivitanova 28,155 .... D3
Portoferraio 8,108 .... C3
Portofino 615 .... B2
Potenza 55,175 .... E4
Pozzuoli 61,856 .... D4
Prato 156,894 .... C3
Putignano 22,361 .... F4
Quartu Sant'Elena 40,506 .... B5
Ragusa 60,871 .... E6
Rapallo 26,457 .... B2
Ravenna 87,582 .... D2
Reggio di Calabria 159,416 .... E5
Reggio nell'Emilia 107,484 .... C2
Rho 50,373 .... B2
Rieti 33,614 .... D3
Rimini 111,991 .... D2
Rome (cap.) 2,605,441 .... F6
Rovereto 31,286 .... C2
Rovigo 41,050 .... C2
Ruvo di Puglia 23,510 .... F4
Salerno 150,252 .... E4
Saluzzo 13,078 .... A2
San Benedetto del Tronto 43,189 .... E3
San Cataldo 20,694 .... D6
San Giovanni in Fiore 19,391 .... F5
Sannicandro Garganico 18,652 .... E4
San Remo 59,872 .... A3
San Severo 53,948 .... E4
Santa Maria Capua Vetere 32,129 .... E4
Santeramo in Colle 21,154 .... F4
San Vito dei Normanni 18,366 .... F4
Saronno 36,732 .... B2
Sassari 104,334 .... B4
Sassuolo 37,515 .... C2
Savona 65,040 .... B2
Schio 30,738 .... C2
Sciacca 35,063 .... D6
Scicli 18,419 .... E6
Senigallia 27,474 .... D3
Sesto Fiorentino 43,307 .... C3
Sestri Levante 19,672 .... B2
Siena 54,982 .... C3
Siracusa (Syracuse) 109,038 .... E6
Sondrio 19,955 .... B1
Sora 20,380 .... D4
Sorrento 15,747 .... E4
Spoleto 21,625 .... D3
Stresa 4,290 .... B2
Sulmona 21,504 .... D3
Syracuse 109,038 .... E6
Taranto 231,441 .... F4
Teramo 35,142 .... D3
Termini Imerese 24,252 .... D6

(continued on following page)

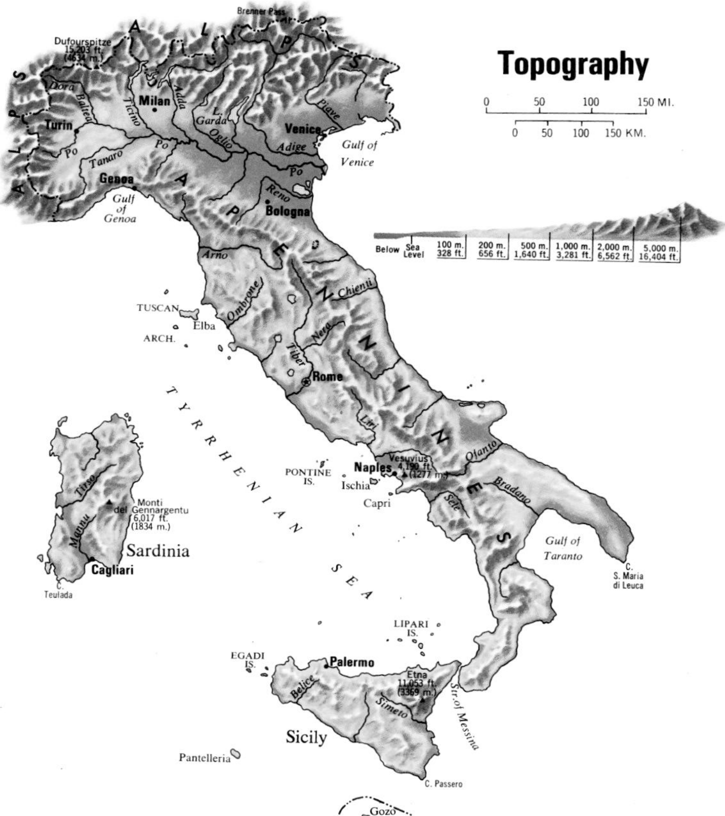
Topography
0 50 100 150 MI.
0 50 100 150 KM.
Below Sea Level
100 m. 328 ft.
200 m. 656 ft.
500 m. 1,640 ft.
1,000 m. 3,281 ft.
2,000 m. 6,562 ft.
5,000 m. 16,404 ft.
Brenner Pass
Dufourspitze 15,203 ft. (4634 m.)
Milan
Turin
Genoa
Gulf of Genoa
Venice
Gulf of Venice
Bologna
Po
Tanaro
Ticino
Adda
Oglio
Adige
Piave
Reno
Arno
Ombrone
Chienti
Tiber
Rome
TUSCAN ARCH.
Elba
PONTINE IS.
Naples
Vesuvius
Ischia
Capri
T Y R R H E N I A N S E A
Gulf of Taranto
Bradano
Sele
Ofanto
C. S. Maria di Leuca
Sardinia
Cagliari
Tirso
Flumendosa
Monti del Gennargentu 6,017 ft. (1834 m.)
C. Teulada
LIPARI IS.
EGADI IS.
Palermo
Etna 11,053 ft. (3369 m.)
Str. of Messina
Belice
Simeto
Sicily
Pantelleria
C. Passero
Gozo
Malta
Lampedusa

Agriculture, Industry and Resources

DOMINANT LAND USE

- Wheat, Rice, Dairy
- Pasture Livestock
- Cereals, Livestock
- Fruit, Truck and Mixed Farming
- Grapes, Wine
- Forests
- Nonagricultural Land

MAJOR MINERAL OCCURRENCES

Ab	Asbestos	K	Potash	Pb	Lead
Al	Bauxite	Lg	Lignite	Py	Pyrites
C	Coal	Mr	Marble	S	Sulfur
Fe	Iron Ore	Na	Salt	Sb	Antimony
G	Natural Gas	O	Petroleum	Zn	Zinc
Hg	Mercury				

⚡ Water Power

▨ Major Industrial Areas

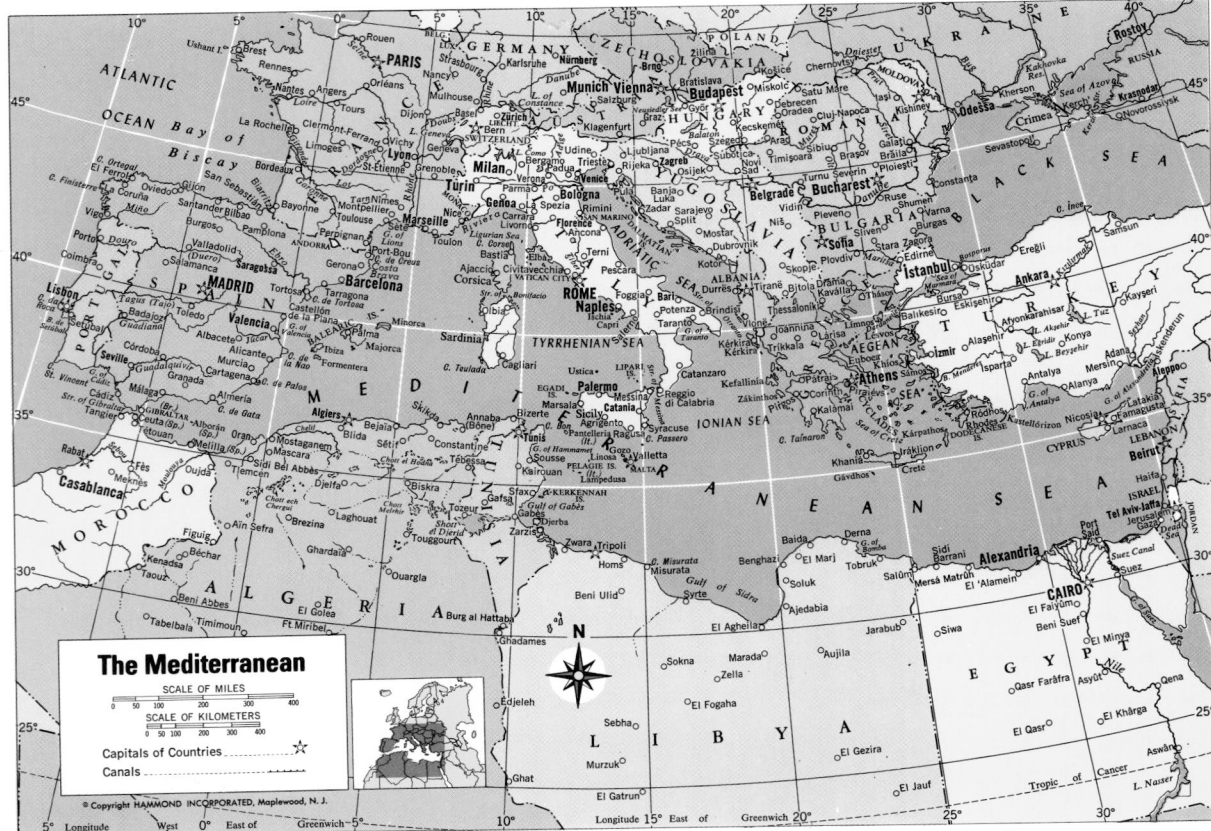

The Mediterranean

SCALE OF MILES
0 50 100   200   300   400

SCALE OF KILOMETERS
0 50 100   200   300   400

Capitals of Countries .... ☆

Canals ....

© Copyright HAMMOND INCORPORATED, Maplewood, N.J.

SWITZERLAND
AREA   15,943 sq. mi. (41,292 sq. km.)
POPULATION   6,647,000
CAPITAL   Bern
LARGEST CITY   Zürich
HIGHEST POINT   Dufourspitze
(Mte. Rosa) 15,203 ft. (4,634 m.)
MONETARY UNIT   Swiss franc
MAJOR LANGUAGES   German, French,
Italian, Romansch
MAJOR RELIGIONS   Protestantism,
Roman Catholicism

LIECHTENSTEIN
AREA   61 sq. mi. (158 sq. km.)
POPULATION   28,000
CAPITAL   Vaduz
LARGEST CITY   Vaduz
HIGHEST POINT   Grauspitze 8,527 ft.
(2,599 m.)
MONETARY UNIT   Swiss franc
MAJOR LANGUAGE   German
MAJOR RELIGION   Roman Catholicism

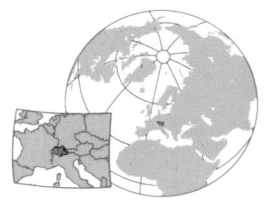
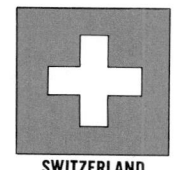

SWITZERLAND

LIECHTENSTEIN

Languages

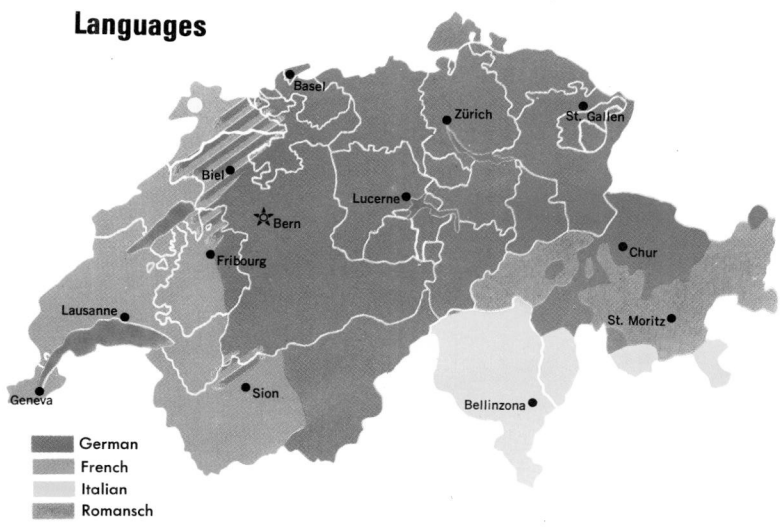

German
French
Italian
Romansch

Switzerland is a multilingual nation with four official languages. 70% of the people speak German, 19% French, 10% Italian and 1% Romansch.

Agriculture, Industry and Resources

DOMINANT LAND USE
- Cereals, Dairy
- Pasture Livestock
- General Farming, Livestock
- Fruit, Truck, Mixed Farming
- Forests
- Nonagricultural Land

Water Power
Major Industrial Areas

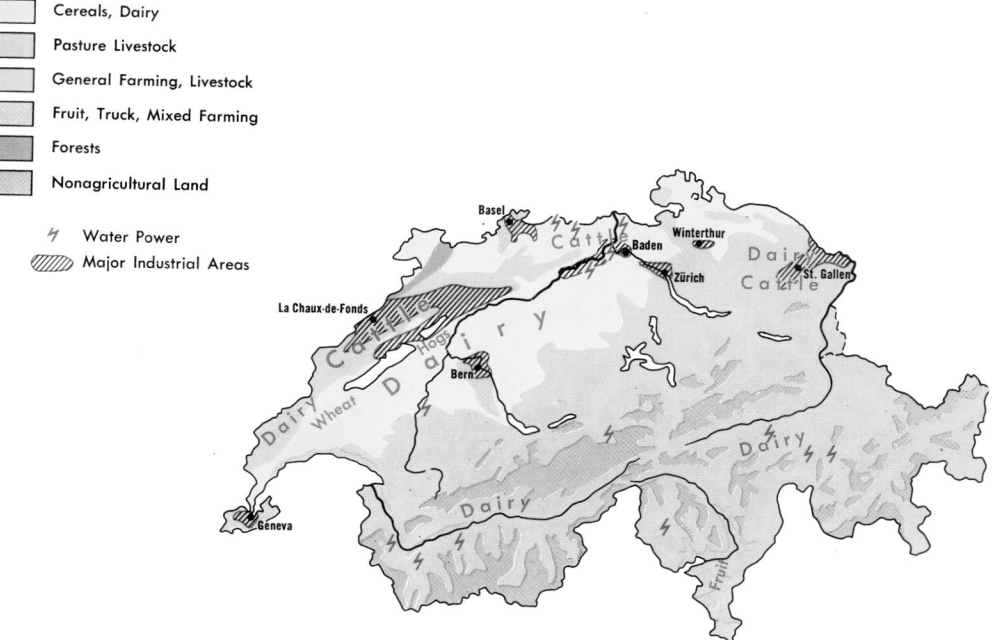

SWITZERLAND

CANTONS

Aargau 453,442 .... F2
Appenzell, Ausser Rhoden 47,611 .... H2
Appenzell, Inner Rhoden 12,844 .... H2
Baselland 219,822 .... E2
Baselstadt 203,915 .... E1
Bern 912,022 .... D2
Fribourg 185,246 .... D3
Geneva (Genève) 349,040 .... B4
Glarus 36,718 .... H3
Graubünden (Grisons) 164,641 .... H3
Jura 64,986 .... D2
Lucerne (Luzern) 296,159 .... F2
Luzern 296,159 .... F2
Neuchâtel 158,368 .... C3
Nidwalden 28,617 .... F3
Obwalden 25,865 .... F3
Sankt Gallen 391,995 .... H2
Schaffhausen 69,413 .... G1
Schwyz 97,354 .... G2
Soleure (Solothurn) 218,102 .... E2
Solothurn 218,102 .... E2
Thurgau 183,795 .... H1
Ticino 265,899 .... G4
Uri 33,883 .... G3
Valais 218,707 .... D4
Vaud 528,747 .... B3

Zug 75,930 .... G2
Zürich 1,122,839 .... G2

CITIES and TOWNS

Aadorf 3,257 .... G2
Aarau 15,788 .... E2
Aarberg 3,212 .... E2
Aarburg 5,354 .... E2
Adelboden 3,276 .... E3
Adliswil 16,418 .... G2
Affoltern am Albis 8,064 .... F2
Aigle 6,233 .... C4
Allschwil 17,952 .... D1
Alpnach 3,556 .... F3
Altdorf 8,230 .... G3
Altstätten 9,260 .... J2
Amriswil 8,790 .... H1
Appenzell 4,781 .... H2
Arbedo-Castione 3,058 .... G4
Arbon 11,333 .... H1
Arosa 2,782 .... J3
Arth 7,795 .... F2
Ascona 4,722 .... G4
Au 5,434 .... J2
Avenches 2,177 .... D3
Baar 15,196 .... F2
Bad Ragaz 3,721 .... H2
Baden 13,870 .... F2
Balerna 3,455 .... G5
Balsthal 5,090 .... E2
Bäretswil 3,145 .... G2
Basel 182,143 .... E1

Basel 364,813 .... E1
Bassecourt 2,942 .... D2
Bauma 3,010 .... G2
Bellinzona 16,743 .... H4
Belp 7,578 .... D3
Bern (cap.) 145,254 .... D3
Bettlach 3,851 .... D2
Bex 4,843 .... D4
Biasca 5,447 .... H4
Biberist 7,519 .... D2
Biel 53,793 .... D2
Binningen 14,195 .... D1
Bischofszell 3,390 .... H1
Bolligen 32,312 .... E3
Boudry 4,488 .... C3
Breitenbach 2,518 .... E2
Bremgarten 4,815 .... F2
Brienz 2,759 .... F3
Brig 9,608 .... F4
Brittnau 2,822 .... E2
Brugg 8,911 .... F2
Bubikon 3,601 .... G2
Buchs 9,066 .... H2
Bülach 12,292 .... G1
Bulle 7,595 .... D3
Buochs 3,742 .... F3
Büren an der Aare 2,761 .... D2
Burgdorf 15,379 .... E2
Bürglen 3,456 .... G3
Bussigny-près-Lausanne 4,909 .... B3
Bütschwil 3,423 .... H2
Carouge 13,100 .... B4
Castagnola 4,430 .... G4
Cham 9,275 .... F2
Château-d'Oex 2,872 .... D4
Châtel-Saint-Denis 3,141 .... C3
Chêne-Bougeries 9,068 .... B4
Chiasso 8,583 .... G5
Chur 32,037 .... J3
Collombey-Muraz 2,982 .... C4
Collonge-Bellerive 4,531 .... B4
Conthey 4,828 .... D4
Courrendlin 2,435 .... D2
Couvet 2,627 .... C3
Davos 10,468 .... J3
Degersheim 3,269 .... H2
Delémont 11,682 .... D2
Derendingen 4,675 .... E2
Dielsdorf 3,767 .... F1
Diepoldsau 3,562 .... J2
Diessenhofen 2,535 .... G1
Dietikon 21,765 .... F2
Disentis-Mustér 2,320 .... G3
Domat-Ems 6,266 .... H3
Dornach 5,442 .... E2
Döttingen 3,264 .... F1
Dübendorf 20,683 .... G2
Düdingen 5,572 .... D3
Dürnten 4,927 .... G2
Ebnat-Kappel 4,950 .... H2
Echallens 2,163 .... C3
Ecublens 7,615 .... B3
Effretikon 14,788 .... G2
Egg 6,074 .... G2
Eggiwil 2,323 .... E3
Egnach 3,397 .... H1
Einsiedeln 9,629 .... G2
Elgg 3,041 .... G2
Emmen 22,392 .... F2
Engelberg 2,963 .... F3
Ennenda 2,512 .... H2
Entlebuch 3,238 .... F3
Erstfeld 4,158 .... G3
Eschenbach 3,661 .... G2
Escholzmatt 3,033 .... E3
Estavayer-le-Lac 3,662 .... C3
Feuerthalen 2,920 .... G1
Flawil 8,575 .... H2
Fleurier 3,573 .... C3
Flims 2,136 .... H3
Flums 4,228 .... H2
Frauenfeld 18,607 .... G1
Freienbach 9,912 .... G2
Fribourg 37,400 .... D3
Frick 3,116 .... E1
Frutigen 5,779 .... E3
Fully 3,926 .... D4
Gais 2,388 .... H2
Gelterkinden 4,954 .... E2

(continued on following page)

Topography

Basel · Rhine · Thur · L. of Constance · Zürich · Limmat · Zürichsee · Zugersee · Vaduz · Scesaplana · Bern · Emme · Simme · L. of Lucerne · Thunersee · Brienzersee · Lausanne · Lake Geneva · Geneva · Rhône · Dufourspitze 15,203 ft. (4634 m.) · Matterhorn · Simplon Pass · Maggiore · L. of Lugano · Great St. Bernard Pass

SWISS PLATEAU · JURA · ALPS · BERNESE OBERLAND · PENNINE ALPS

Scale
0   20   40 MI.
0   20   40 KM.

Below Sea Level	Sea Level	100 m. 328 ft.	200 m. 656 ft.	500 m. 1,640 ft.	1,000 m. 3,281 ft.	2,000 m. 6,562 ft.	5,000 m. 16,404 ft.

Geneva (Genève) 156,505.....B4
Giswil 2,595...................F3
Giubiasco 6,585..............H4
Gland 4,906...................H2
Glarus 5,969..................G2
Glis 3,389.....................J3
Glattfelden 2,753..............E4
Gordola 2,956.................G4
Gossau 14,584................H2
Grabs 4,844...................J2
Grenchen 16,800..............D2
Grindelwald 3,555.............E3
Grosswangen 2,235...........F2
Gstaad.........................D4
Heiden 3,620..................H2
Heimberg 4,107...............E3
Hergiswil 4,254...............F3
Herisau 14,160................H2
Herzogenbuchsee 5,107......E2
Hilterfingen 3,600.............E3
Hinwil 7,554...................G2
Hochdorf 6,034................F2
Horgen 16,577................G2
Huttwil 4,612..................E2
Igis 5,392.....................J3
Ingenbohl 6,232..............G2
Ins 2,608......................D2
Interlaken 4,852...............E3
Jegenstorf 3,541..............D2
Jona 12,156...................H2
Kaltbrunn 2,735...............G2
Kerns 4,200...................F3
Kerzers 2,658.................D3
Kirchberg, Bern 3,966........E2
Kirchberg, St. Gallen 6,398...G2
Klingnau 2,433................F1
Klosters-Serneus 3,487.......J3
Kloten 15,845.................G2
Kölliken 3,080.................F2
Köniz 33,441..................D3
Konolfingen 4,360.............E3
Kreuzlingen 16,101............H1
Kriens 21,097.................F2
Küsnacht 12,766..............G2
Küssnacht am Rigi 8,091......F2
Küttigen 4,356................F2
La Chaux-de-Fonds 37,234....C2
Lachen 5,352..................G2
Lancy 23,527..................B4
Langenthal 13,408............E2
Langnau in Aargau 5,696......F2
Langnau im Emmental 8,821...E3
La Tour-de-Peilz 9,411........C4
Laufen 4,444..................D2
Laupen 2,261..................D3
Lauperswil 2,482..............E3
Lausanne 127,349.............C4
Lauterbrunnen 3,077..........E3
Le Brassus 4,359.............B3
Le Châble 4,541...............D4
Le Chenit (Le Brassus) 4,359..B3
Le Landeron 3,287............C2
Le Locle 12,039...............C2
Le Mont-sur-Lausanne 3,664..C3
Lengnau 4,317................D2
Lenk 2,089....................D4
Lens 2,412....................D4
Lenzburg 7,585...............F2
Leuk 2,983....................E4
Leukerbad 1,070..............E4
Liestal 12,158.................E2
Littau-Sissach 40,800.........E2
Littau 14,996.................F2
Locarno 14,103...............G4
Lucerne 63,278...............F2
Lugano 27,815................G4
Lutry 5,884...................C3
Lützelflüh 3,770...............E3
Luzern (Lucerne) 63,278......F2
Lyss 8,723....................D2
Malters 4,900.................F2
Männedorf 7,833..............G2
Martigny 11,309..............C4

Meilen 10,430.................G2
Meiringen 4,072...............F3
Mellingen 3,285...............F2
Mels 6,235....................H2
Mendrisio 6,590...............G4
Menzingen 3,564..............G2
Menznau 2,248................F2
Meyrin 18,808.................B4
Minusio 5,602.................G4
Möhlin 8,360..................E1
Mollis 2,621...................G2
Monthey 11,285...............C4
Montreux 19,685..............C4
Morges 13,057................B3
Moudon 3,805.................C3
Moutier 7,959.................D2
Mümliswil-Ramiswil 2,386.....E2
Münchenbuchsee 8,395.......D2
Münsingen 9,340..............E3
Muotathal 2,896..............G3
Muri 5,399....................F2
Muri bei Bern 12,285.........D3
Murten 4,558..................D3
Muttenz 16,911...............E1
Näfels 3,766..................G2
Naters 6,662..................E4
Nendaz 4,372.................D4
Netstal 2,642.................H2
Neuchâtel 34,428.............C3
Neuenegg 3,727..............D3
Neuhausen am Rheinfall
    10,662....................G1
Niederbipp 3,165.............E2
Niederurnen 3,438............G2
Nyon 12,842..................B4
Oberägeri 3,563..............G2
Oberburg 2,869...............E2
Oberdiessbach 2,319.........E3
Oberriet 6,222................J2
Obersiggenthal 7,442.........F1
Oberuzwil 4,616..............H2
Oensingen 3,543.............E2
Oftringen 9,006...............E2
Ollon 4,429...................D4
Olten 18,991..................E2
Opfikon 11,444................G2
Orbe 3,985....................C3
Orsières 2,357................D4
Paradiso 3,261...............G5
Payerne 6,713................C3
Peseux 5,212.................C3
Pfäffikon 8,306...............G2
Pfaffnau 2,453................E2
Pieterlen 3,127...............D2
Porrentruy 7,039..............C2
Poschiavo 3,294.............J4
Prangins 2,028...............B4
Pratteln 15,751...............E1
Pully 14,988..................C4
Rafz 2,325....................G1
Rapperswil 7,826.............G2
Regensdorf 12,300............F2
Reichenbach im Kandertal
    2,948.....................E3
Reiden 3,363..................E2
Reinach in Aargau 5,696......F2
Reinach in Baselland 17,813..E2
Renens 16,977...............C3
Rheineck 3,037...............J2
Rheinfelden 9,456............E1
Richterswil 8,672.............G2
Riehen 20,611................E1
Riggisberg 2,196.............D3
Roggwil 3,333................E2
Rolle 3,409...................B4
Romanshorn 7,893............H1
Romont 3,495................C3
Rorschach 9,878.............H2
Rothrist 6,015.................E2
Rüti, Zürich 9,331............G2
Rumlang 5,055...............G2
Ruswil 4,870.................F2
Saanen 5,522.................D4
Sachseln 3,406...............F3

Saint-Blaise 2,788............D2
Sainte-Croix 4,543............B3
Saint-Imier 5,430.............D2
Saint-Légier-La Chiésaz 2,787 C4
Saint-Maurice 3,458..........C4
Saint Moritz 5,900.............J3
Saint Niklaus 2,036...........E4
Saint-Prex 2,937..............B4
Samedan 2,553...............J3
Sankt Gallen 75,847..........H2
Sankt Margrethen 4,935......J2
Sargans 4,267................H2
Sarnen 7,372.................F3
Savièse 4,097.................D4
Saxon 2,394..................D4
Schänis 2,426................H2
Schaffhausen 34,250.........G1
Schattdorf 4,428..............G3
Schiers 2,253.................J2
Schlieren 12,891.............F2
Schönenwerd 4,746..........E2
Schübelbach 4,720...........G2
Schüpfheim 3,537............F3
Schwanden 2,519............H2
Schwyz 12,100...............G2
Sempach 2,237...............F2
Seon 3,826...................F2
Seuzach 4,659................G1
Severen 2,839................H2
Sierre 13,050.................D4
Signau 2,606.................E3
Sigriswil 3,536...............E3
Silenen 2,115.................G3
Simplon 328..................F4
Sion 22,877..................D4
Sirnach 4,122................G2
Sissach 4,564................E2
Solothurn (Soleure) 15,778...D2
Spiez 9,800...................E3
Stäfa 10,558.................G2
Stans 5,681...................F3
Steckborn 3,232.............G1
Steffisburg 12,539............E3
Stein am Rhein 2,507........G1
Suhr 7,366...................F2
Sumiswald 5,070.............E2
Sursee 7,645.................F2
Tafers 2,263..................D3
Tavannes 3,336..............D2
Teufen 5,027.................H2
Thal 4,725....................H2
Thalwil 15,412................G2
Thayngen 3,751..............G1
Therwil 7,311.................E1
Thun 36,891.................E3
Thunstetten 2,567............E2
Thusis 3,605..................H3
Tramelan 4,733..............D2
Turbenthal 2,975.............G2
Uetendorf 4,538..............E3
Unterägeri 5,371.............G2
Unterkulm 2,558..............F2
Unterseen 4,568..............E3
Uster 23,702.................G2
Utzenstorf 3,141.............E2
Uznach 4,269.................H2
Uzwil 9,614...................H2
Vallorbe 3,375................B3
Vechigen 4,036..............E3
Versoix 7,483.................B4
Vevey 16,139.................C4
Vevey-Montreux 60,558......C4
Villars-sur-Glâne 5,788.......D3
Villeneuve 3,573..............C4
Visp 6,383....................E4
Wädenswil 18,485............G2
Wängi 2,909..................G2
Wahlern 5,104................D3
Wald 7,447...................H2
Waldkirch 2,622..............H2
Walenstadt 3,605............H2
Wallisellen 10,887...........G2
Wartau 3,692................H2

Wattwil 7,874.................H2
Weinfelden 8,793.............H1
Wettingen 18,377............F2
Wetzikon 15,859..............G2
Wil 16,245....................H2
Willisau 2,639.................F2
Windisch 7,598...............F1
Winterthur 86,758............G1
Wohlen 12,024...............F2
Wohlen 15,746...............G2
Wohlen bei Bern 7,666.......D3
Wohlusen 3,670..............E2
Worb 11,080.................E3
Wünnewil 3,774..............D3
Yverdon 20,802..............C3
Zell 4,138.....................G2
Zermatt 3,548................E4
Zofingen 8,643...............E2
Zollikofen 8,717..............D3
Zollikon 12,134...............F2
Zug 21,609...................G2
Zürich 369,522...............F2
Zurzach 3,068................F1
Zweisimmen 2,852...........D3

OTHER FEATURES

Aa (riv.).......................F3
Aare (riv.)....................E2
Ägerisee (lake)...............G2
Aiguille d'Argentière (mt.)....C5
Albristhorn (mt.).............D4
Aletschhorn (mt.)............F4
Allaine (riv.).................D2
Areuse (riv.).................C3
Aroser Rothorn (mt.).........J3
Ault (peak)...................H3
Baldeggersee (lake)..........F2
Balmhorn (mt.)...............E4
Bärenhorn (mt.)..............H3
Basodino (mt.)...............G4
Bernese Oberland (reg.)......E3
Bernina (mts.)................J4
Bernina (pass)...............K4
Bernina (peak)...............J4
Bernina (riv.).................J4
Beverin (peak)...............H3
Bielersee (lake)..............D2
Bietschhorn (mt.).............E4
Birs (riv.)....................D2
Blas (peak)...................G3
Blinnenhorn (mt.).............F4
Blümlisalp (mt.)..............E3
Bodensee (Constance) (lake).H1
Borgne (riv.).................D4
Breithorn (mt.)...............E5
Breithorn (mt.)...............E4
Brienzer Rothorn (mt.)........F3
Brienzersee (lake)............E3
Broye (riv.)...................C3
Brule (riv.)...................C3
Buchegg (mts.)...............E3
Buin (peak)...................K3
Bürkelkopf (mt.)..............K3
Bütschelegg (mt.)............D3
Calancasca (riv.).............G4
Campo Tencia (peak)..........G4
Ceneri (mt.)..................G4
Chasseron (mt.)..............C3
Chéserv, Pointe de (mt.)......C4
Cheville (pass)...............D4
Churfirsten (mts.)............H2
Clariden (mt.)................G3
Collon (mt.)..................D5
Constance (Bodensee) (lake).H1
Cornettes de Bise (mts.)......C4
Dammastock (mt.).............F3
Davos (valley)................J3
Dent Blanche (mt.)...........D4
Dent de Lys (mt.).............C4
Dent de Ruth (mt.)............D3
Dent d'Hérens (mt.)..........E5
Dents du Midi (mt.)...........C4
Diablerets (mt.)..............D4

Doldenhorn (mt.)..............E4
Dolent (mt.)..................C5
Dom (mt.)....................E4
Doubs (riv.)..................C2
Drance (riv.).................D4
Dufourspitze (mt.)............E5
Emmental (riv.)...............E3
Engadine (valley).............K3
Err (peak)....................J3
Finsteraarhorn (mt.)..........F3
Finstermünz (pass)...........K3
Fluchthorn (mt.)..............K3
Fluhberg (peak)..............F4
Fort (mt.)....................D4
Friesberg (mt.)...............F3
Furka (pass).................F3
Gelgia (riv.).................H3
Generoso (mt.)...............H5
Geneva (lake)................C4
Giacomo (pass)..............G4

Gibloux (mt.).................D3
Glâne (riv.)..................C3
Glärnisch (mt.)...............H3
Glarus Alps (mts.)............H3
Glatt (riv.)...................G2
Goms (valley)................F4
Grand Combin (mt.)..........D5
Grand Muveran (mt.)..........D4
Grande Dixence (dam)........D4
Grauehörner (mts.)...........H3
Great Saint Bernard (mt.)....D5
Great Saint Bernard (pass)...D5
Great Saint Bernard (tunnel)..D5
Greifensee (lake).............G2
Greina (pass)................G3
Gridone (mt.)................G4
Grimsel (pass)...............F3
Gross Emme (riv.)............E2
Gross Litzner (mt.)...........K3
Hallwilersee (lake)...........F2
Hausstock (mt.)..............H3
Helsenhorn (mt.).............F4

Hinterrhein (riv.)............H3
Hochwang (mt.)..............J3
Hohenstollen (mt.)...........F3
Honegg (mt.)................F3
Hörnli (mt.)..................G2
Ilfis (riv.)...................E3
Inn (riv.)....................K3
Joch (pass)..................F3
Jorat (mt.)...................C3
Joux (lake)..................B3
Jungfrau (mt.)...............E3
Jura (mts.)..................B3
Kaiseregg (mt.)..............D3
Kesch (peak)................J3
Kisten (pass)................H3
Klausen (pass)..............G3
Kleine Emme (riv.)...........F3
La Berra (mt.)...............D3
La Dôle (mt.)................B4
Landquart (riv.).............J3
Le Chasseral (mt.)...........D2
Le Gros Crêt (mt.)...........B3

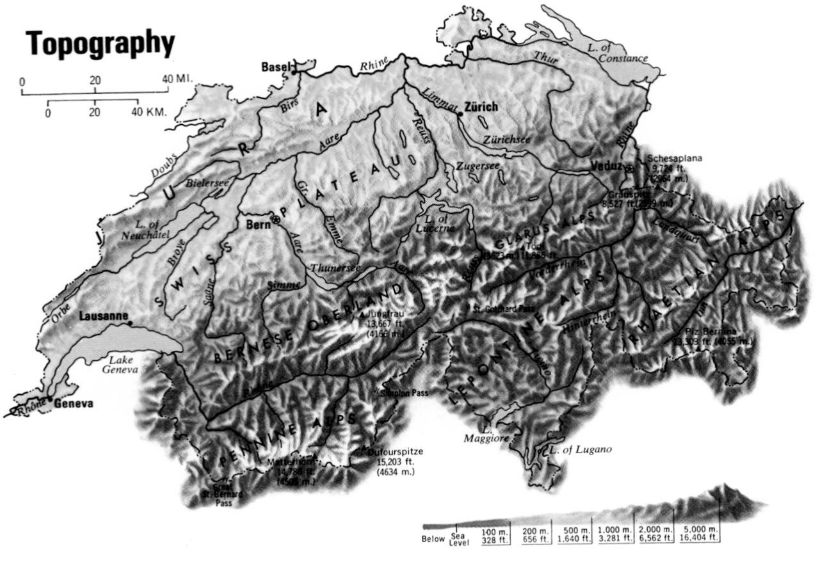

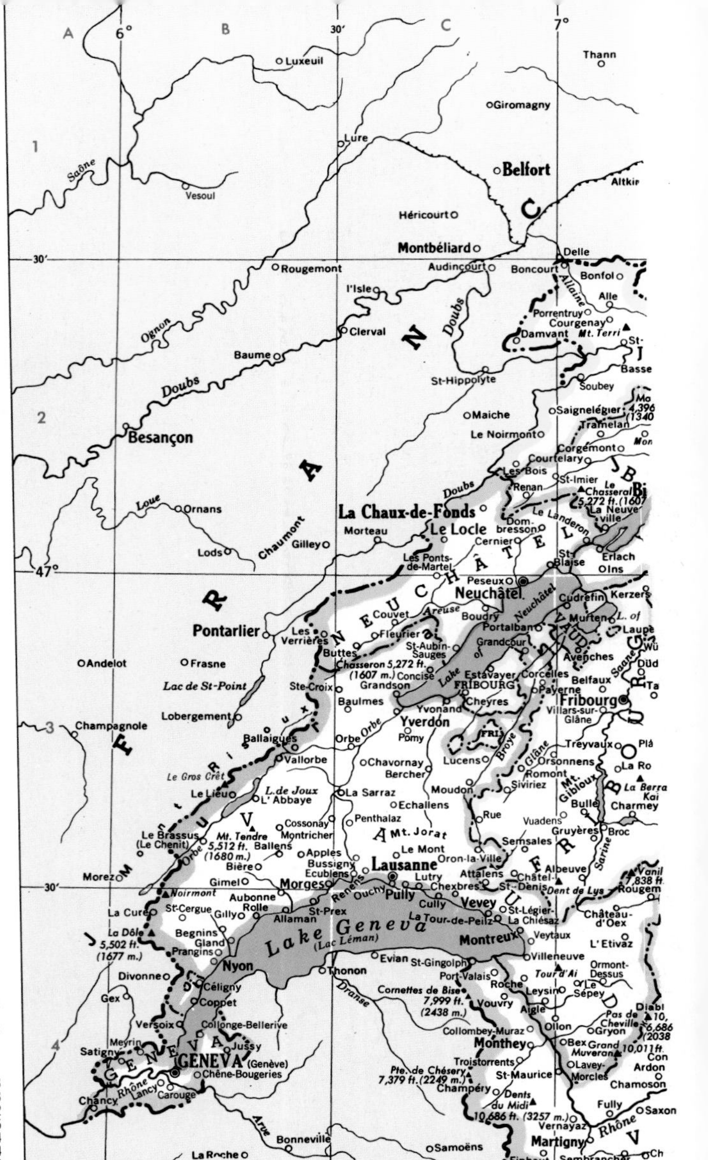

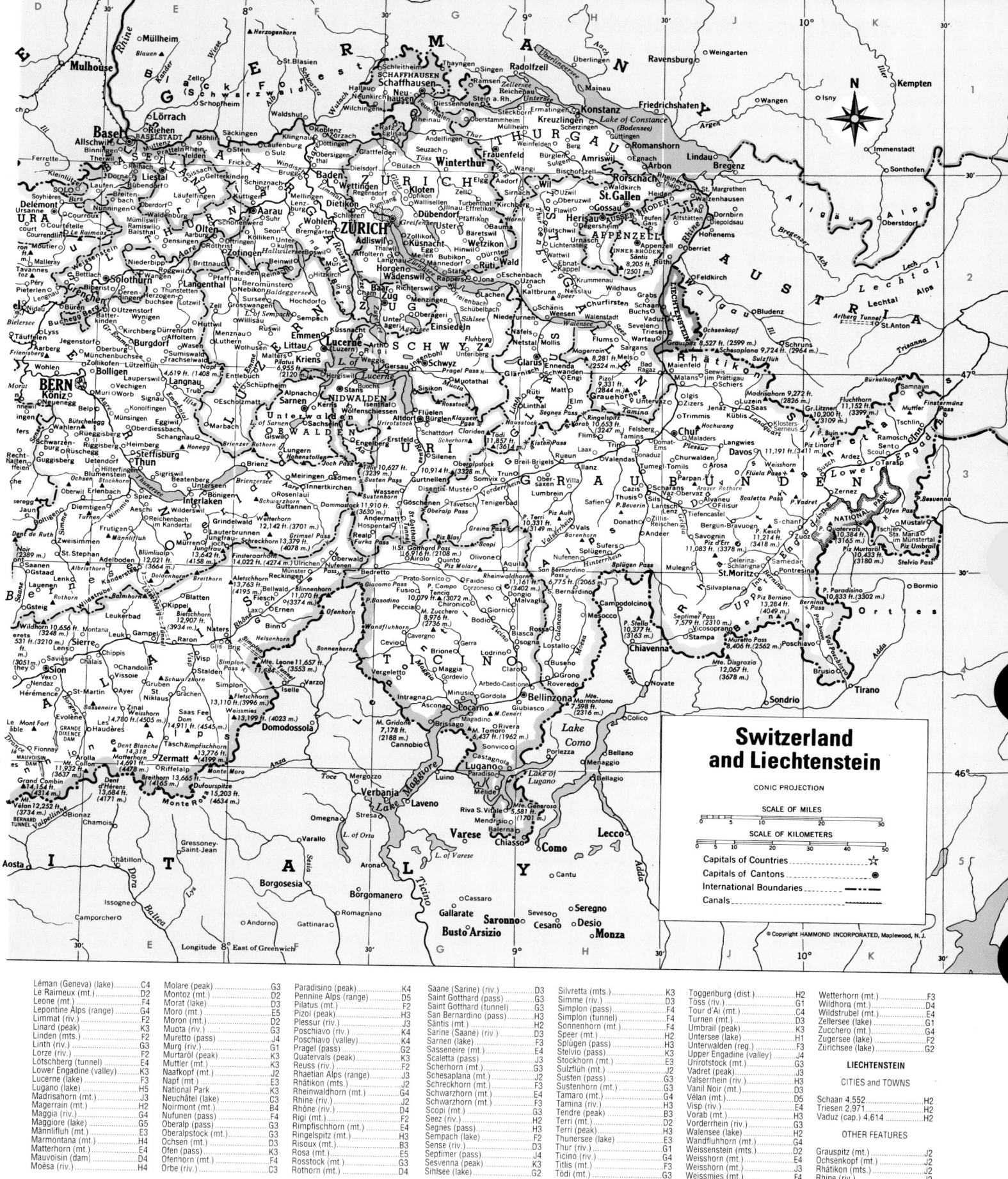

Switzerland and Liechtenstein

CONIC PROJECTION

SCALE OF MILES

SCALE OF KILOMETERS

Capitals of Countries .... ☆
Capitals of Cantons .... ●
International Boundaries .... — · —
Canals ....

© Copyright HAMMOND INCORPORATED, Maplewood, N.J.

Léman (Geneva) (lake)............C4
Le Raimeux (mt.)............D2
Leone (mt.)............F4
Lepontine Alps (range)............G4
Limmat (riv.)............F2
Linard (peak)............K3
Linden (mts.)............F2
Linth (riv.)............G3
Lorze (riv.)............F2
Lötschberg (tunnel)............E4
Lower Engadine (valley)............K3
Lucerne (lake)............F3
Lugano (lake)............H5
Madrisahorn (mt.)............J3
Magerrain (mt.)............H2
Maggia (riv.)............G4
Maggiore (lake)............G5
Männlifluh (mt.)............E3
Marmontana (mt.)............H4
Matterhorn (mt.)............E4
Mauvoisin (dam)............D4
Moësa (riv.)............H4

Molare (peak)............G3
Montoz (mt.)............D2
Morat (lake)............D3
Moro (mt.)............E5
Moron (mt.)............D2
Muota (riv.)............G3
Muretto (pass)............J4
Murg (riv.)............G1
Murtaröl (peak)............K3
Muttler (mt.)............K3
Naafkopf (mt.)............J2
Napf (mt.)............E3
National Park............K3
Neuchâtel (lake)............C3
Noirmont (mt.)............D2
Nufenen (pass)............F4
Oberalp (pass)............G3
Oberalpstock (mt.)............G3
Ochsen (mt.)............D3
Ofen (pass)............K3
Ofenhorn (mt.)............F4
Orbe (riv.)............C3

Paradisino (peak)............K4
Pennine Alps (range)............D5
Pilatus (mt.)............F2
Pizol (peak)............H3
Plessur (riv.)............J3
Poschiavo (riv.)............K4
Poschiavo (valley)............K4
Pragel (pass)............G3
Quatervals (peak)............K3
Reuss (riv.)............F2
Rhaetian Alps (range)............J3
Rhätikon (mts.)............J2
Rheinwaldhorn (mt.)............G4
Rhine (riv.)............F3
Rhône (riv.)............D4
Rigi (mt.)............F3
Rimpfischhorn (mt.)............E4
Ringelspitz (mt.)............H3
Risoux (mt.)............B3
Rosa (mt.)............E5
Rosstock (mt.)............G3
Rothorn (mt.)............D4

Saane (Sarine) (riv.)............D3
Saint Gotthard (pass)............G3
Saint Gotthard (tunnel)............G3
San Bernardino (pass)............H3
Säntis (mt.)............H2
Sarine (Saane) (riv.)............D3
Sarnen (lake)............F3
Sasseneire (mt.)............E4
Scaletta (pass)............J3
Scherhorn (mt.)............G3
Schesaplana (mt.)............J2
Schreckhorn (mt.)............F3
Schwarzhorn (mt.)............E4
Schwarzhorn (mt.)............F3
Scopi (mt.)............G3
Seez (riv.)............H2
Segnes (pass)............H3
Sempach (lake)............F2
Sense (riv.)............D3
Septimer (pass)............J4
Sesvenna (peak)............K3
Sihlsee (lake)............G3

Silvretta (mts.)............K3
Simme (riv.)............E4
Simplon (pass)............F4
Simplon (tunnel)............F4
Sonnenhorn (mt.)............F4
Speer (mt.)............H2
Splügen (pass)............H3
Stelvio (pass)............K4
Stockhorn (mt.)............E3
Sulzfluh (mt.)............J2
Susten (pass)............G3
Sustenhorn (mt.)............G3
Tamaro (mt.)............G4
Tamina (riv.)............H3
Tendre (peak)............C3
Terri (mt.)............H3
Terri (mt.)............G3
Thunersee (lake)............E3
Thur (riv.)............G1
Ticino (riv.)............G4
Titlis (mt.)............F3
Tödi (mt.)............G3

Toggenburg (dist.)............H2
Töss (riv.)............G1
Tour d'Ai (mt.)............D3
Turnen (mt.)............D3
Umbrail (peak)............K3
Untersee (lake)............H1
Unterwalden (reg.)............F3
Upper Engadine (valley)............J4
Urirotstock (mt.)............G3
Vadret (peak)............J3
Valserrhein (riv.)............G4
Vanil Noir (mt.)............D3
Vélan (mt.)............D5
Visp (riv.)............E4
Vorab (mt.)............H3
Vorderrhein (riv.)............G4
Wandfluhhorn (mt.)............G4
Walensee (lake)............H2
Weissenstein (mts.)............D2
Weisshorn (mt.)............E4
Weisshorn (mt.)............J3
Weissmies (mt.)............F4

Wetterhorn (mt.)............F3
Wildhorn (mt.)............D4
Wildstrubel (mt.)............E4
Zellersee (lake)............G1
Zucchero (mt.)............G4
Zugersee (lake)............F2
Zürichsee (lake)............G2

LIECHTENSTEIN

CITIES and TOWNS

Schaan 4,552............H2
Triesen 2,971............H2
Vaduz (cap.) 4,614............H2

OTHER FEATURES

Grauspitz (mt.)............J2
Ochsenkopf (mt.)............J2
Rhätikon (mts.)............J2
Rhine (riv.)............J2

AUSTRIA

PROVINCES

Burgenland 272,274 ....D3
Carinthia 536,727 ....B3
Lower Austria 1,439,137 ....C2
Salzburg 441,842 ....B3
Styria 1,187,512 ....C3
Tirol 586,139 ....A3
Upper Austria 1,270,426 ....B2
Vienna (city) 1,515,666 ....D2
Vorarlberg 305,615 ....A3

CITIES and TOWNS†

Altheim 4,702 ....B2
Althofen 22,015 ....C3
Amstetten 22,015 ....C2
Arnoldstein 6,641 ....B3
Attnang-Puchheim 8,058 ....B2
Bad Aussee 5,047 ....B3
Bad Goisern 6,500 ....B3
Bad Hofgastein 5,960 ....B3
Bad Ischl 13,027 ....B3
Bad Sankt-Leonhard im
  Lavanttal 5,008 ....B3
Baden 23,235 ....D2
Badgastein 5,600 ....B3
Berndorf 8,189 ....C3
Bischofshofen 9,520 ....B3
Bludenz 12,893 ....A3
Bramberg am Wildkogel
  3,410 ....B3
Braunau am Inn 16,192 ....B2
Bregenz 24,683 ....A3
Bruck an der Leitha 7,170 .....D2
Bruck an der Mur 15,086 ....C3
Deutsch Feistritz 3,719 ....C3
Deutschkreutz 3,563 ....D3
Deutsch Landsberg 7,623 ....C3

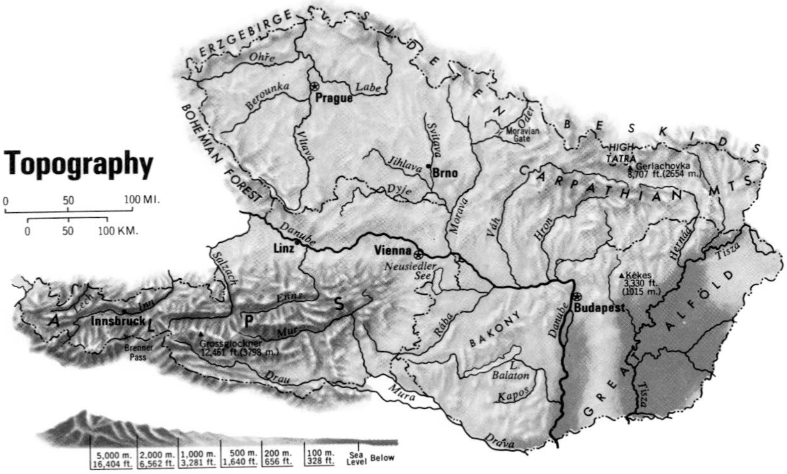

Deutsch Wagram 5,111 ....D2
Dornbirn 38,663 ....A3
Ebensee 9,005 ....B3
Eggenburg 3,729 ....C2
Eisenerz 10,074 ....C3
Eisenkappel-Vellach 3,520 .....C3
Eisenstadt 10,150 ....D3
Enns 9,731 ....C2
Feldbach 4,073 ....C3
Feldkirch 23,876 ....A3
Feldkirchen in Kärnten
  12,181 ....B3
Ferlach 7,658 ....C3
Fieberbrunn 3,926 ....B3
Fohnsdorf 10,360 ....C3
Frankenmarkt 3,166 ....B3
Friesach 7,074 ....C3
Freistadt 6,289 ....C2
Frohnleiten 5,061 ....C3
Fürstenfeld 6,040 ....C3
Gaming 4,099 ....C2
Gänserndorf 4,948 ....D2
Gleisdorf 5,078 ....C3
Gloggnitz 6,290 ....D3
Gmünd 6,457 ....B3
Gmunden 12,720 ....B3
Golling an der Salzach 3,409 ..B3
Götzis 8,740 ....A3
Graz 243,405 ....C3
Grieskirchen 4,813 ....B2
Grosssiegharts 3,374 ....C2
Grünburg 3,630 ....C3
Güssing 3,895 ....C3
Haag 5,095 ....C2
Hainburg an der Donau
  5,749 ....D2
Hainfeld 3,735 ....C2
Hallein 15,404 ....B3
Hartberg 6,048 ....C3
Heidenreichstein 5,351 ....C2
Heiligenblut 1,334 ....B3

Hermagor-Preseggersee
  7,116 ....B3
Herzogenburg 7,313 ....C2
Hohenems 12,669 ....A3
Hollabrunn 10,254 ....D2
Hopfgarten in Nordtirol
  4,956 ....B3
Horn 6,319 ....C2
Imst 6,691 ....A3
Innsbruck 116,110 ....A3
Jenbach 5,725 ....A3
Jennersdorf 4,131 ....C3
Judenburg 11,199 ....C3
Kapfenberg 25,719 ....C3
Kaprun 2,764 ....B3
Kindberg 6,269 ....C3
Kirchdorf an der Krems
  3,708 ....C3
Kitzbühel 7,872 ....B3
Klagenfurt 86,303 ....C3
Klosterneuburg 23,307 ....D2
Knittelfeld 14,153 ....C3
Köflach 12,009 ....C3
Kötschach-Mauthen 3,633 ....B3
Krems an der Donau 23,123 .....C2
Kufstein 13,125 ....B3
Laa an der Thaya 6,485 ....D2
Laakirchen 7,670 ....B3
Landeck 7,325 ....A3
Landskron 10,429 ....B3
Langenlois 6,572 ....C2
Langenwang 4,187 ....C3
Lavamünd 3,824 ....C3
Leibnitz 6,659 ....C3
Lenzing 5,079 ....B3
Leoben 32,006 ....C3
Lienz 11,699 ....B3
Liezen 7,021 ....C3
Lilienfeld 3,030 ....C2
Linz 197,962 ....C2

Lustenau 17,404 ....A3
Mannersdorf am
  Leithagebirge 3,878 ....D2
Marchegg 2,676 ....D2
Matrei in Osttirol 4,298 .....B3
Mattersburg 5,682 ....C3
Mattighofen 4,566 ....B2
Mauthausen 4,353 ....C2
Mauthen-Kötschach 3,633 ....B3
Mayrhofen 3,274 ....A3
Melk 5,074 ....C2
Mistelbach an der Zaya
  10,300 ....D2
Mittersill 5,033 ....B3
Mödling 19,333 ....D2
Mürzzuschlag 10,774 ....C3
Neumarkt am Wallersee
  3,703 ....B3
Neunkirchen 10,780 ....C3
Neusiedl am See 4,154 ....D3
Ober Grafendorf 4,475 ....C2
Oberndorf bei Salzburg 3,838 ..B3
Oberwart 5,973 ....D3
Oberwölz 9,510 ....C3
Paternion 5,914 ....B3
Perg 5,226 ....C2
Pinkafeld 4,802 ....D3
Pöchlarn 3,637 ....C2
Poysdorf 5,658 ....D2
Pregarten 3,823 ....C2
Raabs an der Thaya 3,839 ......C2
Radenthein 7,083 ....B3
Radstadt 3,994 ....B3
Rankweil 9,929 ....A3
Reichenau an der Rax 3,601 ....C3
Retz 4,373 ....C2
Reutte 5,145 ....A3
Ried im Innkreis 10,952 ....C2
Rottenmann 5,425 ....C3
Saalfelden am Steinernen
  Meer 11,436 ....B3

Salzburg 138,213 ....B3
Sankt Johann in Tirol 6,495 ...B3
Sankt Michael im Lungau
  3,246 ....B3
Sankt Michael in
  Obersteiermark 3,604 ....C3
Sankt Paul im Lavanttal
  5,770 ....C3
Sankt Pölten 51,102 ....C2
Sankt Valentin 8,759 ....C2
Sankt Veit an der Glan 12,021 .C3
Schärding 5,784 ....B2
Scheibbs 4,537 ....C2
Schladming 3,930 ....B3
Schrems 6,010 ....C2
Schwarzach im Pongau
  3,607 ....B3
Schwaz 18,859 ....A3
Schwechat 14,844 ....D2
Schwertberg 4,385 ....C2
Sierning 7,891 ....C2
Solbad Hall in Tirol 12,622 ...A3
Spittal an der Drau 14,769 ....B3
Steyr 38,967 ....C2
Stockerau 12,692 ....D2
Tamsweg 5,256 ....B3
Telfs 7,749 ....A3
Ternitz 16,154 ....D3
Traiskirchen 14,102 ....C2
Traun 21,524 ....C2
Trieben 4,471 ....C3
Trofaiach 8,959 ....C3
Tulln 11,287 ....C2
Velden am Wörthersee 7,458 ....C3
Vienna (cap.) 1,515,666 ....D2
Villach 52,744 ....B3
Vöcklabruck 11,039 ....B2
Voitsberg 110,951 ....C3
Völkermarkt 10,900 ....C3
Waidhofen an der Thaya
  5,401 ....C2

Waidhofen an der Ybbs
  11,339 ....C2
Weitensfeld-Flattnitz 5,158 ...C3
Weiz 8,418 ....C3
Wels 51,024 ....C2
Wien (Vienna) (cap.)
  1,515,666 ....D2
Wiener Neustadt 35,050 ....D3
Wilhelmsburg 6,339 ....C2
Wolfsberg 28,182 ....C3
Wörgl 8,644 ....B3
Ybbs an der Donau 5,983 ....C2
Zell am See 7,959 ....B3
Zeltweg 8,722 ....C3
Zistersdorf 5,814 ....D2
Zwettl-Niederösterreich
  11,579 ....C2

OTHER FEATURES

Allgü Alps (mts.) A3
Atter See (lake) B3
Bavarian Alps (mts.) A3
Bodensee (Constance) (lake) ...A3
Brenner (pass) A3
Carnic Alps (mts.) B3
Coglians (mt.) A3
Constance (lake) A3
Danube (riv.) D2
Donau (Danube) (riv.) C2
Drau (riv.) B3
Enns (riv.) C3
Greiner Wald (riv.) C2
Grosser Peilstein (mt.) C2
Grossglockner (mt.) B3
Hochgolling (mt.) B3
Hohe Tauern (range) B3
Hohe Warte (Coglians) (mt.) ...B3
Inn (riv.) B2
Kamp (riv.) C2
Karawanken (range) C3

Lafnitz (riv.) D3
March (riv.) D2
Mühlviertel (reg.) C2
Mur (riv.) C3
Mürz (riv.) C3
Neusiedler See (lake) D3
Niedere Tauern (range) B3
Olsa (riv.) B3
Ötztal Alps (mts.) A3
Parseierspitze (mt.) A3
Raab (riv.) C3
Rhine (riv.) A3
Salzach (riv.) B2
Salzkammergut (reg.) C3
Semmering (pass) C3
Thaya (riv.) C2
Traun (riv.) C2
Traun See (lake) B3
Wildspitze (mt.) A3
Zugspitze (mt.) A3

CZECHOSLOVAKIA

REPUBLICS

Czech Rep. 10,291,927 ....B1
Slovak Rep. 4,991,168 ....E2

REGIONS

Bratislava (city) 380,259 .....D2
Jihočeský 689,229 ....C2
Jihomoravský 2,040,903 ....C1
Praha (city) 1,182,186 ....C1
Severočeský 1,167,231 ....C1
Severomoravský 1,932,722 ......D2
Středočeský 1,151,265 ....C2
Středoslovenský
  1,524,766 ....E2
Východočeský
  1,248,466 ....C1
Východoslovenský
  1,402,252 ....F2
Západočeský 879,925 ....B2
Západoslovenský 1,683,891 .....D2

CITIES and TOWNS

Aš 13,551 ....B1
Austerlitz (Slavkov) 6,316 ....C2
Bánovce nad Bebravou
  15,342 ....E2
Banská Bystrica 66,412 ....E2
Banská Štiavnica 9,180 ....E2
Bardejov 23,741 ....F2

Beneśov 15,172 ....C2
Beroun 23,580 ....B2
Bílina 18,836 ....B1
Blansko 19,508 ....C2
Blatná 7,247 ....B2
Boskovice 12,025 ....C2
Brandýs nad Labem-Stará
  Boleslav 15,071 ....C1
Bratislava 380,259 ....D2
Břeclav 23,978 ....C2
Brezno 17,872 ....E2
Brno 371,463 ....C2
Broumov 7,834 ....D1
Bruntál 17,062 ....D1
Bystřice nad Pernštejnem
  10,044 ....C2
Bystřice pod Hostýnem
  10,359 ....D2
Bytča 11,789 ....E2
Čadca 19,319 ....D3
Čalovo 8,063 ....D3
Čáslav 9,950 ....C2
Česká Kamenice 7,272 ....C1
Česká Lípa 24,924 ....C1
Česká Třebová 17,136 ....C2
České Budějovice 90,415 ....C2
Český Krumlov 13,776 ....C2
(continued)

Topography

0   50   100 MI.
0   50   100 KM.

5,000 m. 2,000 m. 1,000 m. 500 m. 200 m. 100 m. Sea Below
16,404 ft. 6,562 ft. 3,281 ft. 1,640 ft. 656 ft. 328 ft. Level

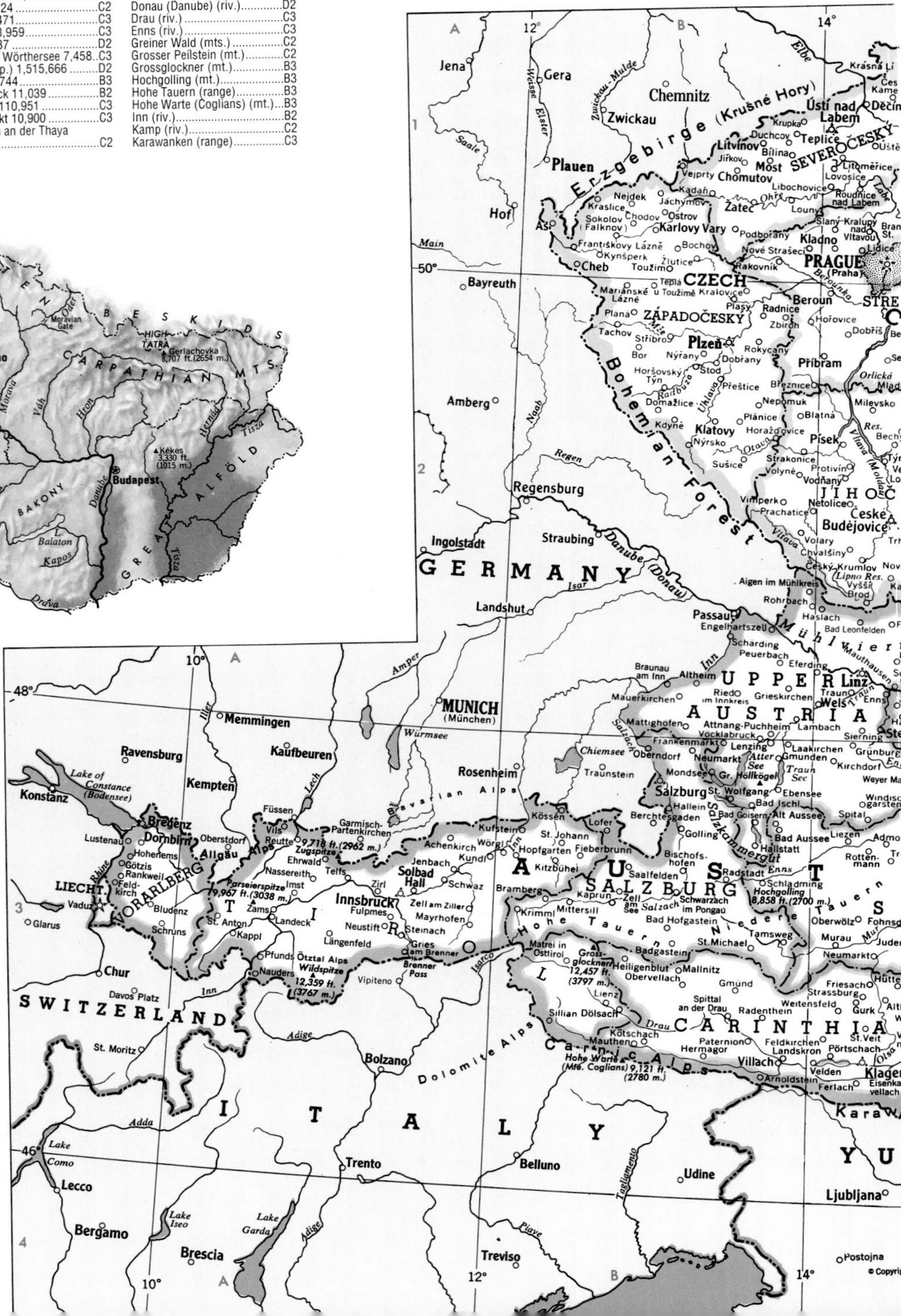

AREA 32,375 sq. mi, (83,851 sq. km.)
POPULATION 7,635,000
CAPITAL Vienna
LARGEST CITY Vienna
HIGHEST POINT Grossglockner
   12,457 ft. (3,797 m.)
MONETARY UNIT schilling
MAJOR LANGUAGE German
MAJOR RELIGION Roman Catholicism

AREA 49,373 sq. mi. (127,876 sq. km.)
POPULATION 15,679,000
CAPITAL Prague
LARGEST CITY Prague
HIGHEST POINT Gerlachovka 8,707 ft.
   (2,654 m.)
MONETARY UNIT koruna
MAJOR LANGUAGES Czech, Slovak
MAJOR RELIGIONS Roman Catholicism,
   Protestantism

AREA 35,919 sq. mi. (93,030 sq. km.)
POPULATION 10,553,000
CAPITAL Budapest
LARGEST CITY Budapest
HIGHEST POINT Kékes 3,330 ft.
   (1,015 m.)
MONETARY UNIT forint
MAJOR LANGUAGE Hungarian
MAJOR RELIGIONS Roman Catholicism,
   Protestantism

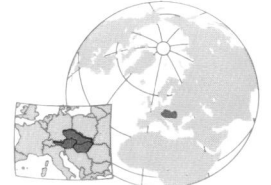

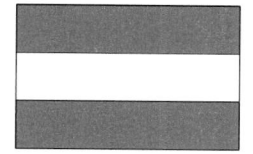

AUSTRIA

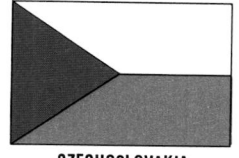

CZECHOSLOVAKIA

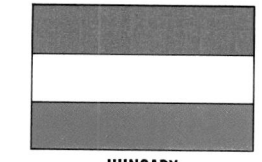

HUNGARY

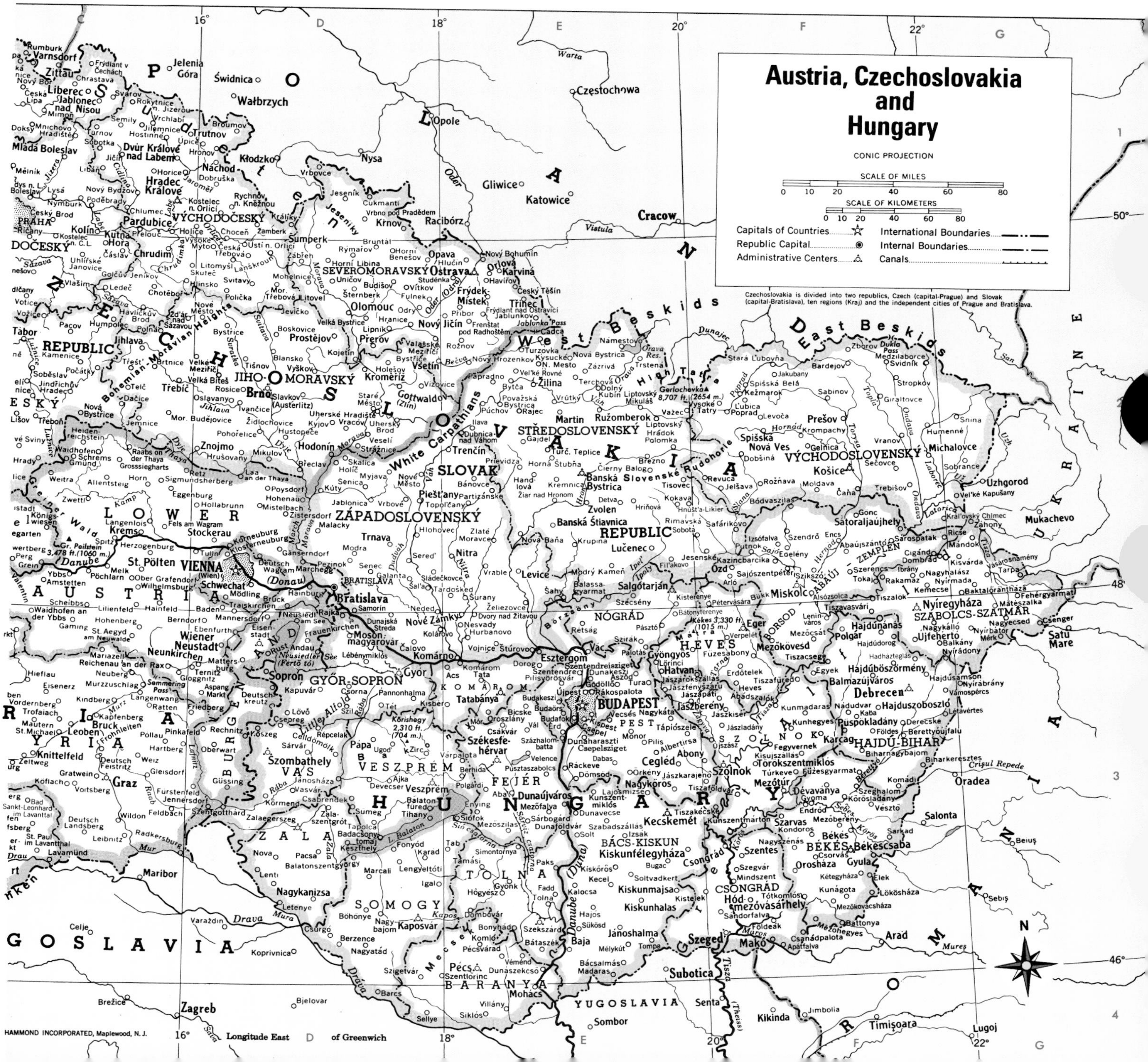

Austria, Czechoslovakia and Hungary

CONIC PROJECTION

SCALE OF MILES
0 10 20   40   60   80

SCALE OF KILOMETERS
0 10 20   40   60   80

Capitals of Countries........ ☆
Republic Capital............... ◉
Administrative Centers...... △

International Boundaries........
Internal Boundaries..............
Canals..................................

Czechoslovakia is divided into two republics, Czech (capital-Prague) and Slovak
(capital-Bratislava), ten regions (Kraj) and the independent cities of Prague and Bratislava.

HAMMOND INCORPORATED, Maplewood, N.J.   Longitude East   of Greenwich

(continued)

Český Těšín 23,389 ... E2
Cheb 31,039 ... B1
Chodov 14,704 ... B1
Chomutov 51,769 ... B1
Chotěboř 8,744 ... C2
Chrastava 7,022 ... C1
Chrudim 20,517 ... C2
Dačice 7,443 ... C2
Děčín 49,682 ... C1
Detva 14,261 ... E2
Dobříš 7,466 ... C2
Dolný Kubín 13,971 ... E2
Domažlice 11,461 ... B2
Dubnica nad Váhom 15,580 ... E2
Duchcov 10,554 ... B1
Dunajská Streda 18,715 ... D3
Dvůr Králové nad Labem 17,270 ... C1
Falknov (Sokolov) 28,523 ... B1
Fil'akovo 10,497 ... E2
Frenštát pod Radhoště 10,434 ... E2
Frýdek-Místek 59,430 ... E2
Frýdlant nad Ostravicí 14,065 ... E2
Frýdlant v. Čechách 7,418 ... C1
Fulnek 8,214 ... D2
Galanta 15,477 ... D2
Gottwaldov 83,983 ... D2
Handlová 17,777 ... E2
Havířov 89,920 ... E2
Havlíčkuv Brod 24,550 ... C2
Hlinsko 10,635 ... C2
Hlohovec 21,148 ... D2
Hlučín 22,581 ... E2
Hodonín 25,485 ... D2
Holešov 13,323 ... D2
Holíč 8,741 ... D2
Hořice v Podkrkonoší 9,251 ... C1
Hradec Králové 95,588 ... C1
Hranice 18,099 ... D2
Hriňová 8,485 ... E2
Hronov 9,609 ... D1
Humenné 27,285 ... F2
Humpolec 10,042 ... C2
Hurbanovo 7,613 ... E3
Ivančice 9,746 ... D2
Jablonec nad Nisou 42,179 ... C1
Jablunkov 15,962 ... E2
Jaroměř 11,562 ... C1
Jeseník 14,314 ... D1
Jičín 16,440 ... C1
Jihlava 51,144 ... C2
Jindřichuv Hradec 20,096 ... C2
Jiřkov 11,980 ... B1
Kadăn 18,420 ... B1
Karlovy Vary 60,950 ... B1
Karviná 78,334 ... E2
Kežmarok 17,570 ... F2
Kladno 71,141 ... B1
Klatovy 21,782 ... B2
Kojetín 8,881 ... D2
Kolárovo 11,295 ... D3
Kolín 30,921 ... C1
Komárno 32,520 ... D3
Košice 202,368 ... F2
Kralupy nad Vltavou 17,528 ... C1
Kraslice 7,371 ... B1
Kremnica 7,168 ... E2
Krnov 25,678 ... D1
Kroměříž 25,887 ... D2
Krupina 7,337 ... E2
Krupka 9,336 ... B1
Kutná Hora 20,927 ... C2
Kyjov 12,632 ... D2
Kysucké Nové Mesto 14,083 ... E2
Lanškroun 10,620 ... D2
Levice 26,132 ... E2
Levoča 11,025 ... F2
Liberec 97,474 ... C1
Lidice ... C1
Lipník nad Bečvou 9,961 ... D2
Liptovský Hrádok 9,197 ... E2
Liptovský Mikuláš 24,520 ... E2
Litoměřice 23,835 ... C1
Litomyšl 10,079 ... D2
Litovel 12,454 ... D2
Litvínov 22,624 ... B1
Louny 20,436 ... B1
Lovosice 11,456 ... C1
Lučenec 26,399 ... E2
Lysá nad Labem 9,113 ... C1
Malacky 15,218 ... D2
Mariánské Lázně 17,932 ... B2
Martin 56,208 ... E2
Mělník 18,941 ... C1
Michalovce 29,765 ... F2
Mikulov 8,472 ... D2
Milevsko 8,852 ... C2
Mimoň 7,437 ... C1
Mladá Boleslav 45,896 ... C1
Mnichovo Hradiště 7,340 ... C1
Modra 7,679 ... D2
Mohelnice 9,405 ... D2
Moravská Třebová 11,543 ... D2
Moravské Budějovice 8,943 ... C2
Most 60,119 ... B1
Myjava 11,668 ... D2
Náchod 19,892 ... D1
Nejdek 9,768 ... B1
Nitra 76,663 ... E2
Nová Baňa 8,321 ... E2
Nové Město na Moravě 11,330 ... D2
Nové Město nad Váhom 18,170 ... D2
Nové Zámky 34,147 ... D3
Nový Bohumín 16,700 ... E2
Nový Bor 10,493 ... C1
Nový Bydžov 9,317 ... C1
Nový Jičín 31,506 ... D2
Nymburk 14,033 ... C1
Odry 10,032 ... D2
Olomouc 102,112 ... D2
Opava 59,384 ... D2
Orlová 31,190 ... E2
Ostrava 322,073 ... E2
Ostrov 19,618 ... B1
Pardubice 91,855 ... C1
Partizánske 23,266 ... E2
Pezinok 17,116 ... D2
Piešt'any 30,487 ... D2
Písek 28,104 ... C2
Plzeň 170,701 ... B2
Poděbrady 13,782 ... C1
Pohořelice 5,125 ... D2
Polička 8,972 ... D2
Poprad 38,077 ... F2
Považská Bystrica 30,444 ... E2
Prachatice 10,354 ... B2
Prague (Praha) (cap.) 1,182,186 ... C1
Přelouč 8,561 ... C1
Přerov 50,265 ... D2
Prešov 71,500 ... F2
Příbor 12,711 ... E2
Příbram 37,854 ... C2
Prievidza 40,813 ... E2
Prostějov 49,599 ... D2
Púchov 17,554 ... E2
Rakovník 16,233 ... B1
Revúca 11,881 ... F2
Říčany u Prahy 10,703 ... C2
Rimavská Sobota 19,699 ... E2
Rokycany 15,041 ... B2
Roudnice nad Labem 13,956 ... C1
Rožňava 18,039 ... F2
Rožnov pod Radhoštěm 15,468 ... E2
Rumburk 10,255 ... C1
Ružomberok 26,396 ... E2
Rychnov nad Kněžnou 8,955 ... D1
Rýmařov 9,927 ... D2
Sabinov 7,008 ... F2
Šafárikovo 7,021 ... F2
Šahy 8,034 ... E2
Šal'a 19,167 ... D2
Samorín 9,677 ... D2
Sedlčany 7,453 ... C2
Semily 8,464 ... C1
Senec 10,772 ... D2
Senica 15,515 ... D2
Sereď 16,071 ... D2
Skalica 13,833 ... D2
Slaný 14,705 ... C1
Slavkov 6,316 ... D2
Snina 13,347 ... G2
Soběslav 8,406 ... C2
Sokolov 28,523 ... B1
Spišská Nová Ves 31,917 ... F2
Staré Město 6,293 ... D2
Šternberk 16,342 ... D2
Strakonice 22,611 ... B2
Stříbro 8,169 ... B2
Stropkov 7,405 ... F2
Studénka 12,497 ... E2
Štúrovo 12,807 ... E3
Šumperk 31,873 ... D2
Šurany 11,320 ... E2
Sušice 11,400 ... B2
Svidník 7,538 ... F2
Svitavy 19,075 ... D2
Tábor 31,867 ... C2
Tachov 12,798 ... B2
Teplice 53,964 ... B1
Tišnov 12,179 ... D2
Topol'čany 31,340 ... E2
Třebíč 30,246 ... C2
Trebišov 14,961 ... F2
Třeboň 8,878 ... C2
Trenčín 47,887 ... E2
Třinec 44,739 ... E2
Trnava 64,062 ... D2
Trutnov 27,648 ... C1
Turnov 13,906 ... C1
Turzovka 6,962 ... E2
Ústí nad Labem 87,909 ... C1
Ústí nad Orlicí 15,945 ... D2
Uherské Hradiště 36,756 ... D2
Uherský Brod 17,459 ... D2
Uničov 12,507 ... D2
Valašské Meziříčí 26,531 ... D2
Varnsdorf 16,356 ... C1
Vel'ké Kapušany 8,459 ... G2
Velké Meziříčí 14,073 ... D2
Veselí nad Moravou 12,464 ... D2
Vimperk 7,257 ... B2
Vítkov 7,543 ... D2
Vlašim 13,284 ... C2
Vodňany 6,989 ... C2
Vráble 7,586 ... E2
Vranov nad Teplou 18,423 ... F2
Vrbno pod Pradědem 6,912 ... D1
Vrchlabí 12,419 ... C1
Vsetín 29,927 ... D2
Vyškov 18,330 ... D2
Vysoké Mýto 10,887 ... D2
Zábřeh 15,184 ... D2
Žatec 19,529 ... B1
Žďár nad Sázavou 25,015 ... C2
Žiar nad Hronom 19,098 ... E2
Žilina 83,016 ... E2
Zlaté Moravce 14,119 ... E2
Zlín (Gottwaldov) 83,983 ... D2
Znojmo 39,271 ... D2
Zvolen 36,538 ... E2

OTHER FEATURES

Bečva (riv.) ... E2
Berounka (riv.) ... C2
Beskids, East (mts.) ... F1
Beskids, West (mts.) ... E2
Bohemian (for.) ... B2
Bohemian-Moravian Heights (hills) ... C2
Chrudimka (riv.) ... C2
Cidlina (riv.) ... C1
Danube (riv.) ... C2
Dudvá (riv.) ... D2
Dukla (pass) ... F2
Dunajec (riv.) ... F2
Dyje (riv.) ... D2
Erzgebirge (mts.) ... B1
Gerlachovka (mt.) ... F2
Hornád (riv.) ... F2
Hron (riv.) ... E2
Ipel' (riv.) ... E2
Jablunka (pass) ... E2
Jeseniky (mts.) ... D1
Jihlava (riv.) ... D2
Jizera (riv.) ... C1
Krušné Hory (Erzgebirge) (mts.) ... B1
Labe (riv.) ... C1
Laborec (riv.) ... F2
Latorica (riv.) ... F2
Lipno (res.) ... C2
Lužnice (riv.) ... C2
Moldau (Vltava) (riv.) ... C2
Morava (riv.) ... D2
Mže (riv.) ... B2
Nitra (riv.) ... E2
Oder (Odra) (riv.) ... D2
Ohře (riv.) ... B1
Ondava (riv.) ... F2
Orava (riv.) ... E2
Orava (riv.) ... E2
Orlice (riv.) ... D1
Orlická (res.) ... C2
Otava (riv.) ... B2
Poprad (riv.) ... F2
Radbuza (riv.) ... B2
Sázava (riv.) ... C2
Slaná (riv.) ... F2
Slovenské Rudohorie (mts.) ... E2
Sudeten (mts.) ... C1
Svitava (riv.) ... D2
Svratka (riv.) ... D2
Tatra, High (riv.) ... F2
Topl'a (riv.) ... F2
Torysa (riv.) ... F2
Úhlava (riv.) ... B2
Už (riv.) ... G2
Váh (riv.) ... D2
Vltava (riv.) ... C2
White Carpathians (mts.) ... E2

HUNGARY

COUNTIES

Bács-Kiskun 553,000 ... E3
Baranya 434,000 ... E4
Békés 416,000 ... F3
Borsod-Abaúj-Zemplén 779,000 ... F2
Budapest (city) 2,104,000 ... E3
Csongrád 457,000 ... F3
Fejér 426,000 ... E3
Győr-Sopron 426,000 ... D3
Hajdú-Bihar 549,000 ... F3
Heves 338,000 ... F3
Komárom 320,000 ... E3
Nógrád 229,000 ... E3
Pest 988,000 ... E3
Somogy 349,000 ... D3
Szabolcs-Szatmár 570,000 ... G3
Szolnok 428,000 ... F3
Tolna 263,000 ... E3
Vas 277,000 ... D3
Veszprém 387,000 ... D3
Zala 311,000 ... D3

CITIES and TOWNS

Abádszalók 6,386 ... F3
Abaújszántó 4,209 ... F2
Abony 15,624 ... E3
Ács 8,423 ... E3
Ajka 34,000 ... D3
Albertirsa 11,252 ... E3
Alsózsolca 5,045 ... F2
Bácsalmás 8,000 ... E3
Baja 41,000 ... E3
Balassagyarmat 20,000 ... E2
Balatonfüred 15,000 ... D3
Balkány 7,667 ... F3
Balmazújváros 17,371 ... F3
Barcs 12,000 ... D4
Bátaszék 7,274 ... E3
Battonya 9,324 ... F3
Békés 22,000 ... F3
Békéscsaba 71,000 ... F3
Berettyóújfalu 18,000 ... F3
Bicske 13,000 ... E3
Bonyhád 15,000 ... E3
Budafok 40,623 ... E3
Budakeszi 10,429 ... E3
Budaörs 22,000 ... E3
Budapest (cap.) 2,104,000 ... E3
Cegléd 40,000 ... E3
Celldömölk 12,000 ... D3
Csepel 71,693 ... E3
Csongrád 21,000 ... F3
Csorna 13,000 ... D3
Dabas 13,075 ... E3
Debrecen 217,000 ... F3
Derecske 9,579 ... F3
Dévaványa 11,208 ... F3
Dombóvár 21,000 ... E3
Dorog 13,000 ... E3
Dunaföldvár 10,318 ... E3
Dunaharaszti 15,788 ... E3
Dunakeszi 29,000 ... E3
Dunaújváros 62,000 ... E3
Edelény 12,000 ... F2
Eger 67,000 ... F3
Egyek 7,956 ... F3
Endrőd 8,136 ... F3
Enying 7,518 ... E3
Érd 44,904 ... E3
Esztergom 30,476 ... E3
Fegyvernek 8,421 ... F3
Fehérgyarmat 9,000 ... G3
Füzesgyarmat 7,097 ... F3
Gödöllő 30,000 ... E3
Gyöngyös 36,000 ... E3
Gyoma 10,392 ... F3
Győr 131,000 ... D3
Gyula 36,000 ... F3
Hadházteglás 13,626 ... F3
Hajdúboszormény 31,000 ... F3
Hajdúdorog 10,118 ... F3
Hajdúnánás 18,000 ... F3
Hajdúsámson 7,492 ... F3
Hajdúszoboszló 24,000 ... F3
Hatvan 25,000 ... E3
Heves 11,000 ... F3
Hódmezővásárhely 54,000 ... F3
Izsák 7,686 ... E3
Jánoshalma 12,534 ... E3
Jászapáti 10,424 ... F3
Jászárokszállás 10,139 ... E3
Jászberény 30,000 ... E3
Jászladány 7,823 ... F3
Kalocsa 20,000 ... E3
Kaposvár 74,000 ... D3
Kapuvár 11,000 ... D3
Karcag 25,000 ... F3
Kazincbarcika 39,000 ... F2
Kecel 10,493 ... E3
Kecskemét 105,000 ... E3
Keszthely 23,000 ... D3
Kisbér 8,000 ... D3
Kiskőrös 15,000 ... E3
Kiskunfélegyháza 35,000 ... E3
Kiskunhalas 32,000 ... E3
Kiskunmajsa 14,439 ... E3
Kispest 65,106 ... E3
Kistelek 8,544 ... E3
Kisújszállás 13,000 ... F3
Kisvárda 17,828 ... G2
Komádi 8,765 ... F3
Komárom 19,955 ... E3
Komló 30,301 ... E3
Kondoros 7,319 ... F3
Körmend 12,000 ... D3
Kőszeg 14,000 ... D3
Kunhegyes 10,116 ... F3
Kunmadaras 7,343 ... F3
Kunszentmárton 12,000 ... F3
Kunszentmiklós 7,952 ... E3
Lajosmizse 12,872 ... E3
Leninváros 19,000 ... F3
Lenti 9,000 ... D3
Létavértes 9,106 ... F3
Lőrinci 10,679 ... E3
Makó 29,000 ... F3
Marcali 13,000 ... D3
Mátészalka 20,000 ... G3
Mélykút 7,640 ... E3
Mezőberény 12,702 ... F3
Mezőhegyes 8,631 ... F3
Mezőkovácsháza 7,000 ... F3
Mezőkövesd 18,000 ... F3
Mezőtúr 21,000 ... F3
Mindszent 8,730 ... F3
Miskolc 210,000 ... F2
Mohács 21,000 ... E4
Monor 16,838 ... E3
Mór 12,066 ... E3
Mosonmagyaróvár 30,000 ... D3
Nádudvar 9,447 ... F3
Nagyatád 15,000 ... D3
Nagyecsed 8,225 ... G3
Nagykálló 11,282 ... F3
Nagykanizsa 55,000 ... D3
Nagykáta 11,922 ... E3
Nagykőrös 27,000 ... E3
Nagyszénás 7,124 ... F3
Nyíradony 7,146 ... F3
Nyírbátor 14,000 ... G3
Nyíregyháza 119,000 ... F3
Orosháza 36,000 ... F3
Oroszlány 22,000 ... E3
Ózd 45,000 ... F2
Paks 26,000 ... E3
Pápa 35,000 ... D3
Pásztó 12,000 ... E3
Pécs 182,000 ... E3
Pilis 9,055 ... E3
Pilisvörösvár 10,217 ... E3
Polgár 9,429 ... F3
Püspökladány 16,000 ... F3
Putnok 7,103 ... F2
Ráckeve 7,534 ... E3
Rákospalota 60,983 ... E3
Sajószentpéter 13,992 ... F2
Salgótarján 49,000 ... E2
Sárbogárd 13,000 ... E3
Sarkad 11,937 ... F3
Sárospatak 15,000 ... F2
Sárvár 16,000 ... D3
Sátoraljaújhely 20,000 ... F2
Siklós 11,000 ... E4
Siófok 24,000 ... E3
Soltvadkert 7,934 ... E3
Sopron 57,000 ... D3
Szabadszállás 8,223 ... E3
Szarvas 19,000 ... F3
Százhalombatta 18,000 ... E3
Szeged 188,000 ... F3
Szeghalom 10,000 ... F3
Székesfehérvár 113,000 ... E3
Szekszárd 39,000 ... E3
Szentendre 20,000 ... E3
Szentes 35,000 ... F3
Szentgotthárd 8,000 ... D3
Szerencs 10,000 ... F2
Szigetvár 13,000 ... D3
Szolnok 81,000 ... F3
Szombathely 87,000 ... D3
Tamási 10,000 ... E3
Tapolca 18,000 ... D3
Tata 26,000 ... E3
Tatabánya 76,000 ... E3
Tiszaföldvár 12,560 ... F3
Tiszafüred 14,000 ... F3
Tiszakécske 12,000 ... F3
Tiszavasvári 14,000 ... F3
Tolna 8,997 ... E3
Törökszentmiklós 24,000 ... F3
Tótkomlós 8,803 ... F3
Tura 8,235 ... E3
Túrkeve 11,000 ... F3
Újfehértó 14,412 ... F3
Újpest 80,384 ... E3
Vác 36,000 ... E3
Várpalota 28,000 ... E3
Vásárosnamény 9,000 ... G2
Vecsés 19,193 ... E3
Veszprém 66,000 ... D3
Vésztő 9,815 ... F3
Zalaegerszeg 63,000 ... D3
Zalaszentgrót 8,000 ... D3
Zirc 11,000 ... D3

OTHER FEATURES

Bakony (mts.) ... D3
Balaton (lake) ... D3
Berettyó (riv.) ... F3
Börzsöny (mts.) ... E3
Bükk (mts.) ... F2
Csepelsziget (isl.) ... E3
Danube (riv.) ... E3
Dráva (riv.) ... D3
Duna (Danube) (riv.) ... E3
Fertő tó (Neusiedler See) (lake) ... D3
Great Alföld (plain) ... F3
Hernád (riv.) ... F2
Ipoly (riv.) ... E2
Kapos (riv.) ... D3
Kékes (mt.) ... E3
Korishegy (mt.) ... D3
Körös (riv.) ... F3
Little Alfold (plain) ... D3
Maros (riv.) ... F3
Mátra (mts.) ... E3
Mecsek (mts.) ... D3
Mura (riv.) ... D3
Rába (riv.) ... D3
Sajó (riv.) ... F2
Sárviz csatorna (canal) ... E3
Sebes Körös (riv.) ... F3
Sió csatorna (canal) ... E3
Szentendreisziget (isl.) ... E3
Tarna (riv.) ... F3
Tisza (riv.) ... F3
Zagyva (riv.) ... F3
Zala (riv.) ... D3

*City and suburbs.
†Population of Austrian cities are communes.

Agriculture, Industry and Resources

DOMINANT LAND USE

- Cereals (chiefly wheat, corn)
- Other Cereals, Livestock, Dairy
- General Farming, Livestock
- General Farming, Truck Farming
- Pasture Livestock
- Grapes, Wine
- Forests
- Nonagricultural Land

MAJOR MINERAL OCCURRENCES

Ag	Silver	Mg	Magnesium
Al	Bauxite	Mn	Manganese
C	Coal	Na	Salt
Cu	Copper	O	Petroleum
Fe	Iron Ore	Pb	Lead
G	Natural Gas	Sb	Antimony
Gr	Graphite	U	Uranium
Hg	Mercury	W	Tungsten
Lg	Lignite	Zn	Zinc

Water Power
Major Industrial Areas

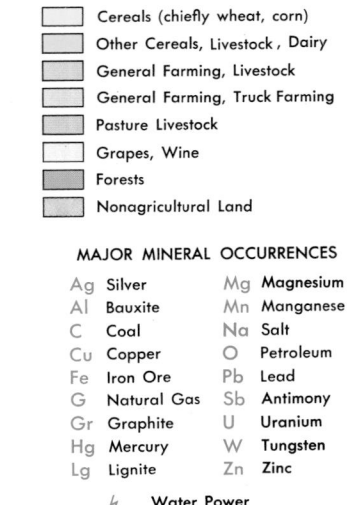

YUGOSLAVIA
AREA 98,766 sq. mi. (255,804 sq. km.)
POPULATION 23,798,000
CAPITAL Belgrade
LARGEST CITY Belgrade
HIGHEST POINT Triglav 9,393 ft. (2,863 m.)
MONETARY UNIT Yugoslav dinar
MAJOR LANGUAGES Serbo-Croation, Slovenian, Macedonian, Montenegrin, Albanian
MAJOR RELIGIONS Eastern Orthodoxy, Roman Catholicism, Islam

ALBANIA
AREA 11,100 sq. mi. (28,749 sq. km.)
POPULATION 3,199,000
CAPITAL Tiranë
LARGEST CITY Tiranë
HIGHEST POINT Korab 9,026 ft. (2,751 m.)
MONETARY UNIT lek
MAJOR LANGUAGE Albanian
MAJOR RELIGIONS Islam, Eastern Orthodoxy, Roman Catholicism

ROMANIA
AREA 91,699 sq. mi. (237,500 sq. km.)
POPULATION 23,249,000
CAPITAL Bucharest
LARGEST CITY Bucharest
HIGHEST POINT Moldoveanul 8,343 ft. (2,543 m.)
MONETARY UNIT leu
MAJOR LANGUAGES Romanian, Hungarian
MAJOR RELIGION Eastern Orthodoxy

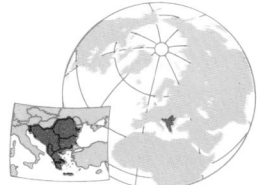

BULGARIA
AREA 42,823 sq. mi. (110,912 sq. km.)
POPULATION 8,981,000
CAPITAL Sofia
LARGEST CITY Sofia
HIGHEST POINT Musala 9,597 ft. (2,925 m.)
MONETARY UNIT lev
MAJOR LANGUAGE Bulgarian
MAJOR RELIGION Eastern Orthodoxy

GREECE
AREA 50,944 sq. mi. (131,945 sq. km.)
POPULATION 9,983,000
CAPITAL Athens
LARGEST CITY Athens
HIGHEST POINT Olympus 9,570 ft. (2,917 m.)
MONETARY UNIT drachma
MAJOR LANGUAGE Greek
MAJOR RELIGION Eastern (Greek) Orthodoxy

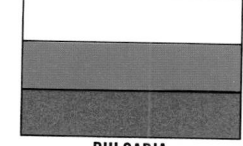
BULGARIA

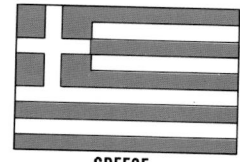
GREECE

YUGOSLAVIA

ALBANIA

ROMANIA

Agriculture, Industry and Resources

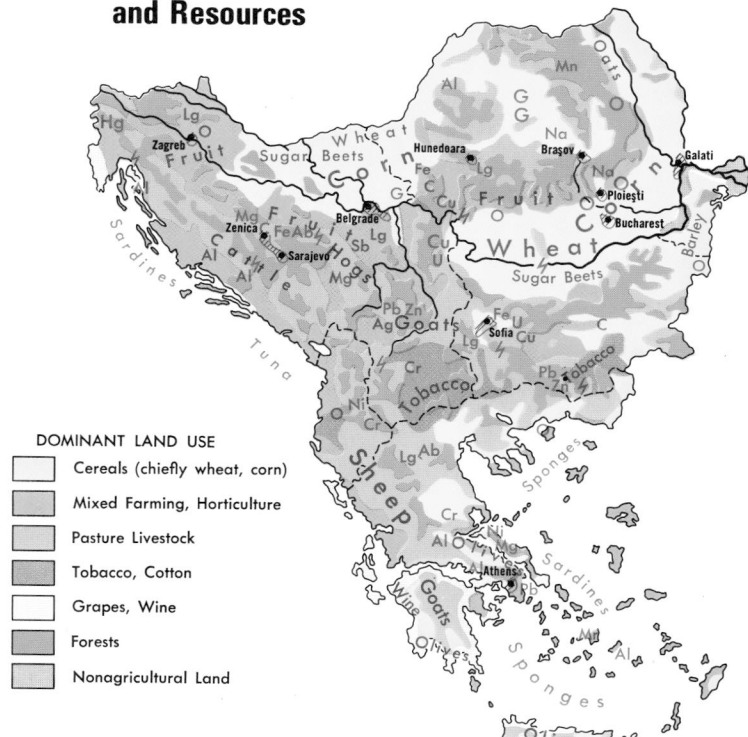

DOMINANT LAND USE

- Cereals (chiefly wheat, corn)
- Mixed Farming, Horticulture
- Pasture Livestock
- Tobacco, Cotton
- Grapes, Wine
- Forests
- Nonagricultural Land

MAJOR MINERAL OCCURRENCES

Ab	Asbestos	Mg	Magnesium
Ag	Silver	Mn	Manganese
Al	Bauxite	Mr	Marble
C	Coal	Na	Salt
Cr	Chromium	Ni	Nickel
Cu	Copper	O	Petroleum
Fe	Iron Ore	Pb	Lead
G	Natural Gas	Sb	Antimony
Hg	Mercury	U	Uranium
Lg	Lignite	Zn	Zinc

⚡ Water Power
▨ Major Industrial Areas

ALBANIA

CITIES and TOWNS

Berat 40,500 ....D5
Delvinë 6,000 ....D6
Durrës (Durazzo) 78,700 ...D5
Elbasan 78,300 ....E5
Fier 40,300 ....D5
Gjirokastër 23,800 ....E5
Kavajë 24,200 ....D5
Korçë 61,500 ....E5
Krujë 9,600 ....D5
Kuçovë (Stalin) 20,600 .....D5
Kukës 9,500 ....E4
Lezhë 6,900 ....D5
Lushnjë 26,900 ....D5
Peshkopi 7,600 ....E5
Pogradec 13,100 ....E5
Sarandë 10,800 ....E6
Shijak 6,200 ....D5
Shkodër 76,300 ....D4
Stalin 20,600 ....D5
Tiranë (Tirana)
  (cap.) 225,700 ....D5
Vlorë 67,700 ....D5

OTHER FEATURES

Adriatic (sea) B4
Drin (riv.) E4
Korab (mt.) E4
Ohrid (lake) E5
Otranto (str.) D5
Prespa (lake) E5
Sazan (isl.) D5
Scutari (lake) D4
Vijosë (riv.) D5

BULGARIA

CITIES and TOWNS

Akhtopol 1,108 ....H4
Ardino 5,498 ....G5
Asenovgrad 47,159 ....G5
Aytos 23,124 ....H4
Balchik 12,764 ....J4
Bansko 10,025 ....G4
Belogradchik 7,198 ....F4
Berkovitsa 16,340 ....F4
Blagoevgrad 65,481 ....F5
Botevgrad 22,659 ....G4
Burgas 182,856 ....H4
Byala 11,017 ....G4
Byala Slatina 16,034 ....G4
Chirpan 20,440 ....G4
Devin 7,985 ....G4
Dimitrovgrad 54,056 ....G4
Dobrich (Tolbukhin) 109,170 ...H4
Dryanovo 10,306 ....G4
Elena 7,629 ....G4
Elin Pelin 6,955 ....F4
Elkhovo 13,655 ....H4
Gabrovo 81,629 ....G4
General-Toshevo 9,274 .....H4
Godech 5,438 ....F4
Gorna Oryakhovitsa 40,895 ...G4
Gotse Delchev 19,836 ......F5
Grudovo 10,736 ....H4
Ikhtiman 13,001 ....F4
Isperikh 11,235 ....H4
Karlovo 28,403 ....G4
Karnobat 22,536 ....H4
Kavarna 12,024 ....J4
Kazanlŭk 61,396 ....G4
Kharmanli 21,050 ....G5
Khaskovo 87,847 ....G4
Kotel 7,985 ....H4
Krumovgrad 6,597 ....G5
Kubrat 10,758 ....H4
Kula 5,163 ....F4
Kŭrdzhali 55,201 ....G5

Kyustendil 53,498 ....F4
Lom 32,307 ....F4
Lovech 48,992 ....G4
Lukovit 10,645 ....G4
Maritsa 8,742 ....H4
Mikhaylovgrad 51,714 .....F4
Momchilgrad 10,189 ....G5
Nesebŭr 8,130 ....H4
Nova Zagora 25,327 ....H4
Novi Pazar 16,314 ....H4
Omurtag 9,505 ....H4
Oryakhovo 14,012 ....F4
Panagyurishte 22,034 ......G4
Pazardzhik 77,603 ....G4
Pernik 94,460 ....F4
Peshtera 18,763 ....G4
Petrich 26,451 ....F5
Pirdop 8,248 ....G4
Pleven 129,863 ....G4
Plovdiv 343,064 ....G4
Pomorie 13,507 ....H4
Popovo 21,236 ....H4
Provadiya 15,762 ....H4
Radomir 16,733 ....F4
Razgrad 49,582 ....H4
Razlog 14,010 ....F5
Rositsa 185,485 ....H4
Ruse 185,485 ....H4
Samokov 27,485 ....F4
Sandanski 24,629 ....F5
Sevlievo 26,560 ....G4
Shumen 100,125 ....H4
Silistra 53,537 ....H3
Simeonovgrad –
  (Maritsa) 8,742 ....H4
Sliven 9,037 ....H4
Smolyan 31,456 ....G5
Smyadovo 5,295 ....H4
Sofia (cap.) 1,121,763 .....F4
Stanke Dimitrov 41,897 ....F4
Stara Zagora 151,163 ......G4
Svilengrad 17,472 ....H5
Svishtov 30,555 ....G4
Teteven 12,784 ....G4
Tolbukhin 109,170 ....H4
Topolovgrad 7,437 ....H4
Troyan 26,179 ....G4
Tŭrgovishte 46,043 ....H4
Tutrakan 12,153 ....H4
Varna 302,816 ....H4
Veliko Tŭrnovo 69,173 .....G4
Vidin 62,541 ....F4
Vratsa 75,180 ....F4
Yambol 90,019 ....H4
Zlatograd 8,780 ....G5

OTHER FEATURES

Arda (riv.) G5
Balkan (mts.) G4
Black (sea) J4
Danube (riv.) H4
Dunav (Danube) (riv.) H4
Emine (cape) J4
Iskŭr (riv.) G4
Kaliakra (cape) J4
Maritsa (riv.) G4
Mesta (riv.) F5
Midzhur (mt.) F4
Musala (mt.) F4
Osŭm (riv.) G4
Rhodope (mts.) G5
Rujen (mt.) F5
Struma (riv.) F5
Timok (riv.) F3
Tundzha (riv.) G4
Vit (riv.) G4

GREECE

REGIONS

Aegean Islands 417,813 ....G6

Athens, Greater 3,027,331 ...F7
Áyion Óros (aut. dist.) 1,732 ...G5
Central Greece and
  Euboea 1,099,841 ....F6
Crete 502,165 ....G8
Epirus 324,541 ....E6
Ionian Islands 182,651 .....D6
Macedonia 2,121,953 ......F5
Pelopónnisos 1,012,528 ....F7
Thessaly 695,654 ....F6
Thrace 345,220 ....G5

CITIES and TOWNS

Agrínion 34,328 ....E6
Aíyina 6,333 ....F7
Aíyion 20,824 ....F6
Alexandroúpolis 34,535 ...G5
Almirós 6,143 ....F6
Amaliás 14,698 ....E7
Amfissa 7,156 ....F6
Argos 20,702 ....F7
Argostólion 6,788 ....E6
Arkhángelos 4,164 ....J7
Árta 18,283 ....E6
Atalándi 5,456 ....F6
Athens (cap.) 885,737 .....F7
Áyios Nikólaos 8,130 ......G8
Candia (Iráklion) 101,634 ...G8
Canea (Khaniá) 40,564 ....G8
Corinth 22,658 ....F7
Dhidhimótikhon 8,374 .....H5
Dráma 36,109 ....F5
Édhessa 16,054 ....F5
Elassón 6,527 ....F6
Ermoúpolis 13,876 ....G7
Fársala 7,094 ....F6
Filiatrá 4,931 ....E7
Flórina 12,562 ....E5
Gargaliánoi 5,371 ....E7
Grevená 7,433 ....E5
Ierápetra 8,575 ....G8
Igoumenítsa 5,879 ....E6
Ioánnina 44,829 ....E6
Iráklion 101,634 ....G8
Itháki 2,037 ....E6
Kalámai 41,911 ....F7
Kalampáka 5,692 ....E6
Kálimnos 10,118 ....H7
Kardhítsa 27,291 ....F6
Karpeníson 5,100 ....E6
Kastéllion (Kissamos) 2,749 ...F8
Kastoría 17,133 ....E5
Katerini 38,016 ....F5
Kaválla 56,375 ....G5
Kérkira 33,561 ....D6
Khalkis 44,867 ....F6
Khaniá 40,564 ....G8
Khíos 24,070 ....G6
Kiáton 7,392 ....F6
Kilkís 11,148 ....F5
Kissamos 2,749 ....F8
Komotiní 34,051 ....G5
Koropí 11,214 ....G7
Kos 11,851 ....H7
Kozáni 30,994 ....F5
Lamía 41,667 ....F6
Langadhás 5,890 ....F5
Lárisa 102,048 ....F6
Lávrion 8,921 ....G7
Leivádhia 16,864 ....F6
Levkás 6,818 ....E6
Litókhoron 6,190 ....F5
Marathón 2,052 ....G6
Megalópolis 4,735 ....F7
Mégara 17,719 ....F6
Mesolóngion 10,164 ....E6
Messíni 6,565 ....E7
Mírina 3,774 ....G6
Mitilíni 24,115 ....H6
Náousa 19,833 ....F5
Návpaktos 9,012 ....F6
Návplion 10,609 ....F7

(continued on following page)

(continued)

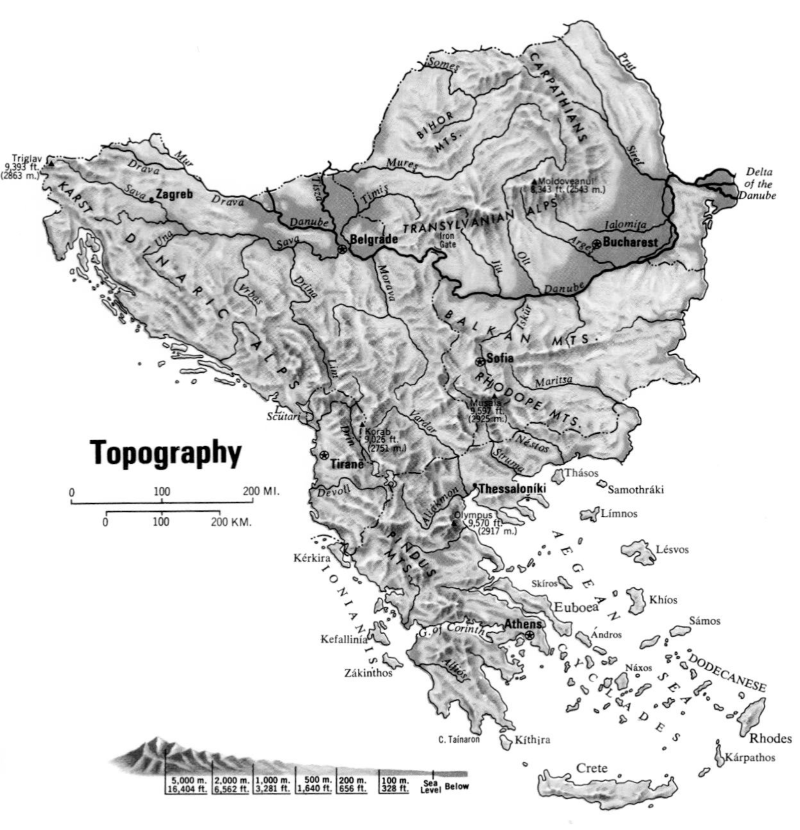
Topography
0 100 200 MI.
0 100 200 KM.
5,000 m. 16,404 ft.
2,000 m. 6,562 ft.
1,000 m. 3,281 ft.
500 m. 1,640 ft.
200 m. 656 ft.
100 m. 328 ft.
Sea Level Below
Triglav 9,393 ft. (2863 m.)
Zagreb
Belgrade
Bucharest
Sofia
Tiranë
Thessaloníki
Athens
Delta of the Danube
CARPATHIANS
BIHOR MTS.
TRANSYLVANIAN ALPS
Moldoveanul 8,343 ft. (2543 m.)
BALKAN MTS.
RHODOPE MTS.
DINARIC ALPS
PINDUS MTS.
KARST
Iron Gate
Musala 9,597 ft. (2925 m.)
Korab 9,026 ft. (2751 m.)
Olympus 9,570 ft. (2917 m.)
Danube
Drava
Sava
Mur
Mureş
Tisza
Timiş
Someş
Prut
Siret
Ialomiţa
Argeş
Olt
Jiu
Morava
Iskur
Maritsa
Vardar
Struma
Néstos
Aliákmon
Drin
Devoll
Lim
Una
Vrbas
Drina
Scutari
Thásos
Samothráki
Límnos
Lésvos
Khíos
Sámos
Skíros
Euboea
Ándros
Náxos
Kérkira
Kefallinía
Zákinthos
G. of Corinth
C. Tainaron
Kíthira
Crete
Rhodes
Kárpathos
AEGEAN SEA
IONIAN SEA
DODECANESE
CYCLADES

Náxos 3,735 G7
Neméa 4,182 F7
Néon Karlóvasi 4,752 H7
Nigríta 6,531 F5
Orestías 12,685 H5
Pátrai 141,529 E6
Piraiévs (Piraeus) 196,389 F7
Pírgos 21,958 E7
Piryí 1,204 G6
Plomárion 3,503 H6
Polikastron 5,635 F5
Políkhnitos 3,342 G6
Políyiros 4,075 F5
Póros 3,605 F7
Préveza 12,662 E6
Psakhná 5,320 F6
Ptolemaís 22,109 E5
Réthimnon 17,736 G8
Rhodes (Ródhos) 40,392 J7
Salamís 20,437 F6
Salonika (Thessaloníki) 406,413 F5
Sámos 5,575 H7
Samothráki 941 G5
Sápai 2,510 G5
Sérrai 45,213 F5
Sérvia 3,369 F5
Siátista 5,702 E5
Sidhirókastron 6,157 F5
Sitía 6,659 H8
Skíathos 3,838 F6
Skíros 2,217 G6
Skópelos 2,668 F6
Souflíon 5,043 H5
Sparta 11,911 F7
Spétsai 3,655 F7
Stilís 4,690 F6
Thásos 2,300 G5
Thessaloníki 406,413 F5
Thíra 1,573 G7
Thívai 18,712 F6
Timbákion 3,864 G8
Tínos 3,879 G7
Tírnavos 10,965 F6
Tríkkala 40,857 E6
Trípolis 21,311 F7
Vartholomión 3,236 E7
Velvendós 3,591 F5
Véria 37,087 F5
Vólos 71,378 F6
Vónitsani 3,627 E6
Vrondádhes 3,979 G6
Xánthi 31,541 G5
Yiannitsá 21,082 F5
Yíthion 4,054 F7
Zante (Zákinthos) 9,764 E7

OTHER FEATURES

Aegean (sea) G6
Akrí (cape) E7
Aktí (pen.) G5
Amorgós (isl.) G7
Anáfi (isl.) G7
Andikíthira (isl.) F8
Ándros (isl.) G7
Arda (riv.) G5
Argolís (gulf) F7
Astipálaia (isl.) H7
Áthos (mt.) G5
Áyios Evstrátios (isl.) G6
Áyios Yeóryios (cape) G5
Cephalonia (Kefallinía) (isl.) E6
Corfu (Kérkira) (isl.) D6
Corinth (gulf) F6
Crete (isl.) G8
Crete (sea) G7
Cyclades (isls.) G7
Día (isl.) G8
Dodecanese (isls.) H8
Euboea (Évvoia) (isl.) G6
Évros (riv.) H5
Gávdhos (isl.) F8
Ídhi (mt.) G8
Ikaría (isl.) G7
Ionian (sea) D7
Íos (isl.) G7
Itháki (Ithaca) (isl.) E6
Kafirévs (cape) G6
Kálimnos (isl.) H7
Kárpathos (isl.) H8
Kásos (isl.) H8
Kassándra (pen.) F6
Kéa (isl.) G7
Kefallinía (isl.) E6
Kérkira (isl.) D6
Khálki (isl.) H7
Khaniá (gulf) G8
Khíos (isl.) G6
Kímilos (isl.) G7
Kiparissía (gulf) E7
Kíthira (isl.) F7
Kíthnos (isl.) G7
Kos (isl.) H7
Kriós (cape) F8
Kríti (Crete) (isl.) G8
Lakonía (gulf) F7
Léros (isl.) H7
Lésvos (isl.) G6
Levítha (isl.) H7
Levkás (isl.) E6
Límnos (isl.) G6
Maléa (cape) F7
Matapan (Taínaron) (cape) F7
Merabéllou (gulf) H8
Mesará (gulf) G8
Messíni (gulf) E7
Míkinos (isl.) G7
Mílos (isl.) G7
Mirtóön (sea) F7
Náxos (isl.) G7
Néstos (riv.) G5
Nísiros (isl.) H7
Northern Sporades (isls.) F6
Olympia (isls.) E7
Olympus (mt.) F5
Parnassus (mt.) F6
Páros (isl.) G7
Pátmos (isl.) H7
Paxoí (isl.) D6
Pindus (mts.) E6
Piniós (riv.) E6
Prespa (lake) E5
Psará (isl.) G6
Psevdhókavos (cape) G6
Rhodes (isl.) H7
Rhodope (mts.) G5
Salonika (Thermaic) (gulf) F6
Sámos (isl.) H7
Samothráki (isl.) G5
Saría (isl.) H8
Saronic (gulf) F7
Sérifos (isl.) G7
Sídheros (cape) H8
Sífnos (isl.) G7
Sími (isl.) H7
Síros (isl.) G7
Sithoniá (pen.) F5
Skíros (isl.) G6
Spátha (cape) F8
Strimón (gulf) G5
Strofádhes (isls.) E7
Taínaron (cape) F7
Thásos (isls.) G5
Thermaic (gulf) F6
Thíra (isl.) G7
Tílos (isl.) H7
Tínos (isl.) G7
Toronaic (gulf) F5
Vardar (riv.) E5
Vólvi (lake) F5
Voïviïs (lake) F6
Voúxa (cape) F8
Zákinthos (Zante) (isl.) E7

ROMANIA

CITIES and TOWNS

Aiud 27,600 F2
Alba Iulia 53,000 F2
Alexandria 43,700 G3
Anina 11,300 E3
Arad 182,000 E2
Babadag 9,000 J3
Bacău 156,200 H2
Baia Mare 123,300 F2
Băileşti 21,500 F3
Balş 17,300 G3
Beiuş 10,100 F2
Bicaz 9,300 G2
Bîrlad 63,800 H2
Bistrita 59,800 G2
Blaj 22,200 F2
Borşa 25,287 G2
Botoşani 84,900 H2
Brad 18,600 F2
Brăila 219,200 H3
Braşov 320,200 G3
Bucharest (Bucureşti) (cap.) 1,929,400 G3
Buhuşi 20,300 H2
Buzău 116,300 H3
Buziaş 8,700 E3
Calafat 17,100 F3
Călăraşi 58,000 H3
Caracal 33,600 G3
Caransebeş 28,800 F3
Carei 25,500 F2
Cernavodă 15,000 J3
Chişineu Criş 9,600 E2
Cîmpia Turzii 25,300 F2
Cîmpina 35,300 G3
Cîmpulung 37,400 G3
Cîmpulung Moldovenesc 20,500 G2
Cisnădie 21,100 G3
Cluj-Napoca 289,800 F2
Comaneşti 18,500 H2
Constanţa 293,900 J3
Corabia 20,300 G4
Costeşti 10,900 G3
Craiova 239,700 F3
Curtea de Argeş 26,900 G3
Darabani 11,500 H1
Dej 36,500 F2
Deva 73,300 F3
Dorohoi 25,700 H2
Drăgăneşti Olt 11,800 G3
Drăgăşani 17,300 G3
Drobeta-Turnu Severin 86,600 F3
Făgăraş 37,200 G3
Fălticeni 24,000 H2
Făurei 3,800 H3
Feteşti 29,600 H3
Focşani 70,700 H3
Găeşti 14,000 G3
Galati 268,000 H3
Gheorghe Gheorghiu-Dej 46,100 H2
Gheorghieni 21,800 G2
Gherla 20,700 G2
Giurgiu 57,000 G4
Hateg 10,200 F3
Hîrlău 8,900 H2
Hîrşova 9,000 J3
Huedin 8,700 F2
Hunedoara 85,700 F3
Huşi 26,000 J2
Iaşi 279,800 H2
Ineu 10,800 E2
Isaccea 5,400 J3
Jimbolia 14,600 E3
Lipova 12,900 E2
Luduş 16,000 G2
Lugoj 50,000 E3
Lupeni 29,100 F3
Mangalia 31,100 J4
Medgidia 45,300 J3
Mediaş 69,000 G2
Miercurea Ciuc 40,400 G2
Mizil 15,200 H3
Moineşti 21,200 H2
Moldova Nouă 17,800 E3
Moreni 18,900 G3
Nădlac 8,500 E2
Năsăud 9,500 G2
Negreşti 7,700 H2
Ocna Mureş 16,200 G2
Odobeşti 8,600 H3
Odorheiu Secuiesc 36,200 G2
Oltenita 26,800 H3
Oradea 192,600 E2
Orăştie 19,900 F3
Oravita 114,300 E3
Orşova 115,800 F3
Panciu 77,900 H3
Paşcani 229,500 H2
Petrila 25,900 F3
Petroşeni 45,600 F3
Piatra Neamt 93,300 H2
Piteşti 143,600 G3
Ploieşti 219,900 H3
Pucioasa 14,100 G3
Rădăuti 26,000 G2
Reghin 33,600 G2
Reşita 96,800 E3
Rîmnicu Sărat 32,400 H3
Rîmnicu Vîlcea 78,900 G3
Roman 62,700 H2
Roşiori de Vede 31,700 G3
Săcele 33,900 G3
Salonta 20,400 E2
Satu Mare 115,600 F2
Sebeş 29,500 F3
Sebiş 6,700 F2
Segarcea 8,700 F3
Sfîntu Gheorghe 57,900 G3
Sfîntu Gheorghe J3
Sibiu 164,200 G3
Sighetu Marmaţiei 40,500 F2
Sighişoara 33,000 G2
Şimleul Silvaniei 15,100 F2
Sinaia 14,700 G3
Sînnicolaul Mare 13,600 E2
Slănic 8,100 G3
Slatina 62,800 G3
Slobozia 39,400 H3
Solca 4,500 G2
Sovata 11,200 G2
Strehaia 11,800 F3
Suceava 76,500 H2
Sulina 5,400 J3
Tăşnad 10,400 F2
Techirghiol 11,800 J3
Tecuci 40,300 H3
Timişoara 288,200 E3
Tîrgovişte 77,500 G3
Tîrgu Frumos 6,900 H2
Tîrgu Jiu 75,200 F3
Tîrgu Mureş 141,300 G2
Tîrgu Neamt 16,600 H2
Tîrgu Ocna 12,800 H2
Tîrgu Secuiesc 19,800 H2
Tîrnăveni 27,900 G2
Toplita 15,200 G2
Tulcea 73,600 J3
Turda 58,700 F2
Turnu Măgurele 33,000 G4
Urlata 11,200 H3
Urziceni 14,300 H3
Vaslui 50,100 H2
Vatra Dornei 17,800 G2
Videle 11,500 G3
Vişeu de Sus 20,800 G2
Zalău 43,300 F2
Zărneşti 25,000 G3
Zimnicea 16,400 G4

OTHER FEATURES

Argeş (riv.) G3
Bîrlad (riv.) H2
Black (sea) J4
Brăila (marshes) H3
Buzău (riv.) H3
Carpathian (mts.) G2
Crişul Alb (riv.) F2
Crişul Repede (riv.) F2
Danube (delta) J3
Danube (riv.) H4
Ialomiţa (marshes) J3
Ialomiţa (riv.) H3
Jijia (riv.) H2
Jiu (riv.) F3
Moldoveanul (mt.) G3
Mureş (riv.) E2
Olt (riv.) G3
Peleaga (mt.) F3
Pietrosul (mt.) G2
Prut (riv.) J2
Siret (riv.) H2
Someş (riv.) F2
Timiş (riv.) E3
Tîrnava Mare (riv.) G2
Transylvanian Alps (mts.) G3

YUGOSLAVIA

INTERNAL DIVISIONS

Bosnia and Hercegovina (rep.) 3,710,965 C3
Croatia (rep.) 4,396,397 C3
Kosovo (aut. reg.) 1,240,919 E4
Macedonia (rep.) 1,623,598 E5
Montenegro (rep.) 527,207 D4
Serbia (rep.) 8,401,673 E3
Slovenia (rep.) 1,697,068 B2
Vojvodina (aut. prov.) 1,953,980 D3

CITIES and TOWNS

Aleksinac 11,943 E4
Apatin 17,501 D3
Arendjelovac 15,659 E3
Bačka Topola 16,028 D3
Banja Luka 85,786 C3
Bar 3,594 D4
Bečej 26,616 E3
Bela Crkva 11,137 E3
Belgrade (cap.) 727,945 E3
Beli Manastir 7,325 D3
Beograde (Belgrade) (cap.) 727,945 E3
Bihać 24,155 B3
Bijeljina 24,888 D3
Bijelo Polje 9,298 D4
Biograd 3,595 B4
Bitola 64,467 E5
Bjelovar 21,019 C3
Bled 4,710 A2
Bor 27,520 E3
Bosanska Dubica 9,191 C3
Bosanska Gradiška 9,742 C3
Bosanska Krupa 8,947 C3
Bosanski Brod 10,113 D3
Bosanski Novi 9,861 C3
Bosanski Šamac 4,949 D3
Brčko 25,575 D3
Bugojno 9,079 C3
Čačak 38,890 E4
Čakovec 11,766 C2
Caribrod (Dimitrovgrad) 5,449 F4
Celje 30,827 B2
Cetinje 12,089 D4
Ćuprija 17,691 E4
Daruvar 8,478 C3
Debar 8,597 E5
Derventa 11,887 C3
Dimitrovgrad 5,449 F4
Djakovica 29,499 E4
Djakovo 15,833 D3
Doboj 18,073 C3
Drvar 6,237 C3
Dubrovnik 31,213 D4
Fiume (Rijeka) 128,883 B3
Foča 9,370 D4
Gevgelija 9,319 F5
Gnjilane 21,359 E4
Gornji Milanovac 11,114 E3
Gospić 8,238 B3
Gostivar 18,805 E5
Gračanica 9,302 D3
Gradačac 7,571 D3
Herceg Novi 6,645 D4
Ivangrad 11,373 D4
Jajce 9,221 C3
Jesenice 16,163 A2
Kanjiža 11,348 D2
Karlovac 47,046 B3
Kavadarci 17,974 F5
Kičevo 14,189 E5
Kikinda 37,392 E3
Knin 7,279 C3
Knjaževac 11,734 F4
Kočani 16,611 F5
Kočevje 7,277 B3
Konjic 9,161 C4
Koper 16,683 A3
Koprivnica 16,398 C2
Kosovska Mitrovica 42,526 E4
Kotor 5,728 D4
Kragujevac 72,080 E3
Kraljevo 28,065 E4
Kranj 26,341 B2
Križevci 8,501 C2
Krško 4,451 B3
Kruševac 29,902 E4
Kumanovo 44,791 E5
Kutina 10,892 C3
Leskovac 46,050 E4
Livno 7,223 C4
Ljubljana 169,064 B3
Loznica 13,513 D3
Makarska 6,589 C4
Maribor 94,976 B2
Modriča 7,406 D3
Mostar 47,821 C4
Murska Sobota 9,665 C2
Negotin 11,325 F3
Nevesinje 3,077 D4
Nikšić 28,940 D4
Niš 128,231 E4
Nova Gradiška 11,765 C3
Novi Pazar 28,696 E4
Novi Sad 143,591 D3
Novo Mesto 9,553 B3
Ogulin 9,975 B3
Ohrid 26,352 E5
Omiš 3,515 C4
Opatija 9,238 B3
Osijek 94,989 D3
Pag 2,318 B3
Pančevo 53,979 E3
Paraćin 21,555 E4
Peć 41,783 E4
Petrinja 12,236 C3
Piran 5,485 A3
Pirot 29,658 F4
Pljevlja 14,459 D4
Pola (Pula) 47,117 A3
Poreč 4,512 A3
Postojna 6,085 B3
Požarevac 33,336 E3
Preševo 7,634 E4
Priboj 12,556 D4
Prijedor 22,379 C3
Prijepolje 7,960 D4
Prilep 48,045 E5
Priština 71,264 E4
Prizren 41,875 E4
Prokuplje 20,617 E4
Ptuj 9,245 B2
Pula 47,117 A3
Radoviš 9,373 F5
Ragusa (Dubrovnik) 31,213 C4
Ravne na Koroškem 6,529 B2
Rijeka 128,883 B3
Rovinj 8,998 A3
Ruma 24,180 D3
Šabac 43,539 D3
Samobor 7,821 B3
Sanski Most 8,718 C3
Sarajevo 245,058 D4
Senj 4,927 B3
Senta 24,694 D3
Šibenik 29,619 C4
Šid 11,867 D3
Sinj 4,705 C4
Sisak 37,215 C3
Sjenica 9,118 E4
Škofja Loka 4,971 B2
Skopje 308,117 E5
Slavonska Požega 18,160 C3
Slavonski Brod 38,829 D3
Smederevo 39,200 E3
Smederevska Palanka 18,837 E3
Sombor 44,210 D3
Split 150,739 C4
Srebrenica 3,101 D3
Sremska Mitrovica 32,569 D3
Štip 27,218 F5
Struga 11,369 E5
Strumica 22,770 F5
Subotica 89,476 D2
Surdulica 7,048 F4
Svetozarevo 27,812 E4
Svilajnac 7,848 E3
Tetovo 35,293 E5
Titograd 54,639 D4
Titovo Užice 35,465 D4
Titov Veles 35,583 E5
Travnik 12,745 C3
Trbovlje 16,393 B2
Trebinje 3,553 D4
Trogir 6,162 C4
Trstenik 7,167 E4
Tržič 4,435 B2
Tuzla 53,836 D3
Ub 3,785 E3
Ulcinj 7,472 D5
Uroševac 22,763 E4
Valjevo 26,655 D3
Varaždin 34,662 C2
Vareš 7,632 D3
Velenje 11,225 B2
Velika Plana 12,664 E3
Veliki Bečkerek (Zrenjanin) 60,201 E3
Vinkovci 29,257 D3
Virovitica 16,389 C3
Visoko 9,365 D4
Vranje 25,909 E4
Vrbas 22,502 D3
Vršac 33,573 E3
Vučitrn 11,701 E4
Vukovar 29,500 D3
Zadar 43,588 B3
Zagreb 561,773 C3
Zaječar 27,724 F4
Zara (Zadar) 43,588 B3
Zenica 49,522 C3
Zrenjanin 60,201 E3
Zvornik 8,498 D3

OTHER FEATURES

Adriatic (sea) B4
Bobotov Kuk (mt.) D4
Bosna (riv.) D3
Brač (isl.) C4
Cazma (riv.) C3
Cres (isl.) B3
Čvrsnica (mt.) C4
Dalmatia (reg.) C4
Danube (riv.) E3
Dinaric Alps (mts.) B3
Drava (riv.) C3
Drina (riv.) D3
Dugi Otok (isl.) B3
Hvar (isl.) C4
Ibar (riv.) E4
Istria (pen.) A3
Kamenjak (cape) A3
Korab (mt.) E5
Korčula (isl.) C4
Kornat (isl.) B4
Krk (isl.) B3
Kupa (riv.) B3
Kvarner (gulf) B3
Lastovo (Lagosta) (isl.) C4
Lim (riv.) D4
Lošinj (isl.) B3
Midzhur (mt.) F4
Mljet (isl.) C4
Morava (riv.) E3
Mur (riv.) B2
Neretva (riv.) D4
Ohrid (lake) E5
Pag (isl.) B3
Palagruža (Pelagosa) (isl.) C4
Prespa (lake) E5
Rab (isl.) B3
Rujen (mt.) F4
Sava (riv.) D3
Scutari (lake) D4
Slavonia (reg.) C3
Šolta (isl.) C4
Tara (riv.) D4
Timok (riv.) F3
Tisa (riv.) E3
Triglav (mt.) A2
Una (riv.) C3
Vardar (riv.) E5
Vis (isl.) C4
Vrbas (riv.) C3
Žirje (isl.) B4

The Balkan States

CONIC PROJECTION

SCALE OF MILES

0 25 50 75 100 125 150 175

SCALE OF KILOMETERS

0 25 50 75 100 125 150 175

Capitals of Countries _____ ☆
Administrative Centers _____ △
International Boundaries _____
Major Internal Boundaries _____
Minor Internal Boundaries ···········
Canals _____

BULGARIA and GREECE are divided into regions and departments, respectively. Because of the scale no attempt has been made to delimit and name these subdivisions; their administrative centers have, however, been designated.
   The larger divisions named in Greece are well-known geographical regions, without administrative function.
   ROMANIA consists of thirty-nine counties and three cities of regional status, Bucharest, Constanța and Petroșeni. Scale does not permit delimiting these counties.
   ALBANIA is divided into twenty-seven districts. Scale does not permit the delimitation of these divisions.
   YUGOSLAVIA is a federation of six republics. The Serbian republic includes an autonomous province (Vojvodina), and an autonomous region (Kosovo).
   More detail shown on following page.

© Copyright HAMMOND INCORPORATED, Maplewood, N.J.

Topography

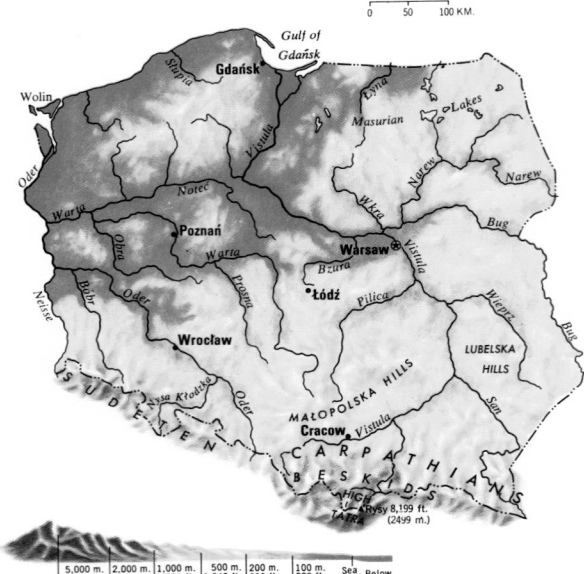

0   50   100 MI.
0   50   100 KM.

Gulf of Gdańsk

Gdańsk

Wolin

Odra

Słupia

Masurian Lakes

Łyna

Nogat

Vistula

Narew

Odra

Warta

Noteć

Wkra

Narew

Bug

Poznań

Warta

Prosna

Bzura

Warsaw

Vistula

Wieprz

Bug

Wrocław

Łódź

Pilica

LUBELSKA HILLS

SUDETEN

Nysa Kłodzka

Odra

MAŁOPOLSKA HILLS

Cracow

Vistula

San

CARPATHIANS

BESKIDS

HIGH TATRA

Rysy 8,199 ft. (2499 m.)

| 5,000 m. 16,404 ft. | 2,000 m. 6,562 ft. | 1,000 m. 3,281 ft. | 500 m. 1,640 ft. | 200 m. 656 ft. | 100 m. 328 ft. | Sea Level | Below |

PROVINCES

Biała Podlaska 304,028	F3
Białystok 687,806	F2
Bielsko 895,357	D4
Bydgoszcz 1,104,048	C2
Chełm 245,484	F3
Ciechanów 425,608	E2
Cracow (Kraków) 1,223,137	E3
Cracow (city) 651,300	E3
Częstochowa 773,365	D3
Elbląg 475,862	D1
Gdańsk 1,417,801	D1
Gorzów 497,342	B2
Jelenia Góra 514,947	B3
Kalisz 706,514	D3
Katowice 3,953,769	D3
Kielce 1,123,691	E3
Konin 465,928	D2
Koszalin 502,750	C1
Krosno 491,471	E4
Legnica 510,000	C3
Leszno 383,315	C3
Łódź 777,800	D3

Łódź (city) 1,139,379	D3
Łomża 344,518	F2
Lublin 1,010,641	F3
Nowy Sącz 690,737	E4
Olsztyn 746,185	E2
Opole 1,010,416	C3
Ostrołęka 393,427	E2
Piła 475,953	C2
Piotrków 638,948	D3
Płock 512,626	D2
Poznań 1,323,368	C2
Przemyśl 404,200	F4
Radom 745,374	E3
Rzeszów 716,317	F4
Siedlce 648,111	F2
Sieradz 408,082	D3
Skierniewice 416,690	E3
Słupsk 410,049	C1
Szczecin 964,298	B2
Tarnobrzeg 594,255	E3
Tarnów 664,953	E4
Toruń 656,421	D2
Wałbrzych 738,092	C3

Warsaw 2,415,950	E2
Warsaw (city) 1,377,100	E2
Włocławek 427,418	D2
Wrocław 1,122,806	C3
Zamość 488,193	F3
Zielona Góra 655,146	B3

CITIES and TOWNS

Aleksandrów Łódzki 19,711	D3
Allenstein (Olsztyn) 160,956	E2
Andrychów 22,387	D4
Augustów 28,307	F2
Auschwitz (Oświęcim) 45,402	D3
Bartoszyce 25,195	E1
Będzin 76,883	D3
Bełchatów 55,632	D3
Biała Podlaska 52,119	F3
Białogard 23,973	C1
Białystok 267,670	F2
Bielawa 34,224	C3
Bielsk Podlaski 26,145	F2

Bielsko-Biała 181,072	D4
Biłgoraj 25,542	F3
Bochnia 28,846	E4
Bogatynia 18,616	B3
Boguszów-Gorce 19,452	B3
Bolesławiec 43,076	B3
Braniewo 17,594	D1
Breslau (Wrocław) 640,557	C3
Brieg (Brzeg) 38,504	C3
Brodnica 26,056	D2
Brzeg 38,504	C3
Busko Zdrój 17,675	E3
Bydgoszcz 380,426	C2
Bytom 229,991	A3
Bytów 16,720	C1
Chełm 64,683	F3
Chełmno 21,506	C2
Chodzież 19,831	C2
Chojnice 37,733	C2
Chorzów 131,850	B4
Chrzanów 42,195	B4
Ciechanów 43,068	E2
Cieszyn 36,682	D4
Cracow 745,568	E3

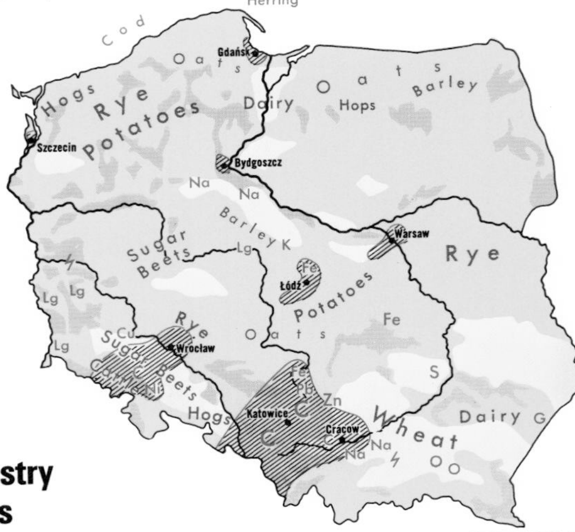

MAJOR MINERAL OCCURRENCES

Ag Silver
C Coal
Cu Copper
Fe Iron Ore
G Natural Gas
K Potash
Lg Lignite

Na Salt
Ni Nickel
O Petroleum
Pb Lead
S Sulfur
Zn Zinc

⚡ Water Power
▨ Major Industrial Areas

DOMINANT LAND USE

☐ Cereals (chiefly wheat)

☐ Rye, Oats, Barley, Potatoes

☐ General Farming, Livestock

☐ Forests

Agriculture, Industry and Resources

Cod
Herring
Hogs Oats
Rye Oats Barley
Potatoes Dairy Hops
Szczecin Na
Bydgoszcz Na
Barley K Warsaw
Sugar Beets Lg Rye
Łódź
Lg Potatoes Fe
Lg Rye Oats S
Sugar Beets Wrocław
Hogs Zn Dairy G
Katowice
Cracow Na
Wheat OO

Republics of Yugoslavia

CONIC PROJECTION

MILES
0 25 50 75 100

KILOMETERS
0 25 50 75 100

Capitals
● National
★ Federal Republics
⊙ Autonomous Provinces

Boundaries
National ———
Federal Republics ········
Autonomous Provinces ········
Canals

Copyright HAMMOND INCORPORATED Maplewood N.J.

AUSTRIA

HUNGARY

ITALY

SLOVENIA

CROATIA

VOJVODINA

ROMANIA

Ljubljana

Zagreb

Novi Sad

Belgrade (Beograd)

BOSNIA AND HERCEGOVINA

Sarajevo

MONTENEGRO

Titograd

KOSOVO

Skopje

MACEDONIA

ALBANIA

Tiranë

GREECE

BULGARIA

Sofia

Thessaloniki

ADRIATIC SEA

Venice (Venezia)

San Marino

ITALY

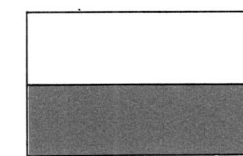

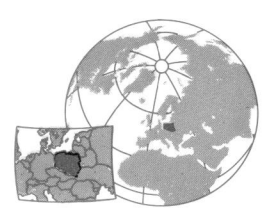

AREA 120,725 sq. mi. (312,678 sq. km.)
POPULATION 37,931,000
CAPITAL Warsaw
LARGEST CITY Warsaw
HIGHEST POINT Rysy 8,199 ft.
 (2,499 m.)
MONETARY UNIT zloty
MAJOR LANGUAGE Polish
MAJOR RELIGION Roman Catholicism

Poland
CONIC PROJECTION

SCALE OF MILES
0 10 20 40 60 80

SCALE OF KILOMETERS
0 10 20 40 60 80

Capitals of Countries ....⍟
Other Capitals ....◉
International Boundaries ___ ___
Internal Boundaries ___ ___
Canals

Poland is divided into 49 provinces (bearing the same name as their capitals) and the autonomous cities of Warsaw, Lódż and Cracow.

© Copyright HAMMOND INCORPORATED, Maplewood, N.J.

ARMENIA

CITIES and TOWNS

Kumayri 120,000 ....E5
Leninakan
  (Kumayri) 120,000 ....E5
Yerevan (cap.) 1,199,000 ....E6

OTHER FEATURES

Caucasus (mts.) E5

AZERBAIJAN

INTERNAL DIVISIONS

Nagorno-Karabakh Aut. Obl.
  188,000 ....E6
Nakhichevan' Aut. Rep.
  295,000 ....E6

CITIES and TOWNS

Baku (cap.) 1,150,000 ....F5
Gyandzhe 278,000 ....E5
Kirovabad (Gyandzhe)
  278,000 ....E6
Lenkoran' 35,505 ....E6

Nakhichevan' 33,279 ....E6
Stepanakert 30,293 ....E6

OTHER FEATURES

Caspian (sea) F6
Caucasus (mts.) E5
Kura (riv.) E6

BELARUS (BELORUSSIA)

CITIES and TOWNS

Baranovichi 159,000 ....C4
Bobruysk 223,000 ....D4
Brest 258,000 ....C4
Gomel' 500,000 ....D4
Grodno 270,000 ....C4
Minsk (cap.) 1,589,000 ....C4
Mogilev 356,000 ....D4
Molodechno 73,000 ....C4
Mozyr' 101,000 ....C4
Pinsk 119,000 ....C4
Vitebsk 350,000 ....D4

OTHER FEATURES

Dnieper (riv.) D5
Dvina, Western (riv.) C4

Western Dvina (riv.) C4

GEORGIA

INTERNAL DIVISIONS

Abkhaz Aut. Rep. 537,000 ....E5
Adzhar Aut. Rep. 393,000 ....E5
South Ossetian Aut. Obl.
  99,000 ....E5

CITIES and TOWNS

Batumi 136,000 ....E5
Kutaisi 235,000 ....E5
Sukhumi 121,000 ....E5
Tbilisi (cap.) 1,260,000 ....E5
Tskhinvali 30,311 ....E5

OTHER FEATURES

Black (sea) D5
Caucasus (mts.) E5

KAZAKHSTAN

CITIES and TOWNS

Abay 34,245 ....H5

Akmolinsk (Tselinograd)
  277,000 ....H4
Aksay 10,010 ....F4
Aktyubinsk 253,000 ....F4
Alekseyevka H4
Alga 12,000 ....F5
Alma-Ata (cap.) 1,128,000 ...H5
Aral'sk 37,722 ....G5
Arkalyk 15,108 ....G4
Arys' 26,414 ....G5
Atbasar 37,228 ....G4
Ayaguz 35,827 ....J5
Balkhash 78,000 ....F5
Balykshi 22,397 ....F5
Baykonyr J5
Charsk 10,100 ....J5
Chelkar 19,377 ....F5
Chilli G5
Chimkent 393,000 ....H5
Chu G4
Derzhavinsk G4
Dossor 10,000 ....F5
Druzhba J5
Dzhambul 307,000 ....H5
Dzhetygara 32,169 ....G4
Dzhezkazgan 109,000 ....G5
Dzhusaly 20,658 ....G5
Ekibastuz 135,000 ....H4
Emba 17,820 ....F5

Fort-Shevchenko 12,000 ......F5
Gur'yev 149,000 ....F5
Kapchagay H5
Karaganda 614,000 ....H5
Karatau 26,962 ....H5
Karazhal 17,702 ....H5
Kentau 52,000 ....G5
Khromtau 10,000 ....F4
Kirovskiy H5
Kokchetav 137,000 ....H4
Kounradskiy 10,000 ....H5
Kul'sary 16,427 ....F5
Kustanay 224,000 ....G4
Kzyl-Orda 153,000 ....G5
Leninogorsk 68,000 ....J4
Leninsk G5
Makinsk 22,850 ....H4
Nikol'skiy (Satpayev)
  32,862 ....G5
Novokazalinsk 34,815 ....G5
Novyy Uzen' 18,073 ....F5
Panfilov 19,173 ....J5
Pavlodar 331,000 ....H4
Petropavlovsk 241,000 ....G4
Rudnyy 124,000 ....G4
Saksaul'skiy G5
Saran' 50,000 ....H5
Sarkand 18,296 ....J5
Saryshagan 10,000 ....H5

Satpayev 32,862 ....G5
Semipalatinsk 334,000 ....J4
Shakhtinsk 50,000 ....H5
Shchuchinsk 40,432 ....H4
Shevchenko 159,000 ....F5
Taldy-Kurgan 119,000 ....H5
Talgar 31,273 ....H5
Tekeli 29,846 ....H5
Temirtau 212,000 ....H4
Tselinograd 277,000 ....H4
Turkestan 67,000 ....G5
Ural'sk 200,000 ....F4
Ushtobe 24,484 ....H5
Ust'-Kamenogorsk
  324,000 ....J5
Yermak 28,133 ....H4
Yermentau 15,276 ....H4
Yesil' 15,000 ....H4
Zaysan 10,000 ....J5
Zyryanovsk 51,000 ....J5

OTHER FEATURES

Alakol' (lake) J5
Altai (mts.) J5
Aral (sea) F5
Balkhash (lake) H5
Bet-Pak-Dala (des.) H5
Caspian (sea) F6

Chu (riv.) H5
Emba (riv.) F5
Ili (riv.) H5
Irtysh (riv.) H4
Ishim (riv.) G4
Mangyshlak (pen.) F5
Sarysu (riv.) G5
Syrdar'ya (riv.) G5
Tengiz (lake) G4
Tobol (riv.) G4
Ulutau (mts.) G5
Ural (riv.) F5
Ust'-Urt (plat.) F5
Zaysan (lake) J5

KYRGYZSTAN (KIRGIZIA)

CITIES and TOWNS

Dzhalal-Abad 55,000 ....H5
Bishkek (cap.) 616,000 ....H5
Frunze (Bishkek)
  616,000 ....H5
Issyk-Kul' H5
Naryn 21,098 ....H5
Osh 213,000 ....H5
Przheval'sk 51,000 ....H5
Rybach'ye (Issyk-Kul') H5
Tokmak H5

(continued)

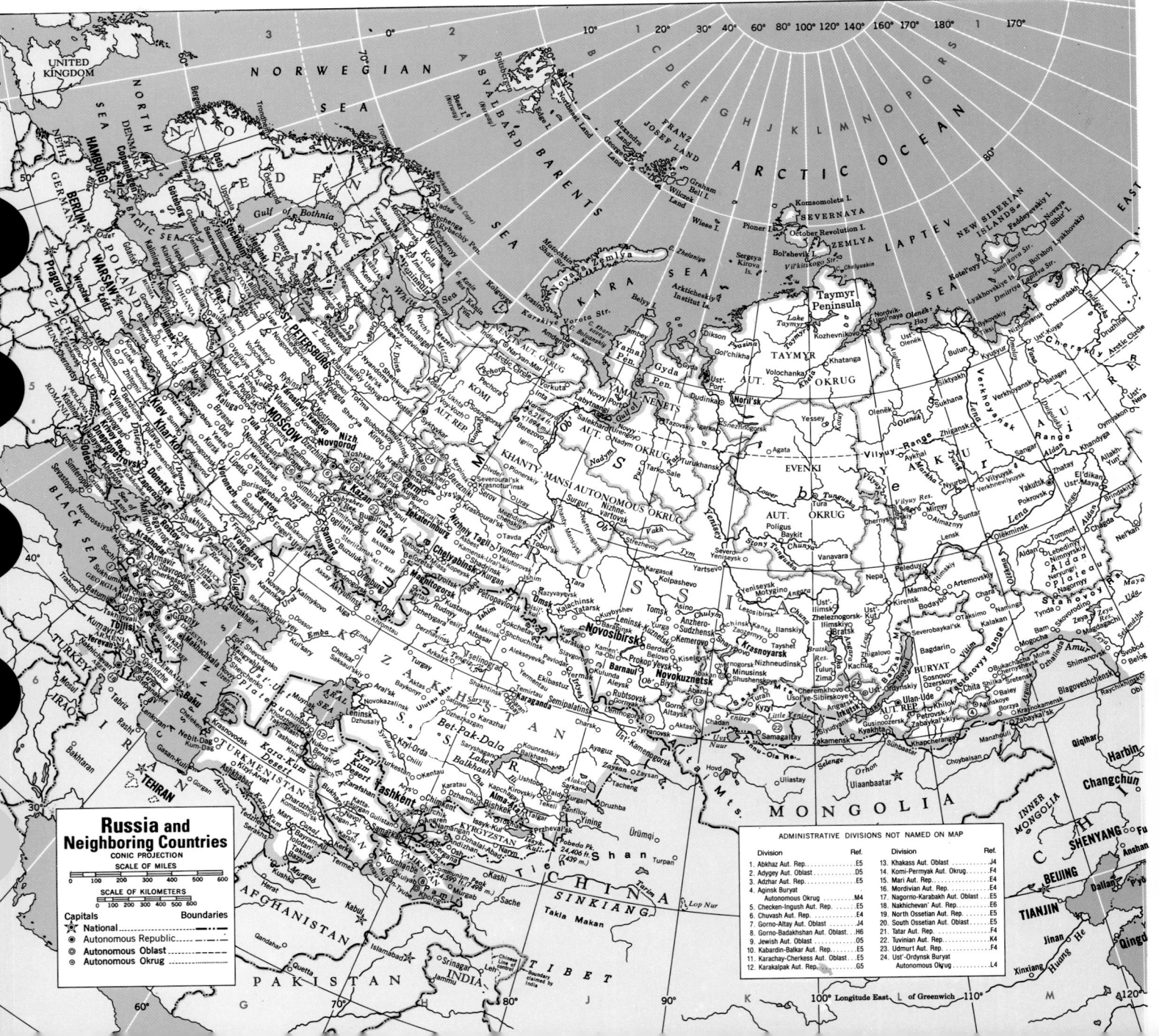

ARMENIA

AZERBAIJAN

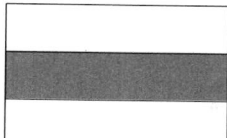
BELARUS

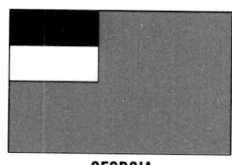
GEORGIA

MOLDOVA

RUSSIA

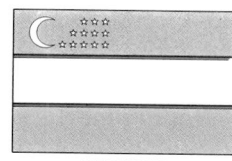
UKRAINE

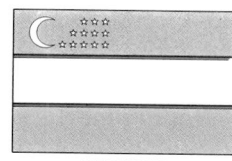
UZBEKISTAN

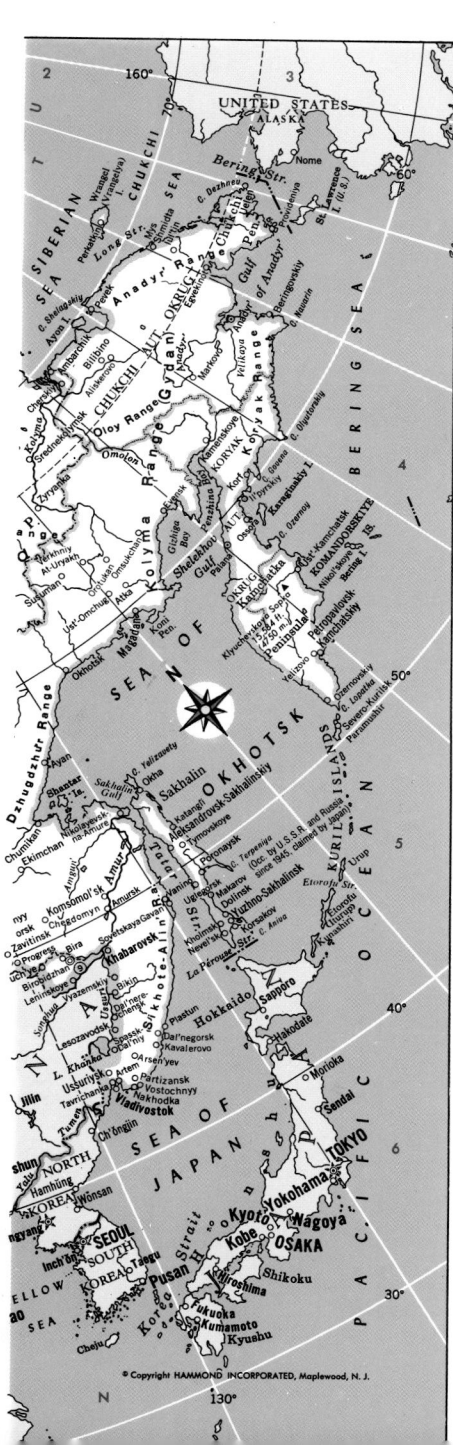

ARMENIA
AREA 11,506 sq. mi. (29,800 sq. km.)
POPULATION 3,283,000
CAPITAL Yerevan
LARGEST CITY Yerevan
HIGHEST POINT Alagez 13,435 ft. (4,095 m.)
MAJOR LANGUAGES Armenian, Azerbaijani, Kurdish, Russian
MAJOR RELIGIONS Eastern (Armenian Apostolic) Orthodoxy, Islam

AZERBAIJAN
AREA 33,436 sq. mi. (86,600 sq. km.)
POPULATION 7,029,000
CAPITAL Baku
LARGEST CITY Baku
HIGHEST POINT Bazardyuzyu 14,653 ft. (4,466 m.)
MAJOR LANGUAGES Azerbaijani, Russian, Armenian
MAJOR RELIGIONS Islam, Eastern (Russian) Orthodoxy

BELARUS (BELORUSSIA)
AREA 80,154 sq. mi. (207,600 sq. km.)
POPULATION 10,200,000
CAPITAL Minsk
LARGEST CITY Minsk
HIGHEST POINT Dzerzhinskaya 1,135 ft. (346 m.)
MAJOR LANGUAGES Belorussian, Russian, Polish, Ukrainian, Yiddish
MAJOR RELIGIONS Eastern (Russian) Orthodoxy, Roman Catholicism, Judaism

GEORGIA
AREA 26,911 sq. mi. (69,700 sq. km.)
POPULATION 5,449,000
CAPITAL Tbilisi
LARGEST CITY Tbilisi
HIGHEST POINT Kazbek 16,512 ft. (5,033 m.)
MAJOR LANGUAGES Georgian, Armenian, Russian, Azerbaijani, Abkhazian, Ossetian
MAJOR RELIGIONS Eastern (Georgian) Orthodoxy, Islam

KAZAKHSTAN
AREA 1,048,300 sq. mi. (2,715,100 sq. km.)
POPULATION 16,538,000
CAPITAL Alma-Ata
LARGEST CITY Alma-Ata
HIGHEST POINT Khan-Tengri 22,951 ft. (6,995 m.)
MAJOR LANGUAGES Kazakh, Russian, German, Ukrainian, Uzbek, Tatar
MAJOR RELIGIONS Islam, Eastern (Russian) Orthodoxy

KYRGYZSTAN (KIRGIZIA)
AREA 76,641 sq. mi. (198,500 sq. km.)
POPULATION 4,291,000
CAPITAL Bishkek (Frunze)
LARGEST CITY Bishkek (Frunze)
HIGHEST POINT Pobeda Peak 24,406 ft. (7,439 m.)
MAJOR LANGUAGES Kirgiz, Russian, Uzbek, Ukrainian, German, Tatar
MAJOR RELIGIONS Islam, Eastern (Russian) Orthodoxy

MOLDOVA
AREA 13,012 sq. mi. (33,700 sq. km.)
POPULATION 4,341,000
CAPITAL Kishinev
LARGEST CITY Kishinev
HIGHEST POINT 1,408 ft. (429 m.)
MAJOR LANGUAGES Moldavian (Romanian), Ukrainian, Russian, Gagauzi, Yiddish
MAJOR RELIGIONS Eastern (Romanian) Orthodoxy, Judaism

RUSSIA
AREA 6,592,812 sq. mi. (17,075,400 sq. km.)
POPULATION 147,386,000
CAPITAL Moscow
LARGEST CITY Moscow
HIGHEST POINT El'brus 18,510 ft. (5,642 m.)
MONETARY UNIT ruble
MAJOR LANGUAGES Russian, Tatar, Ukrainian, Chuvash, Bashkir, Belorussian, Mordvinian, German, Kazakh, Yiddish, Chechen, Udmurt, Ossetian, Buryat, Yakut, Ingush, Tuvan
MAJOR RELIGIONS Eastern (Russian) Orthodoxy, Roman Catholicism, Islam, Judaism, Lamaism, Buddhism, Animism

TAJIKISTAN
AREA 55,251 sq. mi. (143,100 sq. km.)
POPULATION 5,112,000
CAPITAL Dushanbe
LARGEST CITY Dushanbe
HIGHEST POINT Communism Peak 24,599 ft. (7,498 m.)
MAJOR LANGUAGES Tajik, Uzbek, Russian, Tatar, Kirgiz
MAJOR RELIGIONS Islam, Eastern (Russian) Orthodoxy

TURKMENISTAN
AREA 188,455 sq. mi. (488,100 sq. km.)
POPULATION 3,534,000
CAPITAL Ashkhabad
LARGEST CITY Ashkhabad
HIGHEST POINT Rize 9,653 ft. (2,942 m.)
MAJOR LANGUAGES Turkmenian, Russian, Uzbek, Kazakh, Tatar
MAJOR RELIGIONS Islam, Eastern (Russian) Orthodoxy

UKRAINE
AREA 233,089 sq. mi. (603,700 sq. km.)
POPULATION 51,704,000
CAPITAL Kiev
LARGEST CITY Kiev
HIGHEST POINT Goverla 6,762 ft. (2,061 m.)
MAJOR LANGUAGES Ukrainian, Russian, Yiddish, Belorussian, Moldavian (Romanian), Polish, Tatar
MAJOR RELIGIONS Eastern (Ukrainian) Orthodoxy, Roman (Ukrainian Uniate) Catholicism, Judaism

UZBEKISTAN
AREA 173,591 sq. mi. (449,600 sq. km.)
POPULATION 19,906,000
CAPITAL Tashkent
LARGEST CITY Tashkent
HIGHEST POINT Khodzha-Pir'yakh 14,515 ft. (4,424 m.)
MAJOR LANGUAGES Uzbek, Russian, Tajik, Kazakh, Tatar, Karakalpak, Kirgiz, Ukrainian, Turkmenian
MAJOR RELIGIONS Islam, Eastern (Russian) Orthodoxy

Topography

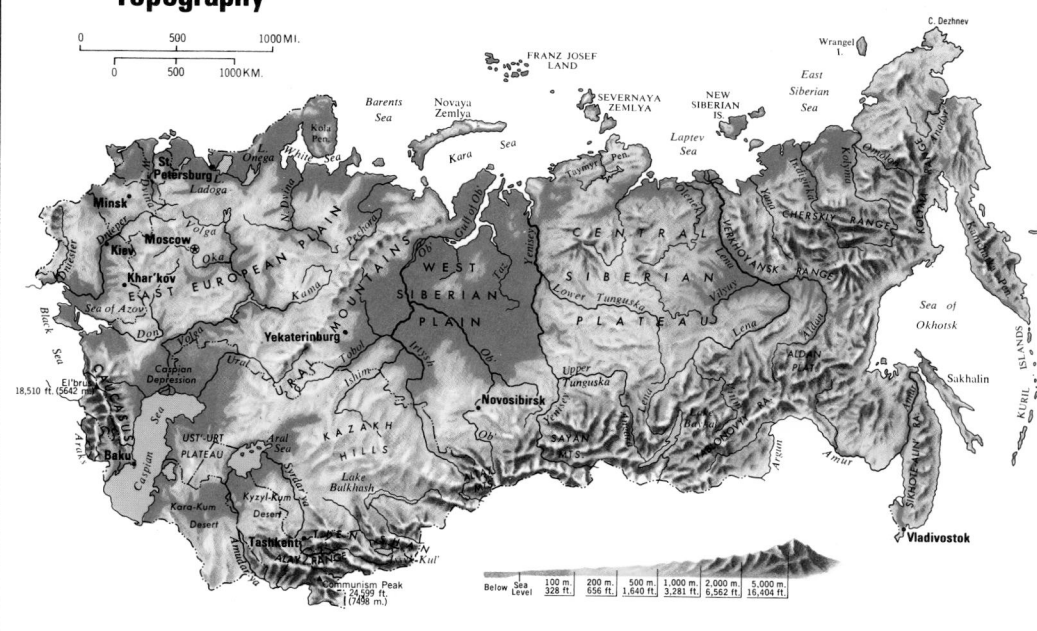

© Copyright HAMMOND INCORPORATED, Maplewood, N.J.

(continued)

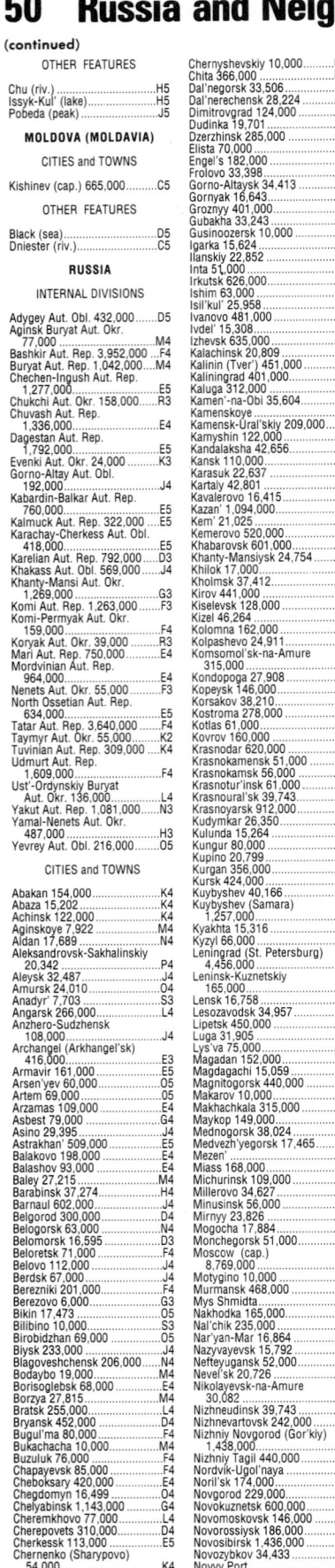

Agriculture, Industry and Resources
(Eastern Europe)

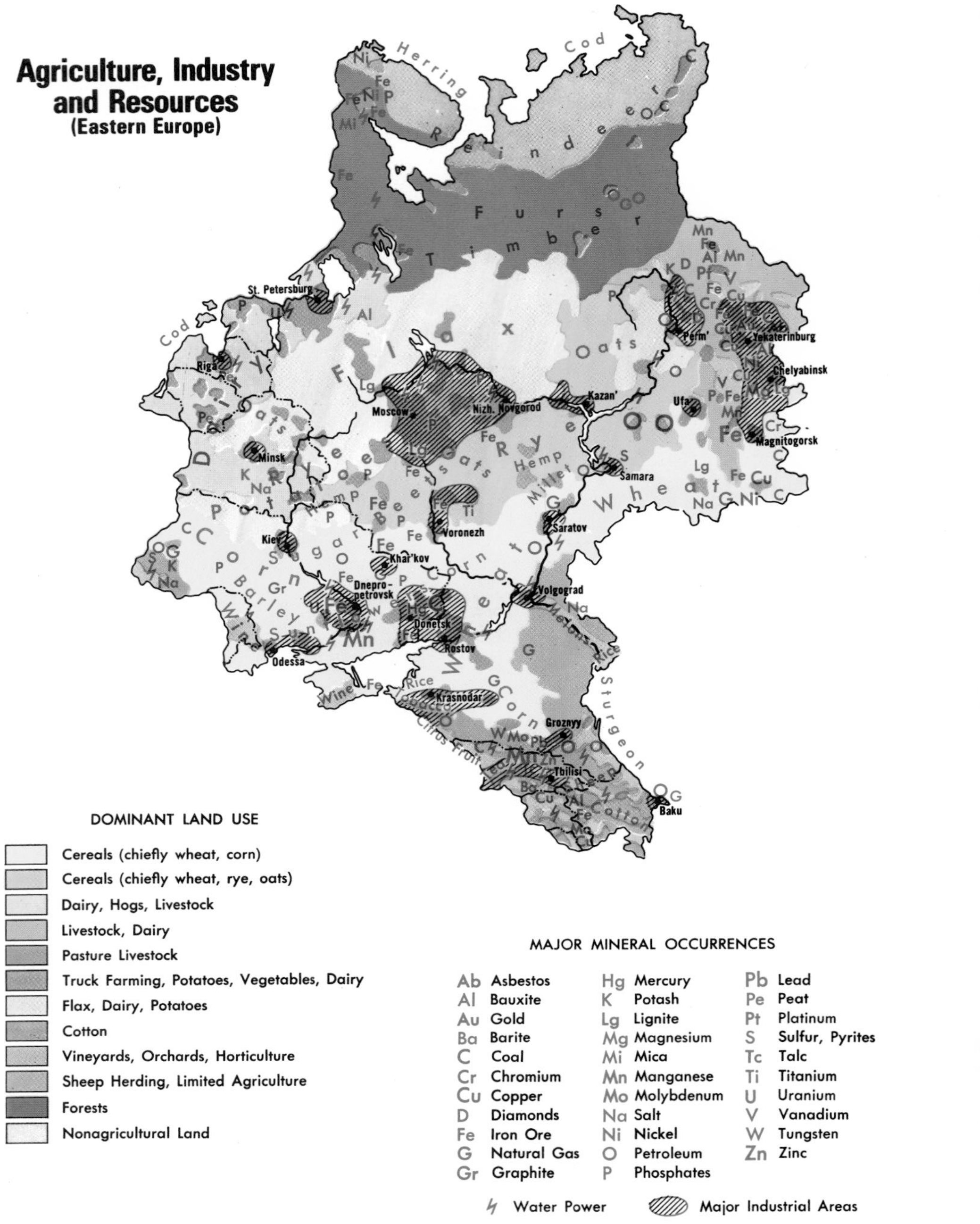

DOMINANT LAND USE

- Cereals (chiefly wheat, corn)
- Cereals (chiefly wheat, rye, oats)
- Dairy, Hogs, Livestock
- Livestock, Dairy
- Pasture Livestock
- Truck Farming, Potatoes, Vegetables, Dairy
- Flax, Dairy, Potatoes
- Cotton
- Vineyards, Orchards, Horticulture
- Sheep Herding, Limited Agriculture
- Forests
- Nonagricultural Land

MAJOR MINERAL OCCURRENCES

Ab	Asbestos	Hg	Mercury	Pb	Lead
Al	Bauxite	K	Potash	Pe	Peat
Au	Gold	Lg	Lignite	Pt	Platinum
Ba	Barite	Mg	Magnesium	S	Sulfur, Pyrites
C	Coal	Mi	Mica	Tc	Talc
Cr	Chromium	Mn	Manganese	Ti	Titanium
Cu	Copper	Mo	Molybdenum	U	Uranium
D	Diamonds	Na	Salt	V	Vanadium
Fe	Iron Ore	Ni	Nickel	W	Tungsten
G	Natural Gas	O	Petroleum	Zn	Zinc
Gr	Graphite	P	Phosphates		

⚡ Water Power   ▨ Major Industrial Areas

Agriculture, Industry and Resources
(Northern Asia)

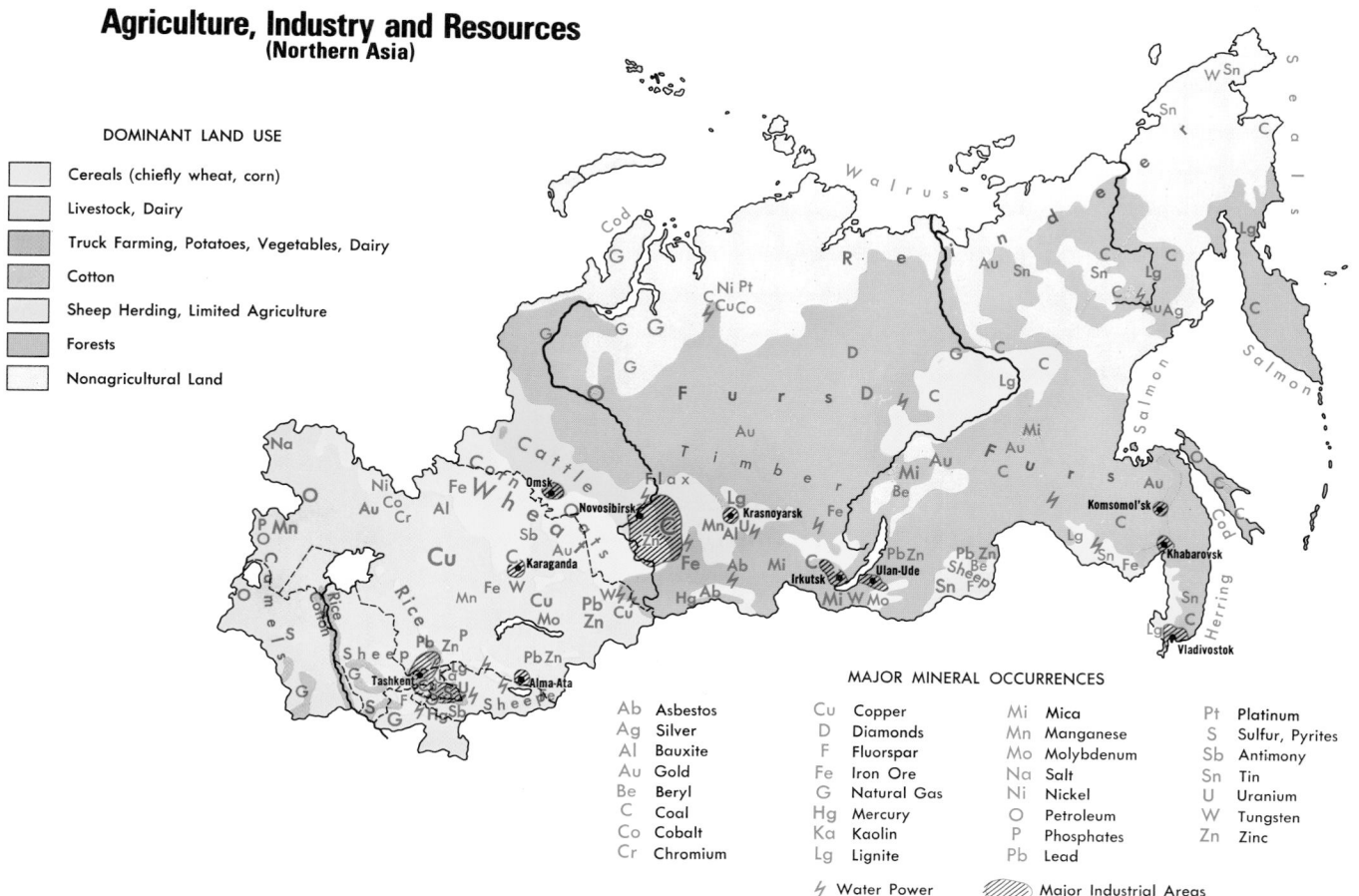

DOMINANT LAND USE

- Cereals (chiefly wheat, corn)
- Livestock, Dairy
- Truck Farming, Potatoes, Vegetables, Dairy
- Cotton
- Sheep Herding, Limited Agriculture
- Forests
- Nonagricultural Land

MAJOR MINERAL OCCURRENCES

Ab	Asbestos	Cu	Copper	Mi	Mica	Pt	Platinum
Ag	Silver	D	Diamonds	Mn	Manganese	S	Sulfur, Pyrites
Al	Bauxite	F	Fluorspar	Mo	Molybdenum	Sb	Antimony
Au	Gold	Fe	Iron Ore	Na	Salt	Sn	Tin
Be	Beryl	G	Natural Gas	Ni	Nickel	U	Uranium
C	Coal	Hg	Mercury	O	Petroleum	W	Tungsten
Co	Cobalt	Ka	Kaolin	P	Phosphates	Zn	Zinc
Cr	Chromium	Lg	Lignite	Pb	Lead		

⚡ Water Power ▨ Major Industrial Areas

Russia and Neighboring Countries
European Part

CONIC PROJECTION

SCALE OF MILES
0   50   100   200   300

SCALE OF KILOMETERS
0   50   100   200   300

National Capitals .... ⭐
Administrative Centers .... △
International boundaries .... ▬▬▬
Aut. Rep., Oblast, Kray boundaries .... ▬▬▬
Autonomous Oblast boundaries .... ┈┈┈
Autonomous Okrug boundaries .... ┈┈┈

© Copyright HAMMOND INCORPORATED, Maplewood, N.J.

Administrative Divisions bear same names as their respective Capitals or Centers, except:

Division	Capital/Center	Grid
Abkhaz Aut. Rep.	Sukhumi	F6
Adygey Aut. Oblast	Maykop	F6
Adzhar Aut. Rep.	Batumi	F6
Bashkir Aut. Rep.	Ufa	J4
Chechen-Ingush Aut. Rep.	Groznyy	G6
Chuvash Aut. Rep.	Cheboksary	G3
Crimean Oblast	Simferopol'	D6
Dagestan Aut. Rep.	Makhachkala	G6
Kabardin-Balkar Aut. Rep.	Nal'chik	F6
Kalmuck Aut. Rep.	Elista	F5
Karachay-Cherkess Aut. Obl.	Cherkessk	F6
Karelian Aut. Rep.	Petrozavodsk	D2
Komi Aut. Rep.	Syktyvkar	H2
Komi-Permyak Aut. Okrug	Kudymkar	H3
Mari Aut. Rep.	Yoshkar-Ola	G3
Mordvinian Aut. Rep.	Saransk	G4
Nagorno-Karabakh Aut. Obl.	Stepanakert	G7
Nenets Aut. Okrug	Nar'yan-Mar	H1
North Ossetian Aut. Rep.	Vladikavkaz	F6
South Ossetian Aut. Obl.	Tskhinvali	F6
Tatar Aut. Rep.	Kazan	G3
Trans-Carpathian Oblast	Uzhgorod	B5
Udmurt Aut. Rep.	Izhevsk	H3
Volyn Oblast	Lutsk	C4

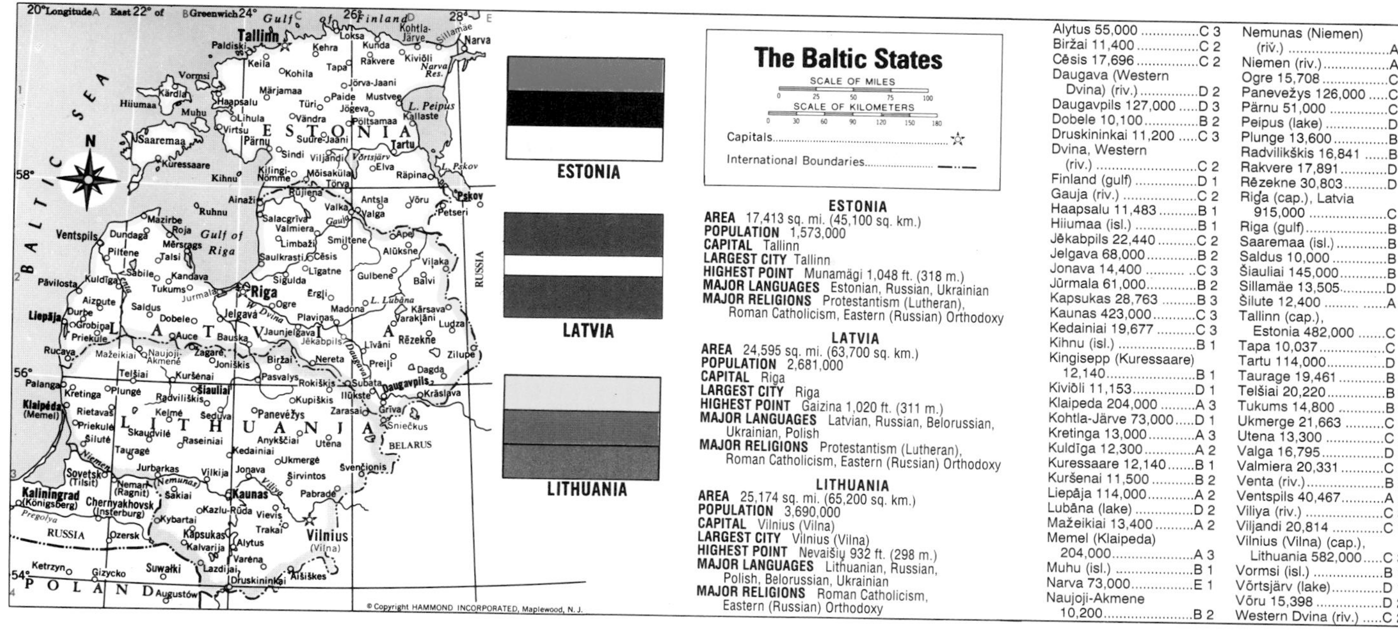

ESTONIA

LATVIA

LITHUANIA

The Baltic States

SCALE OF MILES
SCALE OF KILOMETERS
Capitals ☆
International Boundaries

ESTONIA
AREA 17,413 sq. mi. (45,100 sq. km.)
POPULATION 1,573,000
CAPITAL Tallinn
LARGEST CITY Tallinn
HIGHEST POINT Munamägi 1,048 ft. (318 m.)
MAJOR LANGUAGES Estonian, Russian, Ukrainian
MAJOR RELIGIONS Protestantism (Lutheran), Roman Catholicism, Eastern (Russian) Orthodoxy

LATVIA
AREA 24,595 sq. mi. (63,700 sq. km.)
POPULATION 2,681,000
CAPITAL Riga
LARGEST CITY Riga
HIGHEST POINT Gaizina 1,020 ft. (311 m.)
MAJOR LANGUAGES Latvian, Russian, Belorussian, Ukrainian, Polish
MAJOR RELIGIONS Protestantism (Lutheran), Roman Catholicism, Eastern (Russian) Orthodoxy

LITHUANIA
AREA 25,174 sq. mi. (65,200 sq. km.)
POPULATION 3,690,000
CAPITAL Vilnius (Vilna)
LARGEST CITY Vilnius (Vilna)
HIGHEST POINT Nevaišiu 932 ft. (298 m.)
MAJOR LANGUAGES Lithuanian, Russian, Polish, Belorussian, Ukrainian
MAJOR RELIGIONS Roman Catholicism, Eastern (Russian) Orthodoxy

Alytus 55,000 C 3
Biržai 11,400 C 2
Cēsis 17,696 C 2
Daugava (Western Dvina) (riv.) D 2
Daugavpils 127,000 D 3
Dobele 10,100 B 2
Druskininkai 11,200 C 3
Dvina, Western (riv.) C 2
Finland (gulf) D 1
Gauja (riv.) C 2
Haapsalu 11,483 B 1
Hiiumaa (isl.) B 1
Jēkabpils 22,440 C 2
Jelgava 68,000 B 2
Jonava 14,400 C 3
Jūrmala 61,000 B 2
Kapsukas 28,763 B 3
Kaunas 423,000 C 3
Kedainiai 19,677 C 3
Kihnu (isl.) B 1
Kingisepp (Kuressaare) 12,140 B 1
Kiviõli 11,153 D 1
Klaipeda 204,000 A 3
Kohtla-Järve 73,000 D 1
Kretinga 13,000 A 3
Kuldīga 12,300 A 2
Kuressaare 12,140 B 1
Kuršenai 11,500 B 2
Liepāja 114,000 A 2
Lubāna (lake) D 2
Mažeikiai 13,400 A 2
Memel (Klaipeda) 204,000 A 3
Muhu (isl.) B 1
Narva 73,000 E 1
Naujoji-Akmene 10,200 B 2
Nemunas (Niemen) (riv.) A 3
Niemen (riv.) A 3
Ogre 15,708 C 2
Panevežys 126,000 C 3
Pärnu 51,000 C 1
Peipus (lake) D 1
Plunge 13,600 B 3
Radviliškis 16,841 B 3
Rakvere 17,891 D 1
Rēzekne 30,803 D 2
Rīga (cap.), Latvia 915,000 C 2
Riga (gulf) B 2
Saaremaa (isl.) B 1
Saldus 10,000 B 2
Šiauliai 145,000 B 3
Sillamäe 13,505 D 1
Šilute 12,400 A 3
Tallinn (cap.), Estonia 482,000 C 1
Tapa 10,037 C 1
Tartu 114,000 D 1
Taurage 19,461 B 3
Telšiai 20,220 B 2
Tukums 14,800 B 2
Ukmerge 21,663 C 3
Utena 13,300 C 3
Valga 16,795 D 2
Valmiera 20,331 C 2
Venta (riv.) B 2
Ventspils 40,467 A 2
Viljandi 20,814 C 1
Viliya (riv.) C 3
Vilnius (Vilna) (cap.), Lithuania 582,000 C 3
Vormsi (isl.) B 1
Võrtsjärv (lake) D 1
Võru 15,398 D 2
Western Dvina (riv.) C 2

ARMENIA

CITIES and TOWNS

Kirovakan 162,000 F6
Kumayri 120,000 F6
Leninakan (Kumayri) 120,000 F6
Yerevan (cap.) 1,199,000 F6

OTHER FEATURES

Alagez (mt.) F6
Araks (riv.) G7
Caucasus (mts.) F6
Kapydzhik (mt.) G7
Sevan (lake) G6

AZERBAIJAN

INTERNAL DIVISIONS

Nagorno-Karabakh Aut. Obl. 188,000 G7
Nakhichevan' Aut. Rep. 295,000 F7

CITIES and TOWNS

Baku (cap.) 1,150,000 H6
Gyandzhe 278,000 G6
Kirovabad (Gyandzhe) 278,000 G6
Mingechaur 60,000 G6
Nakhichevan' 33,279 G7
Stepanakert 30,293 G7
Sumgait 231,000 G6

OTHER FEATURES

Apsheron (pen.) H6
Araks (riv.) G7
Caspian (sea) G6
Caucasus (mts.) F6
Kura (riv.) G6

BELARUS (BELORUSSIA)

CITIES and TOWNS

Baranovichi 159,000 C4
Bobruysk 223,000 C4
Borisov 144,000 C4
Brest 258,000 B4
Gomel' 500,000 D4
Grodno 270,000 B4
Lida 73,000 C4
Minsk (cap.) 1,589,000 C4
Mogilev 356,000 C4
Molodechno 82,000 C4
Mozyr' 101,000 C4
Orsha 123,000 D4
Pinsk 119,000 C4
Polotsk 71,000 C3
Rechitsa 67,000 C4
Soligorsk 82,000 C4
Vitebsk 350,000 C3

OTHER FEATURES

Berezina (riv.) C4
Bug (riv.) B4
Dnieper (riv.) D5
Dvina, Western (riv.) C3
Goryn' (riv.) C4
Niemen (riv.) B4
Pripet (marshes) C4
Pripyat' (riv.) C4
Western Dvina (riv.) C3

GEORGIA

INTERNAL DIVISIONS

Abkhaz Aut. Rep. 537,000 F6
Adzhar Aut. Rep. 393,000 F6
South Ossetian Aut. Obl. 99,000 F6

CITIES and TOWNS

Batumi 136,000 F6
Gori 60,000 F6
Kutaisi 235,000 F6
Makaradze (Ozurgeti) 21,679 F6
Ozurgeti 21,679 F6
Poti 45,979 F6
Rustavi 159,000 G6
Sukhumi 121,000 F6
Tbilisi (cap.) 1,260,000 F6
Tiflis (Tbilisi) 1,260,000 F6
Tskhinvali 30,311 F6

OTHER FEATURES

Black (sea) D6
Caucasus (mts.) F6

MOLDOVA (MOLDAVIA)

CITIES and TOWNS

Bel'tsy 159,000 C5
Bendery 130,000 C5
Kishinev (cap.) 665,000 C5
Tighina (Bendery) 130,000 C5
Tiraspol' 182,000 D5

OTHER FEATURES

Black (sea) D6
Dniester (riv.) C5
Prut (riv.) C5

RUSSIA

INTERNAL DIVISIONS

Adygey Aut. Obl. 432,000 F6
Bashkir Aut. Rep. 3,952,000 J4
Chechen-Ingush Aut. Rep. 1,277,000 G6
Chuvash Aut. Rep. 1,336,000 G3
Dagestan Aut. Rep. 1,792,000 G6
Kabardin-Balkar Aut. Rep. 760,000 F6
Kalmuck Aut. Rep. 322,000 F5
Karachay-Cherkess Aut. Obl. 418,000 F6
Karelian Aut. Rep. 792,000 D2
Komi Aut. Rep. 1,263,000 H2
Komi-Permyak Aut. Okr. 159,000 H3
Mari Aut. Rep. 750,000 G3
Mordvinian Aut. Rep. 964,000 G4
Nenets Aut. Okr. 55,000 H1
North Ossetian Aut. Rep. 634,000 F6
Tatar Aut. Rep. 3,640,000 G3
Udmurt Aut. Rep. 1,609,000 H3

CITIES and TOWNS

Akhtubinsk 51,000 G5
Al'met'yevsk 129,000 H3
Archangel (Arkhangel'sk) 416,000 F2
Armavir 161,000 F5
Arzamas 109,000 F3
Astrakhan' 509,000 G5
Azov 79,000 E5
Balakovo 198,000 G4
Balashov 97,000 F4
Bataysk 95,000 E5
Belgorod 300,000 E4
Berezniki 201,000 J3
Borisoglebsk 63,000 F4
Borovichi 63,000 D3
Bryansk 452,000 D4
Bugul'ma 85,000 H4
Buzuluk 76,000 H4
Chapayevsk 86,000 G4
Chaykovskiy 76,000 H3
Cheboksary 420,000 G3
Cherepovets 310,000 E3
Cherkessk 113,000 F6
Chistopol' 65,000 H3
Derbent 78,000 G6
Dimitrovgrad 124,000 G4
Dzerzhinsk 285,000 F3
Elektrostal' 153,000 E3
Elista 80,000 F5
Engel's 182,000 G4
Gatchina 78,000 D3
Glazov 104,000 H3
Groznyy 401,000 G6
Gubkin 70,000 E4
Gukovo 71,000 F5
Gus'-Khrustal'nyy 74,000 F3
Ishimbay 63,000 J4
Ivanovo 481,000 E3
Izhevsk 635,000 H3
Kaliningrad, Kaliningrad 401,000 B4
Kaliningrad, Moscow Oblast 160,000 E3
Kaluga 312,000 E4
Kamensk-Shakhtinskiy 75,000 F5
Kamyshin 122,000 F4
Kazan' 1,094,000 G3
Khasavyurt 72,000 G6
Kimry 60,000 E3
Kineshma 105,000 F3
Kirov 441,000 G3
Kirovo-Chepetsk 83,000 H3
Kislovodsk 114,000 F6
Klintsy 71,000 D4
Kolomna 162,000 E4
Kolpino 142,000 D3
Königsberg (Kaliningrad) 410,000 B4
Kostroma 278,000 F3
Kotlas 66,000 G2
Kovrov 160,000 F3
Krasnodar 620,000 E6
Kropotkin 73,000 F5
Kungur 82,000 J3
Kursk 424,000 E4
Kuznetsk 97,000 G4
Leningrad (St. Petersburg) 4,456,000 C3
Lipetsk 450,000 E4
Lys'va 76,000 J3
Lyubertsy 165,000 E3
Makhachkala 315,000 G6
Maykop 149,000 F6
Michurinsk 109,000 F4
Mineral'nye Vody 72,000 F6
Moscow (Moskva) (cap.) 8,769,000 E3
Murmansk 468,000 D1
Murom 124,000 F3
Mytishchi 154,000 E3
Naberezhnye Chelny 501,000 H3
Nal'chik 235,000 F6
Neftekamsk 107,000 H3
Nevinnomyssk 121,000 F6
Nizhnekamsk 191,000 H3
Nizhniy Novgorod (Gor'kiy) 1,438,000 F3
Novgorod 229,000 D3
Novocherkassk 187,000 F5
Novokuybyshevsk 113,000 G4
Novomoskovsk 146,000 E4
Novorossiysk 186,000 E6
Novoshakhtinsk 106,000 E5
Novotroitsk 106,000 J4
Obninsk 100,000 E3
Oktyabr'skiy 105,000 H4
Ordzhonikidze (Vladikavkaz) 300,000 F6
Orekhovo-Zuyevo 137,000 D3
Orel 337,000 E4
Orenburg 547,000 J4
Orsk 271,000 J4
Penza 483,000 G4
Perm' (Molotov) 1,091,000 J3
Petrozavodsk 270,000 D2
Podol'sk 210,000 E3
Pskov 204,000 C3
Pyatigorsk 129,000 F6
Rostov 1,020,000 F5
Ryazan' 515,000 E4
Rybinsk 252,000 E3
Rzhev 70,000 D3
St. Petersburg 4,456,000 C3
Salavat 150,000 H4
Samara (Kuybyshev) 1,257,000 H4
Saransk 312,000 G4
Sarapul 111,000 H3
Saratov 905,000 G4
Sergiyev Posad 115,000 E3
Serpukhov 144,000 E4
Sevastopol' 356,000 D6
Severodvinsk 249,000 E2
Shakhty 224,000 F5
Shchekino 70,000 E4
Shuya 72,000 F3
Simbirsk 625,000 G4
Smolensk 341,000 D4
Sochi 337,000 E6
Solikamsk 110,000 J3
Stalingrad (Volgograd) 999,000 F5
Staryy Oskol 174,000 E4
Stavropol' 318,000 F5
Sterlitamak 248,000 J4
Stupino 72,000 E4
Syktyvkar 233,000 H2
Syzran' 174,000 G4
Taganrog 291,000 E5
Tambov 305,000 F4
Togliatti (Tol'yatti) 630,000 G4
Tula 540,000 E4
Tver' (Kalinin) 451,000 E3
Ufa 1,083,000 J4
Ukhta 111,000 H2
Ul'yanovsk (Simbirsk) 625,000 G4
Velikiye Luki 114,000 D3
Viipuri (Vyborg) 79,000 C2
Vladikavkaz 300,000 F6
Vladimir 350,000 F3
Volgodonsk 176,000 F5
Volgograd 999,000 F5
Vologda 283,000 F3
Volzhskiy 269,000 G5
Vorkuta 116,000 K1
Voronezh 887,000 E4
Voskresensk 79,000 E3
Votkinsk 103,000 H3
Vyborg 79,000 C2
Vyshniy Volochek 71,000 D3
Yaroslavl' 633,000 E3
Yelets 120,000 E4
Yessentuki 82,000 F6
Yeysk 75,000 E5
Yoshkar-Ola 242,000 G3
Zagorsk (Sergiyev Posad) 115,000 E3
Zelenodol'sk 88,000 G3
Zheleznodorozhnyy 76,000 H2
Zheleznogorsk 74,000 E4

OTHER FEATURES

Azov (sea) E5
Baltic (sea) B3
Barents (sea) E1
Baydarata (bay) L1
Belaya (riv.) H3
Beloye (lake) E2
Black (sea) D6
Bolvanskiy Nos (cape) K1
Caspian (sea) G6
Caucasus (mts.) F6
Central Ural (mts.) J2
Cheshskaya (bay) G1
Chir (riv.) F5
Denezhkin Kamen' (mt.) J2
Desna (riv.) D4
Dnieper (riv.) D5
Dolgiy (isl.) J1
Don (riv.) F5
Dvina (bay) E2
Dvina (riv.) F2
Dykhtau (mt.) F6
El'brus (mt.) F6
Finland (gulf) C3
Ilek (riv.) J4
Il'men' (lake) D3
Imandra (lake) D1
Izhma (riv.) H2
Kama (res.) J3
Kama (riv.) H2
Kandalaksha (gulf) D1
Kanin (pen.) G1
Kanin Nos (cape) F1
Kara (sea) K1
Karskiye Vorota (str.) J1
Kazbek (mt.) F6
Khoper (riv.) F4
Kil'din (isl.) D1
Kinel' (riv.) H4
Kola (pen.) E1
Kolguyev (isl.) G1
Kolva (riv.) J1
Kuban' (riv.) E5
Kubeno (lake) E3
Kuma (riv.) G5
Kuybyshev (res.) G4
Kuyto (lake) D2
Lacha (lake) E2
Ladoga (lake) D2
Lapland (reg.) D1
Lovat' (riv.) D3
Mansel'ka (mts.) C1
Manych-Gudilo (lake) F5
Matveyev (isl.) J1
Medveditsa (riv.) F4
Mezen' (bay) F1
Mezen' (riv.) G1
Mezhdusharskiy (isl.) H1
Moksha (riv.) F4
Moskva (riv.) E3
Msta (riv.) D3
Narodnaya (mt.) J1
Northern Dvina (riv.) F2
North Ural (mts.) K1
Novaya Zemlya (isls.) H1
Oka (riv.) F4
Onega (bay) E2
Onega (lake) E2
Onega (riv.) E2
Payyer (mt.) K1
Pechora (bay) H1
Pechora (riv.) H1
Pechora (sea) H1
Peipus (lake) C3
Pinega (riv.) G2
Ponoy (riv.) E1
Russkiy Zavorot (cape) H1
Rybachiy (pen.) D1
Rybinsk (res.) E3
Samara (riv.) H4
Seg (lake) D2
Solovetskiye (isls.) E1
South Ural (mts.) J4
Suda (riv.) E3
Sukhona (riv.) F2
Sura (riv.) G4
Svir' (riv.) D2
Sysola (riv.) H2
Tel'pos-Iz (mt.) K2
Timan (ridge) G1
Top (lake) D1
Tsil'ma (riv.) H1
Tsimlyansk (res.) F5
Tuloma (riv.) D1
Ufa (riv.) J3
Unzha (riv.) F3
Ural (mts.) J2
Ural (riv.) J4
Usa (riv.) K1
Vaga (riv.) F2
Valday (hills) D3
Vashka (riv.) G2
Vaygach (isl.) K1
Velikaya (riv.) C3
Vetluga (riv.) G3
Vishera (riv.) J2
Vodl (lake) E2
Volga (riv.) G5
Volga-Don (canal) F5
Volgograd (res.) G5
Volkhov (riv.) D3
Vorona (riv.) F4
Vorskla (riv.) E4
Vozhe (lake) F2
Vyatka (riv.) H3
Vychegda (riv.) G2
Vyg (lake) E2
Vym' (riv.) H2
Western Dvina (riv.) C3
White (sea) E1
Yamantau (mt.) J4
Yug (riv.) G2
Yugorskiy (pen.) K1

UKRAINE

INTERNAL DIVISIONS

Crimean Oblast 2,456,000 D6
Trans-Carpathian Obl. 1,252,000 B5
Volyn Oblast 1,062,000 C4

CITIES and TOWNS

Aleksandriya 103,000 D5
Balaklava D6
Belaya Tserkov' 197,000 C5
Belgorod-Dnestrovskiy 51,000 D5
Berdichev 85,000 C5
Berdyansk 132,000 E5
Cherkassy 290,000 D5
Chernigov 296,000 D4
Chernovtsy 257,000 C5
Dneprodzerzhinsk 282,000 D5
Dnepropetrovsk 1,179,000 D5
Donetsk 1,110,000 E5
Drogobych 73,000 B5
Feodosiya 81,000 D5
Gorlovka 337,000 E5
Ivano-Frankovsk 214,000 B5
Izmail 87,000 C5
Kadiyevka (Stakhanov) 112,000 E5
Kalush 64,000 B5
Kamenets-Podol'skiy 102,000 C5
Kerch' 174,000 E5
Khar'kov 1,611,000 E5
Kherson 355,000 D5
Khmel'nitskiy 237,000 C5
Kiev (cap.) 2,587,000 D4
Kirovograd 269,000 D5
Lugansk 497,000 E5
Lutsk 198,000 B4
Lviv (L'vov) (Lwów) 790,000 B5
Makeyevka 430,000 E5
Mariupol' 517,000 E5
Melitopol' 174,000 D5
Mukachevo 82,000 B5
Nikolayev 503,000 D5
Nikopol' 158,000 D5
Odessa 1,115,000 D5
Osipenko (Berdyansk) 132,000 E5
Pavlograd 131,000 E5
Pervomaysk 76,000 D5
Poltava 315,000 D5
Priluki 70,000 D4
Rovno 228,000 C4
Rubezhnoye 68,000 E5
Sevastopol' 356,000 D6
Severodonetsk 131,000 E5
Shostka 82,000 D4
Simferopol' 344,000 D6
Slavyansk 135,000 E5
Smela 70,000 D5
Stakhanov 112,000 E5
Sumy 291,000 E4
Ternopol' 205,000 C5
Uman' 85,000 D5
Uzhgorod 117,000 B5
Vinnitsa 374,000 C5
Voroshilovgrad (Lugansk) 497,000 E5
Yalta 85,000 D6
Yenakiyevo 121,000 E5
Yevpatoriya 108,000 D5
Zaporozh'ye 884,000 E5
Zhitomir 292,000 C4

OTHER FEATURES

Azov (sea) E5
Berezina (riv.) C4
Black (sea) D6
Bug (riv.) B4
Crimea (pen.) D5
Desna (riv.) D4
Dnieper (riv.) D5
Dniester (riv.) C5
Donets (riv.) E5
Goryn' (riv.) C4
Kakhovka (res.) D5
Kiev (res.) C4
Pripet (marshes) C4
Pripyat' (riv.) C4
Prut (riv.) C5
Psel (riv.) D4
Seym (riv.) D4
Vorskla (riv.) E4

Asia

LAMBERT AZIMUTHAL EQUAL-AREA PROJECTION

SCALE OF MILES
0 100 200 400 600 800 1000 1200

SCALE OF KILOMETERS
0 200 400 600 800 1000 1200

Capitals of Countries .... ⊛
Other Capitals .... ⊛
International Boundaries .... ———
Other Boundaries....................... ———
Canals ....

© Copyright HAMMOND INCORPORATED, Maplewood, N.J.

Population Distribution

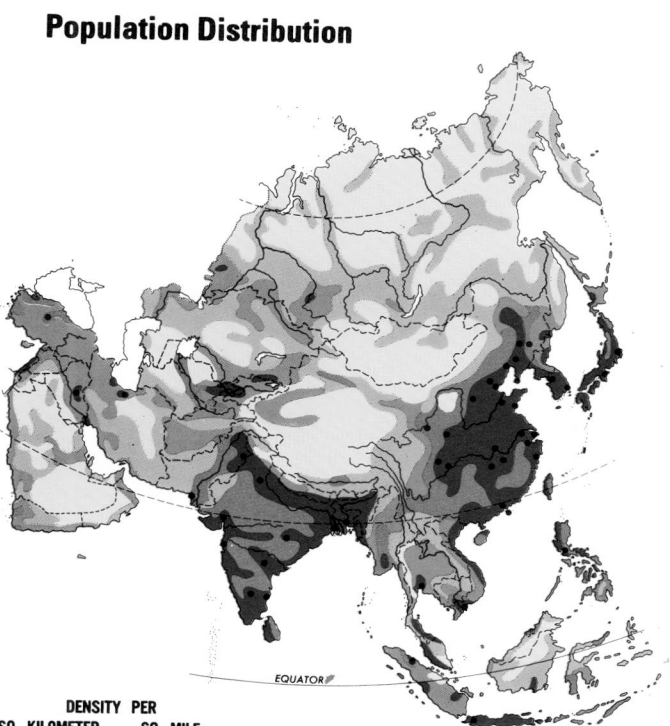

AREA 17,128,500 sq. mi.
(44,362,815 sq. km.)
POPULATION 3,176,000,000
LARGEST CITY Tokyo
HIGHEST POINT Mt. Everest 29,028 ft.
(8,848 m.)
LOWEST POINT Dead Sea -1,296 ft.
(-395 m.)

Vegetation

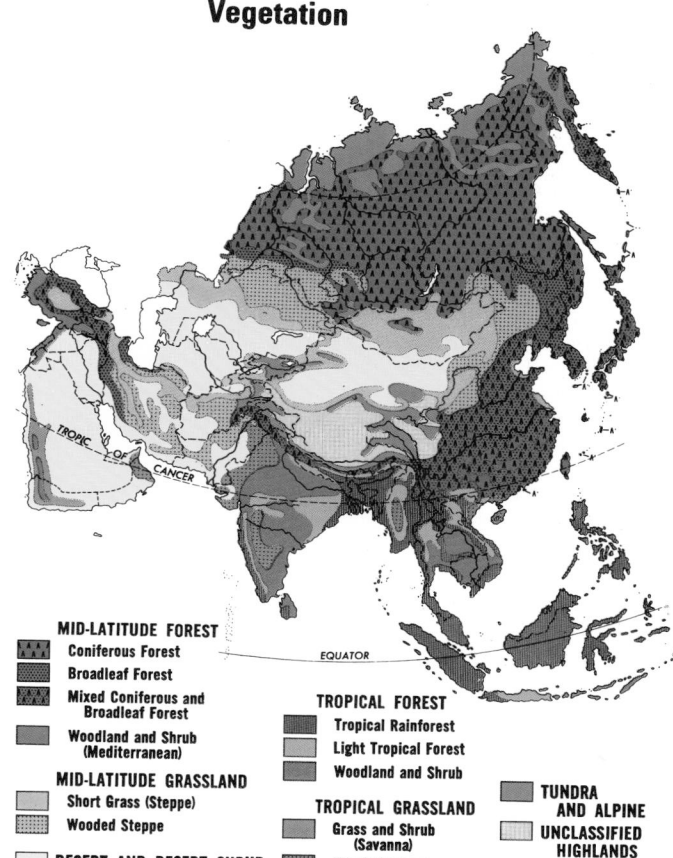

DENSITY PER

SQ. KILOMETER	SQ. MILE
Over 100	Over 260
50-100	130-260
10-50	25-130
1-10	3-25
Under 1	Under 3

• Cities with over 3,000,000
  inhabitants (including suburbs)

MID-LATITUDE FOREST
Coniferous Forest
Broadleaf Forest
Mixed Coniferous and
Broadleaf Forest
Woodland and Shrub
(Mediterranean)

MID-LATITUDE GRASSLAND
Short Grass (Steppe)
Wooded Steppe

DESERT AND DESERT SHRUB

TROPICAL FOREST
Tropical Rainforest
Light Tropical Forest
Woodland and Shrub

TROPICAL GRASSLAND
Grass and Shrub
(Savanna)
Wooded Savanna

TUNDRA AND ALPINE

UNCLASSIFIED HIGHLANDS

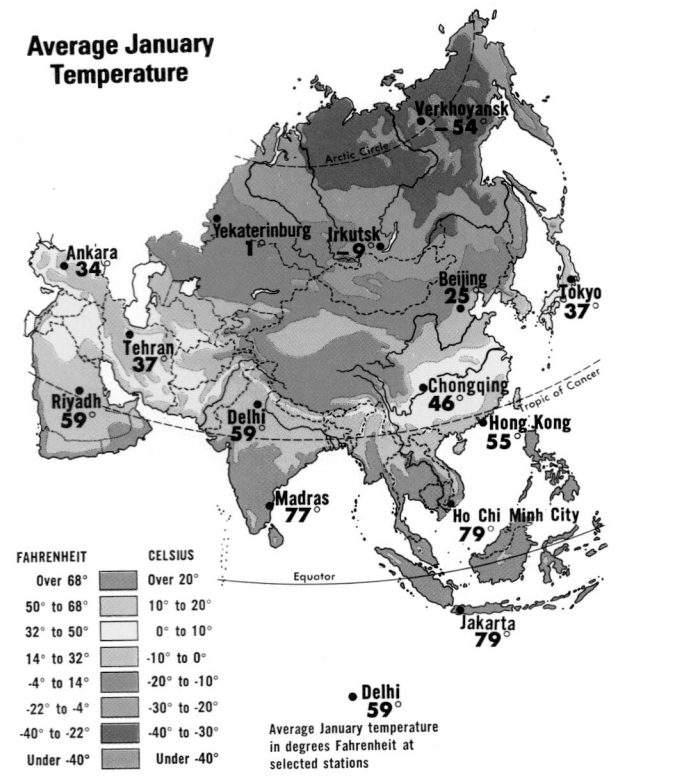

Average January Temperature

Verkhoyansk −54°

Yekaterinburg 1°   Irkutsk −9°

Ankara 34°

Beijing 25°   Tokyo 37°

Tehran 37°

Chongqing 46°   Hong Kong 55°

Riyadh 59°   Delhi 59°

Madras 77°   Ho Chi Minh City 79°

Jakarta 79°

FAHRENHEIT	CELSIUS
Over 68°	Over 20°
50° to 68°	10° to 20°
32° to 50°	0° to 10°
14° to 32°	−10° to 0°
−4° to 14°	−20° to −10°
−22° to −4°	−30° to −20°
−40° to −22°	−40° to −30°
Under −40°	Under −40°

● Delhi 59°
Average January temperature in degrees Fahrenheit at selected stations

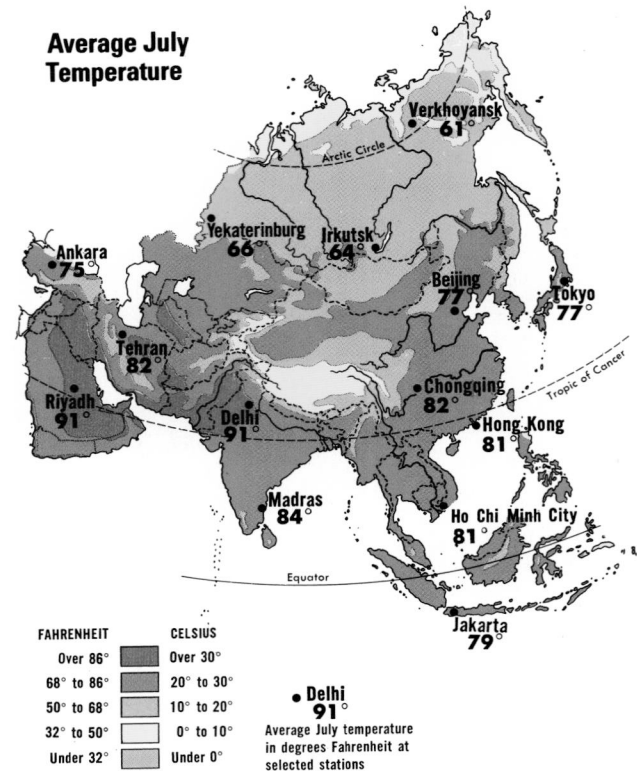

Average July Temperature

Verkhoyansk 61°

Yekaterinburg 66°   Irkutsk 64°

Ankara 75°

Beijing 77°   Tokyo 77°

Tehran 82°

Chongqing 82°   Hong Kong 81°

Riyadh 91°   Delhi 91°

Madras 84°   Ho Chi Minh City 81°

Jakarta 79°

FAHRENHEIT	CELSIUS
Over 86°	Over 30°
68° to 86°	20° to 30°
50° to 68°	10° to 20°
32° to 50°	0° to 10°
Under 32°	Under 0°

● Delhi 91°
Average July temperature in degrees Fahrenheit at selected stations

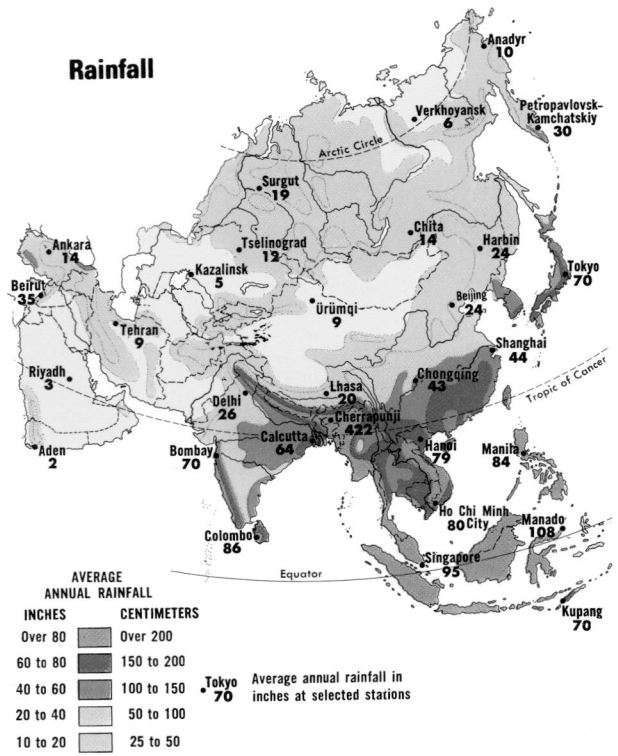

Rainfall

Anadyr 10°

Verkhoyansk 6   Petropavlovsk-Kamchatskiy 30

Surgut 19

Ankara 14   Chita 14   Harbin 24

Beirut 35   Tselinograd 12   Tokyo 70

Kazalinsk 5

Tehran 9   Ürümqi 9   Beijing 24

Riyadh 3   Shanghai 44

Lhasa 20   Chongqing 43

Delhi 26   Cherrapunji 422

Aden 2   Calcutta 64   Hanoi 79   Manila 84

Bombay 70

Ho Chi Minh City 80   Manado 108

Colombo 86

Singapore 95

Kupang 70

AVERAGE ANNUAL RAINFALL	
INCHES	CENTIMETERS
Over 80	Over 200
60 to 80	150 to 200
40 to 60	100 to 150
20 to 40	50 to 100
10 to 20	25 to 50
Under 10	Under 25

● Tokyo 70
Average annual rainfall in inches at selected stations

Vegetation/Relief

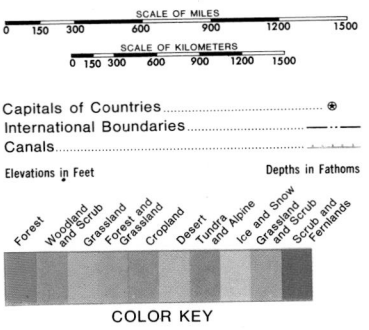

SCALE OF MILES
0 150 300 600 900 1200 1500

SCALE OF KILOMETERS
0 150 300 600 900 1200 1500

Capitals of Countries .... ⊛
International Boundaries .... — · —
Canals ....

Elevations in Feet   Depths in Fathoms

Forest / Woodland and Scrub / Grassland / Forest and Grassland / Cropland / Desert / Tundra and Alpine / Ice and Snow / Grassland and Scrub / Scrub and Fenlands

COLOR KEY

ATLANTIC OCEAN
ICELAND
GREENLAND
Alaska
UNITED STATES
North Pole
ARCTIC OCEAN
NORWEGIAN SEA
Arctic Circle
IRELAND
UNITED KINGDOM
London
NORTH SEA
English Chan.
Bay of Biscay
PORTUGAL
SPAIN
FRANCE
Paris
NORWAY
SWEDEN
FINLAND
Nordkapp
BARENTS SEA
Svalbard (Nor.)
Franz Josef Ld.
Novaya Zemlya
KARA SEA
Severnaya Zemlya
C. Chelyuskin
LAPTEV SEA
New Siberian Is.
EAST SIBERIAN SEA
C. Dezhnev
Bering Str.
BERING SEA
Aleutian Islands
BALTIC SEA
Berlin
POLAND
BELARUS
UKRAINE
Rome
Moscow
Volga
RUSSIA
Siberia
Ob'
Yenisey
Lena
Vilyuy
Yakutsk
Kolyma
Aldan
Kamchatka Peninsula
C. Lopatka
SEA OF OKHOTSK
Sakhalin
Kuril Is.
PACIFIC OCEAN
Ural Mountains
Yekaterinburg
Chelyabinsk
Tobol
Omsk
Irtysh
Novosibirsk
Krasnoyarsk
Angara
Lake Baykal
Irkutsk
Yablonovyy Ra.
Amur
Khabarovsk
Hokkaido
MEDITERRANEAN SEA
BLACK SEA
CASPIAN SEA
CYPRUS
LEBANON
ISRAEL
SYRIA
Cairo
Suez Canal
JORDAN
IRAQ
Baghdad
Tehran
IRAN
KUWAIT
SAUDI ARABIA
Riyadh
BAHRAIN
QATAR
U.A.E.
Persian Gulf
Gulf of Oman
Muscat
OMAN
Rub' al Khali
YEMEN
Aden
Gulf of Aden
Ras Asēr
Socotra
SOMALIA
ETHIOPIA
RED SEA
SUDAN
Nile
Euphrates
KAZAKHSTAN
ARAL SEA
L. Balkhash
Karaganda
UZBEKISTAN
TURKMENISTAN
Ashkhabad
Tashkent
Alma-Ata
KYRGYZSTAN
Syrdar'ya
Amudar'ya
Hindu Kush
AFGHANISTAN
Kabul
Islamabad
Lahore
Helmand
PAKISTAN
Indus
Karachi
K2 (Godwin Austen) 28,250 ft. (8611 m.)
Tarim
Taklimakan
Ürümqi
Altai Mts.
Tien Shan
Kunlun
Tibet
Mt. Everest 29,028 ft. (8848 m.)
MONGOLIA
Ulaanbaatar
Gobi
Great Khingan Ra.
Harbin
Songhua
Vladivostok
Shenyang
N. KOREA
Seoul
S. KOREA
SEA OF JAPAN
Honshu
Tokyo
Nagoya
Osaka
Shikoku
Kyushu
JAPAN
Beijing
Tianjin
Dalian
YELLOW SEA
Huang
Taiyuan
Lanzhou
Xi'an
CHINA
Nanjing
Shanghai
EAST CHINA SEA
Chengdu
Wuhan
Chongqing
Chang
Taipei
Taiwan
Ryukyu Is.
Tropic of Cancer
Guangzhou
HONG KONG (U.K.)
Delhi
New Delhi
Jumna
Kanpur
Ganges
Brahmaputra
INDIA
Ahmadabad
Narbada
Bombay
Godavari
Hyderabad
Kistna
Western Ghats
Bangalore
Madras
Calcutta
BANGLADESH
Dhaka
BURMA
Mekong
Red
Hanoi
Hainan
C. Engaño
Luzon
ARABIAN SEA
BAY OF BENGAL
Rangoon
THAILAND
Bangkok
CAMBODIA
VIETNAM
Ho Chi Minh City
Gulf of Siam
SOUTH CHINA SEA
Manila
PHILIPPINES
Palawan
SULU SEA
Mindanao
Andaman Is.
ANDAMAN SEA
Nicobar Is.
C. Comorin
SRI LANKA (CEYLON)
Colombo
Dondra Head
MALDIVES
MALAYSIA
BRUNEI
CELEBES SEA
Kuala Lumpur
SINGAPORE
Sumatra
Borneo
Celebes
New Guinea
BANDA SEA
INDONESIA
JAVA SEA
FLORES SEA
Jakarta
Java
Surabaya
Timor
TIMOR SEA
Sunda Islands
SEYCHELLES
Equator
COMOROS
INDIAN OCEAN
BRITISH INDIAN OCEAN TERR.
MADAGASCAR
Réunion (Fr.)
MAURITIUS
Tropic of Capricorn
AUSTRALIA
© Copyright HAMMOND INCORPORATED, Maplewood, N. J.
Longitude 70° East of Greenwich

SAUDI ARABIA

KUWAIT

YEMEN

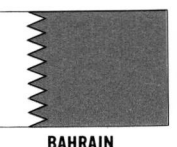
BAHRAIN

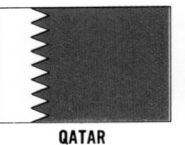
QATAR

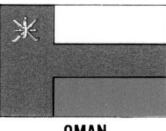
OMAN

AFGHANISTAN

CITIES and TOWNS

Andkhvoy 13,137	H2
Aybak 33,016	J2
Baghlan 75,130	J2
Bamian 7,355	J3
Chaghcharan 2,974	J3

Charikar 25,093	J2
Farah 18,797	H3
Feyzabad 10,142	K2
Gardez 11,415	J3
Ghazni 30,425	J3
Ghurian 12,404	H3
Herat 163,960	H3
Jalalabad 56,384	K3
Kabul (cap.) 905,108	J3

Kalat (Qalat) 5,946	J3
Kandahar (Qandahar) 178,409	J3
Khanabad 26,803	J2
Kholm 28,078	J2
Khowst	J3
Kuhestan	H3
Landay	H3
Lashkar Gah 26,646	H3

Mazar-e Sharif 122,567	J2
Meymaneh 54,954	H2
Pol-e Khomri 31,101	J2
Qalat 5,946	J3
Qal'eh-ye Now 5,340	H3
Qandahar 178,409	J3
Qonduz 107,191	J2
Sar-e Pol 15,699	J2
Sheberghan 54,870	H2

Taloqan 46,202	J2
Zaranj 6,477	H3

OTHER FEATURES

Farah Rud (riv.)	H3
Gowd-e Zerreh (depr.)	H4
Harirud (riv.)	H3
Helmand (riv.)	J3

Hindu Kush (mts.)	J2
Kabul (riv.)	K3
Konar (riv.)	K2
Lurah (riv.)	J3
Margow, Dasht-e (des.)	H3
Murghab (riv.)	H2
Namaksar (salt lake)	H3
Nurestan (reg.)	K2
Paropamisus (mts.)	H3

Qonduz (riv.)	J2
Rigestan (reg.)	H3
Vakhan (reg.)	K2

BAHRAIN

CITIES and TOWNS

Manama (cap.) 88,785	F4

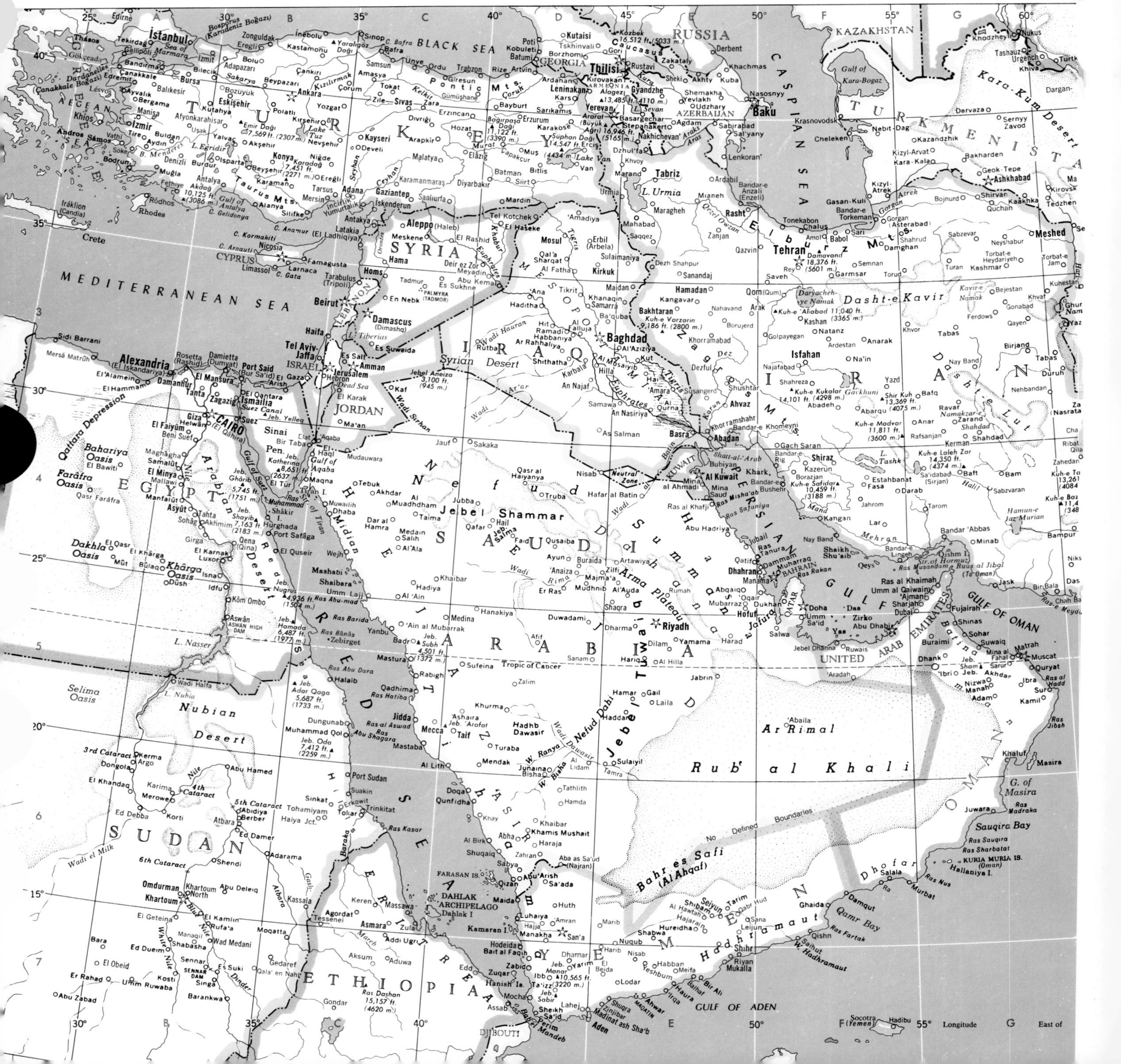

[Map: Near and Middle East showing Turkey, Syria, Iraq, Iran, Saudi Arabia, Egypt, Sudan, Afghanistan, and surrounding regions with the Mediterranean Sea, Black Sea, Caspian Sea, Red Sea, Persian Gulf, and Gulf of Aden]

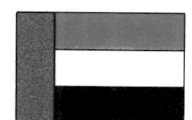

UNITED ARAB EMIRATES

Muharraq 37,732 ....F4

GAZA STRIP

CITIES and TOWNS

Gaza*
118,272 ....B3

IRAN

CITIES and TOWNS

Abadan 296,081 ....E3
Abadeh 16,000 ....F3
Abarqu 8,000 ....F3
Ahvaz 329,006 ....E3
Amol 68,782 ....F2

Anarak 2,038 ....F3	Bejestan 3,823 ....G3
Arak 114,507 ....E3	Birjand 25,854 ....G3
Ardabil 147,404 ....E2	Bojnurd 31,248 ....G2
Ardestan 5,868 ....F3	Borazjan 20,000 ....F4
Asterabad (Gorgan) 88,348....F2	Borazjan 20,000 ....F4
55,978 ....E2	Borujerd 100,103 ....E3
Babol 67,790 ....F2	Chalus 15,000 ....F2
Bafq 5,000 ....G3	Damghan 13,000 ....F2
Baft 6,000 ....G4	Darab 13,000 ....G4
Bakhtaran 290,861 ....E3	Dezful 110,287 ....E3
Bam 22,000 ....G4	
Bandar 'Abbas 89,103 ....G4	
Bandar-e Anzali (Enzeli)	
Bandar-e Bushehr 57,681 ...F4	
Bandar-e Khomeyni 6,000....E3	
Bandar-e Lengeh 4,920 ......F4	
Bandar-e Rig 1,889 ....F4	
Bandar-e Torkeman 13,000...F2	

(continued on following page)

SAUDI ARABIA

AREA   829,995 sq. mi.
           (2,149,687 sq. km.)
POPULATION   14,435,000
CAPITAL   Riyadh
MONETARY UNIT   Saudi riyal
MAJOR LANGUAGE   Arabic
MAJOR RELIGION   Islam

YEMEN

AREA   188,321 sq. mi. (487,792 sq. km.)
POPULATION   10,183,000
CAPITAL   San'a
MONETARY UNIT   Yemeni rial
MAJOR LANGUAGE   Arabic
MAJOR RELIGION   Islam

QATAR

AREA   4,247 sq. mi. (11,000 sq. km.)
POPULATION   422,000
CAPITAL   Doha
MONETARY UNIT   Qatari riyal
MAJOR LANGUAGE   Arabic
MAJOR RELIGION   Islam

KUWAIT

AREA   6,532 sq mi. (16,918 sq. km.)
POPULATION   2,048,000
CAPITAL   Al Kuwait
MONETARY UNIT   Kuwaiti dinar
MAJOR LANGUAGE   Arabic
MAJOR RELIGION   Islam

BAHRAIN

AREA   240 sq. mi. (622 sq. km.)
POPULATION   489,000
CAPITAL   Manama
MONETARY UNIT   Bahraini dinar
MAJOR LANGUAGE   Arabic
MAJOR RELIGION   Islam

OMAN

AREA   120,000 sq. mi. (310,800 sq. km.)
POPULATION   2,000,000
CAPITAL   Muscat
MONETARY UNIT   Omani rial
MAJOR LANGUAGE   Arabic
MAJOR RELIGION   Islam

UNITED ARAB EMIRATES

AREA   32,278 sq. mi. (83,600 sq. km.)
POPULATION   1,206,000
CAPITAL   Abu Dhabi
MONETARY UNIT   dirham
MAJOR LANGUAGE   Arabic
MAJOR RELIGION   Islam

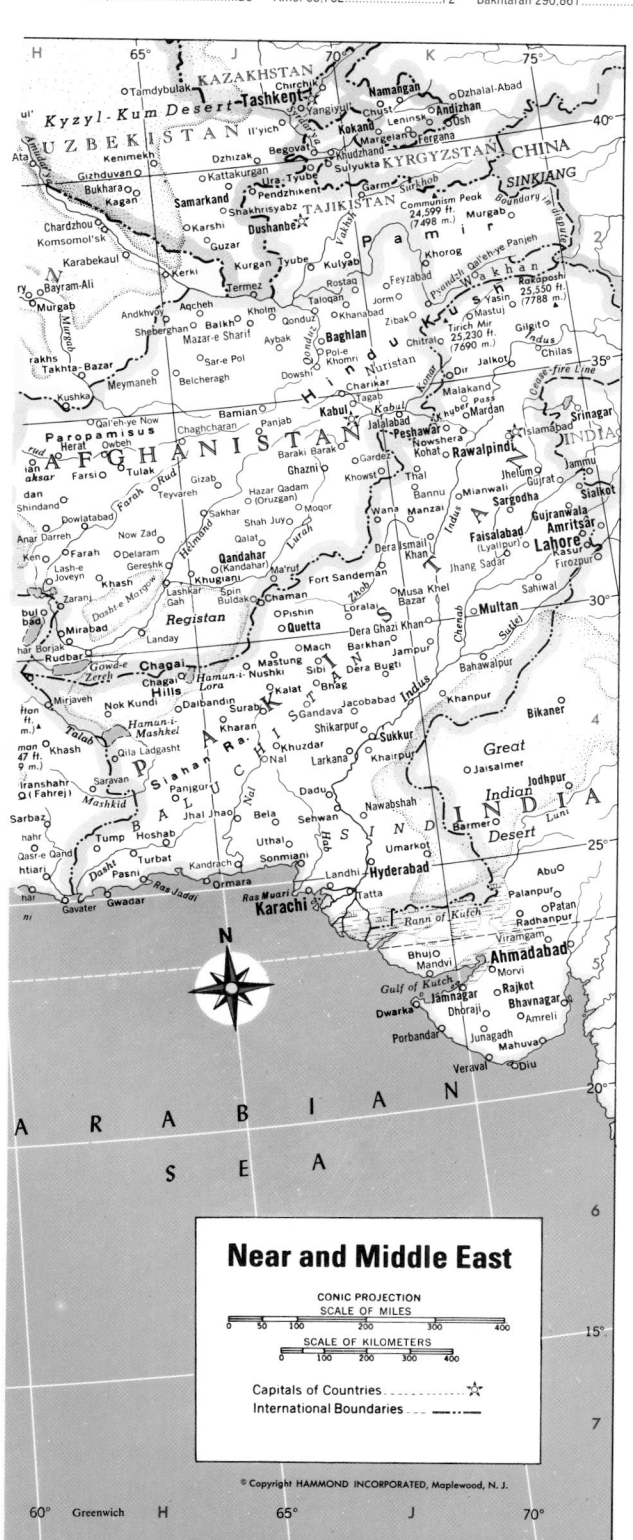

Near and Middle East

CONIC PROJECTION
SCALE OF MILES
0 50 100   200   300   400

SCALE OF KILOMETERS
0 100   200   300   400

Capitals of Countries ....☆
International Boundaries _____

© Copyright HAMMOND INCORPORATED, Maplewood, N.J.

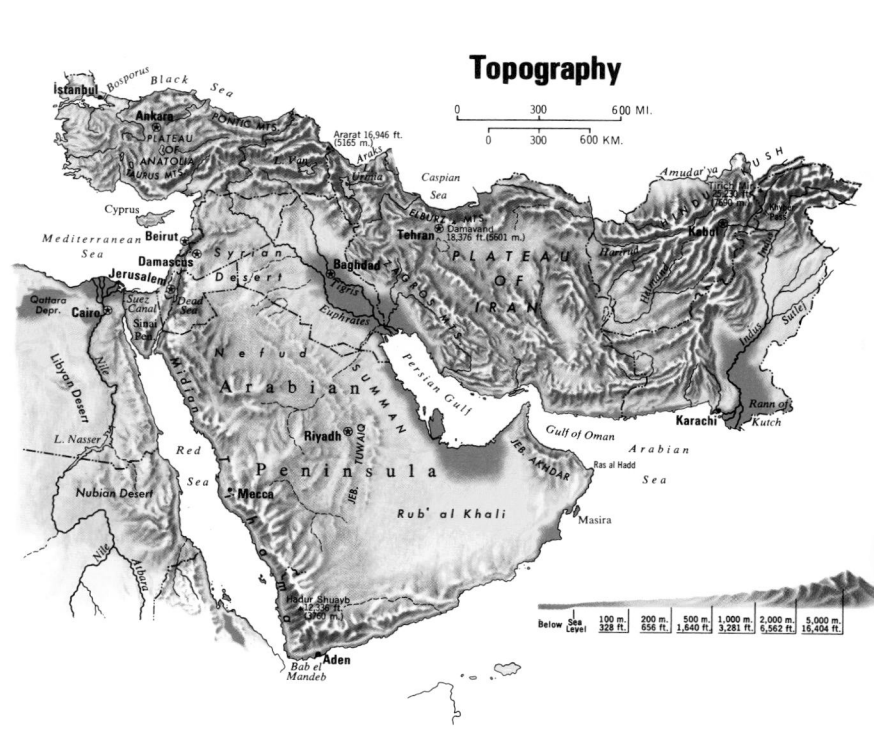

Topography

0   300   600 MI.
0   300   600 KM.

| Below Sea Level | 100 m. 328 ft. | 200 m. 656 ft. | 500 m. 1,640 ft. | 1,000 m. 3,281 ft. | 2,000 m. 6,562 ft. | 5,000 m. 16,404 ft. |

(continued)

Dezh Shahpur 1,384 E2
Enzeli 55,978 E2
Estahbanat 18,187 F4
Fahrej (Iranshahr) 5,000 H4
Fasa 19,000 F4
Ferdows 11,000 G3
Garmsar 4,723 F2
Golpayegan 20,515 F3
Gonabad 8,000 G3
Gorgan 88,348 F2
Hamadan 155,846 E3
Iranshahr 5,000 H4
Isfahan 671,825 F3
Jahrom 38,236 F4
Jask 1,078 G4
Kangan 2,682 F4
Kangavar 9,414 E3
Kashan 84,545 F3
Kashmar 17,000 G2
Kazerun 51,309 F4
Kerman 140,309 G3
Khash 7,439 H4
Khorramabad 104,928 E3
Khorramshahr 146,709 E3
Khvaf 5,000 G3
Khvor 2,912 G3
Khvoy 70,040 E2
Lar 22,000 F4
Mahabad 28,610 E2
Maragheh 60,820 E2
Marand 24,000 E2
Meshed 670,180 H2
Mianeh 28,447 E2
Minab 4,228 G4
Mirjaveh 11,000 H4
Nahavand 24,000 E3
Na'in 5,925 F3
Najafabad 76,236 F3
Nasratabad (Zabol) 20,000 H3
Natanz 4,370 F3
Nehbandan 2,130 G3
Neyshabur 59,101 G2
Nikshahr 1,879 H4
Qasr-e Qand 1,879 H4
Qayen 6,000 G3
Qazvin 138,527 E2
Qom 246,831 F3
Quchan 29,133 G2
Qum (Qom) 246,831 F3
Rafsanjan 21,000 G3
Rasht 187,203 E2
Ravar 5,074 G3
Rey 102,825 F2
Reza'iyeh (Urmia) 163,991 D2
Sabzevar 69,174 G2
Sabzvaran 7,000 G4
Sa'idabad 20,000 G4
Sanandaj 95,834 E2
Saqqez 17,000 E2
Saravan 4,012 H4
Sari 70,936 F2
Saveh 17,565 F2
Semnan 31,058 F2
Shahdad 2,777 G3
Shahreza 34,220 F3
Shahrud 30,767 G2
Shiraz 416,408 F4
Shirvan 11,000 G2
Shushtar 24,000 E3
Sirjan (Sa'idabad) 20,000 G4
Susangerd 21,000 E3
Tabas 10,000 G3
Tabriz 598,576 E2
Tehran (cap.) 4,496,159 F2
Tonekabon 12,000 F2
Torbat-e Heydariyeh 30,106 G2
Torbat-e Jam 13,000 H2
Torud 721 F2
Urmia 163,991 D2
Yazd 135,978 F3
Zabol 20,000 H3
Zahedan 92,628 H4
Zanjan 99,967 E2
Zarand 5,000 G3

OTHER FEATURES

'Aliabad, Kuh-e (mt.) F3
Aras (riv.) E2
Bazman, Kuh-e (mt.) H4
Damavand (mt.) F2
Dez (riv.) E3
Elburz (mts.) F2
Euphrates (riv.) E3
Gavkhuni (lake) F3
Gorgan (riv.) F2
Halil (riv.) G4
Hormuz (str.) G4
Jaz Murian, Hamun-e (marsh) G4
Karun (riv.) E3
Kavir, Dasht-e (salt des.) G3
Kavir-e Namak (salt des.) G3
Khark (isl.) F4
Kukalar, Kuh-e (mt.) F3
Laleh Zar, Kuh-e (mt.) G4
Lut, Dasht-e (salt des.) G3
Madvar, Kuh-e (mt.) F3
Maidani, Ras (cape) G4
Mand Rud (riv.) F4
Mashkid (riv.) H4
Mehran (riv.) F4
Namak, Daryacheh-ye (salt lake) F3
Namakzar-e Shahdad (salt lake) G3
Oman (gulf) G5
Persian (gulf) F4
Qeshm (isl.) G4
Qeys (isl.) F4
Qezel Owzan (riv.) E2
Safidar, Kuh-e (mt.) F4
Shaikh Shu'aib (isl.) F4
Shatt-al-'Arab (riv.) E4
Shir Kuh (mt.) F3
Taftan, Kuh-e (mt.) H4
Talab (riv.) H4
Tashk (lake) F4
Tigris (riv.) E3
Urmia (lake) E2
Varzarin, Kuh-e (mt.) E3
Zagros (mts.) E3

IRAQ

CITIES and TOWNS

Al 'Aziziya 7,450 E3
Al Falluja 38,072 D3
Al Fatha 15,329 D2
Al Musaiyib 15,955 D3
Al Qurna 5,638 E3
'Amara 64,847 E3
'Ana 15,729 D3
An Najaf 128,096 D3
An Nasiriya 60,405 E3
Arbela (Erbil) 90,320 D2
Ar Rahhaliya 1,579 D3
As Salman 1,789 E3
Baghdad (cap.) 502,503 E3
Baghdad* 1,745,328 E3
Baq'uba 34,575 D3
Basra 313,327 E3
Erbil 90,320 D2
Habbaniya 14,405 D3
Haditha 6,870 D3
Hai 16,988 E3
Hilla 84,717 D3
Hit 9,131 D3
Karbal'a 83,301 D3
Khanaqin 23,522 D3
Kirkuk 167,413 D2
Kirkuk* 176,794 D2
Kut 42,116 E3
Mosul 315,157 D2
Qal'a Sharqat 2,434 D2
Ramadi 28,723 D3
Rutba 5,091 D3
Samarra 24,746 D3
Samawa 33,473 D3
Shithatha 2,326 D3
Sulaimaniya 86,822 E2
Tikrit 9,921 D3

OTHER FEATURES

'Ar'ar, Wadi (dry riv.) D3
'Aneiza, Jebel (mt.) C3
Batin, Wadi al (dry riv.) E4
Euphrates (riv.) E3
Hauran, Wadi (dry riv.) D3
Mesopotamia (reg.) D3
Persian (gulf) F4
Shatt-al-'Arab (riv.) E4
Syrian (El Hamad)(des.) D3
Tigris (riv.) E3

KUWAIT

CITIES and TOWNS

Al Kuwait (cap.) 181,774 E4
Mina al Ahmadi E4
Mina Sa'ud E4

OTHER FEATURES

Bubiyan (isl.) E4
Persian (gulf) F4

OMAN

CITIES and TOWNS

'Ibri G5
Matrah 15,000 G5
Muscat (cap.) 7,500 G5
Quryat G5
Raysut (Risut) F6
Salala 4,000 F6
Sohar G5
Suwaiq G5

OTHER FEATURES

Akhdar, Jebel (range) G5
Batina (reg.) G5
Dhofar (reg.) F6
Hadd, Ras al (cape) G5
Hallaniya (isl.) G6
Hormuz (str.) G4
Jibsh, Ras (cape) G5
Kuria Muria (isls.) G6
Madraka, Ras (cape) G6
Masira (gulf) G6
Masira (isl.) G6
Musandam, Ras (cape) G4
Nus, Ras (cape) G6
Oman (gulf) G5
Oman (reg.) G5
Ruus al Jibal (dist.) G4
Sauqira (bay) G6
Sauqira, Ras (cape) G6
Sham, Jebel (mt.) G5
Sharbatat, Ras (cape) G6

QATAR

CITIES and TOWNS

Doha (cap.) 150,000 F4
Dukhan F4
Umm Sa'id F5

OTHER FEATURES

Persian (gulf) F4
Rakan, Ras (cape) F4

SAUDI ARABIA

CITIES and TOWNS

Aba as Sa'ud 47,501 D6
Abha 30,150 D6
Abu 'Arish D6
Abu Hadriya E4
'Ain al Mubarrak C5
Al 'Ain C4
Al Birk D6
Al Hilla E5
Al Lidam D5
Al Muadhdham C4
'Anaiza D4
Artawiya E4
Ayun D4
Badr C5
Bisha D5
Buraida 69,940 D4
Dammam 127,844 F4
Dhaba C4
Dhahran E4
Dilam E5
El Haql C4
Er Ras D4
Hadiya C4
Hafar al Batin E4
Hail 40,502 D4
Hofuf 101,271 E4
Jauf C4
Jidda 561,104 C5
Jizan (Qizan) 32,812 D6
Jubail E4
Jubba D4
Kaf C3
Khaibar, Hejaz C4
Khamis Mushait 49,581 D6
Mastaba C5
Mastura C5
Mecca 366,801 C5
Medina 198,186 D5
Mubarraz 54,325 E4
Najran (Aba as Sa'ud) 47,501 D6
Nisab D4
'Oqair E4
Qadhima C5
Qatif E4
Qizan 32,812 D6
Ra's al Khafji E4
Ras Tanura F4
Riyadh (cap.) 666,840 E5
Rumah E4
Sakaka D4
Shaqra E4
Sufeina D5
Taif 204,857 D5
Tebuk (Tabuk) 74,825 C4
Turaba D5
Umm Lajj C4
Wejh C4
Yenbo C5
Zahran D6
Zalim D5

OTHER FEATURES

Abu-Mad, Ras (cape) C5
'Aneiza, Jebel (mt.) C3
Aqaba (gulf) C4
Arafat, Jebel (mt.) D5
'Ar'ar, Wadi (dry riv.) D3
Arma (plat.) E4
'Asir (reg.) D6
Aswad, Ras al (cape) C5
Bab el Mandeb (str.) D7
Bahr es Safi (des.) E6
Barida, Ras (cape) C5
Batin, Wadi al (dry riv.) E4
Bisha, Wadi (dry riv.) D5
Dahana (des.) E4
Dawasir, Hadhb (range) D5
Dawasir, Wadi (dry riv.) D5
Farasan (isls.) D6
Hatiba, Ras (cape) C5
Hejaz (reg.) C4
Jafura (des.) F5
Mashabi (isl.) C4
Midian (dist.) C4
Misha'ab, Ras (cape) E4
Nefud (des.) D4
Nefud Dahi (des.) D5
Nejd (reg.) D4
Persian (gulf) F4
Ranya, Wadi (dry riv.) D5
Red (sea) C5
Rima, Wadi (dry riv.) D4
Rimal, Ar (des.) F5
Rub al Khali (des.) F5
Safaniya, Ras (cape) E4
Salma, Jebel (mts.) D4
Shaibara (isl.) C4
Shammar, Jebel (plat.) D4
Sirhan, Wadi (dry riv.) C3
Subh, Jebel (mt.) C5
Summan (plat.) E4
Tihama (reg.) C5
Tiran (isl.) C4
Tiran (str.) C4
Tuwaiq, Jebel (range) E5

UNITED ARAB EMIRATES

CITIES and TOWNS

Abu Dhabi (cap.) 347,000 F5
'Ajman G4
Buraimi G5
Dubai F4
Fujairah G4
Jebel Dhanna F5
Ras al Khaimah G4
Ruwais F5
Sharjah F4
Umm al Qaiwain G4

OTHER FEATURES

Das (isl.) F4
Oman (gulf) G5
Yas (isl.) F5
Zirko (isl.) F5

WEST BANK

CITIES and TOWNS

Hebron 38,309 C3

OTHER FEATURES

Dead (sea) C3

YEMEN

CITIES and TOWNS

Aden 240,370 E7
Al Hawtah E6
'Amran D6
Bait al Faqih D7
Balhaf E7
Bir 'Ali E7
Damqut F6
Dhamar 19,467 D7
El Beida 5,975 E7
Hadibu F7
Hajja 5,814 D6
Hodeida 80,314 D7
Hureidha E6
Ibb 19,066 D7
Lodar E7
Luhaiya D6
Madinat ash Sha'b E7
Marib 292 E6
Meifa E7
Mocha D7
Mukalla 45,000 E7
Nisab E7
Qabr Hud E6
Qishn F6
Riyan E7
Sa'ada 4,252 D6
Saihut F6
San'a (cap.) 134,588 D6
Sana F6
Seiyun 20,000 E6
Shabwa E6
Sheikh Sa'id D7
Shibam E6
Shihr E7
Shuqra E7
Ta'izz 78,642 D7
Tarim E6
Yarim D7
Yeshbum E7
Zabid D7

OTHER FEATURES

Bab el Mandeb (str.) D7
Fartak, Ras (cape) F6
Hadhramaut (dist.) E7
Hadhramaut, Wadi (dry riv.) F7
Hanish (isls.) D7
Jebel Manar (mt.) D7
Jebel Sabir (mt.) D7
Kamaran (isl.) D6
Manar, Jebel (mt.) D7
Mandeb, Bab el (str.) D7
Maqatin (ruins) E7
Perim (isl.) D7
Qamr (bay) F6
Ras Fartak (cape) F6
Red (sea) C5
Sabir, Jebel (mt.) D7
Socotra (isl.) F7
Tihama (reg.) C5
Wadi Hadhramaut (dry riv.) F7
Zuqar (isl.) D7

† Population of commune.

* City and suburbs.

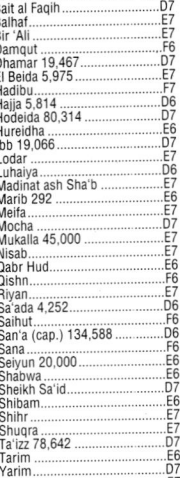

Agriculture, Industry and Resources

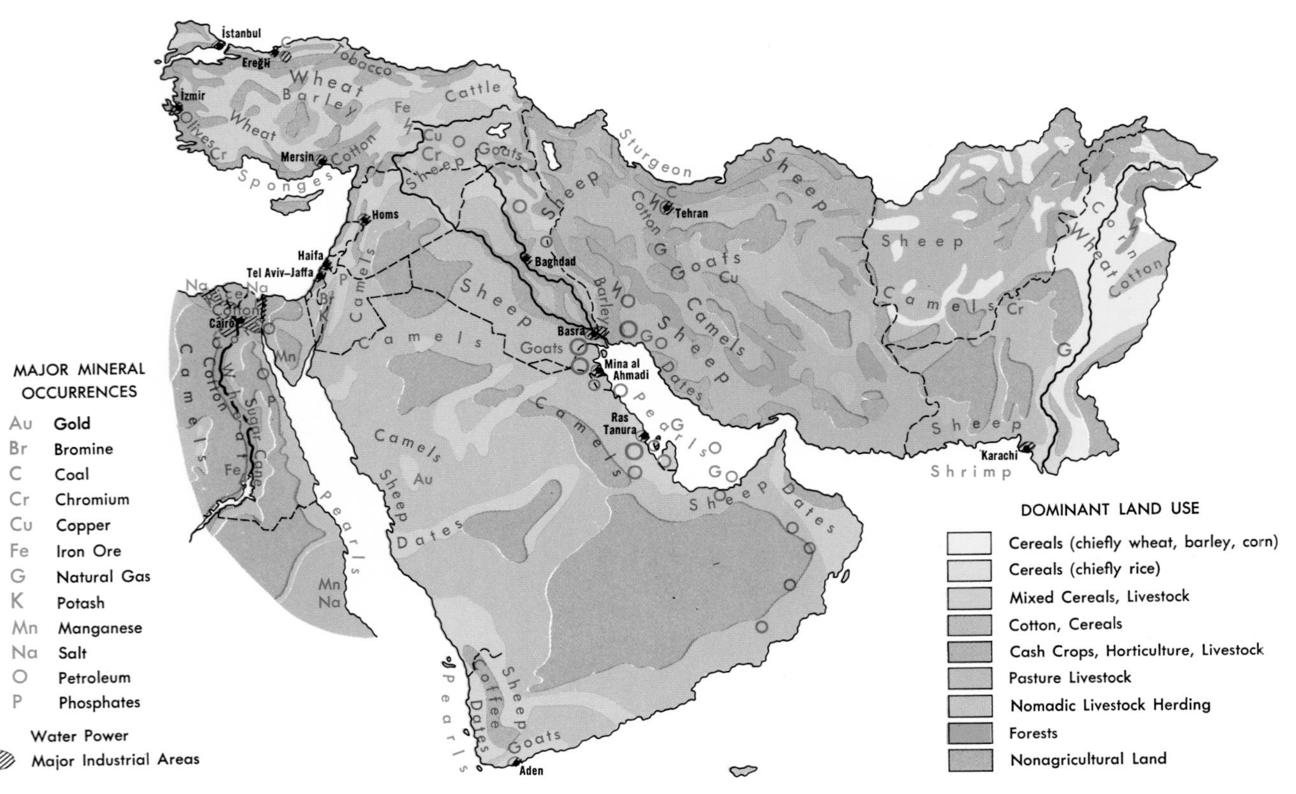

İstanbul
Ereğli
İzmir
Mersin
Homs
Haifa
Tel Aviv–Jaffa
Cairo
Baghdad
Tehran
Basra
Mina al Ahmadi
Ras Tanura
Karachi
Aden
Wheat
Barley
Tobacco
Cattle
Olives
Cotton
Sponges
Sheep
Goats
Camels
Sturgeon
Dates
Pearls
Shrimp
Coffee
Corn
Sugar Cane
MAJOR MINERAL OCCURRENCES
Au Gold
Br Bromine
C Coal
Cr Chromium
Cu Copper
Fe Iron Ore
G Natural Gas
K Potash
Mn Manganese
Na Salt
O Petroleum
P Phosphates
Water Power
Major Industrial Areas
DOMINANT LAND USE
Cereals (chiefly wheat, barley, corn)
Cereals (chiefly rice)
Mixed Cereals, Livestock
Cotton, Cereals
Cash Crops, Horticulture, Livestock
Pasture Livestock
Nomadic Livestock Herding
Forests
Nonagricultural Land

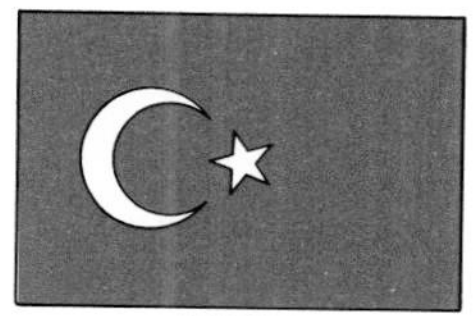

TURKEY

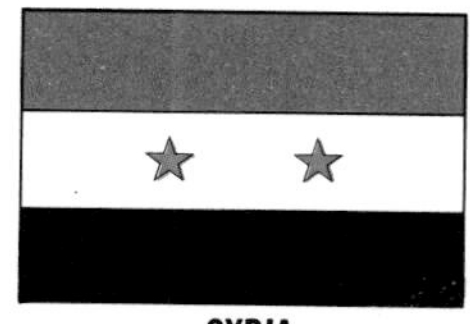

SYRIA

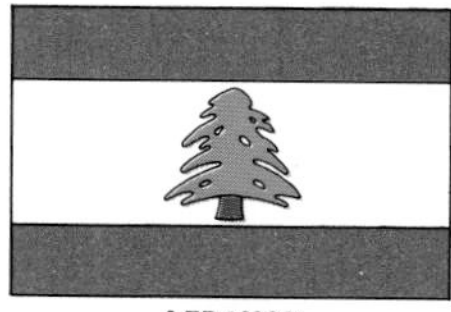

LEBANON

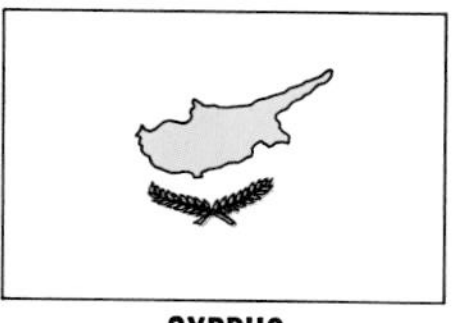

CYPRUS

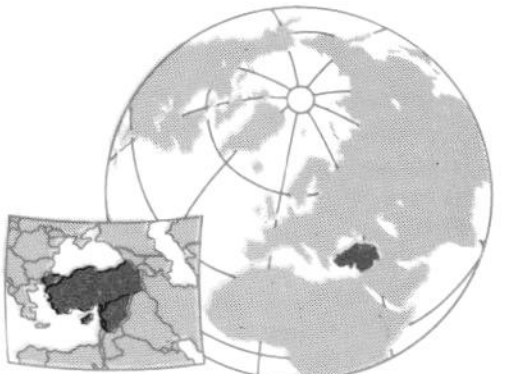

AREA 300,946 sq. mi. (779,450 sq. km.)
POPULATION 56,741,000
CAPITAL Ankara
LARGEST CITY Istanbul
HIGHEST POINT Ararat 16,946 ft. (5,165 m.)
MONETARY UNIT Turkish lira
MAJOR LANGUAGE Turkish
MAJOR RELIGION Islam

AREA 71,498 sq. mi. (185,180 sq. km.)
POPULATION 11,719,000
CAPITAL Damascus
LARGEST CITY Damascus
HIGHEST POINT Hermon 9,232 ft. (2,814 m.)
MONETARY UNIT Syrian pound
MAJOR LANGUAGES Arabic, French, Kurdish, Armenian
MAJOR RELIGIONS Islam, Christianity

AREA 4,015 sq. mi. (10,399 sq. km.)
POPULATION 2,897,000
CAPITAL Beirut
LARGEST CITY Beirut
HIGHEST POINT Qurnet es Sauda 10,131 ft. (3,088 m.)
MONETARY UNIT Lebanese pound
MAJOR LANGUAGES Arabic, French
MAJOR RELIGIONS Christianity, Islam

AREA 3,473 sq. mi. (8,995 sq. km.)
POPULATION 699,000
CAPITAL Nicosia
LARGEST CITY Nicosia
HIGHEST POINT Troödos 6,406 ft. (1,953 m.)
MONETARY UNIT Cypriot pound
MAJOR LANGUAGES Greek, Turkish, English
MAJOR RELIGIONS Eastern (Greek) Orthodoxy,

CYPRUS

CITIES and TOWNS

Famagusta 38,960 .... F5
Kyrenia 3,892 .... E5
Kythrea 3,400 .... E5
Lapithos 3,600 .... E5
Larnaca 19,608 .... E5
Lefka 3,650 .... E5
Limassol 79,641 .... E5
Morphou 9,040 .... E5
Nicosia (cap.) 115,718 .... E5
Paphos 8,984 .... E5
Polis 2,200 .... E5
Rizokarpasso 3,600 .... F5
Yialousa 2,750 .... E5

OTHER FEATURES

Andreas (cape) F5
Arnauti (cape) E5
Famagusta (bay) F5
Gata (cape) E5
Greco (cape) F5
Klides (isls.) F5
Kormakiti (cape) E5
Larnaca (bay) E5
Morphou (bay) E5
Pomos (pt.) E5
Troodos (mt.) E5

LEBANON

CITIES and TOWNS

'Aleih 18,630 .... F6
Amyun 7,926 .... F5
Ba'albek 15,560 .... G5
Beirut (cap.) 474,870 .... F6
Beirut* 938,940 .... F6
Merj 'Uyun 9,318 .... F6
Rasheiya 6,731 .... F6
Saida 32,200 .... F6
Sidon (Saida) 32,200 .... F6
Sur 16,483 .... F6
Tarabulus 127,611 .... F5
Tripoli (Tarabulus) 127,611 .... F5
Tyre (Sur) 16,483 .... F6
Zahle 53,121 .... F6
Zegharta 18,210 .... G5

OTHER FEATURES

Lebanon (mts.) F6
Leontes (Litani) (riv.) F6
Litani (riv.) F6
Sauda, Qurnet es (mt.) G5

SYRIA

PROVINCES

Aleppo 1,316,872 .... G4
Damascus 1,457,934 .... G6
Deir ez Zor 292,780 .... H5
Der'a 230,481 .... G6
El Quneitra 16,490 .... F6
Es Suweida 139,650 .... G6
Hama 514,748 .... G5
Haseke 468,506 .... J4
Homs 546,176 .... G5
Idlib 383,695 .... G5
Latakia 389,552 .... G5
Rashid 243,736 .... H5
Tartus 302,065 .... G5

CITIES and TOWNS

Abu Kemal 6,907 .... J5
'Ain el 'Arab 4,529 .... H4
Aleppo 639,428 .... G4
Azaz 13,923 .... G4
Baniyas 8,537 .... F5
Damascus (cap.) 836,668 .... G6
Damascus* 923,253 .... G6
Deir ez Zor 66,164 .... H5
Der'a 27,651 .... G6
Dimashq (Damascus) (cap.) 836,668 .... G6
Duma 30,050 .... G6
El Bab 27,366 .... G4
El Haseke 32,746 .... J4
El Ladhiqya (Latakia) 125,716 .... F5
El Qaryatein G5
El Quneitra 17,752 .... F6
El Rashid 37,151 .... H5
En Nebk 16,334 .... G5
Es Suweida 29,524 .... G6
Et Tell el Abyad H4
Haffe 4,656 .... G5
Haleb (Aleppo) 639,428 .... G4
Hama 137,421 .... G5
Harim 6,837 .... G4
Homs 215,423 .... G5
Idlib 34,515 .... G5
Izra 3,226 .... G6
Jeble 15,715 .... F5
Jerablus 8,610 .... G4
Jisr esh Shughur 13,131 .... G5
Khan Sheikhun G5
Latakia 125,716 .... F5
Masyaf 7,058 .... G5
Membij 13,796 .... G4
Meskene H5
Meyadin 12,515 .... J5
Qal'at es Salihiye J5
Qamishliye 31,448 .... J4
Quteife 4,993 .... G6
Raqqa (El Rashid) 37,151 .... H5
Safita 9,650 .... G5
Selemiya 21,677 .... G5
Tadmur 10,670 .... H5
Tartus 29,842 .... F5
Telkalakh 6,242 .... F5
Zebdani 10,010 .... G6

OTHER FEATURES

Abdul 'Aziz, Jebel (mts.) J4
'Amrit (ruins) F5
Arwad (Ruad) (isl.) F5
'Asi (Orontes) (riv.) G5
Bahrat Assad (lake) H4
Druz, Jebel ed (mts.) G6
El Furat (riv.) H4
Euphrates (El Furat) (riv.) H4
Hermon (mt.) F6
Khabur (riv.) J5
Orontes (riv.) G5
Palmyra (Tadmor) (ruins) H5
Tigris (riv.) K4

TURKEY

PROVINCES

Adana 1,485,743 .... F4
Adıyaman 367,595 .... H4
Afyonkarahisar 597,516 .... D3
Ağri 368,009 .... K3
Amasya 341,287 .... F2
Ankara 2,854,689 .... E3
Antalya 748,706 .... D4
Artvin 228,997 .... J2
Aydın 652,488 .... B4
Balıkesir 853,177 .... B3
Bilecik 147,001 .... D2
Bingöl 228,702 .... J3
Bitlis 257,908 .... J3
Bolu 471,751 .... D2
Burdur 235,009 .... D4
Bursa 1,148,492 .... C2
Çanakkale 338,091 .... B2
Çankırı 258,436 .... E2
Çorum 571,831 .... F2
Denizli 603,338 .... C4
Diyarbakır 778,150 .... H4
Edirne 363,286 .... B2
Elâzığ 440,808 .... H3
Erzincan 282,022 .... H3
Erzurum 801,809 .... J3
Eskişehir 543,802 .... D3
Gaziantep 808,697 .... G4
Giresun 480,083 .... H2
Gümüşhane 275,191 .... H2
Hakkâri 155,463 .... K4
Hatay 856,271 .... G4
İçel 842,817 .... F4
İsparta 301,166 .... D4
İstanbul 3,264,393 .... C2
İzmir 1,976,763 .... B3
Kahramanmaraş 738,032 .... G4
Kars 700,238 .... K2
Kastamonu 450,946 .... E2
Kayseri 778,383 .... F3
Kırklareli 283,408 .... B2
Kırşehir 240,497 .... F3
Kocaeli 596,899 .... C2
Konya 1,562,139 .... E4
Kütahya 497,089 .... C3
Malatya 669,962 .... H3
Manisa 941,941 .... B3
Mardin 564,967 .... J4
Muğla 438,145 .... C4
Muş 302,406 .... J3
Nevşehir 256,933 .... F3
Niğde 512,071 .... F4
Ordu 713,535 .... G2
Rize 361,258 .... J2
Sakarya 548,747 .... D2
Samsun 1,008,113 .... F2
Siirt 445,483 .... J4
Sinop 276,242 .... F2
Sivas 750,144 .... G3
Tekirdağ 360,742 .... B2
Tokat 624,508 .... G2
Trabzon 731,045 .... H2
Tunceli 157,974 .... H3
Urfa 602,736 .... H4
Uşak 247,224 .... C3
Van 468,646 .... K3
Yozgat 504,433 .... F3
Zonguldak 972,856 .... D2

CITIES and TOWNS

Adalia (Antalya) 176,446 .... D4
Adana 842,845 .... F4
Adapazarı 131,400 .... D2
Adilcevaz 10,342 .... K3
Adıyaman 116,986 .... H4
Afşin 20,084 .... G3
Afyonkarahisar 597,516 .... D3
Ağri (Karaköse) 41,103 .... K3
Ahlat 10,422 .... K3
Akçaabat 13,384 .... H2
Akçadağ 8,015 .... G3
Akçakale 11,184 .... H4
Akçakoca 9,639 .... D2
Akdağmadeni 10,192 .... F3
Akhisar 61,491 .... B3
Aksaray 62,927 .... F3
Akşehir 40,312 .... D3
Akseki 6,815 .... D4
Akyazı 14,795 .... D2
Alaca 15,649 .... F2
Alaçam 11,402 .... F2
Alanya 22,190 .... D4
Alaşehir 25,611 .... C3
Alexandretta (İskenderun) 120,985 .... G4
Alibeyköyü 33,387 .... D6
Altındağ 608,689 .... E2
Altınova 6,980 .... B3
Alucra 8,795 .... H2
Amasya 48,010 .... F2
Anamur 23,025 .... E4
Andırın 6,045 .... G4
Ankara (cap.) 2,203,729 .... E3
Antakya 99,551 .... F4
Antalya 176,446 .... D4
Antioch (Antakya) 99,551 .... F4
Arapkir 8,816 .... H3
Ardahan 14,912 .... K2
Ardeşen 9,582 .... J2
Arhavi 6,801 .... J2
Arsin 6,892 .... H2
Artvin 14,203 .... J2
Aşkale 12,045 .... J3
Avanos 8,927 .... F3
Ayancık 8,257 .... F1
Aybastı 13,517 .... G2
Aydın 37,696 .... B4
Aydıncık 19,371 .... E4
Ayvalık 19,371 .... B3
Babaeski 18,145 .... B2
Bafra 50,213 .... F2
Bahçe 12,366 .... G4
Bakırköy 234,226 .... D6
Balıkesir 124,122 .... B3
Banaz 8,356 .... C3
Bandırma 53,497 .... B2
Bartin 20,728 .... E2
Başkale 9,770 .... K3
Batman 86,172 .... J4
Bayat 5,366 .... F2
Bayburt 22,578 .... J2
Bayındır 12,440 .... B3
Bayramiç 7,854 .... B3
Bergama 34,716 .... B3
Beşiktaş 188,117 .... D6
Besni 15,833 .... G4
Beykoz 94,101 .... D5
Beyoğlu 223,360 .... D6
Beypazarı 16,971 .... D2
Beyşehir 15,845 .... D4
Biga 16,359 .... B2
Bigadiç 8,955 .... C3
Bilecik 15,108 .... D2
Bingöl (Çapakçur) 27,904 .... J3
Birecik 20,412 .... H4
Bismil 19,059 .... J4
Bitlis 27,114 .... J3
Bodrum 32,517 .... B4
Boğazlıyan 10,827 .... F3
Bolu 38,400 .... D2
Bolvadin 30,599 .... D3
Bor 45,480 .... F4
Bornova 60,397 .... B3
Boyabat 14,397 .... F2
Bozdoğan 7,682 .... C4
Bozova 5,510 .... H4
Bozüyük 18,052 .... C3
Bucak 18,852 .... D4
Bulancak 16,089 .... H2
Bulanık 9,140 .... K3
Buldan 10,939 .... C3

(continued on following page)

Agriculture, Industry and Resources

DOMINANT LAND USE

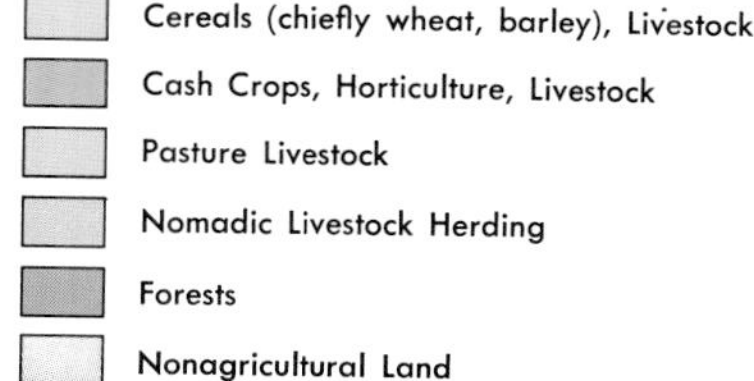

Cereals (chiefly wheat, barley), Livestock
Cash Crops, Horticulture, Livestock
Pasture Livestock
Nomadic Livestock Herding
Forests
Nonagricultural Land

MAJOR MINERAL OCCURRENCES

Ab Asbestos
Al Bauxite
C Coal
Cr Chromium
Cu Copper
Fe Iron Ore
Hg Mercury
Mg Magnesium
Na Salt
O Petroleum
P Phosphates
Pb Lead
Py Pyrites
Sb Antimony
Zn Zinc

Water Power
Major Industrial Areas

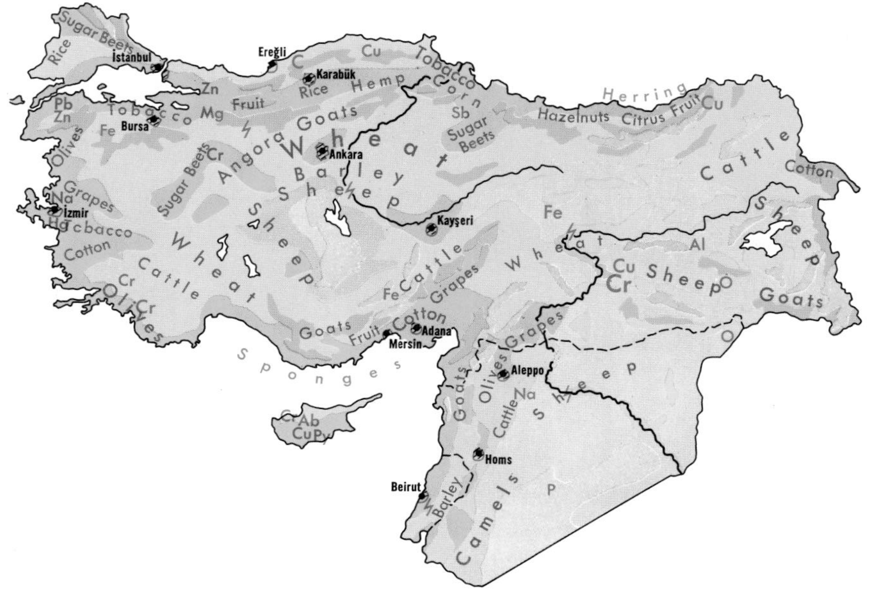

İstanbul
Ereğli
Karabük
Bursa
Ankara
İzmir
Kayseri
Mersin
Adana
Aleppo
Homs
Beirut
Sugar Beets
Rice
Tobacco
Hemp
Fruit
Goats
Wheat
Barley
Sheep
Hazelnuts
Citrus Fruit
Herring
Cattle
Cotton
Olives
Grapes
Sponges
Camels

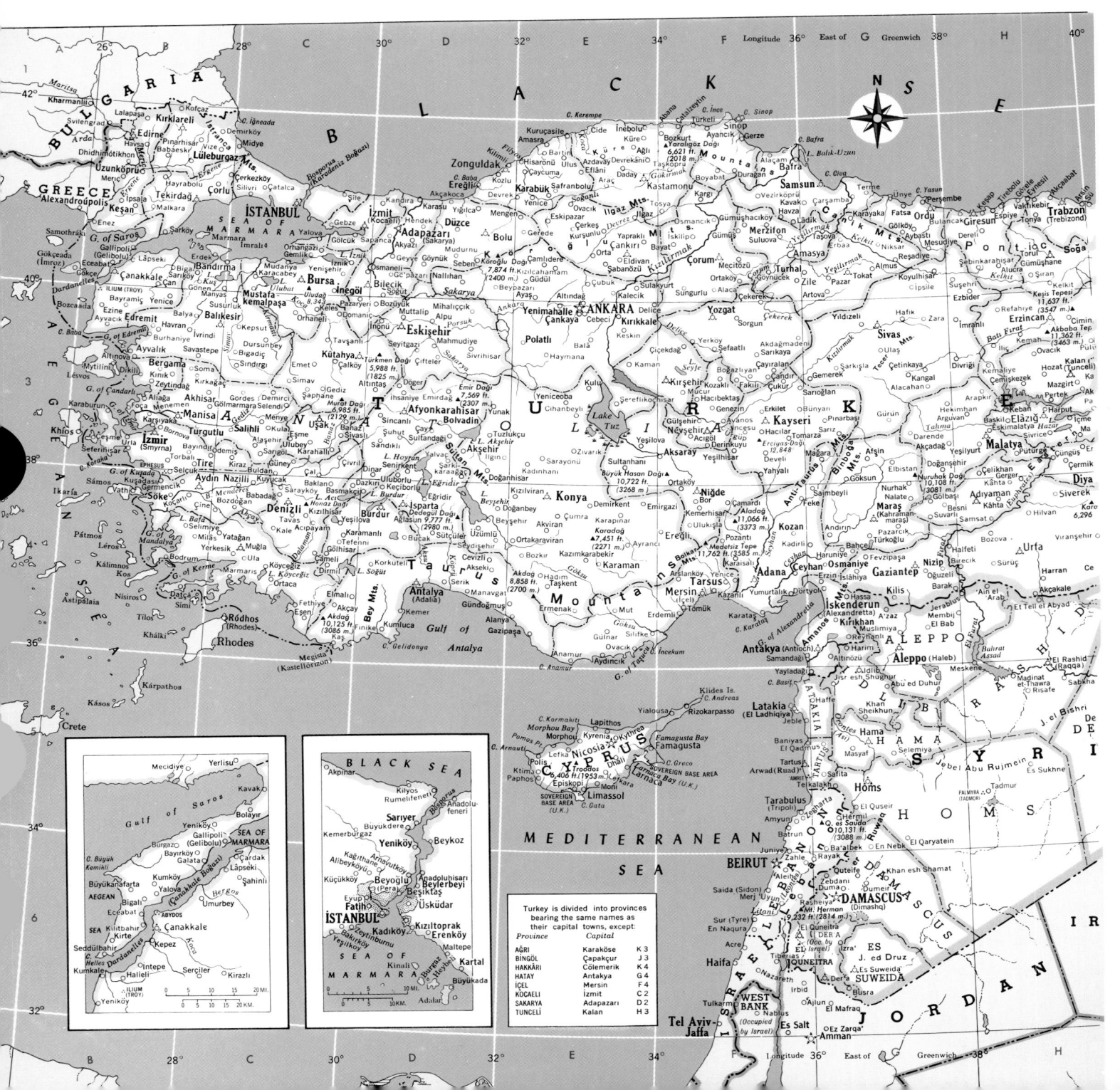

Kaman 19,997 ..... E3
Kandıra 8,142 ..... D2
Kangal 6,644 ..... G3
Karabük 84,975 ..... E2
Karacabey 23,600 ..... C2
Karaköse (Ağri) 41,103 ..... K3
Karakoçan 6,462 ..... H3
Karaman 51,868 ..... E4
Karamanlı 5,904 ..... C4
Karapınar 24,558 ..... E4
Karasu 10,025 ..... D2
Karataş 5,700 ..... F4
Kargı 5,232 ..... F2
Karlıova 5,750 ..... J3
Kars 58,651 ..... K2
Karşıyaka 226,982 ..... B3
Kartal 67,627 ..... D6
Kastamonu 35,636 ..... E2
Kayseri 273,362 ..... F3
Keban 5,172 ..... H3
Keçiborlu 7,843 ..... D4
Kelkit 7,002 ..... H2
Kemalpaşa 10,032 ..... J2
Kemerburgaz 7,234 ..... D5
Kemirhisar 6,205 ..... F4
Kepsut 5,136 ..... C3
Keşan 28,428 ..... B2
Keşap 5,821 ..... H2
Keskin 14,595 ..... E3
Kiğı 6,046 ..... J3
Kilimli 26,649 ..... D2
Kilis 58,686 ..... G4
Kınık 12,034 ..... B3
Kiraz 5,569 ..... C3
Kırıkhan 47,688 ..... G4
Kırıkkale 175,235 ..... E3
Kırkağaç 18,475 ..... B3
Kırklareli 36,183 ..... B2
Kırşehir 50,063 ..... F3
Kızilcahamam 9,604 ..... E2
Kızilhisar 11,119 ..... C4
Kızıltepe 30,530 ..... J4
Koçarlı 5,721 ..... B4
Kocaeli (İzmit) 19,140 ..... D2

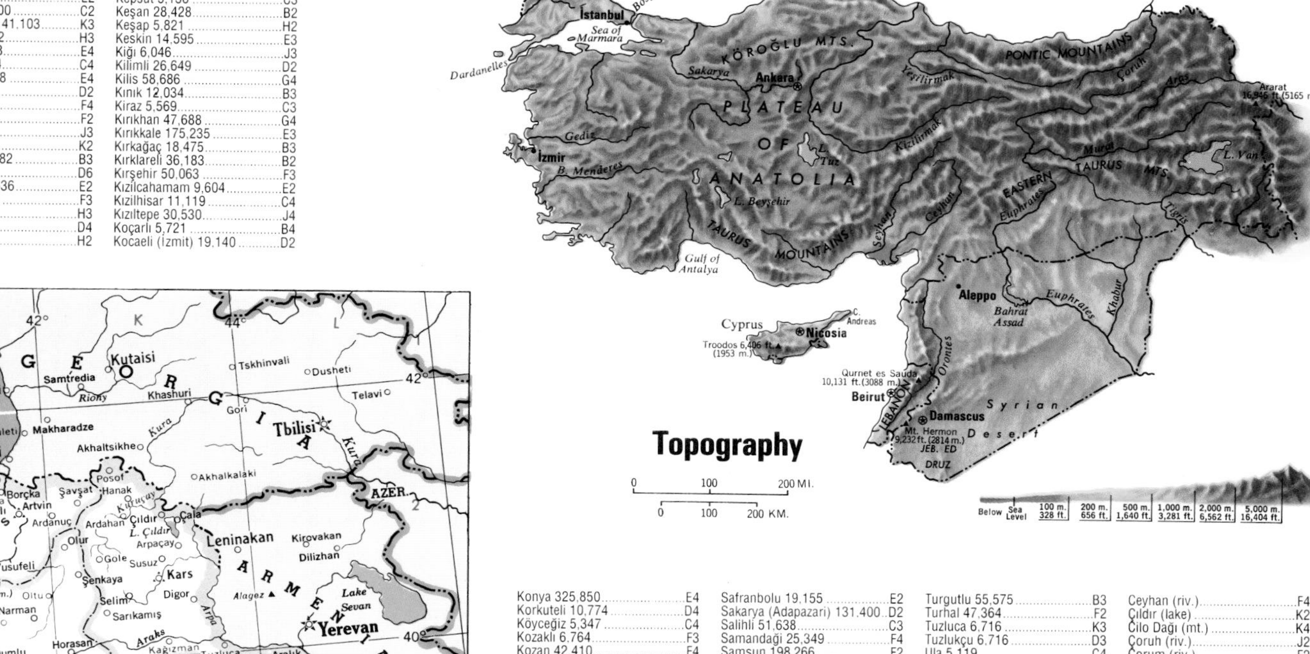

Konya 325,850 ..... E4
Korkuteli 10,774 ..... D4
Köyceğiz 5,347 ..... C4
Kozaklı 6,764 ..... F3
Kozan 42,410 ..... F4
Kozlu 27,322 ..... D2
Kozluk 10,215 ..... J3
Küçükköy 56,411 ..... C6
Kula 12,763 ..... C3
Kulp 5,577 ..... J3
Kulu 12,183 ..... E3
Kumluca 7,977 ..... D4
Kurşunlu 6,678 ..... E2
Kütahya 101,087 ..... C3
Kurtalan 9,748 ..... J3
Kuşadası 14,299 ..... B4
Kuyucak 6,532 ..... C4
Lâdik 7,200 ..... G2
Lice 8,486 ..... J3
Lüleburgaz 35,643 ..... B2
Mağara 5,037 ..... G3
Mahmudiye 5,352 ..... D3
Malatya 184,390 ..... H3
Malazgirt 14,150 ..... K3
Malkara 15,570 ..... B2
Maltepe 66,343 ..... D6
Manavgat 14,392 ..... D4
Manisa 93,970 ..... B3
Maraş (Kahramanmaraş) 177,919 ..... G4
Mardin 37,750 ..... J4
Marmaris 7,710 ..... C4
Mazıdağı 7,941 ..... J4
Mecitözü 5,874 ..... F2
Menemen 22,080 ..... B3
Mersin 215,300 ..... F4
Merzifon 32,031 ..... F2
Mesudiye 5,013 ..... G2
Midyat 20,112 ..... J4
Milâs 20,333 ..... B4
Mucur 9,386 ..... F3
Mudanya 10,556 ..... C2
Mudurnu 5,307 ..... D2
Muğla 27,162 ..... C4
Muradiye 10,036 ..... K3
Muş 40,297 ..... J3
Mustafakemalpaşa 30,099 ..... C3
Mut 14,029 ..... E4
Nallıhan 9,791 ..... D2
Nazilli 64,015 ..... C4
Nevşehir 37,106 ..... F3
Niğde 39,972 ..... F4
Niksar 23,570 ..... G2
Nizip 39,267 ..... G4
Nurhak 5,330 ..... G4
Nusaybin 32,620 ..... J4
Ödemiş 40,652 ..... C3
Oğuzeli 7,826 ..... G4
Oltu 12,288 ..... J2
Ordu 52,080 ..... G2
Orhangazi 18,537 ..... C2
Ortaca 8,604 ..... C4
Ortaköy 8,848 ..... F3
Osmancık 15,304 ..... F2
Osmaneli 6,664 ..... D2
Osmaniye 84,338 ..... G4
Palu 6,842 ..... H3
Pasinler 20,039 ..... J3
Patnos 18,040 ..... K3
Pazarcık 19,821 ..... G4
Pazaryeri 6,005 ..... C3
Pera (Beyoğlu) 94,101 ..... D5
Perşembe 7,190 ..... G2
Pervari 5,021 ..... K4
Pınarbaşı 10,578 ..... G3
Pınarhisar 10,649 ..... B2
Polatlı 43,514 ..... E3
Pozantı 6,297 ..... F4
Refahiye 7,505 ..... H3
Reşadiye 5,588 ..... G2
Reyhanlı 30,843 ..... G4
Rize 41,740 ..... J2
Safranbolu 19,155 ..... E2
Sakarya (Adapazari) 131,400 ..... D2
Salihli 51,638 ..... C3
Samandaği 25,349 ..... F4
Samsun 198,266 ..... F2
Sandıklı 15,966 ..... D3
Sapanca 10,228 ..... D2
Sarayköy 11,009 ..... C4
Sarayönü 8,643 ..... E3
Sarıgöl 7,880 ..... C3
Sarıkamiş 23,331 ..... K2
Sarıkaya 7,297 ..... F3
Sarıköy 4,695 ..... B2
Sarıyer 110,555 ..... D5
Şarkikaraağaç 5,905 ..... D3
Şarkışla 12,611 ..... G3
Şarköy 6,755 ..... B2
Savaştepe 7,110 ..... B3
Savur 6,169 ..... J4
Şebinkarahisar 12,550 ..... H2
Şefaatlı 7,513 ..... F3
Seferihisar 6,506 ..... B3
Selçuk 12,819 ..... B3
Selendi 5,012 ..... C3
Şemdinli 19,677 ..... L4
Senirkent 8,382 ..... D3
Şereflikoçhisar 22,208 ..... E3
Serik 15,662 ..... D4
Seydişehir 30,394 ..... D4
Siirt 42,692 ..... J4
Şile 4,870 ..... C2
Silifke 22,045 ..... E4
Silivri 13,922 ..... C2
Silopi 6,832 ..... K4
Silvan 44,412 ..... J3
Simav 10,775 ..... C3
Sındırgı 8,992 ..... C3
Sinop 18,381 ..... F2
Şiran 6,088 ..... H2
Şırnak 10,947 ..... K4
Sivas 173,831 ..... G3
Sivaslı 4,627 ..... C3
Siverek 30,000 ..... H4
Sivrihisar 9,608 ..... D3
Smyrna (İzmir) 753,749 ..... B3
Söğüt 6,353 ..... D2
Söke 37,362 ..... B4
Solhan 7,170 ..... J3
Soma 30,219 ..... B3
Sorgun 19,623 ..... F3
Şuhut 8,154 ..... D3
Sulakyurt 4,712 ..... E2
Sultandaği 5,115 ..... D3
Sultanhanı 5,112 ..... E3
Suluova 25,682 ..... F2
Sungurlu 24,170 ..... F2
Sürmene 10,152 ..... J2
Sürüç 19,000 ..... H4
Suşehri 11,442 ..... H2
Susurluk 16,113 ..... C3
Tarsus 120,270 ..... F4
Taşkent 7,098 ..... E4
Taşköprü 8,659 ..... F2
Taşova 6,208 ..... G2
Tatvan 40,324 ..... K3
Tavas 10,335 ..... C4
Tavşanlı 23,325 ..... C3
Tekirdağ 51,327 ..... B2
Tercan 5,506 ..... J3
Terme 15,530 ..... G2
Tire 32,242 ..... B3
Tirebolu 9,274 ..... H2
Tokat 60,369 ..... G2
Tomarza 7,733 ..... F3
Tömük 7,660 ..... F4
Tonya 11,010 ..... H2
Tortum 4,280 ..... J2
Torbalı 15,504 ..... B3
Tosya 18,544 ..... F2
Trebizond (Trabzon) 107,412 ..... H2
Tunceli (Kalan) 12,859 ..... H3
Türkoğlu 8,528 ..... G4
Turgutlu 55,575 ..... B3
Turhal 47,364 ..... F2
Tuzluca 6,716 ..... K3
Tuzlukçu 6,716 ..... D3
Ula 5,119 ..... C4
Uluborlu 6,002 ..... D3
Uludere 4,989 ..... K4
Ulukışla 7,841 ..... F4
Ünye 27,946 ..... G2
Urfa 148,434 ..... H4
Ürgüp 6,955 ..... F3
Urla 14,347 ..... B3
Uşak 70,822 ..... C3
Üsküdar 255,899 ..... D6
Uzunköprü 27,706 ..... B2
Vakfıkebir 13,814 ..... H2
Van 93,823 ..... K3
Varto 7,360 ..... J3
Vezirköprü 13,547 ..... F2
Viranşehir 41,934 ..... H4
Vize 9,528 ..... B2
Yahyalı 15,585 ..... F3
Yalova 41,869 ..... C2
Yalvaç 19,986 ..... D3
Yatağan 7,350 ..... C4
Yayladaği 5,300 ..... F5
Yenice, Çanaakkale 4,016 ..... B3
Yenice, İcel 4,106 ..... F4
Yenice, Zonguldak 5,791 ..... E2
Yeniceoba 5,740 ..... E3
Yenimahalle 265,752 ..... E3
Yenişehir 17,013 ..... C2
Yerköy 20,623 ..... F3
Yeşilhisar 11,132 ..... F3
Yeşilova, Burdur 4,393 ..... C4
Yeşilova, Niğde 5,237 ..... E3
Yeşilyurt 7,040 ..... H3
Yıldızeli 11,124 ..... G3
Yozgat 36,220 ..... F3
Yüksekova 11,867 ..... L4
Yunak 7,144 ..... D3
Zara 10,196 ..... G3
Zeytinburnu 126,899 ..... D6
Zile 30,066 ..... G2
Zonguldak 108,661 ..... D2

OTHER FEATURES

Abydos (ruins) B6
Acı (lake) C4
Adalar (isl.) D6
Aegean (sea) A3
Agrı, Büyük (Ararat) (mt.) L3
Akbaba Tepesi (mt.) H3
Akşehir (lake) D3
Aksu (riv.) D4
Alexandretta (gulf) F4
Amanos (mts.) G4
Anatolia (reg.) D3
Ankara (riv.) D3
Antalya (gulf) D4
Anti-Taurus (mts.) G3
Araks (riv.) K2
Ararat (mt.) L3
Arpa (riv.) K2
Baba (cape) A3
Bafra (cape) G2
Banaz (riv.) C3
Batı Fırat (riv.) H3
Bey (mts.) D4
Beyşehir (lake) D4
Bingöl Dağlari (mts.) J3
Black (sea) E1
Bosporus (strait) C2
Burgaz (isl.) D6
Büyük Agrı (Ararat) (mt.) L3
Büyük Hasan Dağı (mt.) E3
Büyük Kemikli (cape) B6
Çanakkale Boğazı (Dardanelles) (str.) B6
Çandarlı (gulf) B3
Çekerek (riv.) F3
Ceyhan (riv.) F4
Çıldır (lake) K2
Cilo Dağı (mt.) K4
Çoruh (riv.) J2
Çorum (riv.) F2
Dalaman (riv.) C4
Dardanelles (strait) B6
Delice (riv.) F3
Devrez (riv.) E2
Dicle (riv.) J4
Eastern Taurus (mts.) J3
Edremit (gulf) B3
Eğridir (lake) D4
Emir Dağı (mt.) D3
Ephesus (ruins) B3
Erciyas-Dağı (mt.) F3
Ergene (riv.) B2
Euphrates (Fırat) (riv.) G4
Filyos (riv.) D2
Fırat (riv.) G4
Gediz (riv.) C3
Gelidonya (cape) D4
Gökçeada (isl.) A2
Gökırmak (riv.) F2
Göksu (riv.) E4
Hakkâri (mts.) K4
Helles (cape) B6
Heybeli (isl.) D6
Hoyran (lake) D3
Ilgaz (mts.) E2
Ilium (ruins) B6
İmroz (Gökçeada) (isl.) A2
İnce (cape) F1
İstranca (mts.) B2
İzmir (gulf) B3
İznik (lake) C2
Kaçkar Dağı (mt.) J2
Karacadağ (mt.) H4
Karadeniz Boğazı (Bosporus) (str.) C2
Karasu-Aras (mts.) J3
Karataş (cape) F4
Kelkit (riv.) G2
Kerme (gulf) B4
Keşiş Tepesi (mt.) H3
Kirmasti (riv.) C3
Kızılırmak (riv.) F2
Köroğlu (mts.) E2
Küre (mts.) E2
Kuş (lake) B2
Kuşada (gulf) B4
Mandalya (gulf) B4
Marmara (isl.) B2
Marmara (sea) C2
Medetsiz Tepe (mt.) F4
Menderes, Büyük (riv.) C4
Meriç (riv.) B2
Murat (riv.) H3
Murat Dağı (mt.) C3
Pontic (mts.) H2
Porsuk (riv.) D3
Prinkipo (Adalar) (isl.) D6
Sakarya (riv.) D2
Saros (gulf) B2
Seyhan (riv.) F4
Simav (riv.) C3
Sinop (cape) F1
Süphan Dağı (mt.) K3
Taşucu (gulf) E4
Taurus (mts.) D4
Tecer (mts.) G3
Tigris (Dicle) (riv.) J4
Troy (Ilium) (ruins) B6
Türkmen Dağ (mt.) D3
Tuz (lake) E3
Ulubat (lake) C2
Uludağ (mt.) C2
Van (lake) K3
Yaralıgöz Dağı (mt.) F2
Yeşilırmak (riv.) G2

*City and suburbs

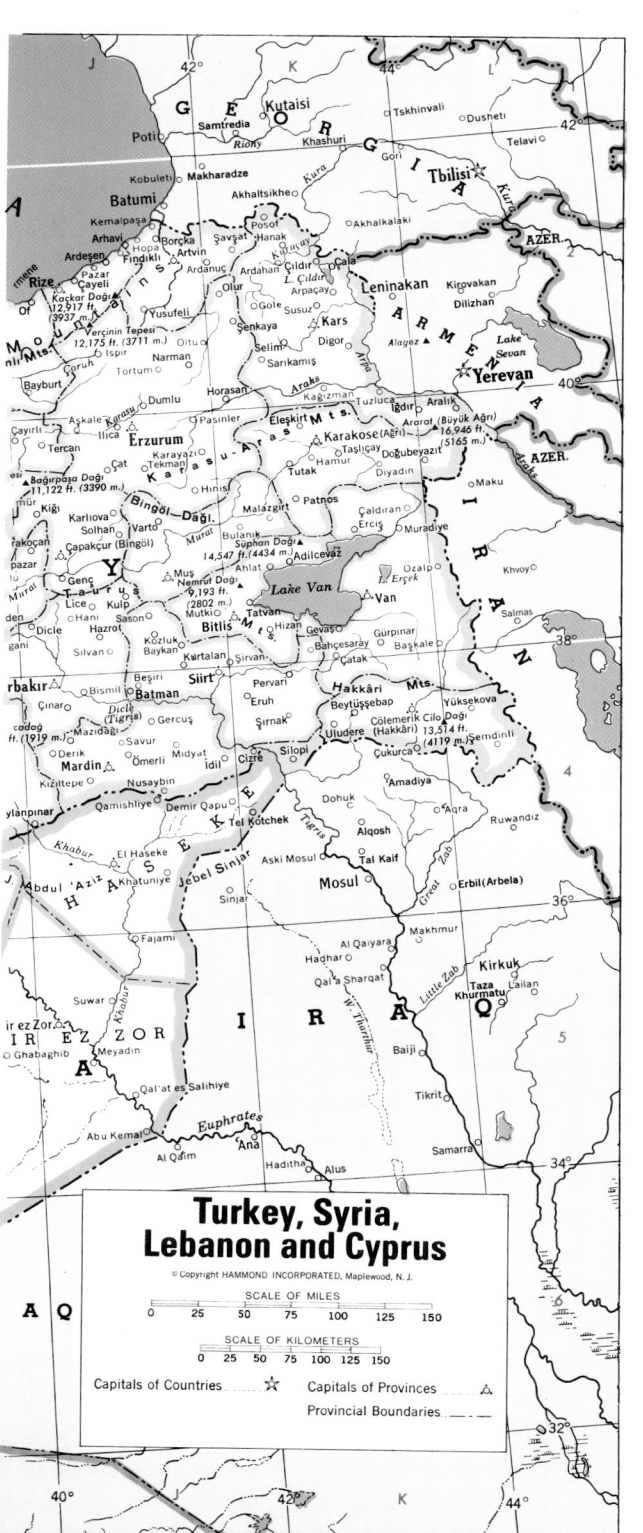

Turkey, Syria, Lebanon and Cyprus

© Copyright HAMMOND INCORPORATED, Maplewood, N. J.

SCALE OF MILES 0 25 50 75 100 125 150

SCALE OF KILOMETERS 0 25 50 75 100 125 150

Capitals of Countries ☆ Capitals of Provinces ⊛ Provincial Boundaries

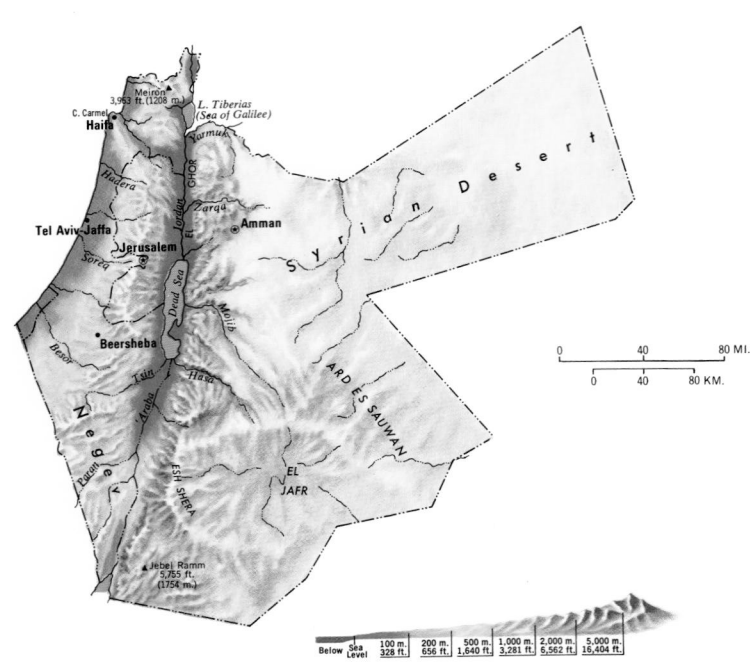

Archaeological Sites in Palestine

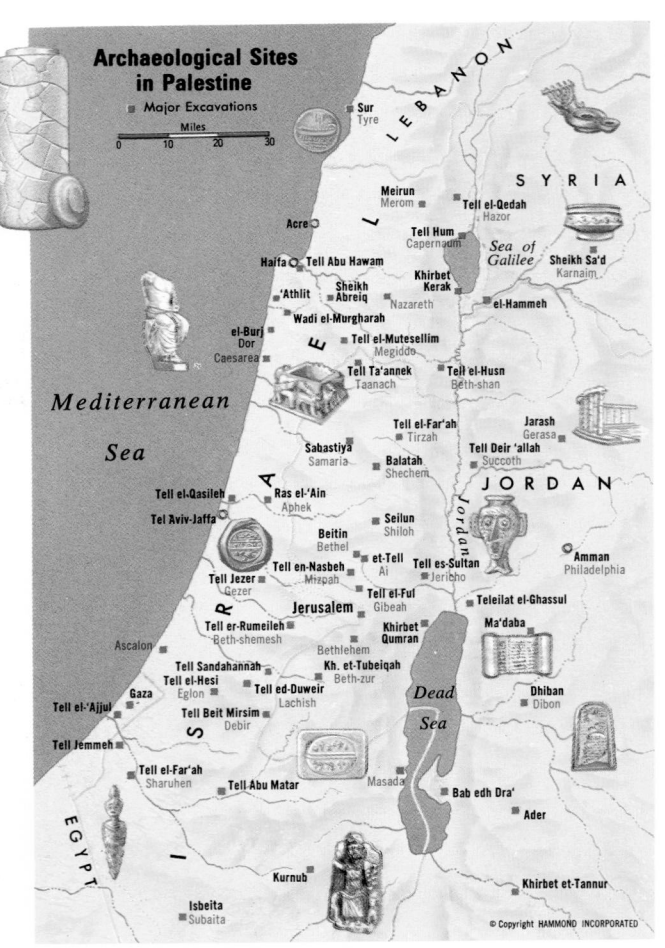

Agriculture, Industry and Resources

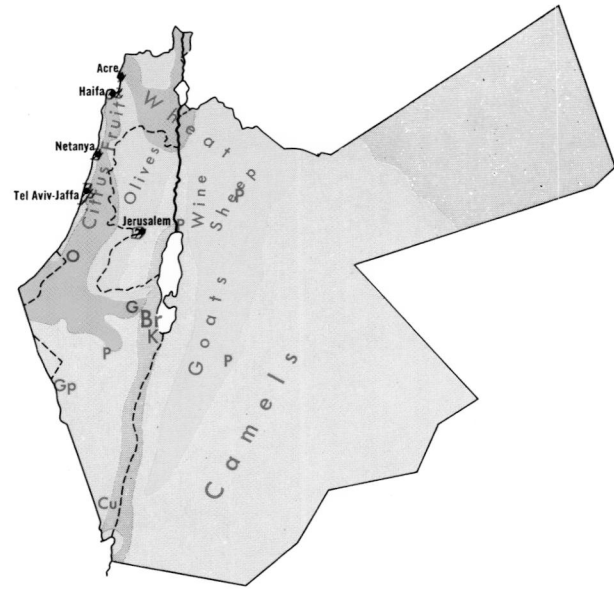

DOMINANT LAND USE

- Cereals, Livestock
- Cash Crops, Horticulture
- Nomadic Livestock Herding
- Nonagricultural Land

MAJOR MINERAL OCCURRENCES

- Br Bromine
- Cu Copper
- G Natural Gas
- Gp Gypsum
- K Potash
- O Petroleum
- P Phosphates

Major Industrial Areas

© Copyright HAMMOND INCORPORATED

ISRAEL

JORDAN

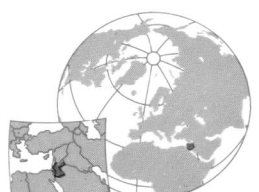

ISRAEL

AREA 7,847 sq. mi. (20,324 sq. km.)
POPULATION 4,625,000
CAPITAL Jerusalem
LARGEST CITY Tel Aviv-Jaffa
HIGHEST POINT Meiran 3,963 ft.
(1,208 m.)
MONETARY UNIT shekel
MAJOR LANGUAGES Hebrew, Arabic
MAJOR RELIGIONS Judaism, Islam,
Christianity

JORDAN

AREA 35,000 sq. mi.
(90,650 sq. km.)
POPULATION 2,779,000
CAPITAL Amman
LARGEST CITY Amman
HIGHEST POINT Jeb. Ramm 5,755 ft.
(1,754 m.)
MONETARY UNIT Jordanian dinar
MAJOR LANGUAGE Arabic
MAJOR RELIGION Islam

GAZA STRIP

CITIES and TOWNS

'Abasan 1,481 ....A5
Bani Suheila 7,561 ....A5
Beit Hanun 4,756 ....A4
Deir el Balah 10,854 ....A5
Deir el Balah* 18,118 ....A5
Gaza 87,793 ....A5
Gaza* 118,272 ....A5
Jabaliya 10,508 ....A4
Jabaliya* 43,604 ....A4
Khan Yunis 29,522 ....A5
Khan Yunis* 52,997 ....A5
Rafah 10,812 ....A5
Rafah* 49,812 ....A5

WEST BANK

CITIES and TOWNS

'Ajja 1,322 ....C3
'Anabta 3,426 ....C3
Anin 914 ....C2
'Anza 807 ....C3
'Aqqaba 1,127 ....C3
'Aqraba 2,501 ....C3
Ariha (Jericho) 5,312 ....C4
'Arraba 4,231 ....C3
'Arura 849 ....C3
'Attil 3,808 ....C3
Beit Fajjar 2,474 ....C4
Beit Hanina 1,177 ....C4
Beit Jala 6,041 ....C4
Beit Lahm
  (Bethlehem) 14,439 ....C4
Beit Sahur 5,380 ....C4
Bethlehem 14,439 ....C4
Biddu 1,259 ....C3
Birqin 2,036 ....C3
Bir Zeit 2,311 ....C4
Burqa 2,477 ....C3
Deir Ballut 1,058 ....C3
Deir Sharaf 973 ....C3
Dhahiriya 4,875 ....B5
Dura 4,954 ....C4
El Bira 9,674 ....C4
El Bira* 13,037 ....C4
El Khalil (Hebron) 38,309 ....C4
Er Rihiya 679 ....C4
Ez Zababida 1,474 ....C3
Halhul 6,041 ....C4
Hebron 38,309 ....C4
Idna 3,713 ....B4
Jaba 2,817 ....C3
Jalama 784 ....C3
Jalbun 914 ....C3
Jenin 8,346 ....C3
Jenin* 13,365 ....C3
Jericho 5,312 ....C4
Jericho* 6,931 ....C4
Jifna 655 ....C4
Kharas 1,364 ....C4
Nablus (Nablus) 41,799 ....C3
Nahhalin 1,109 ....C4
Ni'lin 1,227 ....C4
Qabalan 1,970 ....C3
Qabatiya 6,005 ....C3
Qaffin 2,480 ....C3
Qalqiliya 8,926 ....C3
Qibya 926 ....C4
Rafidiya 1,123 ....C3
Ramallah 12,134 ....C4
Rammun 1,198 ....C4
Rantis 897 ....C3
Salfit 3,201 ....C3
Samu 3,784 ....C5
Shu'fat 14,000 ....C4
Shuweika 2,332 ....C3
Silat Dhahr 2,104 ....C3
Sinjil 1,823 ....C3
Siris 1,335 ....C3
Tammun 2,952 ....C3
Tarqumia 2,412 ....C4
Tubas 5,262 ....C3
Tulkarm 10,255 ....C3
Tulkarm* 15,275 ....C3
Tur 12,200 ....C3
Ya'bad 4,857 ....C3
Yamun 4,384 ....C3
Yatta 7,281 ....C5

OTHER FEATURES

Ebal (mt.) C3
Golan Heights (reg.) D1
Judaea (reg.) C4
Khirhet Qumran (site) C4
Mashash, Wadi (riv.) C4
Samaria (reg.) C3
Tell 'Asur (mt.) C4
West Bank (reg.) C3

JORDAN

GOVERNORATES

Amman 1,000,000 ....D4
El Balqa 113,000 ....D4
El Karak 93,000 ....E5
Irbid 506,000 ....D3
Ma'an 62,000 ....D5

CITIES and TOWNS

'Ajlun⊙ 42,000 ....D3
Amman (cap.) 711,850 ....D4
'Anjara 3,163 ....D3
'Aqaba 15,000 ....D6
Bal'ama 769 ....E3
Baqura 3,042 ....D2
Damiya 483 ....D3
Dana 844 ....E5
Deir Abu Sa'id 1,927 ....D3
El 'Al 492 ....D4
El Husn 3,728 ....D3
El Karak 10,000 ....E4
El Kitta 987 ....D3
El Mafraq 15,500 ....E3
Er Rafid 787 ....D2
Er Ramtha 19,000 ....E2
Er Ruseifa 6,200 ....E3
Es Sahab 2,580 ....E4
Es Salt 24,000 ....D3
Es Sukhna 649 ....E3
Esh Shaubak 4,634 ....D5
Et Tafila 17,000 ....E5
Et Taiyiba 2,606 ....D2
Ez Zarqa 263,400 ....E3
Harima 635 ....D2
Hawara 2,342 ....D2
Hisban 718 ....D4
'Ibbin 1,364 ....D3
Irbid 136,770 ....D2
Jarash 29,000 ....D3
Kitim 1,026 ....D3
Kufrinja 3,922 ....D3
Ma'ad 125 ....D2
Ma'an 9,500 ....E5
Ma'daba 22,600 ....D4
Ma'in 1,271 ....D4
Mazra' D5
Na'ur 2,382 ....D4
Qumeim 955 ....D2
Ra's en Naqb 225 ....E5
Safi E5
Safut 4,210 ....D3
Samar 716 ....D2
Sarih 3,390 ....D2
Subeihi 514 ....D3
Suweilih 3,457 ....D3
Suweima 315 ....D4
Um Jauza 582 ....D3
Wadi es Sir 4,455 ....D4
Wadi Musa 654 ....E5
Waqqas 2,321 ....D2

OTHER FEATURES

'Ajlun, Jebel (range) D3
Aqaba (gulf) D6
'Araba, Wadi (valley) D5
Dead (sea) C4
Hasa, Wadi el (dry riv.) E5
Jordan (riv.) D3
Nebo (mt.) D4
Petra (ruins) D5
Ramm, Jebel (mt.) D5
Shallala, Wadi esh (dry riv.) D3
Shu'eib, Wadi (dry riv.) D3
Zarqa (riv.) D3

* City and suburbs
⊙ Population of subdivision.

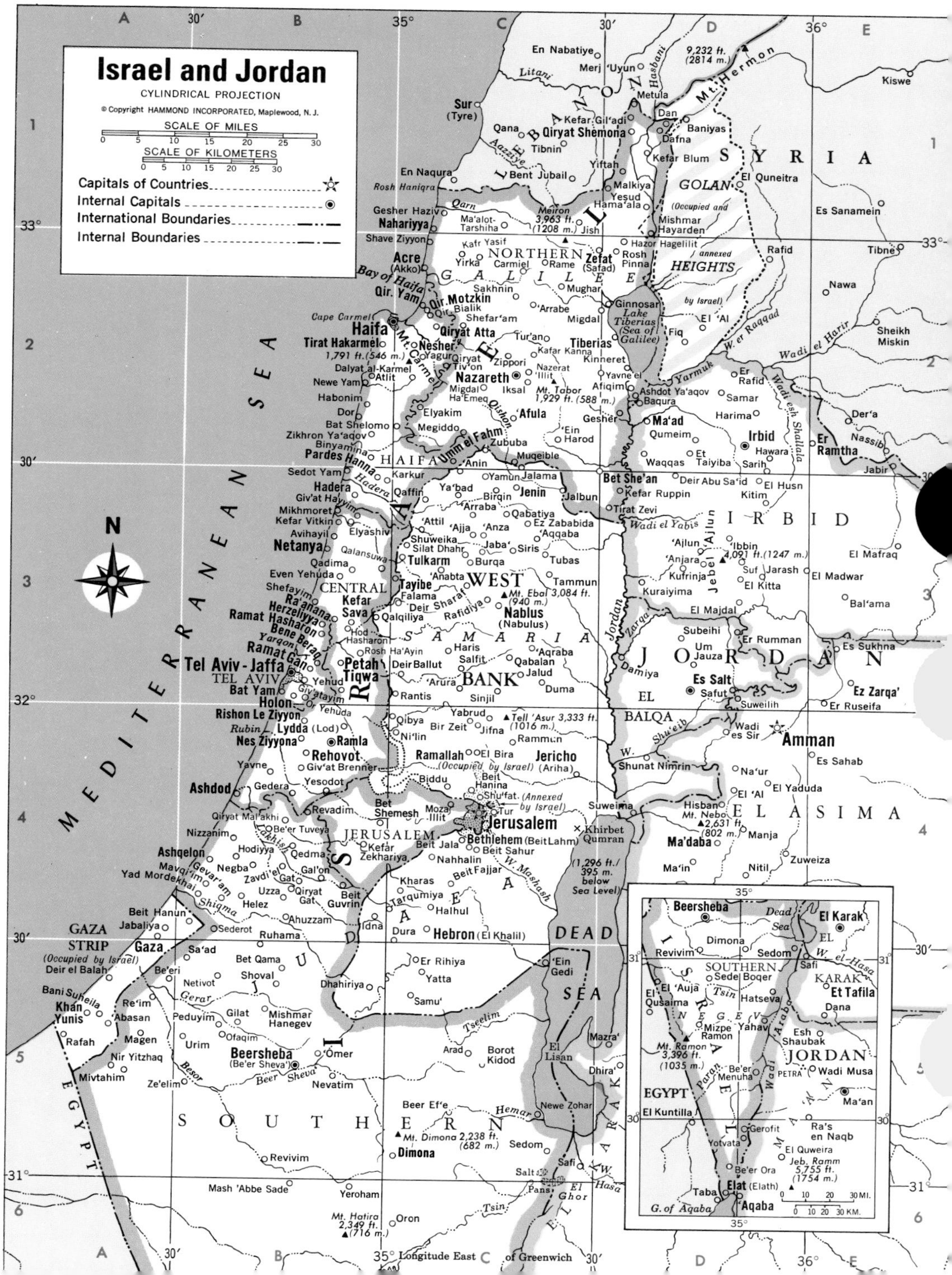

Israel and Jordan

CYLINDRICAL PROJECTION

® Copyright HAMMOND INCORPORATED, Maplewood, N.J.

SCALE OF MILES
0 5 10 15 20 25 30

SCALE OF KILOMETERS
0 5 10 15 20 25 30

Capitals of Countries ....☆
Internal Capitals ....⊙
International Boundaries ....
Internal Boundaries ....

IRAN

INTERNAL DIVISIONS

Azerbaijan, East (prov.)
3,194,543..................E1
Azerbaijan, West (prov.)
1,404,875..................D1
Bakhtaran (prov.) 1,016,199..E3
Bakhtaran (governorate)
394,300....................F4
Bushehr (prov.) 345,427....G6
Central (Markazi) (prov.)
6,921,283..................G3
Esfahan (Isfahan) (prov.)
1,974,938..................H4
Fars (prov.) 2,020,947.....H6
Gilan (prov.) 1,577,800....F2
Hamadan (governorate)
1,086,512..................G3
Hormozgan (prov.) 463,419..J7
Ilam (governorate) 244,222..H4
Isfahan (prov.) 1,974,938...H4
Kerman (prov.) 1,088,045...K6
Khorasan (prov.) 3,266,650..K3
Khuzestan (prov.) 2,176,612..F5
Kohkiluyeh and Boyer
Ahmediyeh (governorate)
244,750....................G5
Kordestan (Kurdistan) (prov.)
781,889....................E3

Lorestan (Luristan)
(governorate) 924,848.....F4
Mazandaran (prov.)
2,384,226..................H2
Semnan (governorate)
485,875....................J3
Sistan and Baluchestan
(prov.) 659,297...........M6
Yazd (governorate) 356,218..J5
Zanjan (governorate) 579,000..F2

CITIES and TOWNS

Abadan 296,081.............F5
Abadeh 16,000.............H5
Abhar 24,000..............F2
Agha Jari 24,195..........F5
Ahar 24,000...............F1
Ahvaz (Ahwaz) 329,006.....F5
Amol 68,782...............H2
Andimeshk 16,000..........F4
Arak 114,507..............G3
Ardabil 147,404...........F1
Asterabad (Gorgan) 88,348..H2
Babol 67,790..............H2
Bakhtaran (Kermanshah)
290,861....................E3
Bam 22,000................L6
Bandar 'Abbas 89,103......J7
Bandar Behesti (Bahar)
1,800......................M8

Bandar-e Anzali (Enzeli)
55,978.....................F2
Bandar-e Bushehr (Bushire)
57,681.....................G6
Bandar-e Khomeyni 6,000...G5
Bandar-e Lingeh 4,920.....J7
Bandar-e Ma'shur 17,000...F5
Bandar-e Torkeman 13,000..H2
Behbehan 39,874...........G5
Behshahr 26,032...........H2
Birjand 25,854............L4
Bojnurd 31,248............K2
Borazjan 20,000...........G6
Borujerd 100,103..........F4
Bostan 4,619..............F5
Chalus 15,000.............G2
Damghan 13,000............J2
Dasht-e Azadegan
(Susangerd) 21,000.......F5
Dizful (Dezful) 110,287...F4
Duzdab (Zahedan) 92,628...M6
Emamshahr (Shahrud)
30,767.....................J2
Enzeli 55,978.............F2
Esfahan (Isfahan) 671,825..G4
Eslamabad 12,000..........F4
Eshtabanat 18,187.........J6
Fahrej (Iranshahr) 5,000...M7
Fasa 19,000...............H6
Ganaveh 9,000.............G6
Garmsar 4,723.............H3

Ghaemshahr 63,289.........H2
Golpayegan 20,515.........G4
Golshan (Tabas) 10,000....K4
Gonbad-e Kavus 59,868.....J2
Gorgan (Gurgan) 88,348....J2
Hamadan 155,846...........F3
Hormoz 2,569..............J7
Iranshahr 5,000...........M7
Isfahan 671,991...........G4
Jahrom 38,236.............H6
Karaj 138,774.............G3
Kashan 84,545.............G3
Kashmar 17,000............L3
Kazerun 51,309............G6
Kazvin (Qazvin) 138,527...F3
Kerman 140,309............K5
Khomeinishar 46,836.......G4
Khorramabad 104,928.......F4
Khorramshahr 146,709......F5
Khvoy (Khoi) 70,040.......D1
Lahijan 25,725............G2
Lar 22,000................J7
Mahabad 28,610............D2
Malayer 28,434............F3
Maragheh 60,820...........E2
Marand 24,000.............D1
Marv Dasht 25,498.........H6
Masjed Soleyman 77,161....F5
Mashhad (Meshed) 670,180..L2
Shahrud 30,767............J2
Miandowab 19,000..........D2
Mianeh 28,447.............E2

Nahavand 24,000...........F3
Najafabad 76,236..........G4
Nasratabad (Zabol) 20,000..M5
Nishapur (Neyshabur) 59,101..L2
Nosratabad 20,000.........L6
Orumiyeh (Urmia) 163,991..D2
Pahlevi (Enzeli) 55,978...F2
Qayen 6,000...............L4
Qazvin 138,527............F3
Quchan 29,133.............L2
Qum (Qom) 246,831.........G3
Rafsanjan 21,000..........K5
Resht (Rasht) 187,203.....F2
Rey 102,825...............G3
Reza'iyeh (Urmia).........D2
Sa'idabad 20,000..........J6
Sabzevar 69,174...........K2
Sakht-Sar 12,000..........G2
Salmas 13,161.............D1
Saqqez 17,000.............E2
Sari 70,936...............H2
Savanat (Estahbanat) 18,187..J6
Saveh 17,565..............G3
Semnan 31,058.............H3
Shahr Kord 24,000.........H4
Shahreza 34,220...........H4
Shahrud 30,767............J2
Shiraz 416,408............H6
Shushtar 24,000...........F4

Sinneh (Sanandaj) 95,834..E3
Sirjan (Sa'idabad) 20,000..J6
Sultanabad (Kashmar)
17,000.....................L3
Susangerd 21,000..........F5
Tabas 10,000..............K4
Tabriz 598,576............D2
Tajrish 157,486...........G3
Tehran (cap.) 4,496,159...G3
Torbat-e Heydariyeh 30,106..L3
Urmia 163,991.............D2
Yazd (Yezd) 135,978.......J5
Zabol 20,000..............M5
Zahedan 92,628............M6
Zenjan (Zanjan) 99,967....F2

OTHER FEATURES

'Arabi (isl.)..............G7
Araks (Aras) (riv.).......E1
Atrak (Atrek) (riv.)......J2
Azerbaijan (reg.).........D1
Bakhtegan (lake)..........J6
Baluchistan (reg.)........M7
Bampur (riv.).............M7
Behistun (ruins)..........E3
Caspian Sea (sea).........G1
Damavand (Demavend)
(mt.)......................H2
Daryacheh-ye Namak
(salt lake)...............G3

Daryacheh-ye Sistan
(salt lake)...............M5
Dasht-e Kavir (salt des.)..J3
Dasht-e Lut (des.)........L5
Dez (riv.)................F4
Elburz (mts.).............G2
Farsi (isl.)..............G7
Gabrik (riv.).............L7
Gamas Ab (riv.)...........E3
Gavkhuni (marsh)..........H4
Gorgan (riv.).............J2
Hamun-e Saberi (lake).....M5
Harirud (riv.)............M3
Hormoz (isl.).............K7
Hormoz (str.).............K7
Jaba Rud (riv.)...........L2
Joveyn (riv.).............K2
Kabir Kuh (mts.)..........E4
Karkheh (riv.)............F5
Karun (riv.)..............F5
Khark (Kharg) (isl.)......G6
Khusf Rud (riv.)..........L4
Khvoleh Lak, Kuh-e (mt.)..H7
Kor (riv.)................H6
Laristan (reg.)...........J7
Makran (reg.).............M8
Mand (riv.)...............H6
Mand (riv.)...............G6
Mashkid (riv.)............N7
Mehran (riv.).............J7
Nahang (riv.).............N7

Namaksar (lake)..................M4
Namakzar-e Shahdad
  (salt lake)......................L5
Oman (gulf).......................M8
Pasargadae (ruins)............H5
Persepolis (ruins)..............H6
Persian (gulf)....................F6
Qaranqu (riv.)...................E2
Qareh Dagh (mts.)............E1
Qareh Su (riv.)..................E1
Qeshm (isl.)......................J7
Qezel Owzam (riv.)...........F2
Ras al Kuh (cape).............K8
Ras-e Meydani (cape).......L8
Safid Rud (riv.)..................F2
Seistan (reg.)....................M5
Shatt-al-'Arab (riv.)............F5
Shelagh (riv.)....................M5
Shirvan (riv.)....................E3
Shur (riv.)..........................J7
Sirri (isl.)...........................J8
Susa (ruins)......................F4
Talab (riv.)........................N6
Talkheh (riv.).....................E1
Tashk (lake)......................J6
Urmia (lake)......................D2
Zagros (mts.)....................E4
Zarineh (riv.).....................E2
Zayandeh (riv.).................H4
Zilbir (riv.)..........................D1
Zohreh (riv.)......................F5

IRAQ
GOVERNORATES

Anbar 535,627..................B4
An Najaf 438,971..............C5
Babil 680,700....................D4
Baghdad 4,038,430..........D4
Basra 1,184,500................E5
Dhi Qar 683,537...............E5
Diyala 650,211..................D4
Dohuk 296,339.................C2
Erbil 657,294....................C3
Karbala' 305,627...............B4
Maysan 395,666...............D5
Muthanna 239,044............D5
Ninawa 1,258,001.............B3
Qadisiya 475,676..............D4
Salahuddin 411,734..........C3
Sulaimaniya 816,406.........D3
Tamin 527,079..................C3
Wasit 455,853...................D4

CITIES and TOWNS

Ad Diwaniya 60,553...........D5
'Afaq 5,390.......................D4
Al 'Aziziya 7,450...............D4
Al Falluja 38,072................C4
Al Fathat† 15,329..............C3
'Ali Gharbi 15,456..............E4
'Ali Sharqi 8,398................E4
Al Kufa 30,862..................D4
Al Musaiyib 15,955............D4
'Amara 64,847..................E5
'Ana 15,729......................B3
An Najaf 128,096..............D5
An Nasiriya 60,405............D5
Arbela (Erbil) 90,320..........D2
Ar Rumaila 1,439..............E5
'Aqra 8,659.......................D2
Az Zubair 41,408...............E5
Ba'quba 34,575.................D4
Basra 313,327...................E5
Dohuk 16,998...................C2
Erbil 90,320.......................D2
Fao 15,399........................F6
Habbaniya 14,405.............C4
Hai 16,988........................E4
Halabja 11,206..................D3
Hilla 84,717.......................D4
Hindiya 16,436..................C4
Hit 9,131...........................C4
Karbal'a 83,301.................C4
Khanaqin 23,522..............D3
Kifri 8,500.........................D3
Kirkuk 167,413..................D3
Kut 42,116........................D4
Mandali 11,262.................D4
Mosul 315,157...................C2
Muqdadiyah 12,181..........D4
N'amaniya 11,943.............D4
Qal'at Diza 6,250...............D2
Ramadi 28,723.................C4
Rumaitha 10,222...............D5
Samarra 24,746................C3
Samawa 33,473................D5
Shatra 18,822...................E5
Sinjar 7,942......................B2
Sulaimaniya 86,822..........D3
Tal Kaif 7,482....................C2
Taza Khurmatu 2,681.......D3
Tikrit 9,921........................C3
Tuz Khurmatu 13,860.......D3
Zakho 14,790...................C2

OTHER FEATURES

Adhaim (riv.).....................D3
Al Hajara (plain)................D5
'Aneiza, Jebel (mt.)...........A4
'Ar'ar, Wadi (dry riv.)........B5
Babylon (ruins).................D4
Batin, Wadi al (dry riv.)......E6
Ctesiphon (ruins)..............D4
Dalmaj, Hor (lake).............D4
Darbandikhan (dam).........D3
Diyala (riv.).......................D4
Euphrates (riv.).................D4
Great Zab (riv.).................C2
Habbaniya, Hor al (lake)....C4
Hammar, Hor al (lake).......E5
Hamrin, Jabal (mts.)..........D3
Hauran, Wadi (dry riv.)......B4
Little Zab (riv.)..................C3
Mesopotamia (reg.)..........B3
Nineveh (ruins).................C2
Razaza (res.)....................C4
Sa'diya, Hor (lake)............E4
Saniya, Hor (lake).............E5
Sha'ib Hisb, Wadi (dry riv.)...C5
Shatt-al-'Arab (riv.)............F5
Sinjar, Jebel (mts.)............B2
Siyah Kuh (mt.).................D2
Suwaiqiya, Hor as (lake)....D4
Tharthar (res.)...................C3
Tharthar, Wadi (dry riv.).....C3
Tigris (riv.).........................E4
Tubal, Wadi al (dry riv.)......B4
Ubaiyidh, Wadi (dry riv.)....B5
Ur (ruins)...........................E5

† Population of commune.

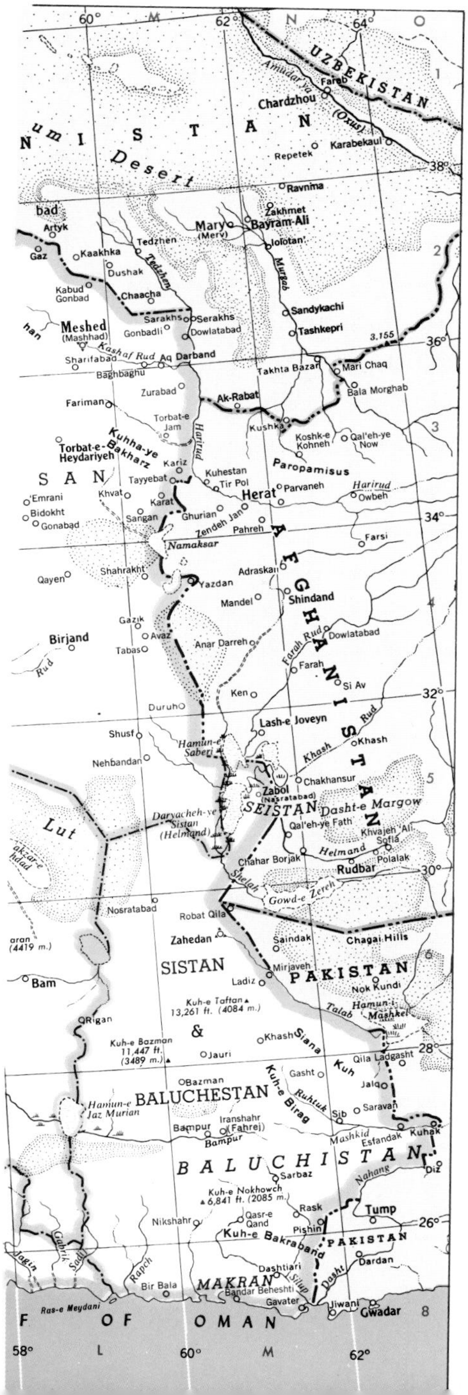

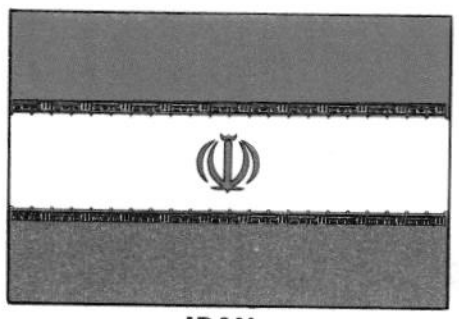

IRAN

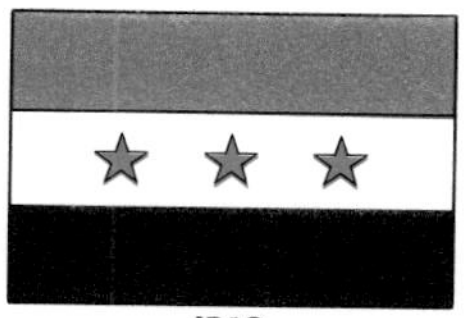

IRAQ

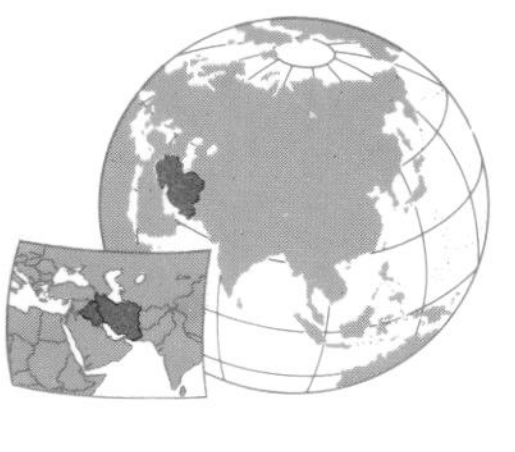

AREA 636,293 sq. mi. (1,648,000 sq. km.)
POPULATION 55,208,000
CAPITAL Tehran
LARGEST CITY Tehran
HIGHEST POINT Damavand 18,376 ft. (5,601 m.)
MONETARY UNIT Iranian rial
MAJOR LANGUAGES Persian, Azerbaijani, Kurdish
MAJOR RELIGION Islam

AREA 172,476 sq. mi. (446,713 sq. km.)
POPULATION 16,335,000
CAPITAL Baghdad
LARGEST CITY Baghdad
HIGHEST POINT Haji Ibrahim 11,811 ft.
  (3.600 m.)
MONETARY UNIT Iraqi dinar
MAJOR LANGUAGES Arabic, Kurdish
MAJOR RELIGION Islam

Topography

0   200   400 MI.
0   200   400 KM.

5,000 m. / 16,404 ft. | 2,000 m. / 6,562 ft. | 1,000 m. / 3,281 ft. | 500 m. / 1,640 ft. | 200 m. / 656 ft. | 100 m. / 328 ft. | Sea Level / Below

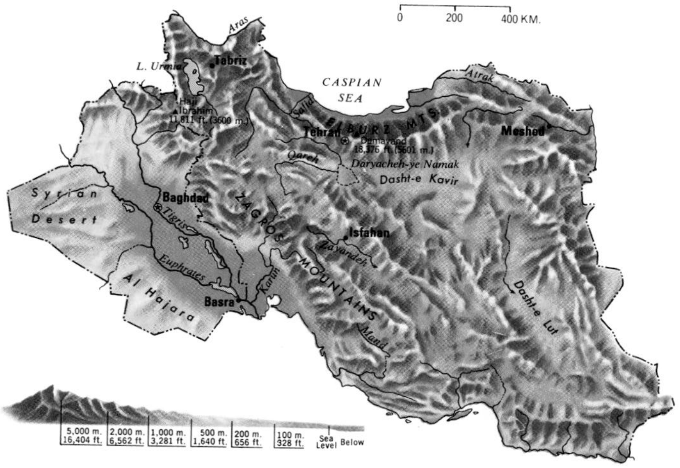

Agriculture, Industry and Resources

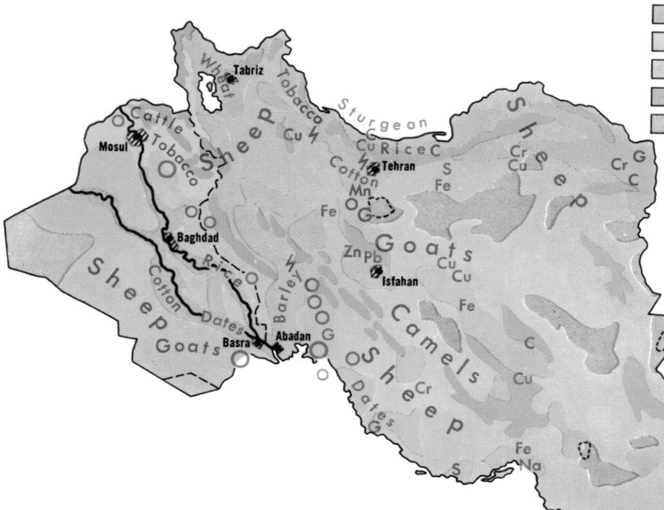

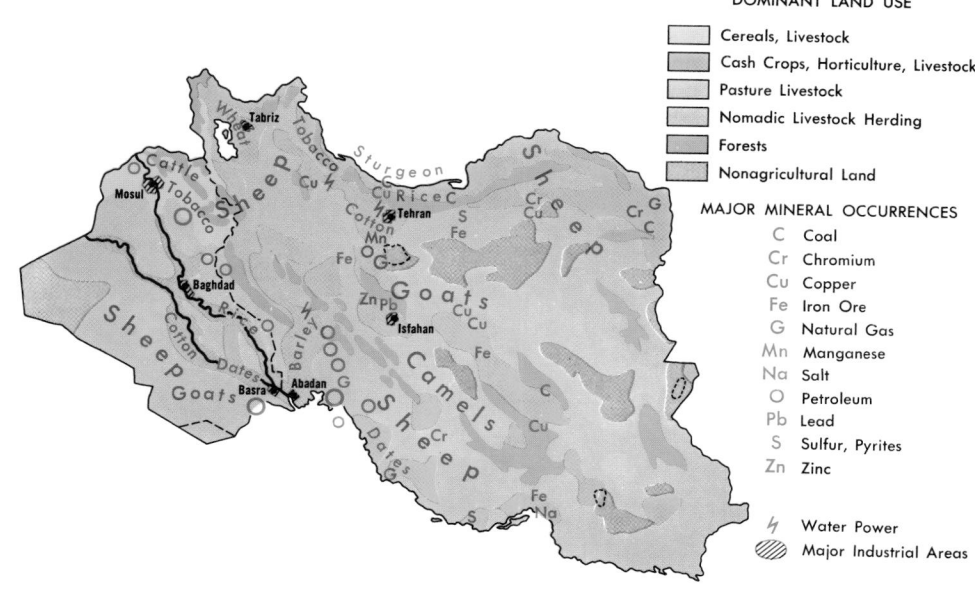

DOMINANT LAND USE

Cereals, Livestock
Cash Crops, Horticulture, Livestock
Pasture Livestock
Nomadic Livestock Herding
Forests
Nonagricultural Land

MAJOR MINERAL OCCURRENCES

C   Coal
Cr Chromium
Cu Copper
Fe Iron Ore
G   Natural Gas
Mn Manganese
Na Salt
O   Petroleum
Pb Lead
S   Sulfur, Pyrites
Zn Zinc

⚡ Water Power
▨ Major Industrial Areas

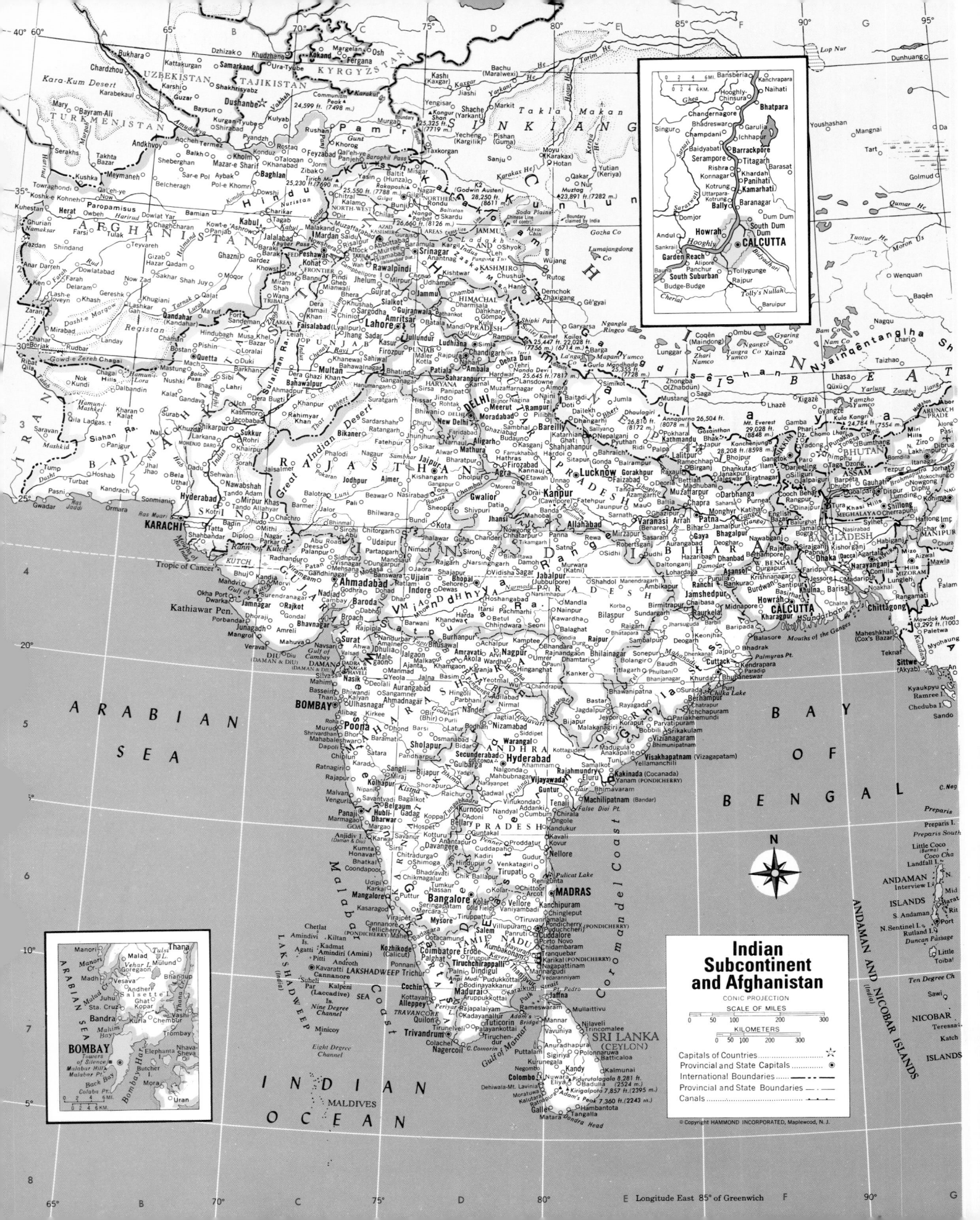

Indian
Subcontinent
and Afghanistan

CONIC PROJECTION

SCALE OF MILES

0   50   100   200   300

KILOMETERS

0   50   100   200   300

Capitals of Countries.............................☆

Provincial and State Capitals.............◉

International Boundaries.....................

Provincial and State Boundaries.......

Canals...

© Copyright HAMMOND INCORPORATED, Maplewood, N.J.

Longitude East 85° of Greenwich

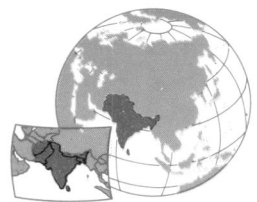

INDIA

AREA 1,269,339 sq. mi. (3,287,588 sq. km.)
POPULATION 843,930,861
CAPITAL New Delhi
LARGEST CITY Calcutta (greater)
HIGHEST POINT Nanda Devi 25,645 ft. (7,817 m.)
MONETARY UNIT Indian rupee
MAJOR LANGUAGES Hindi, English, Bengali, Telugu, Marathi, Tamil, Urdu, Gujarati, Malayalam, Kannada, Oriya, Punjabi, Assamese, Kashmiri, Sindhi
MAJOR RELIGIONS Hinduism, Islam, Christianity, Sikhism, Buddhism, Jainism, Zoroastrianism, Animism

PAKISTAN

AREA 310,403 sq. mi. (803,944 sq. km.)
POPULATION 112,050,000
CAPITAL Islamabad
LARGEST CITY Karachi
HIGHEST POINT K2 (Godwin Austen) 28,250 ft. (8,611 m.)
MONETARY UNIT Pakistani rupee
MAJOR LANGUAGES Urdu, English, Punjabi, Pushtu, Sindhi, Baluchi, Brahui
MAJOR RELIGIONS Islam, Hinduism, Sikhism, Christianity, Buddhism

SRI LANKA (CEYLON)

AREA 25,332 sq. mi. (65,610 sq. km.)
POPULATION 16,806,000
CAPITAL Colombo
LARGEST CITY Colombo
HIGHEST POINT Pidurutalagala 8,281 ft. (2,524 m.)
MONETARY UNIT Sri Lanka rupee
MAJOR LANGUAGES Sinhala, Tamil, English
MAJOR RELIGIONS Buddhism, Hinduism, Christianity, Islam

AFGHANISTAN

AREA 250,775 sq. mi. (649,507 sq. km.)
POPULATION 15,814,000
CAPITAL Kabul
LARGEST CITY Kabul
HIGHEST POINT Nowshak 24,557 ft. (7,485 m.)
MONETARY UNIT afghani
MAJOR LANGUAGES Pushtu, Dari, Uzbek
MAJOR RELIGION Islam

NEPAL

AREA 54,663 sq. mi. (141,577 sq. km.)
POPULATION 18,442,000
CAPITAL Kathmandu
LARGEST CITY Kathmandu
HIGHEST POINT Mt. Everest 29,028 ft. (8,848 m.)
MONETARY UNIT Nepalese rupee
MAJOR LANGUAGES Nepali, Maithili, Tamang, Newari, Tharu
MAJOR RELIGIONS Hinduism, Buddhism

MALDIVES

AREA 115 sq. mi. (298 sq. km.)
POPULATION 206,000
CAPITAL Male
LARGEST CITY Male
HIGHEST POINT 20 ft. (6 m.)
MONETARY UNIT Maldivian rufiyaa
MAJOR LANGUAGE Divehi
MAJOR RELIGION Islam

BHUTAN

AREA 18,147 sq. mi. (47,000 sq. km.)
POPULATION 1,483,000
CAPITAL Thimphu
LARGEST CITY Thimphu
HIGHEST POINT Kula Kangri 24,784 ft. (7,554 m.)
MONETARY UNIT ngultrum
MAJOR LANGUAGES Dzongka, Nepali
MAJOR RELIGIONS Buddhism, Hinduism

BANGLADESH

AREA 55,126 sq. mi. (142,776 sq. km.)
POPULATION 106,507,000
CAPITAL Dhaka
LARGEST CITY Dhaka
HIGHEST POINT Keokradong 4,034 ft. (1,230 m.)
MONETARY UNIT taka
MAJOR LANGUAGES Bengali, English
MAJOR RELIGIONS Islam, Hinduism Christianity

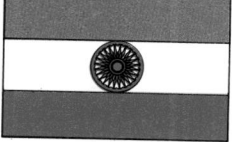

INDIA

PAKISTAN

SRI LANKA (CEYLON)

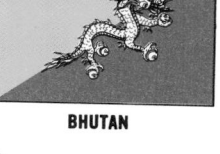

BHUTAN

AFGHANISTAN

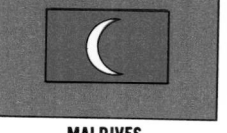

MALDIVES

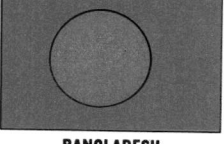

BANGLADESH

NEPAL

AFGHANISTAN

CITIES and TOWNS

Andkhvoy 13,137 ....A1
Aybak 33,016 ....B1
Baghlan 75,130 ....B1
Bamian 7,355 ....B2
Chaghcharan 2,974 ....A2
Charikar 25,093 ....B1
Farah 18,797 ....A2
Feyzabad 10,142 ....C1
Gardez 11,415 ....B2
Gereshk A2
Ghazni 30,425 ....B2
Ghurian 12 404 ....A2
Hazar Qadam B2
Herat 163,960 ....A2
Jalalabad 56,384 ....B2
Kabul (cap.) 905,108 ....B2
Kajat (Qalat) 5,946 ....B2
Kandahar (Qandahar) 178,409 ....B2
Khanabad 26,803 ....B1
Khash.................................A2
Kholm 28,078 ....B1
Khowst B2
Konduz 107,191 ....B1
Kuhestan............................A2
Lashkar Gah 26,646 ....A2
Mazar-e Sharif 122,567 .....B1
Meymaneh 54,954 ....A1
Mirabad A2
Oruzgan (Hazar Qadam) B2
Panjab................................B2
Pol-e Khomri 31,101 ....B1
Qalat 5,946 ....B2
Qal'eh-ye Now 5,340..........A1
Qandahar 178,409 ....B2
Qonduz (Konduz) 107,191 ...B1
Sakhar...............................B1
Sar-e Pol 15,699 ....B1
Sheberghan 54,870 ....B1
Shindand A2
Tagab.................................B2
Taloqan 46,202 ....B1
Zaranj 6,477......................A2

OTHER FEATURES

Baroghil (pass) C1
Chagai (hills).....................A3
Margow, Dasht-e (des.) A2
Farah Rud (riv.) A2
Gowd-e Zereh (depr.) A3
Harirud (riv.) A2
Helmand (riv.)....................B2
Hindu Kush (mts.) B1
Kabul (riv.) C1
Konar (riv.) C1
Konduz (riv.) B1
Lurah (riv.) B2
Namaksar (salt lake) A2
Nuristan (reg.)...................C1

(continued on following page)

Panj (riv.) C1
Paropamisus (range) A2
Qonduz (Konduz) (riv.) B1
Registan (reg.) A2
Tarnak (riv.) B2

BANGLADESH

CITIES and TOWNS

Barisal 159,298 ....G4
Bogra 68,237 ....F4
Chalna Port 14,590 ....F4
Chittagong 1,388,476 ....G4
Comilla 126,130 ....G4
Cox's Bazar G4
Dhaka (cap.) 3,458,602 .....G4
Dinajpur 96,348 ....F3
Faridpur 66,911 ....F4
Habiganj 16,281 ....G4
Jamalpur 89,847 ....F4
Jessore 149,426................F4
Khulna 623,184 ....F4
Kishorganj 52,081 ....G4
Madaripur 58,645 ....G4
Maheshkhali 29,530 ....G4
Mymensingh (Nasirabad) 107,863 ....G4
Narayanganj 196,139 ....G4
Nasirabad 107,863 ....G4
Nawabganj 65,286 ....F4
Noakhali 32,490 ....G4
Pabna 101,080..................F4
Rajshahi 171,600 ....F4
Rangamati 36,490 ....G4
Rangpur 72,829 ....F3
Sirajganj 74,457 ....F4
Sylhet 59,546 ....G4

OTHER FEATURES

Bengal, Bay of (bay) F5
Brahmaputra (riv.)............G3
Ganges (riv.) F3
Ganges, Mouths of the (delta).F3
Mowdok Mual (mt.) G4
Sundarbans (reg.)..............F4

BHUTAN

CITIES and TOWNS

Bumthang 10,000 ....G3
Paro 35,000 ....F3
Punakha 12,000.................G3
Taga Dzong 18,000...........G3
Thimphu (cap.) 50,000 ......G3
Tongsa Dzong 2,500 ....G3

OTHER FEATURES

Chomo Lhari (mt.)..............F3
Himalaya (mts.) E2
Kula Kangri (mt.) G3

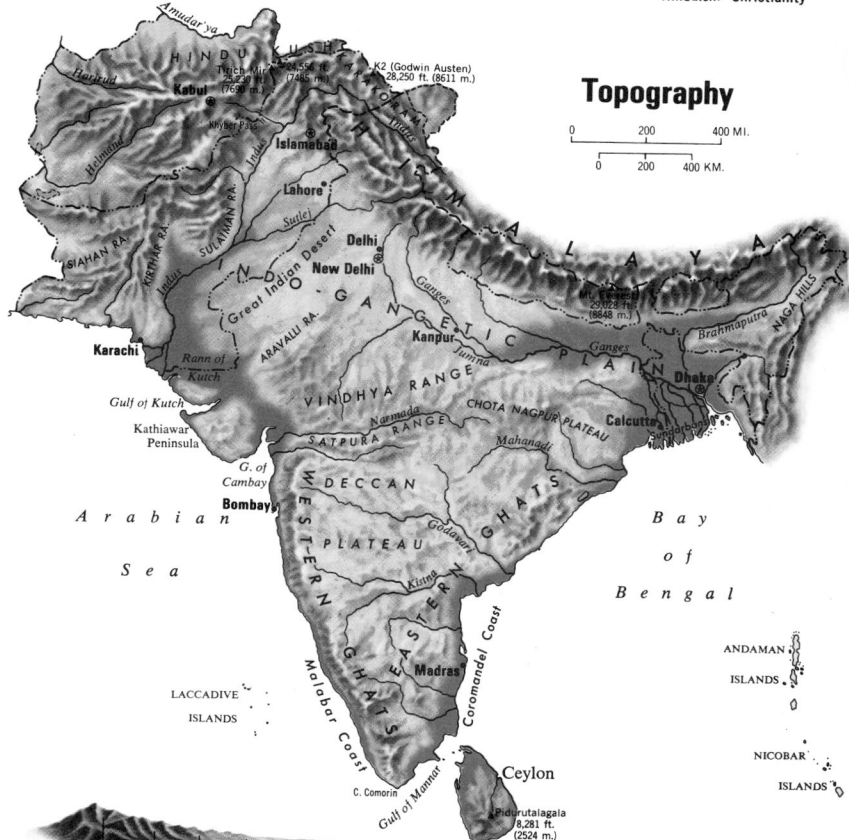

Topography

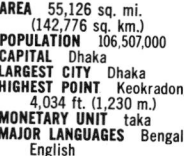

INDIA

INTERNAL DIVISIONS

British India

British India. The provinces of British India were directly administered by Britain. A few areas were leased from the Indian princes.

Indian States. The Indian States, sometimes referred to as the "Native" or "Princely States," were under the nominal control of maharajas or other hereditary princes.

Possessions of Other Countries in India

State or Provincial Boundaries

Other Internal Boundaries

Vidisha 43,212....D4
Vijayawada 544,958....D5
Villupuram 60,242....D6
Viramgam 43,790....C4
Visakhapatnam 594,259....E5
Visnagar 34,863....C4
Vizagapatam (Visakhapatnam) 594,259....E5
Vizianagaram 115,209....E5
Warangal 336,018....D5
Wardha 69,037....D4
Yadgir 32,756....D5
Yanam 8,291....E5
Yeola 24,533....C4

OTHER FEATURES

Abor (hills)....G3
Adam's Bridge (sound)....D7
Agatti (isl.)....C6
Amindiri (isl.)....C6
Amindivi (isls.)....C6
Amini (Amindiri) (isl.)....C6
Anai Mudi (mt.)....D6
Andaman (isls.)....G6
Andaman (sea)....G6
Androth (isl.)....C6
Anjidiv (Angedeva) (isl.)....C6
Arabian (sea)....B5
Back (bay)....B7
Banas (riv.)....D3
Baratang (isl.)....G6
Barren (isl.)....G6
Batti Malv (isl.)....G7
Bengal, Bay of (bay)....F5
Berar (reg.)....D4
Betwa (riv.)....D4
Bhima (riv.)....D5
Bidyadhari (riv.)....F2
Bombay (harbor)....B7
Brahmaputra (riv.)....G3
Butcher (isl.)....B7
Cambay (gulf)....C4
Camorta (isl.)....G7
Cannanore (isls.)....C6
Chambal (riv.)....D3
Chenab (riv.)....C2
Cherial (riv.)....F2
Chetlat (isl.)....C6
Chilka (lake)....F5
Coco (chan.)....G6
Colaba (pt.)....B7
Colair (lake)....E5
Comorin (cape)....D7
Coromandel Coast (reg.)....E6
Daman (dist.)....C4
Damodar (riv.)....F4
Deccan (plat.)....D6

Diu (dist.)....C4
Duncan (passage)....G7
Eastern Ghats (mts.)....D6
Eight Degree (chan.)....C7
Elephanta (isl.)....B7
False Divi (pt.)....E5
Ganga (Ganges) (riv.)....F3
Ganges, Mouths of the (delta)....F4
Ganges (riv.)....F3
Ghaghra (riv.)....E3
Ghea (riv.)....F1
Goa (dist.)....C5
Godavari (riv.)....D5
Golconda (ruins)....D5
Great (chan.)....G7
Great Indian (des.)....C3
Great Nicobar (isl.)....G7
Hagari (riv.)....D6
Himalaya (mts.)....D2
Hindu Kush (mts.)....C1
Hooghly (riv.)....F2
Indira (Pygmalion) (pt.)....G7
Indravati (riv.)....E5
Indus (riv.)....B3
Jhelum (riv.)....C2
Jumna (riv.)....E3
Kachchh (gulf)....B4
Kachchh (reg.)....B4
Kachchh, Rann of (salt marsh)....B4
Kadmat (isl.)....C6
Kalpeni (isl.)....C7
Kamet (mt.)....D2
Kanchenjunga (mt.)....F3
Karakoram (mts.)....D1
Katchall (isl.)....G7
Kathiawar (pen.)....B4
Kaveri (riv.)....D6
Khasi (hills)....G3
Kiltan (isl.)....C6
Kistna (Krishna) (riv.)....D5
Kunlun (range)....D1
Kutch (Kachchh) (reg.)....B4
Kutch (Kachchh), Rann of (salt marsh)....B4
Laccadive (Cannanore) (isls.)....C6
Ladakh (reg.)....D2
Lakshadweep (sea)....C6
Landfall (isl.)....G6
Little Andaman (isl.)....G6
Little Nicobar (isl.)....G7
Luni (riv.)....C3
Mahanadi (riv.)....E4
Mahim (bay)....B7
Malabar (hill)....B7

Malabar (pt.)....B7
Malabar Coast (reg.)....C6
Malad (creek)....B7
Mannar (gulf)....D7
Manori (creek)....B7
Middle Andaman (isl.)....G6
Minicoy (isl.)....C7
Miri (hills)....G3
Mishmi (hills)....H3
Mizo (hill)....G4
Nancowry (isl.)....G7
Nanda Devi (mt.)....D2
Narcondam (isl.)....G6
Narmada (riv.)....D4
Nicobar (isls.)....G7
Nine Degree (chan.)....C7
North Andaman (isl.)....G6
North Sentinel (isl.)....G6
Palk (str.)....D7
Palmyras (pt.)....F4
Pangong Tso (lake)....D2
Penganga (riv.)....D4
Penner (riv.)....D6
Periyar (lake)....D7
Pitti (isl.)....C6
Pulicat (lake)....E6
Pygmalion (pt.)....G7
Ritchies (arch.)....G6
Rutland (isl.)....G6
Salsette (isl.)....B7
Sambhar (lake)....C3
Saraswati (riv.)....F1
Sarsati (riv.)....F1
Satpura (range)....D4
Shipki (pass)....D2
Soda (plains)....D1
Sombrero (chan.)....G7
Son (riv.)....E4
South Andaman (isl.)....G6
Suheli Par (atoll)....C6
Sundarbans (reg.)....F4
Sutlej (riv.)....C3
Tapti (riv.)....D4
Tel (riv.)....E4
Ten Degree (chan.)....G7
Teressa (isl.)....G7
Tillanchong (isl.)....G7
Tolly's Nullah (riv.)....F2
Towers of Silence....B7
Travancore (reg.)....D7
Tulsi (lake)....B6
Tungabhadra (riv.)....D5
Vehar (lake)....B7
Vindhya (range)....D4
Wardha (riv.)....D4
Western Ghats (mts.)....C5
Zaskar (mts.)....D2

MALDIVES

Maldives 143,046....C7

NEPAL

CITIES and TOWNS

Baitadi 128,696....E3
Bhaktapur 40,112....F3
Bhaktapur▲ 110,157....F3
Bhojpur 194,506....F3
Biratnagar 45,100....F3
Dailekh 156,072....E3
Dhankuta 107,649....F3
Doti 166,070....E3
Janakpur 14,294....F3
Jumla▲ 122,753....E3
Kathmandu (cap.) 150,402....E3
Kathmandu▲ 353,752....E3
Lalitpur 59,049....E3
Lalitpur▲ 154,998....E3
Mustang▲ 26,944....E3
Nepalganj 23,523....E3
Palpa 212,633....E3
Pokhara 20,611....E3
Pyuthan▲ 137,338....E3
Ramechhap 157,349....F3
Sallyan▲ 141,457....E3

OTHER FEATURES

Annapurna (mt.)....E3
Bheri (riv.)....E3
Dhaulagiri (mt.)....E3
Everest (mt.)....F3
Himalaya (mts.)....D2
Kanchenjunga (mt.)....F3

PAKISTAN

PROVINCES

Azad Kashmir....C2
Balochistan 4,332,376....B3
Federal Administrated Tribal Areas 2,198,547....C2
Islamabad District 340,286....D1
Northern Areas....C1
North-West Frontier 11,061,328....C2
Punjab 47,292,441....C2
Sindh 19,028,666....B3

CITIES and TOWNS

Abbottabad 66,000....C2
Ahmadpur East 57,000....C3

Attock 40,000....C2
Badin 23,000....B4
Bahawalnagar 74,000....C2
Bahawalpur 178,000....C3
Baltit....C1
Bannu 43,000....C2
Bela 11,000....B3
Bhera 29,000....C2
Bunji....C1
Campbellpore 19,041....C2
Chagai▲ 41,263....A3
Chaman 30,000....B2
Chiniot 106,000....C2
Chitral....C1
Dadu 39,000....B3
Dera Ghazi Khan 103,000....C3
Dera Ismail Khan 68,000....C2
Diplo 7,000....B4
Faisalabad 1,092,000....C2
Fort Sandeman 8,058....B2
Gujranwala 654,000....C2
Gujrat 154,000....C2
Gwadar 17,000....A4
Hunza (Baltit)....C1
Hyderabad 795,000....B3
Islamabad (cap.) 201,000....C2
Jacobabad 80,000....B3
Jhang Sadar 195,000....C2
Jhelum 106,000....C2
Kalat 11,000....B3
Karachi 4,979,000....B4
Kasur 155,000....C2
Khairpur 62,000....B3
Khanewal 89,000....C2
Khanpur 71,000....C3
Kharan Kalat 10,000....A3
Khushab 56,000....C2
Kohat 78,000....C2
Kotri 38,000....B3
Lahore 3,922,000....C2
Larkana 123,000....B3
Leiah 52,000....C2
Loralai 14,000....B2
Lyallpur (Faisalabad) 1,092,000....C2
Mach 8,000....B3
Malakand....C2
Mardan 148,000....C2
Mastung 17,000....B3
Mianwali 59,000....C2
Mirpur Khas 124,000....B3
Multan 730,000....C2
Muzaffarabad....C2
Nagar....D1
Nawabshah 102,000....B3
Nok Kundi 861....A3
Nowshera 75,000....C2
Nushki 11,000....B3

Pasni 18,000....A3
Peshawar 555,000....C2
Pindi Gheb 20,000....C2
Quetta 285,000....B2
Rahimyar Khan 119,000....C3
Rawalpindi 806,000....C2
Risalpur Cantonment 20,000....C2
Rohri 32,000....B3
Sahiwal 152,000....C2
Saidu 15,920....C1
Sargodha 294,000....C2
Shikarpur 88,000....B3
Sialkot 296,000....C2
Sibi 23,000....B3
Skardu....D1
Sonmiani....B3
Sukkur 193,000....B3
Tando Adam 63,000....B3
Tando Allahyar 31,000....B3
Tatta 12,786....B4
Turbat 52,000....A3
Uch 5,483....B3
Wah 122,000....C2
Wana....C2
Yasin....C1

OTHER FEATURES

Aksai Chin (reg.)....D2
Arabian (sea)....B5
Baltistan (reg.)....C1
Baroghil (pass)....C1
Bejhi (riv.)....B3
Bolan (pass)....B3
Chagai (hills)....A3
Chenab (riv.)....C2
Dasht (riv.)....A3
Gilgit (dist.)....C1
Hab (riv.)....B3
Hamun-i-Lora (swamp)....A3
Hamun-i-Mashkel (swamp)....A3
Hindu Kush (mts.)....B1
Indus (riv.)....B3
Indus, Mouths of the (delta)....A4
Jaddi, Ras (pt.)....A4
Jhelum (riv.)....C2
K2 (mt.)....D1
Kabul (riv.)....C2
Kachchh, Rann of (salt marsh)....B4
Karakoram (mts.)....D1
Khyber (pass)....C2
Konar (riv.)....C1
Kutch (Kachchh), Rann of (salt marsh)....B4
Mashkid (riv.)....A3
Mohenjo Daro (ruins)....B3
Muari, Ras (cape)....B4

Nal (riv.)....B3
Nanga Parbat (mt.)....D1
Rakaposhi (mt.)....C1
Ravi (riv.)....C2
Siahan (range)....A3
Sulaiman (range)....C3
Sutlej (riv.)....C3
Talab (riv.)....A3
Taxila (ruins)....C2
Thar (des.)....C3
Tirich Mir (mt.)....C1
Zhob (riv.)....B2

SRI LANKA (CEYLON)

CITIES and TOWNS

Anuradhapura 34,836....E7
Badulla 34,658....E7
Batticaloa 36,761....E7
Colombo (cap.) 618,000....D7
Colombo* 852,098....D7
Dehiwala-Mt. Lavinia 54,785....D7
Galle 72,720....E7
Hambantota 6,908....E7
Jaffna 112,000....E7
Kalmunai 19,176....E7
Kalutara 28,748....E7
Kandy 93,602....E7
Kurunegala 25,189....E7
Mannar 11,157....E7
Matara 36,641....E7
Moratuwa 96,489....D7
Mullaittivu 4,930....E7
Negombo 57,115....D7
Nuwara Eliya 16,347....E7
Polonnaruwa 9,551....E7
Puttalam 17,982....D7
Ratnapura 29,116....D7
Sigiriya 1,446....E7
Tangalla 8,748....E7
Trincomalee 41,780....E7
Vavuniya 15,639....E7

OTHER FEATURES

Adam's (peak)....E7
Adam's Bridge (shoals)....D7
Dondra (head)....E7
Kirigalpota (mt.)....E7
Mannar (gulf)....D7
Palk (str.)....D7
Pedro (pt.)....E6
Pidurutalagala (mt.)....E7

* City and suburbs.
▲ Population of district.

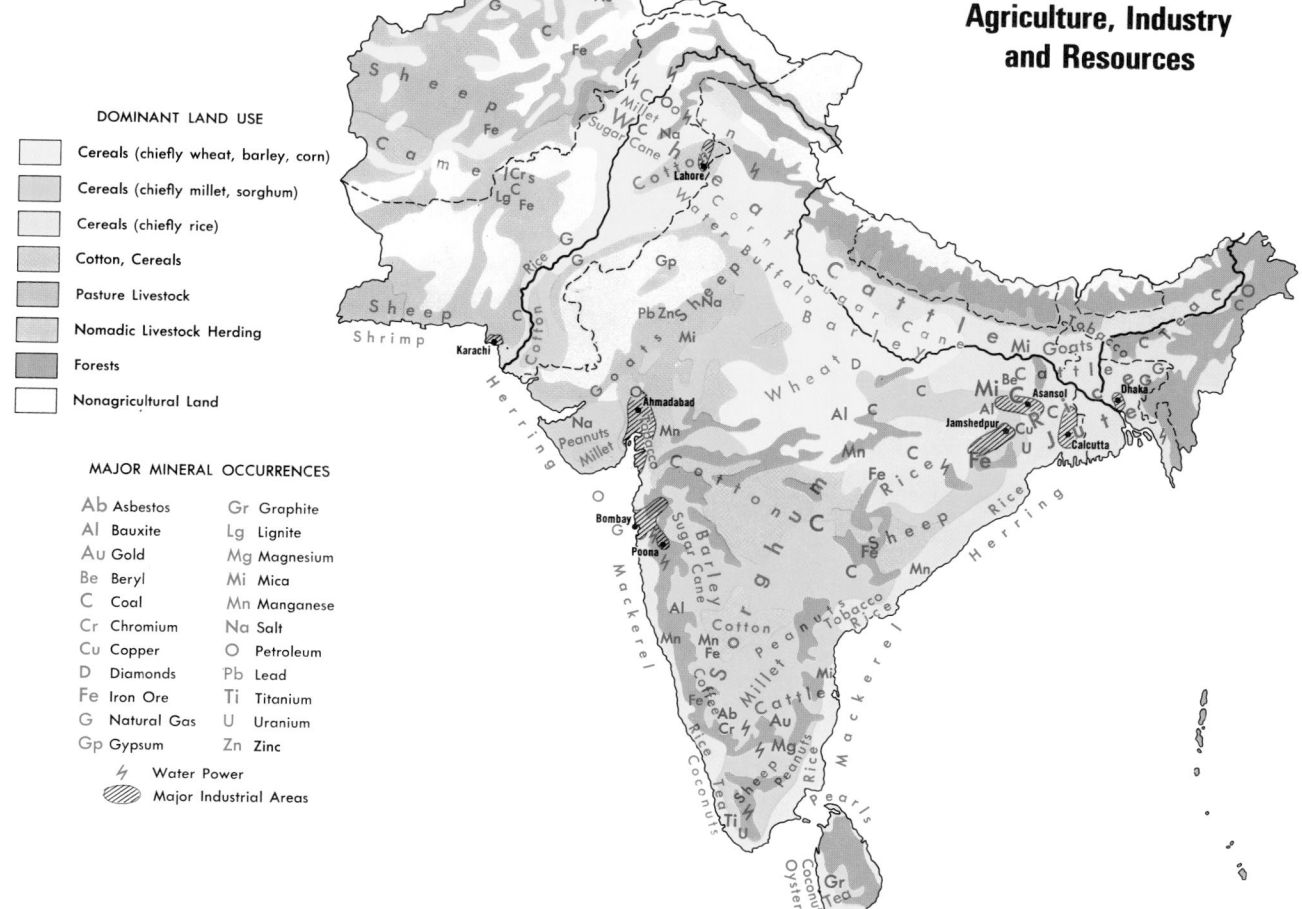

Agriculture, Industry and Resources

DOMINANT LAND USE

- Cereals (chiefly wheat, barley, corn)
- Cereals (chiefly millet, sorghum)
- Cereals (chiefly rice)
- Cotton, Cereals
- Pasture Livestock
- Nomadic Livestock Herding
- Forests
- Nonagricultural Land

MAJOR MINERAL OCCURRENCES

Ab Asbestos
Al Bauxite
Au Gold
Be Beryl
C Coal
Cr Chromium
Cu Copper
D Diamonds
Fe Iron Ore
G Natural Gas
Gp Gypsum

Gr Graphite
Lg Lignite
Mg Magnesium
Mi Mica
Mn Manganese
Na Salt
O Petroleum
Pb Lead
Ti Titanium
U Uranium
Zn Zinc

⚡ Water Power
▨ Major Industrial Areas

Burma, Thailand, Indochina and Malaya

CONIC PROJECTION

SCALE OF MILES

SCALE OF KILOMETERS

International Boundaries . . . .
Division and State Boundaries . . . .
Capitals of Countries . . . .
Division and State Capitals . . . .

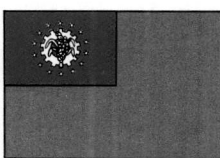

BURMA

THAILAND

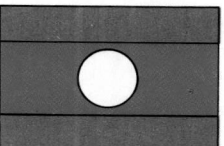

LAOS

CAMBODIA

VIETNAM

MALAYSIA

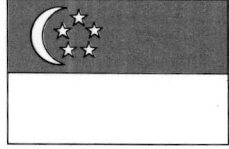

SINGAPORE

BURMA

AREA 261,789 sq. mi. (678,034 sq. km.)
POPULATION 38,541,000
CAPITAL Rangoon
LARGEST CITY Rangoon
HIGHEST POINT Hkakabo Razi 19,296 ft. (5,881 m.)
MONETARY UNIT kyat
MAJOR LANGUAGES Burmese, Karen, Shan, Kachin, Chin, Kayah, English
MAJOR RELIGIONS Buddhism, tribal religions

THAILAND

AREA 198,455 sq. mi. (513,998 sq. km.)
POPULATION 55,448,000
CAPITAL Bangkok
LARGEST CITY Bangkok
HIGHEST POINT Doi Inthanon 8,452 ft. (2,576 m.)
MONETARY UNIT baht
MAJOR LANGUAGES Thai, Lao, Chinese, Khmer, Malay
MAJOR RELIGIONS Buddhism, tribal religions

LAOS

AREA 91,428 sq. mi. (236,800 sq. km.)
POPULATION 3,721,000
CAPITAL Vientiane
LARGEST CITY Vientiane
HIGHEST POINT Phou Bia 9,252 ft. (2,820 m.)
MONETARY UNIT kip
MAJOR LANGUAGE Lao
MAJOR RELIGIONS Buddhism, tribal religions

CAMBODIA

AREA 69,898 sq. mi. (181,036 sq. km.)
POPULATION 8,055,000
CAPITAL Phnom Penh
LARGEST CITY Phnom Penh
HIGHEST POINT 5,948 ft. (1,813 m.)
MONETARY UNIT riel
MAJOR LANGUAGE Khmer (Cambodian)
MAJOR RELIGION Buddhism

VIETNAM

AREA 128,405 sq. mi. (332,569 sq. km.)
POPULATION 64,412,000
CAPITAL Hanoi
LARGEST CITY Ho Chi Minh City (Saigon)
HIGHEST POINT Fan Si Pan 10,308 ft. (3,142 m.)
MONETARY UNIT dong
MAJOR LANGUAGES Vietnamese, Thai, Muong, Meo, Yao, Khmer, French, Chinese, Cham
MAJOR RELIGIONS Buddhism, Taoism, Confucianism, Roman Catholicism, Cao-Dai

MALAYSIA

AREA 128,308 sq. mi. (332,318 sq. km.)
POPULATION 17,377,000
CAPITAL Kuala Lumpur
LARGEST CITY Kuala Lumpur
HIGHEST POINT Mt. Kinabalu 13,455 ft. (4,101 m.)
MONETARY UNIT ringgit
MAJOR LANGUAGES Malay, Chinese, English, Tamil, Dayak, Kadazan
MAJOR RELIGIONS Islam, Confucianism, Buddhism, tribal religions, Hinduism, Taoism, Christianity, Sikhism

SINGAPORE

AREA 226 sq. mi. (585 sq. km.)
POPULATION 2,704,000
CAPITAL Singapore
LARGEST CITY Singapore
HIGHEST POINT Bukit Timah 581 ft. (177 m.)
MONETARY UNIT Singapore dollar
MAJOR LANGUAGES Chinese, Malay, Tamil, English, Hindi
MAJOR RELIGIONS Confucianism, Buddhism, Taoism, Hinduism, Islam, Christianity

Topography

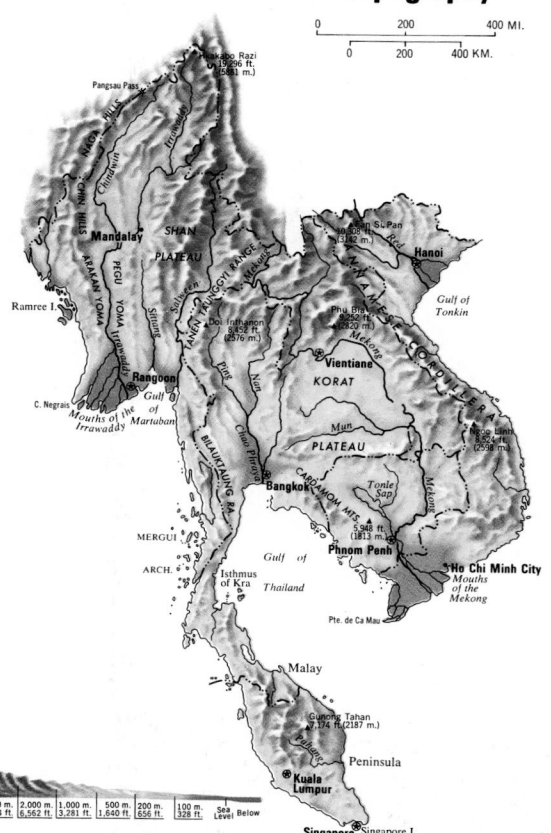

5,000 m. 16,404 ft.	2,000 m. 6,562 ft.	1,000 m. 3,281 ft.	500 m. 1,640 ft.	200 m. 656 ft.	100 m. 328 ft.	Sea Level	Below

BURMA

INTERNAL DIVISIONS

Chin (state) 368,985 ....B2
Irrawaddy (div.) 4,991,057 ...B3
Kachin (state) 903,982 ....C1
Karan (state) 1,057,505 ....C3
Kayah (state) 168,355 ....C3
Magwe (div.) 3,241,103 ....B2
Mandalay (div.) 4,580,923 ....B2
Mon (state) 1,682,041 ....C4
Pegu (div.) 3,800,240 ....C3
Rakhine (state) 1,710,913 ...B3
Rangoon (div.) 3,973,782 .....C3
Sagaing (div.) 3,855,991 ......B1
Shan (state) 3,718,706 ....C2
Tenasserim (div.) 917,628.....C4

CITIES and TOWNS

Akyab (Sittwe) 107,607 ....B2
Allanmyo 15,580 ....B3
Amarapura 11,268 ....B2
Amherst 6,000 ....C3
Bassein 144,092 ....B3
Bhamo 9,821 ....C1
Chauk 24,466 ....B2
Gyobingauk 9,922 ....C3
Henzada 82,531 ....B3
Hmawbi 23,032 ....C3
Insein 143,625......................C3
Kanbalu 3,281 ....B2
Katha 7,648 ....C1
Kawthaung 1,520 ....C5
Kyaikto 13,154 ....C3
Kyangin 6,073 ....B3
Kyaukpadaung 5,480 ....B2
Kyaukpyu 7,335 ....B3
Kyaukse 8,659 ....C2
Labutta 12,982 ....B3
Lashio 69,567 ....C2
Letpadan 15,896 ....C3
Madauk 4,618 ....C3
Magwe 13,270 ....B2
Mandalay 532,895 ....C2
Martaban 5,661 ....C3
Ma-ubin 23,362 ....B3
Maungdaw 3,772 ....B2
Mawlaik 2,993 ....B2
Maymyo 58,059.....................C2
Meiktila 73,210 ....B2
Mergui 67,351 ....C4
Minbu 9,096 ....B2
Minhla 6,470 ....B3
Mogaung 2,920 ....C1
Mogok 8,334 ....C2
Monywa 106,873 ....B2
Moulmein 219,991................C3
Mudon 20,136 ....C3
Myanaung 11,155.................B3
Myaungmya 24,532 ....B3
Myingyan 70,162 ....B2
Myitkyina 12,382 ....C1
Myohaung 6,534...................B2
Okkan 14,443 ....B3
Pakokku 58,132 ....B2
Palaw 5,596 ....C4

Paungde 17,286....................B3
Pegu 150,447 ....C3
Prome (Pye) 36,997 ....B3
Pyapon 19,174.......................B3
Pye 36,997.............................B3
Pyinmana 22,025..................C3
Pyu 10,443 ....C3
Rangoon (cap.) 2,458,712 ...C3
Rathedaung 2,969 ....B2
Sagaing 15,382.....................B2
Sandoway 5,172 ....B3
Shwebo 17,827......................B2
Singu 4,027 ....C2
Sittwe 107,607 ....B2
Syriam 15,296 ....C3
Taungdwingyi 16,233 ....B2
Taunggyi 107,907.................C2
Tavoy 60,435.........................C4
Tharrawaddy 8,977...............C3
Thaton 51,025 ....C3
Thayetmyo 11,649................B3
Thazi 7,531 ....C2
Thongwa 10,829 ....C3
Toungoo 31,589 ....C3
Wakema 20,716 ....B3
Yamethin 11,167 ....C2
Yandoon 15,245 ....B3
Ye 12,852 ....C4
Yenangyaung 57,652 ....B2
Ye-u 5,307 ....B2
Zalun 899..............................B3

OTHER FEATURES

Amya (pass) C4
Andaman (sea) B4
Arakan Yoma (mts.)...............B3
Ataran (riv.) C4
Bengal, Bay of (bay)..............B3
Bentinck (isl.) C5
Bilauktaung (range) C4
Chaukan (pass) C1
Cheduba (isl.) B3
Chin (hills) B2
Chindwin (riv.) B2
Coco (chan.) B4
Combermere (bay).................B3
Daung Kyun (isl.) C4
Dawna (range) C3
Great Coco (isl.)......................B4
Great Tenasserim (riv.)..........C4
Heinze Chaung (bay)..............C4
Heywood (chan.) B3
Hkakabo Razi (mt.) C1
Hka, Nam (riv.) C2
Indawgyi (lake) C1
Inle (lake)...............................C2
Irrawaddy (riv.)......................B3
Irrawaddy, Mouths of the (delta)..............................B4
Kadan Kyun (isl.) C4
Kaladan (riv.) B2
Kalegauk (isl.) C4
Khao Luang (mt.)....................C5
Lanbi Kyun (isl.) C5
Launglon Bok (isls.)...............C4
Letsôk-aw Kyun (isl.) C5
Little Coco (isl.) B4

(continued on following page)

Agriculture, Industry and Resources

DOMINANT LAND USE

- Rice
- Diversified Tropical Crops
- Livestock Grazing, Limited Agriculture
- Tropical Forests

MAJOR MINERAL OCCURRENCES

Ag Silver	Cu Copper	O Petroleum	Sn Tin
Al Bauxite	Fe Iron Ore	P Phosphates	Ti Titanium
Au Gold	G Natural Gas	Pb Lead	W Tungsten
C Coal	Mn Manganese	Sb Antimony	Zn Zinc
Cr Chromium			

⚡ Water Power   Major Industrial Areas

CHINA (MAINLAND)

AREA 3,691,000 sq. mi. (9,559,690 sq. km.)
POPULATION 1,133,682,501
CAPITAL Beijing
LARGEST CITY Shanghai
HIGHEST POINT Mt. Everest 29,028 ft. (8,848 m.)
MONETARY UNIT yuan
MAJOR LANGUAGES Chinese, Chuang, Uigur, Yi, Tibetan, Miao, Mongol, Kazakh
MAJOR RELIGIONS Confucianism, Buddhism, Taoism, Islam

CHINA (TAIWAN)

AREA 13,971 sq. mi. (36,185 sq. km.)
POPULATION 20,204,880
CAPITAL Taipei
LARGEST CITY Taipei
HIGHEST POINT Yü Shan 13,113 ft. (3,997 m.)
MONETARY UNIT new Taiwan yüan (dollar)
MAJOR LANGUAGES Chinese, Formosan
MAJOR RELIGIONS Confucianism, Buddhism, Taoism, Christianity, tribal religions

MONGOLIA

AREA 606,163 sq. mi. (1,569,962 sq. km.)
POPULATION 2,070,000
CAPITAL Ulaanbaatar
LARGEST CITY Ulaanbaatar
HIGHEST POINT Tabun Bogdo 14,288 ft. (4,355 m.)
MONETARY UNIT tughrik
MAJOR LANGUAGES Khalkha Mongolian, Kazakh (Turkic)
MAJOR RELIGION Buddhism

HONG KONG

AREA 403 sq. mi. (1,044 sq. km.)
POPULATION 5,761,000
CAPITAL Victoria
MONETARY UNIT Hong Kong dollar
MAJOR LANGUAGES Chinese, English
MAJOR RELIGIONS Confucianism, Buddhism, Christianity

MACAU

AREA 6 sq. mi. (16 sq. km.)
POPULATION 448,000
CAPITAL Macau
MONETARY UNIT pataca
MAJOR LANGUAGES Chinese, Portuguese
MAJOR RELIGIONS Confucianism, Buddhism, Taoism, Christianity

CHINA (MAINLAND)

CHINA (TAIWAN)

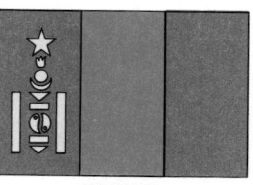

MONGOLIA

CHINA

PROVINCES

Anhui (Anhwei) 49,665,724 ....J5
Chekiang (Zhejiang) 38,884,603 ....K6
Fujian (Fukien) 25,931,106....J6
Gansu (Kansu) 19,569,261 ....E3
Guangdong (Kwangtung) 59,299,220 ....H7
Guangxi Zhuangzu (Kwangsi Chuang Aut. Reg.) 36,420,960 ....G7
Guizhou (Kweiichow) 28,552,997 ....G6
Hainan H8
Hebei (Hopei) 53,005,875 ....J4
Heilongjiang (Heilungkiang) 32,665,546 ....K2
Henan (Honan) 74,422,739 ...H5
Hubei (Hupei) 47,804,150 ....H5
Hunan 54,008,851 ....H6
Inner Mongolian Aut. Reg. (Nei Monggol) 19,274,279 .H3
Jiangsu (Kiangsu) 60,521,114 ....K5
Jiangxi (Kiangsi) 33,184,827 .J6
Jilin (Kirin) 22,560,053 ....L3
Kansu (Gansu) 19,569,261 ....E3
Kiangsu (Jiangxi) 33,184,827 ...J6
Kiangsu (Jiangsu) 60,521,114 ....K5
Kirin (Jilin) 22,560,053 ....L3
Kwangsi Chuang Aut. Reg. (Guangxi Zhuang) 36,420,960 ....G7

Kwangtung (Guangdong) 59,299,220 ....H7
Kweiichow (Guizhou) 28,552,997 ....G6
Liaoning 35,721,693 ....K3
Nei Monggol (Inner Mongolian Aut. Reg.) 19,274,279 ....H3
Ningxia Huizu (Ningsia Hui Aut. Reg.) 3,895,578 ....F3
Qinghai (Tsinghai) 3,895,706..E4
Shaanxi (Shensi) 28,904,423 .G5
Shandong (Shantung) 74,419,054 ....J4
Shanxi (Shansi) 25,251,389 ...H4
Sichuan (Szechwan) 99,713,310 ....F5
Sinkiang-Uigur Aut. Reg. (Xinjiang Uygur) 13,081,631 ...B3
Taiwan 16,609,961 ....K7
Tibet Aut. Reg. (Xizang) 1,892,393 ....B5
Tsinghai (Qinghai) 3,895,706..E4
Xinjian Uygur (Sinkiang-Uigur Aut. Reg.) 13,081,631 ....B3
Xizang (Tibet Aut. Reg.) 1,892,393 ....B5
Yunnan 32,553,817 ....F7
Zhejiang (Chekiang) 38,884,603 ....K6

CITIES and TOWNS

Aihui (Aigun) (Heihe) 73,660..L1
Amoy (Xiamen) 507,390 ......J7
Anqing (Anking) 449,310 .....J5
Anshan 1,195,580 ....K3
Anshun 200,680 ....F5
Anyang 501,390 ....H4
Baicheng, Jilin 276,420 ....K2
Baoding (Paoting) 495,140 ...J4
Baoji (Paoki) 341,240 ....G5
Baotou (Paotow) 1,075,920...G3
Beihai (Pakhoi) 173,740 ....G7
Beijing• (Peking) (cap.) 5,531,460 ....J3
Bengbu (Pengpu) 550,360 ....J5
Canton (Guangzhou, Kwangchow) 3,181,510 ...H7
Changchih (Changzhi) 450,320 ....H4
Changchow (Changzhou) 533,940 ....J5
Changchow (Zhangzhou) 283,490 ....J7
Changchun 1,747,410...........K3
Changde (Changteh) 213,890.H6
Changhua 185,816 ....K7
Changsha 1,066,030............H6
Changteh (Changde) 213,890.H6
Changzhi (Changchih) 450,320 ....H4
Changzhou (Changchow) 533,940 ....K5
Chankiang (Zhanjiang) 853,970 ....H7
Chaotung (Zhaotong) 133,080 ....F6
Chaoyang, Liaoning 206,700...J3
Chefoo (Yantai) 385,180 ....K4
Chengchow (Zhengzhou) 1,404,050 ....H5
Chengde (Chengteh) 326,910..J3
Chengdu (Chengtu) 2,499,000 ....F5
Chengteh (Chengde) 326,910.J3
Chiai 251,840 ....K7
Chifeng 293,460 ....J3
Chinchow (Jinzhou) 599,490..K3
Chinkiang (Zhenjiang) 345,560 ....J5
Chinwangtao (Qinhuangdao) 374,210 ....K4
Chongqing (Chungking) 2,673,170 ....G6
Chüanchow (Quanzhou) 403,180 ....J7
Chuchow (Zhuzhou) 382,950.H6
Chumatien (Zhumadian) 150,440 ....H5
Chungking (Chongqing) 2,673,170 ....G6
Chungshan (Zhongshan) 135,000 ....H7
Conghua 280,250 ....H7
Dafang 962,470 ....G6
Dalian 1,480,240 ....K4
Daqing (Tantung) 545,180.....K3
Daqing 758,430 ....L2
Datong (Tatung) 962,470 .....H3
Datong (Tatung), Shanxi 962,470 ....H3
Da Xian 193,490 ....G5
Dezhou (Tehchow) 258,860 ...J4
Dukou 497,330 ....F6
Fatshan (Foshan) 273,840 ....H7
Fengcheng 995,900 ....K3
Foochow (Fuzhou) 1,111,550..J6

(continued on following page)

China and Mongolia Transportation

Railroads ....
Under Construction ....
Connecting Roads ....
Navigable Rivers ....
Canals ....
Major Seaports ....

© Copyright HAMMOND INCORPORATED, Maplewood, N. J.

Foshan (Fatshan) 273,840 .....H7
Fowyang (Fuyang) 177,850 ...J5
Fushun 1,184,940 ....K3
Fuxin (Fusin) 646,580 ......H3
Fuyang (Fowyang) 177,850 ...J5
Fuzhou (Foochow), Fujian
  1,111,550 ....J6
Fuzhou, Jiangxi 158,300 ....J6
Ganzhou (Kanchow) 362,880 H6
Gejiu (Kokiu) 352,980 ......F7
Guangzhou (Canton)
  3,181,510 ....H7
Guilin (Kweilin) 432,410 ..G6
Guiyang (Kweiyang), Guizhou
  1,350,190 ....J6
Haikou (Hoihow) 263,280 ...H7
Hailar 157,490 ....J2
Hanchung (Hanzhong)
  374,270 ....G5
Handan (Hantan) 929,530 ...H4
Hangzhou (Hangchow)
  1,171,450 ....J5
Hanton (Handan) 929,530 ...H4
Hanzhong (Hanchung)
  374,270 ....G5
Harbin 2,519,120 ....K2
Hebi 336,430 ....H4
Hefei (Hofei) 795,420 ......J5
Hegang (Hokang) 592,470 ...L2
Heihe (Aigun, Aihui) 73,660 ..L1
Hengshui 101,260 ....J4
Hengyang 531,730 ....H6
Hofei (Hefei) 795,420 ......J5
Hohhot (Huhehot) 754,120 ..H3
Hoihow (Haikou) 263,280 ...H7
Hokang (Hegang) 592,470 ...L2
Horqin Youyi Qianqi
  (Ulanhot) 174,050 ....K2
Houma 144,460 ....H4
Hsüchang (Xuchang)
  218,960 ....H5
Huaibei 444,820 ....J5
Huainan 1,029,220 ....J5
Huangshi 375,640 ....J5
Huize 158,380 ....F6
Hunjiang 694,160 ....L3
Huzhou (Wuxing) 925,900 ..K5
Hwainan (Huainan) 1,029,220 J5
Hwangshih (Huangshi)
  375,640 ....J5
Ichang (Yichang) 365,000 ..H5
Ichun (Yichun) 755,830 ....L2
Ipin (Yibin) 245,240 ....F6
Jiamusi (Kiamusze) 540,190 .M2

Ji'an (Kian) 167,550 ....J6
Jiangmen (Kongmoon)
  212,450 ....H7
Jiaozuo (Tsiaotso) 484,370 ..H4
Jiaxing (Kashing) 656,130 ...K5
Jilin (Kirin) 1,808,420 .....L3
Jinan (Tsinan) 1,359,130 ...J4
Jingdezhen (Kingtehchen)
  611,030 ....J6
Jinhua (Kinhwa) 869,490 ...J6
Jining (Tsining), Nei Monggol
  158,570 ....H3
Jining (Tsining), Shandong
  190,420 ....J4
Jinzhou (Chinchow) 599,490 .K3
Jiujiang (Kiukiang) 350,910 ..J6
Jixi (Kisi) 781,800 ....M2
Kaifeng 602,230 ....H5
Kaiyuan, Yunnan 223,420 ...F7
Kalgan (Zhangjiakou)
  617,120 ....J3
Kanchow (Ganzhou) 362,880 .H6
Kaohsiung 1,227,454 ....B2
Karamay 156,970 ....B2
Kashi 256,890 ....A4
Kashing (Jiaxing) 656,130 ..K5
Keelung 347,828 ....B2
Kiamusze (Jiamusi) 540,190 .M2
Kian (Ji'an) 167,550 ....J6
Kingtehchen (Jingdezhen)
  611,030 ....J6
Kinhwa (Jinhua) 869,490 ...J6
Kirin (Jilin) 1,808,420 .....L3
Kisi (Jixi) 781,800 ....M2
Kongmoon (Jiangmen)
  212,450 ....H7
Korla 117,690 ....C3
Kuldja (Yining) 257,280 ....B3
Kunming 1,418,640 ....F6
Kuytun 239,870 ....C3
Kwangchow (Canton)
  3,181,510 ....H7
Kweilin (Guilin) 432,410 ...G6
Kweisui (Hohhot) 754,120 ..H3
Kweiyang (Guiyang)
  1,350,190 ....G6
Lanzhou (Lanchow)
  1,364,480 ....F4
Lengshuijiang 254,590 .....H6
Leshan (Loshan) 958,360 ...F6
Lhasa 83,540 ....D6
Lianyungang (Lienyünkang)
  397,000 ....J5
Liaoyang 646,580 ....K3

Liaoyuan 771,510 ....K3
Linfen 208,210 ....H4
Liuzhou (Liuchow) 581,940 ..G7
Loho (Luohe) 157,670 ....H5
Longyan 346,700 ....J6
Loshan (Leshan) 958,360 ...F6
Loyang (Luoyang) 951,610 ..H5
Lu'an 145,880 ....J5
Luchow (Luzhou) 305,220 ...G6
Lüde (Dalian) 1,480,240 ....K4
Luohe 157,670 ....H5
Luoyang (Loyang) 951,610 ..H5
Luzhou (Luchow) 305,220 ...G6
Ma'anshan 351,880 ....J5
Manchouli (Manzhouli)
  104,260 ....J2
Maoming (Mowming)
  412,540 ....H7
Mianyang, Sichuan 768,500 .G5
Mowming (Maoming)
  412,540 ....H7
Mudanjiang (Mutankiang)
  581,300 ....M3
Mukden (Shenyang)
  3,944,240 ....K3
Nanchang 1,075,710 ....J6
Nanchong (Nanchung)
  228,340 ....G5
Nanjing (Nanking) 2,091,400 .J5
Nanning 889,790 ....G7
Nanpin 407,810 ....J6
Nantong 402,990 ....K5
Nanyang 288,300 ....H5
Neijiang (Neikiang) 270,950 .G6
Ningbo (Ningpo) 478,940 ...K6
Ningpo (Ningbo) 478,940 ...K6
Ningsia (Yinchuan,
  Yinchwan) 354,100 ....G4
Paicheng (Baicheng) 276,420 K2
Pakhoi (Beihai) 173,740 ....G7
Paoki (Baoji) 341,240 ......G5
Paoting (Baoding) 495,140 ..J4
Paotow (Baotou) 1,075,920 ..G3
Peking (Beijing) (cap.)
  5,531,460 ....J4
Pengpu (Bengbu) 550,360 ..J5
Pingtung 189,347 ....K7
Pingxiang, Guangxi
  1,172,370 ....G7
Pingxiang, Jiangxi 76,260 ..H6
Qingdao (Tsingtao)
  1,172,370 ....K4
Qingjiang 234,750 ....J5
Qinhuangdao (Chinwangtao)
  374,210 ....K4
Qinzhou 981,280 ....G7

Qiqihar (Tsitsihar) 1,209,180 ..K2
Qitaihe 283,420 ....M2
Quanzhou (Chüanchow)
  403,180 ....J7
Sanmenxia 147,050 ....H5
Sanming 199,230 ....J6
Shanghai 6,292,960 ....K5
Shangqiu (Shangkiu) 186,760 J5
Shangrao (Shangjao)
  135,160 ....J6
Shantou (Swatow) 717,620 ..J7
Shaoguan (Shiukwan)
  370,550 ....H7
Shaoxing (Shaohing)
  1,091,170 ....K5
Shaoyang 396,600 ....H6
Shashi 238,960 ....H5
Shenyang (Mukden)
  3,944,240 ....K3
Shenzhen 98,060 ....H7
Shiyan 306,830 ....H5
Shuangyashan 400,050 .....M2
Siakuan (Xiaguan) 117,190 ..E6
Sian (Xi'an) 2,185,040 ......G5
Siangfan (Xiangfan) 323,000 H5
Siangtan (Xiangtan) 493,040 .H6
Sienyang (Xianyang) 501,810 G5
Sinchu 208,038 ....K7
Singtai (Xingtai) 334,210 ...H4
Sining (Xining) 566,650 ....F4
Sinsiang (Xinxiang) 525,280 .H4
Sinyang (Xinyang) 240,000 ..H5
Siping (Szeping) 333,850 ...K3
Soochow (Suzhou) 191,710 ..K5
Süchow (Xuzhou) 776,770 ...J5
Suizhong 669,940 ....K3
Suzhou (Soochow) 191,710 ..K5
Swatow (Shantou) 717,620 ..J7
Szeping (Siping) 333,850 ...K3
Tai'an 1,274,770 ....J4
Taichow (Taizhou) 161,200 ..K5
Taichung 565,255 ....K7
Tainan 541,390 ....J7
Taipei 2,108,193 ....K7
Taiyuan 1,745,820 ....H4
Taizhou (Taichow) 161,200 ..K5
Tangshan 1,407,840 ....J4
Tantung (Dandong) 545,180 .K3
Taoyuan 105,841 ....K6
Tatung (Datong) 962,470 ...H3
Tehchow (Dezhou) 258,860 .J4

Tianjin• (Tientsin) 5,142,565 .J4
Tianshui 185,230 ....F5
Tieling 220,850 ....K3
Tientsin• (Tianjin) 5,142,565 .J4
Tianshui (Tianshui) 185,230 .F5
Tongchuan (Tungchwan)
  353,520 ....G5
Tongliao 213,470 ....K3
Tongling 184,060 ....J5
Tsiaotso (Jiaozuo) 484,370 ..H4
Tsinan (Jinan) 1,359,130 ...J4
Tsingkiang (Qingjiang)
  234,750 ....J5
Tsingtao (Qingdao)
  1,172,370 ....K4
Tsining (Jining), Nei Monggol
  158,570 ....H3
Tsining (Jining), Shandong
  190,420 ....J4
Tsitsihar (Qiqihar) 1,209,180 .K2
Tsunyi (Zunyi) 250,670 .....G6
Tungchwan (Tongchuan)
  353,520 ....G5

Tunghwa (Tonghua) 359,960 .L3
Tungliao (Tongliao) 213,470 .K3
Tunxi (Tunki) 103,560 ......J6
Tzekung (Zigong) 866,020 ..F6
Tzpo (Zibo) 2,197,668 ......J4
Ulanhot (Horquin Youyi
  Qianqi) 174,050 ....K2
Ürümqi (Urumchi)
  961,240 ....C3
Wanxian (Wanhsien) 267,000 G5
Weifang 393,410 ....J4
Weihai (Weihaiwei) 205,010 K4
Wenchow (Wenzhou)
  515,650 ....J6
Wenzhou 515,650 ....J6
Wuchow (Wuzhou) 245,250 .H7
Wuchung (Wuzhong)
  245,250 ....G4
Wuhan 3,287,720 ....J5
Wuhu 449,070 ....J5
Wusih (Wuxi) 798,310 ......K5
Wuxi (Wusih) 798,310 ......K5
Wuxing 925,900 ....K5

245,250 ....G4
Wuzhou (Wuchow) 245,250 .H7
Xiaguan (Siakwan) 117,190 .E6
Xiamen (Amoy) 507,390 ....J7
Xi'an (Sian) 2,185,040 ......G5
Xiangfan (Siangfan) 323,000 .H5
Xiangtan (Siangtan) 493,040 .H6
Xianyang (Sienyang) 501,810 G5
Xingtai (Singtai) 334,210 ...H4
Xining (Sining) 566,650 ....F4
Xinxiang (Sinsiang) 525,280 .H4
Xinyang (Sinyang) 240,000 ..H5
Xuchang (Hsüchang) 218,960 H5
Xuzhou (Süchow) 776,770 ...J5
Ya'an 254,420 ....F6
Yangchow (Yangzhou)
  302,090 ....J5
Yangchüan (Yangquan)
  477,570 ....H4
Yangquan (Yangchüan)
  477,570 ....H4
Yangzhou (Yangchow)

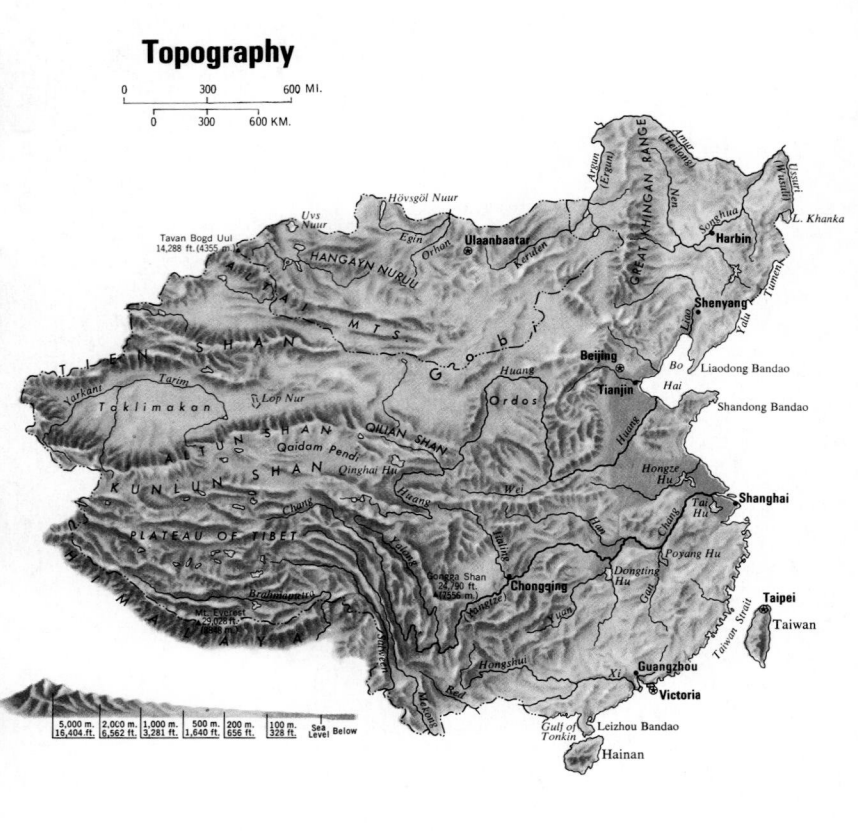

Topography

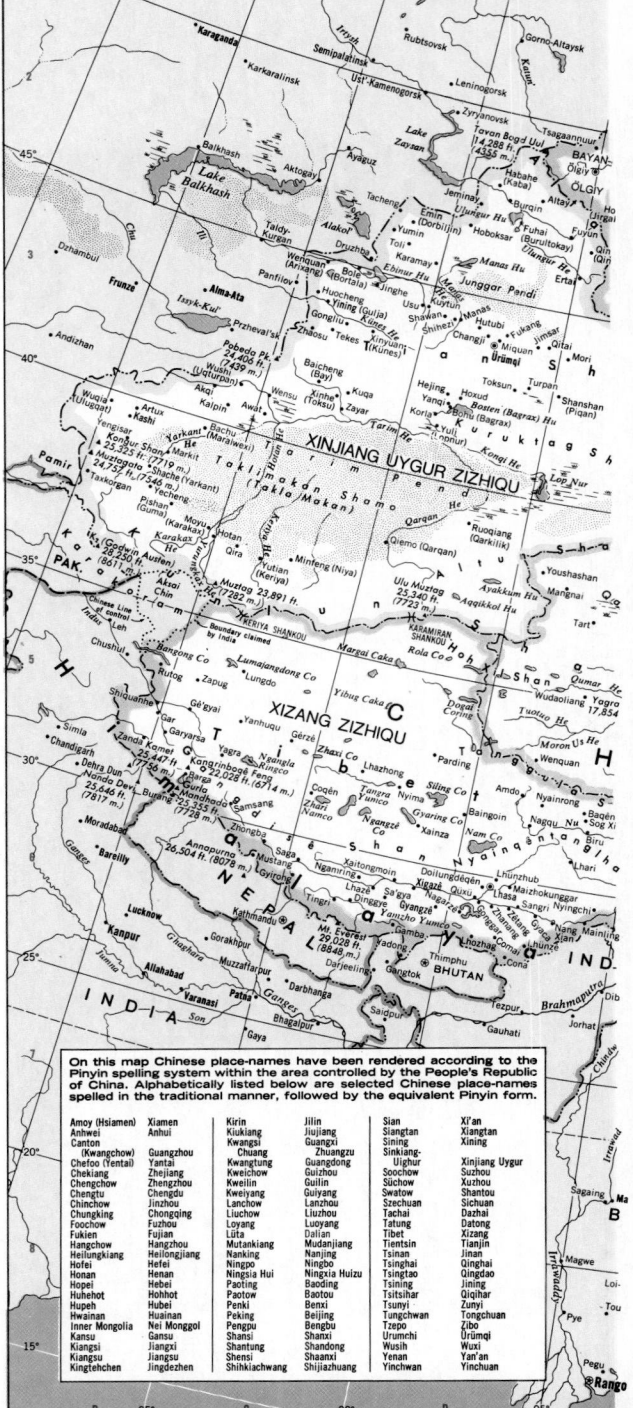

On this map Chinese place-names have been rendered according to the Pinyin spelling system within the area controlled by the People's Republic of China. Alphabetically listed below are selected Chinese place-names spelled in the traditional manner, followed by the equivalent Pinyin form.

Amoy (Hsiamen)	Xiamen	Kirin	Jilin	Sian	Xi'an
Anhwei	Anhui	Kiukiang	Jiujiang	Siangtan	Xiangtan
Canton		Kwangsi	Guangxi	Sining	Xining
(Kwangchow)	Guangzhou	Chuang	Zhuangzu	Sinkiang-	
Chefoo (Yentai)	Yantai	Kwangtung	Guangdong	Uighur	Xinjiang Uygur
Chekiang	Zhejiang	Kweichow	Guizhou	Soochow	Suzhou
Chengtu	Chengdu	Kweilin	Guilin	Süchow	Xuzhou
Chengchow	Zhengzhou	Kweiyang	Guiyang	Swatow	Shantou
Chinchow	Jinzhou	Lanchow	Lanzhou	Szechuan	Sichuan
Chungking	Chongqing	Liuchow	Liuzhou	Tachai	Dazhai
Foochow	Fuzhou	Loyang	Luoyang	Tatung	Datong
Fukien	Fujian	Lüta (Dairen)	Dalian	Tibet	Xizang
Hangchow	Hangzhou	Mutankiang	Mudanjiang	Tientsin	Tianjin
Heilungkiang	Heilongjiang	Nanking	Nanjing	Tsinan	Jinan
Hofei	Hefei	Ningpo	Ningbo	Tsinghai	Qinghai
Honan	Henan	Ningsia Hui	Ningxia Huizu	Tsingtao	Qingdao
Hopei	Hebei	Paoting	Baoding	Tsining	Jining
Huhehot	Hohhot	Paotow	Baotou	Tsitsihar	Qiqihar
Hupeh	Hubei	Penki	Benxi	Tsunyi	Zunyi
Hwainan	Huainan	Peking	Beijing	Tzepo	Zibo
Inner Mongolia	Nei Monggol	Pengpu	Bengbu	Urumchi	Ürümqi
Kansu	Gansu	Shansi	Shanxi	Wusih	Wuxi
Kiangsi	Jiangxi	Shantung	Shandong	Yenan	Yan'an
Kiangsu	Jiangsu	Shensi	Shaanxi	Yinchwan	Yinchuan
Kingtehchen	Jingdezhen	Shihkiachwang	Shijiazhuang		

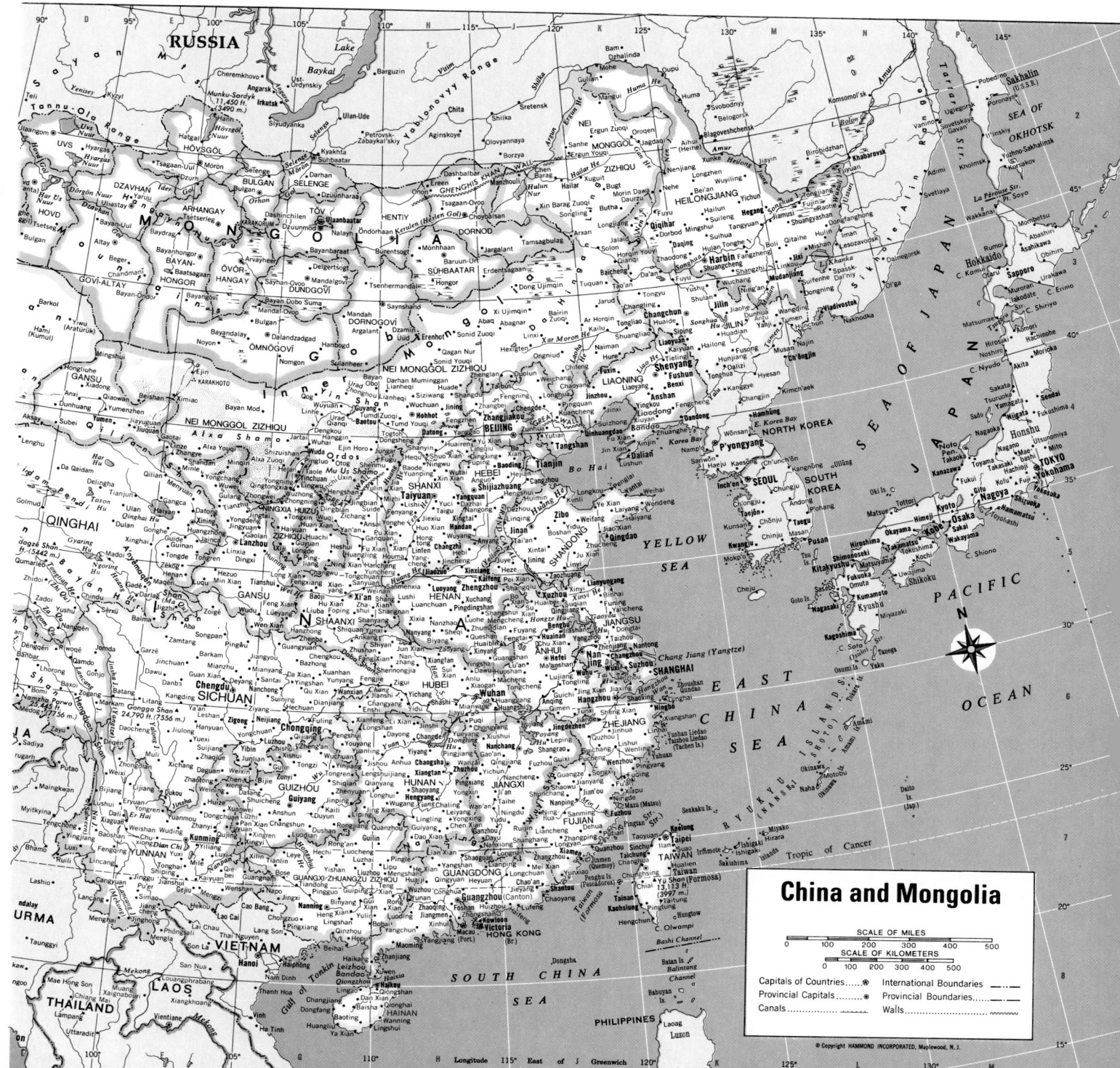

China and Mongolia

SCALE OF MILES
0 100 200 300 400 500

SCALE OF KILOMETERS
0 100 200 300 400 500

Capitals of Countries ......⊛   International Boundaries _____
Provincial Capitals ....⊚   Provincial Boundaries _____
Canals ....   Walls ....

© Copyright HAMMOND INCORPORATED, Maplewood, N.J.

Taiwan (Formosa) (str.) J7	Za Qu (riv.) E5	CITIES and TOWNS
Taizhou (Tachen) (isls.) K6	Zhari Namco (lake) C5	
Takla Makan (Taklimakan	Zhaxi Co (lake) C5	Altay 10,000 ....E2
Shamo) (des.) B4	Zhoushan (arch.) K5	Arvayheer 9,100 ....F2
Tanggula Shan (range) D5		Baatsagaan 800 ....E2
Tangra Yumco (lake) C5	**HONG KONG**	Baruun-Urt 8,200 ....H2
Tarim He (riv.) B3	CITIES and TOWNS	Bayandalay 500 ....F3
Tarim Pendi (basin) B4		Bayangovĭ 400 ....F3
Tian Shan (range) C3	Kowloon* 2,450,187 ....H7	Bayanhongor 11,300 ....E2
Tibet (reg.) B5	Victoria (cap.) 1,183,621 ...H7	Bayan-Ondör 300 ....E3
Tongtian He (Zhi Qu) (riv.)..E5		Bayan-Uul 1,200 ....F2
Tonkin (gulf) G7	**MACAU**	Beger 500 ....E2
Toson Hu (lake) E4	**(MACAO)**	Bulgan, Bulgan 9,800 ....F2
Tumen (riv.) L3	CITIES and TOWNS	Bulgan, Hovd 700 ....J3
Tuotuo He (riv.) D5		Bulgan, Ömnögovĭ 3,100 ....D2
Ulu Muztag (mt.) C4	Macau (Macao) (cap.)	Bürentsogt 3,000 ....H2
Ulungur He (riv.) C2	238,413 ....H7	Chandmanĭ 700 ....E2
Ulungur Hu (lake) C2		Choybalsan 31,000 ....J2
Ussuri (Wusuli Jiang) (riv.).M2	**MONGOLIA**	Dalandzadgad 6,600 ....G3
Wei He (riv.) G5	PROVINCES	Darhan (Darkhan) 56,400 ......G2
Wu Jiang (riv.) G6		Dashbalbar 1,100 ....H2
Wusuli Jiang (Ussuri) (riv.).M2	Arhangay 90,500 ....F2	Dashinchilen 600 ....F2
Wuyi Shan (range) J6	Bayanhongor 64,900 ....E2	Dzamĭn Üüd 1,500 ....H3
Xar Moron He (riv.) J3	Bayan-Ölgiy 73,300 ....C2	Dzüünharaa 8,100 ....G2
Xiang Jiang (riv.) H6	Bayan 45,700 ....F2	Erdenetsagaan 1,500 ....J2
Xi Jiang (riv.) H7	Dornod 51,100 ....H2	Hanh 500 ....F1
Xinyi He (riv.) J5	Dornogovĭ 36,400 ....G3	Hatgal 3,000 ....F1
Yagradagzê Shan (mt.) D4	Dundgovĭ 37,800 ....G2	Hovd (Kobdo Jirgalanta)
Yalong Jiang (riv.) F6	Dzavhan 87,600 ....E2	12,400 ....D2
Yalu (riv.) L3	Govĭ-Altay 59,200 ....E3	Hyargas 1,600 ....E2
Yamzho Yumco (lake) C6	Hentiy 49,900 ....H2	Jibhalanta (Uliastay) 13,000.E2
Yangtze (Chang Jiang) (riv.).K5	Hovd 68,300 ....C2	Kobdo (Hovd) 12,400 ....D2
Yarkant He (riv.) A4	Hövsgöl 89,600 ....E1	Mandalgovĭ 7,000 ....G2
Yellow (Huang He) (riv.) F5	Ömnögovĭ 32,200 ....F3	Mörön (Muren) 10,700 ....F2
Yellow (sea) K4	Övörhangay 84,100 ....F2	Nalayh (Nalaikha) 14,000 .....G2
Yibug Caka (lake) C5	Selenge 53,700 ....H2	Ölgiy (Ulegei) 11,700 ....C2
Yin Shan (mts.) F4	Sühbaatar 44,100 ....H2	Öndörhaan (Undur Khan)
Yuan Jiang (riv.) H6	Töv 74,900 ....G2	7,900 ....H2
Yuhuan (isl.) K6	Uvs 76,300 ....D2	Onon 2,600 ....H2
Yurungkax He (riv.) A4		Saynshand 10,000 ....H3
Yü Shan (mt.) K7		Selenge 1,300 ....F2
Yushan (isls.) K6		

Sühbaatar (Sukhe Bator)	Altai (mts.) C2
35,000 ....G1	Dörgön Nuur (lake) D2
Tsagaan-Ovoo 900 ....H2	Dzavhan Gol (riv.) D2
Tsagaannuur 2,000 ....C2	Ghenghis Khan Wall (ruins)...H2
Tsagaan-Uul 1,700 ....E2	Gobi (des.) G3
Tsetseg 700 ....D2	Hangayn Nuruu (mts.) E2
Tsetserleg 12,400 ....F2	Har Us Nuur (lake) D2
Ulaanbaatar (Ulan Bator)	Herlen Gol (Kerulen) (riv.)...H2
(cap.) 435,400 ....G2	Hovd Gol (riv.) D2
Ulaangom (Ulangom) 14,000 ...D2	Hövsgöl Nuur (lake) F1
Ulegei (Olgiy) 11,700 ....C2	Hyargas Nuur (lake) D2
Uliastay (Jibhalanta) 13,000.E2	Ider Gol (riv.) E2
Urga (Ulaanbaatar) (cap.)	Karakorum (ruins) F2
435,400 ....G2	Kerulen (riv.) H2
	Munku-Sardyk (mt.) F1
OTHER FEATURES	Orhon Gol (riv.) F2
	Selenge Mörön (riv.) G2
Altai (mts.) C2	Tannu-Ola (range) D1
	Tavan Bogd Uul (mt.) C2
	Uvs Nuur (lake) D1

• Population of municipality.
*City and suburbs.

† Populations of mainland cities, excluding Peking (Beijing), Shanghai and Tianjin (Tientsin), courtesy of Kingsley Davis.
Office of Int'l Pop. and Research. Inst. of Int'l Studies Univ. of California.

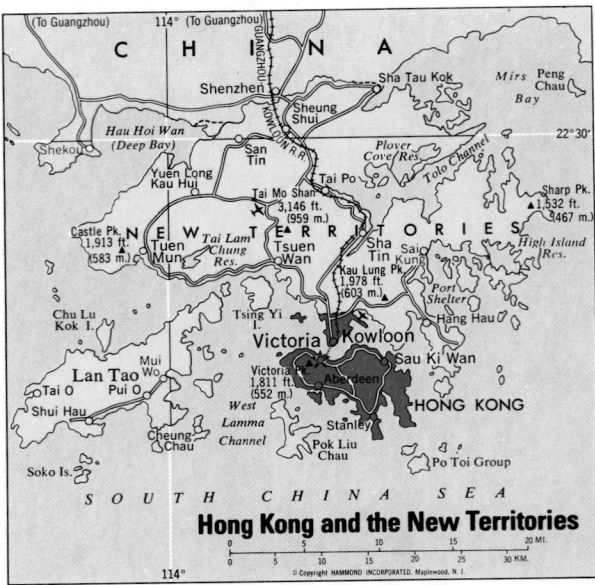

Hong Kong and the New Territories

Agriculture, Industry and Resources

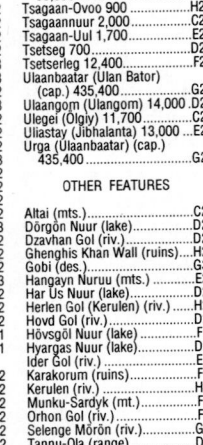

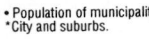

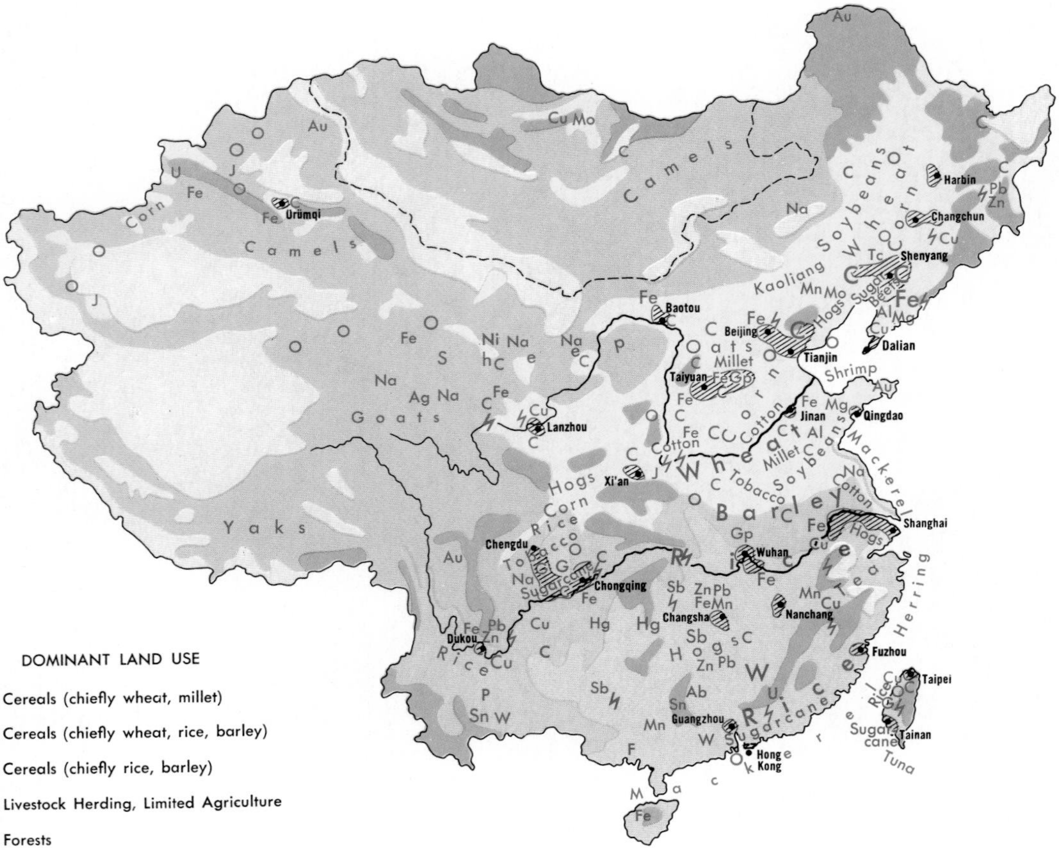

MAJOR MINERAL OCCURRENCES

Ab	Asbestos
Ag	Silver
Al	Bauxite
Au	Gold
C	Coal
Cu	Copper
F	Fluorspar
Fe	Iron Ore
G	Natural Gas
Gp	Gypsum
Hg	Mercury
J	Jade
Mg	Magnesium
Mn	Manganese
Mo	Molybdenum
Na	Salt
Ni	Nickel
O	Petroleum
P	Phosphates
Pb	Lead
Sb	Antimony
Sn	Tin
Tc	Talc
U	Uranium
W	Tungsten
Zn	Zinc

⚡ Water Power

▨ Major Industrial Areas

DOMINANT LAND USE

- Cereals (chiefly wheat, millet)
- Cereals (chiefly wheat, rice, barley)
- Cereals (chiefly rice, barley)
- Livestock Herding, Limited Agriculture
- Forests
- Nonagricultural Land

AREA 145,730 sq. mi. (377,441 sq. km.)
POPULATION 123,116,000
CAPITAL Tokyo
LARGEST CITY Tokyo
HIGHEST POINT Fuji 12,389 ft. (3,776 m.)
MONETARY UNIT yen
MAJOR LANGUAGE Japanese
MAJOR RELIGIONS Buddhism, Shintoism

AREA 46,540 sq. mi. (120,539 sq. km.)
POPULATION 22,419,000
CAPITAL P'yŏngyang
LARGEST CITY P'yŏngyang
HIGHEST POINT Paektu 9,003 ft. (2,744 m.)
MONETARY UNIT won
MAJOR LANGUAGE Korean
MAJOR RELIGIONS Confucianism, Buddhism, Ch'ondogyo

AREA 38,175 sq. mi. (98,873 sq. km.)
POPULATION 42,793,000
CAPITAL Seoul
LARGEST CITY Seoul
HIGHEST POINT Halla 6,398 ft. (1,950 m.)
MONETARY UNIT won
MAJOR LANGUAGE Korean
MAJOR RELIGIONS Confucianism, Buddhism, Ch'ondogyo, Christianity

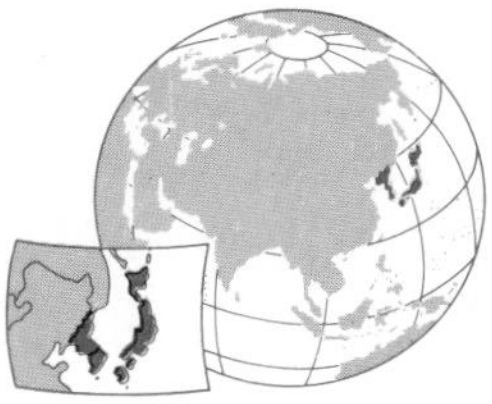

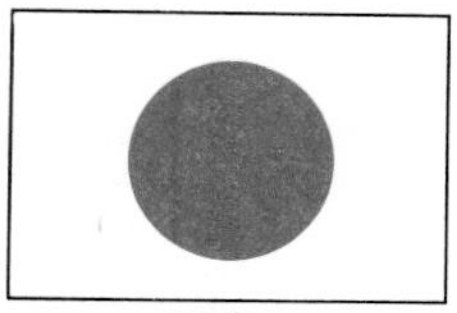

JAPAN

NORTH KOREA

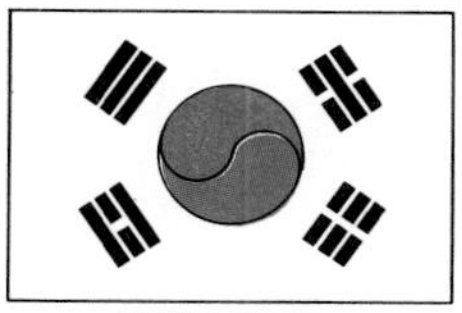

SOUTH KOREA

JAPAN

PREFECTURES

Aichi 6,221,638 ....H6
Akita 1,256,745 ....J4
Aomori 1,523,907 ....K3
Chiba 4,735,424 ....P2
Ehime 1,506,637 ....F7
Fukui 794,354 ....G5
Fukuoka 4,553,461 ....D7
Fukushima 2,035,272 ....K5
Gifu 1,960,107 ....H6
Gumma 1,848,562 ....J5
Hiroshima 2,739,161 ....H6
Hokkaido 5,575,989 ....K2
Hyogo 5,144,892 ....H7
Ibaraki 2,558,007 ....K5
Ishikawa 1,119,304 ....H5
Iwate 1,421,927 ....K4
Kagawa 999,864 ....G6
Kagoshima 1,784,623 ....E8
Kanagawa 6,924,348 ....O2
Kochi 831,275 ....F7
Kumamoto 1,790,327 ....E7
Kyoto 2,527,330 ....J7
Mie 1,686,936 ....H6
Miyagi 2,082,320 ....K4
Miyazaki 1,151,587 ....E8
Nagano 2,083,934 ....J5

CITIES and TOWNS

Abashiri 44,777 ....M1
Ageo 166,243 ....O2
Aizuwakamatsu 114,528 ....J5
Akashi 254,869 ....H8
Akita 284,863 ....J4
Amagasaki 523,650 ....H8

Nagasaki 1,590,564 ....D7
Nara 1,209,365 ....J8
Niigata 2,451,357 ....J5
Oita 1,228,913 ....E7
Okayama 1,871,023 ....F6
Okinawa 1,106,559 ....N6
Osaka 8,473,446 ....J8
Saga 865,574 ....E7
Saitama 5,420,480 ....O2
Shiga 1,079,898 ....J7
Shimane 784,795 ....F6
Shizuoka 3,446,804 ....H6
Tochigi 1,792,201 ....K5
Tokushima 825,261 ....G7
Tokyo 11,618,281 ....O2
Tottori 604,221 ....G6
Toyama 1,103,459 ....H5
Wakayama 1,087,012 ....G6
Yamagata 1,251,917 ....K4
Yamaguchi 1,587,079 ....E6
Yamanashi 804,256 ....J6

Abashiri 44,777 ....M1
Ageo 166,243 ....O2
Aizuwakamatsu 114,528 ....J5
Akashi 254,869 ....H8
Akita 284,863 ....J4
Amagasaki 523,650 ....H8

Amagi 42,863 ....E7
Anan 61,253 ....G7
Aomori 287,594 ....K3
Asahi 35,721 ....K6
Asahikawa 352,619 ....L2
Ashikaga 165,756 ....J5
Ashiya 81,745 ....H8
Atami 50,082 ....H6
Atsugi 145,392 ....O2
Ayabe 42,552 ....J6
Beppu 136,485 ....E7
Chiba 746,430 ....P2
Chichibu 61,285 ....O3
Chigasaki 171,016 ....O3
Chitose 66,788 ....L2
Chofu 180,548 ....O2
Choshi 89,416 ....K6
Daito 116,635 ....J8
Ebetsu 86,349 ....K2
Eniwa 42,911 ....K2
Fuchu, Hiroshima 49,026 ...F6
Fuchu, Tokyo 192,198 ......O2
Fuji 205,751 ....J6
Fujieda 103,225 ....J6
Fujisawa 300,248 ....O3
Fukagawa 35,376 ....L2
Fukuchiyama 63,788 ....G6
Fukue 32,135 ....D7
Fukui 240,962 ....G5
Fukuoka 1,088,588 ....D7

Fukushima 262,837 ....K5
Fukuyama 346,030 ....F6
Funabashi 479,439 ....P2
Furukawa 57,060 ....K4
Gifu 410,357 ....H6
Goshogawara 50,632 ....K3
Habikino 103,181 ....J8
Hachinohe 238,179 ....K3
Hachioji 387,178 ....O2
Hadano 123,133 ....H6
Hagi 53,693 ....E6
Hakodate 320,154 ....K3
Hamada 50,799 ....E6
Hamamatsu 490,824 ....H6
Hanamaki 68,873 ....K4
Hanno 61,179 ....O2
Haramachi 46,052 ....K5
Higashiosaka 521,558 ......J8
Hikone 89,701 ....H6
Himeji 446,256 ....G6
Himi 62,413 ....H5
Hino 145,448 ....O2
Hirakata 353,358 ....J7
Hiratsuka 214,293 ....O3
Hirosaki 175,330 ....K3
Hiroshima 899,399 ....E6
Hitachi 204,596 ....K5
Hitoyoshi 42,236 ....E7
Hofu 111,468 ....E6
Hondo 42,460 ....E7

Honjo 42,962 ....J4
Hyuga 58,347 ....E7
Ibaraki 234,062 ....J7
Ichihara 216,394 ....P3
Ichikawa 364,244 ....P2
Ichinomiya 253,139 ....H6
Ichinoseki 60,214 ....K4
Iida 78,515 ....H6
Iizuka 80,288 ....E7
Ikeda 101,121 ....H7
Ikoma 70,461 ....J8
Imabari 123,234 ....F6
Imari 61,243 ....D7
Ina 56,086 ....H6
Isahaya 83,723 ....D7
Ise 105,621 ....H6
Ishinomaki 120,699 ....K4
Itami 178,228 ....H7
Ito 69,638 ....J6
Itoman 42,239 ....N6
Iwaki 342,074 ....K5
Iwakuni 112,525 ....E6
Iwamizawa 78,311 ....L2
Iwata 75,810 ....H6
Iwatsuki 94,696 ....O2
Izumi 124,323 ....J8
Izumiotsu 67,474 ....J8
Izumisano 90,684 ....G6
Izumo 77,303 ....F6

Joetsu 127,842 ....H5
Joyo 74,350 ....J7
Kadoma 138,902 ....J7
Kaga 65,282 ....H5
Kagoshima 505,360 ....E8
Kaizuka 81,162 ....H8
Kakogawa 212,233 ....G6
Kamaishi 65,250 ....L4
Kamakura 172,629 ....O3
Kameoka 69,410 ....J7
Kanazawa 417,684 ....H5
Kanonji 44,927 ....F6
Kanoya 73,242 ....E8
Kanuma 85,159 ....J5
Karatsu 77,710 ....D7
Kaseda 25,392 ....D8
Kashihara 107,316 ....J8
Kashiwa 239,198 ....P2
Kashiwazaki 83,499 ....J5
Kasugai 244,119 ....H6
Kasukabe 155,555 ....O2
Katsuta 92,621 ....K5
Kawachinagano 78,572 ....J8
Kawagoe 259,314 ....O2
Kawaguchi 379,360 ....J6
Kawanishi 129,834 ....H7
Kawasaki 1,040,802 ....O2
Kesennuma 68,551 ....K4
Kimitsu 77,286 ....O3

Kiryu 132,889 ....J5
Kisarazu 110,711 ....P3
Kishiwada 180,317 ....J8
Kitaibaraki 47,670 ....K5
Kitakami 53,647 ....K4
Kitakyushu 1,065,078 .....E6
Kitami 102,915 ....L2
Kobayashi 40,033 ....E8
Kobe 1,367,390 ....H7
Kochi 300,822 ....F7
Kodaira 154,610 ....O2
Kofu 199,262 ....J6
Koga 56,657 ....J5
Koganei 102,456 ....O2
Komatsu 104,329 ....H5
Koriyama 286,451 ....K5
Koshigaya 223,241 ....P2
Kuki 54,410 ....O2
Kumagaya 136,806 ....J5
Kumamoto 525,662 ....E7
Kurashiki 403,785 ....F6
Kurayoshi 52,270 ....G6
Kure 234,549 ....F6
Kuroiso 46,574 ....K5
Kurume 216,972 ....E7
Kushiro 214,694 ....M2
Kyoto 1,473,065 ....J7
Machida 295,405 ....O2
Maebashi 265,169 ....J5
Maizuru 97,578 ....G6
Masuda 52,756 ....E6
Matsubara 135,841 ....H8
Matsudo 400,863 ....P2
Matsue 135,568 ....F6
Matsumoto 192,085 ....H5
Matsusaka 113,481 ....H6
Matsuto 43,766 ....H5
Matsuyama 401,703 ....F7
Mihara 84,450 ....F6
Miki 70,201 ....H7
Minoo 104,112 ....J7
Mitaka 164,526 ....O2
Mito 215,566 ....K5
Mitsukaido 40,435 ....P2
Miura 48,687 ....O3
Miyako 62,478 ....L4
Miyakonojo 129,009 ....E8
Miyazaki 264,855 ....E8
Mizusawa 55,226 ....K4
Mobara 71,521 ....K6
Mooka 52,764 ....J5
Moriguchi 165,630 ....J7
Morioka 229,114 ....K4
Muko 50,604 ....J7
Muroran 150,199 ....K2
Musashino 136,910 ....O2
Mutsu 47,610 ....K3
Nagahama 54,935 ....H6
Nagano 324,360 ....J5
Nagaoka 180,259 ....J5
Nagaokakyo 71,445 ....J7
Nagasaki 447,091 ....D7
Nago 45,991 ....N6
Nagoya 2,087,902 ....H6
Naha 295,778 ....N6
Nakatsu 63,941 ....E7
Nanao 50,394 ....H5
Nankoku 44,866 ....F7
Nara 297,953 ....J8
Narashino 125,155 ....P2
Naze 49,021 ....O5
Nemuro 42,880 ....M2
Neyagawa 255,859 ....J7
Nichinan 52,949 ....E8
Niigata 457,785 ....J5
Niihama 132,339 ....F6
Niitsu 62,282 ....J5
Nishinomiya 410,329 ......H8
Nobeoka 136,598 ....E7
Noboribetsu 56,503 ....K2
Noda 93,958 ....P2
Nogata 62,595 ....E7
Noshiro 60,674 ....J3
Noto 15,480 ....H5
Numata 47,150 ....J5
Numazu 203,695 ....J6
Obihiro 153,861 ....L2
Oda 38,026 ....F6

(continued on following page)

Agriculture, Industry and Resources

DOMINANT LAND USE

- Cereals, Cash Crops
- Truck Farming, Horticulture
- Mixed Farming, Dairy
- Rice
- Forests, Scrub

MAJOR MINERAL OCCURRENCES

Ag Silver
Au Gold
C Coal
Cu Copper
Fe Iron Ore
G Natural Gas
Gr Graphite
Mg Magnesium

Mn Manganese
Mo Molybdenum
O Petroleum
Pb Lead
Py Pyrites
U Uranium
W Tungsten
Zn Zinc

⚡ Water Power
▨ Major Industrial Areas

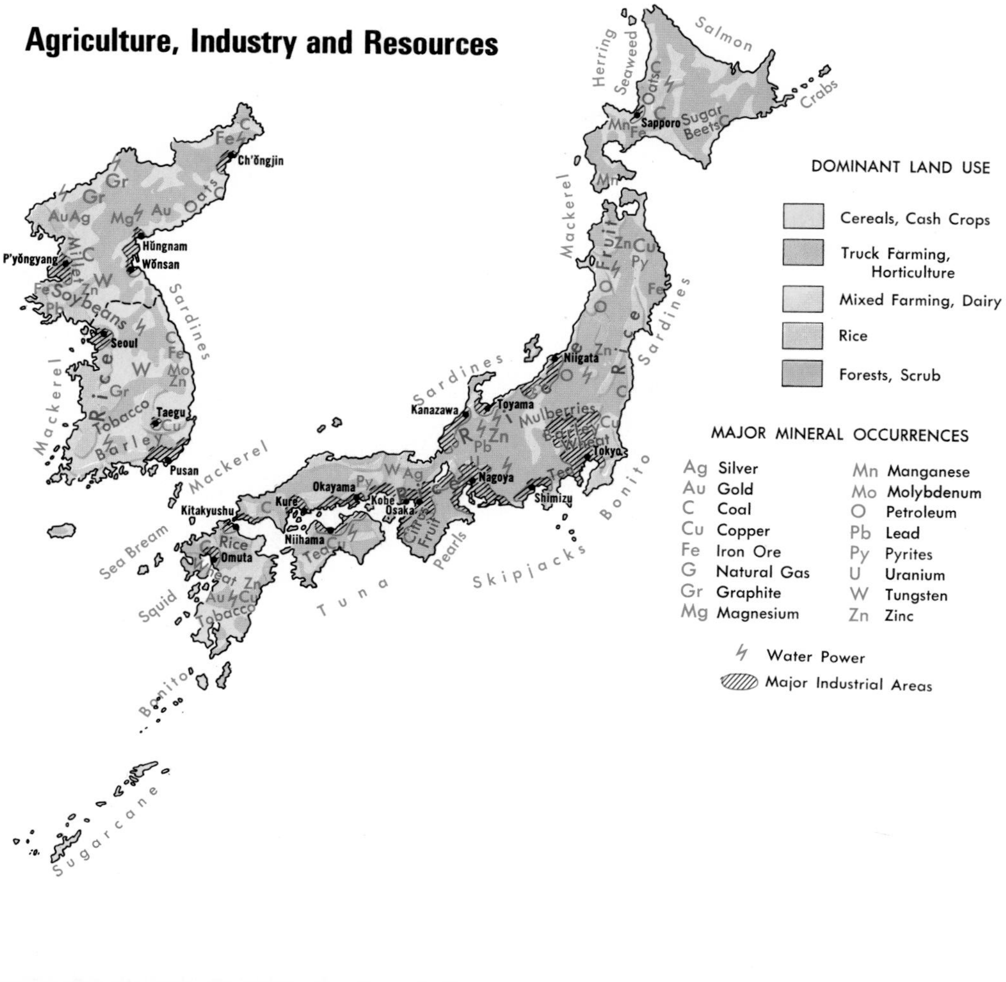

Sata (cape).....E8	Tokachi (riv.).....L2
Shikoku (isl.).....F7	Tokachi (mt.).....L2
Shikotan (isl.).....N2	Tokara (isls.).....O5
Shikotsu (lake).....K2	Tokuno (isl.).....O5
Shimane (pen.).....F6	Tokyo (bay).....O2
Shimokita (pen.).....K3	Tone (riv.).....K6
Shinano (riv.).....J5	Tosa (bay).....F7
Shiono (cape).....H7	Towada (lake).....K3
Shiragami (cape).....J3	Toyama (bay).....H5
Shirane (mt.).....H6	Tsu (isls.).....D6
Shiretoko (cape).....M1	Tsugaru (strait).....K3
Shiriya (cape).....K3	Tsurugi (mt.).....G7
Soya (pt.).....L1	Uchiura (bay).....K2
Suo (sea).....E7	Volcano (isls.).....M4
Suruga (bay).....J6	Wakasa (bay).....G6
Suzu (pt.).....H5	Western Channel (strait).....D6
Takeshima (isls.).....F5	Yaeyama (isls.).....K7
Tanega (isl.).....E8	Yaku (isl.).....E8
Tappi (cape).....K3	Yonaguni (isl.).....K7
Teshio (riv.).....L1	

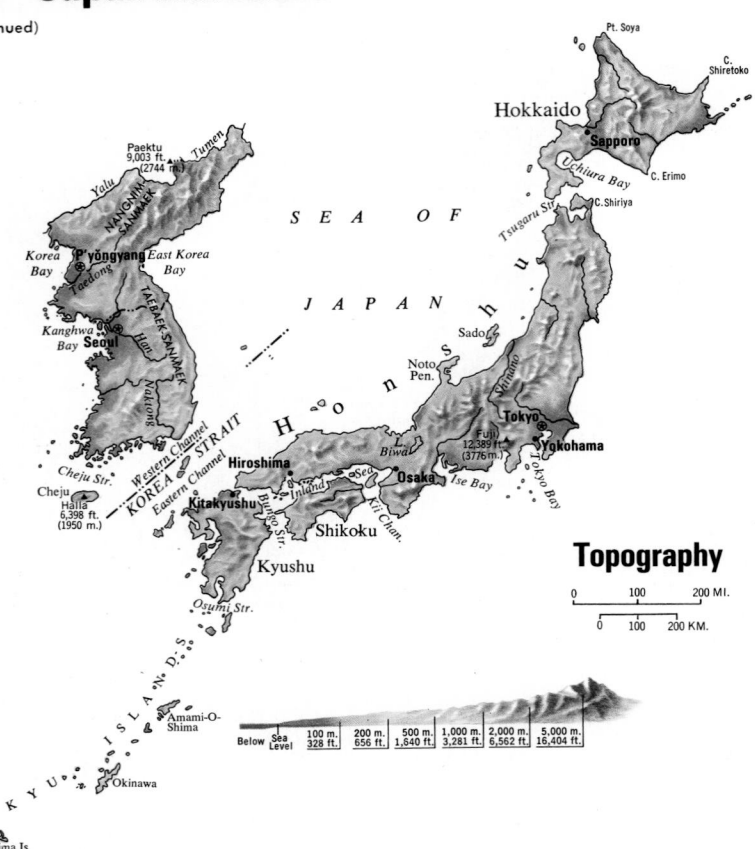

Topography

Below Sea Level	100 m. 328 ft.	200 m. 656 ft.	500 m. 1,640 ft.	1,000 m. 3,281 ft.	2,000 m. 6,562 ft.	5,000 m. 16,404 ft.

0 100 200 MI.
0 100 200 KM.

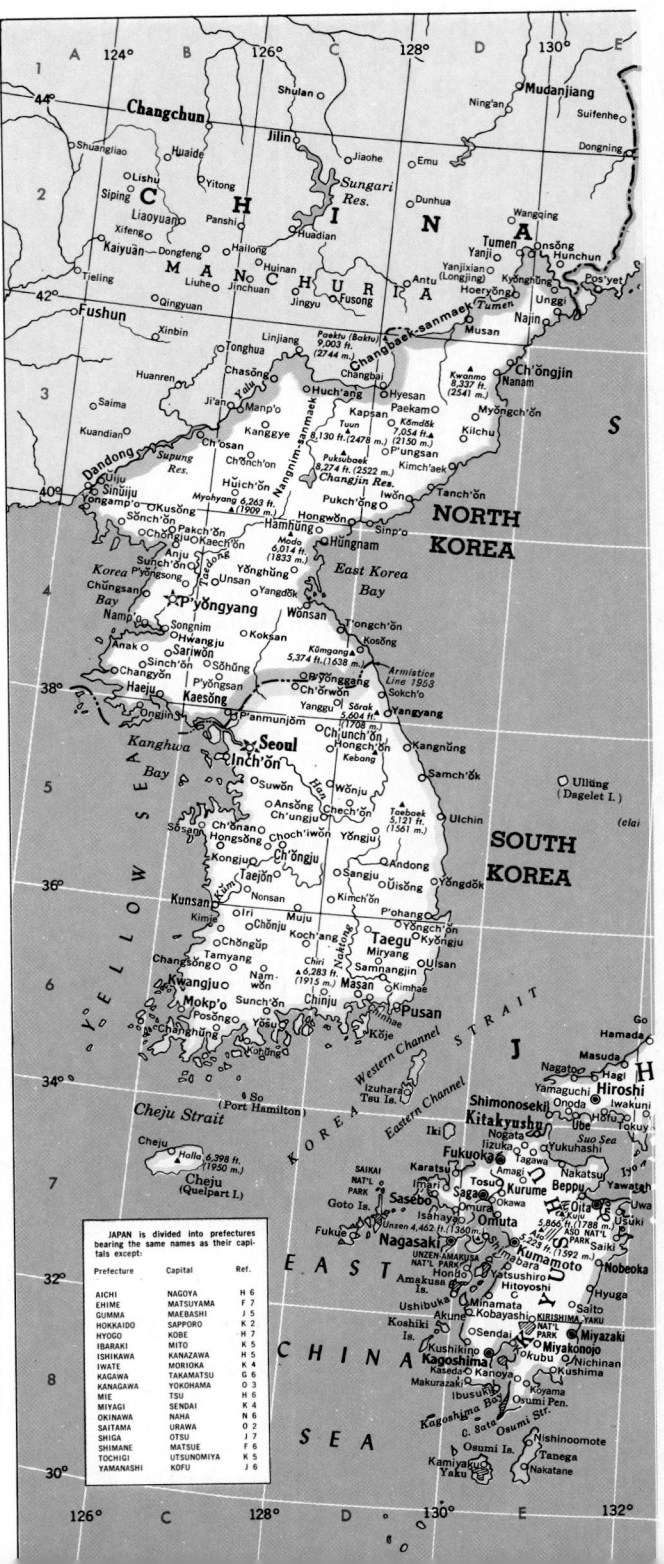

Odate 72,478.....K3	Suwa 50,558.....H6	Yokkaichi 255,442.....H6	Iwaki (mt.).....K3
Odawara 177,467.....J6	Suzuka 156,250.....H6	Yokohama 2,773,674.....O3	Iwate (mt.).....K4
Ofunato 40,023.....J4	Tachikawa 142,675.....O2	Yokosuka 421,107.....O3	Iwo (Iwo Jima) (isl.).....M4
Oga 38,940.....H6	Tagawa 60,077.....E7	Yokote 43,773.....K4	Iwo Jima (isl.).....M4
Ogaki 143,151.....H6	Tajimi 74,311.....H6	Yonago 127,374.....F6	Iyo (sea).....E7
Oita 360,478.....E7	Takaishi 66,815.....H8	Yonezawa 92,823.....K5	Izu (isls.).....J6
Ojiya 44,963.....J5	Takamatsu 316,661.....F6	Yono 72,326.....O2	Izu (pen.).....J6
Okawa 49,537.....E7	Takaoka 175,055.....H5	Yubari 41,715.....L2	Japan (sea).....G4
Okaya 62,210.....H5	Takarazuka 183,628.....H7	Yukuhashi 61,838.....E7	Kagoshima (bay).....E8
Okayama 545,765.....F6	Takasaki 221,429.....J5	Yuzawa 37,800.....K4	Kamui (cape).....K2
Okazaki 262,372.....H6	Takatsuki 340,720.....J7	Zushi 58,479.....O3	Kasumiga (lagoon).....K6
Omagari 41,764.....K4	Takayama 63,813.....H5		Kazan-retto (Volcano) (isls.).....M4
Omiya 354,084.....O2	Takefu 67,104.....G6	**OTHER FEATURES**	Kii (chan.).....G7
Omura 65,638.....E7	Takikawa 51,192.....K2		Kikai (isl.).....O5
Omuta 163,000.....E7	Tanabe, Kyoto 39,198.....J7	Agano (riv.).....J4	Kita Iwo (mt.).....M4
Onaga'va 16,105.....K4	Tanabe, Wakayama 69,575.....G7	Akan National Park.....M2	Kitakami (riv.).....K4
Ono 41,901.....H6	Tateyama 56,257.....K6	Akkeshi (bay).....M2	Komaga (mt.).....K2
Onoda 44,803.....E6	Tendo 52,597.....J4	Amakusa (isls.).....D7	Kuju (mt.).....E7
Onomichi 102,056.....F6	Tenri 64,894.....J8	Amami (isls.).....N5	Kume (isl.).....M6
Osaka 2,648,180.....J8	Teshio 5,281.....K1	Amami-O-Shima (isl.).....N5	Kunashiri (isl.).....M1
Ota 123,115.....J5	Togane 35,603.....K6	Asahi (mt.).....J4	Kutcharo (lake).....M2
Otaru 180,728.....K2	Tokamachi 49,555.....J5	Ashizuri (cape).....F7	Kyushu (isl.).....E7
Otawara 46,662.....J5	Tokorozawa 236,476.....O2	Aso (mt.).....E7	Meakan (mt.).....L2
Otofuke 31,134.....L2	Tokushima 249,343.....G6	Atsumi (bay).....H6	Minami Iwo (isl.).....M5
Oyabe 36,497.....H5	Tokuyama 111,469.....F6	Awaji (isl.).....H8	Miyako (isl.).....L7
Oyama 127,226.....J5	Tokyo (cap.) 8,351,893.....O2	Bandai (mt.).....K5	Mogami (riv.).....K4
Ozu 38,719.....F7	Tokyo* 11,618,281.....O2	Biwa (lake).....H6	Muko (isl.).....M3
Rumoi 36,626.....K2	Tomakomai 151,967.....K2	Bonin (isls.).....M3	Muroto (pt.).....G7
Ryugasaki 43,132.....P2	Tondabayashi 97,495.....J8	Boso (pen.).....K6	Mutsu (bay).....K3
Sabae 59,579.....H5	Tosu 54,254.....E7	Bungo (strait).....F7	Nampo-Shoto (isls.).....M3
Saga 163,765.....E7	Tottori 131,060.....G6	Chichi (isl.).....M3	Nansei Shoto (Ryukyu) (isls.).....L7
Sagamihara 439,300.....O2	Towada 58,886.....K3	Daio (cape).....H6	Nantai (mt.).....J5
Saiki 54,306.....E7	Toyama 305,055.....H5	Daisetsu (mt.).....L2	Nasu (mt.).....J5
Saito 37,836.....E7	Toyohashi 304,273.....H6	Dogo (isl.).....F5	Nemuro (strait).....M1
Sakado 77,335.....O2	Toyonaka 403,174.....J7	Dozen (isls.).....F5	Nii (isl.).....J6
Sakaide 66,226.....G6	Toyota 281,608.....H6	East China (sea).....D8	Nikko National Park.....J5
Sakai 810,106.....J8	Tsu 144,991.....H6	Eastern Channel (strait).....D7	Nojima (cape).....K6
Sakaiminato 37,278.....F6	Tsubame 44,236.....J5	Erimo (cape).....L3	Noto (pen.).....H5
Sakata 102,600.....J4	Tsuchiura 112,517.....J5	Etorofu (isl.).....N1	Nyudo (cape).....J4
Saku 57,361.....J5	Tsuruga 61,844.....G6	Fuji (mt.).....J6	Oga (pen.).....J4
Sakurai 56,439.....J8	Tsuruoka 99,751.....J4	Fuji (riv.).....J6	Ogasawara-gunto (Bonin) (isls.).....M3
Sanda 36,529.....H7	Tsuyama 83,136.....F6	Fuji-Hakone-Izu Nat'l Park.....H6	Okhotsk (sea).....M1
Sanjo 85,275.....J5	Ube 168,958.....E6	Gassan (mt.).....J4	Oki (isls.).....F5
Sapporo 1,401,757.....K2	Ueda 111,540.....J5	Goto (isls.).....D7	Okinawa (isls.).....N6
Sasebo 251,187.....D7	Uji 152,692.....J7	Haha (isl.).....M3	Okinawa (isl.).....N6
Satte 49,704.....O1	Uozu 49,512.....H5	Hachiro (mts.).....J4	Okinoerabu (isl.).....N5
Sawara 49,200.....K6	Urawa 358,185.....O2	Hakken (mt.).....H8	Okushiri (isl.).....K2
Sayama 124,029.....O2	Utsunomiya 377,746.....K5	Haku (mt.).....H5	Oma (cape).....K3
Sendai, Kagoshima 65,645.....E8	Uwajima 71,586.....F7	Harima (sea).....G6	Omono (riv.).....J4
Sendai, Miyagi 664,868.....K4	Wajima 32,662.....H5	Hida (riv.).....H5	Ono (riv.).....E7
Shibata 76,209.....J5	Wakayama 400,802.....G6	Hidaka (mt.).....L2	Ontake (mt.).....H6
Shimabara 46,637.....E7	Wakkanai 53,471.....K1	Hodaka (mt.).....H5	Osaka (bay).....H6
Shimizu 241,576.....J6	Warabi 70,876.....O2	Honshu (isl.).....J5	O-Shima (isl.).....J6
Shimonoseki 268,957.....E6	Yaizu 104,363.....J6	Iki (isl.).....D7	Osumi (isls.).....E8
Shingu 39,993.....H7	Yamagata 237,041.....K4	Inawashiro (lake).....K5	Osumi (strait).....E8
Shiogama 61,040.....K4	Yamaguchi 114,744.....E6	Inubo (cape).....K6	Otakine (mt.).....K5
Shirakawa 43,187.....K5	Yamato 167,935.....O2	Iriomote (isl.).....K7	Rebun (isl.).....K1
Shiroishi 41,205.....K4	Yamatokoriyama 81,266.....J7	Iro (cape).....J6	Rishiri (isl.).....K1
Shizuoka 458,341.....H6	Yamatotakada 61,711.....J8	Ise (bay).....H6	Ryukyu (isls.).....L7
Soka 186,618.....O2	Yao 272,706.....J8	Ishigaki (isl.).....L7	Sado (isl.).....J4
Suita 332,418.....J7	Yatsushiro 108,194.....E7	Ishikari (riv.).....L2	Sagami (bay).....J6
Sukagawa 57,110.....K5	Yawata 64,882.....J7	Ishikari (bay).....K2	Sagami (sea).....J6
Sumoto 44,131.....G6	Yawatahama 43,823.....F7		Sakishima (isls.).....K7

JAPAN is divided into prefectures bearing the same names as their capitals except:

Prefecture	Capital	Ref.
AICHI	NAGOYA	H 6
EHIME	MATSUYAMA	F 7
GUMMA	MAEBASHI	J 5
HOKKAIDO	SAPPORO	K 2
HYOGO	KOBE	H 7
IBARAKI	MITO	K 5
ISHIKAWA	KANAZAWA	H 5
IWATE	MORIOKA	K 4
KAGAWA	TAKAMATSU	F 6
KANAGAWA	YOKOHAMA	O 3
MIE	TSU	H 6
MIYAGI	SENDAI	K 4
OKINAWA	NAHA	N 6
SAITAMA	URAWA	O 2
SHIGA	OTSU	J 7
SHIMANE	MATSUE	F 6
TOCHIGI	UTSUNOMIYA	K 5
YAMANASHI	KOFU	J 6

Yoshino (riv.).................G6

KOREA (NORTH)
CITIES and TOWNS

Anju...............................B4
Ch'ŏngjin 306,000..........E3
Ch'osan.........................C3
Changyŏn......................C3
Chasŏng........................C3
Chŏngju.........................C3
Haeju 140,000................B4
Hamhŭng 484,000..........D3
Heiju (P'yŏngyang) (cap.)..
.................1,250,000......C4
Hongwŏn.......................C3
Hŭich'ŏn........................C3
Hŭngnam.......................C4
Hyesan..........................D3

Kaesŏng 175,000...........C4
Kapsan..........................C3
Kimch'aek 100,000.........D3
Koksan..........................C4
Kosŏng..........................D4
Kusŏng..........................B4
Manp'o...........................C3
Musan...........................D2
Najin..............................E2
Namp'o 140,000.............B4
Nanam...........................D3
Ongjin...........................B5
Onsŏng..........................E2
P'anmunjŏm...................C5
P'ungsan.......................D3
P'yŏngyang (cap.)...........
..................1,250,000.....C4
Pukch'ŏng.....................C3
Sariwŏn.........................B4
Sinp'o............................D4

Sinŭiju 300,000..............B3
Sŏhung..........................C4
Sŏnch'ŏn........................B4
Songnim........................C4
Sunch'ŏn........................B4
Tanch'ŏn........................D3
T'ongch'ŏn.....................C4
Uiju................................B3
Unggi..............................E2
Unsan............................C3
Wŏnsan 275,000............C4
Yangdŏk........................C4
Yŏnghŭng.......................C4
Yŏngampo......................B4

OTHER FEATURES

Baktu (Paektu) (mt.).........C3
Changbaek-sanmaek (mts.)..D2
Changjin (res.)................C3

East Korea (bay)..............D4
Japan (sea)....................G4
Kanghwa (bay)................B5
Korea (bay).....................B4
Kwanmo (mt.).................D3
Nangnim-sanmaek (range)..C3
Paektu (mt.)....................C3
Puksubaek (mt.)..............B3
Supung (res.).................B3
Taedong (riv.).................C4
Tumen (riv.)....................D2
Yalu (riv.)........................C3
Yellow (sea)....................B6

KOREA (SOUTH)
CITIES and TOWNS

Andong 102,024.............D5
Chech'ŏn 74,239............D5

Cheju 167,546................C7
Chinhae 112,098............D6
Chinju 202,753...............D6
Ch'ŏnan 120,618.............C5
Ch'ŏngju 252,985...........C5
Chŏngup 54,864.............C6
Chŏnju 366,997..............C6
Ch'unch'ŏn 155,247........D5
Ch'ungju 113,138............C5
Inch'ŏn 1,084,730..........C5
Iri 145,358......................C6
Kangnŭng 116,903.........D5
Kimch'ŏn 72,229............D5
Kimhae 203,428.............D6
Kimje 221,414................C6
Kohŭng 217,446.............C6
Kongju 39,756................C5
Kunsan 165,318.............C6
Kwangju 727,627............C6
Kyŏngju 122,038............D6

Masan 386,773...............D6
Miryang 42,951...............D6
Mokp'o 221,856..............C6
Namwŏn 50,857.............C6
Nonsan 226,429.............C5
P'anmunjŏm...................C5
P'ohang 201,355............D5
Pusan 3,160,276............D6
Samch'ŏk 42,526............D5
Sangju 52,839................C5
Seoul (cap.) 8,366,756....C5
Sokch'o 65,798...............D5
Sŏsan 38,081.................C5
Sunch'ŏn 114,223...........C6
Suwŏn 310,757..............C5
Taegu 1,607,458.............D6
Taejŏn 651,642...............C5
Ulsan 418,415................D6
Wŏnju 136,961...............D5
Yanggu 277,986.............C4

Yŏngch'ŏn 50,765...........D6
Yŏngju 77,890.................D5
Yŏsu 161,009.................C6

OTHER FEATURES

Cheju 167,546................C7
Dagelet (Ullŭng) (isl.)......E5
East China (sea)..............C8
Halla (mt.)......................C7
Han (riv.)........................C5
Japan (sea)....................G4
Kanghwa (bay)................B5
Kŏje (isl.).......................D6
Korea (strait)..................D6
Naktong (riv.).................D6
Quelpart (Cheju) (isl.).....C7
Ullŭng (isl.)....................E5
Yellow (sea)...................B6

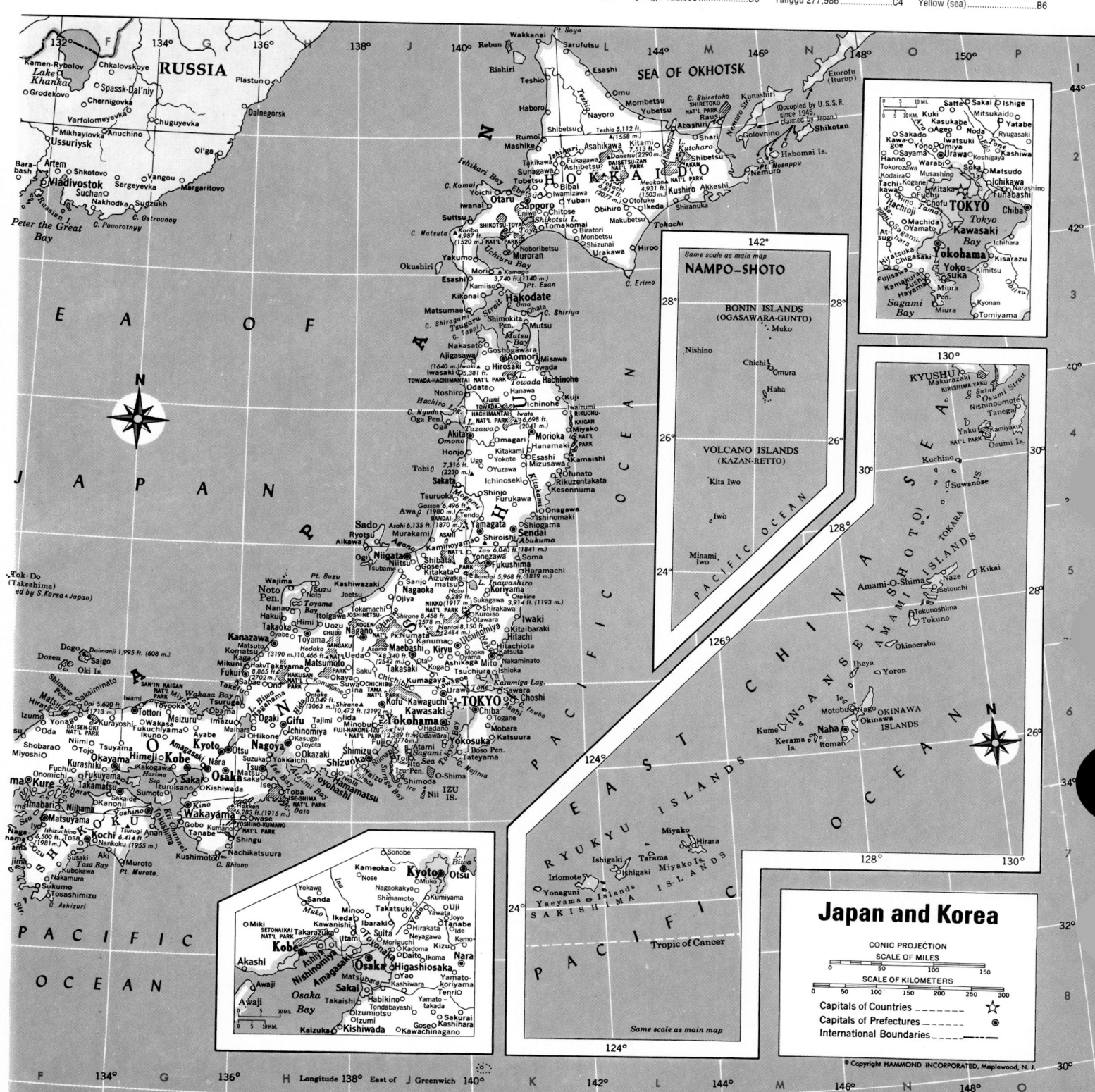

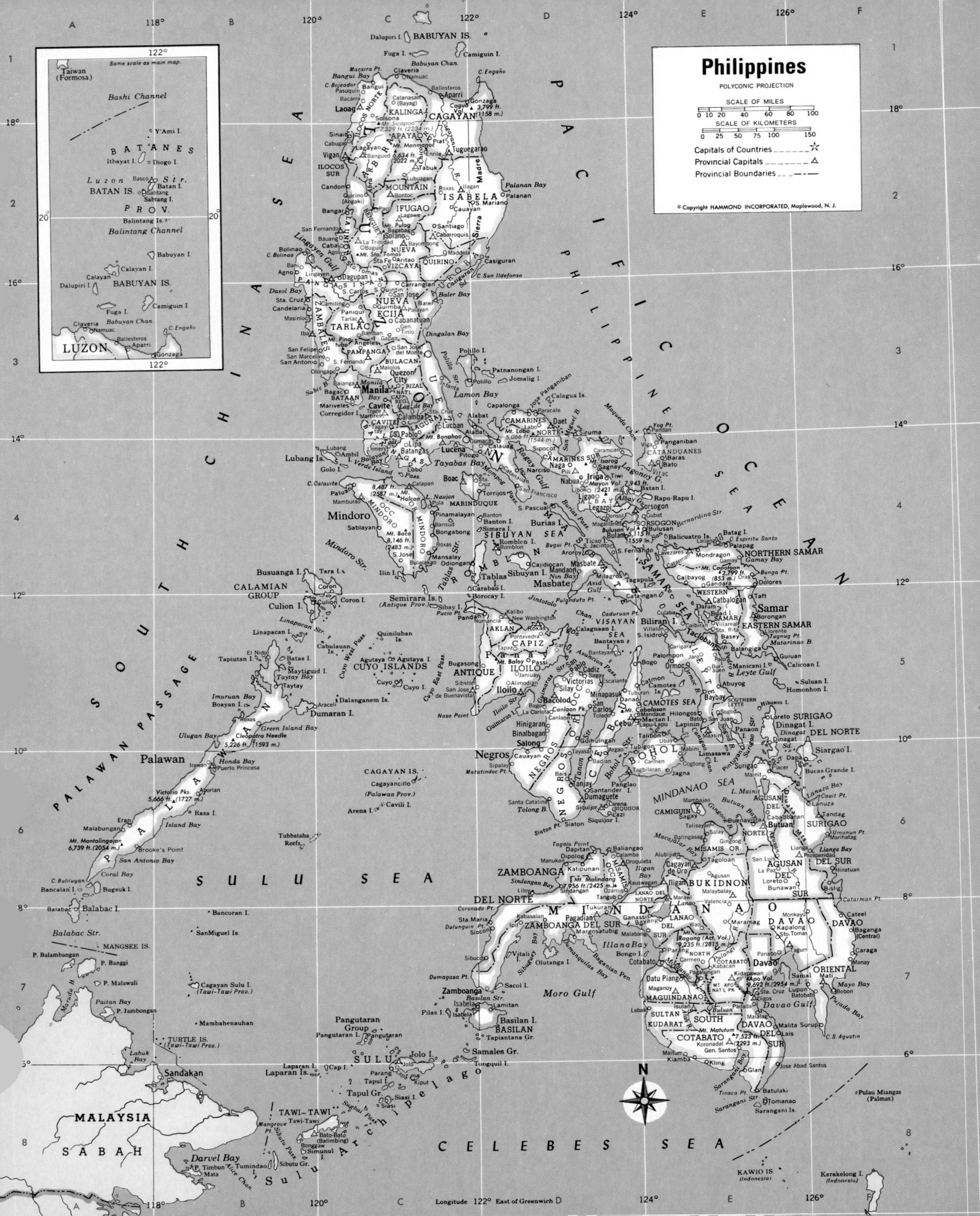

Philippines

POLYCONIC PROJECTION

SCALE OF MILES

SCALE OF KILOMETERS

Capitals of Countries ─────── ☆
Provincial Capitals ─────── △
Provincial Boundaries ──·──·──

© Copyright HAMMOND INCORPORATED, Maplewood, N.J.

PROVINCES

Abra 160,198 . . . C2
Agusan del Norte 365,421 . . E6
Agusan del Sur 631,634 . . . E6
Aklan 324,563 . . . D5
Albay 809,177 . . . D4
Antique 344,879 . . . D5
Aurora 107,145 . . . C3
Basilan 201,407 . . . D7
Bataan 323,254 . . . C3
Batanes 12,091 . . . A2
Batangas 1,174,201 . . . C4
Benguet 354,751 . . . C2
Bohol 806,031 . . . E6
Bukidnon 631,634 . . . E6
Bulacan 1,098,046 . . . C3
Cagayan 711,476 . . . C1
Camarines Norte 368,007 . . . D3
Camarines Sur 1,099,346 . . D4
Camiguin 57,126 . . . E6
Capiz 492,231 . . . D5
Catanduanes 175,247 . . . E4
Cavite 771,320 . . . C3
Cebu 2,091,602 . . . D5
Davao 725,153 . . . E7
Davao del Sur 1,133,599 . . . E7
Davao Oriental 339,931 . . . F7
Eastern Samar 320,637 . . . E5
Ifugao 111,368 . . . C2
Ilocos Norte 390,666 . . . C1
Ilocos Sur 443,591 . . . C2
Iloilo 1,433,641 . . . D5
Isabela 870,604 . . . C2
Kalinga-Apayao 185,063 . . . C1
Laguna 973,104 . . . C3
Lanao del Norte 461,049 . . . E6
Lanao del Sur 404,971 . . . E7
La Union 452,578 . . . C2
Leyte 1,302,648 . . . E5
Maguindanao 536,546 . . . E7
Manila 5,925,884 . . . C3
Marinduque 173,715 . . . C4
Masbate 584,526 . . . D4
Misamis Occidental 386,328 D6
Misamis Oriental 690,032 . . . E6
Mountain 103,052 . . . C2
National Capital Region
(Manila) 5,925,884 . . . C3
Negros Occidental
1,930,301 . . . D6
Negros Oriental 819,399 . . . D6
North Cotabato 564,599 . . . E7
Northern Samar 378,516 . . . E4
Nueva Ecija 1,069,409 . . . C3
Nueva Vizcaya 241,690 . . . C2
Occidental Mindoro 222,431 C4
Oriental Mindoro 448,938 . . . C4
Palawan 371,782 . . . B6
Pampanga 1,181,590 . . . C3
Pangasinan 1,636,057 . . . C3
Quezon 1,129,277 . . . C3
Quirino 83,230 . . . C2
Rizal 555,533 . . . C3
Romblon 193,174 . . . D4
Siquijor 70,300 . . . D6
Sorsogon 500,685 . . . E4
South Cotabato 770,473 . . . E7
Southern Leyte 298,294 . . . E5
Sultan Kudarat 303,784 . . . E7
Sulu 360,588 . . . C7
Surigao del Norte 363,414 . . F5
Surigao del Sur 377,647 . . . F6
Tarlac 638,457 . . . C3
Tawi-Tawi 194,651 . . . B8
Western Samar 501,439 . . . E5
Zambales 444,037 . . . C3
Zamboanga del Norte
588,015 . . . D6
Zamboanga del Sur
1,183,845 . . . D7

AREA 115,707 sq. mi. (299,681 sq. km.)
POPULATION 60,097,000
CAPITAL Manila
LARGEST CITY Manila
HIGHEST POINT Apo 9,692 ft. (2,954 m.)
MONETARY UNIT peso
MAJOR LANGUAGES Pilipino (Tagalog), English, Spanish, Bisayan, Ilocano, Bikol
MAJOR RELIGIONS Roman Catholicism, Islam, Protestantism, tribal religions

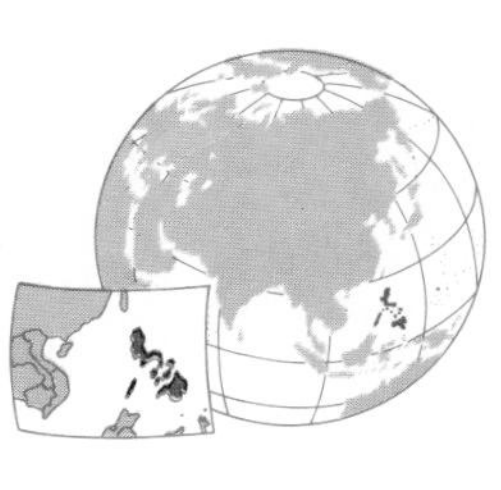

CITIES and TOWNS

Angeles 188,834 . . . C3
Aparri 45,070 . . . C1
Bacolod 262,415 . . . D5
Bagac 13,109 . . . C3
Bago 99,631 . . . D5
Baguio 119,009 . . . C2
Balanga 39,132 . . . C3
Baler 18,349 . . . C3
Balimbing (Bato-Bato)
22,189 . . . C8
Bamban 26,072 . . . C3
Basco 4,341 . . . A2
Batangas 143,570 . . . C4
Bato-Bato 22,189 . . . C8
Baybay 74,640 . . . E5
Bislig 81,615 . . . F6
Boac 37,005 . . . C4
Bontoc 17,091 . . . C2
Burauen 48,058 . . . E5
Butuan 172,489 . . . E6
Cabanatuan 138,298 . . . C3
Cabarroquis 17,450 . . . C2
Cadiz 129,632 . . . D5
Cagayan de Oro 227,312 . . . E6
Calamba 121,175 . . . C3
Calbayog 106,719 . . . E4
Carigara 34,377 . . . E5
Cauayan 70,017 . . . D6
Cavite 87,666 . . . C3
Cebu 490,281 . . . D5
Cotabato 83,871 . . . D7
Dagupan 98,344 . . . C2
Davao 610,375 . . . E7
Digos 70,065 . . . E7
Escalante 71,293 . . . D5
General Santos 149,396 . . . E7
Gingoog 79,937 . . . E6
Guihulngan 84,156 . . . D5
Guimba 58,847 . . . C3
Iba 22,791 . . . B3
Ilagan 79,336 . . . C2
Iligan 167,358 . . . E6
Iloilo 244,827 . . . D5
Infanta 27,914 . . . C3
Jaro 29,739 . . . E5
Jolo 52,429 . . . C8
Koronadal 80,566 . . . E7
Lagawe 15,075 . . . C2
Lapu-Lapu 98,723 . . . E5
Legazpi 99,766 . . . D4
Ligao 69,860 . . . D4
Lingayen 65,187 . . . C2
Lipa 121,166 . . . C4
Lucena 107,880 . . . C4
Maganoy 45,845 . . . E7
Mainit 18,078 . . . E6
Malabang 18,955 . . . D7
Malolos 95,699 . . . C3
Mandaue 110,590 . . . E5
Manila (cap.) 1,630,485 . . . C3
Mariveles 48,594 . . . C3
Mati 78,178 . . . F7
Naga 90,712 . . . D4
Olongapo 156,430 . . . C3
Ormoc 104,978 . . . E5
Ozamis 77,832 . . . D6
Pagadian 80,861 . . . D7
Palo 31,124 . . . E5
Palompon 40,242 . . . E5
Panabo 71,098 . . . E7
Prosperidad 33,824 . . . F6
Puerto Princesa 60,234 . . . B6
Quezon City 1,165,865 . . . C3
Romblon 24,251 . . . D4
Roxas 81,183 . . . D5
Sagay 99,118 . . . D5
San Antonio 42,969 . . . B3
San Carlos, Negros Occ.
91,627 . . . D5
San Carlos Pangasinan
101,243 . . . C3
San Fernando, La Union
68,410 . . . C2
San Fernando, Pampanga
110,891 . . . C3
San Jose 64,254 . . . C3
San Jose del Monte 90,732 . . C3
San Pablo 131,655 . . . C3
Santa Fe 6,338 . . . C2
Santiago 69,877 . . . C2
Silay 111,131 . . . D5
Siquijor 17,533 . . . D6
Surigao 79,745 . . . E6
Tacloban 102,523 . . . E5
Tagaytay 16,322 . . . C3
Tagum 86,201 . . . E7
Tarlac 175,691 . . . C3
Toledo 91,668 . . . D5
Tuguegarao 73,507 . . . C2
Zamboanga 343,722 . . . C7

OTHER FEATURES

Agusan (riv.) . . . E6
Alabat (isl.) . . . D3
Apo (vol.) . . . E7
Babuyan (isl.) . . . B2
Balabac (isl.) . . . A7
Balayan (bay) . . . C4
Balintang (chan.) . . . A2
Baloy (mt.) . . . D5
Bantayan (isl.) . . . D5
Banton (isl.) . . . D4
Bashi (chan.) . . . A1
Basilan (isl.) . . . D7
Batan, Albay (isl.) . . . E4
Batan, Batanes (isl.) . . . B2
Batan (isls.) . . . A2
Bay, Laguna de (lake) . . . C3
Biliran (isl.) . . . E5
Bohol (isl.) . . . E6
Bojeador (cape) . . . C1
Borocay (isl.) . . . D5
Bucas Grande (isl.) . . . F6
Bugsuk (isl.) . . . A6
Buliluyan (cape) . . . A6
Bunga (pt.) . . . E4
Burias (isl.) . . . D4
Busuanga (isl.) . . . B4
Cabalasan (mt.) . . . E5
Cabulauan (isls.) . . . C5
Cagayan (isls.) . . . C6
Cagayan (riv.) . . . C2
Cagayan Sulu (isl.) . . . B7
Cagua (vol.) . . . D1
Calagua (isls.) . . . D3
Calamian Group (isls.) . . . B4
Calayan (isl.) . . . A2
Calicoan (isl.) . . . E5
Camiguin, Cagayan (isl.) . . . B3
Camiguin, Camiguin (isl.) . . . E6
Camotes (isls.) . . . E5
Camotes (sea) . . . E5
Canigao (chan.) . . . E5
Canlaon (peak) . . . D5
Capotoan (mt.) . . . E4
Carabao (isl.) . . . D4
Catanduanes (isl.) . . . E4
Cebu (isl.) . . . D5
Celebes (sea) . . . D8
Cleopatra Needle (mt.) . . . B5
Coron (isl.) . . . C5

Topography

0 100 200 MI.
0 100 200 KM.
BABUYAN IS.
C. Engaño
Lingayen Gulf
C. Bolinao
Luzon
PHILIPPINE
Manila
Bataan Pen.
Manila Bay
Lamon Bay
Catanduanes
Mayon Vol. 7,943 ft.
Mindoro
Marinduque
Sibuyan Sea
Busuanga
CALAMIAN GROUP
Masbate
Samar Sea
Samar
Visayan Sea
Panay
Leyte
Leyte Gulf
Cebu
Palawan
Negros
Bohol
Mindanao Sea
S U L U S E A
Mindanao
Balabac
Moro Gulf
Davao Gulf
Basilan
Jolo
Tawi-Tawi
SULU ARCH.
Tinaca Pt.
Below Sea Level
100 m. 328 ft.
200 m. 656 ft.
500 m. 1,640 ft.
1,000 m. 3,281 ft.
2,000 m. 6,562 ft.
5,000 m. 16,404 ft.

Agriculture, Industry and Resources

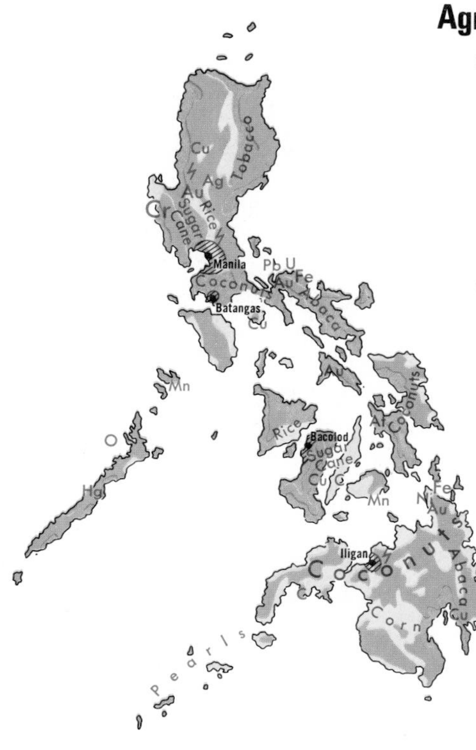

Tobacco
Cu
Ag
Au
Cr
Rice
Sugar Cane
Manila
Pb
U
Fe
Batangas
Mn
O
Hg
Rice
Bacolod
Sugar Cane
Cu
Coconuts
Iligan
Corn
Abaca
Pearls

DOMINANT LAND USE

Cereals (chiefly rice, corn)
Cash Crops
Tropical Forests

MAJOR MINERAL OCCURRENCES

Ag Silver
At Asphalt
Au Gold
C Coal
Cr Chromium
Cu Copper
Fe Iron
Hg Mercury
Mn Manganese
Ni Nickel
O Petroleum
Pb Lead
U Uranium

Water Power
Major Industrial Areas

Corregidor (isl.) . . . C3
Culion (isl.) . . . B5
Cuyo (isl.) . . . C5
Cuyo (isls.) . . . C5
Daram (isl.) . . . E5
Davao (gulf) . . . E7
Dinagat (isl.) . . . E5
Diuata (mts.) . . . E6
Dumanquilas (bay) . . . D7
Dumaran (isl.) . . . C5
Engaño (cape) . . . D1
Espiritu Santo (cape) . . . E4
Fuga (isl.) . . . A3
Guimaras (isl.) . . . D5
Halcon (mt.) . . . C4
Hibuson (isl.) . . . E5
Homonhon (isl.) . . . E5
Honda (bay) . . . B6
Iligan (bay) . . . E6
Ilin (isl.) . . . C4
Illana (bay) . . . D7
Imuruan (bay) . . . B5
Island (bay) . . . B6
Itbayat (isl.) . . . A2
Jintotolo (chan.) . . . D5
Jolo (isl.) . . . C7
Jomalig (isl.) . . . D3
Lagonoy (gulf) . . . E4
Lamon (bay) . . . C3
Lanao (lake) . . . E7
Laparan (isls.) . . . B8
Lapinin (isl.) . . . E5
Leyte (gulf) . . . E5
Leyte (isl.) . . . E5
Limasawa (isl.) . . . E6
Linapacan (isl.) . . . B5
Lingayen (gulf) . . . C2
Lubang (isls.) . . . B4
Luzon (isl.) . . . C3
Luzon (str.) . . . A2
Macajalar (bay) . . . E6
Malindang (mt.) . . . D6
Mangsee (isls.) . . . A7
Manila (bay) . . . C3
Mantalingajan (mt.) . . . A6
Maqueda (chan.) . . . D3
Maraira (pt.) . . . C1
Marinduque (isl.) . . . C4
Masbate (isl.) . . . D4
Mayon (vol.) . . . D4
Maytiguid (isl.) . . . B5
Mindanao (isl.) . . . D7
Mindanao (riv.) . . . E7
Mindoro (isl.) . . . C4
Mindoro (str.) . . . C4
Mompog (passg.) . . . D4
Moro (gulf) . . . D7
Mount Apo National Park . . . E7
Naso (pt.) . . . C5
Negros (isl.) . . . D6
Olutanga (isl.) . . . D7
Pacsan (mt.) . . . C2
Palawan (isl.) . . . B6
Palawan (passg.) . . . A6
Panaon (isl.) . . . E5
Panay (isl.) . . . D5
Panglao (isl.) . . . D6
Pangutaran (isl.) . . . C7
Pangutaran Group (isls.) . . . C7
Patnanongan (isl.) . . . D3
Philippine (sea) . . . D3
Pilas (isl.) . . . C7
Pinatubo (mt.) . . . C3
Polillo (isl.) . . . C3
Pujada (bay) . . . F7
Pulangi (riv.) . . . E7
Ragang (vol.) . . . E7
Ragay (gulf) . . . D4
Rapu-Rapu (isl.) . . . E4
Romblon (isl.) . . . D4
Sabtang (isl.) . . . B2
Sacol (isl.) . . . D7
Samal (isl.) . . . E7
Samales Group (isls.) . . . D7
Samar (isl.) . . . E5
Samar (sea) . . . E4
San Agustin (cape) . . . F7
San Bernardino (str.) . . . E4
San Miguel (bay) . . . D3
San Pedro (bay) . . . E5
Santo Tomas (mt.) . . . C2
Semirara (isls.) . . . C5
Siargao (isl.) . . . F6
Sibay (isl.) . . . C5
Sibuguey (bay) . . . D7
Sibutu Group (isls.) . . . B8
Sibuyan (isl.) . . . D4
Sibuyan (sea) . . . D4
Sierra Madre (mt.) . . . D2
Simunul (isl.) . . . B8
Siquijor (isl.) . . . D6
South China (sea) . . . B3
Subic (bay) . . . C3
Sulu (arch.) . . . B8
Sulu (sea) . . . B6
Suluan (isl.) . . . F5
Surigao (str.) . . . E6
Taal (lake) . . . C4
Tablas (isl.) . . . D4
Tablas (str.) . . . C4
Tagapula (isl.) . . . E4
Tagolo (pt.) . . . D6
Tanon (str.) . . . D6
Tapul (isl.) . . . C8
Tapul Group (isls.) . . . C8
Tara (isl.) . . . C4
Tawi-Tawi (isl.) . . . B8
Tayabas (bay) . . . C4
Ticao (isl.) . . . D4
Tinaca (pt.) . . . E8
Tongquil (isl.) . . . D8
Tumindao (isl.) . . . B8
Turtle (isls.) . . . B7
Verde Island (passg.) . . . C4
Victoria (peaks) . . . B6
Visayan (sea) . . . D5

BRUNEI

CITIES and TOWNS

Bandar Seri Begawan 63,868 E4
Seria 23,511 . . . . . . E5

INDONESIA

CITIES and TOWNS

Adaut J7
Agats K7
Ambon (Amboina) 208,898 . . . H6
Amuntai F6
Amurang G5
Atambua G7
Aubá H7
Baa G8
Bagansiapiapi C5
Balikpapan 280,675 . . . . . . F6
Banda Aceh 72,090 . . . . . . A4
Bandanaira H6
Bandung 1,462,637 . . . . . . H2
Banggai G6
Banjarmasin 381,286 . . . . . . E6
Banyumas J2
Batang J2
Batavia (Jakarta) (cap.) 6,503,449 . . . . . . H1
Baukau H7
Bekasi H2
Belawan B5
Bengkulu 64,783 . . . . . . C6
Beo H5
Biak K6
Binjai 76,464 . . . . . . B5
Bintuhan C6
Blitar 78,503 . . . . . . K2
Bogor 247,409 . . . . . . H2
Bojonegoro J2
Bukittinggi 70,771 . . . . . . B6
Bula J6
Bulukumba G7
Buntok F6
Cianjur H2
Cimahi H2
Cirebon 223,776 . . . . . . H2
Demta L6
Denpasar E7
Dili H7
Djambi (Jambi) 230,373 . . . . . C6
Djokjakarta (Yogyakarta) 398,727 . . . . . . J2
Dobo J7
Donggala F6
Enaratoli K6
Ende G7
Fakfak J6
Garut H2
Gorontalo 97,628 . . . . . . G5
Hollandia (Jayapura) K6
Indramayu H2
Jailolo H5
Jakarta (cap.) 6,503,449 . . . . . H1
Jambi 230,373 . . . . . . C6
Jayapura (Hollandia) K6
Jogjakarta (Yogyakarta) 398,727 . . . . . . J2
Jombang K2
Kaimana J6
Kampung Baru (Tolitoli) G5
Kediri 221,820 . . . . . . K2
Kendari G6
Kepi K7
Ketapang E6
Kokonau K6
Kolonodale G6
Kotabaharu E6
Kotabaru F6
Kotawaringin E6
Kragen K2
Kupang G8
Kutaraja (Banda Aceh) 72,090 . . . . . . A4
Labuha H6
Labuhan G2
Laiwui H6
Larantuka G7
Lekitobi G6
Longiram F5
Madiun 150,562 . . . . . . K2
Magelang 123,484 . . . . . . J2
Majalengka H2
Makassar (Ujung Pandang) 709,038 . . . . . . F7
Malang 511,780 . . . . . . K2
Malili G6
Manado 217,159 . . . . . . G5
Manokwari J6
Maumere G7
Medan 1,378,955 . . . . . . B5
Menggala D6
Merauke K7
Mindiptana L7
Mojokerto 68,849 . . . . . . K2
Muarasiberut B6
Nangatayap E6
Pacitan J2
Padang 480,922 . . . . . . B6
Padangpanjang 34,517 . . . . . . B6
Padangsidempuan B5
Pakanbaru 186,262 . . . . . . C5
Palangkaraya 60,447 . . . . . . E6
Palembang 787,187 . . . . . . D6
Pangkalanbuun E6
Pangkalpinang 90,096 . . . . . . D6
Parepare 86,450 . . . . . . F6
Pasangkayu F6
Pasuruan 95,864 . . . . . . K2
Payakumbuh 78,836 . . . . . . C6
Pekalongan 132,558 . . . . . . J2
Pemalang J2
Pematangsiantar 150,376 . . . . B5
Pinrang F6
Plaju D6
Pontianak 304,778 . . . . . . D6
Probolinggo 100,296 . . . . . . K2
Purbolinggo J2
Raha G6
Rantauprapat C5
Rembang K2
Sabang, Celebes F5
Sabang, Weh 23,821 . . . . . . B4
Salatiga 85,849 . . . . . . J2
Samarinda 264,718 . . . . . . F6
Sampit E6
Sarmi K6
Sawahlunto 13,561 . . . . . . C6
Seba G8
Semarang 1,026,671 . . . . . . J2
Semitau E5
Serui K6
Sibolga 59,897 . . . . . . B5
Sigli B4
Sinabang B5
Singaraja F7
Solo (Surakarta) 469,888 . . . . J2
Solok 31,724 . . . . . . C6
Sorong J6
Sragen J2
Subang H2
Sukabumi 109,994 . . . . . . H2
Sumbawa Besar F7
Sumedang H2
Surabaya 2,027,913 . . . . . . K2
Surakarta 469,888 . . . . . . J2
Tanahmerah K7
Tanjungbalai 41,894 . . . . . . C5
Tanjungkarang 284,275 . . . . . . D7
Tanjungpinang C5
Tanjungselor F5
Tarakan F5
Tebingtinggi 92,087 . . . . . . B5
Tegal 131,728 . . . . . . J2
Telukbayur C6
Tepa H7
Terempa D5
Tjilatjap (Cilicap) H2
Tjirebon (Cirebon) 223,776 . . . H2
Tolitoli G5
Tuban K2
Ujung Pandang 709,038 . . . . . F7
Vikeke H7
Wahai H6
Waigama H6
Wajabula H5
Waren K6
Weda H5
Wonreli H7
Yogyakarta 398,727 . . . . . . J2

OTHER FEATURES

Anambas (isls.) 29,572 . . . . D5
Arafura (sea) J8
Aru (isls.) 34,195 . . . . . . K7
Babar (isl.) H7
Bali (isl.) 2,074,438 . . . . . . F7
Banda (sea) H7
Banggai (arch.) 169,025 . . . G6
Bangka (isl.) 298,017 . . . . . . D6
Banyak (isls.) 1,980 . . . . . . B5
Barisan (mts.) C6
Barito (riv.) E6
Batu (isls.) 16,390 . . . . . . B6
Bawean (isl.) 64,551 . . . . . . K1
Belitung (Billiton) (isl.) 128,694 . . . . . . D6
Berau (bay) J6
Biak (isl.) K6
Billiton (isl.) 128,694 . . . . . . D6
Binongko (isl.) 11,549 . . . . . G7
Bone (gulf) G7
Borneo (isl.) E5
Bosch, van den (cape) J6
Bunguran (Great Natuna) (isl.) D5
Buru (isl.) 23,034 . . . . . . H6
Butung (isl.) 188,173 . . . . . . G6
Celebes (Sulawesi) (isl.) 7,732,383 . . . . . . G5
Celebes (sea) G5
Cenderawasih (bay) K6
Dampier (str.) J6
Digul (riv.) K7
Doberai (pen.) J6
Enggano (isl.) 1,082 . . . . . . C7
Ewab (Kai) (isls.) 108,328 . . J7
Flores (isl.) 860,328 . . . . . . G7
Flores (sea) F7
Frederik Hendrik (Kolepom) (isl.) K7
Geelvink (Cenderawasih) (bay) K6
Great Kai (isl.) 38,748 . . . . . . J7
Halmahera (isl.) 122,521 . . . H5
Irian Jaya (reg.) 923,440 . . . J6
Jambuair (cape) B4
Jamursba (cape) J5
Java (head) C7
Java (isl.) 73,712,411 . . . . . . J2
Java (sea) D6
Jaya, Puncak (mt.) K6
Jayawijaya (range) K6
Jemaja (isl.) 5,628 . . . . . . D5
Kabaena (isl.) G7
Kai (isls.) 108,328 . . . . . . J7
Kalao (isl.) G7
Kalaotoa (isl.) G5
Kalimantan (reg.) 4,956,865. E5
Kangean (isl.) F7
Kapuas (riv.) D6
Karakelong (isl.) H5
Karimata (arch.) 9,398 . . . . . D6
Karimunjawa (isls.) 5,025 . . . J1
Kerinci (mt.) C6
Kisar (isl.) H7
Komodo (isl.) 30,407 . . . . . . F7
Krakatau (Rakata) (isl.) C7
Laut (isl.) 55,711 . . . . . . F6
Leuser (mt.) B5
Lingga (arch.) 46,658 . . . . . D5
Lingga (isl.) 18,027 . . . . . . D6
Lombok (isl.) 1,581,193 . . . . F7
Madura (isl.) 1,509,774 . . . . . K2
Mahakam (riv.) F6
Makassar (str.) F6
Malacca (str.) C5
Mamberamo (riv.) K6
Maoke (mts.) K6
Mapia (isls.) J5
Mentawai (isls.) 30,107 . . . . B6
Misool (isl.) J6
Molucca (sea) H6
Moluccas (isls.) 944,240 . . . H6
Morotai (isl.) 27,333 . . . . . . H5
Muli (str.) K7
Müller (mts.) E5
Muna (isl.) 156,186 . . . . . . G7
Musi (riv.) C6
Natuna (isls.) 23,893 . . . . . . D5
Ngunju (cape) F8
Nias (isl.) 356,093 . . . . . . B5
Numfoor (isl.) J6
Obi (isls.) 12,437 . . . . . . H6
Ombai (str.) H7
Pantar (isl.) 28,259 . . . . . . G7
Perkam (cape) K6
Puting, Borneo (cape) E6
Puting, Sumatra (cape) C7
Raja Ampat Group (isls.) . . . H6
Rakata (isl.) C7
Rantekombola (mt.) F6
Raya (mt.) E6
Riau (arch.) 483,230 . . . . . . C5
Rokan (riv.) C5
Roti (isl.) 76,270 . . . . . . G8
Salawati (isl.) J6
Sangihe (isl.) H5
Sangihe (isls.) 183,000 . . . . G5
Sawu (isls.) 51,002 . . . . . . G8
Sawu (sea) G7
Schouten (isls.) 110,148 . . . K6
Schwaner (mts.) E6
Sebuku (bay) F5
Selatan (cape) E6
Selayar (isl.) 92,342 . . . . . . G7
Semeru (mt.) K2
Siau (isl.) 46,801 . . . . . . H5
Siberut (str.) B6
Simeulue (isl.) 29,147 . . . . . A5
Singkep (isl.) 28,631 . . . . . . D6
Sipura (isl.) 6,051 . . . . . . B6
Slamet (mt.) J2
Sorikmerapi (mt.) B5
South Natuna (isls.) D5
Sudirman (range) K6
Sula (isls.) 36,922 . . . . . . H6
Sulawesi (isl.) 7,732,383 . . . G6
Sumatra (isl.) 19,360,400 . . B5
Sumba (isl.) 291,190 . . . . . . F7
Sumba (str.) F7
Sumbawa (isl.) 621,140 . . . . F7
Sunda (str.) C7
Tahulandang (isl.) 21,493 . . H5
Talaud (isls.) 46,395 . . . . . . H5
Taliabu (isl.) 18,303 . . . . . . G6
Tambelan (isls.) 4,032 . . . . . D5
Tanimbar (isls.) 55,405 . . . . . J7
Tariku (riv.) K6
Tidore (isl.) 28,655 . . . . . . H5
Timor (reg.) 1,435,527 . . . . H7
Timor (sea) H7
Toba (lake) B5
Tolo (gulf) G6
Tomini (gulf) G6
Tukangbesi (isls.) 73,106 . . . G7
Vals (cape) K7
Vogelkop (Doberai) (pen.) . . . J6
Waigeo (isl.) J5
Wakde (isl.) K6
Wangiwangi (isl.) 28,469 . . . G7
We (isl.) B4
Wetar (isl.) H7
Yapen (isl.) 50,888 . . . . . . K6

MALAYSIA

STATES

North Borneo (Sabah) 1,002,608 . . . . . . F3
Sarawak 1,294,753 . . . . . . E5

CITIES and TOWNS

Beaufort 2,709 . . . . . . F4
Bintulu 4,424 . . . . . . E5
Kabong E5
Kampong Sibuti E5
Kapit 1,929 . . . . . . E5
Keningau 2,037 . . . . . . F4
Kota Kinabalu 40,939 . . . . . . F4
Kuching 63,535 . . . . . . E5
Kudat 5,089 . . . . . . F4
Labuan 7,216 . . . . . . E4
Lahad Datu 5,169 . . . . . . F5
Lamag F4
Marudi 4,700 . . . . . . E5
Miri 35,702 . . . . . . E5
Mukah 1,717 . . . . . . E5

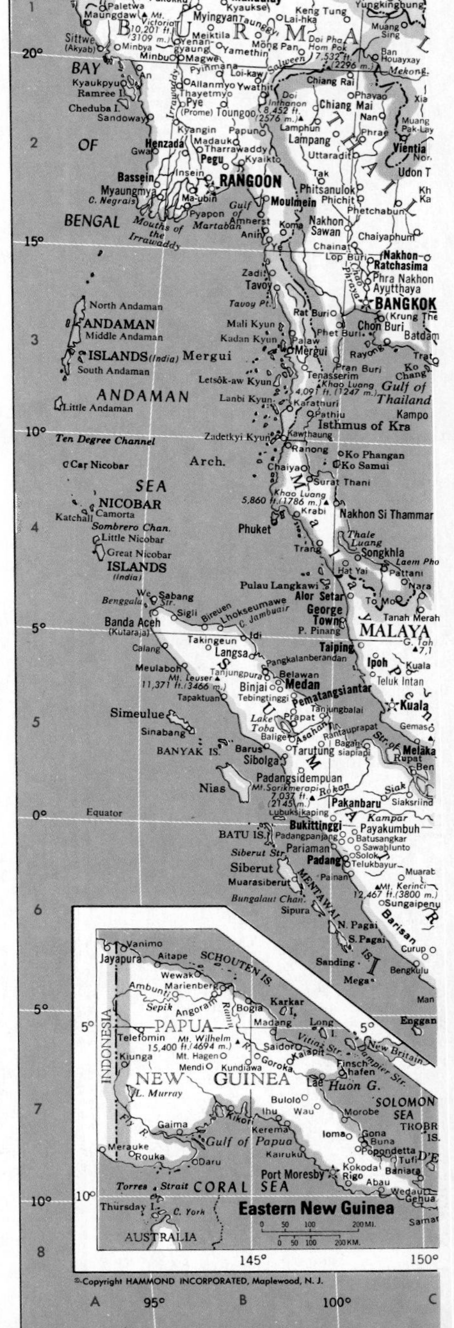

BANGLADESH
BURMA
Mandalay
RANGOON
BAY OF BENGAL
ANDAMAN ISLANDS (India)
ANDAMAN SEA
NICOBAR ISLANDS (India)
THAILAND
BANGKOK
Gulf of Thailand
Isthmus of Kra
MALAYA
Medan
Sumatra
Equator
PAPUA NEW GUINEA
SOLOMON SEA
CORAL SEA
Port Moresby
AUSTRALIA
Eastern New Guinea

Topography

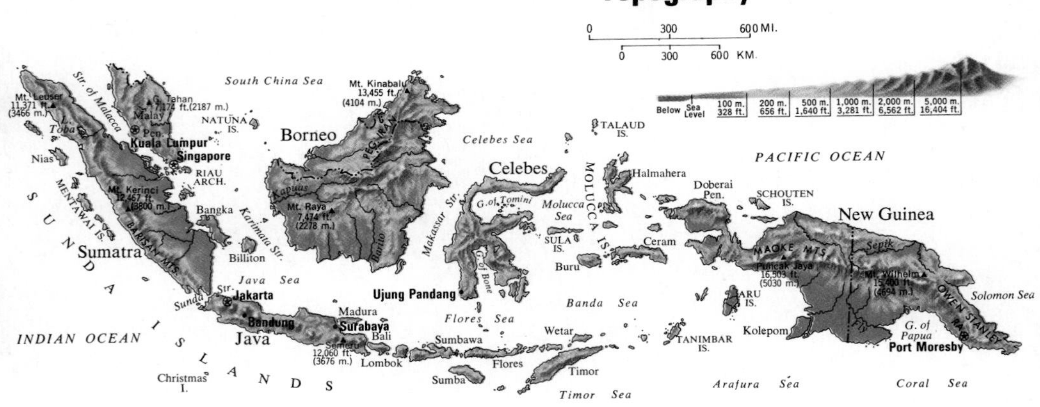

South China Sea
Borneo
Celebes
New Guinea
Sumatra
Java
PACIFIC OCEAN
INDIAN OCEAN
SUNDA ISLANDS
Celebes Sea
Java Sea
Flores Sea
Banda Sea
Timor Sea
Arafura Sea
Coral Sea
Solomon Sea
Kuala Lumpur
Singapore
Jakarta
Bandung
Surabaya
Ujung Pandang
Port Moresby
Halmahera
Timor

Agriculture, Industry and Resources

Singapore
Jakarta
Rubber
Rice
Coconuts
Spices
Pearls
Tobacco
Turtles
Coffee
Tea

DOMINANT LAND USE

Cereals (chiefly rice, corn)
Diversified Tropical Crops
Forests

MAJOR MINERAL OCCURRENCES

Al Bauxite
Au Gold
C Coal
Cu Copper
Fe Iron Ore
G Natural Gas
Mn Manganese
Ni Nickel
O Petroleum
Sn Tin

Major Industrial Areas

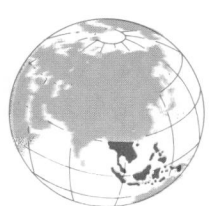

INDONESIA

AREA 788,430 sq. mi. (2,042,034 sq. km.)
POPULATION 179,136,000
CAPITAL Jakarta
LARGEST CITY Jakarta
HIGHEST POINT Puncak Jaya 16,503 ft. (5,030 m.)
MONETARY UNIT rupiah
MAJOR LANGUAGES Bahasa Indonesia, Indonesian and Papuan languages, English
MAJOR RELIGIONS Islam, tribal religions, Christianity, Hinduism

PAPUA NEW GUINEA

AREA 183,540 sq. mi. (475,369 sq. km.)
POPULATION 3,593,000
CAPITAL Port Moresby
LARGEST CITY Port Moresby
HIGHEST POINT Mt. Wilhelm 15,400 ft. (4,694 m.)
MONETARY UNIT kina
MAJOR LANGUAGES pidgin English, Hiri Motu, English
MAJOR RELIGIONS Tribal religions, Christianity

BRUNEI

AREA 2,226 sq. mi. (5,765 sq. km.)
POPULATION 249,000
CAPITAL Bandar Seri Begawan
LARGEST CITY Bandar Seri Begawan
HIGHEST POINT Pagon 6,070 ft. (1,850 m.)
MONETARY UNIT Brunei Dollar
MAJOR LANGUAGES Malay, English, Chinese
MAJOR RELIGIONS Islam, Buddhism, Christianity, tribal religions

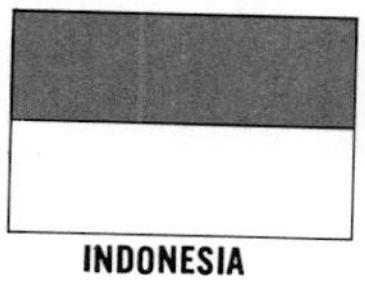

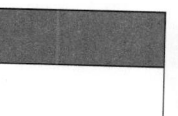

INDONESIA

PAPUA NEW GUINEA

BRUNEI

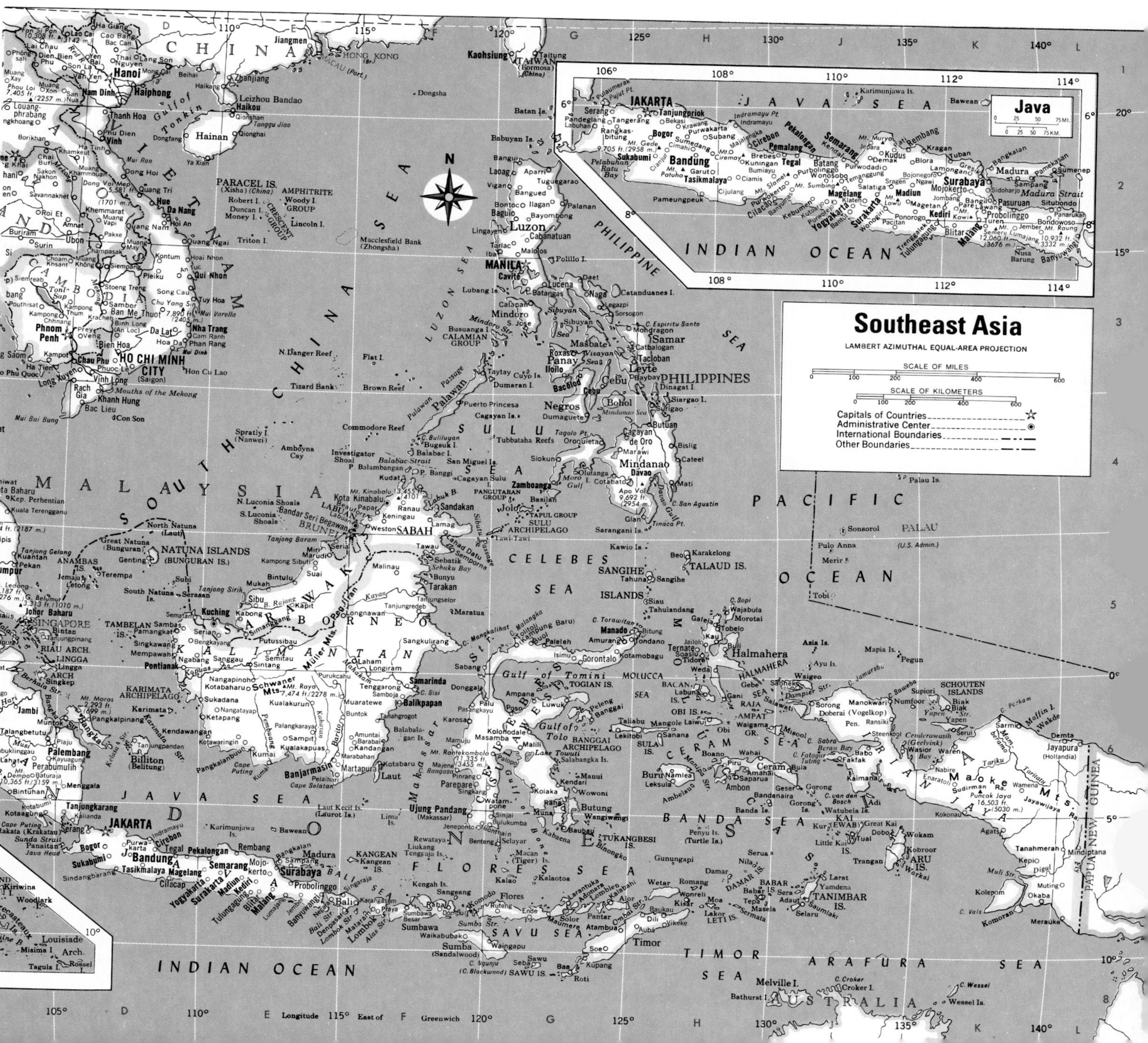

(Map of Southeast Asia showing Indonesia, Malaysia, Philippines, Papua New Guinea, and neighboring regions, with inset maps of Java and a legend for Southeast Asia using Lambert Azimuthal Equal-Area Projection.)

FIJI

AREA 7,055 sq. mi. (18,272 sq. km.)
POPULATION 727,000
CAPITAL Suva
LARGEST CITY Suva
HIGHEST POINT Tomaniivi 4,341 ft. (1,323 m.)
MONETARY UNIT Fijian dollar
MAJOR LANGUAGES Fijian, Hindi, English
MAJOR RELIGIONS Protestantism, Hinduism

KIRIBATI

AREA 291 sq. mi. (754 sq. km.)
POPULATION 64,000
CAPITAL Bairiki (Tarawa)
HIGHEST POINT (on Banaba I.) 285 ft. (87 m.)
MONETARY UNIT Australian dollar
MAJOR LANGUAGES I-Kiribati, English
MAJOR RELIGIONS Protestantism, Roman Catholicism

NAURU

AREA 7.7 sq. mi. (20 sq. km.)
POPULATION 9,000
CAPITAL Yaren (district)
MONETARY UNIT Australian dollar
MAJOR LANGUAGES Nauruan, English
MAJOR RELIGION Protestantism

SOLOMON ISLANDS

AREA 11,500 sq. mi. (29,785 sq. km.)
POPULATION 299,000
CAPITAL Honiara
HIGHEST POINT Mount Popomanatseu 7,647 ft. (2,331 m.)
MONETARY UNIT Solomon Islands dollar
MAJOR LANGUAGES English, pidgin English, Melanesian dialects
MAJOR RELIGIONS Tribal religions, Protestantism, Roman Catholicism

TONGA

AREA 270 sq. mi. (699 sq. km.)
POPULATION 95,000
CAPITAL Nuku'alofa
LARGEST CITY Nuku'alofa
HIGHEST POINT 3,389 ft. (1,033 m.)
MONETARY UNIT pa'anga
MAJOR LANGUAGES Tongan, English
MAJOR RELIGION Protestantism

TUVALU

AREA 9.78 sq. mi. (25.33 sq. km.)
POPULATION 9,000
CAPITAL Fongafale (Funafuti)
HIGHEST POINT 15 ft. (4.6 m.)
MONETARY UNIT Australian dollar
MAJOR LANGUAGES English, Tuvaluan
MAJOR RELIGION Protestantism

Name		Ref
Abaiang (atoll) 3,296		H 5
Abemama (atoll) 2,300		H 5
Adamstown (cap.), Pitcairn Is. 54		N 8
Admiralty (isls.)		E 6
Agaña (cap.), Guam 896		E 4
Agrihan (isl.)		E 4
Ailinglapalap (atoll) 1,385		G 5
Ailuk (atoll) 413		H 4
Aitutaki (atoll) 2,348		K 7
Alofi (cap.), Niue 960		K 7
Alotau 4,310		E 7
Ambrym (isl.) 6,324		G 7
American Samoa 32,297		J 7
Anaa (atoll) 444		M 7
Angaur (isl.) 243		D 5
Apataki (atoll)		M 7
Apia (cap.), W. Samoa 33,100		J 7
Arno (atoll) 1,487		H 6
Arorae (atoll) 1,626		H 6
Atafu (atoll) 577		J 6
Atiu (isl.) 1,225		L 8
Austral (isls.) 5,208		L 8
Avarua (cap.), Cook Is.		D 5
Babelthuap 48,711		D 5
Bairiki (cap.), Kiribati 1,777		J 5
Baker (isl.)		J 5
Banaba (isl.) 2,314		G 6
Banks (isls.) 3,158		G 7
Belep (isls.) 624		G 7
Bellona (reefs)		G 8
Beru (atoll) 2,318		H 6
Bikini (atoll)		G 4
Bismarck (arch.) 218,339		E 6
Bonin (isls.) 1,879		E 3
Bora-Bora (isl.) 2,572		L 7
Bougainville (isl.) 71,761		F 6
Bounty (isls.)		H 10
Bourail 3,149		G 8
Butaritari (atoll) 2,971		H 5
Capitol Hill (cap.), No. Marianas 592		E 4
Caroline (isl.)		M 7
Caroline (isls.)		E 5
Chichi (isl.) 1,879		E 3
Choiseul (isl.) 10,349		F 6
Christmas (Kiritimati) (isl.) 674		L 5
Cook (isls.) 17,695		K 7
Coral (sea)		F 7
Danger (Pukapuka) (atoll) 797		K 7
Daru 7,127		E 7
Disappointment (isls.) 373		N 7
Ducie (isl.)		O 8
Easter (isl.) 1,598		Q 8
Ebon (atoll) 887		G 5
Efate (isl.) 18,038		G 7
Enderbury (isl.)		J 6
Enewetak (Eniwetok) (atoll) 542		G 4
Erromanga (isl.) 945		H 7
Espíritu Santo (isl.) 16,220		G 7
Fais (isl.) 207		E 5
Fakaofo (atoll) 654		J 6
Fanning (Tabuaeran) (isl.) 340		L 5
Faraulep (atoll) 132		E 5
Fatuhiva (isl.) 386		N 7
Fiji 588,068		H 8
Flint (isl.)		L 7
Fly (riv.)		E 7
Fongafale (cap.), Tuvalu		H 6
French Polynesia 137,382		L 8
Funafuti (atoll) 2,120		H 6
Futuna (Hoorn) (isls.) 3,173		J 7
Gambier (isls.) 556		N 8
Gardner (Nukumaroro) (isl.)		J 6
Gilbert (isls.) 47,711		H 6
Greenwich (Kapingamarangi) (atoll) 508		F 5
Guadalcanal (isl.) 46,619		F 7
Guam (isl.) 105,979		E 4
Hall (isls.) 647		F 5
Hawaiian (isls.) 964,691		J 3
Henderson (isl.)		O 8
Hivaoa (isl.) 1,159		N 6
Honiara (cap.), Solomon Is. 14,942		F 6
Hoorn (isls.) 3,173		J 7
Howland (isl.)		J 5
Huahine (isl.) 3,140		L 7
Hull (Orona) (atoll)		J 6
Huon (gulf)		E 6
Ifalik (atoll) 389		E 5
Iwo (isl.)		E 3
Jaluit (atoll) 1,450		G 5
Jarvis (isl.)		K 6
Johnston (atoll) 327		K 4
Kadavu (Kandavu) (isl.) 8,699		H 7
Kanton (atoll)		J 6
Kapingamarangi (atoll) 508		F 5
Kavieng 4,633		E 6
Kermadec (isls.) 5		J 9
Kieta 3,491		F 6
Kimbe 4,662		F 6
Kingman (reef)		K 5
Kiribati 57,500		H 6
Kiritimati (isl.) 674		L 5
Kolonia (cap.), Micronesia 5,549		F 5
Koror (cap.), Belau 6,222		D 5
Kosrae (isl.) 5,491		G 5
Kwajalein (atoll) 6,624		G 5
Lae 61,617		E 6
Lau Group (isls.) 14,452		J 7
Lavongai (isl.)		F 6
Lifu (isl.) 7,585		G 8
Line (isls.)		K 5
Little Makin (atoll) 1,445		H 5
Lord Howe (Ontong Java) (isl.) 1,082		G 6
Lord Howe (isl.) 287		G 9
Lorengau 3,986		E 6
Louisiade (arch.)		F 7
Loyalty (isls.) 14,518		G 8
Luganville 4,935		G 7
Madang 21,335		E 6
Majuro (atoll) (cap.), Marshall Is. 8,583		H 5
Makin (Butaritari) (atoll) 2,971		H 5
Malaita (isl.) 50,912		G 6
Malden (isl.)		L 6
Malekula (isl.) 15,931		G 7
Maloelap (atoll) 763		H 5
Mangaia (isl.) 1,364		L 8
Mangareva (isl.) 556		N 8
Manihiki (atoll) 405		K 7
Manua (isls.) 1,459		K 6
Manus (isl.) 25,844		E 6
Marcus (isl.)		G 8
Maré (isl.) 4,156		G 8
Marianas, Northern 16,780		E 4
Mariana Trench		E 4
Marquesas (isls.) 5,419		N 6
Marshall Islands 30,873		G 4
Marutea (atoll)		N 8
Mata Utu (cap.), Wallis and Futuna 558		J 7
Mauke (isl.) 684		L 8
Melanesia (reg.)		E 6
Micronesia (reg.)		E 4
Micronesia, Federated States of 73,160		F 5
Midway (isls.) 453		J 3
Mili (atoll) 763		H 5
Moen (isl.) 10,351		F 5
Moorea (isl.) 5,788		L 7
Mururoa (isl.)		M 8
Nadi 6,938		H 7
Namonuito (atoll) 783		E 5
Namorik (atoll) 617		G 5
Nanumea (atoll) 844		H 6
Nauru 7,254		G 6
Ndeni (isl.) 4,854		G 7
New Britain (isl.) 148,773		F 6
New Caledonia 133,233		G 8
New Caledonia 118,715		G 8
New Georgia (isl.) 16,472		F 6
New Guinea (isl.)		E 6
New Ireland (isl.) 65,657		F 6
Ngatik (atoll) 560		F 5
Ngulu (atoll) 21		D 5
Niuatoputapu (isl.) 1,650		J 7
Niue (isl.) 3,578		K 7
Niutao (atoll) 866		H 6
Nomoi (isls.) 1,879		F 5
Nonouti (atoll) 2,223		H 6
Norfolk Island (terr.) 2,175		G 8
Northern Marianas 116,780		E 4
Nouméa (cap.), New Caled. 56,078		G 8
Nouméa *74,335		G 8
Nui (atoll) 603		H 6
Nuku'alofa (cap.), Tonga 18,356		J 8
Nukuhiva 1,484		M 6

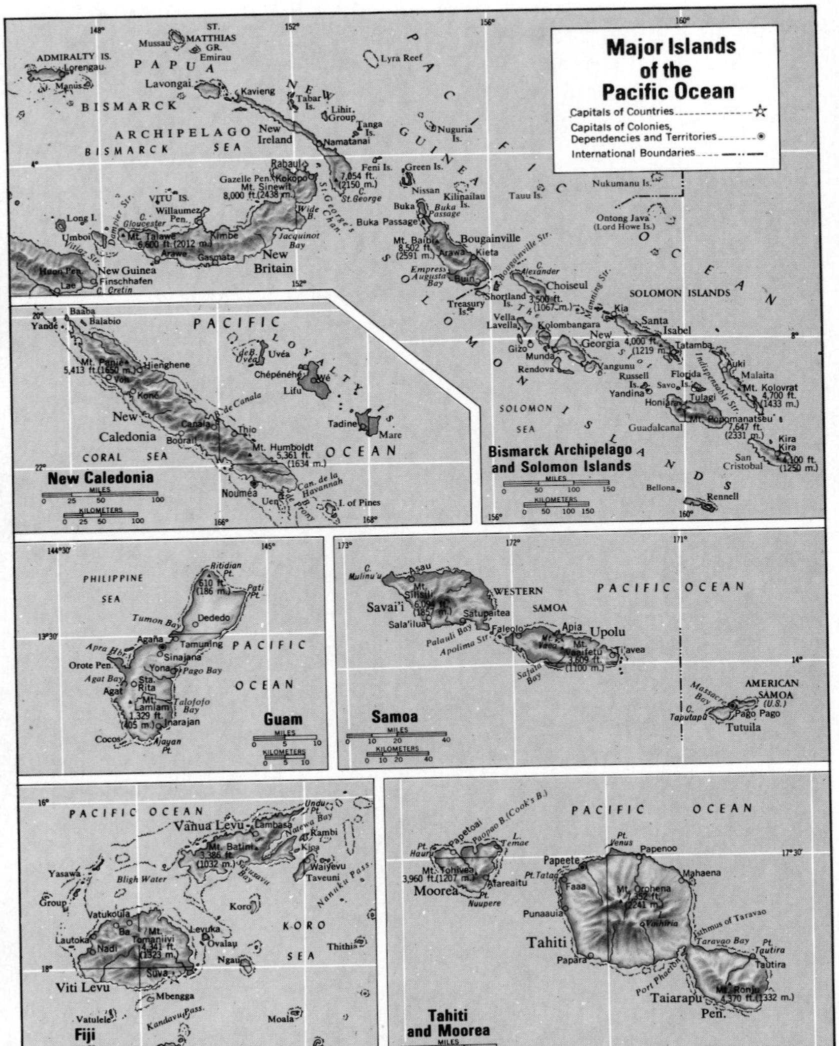

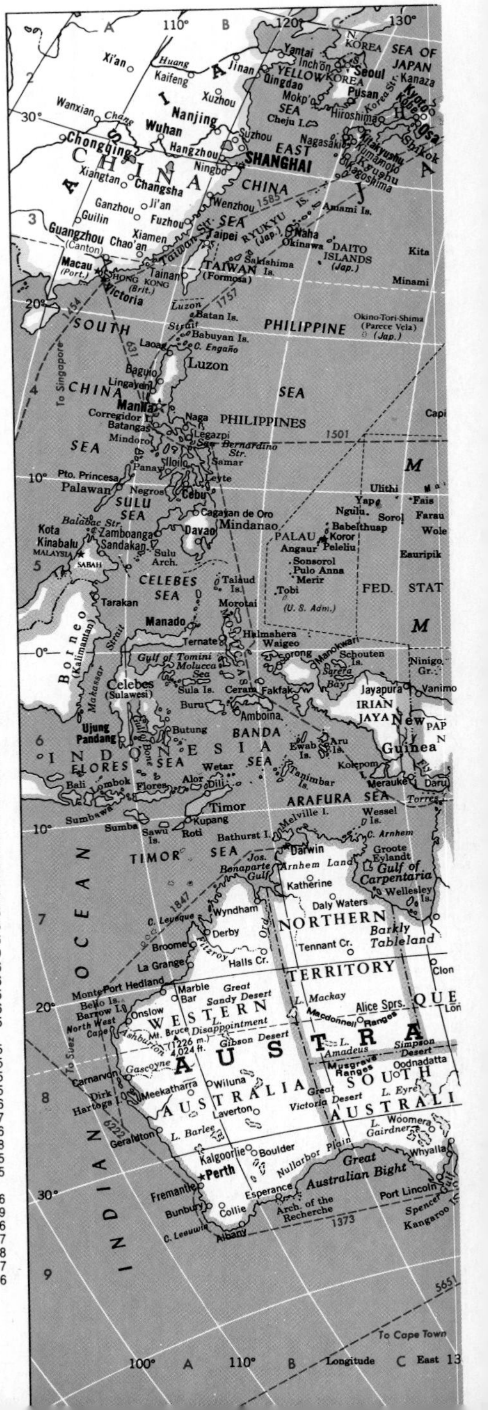

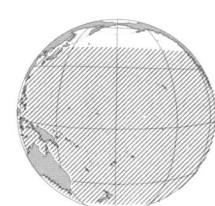

Ocean (Banaba) (isl.) 2,314....G 6
Oeno (isl.)....O 8
Onotoa (isl.) 1,997....H 6
Ontong Java (isl.) 1,082....G 6
Pagan (isl.)....E 4
Pago Pago (cap.), Amer.
  Samoa 3,075....J 7
Palau 12,116....D 5
Palmyra (atoll)....K 5
Papeete (cap.) Fr. Poly.
  22,967....M 7
Papeete *51,987....M 7
Papua (gulf)....E 6
Papua New Guinea
  3,010,727....E 6
Peleliu (isl.) 609....D 5
Penrhyn (Tongareva) (atoll)
  608....L 6
Phoenix (isls.)....J 6
Pines (isl.) 1,095....G 8
Pitcairn (isl.) 54....O 8
Pohnpei (isl.) 19,935....F 5
Polynesia (reg.)....K 7
Popondetta 6,429....E 6
Port Moresby (cap.), Papua
  N.G. 123,624....E 6
Pukapuka (atoll) 797....K 7
Pulap (atoll) 427....E 5
Puluwat (atoll) 441....E 5
Rabaul 14,954....F 6

Raiatea (isl.) 2,517....L 7
Raivavae (isl.) 1,023....M 8
Rakahanga (atoll) 269....K 7
Ralik Chain (isls.)....G 5
Rangiroa (atoll)....M 7
Rapa (isl.) 398....M 8
Rarotonga (isl.) 9,477....K 8
Ratak Chain (isls.)....G 5
Reao (atoll) 424....N 7
Rennell (isl.) 1,132....F 7
Rikitea....N 8
Rimatara (isl.) 813....L 8
Rongelap (atoll) 235....G 4
Rota (isl.) 1,261....E 4
Rotuma (isl.) 2,805....H 7
Rurutu (isl.) 1,555....L 8
Saipan (isl.) 14,549....E 4
Sala y Gómez (isl.)....P 8
Samarai 869....E 7
San Cristobal (isl.) 11,212....G 7
Santa Cruz (isls.) 5,421....G 6
Santa Isabel (isl.) 10,420....G 6
Savai'i (isl.) 43,150....J 7
Senyavin (isls.) 20,035....F 5
Society (isls.) 117,703....L 7
Solomon (isls.)....F 6
Solomon (sea)....F 6
Solomon Islands 221,000....G 6
Starbuck (isl.)....L 6

Suva (cap.) Fiji 63,628....H 7
Suva *117,827....H 7
Swains (isl.) 27....K 7
Sydney (isl.)....K 6
Tabiteuea (atoll) 3,942....H 6
Tabuaeran (atoll) 340....L 5
Tahaa (isl.) 3,513....L 7
Tahiti (isl.) 95,604....L 7
Takaroa (atoll) 337....M 7
Tanna (isl.) 15,715....H 7
Tarawa (atoll) 17,129....H 5
Tasman (sea)....G 9
Teraina (isl.) 458....L 5
Tinian (isl.) 866....E 4
Tokelau (isls.) 1,575....J 6
Tonga 90,128....J 8
Tongareva (atoll) 608....L 6
Tongatapu (isl.) 57,130....J 8
Torres (isls.) 325....G 7
Torres (strait)....E 7
Trobriand (isls.)....F 6
Truk (isls.) 37,488....F 5
Tuamotu (arch.) 9,052....M 7
Tubuai (Austral) (isls.) 5,208....M 8
Tubuai (isl.) 1,419....M 8
Tutuila (isl.) 30,538....J 7
Tuvalu 7,349....H 6
Uapou (isl.) 1,563....M 6
Ujelang (atoll) 309....F 5
Ulithi (atoll) 710....D 4

Upolu (isl.) 114,620....J 7
Uturoa 2,517....L 7
Uvéa (isl.) 2,777....G 7
Vaitupu (atoll) 1,273....H 6
Vanikoro (isl.) 267....G 7
Vanimo 3,071....E 6
Vanua Levu (isl.) 103,122....H 7
Vanuatu 112,596....G 7
Vila (cap.), Vanuatu 4,729....G 7

Vila *14,797....G 7
Viti Levu (isl.) 445,422....H 7
Volcano (isls.)....E 3
Vostok (isl.)....L 7
Wake (isl.) 302....G 4
Wallis (isls.) 6,019....J 7
Wallis and Futuna 9,192....J 7
Washington (Teraina) (atoll)
  458....L 5

Wau 2,349....E 6
Western Samoa 158,130....J 7
Wewak 19,890....E 6
Woleai (atoll) 638....E 5
Wotje (atoll) 535....H 5
Yap (isl.) 6,670....D 5

*City and suburbs.
•Population of urban area.

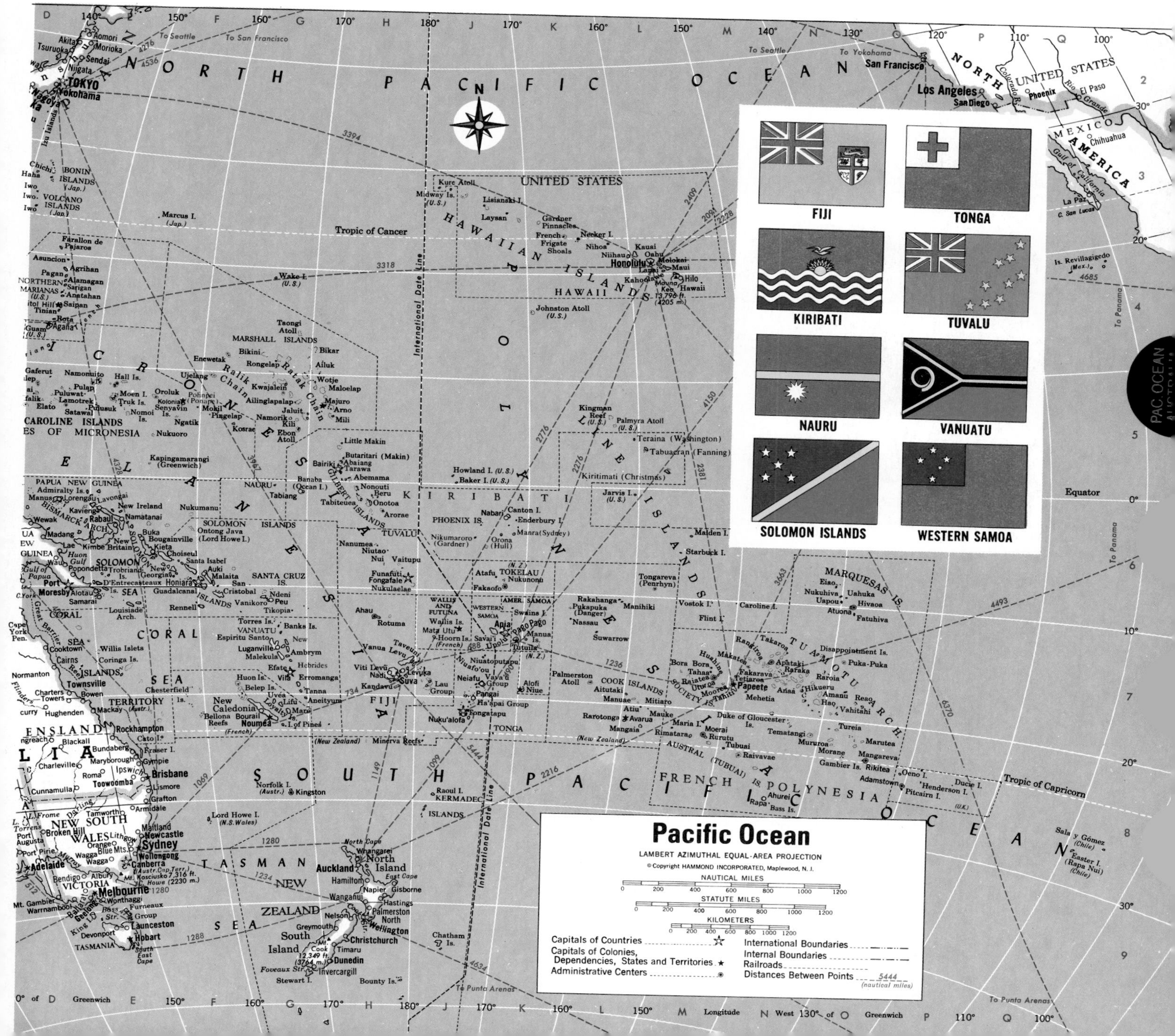

FIJI

TONGA

KIRIBATI

TUVALU

NAURU

VANUATU

SOLOMON ISLANDS

WESTERN SAMOA

Pacific Ocean

LAMBERT AZIMUTHAL EQUAL-AREA PROJECTION

© Copyright HAMMOND INCORPORATED, Maplewood, N.J.

NAUTICAL MILES
0   200   400   600   800   1000   1200

STATUTE MILES
0   200   400   600   800   1000   1200

KILOMETERS
0   200   400   600   800   1000   1200

Capitals of Countries............☆
Capitals of Colonies,
  Dependencies, States and Territories............★
Administrative Centers............⊛

International Boundaries
Internal Boundaries
Railroads
Distances Between Points........5444
  (nautical miles)

Australia

CONIC PROJECTION

MILES
0   50   100   200   300   400   500

KILOMETERS
0 50 100   200   300   400   500

Capital of Country .... ⊛   State & Territorial Capitals .... ◉
International Boundaries ....___ ___   State & Territorial Boundaries ...___ ___

© Copyright HAMMOND INCORPORATED, Maplewood, N.J.

AREA 2,966,136 sq. mi. (7,682,300 sq. km.)
POPULATION 15,602,156
CAPITAL Canberra
LARGEST CITY Sydney
HIGHEST POINT Mt. Kosciusko 7,310 ft.
(2,228 m.)
LOWEST POINT Lake Eyre -39 ft. (-12 m.)
MONETARY UNIT Australian dollar
MAJOR LANGUAGE English
MAJOR RELIGIONS Protestantism,
Roman Catholicism

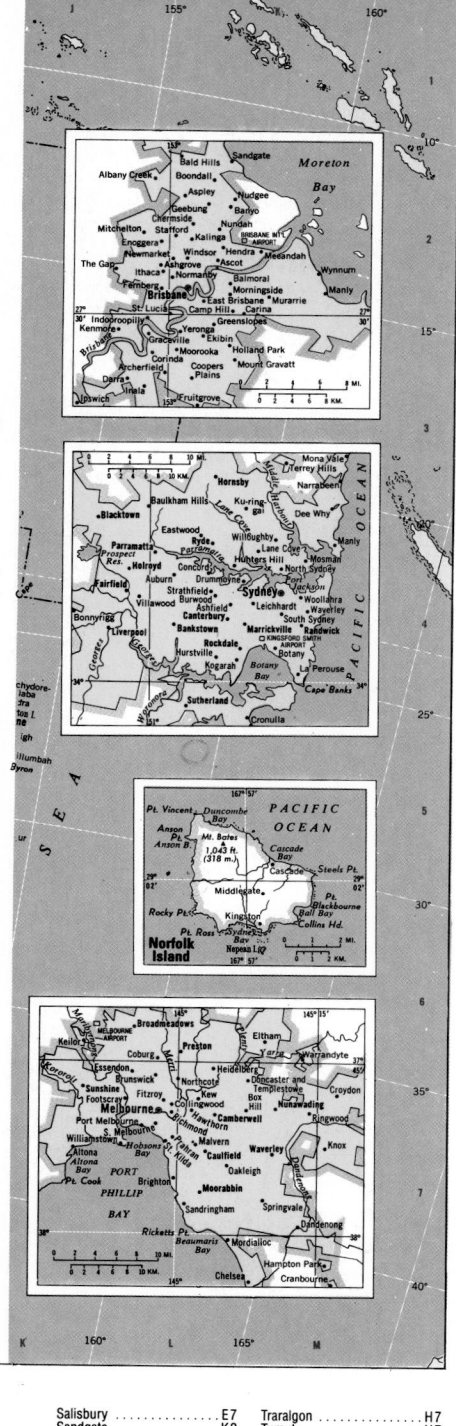

Inset maps (left column):

Brisbane area: Albany Creek, Bald Hills, Sandgate, Moreton Bay, Boondall, Aspley, Nudgee, Geebung, Bayro, Mitchelton, Chermside, Stafford, Nundah, Enoggera, Kalinga, Brisbane Int'l Airport, Newmarket, Windsor, Ascot, Hendra, Meeandah, The Gap, Ithaca, Ashgrove, Wynnum, Fernberg, Normanby, Balmoral, Brisbane, Morningside, Manly, St. Lucia, East Brisbane, Murarrie, Camp Hill, Carina, Indooroopilly, Greenslopes, Kenmore, Yeronga, Ekibin, Gracoville, Moorooka, Holland Park, Corinda, Coopers, Mount Gravatt, Archerfield, Plains, Darra, Inala, Fruitgrove, Ipswich

Sydney area: Mona Vale, Narrabeen, Hornsby, Terrey Hills, Baulkham Hills, Ku-ring-gai, Dee Why, Blacktown, Eastwood, Ryde, Willoughby, Lane Cove, Mosman, Parramatta, Concord, Hunters Hill, North Sydney, Prospect Res., Holroyd, Drummoyne, Port Jackson, Fairfield, Auburn, Strathfield, Burwood, Ashfield, Sydney, Woollahra, Waverley, Canterbury, Leichhardt, South Sydney, Randwick, Bonnyrigg, Liverpool, Bankstown, Marrickville, Rockdale, Kingsford Smith Airport, Botany, Hurstville, Kogarah, Botany Bay, La Perouse, Sutherland, Cape Banks, Cronulla

Norfolk Island: Pt. Vincent, Duncombe Bay, Anson Pt., Anson B., Mt. Bates 1,043 ft. (318 m.), Cascade Bay, Cascade, Steels Pt., Middlegate, Blackbourne, Rocky Pt., Kingston, Ball Bay, Pt. Ross, Sydney B., Collins Hd., Nepean I.

Melbourne area: Melbourne Airport, Broadmeadows, Keilor, Eltham, Coburg, Preston, Yarra, Warrandyte, Essendon, Brunswick, Northcote, Heidelberg, Sunshine, Fitzroy, Doncaster and Templestowe, Croydon, Footscray, Collingwood, Kew, Box Hill, Nunawading, Ringwood, Port Melbourne, Richmond, Hawthorn, Camberwell, S. Melbourne, Malvern, Knox, Williamstown, Prahran, Caulfield, Waverley, Oakleigh, Altona, Brighton, Moorabbin, Hobsons Bay, Pt. Cook, Port Phillip Bay, Sandringham, Springvale, Dandenong, Ricketts Pt., Beaumaris Bay, Mordialloc, Hampton Park, Cranbourne, Chelsea

*City and suburbs.
†Population of met. area.
‡Population of urban area.

Population Distribution

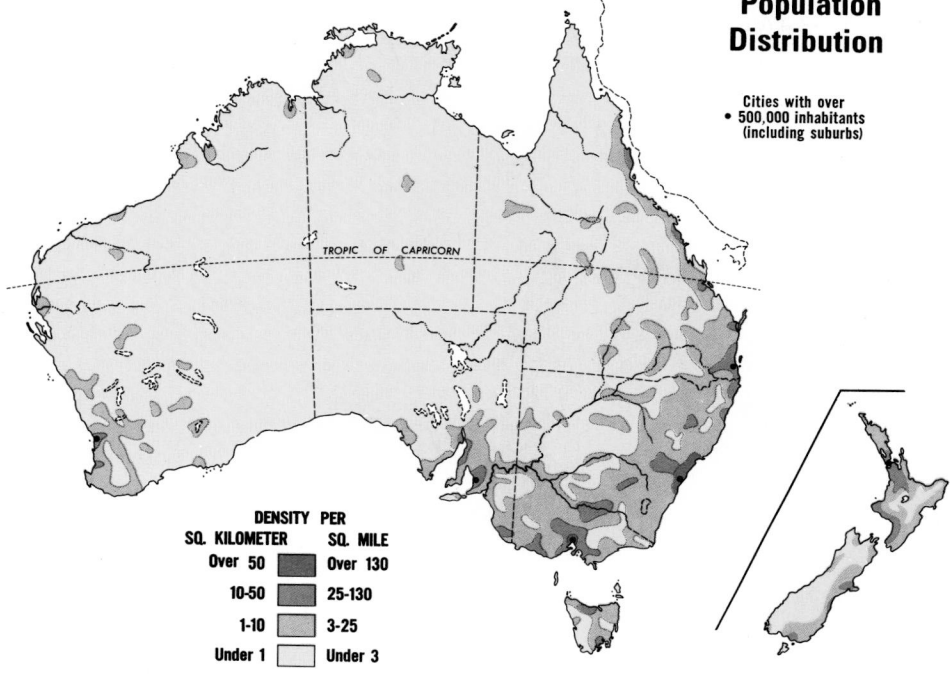

Cities with over
• 500,000 inhabitants
(including suburbs)

DENSITY PER

SQ. KILOMETER	SQ. MILE
Over 50	Over 130
10-50	25-130
1-10	3-25
Under 1	Under 3

TROPIC OF CAPRICORN

Vegetation

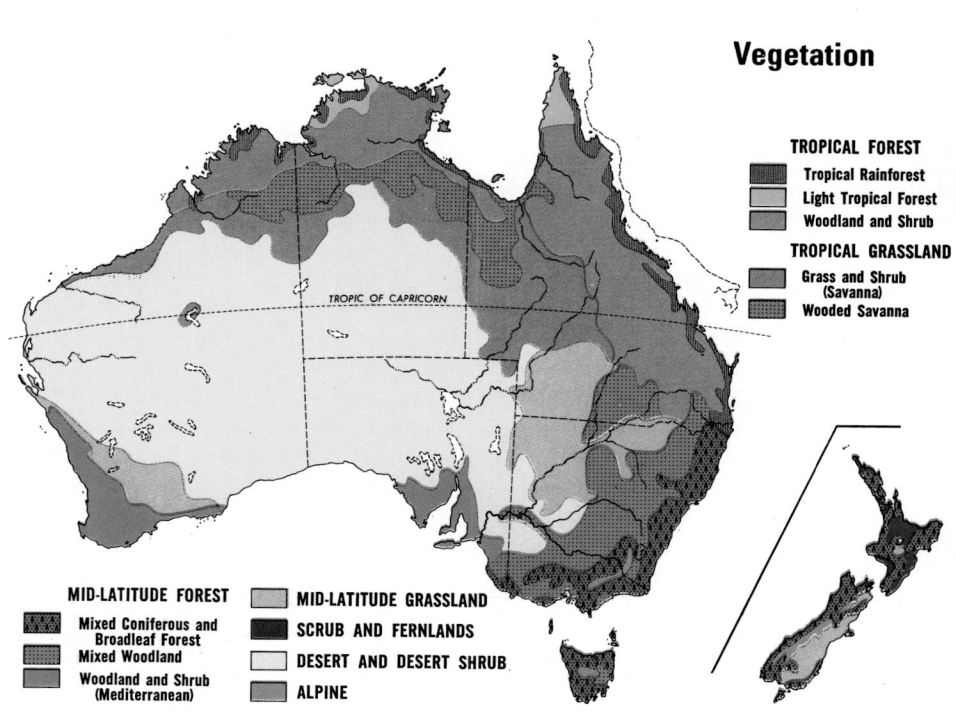

TROPIC OF CAPRICORN

TROPICAL FOREST
- Tropical Rainforest
- Light Tropical Forest
- Woodland and Shrub

TROPICAL GRASSLAND
- Grass and Shrub (Savanna)
- Wooded Savanna

MID-LATITUDE FOREST
- Mixed Coniferous and Broadleaf Forest
- Mixed Woodland
- Woodland and Shrub (Mediterranean)

- MID-LATITUDE GRASSLAND
- SCRUB AND FERNLANDS
- DESERT AND DESERT SHRUB
- ALPINE

Average January Temperature

Darwin 83°
Derby 88°
Onslow 85°
Cairns 81°
Alice Springs 82°
Perth 74°
Kalgoorlie 78°
Albany 63°
Brisbane 77°
Broken Hill 79°
Adelaide 72°
Sydney 70°
Melbourne 67°
Hobart 62°

Auckland 66°
Dunedin 60°

Tropic of Capricorn

FAHRENHEIT	CELSIUS
Over 86°	Over 30°
68° to 86°	20° to 30°
50° to 68°	10° to 20°
32° to 50°	0° to 10°
Under 32°	Under 0°

• Sydney 70°   Average January temperature in degrees Fahrenheit at selected stations

Average July Temperature

Darwin 76°
Derby 72°
Onslow 63°
Cairns 70°
Alice Springs 52°
Perth 55°
Kalgoorlie 52°
Albany 53°
Brisbane 59°
Broken Hill 51°
Adelaide 52°
Sydney 54°
Melbourne 49°
Hobart 46°

Auckland 52°
Dunedin 43°

Tropic of Capricorn

FAHRENHEIT	CELSIUS
Over 68°	20° to 30°
50° to 68°	10° to 20°
32° to 50°	0° to 10°
Under 32°	Under 0°

• Sydney 54°   Average July temperature in degrees Fahrenheit at selected stations

Rainfall

Thursday Island 66
Darwin 60
Derby 23
Cairns 86
Tennant Creek 15
Cloncurry 19
Mackay 63
Onslow 12
South Tropic Line (Tropic of Capricorn)
Alice Springs 12
Geraldton 19
Kalgoorlie 9
William Creek 5
Brisbane 45
Perth 36
Broken Hill 9
Albany 37
Adelaide 20
Albury 29
Sydney 47
Melbourne 26
Hobart 25

Auckland 48
Hokitika 116
Wellington 48
Dunedin 36

AVERAGE ANNUAL RAINFALL	
INCHES	CENTIMETERS
Over 80	Over 200
60 to 80	150 to 200
40 to 60	100 to 150
20 to 40	50 to 100
10 to 20	25 to 50
Under 10	Under 25

• Sydney 47   Average annual rainfall in inches at selected stations

DOMINANT LAND USE

- Cereals (chiefly wheat), Livestock
- Dairy, Truck Farming
- Cash Crops, Horticulture, Fruit
- Pasture Livestock
- Range Livestock
- Forests
- Nonagricultural Land

MAJOR MINERAL OCCURRENCES

Ab	Asbestos	Na	Salt
Ag	Silver	Ni	Nickel
Al	Bauxite	O	Petroleum
Au	Gold	Op	Opals
C	Coal	P	Phosphates
Cu	Copper	Pb	Lead
D	Diamonds	S	Sulfur, Pyrites
Fe	Iron Ore	Sb	Antimony
G	Natural Gas	Sn	Tin
Gp	Gypsum	Ti	Titanium
Lg	Lignite	U	Uranium
Ls	Limestone	W	Tungsten
Mg	Magnesium	Zn	Zinc
Mi	Mica	Zr	Zirconium
Mn	Manganese		

⚡ Water Power
▧ Major Industrial Areas

Agriculture, Industry and Resources

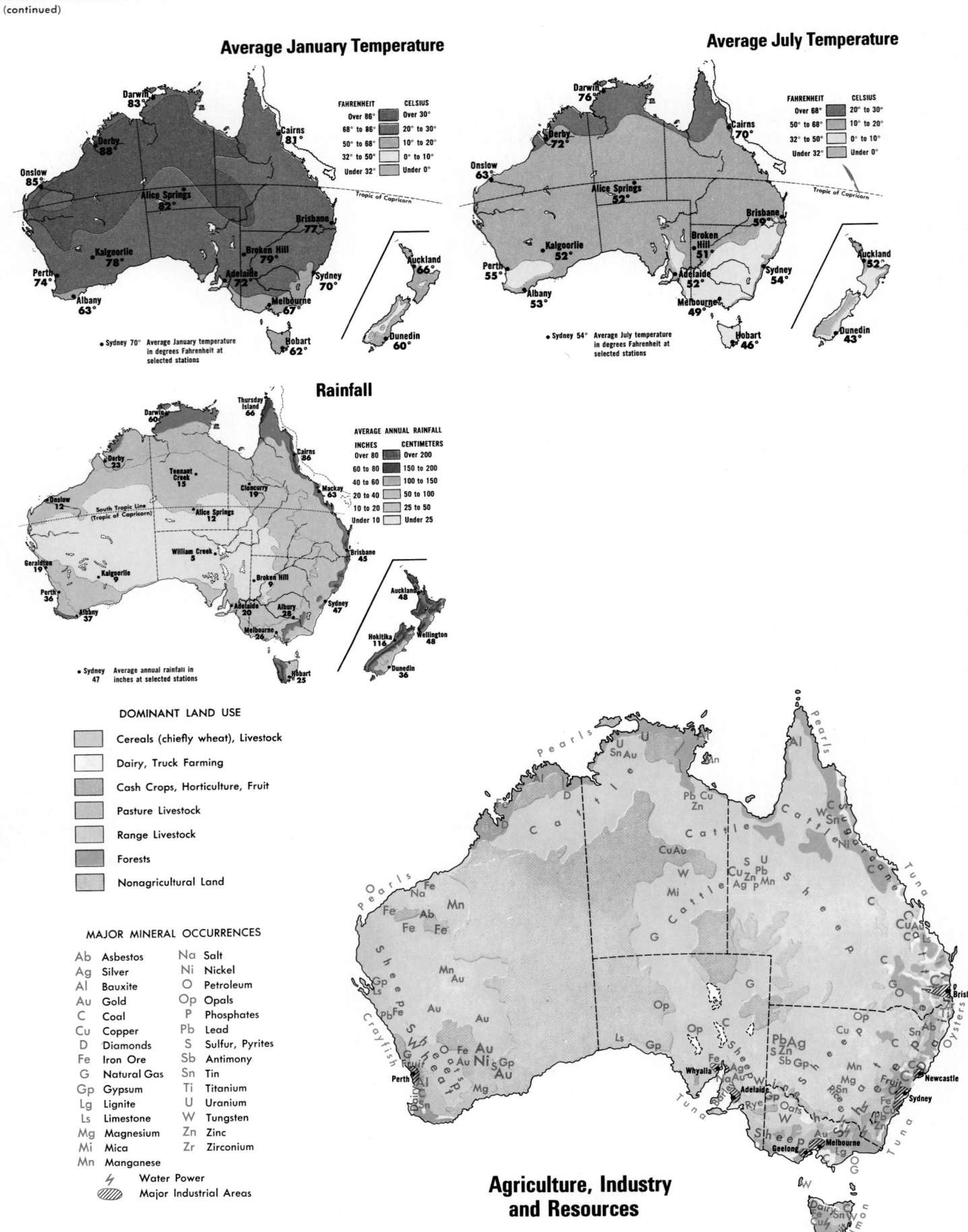

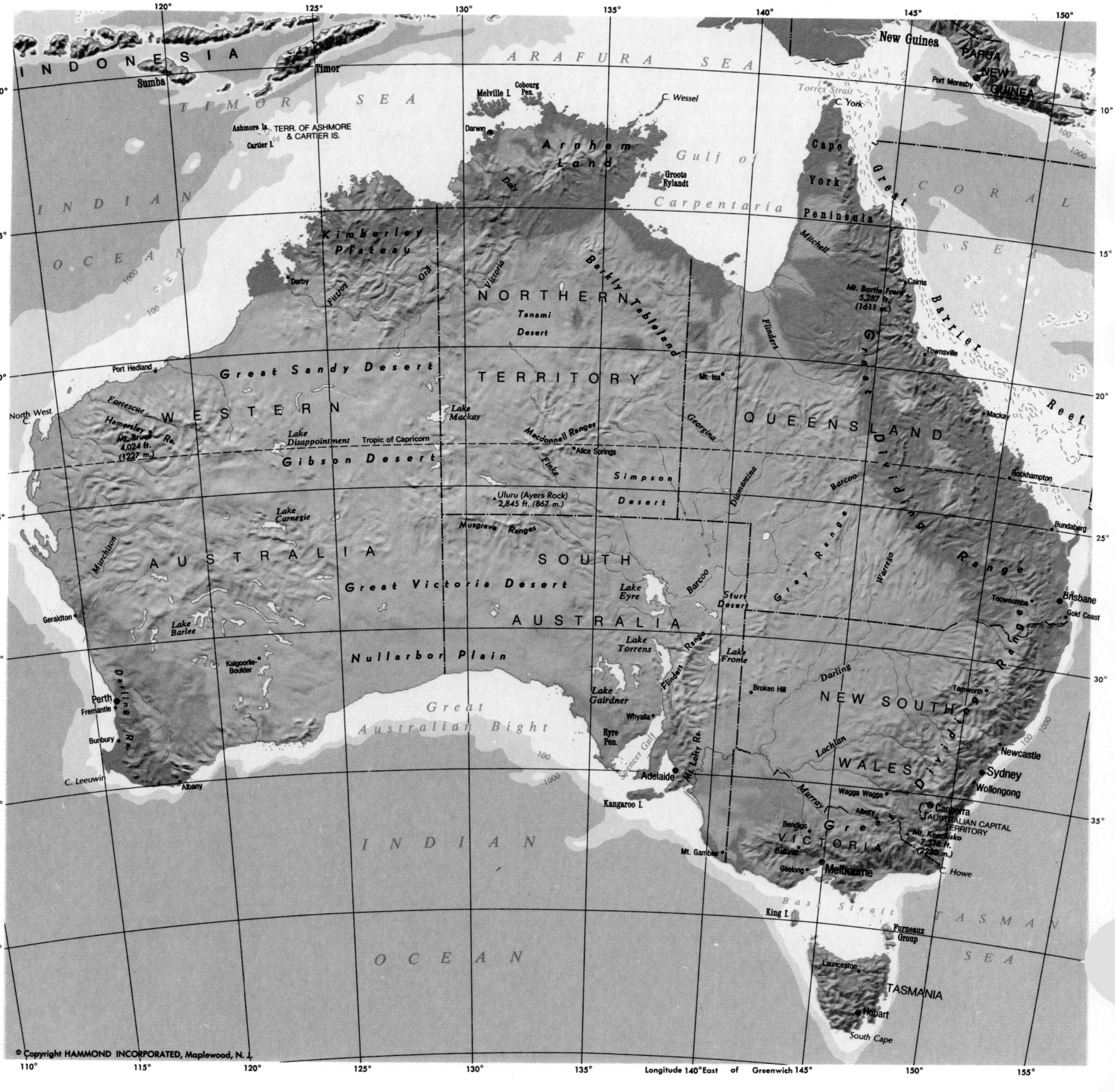

Vegetation/Relief

INDONESIA
Sumba
Timor
ARAFURA SEA
New Guinea
PAPUA NEW GUINEA
Port Moresby

Ashmore Is. TERR. OF ASHMORE & CARTIER IS.
Cartier I.

TIMOR SEA

Melville I.
Cobourg Pen.
C. Wessel
Darwin
Arnhem Land
Gulf of Carpentaria

INDIAN OCEAN

Kimberley Plateau
Derby
Fitzroy
Ord
Victoria
Daly

NORTHERN

Cape York
Great Barrier Reef
CORAL SEA

Port Hedland
North West C.
Great Sandy Desert
TERRITORY
Tanami Desert
Berkly Tableland
Mitchell
Mt. Bartle Frere 5,287 ft. (1611 m.)
Cairns
Townsville

WESTERN
Fortescue
Hamersley Ra.
Mt. Bruce 4,024 ft. (1227 m.)
Lake Disappointment
Tropic of Capricorn
Gibson Desert
Lake Mackay
Macdonnell Ranges
Alice Springs
Finke
Simpson Desert
Mt. Isa
Georgina
QUEENSLAND
Flinders
Mackay
Rockhampton

AUSTRALIA
Lake Carnegie
Uluru (Ayers Rock) 2,845 ft. (867 m.)
Musgrave Ranges
SOUTH
Diamantina
Barcoo
Warrego
Bundaberg

Geraldton
Lake Barlee
Great Victoria Desert
AUSTRALIA
Lake Eyre
Sturt Desert
Grey Range
Brisbane
Toowoomba
Gold Coast

Kalgoorlie-Boulder
Nullarbor Plain
Lake Torrens
Lake Frome
Darling
NEW SOUTH
Tamworth

Perth
Darling Ra.
Fremantle
Bunbury
Lake Gairdner
Flinders Range
Broken Hill
WALES
Lachlan
Newcastle

C. Leeuwin
Albany
Great Australian Bight
Whyalla
Eyre Pen.
Spencer Gulf
Mt. Lofty Ra.
Murray
Wagga Wagga
Albury
Sydney
Wollongong

INDIAN
Adelaide
Kangaroo I.
VICTORIA
Bendigo
Ballarat
Geelong
Melbourne
Canberra AUSTRALIAN CAPITAL TERRITORY
Mt. Kosciusko 7,316 ft. (2230 m.)
C. Howe

OCEAN
Mt. Gambier
King I.
Furneaux Group
Bass Strait
TASMAN SEA

Launceston
TASMANIA
Hobart
South Cape

© Copyright HAMMOND INCORPORATED, Maplewood, N. J.

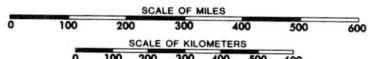

SCALE OF MILES
0 100 200 300 400 500 600
SCALE OF KILOMETERS
0 100 200 300 400 500 600

Capital of Country..⊛
State and Territorial Capitals...........................●
International Boundaries...............................——
State and Territorial Boundaries...............
Elevations in Feet   Depths in Fathoms

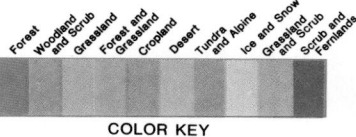

Forest
Woodland and Scrub
Grassland
Forest and Grassland
Cropland
Desert
Tundra and Alpine
Ice and Snow
Grassland and Scrub
Scrub and Fernlands

COLOR KEY

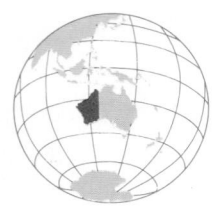

AREA 975,096 sq. mi.
(2,525,500 sq. km.)
POPULATION 1,406,929
CAPITAL Perth
LARGEST CITY Perth
HIGHEST POINT Mt. Bruce 4,024 ft.
(1,227 m.)

Topography

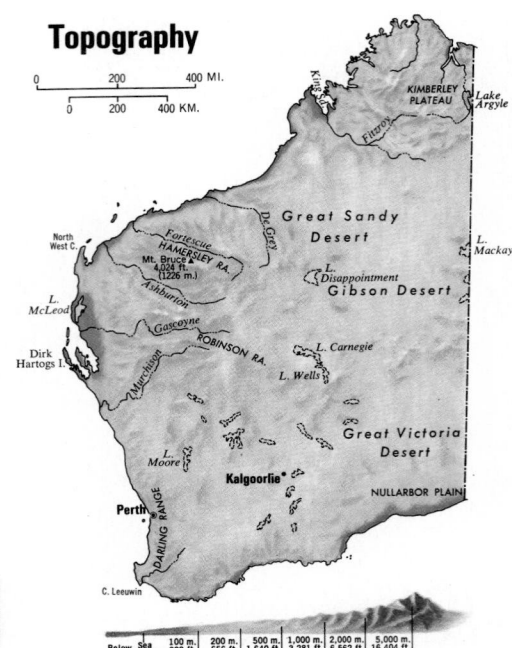

Manjimup 4,150	B6
Marble Bar 357	C3
Margaret River 798	A6
Meekatharra 989	B4
Melville 61,211	A1
Menzies 232	C5
Merredin 3,520	B5
Mingenew 368	A5
Moora 1,677	B5
Morawa 694	B5
Mount Barker 1,519	B6
Mount Magnet 618	B5
Mukinbudin 370	B5
Mullewa 918	A5
Mundijong 356	A2
Nannup 552	B6
Narrogin 4,969	B2
Nedlands 20,257	A1
Newman 5,466	B3
New Norcia	A5
Norseman 1,895	C6
Northam 6,791	B1
Northampton 750	A5
Northcliffe	B6
Nungarin ○332	B5
Onslow 594	A3
Pannawonica 1,170	B3
Paraburdoo 2,357	B3
Pardoo	B3
Pemberton 871	A6
Perenjori 257	A5
Perth (cap.) 809,035	A1
Perth *898,918	A1
Pingelly 937	B2
Pinjarra 1,336	A2
Port Denison-Dongara 1,155	A5
Port Hedland 12,948	B3
Quairading 741	B1
Ravensthorpe 327	B6
Rockingham 24,932	A2
Roebourne 1,688	B3

CITIES and TOWNS

Albany 15,222	B6	Coorow 226	B5
Augusta 588	A6	Corrigin 841	B6
Australind 1,681	A2	Cranbrook 316	B6
Balladonia	D6	Cue 320	B4
Beverley 756	B1	Cuballing ○647	B2
Boddington 367	B2	Cunderdin 731	B5
Boulder-Kalgoorlie 19,848	C5	Dalwallinu 639	B5
Boyanup 365	A2	Dampier 2,471	B3
Bridgetown 1,521	B6	Dandaragan ○1,748	A5
Brookton 595	B2	Darkan 242	B2
Broome 3,666	C2	Denham 402	A4
Bruce Rock 565	B5	Denmark 985	B6
Brunswick Junction 889	A2	Derby 2,933	C2
Bunbury 21,749	A2	Dongara-Port Denison 1,155	A5
Busselton 6,463	A6	Donnybrook 1,197	A2
Canning 52,816	A1	Dwellingup 453	A2
Capel 680	A2	Esperance 6,375	C6
Carnamah 422	A5	Eucla	E5
Carnarvon 5,053	A4	Exmouth 2,583	D2
Collie 7,667	B2	Fitzroy Crossing	D2
Coolgardie 891	C5	Fremantle 22,484	A1
		Geraldton 20,895	A5
		Gingin 382	A1
		Gnowangerup 872	B6

Goldsworthy 923	B3		
Goomalling 600	B1		
Halls Creek 966	D2		
Harvey 2,479	A2		
Hopetoun	C6		
Hyden	B6		
Jarrahdale 315	B2		
Kalbarri 820	A4		
Kalgoorlie 9,145	C5		
Kalgoorlie-Boulder 19,848	C5		
Kambalda 4,463	C5		
Karratha 8,341	B3		
Katanning 4,413	B6		
Kellerberrin 1,091	B5		
Kojonup 544	B6		
Koolyanobbing 277	B5		
Kununurra 2,081	E2		
Kwinana New Town 12,355	A1		
Lake Grace 575	B6		
Laverton 872	C5		
Learmonth	A3		
Leonora 524	C5		
Madura	D5		
Mandurah 10,978	A2		

OTHER FEATURES

Sandstone ○133	B4	Exmouth (gulf)	A3
Shay Gap 853	C3	Fitzroy (riv.)	D2
Southern Cross 798	B5	Flinders (bay)	A6
South Perth 31,524	A1	Forrest River Aboriginal Res.	D1
Stirling 161,858	A1	Fortescue (riv.)	B3
Three Springs 638	A5	Garden (isl)	A1
Tom Price 3,540	B3	Gascoyne (riv.)	B4
Toodyay 560	B1	Geelvink (chan.)	A5
Turkey Creek 212	E2	Geographe (bay)	A6
Wagin 1,488	B2	Geographe (chan.)	A4
Walpole 291	B6	Gibson (des.)	D3
Wandering ○470	B2	Great Australian (bight)	E6
Wanneroo 6,745	A2	Great Sandy (des.)	C3
Waroona 1,462	A2	Great Victoria (des.)	D5
Wickepin 267	B2	Hamersley (range)	B3
Wickham 2,387	B3	Hann (mt.)	D1
Williams 453	B2	Hopkins (lake)	E4
Wiluna 221	C4	Houtman Abrolhos (isls.)	A5
Wittenoom 247	B3	Indian Ocean	A5
Wongan Hills 947	B5	Johnston, The (lakes)	C6
Wundowie 720	A1	Joseph Bonaparte (gulf)	E1
Wyalkatchem 453	B5	Kimberley (plat.)	D2
Wyndham 1,509	E1	King (sound)	C2
Yalgoo ○315	B5	King Leopold (range)	D2
Yampi Sound	C2	Koolan (isl.)	C1
York 1,136	B1	Leeuwin (cape)	A6
		Le Grand (cape)	C6
OTHER FEATURES		Lévêque (cape)	C2
		Londonderry (cape)	D1
Adele (isl.)	C1	Lyons (riv.)	A4
Admiralty (gulf)	D1	Macdonald (lake)	E3
Aloysius (mt.)	E4	Mackay (lake)	E3
Argyle (lake)	E2	McLeod (lake)	A4
Arid (cape)	C6	Minigwal (lake)	C5
Ashburton (riv.)	A3	Monte Bello (isls.)	A3
Augustus (mt.)	B4	Moore (lake)	B5
Austin (lake)	B4	Murchison (riv.)	B4
Australia Aboriginal Res.	E4	Murray (riv.)	A2
Bald (head)	B6	Naturaliste (cape)	A6
Balwina Aboriginal Res.	E3	Naturaliste (chan.)	A4
Barlee (lake)	B5	North West (cape)	A3
Barrow (isl.)	A3	North-West Aboriginal Res.	E4
Beaglebay Aboriginal Res.	C2	Nullarbor (plain)	D5
Bluff Knoll (mt.)	B6	Oakover (riv.)	C3
Bonaparte (arch.)	D1	Ord (mt.)	D2
Bougainville (cape)	D1	Ord (riv.)	E2
Brassey (range)	B3	Percival (lakes)	D3
Bruce (mt.)	B3	Peron (pen.)	A4
Brunswick (bay)	D1	Petermann (ranges)	E4
Buccaneer (arch.)	C2	Rason (lake)	D5
Carey (lake)	C5	Rebecca (lake)	C5
Carnegie (lake)	C4	Recherche (arch.)	C6
Central Aboriginal Res.	E3	Robinson (ranges)	B4
Churchman (mt.)	C1	Roebuck (bay)	C2
Collier (bay)	C1	Rottnest (isl.)	A1
Cosmo Newbery Aboriginal Res.	C5	Saint George (ranges)	D2
Cowan (lake)	C5	Shark (bay)	A4
Cundeelee Aboriginal Res.	C5	Southesk Tablelands	D3
Dale (mt.)	B1	Sturt (creek)	D2
Dampier (arch.)	B3	Swan (riv.)	A1
Dampier Land (reg.)	C2	Timor (sea)	D1
Darling (range)	A1	Tomkinson (ranges)	E4
De Grey (riv.)	B3	Wanna (lakes)	E5
D'Entrecasteaux (pt.)	A6	Warburton Aboriginal Res.	D4
Dirk Hartogs (isl.)	A4	Way (lake)	C4
Disappointment (lake)	C3	Weld (range)	B4
Drysdale (riv.)	D1	Wells (lake)	C4
Dundas (lake)	C6	Whaleback (mt.)	B3
Egerton (mt.)	B4	Wooramel (riv.)	A4
Eighty Mile (beach)	C2	York (sound)	D1
Enid (mt.)	B3		
Esperance (bay)	C6		

○ Population of district.
*Population of met. area.

Western Australia

SCALE OF MILES

KILOMETERS

State Capital ◉
State and Territorial Boundaries _____ — · —

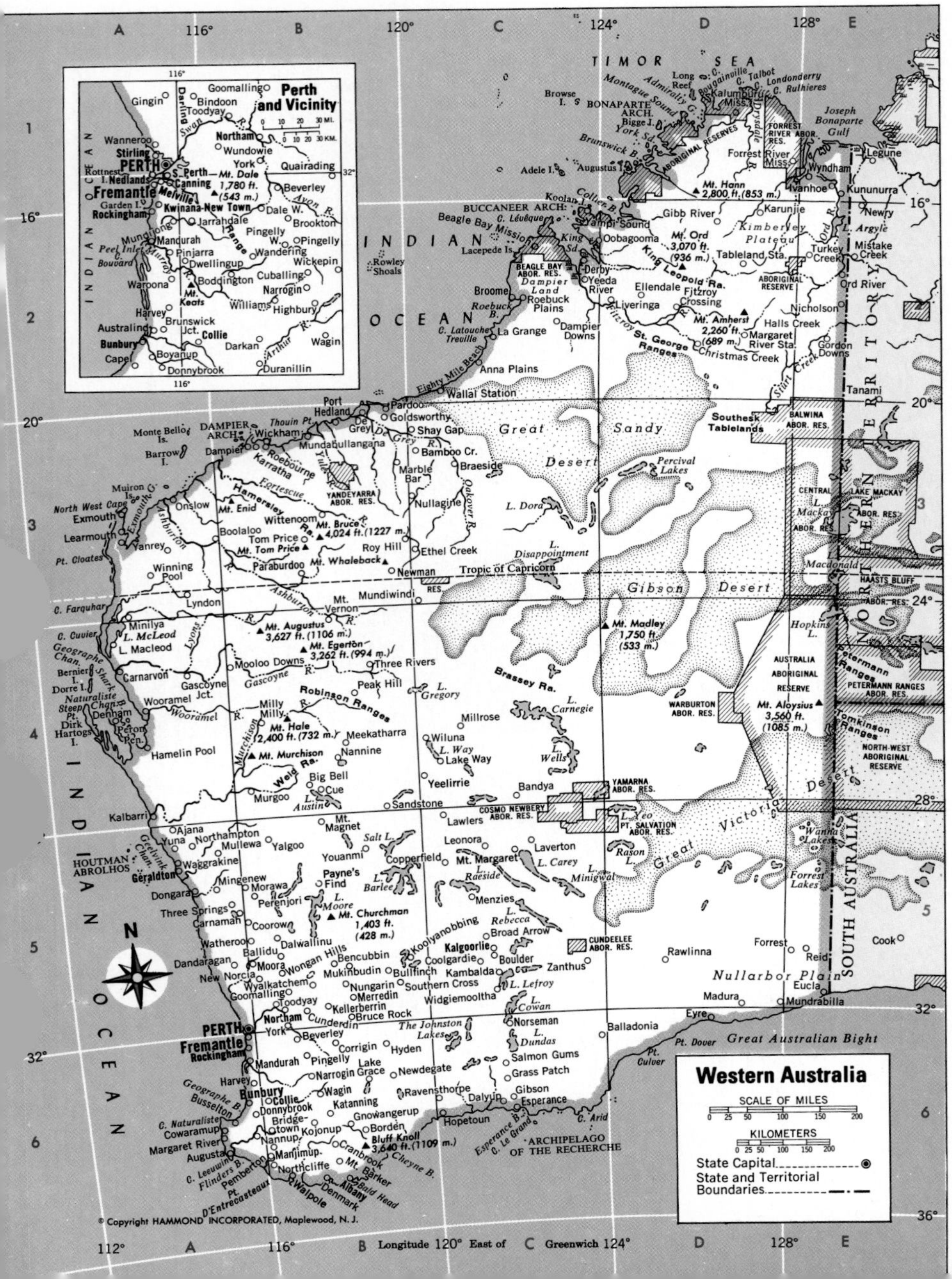

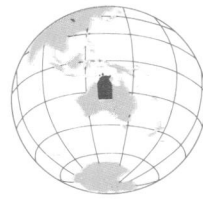

CITIES and TOWNS

Adelaide River B2
Aileron C7
Alice Springs 18,395 .... D7
Alyangula 1,181 .... E2
Angurugu 597 .... E3
Anthony Lagoon D4
Areyonga C8
Arltunga D7
Avon Downs E5
Bamyili-Beswick 685 .... C3
Banka Banka C5
Barrow Creek D6
Batchelor B2
Bathurst Island 1,032 .... B1
Birdum C3
Birrimbah C3
Birrindudu A5
Borroloola 420 .... E4
Bundooma D8
Burramurra E6
Charlotte Waters D8
Claravale B3
Coniston C7
Coolibah B3
Creswell Downs E4
Croker Island Mission C1
Daly River B2
Daly Waters C4
Darwin (cap.) 56,482 .... B2
Docker River 217 .... A8
Elliott C4
Epenarra D6
Erldunda C8
Eva Downs D5
Ewaninga D7
Goulburn Island 277 .... C1
Gove (Nhulunbuy) 3,879 .... E2
Harts Range D7
Hatches Creek D6
Helen Springs C5
Henbury C8
Hermannsburg 541 .... C7
Hooker Creek 671 .... B5
Humpty Doo B2
Katherine 3,737 .... B3
Kildurk A4
Koolpinyah B2
Kulgera C8
Kurundi D6
Lake Nash E6
Larrimah C3
Legune A3
Limbunya B4
Lucy Creek E7
Mainoru C3
Maningrida 702 .... C2
Mataranka C3
Milingimbi 564 .... D2
Mistake Creek A4
Montejinnie C4
Mount Cavenagh C8
Mount Doreen B7
Murray Downs D6
Napperby C7
Newcastle Waters C4
Nhulunbuy 3,879 .... E2
Numbulwar 422 .... D3
Oenpelli 452 .... C2
O. T. Downs D4
Papunya 635 .... B7
Pine Creek 214 .... C2
Plenty River Mine D7
Port Keats 819 .... A3
Powell Creek C5
Rankine Store E5
Robinson River E4
Rockhampton Downs D5
Rodinga D8
Rum Jungle B2
Santa Teresa 479 .... D8
Soudan E6
Stirling Station C6
Tanami A5
Tarlton Downs E7
Tea Tree Well C7
Tempe Downs C8
Tennant Creek 3,118 .... C5
The Granites B6
Top Springs C4
Ucharonidge D4
Umbakumba 247 .... E3
Umbeara C8
Urapunga D3
Utopia D7
Victoria River Downs B4
Warrabri 459 .... D6
Warrego 991 .... C5
Wave Hill B4
White Quartz Hill D7
Willeroo B3
Willowra C6
Wollogorang F4
Yambah C7
Yirrkala 543 .... E2
Yuendumu 687 .... B7

OTHER FEATURES

Amadeus (lake) B8
Arafura (sea) D1
Arnhem (cape) E2
Arnhem Land (reg.) D2
Arnhem Land Aboriginal Res. C2
Arnold (riv.) D3
Barkly Tableland D4
Bathurst (isl.) A1
Beagle (gulf) A2
Beatrice (cape) E3
Bennett (lake) B7
Beswick Aboriginal Res. C3
Bickerton (Isl.) E2
Blaze (pt.) A2
Carpentaria (gulf) E3
Central Wedge (mt.) C7
Clarence (str.) B2
Cobourg (pen.) C1
Conner (mt.) B8
Croker (cape) C1
Daly (riv.) B2
Daly River Aboriginal Res. A2
Davenport (mt.) B7
Dundas (str.) B1
East Alligator (riv.) C2
Ehrenberg (range) B7
Elcho (isl.) D1
Finke (riv.) C8
Fitzmaurice (riv.) B3
Ford (cape) A2
Georgina (riv.) E6
Goulburn (isls.) C1
Goyder (riv.) D2
Groote Eylandt (isl.) 2,230 .... E3
Haasts Bluff Aboriginal Res. B7
Hale (riv.) D8
Hanson (riv.) C6
Hay (dry riv.) E7
Hogarth (mt.) E6
Hopkins (lake) A8
Joseph Bonaparte (gulf) A3
Kata Tjuta (Olga) (mt.) B8
Katherine (riv.) C3
Lake MacKay Aboriginal Res. A6
Lander (riv.) C6
Leisler (mt.) A7
Limmen Bight (riv.) D4
Macdonald (lake) B7
Macdonnell (ranges) C7
MacKay (lake) A7
Mann (riv.) D2
Marshall (riv.) D7
Melville (bay) E2
Melville (isl.) B1
Murchison (range) D6
Napier (mt.) A4
Neale (lake) A8
Newcastle (creek) C4
Nicholson (riv.) E5
Peron (isls.) A2
Petermann (ranges) A8
Petermann Ranges Aboriginal Res. A8
Port Darwin (inlet) B2
Ranken (riv.) E6
Robinson (riv.) E4
Roper (riv.) C3
Sandover (riv.) D6
Simpson (des.) E8
Singleton (mt.) B6
Sir Edward Pellew Group (isls.) E3
South Alligator (riv.) C2
Stanley (mt.) B7
Stewart (cape) D1
Stirling (creek) A4
Sturt (plain) C4
Tanami (des.) C5
Timor (sea) A2
Todd (riv.) D8
Uluru Nat'l Park B8
Vanderlin (isl.) E3
Van Diemen (cape) A1
Van Diemen (gulf) B1
Victoria (riv.) B3
Wagait Aboriginal Res B2
Warwick (chan.) E3
Wessel (cape) E1
Wessel (isls.) E1
West Baines (riv.) A4
White (lake) A6
Woods (lake) C4
Young (mt.) D3
Ziel (mt.) C7

AREA 519,768 sq. mi. (1,346,200 sq. km.)
POPULATION 154,848
CAPITAL Darwin
LARGEST CITY Darwin
HIGHEST POINT Mt. Ziel 4,955 ft. (1,510 m.)

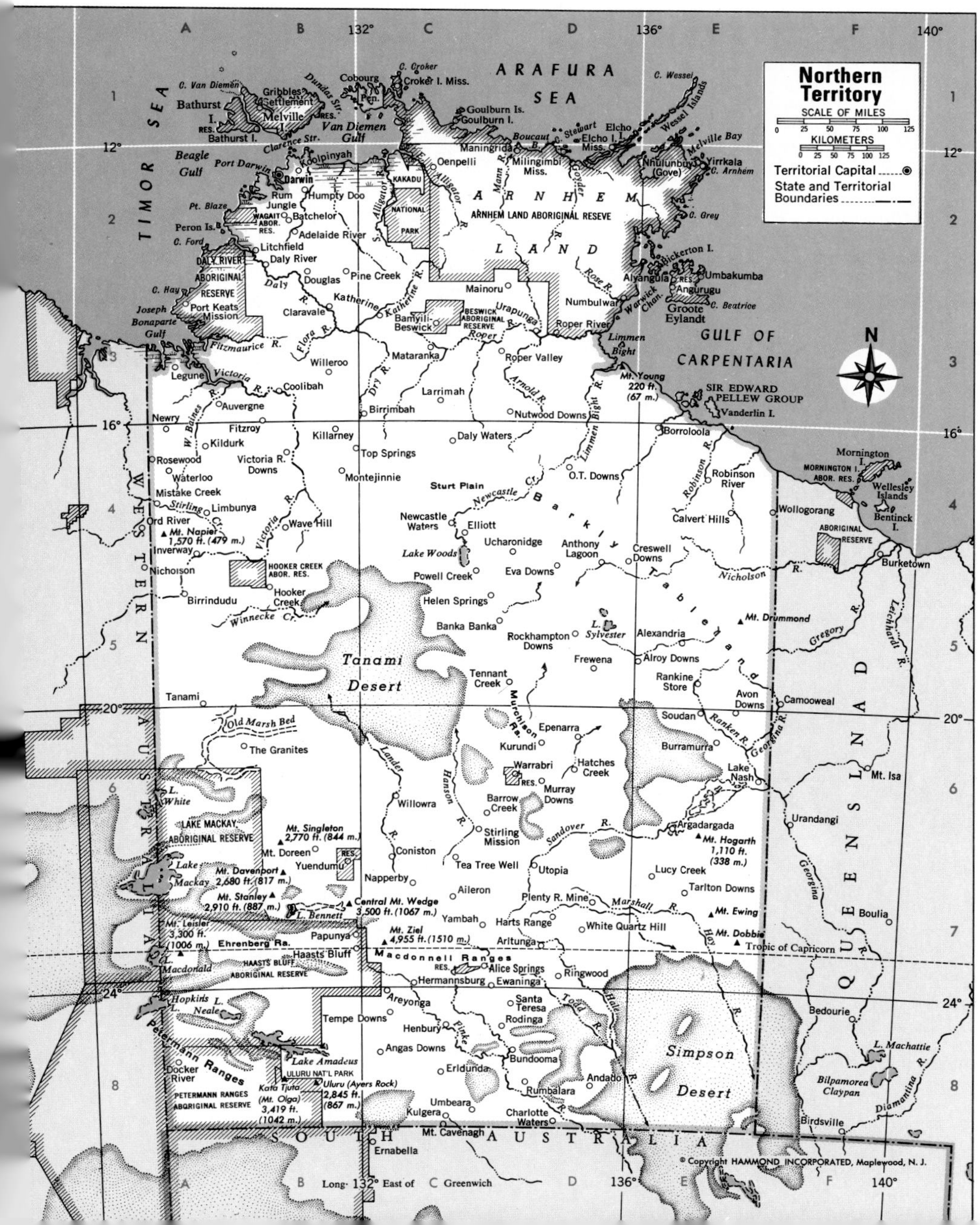

Northern Territory
SCALE OF MILES
0 25 50 75 100 125
KILOMETERS
0 25 50 75 100 125
Territorial Capital
State and Territorial Boundaries
A R A F U R A S E A
T I M O R S E A
GULF OF CARPENTARIA
A R N H E M L A N D
ARNHEM LAND ABORIGINAL RESERVE
Barkly Tableland
Tanami Desert
Simpson Desert
Sturt Plain
Macdonnell Ranges
Darwin
Alice Springs
Katherine
Tennant Creek
Mt. Ziel 4,955 ft. (1510 m.)
Tropic of Capricorn
W E S T E R N A U S T R A L I A
Q U E E N S L A N D
S O U T H A U S T R A L I A
Long. 132° East of Greenwich
© Copyright HAMMOND INCORPORATED, Maplewood, N. J.

Topography

0 100 200 MI.
0 100 200 KM.
Melville I.
Bathurst I.
Cobourg Pen.
C. Croker
Van Diemen Gulf
Beagle Gulf
Darwin
WESSEL IS.
C. Arnhem
Arnhem Land
Groote Eylandt
Limmen Bight
SIR EDWARD PELLEW GROUP
Joseph Bonaparte Gulf
Daly
Katherine
Roper
Victoria
STURT PLAIN
BARKLY TABLELAND
Tanami Desert
Old Marsh Bed
Lander
Sandover
Lake Mackay
Mt. Ziel 4,955 ft. (1510 m.)
EHRENBERG RA.
MACDONNELL RANGES
Hay
Hale
Finke
Lake Amadeus
Simpson Desert
5,000 m. 16,404 ft.
2,000 m. 6,562 ft.
1,000 m. 3,281 ft.
500 m. 1,640 ft.
200 m. 656 ft.
100 m. 328 ft.
Sea Level
Below

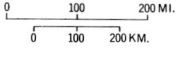

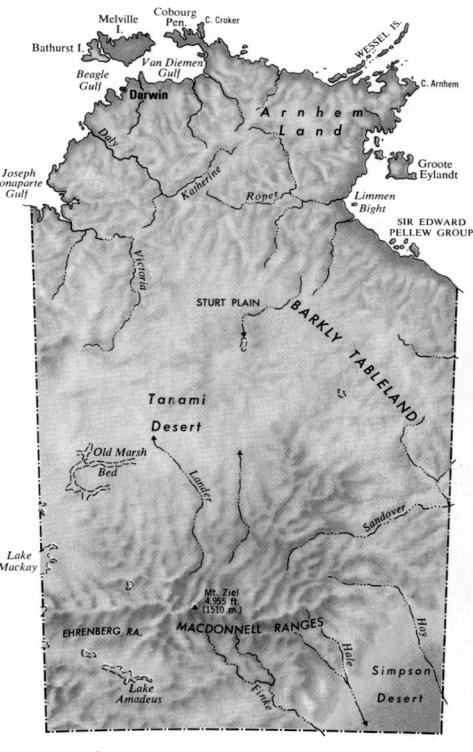

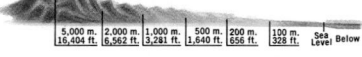

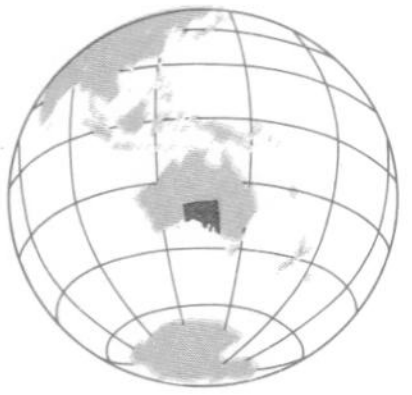

AREA 379,922 sq. mi. (984,000 sq. km.)
POPULATION 1,345,945
CAPITAL Adelaide
LARGEST CITY Adelaide
HIGHEST POINT Mt. Woodroffe 4,970 ft.
(1,515 m.)

Topography

0 100 200 MI.
0 100 200 KM.

Below Sea Level	100 m. 328 ft.	200 m. 656 ft.	500 m. 1,640 ft.	1,000 m. 3,281 ft.	2,000 m. 6,562 ft.	5,000 m. 16,404 ft.

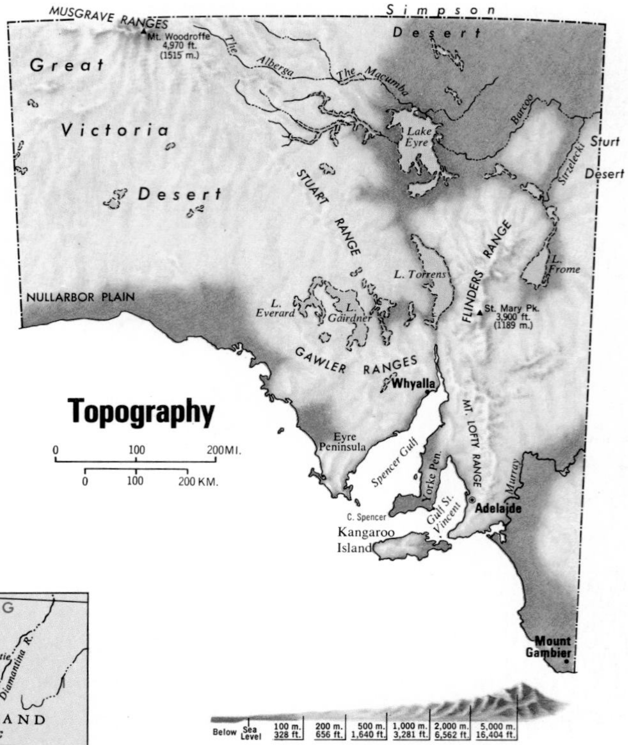

CITIES and TOWNS

Adelaide (cap.) 882,520 .... B6
Adelaide *931,886 .... B6
Andamooka 402 .... E4
Angaston 1,753 .... F6
Balaklava 1,306 .... E5
Barmera 2,014 .... G6
Beachport 357 .... F7
Berri 3,419 .... G6
Birdwood 397 .... C7
Blinman ....
Bordertown 2,138 .... G7
Brighton 19,441 .... A8
Burnside 37,593 .... B8
Burra 1,222 .... F5
Campbelltown 43,084 ...... B7
Ceduna 2,794 .... D5
Clare 2,381 .... F5
Cleve 827 .... E5
Coober Pedy 2,078 .... D3
Cowell 626 .... E5

Crafters-Bridgewater 9,764 .. B8
Crystal Brook 1,240 ...... E5
Cummins 767 .... D6
Edithburgh 359 .... E6
Elizabeth 32,608 .... B7
Elliston ◯1,345 .... D5
Enfield 66,797 .... B7
Gawler 9,433 .... B6
Gladstone 680 .... F5
Glenelg 13,306 .... A8
Gumeracha 387 .... C7
Hahndorf 1,274 .... C8
Hawker 351 .... F4
Hindmarsh 7,593 .... A7
Iron Knob 398 .... E5
Jamestown 1,384 .... F5
Kadina 2,943 .... E5
Kapunda 1,340 .... F6
Keith 1,147 .... G7
Kensington and Norwood
  8,950 .... B8
Kimba 862 .... E5
Kingscote 1,236 .... E6

Kingston 1,325 .... G7
Lameroo 599 .... G6
Laura 504 .... F5
Leigh Creek 1,635 .... F4
Lobethal 1,522 .... C7
Lock 213 .... D5
Loxton 3,100 .... G6
Lyndoch 539 .... C6
Maitland 1,085 .... E6
Mannum 1,984 .... F6
Marion 66,580 .... A8
Marree E3
Meadows 388 .... B8
Meningie 807 .... F6
Millicent 5,255 .... F7
Minlaton 865 .... E6
Mitcham 60,309 .... B8
Moonta 1,751 .... E5
Mount Barker 4,190 .... C8
Mount Gambier 18,193 ..... G7
Murray Bridge 8,664 ...... F6
Nairne 706 .... C8
Nangwarry 758 .... G7

Naracoorte 4,758 .... G7
Noarlunga 60,928 .... A8
Nuriootpa 2,851 .... F6
Oodnadatta D2
Orroroo 604 .... F5
Payneham 16,502 .... B7
Penola 1,205 .... G7
Peterborough 2,575 .... F5
Pinnaroo 731 .... G6
Port Adelaide 35,407 ...... A7
Port Augusta 15,566 .... E5
Port Broughton 587 .... F5
Port Lincoln 9,846 .... E6
Port Pirie 14,695 .... E5
Prospect 18,591 .... B7
Quorn 1,049 .... F5
Renmark 3,475 .... G5
Robe 590 .... F7
Salisbury 86,451 .... B7
Snowtown 492 .... E5
Strathalbyn 1,756 .... F6
Streaky Bay 985 .... D5
Tailem Bend 1,677 .... F6
Tanunda 2,621 .... C6
Tea Tree Gully 67,237 ..... B7
Thebarton 9,208 .... A7
Tumby Bay 933 .... E6
Unley 35,844 .... B8
Uraidla 303 .... B8
Victor Harbor 4,522 .... F6
Virginia 353 .... B7
Waikerie 1,629 .... F6
Wallaroo 2,043 .... E5
West Torrens 45,099 .... A8
Whyalla 30,518 .... E5
Williamstown 495 .... C7
Willunga 667 .... F6
Wilmington 227 .... F6
Woodside 724 .... C8
Woodville 77,634 .... A7
Woomera 1,658 .... E4
Wudinna 572 .... D5
Yorketown 713 .... E6

OTHER FEATURES

Acraman (lake) D5
Alberga, The (riv.) D2
Alexandrina (lake) F6
Anxious (bay) D5
Arckaringa (creek) D2
Barcoo (creek) F3
Birksgate (range) C2
Blanche (lake) F3
Brady (mt.) D3
Cadibarrawirracanna (lake) . D3
Callabonna (lake) F3
Catastrophe (cape) D6
Coffin (bay) D6
Coffin Bay (pen.) D6
Coopers (Barcoo) (creek) .. F3
Coorong, The (lag.) F6
Dey Dey (lake) B3
Encounter (bay) F6
Everard (lake) D4
Everard (ranges) C2
Eyre (pen.) D5
Eyre North (lake) E3
Eyre South (lake) E3
Finke (riv.) C1

Flinders (range) F4
Frome (lake) G4
Gairdner (lake) D4
Gawler (ranges) E5
Gawler (riv.) B6
Gilles (lake) E5
Goyders (lag.) F2
Great Australian (bight) .. A5
Great Victoria (des.) B3
Gregory (lake) F3
Hack (mt.) F4
Hamilton, The (riv.) D2
Harris (lake) D4
Head of Bight (bay) B4
Indian Ocean E7
Investigator (str.) E6
Investigator Group (isls.) . D5
Island (lag.) E4
Jaffa (cape) F7
Kangaroo (isl.) 3,515 ..... E7
Lacepede (bay) F7
Lofty (mt.) B8
Macfarlane (lake) E5
Macumba, The (riv.) E2
Maurice (lake) B3
Meramangye (lake) C3
Morris (mt.) B2
Murray (res.) F6
Musgrave (ranges) B2
Neales, The (riv.) E3
Northumberland (cape) F8
Nukey Bluff (mt.) D5
Nullarbor (plain) A4
Nuyts (arch.) C5
Nuyts (cape) C5
Peera Peera Poolanna (lake) . F2
Saint Mary (peak) F4
Saint Vincent (gulf) F6
Serpentine (lakes) A3
Simpson (des.) E1
Sir Joseph Banks Group
  (isls.) E6
Spencer (cape) E6
Spencer (gulf) E6
Stevenson, The (riv.) D2
Streaky (bay) C5
Strzelecki (creek) G3
Stuart (range) D3
Sturt (des.) G3
The Alberga (riv.) D2
The Coorong (lag.) F6
The Hamilton (riv.) D2
The Macumba (riv.) E2
The Neales (riv.) E3
The Stevenson (riv.) D2
The Warburton (riv.) F2
Thistle (isl.) E6
Torrens (lake) E4
Torrens (riv.) C7
Warburton, The (riv.) F2
Wilkinson (lakes) C3
Woodroffe (mt.) B2
Yalata Aboriginal Res. B4
Yarle (lakes) B4
Yorke (pen.) E6

◯ Population of district.
* Population of met. area.

Adelaide and Vicinity

South Australia
SCALE OF MILES
0 25 50 100 150
KILOMETERS
0 25 50 100 150
State Capital .... ◉
State and Territorial
Boundaries .... ――― ―

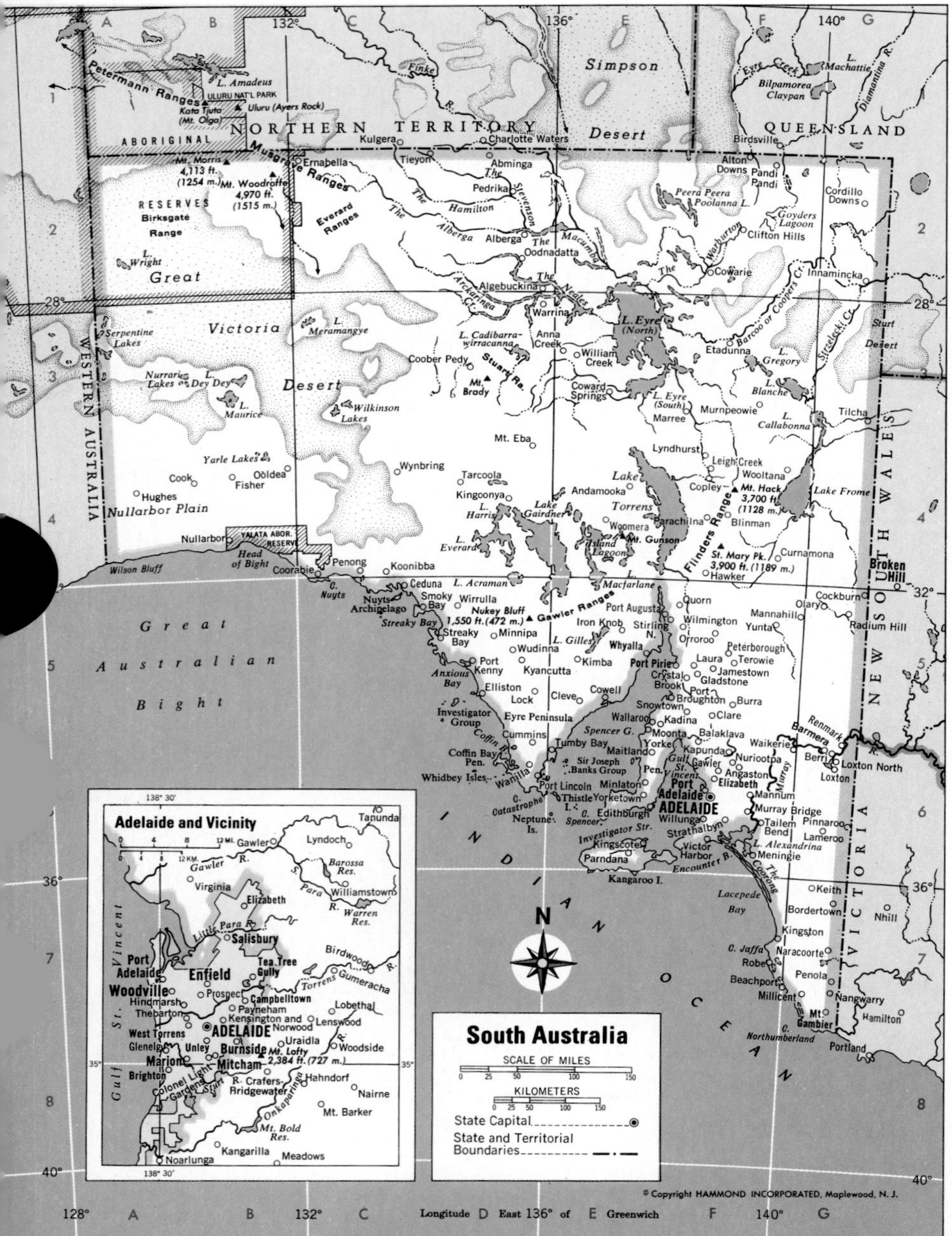

CITIES and TOWNS

Aramac 428	C4
Archerfield 785	D3
Ascot 4,298	E2
Atherton 4,196	C3
Ayr 8,787	C3
Balmoral 2,915	E2
Barcaldine 1,432	C4
Beaudesert 3,780	E6
Biloela 4,643	D5
Birdsville	A5
Blackall 1,609	C5
Blackwater 5,434	D4
Boulia 292	A4
Bowen 7,663	D3
Brisbane (cap.) 689,378	D2
Brisbane *1,028,527	D2
Bucasia 1,356	C4
Bundaberg 32,560	D5
Burketown 210	A3
Cairns 48,557	C3
Caloundra 16,758	E5
Camooweal 251	A3
Camp Hill 8,999	E3
Capella 660	D4
Cardwell 1,249	C3
Charleville 3,523	C5
Charters Towers 6,823	C4
Cherbourg 963	D5
Chermside 6,892	D2
Clermont 1,659	C4
Cloncurry 1,961	B4
Collinsville 2,756	C4
Cooktown 913	C2
Coopers Plains 4,492	D3
Corinda 4,894	D3
Croydon ○255	B3
Cunnamulla 1,627	C5
Dalby 8,784	D5
Dirranbandi 480	D6
East Brisbane 4,853	E3
Eidsvold 613	D5
Emerald 4,628	C4
Esk 676	E5
Gatton 4,190	E5
Gayndah 1,708	D5
Geebung 4,850	E2
Georgetown 319	B3
Gladstone 22,083	D4
Gold Coast 135,437	E6
Goondiwindi 3,576	D6
Gordonvale 2,375	C3
Greenslopes 7,219	E3
Gympie 10,768	E5
Hervey Bay 13,569	E5
Holland Park 7,363	E3
Home Hill 3,138	C3
Hughenden 1,657	B4
Inala 17,383	D3
Indooroopilly 7,959	D3
Ingham 5,598	C3
Injune 407	D5
Innisfail 7,933	C3
Ipswich 68,297	E5
Isisford ○605	C5
Jandowae 781	D5
Jericho ○1,177	C4
Julia Creek 602	B4
Karumba 670	B3
Kilcoy 1,257	E5
Kingaroy 5,134	D5
Longreach 2,971	B4
Mackay 35,361	D4
Mareeba 6,309	C3
Marian 796	C4
Maroochydore-Mooloolaba 17,460	E5
Maryborough 20,111	E5
Mary Kathleen 830	A4
McKinlay ○1,477	B4
Millmerran 1,107	D5
Mitchell 1,171	C5
Mitchelton 5,810	D2
Monto 1,397	D5
Moorooka 8,740	D3
Moranbah 4,362	C9
Mossman 1,614	C3
Mount Isa 23,679	A4
Moura 2,871	D5
Murgon 2,327	D5
Nambour 7,965	E5
Newmarket 3,520	D2
Normanton 926	B3
Nundah 7,358	E2
Proserpine 3,058	D4
Quilpie 694	C5
Ravenshoe 915	C3
Redcliffe 42,223	E5
Richmond 784	B4
Rockhampton 50,146	D4
Roma 5,706	D5
Saint George 2,204	D5
Saint Lucia 6,075	D3
Sandgate 6,776	D2
Sarina 2,815	D4
Springsure 774	D5
Stafford (Stafford Heights) 13,731	D2
Stanthorpe 3,966	D6
Tara 864	D5
Taroom 688	D5
Tewantin-Noosa 9,965	E5
Theodore 643	D5
Thursday Island 2,283	B1
Townsville 86,112	C3
Tully 2,728	C3
Walkerston 1,277	D4
Warwick 8,853	D6
Weipa 2,433	B2
Windsor 6,119	D2
Winton 1,259	B4
Wynnum 10,794	E5
Yeppoon 6,447	D4
Yeronga 4,579	D3

OTHER FEATURES

Albatross (bay)	B2
Archer (riv.)	B2
Balonne (riv.)	D6
Banks (isl.)	B1
Barcoo (creek)	B5
Barkly Tableland	A4
Bartle Frere (mt.)	C3
Beal (range)	B5

AREA 666,872 sq. mi. (1,727,200 sq. km.)
POPULATION 2,587,315
CAPITAL Brisbane
LARGEST CITY Brisbane
HIGHEST POINT Mt. Bartle Frere 5,287 ft. (1,611 m.)

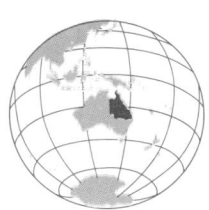

Topography

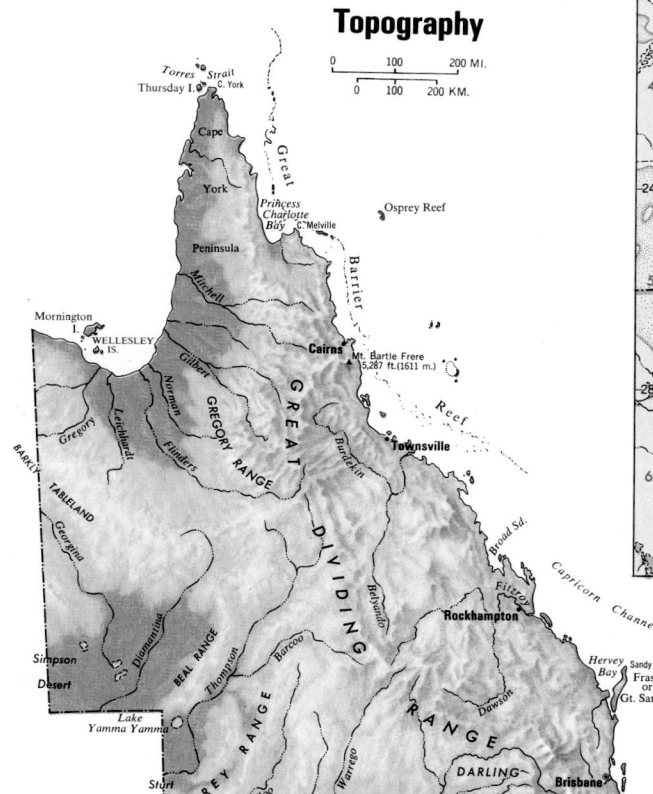

○ Population of district.
*Population of met. area.

Belyando (riv.)	C4	Fitzroy (riv.)	D4	Norman (riv.)	B3		
Broad (sound)	D4	Flinders (riv.)	B3	Northern Peninsula			
Bulloo (lake)	B6	Fraser (isl.)	E5	Aboriginal Res.	B1		
Bulloo (riv.)	B6	Georgina (riv.)	A4	Prince of Wales (isl.)	B1		
Bunker Group (isls.)	E4	Gilbert (riv.)	B3	Princess Charlotte (bay)	C2		
Burdekin (riv.)	C3	Great Dividing (range)	C4	Sandy (cape)	E5		
Cape York (pen.)	B2	Gregory (range)	B3	Selwyn (range)	B4		
Capricorn (chan.)	E4	Gregory (riv.)	A3	Simpson (des.)	A5		
Capricorn Group (isls.)	E4	Grey (range)	B5	Sturt (des.)	B3		
Carnarvon (range)	D5	Hamilton (riv.)	B4	Suttor (riv.)	C4		
Carpentaria (gulf)	A2	Hervey (bay)	E5	Swain (reefs)	E4		
Cloncurry (riv.)	B3	Hinchinbrook (isl.)	C3	Thompson (riv.)	B5		
Coopers (Barcoo) (creek)	B5	Hook (isl.)	D4	Torres (str.)	B1		
Coral (sea)	C1	Leichhardt (riv.)	A3	Warrego (range)	C5		
Culgoa (riv.)	C6	Machattie (lake)	A4	Warrego (riv.)	C5		
Cumberland (isls.)	D4	Macintyre (riv.)	D6	Wellesley (isls.)	A3		
Curtis (isl.)	D4	Maranoa (riv.)	C5	Whitsunday (isl.)	D4		
Darling Downs	D5	Mary (riv.)	E5	Willies (riv.)	C6		
Dawson (riv.)	D5	Melville (cape)	C2	Yamma Yamma (lake)	B5		
Diamantina (riv.)	A5	Mitchell (riv.)	B2	York (cape)	B1		
Drummond (range)	C5	Moreton (bay)	E5				
Duifken (pt.)	B2	Moreton (isl.)	E5				
Endeavour (str.)	B1	Mornington (isl.)	A3				

Cobbadah F2
Coffs Harbour 16,020 . . . . G2
Collarenebri 602 . . . . E1
Collie E2
Comboyne G2
Condobolin 3,355 . . . . D3
Conoble C3
Coogee K3
Coolah 878 . . . . E2
Coolamon 1,088 . . . . D4
Cooma 7,978 . . . . E5
Coonabarabran 3,001 . . . . E2
Coonamble 3,090 . . . . E2
Cootamundra 6,540 . . . . . D4
Copmanhurst ○2,857 . . . . . G1

Coraki 895 . . . . G1
Coramba 202 . . . . G2
Corowa-Wahgunyah 3,390 . D4
Cowra 7,900 . . . . E3
Crescent Head 944 . . . . . . G2
Cronulla J4
Crookwell 2,063 . . . . E4
Cudal 400 . . . . E3
Culburra-Orient Point 2,068 . F4
Culcairn 1,027 . . . . D4
Cullen Bullen 231 . . . . . . F3
Cumnock 252 . . . . E3
Curlewis 487 . . . . F2
Dareton 612 . . . . B4
Darlington Point 599 . . . . . C4
Deepwater 260 . . . . F1

Dee Why K3
Delegate 347 . . . . K3
Delungra 332 . . . . E5
Deniliquin 7,354 . . . . C4
Denman 1,122 . . . . F3
Dorrigo 1,192 . . . . F2
Drummoyne 30,961 . . . . . J3
Dubbo 23,986 . . . . E3
Dunedoo 836 . . . . E3
Dungalear Station D1
Dungog 2,126 . . . . F3
Eden 3,107 . . . . E5
Emmaville 503 . . . . F1
Ermeran Station D3
Eugowra 577 . . . . E3
Evans Head 1,802 . . . . . . G1

NEW SOUTH WALES
AREA 309,498 sq. mi.
(801,600 sq. km.)
POPULATION 5,401,881
CAPITAL Sydney
LARGEST CITY Sydney
HIGHEST POINT Mt. Kosciusko
7,310 ft. (2,228 m.)

VICTORIA
AREA 87,876 sq. mi.
(227,600 sq. km.)
POPULATION 4,019,478
CAPITAL Melbourne
LARGEST CITY Melbourne
HIGHEST POINT Mt. Bogong
6,508 ft. (1,984 m.)

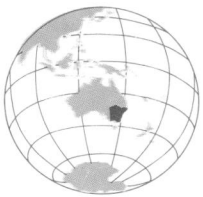

Topography

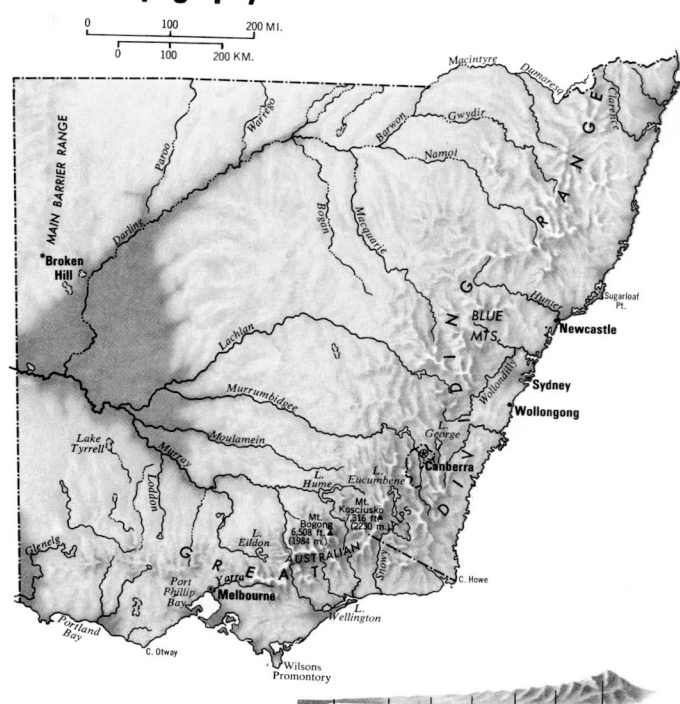

0	100		200 MI.		
0	100		200 KM.		

| Below Sea Level | 100 m. 328 ft. | 200 m. 656 ft. | 500 m. 1,640 ft. | 1,000 m. 3,281 ft. | 2,000 m. 6,562 ft. | 5,000 m. 16,404 ft. |

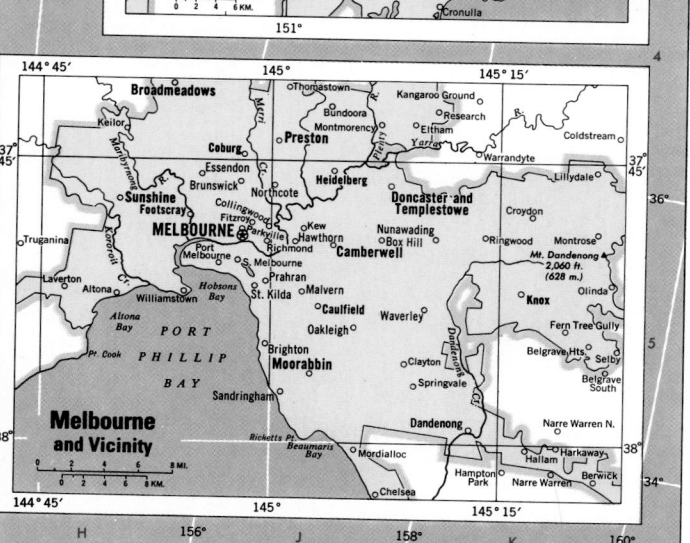

New South Wales and Victoria

SCALE OF MILES
0 25 50 75 100 125 150

SCALE OF KILOMETERS
0 25 50 75 100 125 150

Capital of Country _____ ⊛
State Capitals _____ ★
State and Territorial Boundaries ___

Lord Howe I.

Sydney and Vicinity

Melbourne and Vicinity

Fairfield 129,557 . . . . . . H3
Finley 2,193 . . . . C4
Forbes 8,029 . . . . E3
Forest Hill 1,977 . . . . D4
Forster-Tuncurry 9,261 . . . G3
Frederickton 616 . . . . G2
Ganmain 650 . . . . D4
Gerringong 1,775 . . . . F4
Geurie 290 . . . . E3
Gilgai 257 . . . . F1
Gilgandra 2,700 . . . . E2
Gilgunnia C3
Glen Innes 6,052 . . . . F1
Glenreagh 233 . . . . G2
Gloucester 2,488 . . . . F3
Goodooga 248 . . . . D1
Goolgowi 245 . . . . C3
Gooloogong 221 . . . . E3
Goombalie C1
Goulburn 21,755 . . . . E4
Grafton 17,005 . . . . G1
Grenfell 2,070 . . . . E3
Greta-Branxton 2,849 . . . . F3
Greta East 398 . . . . F3
Griffith 13,187 . . . . C4
Gulargambone 457 . . . . . . E2
Gulgong 1,740 . . . . E3
Gundagai 2,308 . . . . D4
Gunnedah 8,909 . . . . F2
Gunning 438 . . . . E4
Guyra 1,840 . . . . F2
Hanwood 306 . . . . C4
Harrington 1,183 . . . . G2
Hay 2,958 . . . . C4
Henty 883 . . . . D4
Hillston 999 . . . . C3
Holbrook 1,276 . . . . D4
Holroyd 80,116 . . . . H3
Hornsby 111,081 . . . . J3
Howlong 1,072 . . . . D4
Hunters Hill 12,537 . . . . . J3
Hurstville 64,910 . . . . J4
Huskisson 2,296 . . . . F4
Iluka 1,362 . . . . G1
Inverell 9,734 . . . . F1
Ivanhoe 517 . . . . C3
Jerilderie 1,075 . . . . C4
Jindabyne 1,602 . . . . E5
Junee 3,993 . . . . D4
Kandos 1,626 . . . . F3
Karpakora B3
Katoomba-Wentworth Falls 13,942 . . . . F3

Keewong C3
Kempsey 9,037 . . . . G2
Kendall 522 . . . . G2
Khancoban 515 . . . . E5
Kiama 7,717 . . . . F4
Kinalung B3
Kogarah 46,322 . . . . J4
Koorawatha 262 . . . . E4
Kootingal 731 . . . . F2
Ku-ring-gai 101,501 . . . . . J3
Kurri Kurri-Weston 12,795 . F3
Kyogle 3,070 . . . . G1
Lake Cargellico 1,240 . . . . D3
Lane Cove 29,113 . . . . . . J3
Leeton 6,498 . . . . D4
Leichhardt 57,332 . . . . . . J3
Lette B4
Lidcombe J3
Lightning Ridge 1,112 . . . . E1
Lismore 24,033 . . . . G1
Lithgow 12,793 . . . . F3
Liverpool 92,715 . . . . H4
Lockhart 923 . . . . D4
Macksville 2,352 . . . . G2
Maclean 2,593 . . . . G1
Maitland 38,865 . . . . F3
Manildra 582 . . . . E3
Manilla 1,884 . . . . F2
Maroubra K3
Marrickville 83,448 . . . . . . J3
Marsden D3
Marsden Park 518 . . . . . . H3
Marulan 330 . . . . E4
Mathoura 582 . . . . C4
Melrose D3
Mendooran 325 . . . . E2
Menindee 455 . . . . B3
Merimbula 2,899 . . . . E5
Merriwa 943 . . . . F3
Millthorpe 607 . . . . E3
Milpa B2
Milperra H4
Milton 740 . . . . F4
Mittagong 4,266 . . . . F4
Moama C5
Mogil Mogil E1
Molong 1,374 . . . . E3
Mona Vale K2
Moree 10,459 . . . . E1
Morisset 1,593 . . . . F3
Moruya 2,003 . . . . F4
Mosman 26,200 . . . . J3

Moss Vale 4,415 . . . . F4
Mossgiel C4
Moulamein 396 . . . . C4
Mount Arrowsmith A2
Mount Drysdale C2
Mount Hope C3
Mudgee 6,015 . . . . E3
Mullumbimby 2,234 . . . . . G1
Mungindi 707 . . . . E1
Murrumburrah 2,070 . . . . . E4
Murrurundi 861 . . . . F2
Murwillumbah 7,807 . . . . . G1
Muswellbrook 8,548 . . . . . F3
Nabiac 363 . . . . G3
Nambucca Heads 4,053 . . . G2
Narellan 2,104 . . . . F3
Narooma 2,758 . . . . F5
Narrabeen K3
Narrabri 7,296 . . . . E2
Narrandera 5,013 . . . . D4
Narromine 2,994 . . . . E3
New Angledool E1
Newcastle 135,207 . . . . . . F3
Newcastle †389,237 . . . . . F3
Nimmitabel 257 . . . . E5
North Sydney 48,500 . . . . J3
Nowra-Bomaderry 17,887 . . F4
Nundle 235 . . . . F2
Nymboida ○2,044 . . . . G1
Nyngan 2,485 . . . . D2
Oaklands 283 . . . . D4
Oberon 1,937 . . . . E3
Old Bar 970 . . . . G2
Orange 27,626 . . . . E3
Pallamallawa 340 . . . . F1
Pambula 604 . . . . E5
Parkes 9,047 . . . . E3
Parramatta 130,943 . . . . . H3
Peak Hill 1,037 . . . . E3
Penrith 108,720 . . . . F3
Perthville 639 . . . . E3
Picton 1,817 . . . . F4
Pilliga 206 . . . . E2
Popiltah A3
Portland 1,980 . . . . E3
Port Kembla F4
Port Macquarie 19,581 . . . . G2
Queanbeyan 19,383 . . . . . E4
Quirindi 2,851 . . . . F2
Randwick 116,202 . . . . . . J3
Raymond Terrace 7,548 . . . F3
Richmond-Windsor 15,491 . . F3
Rockdale 83,719 . . . . J4

(continued on following page)

Ryde 88,948 ... J3
Rylstone 651 ... E3
Salisbury Downs ... B1
Sawtell 5,970 ... G2
Scone 3,949 ... F3
Shellharbour 41,790 ... F4
Singleton 9,572 ... F3
Smithtown-Gladstone 953 ... G2
South Sydney 30,776 ... J3
South West Rocks 1,314 ... G2
Stephen's Creek ... A2
Strathfield 25,882 ... J3
Stroud 522 ... G3
Sussex Inlet 1,293 ... F4
Sutherland 165,336 ... J4
Sydney (cap.) 2,876,508 ... J3
Sydney †3,204,696 ... J3
Talbingo 481 ... E4
Tamworth 29,657 ... F2
Taralga 272 ... E4
Tarcutta 263 ... D4
Taree 14,697 ... G2
Tathra 1,077 ... F4
Temora 4,350 ... E4
Tenterfield 3,402 ... G1
Terrigal-The Entrance 37,891 ... F3
The Rock 693 ... D4
Thurloo Downs ... B1
Tibbita ... C4
Tibooburra ... B1
Tiltagara ... C2
Tingha 886 ... B1
Tocumwal 1,174 ... F1
Tongo ... C4
Torrowangee ... B2
Tottenham 366 ... A2
Trangie 977 ... D3
Trundle 515 ... D3
Tullamore 324 ... D3
Tumbarumba 1,536 ... D3
Tumut 5,816 ... E4
Tweed Heads ... G1
Ulladulla 6,018 ... F4
Ulmarra 395 ... G1
Ungarie 428 ... D3
Uralla 2,090 ... F2
Urana 419 ... D4
Urbenville 282 ... G1
Urunga 2,045 ... G2
Villawood ... H3
Wagga Wagga 36,837 ... D4
Wakool 278 ... C4
Walcha 1,674 ... F2
Walgett 2,157 ... E2
Walla Walla 593 ... D4

Wallerawang 1,855 ... F3
Wangi-Rathmines 5,106 ... F3
Warialda 1,340 ... F1
Warragamba 1,406 ... F3
Warren 2,153 ... D2
Warringah ○172,653 ... K3
Wauchope 3,645 ... G2
Waverley 61,575 ... J3
Waverley Downs ... B1
Wee Waa 1,904 ... E2
Wellington 5,280 ... E3
Wentworth 1,180 ... A3
Werris Creek 1,924 ... F2
West Wyalong 3,778 ... D3
Wetuppa ... B2
White Cliffs ... B2
Whitton 344 ... D4
Whyjonta ... B1
Wilcannia 982 ... B2
Willoughby 52,120 ... J3
Willow Tree 258 ... F2
Wingham 3,937 ... G2
Wollongong 169,381 ... F4
Wollongong †222,539 ... F4
Woodburn 647 ... G1
Woodenbong 409 ... G1
Woodstock 266 ... E3
Woolgoolga 2,081 ... G2
Wooli 457 ... G1
Woollahra 61,659 ... K3
Wyong 3,902 ... F3
Yallock ... C3
Yalpunga ... A1
Yamba 2,528 ... G1
Yancannia ... B2
Yanco 415 ... D4
Yantara ... B1
Yass 4,283 ... E4
Yenda 697 ... D4
Yeoval 288 ... E3
Young 6,906 ... E4

OTHER FEATURES

Ana Branch, Darling (riv.) ... A3
Australian Alps (mts.) ... D5
Barrington Tops (mt.) ... F2
Barwon (riv.) ... D2
Blue (mts.) ... F3
Bogan (riv.) ... D2
Bondi (beach) ... K3
Botany (bay) ... J4
Bruthen (bay) ... F3
Burrinjuck (res.) ... E4
Byron (cape) ... G1

Carapundy (swamp) ... B1
Castlereagh (riv.) ... E2
Cawndilla (lake) ... A3
Clarence (riv.) ... G1
Colo (riv.) ... F3
Cowal (lake) ... D3
Culgoa (riv.) ... D1
Cuttaburra (creek) ... C1
Darling (riv.) ... B3
Dumaresq (riv.) ... F1
Eucumbene (lake) ... E4
George (lake) ... E4
Georges (riv.) ... H4
Gower (int.) ... J2
Great Dividing (range) ... E3
Green (cape) ... F5
Gunderbooka (ranges) ... C2
Gwydir (riv.) ... E1
Howe (cape) ... F5
Hume (res.) ... D4
Hunter (riv.) ... F3
Kosciusko (mt.) ... E5
Kurnell (pen.) ... J4
Lachlan (range) ... C3
Lachlan (riv.) ... C3
Liverpool (range) ... F2
Lord Howe (isl.) 287 ... J2
Macintyre (riv.) ... E1
Macquarie (lake) ... F3
Macquarie (riv.) ... D2
Main Barrier (range) ... A2
Manning (riv.) ... G2
Marthaguy (creek) ... D2
McPherson (range) ... G1
Menindee (lake) ... B3
Monaro (range) ... E5
Moonie (riv.) ... C4
Moulamein (creek) ... C4
Mount Royal (range) ... F2
Murray (riv.) ... A4
Murrumbidgee (riv.) ... C4
Myall (lake) ... G3
Namoi (riv.) ... E2
Narran (lake) ... D1
New England (range) ... F1
Paroo (riv.) ... C1
Parramatta (riv.) ... J3
Poopeloe (lake) ... C2
Port Jackson (inlet) ... J3
Port Stephens (inlet) ... G3
Richmond (range) ... G1
Richmond (riv.) ... G1
Riverina (reg.) ... C4
Robe (mt.) ... A2
Round, The (mt.) ... G2

Salt, The (lake) ... B2
Shoalhaven (riv.) ... E4
Smoky (cape) ... G2
Snowy (mts.) ... E5
Snowy (riv.) ... E5
Stony (ranges) ... A1
Sturt (mt.) ... A1
Sugarloaf (pt.) ... G3
Talyawalka (creek) ... B3
Tandou (lake) ... B3
Tasman (sea) ... F5
The Round (mts.) ... B2
The Salt (lake) ... B2
Timbarra (riv.) ... G1
Tuggerah (lake) ... F3
Victoria (lake) ... A3
Warrego (riv.) ... C1
Willandra Billabong (creek) ... C3
Wollondilly (riv.) ... E4

VICTORIA

CITIES and TOWNS

Alexandra 1,756 ... C5
Altona 30,909 ... H5
Apollo Bay 921 ... B6
Ararat 8,336 ... B5
Avoca 1,032 ... B5
Bacchus Marsh 6,224 ... C5
Bairnsdale 9,459 ... D5
Ballarat 35,681 ... C5
Ballarat †71,930 ... C5
Balmoral 257 ... A5
Beaufort 1,214 ... B5
Beechworth 3,154 ... D5
Belgrave Heights ... K5
Belgrave South ... K5
Benalla 8,151 ... D5
Bendigo 31,841 ... C5
Bendigo †58,818 ... C5
Berwick 36,181 ... K6
Beulah 290 ... B4
Birchip 895 ... B4
Birregurra 416 ... B6
Boort 863 ... C4
Box Hill 47,579 ... J5
Bright 1,545 ... D5
Brighton 33,697 ... J5
Broadford 1,580 ... C5
Broadmeadows 103,540 ... H4
Brunswick 44,464 ... J5
Bruthen 449 ... D5
Bundoora ... J5
Camberwell 85,883 ... J5

Camperdown 3,545 ... C6
Cann River 345 ... E5
Casterton 1,945 ... A5
Castlemaine 7,583 ... C5
Caulfield 69,922 ... J5
Charlton 1,377 ... B5
Chelsea 26,034 ... J6
Churchill 4,796 ... D6
Clunes 761 ... C5
Cobden 1,453 ... B6
Cobram 3,817 ... C4
Coburg 55,035 ... H5
Cohuna 2,178 ... C4
Colac 10,587 ... C6
Coldstream 1,395 ... K4
Coleraine 1,232 ... A5
Collingwood 15,089 ... J5
Corryong 1,320 ... D5
Craigieburn 4,296 ... C6
Cranbourne 9,400 ... C6
Creswick 2,036 ... C5
Croydon 36,210 ... K5
Dandenong 54,962 ... K5
Darby ... D6
Dartmoor 349 ... A5
Daylesford 2,883 ... C5
Derrinallum 287 ... B5
Dimboola 1,675 ... B5
Donald 1,609 ... B5
Doncaster and Templestowe 90,660 ... H5
Drouin 3,492 ... C6
Dunkeld 402 ... B5
Dunolly 621 ... B5
Eaglehawk 7,355 ... C5
Echuca 7,943 ... C5
Edenhope 827 ... A5
Eildon 737 ... C5
Eltham 34,648 ... J4
Erica 236 ... D5
Essendon 56,380 ... H5
Euroa 2,640 ... C5
Fitzroy 19,112 ... H5
Footscray 49,756 ... H5
Geelong 14,471 ... C6
Geelong †137,173 ... C6
Geelong West 14,823 ... C6
Goroke 370 ... A5
Gunbower 259 ... C4
Hamilton 9,751 ... B5
Hawthorn 30,689 ... J5
Healesville 4,526 ... C5
Heathcote 1,213 ... C5
Heidelberg 64,757 ... J5
Heyfield 1,635 ... D6

Heywood 1,266 ... A6
Hopetoun 1,832 ... B4
Horsham 12,034 ... B5
Inglewood 674 ... B5
Inverloch 1,523 ... C6
Kaniva 956 ... A5
Keilor 81,762 ... H5
Kerang 4,049 ... B4
Kew 28,870 ... J5
Kilmore 1,728 ... C5
Knox 88,902 ... K5
Koroit 1,988 ... B6
Korumburra 2,798 ... D6
Kyabram 5,414 ... C5
Kyneton 3,185 ... C5
Lake Boga 502 ... B4
Lake Bolac 211 ... B5
Lakes Entrance 3,414 ... E5
Lara 4,231 ... C6
Leongatha 3,736 ... D6
Lillydale 62,077 ... K4
Macarthur 322 ... A6
Maffra 3,822 ... D5
Maldon 1,009 ... C5
Mallacoota 726 ... E5
Malvern 43,211 ... J5
Mansfield 1,920 ... D5
Maryborough 7,858 ... B5
Melbourne (cap.) 2,578,759 ... H5
Melbourne †2,722,817 ... H5
Melton 20,599 ... C5
Merbein 1,735 ... A4
Merino 298 ... A5
Mildura 15,763 ... A4
Minyip 567 ... B5
Moe 16,649 ... D6
Montmorency ... J4
Montrose ... K5
Moorabbin 97,810 ... J5
Mooroopna ... C5
Mordialloc 27,869 ... J6
Morea ... C5
Mornington 23,512 ... C6
Mortlake 1,056 ... B6
Morwell 16,491 ... D5
Mount Beauty 1,509 ... D5
Murrayville 313 ... A4
Murtoa 946 ... B5
Myrtleford 2,815 ... D5
Nagambie 1,102 ... C5
Narre Warren North 761 ... K5
Nathalia 1,222 ... C5
Natimuk 482 ... A5
Newtown 10,210 ... C6

Nhill 1,567 ... A5
Northcote 51,235 ... J5
Numurkah 2,713 ... C5
Nunawading 97,052 ... J5
Nyah 351 ... B4
Nyah West 535 ... B4
Oakleigh 55,612 ... J5
Omeo 2,586 ... D5
Orbost 2,586 ... E5
Ouyen 1,527 ... B4
Penshurst 558 ... B5
Porepunkah 268 ... D5
Port Albert 267 ... D6
Port Fairy 2,276 ... B6
Portland 9,353 ... A6
Port Melbourne 8,585 ... H5
Prahran 45,018 ... J5
Preston 84,519 ... J4
Quambatook 359 ... B4
Queenscliff 3,420 ... C6
Rainbow 700 ... A4
Red Cliffs 2,409 ... B4
Richmond 24,506 ... J5
Ringwood 38,665 ... K5
Robinvale 1,751 ... A4
Rochester 2,399 ... C5
Rushworth 994 ... C5
Rutherglen 1,454 ... D5
Saint Arnaud 2,721 ... B5
Saint Kilda 49,366 ... J5
Sale 12,968 ... D6
Sandringham 31,175 ... J5
Sea Lake 943 ... B4
Sebastopol 6,462 ... C5
Seymour 6,494 ... C5
Shepparton-Mooroopna ‡28,373 ... C5
South Barwon 35,307 ... C6
South Melbourne 19,955 ... J5
Springvale 80,186 ... J5
Stawell 6,160 ... B5
Sunbury 11,085 ... C5
Sunshine 94,419 ... H5
Swan Hill 8,398 ... B4
Swifts Creek 288 ... D5
Tallangatta 950 ... D5
Tatura 2,697 ... C5
Templestowe and Doncaster 90,660 ... J5
Terang 2,111 ... B6
Tongala 994 ... C5
Traralgon 18,057 ... D6
Underbool 274 ... A4
Wangaratta 16,202 ... D5
Warburton 2,009 ... C5
Warracknabeal 2,735 ... B5
Warragul 7,712 ... D6
Warrnambool 21,414 ... B6
Waverley 122,471 ... J5
Wedderburn 868 ... B5
Werrimull ... A4
Whittlesea 65,657 ... C5
Willaura 377 ... B5
Williamstown 25,554 ... H5
Winchelsea 825 ... B6
Wodonga 19,208 ... D5
Wonthaggi 4,797 ... C6
Woodend 1,785 ... C5
Wycheproof 938 ... B5
Yallourn 26 ... D6
Yarram 2,085 ... D6
Yarrawonga 3,442 ... C5
Yea 996 ... C5

OTHER FEATURES

Australian Alps (mts.) ... D5
Avoca (riv.) ... B5
Barry (mts.) ... D5
Bogong (mt.) ... D5
Bridgewater (cape) ... A6
Buller (mt.) ... D5
Campaspe (riv.) ... C5
Corangamite (lake) ... B6
Corner (inlet) ... D6
Dandenong (mt.) ... K5
Difficult (mt.) ... B5
Discovery (bay) ... A6
Eildon (lake) ... C5
French (isl.) 123 ... C6
Gippsland (reg.) ... D6
Glenelg (riv.) ... A5
Goulburn (riv.) ... C5
Hindmarsh (lake) ... A5
Hobsons (bay) ... H5
Hopkins (riv.) ... B6
Hume (dam) ... D4
Indian Ocean ... B6
Loddon (riv.) ... C5
Mitchell (riv.) ... D5
Mitta Mitta (riv.) ... D5
Mornington (pen.) ... C6
Mount Emu (creek) ... B5
Murray (riv.) ... A4
Nelson (cape) ... A6
Ninety Mile (beach) ... D6
Otway (cape) ... B6
Ovens (riv.) ... D5
Phillip (isl.) 2,832 ... C6
Portland (bay) ... A6
Port Phillip (bay) ... C6
Rocklands (res.) ... B5
Snowy (riv.) ... E5
South East (pt.) ... D6
Tasman (sea) ... F5
Tyrrell (lake) ... B4
Waratah (bay) ... C6
Wellington (lake) ... D6
Western Port (inlet) ... C6
Wilsons (prom.) ... D6
Wimmera (riv.) ... A5
Yarra (riv.) ... C5

*City and suburbs.
○ Population of district.
†Population of met. area.
‡Population of urban area.

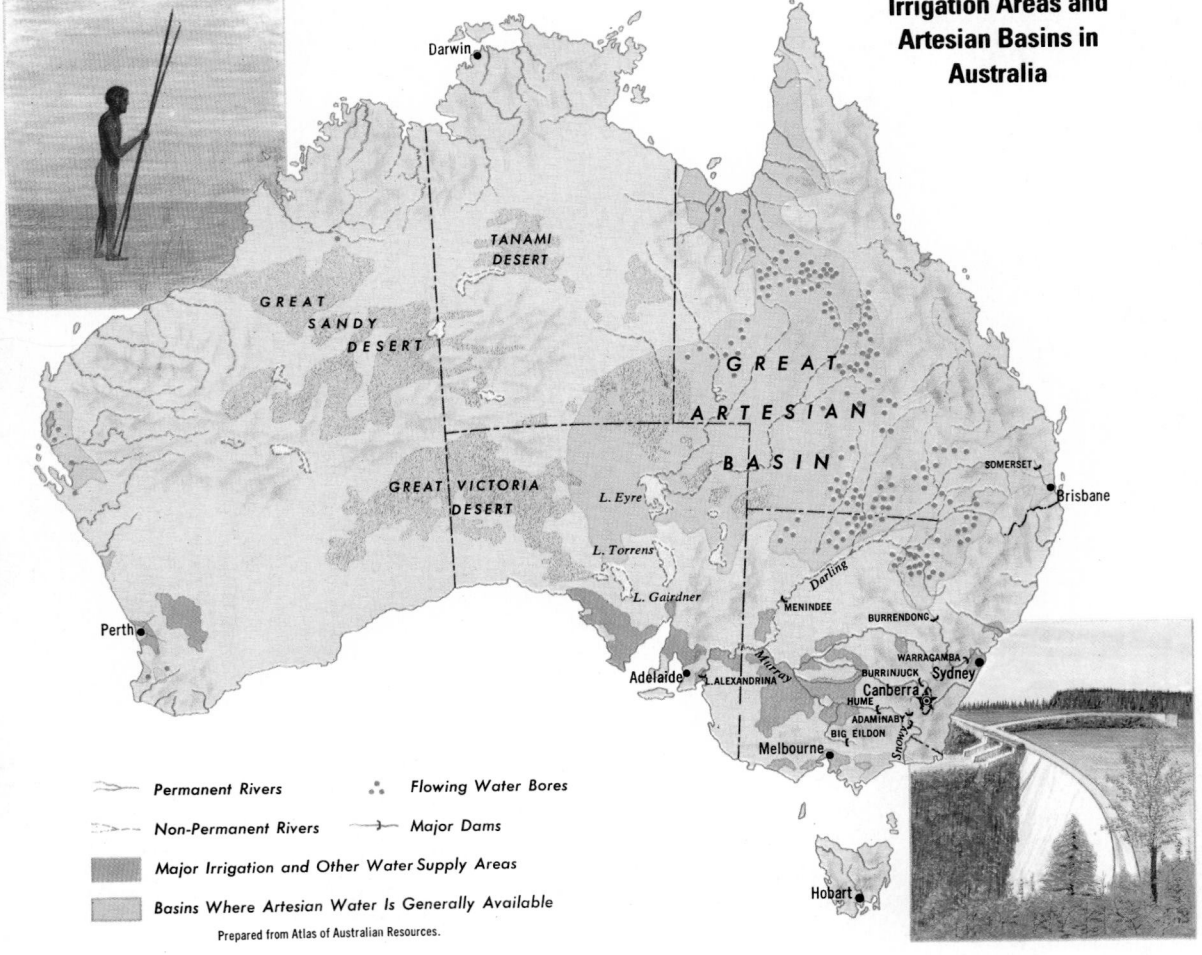

Irrigation Areas and Artesian Basins in Australia

Permanent Rivers
Non-Permanent Rivers
Flowing Water Bores
Major Dams
Major Irrigation and Other Water Supply Areas
Basins Where Artesian Water Is Generally Available

Prepared from Atlas of Australian Resources.

Topography

0   30   60 MI.
0   30   60 KM.

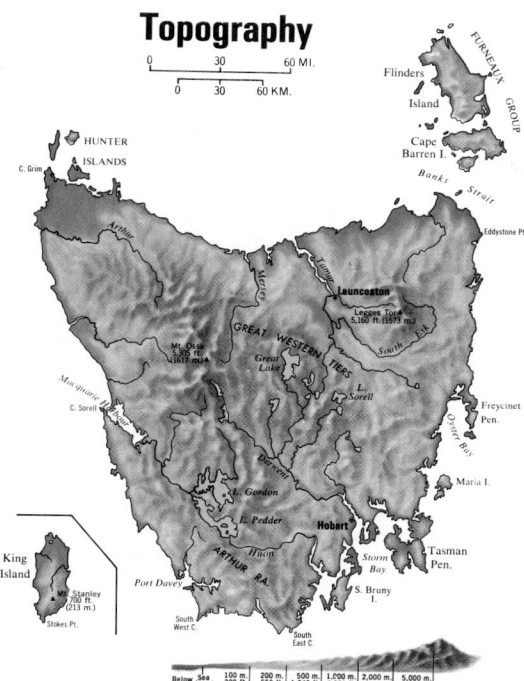

FURNEAUX GROUP
Flinders Island
Cape Barren I.
Banks Strait
HUNTER ISLANDS
C. Grim
Launceston
Legges Tor 5,160 ft. (1573 m.)
GREAT WESTERN TIERS
Mt. Ossa 5,305 ft. (1,617 m.)
Great Lake
Macquarie R.
C. Sorell
L. Gordon
L. Sorell
Eddystone Pt.
Freycinet Pen.
Oyster Bay
Maria I.
ARTHUR RA.
L. Pedder
Huon
Hobart
Storm Bay
Tasman Pen.
Port Davey
South West C.
South East C.

King Island
Mt. Stanley 700 ft. (213 m.)
Stokes Pt.

Below Sea Level | 100 m. 328 ft. | 200 m. 656 ft. | 500 m. 1,640 ft. | 1,000 m. 3,281 ft. | 2,000 m. 6,562 ft. | 5,000 m. 16,404 ft.

TASMANIA

AREA 26,178 sq. mi. (67,800 sq. km.)
POPULATION 436,353
CAPITAL Hobart
LARGEST CITY Hobart
HIGHEST POINT Mt. Ossa 5,305 ft. (1,617 m.)

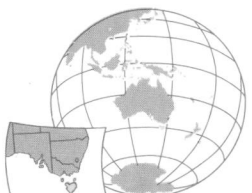

○ Population of district.
*Population of met. area.

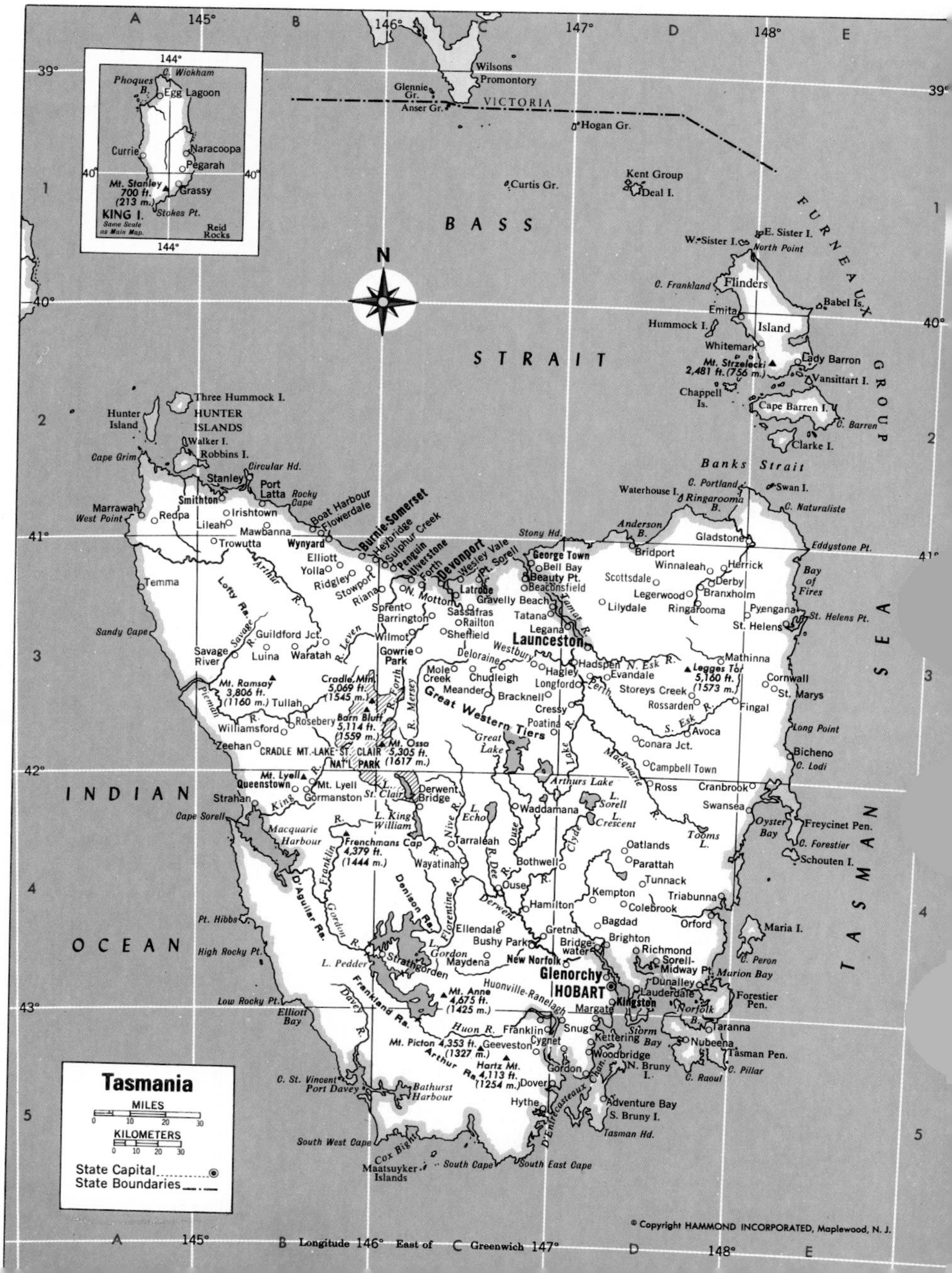

Tasmania
MILES
0 10 20 30
KILOMETERS
0 10 20 30
State Capital . . . . ◉
State Boundaries . . . . _____

© Copyright HAMMOND INCORPORATED, Maplewood, N.J.

New Zealand

CONIC PROJECTION

SCALE OF MILES

SCALE OF KILOMETERS

Capital of Country .... ☆

© Copyright HAMMOND INCORPORATED, Maplewood, N.J.

AREA 103,736 sq. mi. (268,676 sq. km.)
POPULATION 3,389,000
CAPITAL Wellington
LARGEST CITY Auckland
HIGHEST POINT Mt. Cook 12,349 ft.
(3,764 m.)
MONETARY UNIT New Zealand dollar
MAJOR LANGUAGES English, Maori
MAJOR RELIGIONS Protestantism,
Roman Catholicism

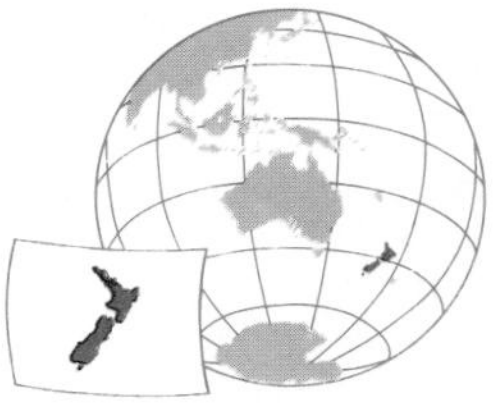

Topography

Three Kings Is.
North Cape
C. Maria van Diemen
Bay of Islands
Kaipara Har.
Great Barrier I.
Coromandel Pen.
Auckland
Bay of Plenty
North
Island
East Cape
L. Taupo
C. Egmont
Mt. Egmont 8,260 ft. (2518 m.)
Ruapehu 9,175 ft. (2796 m.)
Hawke Bay
Mahia Pen.
C. Farewell
Tasman Bay
Cook Strait
Wellington
C. Foulwind
C. Palliser
South
Island
Pegasus Bay
Christchurch
Banks Pen.
Cascade Pt.
Canterbury Plains
Canterbury Bight
SOUTHERN ALPS
Mt. Cook 12,349 ft. (3764 m.)
West Cape
Otago Pen.
Dunedin
Foveaux Str.
Stewart I.

0   75   150 MI.
0   75   150 KM.

Below Sea Level | 100 m. 328 ft. | 200 m. 656 ft. | 500 m. 1,640 ft. | 1,000 m. 3,281 ft. | 2,000 m. 6,562 ft. | 5,000 m. 16,404 ft.

Agriculture, Industry and Resources

Auckland
Wellington
Christchurch
Dunedin

DOMINANT LAND USE

- Mixed Farming, Livestock
- Dairy
- Truck Farming, Horticulture
- Pasture Livestock (chiefly sheep)
- Livestock Herding
- Forests
- Nonagricultural Land

MAJOR MINERAL OCCURRENCES

- C Coal
- G Natural Gas
- J Jade
- Ka Kaolin
- Lg Lignite
- O Petroleum
- U Uranium

⚡ Water Power
▨ Major Industrial Areas

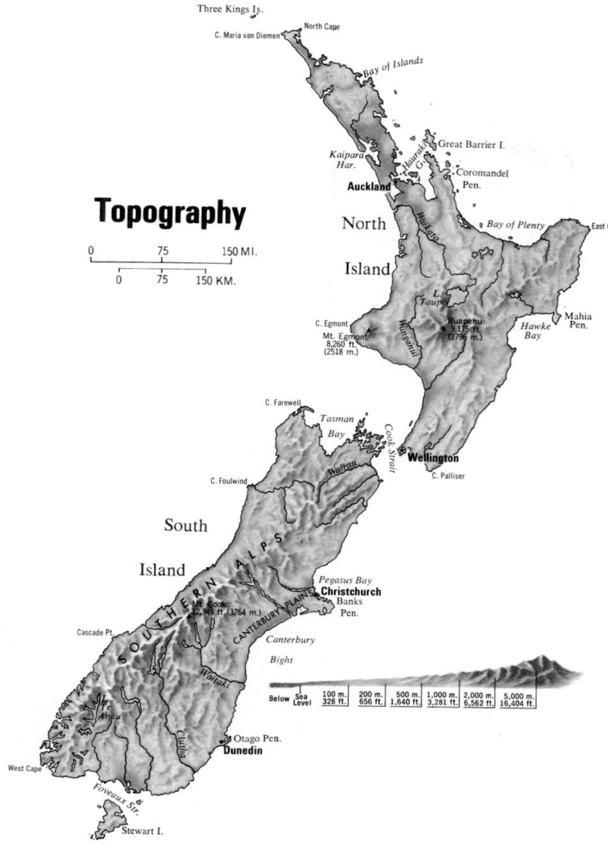

CITIES and TOWNS

Albany 2,001 . . . . B1
Alexandra 4,348 . . . . B6
Ashburton 14,151 . . . . . . C5
Ashhurst 1,906 . . . . E4
Auckland 144,963 . . . . . . B1
Auckland †769,558 . . . . . B1
Balclutha 4,495 . . . . B7
Belmont 2,402 . . . . B1
Birkenhead 21,324 . . . . . B1
Blenheim 17,849 . . . . D4
Bluff 2,720 . . . . B7
Bulls 1,839 . . . . E4
Cambridge 8,514 . . . . E2
Carterton 3,971 . . . . E4
Christchurch 164,680 . . . . D5
Christchurch †289,959 . . . D5
Cromwell 2,364 . . . . B6
Dannevirke 5,663 . . . . . . F4
Dargaville 4,747 . . . . D1
Devonport 10,410 . . . . . . C1
Dunedin 77,176 . . . . C6
Dunedin †107,445 . . . . . . C6
Eastbourne 4,561 . . . . . . B3
East Coast Bays 28,866 . . B1
Edgecumbe 1,929 . . . . . . F2
Ellerslie 5,404 . . . . C1
Eltham 2,411 . . . . E3
Fairfield 1,849 . . . . C6
Featherston 2,458 . . . . . . E4
Feilding 11,522 . . . . E4
Foxton 2,719 . . . . E4
Geraldine 2,128 . . . . C6
Gisborne 29,986 . . . . G3
Gisborne †32,062 . . . . . . G3
Glen Eden 9,406 . . . . B1
Glenfield 3,691 . . . . B1
Gore 9,185 . . . . B7
Green Bay 3,035 . . . . B1
Green Island 6,899 . . . . . C7
Greymouth 8,103 . . . . . . C5
Greytown 1,797 . . . . E4
Half Moon Bay (Oban) 2,448 B7
Hamilton 91,109 . . . . E2
Hamilton †97,907 . . . . . . E2
Hastings 36,083 . . . . F3
Hastings †52,563 . . . . . . F3
Havelock North 8,507 . . . . F3
Hawera 8,400 . . . . E3
Helensville 1,360 . . . . B1
Henderson 6,645 . . . . B1
Heretaunga-Pinehaven 6,171 C2
Hokitika 3,414 . . . . C5
Hornby 8,215 . . . . D5
Howick 13,866 . . . . C1
Huntly 6,534 . . . . E2
Hutt (Upper and Lower) †131,257 . . . . B2
Inglewood 2,839 . . . . E3

Invercargill 49,446 . . . . . B7
Invercargill †53,868 . . . . . B7
Kaiapoi 4,894 . . . . D5
Kaikohe 3,663 . . . . D1
Kaikoura 2,180 . . . . D5
Kaitaia 4,737 . . . . D1
Kawerau 8,593 . . . . F3
Kumeu 3,414 . . . . B1
Levin 14,652 . . . . E4
Lower Hutt 63,245 . . . . . . B2
Lyttelton 3,184 . . . . D5
Manukau 159,362 . . . . . . C1
Marton 4,858 . . . . E4
Masterton 18,785 . . . . . . E4
Mataura 2,345 . . . . B7
Milton 2,193 . . . . B7
Morrinsville 5,080 . . . . . . E2
Mosgiel 9,264 . . . . C6
Motueka 4,693 . . . . D4
Mount Albert 26,462 . . . . B1
Mount Eden 18,305 . . . . . B1
Mount Maunganui 11,391 . E2
Mount Roskill 33,577 . . . . B1
Mount Wellington 19,528 . C1
Murupara 2,964 . . . . F3
Napier 48,314 . . . . F3
Napier †51,330 . . . . F3
Nelson 33,304 . . . . D4
Nelson †43,121 . . . . D4
New Lynn 10,445 . . . . . . B1
New Plymouth 36,048 . . . D3
New Plymouth †44,095 . . . D3
Ngaruawahia 4,435 . . . . . E2
Northcote 10,061 . . . . B1
Oamaru 13,043 . . . . C6
Oban (Half Moon Bay) 2,448 B7
Onehunga 15,386 . . . . . . B1
One Tree Hill 11,078 . . . . B1
Opotiki 3,388 . . . . F3
Orewa 5,552 . . . . B1
Otahuhu 10,298 . . . . C1
Otaki 4,301 . . . . E4
Otorohanga 2,574 . . . . . . E3
Paeroa 3,702 . . . . E2
Pahiatua 2,599 . . . . F4
Paihia 1,740 . . . . D1
Palmerston North 60,105 . E4
Palmerston North †66,691 E4
Papakura 22,473 . . . . C1
Papatoetoe 21,700 . . . . . C1
Patea 1,938 . . . . D7
Petone 8,113 . . . . B2
Picton 3,220 . . . . D4
Pinehaven (Heretaunga-Pinehaven) 6,171 . . . . . . C2
Porirua 41,104 . . . . B2
Port Chalmers 2,917 . . . . C6
Pukekohe 9,070 . . . . E2
Putaruru 4,222 . . . . E3
Queenstown 3,367 . . . . . B6

Raetihi 1,247 . . . . E3
Raglan 1,414 . . . . E2
Rangiora 6,385 . . . . D5
Reefton 1,200 . . . . C5
Riccarton 6,709 . . . . D5
Richmond 6,847 . . . . D4
Riverton 1,479 . . . . B7
Rotorua 38,157 . . . . F3
Rotorua †48,314 . . . . F3
Runanga 1,264 . . . . C5
Russell 932 . . . . E1
Saint Kilda 6,147 . . . . . . C7
Shannon 1,465 . . . . E4
Stratford 5,518 . . . . E3
Taihape 2,586 . . . . E3
Takapuna 64,844 . . . . . . B1
Tapanui 1,042 . . . . B6
Taradale 4,681 . . . . F3
Taumarunui 6,541 . . . . . . E3
Taupo 13,651 . . . . F3
Tauranga 37,099 . . . . F2
Tauranga †53,097 . . . . . . F2
Tawa 12,216 . . . . B2
Te Anau 2,610 . . . . A6
Te Aroha 3,331 . . . . E2
Te Atatu 14,713 . . . . B1
Te Awamutu 7,922 . . . . . E3
Te Kauwhata 842 . . . . . . E2
Te Kuiti 4,795 . . . . E3
Temuka 3,771 . . . . C6
Te Puke 4,577 . . . . F2
Thames 6,456 . . . . E2
The Hermitage C5
Timaru 28,412 . . . . C6
Timaru †29,225 . . . . C6
Titirangi 8,426 . . . . B1
Tokoroa 18,713 . . . . E3
Tuakau 1,982 . . . . E2
Tuatapere 884 . . . . A7
Turangi 5,517 . . . . E3
Upper Hutt 31,405 . . . . . B2
Waihi 3,538 . . . . E2
Waikanae 4,818 . . . . E4
Waikouaiti 858 . . . . C6
Waimate 3,393 . . . . C6
Wainuiomata 19,192 . . . . B3
Waipawa 1,732 . . . . F4
Waipukurau 3,648 . . . . . . F4
Wairoa 5,439 . . . . F3
Waitangi D7
Waitara 6,012 . . . . E3
Waitemata 87,452 . . . . . . B1
Waiuku 3,961 . . . . E2
Wanaka 1,155 . . . . B6
Wanganui 37,012 . . . . . . E3
Wanganui †39,595 . . . . . E3
Warkworth 1,734 . . . . E2
Washdyke 949 . . . . C6
Waverley 1,239 . . . . E3
Wellington (cap.) 135,688 . A3

Wellington †321,004 . . . . A3
Wellsford 1,621 . . . . E2
Westport 4,686 . . . . C4
Whakatane 12,286 . . . . . F2
Whangamata 1,566 . . . . . F2
Whangarei 36,550 . . . . . . E1
Whangarei †40,212 . . . . . E1
Whitianga 1,960 . . . . E2
Winton 2,035 . . . . B7
Woodville 1,647 . . . . F4

OTHER FEATURES

Arthur's (pass) C5
Aspiring (mt.) B6
Banks (pen.) D5
Bream (bay) E1
Brett (cape) E1
Buller (riv.) D4
Campbell (cape) E4
Canterbury (bight) D6
Cascade (pt.) B6
Chatham (isls.) 751 . . . . . D7
Cloudy (bay) E4
Clutha (riv.) B6
Coleridge (lake) C5
Colville (cape) E2
Cook (mt.) C5
Cook (str.) E4
Coromandel (pen.) F2
Devil River (peak) D4
D'Urville (isl.) D4
Dusky (sound) A6
East (cape) G2
Egmont (cape) D3
Egmont (mt.) D3
Ellesmere (lake) D5
Farewell (cape) D4
Foulwind (cape) C4
Fournier (cape) E7
Foveaux (str.) A7
Golden (bay) D4
Great Barrier (isl.) 572 . . . E2
Hauraki (gulf) C1
Hawke (bay) F3
Hikurangi (mt.) G2
Hokianga (harb.) D1
Huiarau (range) F3
Hutt (riv.) C2
Islands (bay) E1
Jackson (bay) B5
Kaikoura (range) D5
Kaimanawa (range) E3
Kaipara (harb.) D2
Karamea (bight) C4
Kawhia (harb.) E2
Kidnappers (cape) F3
Mahia (pen.) G3
Manapouri (lake) A6
Manukau (harb.) B1
Maria van Diemen (cape) . D1
Mataura (riv.) B6
Mercury (isls.) F2
Milford (sound) A6
Needles (cape) E2
Nicholson, Port (inlet) . . . B3
Ninety Mile (beach) D1
North (cape) D1
North (isl.) 2,322,989 . . . . F1
North Taranaki (bight) . . . D3
Otago (pen.) C6
Owen (mt.) D4
Palliser (cape) E4
Pegasus (bay) D5
Pitt (isl.) E7
Plenty (bay) F2
Port Nicholson (inlet) B3
Port Pegasus (inlet) B7
Pukaki (lake) B6
Puysegur (pt.) A7
Rakaia (riv.) C5
Rangitata (riv.) C5
Rangitikei (riv.) E3
Raukumara (range) F3
Reinga (cape) D1
Resolution (isl.) A6
Richmond (range) D4
Rocks (pt.) C4
Rotorua (lake) F2
Ruahine (range) F4
Ruapehu (mt.) E3
Ruapuke (isl.) B7
South (cape) A7
South (isl.) 852,748 . . . . . B5
Southern Alps (range) . . . C5
South Taranaki (bight) . . . D3
Spenser (mts.) D5
Stewart (isl.) 600 . . . . . . A7
Tararua (range) E4
Tasman (bay) D4
Tasman (mts.) D4
Tasman (sea) B4
Taupo (lake) F3
Tauroa (pt.) D1

Te Anau (lake) A6
Tekapo (lake) C5
Terawhiti (cape) A3
Thames (firth) E2
Three Kings (isls.) D1
Turakirae (head) B3
Una (mt.) D5
Waiheke (isl.) 3,223 . . . . . E2
Waikato (riv.) E2
Waimakariri (riv.) D5
Waipa (riv.) E2
Wairau (riv.) D4
Waitaki (riv.) C6
Waitemata (harb.) B1
Wakatipu (lake) B6
Wanaka (lake) B6
Wanganui (riv.) E3
West (cape) A6
Whitcombe (mt.) C5

†Population of urban area.

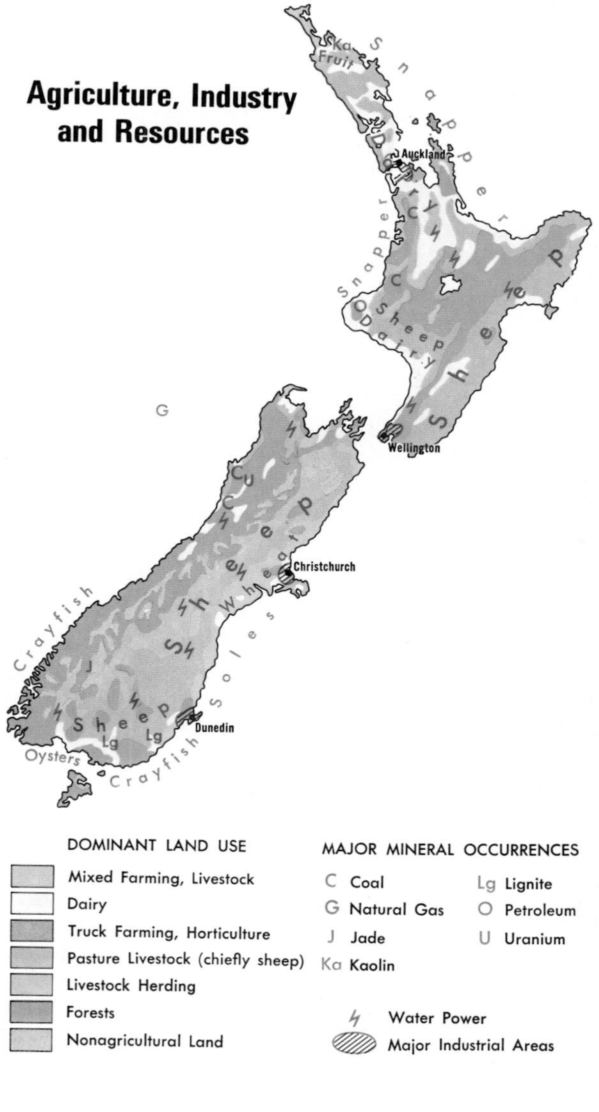

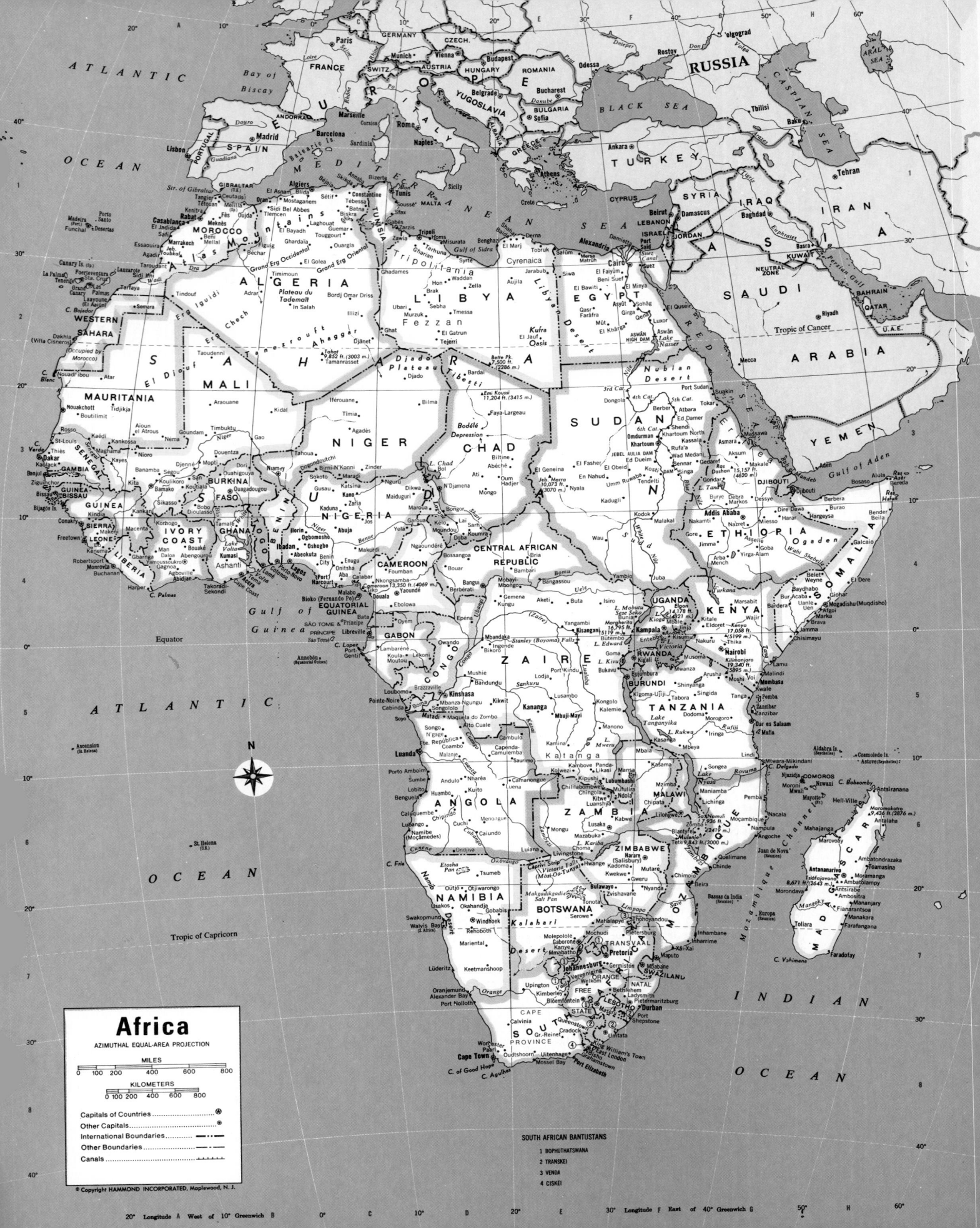

Africa
AZIMUTHAL EQUAL-AREA PROJECTION
MILES
0 100 200 400 600 800
KILOMETERS
0 100 200 400 600 800
Capitals of Countries
Other Capitals
International Boundaries
Other Boundaries
Canals
SOUTH AFRICAN BANTUSTANS
1 BOPHUTHATSWANA
2 TRANSKEI
3 VENDA
4 CISKEI
© Copyright HAMMOND INCORPORATED, Maplewood, N. J.
20° Longitude A West of 10° Greenwich B
0° C 10° D 20° E
30° Longitude F East of 40° Greenwich G
50° H 60°
ATLANTIC OCEAN
ATLANTIC OCEAN
INDIAN OCEAN
MEDITERRANEAN SEA
BLACK SEA
CASPIAN SEA
ARAL SEA
RED SEA
Gulf of Aden
Gulf of Guinea
Mozambique Channel
Bay of Biscay
Persian Gulf
Equator
Tropic of Cancer
Tropic of Capricorn
EUROPE
ASIA
N
FRANCE
GERMANY
CZECH.
SWITZ.
AUSTRIA
HUNGARY
ROMANIA
RUSSIA
ITALY
YUGOSLAVIA
BULGARIA
ALBANIA
GREECE
SPAIN
PORTUGAL
ANDORRA
TURKEY
CYPRUS
SYRIA
LEBANON
ISRAEL
JORDAN
IRAQ
IRAN
KUWAIT
NEUTRAL ZONE
BAHRAIN
QATAR
U.A.E.
SAUDI ARABIA
YEMEN
MOROCCO
ALGERIA
TUNISIA
LIBYA
EGYPT
WESTERN SAHARA
MAURITANIA
MALI
NIGER
CHAD
SUDAN
SENEGAL
GAMBIA
GUINEA-BISSAU
GUINEA
SIERRA LEONE
LIBERIA
IVORY COAST
BURKINA FASO
GHANA
TOGO
BENIN
NIGERIA
CAMEROON
CENTRAL AFRICAN REPUBLIC
EQUATORIAL GUINEA
SÃO TOME & PRINCIPE
GABON
CONGO
ZAIRE
UGANDA
KENYA
RWANDA
BURUNDI
TANZANIA
ETHIOPIA
DJIBOUTI
SOMALIA
ANGOLA
ZAMBIA
MALAWI
MOZAMBIQUE
ZIMBABWE
NAMIBIA
BOTSWANA
SOUTH AFRICA
SWAZILAND
LESOTHO
MADAGASCAR
COMOROS
TRANSVAAL
ORANGE FREE STATE
NATAL
CAPE PROVINCE
SAHARA
Atlas Mountains
Libyan Desert
Nubian Desert
Kalahari Desert
Namib Desert
Tibesti
Ahaggar
Sudd
Katanga
Fezzan
Tripolitania
Cyrenaica
Ogaden
Paris
Munich
Vienna
Budapest
Belgrade
Bucharest
Sofia
Rome
Naples
Madrid
Lisbon
Barcelona
Marseille
Athens
Ankara
Tehran
Baghdad
Damascus
Beirut
Riyadh
Mecca
Baku
Tbilisi
Rostov
Odessa
Rabat
Casablanca
Algiers
Tunis
Tripoli
Cairo
Alexandria
Khartoum
Omdurman
Addis Ababa
Djibouti
Mogadishu (Muqdisho)
Nairobi
Mombasa
Kampala
Kigali
Bujumbura
Dar es Salaam
Dodoma
Kinshasa
Brazzaville
Luanda
Lusaka
Harare (Salisbury)
Bulawayo
Lilongwe
Maputo
Pretoria
Johannesburg
Durban
Cape Town
Port Elizabeth
East London
Bloemfontein
Windhoek
Gaborone
Maseru
Mbabane
Antananarivo
Moroni
Dakar
Banjul
Bissau
Conakry
Freetown
Monrovia
Abidjan
Accra
Lomé
Porto-Novo
Lagos
Abuja
Niamey
Ouagadougou
Bamako
Nouakchott
Yaoundé
Malabo
Libreville
Bangui
N'Djamena
Timbuktu
Kano
Kisangani
Lubumbashi
Asmara
Port Sudan
Aswan
Aswan High Dam
Suez Canal
Canary Is. (Sp.)
Madeira (Port.)
Cape Verde
Ascension (St. Helena)
St. Helena (U.K.)
Annobón (Equatorial Guinea)
Bioko (Fernando Po)
Aldabra Is. (Seychelles)
Bassas da India (Réunion)
Europa (Réunion)
Juan de Nova (Réunion)
L. Chad
L. Victoria
L. Tanganyika
L. Nyasa
L. Turkana
L. Kariba
Victoria Falls
Kilimanjaro 19,340 ft. (5895 m.)
Kenya 17,058 ft. (5199 m.)
Emi Koussi 11,204 ft. (3415 m.)
Tahat 9,852 ft. (3003 m.)
C. of Good Hope
C. Agulhas
C. Verde
C. Blanc
C. Bojador
C. Palmas
C. Lopez
C. Frio
C. Delgado
Ras Hafun

Population Distribution

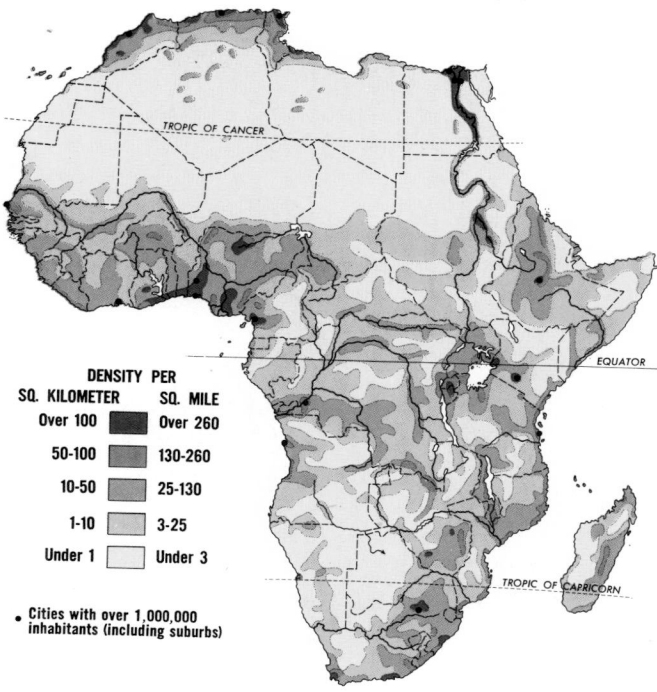

AREA 11,707,000 sq. mi. (30,321,130 sq. km.)
POPULATION 648,000,000
LARGEST CITY Cairo
HIGHEST POINT Kilimanjaro 19,340 ft. (5,895 m.)
LOWEST POINT Lake Assal, Djibouti -512 ft. (-156 m.)

DENSITY PER

SQ. KILOMETER	SQ. MILE
Over 100	Over 260
50-100	130-260
10-50	25-130
1-10	3-25
Under 1	Under 3

• Cities with over 1,000,000 inhabitants (including suburbs)

Vegetation

TROPICAL FOREST
Tropical Rainforest
Light Tropical Forest
Woodland and Shrub

TROPICAL GRASSLAND
Grass and Shrub (Savanna)
Wooded Savanna

MID-LATITUDE FOREST
Mixed Coniferous and Broadleaf Forest
Woodland and Shrub (Mediterranean)

MID-LATITUDE GRASSLAND
Short Grass (Steppe)

RIVER VALLEY AND OASIS

DESERT AND DESERT SHRUB

UNCLASSIFIED HIGHLANDS

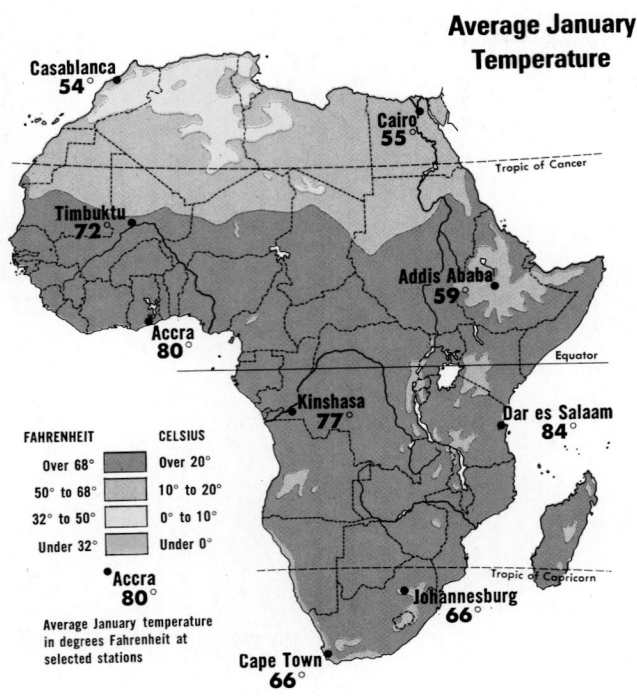

Average January Temperature

Casablanca 54°
Cairo 55°
Timbuktu 72°
Addis Ababa 59°
Accra 80°
Kinshasa 77°
Dar es Salaam 84°
Johannesburg 66°
Cape Town 66°

Tropic of Cancer
Equator
Tropic of Capricorn

FAHRENHEIT	CELSIUS
Over 68°	Over 20°
50° to 68°	10° to 20°
32° to 50°	0° to 10°
Under 32°	Under 0°

• Accra 80°
Average January temperature in degrees Fahrenheit at selected stations

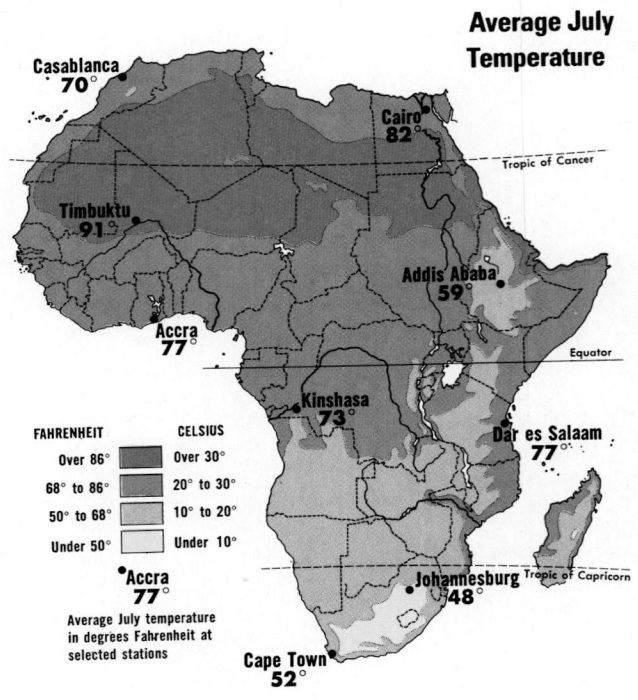

Average July Temperature

Casablanca 70°
Cairo 82°
Timbuktu 91°
Addis Ababa 59°
Accra 77°
Kinshasa 73°
Dar es Salaam 77°
Johannesburg 48°
Cape Town 52°

Tropic of Cancer
Equator
Tropic of Capricorn

FAHRENHEIT	CELSIUS
Over 86°	Over 30°
68° to 86°	20° to 30°
50° to 68°	10° to 20°
Under 50°	Under 10°

• Accra 77°
Average July temperature in degrees Fahrenheit at selected stations

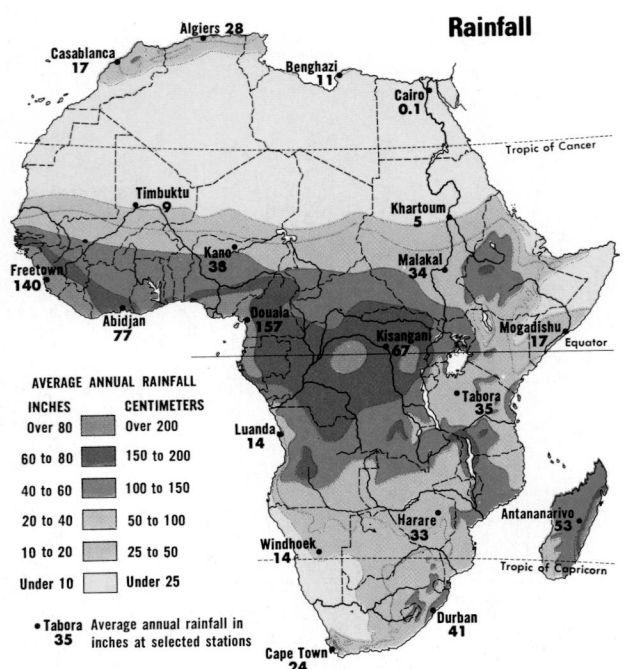

Rainfall

Algiers 28
Casablanca 17
Benghazi 11
Cairo 0.1
Timbuktu 9
Khartoum 5
Kano 38
Malakal 34
Freetown 140
Abidjan 77
Douala 157
Kisangani 67
Mogadishu 17
Tabora 35
Luanda 14
Harare 33
Antananarivo 53
Windhoek 14
Durban 41
Cape Town 24

Tropic of Cancer
Equator
Tropic of Capricorn

AVERAGE ANNUAL RAINFALL

INCHES	CENTIMETERS
Over 80	Over 200
60 to 80	150 to 200
40 to 60	100 to 150
20 to 40	50 to 100
10 to 20	25 to 50
Under 10	Under 25

• Tabora 35
Average annual rainfall in inches at selected stations

Vegetation/Relief

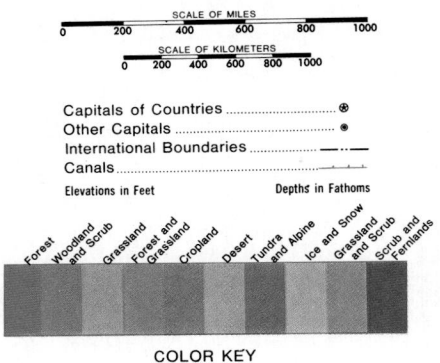

SCALE OF MILES
0 200 400 600 800 1000

SCALE OF KILOMETERS
0 200 400 600 800 1000

Capitals of Countries .... ⊕
Other Capitals .... ⊙
International Boundaries .... — — —
Canals ....

Elevations in Feet   Depths in Fathoms

Forest | Woodland and Scrub | Grassland | Forest and Grassland | Cropland | Desert | Tundra and Alpine | Ice and Snow | Grassland and Scrub | Scrub and Fernlands

COLOR KEY

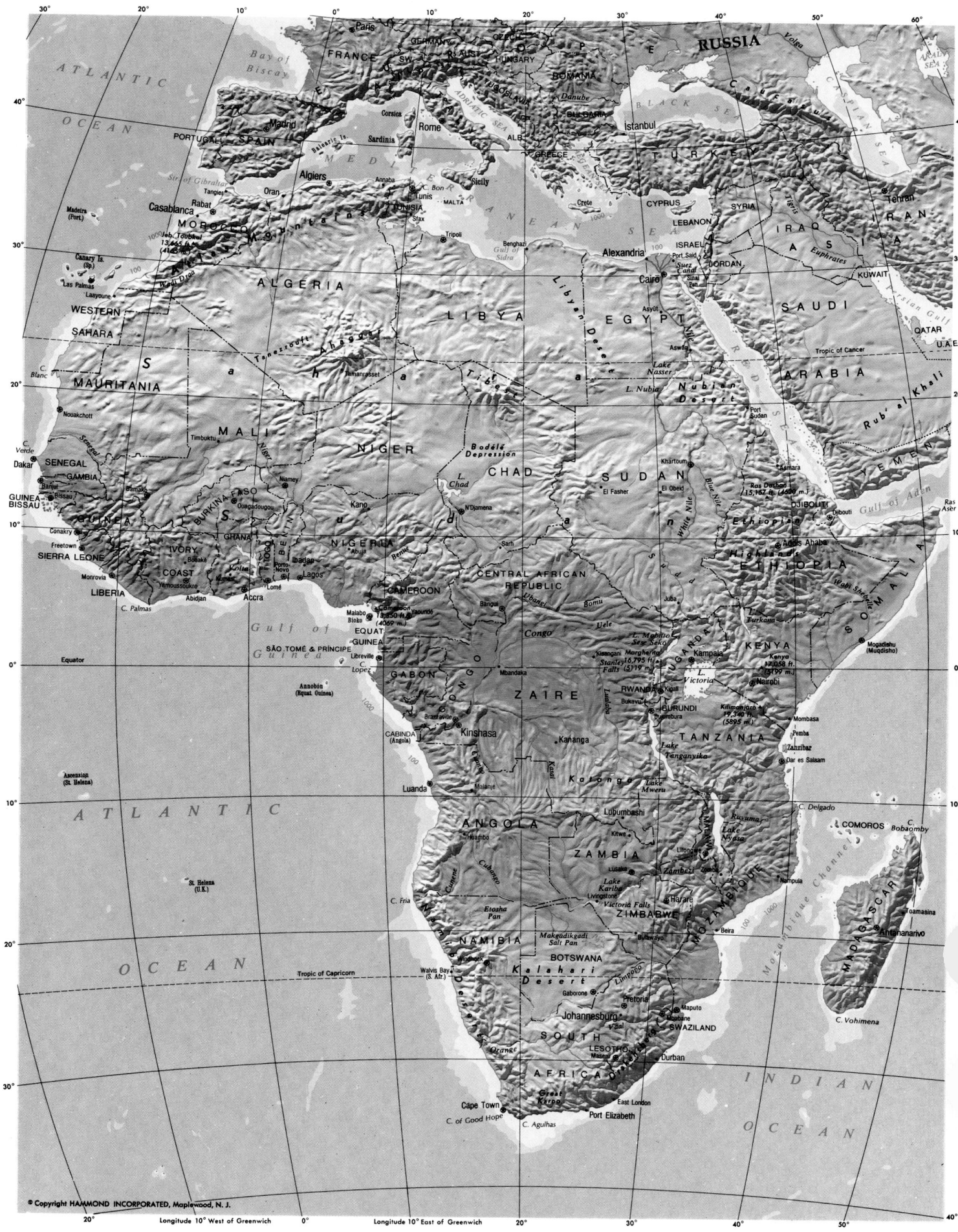

Longitude 10° West of Greenwich   Longitude 10° East of Greenwich

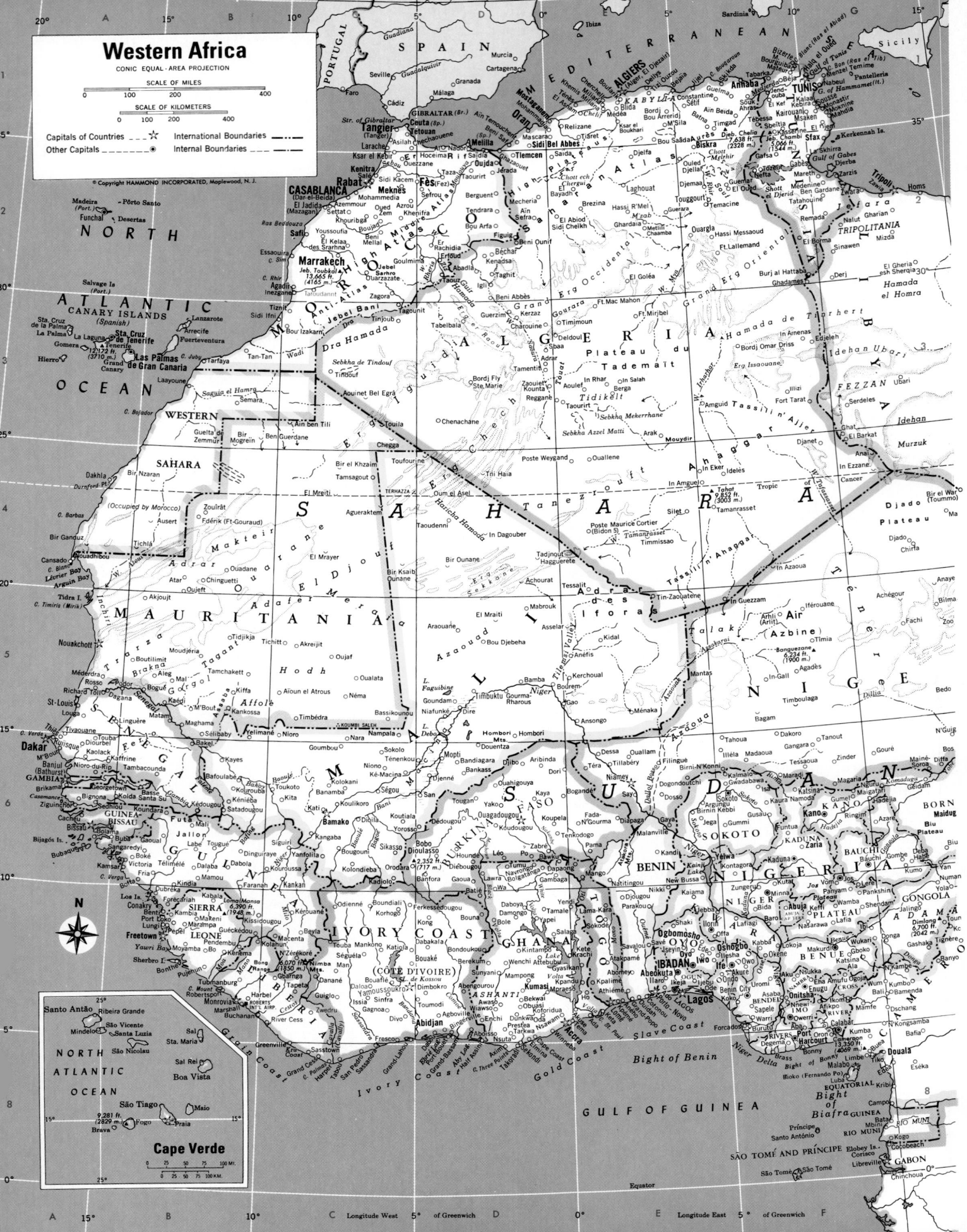

Western Africa
CONIC EQUAL-AREA PROJECTION
SCALE OF MILES
0 100 200 400
SCALE OF KILOMETERS
0 100 200 400
Capitals of Countries
Other Capitals
International Boundaries
Internal Boundaries
© Copyright HAMMOND INCORPORATED, Maplewood, N. J.
SPAIN
PORTUGAL
MEDITERRANEAN SEA
NORTH ATLANTIC OCEAN
CANARY ISLANDS (Spanish)
MOROCCO
ALGERIA
TUNISIA
LIBYA
WESTERN SAHARA
(Occupied by Morocco)
MAURITANIA
MALI
NIGER
SENEGAL
GAMBIA
GUINEA-BISSAU
GUINEA
SIERRA LEONE
LIBERIA
IVORY COAST (CÔTE D'IVOIRE)
BURKINA FASO
GHANA
TOGO
BENIN
NIGERIA
CAMEROON
EQUATORIAL GUINEA
RIO MUNI
GABON
SÃO TOMÉ AND PRÍNCIPE
SAHARA
GULF OF GUINEA
Bight of Benin
Bight of Biafra
Slave Coast
Gold Coast
Ivory Coast
Grain Coast
Tropic of Cancer
Equator
ALGIERS
TUNIS
Tripoli
Rabat
CASABLANCA
Marrakech
Dakar
Banjul (Bathurst)
Bissau
Conakry
Freetown
Monrovia
Abidjan
Yamoussoukro
Accra
Lomé
Porto-Novo
Lagos
Niamey
Bamako
Ouagadougou
Nouakchott
Malabo
Libreville
São Tomé
Longitude West 5° of Greenwich
Longitude East 5° of Greenwich
Cape Verde
Santo Antão
Ribeira Grande
São Vicente
Mindelo
Santa Luzia
São Nicolau
Sal
Sta. Maria
Sal Rei
Boa Vista
NORTH ATLANTIC OCEAN
São Tiago
Maio
Fogo
Praia
Brava
9,281 ft. (2829 m.)

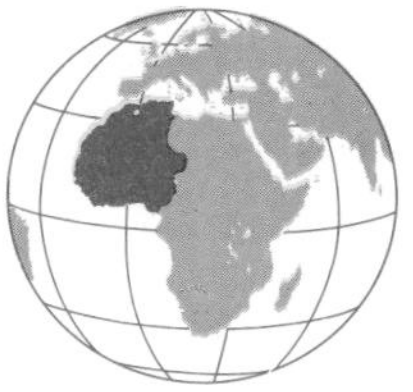

ALGERIA

AREA 919,591 sq. mi. (2,381,740 sq. km.)
POPULATION 22,971,000
CAPITAL Algiers
LARGEST CITY Algiers
HIGHEST POINT Tahat 9,852 ft. (3,003 m.)
MONETARY UNIT Algerian dinar
MAJOR LANGUAGES Arabic, Berber, French
MAJOR RELIGION Islam

BENIN

AREA 43,483 sq. mi. (112,620 sq. km.)
POPULATION 4,591,000
CAPITAL Porto-Novo
LARGEST CITY Cotonou
HIGHEST POINT Atakora Mts. 2,083 ft. (635 m.)
MONETARY UNIT CFA franc
MAJOR LANGUAGES Fon, Somba, Yoruba, Bariba, French, Mina, Dendi
MAJOR RELIGIONS Tribal religions, Islam, Roman Catholicism

CAPE VERDE

AREA 1,557 sq. mi. (4,033 sq. km.)
POPULATION 347,000
CAPITAL Praia
LARGEST CITY Praia
HIGHEST POINT 9,281 ft. (2,829 m.)
MONETARY UNIT Cape Verde escudo
MAJOR LANGUAGE Portuguese
MAJOR RELIGION Roman Catholicism

GAMBIA

AREA 4,127 sq. mi. (10,689 sq. km.)
POPULATION 688,000
CAPITAL Banjul
LARGEST CITY Banjul
HIGHEST POINT 100 ft. (30 m.)
MONETARY UNIT dalasi
MAJOR LANGUAGES Mandingo, Fulani, Wolof, English, Malinke
MAJOR RELIGIONS Islam, tribal religions, Christianity

GHANA

AREA 92,099 sq. mi. (238,536 sq. km.)
POPULATION 13,391,000
CAPITAL Accra
LARGEST CITY Accra
HIGHEST POINT Togo Hills 2,900 ft. (884 m.)
MONETARY UNIT cedi
MAJOR LANGUAGES Twi, Fante, Dagbani, Ewe, Ga, English, Hausa, Akan
MAJOR RELIGIONS Tribal religions, Christianity, Islam

GUINEA

AREA 94,925 sq. mi. (245,856 sq. km.)
POPULATION 6,706,000
CAPITAL Conakry
LARGEST CITY Conakry
HIGHEST POINT Nimba Mts. 6,070 ft. (1,850 m.)
MONETARY UNIT syli
MAJOR LANGUAGES Fulani, Mandingo, Susu, French
MAJOR RELIGIONS Islam, tribal religions

GUINEA-BISSAU

AREA 13,948 sq. mi. (36,125 sq. km.)
POPULATION 943,000
CAPITAL Bissau
LARGEST CITY Bissau
HIGHEST POINT 689 ft. (210 m.)
MONETARY UNIT Guinea-Bissau peso
MAJOR LANGUAGES Balante, Fulani, Crioulo, Mandingo, Portuguese
MAJOR RELIGIONS Islam, tribal religions, Roman Catholicism

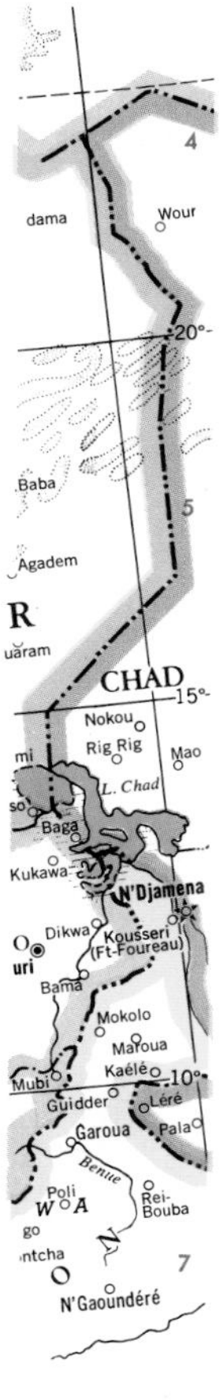

IVORY COAST (CÔTE-D'IVOIRE)

AREA 124,504 sq. mi. (322,465 sq. km.)
POPULATION 9,300,000
CAPITAL Yamoussoukro
LARGEST CITY Abidjan
HIGHEST POINT 5,745 ft. (1,751 m.)
MONETARY UNIT CFA franc
MAJOR LANGUAGES Bale, Bete, Senufu, French, Dioula
MAJOR RELIGIONS Tribal religions, Islam

LIBERIA

AREA 43,000 sq. mi. (111,370 sq. km.)
POPULATION 2,508,000
CAPITAL Monrovia
LARGEST CITY Monrovia
HIGHEST POINT Wutivi 5,584 ft. (1,702 m.)
MONETARY UNIT Liberian dollar
MAJOR LANGUAGES Kru, Kpelle, Bassa, Vai, English
MAJOR RELIGIONS Christianity, tribal religions, Islam

MALI

AREA 464,873 sq. mi. (1,204,021 sq. km.)
POPULATION 7,960,000
CAPITAL Bamako
LARGEST CITY Bamako
HIGHEST POINT Hombori Mts. 3,789 ft. (1,155 m.)
MONETARY UNIT CFA franc
MAJOR LANGUAGES Bambara, Senufu, Fulani, Soninke, French
MAJOR RELIGIONS Islam, tribal religions

MAURITANIA

AREA 419,229 sq. mi. (1,085,803 sq. km.)
POPULATION 1,894,000
CAPITAL Nouakchott
LARGEST CITY Nouakchott
HIGHEST POINT 2,972 ft. (906 m.)
MONETARY UNIT ouguiya
MAJOR LANGUAGES Arabic, Wolof, Tukolor, French
MAJOR RELIGION Islam

MOROCCO

AREA 172,414 sq. mi. (446,550 sq. km.)
POPULATION 24,522,000
CAPITAL Rabat
LARGEST CITY Casablanca
HIGHEST POINT Jeb. Toubkal 13,665 ft. (4,165 m.)
MONETARY UNIT dirham
MAJOR LANGUAGES Arabic, Berber, French
MAJOR RELIGIONS Islam, Judaism, Christianity

NIGER

AREA 489,189 sq. mi. (1,267,000 sq. km.)
POPULATION 7,250,000
CAPITAL Niamey
LARGEST CITY Niamey
HIGHEST POINT Banguezane 6,234 ft. (1,900 m.)
MONETARY UNIT CFA franc
MAJOR LANGUAGES Hausa, Songhai, Fulani, French, Tamashek, Djerma
MAJOR RELIGIONS Islam, tribal religions

NIGERIA

AREA 357,000 sq. mi. (924,630 sq. km.)
POPULATION 104,957,000
CAPITAL Lagos
LARGEST CITY Lagos
HIGHEST POINT Dimlang 6,700 ft. (2,042 m.)
MONETARY UNIT naira
MAJOR LANGUAGES Hausa, Yoruba, Ibo, Ijaw, Fulani, Tiv, Kanuri, Ibibio, English, Edo
MAJOR RELIGIONS Islam, Christianity, tribal religions

SÃO TOMÉ AND PRÍNCIPE

AREA 372 sq. mi. (963 sq. km.)
POPULATION 116,000
CAPITAL São Tomé
LARGEST CITY São Tomé
HIGHEST POINT Pico 6,640 ft. (2,024 m.)
MONETARY UNIT dobra
MAJOR LANGUAGES Bantu languages, Portuguese
MAJOR RELIGIONS Tribal religions, Roman Catholicism

SENEGAL

AREA 75,954 sq. mi. (196,720 sq. km.)
POPULATION 7,113,000
CAPITAL Dakar
LARGEST CITY Dakar
HIGHEST POINT Futa Jallon 1,640 ft. (500 m.)
MONETARY UNIT CFA franc
MAJOR LANGUAGES Wolof, Peul (Fulani), French, Mende, Mandingo, Dida
MAJOR RELIGIONS Islam, tribal religions, Roman Catholicism

SIERRA LEONE

AREA 27,925 sq. mi. (72,325 sq. km.)
POPULATION 4,047,000
CAPITAL Freetown
LARGEST CITY Freetown
HIGHEST POINT Loma Mts. 6,390 ft. (1,947 m.)
MONETARY UNIT leone
MAJOR LANGUAGES Mende, Temne, Vai, English, Krio (pidgin)
MAJOR RELIGIONS Tribal religions, Islam, Christianity

TOGO

AREA 21,622 sq. mi. (56,000 sq. km.)
POPULATION 3,296,000
CAPITAL Lomé
LARGEST CITY Lomé
HIGHEST POINT Agou 3,445 ft. (1,050 m.)
MONETARY UNIT CFA franc
MAJOR LANGUAGES Ewe, French, Twi, Hausa
MAJOR RELIGIONS Tribal religions, Roman Catholicism, Islam

TUNISIA

AREA 63,378 sq. mi. (164,149 sq. km.)
POPULATION 7,465,000
CAPITAL Tunis
LARGEST CITY Tunis
HIGHEST POINT Jeb. Chambi 5,066 ft. (1,544 m.)
MONETARY UNIT Tunisian dinar
MAJOR LANGUAGES Arabic, French
MAJOR RELIGION Islam

BURKINA FASO

AREA 105,869 sq. mi. (274,200 sq. km.)
POPULATION 9,001,000
CAPITAL Ouagadougou
LARGEST CITY Ouagadougou
HIGHEST POINT 2,352 ft. (717 m.)
MONETARY UNIT CFA franc
MAJOR LANGUAGES Mossi, Lobi, French, Samo, Gourounsi
MAJOR RELIGIONS Islam, tribal religions, Roman Catholicism

WESTERN SAHARA

AREA 102,703 sq. mi. (266,000 sq. km.)
POPULATION 174,000
HIGHEST POINT 2,700 ft. (823 m.)
MAJOR LANGUAGE Arabic
MAJOR RELIGION Islam

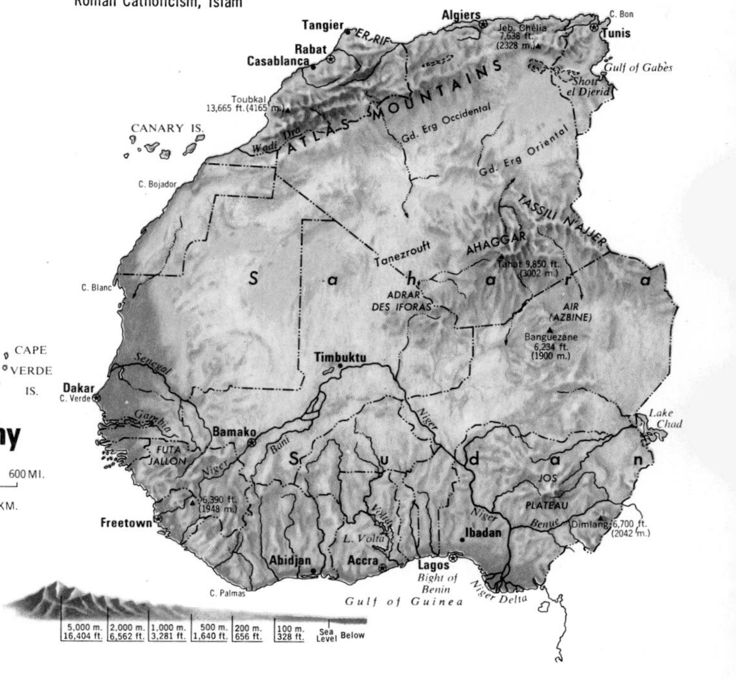

Topography

0   200   400   600 MI.
0   200   400   600 KM.

5,000 m. 2,000 m. 1,000 m. 500 m. 200 m. 100 m. Sea Level Below
16,404 ft. 6,562 ft. 3,281 ft. 1,640 ft. 656 ft. 328 ft.

(continued)

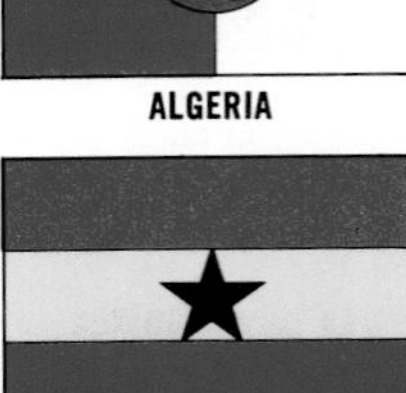
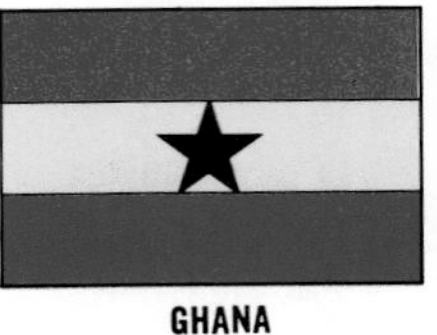
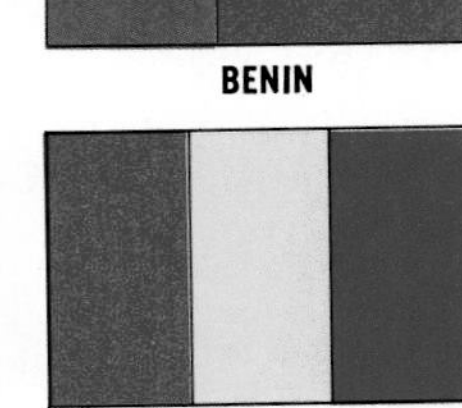
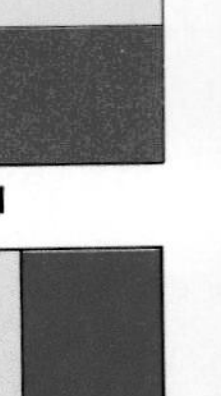
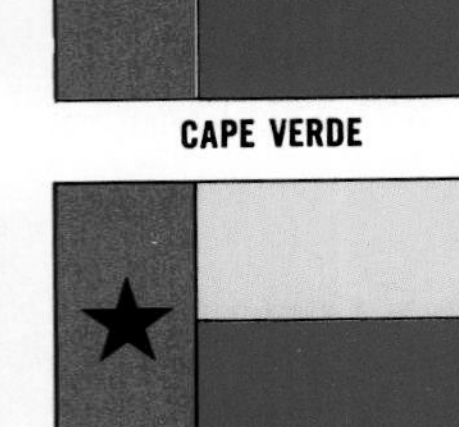
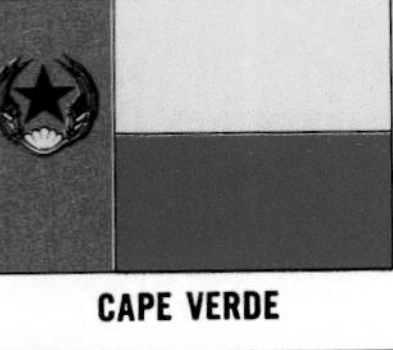

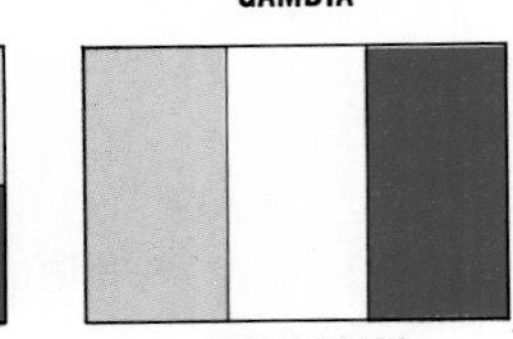
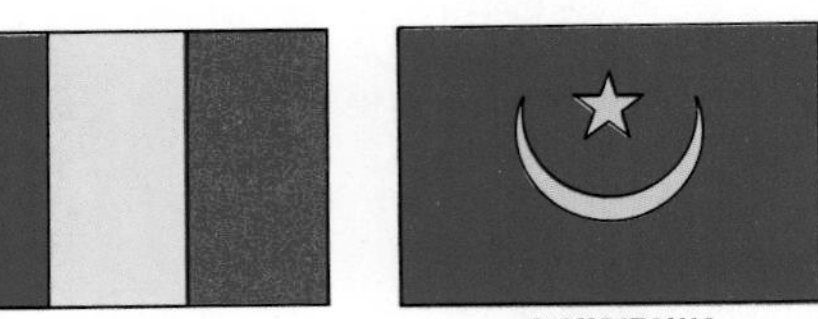
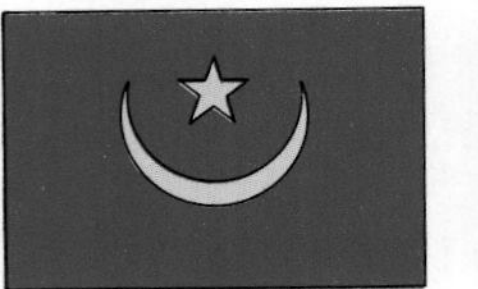
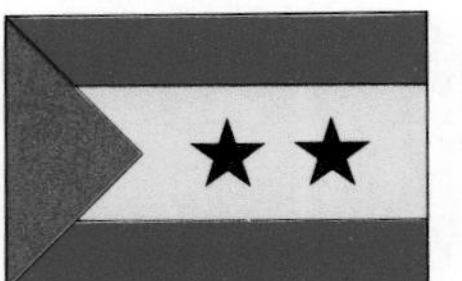
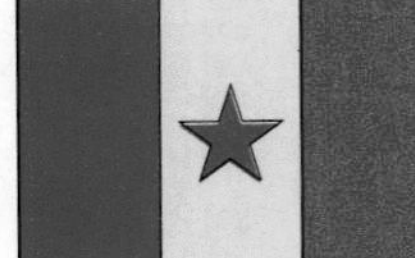
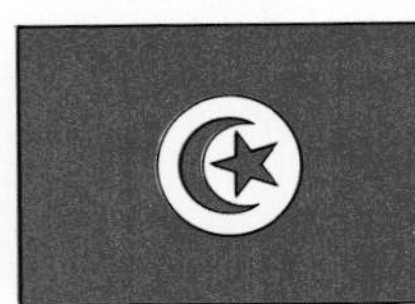

ALGERIA BENIN CAPE VERDE GAMBIA

GHANA GUINEA GUINEA-BISSAU IVORY COAST

LIBERIA MALI MAURITANIA MOROCCO

NIGER NIGERIA SÃO TOMÉ AND PRINCIPE SENEGAL

SIERRA LEONE TOGO TUNISIA BURKINA FASO

ALGERIA

CITIES and TOWNS

Adrar 28,495 ..... D3
Aïn Beïda 67,281 ..... F1
Aïn Sefra 22,400 ..... D2
Aïn Temouchent 48,935 ..... D1
Algiers (cap.) 1,687,579 ..... E1
Annaba 227,795 ..... F1
Aoulef 10,259 ..... E3
Batna 184,833 ..... F1
Béchar 107,042 ..... D2
Bejaïa 118,233 ..... F1
Beni Abbès 7,370 ..... D2
Beni Saf 30,700 ..... D1
Biskra 129,611 ..... F2
Blida 131,615 ..... E1
Bone (Annaba) 227,795 ..... F1
Bordj Bou Arreridj 86,997 ..... E1
Bordj Omar Driss 1,900 ..... F3
Boufarik 54,023 ..... E1
Bougie (Bejaïa) 118,233 ..... F1
Bou Saâda 50,000 ..... E1
Brezina 10,000 ..... E2
Cherchell 32,572 ..... E1
Constantine 449,602 ..... F1
Dellys 29,700 ..... E1
Djelfa 88,929 ..... E2
Djemaa 34,600 ..... F2
El Abiod Sidi Cheikh 15,300 ..... E2
El Asnam 103,998 ..... E1
El Bayadh 44,925 ..... E2
El Djezair (Algiers) (cap.) 1,687,579 ..... E1
El Goléa 24,400 ..... E2
El Oued 73,093 ..... F2
Ghardaïa 62,518 ..... E2
Ghazaouet 29,795 ..... D2
Guelma 84,826 ..... F1
Guerara 22,300 ..... E2
Hassi Messaoud F2
Hassi R'Mel 10,545 ..... E2
In Guezzam 10,304 ..... F5
In Salah 20,733 ..... E3
Jijel 69,274 ..... F1
Khemis Miliana 57,101 ..... E1
Ksar el Boukhari 41,200 ..... E1
Laghouat 71,808 ..... E2
Mascara 70,885 ..... D1
Mecheria 40,251 ..... D2
Médéa 84,062 ..... E1
Metlili Chaamba 21,300 ..... E2
Miliana 36,400 ..... E1
Mohammadia 58,967 ..... D1
Mostaganem 115,302 ..... D1
M'Sila 82,877 ..... E1
Oran 598,525 ..... D1
Orléansville (El Asnam) 103,998 ..... E1
Ouargla 76,270 ..... F2
Ouled Djellal 33,278 ..... F2
Philippeville (Skikda) 128,503 ..... F1
Reggane 10,061 ..... D3
Relizane 83,864 ..... E1
Saïda 84,371 ..... E2
Sétif 185,786 ..... F1
Sidi Bel-Abbes 154,745 ..... D1
Skikda 128,503 ..... F1
Souk Ahras 85,873 ..... F1
Tamanrasset 38,146 ..... F4
Tébessa 111,688 ..... F1
Ténès 26,510 ..... E1
Tiaret 105,562 ..... E1
Timimoun 21,556 ..... E3
Tindouf 6,500 ..... C3
Tizi Ouzou 93,025 ..... E1
Tlemcen 108,145 ..... D2
Touggourt 75,600 ..... F2
Zaouiet Kounta 10,707 ..... D3

OTHER FEATURES

Adrar des Iforas (plat.) E5
Ahaggar (range) F4
Anaï (well) G4
Aouinet Bel Egrâ (well) C3
Atlas (mts.) E2
Aurès (lag.) F1
Azzel Mati, Sebkha (lake) E3
Bougaroun (cape) F1
Chech, Erg (des.) D3
Chelia (mt.) F1
Chelif (riv.) E1
Chergui, Chott Ech (salt lake) E2
Dra, Wadi (dry river) C3
Dra Hamada (plat.) C3
Gourara (oasis) E3
Grand Erg Occidental (des.) E2
Grand Erg Oriental (des.) F2
Guir Hamada (des.) D2
High Plateaus (ranges) D2
Iguidi, Erg (des.) C3
In Ezzane (well) G4
Irharhar, Wadi (dry river) F3
Kabylia (reg.) E1
Mediterranean (sea) E1
Medjerda (riv.) F1
Mekerrhane, Sebkha (salt lake) E3
Melrhir, Chott (salt lake) F2
Mouydir (mts.) E3
Mya, Wadi (dry river) E2
M'zab (oasis) E2
Raoui, Erg er (des.) D3
Rhir, Wadi (dry river) F2
Sahara (des.) E4
Saharan Atlas (ranges) E2
Saoura, Wadi (dry river) D3
Souf (oasis) F2
Tademaït, Plateau du (plat.) E3
Tafassasset, Wadi (dry river) F4
Tahat (mt.) F4
Tamanrasset, Wadi (dry river) E4
Tanezrouft (des.) E4
Tassili N'Ahagger (plat.) E4
Tassili N'Ajjer (plat.) F3
Tidikelt (oasis) E3
Timmissao (well) E4
Tindouf, Sebkha de (salt lake) C3
Tinrhert, Hamada de (des.) F3
Tni Haïa (well) D4
Touat (oasis) E3
Touila (well) C3

BENIN

CITIES and TOWNS

Abomey 38,000 ..... E7
Cotonou 178,000 ..... E7
Grand-Popo E7
Kandi E6
Natitingou 49,000 ..... E6
Ouidah E7
Parakou 21,000 ..... E7
Porto-Novo (cap.) 104,000 ..... E7

OTHER FEATURES

Atakora (mts.) E6
Benin (bight) E8
Guinea (gulf) E8
Mono (riv.) E7
Niger (riv.) E6
Ouémé (riv.) E7
Slave Coast (reg.) E7
Sudan (reg.) E6

BURKINA FASO

CITIES and TOWNS

Banfora 12,358 ..... D6
Bobo Dioulasso 115,063 ..... D6
Bogandé E6
Dédougou D6
Diébougou D6
Djibo D6
Dori D6
Fada-N'Gourma 12,000 ..... E6
Gaoua D6
Kaya 18,000 ..... D6
Koudougou 36,838 ..... D6
Koupela D6
Léo D6
Ouagadougou (cap.) 172,661 ..... D6
Ouahigouya 25,690 ..... D6
Po D6
Tenkodogo E6
Tougan D6
Yako D6
Zabré D6

OTHER FEATURES

Black Volta (Mouhoun) (riv.) D6
Comoé (riv.) D7
Mouhoun (riv.) D6
Nakanbe (riv.) D6
Nazinan (riv.) D6
Oti (riv.) E7
Red Volta (Nazinan) (riv.) D6
Sudan (reg.) D6
White Volta (Nakanbe) (riv.) D6

CAPE VERDE

CITIES and TOWNS

Mindelo 28,797 ..... A7
Praia (cap.) 21,494 ..... B8
Ribeira Grande 1,892 ..... B7
Sal Rei 1,296 ..... B8

OTHER FEATURES

Boa Vista (isl.) B8
Brava (isl.) B8
Fogo (isl.) B8
Maio (isl.) B8
Sal (isl.) B7
Santa Luzia (isl.) B8
Santo Antão (isl.) A7
São Nicolau (isl.) B8
São Tiago (isl.) B8
São Vicente (isl.) B7

GAMBIA

CITIES and TOWNS

Banjul (cap.) 39,476 ..... A6
Basse Santa Su 2,899 ..... B6
Brikama 9,483 ..... A6
Georgetown 2,510 ..... A6

GHANA

CITIES and TOWNS

Accra (cap.) 859,600 ..... D7
Attebubu 9,800 ..... D7
Axim 13,100 ..... D8
Bawku 33,900 ..... D6
Bekwai 11,800 ..... D7
Berekum 21,900 ..... D7
Bolgatanga 31,500 ..... D6
Cape Coast 57,700 ..... D7
Damongo 12,600 ..... D7
Dunkwa 16,900 ..... D7
Elmina 15,600 ..... D8
Ho 37,200 ..... E7
Keta 12,700 ..... E7
Kintampo 14,100 ..... D7
Koforidua 54,400 ..... D7
Kpandu 15,800 ..... D7
Kumasi 348,900 ..... D7
Mampong 19,800 ..... D7
Nsawam 31,900 ..... D7
Obuasi 60,100 ..... D7
Oda 20,957 ..... D7
Prestea 16,300 ..... D7
Salaga 10,600 ..... D7
Sekondi 32,400 ..... D8
Sunyani 36,100 ..... D7
Takoradi 61,500 ..... D8
Tamale 136,800 ..... D7
Tarkwa 22,000 ..... D7
Tema 99,600 ..... E7
Wa 36,000 ..... D6
Wenchi 18,400 ..... D7
Winneba 26,200 ..... D7
Yendi 30,700 ..... D7

OTHER FEATURES

Ashanti (reg.) D7
Benin (bight) E8
Black Volta (riv.) D7
Gold Coast (reg.) D8
Guinea (gulf) E8
Oti (riv.) E7
Red Volta (riv.) D6
Saint Paul (cape) E7
Three Points (cape) D8
Volta (lake) D7
Volta (riv.) E7
White Volta (riv.) D7

GUINEA

CITIES and TOWNS

Boffa B6
Conakry (cap.) 525,671 ..... B7
Dabola B6
Dubréka B7
Fria B6
Kankan 85,310 ..... C6
Kérouané C7
Kindia 79,861 ..... B6
Kissidougou B7
Koundara 6,000 ..... B6
Kouroussa C6
Labé 79,670 ..... B6
Mali B6
N'Zérékoré 23,000 ..... C7
Siguiri C6
Télimélé 12,000 ..... B6
Tougué B6

OTHER FEATURES

Bafing (riv.) B6
Bakoy (riv.) B6
Futa Jallon (lag.) B6
Los (isls.) B7
Milo (riv.) C7
Moa (riv.) B7
Niger (riv.) C6
Nimba (lag.) C7
Verga (cape) B6

GUINEA-BISSAU

CITIES and TOWNS

Bissau (cap.) 109,486 ..... A6
Bolama ◦ 9,133 ..... A6
Bubaque ◦ 8,441 ..... A6
Cacheu ◦ 15,194 ..... A6

OTHER FEATURES

Bijagós (isls.) A6

IVORY COAST

CITIES and TOWNS

Abengourou 31,239 ..... D7
Abidjan 6 85,828 ..... D7
Aboisso 14,272 ..... D7
Agboville 27,192 ..... D7
Bingerville 18,218 ..... D7
Bondoukou 19,111 ..... D7
Bouaflé 15,917 ..... C7
Bouaké 1 73,248 ..... D7
Dabou 23,870 ..... D7
Daloa 60,958 ..... C7
Danané 19,872 ..... C7
Dimbokro 30,986 ..... D7
Divo 37,896 ..... C7
Ferkessédougou 25,307 ..... D7
Gagnoa 42,362 ..... C7
Grand-Bassam 25,808 ..... D7
Grand-Lahou 4,070 ..... C8
Guiglo 10,441 ..... C7
Issia 11,143 ..... C7
Katiola 21,559 ..... C7
Korhogo 47,657 ..... C7
Man 50,315 ..... C7
Odienné 13,864 ..... C7
Port-Bouet 72,616 ..... D7
San Pedro 27,616 ..... C8
Séguéla 12,587 ..... C7
Sinfra 16,399 ..... C7
Tabou 7,255 ..... C8
Toumodi 12,983 ..... D7
Yamoussoukro (cap.) 35,585 ..... C7

OTHER FEATURES

Aby (lag.) D8
Bagoé (riv.) C6
Bandama (riv.) C7
Baoulé (riv.) C6
Black Volta (riv.) D6
Cavally (riv.) C7
Comoé (riv.) D7
Ebrié (lag.) D8
Guinea (gulf) E8
Ivory Coast (reg.) C8
Kossou, Lac de (lake) C7
Nimba (lag.) C7
Sassandra (riv.) C7

LIBERIA

CITIES and TOWNS

Buchanan 23,999 ..... B7
Gbarnga 6,896 ..... C7
Greenville 8,462 ..... C8
Harbel 11,445 ..... B7
Harper 10,627 ..... C8
Monrovia (cap.) 166,507 ..... B7
River Cess 2,041 ..... C7
Robertsport 2,562 ..... B7
Tapeta 3,927 ..... C7
Tubmanburg 14,089 ..... B7
Zwedru 6,094 ..... C7

OTHER FEATURES

Bong (range) B7
Cavalla (riv.) C7
Cestos (riv.) C7
Grain Coast (reg.) B8
Kru Coast (reg.) C8
Mano (riv.) B7
Mount (cape) B7
Nimba (lag.) C7
Palmas (cape) C8
Roberts Field Int'l Airport C7

MALI

CITIES and TOWNS

Ansongo 3,485 ..... E5
Bafoulabé 2,163 ..... B6
Bamako (cap.) 404,022 ..... C6
Banamba 6,776 ..... C6
Bandiagara 8,920 ..... D6
Bankass 3,229 ..... D6
Bougouni 17,246 ..... C6
Bourem 4,538 ..... E5
Dioila 4,953 ..... C6
Dire 8,941 ..... D5
Djenné 10,251 ..... D6
Douentza 6,746 ..... D6
Gao 30,714 ..... E5
Goundam 10,262 ..... D5
Gourma-Rharous 4,671 ..... D5
Kéniéba 4,510 ..... B6
Kadiolo 3,991 ..... C6
Kangaba 3,184 ..... C6
Kati 24,991 ..... C6
Kayes 44,736 ..... B6
Ké-Macina 5,426 ..... C6
Kidal 3,308 ..... E5
Kita 17,538 ..... C6
Kolokani 8,923 ..... C6
Kolondiéba 5,882 ..... C6
Koulikoro 16,376 ..... C6
Koutiala 27,497 ..... C6
Ménaka 3,693 ..... E5
Mopti 53,885 ..... D6
Nara 6,091 ..... C5
Niafunké 6,399 ..... D5
Niono 12,290 ..... C6
Nioro 11,617 ..... C5
San 22,962 ..... D6
Ségou 64,890 ..... C6
Sikasso 47,030 ..... C6
Ténenkou 4,708 ..... C6
Timbuktu (Tombouctou) 20,483 ..... D5
Yanfolila 3,809 ..... C6
Yelimané 1,481 ..... B5
Yorosso 2,390 ..... C6

OTHER FEATURES

Achourat (well) D4
Adrar des Iforas (plat.) E5
Agueraktem (well) C4
Asselar (well) D5
Azaouad (reg.) D5
Azaouak (dry riv.) E5
Bafing (riv.) B6
Bagoé (riv.) C6
Bakoy (riv.) B6
Bani (riv.) C6
Baoulé (dry riv.) C6
Baoulé (riv.) C6
Bir Ksaib Ounane (well) C4
Bir Ounane (well) D4
Chech, Erg (des.) D4
Debo (lake) D5
El Mraiti (well) D5
Faguibine (lake) D5
Faiémé (riv.) B6
Haricha Hamada (des.) D4
Hombori (mts.) D5
In Dagouber (well) D4
Macina (depr.) D6
Niger (riv.) D5
Oum el Asel (well) D4
Sahara (des.) D4
Sekkane, Erg (des.) D4
Senegal (riv.) B5
Sudan (reg.) D6
Tadjnout Hagguerete (well) D4
Terhazza (ruins) C4
Tilemsi (valley) E5
Toufourine (well) C4

MAURITANIA

CITIES and TOWNS

Aïoun el Atrous C5
Akjoujt 8,044 ..... B5
Aleg 6,415 ..... B5
Atar 16,326 ..... B4
Bassikounou C5
Boutilimit 7,261 ..... B5
Fdérik (Fort Gouraud) 2,160 ..... B4
Káedi 20,248 ..... B5
Kiffa 10,629 ..... B5
M'Bout B5
Néma 8,232 ..... C5
Nouadhibou 21,961 ..... A4
Nouakchott (cap.) 134,986 ..... A5
Oualata C5
Rosso 16,466 ..... A5
Sélibaby 5,994 ..... B5
Tidjikja 7,870 ..... B5
Timbédra 5,317 ..... C5
Zouïrât 17,474 ..... B4

OTHER FEATURES

Adafer (reg.) B5
Adrar (reg.) B4
Affolé (reg.) B5
Agueraktem (well) C4
Aïn ben Tili (well) C3
Arguin (bay) A4
Assaba (reg.) B5
Atoui, Wadi (dry riv.) B4
Ben Guerdane (well) B3
Bir el Khzaim (well) C4
Blanc (cape) A4
Brakna (reg.) B5
Chegga (well) C3
Djouf, El (des.) C4
El Mrayer (well) C4
El Mreïti (well) C4
Gorgol (reg.) B5
Hodh (reg.) C5
Iguidi, Erg (des.) C3
Inchiri (reg.) A5
Koumbi Saleh (ruins) C5

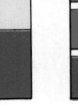

Lévrier (bay) A4
Makteïr (des.) B4
Meraia (reg.) C5
Mirik (Timiris) (cape) A5
Ouarane (reg.) B4
Sahara (des.) C4
Senegal (riv.) B5
Tagant (reg.) B5
Tidra (isl.) A5
Timiris (cape) A5
Touila (well) C3
Trarza (reg.) A5

MOROCCO

CITIES and TOWNS

Agadir 61,192 C2
Al Hoceima 18,686 D1
Azemmour 17,182 C2
Azrou 20,756 C2
Beni Mellal 53,826 C2
Boujad 18,838 C2
Casablanca 1,506,373 C2
Dar-el-Beida (Casablanca) 1,506,373 C2
El Jadida 55,501 C2
El Kelaa des Srarhna 17,163 C2
Er Rachidia 16,775 D2
Essaouira 30,061 C2
Fès (Fez) 325,327 D2
Jerada 30,633 D2
Kenitra 139,206 C2
Khenifra 25,526 C2
Khouribga 73,667 C2
Ksar el Kebir 48,262 C2
Larache 45,710 C1
Marrakech 332,741 C2
Mazagan (El Jadida) 55,501 C2
Meknès 248,369 C2
Mogador (Essaouira) 30,061 B2
Mohammedia 70,392 C2
Nador 32,490 D1
Oued Zem 33,323 C2
Ouezzane 33,267 C2
Oujda 175,532 D2
Port-Lyautey (Kénitra) 139,206 C2
Rabat (cap.) 367,620 C2
Safi 129,113 C2
Saïdia D2
Salé 155,557 C2
Sefrou 28,607 D2
Settat 42,325 C2
Sidi Ifni 13,650 B3
Sidi Kacem 26,831 C2
Tangier (Tanger) 187,894 C1
Tarfaya 1,104 B3
Taroudannt 22,272 C2
Taza 55,157 D2
Tétouan 139,105 C1
Youssoufia 22,435 C2

OTHER FEATURES

Anti-Atlas (ranges) C3
Atlas (mts.) C2
Bani, Jebel (mts.) C3
Beddouza, Ras (cape) C2
Dra, Wadi (dry riv.) C3
Gibraltar (str.) C1
High Atlas (ranges) C2
Juby (cape) B3
Mediterranean (sea) D1
Middle Atlas (ranges) C2
Moulouya (riv.) D2
Rheris, Wadi (dry riv.) D2
Rhir (cape) B2
Rif, Er (range) D2
Sarhro, Jebel (mts.) C2
Sebou (riv.) C2
Sim (cape) B2
Toubkal, Jebel (mt.) C2
Ziz, Wadi (dry riv.) D2

NIGER

CITIES and TOWNS

Agadès 11,000 F5
Arhli (Arlit) F5
Bilma G5
Birni-N'Konni 10,000 E6
Bosso G6
Dakoro F6
Diffa G6
Dosso E6
Filingué 10,000 E6
Gaya 5,000 E6
Gouré G6
Iférouane F5
In-Gall F5
Magaria F6
Mainé-Soro G6
Maradi 45,852 F6
N'Guigmi G6
Niamey (cap.) 225,314 E6
Say E6
Tahoua 31,265 F6
Tanout F6
Tillabéry E6
Zinder 58,436 F6

OTHER FEATURES

Achégour (well) G5
Agadem (well) G5
Air (mts.) F5
Anaye (well) G5
Assakarai (dry riv.) F5
Azaoua (reg.) E5
Azbine (Air) (mts.) F5
Bagam (well) F5
Banguezane (mt.) F5
Bedouaram (well) G5
Chad (lake) G6
Dallol Bosso (dry riv.) E6
Dillia (dry riv.) G5
Djado (plat.) G4
El War (well) G4
In Azaoua (well) F4
Komadugu Yobe (riv.) G6
Mantas (well) E5
Niger (riv.) E6
Rima (riv.) F6
Sahara (des.) F4
Sudan (reg.) F6
Tafassasset, Wadi (dry riv.) F4
Talak (reg.) E5
Ténéré (des.) G5
Timboulaga (well) F5
Tummo (El War) (well) G4
Zoo Baba (well) G5

NIGERIA

STATES

Abuja Capital Territory F7
Anambra 2,300,000 F7
Bauchi 2,496,329 F6
Bendel 2,336,000 F7
Benue 2,641,496 F7
Borno 2,853,553 G6
Cross River 3,633,582 F7
Gongola 1,585,200 G7
Imo 5,000,000 F7
Kaduna 4,098,303 F6
Kano 5,775,000 F6
Kwara 5,240,600 E7
Lagos 1,100,000 E7
Niger 2,900,000 F7
Ogun 1,448,966 E7
Ondo 2,727,676 F7
Oyo 5,208,884 E7
Plateau 1,367,450 F7
Rivers 1,544,314 F8
Sokoto 1,367,450 F6

CITIES and TOWNS

Abeokuta 253,000 E7
Abuja F7
Ado 213,000 E7
Aku F7
Akure F7
Baga G6
Bama G6
Baro F7
Bauchi F6
Benin City 136,000 F7
Biu G6
Bonny F8
Calabar 103,000 F7
Degema F8
Dikwa G6
Ede 182,000 E7
Enugu 187,000 F7
Geidam G6
Gumel F6
Gummi E6
Gusau F6
Ibadan 847,000 E7
Ibi F7
Ife 176,000 E7
Ijebu-Ode E7
Ilesha 224,000 E7
Ilorin 282,000 E7
Iseyin 115,083 E7
Iwo 214,000 E7
Jega E6
Jos F7
Kaduna 202,000 F6
Kano 399,000 F6
Katsina 109,424 F6
Katsina Ala F7
Kontagora F6
Kumo G7
Kuta F7
Lagos (cap.) 1,060,848 E7
Maiduguri 189,000 G6
Maigatari F6
Makurdi F7
Minna F7
Nnewi F7
Nsukka F7
Ogbomosho 432,000 E7
Ondo E7
Onitsha 220,000 F7
Oshogbo 282,000 F7
Owerri F7
Owo F7
Oyo 152,000 E7
Panyam F7
Port Harcourt 242,000 F8
Shaki E7
Shendam F7
Sokoto F6
Toungo G7
Wamba F7
Wukari F7
Yan G7
Yelwa F6
Yola G7
Zaria 224,000 F6

OTHER FEATURES

Adamawa (reg.) G7
Benin (bight) E8
Benue (riv.) F7
Biafra (bight) F8
Biu (plat.) G6
Bonny (bight) F8
Chad (lake) G6
Cross (riv.) F7
Dimlang (mt.) G7
Donga (riv.) G7
Gongola (riv.) G6
Guinea (gulf) E8
Hadejia (riv.) F6
Jos (plat.) F7
Kaduna (riv.) F7
Kainji (res.) E6
Komadugu Yobe (riv.) G6
Niger (delta) F8
Niger (riv.) F7
Osse (riv.) F7
Rima (riv.) F6
Slave Coast (reg.) E7
Sokoto (riv.) F6
Sudan (reg.) F6

PORTUGAL-Madeira

CITIES and TOWNS

Funchal (cap.) 38,340 A2

OTHER FEATURES

Desertas (isls.) A2
Madeira (isl.) A2
Pôrto Santo (isl.) A2

SÃO TOMÉ AND PRINCIPE

CITIES and TOWNS

São Tomé (cap.) 7,681 F8
Santo António 1,618 F8

OTHER FEATURES

Guinea (gulf) E8
Príncipe (isl.) F8
São Tomé (isl.) F8

SENEGAL

CITIES and TOWNS

Bignona 14,537 A6
Dagana 10,506 A5
Dakar (cap.) 798,792 A6
Diourbel 50,618 A6
Kaffrine 11,211 A6
Kaolack 106,899 A6
Kolda 19,302 B6
Louga 35,063 A5
Matam 10,002 B5
M'Bour 37,663 A6
Nioro-du-Rip 7,824 A6
Podor 6,914 B5
Rufisque A6
Saint-Louis 88,404 A5
Tambacounda 25,147 B6
Thiès 117,333 A5
Tivaouane 17,351 A5
Ziguinchor 72,726 A6

OTHER FEATURES

Casamance (riv.) A6
Falémé (riv.) B6
Ferlo (reg.) B6
Gambia (riv.) B6
Senegal (riv.) B5
Verde (cape) A6

SIERRA LEONE

CITIES and TOWNS

Bo 42,216 B7
Bonthe 6,230 B7
Freetown (cap.) 274,000 B7
Kabala 4,610 B7
Kenema 33,880 B7
Makeni 28,684 B7
Moyamba 4,564 B7
Pendembu 2,696 B7
Port Loko 5,809 B7
Pujehun 2,034 B7

OTHER FEATURES

Loma, Mansa (lag.) B7
Mano (riv.) B7
Moa (riv.) B7
Sherbro (isl.) B7
Yawri (bay) B7

SPAIN-Canary Islands, Ceuta and Melilla

CITIES and TOWNS

Arrecife 21,310 B3
Ceuta 60,639 C1
Las Palmas de Gran Canaria 260,368 B3
Melilla 64,942 D1
Santa Cruz de la Palma 10,393 A3
Santa Cruz de Tenerife 74,910 A3

OTHER FEATURES

Canary (isls.) A3
Fuerteventura (isl.) B3
Gomera (isl.) A3
Grand Canary (isl.) A3
Hierro (isl.) A3
Lanzarote (isl.) B3
La Palma (isl.) A3
Tenerife (isl.) A3

TOGO

CITIES and TOWNS

Aného (Anécho) 10,889 E7
Atakpamé 17,440 E7
Dapaong 10,100 E6
Kpalimé 19,801 E7
Lama-Kara 9,400 E7
Lomé (cap.) 148,443 E7
Mango 9,600 E6
Sokodé 29,623 E7

OTHER FEATURES

Benin (bight) E8
Guinea (gulf) E8
Mono (riv.) E7
Oti (riv.) E7
Slave Coast (reg.) E7

TUNISIA

CITIES and TOWNS

Béja 39,226 F1
Ben Gardane 6,593 G2
Bizerte 62,856 F1
El Djem 10,666 G1
El Kef 27,939 F1
Gabès 40,585 F2
Gafsa 42,225 F2
Halq el Oued 41,912 G1
Jendouba 18,127 F1
Kairouan 54,546 F1
Kalaa-Kebira 23,508 F1
Kasserine 22,594 F1
La Goulette (Halq el Oued) 41,912 G1
La Skhirra 4,565 G2
Mahdia 25,711 G1
Mareth 2,185 F2
Mateur 19,645 F1
Médenine 15,826 G2
Menzel Bourguiba 42,111 F1
Menzel Temime 18,857 G1
Moknine 26,035 G1
Monastir 26,759 G1
Msaken 33,559 G1
Nabeul 30,476 G1
Nefta 12,476 F2
Sfax 171,297 G2
Sousse 69,530 G1
Tatahouine 10,399 G2
Tozeur 16,772 F2
Tunis (cap.) 550,404 G1
Zarzis 14,420 G2

OTHER FEATURES

Abiad, Ras el (Blanc) (cape) G1
Blanc (cape) G1
Bon (cape) G1
Chambi, Jebel (mt.) F2
Djerba (isl.) G2
Djerid, Shott el (salt lake) F2
Gabès (gulf) G2
Grand Erg Oriental (des.) F2
Hammamet (gulf) G1
Jefara (reg.) G2
Kerkennah (isls.) G2
Mediterranean (sea) F1
Medjerda (riv.) F1
Tib, Ras el (Bon) (cape) G1
Tunis (gulf) G1

WESTERN SAHARA

CITIES and TOWNS

Dakhla 6,554 A4
El Aaiún (Laayoune) 24,519 B3
Villa Cisneros (Dakhla) 6,554 A4

OTHER FEATURES

Ausert (well) B4
Barbas (cape) A4
Bir Ganduz (well) A4
Bir Nzaran (well) B4
Blanc (cape) A4
Bojador (cape) B3
Durnford (pt.) A4
Guelta de Zemmur (well) B3
Saguia el Hamra (dry riv.) B3
Tichlá (well) B4
Atoui, Wadi (dry riv.) B4

° Population of sub-district or division.

Agriculture, Industry and Resources

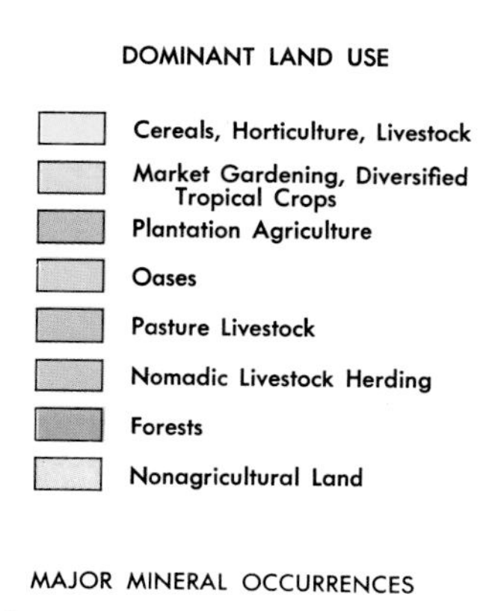

DOMINANT LAND USE
Cereals, Horticulture, Livestock
Market Gardening, Diversified Tropical Crops
Plantation Agriculture
Oases
Pasture Livestock
Nomadic Livestock Herding
Forests
Nonagricultural Land

MAJOR MINERAL OCCURRENCES

Al Bauxite
Au Gold
C Coal
Co Cobalt
Cr Chromium
Cu Copper
D Diamonds
Fe Iron Ore
G Natural Gas
Gn Granite
Gp Gypsum
Hg Mercury
Mn Manganese
Na Salt
O Petroleum
P Phosphates
Pb Lead
Sb Antimony
Sn Tin
Ti Titanium
U Uranium
Zn Zinc

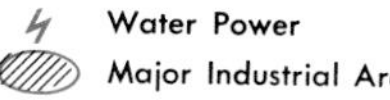

Water Power
Major Industrial Areas

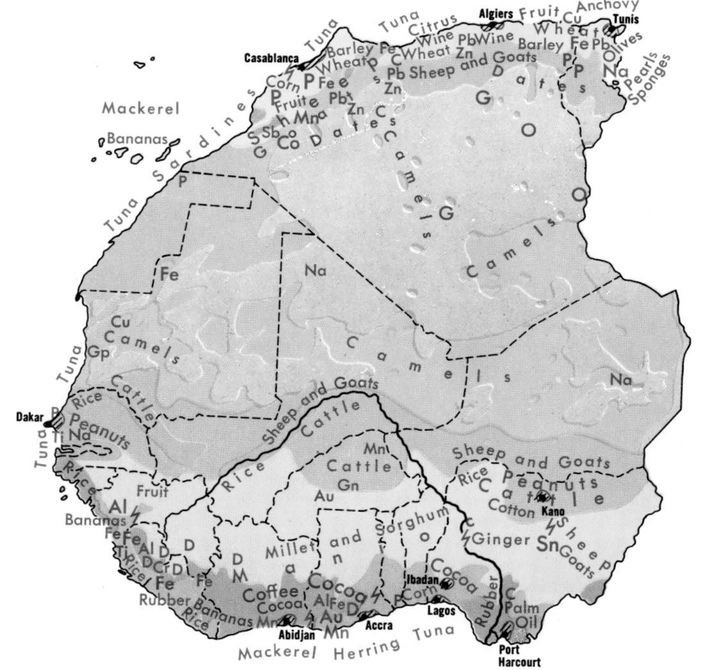

Algiers
Tunis
Casablanca
Dakar
Kano
Ibadan
Lagos
Abidjan
Accra
Port Harcourt
Mackerel
Bananas
Sardines
Tuna
Anchovy
Citrus
Fruit
Wheat
Barley
Wine
Olives
Pearls
Sponges
Sheep and Goats
Dates
Camels
Cattle
Rice
Peanuts
Millet and Sorghum
Cotton
Ginger
Cocoa
Coffee
Rubber
Palm Oil
Herring

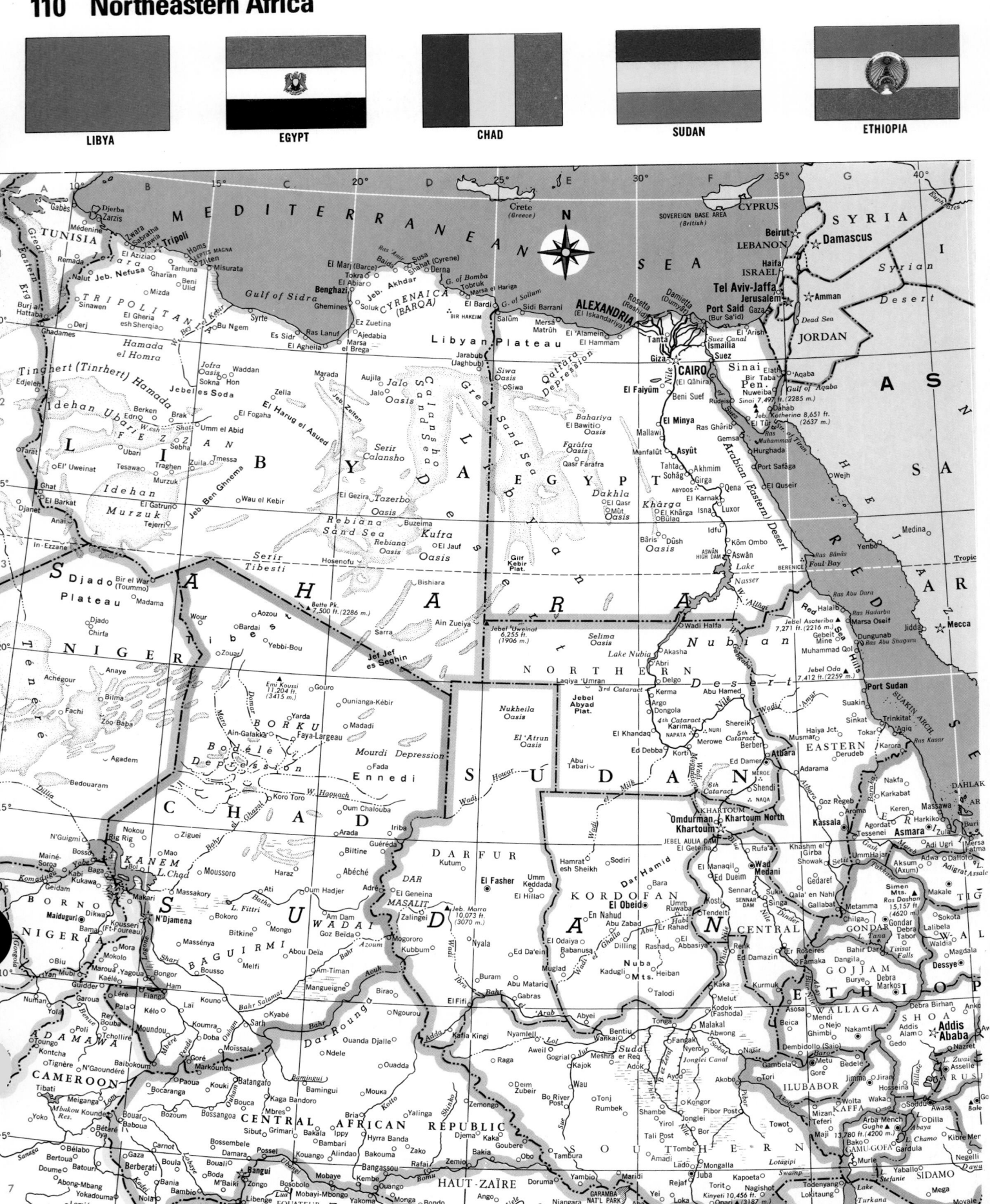

LIBYA
EGYPT
CHAD
SUDAN
ETHIOPIA
MEDITERRANEAN SEA
TUNISIA
SYRIA
LEBANON
ISRAEL
JORDAN
CYPRUS
SOVEREIGN BASE AREA (British)
Crete (Greece)
Tripoli
Benghazi
ALEXANDRIA (El Iskandarîya)
CAIRO (El Qâhira)
Port Said (Bur Sa'id)
Suez
Ismailia
Giza
Beirut
Damascus
Haifa
Tel Aviv-Jaffa
Jerusalem
Amman
Gulf of Sidra
CYRENAICA (BARQA)
TRIPOLITANIA
FEZZAN
Libyan Plateau
Qattara Depression
Great Sand Sea
Calansho Sand Sea
Rebiana Sand Sea
Kufra Oasis
Siwa Oasis
Arabian (Eastern) Desert
Sinai Pen.
Gulf of Aqaba
Gulf of Suez
Lake Nasser
Aswân
Luxor
Asyût
El Minya
Tibesti
BORKU
Bodélé Depression
Ennedi
Mourdi Depression
KANEM
L. Chad
N'Djamena
WADAI
BAGUIRMI
Nubian Desert
NORTHERN
Khartoum
Omdurman
Khartoum North
Port Sudan
Atbara
DARFUR
El Fasher
KORDOFAN
El Obeid
Nuba Mts.
Sudd
CENTRAL
EASTERN
Red Sea Hills
Asmara
Massawa
Mecca
Jidda
Medina
GONDAR
GOJJAM
L. Tana
Addis Ababa
SHOA
WALLAGA
ILUBABOR
KAFFA
GAMU-GOFA
SIDAMO
Lake Turkana
CENTRAL AFRICAN REPUBLIC
Bangui
CAMEROON
NIGERIA
NIGER
ZAIRE
HAUT-ZAÏRE
UGANDA
CONGO
Juba
Malakal
Wau
Tropic of Cancer

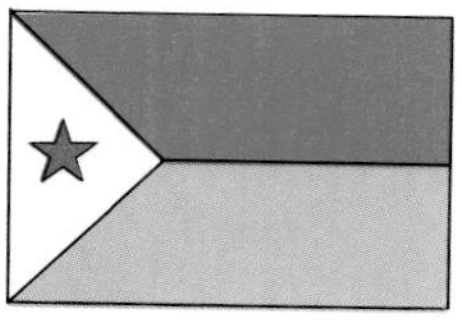

DJIBOUTI

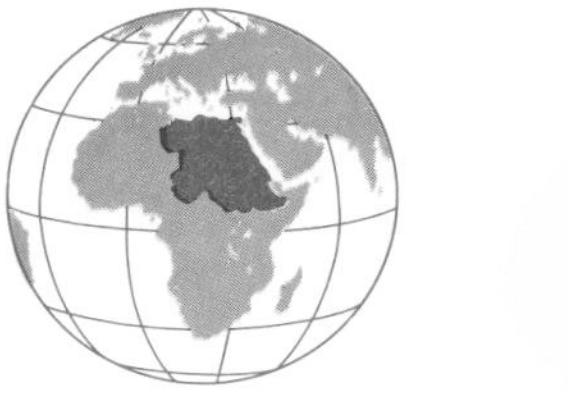

LIBYA

AREA 679,358 sq. mi. (1,759,537 sq. km.)
POPULATION 3,773,000
CAPITAL Tripoli
LARGEST CITY Tripoli
HIGHEST POINT Bette Pk. 7,500 ft. (2,286 m.)
MONETARY UNIT Libyan dinar
MAJOR LANGUAGES Arabic, Berber
MAJOR RELIGION Islam

EGYPT

AREA 386,659 sq. mi. (1,001,447 sq. km.)
POPULATION 53,080,000
CAPITAL Cairo
LARGEST CITY Cairo
HIGHEST POINT Jeb. Katherina 8,651 ft. (2,637 m.)
MONETARY UNIT Egyptian pound
MAJOR LANGUAGE Arabic
MAJOR RELIGIONS Islam, Coptic Christianity

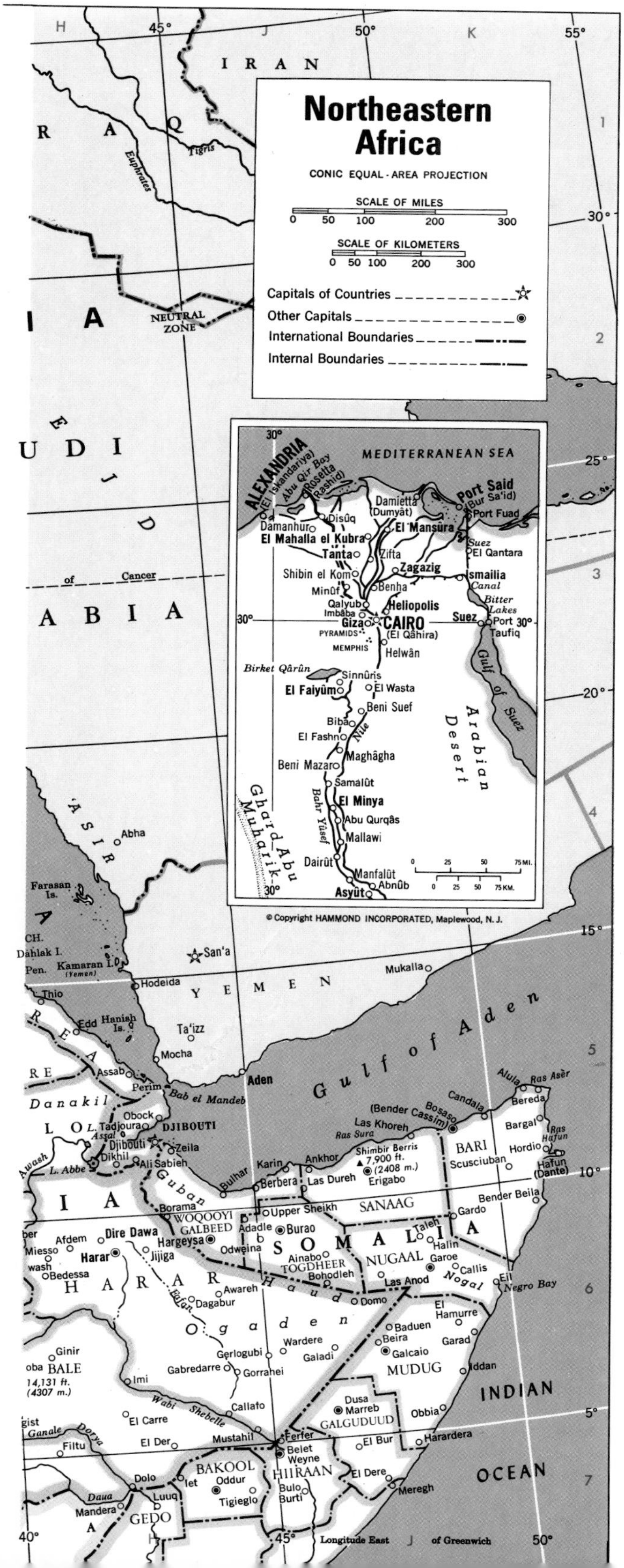

CHAD

AREA 495,752 sq. mi. (1,283,998 sq. km.)
POPULATION 5,538,000
CAPITAL N'Djamena
LARGEST CITY N'Djamena
HIGHEST POINT Emi Koussi 11,204 ft. (3,415 m.)
MONETARY UNIT CFA franc
MAJOR LANGUAGES Arabic, Bagirmi, French, Sara, Massa, Moudang
MAJOR RELIGIONS Islam, tribal religions

SUDAN

AREA 967,494 sq. mi. (2,505,809 sq. km.)
POPULATION 24,485,000
CAPITAL Khartoum
LARGEST CITY Khartoum
HIGHEST POINT Jeb. Marra 10,073 ft. (3,070 m.)
MONETARY UNIT Sudanese pound
MAJOR LANGUAGES Arabic, Dinka, Nubian, Beja, Nuer
MAJOR RELIGIONS Islam, tribal religions

ETHIOPIA

AREA 471,776 sq. mi. (1,221,900 sq. km.)
POPULATION 50,774,000
CAPITAL Addis Ababa
LARGEST CITY Addis Ababa
HIGHEST POINT Ras Dashan 15,157 ft. (4,620 m.)
MONETARY UNIT birr
MAJOR LANGUAGES Amharic, Gallinya, Tigrinya, Somali, Sidamo, Arabic, Ge'ez
MAJOR RELIGIONS Coptic Christianity, Islam

DJIBOUTI

AREA 8,880 sq. mi. (23,000 sq. km.)
POPULATION 456,000
CAPITAL Djibouti
LARGEST CITY Djibouti
HIGHEST POINT Moussa Ali 6,768 ft. (2,063 m.)
MONETARY UNIT Djibouti franc
MAJOR LANGUAGES Arabic, Somali, Afar, French
MAJOR RELIGIONS Islam, Roman Catholicism

Northeastern Africa
CONIC EQUAL - AREA PROJECTION

SCALE OF MILES
0 50 100   200   300

SCALE OF KILOMETERS
0 50 100   200   300

Capitals of Countries _ _ _ _ _ _ _ ☆
Other Capitals _ _ _ _ _ _ _ _ ◉
International Boundaries _ _ _ _ _ _
Internal Boundaries _ _ _ _ _ _

© Copyright HAMMOND INCORPORATED, Maplewood, N.J.

CHAD

CITIES and TOWNS

Abéché 28,100	D5
Abou Deïa	C5
Adré	D5
Am-Timan 4,200	D5
Arada	D4
Ati 7,500	C5
Baibokoum 5,500	C6
Biltine 3,900	D5
Bitkine 5,000	C5
Bokoro 6,500	C5
Bol 2,500	B5
Bongor 14,300	C5
Bousso 4,500	C5
Doba 13,300	C6
Fada	D4
Faya-Largeau 6,800	C4
Fianga 10,000	C6
Goré	C6
Goz Beïda	D5
Guéréda	D4
Iriba	D4
Kélo 16,800	C6
Koumra 17,000	C6
Kouno	C6

Kyabé 5,000	C6
Laï 10,400	C6
Léré	B6
Mangueigne	D5
Mao 4,900	C5
Massakory	C5
Massénya	C5
Melfi	C5
Mogororo	D5
Moïssala 5,100	C6
Mongo 8,300	C5
Moundou 39,600	C6
Moussoro 7,700	C5
N'Djamena (cap.) 179,000	C5
Oum Hadjer 5,600	C5
Ounianga-Kébir	D4
Pala 13,200	B6
Sarh 43,700	C6
Wour	C3
Zouar	C3

OTHER FEATURES

Aouk, Bahr (riv.)	D5
Azoum, Bahr (riv.)	D5
Baguirmi (reg.)	C5
Bahr el Ghazal (dry riv.)	C4
Batha (riv.)	C5

Bodélé (depr.)	C4
Borku (reg.)	C4
Chad (lake)	C5
Emi Koussi (mt.)	C4
Ennedi (plat.)	D4
Fittri (lake)	C5
Kanem (reg.)	C5
Logone (reg.)	C5
Maro (riv.)	C4
Mbéré (dry riv.)	C6
Mourdi (riv.)	D4
Ouham (depr.)	C6
Pendé (riv.)	C6
Sahara (riv.)	C3
Salamat, Bahr (des.)	C6
Shari (riv.)	C5
Sudan (riv.)	C5
Tibesti (mts.)	C4
Wadai (reg.)	D5

DJIBOUTI

CITIES and TOWNS

Ali Sabieh	H5
Dikhil	H5
Djibouti (cap.) 96,000	H5
Obock	H5

Tadjoura	H5

OTHER FEATURES

Abbe (lake)	H5
Aden (gulf)	J5
Bab el Mandeb (strait)	H5

EGYPT

CITIES and TOWNS

Abnûb 39,343	J4
Akhmim 53,234	F2
Alexandria 2,318,655	J2
Aswân 144,377	F3
Asyût 213,983	J4
Benha 88,992	J3
Beni Mazar 39,373	J4
Beni Suef 118,148	J3
Biba 33,074	J4
Bur Sa'id (Port Said) 262,620	K2
Cairo (cap.) 5,084,463	J3
Dairût 31,624	J4
Damanhur 188,927	J3
Damietta 93,546	J3
Disûq 58,650	J3

(continued on following page)

Topography

Topography scale:
0 200 400 600 MI.
0 200 400 600 KM.

5,000 m. / 16,404 ft. — 2,000 m. / 6,562 ft. — 1,000 m. / 3,281 ft. — 500 m. / 1,640 ft. — 200 m. / 656 ft. — 100 m. / 328 ft. — Sea Level — Below

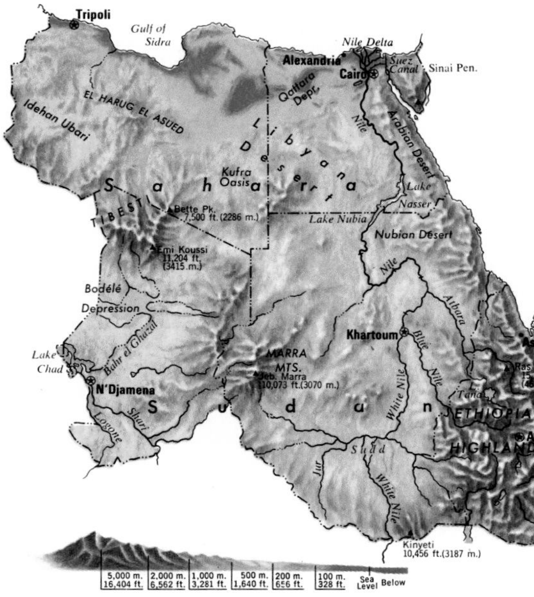

(continued on following page)

Dumyât (Damietta) 93,546.....J3
El 'Alamein E1
El 'Arîsh F1
El Faiyûm 167,081 .....J3
El Fashn 33,506.∘.....J4
El Iskendariya
  (Alexandria) 2,318,655.....J2
El Karnak F2
El Khârga 26,375 .....F2
El Mahalla el Kubra 292,853.....J3
El Mansûra 257,866.....K3
El Minya 146,423 .....J4
El Qahira (Cairo)
  (cap.) 5,084,463.....J3
El Qantara 919 .....K3
El Quseir 12,297 .....F2
El Wasta 17,659 .....J3
Girga 51,110 .....F2
Giza 1,246,713.....J3
Heliopolis J3
Helwan J3
Idfu 34,858.∘.....F2
Ismailia 145,978 .....K3
Isna 34,186 .....F2
Karnak (El Karnak) F2
Kôm Ombo 44,531 .....F2
Luxor 92,748.∘.....F2
Maghâgha 40,802 .....J4
Mallawi 74,256.∘.....J4
Manfalût 41,126 .....J4
Mersâ Matrûh 27,857 .....E1
Minûf 55,131 .....J3
Mût 8,032 .....E2
Port Fuad K3
Port Safâga F2
Port Said 262,620.....K2
Port Taufiq K3
Qalyub 62,739 .....J3
Qena 94,013.∘.....F2
Rashid (Rosetta) 42,962.∘.....J2
Rudeis F2
Salûm 4,161 .....E1
Samalût 48,146 .....J4
Shibin el Kom 102,844.....J3
Sidi Barrani 1,574 .....E1
Sinnûris 42,022 .....J3
Sohâg 101,758.∘.....F2
Suez 194,001.....K3
Tahta 45,242 .....F2
Tanta 284,636 .....J3
Zagazig 202,637.....J3
Zifta 50,410 .....J3

OTHER FEATURES

Abu Qir (bay) J2
Abydos (ruins) F2
Aqaba (gulf) G2
Arabian (des.) F2
Aswân (dam) F3
Aswân High (dam) F3
Bahariya (oasis) E2
Bânâs, Ras (cape) G3
Berenice (ruins) F3

Birket Qârûn (lake) J3
Bitter (lakes) K3
Dakhla (oasis) E2
Eastern (Arabian) (des.) F2
Farâfra (oasis) E2
Foul (bay) G3
Gilf Kebir (plat.) E3
Great Sand Sea (des.) D2
Katherina, Jebel (mt.) F2
Khârga (oasis) F2
Libyan (des.) E2
Libyan (plat.) E2
Mediterranean (sea) E1
Memphis (ruins) J3
Muhammad, Ras (cape) F2
Nasser (lake) F3
Nile (riv.) J3
Pyramids (ruins) J3
Qattara (depr.) E2
Sahara (des.) E3
Sinai (mt.) F2
Sinai (pen.) F2
Siwa (oasis) E2
Suez (canal) K3
Suez (gulf) F2
Tiran (strait) F2
'Uweinat, Jebel (mt.) E3

ETHIOPIA

PROVINCES

Arusi 852,900.....G6
Bale 707,800 .....H6
Eritrea 1,947,600.....G4
Gamu-Gofa 698,800 .....G6
Gojjam 1,750,100.....G5
Gondar 1,355,800.....G5
Harar 3,359,200 .....H6
Ilubabor 688,800 .....F6
Kaffa 1,693,000.....G6
Shoa 5,369,500 .....G6
Sidamo 2,479,800 .....G7
Tigre 1,828,900 .....G5
Wallaga 1,269,100.....G6
Wallo 2,459,900 .....H5

CITIES and TOWNS

Addis Ababa (cap.)
  1,196,300.....G6
Addis Alam 5,500 .....G6
Adigrat 9,400 .....G5
Adi Ugri 12,800 .....G5
Adwa 16,400 .....G5
Aksum 12,800 .....G5
Ankober G6
Arba Mench 7,660 .....G6
Asmara 393,800 .....G4
Assab 16,000 .....H5
Asselle 19,390 .....G6
Awareh H6
Axum (Aksum) 12,800 .....G5
Bahir Dar 25,100 .....G5

Dagabur H6
Dangila G5
Debra Birhan 16,700.....G6
Debra Markos 30,260 .....G5
Debra Tabor 8,700.....G5
Dembidollo 7,600 .....F6
Dessye 49,750.....G5
Dilla 13,800 .....G6
Dire Dawa 63,700.....H6
El Carre H6
Gabredarre H6
Galadi J6
Gambela F6
Gardula 5,800 .....G6
Gerlogubi J6
Ghimbi 8,300 .....G6
Ginir H6
Goba 13,500.....G6
Gondar 38,600.....G5
Gore 8,360 .....G6
Gorrahei H6
Harar 48,440 .....H6
Hosseina 8,500 .....G6
Jijiga 8,000 .....H6
Jimma 47,360 .....G6
Jiran G6
Karkabat G4
Keren G4
Kibre Mengist 8,300 .....G6
Lalibela G5
Magdala G5
Maji G6
Makale 30,780 .....G5
Massawa 19,800 .....G4
Mersa Fatma H5
Metamma G5
Metu 6,860 .....F6
Miesso H6
Mizan Teferi G6
Moyale G7
Murle H6
Mustahil H6
Nakamti 18,310 .....G6
Nakfa G4
Nazret 42,900 .....G6
Negelli 8,800 .....G6
Nejo G6
Saio (Dembidollo) 7,600 .....F6
Soddu 11,900 .....G6
Sokota G5
Tessenei G4
Thio H5
Tori F6
Umm Hajar G4
Waka G6
Waldia 9,600 .....G5
Wardere J6
Wolta G6
Yaballo G7
Zula G4

OTHER FEATURES

Abay (riv.) G5

Abaya (lake) G6
Abbe (lake) H5
Akobo (riv.) F6
Assal (lake) H5
Assale (lake) H5
Atbara (riv.) G4
Awash (riv.) H6
Bale (mt.) G6
Baraka (riv.) G4
Blue Nile (Abay) (riv.) G5
Buri (pen.) H4
Chamo (lake) G6
Dahlak (arch.) H4
Dahlak (isl.) H4
Danakil (reg.) H5
Dawa (riv.) G7
Dinder (riv.) G5
Fafan (riv.) H6
Ganale Dorya (riv.) H6
Gughe (mt.) G6
Haud (reg.) J6
Kasar, Ras (cape) G4
Ogaden (reg.) H6
Omo (riv.) G6
Ras Dashan (mt.) G5
Red (sea) H4
Rudolf (Turkana) (lake) G7
Simen (mts.) G5
Takkaze (riv.) G5
Tana (lake) G5
Tisisat (fall) G5
Turkana (lake) G7
Zwai (lake) G6

LIBYA

CITIES and TOWNS

Ajedabia∘ 53,170.....D1
Aujila∘ 6,695.....D1
Baida∘ 59,765.....D1
Barce (El Marj)∘ 55,444.....D1
Benghazi 286,943 .....C1
Beni Ulid∘ 19,113 .....C1
Brak∘ 16,307 .....B2
Cyrene (Shahat)∘ 17,157.....D1
Derj∘ 2,152 .....B1
Derna∘ 44,145 .....D1
El Abiar∘ 17,685 .....D1
El Agheila 3 .....C1
El Azizia∘ 34,077 .....B1
El Bardi∘ 4,330 .....D1
El Barkat∘ 2,139 .....B3
El Gatrun B3
El Jauf∘ 6,481 .....D3
El Marj∘ 55,444 .....D1
Es Sidr∘ 706 .....C1
Ez Zuetina∘ 7,256 .....D1
Ghadames∘ 6,172 .....A2
Gharian∘ 65,224 .....B1
Ghat∘ 6,924 .....B3
Ghemines∘ 4,313 .....D1
Homs∘ 66,890 .....B1

Hon∘ 2,766 .....C2
Jaghbub (Jarabub)∘ 1,436 .....D2
Jarabub∘ 1,436 .....D2
Marada∘ 3,201 .....C2
Marsa el Brega∘ 2,618 .....D1
Marsa el Hariga∘ 5,043 .....D1
Misurata∘ 102,439 .....C1
Mizda∘ 11,472 .....B1
Murzuk∘ 22,185 .....B2
Nalut∘ 23,535 .....B1
Ras Lanuf∘ 1,990 .....C1
Sabrathaa∘ 30,836 .....B1
Sebha∘ 35,879 .....B2
Shahat∘ 17,157 .....D1
Sinawen∘ 1,549 .....B1
Sokna∘ 3,757 .....C2
Soluk∘ 6,501 .....D1
Syrte∘ 22,797 .....C1
Tarhuna∘ 52,657 .....B1
Tobruk∘ 58,384 .....D1
Tokra∘ 10,714 .....D1
Tripoli (cap.)∘ 550,438 .....B1
Ubari∘ 19,132 .....B2
Waddan∘ 5,347 .....C2
Wau el Kebir C2
Zawia∘ 72,092 .....B1
Zella∘ 72,092 .....C2
Zliten∘ 58,981 .....B1
Zwara∘ 15,078 .....B1

OTHER FEATURES

Akhdar, Jebel (mts.) D1
Barqa (Cyrenaica) (reg.) D1
Ben Ghnema, Jebel (mts.) C2
Bette (peak) C3
Bey el Kebir, Wadi (dry riv.) B1
Bir Hakeim (ruins) D1
Bomba (gulf) D1
Buzeima (well) D3
Calansho Sand Sea (des.) D2
Calansho, Serir (des.) D2
Cyrenaica (reg.) D1
Fezzan (reg.) B2
Great Sand Sea (des.) D2
Harug el Asued, El (mts.) C2
Homra, Hamada el (des.) B2
Idehan Murzuk (des.) B2
Idehan Ubari (des.) B2
Jalo (oasis) D2
Jefara (reg.) B1
Jef Jef es Seghin (plat.) D3
Jofra (oasis) C2
Kufra (oasis) D3
Leptis Magna (ruins) B1
Libyan (des.) D2
Libyan (plat.) D1
Mediterranean (sea) C1
Nefusa, Jebel (mts.) B1
Rebiana (oasis) D3
Rebiana Sand Sea (des.) D3
Sahara (des.) C3
Shati, Wadi esh (dry riv.) B2

Sidra (gulf) C1
Soda, Jebel es (mts.) C2
Tazerbo (oasis) D2
Tibesti, Serir (des.) C3
Tinghert Hamada
  (Tinrhert) (des.) B2
Tripolitania (reg.) B1
'Uweinat, Jebel (mt.) E3
Zelten, Jebel (mts.) D2

SUDAN

PROVINCES

Central F5
Darfur D5
Eastern G4
Khartoum F4
Kordofan E5
Northern E3
Southern E6

CITIES and TOWNS

'Abri F3
Abu Hamed F4
Adok F6
Akobo F6
Amadi F6
Argo F4
Aroma G4
Atbara 66,000 .....F4
Babanusa E5
Bara F5
Bentiu F6
Berber F4
Bor F6
Buram E5
Damazin
  (Ed Damazin) 12,000.....F5
Deim Zubeir E6
Dongola 6,000 .....E4
Dungunab G3
Ed Damazin 12,000 .....F5
Ed Damer 17,000 .....F4
Ed Dueim 27,000 .....F5
El Fasher 52,000 .....D5
El Geneina 33,000 .....D5
El Obeid 90,000 .....E5
El Odaiya E5
Er Nahud 23,000 .....E5
Er Roseires F5
Fashoda (Kodok) F6
Gedaref 92,000 .....G5
Gogrial E6
Goz Regeb G4
Haiya Junction G4
Halaib G3
Jonglei F6
Juba 57,000 .....F7
Kadugli 18,000 .....E5
Kaka F5
Karima F4
Kassala 99,000 .....G4

Kerma F4
Khartoum (cap.) 334,000 .....F4
Khartoum North 151,000 .....F4
Khashm el Girba G4
Kodok F6
Kosti 57,000 .....F5
Kurmuk F5
Kutum D5
Malakal 35,000 .....F6
Maridi F7
Melut F5
Merowe E4
Meshra er Req E6
Mongalla F6
Muglad E5
Muhammad Qol G3
Nagishot F7
Nasir F6
Nyala 60,000 .....D5
Nyamlell E6
Nyerol F6
Omdurman 299,000 .....F4
Opari F7
Pibor Post F6
Port Sudan 133,000 .....G4
Qala'en Nahl F5
Raga E6
Rashad F5
Rejaf F7
Renk F5
Rufa'a F5
Rumbek 17,000 .....E6
Sennar F5
Shambe F6
Shendi F4
Shereik F4
Showak G5
Singa F5
Sinkat G4
Sodiri E5
Suakin G4
Suki F5
Tali Post F6
Talodi F5
Tambura E6
Tendelti F5
Tokar G4
Tombe F6
Tonga F6
Tonj E6
Torit F7
Trinkitat G4
Umm Keddada E5
Umm Ruwaba F5
Wadi Halfa F3
Wad Medani 107,000 .....F5
Wankai E6
Wau 53,000 .....E6
Yambio 7,000 .....E7
Yei F7
Yirol F6
Zalingei D5

OTHER FEATURES

Abu Habl, Wadi (dry riv.) F5
Abu Shagara, Ras (cape) G3
Adda (riv.) D6
Atbara (riv.) G4
Bahr Azoum (riv.) D5
Bahr el 'Arab (riv.) E6
Bahr ez Zeraf (riv.) F6
Blue Nile (riv.) F5
Dar Hamid (reg.) E5
Dar Masalit (reg.) D5
Dinder (riv.) F5
El 'Atrun (oasis) E4
Fifth Cataract (falls) F4
Fourth Cataract (falls) F4
Gabgaba, Wadi (dry riv.) F3
Ghalla, Wadi (dry riv.) E5
Hadarba, Ras (cape) G3
Howar, Wadi (dry riv.) E4
Ibra, Wadi (dry riv.) D5
Jebel Aulia (dam) F4
Jonglei (canal) F6
Jur (riv.) E6
Kinyeti (mt.) F7
Libyan (des.) E3
Lol (dry riv.) E6
Lotagipi Swamp (plain) F6
Marra, Jebel (mt.) D5
Meroe (ruins) F4
Milk, Wadi el (dry riv.) E4
Muqaddam, Wadi (dry riv.) E4
Napata (ruins) F4
Naga (ruins) F4
Nile (riv.) F4
Nuba (mts.) E5
Nubia (lake) F3
Nubian (des.) F3
Nukheila (oasis) E4
Nuri (ruins) F4
Oda, Jebel (mt.) G3
Pibor (riv.) F6
Red (sea) G3
Red Sea (hills) G3
Sahara (des.) E3
Selima (oasis) E3
Sennar (dam) F5
Setit (riv.) G5
Sixth Cataract F4
Sobat (riv.) F6
Suakin (arch.) G4
Sudan (reg.) E5
Sudd (swamp) F6
Sue (riv.) E6
Third Cataract (falls) E4
'Uweinat, Jebel (mt.) E3
White Nile (riv.) F5

∘ Population of sub-district or
  division

Agriculture, Industry and Resources

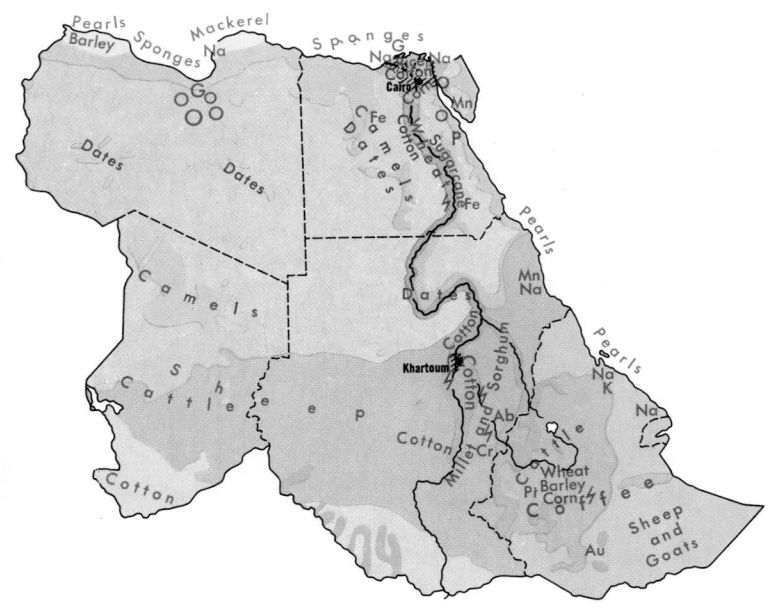

DOMINANT LAND USE

- Cereals, Horticulture, Livestock
- Cash Crops, Mixed Cereals
- Cotton, Cereals
- Market Gardening, Diversified Tropical Crops
- Plantation Agriculture
- Oases
- Pasture Livestock
- Nomadic Livestock Herding
- Forests
- Nonagricultural Land

MAJOR MINERAL OCCURRENCES

Ab	Asbestos	Mn	Manganese
Au	Gold	Na	Salt
Cr	Chromium	O	Petroleum
Fe	Iron Ore	P	Phosphates
G	Natural Gas	Pt	Platinum
K	Potash		

⚡ Water Power

〰 Major Industrial Areas

ANGOLA

AREA 481,351 sq. mi. (1,246,700 sq. km.)
POPULATION 9,747,000
CAPITAL Luanda
LARGEST CITY Luanda
HIGHEST POINT Mt. Moco 8,593 ft. (2,620 m.)
MONETARY UNIT kwanza
MAJOR LANGUAGES Mbundu, Kongo, Lunda, Portuguese
MAJOR RELIGIONS Tribal religions, Roman Catholicism

BURUNDI

AREA 10,747 sq. mi. (27,835 sq. km.)
POPULATION 5,302,000
CAPITAL Bujumbura
LARGEST CITY Bujumbura
HIGHEST POINT 8,858 ft. (2,700 m.)
MONETARY UNIT Burundi franc
MAJOR LANGUAGES Kirundi, French, Swahili
MAJOR RELIGIONS Tribal religions, Roman Catholicism, Islam

CAMEROON

AREA 183,568 sq. mi. (475,441 sq. km.)
POPULATION 11,540,000
CAPITAL Yaoundé
LARGEST CITY Douala
HIGHEST POINT Cameroon 13,350 ft. (4,069 m.)
MONETARY UNIT CFA franc
MAJOR LANGUAGFS Fang, Bamileke, Fulani, Duala, French, English
MAJOR RELIGIONS Tribal religions, Christianity, Islam

CENTRAL AFRICAN REP.

AREA 242,000 sq. mi. (626,780 sq. km.)
POPULATION 2,740,000
CAPITAL Bangui
LARGEST CITY Bangui
HIGHEST POINT Gao 4,659 ft. (1,420 m.)
MONETARY UNIT CFA franc
MAJOR LANGUAGES Banda, Gbaya, Sangho, French
MAJOR RELIGIONS Tribal religions, Christianity, Islam

CONGO

AREA 132,046 sq. mi. (342,000 sq. km.)
POPULATION 1,843,000
CAPITAL Brazzaville
LARGEST CITY Brazzaville
HIGHEST POINT Leketi Mts. 3,412 ft. (1,040 m.)
MONETARY UNIT CFA franc
MAJOR LANGUAGES Kikongo, Bateke, Lingala, French
MAJOR RELIGIONS Christianity, tribal religions, Islam

EQUATORIAL GUINEA

AREA 10,831 sq. mi. (28,052 sq. km.)
POPULATION 341,000
CAPITAL Malabo
LARGEST CITY Malabo
HIGHEST POINT 9,868 ft. (3,008 m.)
MONETARY UNIT CFA franc
MAJOR LANGUAGES Fang, Bubi, Spanish
MAJOR RELIGIONS Tribal religions, Christianity

GABON

AREA 103,346 sq. mi. (267,666 sq. km.)
POPULATION 1,206,000
CAPITAL Libreville
LARGEST CITY Libreville
HIGHEST POINT Ibounzi 5,165 ft. (1,574 m.)
MONETARY UNIT CFA franc
MAJOR LANGUAGES Fang and other Bantu languages, French
MAJOR RELIGIONS Tribal religions, Christianity, Islam

KENYA

AREA 224,960 sq. mi. (582,646 sq. km.)
POPULATION 24,872,000
CAPITAL Nairobi
LARGEST CITY Nairobi
HIGHEST POINT Kenya 17,058 ft. (5,199 m.)
MONETARY UNIT Kenya shilling
MAJOR LANGUAGES Kikuyu, Luo, Kavirondo, Kamba, Swahili, English
MAJOR RELIGIONS Tribal religions, Christianity, Hinduism, Islam

MALAWI

AREA 45,747 sq. mi. (118,485 sq. km.)
POPULATION 8,022,000
CAPITAL Lilongwe
LARGEST CITY Blantyre
HIGHEST POINT Mulanje 9,843 ft. (3,000 m.)
MONETARY UNIT Malawi kwacha
MAJOR LANGUAGES Chichewa, Yao, English, Nyanja, Tumbuka, Tonga, Ngoni
MAJOR RELIGIONS Tribal religions, Islam, Christianity

RWANDA

AREA 10,169 sq. mi. (26,337 sq. km.)
POPULATION 6,274,000
CAPITAL Kigali
LARGEST CITY Kigali
HIGHEST POINT Karisimbi 14,780 ft. (4,505 m.)
MONETARY UNIT Rwanda franc
MAJOR LANGUAGES Kinyarwanda, French, Swahili
MAJOR RELIGIONS Tribal religions, Roman Catholicism, Islam

SOMALIA

AREA 246,200 sq. mi. (637,658 sq. km.)
POPULATION 7,339,000
CAPITAL Mogadishu
LARGEST CITY Mogadishu
HIGHEST POINT Surud Ad 7,900 ft. (2,408 m.)
MONETARY UNIT Somali shilling
MAJOR LANGUAGES Somali, Arabic, Italian, English
MAJOR RELIGION Islam

TANZANIA

AREA 363,708 sq. mi. (942,003 sq. km.)
POPULATION 24,802,000
CAPITAL Dar es Salaam
LARGEST CITY Dar es Salaam
HIGHEST POINT Kilimanjaro 19,340 ft. (5,895 m.)
MONETARY UNIT Tanzanian shilling
MAJOR LANGUAGES Nyamwezi-Sukuma, Swahili, English
MAJOR RELIGIONS Tribal religions, Christianity, Islam

UGANDA

AREA 91,076 sq. mi. (235,887 sq. km.)
POPULATION 17,804,000
CAPITAL Kampala
LARGEST CITY Kampala
HIGHEST POINT Margherita 16,795 ft. (5,119 m.)
MONETARY UNIT Ugandan shilling
MAJOR LANGUAGES Luganda, Acholi, Teso, Nyoro, Soga, Nkole, English, Swahili
MAJOR RELIGIONS Tribal religions, Christianity, Islam

ZAIRE

AREA 905,063 sq. mi. (2,344,113 sq. km.)
POPULATION 34,491,000
CAPITAL Kinshasa
LARGEST CITY Kinshasa
HIGHEST POINT Margherita 16,795 ft. (5,119 m.)
MONETARY UNIT zaire
MAJOR LANGUAGES Tshiluba, Mongo, Kikongo, Kingwana, Zande, Lingala, Swahili, French
MAJOR RELIGIONS Tribal religions, Christianity

ZAMBIA

AREA 290,586 sq. mi. (752,618 sq. km.)
POPULATION 8,073,000
CAPITAL Lusaka
LARGEST CITY Lusaka
HIGHEST POINT Sunzu 6,782 ft. (2,067 m.)
MONETARY UNIT Zambian kwacha
MAJOR LANGUAGES Bemba, Tonga, Lozi, Luvale, Nyanja, English
MAJOR RELIGIONS Tribal religions

ANGOLA

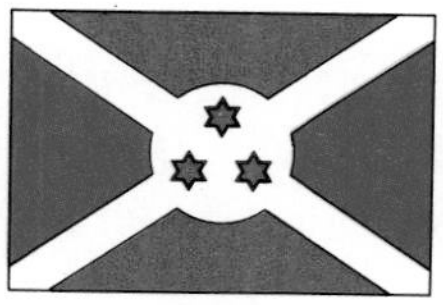

EQUATORIAL GUINEA

SOMALIA

BURUNDI

GABON

TANZANIA

CAMEROON

KENYA

UGANDA

CENTRAL AFRICAN REP.

MALAWI

ZAIRE

CONGO

RWANDA

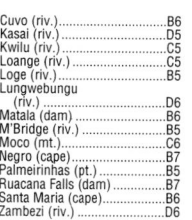

ZAMBIA

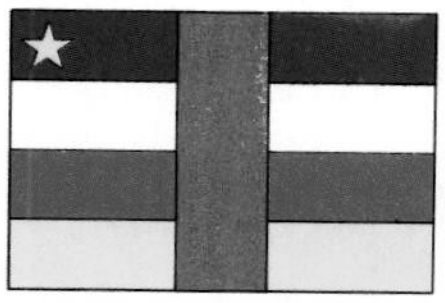

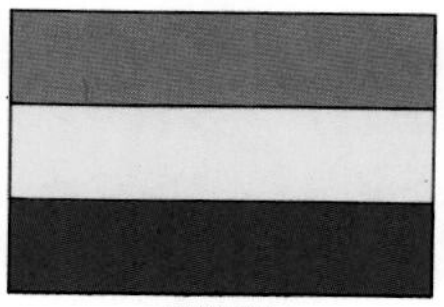

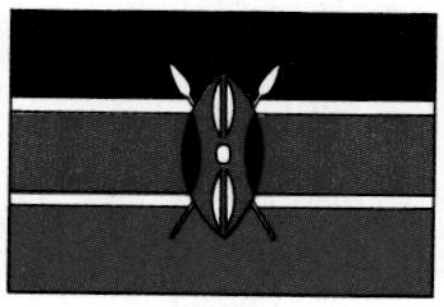

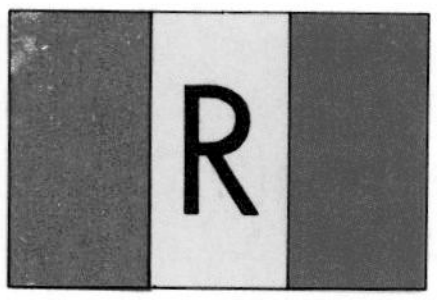

Ebolowa 24,000	B3	Maroua 67,187	B1	Tignère	B2	Cameroon (mt.)	A3
Fort Foureau (Kousseri)		Mbalmayo 22,106	B3	Tiko 13,824	A3	Cross (riv.)	A2
11,627	B1	Meiganga 15,906	B2	Wum 15,149	A2	Dja (riv.)	B3
Foumban 33,944	B2	Moloundou	C3	Yagoua 13,541	B1	Donga (riv.)	A2
Garoua 63,900	B2	Monatélé	B3	Yaoundé (cap.) 313,706	B3	Ivindo (riv.)	B3
Guidder 16,053	B2	Nanga-Eboko	B3	Yoko	B2	Kadei (riv.)	C3
Kousseri 11,627	B1	Ngaoundéré 38,992	B2			Logone (riv.)	C2
Kumba 44,175	A3	Nkongsamba 71,298	B3	OTHER FEATURES		Lom (riv.)	B2
Kumbo 11,699	A3	Poli	B2			Mbakou (res.)	B2
Limbe 27,016	A3	Sangmélima 13,776	B3	Adamawa (reg.)	B2	Mbéré (riv.)	B2
Lomié	B3	Tcholliré	B2	Benué (riv.)	A2	Sanaga (riv.)	B3
Makari	B1	Tibati	B2	Biafra (bight)	A3	Sanga (riv.)	C3

CENTRAL AFRICAN REPUBLIC

CITIES and TOWNS

Alindao 12,295	D2	Berberati 27,285	C3	Grimari 7,308	C2
Baboua 3,999	C2	Birao 3,317	D1	Ippy 10,816	D2
Bambari 31,285	D2	Bocaranga 6,202	C2	Kaga Bandoro 11,876	C2
Bangassou 21,773	D3	Boda 8,771	C2	Kembe 5,051	C3
Bangui (cap.)		Bossangoa 25,150	C2	Mbaïki 12,346	C3
279,792	C3	Bossembele 5,091	C2	Mobaye 4,220	C3
Bania	C3	Bouar 29,528	C2	Ndele 5,858	D2
Batangáfo 12,543	C2	Bouca 8,874	C2	Nola 6,703	C3
		Bozoum 13,573	C2	Obo 3,978	E2
		Bria 14,786	D2	Ouadda 3,009	D2
		Carnot 17,863	C3	Paoua 7,052	C2
		Dekoa 7,663	C2	Zemio 3,259	D2

OTHER FEATURES		
Bamingui (riv.)		C2
Bomu (riv.)		D3
Dar Rounga (reg.)		C2
Gao (mt.)		C2
Kadei (riv.)		C3
Kotto (riv.)		D2
Lobaye (riv.)		C3
Mbéré (riv.)		B2
Ouham (riv.)		C2
Pendé (riv.)		C2

Sangha (riv.)		C3
Shari (riv.)		C2
Shinko (riv.)		D2
Ubangi (riv.)		D2

CONGO
CITIES and TOWNS

Abala		C4
Boundji		C4
Brazzaville (cap.) 298,967		C4

Djambala		B4
Impfondo		C3
Kinkala		B4
Loubomo 29,600		B4
Makoua		C3
Mbinda		B4
Mossaka		C4
Mossendjo		B4
Nkayi 30,600		B4
Ouesso		C3
Owando		C3
Pointe-Noire 141,700		B4

OTHER FEATURES		
Alima (riv.)		B4
Congo (riv.)		C4
Crystal (mts.)		B4
Dja (riv.)		B3
Ivindo (riv.)		B3
Kadei (riv.)		C3
Kouilou (riv.)		B4
Likouala (riv.)		C3
N'Gounie (riv.)		B4
Niari (riv.)		B4

Ogooué (riv.)		A4
Sangha (riv.)		C3
Ubangi (riv.)		C3

EQUATORIAL GUINEA
TERRITORIES

Bioko 78,000		A3
Rio Muni 203,000		B3

CITIES and TOWNS

Bata 270,241		A3
Luba 19,933		A3
Malabo (cap.) 37,237		A3
Mbini 14,503		A3

OTHER FEATURES

Biafra (bight)		A3
Corisco (isl.)		A3
Elobey (isls.)		A3
Fernando Po (Bioko) (isl.)		A3

GABON
CITIES and TOWNS

Bitam 5,936		B3
Cocobeach		A3
Fougamou		B4
Franceville 9,345		B4
Kango		B3
Koula-Moutou 8,032		B4
Lambaréné 17,770		B4
Lastoursville		B4
Libreville (cap.) 105,080		A3
Makokou 5,005		B3
Mayumba		B4
M'Bigou		B4
Médouneu		B3
Mekambo		B3
Mimongo		B4
Minvoul		B3
Moanda 10,709		B4
Mouila 15,016		B4
Mounana		B4
N'Dendé		B4
N'Djolé		B4
Okondja		B4
Omboué		A4
Owendo		A4
Oyem 12,455		B3
Port-Gentil 48,190		A4
Tchibanga 14,001		B4

OTHER FEATURES

Crystal (mts.)		B4
Ibounzi (mt.)		B4
Ivindo (riv.)		B3
Lopez (cape)		A4
N'Dogo (lag.)		A4
N'Gounie (riv.)		B4
N'Komi (lag.)		A4
Ogooué (riv.)		A4
Pongara (pt.)		A3

KENYA
PROVINCES

Central 1,675,647		G4
Coast 944,082		G4
Eastern 1,907,301		G4
Nairobi 509,286		G4
North-Eastern 245,757		G3
Nyanza 2,122,045		F4
Rift Valley 2,210,289		G3
Western 1,328,298		G3

CITIES and TOWNS

Baragoi 2,383		G3
Bunyala		F3
Eldoret 18,196		G3
Embu 3,928		G4
Fort Hall 4,750		G4
Galole 3,609		G4
Garissa		G4
Gilgil 4,178		G4
Isiolo 8,201		G3
Kajiado 1,755		G4
Kakamega 6,244		F3
Kaningo 2,450		G4
Kapenguria 1,790		G3
Kericho 10,144		G4
Kiambu 2,776		G4
Kilifi 2,662		G4
Kisii 6,080		F4
Kisumu 32,431		F3
Kitale 11,573		G3
Kitui 3,071		G4
Kwale 1,092		G4
Lamu 7,403		H4
Lokitaung 4,090		G3
Machakos 6,312		G4
Mado Gashi 1,003		G3
Malindi 10,757		H4
Maralal 3,878		G3
Marsabit 6,635		G3
Migori 2,066		F4
Mombasa 247,073		G4
Nairobi (cap.) 509,286		G4
Naivasha 6,920		G4
Nakuru 47,151		G4
Nanyuki 11,624		G3
Narok 2,608		G4
Ngong 1,583		G4
Nyeri 2,436		G4
Rumuruti 1,484		G3
Thika 18,387		G4
Thomson's Falls 7,602		G4
Vanga		G4
Voi 5,313		G4
Wajir		H3
Wamba 2,650		G3

OTHER FEATURES

Daua (riv.)		H3
Elgon (mt.)		F3
Formosa (bay)		H4
Galana (riv.)		G4
Gedi (ruins)		H4
Kenya (mt.)		G4
Lak Dera (dry riv.)		H3
Lorian (swamp)		G3
Natron (lake)		G4
Nyiru (mt.)		G3
Patta (isl.)		H4
Rudolf (Turkana) (lake)		G3
Tana (riv.)		H4
Tsavo Nat'l Park		G4
Turkana (lake)		G3
Victoria (lake)		F4
Winam (bay)		F4

MALAWI
CITIES and TOWNS

Blantyre 222,153		F7
Chitipa 3,079		F5
Dedza 5,448		F6
Dowa 2,067		F6
Karonga 11,873		F5
Lilongwe (cap.) 102,924		F6
Mangochi 3,341		G6
Mchinji 1,962		F6
Mwanza 2,271		F7
Mzimba 4,962		F6

Ncheu 1,326		F6
Nkhata Bay 4,024		F6
Nkhotakota 10,312		F6
Nsanje 6,091		G7
Rumphi 3,998		F6
Salima 4,646		F6
Thyolo 4,186		F7
Zomba 21,000		G7

OTHER FEATURES

Chilrua (lake)		G7
Malawi (Nyasa) (lake)		F6
Mulanje (mts.)		G7
Nyasa (lake)		F6
Shire (riv.)		G7

RWANDA
CITIES and TOWNS

Butare 21,691		E4
Cyangugu 7,042		E4
Gisenyi 12,436		E4
Kigali (cap.) 117,749		F4
Nyabisindu 8,587		F4

OTHER FEATURES

Kagera Nat'l Park		F4
Karisimbi (mt.)		E4
Kivu (lake)		E4
Ruzizi (riv.)		E4
Virunga (range)		E4

SOMALIA
PROVINCES

Bakool 100,000		H3
Bari 155,000		J1
Bay 302,000		H3
Galguduud 182,000		J2
Gedo 202,800		H3
Hiiraan 147,000		J3
Jubbada Hoose 246,000		H3
Mogadiscio 371,000		J3
Mudug 215,000		J2
Nugaal 85,000		J2
Sanaag 369,000		J1
Shabeellaha Dhexe 237,000		J3
Shabeellaha Hoose 398,000		H3
Togdheer 258,000		J2
Woqooyi Galbeed 440,000		H1

CITIES and TOWNS

Afgoi		J3
Afmadu 2,580		H3
Alula		K1
Ankhor		J1
Balad 1,233		J3
Barawa (Brava) 6,167		H3
Baydhabo 14,962		H3
Belet Weyne 11,426		J3
Bender Cassim		J1
Berbera 12,219		J1
Borama 3,244		H1
Bosaso		J1
Brava 6,167		H3
Bulo Burti 5,247		J3
Bur Acaba		H3
Burao 12,617		J2
Candala		J1
Chisimayu 17,872		H4
Coriole 4,341		H3
Dante (Hafun)		K1
Dusa Mareb		J2
Eil		J2
El Athale (Itala)		J3
Erigabo 4,279		J1

(continued on following page)

Central Africa

CYLINDRICAL EQUAL-AREA PROJECTION

SCALE OF MILES

| 0 | 50 | 100 | 200 | 300 |

SCALE OF KILOMETERS

| 0 | 50 100 | 200 | 300 |

Capitals of Countries .... ☆
Other Capitals .... ◉
International Boundaries _____
Internal Boundaries _____

© Copyright HAMMOND INCORPORATED, Maplewood, N.J.

Topography

| 0 | 200 | 400 | 600 MI. |
| 0 | 200 | 400 | 600 KM. |

| | Below Sea Level | 100 m. 328 ft. | 200 m. 656 ft. | 500 m. 1,640 ft. | 1,000 m. 3,281 ft. | 2,000 m. 6,562 ft. | 5,000 m. 16,404 ft. |

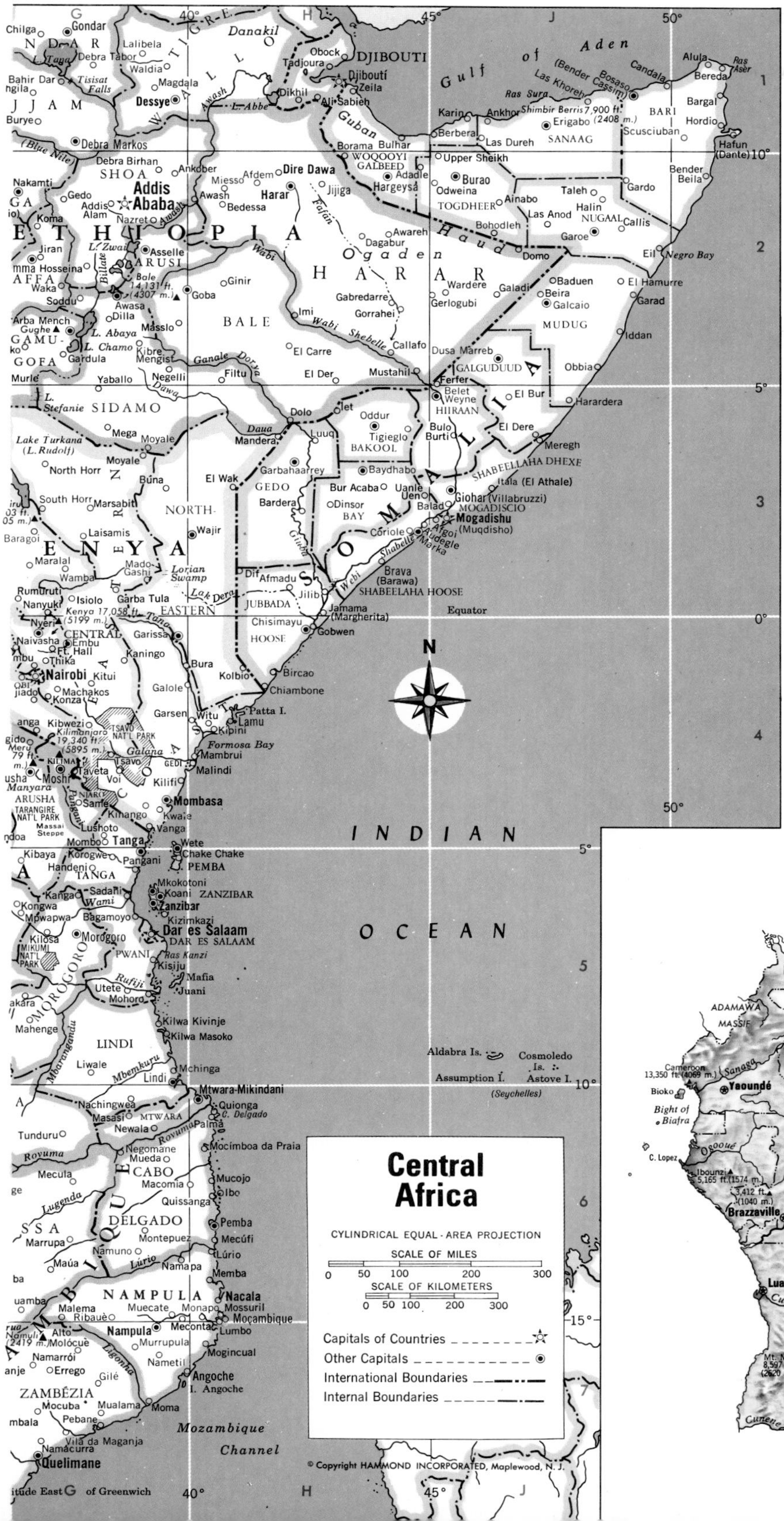

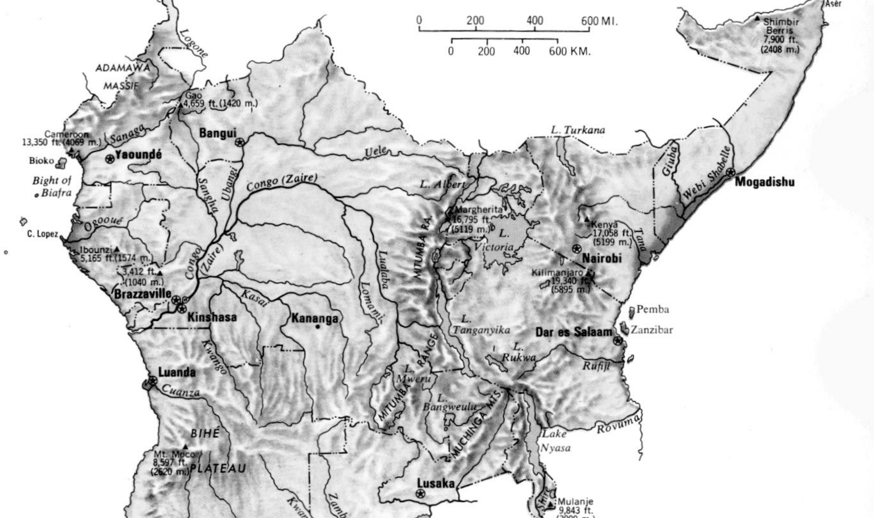

Agriculture, Industry and Resources

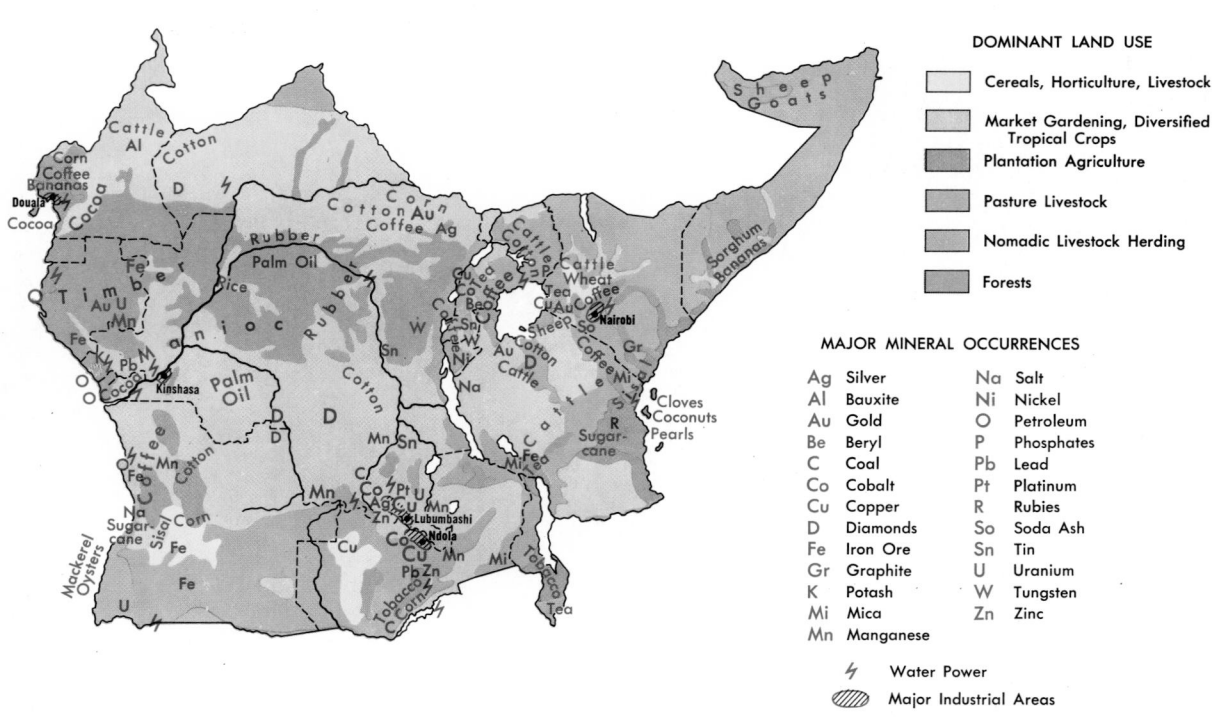

DOMINANT LAND USE

- Cereals, Horticulture, Livestock
- Market Gardening, Diversified Tropical Crops
- Plantation Agriculture
- Pasture Livestock
- Nomadic Livestock Herding
- Forests

MAJOR MINERAL OCCURRENCES

Ag Silver
Al Bauxite
Au Gold
Be Beryl
C Coal
Co Cobalt
Cu Copper
D Diamonds
Fe Iron Ore
Gr Graphite
K Potash
Mi Mica
Mn Manganese

Na Salt
Ni Nickel
O Petroleum
P Phosphates
Pb Lead
Pt Platinum
R Rubies
So Soda Ash
Sn Tin
U Uranium
W Tungsten
Zn Zinc

⚡ Water Power

▨ Major Industrial Areas

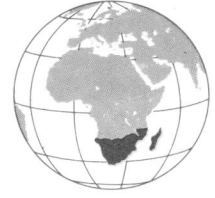

NAMIBIA
AREA 317,827 sq. mi. (823,172 sq. km.)
POPULATION 1,818,000
CAPITAL Windhoek
LARGEST CITY Windhoek
HIGHEST POINT Brandberg 8,550 ft.
   (2,606 m.)
MONETARY UNIT rand
MAJOR LANGUAGES Ovambo, Hottentot,
   Herero, Afrikaans, English
MAJOR RELIGIONS Tribal religions,
   Protestantism

SOUTH AFRICA
AREA 455,318 sq. mi. (1,179,274 sq. km.)
POPULATION 34,492,000
CAPITALS Cape Town, Pretoria
LARGEST CITY Johannesburg
HIGHEST POINT Injasuti 11,182 ft. (3,408 m.)
MONETARY UNIT rand
MAJOR LANGUAGES Afrikaans, English,
   Xhosa, Zulu, Sesotho
MAJOR RELIGIONS Protestantism,
   Roman Catholicism, Islam, Hinduism,
   tribal religions

LESOTHO
AREA 11,720 sq. mi. (30,355 sq. km.)
POPULATION 1,700,000
CAPITAL Maseru
LARGEST CITY Maseru
HIGHEST POINT 11,425 ft. (3,482 m.)
MONETARY UNIT loti
MAJOR LANGUAGES Sesotho, English
MAJOR RELIGIONS Tribal religions,
   Christianity

BOTSWANA
AREA 224,764 sq. mi. (582,139 sq. km.)
POPULATION 1,256,000
CAPITAL Gaborone
LARGEST CITY Francistown
HIGHEST POINT Tsodilo Hill 5,922 ft.
   (1,805 m.)
MONETARY UNIT pula
MAJOR LANGUAGES Setswana, Shona,
   Bushman, English, Afrikaans
MAJOR RELIGIONS Tribal religions,
   Protestantism

MOZAMBIQUE
AREA 303,769 sq. mi. (786,762 sq. km.)
POPULATION 15,326,000
CAPITAL Maputo
LARGEST CITY Maputo
HIGHEST POINT Mt. Binga 7,992 ft.
   (2,436 m.)
MONETARY UNIT metical
MAJOR LANGUAGES Makua, Thonga,
   Shona, Portuguese
MAJOR RELIGIONS Tribal religions,
   Roman Catholicism, Islam

SWAZILAND
AREA 6,705 sq. mi. (17,366 sq. km.)
POPULATION 681,000
CAPITAL Mbabane
LARGEST CITY Manzini
HIGHEST POINT Emlembe 6,109 ft.
   (1,862 m.)
MONETARY UNIT lilangeni
MAJOR LANGUAGES siSwati, English
MAJOR RELIGIONS Tribal religions,
   Christianity

ZIMBABWE
AREA 150,803 sq. mi. (390,580 sq. km.)
POPULATION 9,122,000
CAPITAL Harare
LARGEST CITY Harare
HIGHEST POINT Mt. Inyangani 8,517 ft.
   (2,596 m.)
MONETARY UNIT Zimbabwe dollar
MAJOR LANGUAGES English, Shona,
   Ndebele
MAJOR RELIGIONS Tribal religions,
   Protestantism

MADAGASCAR
AREA 226,657 sq. mi. (587,041 sq. km.)
POPULATION 9,985,000
CAPITAL Antananarivo
LARGEST CITY Antananarivo
HIGHEST POINT Maromokotro 9,436 ft.
   (2,876 m.)
MONETARY UNIT Madagascar franc
MAJOR LANGUAGES Malagasy, French
MAJOR RELIGIONS Tribal religions,
   Roman Catholicism, Protestantism

COMOROS
AREA 719 sq. mi. (1,862 sq. km.)
POPULATION 484,000
CAPITAL Moroni
LARGEST CITY Moroni
HIGHEST POINT Karthala 7,746 ft.
   (2,361 m.)
MONETARY UNIT CFA franc
MAJOR LANGUAGES Arabic, French,
   Swahili
MAJOR RELIGION Islam

MAURITIUS
AREA 790 sq. mi. (2,046 sq. km.)
POPULATION 1,068,000
CAPITAL Port Louis
LARGEST CITY Port Louis
HIGHEST POINT 2,711 ft. (826 m.)
MONETARY UNIT Mauritian rupee
MAJOR LANGUAGES English, French,
   French Creole, Hindi, Urdu
MAJOR RELIGIONS Hinduism, Christianity,
   Islam

SEYCHELLES
AREA 145 sq. mi. (375 sq. km.)
POPULATION 67,000
CAPITAL Victoria
LARGEST CITY Victoria
HIGHEST POINT Mórne Seychellois
   2,993 ft. (912 m.)
MONETARY UNIT Seychellois rupee
MAJOR LANGUAGES English, French,
   Creole
MAJOR RELIGION Roman Catholicism

RÉUNION
AREA 969 sq. mi. (2,510 sq. km.)
POPULATION 570,000
CAPITAL St-Denis

MAYOTTE
AREA 144 sq. mi. (373 sq. km.)
POPULATION 47,300
CAPITAL Dzaoudzi

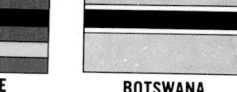
ZIMBABWE

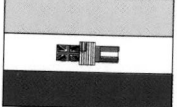
BOTSWANA

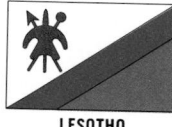
SOUTH AFRICA

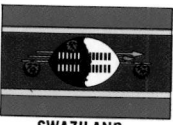
LESOTHO

SWAZILAND

MOZAMBIQUE

COMOROS

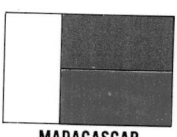
MADAGASCAR

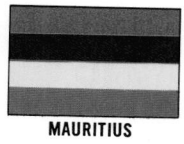
MAURITIUS

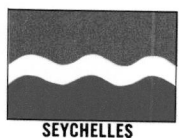
SEYCHELLES

NAMIBIA

Agriculture, Industry and Resources

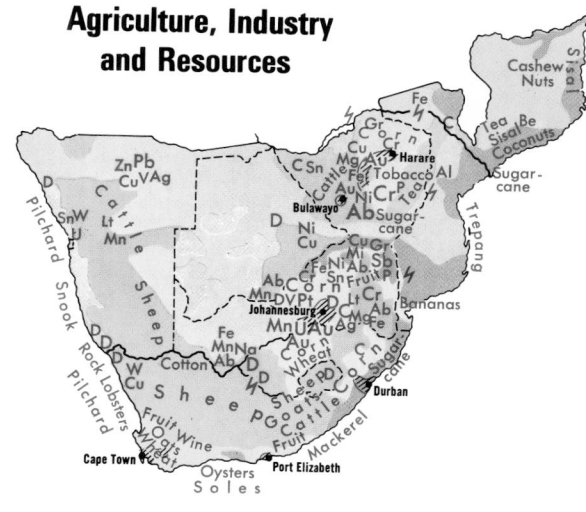

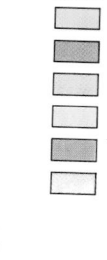

DOMINANT LAND USE

- Cereals, Horticulture, Livestock
- Market Gardening, Diversified Tropical Crops
- Plantation Agriculture
- Pasture Livestock
- Nomadic Livestock Herding
- Forests
- Nonagricultural Land

⚡ Water Power
Major Industrial Areas

MAJOR MINERAL OCCURRENCES

Ab	Asbestos	Cu	Copper	Mn	Manganese	Sb	Antimony
Ag	Silver	D	Diamonds	Na	Salt	Sn	Tin
Al	Bauxite	Fe	Iron Ore	Ni	Nickel	U	Uranium
Au	Gold	Gr	Graphite	P	Phosphates	V	Vanadium
Be	Beryl	Lt	Lithium	Pb	Lead	W	Tungsten
C	Coal	Mg	Magnesium	Pt	Platinum	Zn	Zinc
Cr	Chromium	Mi	Mica				

BOTSWANA

CITIES and TOWNS

Dinokwe 560 ....D4
Francistown 22,000 ....D4
Gaborone (cap.) 21,000 .....D4
Ghanzi 1,198 ....C4
Kanye 10,664 ....D5
Kasane 1,476 ....D3
Lobatse 11,936 ....D5
Mahalapye 12,056 ....D4
Maun 9,614 ....C4
Mochudi 6,945 ....D4
Molepolole 9,448 ....D4
Palapye 5,217 ....D4
Ramotswa 7,991 ....D4
Selebi-Pikwe 20,572 ....D4
Serowe 15,723 ....D4

OTHER FEATURES

Chobe (riv.) C3
Chobe Nat'l Park D3
Dau (lake) C4
Kalahari (des.) C4
Kaukauveld (mts.) C3
Limpopo (riv.) D4
Mababe (depr.) C3
Makgadikgadi (salt pan) D3
Molopo (riv.) C5
Ngami (lake) C4
Ngamiland (reg.) C3
Nossob (riv.) B4
Okovango (riv.) C3
Okovango (swamps) C3
Orange (riv.) B5
Shashe (riv.) D4
Tati (riv.) D4
Tsodilo Hill (mt.) C4
Xau (Dau) (lake) C4

COMOROS

CITIES and TOWNS

Fomboni 3,229 ....G2
Mitsamiouli 3,196 ....G2
Moroni (cap.) 12,000 ....G2
Mutsamudu 7,652 ....G2

OTHER FEATURES

Mwali (Mohéli) (isl.) G2
Njazidja (Grand Comoro) (isl.) G2
Nzwani (Anjouan) (isl.) G2

LESOTHO

CITIES and TOWNS

Leribe 5,200 ....D5

Mafeteng 4,600 ....D5
Maseru (cap.) 71,500 ....D5
Mohaleshoek 3,600 ....D6

MADAGASCAR

PROVINCES

Antananarivo 2,167,973 .....H3
Antsiranana 597,982 ....H2
Fianarantsoa 1,804,365 .....H4
Mahajanga 819,750 ....H3
Toamasina 1,179,660 ....H3
Toliara 1,034,114 ....G4

CITIES and TOWNS

Ambalavao 6,988 ....H4
Ambanja 12,258 ....H2
Ambatolampy 11,539 ....H3
Ambatondrazaka 18,044 ......H3
Ambilobe 9,415 ....H2
Ambodifototra 1,112 ....J3
Ambositra 16,780 ....H4
Andapa 6,275 ....H2
Antalaha 17,541 ....J2
Antananarivo (cap.)
   451,808 ....H3
Antsirabe 32,979 ....H3
Antsiranana 40,443 ....H2
Antsohihy 8,721 ....H2
Arivonimamo 8,497 ....H3
Belo-Tsiribihina 4,403 .....G3
Brickaville (Vohibinany)
   1,741 ....H3
Diégo-Suarez (Antsiranana)
   40,443 ....H2
Faradofay 19,605 ....H5
Farafangana 10,817 ....H4
Fenoarivo, Toamasina 7,696 .H3
Fianarantsoa 68,054 ....H4
Fort-Dauphin (Faradofay)
   19,605 ....H5
Foulpointe H3
Hell-Ville 6,183 ....H2
Ihosy 4,521 ....H4
Maevatanana 7,197 ....H3
Maintirano 6,375 ....G3
Majunga 65,864 ....H3
Manakara 19,768 ....H4
Mananjary 14,638 ....H4
Mandritsara 6,826 ....H3
Maroantsetra 6,645 ....J3
Marovoay 20,253 ....H3
Moramanga 10,806 ....H3
Morombe 6,967 ....G4
Morondava 19,061 ....G4
Port-Bergé 4,734 ....H3
Sambava 6,215 ....J2
Sosumav 10,946 ....H2
Tamatave (Toamasina)
   77,395 ....H3
(continued on following page)

(continued on following page)

Topography

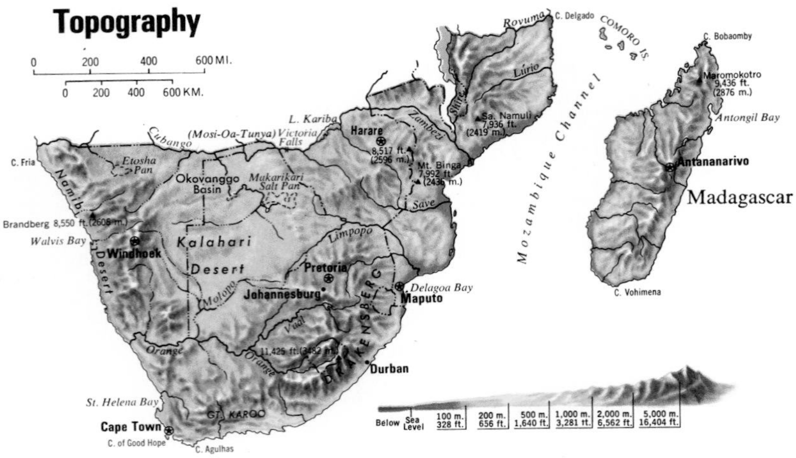
0 200 400 600 MI.
0 200 400 600 KM.
C. Delgado
Rovuma
COMORO IS.
C. Bobaomby
Maromokotro 9,436 ft. (2876 m.)
Antongil Bay
Antananarivo
Madagascar
Mozambique Channel
Lúrio
Shire
Zambezi
Sa. Namuli 7,936 ft. (2419 m.)
Mt. Binga 7,992 ft. (2436 m.)
Save
L. Kariba
Harare
(Mosi-Oa-Tunya) Victoria Falls
Cubango
C. Fria
Etosha Pan
Okovanggo Basin
Makarikari Salt Pan
Brandberg 8,550 ft. (2606 m.)
Walvis Bay
Windhoek
Kalahari
Desert
Limpopo
Pretoria
Johannesburg
Delagoa Bay
Maputo
Molopo
Vaal
Orange
11,425 ft. (3482 m.)
Durban
St. Helena Bay
GT. KAROO
Cape Town
C. of Good Hope
C. Agulhas
C. Vohimena
Below Sea Level
100 m. 328 ft.
200 m. 656 ft.
500 m. 1,640 ft.
1,000 m. 3,281 ft.
2,000 m. 6,562 ft.
5,000 m. 16,404 ft.

Tananarive (Antananarivo) 451,808 ... H3
Tangainony 6,952 ... H4
Toamasina 77,395 ... H3
Toliara (Tuléar) 45,676 ... G4
Tsiroanomandidy 11,444 ... H3
Vangaindrano 3,249 ... H4
Vohibinany 1,741 ... H3
Vohimarina (Vohémar) 4,289 ... J2
Vohipeno 2,736 ... H4

OTHER FEATURES

Alaotra (lake) ... H3
Amber (Bobaomby) (cape) ... H2
Antongil (bay) ... J3
Barren (isls.) ... G3
Betsiboka (riv.) ... H3
Bobaomby (Amber) (cape) ... H2
Boby, Pic (mt.) ... H4
Chesterfield (isl.) ... G3
Ikopa (riv.) ... H3
Itasy (lake) ... H3
Mahajamba (bay) ... H2
Mananara (riv.) ... H4
Mananbao (riv.) ... G3
Mangoky (riv.) ... G4
Mangoro (riv.) ... H3
Maromokotro (mt.) ... H2
Masoala (pen.) ... J3
Menarandra (riv.) ... H4
Mozambique (chan.) ... G3
Nosy Be (isl.) ... H2
Nosy Boraha (isl.) ... J3
Onilahy (riv.) ... G4
Pangalanes (canal) ... H4
Radama (isls.) ... H2
Saint-André (cape) ... G3
Saint-Marie (Nosy Boraha) (isl.) ... J3
Saint-Marie (Vohimena) (cape) ... G5
Saint-Sébastien (cape) ... H2
Sofia (riv.) ... H3
Tsiafajavona (mt.) ... H3
Tsiribihina (riv.) ... G3
Vohimena (cape) ... G5

MAURITIUS

CITIES and TOWNS

Curepipe 52,709 ... G5
Mahébourg 15,463 ... G5
Port Louis (cap.) 141,022 ... G5
Quatre Bornes 51,638 ... G5
Souillac 3,361 ... G5

OTHER FEATURES

Mascarene (isls.) ... F5

MAYOTTE

CITIES and TOWNS

Dzaoudzi (cap.) 196 ... H2

MOZAMBIQUE

PROVINCES

Cabo Delgado 940,000 ... F2
Gaza 999,900 ... E4
Inhambane 977,000 ... E4
Manica 541,200 ... E4
Maputo 491,800 ... E5
Maputo (city) 755,300 ... E5
Nampula 2,402,700 ... F2
Niassa 514,100 ... F2
Sofala 1,055,200 ... E3
Tete 831,000 ... E3
Zambézia 2,500,000 ... F3

CITIES and TOWNS

Angoche 1,714 ... G3
Bartolomeu Dias○ 6,102 ... F4
Beira 46,293 ... F3
Beira* 130,398 ... F3
Chibuto 23,763 ... E4
Chicualacuala 2,050 ... E4
Chimoio 4,507 ... E3
Chinde 742 ... F3
Dona Ana (Mutarara) 686 ... F3
Dondo 2,112 ... F3
Funhalouro○ 42,366 ... E4
Ibo 1,015 ... G2
Inhambane 4,975 ... F4
Inhaminga 1,607 ... F3
Inharrime 856 ... F4
Lichinga 3,011 ... F2
Lumbo○ 11,080 ... G3
Lúrio○ 13,417 ... G2
Mabalane○ 13,158 ... E4
Mabote○ 28,970 ... E4
Machanga○ 15,754 ... F4
Machaze○ 42,255 ... E4
Mandié○ 24,382 ... E3
Mandimba○ 7,634 ... F2
Manhiça○ 1,680 ... E5
Maniamba○ 2,045 ... F2
Maputo (cap.) 755,300 ... E5
Massangena○ 3,301 ... E4
Massinga 517 ... F4
Moçambique 1,730 ... G3
Mocímboa da Praia 935 ... G2
Mocuba 2,293 ... F3
Montepuez 2,837 ... F2
Mualama○ 34,992 ... F3
Mucojo○ 15,867 ... G2
Mueda 1,583 ... F2
Mutarara (Dona Ana) 686 ... F3
Nacala 4,601 ... G2
Nampula 23,072 ... F3
Pafúri○ 2,599 ... E4
Pemba 3,629 ... G2
Quelimane 10,522 ... F3
Quionga○ 3,181 ... G2
Quissico 2,615 ... E4
Songo 2,230 ... E3
Tete 4,549 ... E3
Vila de Sena○ 21,074 ... E3
Xai-Xai 5,234 ... E5

OTHER FEATURES

Angoche (isl.) ... G3
Bazaruto, Ilha do (isl.) ... F4
Binga (mt.) ... E3
Cabora Bassa (dam) ... E3
Changane (riv.) ... E4
Chirua (lake) ... F3
Delagoa (bay) ... E5
Delgado (cape) ... G2
Gorongosa Nat'l Park ... E3
Ligonha (riv.) ... F3
Limpopo (riv.) ... E4
Lugenda (riv.) ... F2
Lúrio (riv.) ... F2
Mazoe (riv.) ... E3
Mozambique (chan.) ... G3
Namuli, Serra (mt.) ... F3
Nyasa (lake) ... E2
Olifants (riv.) ... D4
Rovuma (riv.) ... F2
São Sebastião (pt.) ... F4
Save (riv.) ... E4
Shire (riv.) ... E3
Zambezi (riv.) ... E3

NAMIBIA

CITIES and TOWNS

Aroab 783 ... B5
Aus 767 ... B5
Berseba ... B5
Bethanie 1,207 ... B5
Gibeon ... B5
Gobabis 4,428 ... B4
Grootfontein 4,627 ... B3
Kalkfeld 587 ... B4
Kamanjab 713 ... A3
Karasburg 2,693 ... B5
Karibib 1,653 ... B4
Keetmanshoop 10,297 ... B5
Koes 514 ... B5
Lüderitz 6,642 ... A5
Maltahöhe 1,313 ... B4
Mariental 4,629 ... B4
Okahandja 1,688 ... B4
Omaruru 2,783 ... B4
Ondangwa ... B3
Opuno ... A3
Oranjemund 2,594 ... B5
Oshakati ... B3
Otavi 1,814 ... B3
Otjiwarongo 8,018 ... B4
Outjo 2,545 ... B4
Rehoboth 5,363 ... B4
Rundu 521 ... B3
Stampriet 271 ... B4
Swakopmund 5,681 ... A4
Tsumeb 12,338 ... B3
Usakos 2,334 ... B4
Warmbad 810 ... B5
Windhoek (cap.) 61,369 ... B4
Witvlei 303 ... B4

OTHER FEATURES

Brandberg (mt.) ... A4
Caprivi Strip (reg.) ... C3
Chobe (riv.) ... C3
Cross (cape) ... A4
Cubango (riv.) ... B3
Cunene (riv.) ... A3
Damaraland (reg.) ... B4
Diamond Coast (reg.) ... A5
Elephant (riv.) ... B5
Etosha Pan (salt pan) ... B3
Fish (riv.) ... B5
Fria (cape) ... A3
Great Namaland (reg.) ... B4
Hollam's Bird (isl.) ... A4
Hottentot (bay) ... A5
Kalahari (des.) ... C4
Kaokoveld (reg.) ... A3
Kaukauveld (mts.) ... C3
Kuiseb (riv.) ... B4
Lüderitz (bay) ... A5
Namib (des.) ... A3
Nossob (riv.) ... B4
Okovango (riv.) ... C3
Omatako (riv.) ... B3
Ovamboland (reg.) ... B3
Ruacana Falls (falls) ... A3
Skeleton Coast (reg.) ... A3
Swakop (riv.) ... B4
Ugab (riv.) ... A4
Zambezi (riv.) ... C3

REUNION

CITIES and TOWNS

Le Port 21,564 ... F5
Saint-Benoît 7,778 ... G5
Saint-Denis (cap.) 80,075 ... F5
Saint-Denis* 104,603 ... F5
Saint-Joseph 8,928 ... G6
Saint-Louis 10,252 ... F5
Saint-Pierre 21,817 ... F6

OTHER FEATURES

Bassas da India (isl.) ... F4
Europa (isl.) ... G4
Glorioso (isls.) ... H2
Juan de Nova (isl.) ... G3
Mascarene (isls.) ... F5
Piton des Neiges (mt.) ... G5

SEYCHELLES

CITIES and TOWNS

Anse Boileau† 3,420 ... H5
Anse Royale† 3,182 ... H5
Cascade† 2,600 ... H5
Victoria (cap.) 15,559 ... H5
Victoria* 23,012 ... H5

OTHER FEATURES

Aldabra (isls.) ... H1
Assumption (isl.) ... H1
Astove (isl.) ... H2
Cerf (isl.) ... H5
Cosmoledo (isls.) ... H1
Curieuse (isl.) ... H5
Felicité (isl.) ... J5
Frigate (isl.) ... J5
La Digue (isl.) ... J5
Mahé (isl.) ... H5
Morne Seychellois (mt.) ... H5
North (isl.) ... H5
Praslin (isl.) ... H5
Sainte Anne (isl.) ... H5
Silhouette (isl.) ... H5

SOUTH AFRICA

PROVINCES

Cape Province 5,543,506 ... C6
Natal 5,722,215 ... E5
Orange Free State 1,833,216 ... D5
Transvaal 10,673,033 ... D4

AUTONOMOUS REPUBLICS

Bophuthatswana 1,200,000 ... D5
Ciskei ... D6
Transkei 2,000,000 ... D6
Venda 450,000 ... E4

CITIES and TOWNS

Alberton 23,988 ... H6
Alexandra 57,040 ... H6
Aliwal North 12,311 ... D6
Barberton 12,382 ... E5
Beaufort West 17,862 ... C6
Bellville 49,026 ... F6
Benoni 151,294 ... J6
Bethlehem 29,918 ... D5
Bisho ... D6
Bloemfontein 149,836 ... D5
Boksburg 106,126 ... J6
Brakpan 73,210 ... J6
Brits 12,182 ... D5
Butterworth (Gcuwa) 2,769 ... D6
Cape Town (cap.) 697,514 ... E6
Carltonville 40,641 ... G7
Cradock 20,822 ... D6
De Aar 18,057 ... C6
Dundee 17,162 ... E5
Durban 736,852 ... E5
East London 119,727 ... D6
Edendale 41,194 ... D5
Edenvale 25,126 ... H6
Elsiesrivier 63,706 ... F6
Ermelo 19,036 ... E5
Eshowe 4,552 ... E5
Estcourt 10,922 ... D5
Fort Beaufort 11,640 ... D6
Gcuwa 2,769 ... D6
George 24,625 ... C6
Germiston 221,972 ... H6
Glencoe 10,513 ... E5
Goodwood 31,592 ... F6
Graaff-Reinet 22,392 ... C6
Grahamstown 41,302 ... D6
Grassy Park 32,709 ... E6
Griquatown 2,996 ... C5
Harrismith 16,082 ... D5
Heidelberg 12,521 ... J7
Hermanus 4,956 ... G7
Howick 12,429 ... E5
Johannesburg 654,232 ... H6
Kempton Park 37,205 ... J6
Kimberley 105,258 ... C5
King William's Town 15,798 ... D6
Klerksdorp 63,558 ... D5
Knysna 13,479 ... C6
Kokstad 10,227 ... D6
Kraaifontein 10,286 ... F6
Kroonstad 51,988 ... D5
Krugersdorp 92,725 ... H6
Ladybrand 8,757 ... D5
Ladysmith 28,920 ... D5
Lambert's Bay 3,247 ... B6
Mafikeng (Mafeking) 6,515 ... D5
Matatiele 3,853 ... D6
Messina 21,121 ... D4
Middelburg, Cape Prov. 12,121 ... D6
Middelburg, Transvaal 26,942 ... D5
Milnerton 10,893 ... F6
Mmabatho ... D5
Mossel Bay 17,574 ... C6
Nelspruit 25,092 ... E5
Newcastle 14,407 ... E5
Nigel 41,179 ... J7
Nyanga 15,655 ... F6
Odendaalsrus 15,603 ... D5
Oudtshoorn 26,907 ... C6
Paarl 49,244 ... F6
Parow 60,768 ... F6
Parys 17,447 ... D5
Pietermaritzburg 114,822 ... E5
Pietersburg 27,174 ... D4
Piet Retief 10,056 ... D5
Pinelands 11,769 ... F6
Pinetown 22,721 ... E6
Port Elizabeth 392,231 ... D6
Port Nolloth 2,893 ... B5
Port Saint Johns (Umzimbuvu) 1,817 ... D6
Potchefstroom 57,443 ... D5
Pretoria (cap.) 545,450 ... D5
Queenstown 39,304 ... D6
Randburg 43,257 ... H6
Randfontein 50,481 ... G6
Richards Bay 598 ... E5
Robertson 10,237 ... C6
Roodeport 115,366 ... H6
Rustenburg 22,303 ... D5
Saldanha 4,994 ... B6
Simonstown 12,137 ... E7
Sishen 2,692 ... C5
Somerset East 10,383 ... D6
Somerset West 11,828 ... F6
Soweto 602,043 ... H6
Springs 142,812 ... J6
Standerton 21,038 ... D5

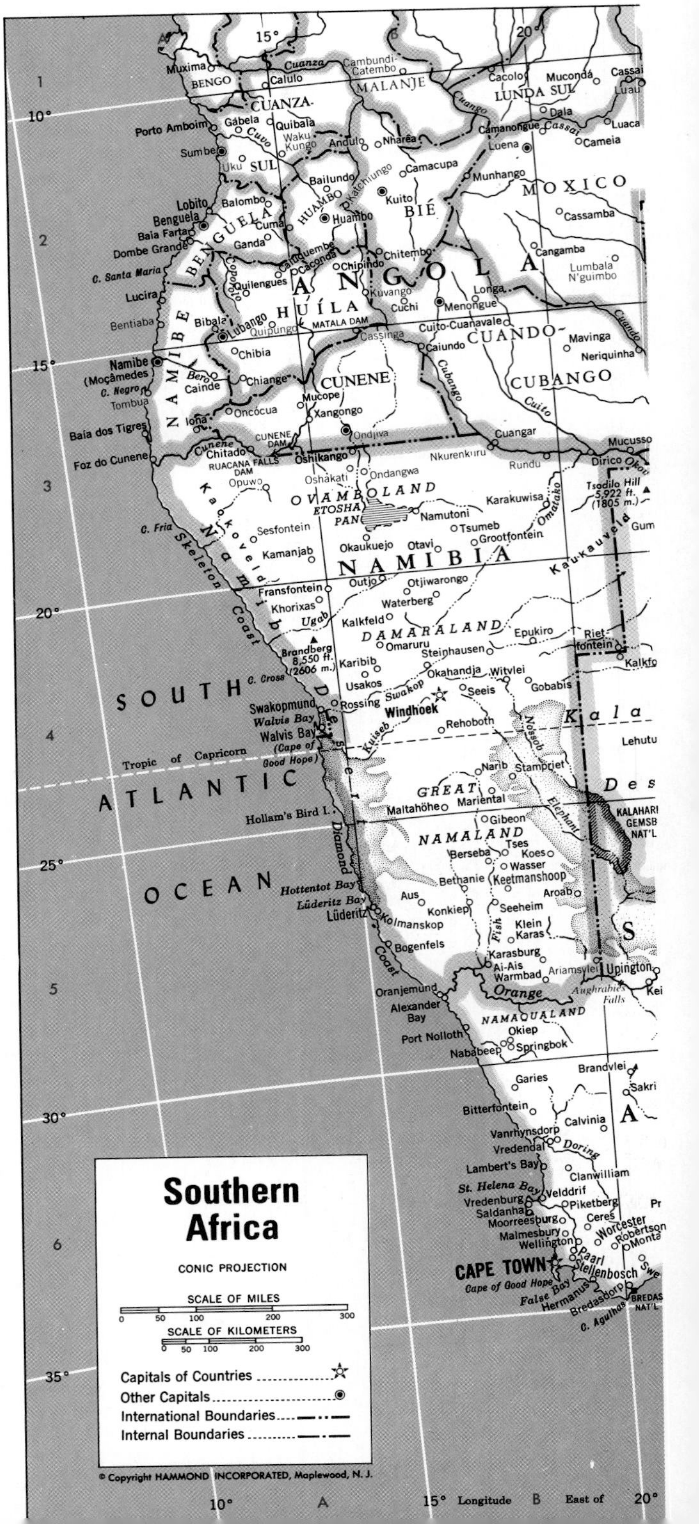
Southern Africa
CONIC PROJECTION
SCALE OF MILES
0 50 100 200 300
SCALE OF KILOMETERS
0 50 100 200 300
Capitals of Countries
Other Capitals
International Boundaries
Internal Boundaries
© Copyright HAMMOND INCORPORATED, Maplewood, N. J.
ANGOLA
NAMIBIA
SOUTH ATLANTIC OCEAN
Tropic of Capricorn
CAPE TOWN
Windhoek
Walvis Bay
Lüderitz
Swakopmund
Longitude
East of

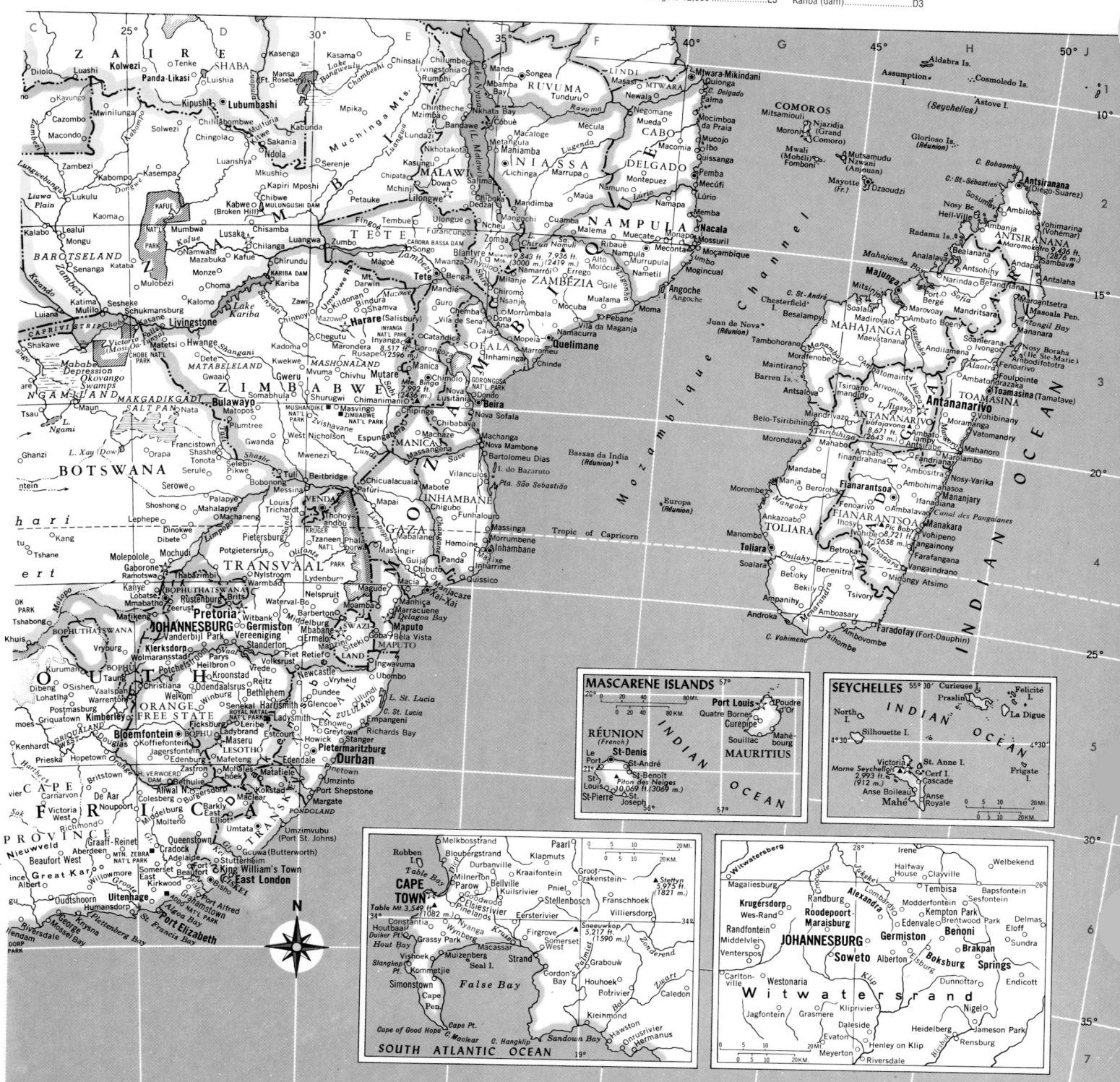

South America

AZIMUTHAL EQUAL-AREA PROJECTION

MILES
0 100 200 400 600

KILOMETERS
0 100 200 400 600

Capitals of Countries .... ⊛
Other Capitals .... ◉
International Boundaries .... ▪▫▪▫
Canals .... ╫╫╫

© Copyright HAMMOND INCORPORATED, Maplewood, N.J.

Population Distribution

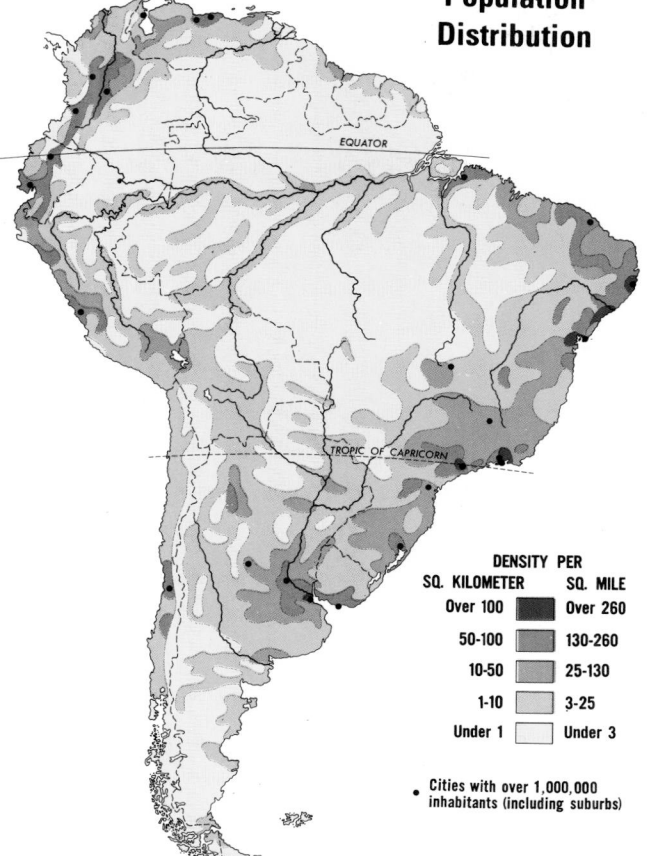

AREA 6,875,000 sq. mi. (17,806,250 sq. km.)
POPULATION 297,000,000
LARGEST CITY São Paulo
HIGHEST POINT Cerro Aconcagua 22,831 ft. (6,959 m.)
LOWEST POINT Salina Grande -131 ft. (-40 m.)

Vegetation

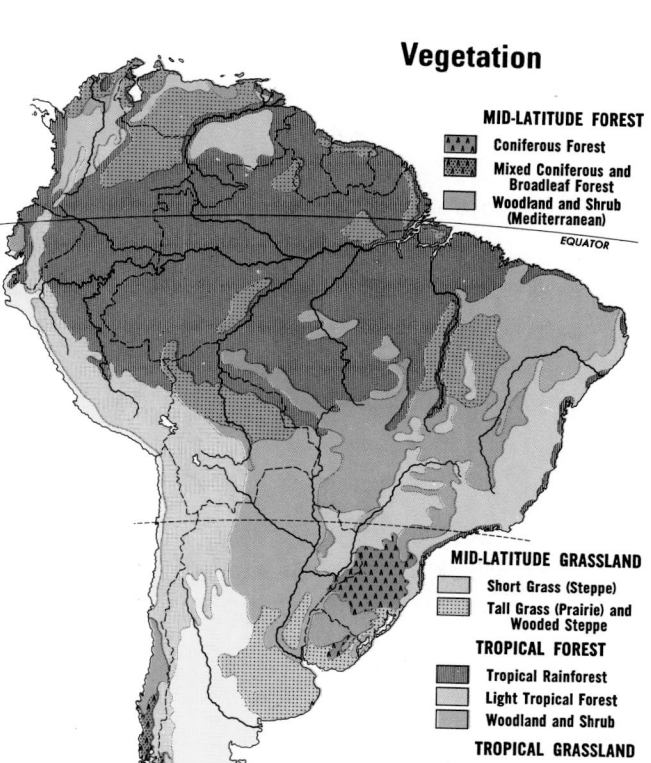

DENSITY PER

SQ. KILOMETER	SQ. MILE
Over 100	Over 260
50-100	130-260
10-50	25-130
1-10	3-25
Under 1	Under 3

• Cities with over 1,000,000 inhabitants (including suburbs)

MID-LATITUDE FOREST
Coniferous Forest
Mixed Coniferous and Broadleaf Forest
Woodland and Shrub (Mediterranean)

MID-LATITUDE GRASSLAND
Short Grass (Steppe)
Tall Grass (Prairie) and Wooded Steppe

TROPICAL FOREST
Tropical Rainforest
Light Tropical Forest
Woodland and Shrub

TROPICAL GRASSLAND
Grass and Shrub (Savanna)
Wooded Savanna

DESERT AND DESERT SHRUB

TUNDRA AND ALPINE

UNCLASSIFIED HIGHLANDS

Average January Temperature

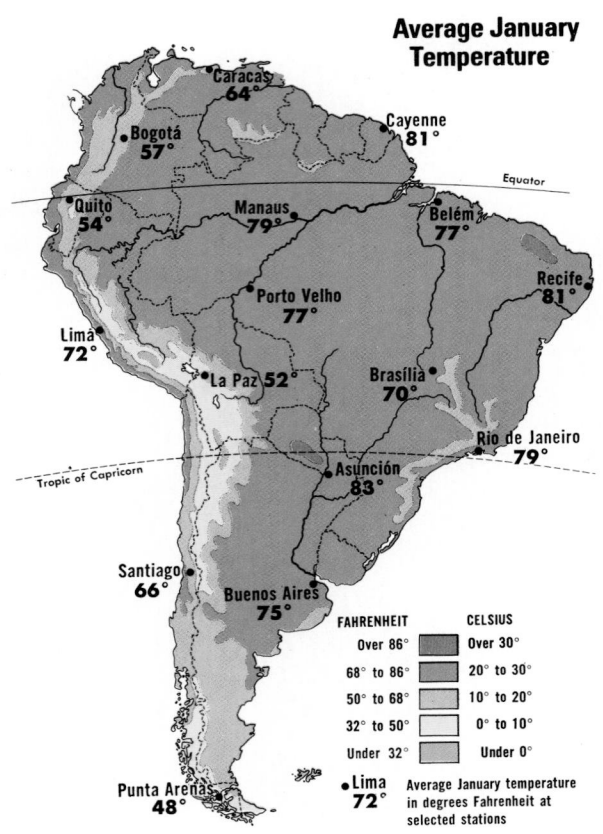

Caracas 64°
Cayenne 81°
Bogotá 57°
Equator
Quito 54°
Manaus 79°
Belém 77°
Porto Velho 77°
Recife 81°
Lima 72°
La Paz 52°
Brasília 70°
Tropic of Capricorn
Asunción 83°
Rio de Janeiro 79°
Santiago 66°
Buenos Aires 75°
Punta Arenas 48°

FAHRENHEIT	CELSIUS
Over 86°	Over 30°
68° to 86°	20° to 30°
50° to 68°	10° to 20°
32° to 50°	0° to 10°
Under 32°	Under 0°

●Lima 72° Average January temperature in degrees Fahrenheit at selected stations

Average July Temperature

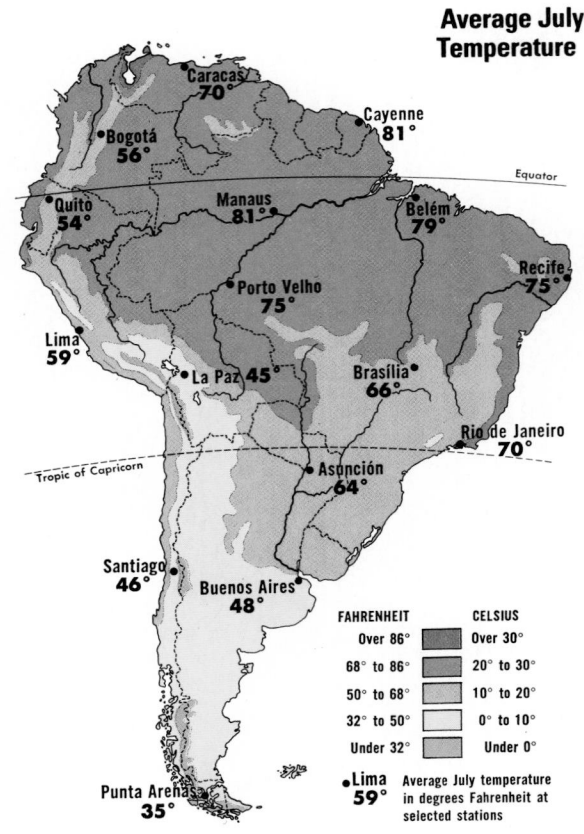

Caracas 70°
Cayenne 81°
Bogotá 56°
Equator
Quito 54°
Manaus 81°
Belém 79°
Porto Velho 75°
Recife 75°
Lima 59°
La Paz 45°
Brasília 66°
Tropic of Capricorn
Asunción 64°
Rio de Janeiro 70°
Santiago 46°
Buenos Aires 48°
Punta Arenas 35°

FAHRENHEIT	CELSIUS
Over 86°	Over 30°
68° to 86°	20° to 30°
50° to 68°	10° to 20°
32° to 50°	0° to 10°
Under 32°	Under 0°

●Lima 59° Average July temperature in degrees Fahrenheit at selected stations

Rainfall

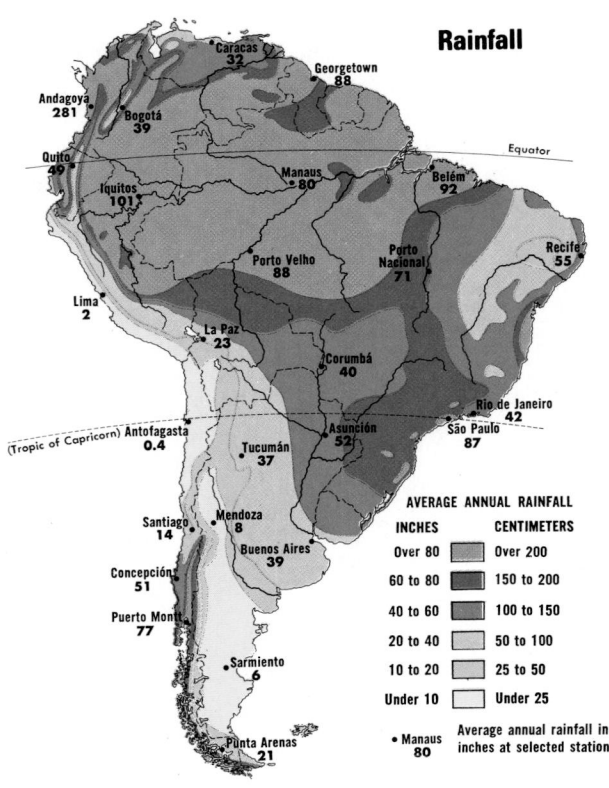

Caracas 32
Georgetown 88
Andagoyá 281
Bogotá 39
Quito 49
Equator
Manaus 80
Belém 92
Iquitos 101
Porto Velho 88
Porto Nacional 71
Recife 55
Lima 2
La Paz 23
Corumbá 40
Rio de Janeiro 42
(Tropic of Capricorn) Antofagasta 0.4
Tucumán 37
Asunción 52
São Paulo 87
Santiago 14
Mendoza 8
Buenos Aires 39
Concepción 51
Puerto Montt 77
Sarmiento 6
Punta Arenas 21

AVERAGE ANNUAL RAINFALL

INCHES	CENTIMETERS
Over 80	Over 200
60 to 80	150 to 200
40 to 60	100 to 150
20 to 40	50 to 100
10 to 20	25 to 50
Under 10	Under 25

● Manaus 80 Average annual rainfall in inches at selected stations

Vegetation/Relief

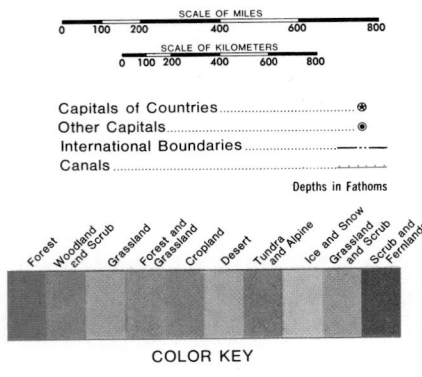

SCALE OF MILES
0 100 200 400 600 800

SCALE OF KILOMETERS
0 100 200 400 600 800

Capitals of Countries .... ⊛
Other Capitals .... ⊛
International Boundaries ....
Canals ....

Depths in Fathoms

Forest | Woodland and Scrub | Grassland | Forest and Grassland | Cropland | Desert | Tundra and Alpine | Ice and Snow | Grassland and Scrub | Scrub and Fernlands

COLOR KEY

CARIBBEAN SEA
G. of Venezuela
ARUBA (Neth.)
NETH. ANTILLES
Curaçao
Bonaire
Willemstad
BARBADOS
GRENADA
West Indies
Tobago
TRINIDAD & TOBAGO
Port of Spain
Trinidad
Pta. Gallinas
Barranquilla
Maracaibo
Caracas
Panamá Canal
Panamá
G. of Panamá
PANAMÁ
L. Maracaibo
Pico Bolívar 16,427 ft. (5007 m.)
Orinoco
Ciudad Guayana
VENEZUELA
Guri Res.
Arauca
Medellín
Magdalena
Cauca
Meta
Bogotá
COLOMBIA
Angel Fall
Caroni
GUYANA
Georgetown
Paramaribo
Cayenne
Mt. Roraima 9,094 ft. (2772 m.)
SURINAME
FRENCH GUIANA
Cali
Orinoco
Pico Phelps (Pico da Neblina) 9,889 ft. (3014 m.)
Vaupés
Branco
Highlands
Jari
Quito
Chimborazo 20,561 ft. (6267 m.)
ECUADOR
Putumayo
Negro
Japurá
Içá
Amazon
Manaus
I. de Marajó
B. de Marajó
Belém
Equator
Guayaquil
Gulf of Guayaquil
Iquitos
Amazon
São Luis
Tocantins
Fortaleza
Teresina
S e l v a s
Yavari
Juruá
Purus
Madeira
Tapajós
Xingu
Pta. Aguja
Ucayali
Marañón
Aripuanã
Teles Pires
Araguaia
Parnaíba
Caatingas
Cabo de São Roque
Natal
Trujillo
Huascarán 22,205 ft. (6768 m.)
BRAZIL
Recife
Maceió
Callao
Lima
Juruena
Tocantins
Guaporé
Mamoré
Beni
Planalto de Brazil
Paraguaçu
Salvador
Cusco
BOLIVIA
Lake Titicaca
Nev. Ancohuma 21,489 ft. (6550 m.)
La Paz
Mato Grosso
Brasília
Goiânia
São Francisco
Jequitinhonha
Grande
Cochabamba
Lake Poopó
Sucre
Arica
Highlands
Campo Grande
Belo Horizonte
Pico da Bandeira 9,482 ft. (2890 m.)
Chaco
Paraguai
Paraná
Grande
PARAGUAY
Tietê
C. de São Tomé
Paraíba
C. Frio
Tropic of Capricorn
Antofagasta
Volcán Llullaillaco 22,057 ft. (6723 m.)
Pilcomayo
Bermejo
São Paulo
Santos
Rio de Janeiro
Asunción
ITAIPU DAM
Curitiba
Iguazú Falls
Iguaçu
I. de San Félix (Chile)
I. San Ambrosio (Chile)
Nev. Ojos del Salado 22,572 ft. (6880 m.)
Salado del Norte
I. de Santa Catarina
CHILE
Paraná
Uruguay
Serra do Mar
Porto Alegre
Córdoba
Santa Fé
Lagoa dos Patos
Cerro Aconcagua 22,831 ft. (6959 m.)
Rosario
Negro
Lagoa Mirim
URUGUAY
Valparaíso
Santiago
Mendoza
I. Robinson Crusoe
I. Alejandro Selkirk
Juan Fernandez Is. (Chile)
Buenos Aires
La Plata
Montevideo
Río de la Plata
C. San Antonio
Salado
Pampas
ATLANTIC OCEAN
PACIFIC OCEAN
Concepción
Colorado
Bahía Blanca
Negro
ARGENTINA
Puerto Montt
Golfo San Matías
Pen. Valdés
Isla de Chiloé
Chubut
Archipiélago de los Chonos
Golfo San Jorge
C. Tres Puntas
Pen. Taitao
Deseado
G. de Penas
Patagonia
Bahía Grande
Falkland Islands (U.K.)
Stanley
Archipiélago Reina Adelaida
Str. of Magellan
Tierra del Fuego
Punta Arenas
Cape Horn
Longitude West of Greenwich
100
1000

124 Venezuela

STATES

| Yaracuy 300,597 | D2 |
| Zulia 1,674,252 | B2 |

CITIES and TOWNS

Amazonas (terr.) 21,696 .....E5
Anzoátegui 683,717 .....F3
Apure 188,717 .....D4
Aragua 891,623 .....E3
Barinas 326,166 .....D3
Bolívar 668,340 .....F4
Carabobo 1,062,268 .....D3
Cojedes 133,991 .....E3
Delta Amacuro (terr.) 48,139 .....H3
Dependencias Federales (terr.) 463 .....E2
Distrito Federal 1,860,637 .....E2
Falcón 503,896 .....D2
Guárico 393,467 .....E3
Lara 945,064 .....C3
Mérida 459,361 .....C3
Miranda 1,421,442 .....E2
Monagas 388,536 .....G3
Nueva Esparta 197,198 .....G2
Portuguesa 424,984 .....D3
Sucre 585,698 .....G2
Táchira 660,234 .....C4
Trujillo 433,735 .....C3

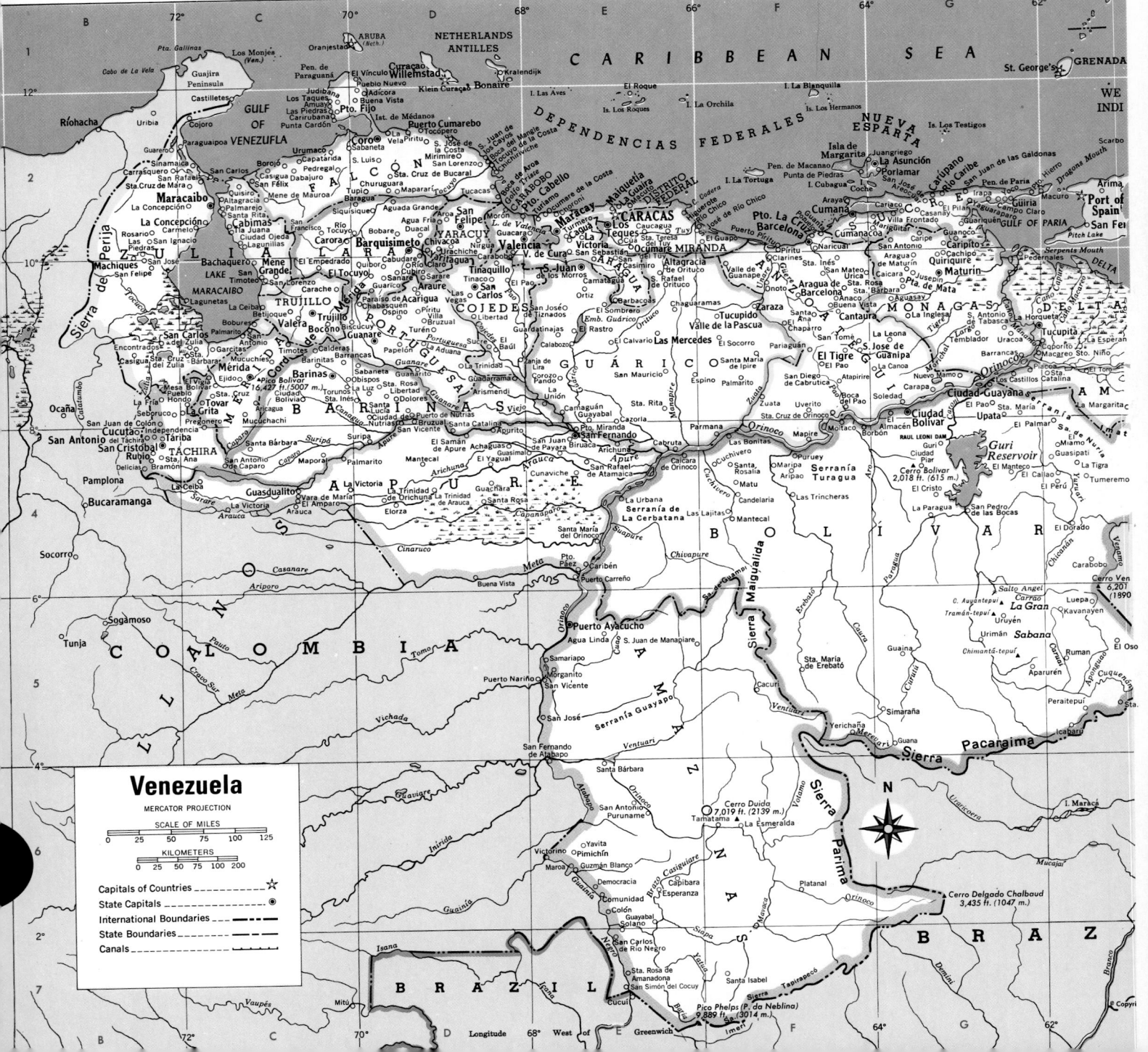

La Leona	G3
La Margarita	H3
Las Lajitas	F4
Las Mercedes 6,739	F3
Las Piedras, Falcón	C2
Las Piedras, Zulia 4,583	B2
Las Trincheras	F4
Las Vegas 3,212	D3
La Tigra	H4
La Trinidad de Arauca	D4
La Vela de Coro 7,172	D2
La Victoria, Apure	C4
La Victoria, Aragua 40,731	E2
Libertad 2,072	D3
Los Castillos	G3
Los Teques 63,106	E2
Macareo Santo Niño	H3
Machiques 18,898	B3
Macuro 1,122	H2
Macuto 11,704	E2
Maiquetía 59,238	E2
Mantecal	F4
Maracaibo 651,574	C2
Maracay 255,134	E2
Mariguitar 5,645	G2

Mene de Mauroa 4,336	C2
Mene Grande 11,498	C3
Mesa Bolívar 956	C3
Mirimire 3,424	D2
Morganito	E5
Morón 19,451	D2
Naricual 1,047	F2
Nirgua 11,918	D2
Nuevo Mamo	G3
Ocumare de la Costa 2,840	E2
Ocumare del Tuy 24,229	E2
Palmarejo	C2
Palmarito, Apure 926	D4
Palmarito, Guárico	F3
Paraguaipoa 3,850	C2
Paraíso de Chabasquén 2,094	D3
Pariaguán 8,173	F3
Parmana	F4
Pedernales	G3
Peraitepuí	H5
Piacoa	H3
Pimichín	E6
Piritu, Anzoátegui 2,479	F2
Piritu, Portuguesa 8,128	D3
Platanal	F6
Porlamar 31,985	G2
Pozuelos 45,391	F2
Pregonero 3,598	C3
Pueblo Hondo	B3
Pueblo Nuevo 3,426	D1
Puerto Ayacucho 10,417	E5
Puerto Cabello 72,103	D2
Puerto Cumarebo 10,064	D2
Puerto Hierro	H2
Puerto La Cruz 63,276	F2
Puerto Miranda	E4
Puerto Píritu 3,495	F2
Punta Cardón 18,182	C2
Punta de Mata 7,777	G3
Punta de Piedras 2,826	F2
Punto Fijo 5,548	C2
Pureuy	F4
Puruname	E6
Quibor 12,216	D3
Quiriquire 7,304	G3
Río Claro 2,460	D3
Rosario	C3
Rubio 19,156	B4
Sabaneta 4,680	D3
Samariapo	E5
San Antonio, Amazonas	E6
San Antonio, Monagas 4,235	G2
San Antonio, Zulia	C3
San Antonio del Táchira 20,342	B4
San Antonio de Tabasca	G3
Sanare 6,717	D3
San Carlos 21,029	D3
San Carlos del Zulia 26,762	C3
San Casimiro 4,843	E3
San Felipe, Yaracuy 43,801	D2
San Felipe, Zulia	B3
San Félix 379	E2
San Fernando 38,960	E4
San Ignacio	B2
San José, Amazonas	E5
San José, Zulia 4,498	B3
San José de Amacuro	H3
San José de Guanipa 22,530	G3
San José de la Costa	D2
San José de Río Chico 3,600	F2

San Juan de Colón	B3
San Juan de los Morros 38,265	E3
San Juan de Manapiare	E5
San Juan de Payara 1,018	E4
San Lorenzo	C3
San Mateo 2,424	F3
San Mauricio	E3
San Pedro de las Bocas	G4
San Rafael 10,910	C2
San Sebastián 5,582	E2
San Simón del Cocuy	E3
Santa Ana, Anzoátegui 3,558	F3
Santa Ana, Táchira 5,116	B4
Santa Bárbara, Amazonas	E6
Santa Bárbara, Barinas 6,155	C4
Santa Bárbara, Monagas 2,034	G3
Santa Bárbara, Zulia	C3
Santa Cruz	C3
Santa Cruz de Bucaral 2,904	D2
Santa Cruz de Mara 5,773	C2
Santa Cruz del Zulia 4,221	B3
Santa Elena 608	H5
Santa Isabel	F7
Santa María, Bolívar	G3
Santa María de Erebató	F5
Santa María de Ipire 3,307	F3
Santa María del Orinoco	E4
Santa Rita, Guárico	E3
Santa Rita, Zulia 15,668	C2
Santa Rosa	D4
Santa Rosa de Amanadona	E7
Santa Teresa 10,220	E2
San Timoteo 3,635	C3
San Tomé	F3
San Vicente	E5
Sarare 4,236	D3
Seboruco 2,616	B3
Simaraña	G5
Sinamaica	B2
Siquisique 3,821	D2
Solano	E6
Soledad 7,108	G3
Suripa	D4
Tamatama	F6
Taríba 15,683	B4
Temblador 5,380	G3
Tia Juana	C2
Timotes 3,229	C3
Tinaco 7,263	D3
Tinaquillo 12,015	D3
Tocuyo de la Costa 4,023	D2

Tovar 12,814	C3
Trujillo 25,921	C3
Tucacas 4,780	D2
Tucupido 9,522	F3
Tucupita 21,417	H3
Tumeremo 5,036	H4
Turén	D3
Turiamo	E2
Turmero 43,832	E2
Upata 22,793	G3
Urachiche 4,759	D2
Urica 1,881	F3
Uriman	G5
Uruyén	G5

Uverito 468	F3
Valencia 367,171	E2
Valera 76,740	C3
Valle de Guanape 3,468	F3
Valle de la Pascua 36,809	F3
Villa Bruzual 14,003	D3
Villa de Cura 27,832	E2
Yaguaraparo 3,931	G2
Yaritagua 21,363	D2
Yavita	E6
Yerichaña	E6
Yoco 2,196	G2
Zanja de Lira	E3
Zaraza 15,480	F3

AREA 352,143 sq. mi. (912,050 sq. km.)
POPULATION 19,246,000
CAPITAL Caracas
LARGEST CITY Caracas
HIGHEST POINT Pico Bolívar 16,427 ft. (5,007 m.)
MONETARY UNIT Bolívar
MAJOR LANGUAGE Spanish
MAJOR RELIGION Roman Catholicism

Topography

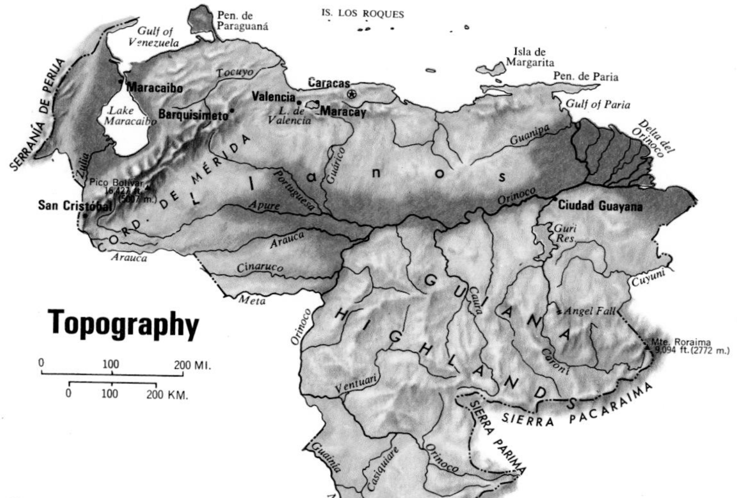

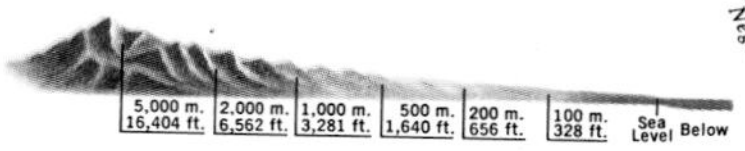

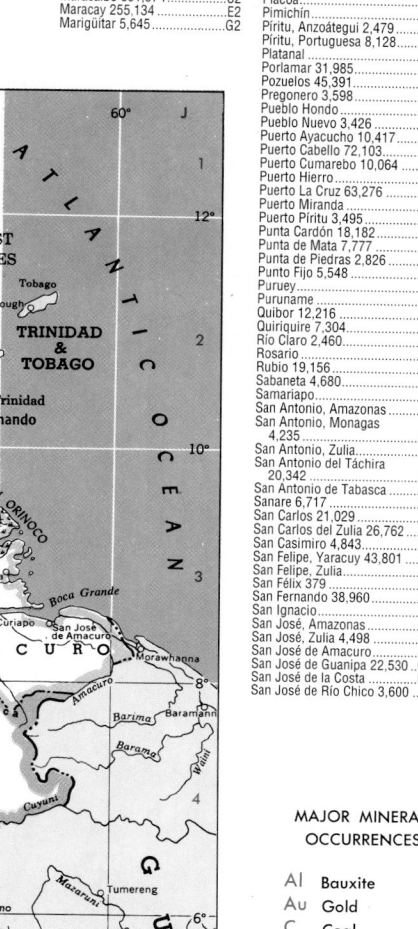

0   100   200 MI.
0   100   200 KM.

5,000 m. 2,000 m. 1,000 m. 500 m. 200 m. 100 m. Sea Below
16,404 ft. 6,562 ft. 3,281 ft. 1,640 ft. 656 ft. 328 ft. Level

OTHER FEATURES

Amacuro (riv.)	H4
Angel (fall)	G5
Aponguao (riv.)	H5
Apure (riv.)	E4
Arauca (riv.)	D4
Arichuna (riv.)	F4
Aro (riv.)	F4
Atabapo (riv.)	E6
Auyantepuí (mt.)	G5
Baria (riv.)	E7
Boca Grande (gulf)	H3
Bolívar, Pico (peak)	C3
Canagua (riv.)	C3
Caño Capure (riv.)	H3
Caño Macareo (riv.)	H3
Caño Mánamo (riv.)	H3
Capanaparo (riv.)	E4
Caparo (riv.)	C4
Carrao (riv.)	G5
Caruai (riv.)	H5
Casiquiare, Brazo (riv.)	E6
Catatumbo (riv.)	B3
Caura (riv.)	F5
Chicanán (riv.)	H4
Chimantá-tepuí (mt.)	G5
Chivapure (riv.)	E4
Cinaruco (riv.)	D4
Coche (isl.)	F2
Codera (cape)	F2
Cojedes (riv.)	D3
Cuao (riv.)	E5
Cubagua (isl.)	F2
Cuchivero (riv.)	F4
Cuquenán (riv.)	H5
Curutú (riv.)	G5
Cuyuni (riv.)	H4
Delgado Chalbaud, Cerro (mt.)	G6
Dragons Mouth (str.)	H2
Duida, Cerro (mt.)	F6
Erebato (riv.)	F5
Guainía (riv.)	E6
Guampí, Sierra de (mts.)	F4
Guanare (riv.)	D3
Guanare Viejo (riv.)	D3
Guárico (res.)	E3
Guárico (riv.)	E3
Guayapo, Serranía (mts.)	E5
Güere (riv.)	F3
Guri (res.)	G4
Imataca, Serranía (mts.)	H4
Imeri, Sierra (mts.)	F7
La Blanquilla (isl.)	F2
La Cerbatana, Serranía de (mts.)	D3
La Gran Sabana (plain)	G5
La Orchila (isl.)	F2

Las Aves (isls.)	E2
La Tortuga (isl.)	F2
Los Hermanos (isls.)	F2
Los Monjes (isls.)	C1
Los Roques (isls.)	E2
Los Testigos (isls.)	G2
Macanao (pen.)	F2
Maigualida, Sierra (range)	F4
Manapire (riv.)	E3
Maracaibo (lake)	C3
Margarita (isl.)	F2
Mavaca (riv.)	F6
Médanos (isth.)	D2
Merevari (riv.)	F5
Mérida, Cordillera de (range)	C3
Meta (riv.)	E4
Morichal Largo (riv.)	G3
Negro (riv.)	E7
Nuria, Sierra de (mts.)	H4
Orinoco (delta)	H3
Orinoco (riv.)	G3
Orituco (riv.)	E3
Pacaraima, Sierra (mts.)	G5
Pao (riv.)	D3
Paragua (riv.)	G4
Paria (gulf)	H2
Paria (pen.)	G2
Parima, Sierra (mts.)	F6
Perijá, Sierra de (mts.)	B2
Phelps (peak)	E7
Portuguesa (riv.)	D3
Raul Leoni (dam)	G4
Roraima (mt.)	H5
Salto Angel (fall)	G5
Sarare (riv.)	C4
Serpents Mouth (passage)	H3
Siapa (riv.)	E7
Suapure (riv.)	E4
Suripá (riv.)	C4
Tapirapecó, Sierra (mts.)	F7
Tigre (riv.)	G3
Tocuco (riv.)	B3
Tocuyo (riv.)	D2
Tramán-tepuí (mt.)	G5
Triste (gulf)	D2
Turagua, Serranía (mts.)	F4
Tuy (riv.)	E2
Unare (riv.)	F3
Valencia (lake)	E2
Venamo (riv.)	H4
Venamo, Cerro (mt.)	H4
Venezuela (gulf)	C2
Ventuari (riv.)	E5
Votomo (riv.)	F6
Yatua (riv.)	E7
Yuruari (riv.)	H4
Zuata (riv.)	F3
Zulia (riv.)	B3

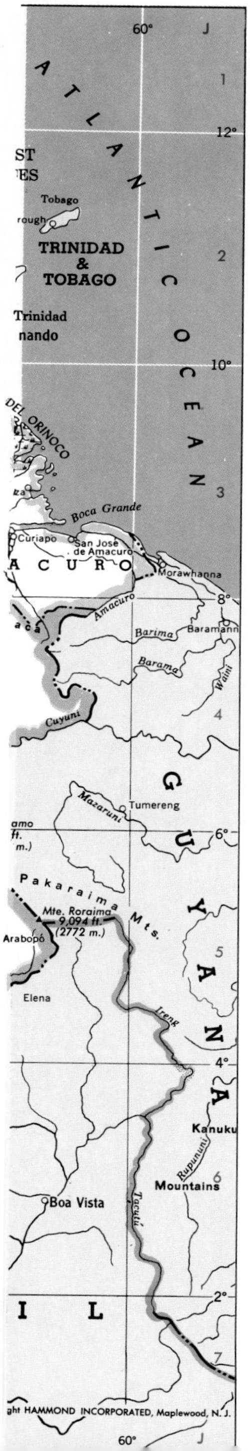

Agriculture, Industry and Resources

MAJOR MINERAL OCCURRENCES

- Al Bauxite
- Au Gold
- C Coal
- D Diamonds
- Fe Iron Ore
- G Natural Gas
- Mn Manganese
- Na Salt
- O Petroleum

⚡ Water Power
〰 Major Industrial Areas

DOMINANT LAND USE

- Diversified Tropical Crops (chiefly plantation agriculture)
- Upland Cultivated Areas
- Upland Livestock Grazing, Limited Agriculture
- Extensive Livestock Ranching
- Forests

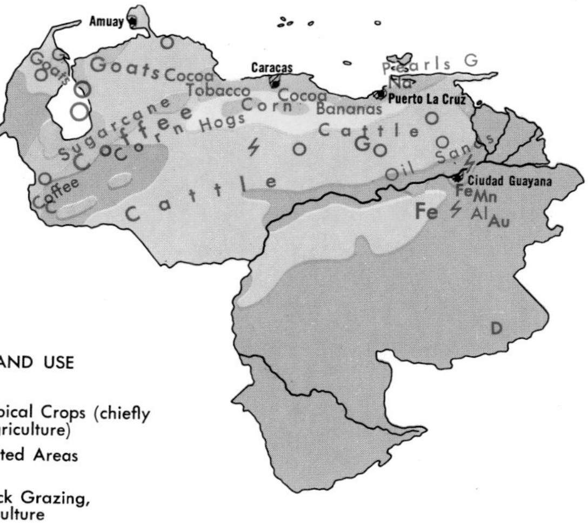

Colombia

MERCATOR PROJECTION

SCALE OF MILES

0 25 50 75 100 125 150

SCALE OF KILOMETERS

0 25 50 75 100 125 150

Capitals of Countries _____ ☆
Other Capitals _____ ◉
International Boundaries _____
Other Boundaries _____
Canals _____

INTENDENCIA DE
SAN ANDRÉS Y PROVIDENCIA
Same scale as main map

© Copyright HAMMOND INCORPORATED, Maplewood, N. J.

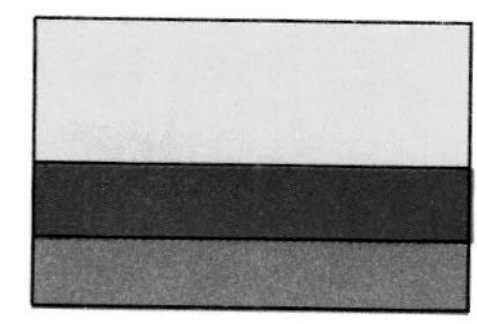

AREA 439,513 sq. mi. (1,138,339 sq. km.)
POPULATION 30,241,000
CAPITAL Bogotá
LARGEST CITY Bogotá
HIGHEST POINT Pico Cristóbal Colón 19,029 ft. (5,800 m.)
MONETARY UNIT Colombian peso
MAJOR LANGUAGE Spanish
MAJOR RELIGION Roman Catholicism

INTERNAL DIVISIONS

Amazonas (comm.) 6,825 D8
Antioquia (dept.) 3,888,067 B4
Arauca (inten.) 19,884 E4
Atlántico (dept.) 958,560 C2
Bolívar (dept.) 802,407 C3
Boyacá (dept.) 1,084,766 D5
Caldas (dept.) 700,954 C5
Caquetá (inten.) 57,103 C7
Casanare (inten.) E5
Cauca (dept.) 603,894 B6
Cesar (dept.) 339,843 D3
Chocó (dept.) 201,915 B4
Córdoba (dept.) 645,478 C3
Cundinamarca (dept.) 1,106,626 C5
Distrito Especial 2,855,065 C5
Guainía (comm.) 1,792 F6
Huila (dept.) 469,834 C6
La Guajira (dept.) 180,520 D2
Magdalena (dept.) 536,122 C3
Meta (dept.) 245,176 D6
Nariño (dept.) 807,112 B7
Norte de Santander (dept.) 693,298 D3
Putumayo (inten.) 22,916 C7
Quindío (dept.) 321,677 C5
Risaralda (dept.) 452,626 B5
San Andrés y Providencia (inten.) 22,719 B1
Santander (dept.) 1,130,977 D4
Sucre (dept.) 354,412 C3
Tolima (dept.) 903,520 C5
Valle del Cauca (dept.) 2,204,722 B6
Vaupés (comm.) 6,923 E7
Vichada (comm.) 2,172 F5

CITIES and TOWNS

Acacías 9,238 D6
Acandí 2,358 B3
Agrado 2,771 C6
Aguachica 16,771 D3
Aguadas 9,995 C5
Agua de Dios 9,689 C5
Agustín Codazzi 28,194 D3
Aipe 3,794 C6
Algeciras 5,022 C6
Amalfi 6,494 C4
Andes 14,957 C5
Anserma 15,559 B5
Antioquia 6,841 B4
Aracataca 7,511 D2
Arauca 7,613 E4
Arjona 29,465 C2
Armenia 180,221 B5
Armero 19,567 C5
Ayapel 7,475 C3
Baranoa 27,394 C2
Baraya 2,581 C6
Barbacoas 4,653 A7
Barbosa 7,960 D5
Barichara 2,548 D4
Barrancabermeja 137,406 C4
Barrancas 2,979 D2
Barranco de Loba 2,215 C3
Barranquilla 896,649 C2
Belén de los Andaquíes 2,190 C7
Bello 206,297 C4
Bogotá (cap.) 3,974,813 D5
Bolívar 13,259 C5
Bucaramanga 341,513 D4
Buenaventura 160,342 B6
Buesaco 2,763 B7
Buga 82,992 B6
Cáceres 7,154 C4
Caicedonia 21,959 C5
Calamar 5,867 C2
Calarcá 29,349 C5
Cali 1,323,944 B6
Campo de la Cruz 13,137 C2
Campoalegre 11,799 C6
Cañasgordas 3,900 B4
Cartagena 491,368 C2
Cartago 92,524 B5
Caucasia 24,138 C4
Cereté 25,890 C3
Cerro de San Antonio 3,394 C2
Chaparral 14,546 C6
Chimichaqua 6,382 D3
Chinácota 4,478 D4
Chinchiná 33,441 C5
Chinú 10,023 C3
Chiquinquirá 21,727 C5
Chiriguaná 6,611 D3
Ciénaga 56,860 C2
Ciénaga de Oro 10,607 C3
Cisneros 7,226 C4
Colombia 2,903 C6
Condoto 4,798 B5
Contratación 3,057 D4
Convención 7,545 D3
Corinto 6,933 B6
Corozal 29,471 C3
Cúcuta 357,026 D4
Cumbal 2,891 B7
Dabeiba 7,600 B4
Dagua 5,392 B6
Duitama 56,390 D5
El Banco 20,756 D3
El Carmen 2,362 D3
El Carmen de Bolívar 30,778 C3
El Cerrito 23,575 B6
El Cocuy 2,740 D4
El Tambo 2,179 B6
Envigado 85,539 C4
Espinal 37,563 C5
Facatativá 44,331 C5
Florencia 66,430 C7
Fonseca 9,988 D2
Fontibón C5
Fresno 8,141 C5
Fundación 29,002 C2
Fusagasugá 41,033 C5
Gamarra 5,071 D3
Garzón 13,783 C6
Gigante 4,880 C6
Girardot 66,385 C5
Gramalote 2,880 D4
Guamal, Meta 2,854 D6
Guamal, Magdalena 4,986 C3
Guapí 5,005 B6
Guateque 6,032 D5
Honda 25,040 C5
Ibagué 269,495 C5
Ipiales 45,419 B7
Istmina 5,575 B5
Itagüí 135,797 C4
Ituango 5,561 C4
La Cruz 4,353 B7
La Dorada 48,572 C5
La Gloria 2,632 D3
La Palma 5,430 C5
La Plata 8,047 C6
La Unión 5,392 B7
Líbano 23,703 C5
Lorica 24,264 C3
Magangué 49,160 C3
Maicao 46,033 D2
Majagual 2,329 C3
Málaga 10,645 D4
Manizales 275,067 C5
Medellín 1,418,554 C4
Mercaderes 3,877 B7
Miraflores 3,584 D5
Miranda 6,439 B6
Mitú 1,637 E7
Mocoa 6,221 B7
Mompós 14,076 C3
Moniquirá 5,711 D5
Montería 157,466 B3
Natagaima 7,772 C6
Neiva 178,130 C6
Ocaña 51,443 D3
Ortega 5,150 C6
Pacho 6,786 C5
Páez 2,098 C6
Paipa 4,260 D5
Palmira 175,186 B6
Pamplona 34,213 D4
Pasto 197,407 B7
Patía 5,306 B6
Paz de Ariporo 2,584 E5
Paz de Río 3,464 D4
Pereira 233,271 C5
Piedecuesta 34,646 D4
Piendamó 5,046 B6
Pitalito 27,104 B7
Pivijay 10,172 C2
Planeta Rica 24,238 C3
Plato 24,895 C3
Popayán 141,964 B6
Pradera 27,152 B6
Puente Nacional 4,317 D5
Puerto Asís 6,364 B7
Puerto Berrío 21,414 C4
Puerto Carreño 2,172 G4
Puerto Colombia 9,255 C2
Puerto Escondido 1,368 B3
Puerto Inírida 1,792 F6
Puerto Leguízamo 3,179 C8
Puerto López 4,948 D5
Puerto Rico 4,853 C7
Puerto Rondón 1,010 E4
Puerto Salgar 6,396 C5
Puerto Tejada 26,573 B6
Puerto Wilches 5,282 D4
Pupiales 2,723 B7
Purificación 8,164 C6
Quibdó 47,950 B5
Remedios 4,681 C4
Remolino 3,408 C2
Restrepo 2,704 D5
Río de Oro 2,985 D3
Riohacha 46,667 D2
Rionegro, Antioquia 22,654 C4
Rionegro, Santander 3,491 D4
Riosucio, Caldas 11,619 C5
Riosucio, Chocó 2,184 B4
Robles 5,422 D2
Rovira 5,105 C5
Sabanalarga 35,786 C2
Sahagún 28,686 C3
Salamina 12,136 C5
Salazar 2,791 D4
Samaniego 4,790 B7
San Agustín 4,532 B7
San Andrés, Antioquia 2,003 C4
San Andrés, San Andrés y Providencia 23,325 A9
San Antero 7,129 C3
Sandoná 7,222 B7
San Gil 24,599 D4
San Jacinto 13,459 C3
San José del Guaviare 4,138 D6
San Juan del César 9,468 D2
San Marcos 26,542 C3
San Martín 8,281 D6
San Onofre 7,899 C3
San Pablo 3,662 B7
San Roque 4,972 C4
San Vicente del Caguán 3,182 C6
Santa Bárbara 11,848 C5
Santa Marta 177,922 D2
Santa Rosa de Cabal 37,112 C5
Santa Rosa de Osos 8,593 C4
Santander 22,644 B6
Sardinata 3,726 D3
Segovia 10,000 C4
Sevilla 31,309 C5
Sibundoy-Las Casas 2,853 B7
Silvia 3,045 B6
Simití 3,062 C4
Sincé 11,909 C3
Sincelejo 120,537 C3
Sitionuevo 5,919 C2
Soatá 4,294 D4
Socorro 15,596 D4
Sogamoso 64,437 D5
Soledad 164,494 C2
Sonsón 15,990 C5
Sopetrán 5,223 C4
Tadó 3,102 B5
Tame 4,811 E4
Tibaná 1,100 D5
Tierralta 7,950 C3
Timaná 4,262 C7
Timbío 4,755 B6
Timbiquí 1,048 B6
Toledo 2,942 D4
Tolú 9,118 C3
Trinidad 729 E5
Tuluá 99,721 B5
Tumaco 45,456 A7
Tunjá 87,851 D5
Túquerres 12,058 B7
Turbaco 28,161 C2
Turbo 25,992 B3
Ubaté 7,716 D5
Uribia 2,193 D2
Urrao 8,577 B4
Valdivia 4,318 C4
Valledupar 142,771 D2
Vélez 8,241 D4
Venadillo 8,383 C5
Villa Rosario 8,668 D4
Villanueva 9,836 D2
Villavicencio 82,869 D5
Villeta 6,507 C5
Yarumal 21,333 C4
Yopal 5,851 D5
Yumbo 43,508 B6
Zapatoca 6,258 D4
Zaragoza 9,660 C4
Zarzal 22,014 B5
Zipaquirá 45,676 D5

OTHER FEATURES

Aguarico (riv.) B7
Aguja, La (cape) C2
Alto Ritacuva (mt.) D4
Amazon (riv.) E9
Ancón de Sardinas (bay) A7
Angostura (falls) E6
Apaporis (riv.) F8
Arauca (riv.) E4
Ariari (riv.) D6
Ariguaní (riv.) D3
Ariporo (riv.) E4
Atabapo (riv.) G6
Atrato (riv.) B4
Baudó, Serranía de (mts.) B5
Caguán (riv.) C7
Cahuinari (riv.) E8
Caquetá (riv.) E8
Caraparaná (riv.) D8
Casanare (riv.) E4
Catatumbo (riv.) D3
Cauca (riv.) B3
Cazueleja, Cerro (mt.) C6
César (riv.) D2
Central, Cordillera (range) C5
Charambirá (pt.) B5
Chicamocha (riv.) D4
Chocó (bay) B6
Corrientes (cape) B5
Cristóbal Colón, Pico (peak) D2
Cuemaní (riv.) D7
Cupica (gulf) B4
Cusachón (isl.) D1
Espada (pt.) E1
Gallinas (pt.) E1
Grande (isl.) B4
Grande, Salto (falls) D8
Guainía (riv.) F6
Guajira (pen.) E1
Guaviare (riv.) F6
Guayabero (riv.) D6
Huila, Nevado del (mt.) C6
Igara-Paraná (riv.) D8
Inírida (riv.) F6
Isana (riv.) F7
La Aguja (cape) C2
La Macarena, Serranía de (mts.) D6
Llanos (plain) D5
Macarena, Serranía de La (mts.) D6
Magdalena (riv.) C3
Manacacías (riv.) D6
Meta (riv.) E5
Metica (riv.) D6
Mira (riv.) A7
Miritiparaná (riv.) E8
Morrosquillo (gulf) C3
Nechí (riv.) C4
Negro (riv.) G7
Occidental, Cordillera (range) B5
Oriental, Cordillera (range) D5
Orinoco (riv.) G5
Orteguaza (riv.) C7
Papurí (riv.) F7
Patía (riv.) B6
Pauto (riv.) E5
Perijá, Serranía de (mts.) D2
Providencia (isl.) B9
Puracé (vol.) B6
Putumayo (riv.) E9
Quitasueño (bank) A8
Roncador (cays) B9
Saldaña (riv.) C6
Salto Grande (falls) D8
San Andrés (isl.) A10
San Jorge (riv.) C3
San Juan (riv.) B5
Santa Marta, Sierra Nevada de (range) D2
Serrana (bank) B9
Serranilla (bank) B8
Sinú (riv.) B3
Sogamoso (riv.) D4
Suárez (riv.) D4
Taraíra (riv.) F8
Tequendama (falls) C5
Tibugá (gulf) B5
Tolima (vol.) C5
Tomo (riv.) F5
Tortugas (gulf) B6
Tunahí, Sierra (mts.) E7
Urabá (gulf) B3
Uva (riv.) E6
Vaupés (riv.) E7
Vela, La (cape) D1
Vichada (riv.) F5
Yarí (riv.) D8
Zapatosa, Ciénaga de (swamp) D3

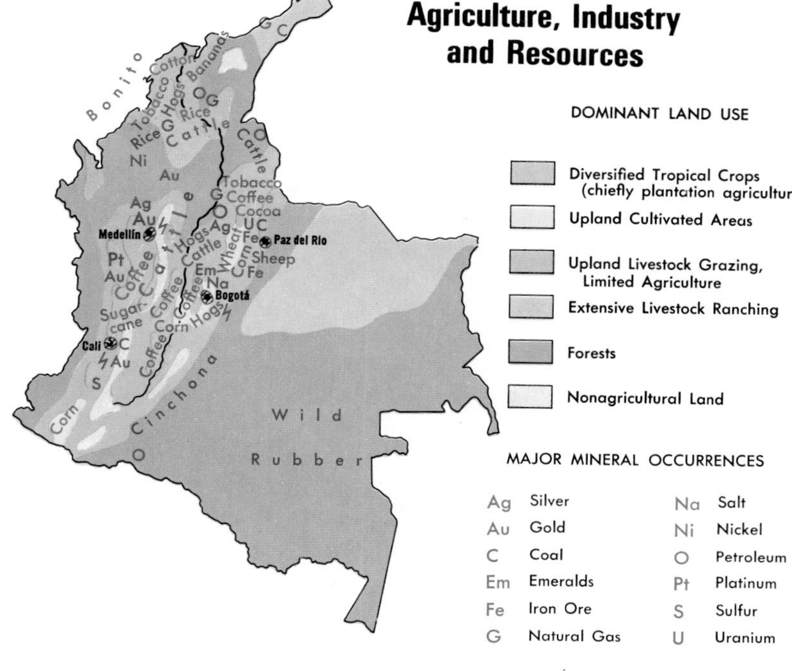
Agriculture, Industry and Resources
DOMINANT LAND USE
Diversified Tropical Crops (chiefly plantation agriculture)
Upland Cultivated Areas
Upland Livestock Grazing, Limited Agriculture
Extensive Livestock Ranching
Forests
Nonagricultural Land
MAJOR MINERAL OCCURRENCES
Ag Silver
Au Gold
C Coal
Em Emeralds
Fe Iron Ore
G Natural Gas
Na Salt
Ni Nickel
O Petroleum
Pt Platinum
S Sulfur
U Uranium
Medellín
Bogotá
Cali
Paz del Rio
Wild Rubber
Cinchona

Water Power

Major Industrial Areas

Topography

0 100 200 MI.
0 100 200 KM.

5,000 m. 16,404 ft. | 2,000 m. 6,562 ft. | 1,000 m. 3,281 ft. | 500 m. 1,640 ft. | 200 m. 656 ft. | 100 m. 328 ft. | Sea Level | Below

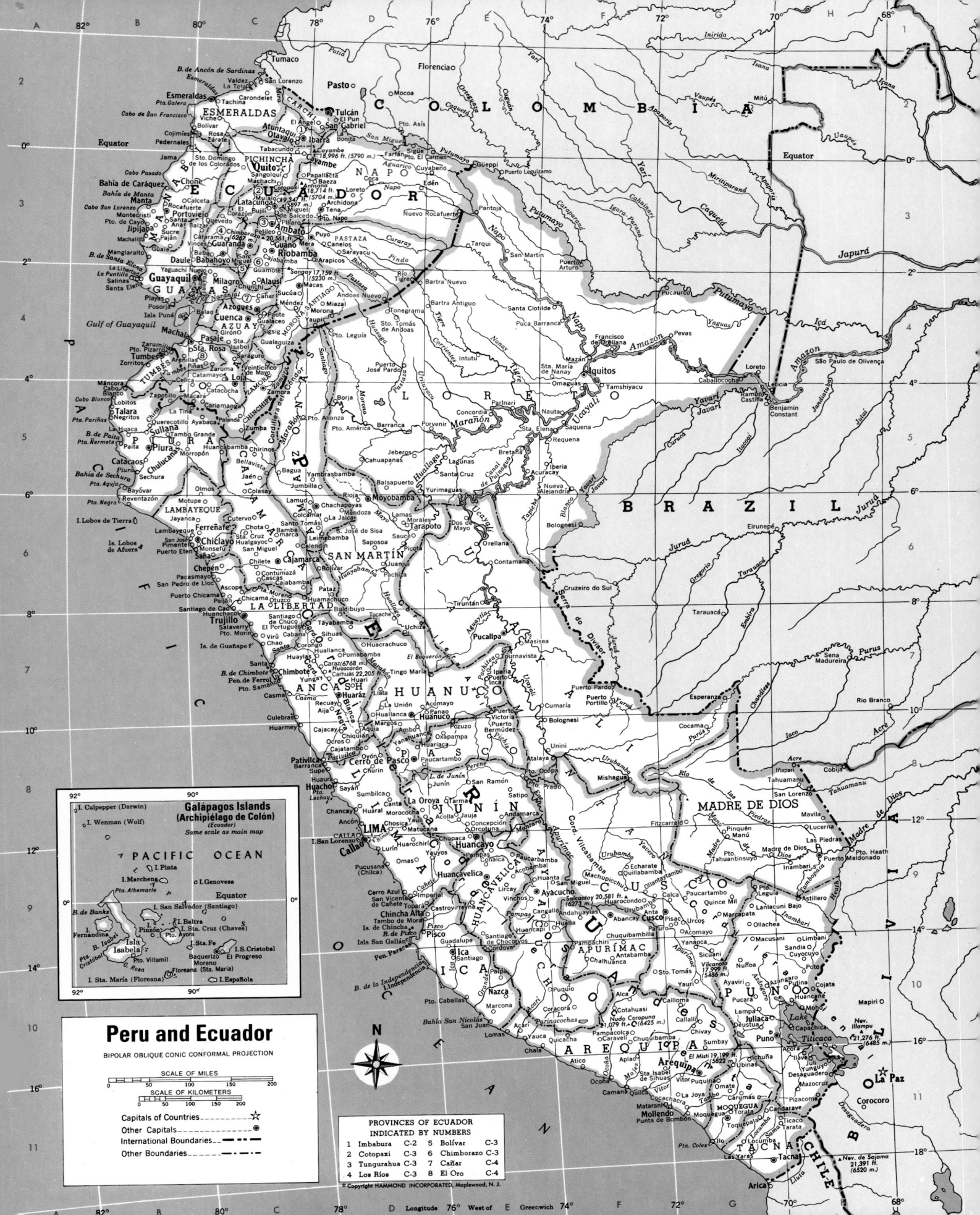
Peru and Ecuador
BIPOLAR OBLIQUE CONIC CONFORMAL PROJECTION
SCALE OF MILES
0 50 100 150 200
SCALE OF KILOMETERS
0 50 100 150 200
Capitals of Countries
Other Capitals
International Boundaries
Other Boundaries
Galápagos Islands (Archipiélago de Colón)
(Ecuador)
Same scale as main map
PACIFIC OCEAN
PROVINCES OF ECUADOR INDICATED BY NUMBERS
1 Imbabura C-2
2 Cotopaxi C-3
3 Tungurahua C-3
4 Los Ríos C-3
5 Bolívar C-3
6 Chimborazo C-3
7 Cañar C-4
8 El Oro C-4
© Copyright HAMMOND INCORPORATED, Maplewood, N. J.
Longitude 76° West of Greenwich
COLOMBIA
ECUADOR
PERU
BRAZIL
BOLIVIA
CHILE
PACIFIC OCEAN
Equator
Quito
Guayaquil
Cuenca
LIMA
Callao
Arequipa
Cusco
Iquitos
Trujillo
Chiclayo
Piura
Huancayo
Puno
Lake Titicaca
La Paz
Tacna
Arica
Amazon
Marañón
Ucayali
Putumayo
Napo
LORETO
SAN MARTÍN
AMAZONAS
CAJAMARCA
LA LIBERTAD
ANCASH
HUÁNUCO
PASCO
JUNÍN
LIMA
ICA
HUANCAVELICA
AYACUCHO
APURÍMAC
CUSCO
MADRE DE DIOS
PUNO
AREQUIPA
MOQUEGUA
TACNA
PIURA
TUMBES
LAMBAYEQUE
UCAYALI

PERU

ECUADOR

PERU
AREA 496,222 sq. mi.
(1,285,215 sq. km.)
POPULATION 22,332,000
CAPITAL Lima
LARGEST CITY Lima
HIGHEST POINT Huascarán 22,205 ft.
(6,768 m.)
MONETARY UNIT inti
MAJOR LANGUAGES Spanish, Quechua,
Aymara
MAJOR RELIGION Roman Catholicism

ECUADOR
AREA 109,483 sq. mi. (283,561 sq. km.)
POPULATION 10,490,000
CAPITAL Quito
LARGEST CITY Guayaquil
HIGHEST POINT Chimborazo 20,561 ft.
(6,267 m.)
MONETARY UNIT sucre
MAJOR LANGUAGES Spanish, Quechua
MAJOR RELIGION Roman Catholicism

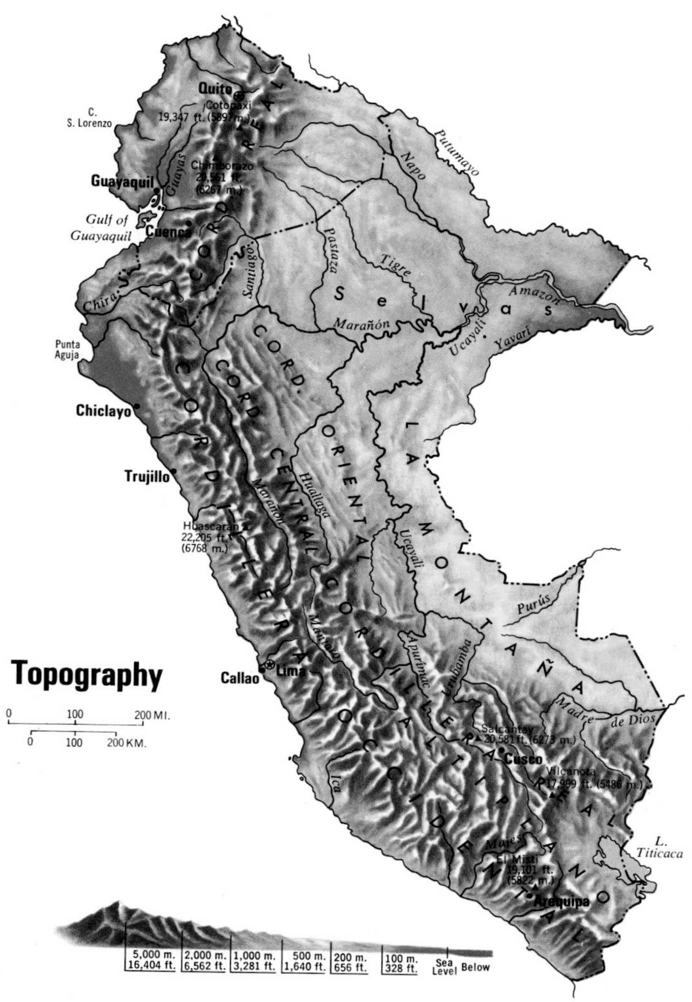

PERU

DEPARTMENTS

Amazonas 256,460	C5
Ancash 815,646	D7
Apurímac 321,936	F10
Arequipa 702,308	F10
Ayacucho 500,732	E9
Cajamarca 1,044,689	C6
Callao (prov.) 446,730	D9
Cusco 829,294	F9
Huánuco 481,924	D7
Huancavelica 346,460	E9
Ica 431,442	E10
Junín 848,993	E8
La Libertad 960,537	C6
Lambayeque 683,425	B6
Lima 4,738,266	D8
Loreto 446,316	E5
Madre de Dios 36,555	G8
Moquegua 99,287	G11
Pasco 221,219	E8
Piura 1,168,442	B5
Puno 893,586	G10
San Martín 319,670	D6
Tacna 133,240	G11
Tumbes 103,979	B4
Ucayali 200,085	E6

CITIES and TOWNS

Abancay 19,807	F9
Acarí 4,907	E10
Acobamba 2,156	E9
Acolla 5,717	E8
Acomayo, Cusco 1,419	G9
Acomayo, Huánuco 2,883	E7
Acora 1,910	H11
Acuracay 1,282	F5
Aija 1,843	D7
Alca 755	F10
Ambo 3,060	D8
Ananea 668	H10
Ancón 8,610	D8
Andahuaylas 7,654	F9
Anta 3,703	F9
Antabamba 2,223	F10
Aplao 1,941	F11
Aquia 970	D8
Arequipa 107,858	G11
Arequipa* 447,431	G11
Ascope 12,070	C6
Atalaya 2,132	E8
Atico 2,316	F11
Ayabaca 4,543	C5
Ayacucho 68,535	F9
Ayaviri 11,067	G10
Azángaro 7,658	H10
Bagua 9,735	C5
Bambamarca 6,867	C6
Barranca, Lima 21,312	C8
Barranca, Loreto 1,351	D5
Bellavista 4,906	C5
Bolívar 1,106	D6
Bretaña 1,035	E5
Buldibuyo 582	D7
Cabana 1,804	C7
Cailloma 1,187	G10
Cajabamba 7,282	C6
Cajamarca 60,280	C6
Cajatambo 1,721	D8
Calca 6,112	G9
Callalli 819	G10
Callao 260,581	D9
Callao* 441,374	D9
Camaná 11,386	F11
Candarave 1,207	G11
Cangallo 1,584	E9
Canta 3,431	D8
Capachica 307	H10
Caraveli 1,827	F10
Caraz 6,376	D7
Carhuás 3,147	D7
Carumás 1,031	G11
Cascas 2,638	C6
Casma 12,725	C7
Castrovirreyna 1,749	E9
Catacaos 30,927	B5
Celendín 8,538	D6
Cerro Azul 2,314	D9
Cerro de Pasco 71,558	D8
Chachapoyas 11,919	D6
Chala 1,646	F10
Chalhuanca 3,071	F10
Chancay 18,993	D8
Chepén 8,279	C6
Chicama 11,160	C6
Chiclayo 280,244	C6
Chilca (Pucusana) 3,329	D9
Chilete 2,537	C6
Chimbote 216,406	C7
Chincha Alta 37,475	D9
Chiquián 3,521	D8
Chirinos 1,061	C5
Chivay 3,296	G10
Chota 8,299	C6
Chulucanas 34,977	B5
Chupaca 5,422	E9
Chuquibamba 2,630	F10
Chuquibambilla 2,147	F9
Churín 1,801	D8
Cocachacra 5,985	G11
Cojata 888	H10
Colasay 721	C5
Colcamar 1,216	D6
Conaica 1,154	E9
Concepción 7,129	E8
Concordia 1,372	C6
Contamana 5,718	E6
Contumazá 2,491	C6
Coracora 4,598	F10
Córdova 453	E10
Corongo 1,762	D7
Cotahuasi 1,301	F10
Cusco (Cuzco) 85,044	F9
Cusco* 171,604	F9
Cutervo 6,890	C6
Cuyocuyo 1,101	H10
Desaguadero 2,682	H11
Deustua 544	G10
Dos de Mayo 574	E6
Echarate 1,071	F9
El Portugués	C7
Esperanza 375	G7
Espinar 6,381	G10
Ferreñafe 22,200	C6
Fitzcarrald	G8
Francisco de Orellana 445	F4
Guadalupe 7,613	C6
Huacho 43,402	D8
Huacrachuco 1,210	D7
Hualgayoc 1,691	C6
Hualla 4,042	F9
Huallanca, Ancash 930	D7
Huallanca, Huánuco 4,806	D7
Huamachuco 8,273	D6
Huancabamba 4,393	C5
Huancané 5,227	H10
Huancapi 2,539	E9
Huancavelica 20,889	E9
Huancayo 165,132	E9
Huanchaco 6,005	C7
Huanta 11,213	E9
Huánuco 52,628	E7
Huaral 34,235	D8
Huaráz 45,116	D7
Huari 2,344	D7
Huariaca 2,671	E8
Huarmey 11,094	C8
Huarochiri 1,828	D9
Huarocondo 2,498	F9
Huaura 9,338	D8
Huaylas 1,344	C7
Iberia 2,307	H9
Ica 111,087	F5
Ichuña 277	G11
Ilave 9,891	H11
Ilo 31,549	G11
Imperial 20,894	D9
Inambari	H9
Iñapari 188	H8
Intutu 746	E4
Iparia 278	E7
Iquitos 173,629	F4
Jaén 24,356	C5
Jauja 14,630	E8
Jayanca 6,401	B6
Jeberos 1,493	D5
Juanjuí 9,324	D6
Juli 5,575	H11
Juliaca 77,976	G10
Jumbilla 1,035	C5
Junín 8,988	E8
Lagunas 4,601	E5
La Huaca 5,161	B5
La Jalca 1,769	D6
La Joya 5,000	G11
Lamas 8,937	D6
Lambayeque 23,746	B6
Lampa 4,319	G10
Lamud 2,405	C6
Lanlacuni Bajo 405	G9
La Oroya 33,305	D8
Las Piedras	H9
Las Yaras 759	G11
La Tina	B5
La Unión 2,828	D7
Leimebamba 1,957	D6
Lima (cap.) 375,957	D8
Lima* 3,968,972	D8
Limbani 728	H10
Lircay 5,213	E9
Llata 2,922	D7
Lobitos 2,975	B5
Lurín 14,405	D9
Machupicchu 544	F9
Macusani 3,389	G10
Madre de Dios 660	G9
Manú 234	G9
Máncora 5,358	B5
Marcapata 369	G9
Marcona 25,962	E10
Margos 1,622	D8
Masisea 1,586	E7
Matarani	F11
Matucana 4,196	D8
Mazocruz 1,580	H11
Mendoza 1,902	D6
Moho 2,560	H10
Mollendo 21,206	F11
Monsefú 17,186	C6
Moquegua 21,488	G11
Morales 4,370	D6
Morococha 11,234	D8
Morropón 7,611	C5
Motupe 3,411	C6
Moyobamba 14,319	D6
Nauta 4,083	F5
Nazca 22,756	E10
Negritos 12,476	B5
Nuñoa 3,613	G10
Ocoña 1,062	F11
Ocros 1,037	D8
Ollachea 1,308	G9
Ollantaytambo 1,500	F9
Olmos 7,946	C5
Omate 1,011	G11
Orcotuna 3,359	E8
Orellana 1,511	E6
Otuzco 5,765	C6
Oxapampa 5,233	E8
Oyón 6,279	D8
Pacasmayo 17,588	C6
Pachiza 889	D6
Paiján 12,699	C6
Paita 18,749	B5
Palpa 3,393	E10
Pampacolca 2,010	F10
Pampas 3,850	E9
Panao 1,363	E7
Paruro 1,727	F9
Paucarbamba 534	E9
Paucartambo, Cusco 1,620	G9
Paucartambo, Pasco 3,497	E8
Pevas 1,347	G4
Picota 2,288	D6
Pimentel 9,129	B6
Pisac 1,566	G9
Pisco 53,414	D9
Piura 186,354	B5
Pomabamba 2,489	D7
Pucallpa 91,953	E7
Pucará 2,268	G10
Pucaurco 628	G4
Pucusana 3,329	D9
Puerto Bermúdez 1,133	E8
Puerto Chicama 3,630	C6
Puerto Eten 2,575	B6
Puerto Inca 1,286	E7
Puerto Maldonado 12,609	H9
Puerto Ocopa 1,088	E8
Puerto Samanco 1,435	C7
Puno 66,477	G10
Punta de Bombón 4,647	F11
Puquina 1,026	G11
Putina 5,414	H10
Querecotillo 10,637	B5
Quillabamba 16,837	F9
Ramón Castilla 1,811	G5
Recuay 2,764	D7
Requena 8,270	F5
Rioja 9,876	D6
Salaverry 5,539	C7
Saña 40,144	C6
Sandia 1,682	H10
San José 4,070	B6
San José de Sisa 3,782	D6
San Miguel, Ayacucho 1,440	F9
San Miguel, Cajamarca 1,798	C6
San Pedro de Lloc 11,463	C6
San Ramón 7,145	E8
Santa 20,490	C7
Santa Clotilde 1,068	E4
Santa Cruz, Cajamarca 2,739	C6
Santa Cruz, Loreto 449	E5
Santiago 5,092	E10
Santiago de Cao 22,119	C6
Santiago de Chuco 5,189	C7
Santo Tomás, Amazonas 1,093	C6
Santo Tomás, Cusco 2,755	G10
San Vicente de Cañete 15,277	D9
Saposoa 4,541	D6
Saquena 2,755	F5
Satipo 9,208	E8
Sauce 2,263	D6
Sayán 5,129	D8
Sechura 11,724	B5
Sicuani 21,176	G10
Sihuas 2,178	D7
Sullana 80,947	B5
Sumbilca 1,155	D8
Supe 10,061	D8
Tacna 92,862	G11
Tahuamanu 2,619	H8
Talara 55,722	B5
Tambo de Mora 2,790	D9
Tambo Grande 10,087	B5
Tamshiyacu 2,040	F5
Tarapoto 33,429	D6
Tarata 2,624	H11
Tarma 34,369	E8
Tayabamba 1,649	D7
Tingo María 25,030	D7
Tocache 5,940	D7
Torata 6,320	G11
Trujillo 354,557	C7
Tumbes 48,187	B4
Uchiza 2,471	D7
Urcos 4,155	G9
Urubamba 4,686	F9
Virú 6,587	C7
Yambrasbamba 277	D5
Yanahuanca 5,109	D8
Yanaoca 1,152	G10
Yauca 1,805	E10
Yauli 1,020	D8
Yauri (Espinar) 6,381	G10
Yauyos 1,296	E9
Yunguyo 7,253	H11
Yurimaguas 22,858	E5
Zarumilla 9,713	B4
Zorritos 4,497	B4

OTHER FEATURES

Acarí (riv.)	E10
Aguaytía (riv.)	E7
Aguja (pt.)	B5
Amazon (riv.)	F4
Andes, Cordillera de los (mts.)	F10
Apurímac (riv.)	F9
Azángaro (riv.)	G10
Azul, Cordillera (range)	E7
Blanca, Cordillera (range)	D7
Blanco (cape)	B5
Boquerón, El (pass)	E7
Cañete (riv.)	D9
Chimbote (bay)	C7
Chincha (isls.)	D9
Chira (riv.)	B5
Cóndor, Cordillera del (range)	C5
Coropuna, Nudo (mt.)	F10
Corrientes (riv.)	E4
Ene (riv.)	E8
Ferrol (pt.)	C7
Grande (riv.)	E10
Guañape (isls.)	C7
Heath (riv.)	H9
Huallaga (riv.)	D5
Huasaga (riv.)	D4
Huascarán (mt.)	D7
Huayabamba (riv.)	D6
Ica (riv.)	E10
Inambari (riv.)	H9
Independencia (bay)	D10
Independencia (isl.)	D10
Junín (lake)	E8
Juruá (riv.)	F7
Lobos de Afuera (isls.)	B6
Lobos de Tierra (isl.)	B6
Locumba (riv.)	G11
Madre de Dios (riv.)	G9
Majes (riv.)	F1
Mantaro (riv.)	E8
Manú (riv.)	G8
Marañón (riv.)	E5
Mayo (riv.)	D6
Misti, El (mt.)	G11
Montaña, La (reg.)	G7
Morona (riv.)	D5
Nanay (riv.)	E4
Napo (riv.)	F4
Negra, Cordillera (range)	D7
Negra (pt.)	B6
Nermete (pt.)	B4
Occidental, Cordillera (range)	F10
Ocoña (riv.)	F11
Oriental, Cordillera (range)	H10
Pachitea (riv.)	E7
Paita (bay)	B5
Pampas (riv.)	E9
Paracas (pt.)	D9
Pariñas (pt.)	B5
Parinacochas (lake)	F10
Pastaza (riv.)	D4
Pativilca (riv.)	D8
Perené (riv.)	E8
Piedras, Las (riv.)	G8
Pisco (bay)	D9
Pisco (riv.)	D9
Piura (riv.)	B5
Purús (riv.)	G7
Putumayo (riv.)	G4
Rímac (riv.)	D8
Salcantay (mt.)	F9
Sama (riv.)	G11
San Gallán (isl.)	D9
San Lorenzo (isl.)	D9
San Nicolás (bay)	E10
Santa (riv.)	C7
Santiago (riv.)	D4
Sechura (bay)	B5
Tambo (riv.)	G11
Tapiche (riv.)	E6
Tigre (riv.)	E4
Titicaca (lake)	H10
Tumbes (riv.)	B4
Ucayali (riv.)	E6
Urubamba (riv.)	F8

Topography

Scale:
0 — 100 — 200 MI.
0 — 100 — 200 KM.

| 5,000 m. 16,404 ft. | 2,000 m. 6,562 ft. | 1,000 m. 3,281 ft. | 500 m. 1,640 ft. | 200 m. 656 ft. | 100 m. 328 ft. | Sea Level | Below |

(continued on following page)

Agriculture, Industry and Resources

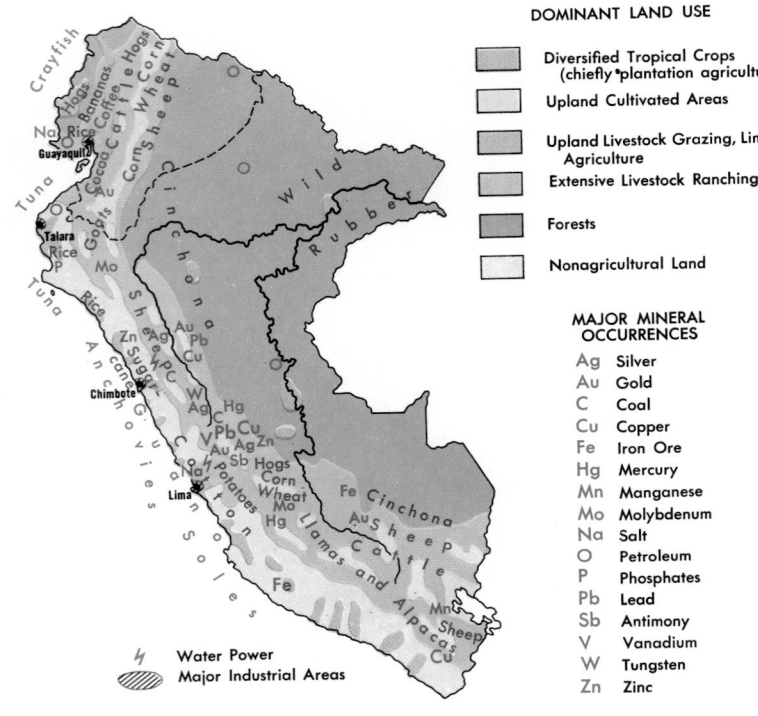

DOMINANT LAND USE

Diversified Tropical Crops
(chiefly plantation agriculture)

Upland Cultivated Areas

Upland Livestock Grazing, Limited
Agriculture

Extensive Livestock Ranching

Forests

Nonagricultural Land

MAJOR MINERAL
OCCURRENCES

Ag Silver
Au Gold
C   Coal
Cu Copper
Fe Iron Ore
Hg Mercury
Mn Manganese
Mo Molybdenum
Na Salt
O   Petroleum
P   Phosphates
Pb Lead
Sb Antimony
V   Vanadium
W   Tungsten
Zn Zinc

⚡ Water Power
▨ Major Industrial Areas

Agriculture, Industry and Resources

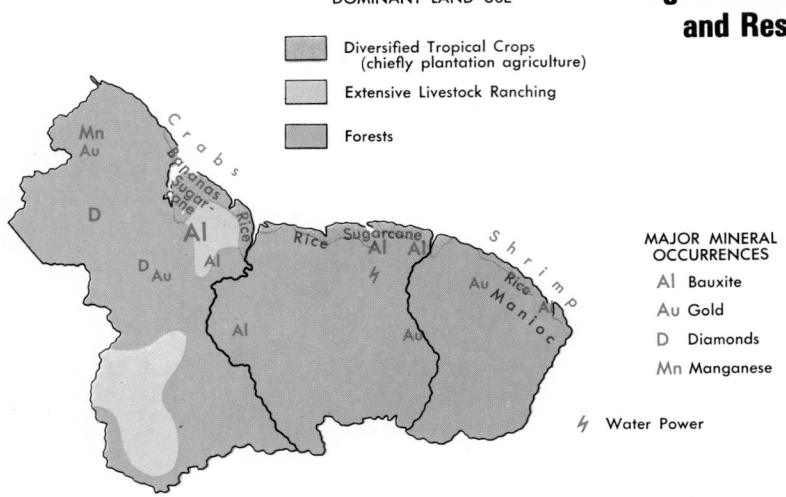

DOMINANT LAND USE

Diversified Tropical Crops
(chiefly plantation agriculture)

Extensive Livestock Ranching

Forests

MAJOR MINERAL
OCCURRENCES

Al Bauxite
Au Gold
D   Diamonds
Mn Manganese

⚡ Water Power

GUYANA
AREA 83,000 sq. mi. (214,970 sq. km.)
POPULATION 1,024,000
CAPITAL Georgetown
LARGEST CITY Georgetown
HIGHEST POINT Mt. Roraima 9,094 ft.
(2,772 m.)
MONETARY UNIT Guyana dollar
MAJOR LANGUAGES English, Hindi
MAJOR RELIGIONS Christianity, Hinduism,
Islam

SURINAME
AREA 55,144 sq. mi. (142,823 sq. km.)
POPULATION 400,000
CAPITAL Paramaribo
LARGEST CITY Paramaribo
HIGHEST POINT Julianatop 4,200 ft. (1,280 m.)
MONETARY UNIT Suriname guilder
MAJOR LANGUAGES Dutch, Hindi, Indonesian
MAJOR RELIGIONS Christianity, Islam,
Hinduism

FRENCH GUIANA
AREA 35,135 sq. mi. (91,000 sq. km.)
POPULATION 90,000
CAPITAL Cayenne
LARGEST CITY Cayenne
HIGHEST POINT 2,723 ft. (830 m.)
MONETARY UNIT French franc
MAJOR LANGUAGE French
MAJOR RELIGIONS Roman Catholicism,
Protestantism

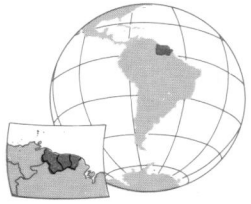

Kamaria (falls) B2	Lelydorp 300 ....D3
Kuyuwini (riv.) B4	Mariënburg 3,500 ....D2
Kwitaro (riv.) B4	Moengo 2,100 ....D3
Leguan (isl.) B2	Nieuw-Amsterdam 1,400 ....D2
Mazaruni (riv.) A2	Nieuw-Nickerie 34,480 ....C2
Moruka (riv.) B2	Paramaribo (cap.) ⊙67,905 ....D2
New (riv.) C4	Paranam D3
Pakaraima (mts.) A3	Totness 1,300 ....C3
Pomeroon (riv.) B2	Uitkijk D3
Potaro (riv.) B3	Wageningen 800 ....C3
Puruni (riv.) B2	Zanderij D3
Roraima (mt.) A3	
Rupununi (riv.) B4	**OTHER FEATURES**
Takutu (riv.) B4	
Venamo (mt.) A3	Bakhuys (mts.) C3
Waini (riv.) B2	Coeroeni (riv.) C4
Wenamu (riv.) A2	Commewijne (riv.) D3

SURINAME
DISTRICTS
Brokopondo 17,763 ....D4	Coppename (riv.) C3
Commewijne 18,740 ....D3	Corantijn (riv.) C3
Coronie 3,251 ....C3	Cottica (riv.) D3
Marowijne 25,911 ....D4	Eilerts de Haan (mts.) C4
Nickerie 35,178 ....C3	Frederik Willem IV (falls) C4
Para 16,635 ....D3	Julianatop (mt.) C4
Paramaribo 102,297 ....D2	Kutari (riv.) C4
Saramacca 13,554 ....C3	Lely (mts.) D3
Suriname 151,585 ....D3	Litani (riv.) D4
	Marowijne (riv.) D3
#### CITIES and TOWNS	Nickerie (riv.) C3
	Orange (mts.) D4
Albina 1,000 ....D3	Saramacca (riv.) D3
Brokopondo D3	Sipaliwini (riv.) C4
Calcutta 1,100 ....C3	Suriname (riv.) D3
Domburg 1,200 ....D3	Tapanahoni (riv.) D4
Groningen 600 ....D2	

*City and suburbs
⊙ Population of sub-district or
·division.
⊙ Population of district

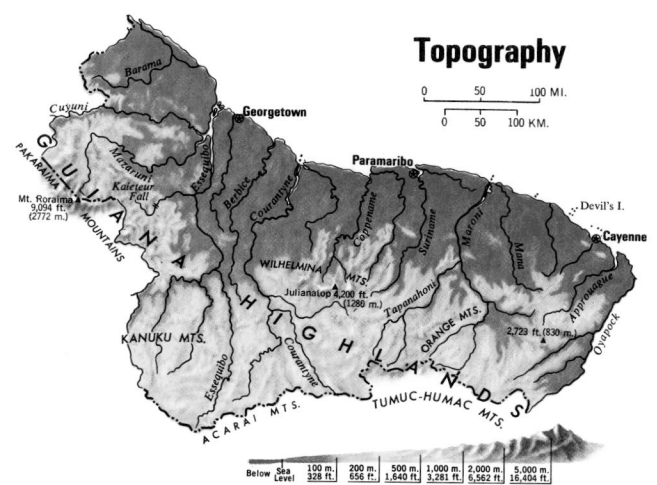
Topography

GUYANA

SURINAME

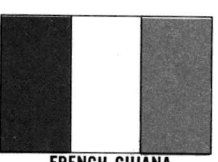
FRENCH GUIANA

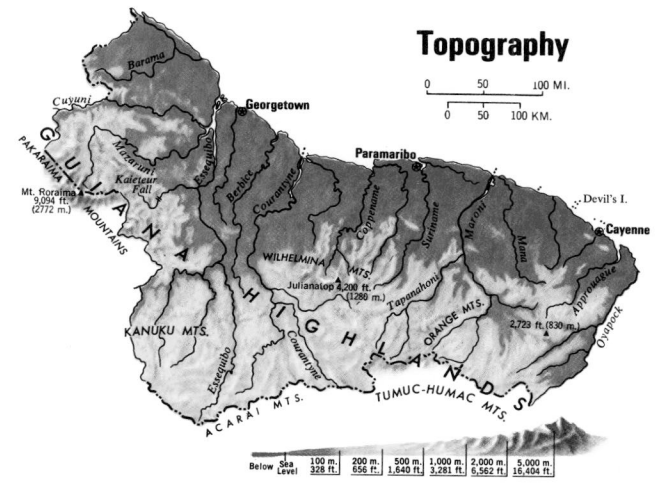

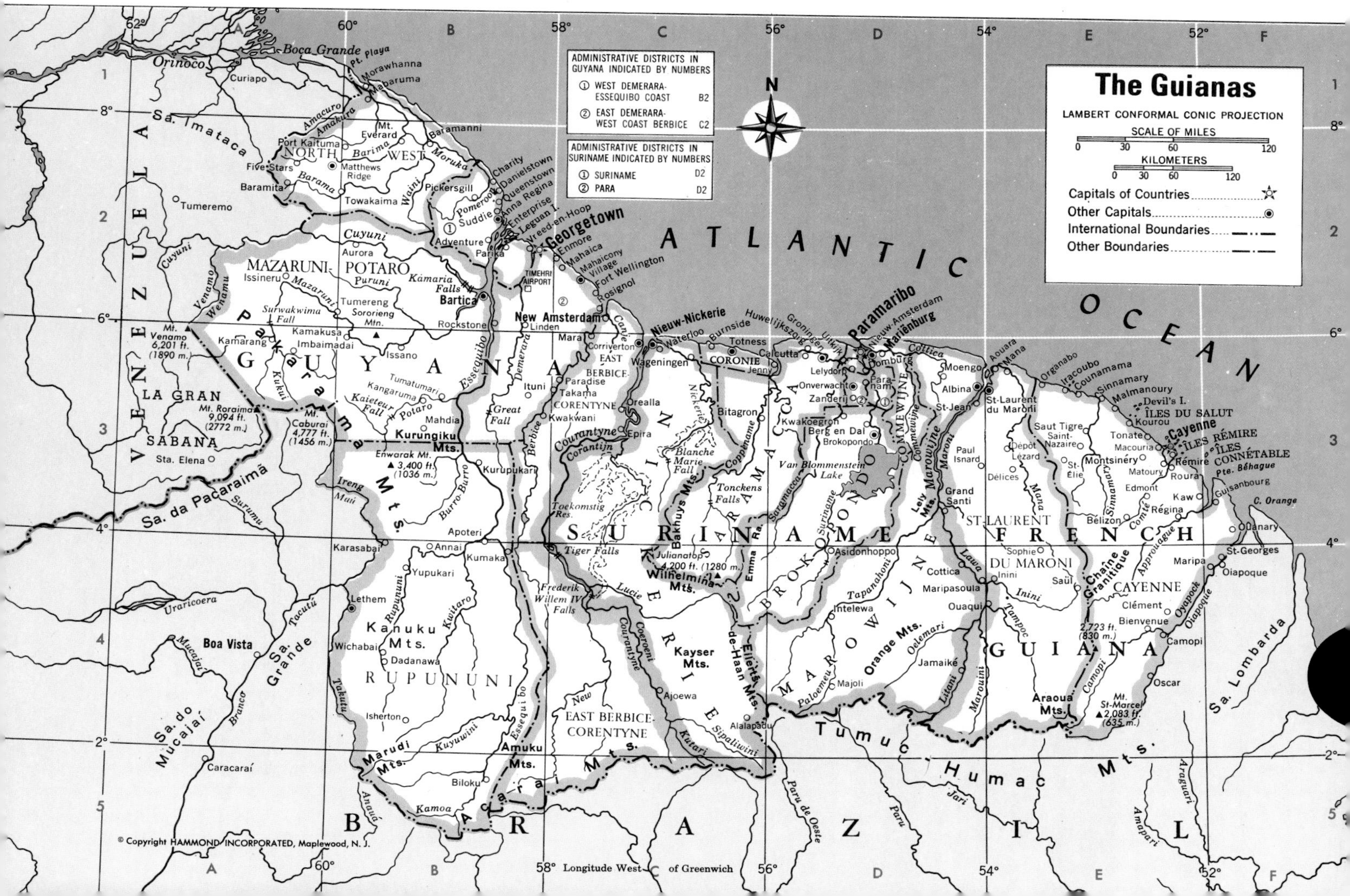

The Guianas
LAMBERT CONFORMAL CONIC PROJECTION
SCALE OF MILES
KILOMETERS

Capitals of Countries ....☆
Other Capitals ....⊙
International Boundaries ....
Other Boundaries ....

ADMINISTRATIVE DISTRICTS IN
GUYANA INDICATED BY NUMBERS
① WEST DEMERARA-
ESSEQUIBO COAST B2
② EAST DEMERARA-
WEST COAST BERBICE C2

ADMINISTRATIVE DISTRICTS IN
SURINAME INDICATED BY NUMBERS
① SURINAME D2
② PARA D2

© Copyright HAMMOND INCORPORATED, Maplewood, N.J.

Brazil

BIPOLAR OBLIQUE CONIC CONFORMAL PROJECTION

SCALE OF MILES
0 50 100 200 300

KILOMETERS
0 50 100 200 300

Capitals of Countries ⊛
State Capitals ⊙
International Boundaries
State Boundaries

Scale 1:14,700,000

© Copyright HAMMOND INCORPORATED, Maplewood, N.J.

BRAZIL
WESTERN PART

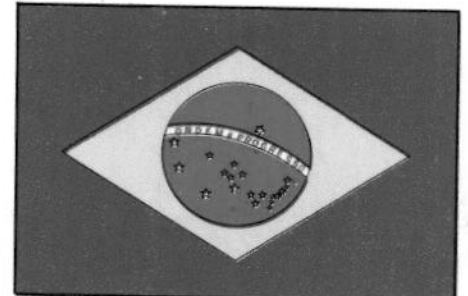

AREA 3,284,426 sq. mi. (8,506,663 sq. km.)
POPULATION 150,368,000
CAPITAL Brasília
LARGEST CITY São Paulo (greater)
HIGHEST POINT Pico da Neblina 9,889 ft. (3,014 m.)
MONETARY UNIT cruzado
MAJOR LANGUAGE Portuguese
MAJOR RELIGION Roman Catholicism

Topography

0 200 400 MI.
0 200 400 KM.

5,000 m. 16,404 ft. | 2,000 m. 6,562 ft. | 1,000 m. 3,281 ft. | 500 m. 1,640 ft. | 200 m. 656 ft. | 100 m. 328 ft. | Sea Level | Below

STATES and TERRITORIES

Acre 301,605 . . . . . G10
Alagoas 1,987,581 . . . . . G5
Amapá (terr.) 175,634 . . . . . D2
Amazonas 1,432,066 . . . . . G9
Bahia 9,474,263 . . . . . F6
Ceará 5,294,876 . . . . . G4
Espírito Santo 2,023,821 . . . F7
Federal District 1,177,393 . . . E6
Goiás 3,865,482 . . . . . D6
Maranhão 4,002,599 . . . . . E4
Mato Grosso 1,141,661 . . . . . B6
Mato Grosso do Sul 1,370,333 . . . . . C7
Minas Gerais 13,390,805 . . . E7
Pará 3,411,868 . . . . . C4
Paraíba 2,772,600 . . . . . G4
Paraná 7,630,466 . . . . . D9
Pernambuco 6,147,102 . . . . . G5
Piauí 2,140,066 . . . . . F4
Rio de Janeiro 11,297,327 . . . F8
Rio Grande do Norte 1,899,720 . . . . . G4
Rio Grande do Sul 7,777,212 . . . . . C10
Rondônia 492,810 . . . . . H10
Roraima (terr.) 79,153 . . . . . H8
Santa Catarina 3,628,751 . . . D9
São Paulo 25,040,698 . . . . . D8
Sergipe 1,141,834 . . . . . G5
Tocantins D5

CITIES and TOWNS

Abaeté 12,861 . . . . . E7
Abaetetuba 33,031 . . . . . D3
Acaraú 7,144 . . . . . F3
Acopiara 10,747 . . . . . G4
Açu 20,544 . . . . . G4
Agudos 18,790 . . . . . *B3
Alagoa Grande 14,204 . . . . . H4
Alagoinhas 76,377 . . . . . G6
Alcobaça 3,430 . . . . . G7
Alegre 9,441 . . . . . *F2
Alegrete 54,786 . . . . . B10
Além Paraíba 23,028 . . . . . *E2
Alenquer 16,477 . . . . . C3
Alfenas 31,815 . . . . . *D2
Altamira 24,846 . . . . . C3
Altos 13,621 . . . . . F4
Amambaí 12,507 . . . . . C8
Amapá 2,676 . . . . . D2
Amarante 6,848 . . . . . F4
Amargosa 11,118 . . . . . F6
Americana 121,794 . . . . . *C3
Amparo 26,970 . . . . . *C3
Anápolis 160,520 . . . . . D7
Anchieta 5,741 . . . . . F8
Andaraí 2,476 . . . . . F6
Andradina 42,036 . . . . . D8
Andrelândia 8,737 . . . . . *D2
Angra dos Reis 24,894 . . . . . *D3
Antonina 11,950 . . . . . *B4
Aparecida 27,265 . . . . . *D3
Apiaí 7,809 . . . . . *B4
Aquidauana 21,514 . . . . . C8
Aracaju 288,106 . . . . . G5
Aracati 20,282 . . . . . G4
Araçatuba 113,486 . . . . . *A2
Araçuaí 12,292 . . . . . F7
Araguari 73,302 . . . . . D7
Araranguá 22,468 . . . . . D10
Araraquara 77,202 . . . . . *B2
Araras 54,323 . . . . . *C3
Araxá 51,339 . . . . . E7
Arcoverde 40,646 . . . . . G5
Areia Branca 12,979 . . . . . G4
Assis 57,217 . . . . . *A3
Avaré 40,716 . . . . . *B3
Bacabal 43,229 . . . . . E4
Bagé 66,743 . . . . . C10
Bahia (Salvador) 1,496,276 . . G6
Baixo Guandu 13,714 . . . . . F7
Balsas 13,566 . . . . . E4
Bambuí 14,172 . . . . . *C2
Barão de Cocais 11,950 . . . . *E1
Barbacena 69,675 . . . . . *E2
Bariri 15,372 . . . . . *B3
Barra 10,809 . . . . . F5
Barra do Corda 19,280 . . . . . E4
Barra do Piraí 51,214 . . . . . *E3
Barra Mansa 123,421 . . . . . *D3
Barras 8,904 . . . . . F4
Barreiras 30,355 . . . . . E6
Barreiros 19,419 . . . . . H5
Barretos 65,294 . . . . . *B2
Batatais 30,478 . . . . . *C2
Baturité 12,388 . . . . . G4
Bauru 178,861 . . . . . *B3
Bebedouro 39,070 . . . . . *B2
Bela Vista 11,936 . . . . . C8
Belém 758,117 . . . . . E3
Belém †1,000,349 . . . . . E3
Belo Horizonte 1,442,483 . . *D1
Belo Horizonte †2,541,788 *D1
Benjamin Constant 6,563 . . . G9
Bento Gonçalves 40,323 . . . C10
Betim 71,599 . . . . . *D2
Bicas 8,611 . . . . . *E2
Birigui 45,348 . . . . . *A2
Blumenau 144,819 . . . . . D9
Boa Esperanca 17,394 . . . . *D2
Boa Vista 43,131 . . . . . H8
Bocaiúva 16,616 . . . . . E7
Bom Conselho 13,196 . . . . . G5
Bom Despacho 22,941 . . . . *D1
Bom Jesus da Lapa 19,978 . . F6
Bom Sucesso 10,331 . . . . . *D2
Borba 5,366 . . . . . H9
Bragança Paulista 61,021 . . *C3
Brasiléia 4,835 . . . . . G10
Brasília (cap.) 411,305 . . . . . E6
Brasília de Minas 10,171 . . . . F7
Brejo 5,859 . . . . . F3
Breves 31,452 . . . . . D3
Brumado 24,663 . . . . . F6
Brusque 37,898 . . . . . D9
Cabedolo 18,581 . . . . . H4
Cabo Frio 40,668 . . . . . *F3
Caçador 25,287 . . . . . D9
Caçapava 45,258 . . . . . *D3
Caçapava do Sul 15,180 . . . . C10
Cáceres 33,472 . . . . . B7
Cachoeira 11,520 . . . . . G6
Cachoeira do Sul 59,967 . . . C10
Cachoeiro de Itapemirim 84,994 . . . . . G8
Caeté 23,331 . . . . . *E1
Caetité 8,823 . . . . . F6
Caiaponia 9,358 . . . . . C7
Caicó 30,777 . . . . . G4
Cajazeiras 30,834 . . . . . G4
Cajuru 9,670 . . . . . *C2
Camaquã 28,078 . . . . . C10
Cambará 13,218 . . . . . *A3
Cambuí 8,552 . . . . . *C3
Cametá 15,539 . . . . . D3
Camocim 19,921 . . . . . F3
Campina Grande 222,229 . . . G4
Campinas 566,517 . . . . . *C3
Campo Belo 30,392 . . . . . *D2
Campo Formoso 10,324 . . . . . F5
Campo Grand 282,844 . . . . . C8
Campo Largo 34,506 . . . . . *B4
Campo Major 24,009 . . . . . F4
Campos 174,218 . . . . . *F2
Cananéia 5,581 . . . . . *C4
Canavieiras 14,076 . . . . . G6
Canindé 18,573 . . . . . G4
Canoas 214,115 . . . . . D10
Canoinhas 25,880 . . . . . D9
Capanema 28,272 . . . . . E3
Capão Bonito 24,081 . . . . . *B4
Caraguatatuba 22,932 . . . . . *D3
Carangola 15,621 . . . . . *E2
Caratinga 39,621 . . . . . *E1
Caravelas 3,704 . . . . . G7
Carazinho 41,913 . . . . . C10
Carolina 10,136 . . . . . E4
Caruaru 137,636 . . . . . G5
Casa Banca 13,739 . . . . . *C2
Cascavel 16,238 . . . . . G4
Cássia 10,701 . . . . . *C2
Castanhal 51,797 . . . . . E3
Castelo 9,162 . . . . . F8
Castro 21,079 . . . . . *B4
Castro Alves 11,286 . . . . . G6
Cataguases 40,659 . . . . . *E2
Catalão 30,516 . . . . . E7
Catanduva 64,813 . . . . . *B2
Catolé do Rocha 12,165 . . . . G4
Caxambu 16,221 . . . . . *D2
Caxias 56,755 . . . . . F4
Caxias do Sul 198,824 . . . . . D10
Ceará (Fortaleza) 648,815 . . . G3
Ceará-Mirim 17,097 . . . . . H4
Ceres 13,671 . . . . . D6
Chapecó 53,198 . . . . . C9
Coari 14,841 . . . . . H9
Codajás 4,923 . . . . . H9
Codó 11,593 . . . . . E4
Colatina 61,057 . . . . . F7
Conceição do Araguaia 18,143 . . . . . D5
Concórdia 17,973 . . . . . D9
Conselheiro Lafaiete 66,262 E2
Corinto 17,056 . . . . . E7
Cornélio Procópio 31,201 . . . D8
Coroatá 16,070 . . . . . F3
coromandel 11,604 . . . . . F7
Corumbá 66,014 . . . . . B7
Coxim 14,876 . . . . . C7
Crateús 29,905 . . . . . F4
Crato 49,244 . . . . . G4
Criciúma 74,003 . . . . . D10
Cristalina 10,521 . . . . . E7
Cruz Alta 53,315 . . . . . C10
Cruzeiro 55,175 . . . . . *D3
Cruzeiro do Sul 11,189 . . . . G10
Cubatão 78,327 . . . . . *C3
Cuiabá 167,894 . . . . . C6
Curitiba 843,733 . . . . . *B4
Curitiba †1,441,743 . . . . . *B4
Currais Novos 25,663 . . . . . G4
Cururupu 10,358 . . . . . E3
Curvelo 37,734 . . . . . E7
Diamantina 20,197 . . . . . F7
Divinópolis 108,344 . . . . . *D2
Dois Córregos 11,811 . . . . . *B3
Dom Pedrito 25,773 . . . . . C10
Dores do Indaiá 13,058 . . . . . E7
Dourados 76,838 . . . . . C8
Duque de Caxias 306,057 . . *E3
Erexim 46,927 . . . . . C9
Esperanca 12,964 . . . . . G4
Esplanada 9,822 . . . . . G5
Estancia 28,250 . . . . . G5
Feira de Santana 225,003 . . . G5
Fernandópolis 39,737 . . . . . *A2
Floriano 35,761 . . . . . F4
Florianópolis 153,547 . . . . . E9
Fonte Boa 3,278 . . . . . G9
Formiga 36,681 . . . . . *D2
Formosa 29,304 . . . . . E6
Fortaleza 648,815 . . . . . G3
Fortaleza †1,581,588 . . . . . G3
Foz do Iguaçu 93,619 . . . . . C9
Franca 143,630 . . . . . *C2
Frutal 22,955 . . . . . *B2
Garanhuns 64,854 . . . . . G5
Garça 26,527 . . . . . *B3
Goiana 30,108 . . . . . H4
Goiânia 703,263 . . . . . D7
Goiás 15,768 . . . . . D6
Governador Valadares 173,699 . . . . . F7
Grajaú 11,147 . . . . . E4
Guaçuí 12,715 . . . . . *F2
Guajará-Mirim 19,992 . . . . . H10
Guarapuava 17,189 . . . . . C9
Guaratinguetá 68,370 . . . . . *D3
Guarujá 67,730 . . . . . *C4
Guarulhos 395,117 . . . . . *C3
Guaxupé 23,637 . . . . . *C2
Guirantinga 8,981 . . . . . C7
Gurupi 27,139 . . . . . D5
Humaitá 10,004 . . . . . H10
Ibaiti 11,352 . . . . . *A3
Ibiá 11,161 . . . . . E7
Ibicaraí 18,202 . . . . . G6
Ibitinga 23,359 . . . . . *B2
Icó 13,007 . . . . . G4
Igarapava 15,342 . . . . . C2
Igarapé-Miri 12,172 . . . . . D3
Iguape 16,827 . . . . . *C4
Iguatu 39,611 . . . . . G4
Ijuí 51,925 . . . . . C10
Ilhéus 71,240 . . . . . G6
Imbituba 9,998 . . . . . D10
Imperatiz 111,818 . . . . . E4
Inhumas 23,455 . . . . . D7
Ipameri 14,163 . . . . . E7
Ipu 12,787 . . . . . F4
Irati 21,956 . . . . . *A4
Itabaiana, Paraíba 17,843 . . . H4
Itabaiana, Sergipe 26,055 . . . G5
Itaberaba 27,590 . . . . . F6
Itabira 57,691 . . . . . F7
Itabirito 22,978 . . . . . *E2
Itabuna 129,938 . . . . . G6
Itacoatiara 26,737 . . . . . B3
Itaituba 19,644 . . . . . C4
Itajaí 78,867 . . . . . D9
Itajubá 53,506 . . . . . *D3
Itanhaem 26,181 . . . . . C4
Itapecerica 10,234 . . . . . *D2
Itapecuru-Mirim 12,216 . . . . F3
Itapemirim 16,829 . . . . . F8
Itaperuna 34,644 . . . . . *F2
Itapetinga 36,897 . . . . . G6
Itapetininga 61,344 . . . . . *B3
Itapeva 36,551 . . . . . *B3
Itapipoca 19,463 . . . . . G3
Itapira 36,308 . . . . . *C3
Itápolis 13,750 . . . . . *B2
Itaporanga 8,988 . . . . . G4
Itaqui 23,136 . . . . . B10
Itararé 24,368 . . . . . *B4
Itatiba 35,537 . . . . . *C3
Itaúna 49,372 . . . . . *D2
Itu 62,211 . . . . . *C3
Ituaçu 1,749 . . . . . F6
Ituiutaba 65,178 . . . . . D7
Itumbiara 56,602 . . . . . D7
Iturama 12,363 . . . . . *A1
Ituverava 21,323 . . . . . *C2
Jaboatão 67,129 . . . . . H5
Jaboticabal 40,276 . . . . . *B2
Jacareí 103,652 . . . . . *D3
Jacarezinho 23,684 . . . . . *A3
Jacobina 26,723 . . . . . F5
Jacupiranga 7,044 . . . . . B4
Jaguaquara 11,336 . . . . . F6
Jaguarão 18,165 . . . . . C11
Jaguariaíva 8,566 . . . . . *B4
Januária 20,484 . . . . . E6
Jataí 40,957 . . . . . D7
Jaú 59,522 . . . . . *B3
Jequié 84,792 . . . . . F6
Jequitinhonha 10,900 . . . . . F7
Ji-Paraná 31,724 . . . . . H10
Joaçaba 16,195 . . . . . D9
João Pessoa 290,424 . . . . . H4
João Pinheiro 17,013 . . . . . E7
Joinvile 217,074 . . . . . D9
Juazeiro 60,940 . . . . . G5
Juazeiro do Norte 125,248 . . F4
Juiz de Fora 299,728 . . . . . *E2
Jundiaí 210,015 . . . . . *C3
Lages 108,768 . . . . . D9
Laguna 27,743 . . . . . D10
Lambari 9,722 . . . . . *D2
Lapa 13,314 . . . . . D9
Laranjeiras do Sul 19,329 . . . C9
Lavras 35,345 . . . . . *D2
Leme 40,155 . . . . . *C3
Leopoldina 28,554 . . . . . *E2
Limeira 137,812 . . . . . *C3
Limoeiro 36,088 . . . . . H4
Limoeiro do Norte 13,112 . . . G4
Linhares 51,575 . . . . . F7
Lins 44,633 . . . . . *B2
Londrina 258,054 . . . . . D8
Lorena 51,276 . . . . . *D3
Luís Correia 3,576 . . . . . F3
Luz 10,068 . . . . . *D1
Luziania 67,284 . . . . . E7
Macaé 39,644 . . . . . *F3
Macaíba 17,036 . . . . . H4
Macapá 89,081 . . . . . D2
Macau 17,543 . . . . . G4
Maceió 376,479 . . . . . H5
Machado 16,164 . . . . . *C2
Mafra 26,226 . . . . . D9
Magé 37,597 . . . . . *E3
Mamanguape 16,321 . . . . . H4
Manacapuru 17,016 . . . . . H9
Manaus 613,068 . . . . . H9
Manhuaçu 22,678 . . . . . *E2
Manhumirim 11,085 . . . . . *E2
Manicoré 9,532 . . . . . H9
Marabá 41,564 . . . . . D4
Maracaju 9,699 . . . . . C8
Maragogipe 13,512 . . . . . G6
Maranguape 20,098 . . . . . G3
Marechal Deodoro 9,400 . . . . H5
Mariana 11,785 . . . . . *E2
Marilia 103,904 . . . . . *A3
Maringá 158,047 . . . . . D8
Mata de São João 23,741 . . . G6
Mato Grosso (Vila Bela da Santíssima Trindade) 1,401 . . . . . B6
Maués 10,846 . . . . . B3
Mineiros 16,844 . . . . . C7
Miracema 15,545 . . . . . *E2
Miracema do Norte D5
Mirassol 25,173 . . . . . *B2
Mococa 33,682 . . . . . *C2
Mogi das Cruzes 122,265 . . . *C3
Mogi-Mirim 41,827 . . . . . *C3
Monte Alegre 10,646 . . . . . C3
Monte Aprazível 9,767 . . . . . *A2
Monteiro 11,051 . . . . . G4
Montenegro 27,246 . . . . . D10
Montes Claros 151,881 . . . . . E7
Morrinhos 20,154 . . . . . D7
Mossoró 118,007 . . . . . G4
Muriaé 50,040 . . . . . *E2
Muzambinho 8,803 . . . . . *C2
Nanuque 34,445 . . . . . F7
Natal 376,552 . . . . . H4
Nazaré 18,068 . . . . . G6
Niquelandia 8,828 . . . . . D6
Niterói 386,185 . . . . . *E3
Nova Cruz 12,824 . . . . . H4
Nova Era 11,126 . . . . . *E1
Nova Friburgo 88,943 . . . . . *E3
Nova Iguaçu 491,802 . . . . . *E3
Nova Lima 35,035 . . . . . *E2
Nova Russas 10,021 . . . . . F4
Novo Hamburgo 132,066 . . . D10
Novo Horizonte 18,439 . . . . *B2
Óbidos 17,143 . . . . . C3
Oeiras 12,406 . . . . . F4
Olimpia 24,376 . . . . . *B2
Olinda 266,392 . . . . . H4
Oliveira 22,642 . . . . . *D2
Oriximiná 12,078 . . . . . C3
Orlândia 22,924 . . . . . *C2
Osasco 376,689 . . . . . *C3
Ourinhos 52,698 . . . . . *B3
Ouro Preto 27,821 . . . . . *E2
Palmares 40,624 . . . . . H5
Palmas 15,823 . . . . . C9
Palmeira 11,521 . . . . . *B4
Palmeira das Missões 23,943 . . . . . C9
Pará (Belém) 758,117 . . . . . E3
Paracatu 29,911 . . . . . E7
Pará de Minas 37,127 . . . . . *D1
Paraguaçu Paulista 17,399 . . . . . D8
Paraíba do Sul 13,510 . . . . . *E3
Paranaíba 21,305 . . . . . D7
Paranaguá 68,366 . . . . . *B4
Paratí 8,684 . . . . . *D3
Parintins 29,369 . . . . . B3
Parnaíba 78,718 . . . . . F3
Passo Fundo 103,121 . . . . . D10
Passos 56,998 . . . . . *C2
Patos 58,735 . . . . . G4
Patos de Minas 59,896 . . . . . E7
Patrocínio 29,520 . . . . . E7
Pau dos Ferros 12,985 . . . . . G4
Paulo Afonso 62,066 . . . . . G5
Pederneiras 18,864 . . . . . *B3
Pedra Azul 13,615 . . . . . F6
Pedreiras 30,843 . . . . . E4
Pedro Segundo 9,693 . . . . . F4
Pelotas 197,092 . . . . . C10
Penápolis 32,168 . . . . . *A2
Penedo 27,064 . . . . . G5
Pernambuco (Recife) 1,184,215 . . . . . H5
Petrolina 73,436 . . . . . G5
Petrópolis 149,427 . . . . . *E3
Picos 33,098 . . . . . F4
Piedade 13,054 . . . . . *C3
Pilar 14,778 . . . . . H5
Pindamonhangaba 51,174 . *D3

(continued on following page)

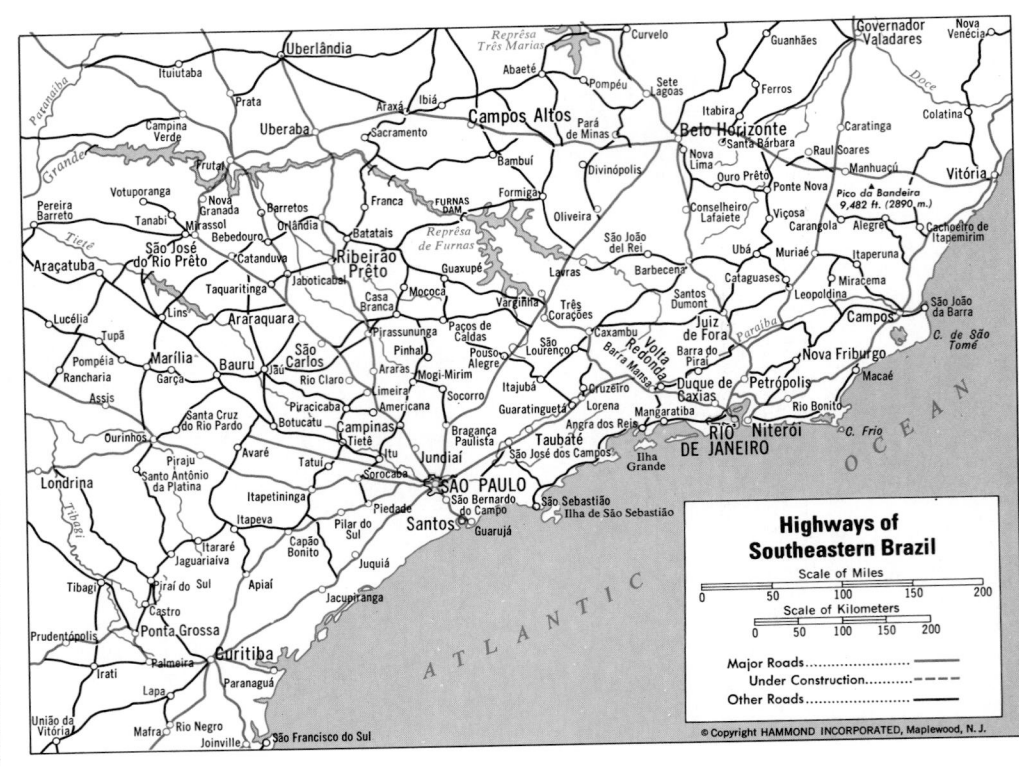

Highways of Southeastern Brazil

Scale of Miles
0   50   100   150   200

Scale of Kilometers
0   50   100   150   200

Major Roads ....
Under Construction ....
Other Roads ....

© Copyright HAMMOND INCORPORATED, Maplewood, N.J.

Agriculture, Industry and Resources

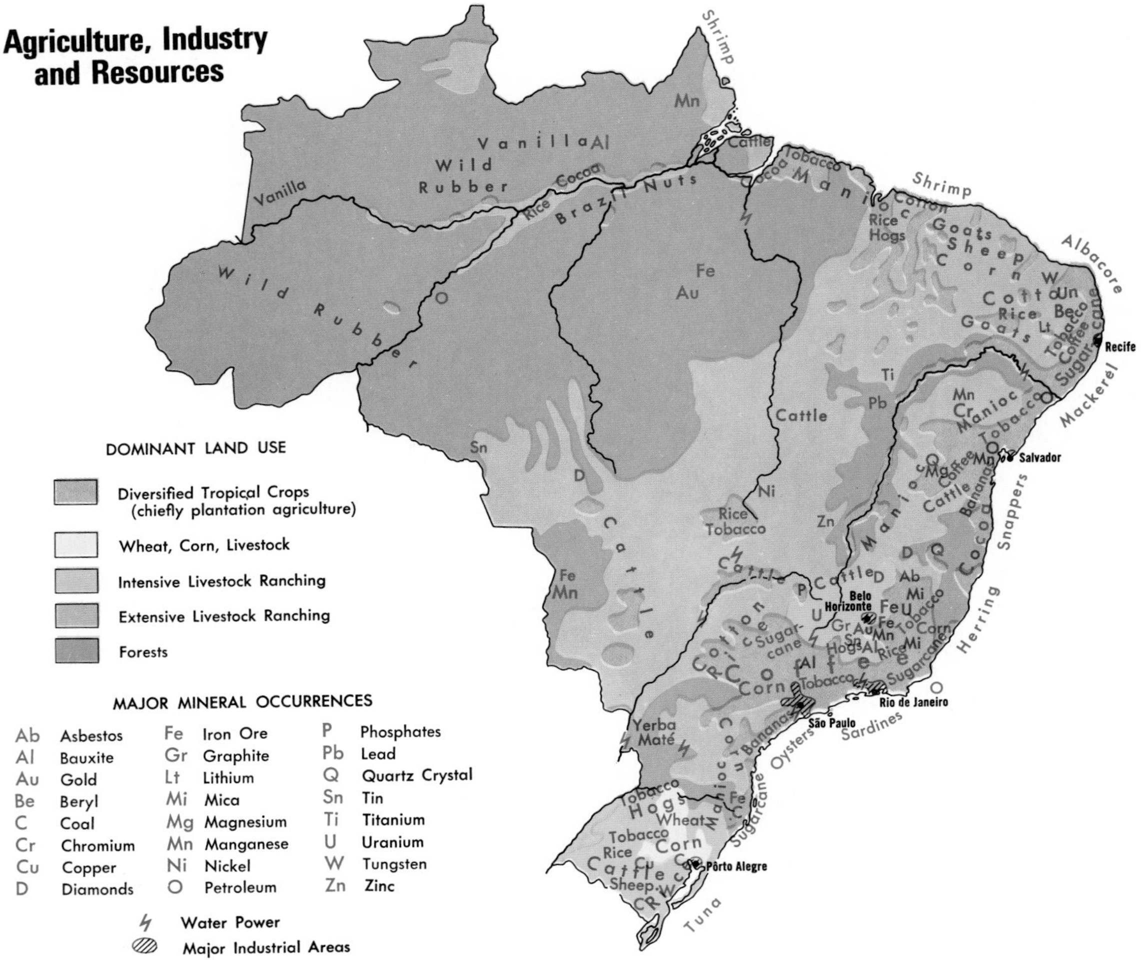

DOMINANT LAND USE

- Diversified Tropical Crops (chiefly plantation agriculture)
- Wheat, Corn, Livestock
- Intensive Livestock Ranching
- Extensive Livestock Ranching
- Forests

MAJOR MINERAL OCCURRENCES

Ab	Asbestos	Fe	Iron Ore	P	Phosphates
Al	Bauxite	Gr	Graphite	Pb	Lead
Au	Gold	Lt	Lithium	Q	Quartz Crystal
Be	Beryl	Mi	Mica	Sn	Tin
C	Coal	Mg	Magnesium	Ti	Titanium
Cr	Chromium	Mn	Manganese	U	Uranium
Cu	Copper	Ni	Nickel	W	Tungsten
D	Diamonds	O	Petroleum	Zn	Zinc

⚡ Water Power

▨ Major Industrial Areas

Brasilia

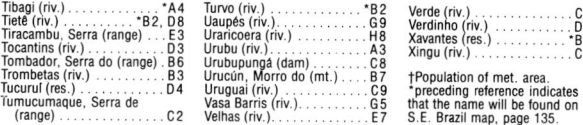

0 .... 5 MI.

0 .... 5 KM.

© Copyright HAMMOND INCORPORATED, Maplewood, N.J.

Southeastern Brazil

POLYCONIC PROJECTION

SCALE OF MILES

0 25 50 100 150

SCALE OF KILOMETERS

0 25 50 100 150

State Capitals.....⊚

State Boundaries.....

© Copyright HAMMOND INCORPORATED, Maplewood, N.J.

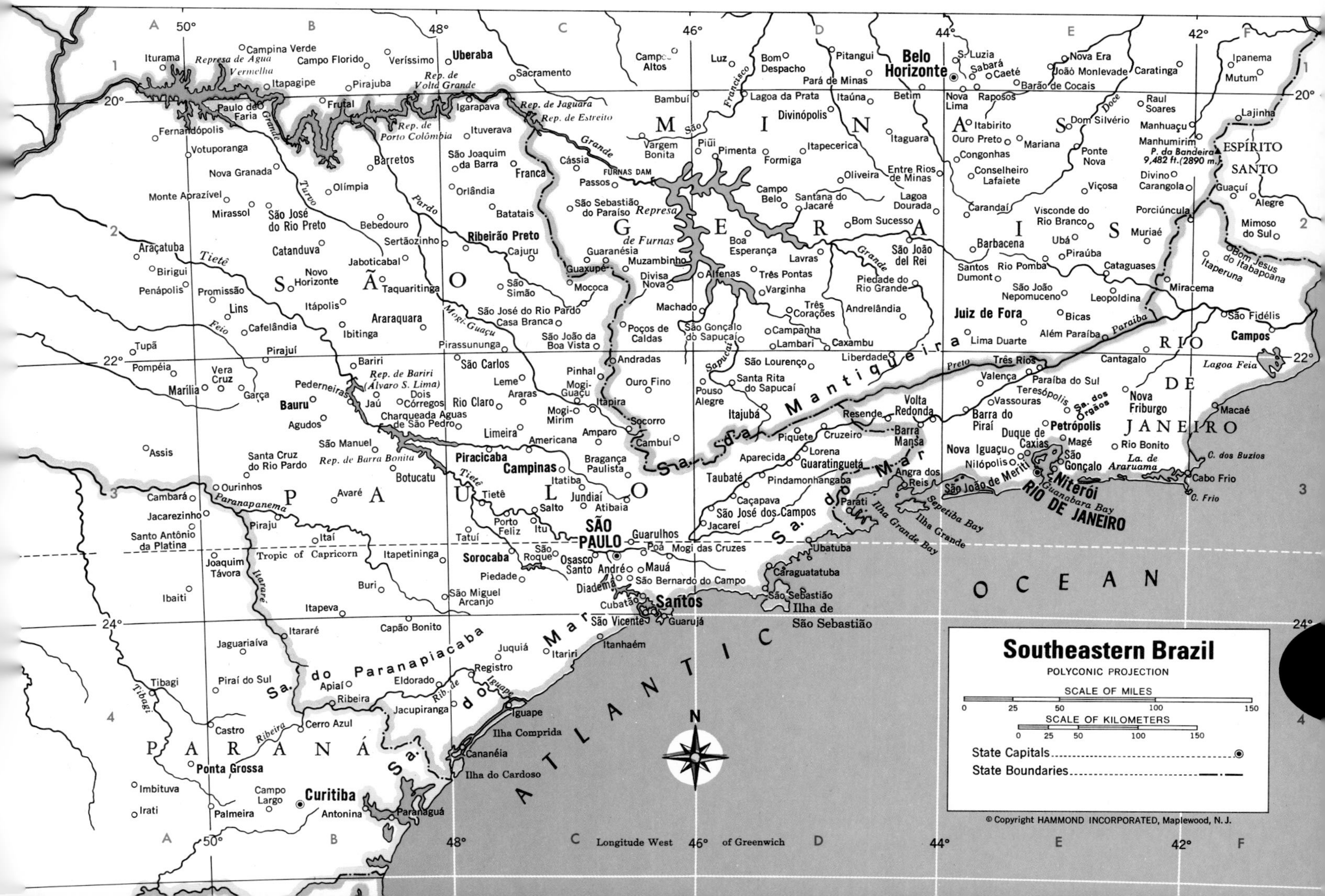

DEPARTMENTS

Beni, El 168,367 ....C3
Chuquisaca 358,516 ....C6
Cochabamba 720,952 ....C5
La Paz 1,465,078 ....A4
Oruro 310,409 ....A6
Pando 34,493 ....B2
Potosí 657,743 ....B7
Santa Cruz 710,724 ....E5
Tarija 187,204 ....D7

CITIES and TOWNS

Achacachi 3,621 ....A5
Aiquile 3,465 ....C6
Alto Seco 3,414 ....D6
Amarete 992 ....A4
Ancoraimes 769 ....A4
Añez (Ascención) D4
Andamarca‡ 5,137 ....B6
Anzaldo 1,056 ....C6
Apolo 1,043 ....A4
Araca‡ 3,537 ....B5

Arampampa 829 ....B5
Arani 2,200 ....C5
Arcopongo‡ 2,223 ....B5
Aroma‡ 873 ....B6
Arque 1,254 ....B5
Ascención (Añez) 2,097 ....D4
Atocha‡ 3,964 ....B7
Ayacucho 729 ....D5
Azurduy 1,234 ....C6
Baures 592 ....D3
Berenguela‡ 2,412 ....A5
Betanzos 1,097 ....C6

Boyuibe 537 ....D7
Cachuela Esperanza 1,073 ...C2
Caiza 838 ....C7
Calamarca 802 ....A5
Callapa 636 ....A5
Camacho‡ 875 ....C7
Camargo 1,609 ....C7
Camatindi‡ 297 ....D7
Camiri 4,969 ....D7
Capinota 1,734 ....B5
Caquiaviri 760 ....A5
Carabuco 626 ....A4

Caracollo 909 ....B5
Caranavi‡ 525 ....B4
Carandaiti 1,403 ....D7
Carmen‡ 845 ....B2
Cataricahua 3,240 ....B6
Cavinas‡ 1,011 ....B3
Chaguaya 643 ....C7
Challana‡ 1,206 ....A4
Challapata 2,529 ....B6
Charagua 1,185 ....D6
Charaña 794 ....A5
Chayanta 1,272 ....B6

Choquecuta‡ 1,976 ....A6
Chulumani 2,362 ....B5
Chuma 931 ....B5
Chuquichambi‡ 1,094 ......B5
Chuquichuqui‡ 1,892 ......C6
Cliza 3,121 ....C5
Cobija 3,650 ....A2
Cocani 658 ....B7
Cocapata‡ 2,855 ....B5
Cochabamba 204,684 .....C5
Cohoni 890 ....B5
Colquechaca 1,070 ....B6

Colquiri 806 ....B5
Comarapa 1,096 ....C5
Concepción 1,056 ....D5
Condo‡ 5,525 ....B6
Conquista‡ 1,162 ....B2
Copacabana 1,981 ....A5
Coripata 1,647 ....B5
Corocoro 4,431 ....A5
Coroico 2,235 ....B5
Cotagaita 1,353 ....C7
Cotoca 915 ....D5
Cuevo 902 ....D7

© Copyright HAMMOND INCORPORATED, Maplewood, N.J.

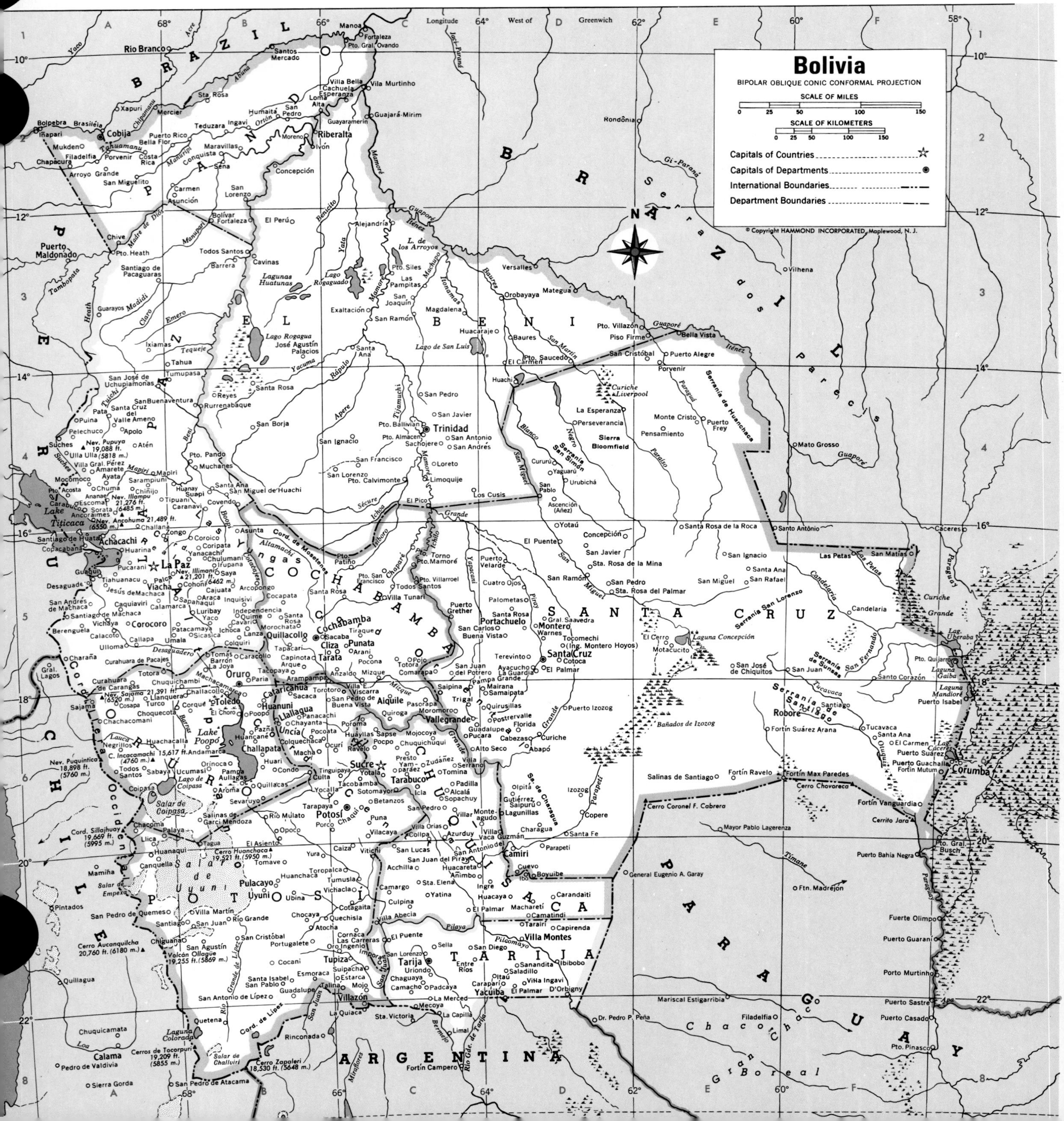

Culpina 981 .... C7
Culta‡ 4,412 .... B6
Curahuara de Pacajes 510 .... A5
El Palmar, Chuquisaca‡ 772 .... D7
El Palmar, Tarija 832 .... D7
El Puente, Santa Cruz‡ 1,185 .... D5
El Puente, Tarija‡ 1,310 .... C7
Entre Ríos 1,011 .... C7
Esmoraca‡ 1,137 .... B7
Estarca‡ 2,331 .... C7
Filadelfia‡ 942 .... A2
Fortaleza‡ 765 .... B3
Fortín Mutum F6
General Saavedra 1,006 .... D5
Guadalupe 2,355 .... C6
Guaqui 2,266 .... A5
Guayaramerín 1,470 .... C2
Huacaraje 673 .... D3
Huachacalla 801 .... A6
Huanay 574 .... B4
Huanchaca B7
Huanuni 5,696 .... B6
Huari 1,070 .... B6
Huarina 1,151 .... A5
Ichoca 591 .... B5
Independencia 1,742 .... B5
Ingeniero Montero Hoyos (Tocomechi) 575 .... D5
Inquisivi 530 .... B5
Irupana 1,937 .... B5
Ivón‡ 772 .... C2
Izozog‡ 2,759 .... D6
Jesús de Machaca 529 .... A5
José Agustín Palacios‡ 2,273 .... B3
La Capilla‡ 1,870 .... C8
Lagunillas 840 .... D6
La Merced‡ 688 .... C8
Lanza 526 .... B5
La Paz (cap.) 635,283 .... B5
Limal‡ 524 .... C8
Llallagua 6,719 .... B6
Llanquera 613 .... A6
Llica 560 .... A6
Loreto 589 .... C4
Macha 1,050 .... B6
Machacamarca 1,746 .... B5
Macharetí‡ 1,164 .... D7
Magdalena 1,724 .... C3
Mairana 508 .... D6
Mecoya‡ 585 .... C8
Mizque 870 .... C5
Mocomoco 977 .... A4
Mojo 469 .... C7
Mojocoya 498 .... C6
Monteagudo 971 .... D6
Montero 2,713 .... D5
Morochata 461 .... B5
Moromoro 556 .... C6
Motacucito‡ 585 .... E5
Ocurí 1,531 .... C6
Orinoca‡ 2,380 .... B6
Orobayaya‡ 1,132 .... D3
Oro Ingenio‡ 945 .... C7
Oruro 124,213 .... B5
Padcaya 324 .... C7
Padilla 2,462 .... C6
Palaya 300 .... A6
Palca 887 .... A5
Palometas‡ 3,453 .... D5
Pampa Aullagas‡ 1,834 .... B6
Pampa Grande 727 .... D5
Panacachi 952 .... B6
Paria 335 .... B5
Pasorapa 1,016 .... C6
Pata 122 .... A4
Patacamaya 1,278 .... B5
Pazña 671 .... B6
Pelechuco 873 .... A4
Pocoata 859 .... B6
Pocona 518 .... C5
Pocpo‡ 2,791 .... C6
Pojo 1,047 .... C5
Poopó 736 .... B6
Porco 817 .... B6
Poroma 171 .... C6
Portachuelo 2,456 .... D5
Portugalete‡ 1,590 .... B7
Porvenir‡ 846 .... A2
Postrervalle 750 .... D6
Potosí 77,397 .... C6
Presto 725 .... C6
Pucara 762 .... C6
Pucarani 1,041 .... A5
Puerto Acosta 1,302 .... A4
Puerto Almacen 358 .... C4
Puerto General Ovando 658 .... C1
Puerto Heath‡ 570 .... A3
Puerto Rico‡ 539 .... B2
Puerto Siles 357 .... C3
Puerto Suárez 1,159 .... F6
Pulacayo 7,984 .... B7
Puna 852 .... C6
Punata 5,014 .... C5
Quechisla 171 .... C7
Queteña 183 .... B8
Quillacas 1,170 .... B6
Quillacollo 9,123 .... B5
Quime 1,256 .... B5
Quiroga‡ 3,467 .... C6
Quirusillas 433 .... D6
Ravelo 907 .... C6
Reyes 1,404 .... B4
Riberalta 6,549 .... C2
Río Grande 281 .... B7
Río Mulato 381 .... B6
Roboré 3,715 .... F6
Rurrenabaque 1,225 .... B4
Sabaya 649 .... A6
Sacaba 2,752 .... C5
Sacaca 1,778 .... B6
Sachojere 401 .... C4
Saipina 573 .... C6
Sajama 231 .... A6
Saladillo‡ 1,315 .... D7
Salinas de Garci Mendoza 335 .... B6
Samaipata 1,656 .... D6
San Agustín‡ 810 .... B7
Sanandita 379 .... D7
San Andrés 399 .... C4
San Andrés de Machaca 101 .... A5
San Antonio, El Beni 436 .... C4
San Antonio de Lípez‡ 177 .... B7
San Antonio del Parapetí 497 .... D7
San Borja 708 .... B4
San Buenaventura 307 .... A4
San Carlos 570 .... D5
San Cristóbal‡ 1,200 .... B7
San Diego‡ 773 .... D7
San Francisco 185 .... C4
San Ignacio, El Beni 1,757 .... C4
San Ignacio, Santa Cruz 1,819 .... E5
San Javier, El Beni 233 .... C4
San Javier, Santa Cruz 564 .... D5
San Joaquín 1,959 .... C3
San José de Chiquitos 1,933 .... E5
San José de Uchupiamonas 277 .... A4
San Juan, Potosí 131 .... B7
San Juan, Santa Cruz‡ 1,482 .... F5
San Juan del Piray 541 .... C7
San Juan del Potrero 263 .... C5
San Lorenzo, El Beni 496 .... C4
San Lorenzo, Pando‡ 317 .... B2
San Lorenzo, Tarija 785 .... C7
San Lucas 925 .... C7
San Matías 887 .... F5
San Miguel 502 .... E5
San Miguel de Huachi 25 .... B4
San Pablo 11 .... B7

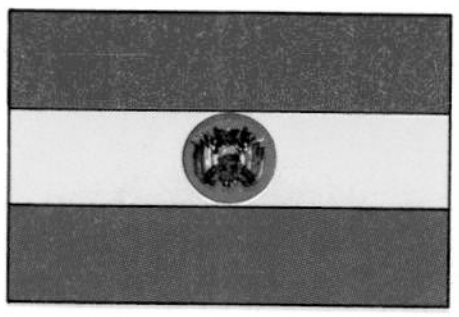

AREA 424,163 sq. mi. (1,098,582 sq. km.)
POPULATION 7,193,000
CAPITALS La Paz, Sucre
LARGEST CITY La Paz
HIGHEST POINT Nevada Ancohuma 21,489 ft. (6.550 m.)
MONETARY UNIT Bolivian peso
MAJOR LANGUAGES Spanish, Quechua, Aymara
MAJOR RELIGION Roman Catholicism

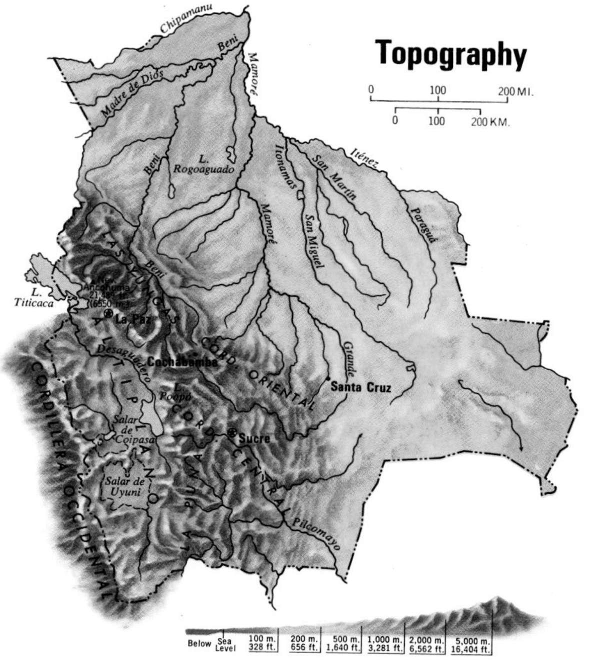

Topography
0 100 200 MI.
0 100 200 KM.
Chipamanu
Beni
Madre de Dios
Mamoré
Iténez
San Martín
Paraguá
L. Rogoaguado
San Miguel
L. Titicaca
La Paz
Cochabamba
Santa Cruz
Sucre
Poopó
Salar de Coipasa
Salar de Uyuni
Desaguadero
Grande
Pilcomayo
CORDILLERA OCCIDENTAL
CORD. ORIENTAL
Below Sea Level
100 m. 328 ft.
200 m. 656 ft.
500 m. 1,640 ft.
1,000 m. 3,281 ft.
2,000 m. 6,562 ft.
5,000 m. 16,404 ft.

San Pedro, Chuquisaca 182 .... C6
San Pedro, El Beni 262 .... C4
San Pedro, Pando‡ 312 .... B2
San Pedro, Santa Cruz 80 .... D5
San Pedro de Buena Vista 1,094 .... C6
San Pedro de Quemes‡ 290 .... A7
San Rafael‡ 1,282 .... E5
San Ramón, El Beni 1,161 .... C3
San Ramón, Santa Cruz 379 .... D5
Santa Ana, El Beni 2,225 .... C3
Santa Ana, La Paz 171 .... B4
Santa Ana, Santa Cruz 275 .... E5
Santa Ana, Santa Cruz 2,225 .... F6
Santa Cruz 254,682 .... D5
Santa Cruz del Valle Ameno 442 .... A4
Santa Elena‡ 4,474 .... C7
Santa Isabel‡ 323 .... B7
Santa Rosa, Cochabamba‡ 942 .... B5
Santa Rosa, Cochabamba‡ 276 .... C5
Santa Rosa, El Beni 765 .... B4
Santa Rosa, Pando‡ 105 .... B2
Santa Rosa, Santa Cruz 995 .... D5
Santa Rosa de la Mina 99 .... D5
Santa Rosa de la Roca 101 .... E5
Santa Rosa del Palmar 441 .... E5
Santiago, Potosí 172 .... A7
Santiago, Santa Cruz 765 .... F6
Santiago de Huata 948 .... A5
Santiago de Machaca 218 .... A5
Santo Corazón‡ 963 .... F5
Sapahaqui 55 .... B5
Sapse‡ 89 .... C6
Sarampiuni 138 .... A4
Saya 339 .... B5
Sena‡ 660 .... B2
Sevaruyo 475 .... B6
Sicasica 1,486 .... B5
Sopachuy 713 .... C6
Sorata 2,087 .... A4
Sotomayor 510 .... C6
Suapi‡ 1,750 .... B4
Suches‡ 231 .... A4
Sucre (cap.) 63,625 .... C6
Suipacha‡ 2,701 .... C7
Tacobamba‡ 6,933 .... C6
Tacopaya 795 .... B5
Talina 122 .... B7
Tapacarí 980 .... B5
Tarabuco 2,833 .... C6
Tarairí‡ 394 .... D7
Tarapaya 357 .... B6
Tarata 3,016 .... C5
Tarija 38,916 .... C7
Teduzara‡ 271 .... B2
Terevinto‡ 3,790 .... D5
Tiahuanacu 1,227 .... A5
Tinguipaya 766 .... C6
Tipuani‡ 1,216 .... B4
Tiraque 1,390 .... C5
Tocomechi 575 .... D5
Todos Santos, Cochabamba 408 .... C5
Todos Santos, Oruro 68 .... A6
Toledo 3,273 .... B6
Tomás Barrón 1,852 .... B5
Tomave 201 .... B7
Tomina 708 .... C6
Toropalca‡ 199 .... B7
Torotoro 1,233 .... C6
Totora C5
Trigal 749 .... C6
Trinidad 14,505 .... C4
Tumupasa 349 .... B4
Tumusla‡ 526 .... C7
Tupiza 8,248 .... C7
Turco 131 .... A6
Ubina‡ 462 .... B7
Ucumasi‡ 1,040 .... B6
Ulla Ulla 52 .... A4
Ulloma 116 .... A5
Umala 481 .... B5
Uncía 4,507 .... B6
Uriondo 860 .... C7
Urubichá 1,369 .... D4
Uyuni 6,968 .... B7
Vallegrande 5,094 .... C6
Versalles 83 .... D3
Viacha 6,607 .... A5
Vichacla 317 .... C7
Vichaya 422 .... A5
Vilacaya 200 .... C6
Villa Abecia 539 .... C7
Villa Bella 88 .... C2
Villa E. Viscarra 658 .... C6
Villa General Pérez 802 .... A4
Villa Ingavi 122 .... D7
Villa Martín 543 .... B7
Villa Montes 3,105 .... D7
Villa Orías 404 .... C6
Villar 322 .... C6
Villa Serrano 1,570 .... C6
Villa Tunari 510 .... C5
Villa Vaca Guzmán 699 .... D6
Villazón 6,261 .... C7
Vitichi 1,515 .... C7
Warnes 1,571 .... D5
Yaco 835 .... B5
Yacuiba 5,027 .... D7
Yamparaéz 725 .... C6
Yanacachi‡ 1,964 .... B5
Yatina‡ 1,850 .... C7
Yocalla‡ 1,814 .... B6
Yotala 1,554 .... C6
Yura 136 .... B7
Zongo 141 .... B5
Zudáñez 1,868 .... C6

OTHER FEATURES

Abuná (riv.) B2
Altamachi (riv.) B5
Ancohuma, Nevada (mt.) A4
Apere (riv.) C4
Arroyas, Los (lake) C3
Barras (riv.) B6
Baures (riv.) D3
Beni (riv.) B4
Benicito (riv.) C3
Bermejo (riv.) C8
Blanco (riv.) D4
Bloomfield, Sierra (mts.) D4
Boopi (riv.) B4
Cáceres (lag.) G6
Candelaria (riv.) F5
Capitán Ustarés, Cerro (mt.) E6
Central, Cordillera (range) C6
Challviri (salt dep.) B8
Chaparé (riv.) C5
Charagua, Sierra de (mts.) D6
Chipamanu (riv.) A2
Chovoreca, Cerro (mt.) F6
Claro (riv.) A3
Coipasa (lake) B6
Coipasa (salt dep.) A6
Colorada (lag.) A8
Concepción (lag.) E5
Coronel F. Gabrera E6
Cotacajes (riv.) B5
Desaguadero (riv.) B5
Emero (riv.) B3
Empexa (salt dep.) A7
Gaiba (lag.) F5
Grande (marsh) F5
Grande (riv.) C4
Grande (riv.) C6
Grande de Lípez (riv.) B7
Guaporé (riv.) C3
Heath (riv.) A3
Huanchaca, Cerro (mt.) B7
Huanchaca, Serranía de (mts.) E4
Huatunas (lag.) B3
Ichilo (riv.) C5
Ichoa (riv.) C4
Illampu, Nevada (mt.) A4
Illimani, Nevada (mt.) B5
Incacamachi, Cerro (mt.) A6
Isiboro (riv.) C5
Iténez (Guaporé) (riv.) C3
Itonamas (riv.) C3
Izozog (swamp) E6
Jara, Cerrito (mt.) F6
Lauca (riv.) A6
Lípez, Cordillera de (range) B8
Liverpool (swamp) D4
Machupo (riv.) C3
Madidi (riv.) A3
Madre de Diós (riv.) A3
Mamoré (riv.) C2
Mandioré (lag.) F6
Manupari (riv.) B3
Manuripi (riv.) B2
Mapiri (riv.) A4
Mizque (riv.) C6
Mosetenes, Cordillera de (range) B5
Negro (riv.) D4
Occidental, Cordillera (range) A6
Ollagüe (vol.) B7
Oriental, Cordillera (range) C5
Ortón (riv.) B2
Otuquis (riv.) F6
Paraguá (riv.) E4
Paraguay (riv.) F7
Paraíso (riv.) E4
Parapetí (riv.) D6
Petas, Las (riv.) F5
Pilaya (riv.) C7
Pilcomayo (riv.) D7
Piray (riv.) D5
Poopó (lake) B6
Pupuya, Nevada (mt.) A4
Puquintica, Nevado (mt.) A6
Rápulo (riv.) C4
Real, Cordillera (range) A5
Rogagua (lake) B3
Rogaguado (lake) C3
Sajama, Nevada (mt.) A6
San Fernando (riv.) F5
San Juan (riv.) C7
San Lorenzo, Serranía (mts.) E5
San Luis (lake) C3
San Martín (riv.) D3
San Miguel (riv.) D4
San Simón, Serranía (mts.) D4
Santiago, Serranía de (mts.) F6
Sécure (riv.) C4
Sillajhuay, Cordillera (mt.) A6
Suches (riv.) A4
Sunsas, Serranía de (mts.) F5
Tahuamanu (riv.) A2
Tarija, Rio Grande de (riv.) C8
Tequeje (riv.) B3
Tijamuchi (riv.) C4
Titicaca (lake) A4
Tocorpuri, Cerros de (mt.) A8
Tucavaca (riv.) F6
Tuichi (riv.) A4
Uberaba (lag.) G5
Uyuni (salt dep.) B7
Yacuma (riv.) B3
Yapacani (riv.) C5
Yata (riv.) C3
Yungas, Las (reg.) B5
Zapaleri, Cerro (mt.) B8

‡Population of canton.

Agriculture, Industry and Resources

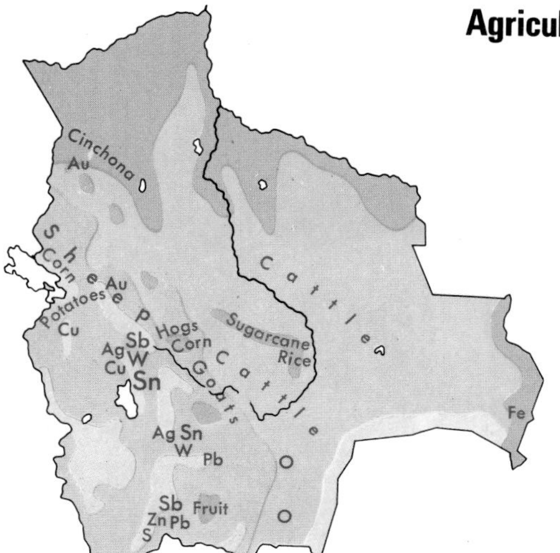

Cinchona
Au
Sheep
Corn
Potatoes
Cu
Ag
Sb
W
Sn
Hogs
Corn
Goats
Sugarcane
Rice
Cattle
Fe
Pb
Fruit
Zn
S

DOMINANT LAND USE

- Diversified Tropical Crops (chiefly plantation agriculture)
- Upland Cultivated Areas
- Upland Livestock Grazing, Limited Agriculture
- Extensive Livestock Ranching
- Forests
- Nonagricultural Land

MAJOR MINERAL OCCURRENCES

Ag	Silver	G	Natural Gas	Sb	Antimony
Au	Gold	O	Petroleum	Sn	Tin
Cu	Copper	Pb	Lead	W	Tungsten
Fe	Iron Ore	S	Sulfur	Zn	Zinc

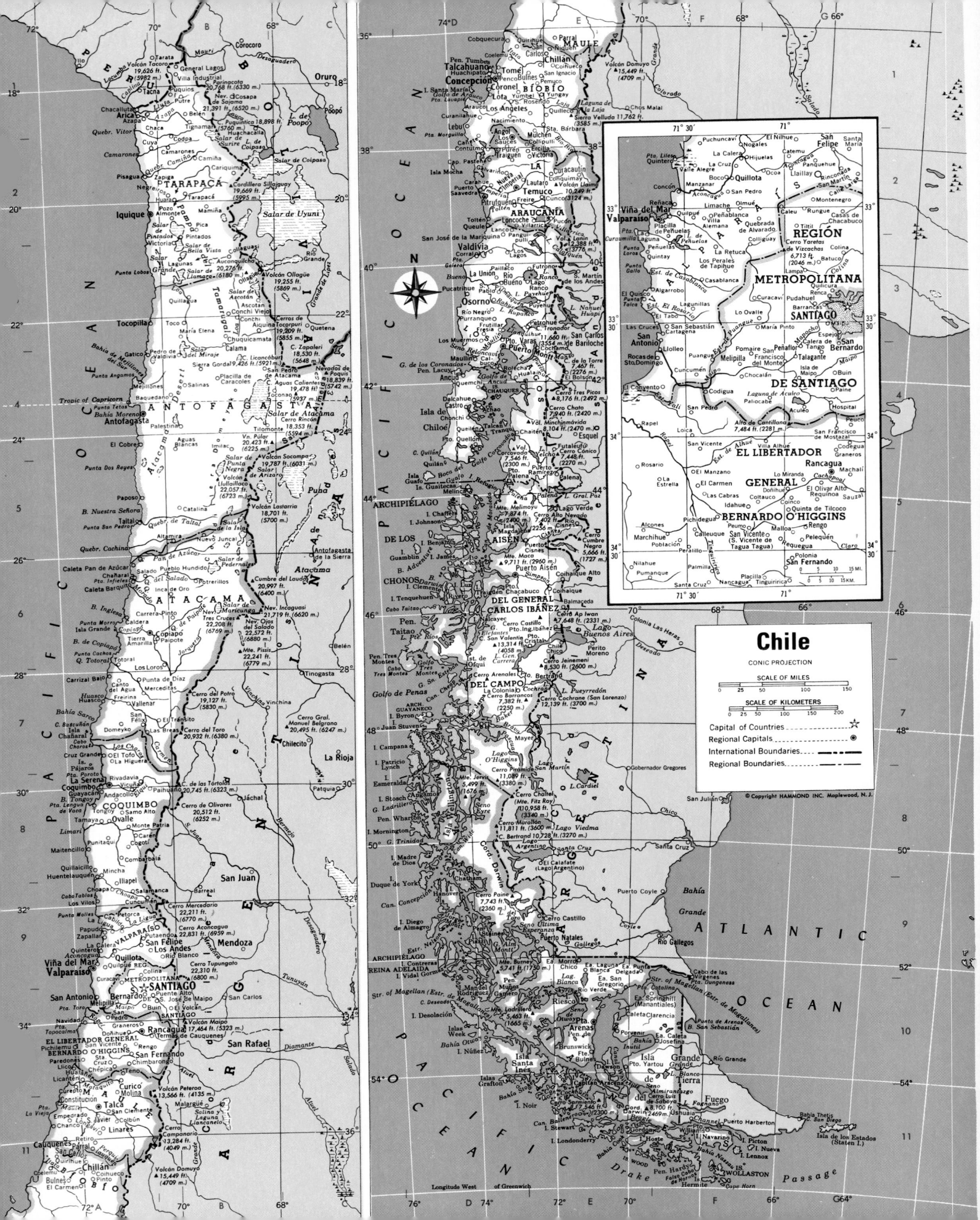

Chile

CONIC PROJECTION

SCALE OF MILES
0 25 50 75 100 125 150

SCALE OF KILOMETERS
0 25 50 75 100 125 150 175 200

Capital of Countries .... ☆
Regional Capitals .... ⊙
International Boundaries .... ─ ─ ─
Regional Boundaries .... ─ · ─ ·

© Copyright HAMMOND INC. Maplewood, N.J.

AREA 292,257 sq. mi. (756,946 sq. km.)
POPULATION 12,961,000
CAPITAL Santiago
LARGEST CITY Santiago
HIGHEST POINT Ojos del Salado 22,572 ft.
(6,880 m.)
MONETARY UNIT Chilean peso
MAJOR LANGUAGE Spanish
MAJOR RELIGION Roman Catholicism

Topography

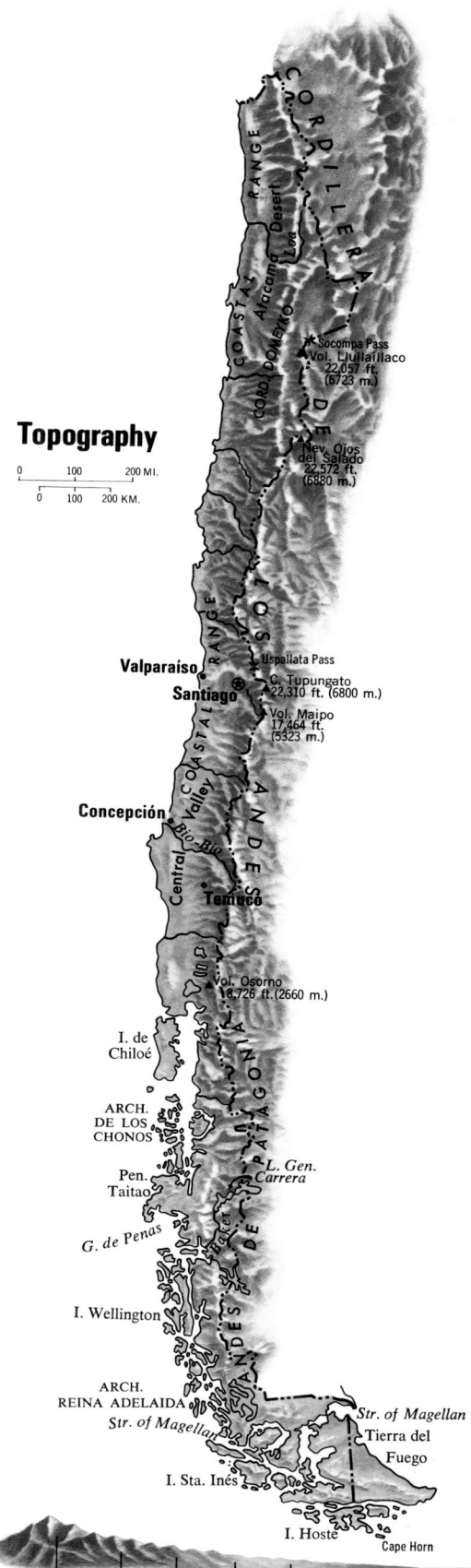

0   100   200 MI.
0   100   200 KM.

5,000 m.	2,000 m.	1,000 m.	500 m.	200 m.	100 m.	Sea
16,404 ft.	6,562 ft.	3,281 ft.	1,640 ft.	656 ft.	328 ft.	Level Below

REGIONS

Aisén del General Carlos
Ibáñez del Campo
65,478 . . . . E6
Antofagasta 341,203 . . . B4
Atacama 183,071 . . . . . B6
Blobio 1,516,552 . . . . . E1
Coquimbo 419,178 . . . . A8
El Libertador General
Bernardo O'Higgins
584,989 . . . . A10
La Araucanía 692,924 . . . E2
Los Lagos 843,430 . . . . D3
Magallanes 132,333 . . . E10
Maule 723,224 . . . . . . A11
Santiago, Región
Metropolitana de (Santiago
Metropolitan Region)
4,294,938 . . . . A9
Tarapacá 273,427 . . . . . B2
Valparaíso 1,204,693 . . . A9

CITIES and TOWNS

Achao ○11,501 . . . . . . D4
Aguas Blancas ○203 . . . B4
Algarrobo ○3,941 . . . . . F3
Ancud ○11,900 . . . . . . D4
Andacollo 6,000 . . . . . . A8
Angol 42,670 . . . . D1
Antofagasta 125,100 . . . A4
Arauco 5,400 . . . . D1
Arica 87,700 . . . . A1
Ascotán B3
Barrancas ○184,241 . . . G3
Belén ○925 . . . . B1
Buin 11,800 . . . . G4
Bulnes 6,900 . . . . E1
Cabildo 5,800 . . . . A9
Calama 45,900 . . . . . . B3
Calbuco ○21,673 . . . . . D4
Caldera ○3,268 . . . . . . A6
Calera de Tango ○6,198 . . G4
Calle Larga ○7,172 . . . . G2
Carahue ○12,733 . . . . . D2
Cartagena ○7,124 . . . . . F3
Casablanca 5,500 . . . . . F3
Casas de Chacabuco . . . G2
Castro 11,200 . . . . D4
Catalina ○1,637 . . . . . . B5
Catemu ○8,728 . . . . . . G2
Cauquenes 20,200 . . . . A11
Cerro Castillo ○537 . . . . E9
Cerro Manantiales F10
Chaitén ○4,067 . . . . . . E4
Chañaral ○36,949 . . . . . A6
Chanco ○12,433 . . . . . A11
Chépica ○11,199 . . . . . A10
Chillán 128,515 . . . . . . A11
Chimbarongo 5,300 . . . . A10
Chonchi ○8,911 . . . . . . D4
Chuquicamata 22,100 . . . B3
Cobquecura ○6,298 . . . . D1
Cochamó ○5,042 . . . . . E3
Codegua ○6,757 . . . . . G4
Codpa ○950 . . . . B1
Coelemu 5,400 . . . . . . D1
Coihaique 32,129 . . . . . E6
Coihueco ○17,276 . . . . A11
Coinco ○4,942 . . . . . . G5
Colbún ○12,924 . . . . . A11
Colina 7,400 . . . . G3
Collipulli 7,200 . . . . . . E2
Coltauco ○11,857 . . . . . F5
Combarbalá ○17,332 . . . A8
Concepción 206,226 . . . D1
Constitución 11,500 . . . A11
Contulmo ○13,987 . . . . D2
Copiapó 45,200 . . . . . . B6
Coquimbo 73,953 . . . . . A8
Coronel 37,300 . . . . . . D1
Corral ○5,533 . . . . D3
Cunco ○18,836 . . . . . . E2
Curacautín 9,800 . . . . . E2
Curacaví 5,800 . . . . . . G3
Curanilahue 13,200 . . . . D1
Curepto ○13,020 . . . . . A10
Curicó 41,300 . . . . A10
Dalcahue ○7,084 . . . . . D4
Domeiko A7
Doñihue ○8,837 . . . . . . G5
El Carmen ○13,226 . . . . A11
El Monte 7,000 . . . . . . G4
El Quisco ○2,152 . . . . . E3
El Tabo ○2,180 . . . . . . F3
El Tofo A7
Empedrado ○7,887 . . . . A11
Ercilla ○8,061 . . . . E2
Estancia Caleta
Josefina ○1,042 . . . . F10
Estancia Morro Chico ○785 . E9
Estancia San Gregorio
○1,156 . . . . E9
Estancia Springhill
(Cerro Manantiales) . . . F10

Freire ○23,313 . . . . . . E2
Freirina ○5,523 . . . . . . A7
Fresia ○15,359 . . . . . . D3
Frutillar ○12,721 . . . . . D3
Futaleufú ○2,366 . . . . . E4
Futrono ○7,109 . . . . . . E3
Galvarino ○9,495 . . . . . D2
General Lagos ○810 . . . . B1
Graneros 8,900 . . . . . . G5
Guayacán A8
Hijuelas ○7,128 . . . . . . F2
Hualañé ○6,912 . . . . . . A10
Huara ○1,934 . . . . B2
Huasco ○4,971 . . . . . . A7
Illapel 12,200 . . . . A8
Inca de Oro 1,406 . . . . . B6
Iquique 64,500 . . . . . . A2
Isla de Maipo ○12,903 . . G4
La Calera 24,600 . . . . . F2
La Cruz ○8,907 . . . . . . F2
La Estrella ○3,707 . . . . F5
Lago Ranco ○12,767 . . . E3
Lagunas ○5,653 . . . . . . B3
La Higuera ○6,991 . . . . A7
La Ligua 7,500 . . . . . . A9
Lampa ○10,220 . . . . . . G3
Lanco 5,200 . . . . D2
Las Cabras ○12,119 . . . F5
La Serena 99,908 . . . . . A8
La Unión 15,200 . . . . . D3
Lautaro 11,900 . . . . . . E2
Lebu 12,500 . . . . D1
Licantén ○6,354 . . . . . A10
Limache 15,200 . . . . . . F2
Linares 37,900 . . . . . . A11
Llay-Llay 9,700 . . . . . . G2
Loica F4
Loncoche ○17,539 . . . . D2
Longaví ○15,909 . . . . . A11
Lonquimay ○9,524 . . . . E2
Los Andes 23,500 . . . . G2
Los Ángeles 49,500 . . . . D1
Los Lagos ○14,934 . . . . D3
Los Muermos ○9,296 . . . D3
Los Sauces ○7,613 . . . . D2
Los Vilos ○10,453 . . . . A9
Lota 48,100 . . . . D1
Machalí 5,800 . . . . G5
Maipú ○117,872 . . . . . G3
Malloa ○9,742 . . . . . . G5
Marchigüe ○4,451 . . . . F5
María Elena 5,900 . . . . B3
María Pinto ○5,980 . . . . G3
Maullín ○14,544 . . . . . D4
Mejillones ○3,333 . . . . A4
Melipilla 23,900 . . . . . . F4
Mincha ○11,329 . . . . . A8
Molina 9,400 . . . . A10
Monte Patria ○18,927 . . A8
Mulchén 13,700 . . . . . . D1
Nacimiento ○17,651 . . . D1
Nancagua ○11,076 . . . . F6
Navidad ○6,618 . . . . . . A10
Negreiros ○1,144 . . . . . B2
Ñiquén ○13,640 . . . . . . E1
Nogales ○18,529 . . . . . F2
Nueva Imperial 8,000 . . . D2
Olivar Alto ○5,414 . . . . G5
Ollagüe B3
Olmué ○8,804 . . . . . . F2
Osorno 68,800 . . . . . . D3
Ovalle 31,700 . . . . A8
Paihuano ○6,048 . . . . . B8
Paillaco 5,200 . . . . D3
Paine ○21,876 . . . . . . G4
Palena ○2,508 . . . . . . E5
Palmilla ○7,965 . . . . . . F6
Panguipulli 5,700 . . . . . E2
Panquehue ○4,230 . . . . G2
Papudo ○2,594 . . . . . . A9
Paredones ○7,404 . . . . A10
Parral 17,000 . . . . A11
Pedro de Valdivia 6,200 . . B4
Pemuco ○7,577 . . . . . . E1
Penco ○33,962 . . . . . . D1
Peñaflor 15,500 . . . . . . G4
Peñuelas F3
Petorca ○8,343 . . . . . . A9
Petrohué E3
Peumo ○11,308 . . . . . . F5
Pica ○1,487 . . . . B2
Pichidegua ○13,550 . . . F5
Pichilemu ○8,042 . . . . . A10
Pinto ○8,687 . . . . A11
Pisagua ○1,880 . . . . . . A2
Pitrufquén 7,800 . . . . . D2
Placilla ○6,441 . . . . . . F6
Porvenir ○4,000 . . . . . E10
Potrerillos 3,800 . . . . . . B6
Pozo Almonte ○1,798 . . B2
Puchuncaví ○7,542 . . . . F2
Pucón 18,000 . . . . E2
Pudahuel G3
Pueblo Hundido 6,200 . . B6
Puente Alto 65,100 . . . . B10
Puerto Aisén 17,848 . . . E6
Puerto Cisnes ○2,800 . . . E5

Puerto Ingeniero
Ibáñez ○1,900 . . . . . E6
Puerto Montt 119,059 . . . E4
Puerto Natales 17,280 . . E9
Puerto Quellón ○7,734 . . D4
Puerto Varas 10,900 . . . E3
Puerto Williams ○949 . . . F11
Pumanque ○3,137 . . . . F6
Punitaqui ○16,167 . . . . A8
Punta Arenas 2,140 . . . . E10
Purén ○11,604 . . . . . . D2
Purranque 5,900 . . . . . D3
Putaendo ○12,806 . . . . A9
Putre ○855 . . . . B1
Puyehue E3
Queilén ○6,055 . . . . . . D4
Quemchi ○6,707 . . . . . D4
Quilicura 8,100 . . . . . . G3
Quillagua B3
Quilleco ○16,043 . . . . . E1
Quillota 36,500 . . . . . . F2
Quilpué 40,600 . . . . . . F2
Quinta de Tilcoco ○6,513 . G5
Quintero 9,900 . . . . . . F2
Quirihue ○11,178 . . . . . E1
Rancagua 140,589 . . . . G5
Renca ○67,168 . . . . . . G3
Rengo 32,400 . . . . G5
Requínoa ○10,730 . . . . G5
Retiro ○15,146 . . . . . . A11
Rinconada San Martín
○4,118 . . . . G2
Río Blanco B9
Río Bueno 9,600 . . . . . D3
Río Negro 5,100 . . . . . D3
Río Verde ○554 . . . . . . E10
Rocas de Santo
Domingo ○4,114 . . . . F4
Rosario ○3,383 . . . . . . F5
Salamanca ○18,741 . . . A9
Samo Alto ○5,689 . . . . A8
San Antonio 46,700 . . . . F3
San Bernardo ○117,766 . . G4
San Carlos 17,000 . . . . E1
San Clemente ○23,273 . . A11
San Felipe 26,100 . . . . . G2
San Fernando 23,600 . . . G6
San Francisco de
Mostazal ○11,439 . . . G4
San Ignacio ○13,523 . . . E1
San Javier 10,800 . . . . A11
San José de
Maipo ○9,601 . . . . . B10
San Pablo ○7,978 . . . . D3
San Pedro 8,255 . . . . . F4
San Pedro de Atacama . . C4
San Rosendo ○14,337 . . E1
Santa Bárbara ○14,345 . . E1
Santa Cruz 8,600 . . . . . F6
Santa María ○8,162 . . . . G2
Santiago (cap.) 3,614,947 . G3
Santiago *3,672,374 . . . G3
San Vicente F4
San Vicente (San Vicente
de Tagua Tagua) ○28,333 . F5
Sierra Gorda ○8,805 . . . B4
Talagante 16,500 . . . . . G4
Talca 133,160 . . . . A11
Talcahuano 148,300 . . . D1
Taltal 6,400 . . . . A5
Tamaya A8
Tarapacá B2
Temuco 197,232 . . . . . E2
Teno ○17,675 . . . . . . A10
Termas de Cauquenes . . B10
Tierra Amarilla ○7,899 . . A6
Tiltil ○9,198 . . . . G2
Toco ○8,734 . . . . B3
Tocopilla 22,000 . . . . . A3
Tocnao C4
Toltén ○16,265 . . . . . . D2
Tomé 29,600 . . . . D1
Traiguén 11,400 . . . . . . D1
Valdivia 115,536 . . . . . D3
Vallenar 26,800 . . . . . . A7
Valparaíso 271,580 . . . . E2

Victoria 16,500 . . . . . . D2
Vicuña 5,100 . . . . A8
Villa Alemana 29,600 . . . F2
Villa Alhué ○5,078 . . . . G4
Villarrica 25,091 . . . . . E2
Viña del Mar 281,361 . . . F2
Yumbel ○21,858 . . . . . E1
Yungay ○10,725 . . . . . E1
Zapallar ○2,894 . . . . . . A9
Zapiga B2

OTHER FEATURES

Aconcagua (riv.) F2
Aculeo (lag.) G4
Adventure (bay) D5
Aguas Calientes, Cerro (mt.) . C4
Almirante Montt (gulf) . . . D9
Ancud (gulf) D4
Angamos (isl.) D8
Angamos (pt.) A4
Ap Iwan, Cerro (mt.) E6
Arauco (gulf) D1
Arenales, Cerro (mt.) . . . D7
Atacama (des.) B4
Atacama, Salar de
(salt dep.) C4
Aucanquilcha, Cerro (mt.) . B3
Azapa, Quebrada (riv.) . . . B1
Baker (riv.) D7
Ballenero (chan.) E11
Bascuñán (cape) A7
Beagle (chan.) E11
Bella Vista, Salar de
(salt dep.) B3
Benjamín (isl.) D5
Bío-Bío (riv.) E2
Blanca (lag.) E10
Blanco (lake) F10
Bravo (riv.) D7
Brunswick (pen.) E10
Bueno (riv.) D3
Buenos Aires (lake) E6
Byron (isl.) D7
Cachapoal (riv.) G5
Cachina, Quebrada (riv.) . . A5
Cachos (pt.) A6
Calafquén (lake) E3
Camarones (riv.) A2
Camiña, Quebrada (riv.) . . B2
Campana (isl.) D7
Campanario, Cerro (mt.) . . A10
Capitán Aracena (isl.) . . . E10
Carmen (riv.) B7
Castillo, Cerro (mt.) D5
Catalina (pt.) F10
Chaffers (isl.) D5
Chaltel, Cerro (mt.) E8
Chañaral (isl.) A7
Chatham (isl.) D9
Chauques (isls.) D4
Cheap (chan.) D7
Chiloé (isl.) 119,286 . . . . D4
Choapa (riv.) A9
Chonos (arch.) D6
Choros (cape) A7
Cisnes (riv.) E5
Clarence (isl.) E10
Clemente (isl.) D6
Cochrane (lake) E7
Cochrane, Cerro (mt.) . . . E7
Cockburn (chan.) E11
Concepción (chan.) D9
Cónico, Cerro (mt.) E4
Contreras (isl.) D9
Cook (isl.) E11
Copiapó (bay) A6
Copiapó (riv.) A6
Corcovado (gulf) D4
Corcovado (vol.) D5
Coronados (gulf) D4
Curaumilla (pt.) A7
Darwin (bay) D6
Darwin, Cordillera (mts.) . . D8
Darwin, Cordillera (mts.) . . E11

(continued on following page)

Agriculture, Industry and Resources

DOMINANT LAND USE

- Cereals, Livestock
- Mediterranean Agriculture (cereals, fruit, livestock)
- Pasture Livestock
- Extensive Livestock Ranching
- Limited Seasonal Grazing
- Forests
- Nonagricultural Land

MAJOR MINERAL OCCURRENCES

Ag	Silver	Hg	Mercury
Au	Gold	Id	Iodine
C	Coal	Mn	Manganese
Cu	Copper	Mo	Molybdenum
Fe	Iron Ore	N	Nitrates
G	Natural Gas	Na	Salt
Gp	Gypsum	O	Petroleum
		S	Sulfur

⚡ Water Power   ▨ Major Industrial Areas

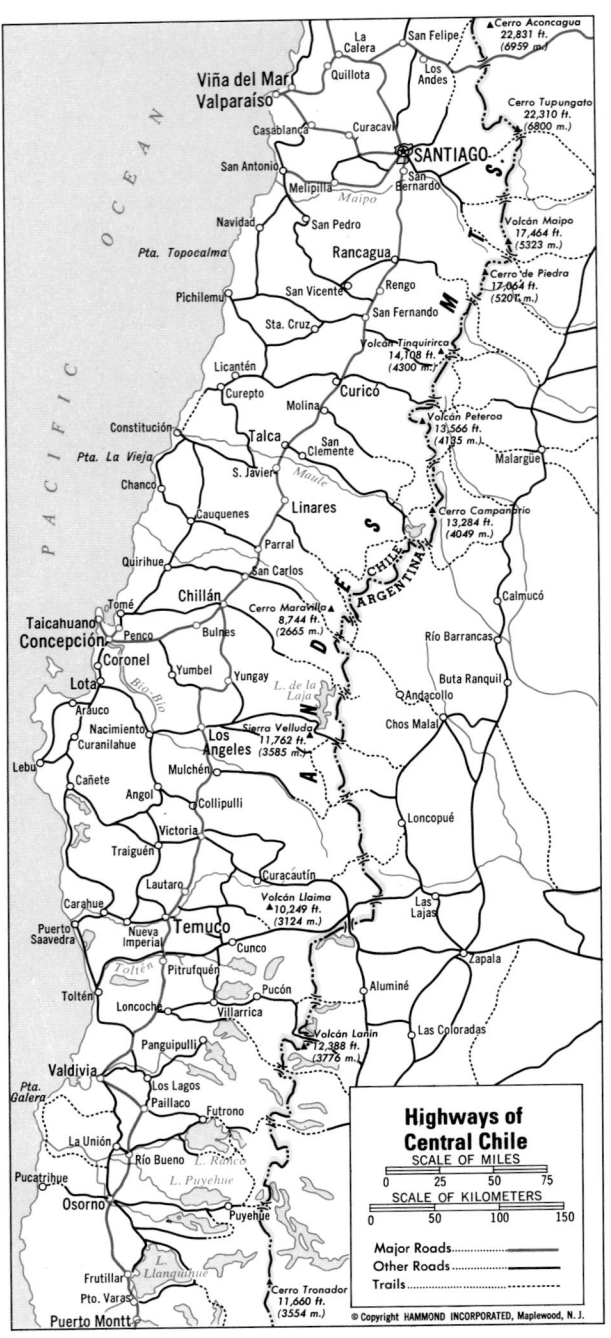

Highways of Central Chile

SCALE OF MILES
0   25   50   75

SCALE OF KILOMETERS
0   50   100   150

Major Roads..............
Other Roads..............
Trails..............

© Copyright HAMMOND INCORPORATED, Maplewood, N.J.

*City and suburbs.
○ Population of commune.

PROVINCES

Buenos Aires 10,796,036 . . . D4
Catamarca 206,204 . . . . C2
Chaco 692,410 . . . . D2
Chubut 262,196 . . . . C5
Córdoba 2,407,135 . . . . D3
Corrientes 657,716 . . . . E2
Distrito Federal 2,908,001 . . H7
Entre Ríos 902,241 . . . . E3
Formosa 292,479 . . . . D1
Jujuy 408,514 . . . . C1
La Pampa 207,132 . . . . C4
La Rioja 163,342 . . . . C2
Mendoza 1,187,305 . . . . . . C4
Misiones 579,579 . . . . F2
Neuquén 241,904 . . . . C4
Río Negro 383,896 . . . . C5
Salta 662,369 . . . . D1
San Juan 469,973 . . . . C3
San Luis 212,837 . . . . C3
Santa Cruz 114,479 . . . . . . C6
Santa Fe 2,457,188 . . . . . . D3
Santiago del Estero 652,318 D2
Tierra del Fuego, Antártida,
  e Islas del Atlántico
  Sur 29,451 . . . . C7
Tucumán 968,066 . . . . C2

CITIES and TOWNS

Abra Pampa 2,929 . . . . C1
Adolfo Alsina 7,707 . . . . . . D4

Aguaray 4,802 . . . . D1
Aguilares 20,286 . . . . C2
Aimogasta 4,640 . . . . C2
Alberti 6,440 . . . . G7
Alcorta 5,818 . . . . F6
Algarrobo del Águila C4
Allen 14,041 . . . . C4
Alpachiri 1,657 . . . . D4
Alta Gracia 30,628 . . . . . . D3
Alumine 1,560 . . . . B4
Alvear 5,419 . . . . E2
Ameghino 2,775 . . . . D3
Añatuya 15,025 . . . . D2
Andalgalá 6,853 . . . . C2
Antofagasta de la Sierra . . . C2
Apóstoles 11,252 . . . . E2
Arrecifes 17,719 . . . . F7
Arroyo Seco 12,886 . . . . . . F6
Ascensión 3,031 . . . . F7
Avellaneda 330,654 . . . . . . G7
Ayacucho 12,363 . . . . E4
Azul 43,582 . . . . E4
Bahía Blanca 220,765 . . . . D4
Bahía Bustamante C6
Bahía Thetis C7
Balcarce 28,985 . . . . E4
Balnearia 4,531 . . . . D3
Baradero 20,103 . . . . G6
Barrancas 3,602 . . . . F6
Barranqueras E2
Barreal 2,739 . . . . C3
Basavilbaso 7,657 . . . . G6
Belén 7,411 . . . . C2

Bella Vista, Corrientes
  14,229 . . . . E2
Bella Vista, Tucumán 9,177 . D2
Bell Ville 26,559 . . . . D3
Bolívar 16,382 . . . . D4
Bovril 4,735 . . . . G5
Bragado 27,101 . . . . F7
Buenos Aires (cap.)
  2,908,001 . . . . H7
Buenos Aires *9,927,404 . . H7
Cafayate 5,048 . . . . C2
Calafate B7
Calchaquí 5,958 . . . . F5
Caleta Olivia 20,141 . . . . . C6
Camarones C5
Campana 51,498 . . . . G6
Cañada de Gómez 24,706 . . F6
Canals 6,627 . . . . D3
Cañuelas 14,831 . . . . G7
Carcarañá 11,121 . . . . F6
Carlos Casares 13,286 . . . . F7
Carlos Tejedor 4,421 . . . . . D4
Carmen de Areco 7,882 . . . F7
Carmen de Patagones
  13,981 . . . . D5
Casilda 23,492 . . . . F6
Castelli 4,507 . . . . H7
Catamarca 88,432 . . . . C2
Caucete 14,512 . . . . C3
Ceres 10,743 . . . . D2
Chabás 5,156 . . . . F6
Chacabuco 26,492 . . . . F7
Chajarí 15,242 . . . . G5

Chamical 6,333 . . . . C3
Charadai 1,078 . . . . D2
Charata 13,070 . . . . D2
Chascomús 21,864 . . . . . . H7
Chepes 4,775 . . . . C3
Chicoana 1,844 . . . . C1
Chilecito 14,010 . . . . C2
Chilvilcoy 43,779 . . . . F7
Choele-Choel 6,191 . . . . . . C4
Chos-Malal 4,823 . . . . C4
Cinco Saltos 15,094 . . . . . . C4
Cipolletti 40,123 . . . . C4
Clorinda 21,008 . . . . E2
Colón, Buenos Aires 16,070 . F6
Colón, Entre Ríos 11,648 . . G6
Colonia Las Heras 3,176 . . . C6
Comandante Fontana 4,468 . D2
Comandante Luis Piedrabuena
  2,492 . . . . C6
Comodoro Rivadavia 96,865 . C6
Concepción 29,359 . . . . . . C2
Concepción de
  la Sierra 2,778 . . . . E2
Concepción del
  Uruguay 46,065 . . . . G6
Concordia 93,618 . . . . G5
Constanza 1,313 . . . . G6
Córdoba 982,018 . . . . D3
Coronda 11,554 . . . . F6
Coronel Brandsen 10,484 . . H7
Coronel Dorrego 10,661 . . . D4
Coronel Pringles 16,592 . . . D4
Coronel Suárez 16,359 . . . . D4

AREA 1,072,070 sq. mi. (2,776,661 sq. km.)
POPULATION 31,929,000
CAPITAL Buenos Aires
LARGEST CITY Buenos Aires
HIGHEST POINT Cerro Aconcagua 22,831 ft.
  (6,959 m.)
MONETARY UNIT austral
MAJOR LANGUAGE Spanish
MAJOR RELIGION Roman Catholicism

Agriculture, Industry and Resources

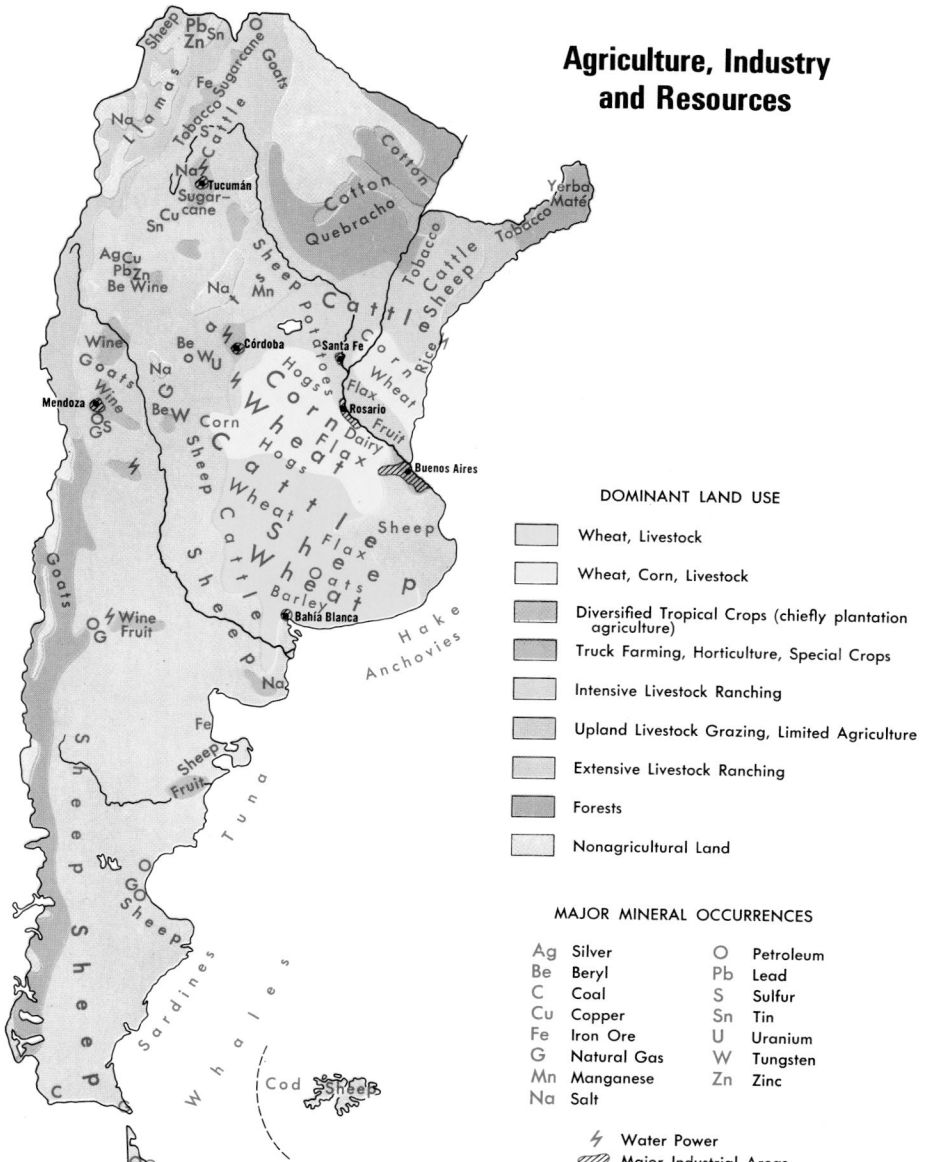

DOMINANT LAND USE

Wheat, Livestock

Wheat, Corn, Livestock

Diversified Tropical Crops (chiefly plantation agriculture)

Truck Farming, Horticulture, Special Crops

Intensive Livestock Ranching

Upland Livestock Grazing, Limited Agriculture

Extensive Livestock Ranching

Forests

Nonagricultural Land

MAJOR MINERAL OCCURRENCES

Ag Silver
Be Beryl
C   Coal
Cu Copper
Fe Iron Ore
G   Natural Gas
Mn Manganese
Na Salt

O   Petroleum
Pb Lead
S   Sulfur
Sn Tin
U   Uranium
W   Tungsten
Zn Zinc

⚡ Water Power
▨ Major Industrial Areas

Coronel Vidal 4,774 . . . . . . E4
Corral de Bustos 8,613 . . . . D3
Corrientes 179,590 . . . . . . E2
Cosquín 13,929 . . . . D3
Crespo 10,668 . . . . F6
Cruz del Eje 23,473 . . . . . . C3
Curuzú Cuatiá 24,955 . . . . . G5
Cutral-Có 25,870 . . . . C4
Daireaux 8,150 . . . . D4
Deán Funes 16,306 . . . . . . D3
Diamante 13,464 . . . . F6
Dolavon 1,778 . . . . C5
Dolores 19,307 . . . . E4
Eduardo Castex 5,397 . . . . D4
El Bolsón 5,001 . . . . B5
Eldorado 22,821 . . . . F2
El Maitén 2,350 . . . . B5
Elortondo 4,939 . . . . F6
El Quebrachal 2,202 . . . . . . D2
Embarcación 9,016 . . . . . . D1
Empedrado 4,732 . . . . E2
Escobar 70,829 . . . . G7
Esperanza 22,838 . . . . F5
Esquel 17,228 . . . . B5
Esquina 10,380 . . . . G5
Famatina 1,237 . . . . C2
Federación 7,259 . . . . G5
Felipe Yofré 1,140 . . . . G4
Fernández 6,062 . . . . D2
Fiambalá 1,201 . . . . C2
Firmat 13,588 . . . . F6
Formosa 95,067 . . . . E2
Fortín Olmos 1,101 . . . . . . F4
Frías 20,901 . . . . D2
Gaiman 2,651 . . . . C5
Gálvez 14,711 . . . . F6
General Acha 7,647 . . . . . . C4
General Alvear, Buenos Aires
  5,481 . . . . F7
General Alvear,
  Mendoza 21,250 . . . . . . C3
General Arenales 3,332 . . . . F7
General Belgrano 10,909 . . . G7
General Conesa 3,566 . . . . C5
General Galarza 3,057 . . . . C6
General Güemes 15,534 . . . D1
General José de
  San Martín 16,296 . . . . . E2
General Juan Madariaga
  13,409 . . . . E4
General La Madrid 5,154 . . . D4
General Las Heras 6,005 . . . G7
General Paz 5,127 . . . . H7
General Pico 30,180 . . . . . . D4
General Ramírez 5,393 . . . . F6
General Roca 38,296 . . . . . C4
General San Martín, Buenos
  Aires 384,306 . . . . G7
General San Martín,
  La Pampa 2,168 . . . . . . D4
General Viamonte 10,112 . . F7
General Villegas 11,307 . . . D4
Gobernador Crespo 2,972 . . F5
Godoy Cruz 141,553 . . . . . C3
Goya 47,357 . . . . G4
Gualeguay 24,883 . . . . G6
Gualeguaychú 51,057 . . . . . G6
Guandacol 1,351 . . . . C2
Hasenkamp 2,804 . . . . F5
Helvecia 3,927 . . . . F5
Hernandarias 3,002 . . . . . . F5
Hernando 8,619 . . . . D3
Huinca Renancó 7,187 . . . . D3
Humahuaca 3,963 . . . . C1
Humberto (Humberto
  Primo) 4,163 . . . . F5
Ibarreta 5,262 . . . . D2
Ibicuy 3,082 . . . . G6
Ingeniero Huergo 3,385 . . . C4
Ingeniero Jacobacci 4,045 . . C5
Ingeniero Luiggi 3,002 . . . . D4
Intendente Alvear 3,640 . . . D4
Itatí 3,269 . . . . E2

Ituzaingó 8,687 . . . . E2
Jáchal 8,832 . . . . C3
Jesús María 17,594 . . . . . . D3
Joaquín V. González 6,054 . . D2
Juárez 11,798 . . . . E4
Jujuy 124,487 . . . . C1
Junín 62,080 . . . . F7
Junín de los Andes 5,638 . . B4
La Banda 46,994 . . . . D2
Laboulaye 16,883 . . . . D3
La Carlota 8,614 . . . . D3
La Cruz 4,132 . . . . E2
La Cumbre 6,110 . . . . C3
La Falda 12,502 . . . . D3
Laguna Paiva 11,129 . . . . . F5
Lanús 465,891 . . . . H7
La Paz, Entre Ríos 14,920 . . G5
La Paz, Mendoza 4,604 . . . C3
La Plata 560,341 . . . . H7
Laprida 6,495 . . . . D4
La Quiaca 8,289 . . . . C1
La Rioja 66,826 . . . . C2
Larroque 3,147 . . . . F5
Las Flores 18,287 . . . . E4
Las Lomitas 4,047 . . . . D1
Las Palmas 5,061 . . . . E2
Las Parejas 7,430 . . . . F6
Las Rosas 9,725 . . . . F6
Las Varillas 10,605 . . . . . . D3
La Toma 4,325 . . . . C3
Lincoln 19,009 . . . . F7
Lobería 8,898 . . . . E4
Lobos 20,798 . . . . G7
Lomas de Zamora 508,620 . G7
Lucas González 3,015 . . . . . G6
Luján 38,919 . . . . G7
Lules 11,391 . . . . C2
Maciel 4,066 . . . . F6
Magdalena 7,135 . . . . H7
Maipú 7,289 . . . . E4
Malabrigo 3,294 . . . . F4
Malargue 9,496 . . . . C4
Maquinchao 1,299 . . . . C5
Marcos Juárez 19,827 . . . . D3
Mar del Plata 407,024 . . . . E4
Máximo Paz 3,216 . . . . F6
Mburucuyá 3,044 . . . . E2
Médanos 4,511 . . . . D4
Mendoza 596,796 . . . . C3
Mercedes, Buenos Aires
  46,581 . . . . G7
Mercedes, Corrientes
  20,603 . . . . G4
Mercedes, San Luis 50,856 . C3
Merlo 293,059 . . . . G7
Metán 18,928 . . . . D2
Miramar 15,473 . . . . E4
Monte Caseros 18,247 . . . . G5
Monte Quemado 4,707 . . . . D2
Monteros 15,832 . . . . C2
Morón 596,769 . . . . G7
Morteros 11,456 . . . . D3
Navarro 7,176 . . . . G7
Necochea 50,939 . . . . E4
Neuquén 90,037 . . . . C4
Nogoyá 15,862 . . . . F6
Norquinco B5
Nueve de Julio 26,608 . . . . F7
Oberá 27,311 . . . . F2
Olavarría 63,686 . . . . D4
Oliva 9,231 . . . . D3
Palo Santo 3,088 . . . . E2
Paraná 159,581 . . . . F5
Paso de Los Libres 24,112 . . E2
Pedro Luro 3,142 . . . . D4
Pehuajó 25,613 . . . . D4
Pellegrini 3,940 . . . . D4
Pergamino 68,989 . . . . F6
Pico Truncado 9,626 . . . . . . C6
Pigüé 10,793 . . . . D4
Pilar 3,805 . . . . F5
Pirané 9,039 . . . . E2
Plaza Huincul 7,988 . . . . . . B4

(continued on following page)

Posadas 139,941 . . . . E2
Presidencia de
la Plaza 4,904 . . . . D2
Presidencia Roque
Sáenz Peña 49,261 . . . . . D2
Puán 4,148 . . . . D4
Puerto Deseado 4,017 . . . . . D6
Puerto Harberton C7
Puerto Iguazú 10,250 . . . . . F2
Puerto Madryn 20,709 . . . . . C5
Puerto Rico 8,195 . . . . D1
Punta Alta 54,375 . . . . D4
Quequén 11,737 . . . . E4
Quimili 8,972 . . . . D2
Quines 3,352 . . . . C3
Quitilipi 9,937 . . . . D2
Rafaela 53,132 . . . . F5
Ramallo 8,248 . . . . F6
Rauch 8,348 . . . . F7
Rawson 12,981 . . . . D5
Reconquista 32,442 . . . . F4
Recreo 3,502 . . . . C2
Resistencia 218,438 . . . . E2
Rinconada D4
Río Colorado 7,361 . . . . D4
Río Cuarto 110,148 . . . . D3
Río Gallegos 43,479 . . . . . . C7
Río Grande 13,271 . . . . C7
Río Segundo 12,839 . . . . . . D3
Río Tercero 34,735 . . . . D3
Rivadavia 10,953 . . . . C3
Rojas 14,247 . . . . F7
Romang 4,017 . . . . F4
Roque Pérez 5,434 . . . . G7
Rosario 954,606 . . . . F6
Rosario de la
Frontera 13,531 . . . . D2
Rosario de Lerma 9,540 . . . . C1
Rosario del Tala 9,552 . . . . . G6
Rufino 15,306 . . . . D3
Saladas 7,345 . . . . E2
Saladillo 14,806 . . . . G7
Salliqueló 5,479 . . . . D4
Salta 260,323 . . . . C1
Salto 18,462 . . . . F7
San Antonio de
Areco 12,932 . . . . G7
San Antonio de
los Cobres 2,357 . . . . C1
San Antonio Oeste 8,690 . . . C5
San Carlos 7,613 . . . . F6
San Carlos de
Bariloche 48,222 . . . . B5
San Cayetano 5,960 . . . . . . E4

San Cristóbal 13,345 . . . . . . F5
San Fernando 128,939 . . . . . G7
San Francisco, Córdoba
58,616 . . . . D3
San Francisco, San Luis
2,448 . . . . C3
San Genaro 2,977 . . . . F6
San Ignacio 3,437 . . . . E2
San Jaime de la
Frontera 2,811 . . . . G5
San Javier 7,557 . . . . F5
San José de Feliciano 4,986 . G5
San Juan 290,479 . . . . C3
San Julián 4,278 . . . . C6
San Justo 14,135 . . . . F5
San Luis 70,632 . . . . C3
San Martín 29,746 . . . . C3
San Martín de
los Andes 9,507 . . . . C5
San Miguel del Monte 8,414 . G7
San Miguel de
Tucumán 496,914 . . . . . . D2
San Nicolás 96,313 . . . . F6
San Pedro, Buenos Aires
27,058 . . . . F6
San Pedro, Jujuy 36,907 . . . D1
San Rafael 70,477 . . . . C3
San Ramón de la
Nva. Orán 32,955 . . . . . . D1
San Salvador 4,342 . . . . G5
San Sebastián C7
Santa Cruz 2,353 . . . . C7
Santa Elena 14,655 . . . . F5
Santa Fe 287,240 . . . . F5
Santa Lucía 4,452 . . . . E2
Santa María 5,380 . . . . C2
Santa Rosa, Córdoba 4,306 . D3
Santa Rosa, La Pampa
51,689 . . . . C4
Santa Rosa, San Luis 2,878 . C3
Santa Victoria D1
Santiago del Estero 148,357 . D2
Santo Tomé, Corrientes
14,352 . . . . F5
Santo Tomé, Santa Fe
35,363 . . . . F5
Sarmiento 6,313 . . . . B6
Sauce 4,677 . . . . G5
Sierra Grande 9,585 . . . . . . C5
Suipacha 4,505 . . . . G7
Sunchales 12,493 . . . . F5
Suncho Corral 3,837 . . . . . . D2
Tafí Viejo 26,625 . . . . C2
Tandil 78,821 . . . . E4

Tapalqué 5,356 . . . . E4
Tartagal 31,367 . . . . D1
Tigre 199,366 . . . . G7
Tinogasta 7,829 . . . . C2
Toay 3,617 . . . . D4
Tornquist 4,696 . . . . D4
Tostado 10,492 . . . . D2
Trelew 52,073 . . . . C5
Trenque Lauquen 22,504 . . . D4
Tres Arroyos 42,118 . . . . . . E4
Trevelin 2,935 . . . . B5
Tunuyán 14,665 . . . . C3
Urdinarrain 5,472 . . . . G6
Ushuaia 10,988 . . . . C7
Valcheta 2,994 . . . . C5
Vedia 6,273 . . . . F7
Veinticinco de Mayo 18,936 . F7
Venado Tuerto 46,775 . . . . . F6
Vera 13,555 . . . . F5
Verónica 5,657 . . . . H7
Viale 5,635 . . . . F5
Vicente López 289,815 . . . . . G7
Victoria 18,883 . . . . F6
Victorica 3,895 . . . . C4
Vicuña Mackenna 5,665 . . . . D3
Viedma 24,338 . . . . D5
Villa Ángela 25,586 . . . . . . D2
Villa Atuel 2,774 . . . . C3
Villa Cañas 7,303 . . . . F6
Villa Constitución 36,157 . . . F6
Villa del Rosario 10,133 . . . . D3
Villa Dolores 21,508 . . . . . . C3
Villa Elisa 4,106 . . . . G6
Villa Federal 9,222 . . . . G5
Villaguay 18,699 . . . . G5
Villa Guillermina 2,971 . . . . D2
Villa Huidobro 4,154 . . . . . . D3
Villa María 67,490 . . . . D3
Villa María Grande 4,517 . . . F5
Villa Nueva 4,604 . . . . D3
Villa Ocampo 9,162 . . . . D2
Villa Regina 14,017 . . . . C4
Villa San José 6,800 . . . . . . G6
Villa San Martín 6,237 . . . . . D2
Vinchina 1,070 . . . . C2
Zapala 18,293 . . . . B4
Zárate 65,504 . . . . G7
Zavalla 3,800 . . . . F6

OTHER FEATURES

Aconcagua, Cerro (mt.) C3
Andes, Cordillera
de los (mts.) C2

Argentino (lake) B7
Arizaro, Salar de (salt dep.) . C2
Arrecifes (riv.) G6
Atacama, Puna de (reg.) C2
Atuel (riv.) C4
Bermejo (riv.) E1
Blanca (bay) D4
Brazo Sur, Pilcomayo (riv.) . . E1
Buenos Aires (lake) B6
Campanario, Cerro (mt.) C4
Chaco Austral (reg.) D2
Chaco Central (reg.) D1
Chico (riv.) C5
Chico (riv.) C6
Chubut (riv.) C5
Colhué Huapi (lake) C6
Colorado (riv.) D4
Cónico, Cerro (mt.) B5
Corrientes (riv.) E2
Coyle (riv.) B7
Delgada (pt.) D5
Desaguadero (riv.) C3
Deseado (riv.) C6
Diamante (riv.) C3
Domuyo (vol.) B4
Dos Bahías (cape)) D6
Dulce (riv.) D2
Dungeness (pt.) C7
El Chocón (res.) C4
Estados, Los (isl.) D7
Fagnano (lake) C7
Famatina, Sierra de (mts.) . . C2
Feliciano (riv.) G5
Gallegos (riv.) B7
General Manuel Belgrano,
Cerro (mt.) C2
Gran Chaco (reg.) D1
Grande (bay) C7
Grande (falls) E3
Grande de Tierra del
Fuego (isl.) C7
Gualeguay (riv.) G5
Guayaquiraró (riv.) G5
Iguazú (falls) F2
Iguazú Nat'l Park E2
Lanín (vol.) B4
Lanín Nat'l Park B4
Lechiguanas (isls.) G6
Lennox (isl.) C8
Limay (riv.) C4
Llancanelo, Salina y
Laguna (salt lake) C4
Llullaillaco (vol.) C1
Magallenes (Magellan) (str.) . C7

Topography

Scale:
0   150   300 MI.
0   150   300 KM.

Tierra del Fuego
Str. of Magellan

5,000 m. 16,404 ft. | 2,000 m. 6,562 ft. | 1,000 m. 3,281 ft. | 500 m. 1,640 ft. | 200 m. 656 ft. | 100 m. 328 ft. | Sea Level | Below

Highways of Central Argentina

MILES
0   25   50   75
KILOMETRES
0   50   100   150

Major Roads . . . .
Other Roads . . . .

© HAMMOND INCORPORATED, Maplewood, N.J.

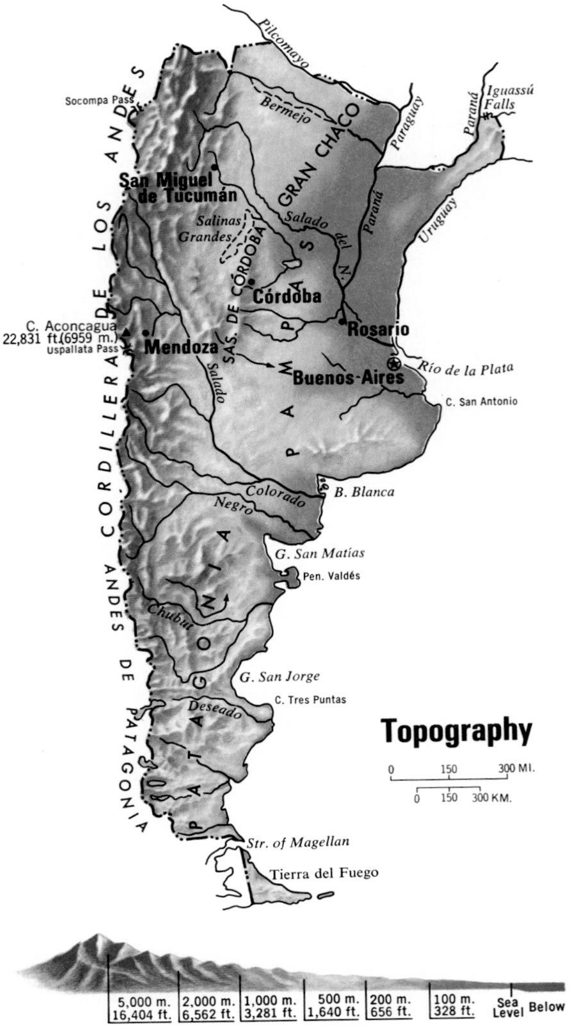

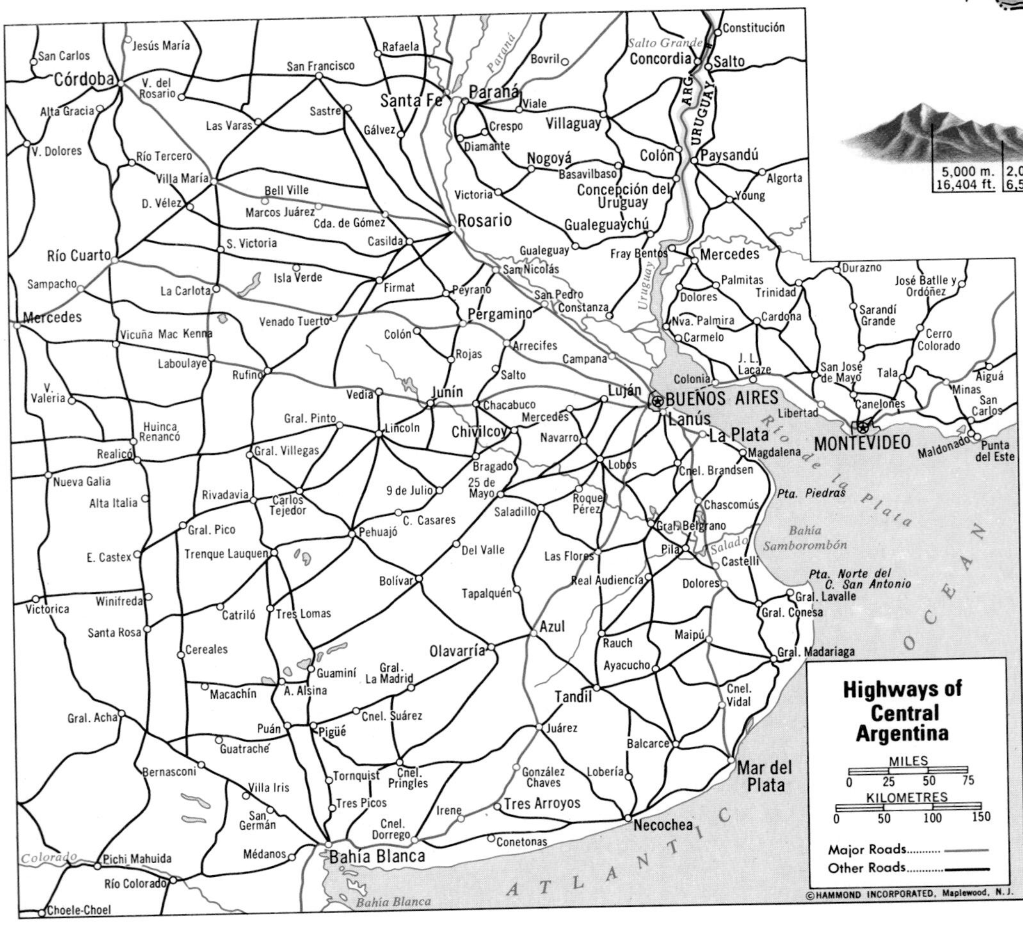

Maipo (vol.) C3
Mar Chiquita (lake) D3
Mendoza (riv.) C3
Mercedario, Cerro (mt.) B3
Mogotes (pt.) E4
Montemayor (plat.) C5
Nahuel Huapi (lake) B5
Nahuel Huapi Nat'l Park B5
Negro (riv.) D4
Neuquén (riv.) C4
Ninfas (pt.) D5
Norte (pt.) D5
Nuevo (gulf) D5
Ojos del Salado, Cerro (mt.) . C2
Pampa de las Tres
Hermanas (plain) C6
Pampas (plain) D4
Paraná (riv.) E2
Patagonia (reg.) C5
Peteroa (vol.) B4
Pilcomayo (riv.) E1
Pissis (mt.) C2
Plata, Río de la (est.) E4
Pueyrredón (lake) B6
Puna de Atacama (reg.) D3
Quinto (riv.) D3
Rincón, Cerro (mt.) C1
Saladillo (riv.) C4
Salado (riv.) H7
Salado (riv.) D2
Salado del Norte (riv.) C2
Salí (riv.) F7
Salto (riv.) E4
Samborombón (bay) E4
San Antonio (cape) D7
San Diego (cape) C6
San Jorge (gulf) C6
San Juan (riv.) C3
San Lorenzo, Cerro (mt.) . . . B6
San Martín (lake) B6
San Matías (gulf) D5
Santa Cruz (riv.) B7

Senguerr (riv.) B6
Staten (Los Estados) (isl.) . . D7
Tarija (riv.) D1
Tercero (riv.) D3
Teuco (riv.) D1
Tierra del Fuego,
Grande de (isl.) C7
Toro, Cerro del (mt.) B2
Tres Puntas (cape) D6
Trinidad (isl.) D4
Tronador (mt.) B5
Tunuyán (riv.) C3
Tupungato, Cerro (mt.) B3
Uruguay (riv.) E3
Valdés (pen.) D5
Viedma (lake) B6
Zapaleri, Cerro (mt.) C1

FALKLAND ISLANDS

CITIES and TOWNS

Stanley (cap.) 1,050 . . . . . . E7

OTHER FEATURES

Adventure (sound) E7
Choiseul (sound) E7
East Falkland (isl.) 1,491 . . . E7
Falkland (isls.) D7
Falkland (sound) D7
George (isl.) E7
Jason (isls.) D7
Lively (isl.) E7
Malvinas (Falkland) (isls.) . . . D7
Pebble (isl.) E7
Saunders (isl.) E7
Weddell (isl.) D7
West Falkland (isl.) 322 . . . . D7

*City and suburbs.

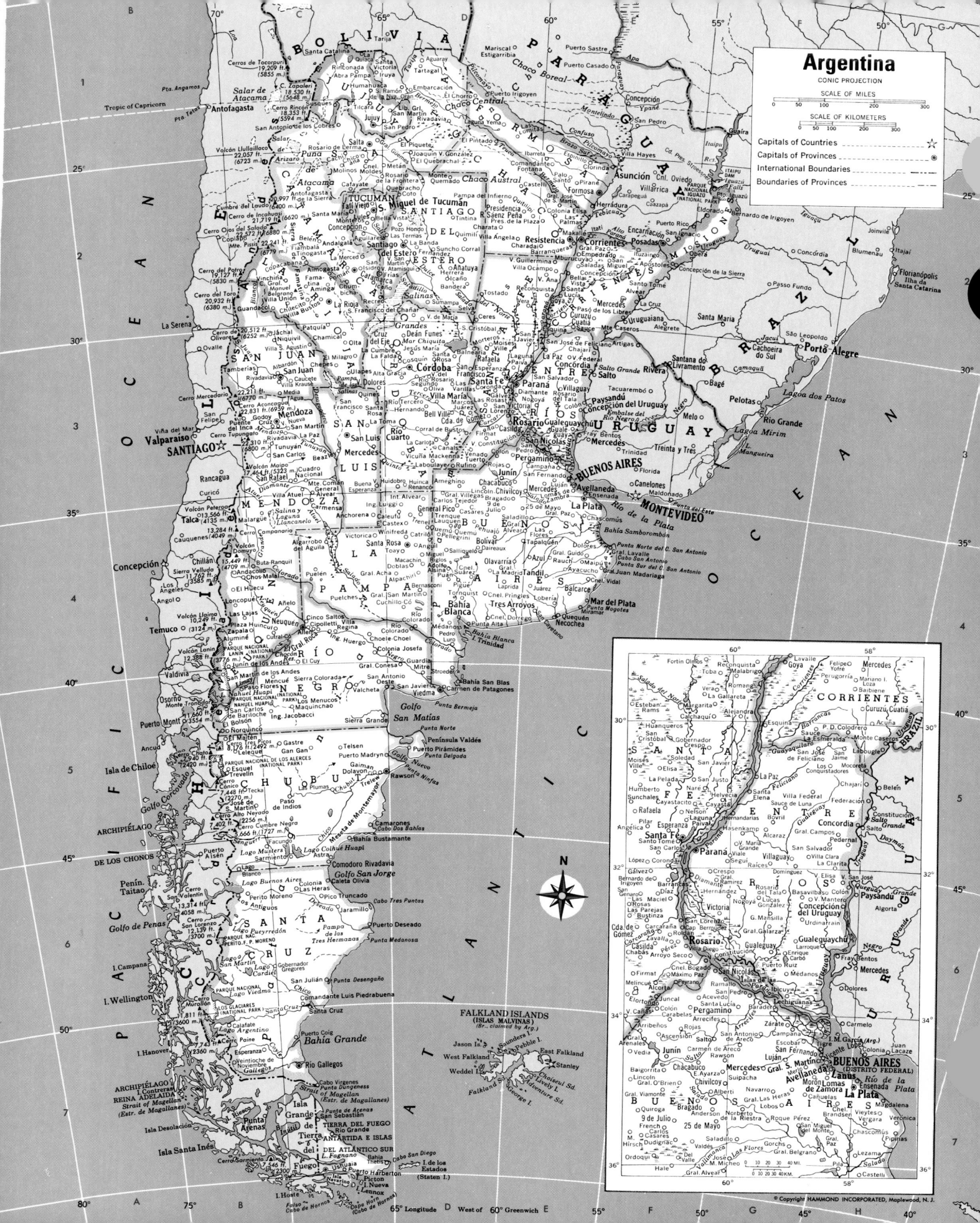

Argentina
CONIC PROJECTION

SCALE OF MILES
0 50 100 200 300

SCALE OF KILOMETERS
0 50 100 200 300

Capitals of Countries .... ☆
Capitals of Provinces .... ◉
International Boundaries ....
Boundaries of Provinces ....

© Copyright HAMMOND INCORPORATED, Maplewood, N.J.

Paraguay

CONIC PROJECTION

SCALE OF MILES
0 20 40 60 80 100 120 140

SCALE OF KILOMETERS
0 20 40 60 80 100 120 140

Capitals of Countries .... ⭐
Capitals of Departments .... ◉
International Boundaries ....
Department Boundaries ....

© Copyright HAMMOND INCORPORATED, Maplewood, N.J.

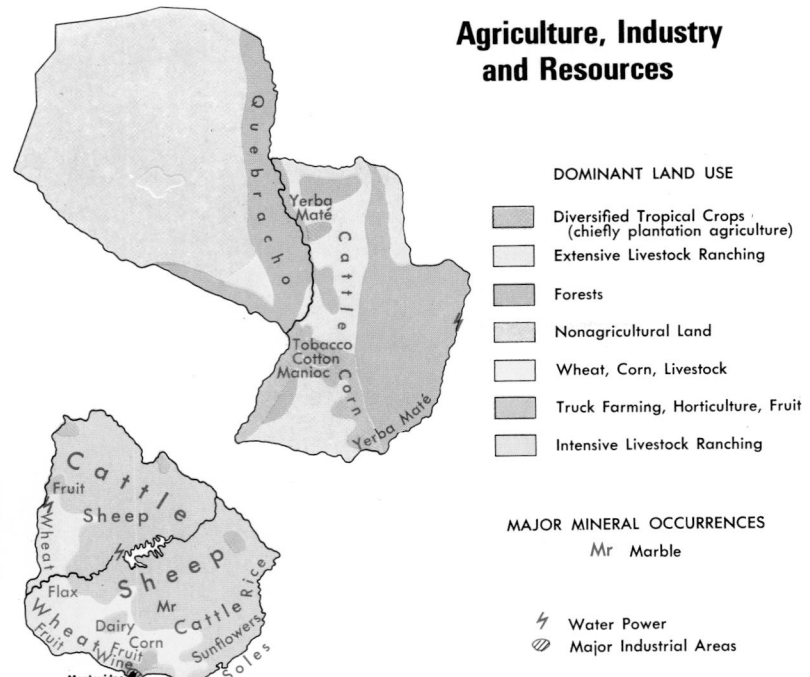

Agriculture, Industry and Resources

DOMINANT LAND USE

- Diversified Tropical Crops (chiefly plantation agriculture)
- Extensive Livestock Ranching
- Forests
- Nonagricultural Land
- Wheat, Corn, Livestock
- Truck Farming, Horticulture, Fruit
- Intensive Livestock Ranching

MAJOR MINERAL OCCURRENCES

Mr Marble

⚡ Water Power
Major Industrial Areas

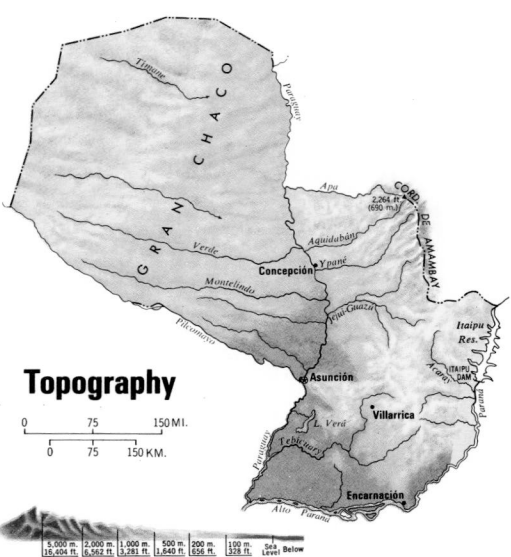

Topography

0 75 150 MI.
0 75 150 KM.

5,000 m. 2,000 m. 1,000 m. 500 m. 200 m. 100 m. Sea Level Below
16,404 ft. 6,562 ft. 3,281 ft. 1,640 ft. 656 ft. 328 ft.

URUGUAY

DEPARTMENTS

Artigas 52,843 ....B1
Canelones 258,195 ....D5
Cerro Largo 71,023 ....E3
Colonia 105,350 ....C5
Durazno 53,635 ....C3
Flores 23,530 ....C4
Florida 63,987 ....D4
Lavalleja 65,823 ....E4
Maldonado 61,259 ....E5
Montevideo 1,202,757 ....B7
Paysandú 88,029 ....B3
Río Negro 46,861 ....B3
Rivera 77,086 ....D2
Rocha 55,097 ....E4
Salto 92,183 ....B2
San José 79,563 ....C5
Soriano 77,906 ....B4
Tacuarembó 76,964 ....D3
Treinta y Tres 43,419 ......E4

CITIES and TOWNS

Aceguá 930 ....E2
Achar 606 ....C3
Agraciada 638 ....A4
Aguas Corrientes 992 .....A6
Aiguá 2,470 ....E5
Algorta 1,372 ....B3
Artigas 29,256 ....C1
Atlántida 2,268 ....B6
Balneario Solís 288 ....B6
Baltasar Brum 1,753 ....B1
Belén 2,129 ....B1
Bella Unión 7,778 ....B1
Bernabé Rivera 540 ....B1
Blanquillo 1,053 ....D3
Cañada Nieto 503 ....B4
Canelones 15,938 ....B6
Cardal 847 ....C4
Cardona 4,126 ....B4
Carlos Reyles 961 ....C3
Carmelo 13,631 ....A4
Carmen 2,318 ....C4
Casupá 2,265 ....D5
Cebollatí 1,233 ....F4
Cerrillos 1,690 ....A6
Cerro Chato,
  Treinta y Tres 1,850 .....D4
Chamizo 486 ....D5
Chuy 4,472 ....F4
Colón, Lavalleja 367 ....E4
Colonia 16,895 ....B5
Colonia Valdense 2,113 ..B5
Conchillas 748 ....B5
Constitución 3,217 ....A2
Costa Azul 453 ....E5
Cufré 430 ....B5
Curtina 723 ....C3
Diez y Nueve (19) de Abril
  308 ....D2
Diez y Ocho (18) de Julio
  742 ....F4
Dolores 12,771 ....A4
Durazno 25,811 ....C4
Egaña 667 ....B6
Empalme Olmos 2,084 ....B6
Estación Atlántida 1,845 .B6
Estación Migues 241 ......C6
Florida 25,030 ....C4
Fraile Muerto 2,468 ....E3
Fray Bentos 19,569 ....A4
Fray Marcos 1,573 ....D5
Garzón 258 ....D5
General Enrique Martínez 973 .F4
Goñi 278 ....C4
Grecco 447 ....B3
Guichón 4,720 ....B3
Ituzaingó 717 ....A6
Javier de Viana 286 ....C1
Joanico 692 ....B6
Joaquín Suárez,
  Canelones 3,517 ....B6
José Batlle y Ordóñez 2,044 ..D4
José Enrique Rodó 1,334 ..C4
José Pedro Varela 3,541 ..E4
Juan L. Lacaze 11,133 ....B5
La Coronilla 571 ....F4
La Cruz 633 ....C4

La Paloma 1,558 ....F5
La Paz, Canelones 14,402 ..B6
Lascano 6,043 ....E4
Las Flores 403 ....D5
Las Piedras 53,983 ....B6
Las Toscas 893 ....E3
Libertad 6,071 ....C5
Lorenzo Geyres 474 ....B3
Mal Abrigo 209 ....C5
Maldonado 22,159 ....D6
Mariscala 1,393 ....E5
Melo 38,260 ....E3
Mercedes 34,667 ....B4
Merinos 403 ....C3
Miguelete 533 ....B5
Migues 2,183 ....C6
Minas 35,433 ....D5
Minas de Corrales 2,518 ..D2
Montes 2,217 ....D5
Montevideo (cap.) 1,173,254. .B7
Nueva Helvecia 8,598 .....B5
Nueva Palmira 6,934 ......A4
Nuevo Berlín 1,970 ....B3
Ombúes de Lavalle 1,689. .B4
Palmitas 1,332 ....B4
Pan de Azúcar 4,862 ....D5
Pando 16,184 ....B6
Paso del Cerro 317 ....C2
Paso de los Toros 13,178 ..C3
Paysandú 62,412 ....A3
Piedras Coloradas 487 ....B3
Piedra Sola 233 ....C3
Piñera 261 ....C3
Piraraja 774 ....D4
Piriápolis 5,221 ....D5
Porvenir 705 ....B3
Progreso 8,257 ....B6
Punta del Este 6,914 ....E6
Quebracho 1,514 ....B2
Reboledo 373 ....D4
Río Branco 5,697 ....F3
Rivera 49,013 ....D1
Rocha 21,612 ....E5
Rodríguez 1,575 ....C5
Rosario 8,302 ....B5
Salto 72,948 ....B2
San Antonio, Canelones
  1,122 ....B6
San Bautista 1,472 ....B6
San Carlos 16,883 ....E5
San Gregorio,
  Tacuarembó 2,892 ....D3
San Jacinto 2,292 ....C6
San Javier 1,583 ....A3
San José de Mayo 28,427. ..C5
San Ramón 6,570 ....D5
Santa Catalina 885 ....B4
Santa Clara de Olimar 2,867 ..D3
Santa Lucía 14,101 ....B6
Santa Rosa 2,736 ....B6
Santiago Vázquez 1,323 ..A7
Sarandí del Yi 6,326 ....D4
Sarandí de Navarro 259 ..C3
Sarandí Grande 5,598 .....C4
Solís 356 ....D5
Solís de Mataojo 1,763 ...D5
Soriano 1,125 ....A4
Tacuarembó 34,152 ....D2
Tala 3,611 ....D5
Tambores 1,534 ....C2
Toledo 3,127 ....B6
Tomás Gomensoro 2,105 .B1
Tranqueras 3,922 ....D2
Treinta y Tres 25,757 ......E4
Trinidad 17,598 ....B4
Tupambaé 1,039 ....E3
Valentines 153 ....E4
Veinticinco (25) de Agosto
  1,891 ....A6
Veinticinco (25) de Mayo
  1,744 ....C5
Velázquez 1,042 ....E5
Vergara 2,822 ....E3
Vichadero 1,989 ....E2
Villa Darwin 507 ....B4
Young 11,080 ....B3
Zapicán 764 ....E4
Zapucay ....

OTHER FEATURES

Arapey Grande (riv.) B2

PARAGUAY

AREA 157,047 sq. mi. (406,752 sq. km.)
POPULATION 4,157,000
CAPITAL Asunción
LARGEST CITY Asunción
HIGHEST POINT Amambay Range
  2,264 ft. (690 m.)
MONETARY UNIT guaraní
MAJOR LANGUAGES Spanish, Guaraní
MAJOR RELIGION Roman Catholicism

Bonete (dam) C3
Brava (pt.) B7
Cañas (range) C2
Caraguatá (riv.) D3
Castillos (lag.) F5
Cebollatí (riv.) F4
Cordobés (riv.) C3
Cuareim (riv.) B1
Cuñapirú, Arroyo (riv.) D2
Daymán (riv.) B2
Durazno, Grande del
  (range) D4
Este (pt.) D6
Grande (range) D4
Haedo (range) C2
India Muerta (riv.) E4
Lobos (isl.) E6
Merín (lag.) F4
Mirador Nacional (mt.) D5
Negra (lag.) B4

Negro (riv.) B4
Negro, Arroyo (riv.) B3
Olimar Grande (riv.) E4
Plata, La (riv.) B5
Polonio (cape) F5
Quequay Grande (riv.) B3
Río Negro (res.) D3
Rocha (lag.) E5
Salto Grande (falls) A2
San José (riv.) C4
San Miguel (swamp) F4
San Salvador (riv.) B4
Santa Ana (range) D2
Santa Lucía (riv.) D5
Santa María (cape) F5
Tacuarembó (riv.) D2
Tacuarí (riv.) E4
Uruguay (riv.) A3
Yaguarón (riv.) F3
Yi (riv.) B4

URUGUAY

AREA 72,172 sq. mi. (186,925 sq. km.)
POPULATION 3,077,000
CAPITAL Montevideo
LARGEST CITY Montevideo
HIGHEST POINT Mirador Nacional 1,644 ft.
  (501 m.)
MONETARY UNIT Uruguayan peso
MAJOR LANGUAGE Spanish
MAJOR RELIGION Roman Catholicism

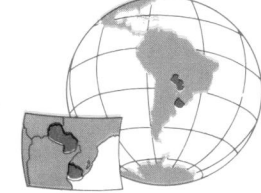

PARAGUAY

URUGUAY

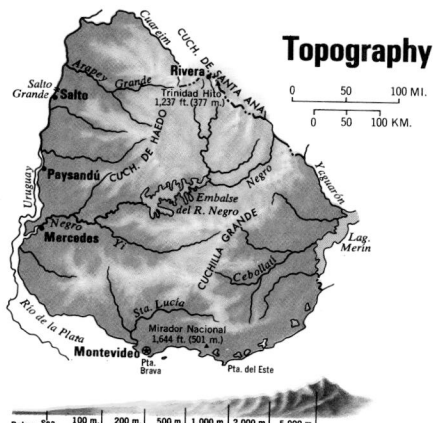

Topography

0   50   100 MI.
0   50   100 KM.

Below Sea Level | 100 m. 328 ft. | 200 m. 656 ft. | 500 m. 1,640 ft. | 1,000 m. 3,281 ft. | 2,000 m. 6,562 ft. | 5,000 m. 16,404 ft.

Uruguay

CONIC PROJECTION

SCALE OF MILES
0   20   40   60
SCALE OF KILOMETERS
0   20   40   60

Capitals of Countries .... ☆
Department Capitals .... ◉
International Boundaries ____ ___
Department Boundaries ____ ___

C Longitude 56° West of D Greenwich 55°

North America

LAMBERT AZIMUTHAL EQUAL-AREA PROJECTION

MILES

0 100 200   400   600   800

KILOMETERS

0 100 200   400   600   800

Capitals of Countries .... ⊛
Other Capitals .... ⊛
International Boundaries .... ___ ___ ___
Other Boundaries .... ___ · ___ · ___

© Copyright HAMMOND INCORPORATED, Maplewood, N. J.

Population Distribution

AREA 9,363,000 sq. mi.
(24,250,170 sq. km.)
POPULATION 427,000,000
LARGEST CITY New York
HIGHEST POINT Mt. McKinley 20,320 ft.
(6,194 m.)
LOWEST POINT Death Valley -282 ft.
(-86 m.)

Vegetation

DENSITY PER

SQ. KILOMETER	SQ. MILE
Over 100	Over 260
50-100	130-260
10-50	25-130
1-10	3-25
Under 1	Under 3

• Cities with over 2,000,000 inhabitants (including suburbs)

MID-LATITUDE FOREST
- Coniferous Forest
- Broadleaf Forest
- Mixed Coniferous and Broadleaf Forest
- Woodland and Shrub (Mediterranean)

MID-LATITUDE GRASSLAND
- Short Grass (Steppe)
- Tall Grass (Prairie)

TROPICAL FOREST
- Tropical Rainforest
- Light Tropical Forest

TROPICAL GRASSLAND
- Wooded Savanna

DESERT AND DESERT SHRUB

TUNDRA AND ALPINE

PERMANENT ICE

Average January Temperature

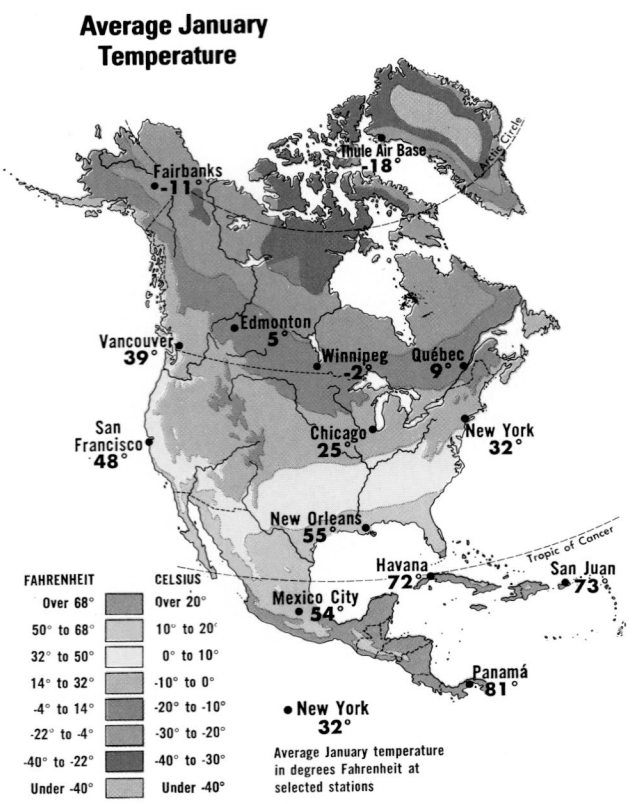

FAHRENHEIT	CELSIUS
Over 68°	Over 20°
50° to 68°	10° to 20°
32° to 50°	0° to 10°
14° to 32°	-10° to 0°
-4° to 14°	-20° to -10°
-22° to -4°	-30° to -20°
-40° to -22°	-40° to -30°
Under -40°	Under -40°

● New York
32°

Average January temperature
in degrees Fahrenheit at
selected stations

Average July Temperature

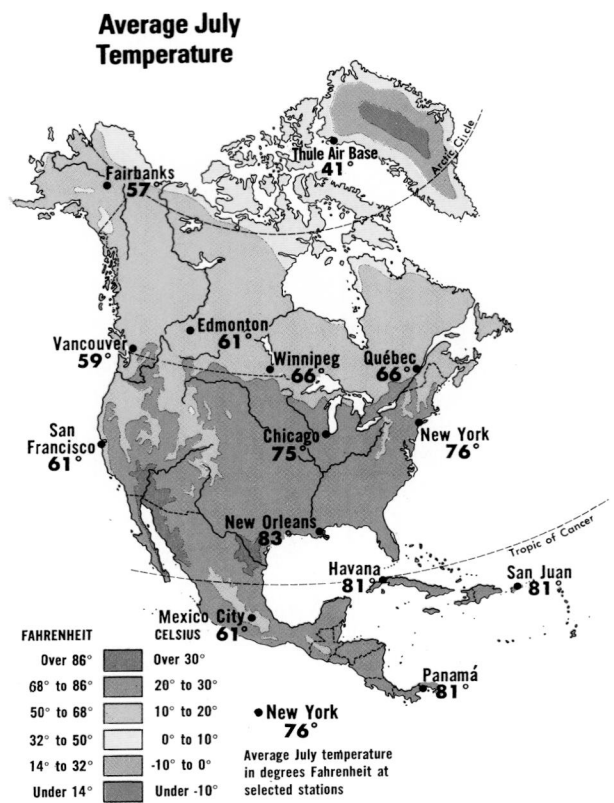

FAHRENHEIT	CELSIUS
Over 86°	Over 30°
68° to 86°	20° to 30°
50° to 68°	10° to 20°
32° to 50°	0° to 10°
14° to 32°	-10° to 0°
Under 14°	Under -10°

● New York
76°

Average July temperature
in degrees Fahrenheit at
selected stations

Rainfall

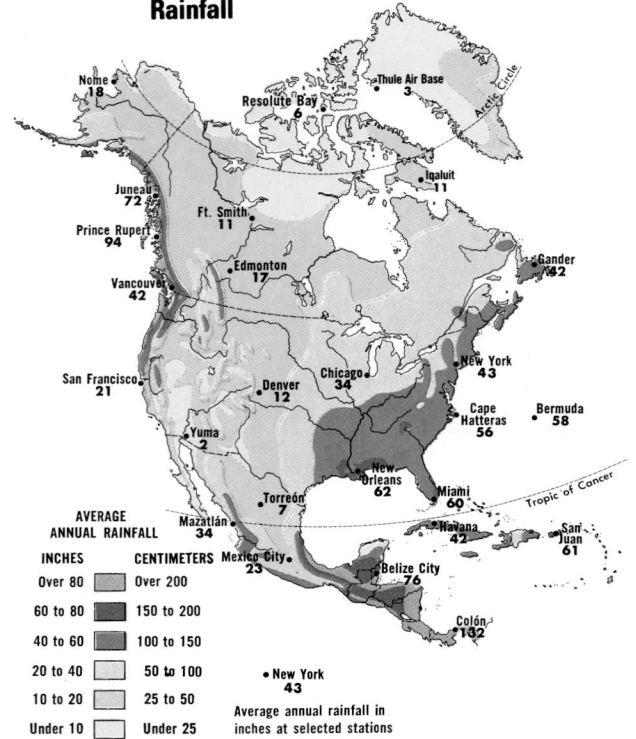

AVERAGE
ANNUAL RAINFALL

INCHES	CENTIMETERS
Over 80	Over 200
60 to 80	150 to 200
40 to 60	100 to 150
20 to 40	50 to 100
10 to 20	25 to 50
Under 10	Under 25

● New York
43

Average annual rainfall in
inches at selected stations

Vegetation/Relief

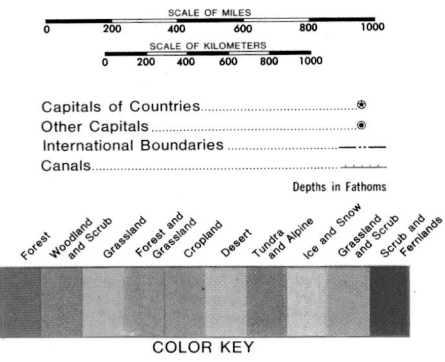

SCALE OF MILES
0   200   400   600   800   1000

SCALE OF KILOMETERS
0   200   400   600   800   1000

Capitals of Countries..................⊕
Other Capitals.............................◉
International Boundaries................— — —
Canals..

Depths in Fathoms

Forest | Woodland and Scrub | Grassland | Forest and Grassland | Cropland | Desert | Tundra and Alpine | Ice and Snow | Grassland and Scrub | Scrub and Fernlands

COLOR KEY

North Pole
EAST SIBERIAN SEA
ARCTIC OCEAN
GREENLAND SEA
RUSSIA
ASIA
BERING SEA
Bering Strait
St. Lawrence I.
Pt. Barrow
BEAUFORT SEA
Queen Elizabeth Islands
GREENLAND (Den.)
ICELAND
Reykjavík
Denmark Strait
Melville I.
Banks I.
Devon I.
Baffin Bay
Victoria I.
Davis Strait
Arctic Circle
Nuuk
C. Farewell
Alaska Pen.
Kodiak I.
Gulf of Alaska
Great Bear L.
Yellowknife
Great Slave L.
L. Athabasca
C. Chidley
Ungava Peninsula
LABRADOR SEA
Alexander Arch.
Prince Rupert
Queen Charlotte Is.
Hudson Bay
CANADA
Laurentian Plateau
Peace
Athabasca
Churchill
Nelson
Newfoundland
Gander
St. John's
C. Race
Vancouver I.
Edmonton
North Saskatchewan
James Bay
Eastmain
Victoria
Vancouver
Calgary
Saskatoon
South
L. Winnipeg
Albany
Gulf of St. Lawrence
Cape Breton I.
Seattle
Regina
Winnipeg
Thunder Bay
Québec
St. John
Halifax
Portland
Missouri
Red
L. Superior
Duluth
Sudbury
Montréal
Ottawa
C. Mendocino
Minneapolis
Mississippi
Huron
Toronto
Boston
C. Cod
Great Salt Lake
Salt Lake City
Great Basin
Snake
North Platte
Milwaukee
L. Michigan
Detroit
Ontario
Buffalo
New York
San Francisco
Omaha
Chicago
L. Erie
Cleveland
Pittsburgh
Philadelphia
Denver
Pikes Peak 14,110 ft. (4301 m.)
Kansas City
Indianapolis
Columbus
Washington
Cincinnati
Ohio
UNITED STATES
St. Louis
Norfolk
Las Vegas
Arkansas
Wichita
Ozark Plateau
C. Hatteras
Colorado
Tulsa
Memphis
Nashville
Mt. Mitchell 6,684 ft. (2037 m.)
Charlotte
Bermuda (U.K.)
Los Angeles
San Diego
Phoenix
Albuquerque
Oklahoma City
Tennessee
Red
Birmingham
Atlanta
Tucson
El Paso
Ciudad Juárez
Fort Worth
Dallas
Lower California
Gulf of California
Jacksonville
San Antonio
Houston
New Orleans
C. Canaveral
Chihuahua
Rio Grande
Tampa
BAHAMAS
Tropic of Cancer
Corpus Christi
Gulf of Mexico
Miami
Nassau
Culiacán
MEXICO
Monterrey
Turks and Caicos Is. (U.K.)
West Indies
C. San Lucas
Havana
CUBA
DOMINICAN REPUBLIC
Tampico
Greater Antilles
Santiago de Cuba
HAITI
Port-au-Prince
Santo Domingo
San Juan
PUERTO RICO
Bay of Campeche
Mérida
Yucatán Pen.
Guadalajara
México City
Popocatépetl 17,887 ft. (5452 m.)
Veracruz
JAMAICA
Kingston
SEA
BELIZE
CARIBBEAN
NETHERLANDS ANTILLES
ARUBA (Neth.)
Curaçao
Bonaire
Willemstad
Acapulco
GUATEMALA
Guatemala
HONDURAS
Tegucigalpa
San Salvador
EL SALVADOR
NICARAGUA
Managua
Caracas
Barranquilla
VENEZUELA
Panama Canal
Panamá
COSTA RICA
San José
PANAMA
SOUTH AMERICA
Bogotá
COLOMBIA
PACIFIC OCEAN
ATLANTIC OCEAN
Longitude 90° West of Greenwich

Topography

0   150   300 MI.

0   150   300 KM.

5,000 m. 2,000 m. 1,000 m. 500 m. 200 m. 100 m. Sea Below
16,404 ft. 6,562 ft. 3,281 ft. 1,640 ft. 656 ft. 328 ft. Level

Monterrey 1,006,221 ....J4	Nuevo Ideal 5,252 ....G4
Morelia 199,099 ....J7	Nuevo Laredo 184,622 ....J3
Moroleón 25,620 ....J6	Oaxaca de Juárez 114,948 ...L8
Motozintla de Mendoza 4,682.N9	Ocampo 4,801 ....K5
Motul de Felipe Carrillo	Ocotlán 35,361 ....K6
Puerto 12,949 ....P6	Ocotlán de Morelos 5,882 ....L8
Muna 5,491 ....P6	Ojinaga 12,757 ....G2
Naica 7,190 ....G2	Ojocaliente 7,582 ....H5
Namiquipa 4,875 ....F2	Ometepec 7,342 ....K8
Nanacamilpa 6,356 ....M1	Oriental 6,009 ....O1
Naranjos 14,732 ....L6	Orizaba 105,150 ....P2
Naucalpan de Juárez 9,425 ...L1	Oxkutzcab 8,182 ....P6
Navojoa 43,817 ....E4	Ozumba de Alzate 6,876 ....M1
Navolato 12,799 ....E4	Pachuca de Soto 83,892 ....K6
Netzahualcóyotl 580,436 ....L1	Padilla 4,581 ....K5
Nochistlán 8,780 ....H6	Palenque 2,595 ....O8
Nogales 14,254 ....E1	Pánuco 14,277 ....P2
Nueva Casas Grandes 20,023..F1	Papantla de Olarte 26,773 ...L6
Nueva Italia de Ruiz 14,718 ...J7	Paraíso 7,561 ....N7
Nueva Rosita 34,706 ....J2	Parral 57,619 ....G3

Parras de la Fuente 18,207 ...H4	
Paso de Ovejas 4,371 ....Q2	
Pátzcuaro 17,299 ....J7	
Pedro Montoya 4,563 ....K6	
Pénjamo 9,245 ....J6	
Pericos 4,445 ....F4	
Perote 12,742 ....O1	
Petatlán 9,419 ....J8	
Peto 8,362 ....P6	
Pichucalco 4,615 ....N8	
Piedras Negras, Coahuila	
41,033 ....J2	
Piedras Negras, Veracruz	
4,099 ....Q2	
Pijijiapan 5,053 ....N9	
Poza Rica de Hidalgo	
152,276 ....L6	
Profesor Rafael Ramírez	
5,338 ....O1	
Progreso 17,518 ....P6	

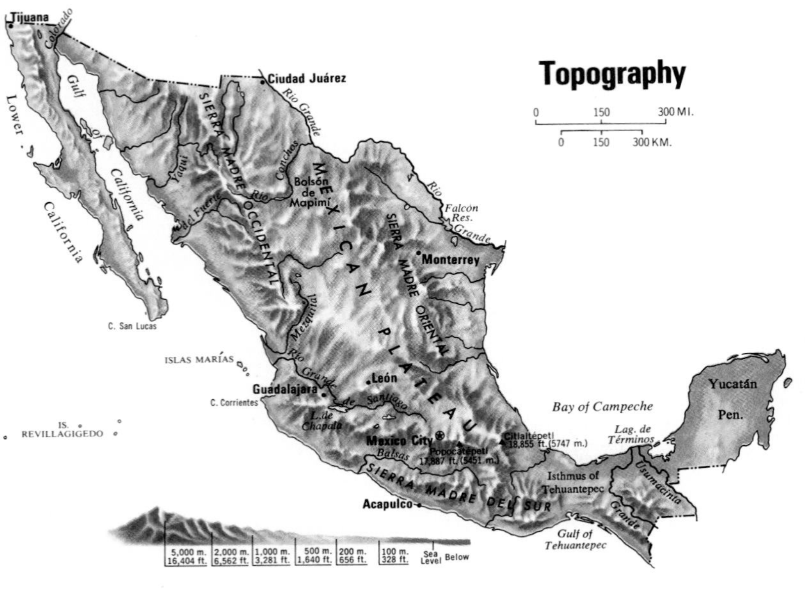

STATES

Aguascalientes 504,300.....H6	Azcapotzalco 534,554 ....L1
Baja California 1,227,400.....B1	Bamoa 5,866 ....E4
Baja California Sur 221,000...C3	Benjamín Hill 5,366 ....D1
Campeche 371,800.........O7	Bernardino de Sahagún
Chiapas 2,097,500.........N8	12,327 ....M1
Chihuahua 1,935,100.......H3	Cabo San Lucas 1,534 ....E5
Coahuila 1,561,000.........G7	Cacahoatán 5,079 ....N9
Colima 339,400 ....L1	Cadereyta Jiménez 13,586...K4
Distrito Federal 9,377,300....L1	Calkiní 6,870 ....O6
Durango 1,160,300.........J6	Calpulálpan 8,659 ....M1
Guanajuato 3,045,600......J6	Calvillo 6,453 ....H6
Guerrero 2,174,200.........J8	Campeche 69,506 ....O7
Hidalgo 1,518,200.........K6	Cananea 17,518 ....D1
Jalisco 4,296,500 ....H6	Canatlán 5,983 ....G4
México 7,542,300 ....K7	Cancún 326 ....Q6
Michoacán 3,049,400.......H7	Cañitas de Felipe Pescador
Morelos 931,400 ....K7	4,885 ....H5
Nayarit 729,500 ....G6	Capulhuac de Mirafuentes
Nuevo León 2,463,500.......K4	8,289 ....K1
Oaxaca 2,517,500..........L8	Cárdenas, San Luis Potosí
Puebla 3,285,300..........L7	12,020 ....K6
Querétaro 730,900.........J6	Cárdenas, Tabasco 15,643 ...N8
Quintana Roo 209,900......P7	Castaños 8,996 ....J3
San Luis Potosí 1,669,900....J5	Catemaco 11,786 ....M7
Sinaloa 1,882,200.........F4	Celaya 79,977 ....J6
Sonora 1,498,100..........D2	Cerritos 10,421 ....J5
Tabasco 1,150,000.........N7	Cerro Azul 20,259 ....L6
Tamaulipas 1,924,900......K4	Chahuites 5,218 ....M8
Tlaxcala 548,500 ....N1	Chalco de Díaz Covarrubias
Veracruz 5,263,800........L7	12,172 ....M1
Yucatán 1,034,300.........P6	Champotón 6,606 ....O7
Zacatecas 1,144,700.......H5	Charcas 10,491 ....J5
	Chetumal 23,685 ....P7
### CITIES and TOWNS	Chiapa de Corzo 8,571 ....N8
	Chiautempan 12,327 ....N1
Acala 11,483..............N8	Chietla 4,602 ....M2
Acámbaro 32,257..........J7	Chihuahua 327,313 ....H3
Acaponeta 11,844..........G5	Chilapa de Álvarez 9,204 .....K8
Acapulco de Juárez 309,254..K8	Chilpancingo de los Bravos
Acatlán de Osorio 7,624......K7	36,193 ....K8
Acatzingo de Hidalgo 6,905...N7	China, Nuevo León 4,958......K4
Acayucan 21,173...........M8	Chocomán 5,114 ....P2
Actopan 11,037............K6	Cholula de Rivadavia 15,399..M1
Agua Dulce 21,060.........M7	Cihuatlán 9,451 ....G7
Agua Prieta 20,754.........E1	Cintalapa de Figueroa 12,036.N8
Aguascalientes 181,277......H6	Ciudad Acuña (Villa Acuña)
Aguililla 5,715.............H7	30,276 ....J2
Ahuacatitlán 6,436.........L1	Ciudad Altamirano 8,694......J7
Ahuacatlán 5,350..........G6	Ciudad Camargo, Chihuahua
Ahumada 6,466............F1	24,030 ....G3
Ajalpan 8,238.............N7	Ciudad Camargo, Tamaulipas
Alamo 9,954..............L6	5,953 ....K3
Aldama 6,047.............J6	Ciudad de Río Grande 11,651.H5
Allende, Coahuila 11,076.....J2	Ciudad del Carmen 34,656 ...N7
Allende, Nuevo León 9,914 ...J4	Ciudad del Maíz 5,241 ....K5
Altamira 6,053.............L5	Ciudad Delicias 52,446 ....G2
Altepexi 6,661............L7	Ciudad Guzmán 48,166 ....H7
Altotonga 6,754...........P1	Ciudad Hidalgo, Chiapas
Alvarado 15,792...........M7	4,105 ....N9
Ameca 21,018.............H6	Ciudad Hidalgo, Michoacán
Amecameca de Juárez	24,692 ....J7
16,276................L1	Ciudad Juárez 424,135........F1
Amozoc de Mota 9,203.......N2	Ciudad Lerdo 19,803..........H4
Anáhuac, Chihuahua 10,886...F2	Ciudad Madero 115,302.......L5
Anáhuac, Nuevo León 8,168 ..J3	Ciudad Mante 51,247.........K5
Apan 13,705..............M1	Ciudad Mendoza 18,696......O2
Apatzingán de la Constitución	Ciudad Miguel Alemán
44,849................J7	11,259 ....K3
Apizaco 21,189............N1	Ciudad Obregón 144,795.....E3
Arandas 18,934............J6	Ciudad Río Bravo 19,803......K4
Arcelia 10,024............J7	Ciudad Satélite 35,083 ....L1
Ario de Rosales 8,774........G7	Ciudad Serdán 9,581 ....O2
Armería 10,616............G7	Ciudad Valles 47,587 ....K5
Arriaga 13,193............N8	Ciudad Victoria 83,897 ....K5
Arteaga 5,324.............H7	Coalcomán de Matamoros
Atlixco 41,967.............M2	4,875 ....H7
Atotonilco el Alto 16,271......H6	Coatepec 21,542 ....L2
Atoyac de Álvarez 8,874......J8	Coatetelco 5,268 ....L2
Autlán de Navarro 20,308.....G7	Coatzacoalcos 69,753 ....M7
Axochiapan 8,283..........M2	Cocorit 4,478 ....E3
	Colima 58,450 ....H7
	Colotlán 6,135 ....H5

Comala 5,592 ....H7	Huejutla 6,854 ....K6
Comalcalco 14,963 ....N7	Huetamo 9,333 ....J7
Comitán de Domínguez	Huimanguillo 7,075 ....N8
21,249 ....O8	Huitzuco de los Figueroa
Compostela 9,801 ....G6	9,406 ....K7
Concepción del Oro 8,144 ....J4	Huixtepec 5,927 ....L8
Contla 7,517 ....N1	Huixtla 15,737 ....N9
Coquimatlán 6,212 ....G7	Hunucmá 8,020 ....O6
Córdoba 78,495 ....P2	Iguala de la Independencia
Cosamaloapan de Carpio	45,355 ....K7
19,766 ....M7	Irapuato 135,596 ....J6
Coscomatepec de Bravo	Isla, Veracruz 8,075 ....M7
6,023 ....P2	Isla Mujeres 2,663 ....Q6
Costa Rica 11,795 ....F4	Ixmiquilpan 6,048 ....K6
Cotija de la Paz 9,178 ....H7	Ixtapa J8
Coyoacán 339,446 ....L1	Ixtapalapa 522,095............L1
Coyotepec 8,888 ....L1	Ixtenco 5,035 ....N1
Coyuca de Benítez 6,328 .....J8	Ixtepec 14,025 ....M8
Cozumel 5,858 ....Q6	Ixtlán del Río 10,986 ....G6
Cuatrociénegas de Carranza	Izamal 9,749 ....P6
5,523 ....H3	Izúcar de Matamoros 21,164..M2
Cuauhtémoc 26,598 ....J7	Jala 4,535 ....G6
Cuautepec de Hinojosa 5,501..K6	Jalapa Enríquez 161,352......P1
Cuautitlán de Romero Rubio	Jalpa 9,904 ....H6
11,439 ....L1	Jalpa de Méndez 4,831 ....N7
Cuautla Morelos 13,946 ......L2	Jáltipan de Morelos 15,170...M8
Cuernavaca 239,813 ....L2	Jerez de García Salinas
Cuitláhuac 4,813 ....P2	20,325 ....H5
Culiacán 228,001 ....F4	Jico 7,269 ....P1
Dolores Hidalgo de la	Jiménez, Chihuahua 18,095...G3
Independencia Naci 16,849..J6	Jojutla de Juárez 14,438 .....L2
Durango 182,633 ....G4	José Cardel 5,396 ....Q1
Dzidzantún 7,064 ....P6	Juan Aldama 9,667 ....H4
Dzitbalché 4,393 ....P6	Juchipila 6,328 ....H6
Ebano 17,492 ....K5	Juchitán de Zaragoza 30,218.M8
Ecatepec de Morelos 11,899..L1	La Barca 18,055 ....H6
Ejutla de Crespo 5,263 ....L8	Lagos de Moreno 33,782 .....J6
Eldorado 8,115 ....F4	La Paz 46,011 ....D5
El Fuerte 7,179 ....E3	La Piedad Cavadas 34,963....H6
El Salto 7,818 ....G5	Las Choapas 20,166 ....M7
Empalme 24,927 ....D2	Las Rosas 7,658 ....N8
Encarnación de Díaz 10,474...H6	León 468,887 ....J6
Ensenada 77,687 ....A1	Lerdo de Tejada 11,628 ......M8
Escárcega 7,248 ....O7	Libres 4,830 ....O1
Escuinapa de Hidalgo 16,442.G5	Linares 24,456 ....K4
Escuintla 4,111 ....N9	Loma Bonita 15,804............M7
Esperanza, Sonora 11,762 ...E3	Loreto 7,132 ....J5
Espita 5,394 ....Q6	Los Mochis 67,953 ....E4
Fortín de las Flores 9,358 ....P2	Los Reyes de Salgado
Francisco I. Madero 12,613...H4	19,452 ....H7
Fresnillo de González	Macuspana 12,293 ....N8
Echeverría 44,475...........H5	Madera 9,759 ....F2
Frontera 10,066 ....N7	Magdalena de Kino 10,281 ...D1
General Terán 5,354 ....K4	Maltrata 5,457 ....O2
Gómez Palacio 79,650........G4	Manzanillo 20,777 ....G7
González 6,440 ....K5	Mapastepec 5,907 ....N9
Guadalajara 1,478,383........H6	Martínez de la Torre 17,203...L6
Guadalupe, Nuevo León	Mascota 5,674 ....G6
51,899 ....J4	Matamoros, Coahuila 15,125.H4
Guadalupe, Zacatecas 13,246.H5	Matamoros, Tamaulipas
Guadalupe Victoria, Durango	165,124 ....L4
7,933 ....G4	Matehuala 28,799 ....J5
Guamúchil 17,151............E4	Matías Romero 13,200........M8
Guanajuato 36,809 ....J6	Maxcanú 6,505 ....O6
Guasave 26,080 ....E4	Mazatlán 147,010............F5
Guaymas 87,492 ....D2	Melchor Múzquiz 18,868 .....H3
Gustavo Díaz Ordaz 10,154...K3	Melchor Ocampo del Balsas
Gutiérrez Zamora 9,099 ......L6	4,766 ....H8
Halachó 4,804 ....O6	Meoquí 12,308 ....G2
Hermosillo 232,691 ....D2	Mérida 233,912 ....P6
Heroica Caborca 20,771 ......C1	Metepec 4,625 ....M2
Heroica Nogales 52,108 ......D1	Mexicali 317,228 ....B1
Hidalgo del Parral (Parral)	Mexico City (cap.) 9,377,300..L1
57,619 ....G3	Miahuatlán de Porfirio Díaz
Huachinango 16,826............K7	5,714 ....L8
Huajuapan de León 13,822 ...L8	Mier 5,636 ....K3
Huamantla 15,565 ....N1	Miguel Auza 9,303 ....H4
Huatabampo 18,799 ....D3	Minatitlán 68,397 ....M8
Huatusco de Chicuellar 9,501.P2	Mineral del Monte 8,887 .....K6
Huauchinango 16,826..........L6	Misantla 8,799 ....P1
Huautla de Jiménez 6,132 ....L7	Monclova 78,134 ....J3
Huejotzingo 8,552 ....M1	Montemorelos 18,642 ....K4

Mexico

CONIC PROJECTION

SCALE OF MILES

0   100   200

SCALE OF KILOMETERS

0   100   200

National Capitals ....★   State Capitals ....⊙

International Boundaries ....–··–   State Boundaries ....·—·—

© Copyright HAMMOND INCORPORATED, Maplewood, N.J.

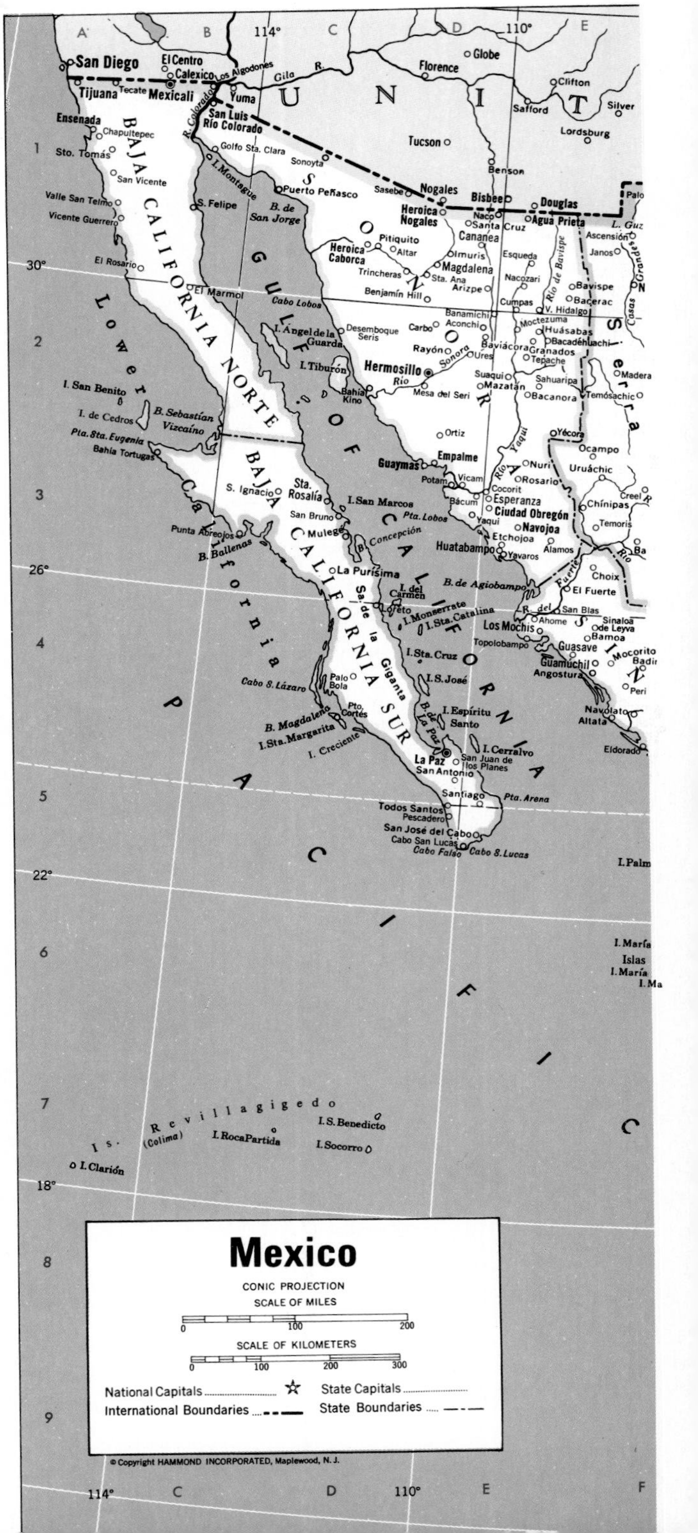

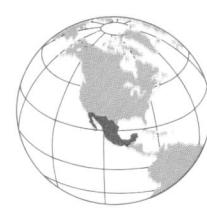

AREA 761,601 sq. mi. (1,972,546 sq. km.)
POPULATION 86,154,000
CAPITAL Mexico City
LARGEST CITY Mexico City
HIGHEST POINT Citlaltépetl 18,855 ft.
  (5,747 m.)
MONETARY UNIT Mexican peso
MAJOR LANGUAGE Spanish
MAJOR RELIGION Roman Catholicism

States Indicated by Numbers
1 Tlaxcala
2 Morelos
3 Distrito Federal
4 México
5 Hidalgo
6 Querétaro
7 Guanajuato
8 Aguascalientes
9 Nayarit
10 Colima

San Luis de la Paz 12,654 ....J6
San Luis Potosí 271,123 ......J5
San Luis Río Colorado
  49,990 ....B1
San Marcos 5,861 ....K8
San Martín de las Pirámides
  4,575 ....M1
San Martín Texmelucan
  23,355 ....M1
San Miguel de Allende 24,286 .J6
San Nicolás de los Garza
  28,803 ....J3
San Pedro de las Colonias
  26,882 ....H4
San Rafael 8,974 ....M1
San Salvador el Seco 7,729 ....O1
Santa Ana 7,020 ....D1
Santa Ana Chiautempan
  (Chiautempan) 12,327 ....N1
Santa Bárbara 16,978 ....F3
Santa María del Río 4,972 .....J6
Santa Rosalía 7,356 ....C3
Santiago Ixcuintla 17,321 .....G6
Santiago Jamiltepec 5,280 .....K8
Santiago Miahuatlán 4,917 .....O2
Santiago Papasquiaro 6,636 ...F4
Santiago Pinotepa Nacional
  9,382 ....K8
Santiago Tuxtla 9,426 ....M7
Saucillo 8,467 ....G2
Sayula 14,339 ....H7
Sayula de Alemán 4,896 ....M8
Silao 31,825 ....J6
Soledad de Doblado 6,612 ......O2
Soledad Díez Gutiérrez 9,622 ..J5
Sombrerete 11,077 ....H5
Tacámbaro de Codallos 9,695 .J7
Tala 15,744 ....H6
Tamazunchale 12,302 ....K6
Tamiahua 6,264 ....L6
Tampico 212,188 ....L5
Tamuín 7,251 ....L6
Tantoyuca 11,902 ....N9
Tapachula 60,620 ....M9
Taxco de Alarcón 27,089 ....K8
Teapa 6,534 ....N8
Tecate 14,738 ....H7
Tecomán 31,625 ....H7
Tecpan de Galeana 8,095 ....J8
Tecuala 12,461 ....G5
Tehuacán 47,497 ....L7
Tehuantepec 16,179 ....M8
Tekax de Alvaro Obregón
  10,326 ....P6
Teloloapan 10,335 ....J7
Temax 4,915 ....P6
Tenancingo de Degollado
  12,807 ....K7
Tenango de Río Blanco
  12,302 ....O2
Tenosique de Pino Suárez
  11,393 ....O8
Teocaltiche 13,745 ....H6

Teocelo 4,572 ....P1
Teotihuacán de Arista 2,238 ...L1
Tepalcingo 5,968 ....M2
Tepatitlán de Morelos 29,292 .H6
Tepatlaxco de Hidalgo 8,833 ..N2
Tepeaca 7,466 ....M1
Tepeapulco 7,027 ....M1
Tepeji del Río 10,365 ....L1
Tepic 108,924 ....G6
Tepoztlán 6,851 ....M1
Tequixquitla 4,825 ....O1
Terán 5,215 ....N8
Texcoco de Mora 18,044 ....L1
Teziutlán 23,948 ....O1
Ticul 14,341 ....P6
Tierra Blanca 22,727 ....L7
Tijuana 363,154 ....A1
Tixtla de Guerrero 10,334 ......K8
Tizayuca 6,262 ....L1
Tizimín 18,343 ....Q6
Tlacolula de Matamoros
  8,300 ....L8
Tlahualilo de Zaragoza 8,951 ..H3
Tlalancaneca 5,090 ....M1
Tlalmanalco de Velásquez
  5,744 ....L1
Tlalnepantla de Comonfort
  45,575 ....L1
Tlalpan 130,719 ....L1
Tlaltenango de Sánchez
  Román 7,698 ....H6
Tlaltizapán 6,384 ....L2
Tlapacoyan 13,172 ....P1
Tlapa de Comonfort 6,676 ......K8
Tlaquepaque 59,760 ....G6
Tlaquiltenango 8,625 ....L2
Tlaxcala de Xicotencatl 9,972 .M1
Tlaxco 4,969 ....N1
Toluca de Lerdo 136,092 ....K7
Tonalá 15,611 ....N8
Topolobampo 4,685 ....E4
Torreón 244,309 ....H4
Tula, Tamaulipas 5,407 ....K5
Tula de Allende 10,720 ....K6
Tulancingo 35,799 ....L1
Tultepec 8,321 ....L1
Tuxpan, Nayarit 20,322 ....G6
Tuxpan, Jalisco 14,693 ....L7
Tuxpan de Rodríguez Cano
  33,901 ....L6
Tuxtepec 17,701 ....L7
Tuxtla Gutiérrez 66,851 ....N8
Tzucabab 4,876 ....P7
Umán 8,371 ....P6
Unión de Tula 6,399 ....G7
Unión Hidalgo 8,658 ....O8
Uruapan del Progreso
  108,124 ....H7
Valladolid 14,663 ....P6
Valle de Allende 4,973 ....G3
Valle de Bravo 7,628 ....J7
Villahermosa 133,181 ....N8
Villanueva 5,895 ....H5
Villa Unión, Sinaloa 6,789 .....F5

Veracruz 255,646 ....Q1
Vicente Guerrero, Durango
  8,451 ....G5
Victor Rosales 7,629 ....H5
Villa Acuña 30,276 ....J2
Villa Cuauhtémoc 6,611 ....L5
Villa de Guadalupe Hidalgo
  88,537 ....L1
Villa Frontera 25,761 ....J3
Villahermosa 133,181 ....N8
Villanueva 5,895 ....H5
Villa Unión, Sinaloa 6,789 .....F5

Villa Vicente Guerrero 18,280 .N1
Xicoténcatl 6,374 ....K5
Xicotepec de Juárez 12,656 ....L6
Xochimilco 116,493 ....L1
Yaqui 8,061 ....D3
Yautepec 13,952 ....L2
Zacahila 7,270 ....L8
Zacapoaxtla 4,527 ....O1
Zacapu 31,989 ....J7
Zacatecas 50,251 ....H5
Zacatelco 14,117 ....N1
Zacatepec 16,839 ....L8

Zacatlán 7,909 ....N1
Zacoalco de Torres 11,343 .....H6
Zamora de Hidalgo 5,775 ......H7
Zaragoza, Coahuila 6,797 ......J2
Zaragoza, Puebla 4,754 ....O1
Zempoala 5,064 ....L1
Zihuatanejo 4,879 ....J8
Zimatlán de Álvarez 5,746 .....L8
Zitácuaro 36,911 ....J7
Zumpango de Ocampo
  12,923 ....L1
Zumpango del Río 8,162 ....J8

OTHER FEATURES

Agiobampo (bay) E3
Aguanaval (riv.) H4
Alacrán (reef) P5
Amistad (res.) J1
Angel de la Guarda (isl.) C2
Antigua (riv.) Q1
Arcas (cay) N6
Arena (pt.) J4
Arenas (cay) O5
Atoyac (riv.) K8
Atoyac (riv.) J7
Babia (riv.) J2
Bacalar (lake) P7
Ballenas (bay) C3
Balsas (riv.) J7
Banderas (bay) G6
Bavispe, Río de (riv.) E1
Blanco (riv.) G2
Bravo (Grande) (riv.) G2
Burro (mts.) J2
California (gulf) D2
Campeche (bank) O6
Campeche (bay) N7
Candelaria (riv.) O8
Carmen (isl.) D3
Carranza, Venustiano (res.) J3
Casas Grandes (riv.) F1
Catoche (cape) Q6
Cedros (isl.) B2
Cerralvo (isl.) E4
Chamela (bay) G7
Chapala (lake) H6
Chetumal (bay) P8
Chichén-Itzá (ruin) P6
Citlaltépetl (mt.) O2
Clarión (isl.) B7
Colorado (riv.) B1
Concepción (bay) D3
Conchos (riv.) G2
Corrientes (cape) F6
Coyuca (riv.) O1
Cozumel (isl.) Q6
Creciente (isl.) D5
Cuitzeo (lake) J7
Delgada (pt.) L7
Dzibichaltún (ruin) P6
El Azúcar (res.) K3
El Chichón (vol.) N8
Espíritu Santo (isl.) D4
Falcón (res.) K3
Falso (cape) D5
Fuerte (riv.) E3
Gigante, Sierra de la (mts.) D4
Grande (Bravo) (riv.) G2
Grande de Santiago (riv.) G6
Grijalva (riv.) N7
Guzmán (lake) F1
Herrero (pt.) P7
Hondo (riv.) P7
Jesús María (reef) L4
La Boquilla (res.) G3
Lacantum (riv.) O8
La Paz (bay) D4
Lobos (cape) C2
Lobos (pt.) D3
Lower California (pen.) C3
Madre (riv.) E3
Madre del Sur, Sierra (mts.) K8
Madre Occidental, Sierra
  (mts.) F3
Madre Oriental, Sierra
  (mts.) J4
Magdalena (bay) C4

Maldonado (pt.) K8
Mapimí (depr.) G3
María Cleófas (isl.) F6
María Madre (isl.) F6
María Magdalena (isl.) F6
Marías, Islas (isls.) F6
Mar Muerto (lag.) N9
Mexico (gulf) N4
Mezcala (riv.) J8
Mezquital (riv.) G5
Mita (isl.) G6
Mitla (ruin) M8
Moctezuma (riv.) K6
Monserrate (isl.) D4
Montague (isl.) B1
Muerto, Mar (lag.) N9
Nauhcampatépetl (mt.) O1
Nayarit, Sierra (mts.) G5
Nazas (riv.) G4
Nohkú (pt.) Q7
Nuevo, Bajo (reef) O6
Orizaba (Citlaltépetl) (mt.) O2
Palenque (ruin) O8
Palmito de la Virgen (isl.) F5
Palmito del Verde (isl.) F5
Pánuco (riv.) K5
Paricutín (vol.) H7
Pátzcuaro (lake) J7
Pérez (isl.) P5
Petacalco (bay) H8
Popocatépetl (mt.) M1
Ramos (riv.) G4
Revillagigedo (isls.) C7
Roca Partida (isl.) C7
Rojo (cape) L6
Sabinas (riv.) J3
San Antonio (reef) L4
San Benedicto (isl.) D7
San Benito (isl.) B2
San Jorge (bay) C1
San José (isl.) D4
San Lázaro (cape) C4
San Lucas (cape) E5
San Marcos (isl.) D3
San Rafael (reef) L4
Santa Ana (reef) N7
Santa Catalina (isl.) D4
Santa Cruz (isl.) D4
Santa Eugenia (pt.) B3
Santa Margarita (isl.) C4
Santa María (lake) F1
Santa María (riv.) F1
Santiaguillo (lake) G4
Sebastián Vizcaíno (bay) B2
Socorro (isl.) D7
Sonora (riv.) D2
Superior (lag.) M9
Teacapán (riv.) F5
Tehuantepec (isth.) M8
Tehuantepec (gulf) M9
Teotihuacán (ruin) M1
Términos (lag.) O7
Tiburón (isl.) C2
Triángulo Este (isl.) N6
Triángulo Oeste (isl.) N6
Tula (riv.) L1
Tula (riv.) F3
Usumacinta (riv.) O8
Uxmal (ruin) P6
Valsequillo (res.) N2
Venustiano Carranza (res.) J3
Verde (riv.) F3
Verde (riv.) L8
Yaqui (riv.) E2
Yucatán (pen.) P7

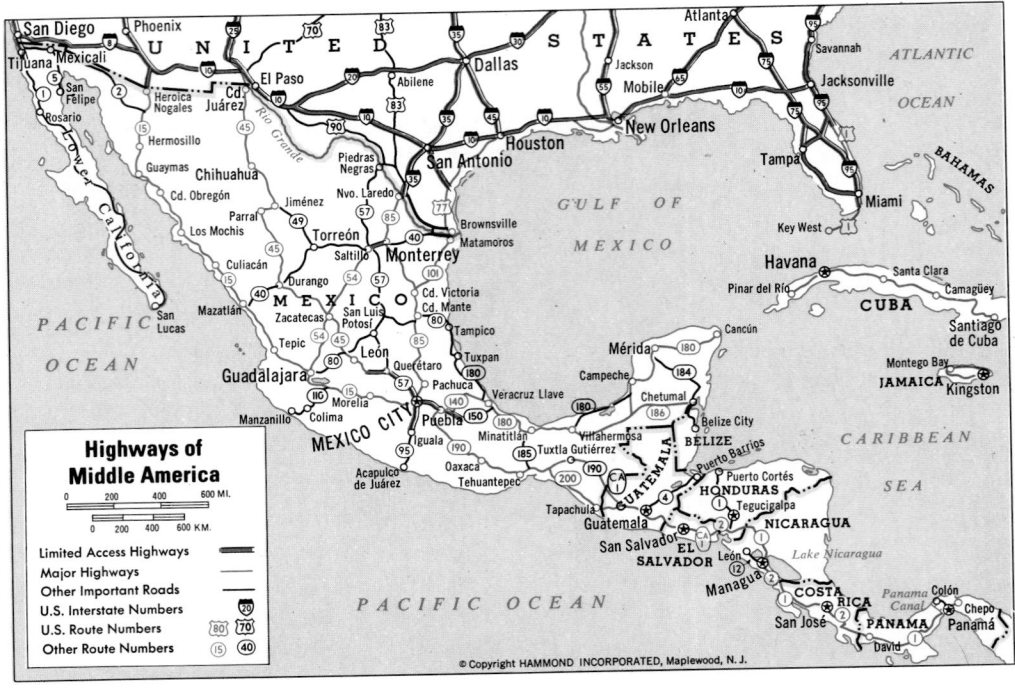

Highways of Middle America

0   200   400   600 MI.
0 200 400 600 K.M.

Limited Access Highways
Major Highways
Other Important Roads
U.S. Interstate Numbers   [20]
U.S. Route Numbers   [80] [70]
Other Route Numbers   [15] [40]

© Copyright HAMMOND INCORPORATED, Maplewood, N.J.

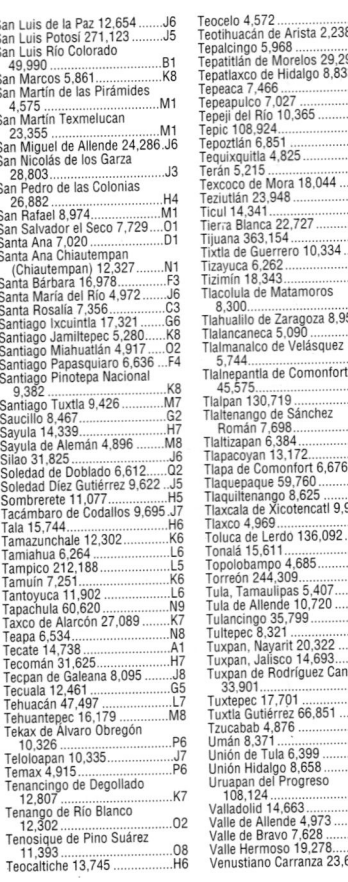

Agriculture, Industry and Resources

DOMINANT LAND USE

Wheat, Livestock
Cereals (chiefly corn), Livestock
Diversified Tropical Cash Crops
Cotton, Mixed Cereals
Livestock, Limited Agriculture
Range Livestock
Forests
Nonagricultural Land

Water Power
Major Industrial Areas

MAJOR MINERAL OCCURRENCES

Ag	Silver	G	Natural Gas	O	Petroleum
Au	Gold	Gr	Graphite	Pb	Lead
C	Coal	Hg	Mercury	S	Sulfur
Cu	Copper	Mn	Manganese	Sb	Antimony
F	Fluorspar	Mo	Molybdenum	Sn	Tin
Fe	Iron Ore	Na	Salt	W	Tungsten
				Zn	Zinc

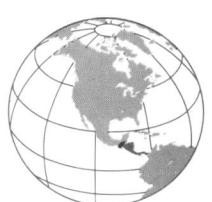

GUATEMALA
AREA 42,042 sq. mi. (108,889 sq. km.)
POPULATION 9,197,000
CAPITAL Guatemala
LARGEST CITY Guatemala
HIGHEST POINT Tajumulco 13,845 ft.
(4,220 m.)
MONETARY UNIT quetzal
MAJOR LANGUAGES Spanish, Quiché
MAJOR RELIGION Roman Catholicism

BELIZE
AREA 8,867 sq. mi. (22,966 sq. km.)
POPULATION 180,000
CAPITAL Belmopan
LARGEST CITY Belize City
HIGHEST POINT Victoria Peak 3,681 ft. (1,122 m.)
MONETARY UNIT Belize dollar
MAJOR LANGUAGES English, Spanish, Mayan
MAJOR RELIGIONS Roman Catholicism, Protestantism

EL SALVADOR
AREA 8,260 sq. mi. (21,393 sq. km.)
POPULATION 5,207,000
CAPITAL San Salvador
LARGEST CITY San Salvador
HIGHEST POINT Santa Ana 7,825 ft.
(2,385 m.)
MONETARY UNIT colón
MAJOR LANGUAGE Spanish
MAJOR RELIGION Roman Catholicism

HONDURAS
AREA 43,277 sq. mi. (112,087 sq. km.)
POPULATION 4,951,000
CAPITAL Tegucigalpa
LARGEST CITY Tegucigalpa
HIGHEST POINT Las Minas 9,347 ft.
(2,849 m.)
MONETARY UNIT lempira
MAJOR LANGUAGE Spanish
MAJOR RELIGION Roman Catholicism

NICARAGUA
AREA 45,698 sq. mi. (118,358 sq. km.)
POPULATION 3,384,000
CAPITAL Managua
LARGEST CITY Managua
HIGHEST POINT Cerro Mocotón 6,913 ft.
(2,107 m.)
MONETARY UNIT córdoba
MAJOR LANGUAGE Spanish
MAJOR RELIGION Roman Catholicism

COSTA RICA
AREA 19,575 sq. mi. (50,700 sq. km.)
POPULATION 2,959,000
CAPITAL San José
LARGEST CITY San José
HIGHEST POINT Chirripó Grande
12,530 ft. (3,819 m.)
MONETARY UNIT colón
MAJOR LANGUAGE Spanish
MAJOR RELIGION Roman Catholicism

PANAMA
AREA 29,761 sq. mi. (77,082 sq. km.)
POPULATION 2,418,000
CAPITAL Panamá
LARGEST CITY Panamá
HIGHEST POINT Vol. Baru 11,401 ft.
(3,475 m.)
MONETARY UNIT balboa
MAJOR LANGUAGE Spanish
MAJOR RELIGION Roman Catholicism

Agriculture, Industry and Resources

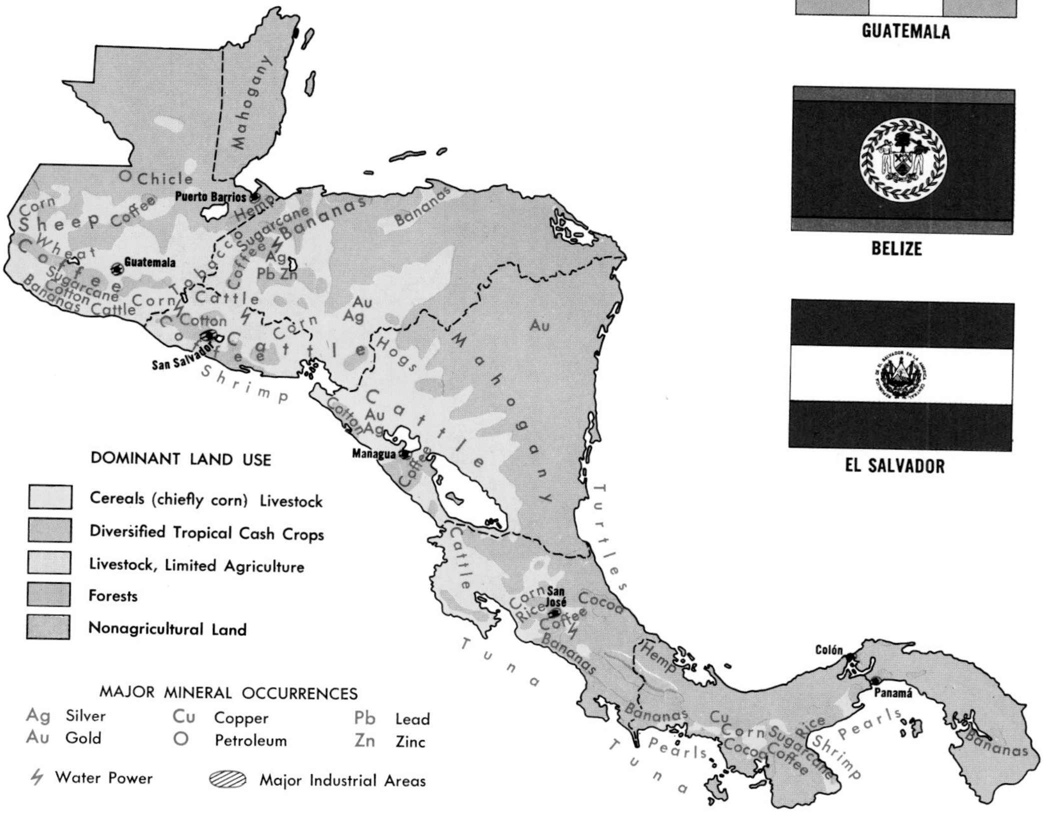

DOMINANT LAND USE
- Cereals (chiefly corn) Livestock
- Diversified Tropical Cash Crops
- Livestock, Limited Agriculture
- Forests
- Nonagricultural Land

MAJOR MINERAL OCCURRENCES
Ag Silver
Au Gold
Cu Copper
O Petroleum
Pb Lead
Zn Zinc

⚡ Water Power   ▨ Major Industrial Areas

GUATEMALA

HONDURAS

BELIZE

NICARAGUA

EL SALVADOR

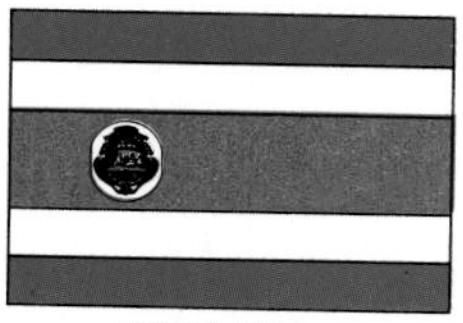

COSTA RICA

PANAMA

(continued on following page)

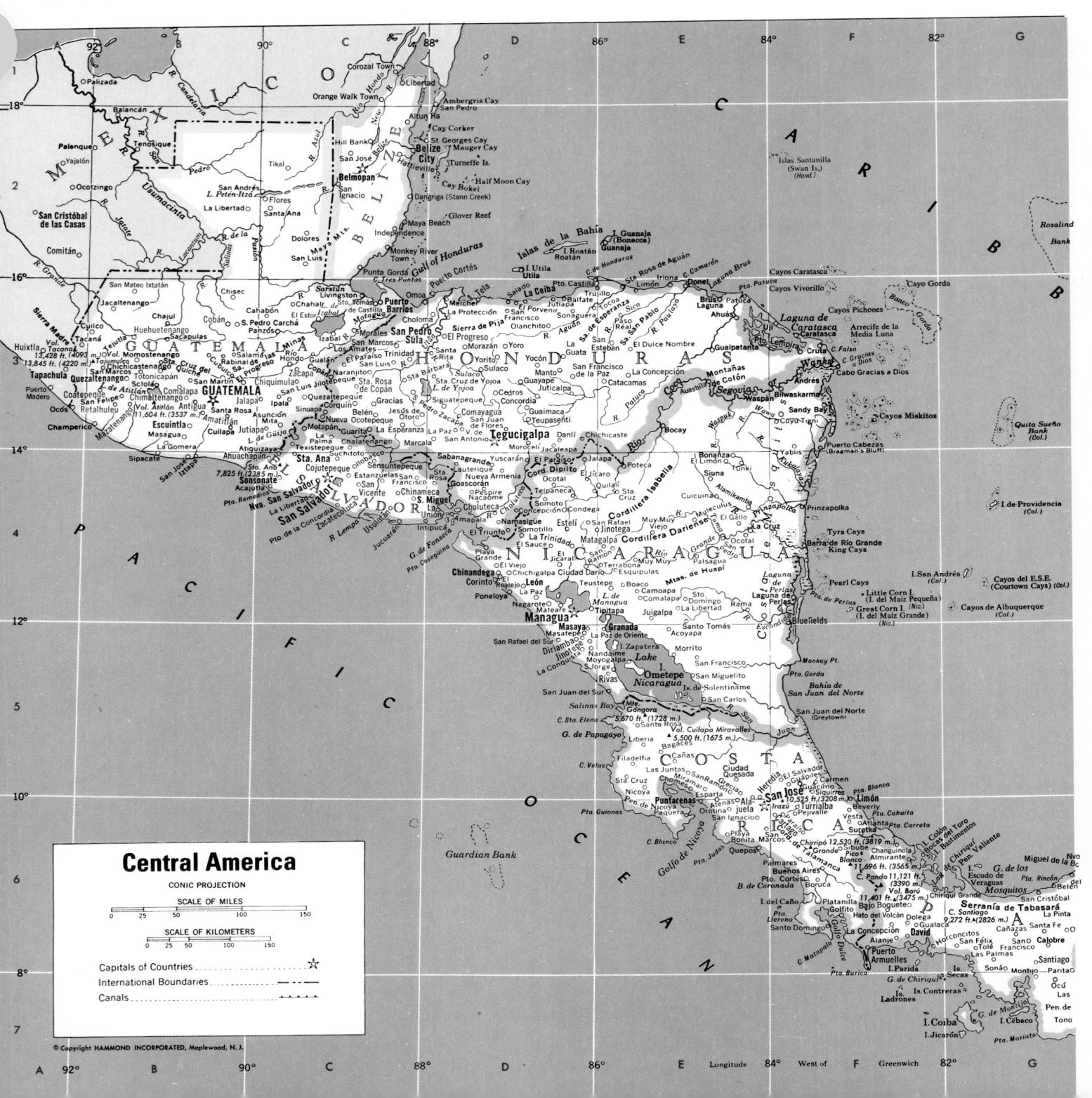

San Pedro (riv.) B2
Sarstún (riv.) C3
Tacaná (vol.) A3
Tajumulco (vol.) B3
Tres Puntas (cape) C3
Usumacinta (riv.) B2

Corquín 2,629 ....C3
Danlí 10,825 ....D3
El Dulce Nombre 1,297 ....E3
El Paraíso 6,709 ....D4
El Paraíso 2,164 ....C3
El Porvenir 1,076 ....D3
El Progreso 28,105 ....D3
El Triunfo 2,925 ....D4
Goascorán 996 ....D4
Gracias 2,299 ....C3
Guaimaca 3,953 ....D3
Guanaja 1,947 ....E2
Guarita 419 ....C3
Guayape 804 ....D3
Jacaleapa 1,609 ....D3
Jesús de Otoro 2,976 ....C3
Jutiapa 1,126 ....D3
Juticalpa 10,075 ....D3
La Ceiba 38,788 ....D3
La Esperanza 2,146 ....C3

HONDURAS

CITIES and TOWNS

Amapala 2,274 ....D4
Brus Laguna 933 ....E3
Catacamas 9,134 ....E3
Cedros 917 ....D3
Choloma 961 ....C3
Choluteca 26,152 ....D4
Comayagua 15,941 ....D3
Concepción de María 579 ....D4
Concordia 646 ....D3

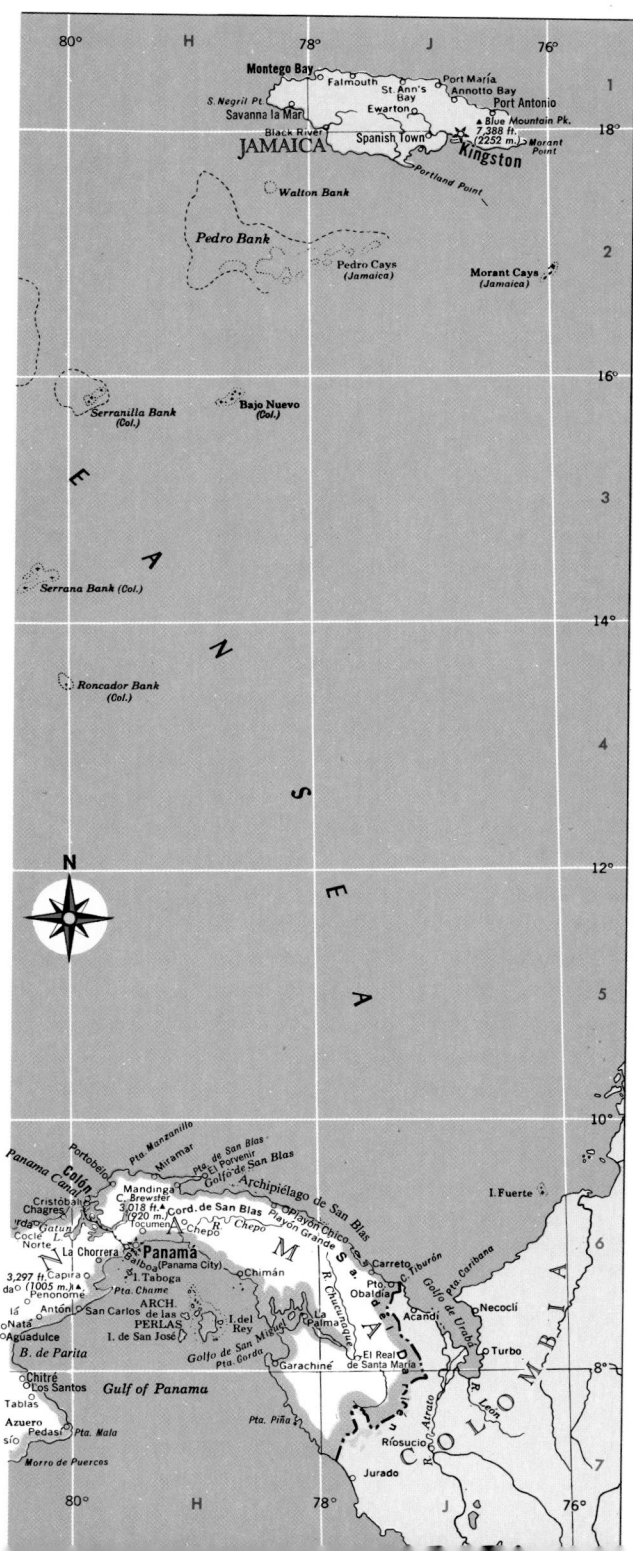

JAMAICA

Montego Bay
Falmouth
S. Negril Pt.
Savanna la Mar
Black River
Spanish Town
Kingston
Port Maria
Annotto Bay
Port Antonio
St. Ann's Bay
Ewarton
Blue Mountain Pk. 7,388 ft. (2252 m.)
Morant Point
Portland Point
Walton Bank
Pedro Bank
Pedro Cays (Jamaica)
Morant Cays (Jamaica)
Serranilla Bank (Col.)
Bajo Nuevo (Col.)
Serrana Bank (Col.)
Roncador Bank (Col.)

CARIBBEAN SEA

N

Portobelo
Pto. Manzanillo
Pta. de San Blas
Pto. el Porvenir
Miramar
Colón
Panama Canal
Cristóbal
Chagres
Gatun
Cord. de San Blas
Archipiélago de San Blas
Mandinga
C. Brewster 3,018 ft. (920 m.)
Tocumen
Cocle del Norte
La Chorrera
Panamá (Panama City)
Capira 3,297 ft. (1005 m.)
Penonomé
Antón
San Carlos de las PERLAS
Natá
Aguadulce
B. de Parita
Chitré
Los Santos
Azuero
Pedasí
Pta. Mala
Morro de Puercos
Gulf of Panama
Chepo
Chimán
I. Taboga
I. del Rey
I. de San José
Golfo de San Miguel
Pta. Garachiné
Playón Chico
Golfo de San Blas
I. Fuerte
Tiburón
Necoclí
Turbo
Golfo de Urabá
Pta. Piña
Ríosucio
Jurado
Pija, Sierra de (mts.)
El Real de Santa María
Sico (riv.)
R. Chucunaque
R. Tuira
Carreto
Pto. Obaldia
Acandí

COLOMBIA

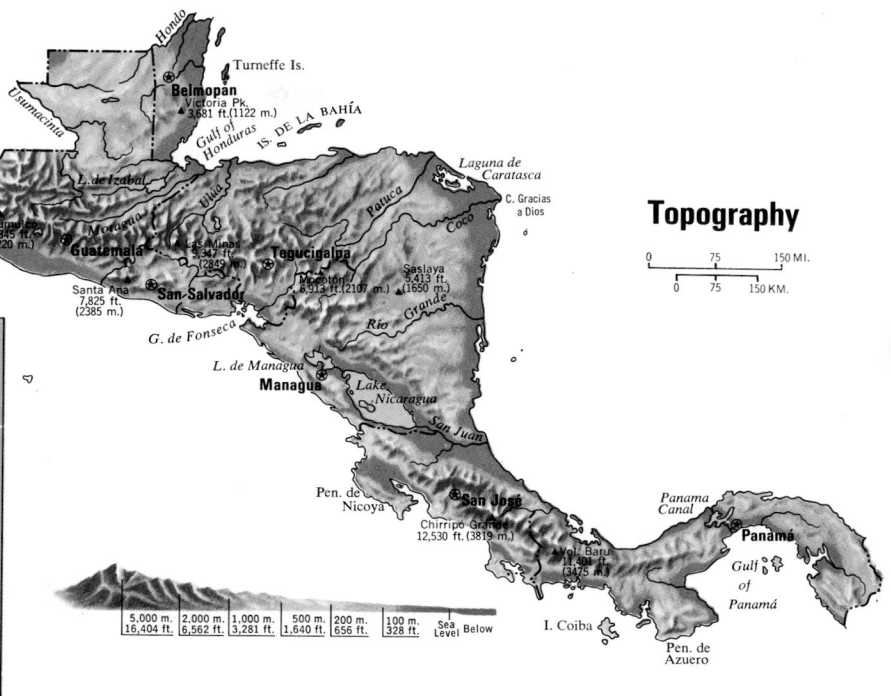

Topography

Victoria Pk. ▲ 3,681 ft. (1122 m.)
Belmopan
Turneffe Is.
Gulf of Honduras
IS. DE LA BAHÍA
Usumacinta
Hondo
Uloa
Patuca
Coco
Laguna de Caratasca
C. Gracias a Dios
Guatemala
13,845 ft. (4220 m.)
Las Minas 9,347 ft. (2849 m.)
Tegucigalpa
Motagua 6,513 ft. (2107 m.)
Saslaya 5,413 ft. (1650 m.)
Santa Ana 7,825 ft. (2385 m.)
San Salvador
Río Grande
G. de Fonseca
L. de Izabal
L. de Managua
Managua
Lake Nicaragua
San Juan
San José
Chirripó Grande 12,530 ft. (3819 m.)
Barú 11,401 ft. (3475 m.)
Panamá
Panama Canal
Gulf of Panamá
I. Coiba
Pen. de Azuero
Pen. de Nicoya

0   75   150 MI.
0   75   150 KM.

| 5,000 m. 16,404 ft. | 2,000 m. 6,562 ft. | 1,000 m. 3,281 ft. | 500 m. 1,640 ft. | 200 m. 656 ft. | 100 m. 328 ft. | Sea Level | Below |

La Paz 6,811 ....D3
Limón 1,704 ....E3
Marcala 3,183 ....C3
Morazán 4,367 ....D3
Morocelí 1,442 ....D3
Nacaome 6,159 ....D4
Namasigüe 816 ....D4
Naranjito 2,770 ....C3
Nueva Armenia 670 ....D4
Nueva Ocotepeque 4,724 ......C3
Olanchito 7,411 ....D3
Omoa 9,161 ....C3
Pespire 1,895 ....D4
Puerto Cortés 25,817 ....D2
Puerto Lempira 727 ....F3
Roatán 1,943 ....D2
Sabanagrande 1,446 ....D4
San Esteban 610 ....D3
San Francisco 1,557 ....D3
San Francisco de la Paz 2,291 D3
San Juan de Flores 1,184 ......D3
San Luis 2,237 ....C3
San Marcos 2,499 ....C3
San Pedro Sula 150,991 ....C3
San Pedro Zacapa 648 ....D3
Santa Bárbara 5,883 ....C3
Santa Cruz de Yojoa 1,848 ....D3
Santa Rita 5,298 ....D3
Santa Rosa de Aguán 1,622 ..E2
Santa Rosa de Copán 12,413 C3
Siguatepeque 12,456 ....D3
Sinuapa 831 ....C3
Sonaguera 2,264 ....D3
Sulaco 1,121 ....D3
Tegucigalpa (cap.) 273,894 ...D3
Tela 19,055 ....D3
Teupasenti 2,003 ....D3
Tocoa 2,803 ....E3
Trinidad 1,598 ....C3
Trujillo 3,961 ....E3
Utila 1,177 ....D2
Villa de San Antonio 2,359 ....D3
Yoro 4,449 ....D3
Yuscarán 1,835 ....D4

OTHER FEATURES

Aguán (riv.) D3
Bahía (isls.) D2
Brus (lag.) E2
Camarón (cape) E2
Caratasca (lag.) F3
Choluteca (riv.) D4
Coco (riv.) E3
Colón (mts.) E3
Esperanza (mts.) E3
Fonseca (gulf) D4
Gorda (bank) F3
Guanaja (isl.) E2
Honduras (cape) E2
Honduras (gulf) D2
Patuca (pt.) E3
Patuca (riv.) E3
Paulaya (riv.) E3
Pija, Sierra de (mts.) D3
Roatán (isl.) D2
San Pablo, Sierra (mts.) E3
Santanilla (Swan) (isls.) F2
Sico (riv.) E3
Sulaco (riv.) D3
Ulúa (riv.) D3
Utila (isl.) D2
Vivorillo (cays) F3
Yojoa (lake) D3

NICARAGUA

CITIES and TOWNS

Acoyapa 2,588 ....E5
Barra de Río Grande F4
Bilwaskarma F3
Bluefields 14,252 ....F4
Boaco 6,372 ....E4
Bonanza E4
Bragmans Bluff
  (Puerto Cabezas) 5,457 .....F3
Cabo Gracias a Dios 3,846 ...F3
Camoapa 4,385 ....E4
Chichigalpa 14,498 ....D4
Chinandega 30,441 ....D4
Ciudad Darío 5,304 ....D4
Comalapa 508 ....E4
Condega 3,414 ....D4
Corinto 13,404 ....D4
Diriamba 10,085 ....D5
El Jícaro 1,669 ....D4
El Jicaral 428 ....D4
El Limón E4
El Realejo 2,229 ....D4
El Sauce 3,202 ....D4
El Viejo 8,507 ....D4
Esquipulas 2,232 ....E4
Estelí 20,222 ....D4
Granada 34,976 ....E5
Greytown
  (San Juan del Norte) 294 ....F5
Jalapa 3,633 ....E4
Jinotega 9,506 ....E4
Jinotepe 12,473 ....D5
Juigalpa 8,497 ....E4
La Conquista 458 ....D5
La Cruz 150 ....E4
La Libertad 1,286 ....E4
La Paz Central 6,175 ....D4
La Paz de Oriente 957 ....E5
La Trinidad 3,548 ....D4
León 55,625 ....D4
Managua (cap.) 398,514 ....D4
Masatepe 6,307 ....D5
Masaya 30,753 ....D5
Matagalpa 21,385 ....E4
Mateare 1,405 ....D4
Morrito 368 ....E4
Moyogalpa 1,551 ....E5
Muy Muy 1,373 ....E4
Nagarote 7,185 ....D4
Nandaime 5,631 ....E5
Ocotal 8,215 ....D4
Palsagua E4
Poneloya D4
Prinzapolka 8,979 ....F4
Puerto Cabezas 5,457 ....F3
Quilalí 1,245 ....E4
Rama 1,341 ....E4
Rivas 10,125 ....E5
San Carlos 2,022 ....E5
San Jorge 2,874 ....E5
San Juan del Norte 294 ....F5
San Juan del Sur 2,393 ....E5
San Miguelito 1,312 ....E5
San Rafael del Norte 1,938 ....E4
San Rafael del Sur 2,914 ....D5
San Ramón 477 ....E4
Santo Domingo 1,949 ....E4
Santo Tomás 2,309 ....E5
Siuna E4
Somotillo 1,864 ....D4
Somoto 5,847 ....D4

Telpaneca 991 ....D4
Terrabona 904 ....E4
Teustepe 1,060 ....E4
Tipitapa 5,758 ....D4
Waspán 1,246 ....E3
Yablis F3

OTHER FEATURES

Coco (riv.) E3
Cosegüina (pt.) D4
Dariense, Cordillera (range) ...E4
Dipilto, Cordillera (range) D4
Escondido (riv.) F4
Fonseca (gulf) D4
Gracias a Dios (cape) F3
Grande (riv.) E4
Great Corn (isl.) F4
Isabelia, Cordillera (range) E4
Kukalaya (riv.) F4
Little Corn (isl.) F4
Managua (lake) D4
Miskitos (cays) F3
Monkey (pt.) F5
Mosquitos, Costa de (reg.) E4
Nicaragua (lake) E5
Ometepe (isl.) E5
Perlas (lag.) F4
Perlas (pt.) F4
Prinzapolca (riv.) E4
Salinas (bay) D5
San Juan (riv.) E5
San Juan del Norte (bay) F5
Segovia (riv.) E3
Tuma (riv.) E4
Tyra (cays) F4
Waspuk (riv.) E3
Wawa (riv.) F4
Zapatera (isl.) E5

PANAMA

CITIES and TOWNS

Aguadulce 10,659 ....G6
Alanje 866 ....F6
Almirante 4,664 ....F6
Antón 4,259 ....G6
Bajo Boquete 2,831 ....F6
Balboa 1,952 ....H6
Bocas del Toro 2,515 ....F6
Calobre 609 ....G6
Cañazas 1,526 ....G6
Capira 1,749 ....H6
Changuinola 9,528 ....F6
Chepo 4,529 ....H6
Chiriquí Grande F6
Chitré 17,156 ....G7
Coclé del Norte G6
Colón 59,832 ....H6
Cristóbal ⊙ 7,959 ....H6
David 50,621 ....F6
Dolega 1,019 ....F6
El Porvenir H6
El Real de Santa María 912 ...J6
Garachiné 1,116 ....G6
Gualaca 1,510 ....F6
Hato del Volcán F6
Horconcitos 1,090 ....F6
La Chorrera 36,971 ....H6
La Concepción 10,460 ....F6
La Palma 164 ....H6
La Pintada 1,100 ....G6
Las Palmas 842 ....G6

Las Tablas 5,230 ....G7
Los Santos 4,644 ....G7
Mandinga 81 ....H6
Montijo 1,152 ....G6
Natá 5,603 ....G6
Ocú 2,353 ....G7
Panamá (cap.) 388,638 ....H6
Panamá⊙ 498,624 ....H6
Parita 1,616 ....G6
Pedasí 934 ....G7
Penonomé 7,389 ....G6
Playón Chico 1,395 ....H6
Portobelo 551 ....H6
Puerto Armuelles 12,488 ....F6
San Carlos 562 ....H6
San Félix 617 ....G6
San Francisco 990 ....G6
Santa Fe 490 ....G6
Santiago 21,809 ....G6
Soná 4,471 ....G6
Tocumen ⊙ 21,745 ....H6
Tolé 1,052 ....G6
Tonosí 891 ....G7

OTHER FEATURES

Azuero (pen.) G7
Barú (vol.) F6
Bastimentos (isl.) G6
Brewster, Cerro (mt.) H6
Burica, Punta (cape) F6
Cébaco (isl.) G7
Chame (pt.) H6
Chepo (riv.) H6
Chiriquí (lag.) G6
Chiriquí (gulf) F7
Chucunaque (riv.) J6
Coiba, Isla de (isl.) F7
Colón, Isla de (isl.) G6
Contreras (isls.) F7
Darién (mts.) J6
Escudo de Veraguas (isl.) G6
Gatun (lake) H6
Gorda (pt.) H6
Jicarón (isl.) G7
Mala, Punta (cape) H7
Mariato, Punta (cape) G7
Montijo (gulf) G7
Mosquitos, Golfo de los
  (gulf) G6
Panama (canal) H6
Panama (gulf) H7
Pando, Cerro (mt.) F6
Parida (isl.) F6
Parita (bay) G6
Perlas (arch.) H6
Rey (isl.) H6
San Blas, Archipiélago de
  (arch.) J7
San Blas, Cordillera de
  (mts.) H6
San Blas, Golfo de (bay) H6
San Blas, Pta. de (pt.) H6
San José (isl.) H6
San Miguel, Golfo de (bay) H6
Santiago, Cerro (mt.) G6
Secas (isls.) G7
Tabasará (mts.) G6
Taboga (isl.) H6
Tiburón (pt.) J6
Valiente (pen.) G6

⊙ City and suburbs
⊛ Population of district

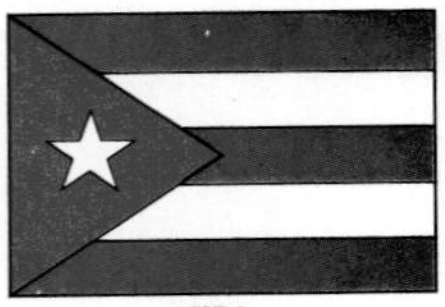

CUBA

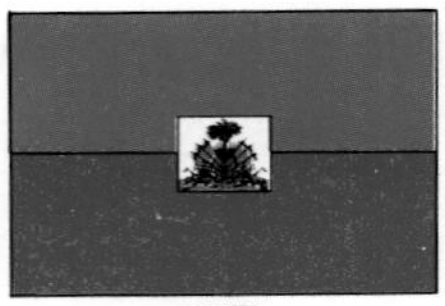

HAITI

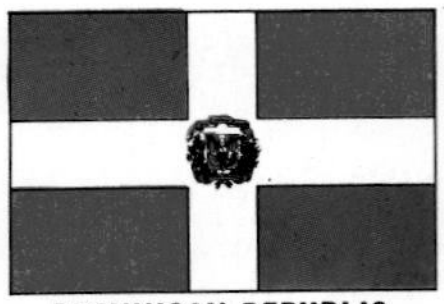

DOMINICAN REPUBLIC

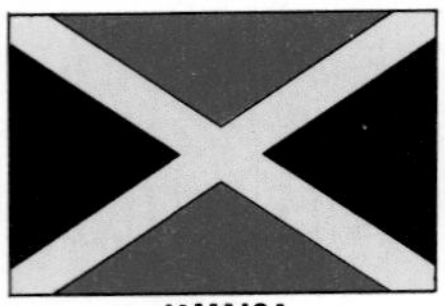

JAMAICA

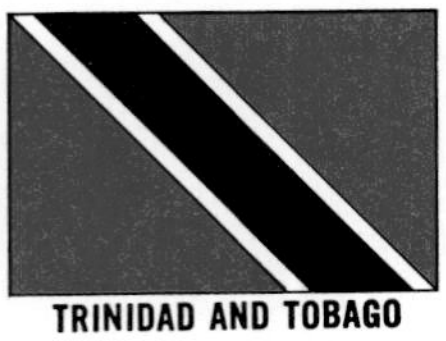

TRINIDAD AND TOBAGO

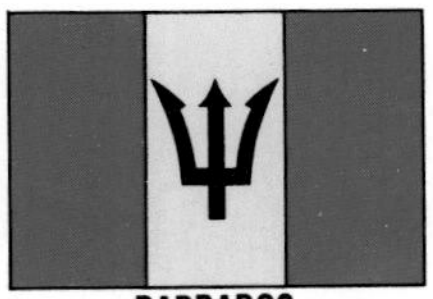

BARBADOS

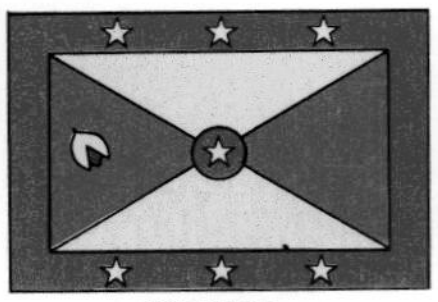

GRENADA

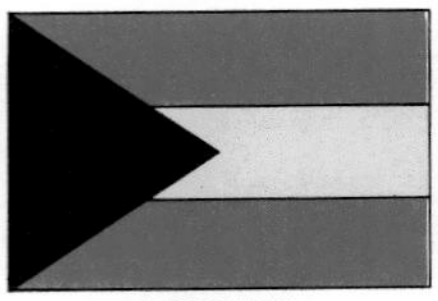

BAHAMAS

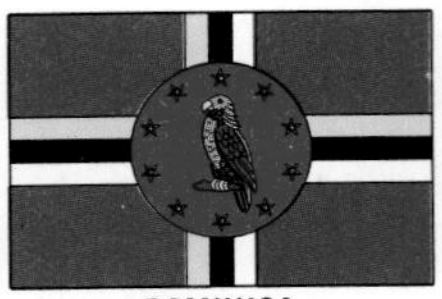

DOMINICA

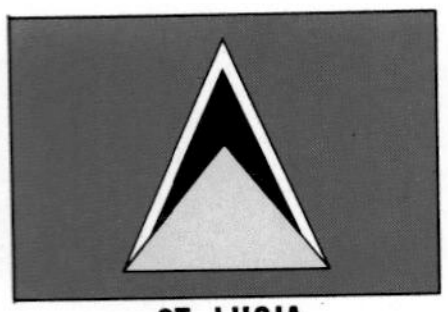

ST. LUCIA

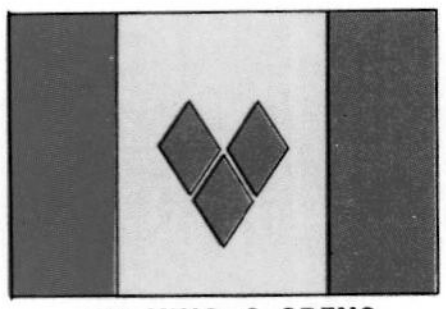

ST. VINC. & GRENS.

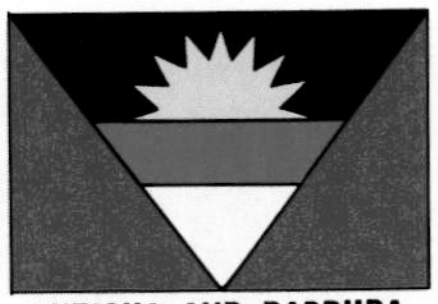

ANTIGUA AND BARBUDA

CUBA
AREA 44,206 sq. mi. (114,494 sq. km.)
POPULATION 10,617,000
CAPITAL Havana
LARGEST CITY Havana
HIGHEST POINT Pico Turquino
6,561 ft. (2,000 m.)
MONETARY UNIT Cuban peso
MAJOR LANGUAGE Spanish
MAJOR RELIGION Roman Catholicism

HAITI
AREA 10,694 sq. mi. (27,697 sq. km.)
POPULATION 5,609,000
CAPITAL Port-au-Prince
LARGEST CITY Port-au-Prince
HIGHEST POINT Pic La Selle 8,793 ft. (2,680 m.)
MONETARY UNIT gourde
MAJOR LANGUAGES Creole French, French
MAJOR RELIGION Roman Catholicism

DOMINICAN REPUBLIC
AREA 18,704 sq. mi. (48,443 sq. km.)
POPULATION 6,867,000
CAPITAL Santo Domingo
LARGEST CITY Santo Domingo
HIGHEST POINT Pico Duarte
10,417 ft. (3,175 m.)
MONETARY UNIT Dominican peso
MAJOR LANGUAGE Spanish
MAJOR RELIGION Roman Catholicism

JAMAICA
AREA 4,411 sq. mi. (11,424 sq. km.)
POPULATION 2,392,000
CAPITAL Kingston
LARGEST CITY Kingston
HIGHEST POINT Blue Mountain Peak
7,402 ft. (2,256 m.)
MONETARY UNIT Jamaican dollar
MAJOR LANGUAGE English
MAJOR RELIGIONS Protestantism,
Roman Catholicism

PUERTO RICO
AREA 3,515 sq. mi. (9,104 sq. km.)
POPULATION 3,522,037
CAPITAL San Juan
MONETARY UNIT U.S. dollar
MAJOR LANGUAGES Spanish, English
MAJOR RELIGION Roman Catholicism

NETHERLANDS ANTILLES
AREA 390 sq. mi. (1,010 sq. km.)
POPULATION 246,000
CAPITAL Willemstad
MONETARY UNIT Antilles guilder
MAJOR LANGUAGES Dutch, Papiamento, English
MAJOR RELIGIONS Roman Catholicism,
Protestantism

BERMUDA
AREA 21 sq. mi. (54 sq. km.)
POPULATION 67,761
CAPITAL Hamilton
MONETARY UNIT Bermuda dollar
MAJOR LANGUAGE English
MAJOR RELIGION Protestantism

ARUBA
AREA 75 sq. mi (193 sq. km.)
POPULATION 66,790
CAPITAL Oranjestad
MONETARY UNIT Aruba guilder
MAJOR LANGUAGES Dutch, Papiamento
MAJOR RELIGION Roman Catholic

Topography

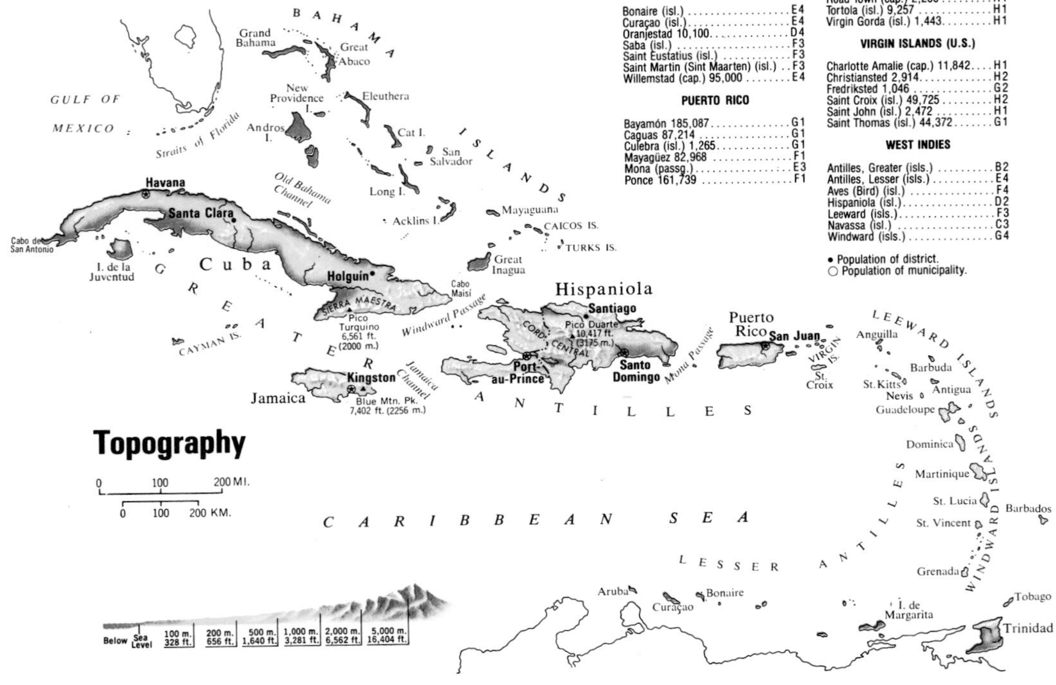

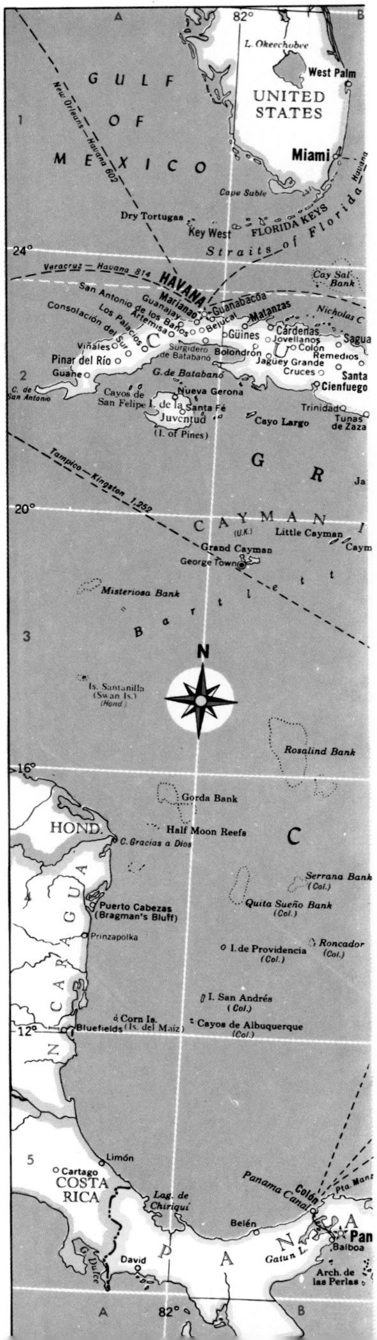

TRINIDAD AND TOBAGO
AREA 1,980 sq. mi. (5,128 sq. km.)
POPULATION 1,212,000
CAPITAL Port of Spain
LARGEST CITY Port of Spain
HIGHEST POINT Mt. Aripo 3,084 ft. (940 m.)
MONETARY UNIT Trinidad and Tobago dollar
MAJOR LANGUAGES English, Hindi
MAJOR RELIGIONS Roman Catholicism,
Protestantism, Hinduism, Islam

SAINT KITTS AND NEVIS

BARBADOS
AREA 166 sq. mi. (430 sq. km.)
POPULATION 256,000
CAPITAL Bridgetown
LARGEST CITY Bridgetown
HIGHEST POINT Mt. Hillaby 1,104 ft.
(336 m.)
MONETARY UNIT Barbadian dollar
MAJOR LANGUAGE English
MAJOR RELIGION Protestantism

BAHAMAS
AREA 5,382 sq. mi. (13,939 sq. km.)
POPULATION 253,000
CAPITAL Nassau
LARGEST CITY Nassau
HIGHEST POINT Mt. Alvernia 206 ft. (63 m.)
MONETARY UNIT Bahamian dollar
MAJOR LANGUAGE English
MAJOR RELIGION Roman Catholicism,
Protestantism

GRENADA
AREA 133 sq. mi. (344 sq. km.)
POPULATION 103,103
CAPITAL St. George's
LARGEST CITY St. George's
HIGHEST POINT Mt. St. Catherine
2,757 ft. (840 m.)
MONETARY UNIT East Caribbean dollar
MAJOR LANGUAGES English, French patois
MAJOR RELIGIONS Roman Catholicism,
Protestantism

DOMINICA
AREA 290 sq. mi. (751 sq. km.)
POPULATION 81,000
CAPITAL Roseau
HIGHEST POINT Morne Diablotin
4,747 ft. (1,447 m.)
MONETARY UNIT Dominican dollar
MAJOR LANGUAGES English, French patois
MAJOR RELIGIONS Roman Catholicism,
Protestantism

West Indies 157

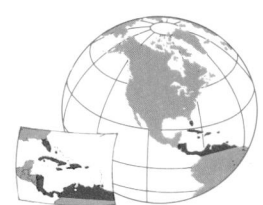

SAINT LUCIA
AREA 238 sq. mi. (616 sq. km.)
POPULATION 148,000
CAPITAL Castries
HIGHEST POINT Mt. Gimie 3,117 ft. (950 m.)
MONETARY UNIT East Caribbean dollar
MAJOR LANGUAGES English, French patois
MAJOR RELIGIONS Roman Catholicism,
Protestantism

SAINT VINCENT AND THE GRENADINES
AREA 150 sq. mi. (388 sq. km.)
POPULATION 124,000
CAPITAL Kingstown
HIGHEST POINT Soufrière 4,000 ft. (1,219 m.)
MONETARY UNIT East Caribbean dollar
MAJOR LANGUAGE English
MAJOR RELIGIONS Protestantism,
Roman Catholicism

ANTIGUA AND BARBUDA
AREA 171 sq. mi. (443 sq. km.)
POPULATION 76,000
CAPITAL St. John's
HIGHEST POINT Boggy Peak 1,319 ft. (402 m.)
MONETARY UNIT East Caribbean dollar
MAJOR LANGUAGE English
MAJOR RELIGION Protestantism

SAINT KITTS & NEVIS
AREA 104 sq. mi. (269 sq. km.)
POPULATION 44,404
CAPITAL Basseterre
HIGHEST POINT Mt. Misery 4,314 ft.
(1,315 m.)
MONETARY UNIT East Caribbean dollar
MAJOR LANGUAGE English
MAJOR RELIGIONS Protestantism,
Roman Catholicism

The West Indies

CONIC PROJECTION

SCALE OF MILES
0 50 100 150 200

SCALE OF KILOMETERS
0 50 100 200 300

Capitals of Countries .... ☆
Other Capitals .... ◉

Puerto Rico

Bermuda Islands

© Copyright HAMMOND INCORPORATED, Maplewood, N.J.

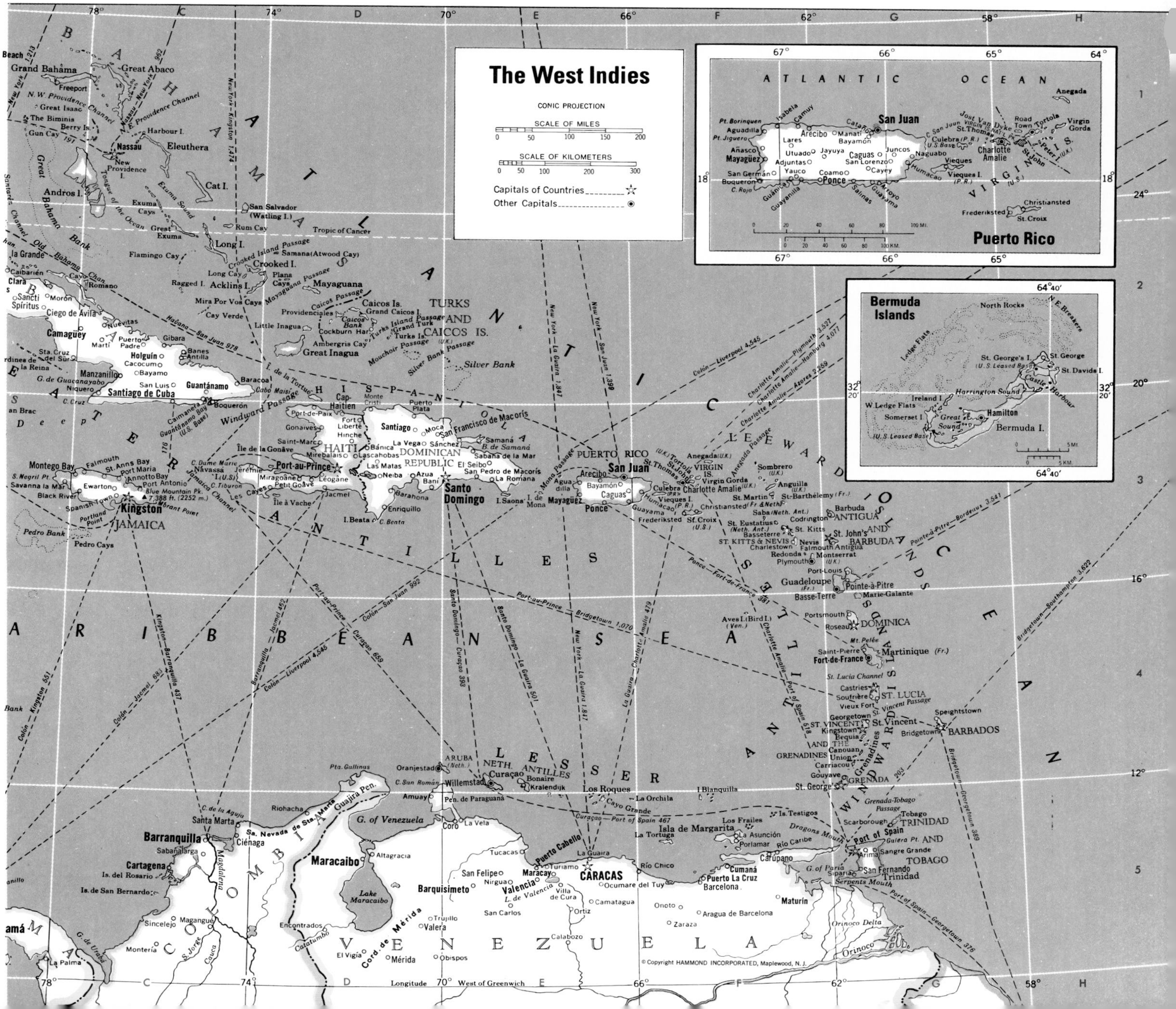

CUBA

PROVINCES

Camagüey, 664,566 . . . . .G2
Ciego de Avila 320,961 . . . . . . .F2
Cienfuegos 326,412 . . . . .E2
Granma 739,335 . . . . .H4
Guantánamo 466,609 . . . . .K4
Holguin 911,034 . . . . .J3
Juventud (municipio especial) 57,879 . . . . .C2
La Habana, Ciudad de Habana 1,924,886 . . . . .C1
La Habana (Havana) 586,029 C1
Las Tunas 436,341 . . . . .H3
Matanzas 557,628 . . . . .D1
Pinar del Río 640,740 . . . . . . .A2
Sancti Spíritus 399,700 . . . . . .F2
Santiago de Cuba 909,506 . . . .H4
Villa Clara 764,743 . . . . .E1

CITIES and TOWNS

Abreus 14,267 . . . . .D2
Agramonte 4,603 . . . . .F2
Aguada de Pasajeros 20,219 . .D1
Alacranes 4,959 . . . . .D1
Alonso Rojas 1,427 . . . . .B2
Alquizar 12,691 . . . . .C1
Altagracia 1,722 . . . . .H4
Alto Songo-La Maya 25,188 . .J 4

Amarillas 2,767 . . . . .D2
Amazonas 1,066 . . . . .F2
Antilla 10,052 . . . . .J3
Arroyo Blanco 1,431 . . . . .F2
Artemisa 45,689 . . . . .B1
Báez 4,178 . . . . .E2
Báguanos 12,678 . . . . .J3
Bahía Honda 16,901 . . . . .B1
Baire 4,879 . . . . .H4
Banao 803 . . . . .F2
Banes 38,905 . . . . .J3
Baracoa 36,702 . . . . .K4
Baraguá 12,633 . . . . .F2
Bauta 26,826 . . . . .C1
Bayamo 109,201 . . . . .H4
Bejucal 15,649 . . . . .C1
Bolondrón 5,840 . . . . .D1
Buenaventura 4,711 . . . . .H3
Buenavista 1,303 . . . . .G2
Buey Arriba 8,017 . . . . .H4
Cabaiguán 36,544 . . . . .F2
Cabañas 4,897 . . . . .B1
Cabezas 5,262 . . . . .C1
Cacocum 14,145 . . . . .H3
Caibarién 32,094 . . . . .E1
Caimanera 6,664 . . . . .K4
Calabazar de Sagua 9,023. . . .E1
Calimete 11,925 . . . . .D1
Camagüey 245,235. . . . . .G3
Camajuaní 26,653 . . . . .E2
Campechuela 20,743 . . . . .G3
Canasí 1,637 . . . . .C1

Candelaria 10,810. . . . . .B1
Cárdenas 65,585 . . . . .D1
Cartagena 2,166 . . . . .D2
Cascajal 3,530 . . . . .E1
Cauto del Embarcadero 949 . . .H4
Cauto el Cristo 1,626 . . . . .J3
Central Amancio Rodríguez 22,506 . . . . .G3
Central Bolivia 6,301 . . . . .G2
Central Brasil 4,904 . . . . .G2
Central Cándido González 3,414 . . . . .G3
Central Colombia 16,799 . . . . .G3
Central Frank País 9,066. . . . . .K3
Central Guatemala 5,584. . . . . .J3
Central Haití 3,609 . . . . .G3
Central Las Reynaldos 3,997 . .J4
Central Loynaz Echevarría 3,245 . . . . .J3
Central Manuel Tames 7,864 . .K4
Céspedes 6,634 . . . . .G2
Chambas 4,877 . . . . .F2
Chaparra 8,428 . . . . .H3
Cidra 3,587 . . . . .D1
Ciego de Ávila 80,010 . . . . . . .F2
Cienfuegos 107,396 . . . . .D2
Colón 47,010 . . . . .D1
Condado 33,115 . . . . .F2
Consolación del Norte 4,681 . .B1
Consolación del Sur 34,334 . . .B2
Contramaestre 44,991 . . . . . . .G3
Corralillo 15,822. . . . . .D1

Cruces 20,324 . . . . .E2
Cueto 23,183 . . . . .J3
Cumanayagua 25,338 . . . . . . .E2
Daiquirí J4
Delicias 10,562 . . . . .H3
Dos Caminos 3,772 . . . . .J4
Dos Ríos 1,786 . . . . .J4
El Caney 3,921 . . . . .J4
El Cobre 3,952 . . . . .J4
El Santo 2,473 . . . . .E1
Encrucijada 23,029 . . . . .E1
Esmeralda 17,205 . . . . .G1
Esperanza 9,241 . . . . .E2
Florencia 6,979 . . . . .F2
Florida 43,881 . . . . .G2
Fomento 17,310 . . . . .F2
Gaspar 2,682 . . . . .F2
Gibara 23,137 . . . . .J3
Guáimaro 29,712 . . . . .G3
Guanabacoa 89,741 . . . . .C1
Guanajay 21,042. . . . . .B1
Guane 14,126 . . . . .A2
Guantánamo 178,129 . . . . . . .K4
Guaro 3,086 . . . . .J3
Guasimal 3,057 . . . . .F2
Guayabal 3,703 . . . . .H3
Guayos 6,753 . . . . .F2
Güines 51,691 . . . . .C1
Güira de Melena 19,851 . . . . . .C1
Guisa 15,182 . . . . .H4
Herradura 3,762 . . . . .B1

Holguín 190,155 . . . . .J3
Ignacio Agramonte 1,487 . . . .G3
Imías 4,491 . . . . .K4
Isabela de Sagua 3,721. . . . . .E1
Jagüey Grande 30,205 . . . . . . .D2
Jamaica 5,128 . . . . .K4
Jaruco 16,844 . . . . .C1
Jatibonico 17,047 . . . . .F2
Jíbaro 1,263 . . . . .F2
Jiguaní 25,069 . . . . .H4
Jobabo 14,899 . . . . .H3
Jovellanos 35,043 . . . . .D1
La Coloma 3,462 . . . . .B2
La Maya-Alto Songo 25,188 . .J4
Las Martinas 4,511. . . . . .A2
Limonar 9,629 . . . . .D1
Los Arabos 10,664 . . . . .E1
Los Palacios 21,884 . . . . .B1
Lugareño 4,396 . . . . .G2
Mabay 6,176 . . . . .H4
Maceo 2,652 . . . . .B1
Majagua 9,110 . . . . .F2
Manacas 5,914 . . . . .E1
Manatí 11,054 . . . . .H3
Manguito 2,739 . . . . .D1
Manicaragua 33,900 . . . . .E2
Mantua 9,165 . . . . .A2
Mapos (Amazonas) 1,066 . . . .F2
Manzanillo 95,420 . . . . .H4
Mariano○127,563. . . . . .C1
Mariel 24,115 . . . . .B1
Martí 11,474. . . . . .D1

Matanzas 103,302 . . . . .C1
Máximo Gómez, Ciego de Ávila 5,116 . . . . .G3
Máximo Gómez, Matanzas 4,970 . . . . .D1
Mayajigua 4,425 . . . . .F2
Mayarí 54,699 . . . . .J3
Mayarí Arriba 2,302 . . . . .J4
Media Luna 13,794 . . . . .G4
Mendoza 2,914 . . . . .A2
Meneses 4,768 . . . . .F2
Minas 17,675 . . . . .G2
Minas de Matahambre 14,976 . . . . .A1
Moa 28,696 . . . . .K3
Morón 40,396 . . . . .F2
Nicaro 9,506 . . . . .J3
Niquero 15,544 . . . . .G4
Nueva Gerona 17,175 . . . . . . .B2
Nuevitas 35,103 . . . . .G2
Orozco 4,256 . . . . .B1
Palma Soriano 66,222 . . . . . . .J4
Palmira 19,680 . . . . .E2
Pedro Betancourt 22,915 . . . . .D1
Perico 20,633 . . . . .D1
Pilón 10,194 . . . . .H4
Pinar del Río 104,598 . . . . . . .B2
Placetas 46,038 . . . . .E2
Primero Enero 14,807 . . . . . . .F2
Puerto Esperanza 3,499 . . . . . .A1
Puerto Padre 46,806 . . . . .H3
Quemado de Güines 11,208 . .E1

Rancho Veloz 3,966 . . . . .D1
Ranchuelo 34,255. . . . . .E2
Regla 38,491 . . . . .C1
Remedios 27,722 . . . . .E2
República Dominicana 2,540 . . . . .F2
Río Cauto 19,550 . . . . .H4
Rodas 16,350 . . . . .E2
Sagua de Tánamo 15,327 . . . .K3
Sagua la Grande 52,315 . . . . .E1
San Andrés 2,127. . . . . .H3
San Antonio de los Baños 28,137 . . . . .C1
San Cristóbal 30,769 . . . . .B1
San Diego de los Baños 1,430 . . . . .B1
San Germán 12,362 . . . . .J3
San José de las Lajas 37,149 . . . . .C1
San José de los Ramos 15,239 . . . . .C1
San Juan y Martínez 13,227 . . .B2
San Luis, Pinar del Río 5,677 . . . . .B2
San Luis, Santiago de Cuba 32,826 . . . . .J4
San Nicolás 12,368 . . . . .C1
San Ramón 2,676 . . . . .H4
Santa Clara 175,113 . . . . .E2
Santa Cruz del Norte 15,239 . . . . .C1

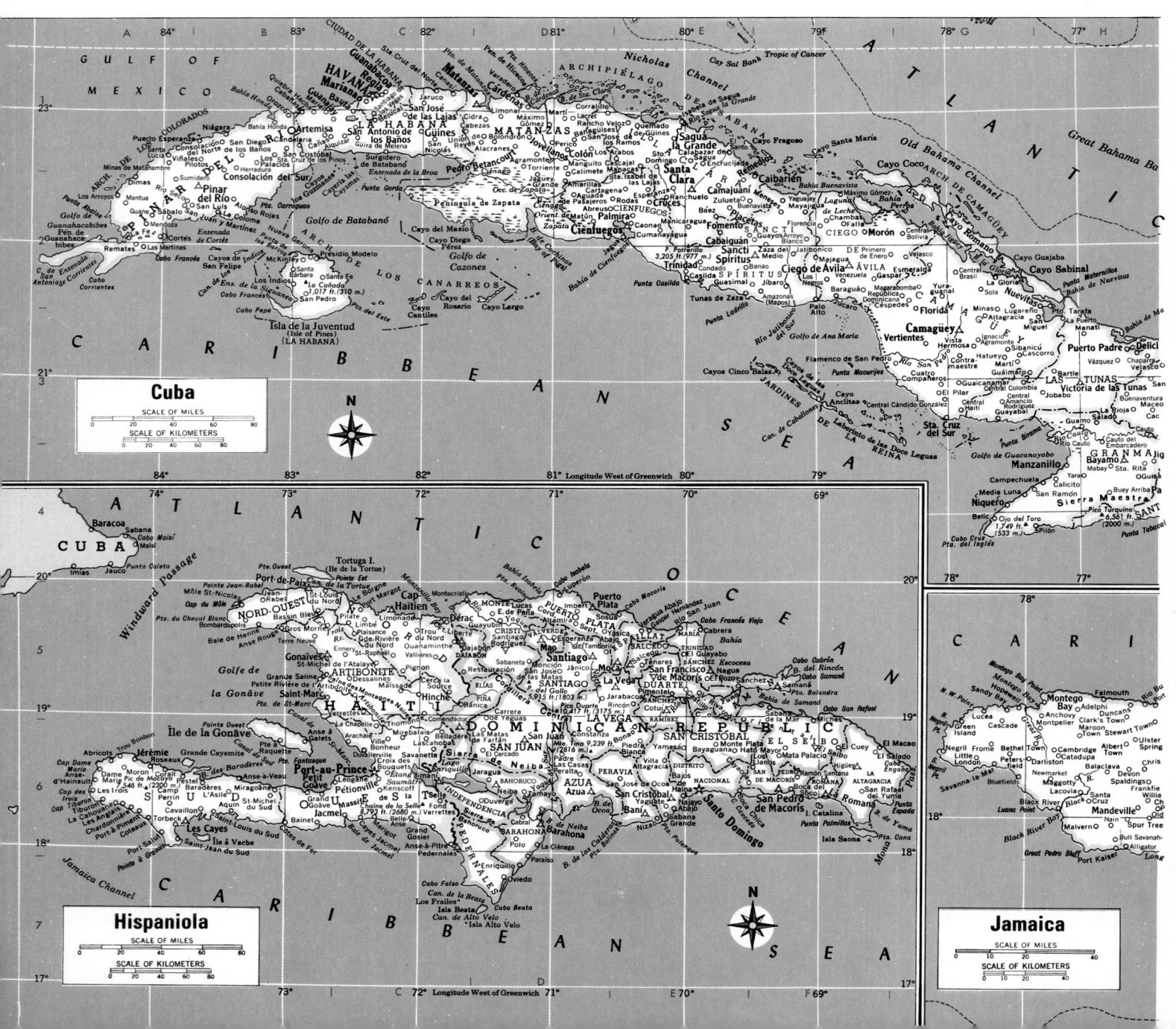

Santa Cruz de los Pinos 3,545 .... B1
Santa Cruz del Sur 27,142 .. G3
Santa Fe 3,925 .... B2
Santa Isabel de las Lajas 7,279 .... E2
Santa Lucía 3,734 .... J3
Santa Rita 6,358 .... H4
Santiago de Cuba 362,432 .J4
Santiago de las Vegas 29,325 .... C1
Santo Domingo 32,950 . E1
Sibanicú 14,252 .... G3
Sola 2,436 .... G2
Sumidero 980 .... A2
Surgidero de Batabanó C1
Tacajó 4,469 .... G3
Torriente 1,759 .... D11
Trinidad 42,080 .... E2
Unión de Reyes 28,422 .. C1
Varadero 14,737 .... D1
Vázquez 3,851 .... H3
Velasco 5,618 .... H3
Venezuela 13,744 .... F2
Vertientes 25,178 .... G3
Victoria de las Tunas 87,522 H3
Viñales 2,049 .... A1
Yaguajay 30,720 .... F2
Yara 238,879 .... H4
Zaza del Medio 7,495 .. E2
Zulueta 5,425 .... E2

OTHER FEATURES

Abalos (pt.) A2
Ana María (gulf) F3
Anclitas (cay) F3
Batabanó (gulf) C2
Birama (pt.) G4
Broa (inlet) C1
Buenavista (bay) F2
Caballones (chan.) F3
Camagüey (arch.) G2
Cantiles (cay) C3
Cárdenas (bay) D1
Carraguao (pt.) B2
Casilda (pt.) E2
Cauto (riv.) H3
Cayamas (cays) C2
Cazones (gulf) D2
Cienfuegos (bay) D2
Cinco Balas (cays) E3
Cochinos (bay) D2
Coco (cay) G1
Corrientes (cape) A2
Corrientes (inlet) A2
Cortés (inlet) B2
Cristal, Sierra del (mts.) .. J3
Cruz (cape) G4
Diego Pérez (cay) C2
Doce Leguas (cays) F3
Este (pt.) C3
Fragoso (cay) F1
Francés (cape) A2

Gorda (pt.) C2
Gran Piedra (mt.) J4
Guacanayabo (gulf) G4
Guajaba (cay) G2
Guanahacabibes (gulf) .. A2
Guanahacabibes (pen.) .. A2
Guantánamo (bay) J4
Guarico (pt.) K3
Guzmanes (cays) B2
Hicacos (pen.) D1
Hicacos (pt.) D1
Honda (bay) B1
Indios (chan.) B1
Inglés (pt.) G4
Jardines de la Reina (arch.) . F3
Jatibonico del Sur (riv.).. F3
Jigüey (bay) G2
Juventud, Isla de la (Pines) (isl.) 57,879 .... B3
Laberinto de las Doce Leguas (cays) F3
Ladrillo (pt.) E3
Largo (cay) F2
Leche (lag.) F2
Los Barcos (cays) E3
Los Canarreos (arch.) C2
Los Colorados (arch.) A1
Lucrecia (cape) J3
Macurijes (pt.) F3
Maestra, Sierra (mts.) .. H4
Maisí (cape) K4
Mangle (pt.) J3
Masío (cay) D1
Matanzas (bay) D1
Nicholas (chan.) E1
Nipe (bay) J3
Nuevitas (bay) H2
Ojo del Toro (mt.) G4
Old Bahama (chan.) G1
Pepe (cape) B3
Perros (cay) G2
Pigs (Cochinos) (bay) .. D2
Pines (Isla de la Juventud) (isl.) 7,879 .... B3
Potrerillo (peak) E2
Quemado (pt.) K4
Romano (cay) G2
Rosario (cay) C2
Sabana (arch.) E1
Sabinal (cay) H2
Sagua la Grande (riv.) .. E1
San Antonio (cape) A2
San Felipe (cays) B2
San Pedro (riv.) G3
Santa Clara (bay) D1
Santa María (cay) F1
Siguanea (bay) B2
Tabacal (pt.) H4
Toa, Cuchillas de (mts.) .. K4
Tortuguilla (pt.) K4
Turquino (peak) H4
Zapata (pen.) C2
Zapata Occidental (swamp). D2
Zapata Oriental (swamp) .. D2

DOMINICAN REPUBLIC
PROVINCES

Azua 142,770 .... D6
Bahoruco 78,636 .... D6
Barahona 137,160 .... D6
Dajabón 57,709 .... D5
Distrito Nacional 1,550,739 . E6
Duarte 235,544 .... E6
Elías Piña 65,384 .... C5
El Seibo 157,866 .... F6
Espaillat 164,017 .... E5
Independencia 38,768 .... D6
La Altagracia 100,112 .. F6
La Romana 109,769 .... F6
La Vega 385,043 .... E6
María Trinidad Sánchez 112,629 .... E5
Monte Cristi 83,407 .... D5
Pedernales 17,006 .... C6
Peravia 168,123 .... E6
Puerto Plata 206,757 .... E5
Salcedo 99,191 .... E5
Samaná 65,699 .... F5
Sánchez Ramírez 126,567 . E5
San Cristóbal 446,132 .... E6
San Juan 239,957 .... D6
San Pedro de Macorís 152,890 .... F6
Santiago 550,372 .... D5
Santiago Rodríguez 55,411 . D5
Valverde 100,319 .... D5

CITIES and TOWNS

Altamira 2,759 .... D5
Azua 31,481 .... D6
Bajos de Haina 33,135 .... E6
Baní 36,705 .... E6
Barahona 49,334 .... D6
Bonao 44,486 .... E6
Cabrera 2,542 .... F5
Comendador 5,962 .... C6
Constanza 15,141 .... D6
Cotuí 16,688 .... E6
Dajabón 8,808 .... D5
El Seibo 13,511 .... F6
Hato Mayor 17,859 .... F6
Higüera 33,501 .... F6
Imbert 5,315 .... D5
Jarabacoa 13,416 .... D5
Jimaní 3,327 .... C6
La Romana 91,571 .... F6
La Vega 52,432 .... E5
Luperón 2,500 .... D5
Mao 33,527 .... D5
Moca 31,176 .... D5
Monción 3,344 .... D5
Nagua 20,912 .... F5
Puerto Plata 45,348 .... E5
Sabana de la Mar 9,983 .. F5
Sabaneta 9,170 .... D5
Samaná 5,023 .... F5
Sánchez 7,919 .... E5
San Cristóbal 58,520 .... E6
San Francisco de Macorís 64,906 .... E5
San Juan 49,764 .... D6
San Pedro de Macorís 78,562 .... F6
Santiago 278,638 .... D5
Santo Domingo (cap.) 1,313,172 .... E6
Tenares 4,065 .... E6
Villa Altagracia 20,890 .. E6

OTHER FEATURES

Alto Velo (chan.) C7
Alto Velo (isl.) D7
Balandra (pt.) F5
Beata (cape) D7
Beata (chan.) C7
Beata (pt.) C7
Cabrón (cape) F5
Calderas (bay) E6
Cana (pt.) F6
Catalina (isl.) F6
Caucedo (capee) E6
Central, Cordillera (range) .. D5
Duarte (peak) D5
Engaño (cape) F6
Enriquillo (lake) C6
Escocesa (bay) F5
Espada (pt.) F6
Falso (cape) C7
Francés Viejo (cape) E5
Gallo (mt.) D5
Isabela (bay) D5
Isabela (cape) D5
Los Frailes (isl.) C7
Macorís (cape) E5
Manzanillo (bay) C5
Mona (passg.) F6
Neiba (bay) D6
Neiba, Sierra de (mts.) .. D6
Ocoa (bay) D6
Oriental, Cordillera (range) . F6
Palenque (pt.) E6
Palmillas (pt.) F6
Rincón (bay) F5
Rucia (pt.) D5
Salinas (pt.) E6
Samaná (bay) F5
Samaná (cape) F5
San Rafael (cape) F5
Saona (isl.) F6
Septentrional, Cordillera (range) D5
Tina (mt.) D6
Yaque del Norte (riv.) D5
Yaque del Sur (riv.) D6
Yuma (bay) F6
Yuna (riv.) E5

HAITI
DEPARTMENTS

Artibonite C5
Nord C5
Nord-Ouest B5
Ouest C6
Sud A6

CITIES and TOWNS

Anse-à-Galets 3,623 .... B6
Anse-d'Hainault 5,220 .... A6
Aquin 3,820 .... B6
Cap-Haïtien 64,406 .... C5
Croix des Bouquets 4,365 .. C6
Dame Marie 4,320 .... A6
Dérac 1,300 .... C5
Dessalines 7,984 .... C5
Fort Liberté 5,012 .... C5
Gonaïves 34,209 .... B5
Grande Rivière du Nord 6,007 .... C5
Gros Morne 4,739 .... B5
Hinche 10,070 .... C5
Jacmel 13,730 .... C6
Jérémie 18,493 .... A6
Kenscoff 2,605 .... C6
Lascahobas 3,805 .... C6
Léogâne 5,782 .... C6
Les Cayes 34,090 .... B6
Limbé 10,476 .... C5
Miragoâne 4,327 .... B6
Mirebalais 6,069 .... C6
Ouanaminthe 7,276 .... C5
Pétionville 35,333 .... C6
Petite Rivière de l'Artibonite 7,559 .... C5
Petit Goâve 7,310 .... B6
Pignon 4,576 .... C5
Port-au-Prince (cap.) 449,831 .... C6
Port-de-Paix 15,540 .... B5
Saint-Louis du Nord 7,203 . C5
Saint-Marc 24,165 .... B5
Saint-Michel de l'Atalaye 7,559 .... C5
Saint-Raaphaël 3,889 .... C5
Trou du Nord 7,637 .... C5
Verrettes 3,670 .... C5

OTHER FEATURES

Artibonite (riv.) C5
Baradères (bay) B6
Cheval Blanc (pt.) B5
Dame Marie (cape) A6
Fantasque (pt.) B6
Gonâve (gulf) B6
Gonâve (isl.) B6
Grande Cayemite (isl.) .. A7
Gravois (pt.) A6
Irois (cape) A6
Jean-Rabel (pt.) B5
Macaya (mt.) A6
Manzanillo (bay) C5
Môle (cape) B5
Noires (mts.) B4
Ouest (pt.) B6
Ouest (pt.) A5
Saint-Marc (chan.) B6
Saint-Marc (pt.) B6
Saumâtre (lake) C6
Selle (peak) C6
Sud (chan.) B6
Tortue (chan.) B5
Tortue (Tortuga) (isl.) .. C4
Tortuga (isl.) C4
Trois-Rivières (riv.) B5
Vache (isl.) B6
Windward (passg.) A5

JAMAICA
CITIES and TOWNS

Alley J7
Alligator Pond H6
Anchovy 2,558 .... H5
Annotto Bay K6
Bamboo 2,971 .... J6
Bath K6
Black River 2,701 .... H6
Bog Walk J6
Bowden K6
Browns Town 5,479 .... J6
Bull Savanna-Junction 5,110 .... H6
Cambridge 2,449 .... H6
Catadupa H6
Christiana H6
Discovery Bay 1,814 .... J5
Falmouth 3,937 .... H5
Green Island G6
Hope Bay K6
Kingston (cap.) 106,791 .. K6
Kingston *516,865 .... J7
Linstead J6
Lucea 3,635 .... G5
Mandeville 14,421 .... H6
May Pen 26,074 .... H6
Montego Bay 43,521 .... H5
Montpelier H6
Morant Bay 7,465 .... K7
Negril G6
Ocho Ríos 5,851 .... J6
Oracabessa J5
Port Antonio 10,538 .... K6
Port Kaiser H7
Port Maria 5,259 .... J6
Port Morant K6
Saint Ann's Bay 7,101 .... J5
Saint Margaret's Bay K6
Savanna-la-Mar 11,759 .. G6
Spanish Town 40,731 .... J6
Williamsfield H6

OTHER FEATURES

Black (riv.) H6
Black River (bay) G6
Blue (mts.) J6
Blue Mountain (peak) K6
Galina (pt.) J6
Grande (riv.) K6
Great (riv.) H6
Great Pedro Bluff (prom.) .. H6
Long (bay) H7
Luana (pt.) G6
Minho (riv.) J6
Montego (bay) G5
Montego Bay ((pt.) G5
North East (pt.) K6
North Negril (pt.) G6
North West (pt.) G5
Old Harbour (bay) J7
Portland (pt.) J7
Sir John's (peak) K6
South East (pt.) K6
South Negril (pt.) G6

*City and Suburbs.
○ Population of municipality.

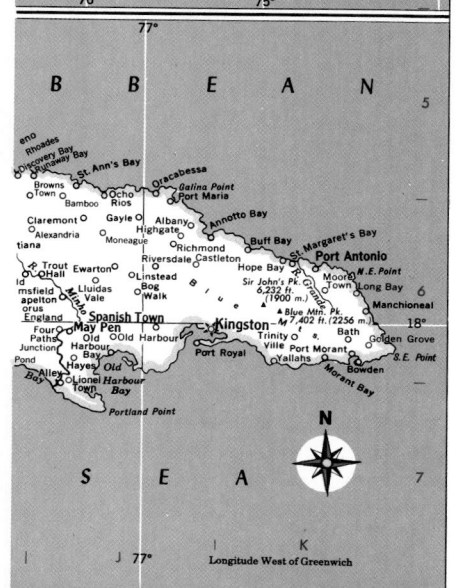

LEGEND

Capitals of Countries _____ ☆
Provincial Capitals _____ △
International Boundaries _____
Provincial Boundaries _____

© Copyright HAMMOND INCORPORATED, Maplewood, N.J.

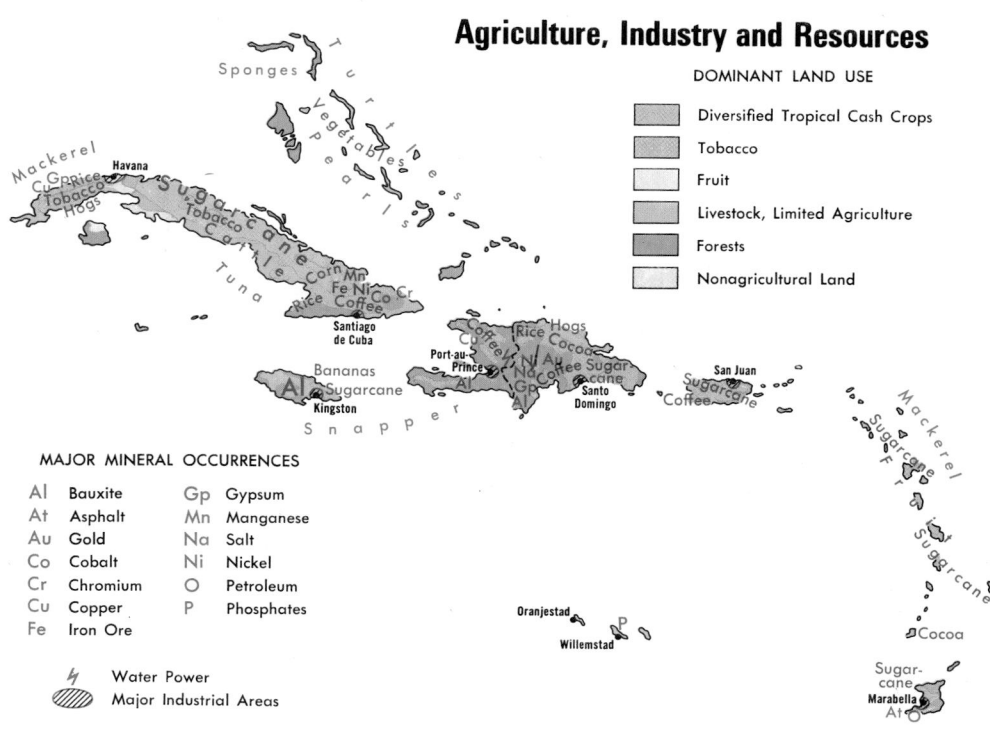

Agriculture, Industry and Resources

DOMINANT LAND USE

Diversified Tropical Cash Crops
Tobacco
Fruit
Livestock, Limited Agriculture
Forests
Nonagricultural Land

MAJOR MINERAL OCCURRENCES

Al	Bauxite	Gp	Gypsum
At	Asphalt	Mn	Manganese
Au	Gold	Na	Salt
Co	Cobalt	Ni	Nickel
Cr	Chromium	O	Petroleum
Cu	Copper	P	Phosphates
Fe	Iron Ore		

⚡ Water Power
Major Industrial Areas

PUERTO RICO

DISTRICTS

Aguadilla A1
Arecibo C1
Bayamón D1
Guayama D2
Humacao E2
Mayagüez B2
Ponce C2
San Juan D1

CITIES and TOWNS

Adjuntas 5,239 B2
Aguada 5,025 A1
Aguadilla 22,039 A1
Aguas Buenas 3,766 E2
Aibonito 9,331 D2
Añasco 5,646 A1
Ángeles ○2,817 B2
Arecibo 48,779 B1
Arroyo 8,435 E3
Bahomamey A1
Bajadero 3,678 C1
Barceloneta 4,502 C1
Barranquitas 3,618 D2
Bayamón 185,087 D1
Boquerón ○3,675 A3
Cabo Rojo 10,292 A2
Caguas 87,214 E2
Caguas †156,819 E2
Camuy 3,834 B1
Carolina 147,835 E1
Cataño 26,243 D1
Cayey 23,305 D2
Ceiba 4,973 F2
Central Aguirre 1,049 D3
Ciales 3,582 C1
Cidra 6,069 D2
Coamo 12,851 D2
Comerío 5,736 D2
Coquí 3,018 D3
Corozal 5,889 D1
Coto Laurel ○5,192 C2
Culebra (Dewey) 938 G1
Dorado 10,203 D1
Ensenada B3
Esperanza 1,130 G2
Fajardo 26,928 F1
Florida 3,641 C1
Guánica 9,628 B3
Guayama 21,097 E3
Guayanilla 6,163 B3
Guaynabo 65,075 D1
Gurabo 7,645 E2
Hatillo 5,019 B1
Hato Rey E1
Hormigueros 12,031 A2
Humacao 19,147 E2
Isabela 12,087 A1
Isabel Segunda 2,330 G2
Jayuya 3,588 C2
Jobos 4,194 D3
Juana Díaz 10,469 C2
Juncos 7,851 E2
Lajas 4,275 A2
Lares 5,224 B2
Las Piedras 4,857 E2
Levittown 31,613 D1
Loíza 3,932 E1
Loíza Aldea E1
Luquillo 4,531 F1
Manatí 17,347 C1
Maricao 1,390 B2
Mayagüez 82,968 A2
Mayagüez †98,155 A2
Moca 3,960 A1
Naguabo 4,135 F2
Naranjito 2,849 D1
Palmer 1,566 F1
Palo Seco 1,172 D1
Parguera A3
Patillas 3,172 E2
Peñuelas 4,235 B2
Playa de Fajardo F1
Playa de Humacao ○5,573 F2
Ponce 161,739 C3
Ponce †168,272 C3
Puerto Nuevo D1
Puerto Real 2,390 A2
Puerto Real (Playa de Fajardo) F1
Punta Santiago (Playa de Humacao) ○5,573 F2
Quebradillas 3,770 B1
Río Blanco 1,433 F2
Río Grande 12,047 E1
Río Piedras E1
Rosario A2
Sabana Grande 7,435 B2
Sabana Seca 11,431 D1
Salinas 6,220 D3
San Antonio 2,681 A1
San Germán 13,054 A2
San Juan (cap.) 424,600 E1
San Juan †1,081,193 E1
San Lorenzo 8,880 E2
San Sebastián 10,619 B1
Santa Isabel 6,948 C3
Santurce E1
Tallaboa 1,059 B3
Toa Alta 4,427 D1
Toa Baja 1,992 D1
Trujillo Alto 41,141 E1
Utuado 11,113 B2
Vega Alta 10,582 D1
Vega Baja 18,233 D1
Vieques (Isabel Segunda) 2,330 G2
Villalba 3,469 C2
Yabucoa 6,797 E2
Yauco 14,594 B2

OTHER FEATURES

Aguadilla (bay) A1
Algarrobo (pt.) A2
Añasco (bay) A1
Arenas (pt.) F2
Bauta (riv.) C2
Bayamón (riv.) D1
Boquerón (bay) A3
Borinquen (pt.) A1
Cabullones (pt.) C3
Caja de Muertos (isl.) C3
Camuy (riv.) B1
Canovanas (riv.) E1
Caonillas (lake) C2
Carite (lake) E2
Carraízo (lake) E1
Cayey, Sierra de (mts.) D2
Central, Cordillera (range) C2
Cerro Gordo (pt.) D1
Coamo (res.) D3
Coamo (riv.) D3
Culebra (isl.) 1,265 G1
Culebrinas (riv.) A1
Culebrita (isl.) G2
El Toro (mt.) F2
El Yunque (mt.) F1
Este (pt.) G2
Fajardo (riv.) F1
Figuras (pt.) E3
Fosforescente (bay) A3
Grande de Añasco (riv.) B2
Grande de Arecibo (riv.) C1
Grande de Loíza (riv.) E1
Grande de Manatí (riv.) C1
Guajataca (lake) B1
Guanajibo (pt.) A2
Guanajibo (riv.) A2
Guánica (lake) B3
Guaniquilla (pt.) A2
Guayabal (lake) C2
Guayanés (pt.) F2
Guayanés (riv.) E2
Guayanilla (bay) B3
Guayo (lake) B2
Guilarte (mt.) B2
Honda (bay) F2
Jacaguas (riv.) C2
Jaicoa, Cordillera (mts.) B1
Jiguero (pt.) A1
Jobos (bay) D3
Lima (pt.) F2
Luquillo, Sierra de (mts.) E2
Manglillo (pt.) B3
Mayagüez (bay) A2
Miquillo (pt.) F1
Molinos (pt.) G1
Mona (passg.) A2
Negra (pt.) G2
Nigua (riv.) D2
Ola Grande (pt.) D3
Palmas Altas (pt.) C1
Patillas (lake) E2
Petrona (pt.) D3
Pirata (mt.) F2
Plata (riv.) D2
Puerca (pt.) F2
Puerto Medio Mundo (bay) F2
Punta, Cerro de (mt.) C2
Ramey A.F.B. A1
Rincón (bay) D3
Rojo (cape) A3
Roosevelt Road Naval Res. F2
Salinas (pt.) D1
San José (lag.) E1
San Juan, Cabezas de (prom.) F1
San Juan Nat'l Hist. Site D1
Soldado (pt.) G2
Sucia (bay) A3
Tanamá (riv.) B1
Toro, El (mt.) F2
Torrecilla (lag.) E1
Tortuguero (lag.) D1
Tuna (pt.) E3
Vacía Talega (pt.) E1
Vieques (isl.) 7,662 G2
Vieques (passg.) F2
Vieques (sound) G2
Yagüez (riv.) A2
Yauco (lake) B2
Yeguas ((pt.) F3

ANTIGUA

CITIES and TOWNS

All Saints 1,796 E11
Cedar Grove 1,460 E11
Falmouth 1,134 E11
Freetown 1,250 E11
Jennings 1,370 D11
Liberta 2,394 E11
Old Road 1,244 D11
Parham 1,570 E11
Saint John's (cap.) 21,814 E11
Willikies 1,843 E11

OTHER FEATURES

Antigua (isl.) 76,213 E11
Boggy (peak) D11
Boon (pt.) E11
Green (isl.) E11
Guiana (isl.) E11
Long (isl.) E11
Saint John's (harb.) C11
Standfast (pt.) E11
Willoughby (bay) E11

ARUBA

CITIES and TOWNS

Aresji D9
Balashi E10
Bubali D10
Bushiribana E10
Druif D1
Oranjestad (cap.) Aruba 10,100 D10
Sint Nicolaas E10
Westpunt D10

OTHER FEATURES

Aruba (isl.) 66,790 E9
Basora (pt.) E10
Jamanota (mt.) E10
Paarden (bay) D10
Palm (beach) D10

BARBADOS

CITIES and TOWNS

Bathsheba B8
Belleplaine B8
Bridgetown (cap.) 7,552 B9
Carlton B8
Cave Hill B9
Checker Hall B8
Codrington B8
Crab Hill B8
Crane C9
Drax Hall B8
Ellerton B9
Greenland B8
Holetown B8
Kendal B8
Lodge Hill B8
Marchfield B9
Mount Standfast B8
Oistins B9
Rose Hill B8
Rouen B9
Saint Lawrence B9
Saint Martins C9
Scarboro B9
Seawell B9
Six Mens B8
Speightstown B8
Spring Hall B8
Welchman Hall B8

OTHER FEATURES

Carlisle (bay) B9
Hillaby (mt.) B8
Long (bay) B9
North (pt.) B8
Oistins (bay) B9
Pelican (isl.) B9
Ragged (pt.) C8
Sam Lord's Castle C9
South (pt.) B9

DOMINICA

CITIES and TOWNS

Barroui 1,480 E6
Castle Bruce 1,975 F6
Coulihaut 1,735 E6
Delice F7
Grand Bay 3,152 F7
Hampstead E5
La Plaine F6
Mahout 2,095 E6
Marigot 3,183 F6
Petit Soufrière F6
Portsmouth 2,329 E5
Rosalie F6
Roseau (cap.) 9,968 E7
Roseau *16,035 E7
Saint Joseph 2,643 E6
Salybia F6
Soufrière E7
Vieille Case E5
Wesley 2,002 F5

OTHER FEATURES

Capuchin (cape) E5
Carib Reserve F6
Clyde (riv.) F6
Crumpton (pt.) F5
Diablotin, Morne (mt.) E6
Dominica (passg.) E5
Douglas (bay) E5
Grand (bay) F7
Jaquet (pt.) E5
Layou (riv.) E6
Martinique (passg.) E7
Micotrin (mt.) F6
Pagoua (bay) F6
Prince Rupert (bay) E5
Scotts (head) E7
Soufrière (bay) E7
Trois Pitons, Morne (mt.) E6

GRENADA

CITIES and TOWNS

Gouyave 2,498 C8
Grand Roy C8
Grenville 1,723 D8
Hermitage D8
La Taste D8
Marquis D8
Mount Tivoli D8
Saint George's (cap.) 6,463 C9
Saint George's *34,624 C9
Sauteurs 605 D8
Victoria 1,673 D8
Woodford C8

OTHER FEATURES

Bedford (pt.) D8
David (pt.) D8
Great Bacolet (pt.) D8
Green (isl.) D8
Grenville (bay) D8
Gros (pt.) C8
Halifax (harb.) C8
Irvin's (bay) D8
Les Tantes (isls.) D7
Molinière (pt.) C8
Prickly (pt.) C9
Ronde (isl.) D7
Saint Catherine (mt.) D8
Saline (pt.) C9
Sinai (mt.) D8
Telescope (pt.) D8

GUADELOUPE

Total Population 329,017

CITIES and TOWNS

Anse-Bertrand 1,921 A5
Baie-Mahault 5,874 A6
Baillif 3,844 A7
Bananier A7
Basse-Terre (cap.) 13,397 A7
Bouillante 1,821 A6
Bourg-des-Saintes 907 A7
Capesterre 7,541 A7
Ferry A6
Gosier 13,741 B6
Gourbeyre 5,637 A7
Goyave 1,709 A6
Grand-Bourg 3,249 B7
Lamentin 2,319 A6
Les Abymes 51,837 B6
Morne-à-l'Eau 9,457 A6
Moule 9,800 B6
Petit-Bourg 5,097 A6
Petit-Canal 1,581 A6
Pigeon A6
Pointe-à-Pitre 25,151 B6
Pointe-Noire 2,180 A6
Port-Louis 4,517 B5
Saint-Claude 6,755 A7
Sainte-Anne 11,527 B6
Sainte-Marguerite B6
Sainte-Marie A6
Sainte-Rose 4,805 A6
Saint-François 3,141 B6
Trois-Rivières 7,881 A7
Vieux-Fort 1,073 B7
Vieux-Habitants 4,065 A7

OTHER FEATURES

Allègre (pt.) A6
Antigues (pt.) A6
Basse-Terre (isl.) 138,777 A6
Châteaux (pt.) B6
Constant, Morne (hill) B7
Désirade, La (isl.) 1,602 B6
Fajou (isl.) A6
Grand Cul-de-Sac Marin (bay) A6
Grande-Terre (isl.) B6
Grande Vigie (pt.) B5
Grand-Îlet (isl.) A7
Guadeloupe (isl.) 167,896 B6
Guadeloupe (passg.) A5
Guadeloupe Nat'l Park A6
Kahouanne (isl.) A6
Marie-Galante (isl.) 13,757 B7
Nord (pt.) B7
Nord-Est (bay) B6
Petit Cul-de-Sac Marin (bay) A6
Petite-Terre (isls.) B6
Saintes (chan.) A7
Saintes (isls.) 2,901 A7
Salée (riv.) A6
Sans Toucher (mt.) A6
Soufrière (mt.) A7
Terre-de-Bas (isl.) 1,427 A7
Terre-de-Haut (isl.) 1,453 A7
Vieux-Fort (pt.) A7

MARTINIQUE

Total Population 330,220

CITIES and TOWNS

Ajoupa-Bouillon 1,569 C5
Basse-Pointe 2,163 C5
Bellefontaine 818 C6
Case-Pilote 1,776 C6
Ducos 4,429 D6
Fond-Saint-Denis 962 C6
Fort-de-France (cap.) 96,649 C6
Grand' Rivière 1,053 C5
Gros-Morne 1,976 D6
La Trinité 3,380 D6
Le Carbet 2,321 C6
Le François 2,940 D6
Le Lamentin 6,872 D6
Le Lorrain 2,024 D6
Le Marin 2,651 D7
Le Morne-Rouge 2,650 C5
Le Prêcheur 1,350 C5
Le Robert 3,610 D6
Le Saint-Esprit 3,947 D6
Les Trois-Îlets 1,484 D6
Le Vauclin 3,054 D6
Macouba 1,142 C5
Marigot 1,765 D5
Rivière-Pilote 1,587 D7
Rivière-Salée 1,859 D7
Sainte-Luce 1,502 D7
Sainte-Marie 3,966 D5
Saint-Joseph 2,052 D6
Saint-Pierre 4,923 C6
Schoelcher 16,412 C6

OTHER FEATURES

Cabet, Pitons du (mt.) C6
Cabrits (isl.) D7
Caravelle (pen.) D6
Cul-de-Sac du Marin (bay) D7
Diable (pt.) D5
Ferré (cape) E7
Fort-de-France (bay) C6
Galion (bay) D6
Lézarde (riv.) D6
Long (isl.) D6
Lorrain (riv.) D5
Martinique (passg.) C5
Pelée (vol.) C5
Pilote (riv.) D7
Ramiers (isl.) C6
Ramville (isl.) D6
Robert (harb.) D6
Rose (pt.) D6
Saint-Martin (cape) C5
Saint-Pierre (bay) C6
Salines (pt.) D7
Salomon (pt.) C7
Vauclin (mt.) D6

NETHERLANDS ANTILLES

CITIES and TOWNS

Ascension F8
Bacuna E8
Boven Bolivia E8
Dokterstuin F8
Emmastad F9
Entrejo E8
Fontein E8
Groot Sint Joris G9
Hato G8
Kralendijk (cap.), Bonaire 2,500 E8
Lagoen E8
Montanja di Reij G9
New Port G9
Noord di Salinja E8
Onima E8
Otrabanda F9
Patrick F8
Rincon E8
Rooi E8
Santa Barbara G9
Santa Catharina G9
Savonet F8
Sint Kruis F8
Sint Martha F8
Sint Michiel F9
Sint Willebrordus F8
Terra Corra E8
Westpunt F8
Willemstad (cap.) 95,000 F9
Willemstad *130,000 F9

OTHER FEATURES

Bonaire (isl.) 8,087 E9
Bullen (bay) F8
Caracas (bay) G9
Curaçao (isl.) 145,430 G7
Goto (lake) D8
Kanon (pt.) G9
Klein Bonaire (isl.) E8
Kudarebe (pt.) D9
Lac (bay) D9
Lacre (pt.) E9
Malmok (mt.) E8
Noord (pt.) D8
Noord (pt.) F8
Pekelmeer (lake) E9
Piscadera (bay) F9
Schottegat (bay) G9
Sint Anna (bay) F9
Sint Christoffel (mt.) F8
Sint Joris (bay) G9
Slag (bay) D8
Vierkant (pt.) E8

SAINT KITTS and NEVIS

CITIES and TOWNS

Basseterre (cap.) 14,725 C10
Cayon C10
Charlestown 1,326 C11
Cotton Ground 471 C11
Dieppe Bay C10
Frigate Bay C10
Gingerland D11
Golden Rock C10
Newcastle D11
Old Road Town C10
Sadlers Village C10
Sandy Point 862 C10
Tabernacle C10
Zion Hill D11

OTHER FEATURES

Brimstone (hill) C10
Dogwood (pt.) D11
Fort (pt.) C11
Great Salt (pond) D10
Heldens (pt.) C10
Horse Shoe (pt.) C11
Misery (mt.) C10
Monkey (hill) C10
Narrows, The (str.) D11
Nevis (isl.) 9,300 D11
Nevis (peak) D11
North Friars (bay) D10
Pinney's (beach) D11
Saint Christopher (Saint Kitts) (isl.) 35,104 D10
South Friars (bay) C10

SAINT LUCIA

CITIES and TOWNS

Anse la Raye •5,007 F6
Canaries •2,075 G6
Castries (cap.) •42,770 G6
Choc G5
Choiseul •6,382 F7
Dauphin G5
Dennery •9,654 G6
Gros Islet •10,329 G5
Laborie •6,944 G7
Marigot G6
Marquis G6
Micoud •12,264 G6
Praslin G6
Soufrière •7,456 F6
Vieux Fort •10,675 G7

OTHER FEATURES

Beaumont (pt.) F6
Canaries, Piton (mt.) G6
Cannelles (pt.) G7
Cannelles (riv.) G6
Cap (pt.) G5
Choc (bay) G5
Fond d'Or (bay) G6
Gimie (mt.) G6
Grand Caille (pt.) F6
Grand Cul de Sac (riv.) G6
Gros Islet (bay) G5
Gros Piton (mt.) G6
La Sorcière (mt.) G6
Maria (isls.) G7
Ministre (pt.) G7
Moule-à-Chique (cape) G7
Petit Piton (mt.) G6
Pigeon (isl.) G5
Port Castries (harb.) G6
Port Praslin (bay) G6
Roseau (riv.) G6
Saint Lucia (chan.) G5
Saint Vincent (chan.) G7
Savannes (bay) G7
Sorcière, La (mt.) G6
Soufrière (bay) F6
Vierge (pt.) G6

SAINT VINCENT and THE GRENADINES

CITIES and TOWNS

Barrouallie 1,298 A9
Calliaqua 627 A9
Camden Park A9
Colonarie A9
Georgetown 1,100 A8
Kingstown (cap.) 17,117 A9
Kingstown *23,330 A9
Layou 1,147 A9
Wallibu A8

OTHER FEATURES

Colonarie (pt.) A9
Cumberland (bay) A8
Dark (head) A8
De Volet (pt.) A8
Espagnol (pt.) A8
Greathead (bay) A9
Kingstown (bay) A9
Owia (bay) A8
Porter (pt.) A8
Richmond (peak) A8
Saint Andrew (mt.) A9
Saint Vincent (passg.) A8
Soufrière (mt.) A8
Yambou (head) A9

TRINIDAD and TOBAGO

CITIES and TOWNS

Arima 11,390 B10
Arouca B10
Basse Terre B11
Biche B10
Blanchisseuse B10
California A11
Carapichaima B10
Caroni B10
Cedros A11
Chaguanas 6,122 B10
Chaguaramas A10
Couva 3,635 B10
Cunapo B10
Flanagin Town B10
Fullarton A11
Fyzabad 1,564 A11
Grande Rivière B10
Guaico B10
Guayaguayare B11
La Brea 1,487 A11
Marabella 18,158 A11
Matelot B10
Matura B10
Mayaro 2,638 B11
Moruga B11
Mucurapo A10
Palo Seco A11
Peñal 3,606 B11
Point Fortin 6,538 A11
Port-of-Spain (cap.) 67,978 A10
Princes Town 8,288 B11
Redhead B10
Rio Claro 2,423 B11
Saint Joseph 4,132 B10
Saint Joseph B11
San Fernando 33,490 A11
San Francique A11
Sangre Grande 8,948 B1
San Juan A10
Sans Souci B10
Siparia 5,773 B11
Tabaquite 2,309 B11
Talparo B10
Toco 1,287 B10
Tunapuna 10,251 B10
Upper Manzanilla B1
Valencia B10
Waterloo A10

OTHER FEATURES

Aripo, El Cerro del (mt.) B10
Boca Grande (passg.) A10
Chacachacare (isl.) A10
Chupara (pt.) B10
Cocos (bay) B10
Dragons Mouth (str.) A10
El Tucuche (mt.) B10
Erin (bay) A11
Galeota (pt.) B11
Galera (pt.) C10
Guapo (bay) A11
Guatuaro (pt.) B11
Icacos (pt.) A11
Maracas (bay) C10
Pitch (lake) A11

VIRGIN ISLANDS (Br.)

CITIES and TOWNS

Road Town (cap.) 2,200 D3
West End C4

OTHER FEATURES

Flanagan (passg.) D4
Frenchman (cay) C4
Great Thatch (isl.) C4
Great Tobago (isl.) B3
Jost Van Dyke (isl.) 135 C3
Little Tobago (isl.) B3
Narrows, The (str.) C4
Norman (isl.) D4
Peter (isl.) D4
Road (bay) D3
Sage (mt.) D4
Sir Francis Drake (chan.) D4
Tortola (isl.) 9,257 D3

VIRGIN ISLANDS (U.S.)

CITIES and TOWNS

Bethlehem E4
Canebay E3
Charlotte Amalie (cap.) 11,842 B4
Christiansted 2,914 F4
Cruz Bay 1,928 C4
Diamond F4
Eastend D4
Emmaus C4
Fredensdal F4
Frederiksted 1,046 E4
Grove Place 3,599 E4
Kingshill F4
Longford F4
Negro Bay E4

OTHER FEATURES

Altona (lag.) F4
Annaly (bay) E3
Baron Bluff (prom.) E3
Bordeaux (mt.) C4
Brass (isls.) A4
Buck (isl.) G3
Buck Island (chan.) F3
Buck Island Reef Nat'l Mon. G3
Butler (bay) E4
Caneel (bay) B4
Capella (isls.) B5
Christiansted Nat'l Hist. Site F4
Coral (bay) C4
Crown (mt.) A4
Dutch Cap (cay) A4
Eagle (mt.) E4
East (pt.) G4
Flanagan (passg.) D4
Flat (cays) A4
Grass (pt.) G4
Great (pond) F4
Great Pond (bay) F4
Green (cay) F4
Hams Bluff (prom.) E3
Hans Lollik (isls.) B4
Hassel (isl.) B4
Jersey (bay) B4
Krause Lagoon (chan.) F4
Leeward (passg.) B4
Long (pt.) B4
Long (pt.) E4
Lovango (cay) C4
Magens (bay) B4
Maho (bay) C4
Narrows, The (str.) C4
Nulliberg (mt.) B4
Perseverance (bay) A4
Picara (pt.) B4
Pillsbury (sound) B4
Privateer (pt.) D4
Pull (pt.) F3
Ram (head) C5
Red (pt.) D4
Reef (bay) C4
Saba (isl.) A4
Saint Croix (isl.) 49,725 G4
Saint James (isls.) B4
Saint John (isl.) 2,472 C4
Saint Thomas (harb.) B4
Saint Thomas (isl.) 44,372 A4
Salt (cay) A4
Salt (riv.) F4
Salt River (bay) F3
Sandy (pt.) D4
Savana (isl.) A4
Southwest (cape) E4
Tague (bay) G4
Thatch (cay) B4
Turner Hole (bay) G4
U.S. Nav. Air Sta. A4
Virgin (str.) A4
Virgin Isls. Nat'l Park C4
Water (isl.) A4
Westend Saltpond (lag.) E4

*City and suburbs.
• Population of district.
†Population of met. area.
○ Population of municipality.

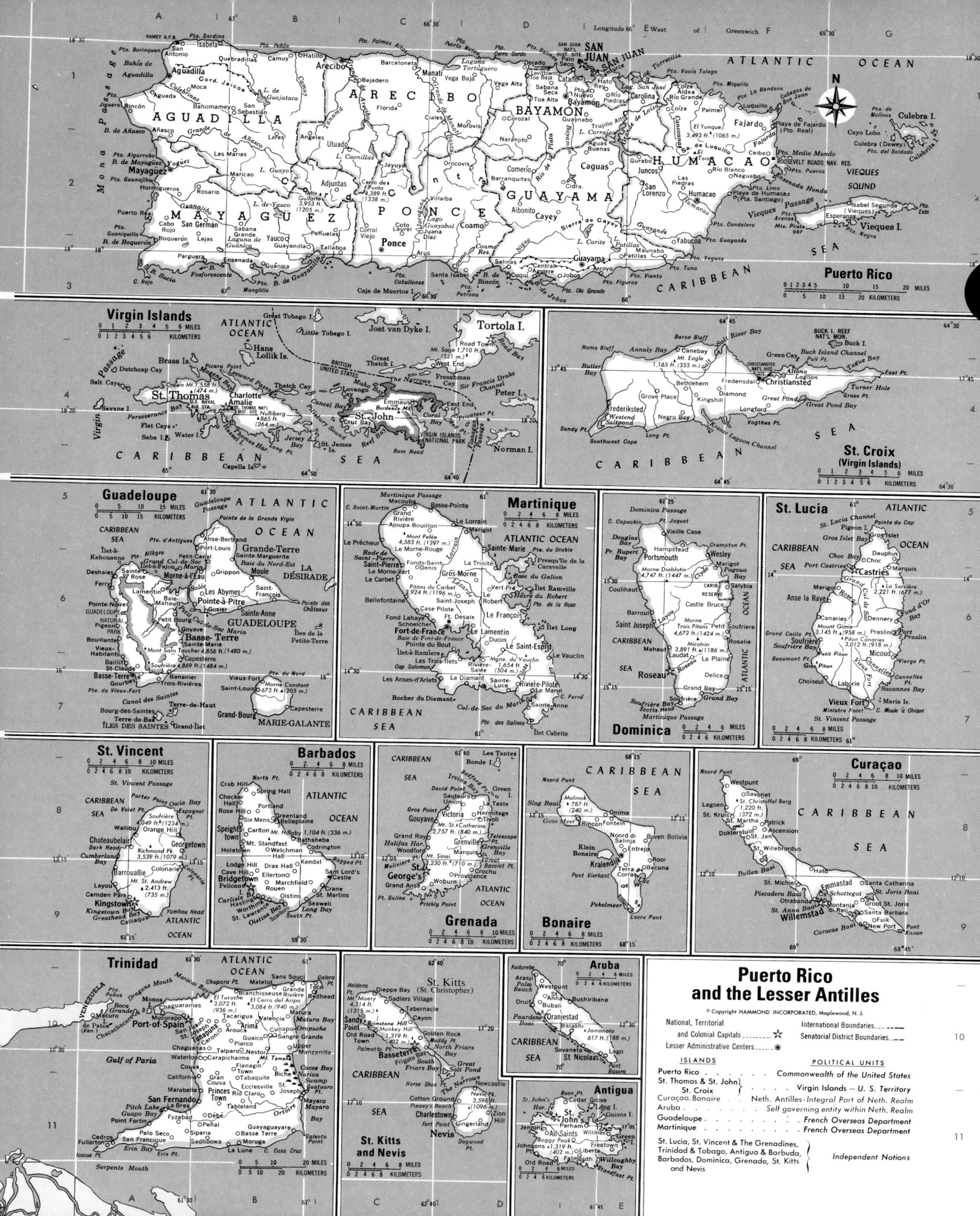
Puerto Rico and the Lesser Antilles
© Copyright HAMMOND INCORPORATED, Maplewood, N. J.
National, Territorial and Colonial Capitals
Lesser Administrative Centers
International Boundaries
Senatorial District Boundaries
ISLANDS
POLITICAL UNITS
Puerto Rico . . . . . Commonwealth of the United States
St. Thomas & St. John, St. Croix . . . Virgin Islands — U. S. Territory
Curaçao, Bonaire . . . Neth. Antilles-Integral Part of Neth. Realm
Aruba . . . . . Self governing entity within Neth. Realm
Guadeloupe . . . . . . French Overseas Department
Martinique . . . . . . French Overseas Department
St. Lucia, St. Vincent & The Grenadines, Trinidad & Tobago, Antigua & Barbuda, Barbados, Dominica, Grenada, St. Kitts and Nevis — Independent Nations
Puerto Rico
ATLANTIC OCEAN
CARIBBEAN SEA
AGUADILLA
ARECIBO
BAYAMON
HUMACAO
MAYAGÜEZ
PONCE
GUAYAMA
Cordillera Central
SAN JUAN
Aguadilla
Mayagüez
Arecibo
Ponce
Caguas
Humacao
Guayama
Vieques I.
Culebra I.
Mona Passage
Vieques Passage
Vieques Sound
El Yunque 3,493 ft. (1065 m.)
Cerro de Punta 4,389 ft. (1338 m.)
Longitude 66° West of Greenwich
Virgin Islands
Tortola I.
St. Thomas
Charlotte Amalie
St. John
Jost van Dyke I.
Virgin Passage
St. Croix (Virgin Islands)
Christiansted
Frederiksted
Guadeloupe
Grande-Terre
Basse-Terre
Pointe-à-Pitre
MARIE-GALANTE
LA DÉSIRADE
ÎLES DES SAINTES
Martinique
Fort-de-France
Mont Pelée 4,583 ft. (1397 m.)
Dominica
Roseau
Portsmouth
Morne Diablotin 4,747 ft. (1447 m.)
St. Lucia
Castries
Vieux Fort
Mount Gimie 3,145 ft. (958 m.)
St. Vincent
Kingstown
Soufrière 4,049 ft. (1234 m.)
Barbados
Bridgetown
Mt. Hillaby 1,104 ft. (336 m.)
Grenada
St. George's
Mt. St. Catherine 2,757 ft. (840 m.)
Bonaire
Kralendijk
Curaçao
Willemstad
Trinidad
Port-of-Spain
San Fernando
Gulf of Paria
Serpents Mouth
Dragons Mouth
VENEZUELA
El Cerro del Aripo 3,084 ft. (940 m.)
St. Kitts (St. Christopher)
Basseterre
Mt. Misery 4,314 ft. (1315 m.)
St. Kitts and Nevis
Nevis
Charlestown
Nevis Pk. 3,596 ft. (1096 m.)
Aruba
Oranjestad
Jamanota 617 ft. (188 m.)
Antigua
St. John's
Boggy Peak 1,319 ft. (402 m.)

Canada
CONIC PROJECTION

SCALE OF MILES
0 50 100   200   300

SCALE OF KILOMETERS
0 50 100 200   300   400   500

Capitals of Countries .... ☆
Provincial & Territorial Capitals .... ★
Administrative Centers .... ◉
International Boundaries ___ ▪ ___ ▪ ___
Provincial Boundaries ___ ___ ___
Regional Boundaries ....

© Copyright HAMMOND INCORPORATED, Maplewood, N. J.

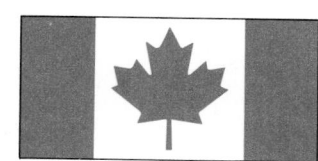

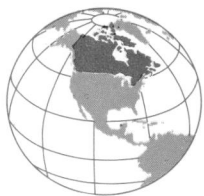

AREA 3,851,787 sq. mi. (9,976,139 sq. km.)
POPULATION 25,309,331
CAPITAL Ottawa
LARGEST CITY Montréal
HIGHEST POINT Mt. Logan 19,524 ft. (5,951 m.)
MONETARY UNIT Canadian dollar
MAJOR LANGUAGES English, French
MAJOR RELIGIONS Protestantism, Roman Catholicism

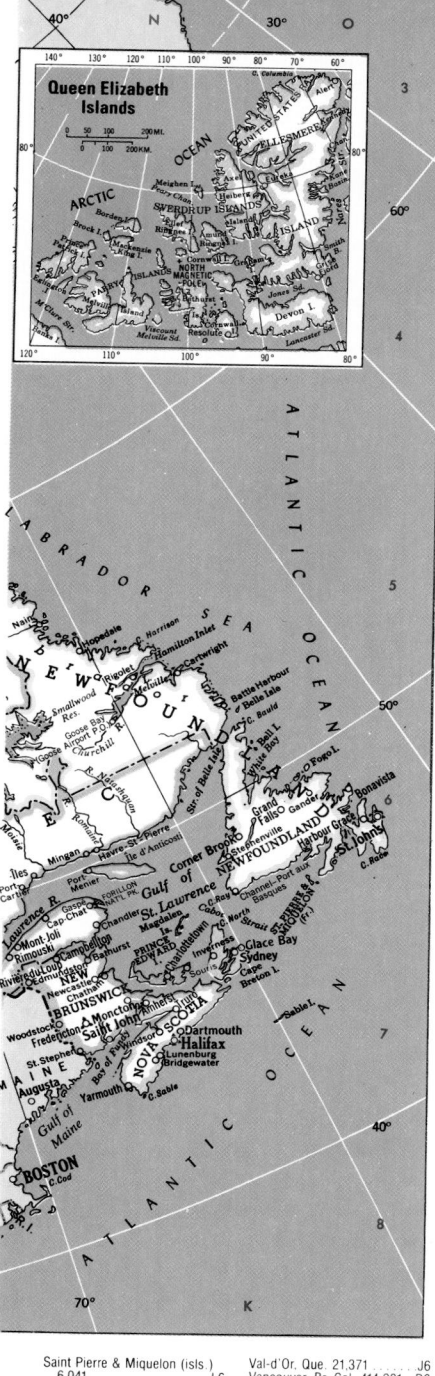

Queen Elizabeth Islands

Population Distribution

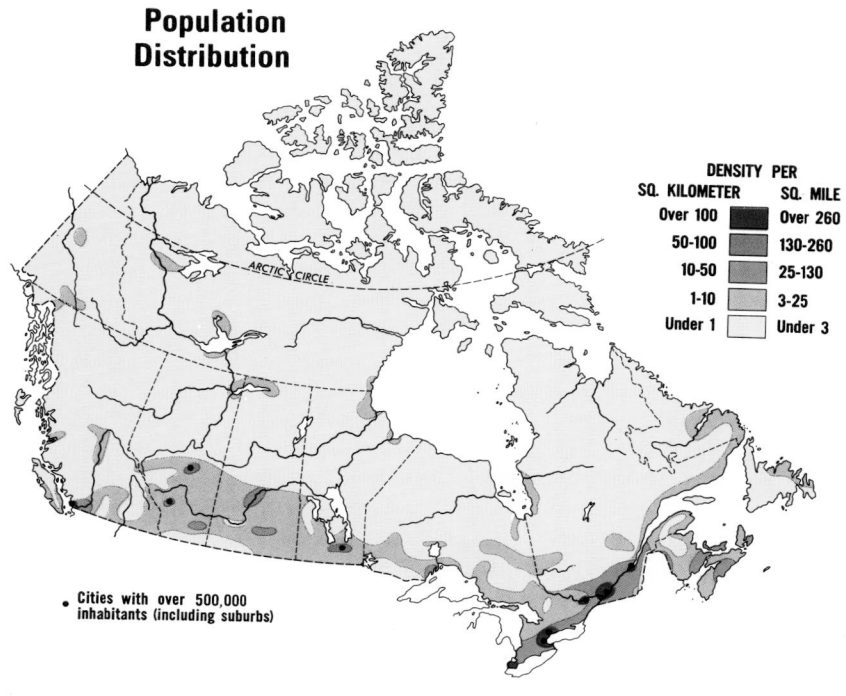

DENSITY PER	
SQ. KILOMETER	**SQ. MILE**
Over 100	Over 260
50-100	130-260
10-50	25-130
1-10	3-25
Under 1	Under 3

• Cities with over 500,000 inhabitants (including suburbs)

Vegetation

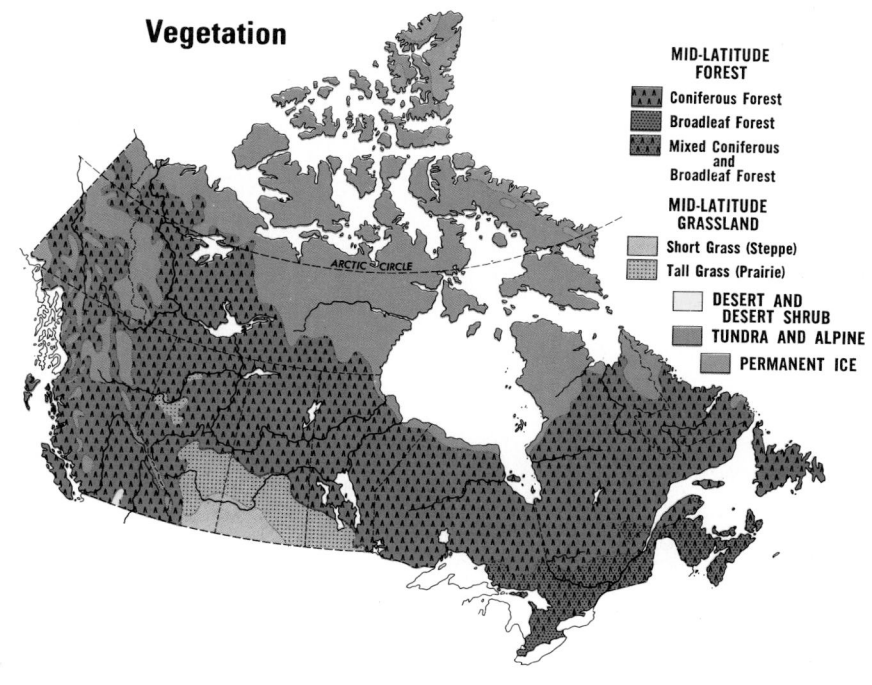

MID-LATITUDE FOREST
Coniferous Forest
Broadleaf Forest
Mixed Coniferous and Broadleaf Forest

MID-LATITUDE GRASSLAND
Short Grass (Steppe)
Tall Grass (Prairie)

DESERT AND DESERT SHRUB
TUNDRA AND ALPINE
PERMANENT ICE

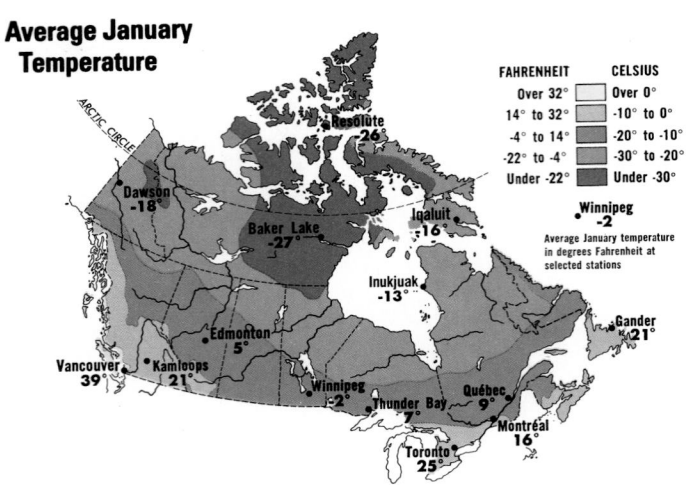

Average January Temperature

FAHRENHEIT	CELSIUS
Over 32°	Over 0°
14° to 32°	-10° to 0°
-4° to 14°	-20° to -10°
-22° to -4°	-30° to -20°
Under -22°	Under -30°

Resolute -26°
Dawson -18°
Baker Lake -27°
Iqaluit -16°
Inukjuak -13°
Edmonton 5°
Gander 21°
Vancouver 39°
Kamloops 21°
Winnipeg -2°
Thunder Bay 7°
Québec 9°
Montréal 16°
Toronto 25°

Winnipeg -2°
Average January temperature in degrees Fahrenheit at selected stations

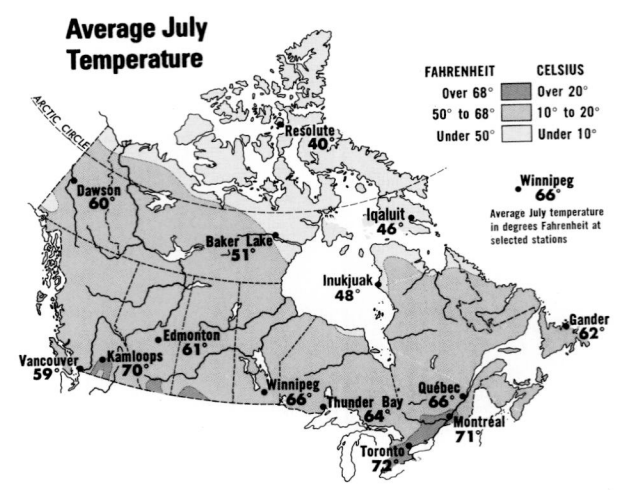

Average July Temperature

FAHRENHEIT	CELSIUS
Over 68°	Over 20°
50° to 68°	10° to 20°
Under 50°	Under 10°

Resolute 40°
Dawson 60°
Baker Lake 51°
Iqaluit 46°
Inukjuak 48°
Edmonton 61°
Gander 62°
Vancouver 59°
Kamloops 70°
Winnipeg 66°
Thunder Bay 64°
Québec 66°
Montréal 71°
Toronto 72°

Winnipeg 66°
Average July temperature in degrees Fahrenheit at selected stations

Agriculture, Industry and Resources

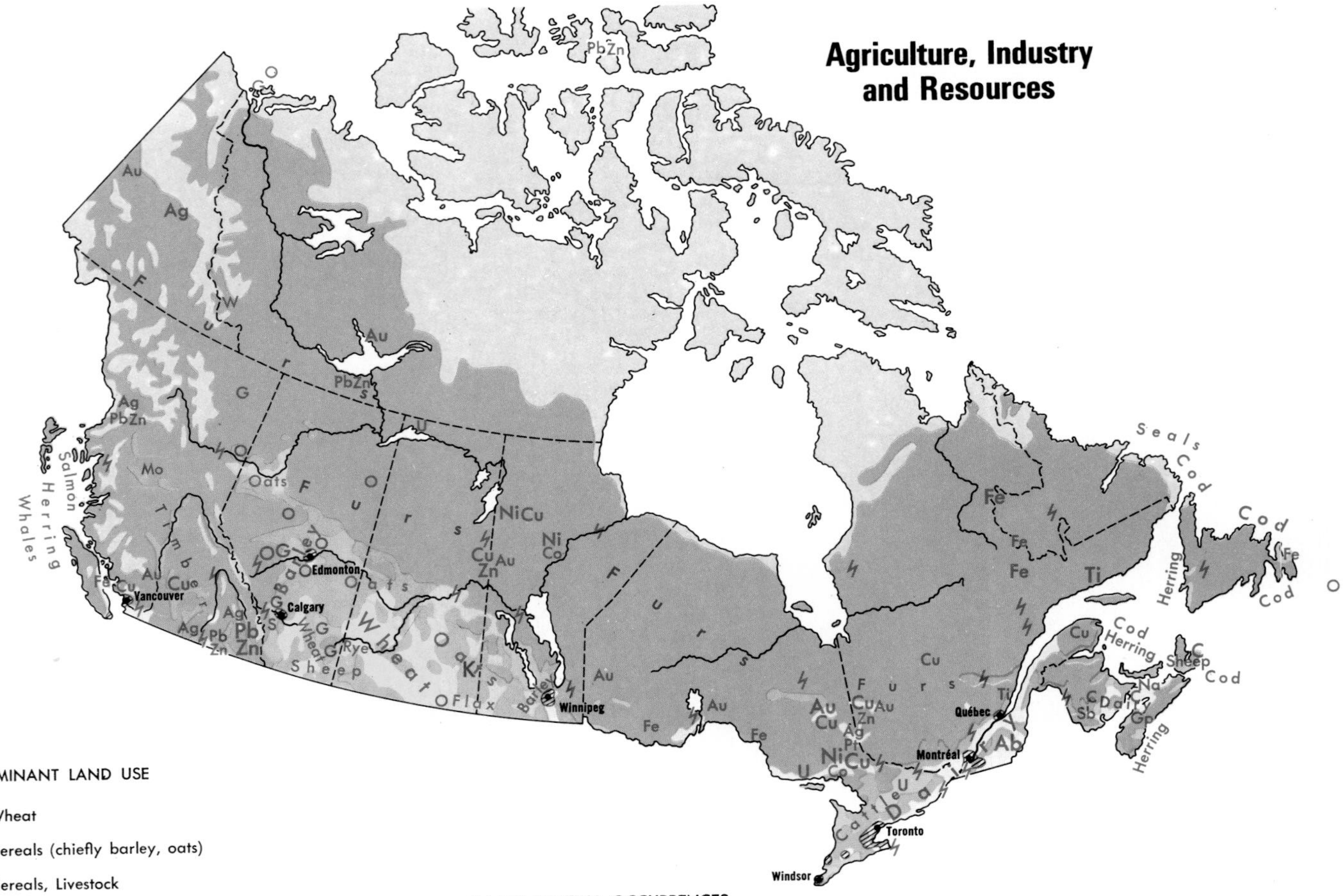

DOMINANT LAND USE

- Wheat
- Cereals (chiefly barley, oats)
- Cereals, Livestock
- General Farming, Livestock
- Dairy
- Fruit, Vegetables
- Pasture Livestock
- Range Livestock
- Forests
- Nonagricultural Land

MAJOR MINERAL OCCURRENCES

Ab Asbestos	Fe Iron Ore	Ni Nickel	Sb Antimony
Ag Silver	G Natural Gas	O Petroleum	Ti Titanium
Au Gold	Gp Gypsum	Pb Lead	U Uranium
C Coal	K Potash	Pt Platinum	W Tungsten
Co Cobalt	Mo Molybdenum	S Sulfur	Zn Zinc
Cu Copper	Na Salt		

⚡ Water Power
Major Industrial Areas

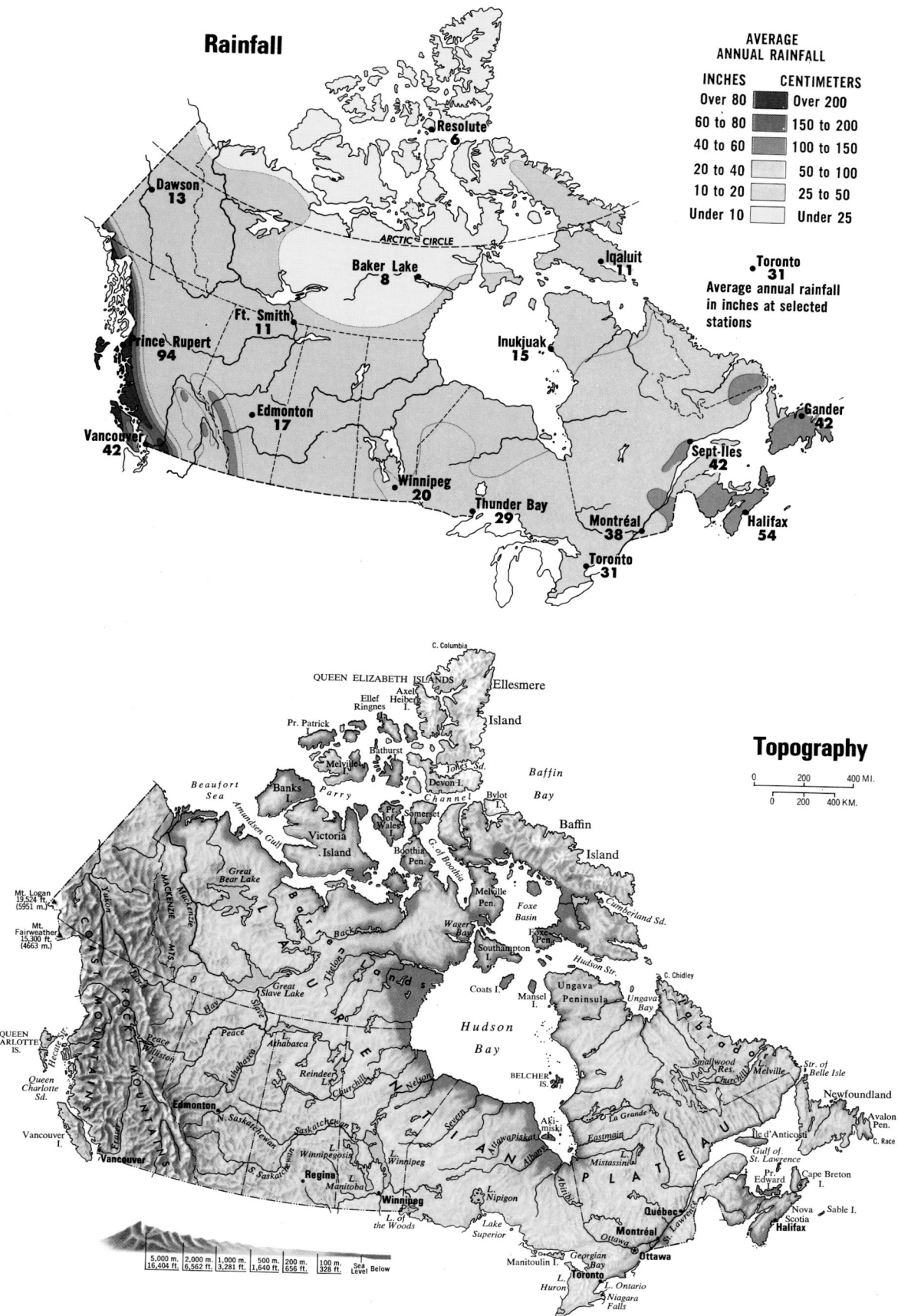

Rainfall

AVERAGE ANNUAL RAINFALL

INCHES		CENTIMETERS
Over 80		Over 200
60 to 80		150 to 200
40 to 60		100 to 150
20 to 40		50 to 100
10 to 20		25 to 50
Under 10		Under 25

Toronto
31
Average annual rainfall
in inches at selected
stations

Resolute
6

Dawson
13

ARCTIC CIRCLE

Baker Lake
8

Iqaluit
11

Ft. Smith
11

Inukjuak
15

Prince Rupert
94

Edmonton
17

Gander
42

Vancouver
42

Sept-Îles
42

Winnipeg
20

Thunder Bay
29

Montréal
38

Halifax
54

Toronto
31

Topography

0   200   400 MI.
0   200   400 KM.

C. Columbia

QUEEN ELIZABETH ISLANDS
Ellesmere

Axel
Heiberg
I.
Ellef
Ringnes
I.

Island

Pr. Patrick

Bathurst

Baffin

Melville

Joh's Sd.

Devon I.

Bay

Beaufort
Sea

Banks
I.

Parry

Bylot
I.

Channel

Amundsen Gulf

P. of
Wales
Somerset

Baffin

Victoria
Island

Boothia
Pen.

G. of Boothia

Island

Mt. Logan
19,524 ft.
(5951 m.)

Great
Bear Lake

Melville
Pen.

Cumberland Sd.

Mt.
Fairweather
15,300 ft.
(4663 m.)

Back

Foxe
Basin

Wager
Bay

QUEEN
CHARLOTTE
IS.

Great
Slave Lake

Southampton

Foxe
Pen.

Hudson Str.

C. Chidley

Queen
Charlotte
Sd.

Peace

Peace

Athabasca

Reindeer
L.

Coats I.

Mansel
I.

Ungava
Peninsula

Ungava
Bay

Liard

Nelson

Churchill

Hudson
Bay

BELCHER
IS.

Smallwood
Res.

L.
Melville

Str. of
Belle Isle

Edmonton

N. Saskatchewan

Saskatchewan

Akimiski

La Grande

Newfoundland

Vancouver
I.

Athabasca

Severn

Attawapiskat

Eastmain

Île d'Anticosti

Avalon
Pen.

C. Race

Vancouver

S. Saskatchewan

L.
Winnipegosis

L.
Winnipeg

Albany

Mistassini

Gulf of
St. Lawrence

Regina

L.
Manitoba

Abitibi

Pr.
Edward

Cape Breton
I.

Winnipeg

L. of
the Woods

L.
Nipigon

Québec

Nova
Scotia

Sable I.

5,000 m.   2,000 m.   1,000 m.   500 m.   200 m.   100 m.   Sea   Below
16,404 ft. 6,562 ft. 3,281 ft. 1,640 ft. 656 ft. 328 ft. Level

Halifax

Lake
Superior

Manitoulin I.

Georgian
Bay

Ottawa

Montréal

Ottawa

Toronto

L.
Huron

L. Ontario

Niagara
Falls

Newfoundland
including Labrador

SCALE

0   25   50   100   150 MI.

0   25   50   100   150 KM.

Capitals of Provinces .... ⊛
Provincial Boundaries .... —·—·—
Provincial Boundary according to
   Imperial Privy Council decision, 1927 .... - - - -

Longitude West of Greenwich

AREA 156,184 sq. mi. (404,517 sq. km.)
POPULATION 568,349
CAPITAL St. John's
LARGEST CITY St. John's
HIGHEST POINT in Torngat Mountains 5,420 ft. (1,652 m.)
SETTLED IN 1610
ADMITTED TO CONFEDERATION 1949
PROVINCIAL FLOWER Pitcher Plant

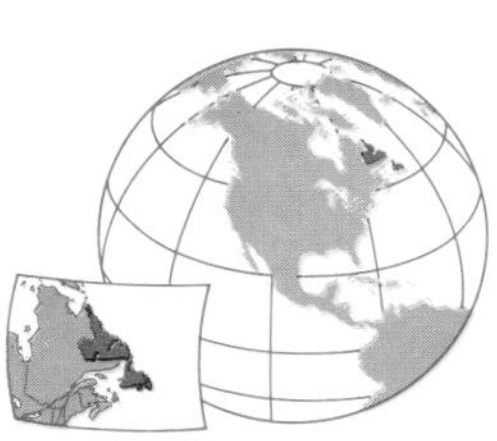

Agriculture, Industry and Resources

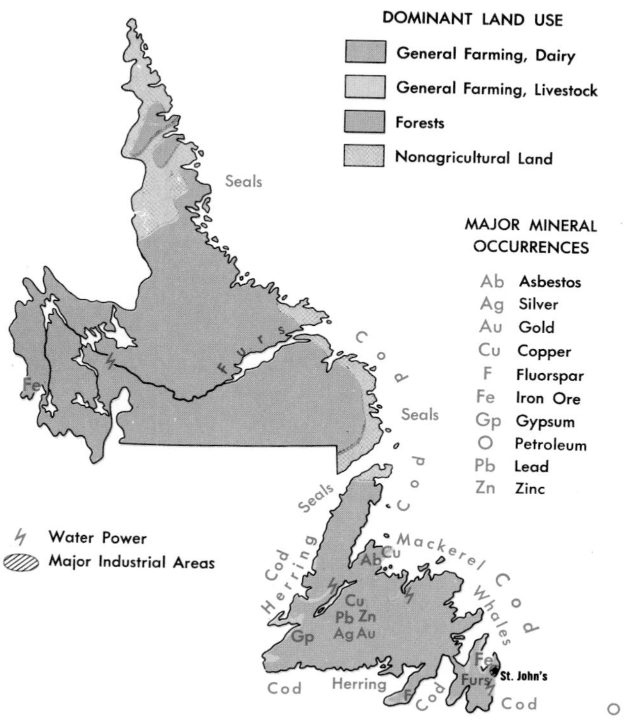
DOMINANT LAND USE
General Farming, Dairy
General Farming, Livestock
Forests
Nonagricultural Land
MAJOR MINERAL OCCURRENCES
Ab Asbestos
Ag Silver
Au Gold
Cu Copper
F Fluorspar
Fe Iron Ore
Gp Gypsum
O Petroleum
Pb Lead
Zn Zinc
Water Power
Major Industrial Areas
Seals
Furs
Cod
Mackerel
Whales
Herring
St. John's

NEWFOUNDLAND

CITIES and TOWNS

Admiral's Beach 362 D2
Admiral's Cove 99 D2
Anchor Point 368 C3
Aquaforte 200 D2
Argentia 93 C2
Arnold's Cove 1,124 C2
Avondale 890 D2
Badger 1,090 C4
Badger's Quay-Valleyfield-Pool's Island 1,566 D4
Baie Verte 2,491 C4
Battle Harbour C3
Bauline 423 D2
Bay Bulls 1,081 D2
Bay de Verde 786 D2
Bay L'Argent 483 D4
Bay Roberts 4,512 D2
Bellburns 147 C3
Belleoram 565 C4
Bellevue 286 D2
Bide Arm 339 C3
Big Pond 167 D2
Birchy Bay 707 D4
Bird Cove 400 C3
Bishop's Falls 4,395 C4
Black Tickle 194 C3
Blackhead Road 1,855 D2
Blaketown 617 D2
Bloomfield 715 D2
Bonavista 4,460 D2
Botwood 4,074 C4
Branch 462 D2
Brigus 898 D2
Broad Cove 198 D2
Brooklyn 197 D2
Brownsdale 199 D2
Buchans 1,655 C4
Bunyan's Cove 590 C2
Burgeo 2,504 C4
Burin 2,904 C4
Burnt Islands 991 C4
Burnt Point 260 D2
Calvert 482 D2
Campbellton 703 D4
Cape Broyle 698 D2
Cape Ray 484 C4
Caplin Cove 150 D2
Carbonear 5,335 D2
Carmanville 966 D4
Cartwright 658 C3
Catalina 1,162 D2
Cavendish 343 D2
Champney's West 141 D2
Chance Cove 498 D2
Change Islands 580 D4
Channel-Port aux Basques 5,988 C4
Chapel Arm 689 D2
Charlottetown 330 D2
Charlottetown 250 C3
Churchill Falls 936 B3
Clarenville 2,878 C2
Clarke's Beach 1,009 D2
Codroy 346 C4
Colinet 318 D2
Colliers 819 D2
Come By Chance 337 C2
Conception Harbour 917 D2
Conche 464 C3
Cook's Harbour 388 C3
Corner Brook 24,339 C4
Cow Head 695 C4
Cox's Cove 980 C4
Cupids 706 D2
Daniell's Harbour 614 C3
Dark Cove 1,344 D4
Davis Inlet 240 B2
Deep Bight 243 C2
Deer Lake 4,348 C4
Dildo 877 D2
Dunville 1,817 D2
Durrell 1,145 D4
Eastport 597 D1
Elliston 527 D2
Embree 846 C4
Englee 998 C3
English Harbour 118 D2
English Harbour West 327 C4
Fermeuse 584 D2
Ferryland 795 D2
Flat Bay 322 C4
Flat Rock 808 D2
Fleur de Lys 616 C3
Flowers Cove 459 C3
Fogo 1,105 D4
Forteau 520 C3
Fortune 2,473 C4
Fox Harbour 280 C3
Fox Harbour 538 D2
François 219 C4
Freshwater 1,276 C2
Freshwater 209 D2
Gambo 2,932 D4
Gander 10,404 D4
Garnish 761 C4
Gaskiers-Point la Haye 505 D2
Gaultois 558 C4
Georges Brook 356 D2
Glenwood 1,129 D4
Glovertown 2,165 C1
Goobies 185 D2
Goose Bay-Happy Valley 7,103 B3
Gooseberry Cove 195 C2
Goose Cove 134 C2
Goose Cove 368 C3
Goulds 4,242 D2
Grand Bank 3,901 C4
Grand Falls 8,765 C4
Grates Cove 275 D2
Green Island Cove 222 C3
Green's Harbour 785 D2
Greenspond 423 D4
Grey River 234 C4
Gull Island 362 D2
Hampden 838 C4
Hant's Harbour 542 D2
Happy Adventure 352 D2
Happy Valley-Goose Bay 7,103 B3
Harbour Breton 2,464 C4
Harbour Deep 278 C3
Harbour Grace 2,988 D2
Harbour Main-Chapel Cove-Lakeview 1,303 D2
Hare Bay 1,520 D4
Hawke's Bay 553 C3
Head of Bay d'Espoir 586 C4
Heart's Content 625 D2
Heart's Delight-Islington 899 D2
Heart's Desire 416 D2
Heatherton 328 C4
Hermitage 863 C4
Hickman's Harbour 479 D2
Hillview 295 D2
Hodge's Cove 438 D2
Holyrood 1,789 D2
Hopedale 425 B2
Howley 456 C4
Isle aux Morts 1,238 C4
Jackson's Arm 623 C4
Jeffrey's 276 C4
Jerseyside 641 B3
Job's Cove 201 D2
Joe Batt's Arm-Barr'd Islands 1,155 D4
Keels 129 D1
Kelligrews (Foxtrap-Greeleytown-Peachtown-Kelligrews) 2,292 D2
Kilbride 5,014 D2
King's Cove 253 D1
King's Point 825 C4
Kippens 1,219 C4
Labrador City 11,538 A3
Lamaline 548 C4
L'Anse-au-Clair 267 C3
L'Anse-au-Loup 589 C3
L'Anse au Meadow 66 C3
La Poile 186 C4
Lark Harbour 783 C4
La Scie 1,422 C4
Lawn 999 C4
Lethbridge 686 D2
Lewisporte 3,963 C4
Little Bay Islands 407 C4
Little Catalina 750 D2
Little Heart's Ease 467 D2
Lodge Bay 124 C3
Long Harbour-Mount Arlington Heights 660 D2
Lourdes 932 C4
Lower Island Cove 415 D2
Lumsden 645 D4
Main Brook 514 C3
Makkovik 347 C2
Markland 344 D2
Mary's Harbour 408 C3
Marystown 6,299 D4
McCallum 243 C4
Melrose 416 D2
Middle Arm, Green Bay 575 C4
Millertown 228 C4
Milltown-Head of Bay d'Espoir 1,376 C4
Milton 258 C2
Mobile 171 D2
Mount Carmel-Mitchell's Brook-St. Catherine's 699 D2
Mount Pearl 11,543 D2
Musgrave Harbour 1,554 D4
Musgravetown 635 C2
Nain 938 B2
New Bonaventure 106 D2
New Chelsea 144 D2
New Harbour 777 D2
Newmans Cove 231 D2
New Perlican 350 D2
Newtown 511 D4
Nippers Harbour 259 C4
Norman's Cove-Long Cove 1,152 D2
Norris Arm 1,216 C4
Norris Point 1,033 C4
North Harbour 151 D2
North River 245 D2
North West Brook 279 C2
North West River 515 B3
O'Donnells 280 D2
Old Bonaventure 111 D2
Old Perlican 709 D2
Paradise 2,861 D2
Parkers Cove 424 D4
Parson's Pond 605 C3
Pasadena 2,685 C4
Patrick's Cove 155 C2
Perry's Cove 141 D2
Peterview 1,119 C4
Petites 108 C4
Petley 147 D2
Petty Harbour-Maddox Cove 853 D2
Picadilly 524 C4
Pinware River 201 C3
Placentia 2,204 C2
Plate Cove 474 D2
Point La Haye 195 D2
Point Lance 141 C2
Point Leamington 848 C4
Point Verde 296 C2
Pollards Point 502 C4
Port au Bras 366 D4
Port au Choix 1,311 C3
Port au Port 603 C4
Port Blandford 702 C2
Port Hope Simpson 581 C3
Port Kirwan 164 D2
Port Rexton 489 D2
Port Saunders 769 C3
Portugal Cove 2,361 D2
Portugal Cove South 371 D2
Port Union 671 D2
Postville 223 B3
Pouch Cove 1,522 D2
Princeton 204 D2
Raleigh 373 C3
Ramea 1,386 C4
Red Bay 316 C3
Red Head Cove 225 D2
Rencontre East 230 C4
Renews-Cappahayden 578 D2
Rigolet 271 C3
Riverhead 431 D2
River of Ponds 304 C3
Robert's Arm 1,005 C4
Rocky Harbour 1,273 C4
Roddickton 1,142 C3
Rose Blanche-Harbour le Cou 975 C4
Rushoon 520 D4
Saint Alban's 1,968 C4
Saint Andrew's 262 C4
Saint Anthony 3,107 C3
Saint Brendan's 468 D4
Saint Bride's 599 C2
Saint George's 1,756 C4
St. John's (cap.) 83,770 D2
Saint Joseph's 262 D2
Saint Lawrence 2,012 C4
Saint Lunaire-Griquet 1,010 C3
Saint Mary's 701 D2
Saint Paul's 454 C4
Saint Phillips 1,365 D2
Saint Shotts 239 D2
Saint Vincent's-Saint Stephens-Peter's River 796 D2
Sally's Cove 100 C4
Salmon Cove 786 D2
Seal Cove 751 C3
Seal Cove-White Bay 498 C4
Seldom-Little Seldom 560 D4
Ship Harbour 265 D2
Shoal Cove 223 C3
Shoal Harbour 1,000 C2
South Branch 264 C4
South Brook, Hall's Bay Dist. 786 C4
South Brook, Humber Dist. 477 C4
Southern Harbour 772 C2
South River 645 D2
Spaniard's Bay 2,125 D2
Springdale 3,501 C4
Stephenville 8,876 C4
Stephenville Crossing 2,172 C4
Summerford 1,198 C4
Summerville 346 D2
Sunnyside 703 D2
Sweet Bay 204 D2
Swift Current 329 C2
Terrenceville 796 D4
Tilting 427 D4
Torbay 3,394 D2
Tors Cove 355 D2
Traytown 383 D1
Trepassey 1,473 D2
Trinity 522 D2
Trinity 375 D4
Trout River 759 C4
Twillingate 1,506 C4
Upper Island Cove 2,025 D2
Victoria 1,870 D2
Wabana 4,254 D2
Wabush 3,155 A3
Wesleyville 1,125 D4
Western Bay 463 D2
West Saint Modeste 273 C3
Whitbourne 1,233 D2
Wild Cove 152 C3
Windsor 5,747 C4
Winterton 753 D2
Witless Bay 907 D2

OTHER FEATURES

Alexis (riv.) C3
Anguille (cape) C4
Annieopscotch (mts.) C4
Ashuanipi (lake) A3
Ashuanipi (riv.) A3
Atikonak (lake) B3
Attikamagen (lake) A3
Avalon (pen.) D2
Barachois Pond Prov. Park C4
Bauld (cape) C3
Bell (isl.) C3
Bell (isl.) D2
Belle Isle (isl.) C3
Belle Isle (str.) C3
Blackhead (bay) D2
Bonavista (bay) D1
Bonavista (cape) D1
Bonne (bay) C4
Branch (riv.) C2
Broyle (cape) D2
Bull Arm (inlet) D2
Burin (pen.) C4
Butter Pot Prov. Park D2
Cabot (str.) B4
Canada (bay) C3
Chidley (cape) B1
Churchill (falls) B3
Churchill (riv.) B3
Cirque (mt.) B2
Clode (sound) D2
Conception (bay) D2
Deep (inlet) B2
Double Mer (lake) C3
Dyke (lake) A3
Eagle (riv.) C3
Espoir (bay) C4
Exploits (riv.) C4
Fogo (isl.) D4
Fortune (bay) C4
Freels (cape) D3
Gander (lake) D4
Gander (riv.) D4
Glover (isl.) C4
Goose (riv.) B3
Grand (lake) B3
Grand (lake) C4
Grates (pt.) D2
Great Colinet (isl.) D2
Grey (isls.) C3
Groais (isl.) C3
Gros Morne (mt.) C4
Gros Morne Nat'l Park C4
Groswater (bay) C3
Hamilton (inlet) C3
Hamilton (sound) D4
Hare (bay) C3
Hawke (hills) D2
Hebron (fjord) B2
Hermitage (bay) C4
Holyrood (bay) D2
Horse (isls.) C3
Horse Chops (head) D2
Humber (riv.) C4
Ingornachoix (bay) C3
Ireland's Eye (isl.) D2
Islands (bay) C4
Kaipokok (bay) B2
Kanairiktok (riv.) B3
Kaumajet (mts.) B2
Kingurutik (mesa) B2
Labrador (reg.) B2
Labrador (sea) C2
La Manche Valley Prov. Park D2
La Poile (bay) C4
Little Mecatina (riv.) B3
Long (isl.) C2
Long (lake) A3
Long (pt.) C4
Long Range (mts.) C4
Main Topsail (mt.) C4
Makkovik (cape) C2
McLelan (str.) B1
Mealy (lake) C3
Meelpaeg (lake) C4
Melville (lake) C3
Menihek (lakes) A3
Merasheen (isl.) C2
Mistaken (pt.) D2
Mistastin (lake) B2
Nachvak (fjord) B2
Naskaupi (riv.) B3
Newfoundland (isl.) C4
Newman (sound) D2
New World (isl.) C4
Norman (cape) C3
North Aulatsivik (isl.) B2
Notre Dame (bay) C4
Okak (bay) B2
Ossokmanuan (res.) B3
Petitsikapau (lake) A3
Pine (cape) D2
Pinware (riv.) C3
Pistolet (bay) C3
Placentia (bay) C2
Ponds (isl.) C3
Port au Port (bay) C4
Port au Port (pen.) C4
Port Manvers (harb.) B2
Race (cape) D2
Ramah (bay) B2
Ramea (isls.) C4
Random (isl.) D2
Random (sound) D2
Ray (cape) C4
Red (isl.) C2
Red Indian (lake) C4
Red Wine (riv.) B3
Rocky (riv.) D2
Round (pond) C4
Saglek (bay) B2
Saint Francis (cape) D2
Saint George (cape) C4
Saint George's (bay) C4
Saint John (bay) C3
Saint John (cape) C3
Saint Lawrence (gulf) B4
Saint Lewis (cape) C3
Saint Mary's (bay) C2
Saint Mary's (cape) C2
Saint Michaels (bay) C3
Salmonier (riv.) D2
Sandwich (bay) C3
Shabogamo (lake) A3
Shoal (bay) D2
Smallwood (res.) B3
Smith (sound) D2
South Aulatsivik (isl.) B2
Spear (cape) D2
Squires Mem. Park C4
Swale (isl.) D1
Terra Nova (riv.) C2
Terra Nova Nat'l Park D2
Territok (cape) B2
Thoresby (mt.) B2
Torbay (pt.) D2
Torngat (mts.) B2
Trespassey (bay) D2
Trinity (bay) D2
Tunungayualok (isl.) B2
Ukasiksalik (isl.) B2
Victoria (lake) C4
White (bay) C3
White Bear (lake) C4
White Handkerchief (cape) B2

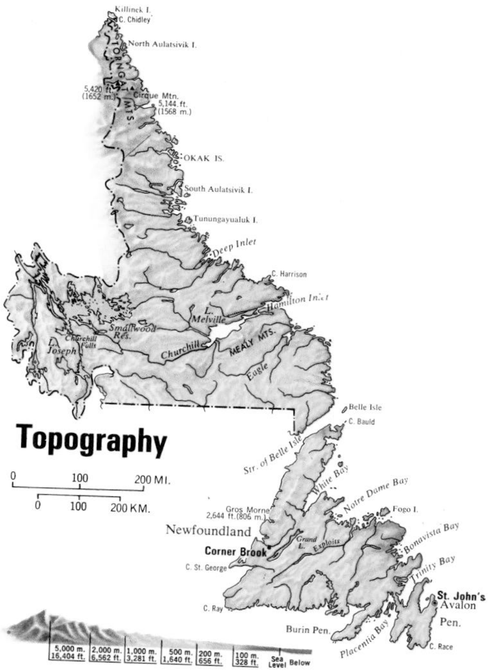
Topography
0 100 200 MI.
0 100 200 KM.
Killinek I.
C. Chidley
North Aulatsivik I.
OKAK IS.
South Aulatsivik I.
Tunungayualuk I.
Deep Inlet
C. Harrison
Hamilton Inlet
Melville
Smallwood Res.
Churchill
MEALY MTS.
Eagle
Belle Isle
C. Bauld
Str. of Belle Isle
White Bay
Notre Dame Bay
Fogo I.
Bonavista Bay
Gros Morne 2,644 ft. (806 m.)
Newfoundland
Corner Brook
C. St. George
C. Ray
Burin Pen.
Trinity Bay
St. John's
Avalon Pen.
Placentia Bay
C. Race
5,000 m. 16,404 ft.
2,000 m. 6,562 ft.
1,000 m. 3,281 ft.
500 m. 1,640 ft.
200 m. 656 ft.
100 m. 328 ft.
Sea Level
Below

SAINT PIERRE and MIQUELON

CITIES and TOWNS

Saint-Pierre (cap.) 5,415 C4

OTHER FEATURES

Miquelon (isl.) 626 C4
Saint Pierre (isl.) 5,415 C4

NOVA SCOTIA

COUNTIES

Annapolis 22,522 .... C 4
Antigonish 18,110 .... F 3
Cape Breton 127,035 .... H 3
Colchester 43,224 .... E 3
Cumberland 35,231 .... C 4
Digby 21,689 .... C 4
Guysborough 12,752 .... F 3
Halifax 288,126 .... D 4
Hants 33,121 .... G 2
Inverness 22,337 .... H 2
Kings 49,739 .... D 4
Lunenburg 45,746 .... D 4
Pictou 50,350 .... F 3
Queens 13,126 .... D 4
Richmond 12,284 .... H 3
Shelburne 17,328 .... C 5
Victoria 8,432 .... H 2
Yarmouth 26,290 .... C 5

CITIES and TOWNS

Alder Point 651 .... H 2
Aldershot .... D 3
Amherst⊚ 9,684 .... D 3
Annapolis Royal⊚ 631 .... C 4
Antigonish⊚ 5,205 .... F 3
Arichat 824 .... H 3
Aylesford 744 .... D 3
Baddeck⊚ 972 .... H 2
Barrington Passage 722 .... C 5
Bear River-Sissibo 854 .... C 4
Beaverbank 1,322 .... E 4
Berwick 1,699 .... D 3
Bridgetown 1,047 .... C 4
Bridgewater 6,669 .... D 4
Brookfield 619 .... E 3
Brooklyn 1,269 .... D 4
Cambridge Station 799 .... D 3
Canning 763 .... D 3
Canso 1,255 .... H 3
Centreville 765 .... D 3
Chéticamp 1,022 .... G 2

Chester 1,131 .... D 4
Chester Basin 639 .... D 4
Church Point 318 .... B 4
Clark's Harbour 1,059 .... C 5
Coldbrook Station 617 .... D 3
Cow Bay 670 .... E 4
Dartmouth 62,277 .... E 4
Debert 618 .... E 3
Digby⊚ 2,558 .... C 4
Dominion 2,856 .... J 2
Donkin 873 .... J 2
Ellershouse-Hartville 662 .... D 4
Elmsdale 1,172 .... E 4
Enfield 1,510 .... E 4
Fall River 1,897 .... E 4
Falmouth 1,110 .... D 3
Glace Bay 21,466 .... J 2
Guysborough⊚ 496 .... G 3
Halifax (cap.)⊚ 114,594 .... E 4
Halifax *277,727 .... E 4
Hantsport 1,395 .... D 3
Herring Cove 1,323 .... E 4
Hilden 1,262 .... E 3

Ingonish 471 .... H 2
Inverness 2,013 .... G 2
Judique 925 .... G 3
Kentville⊚ 4,974 .... D 3
Kingston 1,612 .... E 4
Lakeside 936 .... E 4
Lantz 1,172 .... E 4
Liverpool⊚ 3,304 .... D 4
Lockeport 929 .... D 4
Louisbourg 1,410 .... J 3
Louisdale 979 .... H 3
Lower West Pubnico 790 .... C 5
Lunenburg⊚ 3,014 .... D 4
Mahone Bay 1,228 .... D 4
Meteghan 890 .... B 4
Middleton 1,834 .... D 3
Milford Station 748 .... E 4
Milton 1,678 .... D 4
Mount Uniacke 1,145 .... D 4
Mulgrave 1,099 .... G 3
Musquodoboit Harbour 936 .... E 4
New Glasgow 10,464 .... F 3
New Victoria 1,374 .... H 2

New Waterford 8,808 .... J 2
North Sydney 7,820 .... H 2
Oxford 1,470 .... D 3
Parrsboro 1,799 .... D 3
Pictou⊚ 4,628 .... F 3
Porters Lake 893 .... E 4
Port Hastings 312 .... G 3
Port Hawkesbury 3,850 .... G 3
Port Hood⊚ 701 .... G 2
Port Morien 717 .... J 2
Port Williams 1,227 .... D 3
Prospect 693 .... E 4
Pugwash 648 .... E 3
Reserve Mines 2,472 .... J 2
River Hébert 835 .... D 3
Saint Peters 669 .... H 3
Sandy Point 691 .... C 5
Scotchtown 2,037 .... J 2
Sheet Harbour 819 .... F 4
Shelburne⊚ 2,303 .... C 5
Shubenacadie 984 .... E 3
Springhill 4,896 .... D 3
Stellarton 5,435 .... F 3

Stewiacke 1,174 .... E 3
Sydney⊚ 29,444 .... H 2
Sydney Mines 8,501 .... H 2
Terence Bay 960 .... E 4
Thorburn 1,014 .... F 3
Three Mile Plains 1,355 .... D 4
Timberlea 1,159 .... E 4
Trenton 3,154 .... F 3
Truro⊚ 12,552 .... E 3
Waterville 687 .... D 3
Waverley 1,699 .... E 4
Wedgeport 827 .... C 5
Western Shore 1,712 .... D 4
Westmount 3,097 .... H 2
Westville 4,522 .... F 3
Wileville 746 .... D 4
Windsor⊚ 3,646 .... D 3
Wolfville 3,235 .... D 3
Yarmouth⊚ 7,475 .... B 5

OTHER FEATURES

Advocate (bay) .... D 3

Ainslie (lake) .... G 2
Amet (sound) .... E 3
Andrew (isl.) .... H 3
Annapolis (basin) .... C 4
Annapolis (riv.) .... C 4
Antigonish (harb.) .... G 3
Argos (cape) .... G 3
Aspy (bay) .... H 2
Avon (riv.) .... D 4
Baccaro (pt.) .... C 5
Baddeck (riv.) .... G 4
Barachois (pt.) .... G 4
Barren (isl.) .... G 4
Barrington (bay) .... C 5
Bedford (basin) .... E 4
Berry (head) .... D 4
Bouladerie (isl.) .... H 2
Bras d'Or (lake) .... H 2
Breton (cape) .... J 3
Brier (isl.) .... B 4
Canso (cape) .... G 3
Canso (str.) .... G 3
Cap d'Or (cape) .... D 3

Nova Scotia and Prince Edward Island

SCALE
0 10 20 30 40 50 MI.
0 10 20 30 40 50 KM.

Provincial Capitals .... ⊛ Provincial Boundaries —·—·—
County Seats .... ⊚ County Boundaries — — —

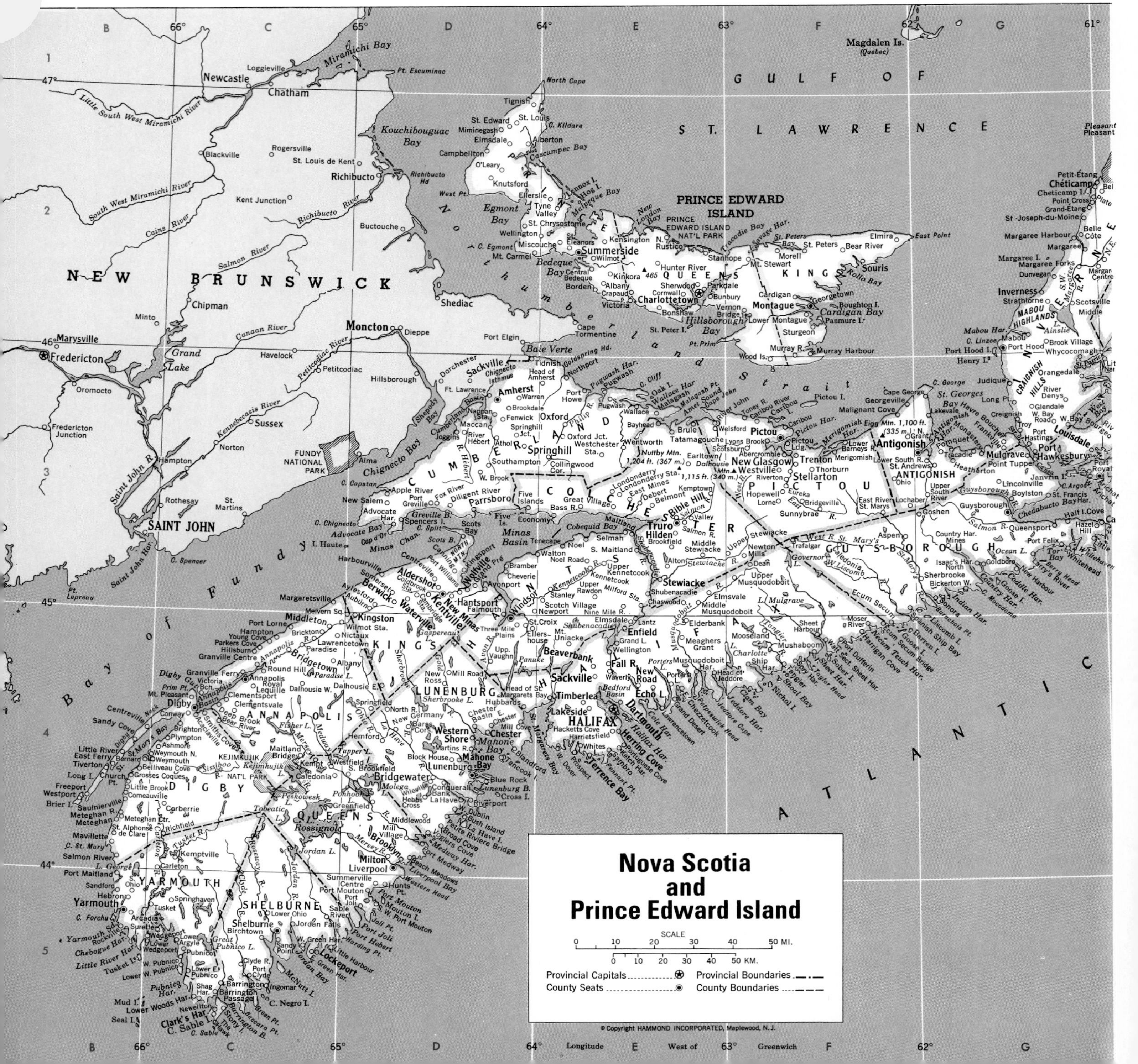

Cape Breton (isl.) .... J 2
Cape Breton Highlands Nat'l
  Park .... H 2
Cape Negro (isl.) .... C 5
Cape Sable (isl.) .... C 5
Capstan (cape) .... D 3
Caribou (isl.) .... F 3
Carleton (riv.) .... C 4
Charlotte (lake) .... F 3
Chebogue (harb.) .... B 5
Chedabucto (bay) .... G 3
Chéticamp (isl.) .... G 2
Chignecto (bay) .... D 3
Chignecto (cape) .... C 3
Chignecto (isth.) .... D 3
Clam (bay) .... F 4
Cliff (cape) .... E 3
Clyde (riv.) .... C 5
Cobequid (bay) .... E 3
Coddle (harb.) .... G 3
Coldspring (head) .... E 3
Cole (harb.) .... E 4
Country (harb.) .... G 3

Craignish (hills) .... G 3
Cross (isl.) .... D 4
Cumberland (basin) .... D 3
Dalhousie (mt.) .... E 3
Dauphin (cape) .... H 2
Digby Gut (chan.) .... C 4
Digby Neck (pen.) .... B 4
East (bay) .... H 3
East (riv.) .... F 3
East Bay (hills) .... H 3
Egmont (cape) .... H 2
Eigg (mt.) .... F 3
Fisher (lake) .... C 4
Five (isls.) .... D 3
Forchu (harb.) .... H 3
Forchu (cape) .... B 5
Framboise Cove (bay) .... H 3
Fundy (bay) .... C 3
Gabarus (bay) .... H 3
Gabarus (cape) .... J 3
Gaspereau (lake) .... D 4
George (cape) .... D 3
George (lake) .... B 5

PRINCE EDWARD ISLAND

AREA 2,184 sq. mi. (5,657 sq. km.)
POPULATION 126,646
CAPITAL Charlottetown
LARGEST CITY Charlottetown
HIGHEST POINT 465 ft. (142 m.)
SETTLED IN 1720
ADMITTED TO CONFEDERATION 1873
PROVINCIAL FLOWER Lady's Slipper

NOVA SCOTIA

AREA 21,425 sq. mi. (55,491 sq. km.)
POPULATION 873,176
CAPITAL Halifax
LARGEST CITY Halifax
HIGHEST POINT Cape Breton Highlands
  1,747 ft. (532 m.)
SETTLED IN 1605
ADMITTED TO CONFEDERATION 1867
PROVINCIAL FLOWER Trailing Arbutus or
  Mayflower

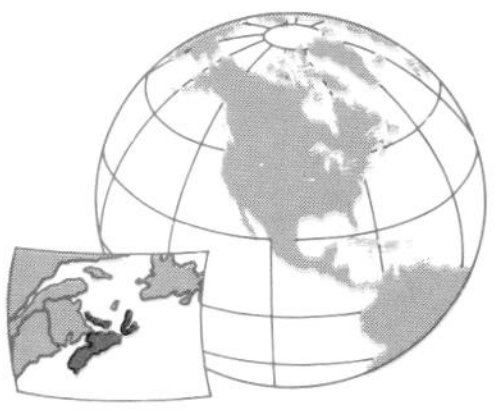

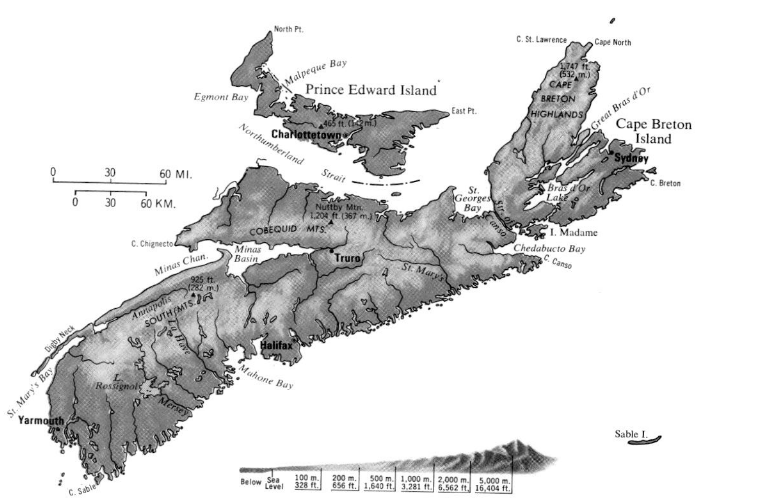

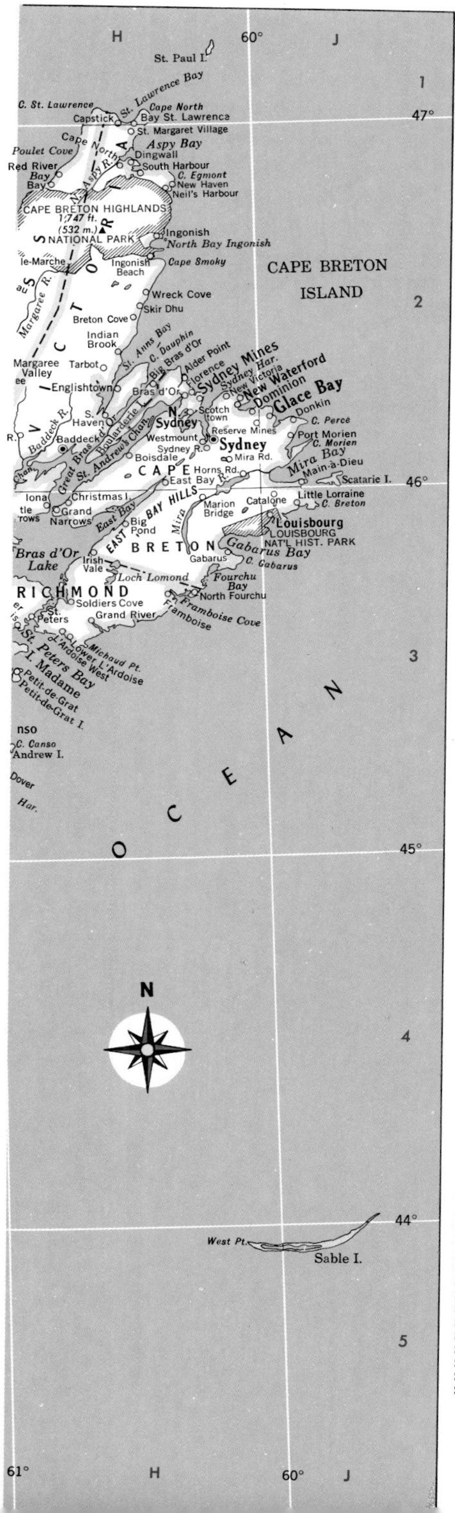

Gold (riv.) .... D 4
Goose (isl.) .... F 4
Goose (isl.) .... G 3
Governor (lake) .... F 3
Great Bras d'Or (chan.) ...... H 2
Great Pubnico (lake) .... C 5
Green (pt.) .... C 5
Greville (bay) .... D 3
Guysborough (riv.) .... F 3
Halifax (harb.) .... E 4
Harding (isl.) .... D 5
Haute (isl.) .... C 3
Hébert (riv.) .... D 3
Henry (isl.) .... G 3
Indian (harb.) .... G 3
Ingonish North (bay) .... H 2
Janvrin (isl.) .... G 3
Jeddore (harb.) .... F 4
John (cape) .... E 3
Joli (pt.) .... D 5
Jordan (bay) .... C 5
Jordan (isl.) .... C 4
Jordan (riv.) .... C 5
Kejimkujik (lake) .... C 4
Kejimkujik Nat'l Park .... C 4
Kennetcook (riv.) .... E 3
La Have (isl.) .... D 4
La Have (riv.) .... D 4
Linzee (cape) .... G 2
Liscomb (isl.) .... G 4
Little River (harb.) .... B 5
Liverpool (harb.) .... D 5
Lomond, Loch (lake) .... H 3
Long (isl.) .... B 4
Louisbourg Nat'l Hist. Park .. J 3
Lunenburg (bay) .... D 4
Mabou (harb.) .... G 2
Mabou Highlands (hills) ...... G 2
Madame (isl.) .... H 3
Mahone (bay) .... D 4
Malagash (pt.) .... E 3
Margaree (isl.) .... F 4
McNutt (isl.) .... C 5
Medway (harb.) .... D 4
Medway (riv.) .... C 4
Merigomish (harb.) .... F 3
Mersey (riv.) .... C 4
Michaud (pt.) .... H 3
Minas (basin) .... D 3
Minas (chan.) .... D 3
Mira (bay) .... J 2
Mira (riv.) .... H 3
Mocodome (cape) .... G 3
Molega (lake) .... D 4
Morien (cape) .... J 2
Mouton (isl.) .... D 5
Mud (isl.) .... B 5
Mulgrave (lake) .... F 3
Musquodoboit (harb.) .... E 4
Necum Teuch (harb.) .... F 4
Nichol (isl.) .... C 4
North (cape) .... H 1
North (mt.) .... D 3
North Aspy (riv.) .... H 2
North Bay Ingonish (bay) .... H 2
North East Margaree (riv.) ... H 2
Northumberland (str.) .... E 2
Nuttby (mt.) .... E 3
Oak (isl.) .... D 4
Ocean (lake) .... G 3
Ohio (riv.) .... D 4
Panuke (lake) .... D 4
Paradise (lake) .... C 4
Pennant (pt.) .... E 4
Percé (cape) .... J 2
Peskowesk (lake) .... C 4
Petit-de-Grat (isl.) .... H 3
Petpeswick (head) .... E 4
Philip (riv.) .... E 3
Pictou (harb.) .... F 3
Pictou (isl.) .... F 3
Pleasant (bay) .... H 2
Ponhook (lake) .... D 4
Porters (lake) .... E 4
Port Hebert (harb.) .... D 5
Port Hood (isl.) .... G 2
Port Joli (harb.) .... D 5
Port Mouton (harb.) .... D 5
Poulet Cove (bay) .... H 2
Prim (pt.) .... C 4
Pubnico (harb.) .... C 5
Pugwash (harb.) .... E 3
Roseway (riv.) .... C 4
Rossignol (lake) .... C 4
Sable (cape) .... C 5
Sable (isl.) .... J 5
Saint Andrews (chan.) .... H 2
Saint Anns (bay) .... H 2
Saint Georges (bay) .... G 3
Saint Lawrence (bay) .... H 1
Saint Lawrence (cape) .... H 1
Saint Margarets (bay) .... E 4
Saint Mary (cape) .... B 4
Saint Marys (bay) .... B 4
Saint Mary's (riv.) .... F 3
Saint Patrick (chan.) .... H 2
Saint Paul (isl.) .... H 1
Saint Peters (bay) .... H 3

Salmon (riv.) .... E 3
Salmon (riv.) .... G 3
Scatarie (isl.) .... J 2
Scots (bay) .... D 3
Seall (isl.) .... B 5
Sheet (harb.) .... F 4
Sherbrooke (lake) .... D 4
Sherbrooke (riv.) .... D 4
Shoal (pt.) .... F 4
Shubenacadie (lake) .... E 4
Shubenacadie (riv.) .... E 3
Sissiboo (riv.) .... C 4
Smoky (cape) .... H 2
Sober (isl.) .... F 4
South West Margaree (riv.) .. G 2
Split (cape) .... D 3
Spry (harb.) .... F 4
Stewiacke (riv.) .... E 3
Sydney (harb.) .... H 2
Tangier (riv.) .... F 4
Taylor (head) .... F 4
Tobeatic (lake) .... C 4
Tor (bay) .... G 3
Tupper (lake) .... D 4
Tusket (isl.) .... B 5

Tusket (riv.) .... C 4
Verte (bay) .... D 2
Wallace (harb.) .... E 3
West (bay) .... G 3
West (pt.) .... H 5
West (riv.) .... F 3
Western (head) .... D 5
West Liscomb (riv.) .... F 3
West Saint Mary's (riv.) ..... F 3
Whitehaven (harb.) .... G 3
Yarmouth (sound) .... B 5

PRINCE EDWARD ISLAND

COUNTIES

Kings 19,215 .... F 2
Prince 42,821 .... D 2
Queens 60,470 .... F 2

CITIES and TOWNS

Alberton 1,020 .... E 2
Bunbury 1,024 .... F 2
Charlottetown (cap.)⊚ 15,282 . E 2

Cornwall 1,838 .... E 2
Georgetown⊚ 737 .... F 2
Kensington 1,143 .... E 2
Miscouche 752 .... D 2
Montague 1,957 .... F 2
Murray Harbour 443 .... F 2
North Rustico 688 .... F 2
O'Leary 736 .... D 2
Parkdale 2,018 .... F 2
Saint Edward 650 .... D 2
Saint Eleanors 2,716 .... E 2
Sherwood 5,681 .... E 2
Souris 1,413 .... F 2
Summerside⊚ 7,828 .... E 2
Tignish 982 .... D 2
Wilmot 1,563 .... E 2

OTHER FEATURES

Bedeque (bay) .... E 2
Boughton (isl.) .... F 2
Cardigan (bay) .... F 2
Cascumpeque (bay) .... D 2
East (pt.) .... G 2
Egmont (bay) .... D 2

Egmont (cape) .... D 2
Hillsborough (bay) .... E 2
Hog (isl.) .... E 2
Kildare (cape) .... E 2
Lennox (isl.) .... E 2
Malpeque (bay) .... E 2
New London (bay) .... E 2
North (pt.) .... E 1
Northumberland (str.) .... D 2
Panmure (isl.) .... F 2
Prim (pt.) .... E 2
Prince Edward Island Nat'l
  Park .... F 2
Rollo (bay) .... F 2
Saint Lawrence (gulf) .... F 2
Saint Peters (bay) .... E 2
Saint Peters (isl.) .... E 2
Savage (harb.) .... F 2
Tracadie (bay) .... F 2
West (pt.) .... D 2
Wood (isls.) .... F 3

⊚County seat.
*Population of metropolitan area.

Agriculture, Industry and Resources

DOMINANT LAND USE

- General Farming, Dairy
- General Farming, Livestock
- Fruits, Vegetables
- Pasture Livestock
- Forests

MAJOR MINERAL OCCURRENCES

Ag Silver
C Coal
Gp Gypsum
Na Salt
O Petroleum
Pb Lead
Zn Zinc

⚡ Water Power
▨ Major Industrial Areas

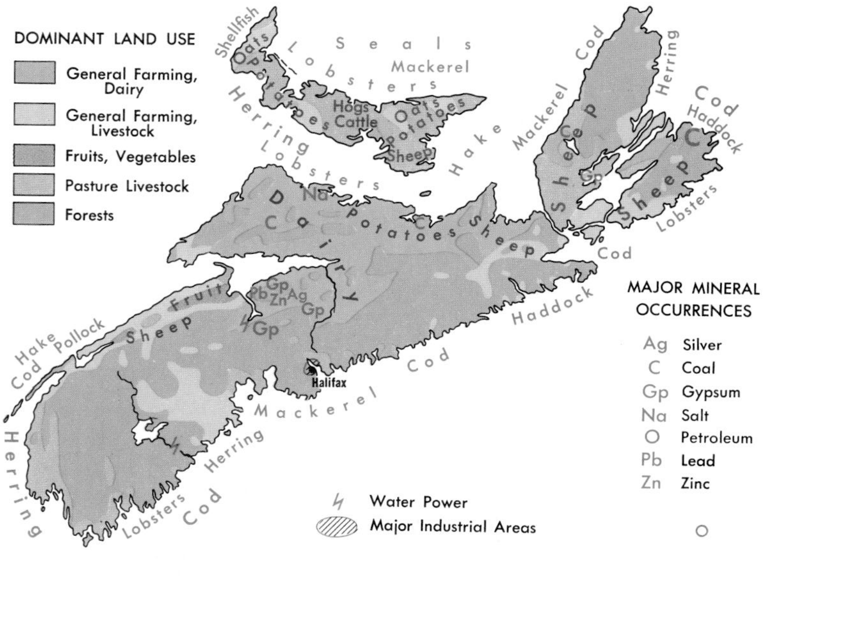

170 New Brunswick

New Brunswick

SCALE
0 5 10   20   30   40 MI.
0 5 10   20   30   40 KM.

Provincial Capitals .... ⊛
County Seats .... ⊚
International Boundaries ----·----
Provincial Boundaries -----------
County Boundaries -------------

© Copyright HAMMOND INCORPORATED, Maplewood, N.J.

Havelock 439 . . . E 3
Hayesville 107 . . . D 2
Hazeldean 108 . . . C 2
Head of Millstream 61 . . . E 3
Hillman 69 . . . C 2
Hillsborough 1,239 . . . F 3
Holmesville 146 . . . C 2
Holtville 222 . . . D 2
Honeydale 77 . . . C 3
Hopewell Cape⊙ 144 . . . F 3
Hopewell Hill 172 . . . F 3
Howard 77 . . . E 2
Howland Ridge 55 . . . C 2
Hoyt 114 . . . D 3
Inkerman 396 . . . F 1
Irishtown 605 . . . F 2
Island View 240 . . . D 3
Jacksonville 363 . . . C 2
Jacquet River 778 . . . E 1
Janeville 204 . . . E 1
Jeanne Mance 89 . . . E 1
Jemseg 228 . . . D 3
Jolicure 96 . . . F 3
Juniper 525 . . . C 2
Kedgwick 1,222 . . . C 1
Keenan Siding 86 . . . E 2
Kent Junction 112 . . . E 2
Kent Lake 57 . . . E 2
Keswick 260 . . . D 3
Kilburn 134 . . . C 2
Killam 60 . . . E 2
Kingsclear 250 . . . D 3
Kingsley 145 . . . D 2
Kirkland 69 . . . C 3
Knowlesville 82 . . . C 2
Kouchibouguac 213 . . . F 2
Lac Baker 292 . . . B 1
Lagacéville 227 . . . E 1
Lake George 170 . . . C 3
Laketon 81 . . . E 2
Lakeville 201 . . . C 2
Lambertville 109 . . . C 3
Lamèque 1,571 . . . F 1
Landry 281 . . . E 1
Laplante 197 . . . E 1
Lavillette 576 . . . E 1
Lawrence Station 229 . . . C 3
Leech 584 . . . E 1
Léger Brook . . . F 2
Légerville 184 . . . F 2
Le Goulet 1,173 . . . F 1
Leonardville 158 . . . C 4
Lepreau 208 . . . D 3
Levesque 77 . . . C 1
Little Cape 513 . . . F 2
Little Shippegan 131 . . . F 1
Loggieville 781 . . . E 1
Lorne 937 . . . D 1
Lower Coverdale 616 . . . F 2
Lower Derby 206 . . . E 2
Lower Durham 52 . . . D 2
Lower Hainesville 66 . . . C 2
Lower Kars 30 . . . E 3
Lower Millstream 184 . . . E 3
Lower Sapin . . . F 2
Lower Southampton . . . C 3
Ludlow 100 . . . D 2
Maces Bay 182 . . . D 3
Madran 247 . . . E 1
Magaguadavic 126 . . . C 3
Maisonnette 757 . . . E 1
Malden 93 . . . G 2
Manners Sutton 159 . . . D 3
Manuels 332 . . . F 1
Mapleview 65 . . . C 2
Marcelville 61 . . . E 2
Martin 104 . . . C 1
Maugerville 249 . . . D 3
Maxwell 64 . . . C 3
McAdam 1,837 . . . C 3
McGivney 156 . . . D 2
McKendrick 608 . . . D 1
McNamee 147 . . . D 2
Meductic 234 . . . C 3
Melrose 121 . . . F 2
Memramcook 276 . . . F 2
Menneval 110 . . . C 1
Midgic Station 208 . . . F 3
Mill Cove 253 . . . D 3
Millerton 130 . . . E 2
Millville 309 . . . C 2
Minto 3,399 . . . D 2
Miscou Centre 554 . . . F 1
Miscou Harbour 106 . . . F 1
Mispec 180 . . . E 3
Moncton 54,743 . . . F 2
Moores Mills 117 . . . C 3
Morrisdale 202 . . . D 3
Moulin-Morneault 459 . . . B 1
Murray Corner 233 . . . G 2
Nackawic 1,357 . . . C 2
Napadogan 103 . . . D 2
Nash Creek 235 . . . D 1
Nashwaak Bridge 142 . . . D 2
Nashwaak Village 258 . . . D 2
Nauwigewauk 139 . . . E 3
Neguac 1,755 . . . E 1
Nelson-Miramichi 1,452 . . . E 2
Newcastle⊙ 6,284 . . . E 2
Newcastle Creek 210 . . . D 2
New Denmark 112 . . . C 1
New Jersey 65 . . . E 1
New Market 143 . . . D 3
New Maryland 485 . . . D 3
New River Beach 33 . . . D 3
Newtown 154 . . . E 3
New Zion 171 . . . D 2
Nicholas Denys 170 . . . D 1
Nictau 30 . . . C 1
Nigadoo 1,075 . . . E 1
Noinville 50 . . . E 2
Nordin 393 . . . E 1
North Head 661 . . . D 4
Norton 1,372 . . . E 3
Notre-Dame 344 . . . F 2
Oak Bay 183 . . . C 3
Oak Point 83 . . . D 3
Oromocto 9,064 . . . D 3
Paquetville 626 . . . E 1
Peel 117 . . . C 2
Pelletier Mills 88 . . . B 1
Pennfield . . . D 3
Penniac 179 . . . D 2
Penobsquis 259 . . . E 3
Perth-Andover⊙ 1,872 . . . C 2
Petitcodiac 1,401 . . . E 3
Petite-Rivière-de-l'Île 549 . . . F 1
Petit Rocher 1,860 . . . E 1
Petit Rocher Sud . . . E 1
Pigeon Hill 595 . . . F 1
Plaster Rock 1,222 . . . C 2
Pocologan 150 . . . D 3
Point de Bute 155 . . . F 3
Pointe-du-Chêne 482 . . . F 2
Pointe-Sapin 331 . . . F 2
Pointe-Verte 1,335 . . . E 1
Pollett River 73 . . . E 3
Pontgrave 229 . . . F 1
Pont-Lafrance 875 . . . E 1
Pont-Landry 444 . . . F 1
Port Elgin 504 . . . F 2
Prime 89 . . . B 1
Prince of Wales 138 . . . D 3
Prince William 225 . . . C 3
Quarryville 205 . . . E 2
Queenstown 112 . . . D 3
Quispamsis 6,022 . . . E 3
Red Bank 141 . . . E 2
Renforth 1,490 . . . E 3
Renous 192 . . . E 2
Rexton 928 . . . F 2
Richardsville . . . D 1
Richibucto⊙ 1,722 . . . E 2
Richibucto Village 442 . . . F 2
Richmond Corner 84 . . . C 2
Riley Brook 126 . . . C 1
Ripples 233 . . . D 3
River de Chute 22 . . . C 2
River Glade 268 . . . E 3
Riverside-Albert 478 . . . F 3
Riverview 14,907 . . . F 2
Rivière-du-Portage 661 . . . F 1
Rivière Verte 1,054 . . . B 1
Robertville 733 . . . E 1
Robichaud 485 . . . F 2
Robinsonville 206 . . . C 1
Rogersville 1,237 . . . E 2
Rollingdam 65 . . . C 3
Rosaireville 86 . . . E 2
Rothesay 1,764 . . . E 3
Rowena 73 . . . C 2
Roy 173 . . . F 2
Royal Road 41 . . . D 2
Rusagonis 231 . . . D 3
Sackville 5,654 . . . F 3
Saint Almo 17 . . . C 2
Saint-André 385 . . . C 1
Saint Andrews⊙ 1,760 . . . C 3
Saint-Antoine 1,217 . . . F 2
Saint Arthur 369 . . . D 1
Saint-Basile 3,214 . . . B 1
Saint-Charles 355 . . . F 2
Saint Croix 86 . . . C 3
Sainte-Anne 329 . . . E 1
Sainte-Anne-de-Kent 337 . . . F 2
Sainte-Anne-de-Madawaska 1,332 . . . B 1
Saint-Édouard-de-Kent 157 . . . F 2
Sainte-Marie-de-Kent 283 . . . F 2
Sainte-Marie-sur-Mer 539 . . . F 1
Sainte-Rose-Gloucester 410 . . . F 1
Saint-François-de-Madawaska 753 . . . B 1
Saint George 1,163 . . . D 3
Saint Hilaire 244 . . . B 1
Saint-Ignace 96 . . . F 2
Saint-Isidore 794 . . . E 1
Saint-Jacques 2,297 . . . B 1
Saint-Jean-Baptiste-de-Restigouche 228 . . . C 1
Saint John⊙ 80,521 . . . E 3
Saint-Joseph 630 . . . F 3
Saint-Joseph-de-Madawaska 173 . . . B 1
Saint-Léolin 799 . . . E 1
Saint Leonard 1,566 . . . C 1
Saint-Louis-de-Kent 1,166 . . . F 2
Saint Margarets 63 . . . E 2
Saint Martin de Restigouche 124 . . . C 1
Saint Martins 530 . . . E 3
Saint-Paul 365 . . . E 2
Saint Quentin 2,334 . . . C 1
Saint-Raphaël-sur-Mer 562 . . . F 1
Saint Sauveur 252 . . . E 1
Saint Stephen 5,120 . . . C 3
Saint Wilfred . . . E 1
Salisbury 1,672 . . . E 2
Salmon Beach 277 . . . E 1
Salmon Creek 38 . . . E 2
Saumarez 690 . . . E 1
Scoudouc 207 . . . F 2
Seal Cove 548 . . . D 4
Shannon 39 . . . E 3
Shediac 4,285 . . . F 2
Shediac Bridge 441 . . . F 2
Sheffield 112 . . . D 3
Sheila 1,172 . . . F 1
Shemogue 199 . . . F 2
Shepody 86 . . . F 3
Shippegan 2,471 . . . F 1
Siegas 227 . . . C 1
Sillikers 292 . . . E 2
Simonds 221 . . . C 2
Sisson Ridge 170 . . . C 2
Six Roads 239 . . . F 1
Smiths Creek 163 . . . E 3
Somerville 326 . . . C 2
South Branch 86 . . . F 2
Springfield, King's 116 . . . E 3
Springfield, York 130 . . . C 2
Stanley 432 . . . D 2
Stickney 232 . . . C 2
Storeytown 140 . . . D 2
Sunny Corner 405 . . . E 2
Sunnyside 87 . . . D 1
Sussex 3,972 . . . E 3
Sussex Corner 1,023 . . . E 3
Tabusintac 231 . . . E 1

AREA 28,354 sq. mi. (73,437 sq. km.)
POPULATION 709,442
CAPITAL Fredericton
LARGEST CITY Saint John
HIGHEST POINT Mt. Carleton 2,690 ft. (820 m.)
SETTLED IN 1611
ADMITTED TO CONFEDERATION 1867
PROVINCIAL FLOWER Purple Violet

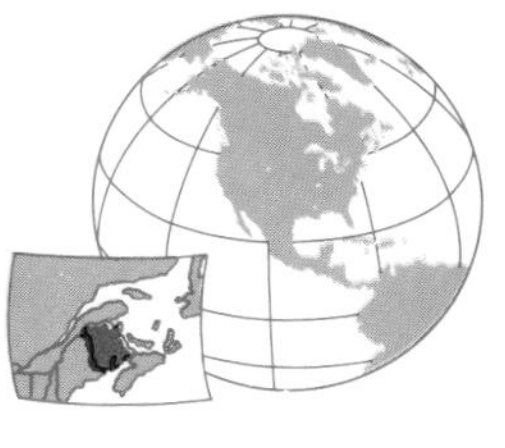

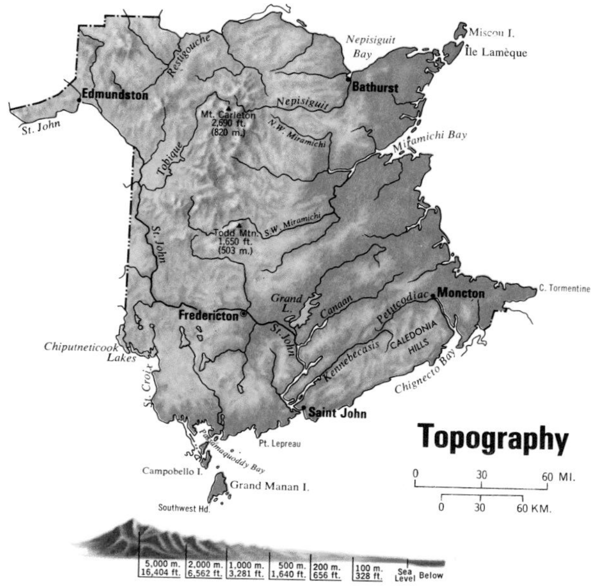

Edmundston
St. John
Restigouche
Nepisiguit Bay
Miscou I.
Île Lamèque
Bathurst
Nepisiguit
Mt. Carleton 2,690 ft. (820 m.)
N.W. Miramichi
Miramichi Bay
Tobique
St. John
Todd Mtn. 1,650 ft. (503 m.)
S.W. Miramichi
Grand L.
Canaan
Petitcodiac
Moncton
C. Tormentine
Fredericton
Chiputneticook Lakes
St. John
Kennebecasis
CALEDONIA HILLS
Chignecto Bay
St. Croix
Saint John
Passamaquoddy Bay
Pt. Lepreau
Campobello I.
Grand Manan I.
Southwest Hd.
0 30 60 MI.
0 30 60 KM.
5,000 m. 16,404 ft.
2,000 m. 6,562 ft.
1,000 m. 3,281 ft.
500 m. 1,640 ft.
200 m. 656 ft.
100 m. 328 ft.
Sea Level
Below

Topography

Agriculture, Industry and Resources

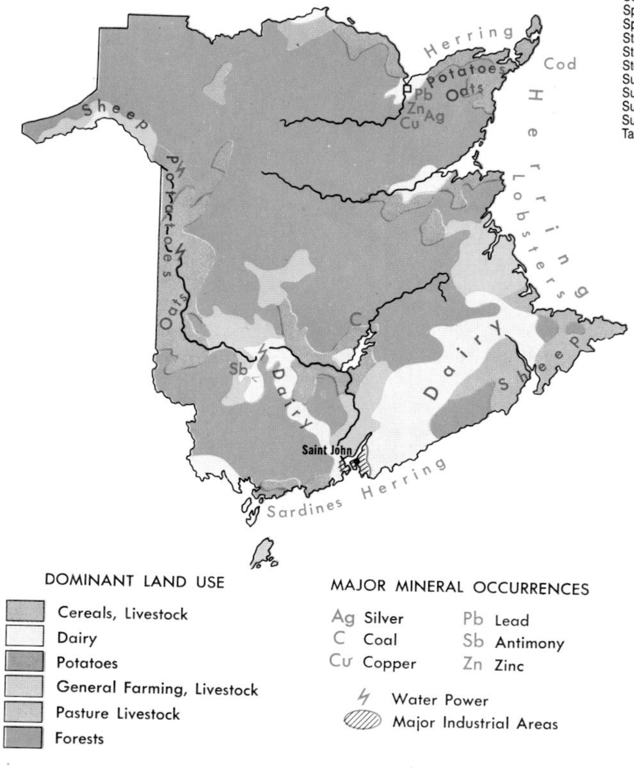

Herring
Cod
Potatoes
Oats
Pb
Zn
Cu
Ag
Sheep
Herring
Lobsters
Potatoes
Oats
C
Dairy
Sheep
Sb
Dairy
Saint John
Herring
Sardines
DOMINANT LAND USE
Cereals, Livestock
Dairy
Potatoes
General Farming, Livestock
Pasture Livestock
Forests
MAJOR MINERAL OCCURRENCES
Ag Silver
C Coal
Cu Copper
Pb Lead
Sb Antimony
Zn Zinc
Water Power
Major Industrial Areas

Taxis River 118 . . . D 2
Tay Creek 161 . . . D 2
Taymouth 301 . . . D 2
Temperance Vale 357 . . . C 2
The Range 58 . . . E 2
Thibault 306 . . . C 1
Tide Head 952 . . . D 1
Tilley 95 . . . C 2
Tobique Narrows 140 . . . C 2
Tracadie 2,452 . . . F 1
Tracy 636 . . . D 3
Turtle Creek 81 . . . F 3
Tweedside 87 . . . C 3
Upham 107 . . . E 3
Upper Blackville 60 . . . E 2
Upper Buctouche 158 . . . F 2
Upper Gagetown 236 . . . D 3
Upper Hainesville 189 . . . C 2
Upper Kent 203 . . . C 2
Upper Maugerville 543 . . . D 3
Upper Mills 153 . . . C 3
Upper Rockport 18 . . . F 3
Upper Sheila 706 . . . E 1
Upper Woodstock 257 . . . C 2
Upsalquitch 112 . . . D 1
Val-Comeau 534 . . . F 1
Val d'Amour 462 . . . D 1
Val Doucet 505 . . . E 1
Verret 637 . . . B 1
Village-Saint-Laurent 187 . . . E 1
Waasis 264 . . . D 3
Wapske 195 . . . C 2
Waterford 120 . . . E 3
Waterville 181 . . . C 2
Waweig . . . C 3
Wayerton 188 . . . E 1
Weaver 86 . . . E 2
Weldon 227 . . . F 3
Welsford 230 . . . D 3
Welshpool 260 . . . D 4
Westfield 1,100 . . . D 3
West Quaco 48 . . . E 3
White Head 185 . . . D 4
White Rapids 238 . . . E 2
Whitney 216 . . . E 2
Wickham 72 . . . D 3
Wicklow 143 . . . C 2
Williamsburg 258 . . . D 2
Williamstown 156 . . . C 2
Willow Grove 509 . . . E 3
Wilmot 57 . . . C 3
Wilson Point 45 . . . F 1
Wilsons Beach 844 . . . D 4
Windsor 43 . . . C 2
Wirral 110 . . . D 3
Woodstock⊙ 4,649 . . . C 2
Woodwards Cove 146 . . . D 4
Youngs Cove 65 . . . E 3
Zealand 458 . . . D 2

OTHER FEATURES

Bald (mt.) . . . C 1
Bartibog (riv.) . . . E 1
Bay du Vin (riv.) . . . E 2
Big Tracadie (riv.) . . . E 1
Buctouche (harb.) . . . F 2
Buctouche (riv.) . . . F 2
Campobello (isl.) . . . D 4
Canaan (riv.) . . . E 2
Carleton (mt.) . . . D 1
Chaleur (bay) . . . E 1
Chignecto (bay) . . . F 3
Chiputneticook (lakes) . . . C 3
Cocagne (isl.) . . . F 2
Cumberland (basin) . . . F 3
Deer (isl.) . . . D 4
Digdeguash (riv.) . . . C 3
Escuminac (bay) . . . D 1
Escuminac (pt.) . . . F 1
Fundy (bay) . . . E 3
Fundy Nat'l Park . . . E 3
Gaspereau (riv.) . . . D 2
Grand (bay) . . . D 3
Grand (lake) . . . C 3
Grand (lake) . . . D 3
Grand Manan (chan.) . . . C 4
Grand Manan (isl.) . . . D 4
Grande (riv.) . . . C 1
Green (riv.) . . . B 1
Hammond (riv.) . . . E 3
Harvey (lake) . . . C 3
Heron (isl.) . . . D 1
Kedgwick (riv.) . . . C 1
Kennebecasis (riv.) . . . E 3
Keswick (riv.) . . . C 2
Kouchibouguac (bay) . . . F 2
Kouchibouguacis (riv.) . . . E 2
Kouchibouguac Nat'l Park . . . F 2
Lamèque (isl.) . . . F 1
Lepreau (riv.) . . . D 3
Little (riv.) . . . D 2
Long (isl.) . . . D 3
Long Reach (inlet) . . . D 3
Maces (bay) . . . D 3
Mactaquac (lake) . . . C 3
Madawaska (riv.) . . . B 1
Magaguadavic (lake) . . . C 3
Magaguadavic (riv.) . . . C 3
Miramichi (bay) . . . E 1
Miscou (isl.) . . . F 1
Miscou (pt.) . . . F 1
Mount Carleton Prov. Park . . . D 1
Musquash (harb.) . . . D 3
Nashwaak (riv.) . . . D 2
Nepisiguit (bay) . . . E 1
Nepisiguit (riv.) . . . D 1
Nerepis (riv.) . . . D 3
Northern (head) . . . D 4
North Sevogle (riv.) . . . D 1
Northumberland (str.) . . . F 2
Northwest Miramichi (riv.) . . . D 1
Oromocto (lake) . . . C 3
Oromocto (riv.) . . . D 3
Passamaquoddy (bay) . . . C 3
Patapédia (riv.) . . . C 1
Petitcodiac (riv.) . . . F 3
Pokemouche (riv.) . . . E 1
Pokesudie (isl.) . . . F 1
Pollett (riv.) . . . E 3
Quaco (head) . . . E 3
Renous (riv.) . . . D 2
Restigouche (riv.) . . . C 1
Richibucto (harb.) . . . F 2
Richibucto (riv.) . . . E 2
Roosevelt Campobello Int'l Park . . . D 4
Saint Croix (riv.) . . . C 3
Saint Francis (riv.) . . . A 1
Saint John (harb.) . . . E 3
Saint John (riv.) . . . C 2
Saint Lawrence (gulf) . . . F 1
Salisbury (bay) . . . F 3
Salmon (riv.) . . . C 1
Salmon (riv.) . . . E 2
Shediac (isl.) . . . F 2
Shepody (bay) . . . F 3
Shippegan (bay) . . . E 1
Shippegan Gully (str.) . . . F 1
South Sevogle (riv.) . . . D 1
Southwest (head) . . . D 4
Southwest Miramichi (riv.) . . . D 2
Spear (cape) . . . G 2
Spednik (lake) . . . C 3
Spencer (cape) . . . E 3
Tabusintac (riv.) . . . E 1
Tabusintac Gully (str.) . . . F 1
Tetagouche (riv.) . . . D 1
Tobique (riv.) . . . C 2
Upsalquitch (riv.) . . . D 1
Utopia (lake) . . . D 3
Verte (bay) . . . G 2
Washademoak (lake) . . . E 3
West (isls.) . . . D 4
White Head (isl.) . . . D 4

⊙County seat.

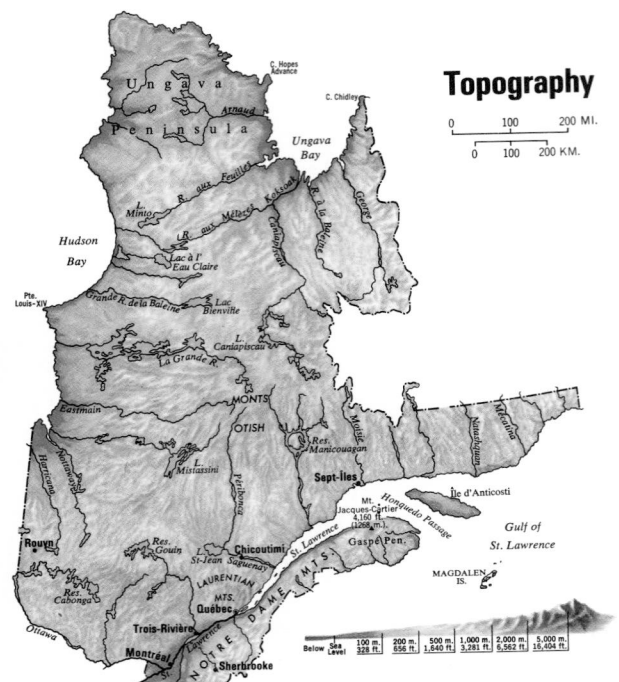

Topography

0   100   200 MI.

0   100   200 KM.

Below Sea Level	100 m. 200 m. 500 m. 1,000 m. 2,000 m. 5,000 m.
	328 ft. 656 ft. 1,640 ft. 3,281 ft. 6,562 ft. 16,404 ft.

COUNTIES

Argenteuil 32,454 .... C 4
Arthabaska 59,277 .... E 4
Bagot 26,840 .... E 4
Beauce 73,427 .... G 3
Beauharnois 54,034 .... C 4
Bellechasse 23,559 .... G 3
Berthier 31,096 .... C 3
Bonaventure 40,487 .... C 2
Brome 17,436 .... E 4
Chambly 307,090 .... J 4
Champlain 119,595 .... E 2
Charlevoix-Est 17,448 .... G 2
Charlevoix-Ouest 14,172 ... G 2
Châteauguay 59,968 .... D 4
Chicoutimi 174,441 .... G 1
Compton 20,536 .... F 4
Deux-Montagnes 71,252 .... C 4
Dorchester 33,949 .... C 3
Drummond 69,770 .... E 4
Frontenac 26,814 .... G 4
Gaspé-Est 41,173 .... D 1
Gaspé-Ouest 18,943 .... C 1
Gatineau 54,229 .... B 3
Hull 131,213 .... B 4
Huntingdon 16,953 .... C 4
Iberville 23,180 .... D 4
Île-de-Montréal 1,760,122 .. H 4
Île-Jésus 268,335 .... H 4
Joliette 60,384 .... C 3
Kamouraska 28,642 .... H 2
Labelle 34,395 .... B 3
Lac-Saint-Jean-Est 47,891 . F 1
Lac-Saint-Jean-Ouest 62,952. E 1
Laprairie 105,962 .... D 4
L'Assomption 109,705 ...... J 3
Lévis 94,104 .... G 2
L'Islet 22,062 .... G 2
Lotbinière 29,653 .... F 3
Maskinongé 20,763 .... D 3
Matane 23,715 .... B 2
Matapédia 23,715 .... B 2
Mégantic 57,892 .... F 3
Missisquoi 36,161 .... D 4
Montcalm 27,557 .... C 3
Montmagny 25,622 .... G 3
Montmorency No. 1 23,048 .. F 2
Montmorency No. 2 6,436 .. G 3
Napierville 13,562 .... C 4
Nicolet 33,513 .... E 3
Papineau 37,975 .... B 4
Pontiac 20,283 .... A 3
Portneuf 58,843 .... F 3
Québec 458,980 .... F 3
Richelieu 53,058 .... D 4
Richmond 40,871 .... E 4
Rimouski 69,099 .... J 1
Rivière-du-Loup 41,250 .... H 2
Rouville 42,391 .... D 4
Saguenay 115,881 .... H 1
Saint-Hyacinthe 55,888 .... D 4
Saint-Jean 55,576 .... D 4
Saint-Maurice 107,703 ..... D 3
Shefford 70,733 .... E 4
Sherbrooke 115,983 .... E 4

CITIES and TOWNS

Acton Vale 4,371 .... D 4
Albanel 992 .... E 1
Alma® 26,322 .... F 1
Amqui® 4,048 .... B 2
Ancienne-Lorette 12,935 .. H 3
Angers ....
Anjou 37,346 .... H 4
Annaville 712 .... E 3
Armagh 878 .... A 3
Arthabaska® 6,827 .... F 3
Arvida .... F 1
Asbestos 7,967 .... E 4
Ascot Corner 847 .... G 4
Audet 760. .... G 4
Ayer's Cliff® 810 .... B 4
Aylmer 26,695 .... B 4
Baie-Comeau 12,866 .... A 1
Baie-d'Urfé 3,674 .... H 4
Baie-Saint-Paul® 3,961 ... G 2
Baie-Trinité 749 .... B 1
Beaconsfield 19,613. .... H 4
Beauceville 4,302 .... G 3
Beauharnois® 7,025. .... D 4
Beaumont 791 .... F 3
Beauport 60,447 .... J 3
Beaupré 2,740. .... G 2
Bécancour® 10,247 .... E 3
Bedford® 2,832 .... E 4
Beebe Plain 1,072 .... E 4
Bélair (Val-Bélair) 12,695 .. H 3
Beloeil 17,540 .... D 4
Bernierville 2,120 .... F 3
Berthier-en-Bas 562 .... G 3
Berthierville® 4,049 .... D 3
Bic 2,994 .... J 1
Biencourt 824 .... J 2
Black Lake 5,148 .... F 3
Blainville 14,682 .... H 4
Boischatel 3,345 .... J 3
Bois-des-Filion 4,943 ..... H 4
Bolduc 1,565. .... G 4
Bonaventure 1,371 .... C 2
Boucherville 29,704 .... J 4
Bromont 2,731. .... E 4
Bromptonville 3,035. .... F 4
Brossard 52,232 .... H 4
Brownsburg 2,875. .... C 4
Buckingham 7,992 .... B 4
Cabano 3,291 .... J 2
Cacouna 1,160 .... H 2
Calumet 729 .... C 4
Candiac 8,502. .... J 4
Cap-à-l'Aigle 819 .... G 2
Cap-Chat 3,464. .... B 1
Cap-de-la-Madeleine 32,626 . E 3
Caplan-Rivière Caplan 1,139. C 2
Cap-Saint-Ignace 1,485. .. G 2
Cap-Santé® 671 .... F 3
Carignan 4,544 .... J 4
Carleton 2,710. .... C 2
Causapscal 2,501 .... B 2
Chambly 12,190 .... J 4
Chambord 961. .... E 1
Chandler 3,946 .... D 2
Charlemagne 4,827 .... H 4
Charlesbourg 68,326 ...... J 3
Charny 8,240 .... J 3
Châteauguay 36,928 ...... H 4
Château-Richer® 3,628 .. F 3
Chénéville 633 .... B 4
Chicoutimi® 60,064 .... G 1
Chicoutimi-Jonquière
*135,172 .... J 3
Chute-aux-Outardes 2,280. A 1
Clermont 3,621 .... G 2
Coaticook 6,271 .... F 4
Coleraine 1,660. .... F 4
Compton 728. .... F 4
Contrecoeur 5,449 .... D 4
Cookshire® 1,480. .... F 4
Coteau-du-Lac® 1,247 .... C 4
Coteau-Landing® 1,386. .. C 4
Côte-Saint-Luc 27,531 .... H 4
Courcelles 608 .... J 3
Courville .... J 3
Cowansville 12,240. .... E 4
Crabtree 1,950 .... D 4
Danville 2,200. .... E 4
Daveluyville 1,257. .... E 3
Deauville 942. .... E 4
Dégelis 3,477 .... J 2
Delisle 4,011 .... F 1
Delson 4,935 .... H 4
Desbiens 1,541. .... E 1
Deschaillons-sur-Saint-
Laurent 950 .... E 3
Deschambault 977 .... E 3
Deschênes .... B 4
Deux-Montagnes 9,944 .. H 4
Didyme 667 .... E 1
Disraëli 3,181 .... F 4
Dolbeau 8,766. .... E 1
Dollard-des-Ormeaux 39,940. H 4
Donnacona 5,731. .... F 3
Dorion 5,749 .... C 4
Dorval 17,727 .... H 4
Dosquet 703 .... F 3
Douville. .... D 4
Drummondville® 27,347 .. E 4
Drummondville-Sud 9,220.. E 4
Dunham 2,887. .... E 4
Durham-Sud 1,045. .... E 4
East Angus 4,016. .... F 4
East Broughton 1,397. ... F 3
East Broughton Station 1,302. F 3
Eastman 612 .... E 4
Entrelacs 1,735. .... C 3
Farnham 6,498 .... E 4
Ferme-Neuve 2,266. ...... B 3
Forestville 4,271 .... H 1
Frampton 684 .... G 3
Francoeur 1,422 .... F 3
Gaspé 17,261 .... D 2
Gatineau 74,988 .... B 4
Giffard. .... J 3
Girardville 1,128 .... E 1
Gracefield 869 .... A 3
Granby 38,069. .... E 4
Grand'Mère 15,442. ...... E 3
Grande-Rivière 4,420. ... D 2
Grandes-Bergeronnes 748. D 1
Grande-Vallée 700 .... D 1
Greenfield Park 18,527 .. J 4
Grenville 1,417. .... C 4
Gros-Morne 672 .... C 1
Hampstead 7,598. .... H 4
Ham-Sud® 62 .... E 4
Hauterive 13,995. .... A 1
Hébertville 2,515. .... F 1
Hébertville-Station 1,442. F 1
Hemmingford 737 .... D 4
Henryville 595 .... D 4
Howick 639 .... D 4
Hudson 4,414 .... C 4
Hull® 56,225. .... B 4
Huntingdon® 3,018. ...... C 4
Île-Perrot 5,945 .... G 4
Iberville® 8,587 .... D 4
Inverness® 329 .... F 3
Joliette® 16,987 .... D 3
Jonquière 60,354 .... F 1
Jonquière-Chicoutimi
*135,172 .... F 1
Kingsey Falls 818 .... E 4
Kirkland 10,476. .... H 4
Knowlton (Lac-Brome)®
4,316. .... E 4
La Baie 20,935 .... G 1
Labelle 1,534. .... C 3
Lac-à-la-Croix 1,017. ..... F 1
Lac-Alouette-Lac-Brière 1,356. D 4
Lac-au-Saumon 1,332. ... B 2
Lac-aux-Sables 838 ...... E 3
Lac-Beaufort .... F 3
Lac-Bouchette 1,703 .... E 1
Lac-Carré 717 .... C 3
Lac-des-Écorces 766 ... B 3
Lac-Drolet 1,120. .... G 4
Lac-Etchemin 2,729 ..... G 3
Lachenaie 8,631 .... H 4
Lachine 37,521 .... H 4
Lachute® 11,729. .... C 4
Lac-Mégantic® 6,119. ... G 4
Lacolle 1,319. .... D 4
Lac-Saint-Charles 5,837. H 3
Lafontaine 4,799. .... C 4
La Guadeloupe 1,692. .. F 4
La Malbaie® 4,030. ...... G 2
Lambton 1,559. .... G 4
L'Annonciation 2,384 ... C 3
Lanoraie (Lanoraie-d'Autry)
1,613. .... D 4
La Pêche 3,961 .... B 4
La Pérade 1,039. .... E 3
La Pocatière 4,560 ...... H 2
La Prairie® 10,627 .... J 4
La Providence .... E 4
Larouche 662. .... F 1
La Salle 76,299 .... H 4
L'Ascension 1,287. ...... F 1
L'Assomption® 4,844 ... F 3
La Station-du-Coteau 892. C 4
Laterrière 788 .... F 1
La Tuque 11,556. .... E 2
Laurentides 1,947. .... D 4
Laurier-Station 1,123 ... F 3
Laurierville 939 .... F 3
Lauzon 13,362. .... J 3
Laval 268,335 .... H 4
Lavaltrie 2,053 .... E 4
L'Avenir 1,116 .... E 4
Lawrenceville 562 .... E 4
Le Moyne 6,137 .... J 4
L'Épiphanie 2,971 .... D 4
Léry 2,239 .... H 4
Lévis® 17,895 .... J 3
Lennoxville 3,922 .... F 4
Les Méchins 803. .... B 1
Linière 1,168 .... G 3
L'Islet 1,070 .... G 2
L'Islet-sur-Mer 774 .... G 2
L'Isle-Verte 1,142 ...... G 1
Longueuil® 124,320 ... J 4
Loretteville 15,060 .... H 3
Lorraine 6,881 .... H 4
Louiseville® 3,735 ..... E 3
Luceville 1,524. .... J 1
Lyster 830 .... E 4
Magog 13,604. .... E 4
Maniwaki® 5,424. ...... B 3
Manseau 626. .... E 4
Maple Grove 2,009. ... H 4
Maria 1,178 .... C 2
Marieville® 4,877 ..... D 4
Mascouche 20,345 ... E 3
Maskinongé 1,005 ... E 3
Masson 4,264 .... B 4
Massueville 671 ...... E 4
Matane® 13,612. ..... B 2
Matapédia 586. .... B 2
Melocheville 1,892. .. C 4
Mercier® 6,352 .... H 4
Metabetchouan 3,406. F 1
Mirabel® 14,080. ..... H 4
Mistassini 6,682 ..... E 1
Montauban 557 ...... E 3
Mont-Carmel 807 ... H 2
Montcerf 570 .... A 3
Montebello 1,229 .... B 4
Mont-Joli 6,359 ..... J 1
Mont-Laurier® 8,405 . B 3
Mont-Louis 756 ..... C 1
Montmagny® 12,405 . G 3
Montréal® 980,354 .. H 4
Montréal *2,828,349 . H 4
Montréal-Est 3,778 .. J 4
Montréal-Nord 94,914 . H 4
Mont-Rolland 1,517 .. C 4
Mont-Royal 19,247 ... H 4
Mont-Saint-Hilaire 10,066. D 4
Morin Heights 592 ... C 4
Murdochville 3,396. .. C 1
Nantes 1,167. .... F 4

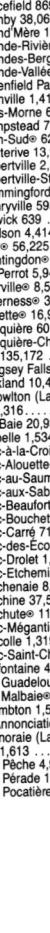

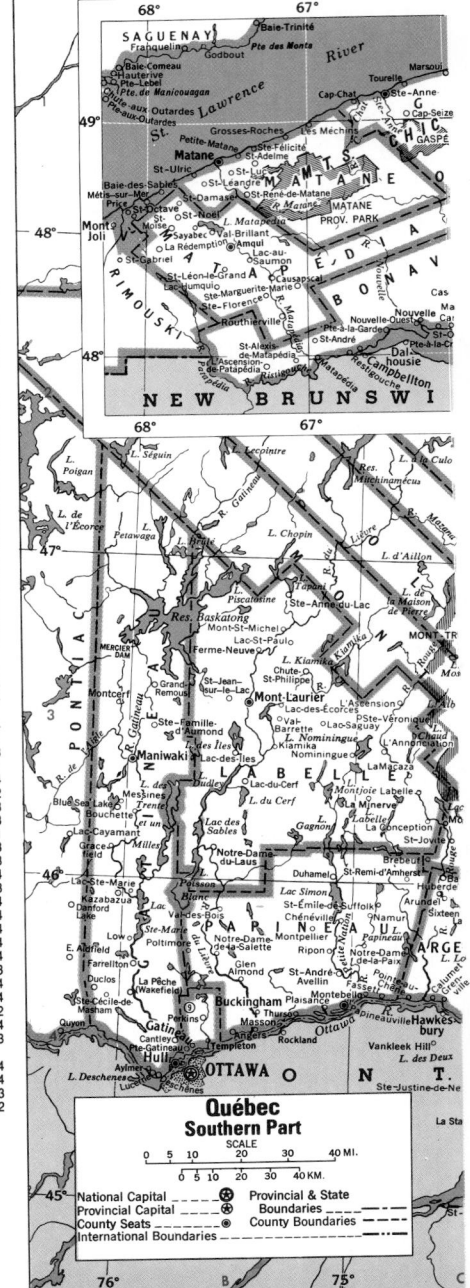

Québec
Southern Part

SCALE

0 5 10   20   30   40 MI.

0 5 10   20   30   40 KM.

National Capital ....⊛
Provincial Capital ....⊕
County Seats ....⊚
International Boundaries _____

Provincial & State
Boundaries _____
County Boundaries _ _ _ _ _

Agriculture, Industry and Resources

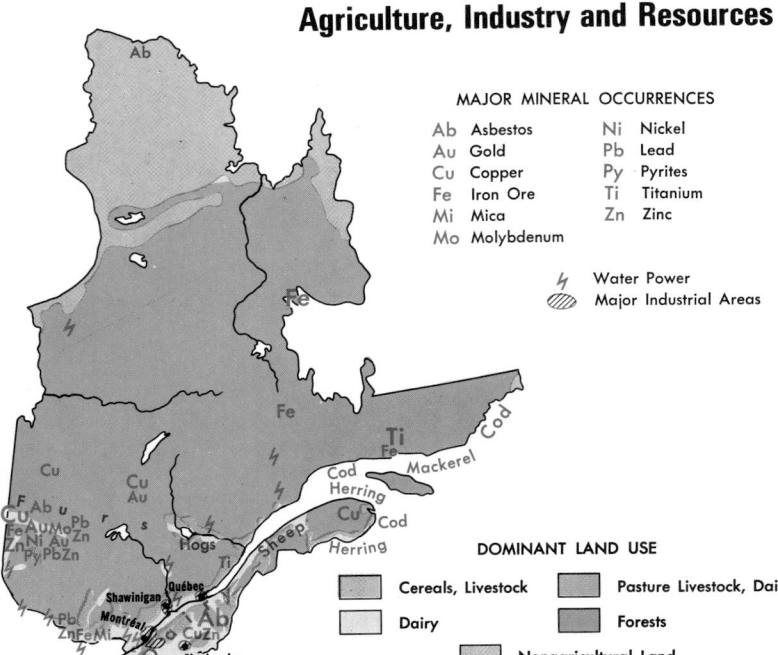

MAJOR MINERAL OCCURRENCES

Ab Asbestos
Au Gold
Cu Copper
Fe Iron Ore
Mi Mica
Mo Molybdenum

Ni Nickel
Pb Lead
Py Pyrites
Ti Titanium
Zn Zinc

⚡ Water Power
▨ Major Industrial Areas

DOMINANT LAND USE

■ Cereals, Livestock
□ Dairy
▨ Nonagricultural Land
■ Pasture Livestock, Dairy
■ Forests

AREA 594,857 sq. mi. (1,540,680 sq. km.)
POPULATION 6,532,461
CAPITAL Québec
LARGEST CITY Montréal
HIGHEST POINT Mont D'Iberville 5,420 ft.
(1,652 m.)
SETTLED IN 1608
ADMITTED TO CONFEDERATION 1867
PROVINCIAL FLOWER White Garden Lily

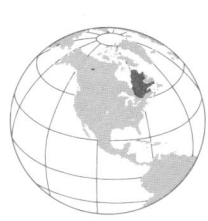

© Copyright HAMMOND INCORPORATED, Maplewood, N.J.

Internal divisions represent Municipal Counties

COUNTIES
indicated by numbers:
1 Iberville ....D 4
2 Napierville ....D 4
3 Rouville ....E 4
4 St-Hyacinthe ....D 4
5 Île-de-Montréal ....H 4
6 Deux-Montagnes ....C 4
7 Soulanges ....C 4
8 Beauharnois ....D 4
9 Hull ....B 4
10 Laprairie ....D 4
11 Richelieu ....D 4
12 Vaudreuil ....C 4

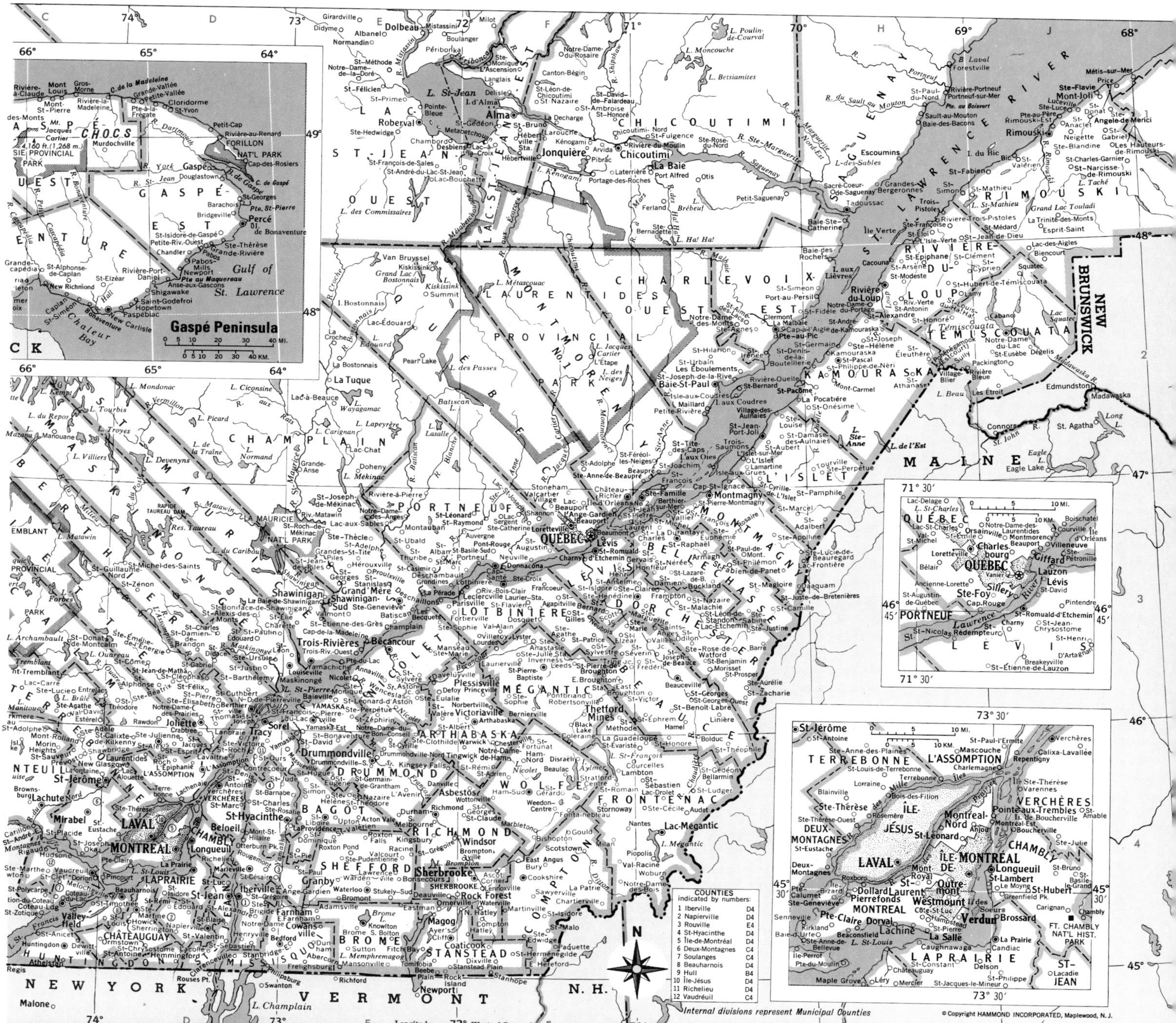

Saint-Eustache 29,716......H 4
Saint-Fabien 1,361 ....J 1
Saint-Félicien 9,058 ....E 1
Saint-Félix-de-Valois® 1,462
1,758 ....G 2
Saint-Ferréol-les-Neiges
1,758 ....G 2
Saint-Flavien 734 ....F 3
Saint-François-de-Sales 831 .E 1
Saint-François-du-Lac® 942 ..E 3
Saint-Fulgence 950 ....G 1
Saint-Gabriel 3,161 ....D 3
Saint-Gabriel-de-Rimouski
779 ....J 1
Saint-Gédéon, Frontenac
1,569 ....E 3
Saint-Gédéon, Lac-St-Jean-E.
1,000 ....F 1
Saint-Georges, Beauce
10,342 ....G 3
Saint-Georges, Champlain
3,344 ....E 3
Saint-Georges-Ouest 6,378 .G 3
Saint-Germain-de-Grantham
1,373 ....E 3
Saint-Gervais 973 ....G 3
Saint-Gilles 912 ....F 3
Saint-Grégoire (Mont-St-
Grégoire) 740 ....D 4
Saint-Henri 1,970 ....G 3
Saint-Honoré, Beauce 1,116 .G 4
Saint-Honoré, Chicoutimi
1,790 ....F 1
Saint-Hubert 60,573 ....J 4
Saint-Hubert-de-Témiscouata
871 ....J 2
Saint-Hyacinthe 38,246 .....D 4
Saint-Isidore 811 ....F 3
Saint-Isidore-de-Laprairie 769 .D 4
Saint-Jacques 2,152 ....D 3
Saint-Jacques-le-Mineur
1,203 ....H 4
Saint-Jean-Chrysostome
6,930 ....J 3
Saint-Jean-de-Dieu 1,377 ...J 1
Saint-Jean-de-Matha 931 ...D 3
Saint-Jean-Port-Joli® 1,813 .G 3
Saint-Jean-sur-Richelieu
35,640 ....D 4
Saint-Jérôme 25,123 ....H 4
Saint-Joachim 1,139 ....G 3
Saint-Joseph-de-Beauce
3,216 ....G 3
Saint-Joseph-de-Sorel 2,545 .D 3
Saint-Jovite 3,841 ....C 3
Saint-Lambert 20,557 ....J 4
Saint-Laurent 65,900 ....H 4

Saint-Lazare 731 ....G 3
Saint-Léonard 79,429 ....H 4
Saint-Léonard-de-Chicoutimi 749 .F 1
Saint-Léon-de-Standon 816 ..G 3
Saint-Léon-le-Grand 722 ....B 2
Saint-Liboire® 746 ....E 4
Saint-Louis-de-Gonzague
615 ....D 4
Saint-Louis-de-Terrebonne
14,142 ....H 4
Saint-Louis-du-Ha! Ha! 809 .H 2
Saint-Luc 8,815 ....D 4
Saint-Luc-de-Matane 598 ...B 1
Saint-Marc-des-Carrières
2,822 ....E 3
Saint-Méthode-de-Frontenac
925 ....F 3
Saint-Michel-de-Bellechasse
963 ....G 3
Saint-Michel-des-Saints
1,584 ....D 3
Saint-Nazaire-de-Chicoutimi
962 ....F 1
Saint-Nérée 970 ....G 3
Saint-Nicolas 5,074 ....H 3
Saint-Noël 666 ....B 1
Saint-Odilon 580 ....G 3
Saint-Omer 718 ....C 2
Saint-Ours 625 ....D 2
Saint-Pacôme 1,996 ....H 2
Saint-Pamphile 3,428 ....H 3
Saint-Pascal® 2,763 ....H 2
Saint-Paul-de-Montminy 602 .G 3
Saint-Paulin 663 ....D 3
Saint-Paul-l'Ermite (Le
Gardeur) 8,312 ....J 4
Saint-Philippe-de-Néri 715 ..H 2
Saint-Pie 1,725 ....E 4
Saint-Pierre 5,305 ....H 4
Saint-Pierre-d'Orléans 880 ..G 3
Saint-Polycarpe 602 ....C 4
Saint-Prime 2,522 ....E 1
Saint-Prosper-de-Dorchester
2,150 ....G 3
Saint-Raphaël® 1,346 ....G 3
Saint-Raymond 3,605 ....F 3
Saint-Rédempteur 4,463 ....J 3
Saint-Régis 1,370 ....C 4
Saint-Rémi 5,074 ....D 4
Saint-Roch-de-l'Achigan
1,160 ....H 4
Saint-Roch-de-Richelieu
1,650 ....D 4
Saint-Romuald-d'Etchemin®
9,849 ....J 3

Saint-Sauveur-des-Monts
2,348 ....C 4
Saint-Siméon 1,152 ....G 2
Saint-Simon 602 ....H 1
Saint-Stanislas 1,443 ....E 3
Saint-Sylvère 1,006 ....E 3
Saint-Timothée 2,113 ....D 4
Saint-Tite 3,031 ....E 3
Saint-Tite-des-Caps 626 ....G 2
Saint-Ubald 1,605 ....E 3
Saint-Ulric 792 ....B 1
Saint-Urbain-de-Charlevoix
1,079 ....G 2
Saint-Victor 1,104 ....G 3
Saint-Zacharie 1,284 ....G 3
Saint-Zotique 1,774 ....C 4
Sault-au-Mouton 828 ....H 1
Sawyerville 939 ....F 4
Sayabec 1,721 ....B 2
Scotstown 762 ....F 4
Senneville 1,221 ....H 4
Shannon 3,488 ....C 4
Shawbridge 942 ....C 4
Shawinigan 23,011 ....E 3
Shawinigan-Sud 11,325 .....E 3
Shawville 1,608 ....A 4
Sherbrooke® 74,075 ....E 4
Sherrington 614 ....D 4
Sillery 12,825 ....J 3
Sorel® 20,347 ....D 3
Squatec 1,000 ....J 2
Stanstead Plain 1,093 ......E 4
Sutton 1,599 ....E 4
Tadoussac® 900 ....H 1
Templeton ....B 4
Terrebonne 11,769 ....H 4
Thetford Mines 19,965 .....F 3
Thurso 2,897 ....B 4
Tourelle (Tourelle-Grand-
Tourelle) 942 ....D 1
Tourville 659 ....H 2
Tracy 12,843 ....D 3
Tring-Jonction 1,315 ....F 3
Trois-Pistoles 4,445 ....H 1
Trois-Rivières 50,466 ......E 3
Trois-Rivières ®111,453 ....E 3
Trois-Rivières-Ouest 13,107 .E 3
Upton 926 ....D 4
Val-Barrette 609 ....B 1
Val-Brillant 687 ....E 4
Valcourt 2,601 ....E 4
Val-David 2,336 ....C 3
Vallée-Jonction 1,200 ......G 3
Valleyfield (Salaberry-de-
Valleyfield) 29,574 ......C 4
Vanier 10,725 ....J 3

Varennes 8,764 ....J 4
Vaudreuil® 7,608 ....C 4
Verchères® 4,473 ....H 4
Verdun 61,287 ....H 4
Victoriaville 21,838 ....E 3
Villeneuve ....J 3
Warwick 2,847 ....E 4
Waterloo® 4,664 ....E 4
Waterville 1,397 ....F 4
Weedon-Centre 1,263 .....F 4
Westmount 20,480 ....H 4
Wickham 2,043 ....E 4
Windsor 5,233 ....F 4
Wottonville 673 ....F 4
Yamachiche 1,258 ....E 3

OTHER FEATURES

Alma (isl.) ....F 1
Aylmer (lake) ....F 4
Baskatong (res.) ....B 3
Batiscan (riv.) ....E 2
Bécancour (riv.) ....F 3
Bonaventure (isl.) ....D 1
Bonaventure (riv.) ....D 1
Brome (lake) ....E 4
Brompton (lake) ....E 4
Cascapédia (riv.) ....C 1
Chaleur (bay) ....C 2
Champlain (lake) ....D 4
Chaudière (riv.) ....F 3
Chic-Chocs (mts.) ....C 1
Chicoutimi (riv.) ....F 1
Coudres (isl.) ....G 2
Deschênes (lake) ....A 4
Deux Montagnes (lake) ....H 4
Ditton (riv.) ....F 4
Forillon Nat'l Park ....D 1
Fort Chambly Nat'l Hist. Park .H 4
Gaspé (bay) ....D 1
Gaspé (cape) ....D 1
Gaspé (pen.) ....C 1
Gaspésie Prov. Park ....C 1
Gatineau (riv.) ....B 3
Iles (isl.) ....C 1
Jacques-Cartier (lake) .....F 2
Jacques-Cartier (mt.) ......F 2
Jacques-Cartier (riv.) ......F 2
Kénogami (lake) ....F 1
Kiamika (lake) ....B 3
La Maurice Nat'l Park ......D 3
Laurentides Prov. Park .....F 2
Lièvre (riv.) ....B 4
Lièvres (isl.) ....H 2
Maskinongé (riv.) ....D 3
Matane (riv.) ....B 1
Matane Prov. Park ....B 1

Matapédia (riv.) ....B 2
Mégantic (lake) ....G 4
Memphremagog (lake) .....E 4
Mercier (dam) ....A 3
Métabetchouane (riv.) .....F 1
Mille Iles (riv.) ....H 4
Montmorency (riv.) ....F 2
Mont-Tremblant Prov. Park ..C 3
Nicolet (riv.) ....E 3
Nominingue (lake) ....B 3
Nord (riv.) ....F 3
Orléans (isl.) ....G 3
Ottawa (riv.) ....B 4
Ouareau (riv.) ....D 3
Ouelle (riv.) ....H 2
Patapédia (riv.) ....B 2
Péribonca (riv.) ....F 1
Petite Nation (riv.) ....B 4
Prairies (riv.) ....H 4
Rimouski (riv.) ....J 1
Ristigouche (riv.) ....B 2
Saguenay (riv.) ....G 1
Sainte-Anne (riv.) ....F 3
Sainte-Anne (riv.) ....E 3
Saint-François (lake) ......F 4
Saint-François (riv.) ....F 4
Saint-Jean (lake) ....E 1
Saint-Lawrence (gulf) ......H 1
Saint Lawrence (riv.) ......H 1
Saint-Louis (lake) ....H 4
Saint-Maurice (riv.) ....E 2
Saint-Pierre (lake) ....E 3
Shawinigan (riv.) ....F 1
Shipshaw (riv.) ....F 1
Soeurs (isl.) ....H 4
Témiscamingue (lake) .....A 3
Tremblant (lake) ....B 3
Trente et un Milles (lake) ..H 1
Verte (isl.) ....E 4
Yamaska (riv.) ....D 4
York (riv.) ....D 1

®County seat.
*Population of metropolitan area.

QUÉBEC, NORTHERN

INTERNAL DIVISIONS

Abitibi 93,529 ....B 2
Abitibi (terr.) ....B 3
Berthier (county) 31,096 ....B 3
Bonaventure (county) 40,487 .D 3
Champlain (county) 119,595 ..C 3
Charlevoix-Est (co.) 17,448 ..C 3

Charlevoix-Ouest (county)
14,172 ....D 3
Chicoutimi (county) 174,441 ..C 2
Gaspé-Est (county) 41,173 ...E 3
Gaspé-Ouest (county) 18,943 .D 3
Gatineau (county) 54,229 ....B 3
Joliette (county) 60,384 .....B 3
Lac-Saint-Jean-Est (county)
47,891 ....C 3
Lac-Saint-Jean-Ouest
(county) 62,952 ....C 2
Maskinongé (county) 20,763 ..C 3
Matane (county) 29,955 .....D 3
Matapédia (county) 23,715 ...D 3
Mistassini (terr.) ....B 2
Montcalm (county) 27,557 ...B 3
Montmorency No. 1 (county)
23,048 ....C 3
Nouveau-Québec (terr.) .....E 1
Pontiac (county) 20,283 .....B 3
Portneuf (county) 58,843 ....C 3
Québec (county) 458,980 ....C 3
Rimouski (county) 69,099 ....D 3
Saguenay (county) 115,881 ..D 3
Saint-Maurice (co.) 107,703 ..C 3
Témiscamingue (co.) 52,570 ..B 3

CITIES and TOWNS

Alma® 26,322 ....C 3
Amos® 9,421 ....B 3
Baie-Comeau 12,866 ....D 3
Baie-du-Poste 1,690 ....C 2
Chicoutimi® 60,064 ....C 3
Gaspé 17,261 ....E 3
Hauterive 13,995 ....D 3
Jonquière 60,354 ....C 3
Lévis 17,895 ....C 3
La Tuque 11,556 ....C 3
Manicouagan ....D 2
Maniwaki 5,424 ....B 3
Matane® 13,612 ....D 3
Mistassini (Baie-du-Poste)
1,690 ....C 2
Mont-Laurier® 8,405 ....B 3
Montmagny® 12,405 ....C 3
New Carlisle 781 ....D 3
Percé® 4,839 ....E 3
Port-Cartier-Ouest ....D 3
Port-Menier 275 ....E 3
Povungnituk 745 ....E 1
Québec (cap.)® 166,474 ....C 3
Rimouski 29,120 ....D 3
Rivière-au-Tonnerre 480 ....D 3
Rivière-du-Loup 13,459 ....D 3
Rouyn 17,224 ....B 3

Sept-Iles 29,262 ....D 3
Shawinigan 23,011 ....C 3
Tadoussac 900 ....C 3
Val d'Or 21,371 ....B 3
Ville-Marie 2,651 ....B 3
Wemindji ....B 2

OTHER FEATURES

Allard (lake) ....E 2
Anticosti (isl.) ....E 3
Baleine, Grand Rivière de la
(riv.) ....B 1
Bell (riv.) ....B 2
Betsiamites (riv.) ....C 2
Bienville (lake) ....C 1
Broadback (riv.) ....B 2
Caborga (res.) ....D 1
Caniapiscau (riv.) ....D 1
Eastmain (riv.) ....C 1
Eau Claire (riv.) ....C 1
Feuilles (riv.) ....D 3
Gaspésie Prov. Park ....D 3
George (riv.) ....D 1
Gouin (res.) ....B 2
Grande Rivière, La (riv.) ...B 2
Honguedo (passage) ....D 3
Hudson (bay) ....A 1
Hudson (str.) ....F 1
Jacques-Cartier (passage) ..D 3
James (bay) ....A 2
Koksoak (riv.) ....D 1
Laurentides Prov. Park .....C 3
Louis-XIV (pt.) ....B 2
Manicouagan (res.) ....D 2
Minto (lake) ....D 1
Mistassini (riv.) ....C 2
Mistassini (lake) ....C 2
Moisie (riv.) ....D 2
Natashquan (riv.) ....E 2
Nottaway (riv.) ....B 2
Nouveau-Québec (crater) ..F 1
Otish (mts.) ....C 3
Ottawa (riv.) ....B 3
Péribonca (riv.) ....C 2
Plétipi (riv.) ....C 2
Saguenay (riv.) ....C 3
Saint-Jean (lake) ....C 3
Saint Lawrence (gulf) ......D 3
Saint Lawrence (riv.) ......D 3
Ungava (bay) ....E 1

®County seat.
*Population of metropolitan area.

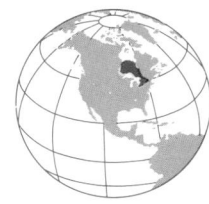

ONTARIO, NORTHERN
INTERNAL DIVISIONS

Algoma (terr. dist.) 133,553...D 3
Cochrane (terr. dist.) 96,875...D 2
Kenora (terr. dist.) 59,421...C 2
Manitoulin (terr. dist.) 11,001...D 3
Nipissing (terr. dist.) 80,268...E 3
Parry Sound (terr. dist.)
  33,528...E 3
Rainy River (terr. dist.) 22,798 B 3
Renfrew (county) 87,484...E 3
Sudbury (reg. munic.)
  159,779...D 3
Sudbury (terr. dist.) 27,068...D 3
Thunder Bay (terr. dist.)
  153,997...C 3
Timiskaming (terr. dist.)
  41,288...D 3

CITIES and TOWNS

Chalk River 1,010...E 3
Elliot Lake 16,723...D 3
Fort Albany 482...D 3
Fort Frances 8,906...B 3
Kapuskasing 12,014...D 2
Kenora⊛ 9,817...B 3
Kirkland Lake 12,219...D 3
Moose Factory 1,452...D 2
Moosonee 1,433...D 2
Nickel Centre 12,318...D 3
North Bay 51,268...E 3
Pembroke 14,026...E 3
Sault Sainte Marie⊛ 82,697...D 3
Sudbury 91,829...D 3
Thunder Bay⊛ 112,486...C 3
Timmins 46,114...D 3
Valley East 20,433...D 3

OTHER FEATURES

Abitibi (lake)...E 3
Abitibi (riv.)...D 2
Albany (riv.)...D 2
Algonquin Prov. Park...E 3
Asheweig (riv.)...C 2
Attawapiskat (riv.)...C 2
Attawapiskat (riv.)...D 2
Basswood (lake)...B 3
Berens (riv.)...A 2
Big Trout (lake)...B 2
Black Duck (riv.)...C 1
Bloodvein (riv.)...A 2
Caribou (isl.)...C 3

Cobham (riv.)...A 2
Eabamet (lake)...C 2
Ekwan (riv.)...C 2
English (riv.)...B 2
Fawn (riv.)...C 2
Finger (lake)...B 2
Georgian (bay)...D 3
Hannah (bay)...D 2
Henrietta Maria (cape)...D 1
Hudson (bay)...D 1
Huron (lake)...D 3
James (bay)...D 2
Kapiskau (riv.)...D 2
Kapuskasing (riv.)...D 3
Kenogami (riv.)...C 2
Kesagami (riv.)...E 2
Lake of the Woods (lake)...B 3
Lake Superior Prov. Park...C 3
Little Current (riv.)...C 2
Long (lake)...C 3
Manitoulin (isl.)...D 3
Mattagami (riv.)...D 3
Michipicoten (isl.)...C 3
Mille Lacs (lake)...B 3
Missinaibi (lake)...D 2
Missinaibi (riv.)...D 2
Missisa (lake)...C 2
Nipigon (lake)...C 3
Nipissing (lake)...E 3
North (chan.)...D 3
North Caribou (lake)...B 2
Nungesser (lake)...B 2
Ogidaki (mt.)...D 3
Ogoki (riv.)...C 2
Opazatika (riv.)...D 3
Opinnagau (riv.)...C 2
Otoskwin (riv.)...B 2
Ottawa (riv.)...E 3
Pipestone (riv.)...B 2
Polar Bear Prov. Park...D 2
Pukaskwa Prov. Park...C 3
Quetico Prov. Park...B 3
Rainy (lake)...B 3
Red (lake)...B 2
Sachigo (riv.)...B 2
Saganaga (lake)...B 3
Saint Ignace (isl.)...C 3
Saint Joseph (lake)...B 2
Sandy (lake)...B 2
Savant (lake)...B 3
Seine (riv.)...B 3
Seul (lake)...B 2
Severn (lake)...B 2
Severn (riv.)...B 2
Shamattawa (riv.)...C 2
Shibogama (lake)...C 2

Sibley Prov. Park...C 3
Slate (isls.)...C 3
Stout (lake)...B 2
Superior (lake)...C 3
Sutton (lake)...D 2
Sutton (riv.)...D 2
Temigami (lake)...D 3
Timiskaming (lake)...E 3
Trout (lake)...B 2
Wabuk (pt.)...D 1
Winisk (lake)...C 2
Winisk (riv.)...C 2
Winnipeg (riv.)...A 2
Woods (lake)...B 3

ONTARIO
INTERNAL DIVISIONS

Algoma (terr. dist.) 133,553...J 5
Brant (county) 104,427...D 4
Bruce (county) 60,020...C 3
Cochrane (terr. dist.) 96,875...J 4
Dufferin (county) 31,145...D 3
Dundas (county) 18,946...J 2
Durham (reg. munic.) 283,639 F 3
Elgin (county) 69,707...C 5
Essex (county) 312,467...B 5
Frontenac (county) 108,133...H 3
Glengarry (county) 20,254...K 2
Grenville (county) 27,176...J 3
Grey (county) 73,824...C 3
Haldimand-Norfolk (reg.
  munic.) 89,456...E 5
Haliburton (county) 11,361...F 2
Halton (reg. munic.) 253,883...E 4
Hamilton-Wentworth (reg.
  munic.) 411,445...D 4
Hastings (county) 106,883...G 3
Huron (county) 56,127...C 4
Kenora (terr. dist.) 59,421...G 5
Kent (county) 107,022...B 5
Lambton (county) 123,445...B 5
Lanark (county) 45,676...H 3
Leeds (county) 53,765...H 3
Lennox and Addington
  (county) 33,040...G 3
Manitoulin (terr. dist.) 11,001..D 2
Middlesex (county) 318,184...C 4
Muskoka (dist. munic.)
  38,370...E 3
Niagara (reg. munic.) 368,288 E 4
Nipissing (terr. dist.) 80,268...F 2
Northumberland (county)
  64,966...G 3

Ottawa-Carleton (reg. munic.)
  546,849...J 2
Oxford (county) 85,920...D 4
Parry Sound (terr. dist.)
  33,528...D 2
Peel (reg. munic.) 490,731...E 4
Perth (county) 66,096...C 4
Peterborough (county)
  102,452...F 3
Prescott (county) 30,365...K 2
Prince Edward (county)
  22,336...G 4
Rainy River (terr. dist.) 22,798 G 5
Renfrew (county) 87,484...G 2
Russell (county) 22,412...J 2
Simcoe (county) 225,071...E 3
Stormont (county) 61,927...K 2
Sudbury (reg. munic.)
  159,779...K 6
Sudbury (terr. dist.) 27,068...J 5
Thunder Bay (terr. dist.)
  153,997...H 5
Timiskaming (terr. dist.)
  41,288...J 5
Toronto (metro. munic.)
  2,137,395...K 4
Victoria (reg. munic.) 47,854...F 3
Waterloo (reg. munic.)
  305,496...D 4
Wellington (county) 129,432...D 4
York (reg. munic.) 252,053...E 4

CITIES and TOWNS

Ailsa Craig 765...C 4
Ajax 25,475...E 4
Alban 342...D 1
Alexandria 3,271...K 2
Alfred 1,057...K 2
Alliston 4,712...E 3
Alvinston 736...B 5
Amherstburg 5,685...A 5
Amherst View 6,110...H 3
Ancaster 14,428...D 4
Angus 3,085...E 3
Apsley 264...F 3
Arkona 473...C 4
Armstrong 378...H 4
Arnprior 5,828...J 2
Aroland 291...H 4
Arthur 1,700...D 4
Astorville 340...E 1
Athens 948...J 3
Atherley 366...E 3
Atikokan 4,452...G 5

Atwood 723...D 4
Aurora 16,267...J 3
Avonmore 273...K 2
Aylmer 5,254...C 5
Ayr 1,295...D 4
Ayton 424...D 3
Bala 577...E 2
Bancroft 2,329...G 2
Barrie 38,423...E 3
Barry's Bay 1,216...G 2
Batawa 430...G 3
Bath 1,071...H 3
Bayfield 649...C 4
Beachburg 682...H 2
Beachville 917...D 4
Beardmore 583...H 5
Beaverton 1,952...E 3
Beeton 1,989...E 3
Belle River 3,568...B 5
Belleville⊛ 34,881...G 3
Belmont 831...C 5
Bethany 365...F 3
Bewdley 508...F 3
Binbrook 306...E 4
Blackstock 720...F 3
Blenheim 4,044...C 5
Blind River 3,444...J 5
Bloomfield 718...G 4
Blyth 926...C 4
Bobcaygeon 1,625...F 3
Bonfield 540...E 1
Bothwell 915...C 5
Bourget 1,057...J 2
Bracebridge⊛ 9,063...E 2
Bradford 7,370...E 3
Braeside 492...H 2
Brampton⊛ 149,030...J 4
Brantford⊛ 74,315...D 4
Bridgenorth 1,633...F 3

Brigden 635...B 5
Brighton 3,147...G 3
Britt 419...D 2
Brockville⊛ 19,896...J 3
Bruce Mines 635...J 5
Brussels 962...C 4
Burford 1,461...D 4
Burgessville 302...D 4
Burk's Falls 922...E 2
Burlington 114,853...E 4
Cache Bay 665...D 1
Caesarea 551...F 3
Calabogie 256...H 2
Caledon 26,645...E 4
Callander 1,158...E 1
Cambridge 77,183...D 4
Campbellford 3,409...G 3
Cannington 1,623...E 3
Capreol 3,845...K 5
Caramat 265...H 5
Cardinal 1,753...J 3
Carleton Place 5,626...H 2
Carlisle 781...D 4
Carlsbad Springs 616...J 2
Carp 707...H 2
Cartier 590...J 5
Casselman 1,675...J 2
Castleton 346...F 3
Chalk River 1,010...G 1
Chapleau 3,243...J 5
Charing Cross 443...B 5
Chatham⊛ 40,952...B 5
Chatsworth 383...D 3
Cherry Valley 289...G 4
Chesley 1,840...C 3
Chesterville 1,430...J 2
Chute-à-Blondeau 365...K 2
City View...J 2
Clarence Creek 796...J 2
Clarksburg 508...D 3

Clifford 645...D 4
Clinton 3,081...C 4
Cobalt 1,759...K 5
Cobden 997...H 2
Coboconk 426...F 3
Coburg⊛ 11,385...F 4
Cochrane⊛ 4,848...K 5
Colborne 1,796...G 4
Colchester 711...B 6
Coldwater 964...E 3
Collingwood 12,064...D 3
Comber 667...B 5
Consecon 295...G 3
Cookstown 918...E 3
Cornwall⊛ 46,144...K 2
Cottam 404...B 5
Courtland 647...D 5
Courtright 1,024...B 5
Crediton 370...C 4
Creemore 1,182...D 3
Crysler 540...J 2
Cumberland 518...J 2
Cumberland Beach-Bramshot-
  Buena Vista 679...E 3
Dashwood 426...C 4
Deep River 5,095...G 1
Delaware 481...C 4
Delhi 4,043...D 5
Delta 360...H 3
Deseronto 1,740...G 3
Douglas 303...H 2
Drayton 809...D 4
Dresden 2,550...B 5
Drumbo 476...D 4
Dryden 6,640...G 4
Dublin 295...C 4
Dubreuilville △988...J 5
Dundalk 1,250...D 3
Dundas 19,586...D 4
Dungannon 284...C 4
Dunnville 11,353...E 5
Durham 2,458...D 3
Dutton 1,115...C 5
Earlton 1,028...K 5
East York 101,974...J 4
Echo Bay 786...J 5
Eden Mills 318...D 4
Eganville 1,245...G 2
Egmondville 465...C 4
Elgin 327...H 3
Elk Lake 526...K 5
Elliot Lake 16,723...B 1
Elmira 7,063...D 4
Elmvale 1,183...D 3
Elmwood 364...C 3
Elora 2,666...D 4
Embro 727...C 4
Embrun 1,883...J 2
Emeryville-Puce 1,611...B 5
Emo 762...F 5
Englehart 1,689...K 5
Enterprise 357...H 3
Erieau 430...C 5
Erin 2,313...D 4
Espanola 5,836...J 5
Essex 6,295...B 5
Etobicoke 298,713...J 4
Everett 570...E 3
Exeter 3,732...C 4
Fauquier 561...J 5
Fenelon Falls 1,701...F 3
Fergus 6,064...D 4
Field 462...E 1
Finch 353...J 2
Fingal 380...C 5
Fitzroy Harbour 446...H 2
Flesherton 565...D 3
Foleyet 484...J 5
Fordwich 365...C 4
Forest 2,671...C 4
Formosa 393...C 4
Fort Erie 24,096...E 5
Fort Frances⊛ 8,906...F 5
Foxboro 597...G 3
Frankford 1,919...G 3
Fraserdale 303...J 5
Freelton 307...D 4
Gananoque 4,863...H 3
Garden Village 270...E 1
Geraldton 2,956...H 5
Glencoe 1,694...C 5
Glen Miller 639...G 3
Glen Robertson 378...K 2
Glen Walter 710...K 2
Goderich⊛ 7,322...C 4
Gogama 652...J 5
Goodwood 335...E 3
Gore Bay⊛ 777...B 2
Gorrie 468...C 4
Grafton 409...G 4
Grand Bend 680...C 4
Grand Valley 1,226...D 4
Granton 315...C 4
Gravenhurst 8,532...E 3
Greely 567...J 2
Green Valley 459...K 2
Grimsby 15,797...E 4
Guelph⊛ 71,207...D 4

(continued on following page)

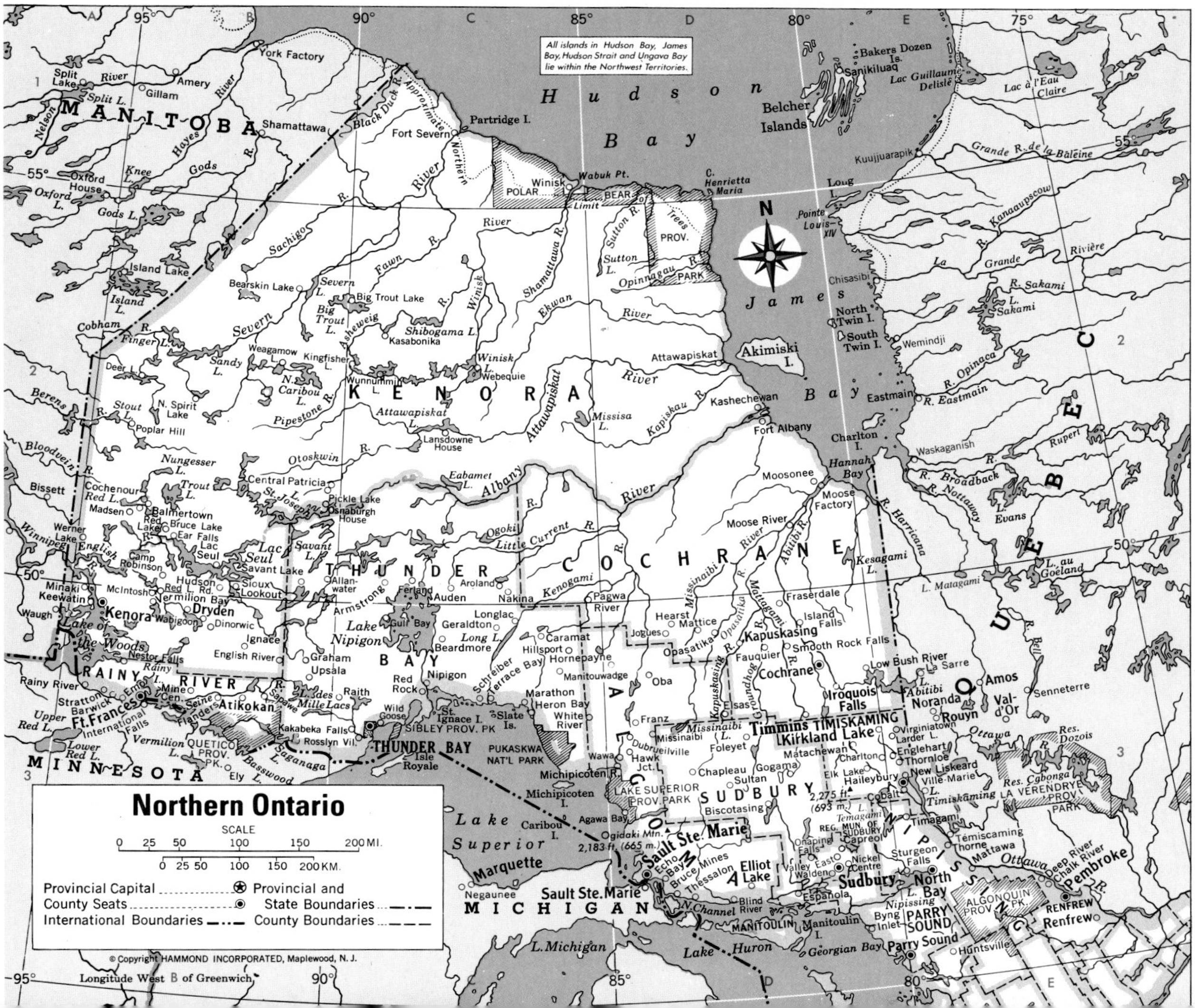

Map facts (right column)

AREA 412,580 sq. mi. (1,068,582 sq. km.)
POPULATION 9,101,694
CAPITAL Toronto
LARGEST CITY Toronto
HIGHEST POINT in Timiskaming Dist.
  2,275 ft. (693 m.)
SETTLED IN 1749
ADMITTED TO CONFEDERATION 1867
PROVINCIAL FLOWER White Trillium

Map

All islands in Hudson Bay, James
Bay, Hudson Strait and Ungava Bay
lie within the Northwest Territories.

Northern Ontario

SCALE
0 25 50   100   150   200 MI.
0 25 50 100   150 200 KM.

Provincial Capital ...⊛
Provincial and
County Seats...⊙
Provincial and
State Boundaries ...
International Boundaries ...

© Copyright HAMMOND INCORPORATED, Maplewood, N.J.

Longitude West B of Greenwich

Haileybury⊙ 4,925 .... K 5
Haldimand 16,866 .... E 5
Haliburton 1,443 .... F 2
Halton Hills 35,190 .... E 4
Hamilton 306,434 .... E 4
Hamilton *542,095 .... E 4
Hanover 6,316 .... C 3
Harriston 1,954 .... D 4
Harrow 2,274 .... B 5
Harrowsmith 599 .... H 3
Harwood 332 .... F 3
Hastings 975 .... G 3
Havelock 1,385 .... G 3
Hawkesbury 9,877 .... K 2
Hawkestone 275 .... E 3
Hawk Junction 349 .... J 5
Hearst 5,533 .... H 5
Hensall 973 .... C 4
Hepworth 393 .... D 3
Hickson 263 .... D 4
Highgate 435 .... C 5
Hillsburgh 1,065 .... D 4
Hillsdale 370 .... E 3
Holland Landing 2,771 .... E 3
Honey Harbour 505 .... E 3
Hornepayne 1,848 .... J 5
Hudson 515 .... G 5
Huntsville 11,467 .... E 2
Huron Park 1,104 .... C 4
Ignace 2,499 .... G 5
Ilderton 301 .... C 4
Ingersoll 8,494 .... C 4
Ingleside 1,400 .... J 2
Innerkip 715 .... D 4
Inverhuron 438 .... C 3
Iron Bridge 821 .... A 1

Iroquois 1,211 .... J 3
Iroquois Falls 6,339 .... J 5
Johnstown 789 .... J 3
Kakabeka Falls 300 .... G 5
Kanata 19,728 .... J 2
Kapuskasing 12,014 .... J 5
Kars 449 .... J 2
Kearney 538 .... E 2
Keene 353 .... F 3
Keewatin 1,863 .... F 5
Kemptville 2,362 .... J 2
Kenora⊙ 9,817 .... F 4
Killaloe Station 634 .... G 2
Killarney 433 .... C 2
Kincardine 5,778 .... C 3
Kingston⊙ 52,616 .... H 3
Kingsville 5,134 .... B 6
Kinmount 262 .... F 2
Kirkland Lake 12,219 .... K 5
Kitchener 139,734 .... D 4
Kitchener *287,801 .... D 4
Komoka 1,152 .... C 5
Lakefield 2,374 .... F 3
Lanark 753 .... H 2
Lancaster 637 .... K 2
Langton 348 .... D 5
Lansdowne 540 .... H 3
Larder Lake 1,084 .... K 5
Latchford 397 .... K 5
Leamington 12,528 .... B 5
Limoges 930 .... J 2
Lincoln 14,196 .... E 4
Linden Beach 579 .... B 6
Lindsay⊙ 13,596 .... F 3
Linwood 450 .... D 4
Lion's Head 467 .... C 2

Lisle 265 .... E 3
Listowel 5,026 .... D 4
Little Britain 265 .... F 3
Little Current 1,507 .... B 2
London 254,280 .... C 5
London *283,668 .... C 5
Longlac 2,431 .... H 5
Long Sault 1,227 .... K 2
L'Orignal 1,819 .... K 2
Lucan 1,616 .... C 4
Lucknow 1,088 .... C 4
Lyn 518 .... J 3
Lynden 451 .... D 4
Lynhurst 685 .... C 5
MacGregor's Bay 861 .... G 2
MacTier 647 .... E 2
Madawaska 264 .... F 2
Madoc 1,249 .... G 3
Maitland 667 .... J 3
Mallorytown 368 .... J 3
Manitouwadge 3,155 .... H 5
Manitowaning 518 .... C 2
Manotick-Hillside Gardens 2,694 .... J 2
Marathon 2,271 .... H 5
Markdale 1,289 .... D 3
Markham 77,037 .... K 4
Markstay 444 .... D 1
Marmora 1,304 .... G 3
Martintown 388 .... K 2
Massey 1,274 .... C 1
Matachewan 444 .... J 5
Matheson 966 .... K 5
Mattawa 2,652 .... F 1
Mattice 803 .... J 5
Maxville 836 .... K 2

Maynooth 277 .... G 2
McGregor 1,145 .... J 2
McKerrow 260 .... C 1
Meaford 4,367 .... D 3
Melbourne 346 .... C 5
Merlin 745 .... C 5
Merrickville 984 .... J 3
Metcalfe 687 .... J 2
Midhurst 1,457 .... E 3
Midland 12,132 .... D 3
Mildmay 928 .... C 3
Milford Bay 401 .... E 2
Millbank 337 .... D 4
Millbrook 927 .... F 3
Milton⊙ 28,067 .... E 4
Milverton 1,463 .... C 4
Minaki 319 .... F 5
Mindemoya 376 .... B 2
Minden⊙ 838 .... F 2
Mississauga 315,056 .... J 4
Mitchell 2,777 .... C 4
Monkton 520 .... C 4
Moonbeam 838 .... J 5
Moorefield 308 .... D 4
Mooretown 344 .... B 5
Moose Creek 393 .... K 2
Morewood 264 .... J 2
Morpeth 284 .... C 5
Morrisburg 2,308 .... J 3
Mount Albert 1,165 .... E 3
Mount Brydges 1,557 .... C 5
Mount Forest 3,474 .... D 4
Mount Hope 557 .... E 4
Munster 1,531 .... J 2
Nakina 936 .... H 4
Nanticoke⊙ 19,816 .... E 5

Napanee 4,803 .... G 3
Navan 419 .... J 2
Neustadt 511 .... D 3
Newboro 260 .... H 3
Newburgh 617 .... H 3
Newbury 441 .... C 5
Newcastle 32,229 .... F 4
New Hamburg 3,923 .... D 4
New Liskeard 5,551 .... K 5
Newmarket⊙ 29,753 .... E 3
Niagara Falls 70,960 .... E 4
Niagara-on-the-Lake 12,186 .... E 4
Nickel Centre 12,318 .... D 1
Nipigon 2,377 .... H 5
Nobel 386 .... D 2
Nobleton 1,861 .... J 3
Noelville 702 .... D 1
North Bay⊙ 51,268 .... E 1
North Gower 818 .... J 2
North York 559,521 .... J 4
Norwich 2,117 .... D 5
Norwood 1,278 .... F 3
Nottawa 960 .... D 3
Oakville 75,773 .... E 4
Oakwood 404 .... F 3
Odessa 849 .... H 3
Oil City 266 .... B 5
Oil Springs 627 .... B 5
Omemee 819 .... F 3
Onaping Falls 6,198 .... J 5
Opasatika 413 .... J 5
Orangeville⊙ 13,740 .... D 4
Orillia 23,955 .... E 3
Osgoode 1,138 .... J 2
Oshawa 117,519 .... F 4
Oshawa *154,217 .... F 4

Ottawa⊙ (cap.), Canada 295,163 .... J 2
Ottawa-Hull ⊙*717,978 .... J 2
Otterville 776 .... D 5
Owen Sound⊙ 19,883 .... D 3
Paincourt 414 .... B 5
Paisley 1,039 .... C 3
Pakenham 367 .... H 2
Palmerston 1,989 .... D 4
Paris 7,485 .... D 4
Parkhill 1,358 .... C 4
Parry Sound⊙ 6,124 .... E 2
Pefferlaw 857 .... E 3
Pelham 11,104 .... E 4
Pembroke⊙ 14,026 .... H 2
Penetanguishene 5,315 .... D 3
Perth⊙ 5,655 .... H 3
Petawawa 5,520 .... H 2
Peterborough⊙ 60,620 .... F 3
Petrolia 4,234 .... B 5
Pickering 37,754 .... K 4
Picton⊙ 4,361 .... G 3
Plantagenet 870 .... K 2
Plattsville 495 .... D 4
Point Edward 2,383 .... F 3
Pontypool 759 .... F 3
Port Burwell 655 .... D 5
Port Carling 629 .... E 2
Port Colborne 19,225 .... E 5
Port Elgin 6,131 .... C 3
Port Franks 547 .... C 4
Port Hope 9,992 .... F 4
Port Lambton 921 .... B 5
Portland 271 .... H 3
Port McNicoll 1,883 .... E 3
Port Perry 4,712 .... E 3

Port Rowan 811 .... D 5
Port Stanley 1,891 .... C 5
Pottageville 286 .... J 3
Powassan 1,169 .... E 1
Prescott⊙ 4,670 .... J 3
Princeton 462 .... D 4
Puce-Emeryville 1,611 .... B 5
Rainy River 1,061 .... F 5
Ramore 382 .... K 5
Rayside-Balfour 15,017 .... H 5
Red Rock 1,260 .... H 5
Renfrew 8,283 .... H 2
Richards Landing 405 .... J 5
Richmond 2,880 .... J 2
Richmond Hill 37,778 .... J 4
Ridgetown 3,062 .... C 5
Ripley 591 .... C 3
River Valley 275 .... D 1
Rockcliffe Park 1,869 .... J 2
Rockland 3,961 .... J 2
Rockwood 1,068 .... D 4
Rodney 1,007 .... C 5
Rosslyn Village 362 .... G 5
Round Lake Centre 255 .... G 2
Russell 1,099 .... J 2
Ruthven 649 .... B 6
Saint Albert 254 .... J 2
Saint Catharines⊙ 124,018 .... E 4
Saint Catharines-Niagara *304,353 .... E 4
Saint Charles 382 .... D 1
Saint Clair Beach 2,845 .... B 5
Saint Clements 890 .... D 4
Saint-Eugène 470 .... K 2
Saint George 865 .... D 4
Saint Isidore de Prescott 746 .... K 2

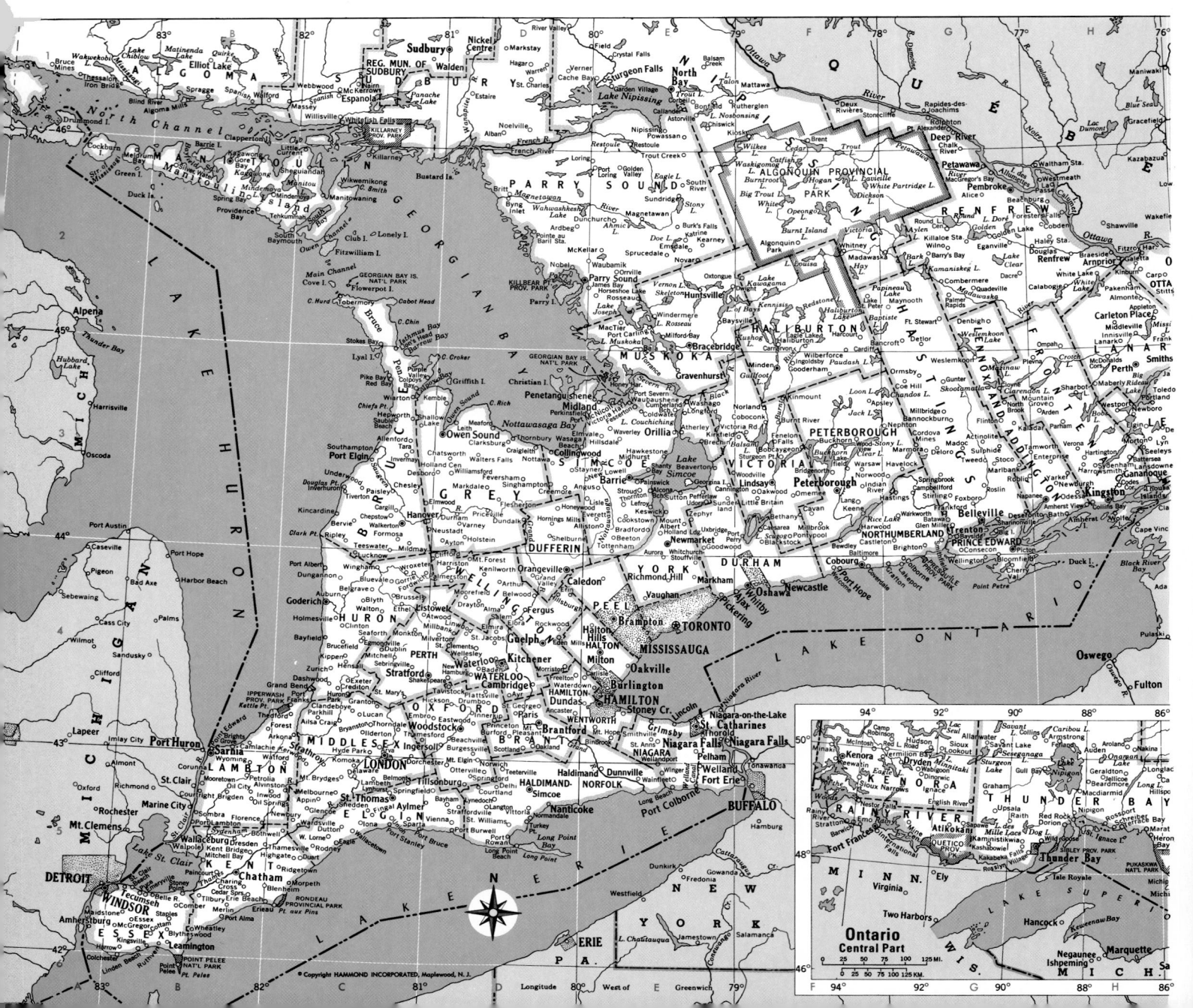

Ontario
Central Part

0 25 50 75 100 125 MI.
0 25 50 75 100 125 KM.

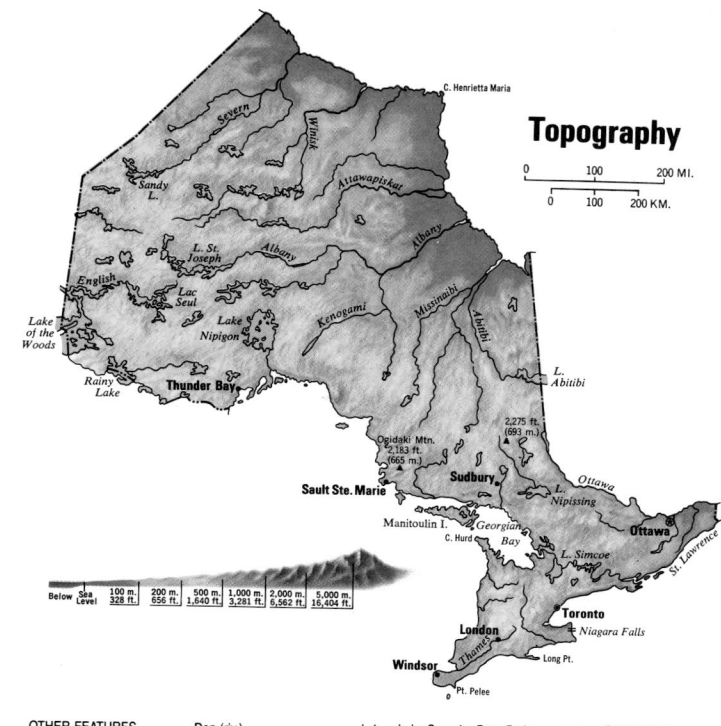

Topography

| Below Sea Level | 100 m. 328 ft. | 200 m. 656 ft. | 500 m. 1,640 ft. | 1,000 m. 3,281 ft. | 2,000 m. 6,562 ft. | 5,000 m. 16,404 ft. |

OTHER FEATURES

⊛County seat.
*Population of metropolitan area.
△Population of town or township.

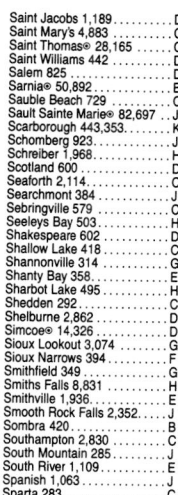

Ontario
Southern Part

SCALE
0 10 20 30 40 50 MI.
0 10 20 30 40 50 KM.

National Capital ⊛	Provincial & State Boundaries
Provincial Capital ⊛	County Boundaries
County Seats ⊛	Canals
International Boundaries	

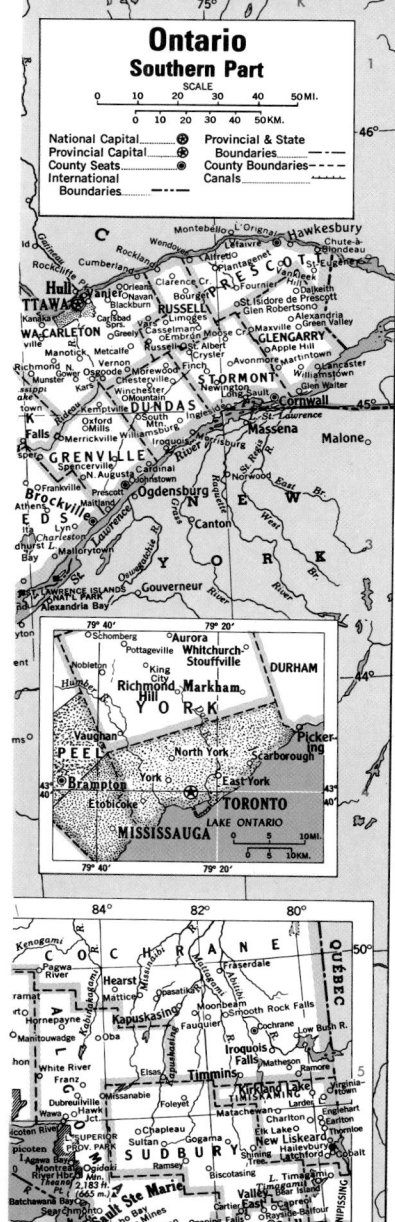

Agriculture, Industry and Resources

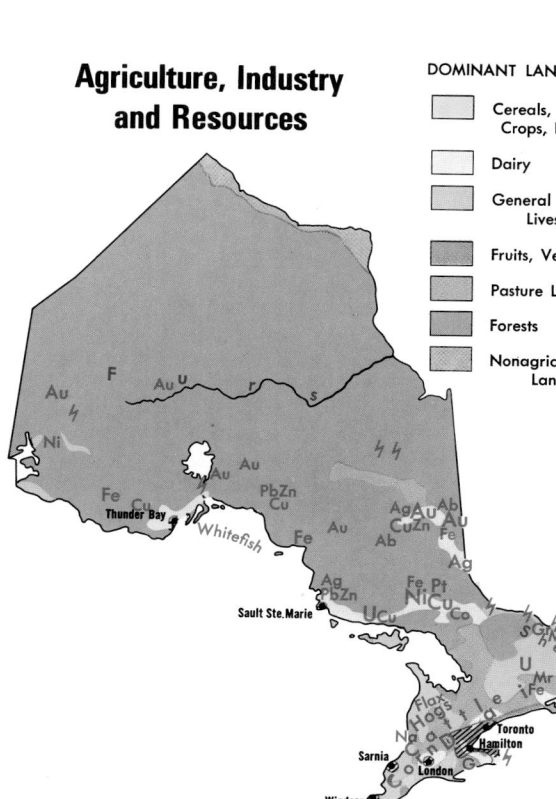

DOMINANT LAND USE

- Cereals, Cash Crops, Livestock
- Dairy
- General Farming, Livestock
- Fruits, Vegetables
- Pasture Livestock
- Forests
- Nonagricultural Land

MAJOR MINERAL OCCURRENCES

Ab	Asbestos	Mg	Magnesium
Ag	Silver	Mr	Marble
Au	Gold	Na	Salt
Co	Cobalt	Ni	Nickel
Cu	Copper	Pb	Lead
Fe	Iron Ore	Pt	Platinum
G	Natural Gas	U	Uranium
Gr	Graphite	Zn	Zinc

⚡ Water Power
▨ Major Industrial Areas

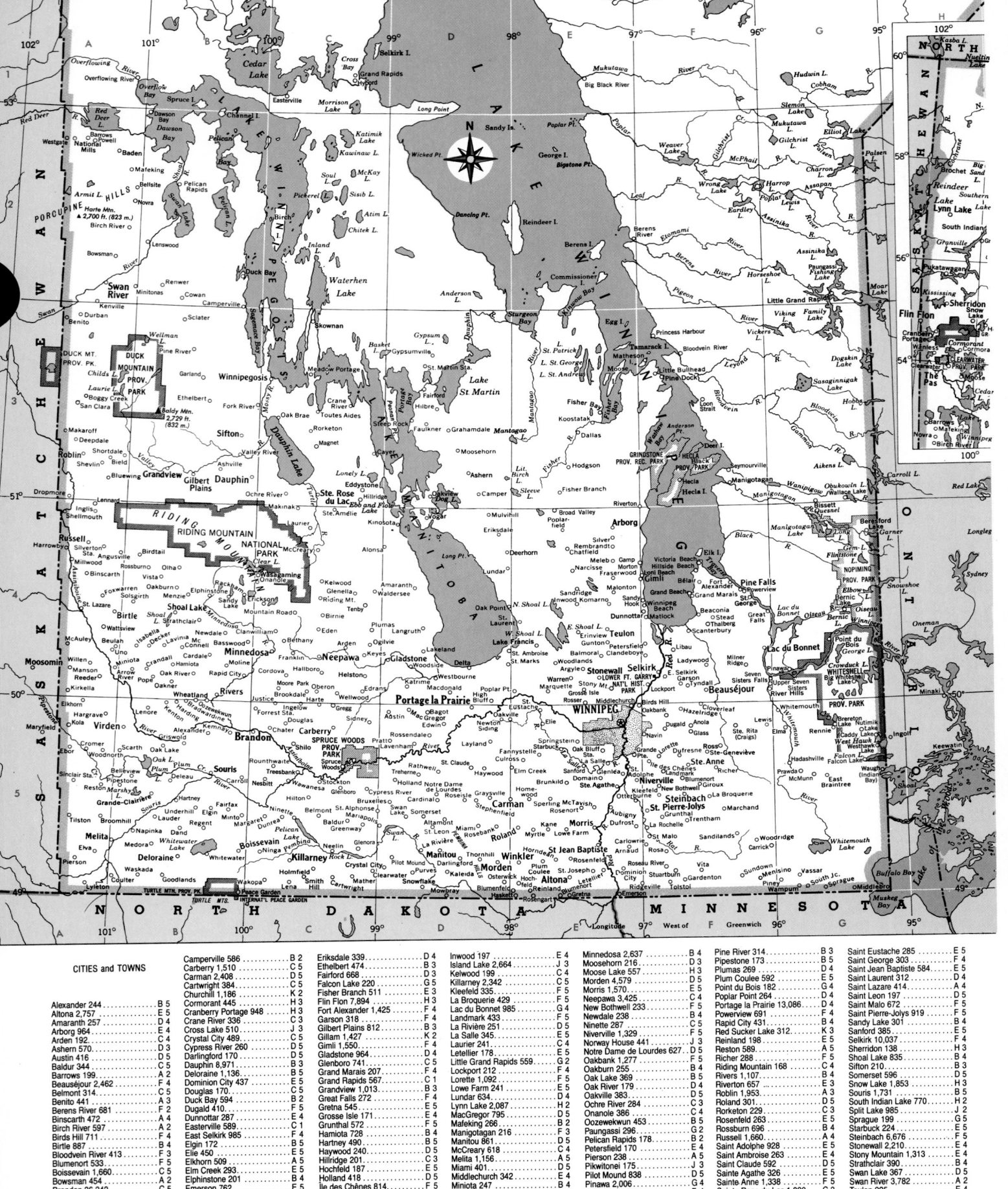

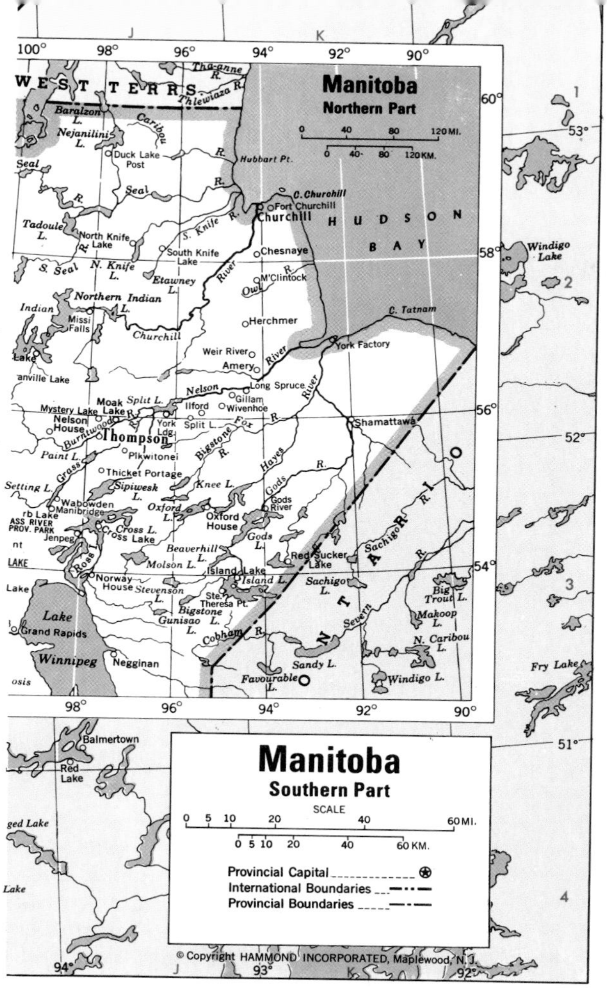

Manitoba
Northern Part

WEST TERRS.

HUDSON BAY

ONTARIO

Manitoba
Southern Part

SCALE
0 5 10 20 40 60 MI.
0 5 10 20 40 60 KM.

Provincial Capital ⊛
International Boundaries
Provincial Boundaries

© Copyright HAMMOND INCORPORATED, Maplewood, N.J.

AREA 250.999 sq. mi. (650,087 sq. km.)
POPULATION 1,063,016
CAPITAL Winnipeg
LARGEST CITY Winnipeg
HIGHEST POINT Baldy Mtn. 2,729 ft. (832 m.)
SETTLED IN 1812
ADMITTED TO CONFEDERATION 1870
PROVINCIAL FLOWER Prairie Crocus

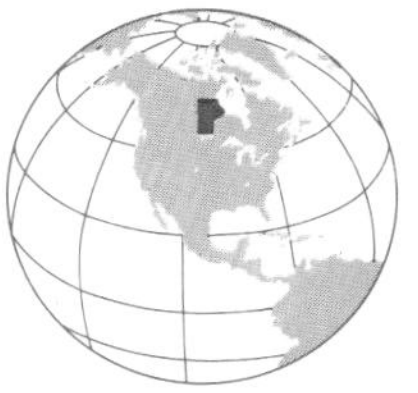

Topography

0 75 150 MI.
0 75 150 KM.

Below Sea Level | 100 m. 328 ft. | 200 m. 656 ft. | 500 m. 1,640 ft. | 1,000 m. 3,281 ft. | 2,000 m. 6,562 ft. | 5,000 m. 16,404 ft.

Agriculture, Industry and Resources

DOMINANT LAND USE

Cereals (chiefly barley, oats)
Cereals, Livestock
Dairy
Livestock
Forests
Nonagricultural Land

MAJOR MINERAL OCCURRENCES

Au Gold
Co Cobalt
Cu Copper
Na Salt

Ni Nickel
O Petroleum
Pb Lead
Pt Platinum
Zn Zinc

Water Power
Major Industrial Areas

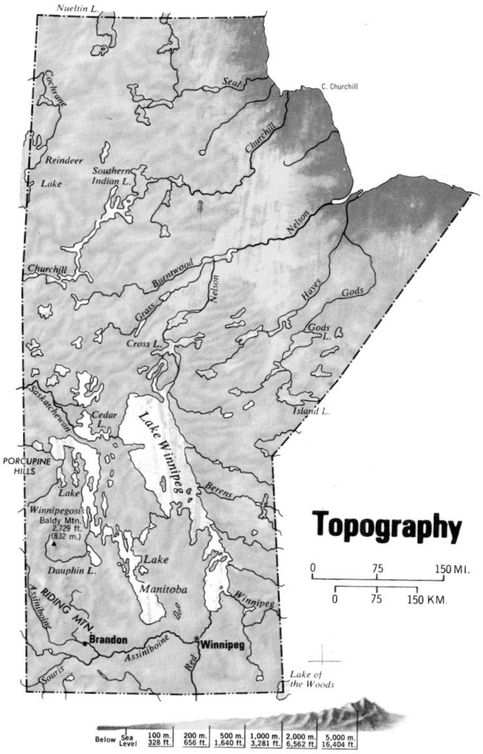

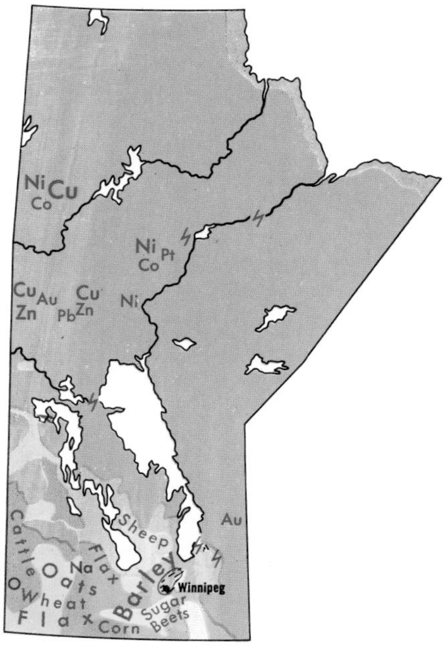

Topography

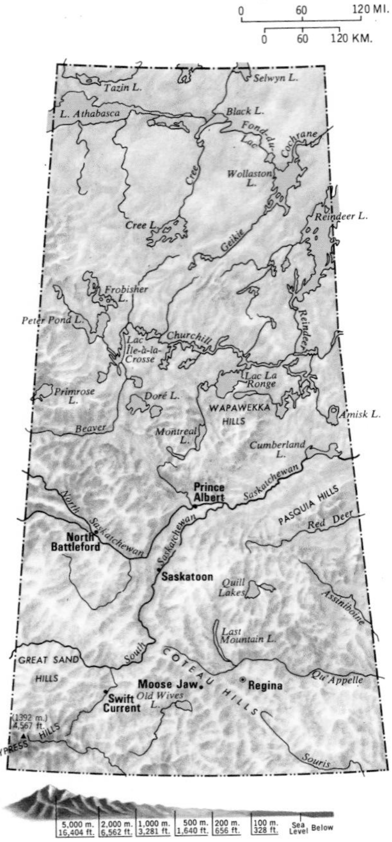

0 60 120 MI.
0 60 120 KM.

5,000 m. 16,404 ft. | 2,000 m. 6,562 ft. | 1,000 m. 3,281 ft. | 500 m. 1,640 ft. | 200 m. 656 ft. | 100 m. 328 ft. | Sea Level | Below

---

Foam Lake 1,452 .... H 4
Fond du Lac 494 .... L 2
Fort Qu'Appelle 1,827 .... H 5
Fox Valley 380 .... B 5
Francis 182 .... H 5
Frobisher 166 .... J 6
Frontier 619 .... C 6
Gainsborough 308 .... K 6
Gerald 197 .... K 5
Glaslyn 430 .... C 2
Glenavon 284 .... J 5
Glen Ewen 168 .... K 6
Goodsoil 263 .... L 4
Govan 394 .... G 4
Grand Coulee 208 .... E 6
Gravelbourg 1,338 .... E 6
Grayson 264 .... J 5
Green Acres 139 .... L 4
Green Lake 634 .... L 4
Grenfell 1,307 .... J 5
Guernsey 198 .... C 5
Gull Lake 1,095 .... C 5
Hafford 557 .... E 3
Hague 625 .... E 3
Hanley 484 .... D 4
Harris 259 .... D 4
Hawarden 137 .... E 4
Hearts Hill ●552 .... B 3
Hepburn 411 .... E 3
Herbert 1,019 .... D 5
Hodgeville 329 .... E 5
Holdfast 297 .... F 5
Hudson Bay 2,361 .... J 3
Humboldt 4,705 .... F 3
Hyas 165 .... J 4
Île-à-la-Crosse 1,035 .... L 3
Imperial 501 .... F 4
Indian Head 1,889 .... H 5
Invermay 353 .... J 4
Ituna 870 .... H 4
Jansen 223 .... G 4
Jasmin ●14 .... H 4
Kamsack 2,688 .... K 4
Kelliher 397 .... H 4
Kelvington 1,054 .... H 3
Kenaston 345 .... E 4
Kennedy 256 .... J 5
Kerrobert 1,141 .... C 4
Kincaid 256 .... D 6
Kindersley 3,969 .... B 4
Kinistino 783 .... F 3
Kipling 1,016 .... J 6
Kisbey 228 .... J 6
Kronau 154 .... G 5
Kyle 516 .... C 5
Lac Pelletier ●586 .... C 5
Lafleche 583 .... E 6
Laird 233 .... E 3
Lake Lenore 361 .... G 3
La Loche 1,632 .... L 3
Lampman 651 .... J 6
Lancer 156 .... C 5
Landis 277 .... C 4
Lang 219 .... G 5
Langenburg 1,324 .... K 5
Langham 1,151 .... E 4
Lanigan 1,732 .... G 4
La Ronge 2,579 .... L 3
Lashburn 813 .... B 3
Leader 1,108 .... B 5
Leask 478 .... E 2
Lebret 274 .... H 5
Lemberg 414 .... H 5
Leoville 393 .... D 2
Leroy 504 .... G 4
Lestock 402 .... H 4
Limerick 164 .... E 6
Lintlaw 234 .... H 3

Lipton 364 .... H 5
Lloydminster 6,034 .... A 2
Loon Lake 369 .... B 1
Loreburn 201 .... E 4
Lucky Lake 333 .... D 5
Lumsden 1,303 .... G 5
Luseland 704 .... B 3
Macdowall 171 .... F 3
Macklin 976 .... A 3
Macoun 190 .... J 6
Maidstone 1,001 .... B 2
Mankota 375 .... D 6
Manor 368 .... J 6
Maple Creek 2,470 .... B 6
Marcelin 238 .... E 3
Margo 153 .... H 4
Marriott ●627 .... D 4
Marsden 229 .... B 3
Marshall 453 .... A 2
Martensville 1,966 .... E 3
Maryfield 431 .... K 6
Maymont 212 .... D 3
McLean 189 .... G 5
Meacham 178 .... F 3
Meadow Lake 3,857 .... C 1
Meath Park 262 .... F 2
Medstead 163 .... C 2
Melfort 6,010 .... G 3
Melville 5,092 .... J 5
Meota 235 .... C 2
Mervin 155 .... C 2
Midale 564 .... H 6
Middle Lake 275 .... F 3
Milden 251 .... D 4
Milestone 667 .... G 5
Montmartre 544 .... H 5
Montreal Lake 448 .... F 1
Moose Jaw 33,941 .... F 5
Moose Range ●679 .... H 3
Moosomin 2,579 .... K 5
Morse 416 .... D 5
Mortlach 293 .... E 5
Mossbank 464 .... E 5
Muenster 385 .... G 3
Naicam 886 .... G 3
Neilburg 354 .... B 3
Neuanlage 144 .... E 3
Neudorf 425 .... J 5
Neuhorst 146 .... E 3
Nipawin 4,376 .... H 2
Nokomis 524 .... G 4
Norquay 552 .... J 4
North Battleford 14,030 .... C 3
North Portal 164 .... J 6
Odessa 232 .... H 5
Ogema 441 .... G 6
Osler 527 .... E 3
Outlook 1,976 .... E 4
Oxbow 1,191 .... J 6
Paddockwood 211 .... F 2
Pangman 227 .... G 6
Paradise Hill 421 .... B 2
Patuanak 173 .... L 3
Paynton 210 .... B 3
Pelican Narrows 331 .... N 3
Pelly 391 .... K 4
Pennant 202 .... C 5
Pense 407 .... G 5
Perdue 472 .... D 3
Pierceland 425 .... K 4
Pilger 150 .... F 3
Pilot Butte 1,255 .... G 5
Pine House 612 .... M 3
Plenty 175 .... C 4
Plunkett 153 .... F 4
Ponteix 769 .... D 6
Porcupine Plain 937 .... H 3
Preeceville 1,243 .... J 4

Prelate 317 .... B 5
Prince Albert 31,380 .... F 2
Prud'homme 222 .... F 3
Punnichy 394 .... H 4
Qu'Appelle 653 .... H 5
Quill Lake 514 .... G 3
Quinton 169 .... G 4
Rabbit Lake 159 .... D 2
Radisson 439 .... D 3
Radville 1,012 .... G 6
Rama 133 .... H 4
Raymore 635 .... G 4
Redvers 859 .... K 6
Regina (cap.) 162,613 .... G 5
Regina ●164,313 .... G 5
Regina Beach 603 .... F 5
Rhein 271 .... J 4
Richmound 188 .... B 5
Riverhurst 193 .... D 5
Rocanville 934 .... K 5
Roche Percé 142 .... J 6
Rockglen 511 .... F 6
Rosetown 2,664 .... D 4
Rose Valley 538 .... H 3
Rosthern 1,609 .... E 3
Rouleau 443 .... G 5
Saint Benedict 157 .... F 3
Saint Brieux 401 .... G 3
Saint Louis 448 .... F 3
Saint Philips ●538 .... K 4
Saint Walburg 802 .... B 2
Saltcoats 549 .... J 4
Sandy Bay 756 .... N 3
Saskatoon 154,210 .... E 3
Saskatoon ●154,210 .... E 3
Sceptre 169 .... B 5
Scott 203 .... C 3
Sedley 373 .... H 5
Semans 344 .... G 4
Shaunavon 2,112 .... C 6
Sheho 285 .... H 4
Shell Lake 220 .... D 2
Shellbrook 1,228 .... E 2
Simpson 231 .... F 4
Sintaluta 215 .... H 5
Smeaton 246 .... G 2
Southey 697 .... G 5
Spalding 337 .... G 3
Spiritwood 926 .... D 2
Spy Hill 354 .... K 5
Springside 533 .... J 4
Star City 527 .... G 3
Stenen 143 .... J 4
Stockholm 391 .... J 5
Stonehenge ●701 .... F 6
Storthoaks 142 .... K 6
Stoughton 716 .... J 6
Strasbourg 842 .... G 4
Sturgis 789 .... J 4
Swift Current 14,747 .... C 5
Tantallon 196 .... K 5
Theodore 473 .... J 4
Timber Bay 152 .... F 1
Tisdale 3,107 .... H 3
Togo 157 .... K 4
Tompkins 275 .... C 5
Torch River ●2,440 .... G 2
Torquay 311 .... H 6
Tramping Lake 178 .... B 3
Tugaske 175 .... E 5
Turnor Lake 166 .... L 1
Turtleford 505 .... B 2
Unity 2,408 .... B 3
Uranium City 2,507 .... L 1
Val Marie 236 .... D 6
Vanguard 261 .... D 6
Vanscoy 298 .... D 4
Vibank 369 .... H 5

Viscount 386 .... F 4
Vonda 313 .... F 3
Wadena 1,495 .... H 4
Wakaw 1,030 .... F 3
Waldeck 292 .... D 5
Waldheim 758 .... E 3
Walpole ●711 .... K 6
Wapella 487 .... K 5
Warman 2,076 .... E 3
Waseca 169 .... B 2
Waskesiu Lake 176 .... F 1
Watrous 1,830 .... F 4
Watson 917 .... G 3
Wawota 622 .... J 6
Weldon 279 .... F 2
Welwyn 170 .... K 5
Weyburn 9,523 .... H 6
White City 602 .... H 2
White Fox 394 .... G 2
Whitewood 1,003 .... J 5
Wilcox 202 .... G 5
Wilkie 1,501 .... C 3
Willow Bunch 494 .... F 6
Willow Creek ●1,218 .... J 5
Windthorst 254 .... J 5
Wiseton 195 .... D 4
Wishart 212 .... H 4
Wollaston Lake 248 .... N 2
Wolseley 904 .... H 5
Wymark 162 .... C 5
Wynyard 2,147 .... G 4
Yarbo 158 .... K 5

Yellow Grass 477 .... H 6
Yorkton 15,339 .... J 4
Young 456 .... F 4
Zenon Park 273 .... H 2

OTHER FEATURES

Allan (hills) .... E 4
Amisk (lake) .... M 4
Antelope (lake) .... C 5
Antler (riv.) .... F 5
Arm (riv.) .... F 3
Assiniboine (riv.) .... J 3
Athabasca (lake) .... C 4
Bad (hills) .... C 4
Bad (hills) .... F 3
Basin (lake) .... F 3
Batoche Nat'l Hist. Site .... E 3
Battle (creek) .... B 6
Battle (riv.) .... C 4
Bear (hills) .... C 4
Beaver (hills) .... H 4
Beaver (riv.) .... L 4
Beaverlodge (lake) .... L 1
Big Muddy (lake) .... G 6
Bigstick (lake) .... B 5
Birch (lake) .... C 2
Bitter (lake) .... B 5
Black (lake) .... M 2
Boundary (plat.) .... B 2
Brightsand (lake) .... B 2
Bronson (lake) .... B 2

CITIES and TOWNS

Abbey 218 .... C 5
Aberdeen 496 .... E 3
Abernethy 300 .... H 5
Air Ronge 557 .... M 3
Alameda 318 .... K 6
Alida 169 .... K 6
Allan 871 .... E 4
Alsask 652 .... B 4
Annaheim 209 .... G 3
Antelope ●231 .... C 5
Arborfield 439 .... H 2
Archerwill 286 .... H 3
Arcola 528 .... J 6
Arlington Beach ●432 .... F 4
Asquith 507 .... D 3
Assiniboia 2,924 .... E 6
Avonlea 442 .... G 5
Baildon ●799 .... F 5
Balcarres 739 .... H 5
Balgonie 777 .... G 5
Batoche .... E 3
Battleford 3,565 .... C 3
Beauval 606 .... L 3
Beechy 279 .... D 5
Bengough 536 .... F 6
Bethune 369 .... F 5
Bienfait 835 .... J 6
Biggar 2,561 .... C 3
Big River 819 .... D 2
Birch Hills 957 .... F 3
Bjorkdale 269 .... H 3
Blaine Lake 653 .... D 3
Borden 197 .... D 3
Brabant Lake 245 .... M 3
Bradwell 168 .... E 4
Bredenbury 467 .... K 5
Briercrest 151 .... F 5
Broadview 840 .... J 5
Brock 184 .... C 4
Browning ●687 .... J 6
Bruno 772 .... F 3
Buchanan 392 .... J 4
Buffalo Gap ●598 .... F 6
Buffalo Narrows 1,088 .... L 3
Burstall 550 .... B 5
Cabri 632 .... C 5
Cadillac 173 .... D 6
Calder 164 .... K 4
Cana ●1,238 .... J 5
Candle Lake 219 .... F 2
Cando 163 .... C 3
Canoe Lake 182 .... L 3
Canora 2,667 .... J 4
Canwood 340 .... E 2
Carievale 246 .... K 6
Carlyle 1,074 .... J 6
Carnduff 1,043 .... K 6
Carrot River 1,169 .... H 2

Central Butte 548 .... E 5
Ceylon 184 .... G 6
Chaplin 389 .... E 5
Chitek Lake 170 .... D 2
Choiceland 543 .... G 2
Christopher Lake 227 .... F 2
Churchbridge 972 .... J 5
Clavet 234 .... E 4
Climax 293 .... C 6
Cochin 221 .... C 2
Codette 236 .... H 2
Coleville 383 .... B 4
Colonsay 594 .... F 4
Connaught Heights ●982 .... G 3
Conquest 256 .... D 4
Consul 153 .... B 6
Coronach 1,032 .... F 6
Craik 565 .... F 4
Craven 206 .... G 5
Creelman 184 .... H 6
Creighton 1,636 .... N 4
Cudworth 947 .... F 3
Cumberland House 831 .... N 3
Cupar 669 .... G 5
Cut Knife 624 .... B 3
Dalmeny 1,064 .... E 3
Davidson 1,166 .... F 4
Debden 403 .... E 2
Delisle 980 .... D 4
Denare Beach 592 .... N 3
Denzil 199 .... B 3
Deschambault Lake 386 .... M 3
Dinsmore 398 .... D 4
Dodsland 272 .... C 4
Domremy 209 .... F 3
Drake 211 .... G 4
Duck Lake 699 .... E 3
Dundurn 531 .... E 4
Dysart 275 .... H 5
Earl Grey 303 .... G 5
Eastend 723 .... C 6
Eatonia 528 .... B 4
Ebenezer 164 .... J 4
Edam 384 .... C 2
Edenwold 143 .... G 5
Elbow 313 .... E 4
Eldorado 229 .... L 2
Elfros 199 .... H 4
Elrose 624 .... D 4
Elstow 143 .... E 4
Endeavour 199 .... J 3
Englefeld 271 .... G 3
Erwood 149 .... J 3
Esterhazy 3,065 .... K 5
Eston 1,413 .... C 4
Estevan 9,174 .... J 6
Eyebrow 168 .... E 5
Fillmore 396 .... H 5
Fleming 141 .... K 5
Flin Flon 367 .... N 4

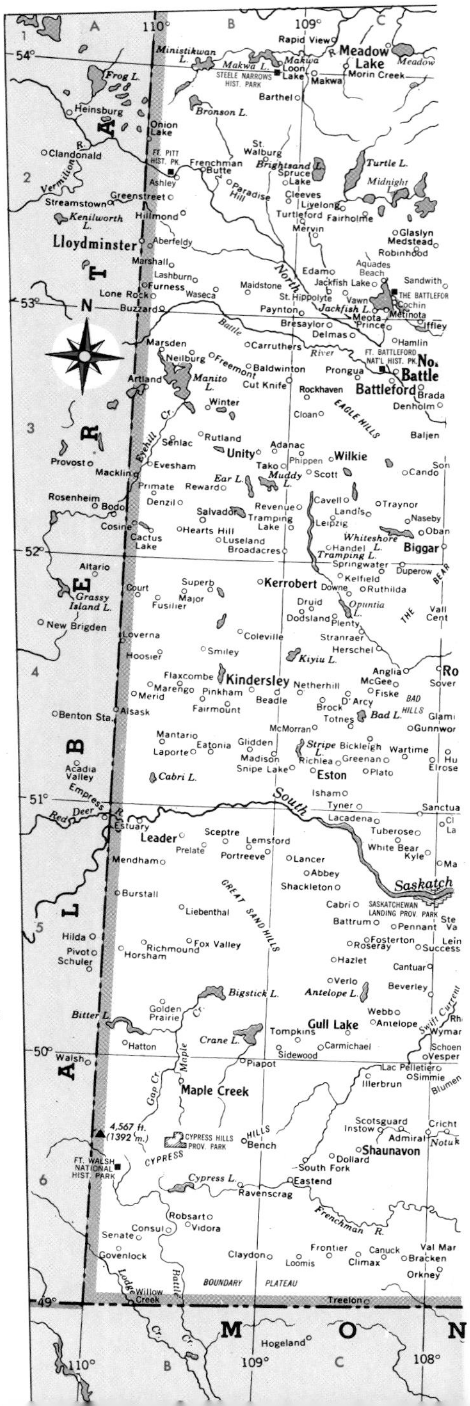

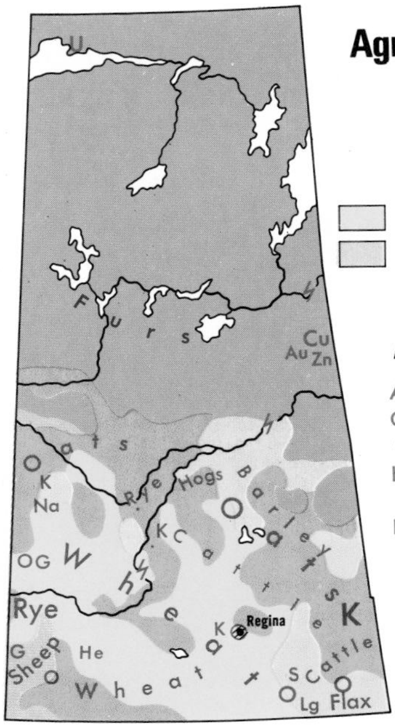

Agriculture, Industry and Resources

DOMINANT LAND USE

Wheat
Cereals (chiefly barley, oats)
Cereals, Livestock
Livestock
Forests

MAJOR MINERAL OCCURRENCES

Au Gold
Cu Copper
G   Natural Gas
He Helium
K   Potash
Lg Lignite
Na Salt
O   Petroleum
S   Sulfur
U   Uranium
Zn Zinc

Water Power
Major Industrial Areas

Buffalo Pound Prov. Park . . . . . F 5
Cabri (lake) . . . . B 4
Cactus (hills) . . . . F 2
Candle (lake) . . . . F 2
Cannington Manor Hist. Park . J 6
Canoe (lake) . . . . L 3
Carrot (riv.) . . . . J 2
Chaplin (lake) . . . . E 5
Chipman (riv.) . . . . M 2
Chitek (lake) . . . . D 2
Churchill (riv.) . . . . M 3
Clearwater (riv.) . . . . L 3
Cochrane (riv.) . . . . N 2
Coteau (lake) . . . . D 4
Cowan (lake) . . . . D 2
Crane (lake) . . . . B 5
Crean (lake) . . . . E 1
Cree (lake) . . . . L 3
Cree (lake) . . . . M 2
Cumberland (lake) . . . . J 1
Cypress (hills) . . . . B 6
Cypress (lake) . . . . B 6
Cypress Hills Prov. Park . . . . B 6
Danielson Prov. Park . . . . E 4
Delaronde (lake) . . . . E 1
Diefenbaker (lake) . . . . E 4
Doré (lake) . . . . E 1
Douglas Prov. Park . . . . E 4
Duck Lake Hist. Park . . . . E 3
Duck Mountain Prov. Park . . . . . . K 4
Eagle (hills) . . . . C 3
Eaglehill (creek) . . . . D 4

Ear (lake) . . . . B 3
Echo Valley Prov. Park . . . . G 5
Etomami (riv.) . . . . J 3
Eyebrow (lake) . . . . E 5
Eyehill (creek) . . . . B 3
Fife (lake) . . . . E 6
File (hills) . . . . H 5
Fir (riv.) . . . . J 2
Fort du Lac (riv.) . . . . M 2
Forrest (lake) . . . . L 3
Fort Battleford Nat'l Hist. Park C 3
Fort Carlton Hist. Park . . . . E 3
Fort Pitt Hist. Park . . . . B 2
Fort Walsh Nat'l Hist. Park . . . . . A 6
Foster (lake) . . . . M 3
Frenchman (riv.) . . . . C 6
Frobisher (lake) . . . . L 3
Gap (creek) . . . . B 6
Gardiner (dam) . . . . D 4
Geikie (riv.) . . . . M 3
Good Spirit (lake) . . . . J 4
Goodspirit Lake Prov. Park . . . . . J 4
Great Sand (hills) . . . . B 5
Green (lake) . . . . D 1
Greenwater Lake Prov. Park . . . . J 3
Haultain (riv.) . . . . L 3
Ile-à-la-Crosse (lake) . . . . L 3
Ironspring (creek) . . . . G 3
Jackfish (lake) . . . . C 2
Katepwa Prov. Park . . . . H 5
Kingsmere (lake) . . . . E 1
Kiyiu (lake) . . . . C 4

Lac La Ronge Prov. Park . . . . M 3
Lanigan (creek) . . . . F 4
Last Mountain (lake) . . . . F 4
Leaf (lake) . . . . J 2
Leech (lake) . . . . J 4
Lenore (lake) . . . . G 3
Little Manitou (lake) . . . . F 4
Lodge (creek) . . . . B 6
Long (lake) . . . . H 6
Loon (creek) . . . . G 4
Makwa (lake) . . . . B 1
Makwa (riv.) . . . . B 2
Manito (lake) . . . . B 3
Maple (creek) . . . . B 5
McFarlane (riv.) . . . . L 2
Meadow (lake) . . . . C 1
Meadow Lake Prov. Park . . . . K 4
Meeting (lake) . . . . D 2
Midnight (lake) . . . . C 2
Ministikwan (lake) . . . . B 1
Missouri Coteau (hills) . . . . F 5
Montreal (lake) . . . . F 1
Moose (riv.) . . . . J 6
Moose Jaw (riv.) . . . . G 5
Moose Mountain (creek) . . . . J 6
Moose Mountain Prov. Park . . . . J 6
Mossy (riv.) . . . . H 1
Muddy (lake) . . . . B 3
Mudjatik (riv.) . . . . L 3
Nipawin Prov. Park . . . . G 1
North Saskatchewan (riv.) . . . . . D 3
Notukeu (creek) . . . . D 6

Oldman (riv.) . . . . L 2
Old Wives (lake) . . . . F 4
Opuntia (lake) . . . . C 4
Overflowing (riv.) . . . . K 2
Pasqua (lake) . . . . J 2
Pasqua (hills) . . . . K 2
Pelican (lake) . . . . E 5
Peter Pond (lake) . . . . L 2
Pheasant (hills) . . . . J 5
Pine Lake Prov. Park . . . . N 3
Pinto (creek) . . . . D 6
Pipestone (creek) . . . . K 6
Pipestone (riv.) . . . . L 2
Ponass (lake) . . . . H 3
Poplar (riv.) . . . . E 6
Porcupine (hills) . . . . K 3
Primrose (lake) . . . . L 3

Primrose Lake Air Weapons
   Range . . . . L 3
Prince Albert Nat'l Park . . . . E 1
Qu'Appelle (riv.) . . . . L 2
Quill (lake) . . . . G 4
Red Deer (lake) . . . . K 3
Red Deer (riv.) . . . . K 3
Reindeer (lake) . . . . M 3
Reindeer (riv.) . . . . N 3
Riou (lake) . . . . M 2
Rivers (lake) . . . . F 6
Ronge, La (lake) . . . . J 3
Rowans Ravine Prov. Park . . . . . F 4
St. Victor Petroglyphs Hist.
   Park . . . . E 6

Saskatchewan (riv.) . . . . H 2
Saskatchewan Landing Prov.
   Park . . . . C 5
Saskeram (riv.) . . . . K 2
Scott (lake) . . . . M 2
Selwyn (lake) . . . . M 2
Souris (riv.) . . . . H 6
South Saskatchewan (riv.) . . . . . C 4
Steele Narrows Hist. Park . . . . . . B 2
Stripe (lake) . . . . C 4
Sturgeon (riv.) . . . . E 2
Swan (lake) . . . . J 3
Swift Current (creek) . . . . D 5
Tazin (lake) . . . . L 2
The Battlefords Prov. Park . . . . . C 2

Thickwood (hills) . . . . D 2
Thunder (hills) . . . . L 4
Tobin (lake) . . . . H 2
Torch (riv.) . . . . H 2
Touchwood (hills) . . . . G 4
Tramping (lake) . . . . C 3
Trout (lake) . . . . L 2
Turtle (lake) . . . . C 2
Twelvemile (lake) . . . . E 6
Vermilion (hills) . . . . E 5
Wapawekka (hills) . . . . M 4
Waskana (creek) . . . . G 5
Waskesiu (lake) . . . . E 2
Watham (riv.) . . . . M 3
Weed (hills) . . . . J 5

White Fox (riv.) . . . . G 2
White Gull (creek) . . . . G 2
Whiteshore (lake) . . . . C 3
Whiteswan (lakes) . . . . F 1
William (riv.) . . . . L 2
Willow Bunch (lake) . . . . F 6
Witchekan (lake) . . . . D 2
Wollaston (lake) . . . . N 2
Wood (mt.) . . . . E 6
Wood (riv.) . . . . E 6
Wood Mountain Hist. Park . . . . . E 6

AREA 251,699 sq. mi. (651,900 sq. km.)
POPULATION 1,009,613
CAPITAL Regina
LARGEST CITY Regina
HIGHEST POINT Cypress Hills 4,567 ft.
   (1,392 m.)
SETTLED IN 1774
ADMITTED TO CONFEDERATION 1905
PROVINCIAL FLOWER Prairie Lily

*Population of metropolitan area.
●Population of rural municipality.

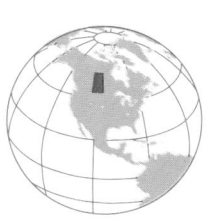

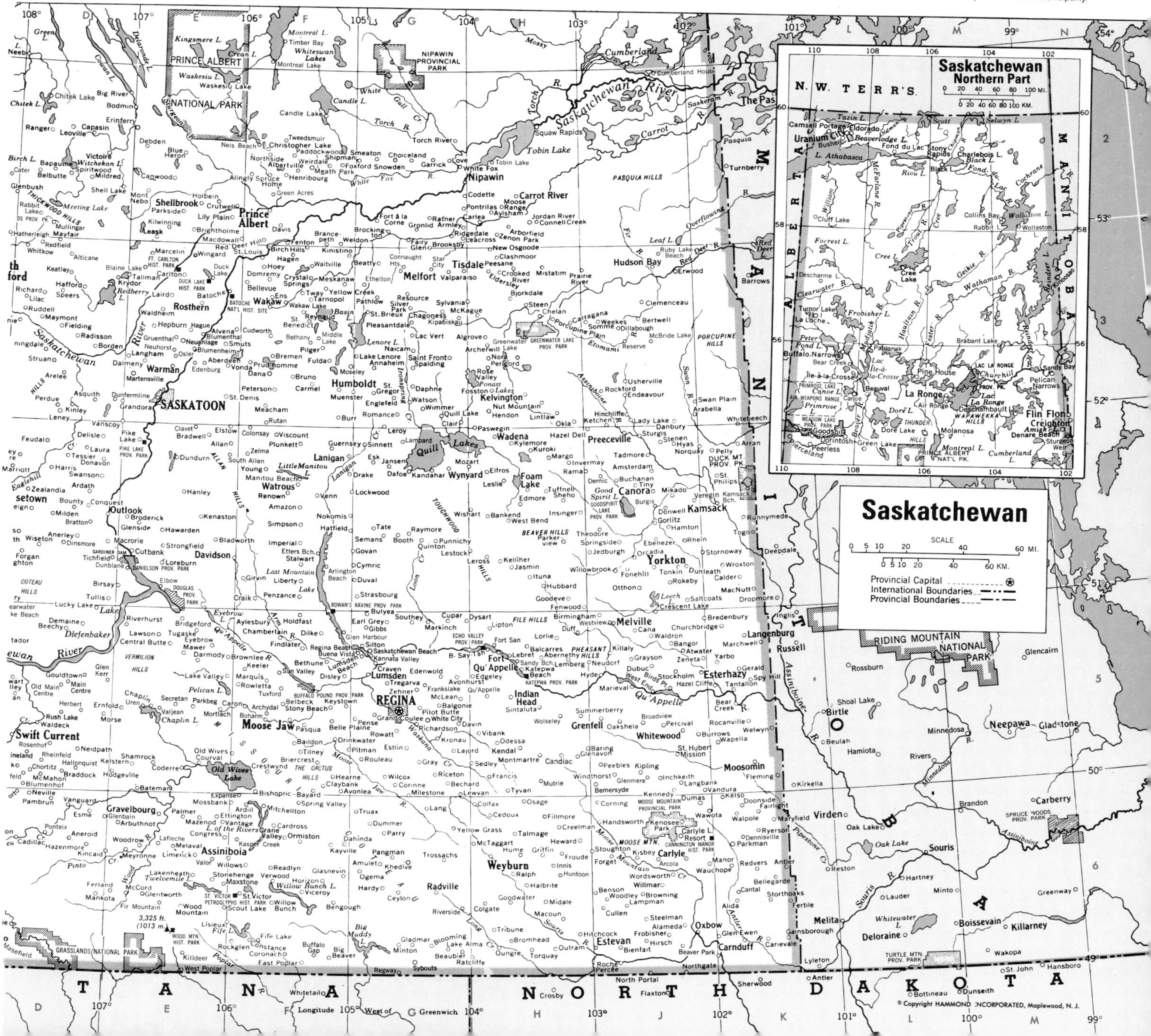

© Copyright HAMMOND INCORPORATED, Maplewood, N.J.

Alberta
Southern Part
SCALE
0 10 20 40 60 80 MI.
0 10 20 40 60 80 KM.
Provincial Capital
International Boundaries
Provincial Boundaries
Alberta
Northern Part
N.W. TERRITORIES
WOOD BUFFALO
NATIONAL PARK
CARIBOU MTS.
BIRCH MOUNTAINS
BUFFALO HEAD HILLS
High Level
Fort Vermilion
Fort Chipewyan
Fort Smith
Fitzgerald
Embarras Portage
Indian Cabins
Steen River
Meander River
Keg River
Paddle Prairie
Rainbow Lake
Zama L.
Hay L.
Habay
Chateh
Rocky Lane
John d'Or Prairie
La Crete
Fox Lake
Garden River
Bitumount
BRITISH COLUMBIA
SASKATCHEWAN
MONTANA
Peace River
Grande Prairie
Dawson Creek
Spirit River
Fairview
Manning
Slave Lake
Lesser Slave Lake
High Prairie
Valleyview
Fox Creek
Swan Hills
Whitecourt
Fort McMurray
THICKWOOD HILLS
Athabasca
Lac La Biche
Cold L.
Grand Centre
Bonnyville
St. Paul
Lloydminster
Vermilion
Vegreville
Redwater
St. Albert
EDMONTON
Sherwood Park
Spruce Grove
Devon
Leduc
Camrose
Wetaskiwin
Wainwright
Hinton
Edson
Jasper
JASPER NATIONAL PARK
WILLMORE WILDERNESS PARK
Grande Cache
Mt. Robson 12,972 ft. (3954 m.)
MT. ROBSON PROV. PARK
WELLS GRAY PROV. PARK
HAMBER PROV. PK.
Drayton Valley
Rocky Mountain House
Red Deer
Ponoka
Lacombe
Stettler
Innisfail
Olds
Three Hills
Drumheller
Hanna
Coronation
BANFF NATIONAL PARK
YOHO NAT'L PARK
KOOTENAY NAT'L PARK
Banff
Canmore
Cochrane
Airdrie
CALGARY
Okotoks
High River
Strathmore
Brooks
Medicine Hat
Vulcan
Claresholm
Fort Macleod
Lethbridge
Taber
Cardston
Pincher Cr.
Coleman
Blairmore
Sparwood
Raymond
Magrath
CYPRESS HILLS PROV. PARK
WATERTON LAKES NAT'L PARK
WATERTON GLACIER INTERNATIONAL PEACE PARK
GLACIER NAT'L PARK
ROCKY MTS.
PORCUPINE HILLS
LIVINGSTONE RA.
Longitude West of Greenwich
© Copyright HAMMOND INCORPORATED, Maplewood, N. J.

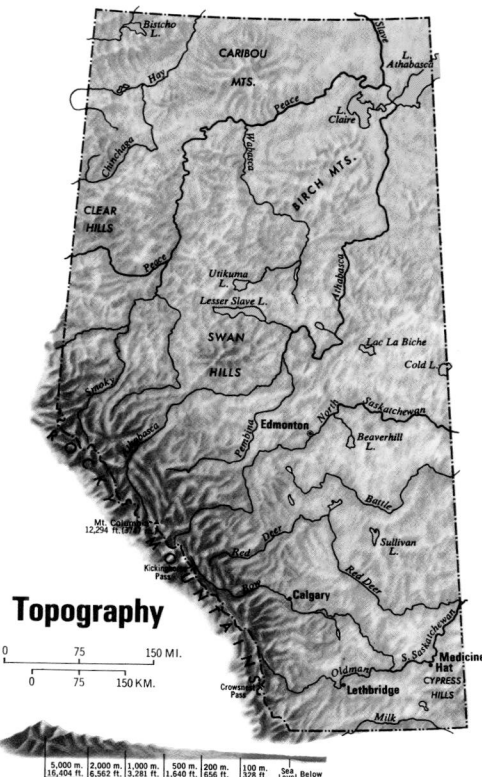

Topography

```
0    75    150 MI.
0    75    150 KM.
```

5,000 m. / 2,000 m. / 1,000 m. / 500 m. / 200 m. / 100 m. / Sea Level
16,404 ft. / 6,562 ft. / 3,281 ft. / 1,640 ft. / 656 ft. / 328 ft. / Below

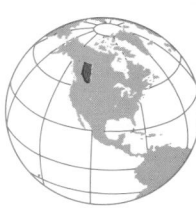

AREA 255,285 sq. mi. (661,185 sq. km.)
POPULATION 2,365,825
CAPITAL Edmonton
LARGEST CITY Edmonton
HIGHEST POINT Mt. Columbia 12,294 ft.
   (3,747 m.)
SETTLED IN 1861
ADMITTED TO CONFEDERATION 1905
PROVINCIAL FLOWER Wild Rose

Rockyford 329 ....D 4
Rocky Mountain House 4,698. C 3
Rosemary 328 ....E 4
Rycroft 649 ....A 2
Ryley 483 ....D 3
Saint Albert 31,996 ....D 3
Saint Paul 4,884 ....E 3
Sangudo 398 ....C 3
Sedgewick 879 ....E 3
Sexsmith 1,180 ....A 2
Shaughnessy 270 ....D 5
Sherwood Park 29,285 ....D 3
Slave Lake 4,506 ....C 2
Smith 216 ....C 2
Smoky Lake 1,074 ....D 2
Spirit River 1,104 ....A 2
Spruce Grove 10,326 ....D 3
Standard 379 ....D 4
Stavely 504 ....D 4
Stettler 5,136 ....D 3
Stirling 688 ....D 5
Stony Plain 4,839 ....D 3
Strathmore 2,986 ....D 4
Strome 281 ....E 3
Sundre 1,742 ....C 4
Swan Hills 2,497 ....C 2
Sylvan Lake 3,779 ....C 3
Taber 5,988 ....E 5
Thorhild 576 ....D 2
Thorsby 737 ....C 3
Three Hills 1,787 ....D 4
Tilley 345 ....E 4
Tofield 1,504 ....D 3
Trochu 880 ....D 4
Turner Valley 1,311 ....C 4
Two Hills 1,193 ....E 3
Valleyview 2,061 ....B 2
Vauxhall 1,049 ....D 4
Vegreville 5,251 ....E 3
Vermilion 3,766 ....E 3
Veteran 314 ....E 3
Viking 1,232 ....E 3
Vilna 345 ....E 2
Vulcan 1,489 ....D 4
Wabamun 662 ....D 3
Wabasca 701 ....C 1
Wainwright 4,266 ....E 3
Warburg 501 ....D 3
Warner 477 ....D 5
Waskatenau 290 ....D 2
Wembley 1,169 ....A 2
Westlock 4,424 ....C 2
Wetaskiwin 9,597 ....D 3
Whitecourt 5,585 ....C 2
Wildwood 441 ....C 3
Willingdon 366 ....E 3
Youngstown 297 ....E 4

OTHER FEATURES

Abraham (lake) ....B 3
Alberta (mt.) ....B 3
Assiniboine (mt.) ....C 4
Athabasca (lake) ....C 5
Athabasca (riv.) ....D 1
Banff Nat'l Park ....B 4
Battle (riv.) ....D 3
Bear (lake) ....A 2
Beaver (riv.) ....E 2
Beaverhill (lake) ....D 3
Behan (lake) ....D 1
Belly (riv.) ....D 5
Berland (riv.) ....A 3
Berry (creek) ....E 4
Biche (lake) ....E 2
Big (isl.) ....B 5
Big Horn (dam) ....B 3

Bighorn (range) ....B 3
Birch (hills) ....A 2
Birch (lake) ....E 3
Birch (mts.) ....B 5
Birch (riv.) ....B 5
Bison (lake) ....B 1
Bittern (lake) ....D 3
Botha (riv.) ....B 1
Bow (riv.) ....D 4
Boyer (riv.) ....A 5
Brazeau (mt.) ....B 3
Brazeau (riv.) ....B 3
Buffalo (lake) ....D 3
Buffalo Head (hills) ....B 5
Burnt (lake) ....C 1
Cadotte (lake) ....B 1
Cadotte (riv.) ....B 1
Calling (lake) ....D 2
Canal (creek) ....E 5
Cardinal (lake) ....B 1
Caribou (mts.) ....B 5
Chinchaga (riv.) ....A 5
Chip (lake) ....C 3
Chipewyan (lake) ....D 1
Chipewyan (riv.) ....D 1
Christina (lake) ....E 2
Christina (riv.) ....E 1
Claire (lake) ....B 5
Clear (hills) ....A 1
Clearwater (lake) ....C 4
Clearwater (riv.) ....C 4
Clyde (lake) ....E 1
Cold (lake) ....E 2
Columbia (mt.) ....B 3
Crowsnest (pass) ....C 5
Cypress (hills) ....E 5
Cypress Hills Prov. Park ....E 5
Dillon (riv.) ....D 1
Dowling (lake) ....D 4
Dunkirk (riv.) ....B 1
Eisenhower (mt.) ....C 4
Elbow (riv.) ....C 4
Elk Island Nat'l Park ....D 3
Ells (riv.) ....C 5
Etzikom Coulee (riv.) ....E 5
Eva (lake) ....B 3
Farrell (lake) ....D 4
Firebag (riv.) ....E 1
Forbes (mt.) ....B 4
Freeman (riv.) ....C 2
Frog (lake) ....E 3
Garson (lake) ....E 1
Gipsy (lake) ....E 1
Gordon (lake) ....E 1
Gough (lake) ....D 4
Graham (lake) ....C 1
Gull (lake) ....C 3
Haig (lake) ....B 1
Hawk (hills) ....B 1
Hay (lake) ....A 5
Hay (riv.) ....A 5

Heart (lake) ....E 2
Highwood (riv.) ....C 4
House (mt.) ....C 2
House (riv.) ....D 2
Iosegun (lake) ....B 2
Iosegun (riv.) ....B 2
Jackfish (riv.) ....B 5
Jasper Nat'l Park ....A 3
Kakwa (riv.) ....A 2
Kickinghorse (pass) ....B 4
Kimiwan (lake) ....B 2
Kirkpatrick (lake) ....E 4
Kitchener (mt.) ....B 3
Legend (lake) ....D 1
Lesser Slave (lake) ....C 2
Liége (riv.) ....D 1
Little Bow (riv.) ....D 4
Little Cadotte (riv.) ....B 1
Little Smoky (riv.) ....B 2
Livingstone (range) ....C 4
Logan (lake) ....E 2
Loon (lake) ....C 1
Loon (riv.) ....C 1
Lubicon (lake) ....C 1
Lyell (mt.) ....B 4
MacKay (riv.) ....D 1
Maligne (lake) ....B 3
Margaret (lake) ....B 5
Marie (lake) ....E 2
Marion (lake) ....D 3
Marten (mt.) ....C 2
McClelland (lake) ....E 1
McGregor (lake) ....D 4
McLeod (riv.) ....B 3
Meikle (riv.) ....A 1
Mikkwa (riv.) ....B 5
Milk (riv.) ....D 5
Mistehae (lake) ....B 2
Muriel (lake) ....E 2
Muskwa (lake) ....C 1
Muskwa (riv.) ....C 1
Namur (lake) ....D 1
Newell (lake) ....E 4
Nordegg (riv.) ....C 3
North Saskatchewan (riv.) ....E 3
North Wabasca (lake) ....D 1
Notikewin (riv.) ....A 1
Oldman (riv.) ....D 5
Otter (lakes) ....B 1
Pakowki (lake) ....E 5
Panny (riv.) ....C 1
Peace (riv.) ....B 1
Peerless (lake) ....C 1
Pelican (lake) ....D 2
Pelican (mts.) ....D 2
Pelican (riv.) ....C 1
Pembina (riv.) ....C 3
Pigeon (lake) ....D 3
Pinehurst (lake) ....E 2
Porcupine (hills) ....C 4
Primrose (lake) ....E 2
Rainbow (lake) ....A 5

Red Deer (lake) ....D 3
Red Deer (riv.) ....D 4
Richardson (riv.) ....C 5
Rocky (mts.) ....B-C 4
Rosebud (riv.) ....D 4
Russell (lake) ....C 1
Saddle (hills) ....A 2
Sainte Anne (lake) ....C 3
Saint Mary (res.) ....D 5
Saint Mary (riv.) ....D 5
Saulteaux (riv.) ....C 2
Seibert (lake) ....E 2
Simonette (riv.) ....A 2
Slave (riv.) ....C 5
Smoky (riv.) ....A 2
Snake Indian (riv.) ....A 3
Snipe (lake) ....B 2
Sounding (creek) ....E 4
South Saskatchewan (riv.) ....E 4
South Wabasca (lake) ....D 2
Spencer (lake) ....E 2
Spray (mts.) ....C 4
Sturgeon (lake) ....B 2
Sullivan (lake) ....D 3
Swan (hills) ....C 2
Swan (riv.) ....C 2
Temple (mt.) ....B 3
The Twins (mt.) ....B 3
Thickwood (hills) ....D 1
Touchwood (lake) ....E 2
Travers (res.) ....D 4
Trout (lake) ....C 1
Trout (riv.) ....C 1
Utikuma (lake) ....C 2
Utikuma (riv.) ....C 1
Utikumasis (lake) ....C 2
Vermilion (riv.) ....E 3
Wabasca (riv.) ....C 1
Wallace (mt.) ....C 2
Wapiti (riv.) ....A 2
Wappau (lake) ....E 2
Watchusk (lake) ....E 1
Waterton-Glacier Int'l Peace Park ....C 5
Waterton Lakes Nat'l Park ....C 5
Whitemud (riv.) ....A 1
Wildhay (riv.) ....B 3
Willmore Wilderness Prov. Park ....A 3
Winagami (lake) ....B 2
Winefred (lake) ....E 2
Winefred (riv.) ....E 2
Wolf (lake) ....E 2
Wolverine (riv.) ....B 1
Wood Buffalo Nat'l Park ....B 5
Yellowhead (pass) ....A 3
Zama (lake) ....A 5

*Population of metropolitan area.

CITIES and TOWNS

Acme 457 ....D 4
Airdrie 8,414 ....C 4
Alberta Beach 485 ....C 3
Alix 837 ....D 3
Andrew 548 ....D 3
Antler Lake 334 ....D 3
Ardmore 224 ....E 2
Arrowwood 156 ....D 4
Athabasca 1,731 ....D 2
Banff 4,208 ....C 4
Barnwell 359 ....D 5
Barons 315 ....D 4
Barrhead 3,736 ....C 2
Bashaw 875 ....D 3
Bassano 1,200 ....D 4
Bawlf 350 ....D 3
Beaumont 2,638 ....D 3
Beaverlodge 1,937 ....A 2
Beiseker 580 ....D 4
Bentley 823 ....C 3
Berwyn 557 ....B 1
Big Valley 360 ....D 3
Black Diamond 1,444 ....C 4
Blackfalds 1,488 ....D 3
Blackfoot 220 ....E 3
Blackie 298 ....D 4
Bon Accord 1,376 ....D 3
Bonnyville 4,454 ....E 2
Bowden 989 ....C 4
Bow Island 1,491 ....E 5
Boyle 638 ....D 2
Bragg Creek 505 ....C 4
Breton 552 ....C 3
Brooks 9,421 ....E 4
Bruce 88 ....E 3
Bruderheim 1,136 ....D 3
Burdett 220 ....E 5
Calgary 592,743 ....C 4
Calgary *592,743 ....C 4
Calmar 1,003 ....D 3
Camrose 12,570 ....D 3
Canmore 3,484 ....C 4
Carbon 434 ....D 4
Cardston 3,267 ....D 5
Carmangay 266 ....D 4
Caroline 436 ....C 3
Carseland 484 ....D 4
Carstairs 1,587 ....C 4
Castor 1,123 ....D 3
Cereal 249 ....E 4
Champion 339 ....D 4
Chauvin 298 ....E 3
Chipman 266 ....D 3
Clairmont 469 ....A 2
Claresholm 3,493 ....D 4
Clive 364 ....D 3
Clyde 364 ....D 2
Coaldale 4,579 ....D 5
Coalhurst 882 ....D 5
Cochrane 3,544 ....C 4
Cold Lake 2,110 ....E 2
College Heights 267 ....D 3
Consort 632 ....E 3
Cooking Lake 218 ....D 3

Coronation 1,309 ....E 3
Coutts 400 ....D 5
Cowley 304 ....D 5
Cremona 382 ....C 4
Crossfield 1,217 ....C 4
Daysland 679 ....D 3
Delburne 574 ....D 3
Desmarais 260 ....D 2
Devon 3,885 ....D 3
Didsbury 3,095 ....C 4
Donalda 280 ....D 3
Donnelly 336 ....B 2
Drayton Valley 5,042 ....C 3
Drumheller 6,508 ....D 4
Duchess 429 ....E 4
East Coulee 218 ....D 4
Eckville 870 ....C 3
Edgerton 387 ....E 3
Edmonton (cap.) 532,246 ....D 3
Edmonton *657,057 ....D 3
Edmonton Beach 280 ....C 3
Edson 5,835 ....B 3
Elk Point 1,022 ....E 2
Elnora 249 ....D 3
Entwistle 462 ....C 3
Erskine 259 ....D 3
Evansburg 779 ....C 3
Exshaw 353 ....C 4
Fairview 2,869 ....A 1
Falher 1,102 ....B 2
Faust 399 ....C 2
Foremost 568 ....E 5
Forestburg 924 ....E 3
Fort Assiniboine 207 ....C 2
Fort Chipewyan 944 ....C 5
Fort Macleod 3,139 ....D 5
Fort McKay 267 ....E 1
Fort McMurray 31,000 ....E 1
Fort Saskatchewan 12,169 ....D 3
Fort Vermilion 752 ....B 5
Fox Creek 1,978 ....C 2
Fox Lake 634 ....B 5
Gibbons 2,276 ....D 3
Gift Lake 428 ....C 2
Girouxville 325 ....B 2
Gleichen 381 ....D 4
Glendon 430 ....E 2
Glenwood 259 ....D 5
Grand Centre 3,146 ....E 2
Grande Cache 4,523 ....A 3
Grande Prairie 24,263 ....A 2
Granum 399 ....D 5
Grimshaw 2,316 ....B 1
Grouard Mission 221 ....C 2
Hanna 2,806 ....E 4
Hardisty 641 ....E 3
Hay Lakes 302 ....D 3
Heisler 212 ....D 3
High Level 2,194 ....A 5
High Prairie 2,506 ....B 2
High River 4,792 ....D 4
Hines Creek 575 ....A 1
Hinton 8,342 ....B 3
Holden 430 ....D 3
Hughenden 267 ....E 3
Hythe 639 ....A 2
Innisfail 5,247 ....D 3

Innisfree 255 ....E 3
Irma 474 ....E 3
Irricana 558 ....D 4
Irvine 360 ....E 5
Jasper 3,269 ....B 3
John d'Or Prairie 437 ....B 5
Joussard 330 ....B 2
Killam 1,005 ....E 3
Kinuso 285 ....C 2
Kitscoty 497 ....E 3
Lac La Biche 2,007 ....E 2
Lacombe 5,591 ....D 3
La Crete 479 ....B 5
Lake Louise 355 ....B 4
Lamont 1,563 ....D 3
Leduc 12,471 ....D 3
Legal 1,022 ....D 3
Lethbridge 54,072 ....D 5
Linden 407 ....D 4
Little Buffalo Lake 253 ....B 1
Lloydminster 8,997 ....E 3
Longview 301 ....C 4
Lougheed 226 ....E 3
Lundbreck 244 ....C 5
Magrath 1,576 ....D 5
Manning 1,173 ....B 1
Mannville 788 ....E 3
Marlboro 211 ....B 3
Marwayne 500 ....E 3
Mayerthorpe 1,475 ....C 3
McLennan 1,125 ....B 2
Medicine Hat 40,380 ....E 4
Milk River 894 ....D 5
Millet 1,120 ....D 3
Mirror 507 ....D 3
Monarch 212 ....D 5
Morinville 4,657 ....D 3
Morrin 244 ....D 4
Mundare 604 ....D 3
Myrnam 397 ....E 3
Nacmine 369 ....D 4
Nampa 334 ....B 1
Nanton 1,641 ....D 4
New Norway 291 ....D 3
New Sarepta 417 ....D 3
Nobleford 534 ....D 5
North Calling Lake 234 ....C 2
Okotoks 3,847 ....C 4
Olds 4,813 ....D 4
Onoway 621 ....C 3
Oyen 975 ....E 4
Peace River 5,907 ....B 1
Penhold 1,531 ....D 3
Picture Butte 1,404 ....D 5
Pincher Creek 3,757 ....D 5
Plamondon 259 ....D 2
Pollockville 19 ....E 4
Ponoka 5,221 ....D 3
Provost 1,645 ....E 3
Rainbow Lake 504 ....A 5
Ralston 357 ....E 4
Raymond 2,837 ....D 5
Redcliff 3,876 ....E 4
Red Deer 46,393 ....D 3
Redwater 1,932 ....D 3
Rimbey 1,685 ....C 3
Robb 230 ....B 3

Agriculture, Industry and Resources

DOMINANT LAND USE

- Wheat
- Cereals (chiefly barley, oats)
- Cereals, Livestock
- Dairy
- Pasture Livestock
- Range Livestock
- Forests
- Nonagricultural Land

MAJOR MINERAL OCCURRENCES

C Coal   O Petroleum
G Natural Gas   S Sulfur
Na Salt

⚡ Water Power
▨ Major Industrial Areas

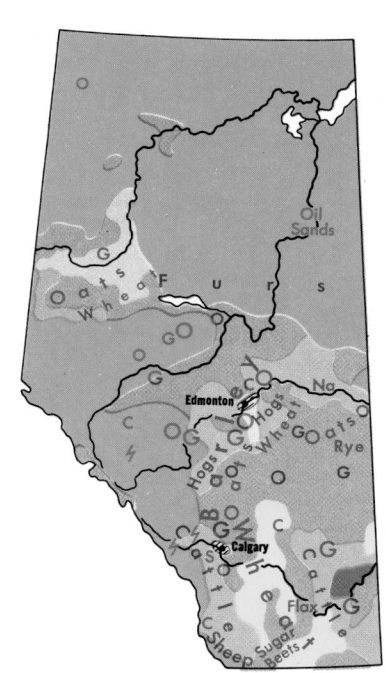

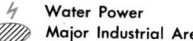

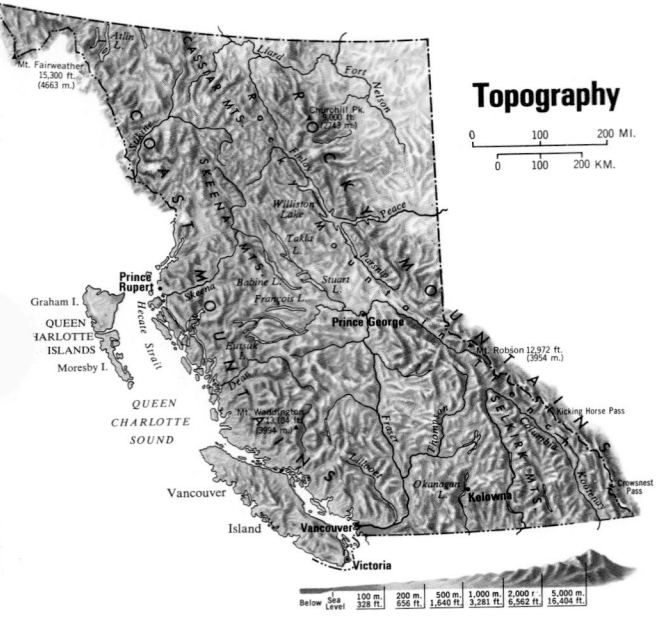

Topography

0 100 200 MI.
0 100 200 KM.

Below Sea Level | 100 m. 328 ft. | 200 m. 656 ft. | 500 m. 1,640 ft. | 1,000 m. 3,281 ft. | 2,000 r. 6,562 ft. | 5,000 m. 16,404 ft.

CITIES and TOWNS

Abbotsford 12,745 ....L 3
Alert Bay 626 ....D 5
Armstrong 2,683 ....H 5
Ashcroft 2,156 ....G 5
Ashton Creek 452 ....H 5
Balfour 472 ....J 5
Barlow 441 ....F 3
Barrière 1,370 ....H 4
Blueberry Creek 635 ....J 5
Blue River 384 ....H 4
Boston Bar 498 ....G 5
Bowen Island 1,125 ....K 3
Brackendale 1,719 ....F 5
Burnaby ○136,494 ....K 3
Burns Lake 1,777 ....D 3
Cache Creek 1,308 ....G 5
Campbell River 15,370 ....K 5
Canal Flats 919 ....K 5
Canyon 698 ....J 5
Cassiar 1,045 ....K 2
Castlegar 6,902 ....J 5
Cawston 785 ....H 5
Central Saanich ○9,890 ....K 3
Chase 1,777 ....H 5
Chemainus 2,069 ....J 3
Cherry Creek 450 ....G 5
Chetwynd 2,553 ....G 2
Chilliwack ○40,642 ....M 3
Clearwater 1,461 ....G 4
Clinton 804 ....G 4
Coldstream ○6,450 ....H 5
Comox 6,607 ....H 2
Coquitlam ○61,077 ....K 3
Courtenay 8,992 ....E 5
Cranbrook 15,915 ....K 5
Creston 4,190 ....J 5
Crofton 1,303 ....J 3
Cultus Lake 481 ....M 3
Cumberland 1,947 ....E 5
Dawson Creek 11,373 ....G 2
Delta ○74,692 ....K 3
Duncan 4,228 ....J 3
Elkford 2,126 ....K 5
Enderby 1,816 ....H 5
Erickson 972 ....J 5
Errington 609 ....J 3
Esquimalt ○15,870 ....K 4
Falkland 478 ....H 5
Fernie 5,444 ....K 5
Forest Grove 444 ....G 4
Fort Fraser 574 ....E 3
Fort Langley 2,326 ....L 3
Fort Nelson 3,724 ....M 2
Fort Saint James 2,284 ....E 3
Fort Saint John 13,891 ....G 2
Fraser Lake 1,543 ....E 3
Fruitvale 1,904 ....J 5
Gabriola 1,627 ....K 3
Galiano 669 ....K 3
Ganges 1,118 ....K 3
Gibsons 2,594 ....K 3
Gold River 2,225 ....D 5
Golden 3,476 ....J 4
Grand Forks 3,486 ....H 5
Granisle 1,430 ....D 3
Greenwood 856 ....H 5
Hagensborg 350 ....D 4
Harrison Hot Springs 569 ....M 3
Hatzic 1,055 ....L 3

Hazelton 393 ....D 2
Hedley 426 ....G 5
Holberg 444 ....C 5
Honeymoon Bay 474 ....J 3
Hope 3,205 ....M 3
Hornby Island 474 ....H 2
Horsefly 430 ....G 4
Houston 1,714 ....D 3
Hudson Hope 984 ....F 2
Invermere 1,969 ....J 4
Kaleden 998 ....H 5
Kamloops 64,048 ....H 5
Kaslo 854 ....J 5
Kelowna 59,196 ....H 5
Kent ○3,394 ....M 3
Keremeos 830 ....G 5
Kimberley 7,375 ....K 5
Kitimat 12,462 ....C 3
Kitsault 554 ....C 2
Kitwanga 369 ....D 2
Lac La Hache 647 ....G 4
Ladysmith 4,558 ....J 3
Lake Cowichan 2,391 ....J 3
Langley 15,124 ....L 3
Lantzville 969 ....G 4
Likely 425 ....G 4
Lillooet 1,725 ....G 5
Lion's Bay 1,078 ....K 3
Logan Lake 2,637 ....G 5
Lumby 1,266 ....H 5
Lytton 428 ....G 5
Mackenzie 5,797 ....F 2
Mackenzie ○5,890 ....F 2
Malakwa 392 ....H 5
Maple Bay 393 ....K 3
Maple Ridge ○32,232 ....L 3
Masset 1,569 ....B 3
Matsqui ○42,001 ....L 3
Mayne 546 ....K 3
McBride 641 ....G 3
Merritt 6,110 ....G 5
Midway 633 ....H 6
Mill Bay 583 ....K 3
Mission ○20,056 ....L 3
Mission City 9,948 ....L 3
Montrose 1,229 ....J 5
Nakusp 1,495 ....J 5
Nanaimo 47,069 ....J 3
Naramata 876 ....H 5
Nelson 9,143 ....J 5
New Denver 642 ....J 5
New Hazelton 792 ....D 2
New Westminster 38,550 ....K 3
Nicomen Island 360 ....L 3
Nootka ....D 5
North Cowichan ○18,210 ....J 3
North Pender Island 906 ....K 3
North Saanich ○6,117 ....K 3
North Vancouver 33,952 ....K 3
North Vancouver ○65,367 ....K 3
Oak Bay ○16,990 ....K 4
Okanagan Falls 1,030 ....H 5
Okanagan Landing 834 ....H 5
Okanagan Mission ....H 5
Old Barkerville 11 ....G 3
Oliver 1,893 ....H 5
One Hundred Mile House 1,925 ....G 4
Osoyoos 2,738 ....H 5
Oyama 430 ....H 5
Parksville 5,216 ....J 3
Peachland ○2,865 ....G 5

Penticton 23,181 ....H 5
Pitt Meadows ○6,209 ....L 3
Port Alberni 19,892 ....H 3
Port Alice 1,668 ....D 5
Port Clements 380 ....B 3
Port Coquitlam 27,535 ....L 3
Port Edward 989 ....B 3
Port Hardy ○3,778 ....D 5
Port McNeill 2,474 ....D 5
Port Moody 14,917 ....L 3
Pouce-Coupé 821 ....G 2
Powell River ○13,423 ....E 5
Prince George 67,559 ....F 3
Prince Rupert 16,197 ....B 3
Princeton 3,051 ....G 5
Qualicum Beach 2,844 ....J 3
Queen Charlotte 1,070 ....A 3
Quesnel 8,240 ....F 4
Radium Hot Springs 419 ....J 5
Revelstoke 5,544 ....H 5
Richmond ○96,154 ....K 3
Roberts Creek 926 ....J 5
Robson 1,008 ....H 6
Rossland 3,967 ....H 5
Royston 754 ....H 2
Saanich ○78,710 ....K 3
Salmo 1,169 ....J 5
Salmon Arm 1,946 ....H 5
Salmon Arm ○10,780 ....H 5
Saltair 1,356 ....J 3
Sandspit 794 ....B 3
Sayward 482 ....D 5
Sechelt 1,096 ....J 2
Shawnigan Lake 419 ....J 3
Shoreacres 555 ....J 5
Sicamous 1,057 ....H 5
Sidney 7,946 ....K 3
Slocan 351 ....J 5
Slocan Park 414 ....J 5
Smithers 4,570 ....D 3
Sointula 567 ....D 5
Sooke 852 ....J 4
Sorrento 659 ....H 5
South Hazelton 500 ....D 2
South Wellington 620 ....J 3
Spallumcheen 4,213 ....H 5
Sparwood 3,267 ....K 5
Sproat Lake 440 ....H 3
Squamish 1,590 ....F 5
Stewart ○1,456 ....C 2
Summerland ○7,473 ....G 5
Surrey ○147,138 ....D 5
Tahsis 1,739 ....D 5
Taylor 956 ....G 2
Telkwa 840 ....D 3
Terrace 8,893 ....C 3
Terrace ○10,914 ....C 3
Thornhill 4,281 ....C 3
Thrums 360 ....J 5
Tofino 705 ....E 5
Trail 9,599 ....J 6
Ucluelet 1,593 ....E 6
Union Bay 601 ....H 2
Valemount 1,130 ....H 4
Vancouver 414,281 ....K 3
Vancouver (Greater)
*1,169,831 ....K 3
Vanderhoof 2,323 ....E 3
Vavenby 479 ....H 4
Vernon 19,987 ....H 5
Victoria (cap.) 64,379 ....K 4
Victoria *233,481 ....K 4
Warfield 1,969 ....J 5
Wasa 345 ....K 5
Wells 417 ....G 3
Westbank 1,271 ....H 5
West Vancouver ○35,728 ....K 3
Westwold 409 ....G 5
Whistler ○1,365 ....F 5
White Rock 13,550 ....K 3
Williams Lake 8,362 ....F 4
Wilson Creek 611 ....J 2
Windermere 611 ....J 5
Winlaw 435 ....J 5
Woss Lake 395 ....D 5
Wynndel 566 ....J 5
Yarrow 1,201 ....M 3
Youbou 965 ....J 3

OTHER FEATURES

Adams (lake) ....H 4
Adams (riv.) ....H 4
Alberni (inlet) ....H 3
Alsek (riv.) ....H 1
Aristazabal (isl.) ....C 4
Assiniboine (mt.) ....K 5
Atlin (lake) ....J 1
Azure (lake) ....G 4
Babine (lake) ....E 3
Babine (riv.) ....D 2
Banks (isl.) ....B 3
Barkley (sound) ....E 6
Beale (cape) ....E 6
Beatton (riv.) ....G 1
Bella Coola (riv.) ....D 4
Bennett, W.A.C. (dam) ....F 2
Birkenhead Lake Prov. Park ....F 5
Bowron Lake Prov. Park ....G 3
Bowser (lake) ....C 2
Brooks (pen.) ....D 5
Browning Entrance (str.) ....B 3
Bryce (mt.) ....J 4
Bugaboo Glacier Prov. Park ....J 4
Bulkley (riv.) ....D 2
Burke (chan.) ....D 4
Burnaby (isl.) ....B 4
Bute (inlet) ....E 5
Caamaño (sound) ....C 4
Calvert (isl.) ....C 4
Canim (lake) ....G 4
Canoe Reach (riv.) ....H 4
Cariboo (mts.) ....G 3
Carpenter (lake) ....F 5
Carp Lake Prov. Park ....F 3
Cassiar (mts.) ....K 2
Castle (mt.) ....A 2
Cathedral Prov. Park ....H 5
Charlotte (lake) ....E 4
Chatham (sound) ....B 3

Chehalis (lake) ....L 3
Chilcotin (riv.) ....F 4
Chilko (lake) ....E 4
Chilko (riv.) ....E 4
Chilkoot (pass) ....J 1
Chuchi (lake) ....F 2
Churchill (peak) ....L 2
Clayoquot (sound) ....D 5
Clearwater (lake) ....G 4
Clearwater (riv.) ....G 4
Coast (mts.) ....D 3
Columbia (lake) ....K 5
Columbia (mt.) ....J 4
Columbia (riv.) ....H 4
Columbia Reach (riv.) ....H 4
Cook (cape) ....C 5
Cowichan (lake) ....J 3
Crowsnest (pass) ....K 5
Cypress Prov. Park ....K 3
Dean (chan.) ....D 4
Dean (riv.) ....D 4
Dease (lake) ....K 2
Dease (riv.) ....K 2
Devils Thumb (mt.) ....A 1
Dixon Entrance (chan.) ....A 3
Douglas (chan.) ....C 3
Duncan (riv.) ....J 5
Dundas (isl.) ....B 3
Elk (riv.) ....K 5
Elk Lakes Prov. Park ....K 5
Eutsuk (lake) ....D 3
Fairweather (mt.) ....H 1
Finlay (riv.) ....E 1

Fitzhugh (sound) ....D 4
Flathead (riv.) ....K 6
Flores (isl.) ....D 5
Fontas (riv.) ....M 2
Forbes (riv.) ....J 4
Fort Nelson (riv.) ....M 2
François (lake) ....D 3
Fraser (lake) ....E 3
Fraser (riv.) ....F 4
Fraser Reach (chan.) ....C 3
Galiano (isl.) ....K 3
Gardner (canal) ....D 3
Garibaldi Prov. Park ....F 5
Georgia (str.) ....E 5
Germansen (lake) ....E 2
Gil (isl.) ....C 3
Glacier Nat'l Park ....J 4
Golden Ears Prov. Park ....L 2
Gordon (riv.) ....J 3
Graham (isl.) ....A 3
Graham Reach (chan.) ....C 3
Grenville (chan.) ....C 3
Halfway (riv.) ....F 2
Hamber Prov. Park ....H 4
Harrison (lake) ....M 2
Hawkesbury (isl.) ....C 3
Hazelton (mts.) ....B 3
Hecate (str.) ....H 4
Hobson (lake) ....G 4
Homathko (riv.) ....E 4
Horsefly (lake) ....G 4
Howe (sound) ....K 3
Hunter (isl.) ....C 4

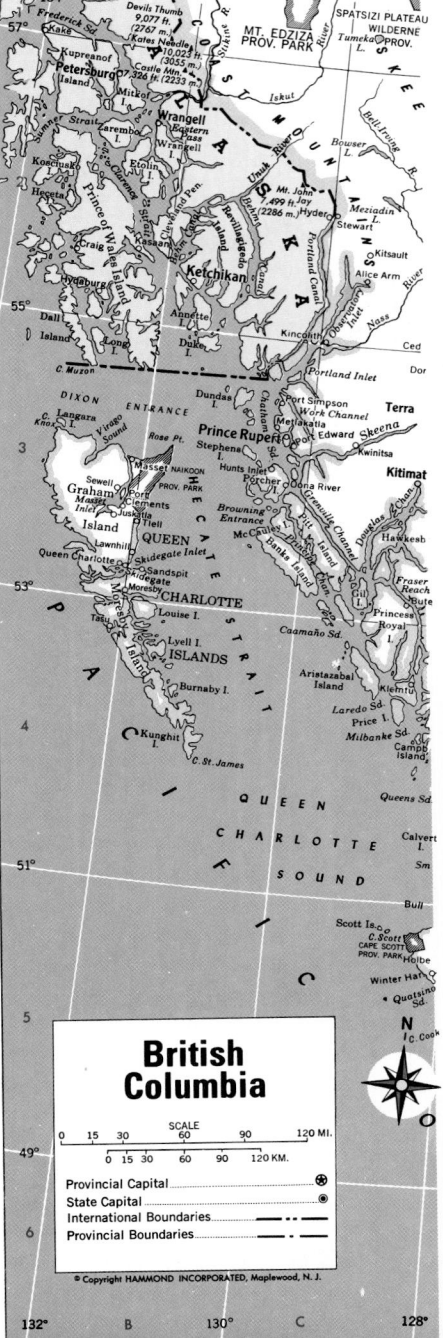

British
Columbia

0 15 30 60 90 120 MI.
0 15 30 60 90 120 KM.

Provincial Capital
State Capital
International Boundaries
Provincial Boundaries

© Copyright HAMMOND INCORPORATED, Maplewood, N.J.

Agriculture, Industry and Resources

DOMINANT LAND USE

Cereals, Livestock
Dairy
Fruits, Vegetables
Pasture Livestock
Forests
Nonagricultural Land

MAJOR MINERAL OCCURRENCES

Ab Asbestos
Ag Silver
Au Gold
C Coal
Cu Copper
Fe Iron Ore
G Natural Gas
Gp Gypsum
Mo Molybdenum
Ni Nickel
O Petroleum
Pb Lead
S Sulfur
Sn Tin
Zn Zinc

⚡ Water Power
〰 Major Industrial Areas

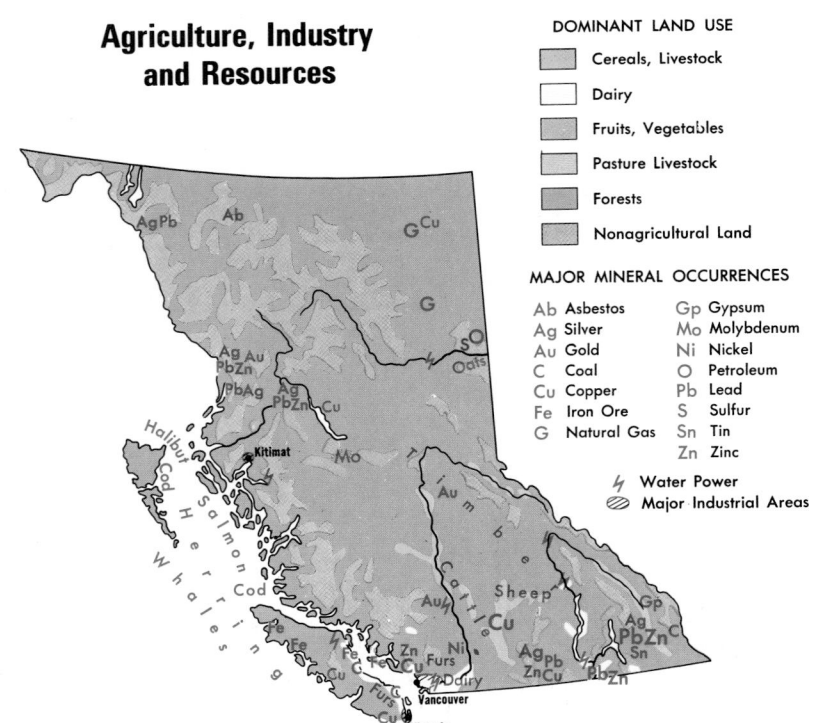

Inzana (lake) ....E 3
Isaac (lake) ....G 3
Iskut (riv.) ....B 2
Jervis (inlet) ....E 5
John Jay (mt.) ....A 1
Johnstone (str.) ....D 5
Juan de Fuca (str.) ....J 4
Kates Needle (mt.) ....A 1
Kechika (riv.) ....L 2
Kenney (dam) ....E 3
Kettle (riv.) ....J 4
Kicking Horse (pass) ....J 4
Kinbasket (lake) ....H 4
King (isl.) ....D 4
Klinaklini (riv.) ....E 4
Kloch (lake) ....E 2
Knight (inlet) ....E 5
Knox (cape) ....A 3
Kokanee Glacier Prov. Park .J 5
Koocanusa (lake) ....K 6
Kootenay (lake) ....J 5
Kootenay (riv.) ....J 5
Kootenay Nat'l Park ....J 4
Kotcho (lake) ....M 2
Kotcho (riv.) ....M 2
Kunghit (isl.) ....B 4
Kyuquot (sound) ....D 5
Langara (isl.) ....A 3
Laredo (sound) ....C 4
Liard (riv.) ....L 2
Lillooet (riv.) ....F 5
Louise (isl.) ....B 4
Lower Arrow (lake) ....H 5

Lyell (isl.) ....B 4
Lyell (mt.) ....J 4
Mabel (lake) ....H 5
Mahood (lake) ....G 4
Malaspina (str.) ....J 2
Manning Prov. Park ....G 5
Masset (inlet) ....A 3
McCauley (isl.) ....B 3
McGregor (riv.) ....G 3
Meziadin (lake) ....C 2
Mica (dam) ....H 4
Milbanke (sound) ....C 4
Moberly (riv.) ....F 2
Monashee (mts.) ....H 4
Moresby (isl.) ....B 4
Morice (lake) ....D 3
Morice (riv.) ....D 3
Mount Assiniboine Prov. Park K 5
Mount Edziza Prov. Park and
   Rec. Area. ....B 1
Mount Revelstoke Nat'l Park H 4
Mount Robson Prov. Park .H 3
Muncho Lake Prov. Park ..L 2
Murray (riv.) ....G 3
Murtle (lake) ....H 4
Muskwa (riv.) ....M 2
Nanika (dam) ....D 3
Nass (riv.) ....C 2
Nation (riv.) ....E 3
Nechako (riv.) ....F 3
Nitinat (lake) ....H 3
Nootka (isl.) ....D 5
Nootka (sound) ....D 5

Nootka (sound) ....D 5
North Thompson (riv.) .....G 4
Observatory (inlet) ....C 2
Okanagan (lake) ....G 5
Okanagan Mtn. Prov. Park ..G 5
Okanagan (riv.) ....H 6
Omineca (mts.) ....E 2
Omineca (riv.) ....E 2
Ootsa (lake) ....D 3
Owikeno (lake) ....D 4
Pacific Rim Nat'l Park .....E 6
Parsnip (riv.) ....F 3
Peace (riv.) ....G 2
Pend Oreille (riv.) ....J 6
Petitot (riv.) ....L 2
Pinchi (lake) ....E 3
Pine (riv.) ....F 2
Pitt (isl.) ....C 3
Pitt (lake) ....F 5
Pitt (riv.) ....L 2
Porcher (isl.) ....B 3
Portland (canal) ....B 2
Portland (inlet) ....C 3
Price (lake) ....D 3
Princess Royal (isl.) .....C 3
Principe (chan.) ....C 3
Prophet (riv.) ....M 2
Purcell (mts.) ....J 5
Quatsino (sound) ....C 5
Queen Charlotte (isls.) ....B 3
Queen Charlotte (sound) ....C 4
Queen Charlotte (str.) ....D 5
Queens (sound) ....C 4
Quesnel (lake) ....G 4

Quesnel (riv.) ....F 4
Rivers (inlet) ....D 4
Robson (mt.) ....H 3
Rocky (mts.) ....F 2
Roderick (isl.) ....C 3
Rose (isl.) ....E 3
Saint James (cape) ....B 4
Salmon (riv.) ....F 3
Salmon Arm (inlet) ....J 2
San Juan (riv.) ....J 4
Schoen Lake Prov. Park ...E 5
Scott (cape) ....C 5
Scott (isls.) ....C 5
Seechelt (inlet) ....J 2
Seechelt (pen.) ....J 2
Selkirk (mts.) ....J 4
Seymour (inlet) ....D 4
Sheslay (riv.) ....J 2
Shuswap (lake) ....H 4
Sikanni Chief (riv.) ....F 1
Silver Star Prov. Park .....H 5
Sir Sandford (mt.) ....H 4
Skagit (riv.) ....G 6
Skeena (mts.) ....C 2
Skeena (riv.) ....C 3
Skidegate (inlet) ....B 3
Slocan (lake) ....J 5
Smith (sound) ....C 4
South Bentinck Arm (inlet) ..D 4
Stave (lake) ....L 3
Stephens (isl.) ....B 3
Stikine (riv.) ....B 1
Stone Mountain Prov. Park .L 2

Strathcona Prov. Park .....E 5
Stuart (lake) ....E 3
Sustut (riv.) ....D 2
Tagish (lake) ....J 1
Tahtsa (lake) ....D 3
Takla (lake) ....E 3
Taku (riv.) ....J 2
Tatlatui (lake) ....D 2
Tatlayoko (lake) ....E 4
Tchentlo (lake) ....E 3
Teslin (riv.) ....K 1
Tetachuck (lake) ....D 3
Texada (isl.) ....J 2
Tezzeron (lake) ....E 3
Thompson (riv.) ....G 5

Three Guardsmen (mt.) ....H 1
Thutade (lake) ....D 2
Tiedemann (mt.) ....E 4
Toad (riv.) ....L 2
Toba (inlet) ....E 5
Tochcha (lake) ....E 3
Top Of The World Prov. Park K 5
Trembleur (lake) ....E 3
Troitsa (lake) ....D 3
Tumeka (lake) ....C 1
Turnagain (riv.) ....K 2
Tuya (riv.) ....K 2
Tweedsmuir Prov. Park ....D 3
Upper Arrow (lake) ....H 5
Valdes (isl.) ....K 3

Vancouver (isl.) ....D 5
Virago (sound) ....A 3
Waddington (mt.) ....E 4
Wapiti (riv.) ....H 3
Wells Gray Prov. Park .....H 4
West Road (riv.) ....E 3
Whitesail (lake) ....D 3
Williston (lake) ....F 2
Work (chan.) ....C 3
Yellowhead (pass) ....H 4
Yoho Nat'l Park ....J 4

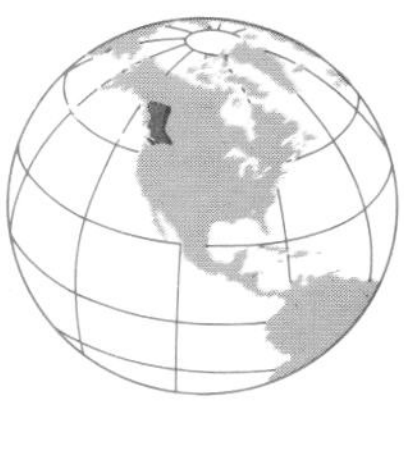

*Population of metropolitan area.
○Population of municipality.

AREA 366,253 sq. mi. (948,596 sq. km.)
POPULATION 2,883,367
CAPITAL Victoria
LARGEST CITY Vancouver
HIGHEST POINT Mt. Fairweather 15,300 ft.
   (4,663 m.)
SETTLED IN 1806
ADMITTED TO CONFEDERATION 1871
PROVINCIAL FLOWER Dogwood

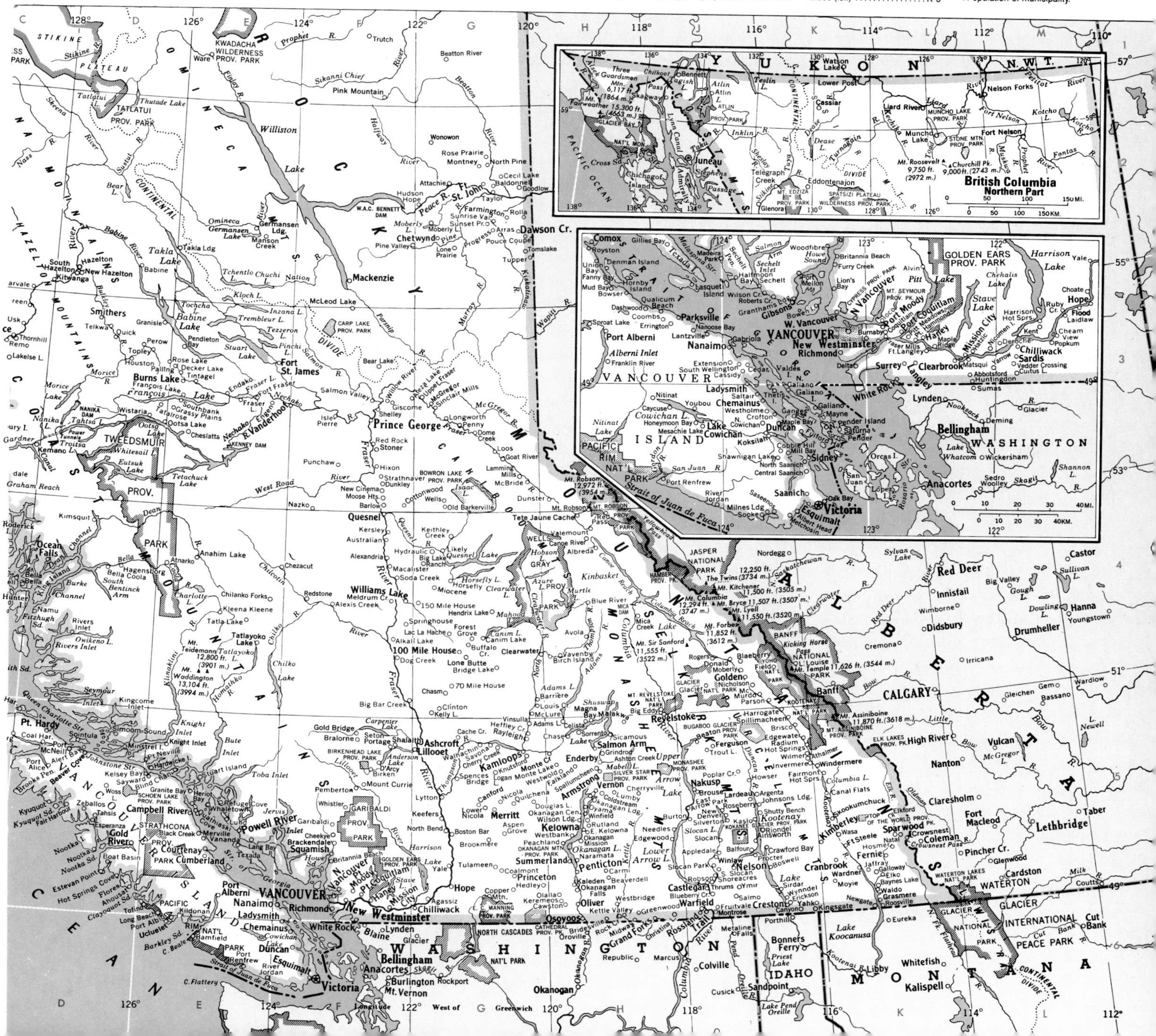

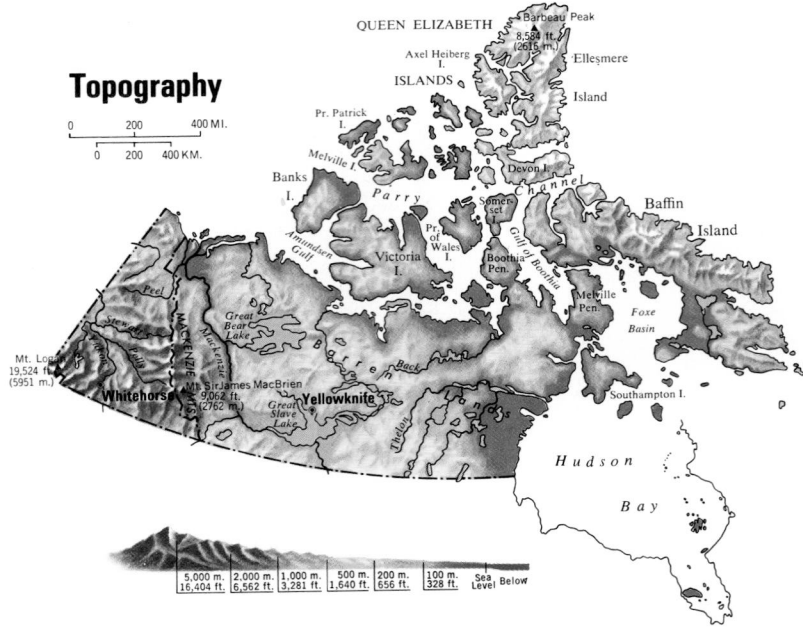

Topography

0   200   400 MI.
0   200   400 KM.

QUEEN ELIZABETH

ISLANDS

| 5,000 m. 16,404 ft. | 2,000 m. 6,562 ft. | 1,000 m. 3,281 ft. | 500 m. 1,640 ft. | 200 m. 656 ft. | 100 m. 328 ft. | Sea Level | Below |

Agriculture, Industry and Resources

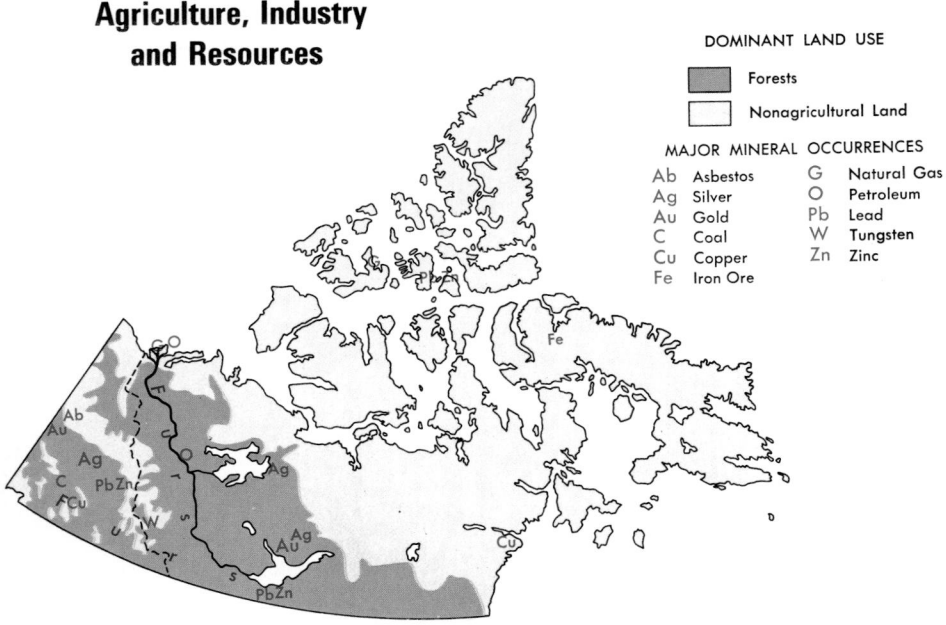

DOMINANT LAND USE

Forests

Nonagricultural Land

MAJOR MINERAL OCCURRENCES

Ab	Asbestos	G	Natural Gas
Ag	Silver	O	Petroleum
Au	Gold	Pb	Lead
C	Coal	W	Tungsten
Cu	Copper	Zn	Zinc
Fe	Iron Ore		

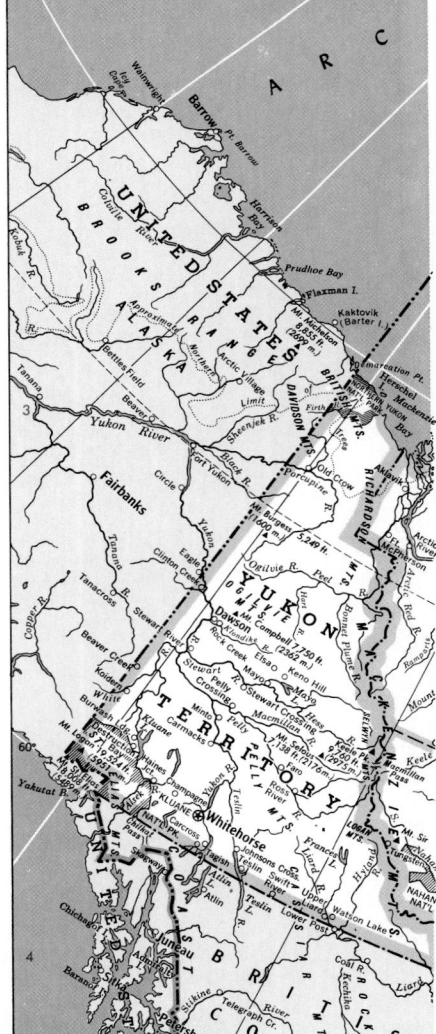

Raanes (pen.)...........K2
Rae (isth.)............K3
Rae (riv.)............G3
Rae (str.)............J3
Ramparts (riv.)........E3
Resolution (isl.)......M3
Richard Collinson (inlet)..G3
Richards (isl.)........E3
Richardson (mts.)......E3
Robeson (chan.)........M1
Roes Welcome (sound)...K3
Rowley (isl.)..........K3
Royal Geographical
  Society (isls.).......J3
Russell (isl.).........J2
Sabine (pen.)..........H2
Salisbury (isl.).......L3
Seahorse (pt.)........L3
Selwyn (lake)..........H4
Sherman (inlet)........J3
Simpson (pen.).........K3
Sir James MacBrien (mt.)..E3
Slave (riv.)..........G3
Smith (bay)...........L2
Smith (cape)..........L3
Smith (sound).........L3
Snare (riv.)..........G3
Snowbird (lake).......H3
Somerset (isl.).......J2
South (bay)...........K3
Southampton (isl.)....K3
South Nahanni (riv.)..E3
Stallworthy (cape)....J1
Steensby (inlet)......L2

Stefansson (isl.)......H2
Sverdrup (chan.)......J1
Sverdrup (isls.)......J2
Takijug (lake)........G3
Talbot (inlet)........L2
Taltson (riv.).........G3
Tathlina (lake).......G3
Tha-anne (riv.).......J3
Thelon (riv.).........H3
Thlewiaza (riv.)......J3
Trout (lake)..........F3
Ungava (bay)..........M4
Vansittart (isl.).....K3
Victoria (isl.).......G2
Victoria (str.).......H3
Viscount Melville (sound)..G2
Wager (bay)...........K3
Wales (isl.)..........K3
Walsingham (cape).....M3
Wellington (chan.)....J2
Wholdaia (lake).......H3
Winter (harb.)........H2
Wollaston (pen.)......G3
Wood Buffalo Nat'l Park..G3
Wynniatt (bay)........G2
Yathkyed (lake).......J3
Yellowknife (riv.)....G3

YUKON TERRITORY

CITIES and TOWNS

Beaver Creek 90........D3
Burwash Landing 73....D3
Carcross 216..........E3

Carmacks •256.........E3
Champagne.............E3
Clinton Creek.........D3
Cowley................E3
Dawson 697............E3
Destruction Bay 45....E3
Elsa 336..............E3
Faro 1,652............E3
Haines Junction •366..E3
Johnson's Crossing 13..E3
Keno Hill 88..........E3
Koidern...............D3
Mayo 398..............E3

Minto.................E3
Old Crow 243..........E3
Pelly Crossing 182....E3
Rock Creek 59.........E3
Ross River 294........E3
Stewart Crossing 20...E3
Stewart River.........D3
Swift River 24........E3
Tagish 89.............E3
Teslin •310...........E3
Upper Liard 130.......F3
Watson Lake •748......F3
Whitehorse (cap.) 14,814..E3

OTHER FEATURES

Alsek (riv.)..........E3
Bonnet Plume (riv.)...E3
British (mts.)........D3
Campbell (mt.)........E3
Cassiar (mts.)........E3
Frances (lake)........E3
Herschel (isl.).......E3
Hess (riv.)...........E3
Hyland (riv.).........F3
Keele (peak)..........E3
Klondike (riv.).......E3
Kluane (lake).........E3

Kluane Nat'l Park.....E3
Liard (riv.)..........E3
Logan (mt.)...........D3
Logan (mts.)..........F3
Mackenzie (mts.)......E3
Macmillan (riv.)......E3
Mayo (lake)...........E3
Northern Yukon Nat'l Pk...E3
Ogilvie (mts.)........E3
Ogilvie (riv.)........E3
Peel (riv.)...........E3
Pelly (mts.)..........E3
Pelly (riv.)..........E3

Porcupine (riv.)......E3
Richardson (mts.).....E3
Rocky (mts.)..........F4
Saint Elias (mt.).....D3
Saint Elias (mts.)....E3
Selous (mt.)..........E3
Selwyn (mts.).........E3
Stewart (riv.)........E3
Teslin (lake).........E4
Teslin (riv.).........E3
White (riv.)..........D3
Yukon (riv.)..........E3
• Population of district.

YUKON TERRITORY

AREA 207,075 sq. mi.
(536,324 sq. km.)
POPULATION 23,504
CAPITAL Whitehorse
LARGEST CITY Whitehorse
HIGHEST POINT Mt. Logan 19,524 ft.
(5,951 m.)
SETTLED IN 1897
ADMITTED TO CONFEDERATION 1898
PROVINCIAL FLOWER Fireweed

NORTHWEST TERRITORIES

AREA 1,304,896 sq. mi. (3,379,683 sq. km.)
POPULATION 52,238
CAPITAL Yellowknife
LARGEST CITY Yellowknife
HIGHEST POINT Mt. Sir James MacBrien
9,062 ft. (2,762 m.)
SETTLED IN 1800
ADMITTED TO CONFEDERATION 1870
PROVINCIAL FLOWER Mountain Avens

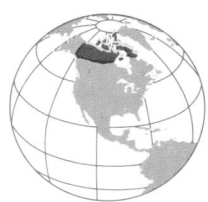

Yukon and Northwest Territories

SCALE
0 50 100   200   300 MI.
0 50 100 200   300 KM.

Territorial Capitals ....⊛
Regional Capitals ....⊛
International Boundaries ....
Provincial & Territorial Boundaries ....
Regional Boundaries ....

All islands in Hudson Bay, James Bay, Hudson Strait
and Ungava Bay lie within the Northwest Territories.

© Copyright HAMMOND INCORPORATED, Maplewood, N.J.

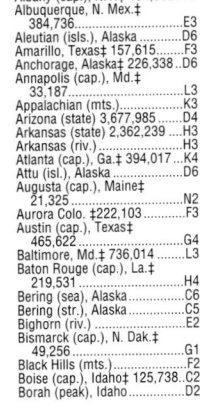

United States

POLYCONIC PROJECTION

SCALE OF MILES

SCALE OF KILOMETERS

Capitals of Countries .... ★
State Capitals .... △
International Boundaries ....

© Copyright HAMMOND INCORPORATED, Maplewood, N.J.

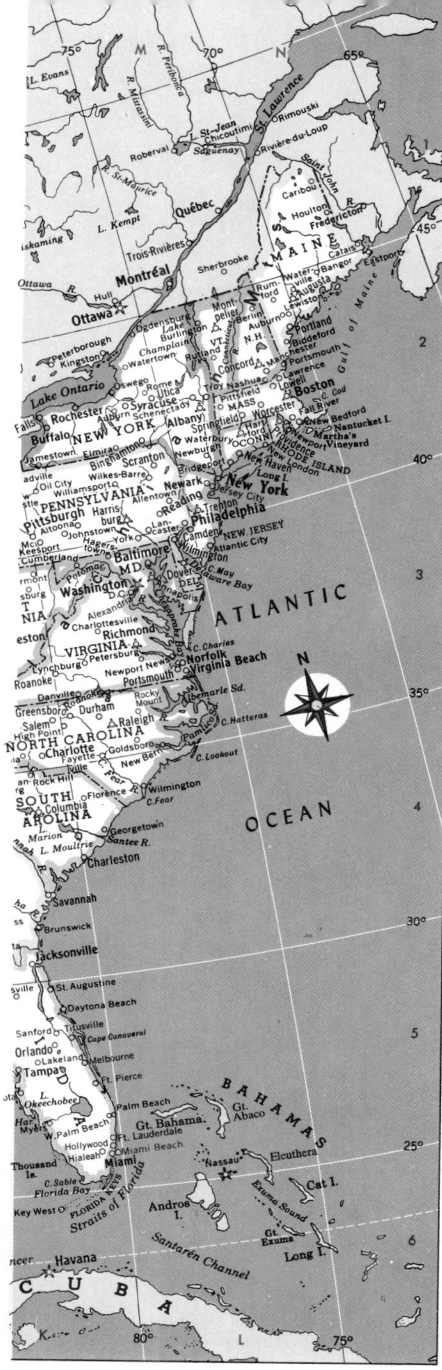

AREA 3,623,420 sq. mi.
(9,384,658 sq. km.)
POPULATION 249,632,692
CAPITAL Washington
LARGEST CITY New York
HIGHEST POINT Mt. McKinley 20,320 ft.
(6,194 m.)
MONETARY UNIT U.S. dollar
MAJOR LANGUAGE English
MAJOR RELIGIONS Protestantism,
Roman Catholicism, Judaism

UNITED

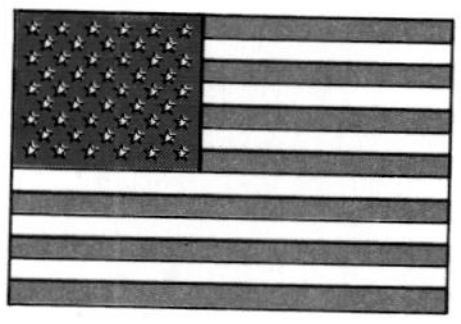

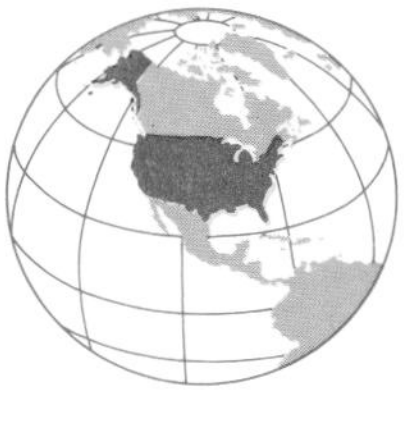

Population Distribution

DENSITY PER	
SQ. KILOMETER	SQ. MILE
Over 100	Over 260
50-100	130-260
10-50	25-130
1-10	3-25
Under 1	Under 3

• Cities with over 1,000,000 inhabitants (including suburbs)

Vegetation

MID-LATITUDE
FOREST
Coniferous Forest
Broadleaf Forest
Mixed Coniferous
and
Broadleaf Forest
Woodland and
Shrub
(Mediterranean)

MID-LATITUDE GRASSLAND
Short Grass (Steppe)
Tall Grass (Prairie)
TROPICAL
RAINFOREST
TROPICAL
GRASSLAND

SWAMP
DESERT AND
DESERT SHRUB
PERMANENT ICE

TUNDRA AND
ALPINE
UNCLASSIFIED

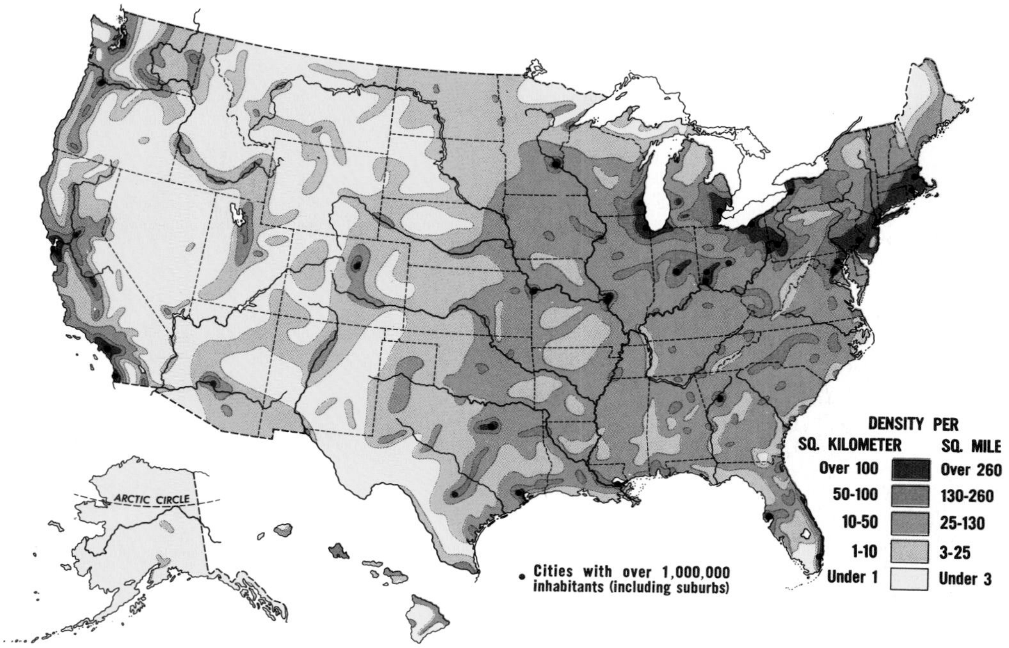

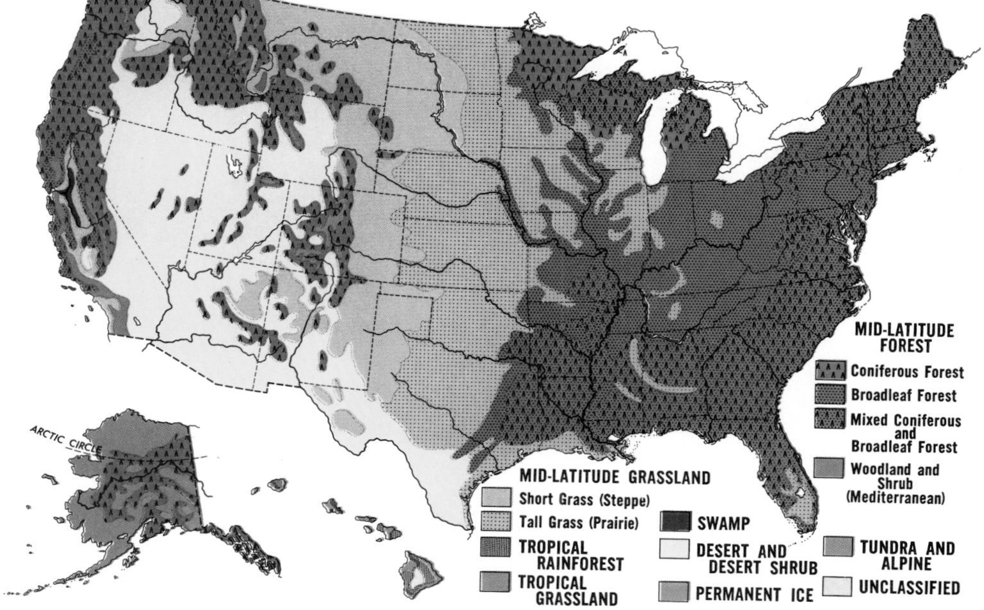

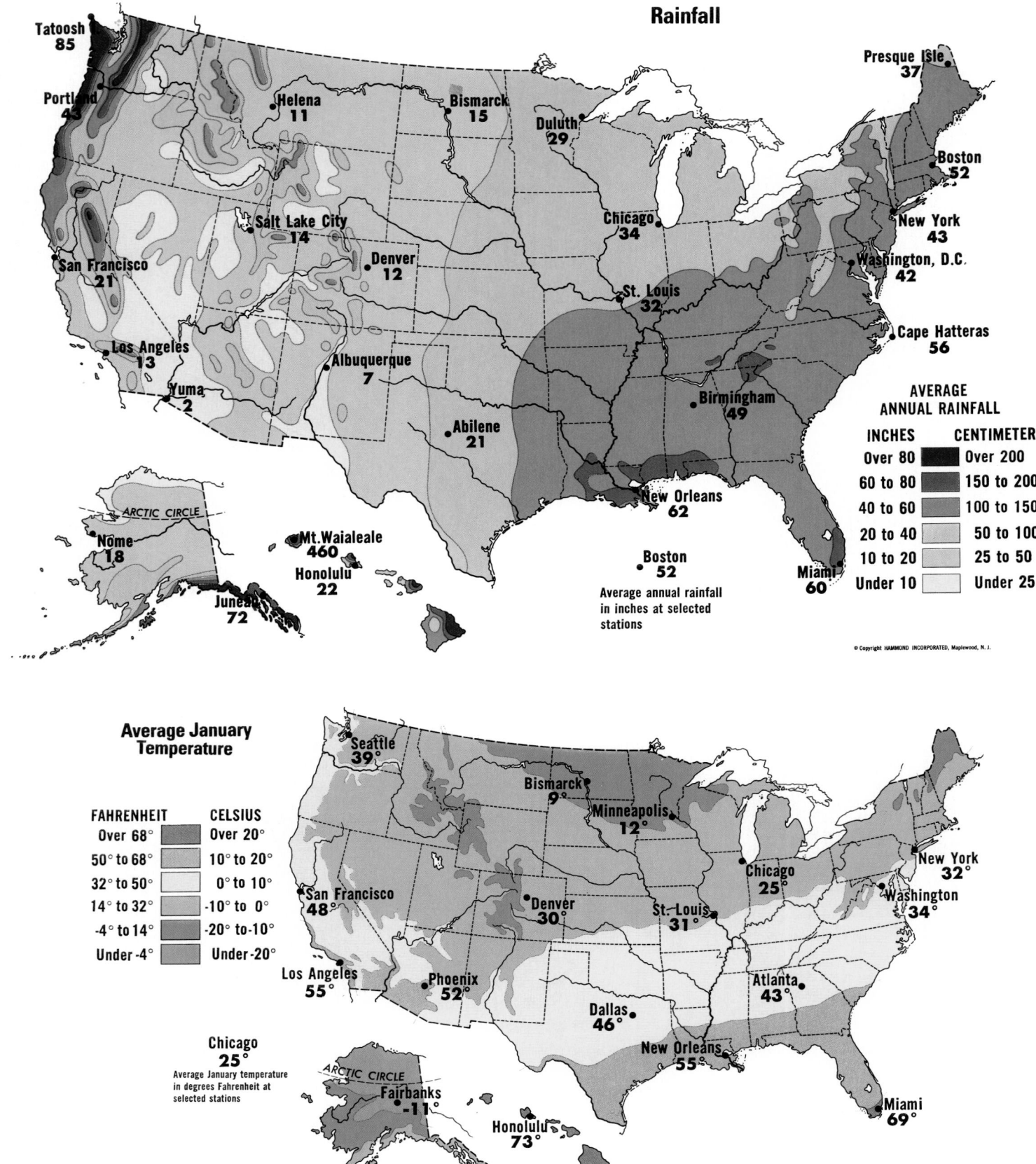

Rainfall

Tatoosh 85
Portland 43
Helena 11
Bismarck 15
Duluth 29
Presque Isle 37
Boston 52
Chicago 34
New York 43
Salt Lake City 14
Washington, D.C. 42
San Francisco 21
Denver 12
St. Louis 32
Cape Hatteras 56
Los Angeles 13
Albuquerque 7
Birmingham 49
Yuma 2
Abilene 21
New Orleans 62
Miami 60

ARCTIC CIRCLE
Nome 18
Mt. Waialeale 460
Honolulu 22
Juneau 72

Boston
52
Average annual rainfall
in inches at selected
stations

AVERAGE
ANNUAL RAINFALL

INCHES	CENTIMETERS
Over 80	Over 200
60 to 80	150 to 200
40 to 60	100 to 150
20 to 40	50 to 100
10 to 20	25 to 50
Under 10	Under 25

© Copyright HAMMOND INCORPORATED, Maplewood, N. J.

Average January Temperature

FAHRENHEIT	CELSIUS
Over 68°	Over 20°
50° to 68°	10° to 20°
32° to 50°	0° to 10°
14° to 32°	-10° to 0°
-4° to 14°	-20° to -10°
Under -4°	Under -20°

Seattle 39°
Bismarck 9°
Minneapolis 12°
New York 32°
San Francisco 48°
Denver 30°
St. Louis 31°
Chicago 25°
Washington 34°
Los Angeles 55°
Phoenix 52°
Atlanta 43°
Dallas 46°
New Orleans 55°
Miami 69°

Chicago
25°
Average January temperature
in degrees Fahrenheit at
selected stations

ARCTIC CIRCLE
Fairbanks -11°
Honolulu 73°

© Copyright HAMMOND INCORPORATED, Maplewood, N. J.

Topography

0 200 400 MI.

0 200 400 KM.

PACIFIC OCEAN

C. Flattery
Seattle
Mt. Rainier 14,410 ft. (4392 m.)
Mt. St. Helens 8,364 ft. (2549 m.)
CASCADE RANGE
BITTERROOT RANGE
Columbia
COLUMBIA PLATEAU
Snake
Fort Peck Lake
Yellowstone
Missouri
GREAT PLAINS
Rainy
Lake Superior
Keweenaw Pen.
St. Lawrence
Gulf of Maine
Lake Sakakawea
Lake Oahe
James
Minneapolis
Wisconsin
Lake Michigan
Lake Huron
Lake Ontario
Lake Champlain
Boston
C. Cod
ROCKY
Great Salt Lake
Great Basin
SIERRA NEVADA
COLORADO
Lake Mead
Denver
Mt. Elbert 14,431 ft. (4399 m.)
N. Platte
Platte
Des Moines
Milwaukee
Chicago
Detroit
Lake Erie
Cleveland
Niagara Falls
New York
Long Island
Philadelphia
ATLANTIC
San Francisco
Central Valley
Ft. Conception
Mojave Desert
SANTA BARBARA IS.
Los Angeles
San Diego
Mt. Whitney 14,495 ft. (4418 m.)
Lake Powell
Grand Canyon
COLORADO PLATEAU
Phoenix
Colorado
Gila
Kansas City
OZARK PLATEAU
St. Louis
Missouri
Ohio
Indianapolis
Washington
ALLEGHENY MTS.
Chesapeake Bay
C. Hatteras
OCEAN
MOUNTAINS
Arkansas
Memphis
Wheeler
Mt. Mitchell 6,684 ft. (2037 m.)
Atlanta
C. Fear
Chattahoochee
Canadian
LLANO ESTACADO
Red
Dallas
Brazos
EDWARDS PLATEAU
Pecos
Colorado
Rio Grande
Houston
GULF COASTAL PLAIN
New Orleans
Mississippi Delta
Jacksonville
C. Canaveral
Okeechobee
The Everglades
Miami
FLORIDA KEYS
Gulf of Mexico

ARCTIC OCEAN

0 200 400 MI.

0 200 400 KM.

BROOKS RANGE
Bering Str.
St. Lawrence I.
Yukon
Mt. McKinley 20,320 ft. (6194 m.)
Anchorage
BERING SEA
Gulf of Alaska
Kodiak I.
ALEXANDER ARCHIPELAGO
Aleutian Islands

HAWAIIAN ISLANDS
PACIFIC OCEAN
Kauai
Oahu
Honolulu
Molokai
Maui
Mauna Kea 13,796 ft. (4205 m.)
Hawaii

0 50 100 MI.

0 50 100 KM.

| 5,000 m. 16,404 ft. | 2,000 m. 6,562 ft. | 1,000 m. 3,281 ft. | 500 m. 1,640 ft. | 200 m. 656 ft. | 100 m. 328 ft. | Sea Level | Below |

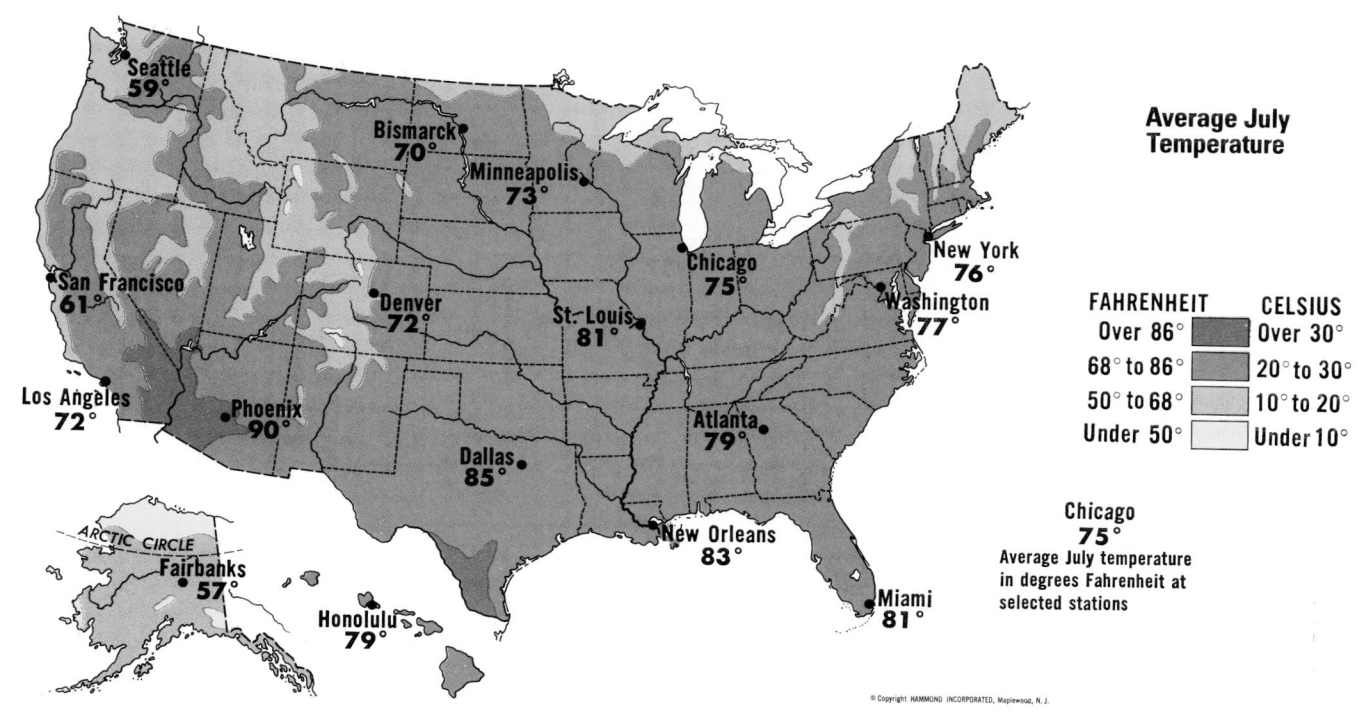

Average July Temperature

Seattle 59°
Bismarck 70°
Minneapolis 73°
San Francisco 61°
Denver 72°
St. Louis 81°
Chicago 75°
New York 76°
Washington 77°
Los Angeles 72°
Phoenix 90°
Dallas 85°
Atlanta 79°
New Orleans 83°
Miami 81°
ARCTIC CIRCLE
Fairbanks 57°
Honolulu 79°

FAHRENHEIT	CELSIUS
Over 86°	Over 30°
68° to 86°	20° to 30°
50° to 68°	10° to 20°
Under 50°	Under 10°

Chicago 75°
Average July temperature in degrees Fahrenheit at selected stations

© Copyright HAMMOND INCORPORATED, Maplewood, N.J.

United States Standard Time Zones

Agriculture, Industry and Resources

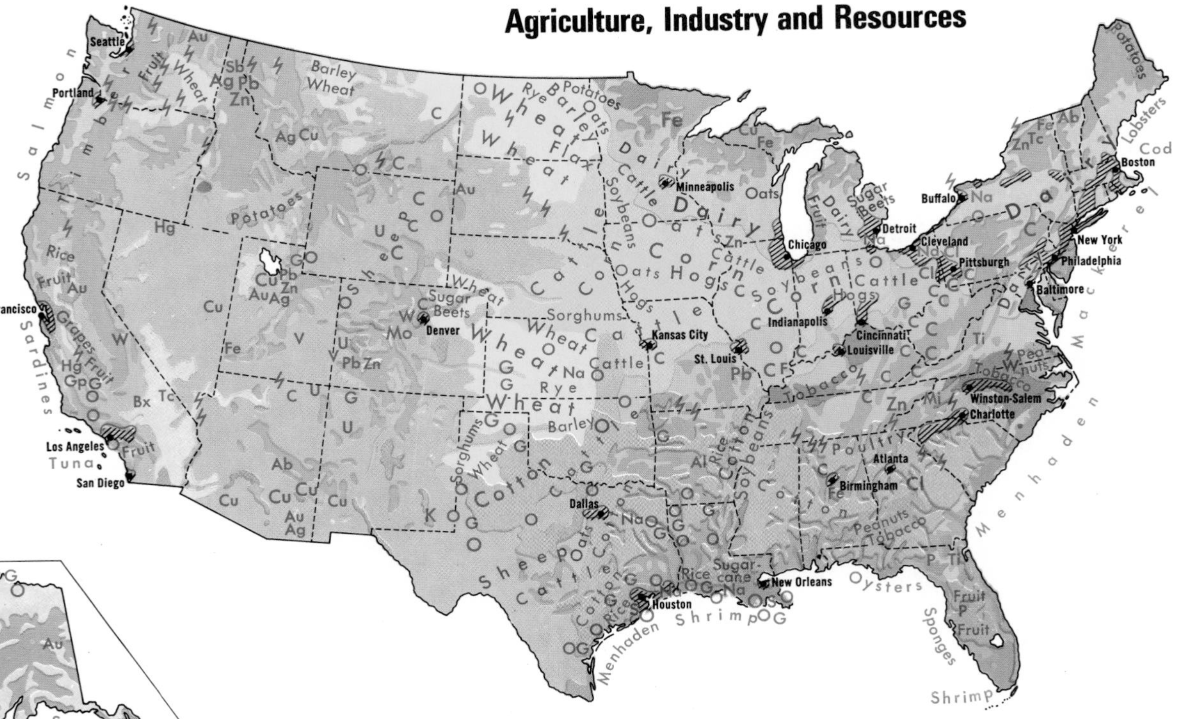

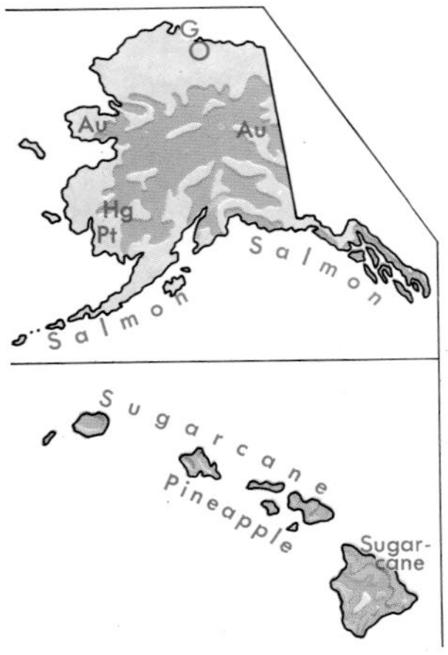

DOMINANT LAND USE

- Wheat and Small Grains
- Feed Grains and Livestock
- Dairy
- General Farming
- Cotton
- Fruit, Truck and Mixed Farming
- Tobacco and General Farming
- Special Crops and General Farming
- Range Livestock
- Forests
- Swampland
- Nonagricultural Land

MAJOR MINERAL OCCURRENCES

Ab	Asbestos	Gp	Gypsum	Sb	Antimony
Ag	Silver	Hg	Mercury	Tc	Talc
Al	Bauxite	K	Potash	Ti	Titanium
Au	Gold	Mi	Mica	U	Uranium
Bx	Borax	Mo	Molybdenum	V	Vanadium
C	Coal	Na	Salt	W	Tungsten
Cl	Clay	O	Petroleum	Zn	Zinc
Cu	Copper	P	Phosphates		
F	Fluorspar	Pb	Lead	⚡	Water Power
Fe	Iron Ore	Pt	Platinum	▨	Major Industrial Areas
G	Natural Gas	S	Sulfur		

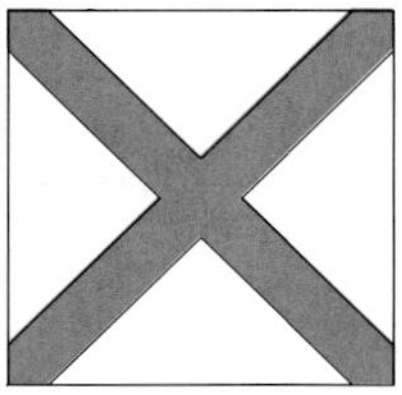

AREA 51,705 sq. mi. (133,916 sq. km.)
POPULATION 4,062,608
CAPITAL Montgomery
LARGEST CITY Birmingham
HIGHEST POINT Cheaha Mtn. 2,407 ft. (734 m.)
SETTLED IN 1702
ADMITTED TO UNION December 14, 1819
POPULAR NAME Heart of Dixie; Cotton State; Yellowhammer State
STATE FLOWER Camellia
STATE BIRD Yellowhammer

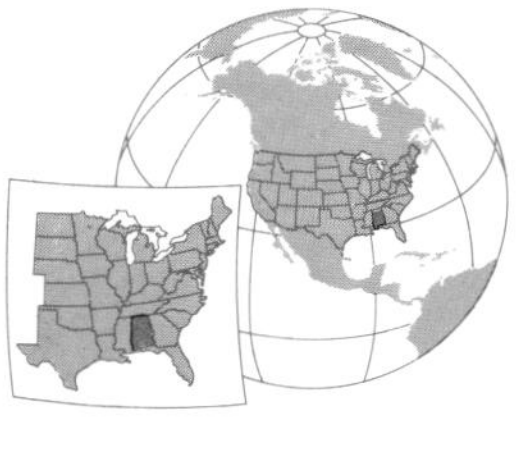

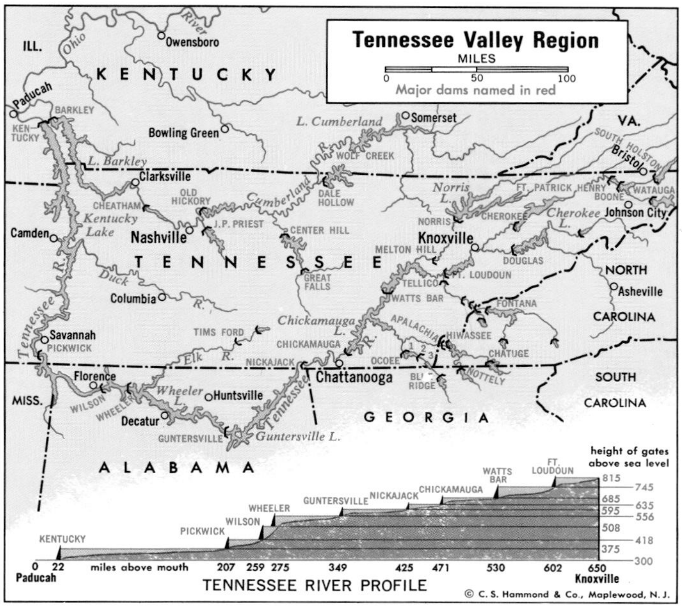

COUNTIES

Autauga 34,222 ....E5
Baldwin 98,280 ....C9
Barbour 25,417 ....H7
Bibb 16,576 ....D5
Blount 39,248 ....E2
Bullock 11,042 ....G6
Butler 21,892 ....E7
Calhoun 116,034 ....G3
Chambers 36,876 ....H5
Cherokee 19,543 ....G2
Chilton 32,458 ....E5
Choctaw 16,018 ....B6
Clarke 27,240 ....C7
Clay 13,252 ....G4
Cleburne 12,730 ....G3
Coffee 40,240 ....G8
Colbert 51,666 ....C1
Conecuh 14,054 ....E8
Coosa 11,063 ....F5
Covington 36,478 ....F8
Crenshaw 13,635 ....F7
Cullman 67,613 ....E2
Dale 49,633 ....G8
Dallas 48,130 ....D6
De Kalb 53,658 ....G2
Elmore 49,210 ....F5
Escambia 35,518 ....D8
Etowah 99,840 ....F2
Fayette 17,962 ....C3
Franklin 27,814 ....C2
Geneva 23,647 ....G8
Greene 10,153 ....C5
Hale 15,498 ....C5
Henry 15,374 ....H7
Houston 81,331 ....H8
Jackson 47,796 ....F1
Jefferson 651,525 ....E3
Lamar 15,715 ....B3
Lauderdale 79,661 ....C1
Lawrence 31,513 ....D1
Lee 87,146 ....H5
Limestone 54,135 ....E1
Lowndes 12,658 ....E6
Macon 24,928 ....G6
Madison 238,912 ....E1
Marengo 23,084 ....C6
Marion 29,830 ....C2
Marshall 70,832 ....F2
Mobile 378,643 ....B9
Monroe 23,968 ....D7
Montgomery 209,085 ....F6
Morgan 100,043 ....E2
Perry 12,759 ....D5
Pickens 20,699 ....B4
Pike 27,595 ....G7
Randolph 19,881 ....H4
Russell 46,860 ....H6
Saint Clair 41,205 ....F3
Shelby 99,358 ....E4
Sumter 16,174 ....B5
Talladega 74,107 ....F4
Tallapoosa 38,826 ....G5
Tuscaloosa 150,522 ....C4
Walker 67,670 ....D3
Washington 16,694 ....B8
Wilcox 13,568 ....D7
Winston 22,053 ....D2

CITIES and TOWNS

Abbeville▲ 3,173 ....H7
Abernant 405 ....D4
Adamsville 4,161 ....D3
Addison 626 ....D2
Adger 400 ....D4
Akron 458 ....C5
Alabaster 14,732 ....E4
Albertville 14,507 ....F2
Aldrich 500 ....E4
Alexander City▲ 14,917 ....G5
Alexandria 464 ....G3
Aliceville 3,009 ....B4
Allgood 464 ....E3
Allsboro 300 ....B1
Alma 500 ....C8
Altoona 960 ....F2
Andalusia▲ 9,269 ....E8
Anderson 339 ....D1
Anniston▲ 26,623 ....G3
Arab 6,321 ....E2
Ardmore 1,090 ....E1
Argo 930 ....E3
Ariton 743 ....G7
Arley 338 ....D2
Ashby 500 ....E4
Ashford 1,926 ....H8
Ashland▲ 2,034 ....G4
Ashville 1,494 ....F3
Athens▲ 16,901 ....E1
Atmore 8,046 ....C8
Attalla 6,859 ....F2
Auburn 33,830 ....H5

Autaugaville 681 ....E6
Avon 462 ....H8
Axis 500 ....B9
Babbie 576 ....F8
Baileyton 352 ....E2
Baker Hill 300 ....H7
Banks 195 ....G7
Barnwell 700 ....C10
Bay Minette▲ 7,168 ....C9
Bayou La Batre 2,456 ....B10
Bear Creek 913 ....C2
Beatrice 454 ....D7
Beaverton 319 ....B3
Belgreen 500 ....C2
Belk 255 ....C3
Bellamy 700 ....B6
Belle Mina 675 ....E1
Bellwood 400 ....G8
Benton 48 ....E6
Berry 1,218 ....C3
Bessemer 33,497 ....D4
Beulah 500 ....H5
Billingsley 150 ....E5
Birmingham▲ 265,968 ....D3
Black 174 ....G8
Blountsville 1,527 ....E2
Blue Mountain 221 ....G3
Blue Springs 108 ....G7
Boaz 6,928 ....F2
Boligee 268 ....C5
Bon Air 91 ....F4
Bon Secour 850 ....C10
Branchville 370 ....F3
Brantley 1,015 ....F7
Brent 2,776 ....D5
Brewton▲ 5,885 ....D8
Bridgeport 2,936 ....G1
Brighton 4,518 ....D4
Brilliant 751 ....C2
Brookside 1,365 ....E3
Brookwood 658 ....D4
Browns 375 ....D6
Brownville 2,386 ....C4
Brundidge 2,472 ....G7
Butler▲ 1,872 ....B6
Cahaba 4,778 ....D6
Calera 2,136 ....E4
Calhoun 950 ....F6
Calvert 600 ....B8
Camden▲ 2,414 ....D7
Camp Hill 1,415 ....G5
Canoe 560 ....D8
Carbon Hill 2,115 ....D3
Cardiff 72 ....E3
Carolina 201 ....F8
Carrollton▲ 1,170 ....B4
Carrville 820 ....G5
Carson 400 ....C8
Castleberry 669 ....D8
Cedar Bluff 1,174 ....G2
Centre▲ 2,893 ....G2
Centreville▲ 2,508 ....D5
Chatom▲ 1,094 ....B8
Chelsea 1,329 ....E4
Cherokee 1,479 ....C1
Chickasaw 6,649 ....B9
Childersburg 4,579 ....F4
Choccolocco 500 ....G3
Choctaw 600 ....B6
Chrysler 400 ....D7
Chunchula 700 ....B9
Citronelle 3,671 ....B8
Clanton▲ 7,669 ....E5
Clayhatchee 411 ....G8
Clayton▲ 1,564 ....G7
Cleveland 739 ....E3
Clio 1,365 ....G7
Coaling 400 ....D4
Coden 600 ....B10
Coffee Springs 294 ....G8
Coffeeville 431 ....B7
Coker 800 ....C4
Collinsville 1,429 ....G2
Columbia 922 ....H8
Columbiana▲ 2,968 ....E4
Coosada 912 ....F5
Cordova 2,623 ....D3
Cottondale 500 ....D4
Cotton Ton 424 ....H6
Cottonwood 1,385 ....H8
County Line 124 ....F4
County Line 199 ....E3
Courtland 803 ....D1
Cowarts 1,400 ....H8
Coy 950 ....D7
Crane Hill 355 ....D2
Creola 1,479 ....B9
Cromwell 650 ....B6
Crossville 1,350 ....G2
Cuba 390 ....B6
Cullman▲ 13,367 ....E2
Cullomburg 325 ....B7
Cusseta 650 ....H5
Dadeville▲ 3,276 ....G5

Daleville 5,117 ....G8
Daphne 11,290 ....C9
Dauphin Island 824 ....B10
Daviston 261 ....G4
Dayton 77 ....C6
De Armanville 350 ....G3
Decatur▲ 48,761 ....D1
Demopolis 7,512 ....C6
Detroit 291 ....B2
Dolomite D4
Dora 2,214 ....D3
Dothan▲ 53,589 ....H8
Double Springs▲ 1,138 ....D2
Douglas 474 ....F2
Dozier 483 ....F7
Dutton 243 ....G1
East Brewton 2,579 ....E8
Eclectic 1,087 ....F5
Edwardsville 118 ....H3
Elba▲ 4,011 ....F8
Elberta 458 ....C10
Eldridge 225 ....C3
Elkmont 389 ....E1
Elmore 600 ....F5
Elrod 746 ....C4
Emelle 44 ....B5
Empire 600 ....D3
Enterprise 20,123 ....G8
Epes 485 ....B5
Ethelsville 52 ....B4
Eufaula 13,220 ....H7
Eunola 199 ....G8
Eutaw▲ 2,281 ....C5
Eva 438 ....E2
Evergreen▲ 3,911 ....E8
Excel 571 ....D8
Fairfield 12,200 ....E4
Fairhope 8,485 ....C10
Fairview 383 ....E2
Falkville 1,337 ....E2
Faunsdale 96 ....C6
Fayette▲ 4,909 ....C3
Five Points 200 ....H4
Flat Rock 750 ....G1
Flomaton 1,811 ....D8
Flint City 1,033 ....D1
Florala 2,075 ....F8
Florence▲ 36,426 ....C1
Foley 4,937 ....C10
Forestdale 10,395 ....E3
Forkland 667 ....C5
Fort Davis 500 ....G6
Fort Deposit 1,240 ....E7
Fort Mitchell 900 ....H6
Fort Payne▲ 11,838 ....G2
Fosters 400 ....C4
Franklin 133 ....E6
Franklin 152 ....D7
Frisco City 1,581 ....D8
Fruitdale 500 ....B8
Fruithurst 177 ....G3
Fulton 384 ....C7
Fultondale 6,400 ....E3
Fyffe 1,094 ....G2
Gadsden▲ 42,523 ....G2
Gainesville 449 ....B5
Gallant 475 ....F2
Gantt 265 ....F8
Gantt's Quarry F4
Garden City 578 ....E2
Gardendale 9,251 ....E3
Gaylesville 149 ....G2
Geiger 270 ....B5
Geneva▲ 4,681 ....G8
Georgiana 1,933 ....E7
Geraldine 801 ....G2
Gilbertown 235 ....B7
Glen Allen 350 ....C3
Glencoe 4,670 ....G3
Glenwood 208 ....F7
Goldville 61 ....G4
Good Hope 1,700 ....E2
Goodsprings 360 ....D3
Goodwater 1,840 ....F4
Gordo 1,918 ....C4
Gordon 493 ....H8
Gorgas 500 ....D3
Goshen 302 ....F7
Gosport 500 ....C7
Grand Bay 3,383 ....B10
Grant 638 ....F1
Graysville 2,241 ....D3
Green Pond 750 ....D4
Greensboro▲ 3,047 ....C5
Greenville▲ 7,492 ....E7
Grimes 443 ....H8
Grove Hill▲ 1,551 ....C7
Gu-Win 243 ....C3
Guin 2,413 ....C3
Gulf Shores 3,261 ....C10
Guntersville▲ 7,038 ....F2
Gurley 1,007 ....F1
Hackleburg 1,161 ....C2
Haleburg 97 ....H8

Haleyville 4,452 ....C2
Hamilton▲ 5,787 ....C2
Hammondville 420 ....G1
Hanceville 2,246 ....E2
Hardaway 600 ....G6
Harpersville 772 ....F4
Hartford 2,448 ....G8
Hartselle 10,795 ....E2
Harvest 1,922 ....E1
Hatchechubbee 840 ....H6
Hatton 950 ....D1
Hayden 385 ....E3
Hayneville▲ 969 ....E6
Hazel Green 2,208 ....E1
Headland 3,266 ....H8
Heath 182 ....F8
Heflin▲ 2,906 ....G3
Heiberger 310 ....D5
Helena 3,918 ....E4
Henagar 1,934 ....G1
Higdon 325 ....G1
Highland Lake 304 ....F3
Hillsboro 587 ....D1
Hobson City 794 ....G3
Hodges 272 ....C2
Hokes Bluff 3,739 ....G3
Hollins 500 ....F4
Holly Pond 602 ....E2
Hollywood 916 ....G1
Holt 4,125 ....D4
Holy Trinity 400 ....H6
Homewood 22,922 ....E4
Hoover 39,788 ....E4
Hope Hull 975 ....F6
Horn Hill 186 ....F8
Hueytown 15,280 ....D4
Huntsville▲ 159,789 ....E1
Hurtsboro 707 ....H6
Hytop 350 ....F1
Ider 671 ....G1
Inverness 2,528 ....G6
Irondale 9,454 ....E3
Jack 519 ....F7
Jackson 789 ....C8
Jacksons Gap 800 ....G5
Jacksonville 10,283 ....G3
Jasper▲ 13,553 ....D3
Jemison 1,898 ....E5
Kansas 230 ....C3
Kellyton 375 ....F5
Kennedy 523 ....B3
Key 400 ....G2

Killen 1,047 ....D1
Kimberly 1,096 ....E3
Kinsey 1,679 ....H8
Kinston 595 ....F8
Lafayette▲ 3,151 ....H5
Lakeview 166 ....G2
Lanett 8,985 ....H5
Langdale 2,034 ....H5
Langston 207 ....G1
Larkinsville 425 ....F1
Lavaca 500 ....B6
Leeds 9,946 ....E3
Leesburg 218 ....G2
Leighton 988 ....D1
Leroy 699 ....B8
Lester 89 ....D1
Level Plains 1,473 ....G8
Lexington 821 ....D1
Libertyville 133 ....F8
Lillian 500 ....D10
Lincoln 2,941 ....F3
Linden▲ 2,548 ....C6
Lineville 2,394 ....G4
Lipscomb 2,892 ....E4
Lisman 481 ....B6
Little River 400 ....C8
Little Shawmut 2,793 ....H5
Littleville 925 ....C1
Livingston▲ 3,530 ....B5
Loachapoka 259 ....G5
Lockhart 484 ....F8
Locust Fork 342 ....E3
Longview 475 ....E4
Louisville 728 ....G7
Lower Peach Tree 926 ....C7
Lowndesboro 139 ....E6
Loxley 1,161 ....C9
Luverne▲ 2,555 ....F7
Lynn 611 ....C2
Madison 14,904 ....E1
Madrid 211 ....H8
Magnolia Springs 800 ....C10
Malvern 570 ....G8
Manchester 400 ....D3
Maplesville 725 ....E5
Margaret 616 ....F3
Marion Junction 400 ....D6
Marion▲ 4,211 ....D5
Maylene 500 ....E4
McCalla 657 ....D4
McCullough 500 ....D8

McIntosh 250 ....B8
McKenzie 464 ....E7
McWilliams 305 ....D7
Memphis 54 ....B4
Mentone 474 ....G1
Meridianville 2,852 ....F1
Midfield 5,559 ....E4
Midland City 1,819 ....H8
Midway 455 ....H6
Mignon 1,548 ....F4
Millbrook 6,050 ....F6
Millerville 345 ....G4
Millport 1,203 ....B3
Millry 781 ....B7
Minter 450 ....D6
Mobile▲ 196,278 ....B9
Monroeville▲ 6,993 ....D7
Monrovia 500 ....E1
Montevallo 4,239 ....E4
Montgomery (cap.)▲ 187,106 ....F6
Montrose 750 ....C9
Moody 4,921 ....F3
Mooresville 54 ....E1
Morris 1,136 ....E3
Morvin 355 ....C7
Moulton▲ 3,248 ....D1
Moundville 1,348 ....C5
Mount Vernon 902 ....B8
Mountain Brook 19,810 ....E4
Mountainboro 261 ....F2
Munford 700 ....F3
Muscle Shoals 9,611 ....C1
Myrtlewood 307 ....C6
Nanafalia 500 ....B6
Napier Field 462 ....H8
Nauvoo 240 ....D3
Nectar 238 ....E3
Needham 99 ....B7
New Brockton 1,184 ....G8
New Hope 2,248 ....F1
New Market 1,094 ....F1
New Site 669 ....G4
Newbern 222 ....C5
Newton 1,580 ....H8
Newville 531 ....H8
North Johns 177 ....D4
Northport 17,366 ....C4
Notasulga 979 ....G5
Oak Grove 436 ....B9
Oak Grove 638 ....E4
Oak Hill 28 ....D7
Oakman 846 ....D3

Odenville 796 ....F3
Ohatchee 1,042 ....G3
Oneonta▲ 4,844 ....E3
Onycha 150 ....F8
Opelika▲ 22,122 ....H5
Opp 6,985 ....F8
Orange Beach 2,253 ....C10
Orrville 234 ....D6
Owens Cross Roads 695 ....E1
Oxford 9,362 ....G3
Ozarka 12,922 ....G8
Paint Rock 214 ....F1
Parrish 1,433 ....D3
Pelham 9,765 ....E4
Pell City▲ 8,118 ....F3
Pennington 302 ....B6
Perdido 500 ....C8
Peterman 600 ....D7
Peterson D4
Petrey 80 ....F7
Phenix City▲ 25,312 ....H6
Phil Campbell 1,317 ....C2
Pickensville 169 ....B4
Piedmont 5,288 ....G3
Pinckard 618 ....G8
Pine Apple 365 ....E7
Pine Hill 481 ....C7
Pinson 10,987 ....E3
Pisgah 652 ....G1
Plantersville 650 ....E5
Pleasant Grove 8,458 ....D4
Point Clear 2,125 ....C10
Pollard 100 ....D8
Powell's Crossroads 636 ....G1
Prattville▲ 19,587 ....E6
Priceville 1,323 ....E1
Prichard 34,311 ....B9
Providence 307 ....C6
Ragland 1,807 ....F3
Rainbow City 7,673 ....F3
Rainsville 3,875 ....G2
Ramer 680 ....F6
Ranburne 447 ....H3
Red Bay 3,451 ....B2
Red Level 588 ....E8
Reece City 657 ....F2
Reform 2,105 ....C4
Remlap 800 ....E3
Renfroe 400 ....F4
Repton 293 ....D8
Republic 500 ....E3
River Falls 710 ....E8

(continued on following page)

Agriculture, Industry and Resources

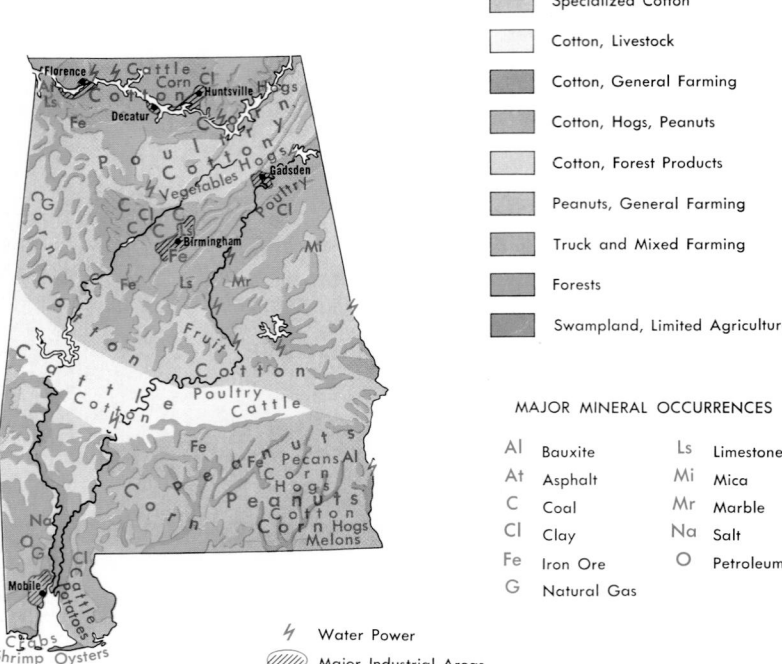

DOMINANT LAND USE

- Specialized Cotton
- Cotton, Livestock
- Cotton, General Farming
- Cotton, Hogs, Peanuts
- Cotton, Forest Products
- Peanuts, General Farming
- Truck and Mixed Farming
- Forests
- Swampland, Limited Agriculture

MAJOR MINERAL OCCURRENCES

Al	Bauxite	Ls	Limestone
At	Asphalt	Mi	Mica
C	Coal	Mr	Marble
Cl	Clay	Na	Salt
Fe	Iron Ore	O	Petroleum
G	Natural Gas		

⚡ Water Power

〰 Major Industrial Areas

Topography

Scale: 0 — 30 — 60 MI.
0 — 30 — 60 KM.

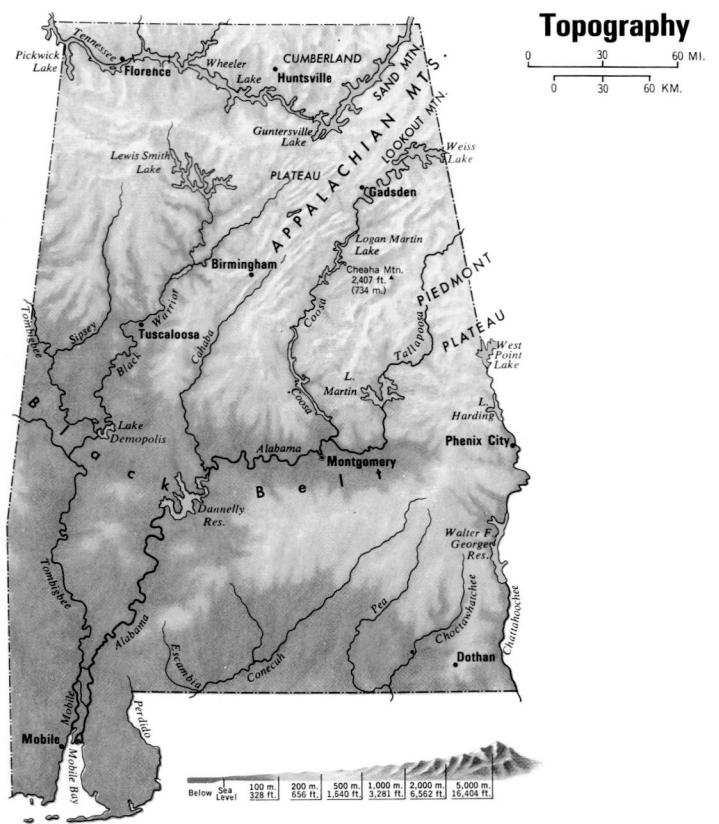

Below Sea Level | 100 m. 328 ft. | 200 m. 656 ft. | 500 m. 1,640 ft. | 1,000 m. 3,281 ft. | 2,000 m. 6,562 ft. | 5,000 m. 16,404 ft.

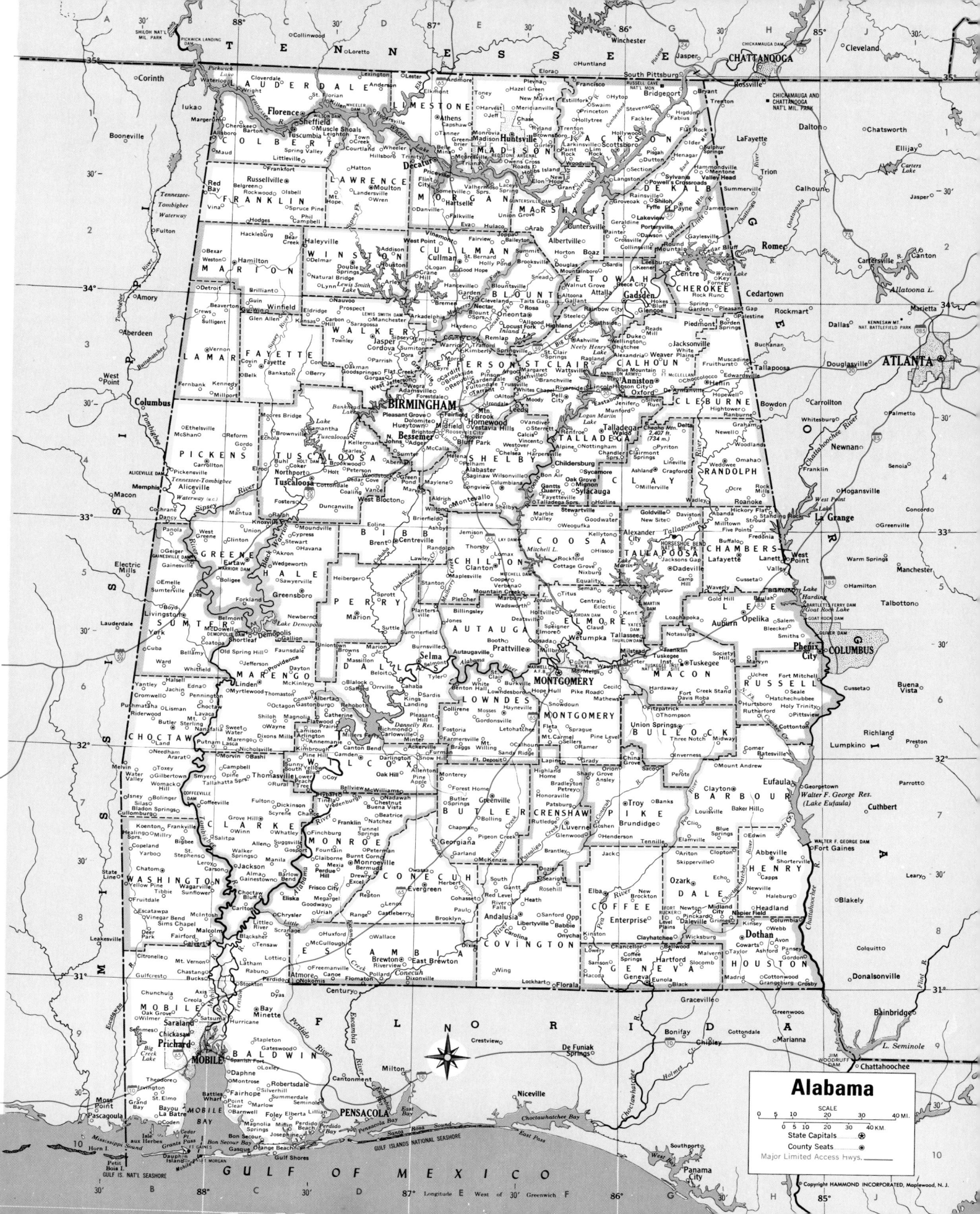

Alabama
SCALE
0 5 10 20 30 40 MI.
0 5 10 20 30 40 KM.
State Capitals
County Seats
Major Limited Access Hwys.
© Copyright HAMMOND INCORPORATED, Maplewood, N. J.
Longitude West of Greenwich
TENNESSEE
GEORGIA
FLORIDA
MISSISSIPPI
GULF OF MEXICO
MOBILE BAY
Choctawhatchee Bay
Pensacola Bay
East Bay
Santa Rosa Sound
Mississippi Sound
GULF ISLANDS NATIONAL SEASHORE
GULF IS. NAT'L SEASHORE
Walter F. George Res. (Lake Eufaula)
Tennessee-Tombigbee Waterway
Lake Martin
Lewis Smith Lake
Weiss Lake
Lake Harding
Cheaha Mtn. 2,407 ft. (734 m.)
LAUDERDALE
LIMESTONE
MADISON
JACKSON
COLBERT
LAWRENCE
MORGAN
MARSHALL
DE KALB
FRANKLIN
WINSTON
CULLMAN
MARION
ETOWAH
CHEROKEE
BLOUNT
LAMAR
FAYETTE
WALKER
JEFFERSON
ST. CLAIR
CALHOUN
CLEBURNE
PICKENS
TUSCALOOSA
SHELBY
TALLADEGA
CLAY
RANDOLPH
BIBB
COOSA
TALLAPOOSA
CHAMBERS
GREENE
HALE
CHILTON
PERRY
AUTAUGA
ELMORE
LEE
SUMTER
MARENGO
DALLAS
MONTGOMERY
MACON
RUSSELL
CHOCTAW
LOWNDES
BULLOCK
WILCOX
BUTLER
CRENSHAW
PIKE
BARBOUR
CLARKE
MONROE
CONECUH
WASHINGTON
COFFEE
DALE
HENRY
ESCAMBIA
COVINGTON
GENEVA
HOUSTON
MOBILE
BALDWIN
MONTGOMERY
BIRMINGHAM
MOBILE
Huntsville
Florence
Decatur
Gadsden
Anniston
Tuscaloosa
Bessemer
Selma
Dothan
Auburn
Opelika
Phenix City
Prichard
CHATTANOOGA
ATLANTA
COLUMBUS
PENSACOLA

Agriculture, Industry and Resources

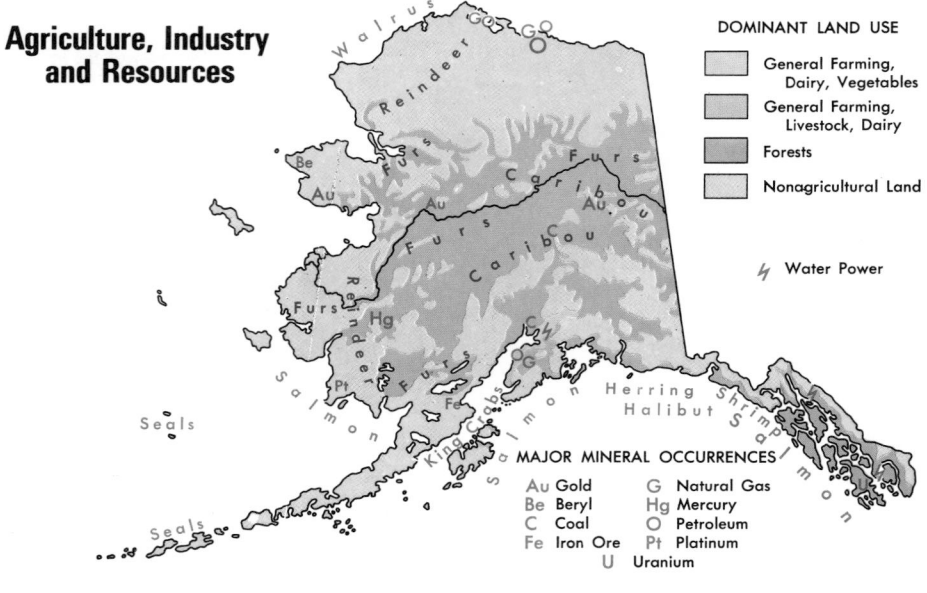

DOMINANT LAND USE

- General Farming, Dairy, Vegetables
- General Farming, Livestock, Dairy
- Forests
- Nonagricultural Land

⚡ Water Power

MAJOR MINERAL OCCURRENCES

Au	Gold	G	Natural Gas
Be	Beryl	Hg	Mercury
C	Coal	O	Petroleum
Fe	Iron Ore	Pt	Platinum
		U	Uranium

Topography

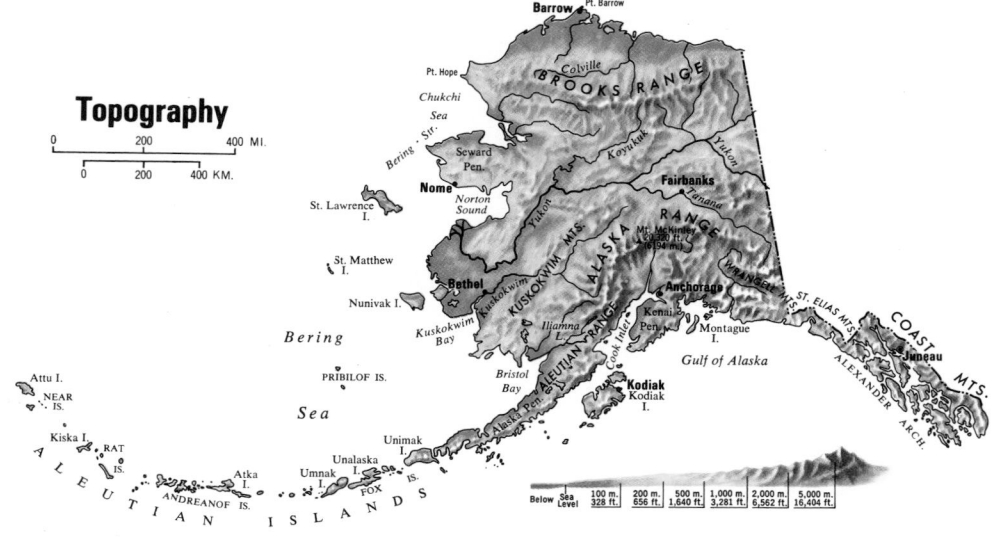

Below Sea Level — 100 m. 328 ft. — 200 m. 656 ft. — 500 m. 1,640 ft. — 1,000 m. 3,281 ft. — 2,000 m. 6,562 ft. — 5,000 m. 16,404 ft.

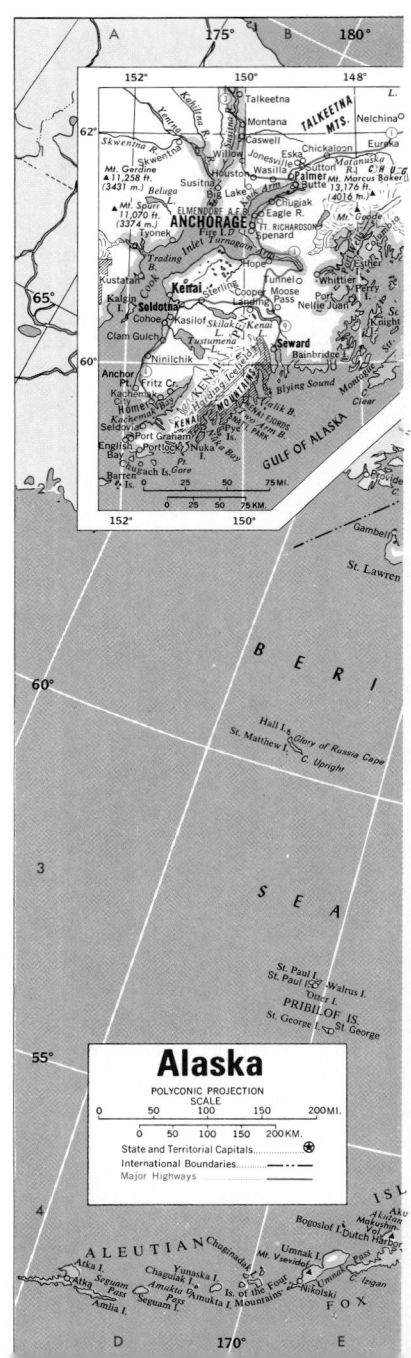

Alaska

POLYCONIC PROJECTION
SCALE

0 50 100 150 200 MI.
0 50 100 150 200 KM.

State and Territorial Capitals..........⊛
International Boundaries.........
Major Highways

Marmot (isl.) H3
Matanuska (riv.) C1
McKinley (mt.) H2
Meade (riv.) G1
Mendenhall (cape) E3
Mentasta (pass) K2
Merrill (pass) H2
Michelson (mtn.) K1
Middleton (isl.) J3
Misty Fjords Nat'l Mon. ...N2
Mitkof (isl.) N2
Montague (isl.) D1
Muir (glac.) M1
Mulchatna (riv.) G2
Muzon (cape) M2
Naknek (lake) G3
Near (isl.) H3
Nelson (isl.) E2
Newenham (cape) F3
Noatak (riv.) F1
Norton (bay) F2
Norton (sound) E2
Nowitna (riv.) H2
Nuka (bay) C2
Nunivak (isl.) C3
Nushagak (riv.) G3
Nuyakuk (lake) G3
Ommaney (cape) M2
Otter (isl.) D3
Pastol (bay) F2
Pavlof (isl.) F3
Pavlof (vol.) F3
Philip Smith (mts.) J1
Porcupine (riv.) K1

Port Clarence (inlet) E1
Port Heiden (inlet) G3
Portland Canal (inlet) N2
Port Moller (inlet) F3
Port Wells (inlet) C1
Pribilof (isls.) D3
Prince of Wales (cape) ...E1
Prince of Wales (isl.) N2
Prince William (sound) ..D1
Prudhoe (bay) J1
Rat (isl.) K4
Redoubt (vol.) H2
Revillagigedo (chan.) N2
Revillagigedo (isl.) N2
Romanzof (cape) E2
Sagavanirktok (riv.) J1
Saint Elias (cape) K3
Saint Elias (mt.) K2
Saint George (isl.) D3
Saint Lawrence (isl.) D2
Saint Matthew (isl.) D2
Saint Paul (isl.) D3
Salisbury (sound) M1
Sanak (isl.) F4
Sanford (mt.) K2
Schwatka (mts.) G1
Seguam (isl.) D4
Selawik (riv.) F1
Semidi (isls.) J3
Semidi (isls.) G3
Semisopochnoi (isl.) K4
Seward (pen.) E1
Sheenjek (riv.) K1
Shelikof (str.) H3

Shemya (isl.) J3
Shishaldin (vol.) J3
Shumagin (isl.) G4
Shuyak (isl.) H3
Sitka (sound) M1
Sitka Nat'l Hist. Park M1
Sitkinak (isl.) H3
Skilak (lake) C1
Skwentna (riv.) A1
Smith (bay) L1
Spencer (cape) L1
Stephens (passage) N1
Stevenson Entrance (str.) ..H3
Stikine (riv.) N2
Stikine (str.) N2
Stony (riv.) G2
Stuart (isl.) F2
Suemez (isl.) M2
Sumner (str.) M2
Susitna (riv.) B1
Sutwik (isl.) G3
Taku (glac.) N1
Taku (riv.) N1
Talkeetna (mts.) J2
Tanaga (isl.) K4
Tanaga (vol.) K4
Tanana (riv.) J2
Taylor (mts.) G2
Tazlina (lake) D1
Tazlina (riv.) D1
Teshekpuk (lake) H1
Tigalda (isl.) F4
Tikchik (lakes) G2
Togiak (bay) F3

Tugidak (isl.) G3
Turnagain Arm (inlet) B1
Tustumena (lake) C1
Two Arm (bay) C2
Ugashik (lakes) G3
Umnak (isl.) E4
Umnak (passage) E4
Unalaska (isl.) E4
Unga (isl.) F3
Unimak (isl.) E4
Unimak (passage) F4
Utukok (riv.) F1
Valley of Ten
  Thousand Smokes G3
Vancouver (mt.) L2
Veniaminof (crater) F3
Vsevidof (mt.) E4
Walrus (isl.) E3
Walrus (isls.) F3
Waring (mts.) G1
West Point (mt.) K2
White (pass) N1
White (riv.) K2
White Mountains Nat'l
  Rec .Area. J1
Witherspoon (mt.) C1
Wrangell (cape) H3
Wrangell (isl.) N2
Wrangell (mts.) K2
Wrangell-St. Elias Nat'l Park ..K2
Yakobi (isl.) M1
Yakutat (bay) K3
Yentna (riv.) A1
Yukon (riv.) F2

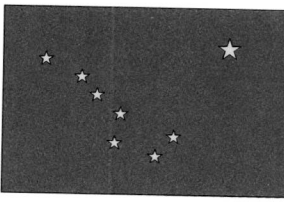
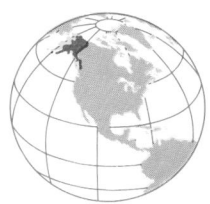

AREA 591,004 sq. mi. (1,530,700 sq. km.)
POPULATION 551,947
CAPITAL Juneau
LARGEST CITY Anchorage
HIGHEST POINT Mt. McKinley 20,320 ft. (6194 m.)
SETTLED IN 1801
ADMITTED TO UNION January 3, 1959
POPULAR NAME Great Land; Last Frontier
STATE FLOWER Forget-me-not
STATE BIRD Willow Ptarmigan

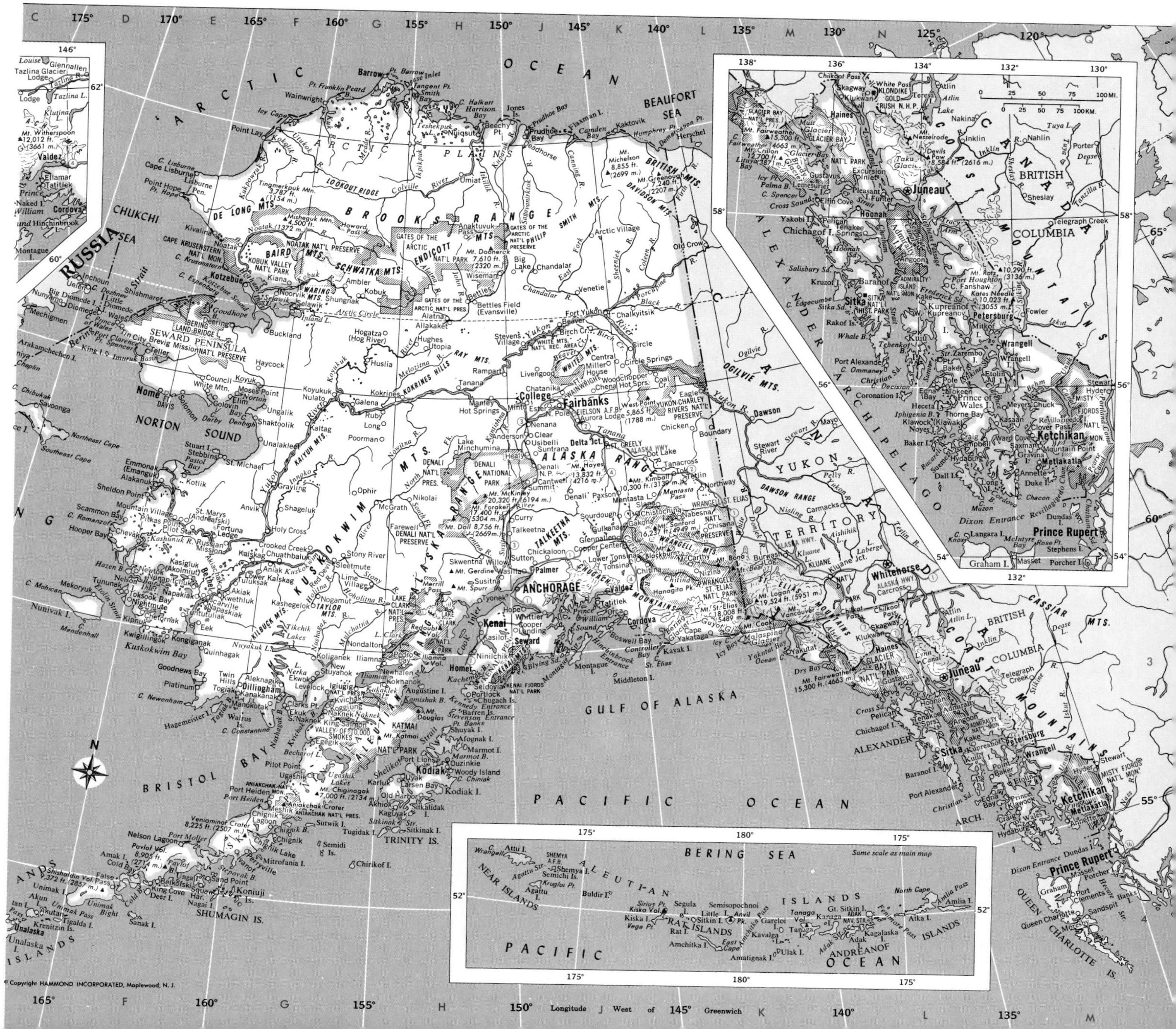

Arizona
SCALE
0 5 10 20 30 40 50 60 MI.
0 5 10 20 30 40 50 60 KM.
State Capitals
County Seats
Major Limited Access Hwys.
© Copyright HAMMOND INCORPORATED, Maplewood, N. J.
Longitude West of Greenwich
114° 113° 112° 111° 110° 109°
37° 36° 35° 34° 33° 32° 31°
A B C D E F
1 2 3 4 5 6 7
U T A H
N E V A D A
C A L I F O R N I A
N E W M E X I C O
M E X I C O
COLORADO
Only point in the UNITED STATES common to four state boundaries.
GLEN CANYON NATIONAL RECREATION AREA
Lake Powell
BRYCE CANYON NAT'L PARK
ZION NAT'L PARK
NATURAL BRIDGES NAT'L MON.
HOVENWEEP NAT'L MON.
UTE MTN. IND. RES.
SHIVWITS IND. RES.
St. George
Hurricane
Kanab
Caliente
Carp
Moapa
MOAPA RIVER IND. RES.
Overton
Dry Lake
Lake Mead
LAKE MEAD NATIONAL RECREATION AREA
HOOVER DAM
Temple Bar
Mt. Navajo 10,416 ft. (3175 m.)
RAINBOW BRIDGE NAT'L MON.
MONUMENT VALLEY
GLEN CANYON DAM
Page
Lees Ferry
Marble Canyon
Colorado City
Fredonia
Cane Beds
Moccasin
KAIBAB INDIAN RES.
PIPE SPRING NAT'L MON.
Littlefield
KAIBAB
Jacob Lake
GRAND CANYON NAT'L PARK
Mt. Trumbull 7,700 ft. (2347 m.)
Mount Trumbull
GRAND CANYON NATIONAL PARK
North Rim
Supai
HAVASUPAI IND. RES.
Grand Canyon
HUALAPAI INDIAN RESERVATION
NAVAJO INDIAN RESERVATION
HOPI INDIAN RESERVATION
PAINTED DESERT
Kaibito
Tonalea
Tuba City
Moenkopi
Cameron
Hotevilla
Kykotsmovi
Shungopavy (Shongopovi)
Second Mesa
Polacca
Keams Canyon
Jeddito
Pinon
Shonto
Kayenta
Dennehotso
Teec Nos Pos
Pastora Pk. 9,412 ft. (2869 m.)
Roof Butte 9,575 ft. (2918 m.)
Many Farms
Lukachukai
CANYON DE CHELLY NAT'L MONUMENT
Tsaile
Chinle
A P A C H E
Steamboat
Ganado
HUBBELL TRADING POST NAT'L HIST. SITE
Cornfields
Klagetoh
Defiance
Window Rock
St. Michaels
Lupton
Houck
Sanders
Chambers
Navajo
Petrified Forest
PETRIFIED FOREST NATIONAL PARK
PAINTED DESERT SECTION
ZUNI IND. RES.
N A V A J O
Dilkon
Indian Wells
Leupp
Winslow
METEOR CRATER
Holbrook
Joseph City
Woodruff
Snowflake
Taylor
Concho
St. Johns
Heber
Aripine
Overgaard
Clay Sprs.
Pinedale
Linden
Show Low
Vernon
Lakeside
Pinetop
McNary
Springerville
Greens Pk. 10,210 ft. (3112 m.)
Eagar
Greer
Nutrioso
Alpine
Baldy Pk. 11,590 ft. (3533 m.)
Cibecue
FORT APACHE INDIAN RESERVATION
Whiteriver
Fort Apache
Maverick
C O C O N I N O
COCONINO PLATEAU
Slate Mtn. 8,209 ft. (2502 m.)
WUPATKI NAT'L MON.
Kendrick Pk. 10,418 ft. (3175 m.)
Humphreys Pk. 12,633 ft. (3851 m.)
O'Leary Pk. 8,925 ft. (2720 m.)
SUNSET CRATER NAT'L MON.
Agassiz Pk. 12,340 ft. (3761 m.)
Government Mtn. 8,347 ft. (2544 m.)
Elden Mtn.
Winona
Flagstaff
WALNUT CANYON NAT'L MON.
Woody Mtn. 8,054 ft. (2455 m.)
Bellemont
Parks
Williams
Ash Fork
Seligman
Nelson
Peach Springs
Mormon Lake
Sedona
Happy Jack
M O H A V E
Kingman
Hualapai Pk. 8,266 ft. (2519 m.)
Hackberry
Valentine
Chloride
Dolan Springs
Katherine
Davis Dam
Bullhead City
Riviera
Oatman
FORT MOHAVE IND. RES.
Needles
Golden Shores
Topock
Yucca
Wikieup
Lake Havasu
Lake Havasu City
CHEMEHUEVI IND. RES.
PARKER DAM
Parker
COLORADO RIVER INDIAN RES.
Poston
Vidal
Rice
Midland
Blythe
Ripley
Ehrenberg
Quartzsite
Bouse
Salome
Wenden
Vicksburg
PICTOGRAPH ROCKS
L A P A Z
Y A V A P A I
Prescott
Paulden
Chino Valley
Clarkdale
Jerome
Clemenceau
Cottonwood
TUZIGOOT NAT'L MON.
Cornville
Rimrock
Lake Montezuma
MONTEZUMA CASTLE NAT'L MON.
Camp Verde
Prescott Valley
Dewey
Humboldt
Cherry
Iron Springs
Skull Valley
Bagdad
Yava
Hillside
Kirkland
Mt. Union 7,971 ft. (2430 m.)
Mayer
Arcosant
Yarnell
Congress
Crown King
Bumble Bee
Black Canyon City
Castle Hot Sprs.
Baker Butte 8,182 ft. (2494 m.)
Pine
Payson
Kohls Ranch
Young
Mazatzal Pk. 7,888 ft. (2404 m.)
G I L A
Tonto Basin
Theodore Roosevelt Lake
Roosevelt
TONTO NAT'L MON.
Globe
Claypool
Miami
Inspiration
Central Hts.
SAN CARLOS INDIAN RESERVATION
San Carlos
Peridot
Coolidge Dam
Rose Pk. 8,789 ft. (2679 m.)
G R E E N L E E
Clifton
Morenci
Plantsite
Duncan
Franklin
G R A H A M
Bylas
Calva
Geronimo
Fort Thomas
Pima
Eden
Thatcher
Safford
Central
Solomon
Klondyke
Mt. Graham 10,713 ft. (3265 m.)
Fort Grant
Bonita
M A R I C O P A
Aguila
Wickenburg
Morristown
Wittmann
Wenden
Tonopah
Wintersburg
Arlington
Buckeye
Palo Verde
Liberty
Avondale
Goodyear
Litchfield Park
Tolleson
Cashion
El Mirage
Surprise
Sun City
Waddell
Peoria
Youngtown
Glendale
PHOENIX
Paradise Valley
Scottsdale
Tempe
Mesa
Chandler
Gilbert
Higley
Fountain Hills
Apache Jct.
Carefree
Cave Creek
Horseshoe Lake
Bartlett Res.
Mt. Ord 7,155 ft. (2181 m.)
FORT McDOWELL IND. RES.
SALT RIVER IND. RES.
Four Pks.
Tortilla Flat
WILLIAMS A.F.B.
LUKE A.F.B.
Superior
Queen Cr.
Florence Jct.
Komatke
GILA RIVER INDIAN RES.
Bapchule
Sacaton
Maricopa
Mobile
Gila Bend
GILA BEND IND. RES.
PAINTED ROCK DAM
Agua Caliente
Sentinel
Stanfield
MARICOPA IND. RES.
P I N A L
Casa Grande
CASA GRANDE NAT'L MON.
Coolidge
Florence
Valley Farms
Randolph
Eloy
Picacho
Arizona City
Red Rock
Oracle
Mammoth
San Manuel
Kearny
Hayden
Winkelman
Riverside Stage Stop
Pinal Pk. 7,850 ft. (2393 m.)
Christmas
Y U M A
Yuma
W. Yuma
Somerton
Gadsden
San Luis
San Luis Río Colorado
YUMA DESERT
COCOPAH IND. RES.
YUMA MARINE CORPS AIR STA.
YUMA PROVING GROUND
LAGUNA DAM
IMPERIAL DAM
Imperial Res.
Laguna Res.
Dome
Roll
Tacna
Wellton
Dateland
Aztec
LECHUGUILLA DESERT
P I M A
Ajo
Why
Gu Achi
PAPAGO INDIAN RESERVATION
Quijotoa
Pisinimo
ORGAN PIPE CACTUS NAT'L MON.
Lukeville
Sonoyta
Kitt Peak 6,875 ft. (2096 m.)
Sells
Topawa
Marana
Mt. Lemmon 9,196 ft. (2803 m.)
Silver Bell
SAGUARO NAT'L MON.
Rillito
Cortaro
Oro Valley
TUCSON
S. Tucson
DAVIS MONTHAN A.F.B.
Tanque Verde
Vail
Rincon Pk. 8,532
SAN XAVIER IND. RES.
Sahuarita
Green Valley
Continental
Greaterville
Amado
Madera Canyon
Sonoita
Elgin
Arivaca
Tubac
TUMACACORI NAT'L MON.
Tumacacori
Carmen
Patagonia
Sasabe
S A N T A   C R U Z
Rio Rico
Nogales
FT. HUACHUCA
Huachuca City
Sierra Vista
Huachuca Pk. 8,406 ft. (2562 m.)
Miller Pk. 9,466 ft. (2885 m.)
Hereford
CORONADO NATIONAL MEMORIAL
Bisbee
Naco
Douglas
Paul Spur
C O C H I S E
Benson
St. David
Pomerene
Dragoon
Willcox
Dos Cabezas
Cochise
Bowie
San Simon
FT. BOWIE NAT'L HIST. SITE
CHIRICAHUA NAT'L MON.
Hilltop
Paradise
Portal
Pearce
Sunsites
Gleeson
Tombstone
Elfrida
McNeal
Fairbank
Heroica Nogales
Agua Prieta
Santa Cruz
Cananea
Mesa del Rio
Fronteras
Imuris
Magdalena
Caborca
Pitiquito
Altar
Río de la Concepción
Puerto Peñasco
Bahía de Adair
I. Montague

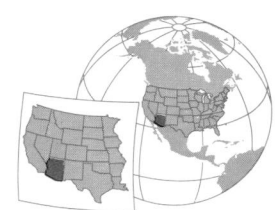

AREA 114,000 sq. mi. (295,260 sq. km.)
POPULATION 3,677,985
CAPITAL Phoenix
LARGEST CITY Phoenix
HIGHEST POINT Humphreys Pk. 12,633 ft.
(3851 m.)
SETTLED IN 1752
ADMITTED TO UNION February 14, 1912
POPULAR NAME Grand Canyon State
STATE FLOWER Saguaro Cactus Blossom
STATE BIRD Cactus Wren

Agriculture, Industry and Resources

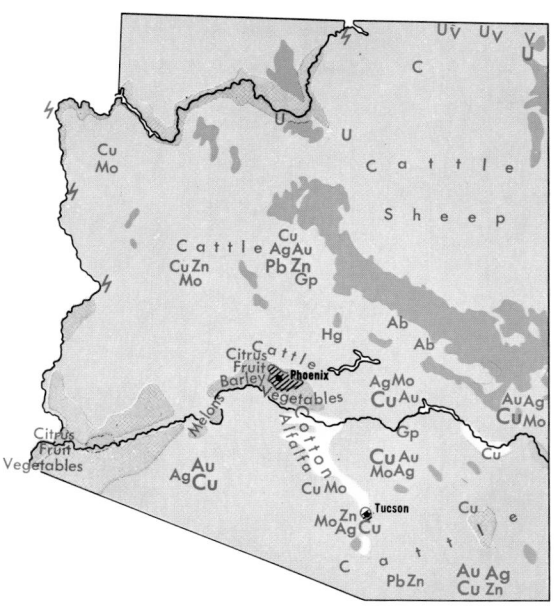

MAJOR MINERAL OCCURRENCES

Ab	Asbestos	Cu	Copper	Pb	Lead
Ag	Silver	Gp	Gypsum	U	Uranium
Au	Gold	Hg	Mercury	V	Vanadium
C	Coal	Mo	Molybdenum	Zn	Zinc

DOMINANT LAND USE

Fruit, Truck and Mixed Farming

Cotton and Alfalfa

General Farming, Livestock, Special Crops

Range Livestock

Forests

Nonagricultural Land

⚡ Water Power

▨ Major Industrial Areas

COUNTIES

Apache 61,591	F3
Cochise 97,624	F7
Coconino 96,591	C3
Gila 40,216	E5
Graham 26,554	E6
Greenlee 8,008	F5
La Paz 13,844	A5
Maricopa 2,122,101	C5
Mohave 93,497	A3
Navajo 77,658	E3
Pima 666,880	D6
Pinal 116,379	D6
Santa Cruz 29,676	E7
Yavapai 107,714	C4
Yuma 106,895	A5

CITIES and TOWNS

Agua Caliente 60	B6
Aguila 900	B5
Ajo 2,919	C6
Alpine 450	F5
Amado 75	D7
Apache Junction 18,100	D5
Arcosanti	C4
Aripine 25	E4
Arivaca 400	D7
Arizona City 1,940	D6
Arizona Sunsites 825	F7
Arlington 950	C5
Ash Fork 800	C3
Avondale 16,169	C5
Aztec 20	B6
Bagdad 1,858	B4
Bapchule 400	D5

Bellemont 210	D3
Benson 3,824	E7
Bisbee▲ 6,288	F7
Black Canyon City 1,811	C4
Blue 50	F5
Bonita 20	E6
Bouse 500	A5
Bowie 600	F6
Buckeye 5,038	C5
Bullhead City (Bullhead City-Riviera) 21,951	A3
Bumble Bee 15	C4
Bylas 1,219	E5
Calva 10	E5
Cameron 493	D3
Camp Verde 6,243	D4
Cane Beds 30	B2
Carefree 1,666	C5
Carmen 200	D7
Casa Grande 19,082	D6
Cashion 3,014	C5
Castle Hot Springs 50	C5
Cave Creek 2,925	D5
Central 300	F6
Central Heights (Central Heights-Midland City) 2,791	E5
Chambers 500	F3
Chandler 90,533	D5
Cherry 20	C4
Chinle 5,059	F2
Chino Valley 4,837	C4
Chloride 225	A3
Christmas 201	E5
Cibecue 1,254	E4
Clarkdale 2,144	C4

Clay Springs 500	E4
Claypool 1,942	E5
Clemenceau 300	C4
Clifton▲ 2,840	F5
Cochise 150	F6
Colorado City 2,426	B2
Concho 100	F4
Congress 800	C4
Continental 250	D7
Coolidge 6,927	D6
Coolidge Dam 42	E5
Cornfields 200	F3
Cornville 2,089	D4
Cortaro 375	D6
Cottonwood 5,918	D4
Crown King 100	C4
Dateland 100	B6
Davis Dam 125	A3
Dennehotso 616	F2
Dewey 100	C4
Dilkon 90	E3
Dolan Springs 1,090	A3
Dos Cabezas 30	F6
Douglas 12,822	F7
Dragoon 150	F6
Duncan 662	F6
Eagar 4,025	F4
Eden 89	F6
Ehrenberg 1,226	A5
El Mirage 5,001	C5
Elfrida 700	F7
Elgin 525	E7
Eloy 7,211	D6
Empire Landing	A4
Fairbank 100	E7
Flagstaff▲ 45,857	D3

(continued on following page)

Topography

0   50   100 MI.

0   50   100 KM.

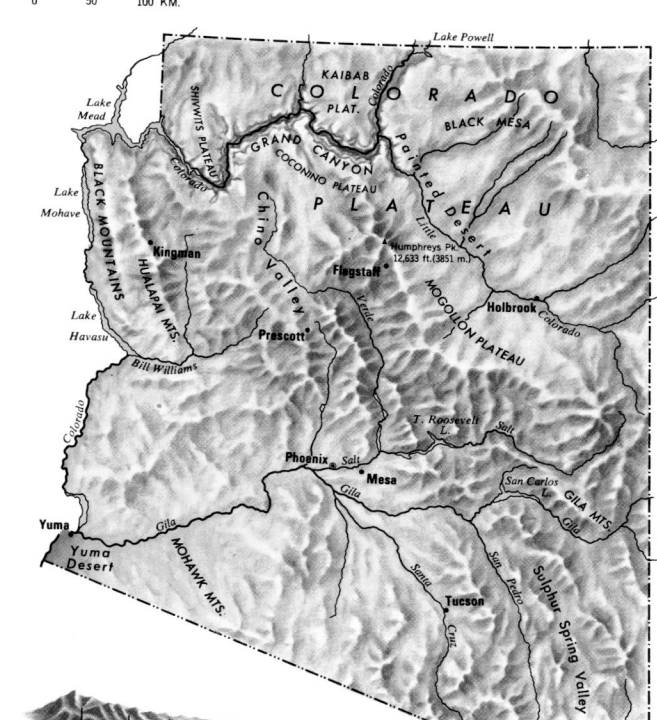

5,000 m. 16,404 ft. | 2,000 m. 6,562 ft. | 1,000 m. 3,281 ft. | 500 m. 1,640 ft. | 200 m. 656 ft. | 100 m. 328 ft. | Sea Level | Below

Florence▲ 7,510 D5
Florence Junction 35 D5
Fort Apache 500 F5
Fort Defiance 4,489 F3
Fort Grant 240 E6
Fort Thomas 450 E5
Fountain Hills 10,030 D5
Franklin 300 F6
Fredonia 1,207 C2
Gadsden 250 A6
Ganado 1,257 F3
Geronimo 25 F5
Gila Bend 1,747 C6
Gilbert 29,188 D5
Gleeson 15 F7
Glendale 148,134 C5
Globe▲ 6,062 E5
Golden Shores A4
Goodyear 6,258 C5
Grand Canyon 1,348 C2
Greaterville 15 E7
Green Valley 13,231 D7
Greer 385 F4
Gu Achi 339 C6
Hackberry 250 B3
Happy Jack 50 D4
Hayden 909 E5
Heber 1,581 E4
Hereford 10 E7
Higley 500 D5
Hillside 100 B4
Hilltop 9 F6
Holbrook▲ 4,686 E4
Hotevilla 869 E3
Houck 900 F3
Huachuca City 1,782 E7
Humboldt 787 C4
Indian Wells 150 E3
Inspiration 500 D5
Iron Springs 175 C4
Jacob Lake 16 C2
Jeddito 20 E3
Jerome 403 C4
Joseph City 650 E4
Kaibito 641 D2
Katherine 102 A3
Kayenta 4,372 E2
Keams Canyon 393 E3
Kearny 2,262 E5
Kingman▲ 12,722 A3
Kirkland 100 C4
Klagetoh 200 F3
Klondyke 86 E6
Kohls Ranch 100 D4
Komatke 1,116 C5
Lake Havasu City 24,363 A4
Lake Montezuma 1,841 D4
Lakeside 1,333 E4
Laveen 800 C5
Lees Ferry 10 D2
Leupp 857 E3
Liberty 150 C5
Linden 50 E4
Litchfield Park 3,303 C5
Littlefield 40 B2
Lukachukai 113 F2
Lukeville 50 C7
Lupton 250 F3
Madera Canyon 75 E7
Mammoth 1,845 E6
Many Farms 1,294 F2
Marana 2,187 D6
Marble Canyon 6 D2
Maricopa 750 C5
Maverick 50 F5
Mayer 810 C4
McNary 355 F4
McNeal 100 F7
Mesa 288,091 D5
Miami 2,018 E5
Mobile 100 C5
Moccasin 150 C2
Moenkopi 924 D2
Morenci 1,799 F5
Mormon Lake 20 D4
Morristown 400 C5
Mount Lemmon 400 E6
Mount Trumbull 14 B2
Naco 750 E7
Navajo 100 F3
Nelson 39 B3
Nogales▲ 19,489 E7
North Rim 50 C2
Nutrioso 500 F5
Oatman 175 A3
Olberg 65 D5
Oracle 3,043 E6
Oraibi 600 E3
Oro Valley 6,670 E6
Overgaard 750 E4
Page 6,598 D2
Palo Verde 500 C5
Paradise 15 F7
Paradise Valley 11,671 D5
Parker 2,897 A4
Parks 175 C3
Patagonia 888 E7
Paul Spur 34 F7
Paulden 350 C4
Payson 8,377 D4
Peach Springs 787 B3
Pearce 700 F7
Peoria 50,618 C5
Peridot 957 E5
Petrified Forest 80 F3
Phoenix (cap.)▲
983,403 C5
Picacho 850 D6
Pima 1,725 F6
Pine 800 D4
Pinedale 400 E4
Pinetop 1,527 F4
Pinon 468 E2
Pisinimo 187 C6
Plantsite F5
Polacca 1,108 E3
Pomerene 365 E6
Portal 72 F7
Poston 480 A4
Prescott▲ 26,455 C4
Prescott Valley 8,858 C4
Quartzsite 1,876 A5
Queen Creek 2,667 D5
Quijotoa 200 C6
Randolph 350 D6
Red Rock 250 D6
Rillito 400 D6
Rimrock 217 D4
Rio Rico 1,407 E7
Riverside Stage Stop 418 D5
Riviera (Riviera-
Bullhead City) A3
Roll 700 A6
Roosevelt 125 D5
Sacaton 1,452 D5
Safford▲ 7,359 F6
Sahuarita 200 E7
Saint David 1,468 E7
Saint Johns▲ 3,294 F4
Saint Michaels 1,119 F3
Salome 800 B5
San Carlos 2,918 E5
San Luis 4,212 A6
San Manuel 4,009 E6
San Simon 400 F6
Sanders 900 F3
Sasabe 50 D7
Scottsdale 130,069 D5
Second Mesa 929 E3
Sedona 7,720 D4
Seligman 510 B3
Sells 2,750 D7
Sentinel 40 B6
Shonto 710 E2
Show Low 5,019 F4
Shungopavy
(Shongopovi) 570 E3
Sierra Vista 32,983 E7
Silver Bell 900 D6
Skull Valley 250 C4
Snowflake 3,510 E4
Solomon 700 F6
Somerton 5,282 A6
Sonoita 220 E7
South Tucson 5,093 D6
Springerville 1,802 F4
Stanfield 150 C6
Stargo 1,038 F5
Steamboat 100 F3
Sun City 38,126 C5
Supai 423 C2
Superior 3,468 D5
Surprise 7,122 C5
Tacna 950 B6
Tanque Verde 850 E6
Taylor 2,418 E4
Teec Nos Pos 317 F2
Tempe 141,865 D5
Temple Bar 84 A2
Thatcher 3,763 F6
Tolleson 4,434 C5
Tombstone 1,220 F7
Tonalea 125 E2
Tonopah 54 B5
Tonto Basin 250 D5
Topawa 500 D7
Topock 325 A4
Tortilla Flat 37 D5
Tsaile 1,043 F2
Tuba City 7,323 D2
Tubac 140 E7
Tucson▲ 405,390 D6
Tumacacori 100 E7
Vail 175 E6
Valentine 120 B3
Valley Farms 240 D6
Vernon 75 F4
Vicksburg 16 B5
Waddell 100 C5
Wellton 1,066 A6
Wenden 400 B5
West Yuma A6
Whiteriver 3,775 E5
Why 65 C6
Wickenburg 4,515 C5
Wikieup 150 B4
Willcox 3,122 F6
Williams 2,532 C3
Window Rock 3,306 F3
Winkelman 676 E6
Winona 25 D3
Winslow 8,190 E3
Wintersburg 400 B5
Wittmann 600 C5
Woodruff 280 E4
Yarnell 800 C4
Yava 40 C4
Young 500 D4
Youngtown 2,542 C5
Yucca 250 A4
Yuma▲ 54,923 A6

OTHER FEATURES

Agassiz (peak) D3
Agua Fria (riv.) C5
Alamo (lake) B4
Apache (lake) D5
Aquarius (range) B4
Aravaipa (creek) E6
Aubrey (cliffs) B3
Baboquivari (mts.) D7
Baker Butte (mt.) D4
Balakai (mesa) F3
Baldy (peak) F5
Bartlett (dam) D5
Bartlett (res.) D5
Big Chino Wash (dry riv.) C3
Big Horn (mts.) B5
Big Sandy (riv.) B4
Bill Williams (riv.) B4
Black (mesa) E2
Black (mts.) A3
Black (riv.) E5
Blue (riv.) F5
Bouse Wash (dry riv.) A4
Buckskin (mts.) B4
Burro (creek) B4
Canyon (lake) D5
Canyon de Chelly Nat'l Mon. F2
Carrizo (creek) E4
Carrizo (mts.) F2
Casa Grande Ruins Nat'l Mon. D6
Castle Dome (mts.) A5
Cataract (creek) C3
Centennial Wash (dry riv.) B5
Cerbat (mts.) A3
Cherry (creek) E4
Chevelon (creek) E4
Chinle (creek) F2
Chinle (valley) F2
Chinle Wash (dry riv.) F2
Chino (valley) C3
Chiricahua (mts.) F6
Chiricahua Nat'l Mon. F6
Chocolate (mts.) A5
Clear (creek) D4
Coconino (plat.) C3
Cocopah Ind. Res. A6
Colorado (riv.) A5
Colorado River Ind. Res. A5
Coolidge (dam) E5
Copper (mts.) B6
Corn (creek) E3
Coronado Nat'l Memorial E7
Cottonwood (cliffs) B3
Cottonwood Wash (dry riv.) E4
Davis (dam) A3
Defiance (plat.) F3
Detrital Wash (dry riv.) A3
Diablo (canyon) D4
Dinnebito Wash (dry riv.) E3
Dot Klish (canyon) E2
Dragoon (mts.) F7
Eagle (creek) F5
East Verde (riv.) D4
Echo (cliffs) D2
Elden (mt.) D3
Fort Apache Ind.Res. E5
Fort Bowie Nat'l Hist. Site F6
Fort Huachuca E7
Fort McDowell Ind. Res. D5
Fort Mohave Ind. Res. A4
Fort Pearce Wash (dry riv.) B2
Fossil (creek) D4
Four Peaks (mt.) D5
Galiuro (mts.) E6
Gila (mts.) A6
Gila (mts.) F5
Gila (riv.) B6
Gila Bend (mts.) B5
Gila Bend Ind. Res. C6
Gila River Ind. Res. C5
Glen Canyon (dam) D2
Glen Canyon Nat'l Rec. Area E1
Gothic (mesa) F2
Government (mt.) C3
Graham (mt.) F6
Grand Canyon Nat'l Park C2
Grand Wash (butte) B2
Grand Wash (riv.) B2
Greens (peak) F4
Growler (mts.) B6
Harcuvar (mts.) B5
Harquahala (mts.) B5
Hassayampa (riv.) C5
Havasu (lake) A4
Havasupai Ind. Res. C2
Hohokam-Pima Nat'l Mon. D5
Hoover (dam) A2
Hopi (buttes) E3
Hopi Ind. Res. E2
Horseshoe (lake) D5
Huachuca (peak) E7
Hualapai (mts.) B4
Hualapai (peak) B3
Hualapai Ind. Res. B3
Hubbell Trading Post
Nat'l Hist. Site F3
Humphreys (peak) D3
Hurricane (cliffs) B2
Imperial (res.) A6
Ives Mesa E3
Juniper (mts.) C3
Kaibab (plat.) C2
Kaibab Ind. Res. C2
Kaibito (plat.) D2
Kanab (creek) C2
Kanab (plat.) C2
Kendrick (peak) D3
Kitt (peak) D7
Kofa (mts.) B5
Laguna (creek) E2
Laguna (res.) A6
Lake Mead Nat'l Rec. Area A2
Lechuguilla (des.) A6
Lemmon (mt.) E6
Little Colorado (riv.) D3
Lukachukai (mts.) F2
Luke A.F.B. C5
Maple (peak) F5
Marble Canyon Nat'l Mon. D2
Maricopa (mts.) C5
Maricopa Ind. Res. C6
Mazatzal (peak) D4
Mead (lake) A2
Meteor (crater) E3
Miller (peak) E7
Moencopi (plat.) D3
Moenkopi Wash (dry riv.) D2
Mogollon (plat.) D4
Mogollon Rim (cliffs) D4
Mohave (lake) A3
Mohave (mts.) A4
Mohawk (mts.) B6
Montezuma Castle Nat'l Mon. D4
Mormon (lake) D4
Mule (mts.) E7
Navajo (creek) D2
Navajo Ind. Res. D2
Navajo Nat'l Mon. E2
Navajo Ord. Depot D3
O'Leary (peak) D3
Oraibi Wash (dry riv.) E3
Ord (mt.) D5
Organ Pipe Cactus Nat'l Mon. C6
Painted (des.) D2
Painted Desert Section
(Petrified Forest) F3
Painted Rock (dam) C5
Papago Ind. Res. C6
Paria (plat.) D2
Paria (riv.) D1
Parker (dam) A4
Pastora (peak) F2
Peloncillo (mts.) F6
Petrified Forest Nat'l Park F4
Pinal (peak) E5
Pinaleno (mts.) F6
Pink (cliffs) E4
Pipe Spring Nat'l Mon. C2
Pleasant (lake) C5
Plomosa (mts.) A5
Polacca Wash (dry riv.) E3
Powell (lake) D1
Pueblo Colorado Wash
(dry riv.) F3
Puerco (riv.) F3
Quajote Wash (dry riv.) D6
Rainbow (plat.) D2
Rincon (peak) E6
Roof Butte (mt.) F2
Rose (peak) F5
Sacramento Wash (dry riv.) A4
Saguaro (lake) D5
Saguaro Nat'l Mon. E6
Salt (riv.) D5
Salt River Ind. Res. D5
San Carlos (lake) E5
San Carlos (riv.) E5
San Carlos Ind. Res. E5
Sand Tank (mt.) C6
San Francisco (riv.) F5
San Pedro (riv.) E6
San Simon (riv.) F6
Santa Catalina (mts.) E6
Santa Cruz (riv.) D6
Santa Maria (riv.) B4
Santa Rosa Wash (dry riv.) D6
San Xavier Ind. Res. D6
Sauceda (mts.) C6
Shivwits (plat.) B2
Shonto (plat.) E2
Sierra Ancha (mts.) D5
Sierra Apache (mts.) E5
Silver (creek) E4
Slate (mt.) D3
Sulphur Spring (valley) F6
Sunset Crater Nat'l Mon. D3
Superstition (mts.) D5
Theodore Roosevelt (lake) D5
Tonto (creek) D4
Tonto Nat'l Mon. D5
Trout (creek) B3
Trumbull (mt.) B2
Tumacacori Nat'l Mon. E7
Tuzigoot Nat'l Mon. D4
Tyson Wash (dry riv.) A5
Uinkaret (plat.) B2
Union (mt.) C4
Verde (riv.) D5
Virgin (mts.) B2
Walker (creek) F2
Walnut Canyon Nat'l Mon. D3
White (riv.) E5
Williams A.F.B. D5
Woody (mt.) D3
Wupatki Nat'l Mon. D3
Yuma (des.) A6
Yuma Proving Ground A6
Zuni (riv.) F4

▲County seat.

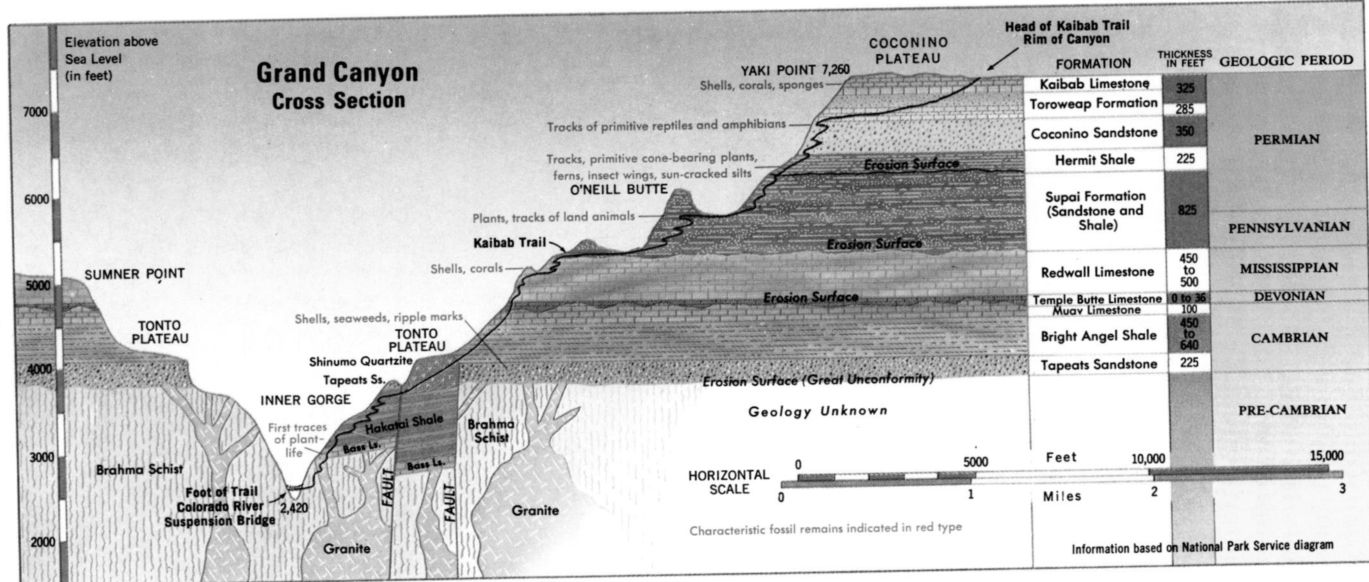
Elevation above Sea Level (in feet)
Grand Canyon
Cross Section
7000
6000
5000
4000
3000
2000
COCONINO PLATEAU
Head of Kaibab Trail
Rim of Canyon
YAKI POINT 7,260
Shells, corals, sponges
Tracks of primitive reptiles and amphibians
Tracks, primitive cone-bearing plants, ferns, insect wings, sun-cracked silts
O'NEILL BUTTE
Plants, tracks of land animals
Kaibab Trail
Shells, corals
Erosion Surface
SUMNER POINT
TONTO PLATEAU
Shells, seaweeds, ripple marks
TONTO PLATEAU
Shinumo Quartzite
Tapeats Ss.
INNER GORGE
First traces of plant-life
Hakatai Shale
Bass Ls.
Brahma Schist
FAULT
Foot of Trail
Colorado River
Suspension Bridge
2,420
Granite
Erosion Surface (Great Unconformity)
Geology Unknown
FORMATION
THICKNESS IN FEET
GEOLOGIC PERIOD
Kaibab Limestone 325
Toroweap Formation 285
Coconino Sandstone 350
Hermit Shale 225
PERMIAN
Supai Formation (Sandstone and Shale) 825
PENNSYLVANIAN
Redwall Limestone 450 to 500
MISSISSIPPIAN
Temple Butte Limestone 0 to 36
DEVONIAN
Muav Limestone 100
Bright Angel Shale 450 to 640
CAMBRIAN
Tapeats Sandstone 225
PRE-CAMBRIAN
HORIZONTAL SCALE
Feet 0 5000 10,000 15,000
Miles 0 1 2 3
Characteristic fossil remains indicated in red type
Information based on National Park Service diagram

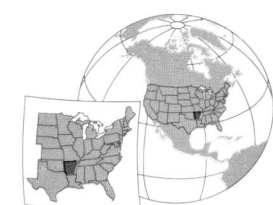

AREA 53,187 sq. mi. (137,754 sq. km.)
POPULATION 2,362,239
CAPITAL Little Rock
LARGEST CITY Little Rock
HIGHEST POINT Magazine Mtn. 2,753 ft. (839 m.)
SETTLED IN 1685
ADMITTED TO UNION June 15, 1836
POPULAR NAME Land of Opportunity
STATE FLOWER Apple Blossom
STATE BIRD Mockingbird

COUNTIES

Arkansas 21,653 .... H5
Ashley 24,319 .... G7
Baxter 31,186 .... F1
Benton 97,499 .... B1
Boone 28,297 .... D1
Bradley 11,793 .... F7
Calhoun 5,826 .... E6
Carroll 18,654 .... C1
Chicot 15,713 .... H7
Clark 21,437 .... D5
Clay 18,107 .... K1
Cleburne 19,411 .... F2
Cleveland 7,781 .... F6
Columbia 25,691 .... D7
Conway 19,151 .... E3
Craighead 68,956 .... J2
Crawford 42,493 .... B2
Crittenden 49,939 .... K3
Cross 19,225 .... J3
Dallas 9,614 .... E6
Desha 16,798 .... H6
Drew 17,369 .... G6
Faulkner 60,006 .... F3
Franklin 14,897 .... C2
Fulton 10,037 .... G1
Garland 73,397 .... D4
Grant 13,948 .... F5
Greene 31,804 .... J1
Hempstead 21,621 .... C6
Hot Spring 26,115 .... E5
Howard 13,569 .... C5
Independence 31,192 .... G2
Izard 11,364 .... G1
Jackson 18,944 .... H2
Jefferson 85,487 .... G5
Johnson 18,221 .... C2
Lafayette 9,643 .... C7
Lawrence 17,457 .... H1
Lee 13,053 .... J4
Lincoln 13,690 .... G6
Little River 13,966 .... B6
Logan 20,557 .... C3
Lonoke 39,268 .... G4
Madison 11,618 .... C1
Marion 12,001 .... E1
Miller 38,467 .... C7
Mississippi 57,525 .... K2
Monroe 11,333 .... H4
Montgomery 7,841 .... C4
Nevada 10,101 .... D6
Newton 7,666 .... D2
Ouachita 30,574 .... E6
Perry 7,969 .... E4
Phillips 28,838 .... J5
Pike 10,086 .... C5
Poinsett 24,664 .... J2
Polk 17,347 .... B5
Pope 45,883 .... D3
Prairie 9,518 .... G4
Pulaski 349,660 ...... F4
Randolph 16,558 ..... H1
Saint Francis 30,858 . J3
Saline 64,183 .... E4
Scott 10,205 .... B4
Searcy 7,841 .... E2
Sebastian 99,590 .. B3
Sevier 13,637 ...... B6
Sharp 14,109 ...... G1
Stone 9,775 .... F2
Union 46,719 ..... E7
Van Buren 14,008 . E2
Washington 113,409 . B2
White 54,676 ...... G3
Woodruff 9,520 .. H3
Yell 17,759 ...... D3

CITIES and TOWNS

Adona 146 .... E3
Alco 200 .... F2
Alexander 201 .... F4
Alicia 157 .... H2
Alix 225 .... C3
Alleene 200 .... B6
Allport 188 .... G4
Alma 2,959 .... B3
Almyra 311 .... H5
Alpena 319 .... D1
Altheimer 972 .... G5
Altus 433 .... C2
Amagon 108 .... H2
Amity 526 .... D5
Antoine 160 .... D5
Arkadelphia▲ 10,014 ..... D5
Arkansas City▲ 523 ...... H6
Armorel 500 .... L2
Ash Flat▲ 667 .... G1
Ashdown▲ 5,150 .... B6
Athens C5
Atkins 2,834 .... E3
Aubrey 204 .... J4
Augusta▲ 2,759 .... H3
Austin 235 .... G4
Avoca 269 .... B1
Bald Knob 2,653 .... G3
Banks 88 .... F6

Barling 4,078 .... B3
Bassett 199 .... K2
Bates 9,187 .... B4
Batesville▲ 8,263 .... G2
Bauxite 412 .... F4
Bay 1,660 .... J2
Bearden 1,021 .... E6
Beaver 57 .... C1
Beebe 4,455 .... G3
Beedeville 183 .... H3
Bella Vista 9,083 ..... B1
Bellefonte 361 .... D1
Belleville 390 .... D3
Ben Lomond 157 .... B6
Benton▲ 18,177 ..... E4
Bentonville▲ 11,257 . B1
Bergman 324 .... E1
Berryville▲ 3,212 .. C1
Bethel Heights 281 . B1
Bethesda 285 ...... G2
Big Flat 93 .... F1
Bigelow 340 ...... E3
Biggers 337 ...... J1
Birdsong 104 .... K3
Birta D3
Biscoe 486 ...... H4
Black Oak 277 ... K2
Black Rock 736 .. H1
Black Springs 97 . C5
Blevins 253 ..... C6
Blue Eye 38 .... D1
Blue Mountain 146 . C3
Bluff City 227 .. D6
Blytheville▲ 22,906 . L2
Bodcaw 161 ... D6
Bonanza 520 .. B3
Bono 1,220 .. J2
Booneville▲ 3,804 . C3
Bradford 874 .. G3
Bradley 585 .. C7
Branch 299 .. C3
Brickeys J4
Brinkley 4,234 . H4
Brookland 919 . J2
Bryant 5,269 .. F4
Buckner 325 .. D7
Bull Shoals 1,534 . E1
Burdette 148 .. L2
Cabot 8,319 .. F4
Caddo Valley 389 . D5
Caldwell 334 .. J3
Cale 70 ...... D6
Calico Rock 938 . F1
Calion 558 ... E7
Camden▲ 14,380 . E6
Cammack Village 828 . E4
Campbell Station 247 . H2
Canfield 365 ...... C7
Caraway 1,178 .... K2
Carlisle 2,253 .... G4
Carthage 452 ..... E5
Casa 200 .... D3
Cash 214 .... J2
Cass 225 ...... C2
Casscoe 297 .. H4
Caulksville 224 . C3
Cave City 1,503 . G2
Cave Springs 465 . B1
Cedarville 375 .. B2
Center Point ... C5
Centerton 491 .. B1
Centerville 300 . D3
Central City 419 . B3
Charleston▲ 2,128 . B3
Cherokee Village (Cherokee
  Village-Hidden Valley)
  4,416 .... G1
Cherry Hill 250 ... B4
Cherry Valley 659 . J3
Chester 125 ..... B2

Danville▲ 1,585 .... D3
Dardanelle▲ 3,722 .... D3
Datto 120 .... J1
De Queen▲ 4,633 .... B5
De Valls Bluff▲ 702 ..... H4
De Witt▲ 3,553 .... H5
Decatur 918 .... A1
Delaplaine 146 .... J1
Delight 311 .... C5
Dell 258 .... K2
Denning 206 .... C3
Dermott 4,715 ...... H7
Des Arc▲ 2,001 .... G4
Diamond City 601 .. E1
Diaz 1,363 .... H2
Dierks 1,263 ..... B5
Donaldson 300 .. E5
Dover 1,055 .... D3
Dryden J2
Dumas 5,520 . H6
Dyer 502 .... B3
Dyess 466 .. K2
Earle 3,393 . K3
East Camden 783 . E6
Edmondson 286 .. K3
El Dorado▲ 23,146 . E7
Elaine 846 ...... J5
Elkins 692 ..... C1
Elm Springs 893 . B1
Emerson 317 ... D7
Emmet 446 .... D6
England 3,351 . G4
Enola 179 .... F3
Eudora 3,155 . H7
Eureka Springs▲ 1,900 . C1
Evening Shade 328 .. G1
Everton 150 ...... E1
Fargo 140 ...... H4
Farmington 1,322 . B1
Fayetteville▲ 42,099 . B1
Felsenthal 95 .... F7
Fifty-Six 156 .... F2
Fisher 245 ..... J2
Flippin 1,006 .. E1
Fordyce▲ 4,729 . F6
Foreman 1,267 . B6
Formosa 224 .. E3
Forrest City▲ 13,364 . J3
Fort Smith▲ 72,798 . B3
Fouke 634 ..... C7
Fountain Hill 195 . G7
Franklin 205 ... G1
Fredonia (Biscoe) 484 . H4
Friendship 160 . E5
Fulton 269 .... C6
Garfield 308 .. C1
Garland City 415 . C7
Garner 191 .. G3
Gassville 1,167 . F1
Gateway 65 .. C1
Genoa 350 .. C7
Gentry 1,726 . A1
Georgetown 126 . G3
Gillett 883 .... H5
Gillham 210 .. B5
Gilmore 331 .. K3
Glenwood 1,354 . C5
Goodwin 225 .. J4
Goshen 589 .. C1
Gosnell 3,783 . K2
Gould 1,470 .. G6
Grady 586 .. G5
Grannis 507 . B5
Gravelly 300 . C4
Gravette 1,412 . B1
Green Forest 2,050 . D1
Greenbrier 2,130 . F3
Greenland 757 . B1
Greenway 212 . K1
Greenwood▲ 3,984 . B3
Greers Ferry 724 . F2
Griffithville 237 . G3
Grubbs 528 .. H2
Guion 93 .... G2
Gum Springs 157 . D5
Gurdon 2,199 . D6
Guy 241 .... F3
Hackett 490 . B3
Halley H6
Hamburg▲ 3,098 . G7
Hampton▲ 1,562 . F6
Hardy 538 .. H1
Harrell 258 . F7
Harrisburg▲ 1,943 . J2
Harrison▲ 9,922 . D1
Hartford 721 . B3
Hartman 498 . C3
Haskell 1,342 . E4
Hatfield 414 . B5
Havana 358 . D3
Haynes 268 . J4
Hazen 1,668 . G4
Heber Springs▲ 5,628 . G2
Hector 478 .. E3
Helena▲ 7,491 . J4
Hensley 500 . F4
Hermitage 639 . F7
Hickory Ridge 436 . J3

Chidester 489 .... D6
Clarendon▲ 2,072 .... H4
Clarkedale 300 .... K3
Clarksville▲ 5,833 .... D3
Cleveland D3
Clinton▲ 2,213 .... F2
Coal Hill 912 .... C3
College City 339 ...... J1
Collins G6
Colt 334 .... J3
Columbus 265 .... C6
Concord 262 .... G2
Conway▲ 26,481 ... F3
Cord 250 .... H2
Corinth 63 ...... C3
Corning▲ 3,323 . J1
Cotter 867 ..... E1
Cotton Plant 1,150 . H3
Cove 346 ..... B5
Coy 142 .... G4
Crawfordsville 617 . K3
Crossett 6,282 . G7
Crystal Springs 215 . D5
Curtis 300 ..... D6
Cushman 428 .. G2
Daisy 122 .... C5
Dalark E5
Damascus 246 . F3

Agriculture, Industry and Resources

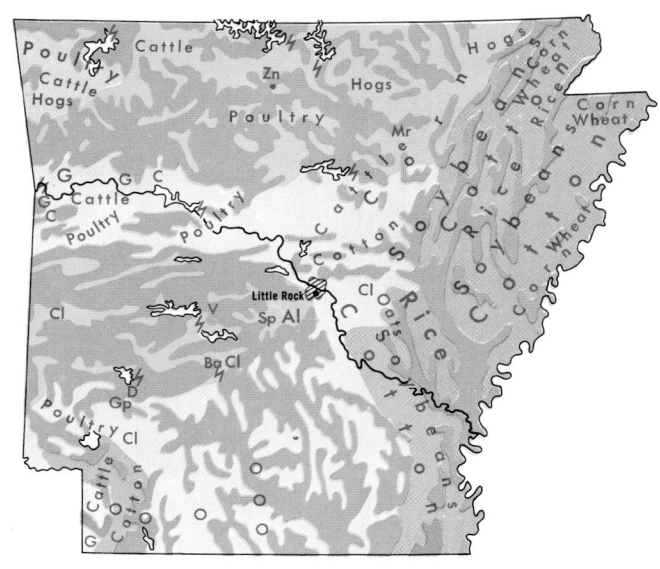

DOMINANT LAND USE

- Fruit and Mixed Farming
- Specialized Cotton
- Cotton, General Farming
- Rice, General Farming
- General Farming, Livestock, Truck Farming, Cotton
- Forests
- Swampland, Limited Agriculture

MAJOR MINERAL OCCURRENCES

Al	Bauxite	Gp	Gypsum
Ba	Barite	Mr	Marble
C	Coal	O	Petroleum
Cl	Clay	Sp	Soapstone
D	Diamonds	V	Vanadium
G	Natural Gas	Zn	Zinc

⚡ Water Power   ▨ Major Industrial Areas

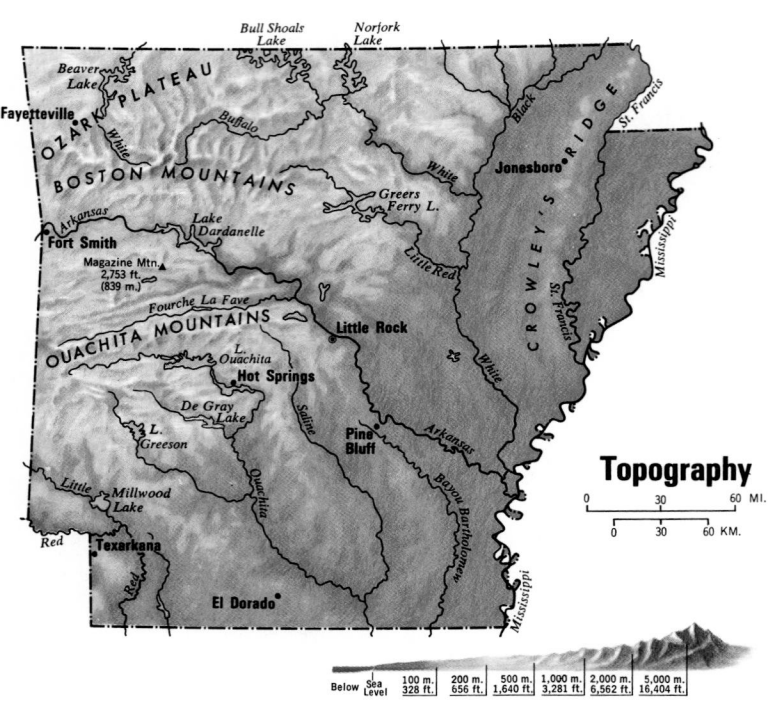

Topography

Bull Shoals Lake • Norfork Lake

Beaver Lake • Fayetteville • OZARK PLATEAU • Buffalo • BOSTON MOUNTAINS • White • Jonesboro • CROWLEY'S RIDGE • St. Francis

Fort Smith • Arkansas • Lake Dardanelle • Greers Ferry L. • Little Red • Black

Magazine Mtn. 2,753 ft. (839 m.) • Fourche La Fave • OUACHITA MOUNTAINS • Little Rock • White • Mississippi

Hot Springs • L. Ouachita • Saline • Francis

De Gray Lake • Pine Bluff • Arkansas

L. Greeson • Ouachita • Bayou Bartholomew

Little • Millwood Lake • Red • Texarkana • El Dorado • Mississippi

| | Below Sea Level | 100 m. 328 ft. | 200 m. 656 ft. | 500 m. 1,640 ft. | 1,000 m. 3,281 ft. | 2,000 m. 6,562 ft. | 5,000 m. 16,404 ft. |

SCALE: 0 30 60 MI. / 0 30 60 KM.

Higden 92 ....F2
Higginson 255 ....G3
Highfill 84 ....B1
Hindsville 69 ....C1
Holly Grove 675 ....H4
Hon 250 ....B4
Hope▲ 9,643 ....C6
Hopper C5
Horatio 793 ....B6
Horseshoe Bend 2,239 ....G1
Hot Springs National Park▲ 32,462 ....D4
Houston 149 ....E3
Hoxie 2,676 ....H1
Hughes 1,810 ....J4
Humnoke 311 ....G4
Humphrey 743 ....G5
Hunter 137 ....H3
Huntington 715 ....B3
Huntsville▲ 1,605 ....C1
Huttig 831 ....F7
Imboden 616 ....H1
Jacksonport 264 ....H2
Jacksonville 29,101 ....F4
Jamestown G2
Jasper▲ 332 ....D1
Jefferson 250 ....F5
Jericho 210 ....K3
Jerusalem 300 ....E3
Jessieville 350 ....D4
Johnson 599 ....B1
Joiner 645 ....K3
Jones Mills 210 ....E5
Jonesboro▲ 46,535 ....J2
Judsonia 1,915 ....G3
Junction City 674 ....E7
Keiser 805 ....K2
Kelso H6
Kensett 1,741 ....G3
Keo 154 ....G4
Kibler 931 ....B3
Kingsland 395 ....F6
Kirby 800 ....C5
Knobel 317 ....J1
Knoxville 239 ....D3
Ladelle G7
Lafe 315 ....J1
Lake City▲ 1,833 ....K2
Lake Frances B1
Lake View 526 ....J5
Lake Village▲ 2,791 ....H7
Lakeview 485 ....E1
Lamar 768 ....D3
Lavaca 1,253 ....B3
Lawson 250 ....F7
Leachville 1,743 ....K2
Lead Hill 283 ....D1
Leola 476 ....E5
Lepanto 2,033 ....K2
Leslie 446 ....E2
Letona 218 ....G3
Lewisville▲ 1,424 ....C7
Lexa 295 ....J4
Lincoln 1,460 ....B2
Little Flock 944 ....B1
Little Rock (cap.)▲ 175,795 ....F4
Lockesburg 608 ....B6
London 825 ....D3
Lonoke▲ 4,022 ....G4
Lonsdale 127 ....E4
Louann 158 ....E7
Lowell 1,224 ....B1

Lundell 250 ....H5
Luxora 1,338 ....K2
Lynn 299 ....H2
Mabelvale 350 ....F4
Madison 1,263 ....J4
Magazine 799 ....C3
Magness 158 ....H2
Magnet Cove 230 ....E5
Magnolia▲ 11,151 ....D7
Malvern▲ 9,256 ....E5
Mammoth Spring 1,097 ....G1
Manila 2,635 ....K2
Mansfield 1,018 ....B3
Marianna▲ 5,910 ....J4
Marie 129 ....K2
Marked Tree 3,100 ....K2
Marmaduke 1,164 ....K1
Marshall▲ 1,318 ....E2
Marvell 1,545 ....J4
Mayflower 1,415 ....F4
Maynard 354 ....J1
McCaskill 75 ....C6
McCrory 1,971 ....H3
McDougal 208 ....K1
McGehee 4,997 ....H6
McNab 95 ....C6
McNeil 686 ....D7
McRae 669 ....G3
Melbourne▲ 1,562 ....G1
Mellwood 250 ....H5
Menifee 355 ....E3
Mena▲ 5,475 ....B4
Midland 220 ....B3
Mineral Springs 1,004 ....C6
Minturn 124 ....H2
Mitchell 513 ....G1
Mitchellville 618 ....H6
Monette 1,115 ....K2
Monroe 250 ....H4
Monticello▲ 8,116 ....G6
Montrose 528 ....H7
Moorefield 160 ....G2
Moro 287 ....H4
Morrilton▲ 6,551 ....E3
Morrison Bluff 84 ....D3
Moscow 325 ....G5
Mount Holly 250 ....E7
Mount Ida▲ 775 ....C4
Mount Pleasant 422 ....G2
Mount Vernon 192 ....F3
Mountain Home▲ 9,027 ....F1
Mountain Pine 866 ....D4
Mountain View▲ 2,439 ....F2
Mountainburg 488 ....B2
Mulberry 1,448 ....B2
Murfreesboro▲ 1,542 ....C5
Nashville▲ 4,639 ....C6
Newhope 300 ....C5
New Jenny Lind 250 ....B3
Newport▲ 7,459 ....H2
Nimmons 96 ....K1
Noble Lake 250 ....G5
Norfork 394 ....F1
Norman 382 ....C5
Norphlet 706 ....E7
Norristown 250 ....D3
North Crossett 3,358 ....G7
North Little Rock 61,741 ....F4
Norvell K3
O'Kean 291 ....J1

Oak Grove 231 ....C1
Oden 126 ....C4
Ogden 264 ....B6
Oil Trough 208 ....G2
Okolona 113 ....D5
Ola 1,090 ....D3
Omaha 207 ....D1
Oppelo 643 ....E3
Osceola▲ 8,930 ....K2
Oxford 562 ....G1
Ozan 69 ....C6
Ozark▲ 3,330 ....C3
Palestine 711 ....J4
Pangburn 630 ....G3
Paragould▲ 18,540 ....J1
Paraloma B6
Paris▲ 3,674 ....C3
Parkdale 393 ....H7
Parkin 1,847 ....J3
Parks 600 ....B4
Patterson 445 ....H3
Pea Ridge 1,620 ....B1
Peach Orchard 197 ....J1
Pearcy 400 ....D5
Perla 145 ....E5
Perry 228 ....E3
Perrytown 248 ....C6
Perryville▲ 1,141 ....E3
Piggott▲ 3,777 ....K1
Pindall 135 ....E1
Pine Bluff▲ 57,140 ....F5
Pineville 220 ....F1
Piney 2,500 ....D3
Plainview 685 ....D4
Pleasant Plains 256 ....G2
Plumerville 832 ....E3
Pocahontas▲ 6,151 ....H1
Pollard 229 ....K1
Poplar Grove 300 ....J4
Portia 521 ....H1
Portland 560 ....H7
Pottsville 984 ....D3
Powhatan 51 ....H1
Poyen 303 ....E5
Prairie Grove 1,761 ....B2
Prattsville 251 ....F5
Prescott▲ 3,673 ....D6
Princeton D6
Pruitt D1
Pyatt 185 ....E1
Quitman 632 ....F3
Ratcliff 180 ....C3
Ratio 250 ....J5
Ravenden 330 ....H1
Ravenden Springs 131 ....H1
Reader 56 ....D6
Readland 225 ....H7
Rector 2,268 ....K1
Redfield 1,082 ....F5
Reed 355 ....H6
Rena B3
Reyno 467 ....J1
Rison▲ 1,258 ....F6
Rivervale 225 ....K2
Rockport 388 ....E5
Roe 135 ....H4
Rogers 24,692 ....B1
Rondo 283 ....J4
Rose Bud 156 ....F3
Rosston 262 ....D6
Russell 180 ....G3
Russellville▲ 21,260 ....D3

Saint Charles 169 ....H5
Saint Francis 201 ....K1
Saint Paul 88 ....C2
Salado 250 ....G2
Salem▲ 1,474 ....G1
Salesville 374 ....F1
Saratoga C6
Scottsville 241 ....D3
Scranton 218 ....C3
Searcy▲ 15,180 ....G3
Sedgwick 86 ....J2
Shannon Hills 1,755 ....F4
Sheridan▲ 3,098 ....F5
Sherrill 55 ....F5
Sherwood 18,893 ....F4
Shirley 363 ....F2
Sidney 271 ....G1
Siloam Springs 8,151 ....B1
Smackover 2,232 ....E7

Smale H4
Smithville 86 ....H1
Snow Lake H5
Snyder 700 ....G7
South Lead Hill 96 ....D1
Sparkman 553 ....E6
Springdale 29,941 ....B1
Springtown B1
Stamps 2,478 ....D7
Star City▲ 2,138 ....G6
Stephens 1,137 ....E7
Steprock 600 ....G3
Strawberry 273 ....H2
Strong 624 ....F7
Stuttgart▲ 10,420 ....H4
Subiaco 538 ....C3
Success 170 ....J1
Sulphur Rock 356 ....H2
Sulphur Springs 523 ....B1

Summit 480 ....E1
Sunset 571 ....K3
Swan Lake G5
Sweet Home 350 ....F4
Swifton 830 ....H2
Taylor 621 ....D7
Texarkana▲ 22,631 ....C7
Thornton 502 ....F6
Tichnor 350 ....H5
Tillar 221 ....H6
Tinsman 69 ....F6
Tollette 316 ....C6
Tontitown 460 ....B1
Traskwood 488 ....E5
Trumann 6,304 ....J2
Tucker 2,020 ....G5
Tuckerman 2,078 ....H2
Tull 313 ....E5
Tupelo 208 ....H3

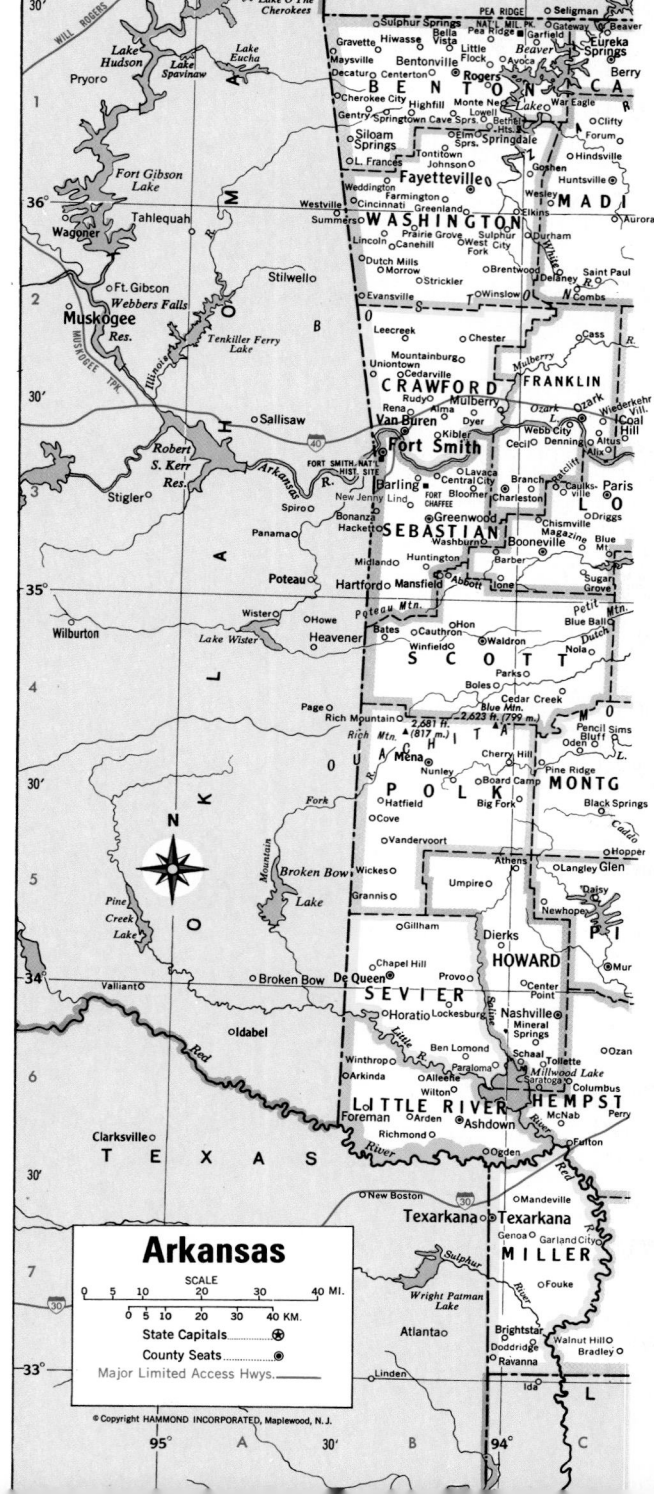

Arkansas

SCALE
0 5 10 20 30 40 MI.
0 5 10 20 30 40 KM.

State Capitals ⊛
County Seats ◉
Major Limited Access Hwys.

© Copyright HAMMOND INCORPORATED, Maplewood, N.J.

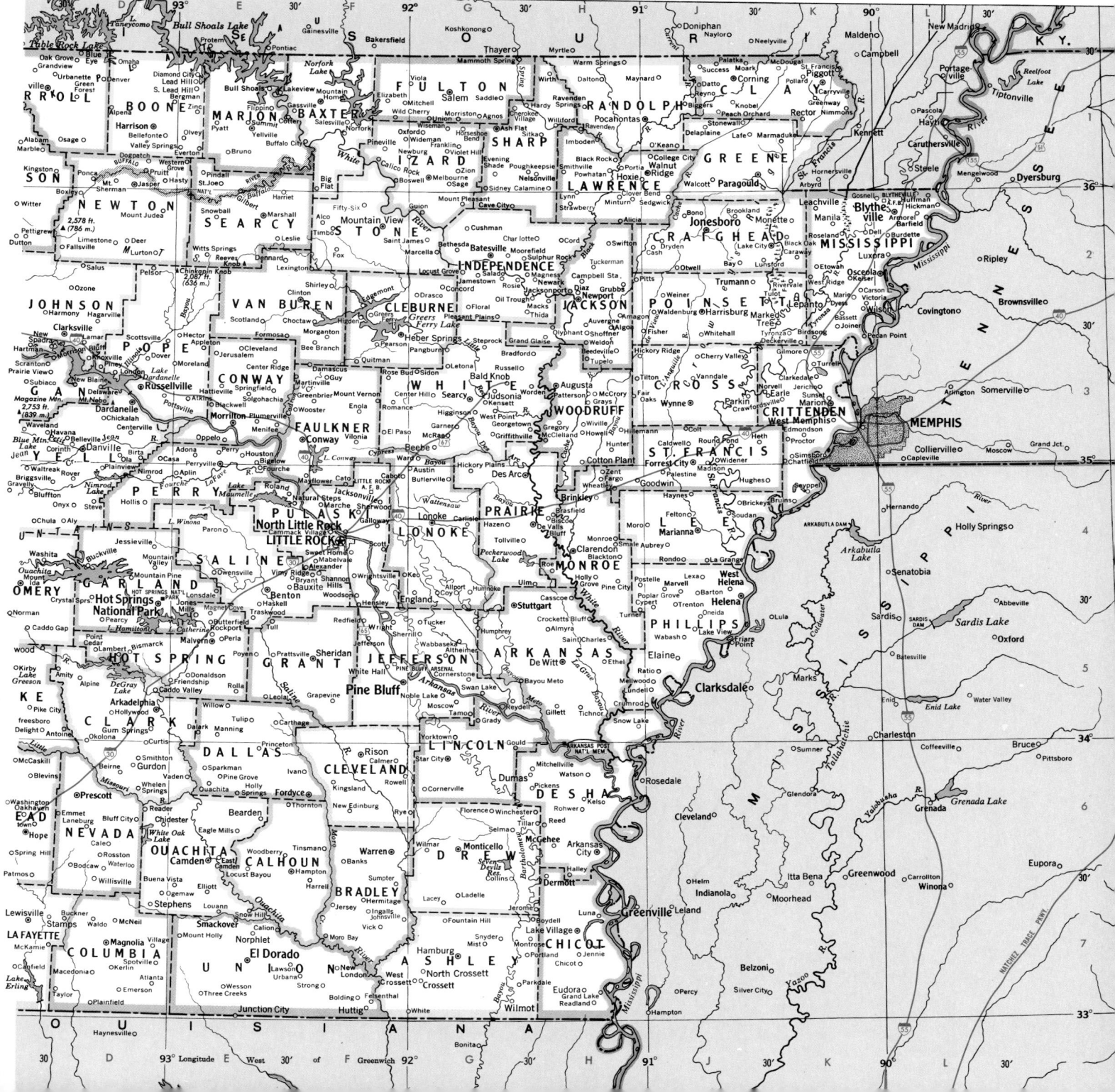

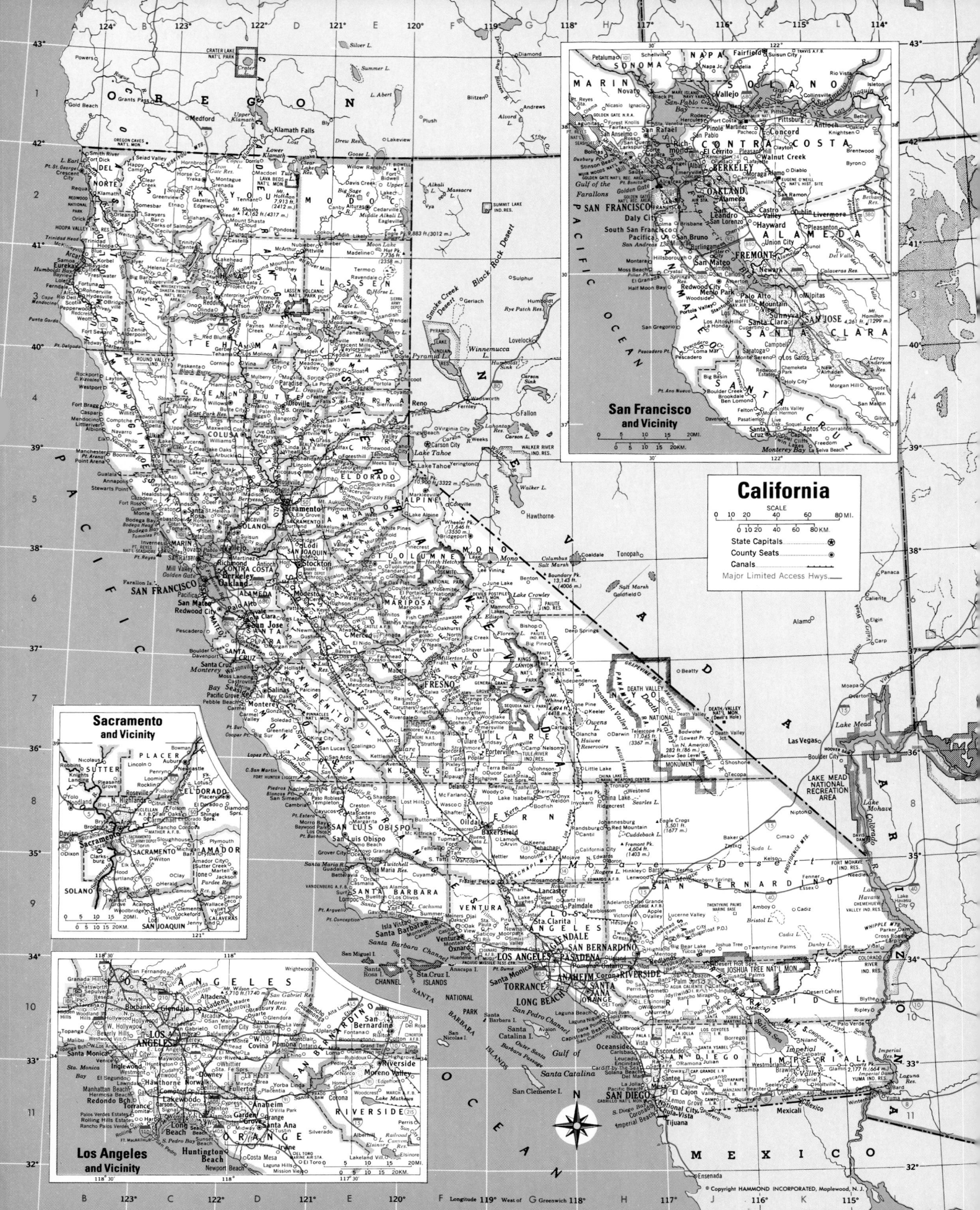
California
SCALE
0 10 20 40 60 80 MI.
0 10 20 40 60 80 KM.
State Capitals
County Seats
Canals
Major Limited Access Hwys.
San Francisco and Vicinity
Sacramento and Vicinity
Los Angeles and Vicinity
O R E G O N
N E V A D A
A R I Z O N A
M E X I C O
P A C I F I C
O C E A N
Sacramento
SAN FRANCISCO
LOS ANGELES
SAN DIEGO
FRESNO
Bakersfield
Stockton
Oakland
San Jose
Long Beach
Santa Barbara
Lake Tahoe
Death Valley National Monument
Lake Mead National Recreation Area
Joshua Tree Nat'l Mon.
Yosemite National Park
Mojave Desert
Channel Islands National Park
Longitude 119° West of Greenwich 118°
© Copyright HAMMOND INCORPORATED, Maplewood, N. J.

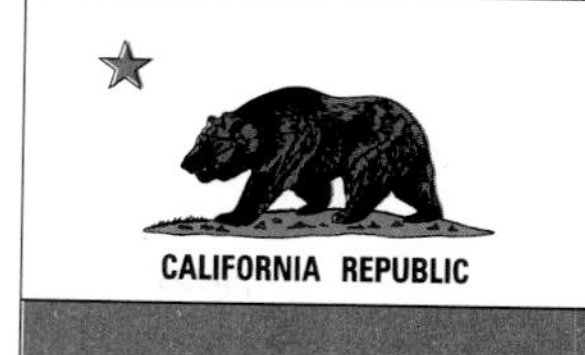

AREA 158,706 sq. mi. (411,049 sq. km.)
POPULATION 29,839,250
CAPITAL Sacramento
LARGEST CITY Los Angeles
HIGHEST POINT Mt. Whitney 14,494 ft. (4418 m.)
SETTLED IN 1769
ADMITTED TO UNION September 9, 1850
POPULAR NAME Golden State
STATE FLOWER Golden Poppy
STATE BIRD California Valley Quail

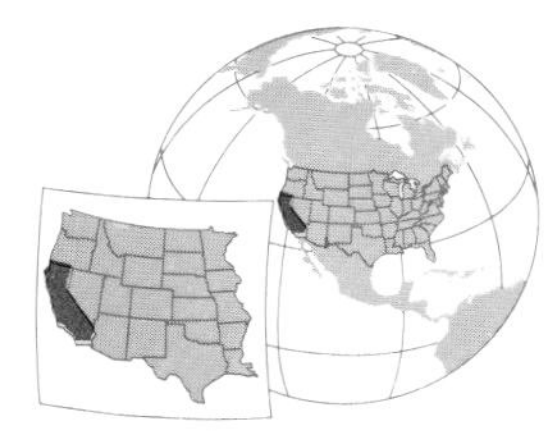

COUNTIES

Alameda 1,279,182 D6
Alpine 1,113 F5
Amador 30,039 E5
Butte 182,120 D4
Calaveras 31,998 E5
Colusa 16,275 C4
Contra Costa 803,732 D6
Del Norte 23,460 B2
El Dorado 125,995 E5
Fresno 667,490 E7
Glenn 24,798 C4
Humboldt 119,118 B3
Imperial 109,303 K1
Inyo 18,281 H7
Kern 543,477 G8
Kings 101,469 E8
Lake 50,631 C4
Lassen 27,598 E3
Los Angeles 8,863,164 G9
Madera 88,090 F6
Marin 230,096 C5
Mariposa 14,302 E6
Mendocino 80,345 B4
Merced 178,403 E6
Modoc 9,678 E2
Mono 9,956 F5
Monterey 355,660 D7
Napa 110,765 C5
Nevada 78,510 E4
Orange 2,410,556 H1
Placer 172,796 E4
Plumas 19,739 E4
Riverside 1,170,413 J1
Sacramento 1,041,219 D5
San Benito 36,697 D7
San Bernardino 1,418,380 J9
San Diego 2,498,016 J1
San Francisco 723,959 J2
San Joaquin 480,628 D5
San Luis Obispo 217,162 E8
San Mateo 649,623 J3
Santa Barbara 369,608 E9
Santa Clara 1,497,577 D6
Santa Cruz 229,734 C6
Shasta 147,036 C3
Sierra 3,318 E4
Siskiyou 43,531 C2
Solano 340,421 D5
Sonoma 388,222 C5
Stanislaus 370,522 D6
Sutter 64,415 D4
Tehama 49,625 C3
Trinity 13,063 B3
Tulare 311,921 G7
Tuolumne 48,456 F5
Ventura 669,016 F9
Yolo 141,092 D5
Yuba 58,228 D4

CITIES and TOWNS

Adelanto 8,517 H9
Alameda 76,459 J2
Alamo 12,277 K2
Albany 16,327 J2
Alhambra 82,106 C10
Alpine 9,695 J11
Alta Loma E10
Altadena 42,658 C10
Alturas▲ 3,231 E2
Amador City 196 C9
Anaheim 266,406 D11
Anderson 8,299 C3
Angels Camp 2,302 E5
Angwin 3,503 C5
Antioch 62,195 L1
Apple Valley 46,079 H9
Aptos 9,061 K4
Arbuckle 1,912 C4
Arcadia 48,290 C10
Arcata 15,197 A3
Arden-Arcade 92,040 B8
Armona 3,122 F7
Arnold 3,788 E5
Aromas 2,275 D7
Arroyo Grande 14,378 E8
Artesia 15,464 C11
Arvin 9,286 G8
Ashland 16,590 K2
Asti 75 C5
Atascadero 23,138 E8
Atherton 7,163 K3
Atwater 22,282 E6
Auberry 1,866 F6
Auburn▲ 10,592 C8
Avalon 2,918 G10
Avenal 9,770 E8
Azusa 41,333 D10
Baker 174,820 J8
Bakersfield▲ 105,611 G8
Baldwin Park 69,330 D10
Banning 20,570 J10
Barstow 21,472 H9
Bayview 1,318 A3
Baywood Park (Baywood Park-Los Osos) 10,933 E8
Beaumont 9,685 J10
Bell 34,365 C11
Bell Gardens 42,355 C11
Bellflower 61,815 C11
Belmont 24,127 J3
Belvedere 2,147 H2
Ben Lomond 7,884 K4
Benicia 24,437 K1
Berkeley 102,724 J2
Bethel Island 2,115 L1
Beverly Hills 31,971 B10
Big Bear City (Sugarloaf Post Office) 4,920 J9
Big Bear Lake 5,351 J9
Big Pine 1,158 G6
Biggs 1,581 D4
Bishop 3,475 G6
Bloomington 15,116 E10
Blue Lake 1,235 B3
Blythe 8,428 L10
Bodfish 1,283 G8
Bolinas 1,098 H1
Boron 2,101 H8
Borrego Springs 2,244 J10
Boulder Creek 6,725 J4
Bowman C7
Brawley 18,923 K11
Brea 32,873 D11
Brentwood 7,563 L2
Bridgeport▲ 525 F5
Brisbane 2,952 J2
Broderick (Broderick-Bryte) 10,194 B8
Bryte (Bryte-Broderick) 10,194 B8
Buellton 3,506 E9
Buena Park 68,784 D11
Burbank 93,643 C10
Burlingame 26,801 J2
Burney 3,423 D3
Buttonwillow 1,301 F8
Cabazon 1,588 J10
Calexico 18,633 K11
California City 5,955 H8
Calipatria 2,690 K10
Calistoga 4,468 C5
Calwa 6,640 F7
Camarillo 52,303 G9
Cambria 5,382 D8
Campbell 36,048 K3
Canoga Park B10
Canyon 7,938 K2
Capistrano Beach 6,168 H10
Capitola 10,171 K4
Cardiff-by-the-Sea 10,054 H10
Carlsbad 63,126 H10
Carmel 4,407 D7
Carmel Valley 4,013 D7
Carmichael 48,702 C8
Carpinteria 13,747 F9
Carson 83,995 C11
Caruthers 1,603 E7
Casitas Springs 1,038 F9
Castro Valley 48,619 K2
Castroville 5,272 D7
Cathedral City 30,085 J10
Cayucos 2,960 E8
Central Valley 4,340 C3
Ceres 26,314 D6
Cerritos 53,240 C11
Chatsworth B10
Chemeketa Park (Chemeketa Park-Redwood Estates) 1,847 K4
Cherryland 11,088 K2
Chester 2,082 D3
Chico 40,079 D4
China Lake 4,275 H8
Chinese Camp 150 E6
Chino 59,682 D10
Chowchilla 5,930 E6
Chula Vista 135,163 J11
Citrus Heights 107,439 C8
Claremont 32,503 D10
Clay 7,317 C9
Clayton 4,325 K2
Clearlake 11,804 C5
Clearlake Oaks 2,419 C4
Cloverdale 4,924 B5
Clovis 50,323 F7
Coachella 16,896 J10
Coalinga 8,212 E7
Colfax 1,306 E4
Colton 40,213 E10
Columbia 1,799 E5
Colusa▲ 4,934 C4
Commerce 12,135 C10
Compton 90,454 C11
Concord 111,348 K1
Corcoran 13,364 F7
Corning 5,870 C4
Corona 76,095 E11
Coronado 26,540 H11
Corralitos 2,513 L4
Corte Madera 8,272 J2
Costa Mesa 96,357 D11
Cotati 5,714 C5
Cottonwood 1,747 C3
Covina 43,207 D10
Crescent City▲ 4,380 A2
Crestline 8,594 H9
Crockett 3,228 J1
Crowley Lake G6
Cudahy 22,817 C11
Culver City 38,793 B10
Cupertino 40,263 K3
Cutler 4,450 F7
Cutten 1,516 A3
Cypress 42,655 D11
Daly City 92,311 H2
Dana Point 31,896 H10
Danville 31,306 K2
Davis 46,209 B8
Death Valley Junction J7
Deer Park 1,825 C5
Del Mar 4,860 H11
Del Rey Oaks 1,661 D7
Del Rosa F10
Delano 22,762 F8
Delhi 3,280 E6
Desert Hot Springs 11,668 J9
Desert View Highlands 2,154 G9
Diamond Springs 2,872 D8
Dinuba 12,743 F7
Dixon 10,401 B9
Dorris 892 D2
Dos Palos 4,196 E6
Downey 91,444 C11
Downieville▲ 500 E4
Duarte 20,688 D10
Dublin 23,229 K2
Dunsmuir 2,129 C2
Durham 4,784 D4
Earlimart 5,881 F8
East Blythe 1,511 L10
East Los Angeles 126,379 C10
Easton 1,877 F7
Edgemont E11
Edison G8
El Cajon 88,693 J11
El Centro▲ 31,384 K11
El Cerrito 4,490 J2
El Dorado 6,395 C8
El Dorado Hills 3,453 C8
El Granada 4,426 H3
El Monte 106,209 D10
El Rio 6,419 F9
El Segundo 15,223 B11
El Toro 62,685 E11
Elk 17,483 B4
Elk Grove 10,959 B9
Emeryville 5,740 J2
Empire D6
Encinitas 55,386 H10
Encino B10
Enterprise C3
Escalon 4,437 E6
Escondido 108,635 J10
Esparto 1,487 C5
Eureka▲ 27,025 A3
Exeter 7,276 F7
Fair Oaks 26,867 C8
Fairfax 6,931 H1
Fairfield▲ 77,211 K1
Fallbrook 22,095 H10
Farmersville 6,235 F7
Felton 5,350 K4
Ferndale 1,331 A3
Fillmore 11,992 G9
Firebaugh 4,429 E7
Florin 24,330 B8
Folsom 29,802 C8
Fontana 87,535 E10
Ford City 3,781 F8
Forest Knolls (Forest Knolls-Lagunitas) H1
Foresthill 1,409 E4
Fort Bragg 6,078 B4
Fortuna 8,788 A3
Foster City 28,176 J2
Fountain Valley 53,691 D11
Fowler 3,208 F7
Frazier Park 2,201 F9
Freedom 8,361 L4
Fremont 173,339 K3
Fresno▲ 354,202 F7
Fullerton 114,144 D11
Galt 8,889 C9
Garden Grove 143,050 D11
Gardena 49,847 C11
Gilroy 31,487 D6
Glen Avon Heights 8,444 E10
Glendale 180,038 C10
Glendora 47,828 D10
Goleta F9
Gonzales 4,660 D7
Goshen 1,809 F7
Granada Hills B10
Grand Terrace 10,946 E10
Grass Valley 9,048 D4
Graton 1,409 C5
Greenacres 7,379 F8
Greenfield 7,464 D7
Greenville 1,396 E3
Gridley 4,631 D4
Groveland 2,753 E6
Grover City 11,656 E8
Guadalupe 5,479 E9
Guerneville 1,966 B5
Gustine 3,931 D6
Half Moon Bay 8,886 H3
Hamilton City 1,811 C4
Hanford▲ 30,897 F7
Harbor City C11
Hawthorne 71,349 C11
Hayfork 2,605 B3
Hayward 111,498 K2
Healdsburg 9,469 B5
Heber 2,566 K11
Hemet 36,094 H10
Hercules 16,829 J1
Herlong 1,188 E3
Hermosa Beach 18,219 B11
Hesperia 50,418 H9
Hidden Hills 1,729 B10
Highgrove 3,175 E10
Highland 34,439 H9
Hillsborough 10,667 J2
Hilmar (Hilmar-Irwin) 3,392 E6
Hollister▲ 19,212 D7
Hollywood C10
Holt 4,820 D6
Holtville 4,399 K11
Home Gardens 7,780 E11
Homeland 3,312 H10
Hughson 3,259 E6
Huntington Beach 181,519 C11
Huntington Park 56,065 C11
Huron 4,766 E7
Idyllwild (Idyllwild-Pine Cove) 2,853 J10
Imperial 4,113 K11
Imperial Beach 26,512 H11
Independence▲ 748 H7
Indian Wells 2,647 J10
Indio 36,793 J10
Inglewood 109,602 B11
Inverness 1,422 B5
Ione 6,516 C9
Irvine 110,330 D11
Isla Vista 20,395 E9
Ivanhoe 3,293 F7
Jackson▲ 3,545 C9
Jamestown 2,178 E6
Joshua Tree 3,898 J9
Julian 1,284 J10
Kelseyville 2,861 C5
Kensington 4,974 J2
Kerman 5,448 E7
Kernville 1,656 G8
Kettleman City 1,411 E7
Keyes 2,878 E6
King City 7,634 D7
Kings Beach 2,796 F4
Kingsburg 7,205 F7
La Canada Flintridge 19,378 C10
La Crescenta (La Crescenta-Montrose) 16,968 C10
La Habra 51,266 D11
La Mesa 52,931 H11
La Mirada 40,452 D11
La Puente 36,955 D10
La Selva Beach 1,603 K4
La Verne 30,897 D10
Lafayette 23,501 K2
Laguna Beach 23,170 G10
Laguna Hills 46,731 D11
Laguna Niguel 44,400 H10
Lagunitas (Lagunitas-Forest Knolls) 1,821 H1
Lake Arrowhead 6,539 H9
Lake Elsinore 18,285 F11
Lake Isabella 3,323 G8
Lakeland Village 5,159 E11
Lakeport▲ 4,390 C4
Lakewood 73,557 C11
Lamont 11,517 G8
Lancaster 97,291 G9
Larkspur 11,070 H1
Lathrop 6,841 D6
Laton 1,415 F7
Lawndale 27,331 B11
Le Grand 1,205 E6
Lemon Grove 23,984 J11
Lemoore 13,622 F7
Lenwood 3,190 H9
Leucadia 9,478 H10
Lewiston 1,187 C3
Lincoln 7,248 B8
Linda 13,033 D4
Linden 1,339 D5
Lindsay 8,338 F7
Live Oak 11,482 K4
Live Oak 3,103 D4
Live Oak 4,320 K4
Livermore 56,741 L2
Livingston 7,317 E6
Locke 2,722 B9
Lockeford 1,852 C9
Lodi 51,874 C9
Loma Linda 17,400 F10
Lomita 19,382 C11
Lompoc 37,649 E9
Lone Pine 1,818 H7
Long Beach 429,433 C11
Loomis 5,705 C8
Los Alamitos 11,676 D11
Los Altos 26,303 K3
Los Altos Hills 7,514 J3
Los Angeles▲ 3,485,398 C10
Los Banos 14,519 E6
Los Gatos 27,357 K4
Los Molinos 1,709 D3
Los Osos (Los Osos-Baywood Park) 10,933 E8
Lost Hills 1,212 F8
Lower Lake 1,217 C5
Lucerne 2,011 C4
Lynwood 61,945 C11
Madera▲ 29,281 E7
Magalia 8,987 D4
Mammoth Lakes 4,785 G6
Manhattan Beach 32,063 B11
Manteca 40,773 D6
Maricopa 1,193 F8
Marina 26,436 D7
Mariposa▲ 1,152 F6
Markleeville▲ 500 F5
Martinez▲ 31,808 K1
Marysville▲ 12,324 D4
Maywood 27,850 C10
McCloud 1,555 C2
McFarland 7,005 F8
McKinleyville 10,749 A3
Mecca 1,966 K10
Meiners Oaks (Meiners Oaks-Mira Monte) 3,329 F9
Mendota 6,821 E7
Menlo Park 28,040 J3
Mentone 5,675 H9
Merced▲ 56,216 E6
Mill Valley 13,038 H2
Millbrae 20,412 J2
Milpitas 50,686 L3
Mira Loma 15,786 E10
Mission Viejo 72,820 D11
Modesto▲ 164,730 D6
Mojave 3,763 G8
Monrovia 35,761 D10
Montague 1,415 C2
Montara 2,552 H3
Montclair 28,434 D10
Monte Sereno 3,287 K4
Montebello 59,564 C10
Monterey 31,954 D7
Monterey Park 60,738 C10
Montrose (Montrose-La Crescenta) C10
Moorpark 25,494 G9
Moraga 15,852 K2
Moreno Valley 118,779 H10
Morgan Hill 23,928 L4
Morro Bay 9,664 D8
Moss Beach 3,002 H3
Mount Shasta 3,460 C2
Mountain View 67,460 K3
Mulberry 1,946 D4
Murphys 1,517 E5
Murrieta 1,628 H10
Muscoy 7,541 E10
Napa▲ 61,842 C5
National City 54,249 J11
Needles 5,191 L9
Nevada City▲ 2,855 D4
Newark 37,861 K3
Newhall 12,029 G9
Newman 4,151 D6
Newport Beach 66,643 D11
Nipomo 7,109 E8
Norco 23,302 E11
North Edwards 1,259 H8
North Highlands 42,105 B8
Norwalk 94,279 C11
Novato 47,585 H1
Oak View 3,606 F9
Oakdale 11,961 E6
Oakhurst 2,602 F6
Oakland▲ 372,242 J2
Oakley 18,374 L1
Oceano 6,169 E8
Oceanside 128,398 H10
Oildale 26,553 F8
Ojai 7,613 F9
Ontario 133,179 D10
Opal Cliffs 5,940 K4
Orange 110,658 D11
Orange Cove 5,604 F7
Orinda 16,642 J2
Orland 5,052 C4
Orosi 5,486 F7
Oroville▲ 11,960 D4
Oxnard 142,216 F9
Pacheco (Pacheco-Vine Hill) 3,325 K1
Pacific Grove 16,117 C7
Pacifica 37,670 H2
Pajaro 3,332 D7
Palermo 5,260 D4
Palm Desert 23,252 J10
Palm Springs 40,181 J10
Palmdale 68,842 G9
Palo Alto 55,900 K3
Palos Verdes Estates 13,512 B11
Paradise 25,408 D4
Paramount 47,669 C11
Parlier 7,938 F7
Pasadena 131,591 C10
Paso Robles 18,583 E8
Patterson 8,626 D6
Pebble Beach C7
Pedley 8,869 E10
Perris 21,460 F11
Petaluma 43,184 H1
Pico Rivera 59,177 C10
Piedmont 10,602 J2
Pine Valley 1,297 J11
Pinole 17,460 J1
Piru 1,157 G9
Pismo Beach 7,669 E8
Pittsburg 47,564 L1
Pixley 2,457 F8
Placentia 41,259 D11
Placerville▲ 8,355 C8
Planada 3,531 E6
Pleasant Hill 31,585 K2
Pleasanton 50,553 L2
Pollock Pines 4,291 E5
Pomona 131,723 D10
Poplar (Poplar-Cotton Center) 1,901 F7

(continued on following page)

Topography

KLAMATH MTS.
Mt. Shasta 14,162 ft. (4317 m.)
Goose L.
Cape Mendocino
Eureka
Shasta L.
Lassen Pk. 10,457 ft. (3187 m.)
Honey L.
COAST RANGES
SIERRA NEVADA
Sacramento
Donner Pass
L. Tahoe
Clear L.
Mono L.
Pt. Reyes
San Francisco
San Francisco Bay
Oakland
Stockton
San Jose
DIABLO RANGE
Monterey Bay
Fresno
Mt. Whitney 14,494 ft. (4418 m.)
Death Valley
Owens L.
Pt. Sur
SANTA LUCIA RA.
Tulare L.
Bakersfield
Buena Vista L.
Mojave Desert
L. Havasu
Pt. Arguello
Los Angeles
Riverside
Long Beach
Sta. Rosa I.
Sta. Cruz I.
SANTA BARBARA IS.
Sta. Catalina I.
San Clemente I.
San Diego
Salton Sea
Imperial Valley
Colorado R.

0 50 100 MI.
0 50 100 KM.

5,000 m. 16,404 ft. | 2,000 m. 6,562 ft. | 1,000 m. 3,281 ft. | 500 m. 1,640 ft. | 200 m. 656 ft. | 100 m. 328 ft. | Sea Level | Below

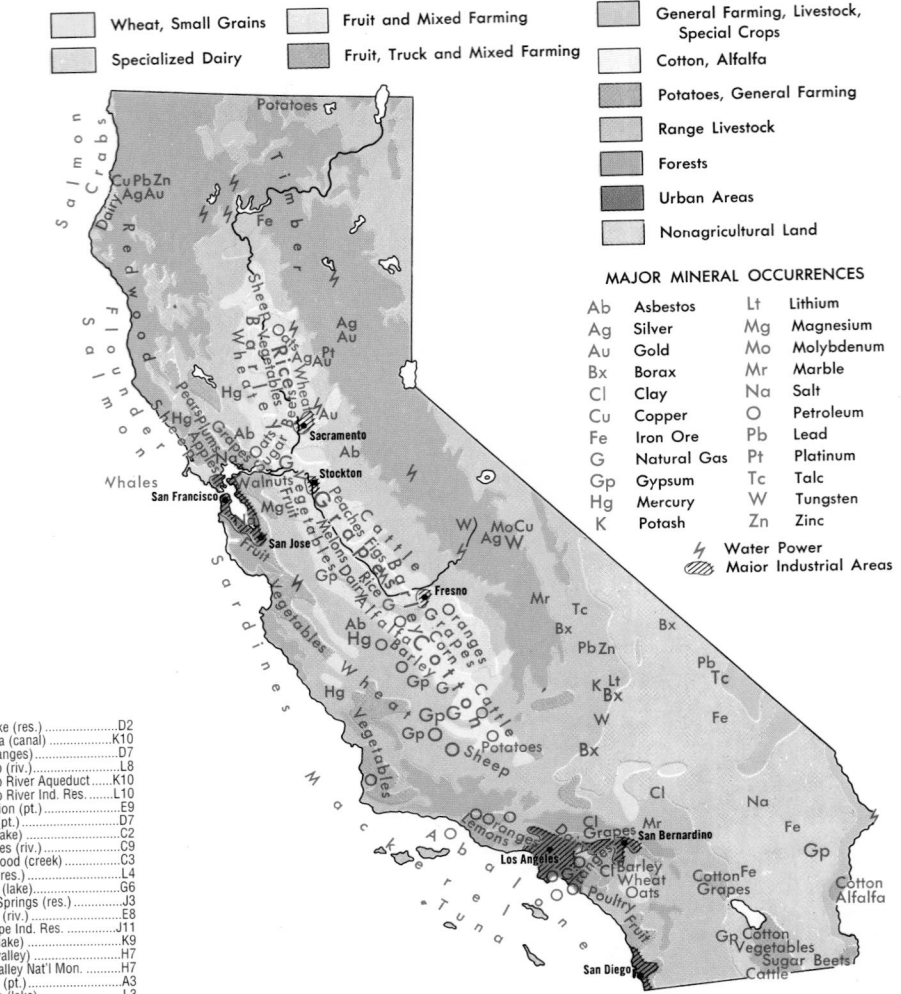

Agriculture, Industry and Resources

DOMINANT LAND USE

Wheat, Small Grains
Specialized Dairy
Fruit and Mixed Farming
Fruit, Truck and Mixed Farming
General Farming, Livestock, Special Crops
Cotton, Alfalfa
Potatoes, General Farming
Range Livestock
Forests
Urban Areas
Nonagricultural Land

MAJOR MINERAL OCCURRENCES

Ab	Asbestos	Lt	Lithium
Ag	Silver	Mg	Magnesium
Au	Gold	Mo	Molybdenum
Bx	Borax	Mr	Marble
Cl	Clay	Na	Salt
Cu	Copper	O	Petroleum
Fe	Iron Ore	Pb	Lead
G	Natural Gas	Pt	Platinum
Gp	Gypsum	Tc	Talc
Hg	Mercury	W	Tungsten
K	Potash	Zn	Zinc

Water Power
Major Industrial Areas

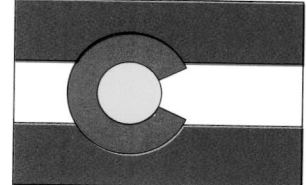

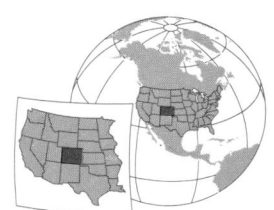

AREA 104,091 sq. mi. (269,596 sq. km.)
POPULATION 3,307,912
CAPITAL Denver
LARGEST CITY Denver
HIGHEST POINT Mt. Elbert 14,433 ft. (4399 m.)
SETTLED IN 1858
ADMITTED TO UNION August 1, 1876
POPULAR NAME Centennial State
STATE FLOWER Rocky Mountain Columbine
STATE BIRD Lark Bunting

COUNTIES

Adams 265,038....................L3
Alamosa 13,617....................H7
Arapahoe 391,511....................L3
Archuleta 5,345....................E8
Baca 4,556....................O8
Bent 5,048....................N7
Boulder 225,339....................J2
Chaffee 12,684....................G5
Cheyenne 2,397....................O5
Clear Creek 7,619....................H3
Conejos 7,453....................G8
Costilla 3,190....................J8
Crowley 3,946....................M6
Custer 1,926....................J6
Delta 20,980....................D5
Denver 467,610....................K3
Dolores 1,504....................C7
Douglas 60,391....................K4
Eagle 21,928....................F3
El Paso 397,014....................K5
Elbert 9,646....................L4
Fremont 32,273....................J5
Garfield 29,974....................C3
Gilpin 3,070....................H3
Grand 7,966....................G2
Gunnison 10,273....................E5
Hinsdale 467....................E7
Huerfano 6,009....................K7
Jackson 1,605....................G1
Jefferson 438,430....................J3
Kiowa 1,688....................O6
Kit Carson 7,140....................O4
La Plata 32,284....................D8
Lake 6,007....................G4
Larimer 186,136....................H1
Las Animas 13,765....................L8
Lincoln 4,529....................M5
Logan 17,567....................N1
Mesa 93,145....................B5
Mineral 558....................F7
Moffat 11,357....................C1
Montezuma 18,672....................B8
Montrose 24,423....................C6
Morgan 21,939....................M2
Otero 20,185....................M7
Ouray 2,295....................D6
Park 7,174....................H4
Phillips 4,189....................P1
Pitkin 12,661....................F4
Prowers 13,347....................P7
Pueblo 123,051....................K6
Rio Blanco 5,972....................C3
Rio Grande 10,770....................G7
Routt 14,088....................E1
Saguache 4,619....................G6
San Juan 745....................D7
San Miguel 3,653....................C6
Sedgwick 2,690....................P1

Summit 12,881....................G3
Teller 12,468....................J5
Washington 4,812....................N3
Weld 131,821....................L1
Yuma 8,954....................P2

CITIES and TOWNS

Agate 90....................M4
Aguilar 520....................K8
Akron▲ 1,599....................N2
Alamosa▲ 7,579....................H8
Allenspark 200....................J2
Alma 148....................G4
Almont 135....................F5
Amherst 85....................P1
Anton 875....................N3
Antonito 1,103....................H8
Arapahoe 300....................P5
Arlington 37....................N6
Arriba 220....................N4
Arriola 5,672....................B8
Arvada 89,235....................J3
Aspen▲ 5,049....................F4
Atwood 100....................N1
Ault 1,107....................K1
Aurora 222,103....................K3
Austin....................D5
Avon 1,798....................F3
Avondale 750....................L6
Bailey 150....................H4
Barnesville 20....................L2
Basalt 1,128....................E4
Bayfield 1,090....................D8
Bedrock 45....................B6
Beecher Island 5....................P3
Bellvue 250....................J1
Bennett 1,757....................L3
Berthoud 2,990....................J2
Berthoud Pass 40....................H3
Bethune 173....................P4
Beulah 650....................K6
Black Forest 8,143....................K4
Black Hawk 227....................J3
Blanca 272....................H8
Blue River 440....................G4
Bonanza 16....................G6
Boncarbo 200....................K8
Bond 65....................F3
Boone 341....................L6
Boulder▲ 83,312....................J2
Bowie 18....................D5
Boyero 12....................N5
Brandon 30....................P6
Branson 58....................M8
Breckenridge▲ 1,285....................G4
Briggsdale 85....................L1
Brighton▲ 14,203....................K3
Bristol 200....................P6
Brookside 183....................J6

Broomfield 24,638....................J3
Brush 4,165....................M2
Buckingham 5....................L1
Buena Vista 1,752....................G5
Buffalo Creek 150....................J4
Burlington▲ 2,941....................P4
Burns 100....................F3
Byers 1,065....................L3
Cahone 200....................B7
Calhan 562....................L4
Campo 121....................O8
Canon City▲ 12,687....................J6
Capulin 600....................G8
Carbondale 3,004....................E4
Carr 49....................K1
Cascade 1,479....................K5
Castle Rock▲ 8,708....................K4
Cedaredge 1,380....................D5
Center 1,963....................G7
Central City▲ 335....................J3
Chama 239....................J8
Cheraw 265....................N6
Cheyenne Wells▲ 1,128....................P5
Chimney Rock 76....................E8
Chivington 20....................O6
Chromo 115....................F8
Cimarron 50....................D6
Clark 20....................F1
Clifton 12,671....................C4
Climax 975....................G4
Coal Creek 157....................J6
Coaldale 153....................H6
Coalmont 50....................F1
Cokedale 116....................K8
Collbran 228....................C4
Colona 54....................D6
Colorado City 1,149....................K6
Colorado Springs▲ 281,140....................K5
Columbine 23,969....................E1
Commerce City 16,466....................K3
Como 30....................H4
Conejos▲ 200....................G8
Cope 110....................O3
Cornish 15....................L2
Cortez▲ 7,284....................B8
Cotopaxi 250....................H6
Cowdrey 80....................G1
Craig▲ 8,091....................D2
Crawford 221....................D5
Creede▲ 362....................E7
Crested Butte 878....................E5
Crestone 39....................H7
Cripple Creek▲ 584....................J5
Crook 148....................O1
Crowley 225....................M6
Cuchara 43....................J8
Dacono 2,228....................K2
Dailey 20....................O1
De Beque 257....................C4
Deckers 4....................J4

Deer Trail 476....................M3
Del Norte▲ 1,674....................G7
Delhi 10....................M7
Delta▲ 3,789....................D5
Deora 2....................O7
Denver (cap.)▲ 467,610....................K3
Dillon 553....................H3
Dinosaur 324....................B2
Divide 700....................J5
Dolores 866....................C8
Dove Creek 643....................A7
Doyleville 75....................F6
Drake 300....................J2
Durango▲ 12,430....................D8
Eads▲ 780....................O6
Eagle▲ 1,580....................F3
Eaton 1,959....................K1
Eckley 211....................P2
Edgewater 4,613....................J3
Edwards 250....................F3
Egnar 50....................B7
Elbert 200....................L4
Eldora 100....................H3
Elizabeth 818....................K4
Elk Springs 18....................C2
Empire 401....................H3
Englewood 29,387....................K3
Erie 1,258....................K2
Estes Park 3,184....................J2
Eureka 25....................D7
Evans 5,877....................K2
Evergreen 7,582....................J3
Fairplay▲ 387....................H4
Farisita 116....................J7
Federal Heights 9,342....................J3
Firestone 1,358....................K2
Firstview 6....................O5
Flagler 564....................N4
Fleming 344....................O1
Florence 2,987....................J6
Florissant 130....................J5
Fort Collins▲ 87,758....................J1
Fort Garland 700....................H7
Fort Lupton 5,159....................K2
Fort Lyon 500....................N6
Fort Morgan▲ 9,068....................M2
Fountain 9,984....................K5
Fowler 1,154....................L6
Foxton 12....................J4
Franktown 200....................K4
Fraser 575....................H3
Frederick 988....................K2
Freshwater (Guffey) 24....................H5
Frisco 1,601....................G3
Fruita 4,045....................B4
Galeton 200....................K1
Garcia 75....................J8
Gardner 100....................J7
Garfield 30....................G5
Gateway 7,510....................B5

Genoa 167....................N4
Georgetown▲ 891....................H3
Gilcrest 1,084....................K2
Gill 250....................L2
Gilman 160....................G3
Glade Park 100....................B5
Glen Haven 110....................H2
Glendevey 50....................H1
Glenwood Springs▲ 6,561....................E4
Golden▲ 13,116....................J3
Goodrich 85....................M2
Gould 12....................G2
Granada 513....................P6
Granby 966....................H2
Grand Junction ▲ 29,034....................B4
Grand Lake 259....................H2
Granite 47....................G4
Grant 50....................H4
Greeley▲ 60,536....................K2
Green Mountain Falls 663....................K5
Greenland 21....................K4
Greystone 2....................B1
Grover 135....................L1
Guffey 24....................H5
Gulnare 6....................K8
Gunnison▲ 4,636....................E5
Gypsum 1,750....................F3
Hale 4....................P3
Hamilton 100....................D2
Hartman 108....................P6
Hartsel 95....................H4
Hasty 150....................O6
Haswell 62....................N6
Haxtun 952....................O1
Hayden▲ 1,444....................E2
Hereford 50....................L1
Hesperus 250....................C8
Hillrose 169....................N2
Hillside 79....................H6
Hoehne 400....................L8
Holly 877....................P6
Holyoke▲ 1,931....................P1
Hooper 112....................H7
Hot Sulphur Springs▲ 347....................H2
Hotchkiss 744....................D5
Howard 200....................H6
Hoyt 60....................L2
Hudson 918....................K2
Hugo▲ 660....................N4
Hygiene 450....................J2
Idaho Springs 1,834....................H3
Idalia 125....................P3
Ignacio 720....................D8
Iliff 174....................N1
Jamestown 251....................J2
Jansen 267....................K8
Jaroso 50....................H8
Jefferson 50....................H4
Joes 100....................O3
Johnstown 1,579....................K2

Julesburg▲ 1,295....................P1
Karval 51....................N5
Keenesburg 570....................L2
Keota 5....................L1
Kersey 980....................L2
Kim 76....................N8
Kiowa▲ 275....................L4
Kirk 30....................P3
Kit Carson 305....................O5
Kremmling 1,166....................G2
Kutch 2....................M5
La Garita 10....................G7
La Jara 725....................H8
La Junta▲ 7,637....................M7
La Salle 1,783....................K2
La Veta 726....................J8
Lafayette 14,548....................K3
Laird 101....................P2
Lake City▲ 223....................E6
Lake George 500....................J5
Lakewood 126,481....................J3
Lamar▲ 8,343....................O6
Laporte 950....................J1
Larkspur 232....................K4
Las Animas▲ 2,481....................N6
Lasauces 150....................H8
Lavalley 237....................J8
Lawson 108....................H3
Lay 40....................D2
Lazear 60....................D5
Leadville▲ 2,629....................G4
Lebanon 50....................B8
Lewis 150....................B8
Limon 1,831....................M4
Lincoln Park 3,728....................J6
Lindon 60....................N3
Littleton▲ 33,685....................K3
Livermore 150....................J1
Lochbuie 1,168....................K2
Log Lane Village 667....................M2
Loma 265....................B4
Longmont 42,942....................J2
Longview 110....................J4
Louisville 12,361....................J3
Louviers 300....................K4
Loveland 37,352....................J2
Lucerne 135....................K2
Lycan 4....................P7
Lyons 1,227....................J2
Mack 380....................B4
Maher 75....................D5
Malta 200....................G4
Manassa 988....................H8
Mancos 842....................C8
Manitou Springs 4,535....................J5
Manzanola 437....................M6
Marble 64....................E4
Marvel 176....................C8
Masonville 200....................J2
Masters 50....................L2

(continued on following page)

Agriculture, Industry and Resources

DOMINANT LAND USE

- Specialized Wheat
- Wheat, Range Livestock
- Wheat, Grain Sorghums, Range Livestock
- Dry Beans, General Farming
- Sugar Beets, Dry Beans, Livestock, General Farming
- Fruit, Mixed Farming
- General Farming, Livestock, Special Crops
- Range Livestock
- Forests
- Urban Areas
- Nonagricultural Land

MAJOR MINERAL OCCURRENCES

Ag Silver
Au Gold
Be Beryl
C   Coal
Cl Clay
Cu Copper
F   Fluorspar
Fe Iron Ore
G   Natural Gas

Mi Mica
Mo Molybdenum
Mr Marble
O   Petroleum
Pb Lead
U   Uranium
V   Vanadium
W   Tungsten
Zn Zinc

⚡ Water Power
▨ Major Industrial Areas

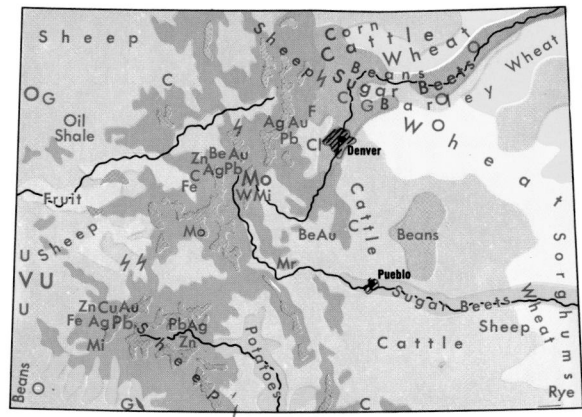

Topography

0   50   100 MI.

0   50   100 KM.

Below Sea Level | 100 m. 328 ft. | 200 m. 656 ft. | 500 m. 1,640 ft. | 1,000 m. 3,281 ft. | 2,000 m. 6,562 ft. | 5,000 m. 16,404 ft.

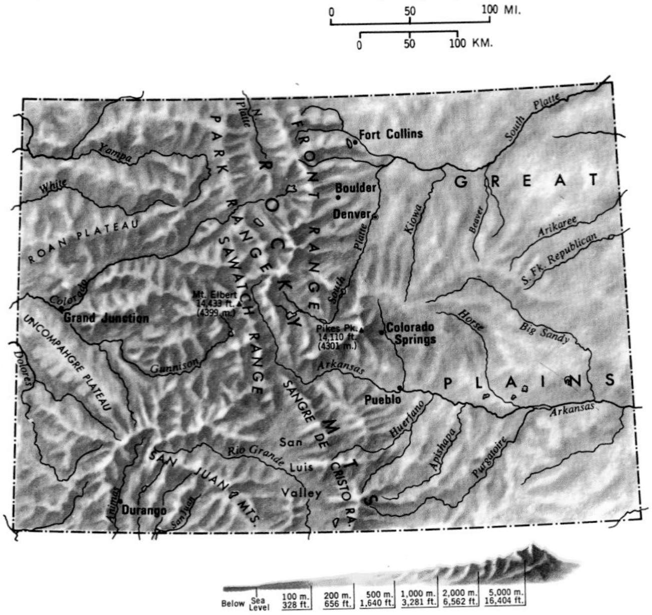

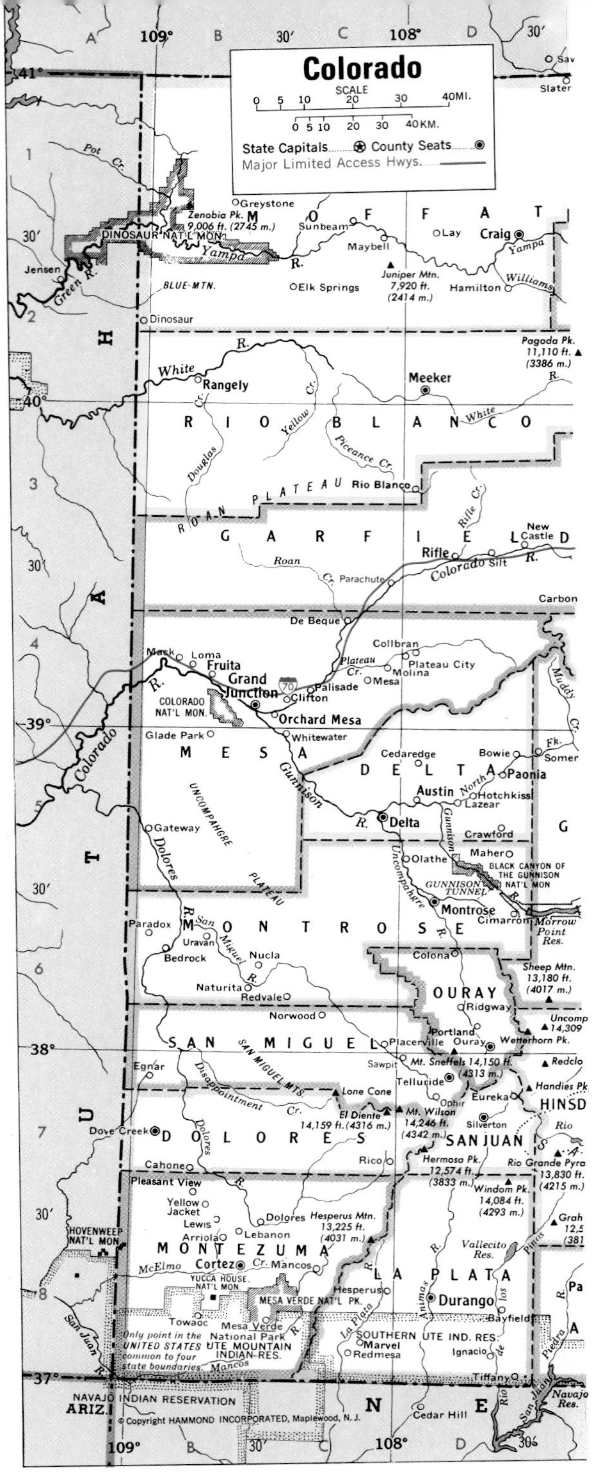

Matheson 120 ....M4
Maybell 130 ....C2
McClave 125 ....O6
McCoy 62 ....F3
Mead 456 ....K2
Meeker▲ 2,098 ....D2
Meredith 47 ....F4
Merino 238 ....N2
Mesa 120 ....C4
Mesa Verde National Park 45 ...C8
Mesita 70 ....H8
Milliken 1,605 ....K2
Milner 196 ....F2
Minturn 1,066 ....G3
Model 200 ....L8
Moffat 99 ....H6
Molina 200 ....D4
Monte Vista 4,324 ....G7
Montezuma 63 ....H3
Montrose▲ 8,854 ....D6
Monument 1,020 ....K4
Morrison 465 ....J3
Mosca 100 ....H7
Nathrop 150 ....H5
Naturita 434 ....B6
Nederland 1,099 ....H3
New Castle 679 ....E3
New Raymer 80 ....M1
Ninaview 2 ....N7
Niwot 2,666 ....J2
North Avondale 110 ....L6
North La Junta 1,076 ....N7
Northglenn 27,195 ....K3
Norwood 429 ....C6
Nucla 656 ....B6
Nunn 324 ....K1
Oak Creek 673 ....F2
Ohio 100 ....E5
Olathe 1,263 ....D5
Olney Springs 340 ....M6
Ophir 69 ....D7
Orchard 2,218 ....L2
Orchard Mesa 5,977 ....C4
Ordway▲ 1,025 ....M6
Ortiz 163 ....H8
Otis 451 ....O2
Ouray▲ 644 ....D6
Ovid 349 ....P1
Padroni 100 ....N1
Pagosa Junction 15 ....E8
Pagosa Springs▲ 1,207 ....E8
Palisade 1,871 ....C4
Palmer Lake 1,480 ....J4
Paoli 75 ....P1
Paonia 1,403 ....D5
Parachute 658 ....C4
Paradox 250 ....B6
Parkdale 21 ....H6
Parker 5,450 ....K4
Parlin 100 ....F6
Parshall 80 ....G2
Peetz 191 ....N1
Penrose 2,235 ....K6
Peyton 250 ....K4
Phippsburg 300 ....F2
Pierce 823 ....K1
Pine 100 ....J4
Pinecliffe 375 ....J3
Pinon 50 ....K6
Pitkin 53 ....F5
Placerville 50 ....D6
Plateau City 35 ....D4
Platner 30 ....N2
Platteville 1,515 ....K2
Pleasant View 300 ....B7
Poncha Springs 244 ....G6
Portland L6
Portland 17 ....K6
Powderhorn 100 ....E6
Pritchett 153 ....O8
Proctor 25 ....N1
Pryor 50 ....K8
Pueblo▲ 98,640 ....K6
Radium 22 ....G3
Ramah 94 ....L4
Rand 50 ....G2
Rangely 2,278 ....B2
Raymer (New Raymer) 80 ...M1
Red Cliff 297 ....G4
Red Feather Lakes ¹50 ....H1
Red Mesa 100 ....C8
Red Wing 200 ....J7
Redstone 115 ....E4
Redvale 300 ....B6
Rico 92 ....C7
Ridgway 423 ....D6
Rifle 4,636 ....C3
Rio Blanco 4 ....J6
Rockvale 321 ....K6
Rocky Ford 4,162 ....M6
Roggen 100 ....L2
Romeo 341 ....G8
Rush 40 ....L5
Rye 168 ....K7
Saguache▲ 584 ....G6
Saint Elmo 75 ....G5
Salida▲ 4,737 ....H6
San Acacio 50 ....J8
San Isabel 8 ....K7
San Luis▲ 800 ....J8
San Pablo 150 ....J8
Sanford 750 ....H8
Sargents 31 ....F6
Sawpit 36 ....D7
Security (Security-Widefield)
    18,768 ....K5
Sedalia 200 ....K4
Sedgwick 183 ....O1
Segundo 200 ....J8
Seibert 181 ....O4
Severance 106 ....K1
Shawnee 100 ....H4
Sheridan 4,976 ....J3
Sheridan Lake 95 ....P6
Silt 1,095 ....D4
Silver Cliff 322 ....J6
Silver Plume 134 ....H3
Silverthorne 1,768 ....G3
Silverton▲ 716 ....D7
Simla 481 ....M4
Slater 10 ....E1
Snowmass 1,449 ....E4
Snyder 200 ....M2
Somerset 200 ....E5
South Fork 500 ....F7
Springfield▲ 1,475 ....O8
Starkville 104 ....L8
Steamboat Springs▲ 6,695 ...F2
Sterling 10,362 ....N1
Stoneham 35 ....M1
Stonington 27 ....P8
Strasburg 1,005 ....L3
Stratton 649 ....O4
Sugar City 252 ....M6
Sunbeam 19 ....C1
Superior 255 ....J3
Swink 584 ....M7
Tabernash 250 ....H3
Telluride▲ 1,309 ....D7
Tennessee Pass 5 ....H6
Texas Creek 80 ....H6
Thatcher 50 ....L7
Thornton 55,031 ....K3
Tiffany 24 ....D8
Timnath 190 ....M7
Timpas 25 ....M7
Tincup 18 ....F5
Toponas 55 ....F2
Towaoc 700 ....B8
Towner 61 ....P6
Trinchera 30 ....M8
Trinidad▲ 8,580 ....L8
Truckton 10 ....L5
Twin Lakes 40 ....G4
Two Buttes 63 ....P7
Tyrone 9 ....L8
Uravan 500 ....B6
Utleyville 2 ....O8
Vail 3,659 ....G3
Valdez 12 ....K8
Vernon 50 ....P3
Victor 258 ....J5
Vilas 105 ....P8
Villa Grove 37 ....G6
Villegreen 6 ....M8
Vineland 200 ....K6
Virginia Dale 2 ....J1
Vona 100 ....O4
Wagon Wheel Gap 20 ....F7
Walden▲ 890 ....G1
Walsenburg▲ 3,300 ....K7
Walsh 692 ....P8
Ward 159 ....H2
Weldona 200 ....M2
Wellington 1,340 ....K1
Westcliffe▲ 312 ....H6
Westcreek 2 ....J4
Westminster 74,625 ....J3
Weston 150 ....K8
Wetmore 150 ....J6
Wheat Ridge 29,419 ....J3
Whitewater 300 ....C5
Wiggins 499 ....L2
Wild Horse 13 ....N5
Wiley 406 ....O6
Williamsburg 253 ....J6
Windsor 5,062 ....J2
Winter Park 528 ....H3
Wolcott 30 ....F3
Woodland Park 4,610 ....J4
Woodrow 24 ....M3
Woody Creek 400 ....F4
Wray 1,998 ....P2
Yampa 317 ....F2
Yellow Jacket 115 ....B7
Yoder 25 ....L5
Yuma 3,137 ....O2

OTHER FEATURES

Adams (mt.) H6
Adobe Creek (res.) N6
Air Force Academy 9,062 ....K5
Alamosa (creek) G8
Alva B. Adams (tunnel) H2
Animas (riv.) D8
Antero (mt.) H5
Antero (res.) H5
Antora (peak) G6
Apishapa (riv.) L8
Arapaho Nat'l Rec. Area G2
Arapahoe (peak) H2
Arikaree (riv.) O3
Arkansas (riv.) P6
Arkansas Divide (mts.) L4
Baker (mt.) H2
Bald (mt.) H4
Bear (creek) P8
Beaver (creek) M3
Bennett (peak) G7
Bent's Old Fort
    Nat'l Hist. Site M6
Big Grizzly (creek) G1
Big Sandy (creek) N4
Big Thompson (riv.) H2
Bijou (creek) L3
Black Canyon of the Gunnison
    Nat'l Mon. D5
Black Squirrel (creek) L5
Blanca (peak) H7
Blue (mt.) B2
Blue (riv.) G3
Blue Mesa (res.) E5
Bonny (res.) P3
Box Elder (creek) K4
Cache la Poudre (riv.) H1
Cameron (peak) H1
Carbon (peak) E5
Castle (peak) F5
Cebolla (creek) E6
Cedar (creek) M1
Chacuaco (creek) M8
Cheesman (lake) J4
Clay (peak) O7
Elk (riv.) F2
Empire (res.) L2
Ent A.F.B. K5
Ethel (mt.) F1
Evans (mt.) H3
Florissant Fossil Beds
    Nat'l Mon. J5
Fort Carson 11,309 ....K5
Fountain (creek) K5
Frenchman (creek) P1
Del Norte▲ (peak) F7
De Weese (plat.) J6
Dinosaur Nat'l Mon. B2
Disappointment (creek) B5
Dolores (riv.) B3
Douglas (creek) B3
Eagle (riv.) E3
Elbert (mt.) G4
El Diente (peak) C7
Eleven Mile Canyon (res.) H5
Frenchman, North Fork
    (creek) O1
Frenchman, South Fork
    (creek) O1
Front (range) H1
Gore (range) G3
Graham (peak) E8
Granby (lake) G3
Great Sand Dunes Nat'l Mon. ...H7
Green (riv.) A2
Green Mountain (res.) G3
Gunnison (riv.) D6
Gunnison (tunnel) D6
Gunnison, North Fork (riv.) ...D5
Handies (peak) E7
Harvard (mt.) G5
Hermosa (peak) D7
Hesperus (mt.) C8
Holy Cross (mt.) F4
Horse (creek) M5
Horse Creek (res.) N6
Horsetooth (res.) J1
Hovenweep Nat'l Mon. A8
Huerfano (riv.) L7
Illinois (riv.) G1
Jackson Lake (res.) L2
James (peak) H3
John Martin (res.) N6
Juniper (creek) C1
Kiowa (creek) L3
Kit Carson (mt.) H7
La Garita (mts.) F7
Lake Fork, Gunnison (riv.) ...E6
Landsman (creek) P4
La Plata (peak) G4
La Plata (riv.) C8
Laramie (mts.) H1
Laramie (riv.) H1
Lincoln (mt.) G4
Lone Cone (mt.) C7

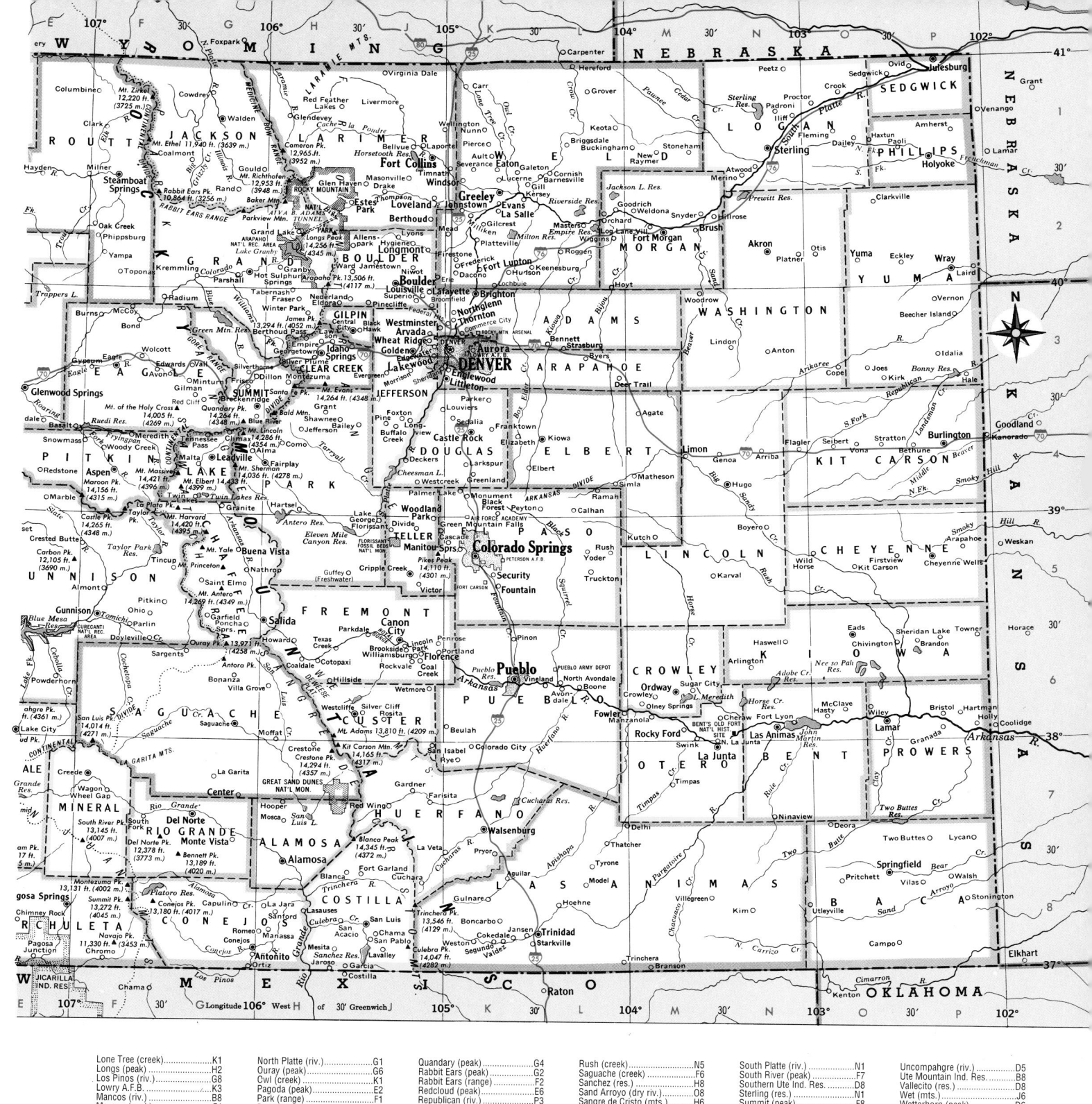

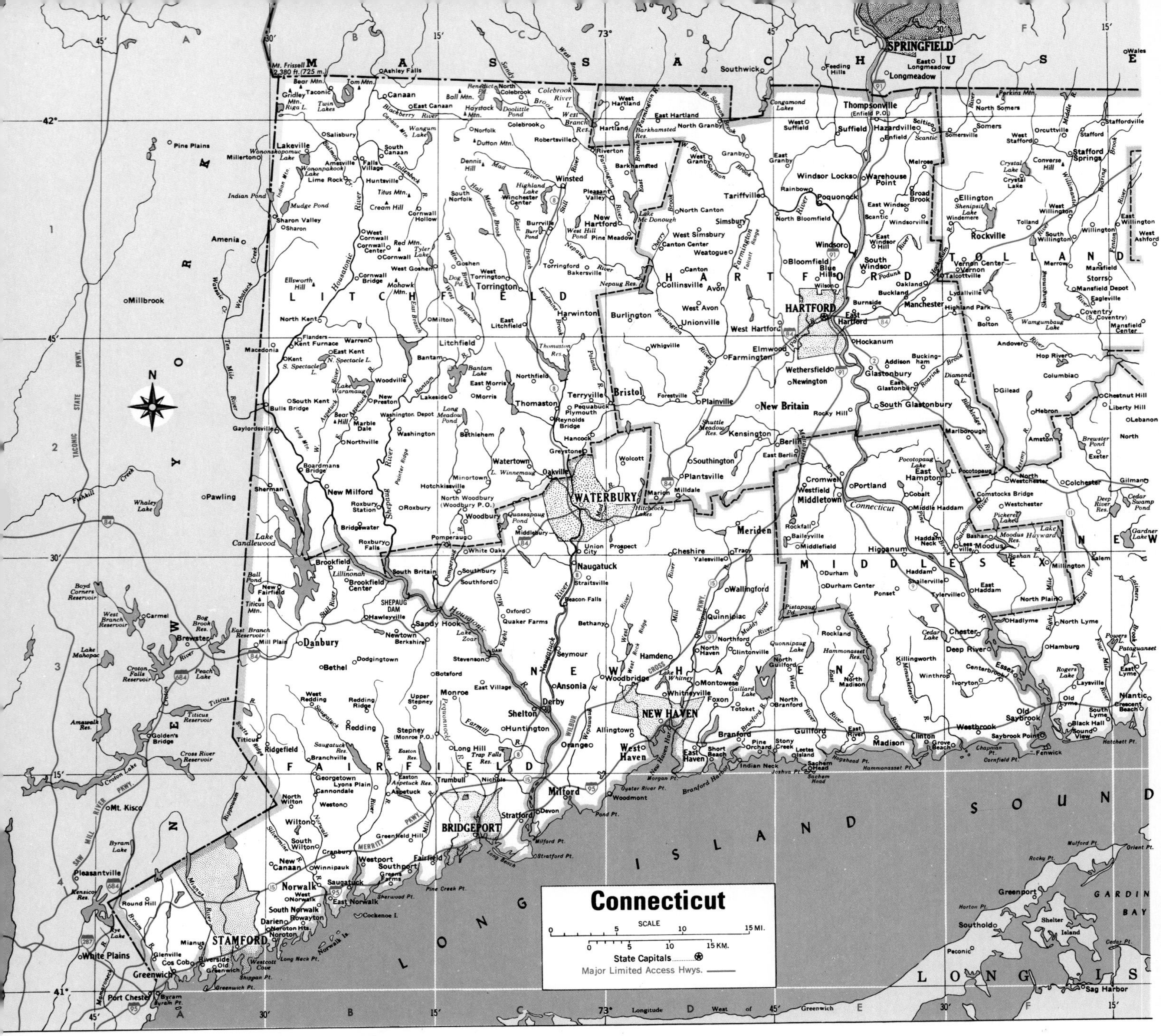

Connecticut

SCALE
0   5   10   15 MI.
0   5   10   15 KM.

⊗ State Capitals
— Major Limited Access Hwys.

Longitude West of 45° Greenwich

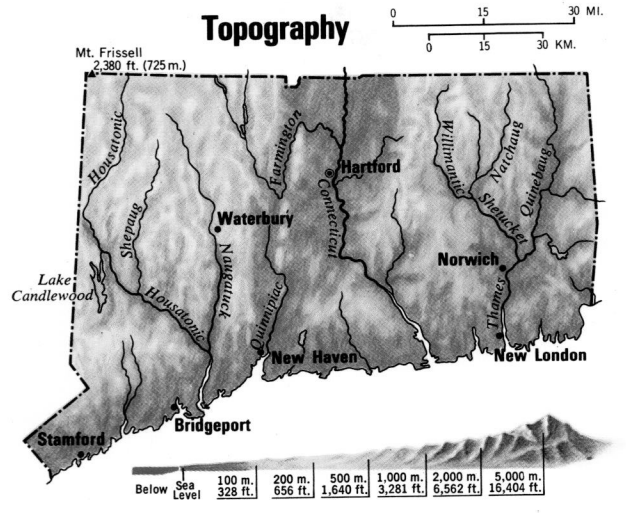

Topography

Mt. Frissell
2,380 ft. (725 m.)

0   15   30 MI.
0   15   30 KM.

Below Sea Level | 100 m. 328 ft. | 200 m. 656 ft. | 500 m. 1,640 ft. | 1,000 m. 3,281 ft. | 2,000 m. 6,562 ft. | 5,000 m. 16,404 ft.

COUNTIES

Fairfield 827,645	B3
Hartford 851,783	D1
Litchfield 174,092	B1
Middlesex 143,196	E3
New Haven 804,219	D3
New London 254,957	G2
Tolland 128,699	F1
Windham 102,525	H1

CITIES and TOWNS

Abington 600	G1
Addison 700	E2
Allingtown	D3
Amston 900	F2
Andover • 2,540	F2
Ansonia 18,403	C3
Ashford P.O. (Warrenville) 500	G1
Ashford • 3,765	G1
Avon 1,434	D1
Avon • 13,937	D1
Bakersville 750	C1
Ballouville 800	H1
Baltic 757	G2
Bantam 757	B2
Barkhamsted • 3,369	D1
Beacon Falls 5,083	C3
Berkshire 500	B3
Berlin • 16,787	E2
Bethany • 4,608	C3
Bethel 8,835	B3
Bethel • 17,541	B3
Bethlehem 1,762	C2
Bethlehem • 3,071	C2
Bloomfield • 19,483	E1
Blue Hills 3,206	E1
Bolton • 4,575	F1
Branchville 600	B3
Branford 5,688	D3
Branford • 27,603	D3
Bridgeport 141,686	C4
Bridgewater • 1,654	B2
Bristol 60,640	D2
Broad Brook 3,585	E1
Brookfield • 14,113	B3
Brookfield Center	B3
Brooklyn • 6,681	H1
Buckingham 800	F2
Burlington • 7,026	D1
Burnside	E1
Byram	A4
Canaan 1,057	B1
Canaan • 1,194	B1
Canterbury • 4,467	H2
Canton 1,680	D1
Canton • 8,268	D1
Center Groton 600	G3
Centerbrook 800	F3
Central Village 950	H2
Chaplin • 2,048	G1
Cheshire 5,759	D2
Cheshire • 25,684	D2
Chester 1,563	F3
Chester • 3,417	F3
Clinton 3,439	E3
Clinton • 12,767	E3
Clintonville	D3
Cobalt 700	E2
Colchester 3,212	F2
Colchester • 10,980	F2
Colebrook • 1,365	C1
Collinsville 2,591	D1
Columbia • 4,510	F2
Cornwall • 1,414	B1
Cos Cob	A4
Coventry 3,769	F1
Coventry • 10,063	F1
Cranbury 700	B4
Cromwell • 12,286	E2
Crystal Lake 1,175	F1
Danbury 65,585	B3
Danielson 4,441	H1
Darien • 18,196	B4
Dayville	H1
Deep River 2,520	F3
Deep River • 4,332	F3
Derby 12,199	C3
Devon	C4
Durham 2,650	E3
Durham • 5,732	E3
Durham Center 500	E3
East Berlin 950	E2
East Brooklyn 1,481	H1
East Canaan 800	B1
East Granby • 4,302	E1
East Haddam • 6,676	F3
East Hampton 2,167	E2
East Hampton • 10,428	E2
East Hartford 50,452	E1
East Hartland 900	D1
East Haven • 26,144	D3
East Killingly 900	H1
East Lyme • 15,340	G3
East Morris 800	C2
East Norwalk	B4
East Putnam 500	H1
East River 500	E3
East Windsor • 10,081	E1
East Windsor Hill 500	E1
Eastford • 1,314	G1
Easton • 6,303	B4
Ellington • 11,197	F1
Elmwood	D2
Enfield 8,151	E1
Enfield • 45,532	E1
Essex 2,500	F3
Essex • 5,904	F3
Fabyan 600	G1
Fairfield 53,418	B4
Falls Village 600	B1
Farmington • 20,608	D2
Fenwick 89	F3
Forestville	D2
Foxon	D3
Franklin • 1,810	G2

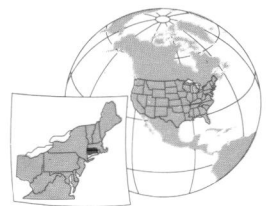

AREA 5,018 sq. mi. (12,997 sq. km.)
POPULATION 3,295,669
CAPITAL Hartford
LARGEST CITY Bridgeport
HIGHEST POINT Mt. Frissell (S. Slope) 2,380 ft. (725 m.)
SETTLED IN 1635
ADMITTED TO UNION January 9, 1788
POPULAR NAME Constitution State; Nutmeg State
STATE FLOWER Mountain Laurel
STATE BIRD Robin

Milldale 975	D2	Poquonock Bridge 2,770	G3	Thompson • 8,668	H1	Colebrook River (lake)	C1
Milton 600	C1	Portland 5,645	E2	Thompsonville 8,458	E1	Congamond (lakes)	E1
Mohegan 700	G3	Portland • 8,418	E2	Tolland 11,001	F1	Connecticut (riv.)	E2
Monroe • 16,896	C3	Preston 5,006	H2	Torringford	C1	Dennis (hill)	C1
Monroe P.O. (Stepney)	B3	Prospect • 7,775	D2	Torrington 33,687	C1	Easton (res.)	B3
Montowese	D3	Putnam 6,835	H1	Totoket 950	D3	Eight Mile (riv.)	F3
Montville 1,711	G3	Putnam • 9,031	H1	Trumbull • 32,016	C4	Farmington (riv.)	D1
Montville • 16,673	G3	Putnam Heights 500	H1	Uncasville 1,597	G3	French (riv.)	H1
Moodus 1,170	F2	Quaker Hill 2,052	G3	Union • 612	G1	Frissell (mt.)	B1
Moosup 3,289	H2	Quinebaug 1,031	H1	Union City	D1	Gaillard (lake)	D3
Morningside Park	G3	Quinnipiac	D3	Unionville	D1	Gardner (lake)	G2
Morris • 2,039	C2	Redding • 7,927	B3	Vernon Center	F1	Hammonasset (pt.)	E3
Mystic 2,618	H3	Redding Ridge 550	B3	Vernon • 29,841	F1	Hammonasset (riv.)	E3
Naugatuck 30,625	C3	Ridgefield 6,363	B3	Versailles 540	G2	Haystack (mt.)	C1
New Canaan • 17,864	B4	Ridgefield • 20,919	B3	Voluntown • 2,113	H2	Highland (lake)	C1
New Fairfield • 12,911	B3	Riverside	A4	Wallingford 17,827	D3	Hockanum (riv.)	E1
New Hartford 1,269	C1	Rockfall 900	E2	Wallingford • 40,822	D3	Hop (riv.)	F1
New Hartford • 5,769	C1	Rockville	F1	Warehouse Point	E1	Housatonic (riv.)	C3
New Haven 130,474	D3	Rocky Hill 16,554	E2	Warren • 1,226	B2	Lillinonah (lake)	B3
New London 28,540	G3	Rogers 650	H1	Washington • 3,905	B2	Little (riv.)	G2
New Milford 5,775	B2	Round Hill 900	A4	Washington Depot 900	B2	Long Island (sound)	C4
New Milford • 23,629	B2	Rowayton	B4	Waterbury 108,961	C2	Mad (riv.)	C1
New Preston 1,217	B2	Roxbury • 1,825	B2	Waterford 2,736	G3	Mashapaug (lake)	G1
Newington • 29,208	E2	Salem • 3,310	F3	Waterford • 17,930	G3	Mason (isl.)	H3
Newtown 1,800	B3	Salisbury • 4,090	B1	Watertown • 20,456	C2	Mattabesset (riv.)	E2
Newtown • 20,779	B3	Sandy Hook	B3	Wauregan 1,079	H1	Mianus (riv.)	A4
Niantic 3,048	G3	Saugatuck	B4	Weatogue 2,521	D1	Mohawk (mt.)	B1
Nichols	C4	Saybrook Point 700	F3	West Avon	D1	Moosup (riv.)	H2
Noank 1,406	G3	Scantic 500	E1	West Granby 567	D1	Mount Hope (riv.)	G1
Norfolk • 2,060	C1	Scotland • 1,215	G2	West Hartford • 60,110	D1	Mudge (pond)	B1
Noroton	B4	Seymour • 14,288	C3	West Haven 54,021	D3	Mystic (riv.)	H3
Noroton Heights	B4	Sharon • 2,928	B1	West Mystic 3,595	H3	Natchaug (riv.)	G1
North Bloomfield 500	E1	Shelton 35,418	C3	West Norwalk 950	B4	Naugatuck (riv.)	C3
North Branford • 12,996	E3	Sherman • 2,809	B2	West Simsbury 2,149	D1	Nepaug (res.)	C1
North Franklin 500	G2	Short Beach	D3	West Suffield	E1	Niantic (riv.)	G3
North Granby 1,455	D1	Simsbury 5,577	D1	Westbrook 2,060	F3	Norwalk (riv.)	B4
North Grosvenor Dale 1,705	H1	Simsbury • 22,023	D1	Westbrook • 5,414	F3	Pachaug (pond)	H2
North Guilford	E3	Somers 1,643	F1	Westfield	E2	Pawcatuck (riv.)	H3
North Haven • 22,249	D3	Somers • 9,108	F1	Weston • 8,648	B4	Pequabuck (riv.)	D2
North Lyme	F3	Somersville 750	F1	Westport • 24,410	B4	Pequonnock (riv.)	C3
North Stonington • 4,884	H3	South Coventry (Coventry)		Wethersfield • 25,651	E2	Pocotopaug (lake)	E2
North Wilton 900	B4	1,257	F1	Whitneyville	D3	Quaddick (res.)	H1
North Woodbury 900	C2	South Glastonbury	E2	Willimantic 14,746	G2	Quinebaug (riv.)	H2
Northfield 600	C2	South Killingly 500	H1	Willington • 5,979	F1	Quinnipiac (riv.)	D3
Northford	D3	South Norwalk	B4	Wilton 15,989	B4	Rippowam (riv.)	A4
Northville 700	B2	South Wilton	B4	Winchester • 11,524	C1	Sachem (head)	E4
Norwalk 78,331	B4	South Windham 1,644	G2	Windham • 22,039	G2	Salmon (brook)	D1
Norwich 37,391	G2	South Windsor • 22,090	E1	Windsor 17,517	E1	Salmon (riv.)	F2
Norwichtown	G2	South Woodstock 1,112	G1	Windsor • 27,817	E1	Saugatuck (res.)	B3
Oakdale 608	G3	Southbury • 15,818	C3	Windsor Locks • 12,358	E1	Scantic (riv.)	E1
Oakville 8,741	C2	Southington • 38,518	D2	Winnipauk 650	B4	Shenipsit (lake)	F1
Occum	G2	Southport	B4	Winsted 8,254	C1	Shepaug (riv.)	B2
Old Greenwich	A4	Stafford • 11,091	F1	Winthrop 750	E3	Shetucket (riv.)	G2
Old Lyme • 6,535	F3	Stafford Springs 4,100	F1	Wolcott • 13,700	D2	Silvermine (riv.)	B4
Old Mystic 600	H3	Staffordville 500	G1	Woodbridge • 7,924	D3	Spectacle (lakes)	B2
Old Saybrook 1,820	F3	Stamford 108,056	A4	Woodbury 1,212	C2	Still (riv.)	B3
Old Saybrook • 9,552	F3	Stepney	B3	Woodbury • 8,131	C2	Still (riv.)	C1
Oneco 550	H2	Sterling • 2,357	H2	Woodmont 1,770	D4	Talcott (range)	D1
Orange • 12,830	C3	Stonington 1,100	H3	Woodstock • 6,008	H1	Thames (riv.)	G3
Oxford • 8,685	C3	Stonington • 16,919	H3	Yalesville	D3	Thomaston (res.)	C2
Pawcatuck 5,289	H3	Stony Creek	E3	Yantic	G2	Titicus (riv.)	A3
Pequabuck 642	C2	Storrs 12,198	F1			Trap Falls (res.)	C3
Plainfield 2,856	H2	Stratford • 49,389	C4	OTHER FEATURES		Twin (lakes)	B1
Plainfield • 14,363	H2	Suffield 1,353	E1			Wamgumbaug (lake)	F1
Plainville • 17,392	D2	Suffield • 11,427	E1	Aspetuck (res.)	B4	Waramaug (lake)	B2
Plantsville	D2	Taftville	G2	Bantam (lake)	C2	West Rock Ridge (hills)	D3
Pleasure Beach 1,356	G3	Talcottville 875	F1	Barkhamsted (res.)	D1	Willimantic (riv.)	F1
Plymouth • 11,822	C2	Tariffville 1,477	D1	Bear (mt.)	B1	Wononskopomuc (lake)	B1
Pomfret • 3,102	H1	Terryville 5,426	C2	Byram (riv.)	A4	Yantic (riv.)	G2
Poquonock	E1	Thamesville	G2	Candlewood (lake)	A2		
		Thomaston • 6,947	C2	Coast Guard Academy	G3	• Population of town or township	

Gales Ferry 1,191	G3	Ivoryton	F3
Gaylordsville 960	A2	Jewett City 3,349	H2
Georgetown 1,694	B4	Kensington 8,306	D2
Glastonbury 7,082	E2	Kent • 2,918	B2
Glastonbury • 27,901	E2	Killingly • 15,889	H1
Glenville	A4	Killingworth • 4,814	E3
Goshen • 2,329	C1	Lake Pocotopaug 3,029	F2
Granby 1,912	D1	Lakeville	B1
Granby • 9,369	D1	Lebanon • 6,041	G2
Greenfield Hill	B4	Ledyard • 14,913	G3
Greenwich • 58,441	A4	Leetes Island 500	E3
Grosvenor Dale 700	H1	Lisbon • 3,790	G2
Groton 9,837	G3	Litchfield 1,378	C2
Groton • 45,144	G3	Litchfield • 8,365	C2
Guilford 2,588	E3	Long Hill	C3
Guilford • 19,848	E3	Lords Point 500	H3
Haddam • 6,769	D3	Lyons Plain 700	B4
Hamden • 52,434	D3	Madison 2,139	E3
Hampton • 1,578	G1	Madison • 15,485	E3
Hanover 500	G2	Manchester 31,058	E1
Hartford (cap.) 139,739	E1	Manchester • 51,618	E1
Hartland • 1,866	D1	Mansfield • 21,103	F1
Harwinton 3,293	C1	Mansfield Center 1,043	G1
Harwinton • 5,228	C1	Marion 900	D2
Hawleyville 600	B3	Marlborough 1,039	F2
Hazardville 5,179	E1	Marlborough • 5,535	F2
Hebron • 7,079	F2	Meriden 59,479	D2
Higganum 1,692	E2	Middlebury • 6,145	C2
Highland Park 500	F1	Middlefield • 3,925	E2
Hockanum	E1	Middletown 42,762	E2
Huntington	C3	Milford 48,168	C4
Indian Neck	D3	Mill Plain 750	A3

Agriculture, Industry and Resources

DOMINANT LAND USE

Specialized Dairy

Dairy, Poultry, Mixed Farming

Forests

Urban Areas

MAJOR MINERAL OCCURRENCES

Cl Clay   Mi Mica

Major Industrial Areas

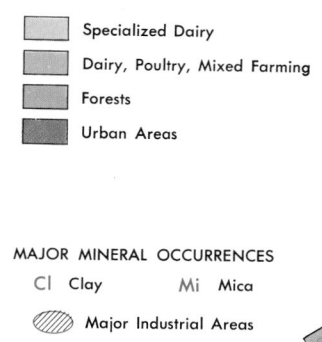

Florida

SCALE

0 5 10 20 30 40 50 MI.
0 5 10 20 30 40 50KM.

State Capitals .... ⊛
County Seats .... ⊙
Canals ....
Major Limited Access Hwys. ....

Western Part of Florida

Same scale as main map

© Copyright HAMMOND INCORPORATED, Maplewood, N.J.

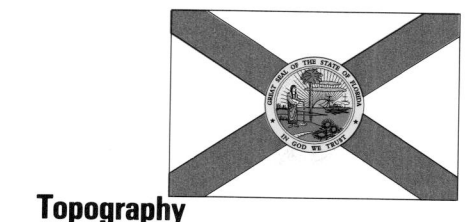

AREA 58,664 sq. mi. (151,940 sq. km.)
POPULATION 13,003,362
CAPITAL Tallahassee
LARGEST CITY Jacksonville
HIGHEST POINT (Walton County) 345 ft. (105 m.)
SETTLED IN 1565
ADMITTED TO UNION March 3, 1845
POPULAR NAME Sunshine State; Peninsula State
STATE FLOWER Orange Blossom
STATE BIRD Mockingbird

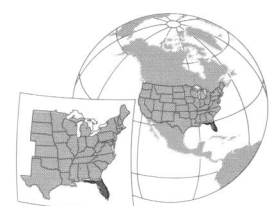

Topography

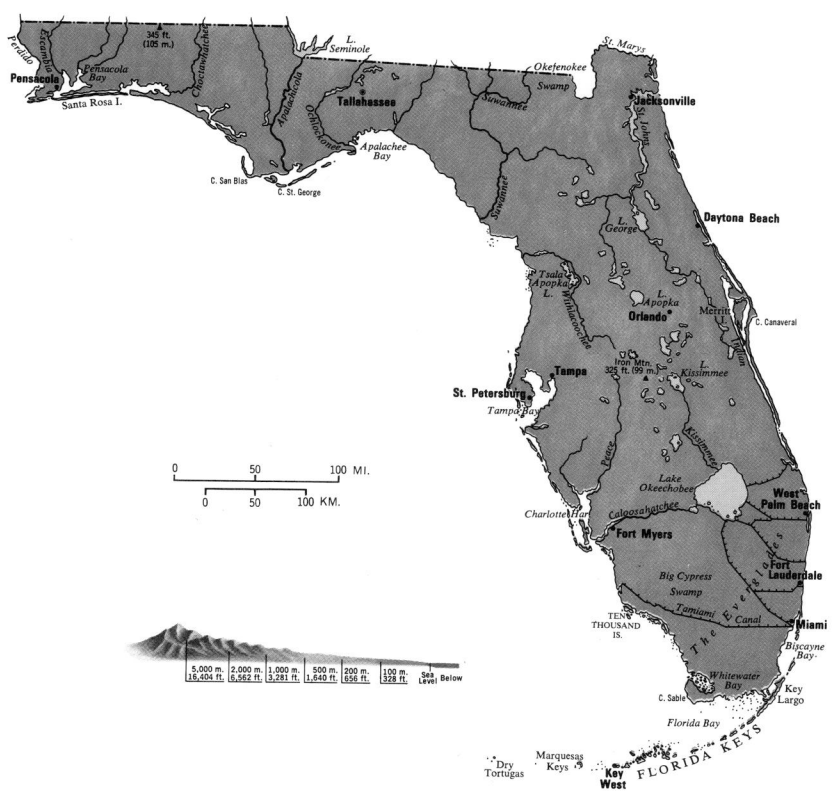

Daytona Beach 2,335 ....F2	Hastings 595 ....E2
Daytona Beach Shores 1,324 ..F2	Havana 1,654 ....B1
De Bary 7,176 ....E3	Hawthorne 1,305 ....D2
De Funiak Springs▲ 5,120 ...C6	Hernando 2,103 ....D3
De Land 16,491 ....E2	Hialeah 188,004 ....B4
De Leon Springs 1,481 ....E2	Hialeah Gardens 7,713 ....B4
Deer Park 250 ....E4	High Point 2,288 ....B3
Deerfield Beach 46,325 ....F5	High Springs 3,144 ....D2
Delray Beach 47,181 ....F5	Highland Beach 3,209 .....F5
Deltona 50,828 ....E3	Highland City 1,919 ....E4
Destin 8,080 ....C6	Highland Park 155 ....E4
Doctors Inlet 800 ....E1	Hiland Park 3,865 ....C6
Dover 2,606 ....D4	Hillcrest Heights 221 .....E4
Dowling Park 250 ....C1	Hilliard 1,751 ....E1
Dundee 2,335 ....E3	Hillsboro Beach 1,748 ....F5
Dunnellon 1,624 ....D2	Hinson 250 ....B1
Dunedin 34,012 ....B2	Hobe Sound 11,507 ....F4
Eagle Lake 1,758 ....E4	Holder 350 ....D3
Earleton 350 ....D2	Hollister 980 ....E2
East Lake-Orient Park 6,171 ..C2	Holly Hill 11,141 ....E2
East Naples 22,951 ....E5	Hollywood 121,697 ....B4
East Palatka 1,989 ....E2	Holmes Beach 4,810 ......D4
Eastpoint 1,577 ....B2	Holt 850 ....C6
Eatonville 2,170 ....E3	Homestead 26,866 ....F6
Ebro 255 ....C6	Homosassa 2,113 ....D3
Edgewater 15,337 ....F3	Homosassa Springs 6,271 ..D3
Edgewood 1,062 ....E3	Horseshoe Beach 252 .....C2
Egypt Lake 14,580 ....C2	Hosford 750 ....B1
El Portal 2,457 ....B4	Howey In The Hills 724 ..E3
Elfers 12,356 ....D3	Hudson 7,344 ....D3
Elkton 240 ....E2	Hurlburt B6
Englewood 15,025 ....D5	Hypoluxo 830 ....F5
Ensley 16,362 ....B6	Immokalee 14,120 ....E5
Espanola 300 ....E2	Indialantic 2,844 ....F3
Estero 3,177 ....E5	Indian Creek 44 ....B4
Esto 253 ....C5	Indian Harbour Beach 6,933 ..F3
Eustis 12,967 ....E3	Indian River Shores 2,278 ..F4
Everglades City 524 ....E6	Indian Rocks Beach 3,963 ..B3
Fairbanks 300 ....D2	Indian Shores 1,405 ......B3
Fairfield 450 ....D2	Indiantown 4,794 ....F4
Fanning Springs 493 ....C2	Inglis 1,241 ....D2
Felda 500 ....E5	Intercession City 600 .....E3
Fellsmere 2,179 ....F4	Interlachen 1,160 ....E2
Fernandina Beach▲ 8,765 ...E1	Inverness▲ 5,797 ....D3
Five Points 1,136 ....D1	Islamorada 1,220 ....F7
Flagler Beach 3,820 ....E2	Islandia 13 ....F6
Florahome 400 ....E2	Jacksonville Beach 17,839 ..E1
Floral City 2,609 ....D3	Jacksonville▲ 672,971 ....E1
Florida City 5,806 ....F6	Jasmine Estates 17,136 ...D3
Florida Ridge 12,218 ....F4	Jasper▲ 2,099 ....D1
Foley 525 ....C1	Jay 666 ....B5
Fort Denaud 600 ....E5	Jennings 712 ....C1
Fort Green 300 ....E4	Jensen Beach 9,884 ....F4
Fort Lauderdale▲ 149,377 ..C4	June Park 4,080 ....F3
Fort McCoy 600 ....E2	Juno Beach 2,121 ....F5
Fort Meade 4,976 ....E4	Jupiter 24,986 ....F5
Fort Myers Beach 9,284 .....E5	Jupiter Island 549 ....F4
Fort Myers▲ 45,206 ....E5	Kathleen 2,743 ....D3
Fort Ogden 900 ....E4	Kenansville 650 ....F4
Fort Pierce▲ 36,830 ....F4	Kendall 87,271 ....B5
Fort Walton Beach 21,471 ...C6	Kenneth City 4,462 ....B3
Fort White 268 ....D2	Key Biscayne 8,854 ....B5
Fountain 900 ....B1	Key Colony Beach 977 ....F7
Freeport 843 ....C6	Key Largo 11,336 ....F6
Frink 275 ....D6	Key West▲ 24,832 ....E7
Frostproof 2,808 ....E4	Keystone Heights 1,315 ...E2
Fruitland Park 2,754 ....D3	Kinard 295 ....C6
Fruitville 9,808 ....D4	Kissimmee▲ 30,050 ....E3
Gainesville▲ 84,770 ....D2	La Belle▲ 2,703 ....E5
Geneva 1,120 ....E3	La Crosse 122 ....D2
Georgetown 687 ....E2	Lacoochee 2,072 ....D3
Gibsonton 7,706 ....C3	Lady Lake 8,071 ....E3
Gifford 6,278 ....F4	Lake Alfred 3,622 ....E3
Glen Saint Mary 462 ....D1	Lake Buena Vista 1,776 ...E3
Glenwood 400 ....E2	Lake Butler▲ 2,116 ....D1
Golden Beach 774 ....C4	Lake Carroll 13,012 ....C2
Golden Gate 14,148 ....E5	Lake Como 340 ....E2
Golf 234 ....F5	Lake Forest B4
Gomez 400 ....F4	Lake Harbor 600 ....F5
Gonzalez 7,669 ....B6	Lake Helen 2,344 ....E3
Goodland 600 ....E6	Lake Jem 314 ....E3
Goulding 4,159 ....B6	Lake Magdalene 15,973 ..D3
Goulds 7,284 ....F6	Lake Mary 5,929 ....E3
Graceville 2,675 ....D5	Lake Monroe 600 ....E3
Graham 225 ....D2	Lake Park 6,704 ....F5
Grand Ridge 536 ....A1	Lake Placid 1,158 ....E4
Grandin 250 ....E2	Lake Wales 9,670 ....E4
Grant 500 ....F4	Lake Worth 28,564 ....G5
Green Cove Springs▲ 4,497 ..E2	Lakeland 70,576 ....D3
Greenacres City 18,683 .....F5	Lakeport 375 ....E4
Greensboro 586 ....B1	Lakewood 7,211 ....C5
Greenville 950 ....C1	Land O'Lakes 7,892 ....D3
Greenwood 474 ....A1	Lantana 8,392 ....F5
Gretna 1,981 ....B1	Lauderdale Lakes 27,341 ..B3
Grove City 2,374 ....D5	Lauderdale-by-the-Sea 2,990 ..C3
Groveland 2,300 ....E3	Lauderhill 49,708 ....B3
Gulf Breeze 5,530 ....B6	Laurel 8,245 ....D4
Gulf Hammock 325 ....D2	Laurel Hill 543 ....C5
Gulf Harbors D3	Lawtey 676 ....D1
Gulf Stream 690 ....F5	Layton 183 ....F7
Gulfport 11,727 ....B3	Lazy Lake 33 ....B3
Haines City 11,683 ....E3	Lecanto 1,243 ....D3
Hallandale 30,996 ....B4	Lee 306 ....C1
Hampton 296 ....D2	Leesburg 14,903 ....E3
Harlem 2,826 ....F5	(continued on following page)
Harold 500 ....B6	

COUNTIES

Alachua 181,596 ....D2	Manatee 211,707 ....D4
Baker 18,486 ....D1	Marion 194,833 ....D2
Bay 126,994 ....C6	Martin 100,900 ....F4
Bradford 22,515 ....D2	Monroe 78,024 ....E7
Brevard 398,978 ....F3	Nassau 43,941 ....E1
Broward 1,255,488 ....F5	Okaloosa 143,776 ....C6
Calhoun 11,011 ....C6	Okeechobee 29,627 ....F4
Charlotte 110,975 ....E5	Orange 677,491 ....E3
Citrus 93,515 ....D3	Osceola 107,728 ....E3
Clay 105,986 ....E2	Palm Beach 863,518 ....F5
Collier 152,099 ....E5	Pasco 281,131 ....D3
Columbia 42,613 ....D1	Pinellas 851,659 ....D4
Dade 1,937,094 ....F6	Polk 405,382 ....E4
De Soto 19,039 ....E4	Putnam 65,070 ....E2
Dixie 10,585 ....C2	Saint Johns 51,303 ....E2
Duval 672,971 ....E1	Saint Lucie 87,182 ....F4
Escambia 262,798 ....B6	Santa Rosa 81,608 ....B6
Flagler 28,701 ....E2	Sarasota 277,776 ....D4
Franklin 8,967 ....B2	Seminole 287,529 ....E3
Gadsden 41,105 ....B1	Sumter 31,577 ....D3
Gilchrist 9,667 ....D2	Suwannee 26,780 ....C1
Glades 7,591 ....E5	Taylor 17,111 ....C1
Gulf 11,504 ....D7	Union 10,252 ....D1
Hamilton 10,930 ....D1	Volusia 370,712 ....E2
Hardee 19,499 ....E4	Wakulla 14,202 ....B1
Hendry 25,773 ....E5	Walton 27,760 ....C6
Hernando 101,115 ....D3	Washington 16,919 ....C6
Highlands 68,432 ....E4	
Hillsborough 834,054 ......D3	## CITIES and TOWNS
Holmes 15,778 ....C5	
Indian River 90,208 ....F4	Alachua 4,529 ....D2
Jackson 41,375 ....D5	Alford 472 ....D6
Jefferson 11,296 ....C1	Altamonte Springs 34,879 ..E3
Lafayette 5,578 ....C1	Altha 497 ....A1
Lake 152,104 ....E3	Altoona 800 ....E2
Lee 335,113 ....E5	Alturas 900 ....E4
Leon 192,493 ....B1	Alva 1,036 ....E5
Levy 25,923 ....D2	Anna Maria 1,744 ....D4
Liberty 5,569 ....B1	Anthony 500 ....D2
Madison 16,569 ....C1	Apalachicola▲ 2,602 ......A2
	Apollo Beach 6,025 ....D4
	Apopka 13,512 ....E3

Arcadia▲ 6,488 ....E4	Bostwick 500 ....E2	Chiefland 1,917 ....D2
Archer 1,372 ....D2	Boulogne E1	Chipley▲ 3,866 ....D6
Aripeka 450 ....D3	Bowling Green 1,836 ....E4	Chokoloskee 600 ....E6
Astatula 981 ....E3	Boynton Beach 46,194 ....F5	Christmas 800 ....E3
Astor 1,273 ....E2	Bradenton Beach 1,657 ....D4	Cinco Bayou 322 ....B6
Atlantic Beach 11,636 ....E1	Bradenton▲ 43,779 ....D4	Citra 500 ....D2
Auburndale 8,858 ....E4	Bradley 1,108 ....D4	Clarksville 350 ....D6
Avon Park 8,042 ....E4	Brandon 57,985 ....D4	Clearwater▲ 98,784 ....B2
Azalea Park 8,926 ....E4	Branford 670 ....D2	Clermont 6,910 ....E3
Babson Park 1,125 ....E4	Briny Breezes 400 ....G5	Cleveland 2,896 ....E5
Bagdad 1,457 ....B6	Bristol▲ 937 ....B1	Clewiston 6,085 ....E5
Baker 500 ....C6	Broadview Park-Rock Hill	Cocoa 17,722 ....F3
Bal Harbour 3,045 ....C4	6,022 ....B4	Cocoa Beach 12,123 ....F3
Baldwin 1,450 ....E1	Bronson▲ 875 ....D2	Coconut Creek 27,485 .....F5
Barberville 500 ....E2	Brooker 312 ....D2	Coleman 857 ....D3
Bartow▲ 14,716 ....E4	Brooksville▲ 7,440 ....D3	Compass Lake 296 ....D6
Bascom 90 ....A1	Browardale 6,257 ....B4	Concord 300 ....B1
Basinger 300 ....F4	Browns Village B5	Cooper City 20,791 ....B4
Bay Harbor Islands 4,703 ..B4	Bruce 221 ....B5	Copeland 350 ....E6
Bay Lake E3	Bunche Park 4,388 ....B4	Coral Cove 2,042 ....D4
Bay Pines 4,171 ....B3	Bunnell▲ 1,873 ....E2	Coral Gables 40,091 ....B5
Bayshore 17,062 ....E5	Bushnell▲ 1,998 ....D3	Coral Springs 79,443 ......F5
Bayshore Gardens 14,945 ..D4	Callahan 946 ....E1	Cornwell 700 ....E4
Bee Ridge 6,406 ....D4	Callaway 12,253 ....D6	Cortez 4,509 ....D4
Bell 267 ....D2	Campbellton 202 ....D6	Cottagehill 300 ....B6
Belle Glade 16,177 ....F5	Canal Point 900 ....F5	Cottondale 900 ....D6
Belle Glade Camp 1,616 ..F5	Candler 275 ....E2	Crawfordville▲ 1,110 .....B1
Belle Isle 5,272 ....E3	Cantonment B6	Crescent City 1,859 ....E2
Belleair 3,968 ....B2	Cape Canaveral 8,014 ....F3	Crestview▲ 9,886 ....C6
Belleair Beach 2,070 .....B2	Cape Coral 74,991 ....E5	Cross City▲ 2,041 ....C2
Belleair Bluffs 2,128 .....B3	Carol City 53,331 ....B4	Cross Creek D2
Belleair Shore 80 ....B3	Carrabelle 1,200 ....B2	Crystal Lake 5,300 ....D4
Belleview 2,666 ....D2	Carville 631 ....C6	Crystal River 4,044 ....D3
Beverly Beach 312 ....E2	Cassadaga 350 ....E2	Crystal Springs 800 ....D3
Biscayne Park 3,068 .....B4	Casselberry 18,911 ....E3	Cutler Ridge 21,268 ....F6
Bithlo 4,834 ....E3	Cedar Grove 1,479 ....D6	Cypress 9,188 ....A1
Blountstown▲ 2,404 .....A1	Cedar Key 668 ....C2	Cypress Gardens 8,043 ....E3
Boca Grande 900 ....D5	Center Hill 735 ....D3	Cypress Quarters 1,343 ...F4
Boca Raton 61,492 ....F5	Century 1,989 ....B5	Dade City▲ 5,633 ....D3
Bokeelia 750 ....D5	Charlotte Harbor 3,327 ....E5	Dania 13,024 ....B4
Bonifay▲ 2,612 ....C5	Chattahoochee 4,382 ....B1	Davenport 1,529 ....E3
Bonita Sings 5,435 ....E5	Cherry Lake Farms 400 ....C1	Davie 47,217 ....B4
		Day 61,921 ....C1

(continued)

Lehigh Acres 13,611 E5
Leisure City 19,379 F6
Leonia 350 C5
Leto 9,003 C2
Lighthouse Point 10,378 F5
Live Oak▲ 6,332 D1
Lloyd 500 C1
Lochloosa 400 E2
Longboat Key 5,937 D4
Longwood 13,316 E3
Lorida 950 E4
Loughman 1,214 E3
Lowell 250 D2
Loxahatchee 950 F5
Lutz 10,552 D3
Lynn Haven 9,298 C6
Macclenny▲ 3,966 D1
Madeira Beach 4,225 B3
Madison▲ 3,345 C1
Maitland 9,110 E3
Malabar 1,977 F3
Malone 765 A1
Mango 8,700 D4
Marathon 8,857 E7
Marco (Marco Island) 9,493 E6
Margate 42,985 F5
Marianna▲ 6,292 A1
Marineland 21 E2
Mary Esther 4,139 B6
Masaryktown 389 D3
Mascotte 1,761 E3
Mayo▲ 917 C1
McDavid 500 B5
McIntosh 411 D2
Medley 663 B4
Melbourne 59,646 F3
Melbourne Beach 3,021 F3
Melrose 6,477 D2
Melrose Park 5,672 B4
Memphis 6,760 D4
Merritt Island 32,886 F3
Mexico Beach 992 D6
Miami Beach 92,639 C5
Miami Lakes 12,750 B4
Miami Shores 10,084 B4
Miami Springs 13,268 B5
Miami▲ 358,548 B5
Micanopy 612 D2
Micco 8,757 F4
Miccosukee 300 B1
Middleburg 6,223 E1
Midway 852 B1
Milligan 950 C6
Milton▲ 7,216 B6
Mims 9,412 F3
Minneola 1,515 E3
Miramar 40,663 B4
Molino 1,207 B6
Montbrook 250 D2
Monticello▲ 2,573 C1
Montverde 890 E3
Moore Haven▲ 1,432 E5
Mossy Head 280 C6
Mount Dora 7,196 E3
Mulberry 2,988 E4
Murdock 272 D4
Myakka City 672 D4
Myrtle Grove 17,402 B6
Naples Park 8,002 E5
Naples▲ 19,505 E5
Naranja 5,790 F6
Neptune Beach 6,816 E1
New Port Richey 14,044 D3
New Smyrna Beach 16,543 F2
Newberry 1,644 D2
Niceville 10,507 C6
Nichols 300 E4
Nocatee 950 E4
Nokomis 3,448 D4
Noma 207 C5
Norland 22,109 B4
North Bay Village 5,383 B4
North Fort Myers 30,027 E5
North Lauderdale 26,506 B3
North Miami 49,998 B4
North Miami Beach 35,359 C4
North Naples 13,422 E5
North Palm Beach 11,343 F5
North Port 11,973 D4
North Redington Beach 1,135 B3
Oak Hill 917 F3
Oakland 700 E3
Oakland Park 1,743 B3
Ocala▲ 42,045 D2
Ocean Breeze Park 519 F4
Ocean Ridge 1,570 F5
Ochopee 750 E6
Ocoee 12,778 E3
Odessa 500 D3
Ojus 15,519 B4
Okahumpka 900 D3
Okeechobee▲ 4,943 F4
Oklawaha 700 E2
Old Town 850 C2
Oldsmar 8,361 B2
Olustee 400 D1
Ona E4
Oneco 6,417 D4
Opa Locka 14,460 B4
Orange 5,347 B1
Orange City 2,795 E3
Orange Lake 900 D2
Orange Park 9,488 E1
Orange Springs 500 E2
Orchid 10 F4
Orlando▲ 164,693 E3
Ormond Beach 29,721 E2
Ormond-by-the-Sea 7,665 E2
Osprey 2,597 D4
Osteen 875 E3
Otter Creek 136 D2
Oviedo 11,114 E3
Oxford D3
Ozona 900 D3
Pace 6,277 B6
Pahokee 6,822 F5
Palatka▲ 10,201 E2
Palm Bay 62,632 F3
Palm Beach 9,814 G5
Palm Beach Gardens 22,965 F5
Palm Beach Shores 1,040 G5
Palm City 3,925 F4
Palm Coast 14,287 E2
Palm Harbor 50,256 D3
Palm River-Clair Mel 14,447 C3
Palm Shores 210 F3
Palm Springs 9,763 F5
Palmetto 9,268 D4
Panacea 950 B1
Panama City Beach 4,051 C6
Panama City▲ 34,378 C6
Parker 4,598 C6
Parkland 3,558 F5
Parrish 950 D4
Paxton 600 C5
Pembroke Park 4,933 B4
Pembroke Pines 65,452 B4
Penney Farms 609 E2
Pennsuco 15 B4
Pensacola▲ 58,165 B6
Perrine 15,576 F6
Perry▲ 7,151 C1
Pierce 500 E4
Pierson 2,988 E2
Pine Hills 35,322 E3
Pineland 700 D5
Pinellas Park 43,426 B3
Placida 250 D5
Plant City 22,754 D3
Plantation 1,885 B4
Plymouth 950 E3
Polk City 1,439 E3
Pomona Park 663 E2
Pompano Beach 72,411 F5
Ponce Inlet 1,704 F2
Ponce de Leon 406 C6
Ponte Vedra Beach E1
Port Charlotte 41,535 D5
Port Mayaca 400 F5
Port Orange 35,317 F2
Port Richey 2,523 D3
Port Saint Joe 4,044 D6
Port Saint Lucie 55,866 F4
Port Salerno 7,786 F4
Portland 300 C6
Princeton 7,073 F6
Progress Village C3
Punta Gorda▲ 10,747 E5
Quincy▲ 7,444 B1
Raiford 198 D1
Raleigh 275 D2
Red Bay 300 C6
Reddick 554 D2
Redington Beach 1,626 B3
Redington Shores 2,366 B3
Richland 250 D3
Richmond Heights 8,583 F6
Riverland 5,919 B4
Riverview 6,478 D4
Riviera Beach 27,639 G5
Rockledge 16,023 F3
Roseland 1,379 F4
Round Lake 275 D6
Ruskin 6,046 C3
Safety Harbor 15,124 B2
Saint Augustine Beach 3,657 E2
Saint Augustine▲ 11,692 E2
Saint Catherine 486 D3
Saint Cloud 12,453 E3
Saint James City 1,904 D5
Saint Leo 1,009 D3
Saint Lucie 584 F4
Saint Marks 307 B1
Saint Petersburg 238,629 B3
Saint Petersburg Beach 9,200 B3
Samoset 3,119 D4
Samsula (Samsula-Spruce
Creek) 3,404 E2
San Antonio 776 D3
San Mateo 975 E2
Sanderson 800 D1
Sanford▲ 32,387 E3
Sanibel 5,468 D5
Sarasota Springs 16,088 D4
Sarasota▲ 50,961 D4
Satellite Beach 9,889 F3
Satsuma 610 E2
Scottsmoor 900 F3
Sea Ranch Lakes 619 C3
Sebastian 10,205 F4
Sebring▲ 8,900 E4
Seffner 5,371 D4
Seminole 9,251 B3
Seville 500 E2
Sewalls Point 1,187 F4
Shalimar 341 C6
Sharpes 3,348 F3
Siesta Key 7,772 D4
Silver Springs 6,421 D2
Sneads 1,746 B1
Sopchoppy 367 B1
Sorrento 500 E3
South Bay 3,558 F5
South Daytona 12,482 F2
South Miami 10,404 B5
South Miami Heights 30,030 F6
South Pasadena 5,644 B3
South Patrick Shores 10,249 F3
South Venice 11,951 D4
Southport 1,992 C6
Sparr 902 D2
Springfield 8,715 D6
Starke▲ 5,226 D2
Steinhatchee 800 C2
Stuart▲ 11,936 F4
Summerfield 780 D2
Summerland Key 350 E7
Sun City 8,326 D4
Sun City Center 5,605 C3
Sunny Isles 11,772 C4
Sunnyside 1,008 C6
Sunrise 64,407 B4
Surfside 4,108 B4
Suwannee 365 C2
Sweetwater 13,909 B5
Switzerland 3,906 E1
Taft 900 E3
Tallahassee (cap.)▲ 124,773 B1
Tamarac 44,822 B3
Tampa▲ 280,015 C2
Tarpon Springs 17,906 D3
Tavares▲ 7,383 E3
Tavernier 2,433 F6
Telogia 400 B1
Temple Terrace 16,444 C2
Tequesta 4,499 F5
Terra Ceia 450 D4
Thonotosassa 900 D3
Tice 3,971 E5
Titusville▲ 39,394 F3
Town'n Country 60,946 B2
Treasure Island 7,266 B3
Trenton▲ 1,287 D2
Trilby 930 D3
Umatilla 2,350 E3
University 23,760 C2
Valparaiso 4,672 C6
Venice 16,922 D4
Venus 500 E4
Vernon 778 C6
Vero Beach▲ 17,350 F4
Villa Tasso 365 C6
Virginia Gardens 2,212 B5
Wabasso 1,145 F4
Wacissa 350 B1
Wakulla 225 B1
Waldo 1,017 D2
Walnut Hill 500 B5
Ward Ridge 104 D7
Warrington 16,040 B6
Watertown 3,340 D1
Wauchula▲ 3,253 E4
Wausau 313 D6
Waverly 2,071 E4
Webster 746 D3
Weeki Wachee 53 D3
Weirsdale 995 D3
Welaka 533 E2
Wellborn 500 D1
West Bay 500 C6
West Eau Gallie 2,591 F3
West Melbourne 8,399 F3
West Miami 5,727 B5
West Palm Beach▲ 67,643 F5
West Pensacola 22,107 B6
Westville 257 C6
Westwood Lakes 11,522 B5
Wewahitchka▲ 1,779 D6
White City 4,645 F4
White Springs 704 D1
Wildwood 3,421 D3
Williston 2,179 D2
Wilton Manors 11,804 B3
Wimauma 2,932 D4
Windermere 1,371 E3
Winter Beach 300 F4
Winter Garden 9,745 E3
Winter Haven 24,725 E3
Winter Park 22,242 E3
Winter Springs 22,151 E3
Woodville 2,760 B1
Worthington Springs 178 D2
Yalaha 1,168 E3
Yankeetown 635 D2
Youngstown 900 D6
Yulee 6,915 E1
Zellwood 1,760 E3
Zephyrhills 8,220 D3
Zolfo Springs 1,219 E4

OTHER FEATURES

Alapaha (riv.) C1
Alligator (lake) E3
Amelia (isl.) E1
Anastasia (isl.) E2
Anclote (keys) D3
Apalachee (bay) B2
Apalachicola (bay) B2
Apalachicola (riv.) A1
Apopka (lake) E3
Arbuckle (lake) E4
Aucilla (riv.) C1
Banana (riv.) F3
Beresford (lake) E3
Big Cypress (swamp) E5
Big Cypress Nat'l Preserve E5
Biscayne (bay) F6
Biscayne (key) B5
Biscayne Nat'l Park F6
Blackwater (riv.) B6
Blue Cypress (lake) F4
Boca Chica (key) E7
Boca Ciega (key) B3
Boca Grande (key) D7
Bryant (lake) E2
Caloosahatchee (riv.) E5
Canaveral (cape) F3
Captiva (isl.) D5
Casey (key) D4
Castillo de San Marcos
Nat'l Mon. E2
Cecil Field Naval Air Sta. E1
Charlotte (harb.) D5
Chattahoochee (riv.) B1
Chipola (riv.) D6
Choctawhatchee (riv.) C6
Crescent (lake) E2
Cumberland Island
Nat'l Seashore E1
Cypress (lake) E3
De Soto Nat'l Mem. D4
Dead (lake) D6
Dexter (lake) E2
Dog (isl.) B2
Dorr (lake) E2
Dry Tortugas (keys) D7
Dumfoundling (bay) C4
East (pt.) E6
Eglin A.F.B 8,347 C6
Egmont (key) D4
Elliott (key) F6
Escambia (riv.) B6
Estero (isl.) E5
Eureka (res.) E2
Everglades, The (swamp) F6
Everglades Nat'l Park E6
Fenholloway (riv.) C1
Florida (bay) F6
Florida (cape) F6
Florida (keys) E7
Florida (strs.) F7
Fort Caroline Nat'l Mem. E1
Fort Jefferson Nat'l Mon. C7
Fort Matanzas Nat'l Mon. E2
Gasparilla (isl.) D5
George (lake) E2
Grassy (key) F7
Gulf Islands Nat'l Seashore B6
Harney (lake) F3
Hart (lake) E3
Hillsborough (bay) C3
Hillsborough (canal) F5
Hillsborough (riv.) C2
Homestead A.F.B 5,153 F6
Homosassa (isls.) D3
Iamonia (lake) B1
Indian (riv.) F3
Iron (mt.) E4
Istokpoga (lake) E4
Jackson (lake) B1
Jackson (lake) E4
Jacksonville Naval Air Sta. E1
John F. Kennedy
Space Center F3
June in Winter (lake) E4
Kerr (lake) E2
Key Largo (key) F6
Key Vaca (key) E7
Key West Naval Air Sta. E7
Kissimmee (lake) E4
Kissimmee (riv.) E4
Largo (key) F6
Levy (lake) D2
Lochloosa (lake) D2
Long (key) B3
Long (key) F7
Longboat (key) D4
Lower Matecumbe (key) F7
Lowery (lake) E3
MacDill A.F.B. C3
Manatee (riv.) D4
Marco (isl.) E6
Marian (lake) E4
Marquesas (keys) D7
Matanzas (inlet) E2
Mayport Naval Air Sta. E1
McCoy A.F.B. E3
Merritt (isl.) F3
Mexico (gulf) C4
Miami (canal) F5
Miami (riv.) B5
Miccosukee (lake) B1
Monroe (lake) E3
Mosquito (lag.) F3
Mullet (key) D4
Myakka (riv.) D4
Nassau (riv.) E1
Nassau (sound) E1
New (riv.) B1
New (riv.) D1
Newnans (lake) D2
North Merritt (isl.) F3
North New River (canal) F5
Ochlockonee (riv.) B1
Okaloacoochee Slough
(swamp) E5
Okeechobee (lake) F5
Okefenokee (swamp) D1
Oklawaha (riv.) E2
Old Rhodes (key) F6
Old Tampa (bay) B3
Olustee (riv.) D1
Orange (lake) D2
Patrick A.F.B. F3
Peace (riv.) E4
Pensacola (bay) B6
Pensacola Naval Air Sta. B6
Perdido (riv.) B6
Pine (isl.) D5
Pine Island (sound) D5
Pinellas (pt.) B3
Piney (isl.) B1
Piney (pt.) C2
Placid (lake) E4
Plantation (key) F7
Poinsett (lake) F3
Ponce de Leon (bay) E6
Port Everglades (harb.) C4
Port Tampa (harb.) B3
Raccoon (pt.) D3
Reedy (lake) E4
Romano (cape) E6
Sable (cape) E6
Saint Andrew (pt.) D6
Saint George (cape) A2
Saint George (isl.) B2
Saint George (sound) B2
Saint Johns (riv.) E2
Saint Joseph (bay) D6
Saint Joseph (pt.) D6
Saint Lucie (canal) F4
Saint Lucie (inlet) F4
Saint Marys (riv.) D1
Saint Marys Entrance (inlet) E1
Saint Vincent (isl.) D7
San Blas (cape) D7
Sand (key) B3
Sands (key) F6
Sanibel (isl.) D5
Santa Fe (lake) D2
Santa Fe (riv.) D2
Santa Rosa (isl.) B6
Santa Rosa (sound) B6
Sarasota (pt.) D4
Seminole (lake) B1
Seminole Ind. Res. E4
Seminole Ind. Res. E5
Shark (pt.) E6
Shoal (riv.) C6
Snake Creek (canal) B4
South New River (canal) F5
Stafford (lake) D2
Sugarloaf (key) E7
Suwannee (riv.) C2
Suwannee (sound) C2
Talbot (isl.) E1
Talquin (lake) B1
Tamiami (canal) E5
Tampa (bay) D4
Ten Thousand (isls.) E6
Torch (key) E7
Treasure (isl.) B3
Tsala Apopka (lake) D3
Tyndall A.F.B. C6
Upper Matecumbe (key) F7
Vaca (key) E7
Virginia (key) B5
Waccasassa (bay) D2
Waccasassa (riv.) D2
Washington (lake) F3
Weir (lake) E2
Weohyakapka (lake) E4
West Palm Beach (canal) F5
Whitewater (bay) F6
Whiting Field Naval Air Sta. B6
Wimico (lake) A2
Winder (lake) F3
Withlacoochee (riv.) C1
Withlacoochee (riv.) D2
Yale (lake) E3
Yellow (riv.) B6

▲County seat

Agriculture, Industry and Resources

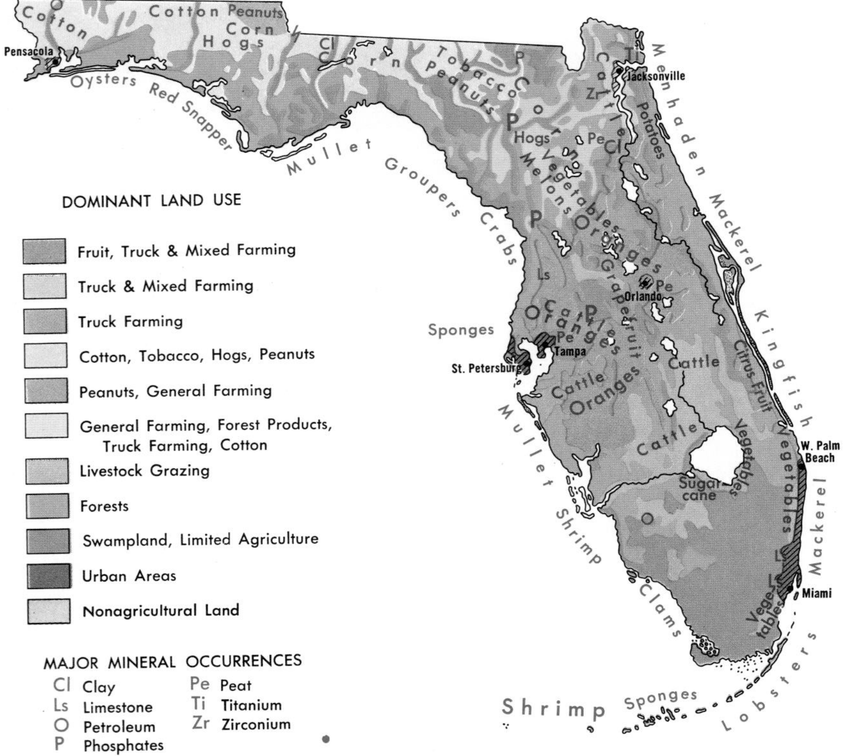

Cotton
Cotton Peanuts
Corn
Hogs
Pensacola
Oysters
Red Snapper
Mullet
Groupers
Crabs
Tobacco
Peanuts
Cattle
Potatoes
Jacksonville
Menhaden
Hogs
Melons
Vegetables
Oranges
Grapefruit
Orlando
Mackerel
Kingfish
Sponges
Tampa
St. Petersburg
Citrus Fruit
Vegetables
W. Palm Beach
Sugar cane
Shrimp
Miami
Clams
Lobsters
DOMINANT LAND USE
Fruit, Truck & Mixed Farming
Truck & Mixed Farming
Truck Farming
Cotton, Tobacco, Hogs, Peanuts
Peanuts, General Farming
General Farming, Forest Products, Truck Farming, Cotton
Livestock Grazing
Forests
Swampland, Limited Agriculture
Urban Areas
Nonagricultural Land
MAJOR MINERAL OCCURRENCES
Cl Clay
Ls Limestone
O Petroleum
P Phosphates
Pe Peat
Ti Titanium
Zr Zirconium
Water Power
Major Industrial Areas

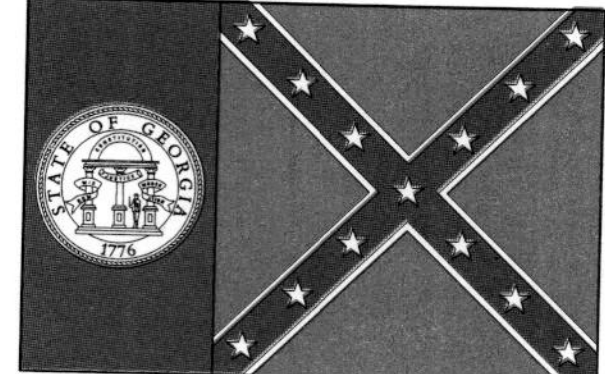

AREA 58,910 sq. mi. (152,577 sq. km.)
POPULATION 6,508,419
CAPITAL Atlanta
LARGEST CITY Atlanta
HIGHEST POINT Brasstown Bald 4,784 ft. (1458 m.)
SETTLED IN 1733
ADMITTED TO UNION January 2, 1788
POPULAR NAME Empire State of the South; Peach State
STATE FLOWER Cherokee Rose
STATE BIRD Brown Thrasher

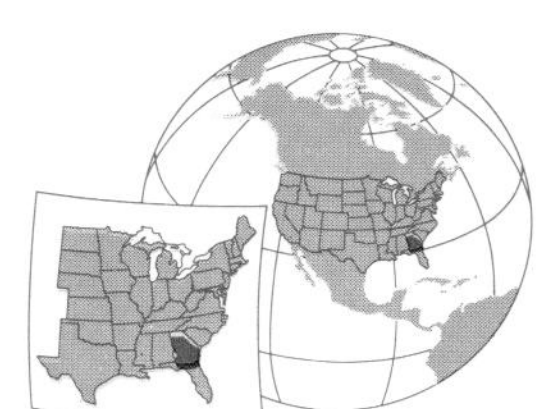

COUNTIES

Appling 15,744 H7
Atkinson 6,213 G8
Bacon 9,566 G7
Baker 3,615 D8
Baldwin 39,530 F4
Banks 10,308 E2
Barrow 29,721 E2
Bartow 55,911 C2
Ben Hill 16,245 F7
Berrien 14,153 F8
Bibb 149,967 E5
Bleckley 10,430 F6
Brantley 11,077 J8
Brooks 15,398 E9
Bryan 15,438 K6
Bulloch 43,125 J6
Burke 20,579 J4
Butts 15,326 E4
Calhoun 5,013 C7
Camden 30,167 J9
Candler 7,744 H6
Carroll 71,422 B3
Catoosa 42,464 B1
Charlton 8,496 H9
Chatham 216,935 K6
Chattahoochee 16,934 C6
Chattooga 22,242 B1
Cherokee 90,204 D2
Clarke 87,594 F3
Clay 3,364 B7
Clayton 182,052 D3
Clinch 6,160 G9
Cobb 447,745 C3
Coffee 29,592 G8
Colquitt 36,645 E8
Columbia 66,031 H3
Cook 13,456 F8
Coweta 53,853 C4
Crawford 8,991 E5
Crisp 20,011 E7
Dade 13,147 A1
Dawson 9,429 D2
De Kalb 483,024 D3
Decatur 25,511 C9
Dodge 17,607 F6
Dooly 9,901 E6
Dougherty 96,311 D7
Douglas 71,120 C3
Early 11,854 C8
Echols 2,334 G9
Effingham 25,687 K6
Elbert 18,949 G2
Emanuel 20,546 H5
Evans 8,724 J6
Fannin 15,992 D1
Fayette 62,415 C4
Floyd 81,251 B2
Forsyth 44,083 D2
Franklin 16,650 F2
Fulton 648,951 D3
Gilmer 13,368 D1
Glascock 2,357 G4
Glynn 62,496 J8
Gordon 35,072 C2
Grady 20,279 D9
Greene 11,793 F3
Gwinnett 352,910 D2
Habersham 27,621 E1
Hall 95,428 E2
Hancock 8,908 G4
Haralson 21,966 B3
Harris 17,788 C5
Hart 19,712 G2
Heard 8,628 B4
Henry 58,741 D4
Houston 89,208 E6
Irwin 8,649 F7
Jackson 30,005 E2
Jasper 8,453 E4
Jeff Davis 12,032 G7
Jefferson 17,408 H4
Jenkins 8,247 J5
Johnson 8,329 G5
Jones 20,739 E5
Lamar 13,038 D4
Lanier 5,531 F8
Laurens 39,988 G6
Lee 16,250 D7
Liberty 52,745 J7
Lincoln 7,442 H3
Long 6,202 J7
Lowndes 75,981 F9
Lumpkin 14,573 D1
Macon 13,114 D6
Madison 21,050 F2
Marion 5,590 C6
McDuffie 20,119 H4
McIntosh 8,634 K7
Meriwether 22,411 C4
Miller 6,280 C8
Mitchell 20,275 D8
Monroe 17,113 E4
Montgomery 7,163 G6
Morgan 12,883 F3
Murray 26,147 C1
Muscogee 179,278 C6
Newton 41,808 E3
Oconee 17,618 F3
Oglethorpe 8,929 F3
Paulding 41,611 C3
Peach 21,189 E5
Pickens 14,432 D2
Pierce 13,328 H8
Pike 10,224 D4
Polk 33,815 B3
Pulaski 8,108 E6
Putnam 14,137 F4
Quitman 2,209 B7
Rabun 11,648 F1
Randolph 8,023 C7
Richmond 189,719 H4
Rockdale 54,091 D3
Schley 3,588 D6
Screven 13,842 J5
Seminole 9,010 C9
Spalding 54,457 D4
Stephens 23,257 F1
Stewart 5,654 C6
Sumter 30,228 D6
Talbot 6,524 C5
Taliaferro 1,915 G3
Tattnall 17,722 H6
Taylor 7,642 D5
Telfair 11,000 G7
Terrell 10,653 D7
Thomas 38,986 E9
Tift 34,998 E7
Toombs 24,072 H6
Towns 6,754 E1
Treutlen 5,994 G6
Troup 55,536 B4
Turner 8,703 E7
Twiggs 9,806 F5
Union 11,993 E1
Upson 26,300 D5
Walker 58,340 B1
Walton 38,586 E3
Ware 35,471 H8
Warren 6,078 G4
Washington 19,112 G4
Wayne 22,356 J7
Webster 2,263 C6
Wheeler 4,903 G6
White 13,006 E1
Whitfield 72,462 B1
Wilcox 7,008 F7
Wilkes 10,597 G3
Wilkinson 10,228 F5
Worth 19,745 E8

CITIES and TOWNS

Abbeville▲ 907 F7
Acworth 4,519 C2
Adairsville 2,131 C2
Adel▲ 5,093 F8
Adrian 615 G5
Ailey 579 G6
Alamo▲ 855 G6
Alapaha 812 F8
Albany▲ 78,122 D7
Aldora 127 D4
Allenhurst 594 J7
Allentown 273 F5
Alma▲ 3,663 G7
Alpharetta 13,002 D2
Alston 160 H6
Alto 651 E2
Alvaton 91 C4
Ambrose 288 G7
Americus▲ 16,512 D6
Andersonville 277 D6
Appling▲ 150 H3
Arabi 433 E7
Aragon 902 B2
Arcade 697 E2
Arco 6,189 J8
Argyle 206 G8
Arlington 1,513 C8
Armuchee 600 B2
Arnoldsville 275 F3
Ashburn▲ 4,827 E7
Athens▲ 45,734 F3
Atlanta (cap.)▲ 394,017 K1
Attapulgus 380 D9
Auburn 3,139 E2
Augusta▲ 44,639 J4
Austell 4,173 J1
Avalon 159 F1
Avera 215 G4
Avondale Estates 2,209 L1
Baconton 623 D8
Bainbridge▲ 10,712 C9
Baldwin 1,439 E2
Ball Ground 905 D2
Barnesville▲ 4,747 D4
Barney 146 E8
Bartow 292 G5
Barwick 385 E9
Baxley▲ 3,841 H7
Bellville 192 H6
Belvedere 18,089 L1
Benevolence 138 C7
Berkeley Lake 791 D3
Berlin 480 E8
Bethlehem 348 E3
Between 82 E3
Bibb City 597 B5
Bishop 158 F3
Blackshear▲ 3,263 H8
Blairsville▲ 564 E1
Blakely▲ 5,595 C8
Bloomingdale 2,271 K6
Blue Ridge▲ 1,336 D1
Bluffton 138 C7
Blythe 300 H4
Bogart 1,018 E3
Boston 1,395 E9
Bostwick 307 E3
Bowdon 1,981 B3
Bowersville 311 F2
Bowman 791 G2
Box Springs 518 C5
Braselton 418 E2
Braswell 247 C3
Bremen 4,356 B3
Brinson 238 C9
Bronwood 513 D7
Brookfield 600 F8
Brookhaven K1
Brooklet 1,013 J6
Brooks 328 D4
Broxton 1,211 G7
Brunswick▲ 16,433 K8
Buchanan▲ 1,009 B3
Buckhead 176 F3
Buena Vista▲ 1,472 D6
Buford 8,771 D2
Butler▲ 1,673 D5
Byromville 452 E6
Byron 2,276 E5
Cadwell 458 G6
Cairo▲ 9,035 D9
Calhoun▲ 7,135 C1
Calvary 500 D9
Camak 220 G4
Camilla▲ 5,008 D8
Campton E3
Canon 737 F2
Canton▲ 4,817 C2
Carl 263 E3
Carlton 282 F2
Carnesville▲ 514 F2
Carrollton▲ 16,029 C3
Carters 12,035 C1
Cartersville▲ 9,247 C2
Cataula 500 C5
Cave Spring 950 B2
Cecil 376 F8
Cedar Grove A1
Cedartown▲ 7,978 B2
Center 3,251 F2
Centerville 2,622 E5
Centralhatchee 301 B4
Chalybeate Springs 265 C5
Chamblee 7,668 K1
Charles H6
Chatsworth▲ 2,865 C1
Chauncey 312 F6
Chester 1,072 F6
Chickamauga 2,149 B1
Chula 500 E7
Clarkesville▲ 1,151 F1
Clarkston 5,385 L1
Claxton▲ 2,464 J6
Clayton▲ 1,613 F1
Clermont 402 E2
Cleveland▲ 1,653 E1
Climax 226 D9
Clyattville 500 F9
Cobb 338 E7
Cobbtown 494 H6
Cochran▲ 4,390 F6
Cohutta 529 C1
Colbert 443 F2
Coleman 137 C7
Colemans Lake H5
College Park 20,457 K2
Collins 528 H6
Colquitt▲ 1,991 C8
Columbus▲ 179,278 C6
Comer 939 F2
Commerce 4,108 E2
Concord 211 D4
Conley 5,528 K2
Constitution K2
Conyers▲ 7,380 D3
Coolidge 610 E8
Coosa 600 B2
Cordele▲ 10,321 E7
Corinth 136 B4
Cornelia 3,219 E1
Cotton 122 D8
Covington▲ 10,026 E3
Crandall C1
Crawford 694 F3
Crawfordville▲ 577 G3
Crosland E8
Crystal Springs 500 B2
Culloden 242 D5
Cumming▲ 2,828 D2
Cusseta▲ 1,107 C6
Cuthbert▲ 3,730 C7
Dacula 2,217 E3
Dahlonega▲ 3,086 D1
Daisy 138 J6
Dallas▲ 2,810 C3
Dalton▲ 21,761 C1
Damascus 290 C8
Danielsville▲ 318 F2
Danville 480 F5
Darien▲ 1,783 K8
Dasher 659 F9
Davisboro 407 G5
Dawson▲ 5,295 D7
Dawsonville▲ 467 D2
De Soto 258 D7
Dearing 547 H4
Decatur▲ 17,336 K1
Deenwood 2,055 H8
Deepstep 111 G4
Demorest 1,088 F1
Denton 335 G7
Dexter 475 G6
Dickey C7
Dillard 199 F1
Dixie 259 E9
Dock Junction (Arco) J8
Doerun 899 E8
Donalsonville▲ 2,761 C8
Dooling 28 E6
Doraville 7,626 K1
Douglas▲ 10,464 G7
Douglasville▲ 11,635 C3
Dry Branch 700 F5
Du Pont 177 G9
Dublin▲ 16,312 G5
Ducktown D2
Dudley 430 F5
Duluth 9,029 D2
Dunwoody 26,302 K1
Durand 206 C5
East Dublin 2,524 G5
East Ellijay 303 C1
East Juliette E4
East Newnan 1,173 C4
East Point 34,402 K2
Eastman▲ 5,153 F6
Eastville E3
Eatonton▲ 4,737 F4
Eden 990 K6
Edge Hill 22 G4
Edison 1,182 C7
Elberta 1,559 E5
Elberton▲ 5,682 G2
Elizabeth 950 J1
Ellabell 500 K6
Ellaville▲ 1,724 D6
Ellenton 227 E8
Ellenwood L2
Ellerslie 700 C5
Ellijay▲ 1,178 C1
Emerson 1,201 C2
Enigma 611 F8
Ephesus 324 B4

(continued on following page)

Agriculture, Industry and Resources

DOMINANT LAND USE

- Specialized Cotton
- Cotton, General Farming
- Cotton, Tobacco, Hogs, Peanuts
- Peanuts, General Farming
- General Farming, Livestock, Fruit, Tobacco
- General Farming, Forest Products, Cotton, Truck Farming
- Forests
- Swampland, Limited Agriculture
- Urban Areas

MAJOR MINERAL OCCURRENCES

- Al Bauxite
- Ba Barite
- C Coal
- Cl Clay
- Fe Iron Ore
- Gn Granite
- Mi Mica
- Mn Manganese
- Mr Marble
- Sl Slate
- Tc Talc
- Ti Titanium

Water Power

Major Industrial Areas

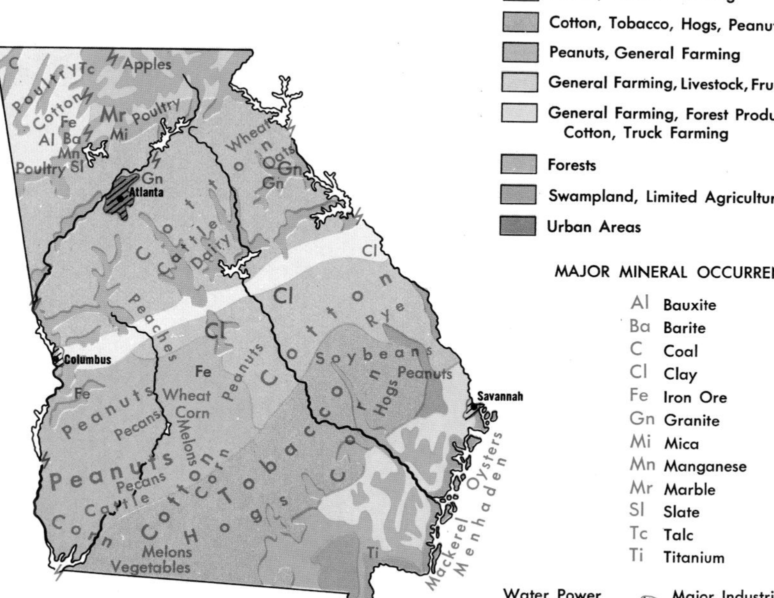

Eton 315...C1
Euharlee 850...C2
Evans 13,713...H3
Experiment 3,762...D4
Fair Oaks 6,996...J1
Fairburn 4,013...J2
Fairmount 657...C2
Fargo 800...G9
Farmington...F3
Farrar...E4
Fayetteville▲ 5,827...C4
Felton 500...B3
Finleyson 101...F6
Fitzgerald▲ 8,612...F7
Fleming 279...K7
Flemington 440...K7
Flippen 600...D3
Flovilla 602...E4
Flowery Branch 1,251...D2
Floyd...H9
Folkston▲ 2,285...H9
Forest Park 16,925...K2
Forsyth▲ 4,268...E4
Fort Gaines▲ 1,248...C7
Fort Oglethorpe 5,880...B1
Fort Valley▲ 8,198...E5
Franklin Springs 475...F2
Franklin▲ 876...B4
Funston 248...E8
Gainesville▲ 17,885...E2
Garden City 7,410...K6
Garfield 255...H5
Gay 133...C4
Geneva 182...C5
Georgetown▲ 913...B7
Gibson▲ 679...G4
Gillsville 113...E2
Gilmore...J1
Girard 195...J4
Glenn 3,676...B4
Glennville 4,144...J7
Glenwood 824...G6
Glenwood 881...L1
Glynco...J8
Good Hope 181...E3
Gordon 2,468...F5
Grantville 1,180...C4
Gray▲ 2,189...E3
Grayson 529...D3
Graysville 193...B1
Greensboro▲ 2,860...F3
Greenville▲ 1,167...C4
Griffin▲ 21,347...H4
Grovetown 3,596...J7
Gumbranch 291...K6
Guyton 740...F4
Haddock 800...D3
Hagan 787...J6
Hahira 1,353...F9
Hamilton▲ 454...C5

Hampton 2,694...D4
Hapeville 5,483...K2
Haralson 139...C4
Hardwick (Midway-Hardwick) 8,977...F4
Harlem 2,199...H4
Hartwell▲ 4,555...G2
Hawkinsville▲ 3,527...E6
Hazlehurst▲ 4,202...G7
Helen 300...E1
Helena 1,256...G6
Hephzibah 2,466...H4
Hiawassee▲ 547...E1
Higgston 274...J5
Hilltonia 402...J7
Hinesville▲ 21,603...J7
Hiram 1,389...C2
Hoboken 440...H8
Hogansville 2,976...C4
Holly Springs 2,406...D2
Homeland 981...H9
Homer▲ 742...F2
Homerville▲ 2,560...G8
Hoschton 642...E2
Howell...F9
Hull 156...F2
Ideal 554...D6
Ila 297...F2
Indian Springs 1,273...E4
Industrial City 1,054...C1
Inman 300...? ...
Iron City 503...C8
Irwinton▲ 641...F5
Isle of Hope 975...K7
Ivey 1,053...F5
Jackson▲ 4,076...D4
Jacksonville 128...G7
Jakin 137...C8
Jasper▲ 1,772...D2
Jefferson▲ 2,763...E2
Jeffersonville▲ 1,545...F5
Jenkinsburg 213...E4
Jersey 149...E3
Jesup▲ 8,958...J7
Jonesboro▲ 3,635...E4
Juliette 600...E4
Junction City 182...D5
Juno 522...? ...
Kennesaw 8,936...H4
Keysville 284...H4
Kingsland 4,699...J9
Kingston 616...C2
Kite 297...G5
Knoxville▲ 75...E5
La Fayette▲ 6,313...B1
La Grange▲ 25,597...B4
Lake City 2,733...K2
Lake Park 500...F9
Lakeland▲ 2,467...F8

Lavonia 1,840...F2
Lawrenceville▲ 16,848...D3
Leary 701...C8
Lebanon 800...D2
Leesburg▲ 1,452...D7
Leland...J1
Lenox 783...F8
Leslie 445...D6
Lexington▲ 230...F3
Lilburn 9,301...D3
Lilly 138...E6
Lincoln Park 1,755...D5
Lincolnton▲ 1,476...G3
Lindale 4,187...B2
Linwood 342...B1
Lithia Springs 11,403...C3
Lithonia 2,448...D3
Lizella 915...E5
Locust Grove 1,681...D4
Loganville 3,180...E3
Lollie...G6
Lone Oak 161...C4
Lookout Mountain 1,636...B1
Louisville▲ 2,429...H4
Lovejoy 754...D4
Lovett...G5
Ludowici▲ 1,291...J7
Lula 1,018...E2
Lumber City 1,429...G7
Lumpkin▲ 1,250...C6
Luthersville 741...C4
Lyerly 493...B1
Lyons▲ 4,502...H6
Mableton 25,725...J1
Macon▲ 106,612...E5
Madison▲ 3,483...F3
Manassas 123...H6
Manchester 4,104...C5
Mansfield 341...E3
Marietta▲ 44,129...J1
Marlow 500...D6
Marshallville 1,457...D6
Martin 243...F2
Martinez 33,731...H3
Matthews...H4
Maxeys 180...F3
Maysville 728...E2
McCaysville 1,065...D1
McDonough▲ 2,929...D4
McIntosh 500...K7
McIntyre 552...F5
McRae▲ 3,007...G6
Meansville 250...D4
Mechanicsville...L1
Meigs 1,120...D8
Meldrim 510...K6
Menlo 538...B2
Merrillville...E9
Metcalf...E9
Metter▲ 3,707...H6

Middleton...G2
Midville 620...H5
Midway 863...K7
Milan 1,056...G6
Milledgeville▲ 17,727...F4
Millen▲ 3,808...J5
Milner 321...D4
Milstead...D3
Mineral Bluff 153...D1
Mitchell 181...G4
Modoc...H5
Molena 439...D4
Monroe▲ 9,759...E3
Monticello▲ 2,289...E4
Montrose 117...F5
Moreland 366...C4
Morgan▲ 252...C7
Morganton 295...D1
Morven 536...E9
Mount Airy 543...F1
Mount Berry...B2
Mount Bethel...K1
Mount Vernon▲ 1,914...G6
Mount Zion 511...B3
Mountain City 784...F1
Mountain Park 554...D2
Mountain View...K2
Mountville 168...C4
Murrayville 550...E2
Nahunta▲ 1,049...H8
Nashville▲ 4,782...F8
Naylor 111...F9
Nelson 486...D2
New Holland 950...E2
Newborn 404...E3
Newington 319...J5
Newnan▲ 12,497...C4
Newton▲ 762...D8
Nicholls 1,003...G7
Nicholson 535...F2
Norcross 5,947...D3
Norman Park 711...E8
Normantown...H6
North Canton 950...C2
North High Shoals 268...F3
Norwood 238...G4
Nunez 135...H5
Oak Park 269...H6
Oakfield 113...E7
Oakman 150...C1
Oakwood 1,464...E2
Ochlocknee 588...E9
Ocilla▲ 3,182...F7
Oconee 234...G5
Odessadale 142...C4
Odum 388...H7
Oglethorpe▲ 1,302...D6

Ohoopee...H6
Oliver 242...J5
Omaha 116...C6
Omega 912...E8
Orchard Hill 239...D4
Oxford 1,945...E3
Palmetto 2,612...C3
Panthersville 9,874...L1
Parrott 140...D7
Patterson 626...H8
Pavo 774...E9
Payne 192...E5
Peachtree City 19,027...C4
Pearson▲ 1,714...G8
Pelham 3,869...D8
Pembroke▲ 1,503...J6
Pendergrass 298...F3
Penfield...F3
Perry▲ 9,452...E6
Phillipsburg 1,044...E8
Piedmont...D4
Pine Lake 810...D3
Pine Mountain 875...C5
Pine Park...D9
Pinehurst 388...E6
Pineora 387...K6
Pineview 594...F6
Pitts 214...E7
Pittsburg...F6
Plainfield 128...F6
Plains 711...D6
Plainville 231...C2
Pocotalago...F2
Pooler 4,453...K6
Port Wentworth 4,012...K6
Portal 522...J5
Porterdale 1,278...E3
Poulan 962...E8
Powder Springs 6,893...C3
Preston▲ 388...C6
Primrose 30...C4
Pulaski 264...J6
Putney 3,108...D8
Quitman▲ 5,292...E9
Raleigh...C5
Ranger 153...C2
Ray City 603...F8
Rayle 107...G3
Rebecca 148...E7
Red Oak 501...J2
Reidsville▲ 2,469...H6
Remerton 463...F9
Reno...D9
Rentz 364...G6
Resaca 244...C1
Rest Haven 176...E2
Reynolds 1,166...D5
Rhine 466...F7
Riceboro 745...K7

Richland 1,668...C6
Richmond Hill 2,934...K7
Riddleville 79...G5
Rincon 2,697...K6
Ringgold▲ 1,675...B1
Riverdale 9,359...K2
Riverside 74...B2
Riverside 99...E8
Roberta▲ 939...E5
Rochelle 1,510...F7
Rockmart 3,356...B2
Rocky Face 500...C1
Rocky Ford 197...J5
Rocky Mount 56...C4
Rome▲ 30,326...B2
Roopville 248...B4
Rossville 3,601...B1
Roswell 47,923...D2
Royston 2,758...F2
Ruckersville...G2
Russell 871...E3
Rutledge 659...E3
Saint George 600...H9
Saint Marks 36...H5
Saint Marys 8,187...J9
Saint Simons Island 12,026...K8
Sale City 324...D8
Sandersville▲ 6,290...G5
Sandy Springs 67,842...K1
Santa Claus 154...H6
Sardis 1,116...C4
Sargent 800...D7
Savannah▲ 137,560...L6
Scotland 244...G5
Scott 8,636...L1
Scottdale 8,770...L1
Screven 819...H7
Sea Island 600...K8
Senoia 956...C4
Seville 209...E7
Shady Dale 180...E4
Shannon 1,703...B2
Sharon 94...G3
Sharpsburg 224...C7
Shellman 1,162...C7
Shiloh 329...C5
Siloam 329...F3
Silver Creek 500...B2
Six Flags Over Georgia...J1
Smithonia...F2
Smithville 804...D7
Smyrna 30,981...K1
Snellville 12,084...D3
Social Circle 2,755...E3
Soperton▲ 2,797...G6
Sparks 1,205...F8
Sparta▲ 1,710...F4
Spring Place 246...C1
Springfield▲ 1,415...K6
Stapleton 330...H4
Statenville▲ 700...G9
Statesboro▲ 15,854...J6
Statham 1,360...E3
Stillmore 615...H6
Stockbridge 3,359...D3
Stockton 532...F9
Stone Mountain 6,494...D3
Stonewall 950...J2
Sugar Hill 4,557...E2
Sugar Valley...C1
Summertown 153...H5
Summerville▲ 5,025...B2
Sumner 209...E7
Sunny Side 215...D4
Surrency 253...H7
Suwanee 2,412...D2
Swainsboro▲ 7,361...H5
Sycamore 417...E7
Sylvania▲ 2,871...J5
Sylvester▲ 5,702...E7
Talbotton▲ 1,046...C5
Talking Rock 62...D1
Tallapoosa 2,805...B3
Tallulah Falls 147...E1
Talmo 189...E2
Tarrytown 130...H6
Tate 950...C2
Taylorsville 269...C2
Tazewell...D6
Tell...J2
Temple 1,870...B3
Tennille 1,552...G5
The Rock 88...D5
Thomaston▲ 9,127...D5
Thomasville▲ 17,457...E9
Thomson▲ 6,862...H4
Thunderbolt 2,786...L7
Tifton▲ 14,215...F7
Tiger 301...F1
Tignall 711...G3
Toccoa▲ 8,266...F1
Toco Hills...K1
Toomsboro 617...F5
Towns...G7
Trenton▲ 1,994...A1
Trion 1,661...B1
Tunnel Hill 970...C1
Turin 189...C4
Twin City 1,466...H5
Ty Ty 579...E8
Tybee Island 2,842...L6
Tyrone 2,724...C4
Unadilla 1,620...E6
Union City 8,375...J2
Union Point 1,753...F3
Unionville 2,710...F8
Uvalda 561...H6
Valdosta▲ 39,806...F9
Van Wert 303...B3
Vanna...F2
Varnell 358...C1
Vernonburg 74...K7
Vidalia 11,078...H6
Vidette...H4

Vienna▲ 2,708...E6
Villa Rica 6,542...C3
Vinings 7,417...K1
Waco 461...B3
Wadley 2,473...H5
Waleska 700...D2
Walnut Grove 458...E3
Walthourville 2,024...J7
Waresboro 582...H8
Warm Springs 407...C5
Warner Robins 43,726...E5
Warrenton▲ 2,056...G4
Warwick 501...E7
Watkinsville▲ 1,600...E3
Waverly 769...J8
Waverly Hall 913...C5
Waycross▲ 16,410...H8
Waynesboro▲ 5,701...J4
Welcome All...J2
Wesley...H6
West Point 3,571...B5
Weston 42...C7
Whigham 605...D9
White 542...C2
White Plains 286...F4
White Sulphur Springs 118...C5
Whitesburg 643...B4
Willacoochee 1,205...G8
Williamson 295...D4
Wilmington Island 11,230...L7
Winder▲ 7,373...E3
Winterville 876...F3
Woodbine▲ 1,212...J9
Woodbury 1,429...C5
Woodland 552...D5
Woodstock 4,361...D2
Woodville 415...F3
Woolsey 120...D4
Wrens 2,414...H4
Wrightsville▲ 2,331...G5
Yatesville 409...D5
Young Harris 611...E1
Zebulon▲ 1,035...D4

OTHER FEATURES

Alapaha (riv.)...F7
Allatoona (lake)...C2
Altamaha (riv.)...H7
Andersonville Nat'l Hist. Site...D6
Atlanta Naval Air Sta....J1
Banks (lake)...F9
Bartletts Ferry (dam)...B5
Blackshear (lake)...H8
Blue Ridge (mts.)...D1
Brasstown Bald (mt.)...E1
Burton (lake)...E1
Carters (lake)...C1
Chattahoochee (riv.)...B8
Chattahoochee River Nat'l Rec. Area...K1
Chattooga (riv.)...A2
Chattooga (riv.)...F1
Chatuge (lake)...E1
Chickamauga and Chattanooga Nat'l Mil. Park...B1
Coosa (riv.)...A2
Coosawattee (riv.)...C1
Cumberland (isl.)...K9
Cumberland Island Nat'l Seashore...K9
Dobbins A.F.B....J1
Doboy (sound)...K8
Etowah (riv.)...C2
Flint (riv.)...D8
Fort Benning...B6
Fort Frederica Nat'l Mon....K8
Fort Gordon 9,140...H4
Fort McPherson...K1
Fort Pulaski Nat'l Mon....L6
Fort Stewart 13,774...J7
Goat Rock (lake)...B5
Harding (lake)...B5
Hartwell (lake)...G2
Jekyll (isl.)...K8
Jimmy Carter Nat'l Hist. Site...D6
Kennesaw Mtn. Nat'l Battlefield Park...J1
Martin Luther King, Jr., Nat'l Hist. Site...K1
Moody A.F.B. 1,288...F9
Morgan Falls (dam)...K1
Nottely (lake)...E1
Ochlockonee (riv.)...D10
Ocmulgee (riv.)...E5
Ocmulgee Nat'l Mon....F5
Oconee (riv.)...F5
Ogeechee (riv.)...J5
Okefenokee (swamp)...H9
Oliver (lake)...B5
Oostanaula (riv.)...B2
Ossabaw (sound)...K7
Rabun (lake)...E1
Robins A.F.B. 3,092...F5
Saint Andrew (sound)...K9
Saint Catherines (isl.)...K7
Saint Mary's (riv.)...J9
Saint Simons (isl.)...K8
Sapelo (isl.)...K8
Satilla (riv.)...G8
Savannah (riv.)...K5
Sea (isls.)...K9
Seminole (lake)...B9
Sidney Lanier (lake)...D2
Sinclair (lake)...F4
Skidaway (isl.)...L7
Springer (mt.)...D1
Strom Thurmond (lakes)...H3
Suwannee (riv.)...G10
Walter F. George (res.)...B7
Wassaw (sound)...L7
Weiss (lake)...A2
West Point (lake)...B4

▲County seat

Map labels: Brasstown Bald 4,784 ft. (1458 m.), BLUE RIDGE, PIEDMONT PLATEAU, FALL LINE HILLS, COASTAL PLAIN, SEA ISLANDS, Hartwell Lake, Sidney Lanier, Allatoona L., West Point Lake, L. Sinclair, L. Harding, Walter F. George Res., L. Seminole, Strom Thurmond Lake, Okefenokee Swamp

Cities: Atlanta, Athens, Augusta, Macon, Columbus, Albany, Valdosta, Savannah

Rivers: Oostanaula, Etowah, Chattahoochee, Coosa, Flint, Oconee, Ocmulgee, Ogeechee, Savannah, Canoochee, Altamaha, Ochlockonee, Withlacoochee, Alapaha, Satilla, St. Marys, Suwannee

Scale: 0 40 80 MI. / 0 40 80 KM.

Elevation legend: 5,000 m. 16,404 ft. | 2,000 m. 6,562 ft. | 1,000 m. 3,281 ft. | 500 m. 1,640 ft. | 200 m. 656 ft. | 100 m. 328 ft. | Sea Level | Below

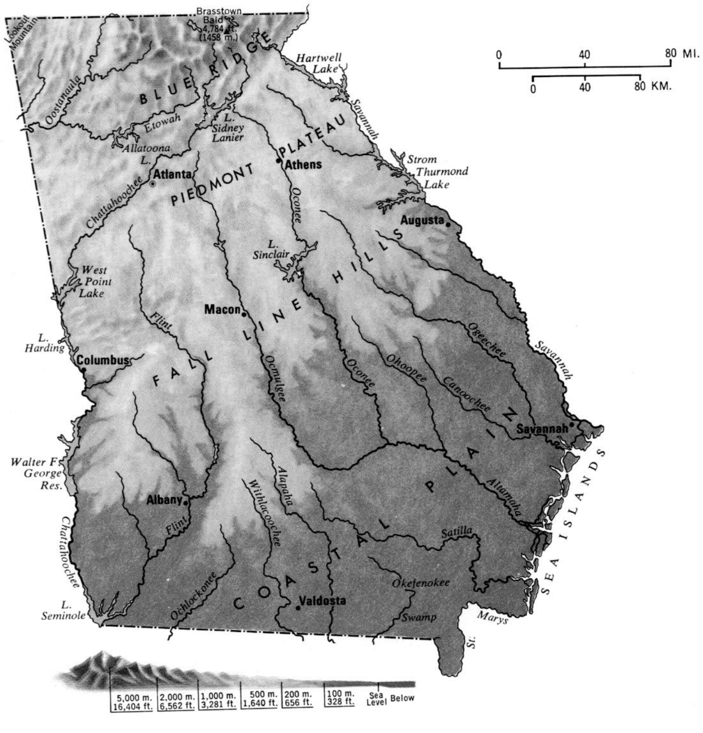

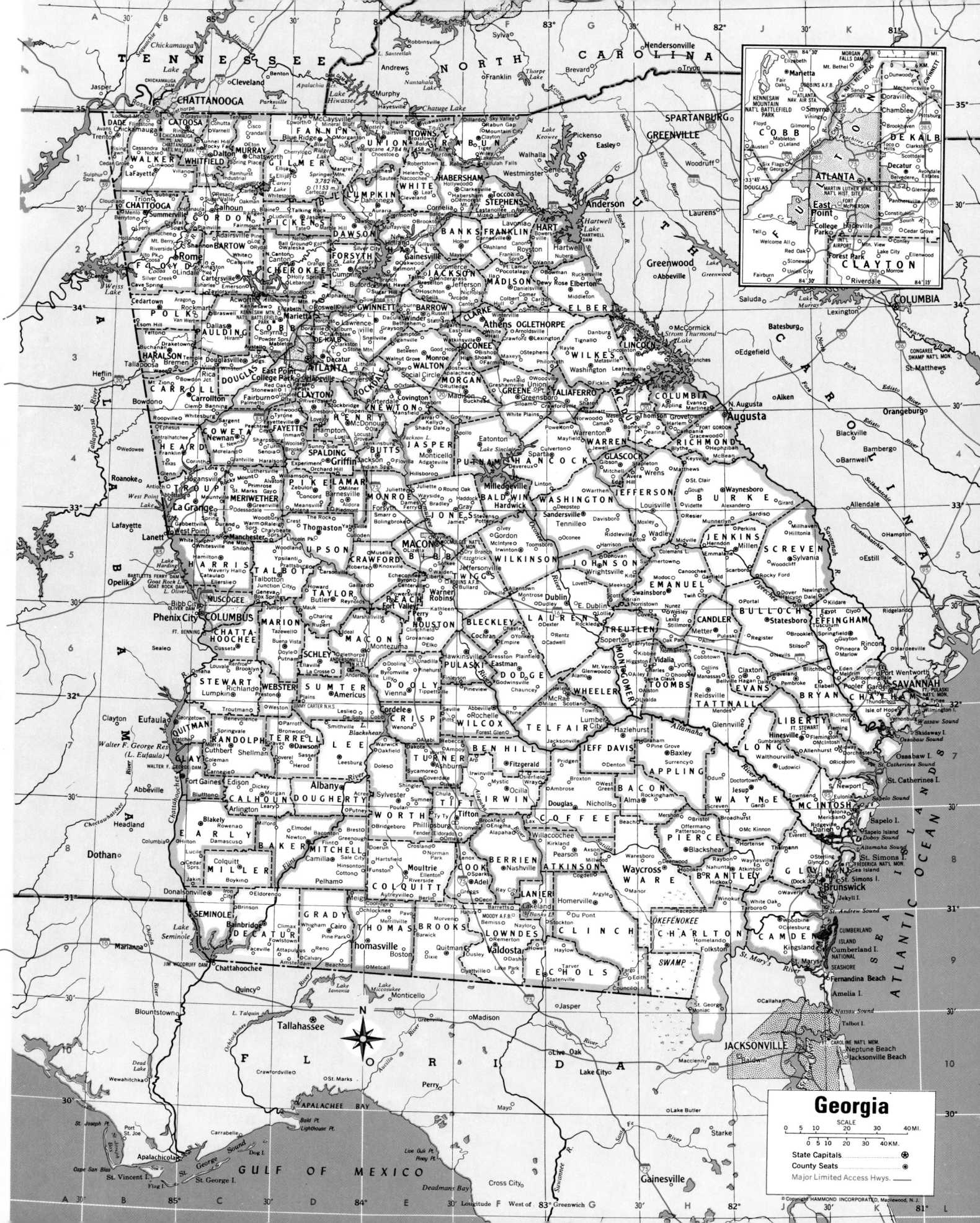

Georgia

SCALE

0 5 10   20   30   40 MI.

0 5 10   20   30   40 KM.

State Capitals .... ⊛

County Seats .... ⊙

Major Limited Access Hwys. ————

COUNTIES

Hawaii 120,317 ....K7
Honolulu 836,231 ....D3
Kalawao 130 ....G1
Kauai 51,177 ....A1
Maui 100,374 ....J1

CITIES and TOWNS

Aiea 8,906 ....B3
Aina Haina F2
Ala Moana C4
Anahola 1,181 ....C1
Barbers Point 2,218 .....E2
Captain Cook 2,595 ......G5
Eleele 1,489 ....C2
Ewa 14,315 ....A4
Ewa Beach 14,369 ....A4
Haena 200 ....C1
Haiku 4,509 ....J2
Haina 333 ....H3
Hakalau J4
Halawa Heights B3
Halawa, Hawaii 50 ....G3
Haleiwa 2,442 ....E1
Haliimaile 841 ....J2
Hana 683 ....K2
Hanalei 461 ....C1

Hanamaulu 3,611 ....C1
Hanapepe 1,395 ....C2
Hauula 3,479 ....E1
Hawaii Kai F2
Hawaii National Park 250 .J6
Hawi 924 ....G3
Hickam Housing 6,553 ....B4
Hilo▲ 37,808 ....J5
Holualoa 3,834 ....G5
Honaunau 2,373 ....G6
Honohina 125 ....J4
Honokaa 2,186 ....H3
Honokahua 309 ....H1
Honokohau 200 ....G5
Honokohau 309 ....J1
Honolulu (cap.)▲ 365,272 .C4
Honouliuli 600 ....A4
Hoolehua G5
Huehue 100 ....G5
Hulopoe Bay H2
Humuula 50 ....H5
Iroquois Point 4,188 ....A4
Iwilei C4
Kaaawa 1,138 ....F1
Kahakuloa 75 ....J1
Kahala D5
Kahaluu 3,068 ....E2
Kahuku 2,063 ....E1

Kahului 16,889 ....J2
Kailua (Kailua Kona),
  Hawaii 9,126 ....F5
Kailua Kona F5
Kailua, Oahu 36,818 .....F2
Kaimuki D4
Kainaliu 512 ....G1
Kalae 150 ....G1
Kalaheo 3,592 ....C2
Kalaoa 4,490 ....G5
Kalapana 75 ....J6
Kalaupapa▲ 170 ....G1
Kalihi 435 ....H1
Kamalo 60 ....H1
Kamuela 1,179 ....G4
Kaneohe 35,448 ....F2
Kapaa 8,149 ....D1
Kapaahu 850 ....J6
Kapaau 1,083 ....G3
Kapalama C4
Kapoho 300 ....K5
Kapulena 125 ....H4
Kaumakani 803 ....C2
Kaumalapau Harbor G2
Kaunakakai 2,658 ....G1
Kaupakulua 600 ....K2
Kaupo 65 ....K2
Kawaihae 50 ....G4
Kawailoa 200 ....E1
Keaau 1,584 ....J5

Kealakekua 1,453 ....G5
Kealia 550 ....D1
Kealia, Kauai 300 ....D1
Keanae 280 ....K2
Keauhou F5
Kekaha 3,506 ....C2
Keokea 500 ....G6
Keokea 750 ....J2
Kihei 11,107 ....J2
Kilauea 1,685 ....C1
Kipahulu 75 ....K2
Koali 60 ....K2
Kohala (Kapaau) G3
Kokomo 500 ....K2
Koloa 1,791 ....C2
Koloa Landing C2
Kualapuu 1,661 ....G1
Kukaiau 75 ....H4
Kukuihaele 316 ....H3
Kula 800 ....J2
Kunia 550 ....E2
Kurtistown 910 ....J5
Lahaina 9,073 ....H2
Laie 5,577 ....E1
Lanai City 2,400 ....H2
Laupahoehoe 508 ....J4
Lawai 1,787 ....C2
Lower Paia 1,500 ....J1
Maalaea 443 ....J2

Maili 6,059 ....D2
Makaha 7,990 ....D2
Makaiwa H2
Makakilo 9,828 ....E2
Makapala G3
Makawao 5,405 ....K2
Makaweli 500 ....B2
Makena 100 ....J2
Makiki C4
Mana B2
Manele Bay H2
Maunaloa 405 ....G1
Maunawili 4,847 ....F2
Mililani Town 29,359 ....E2
Miloli 120 ....G6
Moiliili C4
Mokapu 11,615 ....F2
Mokuleia 1,776 ....D1
Mountain View 3,075 .....J5
Naalehu 1,027 ....H7
Nanakuli 9,575 ....D2
Napili-Honokowai 4,332 ..H1
Ninole 75 ....J4
Olowalu 750 ....H2
Ookala 401 ....J4
Opihikao 125 ....K6
Paauilo 620 ....H4
Paauhau 350 ....H4
Pacific Heights 5,305 ...C4
Pacific Palisades E2

Pahala 1,520 ....H6
Pahoa 1,027 ....J5
Paia 2,091 ....J2
Papa 1,634 ....G3
Papaaloa J4
Papaikou 1,567 ....J5
Paukaa 495 ....J5
Pauwela 468 ....K2
Peahi 308 ....K2
Pearl City 30,993 ....E2
Pepeekeo 1,813 ....J4
Poipu 975 ....C2
Princeville 1,244 ....C1
Puako 397 ....G4
Puhi 1,210 ....C2
Pukalani 5,879 ....J2
Punaluu 672 ....H7
Puuanahulu 56 ....G4
Puuiki 75 ....K2
Puunene 572 ....J2
Puunui C4
Puuwai 200 ....A2
Schofield Barracks 19,597 .E2
Spreckelsville 350 ......J1
Sunset Beach E1
Ulumalu 201 ....K2
Ulupalakua 75 ....J2
Volcano 1,516 ....J6
Waiakoa J2

Waialae D4
Waialua, Oahu 3,943 .....E1
Waianae 8,758 ....D2
Waihee 4,004 ....J2
Waikane 717 ....E2
Waikapu 729 ....J2
Waikiki 50 ....H4
Waikiki C4
Wailea, Hawaii 150 ......J4
Wailea-Makena, Maui 3,799 .J4
Wailua 2,018 ....D2
Wailuku▲ 10,688 ....J2
Waimalu 29,967 ....B3
Waimanalo 3,508 ....F2
Waimanalo Beach 4,185 ...F2
Waimea (Kamuela), Hawaii
  1,840 ....G3
Waimea 200 ....E1
Waimea, Kauai 5,972 .....B2
Wainaku 1,243 ....J5
Wainiha 175 ....C1
Waiohinu 200 ....G7
Waipahu 31,435 ....A3
Waipio 11,812 ....H3
Waipio Acres 5,304 ......E2
Whitmore Village 3,373 ..E1

OTHER FEATURES

Alalakeiki (chan.) J3

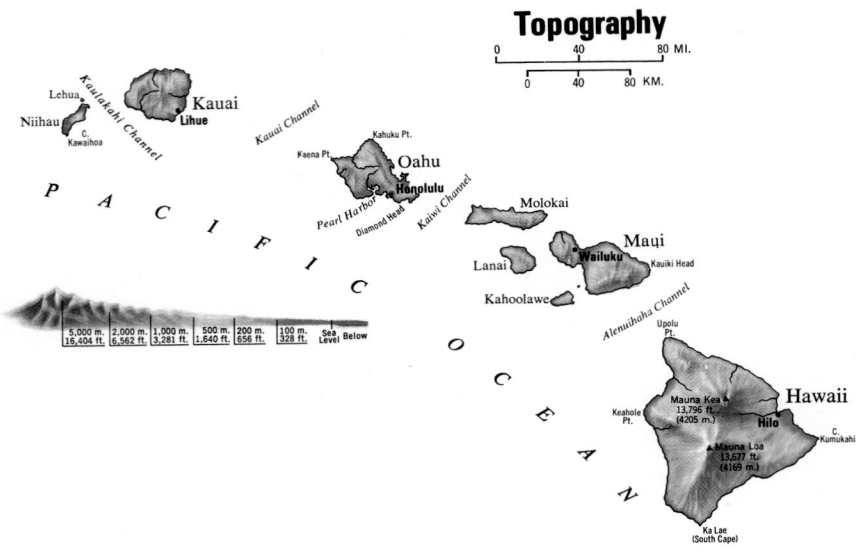

Topography

0   40   80 MI.
0   40   80 KM.

5,000 m. / 2,000 m. / 1,000 m. / 500 m. / 200 m. / 100 m. / Sea Level / Below
16,404 ft. / 6,562 ft. / 3,281 ft. / 1,640 ft. / 656 ft. / 328 ft.

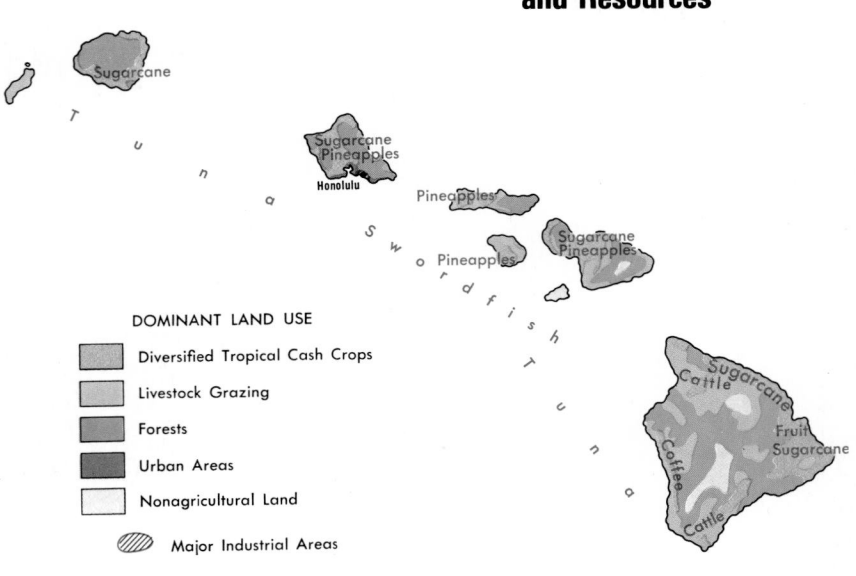

Agriculture, Industry and Resources

DOMINANT LAND USE

- Diversified Tropical Cash Crops
- Livestock Grazing
- Forests
- Urban Areas
- Nonagricultural Land
- Major Industrial Areas

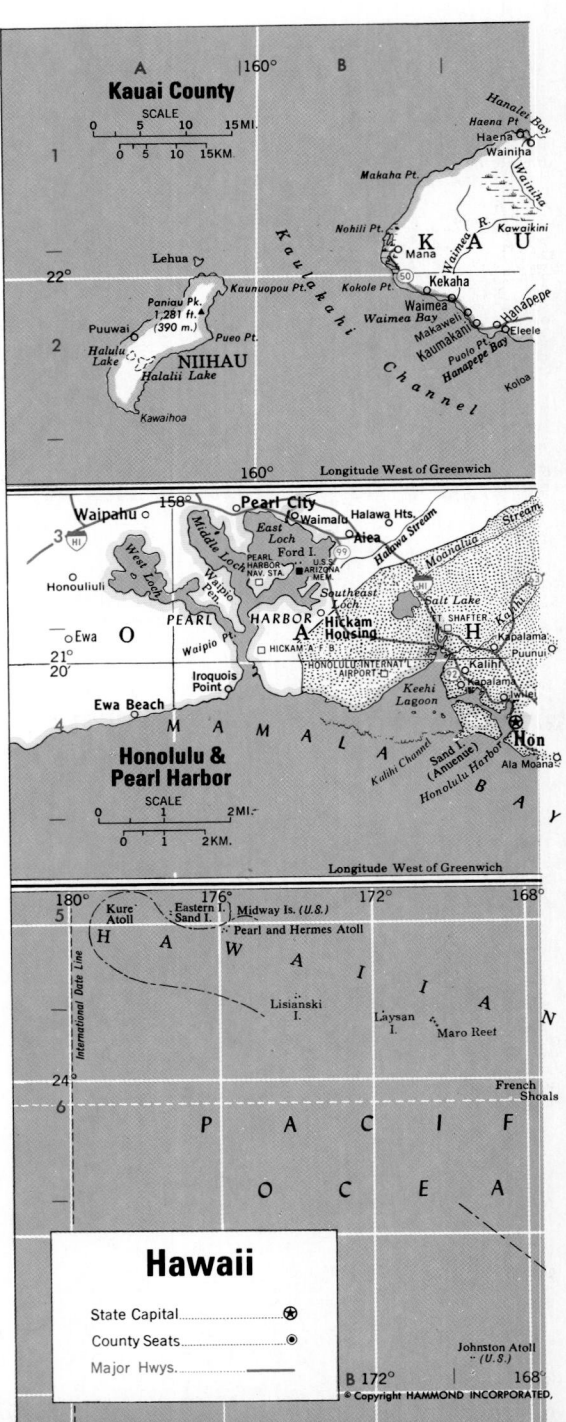

Kauai County

SCALE
0   5   10   15 MI.
0   5   10   15KM.

Honolulu & Pearl Harbor

SCALE
0   1   2MI.
0   1   2KM.

Hawaii

State Capital .... ✪
County Seats .... ◉
Major Hwys. .... ───

© Copyright HAMMOND INCORPORATED

Alenuihaha (chan.) E7
Anuenue (Sand) (isl.).........C4
Auau (chan.) H2
Barbers Point Naval Air Sta...E2
Diamond (head) C5
East Loch (inlet) B3
Ford (isl.) B3
Fort Shafter 2,952 ....C3
French Frigate (shoals) C6
Gardner Pinnacles (isls.)......C6
Halalii (lake) A2
Halawa (bay) H1
Haleakala (crater) K2
Haleakala Nat'l Park K2
Hawaii (isl.) H5
Hawaii Volcanoes Nat'l Park ..H6
Hickam A.F.B. B4
Hilo (bay) J5
Honolulu (harb.) C4
Honolulu Int'l Airport B4
Ilio (pt.) G1
Kaala (mt.) D1
Kahala (mt.) D1
Kahana (bay) E1
Kaiwi (chan.) F6
Ka Lae (cape) G7
Kalaupapa Nat'l Hist. Park ...H1
Kalohi (chan.) G1
Kaloko-Honokohau
  Nat'l Hist. Park F5

Kamakou (peak) H1
Kanapou (bay) J3
Kaneohe Bay U.S.M.C.
  Air Station F2
Kau (des.) J6
Kauai (chan.) E6
Kauai (isl.) C1
Kauiki (head) K2
Kaula (isl.) D6
Kaulakahi (chan.) B2
Kawaihae (bay) G4
Kawaihoa (pt.) A2
Kawaikini (peak) C1
Keahi (pt.) A4
Kealaikahiki (chan.) H3
Kealakekua (bay) F6
Keanapapa (pt.) G2
Keehi (lag.) B4
Kiholo (bay) G4
Kilauea (crater) H6
Kohala (mts.) G4
Koko (head) D4
Konahuanui (peak) D3
Koolau (range) D2
Kumukahi (cape) K5
Kure (atoll) A5
Laau (pt.) G1
Lanai (isl.) G1
Lanaihale (mt.) H2
Laysan (isl.) B6

Lisianski (isl.) B5
Lua Makika (mt.) J3
Maalaea (bay) J2
Makahuena (pt.) C2
Makapuu (pt.) F2
Mamala (bay) B4
Manana (isl.) F2
Maro (reef) C6
Mauna Kea (mt.) H4
Mauna Loa (mt.) G6
Middle Loch (inlet) A3
Moanalua (stream) B3
Mokapu (pen.) F2
Mokuaweoweo (crater) H6
Molokai (isl.) G1
Molokini (isl.) J2
Nawiliwili (bay) D2
Necker (isl.) D6
Nihoa (isl.) D6
Niihau (isl.) A2
Oahu (isl.) E1
Pailolo (chan.) H1
Palolo (stream) D4
Paniau (peak) A2
Pearl (harb.) A3
Pearl and Hermes (atoll) B5
Pearl Harbor Naval Sta. B3
Punchbowl (hill) C4

Puolo (pt.) C2
Puuhonua O Honaunau
  Nat'l Hist. Park F6
Puu Keahiakahoe (mt.) D3
Puukohola Heiau
  Nat'l Hist. Park G4
Puu Kukui (mt.) J2
Red Hill (mt.) K2
Roundtop (mt.) C4
Salt (lake) B4
Sand (isl.) B4
South (Ka Lae) (cape) G7
Southeast Loch (inlet) B3
Sugarloaf (hill) D4
Tantalus (mt.) D4
Upolu (pt.) G3
U.S.S. Arizona Memorial......B3
Waialeale (mt.) C1
Waikiki (beach) C4
Wailuku (riv.) J5
Waimea (bay) B2
Waimea (riv.) C1
Wainiha (riv.) C1
Waipio (bay) H3
Waipio (pen.) A3
Waipio (pt.) A4
West Loch (inlet) A3
Wheeler A.F.B. 2,600 ....E1

▲County seat

HAWAII

AREA 6,471 sq. mi. (16,760 sq. km.)
POPULATION 1,115,274
CAPITAL Honolulu
LARGEST CITY Honolulu
HIGHEST POINT Mauna Kea 13,796 ft. (4205 m.)
SETTLED IN —
ADMITTED TO UNION August 21, 1959
POPULAR NAME Aloha State
STATE FLOWER Hibiscus
STATE BIRD Nene (Hawaiian Goose)

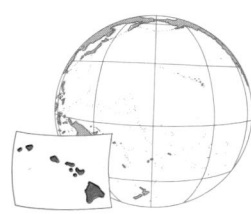

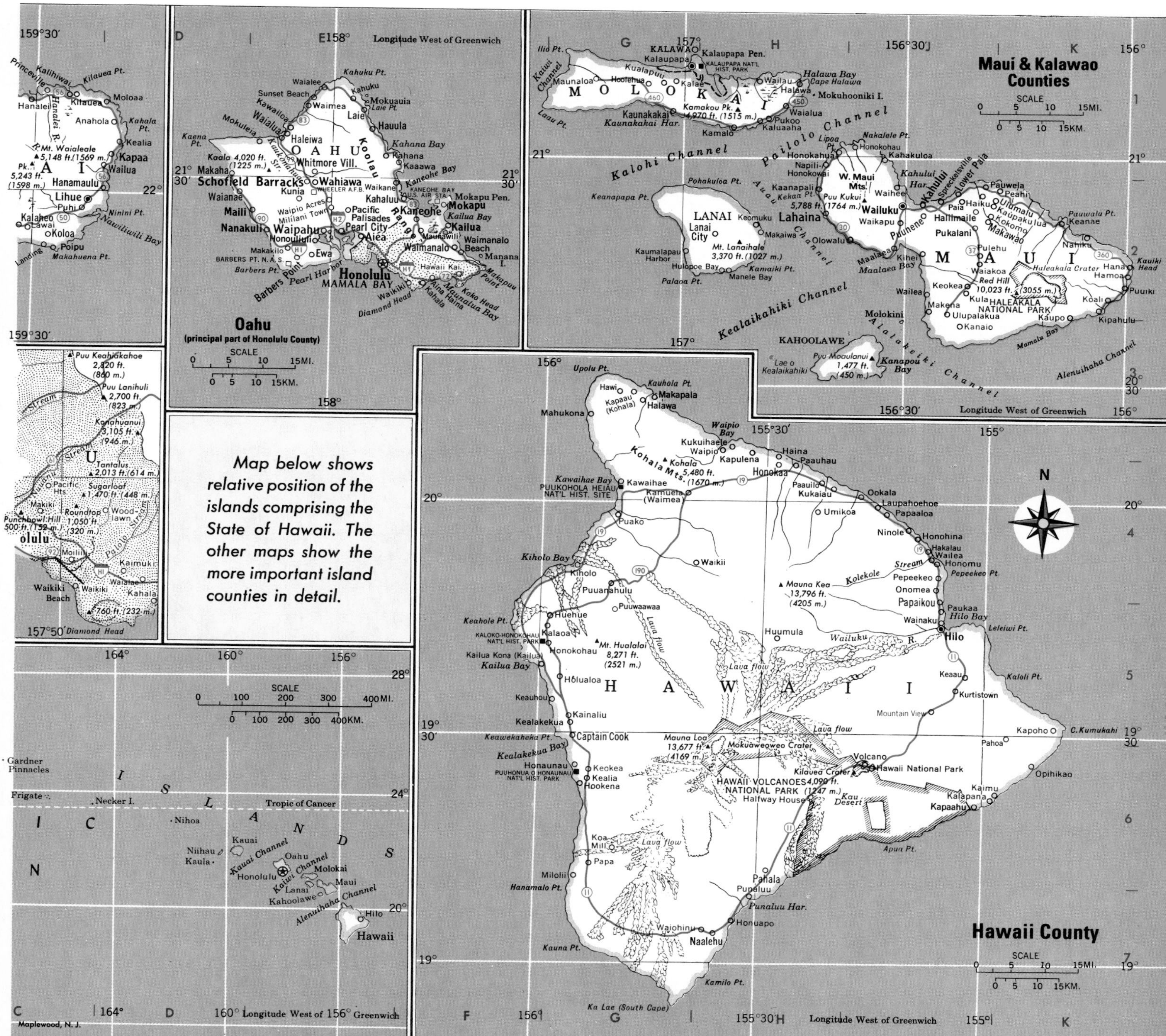

Oahu
(principal part of Honolulu County)

Map below shows relative position of the islands comprising the State of Hawaii. The other maps show the more important island counties in detail.

Maui & Kalawao Counties

Hawaii County

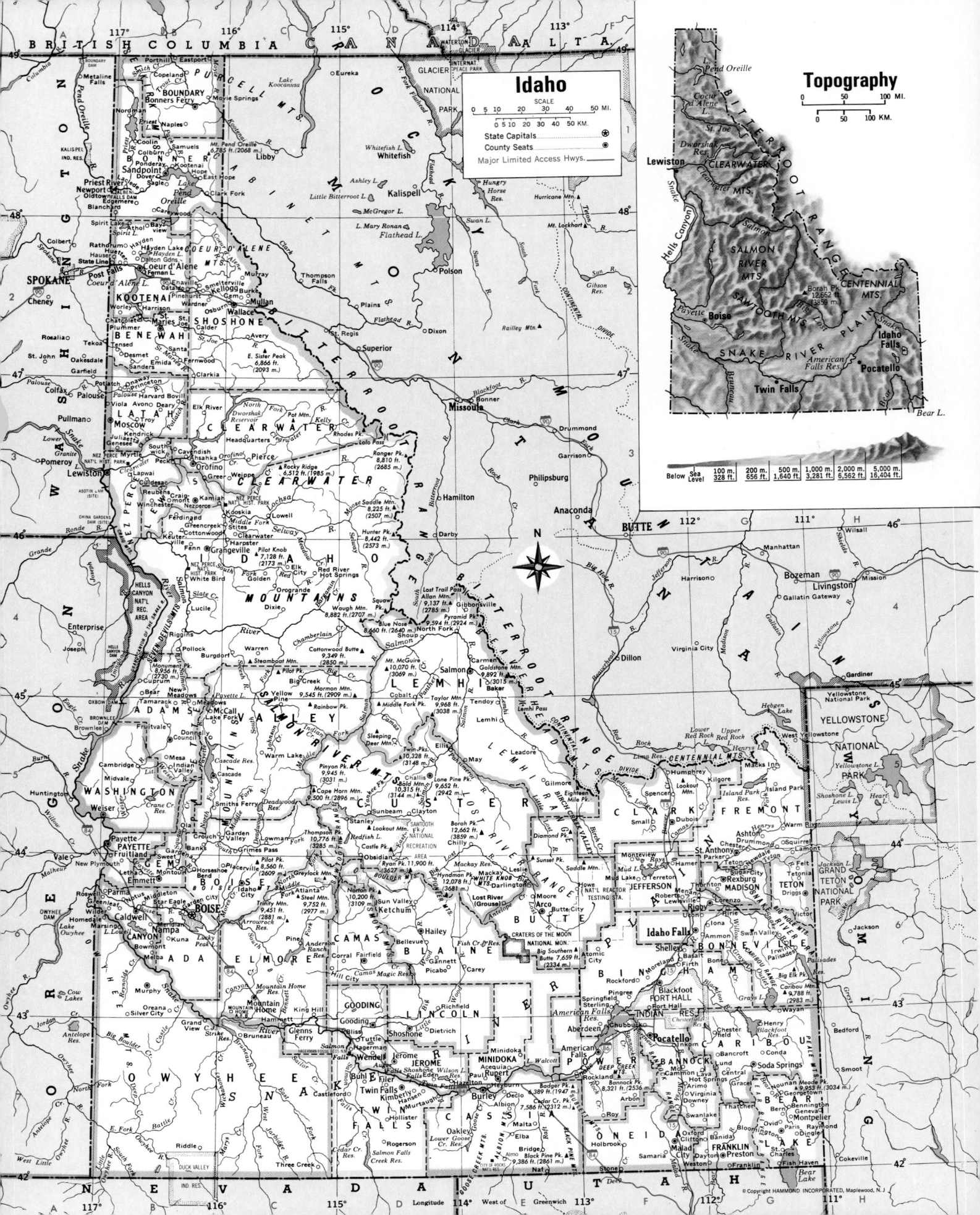

Idaho

SCALE
0 5 10 20   30   40   50 MI.
0 5 10 20 30 40 50 KM.

State Capitals............⊛
County Seats..............◉
Major Limited Access Hwys.

Topography

0   50   100 MI.
0   50   100 KM.

| Below Sea Level | 100 m. 328 ft. | 200 m. 656 ft. | 500 m. 1,640 ft. | 1,000 m. 3,281 ft. | 2,000 m. 6,562 ft. | 5,000 m. 16,404 ft. |

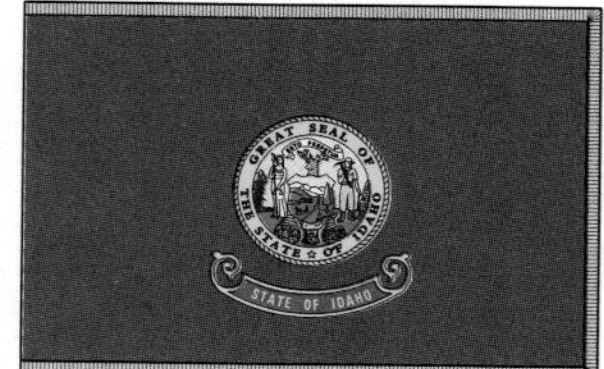

AREA 83,564 sq. mi. (216,431 sq. km.)
POPULATION 1,011,986
CAPITAL Boise
LARGEST CITY Boise
HIGHEST POINT Borah Pk. 12,662 ft. (3859 m.)
SETTLED IN 1842
ADMITTED TO UNION July 3, 1890
POPULAR NAME Gem State
STATE FLOWER Syringa
STATE BIRD Mountain Bluebird

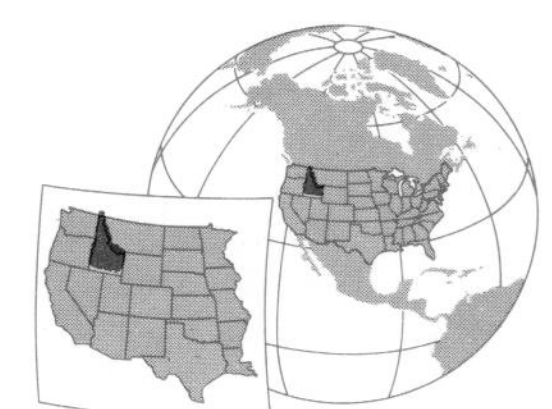

COUNTIES

Ada 205,775 ... B6
Adams 3,254 ... B5
Bannock 66,026 ... F7
Bear Lake 6,084 ... G7
Benewah 7,937 ... B2
Bingham 37,583 ... F6
Blaine 13,552 ... D6
Boise 3,509 ... C6
Bonner 26,622 ... B1
Bonneville 72,207 ... G6
Boundary 8,332 ... B1
Butte 2,918 ... E6
Camas 727 ... D6
Canyon 90,076 ... B6
Caribou 6,963 ... G7
Cassia 19,532 ... E7
Clark 762 ... F5
Clearwater 8,505 ... C3
Custer 4,133 ... D5
Elmore 21,205 ... C6
Franklin 9,232 ... G7
Fremont 10,937 ... G5
Gem 11,844 ... B6
Gooding 11,633 ... D6
Idaho 13,783 ... C4
Jefferson 16,543 ... F6
Jerome 15,138 ... D7
Kootenai 69,795 ... B2
Latah 30,617 ... B3
Lemhi 6,899 ... D4
Lewis 3,516 ... B3
Lincoln 3,308 ... D6
Madison 23,674 ... G6
Minidoka 19,361 ... E7
Nez Perce 33,754 ... B3
Oneida 3,492 ... F7
Owyhee 8,392 ... B7
Payette 16,434 ... B5
Power 7,086 ... F7
Shoshone 13,931 ... B2
Teton 3,439 ... G6
Twin Falls 53,580 ... D7
Valley 6,109 ... C5
Washington 8,550 ... B5

CITIES and TOWNS

Aberdeen 1,406 ... F7
Acequia 106 ... E7
Ahsahka 160 ... B3
Albion 305 ... E7
American Falls▲ 3,757 ... E7
Ammon 5,002 ... G6
Arco▲ 1,016 ... E6
Arimo 311 ... F7
Ashton 1,114 ... G5
Athol 346 ... B2
Atomic City 25 ... F6
Bancroft 393 ... G7
Basalt 407 ... F6
Bayview 350 ... B2
Bellevue 1,275 ... D6
Bern 154 ... G7
Blackfoot▲ 9,646 ... F6
Bliss 185 ... D7
Bloomington 197 ... G7
Boise (cap.)▲ 102,160 ... B6
Bonners Ferry▲ 2,193 ... B1
Bovill 256 ... B3
Bruneau 160 ... C7
Buhl 3,516 ... D7
Burgdorf ... B4
Burke 150 ... C2
Burley▲ 8,702 ... E7
Butte City 59 ... E6
Calder 200 ... B2
Caldwell▲ 18,400 ... B6
Cambridge 374 ... B5
Carey 800 ... E6
Cascade▲ 877 ... C5
Castleford 179 ... C7
Cataldo 150 ... B2
Challis▲ 1,073 ... D5
Chatcolet 72 ... B2
Chester 300 ... G5
Chilly ... E5
Chubbuck 7,791 ... F7
Clark Fork 448 ... B1
Clarkia 175 ... B2
Clayton 26 ... D5
Clifton 228 ... F7
Coeur d'Alene▲ 24,563 ... B2
Colburn 250 ... B1
Conda 200 ... G7
Coolin 150 ... B1
Cottonwood 822 ... B3
Council▲ 831 ... B5
Craigmont 542 ... B3
Crouch 75 ... B5
Culdesac 280 ... B3
Dalton Gardens 1,951 ... B2
Dayton 357 ... F7
Deary 529 ... B3
Declo 279 ... E7
Dietrich 127 ... D7
Dingle 300 ... G7
Donnelly 135 ... B5
Dover 294 ... B1
Downey 626 ... F7
Driggs▲ 846 ... G6
Drummond 37 ... G5
Dubois▲ 420 ... F5
Eagle 3,327 ... B6
East Hope 215 ... B1
Eden 314 ... D7
Elk City 500 ... C4
Elk River 149 ... B3
Emida 175 ... B2
Emmett▲ 4,601 ... B6
Fairfield▲ 371 ... D6
Ferdinand 135 ... B3
Fernan Lake 178 ... B2
Fernwood 608 ... B2
Filer 1,511 ... D7
Firth 429 ... F6
Fort Hall 2,681 ... F6
Franklin 478 ... G7
Fruitland 2,400 ... B6
Fruitvale 200 ... B5
Garden City 6,369 ... B6
Garden Valley 250 ... C5
Genesee 725 ... B3
Geneva 220 ... G7
Georgetown 558 ... G7
Gilmore ... E5
Glenns Ferry 1,304 ... C7
Gooding▲ 2,820 ... D7
Grace 973 ... G7
Grand View 330 ... B7
Grangeville▲ 3,226 ... B4
Greenleaf 648 ... B6
Grimes Pass ... C5
Hagerman 600 ... D7
Hailey▲ 3,687 ... D6
Hamer 79 ... F6
Hammett 180 ... C7
Hansen 848 ... D7
Harrison 226 ... B2
Hauser 380 ... A2
Hayden 3,744 ... B2
Hayden Lake 338 ... B2
Hazelton 394 ... E7
Headquarters 165 ... C3
Heise 84 ... G6
Heyburn 2,714 ... E7
Hollister 144 ... D7
Homedale 1,963 ... A6
Hope 99 ... B1
Horseshoe Bend 643 ... B6
Huetter 82 ... B2
Idaho City▲ 322 ... C6
Idaho Falls▲ 43,929 ... F6
Inkom 769 ... F7
Iona 1,049 ... G6
Irwin 108 ... G6
Island Park 159 ... G5
Jerome▲ 6,529 ... D7
Juliaetta 488 ... B3
Kamiah 1,157 ... B3
Kellogg 2,591 ... B2
Kendrick 325 ... B3
Ketchum 2,523 ... D6
Kimberly 2,367 ... D7
Kooskia 692 ... C3
Kootenai 327 ... B1
Kuna 1,955 ... B6
Laclede 400 ... B1
Lake Fork 250 ... B5
Lapwai 932 ... B3
Lava Hot Springs 420 ... F7
Leadore 74 ... E5
Lewiston▲ 28,082 ... A3
Lewisville 471 ... F6
Lost River (Grouse) 29 ... E6
Lowman 180 ... C5
Mackay 574 ... E6
Macks Inn 200 ... G5
Malad City▲ 1,946 ... F7
Malta 171 ... E7
Marsing 798 ... B6
McCall 2,005 ... C5
McCammon 722 ... F7
Meadows 250 ... B5
Melba 252 ... B6
Menan 601 ... F6
Meridian 9,596 ... B6
Middleton 1,851 ... B6
Midvale 110 ... B5
Minidoka 67 ... E7
Monteview 200 ... F6
Montpelier 2,656 ... G7
Moore 190 ... E6
Moreland 600 ... F6
Moscow▲ 18,519 ... B3
Mountain Home▲ 7,913 ... C6
Moyie Springs 415 ... B1
Mud Lake 179 ... F6
Mullan 821 ... C2
Murphy▲ 200 ... B6
Murtaugh 114 ... D7
Nampa 28,365 ... B6
Naples 250 ... B1
New Meadows 534 ... B4
New Plymouth 1,313 ... B6
Newdale 377 ... G6
Nezperce▲ 453 ... B3
Nordman 300 ... B1
North Fork 250 ... D4
Notus 380 ... B6
Oakley 635 ... D7
Ola 175 ... B5
Oldtown 151 ... A1
Onaway 203 ... B3
Orofino▲ 2,868 ... B3
Osburn 1,579 ... B2
Oxford 44 ... F7
Paris▲ 581 ... G7
Parker 288 ... G6
Parma 1,597 ... B6
Patterson 4 ... E5
Paul 901 ... E7
Payette▲ 5,592 ... B5
Pearl 8 ... B6
Peck 160 ... B3
Pierce 746 ... C3
Pinehurst 1,722 ... B2
Placerville 14 ... C6
Plummer 804 ... B2
Pocatello▲ 46,080 ... F7
Ponderay 449 ... B1
Post Falls 7,349 ... A2
Potlatch 790 ... A3
Preston▲ 3,710 ... G7
Priest River 1,560 ... A1
Rathdrum 2,000 ... A2
Reubens 46 ... B3
Rexburg▲ 14,302 ... G6
Richfield 383 ... D6
Rigby▲ 2,681 ... F6
Riggins 443 ... B4
Ririe 596 ... G6
Roberts 557 ... F6
Rockland 264 ... F7
Rupert▲ 5,455 ... E7
Sagle 600 ... B1
Saint Anthony▲ 3,010 ... G6
Saint Charles 211 ... G7
Saint Maries▲ 2,442 ... B2
Salmon▲ 2,941 ... D4
Samuels 467 ... B1
Sandpoint▲ 5,203 ... B1
Shelley 3,536 ... F6
Shoshone▲ 1,249 ... D7
Silver City 1 ... B6
Smelterville 464 ... B2
Soda Springs▲ 3,111 ... G7
Spencer 11 ... F5
Spirit Lake 790 ... A2
Stanley 71 ... D5
Star 500 ... B6
State Line 26 ... A2
Stites 204 ... C3
Sugar City 1,275 ... G6
Sun Valley 938 ... D6
Swan Valley 141 ... G6
Sweet 290 ... B6
Tendoy 155 ... E5
Tensed 90 ... B2
Terreton 400 ... F6
Teton 570 ... G6
Tetonia 132 ... G6
Thatcher 300 ... G7
Thornton 177 ... G6
Troy 699 ... B3
Twin Falls▲ 27,591 ... D7
Ucon 895 ... F6
Victor 292 ... G6
Wallace▲ 1,010 ... C2
Wardner 246 ... B2
Warm Lake 200 ... C5
Warm River 9 ... G5
Wayan 175 ... G7
Weippe 532 ... C3
Weiser▲ 4,571 ... B5
Wendell 1,963 ... D7
Weston 390 ... F7
White Bird 108 ... B4
Wilder 1,232 ... A6
Winchester 262 ... B3
Worley 182 ... B2

OTHER FEATURES

Albeni Falls (dam) ... B1
Albion (mts.) ... E7
Allan (mt.) ... D4
American Falls (res.) ... F6
Anderson Ranch (res.) ... C6
Antelope (creek) ... E6
Arrowrock (res.) ... C6
Auger (falls) ... D7
Badger (peak) ... E7
Bald (mt.) ... D5
Bannock (creek) ... F7
Bannock (peak) ... F7
Bannock (range) ... F7
Bargamin (creek) ... C4
Battle (creek) ... B7
Bear (lake) ... G7
Bear (riv.) ... G7
Bear River (range) ... G7
Beaver (creek) ... F5
Beaverhead (mts.) ... E4
Big (creek) ... C4
Big Boulder (creek) ... B7
Big Elk (peak) ... G6
Big Hole (mts.) ... G6
Big Lost (riv.) ... E6
Big Southern (butte) ... E6
Big Wood (riv.) ... D6
Birch (creek) ... F5
Birch Creek (valley) ... E5
Bitterroot (range) ... D3
Blackfoot (res.) ... G7
Black Pine (mts.) ... E7
Blue Nose (mt.) ... D4
Boise (mts.) ... B6
Boise (riv.) ... B6
Borah (peak) ... E5
Boulder (mts.) ... D6
Brownlee (dam) ... B5
Bruneau (riv.) ... C7
Camas (creek) ... D5
Camas (creek) ... D6
Camas (creek) ... F5
Canyon (creek) ... C6
Cape Horn (mt.) ... C5
Caribou (mt.) ... G6
Caribou (range) ... G6
Cascade (res.) ... C5
Castle (creek) ... B7
Castle (peak) ... D5
Cedar Creek (peak) ... E7
Cedar Creek (res.) ... D7
Centennial (mts.) ... F5
Chesterfield (res) ... F7
Clearwater (mts.) ... C3
Clearwater (riv.) ... B3
Coeur d'Alene (lake) ... B2
Coeur d'Alene (mts.) ... C2
Coeur d'Alene (riv.) ... B2
Cottonwood (butte) ... C4
Craig (mts.) ... B4
Crane Creek (res.) ... B5
Craters of the Moon Nat'l Mon. ... E6
Deadwood (res.) ... C5
Deep (creek) ... B7
Deep (creek) ... F7
Deep Creek (mts.) ... F7
Diamond (peak) ... E5
Duck Valley Ind. Res. ... B7
Dworshak (res.) ... C3
East Sister (peak) ... C2
Eighteen Mile (peak) ... E5
Fish Creek (res.) ... E6
Fort Hall Ind. Res. ... F6
Goldstone (mt.) ... E4
Goose (creek) ... E7
Goose Creek (mts.) ... E7
Grand Canyon of the Snake River (canyon) ... B4
Grays (lake) ... G6
Grays Lake Outlet (creek) ... G6
Greylock (mt.) ... C6
Hayden (lake) ... B2
Hells (canyon) ... B4
Hells Canyon Nat'l Rec. Area ... B4
Henrys (lake) ... G5
Henrys Fork, Snake (riv.) ... G5
Hunter (peak) ... D3
Hyndman (peak) ... D6
Indian (creek) ... C5
Island Park (res.) ... G5
Jarbidge (riv.) ... C7
Johnson (creek) ... C5
Jordan (creek) ... A7
Kootenai (riv.) ... C1
Lemhi (pass) ... E5
Lemhi (range) ... E5
Lemhi (riv.) ... E5
Little Lost (riv.) ... E5
Little Owyhee (riv.) ... B7
Little Salmon (riv.) ... B4
Little Weiser (riv.) ... B5
Little Wood (riv.) ... D6
Lochsa (riv.) ... C3
Lolo (creek) ... C3
Lolo (pass) ... D3
Lone Pine (peak) ... D5
Lookout (mt.) ... D5
Lookout (mt.) ... F5
Lost River (range) ... E5
Lost Trail (pass) ... D4
Lowell (lake) ... B6
Lower Goose Creek (res.) ... D7
Lower Granite (lake) ... A3
Lucky Peak (lake) ... B6
Mackay (res.) ... E6
Magic (res.) ... D6
Malad (riv.) ... F7
Marsh (creek) ... F7
McGuire (mt.) ... D4
Meade (peak) ... G7
Meadow (creek) ... C4
Medicine Lodge (creek) ... F5
Middle Fork (peak) ... D5
Monument (peak) ... B4
Moose (creek) ... D3
Mores (creek) ... C6
Mormon (mt.) ... C4
Mountain Home (res.) ... C6
Mountain Home A.F.B. 5,936 ... C6
Moyie (riv.) ... B1
Mud (lake) ... F6
National Reactor Testing Sta. ... F6
Nez Perce Nat'l Hist. Park ... C3
Norton (peak) ... D6
Orofino (creek) ... C3
Owyhee (mts.) ... B6
Owyhee, East Fork (riv.) ... B7
Oxbow (dam) ... B5
Pack (riv.) ... B1
Pahsimeroi (riv.) ... E5
Palisades (res.) ... G6
Palouse (riv.) ... B3
Panther (creek) ... D4
Payette (lake) ... C4
Payette (mts.) ... B5
Payette (riv.) ... B6
Peale (mts.) ... G7
Pend Oreille (lake) ... B1
Pend Oreille (mt.) ... B1
Pend Oreille (riv.) ... A1
Pilot (peak) ... C4
Pilot (peak) ... C6
Pilot Knob (mt.) ... C4
Pinyon (peak) ... C5
Pioneer (mts.) ... D6
Pot (mt.) ... C3
Potlatch (riv.) ... B3
Priest (lake) ... B1
Priest (riv.) ... B1
Purcell (mts.) ... B1
Pyramid (peak) ... E4
Raft (riv.) ... E7
Rainbow (mt.) ... C5
Ranger (peak) ... D3
Rays (lake) ... F6
Red (riv.) ... C4
Redfish (lake) ... D5
Reynolds (creek) ... B6
Rhodes (peak) ... D3
Rock (creek) ... F7
Rocky (mts.) ... D1
Rocky Ridge (mt.) ... C3
Ryan (peak) ... D6
Saddle (mt.) ... D3
Saddle (mt.) ... F6
Sailor (creek) ... C7
Saint Joe (riv.) ... B2
Saint Maries (riv.) ... B2
Salmon (falls) ... C7
Salmon (riv.) ... B4
Salmon Falls (creek) ... D7
Salmon Falls Creek (res.) ... D7
Salmon River (mts.) ... C5
Sawtooth (range) ... C6
Sawtooth Nat'l Rec. Area ... D5
Secesh (riv.) ... C4
Selkirk (mts.) ... B1
Selway (riv.) ... C3
Seven Devils (mts.) ... B4
Shoshone (falls) ... D7
Sleeping Deer (mt.) ... D5
Smith (creek) ... B1
Smoky (mts.) ... D6
Snake (riv.) ... A3
Snake River (plain) ... D7
Snake River (range) ... G6
Spirit (lake) ... B2
Squaw (creek) ... B5
Squaw (peak) ... D4
Steamboat (mt.) ... C4
Steel (mt.) ... C6
Strike, C.J. (res.) ... C7
Sublett (mts.) ... E7
Sunset (peak) ... E6
Taylor (mt.) ... D5
Teton (riv.) ... G6
Thompson (peak) ... C5
Trinity (mt.) ... C6
Trout (creek) ... B1
Twin (falls) ... D7
Twin Peaks (mt.) ... D5
Walcott (lake) ... E7
Waugh (mt.) ... D4
Weiser (riv.) ... B5
White Knob (mts.) ... E6
Wickahoney (creek) ... C7
Willow (creek) ... G6
Wilson Lake (res.) ... D7
Yankee Fork, Salmon (riv.) ... D5
Yellowstone Nat'l Park ... H5

▲County seat

Agriculture, Industry and Resources

DOMINANT LAND USE

Wheat, General Farming
Wheat, Peas
Specialized Dairy
Potatoes, Beans, Sugar Beets, Livestock, General Farming
General Farming, Dairy, Hay, Sugar Beets
General Farming, Livestock, Special Crops
General Farming, Dairy, Range Livestock
Range Livestock
Forests

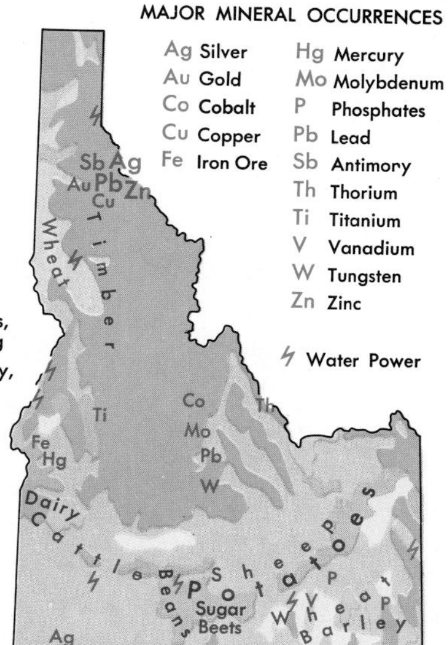
MAJOR MINERAL OCCURRENCES
Ag Silver
Au Gold
Co Cobalt
Cu Copper
Fe Iron Ore
Hg Mercury
Mo Molybdenum
P Phosphates
Pb Lead
Sb Antimony
Th Thorium
Ti Titanium
V Vanadium
W Tungsten
Zn Zinc
Water Power
Wheat
Timber
Dairy
Cattle
Beans
Sugar Beets
Sheep
Potatoes
Wheat
Barley

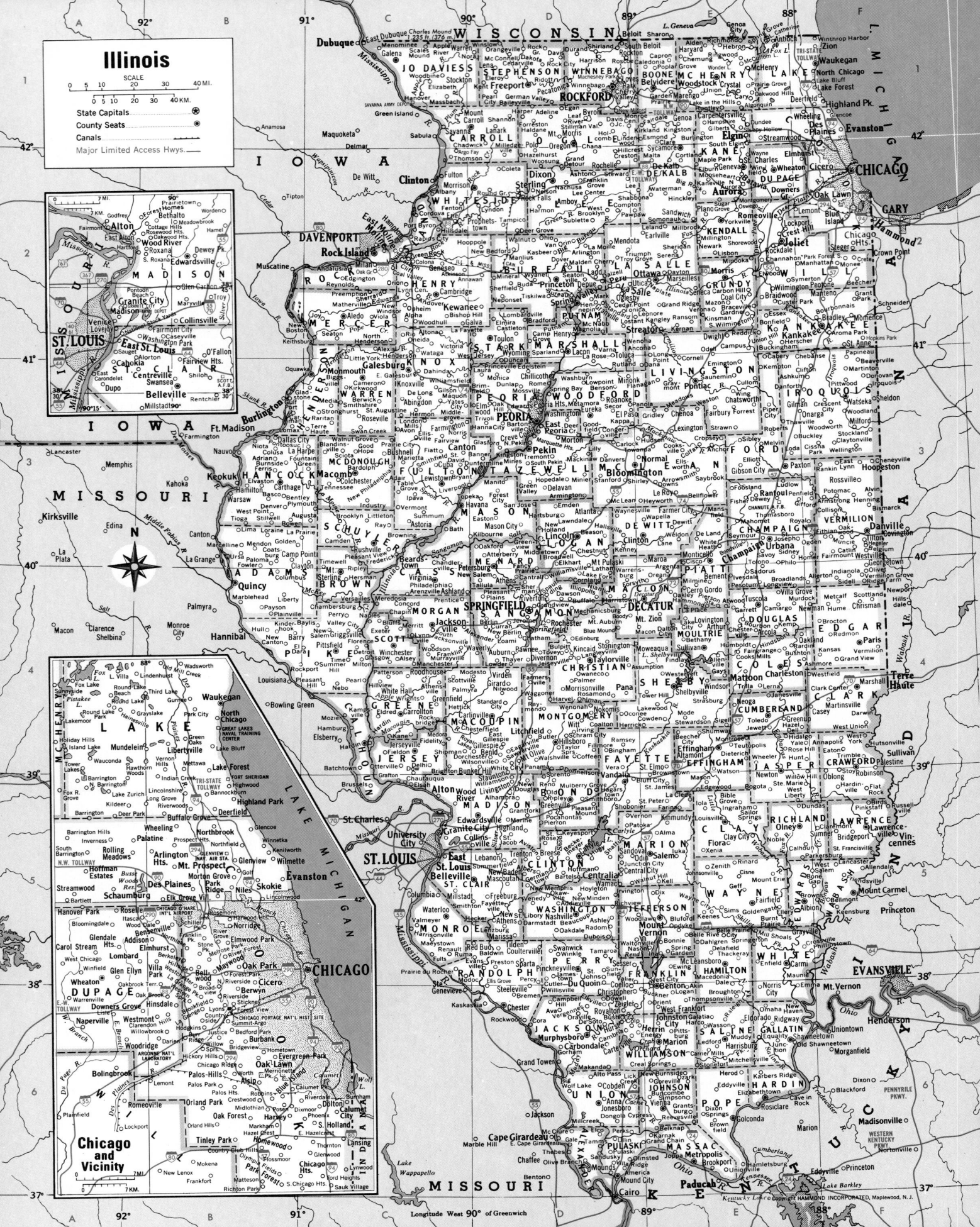

Illinois
SCALE
0 5 10 20 30 40 MI.
0 5 10 20 30 40 KM.
State Capitals
County Seats
Canals
Major Limited Access Hwys.
WISCONSIN
IOWA
MISSOURI
KENTUCKY
INDIANA
LAKE MICHIGAN
JO DAVIESS
STEPHENSON
WINNEBAGO
BOONE
MC HENRY
LAKE
CARROLL
OGLE
DE KALB
KANE
DU PAGE
COOK
WHITESIDE
LEE
KENDALL
WILL
ROCK ISLAND
HENRY
BUREAU
LA SALLE
GRUNDY
MERCER
STARK
PUTNAM
MARSHALL
KANKAKEE
KNOX
LIVINGSTON
IROQUOIS
WARREN
PEORIA
WOODFORD
HENDERSON
HANCOCK
MC DONOUGH
FULTON
TAZEWELL
MC LEAN
FORD
VERMILION
CHAMPAIGN
SCHUYLER
MASON
LOGAN
DE WITT
PIATT
ADAMS
BROWN
CASS
MENARD
MACON
MORGAN
SANGAMON
SCOTT
PIKE
DOUGLAS
MOULTRIE
EDGAR
COLES
CHRISTIAN
SHELBY
CALHOUN
GREENE
MACOUPIN
MONTGOMERY
CUMBERLAND
CLARK
JERSEY
FAYETTE
EFFINGHAM
JASPER
CRAWFORD
BOND
MADISON
CLAY
RICHLAND
LAWRENCE
CLINTON
MARION
ST. CLAIR
WASHINGTON
JEFFERSON
WAYNE
EDWARDS
WABASH
MONROE
RANDOLPH
PERRY
FRANKLIN
HAMILTON
WHITE
JACKSON
WILLIAMSON
SALINE
GALLATIN
UNION
JOHNSON
POPE
HARDIN
ALEXANDER
PULASKI
MASSAC
SPRINGFIELD
CHICAGO
ROCKFORD
PEORIA
DECATUR
ST. LOUIS
DAVENPORT
EVANSVILLE
Longitude West 90° of Greenwich
© Copyright HAMMOND INCORPORATED, Maplewood, N. J.
Chicago and Vicinity

ILLINOIS

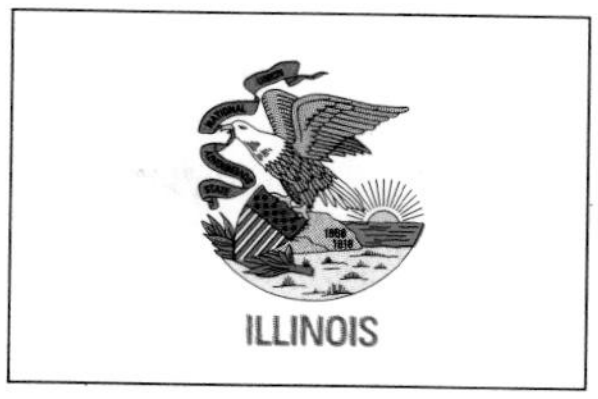

AREA 56,345 sq. mi. (145,934 sq. km.)
POPULATION 11,466,682
CAPITAL Springfield
LARGEST CITY Chicago
HIGHEST POINT Charles Mound 1,235 ft. (376 m.)
SETTLED IN 1720
ADMITTED TO UNION December 3, 1818
POPULAR NAME Prairie State; Land of Lincoln
STATE FLOWER Native Violet
STATE BIRD Cardinal

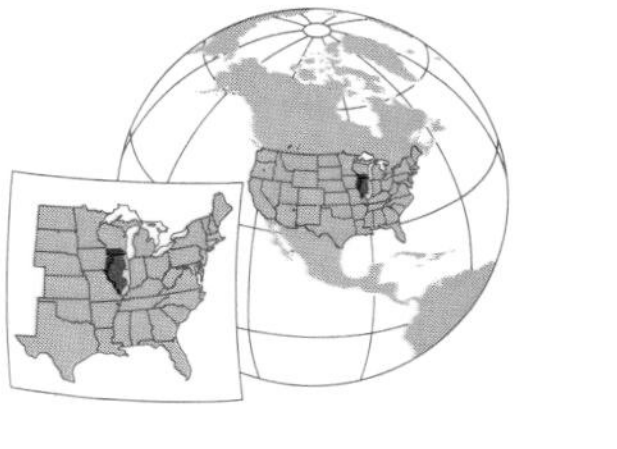

COUNTIES

Adams 66,090 ....B4
Alexander 10,626 ....D6
Bond 14,991 ....D5
Boone 30,806 ....E1
Brown 5,836 ....C4
Bureau 35,688 ....D2
Calhoun 5,322 ....C4
Carroll 16,805 ....D1
Cass 13,437 ....C4
Champaign 173,025 ....E3
Christian 34,418 ....D4
Clark 15,921 ....F4
Clay 14,460 ....E5
Clinton 33,944 ....D5
Coles 51,644 ....E4
Cook 5,105,067 ....F2
Crawford 19,464 ....F4
Cumberland 10,670 ....E4
De Kalb 74,624 ....E2
De Witt 16,516 ....E3
Douglas 19,464 ....E4
Du Page 658,858 ....E2
Edgar 19,595 ....F4
Edwards 7,440 ....E5
Effingham 31,704 ....E4
Fayette 20,893 ....D4
Ford 14,275 ....E3
Franklin 40,319 ....E6
Fulton 38,080 ....C3
Gallatin 6,909 ....E6
Greene 15,317 ....C4
Grundy 32,337 ....E2
Hamilton 8,499 ....E5
Hancock 21,373 ....B3
Hardin 5,189 ....E6
Henderson 8,096 ....C2
Henry 51,159 ....C2
Iroquois 30,787 ....F3
Jackson 61,067 ....D6
Jasper 10,609 ....E4
Jefferson 37,020 ....E5
Jersey 20,539 ....C4
Jo Daviess 21,821 ....C1
Johnson 11,347 ....E6
Kane 317,471 ....E2
Kankakee 96,255 ....F2
Kendall 39,413 ....E2
Knox 56,393 ....C3
La Salle 106,913 ....E2
Lake 516,418 ....E1
Lawrence 15,972 ....F5
Lee 34,392 ....D2
Livingston 39,301 ....E3
Logan 30,798 ....D3
Macon 117,206 ....E4
Macoupin 47,679 ....D4
Madison 249,238 ....D5
Marion 41,561 ....E5
Marshall 12,846 ....D2
Mason 16,269 ....D3
Massac 14,752 ....E6
McDonough 35,244 ....C3
McHenry 183,241 ....E1
McLean 129,180 ....E3
Menard 11,164 ....D3
Mercer 17,290 ....C2
Monroe 22,422 ....C5
Montgomery 30,728 ....D4
Morgan 36,397 ....C4
Moultrie 13,930 ....E4
Ogle 45,957 ....D1
Peoria 182,827 ....D3
Perry 21,412 ....D5
Piatt 15,548 ....E4
Pike 17,577 ....C4
Pope 4,373 ....E6
Pulaski 7,523 ....D6
Putnam 5,730 ....D2
Randolph 34,583 ....D5
Richland 16,545 ....E5
Rock Island 148,723 ....C2
Saint Clair 267,531 ....C5
Saline 26,551 ....E6
Sangamon 178,386 ....D4
Schuyler 7,498 ....C3
Scott 5,644 ....C4
Shelby 22,261 ....E4
Stark 6,534 ....D2
Stephenson 48,052 ....D1
Tazewell 123,692 ....D3
Union 17,619 ....D6
Vermilion 88,257 ....F3
Wabash 13,111 ....F5
Warren 19,181 ....C3
Washington 14,965 ....D5
Wayne 17,241 ....E5
White 16,522 ....E5
Whiteside 60,186 ....D2
Will 357,313 ....F2
Williamson 57,733 ....D6
Winnebago 252,913 ....D1
Woodford 32,653 ....D3

CITIES and TOWNS

Abingdon 3,597 ....C3
Addison 32,058 ....B5
Albany 835 ....C2
Albers 700 ....D5
Albion▲ 2,116 ....E5
Aledo▲ 3,681 ....C2
Alexis 908 ....C2
Algonquin 11,663 ....E1
Alhambra 709 ....D5
Allendale 476 ....F5
Alorton 2,960 ....B2
Alpha 753 ....C2
Alsip 18,227 ....B6
Altamont 2,296 ....E4
Alton 32,905 ....A2
Altona 559 ....C2
Amboy 2,377 ....D2
Andalusia 1,052 ....C2
Andover 579 ....C2
Anna 4,805 ....D6
Annawan 802 ....C2
Antioch 6,105 ....E1
Arcola 2,678 ....E4
Arenzville 432 ....C4
Argenta 940 ....E4
Arlington Heights 75,460 ..B5
Aroma Park 690 ....F2
Arthur 2,112 ....E4
Ashkum 650 ....E3
Ashland 1,257 ....C4
Ashley 583 ....D5
Ashmore 800 ....F4
Ashton 1,042 ....D2
Assumption 1,244 ....E4
Astoria 1,205 ....C3
Athens 1,404 ....D4
Atkinson 950 ....C2
Atlanta 1,616 ....D3
Atwood 1,253 ....E4
Auburn 3,724 ....D4
Augusta 614 ....C3
Aurora 99,581 ....E2
Ava 674 ....D6
Aviston 924 ....D5
Avon 957 ....C3
Baldwin 426 ....D6
Bannockburn 1,388 ....B5
Barrington 9,504 ....A5
Barrington Hills 4,202 ....A5
Barry 1,391 ....C4
Bartlett 19,373 ....A5
Bartonville 5,643 ....D3
Batavia 17,076 ....E2
Beardstown 5,270 ....C3
Beckemeyer 1,070 ....D5
Bedford Park 566 ....B6
Beecher 2,032 ....F2
Beecher City 437 ....E4
Belgium 511 ....F3
Belleville▲ 42,785 ....B3
Bellwood 20,241 ....B5
Belvidere▲ 15,958 ....E1
Bement 1,668 ....E4
Benld 1,604 ....D4
Bensenville 17,767 ....B5
Benton▲ 7,216 ....E6
Berkeley 5,137 ....B5
Berwyn 45,426 ....B6
Bethalto 9,507 ....D5
Bethany 1,369 ....E4
Blandinsville 762 ....C3
Bloomingdale 16,614 .....A5
Bloomington▲ 51,972 ....D3
Blue Island 21,203 ....B6
Blue Mound 1,161 ....D4
Bluffs 774 ....C4
Bluford 747 ....E5
Bolingbrook 40,843 ....A6
Bourbon 13,934 ....E4
Bourbonnais 13,280 ....F2
Bowen 462 ....B3
Braceville 587 ....E2
Bradford 678 ....D2
Bradley 10,792 ....F2
Braidwood 3,584 ....E2
Breese 3,567 ....D5
Bridgeport 2,118 ....F5
Bridgeview 14,402 ....B6
Brighton 2,270 ....C4
Brimfield 797 ....D3
Broadview 8,713 ....B6
Brookfield 18,876 ....B6
Brooklyn (Lovejoy) 1,144 ..A2
Brookport 1,070 ....E6
Brownstown 668 ....E5
Buckley 557 ....F3
Buckner 478 ....E6
Buda 563 ....D2
Buffalo 503 ....D4
Buffalo Grove 36,427 .....B5
Bunker Hill 1,722 ....D4
Burbank 27,600 ....B6
Burnham 3,916 ....C6
Burr Ridge 7,669 ....B6
Bushnell 3,288 ....C3
Byron 2,284 ....D1
Cahokia 17,550 ....A3
Cairo▲ 4,846 ....D6
Calumet City 37,840 ......C6
Calumet Park 8,418 ....C6
Cambria 1,230 ....D6
Cambridge▲ 2,124 ....C2
Camp Point 1,230 ....B3
Canton 13,922 ....C3
Capron 682 ....E1
Carbon Cliff 1,492 ....C2
Carbondale 27,033 ....D6
Carlinville▲ 5,416 ....D4
Carlyle▲ 3,474 ....D5
Carmia 5,564 ....E5
Carol Stream 31,716 ......A5
Carpentersville 23,049 ...E1
Carrier Mills 2,268 ....E6
Carrollton▲ 2,507 ....C4
Carterville 3,630 ....D6
Carthage▲ 2,657 ....B3
Cary 10,043 ....E1
Casey 2,914 ....F4
Caseyville 4,419 ....B2
Catlin 2,173 ....F3
Cave in Rock 381 ....E6
Cedarville 751 ....D1
Central City 1,390 ....D5
Centralia 14,274 ....D5
Centreville 7,489 ....B3
Cerro Gordo 1,436 ....E4
Chadwick 557 ....D1
Champaign 63,502 ....E3
Chandlerville 691 ....D4
Channahon 4,266 ....E2
Chapin 632 ....C4
Charleston▲ 20,398 ....E4
Chatham 6,074 ....D4
Chatsworth 1,186 ....E3
Chebanse 1,082 ....F3
Chenoa 1,732 ....E3
Cherry 487 ....D2
Cherry Valley 1,615 ....D1
Chester▲ 8,194 ....D6
Chicago Heights 33,072 ..C6
Chicago Ridge 13,643 ....B6
Chicago▲ 2,783,726 ......C5
Chillicothe 5,959 ....D3
Chrisman 1,136 ....F4
Christopher 2,774 ....D6
Cicero 67,436 ....B5
Cisne 645 ....E5
Cissna Park 805 ....F3
Clarendon Hills 6,994 .....B6
Clay City 929 ....E5
Clayton 762 ....C3
Clifton 1,347 ....F3
Clinton▲ 7,437 ....E3
Coal City 3,907 ....E2
Coal Valley 2,683 ....C2
Cobden 1,090 ....D6
Coffeen 736 ....D4
Colchester 1,645 ....C3
Colfax 854 ....E3
Collinsville 22,446 ....B2
Colona 2,237 ....C2
Columbia 5,524 ....C5
Cordova 638 ....C2
Cornell 556 ....E3
Cortland 963 ....E2
Coulterville 984 ....D5
Country Club Hills 15,431 ..B6
Countryside 5,716 ....B6
Cowden 599 ....E4
Creal Springs 791 ....E6
Crescent City 541 ....F3
Crest Hill 10,643 ....E2
Creston 549 ....D2
Crestwood 10,823 ....B6
Crete 6,773 ....F2
Creve Coeur 5,938 ....D3
Crossville 805 ....F5
Crystal Lake 24,512 ....E1
Cuba 1,440 ....C3
Cullom 568 ....E3
Cutler 523 ....D5
Dahlgren 512 ....E5
Dakota 549 ....D1
Dallas City 1,037 ....B3
Dalton City 573 ....E4
Dalzell 587 ....D2
Danforth 457 ....E3
Danvers 981 ....D3
Danville▲ 33,828 ....F3
Darien 18,341 ....A6
Davis 541 ....D1
Dawson 536 ....D4
De Kalb 34,925 ....E2
De Land 458 ....E4
De Soto 1,500 ....D6
Decatur▲ 83,885 ....E4
Deer Creek 630 ....D3
Deer Park 2,887 ....A5
Deerfield 17,327 ....B5
Delavan 1,642 ....D3
Depue 1,729 ....D2
Des Plaines 53,223 ....B5
Dieterich 568 ....E4
Divernon 1,178 ....D4
Dix 456 ....E5
Dixmoor 3,647 ....C6
Dixon▲ 15,144 ....D2
Dolton 23,930 ....C6
Dongola 728 ....D6
Dow 465 ....C4
Dowell 480 ....D6
Downers Grove 46,858 ...A6
Downs 620 ....E3
Du Quoin 6,697 ....D5
Dundee (East and West
  Dundee) 6,169 ....E1
Dunlap 851 ....D3
Dupo 3,164 ....A3
Durand 1,100 ....D1
Dwight 4,230 ....E2
Earlville 1,435 ....E2
East Alton 7,063 ....A2
East Cape Girardeau 451 ..D6
East Carondelet 630 ....A3
East Dubuque 1,914 ....C1
East Dundee (Dundee) 2,721 ..E1
East Galesburg 813 ....C3
East Hazelcrest 1,570 .....C6
East Moline 20,147 ....C2
East Peoria 21,378 ....D3
East Saint Louis 40,944 ..A2
Edgewood 502 ....E5
Edinburg 982 ....D4
Edwards 14,579 ....D3
Edwardsville▲ 12,480 ....B2
Effingham▲ 11,851 ....E4
El Paso 2,499 ....D3
Elburn 1,275 ....E2
Eldorado 4,536 ....E6
Elgin 77,010 ....E1
Elizabeth 641 ....C1
Elizabethtown▲ 427 ......E6
Elk Grove Village 33,429 ..B5
Elkhart 475 ....D3
Elkville 958 ....D6
Elmhurst 42,029 ....B5
Elmwood 1,841 ....D3
Elmwood Park 23,206 ....B5
Elsah 851 ....C5
Elwood 951 ....E2
Emden 459 ....D3
Energy 1,106 ....E6
Enfield 683 ....E5
Equality 748 ....E6
Erie 1,572 ....C2
Essex 482 ....E2
Eureka▲ 4,435 ....D3
Evanston 73,233 ....B5
Evansville 844 ....D5
Evergreen Park 20,874 ...B6
Fairbury 3,643 ....E3
Fairfield▲ 5,439 ....E5
Fairmont 2,894 ....A2
Fairmont City 2,140 ....B2
Fairmount 678 ....F3
Fairview 510 ....C3
Fairview Heights 14,351 ..B3
Farina 575 ....E5
Farmer City 2,114 ....E3
Farmersville 698 ....D4
Farmington 2,535 ....C3
Findlay 787 ....E4
Fisher 1,526 ....E3
Fithian 512 ....F3
Flanagan 887 ....E3
Flat Rock 421 ....F4
Flora 5,054 ....E5
Flossmoor 8,651 ....B6
Ford Heights 4,259 ....C6
Forest Homes 1,701 ....B2
Forest Park 14,918 ....B5
Forest View 743 ....B6
Forrest 1,124 ....E3
Forreston 1,361 ....D1
Forsyth 1,275 ....D4
Fox Lake 7,478 ....A4
Fox River Grove 3,551 ....A5
Frankfort 7,180 ....F2
Franklin 634 ....C4
Franklin Grove 968 ....D2
Franklin Park 18,485 ......B5
Freeburg 3,115 ....C3
Freeport▲ 25,840 ....D1
Fulton 3,698 ....C2
Galatia 983 ....E6
Gale 3,647 ....D6
Galena▲ 3,876 ....C1
Galesburg▲ 33,530 ....C3
Galva 2,742 ....D2
Gardner 1,237 ....E2
Geneseo 5,990 ....C2
Geneva▲ 12,617 ....E2
Genoa 3,083 ....E1
Georgetown 3,678 ....F4
German Valley 480 ....D1
Germantown 1,167 ....D5
Gibson City 3,498 ....E3
Gifford 845 ....E3
Gilberts 987 ....E1
Gillespie 3,645 ....D4
Gilman 1,816 ....E3
Glasford 1,115 ....D3
Glen Carbon 7,731 ....B2
Glen Ellyn 24,944 ....A5
Glencoe 8,499 ....B5
Glendale Heights 27,973 ..A5
Glenview 37,093 ....B5
Glenwood 9,289 ....C6
Godfrey 5,436 ....A2
Golconda▲ 823 ....E6
Golden 565 ....B3
Golf 454 ....B5
Goodfield 454 ....D3
Goreville 872 ....D6
Grafton 918 ....C5
Grand Ridge 560 ....E2
Grand Tower 775 ....D6
Grandview 1,647 ....D4
Granite City 32,862 ....A2
Grant Park 1,024 ....F2
Granville 1,407 ....D2
Grayslake 7,388 ....B4
Grayville 2,043 ....E5
Green Oaks 2,101 ....B4
Green Rock 2,615 ....C2
Green Valley 745 ....D3
Greenfield 1,162 ....C4
Greenup 1,616 ....E4
Greenview 848 ....D3
Greenville▲ 4,806 ....D5
Gridley 1,304 ....E3
Griggsville 1,218 ....C4
Gurnee 13,701 ....B4
Hamel 530 ....B2
Hamilton 3,281 ....B3
Hammond 527 ....E4
Hampshire 1,843 ....E1
Hampton 1,601 ....C2
Hanna City 1,205 ....D3
Hanover 908 ....C1
Hanover Park 32,895 .....A5
Hardin▲ 1,071 ....C4
Harrisburg▲ 9,289 ....E6
Harristown 1,319 ....D4
Hartford 1,676 ....A2
Harvard 5,975 ....E1
Harwood Heights 7,680 ..B5
Havana▲ 3,610 ....D3
Hawthorn Woods 4,423 ..A5
Hazel Crest 13,334 ....B6
Hebron 809 ....E1
Hecker 534 ....D5
Hegeler 1,853 ....F3
Hennepin▲ 669 ....D2
Henry 2,591 ....D2
Herrick 466 ....D4
Herrin 10,857 ....E6
Herscher 1,278 ....E2
Heyworth 1,627 ....E3
Hickory Hills 13,021 ....B6
Highland 7,525 ....D5
Highland Park 30,575 .....B5
Highwood 5,331 ....B5
Hillcrest 828 ....D1
Hillsboro▲ 4,400 ....D4
Hillsdale 489 ....C2
Hillside 7,672 ....B5
Hinckley 1,582 ....E2
Hinsdale 16,029 ....B6
Hodgkins 1,963 ....B6
Hoffman 492 ....D5
Hoffman Estates 46,561 ..A5
Holiday Hills 807 ....A4
Homer 1,264 ....F3
Hometown 4,769 ....B6
Homewood 19,278 ....B6
Hoopeston 5,871 ....F3
Hopedale 805 ....D3
Hopkins Park 601 ....F2
Hoyleton 508 ....D5
Hudson 1,006 ....E3
Hull 514 ....B4
Humboldt 470 ....E4
Hunt 2,453 ....E4
Huntley 1,646 ....E1
Hurst 842 ....D6
Hutsonville 622 ....F4
Illiopolis 934 ....D4
Ina 489 ....E5
Industry 571 ....C3
Inverness 6,503 ....A5
Ipava 483 ....C3
Irving 516 ....D4
Irvington 827 ....D5
Island Lake 4,449 ....A4
Itasca 6,947 ....B5
Jacksonville▲ 19,324 .....C4
Jerome 1,206 ....D4
Jerseyville▲ 7,382 ....C4
Johnston City 3,706 ....E6
Joliet▲ 76,836 ....E2
Jonesboro▲ 1,728 ....D6
Joppa 492 ....E6
Joy 452 ....C2
Junction City 539 ....D5
Justice 11,137 ....B6

(continued on following page)

Topography

5,000 m. / 16,404 ft. 2,000 m. / 6,562 ft. 1,000 m. / 3,281 ft. 500 m. / 1,640 ft. 200 m. / 656 ft. 100 m. / 328 ft. Sea Level Below

0 ____ 40 ____ 80 MI.

0 ____ 40 ____ 80 KM.

Charles Mound 1,235 ft. (376 m.) ▲
Rockford
Fox L.
Evanston
Chicago
Rock Island
Joliet
Peoria
Champaign
Quincy
Springfield
Decatur
East St. Louis
Carlyle L.
Rend L.

Mississippi
Pecatonica
Rock
Green
Spoon
Illinois
Fox
Des Plaines
Kankakee
Vermillion
La Moine
Mackinaw
Sangamon
Sugar
Salt
Macoupin
Silver
Kaskaskia
Shoal
Little Wabash
Skillet Fk.
Wabash
Big Muddy
Saline
Embarrass
Ohio

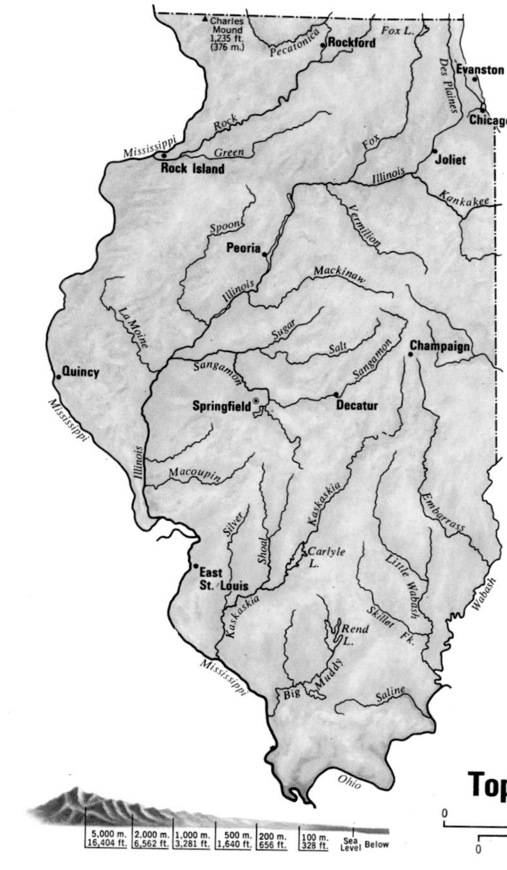

Agriculture, Industry and Resources

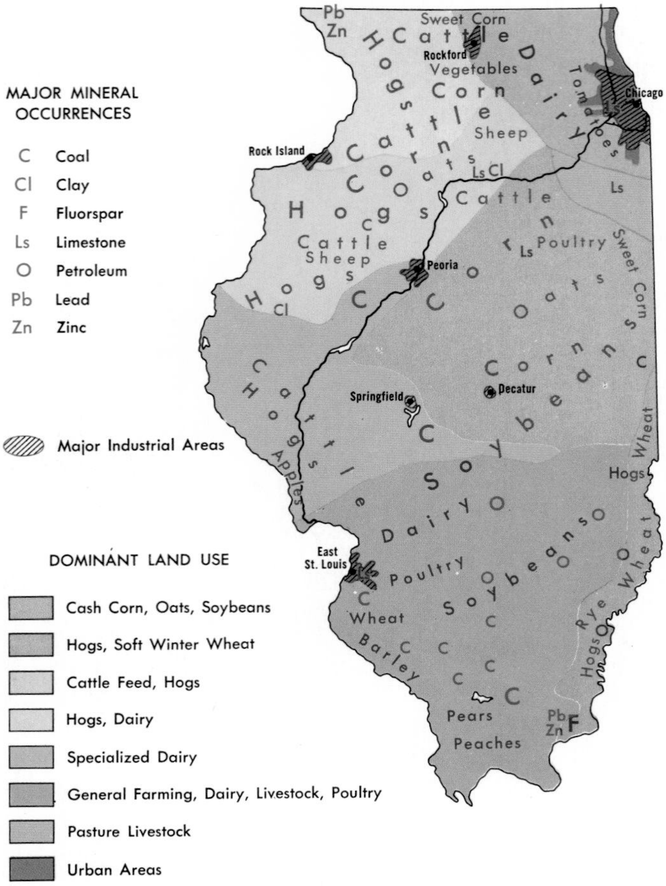
MAJOR MINERAL OCCURRENCES
C Coal
Cl Clay
F Fluorspar
Ls Limestone
O Petroleum
Pb Lead
Zn Zinc
Major Industrial Areas
DOMINANT LAND USE
Cash Corn, Oats, Soybeans
Hogs, Soft Winter Wheat
Cattle Feed, Hogs
Hogs, Dairy
Specialized Dairy
General Farming, Dairy, Livestock, Poultry
Pasture Livestock
Urban Areas
Sweet Corn
Cattle
Rockford
Dairy
Vegetables
Tomatoes
Chicago
Corn
Hogs
Sheep
Oats
Rock Island
Cattle
Peoria
Poultry
Sweet Corn
Springfield
Decatur
Soybeans
Wheat
Apples
East St. Louis
Barley
Rye
Pears
Peaches

Kane 456 C4
Kankakee▲ 27,575 F2
Kansas 887 F4
Karnak 581 E6
Kaskaskia 32 C6
Keithsburg 747 B2
Kenilworth 2,402 B5
Kewanee 12,969 C2
Keyesport 440 D5
Kildeer 2,257 A5
Kincaid 1,353 D4
Kingston 562 E1
Kinmundy 879 E5
Kirkland 1,011 E1
Kirkwood 884 C3
Knoxville 3,243 C3
La Grange 15,362 B6
La Grange Park 12,861 B5
La Harpe 1,407 C3
La Moille 654 D2
La Salle 9,717 E2
Lacon▲ 1,986 D2
Ladd 1,283 D2
Lake Barrington 3,855 A5
Lake Bluff 5,513 B4
Lake Catherine 1,515 E1
Lake Forest 17,836 B4
Lake Villa 2,857 A4
Lake Zurich 14,947 A5
Lake in the Hills 5,866 E1
Lakemoor 1,322 A4
Lakewood 1,609 E4
Lanark 1,382 D1
Lansing 28,086 C6
Latham 482 D4
Lawrenceville▲ 4,897 F5
Le Roy 2,777 E3
Leaf River 546 D1
Lebanon 3,688 D5
Leland 862 E2
Lemont 7,348 B6
Lena 2,605 D1
Lenzburg 510 D5
Lewistown▲ 2,572 C3
Lexington 1,809 E3
Liberty 541 B4
Libertyville 19,174 B4
Lincoln▲ 15,418 D3
Lincolnshire 4,931 B5
Lincolnwood 11,365 B5
Lindenhurst 8,038 B4
Lisle 19,512 A6
Litchfield 6,883 D4
Livingston 928 D5
Loami 802 D4
Lockport 9,401 B6
Lomax 473 B3
Lombard 39,408 B5
London Mills 485 C3
Long Grove 4,740 B5
Lostant 510 D2
Louisville▲ 1,098 E5
Lovejoy 1,233 A2
Loves Park 15,462 E1
Lovington 1,143 E4
Lyndon 615 D2
Lynwood 6,535 C6
Lyons 9,828 B6
Machesney Park 19,033 D1
Mackinaw 1,331 D3
Macomb▲ 19,952 C3
Macon 1,282 E4
Madison 4,629 A2
Mahomet 3,103 E3
Malta 865 E2
Manhattan 2,059 F2
Manito 1,711 D3
Mansfield 929 E3
Manteno 3,488 F2
Maple Park 641 E2
Marengo 4,768 E1
Marine 972 D5
Marion▲ 14,545 E6
Marissa 2,375 D5
Markham 13,136 B6
Maroa 1,602 E3
Marquette Heights 3,077 D3
Marseilles 4,811 E2
Marshall▲ 3,555 F4
Martinsville 1,161 F4
Maryville 2,576 B2
Mascoutah 5,511 D5
Mason City 2,323 D3
Matherville 708 C2
Matteson 11,378 B6
Mattoon 18,441 E4
Maywood 27,139 B5
Mazon 764 E2
McCullom Lake 1,033 E1
McHenry 16,177 E1
McLean 797 D3
McLeansboro▲ 2,677 E5
Meadowbrook 1,082 B2
Mechanicsburg 538 D4
Medora 420 C4
Melrose Park 20,859 B5
Melvin 466 E3
Mendon 854 B3
Mendota 7,018 D2
Meredosia 1,134 C4
Merrionette Park 2,065 B6
Metamora 2,520 D3
Metropolis▲ 6,734 E6
Middletown 436 D3
Midlothian 14,372 B6
Milan 5,831 C2
Milford 1,512 F3
Milledgeville 1,076 D1
Millington 470 E2
Millstadt 2,566 B3
Minier 1,155 D3
Minonk 1,982 D3
Minooka 2,561 E2
Mokena 6,128 B6
Moline 43,202 C2
Momence 2,968 F2
Monee 1,044 F2
Monmouth▲ 9,489 C3
Montgomery 4,267 E2
Monticello▲ 4,549 E3
Morris▲ 10,270 E2
Morrison▲ 4,363 C2
Morrisonville 1,113 D4
Morton 13,799 D3
Morton Grove 22,408 B5
Mound City▲ 765 D6
Mounds 1,407 D6
Mount Auburn 544 D4
Mount Carmel▲ 8,287 F5
Mount Carroll▲ 1,726 D1
Mount Morris 2,919 D1
Mount Olive 2,126 D4
Mount Prospect 53,170 B5
Mount Pulaski 1,610 D3
Mount Sterling▲ 1,922 C4
Mount Vernon▲ 16,988 E5
Mount Zion 4,522 E4
Moweaqua 1,785 E4
Mulberry Grove 660 D5
Mundelein 21,215 A4
Murphysboro▲ 9,176 D6
Murrayville 673 C4
Naperville 85,351 A6
Naplate 609 E2
Nashville▲ 3,202 D5
Nauvoo 1,108 B3
Neoga 1,678 E4
Neponset 529 D2
New Athens 2,010 D5
New Baden 2,602 D5
New Berlin 797 D4
New Boston 620 B2
New Haven 459 E6
New Lenox 9,627 B6
New Millford 463 D1
New Windsor C2
Newark 840 E2
Newman 960 F4
Newton▲ 3,154 E5
Niantic 647 D4
Niles 28,284 B5
Noble 756 E5
Nokomis 2,534 D4
Normal 40,023 E3
Norridge 14,459 B5
Norris City 1,341 E6
North Aurora 5,940 E2
North Barrington 1,787 A5
North Chicago 34,978 B4
North Pekin 1,556 D3
North Riverside 6,005 B5
North Utica (Utica) 848 E2
Northbrook 32,308 B5
Northfield 4,635 B5
Northlake 12,505 B5
O'Fallon 16,073 B2
Oak Brook 9,178 B6
Oak Forest 26,203 B6
Oak Grove 626 C2
Oak Lawn 56,182 B6
Oak Park 53,648 B5
Oakbrook Terrace 1,907 B5
Oakland 996 F4
Oakwood 1,533 F3
Oakwood Hills 1,498 E1
Oblong 1,616 F5
Odell 1,030 E2
Odin 1,150 D5
Ogden 671 F3
Oglesby 3,619 D2
Ohio 426 D2
Okawville 1,274 D5
Olney▲ 8,664 E5
Olympia Fields 4,248 B6
Onarga 1,281 F3
Oneida 723 C2
Oquawka▲ 1,442 B3
Orangeville 451 D1
Oreana 847 E4
Oregon▲ 3,891 D1
Orient 428 E6
Orion 1,821 C2
Orland Hills 5,510 B6
Orland Park 35,720 B6
Oswego 3,876 E2
Ottawa▲ 17,451 E2
Palatine 39,253 B5
Palestine 1,619 F4
Palmyra 722 C4
Palos Heights 11,478 B6
Palos Hills 17,803 B6
Palos Park 4,199 B6
Pana 5,796 D4
Paris▲ 8,987 F4
Park City 4,677 B4
Park Forest 24,656 B6
Park Forest South 6,245 F2
Park Ridge 36,175 B5
Patoka 656 D5
Pawnee 2,384 D4
Pawpaw 791 E2
Paxton▲ 4,289 E3
Payson 1,114 B4
Pearl City 670 D1
Pecatonica 1,760 D1
Pekin▲ 32,254 D3
Peoria Heights 6,930 D3
Peoria▲ 113,504 D3
Peotone 2,947 F2
Percy 925 D5
Perry 491 C4
Peru 9,302 D2
Pesotum 558 E4
Petersburg▲ 2,261 D4
Philo 1,028 E3
Phoenix 2,217 C6
Pierron 554 D5
Pinckneyville▲ 3,372 D5
Piper City 760 E3
Pittsburg 602 E6
Pittsfield▲ 4,231 C4
Plainfield 4,557 A6
Plano 5,104 E2
Pleasant Hill 1,030 C4
Pleasant Plains 701 D4
Plymouth 521 C3
Pocahontas 837 D5
Polo 2,514 D1
Pontiac▲ 11,428 E3
Pontoon Beach 4,013 A2
Poplar Grove 743 E1
Port Byron 1,002 C2
Posen 4,226 B6
Potomac 753 F3
Prairie City 497 C3
Prairie Grove 654 E1
Prairie du Rocher 540 C5
Preston 2,750 D5
Princeton▲ 7,197 D2
Princeville 1,421 D3
Prophetstown 1,749 D2
Prospect Heights 15,239 B5
Quincy▲ 39,681 B4
Ramsey 963 D4
Rankin 619 F3
Ransom 438 E2
Rantoul 17,212 E3
Rapids City 932 C2
Ray 820 C3
Raymond 957 D4
Red Bud 2,918 D5
Reynolds 583 C2
Richmond 1,016 E1
Richton Park 10,523 B6
Ridge Farm 939 F4
Ridgway 1,103 E6
River Forest 11,669 B5
River Grove 9,961 B5
Riverdale 13,671 C6
Riverside 8,774 B6
Riverton 2,638 D4
Riverwoods 2,868 B5
Roanoke 1,910 D3
Robbins 7,498 B6
Robinson▲ 6,740 F5
Rochelle 8,769 D2
Rochester 2,676 D4
Rock Falls 9,654 D2
Rock Island▲ 40,552 C2
Rockdale 1,709 E2
Rockford▲ 139,426 D1
Rockton 2,928 E1
Rolling Meadows 22,591 A5
Rome 1,902 D3
Romeoville 14,074 B6
Roodhouse 2,139 C4
Roscoe 2,079 D1
Roselle 20,819 A5
Rosemont 3,995 B5
Roseville 1,151 C3
Rosewood Heights 4,821 B2
Rosiclare 1,378 E6
Rossville 1,334 F3
Round Lake 3,550 A4
Round Lake Beach 16,434 A4
Round Lake Park 4,045 A4
Roxana 1,562 B2
Royalton 1,191 D6
Rushville▲ 3,229 C3
Sadorus 469 E4
Saint Anne 1,153 F2
Saint Charles 22,501 E2
Saint David 603 C3
Saint Elmo 1,473 E4
Saint Francisville 851 F5
Saint Jacob 752 D5
Saint Joseph 2,052 E3
Saint Libory 525 D5
Salem▲ 7,470 E5
San Jose 519 D3
Sandoval 1,535 D5
Sandwich 5,567 E2
Sauk Village 9,926 C6
Savanna 3,819 C1
Savoy 2,674 E3
Saybrook 767 E3
Schaumburg 68,586 A5
Schiller Park 11,189 B5
Schram City 692 D4
Seneca 1,878 E2
Sesser 2,087 D5
Shabbona 897 E2
Shannon 887 D1
Shawneetown▲ 1,575 E6
Sheffield 951 D2
Shelbyville▲ 4,943 E4
Sheldon 1,109 F3
Sheridan 1,288 E2
Sherman 2,080 D4
Sherrard 697 C2
Shiloh 2,655 B3
Shipman 624 C4
Shorewood 6,264 E2
Sidell 584 F4
Sidney 1,027 E3
Silvis 6,926 C2
Skokie 59,432 B5
Sleepy Hollow 3,241 E1
Smithton 1,587 C5
Somonauk 1,263 E2
Sorento 596 D5
South Barrington 2,937 A5
South Beloit 4,072 E1
South Chicago Heights 3,597 C6
South Elgin 7,474 E2
South Holland 22,105 C6
South Jacksonville 3,187 C4
South Pekin 1,184 D3
South Roxana 1,961 B2
South Wilmington 698 E2
Sparta 4,853 D5
Spaulding 440 D4
Spring Bay 439 D3
Spring Grove 1,066 E1
Spring Valley 5,246 D2
Springfield (cap.)▲ 105,227 D4
Stanford 620 D3
Staunton 4,806 D5
Steeleville 2,059 D6
Steger 8,584 F2
Sterling 15,132 D2
Stewardson 660 E4
Stickney 5,678 B6
Stillman Valley 848 D1
Stockton 1,871 C1
Stone Park 4,383 B5
Stonington 1,006 D4
Strasburg 473 E4
Streamwood 30,987 A5
Streator 14,121 E2
Stronghurst 799 C3
Sugar Grove 2,005 E2
Sullivan▲ 4,354 E4
Summerfield 509 D5
Summit-Argo 10,110 B6
Sumner 1,083 F5
Sunnyside 1,529 A4
Swansea 8,201 B3
Sycamore▲ 9,708 E2
Tallula 598 D4
Tamaroa 780 D5
Tamms 748 D6
Tampico 833 D2
Taylor Springs 670 D4
Taylorville 11,133 D4
Teutopolis 1,417 E4
Thayer 730 D4
Thebes 461 D6
Third Lake 1,248 B4
Thomasboro 1,250 E3
Thompsonville 602 E6
Thomson 538 C2
Thornton 2,778 C6
Tilden 919 D5
Tilton 2,729 F3
Tinley Park 37,121 B6
Tiskilwa 830 D2
Toledo▲ 1,199 E4
Tolono 2,605 E3
Toluca 1,315 D2
Tonica 715 E2
Toulon▲ 1,328 D2
Tovey 533 D4
Towanda 856 E3
Tower Hill 601 E4
Tower Lakes 1,333 A4
Tremont 2,088 D3
Trenton 2,481 D5
Troy 6,046 B2
Tuscola▲ 4,155 E4
Union 542 E1
Urbana▲ 36,344 E3
Ursa 506 B3
Utica E2
Valier 708 D5
Valmeyer 897 C5
Vandalia▲ 6,114 D5
Venice 3,571 A2
Vermont 806 C3
Vernon Hills 15,319 B4
Versailles 480 C4
Vienna▲ 1,446 E6
Villa Grove 2,734 E4
Villa Park 22,253 B5
Viola 964 C2
Virden 3,635 D4
Virginia▲ 1,767 C4
Wadsworth 1,826 B4
Walnut 1,463 D2
Wamac 1,501 D5
Wapella 608 E3
Warren 1,550 C1
Warrensburg 1,274 D4
Warrenville 11,333 A6
Warsaw 1,882 B3
Washburn 1,075 D3
Washington 10,099 D3
Washington Park 7,431 B2
Wataga 879 C2
Waterloo▲ 5,072 C5
Waterman 1,074 E2
Watseka▲ 5,424 F3
Watson 646 E4
Wauconda 6,294 A4
Waukegan▲ 69,392 B4
Waverly 1,402 D4
Wayne 1,541 E2
Wayne City 1,099 E5
Waynesville 440 D3
Wenona 950 E2
West Chicago 14,796 A5
West City 747 E5
West Dundee (Dundee) 3,728 E1
West Frankfort 8,526 E6
West Salem 1,042 F5
Westchester 17,301 B5
Western Springs 11,984 B6
Westfield 676 F4
Westmont 21,228 B6
Westville 3,387 F3
Wheaton▲ 51,464 A5
Wheeling 29,911 B5
White Hall 2,814 C4
Williamsfield 571 C3
Williamsville 1,140 D4
Willisville 577 D6
Willow Springs 4,509 B6
Willowbrook 1,808 B6
Wilmette 26,690 B5
Wilsonville 609 D4
Winchester▲ 1,769 C4
Windsor (New Windsor) 774 C2
Windsor 1,228 E4
Winfield 7,096 A5
Winnebago 1,840 D1
Winnetka 12,174 B5
Winthrop Harbor 6,240 F1
Witt 866 D4
Wonder Lake 1,024 E1
Wood Dale 12,425 B5
Wood River 11,490 B2
Woodhull 808 C2
Woodlawn 582 D5
Woodridge 26,256 B6
Woodson 472 C4
Woodstock▲ 14,353 E1
Worden 896 B2
Worth 11,208 B6
Wyanet 1,017 D2
Wyoming 1,462 D2
Yates City 760 C3
Yorkville▲ 3,925 E2
Zeigler 1,746 D6
Zion 19,775 F1

OTHER FEATURES

Apple (creek) C4
Apple (riv.) C1
Argonne Nat'l Laboratory B6
Big Bureau (riv.) D2
Big Muddy (riv.) D6
Bonpas (creek) F5
Cache (riv.) D6
Calumet (lake) C6
Carlyle (lake) D5
Chanute A.F.B. E3
Charles Mound (hill) C1
Chicago Portage Nat'l Hist. Site B6
Crab Orchard (lake) E6
Des Plaines (riv.) A6
Du Page (riv.) E2
Edwards (riv.) C2
Embarras (riv.) E4
Fort Sheridan B5
Fox (lake) A4
Fox (riv.) E2
Fox (riv.) E5
Glenview Naval Air Sta. B5
Granite City Army Depot A2
Great Lakes Naval Trng. Ctr. B4
Green (riv.) D2
Henderson (riv.) C2
Illinois (riv.) C4
Illinois-Mississippi (canal) C2
Iroquois (riv.) F3
Kankakee (riv.) F2
Kaskaskia (riv.) E4
La Moine (riv.) C3
Little Wabash (riv.) E5
Mackinaw (riv.) E3
Macoupin (riv.) C4
Michigan (lake) F1
Mississippi (riv.) C5
O'Hare International Airport B5
Ohio (riv.) E6
Plum (riv.) C1
Pope (creek) C2
Rend (lake) D5
Rock (creek) D2
Rock (riv.) C2
Saline (riv.) E6
Salt (creek) D3
Sangamon (riv.) C3
Savanna Army Depot C1
Scott A.F.B. 7,245 B3
Shelbyville (lake) E4
Shoal (creek) D5
Spoon (riv.) C3
Wabash (riv.) F5

▲County seat

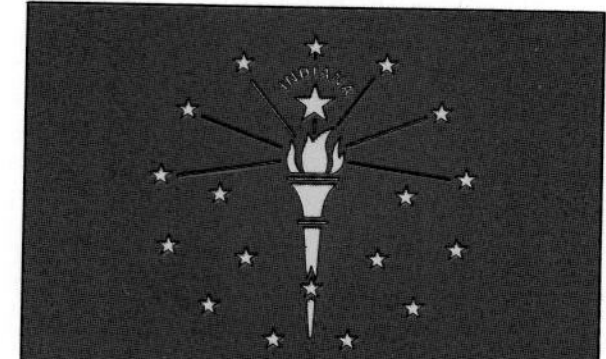

AREA 36,185 sq. mi. (93,719 sq. km.)
POPULATION 5,564,228
CAPITAL Indianapolis
LARGEST CITY Indianapolis
HIGHEST POINT 1,257 ft. (383 m.) (Wayne County)
SETTLED IN 1730
ADMITTED TO UNION December 11, 1816
POPULAR NAME Hoosier State
STATE FLOWER Peony
STATE BIRD Cardinal

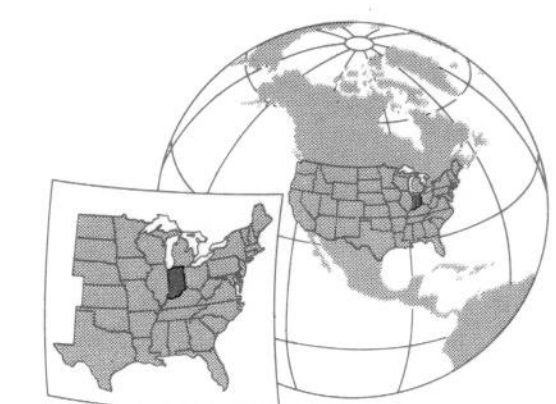

COUNTIES

Adams 31,095 ....H3
Allen 300,836 ....G2
Bartholomew 63,657 ....F6
Benton 9,441 ....C3
Blackford 14,067 ....G4
Boone 38,147 ....E4
Brown 14,080 ....E6
Carroll 18,809 ....D3
Cass 38,413 ....E3
Clark 87,777 ....F8
Clay 24,705 ....C6
Clinton 30,974 ....E4
Crawford 9,914 ....E8
Daviess 27,533 ....C7
De Kalb 35,324 ....H2
Dearborn 38,835 ....H6
Decatur 23,645 ....G6
Delaware 119,659 ....G4
Dubois 36,616 ....D8
Elkhart 156,198 ....F1
Fayette 26,015 ....G5
Floyd 64,404 ....F8
Fountain 17,808 ....C4
Franklin 19,580 ....G6
Fulton 18,840 ....E2
Gibson 31,913 ....B8
Grant 74,169 ....F3
Greene 30,410 ....D6
Hamilton 108,936 ....E4
Hancock 45,527 ....F5
Harrison 29,890 ....E8
Hendricks 75,717 ....D5
Henry 48,139 ....G5
Howard 80,827 ....E4
Huntington 35,427 ....G3
Jackson 37,730 ....E7
Jasper 24,960 ....C2
Jay 21,512 ....G4
Jefferson 29,797 ....G7
Jennings 23,661 ....F7
Johnson 88,109 ....E6
Knox 39,884 ....C7
Kosciusko 65,294 ....F2
LaPorte 108,632 ....D1
Lagrange 29,477 ....G1
Lake 475,594 ....C2
Lawrence 42,836 ....E7
Madison 130,669 ....F4
Marion 797,159 ....E5
Marshall 42,182 ....E2
Martin 10,369 ....D7
Miami 36,897 ....E3
Monroe 108,978 ....D6
Montgomery 34,436 ....D4
Morgan 55,920 ....E6
Newton 13,551 ....C3
Noble 37,877 ....G2
Ohio 5,315 ....H7
Orange 18,409 ....E7
Owen 17,281 ....D6
Parke 15,410 ....C5
Perry 19,107 ....D8
Pike 12,509 ....C8
Porter 128,932 ....C2
Posey 25,968 ....B8
Pulaski 12,643 ....D2
Putnam 30,315 ....D5
Randolph 27,148 ....G4
Ripley 24,616 ....G6
Rush 18,129 ....G5
Saint Joseph 241,617 ....E1
Scott 20,991 ....F7
Shelby 40,307 ....F5
Spencer 19,490 ....C9
Starke 22,747 ....D2
Steuben 27,446 ....G1
Sullivan 18,993 ....C6
Switzerland 7,738 ....G7
Tippecanoe 130,598 ....D4
Tipton 16,119 ....E4
Union 6,976 ....H5
Vanderburgh 165,058 ....B8
Vermillion 16,773 ....C5
Vigo 106,107 ....C6
Wabash 35,069 ....F3
Warren 8,176 ....C4
Warrick 44,920 ....C8
Washington 23,717 ....E7
Wayne 71,951 ....G5
Wells 25,948 ....G3
White 23,265 ....D3
Whitley 27,651 ....F2

CITIES and TOWNS

Abington 200 ....H5
Adams 250 ....F6
Adamsboro 325 ....E3
Advance 520 ....D5
Akron 1,001 ....E2
Alamo 112 ....C5
Albany 2,357 ....G4
Albion▲ 1,823 ....G2
Alexandria 5,709 ....F4
Altona 156 ....G2
Ambia 249 ....C4
Amboy 370 ....F3
Americus 150 ....D3
Amity 200 ....E6
Amo 380 ....D5
Anderson▲ 59,459 ....F4
Andersonville 225 ....G5
Andrews 1,118 ....F3
Angola▲ 5,824 ....G1
Anthony 130 ....G4
Arcadia 1,468 ....E4
Arcola 300 ....G2
Ardmore 800 ....E1
Argos 1,642 ....E2
Arlington 500 ....F5
Ashley 767 ....G1
Athens 145 ....E2
Atlanta 703 ....E4
Attica 3,457 ....C4
Atwood 300 ....F2
Auburn▲ 9,379 ....G2
Aurora 3,825 ....H6
Austin 4,310 ....F7
Avilla 1,366 ....G2
Avoca 400 ....D7
Azalia 194 ....F6
Bainbridge 682 ....D5
Bargersville 1,681 ....E5
Batesville 4,720 ....G6
Battle Ground 806 ....D3
Bear Branch 150 ....G7
Bedford▲ 13,817 ....E7
Beech Grove 13,383 ....E5
Bellmore 160 ....C5
Bennetts Switch 138 ....E3
Benton 220 ....F2
Berne 3,559 ....H3
Bethany 90 ....E5
Beverly Shores 622 ....D1
Bicknell 3,357 ....C7
Bippus 300 ....F3
Birdseye 472 ....D8
Black Oak C1
Blanford 500 ....B5
Blocher 400 ....F7
Bloomfield▲ 2,592 ....D6
Blooming Grove 300 ....G5
Bloomingdale 341 ....C5
Bloomington▲ 60,633 ....D6
Blountsville 155 ....G4
Blue Ridge 219 ....F5
Bluffton▲ 9,020 ....G3
Boggstown 200 ....F5
Boone Grove 220 ....C2
Boonville▲ 6,724 ....C8
Borden F8
Boston 159 ....H5
Boswell 767 ....C3
Bourbon 1,672 ....E2
Bowling Green 200 ....D6
Bradford 350 ....E8
Brazil▲ 7,640 ....C5
Bremen 4,725 ....E2
Bridgeton 250 ....C5
Bright 3,945 ....H6
Brimfield 292 ....G2
Bringhurst 275 ....E3
Bristol 1,133 ....F1
Brook 899 ....C3
Brooklyn 1,162 ....E5
Brooksburg 79 ....G7
Brookston 1,804 ....D3
Brookville▲ 2,529 ....G6
Brownsburg 7,628 ....E5
Brownstown▲ 2,872 ....F7
Brownsville 250 ....H5
Bruceville 471 ....C7
Bryant 273 ....G3
Buck Creek 225 ....D4
Buckskin 200 ....C8
Buffalo 500 ....D3
Bunker Hill 1,010 ....E3
Burket 200 ....F2
Burlington 568 ....E4
Burnettsville 401 ....D3
Burney 300 ....F6
Burns City 140 ....D7
Burns Harbor 788 ....C1
Burrows 250 ....E3
Butler 2,601 ....H2
Butlerville 300 ....F6
Byron 200 ....C5
Cadiz 202 ....G5
Cambridge City 2,091 ....G5
Camden 607 ....D3
Cammack 250 ....G4
Campbellsburg 606 ....E7
Cannelburg 97 ....C7
Cannelton▲ 1,786 ....D9
Carbon 350 ....C5
Carefree 26 ....E8
Carlisle 613 ....C7
Carmel 25,380 ....E5
Cartersburg 300 ....E5
Carthage 887 ....F5
Cassville 159 ....E3
Cates 125 ....C4
Cayuga 1,083 ....C5
Cedar Grove 246 ....H6
Cedar Lake 8,885 ....C2
Celestine 150 ....D8
Centenary 150 ....B5
Center 278 ....E4
Centerpoint 242 ....C6
Centerton 250 ....E5
Centerville 2,398 ....H5
Chalmers 525 ....D3
Chandler 3,099 ....C8
Chapel Hill 175 ....E6
Charlestown 5,889 ....F8
Charlottesville 300 ....F5
Chelsea 200 ....F7
Chester 2,730 ....H5
Chesterfield 2,701 ....F4
Chesterton 9,124 ....D1
Chili 280 ....F3
Chrisney 511 ....C8
Churubusco 1,781 ....G2
Cicero 3,268 ....E4
Clarks Hill 716 ....D4
Clarksburg 300 ....G6
Clarksville 19,833 ....F8
Clay City 929 ....C6
Claypool 411 ....F2
Clayton 610 ....D5
Clear Creek 200 ....E6
Clear Lake 272 ....H1
Clifford 308 ....F6
Clinton 5,040 ....C5
Cloverdale 1,681 ....D5
Cloverland 175 ....C6
Clymers 150 ....E3
Coal City 225 ....D6
Coalmont 450 ....C6
Coatesville 469 ....D5
Coesse 150 ....G2
Colburn 300 ....D3
Colfax 727 ....D4
Collegeville 993 ....C3
Columbia City▲ 5,706 ....G2
Columbus▲ 31,802 ....E6
Commiskey 150 ....F7
Connersville▲ 15,550 ....G5
Converse 1,144 ....F3
Correct 131 ....G7
Cortland 175 ....F7
Corunna 241 ....G2
Cory 2,661 ....C6
Corydon▲ 2,724 ....E8
Covington▲ 2,747 ....C4
Cowan 428 ....G4
Craigville 130 ....G3
Crandall 147 ....E8
Crane 216 ....D7
Crawfordsville▲ 13,584 ....D4
Cromwell 520 ....F2
Cross Plains 254 ....G7
Crothersville 1,687 ....F7
Crown Point▲ 17,728 ....C2
Crumstown 175 ....E1
Culver 1,404 ....E2
Cumberland 1,624 ....F5
Cutler 140 ....D4
Cynthiana 669 ....B8
Dale 1,553 ....D8
Daleville 1,681 ....F4
Dana 612 ....C5
Danville▲ 4,345 ....D5
Darlington 740 ....D4
Darmstadt 1,346 ....B8
Dayton 996 ....D4
Decatur▲ 8,644 ....H3
Decker 281 ....B7
Deer Creek 250 ....E3
Deerfield 300 ....H4
Delaware 135 ....G6
Delong 156 ....E2
Delphi▲ 2,531 ....D3
Demotte 2,482 ....C2
Denham 140 ....D2
Denver 504 ....E3
Depauw 150 ....E8
Deputy 200 ....F7
Desoto 385 ....G4
Dillsboro 1,200 ....G6
Donaldson 320 ....E2
Doolittle Mills 200 ....D8
Dublin 805 ....G5
Dubois 550 ....D8
Dugger 936 ....C6
Dundee 160 ....F4
Dune Acres 263 ....C1
Dunkirk 2,739 ....G4
Dunlap 5,705 ....F1
Dunreith 205 ....F5
Dupont 391 ....G7
Dyer 10,923 ....C1
Eagletown 306 ....E4
Earl Park 443 ....C3
East Chicago 33,892 ....C1
East Enterprise 250 ....H7
East Germantown (Pershing) 372 ....G5
Eaton 1,614 ....G4
Economy 151 ....G5
Edgewood 2,057 ....F4
Edinburgh 4,536 ....E6
Edwardsport 380 ....C7
Edwardsville 700 ....F8
Elberfeld 635 ....C8
Elizabeth 153 ....F8
Elizabethtown 495 ....F6
Elkhart 43,627 ....F1
Ellettsville 3,275 ....D6
Elnora 679 ....C7
Elrod 200 ....G6
Elston 500 ....D4
Elwood 9,494 ....F4
Eminence 200 ....D5
English▲ 614 ....E8
Etna 578 ....F2
Etna Green 522 ....E2
Eugene 400 ....B5
Evansville▲ 126,272 ....C9
Everton 500 ....G5
Fair Oaks 175 ....C2
Fairbanks 165 ....B6
Fairland 1,348 ....F5
Fairmount 3,130 ....F4
Fairview 1,446 ....G7
Fairview Park 1,545 ....C5
Farmersburg 1,159 ....C6
Farmland 1,412 ....G4
Fayetteville 180 ....D7
Ferdinand 2,318 ....D8
Fillmore 497 ....D5
Finly 400 ....F5
Fishers 7,508 ....E5
Flat Rock 323 ....F6
Flora 2,179 ....E3
Florence 155 ....H7
Floyds Knobs 500 ....F8
Fontanet 325 ....C5
Forest 400 ....E4
Fort Branch 2,447 ....B8
Fort Wayne▲ 173,072 ....G2
Fortville 2,690 ....F5
Fountain 766 ....C4
Fountain City 839 ....H5
Fountaintown 225 ....F5
Fowler▲ 2,333 ....C3
Fowlerton 306 ....F4
Francesville 969 ....D3
Francisco 560 ....B8
Frankfort▲ 14,754 ....E4
Franklin▲ 12,907 ....E6
Frankton 1,736 ....F4
Fredericksburg 155 ....E8
Freelandville 600 ....C7
Freetown 600 ....E7
Fremont 1,407 ....H1
French Lick 2,087 ....D7
Fulton 371 ....E3
Galena 1,231 ....F8
Galveston 1,609 ....E3
Garrett 5,349 ....G2
Gary 116,646 ....C1
Gas City 6,296 ....F4
Gaston 979 ....G4
Geneva 1,280 ....H3
Gentryville 277 ....C8
Georgetown 2,092 ....F8
Gessie 144 ....C4
Glenwood 285 ....G5
Glezen 300 ....C8
Goldsmith 235 ....E4
Goodland 1,033 ....C3
Goshen▲ 23,797 ....F1
Gosport 764 ....D6
Grabill 751 ....H2
Grandview 761 ....C9
Granger 20,241 ....E1
Grantsburg 189 ....E8
Gravelton 150 ....F2
Greencastle▲ 8,984 ....D5
Greendale 3,881 ....H6
Greenfield▲ 11,657 ....F5

(continued on following page)

Agriculture, Industry and Resources

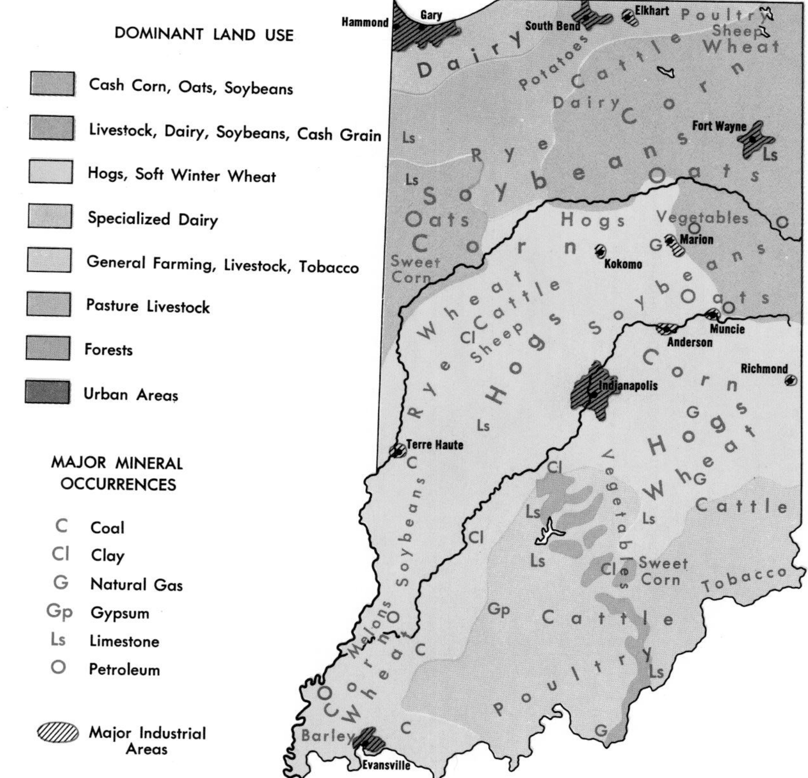
DOMINANT LAND USE
Cash Corn, Oats, Soybeans
Livestock, Dairy, Soybeans, Cash Grain
Hogs, Soft Winter Wheat
Specialized Dairy
General Farming, Livestock, Tobacco
Pasture Livestock
Forests
Urban Areas
MAJOR MINERAL OCCURRENCES
C Coal
Cl Clay
G Natural Gas
Gp Gypsum
Ls Limestone
O Petroleum
Major Industrial Areas
Hammond
Gary
South Bend
Elkhart
Fort Wayne
Kokomo
Marion
Muncie
Anderson
Indianapolis
Richmond
Terre Haute
Evansville
Dairy
Poultry
Sheep
Wheat
Potatoes
Cattle
Corn
Rye
Soybeans
Oats
Sweet Corn
Hogs
Vegetables
Tobacco
Melons
Barley

Greens Fork 416 ....H5
Greensboro 204 ....G5
Greensburg▲ 9,286 ....G6
Greentown 2,172 ....E4
Greenville 508 ....F8
Greenwood 26,265 ....E5
Griffin 171 ....B8
Griffith 17,916 ....C1
Grovertown 150 ....D2
Gwynneville 250 ....F5
Hagerstown 1,835 ....G5
Hamilton 684 ....H1
Hamlet 789 ....D2
Hammond 84,236 ....B1
Hanna 150 ....D2
Hardinsburg 322 ....E8
Harlan 840 ....H2
Harmony 645 ....C5
Harrodsburg 400 ....D6
Hartford City▲ 6,960 ....F4
Hartsville 391 ....F6
Hatfield 800 ....C9
Haubstadt 1,455 ....B8
Hayden 300 ....F7
Haysville 600 ....D8
Hazelwood 650 ....D5
Hazleton 357 ....C2
Hebron 3,183 ....E6
Helmsburg 150 ....E7
Heltonville 400 ....E7
Hemlock 300 ....F4
Henryville 1,132 ....F7
Hibbard 150 ....E2
Highland 23,696 ....B1
Hillisburg 180 ....E4
Hillsboro 499 ....C4
Hillsdale 500 ....C5
Hoagland 600 ....H3
Hobart 21,822 ....C1
Hobbs 200 ....F4
Holland 675 ....C8
Hollandsburg 150 ....C5
Holton 451 ....G6
Homer 235 ....F5
Hope 2,171 ....F6
Hortonville 240 ....E4
Houston 200 ....E6
Howe 800 ....G1
Hudson 438 ....G1
Hudson Lake 1,347 ....D1
Huntertown 1,330 ....G2
Huntingburg 5,242 ....D8
Huntington▲ 16,389 ....G3
Huntsville 1,200 ....G4
Huron 250 ....D7
Hymera 771 ....C6
Idaville 655 ....D3
Independence 150 ....C4
Indian Village 142 ....E1
Indianapolis (cap.)▲ 741,952 ....F5
Ingalls 889 ....F5
Inglefield 378 ....B8
Inwood 150 ....E2
Ireland 600 ....C8
Jamestown 764 ....D5
Jasonville 2,200 ....C6
Jasper▲ 10,030 ....D8
Jefferson 21,841 ....D4
Jeffersonville▲ 21,220 ....F8
Jolietville 300 ....E4
Jonesboro 2,073 ....F4
Jonesville 221 ....F6
Kempton 362 ....E4
Kendallville 7,773 ....G2
Kennard 382 ....G5
Kent 1,798 ....F7
Kentland▲ 1,936 ....C3
Kewanna 542 ....E2
Keystone 204 ....F2
Kimmell 300 ....G2
Kingman 561 ....C4
Kingsbury 258 ....D1
Kingsford Heights 1,486 ....E4
Kirklin 707 ....E4
Knightstown 2,048 ....F5
Knightsville 740 ....C5
Knox▲ 3,705 ....D2
Kokomo▲ 44,962 ....E4
Koontz Lake 1,615 ....C2
Kouts 1,603 ....C2
La Crosse 677 ....D2
La Fontaine 909 ....F3
Ladoga 1,124 ....D5
Lafayette▲ 43,764 ....D4
Lagrange▲ 2,382 ....F1
Lagro 496 ....F3
Lake Bruce 160 ....E2
Lake James 400 ....H1
Lake Station 13,899 ....C1
Lake Village 900 ....C2
Laketon 500 ....F3
Lakeville 655 ....E1
Lancaster 275 ....F7
Landess 150 ....F3
Lanesville 512 ....E8
Laotto 361 ....G2
Lapaz 562 ....E2
Lapel 1,742 ....F4
LaPorte▲ 21,507 ....D1
Laconia 75 ....E8
Larwill 219 ....G2
Laurel 544 ....G6
Lawrence 26,763 ....F5
Lawrenceburg▲ 4,375 ....H6
Leavenworth 320 ....E8
Lebanon▲ 12,059 ....D4
Lee 584 ....F2
Leesburg 629 ....F2
Leesville 164 ....E7
Leiters Ford 280 ....E2
Leo 500 ....G2
Leopold 175 ....D8
Leroy 400 ....C2
Letts 247 ....F6
Lewis 437 ....C6
Lewisville 577 ....G5

Lexington F7
Liberty Center 275 ....G3
Liberty Mills 200 ....F2
Liberty▲ 2,051 ....H5
Ligonier 3,443 ....F2
Lincoln City 160 ....C8
Lincolnville 150 ....F3
Linden 718 ....D4
Linn Grove 175 ....H3
Linton 5,814 ....C6
Linwood 157 ....F4
Lisbon 200 ....G2
Little York 155 ....F7
Livonia 136 ....E7
Lizton 410 ....D5
Logan 16,812 ....E3
Logansport▲ 17,731 ....D1
Long Beach 2,044 ....D7
Loogootee 2,884 ....G4
Losantville 253 ....G4
Lowell 6,430 ....C2
Lucerne 135 ....E3
Lydick C9
Lyford 400 ....C5
Lynn 1,183 ....H4
Lynnville 640 ....C8
Lyons 753 ....C7
Mackey 89 ....C8
Madison▲ 12,006 ....G7
Majenica 150 ....G3
Manchester 250 ....H6
Manilla 350 ....F5
Mansfield 200 ....C5
Marco 150 ....C7
Marengo 856 ....E8
Mariah Hill 300 ....D8
Marietta 234 ....F6
Marion▲ 32,618 ....F3
Markle 1,208 ....G3
Markleville 412 ....F5
Marshall 379 ....C5
Martinsburg 200 ....E8
Martinsville▲ 11,677 ....D6
Matthews 571 ....E4
Mauckport 95 ....E8
Maxinkuckee 150 ....E2
Maxwell 300 ....F5
Mays 156 ....F5
McCordsville 684 ....C5
Mecca 331 ....C5
Mechanicsburg 150 ....G5
Medaryville 689 ....D2
Medora 805 ....E7
Mellott 222 ....C4
Memphis 300 ....F8
Mentone 912 ....F2
Merom 257 ....B6
Merrillville 27,257 ....C2
Metamora 350 ....G6
Metz 200 ....H1
Mexico 1,003 ....E3
Miami 350 ....E3
Michiana Shores 378 ....D1
Michigan City 33,822 ....C1
Michigantown 472 ....E4
Middlebury 2,004 ....F1
Middletown 2,333 ....F4
Midland 250 ....C6
Milan 1,529 ....G6
Milford 126 ....F2
Milford 177 ....D4
Mill Creek 208 ....F1
Millersburg 854 ....G2
Millhousen 151 ....G6
Milltown 917 ....E8
Milroy 750 ....G6
Milton 634 ....G5
Mishawaka 42,608 ....E1
Mitchell 4,669 ....D7
Modoc 218 ....G4
Mongo 225 ....G1
Monon 1,585 ....D3
Monroe 788 ....H3
Monroe City 538 ....C7
Monroeville 1,232 ....H3
Monrovia 800 ....E5
Monterey 230 ....E2
Montezuma 1,134 ....C5
Montgomery 351 ....C7
Monticello▲ 5,237 ....D3
Montmorenci 300 ....D4
Montpelier 1,880 ....G3
Mooreland 465 ....G5
Moores Hill 649 ....G6
Mooresville 5,541 ....E5
Morgantown 978 ....E6
Morocco 1,044 ....C3
Morris 980 ....G6
Morristown 989 ....F5
Mount Auburn 138 ....G5
Mount Ayr 151 ....C3
Mount Carmel 108 ....H6
Mount Etna 111 ....F3
Mount Summit 238 ....G4
Mount Vernon▲ 7,217 ....B9
Mulberry 1,262 ....D4
Muncie▲ 71,035 ....G4
Munster 19,949 ....B1
Murray 136 ....G3
Nabb 150 ....F7
Napoleon 238 ....G6
Nappanee 5,510 ....F2
Nashville▲ 873 ....E6
Needmore 200 ....E7
New Albany▲ 36,322 ....F8
New Amsterdam 30 ....E8
New Carlisle 1,446 ....E1
New Castle▲ 17,753 ....G5
New Chicago 2,066 ....C1
New Goshen 500 ....B5
New Harmony 846 ....B8
New Haven 9,320 ....H2
New Lebanon 150 ....C6
New Lisbon 300 ....G5
New London 200 ....E4

New Marion 200 ....G6
New Market 614 ....D5
New Middleton 82 ....E8
New Palestine 671 ....F5
New Paris 1,007 ....F2
New Pekin 1,095 ....F7
New Point 296 ....G6
New Providence (Borden) 270 ....F8
New Richmond 312 ....D4
New Ross 331 ....D5
New Salem 200 ....G5
New Salisbury 350 ....E8
New Trenton 200 ....H6
New Washington 800 ....F7
New Waverly 162 ....E3
New Whiteland 4,097 ....E5
New Winchester 180 ....D5
Newbern 150 ....F6
Newberry 207 ....C6
Newburgh 2,880 ....C9
Newport▲ 627 ....C5
Newtonville 136 ....D8
Newtown 243 ....C4
Newville 150 ....H2
Noblesville▲ 17,655 ....F4
North Grove 91 ....F3
North Judson 1,582 ....D2
North Liberty 1,366 ....E1
North Manchester 6,383 ....F3
North Salem 499 ....D5
North Terre Haute 4,331 ....C5
North Vernon 5,311 ....F6
North Webster 881 ....F2
Norway 300 ....D3
Notre Dame E1
Nulltown 235 ....F6
Oakford 325 ....E4
Oakland City 2,810 ....C8
Oaktown 655 ....C7
Oakville 220 ....G4
Odon 1,475 ....C7
Ogden Dunes 1,499 ....C1
Oldenburg 715 ....G6
Onward 63 ....E3
Oolitic 1,424 ....E7
Ora 200 ....D2
Orange 200 ....G5
Orestes 458 ....F4
Orland 361 ....G1
Orleans 2,083 ....D7
Osceola 1,999 ....E1
Osgood 1,688 ....G6
Ossian 2,428 ....G3
Oswego 150 ....F2
Otisco 425 ....F7
Otterbein 1,291 ....C4
Otwell 600 ....C8
Owensburg 200 ....D7
Owensville 1,053 ....B8
Oxford 1,273 ....C3
Packerton 150 ....F2
Palestine 800 ....E8
Palmyra 621 ....E8
Paoli▲ 3,542 ....E7
Paragon 515 ....D6
Parker City 1,323 ....G4
Patoka 704 ....C8
Patricksburg 250 ....D6
Patriot 190 ....H7
Paxton 200 ....C6
Pekin 950 ....E7
Pendleton 2,309 ....F5
Pennville 637 ....G4
Perkinsville 175 ....F4
Perrysville 443 ....C4
Pershing 425 ....E2
Pershing G5
Peru▲ 12,843 ....E3
Petersburg▲ 2,449 ....C7
Petroleum 212 ....G3
Pierceton 1,030 ....F2
Pilot Knob 150 ....E8
Pimento 150 ....C6
Pine Lake 1,676 ....D1
Pine Village 134 ....C4
Pittsboro 815 ....D5
Pittsburg 175 ....D3
Plainfield 10,433 ....E5
Plainville 444 ....C7
Pleasant Lake 800 ....H1
Pleasant Mills 175 ....H3
Plymouth▲ 8,303 ....E2
Poe 162 ....H3
Poland 230 ....C6
Poneto 236 ....G3
Portage 29,060 ....C1
Porter 3,118 ....C1
Portland▲ 6,483 ....H4
Poseyville 1,089 ....B8
Pottawattomie Park 281 ....C1
Prairie Creek 275 ....C6
Prairieton 200 ....B6
Preble 150 ....H3
Princes Lakes 1,055 ....E6
Princeton▲ 8,127 ....B8
Providence 250 ....E6
Putnamville 250 ....D5
Quincy 250 ....D6
Ragsdale 135 ....C7
Ramsey 550 ....E8
Ray 200 ....H1
Rays Crossing 157 ....F5
Reddington 400 ....F6
Redkey 1,383 ....G4
Reelsville 210 ....D5
Remington 1,247 ....C3
Rensselaer▲ 5,045 ....D3
Reynolds 528 ....D3
Richland 500 ....C7
Richmond▲ 38,705 ....H5
Ridgeville 808 ....G4
Rigdon 150 ....F4
Riley 232 ....C6
Rising Sun▲ 2,311 ....H7
Roachdale 902 ....D5

Roann 447 ....F3
Roanoke 1,018 ....G3
Rochester▲ 5,969 ....E2
Rockfield 300 ....D3
Rockport▲ 2,315 ....C9
Rockville▲ 2,706 ....C5
Rolling Prairie 550 ....D1
Rome 1,138 ....D9
Rome City 1,319 ....G1
Romney 250 ....D4
Rosedale 783 ....C5
Roseland 706 ....E1
Roselawn 200 ....C2
Rossville 1,475 ....D4
Royal Center 859 ....E3
Royerton 300 ....G4
Rushville▲ 5,533 ....G5
Russellville 336 ....D5
Russiaville 988 ....E4
Saint Anthony 470 ....D8
Saint Bernice 500 ....C5
Saint Henry 560 ....D8
Saint Joe 452 ....H2
Saint John 4,921 ....C2
Saint Leon 493 ....H6
Saint Louis Crossing 150 ....F6
Saint Mary-of-the-Woods 920 ....B6
Saint Marys E1
Saint Meinrad 910 ....D8
Saint Paul 1,032 ....F6
Saint Peter 175 ....H6
Saint Philip 400 ....B9
Saint Wendel 300 ....B8
Salamonia 138 ....H4
Salem▲ 5,619 ....H3
Salem▲ 5,290 ....E7
Saltillo 117 ....E7
San Pierre 325 ....D2
Sandborn 455 ....C7
Santa Claus 927 ....D8
Saratoga 266 ....H4
Sardinia 133 ....F6
Schererville 19,926 ....C2
Schneider 310 ....C2
Schnellville 250 ....D8
Scipio 200 ....F6
Scott 5,334 ....F1
Scottsburg▲ 5,068 ....F7
Sedalia 160 ....E4
Seelyville 1,090 ....C6
Sellersburg 5,745 ....F8
Selma 800 ....G4
Servia 212 ....F3
Seymour 15,576 ....F7
Shadeland 1,674 ....C4
Shamrock Lakes 207 ....G4
Sharpsville 769 ....E4
Shelburn 1,147 ....C6
Shelby 15,336 ....C2
Shelbyville▲ 14,989 ....F6
Shepardsville 325 ....B5
Sheridan 2,046 ....E4
Shideler 275 ....G4
Shipshewana 524 ....F1
Shirley 817 ....F5
Shirley City (Woodburn) H2
Shoals▲ 853 ....D7
Sidney 167 ....F2
Silver Lake 528 ....F2
Sims 250 ....E4
Smith Valley E5
Smithville 500 ....D6
Solsberry 200 ....D6
Somerset 350 ....F3
Somerville 223 ....C8
South Bend▲ 105,511 ....E1
South Milford 270 ....G1
South Whitley 1,482 ....F2
Southport 1,969 ....E5
Spartanburg 201 ....H4
Speed 13,092 ....F8
Speedway 12,641 ....E5
Spelterville 200 ....C5
Spencer▲ 2,609 ....D6
Spencerville 400 ....G2
Spiceland 757 ....G5
Spring Grove 420 ....H5
Spring Lake 216 ....F5
Springport 194 ....G4
Springville 279 ....D7
Spurgeon 149 ....C8
Stanford 200 ....D6
Star City 361 ....D3
State Line 182 ....C4
Staunton 592 ....C6
Stendal 175 ....C8
Stewartsville 225 ....B8
Stilesville 298 ....D5
Stillwell 225 ....D1
Stinesville 204 ....D6
Stockwell 310 ....D4
Straughn 318 ....G5
Stroh 300 ....G1
Sullivan▲ 4,663 ....C6
Sulphur 257 ....D8
Sulphur Springs 345 ....G4
Sumava Resorts 300 ....C2
Summitville 1,010 ....F4
Sunman 623 ....G6
Swayzee 1,059 ....F4
Sweetser 924 ....F4
Switz City 257 ....C6
Syracuse 2,729 ....F2
Talma 170 ....E2
Taylorsville 1,044 ....F6
Tell City 8,088 ....D9
Tennyson 267 ....C8
Terhune 150 ....E4
Terre Haute▲ 57,483 ....C6
Thayer 350 ....C2
Thorntown 1,506 ....D4
Tippecanoe 320 ....E2
Tipton▲ 4,751 ....E4
Tocsin 160 ....G3
Topeka 912 ....F1

Town of Pines 789 ....D1
Trafalgar 531 ....E6
Trail Creek 2,463 ....D1
Tri Lakes 3,299 ....G2
Troy 465 ....D9
Tunnelton 150 ....E7
Twelve Mile 240 ....E3
Tyner 245 ....E2
Underwood 550 ....F7
Union 3,612 ....C8
Union City 3,908 ....H4
Union Mills 650 ....D2
Uniondale 289 ....G3
Unionville 225 ....E6
Universal 392 ....C5
Upland 3,295 ....F4
Urbana 400 ....F3
Utica 411 ....F8
Valeene 150 ....E8
Vallonia 550 ....E7
Valparaiso▲ 24,414 ....C2
Van Buren 934 ....F3
Veedersburg 2,192 ....C4
Velpen 375 ....C8
Vera Cruz 83 ....G3
Vernon▲ 370 ....F7
Versailles▲ 1,791 ....G6
Vevay▲ 1,393 ....G7
Vicksburg 175 ....C7
Vienna 175 ....F7
Vincennes▲ 19,859 ....C7
Wabash▲ 12,127 ....F3
Wadesville 450 ....B8
Wakarusa 1,667 ....F1
Waldron 850 ....F6
Walesboro 214 ....F6
Walkerton 2,061 ....D2
Wallace 89 ....C4
Wallen 945 ....G2
Walton 1,053 ....E3
Wanatah 852 ....D2
Warren 1,185 ....G3
Warrington 200 ....F5
Warsaw▲ 10,968 ....F2
Washington▲ 10,838 ....C7
Waterloo 2,040 ....G2
Watson 200 ....F8
Waveland 760 ....D5
Wawaka 320 ....G2
Wawasee 600 ....F2
Wawpecong 175 ....F3
Waynetown 911 ....C4
Webster 350 ....H5
West Baden Springs 675 ....D7
West College Corner 686 ....H5
West Harrison 318 ....H6
West Lafayette 25,907 ....D4
West Lebanon 760 ....C4
West Middleton 327 ....E4
West Terre Haute 2,495 ....B6
Westfield 3,304 ....E4
Westphalia 300 ....C7
Westpoint 375 ....C4
Westport 1,478 ....F6
Westville 5,255 ....D1
Wheatfield 621 ....C2

Wheatland 439 ....C7
Wheeler 540 ....C1
Wheeling 180 ....G4
Wheeling 500 ....C8
Whiteland 2,446 ....E5
Whitestown 476 ....E5
Whitewater 111 ....H5
Whiting 5,155 ....F5
Wilkinson 446 ....F5
Williams 425 ....D7
Williamsport▲ 1,798 ....C4
Willow Branch 145 ....F5
Wilmington 600 ....H6
Winamac▲ 2,262 ....D2
Winchester▲ 5,095 ....G4
Windfall 779 ....F4
Windsor 150 ....G4
Wingate 275 ....C4
Winona Lake 4,053 ....F2
Winslow 875 ....C8
Wirt 150 ....G7
Wolcott 886 ....C3
Wolcottville 879 ....G1
Wolflake 230 ....G2
Woodburn 1,321 ....H2
Woodland 400 ....E1
Woodlawn Heights 109 ....F4
Worthington 1,473 ....C6
Wyandotte 26 ....E8
Wyatt 250 ....E1
Yankeetown 250 ....C9
Yeoman 131 ....D3
Yoder 250 ....G3
Yorktown 4,106 ....G4
Young America 259 ....E3
Youngstown 350 ....C6
Zanesville 575 ....G3
Zenas 225 ....F6
Zionsville 5,281 ....E5

OTHER FEATURES

Anderson (riv.) D8
Bass (lake) F2
Beanblossom (creek) D6
Big (creek) F5
Big Blue (riv.) C3
Big Pine (creek) C4
Big Raccoon (creek) C5
Big Walnut (creek) D5
Blue (riv.) E8
Brookville (lake) G6
Buck (creek) E8
Busseron (creek) C7
Camp (creek) E6
Cedar (creek) G2
Clifty (creek) F6
Coal (coal) C4
Crooked (creek) D2
Cypress (pond) B8
Deer (creek) E3
Deer (creek) D5
Eel (riv.) C6
Eel (riv.) F3
Elkhart (riv.) F1

Fawn (riv.) G1
Flatrock (creek) F5
Fort Benjamin Harrison F5
Freeman (lake) D3
Geist (res.) F5
George Rogers Clark Nat'l Hist. Park B7
Graham (creek) F7
Grissom A.F.B. 4,271 ....E3
Huntington (lake) F3
Indian (creek) D6
Indian (creek) E8
Indiana Dunes Nat'l Lakeshore C1
Iroquois (riv.) B3
Jefferson Proving Ground G7
Kankakee (riv.) C2
Lemon (lake) C2
Lincoln Boyhood Nat'l Mem. C8
Little (riv.) G3
Little Elkhart (riv.) F1
Little Pigeon (creek) C9
Little Vermilion (riv.) B5
Lost (riv.) D7
Maria (creek) C7
Maumee (riv.) H2
Maxinkuckee (lake) E2
Michigan (lake) C1
Mill (creek) D5
Mississinewa (lake) F3
Mississinewa (riv.) E4
Monroe (lake) E6
Morse (res.) E4
Muscatatuck (riv.) E7
Ohio (riv.) B9
Patoka (riv.) C8
Pigeon (creek) C8
Pigeon (riv.) F1
Pipe (creek) F4
Prairie (creek) C7
Richland (creek) D6
Saint Joseph (riv.) E1
Saint Joseph (riv.) H2
Saint Marys (lake) H3
Saint Marys (riv.) H3
Salamonie (lake) F3
Salamonie (riv.) G4
Salt (creek) E6
Sand (creek) D3
Shafer (lake) D3
Silver (lake) B3
Sugar (creek) B3
Sugar (creek) C5
Sugar (creek) F5
Tippecanoe (riv.) D3
Vermilion (riv.) B4
Vernon Fork (creek) B7
Wabash (riv.) C7
Wawasee (lake) F2
White (riv.) B8
White, East Fork (riv.) C7
White, West Fork (riv.) C7
Whitewater (riv.) H6
Wildcat (creek) E4

▲County seat

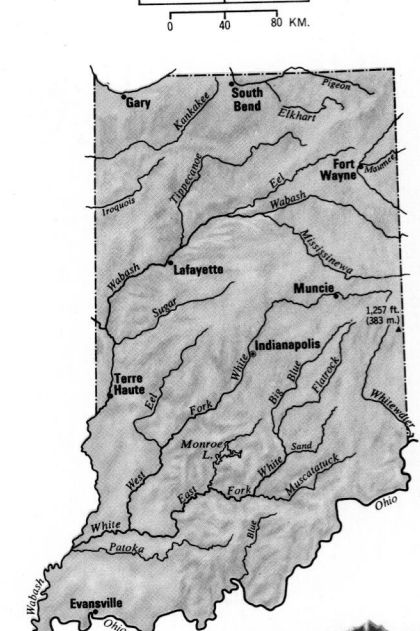

Topography

0   40   80 MI.

0   40   80 KM.

Gary
South Bend
Elkhart
Kankakee
Fort Wayne
Iroquois
Maumee
Wabash
Tippecanoe
Eel
Lafayette
Muncie
1,257 ft. (383 m.)
Indianapolis
Terre Haute
Sugar
White
Monroe L.
Big
Flatrock
Blue
Whitewater
West Fork
East Fork
White
Sand
Muscatatuck
Patoka
White
Ohio
Wabash
Evansville
Ohio

| Below Sea Level | 100 m. 328 ft. | 200 m. 656 ft. | 500 m. 1,640 ft. | 1,000 m. 3,281 ft. | 2,000 m. 6,562 ft. | 5,000 m. 16,404 ft. |

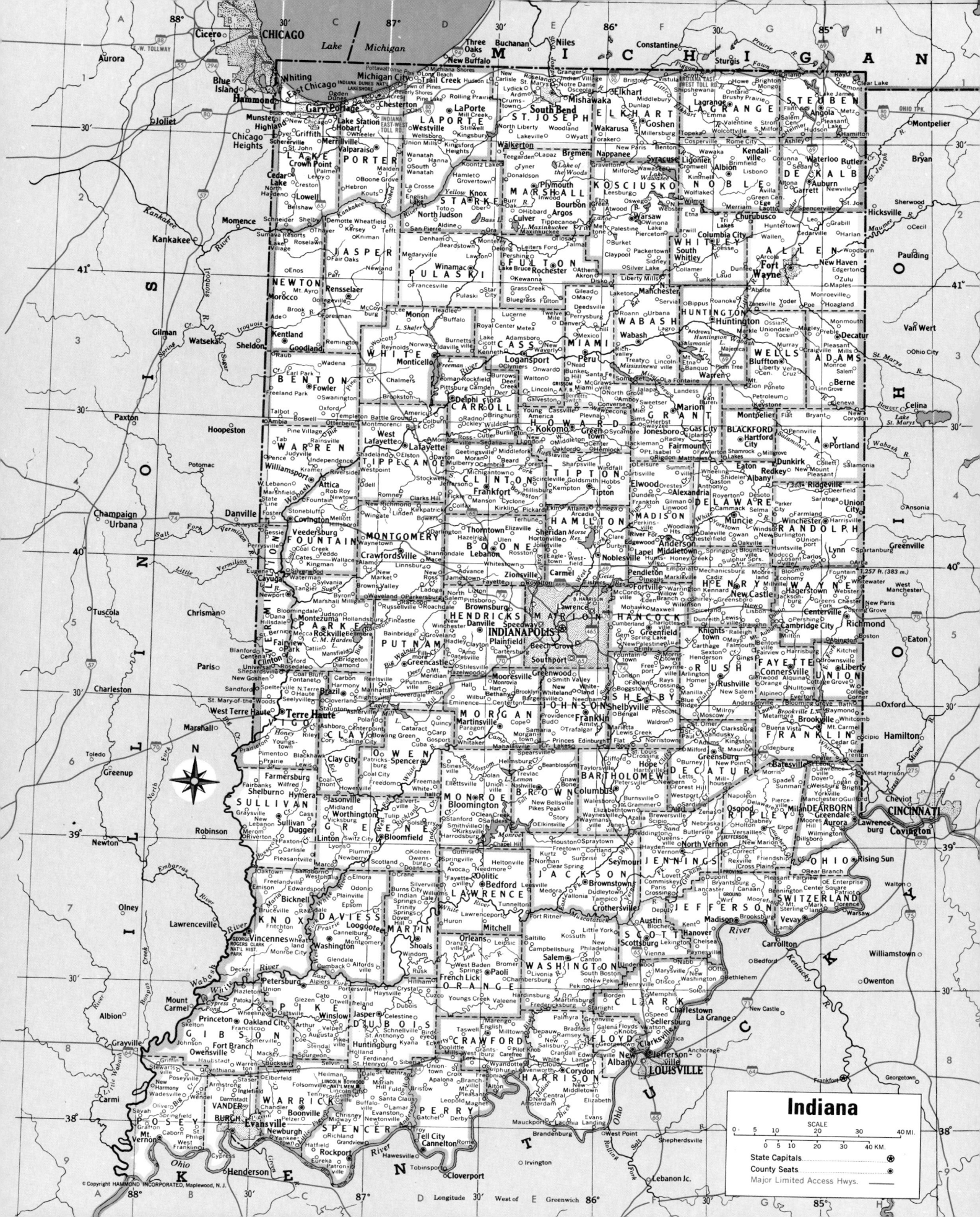
Indiana
SCALE
0 5 10 20 30 40 MI.
0 5 10 20 30 40 KM.
State Capitals
County Seats
Major Limited Access Hwys.
© Copyright HAMMOND INCORPORATED, Maplewood, N.J.
Longitude 30′ West of Greenwich 86°
MICHIGAN
ILLINOIS
OHIO
KENTUCKY
Lake Michigan
CHICAGO
INDIANAPOLIS
CINCINNATI
LOUISVILLE
LAKE
PORTER
LAPORTE
ST. JOSEPH
ELKHART
LAGRANGE
STEUBEN
NEWTON
JASPER
STARKE
MARSHALL
KOSCIUSKO
NOBLE
DE KALB
PULASKI
FULTON
WHITLEY
ALLEN
BENTON
WHITE
CASS
MIAMI
WABASH
HUNTINGTON
WELLS
ADAMS
WARREN
TIPPECANOE
CARROLL
HOWARD
GRANT
BLACKFORD
JAY
FOUNTAIN
MONTGOMERY
CLINTON
TIPTON
MADISON
DELAWARE
RANDOLPH
VERMILLION
PARKE
BOONE
HAMILTON
HENRY
WAYNE
HENDRICKS
MARION
HANCOCK
PUTNAM
VIGO
CLAY
MORGAN
JOHNSON
SHELBY
RUSH
FAYETTE
UNION
OWEN
FRANKLIN
DECATUR
BARTHOLOMEW
BROWN
MONROE
GREENE
SULLIVAN
DEARBORN
RIPLEY
JENNINGS
JACKSON
LAWRENCE
DAVIESS
KNOX
MARTIN
OHIO
SWITZERLAND
JEFFERSON
SCOTT
WASHINGTON
ORANGE
DUBOIS
PIKE
GIBSON
CLARK
FLOYD
HARRISON
CRAWFORD
PERRY
SPENCER
WARRICK
VANDERBURGH
POSEY

COUNTIES

Adair 8,409	E6
Adams 4,866	D6
Allamakee 13,855	L2
Appanoose 13,743	H7
Audubon 7,334	D5
Benton 22,429	J4
Black Hawk 123,798	J3
Boone 25,186	F5
Bremer 22,813	J3
Buchanan 20,844	K4
Buena Vista 19,965	C3
Butler 15,731	H3
Calhoun 11,508	D4
Carroll 21,423	D5
Cass 15,128	D6
Cedar 17,381	L5
Cerro Gordo 46,733	G2
Cherokee 14,098	B3
Chickasaw 13,295	J2
Clarke 8,287	F6
Clay 17,585	C2
Clayton 19,054	L3

Clinton 51,040	M5
Crawford 16,775	C4
Dallas 29,755	E5
Davis 8,312	J7
Decatur 8,338	F7
Delaware 18,035	L4
Des Moines 42,614	L7
Dickinson 14,909	C2
Dubuque 86,403	M4
Emmet 11,569	D2
Fayette 21,843	H2
Floyd 17,058	G3
Franklin 11,364	G3
Fremont 8,226	B7
Greene 10,045	E5
Grundy 12,029	H4
Guthrie 10,935	D5
Hamilton 16,071	F4
Hardin 19,094	G4
Harrison 14,730	B5
Henry 19,226	K6
Howard 9,809	J2
Humboldt 10,756	E3
Ida 8,365	C4

Iowa 14,630	J5
Iowa 2,913,808	J5
Jackson 19,950	M4
Jasper 34,795	G5
Jefferson 16,310	K6
Johnson 96,119	L4
Jones 19,444	L4
Keokuk 11,624	J6
Kossuth 18,591	E2
Lee 38,687	L7
Linn 168,767	K4
Louisa 11,592	L6
Lucas 9,070	G6
Lyon 11,952	A2
Madison 12,483	E6
Mahaska 21,522	H6
Marion 30,001	G6
Marshall 38,276	G4
Mills 13,202	B6
Mitchell 10,928	H2
Monona 10,034	B4
Monroe 8,114	H7
Montgomery 12,076	C6
Muscatine 39,907	L5

O'Brien 16,972	B2
Osceola 7,267	B2
Page 16,870	C7
Palo Alto 10,669	D2
Plymouth 23,388	A3
Pocahontas 9,525	D3
Polk 327,140	F5
Pottawattamie 82,628	B6
Poweshiek 19,033	H5
Ringgold 5,420	E7
Sac 12,324	C4
Scott 150,979	M5
Shelby 13,230	C5
Sioux 29,903	A2
Story 74,252	G4
Tama 17,419	H4
Taylor 7,114	D7
Union 7,007	E6
Van Buren 7,676	K7
Wapello 35,687	H6
Warren 36,033	F6
Washington 19,612	K6
Wayne 7,067	G7
Webster 40,342	E4

Winnebago 12,122	F2
Winneshiek 20,847	K2
Woodbury 98,276	B4
Worth 7,991	G2
Wright 14,269	F3

CITIES and TOWNS

Ackley 1,696	G3
Adair 894	D6
Adel▲ 3,304	E5
Afton 953	E6
Agency 616	J7
Ainsworth 506	K6
Akron 1,450	A3
Albert City 779	H6
Albia▲ 3,870	H6
Albion 585	H4
Alburnett 456	K4
Alden 855	G4
Alexander 170	G3
Algona▲ 6,015	E2
Alleman 340	F5
Allerton 599	G7

Allison▲ 1,000	H3
Alta 1,820	C3
Alta Vista 246	J2
Alton 1,063	A3
Altoona 7,191	G5
Alvord 204	A2
Amana 300	K5
Anamosa▲ 5,100	L4
Andrew 319	M4
Anita 1,068	D6
Ankeny 18,482	F5
Anthon 638	B4
Aplington 1,034	H3
Arcadia 485	C4
Arion 148	B5
Arlington 465	K3
Armstrong 1,025	D2
Arnolds Park 953	C2
Arthur 272	C4
Asbury 2,013	M4
Ashton 462	B2
Atalissa 357	L5
Atkins 637	K4

Atlantic 7,432	D6
Auburn 283	D4
Audubon▲ 2,524	D5
Aurelia 1,034	C3
Aurora 196	K3
Avoca 1,497	C6
Ayrshire 195	D2
Badger 569	E3
Bagley 303	E5
Baldwin 137	M4
Bancroft 857	E2
Barnes City 221	H6
Barnum 174	E4
Batavia 520	J7
Battle Creek 818	B4
Baxter 938	G5
Bayard 511	D5
Beacon 509	H6
Beaman 183	H4
Bedford▲ 1,528	D7
Belle Plaine 2,834	J5
Bellevue 2,239	M4
Belmond 2,500	F3
Bennett 395	L5

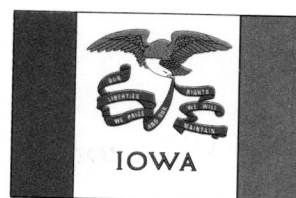

IOWA

AREA 56,275 sq. mi. (145,752 sq. km.)
POPULATION 2,787,424
CAPITAL Des Moines
LARGEST CITY Des Moines
HIGHEST POINT (Osceola Co.) 1670 ft.
(509 m.)
SETTLED IN 1788
ADMITTED TO UNION December 28, 1846
POPULAR NAME Hawkeye State
STATE FLOWER Wild Rose
STATE BIRD Eastern Goldfinch

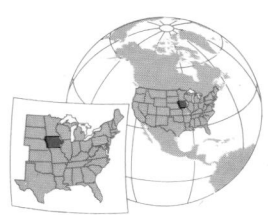

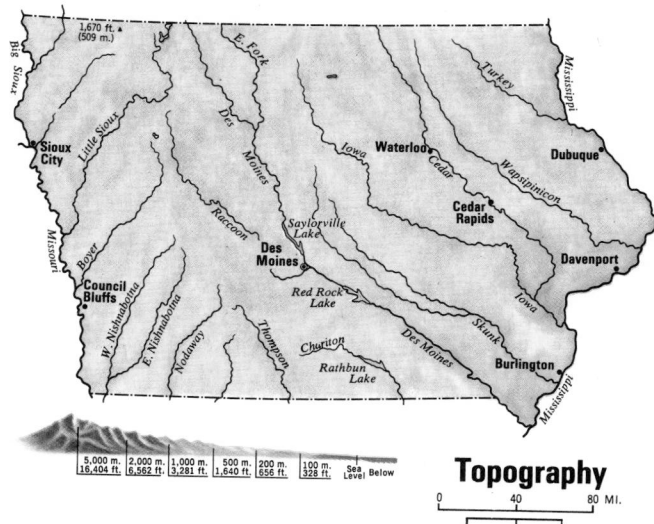

Topography

(continued on following page)

Agriculture, Industry and Resources

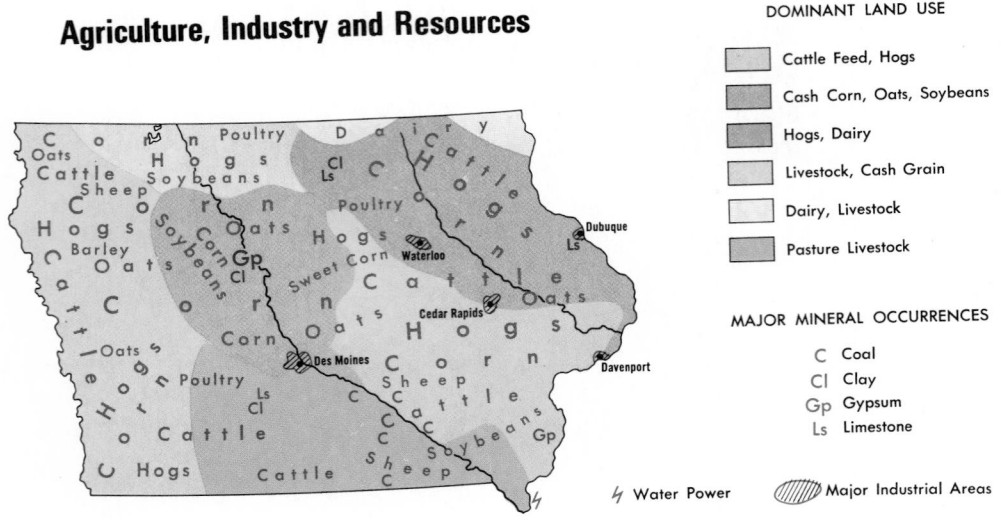

DOMINANT LAND USE

- Cattle Feed, Hogs
- Cash Corn, Oats, Soybeans
- Hogs, Dairy
- Livestock, Cash Grain
- Dairy, Livestock
- Pasture Livestock

MAJOR MINERAL OCCURRENCES

- C   Coal
- Cl   Clay
- Gp   Gypsum
- Ls   Limestone

⚡ Water Power   Major Industrial Areas

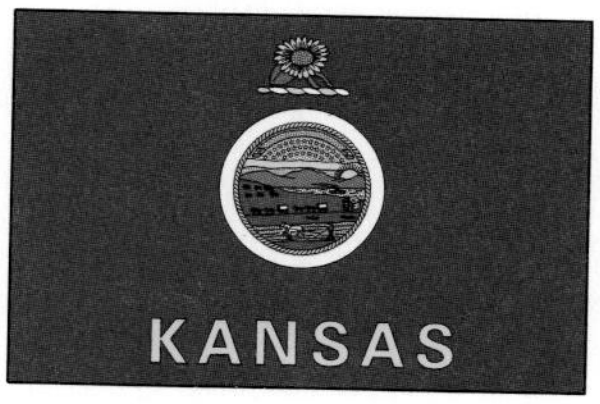

AREA 82,277 sq. mi. (213,097 sq. km.)
POPULATION 2,485,600
CAPITAL Topeka
LARGEST CITY Wichita
HIGHEST POINT Mt. Sunflower 4,039 ft. (1231 m.)
SETTLED IN 1831
ADMITTED TO UNION January 29, 1861
POPULAR NAME Sunflower State
STATE FLOWER Sunflower
STATE BIRD Western Meadowlark

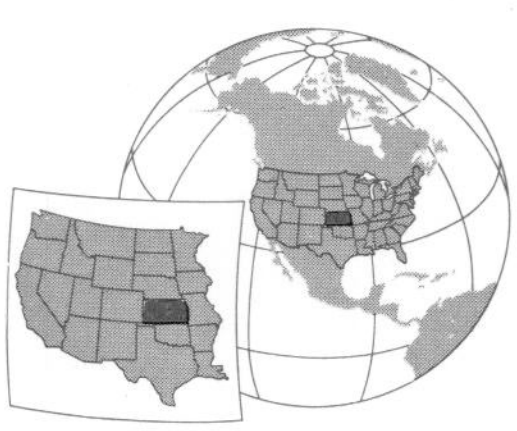

Agriculture, Industry and Resources

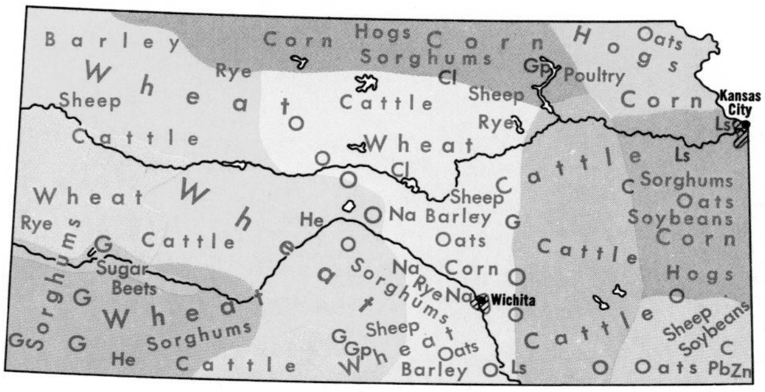

DOMINANT LAND USE

- Specialized Wheat
- Wheat, General Farming
- Wheat, Range Livestock
- Wheat, Grain Sorghums, Range Livestock
- Cattle Feed, Hogs
- Livestock, Cash Grain
- Livestock, Cash Grain, Dairy
- General Farming, Livestock, Cash Grain
- General Farming, Livestock, Special Crops
- Range Livestock

MAJOR MINERAL OCCURRENCES

C	Coal	Ls	Limestone
Cl	Clay	Na	Salt
G	Natural Gas	O	Petroleum
Gp	Gypsum	Pb	Lead
He	Helium	Zn	Zinc

Major Industrial Areas

COUNTIES

Allen 15,654 G4
Anderson 7,803 G3
Atchison 16,932 G2
Barber 5,874 D4
Barton 29,382 D3
Bourbon 14,966 H4
Brown 11,128 G2
Butler 50,580 F4
Chase 3,021 F3
Chautauqua 4,407 F4
Cherokee 21,374 H4
Cheyenne 3,243 A2
Clark 2,418 C4
Clay 9,158 E2
Cloud 11,023 E2
Coffey 8,404 G3
Comanche 2,313 C4
Cowley 36,915 F4
Crawford 35,568 H4
Decatur 4,021 B2
Dickinson 18,958 E3
Doniphan 8,134 G2
Douglas 81,798 G3
Edwards 3,787 C4
Elk 3,327 F4
Ellis 26,004 C3
Ellsworth 6,586 D3
Finney 33,070 B3
Ford 27,463 C4
Franklin 21,994 G3
Geary 30,453 F3
Gove 3,231 B3
Graham 3,543 C2
Grant 7,159 A4
Gray 5,396 B4
Greeley 1,774 A3
Greenwood 7,847 F4
Hamilton 2,388 A3
Harper 7,124 D4
Harvey 31,028 E3
Haskell 3,886 B4
Hodgeman 2,177 C3
Jackson 11,525 G2
Jefferson 15,905 G2
Jewell 4,251 D2
Johnson 355,054 H3
Kearny 4,027 A3
Kingman 8,292 D4
Kiowa 3,660 C4
Labette 23,693 G4
Lane 2,375 B3
Leavenworth 64,371 G2
Lincoln 3,653 D2
Linn 8,254 H3
Logan 3,081 A3
Lyon 34,732 F3
Marion 12,888 E3
Marshall 11,705 F2
McPherson 27,268 E3
Meade 4,247 B4
Miami 23,466 H3
Mitchell 7,203 D2
Montgomery 38,816 G4
Morris 6,198 F3
Morton 3,480 A4
Nemaha 10,446 F2
Neosho 17,035 G4
Ness 4,033 C3
Norton 5,947 C2
Osage 15,248 G3
Osborne 4,867 D2
Ottawa 5,634 E2
Pawnee 7,555 C3
Phillips 6,590 C2
Pottawatomie 16,128 F2
Pratt 9,702 D4
Rawlins 3,404 A2
Reno 62,389 D4
Republic 6,482 E2
Rice 10,610 D3
Riley 67,139 F2
Rooks 6,039 C2
Rush 3,842 C3
Russell 7,835 D3
Saline 49,301 E3
Scott 5,289 B3
Sedgwick 403,662 E4
Seward 18,743 B4
Shawnee 160,976 G2
Sheridan 3,043 B2
Sherman 6,926 A2
Smith 5,078 D2
Stafford 5,365 D3
Stanton 2,333 A4
Stevens 5,048 A4
Sumner 25,841 E4
Thomas 8,258 A2
Trego 3,694 C3
Wabaunsee 6,603 F3
Wallace 1,821 A3
Washington 7,073 E2
Wichita 2,758 A3
Wilson 10,289 G4
Woodson 4,116 G4
Wyandotte 161,993 H2

CITIES and TOWNS

Abbyville 123 D4
Abilene▲ 6,242 E3
Ada 120 E2
Admire 147 F3
Agenda 81 E2
Agra 322 C2
Alamota 50 B3
Albert 229 C3
Alden 182 D3
Alexander 85 C3
Aliceville 60 G3
Allen 191 F3
Alma▲ 871 F2
Almena 423 C2
Alta Vista 477 F3
Altamont 1,048 G4
Alton 115 D2
Altoona 456 G4
Americus 891 F3
Ames 65 E2
Andale 566 E4
Andover 4,047 E4
Angola 55 G4
Anthony▲ 2,516 D4
Arcadia 338 H4
Argonia 529 E4
Arkansas City 12,762 E4
Arlington 457 D4
Arma 1,542 H4
Ash Valley 50 C3
Ashland▲ 1,032 C4
Assaria 387 E3
Atchison▲ 10,656 G2
Athol 86 D2
Atlanta 232 F4
Attica 716 D4
Atwood▲ 1,388 B2
Auburn 908 G3
Augusta 7,876 F4
Aurora 101 E2
Axtell 432 F2
Baileyville 130 F2
Baldwin City 2,961 G3
Barnard 129 D2
Barnes 167 F2
Bartlett 107 G4
Basehor 1,591 G2
Bassett 20 G4
Bavaria 100 E3
Baxter Springs 4,351 H4
Bazine 373 C3
Beagle 88 G3
Beattie 221 F2
Beaumont 112 F4
Beaver 57 D3
Beeler 80 B3
Belle Plaine 1,649 E4
Belleville▲ 2,517 E2
Beloit▲ 4,066 D2
Belpre 116 C4
Belvue 207 F2
Bendena 125 G2
Benedict 16 G4
Bennington 568 E2
Bentley 360 E4
Benton 669 E4
Bern 190 F2
Berryton 150 G3
Beverly 131 E2
Big Bow 55 A4
Bird City 467 A2
Bison 252 C3
Blaine 50 F2
Bloom 65 C4
Blue Mound 251 H3
Blue Rapids 1,131 F2
Bluff City 69 E4
Bogue 150 C2
Bonner Springs 6,413 H2
Brazilton 91 H4
Bremen 60 F2
Brewster 296 A2
Bridgeport 95 E3
Bronson 343 H4
Brookville 226 E3
Brownell 44 C3
Bucklin 710 C4
Bucyrus 135 H3
Buffalo 293 G4
Buhler 1,277 E3
Bunker Hill 111 D3
Burden 518 F4
Burdett 248 C3
Burdick 100 F3
Burlingame 1,074 G3
Burlington▲ 2,735 G3
Burns 226 F3
Burr Oak 278 D2
Burrton 866 E3
Bushong 57 F3
Bushton 341 D3
Byers 46 D4
Caldwell 1,351 E4
Cambridge 74 F4
Caney 2,062 G4
Canton 794 E3
Carbondale 1,526 G3
Carlton 39 E3
Carlyle 75 G4
Cassoday 95 F3
Catharine 121 C3
Cawker City 588 D2
Cedar 25 D2
Cedar Point 39 F3
Cedar Vale 760 F4
Centerville 104 H3
Centralia 452 F2
Chanute 9,488 G4
Chapman 1,264 E3
Chase 577 D3
Chautauqua 132 F4
Cheney 1,560 E4
Cherokee 651 H4
Cherryvale 2,464 G4
Chetopa 1,357 G4
Chicopee 300 H4
Cimarron▲ 1,626 B4
Circleville 153 G2
Claflin 678 D3
Clay Center▲ 4,613 E2
Clayton 91 B2
Clearview City G3
Clearwater 1,875 E4
Clifton 561 E2
Climax 57 F4
Clyde 793 E2
Coats 127 D4
Codell 90 C2
Coffeyville 12,917 G4
Colby▲ 5,396 A2
Coldwater▲ 939 C4
Collyer 144 B2
Colony 447 G3
Columbus▲ 3,268 H4
Colwich 1,091 E4
Concordia▲ 6,167 E2
Conway 1,384 E3
Conway Springs 1,313 E4
Coolidge 90 A3
Copeland 290 B4
Corning 142 F2
Cottonwood Falls▲ 889 F3
Council Grove▲ 2,228 F3
Courtland 343 E2
Coyville 78 G4
Crestline 85 H4
Cuba 242 E2
Cullison 120 D4
Culver 162 E3
Cummings 150 G2
Cunningham 535 D4
Damar 112 C2
Danville 56 E4
De Soto 2,291 H3
Dearing 428 G4
Deerfield 677 A4
Delia 172 G2
Delphos 494 E2
Denison 225 G2
Dennis 96 G4
Denton 166 G2
Derby 14,699 E4
Detroit 90 E3
Devon 108 H4
Dexter 320 F4
Dighton▲ 1,361 B3
Dodge City▲ 21,129 B4
Dorrance 195 D3
Douglass 1,722 F4
Dover 192 G3
Downs 1,119 D2
Dresden 73 B2
Dunlap 65 F3
Durham 119 E3
Dwight 365 F3
Earlton 69 G4
Eastborough 896 E4
Easton 405 G2
Edgerton 1,244 H3
Edmond 37 C2
Edna 438 G4
Edson 55 A2
Edwardsville 3,979 H2
Effingham 540 G2
El Dorado▲ 11,504 F4
Elbing 184 E3
Elgin 118 F4
Elk City 334 G4
Elk Falls 122 F4
Elkhart▲ 2,318 A4
Ellinwood 2,329 D3
Ellis 1,814 C3
Ellsworth▲ 2,294 D3
Elmdale 83 F3
Elmont 112 G2
Elsmore 91 G4
Elwood 1,079 H2
Elyria 100 E3
Emmett 165 F2
Emporia▲ 25,512 F3
Englewood 96 C4
Ensign 192 B4
Enterprise 865 E3
Erie▲ 1,276 G4
Esbon 167 D2
Eskridge 518 F3
Eudora 3,006 G3
Eureka▲ 2,974 F4
Everest 310 G2
Fairview 306 G2
Fairway 4,173 H2
Fall River 113 G4
Falun 89 E3
Farlington 80 H4
Florence 636 E3
Fontana 131 H3
Ford 247 C4
Formoso 128 D2
Fort Dodge 400 C4
Fort Leavenworth H2
Fort Scott▲ 8,362 H4
Fowler 571 B4
Frankfort 927 F2
Franklin 400 H4
Frederick 18 D3
Fredonia▲ 2,599 G4
Freeport 8 E4
Frontenac 2,588 H4
Fulton 191 H4
Galatia 47 D3
Galena 3,308 H4
Galesburg 160 G4
Galva 651 E3
Garden City▲ 24,097 B4
Garden Plain 731 E4
Gardner 3,191 H3
Garfield 236 C3
Garland 112 H4
Garnett▲ 3,210 G3
Gas 505 G4
Gaylord 173 D2
Gem 104 B2
Geneseo 382 D3
Geuda Springs 219 E4
Girard▲ 2,794 H4
Glade 101 C2
Glasco 556 E2
Glen Elder 448 D2
Goddard 1,804 E4
Goessel 506 E3
Goff 156 G2
Goodland▲ 4,983 A2
Gorham 284 D3
Gove▲ 103 B3
Grainfield 357 B2
Grandview Plaza 1,233 F2
Grantville 220 G2
Great Bend▲ 15,427 D3
Greeley 339 G3
Green 150 E2
Greenleaf 353 E2
Greensburg▲ 1,792 C4
Grenola 256 F4
Gridley 356 G3

(continued on following page)

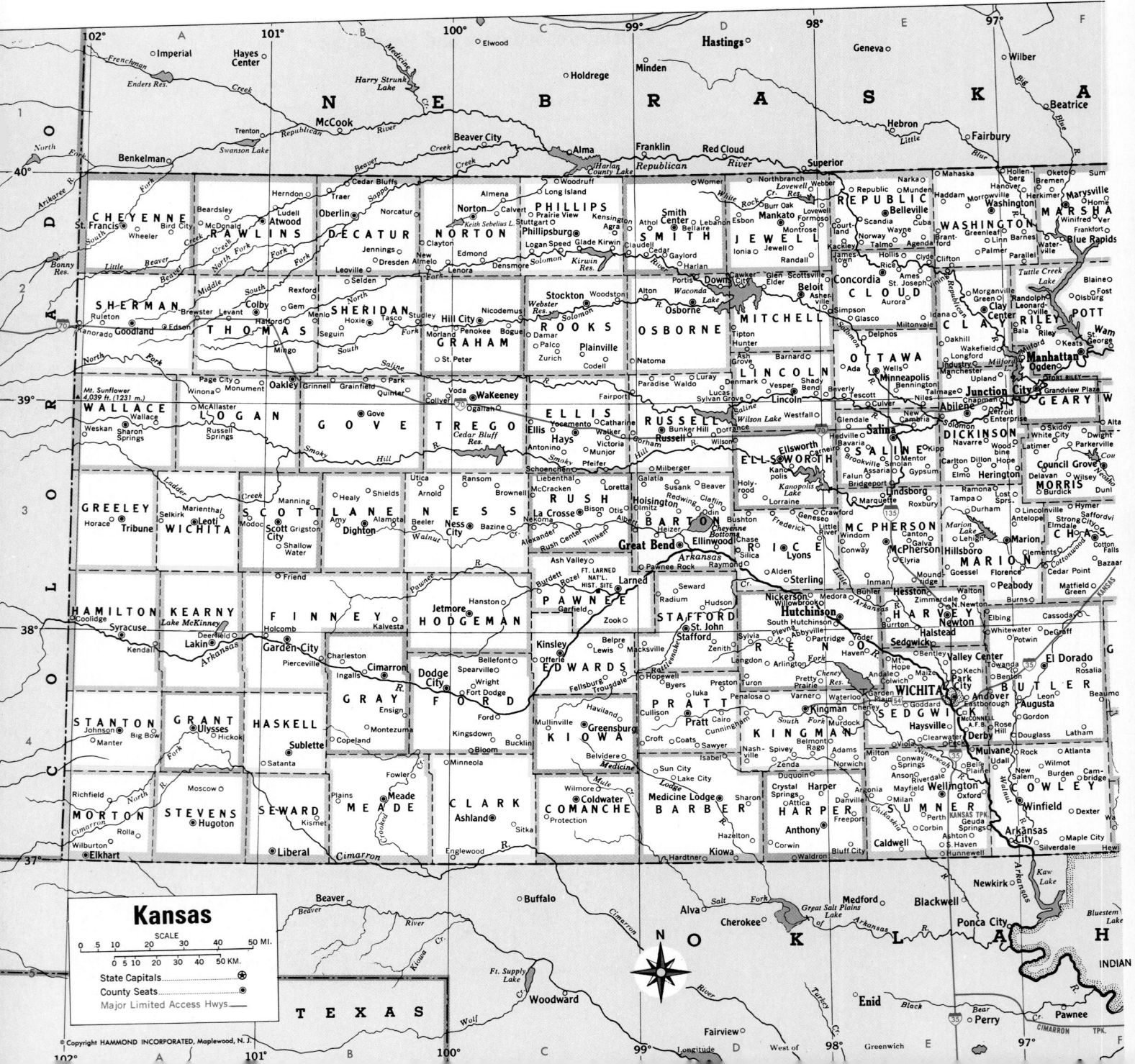

Kansas

SCALE

State Capitals .... ⊛
County Seats .... ◉
Major Limited Access Hwys. ───

© Copyright HAMMOND INCORPORATED, Maplewood, N.J.

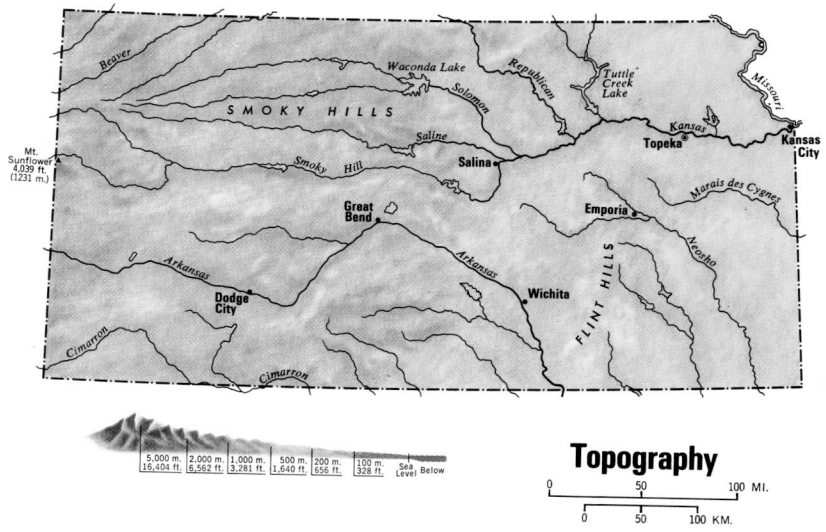

Topography

KENTUCKY

COUNTIES

Adair 15,360 L6
Allen 14,628 J7
Anderson 14,571 M5
Ballard 7,902 C6
Barren 34,001 K7
Bath 9,692 O4
Bell 31,506 O7
Boone 57,589 M3
Bourbon 19,236 N4
Boyd 51,150 R4
Boyle 25,641 M5
Bracken 7,766 N3
Breathitt 15,703 P5
Breckinridge 16,312 J5
Bullitt 47,567 K5
Butler 11,245 H6
Caldwell 13,232 F6
Calloway 30,735 E7
Campbell 83,866 N3
Carlisle 5,238 C7
Carroll 9,292 L3
Carter 24,340 P4
Casey 14,211 M6
Christian 68,941 F7
Clark 29,496 N4
Clay 21,746 O6
Clinton 9,135 L7
Crittenden 9,196 E6
Cumberland 6,784 L7
Daviess 87,189 G5
Edmonson 10,357 J6
Elliott 6,455 P4
Estill 14,614 O5
Fayette 225,366 M5
Fleming 12,292 O4
Floyd 43,586 R5
Franklin 43,781 M4
Fulton 8,271 C7
Gallatin 5,393 M3
Garrard 11,579 M5
Grant 15,737 M3
Graves 33,550 D7
Grayson 21,050 J5
Green 10,371 K6
Greenup 36,742 R3
Hancock 7,864 H5
Hardin 89,240 K5
Harlan 36,574 P7
Harrison 16,248 N4
Hart 14,890 K6
Henderson 43,044 F5
Henry 12,823 L4
Hickman 5,566 C7
Jackson 11,955 N6
Jefferson 664,937 K4
Jessamine 30,508 M5
Johnson 23,248 R5
Kenton 142,031 M3
Knott 17,906 R6
Knox 29,676 O7
Larue 11,679 K5
Laurel 43,438 N6
Lawrence 13,998 R4
Lee 7,422 O5
Leslie 13,642 P6
Letcher 27,000 R6
Lewis 13,029 P3
Lincoln 20,045 M6
Livingston 9,062 E6
Logan 24,416 H7
Lyon 6,624 E7
Madison 57,508 N5
Magoffin 13,077 P5
Marion 16,499 L5
Marshall 27,205 E7
Martin 12,526 R5
Mason 16,666 O3
McCracken 62,879 D6
McCreary 15,603 N7
McLean 9,628 G5
Meade 24,170 J5
Menifee 5,092 O5
Mercer 19,148 M5
Metcalfe 8,963 K7
Monroe 11,401 K7
Montgomery 19,561 O4
Morgan 11,648 P5
Muhlenberg 31,318 G6
Nelson 29,710 K5
Nicholas 6,725 N4
Ohio 21,105 H6
Oldham 33,263 L4
Owen 9,035 M3
Owsley 5,036 O6
Pendleton 12,036 N3
Perry 30,283 P6
Pike 72,583 S6
Powell 11,686 O5
Pulaski 49,489 M6
Robertson 2,124 N3
Rockcastle 14,803 N6
Rowan 20,353 P4
Russell 14,716 L6
Scott 23,867 M4
Shelby 24,824 L4
Simpson 15,145 H7
Spencer 6,801 L4
Taylor 21,146 L6
Todd 10,940 G7
Trigg 10,361 F7
Trimble 6,090 L3
Union 16,557 F5
Warren 76,673 H6
Washington 10,441 L5
Wayne 17,468 M7
Webster 13,955 F5
Whitley 33,326 N7
Wolfe 6,503 O5
Woodford 19,955 M4

CITIES and TOWNS

Adairville 906 H7
Ages 500 P7
Albany▲ 2,062 L7
Alexandria▲ 5,592 N3
Allen 229 R5
Allensville 218 G7
Amburgey 500 R6
Anchorage 2,082 L2
Annville 470 O6
Arjay 975 O7
Arlington 449 D7
Ashland 23,622 R4
Auburn 1,273 H7
Audubon Park 1,520 J2
Augusta 1,336 N3
Austin 500 K7
Auxier 900 R5
Bancroft 582 K1
Banner 950 R5
Barbourmeade 1,402 K1
Barbourville▲ 3,658 O7
Bardstown▲ 6,801 L5
Bardwell▲ 819 D7
Barlow 706 D6
Baskett 550 F5
Beattyville▲ 1,131 O5
Beauty 800 S5
Beaver Dam 2,904 H6
Bedford▲ 761 L3
Bee Spring 500 J6
Beechwood Village 1,263 K2
Belcher 500 S6
Belfry 800 S5
Bellemeade 927 L2
Bellevue 6,997 S1
Benham 717 R7
Benton▲ 3,899 E7
Berea 9,126 N5
Berry 240 N3
Betsy Layne 975 R5
Big Creek 700 O6
Blaine 271 R4
Blandville 95 D7
Bloomfield 845 L5
Blue Ridge Manor 565 L2
Boldman 510 R5
Bonnieville 300 K6
Bonnyman 800 P6
Boone 232 N5
Booneville▲ 191 O6
Bowling Green▲ 40,641 H7
Bradford 199 N3
Bradfordsville 331 L6
Brandenburg▲ 1,857 J4
Bremen 267 G6
Briensburg E7
Broadfields 273 K2
Brodhead 1,140 N6
Bromley 1,137 S2
Brooks 2,464 K4
Brooksville▲ 670 N3
Brownsboro Farm 670 L1
Brownsville 897 J6
Buechel 7,081 K2
Buffalo K6
Bulan 800 P6
Burgin 1,009 M5
Burkesville▲ 1,815 L7
Burlington▲ 6,070 R2
Burnside 695 M6
Butler 625 N3
Cadiz▲ 2,148 F7
Calhoun▲ 854 G5
California 130 N3
Calvert City 2,531 E6
Camargo 1,022 O4
Campbellsburg 604 L3
Campbellsville▲ 9,577 L6
Campton▲ 484 O5
Caney 549 P5
Caneyville 642 J6
Cannel City 600 P5
Carlisle▲ 1,639 N4
Carrollton▲ 3,715 L3
Carter P4
Catlettsburg▲ 2,231 R4
Cave City 1,953 K6
Cawood 800 P7
Center 383 K6
Centertown 462 G6
Centerville S6
Central City 4,979 G6
Cerulean F7
Clarkson 611 J6
Clay 1,173 F6
Clay City 1,258 O5
Clearfield 1,250 P4
Clinton▲ 1,547 D7
Clover Bottom 600 N5
Cloverport 1,207 H5
Coal Run 262 R5
Cold Spring 2,880 T2
Columbia▲ 3,845 L6
Columbus 252 C7
Combs 900 P6
Corbin 7,419 N7
Corinth 137 M3
Corydon 790 F5
Covington 43,264 S2
Crab Orchard 825 M6
Crescent Springs 2,179 R2
Crestview 356 S2
Crestview Hills 2,546 R2
Crestwood 1,435 L4
Crittenden 731 M3
Crofton 699 G6
Cumberland 3,112 R6
Cynthiana▲ 6,497 N4
Danville▲ 12,420 M5
Dawson Springs 3,129 F6
Dayton 6,576 T1
Devondale 1,164 K2
Dexter E7
Dixon▲ 552 F5
Dorton 750 R6
Douglass Hills 5,549 L2
Dover 297 O3
Drakesboro 565 H6
Dry Ridge 1,601 M3
Earlington 1,833 F6
East Bernstadt 550 N6
Echols 576 H6
Eddyville▲ 1,889 E6
Edgewood 8,143 S2
Edmonton▲ 1,477 K7
Elizabethtown▲ 18,167 K5
Elkhorn City 813 S6
Elkton▲ 1,789 G7
Elsmere 6,847 R2
Eminence 2,055 L4
Eolia 875 R6
Erlanger 15,979 R2
Essie 650 P6
Eubank 354 M6
Evarts 1,063 P7
Ewing 268 O4
Fairdale 6,563 K4
Fairfield 142 L5
Fairview 119 G7
Fairview 198 S2
Fallsburg R4
Falmouth▲ 2,378 N3
Fancy Farm 800 D7
Farmington 600 D7
Fedscreek 950 S6
Ferguson 934 M6
Fincastle 838 L1
Flat 7,799 O5
Flat Lick 600 O7
Flatwoods 8,354 R4
Fleming (Fleming-Neon) 759 R6
Flemingsburg▲ 3,071 O4
Florence 18,624 R2
Ford 522 N5
Fordsville 561 H5
Forest Hills 454 L2
Fort Knox 21,495 K5
Fort Mitchell 7,438 S2
Fort Thomas 16,032 S2
Fort Wright 6,570 S2
Fountain Run 259 K7
Frankfort (cap.)▲ 25,968 M4
Franklin▲ 7,607 J7
Fredonia 490 E6
Frenchburg▲ 625 O5
Fullerton 950 P3
Fulton 3,078 D7
Gamaliel 462 K7
Garrison 700 P3
Georgetown▲ 11,414 M4
Germantown 213 O3
Ghent 365 L3
Gilbertsville E7
Glasgow▲ 12,351 J7
Glencoe 257 M3
Glenview 653 K1
Goose Creek 321 L1
Goshen 2,447 K4
Gramoor 1,167 K1
Grand Rivers 351 E7
Gray 2,911 O7
Grayson▲ 3,510 R4
Greensburg▲ 1,990 K6
Greenup▲ 1,158 R3
Greenville▲ 4,689 G6
Guthrie 1,504 G7
Hammond 510 O7
Hanson 450 G6
Hardin 595 E7
Hardinsburg▲ 1,906 H5
Hardy 900 S5
Harlan▲ 2,686 P7
Harold 520 R5
Harrodsburg▲ 7,335 M5
Hartford▲ 2,532 H6
Hatfield 700 S5
Hawesville▲ 998 H5
Hazard▲ 5,416 P6
Hazel 460 E7
Hebron 930 R2
Helton 600 P7
Henderson▲ 25,945 F5
Hickman▲ 2,689 C7
Hickory 152 D7
Highland Heights 4,223 T2
Hima 600 O6
Himyar 545 O7
Hindman▲ 798 R6
Hiseville 220 K6
Hitchins 750 R4
Hodgenville▲ 2,721 K5
Hollow Creek 991 K4
Hopkinsville▲ 29,809 F7
Horse Cave 2,284 K6
Houston Acres 496 K2
Hustonville 313 M6
Hyden▲ 375 P6
Independence▲ 10,444 M3
Indian Hills 1,074 K1
Inez▲ 511 S5
Irvine▲ 2,836 O5
Irvington 1,180 J5
Island 446 G6
Ivel 850 R5
Jackson▲ 2,466 P5
Jamestown▲ 1,641 L7
Jeff 23,221 P6
Jeffersontown 15,795 L2
Jeffersonville 1,854 O5
Jenkins 2,751 R6
Junction City 1,983 M5
Keavy 900 N6
Keene 393 M5
Kenton 358 N3
Kenton Vale 145 S2
Kenvir 800 P7
Kevil 337 D6
King 399 O7
Kingsley 464 K2
Kitts 800 P7
Kuttawa 535 E6
La Center 1,040 C6
La Fayette 106 F7
La Grange▲ 3,853 L4
Lackey R6
Lake 3,131 O6
Lakeside Park 3,062 R2
Lancaster▲ 3,421 M5
Lawrenceburg▲ 5,911 M4
Leatherwood 800 P6
Lebanon Junction 1,741 K5
Lebanon▲ 5,695 L5
Leitchfield▲ 4,965 J6
Lejunior 597 P7
Lewisburg 772 G6
Lewisport 1,778 H5
Lexington▲ 204,165 N4
Liberty▲ 1,937 M6
Littcarr 645 R6
Livermore 1,534 G5
Livingston 241 N6
Lockport 84 M4
London▲ 5,757 N6
Lone Oak 465 D6
Lookout 600 S6
Lookout Heights S2
Loretto 820 L5
Lothair 600 P6
Louisa▲ 1,990 R4
Louisville▲ 269,063 J2
Loyall 1,100 P7
Ludlow 4,736 S2
Lynch 1,166 R7
Mackville 200 L5
Madisonville▲ 16,200 F6
Majestic 600 S5
Manchester▲ 1,634 O6
Marion▲ 3,320 E6
Marshes Siding 800 M7
Martha 650 R4
Martin 694 R5
Mary 177 O5
Mason 1,119 M3
Mayfield▲ 9,935 D7
Maysville▲ 7,169 O3
McAndrews 975 S5
McCarr 592 S5
McHenry 414 H6
McKee▲ 870 O6
McRoberts 1,101 R6
McVeigh 650 S5
Meadow Vale 798 L1
Meally 550 R5
Melbourne 660 T2
Mentor 169 N3
Meta 600 S5
Middlesboro 11,328 O7
Middletown 5,016 L2
Midway 1,290 M4
Millersburg 937 N4
Millstone 550 R6
Milton 563 L3
Minor Lane Heights 1,675 K4
Monterey 164 M4
Monticello▲ 5,357 M7
Moorland 467 L2
Morehead▲ 8,357 P4
Morgan 3,776 N3
Morganfield▲ 3,781 E5
Morgantown▲ 2,284 H6
Mortons Gap 987 F6
Mount Olivet▲ 384 N3
Mount Sterling▲ 5,362 N4
Mount Vernon▲ 2,654 N6
Mount Washington 5,226 K4
Mouthcard 900 S6
Muldraugh 1,376 J5
Munfordville▲ 1,556 J6
Murray▲ 14,439 E7
Nebo 227 F6
Neon (Neon-Fleming) R6
New Castle▲ 893 L4
New Concord 800 E7
New Haven 796 K5
New Hope L5
Newport 18,871 S2
Nicholasville▲ 13,603 N5
North Middletown 602 N4
Northfield 898 K1
Nortonville 1,209 G6
Oak Grove 2,863 G7
Oakland 202 J6
Oil Springs 900 P5
Okolona 18,902 K4
Oldtown 570 R4
Olive Hill 1,809 P4
Owensboro▲ 53,549 G5
Owenton▲ 1,306 M3
Owingsville▲ 1,491 O4
Paducah▲ 27,256 D6
Paintsville▲ 4,354 R5
Paris▲ 8,730 N4
Park City 549 J6
Park Hills 3,321 S2
Parksville 560 M5
Parkway Village 707 J2
Pembroke 640 G7
Perryville 815 M5
Petersburg M2
Pewee Valley 1,283 L4
Phelps 1,298 S6
Philpot 700 H5
Pikeville▲ 6,324 S6
Pine Knot 1,549 M7
Pineville▲ 2,198 O7
Pittsburg N6
Plantation 830 K1
Pleasure Ridge Park 25,131 J4
Pleasureville 761 L4
Plum Springs 361 J7
Powderly 748 G6
Premium 729 R6
Preston 3,558 O4
Prestonsburg▲ 4,011 R5
Prestonville 205 L3
Princeton▲ 6,940 F6
Prospect 2,788 K4
Providence 4,123 F6
Raceland 2,256 R3
Radcliff 19,772 K5
Ravenna 804 O5
Raywick 157 L5
Richmond▲ 21,155 N5
Riverwood 506 K1
Robards 701 F5
Rochester 191 H6
Rockholds 775 N7
Rockport 385 H6
Rolling Fields 593 K2
Rolling Hills 1,135 L1
Russell 4,014 R3
Russell Springs 2,363 L6
Russellville▲ 7,454 H7
Ryland Heights 279 M3
Sacramento 563 G6
Sadieville 255 M4
Saint Charles 316 F6
Saint Matthews 15,800 K2

Agriculture, Industry and Resources

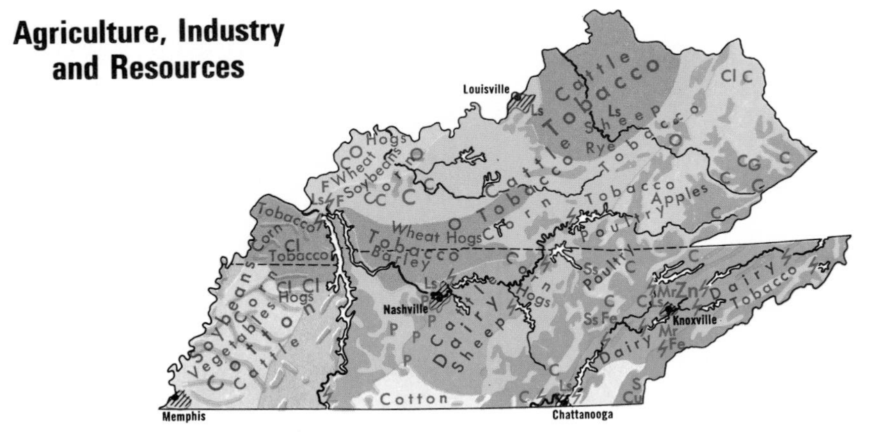

DOMINANT LAND USE

- Hogs, Soft Winter Wheat
- Tobacco, General Farming
- General Farming, Livestock, Tobacco
- General Farming, Livestock, Dairy
- General Farming, Livestock, Fruit, Tobacco
- Specialized Cotton
- Cotton, General Farming
- Cotton, Livestock
- Forests
- Swampland, Limited Agriculture

MAJOR MINERAL OCCURRENCES

C Coal
Cl Clay
Cu Copper
F Fluorspar
Fe Iron Ore
G Natural Gas
Ls Limestone
Mr Marble
O Petroleum
P Phosphates
S Pyrites
Ss Sandstone
Zn Zinc

Water Power
Major Industrial Areas

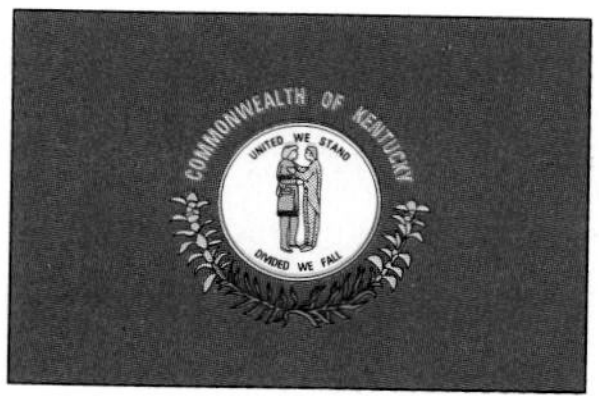

KENTUCKY

KENTUCKY

AREA 40,409 sq. mi. (104,659 sq. km.)
POPULATION 3,698,969
CAPITAL Frankfort
LARGEST CITY Louisville
HIGHEST POINT Black Mtn. 4,145 ft. (1263 m.)
SETTLED IN 1774
ADMITTED TO UNION June 1, 1792
POPULAR NAME Bluegrass State
STATE FLOWER Goldenrod
STATE BIRD Cardinal

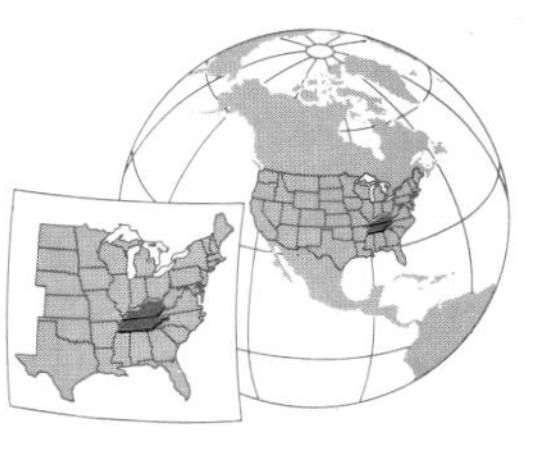

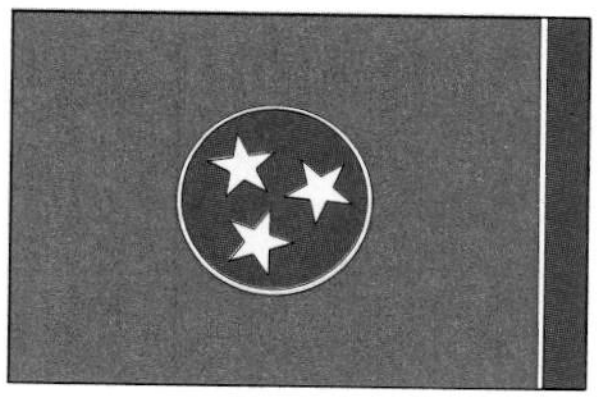

TENNESSEE

TENNESSEE

AREA 42,144 sq. mi. (109,153 sq. km.)
POPULATION 4,896,641
CAPITAL Nashville
LARGEST CITY Memphis
HIGHEST POINT Clingmans Dome 6,643 ft. (2025 m.)
SETTLED IN 1757
ADMITTED TO UNION June 1, 1796
POPULAR NAME Volunteer State
STATE FLOWER Iris
STATE BIRD Mockingbird

Saint Regis Park 1,756 K2
Salem 770 E6
Salt Lick 342 O4
Salyersville▲ 1,917 P5
Sanders 231 M3
Sandy Hook▲ 548 P4
Sardis 171 O3
Science Hill 628 M6
Scottsville▲ 4,278 J7
Sebree 1,510 F5
Seco R6
Sedalia D7
Seneca Gardens 684 K2
Sextons Creek 975 O6
Sharpsburg 315 O4
Shelbyville▲ 6,238 L4
Shepherdsville▲ 4,805 K4
Shively 15,535 K4
Silver Grove 1,102 T2
Simpson 907 P5
Simpsonville 642 L4
Slaughters 235 F6
Smilax 987 P6
Smithfield 115 L4
Smithland▲ 384 E6
Smiths Grove 703 J6
Somerset▲ 10,733 M6
Sonora 295 K5
South 202 J6
South Carrollton 262 G6
South Portsmouth 900 P3
South Shore 1,318 R3
South Williamson 1,016 S5
Southgate 3,266 T2
Sparta 133 M3
Spottsville 914 G5
Springfield▲ 2,875 L5
Springlee 451 K2
Staffordsville 700 R5
Stamping Ground 698 M4
Stanford▲ 2,686 M5
Stanton▲ 2,795 O5
Stearns 1,550 N7
Stone 900 S5
Strathmoor Village 361 K2
Sturgis 2,184 F5
Tateville 680 M7
Taylor Mill 5,530 S2
Taylorsville▲ 774 L4
Thealka 600 R5
Thornhill 146 K1
Tollesboro 808 O3
Tompkinsville▲ 2,861 K7
Trenton 378 G7
Tyner 590 O6
Union 1,001 M3
Uniontown 1,008 F5
Upton 719 K6
Valley Station 22,840 K4
Van 1,050 R6
Van Lear 2,035 R5
Vanceburg▲ 1,713 P3
Verda 1,133 P7
Versailles▲ 7,269 M4
Vicco 244 P6
Villa Hills 7,739 R2
Vine Grove 3,586 K5
Virgie 600 R6
Visalia 190 N3
Wallins Creek 261 O7
Walton 2,034 M3
Warfield 364 S5
Warsaw▲ 1,202 M3
Washington 795 O3
Water Valley 321 D7
Waverly 345 F5
Wayland 359 R6
Weeksbury 850 R6
Wellington 593 O5
Wellington 653 K2
West Buechel 1,587 K2
West Liberty▲ 1,887 P5
West Point 1,216 J4
West Somerset 850 M6
Westwood 734 R4
Westwood 826 L1
Wheatcroft 206 F5
Wheelwright 721 R6
White Plains 598 G6
Whitesburg▲ 1,636 R6
Whitesville 682 H5
Whitley City▲ 1,133 N7
Wickliffe▲ 851 C7
Wilders 633 S2
Willard R4
Williamsburg▲ 5,493 N7
Williamstown▲ 3,023 M3
Willisburg 223 L5
Wilmore 4,215 M5
Winchester▲ 15,799 N5
Windy Hills 2,452 K1
Wingo 568 D7
Winston Park S2
Wolf Creek 600 J4
Woodbine 900 N7
Woodburn 343 J7
Woodbury 117 H6
Woodland Hills 714 L2
Woodlawn (Oakdale) 308 D6
Woodlawn 331 T2
Woodlawn Park 1,099 K2
Wooton 750 P6
Worthington 1,751 R3
Worthville 191 L3
Wurtland 1,221 R3
Zebulon 750 S5

OTHER FEATURES

Abraham Lincoln Birthplace Nat'l Hist. Site K5
Barkley (dam) E6
Barkley (lake) F7
Barren (riv.) H6
Barren River (lake) J7
Beech Fork (riv.) L5
Big Sandy (riv.) R4
Black (mt.) R7
Buckhorn (lake) O6
Chaplin (riv.) L5
Clarks, East Fork (riv.) E7
Cove Run (lake) P4
Cumberland (lake) M7
Cumberland (mt.) P7
Cumberland (riv.) K8
Cumberland Gap Nat'l Hist. P7
Dale Hollow (lake) L7
Dewey (lake) R5
Dix (riv.) M5
Drakes (creek) J7
Dry (creek) R2
Eagle (creek) M3
Fishtrap (lake) S6
Fort Campbell G7
Grayson (lake) P4
Green (riv.) G6
Green River (lake) L6
Herrington (lake) M5
Hinkston (creek) N4
Kentucky (dam) E7
Kentucky (lake) E8
Kentucky (riv.) M3
Land Between The Lakes Rec. Area E7
Laurel River (lake) N6
Lexington Blue Grass Army Depot N4
Licking (riv.) N3
Mammoth Cave Nat'l Park J6
Mayfield (creek) C7
Mississippi (riv.) 10
Mud (riv.) H7
Nolin (lake) K6
Nolin (riv.) J6
Obion (creek) C7
Ohio (riv.) F5
Paint Lick (riv.) M5
Panther (creek) G5
Pine (mt.) F1
Pond (riv.) G6
Red (riv.) G7
Red (riv.) O5
Rockcastle (riv.) N6
Rolling Fork (riv.) K5
Rough (riv.) H5
Rough River (lake) J5
Salt (riv.) K5
Tennessee (riv.) D6
Tradewater (riv.) F6
Tug Fork (riv.) S5

TENNESSEE

COUNTIES

Anderson 68,250 N8
Bedford 30,411 J9
Benton 14,524 E8
Bledsoe 9,669 L9
Blount 85,969 O9
Bradley 73,712 M1
Campbell 35,079 N8
Cannon 10,467 J9
Carroll 27,514 E9
Carter 51,505 S8
Cheatham 27,140 G8
Chester 12,819 D1
Claiborne 26,137 O8
Clay 7,238 K7
Cocke 29,141 P9
Coffee 40,339 J9
Crockett 13,378 C9
Cumberland 34,736 L9
Davidson 510,784 H8
De Kalb 13,589 K9
Decatur 10,472 E9
Dickson 35,061 G8
Dyer 34,854 C8
Fayette 25,559 C1
Fentress 14,669 M8
Franklin 34,725 J1
Gibson 46,315 D9
Giles 25,741 G1
Grainger 17,095 O8
Greene 55,853 R8
Grundy 13,362 K1
Hamblen 50,480 P8
Hamilton 285,536 L1
Hancock 6,739 P7
Hardeman 23,377 C1
Hardin 22,633 E1
Hawkins 44,565 P8
Haywood 19,437 C9
Henderson 21,844 E9
Henry 27,888 E8
Hickman 16,754 G9
Houston 7,018 F8
Humphreys 15,795 F8
Jackson 9,297 K8
Jefferson 33,016 P8
Johnson 13,766 T7
Knox 335,749 O9
Lake 7,129 B8
Lauderdale 23,491 B9
Lawrence 35,303 G1
Lewis 9,247 F9
Lincoln 28,157 H1
Loudon 31,255 N9
Macon 15,906 J7
Madison 77,982 D9
Marion 24,860 K1
Marshall 21,539 H1
Maury 54,812 G9
McMinn 42,383 M1
McNairy 22,422 D1
Meigs 8,033 M9
Monroe 30,541 N1
Montgomery 100,498 G8
Moore 4,721 J1
Morgan 17,300 M8
Obion 31,717 C8
Overton 17,636 L8
Perry 6,612 F9
Pickett 4,548 M7
Polk 13,643 N1
Putnam 51,373 K8
Rhea 24,344 M9
Roane 47,227 M9
Robertson 41,494 H7
Rutherford 118,570 J9
Scott 18,358 M8
Sequatchie 8,863 L1
Sevier 51,043 O9
Shelby 826,330 B1
Smith 14,143 J8
Stewart 9,479 F7
Sullivan 143,596 S7
Sumner 103,281 J8
Tipton 37,568 B9
Trousdale 5,920 J8
Unicoi 16,549 S8
Union 13,694 O8
Van Buren 4,846 L9
Warren 32,992 K9
Washington 92,315 R8
Wayne 13,935 F1
Weakley 31,972 D8
White 20,090 L9
Williamson 81,021 H9
Wilson 67,675 J8

CITIES and TOWNS

Adams 587 G7
Adamsville 1,745 E10
Afton 800 R8
Alamo▲ 2,426 C9
Alcoa 6,400 N9
Alexandria 730 J8
Algood 2,399 K8
Allardt 609 M8
Allons 600 L8
Altamont▲ 679 K10
Apison 750 L10
Ardmore 866 H10
Arlington 1,541 B10
Armathwaite 700 M8
Arthur 500 O7
Ashland City▲ 2,552 G8
Athens▲ 12,054 M10
Atoka 659 B10
Atwood 1,066 D9
Auburntown 240 J9
Baileyton 309 R8
Banner Hill 1,717 R8
Bartlett 26,989 B10
Bath Springs 800 E10
Baxter 1,289 K8
Bean Station 500 P8
Beechgrove 550 J9
Beersheba Springs 596 K10
Bell Buckle 326 J9
Belle Meade 2,839 H8
Bells 1,643 C9
Benton▲ 992 M10
Berry Hill 802 H8
Berry's Chapel 2,703 H9
Bethel Springs 755 D10
Big Sandy 505 E8
Birchwood 550 M10
Blaine 1,326 O8
Bloomingdale 10,953 R7
Bloomington Springs 800 K8
Blountville▲ 2,605 S7
Bluff City 1,390 S8
Bolivar▲ 5,969 C10
Braden 354 B10
Bradford 1,154 D8
Braemar S8
Brentwood 16,392 H8
Briceville 850 N8
Brighton 717 B10
Bristol 23,421 S7
Brownsville▲ 10,019 C9
Bruceton 1,586 E8
Buena Vista 500 E9
Bulls Gap 659 P8
Burlison 394 B9
Burns 1,127 G8
Butler 500 T8
Byrdstown▲ 998 L7
Calhoun 552 M10
Camden▲ 3,643 E8
Carthage▲ 2,386 K8
Caryville 1,751 N8
Castalian Springs 650 J8
Cedar Hill 347 H7
Celina▲ 1,493 K7
Centertown 332 K9
Centerville▲ 3,616 G9
Chapel Hill 833 H9
Charleston 653 M10
Charlotte▲ 854 G8
Chattanooga▲ 152,466 K10
Chuckey 500 R8
Church Hill 4,834 R7
Clairfield 650 O7
Clarksburg 321 E9
Clarksville▲ 75,494 G7
Cleveland▲ 30,354 M10
Clifton 620 F10
Clinton▲ 8,972 N8
Coalfield 712 N8
Coalmont 813 K10
Cokercreek 500 N10
College Grove 580 H9
Collegedale 5,048 M10
Collierville 14,427 B10
Collinwood 1,014 F10
Colonial Heights 6,716 R8
Columbia▲ 28,583 G9
Concord 8,569 N9
Cookeville▲ 21,744 L8
Copperhill 362 N10
Cordova 600 B10
Cornersville 683 H10
Corryton 500 O8
Counce 975 E10
Covington▲ 7,487 B9
Cowan 1,738 K10
Crab Orchard 876 M9
Crockett Mills 500 C9
Cross Plains 1,025 H7
Crossville▲ 6,930 L9
Crump 2,028 E10
Cumberland City 319 F8
Cumberland Gap 210 O8
Cypress Inn 500 F10
Dandridge▲ 1,540 O8
Dayton▲ 5,671 L9
Decatur▲ 1,361 M9
Decaturville▲ 879 E9
Dechard 2,196 J10
Dickson 8,791 G8
Dover▲ 1,341 F8
Dowelltown 308 K8
Doyle 345 K9
Dresden▲ 2,488 D8
Drummonds 800 A10
Duck River 750 G9
Ducktown 421 N10
Dunlap▲ 3,731 L10
Dyer 2,204 D8
Dyersburg▲ 16,317 C8
Eads 550 B10
Eagleton Village 5,169 O9
Eagleville 462 H9
East Ridge 21,101 L11
Eastview 563 D10
Elgin 700 M8
Elizabethton▲ 11,931 S8
Elk Valley 750 N7
Elkton 448 H10
Ellendale 850 B10
Embreeville Junction R8
Emory Gap 500 M9
Englewood 1,611 M10
Enville 211 E10
Erin▲ 1,586 F8
Erwin▲ 5,015 S8
Estill Springs 1,408 J10
Ethridge 565 G10
Etowah 3,815 M10
Eva 500 E8
Fairfield 2,209 J9
Fairview 4,210 G9
Fall Branch 1,203 R8
Farner 750 N10
Fayetteville▲ 6,921 H10
Finger 279 D10
Finley 1,014 B8
Flintville 500 H10
Forest Hills 4,231 H8
Fort Pillow 700 B9
Fowlkes 700 C9
Franklin▲ 20,098 H9
Friendship 467 C9
Friendsville 792 N9
Gadsden 561 D9
Gainesboro▲ 1,002 K8
Gallatin▲ 18,794 H8
Gallaway 762 B10
Garland 194 B9
Gates 608 C9
Gatlinburg 3,417 O9
Germantown 32,893 B10
Gibson 281 D9
Gilt Edge 447 B9
Gleason 1,402 D8
Goodlettsville 8,177 H8
Gordonsville 891 K8
Grand Junction 365 C10
Grandview M9
Graysville 1,301 L10
Greenback 611 N9
Greenbrier 2,873 H8
Greeneville▲ 13,532 R8
Greenfield 2,105 D8
Grimsley 650 L8
Gruetli 1,810 K10
Guys 497 D10
Habersham 750 N8
Halls 2,431 C9
Halls Crossroads O8
Hampshire 788 G9
Hampton 2,236 S8
Harriman 7,119 M9
Harris 7,191 C8
Harrison 6,206 L10
Harrogate (Shawanee) 2,657 O8
Hartsville▲ 2,188 J8
Helenwood 675 M8
Henderson▲ 4,760 D10
Hendersonville 32,188 H8
Henning 802 B9
Henry 317 E8
Hickory Valley 159 C10
Hixson L10
Hohenwald▲ 3,760 F9
Hollow Rock 902 E8
Hornbeak 445 C8
Hornsby 313 D10
Humboldt 9,651 D9
Huntingdon▲ 4,180 E8
Huntland 885 J10
Huntsville▲ 660 N8
Hurricane Mills 850 F9
Iron City 402 F10
Jacksboro▲ 1,568 N8
Jackson▲ 48,949 D9
Jamestown▲ 1,862 M8
Jasper▲ 2,780 K10
Jefferson City 5,494 P8
Jellico 2,447 N7
Johnson City 49,381 S8
Jones 3,091 C9
Jonesborough▲ 2,829 R8
Karns 1,458 N9
Kenton 1,366 C8
Kimball 1,243 K10
Kimberlin Heights 500 O9
Kingsport 36,365 R7
Kingston Springs 1,529 G8
Kingston▲ 4,552 N9
Knoxville▲ 165,121 O9
Kodak 700 O9
La Follette 7,192 N8
La Grange 167 C10
La Vergne 7,499 H9
Laager 675 K10
Lafayette▲ 3,641 J7
Lake City 2,166 N8
Lakeland 1,204 B10
Lakesite 732 L10
Lakewood 2,009 H8
Lawrenceburg▲ 10,412 G10
Lebanon▲ 15,208 J8
Lenoir City 6,147 N9
Leoma 600 G10
Lewisburg▲ 9,879 H10
Lexington▲ 5,810 E9
Liberty 391 K8
Linden▲ 1,099 F9
Livingston▲ 3,809 L8
Lobelville 830 F9
Long Island S7
Lookout Mountain 1,901 L11
Loretto 1,515 G10
Loudon▲ 4,026 N9
Louisville 500 N9
Luttrell 812 O8
Lutts 740 F10
Lyles 500 G9
Lynchburg▲ 668 J10
Lynnville 344 G10
Madisonville▲ 3,033 N9
Malesus 600 D9
Manchester▲ 7,709 J10
Martel 500 N9
Martin 8,600 D8
Maryville▲ 19,208 O9
Mascot 2,138 O8
Mason 337 B10
Maury City 782 C9
Maynardville▲ 1,298 O8
McDonald 500 M10
McEwen 1,442 F8
McKenzie 5,168 E8
McLemoresville 280 D9
McMinnville▲ 11,194 K9
Medina 658 D9
Medon 137 D10
Memphis▲ 610,337 B10
Michie 677 E10
Middleton 536 D10
Midway 2,953 P8
Milan 7,512 D9
Milledgeville 279 E10
Milligan College 600 S8
Millington 17,866 B10
Minor Hill 372 G10
Mitchellville 193 J7
Monteagle 1,138 K10
Monterey 2,559 L8
Morley 600 N7
Morrison 570 K9
Morrison City 2,032 R7
Morristown▲ 21,385 P8
Moscow 384 C10
Mosheim 1,451 R8
Mount Carmel 4,082 R8
Mount Juliet 5,389 H8
Mount Pleasant 4,278 G9
Mountain City▲ 2,169 T8
Munford 2,326 B10
Murfreesboro▲ 44,922 J9
Murray Lake Hills L10
Nashville (cap.)▲ 488,374 H8
Neubert 800 O9
New Hope 854 K11
New Johnsonville 1,643 E8
New Market 1,086 O8
New Tazewell 1,864 O8
Newbern 2,515 C8
Newport▲ 7,123 P9
Niota 745 M9
Norma 118 N8
Normandy 118 J10
Norris 1,303 N8
Oak Hill 4,301 H8
Oak Ridge 27,310 N8
Oakdale 268 M9
Oakland 392 B10
Obion 1,241 C8
Oliver Springs 3,433 N8
Oneida 3,502 N7
Ooltewah 4,903 M10
Orebank 1,284 R7
Orlinda 469 H7
Orme 150 K10
Pall Mall 750 M7
Palmer 769 K10
Paris▲ 9,332 E8
Parrotsville 121 P8
Parsons 2,033 E9
Pegram 1,371 H8
Petersburg 514 H10
Petros 1,286 M8
Philadelphia 463 M9
Pickwick Dam 650 E10
Pigeon Forge 3,027 O9
Pikeville▲ 1,771 L9
Piperton 612 B10
Pittman Center 478 P9
Pleasant Hill 494 L9
Pleasant View 625 G8
Portland 5,165 H7
Powder Springs 600 O8
Powell 7,534 N8
Powells Crossroads 1,098 L10
Primm Springs 750 G9
Pulaski▲ 7,895 G10
Puryear 592 E8
Ramer 337 D10
Red Bank 12,322 L10
Red Boiling Springs 905 K7
Rheatown R8
Ridgely 1,775 B8
Ridgeside 400 L10
Ripley▲ 6,188 B9
Rives 344 C8
Roan Mountain 1,220 S8
Rockford 646 O9
Rockwood 5,348 M9
Rogersville▲ 4,149 P8
Rosemark 950 B10
Rossville 291 B10
Russellville 1,069 P8
Rutherford 1,303 C8
Rutledge▲ 903 P8
Saint Joseph 789 G10
Sale Creek 900 L10
Saltillo 383 E10
Samburg 374 C8
Sardis 305 E10
Saulsbury 106 C10
Saundersville H8
Savannah▲ 6,547 E10
Scotts Hill 594 E10
Selmer▲ 3,838 D10
Sequatchie 800 K10
Sevierville▲ 7,178 P9
Sewanee 2,128 K10
Seymour 7,026 O9
Sharon 1,047 D8
Shelbyville▲ 14,049 H10
Sherwood 900 K10
Signal Mountain 7,034 L10
Smithville▲ 3,791 K9
Smyrna 13,647 H9
Sneedville▲ 1,446 P7
Soddy-Daisy (Daisy-Soddy) 8,240 L10
Somerville▲ 2,047 C10
South Carthage 851 K8
South Cleveland 5,372 M10
South Clinton 1,671 N8
South Fulton 2,688 D8
South Pittsburg 3,295 K10
Southside 800 G8
Sparta▲ 4,681 K9
Spencer▲ 1,125 L9
Spring City 2,199 M9
Spring Hill 1,464 H9
Springfield▲ 11,227 H8
Stanton 487 C10
Stantonville 264 E10
Strawberry Plains 680 O8
Sullivan Gardens 2,513 R8
Summertown 850 G10
Surgoinsville 1,499 R8
Sweetwater 5,066 N9
Talbott 975 P8
Tazewell▲ 2,150 O8
Tellico Plains 657 N10
Ten Mile 700 M9
Tennessee Ridge 1,271 F8
Tiftona L11
Tipton 2,149 B10
Tiptonville▲ 2,438 B8
Toone 279 D10
Townsend 329 O9
Tracy City 1,556 K10
Treadway 712 P8
Trenton▲ 4,836 D9
Trezevant 874 D8
Trimble 694 C8
Troy 1,047 C8
Tullahoma 16,761 J10
Tusculum 1,918 R8
Union City▲ 10,513 C8
Vanleer 369 G8
Victoria 800 K10
Viola 123 K9
Vonore 605 N9
Walden 1,523 L10
Walterhill 1,043 J9
Wartburg▲ 932 M8
Wartrace 494 J9

(continued on following page)

Topography

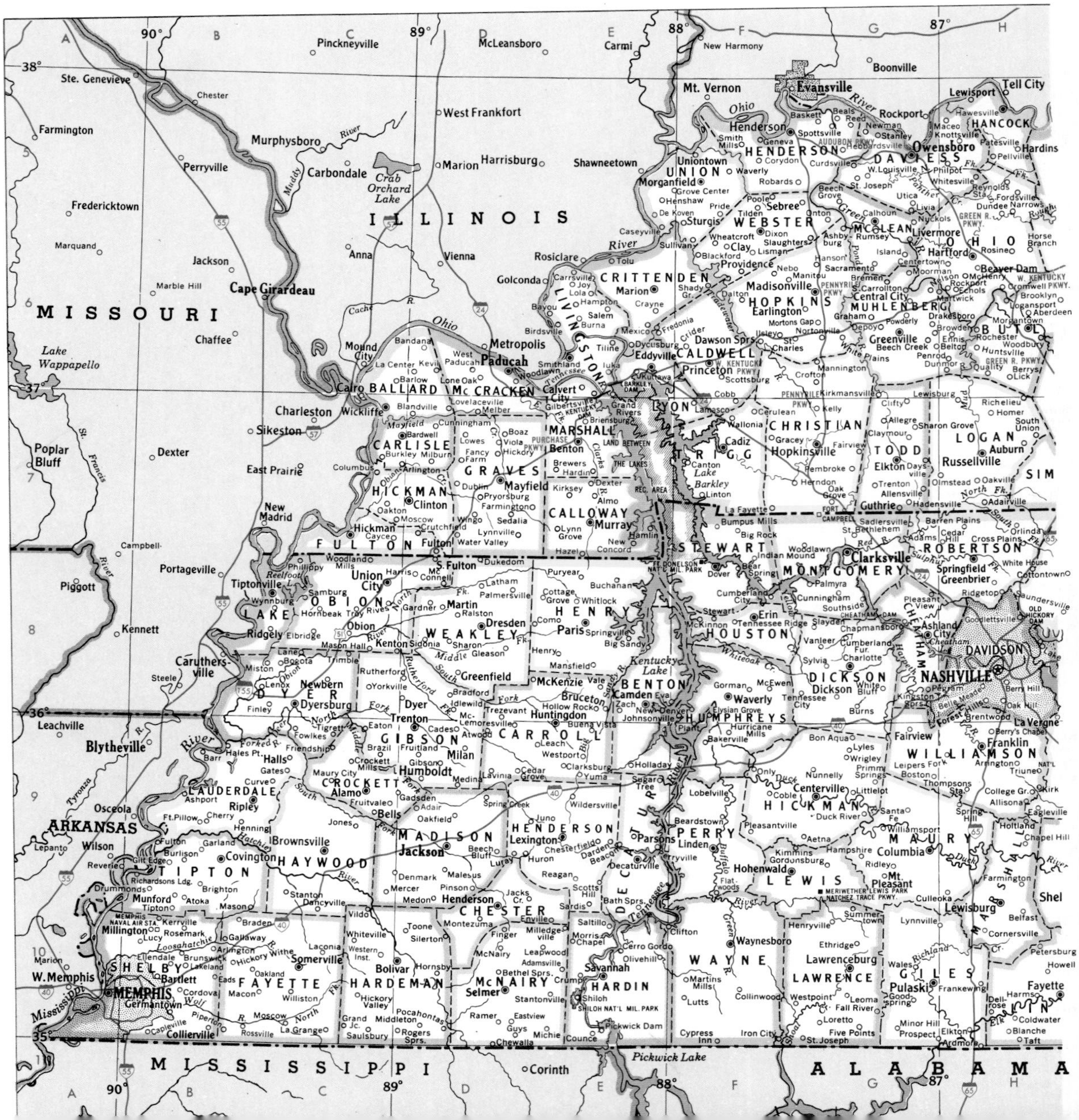

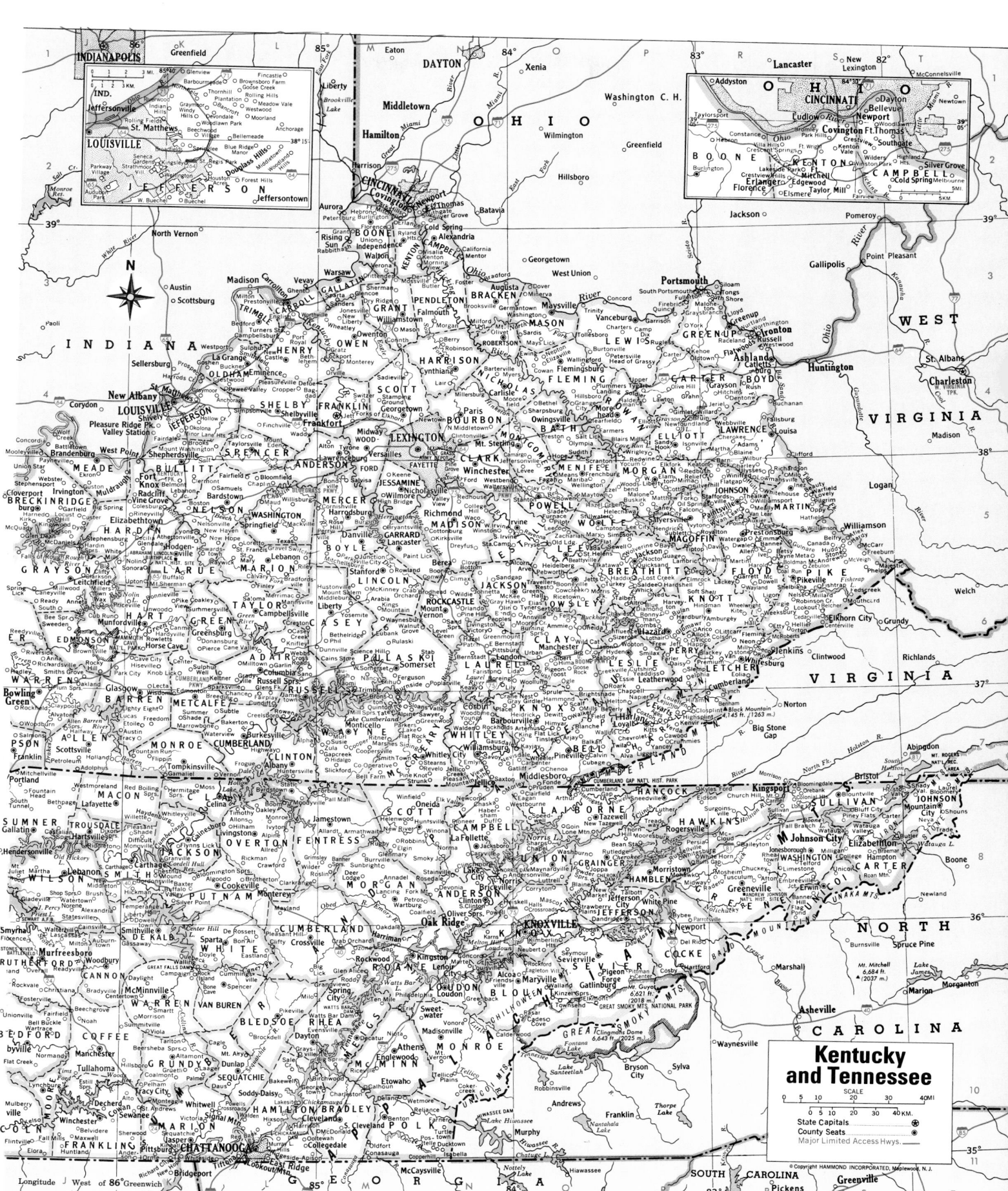

Kentucky and Tennessee

SCALE

0 5 10 20 30 40 MI.
0 5 10 20 30 40 KM.

State Capitals ●
County Seats ○
Major Limited Access Hwys.

© Copyright HAMMOND INCORPORATED, Maplewood, N.J.

Topography

0   40   80 MI.

0   40   80 KM.

5,000 m. | 2,000 m. | 1,000 m. | 500 m. | 200 m. | 100 m. | Sea Level | Below
16,404 ft. | 6,562 ft. | 3,281 ft. | 1,640 ft. | 656 ft. | 328 ft.

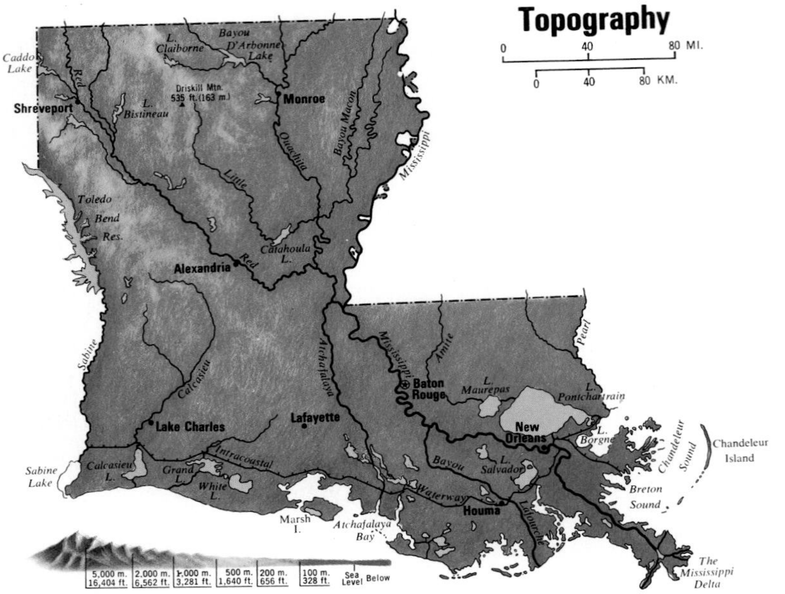

PARISHES

Acadia 56,427 ....F6
Allen 21,390 ....E5
Ascension 50,068 ....L3
Assumption 22,084 ....H7
Avoyelles 41,393 ....G4
Beauregard 29,692 ....D5
Bienville 16,387 ....D2
Bossier 80,721 ....C1
Caddo 252,437 ....C1
Calcasieu 167,223 ....D6
Caldwell 10,761 ....F2
Cameron 9,336 ....D7
Catahoula 12,287 ....G3
Claiborne 17,095 ....D1
Concordia 22,981 ....G4
De Soto 25,727 ....C2
East Baton Rouge 366,191 ...K1
East Carroll 11,772 ....H1
East Feliciana 19,015 ......H5
Evangeline 33,343 ....F5
Franklin 24,141 ....G2
Grant 16,703 ....E4
Iberia 63,752 ....G7
Iberville 32,159 ....J6
Jackson 17,321 ....E2
Jefferson 454,592 ....L6
Jefferson Davis 32,168 .....E6
La Salle 17,004 ....F6
Lafayette 150,017 ....F6
Lafourche 82,483 ....J7
Lincoln 39,763 ....E1
Livingston 58,806 ....L2
Madison 15,682 ....H2
Morehouse 34,803 ....G1
Natchitoches 39,863 ....D3
Orleans 557,927 ....L6
Ouachita 139,241 ....F2
Plaquemines 26,049 ....L8
Pointe Coupee 24,045 ....G5
Rapides 135,282 ....E4
Red River 10,433 ....D2
Richland 20,537 ....G2
Sabine 25,280 ....C3
Saint Bernard 64,097 ....L7
Saint Charles 37,259 ....K7
Saint Helena 9,827 ....J5
Saint James 21,495 ....L3
Saint John the Baptist
   31,924 ....M3
Saint Landry 84,128 ....F5
Saint Martin 40,214 ....G6
Saint Mary 64,253 ....H7
Saint Tammany 110,869 ......L6
Tangipahoa 80,698 ....K5
Tensas 8,525 ....H2
Terrebonne 94,393 ....J8
Union 21,167 ....F1
Vermilion 48,458 ....F7
Vernon 53,475 ....D4
Washington 44,207 ....K5
Webster 43,631 ....D1
West Baton Rouge 19,086 ....H6
West Carroll 12,922 ....H1
West Feliciana 12,186 ......H5
Winn 17,253 ....E3

CITIES and TOWNS

Abbeville▲ 11,187 ....F7
Abita Springs 1,296 ....L6
Acme 235 ....G4
Acy 570 ....L3
Addis 1,222 ....J2
Adeline 200 ....G7

Akers 150 ....N2
Albany 645 ....M1
Alberta 150 ....D2
Alexandria▲ 49,188 ....E4
Allen 175 ....D3
Alto 132 ....G2
Alton 500 ....L6
Amelia 2,447 ....H7
Amite▲ 4,301 ....K5
Anacoco 823 ....D4
Anandale F4
Andrew 100 ....F6
Angie 235 ....L5
Angola 600 ....G5
Ansley 100 ....E2
Arabi 8,787 ....P4
Arbroth 250 ....E1
Arcadia▲ 3,079 ....E1
Archibald 425 ....G3
Archie 280 ....K5
Arcola 200 ....G6
Arnaudville 1,444 ....G6
Ashland 289 ....D2
Athens 278 ....E1
Atlanta 118 ....E3
Avery Island 500 ....G7
Bains 400 ....H5
Baker 13,233 ....K1
Baldwin 2,379 ....H7
Ball 3,305 ....F4
Bancroft 114 ....D5
Baptist 150 ....M1
Barataria 1,160 ....L7
Basile 1,808 ....E5
Baskin 243 ....G2
Bastrop▲ 13,916 ....G1
Batchelor 500 ....G5
Baton Rouge (cap.)▲ 219,531 .K2
Bayou Barbary 200 ....M2
Bayou Cane 15,876 ....J7
Bayou Goula 850 ....J3
Bayou Vista 4,733 ....H7
Baywood 100 ....K1
Beaver 350 ....E5
Beekman 150 ....G1
Bel 150 ....D6
Belcher 249 ....C1
Bell City 400 ....D6
Belle Alliance H6
Belle Chasse 8,512 ....O4
Belle D'Eau 120 ....H6
Belle Rose 900 ....K3
Bellwood 150 ....D3
Belmont 350 ....C3
Benson 200 ....C3
Bentley 120 ....E3
Benton▲ 2,047 ....C1
Bernice 1,543 ....E1
Bertrandville 175 ....L7
Berwick 4,375 ....H7
Bethany 300 ....B2
Bethany D2
Bienville 316 ....C1
Blanchard 1,175 ....C1
Bogalusa 14,280 ....L5
Bolinger 200 ....G1
Bonita 265 ....G1
Boothville 300 ....M8
Bordelonville 350 ....G4
Bosco 480 ....F2
Bossier City 52,721 ....C1
Boudreaux 275 ....J8
Bourg 2,073 ....J7
Boutte 2,702 ....N4
Boyce 1,361 ....E4
Braithwaite 350 ....P4
Branch 200 ....F6

Breaux Bridge 6,515 ....G6
Brittany 475 ....L3
Broussard 3,213 ....G6
Brusly 1,824 ....J2
Bryceland 103 ....E2
Buckeye 280 ....E4
Bunkie 5,044 ....F5
Buras (Buras-Triumph) 4,137 .L8
Burnside 500 ....L3
Bush 275 ....L5
Cade 175 ....G6
Calcasieu 400 ....D6
Calhoun 200 ....F2
Calumet 100 ....H7
Calvin 207 ....E3
Cameron▲ 2,041 ....D7
Campti 929 ....D3
Cankton 325 ....F6
Carencro 5,429 ....G6
Carlisle 975 ....L7
Carville 1,108 ....K3
Castor 196 ....D2
Cecelia 550 ....G6
Center Point 850 ....F4
Centerville 600 ....H7
Central 546 ....L3
Chacahoula 150 ....J7
Chalmette▲ 31,860 ....P4
Charenton 1,584 ....H7
Chase 200 ....G2
Chataignier 281 ....F5
Chatham 557 ....F2
Chauvin 3,375 ....J8
Cheneyville 1,005 ....F4
Chopin 175 ....E4
Choudrant 557 ....F1
Church Point 4,677 ....F6
Clarence 577 ....E3
Clarks 650 ....F2
Clay 400 ....H3
Clayton 917 ....H3
Clear Lake 100 ....E3
Clinton▲ 1,904 ....J5
Clio 125 ....M2
Cloutierville 100 ....E3
Colfax▲ 1,696 ....E3
Collinston 375 ....G1
Columbia▲ 386 ....F2
Convent▲ 400 ....L3
Converse 350 ....C3
Corey 110 ....F2
Cotton Valley 1,130 ....D1
Cottonport 2,600 ....F5
Couchwood 150 ....D1
Coushatta▲ 1,845 ....D2
Covington▲ 7,691 ....K5
Cow Island 200 ....F7
Cravens 200 ....E5
Creole 175 ....D7
Crescent 300 ....J2
Creston 135 ....E3
Crowley▲ 13,983 ....F6
Crowville 400 ....G2
Cullen 1,642 ....D1
Curtis 110 ....C2
Cut Off 5,325 ....K7
Dalcour 275 ....P4
Danville 100 ....E2
Darrow 500 ....K3
Davant 600 ....L7
De Quincy 3,474 ....D6
De Ridder▲ 9,868 ....D5
Deerford 100 ....K1
Delcambre 1,978 ....G7
Delhi 3,169 ....H2
Delta 234 ....J2

Denham Springs 8,381 ....L2
Des Allemands 2,504 ....N4
Destrehan 8,031 ....N4
Deville 1,113 ....F4
Diamond 370 ....L7
Dixie 330 ....C1
Dixie Inn 347 ....D1
Dodson 350 ....E2
Donaldsonville▲ 7,949 ....K3
Donner 500 ....J7
Downsville 101 ....F1
Doyline 884 ....D1
Dry Creek 300 ....D5
Dry Prong 380 ....E3
Dubach 843 ....E1
Dubberly 253 ....D1
Dulac 3,273 ....J8
Dunn 225 ....G2
Duplessis 500 ....K2
Duson 1,465 ....F6
East Hodge 421 ....E2
East Point 100 ....D2
Easton 365 ....F5
Echo 525 ....F4
Edgard▲ 2,753 ....M3
Edgefield 207 ....D2
Edgerly 250 ....C6
Effie 300 ....F4
Elizabeth 414 ....E5
Elm Grove 100 ....C2
Elm Park 200 ....H5
Elmer 200 ....E4
Elton 1,277 ....E6
Empire 2,654 ....L8
Enterprise 375 ....G3
Epps 541 ....G1
Erath 2,428 ....F7
Eros 177 ....F2
Erwinville 790 ....H5
Esther 745 ....F7
Estherwood 745 ....F6
Ethel 250 ....H5
Eunice 11,162 ....F6
Eva 100 ....G4
Evangeline 400 ....F6
Evans 500 ....D5
Evergreen 283 ....G3
Extension 950 ....G3
Fairbanks 300 ....F1
Farmerville▲ 3,334 ....F1
Fenton 365 ....E6
Ferriday 4,111 ....G3
Fields 125 ....D5
Fisher 277 ....D4
Flatwoods 360 ....E4
Flora 300 ....D3
Florien 626 ....D4
Fluker 400 ....K5
Folsom 469 ....L5
Forbing 100 ....C2
Fordoche 869 ....H5
Forest 263 ....G1
Forest Hill 408 ....E4
Fort Jesup 100 ....D3
Fort Necessity 150 ....G2
Franklin▲ 9,004 ....G7
Franklinton▲ 4,007 ....K5
French Settlement 829 ......L3
Frierson 700 ....C2
Frost 500 ....L2
Fryeburg 150 ....D2
Fullerton 120 ....D4
Galliano 4,294 ....K8
Galvez 200 ....L2
Garden City 225 ....H7
Garyville 3,181 ....M3

(continued)

Louisiana

SCALE
0 5 10   20   30   40 MI.
0 5 10 20 30 40 KM.

State Capitals ....⊛
Parish Seats ....◉
Canals ....
Major Limited Access Hwys. ▬▬▬

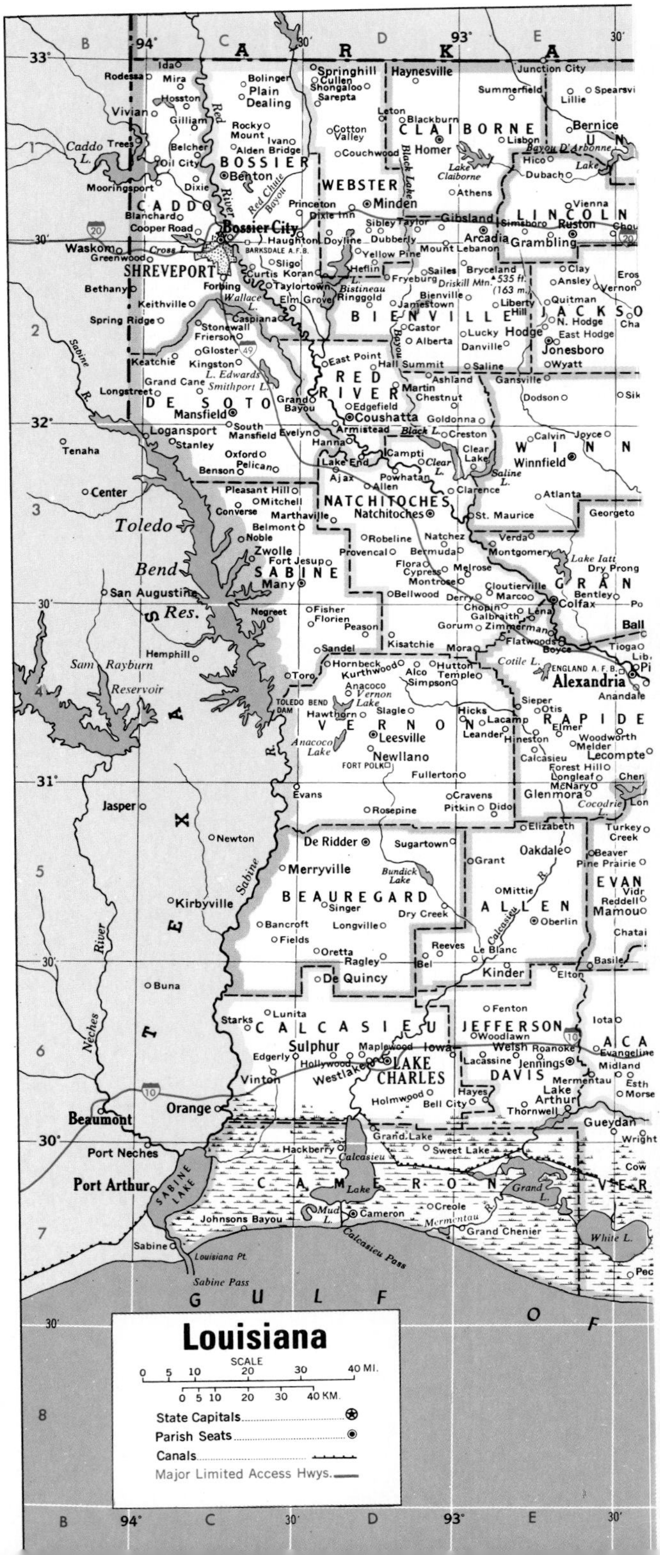

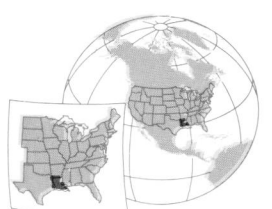

AREA 47,752 sq. mi. (123,678 sq. km.)
POPULATION 4,238,216
CAPITAL Baton Rouge
LARGEST CITY New Orleans
HIGHEST POINT Driskill Mtn. 535 ft. (163 m.)
SETTLED IN 1699
ADMITTED TO UNION April 30, 1812
POPULAR NAME Pelican State
STATE FLOWER Magnolia
STATE BIRD Eastern Brown Pelican

New Orleans, Baton Rouge and Vicinity

Longitude 91° West of Greenwich

© Copyright HAMMOND INCORPORATED, Maplewood, N.J.

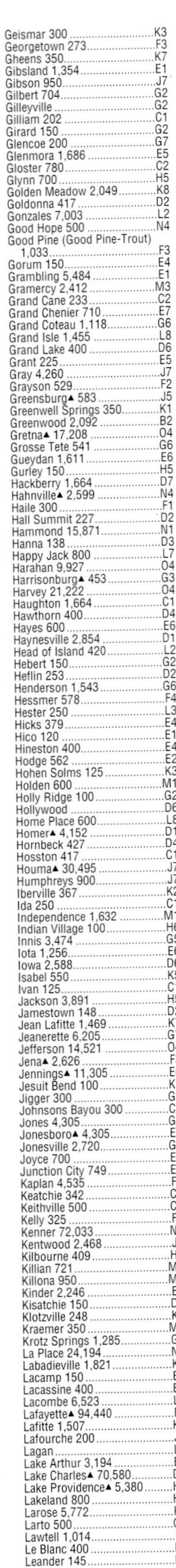

Geismar 300 K3
Georgetown 273 F3
Gheens 350 K7
Gibsland 1,354 E1
Gibson 950 J7
Gilbert 704 G2
Gilleyville G2
Gilliam 202 C1
Girard 150 G2
Glencoe 200 G7
Glenmora 1,686 E5
Gloster 780 C2
Glynn 700 H5
Golden Meadow 2,049 K8
Goldonna 417 D2
Gonzales 7,003 L2
Good Hope 500 N4
Good Pine (Good Pine-Trout) 1,033 F3
Gorum 150 E4
Grambling 5,484 E1
Gramercy 2,412 M3
Grand Cane 233 C2
Grand Chenier 710 E7
Grand Coteau 1,118 G6
Grand Isle 1,455 L8
Grand Lake 400 D6
Grant 225 E5
Gray 4,260 J7
Grayson 529 F2
Greensburg▲ 583 J5
Greenwell Springs 350 K1
Greenwood 2,092 B2
Gretna▲ 17,208 O4
Grosse Tete 541 G6
Gueydan 1,611 E6
Gurley 150 H5
Hackberry 1,664 D7
Hahnville▲ 2,599 N4
Haile 300 F1
Hall Summit 227 D2
Hammond 15,871 N1
Hanna 138 D3
Happy Jack 800 L7
Harahan 9,927 O4
Harrisonburg▲ 453 G3
Harvey 21,222 O4
Haughton 1,664 C1
Hawthorn 400 D4
Hayes 600 E6
Haynesville 2,854 D1
Head of Island 420 L2
Hebert 150 G2
Heflin 253 D2
Henderson 1,543 G6
Hessmer 578 F4
Hester 250 L3
Hicks 379 E4
Hico 120 E1
Hineston 400 E4
Hodge 562 E2
Hohen Solms 125 K3
Holden 600 M1
Holly Ridge 100 G2
Hollywood D6
Home Place 600 L8
Homer▲ 4,152 D1
Hornbeck 427 D4
Hosston 417 C1
Houma▲ 30,495 J7
Humphreys 900 J7
Iberville 367 K2
Ida 250 C1
Independence 1,632 M1
Indian Village 100 H6
Innis 3,474 G5
Iota 1,256 E6
Iowa 2,588 D6
Isabel 550 K5
Ivan 125 C1
Jackson 3,891 H5
Jamestown 148 D2
Jean Lafitte 1,469 K7
Jeanerette 6,205 G7
Jefferson 14,521 O4
Jena▲ 2,626 F3
Jennings▲ 11,305 E6
Jesuit Bend 100 K7
Jigger 300 G2
Johnsons Bayou 300 C7
Jones 4,305 G1
Jonesboro▲ 4,305 E2
Jonesville 2,720 G3
Joyce 700 E3
Junction City 749 E1
Kaplan 4,535 F6
Keatchie 342 C2
Keithville 500 C2
Kelly 325 F3
Kenner 72,033 N4
Kentwood 2,468 J5
Kilbourne 409 H1
Killian 721 M2
Killona 950 M4
Kinder 2,246 E6
Kisatchie 150 D4
Klotzville 248 K3
Kraemer 350 M4
Krotz Springs 1,285 G5
La Place 24,194 N3
Labadieville 1,821 K4
Lacamp 150 E4
Lacassine 400 E6
Lacombe 6,523 L6
Lafayette▲ 94,440 F6
Lafitte 1,507 K7
Lafourche 200 J7
Lagan L7
Lake Arthur 3,194 E6
Lake Charles▲ 70,580 D6
Lake Providence▲ 5,380 H1
Lakeland 800 H5
Larose 5,772 H7
Larto 500 G4
Lawtell 1,014 F5
Le Blanc 400 E5
Leander 145 E4

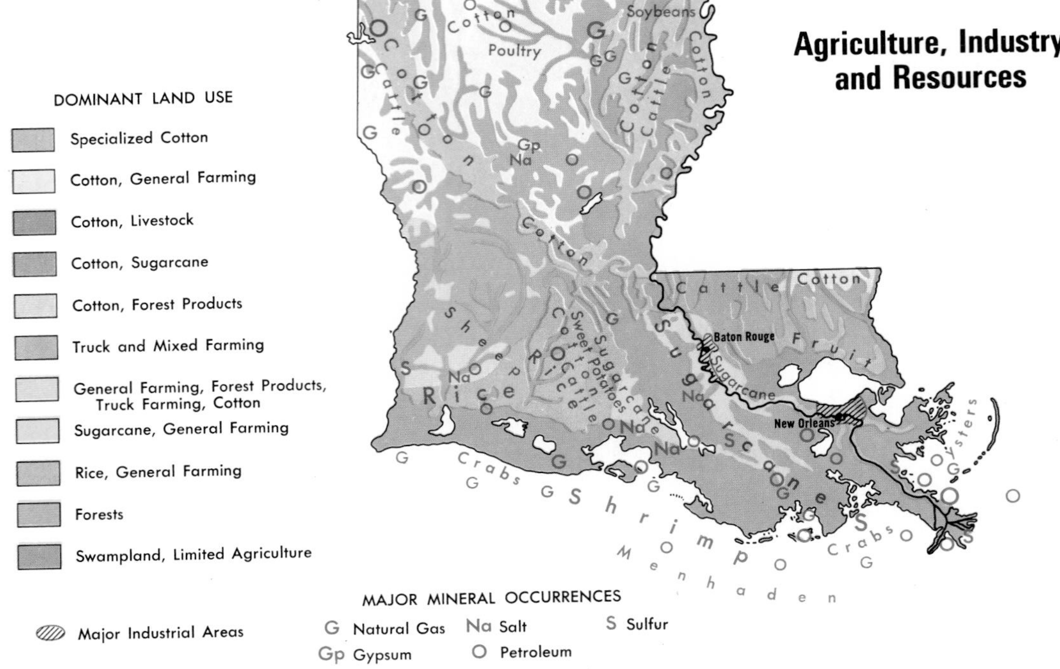
Agriculture, Industry and Resources
DOMINANT LAND USE
Specialized Cotton
Cotton, General Farming
Cotton, Livestock
Cotton, Sugarcane
Cotton, Forest Products
Truck and Mixed Farming
General Farming, Forest Products, Truck Farming, Cotton
Sugarcane, General Farming
Rice, General Farming
Forests
Swampland, Limited Agriculture
Major Industrial Areas
MAJOR MINERAL OCCURRENCES
G Natural Gas
Na Salt
S Sulfur
Gp Gypsum
O Petroleum
Soybeans
Cotton
Poultry
Cattle
Sheep
Rice
Sweet Potatoes
Sugarcane
Fruit
Baton Rouge
New Orleans
Oysters
Crabs
Shrimp
Menhaden

Lebeau 200 F5
Lecompte 1,661 F4
Leesville▲ 7,638 D4
Lena 300 E4
Leonville 825 G6
Leton 125 D1
Lettsworth 200 G5
Lewisburg 265 F6
Libuse 500 F4
Lillie 145 E1
Linville 150 F1
Lisbon 160 E1
Lismore 380 G3
Little Farms N4
Livingston▲ 999 L1
Livonia 970 G5
Lobdell 200 J1
Lockport 2,503 K7
Logansport 1,390 C3
Lonepine 850 F5
Longstreet 189 B2
Longville 300 D5
Loranger 250 N1
Loreauville 860 G6
Lottie 400 G5
Lucky 342 E2
Lucy 825 M3
Luling 2,803 N4
Lunita 100 C6
Lutcher 3,907 L3
Madisonville 659 K6
Mamou 3,483 F5
Mandeville 7,083 L6
Mangham 598 G2
Mansfield▲ 5,389 C2
Mansura 1,601 G4
Many▲ 3,112 C3
Maplewood D6
Maringouin 1,149 G6
Marion 775 F1
Marksville▲ 5,526 G4
Marrero 36,671 O4
Marthaville 150 D3
Martin 545 D2
Mathews 3,009 J7
Maurepas 200 M2
Maurice 432 F6
Mayna 122 G4
McCall 150 K3
McNary 248 E5
Melder 150 E4
Melrose 500 E3
Melville 1,562 G5
Mer Rouge 586 G1
Mermentau 760 E6
Merryville 1,235 D5
Metairie 149,428 O4
Midland 560 F6
Milton 450 F6
Mimosa Park 4,516 N4
Minden▲ 13,661 D1
Mira 354 C1
Mitchell 155 C3
Mix 150 G5
Modeste 225 K3
Monroe▲ 54,909 F1
Montegut 1,784 J8
Monterey 800 G4
Montgomery 645 E3
Montpelier 247 M1
Montz 200 M3

Mooringsport 873 B1
Mora 427 E4
Moreauville 919 G4
Morgan City 14,531 H7
Morganza 759 G5
Morrow 600 F5
Morse 782 F6
Mound 16 H2
Mount Airy 700 M3
Mount Hermon 170 K5
Mount Lebanon 102 D2
Myrtle Grove 100 K7
Nairn 500 L8
Napoleonville▲ 802 K4
Natalbany 1,289 N1
Natchez 434 D3
Natchitoches▲ 16,609 D3
Nebo 200 F3
Negreet 400 C4
New Era 200 G4
New Iberia▲ 31,828 G6
New Orleans▲ 496,938 O4
New Roads▲ 5,303 G5
New Sarpy 2,946 N4
Newellton 1,576 H2
Newllano 2,660 D4
Noble 225 C3
Norco 3,385 N3
North Hodge 477 E2
Norwood 317 H5
Oak Grove▲ 2,126 H1
Oak Ridge 174 G1
Oakdale 6,832 E5
Oberlin▲ 1,808 E5
Odenburg 175 G5
Oil City 1,282 C1
Olivier 300 G7
Olla 1,410 F3
Opelousas▲ 18,151 G5
Oretta 110 D5
Oscar 650 H5
Otis 400 E4
Oxford 125 C3
Paincourtville 1,550 K3
Palmetto 229 G5
Paradis 750 M4
Parhams 100 G4
Parks 400 G6
Patoutville 230 G7
Patterson 4,736 H7
Paulina 500 L3
Pearl River 1,507 L6
Peason 120 D4
Pecan Island 480 F7
Pelican 250 C3
Perry 230 F7
Perryville 100 G1
Phoenix 525 L7
Pilottown 175 M8
Pine Grove 570 J5
Pine Prairie 713 E5
Pineville 12,251 F4
Pioneer 116 H1
Pitkin 600 E5
Plain Dealing 1,074 C1
Plaquemine▲ 7,186 J2
Plattenville 205 K4
Plaucheville 187 G5
Pleasant Hill 824 C3
Pointe a la Hache▲ 750 L7
Pollock 330 F3

Ponchatoula 5,425 N2
Port Allen▲ 6,277 J2
Port Barre 2,144 G5
Port Hudson 200 J1
Port Sulphur 3,523 L8
Port Vincent 446 L2
Powhatan 147 D3
Prairieville 500 K2
Pride 100 K1
Princeton 350 C1
Provencal 538 D3
Quitman 162 E2
Raceland 5,564 J7
Rayne 8,502 F6
Rayville▲ 4,411 G2
Reddell 500 F5
Reeves 188 D5
Reggio 400 L7
Remy 850 L3
Reserve 8,847 M3
Richmond 447 H2
Richwood 1,253 F2
Ridgecrest 804 G3
Ringgold 1,655 D2
Rio 400 L5
Roanoke 800 E6
Robeline 149 D3
Robert 600 N1
Rocky Mount 150 C1
Rodessa 294 B1
Rogers 150 F3
Romeville 133 L3
Rosa 300 G5
Rosedale 807 G6
Roseland 1,093 J5
Rosepine 1,135 D5
Ruby 400 F4
Ruston▲ 20,027 E1
Saint Amant 900 L2
Saint Benedict 190 K5
Saint Bernard 750 L7
Saint Francisville▲ 1,700 H5
Saint Gabriel 975 K2
Saint James 600 L3
Saint Joseph▲ 1,517 H3
Saint Landry 550 F5
Saint Martinville▲ 7,137 G6
Saint Maurice 560 E3
Saint Rose 6,259 N4
Saint Tammany 150 L6
Saline 272 E2
Samtown F4
Sarepta 886 D1
Schriever 4,958 J7
Scotlandville 15,113 J1
Scott 4,912 F6
Seymourville 2,891 J2
Shongaloo 161 D1
Shreveport▲ 198,525 C2
Sibley 997 D1
Sicily Island 421 G3
Sieper 226 E4
Sikes 120 F2
Simmesport 2,092 G5
Simpson 536 D4
Simsboro 634 E1
Singer 250 D5
Slagle 650 D4
Slaughter 827 H5
Slidell 24,124 L6
Smoke Bend 300 K3

Sondheimer 225 H1
Sorrento 1,119 L3
South Mansfield 407 C3
Spearsville 132 E1
Springfield 439 M2
Springhill 5,668 D1
Standard 190 F3
Stanley 131 C3
Starks 750 C6
Start 200 G2
Sterlington 1,140 F1
Stonewall 1,266 C2
Sugartown 375 D5
Sulphur 20,125 D6
Summerfield 170 E1
Sun 429 L5
Sunset 2,201 F6
Sunshine 900 K2
Supreme 1,020 K4
Swartz 3,698 G1
Sweet Lake 300 D7
Talisheek 315 L5
Tallulah▲ 8,526 H2
Tangipahoa 569 J5
Taylor 500 D1
Taylortown 150 C2
Temple 250 E4
Tendal 200 H2
Terry Town 23,548 O4
Theriot 450 J8
Thibodaux▲ 14,035 J7
Tickfaw 565 M1
Tioga 457 F4
Toro 100 C4
Transylvania 400 H1
Trees 327 B1
Triumph (Triumph-Buras) 4,137 L8
Trout (Trout-Good Pine) 1,033 F3
Tullos 427 F3
Tunica 500 G5
Turkey Creek 283 F5
Union 665 L3
Urania 782 F3
Vacherie 2,169 L3
Valverda 200 G5
Varnado 236 L5
Venice 900 M8
Vernon 150 E2
Vick 500 F4
Vidalia▲ 4,953 G3
Vienna 404 E1
Ville Platte▲ 9,037 F5
Vinton 3,154 C6
Violet 8,574 P4
Vivian 4,156 B1
Wadesboro 125 M2
Wakefield 400 H5
Walker 3,727 L1
Wallace 200 M3
Walters 500 G3
Warden 130 H1
Wardville F4
Washington 1,253 G5
Waterproof 1,080 H3
Watson 800 L1
Waverly 350 H2
Weeks 400 G7
Welcome 450 L3
Welsh 3,299 E6
West Monroe 14,096 F1

West Pointe a la Hache 250 L7
Westlake 5,007 D6
Westwego 11,218 O4
Weyanoke 500 H5
White Castle 2,102 J3
Whitehall 380 M2
Whiteville 150 F5
Wildsville 800 G3
Wills Point 150 L7
Wilson 707 H5
Winnfield▲ 6,138 E3
Winnsboro▲ 5,755 G2
Wisner 1,153 G3
Woodhaven M1
Woodlawn 150 E6
Woodworth 754 E4
Youngsville 1,195 G6
Zachary 9,036 K1
Zwolle 1,779 C3

OTHER FEATURES

Allemands (lake) M4
Alligator (pt.) L6
Amite (riv.) L2
Anacoco (lake) D4
Atchafalaya (bay) H8
Atchafalaya (riv.) G6
Barataria (bay) L8
Barataria (passage) L8
Barksdale A.F.B. C2
Bayou D'Arbonne (lake) E1
Bird (isl.) M8
Bistineau (lake) D2
Black (lake) D3
Black Lake (bayou) D1
Boeuf (lake) J7
Boeuf (riv.) G1
Bonnet Carré Spillway and Floodway N3
Borgne (lake) L7
Boudreau (bay) M7
Boudreaux (lake) J8
Breton (isl.) M8
Breton (sound) M7
Bundick (lake) D5
Caddo (lake) B1
Caillou (bay) J8
Calcasieu (lake) D7
Calcasieu (passage) D7
Calcasieu (riv.) E5
Catahoula (lake) F4
Cataouatche (lake) N4
Cat Island (chan.) M6
Cat Island (passage) J8
Chandeleur (isls.) N7
Chandeleur (sound) M7
Chenier (lake) F2
Chicot (pt.) M7
Claiborne (lake) E1
Clear (lake) D3
Cocodrie (lake) E5
Cotile (lake) E4
Cross (lake) C2
Curlew (isls.) M7
Dernieres (isls.) J8
Door (pt.) M6
Driskill (mt.) E2
Drum (bay) M7
East (bay) M8
East Cote Blanche (bay) G7
Edwards (lake) C2
Eloi (bay) M7
England A.F.B. E4
Fields (lake) J7
Fort Polk 14,730 D4
Free Mason (isls.) M7
Garden Island (bay) M8
Grand (lake) E7
Grand (lake) H7
Grand Terre (isls.) L8
Iatt (lake) E3
Jean Lafitte Nat'l Hist. Park P4
Lafourche (bayou) K8
Little (riv.) F3
Louisiana (pt.) C7
Macon (bayou) H1
Main (passage) M8
Manchac (passage) N2
Marsh (isl.) G7
Maurepas (lake) M2
Mermentau (riv.) E7
Mexico (gulf) F8
Mississippi (delta) M8
Mississippi (riv.) H3
Mississippi (sound) M6
Mississippi River Gulf Outlet (canal) L7
Mozambique (pt.) M7
Mud (lake) D7
Naval Air Sta. O4
North (isls.) M7
North (pass) N8
North (pt.) M7
Northeast (pass) M8
Ouachita (riv.) F1
Palourde (lake) H7
Pearl (riv.) L5
Point au Fer (isl.) H8
Point au Fer (pt.) H8
Pontchartrain (lake) O3
Pontchartrain Causeway O3
Poverty Pt. Nat'l Mon H1
Raccoon (pt.) H8
Red (riv.) G4
Sabine (lake) C7
Sabine (passage) C7
Sabine (riv.) C5
Saline (lake) E3
Salvador (lake) K7
Smithport (lake) C2
South (pass) M8
South (pt.) G8
Southeast (pass) M8
Southwest (pass) L8
Tangipahoa (riv.) N1
Tensas (riv.) G3
Terrebonne (bay) J8
Tickfaw (riv.) M1
Timbalier (bay) K8
Timbalier (isl.) K8
Toledo Bend (res.) C3
Turkey Creek (lake) G3
Vermilion (bay) F7
Vernon (lake) D4
Verret (lake) H7
Wallace (lake) C2
West (bay) M8
West Cote Blanche (bay) G7
White (lake) E7

▲ Parish seat

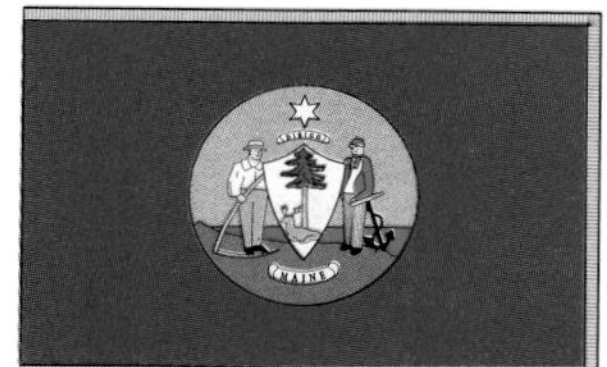

AREA 33,265 sq. mi. (86,156 sq. km.)
POPULATION 1,233,223
CAPITAL Augusta
LARGEST CITY Portland
HIGHEST POINT Katahdin 5,268 ft. (1606 m.)
SETTLED IN 1624
ADMITTED TO UNION March 15, 1820
POPULAR NAME Pine Tree State
STATE FLOWER White Pine Cone & Tassel
STATE BIRD Chickadee

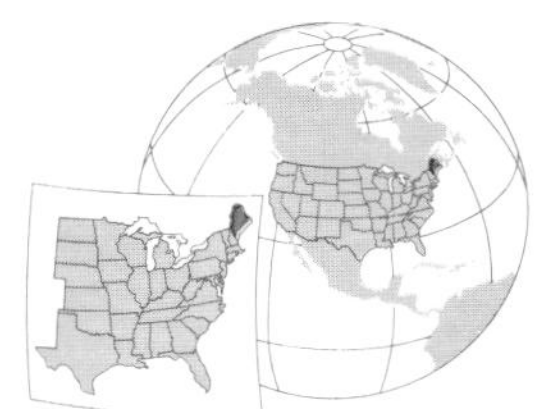

COUNTIES

Androscoggin 105,259 C7
Aroostook 86,936 F2
Cumberland 243,135 C8
Franklin 29,008 B5
Hancock 46,948 G6
Kennebec 115,904 D7
Knox 36,310 E7
Lincoln 30,357 D7
Oxford 52,602 B7
Penobscot 146,601 F5
Piscataquis 18,653 E4
Sagadahoc 33,535 D7
Somerset 49,767 C4
Waldo 33,018 E6
Washington 35,308 H6
York 164,587 B9

CITIES and TOWNS

Abbot Village• 576 D5
Acton 850 B8
Acton• 1,727 B8
Addison 350 H6
Addison• 1,114 H6
Albion• 1,736 E6
Alexander• 478 H5
Alfred 1,890 B9
Alfred• 2,238 B9
Allagash• 359 F1
Alna• 571 D7
Alton• 771 F5
Amherst• 226 G6
Andover 350 B6
Andover• 953 B6
Anson 950 D6
Anson• 2,382 D6
Appleton• 1,069 E7
Argyle 202 F5
Ashland 750 G2
Ashland• 1,542 G2
Athens 300 D6
Athens• 897 D6
Atkinson• 332 E5
Auburn▲ 24,309 C7
Augusta (cap.)▲ 21,325 D7
Aurora• 82 G6
Bailey Island 500 D8
Bancroft H4
Bancroft• 66 H4
Bangor▲ 33,181 F6
Bar Harbor 2,685 G7
Bar Harbor• 2,768 G7
Bar Mills 800 C8
Baring 235 J5
Baring• 275 J5
Bass Harbor 450 G7
Bath▲ 9,799 D8
Bayside F7
Beals• 667 H7
Beddington• 43 H6
Belfast▲ 6,355 F7
Belgrade 950 D7
Belgrade• 2,375 D7
Belgrade Lakes 700 D6
Belmont• 652 E7
Benedicta• 225 G4
Benton• 2,312 D6
Berwick 2,378 B9
Berwick• 5,995 B9
Bethel 750 B7
Bethel• 2,329 B7
Biddeford 20,710 B9
Biddeford Pool 500 C9
Bingham 1,074 D5
Bingham• 1,071 D5
Birch Harbor 300 H7
Blaine-Mars Hill 1,921 H2
Blaine• 784 H2
Blanchard 78 D5
Blue Hill 850 F7
Blue Hill• 1,941 F7
Bolsters Mills 150 B7
Boothbay 200 D8
Boothbay• 2,648 D8
Boothbay Harbor 1,267 D8
Bowdoinham• 2,192 D7
Bowerbank• 72 E5
Bradford 150 F5
Bradford• 1,103 F5
Bradley• 1,136 F6
Brewer 9,021 F6
Bridgewater• 647 H3
Bridgton 1,639 B7
Bridgton• 2,195 B7
Brighton• 94 D5
Bristol 450 D8
Bristol• 2,326 D8
Brooklin• 785 F7
Brooks 900 E6
Brooksville• 760 F7
Brookton 175 H4
Brownfield 300 B8
Brownfield• 1,034 B8
Brownville 600 E5
Brownville• 1,506 E5
Brownville Junction 950 E5
Brunswick 10,990 C8
Brunswick• 14,683 C8
Bryant Pond 600 B7
Buckfield• 1,566 C7
Bucks Harbor 300 J6
Bucksport 2,853 F6
Bucksport• 2,989 F6
Burlington• 360 G5
Burnham• 961 E6
Buxton• 6,494 C8
Byron• 111 B6
Calais 3,963 J5
Cambridge• 490 E5
Camden 3,743 F7
Camden• 4,022 F7
Canaan• 1,636 D6
Canton• 951 C7
Cape Neddick 2,193 B9
Cape Porpoise 500 C9
Caratunk 98 C5
Cardville 223 F5
Caribou 9,415 G2
Carmel• 1,906 E6
Carrabassett Valley• 325 C5
Carroll• 185 G5
Carthage• 458 C6
Cary• 235 H4
Casco 400 B7
Casco• 3,018 B7
Castine• 1,161 F7
Centerville• 30 H6
Chapman• 422 G2
Charleston• 1,187 F5
Charlotte• 271 J5
Chebeague Island 900 C8
Chelsea• 2,497 D7
Cherryfield• 1,183 H6
Chester• 442 F5
Chesterville• 1,012 C6
China 2,918 E7
China• 3,713 E7
Chisholm 1,653 C7
Clifton• 607 G6
Clinton 1,305 D6
Clinton• 1,485 D6
Columbia• 437 H6
Columbia Falls• 552 H6
Cooper• 124 H6
Coopers Mills 200 E7
Corea 375 H7
Corinna• 2,196 E6
Cornish• 1,178 B8
Cornville• 1,008 D6
Costigan 200 F5
Cranberry Isles• 189 G7
Crawford• 89 H5
Crescent Lake 325 C7
Criehaven F8
Crouseville 450 G2
Crystal• 303 G4
Cumberland Center 2,015 C8
Cumberland Center• 1,890 C8
Cundys Harbor 150 D8
Cushing• 988 E7
Cutler 400 J6
Cutler• 779 J6
Damariscotta• 1,811 E7
Damariscotta-Newcastle 1,567 E7
Danforth 650 H4
Danforth• 710 H4
Deblois• 73 H6
Dedham• 1,229 F6
Deer Isle 600 F7
Deer Isle• 1,829 F7
Denmark• 855 B8
Dennysville• 355 J6
Derby 300 E5
Detroit• 751 E6
Dexter 3,118 E5
Dexter• 2,650 E5
Dixfield 1,725 C6
Dixfield• 1,300 C6
Dixmont• 1,007 E6
Dover-Foxcroft▲ 2,974 E5
Dover-Foxcroft• 3,077 E5
Dresden• 1,332 D7
Dry Mills 700 C8
Dryden 675 C6
Dyer Brook• 243 G3
Eagle Lake 675 F1
Eagle Lake• 942 F1
East Andover 250 B6
East Baldwin 175 B8
East Blue Hill 150 G7
East Boothbay 800 D8
East Corinth 525 F5
East Dixfield 250 C6
East Eddington 200 F6
East Hiram 198 B8
East Holden 600 F6
East Lebanon 950 B9
East Limington 200 B8
East Livermore 500 C7
East Machias 850 J6
East Machias• 1,218 J6
East Madison 400 D6
East Millinocket 2,361 F4
East Millinocket• 2,075 F4
East Parsonfield 400 B8
East Peru 200 C7
East Poland 200 C7
East Stoneham 300 B7
East Sullivan 496 G6
East Vassalboro 300 D7
East Waterboro 365 B8
East Wilton 650 C6
Easton• 1,291 H2
Eastport 1,965 K6
Eddington 250 F6
Eddington• 1,947 F6
Edgecomb• 993 D8
Edmunds 430 J6
Eliot• 5,329 B9
Ellsworth▲ 5,975 F6
Enfield 150 F5
Enfield• 1,476 F5
Etna• 977 E6
Eustis• 616 B5
Exeter• 937 E6
Fairbanks 400 C6
Fairfield 3,169 D6
Fairfield Center 975 D6
Fairfield• 2,794 D6
Falmouth 1,655 C8
Falmouth• 7,610 C8
Farmingdale 2,014 D7
Farmingdale• 2,070 D7
Farmington▲ 3,583 C6
Farmington• 4,197 C6
Farmington Falls 500 C6
Fayette• 855 C7
Five Islands 225 D8
Fort Fairfield 2,282 H2
Fort Fairfield• 1,729 H2
Fort Kent 2,375 F1
Fort Kent• 2,123 F1
Fort Kent Mills 200 F1
Foxcroft 2,974 E5
Frankfort• 1,020 F6
Franklin 350 G6
Franklin• 1,141 G6
Freedom• 593 E6
Freeport 1,906 C8
Freeport• 1,829 C8
Frenchboro• 44 G7
Frenchville 980 G1
Frenchville• 1,338 G1
Friendship 700 E7
Friendship• 1,099 E7
Fryeburg 1,644 A7
Fryeburg• 1,580 A7
Gardiner• 6,746 D7
Garland 300 E5
Garland• 1,064 E5
Georgetown 190 D8
Georgetown• 914 D8
Gilead• 204 B7
Glen Cove 250 E7
Glenburn• 3,198 F6
Goodwins Mills 340 B8
Goose Rocks Beach 200 C9
Gorham 4,052 C8
Gorham• 3,618 C8
Gouldsboro 498 H7
Gouldsboro• 1,986 H7
Grand Isle 600 G1
Grand Isle• 558 G1
Grand Lake Stream• 174 H5
Gray 525 C8
Gray• 5,904 C8
Great Pond• 59 G6
Greene• 3,661 C7
Greenville• 1,839 D5
Greenville 1,601 D5
Greenville Junction 650 D5
Guilford 1,235 E5
Guilford• 1,082 E5
Hallowell 2,534 D7
Hamlin• 204 H1
Hampden 3,538 F6
Hampden• 3,895 F6
Hampden Highlands 950 F6
Hancock• 1,757 G6
Hanover• 272 B7
Harmony 450 D6
Harmony• 838 D6
Harpswell• 5,012 D8
Harrington• 893 H6
Harrison• 1,951 B7
Hartford• 722 C7
Hartland 1,041 D6
Hartland• 1,038 D6
Haynesville• 243 G4
Hebron• 878 C7
Hermon• 3,755 F6
Highland Lake 600 C8
Hiram 175 B8
Hiram• 1,260 B8
Hodgdon• 1,257 H3
Hollis Center• 2,892 B8
Hope 175 E7
Hope• 1,017 E7
Houlton▲ 5,730 H3
Houlton• 5,627 H3
Howland 1,502 F5
Howland• 1,304 F5
Hudson• 1,048 F5
Hulls Cove 200 G7
Island Falls• 897 G3
Isle Au Haut• 57 F7
Islesboro 200 F7
Islesboro• 579 F7
Jackman 700 C4
Jackman• 920 C4
Jacksonville 200 J6
Jay 850 C7
Jay• 5,080 C7
Jefferson• 2,111 D7
Jonesboro• 585 J6
Jonesport 1,050 H6
Jonesport• 1,525 H6
Keegan 450 G1
Kenduskeag• 1,234 E6
Kennebunk 3,294 B9
Kennebunk• 4,206 B9
Kennebunk Beach 200 C9
Kennebunkport 1,685 C9
Kennebunkport• 1,100 C9
Kents Hill 300 D7
Kezar Falls 680 B8
Kingfield• 1,114 C6
Kingman 246 G4
Kingsbury• 13 D5
Kittery 5,465 B9
Kittery• 5,151 B9
Kittery Point 1,093 B9
Knox• 681 E6
Lagrange 250 F5
Lagrange• 509 F5
Lake View• 23 F5
Lamoine• 1,311 G7
Lee• 832 G5
Leeds• 1,669 C7
Levant• 1,627 F6
Lewiston 39,757 C7
Liberty 200 E7
Liberty• 790 E7
Lille 300 G1
Limerick• 1,688 B8
Limestone 1,334 H2
Limestone• 1,245 H2
Limington• 2,796 B8
Lincoln 3,524 G5
Lincoln• 3,399 G5
Lincoln Center 325 G5
Lincolnville 800 E7
Lincolnville• 1,809 E7
Lincolnville Center 200 E7
Linneus• 810 H3
Lisbon• 9,457 C7
Lisbon Falls 4,674 D7
Lisbon-Lisbon Center 1,865 C7
Litchfield• 2,650 D7
Little Deer Isle 475 F7
Little Falls-South Windham 1,715 C8
Littleton• 956 H3
Livermore 280 C7
Livermore• 1,950 C7
Livermore Falls 2,441 C7
Livermore Falls• 1,935 C7
Locke Mills 600 B7
Lovell 180 B7
Lovell• 888 B7
Lowell• 267 F5
Lubec 900 K6
Lubec• 1,853 K6
Ludlow• 430 G3
Machias▲ 1,277 J6
Machias• 1,773 J6
Machiasport 374 H6
Machiasport• 1,166 H6
Macwahoc• 114 G4
Madawaska 4,165 G1
Madawaska• 3,653 G1
Madison 2,788 D6
Madison• 2,956 D6
Madrid• 178 B6
Manchester• 2,099 D7
Mapleton• 1,853 G2
Mars Hill• 1,760 H2
Mars Hill-Blaine 1,717 H2
Masardis• 305 G3

(continued on following page)

Agriculture, Industry and Resources

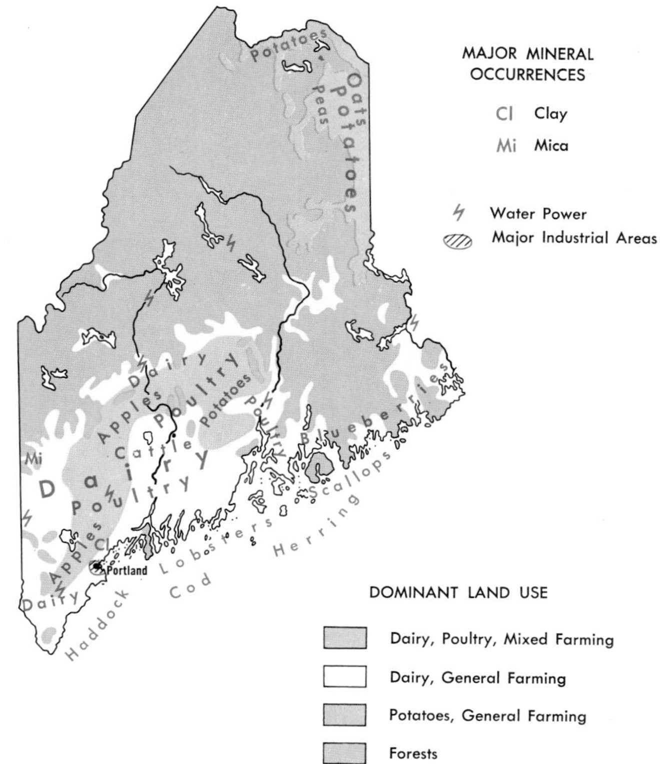
Potatoes
Oats
Peas
Potatoes
Dairy
Poultry
Potatoes
Apples
Cattle
Dairy
Poultry
Blueberries
Scallops
Mi
Cl
Apples
Dairy
Portland
Lobsters
Herring
Cod
Haddock
MAJOR MINERAL OCCURRENCES
Cl Clay
Mi Mica
Water Power
Major Industrial Areas

DOMINANT LAND USE

Dairy, Poultry, Mixed Farming
Dairy, General Farming
Potatoes, General Farming
Forests

(continued)

Matinicus 66 F8
Mattawamkeag• 830 G5
Mechanic Falls 2,198 C7
Mechanic Falls• 2,388 C7
Meddybemps• 133 J5
Medford 194 F5
Medway• 1,922 G4
Mercer• 593 D6
Mexico 3,207 B6
Mexico• 2,302 B6
Milbridge• 1,305 H6
Milford 1,688 F6
Milford• 2,228 F6
Millinocket• 6,922 F4
Milo 2,255 F5
Milo• 2,129 F5
Minot 250 C7
Minot• 1,664 C7
Minturn 150 G7
Monhegan• 88 E8
Monmouth 500 D7
Monmouth• 3,353 C7
Monroe• 802 E6
Monson• 744 E5
Monticello• 872 H3
Montville• 877 E7
Moody 500 B9
Moose River• 233 C4
Morrill• 644 E7
Mount Desert 150 G7
Mount Desert• 1,899 G7
Mount Vernon• 1,362 D7
Naples• 2,860 B8
New Gloucester 400 C8
New Gloucester• 3,916 C8
New Harbor 850 E8
New Limerick• 524 G3
New Portland 300 C6
New Portland• 789 C6
New Sharon• 1,175 C6
New Sweden 175 G2
New Sweden• 715 G2
New Vineyard• 661 C6
Newburgh• 1,317 F6
Newcastle• 1,538 D7
Newcastle-Damariscotta 1,411 E7
Newfield 200 B8
Newfield• 1,042 B8
Newport 1,748 E6
Newport• 1,843 E6
Newry• 316 B6
Nobleboro• 1,455 D7
Norridgewock 1,318 D6
Norridgewock• 1,496 D6
North Anson 950 D6
North Belgrade 300 D7
North Berwick 1,436 B9
North Berwick• 1,568 B9
North Bridgton 300 B7
North Cutler 153 J6
North Fryeburg 250 B7
North Haven 400 F7
North Haven• 332 F7
North Jay 800 C6
North Limington 400 B8
North Livermore 250 C7
North Lubec 250 J6
North New Portland 500 C6
North Penobscot 403 F7
North Raymond 225 C8
North Turner 350 C7
North Vassalboro 950 D7
North Waldoboro 250 E7
North Waterboro 200 B8
North Waterford 390 B7
North Wayne 175 C7
North Whitefield 300 D7
North Windham 4,077 C8
North Yarmouth 500 C8
North Yarmouth• 2,429 C8
Northeast Harbor 800 G7
Northfield• 99 H6
Northport• 1,201 E7
Norway 2,653 B7
Norway• 3,023 B7
Oakfield• 846 G3
Oakland 3,387 D6
Oakland• 3,510 D6
Ocean Park 200 C9
Ogunquit 974 B9
Olamon 150 F5
Old Orchard Beach 6,023 C9
Old Orchard Beach• 7,789 C9
Old Town 8,317 F6
Oquossoc 150 B6
Orient• 157 H4
Orland 200 F6
Orland• 1,805 F6
Orono 9,891 F6
Orono• 9,789 F6
Orrington 250 F6
Orrington• 3,309 F6
Orrs Island 600 D8
Otisfield• 1,136 B7
Otter Creek 260 G7
Owls Head• 1,574 F7
Oxbow• 69 G3
Oxford 550 B7
Oxford• 1,284 B7
Palermo• 1,021 E7
Palmyra• 1,867 E6
Paris• 4,492 B7
Parkman• 790 D5
Passadumkeag• 428 F5
Patten 1,057 F4
Patten• 1,256 F4
Pejepscot 200 D8
Pemaquid 200 E8
Pembroke 300 J6
Pembroke• 852 J6
Penobscot 150 F7
Penobscot• 1,131 F7
Perham• 395 G2
Perry• 758 J6
Peru• 1,541 C6
Phillips• 1,148 C6
Phippsburg 1,527 D8
Phippsburg• 1,815 D8
Pine Point 650 C8
Pittsfield 3,117 E6
Pittsfield• 3,222 E6
Pittston• 2,444 D7
Plymouth• 1,152 E6
Poland 500 C7
Poland• 4,342 C7
Port Clyde 400 E8
Portage• 562 G2
Porter 225 B8
Porter• 1,301 B8
Portland▲ 64,358 C8
Pownal• 1,262 C8
Prentiss• 245 G5
Presque Isle 10,550 H2
Princeton• 973 H5
Prospect• 542 F6
Prospect Harbor 445 H7
Randolph• 1,949 D7
Rangeley 900 B6
Rangeley• 103 B6
Raymond 550 B8
Raymond• 3,311 B8
Readfield 300 D7
Readfield• 2,033 D7
Red Beach 210 J5
Richmond 1,578 D7
Richmond• 1,775 D7
Richmond Corner 200 D7
Ripley• 445 E5
Robbinston 200 J5
Robbinston• 495 J5
Robinsons 160 H3
Rockland▲ 7,972 E7
Rockport 875 E7
Rockport• 2,854 E7
Rockville 250 E7
Rockwood 265 D4
Rome• 758 D6
Roque Bluffs• 234 H6
Round Pond 400 E8
Roxbury• 437 B6
Rumford 6,256 B6
Rumford• 5,419 B6
Rumford Center 325 B7
Rumford Point 320 B6
Sabattus 1,234 C7
Sabattus• 3,696 C7
Saco 15,181 C8
Saint Agatha• 1,035 G1
Saint Albans• 1,400 E6
Saint David 915 G1
Saint Francis• 839 E1
Saint George 700 E7
Saint George• 1,948 E7
Saint John• 322 F1
Sandy Point 350 F7
Sanford 10,268 B9
Sanford• 10,296 B9
Sangerville• 1,398 E5
Scarborough 2,280 C8
Scarborough• 2,586 C8
Seal Cove 215 G7
Seal Harbor 500 G7
Searsmont 400 E7
Searsmont• 938 E7
Searsport 1,348 F7
Searsport• 1,151 F7
Sebago Lake 800 B8
Sebec• 554 E5
Seboeis• 40 F5
Sedgwick• 905 F7
Shapleigh• 1,911 B8
Shawmut 500 D6
Sheepscott 150 D7
Sheridan 300 F2
Sherman 1,021 G4
Sherman• 1,027 G4
Sherman Mills 600 G4
Sherman Station 650 F4
Shirley Mills 242 D5
Shirley Mills• 208 D5
Sidney• 2,593 D7
Sinclair• 264 G1
Skowhegan▲ 6,517 D6
Skowhegan• 6,990 D6
Smithfield• 865 D6
Smyrna Mills• 354 G3
Soldier Pond 500 F1
Solon• 916 D6
Somerville• 458 E7
Somesville (Mount Desert) 150 D7
Sorrento• 295 G7
South Berwick 2,120 B9
South Berwick• 5,877 B9
South Bridgton 373 B8
South Bristol• 825 D8
South Casco 750 B8
South China 225 D7
South Eliot 3,112 B9
South Harpswell 650 C8
South Hiram 350 B8
South Hope 200 E7
South La Grange 150 F5
South Lebanon 200 A9
South Lincoln 150 F5
South Monmouth 400 D7
South Orrington 400 F6
South Paris▲ 2,320 B7
South Penobscot 150 F7
South Portland 23,163 C8
South Sanford 3,929 B9
South Thomaston• 1,227 E7
South Waldoboro 300 E7
South Waterford 300 B7
South Windham (Little Falls-South Windham) C8
Southport 400 D8
Southport• 645 D8
Southwest Harbor 1,052 G7
Southwest Harbor• 1,952 G7
Springfield• 406 G5
Springvale 3,542 B9
Stacyville 155 F4
Stacyville• 480 F4
Standish 700 B8
Standish• 7,678 B8
Starks• 508 D6
Steep Falls 500 B8
Stetson• 847 E6
Steuben 190 H6
Steuben• 1,084 H6
Stillwater 700 F6
Stockholm• 286 G1
Stockton Springs 500 F7
Stockton Springs• 1,383 F7
Stonington• 1,252 F7
Stow• 283 A7
Stratton 600 B5
Strong• 1,217 C6
Sullivan• 1,118 G6
Sumner• 761 C7
Sunset 165 F7
Surry• 1,004 F7
Swans Island• 348 G7
Swanville• 1,130 E6
Sweden• 222 B7
Temple• 560 C6
Tenants Harbor 900 E8
Thomaston 2,348 E7
Thomaston• 2,445 E7
Thorndike• 702 E6
Topsfield• 235 H5
Topsham 4,657 D8
Topsham• 6,147 D8
Tremont 175 G7
Tremont• 1,324 G7
Trenton• 1,060 G7
Trevett 400 D8
Troy• 802 E6
Turner 400 C7
Turner• 4,315 C7
Union 300 E7
Union• 1,989 E7
Unity• 36 E6
Upper Frenchville 405 G1
Upton• 70 B6
Van Buren 3,282 G1
Van Buren• 2,759 G1
Vanceboro• 201 J4
Vassalboro• 3,679 D7
Veazie• 1,633 F6
Vienna• 417 D6
Vinalhaven• 1,072 F7
Waite• 119 H5
Waldo• 626 E7
Waldoboro 1,195 E7
Waldoboro• 1,420 E7
Walnut Hill 400 C8
Waltham• 276 G6
Warren 770 E7
Warren• 3,192 E7
Washburn 1,221 G2
Washburn• 1,880 G2
Washington• 1,185 E7
Waterboro 700 B8
Waterboro• 4,510 B8
Waterford• 1,299 B7
Waterville 17,173 D6
Wayne 175 C7
Wayne• 1,029 D7
Weeks Mills 235 E7
Weld• 430 C6
Wellington• 270 D5
Wells 950 B9
Wells• 7,778 B9
Wells Beach 600 B9
Wesley• 146 H6
West Baldwin 198 B8
West Bath• 1,716 D8
West Bethel 160 B7
West Brooksville 156 F7
West Buxton 185 B8
West Enfield 609 F5
West Farmington 700 C6
West Forks• 63 D5
West Franklin 350 G6
West Gouldsboro 225 G7
West Jonesport 400 H6
West Kennebunk 750 B9
West Lubec 275 J6
West Minot 400 C7
West Newfield 300 B8
West Paris• 1,514 B7
West Peru 700 C7
West Poland 250 C7
West Rockport 350 E7
West Scarborough 500 C8
West Tremont 250 G7
Westbrook 16,121 C8
Westfield• 589 G3
Weston• 207 H4
Whitefield 550 D7
Whitefield• 1,931 D7
Whiting• 407 J6
Whitneyville• 241 H6
Willimantic• 170 E5
Wilton 4,382 C6
Wilton• 2,453 C6
Windsor• 1,895 D7
Winn 250 G5
Winn• 479 G5
Winslow 5,903 D6
Winslow• 5,436 D6
Winter Harbor• 1,157 G7
Winterport 1,126 F6
Winterport• 1,274 F6
Winterville• 217 F2
Winthrop 3,264 C7
Winthrop• 2,819 C7
Wiscasset 975 D7
Wiscasset• 1,233 D7
Woodland• 1,287 H5
Woolwich• 2,570 D8
Wyman Dam 300 D5
Yarmouth 2,981 C8
Yarmouth• 3,338 C8
York 4,530 B9
York Beach 900 B9
York Harbor 2,555 B9
York• 9,818 B9

OTHER FEATURES

Abraham (mt.) C5
Acadia Nat'l Park G7
Allagash (lake) D3
Allagash (riv.) E2
Androscoggin (riv.) C7
Aroostook (riv.) G2
Attean (pond) C4
Baker (lake) D3
Baskahegan (lake) H5
Bear (riv.) B6
Big (brook) E2
Big (lake) H5
Big Black (riv.) D2
Bigelow (bight) C9
Big Spencer (mt.) E4
Black (pond) D3
Blue (mt.) C6
Blue Hill (bay) G7
Bog (lake) H6
Brassua (lake) D4
Casco (bay) C8
Cathance (lake) J6
Caucomgomoc (lake) D3
Center (pond) E5
Chamberlain (lake) E3
Chemquasabamticook (lake) D3
Chesuncook (lake) E3
Chiputneticook (lakes) H4
Clayton (lake) D2
Clifford (lake) H5
Cold Stream (pond) G5
Crawford (lake) H5
Cross (isl.) J6
Cross (lake) G1
Cupsuptic (riv.) B5
Dead (riv.) C5
Deer (isl.) F7
Duck (isls.) G7
Eagle (lake) E3
Eagle (lake) F1
East Machias (riv.) H6
East Musquash (lake) H5
Elizabeth (cape) C8
Ellis (pond) B6
Ellis (riv.) B6
Embden (pond) D6
Endless (lake) F5
Englishman (bay) J6
Eskutassis (pond) G5
Fifth (lake) H5
Fish (riv.) F2
Fish River (lake) F2
Flagstaff (lake) C5
Fourth (lake) H5
Frenchman (bay) G7
Gardner (lake) J6
Georges (isls.) E8
Graham (lake) G6
Grand (lake) H4
Grand Falls (lake) H5
Grand Lake Seboeis (lake) F3
Grand Manan (chan.) K6
Great Moose (lake) D6
Great Wass (isl.) J7
Green (isl.) F8
Harrington (lake) E4
Haut (isl.) G7
Indian (pond) D4
Islesboro (isl.) F7
Jo-Mary (lakes) E4
Katahdin (mt.) F4
Kennebec (riv.) D7
Kezar (lake) B7
Kezar (pond) B7
Kingsbury (pond) D5
Little Black (riv.) E1
Little Madawaska (riv.) G2
Lobster (lake) E4
Long (lake) B7
Long (lake) E2
Long (lake) G1
Long (pond) C4
Long (pond) D6
Long (pond) E5
Long Falls (dam) C5
Longfellow (mts.) B6
Loon (lake) D3
Loring A.F.B. 7,829 H2
Lower Roach (pond) E4
Lower Sysladobsis (lake) G5
Machias (bay) J6
Machias (riv.) F2
Machias (riv.) H6
Machias Seal (isl.) J7
Madagascal (pond) G5
Marshall (isl.) G7
Matinicus Rock (isl.) F8
Mattamiscontis (lake) F4
Mattawamkeag (lake) G4
Mattawamkeag (riv.) G4
Meddybemps (lake) J5
Metinic (isl.) E8
Millinocket (lake) F3
Millinocket (lake) F4
Molunkus (lake) G4
Monhegan (isl.) E8
Moose (pond) B7
Moose (riv.) D4
Moosehead (lake) D4
Mooseleuk (stream) F2
Mooselookmeguntic (lake) B6
Mopang (lake) H6
Mount Desert (isl.) G7
Mount Desert Rock (isl.) G8
Moxie (lake) D5
Munsungan (lake) E3
Muscongus (bay) E8
Musquacook (lakes) E2
Nahmakanta (lake) E4
Nicatous (lake) G5
Nollesemic (lake) F4
Old (stream) H6
Onawa (lake) E5
Parlin (pond) C4
Parmachenee (lake) B5
Passamaquoddy (bay) J5
Passamaquoddy Ind. Res. J6
Pemadumcook (lake) E4
Penobscot (bay) F7
Penobscot (lake) C4
Penobscot (riv.) F5
Penobscot Ind. Res. F6
Pierce (pond) C5
Piscataqua (riv.) B9
Piscataquis (riv.) E5
Pleasant (lake) E3
Pleasant (lake) G3
Pleasant (lake) H5
Pleasant (riv.) H6
Pocomoonshine (lake) H5
Portage (lake) F2
Presque Isle A.F.B. G2
Priestly (lake) E2
Pushaw (lake) F6
Ragged (isl.) F8
Ragged (lake) E4
Rainbow (lake) E4
Rangeley (lake) B6
Richardson (lakes) B6
Rocky (lake) J6
Round (pond) E2
Rowe (lake) F2
Saco (riv.) B8
Saint Croix (riv.) J5
Saint Croix Island Nat'l Mon. J5
Saint Francis (riv.) E1
Saint Froid (lake) F2
Saint John (pond) D3
Saint John (riv.) G1
Salmon Falls (riv.) B9
Sandy (riv.) C6
Schoodic (lake) F5
Scraggly (lake) F3
Scraggly (lake) H5
Seal (isl.) F8
Sebago (lake) B8
Sebasticook (lake) E6
Seboeis (lake) F5
Seboeis (riv.) F3
Seboomook (lake) D4
Shallow (lake) E3
Small (cape) D8
Sourdnahunk (lake) F3
Spencer (pond) D4
Spencer (stream) C5
Spider (lake) E3
Squa Pan (lake) G2
Square (lake) G1
Sunday (riv.) B6
Swift (riv.) B6
Sysladobsis, Lower (lake) G5
Third (lake) H5
Twin (lakes) F4
Umbagog (lake) A6
Umcalcus (lake) G3
Umsaskis (lake) E2
Union, West Branch (riv.) G6
Vinalhaven (isl.) F7
Wassataquoik (stream) F4
Webb (lake) C6
Webster (brook) E3
West Grand (lake) H5
West Musquash (lake) H5
West Quoddy (head) K6
Wilson (ponds) E5
Winnecook (lake) E6
Wooden Ball (isl.) F8
Wyman (lake) C5
Wytopitlock (lake) G4

▲County seat.
•Population of town or township.

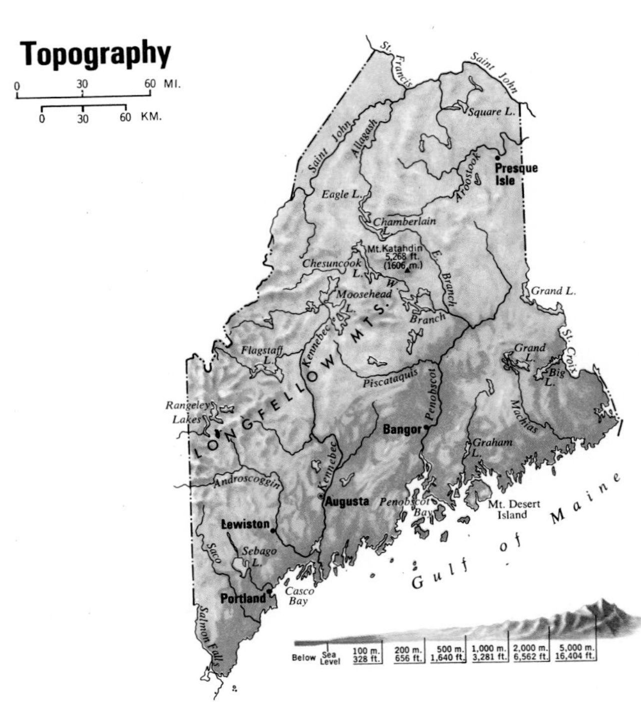
Topography
0 30 60 MI.
0 30 60 KM.
St. Francis
Saint John
Square L.
Saint John
Allagash
Aroostook
Presque Isle
Eagle L.
Chamberlain
Mt. Katahdin 5,268 ft. (1606 m.)
Chesuncook L.
E. Branch
Moosehead L.
W. Branch
Grand L.
St. Croix
Flagstaff L.
Kennebec
LONGFELLOW MTS.
Piscataquis
Penobscot
Grand L.
Big L.
Rangeley Lakes
Machias
Bangor
Graham L.
Androscoggin
Kennebec
Augusta
Penobscot Bay
Mt. Desert Island
Lewiston
Gulf of Maine
Sebago L.
Saco
Portland
Casco Bay
Salmon Falls
Below Sea Level
100 m. 328 ft.
200 m. 656 ft.
500 m. 1,640 ft.
1,000 m. 3,281 ft.
2,000 m. 6,562 ft.
5,000 m. 16,404 ft.

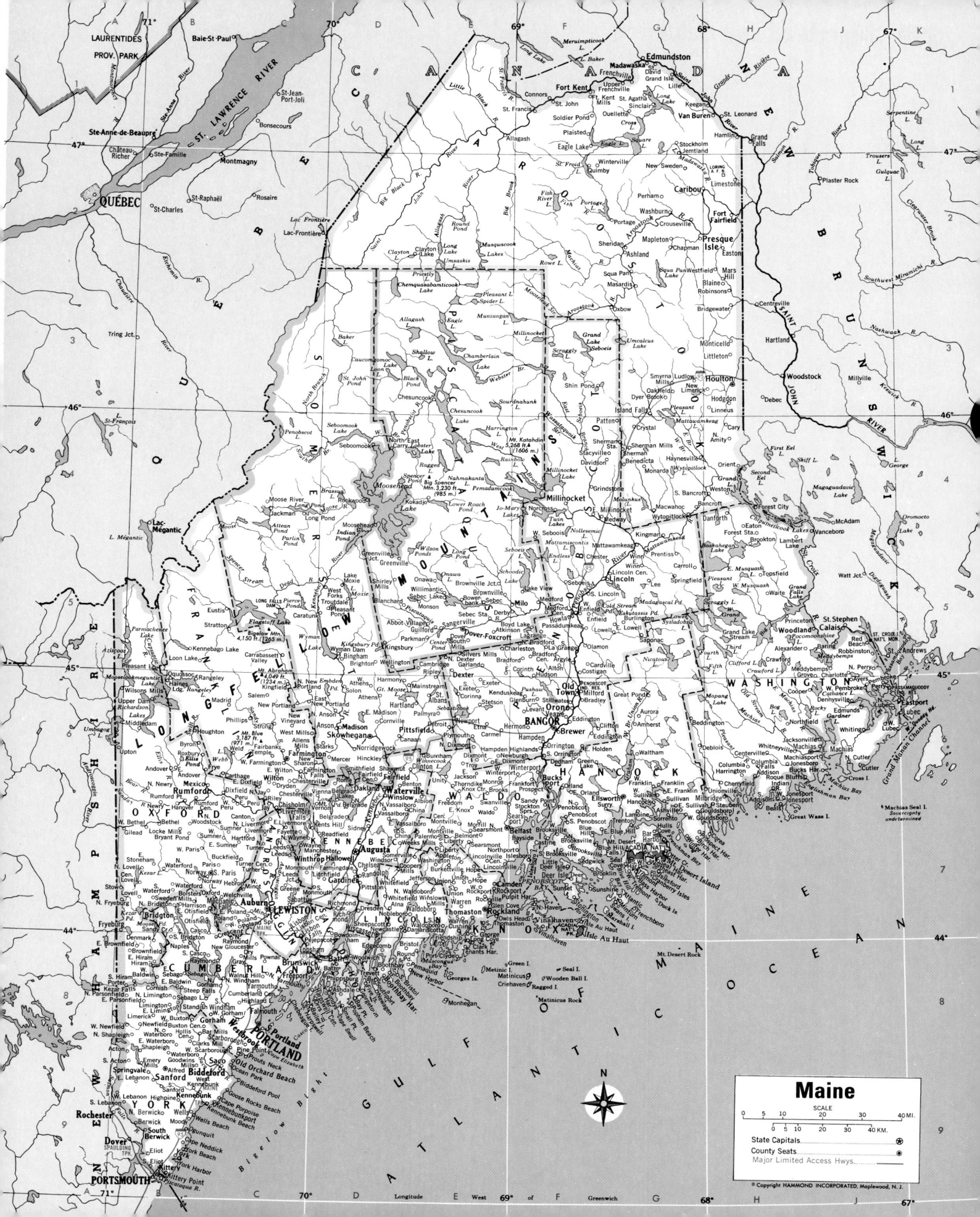

Maine

SCALE

0 5 10 20 30 40 MI.
0 5 10 20 30 40 KM.

State Capitals.............................⊛
County Seats...............................◉
Major Limited Access Hwys.............

© Copyright HAMMOND INCORPORATED, Maplewood, N.J.

MARYLAND

COUNTIES

(continued)

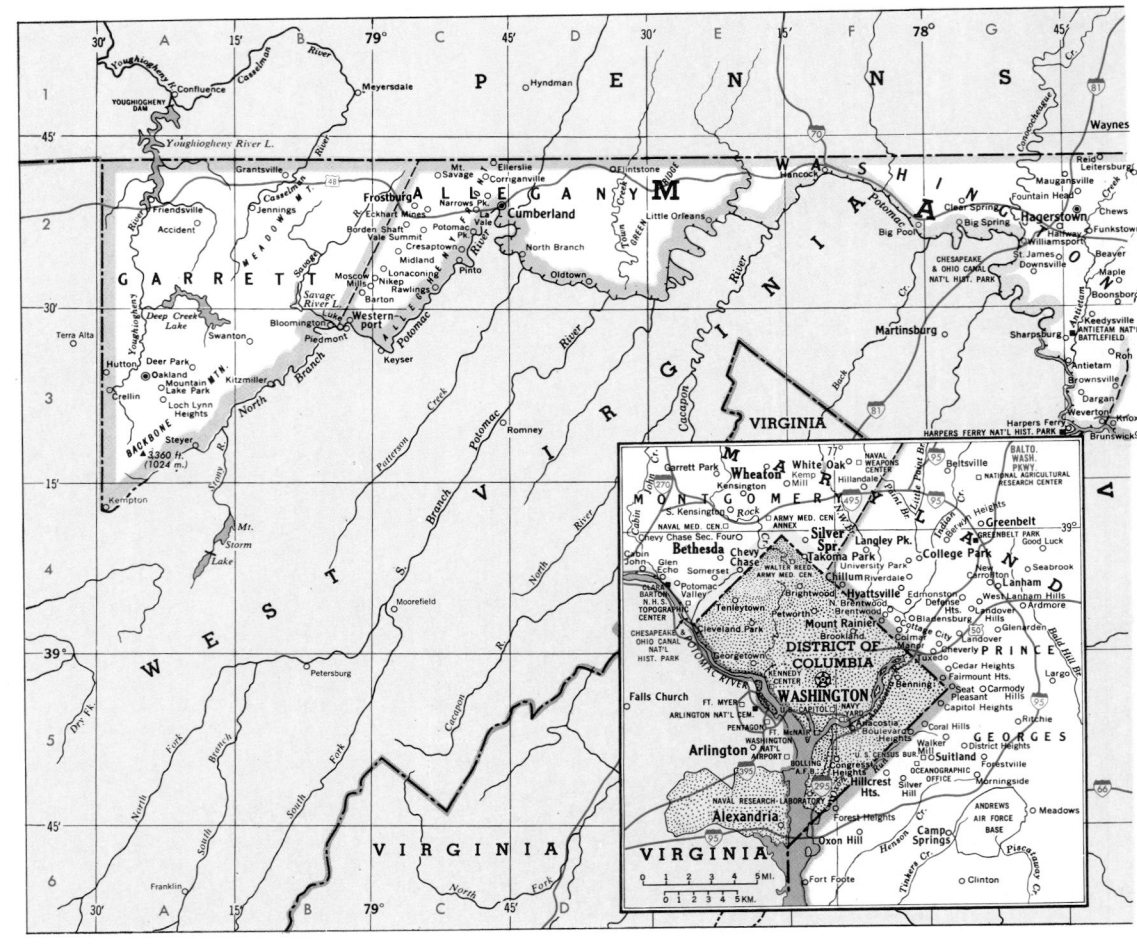

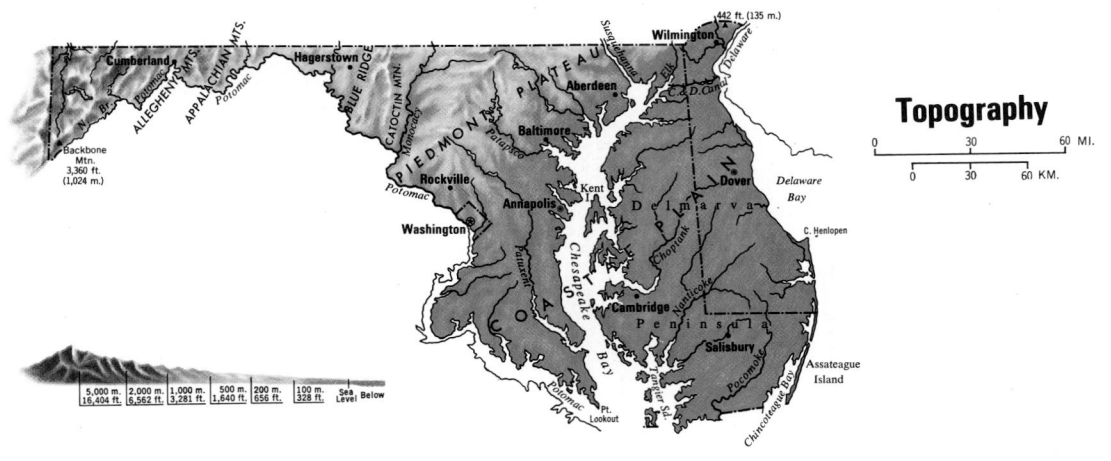

Topography

MARYLAND
AREA 10,460 sq. mi. (27,091 sq. km.)
POPULATION 4,798,622
CAPITAL Annapolis
LARGEST CITY Baltimore
HIGHEST POINT Backbone Mtn. 3,360 ft. (1024 m.)
SETTLED IN 1634
ADMITTED TO UNION April 28, 1788
POPULAR NAME Old Line State; Free State
STATE FLOWER Black-eyed Susan
STATE BIRD Baltimore Oriole

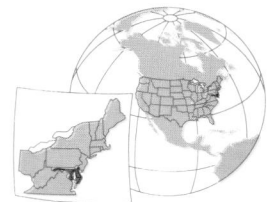

DELAWARE
AREA 2,044 sq. mi. (5,294 sq. km.)
POPULATION 668,696
CAPITAL Dover
LARGEST CITY Wilmington
HIGHEST POINT Ebright Road 442 ft. (135 m.)
SETTLED IN 1627
ADMITTED TO UNION December 7, 1787
POPULAR NAME First State; Diamond State
STATE FLOWER Peach Blossom
STATE BIRD Blue Hen Chicken

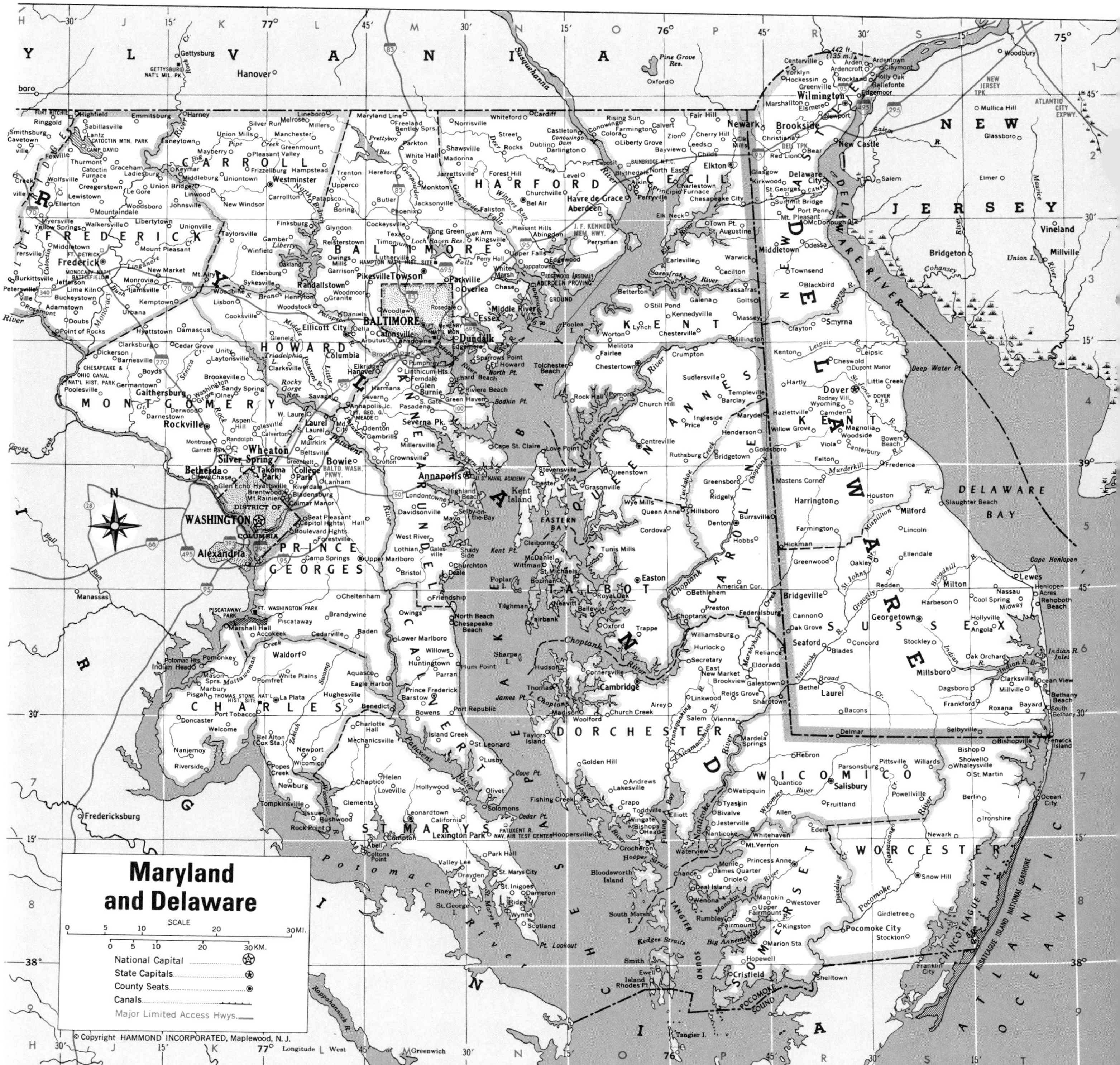

Maryland and Delaware

SCALE

0 5 10 20 30 MI.
0 5 10 20 30 KM.

National Capital
State Capitals
County Seats
Canals
Major Limited Access Hwys.

246 Maryland and Delaware

(continued)

Joppatowne 11,084 N3
Keedysville 464 H3
Kemp Mill F3
Kemptown 250 J3
Kennedyville 225 P3
Kensington 1,713 E4
Keymar 200 K2
Kingsville 3,550 N3
Kitzmiller 275 B3
Knoxville 500 H3
La Plata▲ 5,841 L6
La Vale (La Vale-Narrows Park) 4,694 C2
Landover 5,052 G4
Landover Hills 2,074 G4
Langley Park 17,474 F4
Lanham (Lanham-Seabrook) 16,792 G4
Lansdowne (Lansdowne-Baltimore Highlands) 15,509 M3
Largo 9,475 G5
Laurel 19,438 L4
Laytonsville 248 K4
Le Gore 500 J2
Leeds 177 P2
Leitersburg 350 H2
Leonardtown▲ 1,475 M7
Level 250 O2
Lewistown 600 J2
Lexington Park 9,943 M7
Libertytown 400 J3
Lime Kiln 230 J3
Lineboro 300 L2
Linkwood 250 P6
Linthicum Heights 7,547 M4
Little Orleans 600 E2
Loch Lynn Heights 461 A3
Lonaconing 1,122 C2
Londontowne 6,992 M5
Long Green 1,626 M3
Loveville 600 M7
Luke 184 B3
Lutherville (Lutherville-Timonium) 16,442 M3
Madison 350 O6
Manchester 2,810 L2
Manokin 270 P8
Mapleville 200 H2
Marbury 1,244 K6
Mardela Springs 360 P7
Marion Station 400 R8
Marshall Hall 325 K6
Marydel 143 P4
Maryland City 6,813 L4
Maryland Line 281 M2
Massey 280 P3
Maugansville 1,707 H2
Mayo 2,537 M5
McDaniel 275 N5
Meadows 200 G5
Mechanicsville 784 M7
Middle River 24,616 N3
Middleburg 200 K2
Middletown 1,834 J3
Midland 574 C2
Millersville 380 M4
Millington 409 P3
Monkton 307 M2
Montrose K4
Morningside 930 G5
Moscow Mills 260 B2
Mount Airy 3,730 K3
Mount Pleasant 400 J3
Mount Rainier 7,954 F4
Mount Savage 1,640 C2
Mount Vernon 900 P8
Mountain Lake Park 1,938 A3
Mountaindale 400 J2
Muirkirk 950 L4
Myersville 464 H3
Nanjemoy 238 K7
Nanticoke 450 P7
Narrows Park (Narrows Park-La Vale) C2
Neavitt 300 N6
New Carrollton 12,002 G4
New Market 328 J3
New Windsor 757 K2
Newark 900 S7
Newburg 550 L7
Nikep 200 C2
North Beach 1,173 N6
North Brentwood 512 F4
North East 1,913 P2
North Potomac 18,456 K4
Oakland 2,242 L3
Oakland▲ 1,741 A3
Ocean City 5,146 T7
Odenton 12,833 M4
Oella 600 L3
Oldtown 200 D2
Olivet 200 N7
Olney 23,019 K4
Orchard Beach 200 M4
Overlea 12,137 N3
Owings 9,474 M6
Owings Mills 9,526 L3
Oxford 699 O6
Oxon Hill 35,794 F6
Park Hall 775 N8
Parkton 290 M2
Parkville 31,617 M3
Parran 200 M6
Parsonsburg 200 R7
Pasadena 10,012 M4
Perry Hall 22,723 N3
Perryman 2,160 O3
Perryville 2,456 O2
Petersville 320 H3
Phoenix 165 M2
Pikesville 24,815 M3
Piney Point 950 M8
Pinto 175 C2
Piscataway 500 L6
Pisgah 650 K6
Pittsville 602 S7
Pleasant Hills 2,591 N3
Pleasant Valley 200 L2
Plum Point 200 N6
Pocomoke City 3,922 R8
Point of Rocks 210 J3
Pomfret 600 L6
Pomonkey 410 K6
Poolesville 3,796 J4
Port Deposit 685 O2
Potomac Heights 1,524 K6
Potomac Park (Potomac Park-Bowling Green) 2,275 C2
Potomac Valley E4
Powellville 400 S7
Preston 437 P6
Prince Frederick▲ 1,885 M6
Princess Anne▲ 1,666 P8
Pumphrey 5,483 M4
Quantico 200 R7
Queen Anne 250 O5
Queenstown 453 O5
Randallstown 26,277 L3
Randolph K4
Rawlings 500 C2
Reid 320 H2
Reisterstown 19,314 L3
Ridge 1,034 N8
Ridgely 933 P5
Ringgold 200 H2
Rising Sun 1,263 O2
Ritchie 950 G5
Riverdale 5,185 F4
Riviera Beach 11,376 N4
Rock Hall 1,584 O4
Rocks 450 N2
Rockville▲ 44,835 K4
Rohrersville 525 H3
Rosedale 18,703 M3
Rosemont 256 H3
Royal Oak 600 O6
Rumbley 200 P8
Sabillasville 450 J2
Saint Inigoes 750 N8
Saint Leonard 244 N7
Saint Marys City N8
Saint Michaels 1,301 N5
Salisbury▲ 20,592 R7
Sandy Spring (Sandy Spring-Ashton) 2,659 K4
Savage (Savage-Guilford) 9,669 L4
Scotland 475 N8
Seabrook (Seabrook-Lanham) G4
Seat Pleasant 5,359 G5
Secretary 528 P6
Selby-on-the-Bay 3,101 N5
Severn 24,499 M4
Severna Park 25,879 M4
Shady Side 4,107 M5
Sharpsburg 659 G3
Sharptown 609 R6
Silver Run 350 K2
Silver Spring 76,046 F4
Smithsburg 1,221 H2
Snow Hill▲ 2,217 S8
Solomons 250 N7
Somerset 993 E4
South Gate 27,564 M4
South Kensington 8,777 E4
South Laurel 18,591 L4
Sparrows Point N4
Stevensville 1,862 N5
Still Pond 350 O3
Stockton 400 S8
Street 200 N2
Sudlersville 428 P4
Suitland (Suitland-Silver Hill) 35,111 F5
Swanton 223 A3
Sykesville 2,303 K3
Takoma Park 16,700 F4
Taneytown 3,695 K2
Taylors Island 400 N7
Texas 300 M3
Thurmont 3,398 J2
Tilghman 979 N6
Timonium (Timonium-Lutherville) M3
Toddville 500 O7
Tompkinsville 200 L7
Towson▲ 49,445 M3
Trappe 974 O6
Tuxedo 500 G5
Union Bridge 910 K2
Union Mills 225 K2
Uniontown 250 K2
Unionville 200 K3
University Park 2,243 F4
Upper Fairmount 500 P8
Upper Falls 550 N3
Upper Marlboro▲ 745 M5
Upperco 500 L2
Vale Summit 175 C2
Valley Lee 600 M8
Vienna 264 P7
Waldorf 15,058 L6
Walker Mill 10,920 F5
Walkersville 4,145 J3
Warwick 550 P3
Washington Grove 434 K4
Welcome 438 K7
Wenona 270 P8
West Lanham Hills 350 G4
West Laurel 4,151 L4
West River 300 M5
Westernport 2,454 B3
Westminster▲ 13,068 L2
Westover 450 R8
Wheaton (Wheaton-Glenmont) 53,720 E3
White Hall 360 M2
White Marsh 8,183 N3
White Oak 18,671 F3
White Plains 3,560 L6
Whiteford 500 N2
Wicomico 210 L7
Willards 708 S7
Williamsport 2,103 G2
Willows 250 M6
Winfield 200 K3
Wingate 225 O7
Wittman 544 N5
Woodbine 872 K3
Woodlawn 5,329 M3
Woodmoor L3
Woodsboro 513 J2
Woolford 330 O7
Worton 200 O3
Wye Mills 315 O5
Wynne 450 N8
Yellow Springs 940 H3
Zion 225 P2

OTHER FEATURES

Aberdeen Proving Ground 5,267 N3
Allegheny Front (mts.) C2
Andrews A.F.B. 10,228 G5
Antietam (creek) H2
Antietam Nat'l Battlefield H3
Back (riv.) N4
Backbone (mt.) A3
Bainbridge N.T.C. O2
Bald Hill Branch (riv.) G4
Big Annemessex (riv.) P8
Big Pipe (creek) K2
Bloodsworth (isl.) O8
Blue Ridge (mts.) H3
Bodkin (pt.) N4
Bush (creek) J3
Cabin John (creek) D4
Camp David J2
Casselman (riv.) B2
Catoctin (creek) H3
Catoctin Mt. Park J2
Cedar (pt.) N7
Census Bureau F5
Chesapeake (bay) N7
Chesapeake and Delaware (canal) R2
Chesapeake and Ohio Canal Nat'l Hist. Park J4
Chester (riv.) O4
Chicamacomico (riv.) P7
Chincoteague (bay) S8
Choptank (riv.) O6
Clara Barton Nat'l Hist. Site E4
Conococheague (bay) G1
Conowingo (dam) O2
Cove (pt.) N7
Deep Creek (lake) A3
Deer (creek) N2
Dividing (creek) R8
Eastern (bay) N5
Elk (riv.) P3
Fishing (bay) O7
Fort Detrick J3
Fort George G. Meade 12,509 L4
Fort McHenry Nat'l Mon. M3
Fort Ritchie 1,249 H2
Fort Washington Park L6
Great Seneca (creek) J4
Greenbelt Park G4
Green Ridge (mts.) E2
Gunpowder (riv.) N3
Gunpowder Falls (creek) M2
Hampton Nat'l Hist. Site M3
Harpers Ferry Nat'l Hist. Park G3
Henson (creek) F6
Honga (riv.) O7
Hooper (str.) O8
Indian (creek) G4
James (pt.) N6
Kedges (strs) O8
Kent (isl.) N5
Kent (pt.) N5
Liberty (lake) L3
Linganore (creek) J3
Little Choptank (riv.) N6
Little Gunpowder Falls (creek) M2
Little Paint Branch (riv.) F4
Little Patuxent (riv.) L4
Loch Raven (res.) M3
Lookout (pt.) N8
Manokin (riv.) P8
Marshyhope (creek) P6
Mattawoman (creek) K6
Meadow (mt.) B2
Middle Patuxent (riv.) L3
Monocacy (riv.) J3
Monocacy Nat'l Battlefield J3
Nanticoke (riv.) P7
Nassawango (creek) S8
National Agricultural Research Center G3
Naval Academy, U.S. 5,420 N5
Naval Medical Center E4
Naval Weapons Center F3
North (pt.) N4
Oceanographic Office F5
Oxon Run (riv.) F5
Paint Branch (riv.) F4
Patapsco (riv.) M4
Patuxent (riv.) M7
Patuxent River Nav. Air Test Ctr. N7
Piscataway (creek) G6
Piscataway Park K6
Pocomoke (riv.) S8
Pocomoke (sound) P9
Pooles (isl.) O3
Poplar (isl.) N5
Potomac (riv.) M8
Prettyboy (res.) M2
Rock (creek) K4
Rocky Gorge (res.) L4
Saint George (isl.) M8
Saint Marys (riv.) N8
Sassafras (riv.) P3
Savage (riv.) B2
Savage River (lake) B2
Severn (riv.) N4
Sharps (isl.) N6
Smith (isl.) O8
South Marsh (isl.) O8
Susquehanna (riv.) N1
Tangier (sound) P8
Thomas Stone Nat'l Hist. Site K6
Tinkers (creek) F6
Topographic Center E4
Town (creek) D2
Transquaking (riv.) P7
Triadelphia (lake) L4
Tuckahoe (creek) P5
Walter Reed Army Medical Center Annex E4
Wicomico (riv.) L7
Wicomico (riv.) R7
Winters Run (creek) N2
Youghiogheny (riv.) A3
Youghiogheny River (lake) A2
Zekiah Swamp (riv.) L7

DELAWARE

COUNTIES

Kent 110,993 R4
New Castle 441,946 R2
Sussex 113,229 S6

CITIES and TOWNS

Arden 477 R1
Ardencroft 282 R1
Ardentown 325 S1
Bear 200 R2
Bellefonte 1,243 S1
Bethany Beach 326 T6
Bethel 178 R6
Blades 834 R6
Bowers Beach 198 S4
Bridgeville 1,210 R6
Brookside 15,307 R2
Camden 1,899 R4
Centerville 800 R1
Cheswold 321 R4
Christiana 500 R2
Clarksville 350 T6
Claymont 9,800 S1
Clayton 1,163 R3
Concord 200 R6
Cool Spring 200 T6
Dagsboro 398 S6
Delaware City 1,682 R2
Delmar 962 R7
Dover (cap.)▲ 27,630 R4
Dupont Manor 1,059 R4
Edgemoor 5,853 S1
Ellendale 313 S5
Elsmere 5,935 R2
Farmington 122 R5
Felton 683 R4
Fenwick Island 186 T7
Frankford 591 S6
Frederica 761 S4
Georgetown▲ 3,732 S6
Glasgow 350 R2
Greenville 230 R1
Greenwood 578 R5
Harbeson 300 S6
Harrington 2,311 R5
Hockessin 950 R1
Houston 487 S5
Kenton 232 R4
Kirkwood 350 R2
Laurel 3,226 R6
Leipsic 236 S4
Lewes 2,295 T5
Lincoln 757 S5
Little Creek 167 S4
Magnolia 211 R4
Middletown 3,834 R3
Midway 250 T6
Milford 6,040 S5
Millsboro 1,643 S6
Millville 206 T6
Milton 1,417 S5
New Castle 4,837 R2
Newark 25,098 P2
Newport 1,240 R2
Oak Orchard 350 T6
Ocean View 606 T6
Odessa 303 R3
Port Penn 300 R2
Rehoboth Beach 1,234 T6
Rodney Village 1,745 R4
Roxana 250 T6
Saint Georges 450 R2
Seaford 5,689 R6
Selbyville 1,335 S7
Smyrna 5,231 R3
South Bethany 148 T6
Townsend 322 R3
Viola 153 R4
Wilmington▲ 71,529 R2
Woodside 140 R4
Wyoming 977 R4

OTHER FEATURES

Broad (creek) R6
Broadkill (riv.) S5
Chesapeake and Delaware (canal) R2
Choptank (riv.) P5
Deep Water (pt.) S4
Delaware (bay) T5
Delaware (riv.) R3
Dover A.F.B. S4
Henlopen (cape) T5
Indian (riv.) S6
Indian River (bay) T6
Indian River (inlet) T6
Leipsic (riv.) R4
Mispillion (riv.) S5
Murderkill (riv.) R5
Nanticoke (riv.) R6
Saint Jones (riv.) R4
Smyrna (res.) R3

DISTRICT OF COLOMBIA

CITIES and TOWNS

Georgetown E5
Washington D.C. (cap), U.S. 609,909 F5

OTHER FEATURES

Anacostia (riv.) F5
Bolling A.F.B. F5
Fort Lesley J. McNair E5
Kennedy Center A5
Naval Yard F5
U.S. Capitol F5
Walter Reed Army Med. Ctr. E4

▲County seat.

Agriculture, Industry and Resources

DOMINANT LAND USE

- Dairy, General Farming
- Fruit and Mixed Farming
- Truck and Mixed Farming
- Tobacco, General Farming
- Forests
- Swampland, Limited Agriculture
- Urban Areas

MAJOR MINERAL OCCURRENCES

- C Coal
- Cl Clay
- G Natural Gas
- Ls Limestone

- Water Power
- Major Industrial Areas

MASSACHUSETTS

AREA 8,284 sq. mi. (21,456 sq. km.)
POPULATION 6,029,051
CAPITAL Boston
LARGEST CITY Boston
HIGHEST POINT Mt. Greylock 3,491 ft. (1064 m.)
SETTLED IN 1620
ADMITTED TO UNION February 6, 1788
POPULAR NAME Bay State; Old Colony
STATE FLOWER Mayflower
STATE BIRD Chickadee

RHODE ISLAND

AREA 1,212 sq. mi. (3,139 sq. km.)
POPULATION 1,005,984
CAPITAL Providence
LARGEST CITY Providence
HIGHEST POINT Jerimoth Hill 812 ft. (247 m.)
SETTLED IN 1636
ADMITTED TO UNION May 29, 1790
POPULAR NAME Little Rhody; Ocean State
STATE FLOWER Violet
STATE BIRD Rhode Island Red

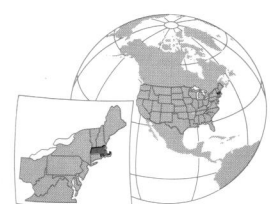

Agriculture, Industry and Resources

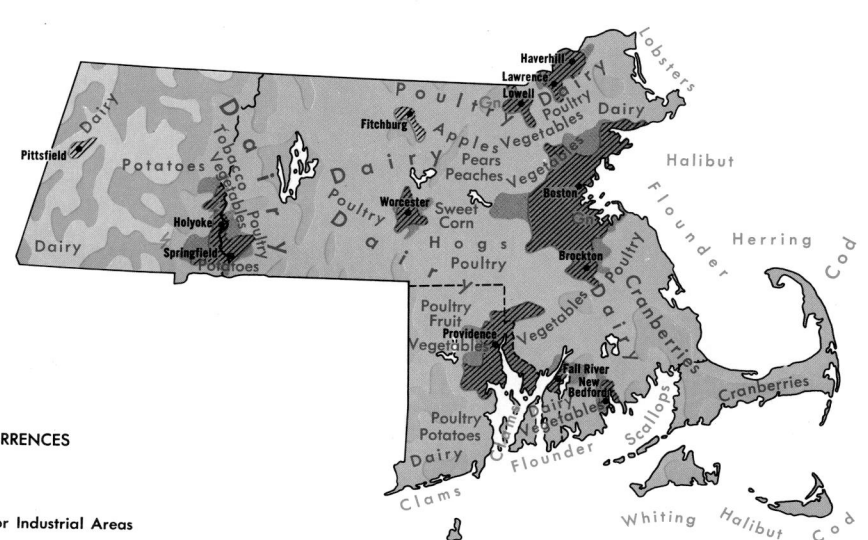

DOMINANT LAND USE

- Specialized Dairy
- Dairy, Poultry, Mixed Farming
- Forests
- Urban Areas

MAJOR MINERAL OCCURRENCES

Gn Granite

⚡ Water Power   ▨ Major Industrial Areas

Vineyard Haven 1,762 M7
Waban B7
Wakefield• 24,825 C5
Wales• 1,566 F4
Walpole 5,495 B8
Walpole• 20,212 B8
Waltham 57,878 B6
Ware 6,533 E3
Ware• 9,808 E3
Wareham 19,232 L5
Wareham• 18,457 L5
Wareham Center 2,607 L5
Warren 1,516 F4
Warren• 4,437 F4
Warwick• 740 E2
Washington• 615 B3
Watertown• 33,284 C6
Waverley B6
Wayland• 11,874 A7
Webster 11,849 G4
Webster• 16,196 G4
Wellesley• 26,615 B7
Wellesley Hills B7
Wellfleet• 2,493 O5
Wendell• 899 E2
Wenham• 4,212 L2
West Acton 975 H3
West Barnstable 1,508 N6
West Boxford 950 K2
West Boylston• 6,611 G3
West Bridgewater• 6,389 K4
West Brookfield 1,419 F4
West Brookfield• 3,532 F4
West Chatham 1,504 O6
West Chelmsford J2
West Concord 5,761 A6
West Dennis 2,307 O6
West Falmouth 1,752 M6
West Groton 950 H2
West Hanover L4
West Harwich 883 O6
West Mansfield 950 K5
West Medway J4
West Newbury• 3,421 L1
West Newton B7
West Springfield• 27,537 D4
West Stockbridge• 1,483 A3
West Tisbury• 1,704 M7
West Townsend 950 H2
West Upton-Upton H4
West Wareham 2,059 L5
West Warren F4
West Yarmouth 5,409 N6
Westborough 3,917 H3
Westborough• 14,133 H3
Westfield• 38,372 D4
Westford• 16,392 J2
Westhampton• 1,327 C3
Westminster• 6,191 G2
Weston• 10,200 B6
Westport 13,852 K6
Westport• 13,763 K6
Westwood• 12,557 B8
Weymouth 54,063 D8
Whately• 1,375 D3
Whitinsville 5,639 H4
Whitman• 13,240 L4
Wilbraham 3,352 E4
Wilbraham• 12,635 E4
Williamsburg• 2,515 C3
Williamstown 4,791 B2
Williamstown• 8,220 B2
Wilmington• 17,654 C5
Winchendon 4,316 F2
Winchendon• 8,805 F2
Winchester• 20,267 C6
Windsor• 770 B2
Winthrop• 18,127 D6
Woburn 35,943 C6
Woods Hole 1,080 M6
Worcester▲ 169,759 H3
Worthington• 1,156 C3
Wrentham• 9,006 J4
Yarmouth Port 4,271 N6
Yarmouth• 21,174 O6

OTHER FEATURES

Adams Nat'l Hist. Site D7
Agawam (riv.) M5
Allerton (pt.) E7
Ann (cape) M2
Ashmere (lake) B3
Assabet (riv.) H3
Assawompset (pond) L5
Batchelor (brook) D3
Berkshire (hills) B4
Big (pond) B4
Bigelow (bight) M1
Blackstone (riv.) G3
Blue (hills) C8
Boston (bay) E6
Boston (harb.) D7
Boston Nat'l Hist. Park D6
Brewster (isls.) E7
Buel (lake) A4
Buzzards (bay) L7
Cambridge (res.) B6
Cape Cod (bay) N5
Cape Cod (canal) N5
Cape Cod Nat'l Seashore P5
Chappaquiddick (isl.) N7
Charles (riv.) C7
Chicopee (riv.) D4
Cobble Mountain (res.) C4
Cochituate (lake) A7
Cod (cape) O4
Concord (riv.) J2
Congamond (lakes) D4
Connecticut (riv.) D2
Cuttyhunk (isl.) L7
Deer (isl.) E7
Deerfield (riv.) C2
East (pt.) E6
East Chop (pt.) M7
Eastern (pt.) M2
Elizabeth (isls.) L7
Everett (mt.) A4
Falls (riv.) D2
Fort Devens 8,973 H2
Fresh (pond) C6
Gammon (pt.) N6
Gay Head (prom.) L7
Grace (mt.) E2
Great (pt.) O7
Green (riv.) B2
Greylock (mt.) B2
Gurnet (pt.) M4
Hingham (bay) E7
Holyoke (range) D3
Hoosac (mts.) B2
Hoosic (riv.) A1
Housatonic (riv.) A4
Ipswich (riv.) L2
John F. Kennedy Nat'l Hist. Site C7
Knightville (res.) C3
Laurence G. Hanscom Field B6
Little (riv.) C4
Logan Int'l Airport D7
Long (isl.) E7
Long (pt.) O4
Long (pond) L5
Longfellow Nat'l Hist. Site C6
Lowell Nat'l Hist. Park J2
Maine (gulf) M2
Manhan (riv.) D4
Manomet (pt.) N5
Marblehead (neck) F6
Martha's Vineyard (isl.) M7
Massachusetts (bay) M4
Merrimack (riv.) K1
Mill (riv.) C3
Mill (riv.) D3
Millers (riv.) E2
Minute Man Nat'l Hist. Park B6
Mishaum (pt.) L6
Monomonac (lake) G2
Monomoy (isl.) O6
Monomoy (pt.) O6
Mount Hope (bay) K6
Muskeget (chan.) N7
Muskeget (isl.) N7
Mystic (lake) C6
Mystic (riv.) C6
Nahant (bay) E6
Nantucket (isl.) O8
Nantucket (sound) N6
Nashawena (isl.) L7
Nashua (riv.) H3
Naushon (isl.) L7
Neponset (riv.) C8
Nomans Land (isl.) L7
Nonamesset (isl.) M6
North (riv.) D2
North (riv.) L4
Onota (lake) A3
Otis (res.) B4
Otis A.F.B. M6
Pasque (isl.) L7
Plum (isl.) L2
Plymouth (bay) M5
Poge (cape) N7
Pontoosuc (lake) A3
Quabbin (res.) E3
Quaboag (riv.) F4
Quincy (bay) D7
Quinebaug (riv.) F4
Race (pt.) N4
Salem Maritime Nat'l Hist. Site E5
Saugus Iron Works Nat'l Hist. Site D6
Shawshine (riv.) K2
Silver (lake) L4
South (riv.) D2
South Weymouth Nav. Air Sta. E8
Springfield Armory Nat'l Hist. Site D4
Squibnocket (pt.) M7
Stillwater (riv.) G3
Sudbury (res.) H3
Sudbury (riv.) A6
Swift (riv.) E4
Taconic (mts.) A2
Taunton (riv.) K5
Thompson (isl.) D7
Toby (mt.) E3
Tom (mt.) D4
Tuckernuck (isl.) N7
Vineyard (sound) L7
Wachusett (mt.) G3
Wachusett (res.) G3
Walden (pond) A6
Ware (riv.) F3
Watuppa (pond) K6
Webster (lake) G4
Wellfleet (harb.) O5
West (riv.) H4
West Chop (pt.) M7
Westfield (riv.) C3
Westover A.F.B. D4
Weweantic (riv.) L5
Whitman (riv.) G2
Winter I. Coast Guard Air Sta. E5

RHODE ISLAND

COUNTIES

Bristol 48,859 J6
Kent 161,135 H6
Newport 87,194 K6
Providence 596,270 H5
Washington 110,006 H7

CITIES and TOWNS

Anthony H6
Apponaug J6
Arctic J6
Arnold Mills J5
Ashaway 1,584 G7
Ashton J5
Barrington• 15,849 J6
Block Island• H8
Bradford 1,604 H7
Bristol▲• 21,625 J6
Centerdale H5
Central Falls 17,637 J5
Charlestown 6,478 H7
Conimicut J6
Coventry (Washington) 31,083 H6
Coventry Center H6
Cranston 76,060 J5
East Greenwich▲• 11,865 H6
East Providence 50,380 J5
Esmond H5
Exeter• 5,461 H6
Georgiaville H5
Greenville 8,303 H5
Harrisville 1,654 H5
Hillsgrove J6
Hope Valley 1,446 H6
Hopkinton• 6,873 H7
Island Park J6
Jamestown 4,999 J6
Jamestown• 4,040 J6
Kingston 6,504 J7
La Fayette H6
Little Compton• 3,339 K6
Lonsdale J5
Manville H5
Middletown• 19,460 J6
Narragansett 14,985 J7
Narragansett• 12,088 J7
Natick H6
New Shoreham (Block Island)• 836 H8
Newport▲ 28,227 J7
North Kingstown• 23,786 J6
North Providence• 32,090 J5
North Tiverton K6
Norwood J6
Oakland Beach J6
Pascoag 5,011 H5
Pawtucket 72,644 J5
Peace Dale-Wakefield 7,134 J7
Pontiac J6
Portsmouth• 16,857 J6
Providence (cap.)▲ 160,728 H5
Riverside J5
Rumford J5
Tiverton 7,259 K6
Tiverton• 14,312 K6
Valley Falls 11,175 J5
Wakefield-Peace Dale 7,134 J7
Warren• 11,385 J6
Warwick 85,427 J6
Watch Hill 300 G7
West Kingston 950 H7
West Warwick 29,268 H6
Westerly▲ 16,477 G7
Westerly• 21,605 G7
Woonsocket▲ 43,877 J4

OTHER FEATURES

Black Rock (pt.) H8
Block (isl.) H8
Block Island (sound) H8
Brenton (pt.) J7
Conanicut (isl.) J6
Dickens (pt.) H8
Durfee (hill) G5
Grace (pt.) H8
Jerimoth (hill) G5
Judith (pt.) J7
Mount Hope (bay) K6
Narragansett (bay) J6
Noyes (pt.) H7
Pawcatuck (riv.) G7
Prudence (isl.) J6
Rhode Island (isl.) J6
Rhode (sound) J7
Roger Williams Nat'l Mem. J5
Sakonnet (pt.) K7
Sakonnet (riv.) K7
Sandy (pt.) H8
Scituate (res.) H5
Touro Synagogue Nat'l Hist. Site J7
Watch Hill (pt.) G7

▲County seat or Shire town
•Population of town or township

Massachusetts and Rhode Island

SCALE 0 5 10 15 20 MI.
0 5 10 15 20 KM.

State Capitals
County Seats (Shire Towns)
Canals
Major Limited Access Hwys.

Topography

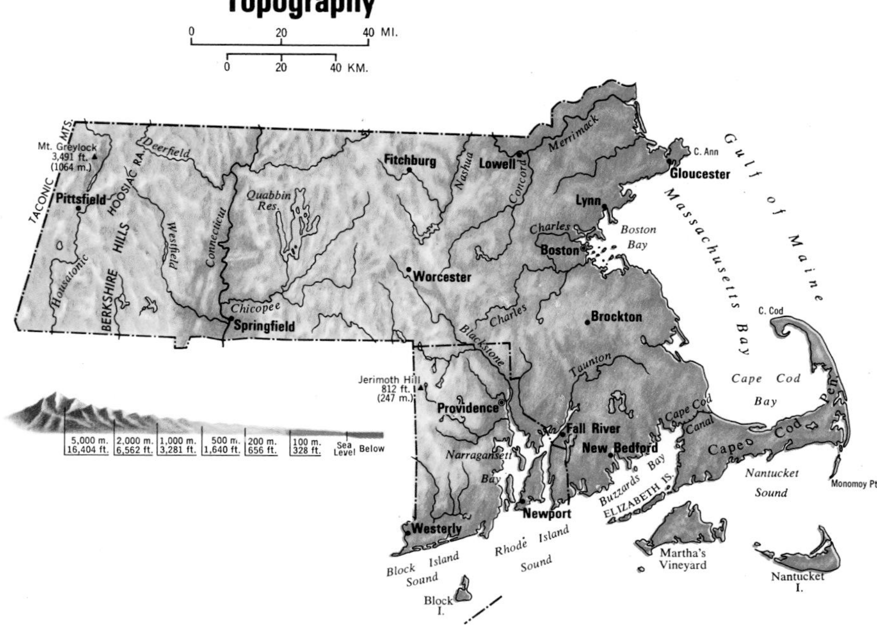
0 20 40 MI.
0 20 40 KM.
Mt. Greylock 3,491 ft. (1064 m.)
TACONIC MTS.
Pittsfield
HOOSAC RA.
BERKSHIRE HILLS
Housatonic
Westfield
Deerfield
Connecticut
Quabbin Res.
Chicopee
Springfield
Fitchburg
Nashua
Lowell
Concord
Merrimack
C. Ann
Gloucester
Lynn
Charles
Boston
Boston Bay
Worcester
Blackstone
Charles
Brockton
Taunton
Jerimoth Hill 812 ft. (247 m.)
Providence
Narragansett Bay
Fall River
New Bedford
Buzzards Bay
ELIZABETH IS.
Westerly
Newport
Block Island Sound
Rhode Island Sound
Block I.
Martha's Vineyard
Nantucket I.
Nantucket Sound
Cape Cod
Canal
Cape Cod Bay
C. Cod
Monomoy Pt.
Gulf of Maine
Massachusetts Bay
5,000 m. 16,404 ft.
2,000 m. 6,562 ft.
1,000 m. 3,281 ft.
500 m. 1,640 ft.
200 m. 656 ft.
100 m. 328 ft.
Sea Level
Below

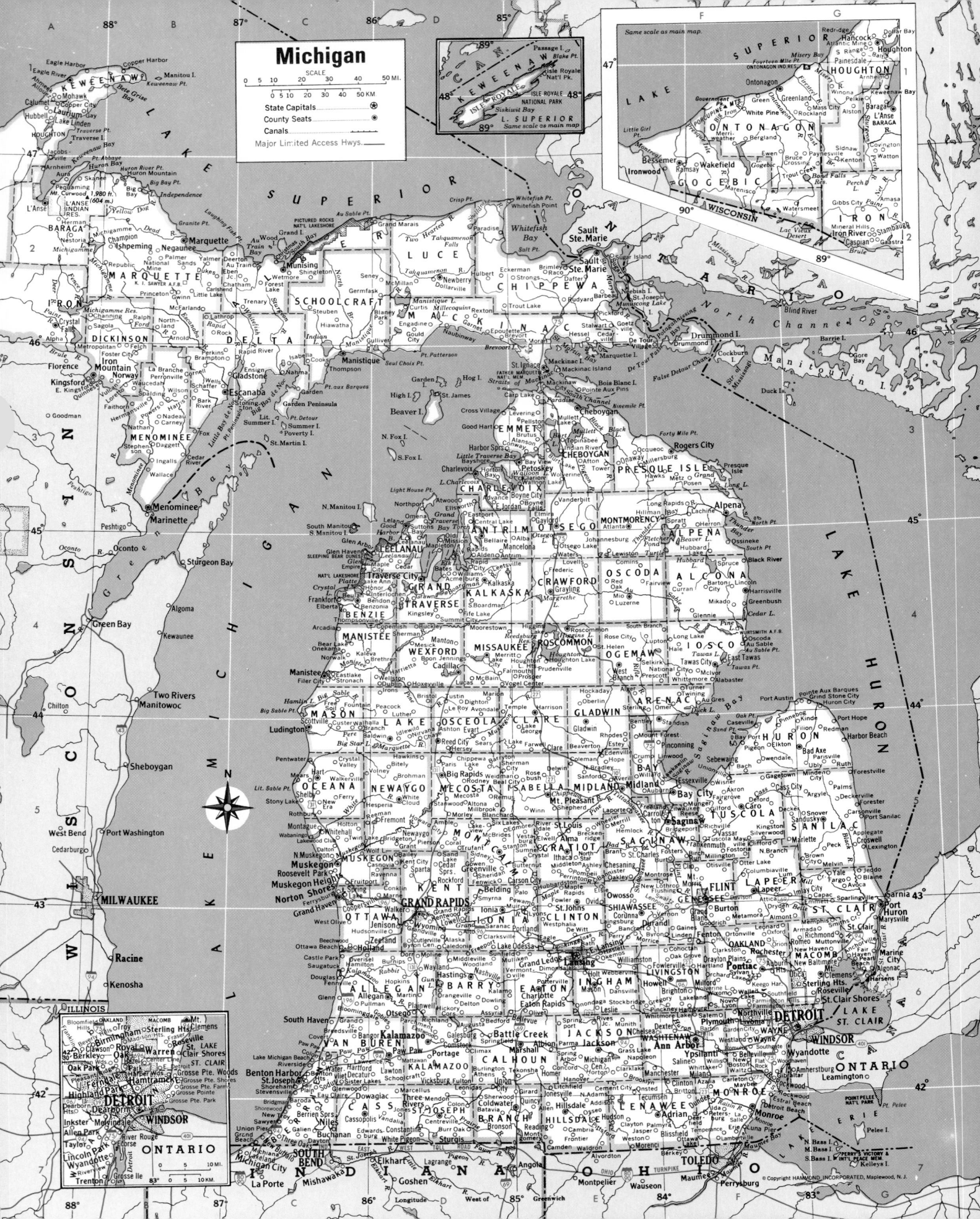
Michigan
SCALE
0 5 10 20 30 40 50 MI.
0 5 10 20 30 40 50 KM.
State Capitals
County Seats
Canals
Major Limited Access Hwys.
Same scale as main map.
LAKE SUPERIOR
LAKE MICHIGAN
LAKE HURON
LAKE ST. CLAIR
LAKE ERIE
North Channel
Manitoulin I.
Green Bay
Saginaw Bay
Grand Traverse Bay
Whitefish Bay
Straits of Mackinac
ONTARIO
WISCONSIN
ILLINOIS
INDIANA
OHIO
CAN.
KEWEENAW
ISLE ROYALE
ISLE ROYALE NATIONAL PARK
L. SUPERIOR
HOUGHTON
ONTONAGON
GOGEBIC
IRON
BARAGA
MARQUETTE
ALGER
LUCE
CHIPPEWA
SCHOOLCRAFT
MACKINAC
DELTA
DICKINSON
MENOMINEE
EMMET
CHEBOYGAN
PRESQUE ISLE
CHARLEVOIX
ANTRIM
OTSEGO
MONTMORENCY
ALPENA
LEELANAU
GRAND TRAVERSE
KALKASKA
CRAWFORD
OSCODA
ALCONA
BENZIE
MANISTEE
WEXFORD
MISSAUKEE
ROSCOMMON
OGEMAW
IOSCO
MASON
LAKE
OSCEOLA
CLARE
GLADWIN
ARENAC
HURON
OCEANA
NEWAYGO
MECOSTA
ISABELLA
MIDLAND
BAY
TUSCOLA
SANILAC
MUSKEGON
MONTCALM
GRATIOT
SAGINAW
OTTAWA
KENT
IONIA
CLINTON
SHIAWASSEE
GENESEE
LAPEER
ST. CLAIR
ALLEGAN
BARRY
EATON
INGHAM
LIVINGSTON
OAKLAND
MACOMB
VAN BUREN
KALAMAZOO
CALHOUN
JACKSON
WASHTENAW
WAYNE
CASS
ST. JOSEPH
BRANCH
HILLSDALE
LENAWEE
MONROE
Lansing
Detroit
Grand Rapids
Flint
Saginaw
Bay City
Kalamazoo
Ann Arbor
Battle Creek
Jackson
Muskegon
Traverse City
Marquette
Sault Ste. Marie
Escanaba
Alpena
Port Huron
Milwaukee
Green Bay
Toledo
South Bend
Windsor
Sarnia
POINT PELEE NAT'L PARK
PICTURED ROCKS NAT'L LAKESHORE
SLEEPING BEAR DUNES NAT'L LAKESHORE
© Copyright HAMMOND INCORPORATED, Maplewood, N. J.

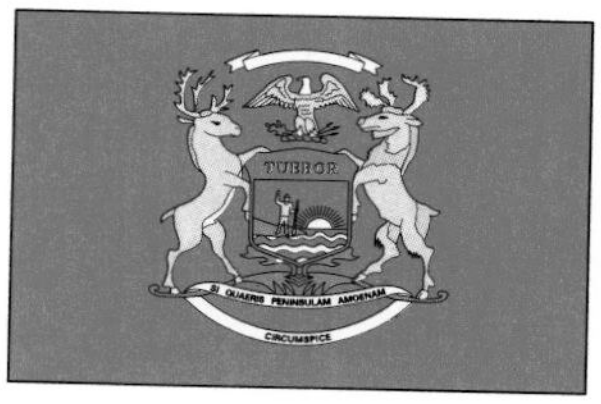

AREA 58,527 sq. mi. (151,585 sq. km.)
POPULATION 9,328,784
CAPITAL Lansing
LARGEST CITY Detroit
HIGHEST POINT Mt. Curwood 1,980 ft. (604 m.)
SETTLED IN 1650
ADMITTED TO UNION January 26, 1837
POPULAR NAME Wolverine State
STATE FLOWER Apple Blossom
STATE BIRD Robin

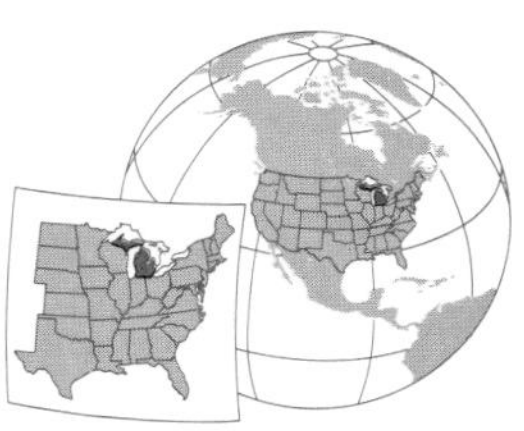

Topography

0 50 100 MI.
0 50 100 KM.

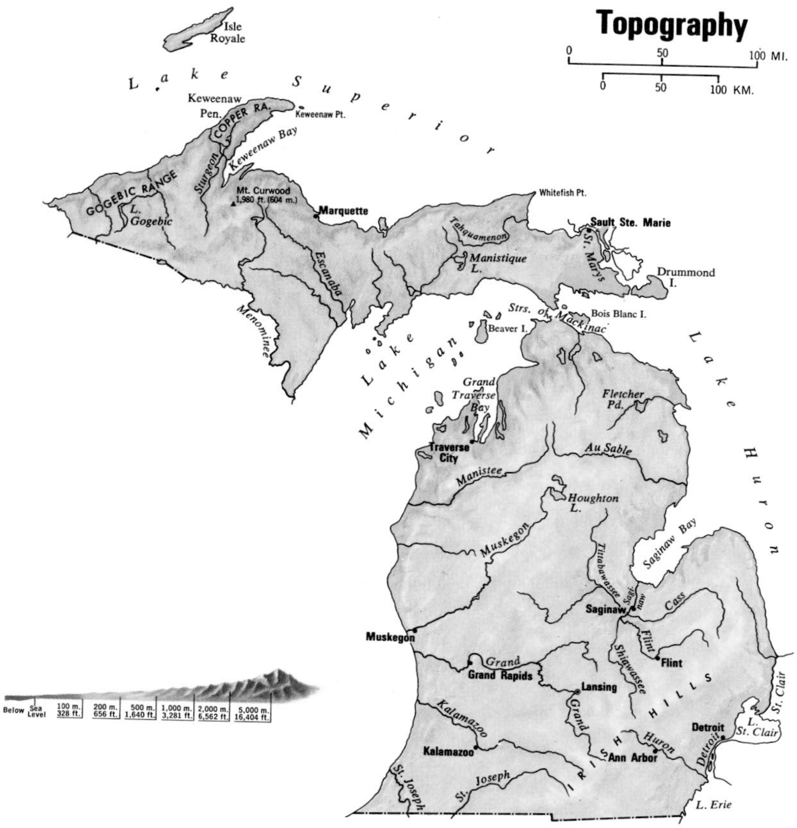

COUNTIES

Alcona 10,145 ....F4
Alger 8,972 ....C2
Allegan 90,509 ....D6
Alpena 30,605 ....F4
Antrim 18,185 ....D3
Arenac 14,931 ....F4
Baraga 7,954 ....F4
Barry 50,057 ....D6
Bay 111,723 ....E5
Benzie 12,200 ....C4
Berrien 161,378 ....C7
Branch 41,502 ....D7
Calhoun 135,982 ....D6
Cass 49,477 ....C7
Charlevoix 21,468 ....D3
Cheboygan 21,398 ....E3
Chippewa 34,604 ....E2
Clare 24,952 ....E5
Clinton 57,883 ....E6
Crawford 12,260 ....E4
Delta 37,780 ....C2
Dickinson 26,831 ....B2
Eaton 92,879 ....E6
Emmet 25,040 ....E3
Genesee 430,459 ....F5
Gladwin 21,896 ....E4
Gogebic 18,052 ....F2
Grand Traverse 64,273 ...D4
Gratiot 38,982 ....E5
Hillsdale 43,431 ....E7
Houghton 35,446 ....G1
Huron 34,951 ....F5
Ingham 281,912 ....E6
Ionia 57,024 ....D6
Iosco 30,209 ....F4
Iron 13,175 ....G2
Isabella 54,624 ....E5
Jackson 149,756 ....E6
Kalamazoo 223,411 ......D6
Kalkaska 13,497 ....D4
Kent 500,631 ....D5
Keweenaw 1,701 ....A1
Lake 8,583 ....D5
Lapeer 74,768 ....F5
Leelanau 16,527 ....D4
Lenawee 91,476 ....E7
Livingston 115,645 ......F6
Luce 5,763 ....D2
Mackinac 10,674 ....D2
Macomb 717,400 ....G6
Manistee 21,265 ....C4
Marquette 70,887 ....B2
Mason 25,537 ....C4
Mecosta 37,308 ....D5
Menominee 24,920 ....B3
Midland 75,651 ....E5
Missaukee 12,147 ....D4
Monroe 133,600 ....F7
Montcalm 53,059 ....D5
Montmorency 8,936 ......E3
Muskegon 158,983 ....C5
Newaygo 38,202 ....D5
Oakland 1,083,592 ....F6
Oceana 22,454 ....C5
Ogemaw 18,681 ....E4
Ontonagon 8,854 ....F1
Osceola 20,146 ....D5
Oscoda 7,842 ....E4
Otsego 17,957 ....E3
Ottawa 187,768 ....C6
Presque Isle 13,743 .....F3
Roscommon 19,776 ......E4
Saginaw 211,946 ....E5
Saint Clair 138,802 ......G6
Saint Joseph 56,083 .....D7
Sanilac 39,928 ....G5
Schoolcraft 8,302 ....C2
Shiawassee 69,770 ......E6
Tuscola 55,498 ....F5
Van Buren 66,814 ....C6
Washtenaw 282,937 .....F6
Wayne 2,111,687 ....F6
Wexford 26,360 ....D4

CITIES and TOWNS

Addison 632 ....E7
Adrian▲ 22,097 ....F7
Akron 477 ....F5
Alabaster 46 ....F4
Alanson 677 ....E3
Albion 10,066 ....E6
Algonac 4,551 ....G6
Allegan▲ 4,547 ....D6
Allen 201 ....E7
Allen Park 31,092 ....B7
Alma 9,034 ....E5
Almont 2,354 ....F6
Alpena▲ 11,354 ....F3
Alpha 219 ....A2
Anchorville 3,202 ....G6
Ann Arbor▲ 109,592 ....F6
Applegate 297 ....G5
Arcadia 780 ....C4

Armada 1,548 ....G6
Ashley 518 ....E5
Athens 990 ....D6
Atlanta▲ 475 ....E3
Atlantic Mine 809 ......G1
Au Gres 838 ....F4
Au Sable 1,542 ....F4
Auburn 1,855 ....F5
Auburn Heights 7,500 ...F6
Augusta 927 ....D6
Averill 800 ....E5
Bad Axe▲ 3,484 ....G5
Baldwin▲ 821 ....D5
Bancroft 599 ....E6
Bangor 1,922 ....C6
Baraga 1,231 ....G1
Bark River 800 ....B3
Baroda 657 ....C7
Barryton 393 ....D5
Barton Hills 320 ....F6
Battle Creek 53,540 .....D6
Bay City▲ 38,936 ......F5
Bay Port 750 ....F5
Beal City 345 ....D5
Bear Lake 339 ....C4
Beaverton 1,150 ....E5
Beechwood 2,676 ....C6
Belding 5,969 ....D5
Bellaire▲ 1,104 ....D4
Belleville 3,270 ....F6
Bellevue 1,401 ....E6
Benton Harbor 12,818 ...C6
Benton Heights 5,465 ...C6
Benzonia 449 ....D4
Berkley 16,960 ....B6
Berrien Springs 1,927 ...C7
Bessemer▲ 2,272 ......F2
Beulah▲ 421 ....C4
Beverly Hills 10,610 ....B6
Big Rapids▲ 12,603 ....D5
Birch Run 992 ....F5
Birmingham 19,997 .....B6
Bitely 750 ....D5
Blissfield 3,172 ....F7
Bloomfield Hills 4,288 ..B6
Bloomingdale 503 ......C6
Boyne City 3,478 ....D3
Boyne Falls 369 ....E3
Breckenridge 1,301 .....E5
Breedsville 213 ....C6
Bridgeport 8,569 ....F5
Bridgman 2,140 ....C7
Brighton 5,686 ....F6
Britton 694 ....F6
Bronson 2,342 ....D7
Brooklyn 1,027 ....E6
Brown City 1,244 ....G5
Buchanan 4,992 ....C7
Buckley 402 ....D4
Burlington 294 ....D6
Burr Oak 882 ....D7
Burt 1,169 ....F5
Burton 27,617 ....F6
Byron 573 ....E6
Byron Center 900 ......D6
Cadillac▲ 10,104 ......D4
Caledonia 885 ....D6
Calumet 818 ....A1
Camden 482 ....E7
Capac 1,583 ....G5
Carleton 2,770 ....F6
Carney 197 ....B3
Caro▲ 4,054 ....F5
Carrollton 6,521 ....F5
Carson City 1,158 ......E5
Carsonville 583 ....G5
Caseville 857 ....F5
Casnovia 376 ....D5
Caspian 1,031 ....G2
Cass City 2,276 ....F5
Cassopolis▲ 1,822 .....C7
Cedar Springs 2,600 ...D5
Cement City 493 ....E6
Center Line 9,026 ......B6
Central Lake 954 ....D3
Centreville▲ 1,516 .....D7
Charlevoix▲ 3,116 .....D3
Charlotte▲ 8,083 ......E6
Chatham 268 ....B2
Cheboygan▲ 4,999 ....E3
Chelsea 3,772 ....E6
Chesaning 2,567 ....E5
Clare 3,021 ....E5
Clarkston 1,005 ....F6
Clarksville 360 ....D6
Clawson 13,874 ....B6
Clayton 384 ....E7
Clifford 354 ....F5
Climax 677 ....D6
Clinton 2,475 ....F6
Clio 2,629 ....F5
Coldwater▲ 9,607 .....D7
Coleman 1,237 ....E5
Coloma 1,679 ....C6
Colon 1,224 ....D7
Columbiaville 934 ......F5

Comstock • 11,162 ......D6
Concord 944 ....E6
Constantine 2,032 ......D7
Coopersville 3,421 .....C5
Copemish 222 ....D4
Copper City 198 ....A1
Corunna▲ 3,091 ....E6
Croswell 2,174 ....G5
Crystal 800 ....E5
Crystal Falls▲ 1,922 ...A2
Curtis 800 ....D2
Custer 312 ....C5
Cutlerville 11,228 ......D6
Daggett 260 ....B3
Dansville 437 ....E6
Davison 5,693 ....F5
De Tour Village 407 ....E3
De Witt 3,964 ....E6
Dearborn 89,286 ....B7
Dearborn Heights 60,838 .B7
Decatur 1,760 ....C6
Deckerville 1,015 ......G5
Deerfield 922 ....F7
Detroit Beach 2,113 ....F7
Detroit▲ 1,027,974 ....B7
Dexter 1,497 ....F6
Dimondale 1,247 ....E6
Dollar Bay 950 ....G1
Douglas 1,040 ....C6
Dowagiac 6,409 ....C6
Drayton Plains ....
Drummond Island • 746 .F3
Dryden 628 ....F6
Dundee 2,664 ....F7
Durand 4,283 ....E6
Eagle River▲ 20 ....A1
East Detroit 35,283 ....B6
East Grand Rapids 10,807 .D6

East Jordan 2,240 ......D3
East Kingsford A3
East Lansing 50,677 ....E6
East Tawas 2,887 ......F4
Eastlake 473 ....C4
Eastwood 6,340 ....D6
Eaton Rapids 4,695 ....E6
Eau Claire 494 ....C6
Ecorse 12,180 ....B7
Edmore 1,126 ....E5
Edwardsburg 1,142 .....C7
Elberta 478 ....C4
Elk Rapids 1,626 ....D4
Elkton 958 ....F5
Ellsworth 418 ....D3
Elsie 957 ....E5
Emmett 297 ....G6
Empire 306 ....C4
Erie 750 ....F7
Escanaba▲ 13,659 .....C3
Essexville 4,088 ....F5
Estral Beach 430 ....F7
Evart 1,744 ....D5
Ewen 821 ....F2
Fair Haven 1,505 ....G6
Fair Plain 8,051 ....C6
Fairgrove 592 ....F5
Farmington 10,132 .....F6
Farmington Hills 74,652 .F6
Farwell 851 ....E5
Fennville 1,023 ....C6
Fenton 8,444 ....F6
Ferndale 25,084 ....B6
Ferrysburg 2,919 ......C5
Fife Lake 394 ....D4
Flat Rock 7,290 ....F6
Flint▲ 140,761 ....F5
Flushing 8,542 ....F5

Fountain 165 ....C4
Fowler 912 ....E5
Fowlerville 2,648 ....E6
Frankenmuth 4,408 .....F5
Frankfort▲ 1,546 ......C4
Franklin 2,626 ....B6
Fraser 13,899 ....B6
Freeland 1,421 ....E5
Freeport 458 ....D6
Fremont 3,875 ....D5
Fruitport 1,090 ....C5
Gaastra 376 ....G2
Gagetown 337 ....F5
Gaines 427 ....E6
Galesburg 1,863 ....D6
Galien 596 ....C7
Garden 268 ....C3
Garden City 31,846 ....F6
Gaylord▲ 3,256 ....E3
Gibraltar 4,297 ....F6
Gladstone 4,565 ....C3
Gladwin▲ 2,682 ....E5
Gobles 769 ....D6
Goodrich 916 ....F6
Grand Blanc 7,760 .....F6
Grand Haven▲ 11,951 ..C5
Grand Ledge 7,579 ....E6
Grand Rapids▲ 189,126 .D5
Grandville 15,624 ......D6
Grant 764 ....D5
Grass Lake 903 ....E6
Grayling▲ 1,944 ....E4
Greenville 8,101 ....D5
Grosse Ile 9,781 ....B7
Grosse Pointe 5,681 ....B7
Grosse Pointe Farms 10,092 .B6
Grosse Pointe Park 12,857 .B7
Grosse Pointe Shores 2,955 .B6

Grosse Pointe Woods 17,715 .B6
Gulliver 962 ....D2
Gwinn 2,370 ....B2
Hamilton 950 ....C6
Hamtramck 18,372 .....B6
Hancock 4,547 ....G1
Hanover 481 ....E6
Harbor Beach 2,089 ....G5
Harbor Springs 1,540 ...D3
Harper Woods 14,903 ...B6
Harrison▲ 1,835 ....E4
Harrisville▲ 470 ....F4
Hart▲ 1,942 ....C5
Hartford 2,341 ....C6
Haslett 10,230 ....E6
Hastings▲ 6,549 ......D6
Hazel Park 20,051 .....B6
Hemlock 1,601 ....E5
Hermansville 950 ......B3
Hersey 354 ....D5
Hesperia 846 ....D5
Highland Park 20,121 ..B6
Hillman 643 ....F3
Hillsdale▲ 8,170 ......E7
Holland 30,745 ....C6
Holly 5,595 ....F6
Holt 11,744 ....E6
Homer 1,758 ....E6
Honor 292 ....D4
Hopkins 546 ....D6
Houghton Lake 3,353 ...E4
Houghton Lake Heights .E4
Houghton▲ 7,498 .....G1
Howard City 1,351 .....D5
Howell▲ 8,184 ....E6
Hubbardston 404 ....E5
Hubbell 1,174 ....A1
Hudson 2,580 ....E7

Hudsonville 6,170 ......D6
Huntington Woods 6,419 .B6
Ida 970 ....F7
Imlay City 2,921 ....F5
Indian River 950 ....E3
Inkster 30,772 ....B7
Interlochen 600 ....D4
Ionia▲ 5,935 ....D6
Iron Mountain▲ 8,525 ..B3
Iron River 2,095 ....G2
Ironwood 6,849 ....F2
Ishpeming 7,200 ....B2
Isle Royale National Park .E1
Ithaca▲ 3,009 ....E5
Jackson▲ 37,446 ......E6
Jenison 17,882 ....D6
Jonesville 2,283 ....E6
Kalamazoo▲ 80,277 ....D6
Kaleva 484 ....C4
Kalkaska▲ 1,952 ......D4
Keego Harbor 2,932 ....F6
Kent City 899 ....D5
Kentwood 37,826 ......D6
Kinde 473 ....G5
Kingsford 5,480 ....A3
Kingsley 738 ....D4
Kingston 439 ....F5
L'Anse▲ 2,151 ....G1
Laingsburg 1,148 ......E6
Lake Ann 217 ....D4
Lake City▲ 858 ....D4
Lake George 950 ....E5
Lake Linden 1,203 .....A1
Lake Michigan Beach 1,694 .C6
Lake Odessa 2,256 .....D6
Lake Orion 3,057 ......F6
Lakeview 1,108 ....E5
Lakewood Club 659 .....C5

(continued on following page)

Lambertville 7,860 ....F7
Lansing (cap.) 127,321 ....E6
Lapeer▲ 7,759 ....F5
Laurium 2,268 ....A1
Lawrence 915 ....C6
Lawton 1,685 ....D6
Le Roy 251 ....D4
Leland 776 ....D3
Lennon 534 ....E5
Leonard 357 ....F6
Leslie 1,872 ....E6
Levering 967 ....E3
Lexington 779 ....G5
Lincoln 824 ....F4
Lincoln Park 41,832 ....B7
Linden 2,415 ....F6
Litchfield 1,317 ....E6
Little Lake 975 ....B2
Livonia 100,850 ....D6
Lowell 3,983 ....D5
Ludington▲ 8,507 ....C5
Luna Pier 1,507 ....F7
Luther 343 ....D4
Lyons 824 ....E5
Mackinac Island 469 ....E3
Mackinaw City 875 ....E3
Madison Heights 32,196 ....B6
Mancelona 1,370 ....E4
Manchester 1,753 ....E6
Manistee▲ 6,734 ....C4
Manistique▲ 3,456 ....C3
Manton 1,161 ....D4
Maple Rapids 680 ....E5
Marcellus 1,193 ....D6
Marine City 4,556 ....G6
Marion 807 ....D4
Marlette 1,924 ....G5
Marquette▲ 21,977 ....B2
Marshall▲ 6,891 ....E6
Martin 462 ....D6
Marysville 8,515 ....G6
Mason▲ 6,768 ....E6
Mass City 850 ....G1
Mattawan 2,456 ....D6
Maybee 500 ....F6
Mayville 1,010 ....F5
McBain 692 ....D4
McBrides 252 ....D5
Mecosta 393 ....D5
Melvindale 11,216 ....B7
Memphis 1,221 ....G5
Mendon 920 ....D6
Menominee▲ 9,398 ....B3
Merrill 755 ....E5
Mesick 406 ....D4
Metamora 447 ....F6
Michiana 164 ....C7
Michigan Center 4,863 ....E6
Middleville 1,966 ....D6
Midland▲ 38,053 ....E5
Milan 4,040 ....F6
Milford 5,511 ....F6
Millersburg 250 ....F3

Millington 1,114 ....F5
Minden City 233 ....G5
Mineral Hills 200 ....G2
Mio▲ 1,886 ....E4
Mohawk 800 ....A1
Monroe▲ 22,902 ....F7
Montague 2,276 ....C5
Montgomery 388 ....E7
Montrose 1,811 ....F5
Morenci 2,342 ....E7
Morley 528 ....D5
Morrice 630 ....E6
Mount Clemens▲ 18,405 ....G6
Mount Morris 3,292 ....F5
Mount Pleasant▲ 23,285 ....E5
Muir 667 ....E5
Mulliken 590 ....E6
Munising▲ 2,783 ....C2
Muskegon▲ 40,283 ....C5
Muskegon Heights 13,176 ....C5
Napoleon 1,332 ....E6
Nashville 1,654 ....E6
Naubinway 850 ....D2
Negaunee 4,741 ....B2
New Baltimore 5,798 ....G6
New Boston 1,200 ....B7
New Buffalo 2,317 ....C7
New Era 520 ....C5
New Haven 2,331 ....G6
New Lothrop 596 ....F5
Newaygo 1,336 ....D5
Newberry▲ 1,873 ....D2
Niles 12,458 ....C7
North Adams 512 ....E7
North Branch 1,023 ....F5
North Muskegon 3,919 ....C5
Northport 605 ....D3
Northville 6,226 ....F6
Norton Shores 21,755 ....C5
Norway 2,910 ....B3
Novi 32,998 ....F6
Oak Park 30,462 ....B6
Oakley 362 ....E5
Okemos 20,216 ....E6
Olivet 1,604 ....E6
Omer 385 ....F4
Onaway 1,039 ....E3
Onekama 515 ....C4
Onsted 801 ....E6
Ontonagon▲ 2,040 ....F1
Orchard Lake 1,798 ....F6
Ortonville 1,252 ....F6
Oscoda 1,061 ....F4
Ossineke 1,091 ....F4
Otisville 724 ....F5
Otsego 3,937 ....D6
Otter Lake 474 ....F5
Ovid 1,442 ....E5
Owendale 285 ....F5
Owosso 16,322 ....E5
Oxford 2,929 ....F6
Parchment 1,958 ....D6
Parma 809 ....E6

Paw Paw Lake 3,782 ....C6
Paw Paw▲ 3,169 ....D6
Pearl Beach 3,394 ....G6
Peck 558 ....G5
Pellston 583 ....E3
Pentwater 1,050 ....C5
Perrinton 393 ....E5
Perry 2,163 ....E6
Petersburg 1,201 ....F6
Petoskey▲ 6,056 ....E3
Pewamo 520 ....E5
Pierson 207 ....F5
Pigeon 1,207 ....F5
Pinckney 1,603 ....F6
Pinconning 1,291 ....F5
Plainwell 4,057 ....D6
Pleasant Ridge 2,775 ....B6
Plymouth 9,560 ....F6
Pontiac▲ 71,166 ....F6
Port Austin 815 ....F4
Port Hope 313 ....G4
Port Huron▲ 33,694 ....G5
Port Sanilac 656 ....G5
Portage 41,042 ....D6
Portland 3,889 ....E6
Posen 263 ....F3
Potterville 1,523 ....E6
Powers 271 ....B3
Prescott 314 ....F4
Prudenville 1,513 ....E4
Quincy 1,680 ....E7
Quinnesec 1,254 ....A3
Ramsay 2 ....F2
Rapid River 950 ....C3
Ravenna 919 ....D5
Reading 1,127 ....E7
Reed City▲ 2,379 ....D5
Reese 1,414 ....F5
Republic 465 ....B2
Richland 465 ....D6
Richmond 4,141 ....G6
River Rouge 11,314 ....B7
Riverview 13,894 ....B7
Rochester 7,130 ....F6
Rockford 3,750 ....D5
Rockwood 3,141 ....F6
Rogers City▲ 3,642 ....F3
Romeo 3,520 ....F6
Romulus 22,897 ....F6
Roosevelt Park 3,885 ....C5
Roscommon▲ 858 ....E4
Rose City 686 ....E4
Rosebush 333 ....E5
Roseville 51,412 ....B6
Rothbury 407 ....C5
Royal Oak 65,410 ....B6
Rudyard 950 ....E2
Saginaw▲ 69,512 ....F5
Saint Charles 2,144 ....E5
Saint Clair 5,116 ....G6
Saint Clair Shores 68,107 ....B6
Saint Ignace▲ 2,568 ....E3
Saint James • 240 ....D3

Saint Johns▲ 7,284 ....E6
Saint Joseph▲ 9,214 ....C6
Saint Louis 3,828 ....E5
Saline 6,660 ....F6
Sand Lake 456 ....D5
Sandusky▲ 2,403 ....G5
Sanford 889 ....E5
Saranac 1,461 ....D6
Saugatuck 954 ....C6
Sault Sainte Marie▲ 14,689 ....E2
Schoolcraft 1,517 ....D6
Scottville 1,287 ....C5
Sebewaing 1,923 ....F5
Shelby 1,871 ....C5
Shepherd 1,413 ....E5
Sheridan 730 ....D5
Sherwood 320 ....D6
Shoreham 737 ....C6
Shorewood 1,735 ....C7
South Haven 5,563 ....C6
South Lyon 5,857 ....F6
South Monroe 5,266 ....F7
South Range 745 ....G1
South Rockwood 1,221 ....F7
Southfield 75,728 ....F6
Southgate 30,771 ....F6
Sparlingville 1,974 ....G6
Sparta 3,968 ....D5
Spring Arbor 2,010 ....E6
Spring Lake 2,537 ....C5
Springfield 5,582 ....D6
Springport 707 ....E6
Stambaugh 1,281 ....G2
Standish▲ 1,377 ....F5
Stanton▲ 1,504 ....D5
Stanwood 174 ....D5
Stephenson 904 ....B3
Sterling 520 ....F4
Sterling Heights 117,810 ....B6
Stevensville 1,230 ....C6
Stockbridge 1,202 ....E6
Sturgis 10,130 ....D7
Sunfield 610 ....E6
Suttons Bay 561 ....D3
Swartz Creek 4,851 ....F6
Sylvan Lake 1,884 ....F6
Tawas City▲ 2,009 ....F4
Taylor 70,811 ....F6
Tecumseh 7,462 ....E7
Tekonsha 722 ....E6
Temperance 6,542 ....F7
Thompsonville 416 ....C4
Three Oaks 1,786 ....C7
Three Rivers 7,413 ....D7
Traverse City▲ 15,155 ....D4
Trenton 20,586 ....B7
Troy 72,884 ....B6
Tustin 236 ....D4
Twin Lake 1,328 ....C5
Twining 169 ....F4
Ubly 821 ....G5
Union City 1,767 ....D6
Union Pier 1,039 ....C7

Unionville 590 ....F5
Utica 5,081 ....F6
Vandalia 357 ....D7
Vanderbilt 605 ....E3
Vassar 2,559 ....F5
Vermontville 776 ....E6
Vernon 913 ....E5
Vicksburg 2,216 ....D6
Wakefield 2,318 ....F2
Waldron 581 ....E7
Walker 17,279 ....D5
Walkerville 262 ....C5
Walled Lake 6,278 ....F6
Warren 144,864 ....B6
Watersmeet 850 ....G2
Watervliet 1,867 ....C6
Wayland 2,751 ....D6
Wayne 19,899 ....F6
Webberville 1,698 ....E6
Weidman 696 ....D5
Wells B3
West Branch▲ 1,914 ....E4
Westland 84,724 ....F6
Westphalia 780 ....E5
White Cloud▲ 1,147 ....D5
White Pigeon 1,458 ....D7
White Pine 1,142 ....F1
Whitehall 3,027 ....C5
Whitmore Lake 3,251 ....F6
Whittemore 463 ....F4
Williamston 2,922 ....E6
Wixom 8,550 ....F6
Wolf Lake 4,110 ....D5
Wolverine 364 ....E3
Wolverine Lake 4,727 ....F6
Woodhaven 11,631 ....F6
Woodland 466 ....D6
Wyandotte 30,938 ....B7
Wyoming 63,891 ....D5
Yale 1,977 ....G5
Ypsilanti 24,846 ....F6
Zeeland 5,417 ....C6
Zilwaukee 1,850 ....F5

OTHER FEATURES

Abbaye (pt.) B2
Au Sable (pt.) C4
Au Sable (pt.) F4
Au Sable (riv.) E4
Au Train (bay) C2
Bad (riv.) C3
Barques (pt.) G4
Beaver (isl.) D3
Beaver (isl.) F4
Belle (riv.) G6
Bete Grise (bay) B1
Big Bay (pt.) B2
Big Bay de Noc (bay) C3
Big Iron (riv.) F1
Big Sable (pt.) C4
Big Sable (riv.) C4
Big Star (lake) C5

Black (lake) E3
Black (riv.) E3
Black (riv.) G5
Blake (pt.) E1
Boardman (riv.) D4
Bois Blanc (isl.) E3
Bond Falls (res.) F2
Brevoort (lake) D3
Brule (riv.) A3
Burt (lake) E3
Cass (riv.) F5
Cedar (lake) F4
Charlevoix (lake) D3
Chippewa (riv.) E5
Crisp (pt.) D2
Crystal (lake) C4
Curwood (mt.) A2
Dead (riv.) B2
Deer (lake) E3
De Tour (passage) E3
Detour (pt.) B7
Detroit (riv.) B7
Drummond (isl.) F3
Duck (lake) D4
Elk (lake) D4
Erie (lake) G7
Escanaba (riv.) B2
False Detour (chan.) F3
Father Marquette Nat'l Mem. E3
Fawn (riv.) D7
Fence (riv.) A2
Firesteel (riv.) G1
Fletcher (pond) F4
Flint (riv.) F5
Ford (riv.) B2
Forty Mile (pt.) F3
Fourteen Mile (pt.) F1
Garden (isl.) D3
Garden (pen.) C3
Glen (lake) C4
Gogebic (lake) F2
Good Harbor (bay) D3
Government (peak) F1
Grand (isl.) C2
Grand (lake) F3
Grand (riv.) D6
Grand Traverse (bay) D3
Granite (pt.) B2
Green (bay) B4
Gun (lake) D6
Hamlin (lake) C4
Higgins (lake) E4
High (isl.) D3
Houghton (lake) E4
Hubbard (lake) F4
Huron (bay) A2
Huron (isl.) A2
Huron (riv.) G4
Huron (riv.) F6
Huron River (pt.) B2
Independence (lake) B2
Indian (lake) C3
Isle Royale (isl.) D1

Isle Royale Nat'l Park E1
Kalamazoo (riv.) C6
Keweenaw (bay) A1
Keweenaw (pt.) B1
K.I. Sawyer A.F.B. 6,577 ....B2
L'Anse Ind. Res. A2
Laughing Fish (pt.) B2
Leelanau (lake) D4
Light House (pt.) D3
Little Bay de Noc (bay) B3
Little Girl (riv.) E1
Little Sable (pt.) C5
Little Summer (isl.) C3
Little Traverse (bay) D3
Long (lake) E6
Lookingglass (riv.) E6
Mackinac (isl.) E3
Mackinac (str.) E3
Manistee (riv.) C4
Manistique (riv.) D2
Manistique (riv.) C2
Maple (isl.) B1
Maple (riv.) E5
Margrethe (lake) E4
Marquette (isl.) E3
Maumee (bay) F7
Menominee (riv.) B3
Michigamme (lake) A2
Michigamme (res.) B2
Michigamme (riv.) B2
Michigan (lake) B5
Mill (creek) G5
Millecoquins (lake) D2
Misery (bay) G1
Misery (riv.) G1
Montreal (riv.) F1
Mullett (lake) E3
Munuscong (lake) E2
Muskegon (riv.) C5
Neebish (isl.) E2
Net (riv.) G2
Ninemile (pt.) F2
North (chan.) E2
North (pt.) F3
North Fox (isl.) D3
North Manitou (isl.) C3
Oak (pt.) F5
Ontonagon (riv.) G1
Ontonagon Ind. Res. F1
Otsego (lake) A2
Paint (riv.) A2
Paradise (lake) E3
Passage (isl.) E1
Patterson (pt.) D3
Paw Paw (riv.) C6
Peninsula (pt.) C3
Perch (lake) G2
Perch (lake) G2
Pere Marquette (riv.) D5
Pictured Rocks (cliff) C2
Pictured Rocks
  Nat'l Lakeshore C2
Pigeon (riv.) D7
Pigeon (riv.) E3
Pine (riv.) D4
Pine (riv.) E5
Platte (riv.) C4
Porcupine (mts.) F1
Potagannissing (bay) F2
Poverty (isl.) C3
Prairie (riv.) D7
Presque Isle (riv.) F1
Rabbit (riv.) D6
Raisin (riv.) F7
Rapid (riv.) B2
Reedsburg (res.) E4
Rifle (riv.) F4
Royale (isl.) E1
Saginaw (bay) F5
Saginaw (riv.) F5
Saint Clair (lake) G6
Saint Clair (riv.) G6
Saint Joseph (riv.) C7
Saint Martin (bay) E2
Saint Martin (isl.) C3
Saint Marys (riv.) E2
Salt (riv.) E2
Sand (riv.) B2
Seul Choi (pt.) D3
Shelldrake (riv.) D2
Shiawassee (riv.) E5
Siskiwit (bay) E1
Sleeping Bear Dunes
  Nat'l Lakeshore C4
South (bay) C2
South (pt.) F4
South (chan.) E3
South Fox (isl.) D3
South Manitou (isl.) C3
Sturgeon (riv.) C2
Sugar (isl.) E2
Summer (isl.) C3
Superior (lake) C2
Tahquamenon (falls) D2
Tahquamenon (riv.) D2
Tawas (lake) F4
Tawas (pt.) F4
Thunder (bay) F3
Thunder Bay (riv.) F3
Tittabawassee (riv.) E5
Torch (lake) D3
Traverse (lake) A1
Traverse (pt.) A1
Turtle (lake) F4
Two Hearted (riv.) D2
Vieux Desert (lake) G2
Walloon (lake) E3
White (riv.) C5
Whitefish (bay) E2
Whitefish (pt.) E2
Whitefish (riv.) C2
Wood (isl.) C2
Wurtsmith A.F.B. 5,080 ....F4
Yellow Dog (riv.) B2

▲ County Seat
• Population of town or township

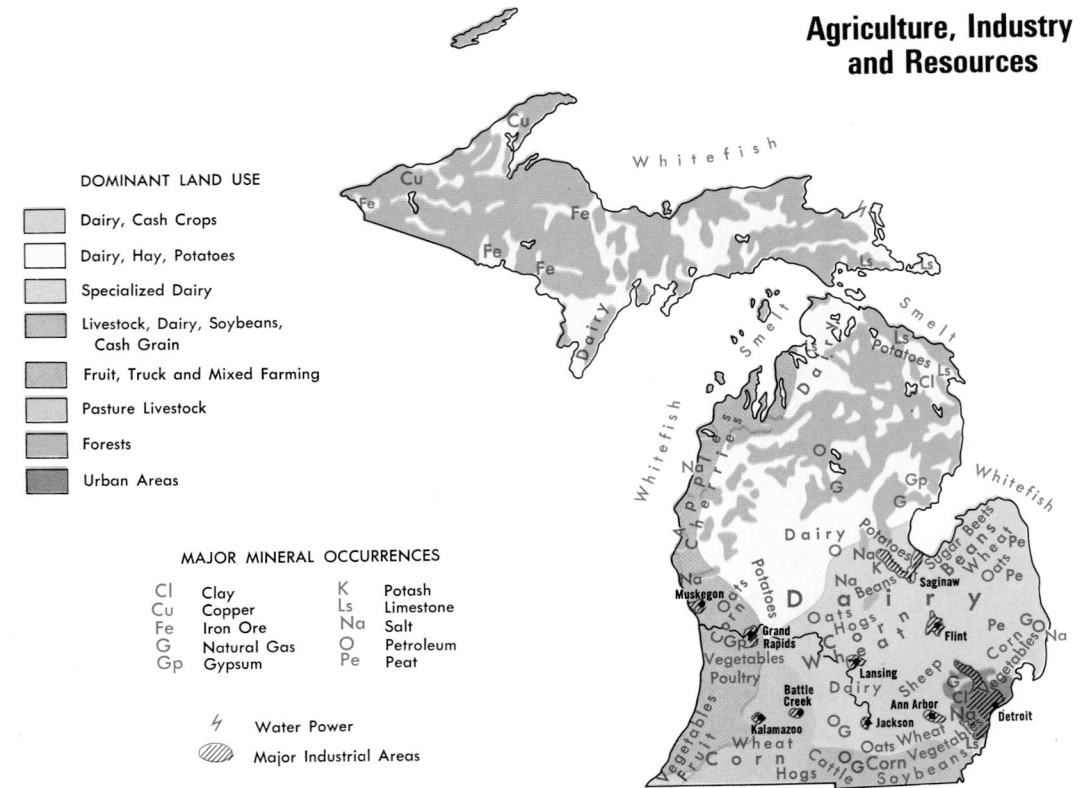

Agriculture, Industry and Resources

DOMINANT LAND USE

Dairy, Cash Crops
Dairy, Hay, Potatoes
Specialized Dairy
Livestock, Dairy, Soybeans, Cash Grain
Fruit, Truck and Mixed Farming
Pasture Livestock
Forests
Urban Areas

MAJOR MINERAL OCCURRENCES

Cl Clay
Cu Copper
Fe Iron Ore
G Natural Gas
Gp Gypsum
K Potash
Ls Limestone
Na Salt
O Petroleum
Pe Peat

Water Power
Major Industrial Areas

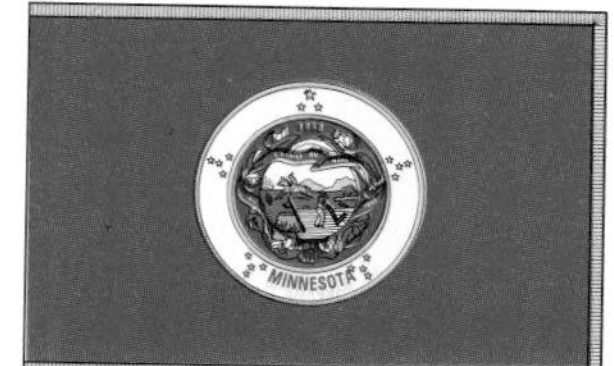

AREA 84,402 sq. mi. (218,601 sq. km.)
POPULATION 4,387,029
CAPITAL St. Paul
LARGEST CITY Minneapolis
HIGHEST POINT Eagle Mtn. 2,301 ft. (701 m.)
SETTLED IN 1805
ADMITTED TO UNION May 11, 1858
POPULAR NAME North Star State; Gopher State
STATE FLOWER Pink & White Lady's-Slipper
STATE BIRD Common Loon

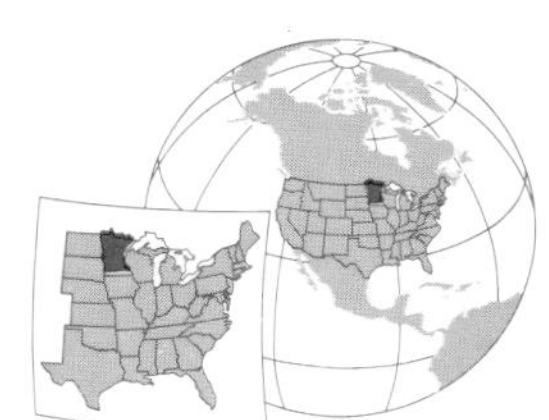

COUNTIES

Aitkin 12,425 E4
Anoka 243,641 E5
Becker 27,881 C4
Beltrami 34,384 C2
Benton 30,185 D5
Big Stone 6,285 B5
Blue Earth 54,044 D6
Brown 26,984 D6
Carlton 29,259 F4
Carver 47,915 E6
Cass 21,791 D4
Chippewa 13,228 C5
Chisago 30,521 F5
Clay 50,422 B4
Clearwater 8,309 C3
Cook 3,868 H3
Cottonwood 12,694 C6
Crow Wing 44,249 D4
Dakota 275,227 E6
Dodge 15,731 F7
Douglas 28,674 C5
Faribault 16,937 D7
Fillmore 20,777 F7
Freeborn 33,060 E7
Goodhue 40,690 F6
Grant 6,246 B5
Hennepin 1,032,431 E5
Houston 18,497 G7
Hubbard 14,939 D3
Isanti 25,921 E5
Itasca 40,863 E3
Jackson 11,677 C7
Kanabec 12,802 E5
Kandiyohi 38,761 C5
Kittson 5,767 B2
Koochiching 16,299 E2
Lac qui Parle 8,924 B6
Lake 10,415 G3
Lake of the Woods 4,076 D2
Le Sueur 23,239 E6
Lincoln 6,890 B6
Lyon 24,789 C6
Mahnomen 5,044 C3
Marshall 10,993 B2
Martin 22,914 D7
McLeod 32,030 D6
Meeker 20,846 D5
Mille Lacs 18,670 E5
Morrison 29,604 D4
Mower 37,385 F7
Murray 9,660 C6
Nicollet 28,076 D6
Nobles 20,098 C7
Norman 7,975 B3
Olmsted 106,470 F7
Otter Tail 50,714 C4
Pennington 13,306 B2
Pine 21,264 F4
Pipestone 10,491 B6
Polk 32,498 B3
Pope 10,745 C5
Ramsey 485,765 E5
Red Lake 4,525 B3
Redwood 17,254 C6
Renville 17,673 C6
Rice 49,183 E6
Rock 9,806 B7
Roseau 15,026 C2
Saint Louis 222,229 F3
Scott 57,846 E6
Sherburne 41,945 E5
Sibley 14,366 D6
Stearns 118,791 D5
Steele 30,729 E7
Stevens 10,634 B5
Swift 10,724 C5
Todd 23,363 D4
Traverse 4,463 B5
Wabasha 19,744 F6
Wadena 13,154 D4
Waseca 18,079 E6
Washington 145,896 F5
Watonwan 11,682 D7
Wilkin 7,516 B4
Winona 47,828 G6
Wright 68,710 D5
Yellow Medicine 11,684 B6

CITIES and TOWNS

Ada▲ 1,708 B3
Adams 756 F7
Adrian 1,141 C7
Afton 2,645 F6
Aitkin▲ 1,698 E4
Akeley 393 D3
Albany 1,548 D5
Albert Lea▲ 18,310 E7
Alberta 136 B5
Albertville 1,251 E5
Alborn 500 F4
Alden 623 E7
Aldrich 70 C4
Alexandria▲ 7,838 C5
Alpha 105 D7
Altura 349 G6
Alvarado 356 B2
Amboy 517 D7
Andover 15,216 E5
Annandale 2,054 D5
Anoka▲ 17,192 E5
Apple Valley 34,598 G6
Appleton 1,552 C5
Arco 104 B6
Argyle 636 B2
Arlington 1,886 D6
Arnold 2,891 F4
Ashby 469 C4
Askov 343 F4
Atwater 1,053 D5
Audubon 411 C4
Aurora 1,965 F3
Austin▲ 21,907 E7
Avoca 150 C7
Avon 970 D5
Babbitt 1,562 G3
Backus 240 D4
Badger 381 B2
Bagley▲ 1,388 C3
Balaton 737 C6
Barnesville 2,066 B4
Barnum 482 F4
Barrett 350 B5
Barry 40 B5
Battle Lake 698 C4
Baudette▲ 1,146 D2
Baxter 3,695 D4
Bayport 3,200 F5
Beardsley 297 B5
Beaver Bay 147 G3
Beaver Creek 249 B7
Becker 902 E5
Bejou 110 B3
Belgrade 700 C5
Belle Plaine 3,149 E6
Bellechester 110 F6
Bellingham 247 B5
Beltrami 137 B3
Belview 383 C6
Bemidji▲ 11,245 D3
Bena 147 D3
Benson▲ 3,235 C5
Bertha 507 C4
Bethel 394 E5
Big Falls 341 E2
Big Lake 3,113 E5
Bigelow 232 C7
Bigfork 384 E3
Bingham Lake 155 C7
Bird Island 1,326 D6
Biscay 113 D6
Biwabik 1,097 F3
Blackduck 718 D3
Blaine 38,975 G5
Blomkest 183 D6
Blooming Prairie 2,043 E7
Bloomington 86,335 G6
Blue Earth▲ 3,745 D7
Bluffton 187 C4
Bock 115 E5
Borup 119 B3
Bovey 662 E3
Bowlus 260 D5
Boy River 43 D3
Boyd 251 C6
Braham 1,139 E5
Brainerd▲ 12,353 D4
Branch 2,400 F5
Brandon 441 C5
Breckenridge▲ 3,708 B4
Breezy Point 432 D4
Brewster 532 C7
Bricelyn 426 E7
Brook Park 125 F5
Brooklyn Center 28,887 G5
Brooklyn Park 56,381 G5
Brooks 158 B3
Brookston 107 F4
Brooten 589 C5
Browerville 782 D4
Browns Valley 804 B5
Brownsdale 695 F7
Brownsville 415 G7
Brownton 781 D6
Bruno 89 F4
Buckman 201 D5
Buffalo Lake 734 D6
Buffalo▲ 6,856 E5
Buhl 915 F3
Burnsville 51,288 E6
Burtrum 172 D5
Butterfield 509 D7
Byron 2,441 F6
Caledonia▲ 2,846 G7
Callaway 212 C3
Calumet 382 E3
Cambridge▲ 5,094 E5
Campbell 233 B4
Canby 1,826 B6
Cannon Falls 3,232 F6
Canton 362 F7
Carlos 361 C5
Carlton▲ 923 F4
Carver 744 E6
Cass Lake 923 D3
Cedar Mills 80 D6
Center City▲ 451 F5
Centerville 1,633 E5
Ceylon 461 D7
Champlin 16,849 G5
Chandler 316 C7
Chanhassen 11,732 F6
Chaska▲ 11,339 F6
Chatfield 2,226 F7
Chickamaw Beach 132 D4
Chisago City 2,009 E5
Chisholm 5,290 E3
Chokio 521 B5
Circle Pines 4,704 G5
Clara City 1,307 C6
Claremont 530 E6
Clarissa 637 C4
Clarkfield 924 C6
Clarks Grove 675 E7
Clear Lake 315 E5
Clearbrook 560 C3
Clearwater 597 D5
Clements 191 D6
Cleveland 699 E6
Climax 264 B3
Clinton 574 B5
Clitherall 109 C4
Clontarf 172 C5
Cloquet 10,885 F4
Coates 186 E6
Cobden 62 D6
Cohasset E3
Cokato 2,180 D5
Cold Spring 2,459 D5
Coleraine 1,041 E3
Cologne 563 E6
Columbia Heights 18,910 G5
Comfrey 433 D6
Comstock 123 B4
Conger 143 E7
Cook 680 F3
Coon Rapids 52,978 G5
Corcoran 5,199 F5
Correll 60 B5
Cosmos 610 D6
Cottage Grove 22,935 F6
Cotton 982 F3
Cottonwood 924 C6
Courtland 412 D6
Cromwell 221 F4
Crookston▲ 8,119 B3
Crosby 2,073 D4
Crosslake 1,132 E4
Crystal 23,788 G5
Currie 303 C6
Cuyuna 172 E4
Cyrus 328 C5
Dakota 360 G7
Dalton 234 C4
Danube 562 C6
Danvers 98 C5
Darfur 128 D6
Darwin 252 D5
Dassel 1,082 D5
Dawson 1,626 B6
Day 4,443 E5
Dayton 4,070 E5
De Graff 149 C5
Deephaven 3,653 G5
Deer Creek 303 C4
Deer River 838 E3
Deerwood 524 E4
Delano 2,709 E5
Delavan 245 D7
Delhi 69 C6
Dellwood 887 F5
Denham 36 F4
Dennison 152 E6
Dent 177 C4
Detroit Lakes▲ 6,635 C4
Dexter 303 F7
Dilworth 2,562 B4
Dodge Center 1,954 F6
Donaldson 57 B2
Donnelly 221 B5
Doran 78 B4
Dover 416 F7
Dovray 60 C6
Duluth▲ 85,493 F4
Dumont 126 B5
Dundas 473 E6
Dundee 107 C7
Dunnell 187 D7
Eagan 47,409 G6
Eagle Bend 524 D4
Eagle Lake 1,703 E6
East Bethel 8,050 E5
East Grand Forks 8,658 B3
East Gull Lake 687 D4
Easton 229 E7
Echo 304 C6
Eden Prairie 39,311 G6
Eden Valley 732 D5
Edgerton 1,106 B7
Edina 46,070 G5
Effie 130 E3
Eitzen 221 G7
Elba 220 F6
Elbow Lake▲ 1,186 B5
Elgin 733 F6
Elizabeth 152 B4
Elk River▲ 11,143 E5
Elko 223 E6
Elkton 142 F7
Ellendale 549 E7
Ellsworth 580 C7
Elmdale 130 D5
Elmore 709 D7
Elrosa 205 C5
Ely 3,968 G3
Elysian 445 E6
Emily 613 E4
Emmons 439 E7
Erhard 181 B4
Erskine 422 B3
Esko 500 F4
Evan 83 D6
Evansville 566 C4
Eveleth 4,064 F3
Excelsior 2,367 E6
Eyota 1,448 F7
Fairfax 1,276 D6
Fairmont▲ 11,265 D7
Falcon Heights 5,380 G5
Faribault▲ 17,085 E6
Farmington 5,940 E6
Farwell 74 C5
Federal Dam 118 D3
Felton 211 B3
Fergus Falls▲ 12,362 B4
Fertile 853 B3
Fifty Lakes 299 D4
Finlayson 242 F4
Fisher 413 B3
Flensburg 213 D5
Floodwood 574 E4
Florence 53 B6
Florenton 635 F3
Foley▲ 1,854 D5
Forada 171 C5
Forest Lake 5,833 F5
Foreston 354 E5
Fort Ripley 92 D4
Fosston 1,529 C3
Fountain 327 F7
Foxhome 160 B4
Franklin 512 D6
Frazee 1,176 C4
Freeborn 301 E7
Freeport 556 D5
Fridley 28,335 G5
Frost 236 D7
Fulda 1,212 C7
Garfield 203 C5
Garrison 138 E4
Garvin 149 C6
Gary 200 B3
Gaylord▲ 1,935 D6
Geneva 444 E7
Genola 85 D5
Georgetown 107 B3
Ghent 316 C6
Gibbon 712 D6
Gilbert 1,934 F3
Gilman 192 E5
Glen 4,648 E4
Glencoe▲ 4,396 D6
Glenville 778 E7
Glenwood▲ 2,573 C5
Glyndon 862 B4
Golden Valley 20,971 G5
Gonvick 302 C3
Good Thunder 561 D6
Goodhue 533 F6
Goodridge 115 C2
Goodview 2,878 G6
Graceville 671 B5
Granada 374 D7
Grand Marais▲ 1,171 G2
Grand Meadow 967 F7
Grand Rapids▲ 7,976 E3
Granite Falls▲ 3,083 C6
Grasston 119 E5
Green Isle 239 E6
Greenbush 800 B2
Greenfield 1,450 F5
Greenwald 209 D5
Grey Eagle 353 D5
Grove City 547 D5
Grygla 220 C2
Gully 128 C3
Hackensack 245 D4
Hadley 94 C7
Hallock▲ 1,304 A2
Halma 73 B2
Halstad 611 B3
Ham Lake 8,924 E5
Hamburg 492 D6
Hamel F5
Hammond 205 F6
Hampton 363 E6
Hancock 723 C5
Hanley Falls 246 C6
Hanover 787 E5
Hanska 443 D6
Harding 76 E4
Hardwick 234 B7
Harmony 1,081 F7
Harris 843 F5
Hartland 270 E7
Hastings▲ 15,445 F6
Hatfield 66 B7
Hawley 1,655 B4
Hayfield 1,283 F7
Hayward 246 E7
Hazel Run 81 C6
Hector 1,145 D6
Heidelberg 73 E6
Henderson 746 E6
Hendricks 684 B6
Hendrum 309 B3
Henning 738 C4
Henriette 78 E5
Herman 485 B5
Hermantown 6,761 F4
Heron Lake 730 C7
Hewitt 269 C4
Hibbing 18,046 F3

(continued on following page)

Agriculture, Industry and Resources

DOMINANT LAND USE

- Wheat, General Farming
- Dairy, Livestock
- Dairy, Hay, Potatoes
- Cattle Feed, Hogs
- Livestock, Cash Grain
- Forests
- Swampland, Limited Agriculture
- Urban Areas

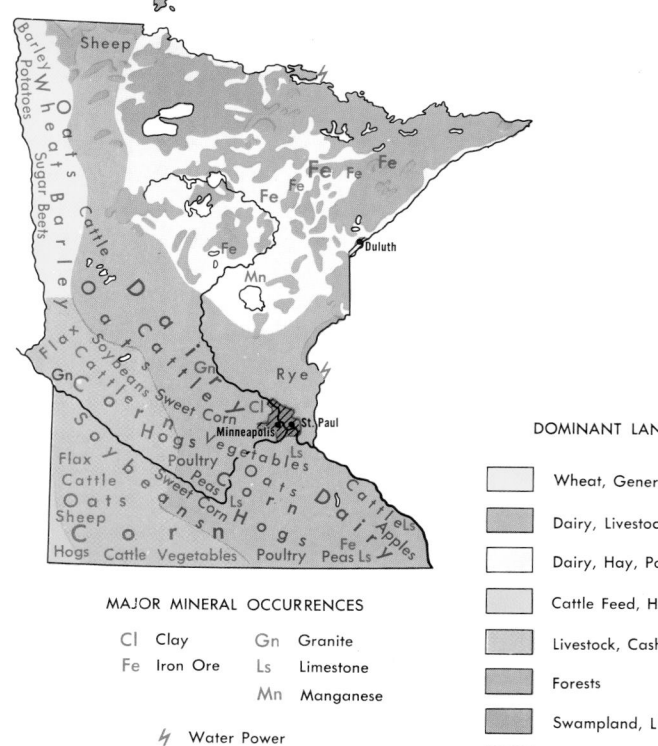

MAJOR MINERAL OCCURRENCES

Cl Clay
Fe Iron Ore
Gn Granite
Ls Limestone
Mn Manganese

Water Power
Major Industrial Areas

Hill City 469 ....E4
Hillman 45 ....E4
Hills 607 ....B7
Hinckley 946 ....E4
Hitterdal 242 ....B4
Hoffman 576 ....C5
Hokah 687 ....G7
Holdingford 561 ....D5
Holland 216 ....B6
Hollandale 289 ....E7
Holloway 123 ....C5
Holt 88 ....B2
Hopkins 16,534 ....G5
Houston 1,013 ....G7
Howard Lake 1,343 ....D5
Hoyt Lakes 2,348 ....F3
Hugo 4,417 ....E5
Humboldt 74 ....A2
Hutchinson 11,523 ....D6
Ihlen 101 ....B7
Independence 2,822 ....E5
Indus E2
International Falls▲ 8,325 ....E2
Inver Grove Heights 22,477 ....C7
Iona 158 ....C7
Iron 133 ....F3
Ironton 553 ....D4
Isanti 1,228 ....E5
Island View 150 ....E2
Isle 566 ....E4
Ivanhoe▲ 751 ....B6
Jackson▲ 3,559 ....C7
Janesville 1,969 ....E6
Jasper 599 ....B7
Jeffers 443 ....C6
Jenkins 262 ....D4
Johnson 46 ....B5
Jordan 2,909 ....E6
Kandiyohi 506 ....D5
Karlstad 881 ....B2
Kasota 655 ....D6
Kasson 3,514 ....F6
Keewatin 1,118 ....E3
Kelliher 348 ....D2
Kellogg 423 ....G6
Kelly Lake 900 ....F3
Kennedy 337 ....A2
Kenneth 81 ....B7
Kensington 295 ....C5
Kent 131 ....B4
Kenyon 1,552 ....E6
Kerkhoven 732 ....C5
Kerrick 56 ....F4
Kettle River 190 ....F4
Kiester 606 ....E7
Kilkenny 167 ....E6
Kimball 690 ....D5
Kingston 131 ....D5
Kinney 257 ....F3
La Crescent 4,311 ....G7
La Prairie 438 ....E3
La Salle 98 ....D6
Lafayette 462 ....D6
Lake Benton 693 ....B6
Lake Bronson 272 ....B2
Lake City 4,391 ....F6
Lake Crystal 2,084 ....D6
Lake Elmo 5,903 ....F6
Lake Henry 90 ....D5
Lake Lillian 229 ....C6
Lake Park 638 ....B4
Lake Saint Croix Beach 1,078 ..F6

Lake Shore 693 ....D4
Lake Wilson 319 ....B7
Lakefield 1,679 ....C7
Lakeland 2,000 ....F6
Lakeville 24,854 ....E6
Lamberton 972 ....C6
Lancaster 342 ....B2
Lanesboro 858 ....G7
Laporte 101 ....D3
Lastrup 112 ....D4
Lauderdale 2,700 ....G5
Le Center▲ 2,006 ....E6
Le Roy 904 ....F7
Le Sueur 3,714 ....E6
Lengby 112 ....C3
Leonard 26 ....C3
Leonidas 70 ....F3
Lester Prairie 1,180 ....D6
Lewiston 1,298 ....G7
Lewisville 255 ....D7
Lexington 2,279 ....G5
Lilydale 506 ....G5
Lindstrom 2,461 ....E5
Lino Lakes 8,807 ....G5
Lismore 248 ....B7
Litchfield▲ 6,041 ....D5
Little Falls▲ 7,232 ....D5
Little Rock 714 ....D5
Littlefork 838 ....E2
Long Beach 204 ....C5
Long Lake 1,984 ....F5
Long Prairie▲ 2,786 ....D5
Longville 224 ....D4
Lonsdale 1,252 ....E6
Loretto 404 ....F5
Louisburg 42 ....B5
Lowry 233 ....C5
Lucan 235 ....C6
Luverne▲ 4,382 ....B7
Lyle 504 ....F7
Lynd 287 ....C6
Mabel 745 ....G7
Madelia 2,237 ....D6
Madison Lake 643 ....E6
Madison▲ 1,951 ....B5
Magnolia 155 ....B7
Mahnomen▲ 1,154 ....C3
Mahtomedi 5,569 ....E5
Manchester 69 ....E7
Manhattan Beach 61 ....D4
Mankato▲ 31,477 ....E6
Mantorville▲ 874 ....F6
Maple Grove 38,736 ....G5
Maple Lake 1,394 ....D5
Maple Plain 2,005 ....F5
Mapleton 1,526 ....E6
Mapleview 206 ....E7
Maplewood 30,954 ....E3
Marble 618 ....E3
Marietta 211 ....B5
Marine on Saint Croix 602 ....F5
Marshall▲ 12,023 ....C6
Mayer 471 ....E6
Maynard 419 ....C5
Mazeppa 722 ....F6
McGrath 62 ....E4
McGregor 376 ....E4
McIntosh 665 ....C3
McKinley 116 ....F3
Meadowlands 92 ....F3
Medford 733 ....E6
Medicine Lake 385 ....G5

Medina (Hamel) 3,096 ....F5
Meire Grove 124 ....C5
Melrose 2,561 ....D5
Menahga 1,076 ....C4
Mendota 164 ....G5
Mendota Heights 9,431 ....G6
Mentor 94 ....B3
Middle River 285 ....B2
Miesville 135 ....F6
Milaca▲ 2,182 ....E5
Milan 353 ....C5
Millerville 104 ....C4
Millville 163 ....F6
Milroy 297 ....C6
Minneapolis▲ 368,383 ....G5
Minneiska 127 ....G6
Minneota 1,417 ....C6
Minnesota City 258 ....G6
Minnesota Lake 681 ....E7
Minnetonka 48,370 ....F5
Minnetrista 3,439 ....F5
Mizpah 100 ....D2
Montevideo▲ 5,499 ....C5
Montgomery 2,399 ....E6
Monticello 4,941 ....E5
Montrose 1,008 ....E5
Moorhead▲ 32,295 ....B4
Moose Lake 1,206 ....F4
Mora▲ 2,905 ....E5
Morgan 965 ....C6
Morris▲ 5,613 ....C5
Morristown 784 ....E6
Morton 448 ....C6
Motley 441 ....D4
Mound 9,634 ....E6
Mounds View 12,541 ....G5
Mountain Iron 3,362 ....F3
Mountain Lake 1,906 ....D7
Murdock 282 ....C5
Myrtle 72 ....E7
Nashua 63 ....B4
Nashwauk 1,026 ....E3
Nassau 83 ....B5
Naytahwaush 378 ....C3
Nelson 177 ....C5
Nerstrand 210 ....E6
Nevis 375 ....D4
New Auburn 363 ....D6
New Brighton 22,207 ....G5
New Germany 353 ....E6
New Hope 21,853 ....G5
New London 971 ....D5
New Market 227 ....E6
New Munich 314 ....D5
New Prague 3,569 ....E6
New Richland 1,237 ....E7
New Trier 96 ....F6
New Ulm▲ 13,132 ....D6
New York Mills 940 ....C4
Newfolden 345 ....B2
Newport 3,720 ....F6
Nicollet 795 ....D6
Nielsville 100 ....B3
Nimrod 65 ....D4
Nisswa 1,391 ....D4
Norcross 86 ....B5
North Branch 1,867 ....F5
North Mankato 10,164 ....D6
North Oaks 3,386 ....G5
North Redwood 203 ....D6
North Saint Paul 12,376 ....G5

Northfield 14,684 ....E6
Northome 283 ....D3
Northrop 276 ....D7
Norwood 1,351 ....E6
Oak Park 3,486 ....E5
Oakdale 18,374 ....B5
Odessa 155 ....B5
Odin 102 ....D7
Ogema 164 ....C3
Ogilvie 510 ....E5
Okabena 223 ....C7
Oklee 441 ....C3
Olivia▲ 2,623 ....C6
Onamia 676 ....E4
Ormsby 159 ....D7
Oronoco 727 ....F6
Orr 265 ....F2
Ortonville▲ 2,205 ....B5
Osakis 1,256 ....C5
Oslo 362 ....A2
Osseo 2,704 ....G5
Ostrander 276 ....F7
Ottertail 313 ....C4
Owatonna▲ 19,386 ....E6
Palisade 144 ....E4
Park Rapids▲ 2,863 ....D4
Parkers Prairie 956 ....C4
Payne 2,275 ....F3
Paynesville 2,140 ....D5
Pease 178 ....E5
Pelican Lakes (Breezy Point) D4

Pelican Rapids 1,886 ....B4
Pemberton 228 ....E7
Pengilly 625 ....E3
Pennock 476 ....C5
Pequot Lakes 843 ....D4
Perham 2,075 ....C4
Perley 132 ....B3
Peterson 259 ....G7
Pierz 1,014 ....D5
Pillager 306 ....D4
Pine City▲ 2,613 ....F5
Pine Island 2,125 ....F6
Pine River 871 ....D4
Pipestone▲ 4,554 ....B7
Plainview 2,768 ....F6
Plato 355 ....D6
Pleasant Lake 79 ....D5
Plummer 277 ....B3
Plymouth 50,889 ....F5
Ponemah 704 ....D2
Porter 210 ....B6
Preston▲ 1,530 ....F7
Princeton 3,719 ....E5
Prinsburg 502 ....C6
Prior Lake 11,482 ....E6
Proctor 2,974 ....F4
Quamba 124 ....E5
Racine 288 ....F7
Ramsey 12,408 ....G5
Randall 571 ....D4
Randolph 331 ....E6
Ranier 199 ....E2
Ray 723 ....E2
Raymond 723 ....C5
Red Lake Falls▲ 1,481 ....B3
Red Wing▲ 15,134 ....F6
Redby 787 ....D2
Redwood Falls▲ 4,859 ....C6
Regal 51 ....D5
Remer 342 ....E3

Renville 1,315 ....C6
Revere 117 ....C6
Rice 610 ....D5
Richfield 35,710 ....G6
Richmond 965 ....D5
Richville 121 ....C4
Riverton 122 ....D4
Robbinsdale 14,396 ....G5
Rochester▲ 70,745 ....F6
Rock Creek 1,040 ....F5
Rockford 2,665 ....F5
Rockville 579 ....D5
Rogers 698 ....F5
Rollingstone 697 ....G6
Ronneby 58 ....E5
Roosevelt 180 ....C2
Roscoe 141 ....D5
Rose Creek 363 ....F7
Roseau▲ 2,396 ....C2
Rosemount 8,622 ....G6
Roseville 33,485 ....G5
Rothsay 443 ....B4
Round Lake 463 ....C7
Royalton 802 ....D5
Rush City 1,497 ....F5
Rushford 1,485 ....G7
Rushmore 381 ....C7
Russell 394 ....C6
Ruthton 328 ....B6
Rutledge 152 ....F4
Sabin 495 ....B4
Sacred Heart 603 ....C6
Saint Anthony 7,727 ....G5
Saint Anthony 81 ....D5
Saint Bonifacius 1,180 ....F5
Saint Charles 2,642 ....F7
Saint Clair 633 ....E6
Saint Cloud 48,812 ....D5
Saint Francis 2,538 ....E5
Saint Hilaire 298 ....B2
Saint James▲ 4,364 ....D7
Saint Joseph 3,294 ....D5
Saint Leo 101 ....C6
Saint Louis Park 43,787 ....G5
Saint Martin 274 ....D5
Saint Michael 2,506 ....E5
Saint Paul (cap.)▲ 272,235 ....G6
Saint Paul Park 4,965 ....G6
Saint Peter▲ 9,421 ....E6
Saint Rosa 75 ....D5
Saint Stephen 607 ....D5
Saint Vincent 116 ....A2
Sanborn 459 ....C6
Sandstone 2,057 ....F4
Sargeant 78 ....F7
Sartell 5,393 ....D5
Sauk Centre 3,581 ....C5
Sauk Rapids 7,825 ....D5
Savage 9,906 ....G6
Scanlon 878 ....F4
Seaforth 87 ....C6
Sebeka 662 ....C4
Sedan 63 ....C5
Shafer 368 ....F5
Shakopee▲ 11,739 ....F6
Shelly 225 ....B3
Sherburn 1,105 ....D7
Shevlin 157 ....C3
Shoreview 24,587 ....G5
Shorewood 5,917 ....F5
Silver Bay 1,894 ....G3
Silver Lake 764 ....D6
Skyline 272 ....D6
Slayton▲ 2,147 ....C7
Sleepy Eye 3,694 ....D6
Sobieski 199 ....D5
Solway 74 ....C3
Soudan 900 ....F3
South Haven 193 ....D5
South International Falls
 2,806 ....E2
South Saint Paul 20,197 ....G6
Spicer 1,020 ....C5
Spring Grove 1,153 ....G7
Spring Hill 77 ....D5
Spring Lake 6,532 ....E5
Spring Lake Park 6,477 ....G5
Spring Park 1,571 ....F5
Spring Valley 2,461 ....F7
Springfield 2,173 ....C6
Squaw Lake 139 ....D3
Stacy 1,081 ....E5
Staples 2,754 ....D4
Starbuck 1,143 ....C5
Steen 176 ....B7
Stephen 707 ....A2
Stewart 566 ....D6
Stewartville 4,520 ....F7
Stillwater▲ 13,882 ....F5
Stockton 529 ....G6
Storden 283 ....C6
Strandquist 98 ....B2
Strathcona 40 ....B2
Sturgeon Lake 230 ....F4
Sunburg 117 ....C5
Sunfish Lake 413 ....G5
Swanville 324 ....D5
Taconite 310 ....E3
Tamarack 53 ....F4
Taopi 83 ....F7
Taunton 175 ....B6
Taylors Falls 694 ....F5
Tenstrike 184 ....D3
Thief River Falls▲ 8,010 ....B2
Thomson 132 ....F4
Tintah 74 ....B5
Tonka Bay 1,472 ....F5
Tower 502 ....F3
Tracy 2,059 ....C6
Trail 67 ....C3
Trimont 745 ....D7
Trommald 80 ....D4
Trosky 120 ....B7
Truman 1,292 ....D7
Turtle River 62 ....D3
Twin Lakes 154 ....E7
Twin Valley 821 ....B3

Two Harbors▲ 3,651 ....G3
Tyler 1,257 ....B6
Ulen 547 ....B3
Underwood 284 ....C4
Upsala 371 ....D5
Urbank 73 ....C4
Utica 220 ....G7
Vadnais Heights 11,041 ....G5
Vergas 287 ....C4
Vermillion 510 ....F6
Verndale 560 ....D4
Vernon Center 339 ....D7
Vesta 302 ....C6
Victoria 2,354 ....F6
Viking 103 ....B2
Villard 247 ....C5
Vining 84 ....C4
Virginia 9,410 ....F3
Wabasha▲ 2,384 ....G6
Wabasso 684 ....C6
Waconia 3,498 ....E6
Wadena▲ 4,131 ....C4
Wahkon 197 ....E4
Waite Park 5,020 ....D5
Waldorf 243 ....E7
Walker▲ 950 ....D4
Walnut Grove 625 ....C6
Walters 86 ....E7
Waltham 170 ....F7
Wanamingo 847 ....F6
Wanda 103 ....C6
Warba 137 ....E3
Warren▲ 1,813 ....B2
Warroad 1,679 ....C1
Waseca▲ 8,385 ....E6
Watertown 2,408 ....E6
Waterville 1,771 ....E6
Watkins 849 ....D5
Watson 211 ....C5
Waubun 330 ....C3
Waverly 600 ....E5
Wayzata 3,806 ....G5
Welcome 790 ....D7
Wells 2,465 ....E7
Wendell 159 ....B4
West Concord 871 ....F6
West Saint Paul 19,248 ....G5
West Union 54 ....C5
Westbrook 853 ....C6
Westport 47 ....C5
Whalan 97 ....G7
Wheaton▲ 1,615 ....B5
White Bear Lake 24,704 ....G5
White Earth 319 ....C3
Wilder 83 ....C7
Willernie 584 ....G5
Williams 212 ....D2
Willmar▲ 17,531 ....C5
Willow River 284 ....F4
Wilmont 351 ....C7
Wilton 171 ....C3
Windom▲ 4,283 ....C7
Winger 167 ....B3
Winnebago 1,565 ....D7
Winona▲ 25,399 ....G6
Winsted 1,581 ....D6
Winthrop 1,279 ....D6
Winton 169 ....F3
Wolf Lake 35 ....C4
Wolverton 158 ....B4
Wood Lake 406 ....C6
Woodbury 20,075 ....F6
Woodstock 159 ....B7
Worthington▲ 9,977 ....C7
Wright 144 ....E4
Wykoff 493 ....F7
Wyoming 2,142 ....F5
Young America 1,354 ....E6
Zemple 63 ....E3
Zim 1,350 ....F3
Zumbro Falls 237 ....F6
Zumbrota 2,312 ....F6

OTHER FEATURES

Ash (riv.) F2
Bald Eagle (lake) G3
Basswood (lake) G2
Battle (riv.) D3
Baudette (riv.) D2
Bear (riv.) E3
Bemidji (lake) D3
Benton (lake) B6
Big Fork (riv.) E2
Big Sandy (lake) E4
Big Stone (lake) B5
Birch (lake) G3
Black (riv.) D2
Blue Earth (riv.) D7
Bois de Sioux (riv.) B4
Bowstring (lake) E3
Buffalo (riv.) B4
Burntside (lake) F3
Cass (lake) D3
Cedar (riv.) E7
Chippewa (riv.) C5
Christina (lake) C4
Clearwater (riv.) C3
Cloquet (riv.) F4
Cobb (riv.) E7
Cottonwood (riv.) C6
Crooked (creek) F4
Crooked (lake) G2
Crow (riv.) F5
Crow Wing (riv.) D4
Cuyuna (range) D4
Dead (lake) C4
Deer (lake) E3
Des Moines (riv.) C7
Eagle (mt.) G2
East Swan (riv.) F3
Elbow (lake) D3
Emily (lake) D4
Fond du Lac Ind. Res. F4
Grand Portage Ind. Res. G2
Grand Portage Nat'l Mon. G2

Green (lake) D5
Greenwood (lake) G3
Gull (lake) D4
Heron (lake) C7
Hill (riv.) C3
Independence (lake) F5
Isabella (lake) G3
Itasca (lake) C3
Kabetogama (lake) E2
Kanaranzi (creek) C7
Kettle (riv.) F4
Knife (lake) G2
La Croix (lake) F2
Lac qui Parle (lake) C5
Lac qui Parle (riv.) B6
Lake of the Woods (lake) D1
Leaf (riv.) C4
Leech (lake) D3
Leech Lake Ind. Res. D3
Lida (lake) C4
Little Fork (riv.) E2
Little Rock (creek) B2
Long (lake) F3
Long (lake) B3
Long Prairie (riv.) C5
Lost (riv.) C3
Lower Red (lake) C2
Maple (lake) B3
Maple (riv.) E7
Marsh (lake) B5
Mary (lake) C2
Mesabi (range) E3
Middle (riv.) B2
Mille Lacs Ind. Res. E4
Mille Lacs (lake) E4
Miltona (lake) C4
Minneapolis-Saint Paul
 Airport G5
Minnesota (riv.) E6
Minnetonka (lake) F5
Minnewaska (lake) C5
Misquah (hills) F2
Mississippi (riv.) G7
Moose (lake) C2
Mud (riv.) C2
Mud (lake) C2
Muskeg (bay) B5
Mustinka (riv.) B5
Nemadji (riv.) F4
Nett (lake) E2
Nett Lake Ind. Res. E2
North (lake) F1
Otter Tail (lake) C4
Otter Tail (riv.) C4
Partridge (riv.) F3
Pelican (lake) C4
Pelican (lake) D4
Pelican (lake) F2
Pelican (riv.) B4
Pelican (riv.) D4
Pepin (lake) F6
Pigeon (riv.) G2
Pike (riv.) F3
Pipestone Nat'l Mon. B6
Pokegama (lake) E3
Pomme de Terre (riv.) C5
Poplar (riv.) F3
Prairie (riv.) E3
Rainy (lake) E2
Rainy (riv.) D2
Rapid (riv.) D2
Redeye (riv.) D4
Red (lake) C2
Red (riv.) B2
Red River of the North (riv.) A2
Redeye (riv.) D4
Redwood (riv.) C6
Reno (riv.) C4
Rice (lake) C5
Rock (riv.) B7
Root (riv.) G7
Roseau (riv.) B2
Rum (riv.) E5
Saganaga (lake) H2
Saint Croix (riv.) F5
Saint Louis (riv.) F4
Sand (creek) F5
Sand Hill (riv.) B3
Sarah (lake) F5
Schoolcraft C3
Shakopee (creek) C5
Shell (riv.) C4
Shetek (lake) C6
Sleepy Eye (creek) C6
Snake (riv.) A2
Snake (riv.) E4
South Fowl (lake) G1
Star (lake) C4
Sturgeon (riv.) F3
Superior (lake) G3
Swan (lake) D6
Tamarac (riv.) A2
Tamarack (riv.) D2
Thief (lake) C2
Thief (riv.) B2
Traverse (lake) B5
Trout (lake) F2
Two Rivers (riv.) A1
Upper Red (lake) D2
Vermilion (lake) F3
Vermilion (range) F2
Vermilion (riv.) F2
Voyageurs Nat'l Park E2
Wabatawangang (lake) D3
West Swan (riv.) F3
White Earth Ind. Res. C3
Whiteface (riv.) F3
Whitefish (lake) D4
White Iron (lake) G3
Wild Rice (lake) F4
Wild Rice (riv.) B3
Willow (riv.) E4
Winnibigoshish (lake) D3
Woods (lake) D1
Zumbro (riv.) F6

▲County seat

Topography

0   50   100 MI.
0   50   100 KM.

Lake of the Woods, Rainy Lake, Upper Red Lake, Lower Red Lake, Wild Rice, L. Itasca, Little Fork, Vermilion Ra., Eagle Mtn. 2,301 ft. (701 m.), Lake Superior, Mesabi Range, Misquah Hills, Hibbing, Leech Lake, Duluth, Moorhead, Crow Wing, Cuyuna Range, Mille Lacs Lake, Chippewa, Rum, St. Croix, St. Cloud, Big Stone Lake, Lake Traverse, Minneapolis, St. Paul, Minnesota, Lake Pepin, Mankato, Zumbro, Des Moines, Rochester, Root, Mississippi

Below Sea Level | 100 m. 328 ft. | 200 m. 656 ft. | 500 m. 1,640 ft. | 1,000 m. 3,281 ft. | 2,000 m. 6,562 ft. | 5,000 m. 16,404 ft.

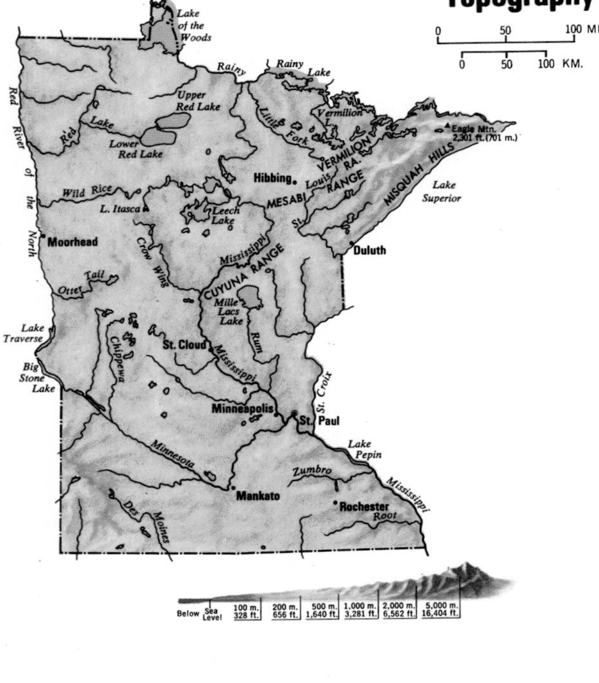

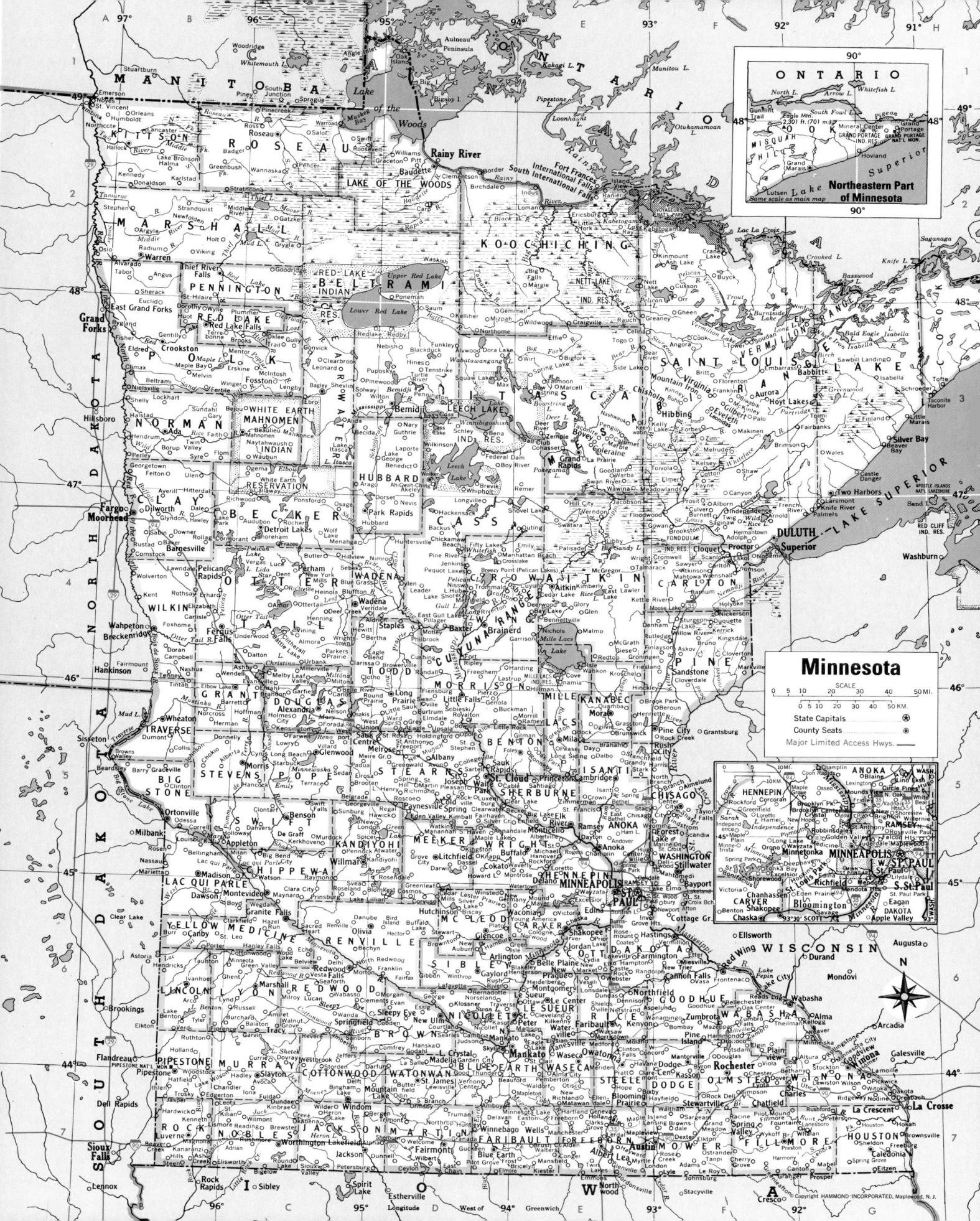
Minnesota
SCALE
0 5 10 20 30 40 50 MI.
0 5 10 20 30 40 50 KM.
State Capitals
County Seats
Major Limited Access Hwys.
Northeastern Part of Minnesota
Same scale as main map
ONTARIO
Lake Superior
COOK
GRAND PORTAGE IND. RES.
GRAND PORTAGE NAT'L MON.
MANITOBA
ONTARIO
CANADA
NORTH DAKOTA
SOUTH DAKOTA
IOWA
WISCONSIN
LAKE SUPERIOR
Lake of the Woods
Upper Red Lake
Lower Red Lake
Leech Lake
Mille Lacs Lake
RED LAKE INDIAN RES.
WHITE EARTH INDIAN RESERVATION
LEECH LAKE IND. RES.
NETT LAKE IND. RES.
MILLE LACS IND. RES.
FOND DU LAC IND. RES.
VOYAGEURS NAT'L PARK
APOSTLE ISLANDS NAT'L LAKESHORE
RED CLIFF IND. RES.
PIPESTONE NAT'L MON.
CUYUNA RANGE
MESABI RANGE
VERMILION RANGE
KITTSON
ROSEAU
LAKE OF THE WOODS
MARSHALL
KOOCHICHING
PENNINGTON
BELTRAMI
RED LAKE
POLK
CLEARWATER
ITASCA
SAINT LOUIS
LAKE
NORMAN
MAHNOMEN
HUBBARD
CASS
CLAY
BECKER
WADENA
CROW WING
AITKIN
CARLTON
WILKIN
OTTER TAIL
TODD
MORRISON
MILLE LACS
KANABEC
PINE
GRANT
DOUGLAS
TRAVERSE
STEVENS
POPE
STEARNS
BENTON
SHERBURNE
ISANTI
CHISAGO
BIG STONE
SWIFT
KANDIYOHI
MEEKER
WRIGHT
ANOKA
WASHINGTON
HENNEPIN
RAMSEY
LAC QUI PARLE
CHIPPEWA
YELLOW MEDICINE
RENVILLE
McLEOD
CARVER
SCOTT
DAKOTA
SIBLEY
LINCOLN
LYON
REDWOOD
NICOLLET
LE SUEUR
RICE
GOODHUE
WABASHA
BROWN
PIPESTONE
MURRAY
COTTONWOOD
WATONWAN
BLUE EARTH
WASECA
STEELE
DODGE
OLMSTED
WINONA
ROCK
NOBLES
JACKSON
MARTIN
FARIBAULT
FREEBORN
MOWER
FILLMORE
HOUSTON
ST. PAUL
MINNEAPOLIS
Duluth
Rochester
St. Cloud
Mankato
Bemidji
Brainerd
Moorhead
Fargo
Grand Forks
International Falls
Hibbing
Virginia
Winona
Red Wing
Sioux Falls
La Crosse
Superior
Longitude West of Greenwich
© Copyright HAMMOND INCORPORATED, Maplewood, N.J.

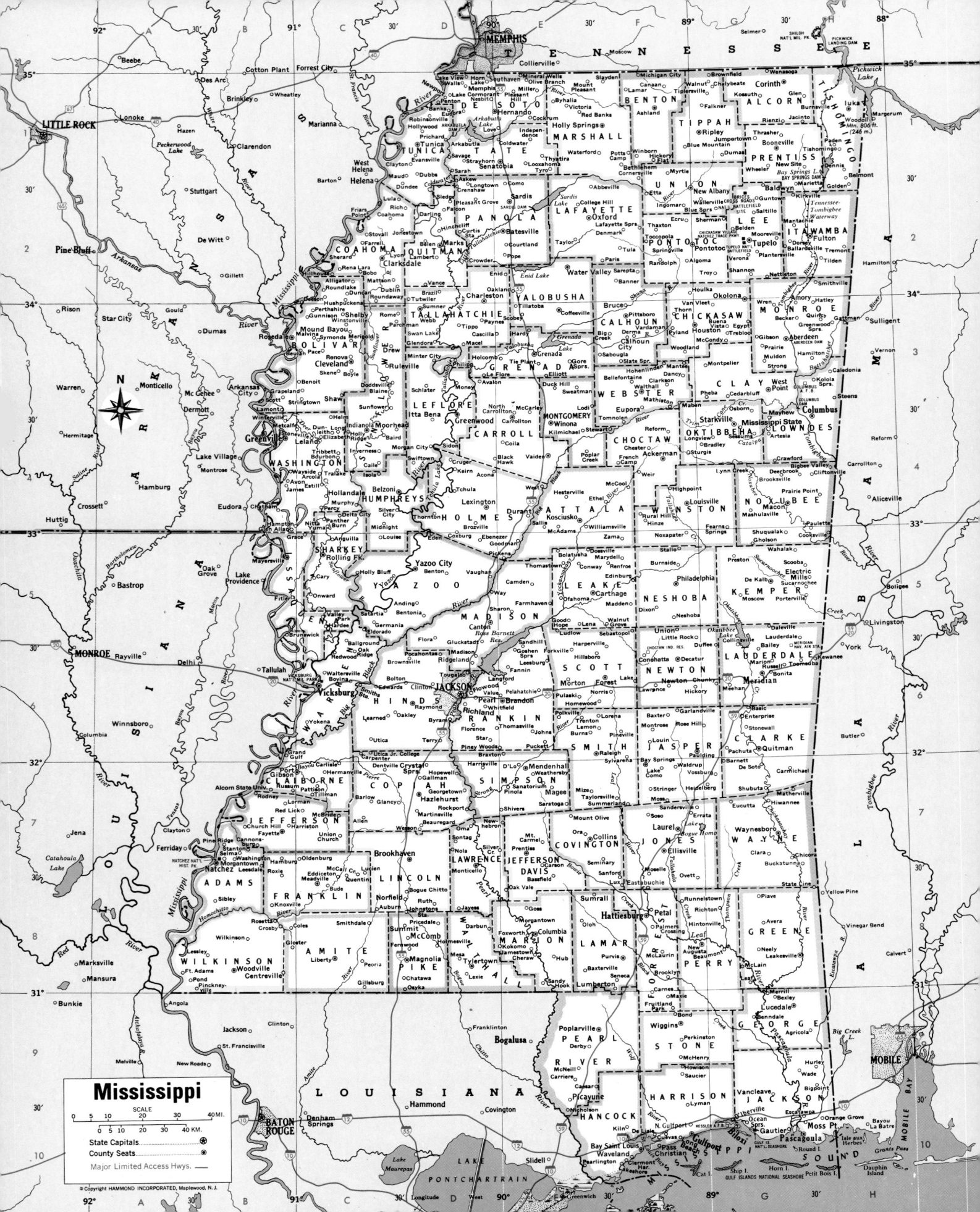

Mississippi

SCALE

| 0 | 5 | 10 | 20 | 30 | 40 MI. |

| 0 | 5 | 10 | 20 | 30 | 40 KM. |

● State Capitals ⊛

○ County Seats ⊛

Major Limited Access Hwys. ——

© Copyright HAMMOND INCORPORATED, Maplewood, N.J.

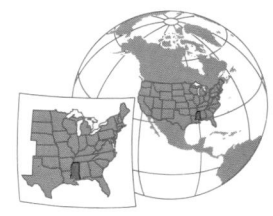

AREA 47,689 sq. mi. (123,515 sq. km.)
POPULATION 2,586,443
CAPITAL Jackson
LARGEST CITY Jackson
HIGHEST POINT Woodall Mtn. 806 ft.
(246 m.)
SETTLED IN 1716
ADMITTED TO UNION December 10, 1817
POPULAR NAME Magnolia State
STATE FLOWER Magnolia
STATE BIRD Mockingbird

COUNTIES

Adams 35,356 ....B8
Alcorn 31,722 ....G1
Amite 13,328 ....C8
Attala 18,481 ....D4
Benton 8,046 ....F1
Bolivar 41,875 ....C3
Calhoun 14,908 ....F3
Carroll 9,237 ....E4
Chickasaw 18,085 ....G3
Choctaw 9,071 ....F4
Claiborne 11,370 ....C7
Clarke 17,313 ....G6
Clay 21,120 ....G3
Coahoma 31,665 ....C2
Copiah 27,592 ....D7
Covington 16,527 ....E7
De Soto 53,930 ....E1
Forrest 68,314 ....F8
Franklin 8,377 ....C8
George 16,673 ....G9
Greene 10,220 ....G8
Grenada 21,555 ....E3
Hancock 31,760 ....E10
Harrison 165,365 ....F10
Hinds 254,441 ....D6
Holmes 21,604 ....D4
Humphreys 12,134 ....C4
Issaquena 1,909 ....B5
Itawamba 20,017 ....H2
Jackson 115,243 ....G9
Jasper 17,114 ....F6
Jefferson 8,653 ....B7
Jefferson Davis 14,051 .....E7
Jones 62,031 ....F7
Kemper 10,356 ....G5
Lafayette 31,826 ....E2
Lamar 30,424 ....E8
Lauderdale 75,555 ....G6
Lawrence 12,458 ....D7
Leake 18,436 ....E5
Lee 65,581 ....G2
Leflore 37,341 ....D3
Lincoln 30,278 ....D8
Lowndes 59,308 ....H4
Madison 53,794 ....D5
Marion 25,544 ....E8
Marshall 30,361 ....E1
Monroe 36,582 ....H3
Montgomery 12,388 ....E4
Neshoba 24,800 ....F5
Newton 20,291 ....F6
Noxubee 12,604 ....G4
Oktibbeha 38,375 ....G4
Panola 29,996 ....E2
Pearl River 38,714 ....E9
Perry 10,865 ....G8
Pike 36,882 ....D8
Pontotoc 22,237 ....F2
Prentiss 23,278 ....G1
Quitman 10,490 ....D2
Rankin 87,161 ....E6
Scott 24,137 ....E6
Sharkey 7,066 ....C5
Simpson 23,953 ....E7
Smith 14,798 ....E6
Stone 10,750 ....F9
Sunflower 32,867 ....C3
Tallahatchie 15,210 ....D3
Tate 21,432 ....E1
Tippah 19,523 ....G1
Tishomingo 17,683 ....H1
Tunica 8,164 ....D1
Union 22,085 ....F2
Walthall 14,352 ....D8
Warren 47,880 ....C6
Washington 67,935 ....C4
Wayne 19,517 ....G7
Webster 10,222 ....F3
Wilkinson 9,678 ....B8
Winston 19,433 ....F4
Yalobusha 12,033 ....E2
Yazoo 25,506 ....D5

CITIES and TOWNS

Abbeville 399 ....F2
Aberdeen▲ 6,837 ....H3
Ackerman▲ 1,573 ....F4
Acona 200 ....D4
Agricola 200 ....G9
Alcorn State University B7
Algoma 420 ....G2
Alligator 187 ....C2
Amory 7,093 ....H3
Anguilla 883 ....C5
Arcola 564 ....C4
Arkabutla 400 ....D1
Artesia 484 ....G4
Ashland▲ 490 ....F1
Askew 300 ....D1
Auburn 500 ....C8
Avalon 100 ....D3
Avera 150 ....G8
Avon 400 ....C4
Bailey 320 ....G6
Baird 150 ....C4
Baldwyn 3,204 ....G2
Ballardsville 105 ....H2
Banks 100 ....D1
Banner 120 ....F2
Bassfield 249 ....E8
Batesville▲ 6,403 ....E2
Baxterville 100 ....E8
Bay Saint Louis▲ 8,063 ...F10
Bay Springs▲ 1,729 ....G8
Beaumont 1,054 ....G8
Beauregard 206 ....D7
Becker 300 ....G3
Belden 241 ....G2
Belen 400 ....D2
Bellefontaine 400 ....F3
Belmont 1,554 ....H1
Belzoni▲ 2,536 ....C4
Benndale 500 ....G9
Benoit 641 ....C3
Benton 390 ....D5
Bentonia 518 ....D5
Bethlehem 210 ....F1
Beulah 460 ....B3
Bexley 130 ....G9
Big Creek 123 ....F3
Bigbee Valley 370 ....H4
Bigpoint 350 ....H9
Biloxi 46,319 ....G10
Blue Mountain 667 ....G1
Blue Springs 140 ....G2
Bobo 200 ....C2
Bogue Chitto 689 ....D8
Bolatusha 87 ....E5
Bolton 637 ....D6
Bond 350 ....F9
Bonita 300 ....G6
Bourbon 200 ....C4
Boyle 651 ....C3
Brandon▲ 11,077 ....E6
Braxton 141 ....D6
Brazil 229 ....D2
Brookhaven▲ 10,243 ....D8
Brooklyn 450 ....F8
Brooksville 1,098 ....G4
Brownfield 125 ....G1
Brownsville 200 ....D4
Brozville 150 ....D4
Bruce 2,127 ....F3
Brunswick 90 ....C5
Buckatunna 500 ....G7
Bude 969 ....C8
Burns 949 ....E6
Burnsville 889 ....H1
Byhalia 955 ....E1
Byram 250 ....D6
Caesar 80 ....E9
Caledonia 821 ....H3
Calhoun City 1,838 ....F3
Camden 150 ....E5
Canaan 200 ....F1
Cannonsburg 240 ....B7
Canton▲ 10,062 ....D5
Carlisle 425 ....C7
Carpenter 200 ....C6
Carriere 900 ....E9
Carrollton▲ 221 ....E4
Carson 400 ....E7
Carthage▲ 3,819 ....E5
Cary 382 ....C5
Cascilla 230 ....D3
Cedarbluff 175 ....G3
Centreville 1,771 ....B8
Chalybeate 350 ....G1
Charleston▲ 2,328 ....D3
Chatawa 300 ....D8
Chatham 150 ....B4
Cheraw 100 ....E8
Chunky 292 ....G6
Church Hill 350 ....B7
Clara 275 ....G7
Clarksdale▲ 19,717 ....D2
Clarkson 100 ....F3
Cleveland▲ 15,384 ....C3
Clermont Harbor 550 ....F10
Cliftonville 280 ....H4
Clinton 21,847 ....D6
Cockrum 150 ....E1
Coffeeville▲ 825 ....E3
Coldwater 1,502 ....E1
Coles 150 ....C8
College Hill 150 ....E2
Collins▲ 2,541 ....E7
Collinsville 1,364 ....G6
Columbia▲ 6,815 ....E8
Columbus▲ 23,799 ....H3
Como 1,387 ....E1
Conehatta 925 ....F6
Corinth▲ 11,820 ....G1
Courtland 329 ....E2
Coxburg 300 ....D5
Crawford 668 ....G4
Crenshaw 978 ....D2
Crosby 465 ....B8
Crowder 758 ....D2
Cruger 548 ....D4
Crystal Springs 5,643 ......D7
Cuevas 200 ....F10
Curtis Station 350 ....D2
D'Iberville 6,566 ....G10
D'Lo 421 ....E7
Daleville 210 ....G5
Dancy 116 ....F3
Darbun 100 ....D8
Darling 275 ....D2
De Kalb▲ 1,073 ....G5
De Lisle 450 ....F10
De Soto 150 ....G7
Decatur▲ 1,248 ....F6
Delta City 310 ....C4
Dennis 150 ....H1
Dentville 175 ....C7
Derby 298 ....E9
Derma 959 ....F3
Dixon 125 ....F5
Doddsville 149 ....C3
Dorsey 100 ....H2
Drew 2,349 ....C3
Dublin 100 ....C2
Duck Hill 586 ....E3
Duffee 175 ....G6
Dumas 407 ....G1
Duncan 416 ....C2
Dundee 600 ....D1
Dunleith 140 ....C4
Durant 2,838 ....E4
Eastabuchie 200 ....F8
Ebenezer 200 ....D5
Ecru 696 ....F2
Eden 88 ....D5
Edinburg 200 ....F5
Edwards 1,279 ....C6
Egypt 100 ....G3
Electric Mills 100 ....G5
Elizabeth 500 ....C4
Elliott 200 ....E3
Ellisville▲ 3,634 ....F7
Enid 100 ....E2
Enterprise 477 ....G6
Errata 85 ....F7
Escatawpa 3,902 ....G10
Estill 100 ....C4
Ethel 454 ....F4
Eudora 200 ....D1
Eupora 2,145 ....F3
Falcon 167 ....D2
Falkner 232 ....G1
Fannin 250 ....E6
Farrell 300 ....C2
Fayette▲ 1,853 ....B7
Fernwood 500 ....D8
Fitler 175 ....B5
Flora 1,482 ....D5
Florence 1,831 ....D6
Flowood 2,860 ....D6
Forest▲ 5,060 ....F6
Forkville 185 ....E6
Foxworth 800 ....E8
French Camp 320 ....F4
Friars Point 1,334 ....C2
Fulton▲ 3,387 ....H2
Gallman D7
Garlandville 150 ....F6
Gattman 120 ....H3
Gautier 10,088 ....G10
Georgetown 332 ....D7
Glen 165 ....H1
Glen Allan 650 ....B4
Glendora 220 ....D3
Gloster 1,323 ....B8
Gluckstadt 150 ....D5
Golden 202 ....H2
Good Hope 125 ....E5
Goodman 1,256 ....E5
Gore Springs 125 ....E3
Goshen Springs 100 ....E6
Goss 100 ....E8
Grace 325 ....C5
Grapeland 200 ....B3
Greenville▲ 45,226 ....B4
Greenwood Springs 170 ..H3
Greenwood▲ 18,906 ....D4
Grenada▲ 10,864 ....E3
Gulfport▲ 40,775 ....F10
Gunnison 611 ....C3
Guntown 692 ....G2
Hamburg 150 ....B7
Hamilton 500 ....H3
Hampton 200 ....B4
Hardee 100 ....C5
Harperville 200 ....E6
Harriston 500 ....C7
Harrisville 500 ....D7
Hatley 529 ....H3
Hattiesburg▲ 41,882 ....F8
Hazlehurst▲ 4,221 ....D7
Heidelberg 981 ....F7
Helm 80 ....C4
Hermanville 750 ....C7
Hernando▲ 3,125 ....E1
Hickory 493 ....F6
Hickory Flat 535 ....F1
Hillsboro 800 ....E6
Hintonville 300 ....F8
Hiwannee 250 ....G7
Hohenlinden 96 ....F3
Hollandale 3,576 ....C4
Holly Bluff 700 ....C5
Holly Ridge 350 ....C4
Holly Springs▲ 7,261 ......F1
Hollywood 80 ....D1
Hopewell 250 ....D7
Horn Lake 9,069 ....D1
Houlka G2
Houston▲ 3,903 ....G3
Howison 300 ....F9
Hub 80 ....E8
Hurley 500 ....H9
Independence 150 ....E1
Indianola▲ 11,809 ....C4
Ingomar 150 ....F2
Inverness 1,174 ....C4
Isola 732 ....C4
Itta Bena 2,377 ....D4
Iuka▲ 3,122 ....H1
Jackson (cap.)▲ 196,637 ..D6
James 100 ....B4
Jayess 200 ....D8
Johns 90 ....E6
Jonestown 1,467 ....D2
Jumpertown 438 ....G1
Kewanee 250 ....H6
Kilmichael 826 ....E4
Kiln 1,262 ....F10
Kirkville 200 ....H2
Kokomo 250 ....E8
Kolola Springs 100 ....H3
Kosciusko▲ 6,986 ....E4
Kossuth 245 ....G1
Lafayette Springs 80 ....F2
Lake 369 ....F6
Lake Como 150 ....F7
Lake Cormorant 300 ....D1
Lake View 125 ....D1
Lakeshore 550 ....F10
Lamar 200 ....F1
Lambert 1,131 ....D2
Lamont 400 ....B3
Langford 100 ....D6
Lauderdale 600 ....G5
Laurel▲ 18,827 ....F7
Lawrence 250 ....F6
Le Flore 99 ....C4
Leaf 250 ....G8
Leakesville▲ 1,129 ....G8
Learned 111 ....C6
Leland 6,366 ....C4
Lemon 90 ....C4
Lena 175 ....E5
Lessley 100 ....B8
Lexington▲ 2,227 ....D4
Liberty▲ 624 ....C8
Long 15,804 ....D2
Long Beach 7,967 ....F10
Longtown 150 ....D1
Longview 800 ....D4
Looxahoma 200 ....E1
Lorena 90 ....E6
Lorman 350 ....B7
Louin 289 ....F6
Louise 343 ....C5
Louisville▲ 7,169 ....G4
Lucedale▲ 2,592 ....G9
Ludlow 350 ....E5
Lula 224 ....C2
Lumberton 2,121 ....E8
Lyman 1,117 ....F10
Lyon 446 ....D2
Maben 752 ....F3
Macon▲ 2,256 ....G4
Madden 450 ....F5
Madison 7,471 ....D6
Magee 3,607 ....E7
Magnolia▲ 2,245 ....D8
Malvina 100 ....C3
Mantachie 651 ....H2
Mantee 134 ....F3
Marietta 287 ....H2
Marion 1,359 ....G6
Marks▲ 1,758 ....D2
Marydell 99 ....F5
Mashulaville 227 ....G4
Matherville 150 ....G7
Mattiston 818 ....D3
Mattson 200 ....C2
Maxie 233 ....F9
Mayersville▲ 329 ....B5
Mayhew 150 ....G4
McAdams 350 ....E4
McCall Creek 250 ....C7
McCarley 250 ....E4
McComb 11,591 ....D8
McCondy 150 ....G3
McCool 169 ....F4
McHenry 660 ....F9
McLain 536 ....G8
McLaurin 100 ....F8
McNeill 800 ....E9
Meadville▲ 453 ....C8
Meehan 100 ....G6
Mendenhall▲ 2,463 ....E7
Meridian▲ 41,036 ....G6
Merigold 572 ....C3
Merrill 100 ....G9
Metcalfe 1,092 ....B4
Michigan City 350 ....F1
Midnight 500 ....C4
Mineral Wells 250 ....C4
Minter City 150 ....D3
Mississippi State G4
Mize 312 ....E7
Money 350 ....D3
Monticello▲ 1,755 ....D7
Montpelier 175 ....G3
Montrose 106 ....F6
Mooreville 200 ....G2
Moorhead 2,417 ....C4
Morgan City 139 ....D4
Morgantown 32,880 ....B7
Morgantown 325 ....E8
Morton 3,212 ....E6
Moselle 525 ....F8
Moss 17,837 ....F7
Moss Point 18,998 ....G10
Mound Bayou 2,222 ....C3
Mount Olive 914 ....E7
Mount Pleasant 250 ....E1
Murphy 100 ....C4
Myrtle 358 ....F1
Natchez▲ 19,460 ....B7
Neely 270 ....G8
Nesbit 366 ....D1
Neshoba 250 ....F5
Nettleton 2,462 ....G2
New Albany▲ 6,775 ....F2
New Augusta▲ 668 ....F8
New Houlka (Houlka) 558 ..G2
New Site 100 ....H1
Newbebron 470 ....D7
Newton 3,701 ....F6
Nicholson 400 ....E10
Nitta Yuma 150 ....C4
Nola 120 ....E7
North Carrollton 578 ....E3
North Gulfport 4,966 ....F10
Noxapater 441 ....F5
Oak Ridge 350 ....C6
Oak Vale E8
Oakland 553 ....E2
Oakley 133 ....D6
Ocean Springs 14,658 .....G10
Ofahoma 350 ....E5
Okolona▲ 3,267 ....G2
Olive Branch 3,567 ....E1
Oloh 93 ....E8
Oma 200 ....D7
Ora 15,676 ....E7
Orange Grove H10
Osyka 483 ....D8
Ovett 600 ....F8
Oxford▲ 9,984 ....F2
Pace 354 ....C3
Pachuta 268 ....G6
Paden 123 ....H1
Palmers Crossing 2,765 ..F8
Panther Burn 300 ....C4
Parchman 200 ....D3
Paris 253 ....F2
Pascagoula▲ 25,899 ....G10
Pass Christian 5,557 ....F10
Pattison 540 ....C7
Paulding▲ 630 ....F6
Paulette 250 ....H4
Paynes 100 ....D3
Pearl 19,588 ....D6
Pearlington 1,603 ....E10
Pelahatchie 1,553 ....E6
Penton 175 ....D1
Peoria 100 ....C8
Perkinston 950 ....F9
Petal 7,883 ....F8
Pheba 280 ....G3
Philadelphia▲ 6,758 ....F5
Philipp 975 ....D3
Piave 150 ....G8
Picayune 10,633 ....E9
Pickens 1,285 ....E5
Pine Ridge 175 ....B7
Pineville 80 ....F6
Piney Woods 450 ....D6
Pinola E7
Pittsboro▲ 277 ....F3
Plantersville 1,046 ....G2
Pleasant Grove 100 ....D2
Pleasant Hill 400 ....E1
Polkville 129 ....E6

(continued on following page)

Topography

0   40   80 MI.

0   40   80 KM.

Pickwick Lake
Woodall Mtn. 806 ft. (246 m.)
Arkabutla Lake
Sardis Lake
Enid Lake
Tupelo
Grenada Lake
Columbus
Greenville
Tallahatchie
Yazoo
Big Black
Ross Barnett Res.
Pearl
Meridian
Vicksburg
Jackson
Mississippi
Big Black
Natchez
Homochitto
Bogue Chitto
Leaf
Chickasawhay
Hattiesburg
Tallahala
Wolf
Pearl
Gulfport
Biloxi
Pascagoula
Mississippi Sound

5,000 m. 16,404 ft. | 2,000 m. 6,562 ft. | 1,000 m. 3,281 ft. | 500 m. 1,640 ft. | 200 m. 656 ft. | 100 m. 328 ft. | Sea Level | Below

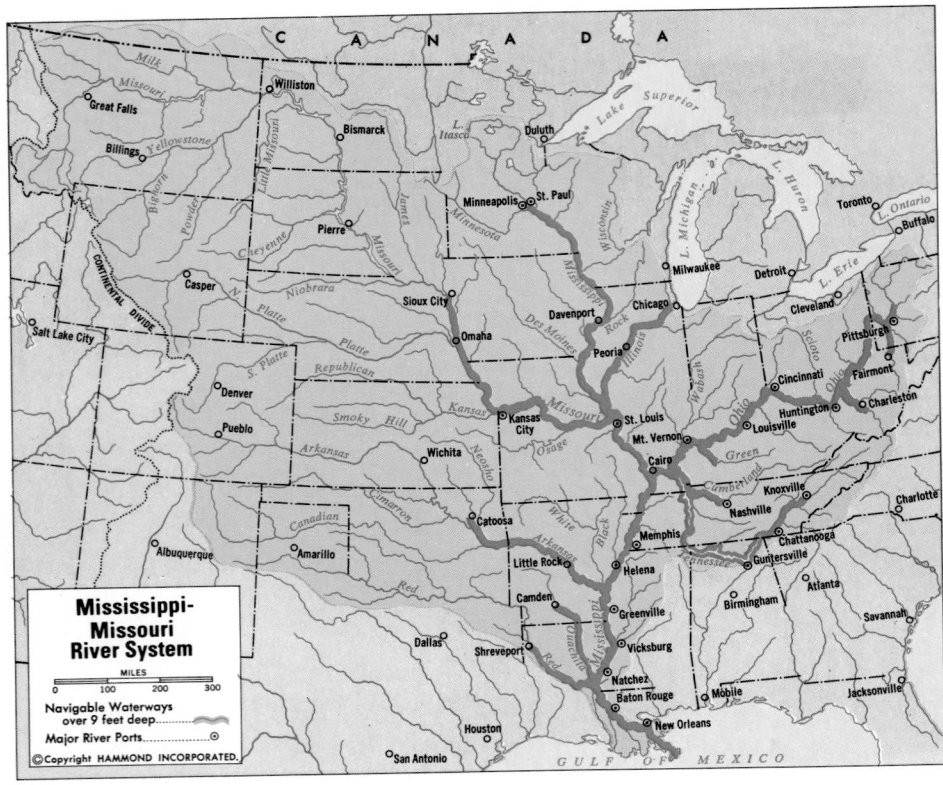

Mississippi-Missouri River System

MILES
0   100   200   300

Navigable Waterways over 9 feet deep.
Major River Ports......⊚
©Copyright HAMMOND INCORPORATED.

Agriculture, Industry and Resources

DOMINANT LAND USE

Specialized Cotton

Cotton, Livestock

Cotton, General Farming

Cotton, Forest Products

Truck and Mixed Farming

Forests

Swampland, Limited Agriculture

MAJOR MINERAL OCCURRENCES

Cl Clay
Fe Iron Ore
G Natural Gas
O Petroleum
▨ Major Industrial Areas

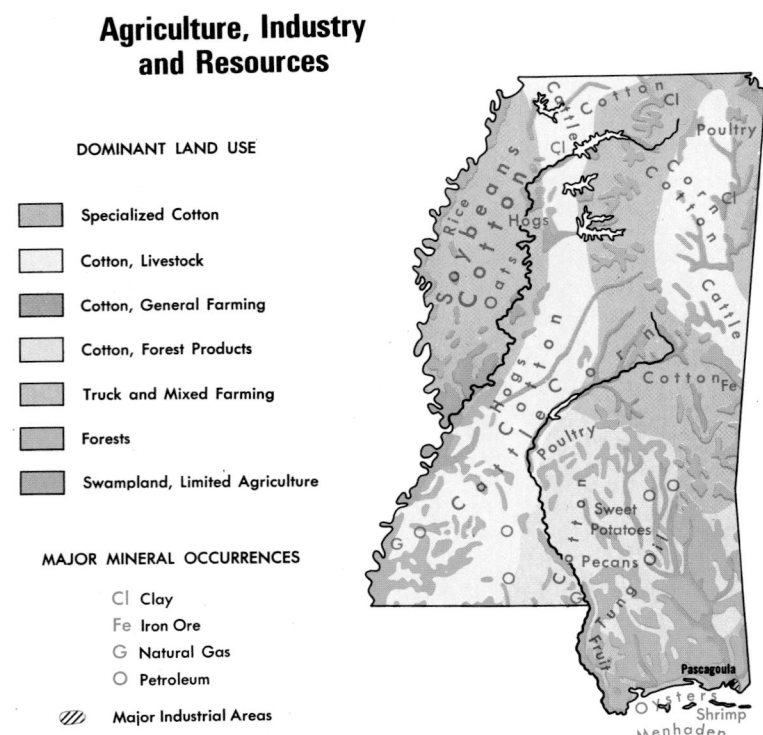

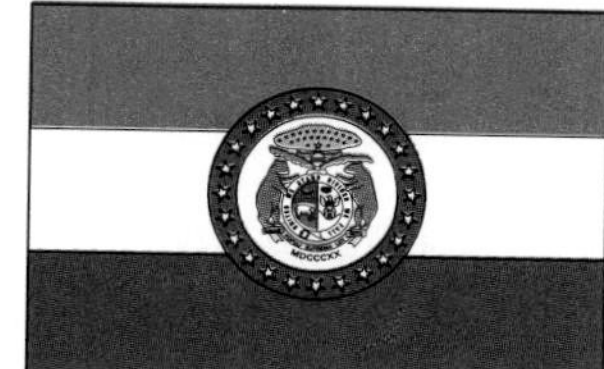

AREA 69,697 sq. mi. (180,515 sq. km.)
POPULATION 5,137,804
CAPITAL Jefferson City
LARGEST CITY St. Louis
HIGHEST POINT Taum Sauk Mtn. 1,772 ft. (540 m.)
SETTLED IN 1764
ADMITTED TO UNION August 10, 1821
POPULAR NAME Show Me State
STATE FLOWER Hawthorn
STATE BIRD Bluebird

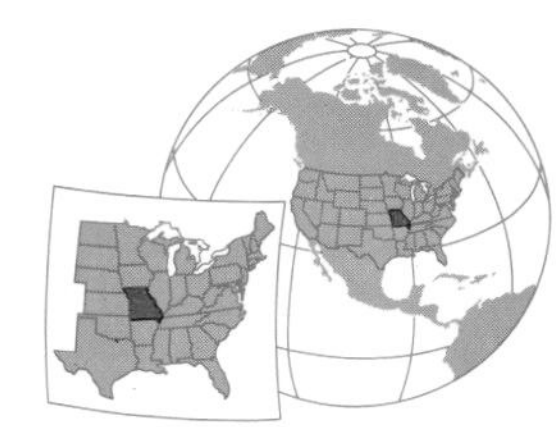

COUNTIES

Adair 24,577 G2
Andrew 14,632 C3
Atchison 7,457 B2
Audrain 23,599 J4
Barry 27,547 E9
Barton 11,312 D7
Bates 15,025 D6
Benton 13,859 F6
Bollinger 10,619 M8
Boone 112,379 H4
Buchanan 83,083 C3
Butler 38,765 M9
Caldwell 8,380 E3
Callaway 32,809 J5
Camden 27,495 G6
Cape Girardeau 61,633 N8
Carroll 10,748 F4
Carter 5,515 L9
Cass 63,808 D5
Cedar 12,093 E7
Chariton 9,202 F3
Christian 32,644 F9
Clark 7,547 J2
Clay 153,411 D4
Clinton 16,595 D3
Cole 63,579 H6
Cooper 14,835 G5
Crawford 19,173 K7
Dade 7,449 E8
Dallas 12,646 F7
Daviess 7,865 E3
De Kalb 8,222 D3
Dent 13,702 J7
Douglas 11,876 G9
Dunklin 33,112 M1
Franklin 80,603 K6
Gasconade 14,006 J6
Gentry 6,848 D2
Greene 207,949 F8
Grundy 10,536 E2
Harrison 8,469 E2
Henry 20,044 E6
Hickory 7,335 F7
Holt 6,034 B2
Howard 9,631 G4
Howell 31,447 J9
Iron 10,726 L7
Jackson 633,232 R5
Jasper 90,465 D8
Jefferson 171,380 L6
Johnson 42,514 E5
Knox 4,482 H2
Laclede 27,158 G7
Lafayette 31,107 E4
Lawrence 30,236 E8
Lewis 10,233 J2
Lincoln 28,892 L4
Linn 13,885 F3
Livingston 14,592 E3
Macon 15,345 G3
Madison 11,127 M8
Maries 7,976 J6
Marion 27,682 J3
McDonald 16,938 D9
Mercer 3,723 E2
Miller 20,700 H6
Mississippi 14,442 O9
Moniteau 12,298 G5
Monroe 9,104 H3
Montgomery 11,355 K5
Morgan 15,574 G6
New Madrid 20,928 N9
Newton 44,445 D9
Nodaway 21,709 C2
Oregon 9,470 K9
Osage 12,018 J6
Ozark 8,598 H9
Pemiscot 21,921 N1
Perry 16,648 N7
Pettis 35,437 F5
Phelps 35,248 J7
Pike 15,969 K4
Platte 57,867 C4
Polk 21,826 F7
Pulaski 41,307 H7
Putnam 5,079 F2
Ralls 8,476 J3
Randolph 24,370 G3
Ray 21,971 E4
Reynolds 6,661 L8
Ripley 12,303 L9
Saint Charles 144,107 M2
Saint Clair 8,622 E6
Saint Francois 42,600 M7
Saint Louis 974,180 O3
Saint Louis (city county) 452,801 P3
Sainte Genevieve 15,180 M7
Saline 23,523 F4
Schuyler 4,236 G2
Scotland 4,822 H2
Scott 39,376 N8
Shannon 7,613 K8
Shelby 6,942 H3
Stoddard 28,895 N9
Stone 19,078 F9
Sullivan 6,326 F2
Taney 25,561 F9
Texas 21,476 J8
Vernon 19,041 D7
Warren 19,534 K5
Washington 20,380 L7
Wayne 11,543 L8
Webster 23,753 G8
Worth 2,440 D2
Wright 16,758 H8

CITIES and TOWNS

Adrian 1,582 D6
Advance 1,139 N8
Affton 21,106 P4
Agency 642 C3
Alba 465 D8
Albany▲ 1,958 D2
Alexandria 341 K2
Alma 446 E4
Altamont 188 D3
Altenburg 307 O7
Alton▲ 692 K9
Amazonia 257 C3
Amoret 212 C6
Amsterdam 237 D6
Anderson 1,432 D9
Annapolis 363 L8
Anniston 288 O9
Appleton City 1,280 D6
Arbyrd 597 M10
Arcadia 609 L7
Archie 799 D5
Argyle 178 J6
Armstrong 310 G4
Arnold 18,828 M6
Asbury 220 C8
Ash Grove 1,128 E8
Ashland 1,252 H5
Atlanta 411 H3
Augusta 263 L5
Aurora 6,459 E9
Auxvasse 821 J4
Ava▲ 2,938 G9
Avondale 550 P5
Bakersfield 292 H9
Ballwin 21,816 N3
Baring 182 H2
Barnard 234 C2
Barnett 215 G6
Bates City 197 E5
Battlefield 1,526 F8
Bel-Nor 2,935 P2
Bel-Ridge 3,199 P2
Bell City 469 N8
Bella Villa 708 R4
Belle 1,218 J6
Bellefontaine 10,922 N2
Bellefontaine Neighbors 12,082 R2
Bellflower 413 K4
Belton 18,150 C5
Benton City 139 J4
Benton▲ 575 O8
Berger 247 K5
Berkeley 12,450 P2
Bernie 1,847 M9
Bertrand 692 O9
Bethany▲ 3,005 E2
Beverly 660 O4
Bevier 643 G3
Billings 989 F8
Birch Tree 599 K9
Birmingham 222 R5
Bismarck 1,579 L7
Black 6,128 L7
Black Jack 5,293 R1
Blackburn 308 F4
Blackwater 221 G5
Blairstown 185 E5
Bland 651 J6
Blodgett 202 O8
Bloomfield▲ 1,800 M9
Bloomsdale 353 M6
Blue Springs 40,153 R6
Bogard 228 E4
Bolckow 253 C2
Bolivar▲ 6,845 F7
Bonne Terre 3,871 L7
Boonville▲ 7,095 G5
Bosworth 334 F4
Bourbon 1,188 K6
Bowling Green▲ 2,976 K4
Brandsville 167 J9
Branson 3,706 F9
Brashear 318 H2
Braymer 886 E3
Breckenridge 418 E3
Breckenridge Hills 5,404 O2
Brentwood 8,150 P3
Bridgeton 17,779 O2
Bridgeton Terrace 334 O2
Bronaugh 211 C7
Brookfield 4,888 F3
Browning 331 F2
Brunswick 1,074 F4
Bucklin 616 G3
Buckner 2,873 R5
Buffalo▲ 2,414 F7
Bunceton 341 G5
Bunker 390 K8
Burlington Junction 634 B2
Butler▲ 4,099 D6
Butterfield 248 E9
Cabool 2,006 H8
Cainsville 387 E2
Cairo 282 H4
Caledonia 142 L7
Calhoun 450 E6
California▲ 3,465 H5
Callao 332 G3
Calverton Park 1,404 P2
Camden 238 D4
Camden Point 373 C4
Camdenton▲ 2,561 G6
Cameron 4,831 D3
Campbell 2,165 M9
Canalou 319 N9
Canton 2,623 J2
Cape Girardeau 34,438 O8
Cardwell 792 M10
Carl Junction 4,123 C8
Carrollton▲ 4,406 E4
Carterville 2,013 D8
Carthage▲ 10,747 D8
Caruth 7,389 N10
Caruthersville▲ 7,958 N10
Carytown 149 D8
Cassville▲ 2,371 E9
Cedar City 427 H5
Cedar Hill Lakes 227 L6
Center 552 J3
Centertown 356 H5
Centerview 214 E5
Centerville▲ 89 L8
Centralia 3,414 H4
Chaffee 3,059 N8
Chamois 449 J5
Charlack 1,388 P2
Charleston▲ 5,085 O9
Chesterfield 37,991 N2
Chilhowee 335 E5
Chillicothe▲ 8,804 E3
Chula 183 F3
Circle City 154 N9
Clarence 1,026 H3
Clark 257 H4
Clarksburg 358 G5
Clarksdale 287 D3
Clarkson Valley 2,508 N3
Clarksville 480 K4
Clarkton 1,113 M10
Claycomo 1,668 P5
Clayton▲ 13,874 P3
Clearmont 175 C1
Cleveland 506 C5
Clever 580 F8
Clinton▲ 8,703 E6
Cobalt City 254 M7
Cole Camp 1,054 F6
Collins 144 E7
Columbia▲ 69,101 H5
Commerce 173 O8
Conception Junction 236 C2
Concord 19,859 P4
Concordia 2,160 E5
Conway 629 G7
Cool Valley 1,407 P2
Cooter 451 N10
Corder 485 E4
Cottleville 2,936 M2
Country Club Village 1,234 C3
Cowgill 257 E3
Craig 346 B2
Crane 1,218 E9
Creighton 289 D6
Crestwood 11,234 O3
Creve Coeur 12,304 O2
Crocker 1,077 H7
Cross Timbers 168 F6
Crystal City 4,088 M6
Crystal Lake Park 506 O3
Cuba 2,537 K6
Curryville 261 K4
Dadeville 220 E8
De Kalb 222 C3
De Soto 5,993 L6
Dearborn 480 C3
Deepwater 441 E6
Dellwood 5,245 R2
Delta 450 N8
Des Arc 173 L8
Des Peres 8,395 O3
Desloge 4,150 M7
Dexter 7,559 N9
Diamond 775 D9
Diehlstadt 145 N9
Diggins 258 G8
Dixon 1,585 H6
Doniphan▲ 1,713 L9
Doolittle 599 J7
Downing 359 H2
Drexel 936 C6
Dudley 271 M9
Duenweg 940 D8
Duquesne 1,229 D8
Eagleville 275 D2
East Lynne 289 D5
East Prairie 3,416 O9
Easton 232 C3
Edgar Springs 215 J7
Edgerton 565 C3
Edina▲ 1,283 H2
Edmundson 1,111 O2
El Dorado Springs 3,830 E7
Eldon 4,419 G6
Ellington 994 L8
Ellisville 7,545 M3
Ellsinore 405 L9
Elmo 179 B1
Elsberry 1,898 L4
Elvins 1,391 L7
Eminence▲ 582 K8
Emma 194 F5
Eolia 389 L4
Essex 531 N9
Esther 1,071 M7
Eugene 141 H6
Eureka 4,683 M4
Everton 325 E8
Ewing 463 J2
Excelsior Springs 10,354 R4
Exeter 597 D9
Fair Grove 919 F8
Fair Play 442 E7
Fairfax 699 B2
Fairview 298 D9
Farber 418 J4
Farley 217 O4
Farmington▲ 11,598 M7
Fayette▲ 2,888 G4
Fenton 3,346 O4
Ferguson 22,286 P2
Ferrelview 338 O4
Festus 8,105 M6
Fillmore 256 C2
Fisk 422 M9
Flat 4,823 J7
Flat River 4,443 M7
Fleming 130 D4
Flemington 141 F7
Flinthill 219 L5
Florissant 51,206 P1
Foley 209 L4
Fordland 523 G8
Forest City 380 B3
Foristell 144 L5
Forsyth▲ 1,175 F9
Foster 161 D6
Frankford 396 K4
Franklin 181 G4
Fredericktown▲ 3,950 M7
Freeburg 446 J6
Freeman 480 C5
Freistatt 166 E8
Fremont 201 K9
Frohna 162 N7
Frontenac 3,374 O3
Fulton▲ 10,033 J5
Gainesville▲ 659 G9
Galena▲ 401 F9
Gallatin▲ 1,864 E3
Galt 296 F2
Garden City 1,225 D5
Gasconade 253 J5
Gerald 888 K6
Gideon 1,104 N10
Gilliam 212 F4
Gilman City 393 D2
Gladstone 26,243 P5
Glasgow 1,295 G4
Glenaire 597 R5
Glendale 5,945 P3
Glenwood 195 G1
Golden 794 E9
Golden City 900 D8
Goodman 1,094 C9
Gordonville 345 N8
Gower 1,249 C3
Graham 204 C2
Grain Valley 1,898 S6
Granby 1,945 D9
Grandin 233 L9
Grandview 24,967 P6
Grant City▲ 998 D2
Grantwood 904 O4
Gray Summit 2,505 L6
Green Castle 285 G2
Green City 671 F2
Green Ridge 452 F5
Greenfield▲ 1,416 E8
Greentop 425 H2
Greenville▲ 437 M8
Greenwood 1,505 R6
Hale 480 F3
Half Way 157 F7
Hallsville 917 H4
Halltown 161 E8
Hamilton 1,737 E3
Hanley Hills 2,325 P2
Hannibal 18,004 K3
Hardin 598 E4
Harrisburg 169 H4
Harrisonville▲ 7,683 D5
Hartville▲ 495 G8
Hawk Point 472 K5
Hayti 3,280 N10
Hayti Heights 893 N10
Haywood City 263 N9
Hazelwood 15,324 P2
Henrietta 412 E4
Herculaneum 2,263 M6
Hermann▲ 2,754 K5
Hermitage▲ 512 F7
Higbee 639 H4
Higginsville 4,693 E4
High Hill 204 K5

(continued on following page)

Agriculture, Industry and Resources

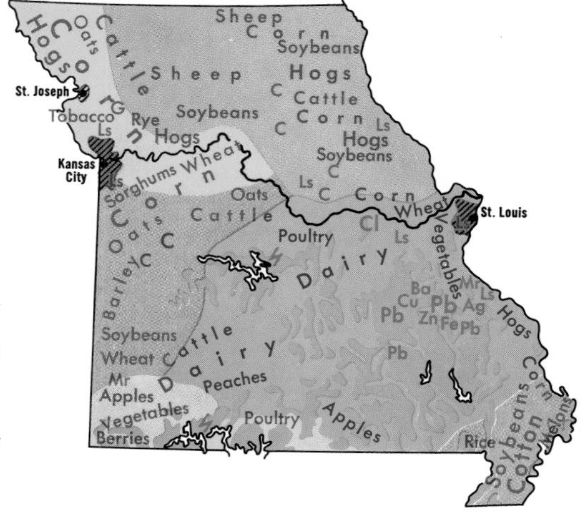

DOMINANT LAND USE

- Cattle Feed, Hogs
- Livestock, Cash Grain, Dairy
- Pasture Livestock
- Specialized Cotton
- General Farming, Dairy, Livestock, Poultry
- General Farming, Livestock, Truck Farming, Cotton
- Fruit and Mixed Farming
- Forests
- Urban Areas

MAJOR MINERAL OCCURRENCES

Ag	Silver	G	Natural Gas
Ba	Barite	Ls	Limestone
C	Coal	Mr	Marble
Cl	Clay	Pb	Lead
Cu	Copper	Zn	Zinc
Fe	Iron Ore		

Water Power   Major Industrial Areas

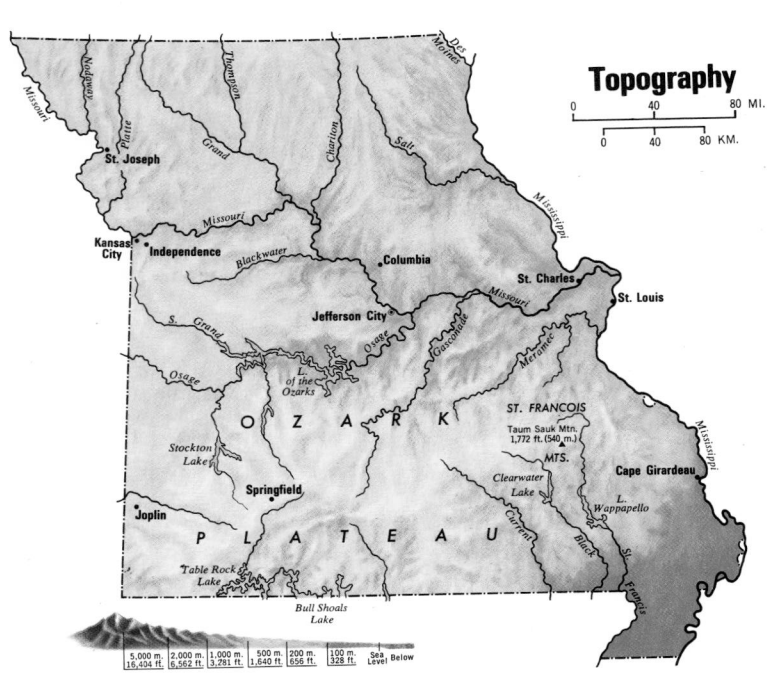

Topography

0   40   80 MI.

0   40   80 KM.

5,000 m. · 2,000 m. · 1,000 m. · 500 m. · 200 m. · 100 m. · Sea Level · Below
16,404 ft. · 6,562 ft. · 3,281 ft. · 1,640 ft. · 656 ft. · 328 ft.

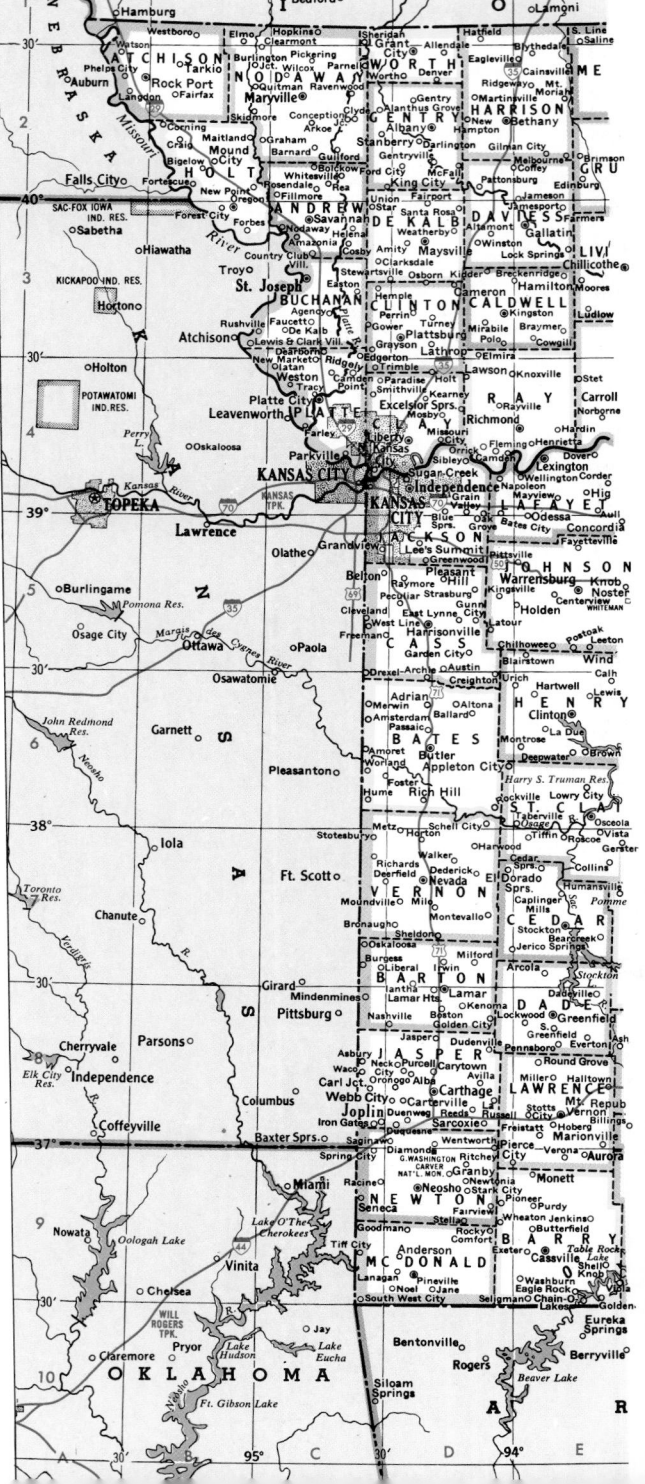

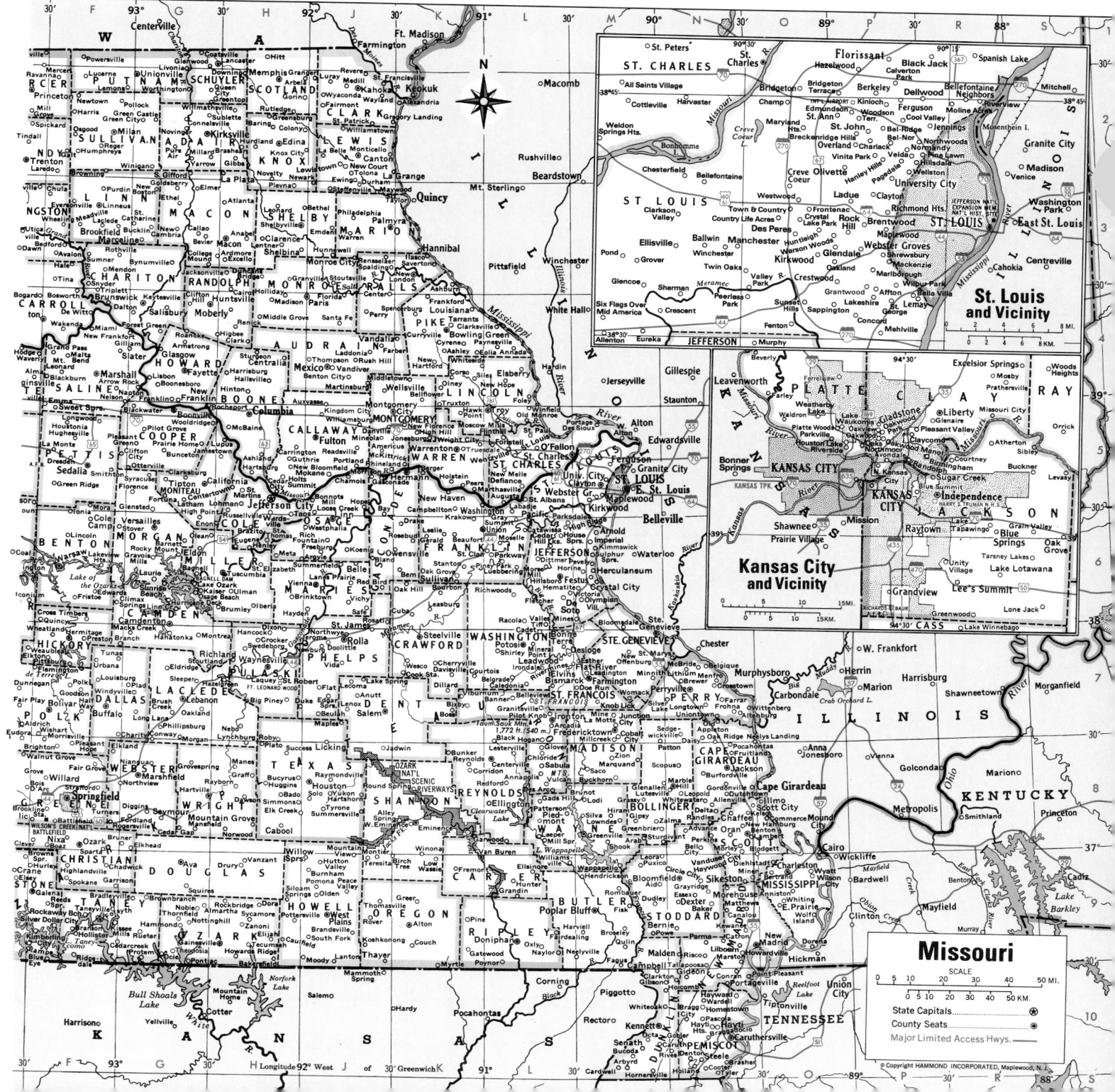

Agriculture, Industry and Resources

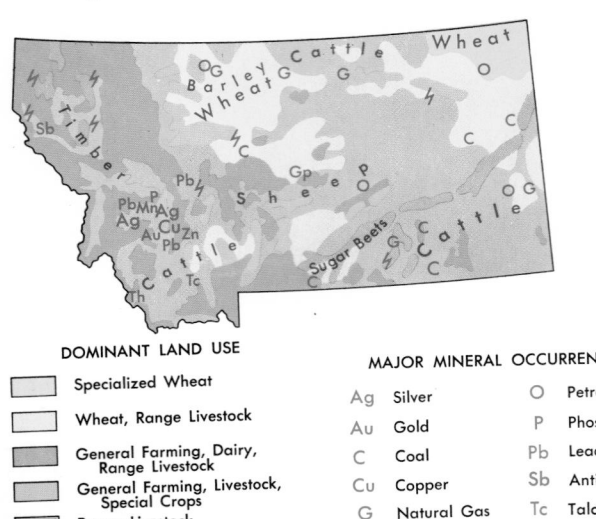

DOMINANT LAND USE

▢	Specialized Wheat
▢	Wheat, Range Livestock
▢	General Farming, Dairy, Range Livestock
▢	General Farming, Livestock, Special Crops
▢	Range Livestock
▢	Sugar Beets, Beans, Livestock, General Farming
▢	Forests

MAJOR MINERAL OCCURRENCES

Ag	Silver		O	Petroleum
Au	Gold		P	Phosphates
C	Coal		Pb	Lead
Cu	Copper		Sb	Antimony
G	Natural Gas		Tc	Talc
Gp	Gypsum		Th	Thorium
Mn	Manganese		Zn	Zinc
⚡	Water Power			

COUNTIES

Beaverhead 8,424	C5
Big Horn 11,337	J5
Blaine 6,728	G2
Broadwater 3,318	E4
Carbon 8,080	G5
Carter 1,503	M5
Cascade 77,691	E3
Chouteau 5,452	F3
Custer 11,697	L4
Daniels 2,266	L2
Dawson 9,505	M3
Deer Lodge 10,278	C5
Fallon 3,103	M4
Fergus 12,083	G3
Flathead 59,218	B2
Gallatin 50,463	E5
Garfield 1,589	J3
Glacier 12,121	C2
Golden Valley 912	G4
Granite 2,548	C4
Hill 17,654	F2
Jefferson 7,939	D4
Judith Basin 2,282	F4
Lake 21,041	B3
Lewis and Clark 47,495	D3
Liberty 2,295	E2
Lincoln 17,481	A2
Madison 5,989	D5
McCone 2,276	L3
Meagher 1,819	F4
Mineral 3,315	B3
Missoula 78,687	C3
Musselshell 4,106	H4
Park 14,562	F5
Petroleum 519	H3
Phillips 5,163	J2
Pondera 6,433	D2
Powder River 2,090	L5
Powell 6,620	D4
Prairie 1,383	B4
Ravalli 25,010	B4
Richland 10,716	M3
Roosevelt 10,999	L2
Rosebud 10,505	K4
Sanders 8,669	A3
Sheridan 4,732	M2
Silver Bow 33,941	D5
Stillwater 6,536	G5
Sweet Grass 3,154	G5
Teton 6,271	D3
Toole 5,046	E2
Treasure 874	J4
Valley 8,239	K2
Wheatland 2,246	G4
Wibaux 1,191	M4
Yellowstone 113,419	H4

CITIES and TOWNS

Absarokee 1,067	G5
Acton 50	H5
Alberton 354	B3
Alder 120	D5
Alzada 52	M5
Amsterdam 130	E5
Anaconda-Deer Lodge County▲	C4
Angela 50	K4
Antelope 83	M2
Apgar 25	B2
Arlee 489	B3
Armington 75	F3
Ashland 484	K5
Augusta 497	D3
Avon 125	C2
Babb 150	C2
Bainville 165	M2
Baker▲ 1,818	M4
Ballantine 380	H5
Bannack 2	D4
Basin 350	D4
Bearcreek 37	G5
Becket 35	H5
Belfry 300	G5
Belgrade 3,411	E5
Belt 571	F3
Big Arm 250	B3
Big Sandy 740	G2
Big Sky 50	E5
Big Timber▲ 1,557	G5
Bigfork 1,080	B2
Billings▲ 81,151	H5
Birney 100	K5
Black Eagle 1,500	E3
Blackfoot 100	D2
Bloomfield 28	M3
Bonner-West Riverside 1,669	C4
Boulder▲ 1,316	E4
Box Elder 300	F2
Boyd 32	G5
Bozeman▲ 22,660	E5
Brady 450	E2
Bridger 692	H5
Broadus▲ 572	L5
Broadview 133	H4
Brockton 365	M2
Brockway 55	L3
Browning 1,170	C2
Busby 409	J5
Butte-Silver Bow County▲ 33,336	D5
Bynum 49	D3
Camas Prairie 160	B3
Cameron 150	E5
Canyon Creek 100	D4
Canyon Ferry 100	E4
Cardwell 34	E5
Carter 70	K4
Cartersville 115	K4
Cascade 729	E3
Charlo 358	B3
Chester▲ 942	E2
Chinook▲ 1,512	G2
Choteau▲ 1,741	D3
Christina 60	G3
Circle▲ 805	L3
Clancy 550	E4
Clinton 250	C4
Clyde Park 282	F5
Coffee Creek 62	F3
Colstrip 3,035	K5
Columbia Falls 2,942	B2
Columbus▲ 1,573	G5
Condon 300	C3
Conner 450	B5
Conrad▲ 2,891	D2
Cooke City 120	G5
Coram 450	C2
Corvallis 500	C4
Craig 100	D3
Crane 163	M3
Creston 60	C2
Crow Agency 1,446	J5
Culbertson 796	M2
Custer 300	J4
Cut Bank▲ 3,329	D2
Dagmar 35	M2

Montana

SCALE
0 5 10   20   40   60 MI.
0 5 10 20   40   60KM.

⊛ State Capitals
◉ County Seats
Major Limited Access Hwys.

Topography

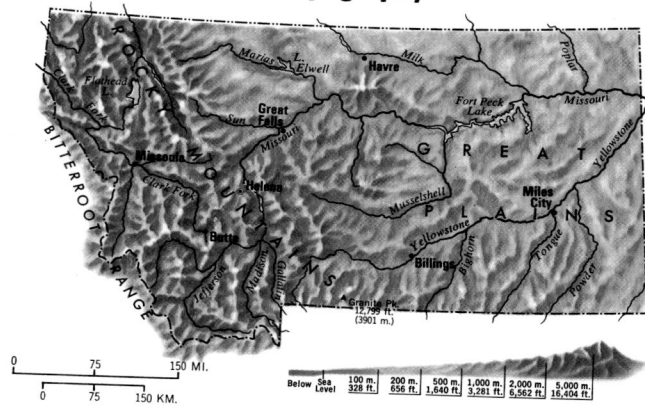

0   75   150 MI.
0   75   150 KM.

Below Sea Level | 100 m. 328 ft. | 200 m. 656 ft. | 500 m. 1,640 ft. | 1,000 m. 3,281 ft. | 2,000 m. 6,562 ft. | 5,000 m. 16,404 ft.

MONTANA

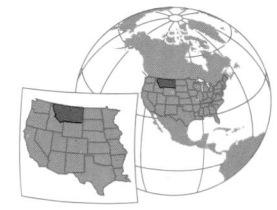

AREA 147,046 sq. mi. (380,849 sq. km.)
POPULATION 803,655
CAPITAL Helena
LARGEST CITY Billings
HIGHEST POINT Granite Pk. 12,799 ft. (3901 m.)
SETTLED IN 1809
ADMITTED TO UNION November 8, 1889
POPULAR NAME Treasure State; Big Sky Country
STATE FLOWER Bitterroot
STATE BIRD Western Meadowlark

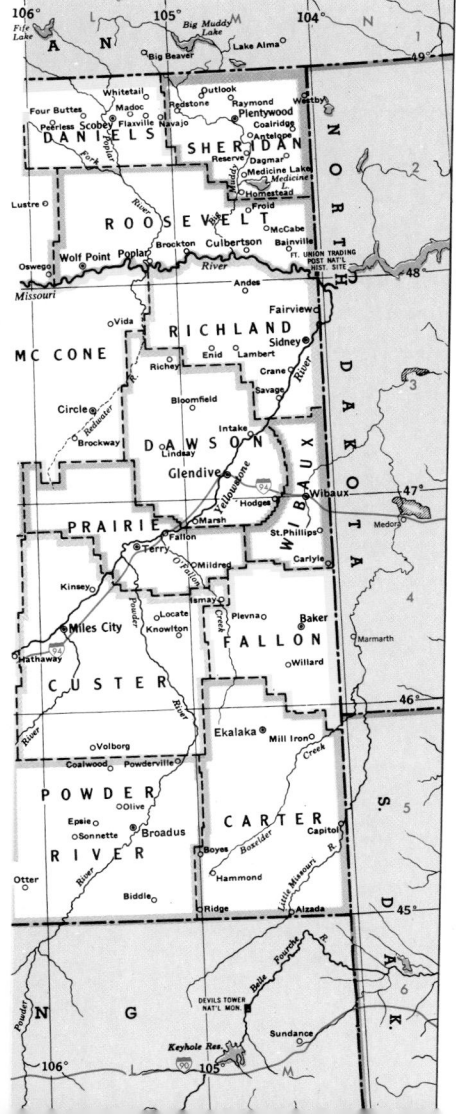

Darby 625 ....B4
Dayton 140 ....B3
De Borgia 300 ....A3
Decker 150 ....K5
Deer Lodge▲ 3,378 .....D4
Dell 29 ....D6
Delpine 33 ....D5
Denton 350 ....G3
Dillon▲ 3,991 ....D5
Divide 275 ....D5
Dixon 550 ....B3

Dodson 137 ....H2
Drummond 264 ....D4
Dupuyer 105 ....D2
Dutton 392 ....E3
East Glacier Park 326 ...C2
East Helena 1,538 ......E4
Edgar 220 ....H5
Ekalaka▲ 439 ....M5
Elliston 250 ....D4
Elmo 250 ....B3
Emigrant 80 ....F5

Ennis 773 ....E5
Epsie 60 ....L5
Essex 48 ....C2
Eureka 1,043 ....B2
Fairfield 660 ....D3
Fairview 869 ....M3
Fallon 225 ....L4
Flaxville 88 ....L2
Florence 700 ....B4
Floweree 48 ....E3
Forestgrove 100 ....H3
Forsyth▲ 2,178 ....K4
Fort Belknap 422 ......H2
Fort Benton▲ 1,660 ....F3
Fort Peck 325 ....K2
Fort Shaw 200 ....E3
Fort Smith 300 ....J5
Fortine 250 ....A2
Four Buttes 50 ....L2
Frazer 403 ....K2
Frenchtown 300 ....B3
Froid 195 ....M2
Fromberg 370 ....H5
Galata 100 ....E2
Galen 210 ....D4
Gallatin Gateway 600 ..E5
Gardiner 600 ....F5
Garneill 61 ....G4
Garrison 300 ....D4
Garryowen 200 ....J5
Geraldine 299 ....F3
Geyser 125 ....F3
Gildford 250 ....F2
Glasgow▲ 3,572 ......K2
Glen 4,802 ....D5
Glendive▲ 5,978 ......M3
Goldcreek 100 ....D4
Grant 25 ....C5
Grantsdale 500 ....B4
Grass Range 159 .....H3
Great Falls▲ 55,097 ...E3
Greenough 120 ....C4
Greycliff 37 ....G5
Hall 130 ....C4
Hamilton▲ 2,737 .....B4
Hardin▲ 2,940 ....J5
Harlem 882 ....H2
Harlowton▲ 1,049 ...F4
Harrison 94 ....E5
Hathaway 55 ....K4
Haugan 90 ....A3
Havre▲ 10,201 .....G2
Hays 333 ....H2
Heart Butte 499 ....C2
Helena (cap.)▲ 24,569 .E4
Helmville 250 ....C4
Heron 79 ....A3
Highwood 150 ......F3
Hilger 38 ....G3
Hingham 181 ....F2
Hinsdale 260 ......K2
Hobson 226 ....G4
Hodges 50 ....M4
Hogeland 35 ......H2
Homestead 50 ....M2
Hot Springs 411 ..B3
Hungry Horse 700 ..C2
Huntley 250 ....H5
Huson 97 ....B3
Hysham▲ 361 ....J4
Ingomar 48 ......J4
Intake 60 ....M3
Inverness 150 ...F2
Jackson 210 ....C5
Jardine 30 ......F5
Jeffers 70 ....E5
Jefferson City 162 ..E4
Jefferson Island 25 ..E5
Joliet 522 ....H5
Joplin 300 ....F2
Jordan▲ 494 ...J3
Judith Gap 133 ..G4
Kalispell▲ 11,917 ..B2
Kevin 185 ....D2
Kila 350 ....B2
Kinsey 100 ......L4
Kirby 30 ....J5
Klein 250 ....H4

Kremlin 304 ....F2
Lakeside 663 ....B2
Lakeview 28 ....E6
Lambert 203 ....M3
Lame Deer 1,918 ....K5
Landusky 40 ....H3
Laurel 5,686 ....H5
Laurin 60 ....D5
Lavina 151 ....H4
Lewistown▲ 6,051 ..G3
Libby▲ 2,532 ....A2
Lima 265 ....D6
Lincoln 473 ....D4
Lindsay 50 ....L3
Livingston▲ 6,701 ..F5
Locate 55 ....L4
Lodge Grass 517 ..J5
Lodge Pole 292 ...H2
Logan 53 ....E5
Lohman 25 ....G2
Lolo 2,746 ....B4
Lolo Hot Springs 25 ..B4
Loma 200 ....F3
Lonepine 50 .....B3
Lothair 29 ......E2
Maltana 2,340 ...J2
Manhattan 1,034 ..E5
Marion 450 ......B2
Martinsdale 75 ..F4
Marysville 76 ...D4
Maxville 44 .....C4
McAllister 55 ...E5
McLeod 150 ....G5
Medicine Lake 357 ..M2
Melrose 300 ....D5
Melstone 166 ..H4
Melville 700 ...F4
Miles City▲ 8,461 ..L4
Mill Iron 66 ...M5
Milltown 300 ..C4
Missoula▲ 42,918 ..C4
Moccasin 57 ...F3
Molt 31 ....H5
Monarch 120 ..F3
Moore 211 .....G4
Musselshell 117 ..H4
Myers 120 .....J4
Nashua 375 ...K2
Neihart 53 ....F4
Nibbe 30 .....H4
Norris 55 .....E5
North Havre 1,230 ..G2
Noxon 800 ....A3
Nye 50 ....G5
Oilmont 50 ...E2
Olney 200 ....B2
Opheim 145 ..K2
Oswego 75 ...L2
Outlook 109 ..M2
Ovando 300 ..C3
Pablo 1,298 ..B3
Paradise 400 ..B3
Park City 800 ..H5
Peerless 110 ..L2
Pendroy 100 ..D2
Perma 50 .....B3
Philipsburg▲ 925 ..C4
Plains 992 ....B3
Plentywood▲ 2,136 ..M2
Plevna 140 ...M4
Polaris 53 ....C5
Polson▲ 3,283 ..B3
Pompeys Pillar 300 ..J5
Pony 130 .....E5
Poplar 881 ....L2
Pomac 80 ....E5
Power 159 ....E3
Pray 40 ....F5
Proctor 150 ..B3
Pryor 654 ....H5
Radersburg 104 ..E4
Ramsay 95 ...D4
Rapelje 50 ...G5
Ravalli 150 ..B3
Raymond 26 ..M2
Raynesford 35 ..F3
Red Lodge▲ 1,958 ..G5
Redstone 40 ..M2
Reedpoint 160 ..G5

Regina 83 ....J3
Reserve 80 ....M2
Rexford 132 ....A2
Richey 259 ....L3
Richland 48 ....K2
Ringling 102 ....F4
Roberts 312 ....G5
Rocky Boy 150 ......G2
Rollins 200 ....B3
Ronan 1,547 ....B3
Roscoe 40 ....G5
Rosebud 259 ....K4
Roundup▲ 1,808 ...H4
Roy 200 ....H3
Rudyard 450 ....F2
Ryegate▲ 260 ......G4
Saco 261 ....J2
Saint Ignatius 778 ...C3
Saint Regis 500 ....A3
Saint Xavier 200 ...J5
Saltese 90 ....A3
Sand Coulee 600 ...E3
Sanders 50 ....J4
Santa Rita 120 ....D2
Savage 300 ....M3
Scobey▲ 1,154 ....L2
Seeley Lake 900 ..C3
Shawmut 66 ....G4
Sheffield 49 ....K4
Shelby▲ 2,763 ....E2
Shepherd 200 .....H5
Sheridan 652 .....D5
Sidney▲ 5,217 ....M3
Silesia 90 ....H5
Silver Star 125 ..D5
Simms 200 ......E3
Simpson 70 .....F2
Somers 700 .....B2
Sonnette 42 .....L5
Springdale 45 ...F5
Square Butte 48 ..F3
Stanford▲ 529 ...F3
Stark 51 ....B3
Stevensville 1,221 ..C4
Stockett 500 ....E3
Stryker 96 ......B2
Suffolk 45 .....G3
Sula 200 ......B5
Sun River 300 ..E3
Sunburst 437 ..E2
Superior▲ 881 ..B3
Swan Lake 100 ..C3
Sweetgrass 250 ..E2
Terry▲ 659 ....L4
Thompson Falls▲ 1,319 ..A3
Three Forks 1,203 ..E5
Thurlow 84 ...K4
Toston 70 ....E4
Townsend▲ 1,635 ..E4
Trego 50 ....B2
Trident 50 ...E5
Trout Creek 300 ..A3
Troy 953 ....A2
Turner 150 ..H2
Twin Bridges 374 ..D5
Twodot 285 ..F4
Ulm 450 ....E3
Utica 30 ....F4
Valier 519 ..D2
Vananda 50 ..K4
Vandalia 35 ..J2
Vaughn 2,270 ..E3
Vida 50 .....L3
Virgelle 28 ..F2
Virginia City▲ 142 ..E5
Volborg 150 ..L5
Wagner 32 ...H2
Walkerville 605 ..D4
Warmsprings 500 ..D4
Waterloo 50 ..D5
West Glacier 150 ..C2
West Yellowstone 913 ..E6
Westby 253 ..M2
White Sulphur Springs▲ 963 ..E4
Whitefish 4,368 ..B2
Whitehall 1,067 ..D5
Whitetail 150 ..L2
Whitewater 100 ..J2

Whitlash 50 ....E2
Wibaux▲ 628 ....M3
Wickes 60 ....D4
Willow Creek 150 ...E5
Wilsall 250 ....F5
Windham 63 ....F3
Winifred 150 ....G3
Winnett▲ 188 ....H4
Winston 120 ....E4
Wisdom 140 ....C5
Wise River 150 ......C5
Wolf Creek 500 .....D3
Wolf Point▲ 2,880 ..L2
Woodside 75 ....B4
Worden 600 ....H5
Wyola 350 ....J5
Zurich 60 ....G2

OTHER FEATURES

Absaroka (range) F5
Allen (mt.) C2
Arrow (creek) F3
Ashley (lake) B2
Battle (creek) G1
Bearhat (mt.) C2
Bears Paw (mts.) G2
Beartooth (mts.) G5
Beaver (creek) H5
Beaverhead (riv.) D5
Benton (lake) E3
Big (lake) G5
Big Belt (mts.) E4
Big Dry (creek) K3
Big Hole (riv.) C5
Big Hole Nat'l Battlefield ..C5
Bighorn (lake) H5
Bighorn (riv.) J5
Bighorn Canyon Nat'l
  Rec. Area H5
Big Muddy (riv.) M2
Big Porcupine (creek) ..J4
Birch (creek) D2
Birch Creek (res.) ..D2
Bitterroot (range) ...B4
Bitterroot (riv.) B4
Blackfeet Ind. Res. ..D2
Blackfoot (riv.) C4
Blackmore (mt.) F5
Bowdoin (lake) J2
Boxelder (creek) ...H3
Boxelder (creek) ...M5
Bynum (res.) D2
Cabinet (mts.) A2
Canyon Ferry (lake) ..E4
Clark Canyon (res.) ..D6
Clark Fork (riv.) ...A3
Clarks Fork, Yellowstone
  (riv.) G6
Cottonwood (creek) ..E2
Cow (creek) H3
Crazy (peak) F4
Crow Ind. Res. H5
Cut Bank (creek) D2
Douglas (creek) K5
Earthquake (lake) ...E6
Electric (peak) F5
Elwell (lake) E2
Emigrant (peak) F5
Ennis (lake) E5
Flathead (lake) B2
Flathead (riv.) B2
Flathead, North Fork (riv.) ..B2
Flathead, South Fork (riv.) ..C3
Flathead Ind. Res. ..B3
Flatwillow (creek) ..H4
Fort Belknap Ind. Res. ..H2
Fort Peck (lake) ...K3
Fort Union Trading Post
  Nat'l Hist. Site ..N2
Frances (lake) D2
Freezeout (lake) ...D3
Frenchman (riv.) ..J1
Fresno (res.) F2
Gallatin (peak) ...E5
Gallatin (riv.) ...E5
Georgetown (lake) ..C4
Gibson (res.) D3
Glacier Nat'l Park ..C2

Granite (peak) F5
Grant-Kohrs Ranch
  Nat'l Hist. Site D4
Hauser (lake) E4
Haystack (peak) A3
Hebgen (lake) E6
Helena (lake) E4
Holter (lake) D4
Hungry Horse (res.) ..C2
Hurricane (mt.) D2
Hyalite (peak) E5
Jackson (mt.) C2
Jefferson (riv.) D5
Judith (riv.) G3
Koocanusa (lake) A2
Kootenai (riv.) A2
Lemhi (pass) C6
Lewis and Clark (range) ..C3
Lima (res.) D6
Little Bighorn (riv.) ..J5
Little Bitterroot (lake) ..B2
Little Dry (creek) ..K3
Little Missouri (riv.) ..M5
Lockhart (mt.) D3
Lodge (creek) G1
Lolo (pass) B4
Lone (mt.) E5
Lost Trail (pass) ..B5
Lower Red Rock (lake) ..E6
Lower Saint Mary (lake) ..C2
Madison (riv.) E5
Malmstrom A.F.B. 5,938 ..E3
Marias (riv.) D2
Martinsdale (res.) ..F4
Mary Ronan (lake) ..B3
McDonald (lake) ...B2
McGloughlin (peak) ..C4
McGregor (lake) B3
Medicine (lake) ...M2
Milk (riv.) J2
Mission (range) ...C3
Missouri (riv.) ...L3
Musselshell (riv.) ..J3
Nelson (res.) J2
Ninepipe (res.) ...C3
Northern Cheyenne
  Indian Reservation ..K5
O'Fallon (creek) ..L4
Pishkun (res.) D3
Poplar (riv.) L2
Porcupine (creek) ..K2
Powder (riv.) L4
Purcell (mts.) A2
Railley (mt.) C3
Red Rock (lakes) ..E6
Red Rock (riv.) ...D6
Redwater (riv.) ...L3
Rock (creek) C4
Rocky (mts.) D4
Rocky Boy's Ind. Res. ..G2
Rosebud (creek) ..K4
Ruby (riv.) D5
Ruby River (res.) ..D5
Sage (creek) F2
Saint Mary (lake) ..C2
Saint Mary (riv.) ..C1
Sandy (creek) ...F2
Sheep (mt.) C2
Shields (riv.) ...F4
Siyeh (mt.) C2
Smith (riv.) E3
Sphinx (mt.) ...E5
Stillwater (riv.) ..G5
Stimson (mt.) ..C2
Sun (riv.) D3
Swan (lake) C3
Teton (riv.) ...D2
Tongue (riv.) ..K5
Upper Red Rock (lake) ..E6
Ward (peak) ...C2
Waterton-Glacier Int'l
  Peace Park C2
Whitefish (lake) ..B2
Willow (creek) ...E2
Willow Creek (res.) ..D3
Yellowstone (riv.) ..M3
Yellowstone National Park ..F6

▲County seat

Agriculture, Industry and Resources

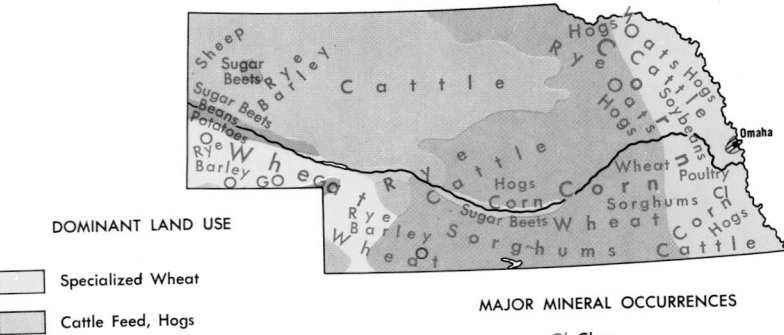

DOMINANT LAND USE

- Specialized Wheat
- Cattle Feed, Hogs
- Livestock, Cash Grain
- General Farming, Livestock, Special Crops
- Sugar Beets, Dry Beans, Livestock, General Farming
- Range Livestock

MAJOR MINERAL OCCURRENCES

- Cl Clay
- G Natural Gas
- O Petroleum
- ⚡ Water Power
- Major Industrial Areas

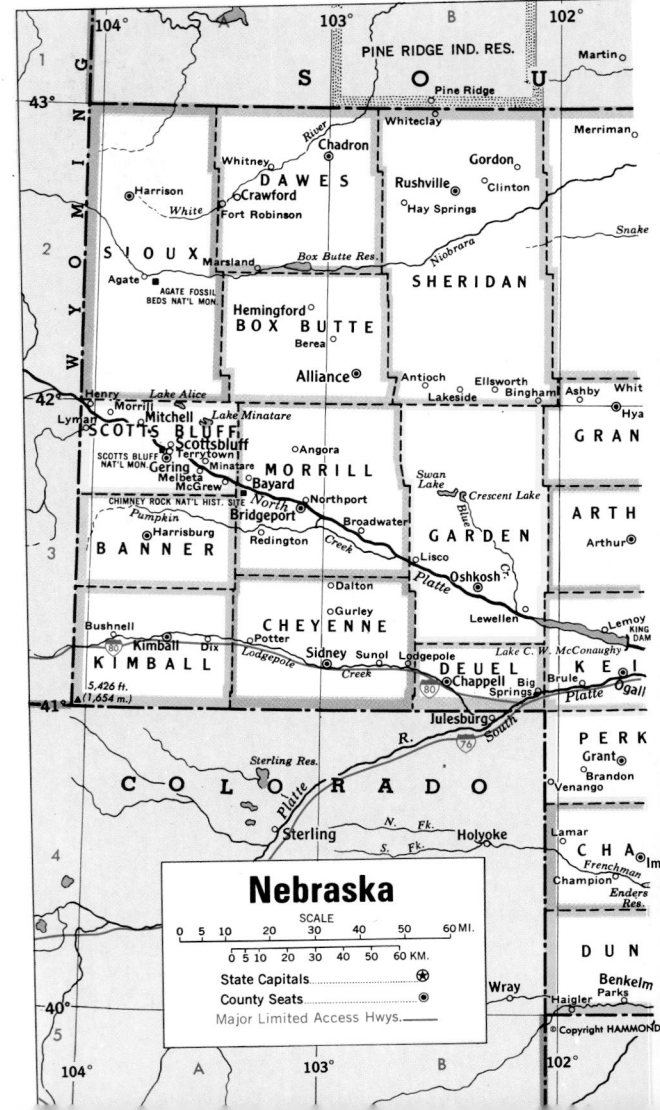

Nebraska

SCALE

0 5 10   20   30   40   50   60 MI.

0 5 10 20 30 40 50 60 KM.

State Capitals............⊛

County Seats............◉

Major Limited Access Hwys.

© Copyright HAMMOND

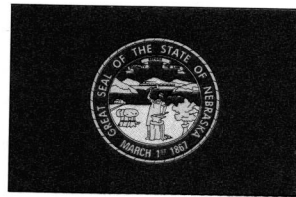

AREA 77,355 sq. mi. (200,349 sq. km.)
POPULATION 1,584,617
CAPITAL Lincoln
LARGEST CITY Omaha
HIGHEST POINT (Kimball Co.) 5,246 ft. (1654 m.)
SETTLED IN 1847
ADMITTED TO UNION March 1, 1867
POPULAR NAME Cornhusker State
STATE FLOWER Goldenrod
STATE BIRD Western Meadowlark

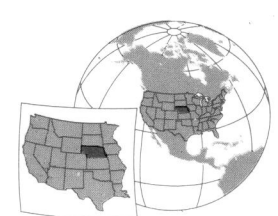

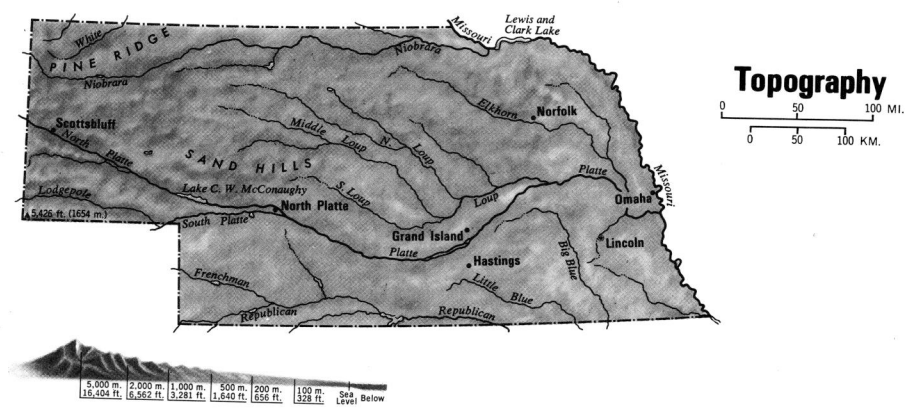

Topography

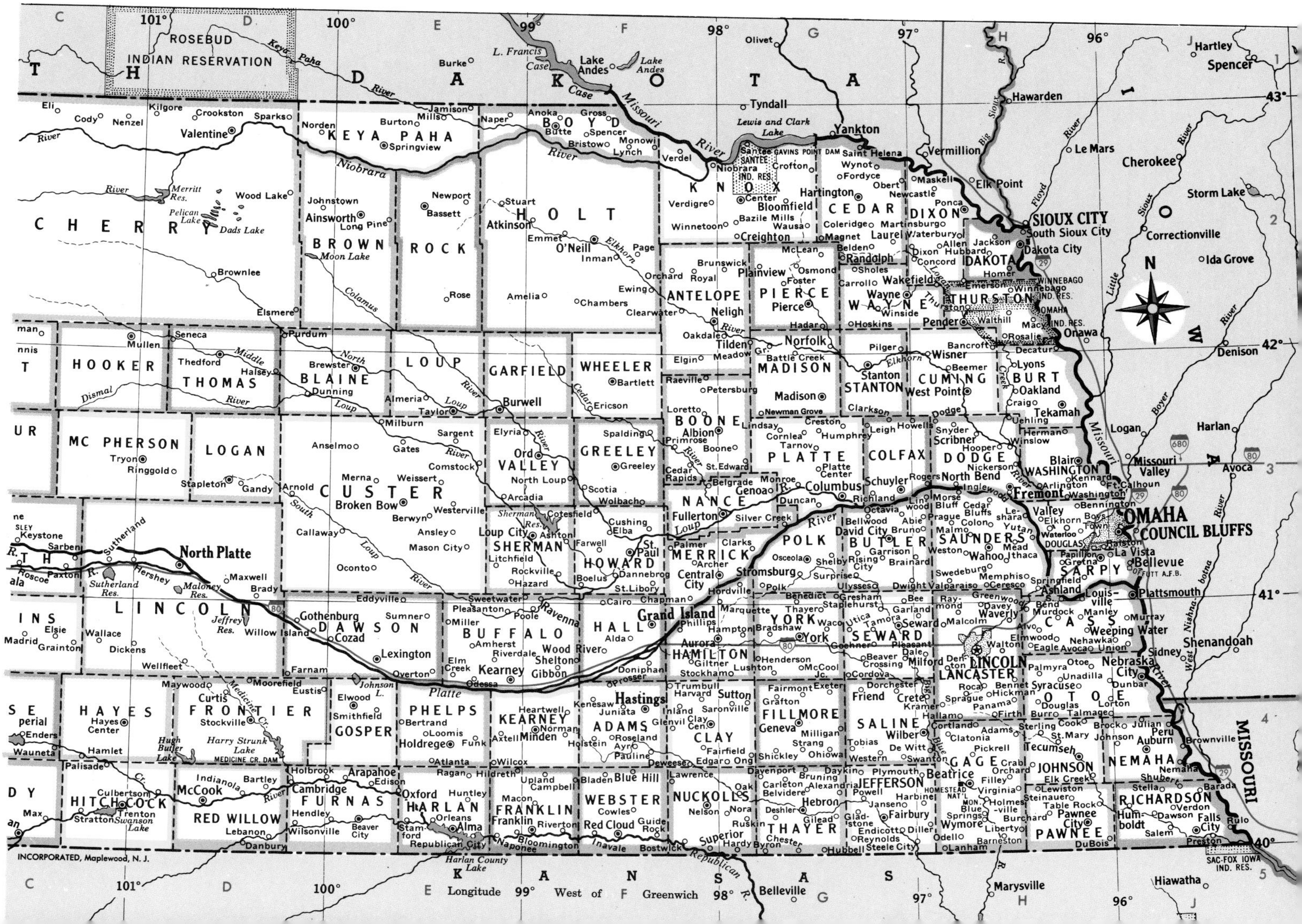

INCORPORATED, Maplewood, N.J.

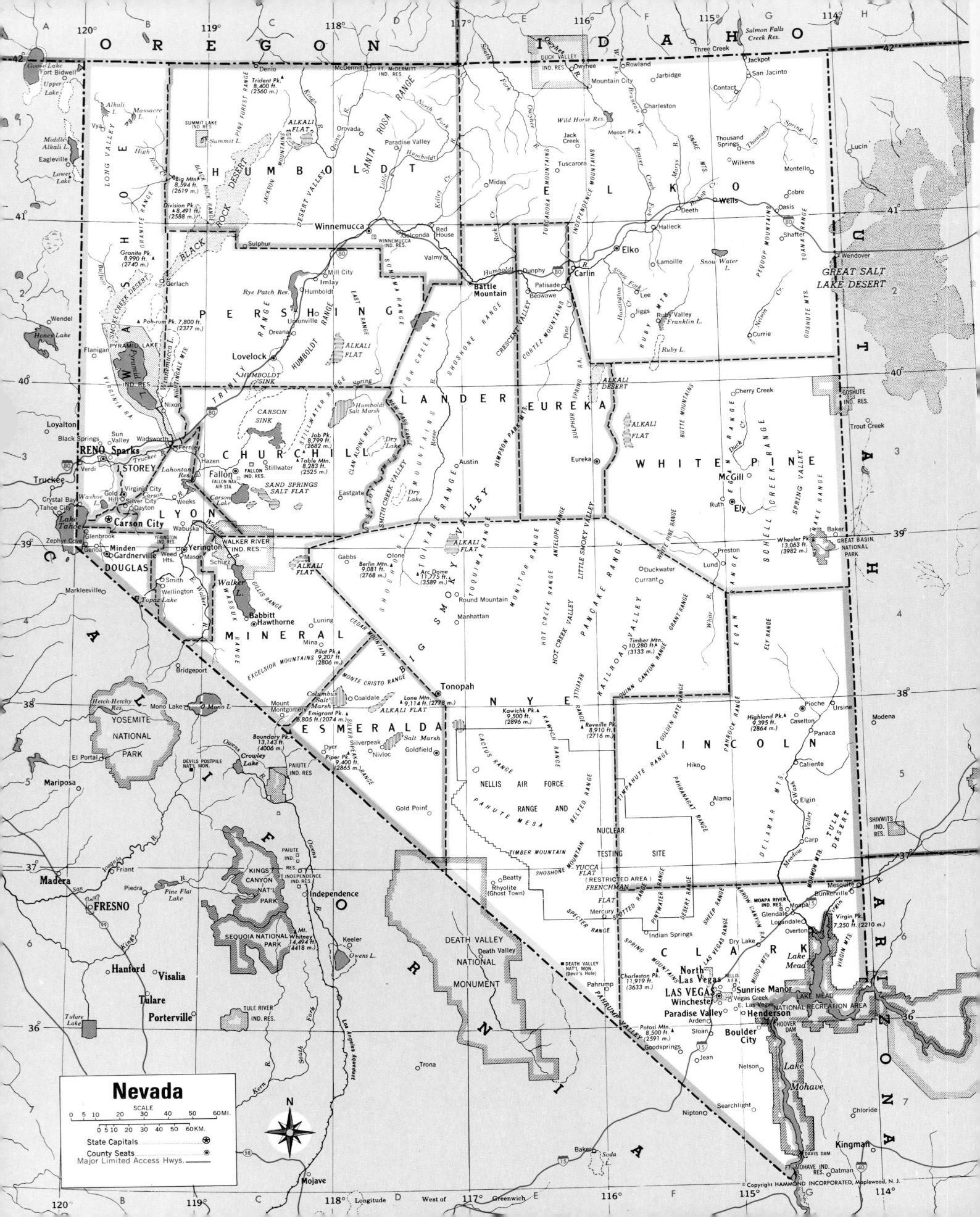

Nevada
SCALE
0 5 10 20 30 40 50 60 MI.
0 5 10 20 30 40 50 60 KM.
State Capitals
County Seats
Major Limited Access Hwys.
OREGON
IDAHO
UTAH
ARIZONA
CALIFORNIA
HUMBOLDT
WASHOE
PERSHING
ELKO
LANDER
EUREKA
WHITE PINE
CHURCHILL
STOREY
LYON
DOUGLAS
MINERAL
ESMERALDA
NYE
LINCOLN
CLARK
Carson City
RENO
Sparks
Winnemucca
Elko
Ely
Tonopah
Las Vegas
North Las Vegas
Henderson
Boulder City
Lovelock
Fallon
Yerington
Minden
Gardnerville
Hawthorne
Goldfield
Pioche
Eureka
Austin
Battle Mountain
Virginia City
Wells
Carlin
McGill
Mesquite
Lake Tahoe
Pyramid Lake
Walker L.
Lake Mead
Lake Mohave
Humboldt R.
Black Rock Desert
Great Salt Lake Desert
Great Basin National Park
Nellis Air Force Range and Nuclear Testing Site
Death Valley National Monument
Yosemite National Park
Sequoia National Park
Kings Canyon Nat'l Park
Lake Mead National Recreation Area
Hoover Dam
Davis Dam
Boundary Pk. 13,143 ft. (4006 m.)
Wheeler Pk. 13,063 ft. (3982 m.)
Charleston Pk. 11,919 ft. (3633 m.)
Mt. Whitney 14,494 ft. (4418 m.)
Toiyabe Range
Toquima Range
Shoshone Mountains
Ruby Mts.
Spring Mountains
Big Smoky Valley
Pahrump Valley
Salmon Falls Creek Res.
Goose Lake
Honey Lake
Mono Lake
Owens L.
FRESNO
Madera
Bishop
Mojave
Kingman
Bridgeport
Truckee
Independence
Trona
Baker
Nipton
Searchlight
120°
119°
118°
117°
116°
115°
114°
42°
41°
40°
39°
38°
37°
36°
Longitude West of Greenwich
© Copyright HAMMOND INCORPORATED, Maplewood, N. J.

AREA 110,561 sq. mi. (286,353 sq. km.)
POPULATION 1,206,152
CAPITAL Carson City
LARGEST CITY Las Vegas
HIGHEST POINT Boundary Pk. 13,143 ft. (4006 m.)
SETTLED IN 1850
ADMITTED TO UNION October 31, 1864
POPULAR NAME Silver State; Sagebrush State
STATE FLOWER Sagebrush
STATE BIRD Mountain Bluebird

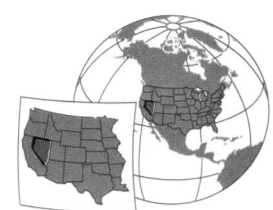

MAJOR MINERAL OCCURRENCES

Ag Silver
Au Gold
Ba Barite
Cu Copper
Gp Gypsum
Hg Mercury
Lt Lithium
Mg Magnesium
Mo Molybdenum
Na Salt
O   Petroleum
Pb Lead
S   Sulfur
W   Tungsten   ⚡ Water Power
Zn Zinc

DOMINANT LAND USE

- General Farming, Dairy, Livestock
- General Farming, Livestock, Special Crops
- Range Livestock
- Forests
- Nonagricultural Land

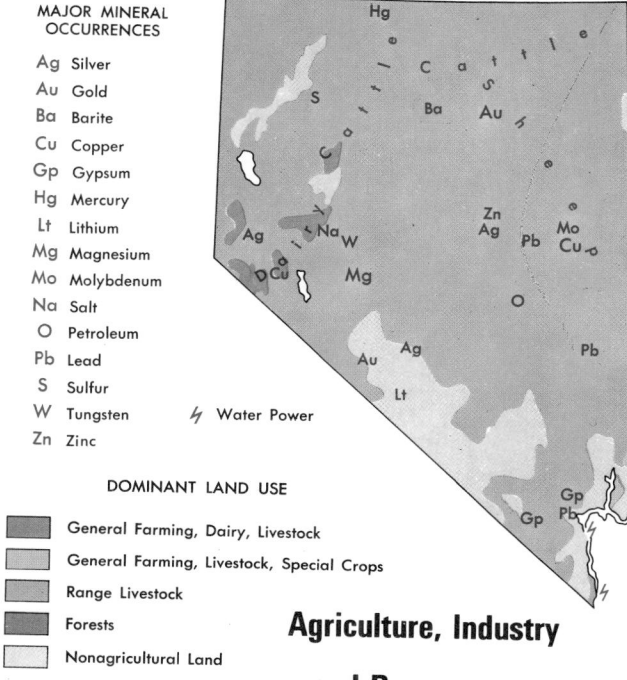

Agriculture, Industry and Resources

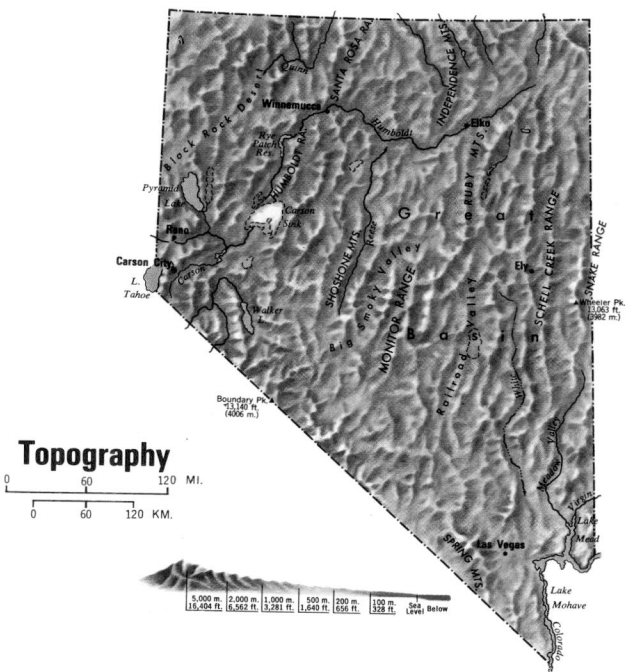

Topography

0   60   120 MI.
0   60   120 KM.

5,000 m. 2,000 m. 1,000 m. 500 m. 200 m. 100 m. Sea Level Below
16,404 ft. 6,562 ft. 3,281 ft. 1,640 ft. 656 ft. 328 ft.

COUNTIES

Carson City (city) 40,443 ....B3
Churchill 17,938 ....C3
Clark 741,459 ....F6
Douglas 27,637 ....B4
Elko 33,530 ....F1
Esmeralda 1,344 ....D5
Eureka 1,547 ....E3
Humboldt 12,844 ....C1
Lander 6,266 ....D3
Lincoln 3,775 ....F5
Lyon 20,001 ....B3
Mineral 6,475 ....C4
Nye 17,781 ....E4
Pershing 4,336 ....C2
Storey 2,526 ....B3
Washoe 254,667 ....B2
White Pine 9,264 ....F3

CITIES and TOWNS

Alamo 300 ....F5
Austin 300 ....E3
Babbitt C4
Baker 140 ....G3
Battle Mountain▲ 3,542 ....E2
Beatty 1,623 ....E5
Beowawe 77 ....E2
Black Springs 180 ....B3
Boulder City 12,567 ....G7
Bunkerville 300 ....G6
Caliente 1,111 ....G5
Carlin 2,220 ....E2
Carp 30 ....G5
Carson City (cap.) 40,443 ....B3
Caselton G5
Cherry Creek 80 ....G3
Coaldale 31 ....D4
Crystal Bay 6,225 ....A3
Currant 30 ....F4
Dayton 2,217 ....B3
Deeth 125 ....F1
Denio 35 ....C1
Duckwater 80 ....F4
Dunphy 25 ....E2
Dyer 56 ....C5
East Las Vegas 11,087 ....F6
Elko▲ 14,736 ....F2
Ely▲ 4,756 ....G3
Eureka▲ 300 ....E3
Fallon▲ 6,438 ....C3
Fernley 5,164 ....B3
Gabbs 667 ....D4
Gardnerville 2,177 ....B4
Genoa 254 ....B4
Gerlach 400 ....B2
Glenbrook 800 ....B3
Glendale 75 ....G6
Golconda 275 ....D2
Gold Hill 80 ....B3
Goldfield▲ 500 ....D5
Goodsprings 80 ....F7
Halleck 68 ....F2
Hawthorne▲ 4,162 ....C4
Hazen 76 ....C3
Henderson 64,942 ....G6
Hiko 210 ....F5
Imlay 90 ....C2
Indian Springs 1,164 ....F6
Jack Creek E1
Jackpot 400 ....G1
Jean 125 ....F7
Lamoille 100 ....F2
Las Vegas▲ 258,295 ....F6
Lee 125 ....F2
Logandale 410 ....G6
Lovelock▲ 2,069 ....C2
Lund 380 ....F4
Luning 90 ....C4
Manhattan 93 ....E4
Mason 200 ....B4
McDermitt 373 ....D1
McGill 1,258 ....G3
Mercury 900 ....E6
Mesquite 1,871 ....G6
Mina 450 ....C4
Minden▲ 1,441 ....B4
Moapa 3,444 ....G6
Montello 100 ....G1
Mountain City 100 ....F1
Nelson 75 ....G7
Nixon 400 ....B3
North Las Vegas 47,707 ....F6
Oreana 45 ....C2
Orovada 200 ....D1
Overton 1,111 ....G6
Owyhee 908 ....F1
Pahrump 7,424 ....E6
Panaca 650 ....G5
Paradise Valley 115 ....D1
Paradise Valley 84,818 ....F6
Pioche▲ 850 ....G5
Preston 50 ....G4
Reno▲ 133,850 ....B3
Round Mountain 400 ....E4

Ruby Valley 150 ....F2
Ruth 455 ....F3
Schurz 617 ....C4
Searchlight 500 ....F7
Silver City 150 ....B3
Silverpeak 100 ....D5
Sloan 30 ....F7
Smith 1,033 ....B4
Sparks 53,367 ....B3
Stillwater 150 ....C3
Sulphur C2
Sun Valley 11,391 ....B3
Sunrise Manor 95,362 ....F6
Thousand Springs G1
Tonopah▲ 3,616 ....D4
Ursine 45 ....G5
Valmy 200 ....D2
Vegas Creek G6
Verdi 100 ....B3
Virginia City▲ 750 ....B3
Wabuska 150 ....B3
Wadsworth 640 ....B3
Wellington 505 ....B4
Wells 1,256 ....G1
Winchester 23,365 ....F6
Winnemucca▲ 6,134 ....D2
Yerington▲ 2,367 ....B4
Zephyr Cove 1,434 ....A3

OTHER FEATURES

Alkali (lake) B1
Antelope (range) E3
Arc Dome (mt.) D4
Arrow Canyon (range) G6
Beaver Creek Fork,
  Humboldt (riv.) F1
Belted (range) E5
Berlin (mt.) D4
Big (mt.) B1
Big Smoky (valley) D4
Bishop (creek) F1
Black Rock (des.) B2
Black Rock (range) B1
Boundary (peak) C5
Buffalo (creek) B2
Butte (mts.) F3
Cactus (range) E5
Carson (lake) C3
Carson (riv.) B3
Carson (sink) C3
Cedar (mt.) D4
Charleston (peak) F6
Clan Alpine (mts.) D3
Columbus (salt marsh) C4
Cortez (mts.) E2
Crescent (valley) E2
Davis (dam) G7
Death Valley Nat'l Mon. E6
Delamar (mts.) G5
Desatoya (mts.) D3
Desert (range) F6
Desert (valley) C1
Devil's Hole (Death Valley
  Nat'l Mon.) E6
Division (peak) B1
Duck (creek) G3
Duck Valley Ind. Res. E1
East (range) D2
East Walker (riv.) B4
Egan (range) G4
Ely (range) G4
Emigrant (peak) C5
Excelsior (mts.) C4
Fallon Ind. Res. C3
Fallon Nav. Air Sta. C3
Fish Creek (mts.) D2
Fort McDermitt Ind. Res. D1
Fort Mohave Ind. Res. G7
Franklin (lake) F2
Frenchman Flat (basin) F6
Gillis (range) C4
Golden Gate (range) F5
Goshute (mts.) G2
Goshute Ind. Res. G3
Granite (peak) B2
Granite (range) B2
Grant (range) F4
Great Basin Nat'l Park G4
Great Salt Lake (des.) H2
High Rock (creek) B1
Highland (peak) G5
Hoover (dam) G7
Hot Creek (range) E4
Hot Creek (valley) E4
Humboldt (range) C2
Humboldt (riv.) E2
Humboldt (salt marsh) D3
Humboldt (sink) C2
Huntington (creek) F2
Independence (mts.) E1
Jackson (mts.) C1
Job (peak) C3
Kawich (range) E5
Kelley (creek) D1
Kings (riv.) C1
Lahontan (res.) B3

Lake Mead
  National Rec. Area G6
Las Vegas (riv.) F6
Little Humboldt (riv.) D1
Little Smoky (valley) E4
Lone (mt.) D4
Long (valley) B1
Marys (riv.) F1
Mason (range) F1
Massacre (lake) B1
Mead (lake) G6
Meadow Valley Wash (riv.) G5
Moapa River Ind. Res. G6
Mohave (lake) G7
Monitor (range) E4
Monte Cristo (range) D4
Mormon (mts.) G5
Muddy (mts.) G6
Nellis A.F.B. 8,377 ....F6
Nellis Air Force Range and
  Nuclear Test Site E5
Nelson (creek) G2
New Pass (range) D3
Nightingale (mts.) B2
Owyhee (riv.) E1
Pahranagat (range) F5
Pahrock (range) F5
Pah-rum (peak) B2
Pahrump (valley) F6
Pahute (mesa) E5
Pancake (range) F4
Pequop (mts.) G2
Pilot (peak) C4
Pine (creek) E2
Pine Forest (range) C1
Pintwater (range) F6
Piper (peak) D5
Potosi (mt.) F7
Pyramid (lake) B2
Pyramid Lake Ind. Res. B2
Quinn (riv.) D1
Quinn Canyon (range) F4
Railroad (valley) F4
Reese (riv.) D3
Reveille (peak) E5
Reveille (range) E4
Ruby (lake) F2
Ruby (mts.) F2
Rye Patch (res.) C2
Sand Springs (salt flat) C3
Santa Rosa (range) D1
Schell Creek (range) G3
Sheep (range) F6
Shoshone (mt.) E6
Shoshone (mts.) D3
Shoshone (range) E2
Silver Peak (range) D5
Simpson Park (mts.) E3
Smith Creek (valley) D3
Smoke Creek (des.) B2
Snake (mts.) F1
Snake (range) G3
Snow Water (lake) G2
Sonoma (range) D2
Specter (range) E6
Spotted (range) F6
Spring (creek) D2
Spring (mts.) F6
Spring (valley) G3
Stillwater (range) C3
Sulphur Spring (range) E3
Summit (lake) C1
Summit Lake Ind. Res. B1
Table (mt.) C3
Tahoe (lake) B3
Thousand Spring (creek) G1
Timber (mt.) E5
Timber (mt.) F4
Timpahute (range) F5
Toana (range) G2
Toiyabe (range) D3
Topaz (lake) B4
Toquima (range) E4
Trident (peak) C1
Trinity (range) C2
Truckee (riv.) B3
Tule (des.) G5
Tuscarora (mts.) E1
Virgin (mts.) G6
Virgin (peak) G6
Virgin (riv.) G6
Virginia (range) B3
Walker (lake) C4
Walker (riv.) C3
Walker River Ind. Res. C3
Washoe (lake) B3
Wassuk (range) C4
Wheeler (peak) G4
White (riv.) F4
White Pine (range) F3
Wild Horse (res.) E1
Winnemucca (lake) B2
Winnemucca Ind. Res. D2
Yerington Ind. Res. B3
Yucca Flat (basin) E6

▲County seat

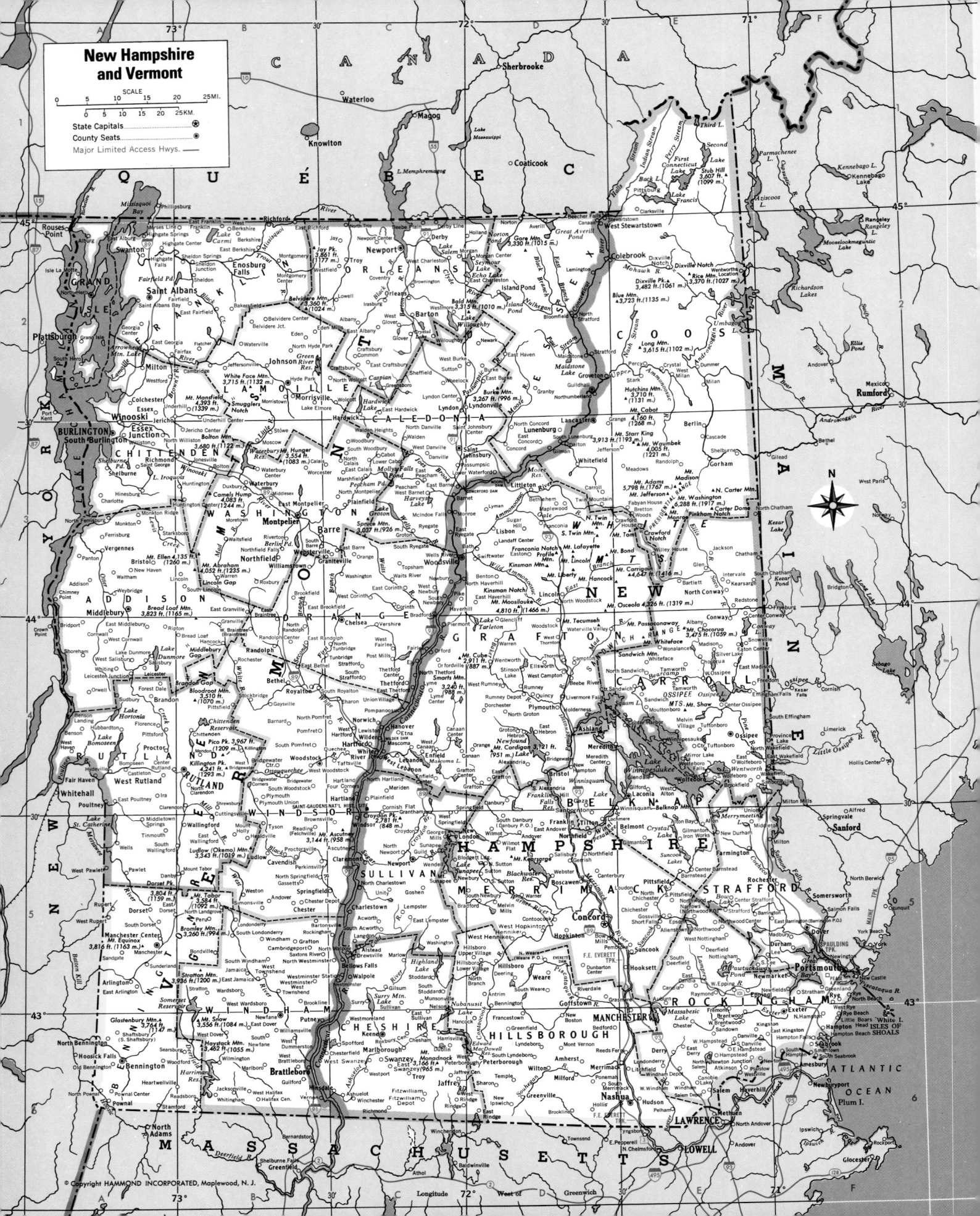
New Hampshire and Vermont
SCALE
0 5 10 15 20 25 MI.
0 5 10 15 20 25 KM.
State Capitals
County Seats
Major Limited Access Hwys.
CANADA
QUÉBEC
NEW YORK
MAINE
MASSACHUSETTS
ATLANTIC OCEAN
NEW HAMPSHIRE
GRAND ISLE
FRANKLIN
ORLEANS
ESSEX
LAMOILLE
CALEDONIA
CHITTENDEN
WASHINGTON
ADDISON
ORANGE
RUTLAND
WINDSOR
BENNINGTON
WINDHAM
COOS
GRAFTON
CARROLL
BELKNAP
SULLIVAN
MERRIMACK
STRAFFORD
CHESHIRE
HILLSBOROUGH
ROCKINGHAM
WHITE MTS.
GREEN MTS.
Sherbrooke
Magog
Knowlton
Waterloo
Coaticook
Plattsburgh
Burlington
South Burlington
Saint Albans
Swanton
Montpelier
Barre
Newport
Rutland
Bennington
Brattleboro
Middlebury
Concord
Manchester
Nashua
Portsmouth
Lawrence
Lowell
Haverhill
Keene
Laconia
Dover
Rochester
Rumford
Sanford
Berlin
Lake Champlain
Lake Memphremagog
Lake Winnipesaukee
Connecticut R.
Mt. Washington 6,288 ft. (1917 m.)
Mt. Mansfield 4,393 ft. (1339 m.)
Killington Pk. 4,241 ft. (1293 m.)
Mt. Monadnock 3,166 ft. (965 m.)
45°
44°
43°
73°
72°
71°
Longitude West of Greenwich
© Copyright HAMMOND INCORPORATED, Maplewood, N. J.

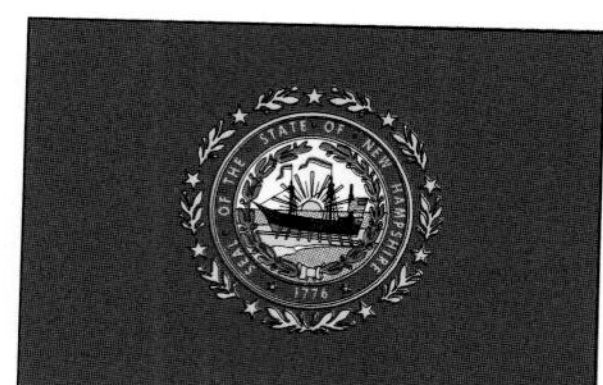

NEW HAMPSHIRE

AREA 9,279 sq. mi. (24,033 sq. km.)
POPULATION 1,113,915
CAPITAL Concord
LARGEST CITY Manchester
HIGHEST POINT Mt. Washington 6,288 ft. (1917 m.)
SETTLED IN 1623
ADMITTED TO UNION June 21, 1788
POPULAR NAME Granite State
STATE FLOWER Purple Lilac
STATE BIRD Purple Finch

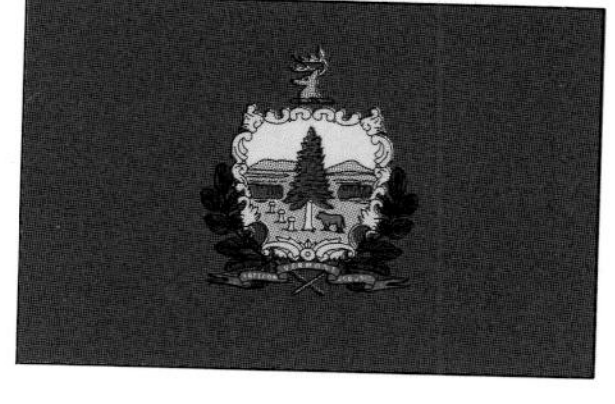

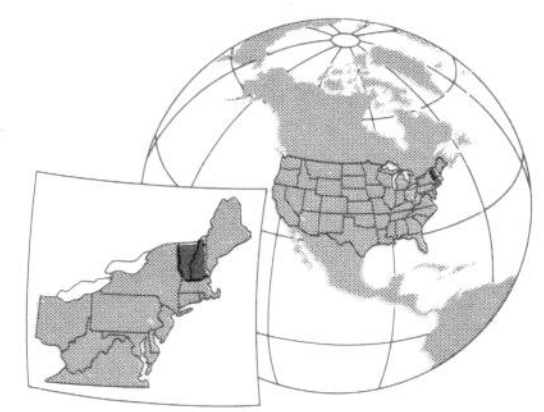

VERMONT

AREA 9,614 sq. mi. (24,900 sq. km.)
POPULATION 564,964
CAPITAL Montpelier
LARGEST CITY Burlington
HIGHEST POINT Mt. Mansfield 4,393 ft. (1339 m.)
SETTLED IN 1764
ADMITTED TO UNION March 4, 1791
POPULAR NAME Green Mountain State
STATE FLOWER Red Clover
STATE BIRD Hermit Thrush

Topography

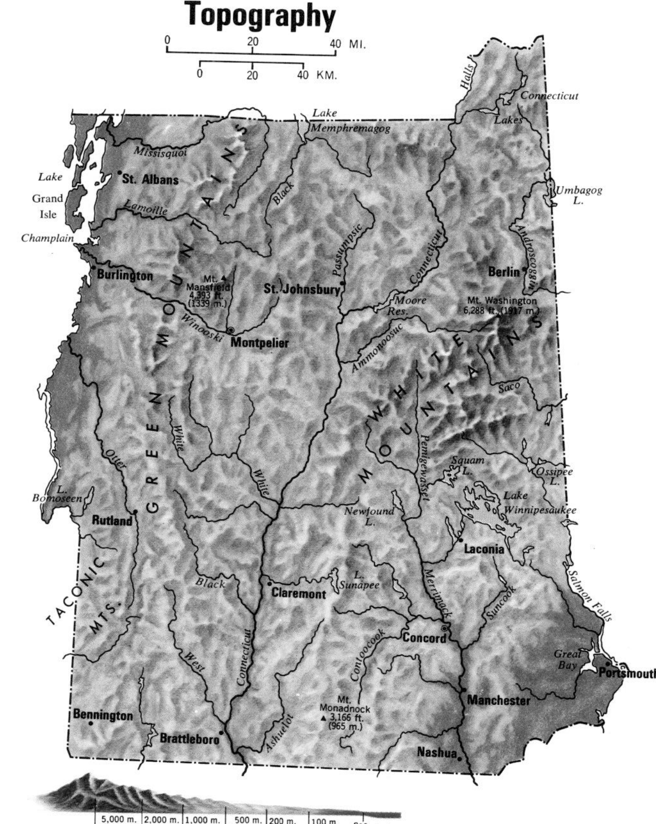

NEW HAMPSHIRE

COUNTIES

Belknap 49,216 ..... D4
Carroll 35,410 ..... E4
Cheshire 70,121 ..... C6
Coos 34,828 ..... E2
Grafton 74,929 ..... D4
Hillsborough 336,073 ..... D6
Merrimack 120,005 ..... D5
Rockingham 245,845 ..... E5
Strafford 104,233 ..... E5
Sullivan 38,592 ..... C5

CITIES and TOWNS

Acworth• 776 ..... C5
Albany• 536 ..... E4
Alexandria• 1,190 ..... D4
Allenstown• 4,649 ..... E5
Alstead• 1,721 ..... C5
Alton Bay 500 ..... E5
Alton• 3,286 ..... E5
Amherst• 9,068 ..... D6
Andover• 1,883 ..... D5
Antrim 1,325 ..... D5
Antrim• 2,360 ..... D5
Ashland 1,915 ..... D4
Ashland• 1,807 ..... D4
Ashuelot 810 ..... C6
Atkinson• 5,188 ..... E6
Auburn• 4,085 ..... E5
Barnstead• 3,100 ..... E5
Barrington• 6,164 ..... F5
Bartlett• 2,290 ..... E3
Bath• 784 ..... D3
Bedford• 12,563 ..... D6
Beebe River 355 ..... D4
Belmont• 5,796 ..... E5
Bennington• 1,236 ..... D5
Benton• 330 ..... D3
Berlin 11,824 ..... E3
Bethlehem• 2,033 ..... D3
Boscawen• 3,586 ..... D5
Bow Mills 802 ..... D5
Bradford• 1,405 ..... D5
Brentwood• 2,590 ..... E6
Bretton Woods E3
Bridgewater• 796 ..... D4
Bristol 1,483 ..... D4
Bristol• 2,537 ..... D4
Brookfield• 518 ..... E4
Brookline• 2,410 ..... D6
Campton• 2,377 ..... D4
Canaan• 3,045 ..... C4
Candia• 3,557 ..... E5
Canobie Lake 500 ..... E6
Canterbury• 1,687 ..... D5
Carroll• 528 ..... D3
Cascade 350 ..... E3
Center Barnstead 400 ..... E5
Center Conway 558 ..... E4
Center Harbor• 996 ..... E4
Center Ossipee• 800 ..... E4
Center Tuftonboro 300 ..... E4
Charlestown 1,173 ..... C5
Charlestown• 4,630 ..... C5
Chatham• 268 ..... E3
Chester• 2,691 ..... E6
Chesterfield• 3,112 ..... C6
Chichester• 1,942 ..... E5
Chocorua 575 ..... E4
Claremont 13,902 ..... C5
Clarksville• 232 ..... E1
Colebrook 2,444 ..... E2
Colebrook• 2,459 ..... E2
Concord• (cap.) 36,006 ..... D5
Contoocook 1,334 ..... D5
Conway 1,604 ..... E4
Conway• 7,940 ..... E4
Cornish Flat 450 ..... C4
Croydon• 627 ..... C5
Dalton• 827 ..... D3
Danbury• 881 ..... D4
Danville• 2,534 ..... E6
Deerfield• 3,124 ..... E5
Deering• 1,707 ..... D5
Derry 20,446 ..... E6
Derry• 29,603 ..... E6
Dorchester• 392 ..... D4
Dover▲ 25,042 ..... F5
Dublin• 1,474 ..... C6
Dummer• 327 ..... E2
Durham 9,236 ..... F5
Durham• 11,818 ..... F5
East Andover 500 ..... D5
East Hampstead 900 ..... E6
East Kingston• 1,352 ..... F6
East Lempster 300 ..... C5
East Sullivan 300 ..... C6
East Swanzey 500 ..... C6
East Wolfeboro 400 ..... E4
Easton• 223 ..... D3
Eaton (Eaton Center) 362 ..... E4
Ellsworth• 74 ..... D4
Enfield 1,560 ..... C4
Enfield• 3,979 ..... C4
Epping 1,384 ..... E5
Epping• 5,162 ..... E5
Epsom• 3,591 ..... E5
Errol• 292 ..... E2
Etna 550 ..... C4
Exeter▲ 9,556 ..... F6
Exeter• 12,481 ..... F6
Farmington 3,567 ..... E5
Farmington• 5,739 ..... E5
Fitzwilliam• 2,011 ..... C6
Fitzwilliam Depot 350 ..... C6
Francestown• 1,217 ..... D6
Franconia• 811 ..... D3
Franklin 8,304 ..... D5
Freedom• 935 ..... E4
Fremont• 2,576 ..... E6
Georges Mills 375 ..... C5
Gerrish 500 ..... D5
Gilford• 5,867 ..... E4
Gilmanton• 2,609 ..... E5
Gilmanton Iron Works 300 ..... E5
Gilsum• 745 ..... C5
Glen 600 ..... E3
Goffstown• 14,621 ..... D5
Gorham 1,910 ..... E3
Gorham• 3,173 ..... E3
Goshen• 742 ..... C5
Grafton• 923 ..... D4
Grantham• 1,247 ..... C5
Grasmere 400 ..... D5
Greenfield• 1,519 ..... D6
Greenland• 2,768 ..... F5
Greenville 1,135 ..... D6
Greenville• 2,231 ..... D6
Groton• 318 ..... D4
Groveton 1,255 ..... D2
Guild 500 ..... C5
Hampstead• 6,732 ..... E6
Hampton 7,989 ..... F6
Hampton• 12,278 ..... F6
Hampton Beach 975 ..... F6
Hampton Falls• 1,503 ..... F6
Hancock• 1,604 ..... C6
Hanover 6,538 ..... C4
Hanover• 9,212 ..... C4
Harrisville• 981 ..... C6
Haverhill• 4,164 ..... C3
Hebron• 386 ..... D4
Henniker 1,693 ..... D5
Henniker• 4,151 ..... D5
Hill• 814 ..... D4
Hillsboro 1,826 ..... D5
Hillsboro• 4,498 ..... D5
Hinsdale 1,718 ..... C6
Hinsdale• 3,936 ..... C6
Holderness• 1,694 ..... D4
Hollis• 5,705 ..... D6
Hooksett 2,573 ..... E5
Hooksett• 8,767 ..... E5
Hopkinton• 4,806 ..... D5
Hudson 7,626 ..... E6
Hudson• 19,530 ..... E6
Intervale 725 ..... E3
Jackson• 678 ..... E3
Jaffrey 2,558 ..... C6
Jaffrey• 5,361 ..... C6
Jaffrey Center 340 ..... C6
Jefferson• 965 ..... D3
Kearsarge 350 ..... E3
Keene▲ 22,430 ..... C6
Kingston• 5,591 ..... E6
Laconia▲ 15,743 ..... E4
Lancaster▲ 1,859 ..... D3
Lancaster• 3,522 ..... D3
Landaff• 350 ..... D3
Langdon• 580 ..... C5
Lebanon 12,183 ..... C4
Lee• 3,729 ..... F5
Lempster• 947 ..... C5
Lincoln• 1,229 ..... D3
Lisbon 1,246 ..... D3
Lisbon• 1,664 ..... D3
Litchfield• 5,516 ..... E6
Littleton 4,633 ..... D3
Littleton• 5,827 ..... D3
Lochmere 300 ..... D5
Londonderry• 19,781 ..... E6
Loudon• 4,114 ..... E5
Lyman• 388 ..... D3
Lyme• 1,496 ..... C4
Lyndeborough• 1,294 ..... D6
Madbury• 1,404 ..... F5
Madison• 1,704 ..... E4
Manchester 99,567 ..... E6
Marlborough 1,211 ..... C6
Marlborough• 1,927 ..... C6
Marlow• 650 ..... C5
Melvin Village 450 ..... E4
Meredith 1,654 ..... D4
Meredith• 4,837 ..... D4
Meriden 800 ..... C4
Merrimack• 22,156 ..... D6
Middleton• 1,183 ..... E5
Milan• 1,295 ..... E2
Milford 8,015 ..... D6
Milford• 11,795 ..... D6
Milton• 3,691 ..... F5
Milton Mills 450 ..... F4
Mirror Lake 350 ..... E4
Monroe• 746 ..... C3
Mont Vernon• 1,812 ..... D6
Moultonboro• 2,956 ..... E4
Nashua▲ 79,662 ..... D6
Nelson• 535 ..... C5
New Boston• 3,214 ..... D6
New Castle• 840 ..... F5
New Durham• 1,974 ..... E5
New Hampton• 1,606 ..... D4
New Ipswich• 4,014 ..... D6
New London 3,180 ..... D5
New London• 2,935 ..... D5
Newbury• 1,347 ..... C5
Newfields• 888 ..... F5
Newington• 990 ..... F5
Newmarket 4,917 ..... F5
Newmarket• 7,157 ..... F5
Newport▲ 3,772 ..... C5
Newport• 6,110 ..... C5
Newton Junction 450 ..... E6
Newton• 3,473 ..... E6
North Chichester 450 ..... E5
North Conway 2,032 ..... E3
North Hampton• 3,637 ..... F6
North Haverhill 400 ..... D3
North Stratford 600 ..... D2
North Walpole 950 ..... C5
North Weare 400 ..... D5
North Woodstock 750 ..... D3
Northfield-Tilton D5
Northfield• 4,263 ..... D5
Northumberland• 2,492 ..... D2
Northwood• 3,124 ..... E5
Northwood Narrows 325 ..... E5
Nottingham• 2,939 ..... E5
Orange• 237 ..... D4
Orford• 1,008 ..... C4
Ossipee 3,309 ..... E4
Pelham• 9,408 ..... E6
Pembroke• 6,561 ..... E5
Peterborough 2,685 ..... D6
Peterborough• 5,239 ..... D6
Piermont• 624 ..... C4
Pike 433 ..... C3
Pittsburg• 901 ..... E1
Pittsfield 1,717 ..... E5
Pittsfield• 3,701 ..... E5
Plainfield• 2,056 ..... C4
Plaistow• 7,316 ..... E6
Plymouth 3,967 ..... D4
Plymouth• 5,811 ..... D4
Portsmouth 25,925 ..... F5
Randolph• 371 ..... E3
Raymond 2,516 ..... E5
Raymond• 8,713 ..... E5
Redstone 300 ..... E3
Richmond• 877 ..... C6
Rindge• 4,941 ..... C6
Rochester 26,630 ..... E5
Roxbury• 248 ..... C6
Rumney• 1,446 ..... D4
Rye• 4,612 ..... F5
Rye Beach 600 ..... F6
Rye North Beach 700 ..... F5
Salem• 25,746 ..... E6
Salem Depot 975 ..... E6
Salisbury• 1,061 ..... D5
Salmon Falls 950 ..... F5
Sanbornton• 2,136 ..... D5
Sanbornville 750 ..... F4
Sandown• 4,060 ..... E6
Sandwich• 1,066 ..... E4
Seabrook• 6,503 ..... F6
Sharon• 299 ..... D6
Shelburne 437 ..... E3
Shelburne• 318 ..... E3
Silver Lake 350 ..... E4
Somersworth 11,249 ..... F5
South Deerfield 500 ..... E5
South Hampton• 740 ..... F6
South Lyndeboro 300 ..... D6
South Merrimack 650 ..... D6
South Seabrook 500 ..... F6
South Weare 400 ..... D5
Spofford 750 ..... C6
Springfield• 788 ..... C4
Stark• 518 ..... E2
Stewartstown• 1,048 ..... E2
Stoddard• 622 ..... C5
Strafford• 2,965 ..... E5
Stratford• 927 ..... D2
Stratham• 4,955 ..... F5
Sugar Hill• 464 ..... D3
Sullivan• 706 ..... C5
Sunapee• 2,559 ..... C5
Suncook 5,214 ..... E5
Surry• 667 ..... C5
Sutton• 1,457 ..... D5
Swanzey• 6,236 ..... C6
Tamworth• 2,165 ..... E4
Temple• 1,194 ..... D6
Thornton• 1,505 ..... D4
Tilton-Northfield 3,081 ..... D5
Tilton• 3,240 ..... D5
Troy 2,097 ..... C6
Troy• 2,131 ..... C6
Tuftonboro• 1,842 ..... E4
Twin Mountain 500 ..... D3
Unity• 1,341 ..... C5
Wakefield• 3,057 ..... F4
Walpole• 3,210 ..... C5
Warner• 2,250 ..... D5
Warren• 820 ..... D4
Washington• 628 ..... C5
Waterville Valley• 151 ..... D4
Weare• 6,193 ..... D5
Webster• 1,405 ..... D5
Wentworth• 630 ..... D4
Wentworths Location 53 ..... E2
West Campton 400 ..... D4
West Epping 400 ..... E5
West Henniker 500 ..... D5
West Lebanon C4
West Milan 350 ..... E2
West Rye 350 ..... F6
West Stewartstown 700 ..... E2
West Swanzey 1,055 ..... C6
Westmoreland• 1,596 ..... C6
Westville 750 ..... E6
Whitefield 1,041 ..... D3
Whitefield• 1,909 ..... D3
Wilmot Flat 450 ..... D5
Wilmot• 935 ..... D5
Wilton 1,165 ..... D6
Wilton• 3,122 ..... D6
Winchester• 1,735 ..... C6
Windham• 9,000 ..... E6
Winnisquam 500 ..... E5
Wolfeboro 2,783 ..... E4
Wolfeboro• 4,807 ..... E4
Wolfeboro Falls 600 ..... E4
Woodstock• 1,167 ..... D4
Woodsville▲ 1,122 ..... C3

OTHER FEATURES

Adams (mt.) E3
Ammonoosuc (riv.) D3
Androscoggin (riv.) E2
Ashuelot (riv.) C6
Back (lake) E1
Baker (riv.) D4
Bearcamp (riv.) E4
Beaver (brook) E6
Belknap (mt.) E5
Blackwater (res.) D5
Blue (mt.) E2
Bond (mt.) E3
Bow (lake) E5
Cabot (mt.) E2
Cannon (mt.) D3
Cardigan (mt.) D4
Carrigain (mt.) E3
Carter Dome (mt.) E3
Chocorua (mt.) E4
Cocheco (riv.) E5
Cold (riv.) C5
Comerford (dam) D3
Connecticut (riv.) B6
Contoocook (riv.) D6
Conway (lake) E4
Crawford Notch (pass) E3
Croydon (peak) C5
Croydon Branch, Sugar (riv.) C5
Crystal (lake) E5
Cube (mt.) D4
Dixville (peak) E2
Dixville Notch (pass) E2
Edward MacDowell (res.) D6
Ellis (riv.) E3
Everett (dam) D5
Exeter (riv.) E6
First Connecticut (lake) E1
Francis (lake) E1
Franconia Notch (pass) D3
Franklin Falls (res.) D4
Gale (riv.) D3
Great (bay) F5
Halls (stream) E1
Hancock (mt.) D3
Highland (lake) C5
Hutchins (mt.) E2
Indian (stream) E1
Jefferson (mt.) E3
Kearsarge (mt.) D5
Kinsman (mt.) D3
Kinsman Notch (pass) D3
Lafayette (mt.) D3
Lamprey (riv.) E5
Liberty (mt.) D3
Lincoln (mt.) D3
Long (mt.) E2
Mad (riv.) D4
Madison (mt.) E3
Mascoma (lake) C4
Massabesic (lake) E6
Merrimack (riv.) D5
Merrymeeting (lake) E5
Mohawk (riv.) E2
Monadnock (mt.) C6
Monroe (mt.) E3
Moore (dam) D3
Moore (res.) D3
Moosilauke (mt.) D3
Nash (stream) E2
Newfound (lake) D4
North Carter (mt.) E3
North Twin (mt.) D3
Nubanusit (lake) C5
Osceola (mt.) E3
Ossipee (lake) E4
Ossipee (mts.) E4
Ossipee (riv.) F4
Passaconaway (mt.) E4
Pawtuckaway (pond) E5
Pease A.F.B. F5
Pemigewasset (riv.) D4
Perry (stream) E1
Pine (riv.) E4
Pinkham Notch (pass) E3
Piscataqua (riv.) F5
Piscataquog (riv.) D5
Presidential (range) E3
Rice (mt.) E2
Saco (riv.) E3

Agriculture, Industry and Resources

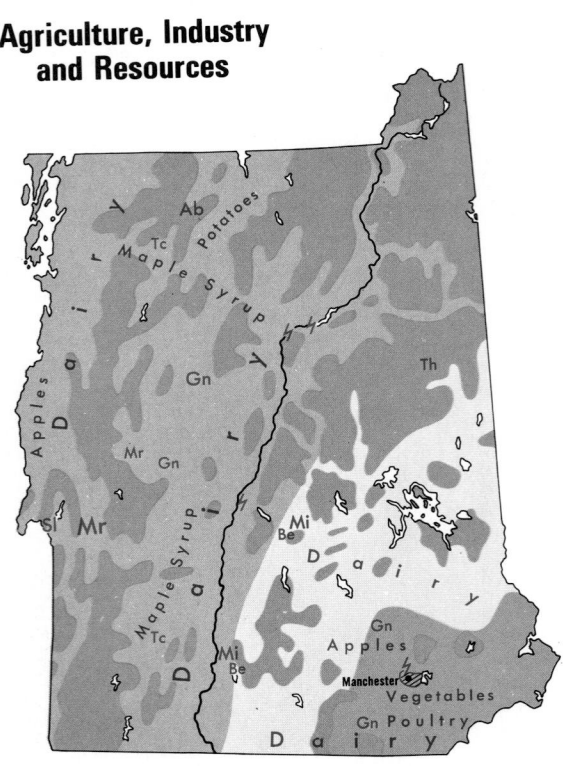

DOMINANT LAND USE

- Specialized Dairy
- Dairy, General Farming
- Dairy, Poultry, Mixed Farming
- Forests

⚡ Water Power

▨ Major Industrial Areas

MAJOR MINERAL OCCURRENCES

Ab	Asbestos	Mr	Marble
Be	Beryl	Sl	Slate
Gn	Granite	Tc	Talc
Mi	Mica	Th	Thorium

Saint-Gaudens Nat'l Hist. Site..B4
Salmon Falls (riv.)..........F5
Sandwich (mt.)...............E4
Sandwich (range).............E1
Second (lake)................E4
Shaw (mt.)...................E4
Shoals (isls.)...............F6
Smarts (mt.).................C4
Souhegan (riv.)..............D6
South Twin (mt.).............D3
Squam (lake).................E4
Starr King (mt.).............E3
Stub Hill (mt.)..............E1
Sugar (riv.).................C5
Sunapee (lake)...............C5
Suncook (lakes)..............E5
Suncook (riv.)...............E5
Surry Mountain (lake)........C5
Tarleton (lake)..............D4
Tecumseh (mt.)...............D4
Third (lake).................E1
Tom (mt.)....................E3
Umbagog (lake)...............E2
Upper Ammonoosuc (riv.)......E2
Warner (riv.)................D5
Washington (mt.).............E3
Waumbek (mt.)................E3
Wentworth (lake).............E4
White (isl.).................F6
White (mts.).................E3
Whiteface (mt.)..............E4
Wild Ammonoosuc (riv.).......D3
Wilder (dam).................C4
Winnipesaukee (lake).........E4
Winnipesaukee (riv.).........D5
Winnisquam (lake)............D4

AREA 7,787 sq. mi. (20,168 sq. km.)
POPULATION 7,748,634
CAPITAL Trenton
LARGEST CITY Newark
HIGHEST POINT High Point 1,803 ft. (550 m.)
SETTLED IN 1617
ADMITTED TO UNION December 18, 1787
POPULAR NAME Garden State
STATE FLOWER Purple Violet
STATE BIRD Eastern Goldfinch

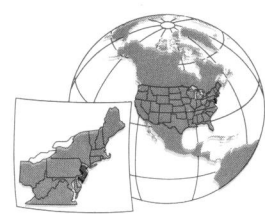

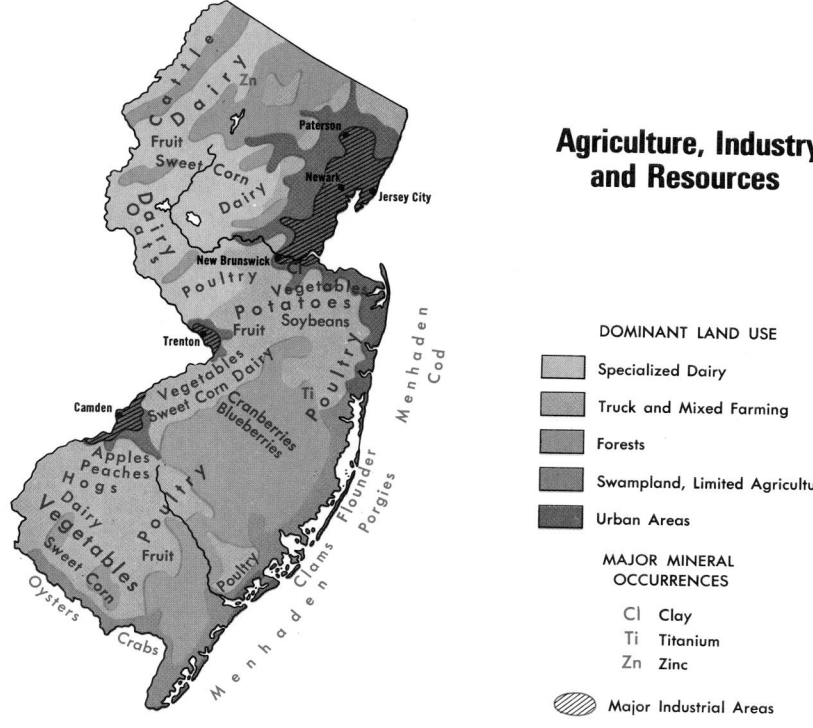

Agriculture, Industry and Resources

DOMINANT LAND USE

- Specialized Dairy
- Truck and Mixed Farming
- Forests
- Swampland, Limited Agriculture
- Urban Areas

MAJOR MINERAL OCCURRENCES

- Cl Clay
- Ti Titanium
- Zn Zinc

Major Industrial Areas

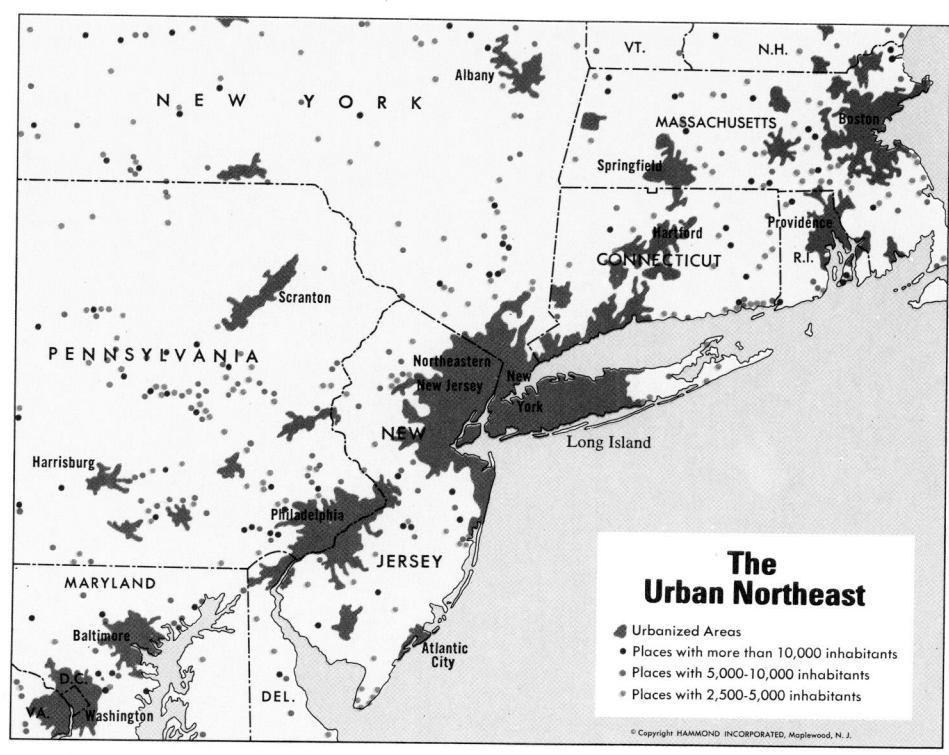

The Urban Northeast

- Urbanized Areas
- Places with more than 10,000 inhabitants
- Places with 5,000-10,000 inhabitants
- Places with 2,500-5,000 inhabitants

© Copyright HAMMOND INCORPORATED, Maplewood, N. J.

COUNTIES

Atlantic 224,327	D5
Bergen 825,380	E2
Burlington 395,066	D4
Camden 502,824	D4
Cape May 95,089	D5
Cumberland 138,053	C5
Essex 778,206	E2
Gloucester 230,082	C4
Hudson 553,099	E2
Hunterdon 107,776	D2
Mercer 325,824	D3
Middlesex 671,780	E3
Monmouth 553,124	E3
Morris 421,353	D2
Ocean 433,203	E4
Passaic 453,060	E1
Salem 65,294	C4
Somerset 240,279	D2
Sussex 130,943	D1
Union 493,819	E2
Warren 91,607	C2

CITIES and TOWNS

Aberdeen 17,235	E3
Absecon 7,298	D5
Allamuchy 600	D2
Allendale 5,900	B1
Allenhurst 759	F3
Allentown 1,828	D3
Allenwood	E3
Alloway 1,371	C4
Alpha 2,530	C2
Alpine 1,716	C1
Andover 700	D2
Annandale 1,074	D2
Ashland	B3
Asbury Park 16,799	F3
Atlantic City 37,986	E5
Atlantic Highlands 4,629	F3
Audubon 9,205	B3
Audubon Park 1,150	B3
Augusta 500	D1
Aura 500	C4
Avalon 1,809	D5
Avenel 15,504	E2
Avon By The Sea 2,165	E3
Barnegat 1,160	E4
Barnegat Light 675	E4
Barrington 6,774	B3
Basking Ridge	D2
Bay Head 1,226	E3
Bayonne 61,444	B2
Beach Haven 1,475	E4
Beach Haven Crest 500	E4
Beach Haven Terrace 500	E4
Beachwood 9,324	E4
Bedminster • 2,469	D2
Belford	E3
Belle Mead	D3
Belleplain 500	D5
Belleville 34,213	B2
Bellmawr 12,603	B3
Belmar 5,877	E3
Belvidere▲ 2,669	C2
Bergenfield 24,458	C1
Berkeley Heights • 11,980	E2
Berlin 5,672	D4
Bernardsville 6,597	D2
Beverly 2,973	D3
Blackwood 5,120	C4
Blackwood Terrace	C4
Blairstown • 4,360	C2
Bloomfield 45,061	B2
Bloomingdale 7,530	E1
Bloomsbury 890	C2
Bogota 7,824	B2
Boonton 8,343	E2
Bordentown 4,341	D3
Bound Brook 9,487	D2
Bradley Beach 4,475	F3
Branchville 851	D1
Brant Beach 500	E4
Breton Woods	E3
Brick • 66,473	E3
Bridgeport 750	B3
Bridgeton▲ 18,942	C5
Bridgewater • 29,175	D2
Brielle 4,406	E3
Brigantine 11,354	E5
Brooklawn 1,805	B3
Brookside	D2
Browns Mills 11,429	D4
Budd Lake 7,272	D2
Buena 4,441	D4
Burlington 9,835	D3
Butler 7,392	E2
Caldwell 7,549	B2
Califon 1,073	D2
Camden▲ 87,492	B3
Candlewood 6,750	E3
Cape May 4,668	D6
Cape May Court House▲ 4,426	D5

Cape May Point 248	D6
Carlstadt 5,510	B2
Carneys Point 7,686	C4
Carteret 19,025	E2
Cedar Brook 600	D4
Cedar Grove▲ 12,053	B2
Cedar Knolls	E2
Cedarville 900	C5
Cedarwood Park	E3
Chatham 8,007	E2
Chatsworth 700	D4
Cheesequake	E3
Cherry Hill • 69,319	B3
Chesilhurst 1,526	D4
Chester 1,214	D2
Chesterfield • 3,867	D3
Cinnaminson • 14,583	B3
Clark • 14,629	A3
Clarksboro	C4
Clarksburg 800	E3
Clayton 6,155	C4
Clementon 5,601	B3
Cliffside Park 20,393	C2
Cliffwood	E3
Clifton 71,742	B2
Clinton 2,054	D2
Closter 8,094	C1
Cold Spring 500	D6
Collingswood 15,289	B3
Cologne 800	D4
Colonia 18,238	E2
Colts Neck 950	E3
Columbia 600	C2
Columbus 800	D3
Convent Station	E2
Corbin City 412	D5
Cranberry Lake 500	D2
Cranbury 1,255	E3
Cranford • 22,624	E2
Cresskill 7,558	C1
Dayton 4,321	D3
Deal 1,179	E3
Deepwater 800	C4
Delanco • 3,316	D3
Delran • 14,811	B3
Demarest 4,800	C1
Dennisville 890	D5
Denville • 14,380	E2
Deptford • 23,473	B4
Dividing Creek 500	C5
Dorchester 500	D5
Dorothy 900	D5
Dover 15,115	D2
Dumont 17,187	C1
Dunellen 6,528	D2
East Brunswick • 43,548	E3
East Hanover • 9,926	E2
East Keansburg	E3
East Millstone 950	D3
East Newark 2,157	B2
East Orange 73,552	B2
East Rutherford 7,902	B2
Eatontown 13,800	E3
Edgewater 5,001	C2
Edgewater Park • 8,388	D3
Edison • 88,680	E2
Egg Harbor City 4,583	D4
Elberon	F3
Elizabeth▲ 110,002	B2
Elmer 1,571	C4
Elmwood Park 17,623	B2
Elwood 1,538	D4
Emerson 6,930	B1
Englewood 24,850	C2
Englewood Cliffs 5,634	C2
English Creek 500	D5
Englishtown 1,268	E3
Essex Fells 2,363	B2
Estell Manor 1,404	D5
Ewan 610	C4
Ewing 34,185	D3
Fair Haven 5,270	E3
Fair Lawn 30,548	B1
Fairfield • 7,615	A2
Fairton 1,359	C5
Fairview 10,733	C2
Fanwood 7,115	E2
Far Hills 657	D2
Farmingdale 1,462	E3
Fieldsboro 579	D3
Flagtown 800	D2
Flanders	D2
Flemington▲ 4,047	D2
Florence-Roebling 8,564	D3
Florham Park 8,521	E2
Folsom 2,181	D4
Fords 14,392	E2
Forked River 4,243	E4
Fort Lee 31,997	C2
Franklin 4,977	D1
Franklin Lakes 9,873	B1
Franklin Park • 31,358	D3
Franklinville	C4
Freehold▲ 10,742	E3
Frenchtown 1,528	C2
Garfield 26,727	B2

(continued on following page)

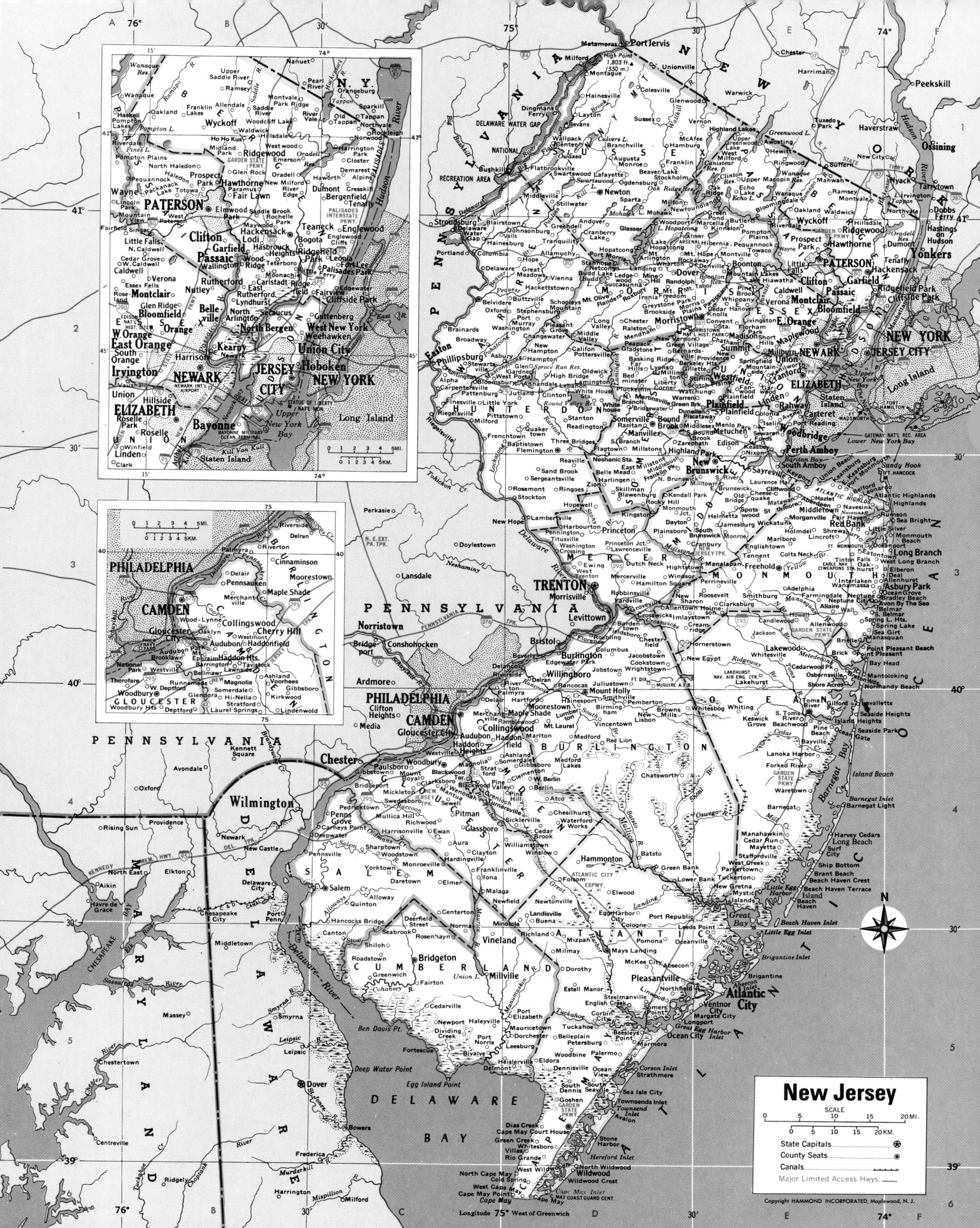

New Jersey
SCALE
0 5 10 15 20 MI.
0 5 10 15 20 KM.
State Capitals
County Seats
Canals
Major Limited Access Hwys.
Copyright HAMMOND INCORPORATED, Maplewood, N. J.
Longitude 75° West of Greenwich
PENNSYLVANIA
NEW YORK
DELAWARE
MARYLAND
ATLANTIC OCEAN
DELAWARE BAY
N.Y.
TRENTON
NEWARK
JERSEY CITY
PATERSON
ELIZABETH
CAMDEN
PHILADELPHIA
NEW YORK
Wilmington
Atlantic City
New Brunswick
Perth Amboy
Trenton
Long Island
Staten Island
SUSSEX
PASSAIC
BERGEN
MORRIS
ESSEX
HUDSON
UNION
WARREN
HUNTERDON
SOMERSET
MIDDLESEX
MERCER
MONMOUTH
OCEAN
BURLINGTON
CAMDEN
GLOUCESTER
SALEM
CUMBERLAND
ATLANTIC
CAPE MAY
DELAWARE WATER GAP NATIONAL RECREATION AREA
High Point 1,803 ft. (550 m.)
Port Jervis
Newton
Morristown
Somerville
Flemington
Belvidere
Freehold
Toms River
Mount Holly
Woodbury
Salem
Bridgeton
Cape May Court House
Cape May
Sandy Hook
Barnegat Inlet
Little Egg Inlet
Vineland
Millville
Dover

New Mexico

SCALE
0 5 10 20 30 40 50 60 MI.
0 5 10 20 30 40 50 60 KM.

State Capitals ⊛
County Seats ◉
Major Limited Access Hwys.

© Copyright HAMMOND INCORPORATED, Maplewood, N.J.

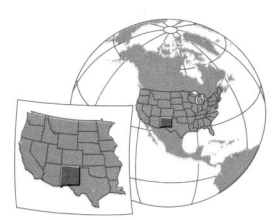

AREA 121,593 sq. mi. (314,926 sq. km.)
POPULATION 1,521,779
CAPITAL Santa Fe
LARGEST CITY Albuquerque
HIGHEST POINT Wheeler Pk. 13,161 ft.
    (4011 m.)
SETTLED IN 1605
ADMITTED TO UNION January 6, 1912
POPULAR NAME Land of Enchantment
STATE FLOWER Yucca
STATE BIRD Road Runner

Espanola 8,389	C3
Estancia▲ 792	D4
Eunice 2,676	F6
Fairacres 700	C6
Farmington 33,997	A2
Faywood 100	B6
Fence Lake 150	A4
Fierro 200	A6
Flora Vista 1,021	A2
Floyd 117	F4
Folsom 71	F2
Fort Bayard 400	A6
Fort Stanton 80	D5
Fort Sumner▲ 1,269	E4
Fort Wingate 800	A3
Fruitland 800	A2
Galisteo 125	D3
Gallina 420	C2
Gallup▲ 19,154	A3
Garnerco 800	A3
Garfield 600	B6
Garita 66	E3
Gila 350	A6
Glencoe 125	D5
Glenwood 220	A5
Glorieta 300	D3
Golden 100	C3
Grady 110	F4
Grants▲ 8,626	B3
Guadalupita 300	D2
Hachita 75	A7
Hagerman 961	E5
Hanover 300	A6
Hatch 1,136	B6
Hernandez 500	C2
High Rolls-Mountain	
Park 555	D5
Hillsboro 175	B6
Hobbs 29,115	F6
Holman 400	D2
Hondo 425	D5
Hope 101	E6
Hot Springs▲ (Truth or	
Consequences) 6,221	B5
House 85	F4
Humble City 65	F6
Hurley 1,534	A6
Ilfeld 68	D3
Isleta 1,703	C4
Jal 2,156	F6
Jarales 700	C4
Jemez Pueblo 1,301	C3
Jemez Springs 413	C3
Kenna 100	F5
Kirtland 3,552	A2
La Cueva 200	D3
La Jara 210	B2
La Luz 1,625	C6
La Madera 200	C2
La Mesa 900	C7
La Plata 150	A2
La Union 200	C7
Laguna 434	B3
Lajoya 97	C4
Lake Arthur 336	E5
Lamy 66	D3
Las Cruces▲ 62,126	C6
Las Vegas▲ 14,753	D3
Ledoux 300	D3
Lemitar 800	B4
Lincoln 100	D5
Lindrith 349	C2
Llano 325	D2
Loco Hills 375	F6
Logan 870	F3

Lordsburg▲ 2,951	A6
Los Alamos▲ 11,455	C3
Los Lunas▲ 6,013	C4
Los Ojos	C2
Los Ranchos de Albuquerque	
3,955	C3
Loving 1,243	E6
Lovington▲ 9,322	F6
Lumberton 175	C2
Luna 200	A5
Magdalena 861	B4
Malaga 300	E6
Manuelito 200	A3
Manzano 65	C4
Maxwell 247	E2
Mayhill 300	D6
McAlister 320	F4
McDonald 65	F5
McIntosh 325	C4
Meadow Vista 3,377	C7
Melrose 662	F4
Mentmore 315	A3
Mescalero 1,159	D5
Mesilla 1,975	C6
Mesilla Park	C6
Mesquite 500	C6
Mexican Springs 242	A3
Miami 112	E2
Milan 1,911	B3
Mimbres 300	B6
Montezuma 250	D3
Monticello 125	B5
Monument 300	F6
Mora▲	D2
Moriarty 1,399	D4
Mosquero▲ 164	F3
Mountainair 926	C4
Mule Creek 62	A6
Nambe 1,246	D3
Nara Visa 250	F3
Navajo 1,985	A3
New Laguna 250	B3
Newcomb 388	A2
Newkirk 54	E3
Nogal 150	D5
Ocate 75	D2
Oil Center 236	F6
Ojo Caliente 600	D2
Ojo Feliz 133	E2
Ojo Sarco 380	D2
Organ 300	C6
Orogrande 80	C7
Otis 200	E6
Paguate 492	B3
Pecos 1,012	D3
Pena Blanca 300	C3
Penasco 648	D2
Peralta 3,182	C4
Petaca 84	C2
Picacho 100	D5
Pie Town 90	A4
Pinos Altos 250	A6
Placitas 1,611	C3
Pleasanton 70	A5
Pojoaque 1,037	C3
Ponderosa 300	C3
Portales▲ 10,690	F4
Prewitt 300	B3
Puerto de Luna 175	E4
Questa 1,707	D2
Radium Springs 150	C6
Rainsville 350	D2
Ramah 574	A3
Ranchos de Taos 1,779	D2
Raton▲ 7,372	E2

Red River 387	D2
Regina 80	B2
Rehoboth 200	A3
Reserve▲ 319	A5
Ribera 84	D3
Rincon 300	C6
Rio Rancho 32,505	C3
Rociada 140	D3
Rodarte 650	D2
Rodeo 200	A7
Roswell▲ 44,654	E5
Rowe 290	D3
Roy 362	E3
Ruidoso 4,600	D5
Ruidoso Downs 920	D5
Rutheron 95	C2
Salem 400	B6
San Acacia 286	B4
San Antonio 359	B5
San Cristobal 350	D2
San Felipe Pueblo 1,557	C3
San Fidel 150	B3
San Ildefonso 447	C3
San Jon 277	F3
San Jose 150	D3
San Juan Pueblo 4,107	C2
San Lorenzo 200	B6
San Mateo 200	B3
San Miguel 400	C6
San Patricio 300	D5
San Rafael 300	A3
San Ysidro 233	C3
Santa Cruz 2,504	D2
Santa Fe (cap.)▲ 55,859	C3
Santa Rita 600	A6
Santa Rosa▲ 2,263	E4
Santo Domingo Pueblo 2,866	C3
Sapello 600	D3
Seboyeta 125	B3
Sedan 60	F2
Sena 150	D3
Serafina 225	D3
Sherman 100	B6
Shiprock 7,687	A2
Silver City▲ 10,683	A6
Socorro▲ 8,159	C4
Soham 104	D3
Solano 114	E3
Springer 1,262	E2
Sunspot 78	D6
Taiban 120	F4
Tajique 145	C4
Taos▲ 4,065	D2

Tatum 768	F5
Tesuque 1,490	C3
Texico 966	F4
Thoreau 1,099	A3
Tierra Amarilla▲ 850	C2
Tijeras 340	C3
Tinnie 100	D5
Toadlena 200	A3
Tohatchi 661	A3
Tome 500	C4
Torreon 200	C4
Trampas 76	D2
Trementina 80	E3
Tres Piedras 200	D2
Truchas 275	D2
Trujillo 148	E3
Truth or Consequences▲	
6,221	B5
Tucumcari▲ 6,831	F3
Tularosa 2,615	C5
Tyrone 100	A6
University Park 4,520	C6
Ute Park 67	D2
Vadito 283	D2
Vado 325	C6
Valdez 300	D2
Valencia 3,917	C4
Vallecitos 450	C2
Vanadium 150	A6
Vaughn 633	D4
Velarde 950	D2
Vermejo Park 85	D2
Villanueva 500	D3
Virden 108	A6
Wagon Mound 319	E2
Waterflow 475	A2
Watrous 175	D3
White Horse Lake	B3
White Rock 6,192	C3
White Sands Missile Range	
2,616	C6
Willard 183	D4
Williamsburg 456	B5
Yeso 200	E4
Youngsville 125	C2
Zia Pueblo 637	C3
Zuni 5,551	A3

OTHER FEATURES

Abiquiu (res.)	C2
Alamosa (riv.)	B5
Animas (riv.)	B1
Avalon (res.)	E6
Aztec Ruins Nat'l Mon.	A2

Baldy (peak)	D3
Bandelier Nat'l Mon.	C3
Big Burro (mts.)	A6
Black (mt.)	A6
Black (range)	B5
Blanco (creek)	F4
Bluewater (creek)	B4
Bluewater (creek)	D6
Bluewater (lake)	A3
Boulder (lake)	C2
Brazos (peak)	C2
Burford (lake)	C2
Caballo (res.)	B6
Canadian (riv.)	F3
Cannon A.F.B. 3,312	F4
Canyon Blanco (creek)	B2
Capitan (mts.)	D5
Capitan (peak)	D5
Capulin Volcano Nat'l Mon.	E2
Carlsbad Caverns Nat'l Park	E6
Carrizo (creek)	F2
Chaco (mesa)	B3
Chaco (riv.)	A2
Chaco Culture Nat'l Hist. Park	B2
Chico Arroyo (creek)	B3
Chivato (mesa)	B3
Chupadera (mesa)	C5
Chuska (mts.)	A3
Cimarron (riv.)	E2
Colorado, Arroyo (riv.)	B4
Compañero, Arroyo (creek)	B2
Conchas (lake)	E3
Conchas (riv.)	E3
Cookes (range)	B6
Corrumpa (creek)	F2
Costilla (peak)	D2
Cuchillo Negro (creek)	B5
Cuervo (creek)	E3
Dark Canyon (creek)	E6
Datil (mts.)	B4
Dry Cimarron (riv.)	F2
Eagle Nest (lake)	D2
Elephant Butte (res.)	B5
El Morro Nat'l Mon.	A3
El Rito (riv.)	C2
Fifteenmile Arroyo (creek)	D4
Florida (mts.)	B7
Fort Bliss Mil. Res.	C6
Fort Union Nat'l Mon.	E3
Gallinas (mts.)	B4
Gallinas (riv.)	E3
Gila (riv.)	A6
Gila Cliff Dwellings Nat'l Mon.	A5
Grouse (mt.)	A5
Guadalupe (mts.)	D6

Hatchet (mts.)	A7
Holloman A.F.B. 5,891	C6
Hueco (mts.)	D6
Jemez (mts.)	C3
Jemez Canyon (res.)	C3
Jicarilla Ind. Res.	B2
Jornada del Muerto (valley)	C5
Kirtland A.F.B.	C3
Ladron (mts.)	B4
La Plata (riv.)	A1
Lake Avalon (res.)	E6
Largo, Cañon (creek)	B2
Las Animas (creek)	B5
Llano Estacado	
(Staked) (plain)	F5
Lucero (lake)	C6
Macho, Arroyo del (creek)	D5
Magdalena (mts.)	B4
Manzano (mts.)	C4
Manzano (peak)	C4
McMillan (lake)	E6
Mescalero (ridge)	F6
Mescalero Apache Ind. Res.	D5
Mimbres (mts.)	B6
Mimbres (riv.)	B6
Mogollon (mts.)	A5
Mogollon Baldy (peak)	A5
Montosa (mesa)	E3
Mora (riv.)	E3
Nacimiento (mts.)	C3
Nacimiento (peak)	C2
Navajo (res.)	B2
Navajo Ind. Res.	A2
North Truchas (peak)	D3
Ocate (creek)	E3
O'Keeffe Nat'l Hist. Site	C2
Oscura (mts.)	C5
Osha (peak)	C4
Padilla (creek)	D5
Pajarito (creek)	A2
Pecos (riv.)	E5
Pecos Nat'l Mon.	D3
Peloncillo (mts.)	A6
Perro (lake)	D4
Pinos, Rio de los (riv.)	C2
Pintada Arroyo (creek)	E4
Playas (lake)	A7
Potrillo (mts.)	B7
Pueblo Ind. Res.	B4
Pueblo Ind. Res.	B6
Pueblo Ind. Res.	D2
Pueblo Ind. Res.	D3
Puerco (riv.)	A3
Red Bluff (lake)	E7

Revuelto (creek)	F3
Rio Brazos (riv.)	C2
Rio Chama (riv.)	C2
Rio Felix (riv.)	E5
Rio Grande (riv.)	C5
Rio Hondo (riv.)	E5
Rio Penasco (riv.)	E6
Rio Puerco (riv.)	C4
Rio Salado (riv.)	B4
Rocky (mts.)	C1
Sacramento (mts.)	D6
Salinas Pueblo Missions	
Nat'l Mon.	C4
Salt (creek)	E5
Salt (lake)	F4
San Agustin (plains)	B5
San Andres (mts.)	C6
San Antonio (mt.)	C2
Sandia (peak)	C3
San Francisco (riv.)	A5
San Juan (riv.)	B3
San Jose (riv.)	B3
Sangre de Cristo (mts.)	D3
San Mateo (mts.)	B5
Seven Rivers (riv.)	E6
Ship Rock (peak)	A2
Sierra Blanca (creek)	C5
Staked (Llano Estacado)	
(plain)	F5
Sumner (lake)	E4
Taylor (mt.)	B3
Tecolote (creek)	D3
Tequesquite (creek)	F2
Thompson (peak)	D3
Tierra Blanca (creek)	B6
Tramperos (creek)	F2
Tularosa (valley)	C6
Ute (creek)	F3
Ute (peak)	D2
Ute (res.)	F3
Ute Mountain Ind. Res.	A1
Vermejo (riv.)	E2
Wheeler (peak)	D2
White Sands (des.)	C5
White Sands Missile Range	C6
White Sands Nat'l Mon.	C6
Whitewater Baldy (peak)	A5
Wingate Army Depot	A3
Yeso (creek)	E4
Zuni (mts.)	A3
Zuni (riv.)	A3
Zuni-Cibola Nat'l Hist. Park	A3
Zuni Ind. Res.	A3

▲County seat

Topography

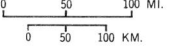

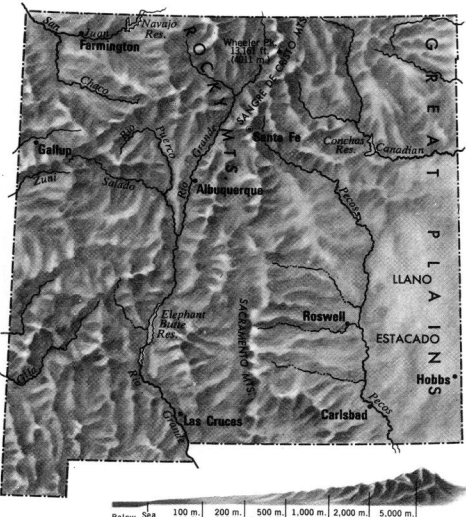

Agriculture, Industry and Resources

DOMINANT LAND USE

- Wheat, Grain Sorghums, Range Livestock
- General Farming, Livestock, Special Crops
- General Farming, Livestock, Cash Grain
- Dry Beans, General Farming
- Cotton, Forest Products
- Range Livestock
- Forests
- Nonagricultural Land

MAJOR MINERAL OCCURRENCES

Ag	Silver	Gp	Gypsum
Au	Gold	K	Potash
C	Coal	Mo	Molybdenum
Cu	Copper	Mr	Marble
G	Natural Gas	Na	Salt

O	Petroleum	U	Uranium
		V	Vanadium
Pb	Lead	Zn	Zinc
		⚡	Water Power

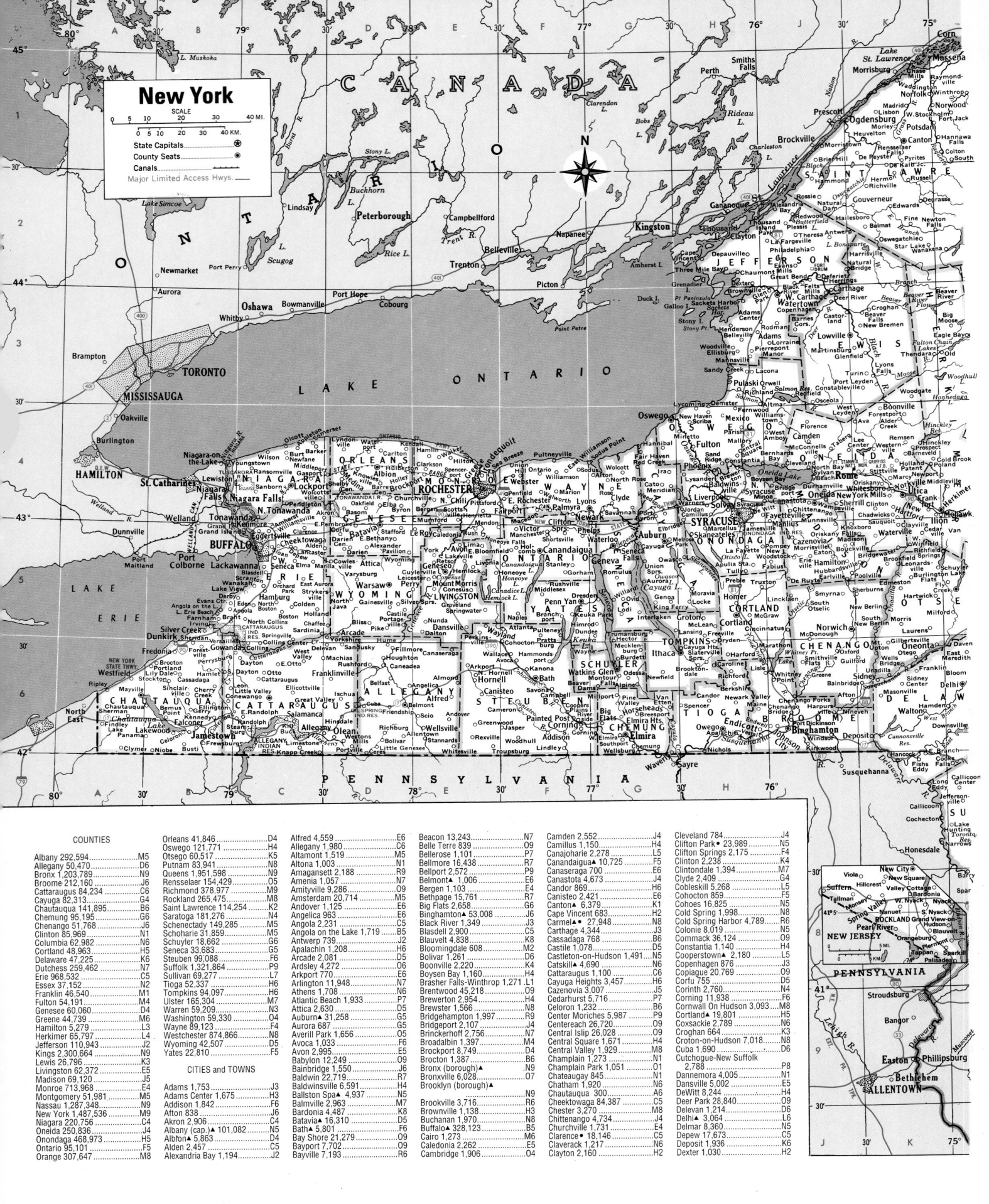

New York

SCALE
0 5 10 20 30 40 MI.
0 5 10 20 30 40 KM.

State Capitals.............⊛
County Seats.............◉
Canals....................
Major Limited Access Hwys.....

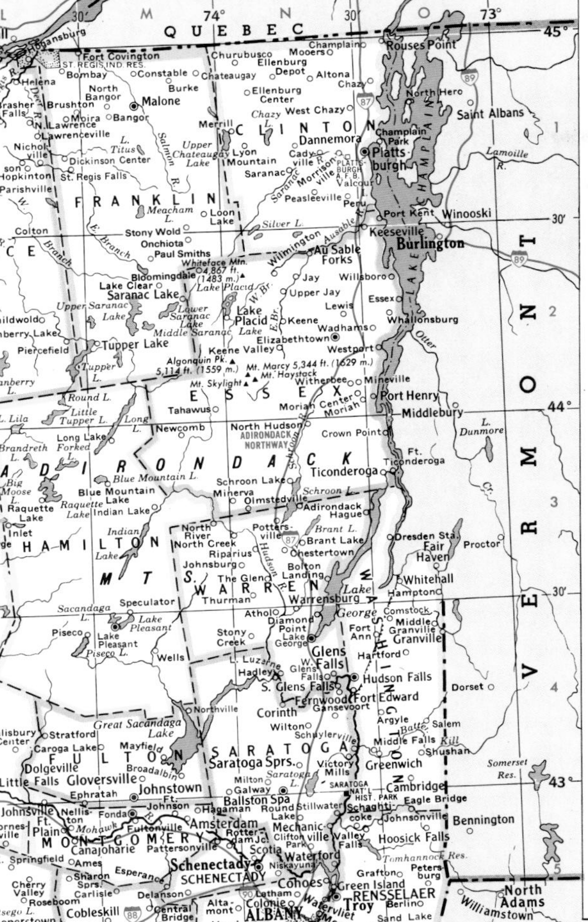

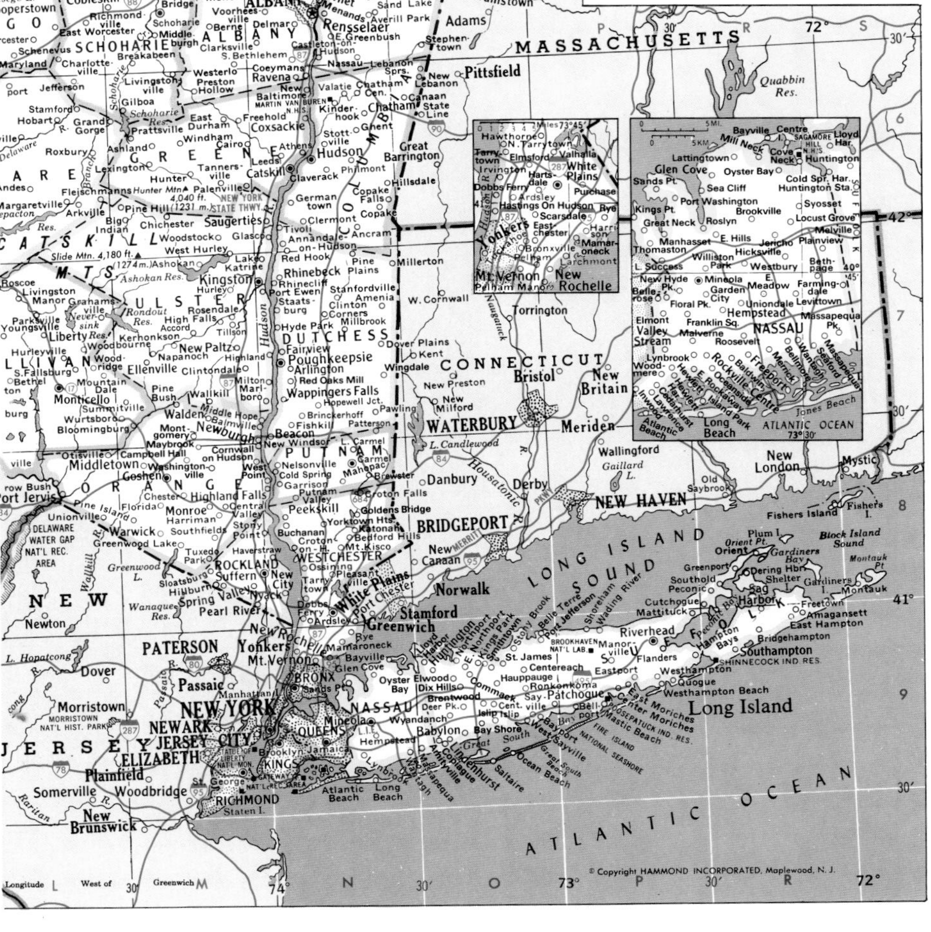

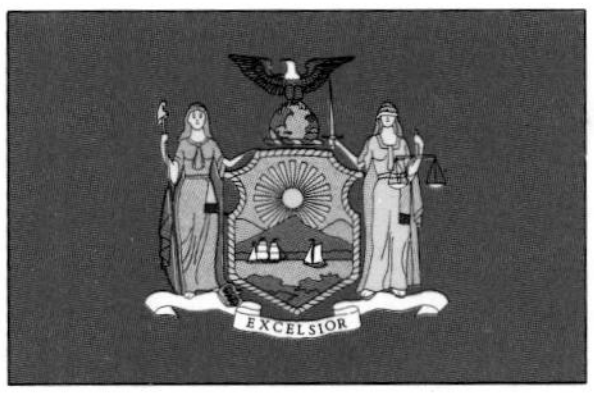

AREA 49,108 sq. mi. (127,190 sq. km.)
POPULATION 18,044,505
CAPITAL Albany
LARGEST CITY New York
HIGHEST POINT Mt. Marcy 5,344 ft.
  (1629 m.)
SETTLED IN 1614
ADMITTED TO UNION July 26, 1788
POPULAR NAME Empire State
STATE FLOWER Rose
STATE BIRD Bluebird

Topography

0   50   100 MI.
0   50   100 KM.

5,000 m. | 2,000 m. | 1,000 m. | 500 m. | 200 m. | 100 m. | Sea | Below
16,404 ft. | 6,562 ft. | 3,281 ft. | 1,640 ft. | 656 ft. | 328 ft. | Level

© Copyright HAMMOND INCORPORATED, Maplewood, N.J.

Dix Hills 25,849	O9
Dobbs Ferry 9,940	O6
Dolgeville 2,452	L4
Dover Plains 1,847	O7
Dryden 1,908	H6
Dundee 1,588	F5
Dunkirk 13,989	B5
Earlville 883	J5
East Aurora 6,647	C5
East Greenbush 3,784	N5
East Hampton 1,402	R9
East Hills 6,746	R7
East Meadow 36,909	R7
East Moriches 4,021	P9
East Northport 20,411	O9
East Rochester 6,932	F4
East Rockaway 10,152	R7
East Syracuse 3,343	H4
Eastchester 18,537	P6
Eden 3,088	C5
Elba 703	D4
Elbridge 1,099	G5
Elizabethtown 659	N2
Ellenville 4,243	M7
Elma 2,452	C5
Elmira Heights 4,359	G6
Elmira 33,724	G6
Elmont 28,612	P7
Elmsford 3,938	O6
Elwood 10,916	O9
Endicott 13,531	H6
Endwell 12,602	H6
Evans Mills 661	J2
Fair Haven 895	G4
Fairport 5,943	F4
Fairview 4,811	N7
Falconer 2,653	B6
Farmingdale 8,022	R7
Fayetteville 4,248	J4
Fernwood 3,640	N4
Fishkill 1,957	N7
Flanders-Riverside 5,400	P9
Floral Park 15,947	P7
Florida 2,497	M8
Fonda▲ 1,007	M5
Forestville 738	B6
Fort Covington ● 1,804	M1
Fort Edward 3,561	O4
Fort Johnson 615	M5
Fort Plain 2,416	L5
Frankfort 2,693	K4
Franklin Square 28,205	R7
Franklinville 1,739	D6
Fredonia 10,436	B6
Freeport 39,894	R7
Frewsburg 1,817	B6
Friendship 1,423	D6
Fulton 12,929	H4
Fultonville 748	M5
Garden City 21,686	R7
Gasport 1,336	C4
Geneseo▲ 7,187	E5
Geneva 14,143	G5
Glasco 1,538	M6
Glen Cove 24,149	R6
Glens Falls 15,023	N4
Gloversville 16,656	M4
Golden's Bridge 1,589	N8
Goshen▲ 5,255	M8
Gouverneur 4,604	K2
Gowanda 2,901	B6
Granville 2,646	O4
Great Neck 8,745	P6
Greece 15,632	E4
Green Island 2,490	N5
Greene 1,812	J6
Greenport 2,070	P8
Greenwich 1,961	O4
Greenwood Lake 3,208	M8
Groton 2,398	H5
Hadley-Lake Luzerne 1,988	N4
Hagaman 1,377	M5
Hamburg 10,442	C5
Hamilton 3,790	J5
Hammondsport 929	F6
Hampton Bays 7,893	R9
Hancock 1,330	K7
Hannibal 680	G4
Harriman 2,288	M8
Harrison 23,308	P6
Harrisville 703	K2
Hartsdale 9,587	P6
Hastings On Hudson 8,000	O6
Hauppauge 19,750	O9
Haverstraw 9,438	M8
Hawthorne 4,764	O6
Hempstead 49,453	R7
Herkimer▲ 7,945	L4
Heuvelton 771	K1
Hewlett 6,620	P7
Hewlett Harbor 1,193	P7
Hicksville 40,174	R7
Highland 4,492	M7
Highland Falls 3,937	M8
Hillburn 892	M8
Hillcrest 6,447	K8
Hilton 5,216	E4
Holcomb 790	F5
Holland 1,288	C5
Holley 1,890	D4
Homer 3,476	H5
Honeoye Falls 2,340	F5
Hoosick Falls 3,490	O5
Hopewell Junction 1,786	N7
Hornell 9,877	E6
Horseheads 6,802	G6
Houghton 1,740	D6
Hudson Falls▲ 7,651	O4
Hudson▲ 8,034	N6
Huntington 18,243	R6

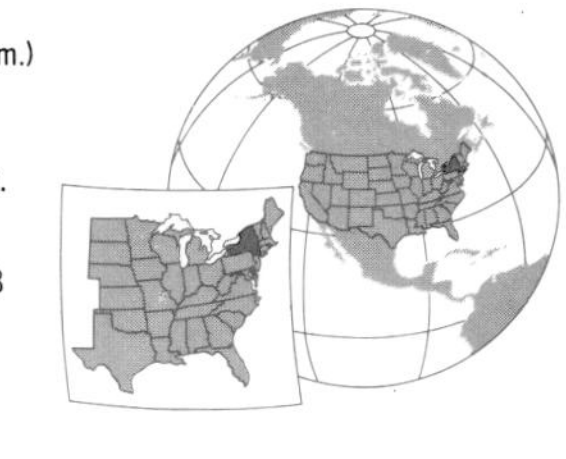

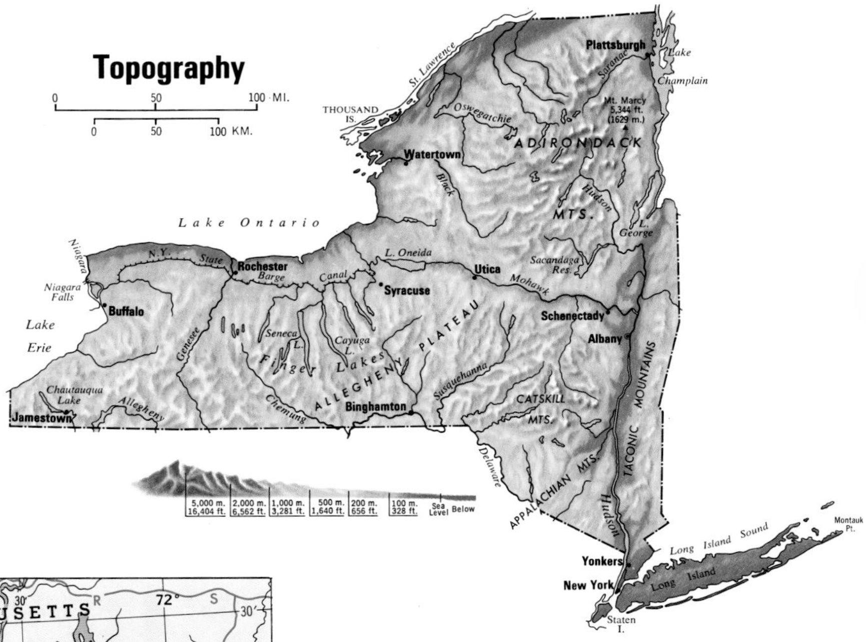

(continued on following page)

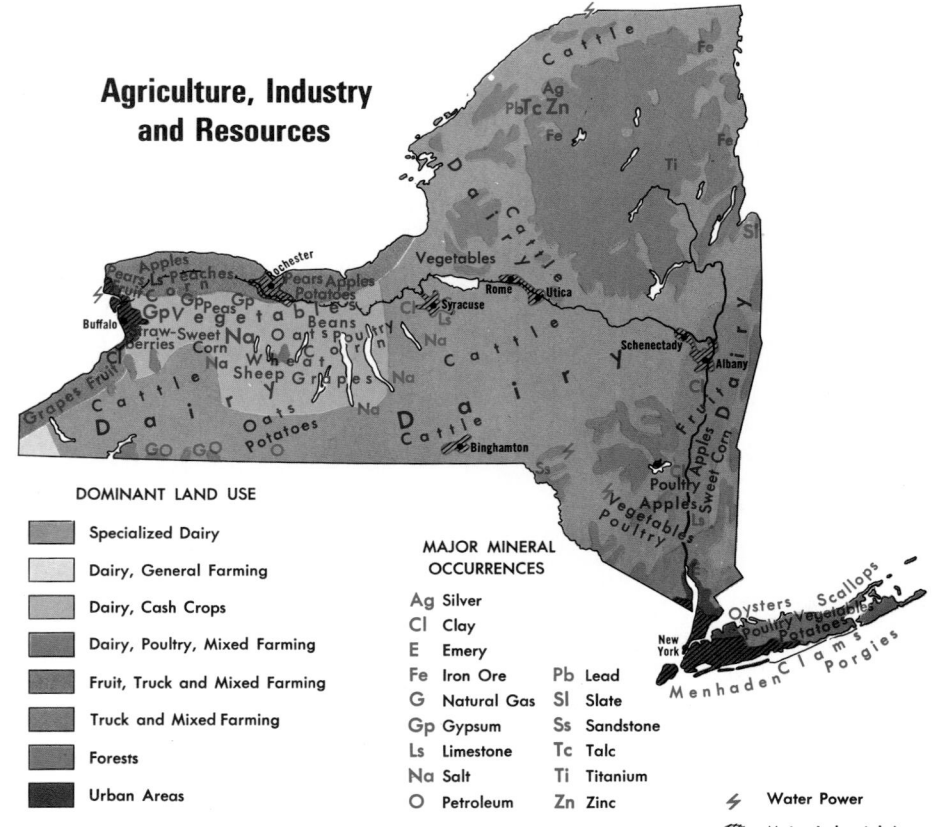

Agriculture, Industry and Resources

DOMINANT LAND USE

- Specialized Dairy
- Dairy, General Farming
- Dairy, Cash Crops
- Dairy, Poultry, Mixed Farming
- Fruit, Truck and Mixed Farming
- Truck and Mixed Farming
- Forests
- Urban Areas

MAJOR MINERAL OCCURRENCES

- Ag Silver
- Cl Clay
- E Emery
- Fe Iron Ore
- G Natural Gas
- Gp Gypsum
- Ls Limestone
- Na Salt
- O Petroleum
- Pb Lead
- Sl Slate
- Ss Sandstone
- Tc Talc
- Ti Titanium
- Zn Zinc

⚡ Water Power

Major Industrial Areas

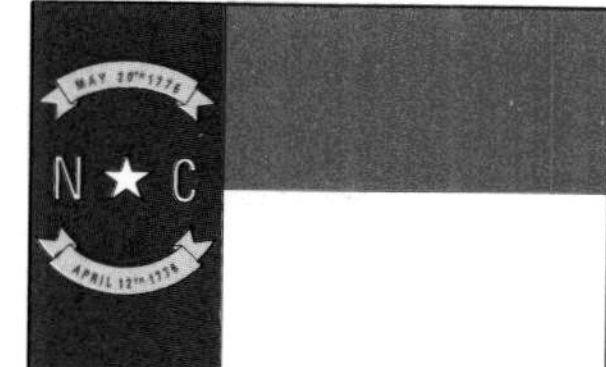

N ★ C
MAY 20th 1775
APRIL 12th 1776

AREA 52,669 sq. mi. (136,413 sq. km.)
POPULATION 6,657,630
CAPITAL Raleigh
LARGEST CITY Charlotte
HIGHEST POINT Mt. Mitchell 6,684 ft. (2037 m.)
SETTLED IN 1650
ADMITTED TO UNION November 21, 1789
POPULAR NAME Tarheel State
STATE FLOWER Flowering Dogwood
STATE BIRD Cardinal

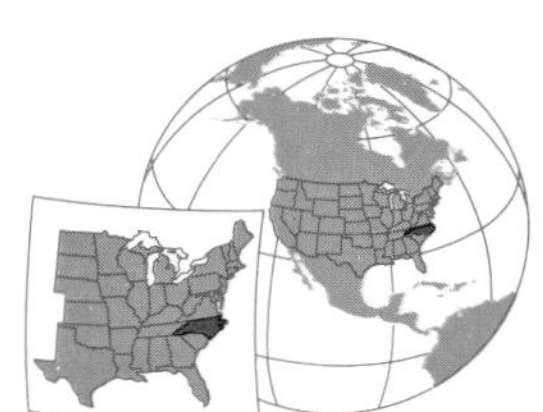

Great Smoky Mountains

MILES 0 5 10 15

© HAMMOND INCORPORATED

COUNTIES

Alamance 108,213 ..... L3
Alexander 27,544 ..... G3
Alleghany 9,590 ..... G1
Anson 23,474 ..... J4
Ashe 22,209 ..... F2
Avery 14,867 ..... F2
Beaufort 42,283 ..... R4
Bertie 20,388 ..... P2
Bladen 28,663 ..... M5
Brunswick 50,985 ..... N6
Buncombe 174,821 ..... D3
Burke 75,744 ..... F3
Cabarrus 98,935 ..... H4
Caldwell 70,709 ..... F3
Camden 5,904 ..... S2
Carteret 52,556 ..... R5
Caswell 20,693 ..... L2
Catawba 118,412 ..... G3
Chatham 38,759 ..... L3
Cherokee 20,170 ..... A4
Chowan 13,506 ..... R2
Clay 7,155 ..... B4
Cleveland 84,714 ..... F4
Columbus 49,587 ..... M6
Craven 81,613 ..... P4
Cumberland 274,566 ..... M4
Currituck 13,736 ..... S2
Dare 22,746 ..... T3
Davidson 126,677 ..... J3
Davie 27,859 ..... H3
Duplin 39,995 ..... O5
Durham 181,835 ..... M3
Edgecombe 56,558 ..... O3
Forsyth 265,878 ..... J2
Franklin 36,414 ..... N2
Gaston 175,093 ..... G4
Gates 9,305 ..... R2
Graham 7,196 ..... B4
Granville 38,345 ..... M2
Greene 15,384 ..... O3
Guilford 347,420 ..... K3
Halifax 55,516 ..... O2
Harnett 67,822 ..... M4
Haywood 46,942 ..... C3
Henderson 69,285 ..... D4
Hertford 22,523 ..... P2
Hoke 22,856 ..... L4
Hyde 5,411 ..... S3
Iredell 92,931 ..... H3
Jackson 26,846 ..... C4
Johnston 81,306 ..... N4
Jones 9,414 ..... P4
Lee 41,374 ..... L4
Lenoir 57,274 ..... O4
Lincoln 50,319 ..... G3
Macon 23,499 ..... B4
Madison 16,953 ..... D3
Martin 25,078 ..... P3
McDowell 35,681 ..... E3
Mecklenburg 511,433 ..... H4
Mitchell 14,433 ..... E2
Montgomery 23,346 ..... K4
Moore 59,013 ..... L4
Nash 76,677 ..... O2
New Hanover 120,284 ..... O6
Northampton 20,798 ..... P2
Onslow 149,838 ..... P5
Orange 93,851 ..... L2
Pamlico 11,372 ..... R4
Pasquotank 31,298 ..... S2
Pender 28,855 ..... O5
Perquimans 10,447 ..... S2
Person 30,180 ..... M2
Pitt 107,924 ..... P3
Polk 14,416 ..... E4
Randolph 106,546 ..... K3
Richmond 44,518 ..... K4
Robeson 105,179 ..... L5
Rockingham 86,064 ..... K2
Rowan 110,605 ..... H3
Rutherford 56,918 ..... E4
Sampson 47,297 ..... N4
Scotland 33,754 ..... L5
Stanly 51,765 ..... J4
Stokes 37,223 ..... J2
Surry 61,704 ..... H2
Swain 11,268 ..... B3
Transylvania 25,520 ..... D4
Tyrrell 3,856 ..... S3
Union 84,211 ..... H4
Vance 38,892 ..... N2
Wake 423,380 ..... M3
Warren 17,265 ..... N2
Washington 13,997 ..... R3
Watauga 36,952 ..... F2
Wayne 104,666 ..... N4
Wilkes 59,393 ..... G2
Wilson 66,061 ..... O3
Yadkin 30,488 ..... H2
Yancey 15,419 ..... E3

CITIES and TOWNS

Abbottsburg 425 ..... M5
Aberdeen 2,700 ..... L4
Acme N6
Advance J3
Ahoskie 4,391 ..... P2
Alamance 258 ..... K2
Alarka 900 ..... C4
Albemarle▲ 14,939 ..... J4
Alexander Mills 662 ..... F4
Alliance 583 ..... R4
Altamahaw 1,076 ..... L2
Andrews 2,551 ..... B4
Angier 2,235 ..... M4
Ansonville 614 ..... J4
Apex 4,968 ..... M3
Arapahoe 430 ..... R4
Archdale 6,913 ..... K3
Arlington 795 ..... H2
Ash 16,362 ..... N6
Asheboro▲ 15,252 ..... K3
Asheville▲ 61,607 ..... D3
Askewville 201 ..... R2
Atkinson 275 ..... N5
Atlantic 1,938 ..... S5
Atlantic Beach 941 ..... R5
Aulander 1,209 ..... P2
Aurora 654 ..... R4
Autryville 166 ..... M4
Avon 500 ..... U4
Avondale F4
Ayden 4,740 ..... P4
Badin 1,481 ..... J4
Bahama 280 ..... M2
Bailey 553 ..... N3
Bakersville▲ 332 ..... E2
Balfour 1,118 ..... E4
Banner Elk 933 ..... F2
Bannertown 1,028 ..... H1
Barco 325 ..... T2
Barker Heights 1,137 ..... D4
Bat Cave 450 ..... E4
Bath 154 ..... R4
Battleboro 447 ..... O2
Bayboro▲ 733 ..... R4
Bear Creek 500 ..... L3
Beargrass 77 ..... P3
Beaufort▲ 3,808 ..... R5
Belhaven 2,269 ..... R3
Bellarthur 350 ..... O3
Belmont 8,434 ..... H4
Belvidere 275 ..... S2
Belville 66 ..... N6
Belwood 631 ..... F4
Benham 400 ..... G2
Bennett 254 ..... K3
Benson 2,810 ..... N4
Bessemer City 4,698 ..... G4
Beta 500 ..... C4
Bethel 1,842 ..... P3
Beulaville 933 ..... O5
Biltmore Forest 1,327 ..... E3
Biscoe 1,484 ..... K4
Black Creek 615 ..... O3
Black Mountain 5,418 ..... E3
Bladenboro 1,821 ..... M5
Blowing Rock 1,257 ..... F2
Boardman 250 ..... M6
Boger City 1,373 ..... G4
Boiling Spring Lakes 1,650 ..... N7
Boiling Springs 2,445 ..... F4
Bolivia▲ 228 ..... N6
Bolton 531 ..... N6
Bonlee 300 ..... L3
Boomer 250 ..... G2
Boone▲ 12,915 ..... F2
Boonville 1,009 ..... H2
Brevard▲ 5,388 ..... D4
Bridgeton 453 ..... R4
Broadway 973 ..... L4
Brookford 451 ..... G3
Browns Summit 500 ..... K2
Brunswick 302 ..... M6
Bryson City▲ 1,145 ..... C4
Buies 2,085 ..... L5
Buies Creek 1,939 ..... M4
Bullock 525 ..... M2
Bunn 364 ..... N3
Bunnlevel M4
Burgaw▲ 1,807 ..... N5
Burlington 39,498 ..... K2
Burnsville▲ 1,482 ..... E3
Butner 4,679 ..... M2
Buxton 700 ..... U4
Bynum 312 ..... L3
Calabash 1,210 ..... M7
Calypso 481 ..... N4
Camden▲ 300 ..... S2
Cameron 215 ..... L4
Candler 950 ..... D3
Candor 748 ..... K4
Canton 3,790 ..... D3
Cape Carteret 1,008 ..... P5
Carolina Beach 3,630 ..... O6
Carrboro 11,553 ..... L3
Carthage▲ 976 ..... K4
Cary 43,858 ..... M3
Casar 328 ..... F3
Cashiers 553 ..... C4
Castalia 261 ..... O2
Castle Hayne 1,182 ..... O6
Caswell Beach 175 ..... N7
Catawba 467 ..... G3
Catharine Lake 500 ..... O5
Cedar Falls 400 ..... K3
Cedar Grove 250 ..... L2
Cedar Island 310 ..... S5
Cedar Mountain 250 ..... D4
Centerville 115 ..... N2
Cerro Gordo 227 ..... M6
Chadbourn 2,005 ..... M6
Chadwick Acres 15 ..... P6
Chapel Hill 38,719 ..... L3
Charlotte▲ 395,934 ..... H4
Cherokee 975 ..... C4
Cherry 4,756 ..... R3
Cherryville 4,844 ..... G4
China Grove 2,732 ..... H3
Chinquapin 280 ..... O5
Chocowinity 624 ..... P4
Claremont 980 ..... G3
Clarendon 300 ..... M6
Clark 739 ..... P4
Clarkton 664 ..... M6
Clayton 4,756 ..... N3
Clemmons 6,020 ..... J2
Cleveland 696 ..... H3
Cliffside 950 ..... F4
Climax 475 ..... K3
Clinton▲ 8,204 ..... N5
Clyde 1,041 ..... D3
Coats 1,493 ..... M4
Cofield 407 ..... R2
Coinjock 650 ..... S2
Colerain 139 ..... R2
Collettsille 275 ..... F3
Columbia▲ 836 ..... S3
Columbus▲ 812 ..... E4
Comfort 325 ..... O5
Como 71 ..... P1
Concord▲ 27,347 ..... H4
Conetoe 292 ..... O3
Connellys Springs 500 ..... F3
Conover 5,465 ..... G3
Conway 759 ..... P2
Cooleemee 971 ..... H3
Cornelius 2,581 ..... H4
Council M6
Cove City 497 ..... P4
Cramerton 2,371 ..... G4
Creedmoor 1,504 ..... M2
Creswell 361 ..... S3
Crisp 435 ..... O3
Crossnore 271 ..... F2
Cruso 800 ..... D4
Culberson A4
Cullowhee 4,029 ..... C4
Cumberland 400 ..... M5
Currie 294 ..... N6
Currituck▲ 700 ..... T2
Dallas 3,012 ..... G4
Dalton 400 ..... J2
Danbury▲ 119 ..... J2
Davidson 4,046 ..... H4
Davis 612 ..... R5
Delco 450 ..... N6
Denton 1,292 ..... J3
Dillsboro 95 ..... C4
Dobson▲ 1,195 ..... H2
Dortches 840 ..... O2
Dover 451 ..... P4
Drexel 1,746 ..... F3
Dublin 246 ..... M5
Dudley N4
Dulah 350 ..... M6
Dundarrach L5
Dunn 8,336 ..... M4
Durham▲ 136,611 ..... M2
Dysartsville 950 ..... F3
Eagle Springs 280 ..... K4
Earl 230 ..... F4
East Arcadia 468 ..... N6
East Bend 619 ..... H2
East Flat Rock 3,218 ..... E4
East Laurinburg 302 ..... L5
East Marion 1,851 ..... F3
East Spencer 2,055 ..... J3
Eden 15,238 ..... K1
Edenton▲ 5,268 ..... R2
Edward R4
Efland 600 ..... L2
Elizabeth City▲ 14,292 ..... S2
Elizabethtown▲ 3,704 ..... M5
Elk Park 486 ..... E2
Elkin 3,790 ..... H2
Ellenboro 514 ..... F4
Ellerbe 1,132 ..... K4
Elm City 1,624 ..... O3
Elon College 4,394 ..... L2
Emerald Isle 2,434 ..... P5
Enfield 3,082 ..... O2
Engelhard 500 ..... T3
Enka 5,567 ..... D3
Ernul 350 ..... P4
Erwin 4,061 ..... M4
Ether 425 ..... K4
Etowah 1,997 ..... D4
Eure 282 ..... R2

(continued on following page)

Agriculture, Industry and Resources

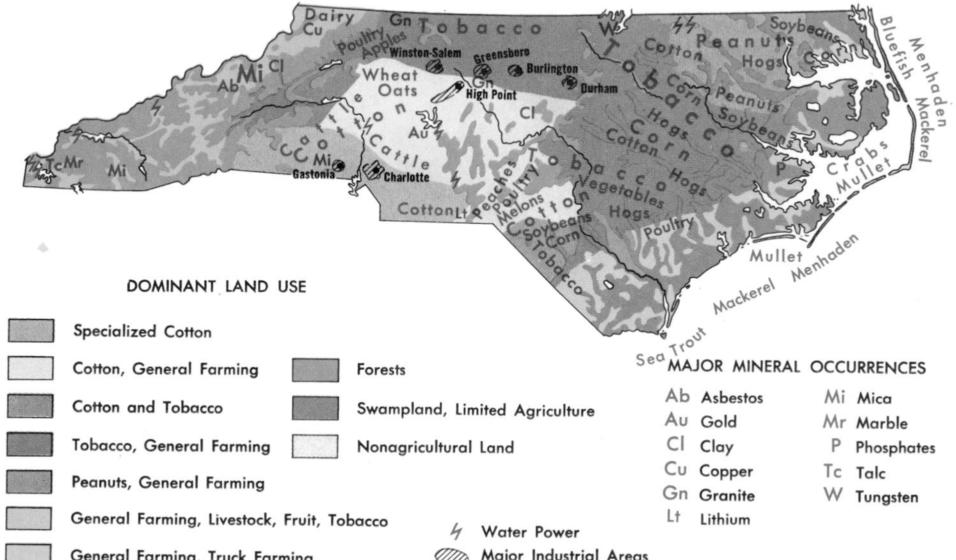

Winston-Salem
Greensboro
Burlington
Durham
High Point
Gastonia
Charlotte
Bluefish
Menhaden
Mackerel
Crabs
Mullet
Sea Trout
DOMINANT LAND USE
Specialized Cotton
Cotton, General Farming
Cotton and Tobacco
Tobacco, General Farming
Peanuts, General Farming
General Farming, Livestock, Fruit, Tobacco
General Farming, Truck Farming, Tobacco, Livestock
Forests
Swampland, Limited Agriculture
Nonagricultural Land
MAJOR MINERAL OCCURRENCES
Ab Asbestos
Au Gold
Cl Clay
Cu Copper
Gn Granite
Lt Lithium
Mi Mica
Mr Marble
P Phosphates
Tc Talc
W Tungsten
Water Power
Major Industrial Areas

Topography

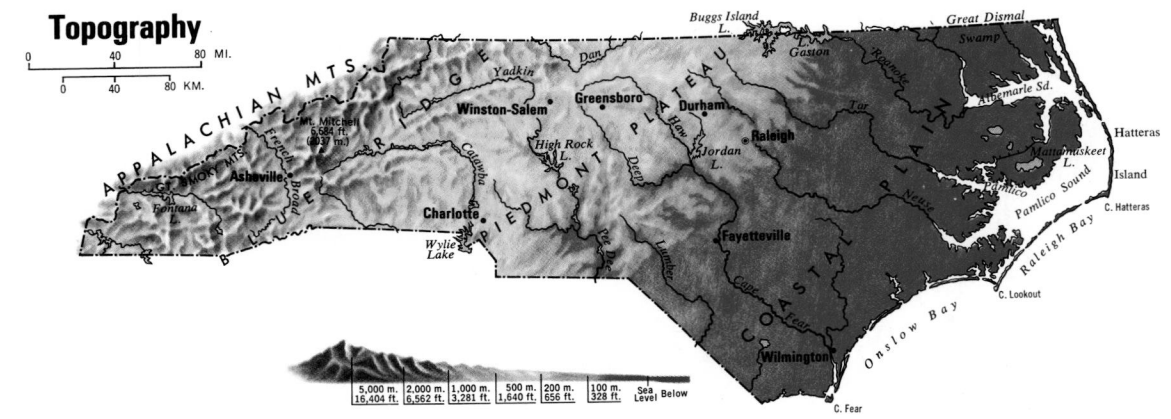

0   40   80 MI.
0   40   80 KM.

5,000 m. / 16,404 ft. 2,000 m. / 6,562 ft. 1,000 m. / 3,281 ft. 500 m. / 1,640 ft. 200 m. / 656 ft. 100 m. / 328 ft. Sea Level Below

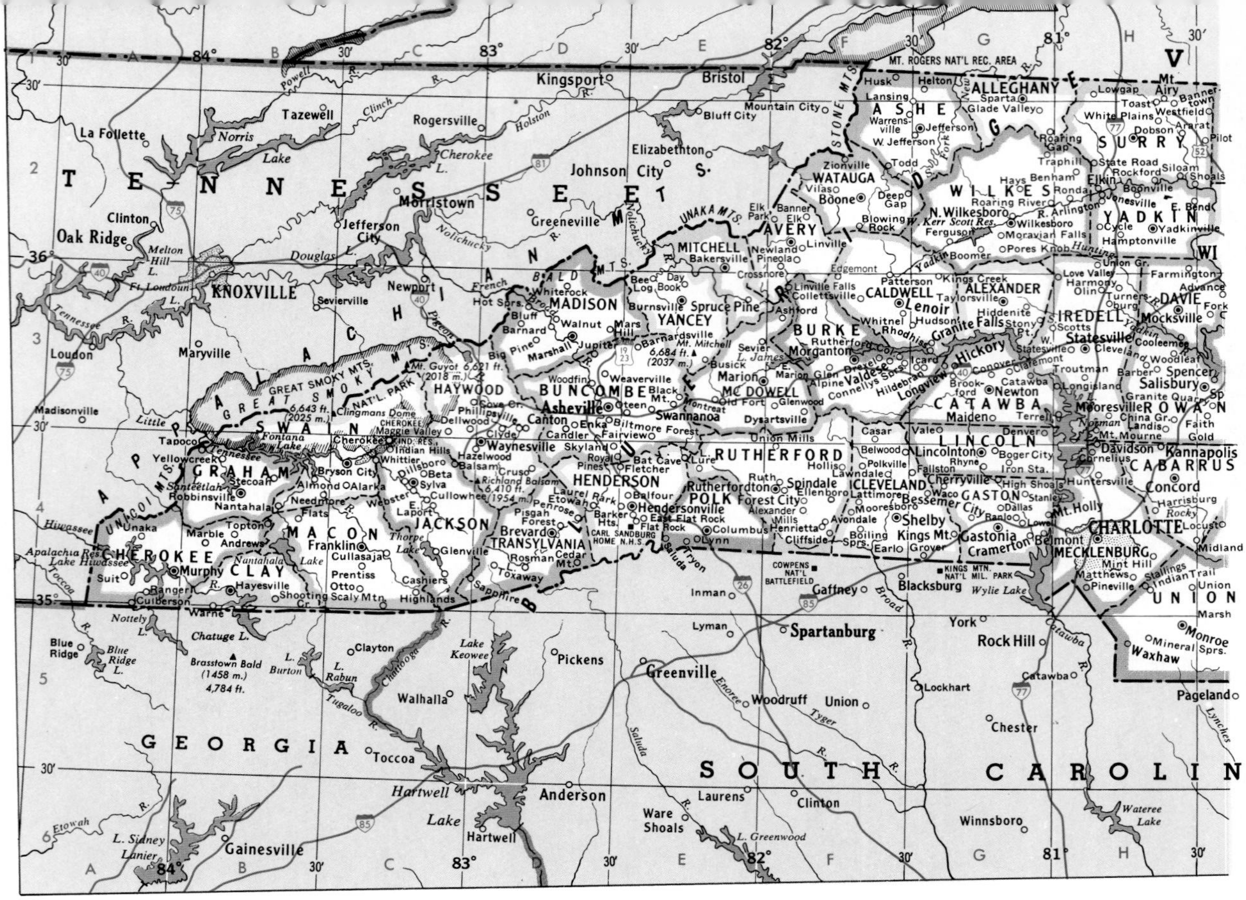

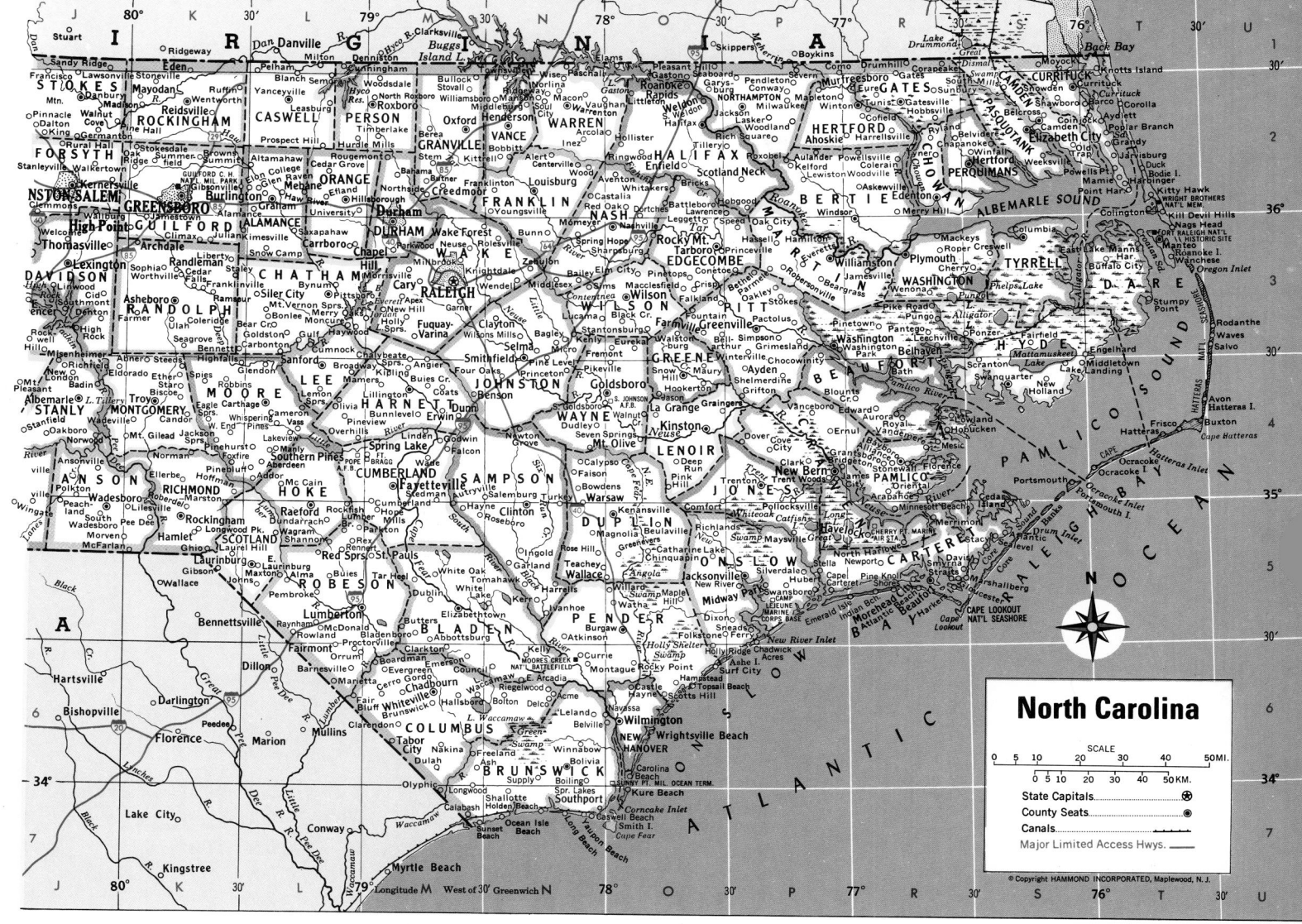

Rhodhiss 638 ....F3
Rich Square 1,058 ....P2
Richfield 535 ....J4
Richlands 996 ....O5
Ridgeway 500 ....N2
Riegelwood 459 ....N6
Roanoke Rapids 15,722 ....O2
Roaring Gap 450 ....H2
Roaring River 287 ....G2
Robbins 970 ....K4
Robbinsville▲ 709 ....B4
Robersonville 1,940 ....P3
Rockingham 9,399 ....K5
Rockwell 1,598 ....J3
Rocky Mount 48,997 ....O3
Rocky Point 975 ....O6
Rolesville 572 ....N3
Ronda 367 ....H2
Roper 669 ....R3
Rose Hill 1,287 ....N5
Roseboro 1,441 ....M5
Rosman 385 ....D4
Rougemont 400 ....L2
Rowland 1,139 ....L5
Roxboro 7,332 ....M2
Roxobel 244 ....P2
Royal 4,418 ....R4
Royal Pines D4
Ruffin 680 ....K2
Rural Hall 1,652 ....J2
Ruth 366 ....E4
Rutherford College 1,126 ....F3
Rutherfordton▲ 3,617 ....E4
Saint Pauls 1,992 ....M5
Salemburg 409 ....N4
Salisbury▲ 23,087 ....H3
Saluda 488 ....D4
Sandy Ridge 500 ....J1
Sanford 14,475 ....L4
Sapphire 350 ....D4
Saxapahaw 1,178 ....L3
Scaly Mountain 250 ....D4
Scotland Neck 2,575 ....P2
Scotts 500 ....H3
Scranton 250 ....S4
Seaboard 791 ....O1
Seagrove 244 ....K3

Sealevel 600 ....S5
Selma 4,600 ....N3
Semora 500 ....L2
Seven Springs 163 ....O4
Severn 260 ....P2
Sevier 302 ....E3
Shallotte 965 ....N7
Sharpsburg 1,536 ....O3
Shawboro 300 ....S2
Shelby▲ 14,669 ....G4
Shoals 350 ....J2
Shooting Creek 250 ....B4
Siler City 4,808 ....L3
Silverdale 250 ....P5
Simpson 410 ....P3
Sims 124 ....N3
Skyland D4
Smithfield▲ 7,540 ....N3
Smyrna 291 ....R5
Sneads Ferry 2,031 ....P5
Snow Hill▲ 1,378 ....O4
Sophia 350 ....K3
South Goldsboro 2,531 ....N4
South Mills 950 ....S2
South Wadesboro ....
South Weldon 1,640 ....O2
Southern Pines 9,129 ....L4
Southmont 950 ....J3
Southport 2,369 ....N7
Sparta▲ 1,957 ....G1
Speed 88 ....P3
Spencer 3,219 ....H3
Spindale 4,040 ....E4
Spring Hope 1,221 ....N3
Spring Lake 7,524 ....M4
Spruce Pine 2,010 ....E3
Stacy 410 ....S5
Staley 204 ....K3
Stallings 2,132 ....H4
Stanfield 517 ....J4
Stanley 2,823 ....G4
Stanleyville 4,779 ....J2
Stantonsburg 782 ....O3
Star 775 ....K4
Statesville▲ 17,567 ....H3
Stecoah 250 ....B4
Stedman 577 ....M4

Stella 700 ....P5
Stem 249 ....M2
Stokes 2,134 ....P3
Stokesdale 1,070 ....J2
Stoneville 1,109 ....K2
Stonewall 279 ....R4
Stony Point 1,286 ....G3
Stovall 409 ....M2
Stumpy Point 250 ....T3
Suit 350 ....M2
Summerfield 2,051 ....K2
Sunbury 400 ....R2
Sunset Beach 311 ....N7
Supply 300 ....N6
Surf City 970 ....O6
Swannanoa 3,538 ....E3
Swanquarter▲ 550 ....S4
Swansboro 1,165 ....P5
Sylva▲ 1,809 ....C4
Tabor City 2,330 ....M6
Tar Heel 115 ....M5
Tarboro▲ 11,037 ....O3
Taylorsville▲ 1,566 ....G3
Teachey 244 ....N5
Terrell 319 ....G3
Thomasville 15,915 ....J3
Tillery 400 ....O2
Timberlake 500 ....M2
Toast 2,125 ....H2
Todd F2
Topsail Beach 346 ....O6
Traphill 550 ....G2
Trenton▲ 248 ....P4
Troutman 1,493 ....H3
Troy▲ 3,404 ....K4
Tryon 1,680 ....E4
Turkey 234 ....N4
Tyner 264 ....R2
Ulah 546 ....K3
Union Grove 614 ....H2
Union Mills 500 ....E3
Valdese 3,914 ....F3
Vanceboro 946 ....P4
Vandemere 299 ....R4
Vass 670 ....L4
Waco 320 ....G4

Wade 238 ....M4
Wadesboro▲ 3,645 ....J5
Wagram 480 ....L5
Wake Forest 5,769 ....M3
Walkertown 1,200 ....J2
Wallace 2,939 ....N5
Wallburg 300 ....J3
Walnut 1,088 ....D3
Walnut Cove 1,147 ....J2
Walnut Creek 623 ....O4
Walstonburg 188 ....O3
Wanchese 1,380 ....T3
Warrensville F2
Warrenton▲ 949 ....N2
Warsaw 2,859 ....N4
Washington Park 403 ....R3
Washington▲ 9,075 ....R3
Watha 99 ....O5
Waxhaw 1,294 ....H5
Waynesville▲ 6,758 ....D4
Weaverville 2,107 ....D3
Webster 410 ....C4
Weeksville 500 ....S2
Welcome 3,377 ....J3
Weldon 1,392 ....O2
Wendell 2,822 ....N3
Wentworth▲ 150 ....K2
West End 950 ....K4
West Jefferson 1,002 ....F2
West Statesville G3
Westfield 450 ....J2
Whispering Pines 1,243 ....L4
Whitakers 860 ....O2
White Lake 390 ....M5
White Plains 1,027 ....H2
Whiteville▲ 5,078 ....M6
Whitnel 975 ....F3
Wilkesboro▲ 2,573 ....G2
Willard 300 ....O5
Williamston▲ 59 ....P3
Williamston 5,503 ....P3
Wilmington▲ 55,530 ....N6
Wilson▲ 36,930 ....O3
Wilsons Mills N3
Windsor▲ 2,056 ....P2
Winfall 501 ....R2
Wingate 2,821 ....J5

Winston-Salem▲ 143,485 ....J2
Winterville 2,816 ....P3
Winton▲ 796 ....P2
Wise 550 ....N2
Wood 2,736 ....N2
Woodfin 3,260 ....D3
Woodland 760 ....P2
Woodleaf 550 ....H3
Worthville 350 ....K3
Wrightsville Beach 2,937 ....O6
Yadkinville▲ 2,525 ....H2
Yanceyville▲ 1,973 ....L2
Yaupon Beach 734 ....N7
Youngsville 424 ....N2
Zebulon 3,173 ....N3

OTHER FEATURES

Albemarle (sound) S2
Alligator (lake) S3
Alligator (riv.) S3
Angola (swamp) O5
Apalachia (lake) A4
Appalachian (mts.) D2
Ashe (isl.) P6
Bald (mts.) D3
Black (riv.) N5
Blue Ridge (mts.) E3
Bodie (isl.) T2
Broad (riv.) E4
Buggs Island (lake) M1
Camp Lejeune
  Marine Corps Base P5
Cape Fear (riv.) N6
Cape Hatteras Nat'l Seashore ..T4
Carl Sandburg Home
  Nat'l Hist. Site D4
Catawba (lake) G4
Catawba (riv.) G3
Catfish (lake) P5
Chatuge (lake) B5
Cherokee Ind. Res. C3
Cherry Point Marine Air Sta. R5
Chowan (riv.) R2
Clingmans Dome (mt.) C3
Contentnea (creek) N3
Core (banks) S5

Core (sound) S5
Corncake (inlet) O7
Croatan (sound) T3
Currituck (sound) T2
Dan (riv.) L1
Deep (riv.) K3
Drum (inlet) S5
Fear (cape) O7
Fishing (creek) O2
Fontana (lake) B4
Fort Bragg 34,744 ....M4
Fort Raleigh Nat'l Hist. Site T3
French Broad (riv.) D3
Gaston (res.) O2
Great (lake) P5
Great Dismal (swamp) S1
Great Smoky (mts.) B3
Great Smoky Mts. Nat'l Park B3
Green (swamp) N6
Guyot (mt.) C3
Hatteras (cape) U4
Hatteras (inlet) T4
Hatteras (isl.) U4
Haw (riv.) K2
High Rock (lake) J3
Hiwassee (lake) A4
Hiwassee (riv.) A4
Holly Shelter (swamp) O6
Hunting (riv.) H2
Hyco (riv.) L2
James (lake) E3
Jordan, B. Everett (lake) M3
Lanes (creek) J5
Little (riv.) N3
Little (riv.) L4
Little Pee Dee (riv.) L6
Little Tennessee (riv.) B4
Long (bay) P5
Lookout (cape) S5
Lumber (riv.) L6
Mattamuskeet (lake) S3
Meherrin (riv.) P1
Mitchell (mt.) E3
Moores Creek
  Nat'l Battlefield N6
Nantahala (lake) B4
Neuse (riv.) R5

New (riv.) O5
New, South Fork (riv.) G2
New River (inlet) P6
Nolichucky (riv.) E2
Norman (lake) H3
North East Cape Fear (riv.) O4
Ocracoke (inlet) T5
Ocracoke (isl.) T4
Onslow (bay) P6
Oregon (inlet) U3
Pamlico (riv.) R4
Pamlico (sound) S4
Pee Dee (riv.) J4
Phelps (lake) S3
Pigeon (riv.) C3
Pope A.F.B. 2,857 ....L4
Portsmouth (isl.) T5
Pungo (lake) R3
Pungo (riv.) R4
Raleigh (bay) S5
Richland Balsam (mt.) D4
Roanoke (isl.) T3
Roanoke (riv.) P2
Rocky (riv.) H4
Santeetlah (lake) B4
Seymour Johnson A.F.B. N4
Six Run (creek) N4
Smith (isl.) O7
South (riv.) M5
South Yadkin (riv.) H3
Stone (riv.) G2
Sunny Point
  Mil. Ocean Term. O6
Tar (riv.) O3
Thorpe (lake) C4
Tillery (lake) J4
Trent (riv.) P4
Unaka (mts.) A4
Unicoi (mts.) A4
Waccamaw (lake) N6
Waccamaw (riv.) M7
Whiteoak (swamp) P5
W. Scott Kerr (res.) G2
Wright Brothers Nat'l Mem. ..T2
Yadkin (riv.) J3

▲County seat.

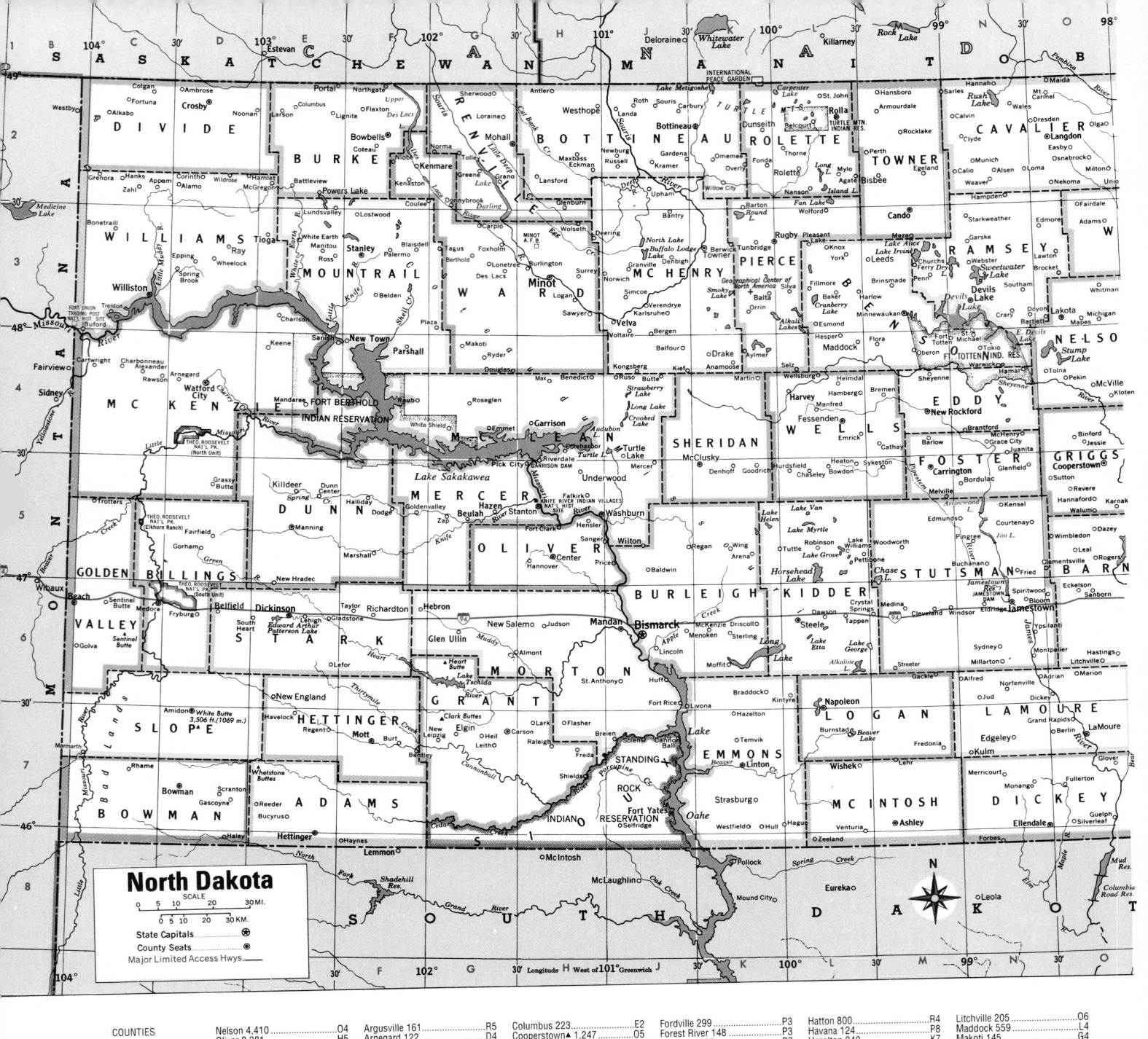

North Dakota

SCALE
0 5 10   20   30 MI.
0 5 10   20   30 KM.

State Capitals .... ⊛
County Seats .... ◉
Major Limited Access Hwys. ▬

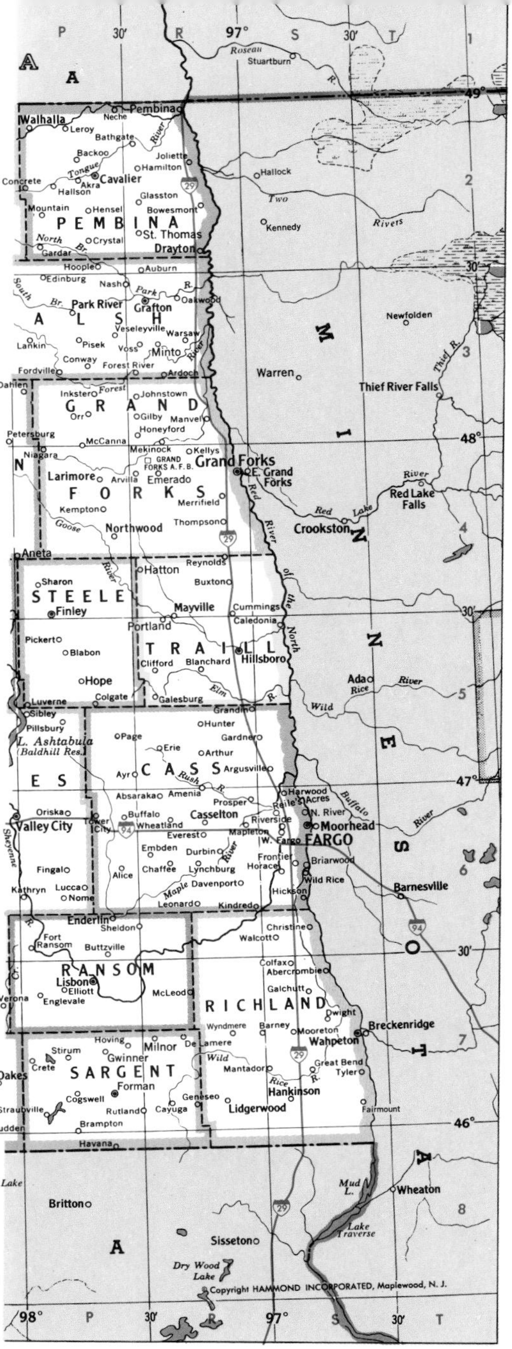

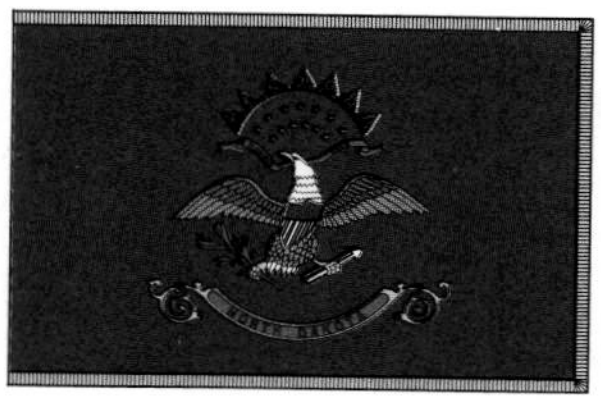

AREA 70,702 sq. mi. (183,118 sq. km.)
POPULATION 641,364
CAPITAL Bismarck
LARGEST CITY Fargo
HIGHEST POINT White Butte 3,506 ft.
(1069 m.)
SETTLED IN 1780
ADMITTED TO UNION November 2, 1889
POPULAR NAME Flickertail State; Sioux State
STATE FLOWER Wild Prairie Rose
STATE BIRD Western Meadowlark

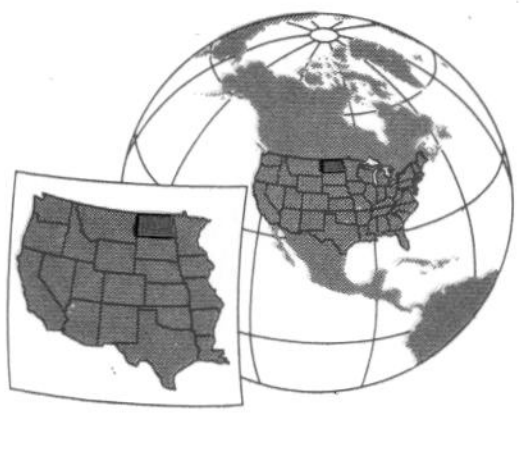

Topography

Towner▲ 669	K3
Turtle Lake 681	J4
Tuttle 160	L5
Underwood 976	H5
Upham 205	J2
Valley City▲ 7,163	P6
Velva 968	J3
Verona 103	O7
Wahpeton▲ 8,751	S7
Walcott 178	R6
Walhalla 1,131	P2
Washburn 1,506	J5
Watford City▲ 1,784	D4
West Fargo 12,287	S6
Westhope 578	H2
White Shield 274	G4
Wildrose 193	D2
Williston▲ 13,131	C3
Willow City 281	K2
Wilton 728	J5
Wimbledon 275	O5
Wing 208	K5
Wishek 1,171	L7
Woodworth 102	M5
Wyndmere 501	R7
Zap 287	G5
Zeeland 197	L8

OTHER FEATURES

Alkali (lakes)	L3	Fan (lake)	L2	Little Missouri (riv.)	D4	Smoky (lake)	K3
Alkaline (lake)	L6	Forest (riv.)	P3	Little Muddy (riv.)	C3	Souris (riv.)	J2
Apple (creek)	J6	Fort Berthold Ind. Res.	E4	Long (lake)	J4	Spring (creek)	E5
Arrowwood (lake)	N5	Fort Totten Ind. Res.	N4	Long (lake)	K6	Standing Rock Ind. Res.	J7
Ashtabula (Baldhill Res.) (lake)	P5	Fort Union Trading Post Nat'l Hist. Site	B3	Long (lake)	L2	Strawberry (lake)	J4
Audubon (lake)	H4	Garrison (dam)	H5	Maple (riv.)	O8	Stump (lake)	O4
Bad Lands (reg.)	C7	George (lake)	L6	Maple (riv.)	R6	Sweetwater (lake)	N3
Baldhill (Ashtabula Lake) (res.)	P5	Goose (riv.)	P4	Metigoshe (lake)	K2	Theodore Roosevelt Nat'l Park	C5
Bear (creek)	O7	Grand, North Fork (riv.)	E8	Minot A.F.B. 9,095	H3	Theodore Roosevelt Nat'l Park	D4
Beaver (creek)	K7	Grand Forks A.F.B.9,343	R4	Missouri (riv.)	H5	Theodore Roosevelt Nat'l Park	D6
Beaver (creek)	B5	Green (riv.)	D5	Muddy (creek)	G6	Thirty Mile (creek)	F6
Beaver (lake)	L7	Grove (lake)	L3	Myrtle (lake)	L5	Tongue (riv.)	P2
Buffalo Lodge (lake)	J3	Heart (butte)	G6	North (lake)	J3	Tschida (lake)	G6
Cannonball (riv.)	G7	Heart (riv.)	F6	Oahe (lake)	J7	Turtle (lake)	H4
Carpenter (lake)	L2	Helen (lake)	K5	Oak (creek)	J8	Turtle (mts.)	K2
Cedar (creek)	G7	Horsehead (lake)	L5	Park (riv.)	R3	Turtle Mountain Ind. Res.	L2
Chase (lake)	M5	International Peace Garden	K1	Patterson, Edward A. (lake)	E6	Upper Des Lacs (lake)	F2
Cherry (creek)	D4	Irvine (lake)	M3	Pembina (riv.)	O1	Van (lake)	L5
Clark (buttes)	G6	Island (lake)	L2	Pipestem (riv.)	M5	Whetstone (buttes)	E7
Coteau du Missouri (plain)	G3	James (riv.)	N6	Porcupine (creek)	J7	White Butte (buttes)	D7
Cranberry (lake)	L3	Jamestown (res.)	N6	Red River of the North (riv.)	S4	White Earth (riv.)	E3
Crooked (lake)	J4	Jim (lake)	N6	Round (lake)	K3	Wild Rice (riv.)	R7
Cut Bank (creek)	H2	Knife (riv.)	G5	Rush (lake)	N2	Yellowstone (riv.)	B4
Darling (lake)	G2	Knife R. Indian Villages Nat'l Hist. Site	H5	Rush (lake)	R5	
Deep (riv.)	J1	Little Deep (creek)	G2	Sakakawea (lake)	G5	
Des Lacs (riv.)	G3	Little Knife (riv.)	F3	Sentinel (butte)	C6	
Devils (lake)	N3			Shell (creek)	F3	
Dry (lake)	M3			Sheyenne (riv.)	O6	
East Devils (lake)	N4					
Egg (creek)	H3					
Elm (riv.)	N8					
Elm (riv.)	R5					
Etta (lake)	L6					

▲County seat

Copyright HAMMOND INCORPORATED, Maplewood, N.J.

New Leipzig 326	G7	Rocklake 221	M2
New Rockford▲ 1,604	N4	Rolette 623	L2
New Salem 909	G6	Rolla▲ 1,286	L2
New Town 1,388	F4	Rugby▲ 2,909	L3
Newburg 104	J2	Rutland 212	P7
Noonan 231	D2	Ryder 121	G4
Northwood 1,166	P4	Saint John 368	L2
Oakes 1,775	O7	Saint Thomas 444	R2
Oberon 103	M4	Sanborn 164	O6
Oriska 103	P6	Sanish	E4
Osnabrock 214	O2	Sawyer 319	H3
Page 266	P5	Scranton 294	D7
Palermo 95	F3	Selfridge 242	J7
Park River 1,725	P3	Sharon 119	P4
Parshall 943	F4	Sheldon 149	P6
Pekin 101	O4	Sherwood 286	G2
Pembina 642	R2	Sheyenne 272	M4
Petersburg 219	P3	Souris 97	J2
Pick City 203	G5	South Heart 322	D6
Pisek 130	P3	Stanley▲ 1,371	F3
Plaza 193	G3	Stanton▲ 517	H5
Portal 192	E2	Starkweather 197	N3
Portland 602	P5	Steele▲ 762	L6
Powers Lake 408	E2	Strasburg 553	K7
Ray 603	D3	Streeter 161	M6
Reeder 252	E7	Surrey 856	H3
Regent 268	E7	Sykeston 167	M5
Reile's Acres 210	S6	Tappen 239	L6
Reynolds 299	R4	Taylor 163	F6
Rhame 186	C7	Thompson 930	R4
Richardton 625	F6	Tioga 1,278	E3
Riverdale 283	H4	Tolna 230	O4
Riverside 465	S6	Tower City 233	P6

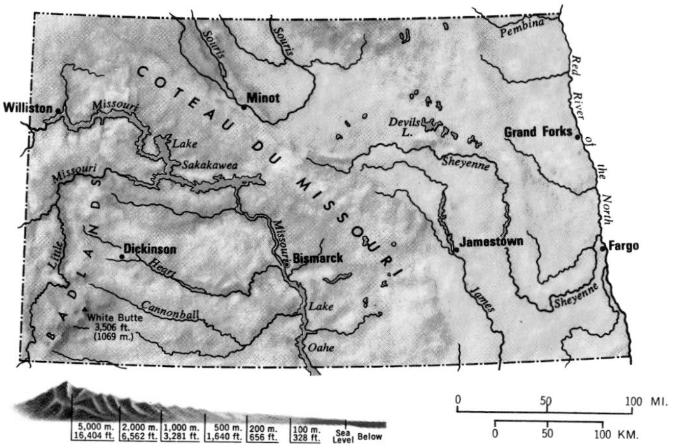

Agriculture, Industry and Resources

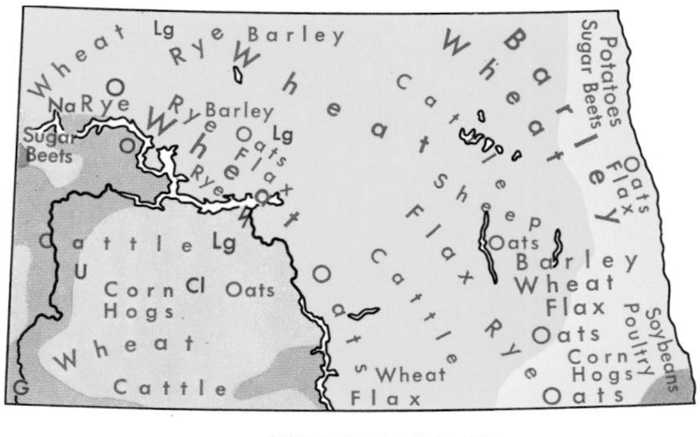

DOMINANT LAND USE

- Specialized Wheat
- Wheat, General Farming
- Wheat, Range Livestock
- Livestock, Cash Grain
- Sugar Beets, Dry Beans, Livestock, General Farming
- Range Livestock
- ⚡ Water Power

MAJOR MINERAL OCCURRENCES

- Cl Clay
- G Natural Gas
- Lg Lignite
- Na Salt
- O Petroleum
- U Uranium

Ohio

SCALE
0 5 10   20   30   40 MI.
0 5 10   20   30   40 KM.

State Capitals............................⊛
County Seats.............................◉
Major Limited Access Hwys.

© Copyright HAMMOND INCORPORATED, Maplewood, N.J.

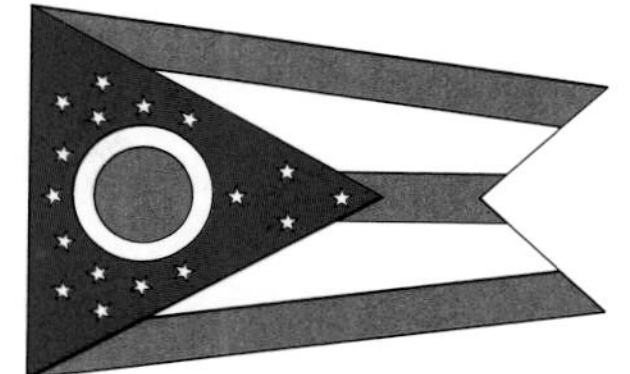

AREA 41,330 sq. mi. (107,045 sq. km.)
POPULATION 10,887,325
CAPITAL Columbus
LARGEST CITY Cleveland
HIGHEST POINT Campbell Hill 1,550 ft. (472 m.)
SETTLED IN 1788
ADMITTED TO UNION March 1, 1803
POPULAR NAME Buckeye State
STATE FLOWER Scarlet Carnation
STATE BIRD Cardinal

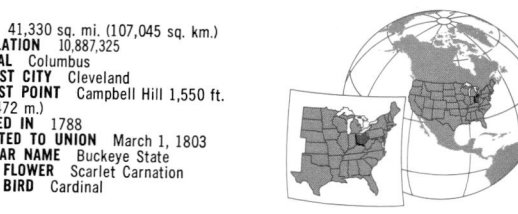

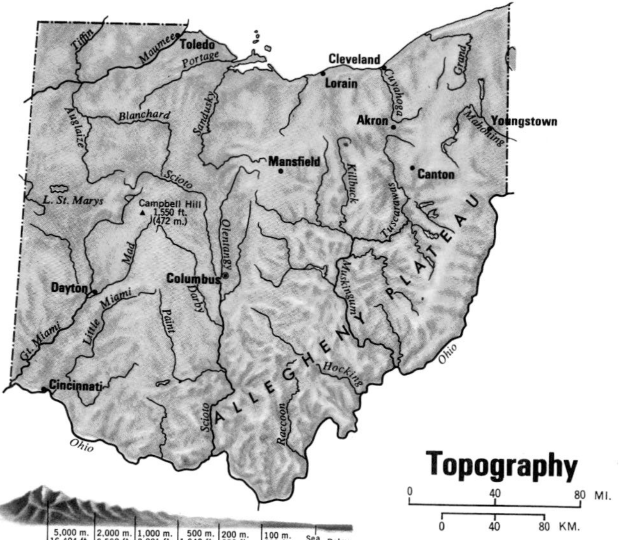
Tiffin
Maumee
Toledo
Portage
Cleveland
Lorain
Cuyahoga
Grand
Akron
Youngstown
Mahoning
Blanchard
Sandusky
Auglaize
Mansfield
Canton
Killbuck
Tuscarawas
L. St. Marys
Campbell Hill ▲ 1,550 ft. (472 m.)
Scioto
Olentangy
Mad
Columbus
Dayton
Darby
Little Miami
Paint
Gt. Miami
Muskingum
ALLEGHENY PLATEAU
Hocking
Cincinnati
Raccoon
Ohio
Topography
0 40 80 MI.
0 40 80 KM.
5,000 m. 16,404 ft.
2,000 m. 6,562 ft.
1,000 m. 3,281 ft.
500 m. 1,640 ft.
200 m. 656 ft.
100 m. 328 ft.
Sea Level
Below

COUNTIES

Adams 25,371 D8
Allen 109,755 B4
Ashland 47,507 F4
Ashtabula 99,821 J2
Athens 59,549 F7
Auglaize 44,585 B4
Belmont 71,074 J5
Brown 34,966 C8
Butler 291,479 A7
Carroll 26,521 H4
Champaign 36,019 C5
Clark 147,548 C6
Clermont 150,187 B7
Clinton 35,415 C7
Columbiana 108,276 J4
Coshocton 35,427 G5
Crawford 47,870 E4
Cuyahoga 1,412,140 G3
Darke 53,619 A5
Defiance 39,350 A3
Delaware 66,929 D5
Erie 76,779 E3
Fairfield 103,461 E6
Fayette 27,466 D6
Franklin 961,437 E5
Fulton 38,498 B2
Gallia 30,954 F8
Geauga 81,129 H3
Greene 136,731 C6
Guernsey 39,024 H5
Hamilton 866,228 A7
Hancock 65,536 C3
Hardin 31,111 C4
Harrison 16,085 H5
Henry 29,108 B3
Highland 35,728 C7
Hocking 25,533 F6
Holmes 32,849 G4
Huron 56,240 E3
Jackson 30,230 E7
Jefferson 80,298 J5
Knox 47,473 F5
Lake 215,499 H2
Lawrence 61,834 E8
Licking 128,300 F5
Logan 42,310 C5
Lorain 271,126 F3
Lucas 462,361 C2
Madison 37,068 D6
Mahoning 264,806 J4
Marion 64,274 D4
Medina 122,354 G3
Meigs 22,987 F7
Mercer 39,443 A4
Miami 93,182 B5
Monroe 15,497 H6
Montgomery 573,809 B6
Morgan 14,194 G6
Morrow 27,749 E4
Muskingum 82,068 G5
Noble 11,336 G6
Ottawa 40,029 D2
Paulding 20,488 A3
Perry 31,557 F6
Pickaway 48,255 D6
Pike 24,249 D7
Portage 142,585 H3
Preble 40,113 A6
Putnam 33,819 B3
Richland 126,137 E4
Ross 69,330 D7
Sandusky 61,963 D3
Scioto 80,327 D8
Seneca 59,733 D3
Shelby 44,915 B5
Stark 367,585 H4
Summit 514,990 G3
Trumbull 227,813 J3
Tuscarawas 84,090 H5
Union 31,969 D5
Van Wert 30,464 A4
Vinton 11,098 E7
Warren 113,909 B7
Washington 62,254 H7
Wayne 101,461 G4
Williams 36,956 A2
Wood 113,269 C3
Wyandot 22,254 D4

CITIES and TOWNS

Aberdeen 1,329 C8
Ada 5,413 C4
Adamsville 151 G5
Addyston 1,198 B9
Adelphi 398 E7
Adena 842 J5
Akron▲ 223,019 G3
Albany 795 F7
Alexandria 468 E5
Alger 864 C4
Alliance 23,376 H4
Alvordton 298 A2
Amanda 729 E6
Amberley 3,108 C9
Amelia 1,837 D10
Amesville 250 F7
Amherst 10,332 F3
Amsterdam 669 J5
Andover 1,216 J2
Anna 1,164 B5
Ansonia 1,279 A5
Antioch 68 H6
Antwerp 1,677 A3
Apple Creek 860 G4
Aquilla 360 H2
Arcadia 546 D3
Arcanum 1,953 A6
Archbold 3,440 B2
Arlington 1,267 C4
Arlington Heights 1,084 C9
Ashland▲ 20,079 F4
Ashley 1,059 E5
Ashtabula 21,633 J2
Ashville 2,254 E6
Athalia 346 F8
Athens▲ 21,265 F7
Attica 944 E3
Aurora 9,192 H3
Austintown 32,371 J3
Avon 7,337 F3
Avon Lake 15,066 F2
Bailey Lakes 367 F4
Bainbridge 968 D7
Bairdstown 130 C3
Ballville 3,083 D3
Baltic 659 G5
Baltimore 2,971 E6
Barberton 27,623 G4
Barnesville 4,326 H6
Barnhill 313 H5
Barton 1,039 J5
Batavia▲ 1,700 B7
Batesville 95 H6
Bay View 739 E3
Bay Village 17,000 G9
Beach City 1,051 G4
Beachwood 10,677 J9
Beallsville 464 J6
Beaver 336 E7
Beavercreek 33,626 C6
Beaverdam 467 C4
Bedford 14,822 H9
Bedford Heights 12,131 J9
Bellaire 6,028 J5
Bellbrook 6,511 C6
Belle Center 796 C4
Belle Valley 267 G6
Bellefontaine▲ 12,142 C5
Bellevue 8,146 E3
Bellville 1,568 E4
Belmont 471 J5
Belmore 161 B3
Beloit 1,037 J4
Belpre 6,796 G7
Bentleyville 674 J9
Benton 351 G4
Benton Ridge 343 C4
Berea 19,051 G10
Bergholz 713 J4
Berkey 264 C2
Berlin 691 G4
Berlin Heights 756 F3
Bethel 2,407 B8
Bethesda 1,161 H5
Bettsville 752 D3
Beverly 1,444 G6
Bexley 13,088 E6
Blakeslee 128 A2
Blanchester 4,206 B7
Bloomdale 632 D3
Bloomingburg 769 D6
Bloomingdale 227 J5
Bloomville 949 D3
Blue Ash 11,860 C9
Bluffton 3,367 C4
Boardman 38,596 J3
Bolivar 914 G4
Boston Heights 733 J10
Botkins 1,340 B5
Bowerston 343 H5
Bowersville 225 C6
Bowling Green▲ 28,176 C3
Bradford 2,005 B5
Bradner 1,093 C3
Brady Lake 490 H3
Brecksville 11,818 H10
Bremen 1,386 F6
Brewster 2,307 G4
Brice 109 E6
Bridgeport 2,318 J5
Bridgetown 11,748 B9
Brilliant 1,672 J5
Brimfield 3,223 H3
Broadview Heights 12,219 H10
Brook Park 22,865 G9
Brookfield 1,396 J3
Brooklyn 11,706 H9
Brooklyn Heights 1,450 H9
Brookside 703 J5
Brookville 4,621 B6
Broughton 151 B3
Brunswick 28,230 G3
Bryan▲ 8,348 A3
Buchtel 640 F7
Buckeye Lake 2,986 F6
Buckland 239 B4
Bucyrus▲ 13,496 E4
Burbank 289 F4
Burgoon 224 D3
Burkettsville 268 A5
Burlington 3,003 F9
Burton 1,349 H3
Butler 968 F4
Butlerville 188 B7
Byesville 2,435 G6
Cadiz▲ 3,439 J5
Cairo 473 B4
Calcutta 1,212 J4
Caldwell▲ 1,786 G6
Caledonia 644 D4
Cambridge▲ 11,748 G5
Camden 2,210 A6
Campbell 10,038 J3
Canal Fulton 4,157 H4
Canal Winchester 2,617 E6
Canfield 5,409 J3
Canton▲ 84,161 H4
Cardington 1,770 E5
Carey 3,684 D4
Carlisle 4,872 B6
Carroll 558 E6
Carrollton▲ 3,042 J4
Casstown 246 B5
Castalia 915 E3
Castine 163 A6
Catawba 268 C6
Cecil 249 A3
Cedarville 3,210 C6
Celina▲ 9,650 A4
Centerburg 1,323 E5
Centerville 128 B6
Chagrin Falls 4,146 J9
Chardon▲ 4,446 H2
Chatfield 206 E4
Chauncey 980 F7
Cherry Fork 178 C8
Cherry Grove 4,972 C10
Chesapeake 1,073 E9
Cheshire 250 F8
Chester 309 G7
Chesterhill 395 G6
Chesterland 2,078 H2
Chesterville 286 E5
Cheviot 9,616 B9
Chickasaw 378 A5
Chillicothe▲ 21,923 E7
Chilo 130 B8
Christiansburg 599 C5
Cincinnati▲ 364,040 B9
Circleville▲ 11,666 D6
Clarington 406 J6
Clark 523 G5
Clarksburg 483 D7
Clarksville 485 C7
Clay Center 289 D2
Clayton 713 B6
Cleveland Heights 54,052 H9
Cleveland▲ 505,616 H9
Cleves 2,208 B9
Clinton 1,175 G4
Cloverdale 270 B3
Clyde 5,776 E3
Coal Grove 2,251 E9
Coalton 553 E7
Coldwater 4,335 A5
College Corner 379 A6
Columbiana 4,961 J4
Columbus (cap.)▲ 632,910 E6
Columbus Grove 2,231 B4
Commercial Point 405 D6
Conesville 420 G5
Congress 162 F4
Conneaut 13,241 J2
Continental 1,214 B3
Convoy 1,200 A4
Coolville 663 G7
Corning 703 F6
Cortland 5,666 J3
Corwin 225 B6
Coshocton▲ 12,193 G5
Cove 6,669 E8
Covedale 5,830 B10
Covington 2,603 B5
Craig Beach 1,402 H3
Crestline 4,934 E4
Creston 1,848 G3
Cridersville 1,885 B4
Crooksville 2,601 F6
Crown City 445 F8
Cumberland 318 G6
Custar 209 C3
Cuyahoga Falls 48,950 G3
Cuyahoga Heights 682 H9
Cygnet 560 C3
Dalton 1,377 G4
Danville 1,001 F5
Darbydale 825 D6
Darbyville 272 D6
Dayton▲ 182,044 B6
Deer Park 6,181 C9
Deersville 86 H5
Defiance▲ 16,768 B3
Degraff 1,331 C5
Delaware▲ 20,030 E5
Dellroy 314 H4
Delphos 7,093 B4
Delta 2,849 B2
Dennison 3,282 H5
Dent 6,416 B9
Deshler 1,876 C3
Devola 2,736 H7
Dexter City 161 G6
Dillonvale 857 J5
Dover 11,329 G4
Doylestown 2,668 G4
Dresden 1,581 G5
Dublin 16,366 D5
Dunkirk 869 C4
Dupont 279 B3
East Canton 1,742 H4
East Cleveland 33,096 H9
East Liverpool 13,654 J4
East Palestine 5,168 J4
East Sparta 771 H4
Eastlake 21,161 J8
Eaton Estates 1,586 G3
Eaton▲ 7,396 A6
Edgerton 1,896 A3
Edgewood 5,189 J2
Edison 488 E4
Edon 880 A2
Eldorado 549 A6
Elgin 71 A4
Elida 1,486 B4
Elmore 1,334 D3
Elmwood Place 2,937 B9
Elyria▲ 56,746 F3
Empire 364 J5
Englewood 11,432 B6
Euclid 54,875 J9
Evendale 3,175 C9
Fairborn 31,300 B6
Fairfax 2,029 C9
Fairfield 39,729 A7
Fairlawn 5,779 G3
Fairport Harbor 2,978 H2
Fairview Park 18,028 G9
Farmer 932 A3
Farmersville 950 A6
Fayette 1,248 B2
Fayetteville 393 C7
Felicity 856 B8
Findlay▲ 35,703 C3
Fletcher 545 B5
Florida 304 B3
Flushing 1,042 J5
Forest 1,594 C4
Forest Park 18,609 B9
Forestville 9,185 C10
Fort Jennings 436 B4
Fort Loramie 1,042 B5
Fort McKinley 9,740 B6
Fort Recovery 1,313 A5
Fort Shawnee 4,128 B4
Fostoria 14,983 D3
Frankfort 1,065 D7
Franklin 11,026 B6
Franklin Furnace 1,212 E8
Frazeysburg 1,165 F5
Fredericksburg 502 G4
Fredericktown 2,443 F5
Freeport 475 H5
Fremont▲ 17,648 D3
Fulton 325 E5
Fultonham 178 F6
Gahanna 27,791 E5
Galena 361 E5
Galion 11,859 E4
Gallipolis▲ 4,831 F8
Gambier 2,073 F5
Garfield Heights 31,739 J9
Garrettsville 2,014 H3
Gates Mills 2,508 J9
Geneva 6,597 J2
Geneva-on-the-Lake 1,626 H2
Genoa 2,262 D2
Georgetown▲ 3,627 C8
Germantown 4,916 B6
Gettysburg 539 A5
Gibsonburg 2,579 D3
Gilboa 208 C3
Girard 11,304 J3
Glandorf 829 B3
Glendale 2,445 C9
Glenford 208 F6
Glenmont 233 F4
Glenwillow 455 J10
Glouster 2,001 F6
Gnadenhutten 1,226 G5
Golf Manor 4,154 C9
Gordon 206 B6
Grafton 3,344 F3
Grand Rapids 955 C3
Grand River H2
Grandview 1,301 H7
Grandview Heights 7,010 D6
Granville 4,353 E5
Gratiot 195 F6
Gratis 998 A6
Green Camp 393 D4
Green Springs 1,446 E3
Greenfield 5,172 D7
Greenhills 4,393 B9
Greensburg 3,306 G4
Greentown 1,856 H4
Greenville▲ 12,863 A5
Greenwich 1,442 E3
Groesbeck 6,684 B9
Grove City 19,661 D6
Groveport 2,948 E6
Grover Hill 518 B3
Hamden 877 F7
Hamersville 586 C8
Hamilton▲ 61,368 A7
Hamler 623 B3
Hanging Rock 306 E8
Hanover 803 F5
Hanoverton 434 J4
Harbor View 122 C2
Harpster 233 D4
Harrisburg 340 D6
Harrison 7,518 A9
Harrisville 308 J5
Harrod 537 C4
Hartford 418 J3
Hartford 444 E5
Hartville 2,031 H4
Harveysburg 437 C7
Haskins 549 C3
Haviland 210 A3
Hayesville 457 F4
Heath 7,231 F5
Hebron 2,076 E6
Helena 267 D3
Hemlock 203 F6
Hicksville 3,664 A3
Higginsport 298 C8
Highland 275 C7
Highland Heights 6,249 J9
Hilliard 11,796 D5
Hillsboro▲ 6,235 C7
Hiram 1,330 H3
Holgate 1,290 B3
Holland 1,210 C2
Hollansburg 300 A5
Holloway 354 H5
Holmesville 419 G4
Hopedale 685 J5
Hoytville 301 C3
Hubbard 8,248 J3
Huber Heights 38,696 B6
Hudson 5,159 H3
Hunting Valley 799 J9
Huntsville 343 C5
Huron 7,030 E3
Independence 6,500 H9
Indian Hill 5,383 C9
Irondale 382 J4
Ironton▲ 12,751 E8
Ithaca 119 A6
Jackson Center 1,398 B5
Jackson▲ 6,144 E7
Jacksonville 544 F7
Jamestown 1,794 C6
Jefferson (West Jefferson) 3,331 D6
Jefferson▲ 2,952 J2
Jeffersonville 1,281 C6
Jenera 285 C4
Jeromesville 582 F4
Jerry City 517 C3
Jerusalem 144 H6
Jewett 778 H5
Johnstown 3,237 E5
Junction City 770 F6
Kalida 947 B4
Kelleys Island 172 E2
Kent 28,835 H3
Kenton▲ 8,356 C4
Kettering 60,569 B6
Kettlersville 194 B5
Killbuck 809 G5
Kimbolton 134 G5
Kingston 1,153 E7
Kingsville 1,243 J2
Kipton 283 F3
Kirby 155 D4
Kirkersville 563 E6
Kirtland 5,881 H2
Kirtland Hills 628 H2
La Rue 802 D4
Lafayette 449 C4
Lagrange 1,199 F3
Lakeline 210 J8
Lakemore 2,684 H3
Lakeview 1,056 C4
Lakewood 59,718 G9
Lancaster▲ 34,507 E6
Latty 205 A3
Laura 483 B6
Laurelville 605 E7
Lawrenceville 304 C6
Lebanon▲ 10,453 B7
Leesburg 1,063 D7
Leesville 156 H5
Leetonia 2,070 J4
Leipsic 2,203 C3
Lewisburg 1,584 A6
Lewisville 261 H6
Lexington 4,124 E4
Liberty Center 1,084 B3
Lima▲ 45,549 B4
Limaville 152 H4
Lincoln Heights 4,805 C9
Lindsey 529 D3
Linndale 159 G9
Lisbon▲ 3,037 J4
Lithopolis 563 E6
Lockbourne 173 E6
Lockington 214 B5
Lockland 4,357 C9
Lodi 3,042 F3
Logan▲ 6,725 F6
London▲ 7,807 C6
Lorain 71,245 F3
Lordstown 3,404 J3
Lore City 384 H6
Loudonville 2,915 F4
Louisville 8,087 H4
Loveland 9,990 D9
Lowell 617 H6
Lowellville 1,349 J3
Lower Salem 103 H6
Lucas 730 F4
Lucasville 1,575 E8
Luckey 848 D3
Ludlow Falls 300 B6
Lynchburg 1,212 C7
Lyndhurst 15,982 J9
Lyons 579 B2
Macedonia 7,509 J10
Mack 2,816 B9
Macksburg 218 G6
Madeira 9,141 C9
Madison 2,477 H2
Magnetic Springs 373 D5
Magnolia 937 H4
Maineville 359 C9
Malinta 294 B3

(continued on following page)

Agriculture, Industry and Resources

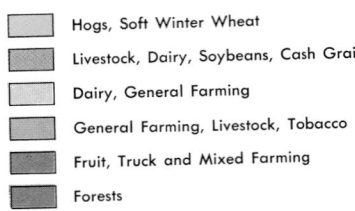

DOMINANT LAND USE

- Hogs, Soft Winter Wheat
- Livestock, Dairy, Soybeans, Cash Grain
- Dairy, General Farming
- General Farming, Livestock, Tobacco
- Fruit, Truck and Mixed Farming
- Forests
- Urban Areas

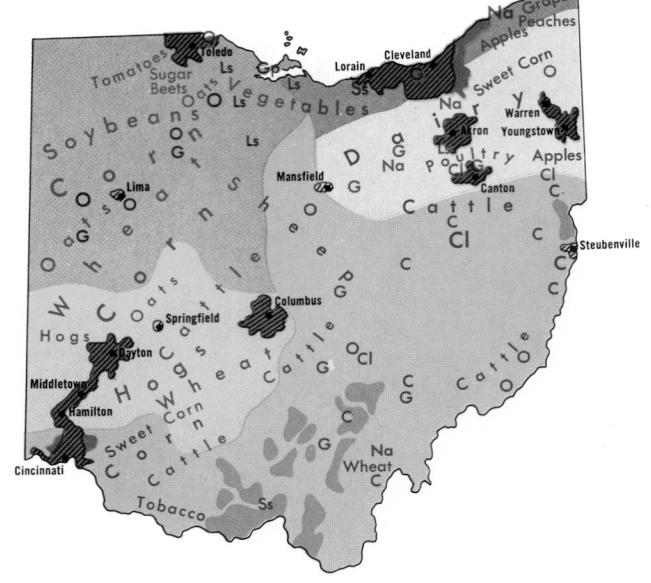

MAJOR MINERAL OCCURRENCES

C	Coal
Cl	Clay
G	Natural Gas
Gp	Gypsum
Ls	Limestone
Na	Salt
O	Petroleum
Ss	Sandstone

Major Industrial Areas

AREA 69,956 sq. mi. (181,186 sq. km.)
POPULATION 3,157,604
CAPITAL Oklahoma City
LARGEST CITY Oklahoma City
HIGHEST POINT Black Mesa 4,973 ft. (1516 m.)
SETTLED IN 1889
ADMITTED TO UNION November 16, 1907
POPULAR NAME Sooner State
STATE FLOWER Mistletoe
STATE BIRD Scissor-tailed Flycatcher

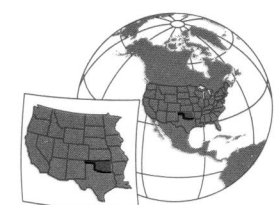

COUNTIES

Adair 18,421	S3
Alfalfa 6,416	K1
Atoka 12,778	O6
Beaver 6,023	E1
Beckham 18,812	G4
Blaine 11,470	K3
Bryan 32,089	O7
Caddo 29,550	K4
Canadian 74,409	K3
Carter 42,919	M6
Cherokee 34,049	R3
Choctaw 15,302	P6
Cimarron 3,301	A1
Cleveland 174,253	M4
Coal 5,780	O5
Comanche 111,486	K5
Cotton 6,651	K6
Craig 14,104	R1
Creek 60,915	O3
Custer 26,897	H3
Delaware 28,070	S2
Dewey 5,551	H2
Ellis 4,497	G2
Garfield 56,735	L2
Garvin 26,605	M5
Grady 41,747	L5
Grant 5,689	L1
Greer 6,559	G5
Harmon 3,793	G5
Harper 4,063	G1
Haskell 10,940	R4
Hughes 13,023	O4
Jackson 28,764	H5
Jefferson 7,010	L6
Johnston 10,032	N6
Kay 48,056	M1
Kingfisher 13,212	L3
Kiowa 11,347	J5
Latimer 10,333	R5
Le Flore 43,270	S5
Lincoln 29,216	N3
Logan 29,011	M3
Love 8,157	M7
Major 8,055	K2
Marshall 10,829	N6
Mayes 33,366	R2
McClain 22,795	L5
McCurtain 33,433	S6
McIntosh 16,779	P4
Murray 12,042	M6
Muskogee 68,078	R3
Noble 11,045	M2
Nowata 9,992	P1
Okfuskee 11,551	O3
Oklahoma 599,611	M3
Okmulgee 36,490	P3
Osage 41,645	O1
Ottawa 30,561	S1
Pawnee 15,575	N2
Payne 61,507	N2
Pittsburg 40,581	P5
Pontotoc 34,119	N5
Pottawatomie 58,760	N4
Pushmataha 10,997	R6
Roger Mills 4,147	G3
Rogers 55,170	P2
Seminole 25,412	N4
Sequoyah 33,828	L6
Stephens 42,299	L5
Texas 16,419	C1
Tillman 10,384	J6
Tulsa 503,341	P2
Wagoner 47,883	P3
Washington 48,066	P1
Washita 11,441	J4
Woods 9,103	J1
Woodward 18,976	H2

CITIES and TOWNS

Achille 491	O7
Ada▲ 15,820	N5
Adair 685	R2
Adams 150	D1
Adamson 150	P5
Addington 100	L6
Afton 915	S1
Agra 334	N3
Akins 250	S3
Albany 65	O7
Albert 100	K4
Albion 88	R5
Alderson 395	P5
Alex 639	L5
Alfalfa 70	J4
Aline 295	K1
Allen 972	O5
Altus▲ 21,910	H5
Alva▲ 5,495	J1
Amber 418	L4
Ames 268	K2
Amorita 56	K1
Anadarko▲ 6,586	K4
Antlers▲ 2,524	P6
Apache 1,591	K5
Apperson 30	N1
Aqua Park	R3
Arapaho♦ 802	H3
Arcadia 320	M3
Ardmore▲ 23,079	M6
Arkoma 2,393	T4
Arnett▲ 547	G2
Asher 449	N5
Ashland 56	O5
Atoka▲ 3,298	O6
Atwood 225	O5
Avant 369	O2
Avard 37	J1
Avery 35	N3
Bache 100	P5
Bacone 786	R3
Baker 70	D1
Balko 100	E1
Barnsdall 1,316	O1
Baron 300	S3
Bartlesville▲ 34,256	O1
Battiest 250	S6
Bearden 142	O4
Beaver▲ 1,584	F1
Beggs 1,150	P3
Belzoni 50	R6
Bengal 300	R5
Bennington 251	P7
Bentley 75	O6
Berlin 50	G4
Bernice 330	S1
Bessie 248	H4
Bethany 20,075	L3
Bethel 2,505	S6
Bethel Acres 2,314	M4
Big Cabin 271	R1
Billings 555	M1
Binger 724	K4
Bison 103	L2
Bixby 9,502	P3
Blackburn 110	N2
Blackgum 150	S3
Blackwell 7,538	M1
Blair 922	H5
Blanchard 1,922	L4
Blanco 215	P5
Blocker 135	P4
Blue 175	O7
Bluejacket 247	R1
Boggy Depot 100	O6
Boise City▲ 1,509	B1
Bokchito 576	O6
Bokhoma 35	S7
Bokoshe 403	S4
Boley 908	O4
Boswell 643	P6
Bowlegs 398	N4
Bowring 115	O1
Boyd 10	E1
Boynton 391	P3
Braden 15	S4
Bradley 166	L5
Braggs 308	R3
Braman 251	M1
Bray 925	L5
Breckinridge 261	L2
Briartown 55	R4
Bridgeport 137	K3
Brinkman	G4
Bristow 4,062	O3
Broken Arrow 58,043	P2
Broken Bow 3,961	S7
Bromide 162	N6
Brooksville 69	M4
Bryant 74	P4
Buffalo▲ 1,312	G1
Bunch 64	S3
Burbank 165	N1
Burlington 169	K1
Burneyville 150	M7
Burns Flat 1,027	H4
Butler 341	H3
Byars 263	N5
Byng 598	N5
Byron 57	K1
Cache 2,251	J5
Caddo 918	O6
Cairo 50	O5
Calera 1,536	O7
Calumet 560	K3
Calvin 251	O5
Camargo 185	H2
Cameron 327	T4
Canadian 261	P4
Canadian City	L4
Caney 184	O6
Canton 632	J2
Canute 538	H4
Capron 38	J1
Cardin 165	S1
Carmen 459	J1
Carney 1,593	J4
Carney 558	N3
Carrier 171	K2
Carter 286	H4
Cartersville 79	S4
Cashion 430	L3
Castle 94	O4
Catoosa 2,954	P2
Cement 642	K5
Center 100	N5
Centrahoma 106	O5
Centralia	R1
Chandler▲ 2,596	N3
Chattanooga 437	J6
Checotah 3,290	R4
Chelsea 1,620	P1
Cherokee▲ 1,787	K1
Chester 104	J2
Cheyenne▲ 948	G3
Chickasha▲ 14,988	L4
Chilocco 400	M1
Choctaw 8,545	M3
Chouteau 1,771	R2
Christie 375	S3
Cimarron 71	L3
Claremore▲ 13,280	P2
Clarita 72	O6
Clayton 636	R5
Clearview 47	O4
Clemscot 52	L6
Cleo Springs 359	K2
Cleora 45	S1
Cleveland 3,156	O2
Clinton 9,298	H3
Cloud Chief 12	J4
Cloudy 175	R6
Coalgate▲ 1,895	O5
Cogar 40	K4
Colbert 1,043	O7
Colcord 628	S2
Cold Springs 24	J5
Cole 355	L4
Coleman 200	O6
Collinsville 3,612	P2
Colony 163	J4
Comanche 1,695	L6
Commerce 2,426	R1
Concho 300	L3
Connerville 150	N6
Cooperton 15	J5
Copan 809	P1
Cordell▲	H4
Corinne 100	R6
Corn 548	J4
Cornish 164	L6
Council Hill 139	P3
Countyline 550	L6
Courtney 12	L7
Covington 590	L2
Coweta 6,159	P3
Cowlington 756	S4
Cox City 285	L5
Coyle 289	M3
Crawford 53	G2
Crescent 1,236	L3
Cromwell 268	N4
Crowder 339	P4
Cumberland 100	N6
Curtis 30	H2
Cushing 7,218	N3
Custer City 443	J3
Cyril 1,072	K5
Dacoma 182	J1
Daisy 250	P5
Dale 160	M4
Darwin 50	P6
Davenport 979	N3
Davidson 473	J6
Davis 2,543	M5
Deer Creek 124	L1
Del City 23,928	L4
Dela 434	P6
Delaware 544	P1
Delhi 41	G4
Depew 502	O3
Devol 165	J6
Dewar 921	P4
Dewey 3,326	P1
Dibble 181	L4
Dickson 942	M6
Dill City 622	H4
Disney 750	S2
Dougherty 138	M6
Douglas 55	L2
Douthat 30	S1
Dover 376	L3
Dow 300	P5
Driftwood	K1
Drummond 408	L2
Drumright 2,799	N3
Duke (E. Duke) 360	G5
Duncan▲ 21,732	L5
Durant▲ 12,823	O6
Durham 30	G3
Dustin 429	O4
Eagle City 56	J3
Eagletown 650	S6
Eakly 277	K4
Earlsboro 535	N4
Edmond 52,315	M3
El Reno▲ 15,414	K3
Eldorado 573	G6
Elgin 975	K5
Elk City 10,428	G4
Elmer 132	H6
Elmore City 493	M5
Elmwood 300	F1
Empire City 219	L6
Enid▲ 45,309	L2
Enterprise 130	R4
Erick 1,083	G4
Eucha 210	S2
Eufaula▲ 2,652	P4
Fair Oaks 1,133	P2
Fairfax 1,749	N1
Fairland 916	S1
Fairmont 129	L2
Fairview▲ 2,936	J2
Fallis 49	M3
Fanshawe 331	S5
Fargo 299	G2
Farris 100	P6
Faxon 127	J6
Fay 140	J3
Featherston 75	P4
Felt 120	A1
Fillmore 60	N6
Finley 350	R6
Fittstown 500	N5
Fitzhugh 196	N5
Fleetwood 12	L7
Fletcher 1,002	K5
Foraker 25	O1
Forest Park 1,249	M3
Forgan 489	E1
Fort Cobb 663	K4
Fort Gibson 3,359	R3
Fort Supply 369	G1
Fort Towson 568	R7
Foss 148	H4
Foster 100	M5
Fox 400	M6
Foyil 86	R2
Francis 346	N5
Frederick▲ 5,221	H6
Freedom 264	H1
Gage 473	G2
Gans 218	S4
Garber 959	M2
Garvin 128	S7
Gate 159	F1
Geary 1,347	K3
Gene Autry 97	N6
Geronimo 990	K6
Gerty 95	O5
Glencoe 473	M2
Glenpool 6,688	P3
Glover 244	S6
Golden 300	S6
Goldsby 816	L4
Goltry 297	K1
Goodwater 240	S7
Goodwell 1,065	C1
Gore 690	R3
Gotebo 370	J4
Gould 237	G5
Gowen 75	R5
Gracemont 339	K4
Grady 85	L6
Graham 200	M6
Grainola 58	N1
Grand Lake Towne 58	S1
Grandfield 1,224	J6
Granite 1,844	H5
Grant	R7
Gray Horse 60	N1
Grayson 66	P3
Greenfield 200	K3
Griggs 15	B1
Grove 4,020	S1
Guthrie▲ 10,518	M3
Guymon▲ 7,803	D1
Haileyville 918	P5
Hall Park 1,090	M4
Hallett 159	N2
Hammon 611	H3
Hanna 99	P4
Hanson 250	S4
Harden City 250	N5
Hardesty 228	D1
Hardy	N1
Harjo 35	N4
Harmon 27	G2
Harrah 4,206	M4
Harris 192	S7
Hartshorne 2,120	R5
Haskell 2,143	P3
Hastings 164	K6
Haworth 293	S7
Haywood 175	P5
Headrick 183	H5
Healdton 2,872	M6
Heavener 2,601	S5
Helena 1,043	K1
Hendrix 108	O7
Hennepin 300	M5
Hennessey 1,902	L2
Henryetta 5,872	O4
Herd 18	O1
Hess 29	H6
Hester 25	H5
Hickory 77	N5
Hillsdale 96	K1
Hinton 1,233	K4
Hitchcock 139	K3
Hitchita 118	P3
Hobart▲ 4,305	J5
Hockerville 125	S1
Hodgen 150	S5
Hoffman 175	P4
Holdenville▲ 4,792	O4
Hollis▲ 2,584	G5
Hollister 59	J6
Homestead 35	K2
Hominy 2,342	O2
Honobia 80	R5
Hooker 1,551	D1
Hoot Owl 5	R2
Hopeton 42	J1
Howe 510	S5
Hoyt 160	R4
Hugo▲ 5,978	P7
Hulah 50	O1
Hulbert 499	R3
Humphreys 68	G5
Hunter 218	L1
Hydro 970	J3
Idabel▲ 6,957	S7
Indiahoma 337	J5

(continued on following page)

Agriculture, Industry and Resources

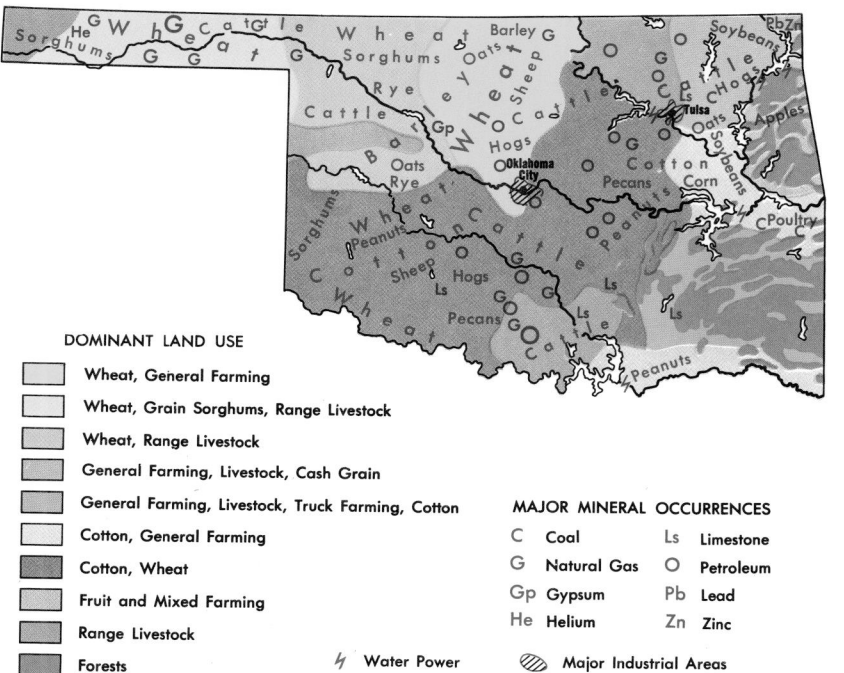

DOMINANT LAND USE

- Wheat, General Farming
- Wheat, Grain Sorghums, Range Livestock
- Wheat, Range Livestock
- General Farming, Livestock, Cash Grain
- General Farming, Livestock, Truck Farming, Cotton
- Cotton, General Farming
- Cotton, Wheat
- Fruit and Mixed Farming
- Range Livestock
- Forests

MAJOR MINERAL OCCURRENCES

C	Coal	Ls	Limestone
G	Natural Gas	O	Petroleum
Gp	Gypsum	Pb	Lead
He	Helium	Zn	Zinc

⚡ Water Power   ▨ Major Industrial Areas

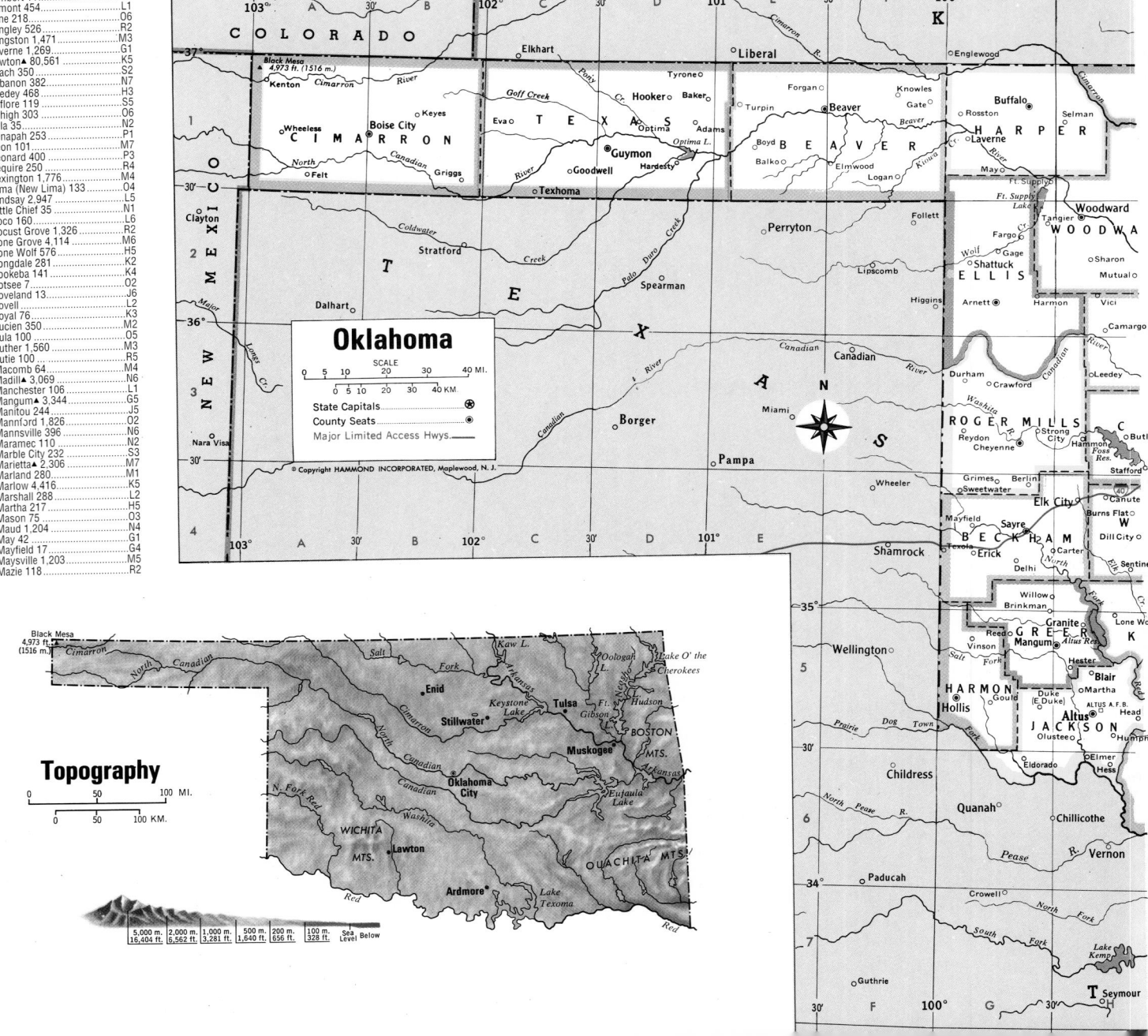

Oklahoma

SCALE
0 5 10 20 30 40 MI.
0 5 10 20 30 40 KM.

State Capitals ⊛
County Seats ◉
Major Limited Access Hwys. ────

© Copyright HAMMOND INCORPORATED, Maplewood, N.J.

Topography

0 50 100 MI.
0 50 100 KM.

5,000 m. 2,000 m. 1,000 m. 500 m. 200 m. 100 m. Sea Below
16,404 ft. 6,562 ft. 3,281 ft. 1,640 ft. 656 ft. 328 ft. Level

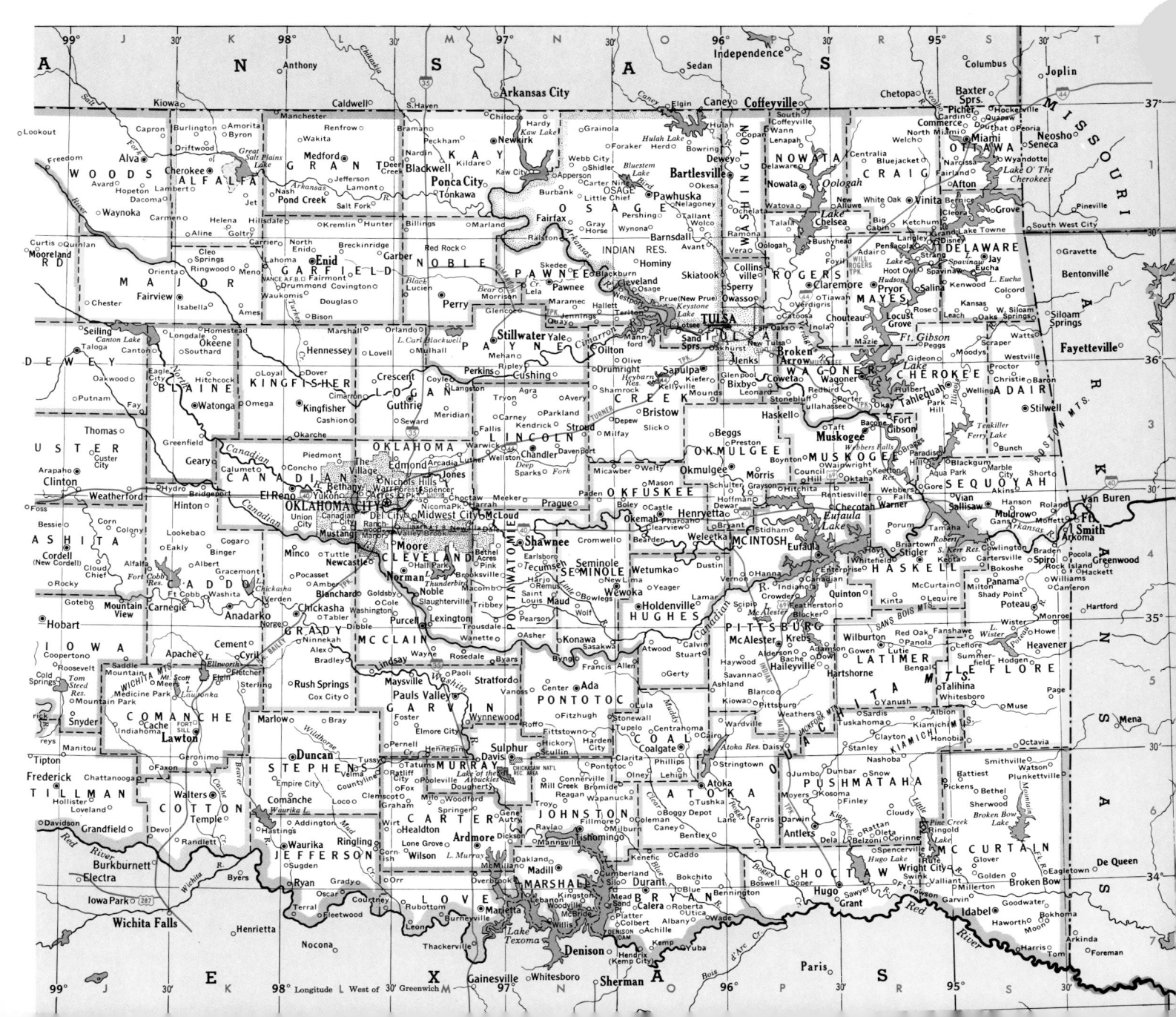

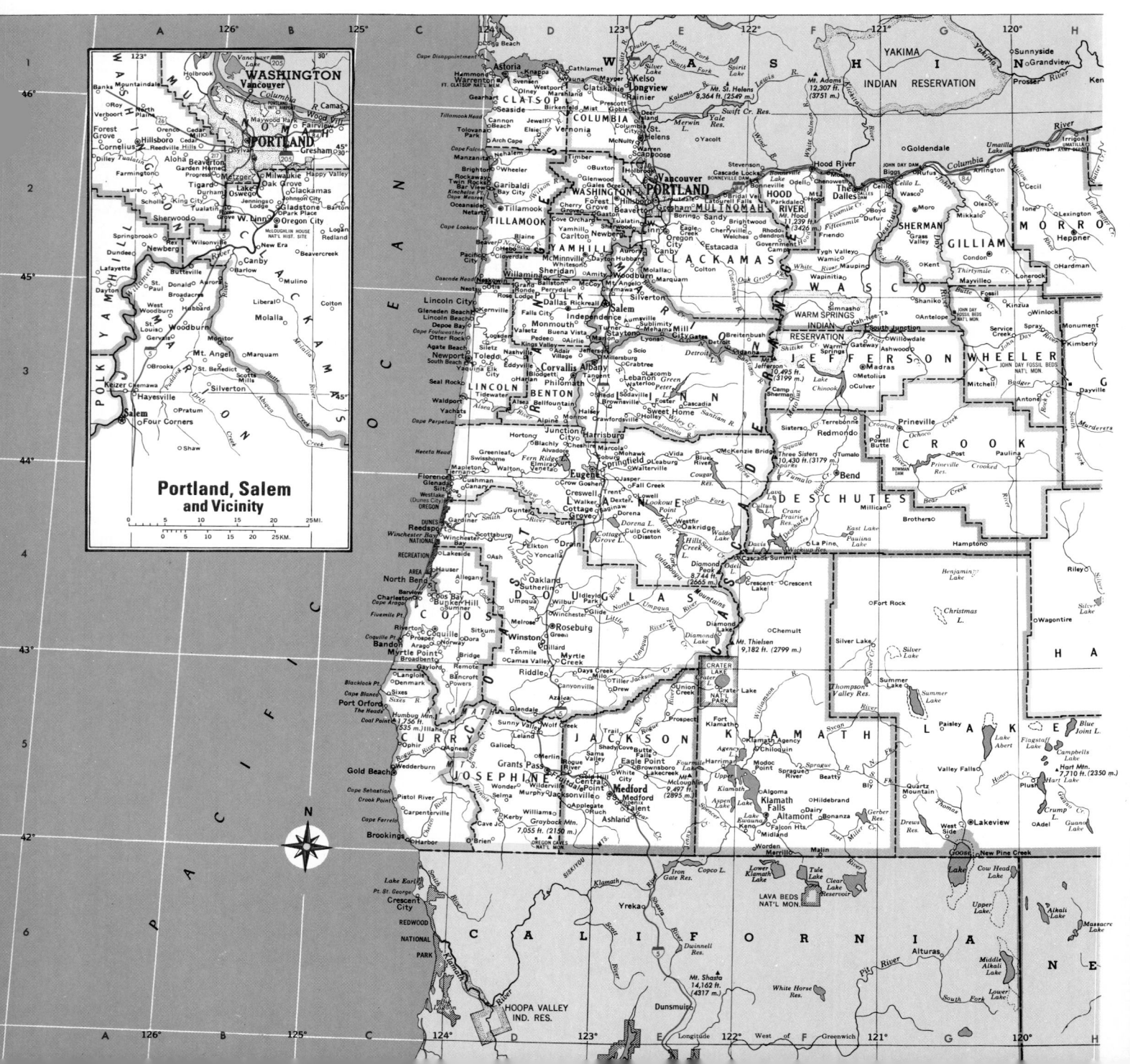

STATE OF OREGON
1859

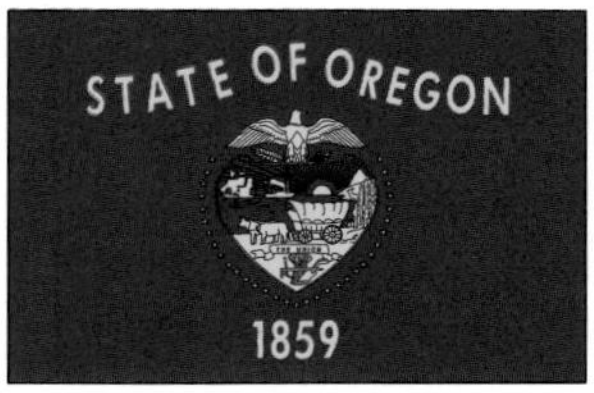

AREA 97,073 sq. mi. (251,419 sq. km.)
POPULATION 2,853,733
CAPITAL Salem
LARGEST CITY Portland
HIGHEST POINT Mt. Hood 11,239 ft. (3426 m.)
SETTLED IN 1810
ADMITTED TO UNION February 14, 1859
POPULAR NAME Beaver State
STATE FLOWER Oregon Grape
STATE BIRD Western Meadowlark

Crabtree 200	E3
Crane 84	J4
Crater Lake 36	E5
Crawfordsville 350	E3
Crescent 750	F4
Crescent Lake 120	F4
Creswell 2,431	D4
Crow 200	D4
Culp Creek 600	E4
Culver 570	F3
Curtin 350	D4
Cushman 175	D4
Dairy 80	F5
Dale 85	J3
Dallas▲ 9,422	D3
Dalles, The▲ 11,060	F2
Danner 12	K5
Days Creek 550	D5
Dayton 1,526	A3
Dayville 144	H3
Deer Island 225	E2
Denmark 15	C5
Depoe Bay 870	C3
Detroit 331	E3
Dexter 500	E4
Diamond 6	J4
Diamond Lake 56	E4
Dillard 602	D4
Dilley 250	A2
Disston 123	E4
Donald 316	A3
Dora 100	D4
Dorena 200	E4
Drain 1,011	D4
Drew 60	E5
Drewsey	J4
Dufur 527	F2
Dundee 1,663	A2
Dunes City (Westlake)	C4
Durham 748	A2
Durkee 158	K3
Eagle Creek 250	E2
Eagle Point 3,008	E5
Echo 499	H2
Eddyville 564	D3
Elgin 1,586	K2
Elk City 30	D3
Elkton 172	D4

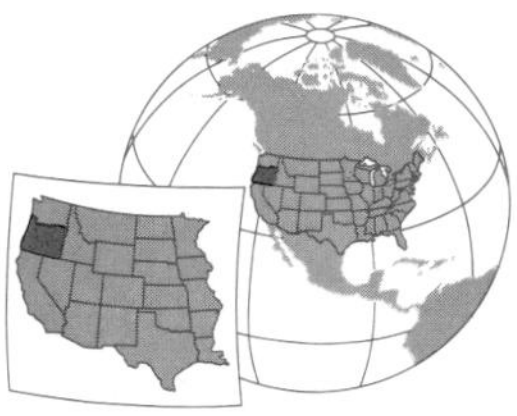

Topography

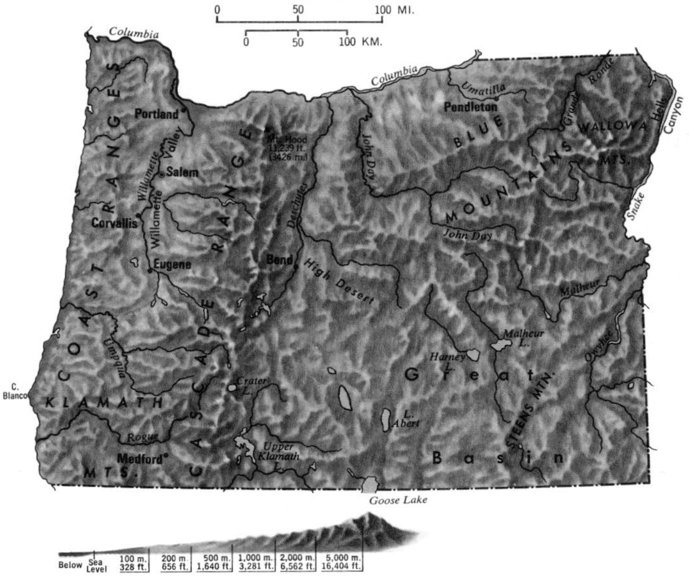

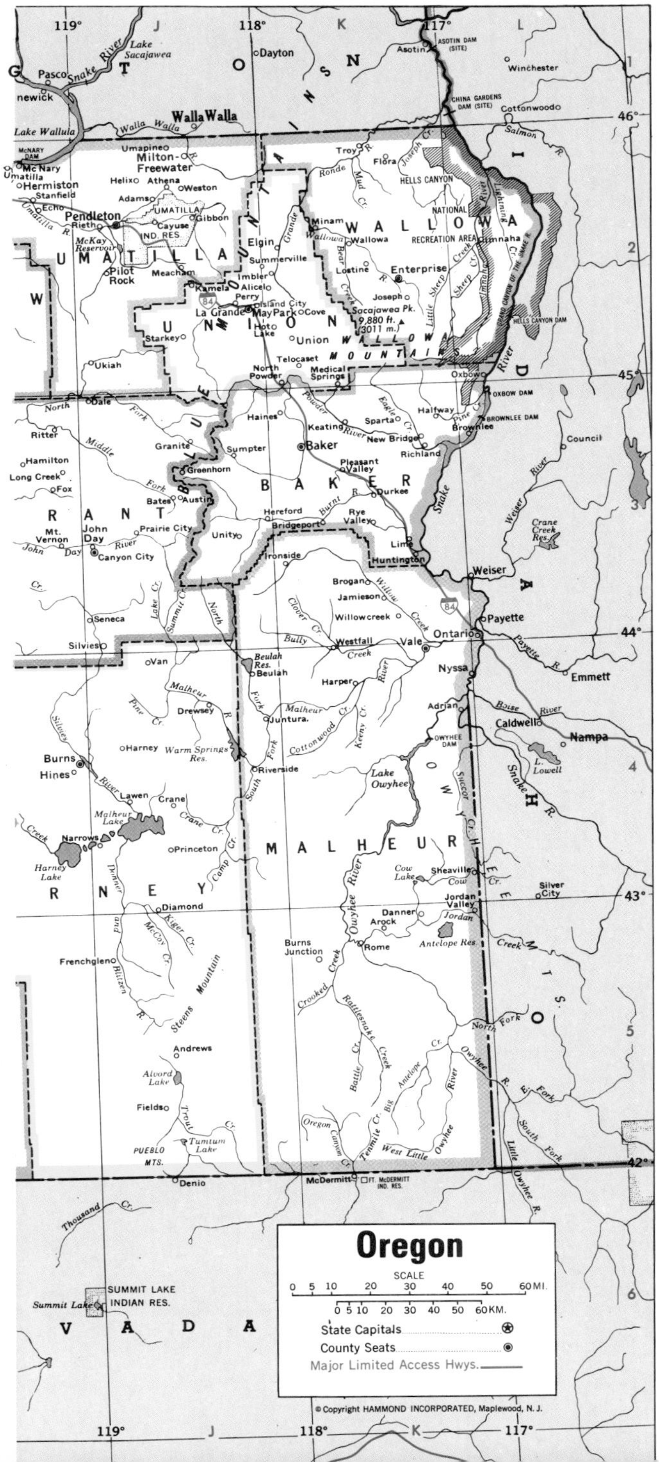

Elmira 900	D3
Elsie 30	D2
Enterprise▲ 1,905	K2
Estacada 1,419	E2
Eugene▲ 112,669	D3
Fairview 2,391	B2
Falcon Heights	F5
Fall Creek 58	E4
Falls City 818	D3
Farmington 100	A2
Fields 150	J5
Flora 45	K2
Florence 5,162	C4
Forest Grove 13,559	A2
Fort Klamath 200	E5
Fort Rock 150	G4
Fossil▲ 399	G2
Foster 850	E3
Four Corners 12,156	A3
Fox 30	H3
Frenchglen 45	H5
Fruitdale-Harbeck 4,733	D5
Gales Creek 150	D2
Galice 30	D5
Garden Home-Whitford 6,652	A2
Gardiner 750	C4
Garibaldi 877	D2
Gaston 563	D2
Gates 499	E3
Gateway 108	F3
Gaylord 80	C5
Gearhart 1,027	C1
Gervais 992	A3
Gibbon 300	J2
Gladstone 10,152	B2
Glenada 300	C4
Glendale 707	D5
Gleneden Beach 400	C3
Glenwood 225	D2
Glide 470	D4
Goble 108	E1
Gold Beach▲ 1,546	C5
Gold Hill 964	D5
Goshen 200	D4
Government Camp 230	F2
Grand Ronde 289	D2
Granite 8	J3
Grants Pass▲ 17,488	D5
Grass Valley 160	G2
Green 5,076	D4
Greenhorn 0	J3
Greenleaf 60	D3
Gresham 68,235	B2
Gunter 8	D4
Haines 405	J3
Halfway 311	K3
Halsey 667	D3
Hamilton 12	H3
Hammond 589	C1
Hampton 24	G4
Happy Valley 1,519	B2
Harbor 2,143	C5
Hardman	H2
Harlan 200	D3
Harney 15	J4
Harper 400	K4
Harriman 250	E5
Harrisburg 1,939	D3
Hauser 400	C4
Hayesville 14,318	A3
Hebo 400	D2
Helix 150	J2
Heppner▲ 1,412	H2
Hereford 128	K3
Hermiston 10,040	H2
Hildebrand 50	F5
Hillsboro▲ 37,520	A2
Hines 1,452	H4
Holbrook 494	A1
Holley 75	E3
Hood River▲ 4,632	F2
Horton 175	D3
Hubbard 1,881	A3
Huntington 522	K3
Idanha 289	F3
Idleyld Park 300	D4
Illahe 30	C5
Imbler 299	J2
Imnaha 150	L2
Independence 4,425	D3
Ione 255	H2
Ironside 50	K3
Irrigon 737	H2
Island City 696	K2
Jacksonville 1,896	D5
Jamieson 120	K3
Jasper 231	E3
Jefferson 1,805	D3
Jennings Lodge 6,530	B2
Jewell 10	D2
John Day 2,012	J3
Johnson City 586	B2
Jordan Valley 364	K5
Junction City 3,670	D3
Juntura	K4
Kah-Nee-Ta 100	F3
Kamela 11	J2
Keizer 21,884	A3
Keno 500	F5
Kent 200	G2
Kerby 650	D5
Kernville 450	D3
Kimberly 14	H3
King City 2,060	A2
Kings Valley 50	D3
Klamath Agency 10	F5
Klamath Falls▲ 17,737	F5
Knappa 950	D1
La Grande▲ 11,766	J2
La Pine 850	F4
Lacomb 425	E3
Lafayette 1,292	A2
Lake Oswego 30,576	B2
Lakecreek 160	E5
Lakeside 1,437	C4
Lakeview▲ 2,526	G5
Langlois 150	C5
Latourell Falls 40	E2
Lawen 95	J4
Leaburg 150	E3
Lebanon 10,950	E3
Leland 70	D5
Lexington 286	H2
Liberal 300	B3
Lime 25	K3
Lincoln Beach 1,507	C3
Lincoln City 5,892	C3
Logan 450	D3
Logsden 55	D3
Lonerock 11	H2
Long Creek 249	H3
Lostine 231	K2
Lowell 785	E4
Lyons 938	E3
Madras▲ 3,443	F3
Malin 725	F5
Manzanita 513	C2
Mapleton 950	C3
Marcola 900	E3
Marion 300	D3
Marquam 40	B3
Marshland 30	D1
Maupin 456	F2
May Park	J2
Mayger 35	D1
Mayville 25	G2
Maywood Park 781	B2
McCoy 40	D2
McKenzie Bridge 500	E3
McMinnville▲ 17,894	D2
McNary 330	H2
McNulty 1,805	E2
Meacham 150	J2
Medford▲ 46,951	E5
Mehama 250	D4
Melrose 30	D4
Merlin 500	D5
Merrill 837	F5
Metolius 513	F3
Metzger 3,149	A2
Midland 520	F5
Mikkalo 40	G2
Mill City 1,555	E3
Millersburg 715	E3
Milo 85	D4
Milton-Freewater 5,533	J2
Milwaukie 18,692	B2
Mist 40	D1
Mitchell 163	G3
Modoc Point 65	F5
Mohawk 50	E3
Molalla 3,651	B3
Monitor 82	B3
Monmouth 6,288	D3
Monroe 448	D3
Monument 162	H3
Moro▲ 292	G2
Mosier 244	F2
Mount Angel 2,778	B3
Mount Hood 2,234	F2
Mount Vernon 538	H3
Mountaindale 25	A1
Muling 720	B2
Murphy 500	D5
Myrtle Creek 3,063	D4
Myrtle Point 2,712	C4
Nashville 23	D3
Nehalem 232	D2
Neotsu 300	C2
Neskowin 250	D2
Netarts 975	C2
New Bridge 28	K3
New Era 27	B2
New Pine Creek 400	G5
Newberg 13,086	A2
Newport▲ 8,437	C3
North Bend 9,614	C4
North Plains 972	A2
North Powder 448	K2
Norway 150	C4
Nyssa 2,629	K4
O'Brien 850	D5
Oak Grove 12,576	B2
Oakland 844	D4
Oakridge 3,063	E4
Oceanside 300	C2
Odell 450	F2
Olex 40	G2
Olney 75	D1
Ontario 9,392	K3
Ophir 275	C5
Oregon City▲ 14,698	B2
Orenco 220	A2
Otis 200	D2
Otter Rock 450	C3
Oxbow 100	L2
Pacific City 500	C2
Paisley 350	G5
Park Place 500	B2
Parkdale 350	F2
Paulina 80	G3
Pedee 45	D3
Pendleton▲ 15,126	J2
Perry 50	J2
Perrydale 200	D2

(continued on following page)

Oregon

SCALE
0 5 10   20   30   40   50   60 MI.
0 5 10   20   30   40   50   60 KM.

State Capitals ... ✪
County Seats ... ⊛
Major Limited Access Hwys. ...

© Copyright HAMMOND INCORPORATED, Maplewood, N.J.

Agriculture, Industry and Resources

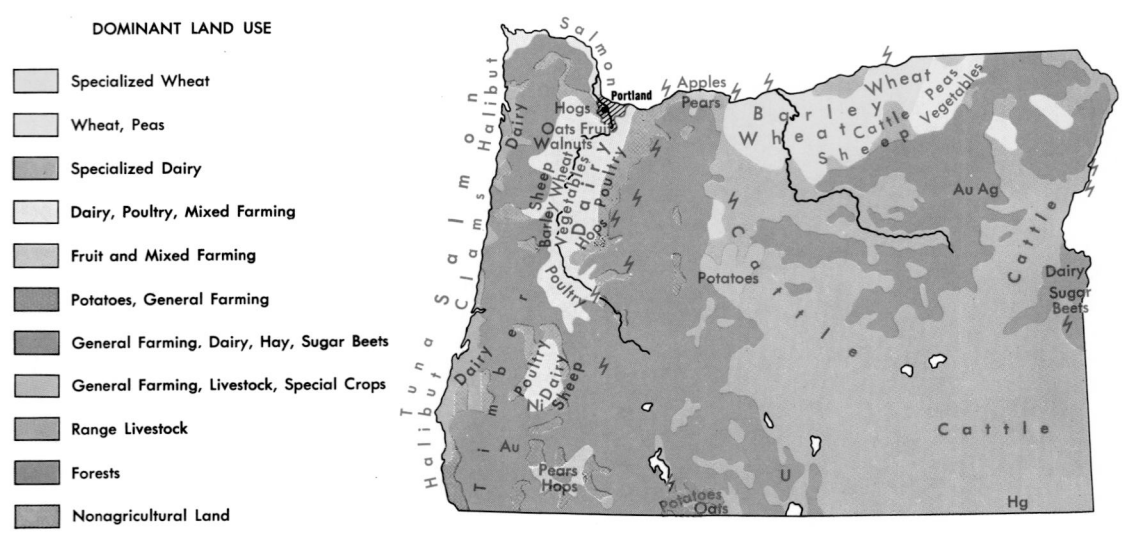

DOMINANT LAND USE

- Specialized Wheat
- Wheat, Peas
- Specialized Dairy
- Dairy, Poultry, Mixed Farming
- Fruit and Mixed Farming
- Potatoes, General Farming
- General Farming, Dairy, Hay, Sugar Beets
- General Farming, Livestock, Special Crops
- Range Livestock
- Forests
- Nonagricultural Land

MAJOR MINERAL OCCURRENCES

Ag Silver   Hg Mercury

Au Gold   Ni Nickel

U Uranium

⚡ Water Power

▨ Major Industrial Areas

DOMINANT LAND USE

- Specialized Dairy
- Dairy, General Farming
- Fruit and Mixed Farming
- Fruit, Truck and Mixed Farming
- General Farming, Livestock, Tobacco
- General Farming, Livestock, Fruit, Tobacco
- Forests
- Urban Areas

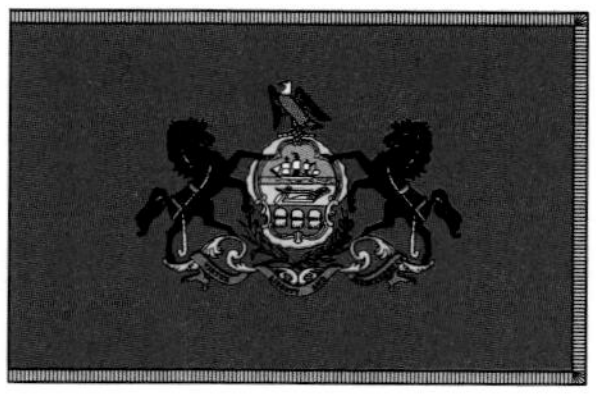

AREA 45,308 sq. mi. (117,348 sq. km.)
POPULATION 11,924,710
CAPITAL Harrisburg
LARGEST CITY Philadelphia
HIGHEST POINT Mt. Davis 3,213 ft. (979 m.)
SETTLED IN 1682
ADMITTED TO UNION December 12, 1787
POPULAR NAME Keystone State
STATE FLOWER Mountain Laurel
STATE BIRD Ruffed Grouse

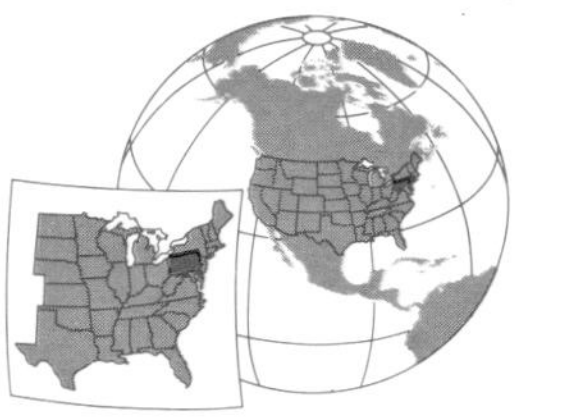

MAJOR MINERAL OCCURRENCES

C Coal
Cl Clay
Co Cobalt
Fe Iron Ore
G Natural Gas
Ls Limestone
O Petroleum
Sl Slate
Ss Sandstone
Zn Zinc

Water Power
Major Industrial Areas

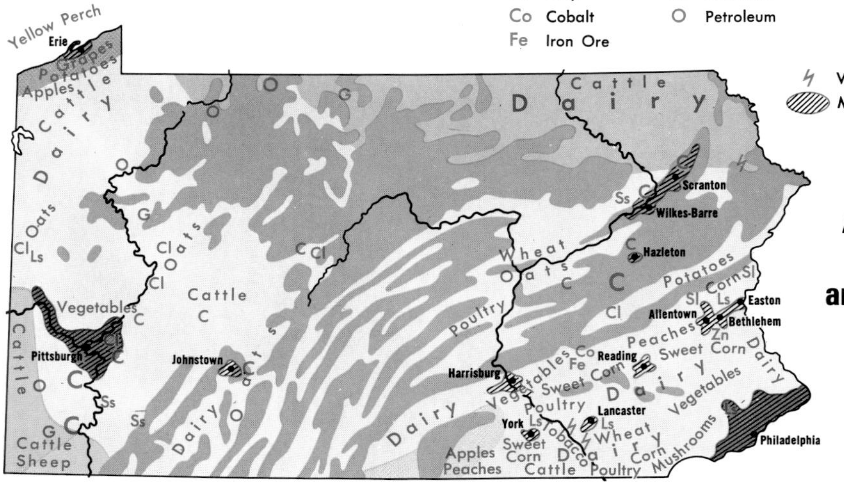

Agriculture, Industry and Resources

COUNTIES

Adams 78,274 ....H6
Allegheny 1,336,449 ....B5
Armstrong 73,478 ....D4
Beaver 186,093 ....B4
Bedford 47,919 ....E6
Berks 336,523 ....K5
Blair 130,542 ....F4
Bradford 60,967 ....J2
Bucks 541,174 ....M5
Butler 152,013 ....C4
Cambria 163,029 ....E4
Cameron 5,913 ....F3
Carbon 56,846 ....L4
Centre 123,786 ....G4
Chester 376,396 ....L6
Clarion 41,699 ....D3
Clearfield 78,097 ....F3
Clinton 37,182 ....G3
Columbia 63,202 ....K3
Crawford 86,169 ....B2
Cumberland 195,257 ....H5
Dauphin 237,813 ....J5
Delaware 547,651 ....M6
Elk 34,878 ....E3
Erie 275,572 ....B2
Fayette 145,351 ....C6
Forest 4,802 ....D2
Franklin 121,082 ....G6
Fulton 13,837 ....F6
Greene 39,550 ....B6
Huntingdon 44,164 ....F5
Indiana 89,994 ....D4
Jefferson 46,083 ....D3
Juniata 20,625 ....H4
Lackawanna 219,039 ....L3
Lancaster 422,822 ....K5
Lawrence 96,246 ....B4
Lebanon 113,744 ....K5
Lehigh 291,130 ....L4
Luzerne 328,149 ....L3
Lycoming 118,710 ....H3
McKean 50,635 ....E2
Mercer 121,003 ....B3
Mifflin 46,197 ....G4
Monroe 95,709 ....M3
Montgomery 678,111 ....M5
Montour 17,735 ....J3
Northampton 247,105 ....M4
Northumberland 96,771 ....J4
Perry 41,172 ....H5
Philadelphia (city county)
1,688,210 ....M6
Pike 27,966 ....M3
Potter 16,717 ....G2
Schuylkill 152,585 ....K4
Snyder 36,680 ....H4
Somerset 78,218 ....D6
Sullivan 6,104 ....J3
Susquehanna 40,380 ....L2
Tioga 41,126 ....H2
Union 36,176 ....H4
Venango 59,381 ....C3
Warren 45,050 ....D2
Washington 204,584 ....B5
Wayne 39,944 ....M2
Westmoreland 370,321 ....D5
Wyoming 28,076 ....K2
York 339,574 ....J6

CITIES and TOWNS

Abbottstown 539 ....J6
Abington• 58,836 ....M5
Adamstown 1,108 ....K5
Akron 3,869 ....K5
Albion 1,575 ....B2
Alburtis 1,415 ....L5
Aldan 4,549 ....M7
Alexandria 411 ....F4
Aliquippa 13,374 ....B4
Allentown▲ 105,090 ....L4
Allison Park 10,000 ....C4
Altoona 51,881 ....F4
Ambler 6,609 ....M5
Ambridge 8,133 ....B4
Annville 4,294 ....J5
Apollo 1,895 ....C4
Archbald 6,291 ....F6
Ardmore 12,646 ....M6
Arendtsville 693 ....H6
Arnold 6,113 ....C4
Ashland 3,859 ....K4
Ashley 3,291 ....E7
Aspinwall 2,880 ....C6
Atglen 825 ....K6
Athens 3,468 ....K2
Atlas 1,162 ....K4
Auburn 913 ....K4
Austin 569 ....F2
Avalon 5,784 ....B6
Avella 900 ....B5
Avis 1,506 ....H3
Avoca 2,897 ....F7
Avondale 954 ....L6
Avonmore 1,089 ....C4
Baden 5,074 ....B4
Bala-Cynwyd N6
Baldwin 21,923 ....B7
Bally 973 ....L5
Bangor 5,383 ....M4
Barnesboro 2,530 ....E4
Bath 2,358 ....M4
Beallsville 530 ....C5
Beaver Falls 10,687 ....B4
Beaver Meadows 985 ....L4
Beaver▲ 5,028 ....B4
Beaverdale 1,187 ....E5
Beavertown 853 ....H4
Bedford▲ 3,137 ....F5
Beech Creek 716 ....G3
Belle Vernon 1,213 ....C5
Bellefonte▲ 6,358 ....G4
Belleville 1,589 ....G4
Bellevue 9,126 ....B6
Bellwood 1,976 ....F4
Ben Avon 2,096 ....B6
Bendersville 560 ....H6
Bentleyville 2,673 ....B5
Benton 958 ....K3
Berlin 2,064 ....E6
Bernville 789 ....K5
Berrysburg 376 ....J4
Berwick 10,976 ....K3
Berwyn Devon 5,019 ....L5
Bessemer 1,196 ....B4
Bethel Park 33,823 ....B7
Bethlehem 71,428 ....M4
Big Run 699 ....E4
Biglerville 993 ....H6
Birdsboro 4,222 ....L5
Black Lick 1,100 ....D4
Blairsville 3,595 ....D5
Blakely 7,222 ....F6
Blawnox 1,626 ....C6
Bloomfield (New Bloomfield)▲
1,092 ....H5
Blooming Valley 391 ....B2
Bloomsburg▲ 12,439 ....J3
Blossburg 1,571 ....H2
Boalsburg 2,206 ....G4
Bobtown 1,008 ....B6
Boiling Springs 1,978 ....H5
Bolivar 544 ....D5
Boothwyn 5,069 ....L7
Boswell 1,485 ....E5
Bowmanstown 888 ....L4
Boyertown 3,759 ....L5
Brackenridge 3,784 ....C4
Braddock 4,682 ....C7
Bradford 9,625 ....E2
Brentwood 10,823 ....B7
Briar Creek 616 ....K3
Brickerville 1,268 ....K5
Bridgeport 4,292 ....M5
Bridgeville 5,445 ....B5
Bridgewater 751 ....B4
Brisbin 369 ....F4
Bristol 10,405 ....N5
Bristol• 587,330 ....N5
Broad Top 331 ....F5
Brockway 2,207 ....E3
Brodheadsville 1,389 ....M4
Brookhaven 8,567 ....M7
Brookville▲ 4,184 ....D3
Broomall 10,930 ....M6
Brownstown 937 ....K5
Brownsville 3,164 ....C5
Bruin 646 ....C3
Bryn Athyn 1,081 ....M5
Bryn Mawr 3,271 ....M5
Burgettstown 1,634 ....A5
Burlington 479 ....J2
Burnham 2,197 ....H4
Burnside 350 ....E4
Butler▲ 15,714 ....C4
Cadogan• 459 ....C4
Cairnbrook 1,081 ....E5
California 5,748 ....C5
Callery 420 ....C4
Cambridge Springs 1,837 ....C2
Camp Hill 7,831 ....H5
Canonsburg 9,200 ....B5
Canton 1,966 ....J2
Carbondale 10,664 ....L2
Carlisle▲ 18,419 ....H5
Carmichaels 532 ....B6
Carnegie 9,278 ....B7
Carroll Valley 1,457 ....H6
Carrolltown 1,286 ....E4
Castle Shannon 9,135 ....B7
Catasauqua 6,662 ....M4
Catawissa 1,683 ....K4
Centerville 4,207 ....B6
Central City 1,246 ....E5
Centre Hall 1,203 ....G4
Chalfont 3,069 ....M5
Chambersburg▲ 16,647 ....G6
Charleroi 5,014 ....C5
Cheltenham• 35,509 ....M5
Cherry Tree 431 ....E4
Chester 41,856 ....L7
Chester Heights 2,273 ....L7
Chester Hill 945 ....F4
Cheswick 1,971 ....C6
Chicora 1,058 ....C4
Christiana 1,045 ....K6
Churchill 3,883 ....C7
Clairton 9,656 ....C7
Clarendon 650 ....D2
Clarion▲ 6,457 ....D3
Clark (Clarksville) 610 ....B3
Clarks Green 1,603 ....F6
Clarks Summit 5,433 ....F6
Claysburg 1,399 ....F5
Claysville 962 ....B5
Clearfield▲ 6,633 ....F3
Clifton Heights 7,111 ....M7
Clintonville 520 ....C3
Clymer 1,499 ....E4
Coalport 578 ....E4
Coatesville 11,038 ....L5
Cochranton 1,174 ....B2
Codorus (Jefferson) 685 ....J6
Cokeburg 724 ....B5
Collegeville 4,227 ....M5
Collingdale 9,175 ....N7
Columbia 10,701 ....K5
Colver 1,024 ....E4
Colwyn 2,613 ....N7
Confluence 873 ....D6
Conneaut Lake 699 ....B2
Conneautville 822 ....A2
Connellsville 9,229 ....C5
Connoquenessing 507 ....B4
Conshohocken 8,064 ....M5
Conway 2,424 ....B4
Conyngham 2,060 ....K3
Coopersburg 2,599 ....M5
Cooperstown 506 ....C2
Coplay 3,267 ....L4
Coraopolis 6,747 ....B4
Cornwall 3,231 ....K5
Corry 7,216 ....C2
Coudersport▲ 2,854 ....G2
Crabtree 900 ....D5
Crafton 7,188 ....B7
Cranesville 598 ....B2
Cresson 1,784 ....E5
Cressona 1,694 ....K4
Cross Roads 322 ....J6
Curwensville 2,924 ....E4
Dale 1,642 ....E5
Dallas 2,567 ....E7
Dallastown 3,974 ....J6
Dalton 1,369 ....L2
Danville▲ 5,165 ....J4
Darby 10,955 ....M7
Dauphin 845 ....J5
Dayton 572 ....D4
Delaware Water Gap 733 ....M4
Delmont 2,041 ....D5
Delta 761 ....K6
Denver 2,861 ....K5
Derry 2,950 ....D5
Dickson City 6,276 ....F7
Dillsburg 1,925 ....J5
Donora 5,928 ....C5
Dormont 9,772 ....B7
Dover 1,884 ....J6
Downingtown 7,749 ....L5
Doylestown▲ 8,575 ....M5
Dravosburg 2,377 ....C7
Drexel Hill 29,744 ....M6
Drifton 1,786 ....L3
DuBois 8,286 ....E3
Dublin 1,985 ....M5
Duboistown 1,201 ....H3
Dunbar 1,213 ....C6
Duncannon 1,450 ....H5
Duncansville 1,309 ....F5
Dunmore 15,403 ....F7
Dupont 2,984 ....F7
Duquesne 8,525 ....C7
Duryea 4,869 ....F7
Dushore 738 ....K2
East Bangor 1,006 ....M4
East Berlin 1,175 ....J6
East Berwick 2,128 ....K3
East Brady 1,047 ....C3
East Butler 725 ....C4
East Conemaugh 1,470 ....E5
East Faxon 3,951 ....J3
East Greenville 3,117 ....L5
East Lansdowne 2,691 ....M7
East Petersburg 4,197 ....K5
East Pittsburgh 2,160 ....C7
East Prospect 558 ....J6
East Stroudsburg 8,781 ....M4
East Washington 2,126 ....B5
Easton▲ 26,276 ....M4
Eau Claire 371 ....C3
Ebensburg▲ 3,872 ....E5
Economy 9,519 ....B4
Eddystone 2,446 ....M7
Edgewood 2,719 ....B7
Edgeworth 1,670 ....B4
Edinboro 7,736 ....B2
Edwardsville 5,399 ....E7
Elderton 371 ....D4
Eldred 869 ....F2
Elizabeth 1,610 ....C5
Elizabethtown 9,952 ....J5
Elizabethville 1,467 ....J4
Elkland 1,849 ....H1
Ellsworth 1,048 ....B5
Ellwood City 8,894 ....B4
Elverson 470 ....L5
Elysburg 1,890 ....K4
Emigsville 2,580 ....J5
Emlenton 834 ....C3
Emmaus 11,157 ....M4
Emporium▲ 2,513 ....F2
Emsworth 2,892 ....B6
Enola 5,961 ....J5
Enon Valley 355 ....B4
Ephrata 12,133 ....K5
Erie▲ 108,718 ....B1
Ernest 492 ....D4
Espy 1,430 ....K4
Etna 4,200 ....B6
Etters (Goldsboro) 477 ....J5
Evans City 2,054 ....B4
Everett 1,777 ....F5
Everson 939 ....C5
Exeter 5,691 ....F7
Export 981 ....C5
Factoryville 1,310 ....L2
Fairchance 1,918 ....C6
Fairfield 524 ....H6
Fairless Hills 9,026 ....N5
Falls Creek 1,087 ....E3
Farrell 6,841 ....A3
Fawn Grove 489 ....J6
Fayette City 713 ....C5
Fayetteville 3,033 ....G6
Felton 438 ....J6
Ferndale 2,020 ....E5
Finleyville 446 ....B5
Fleetwood 3,478 ....L5
Fleming (Unionville) 361 ....G4
Flemington 1,321 ....G3
Folcroft 7,506 ....M7
Folsom 8,173 ....M7
Ford City 3,413 ....D4
Ford Cliff 450 ....D4
Forest City 1,846 ....L2
Forest Hills 7,335 ....C7
Forty Fort 5,049 ....F7
Fountain Hill 4,637 ....L4
Fox Chapel 5,319 ....C6
Frackville 4,700 ....K4
Franklin▲ 7,329 ....C3
Franklintown 373 ....H5
Fredericksburg 1,269 ....B2
Fredericktown 1,052 ....C6
Fredonia 683 ....B3
Freeburg 640 ....H4
Freedom 1,897 ....B4
Freeland 3,909 ....L3
Freemansburg 1,946 ....M4
Freeport 1,983 ....C4
Galeton 1,370 ....G2
Gallitzin 2,003 ....E4
Gap 1,226 ....L6
Garden View 2,687 ....H3
Garrett 520 ....D6
Geistown 2,749 ....E5
Gettysburg▲ 7,025 ....H6
Gilberton 953 ....K4
Girard 2,879 ....B2
Girardville 1,889 ....K4
Glassport 5,582 ....C7
Glen Lyon 2,082 ....E7
Glen Rock 1,688 ....J6
Glenolden 7,260 ....M7
Glenside 8,704 ....M5
Grampian 395 ....E4
Gratz 696 ....J4
Great Bend 704 ....L2
Greencastle 3,600 ....G6
Greensburg▲ 16,318 ....D5
Greentree 4,905 ....B7
Greenville 6,734 ....B3
Grove City 8,240 ....B3
Halifax 911 ....J5
Hallstead 1,274 ....L2
Hamburg 3,987 ....L4
Hanover 14,399 ....J6
Harmony 1,054 ....B4
Harrisburg (cap.)▲ 52,376 ....H5
Harrisville 862 ....B3
Harveys Lake 2,746 ....E7
Hastings 1,431 ....E4
Hatboro 7,382 ....M5
Hatfield 2,650 ....M5
Haverford• 52,371 ....M6
Havertown M6
Hawley 1,244 ....M3
Hawthorn 528 ....D3
Hazleton 24,730 ....L4
Heidelberg 1,238 ....B7
Hellam (Hallam) 1,428 ....J6
Hellertown 5,662 ....M4
Herndon 422 ....J4
Hershey 11,860 ....J5
Highland Park 1,583 ....H4
Highspire 2,668 ....J5
Hollidaysburg▲ 5,624 ....F5
Homer City 1,809 ....D4
Homestead 4,179 ....B7
Honesdale▲ 4,972 ....M2
Honey Brook 1,184 ....L5
Hooversville 731 ....E5
Hop Bottom 345 ....L2
Hopwood 2,021 ....C6
Houston 1,445 ....B5
Houtzdale 1,204 ....F4
Howard 749 ....G3
Hughestown 1,734 ....F7
Hughesville 2,049 ....J3
Hummelstown 3,981 ....J5
Huntingdon▲ 6,843 ....G5
Hyde 1,643 ....F4
Hyde Park 542 ....D4
Hydetown 681 ....C2
Hyndman 1,019 ....E6
Imperial-Enlow 3,449 ....B5
Indian Lake 388 ....E5
Indiana▲ 15,174 ....D4
Industry 2,124 ....B4
Ingram 3,901 ....B7
Irvona 666 ....E4
Irwin 4,604 ....C5
Jacobus 1,370 ....J6
Jamestown 761 ....A3
Jeannette 11,221 ....C5
Jenkintown 4,574 ....M5
Jennerstown 635 ....D5
Jermyn 2,263 ....L2
Jerome 1,074 ....D5
Jersey Shore 4,353 ....H3
Jessup 4,605 ....F6
Jim Thorpe (Mauch Chunk)▲
5,048 ....L4

(continued on following page)

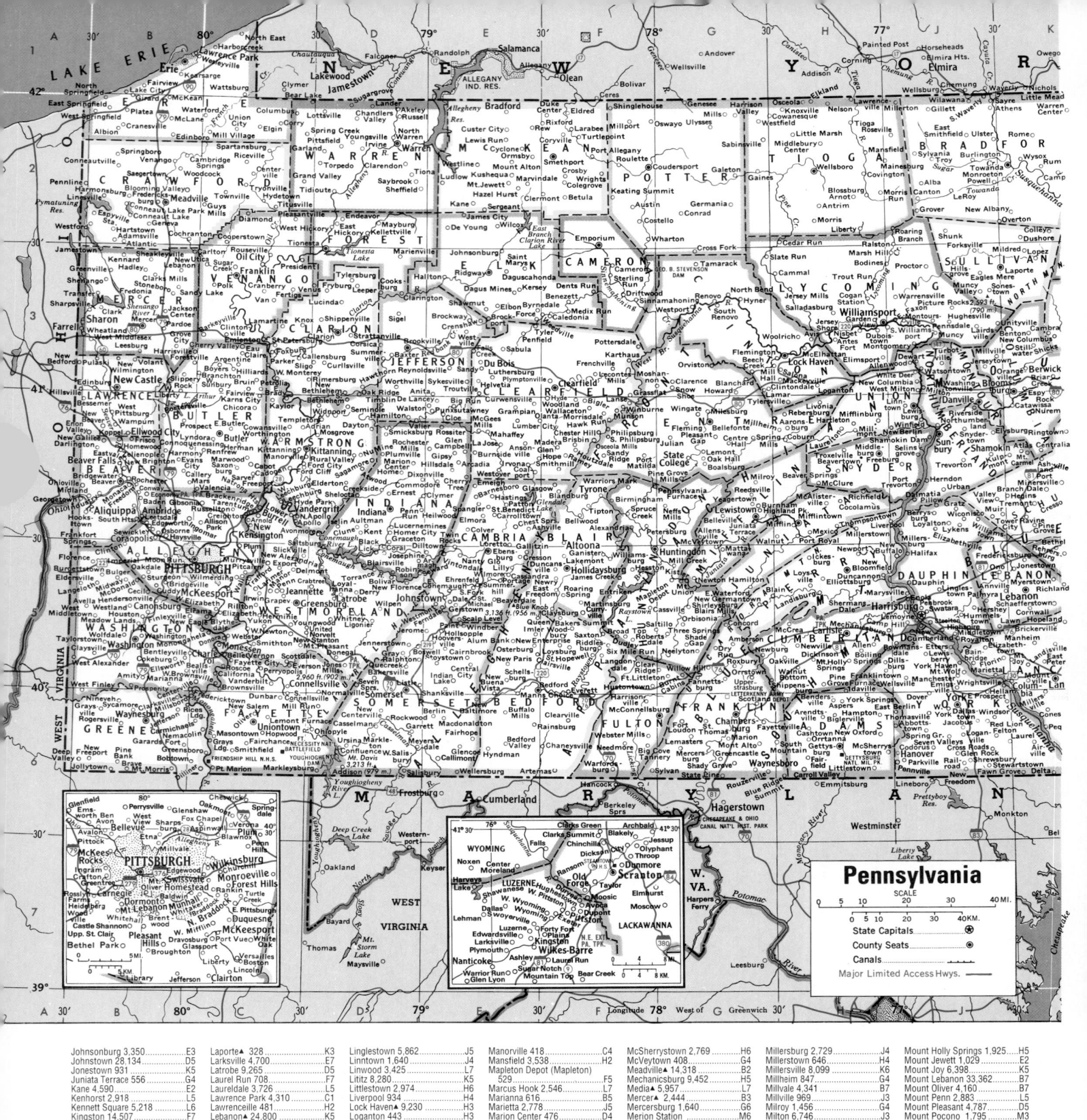

Petersburg 469	G4
Philadelphia▲ 1,585,577	N6
Philipsburg 3,048	F4
Phoenixville 15,066	L5
Picture Rocks 660	J3
Pillow 341	J4
Pine Grove 2,118	K4
Pine Grove Mills 1,129	G4
Pitcairn 4,087	C5
Pittsburgh▲ 369,879	B7
Pittston 9,389	F7
Plains 4,694	F7
Platea 467	B2
Pleasant Gap 1,699	G4
Pleasant Hills 8,884	B7
Plum 25,609	C5
Plumville 390	D4
Plymouth 7,134	F7
Plymptonville 1,074	E3
Pocono Pines 824	M3
Point Marion 1,344	C6
Polk 1,267	C3
Port Allegany 2,391	F2
Port Carbon 2,134	K4
Port Matilda 669	F4
Port Royal 836	H4
Port Vue 4,641	C7
Portage 3,105	E5
Portland 516	M4
Pottstown 21,831	L5
Pottsville▲ 16,603	K4
Prospect 1,122	B4
Prospect Park 6,764	M7
Punxsutawney 6,782	E4
Quakertown 8,982	M5
Quarryville 1,642	K6
Ramey 536	F4
Rankin 2,503	C7
Reading▲ 78,380	L5
Reamstown 2,649	K5
Red Hill 1,794	L5
Red Lion 6,130	J6
Reedsville 1,023	G4
Renovo 1,526	G3
Reynoldsville 2,818	D3
Rices Landing 457	C6
Richland 1,457	K5
Richlandtown 1,195	M5
Ridgway▲ 4,793	E3
Ridley Park 7,592	M7
Riegelsville 912	M4
Rimersburg 1,053	D3
Ringtown 853	K4
Riverside 1,991	J4
Roaring Spring 2,615	F5
Robesonia 1,944	K5
Rochester 4,156	B4
Rockledge 2,679	M5
Rockwood 1,014	D6
Rome 475	K2
Roscoe 872	C6
Rose Valley 982	L7
Roseto 1,555	M4
Rosslyn Farms 483	C7
Rouseville 583	C3
Rouzerville 1,188	G6
Royalton 1,120	J5
Royersford 4,458	L5
Rural Valley 957	D4
Russellton 1,691	C4
Rutledge 843	M7
Saegertown 1,066	B2
Saint Clair 3,524	K4
Saint Marys 5,511	E3
Saint Michael-Sidman 1,189	E5
Saint Petersburg 349	C3
Salisbury 716	D6
Saltillo 347	G5
Saltsburg 990	D5
Sandy 1,795	E3
Sandy Lake 722	B3
Saxonburg 1,345	C4
Saxton 838	F5
Sayre 5,791	K2
Scalp Level 1,158	E5

Schnecksville 1,780	L4
Schuylkill Haven 5,610	K4
Schwenksville 1,326	L5
Scottdale 5,184	C5
Scranton▲ 81,805	F7
Selinsgrove 5,384	J4
Sellersville 4,479	M5
Seven Valleys 483	J6
Seward 522	E5
Sewickley 4,134	B4
Shamokin 9,184	J4
Shamokin Dam 1,690	J4
Sharon 17,493	B3
Sharon Hill 5,771	N7
Sharpsburg 3,781	B6
Sharpsville 4,729	A3
Sheffield 1,294	D2
Shenandoah 6,221	K4
Shickshinny 1,108	K3
Shillington 5,062	K5
Shinglehouse 1,243	F2
Shippensburg 5,331	H5
Shippenville 474	D3
Shoemakersville 1,443	K4
Shrewsbury 2,672	J6
Sinking Spring 2,467	K5
Skippack 2,042	M5
Slatington 4,678	L4
Slickville 1,178	C5
Sligo 706	C3
Slippery Rock 3,008	B3
Smethport▲ 1,734	F2
Smithfield 1,000	C6
Smithton 388	C5
Snow Shoe 800	G3
Snydertown 416	J4
Somerset▲ 6,454	D6
Souderton 5,957	M5
South Bethlehem 479	D4
South Connellsville 2,204	C6
South Fork 1,197	E5
South Heights 647	B4
South Philipsburg 438	F4
South Renovo 579	G3
South Waverly 1,049	J2
South Williamsport 6,496	J3
Spangler 2,068	E4
Spartansburg 403	C2
Spring City 3,433	L5
Spring Grove 1,863	J6
Springboro 597	B2
Springdale 3,992	C5
Springfield 24,160	M7
State College 38,923	G4
State Line 1,253	H6
Steelton 5,152	J5
Stewartstown 1,308	K6
Stockertown 641	M4
Stoneboro 1,091	B3
Stowe 3,598	L5
Stoystown 389	E5
Strasburg 2,568	K6
Strattanville 490	D3
Strausstown 353	K5
Stroudsburg▲ 5,312	M4
Sturgeon 1,312	B5
Sugar Creek 5,532	C3
Sugar Notch 1,044	E7
Sugargrove 630	D1
Summerhill 614	E5
Summerville 675	D3
Summit Hill 3,332	L4
Sunbury▲ 11,591	J4
Susquehanna 1,994	L2
Swarthmore 6,157	M7
Swatara 18,796	J5
Swissvale 10,637	C7
Swoyerville 5,630	E7
Sykesville 1,387	E3
Tamaqua 7,943	L4
Tarentum 5,674	C4
Tatamy 873	M4
Taylor 6,941	F7
Telford 4,238	M5
Temple 1,491	L5

Terre Hill 1,282	L5
Thompsontown 582	H4
Three Springs 422	G5
Throop 4,070	F7
Tidioute 791	D2
Tioga 638	H2
Tionesta▲ 623	D2
Tipton 1,194	F4
Titusville 6,434	C2
Topton 1,987	L5
Towanda▲ 3,242	J2
Tower City 1,518	J4
Townville 358	C2
Trafford 3,537	C5
Trainer 2,271	L7
Tremont 1,814	K4
Tresckow 1,033	K4
Trevorton 2,058	J4
Troy 1,262	J2
Trumbauersville 894	M5
Tullytown 2,339	N5
Tunkhannock▲ 2,251	L2
Turbotville 675	J3
Turtle Creek 6,556	C7
Tyrone 5,743	F4
Ulysses (Lewisville) 653	G2
Union City 3,537	C2
Uniontown▲ 12,034	C6
Upland 3,334	L7
Upper Darby ● 84,054	M6
Upper Saint Claire ● 19,023	B7
Valencia 364	C4
Valley Forge 400	L5
Valley View 1,749	J4
Vanderbilt 635	C5
Vandergrift 5,904	C4
Vandling 660	M2
Verona 3,260	C6
Versailles 2,150	C7
Villanova	M6
Vintondale 582	E5
Wall 853	C5
Walnutport 2,055	L4
Wampum 666	B4
Warren▲ 11,122	D2
Warrior Run 656	E7
Washington▲ 15,864	B5
Waterford 1,492	B2
Watsontown 2,311	J3
Wattsburg 486	C1
Wayne	M6
Waynesboro 9,578	G6
Waynesburg▲ 4,270	B6
Weatherly 2,640	L4
Wellsboro▲ 3,430	H2
Wernersville 1,934	K5
Wesleyville 3,655	C1
West Brownsville 1,170	C5
West Chester▲ 18,041	L6
West Elizabeth 634	C7
West Grove 2,128	L6
West Hazleton 4,136	K4
West Kittanning 1,253	C4
West Lawn 1,606	K5
West Leechburg 1,359	C4
West Middlesex 982	B3
West Mifflin 23,644	C7
West Newton 3,152	C5
West Pittsburg 1,183	B3
West Pittston 5,590	F7
West View 7,734	B6
West Wyoming 3,117	E7
West York 4,283	J6
Westfield 1,119	H2
Westmont 5,789	D5
Westover 446	E4
Wheatland 760	B3
Whitaker 1,416	C7
White Haven 1,132	L3
White Oak 8,761	C7
Whitehall 14,451	B7
Wiconisco 1,321	J4
Wilkes-Barre▲ 47,523	F7

Wilkinsburg 21,080	C7
Williamsburg 1,456	F5
Williamsport▲ 31,933	H3
Williamstown 1,509	J4
Willow Grove 16,325	M5
Wilmerding 2,421	C5
Wilson 7,830	M4
Windber 4,756	E5
Windgap 2,651	M4
Windsor 1,355	J6
Wolfdale 2,906	B5
Womelsdorf 2,270	K5
Woodlyn 10,151	M7
Worthington 713	C4
Wrightsville 2,396	J5
Wyalusing 686	K2
Wyoming 3,255	E7
Wyomissing 7,332	K5
Yardley 2,288	N5
Yeadon 11,980	N7
Yeagertown 1,150	G4
York Haven 758	J5
York Springs 547	H6
York▲ 42,192	J6
Youngsville 1,775	D2
Youngwood 3,372	D5
Zelienople 4,158	B4

OTHER FEATURES

Allegheny (res.)	E2
Allegheny (riv.)	D2
Allegheny Front (mts.)	E5
Appalachian (mts.)	H4
Ararat (mt.)	M2
Arthur (lake)	C4
Beaver (riv.)	B4
Blue (mt.)	G5
Blue Knob (mt.)	E5
Casselman (riv.)	D6
Clarion (riv.)	D3
Conemaugh (riv.)	D5
Conemaugh River (lake)	D4
Conewango (creek)	D1
Davis (lake)	D6
Delaware (riv.)	N3
Delaware Water Gap	
Nat'l Rec.	N3
Erie (lake)	B1
Fort Necessity Nat'l	
Battlefield	C6
George B. Stevenson (lake)	G3
Gettysburg Nat'l Mil. Park	H6
Glendale (lake)	E4
Juniata (riv.)	G4
Laurel Hill (mt.)	D5
Lehigh (riv.)	L3
Letterkenny Army Depot	G6
Licking (creek)	F6
Little Tinicum (isl.)	M7
Lycoming (creek)	H3
Monongahela (riv.)	C6
North (mt.)	K3
Ohio (riv.)	A4
Oil (creek)	C2
Pine (creek)	H2
Pine Grove (creek)	K6
Pocono (mts.)	M3
Pymatuning (res.)	A2
Redbank (creek)	E3
Schuylkill (riv.)	M5
Shenango River (lake)	B3
Sinnemahoning (creek)	F3
South (mt.)	H6
Steamtown Nat'l Hist. Site	F7
Susquehanna (riv.)	K6
Tioga (riv.)	H1
Tionesta Creek (lake)	D3
Towanda (creek)	J2
Tuscarora (mt.)	G5
Wallenpaupack (lake)	M3
Youghiogheny River (lake)	D6

▲County seat
● Population of town or township

Topography

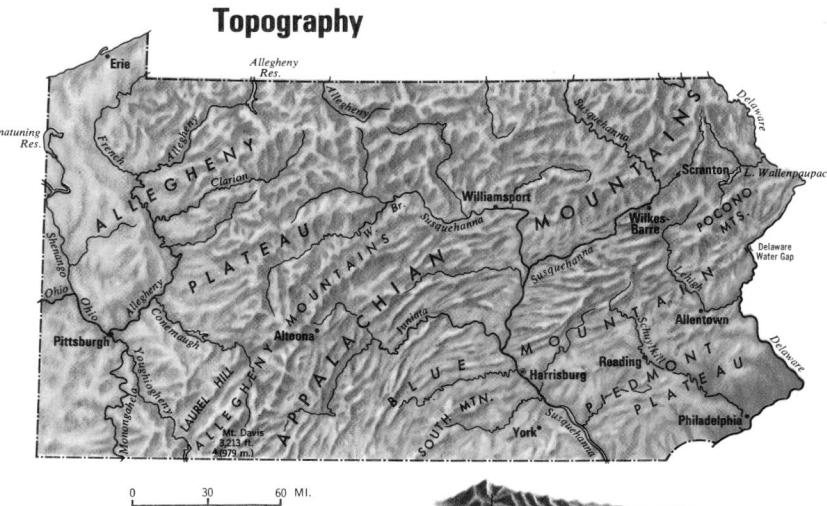

5,000 m. 16,404 ft.	2,000 m. 6,562 ft.	1,000 m. 3,281 ft.	500 m. 1,640 ft.	200 m. 656 ft.	100 m. 328 ft.	Sea Level	Below

New Beaver 1,736	B4
New Berlin 892	J4
New Bethlehem 1,151	D3
New Bloomfield▲	H5
New Brighton 6,854	B4
New Britain 2,174	M5
New Castle▲ 28,334	B3
New Cumberland 7,665	J5
New Eagle 2,172	B5
New Florence 854	D5
New Freedom 2,920	J6
New Galilee 500	A4
New Holland 4,484	K5
New Hope 1,400	N5
New Kensington 15,894	C4
New Milford 953	L2
New Oxford 1,617	H6
New Philadelphia 1,283	K4
New Salem (Delmont) 669	D5
New Stanton 2,081	C5
New Wilmington 2,706	B3
Newport 1,568	H5
Newtown 2,565	N5
Newtown Square ● 11,775	L6

Newville 1,349	H5
Nicholson 857	L2
Norristown▲ 30,749	M5
North Apollo 1,391	C4
North Braddock 7,036	C7
North Catasauqua 2,867	L4
North East 4,617	C1
North Wales 3,802	M5
North Warren 1,232	D2
Northampton 8,717	M4
Northumberland 3,860	J4
Norvelt 2,541	D5
Norwood 6,162	M7
Nuangola 701	E7
Oakdale 1,752	B5
Oakland 641	L2
Oakmont 6,961	C6
Ohioville 3,865	B4
Oil City 11,949	C3
Old Forge 8,834	F7
Oliver 3,271	C6
Olyphant 5,222	F7
Orangeville 504	K3
Orbisonia 447	G5

Orwigsburg 2,780	K4
Osborne 565	B4
Osceola Mills 1,310	F4
Oxford 3,769	K6
Paint 1,091	E5
Palmerton 5,394	L4
Palmyra 6,910	J5
Paoli 5,603	M5
Paradise 1,107	K5
Parker 853	C3
Parkesburg 2,981	L6
Parkside 2,369	M7
Parkville 6,014	J6
Patton 2,206	E4
Pen Argyl 3,492	M4
Penbrook 2,791	J5
Penn 511	C5
Penn Hills 51,430	C7
Penn Wynne 5,807	M6
Penndel 2,703	N5
Pennsburg 2,460	M5
Pennville 1,559	J6
Perkasie 7,878	M5
Perryopolis 1,833	C5

© Copyright HAMMOND INCORPORATED, Maplewood, N.J.

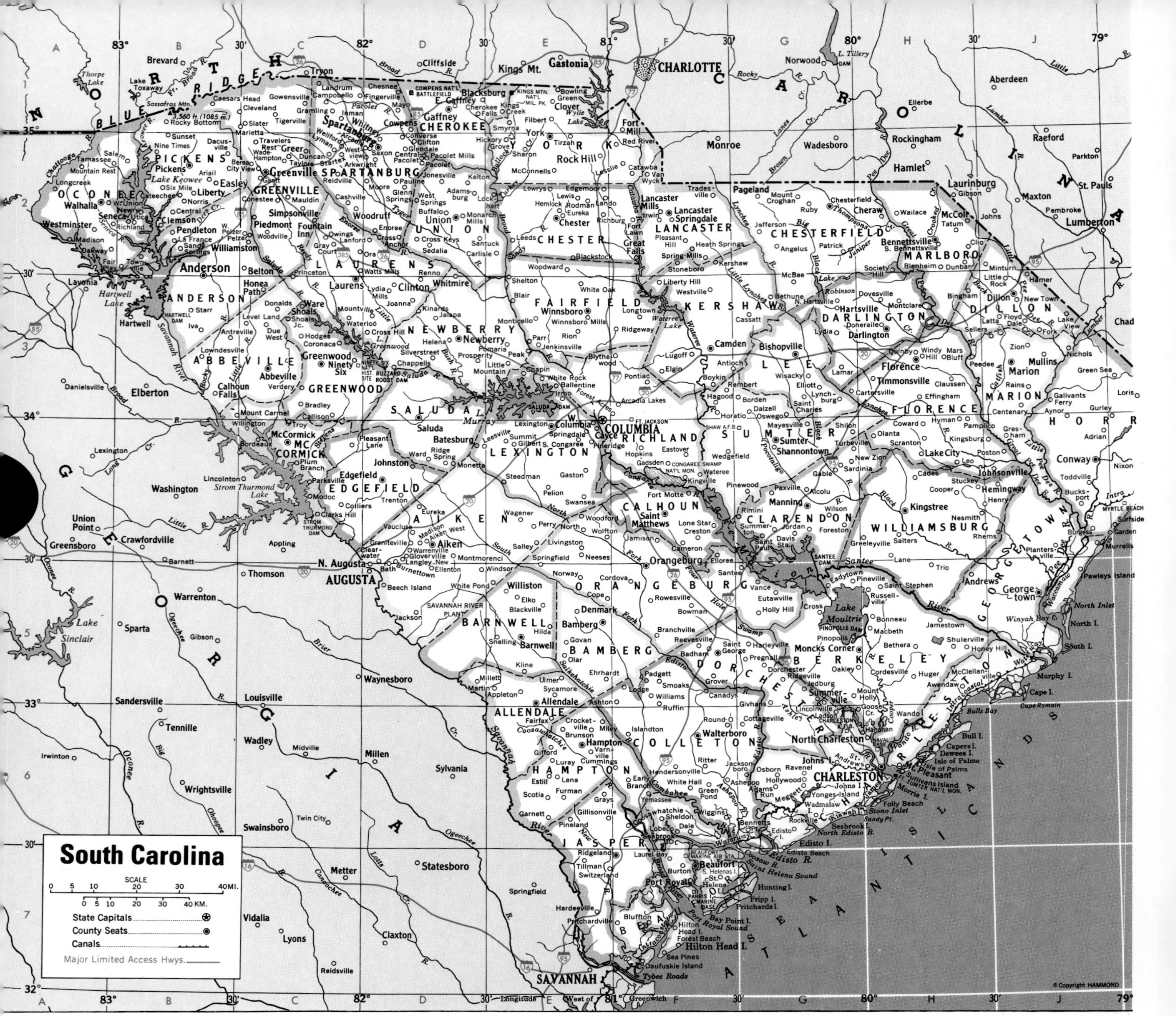
South Carolina
SCALE
0 5 10 20 30 40 MI.
0 5 10 20 30 40 KM.
State Capitals
County Seats
Canals
Major Limited Access Hwys.
© Copyright HAMMOND
Longitude West of 81° Greenwich

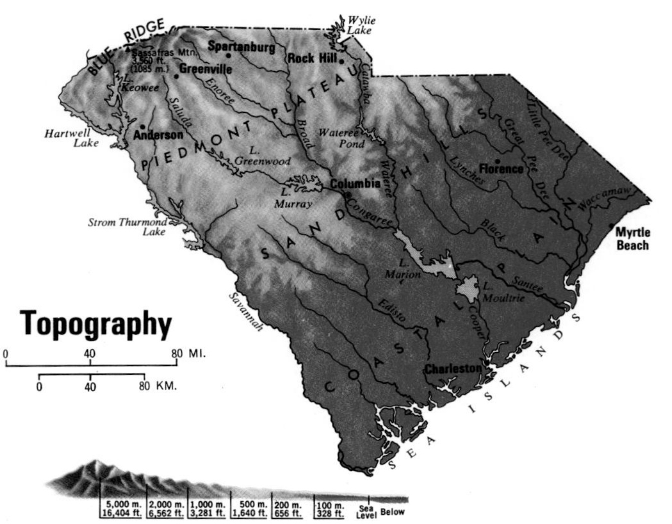
Topography
0 40 80 MI.
0 40 80 KM.
5,000 m. 16,404 ft.
2,000 m. 6,562 ft.
1,000 m. 3,281 ft.
500 m. 1,640 ft.
200 m. 656 ft.
100 m. 328 ft.
Sea Level
Below

COUNTIES

Abbeville 23,862 ..... B3
Aiken 120,940 ..... D4
Allendale 11,722 ..... E6
Anderson 145,196 ..... B2
Bamberg 16,902 ..... E5
Barnwell 20,293 ..... E5
Beaufort 86,425 ..... F7
Berkeley 128,776 ..... G5
Calhoun 12,753 ..... F4
Charleston 295,039 ..... H6
Cherokee 44,506 ..... D1
Chester 32,170 ..... E2
Chesterfield 38,577 ..... G2
Clarendon 28,450 ..... G4
Colleton 34,377 ..... F6
Darlington 61,851 ..... H3
Dillon 29,114 ..... J3
Dorchester 83,060 ..... G5
Edgefield 18,375 ..... D4
Fairfield 22,295 ..... E3
Florence 114,344 ..... H3
Georgetown 46,302 ..... J5
Greenville 320,167 ..... C2
Greenwood 59,567 ..... C3
Hampton 18,191 ..... E6
Horry 144,053 ..... J4
Jasper 15,487 ..... E6
Kershaw 43,599 ..... F3
Lancaster 54,516 ..... F2
Laurens 58,092 ..... D2
Lee 18,437 ..... G3
Lexington 167,611 ..... E4
Marion 33,899 ..... J3
Marlboro 29,361 ..... H2
McCormick 8,868 ..... C4
Newberry 33,172 ..... D3
Oconee 57,494 ..... A2
Orangeburg 84,803 ..... F5
Pickens 93,894 ..... B2
Richland 285,720 ..... F4
Saluda 16,357 ..... D3
Spartanburg 226,800 ..... D2
Sumter 102,637 ..... G4
Union 30,337 ..... D2
Williamsburg 36,815 ..... H4
York 131,497 ..... E2

CITIES and TOWNS

Abbeville▲ 5,778 ..... C3
Adams Run 500 ..... G6
Adamsburg 300 ..... D2
Aiken West 3,083 ..... D4
Aiken▲ 19,872 ..... D4
Alcolu 600 ..... G4
Allendale▲ 4,410 ..... E5
Allsbrook 100 ..... K3
Anderson 26,184 ..... B2
Andrews 3,050 ..... H5
Antioch 500 ..... F3
Antreville 500 ..... B3
Appleton 200 ..... E5
Arcadia 899 ..... C2
Arcadia Lakes 611 ..... F3
Ariail 2,419 ..... B2
Arkwright 2,623 ..... C2
Atlantic Beach 446 ..... K4
Awendaw 200 ..... H5
Aynor 470 ..... J3
Ballentine 550 ..... E3
Bamberg▲ 3,843 ..... E5
Barnwell▲ 5,255 ..... E5
Batesburg 4,082 ..... D4
Bath 2,242 ..... D5
Beaufort▲ 9,576 ..... F7
Beech Island 400 ..... D5
Belton 4,646 ..... C2
Bennettsville 9,345 ..... H2
Berea 13,535 ..... C2
Bethera 265 ..... H5
Bethune 405 ..... G3
Bingham 200 ..... H3
Bishopville▲ 3,560 ..... G3
Blacksburg 1,907 ..... D1
Blackville 2,688 ..... E5
Blenheim 191 ..... H2
Bluffton 738 ..... F7
Blythewood 164 ..... E3
Bonneau 374 ..... H5
Bowman 1,063 ..... F5
Boykin 350 ..... F3
Branchville 1,107 ..... F5
Brunson 587 ..... E6
Bucksport 1,022 ..... J4
Buffalo 1,569 ..... D2
Burgess 250 ..... J4
Burnettown 493 ..... D5
Burton 6,917 ..... F7
Calhoun Falls 2,328 ..... B3
Camden▲ 6,696 ..... F3
Cameron 504 ..... F4
Campobello 465 ..... C1
Canadys 130 ..... F5
Carlisle 470 ..... D2
Cashville 200 ..... C2
Catawba 607 ..... F2
Cateechee 225 ..... B2
Cayce 11,163 ..... E4
Centenary 700 ..... J3
Central 2,438 ..... B2
Central Pacolet 257 ..... D2
Chapin 282 ..... D3
Chappells 45 ..... D3
Charleston▲ 80,414 ..... G6
Cheraw 5,505 ..... H2
Cherokee Falls 250 ..... D1
Chesnee 1,280 ..... D1
Chester▲ 7,158 ..... E2
Chesterfield▲ 1,373 ..... G2
City View 1,490 ..... C2
Clarks Hill 200 ..... C4
Claussen 500 ..... H3
Clearwater 4,731 ..... D4
Clemson 11,096 ..... B2
Cleveland 800 ..... C1
Clifton 950 ..... D2
Clinton 7,987 ..... D3
Clio 882 ..... H2
Clover 3,422 ..... E1
Columbia (cap.)▲ 98,052 ..... F4

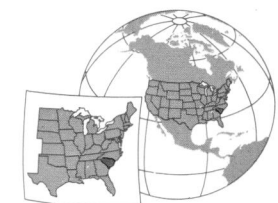

AREA 31,113 sq. mi. (80,583 sq. km.)
POPULATION 3,505,707
CAPITAL Columbia
LARGEST CITY Columbia
HIGHEST POINT Sassafras Mtn. 3,560 ft.
(1085 m.)
SETTLED IN 1670
ADMITTED TO UNION May 23, 1788
POPULAR NAME Palmetto State
STATE FLOWER Carolina (Yellow)
Jessamine
STATE BIRD Carolina Wren

Fayetteville
Cape
Elizabethtown
Whiteville
bourn
L. Waccamaw
Allsbrook
Longs
Shallotte
Waccamaw
Wampee
ville
Little River
North Myrtle Beach
Myrtle Beach
A.F.B.
Beach
City Beach
Inlet

INCORPORATED, Maplewood, N. J.

Edisto Beach 340	G7	Langley 1,714	D4
Edisto Island 900	G6	Latta 1,565	J3
Effingham 300	H3	Laurel Bay 4,972	F7
Ehrhardt 442	E5	Laurens▲ 9,694	C3
Elgin 622	F3	Leesville 2,025	E4
Elko 214	E5	Lena 275	E4
Elliott 500	G3	Lesslie 1,102	E2
Elloree 939	F4	Level Land 100	C3
Enoree 1,107	D2	Lexington▲ 3,289	E4
Estill 2,387	E6	Liberty 3,228	B2
Eureka 1,738	E2	Lincolnville 716	G6
Eutawville 350	G5	Little Mountain 235	E3
Fair Play 500	A2	Little River 3,470	K4
Fairfax 2,317	E6	Little Rock 500	J3
Filbert 203	E1	Livingston 171	E4
Fingerville 320	D1	Lobeco 345	F7
Florence▲ 29,813	H3	Lockhart 58	E2
Floyd Dale 450	J3	Lodge 147	E5
Folly Beach 1,398	H6	Longcreek 200	A2
Forest Acres 7,197	E3	Longtown 400	F3
Forest Beach 500	F7	Loris 2,067	K3
Foreston 300	G4	Lowndesville 162	B3
Fort Lawn 718	F2	Lowrys 200	E2
Fort Mill 4,930	F1	Lugoff 3,211	F3
Fort Motte 700	F4	Luray 102	E6
Fountain Inn 4,388	C2	Lydia 500	G3
Furman 260	E6	Lydia Mills 925	D3
Gable 230	G4	Lyman 2,271	C2
Gadsden 500	F4	Lynchburg 475	G3
Gaffney▲ 13,145	D1	Madison	A2
Gantt 13,891	C2	Madison 1,150	D4
Garden City Beach 300	K4	Manning▲ 4,428	G4
Garnett 500	E6	Marietta-Slater	C1
Gaston 984	E4	Marion▲ 7,658	J3
Georgetown▲ 9,517	J5	Mars Bluff 500	H3
Gifford 313	E6	Mauldin 11,587	C2
Gilbert 324	E4	Mayesville 694	G4
Gillisonville 350	E6	Mayo 1,569	D1
Givhans 400	G5	McBee 715	G3
Glendale 1,049	D2	McClellanville 333	H5
Glenn Springs 350	D2	McColl 2,685	H2
Gloverville 2,753	D4	McConnells 157	E2
Goose Creek 24,692	H6	McCormick▲ 1,659	C4
Govan 84	E5	Meggett 787	G6
Gowensville 200	C1	Modoc 300	C4
Gramling 400	C1	Monarch Mills 2,353	D2
Graniteville 1,158	D4	Moncks Corner▲ 5,607	G5
Gray Court 914	C2	Monetta 285	D4
Great Falls 2,997	F2	Montmorenci 500	D4
Greeleyville 464	H4	Moore 500	D2
Greenville▲ 58,282	C2	Mount Carmel 117	C3
Greenwood▲ 20,807	C3	Mount Croghan 131	G2
Greer 10,322	C2	Mount Holly 200	H5
Gresham 350	J4	Mount Pleasant 30,108	H6
Gurley 425	J3	Mountain Rest 500	A2
Hamer 588	J3	Mullins 5,910	J3
Hampton▲ 2,997▲	E6	Murrells Inlet 3,334	K4
Hanahan 13,176	H6	Myrtle Beach 24,848	K4
Hardeeville 1,583	E7	Neeses 410	E4
Harleyville 633	G5	Nesmith 350	H4
Hartsville 8,372	G3	New Ellenton 2,515	D5
Heath Springs 907	F2	New Town 950	J3
Helena 300	D3	New Zion 200	H4
Hemingway 829	J4	Newberry▲ 10,542	D3
Hemlock (Eureka)	E2	Newry 400	B2
Hickory Grove 287	E2	Nichols 528	J3
Hilda 342	E5	Ninety Six 2,099	C3
Hilton Head Island 23,694	F7	Norris 884	B2
Hodges 125	C3	North 809	E4
Holly Hill 1,478	G5	North Augusta 15,351	C5
Hollywood 2,094	G6	North Charleston 70,218	G6
Honea Path 3,841	C3	North Hartsville 2,906	G3
Hopkins 300	F4	North Myrtle Beach 8,636	K4
Horatio 500	F3	Norway 401	E5
Huger 500	H5	Oakley 250	G5
Inman 1,742	C1	Olanta 687	H4
Irmo 11,280	D3	Olar 391	E5
Irwin 1,296	F2	Ora 13,739	D2
Isle of Palms 3,680	H6	Orangeburg▲ 14,933	F4
Iva 1,174	B3	Oswego 500	G3
Jackson 1,681	D5	Pacolet 1,736	D2
Jacksonboro 475	G6	Pacolet Mills 696	D2
Jamestown 84	H5	Pageland 2,666	G2
Jedburg 900	G5	Pamplico 1,314	H4
Jefferson 745	G2	Parksville 193	C4
Joanna 1,735	D3	Parr 7,172	E3
Johns Island 200	H6	Patrick 368	G2
Johnsonville 1,415	J4	Pauline 750	D2
Johnston 2,688	D4	Pawleys Island 176	J5
Jonesville 1,205	D2	Paxville 218	G4
Kershaw 1,814	G2	Peak 78	E3
Kinards 300	D3	Peedee 350	H3
Kingsburg 300	H4	Pelion 336	E4
Kingstree▲ 3,858	H4	Pelzer 81	B2
Kingville 500	F4	Pendleton 3,314	B2
Kline 285	E5	Perry 241	E4
La France 875	B2	Pickens▲ 3,042	B2
Ladson 13,540	G6	Piedmont 4,143	C2
Lake City 7,153	H4	Pineland 800	E6
Lake View 872	J3	Pineridge 1,731	E4
Lamar 1,125	G3	Pineville 900	H5
Lancaster Mills 2,096	F2	Pinewood 600	G4
Lancaster▲ 8,914	F2	Pinopolis 788	G5
Lando 250	E2	Plantersville 231	J4
Landrum 2,347	C1	Plum Branch 101	C4
Lane 523	H5	Pomaria 267	E3

Port Royal 2,985	F7	Stuckey 311	H4
Poston 250	J4	Sullivans Island 1,623	H6
Princeton 500	C2	Summerton 975	G4
Prosperity 1,116	D3	Summerville 22,519	G5
Quinby 865	H3	Summit 242	E4
Rains 450	J3	Sumter▲ 41,943	G4
Ravenel 2,165	G6	Surfside Beach 3,845	K4
Red River	F5	Swansea 527	E4
Reevesville 244	F5	Sycamore 208	E5
Reidville	F5	Tamassee 320	A2
Rembert 500	G3	Tatum 49	H2
Richburg 405	F2	Taylors 19,619	C2
Ridge Spring 861	D4	Tigerville 975	C1
Ridgeland▲ 1,071	E7	Tillman 225	E7
Ridgeville 1,625	G5	Timmonsville 2,182	H3
Ridgeway 407	F3	Toddville 200	J4
Rimini 525	G4	Townville 300	B2
Rion 300	E3	Tradesville 500	F2
Ritter 300	F6	Travelers Rest 3,069	C2
Rock Hill 41,643	F2	Trenton 303	D4
Rodman 500	D4	Trio 400	H5
Rowesville 316	F5	Troy 140	C4
Ruby 300	G2	Turbeville 698	G4
Ruffin 400	F6	Ulmer 90	E5
Saint Andrews 26,692	G6	Union▲ 9,836	D2
Saint George▲ 2,077	F5	Utica 1,478	B2
Saint Matthews▲ 2,345	F4	Vance 214	G5
Saint Paul 725	G4	Varnville 1,970	E6
Saint Stephen 1,697	H5	Vaucluse 606	D7
Salem 192	A2	Wade-Hampton 20,014	C2
Salley 451	D4	Wagener 731	E4
Salters 300	H4	Walhalla▲ 3,755	A2
Saluda▲ 2,798	D4	Wallace 500	H2
Santee 638	F5	Walterboro▲ 5,492	F6
Sardinia 225	G4	Wampee 200	K4
Saxon 4,002	D2	Wando 500	H6
Scotia 182	E6	Ward 132	D4
Scranton 300	H4	Ware Shoals 2,497	C3
Sea Pines 500	F7	Warrenville 1,029	D4
Seabrook 948	F6	Waterloo 122	D3
Sellers 358	H3	Watts Mill 1,535	D2
Seneca 7,726	A2	Wedgefield 550	G4
Shannontown	G4	Wellford 2,511	C2
Sharon 270	E2	West Columbia 10,588	E4
Sheldon 225	F6	West Pelzer 989	B2
Shulerville 375	H5	West Springs 500	D2
Silverstreet 156	D3	West Union 260	A2
Simpsonville 11,708	C2	Westminster 3,120	A2
Six Mile 562	B2	Westview 1,999	C2
Slater-Marietta 2,245	C1	Westville 440	F3
Smoaks 172	F5	White Pond 200	D5
Smyrna 57	E1	White Rock 600	E3
Snelling 125	E4	Whitmire 1,702	D2
Society Hill 686	H2	Whitney 4,052	D1
South Bennettsville 1,065	H2	Williams 188	F5
South Congaree 2,406	E4	Williamston 3,876	C2
Spartanburg▲ 43,467	C1	Williston 3,099	E5
Spring Mills 1,419	F2	Windsor 124	D5
Springdale 2,643	F2	Windy Hill 1,622	K4
Springdale 2,985	E4	Winnsboro Mills 2,275	E3
Springfield 523	E4	Winnsboro▲ 3,475	E3
Starr 164	B3	Wisacky 250	G3
Startex 1,162	C2		

Woodford 200	E4	Little (riv.)	D3
Woodruff 4,365	D2	Little Lynches (riv.)	G3
Woodville	C2	Little Pee Dee (riv.)	J4
Yemassee 728	F6	Little River (inlet)	L4
Yonges Island 500	G6	Lumber (riv.)	J3
York▲ 6,709	E1	Lynches (riv.)	H3
		Marion (lake)	G5
OTHER FEATURES		Morris (isl.)	H6
		Moultrie (lake)	H5
Ashepoo (riv.)	F6	Murphy (isl.)	J5
Ashley (riv.)	G6	Murray (lake)	D4
Bay Point (isl.)	F7	Myrtle Beach A.F.B.	K4
Beaufort Marine Air Sta.	F7	Naval Base	H6
Big Black (creek)	G2	New (riv.)	E7
Black (riv.)	H4	Ninety Six Nat'l Hist. Site	C3
Blue Ridge (mts.)	B1	North (inlet)	J5
Broad (riv.)	D2	North (isl.)	J5
Broad (riv.)	F7	North Edisto (riv.)	G6
Buck (creek)	J3	Pacolet (riv.)	D1
Bull (isl.)	H6	Palms, Isle of (isl.)	H6
Bullock (creek)	E2	Parris Island Marine Base	F7
Bulls (bay)	H6	Pee Dee (riv.)	J4
Bush (riv.)	D3	Pocotaligo (riv.)	G4
Buzzard Roost (dam)	D3	Port Royal (sound)	F7
Cape (riv.)	J5	Pritchards (isl.)	G7
Capers (isl.)	H6	Reedy (riv.)	C2
Catawba (riv.)	F2	Robinson (lake)	G3
Catfish (creek)	J3	Romain (cape)	J6
Chattooga (riv.)	A2	Saint Helena (isl.)	J5
Combahee (riv.)	F6	Saint Helena (sound)	G7
Congaree (riv.)	F4	Salkehatchie (riv.)	E5
Congaree Nat'l Mon.	F4	Saluda (riv.)	D3
Cooper (riv.)	H6	Sandy (pt.)	H6
Coosaw (riv.)	G7	Sandy (riv.)	E2
Coosawhatchie (riv.)	E6	Santee (dam)	G4
Cowpens Nat'l Battlefield	D1	Santee (riv.)	H5
Crooked (creek)	H2	Sassafras (mt.)	B1
Deep (creek)	H2	Savannah (riv.)	E6
Dewees (isl.)	H6	Savannah River Plant	D5
Donaldson A.F.B.	C2	Sea (isls.)	G7
Edisto (isl.)	G6	Seabrook (isl.)	G6
Edisto (isl.)	G7	Seneca (riv.)	B2
Enoree (riv.)	C2	Shaw A.F.B.	G4
Fort Jackson	F4	South (isl.)	J5
Fort Sumter Nat'l Mon.	H6	Stevens (creek)	C4
Four Hole Swamp (creek)	F5	Stono (inlet)	H6
Fripp (isl.)	G7	Strom Thurmond (dam)	C4
Great Pee Dee (riv.)	J4	Strom Thurmond (lake)	C4
Greenwood (lake)	D3	Thompsons (creek)	G2
Hartwell (dam)	B3	Tugaloo (riv.)	A2
Hartwell (lake)	A3	Turkey (creek)	E2
Hilton Head (isl.)	F7	Tybee Roads (chan.)	F7
Hunting (isl.)	G7	Tyger (riv.)	D2
Intracoastal Waterway	H5	Waccamaw (riv.)	J5
James (isl.)	H6	Wadmalaw (isl.)	G6
Johns (isl.)	G6	Wando (riv.)	H6
Juniper (creek)	H2	Wateree (lake)	F3
Keowee (lake)	B2	Winyah (bay)	J5
Keowee (riv.)	B2	Wylie (lake)	E1
Kiawah (isl.)	G6		
Kings Mountain		▲County seat	
Nat'l Mil. Park	E1		
Little (riv.)	C3		

Conestee 500	C2	Huger 500	H5
Converse 1,173	D2	Inman 1,742	C1
Conway▲ 9,819	J4	Irmo 11,280	D3
Coosawhatchie 250	F6	Irwin 1,296	F2
Cope 124	E5	Isle of Palms 3,680	H6
Cordesville 300	H5	Iva 1,174	B3
Cordova 135	E4	Jackson 1,681	D5
Coronaca 200	C3	Jacksonboro 475	G6
Cottageville 572	G6	Jamestown 84	H5
Coward 532	H4	Jedburg 900	G5
Cowpens 2,176	D1	Jefferson 745	G2
Cross 469	G5	Joanna 1,735	D3
Cross Anchor 350	D2	Johns Island 200	H6
Cross Hill 604	D3	Johnsonville 1,415	J4
Cross Keys 250	D2	Johnston 2,688	D4
Cummings 275	E6	Jonesville 1,205	D2
Dacusville 350	B2	Kershaw 1,814	G2
Dale 500	F6	Kinards 300	D3
Dalzell 625	G3	Kingsburg 300	H4
Darlington▲ 7,311	H3	Kingstree▲ 3,858	H4
Davis Station 300	G4	Kingville 500	F4
Denmark 3,762	E5	Kline 285	E5
Dillon▲ 6,829	J3	La France 875	B2
Donalds 326	C3	Ladson 13,540	G6
Doneraile 1,276	H3	Lake City 7,153	H4
Dorchester 400	G5	Lake View 872	J3
Due West 1,220	C3	Lamar 1,125	G3
Duncan 2,152	C2	Lancaster Mills 2,096	F2
Easley 15,195	B2	Lancaster▲ 8,914	F2
East Gaffney 3,278	D1	Lando 250	E2
Eastover 1,044	F4	Landrum 2,347	C1
Edgefield 2,563▲	C4	Lane 523	H5
Edgemoor 500	E2		

Agriculture, Industry and Resources

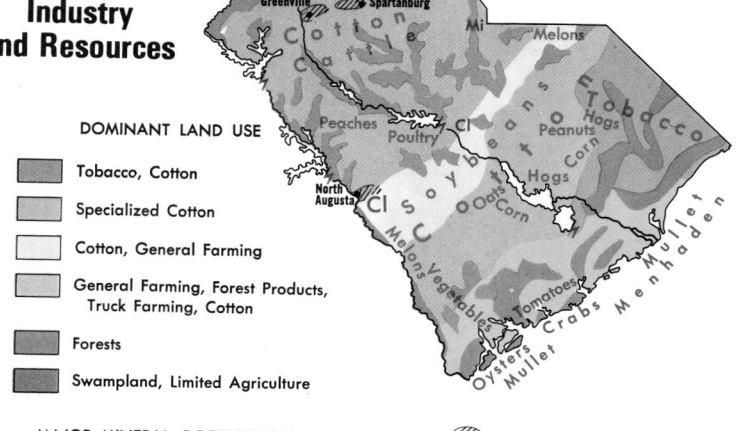

DOMINANT LAND USE

Tobacco, Cotton

Specialized Cotton

Cotton, General Farming

General Farming, Forest Products, Truck Farming, Cotton

Forests

Swampland, Limited Agriculture

MAJOR MINERAL OCCURRENCES

Cl Clay

Mi Mica

Major Industrial Areas

Water Power

COUNTIES

Aurora 3,135	M6
Beadle 18,253	N5
Bennett 3,206	F7
Bon Homme 7,089	O7
Brookings 25,207	R5
Brown 35,580	N2
Brule 5,485	L6
Buffalo 1,759	L5
Butte 7,914	B4
Campbell 1,965	J2
Charles Mix 9,131	M7
Clark 4,403	O4
Clay 13,186	P8
Codington 22,698	P4
Corson 4,195	G2
Custer 6,179	B6
Davison 17,503	N6
Day 6,978	O3
Deuel 4,522	R4
Dewey 5,523	G3
Douglas 3,746	N7
Edmunds 4,356	L3
Fall River 7,353	B7
Faulk 2,744	L3
Grant 8,372	R4
Haakon 2,624	F5
Hamlin 4,974	P4
Hand 4,272	L4
Hanson 2,994	O6
Harding 1,669	B2
Hughes 14,817	J5
Hutchinson 8,262	O7
Hyde 1,696	K4
Jackson 2,811	F6
Jerauld 2,425	M5
Jones 1,324	H6
Kingsbury 5,925	P5
Lake 10,550	P5
Lawrence 20,655	B5
Lincoln 15,427	R7
Lyman 3,638	J6

Marshall 4,844	O2
McCook 5,688	P6
McPherson 3,228	L2
Meade 21,878	D5
Mellette 2,137	H6
Miner 3,272	O5
Minnehaha 123,809	R6
Moody 6,507	R5
Perkins 3,932	D3
Potter 3,190	J3
Roberts 9,914	P2
Sanborn 2,833	N5
Shannon 9,902	D7
Spink 7,981	N4
Stanley 2,453	H5
Sully 1,589	J4
Todd 8,352	H7
Tripp 6,924	K7
Turner 8,576	P7
Union 10,189	R8
Walworth 6,087	J3

Yankton 19,252	P7
Ziebach 2,220	F4

CITIES and TOWNS

Aberdeen▲ 24,927	M3
Agar 82	J4
Akaska 52	J3
Albee 15	S3
Alcester 843	R7
Alexandria▲ 518	O6
Allen 300	F7
Alpena 251	N5
Altamont 48	R4
Amherst 75	O2
Andover 106	O3
Ardmore 16	B7
Arlington 908	P5
Armour▲ 854	N7
Artas 28	K2
Artesian 217	O6
Ashton 148	N3

Astoria 155	S4
Aurora 619	R5
Avon 576	N8
Badger 114	P5
Baltic 666	R6
Bancroft 30	O4
Barnard 65	N2
Batesland 124	E7
Bath 175	N3
Belle Fourche▲ 4,335	B4
Belvidere 159	G6
Beresford 1,849	R7
Big Stone City 669	S3
Bison▲ 451	E2
Black Hawk 1,995	C5
Blunt 342	J4
Bonesteel 297	M7
Bowdle 589	K3
Box Elder 2,680	C5
Bradley 117	O3
Brandon 3,543	R6
Brandt 123	R4

Brentford 69	N3
Bridgewater 533	P6
Bristol 419	O3
Britton▲ 1,394	O2
Broadland 40	N4
Brookings▲ 16,270	R5
Bruce 235	R5
Bryant 374	P4
Buffalo Gap 173	C6
Buffalo▲ 488	B2
Bullhead 179	G2
Burbank 90	R8
Burke▲ 756	L7
Bushnell 81	R5
Butler 17	O3
Camp Crook 146	B2
Canistota 608	P6
Canning 40	L5
Canova 172	O6
Canton▲ 2,787	R7
Caputa 50	D5

Carthage 221	O5
Castlewood 549	R4
Cavour 166	N5
Center 887	P6
Centerville 892	R7
Central City 185	B5
Chamberlain▲ 2,347	L6
Chancellor 276	R7
Chelsea 33	M3
Cherry Creek 500	F4
Chester 375	R6
Claire City 85	P2
Claremont 135	N2
Clark▲ 1,292	O4
Clear Lake▲ 1,247	R4
Colman 482	R6
Colome 309	K7
Colton 657	P6
Columbia 133	N2
Conde 203	N3
Corona 118	R3
Corsica 619	N7

AREA 77,116 sq. mi. (199,730 sq. km.)
POPULATION 699,999
CAPITAL Pierre
LARGEST CITY Sioux Falls
HIGHEST POINT Harney Pk. 7,242 ft.
  (2207 m.)
SETTLED IN 1856
ADMITTED TO UNION November 2, 1889
POPULAR NAME Coyote State; Sunshine
  State
STATE FLOWER Pasqueflower
STATE BIRD Ring-necked Pheasant

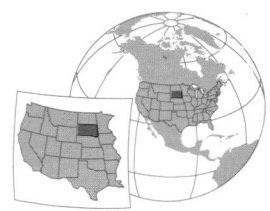

Topography

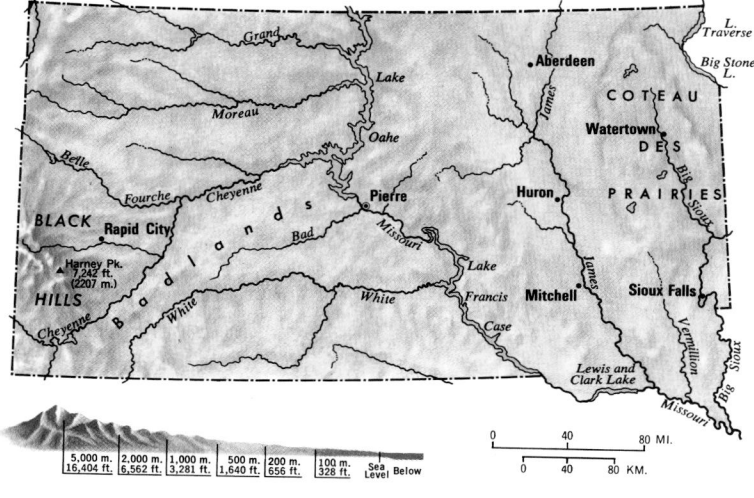

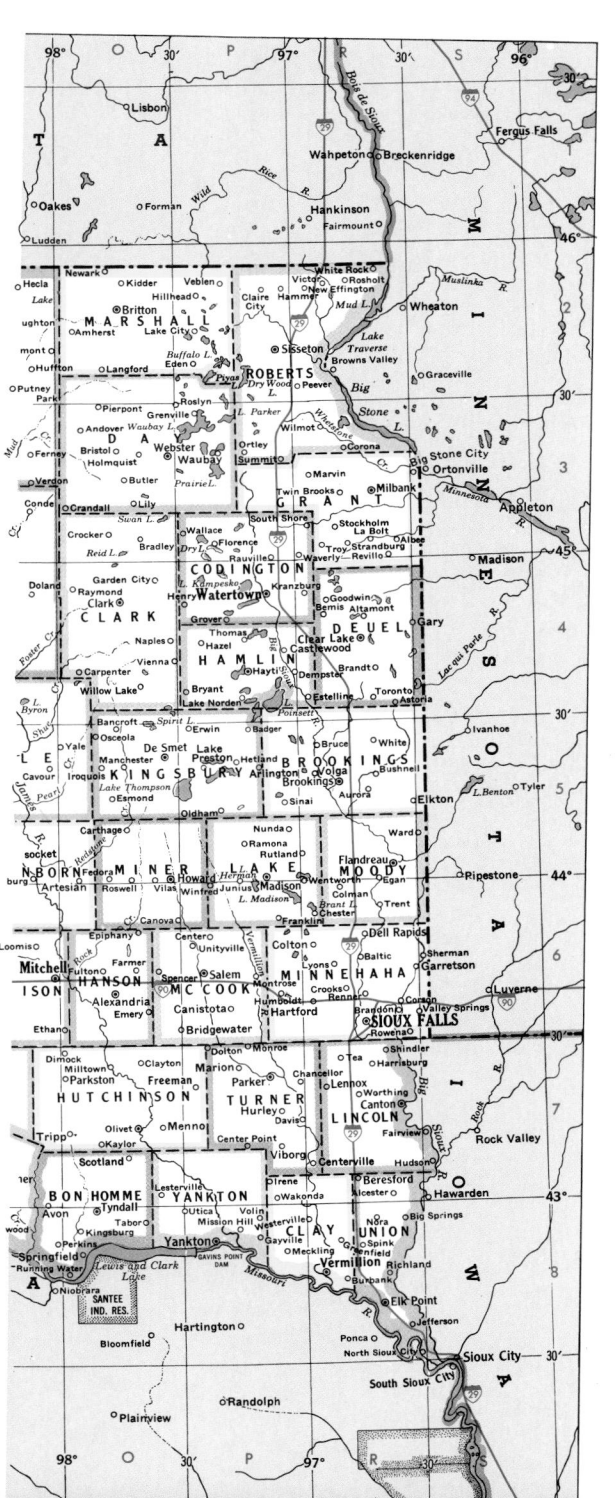

The Black Hills

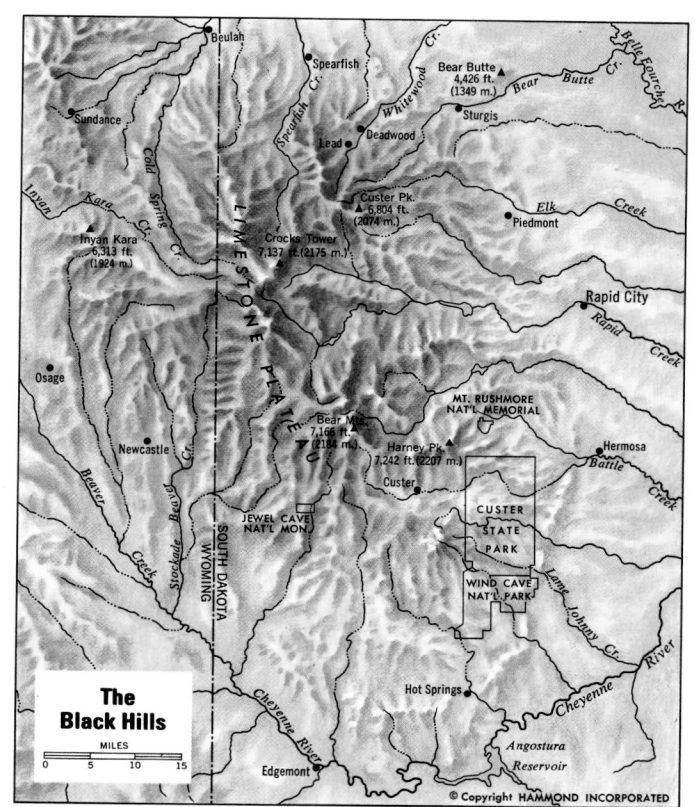

© Copyright HAMMOND INCORPORATED

Agriculture, Industry and Resources

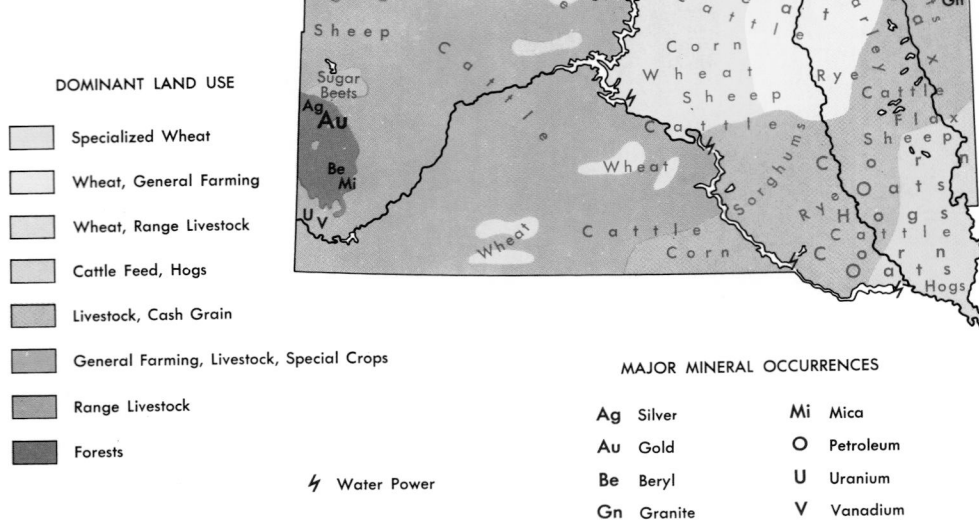

DOMINANT LAND USE

☐ Specialized Wheat

☐ Wheat, General Farming

☐ Wheat, Range Livestock

☐ Cattle Feed, Hogs

☐ Livestock, Cash Grain

☐ General Farming, Livestock, Special Crops

☐ Range Livestock

☐ Forests

⚡ Water Power

MAJOR MINERAL OCCURRENCES

Ag Silver   **Mi** Mica

Au Gold   **O** Petroleum

Be Beryl   **U** Uranium

Gn Granite   **V** Vanadium

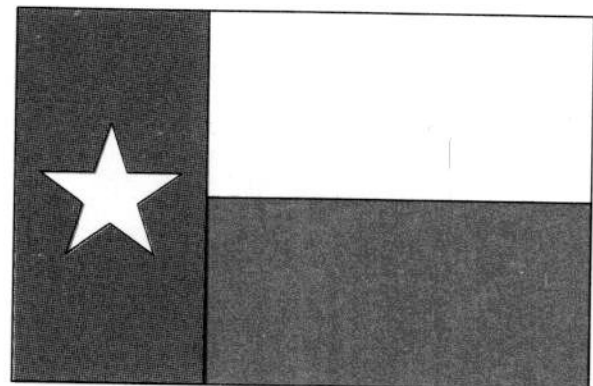

AREA 266,807 sq. mi. (691,030 sq. km.)
POPULATION 17,059,805
CAPITAL Austin
LARGEST CITY Houston
HIGHEST POINT Guadalupe Pk. 8,749 ft. (2667 m.)
SETTLED IN 1686
ADMITTED TO UNION December 29, 1845
POPULAR NAME Lone Star State
STATE FLOWER Bluebonnet
STATE BIRD Mockingbird

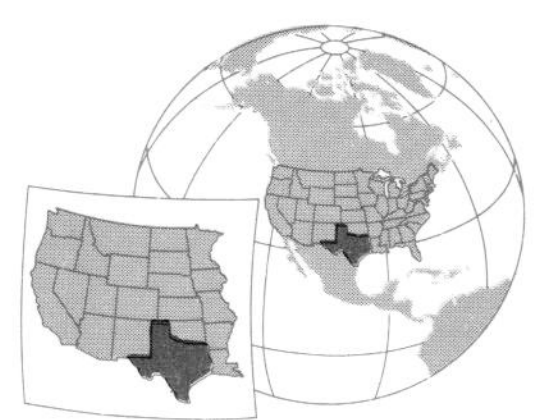

COUNTIES

Anderson 48,024 ... J6
Andrews 14,338 ... B5
Angelina 69,884 ... K6
Aransas 17,892 ... H10
Archer 7,973 ... F4
Armstrong 2,021 ... C3
Atascosa 30,533 ... F9
Austin 19,832 ... H8
Bailey 7,064 ... B3
Bandera 10,562 ... E8
Bastrop 38,263 ... G7
Baylor 4,385 ... E4
Bee 25,135 ... G9
Bell 191,088 ... G6
Bexar 1,185,394 ... F8
Blanco 5,972 ... F8
Borden 799 ... C5
Bosque 15,125 ... G6
Bowie 81,665 ... K4
Brazoria 191,707 ... J8
Brazos 121,862 ... H7
Brewster 8,681 ... A8
Briscoe 1,971 ... C3
Brooks 8,204 ... F11
Brown 34,371 ... F6
Burleson 13,625 ... H7
Burnet 22,677 ... F7
Caldwell 26,392 ... G8
Calhoun 19,053 ... H9
Callahan 11,859 ... E5
Cameron 260,120 ... G11
Camp 9,904 ... K5
Carson 6,576 ... C2
Cass 29,982 ... K4
Castro 9,070 ... B3
Chambers 20,088 ... K8
Cherokee 41,049 ... J6
Childress 5,953 ... D3
Clay 10,024 ... F4
Cochran 4,377 ... B4
Coke 3,424 ... D6
Coleman 9,710 ... E6
Collin 264,036 ... H4
Collingsworth 3,573 ... D3
Colorado 18,383 ... H8
Comal 51,832 ... F8
Comanche 13,381 ... F5
Concho 3,044 ... E6
Cooke 30,777 ... G4
Coryell 64,213 ... G6
Cottle 2,247 ... D3
Crane 4,652 ... B6
Crockett 4,078 ... C7
Crosby 7,304 ... C4
Culberson 3,407 ... C11
Dallam 5,461 ... B1
Dallas 1,852,810 ... H5
Dawson 14,349 ... C5
De Witt 18,903 ... G9
Deaf Smith 19,153 ... B3
Delta 4,857 ... J4
Denton 273,525 ... G4
Dickens 2,571 ... D4
Dimmit 10,433 ... E9
Donley 3,696 ... D2
Duval 12,918 ... F10
Eastland 18,488 ... F5
Ector 118,934 ... B6
Edwards 2,266 ... D7
El Paso 591,610 ... A10
Ellis 85,167 ... H5
Erath 27,991 ... F5
Falls 17,712 ... H6
Fannin 24,804 ... H4
Fayette 20,095 ... H8
Fisher 4,842 ... D5
Floyd 8,497 ... C3
Foard 1,794 ... E3
Fort Bend 225,421 ... J8
Franklin 7,802 ... J4
Freestone 15,818 ... H6
Frio 13,472 ... E9
Gaines 14,123 ... B5
Galveston 217,399 ... K8
Garza 5,143 ... C4
Gillespie 17,204 ... F7
Glasscock 1,447 ... C6
Goliad 5,980 ... G9
Gonzales 17,205 ... G8
Gray 23,967 ... D2
Grayson 95,021 ... H4
Gregg 104,948 ... K5
Grimes 18,828 ... J7
Guadalupe 64,873 ... G8
Hale 34,671 ... C3
Hall 3,905 ... D3
Hamilton 7,733 ... F6
Hansford 5,848 ... C1
Hardeman 5,283 ... E3
Hardin 41,320 ... K7
Harris 2,818,199 ... J8
Harrison 57,483 ... K5
Hartley 3,634 ... B2
Haskell 6,820 ... E4
Hays 65,614 ... F7
Hemphill 3,720 ... D2
Henderson 58,543 ... J5
Hidalgo 383,545 ... F11
Hill 27,146 ... G5
Hockley 24,199 ... B4
Hood 28,981 ... G5
Hopkins 28,833 ... J4
Houston 21,375 ... J6
Howard 32,343 ... C5
Hudspeth 2,915 ... B10
Hunt 64,343 ... H4
Hutchinson 25,689 ... C2
Irion 1,629 ... C6
Jack 6,981 ... F4
Jackson 13,039 ... H9
Jasper 31,102 ... K7
Jeff Davis 1,946 ... C11
Jefferson 239,397 ... K8
Jim Hogg 5,109 ... F11
Jim Wells 37,679 ... F10
Johnson 97,165 ... G5
Jones 16,490 ... E5
Karnes 12,455 ... G9
Kaufman 52,220 ... H5
Kendall 14,589 ... F8
Kenedy 460 ... G11
Kent 1,010 ... D4
Kerr 36,304 ... E7
Kimble 4,122 ... E7
King 354 ... D4
Kinney 3,119 ... D8
Kleberg 30,274 ... G10
Knox 4,837 ... E4
La Salle 5,254 ... E9
Lamar 43,949 ... J4
Lamb 15,072 ... B3
Lampasas 13,521 ... F6
Lavaca 18,690 ... H8
Lee 12,854 ... H7
Leon 12,665 ... J6
Liberty 52,726 ... K7
Limestone 20,946 ... H6
Lipscomb 3,143 ... D1
Live Oak 9,556 ... F9
Llano 11,631 ... F7
Loving 107 ... A6
Lubbock 222,636 ... C4
Lynn 6,758 ... C4
Madison 10,931 ... J6
Marion 9,984 ... K5
Martin 4,956 ... C5
Mason 3,423 ... E7
Matagorda 36,928 ... H9
Maverick 36,378 ... D9
McCulloch 8,778 ... E6
McLennan 189,123 ... G6
McMullen 817 ... F9
Medina 27,312 ... E8
Menard 2,252 ... E7
Midland 106,611 ... B6
Milam 22,946 ... H7
Mills 4,531 ... F6
Mitchell 8,016 ... D5
Montague 17,274 ... G4
Montgomery 182,201 ... J7
Moore 17,865 ... C2
Morris 13,200 ... K4
Motley 1,532 ... D3
Nacogdoches 54,753 ... K6
Navarro 39,926 ... H5
Newton 13,569 ... L7
Nolan 16,594 ... D5
Nueces 291,145 ... G10
Ochiltree 9,128 ... D1
Oldham 2,278 ... B2
Orange 80,509 ... L7
Palo Pinto 25,055 ... F5
Panola 22,035 ... K5
Parker 64,785 ... G5
Parmer 9,863 ... B3
Pecos 14,675 ... B7
Polk 30,687 ... K7
Potter 97,874 ... C2
Presidio 6,637 ... C12
Rains 6,715 ... J5
Randall 89,673 ... C2
Reagan 4,514 ... C6
Real 2,412 ... E8
Red River 14,317 ... J4
Reeves 15,852 ... D11
Refugio 7,976 ... G9
Roberts 1,025 ... D2
Robertson 15,511 ... H6
Rockwall 25,604 ... H5
Runnels 11,294 ... E6
Rusk 43,735 ... K5
Sabine 9,586 ... L6
San Augustine 7,999 ... K6
San Jacinto 16,372 ... J7
San Patricio 58,749 ... G10
San Saba 5,401 ... F6
Schleicher 2,990 ... D7
Scurry 18,634 ... D5
Shackleford 3,915 ... E5
Shelby 22,034 ... K6
Sherman 2,858 ... C1
Smith 151,309 ... J5
Somervell 5,360 ... G5
Starr 40,518 ... F11
Stephens 9,010 ... F5
Sterling 1,438 ... C6
Stonewall 2,013 ... D4
Sutton 4,135 ... D7
Swisher 8,133 ... C3
Tarrant 1,170,103 ... G5
Taylor 119,655 ... E5
Terrell 1,410 ... B7
Terry 13,218 ... B4
Throckmorton 1,880 ... E4
Titus 24,009 ... K4
Tom Green 98,458 ... D6
Travis 576,407 ... G7
Trinity 11,445 ... J6
Tyler 16,646 ... K7
Upshur 31,370 ... K5
Upton 4,447 ... B6
Uvalde 23,340 ... E8
Val Verde 38,721 ... C8
Van Zandt 37,944 ... J5
Victoria 74,361 ... H9
Walker 50,917 ... J7
Waller 23,390 ... J8
Ward 13,115 ... A6
Washington 26,154 ... H7
Webb 133,239 ... E10
Wharton 39,955 ... H8
Wheeler 5,879 ... D2
Wichita 122,378 ... F3
Wilbarger 15,121 ... E3
Willacy 17,705 ... G11
Williamson 139,551 ... G7
Wilson 22,650 ... F8
Winkler 8,626 ... A6
Wise 34,679 ... G4
Wood 29,380 ... J5
Yoakum 8,786 ... B4
Young 18,126 ... F4
Zapata 9,279 ... E11
Zavala 12,162 ... E9

CITIES and TOWNS

Abernathy 2,720 ... B4
Abilene▲ 106,654 ... E5
Addison 8,783 ... G2
Alamo 8,210 ... F11
Alamo Heights 6,502 ... K10
Albany▲ 1,962 ... E5
Alice▲ 19,788 ... F10
Allen 18,309 ... H1
Alpine▲ 5,637 ... D12
Alvarado 2,918 ... G5
Alvin 19,220 ... J3
Amarillo▲ 157,615 ... C2
Anahuac▲ 1,993 ... K8
Anderson▲ 500 ... J7
Andrews▲ 10,678 ... B5
Angleton▲ 17,140 ... J8
Anson▲ 2,644 ... E5
Anthony 3,328 ... A10
Aransas Pass 7,180 ... G10
Archer City▲ 1,748 ... F4
Arlington 261,721 ... F2
Aspermont▲ 1,214 ... D4
Athens▲ 10,967 ... J5
Atlanta 6,118 ... K4
Austin (cap.)▲ 465,622 ... G7
Azle 8,868 ... E2
Bacliff 5,549 ... K2
Baird▲ 1,658 ... E5
Balch Springs 17,406 ... H2
Balcones Heights 3,022 ... J10
Ballinger▲ 3,975 ... E6
Bandera▲ 877 ... F8
Barrett 3,052 ... K1
Bastrop▲ 4,044 ... G7
Bay City▲ 18,170 ... H9
Baytown 63,850 ... L2
Beaumont▲ 114,323 ... K7
Bedford 43,762 ... F2
Beeville▲ 13,547 ... G9
Bellaire 13,842 ... J2
Bellmead 8,336 ... H6
Bellville▲ 3,378 ... H8
Belton▲ 12,476 ... G7
Benavides 1,788 ... F10
Benbrook 19,564 ... E2
Benjamin▲ 225 ... E4
Big Lake▲ 3,672 ... C6
Big Spring▲ 23,093 ... C5
Bishop 3,337 ... G10
Bloomington 1,888 ... H9
Blue Mound 2,133 ... E2
Boerne▲ 4,274 ... J10
Bonham▲ 6,686 ... H4
Borger 15,675 ... C2
Boston▲ 400 ... K4
Bowie 4,990 ... G4
Brackettville▲ 1,740 ... D8
Brady▲ 5,946 ... E6
Brazoria 2,717 ... J9
Breckinridge▲ 5,665 ... F5
Brenham▲ 11,952 ... H7
Briar 3,899 ... E1
Bridge City 8,034 ... L7
Bridgeport 3,581 ... G4
Brookshire 2,922 ... J8
Brownfield▲ 9,560 ... B4
Brownsville▲ 98,962 ... G12
Brownwood▲ 18,387 ... F6
Bryan▲ 55,002 ... H7
Buda 1,795 ... G7
Buna 2,127 ... L7
Bunker Hill Village 3,391 ... J1
Burkburnett 10,145 ... F3
Burleson 16,113 ... F3
Burnet▲ 3,423 ... F7
Caldwell▲ 3,181 ... H7
Cameron▲ 5,580 ... H7
Canadian▲ 2,417 ... D2
Canton▲ 2,949 ... J5
Canutillo 4,442 ... A10
Canyon▲ 11,365 ... C3
Carrizo Springs▲ 5,745 ... E9
Carrollton 82,169 ... G2
Carthage▲ 6,496 ... K5
Castle Hills 4,198 ... J10
Castroville 2,159 ... J11
Cedar Hill 19,976 ... G3
Cedar Park 5,161 ... G7
Center▲ 4,950 ... K6
Centerville▲ 812 ... H6
Channelview 25,564 ... K1
Channing▲ 277 ... B2
Childress▲ 5,055 ... D3
Cisco 3,813 ... E5
Clarendon▲ 2,067 ... C3
Clarksville▲ 4,311 ... K4
Claude▲ 1,199 ... C2
Clear Lake Shores 1,096 ... K2
Cleburne▲ 22,205 ... G5
Cleveland 7,124 ... K7
Clifton 3,195 ... G6
Clute 8,910 ... J9
Clyde 3,002 ... E5
Cockrell Hill 3,746 ... G2
Coldspring▲ 538 ... J7
Coleman▲ 5,410 ... E6
College Station▲ 52,456 ... H7
Colleyville 12,724 ... F2
Colorado City▲ 4,749 ... C5
Columbus▲ 3,367 ... H8
Comanche▲ 4,087 ... F6
Commerce 6,825 ... J4
Conroe▲ 27,610 ... J7
Converse 8,887 ... K11
Cooper▲ 2,153 ... J4
Coppell 16,881 ... G2
Copperas Cove 24,079 ... G6
Corpus Christi▲ 257,453 ... G10
Corsicana▲ 22,911 ... H5
Cotulla▲ 3,694 ... E9
Crane▲ 3,533 ... B6
Crockett▲ 7,024 ... J6
Crosby 1,811 ... J8
Crosbyton▲ 2,026 ... C4
Crowell▲ 1,230 ... E4
Crowley 6,974 ... E3
Crystal City▲ 8,263 ... E9
Cuero▲ 6,700 ... G8
Daingerfield▲ 2,572 ... K4
Dalhart▲ 6,246 ... B1
Dallas▲ 1,006,877 ... G2
Dalworthington Gardens 1,758 ... F2
Dayton 5,151 ... J7
De Kalb 1,976 ... K4
De Leon 2,190 ... F5
De Soto 30,544 ... G3
Decatur▲ 4,252 ... G4
Deer Park 27,652 ... K2
Del Rio▲ 30,705 ... D8
Denison 21,505 ... H4
Denton▲ 66,270 ... G4
Denver City 5,145 ... B4
Devine 3,928 ... E8
Diboll 4,341 ... K6
Dickens▲ 322 ... D4
Dickinson 9,497 ... K3
Dilley 2,632 ... E9
Dimmitt▲ 4,408 ... B3
Donna 12,652 ... F11
Double Oak 1,664 ... F1

(continued on following page)

Agriculture, Industry and Resources

DOMINANT LAND USE

- Wheat, Grain Sorghums, Range Livestock
- Cotton, Wheat
- Specialized Cotton
- Cotton, General Farming
- Cotton, Forest Products
- Cotton, Range Livestock
- Rice, General Farming
- Peanuts, General Farming
- General Farming, Livestock, Cash Grain
- General Farming, Forest Products, Truck Farming, Cotton
- Fruit, Truck and Mixed Farming
- Range Livestock
- Forests
- Swampland, Limited Agriculture
- Nonagricultural Land
- Urban Areas

MAJOR MINERAL OCCURRENCES

At Asphalt
Cl Clay
Fe Iron Ore
G Natural Gas
Gn Granite
Gp Gypsum
Gr Graphite
He Helium
Ls Limestone
Na Salt
O Petroleum
S Sulfur
Tc Talc
U Uranium

Water Power
Major Industrial Areas

Dublin 3,190 F5
Dumas▲ 12,871 C2
Duncanville 35,748 G3
Eagle Lake 3,551 H8
Eagle Pass▲ 20,651 D9
Eastland▲ 3,690 F5
Edcouch 2,878 G11
Edgecliff 2,715 E2
Edinburg▲ 29,885 F11
Edna▲ 5,343 H9
El Campo 10,511 H8
El Lago 3,269 K2
El Paso▲ 515,342 A10
Eldorado▲ 2,019 D7
Electra 3,113 F4
Elgin 4,846 G7
Elsa 5,242 G11
Emory▲ 963 J5
Ennis 13,883 H5
Euless 38,149 F2
Everman 5,672 F3
Fabens 5,599 B10
Fairfield▲ 3,234 H6
Falfurrias▲ 5,788 F10
Farmers Branch 24,250 G2
Farmersville 2,640 H4
Farwell▲ 1,373 A3
Ferris 2,212 H3
Floresville▲ 5,247 K11
Flower Mound 15,527 F1
Floydada▲ 3,896 C3
Forest Hill 11,482 F2
Forney 4,070 H5
Fort Davis▲ 900 D11
Fort Stockton▲ 8,524 A7
Fort Worth▲ 447,619 F2
Franklin▲ 1,336 H7
Fredericksburg▲ 6,934 E7
Fredonia 50 E7
Freeport 11,389 J9
Freer 3,271 F10
Fresno 3,182 J2
Friendswood 22,814 J2
Friona 3,688 B3
Frisco 6,141 H4
Fritch 2,335 C2
Gail▲ 171 C5
Gainesville▲ 14,256 G4
Galena Park 10,033 J1
Galveston▲ 59,070 L3
Ganado 1,701 H8
Garden City▲ 350 C6
Garland 180,650 H2
Gatesville▲ 11,492 G6
George West▲ 2,586 F9
Georgetown▲ 14,842 G7
Giddings▲ 4,093 H7
Gilmer▲ 4,822 J5
Gladewater 6,027 K5
Glen Rose▲ 1,949 G5
Glenn Heights 4,564 G2
Goldthwaite▲ 1,658 F6
Goliad▲ 1,946 G9
Gonzales▲ 6,527 G8
Graham▲ 8,986 F4
Granbury▲ 4,045 G5
Grand Prairie 99,616 G2
Grand Saline 2,630 J5
Grapevine 29,202 F2
Greenville▲ 23,071 H4
Groesbeck▲ 3,185 H6
Groves 16,513 L8
Groveton▲ 1,071 J7
Guthrie▲ 170 D4
Hale Center 2,067 C3
Hallettsville▲ 2,718 G8
Hallsville 2,288 K5
Haltom City 32,856 F2
Hamilton▲ 2,937 G6
Hamlin 2,791 E5
Harlingen 48,735 G11
Haskell▲ 3,362 E4
Hearne 5,132 H7
Hebbronville▲ 4,465 F10
Hedwig Village 2,616 H1
Hemphill▲ 1,182 L6
Hempstead▲ 3,551 J7
Henderson▲ 11,139 K5
Henrietta▲ 2,896 F4
Hereford▲ 14,745 B3
Hickory Creek 1,893 F1
Hidalgo 3,292 F11
Highland Park 8,739 G2
Highland Village 7,027 F1
Highlands 6,632 K1
Hillsboro▲ 7,072 G5
Hitchcock 5,868 K3
Hollywood 3,231 K10
Hondo▲ 6,018 E8
Honey Grove 1,681 J4
Hooks 2,684 K4
Houston▲ 1,630,553 J2
Howe 2,173 H4
Hughes Springs 1,938 K5
Humble 12,060 J7
Hunters Creek Village 3,954 J1
Huntington 1,794 K6
Huntsville▲ 27,925 J7
Hurst 33,574 F2
Hutchins 2,719 G3
Idalou 2,074 C4
Iowa Park 6,072 F4
Irving 155,037 G2
Italy 1,699 H5
Jacinto City 9,343 J1
Jacksboro▲ 3,350 F4
Jacksonville 12,765 J5
Jasper▲ 6,959 L7
Jayton▲ 608 D4
Jefferson▲ 2,199 K5
Jersey Village 4,826 J1
Johnson City▲ 932 F7
Jones Creek 2,160 J9
Jourdanton▲ 3,220 F9
Junction▲ 2,654 E7
Karnes City▲ 2,916 G9
Katy 8,005 J8
Kaufman▲ 5,238 H5
Keene 3,944 G5
Keller 13,683 F2
Kenedy 3,763 G9
Kennedale 4,096 F3
Kerens 1,702 H5
Kermit▲ 6,875 B6
Kerrville▲ 17,384 E7
Kilgore 11,066 K5
Killeen 63,535 G6
Kingsland 2,725 F7
Kingsville▲ 25,276 G10
Kirby 8,326 K11
Kirbyville 1,871 K7
Kountze▲ 2,056 K7
Kyle 2,225 G8
La Feria 3,495 G11
La Grange▲ 3,951 G8
La Joya 2,604 F11
La Marque 14,120 K3
La Porte 27,910 K2
Lake Dallas 3,656 G1
Lake Jackson 22,776 J8
Lake Worth 4,591 E2
Lamesa▲ 10,809 C5
Lampasas▲ 6,382 F6
Lancaster 22,117 G3
Laredo▲ 122,899 E10
League City 30,159 K2
Leakey▲ 399 E8
Leon Valley 9,581 J10
Leonard 1,744 H4
Levelland▲ 13,986 B4
Lewisville 46,521 G1
Liberty▲ 7,733 K7
Lindale 2,428 J5
Linden▲ 2,375 K4
Lipscomb▲ 52 D1
Littlefield▲ 6,489 B4
Live Oak 10,023 K10
Livingston▲ 5,019 K7
Llano▲ 2,962 F7
Lockhart▲ 9,205 G8
Lockney 2,207 C3
Lomax 2,991 K2
Longview▲ 70,311 K5
Los Fresnos 2,473 G11
Lubbock▲ 186,206 C4
Lucas 2,205 H1
Lufkin▲ 30,206 K6
Luling 4,661 G8
Lumberton 6,640 K7
Lyford 1,674 G11
Lytle 2,255 J11
Mabank 1,739 H5
Madisonville▲ 3,569 J7
Malakoff 2,038 H5
Mansfield 15,607 F3
Manvel 3,733 J3
Marble Falls 4,007 F7
Marfa▲ 2,424 C12
Marlin▲ 6,386 H6
Marshall▲ 23,682 K5
Mart 2,004 H6
Mason▲ 2,041 E7
Matador▲ 790 D3
Mathis 5,423 G9
McAllen 84,021 F11
McCamey 2,493 B6
McGregor 4,683 G6
McKinney▲ 21,283 H4
Memphis▲ 2,465 D3
Menard▲ 1,606 E7
Mentone▲ 50 D10
Mercedes 12,694 F12
Meridian▲ 1,390 G6
Merkel 2,469 E5
Mertzon▲ 778 C6
Mesquite 101,484 H2
Mexia 6,933 H6
Miami▲ 675 D2
Midland▲ 89,443 C6
Midlothian 5,141 G5
Mineola 4,321 J5
Mineral Wells 14,870 F5
Mission 28,653 F11
Missouri City 36,176 J2
Monahans▲ 8,101 B6
Montague▲ 1,253 G4
Morton▲ 2,597 B4
Mount Pleasant▲ 12,291 K4
Mount Vernon▲ 2,219 J4
Muleshoe▲ 4,571 B3
Nacogdoches▲ 30,872 J6
Nash 2,162 K4
Nassau Bay 4,320 K2
Navasota 6,296 J7
Nederland 16,192 K8
Needville 2,199 J8
New Boston 5,057 K4
New Braunfels▲ 27,334 K10
Newton▲ 1,885 L7
Nixon 1,995 G8
Nocona 2,870 G4
North Richland Hills 45,895 F2
Odessa▲ 89,699 B6
Olmos Park 2,161 K11
Olney 3,519 F4
Olton 2,116 B3
Orange▲ 19,381 L7
Overton 2,105 K5
Ovilla 2,027 G3
Ozona▲ 3,181 C7
Paducah▲ 1,788 D4
Paint Rock▲ 227 E6
Palacios 4,418 H9
Palestine▲ 18,042 J6
Palo Pinto▲ 350 F5
Pampa▲ 19,959 D2
Panhandle▲ 2,353 C2
Pantego 2,371 F2
Paris▲ 24,699 J4
Pasadena 119,363 J2
Pearland 18,697 J2
Pearsall▲ 6,924 E9
Pecos▲ 12,069 D10
Perryton▲ 7,607 D1
Pflugerville 4,444 G7
Pharr 32,921 F11
Pickton 1,729 C2
Pilot Point 2,538 H4
Piney Point Village 3,197 J1
Pittsburg▲ 4,007 J4
Plains▲ 1,422 B4
Plainview▲ 21,700 C3
Plano 128,713 G1
Pleasanton 7,678 F9
Port Aransas 2,233 H10
Port Arthur 58,724 K8
Port Isabel 4,467 G11
Port Lavaca▲ 10,886 H9
Port Neches 12,974 K7
Portland 12,224 G10
Post▲ 3,768 C4
Poteet 3,206 F8
Prairie View 4,004 J7
Premont 2,914 F10
Presidio 3,072 C12
Quanah▲ 3,413 E3
Queen City 1,748 L4
Quitman▲ 1,684 J5
Ralls 2,172 C4
Ranger 2,803 F5
Rankin▲ 1,011 B6
Raymondville▲ 8,880 G11
Red Oak 3,124 H5
Refugio▲ 3,158 G9
Reno 1,784 E2
Richardson 74,840 G2
Richland Hills 7,978 F2
Richmond▲ 9,801 J8
Rio Grande City▲ 9,891 F11
Rio Hondo 1,793 G11
River Oaks 6,580 E2
Robert Lee▲ 1,276 D6
Robstown 12,849 G10
Roby▲ 616 D5
Rockdale 5,235 G7
Rockport▲ 4,753 H9
Rocksprings▲ 1,339 D8
Rockwall▲ 10,486 H5
Roma-Los Saenz 3,384 E11
Rosenberg 20,183 J8
Rotan 1,913 D5
Round Rock 30,923 G7
Rowlett 23,260 H2
Royse City 2,206 H4
Rusk▲ 4,366 J6
Sachse 5,346 H2
Saginaw 8,551 E2
San Angelo▲ 84,474 D6
San Antonio▲ 935,933 J11
San Augustine▲ 2,337 K6
San Benito 20,125 G12
San Diego▲ 4,983 F10
San Elizario 4,385 A10
San Juan 10,815 F11
San Leon 3,328 L2
San Marcos▲ 28,743 F8
San Saba▲ 2,626 F6
Sanderson▲ 1,128 B7
Sanger▲ 3,508 G4
Sansom Park Village 3,921 E2
Santa Fe 8,429 K3
Sarita▲ 200 G10
Schertz 10,555 K10
Schulenburg 2,455 H8
Seabrook 6,685 K2
Seagoville 8,969 H3
Seagraves 2,398 B5
Sealy 4,541 H8
Seguin▲ 18,853 G8
Seminole▲ 6,342 K10
Seymour▲ 3,185 E4
Shamrock 2,286 D2
Shepherd 1,812 K7
Sherman▲ 31,601 H4
Shiner 2,074 G8
Sierra Blanca▲ 800 B11
Silsbee 6,368 K7
Silverton▲ 779 C3
Sinton▲ 5,549 G9
Slaton 6,078 C4
Smithville 3,196 G7
Snyder▲ 12,195 D5
Sonora▲ 2,751 D7
South Houston 14,207 J2
South Padre Island 1,677 F11
Spearman▲ 3,197 C1
Spring 33,111 J7
Spring Valley 3,392 J1
Stafford 8,397 J2
Stamford 3,817 E5
Stanton▲ 2,576 C5
Stephenville▲ 13,502 F5
Sterling City▲ 1,096 D6
Stinnett▲ 2,166 C2
Stratford▲ 1,781 C1
Sugar Land 24,529 J8
Sulphur Springs▲ 14,062 J4
Sundown 1,759 B4
Sunnyvale 2,228 H2
Sweeny 3,297 J8
Sweetwater▲ 11,967 D5
Taft 3,222 G9
Tahoka▲ 2,868 C4
Taylor 11,472 G7
Taylor Lake Village 3,394 K2
Teague 3,268 H6
Temple 46,109 G6
Terlingua 100 D12
Terrell 12,490 H5
Terrell Hills 4,592 K11
Texarkana 31,656 L4
Texas City 40,822 K3
Texhoma 291 C1
The Colony 22,113 G1
Three Rivers 1,889 F9
Throckmorton▲ 1,036 F4
Tilden▲ 450 F9
Tomball 6,370 J7
Trinity 2,648 J7
Tulia▲ 4,699 C3
Tyler▲ 75,450 J5
Universal City 13,057 K10
University Park 22,259 F2
Uvalde▲ 14,729 E8
Van 1,854 J5
Van Alstyne 2,090 H4
Van Horn▲ 2,930 C11
Vega▲ 840 B2
Vernon▲ 12,001 E3
Victoria▲ 55,076 H9
Vidor 10,935 L7
Waco▲ 103,590 G6
Wake Village 4,757 K4
Waskom 1,812 L5
Watauga 20,009 F2
Waxahachie▲ 18,168 H5
Weatherford▲ 14,804 G5
Webster 4,678 K2
Weimar 2,052 H8
Wellington▲ 2,456 D3
Weslaco 21,877 F11
West 2,515 G6
West Columbia 4,372 J8
West Orange 4,187 L7
West University Place 12,920 J2
Westworth 2,350 E2
Wharton▲ 9,011 J8
Wheeler▲ 1,393 D2
White Oak 5,136 K5
White Settlement 15,472 E2
Whitesboro 3,209 H4
Whitewright 1,713 H4
Wichita Falls▲ 96,259 F4
Willis 2,764 J7
Wills Point 2,986 J5
Wilmer 2,479 H3
Windcrest 5,331 K11
Winnie 2,238 K8
Winnsboro 2,904 J5
Winters 2,905 E6
Wolfforth 1,941 C4
Woodsboro 1,731 G9
Woodville▲ 2,636 K7
Wylie 8,716 H1
Yoakum 5,611 G8
Yorktown 2,207 G9
Zapata▲ 7,119 E11

OTHER FEATURES

Alibates Flint Quarries Nat'l Mon. C2
Amistad (res.) C8
Amistad Nat'l Rec. Area D8
Angelina (riv.) K6
Apache (mts.) C11
Aransas (passage) H10
Arlington (lake) F2
Baffin (bay) G10
Balcones Escarpment (plat.) E8
Benbrook (lake) E3
Bergstrom A.F.B. G7
Big Bend Nat'l Park A8
Big Thicket Nat'l Preserve K7
Bolivar (pen.) K8
Brazos (riv.) H7
Brooks A.F.B. K11
Brownwood (lake) E6
Buchanan (lake) F7
Caddo (lake) L5
Calaveras (lake) K11
Canadian (riv.) D1
Carrizo (creek) A1
Carswell A.F.B. E2
Cathedral (mt.) D12
Cavallo (passage) H9
Cedar (lake) B5
Cerro Alto (mt.) B10
Chamizal Nat'l Mon. A10
Chinati (mts.) C12
Chinati (peak) C12
Chisos (mts.) A8
Cibolo (creek) K11
Clear Fork, Brazos (riv.) D5
Coldwater (creek) B1
Colorado (riv.) F7
Copano (bay) G9
Corpus Christi (lake) F9
Corpus Christi N.A.S. G10
Cottonwood Draw (dry riv.) C10
Davis (mts.) C11
Deep (creek) C5
Delaware (creek) C10
Delaware (mts.) C10
Denison (dam) H4
Devils (riv.) D7
Double Mountain Fork, Brazos (riv.) C4
Dyess A.F.B. D5
Eagle (peak) C11
Eagle Mountain (lake) E2
Edwards (plat.) C7
Elephant (mt.) D12
Elm Fork, Trinity (riv.) G2
Emory (peak) A8
Falcon (res.) E11
Finlay (mts.) B10
Fort Bliss 13,915 A10
Fort Davis Nat'l Hist. Site D11
Fort Hood 35,580 G6
Fort Sam Houston K11
Frio (riv.) E8
Galveston (bay) L2
Galveston (isl.) K8
Glass (mts.) A7
Goodfellow A.F.B. D6
Grapevine (lake) F2
Guadalupe (mts.) C10
Guadalupe (peak) B10
Guadalupe (riv.) G8
Guadalupe Mountains Nat'l Park C10
Houston (lake) J8
Houston Ship (chan.) K2
Howard (creek) C7
Hubbard Creek (lake) F5
Hueco (mts.) B10
Intracoastal Waterway J9
Johnson Draw (dry riv.) C7
Kelly A.F.B. J11
Kemp (lake) E4
Kingsville N.A.S. G10
Kiowa (creek) D1
Lackland A.F.B. 9,352 J11
Lake Meredith Nat'l Rec. Area C2
Lampasas (riv.) G6
Laughlin A.F.B. 2,556 D8
Lavon (lake) H1
Leon (riv.) F6
Livermore (mt.) C11
Livingston (lake) K7
Llano (riv.) D7
Llano Estacado (plain) B4
Locke (mt.) D11
Los Olmos (creek) F10
Los Olmos (creek) F11
Lyndon B. Johnson Nat'l Hist. Site F7
Lyndon B. Johnson Space Ctr. K2
Madre (lag.) G11
Maravillas (creek) A7
Matagorda (bay) H9
Matagorda (isl.) H9
Matagorda (pen.) J9
Medina (lake) E8
Medina (riv.) J11
Mexico (gulf) K9
Middle Concho (riv.) C6
Mountain Creek (lake) G2
Mustang (creek) A1
Mustang (isl.) G10
Mustang Draw (dry riv.) B5
Navasota (riv.) H7
Navidad (riv.) H8
Neches (riv.) K6
North Concho (riv.) C6
North Pease (riv.) D3
Nueces (riv.) F9
Padre (isl.) G10
Padre Island Nat'l Seashore G11
Palo Duro (creek) B2
Palo Duro (creek) C1
Pease (riv.) D3
Pecos (riv.) C7
Pedernales (riv.) F7
Possum Kingdom (lake) F5
Prairie Dog Town Fork, Red (riv.) C3
Quitman (mts.) B11
Randolph A.F.B. K10
Ray Hubbard (lake) H2
Red (riv.) F3
Red Bluff (lake) D10
Reese A.F.B. B4
Rio Grande (riv.) D9
Rita Blanca (creek) B2
Sabine (riv.) L7
Salt Fork, Red (riv.) D3
Sam Rayburn (res.) K6
San Antonio (bay) H9
San Antonio (mt.) B10
San Antonio Missions Nat'l Hist. Park J11
San Francisco (creek) B8
San Luis (passage) K8
San Martine Draw (dry riv.) C11
San Saba (riv.) D7
Santa Isabel (creek) E10
Santiago (mts.) A8
Santiago (peak) D12
Sheppard A.F.B. F3
Sierra Diablo (mts.) C10
Sierra Vieja (mts.) C11
Staked (Llano Estacado) (plain) B4
Stamford (lake) E4
Stockton (plat.) B7
Sulphur (riv.) J4
Sulphur Draw (dry riv.) B4
Sulphur Springs (creek) B4
Tenmile (creek) G3
Terlingua (creek) D12
Texoma (lake) H3
Thomas (lake) C5
Tierra Blanca (creek) B3
Toledo Bend (res.) L6
Toyah (creek) D11
Toyah (lake) A6
Travis (lake) G7
Trinity (bay) L2
Trinity (riv.) H5
Trinity, West Fork (riv.) G2
Trujillo (creek) A2
Washita (riv.) D2
West (bay) K3
White (riv.) C3
White River (lake) C4
White Rock (creek) G2
Wichita (riv.) F4
Wolf (creek) D1
Worth (lake) E2
Wright Patman (lake) K4

▲County seat

Texas

Western Part of Texas
Same scale as main map

State Capitals ⊛
County Seats ⊙
Major Limited Access Hwys.

© Copyright HAMMOND INCORPORATED, Maplewood, N.J.

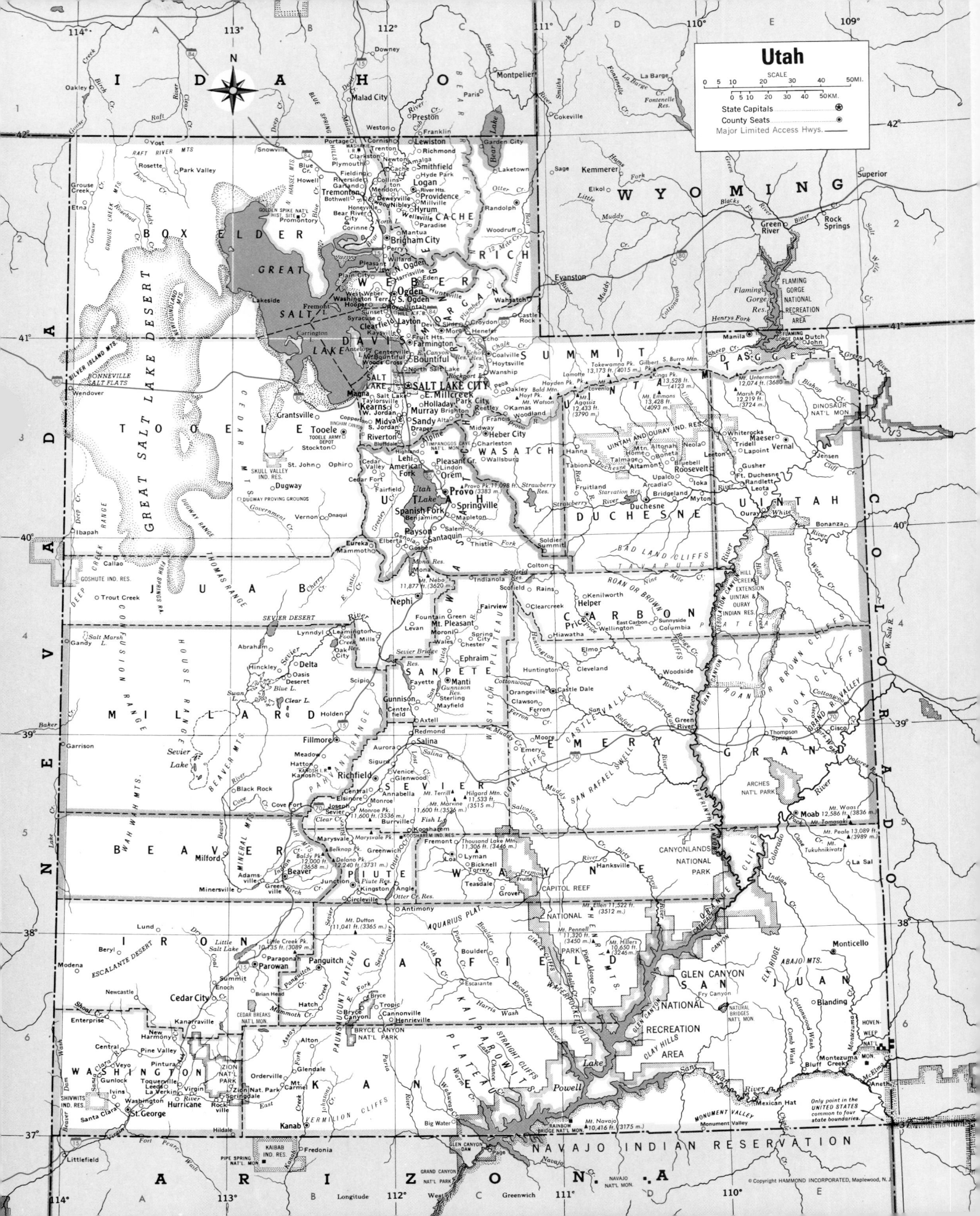

Utah
SCALE
0 5 10 20 30 40 50 MI.
0 5 10 20 30 40 50 KM.
State Capitals
County Seats
Major Limited Access Hwys.
IDAHO
WYOMING
COLORADO
NEVADA
ARIZONA
BOX ELDER
CACHE
RICH
WEBER
MORGAN
DAVIS
SUMMIT
DAGGETT
SALT LAKE
TOOELE
UTAH
WASATCH
UINTAH
DUCHESNE
JUAB
SANPETE
CARBON
MILLARD
SEVIER
EMERY
GRAND
BEAVER
PIUTE
WAYNE
IRON
GARFIELD
SAN JUAN
WASHINGTON
KANE
GREAT SALT LAKE
GREAT SALT LAKE DESERT
SALT LAKE CITY
Ogden
Provo
Logan
Brigham City
Vernal
Price
Moab
Cedar City
St. George
Kanab
Monticello
Blanding
FLAMING GORGE NATIONAL RECREATION AREA
DINOSAUR NAT'L MON.
ARCHES NAT'L PARK
CANYONLANDS NATIONAL PARK
CAPITOL REEF NATIONAL PARK
GLEN CANYON NATIONAL RECREATION AREA
BRYCE CANYON NAT'L PARK
ZION NAT'L PARK
CEDAR BREAKS NAT'L MON.
NATURAL BRIDGES NAT'L MON.
RAINBOW BRIDGE NAT'L MON.
Lake Powell
NAVAJO INDIAN RESERVATION
UINTA MTS.
HENRY MTS.
ABAJO MTS.
Only point in the UNITED STATES common to four state boundaries.
Longitude West of Greenwich
© Copyright HAMMOND INCORPORATED, Maplewood, N.J.

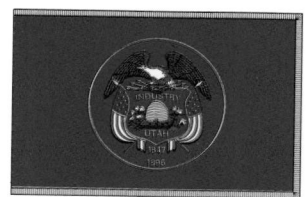

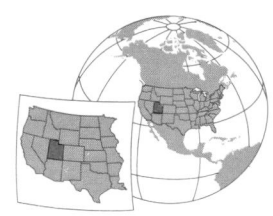

AREA 84,899 sq. mi. (219,888 sq. km.)
POPULATION 1,727,784
CAPITAL Salt Lake City
LARGEST CITY Salt Lake City
HIGHEST POINT Kings Pk. 13,528 ft. (4123 m.)
SETTLED IN 1847
ADMITTED TO UNION January 4, 1896
POPULAR NAME Beehive State
STATE FLOWER Sego Lily
STATE BIRD Sea Gull

COUNTIES

Beaver 4,765.................A5
Box Elder 36,485...........A2
Cache 70,183................C2
Carbon 20,228..............D4
Daggett 690.................E3
Davis 187,941..............B3
Duchesne 12,645...........D3
Emery 10,332...............D4
Garfield 3,980..............C6
Grand 6,620.................E5
Iron 20,789.................A6
Juab 5,817..................A4
Kane 5,169..................B6
Millard 11,333..............A4
Morgan 5,528...............C2
Piute 1,277.................B5
Rich 1,725..................C2
Salt Lake 725,956..........B3
San Juan 12,621............E6
Sanpete 16,259.............C4
Sevier 15,431...............C5
Summit 15,518..............C3
Tooele 26,601...............A3
Uintah 22,211...............E3
Utah 263,590................C3
Wasatch 10,089.............C3
Washington 48,560.........A6
Wayne 2,177................C5
Weber 158,330..............B2

CITIES and TOWNS

Alpine 3,492................C3
Alta 397....................C3
Amalga 366.................C2
American Fork 14,696.......C3
Annabella 487...............B5
Aurora 851...................B5
Bear River City 700..........B2
Beaver▲ 1,998...............B5
Bicknell 327.................C5
Big Water 326...............C6
Blanding 3,162..............E6
Bluffdale 2,152.............B3
Bountiful 36,659............C3
Brigham City▲ 15,644.......C2
Brighton 150................C3
Castle Dale 1,704...........D4
Castle Rock.................C2
Cedar City 13,443...........A6
Cedar Fort 284..............B3
Centerfield 766.............C4
Centerville 11,500..........C3
Charleston 336..............C3
Circleville 417..............B5
Clarkston 645...............B2

Clearfield 21,435...........B2
Cleveland 522..............D4
Coalville▲ 1,065............C3
Corinne 639.................B2
Delta 2,998.................B4
Deweyville 318..............B2
Draper 7,257................C3
Duchesne▲ 1,308...........D3
Dugway 1,761...............B3
East Carbon 1,270..........D4
East Millcreek 21,184.......C3
Elmo 267....................D4
Elsinore 608................B5
Elwood 575.................B2
Emery 300..................D4
Enoch 1,947................A6
Enterprise 936..............A6
Ephraim 3,363..............C4
Eureka 562.................B4
Fairview 960................C4
Farmington▲ 9,028.........C4
Ferron 1,606................D4
Fielding 422................B2
Fillmore▲ 1,956............B5
Fort Duchesne 655..........E3
Fountain Green 578.........C4
Francis 381.................C3
Fruit Heights 3,900.........C2
Garden City 193.............C2
Garland 1,637..............B2
Genola 803.................C3
Glendale 282...............B6
Glenwood 437..............C5
Goshen 578.................C3
Grantsville 4,500...........B3
Green River 866............E4
Gunnison 1,298.............C4
Harrisville 3,004............C2
Heber City▲ 4,782.........C3
Helper 2,148................D4
Henefer 554................C2
Highland 5,002.............C3
Hildale 1,325...............A6
Hinckley 658................B4
Holden 402.................B4
Holladay 22,189............C3
Honeyville 1,112............B2
Hooper 3,468...............B2
Howell 237..................B2
Huntington 1,875...........C4
Huntsville 561..............C2
Hurricane 3,915............A6
Hyde Park 2,190............C2
Hyrum 4,829...............C2
Ivins 1,630..................A6
Joseph 198.................B5
Junction▲ 132..............B5

Kamas 1,061................C3
Kanab▲ 3,289..............B6
Kanarraville 228.............A6
Kanosh 386.................B5
Kaysville 13,961............B2
Kearns 28,374..............B3
Koosharem 266.............B5
La Verkin 1,771.............A6
Laketown 261...............C2
Layton 41,784..............C2
Leamington 253.............B4
Leeds 254..................A6
Lehi 8,475..................C3
Levan 416..................C4
Lewiston 1,532.............C2
Lindon 3,818...............C3
Loa▲ 444..................C5
Logan▲ 32,762.............C2
Lyman 198..................C5
Maeser 2,598...............E3
Magna 17,829..............B3
Manila▲ 207................E3
Manti▲ 2,268..............C4
Mantua 665.................C2
Mapleton 3,572............C3
Marysvale 364..............B5
Mayfield 438...............C4
Meadow 250................B5
Mendon 684................B2
Mexican Hat 259...........E6
Midvale 11,886.............B3
Midway 1,554..............C3
Milford 1,107...............A5
Millville 1,202..............C2
Minersville 608.............A5
Moab▲ 3,971..............E5
Mona 584..................C4
Monroe 1,472..............B5
Montezuma Creek 345......E6
Monticello▲ 1,806.........E6
Morgan▲ 2,023.............C2
Moroni 1,115...............C4
Mount Pleasant 2,092......C4
Murray 31,282..............C3
Myton 468.................D3
Neola 511..................D3
Nephi▲ 3,515..............C4
Newton 659.................C2
Nibley 1,167...............C2
North Ogden 11,668........C2
North Salt Lake 6,474......C3
Oak City 587...............B4
Oakley 522.................C3
Ogden▲ 63,909............C2
Orangeville 1,459..........C4
Orderville 422..............B6
Orem 67,561...............C3
Panguitch▲ 1,444.........B6

Paradise 561................C2
Paragonah 307.............B6
Park City 4,468............C3
Parowan▲ 1,873...........B6
Payson 9,510...............C3
Perry 1,211.................C2
Plain City 2,722............B2
Pleasant Grove 13,476.....C3
Pleasant View 3,603........B2
Plymouth 267...............B2
Price▲ 8,712...............D4
Providence 3,344...........C2
Provo▲ 86,835.............C3
Randlett 283................E3
Randolph▲ 488............C2
Redmond 648...............C4
Richfield▲ 5,593...........B5
Richmond 1,955............C2
River Heights 1,274........C2
Riverton 11,261.............B3
Roosevelt 3,915............D3
Roy 24,603.................C2
Saint George▲ 28,502.....A6
Salem 2,284................C3
Salina 1,943................C5
Salt Lake City (cap.)▲
  159,936...................C3
Sandy 75,058...............C3
Santa Clara 2,322..........A6
Santaquin 2,386............C4
Scipio 291..................B4
Sigurd 385..................B5
Smithfield 5,566............C2
South Jordan 12,220........B3
South Ogden 12,105........C2
South Salt Lake 10,129.....C3
Spanish Fork 11,272........C3
Spring City 715.............C4
Springdale 275..............B6
Springville 13,950..........C3
Stockton 426...............B3
Sunnyside 339.............D4
Sunset 5,128...............B2
Syracuse 4,658.............B2
Taylorsville-Bennion 52,351..B3
Tooele▲ 13,887............B3
Toquerville 488............A6
Tremonton 4,264...........B2
Trenton 464................B2
Tropic 374..................B6
Uintah 760..................C2
Vernal▲ 6,644.............E3
Wallsburg 252..............C3
Washington 4,198..........A6
Washington Terrace 8,189...B2
Wellington 1,632...........D4
Wellsville 2,206............C2
Wendover 1,127............A3

West Bountiful 4,477........B3
West Jordan 42,892.........B3
Whiterocks 312.............E3
Willard 1,298...............B2
Woods Cross 5,384.........B3

OTHER FEATURES

Abajo (mts.)................E6
Agassiz (mt.)...............D3
Antelope (isl.)..............B3
Aquarius (plat.)............C5
Arches Nat'l Park..........E5
Assay (creek)...............B6
Bad Land (cliffs)...........D4
Baldy (peak)...............B5
Bear (lake)..................C2
Bear (riv.).................B2
Beaver (mts.)..............A5
Beaver (riv.)...............A5
Beaver Dam Wash (creek)..A6
Birch (creek)...............C4
Blue (creek)................B2
Bonneville (salt flats)......A3
Book (cliffs)...............E4
Bryce Canyon Nat'l Park...B6
Canyonlands Nat'l Park....D5
Capitol Reef Nat'l Park....C5
Castle (valley).............D4
Cedar (mts.)...............B3
Cedar Breaks Nat'l Mon....B6
Chalk (creek)...............C3
Chinle (creek)..............E6
Clear (lake)................B4
Cliff (creek)................C5
Coal (cliffs)................E5
Colorado (riv.)..............E5
Confusion (range)..........A4
Cottonwood (creek)........C4
Cub (creek).................C1
Deep (creek)...............B1
Deep Creek (range)........A4
Delano (peak)..............B5
Desolation (canyon)........E4
Dinosaur Nat'l Mon.........E3
Dirty Devil (riv.)...........D5
Dolores (riv.)...............E5
Dry Coal (creek)...........A6
Duchesne (riv.)............D3
Dugway (range).............A3
Dugway Proving Grounds...B3
Dutton (mt.)...............B5
East Canyon (res.).........C3
Echo (res.).................C3
Elk (ridge).................E6
Ellen (mt.).................D5
Emmons (mt.)..............D3
Escalante (des.)............A6

West Bountiful 4,477........B3

Escalante (riv.)............C6
Fish (lake).................C5
Fish Springs (range).......A4
Flaming Gorge (res.)......E3
Flaming Gorge Nat'l
  Rec. Area.................E2
Fool Creek (res.)..........B4
Fremont (isl.)..............B2
Fremont (riv.)..............C5
Glen Canyon Nat'l Rec. Area..D6
Golden Spike Nat'l Hist. Site..B2
Goshute Ind. Res...........A4
Government (creek).........B3
Gray (canyon)..............D4
Great Salt (lake)...........B2
Great Salt Lake (des.)......A3
Greeley (creek)............B3
Green (riv.)................D4
Grouse (creek)............A2
Grouse Creek (mts.).......A2
Gunnison (res.)............C4
Henry (mts.)...............D6
Hilgard (mt.)...............D6
Hill (creek)................E4
Hill A.F.B..................C2
Hill Creek Extension, Uintah
  and Ouray Ind. Res.......E4
Hillers (mt.)...............D6
House (range)..............A4
Hovenweep Nat'l Mon......E6
Hoyt (peak)................C3
Huntington (creek).........C4
Indian (creek)..............B5
Jordan (riv.)...............B3
Kaiparowits (plat.)........C6
Kanab (creek)..............B7
Kanosh Ind. Res...........B5
Kings (peak)...............D3
Koosharem Ind. Res.......C5
Little Creek (peak).........B6
Little Salt (lake)...........A6
Malad (riv.)................B1
Marsh (peak)...............E3
Marvine (mt.)..............C5
Mineral (mts.)..............B5
Mona (res.)................C3
Monroe (peak)..............B5
Montezuma (creek).........E6
Monument (valley)........D6
Muddy (creek)..............C4
Natural Bridges Nat'l Mon..E6
Navajo (mt.)...............D7
Navajo Ind. Res............D7
Nebo (mt.).................C4
Newfoundland (mts.)......A2
Nine Mile (creek)..........D3
North (lake)................B2
Orange (cliffs).............D5

Otter (creek)...............C5
Otter Creek (res.)..........C5
Paria (riv.).................B6
Paunsaugunt (plat.)........B6
Pahvant (range)............B5
Peale (mt.)................E5
Pennell (mt.)...............D6
Piute (res.)................B5
Plumber (creek)............C2
Powell (lake)...............D6
Price (riv.).................D4
Provo (peak)...............C3
Provo (riv.)................C3
Raft River (mts.)...........A2
Rainbow Bridge Nat'l Mon...C6
Roan (cliffs)................E4
Rockport (lake)............C3
Salvation (creek)..........C5
San Juan (riv.)............D6
San Pitch (riv.)............C4
San Rafael (riv.)...........D4
San Rafael Swell (mts.)....D5
Santa Clara (riv.)..........A6
Sevier (des.)...............B4
Sevier (lake)...............A5
Sevier (riv.)................B4
Silver Bridge (res.)........C4
Shivwits Ind. Res..........A6
Silver Island (mts.).........A3
Skull Valley Ind. Res.......B3
Spanish Fork (riv.)........C3
Strait (cliffs)..............C6
Strawberry (res.)..........C3
Strawberry (riv.)..........D3
Swan (lake)................B4
Tavaputs (plat.)...........D4
Thomas (range)............A4
Thousand Lake (mt.).......C5
Timpanogos Cave Nat'l Mon...C3
Tokewamna (peak).........D3
Tooele Army Depot........B3
Two Water (creek).........E4
Uinta (mts.)...............D3
Uinta (riv.)................D3
Uintah and Ouray Ind. Res..D3
Utah (lake).................C3
Virgin (riv.)................A6
Waas (mt.)................E5
Wah Wah (mts.)............A5
Wasatch (range)...........C3
Washakie Ind. Res.........B2
Waterpocket Fold (cliffs)...D6
Weber (riv.)...............C3
White (riv.)................E3
Willow (creek)............E4
Zion Nat'l Park............A6

▲County seat

Agriculture, Industry and Resources

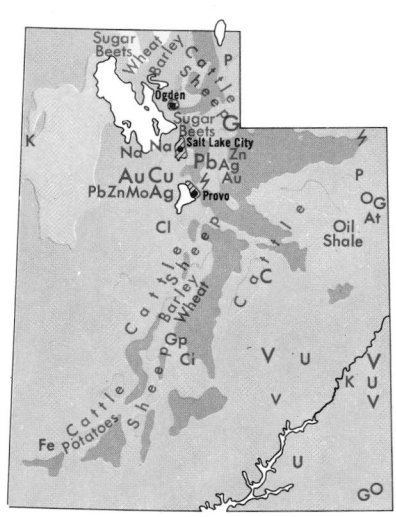

DOMINANT LAND USE

Wheat, General Farming

General Farming, Livestock, Special Crops

Range Livestock

Forests

Nonagricultural Land

MAJOR MINERAL OCCURRENCES

Ag Silver
At Asphalt
Au Gold
C Coal
Cl Clay
Cu Copper

Fe Iron Ore
G Natural Gas
Gp Gypsum
K Potash
Mo Molybdenum
Na Salt

O Petroleum
P Phosphates
Pb Lead
U Uranium
V Vanadium
Zn Zinc

 Water Power

Major Industrial Areas

Topography

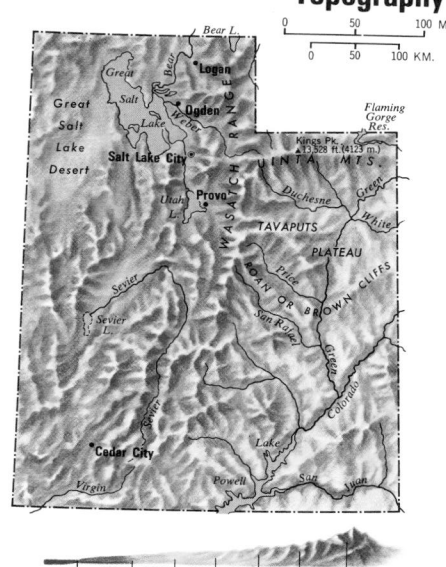

| Below Sea Level | 100 m. 328 ft. | 200 m. 656 ft. | 500 m. 1,640 ft. | 1,000 m. 3,281 ft. | 2,000 m. 6,562 ft. | 5,000 m. 16,404 ft. |

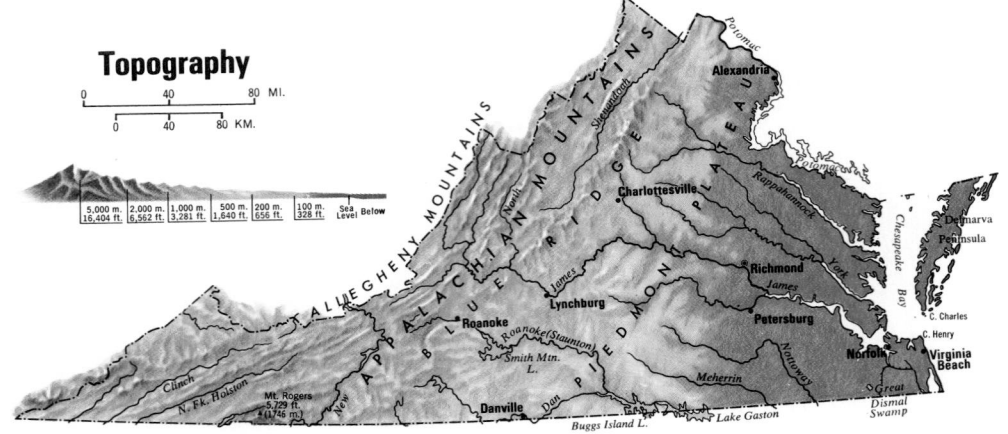

Topography

5,000 m. | 2,000 m. | 1,000 m. | 500 m. | 200 m. | 100 m. | Sea | Below
16,404 ft. | 6,562 ft. | 3,281 ft. | 1,640 ft. | 656 ft. | 328 ft. | Level |

© Copyright HAMMOND INCORPORATED, Maplewood, N.J.

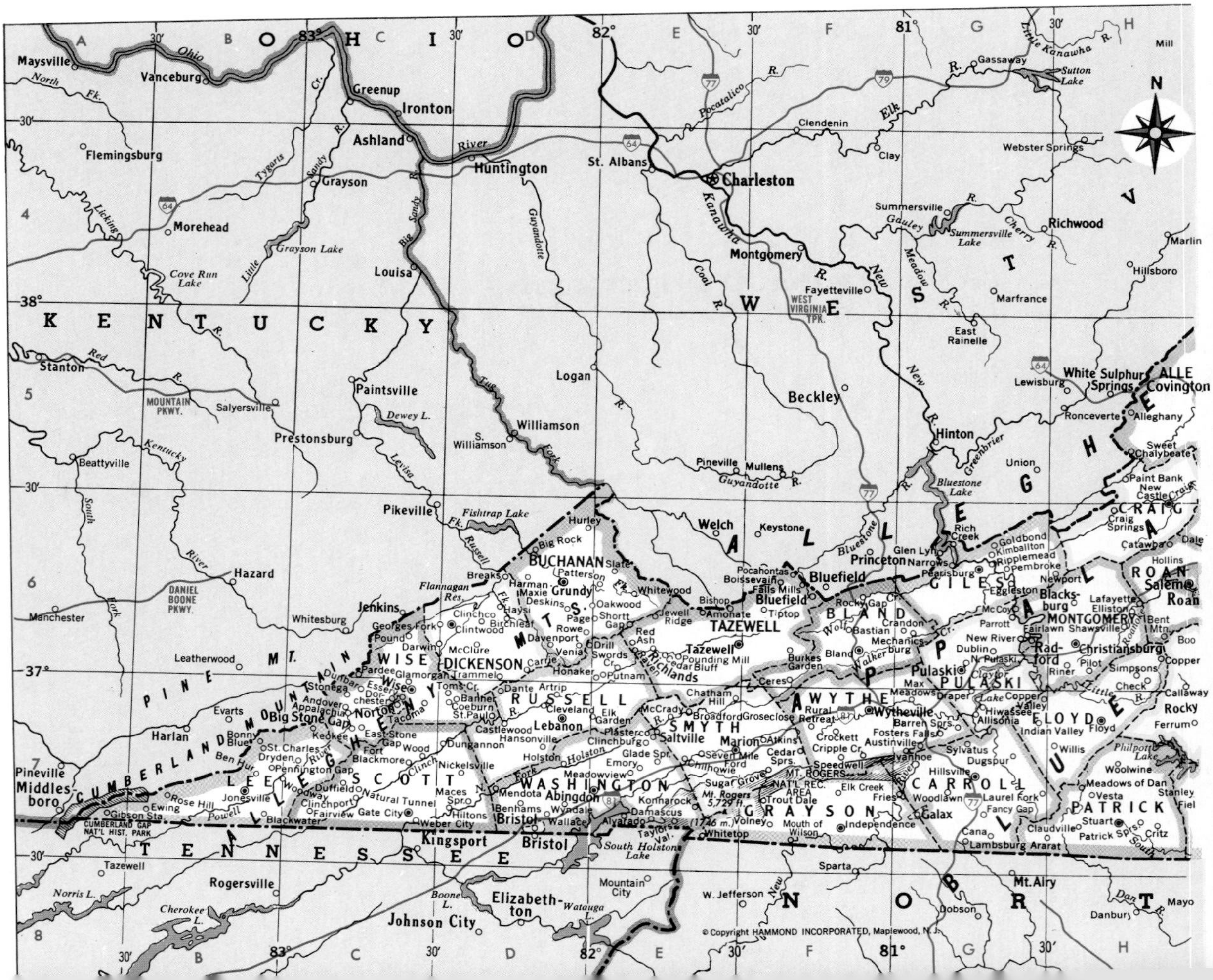

AREA 40,767 sq. mi. (105,587 sq. km.)
POPULATION 6,216,568
CAPITAL Richmond
LARGEST CITY Norfolk
HIGHEST POINT Mt. Rogers 5,729 ft. (1746 m.)
SETTLED IN 1607
ADMITTED TO UNION June 26, 1788
POPULAR NAME Old Dominion
STATE FLOWER Dogwood
STATE BIRD Cardinal

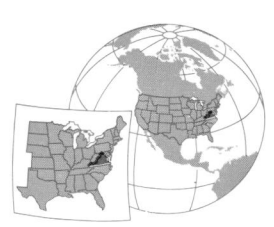

(continued on following page)

Agriculture, Industry and Resources

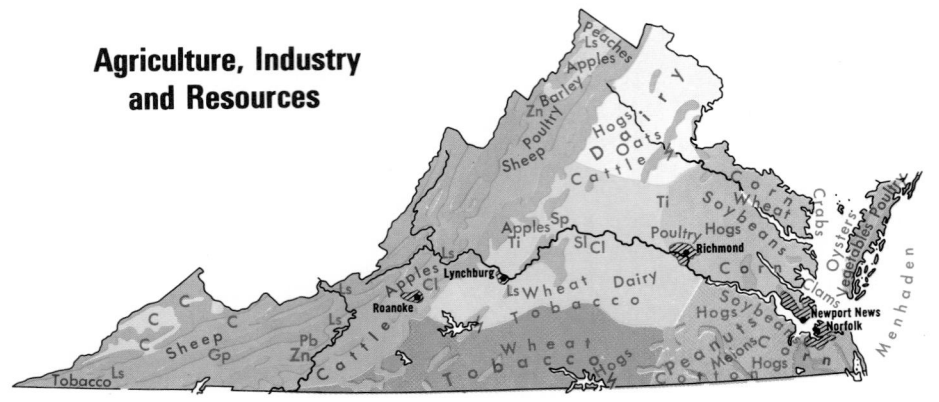

DOMINANT LAND USE

- ☐ Dairy, General Farming
- General Farming, Livestock, Dairy
- General Farming, Livestock, Tobacco
- General Farming, Livestock, Fruit, Tobacco
- General Farming, Truck Farming, Tobacco, Livestock
- Tobacco, General Farming
- Peanuts, General Farming
- Fruit and Mixed Farming
- Truck and Mixed Farming
- Forests
- Swampland, Limited Agriculture

MAJOR MINERAL OCCURRENCES

C	Coal	Sl	Slate
Cl	Clay	Sp	Soapstone
Gp	Gypsum	Ti	Titanium
Ls	Limestone	Zn	Zinc
Pb	Lead		

⚡ Water Power
▨ Major Industrial Areas

Haysi 222	D6	
Healing Springs 175	J5	
Heathsville▲ 300	P5	
Henry 300	J7	
Herndon 16,139	O3	
Highland Springs 13,823	O5	
Hillsville▲ 2,008	G7	
Hiltons 300	C7	
Hiwassee 250	G7	
Hoadly 400	O3	
Hollins College 12,295	H6	
Honaker 950	C6	
Hopewell (I.C.) 23,101	O6	
Horntown 400	T5	
Hot Springs 200	J4	
Huddleston 200	K6	
Hume 350	N3	
Huntington 7,489	S3	
Hurley 850	D6	
Hurt 1,294	K6	
Independence▲ 988	F7	
Indian Valley 300	G7	
Iron Gate 417	J5	
Irvington 496	R5	
Isle of Wight▲ 185	P7	
Ivanhoe 900	G7	
Ivor 324	P7	
Ivy 900	L4	
Jamestown 12	P6	
Jamesville 500	S5	
Jarratt 556	O7	
Jefferson 25,782	N5	
Jefferson Manor	S3	
Jeffersonton 300	N3	
Jewell Ridge 600	E6	
Jonesville▲ 927	B7	
Keeling 680	K7	
Keezletown 975	L4	
Keller 235	S5	
Kenbridge 1,264	M7	
Kents Store 130	M5	
Keokee 300	C7	
Keswick 300	M4	
Keysville 800	M6	
Kilmarnock 1,109	R5	
King George▲ 575	O4	
King William▲ 100	O5	
King and Queen Court House▲ 500	P5	
Kinsale 250	P5	
La Crosse 549	M7	

Lacey Spring 140	L3	
Ladysmith 360	N4	
Lafayette-Elliston	H6	
Lake Barcroft 8,686	S3	
Lakeside 12,081	O5	
Lambsburg 800	G7	
Lancaster▲ 110	R5	
Laurel Fork 300	G7	
Lawrenceville▲ 1,486	N7	
Lebanon Church 300	L2	
Lebanon▲ 3,206	D7	
Leesburg▲ 16,202	N2	
Lewisetta 125	R4	
Lexington (I.C.)▲ 6,959	J5	
Lincolnia 13,041	S3	
Linden 320	M3	
Linville 500	L3	
Little Plymouth 195	P5	
Lively 400	R5	
Loretto 150	O4	
Lorton 15,385	O3	
Louisa▲ 1,088	M4	
Lovettsville 749	N2	
Lovingston▲ 600	L5	
Lowesville 500	K5	
Lowmoor 700	J4	
Lucketts 500	N2	
Lunenburg▲ 13	M7	
Luray▲ 4,587	M3	
Lynch Station 500	K6	
Lynchburg (I.C.) 66,049	K5	
Machipongo 400	S6	
Madison Heights 11,700	K5	
Madison▲ 267	M4	
Manakin-Sabot 200	N5	
Manassas (I.C.)▲ 27,957	O3	
Manassas Park (I.C.) 6,734	O3	
Mannboro 175	N6	
Manquin-576	O5	
Mantua 6,804	S3	
Mappsville 700	T5	
Marion▲ 6,630	E7	
Markham 300	N3	
Marshall 800	N3	
Martinsville (I.C.)▲ 16,162	J7	
Massies Mill 225	K5	
Mathews▲ 300	R6	
Matoaca 1,967	N6	
Mattaponi 300	P5	
Maurertown 158	L2	
Max Meadows 782	G6	

McClure 300	D6	
McCoy 600	G6	
McGaheysville 600	L4	
McKenney 386	N7	
McLean 38,168	S2	
Meadows of Dan 150	H7	
Meadowview-Emory 2,292	C7	
Mechanicsburg 350	G6	
Mechanicsville 22,027	O5	
Meherrin 400	M6	
Melfa 428	S5	
Mendota 375	D7	
Merrifield 8,399	S3	
Middlebrook 125	K4	
Middleburg 549	B3	
Middletown 841	M2	
Midland 600	N3	
Midlothian 950	N6	
Milford 650	O4	
Millboro 400	J5	
Millboro Springs 200	J4	
Millwood 400	N2	
Mine Run 450	N4	
Mineral 471	N4	
Mobjack 210	R6	
Modest Town 225	T5	
Mollusk 800	R5	
Moneta 300	J6	
Monroe 500	K5	
Monterey▲ 222	K4	
Montross▲ 359	P4	
Montvale 900	J6	
Morattico 225	R5	
Moseley 200	N6	
Mount Crawford 228	L4	
Mount Holly 200	P4	
Mount Jackson 1,583	L3	
Mount Sidney 500	L4	
Mount Solon 124	K4	
Mount Vernon 27,485	O3	
Mouth of Wilson 400	F7	
Mustoe 150	K4	
Naruna 175	L6	
Nassawadox 564	S6	
Nathalie 200	L7	
Natural Bridge 200	J5	
Natural Bridge Sta. 450	K5	
Naxera 300	R6	
Nellysford 290	L5	
New Baltimore 125	N3	

New Castle▲ 152	H5	
New Church 427	S5	
New Hope 200	L4	
New Kent▲ 25	P5	
New Market 1,435	L3	
New River 500	G6	
Newington 17,965	S3	
Newport 600	H6	
Newport News (I.C.) 170,045	P6	
Newsoms 337	O7	
Nickelsville 411	D7	
Nokesville 520	N3	
Nora 550	D6	
Norfolk (I.C.) 261,229	R7	
Norge 750	P6	
North Garden 300	L5	
North Pulaski 1,405	G6	
North Springfield 8,996	S3	
Norton (I.C.) 4,247	C7	
Nottoway▲ 170	M6	
Oak Hall 221	S5	
Oakpark 150	M4	
Oakton 24,610	R3	
Oakwood 715	E6	
Occoquan 361	O3	
Onancock 1,434	S5	
Onley 532	S5	
Orange▲ 2,582	M4	
Owenton 400	O5	
Oyster 200	S6	
Paint Bank 235	H5	
Painter 259	S5	
Palmyra▲ 250	M5	
Pamplin 273	L6	
Pardee 190	C6	
Parksley 779	S5	
Parrott 750	G6	
Patrick Springs 800	H7	
Peaks 500	D6	
Pearisburg▲ 2,064	G6	
Pembroke 1,064	G6	
Penhook 500	J7	
Pennington Gap 1,922	C7	
Petersburg (I.C.) 38,386	N6	
Phenix 260	L6	
Philomont 265	N2	
Pilot 360	H6	
Pimmit 6,658	S2	
Piney River 778	L5	
Pittsville 600	K7	
Pleasant Valley 150	L4	
Pocahontas 513	D6	
Poquoson 11,005	R6	
Port Royal 204	O4	
Portsmouth (I.C.) 103,907	R7	
Potomac Beach 200	P4	
Pound 995	C6	
Pounding Mill 399	E6	
Powhatan▲ 600	N5	
Prince George▲ 150	O6	
Prospect 275	L6	
Providence Forge 500	P6	
Pulaski▲ 9,985	G6	
Pungoteague 500	S5	
Purcellville 1,744	N2	
Purdy 350	N7	
Quantico 670	O3	
Quicksburg 160	L3	
Quinby 350	S5	
Radford (I.C.) 15,940	G6	
Radiant 250	M4	
Randolph 150	L7	
Raphine 500	K5	
Rapiden 176	M4	

Raven 2,640	E6	
Rawlings 200	N7	
Rectortown 225	N3	
Red Ash 300	E6	
Red Hill 12,675	E7	
Red House 150	L6	
Red Oak 250	L7	
Reedville 400	R5	
Reliance 150	M3	
Remington 460	N3	
Republican Grove 125	K7	
Reston 48,556	R2	
Rice 194	M6	
Rich Creek 746	G6	
Richlands 4,456	E6	
Richmond (cap.) (I.C.)▲ 203,056	O5	
Ridgeway 752	J7	
Riner 360	H6	
Ringgold 150	K7	
Ripplemead 600	G6	
Riverton 500	M3	
Rixeyville 150	M3	
Roanoke (I.C.) 96,397	H6	
Rockville 290	N5	
Rocky Gap 200	F6	
Rocky Mount▲ 4,098	J7	
Rose Hill 12,675	B7	
Rosedale 760	E7	
Roseland 300	K5	
Round Hill 514	N2	
Rowe 150	D6	
Ruby 188	N3	
Rural Retreat 972	F7	
Rushmere▲ 1,064	P6	
Rustburg▲ 650	K6	
Ruther Glen 200	O5	
Ruthville 300	P6	
Saint Charles 206	B7	
Saint Paul 1,007	D7	
Saint Stephens Church 500	O5	
Salem (I.C.)▲ 23,756	H6	
Saltville 2,376	E7	
Saluda▲ 150	P5	
Sandy Hook 700	M5	
Saxis 367	S5	
Schuyler 250	L7	
Scottsburg 152	L7	
Scottsville 239	L5	
Sealston 200	O4	
Sebrell 160	O7	
Sedley 523	P7	
Selma 500	J5	
Seven Corners 7,280	S3	
Seven Mile Ford 425	E7	
Shanghai 150	P5	
Shawsville 1,260	H6	
Shenandoah 2,213	L4	
Shiloh 150	L5	
Shipman 350	L5	
Simpsons 150	H6	
Singers Glen 155	K3	
Skippers 150	N7	
Skipwith 128	L7	
Smithfield 4,686	P6	
Snell 300	N4	
Somerset 200	M4	
South Boston (I.C.) 6,997	L7	
South Hill 4,217	M7	
Sparta 485	O4	
Speedwell 650	F7	
Spencer 500	J7	
Sperryville 500	M3	
Spotsylvania▲ 350	N4	
Springfield 23,706	S3	

Stafford▲ 750	O4	
Stanardsville▲ 257	L4	
Stanley 1,186	L3	
Stanleytown 1,563	H7	
Star Tannery 500	L2	
Staunton (I.C.)▲ 24,461	K4	
Steeles Tavern 200	K5	
Stephens City 1,186	M2	
Sterling 20,512	O2	
Stevensburg 125	N4	
Stonega 275	C7	
Stony Creek 271	N7	
Strasburg 3,762	M3	
Stuart▲ 965	H7	
Stuarts Draft 5,087	L4	
Studley 500	O5	
Suffolk (I.C.) 52,141	P7	
Sugar Grove 1,027	E7	
Surry▲ 192	P6	
Susan 500	R6	
Sussex▲ 75	O7	
Sutherlin 180	K7	
Sweet Briar 900	K5	
Swords Creek 315	E6	
Sylvatus 200	G7	
Tacoma 150	C7	
Tangier 659	R5	
Tappahannock▲ 1,550	O5	
Tazewell▲ 4,176	E6	
Temperanceville 400	T5	
Thaxton 450	J6	
The Plains 219	N3	
Thornburg 135	N4	
Timberville 1,596	L3	
Tiptop 175	F6	
Toano 950	P6	
Toms Brook 227	L3	
Townsend 525	R6	
Trammel 450	D6	
Triangle 4,740	O3	
Triplett 300	N7	
Trout Dale 248	F7	
Troutville 455	J6	
Tyro 125	K5	
Union Hall 125	J6	
Unionville 500	N4	
Upperville 250	N2	
Urbanna 529	P5	
Valentines 400	N7	
Vansant 1,187	D6	
Vera 150	L6	
Vernon Hill 250	K7	
Verona 3,479	K4	
Vesta 350	H7	
Vesuvius 500	K5	
Victoria 1,830	M6	
Vienna 14,852	R2	
Vinton 7,665	H6	
Virgilina 161	L7	
Virginia Beach (I.C.) 393,069	S7	
Wachapreague 291	S5	
Wakefield 1,070	O7	
Walkerton 985	O5	
Warm Springs▲ 325	J4	
Warrenton▲ 4,830	N3	
Warsaw▲ 961	P5	
Washington▲ 198	M3	
Water View 265	P5	
Waterford 350	N2	
Waverly 2,223	O6	
Waynesboro (I.C.) 18,549	K4	
Weber City 1,377	C7	
Weems 500	R5	
Weirwood 300	S6	
West Augusta 325	K4	
West Point 2,938	P5	
West Springfield 28,126	S3	
Weyers Cave 300	L4	
White Hall 250	L4	
White Stone 372	R5	
Whitetop 860	E7	
Whitewood 350	D6	
Wicomico Church 500	R5	
Wilderness 300	N4	
Williamsburg (I.C.)▲ 11,530	P6	
Williamsville 145	J4	
Willis 170	H7	
Willis Wharf 360	S5	
Winchester (I.C.)▲ 21,947	M2	
Windsor 1,025	P7	
Wirtz 500	J6	
Wise (I.C.)▲ 3,193	C7	
Wolftown 350	M4	
Woodberry Forest 450	M4	
Woodbridge 26,401	O3	
Woodlawn 1,689	G7	
Woodstock▲ 3,182	L3	
Woodville 400	M3	
Woodway 400	C7	
Woolwine 150	H7	
Wylliesburg 213	L7	
Wytheville▲ 8,038	G7	
Zuni 300	P7	

OTHER FEATURES

Aarons (creek)	L7	
Allegheny (mts.)	H5	
Anna (lake)	N4	
Appalachian (mts.)	J5	
Appomattox (riv.)	M6	
Appomattox Court House Nat'l Hist. Park	K6	
Arlington Nat'l Cemetery	T3	
Assateague Island Nat'l Seashore	T4	
Back (bay)	S7	
Back (creek)	K7	
Banister (riv.)	K7	
Big Otter (riv.)	K6	
Blackwater (riv.)	J6	
Blackwater (riv.)	O7	
Blue Ridge (mts.)	J5	
Bluestone (lake)	G5	
Booker T. Washington Nat'l Mon.	J6	
Buggs Island (lake)	L8	

Bull Run (creek)	N3	
Cedar (isl.)	S5	
Central Intelligence Agency (C.I.A.)	S2	
Charles (cape)	R6	
Chesapeake (bay)	R5	
Chesapeake and Ohio Canal Nat'l Hist. Park	O2	
Chincoteague (bay)	T4	
Chincoteague (inlet)	T5	
Claytor (lake)	G6	
Clinch (riv.)	C7	
Cobb (isl.)	S6	
Colonial Nat'l Hist. Park	P6	
Cowpasture (riv.)	J4	
Craig (creek)	H5	
Cub (creek)	L6	
Cumberland (mt.)	B7	
Cumberland Gap Nat'l Hist. Park	A7	
Dan (riv.)	K7	
Drummond (lake)	P7	
Fishermans (isl.)	S6	
Flannagan (res.)	C6	
Flat (creek)	M6	
Fort A.P. Hill	O4	
Fort Belvoir 8,590	O3	
Fort Eustis	P6	
Fort Lee 6,595	O6	
Fort Monroe	R6	
Fort Myer	T2	
Fort Pickett	N6	
Fort Story	S7	
Gaston (lake)	M8	
George Washington Birthplace Nat'l Mon.	P4	
Goose (creek)	J6	
Goose (creek)	N3	
Great Machipongo (inlet)	S6	
Great North (mt.)	L2	
Hampton Roads (est.)	R7	
Henry (cape)	R7	
Hog (isl.)	S6	
Hog Island (bay)	S6	
Holston, North Fork (riv.)	D7	
Hyco (riv.)	K8	
Jackson (riv.)	J4	
James (riv.)	O6	
Jamestown Nat'l Hist. Site	P6	
John H. Kerr (dam)	M7	
Langley A.F.B.	R6	
Leesville (lake)	K6	
Levisa Fork (riv.)	C5	
Little (inlet)	S6	
Little (isl.)	H7	
Little (riv.)	N5	
Manassas Nat'l Battlefield Pk.	N3	
Massanutten (mt.)	L3	
Mattaponi (riv.)	O5	
Mattaponi Ind. Res.	P5	
Maury (riv.)	K3	
Meherrin (riv.)	M7	
Metompkin (inlet)	T5	
Metompkin (isl.)	T5	
Mobjack (bay)	R6	
Mount Rogers Nat'l Rec. Area	F7	
New (inlet)	S6	
New (inlet)	F8	
Ni (riv.)	N4	
North Anna (riv.)	M4	
Nottoway (riv.)	O7	
Oceana N.A.S.	S7	
Pamunkey (riv.)	O5	
Pamunkey Ind. Res.	P5	
Parramore (isl.)	S5	
Pentagon	T3	
Petersburg Nat'l Battlefield	O6	
Philpott (lake)	H7	
Piankatank (riv.)	P5	
Pigg (riv.)	J7	
Po (riv.)	N4	
Pocomoke (sound)	S5	
Potomac (riv.)	O4	
Powell (riv.)	B7	
Quantico Marine Corps Air Sta.	O4	
Quinby (inlet)	S6	
Rapidan (riv.)	M4	
Rappahannock (riv.)	P4	
Red Hill Patrick Henry Nat'l Mem.	L6	
Richmond Nat'l Battlefield Pk.	O6	
Rivanna (riv.)	M5	
Roanoke (riv.)	N8	
Rogers (mt.)	E7	
Russell Fork (riv.)	C5	
Sand Shoal (isl.)	S6	
Shenandoah (mt.)	K3	
Shenandoah (riv.)	N2	
Shenandoah Nat'l Park	L3	
Ship Shoal (isl.)	S6	
Slate (riv.)	L5	
Smith (isl.)	S6	
Smith (riv.)	J7	
Smith Mountain (lake)	J6	
South Anna (riv.)	N5	
South Holston (lake)	E7	
South Mayo (riv.)	H7	
Stony (creek)	N6	
Swift (creek)	O6	
Tangier (isl.)	R5	
Tangier (sound)	S5	
Tug Fork (riv.)	D5	
U.S. Naval Base	R7	
Vint Hill Farms Mil. Res.	N3	
Wachapreague (inlet)	T6	
Walker (creek)	F6	
Wallops (isl.)	T5	
Willis (riv.)	M5	
Wolf (creek)	F6	
Wolf Trap Farm Park	S2	
York (riv.)	P6	

I.C. Independent City
▲County seat

AREA 68,139 sq. mi. (176,480 sq. km.)
POPULATION 4,887,941
CAPITAL Olympia
LARGEST CITY Seattle
HIGHEST POINT Mt. Rainier 14,410 ft. (4392 m.)
SETTLED IN 1811
ADMITTED TO UNION November 11, 1889
POPULAR NAME Evergreen State
STATE FLOWER Western Rhododendron
STATE BIRD Willow Goldfinch

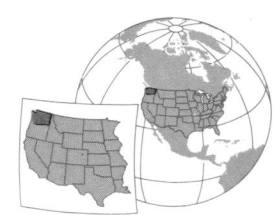

COUNTIES

Adams 13,603 ....G3
Asotin 17,605 ....H4
Benton 112,560 ....F4
Chelan 52,250 ....E3
Clallam 56,464 ....B2
Clark 238,053 ....C5
Columbia 4,024 ....H4
Cowlitz 82,119 ....C4
Douglas 26,205 ....F3
Ferry 6,295 ....G2
Franklin 37,473 ....G4
Garfield 2,248 ....H4
Grant 54,758 ....F3
Grays Harbor 64,175 ....B3
Island 60,195 ....C2
Jefferson 20,146 ....B3
King 1,507,319 ....C3
Kitsap 189,731 ....C3
Kittitas 26,725 ....E3
Klickitat 16,616 ....E5
Lewis 59,358 ....C4
Lincoln 8,864 ....G3
Mason 38,341 ....B3
Okanogan 33,350 ....F2
Pacific 18,882 ....B4
Pend Oreille 8,915 ....H2
Pierce 586,203 ....C3
San Juan 10,035 ....C2
Skagit 79,555 ....D2
Skamania 8,289 ....D5
Snohomish 465,642 ....D2
Spokane 361,364 ....H3
Stevens 30,948 ....H2
Thurston 161,238 ....C4
Wahkiakum 3,832 ....B4
Walla Walla 48,439 ....G4
Whatcom 127,780 ....D2
Whitman 38,775 ....H4
Yakima 188,823 ....E4

CITIES and TOWNS

Aberdeen 16,565 ....B3
Acme 500 ....C2
Addy 180 ....H2
Airway Heights 1,971 .....H3
Albion 632 ....H4
Alder 300 ....C4
Algona 1,694 ....C3
Allyn 80 ....C3
Almira 310 ....G3
Aloha 140 ....A3
Amanda Park 495 ....A3
Amboy 480 ....C5
Anacortes 11,451 ....C2
Appleton 120 ....D5
Ardenvoir 150 ....E3
Ariel 386 ....C5
Arlington 4,037 ....C2
Ashford 300 ....C4
Asotin▲ 981 ....H4
Auburn 33,102 ....C3
Azwell 152 ....F3
Bainbridge Island-Winslow
  (Winslow) A2
Baring 200 ....D3
Battle Ground 3,758 ......C5
Bay Center 187 ....A4
Bay City 187 ....B4
Beaux Arts Village 303 ...B2
Beaver 450 ....B2
Belfair 500 ....C3
Bellevue 86,874 ....B2
Bellingham▲ 52,179 ......C2
Benton City 1,806 ....F4
Beverly 200 ....F4
Biglake 105 ....C2
Bingen 645 ....D5
Black Diamond 1,422 .....D3
Blaine 2,489 ....C2
Blanchard 125 ....C2
Bonney Lake 7,494 ....C3
Bothell 12,345 ....B1
Bow 200 ....C2
Boyds 125 ....G2
Bremerton 38,142 ....C3
Brewster 1,633 ....F2
Bridgeport 1,498 ....F3
Brier 5,633 ....C3
Brinnon 500 ....B3
Brownstown 200 ....E4
Brush Prairie 2,650 ......C5
Bryn Mawr-Skyway 12,514 .B2
Buckley 3,516 ....C3
Bucoda 536 ....C4
Buena 590 ....E4
Burbank 1,745 ....G4
Burien 25,089 ....A2
Burley 300 ....C3
Burlington 4,349 ....C2
Burton 650 ....C3
Camas 6,442 ....C5
Carbonado 495 ....D3
Carlsborg 500 ....B2
Carlton 410 ....F2
Carnation 1,243 ....D3
Carson 500 ....D5
Cashmere 2,544 ....E3
Castle Rock 2,067 ....B4
Cathlamet▲ 508 ....B4
Cedar Falls 200 ....D3
Central Park 2,669 ....B3
Centralia 12,101 ....C4
Chattaroy 250 ....H3
Chehalis▲ 6,527 ....C4
Chelan 2,969 ....E3
Chelan Falls 250 ....E3
Cheney 7,723 ....H3
Chewelah 1,945 ....H2
Chimacum 275 ....C3
Chinook 928 ....A4
Cinebar 200 ....C4
Clallam Bay 600 ....A2
Clarkston 6,753 ....H4
Clayton 175 ....H3
Cle Elum 1,778 ....E3
Clearlake 750 ....C2
Clearwater 194 ....A3
Clinton 1,564 ....C3
Clyde F4
Clyde Hill 2,972 ....B2
Coalfield 500 ....B2
Colbert 225 ....H3
Colby 150 ....A2
Colfax▲ 2,713 ....H4
College Place 6,308 .....G4
Colton 325 ....H4
Columbia Heights 2,515 .C4
Colville▲ 4,360 ....H2
Conconully 153 ....F2
Concrete 735 ....D2
Connell 2,005 ....G4
Conway 150 ....C2
Copalis Beach 600 ....A3
Copalis Crossing 500 ....B3
Cosmopolis 1,372 ....B4
Coulee City 568 ....F3
Coulee Dam 1,087 ....G3
Coupeville▲ 1,377 ....C2
Creston 230 ....G3
Cumberland 250 ....D3
Curlew 168 ....G2
Cusick 195 ....H2
Custer 200 ....C2
Dallesport 600 ....D5
Danville 215 ....G2
Darrington 1,042 ....D2
Davenport▲ 1,502 ....G3
Dayton▲ 2,468 ....H4
Deer Harbor 400 ....C2
Deer Park 2,278 ....H3
Deming 200 ....C2
Des Moines 17,283 ......B2
Dishman 9,671 ....H3
Dixie 210 ....G4
Doe Bay 150 ....C2
Doty 245 ....B4
Dryad 125 ....B4
Dryden 500 ....E3
Du Pont 592 ....C3
Dungeness 675 ....B2
Duvall 2,770 ....D3
East Olympia 300 ....B4
East Wenatchee 2,701 ...E3
Easton 250 ....D3
Eastsound 800 ....B2
Eatonville 1,374 ....C4
Edison 250 ....C2
Edmonds 30,744 ....C3
Edwall 150 ....H3
Electric City 910 ....F3
Ellensburg▲ 12,361 .....E3
Elma 3,011 ....B3
Elmer City 290 ....G2
Eltopia 200 ....G4
Endicott 320 ....H4
Enetai 2,638 ....A2
Entiat 449 ....E3
Enumclaw 7,227 ....D3
Ephrata▲ 5,349 ....F3
Erlands Point 1,254 .....A2
Ethel 180 ....C4
Everett▲ 69,961 ....C3
Everson 1,490 ....C2
Fairfield 446 ....H3
Fairview-Sumach 2,749 ..E4
Fall City 1,582 ....D3
Farmington 126 ....H3
Ferndale 5,398 ....C2
Fife 3,864 ....C3
Finley 4,897 ....F4
Fircrest 5,258 ....C3
Fords Prairie 2,480 ......B4
Forks 2,862 ....A3
Four Lakes 500 ....H3
Frances 144 ....B4
Freeland 1,278 ....C2
Freeman 150 ....H3
Friday Harbor▲ 1,492 ...B2
Fruitland 150 ....G2
Fruitvale 4,125 ....E4
Galvin 250 ....B4
Garfield 544 ....H3
Garrett 1,004 ....G4
Geiger Heights H3
George 253 ....F3
Gig Harbor 3,236 ....C3
Glacier 150 ....D2
Glenoma 500 ....C4
Glenwood 626 ....D4
Gold Bar 1,078 ....D3
Goldendale▲ 3,319 ......E5
Gorst 750 ....C3
Grand Coulee 984 ......G3
Grand Mound 1,394 .....C4
Grandview 7,169 ....F4
Granger 2,053 ....E4
Granite Falls 1,060 .....D2
Grapeview 250 ....C3
Grayland 750 ....A4
Grays River 350 ....B4
Greenacres 4,626 ....J3
Greenbank 600 ....C2
Hadlock-Irondale 2,742 .C2
Hamilton 228 ....D2
Hansville 250 ....A2
Harper 300 ....A2
Harrah 341 ....E4
Harrington 449 ....G3
Hartline 176 ....F3
Hatton 71 ....F4
Heisson 200 ....C5
Hobart 500 ....B3
Hoodsport 500 ....B3
Hoquiam 8,972 ....B4
Humptulips 275 ....A3
Humptulips 200 ....G2
Hunts Point 513 ....B2
Husum 200 ....D5
Ilwaco 815 ....A4
Inchelium 393 ....G2
Index 139 ....D3
Indianola 1,729 ....A1
Ione 507 ....H2
Issaquah 7,786 ....C3
Joyce 375 ....B2
Juanita 17,232 ....B1
Kahlotus 167 ....H4
Kalama 1,210 ....C4
Kapowsin 500 ....C3
Keller 195 ....G2
Kelso▲ 11,820 ....C4
Kenmore 8,917 ....B1
Kennewick 42,155 ......F4
Kent 37,960 ....C3
Kettle Falls 1,272 ......H2
Keyport 900 ....A2
Kingston 1,270 ....C3
Kiona 230 ....F4
Kirkland 40,052 ....B2
Kittitas 843 ....E4
Klickitat 750 ....D5
Krupp (Marlin) 53 .....F3
La Center 451 ....C5
La Conner 656 ....C2
La Push 500 ....A3
Lacey 19,279 ....C3
Lacrosse 336 ....H4
Lake Forest Park 4,031 .B1
Lake Stevens 3,380 ....C2
Lakewood 58,412 .....C2
Lamont 91 ....H3
Langley 845 ....C2
Latah 175 ....H3
Laurel 972 ....C2
Leavenworth 1,692 ....E3
Lebam 275 ....B4
Liberty Lake 2,015 ....J3
Lind 472 ....G4
Littlerock 850 ....B4
Long Beach 1,236 .....A4
Longbranch 640 ....C3
Longview 31,499 ......B4
Loomis 150 ....F2
Loon Lake 500 ....H2
Lummi Island 675 .....C2
Lyle 580 ....D5
Lyman 275 ....D2
Lynden 5,709 ....C2
Lynnwood 28,695 .....C3
Mabton 1,482 ....E4
Malaga 125 ....E3
Malden 189 ....H3
Malo 240 ....G2
Malone 175 ....B4
Malott 350 ....F2
Manchester 4,031 ....A2
Mansfield 311 ....F3
Manson 220 ....E3
Maple Falls 300 ......D2
Maple Valley 1,211 ....C3
Marblemount 300 .....D2
Marcus 135 ....H2
Marietta-Alderwood 2,766 .C2
Markham 117 ....B4
Marlin F3
Marysville 10,328 ....C2
Matlock 255 ....B3
Mattawa 941 ....F4
McCleary 1,235 ......B3
McKenna 300 ....C4
Mead H3
Medical Lake 3,664 ...H3
Medina 2,981 ....B2
Menlo 237 ....B4
Mercer Island (city)
  20,816 ....B2
Mesa 252 ....G4
Metaline 198 ....H2
Metaline Falls 210 ...H2
Mica 105 ....H3
Milan 150 ....H3
Millwood 1,559 ......H3
Milton 4,995 ....C3
Mineral 550 ....C4
Moclips 500 ....A3
Monitor 650 ....E3
Monroe 4,278 ....D3
Montesano▲ 3,064 ....B4
Moses Lake 11,235 ...F3
Mossyrock 452 ....C4
Mount Vernon▲ 17,647 .C2
Mountlake Terrace 19,320 .B1
Moxee City 814 ....E4
Mukilteo 7,007 ....C3
Naches 596 ....E4
Nahcotta 200 ....A4
Napavine 745 ....C4
Naselle 500 ....B4
Navy Yard City 2,905 ..A2
Neah Bay 916 ....A2
Neilton 250 ....B3
Nespelem 291 ....G2
Newhalem 350 ....D2
Newman Lake 102 .....J3
Newport▲ 1,691 ....H2
Nine Mile Falls 150 ...H3
Nisqually 558 ....C3
Nooksack 584 ....C2
Nordland 706 ....C2
Normandy Park 6,709 .A2
North Bend 2,578 ....D3
North Bonneville 411 ..C5
Northport 308 ....H2
Oak Harbor 17,176 ...C2
Oakesdale 346 ....H3
Oakville 493 ....B4

Agriculture, Industry and Resources

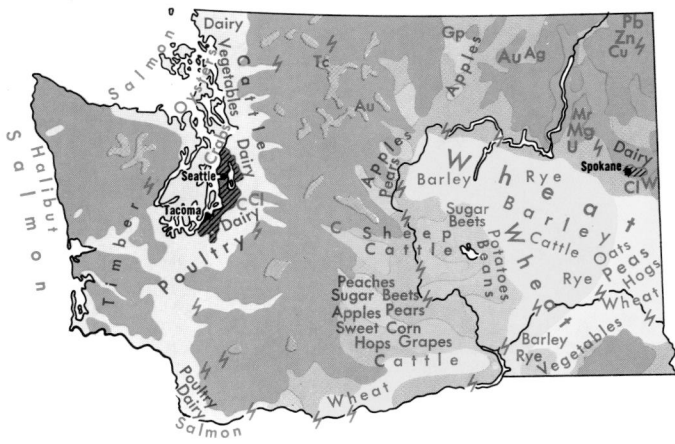

DOMINANT LAND USE

Specialized Wheat

Wheat, Peas

Dairy, Poultry, Mixed Farming

Fruit and Mixed Farming

General Farming, Dairy, Range Livestock

General Farming, Livestock, Special Crops

Range Livestock

Forests

Urban Areas

Nonagricultural Land

MAJOR MINERAL OCCURRENCES

Ag Silver
Au Gold
C   Coal
Cl Clay
Cu Copper
Gp Gypsum
Mg Magnesium

Mr Marble
Pb Lead
Tc Talc
U   Uranium
W   Tungsten
Zn Zinc

⚡ Water Power
▨ Major Industrial Areas

(continued on following page)

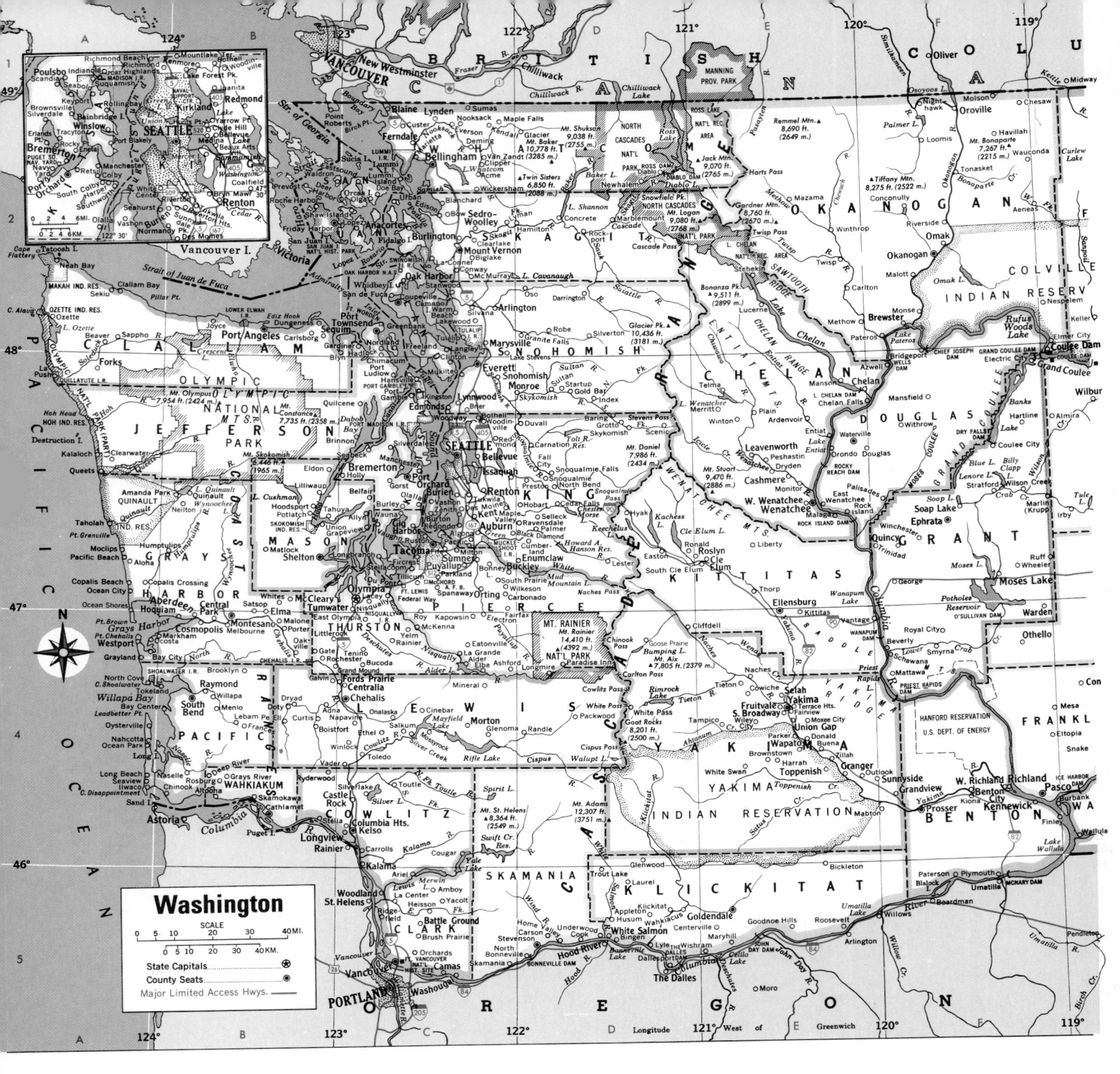

Washington

SCALE

0 5 10 20 30 40 MI.

0 5 10 20 30 40 KM.

State Capitals............⊛
County Seats.............⊛
Major Limited Access Hwys._____

Topography

| Below Sea Level | 100 m. 328 ft. | 200 m. 656 ft. | 500 m. 1,640 ft. | 1,000 m. 3,281 ft. | 2,000 m. 6,562 ft. | 5,000 m. 16,404 ft. |

0   40   80 MI.
0   40   80 KM.

© Copyright HAMMOND INCORPORATED, Maplewood, N.J.

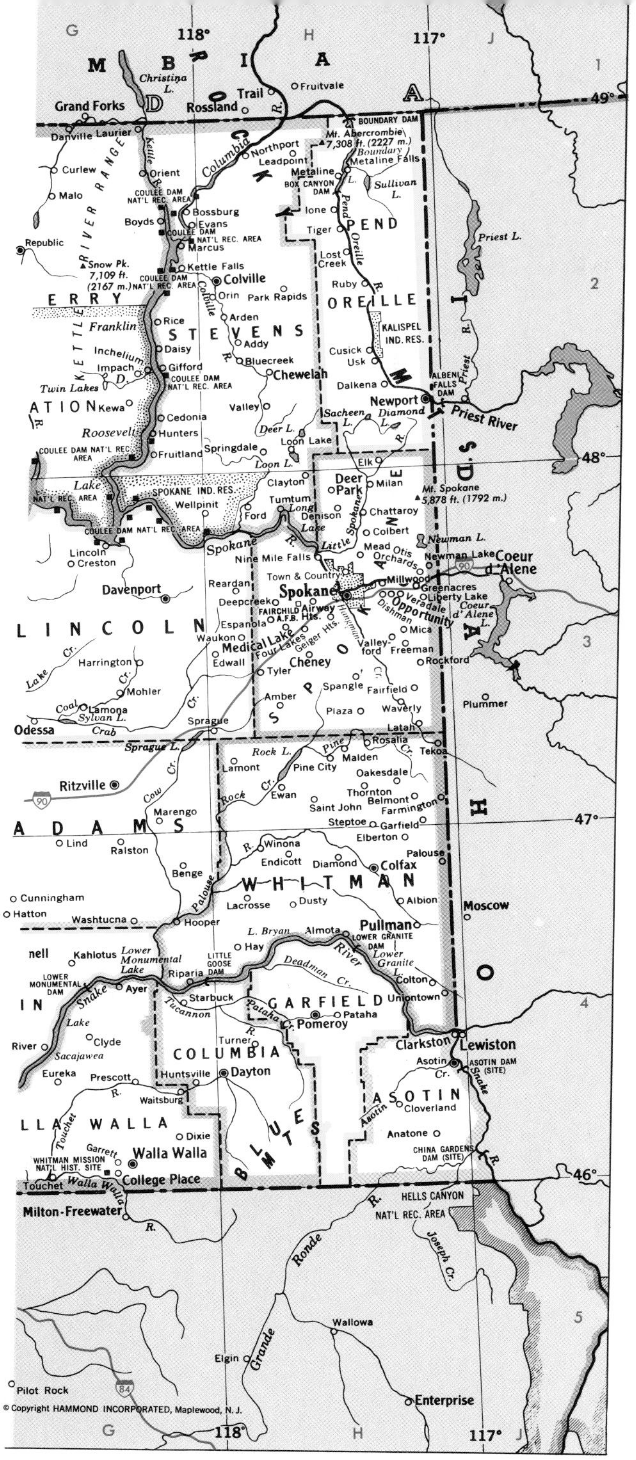

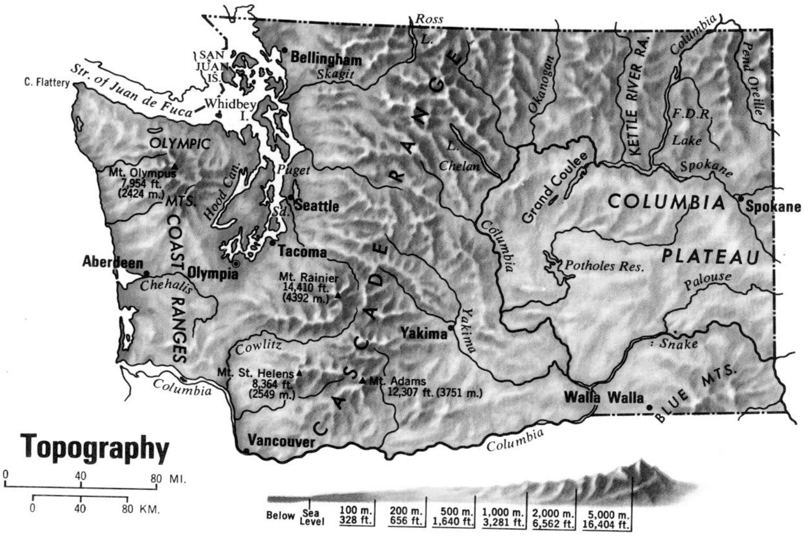

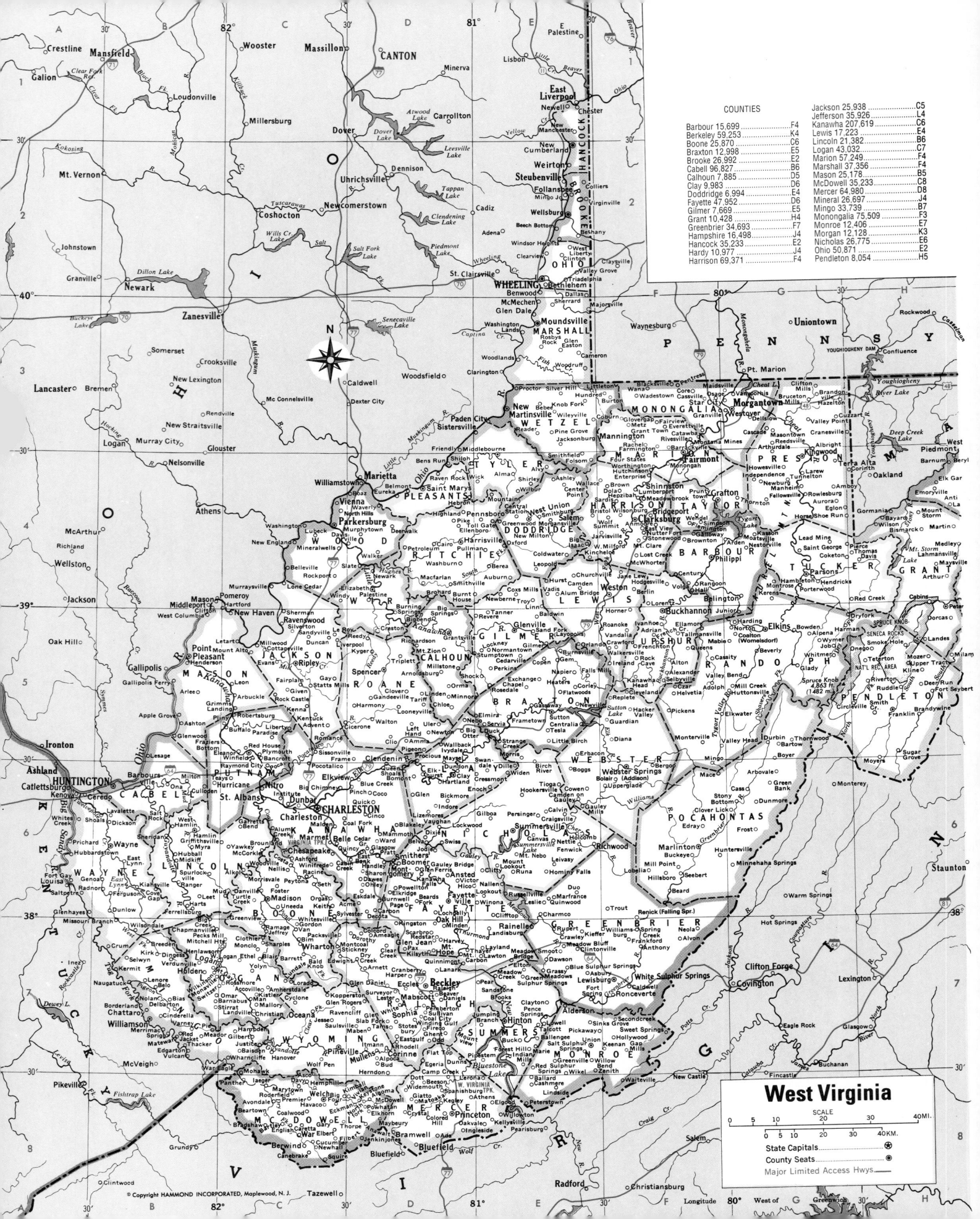

West Virginia

COUNTIES

County	Population	Grid
Barbour	15,699	F4
Berkeley	59,253	K4
Boone	25,870	C6
Braxton	12,998	E5
Brooke	26,992	E2
Cabell	96,827	B6
Calhoun	7,885	D5
Clay	9,983	D6
Doddridge	6,994	E4
Fayette	47,952	D6
Gilmer	7,669	E5
Grant	10,428	H4
Greenbrier	34,693	F7
Hampshire	16,498	J4
Hancock	35,233	E2
Hardy	10,977	J4
Harrison	69,371	F4
Jackson	25,938	C5
Jefferson	35,926	L4
Kanawha	207,619	C6
Lewis	17,223	E4
Lincoln	21,382	B6
Logan	43,032	C7
Marion	57,249	F4
Marshall	37,356	E2
Mason	25,178	B5
McDowell	35,233	C8
Mercer	64,980	D8
Mineral	26,697	J4
Mingo	33,739	B7
Monongalia	75,509	F3
Monroe	12,406	E7
Morgan	12,128	J4
Nicholas	26,775	E6
Ohio	50,871	E2
Pendleton	8,054	H5

SCALE

| 0 | 5 | 10 | 20 | 30 | 40 MI. |
| 0 | 5 | 10 | 20 | 30 | 40 KM. |

State Capitals.................⊛
County Seats.................◉
Major Limited Access Hwys.____

Pleasants 7,546..........D4
Pocahontas 9,008..........F6
Preston 29,037..........G4
Putnam 42,835..........C6
Raleigh 76,819..........D7
Randolph 27,803..........G5
Ritchie 10,233..........D4
Roane 15,120..........D5
Summers 14,204..........E7
Taylor 15,144..........F4
Tucker 7,728..........F4
Tyler 9,796..........E4
Upshur 22,867..........F5
Wayne 41,636..........B6
Webster 10,729..........F6
Wetzel 19,258..........E3
Wirt 5,192..........D4
Wood 86,915..........D4
Wyoming 28,990..........C7

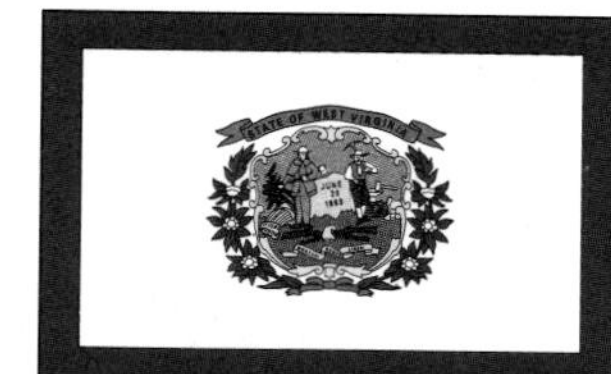

AREA 24,231 sq. mi. (62,758 sq. km.)
POPULATION 1,801,625
CAPITAL Charleston
LARGEST CITY Charleston
HIGHEST POINT Spruce Knob 4,863 ft. (1482 m.)
SETTLED IN 1774
ADMITTED TO UNION June 20, 1863
POPULAR NAME Mountain State
STATE FLOWER Big Rhododendron
STATE BIRD Cardinal

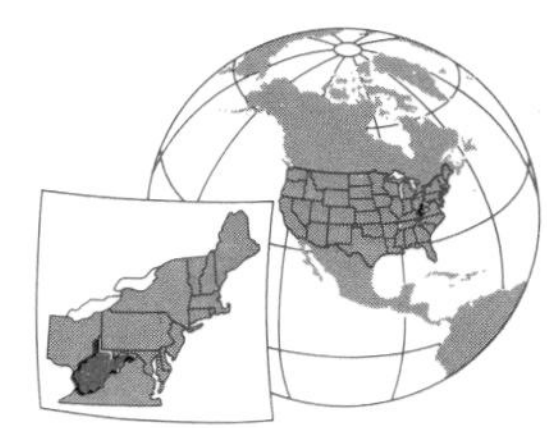

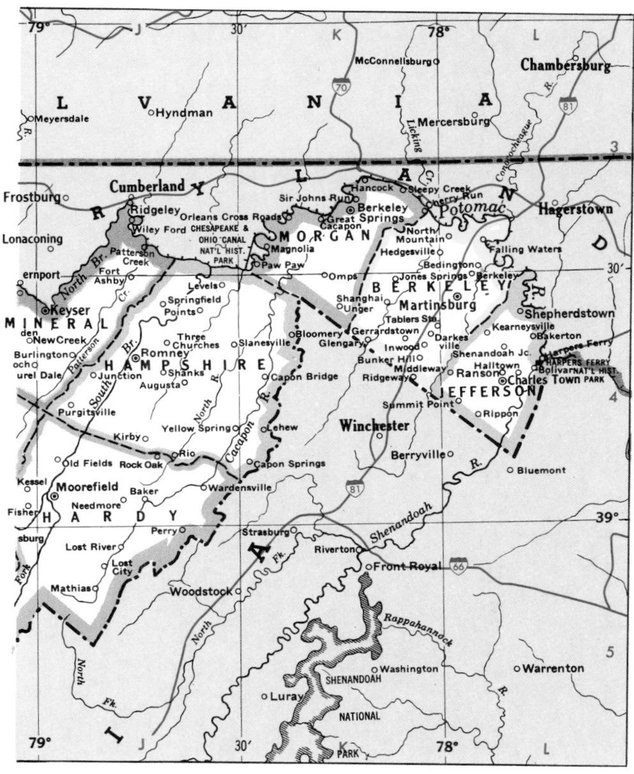

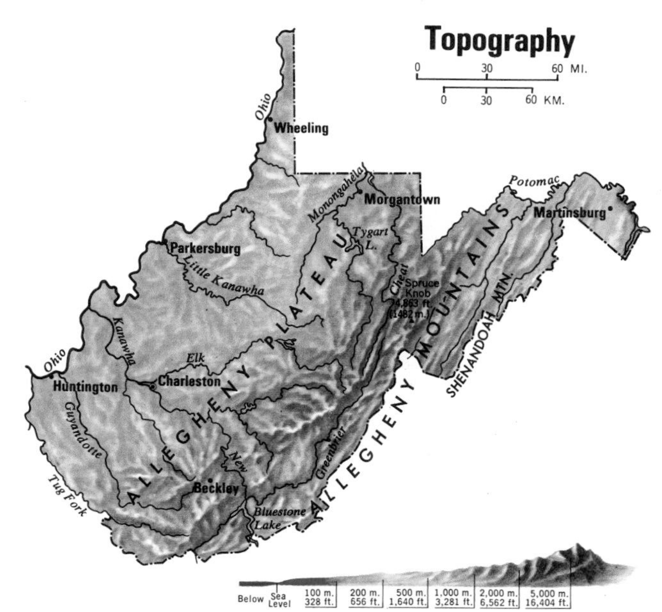

CITIES and TOWNS

Accoville 975..........C7
Acme 165..........D6
Ada 250..........D8
Addison▲ (Webster Springs) 674..........F6
Adrian 510..........F5
Albright 195..........G3
Alderson 1,152..........E7
Algoma 200..........D8
Alkol 500..........C6
Alma 197..........E4
Alpoca 200..........D7
Alum Bridge 150..........F5
Alum Creek 1,602..........C6
Alvy 150..........E4
Ameagle 230..........D7
Amherstdale 1,057..........C7
Amma 200..........D5
Anawalt 329..........D8
Anmoore 686..........F4
Ansted 1,643..........D6
Apple Grove 900..........B5
Arbovale 610..........G6
Arden 130..........G4
Arnett 300..........D7
Arnoldsburg 175..........D5
Arthur 350..........H4
Arthurdale 1,063..........G3
Asbury 280..........E7
Asco 175..........C8
Ashford 400..........C6
Ashton 259..........B5
Athens 741..........E8
Auburn 89..........E4
Augusta 750..........J4
Aurora 250..........G4
Avondale 250..........C8
Baisden 500..........C7
Baker 200..........J4
Bakerton 125..........L4
Bald Knob 356..........C7
Ballard 220..........E8
Ballengee 170..........E7
Bancroft 381..........C5
Barboursville 2,774..........B6
Barnabus 750..........C7
Barrackville 1,443..........F3
Barrett 950..........C7
Bartley 900..........C8
Bartow 500..........G5
Bayard 414..........H4
Beards Fork 400..........D6
Beartown 500..........C8
Beaver (Glen Hedrick) 1,244..........D7
Bebee 125..........E3
Beckley▲ 18,296..........D7
Bedington 150..........L3
Beech Bottom 415..........E2
Beeson 300..........D8
Belington 1,850..........F4
Belle 1,421..........C6
Belmont 912..........D4
Belva 275..........D6
Benwood 1,669..........E2
Bergoo 220..........F6
Berkeley 600..........L4
Berkeley Springs▲ 789..........K3
Berwind 615..........C8
Bethany 1,139..........E2
Bethlehem 2,694..........E2
Beverly 696..........G5
Bickmore 300..........D6
Big Chimney 450..........C6
Big Creek 500..........B7
Big Four 150..........C8
Big Otter 150..........D5
Big Springs 485..........D5
Bim 500..........C7
Birch River 650..........E6
Blacksville 168..........F3
Blair 800..........C7
Bloomery 200..........K4
Blue Creek 650..........D6
Bluefield 12,756..........D8
Boaz 1,137..........D4
Boggs 131..........E6
Bolair 450..........F6
Bolivar 1,013..........L4
Bomont 170..........D6
Boomer 1,051..........D6
Borderland 250..........B7
Bowden 135..........G5
Bradshaw 394..........C8
Bramwell 620..........D8
Brandonville 73..........G3
Brandywine 300..........H5
Breeden 600..........B7
Bridgeport 6,739..........F4
Brooks 196..........E7
Brounland 900..........C6
Brownton 400..........F4
Bruceton Mills 132..........G3
Buck 150..........E7
Buckhannon▲ 5,909..........F5
Bud 400..........D7
Buffalo 969..........C5
Bunker Hill 600..........K4
Burlington 300..........J4
Burning Springs 137..........D5
Burnsville 495..........E5
Burnt House 175..........D4
Burnwell 140..........D6
Burton 200..........F3
Cabin Creek 900..........C6
Cabins 300..........H4
Cairo 290..........D4
Caldwell 795..........F7
Calvin 400..........E6
Camden on Gauley 171..........E6
Cameron 1,177..........E3
Camp Creek 200..........D7
Canebrake 300..........C8
Canvas 300..........E6
Capon Bridge 192..........K4
Capon Springs 580..........K4
Carbon 300..........D6
Caretta 650..........C8
Cass 148..........G6
Cassity 150..........F5
Cassville 1,458..........F3
Catawba 186..........F3
Cedar Grove 1,213..........D6
Center Point 250..........E4
Central Station 200..........E4
Ceredo 1,916..........F4
Chapmanville 1,110..........B7
Charles Town▲ 3,122..........L4
Charleston (cap.)▲ 57,287..........C6
Charmco 800..........E6
Chattaroy 1,182..........B7
Chesapeake 1,896..........C6
Chester 2,905..........E1
Christian 200..........C7
Cinco 500..........D6
Circleville 180..........H5
Clarksburg▲ 18,059..........F4
Clay▲ 592..........D6
Clear Creek 300..........D7
Clearview 622..........E2
Clendenin 1,203..........D5
Clifton 325..........B5
Clifton Mills 136..........G3
Clifty 250..........E6
Clinton 350..........E2
Clintonville 250..........E7
Clio 300..........D5
Clothier 900..........C7
Clover 350..........D5
Clover Lick 250..........F6
Coal City 1,876..........D7
Coal Fork 2,100..........D6
Coalton 277..........G5
Coalwood 650..........C8
Coburn 230..........F3
Colcord 600..........D7
Colliers 864..........E2
Colored Hill 900..........D8
Core 250..........F3
Corinne 900..........D7
Corinth 195..........H4
Costa 250..........C6
Cottageville 300..........C5
Cove Gap 650..........B6
Cowen 549..........E6
Coxs Mills 275..........E4
Craigsville 1,955..........E6
Cranberry 315..........D7
Crawley 395..........E7
Crum 500..........B7
Crystal 150..........D8
Cucumber 274..........C8
Culloden 2,907..........B6
Cyclone 500..........C7
Dallas 450..........E2
Daniels 1,714..........D7
Danville 595..........C6
Darkesville 150..........L4
Davis 799..........H4
Davisville 200..........C4
Davy 403..........C8
Dawes 800..........D6
Dawson 300..........E7
Decota 800..........D6
Deerwalk 150..........D4
Delbarton 705..........B7
Dellslow 300..........G3
Diana 300..........F5
Dickson 200..........B6
Dille 300..........E6
Dingess 600..........B7
Dixie 985..........D6
Dola 200..........F4
Dorothy 400..........D7
Dry Creek 441..........D7
Dryfork 425..........H5
Dunbar 8,697..........C6
Dunlow 169..........B6
Dunmore 280..........G6
Durbin 278..........G5
East Bank 892..........D6
East Lynn 150..........B6
East View 1,222..........F4
Eastgulf 300..........D7
Eccles 1,162..........D7
Eckman 750..........C8
Edgarton 415..........B7
Edray 175..........F6
Egeria 150..........D7
Elbert 400..........C8
Eleanor 1,256..........C5
Elizabeth▲ 900..........D4
Elk Garden 261..........H4
Elkhorn 150..........D8
Elkins▲ 7,420..........G5
Elkridge 500..........D6
Elkview 1,047..........C6
Ellenboro 453..........F5
Elton 200..........E7
English 500..........C8
Enterprise 1,058..........F4
Erbacon 350..........E6
Eskdale 400..........D6
Ethel 450..........C7
Evans 400..........C5
Everettville 175..........F3
Fairmont 20,210..........F4
Fairplain 200..........C5
Fairview 513..........F3
Falling Spring (Renick) 191..........F6
Falling Waters 130..........L3
Farmington 414..........F3
Fayetteville▲ 2,182..........D6
Fenwick 500..........E6
Ferguson 150..........B6
Ferrellsburg 300..........B6
Filbert 130..........D8
Fireco 200..........D7
Fisher 500..........H4
Flat Top 550..........D7
Flatwoods 324..........E5
Flemington 352..........F4
Follansbee 3,339..........E2
Folsom 360..........E4
Forest Hill 314..........E7
Fort Ashby 1,288..........J4
Fort Gay 852..........A6
Fort Seybert 200..........H5
Fort Spring 250..........E7
Foster 500..........C6
Four States 500..........F4
Frametown 150..........E5
Frankford 200..........F7
Franklin▲ 914..........H5
Fraziers Bottom 250..........B5
French Creek 200..........F5
Friendly 146..........D3
Gallipolis Ferry 325..........B5
Galloway 500..........F4
Gandeeville 150..........D5
Gap Mills 300..........F7
Gary 1,355..........C8
Gassaway 946..........E5
Gauley Bridge 691..........D6
Gauley Mills 165..........E6
Gay 300..........C5
Gerrardstown 240..........K4
Ghent 500..........D7
Giatto 400..........D8
Gilbert 456..........C7
Gilboa 500..........E6
Glady 175..........G5
Glasgow 906..........D6
Glen 175..........D6
Glen Dale 1,612..........E3
Glen Daniel 300..........D7
Glen Ferris 200..........D6
Glen Hedrick (Beaver)..........B7
Glen Jean..........D7
Glen Rogers 500..........D7
Glen White 300..........D7
Glengary 250..........K4
Glenhayes 175..........A6
Glenville▲ 1,923..........E5
Glenwood 400..........B5
Gordon 300..........C7
Grafton▲ 5,524..........G4
Grant Town 694..........F3
Grantsville▲ 671..........D5
Granville 798..........F3
Great Cacapon 750..........K3
Green Bank 115..........G6
Green Sulphur Springs 225..........E7
Greenview 250..........C6
Greenwood 750..........E4
Griffithsville 300..........B6
Grimms Landing 350..........B5
Guardian 175..........F5
Hacker Valley 440..........F5
Halltown 375..........L4
Hambleton 265..........G4
Hamlin▲ 1,030..........B6
Hampden 300..........C7
Hancock 175..........K3
Handley 334..........D6
Hanover 300..........C7
Harman 128..........G5

(continued on following page)

DOMINANT LAND USE

Agriculture, Industry and Resources

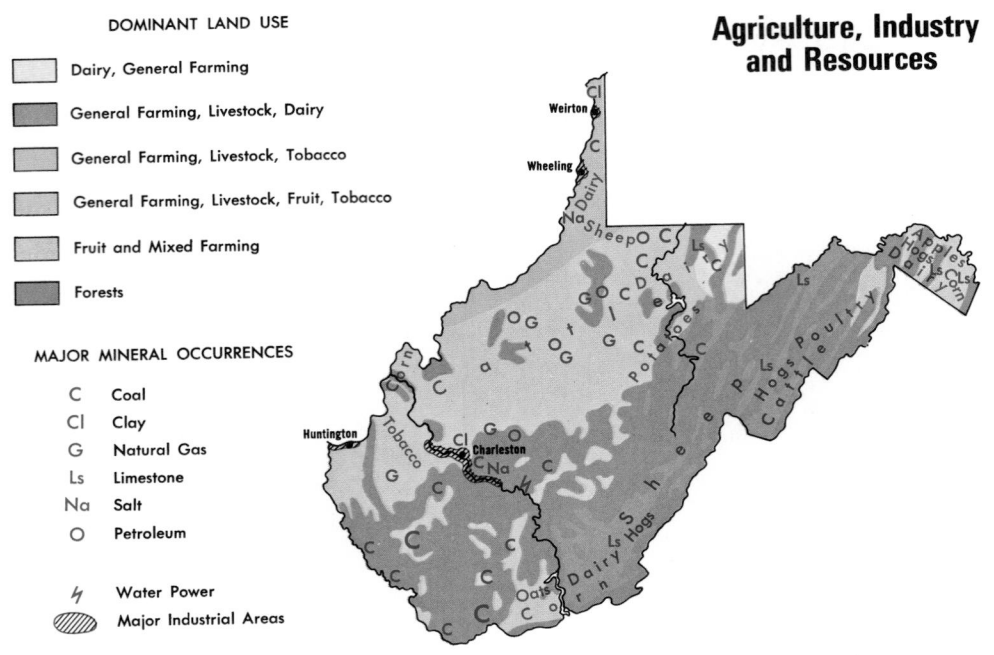

- Dairy, General Farming
- General Farming, Livestock, Dairy
- General Farming, Livestock, Tobacco
- General Farming, Livestock, Fruit, Tobacco
- Fruit and Mixed Farming
- Forests

MAJOR MINERAL OCCURRENCES

- C Coal
- Cl Clay
- G Natural Gas
- Ls Limestone
- Na Salt
- O Petroleum
- ⚡ Water Power
- Major Industrial Areas

Harmony 600 ....D5	Landisburg 250 ....E7	Mill Creek 685 ....G5	Orma D5	Rivesville 1,064 ....F3	Tallmansville 140 ....F5	Williamstown 2,774 ....C4
Harper 400 ....D7	Landville 400 ....C7	Mill Point 148 ....F6	Osage 183 ....F3	Robertsburg 140 ....C5	Tanner 375 ....E4	Wilsonburg 350 ....F4
Harpers Ferry 308 ....L4	Lavalette 600 ....B6	Millstone 850 ....D5	Packsville 225 ....C7	Rock Cave 400 ....F5	Teays 200 ....B6	Wilsondale 250 ....B7
Harrisville▲ 1,839 ....E4	Layland 500 ....E7	Millwood 800 ....C5	Paden City 2,862 ....D3	Roderfield 900 ....C8	Terra Alta 1,713 ....H4	Windsor Heights 800 ....E2
Hartford 487 ....C4	Layopolis (Sand Fork) E5	Milton 2,242 ....B6	Page 600 ....D6	Romney▲ 1,966 ....J4	Tesla 300 ....E5	Winfield▲ 1,164 ....C5
Harts 2,332 ....B6	Leet 175 ....B6	Minden 800 ....D7	Panther 450 ....C8	Roncevere 1,754 ....F7	Thacker 525 ....B7	Winifrede 750 ....C6
Harvey 300 ....D7	Left Hand 700 ....D5	Mineralwells 1,698 ....C4	Parkersburg▲ 33,862 ....D4	Rosedale 400 ....E5	Thomas 573 ....H4	Winona 250 ....E6
Havaco 350 ....C8	Leivasy 200 ....E6	Mingo 350 ....F5	Parsons▲ 1,453 ....G4	Rossmore 200 ....C7	Thornton 200 ....G4	Wolf Pen 175 ....C7
Heaters 440 ....E5	Lenore 800 ....B7	Minnora 500 ....D5	Patterson Creek 157 ....J3	Rowlesburg 648 ....G4	Thorpe 600 ....D8	Wolf Summit 750 ....F4
Hedgesville 227 ....K3	Leon 145 ....C5	Missouri Branch 250 ....A7	Paw Paw 538 ....K3	Runa 150 ....D7	Three Churches 350 ....J4	Woodlands 200 ....E3
Helvetia 130 ....F5	Lerona 550 ....D8	Mitchell Heights 265 ....B7	Pax 167 ....D7	Rupert 1,104 ....E7	Thurmond 39 ....D7	Woodville 300 ....C6
Hemphill 700 ....C8	Lesage 600 ....B5	Moatsville 150 ....G4	Pecks Mill 350 ....B7	Russellville 280 ....E6	Tioga 825 ....E6	Worthington 233 ....F4
Henderson 549 ....B5	Leslie 350 ....E6	Monaville 950 ....B7	Pemberton 300 ....D7	Saint Albans 11,194 ....C6	Triadelphia 835 ....E2	Yawkey 985 ....C6
Hendricks 303 ....G4	Lester 420 ....D7	Monclo 242 ....C7	Pence Springs 300 ....E7	Saint George 150 ....G4	Troy 110 ....E4	Yellow Spring 280 ....J4
Henlawson 900 ....B7	Letart 350 ....C5	Monomgah 1,132 ....F4	Pennsboro 1,282 ....E4	Saint Marys▲ 2,148 ....D4	Tunnelton 331 ....G4	Yolyn 400 ....C7
Hepzibah 600 ....F4	Levels 180 ....J4	Montana Mines 200 ....F3	Pentress 250 ....F3	Salem 2,063 ....E4	Turtle Creek 566 ....C6	
Herndon 500 ....D7	Lewisburg▲ 3,598 ....E7	Montcoal 150 ....D7	Petersburg▲ 2,360 ....H5	Salt Rock 350 ....B6	Uneeda 700 ....C6	**OTHER FEATURES**
Hico 750 ....D6	Liberty 150 ....C5	Monterville 250 ....F5	Peterstown 550 ....E8	Sand Fork 196 ....E5	Unger 300 ....K4	
Hillsboro 188 ....F6	Lindside 225 ....E8	Montgomery 2,449 ....D6	Peytona 175 ....C6	Sandstone 300 ....E7	Union▲ 566 ....E7	Big Sandy (riv.) A6
Hinton▲ 3,433 ....E7	Linn 165 ....E4	Montrose 140 ....G4	Philippi▲ 3,132 ....G4	Sandyville 500 ....C5	Upper Tract 155 ....H5	Bluestone (lake) E7
Hodgesville 200 ....F4	Little Birch 400 ....E5	Moorefield▲ 2,148 ....H5	Pickaway 225 ....E7	Saulsville 250 ....C7	Upperglade 750 ....F6	Buckhannon (riv.) F5
Holcomb 200 ....E6	Littleton 198 ....F3	Morgansville 164 ....E4	Pickens 240 ....F5	Scarbo 800 ....D7	Vadis 130 ....E4	Cacapon (riv.) J4
Holden 1,246 ....B7	Lizemores 400 ....D6	Morgantown▲ 25,879 ....F4	Pie 250 ....B7	Selwyn 500 ....B7	Valley Bend 950 ....F5	Cheat (riv.) G3
Hollywood 150 ....F5	Lochgelly 250 ....D6	Morrisvale 500 ....C6	Piedmont 1,094 ....H4	Seth 950 ....C6	Valley Grove 569 ....E2	Cherry (riv.) E6
Hominy Falls 175 ....E6	Lockney 190 ....D5	Moundsville▲ 10,753 ....E3	Pinch 2,695 ....C6	Shanghai 200 ....K4	Valley Head 900 ....G5	Chesapeake and Ohio Canal
Hookersville 250 ....E6	Lockwood 300 ....D6	Mount Alto 300 ....C5	Pine Grove 701 ....E3	Shanks 500 ....J4	Van 800 ....C7	Nat'l Hist. Park J3
Horse Shoe Run 500 ....G4	Logan▲ 2,206 ....B7	Mount Carbon 450 ....D7	Pineville▲ 865 ....C7	Sharon 450 ....D6	Varney 750 ....B7	Clear Fork, Guyandotte (riv.) C7
Howesville 600 ....G4	Lookout 200 ....E6	Mount Clare 950 ....F4	Pliny 900 ....B5	Sharples 250 ....C7	Vaughan 375 ....D6	Coal (riv.) C6
Hubball 145 ....B6	Lorado 400 ....C7	Mount Gay 4,366 ....C6	Poca 1,124 ....C6	Shenandoah Junction 600 ....L4	Verdunville 950 ....B7	Dry Fork (riv.) C8
Hundred 386 ....E3	Lorentz 200 ....F4	Mount Hope 1,573 ....D7	Pocotalico 2,420 ....C6	Shepherdstown 1,287 ....L4	Victor 500 ....D6	Dry Fork (riv.) G5
Huntington 54,844 ....A6	Lost City 130 ....J5	Mount Lookout 500 ....E6	Point Pleasant▲ 4,996 ....B5	Sheridan 160 ....B6	Vienna 10,862 ....D4	East Lynn (lake) B6
Hurricane 4,461 ....C6	Lost Creek 413 ....F4	Mount Nebo 535 ....E6	Points 250 ....J4	Sherrard 400 ....E3	Vivian 500 ....D8	Elk (riv.) C6
Hutchinson 285 ....F4	Lost River 500 ....J5	Mount Storm 500 ....H4	Powellton 1,905 ....D6	Shinnston 2,543 ....F4	Vulcan 130 ....B7	Fish (creek) E3
Huttonsville 211 ....G5	Lowell 140 ....E7	Mount Zion 350 ....D5	Powhatan 400 ....D8	Shirley 275 ....E4	Wadestown 300 ....F3	Gauley (riv.) D6
Iaeger 551 ....C8	Lubeck 1,579 ....C4	Mountain 200 ....C7	Pratt 640 ....D6	Shoals 150 ....B6	Waiteville 230 ....F8	Greenbrier (riv.) F6
Independence 600 ....G4	Lumberport 1,014 ....F4	Mud 143 ....C6	Premier 400 ....C8	Shock 200 ....D5	Walkersville 135 ....F5	Guyandotte (riv.) B6
Indian Mills 150 ....E7	Lundale 525 ....C7	Mullens 2,006 ....D7	Prichard 500 ....A6	Silverton 250 ....C5	Wallace 325 ....E4	Harpers Ferry Nat'l Hist. Park L4
Indore 300 ....D6	Maben 450 ....D7	Murphytown 600 ....D4	Princeton▲ 7,043 ....D8	Simpson 250 ....F4	Wallback 150 ....D5	Hughes (riv.) D4
Inwood 1,360 ....K4	Mabie 550 ....F5	Nallen 250 ....E6	Procious 600 ....D5	Sinks Grove 156 ....F7	Walton 550 ....D5	Kanawha (riv.) C5
Itmann 600 ....D7	Mabscott 1,543 ....D7	Napier 158 ....E5	Proctor 350 ....E3	Sissonville 4,290 ....C5	Wana 150 ....F3	Little Kanawha (riv.) D5
Ivanhoe 200 ....F5	Macfarlan 436 ....D4	Naugatuck 500 ....B7	Pruntytown 145 ....F4	Sistersville 1,797 ....D3	War 1,081 ....C8	Meadow (riv.) E6
Ivydale 800 ....D5	Madison▲ 3,051 ....C6	Nebo 200 ....D5	Pullman 109 ....E4	Slab Fork 210 ....D7	Ward 850 ....D6	Mill (creek) C5
Jacksonburg 400 ....E3	Maidsville 500 ....F3	Nellis 600 ....C6	Purgitsville 450 ....J4	Slanesville 250 ....K4	Wardensville 140 ....J4	Monongahela (riv.) G3
Jane Lew 439 ....F4	Malden 900 ....C6	Neola 300 ....F7	Quick 400 ....C6	Smithburg 130 ....E4	Washington 1,030 ....D4	Mount Storm (lake) H4
Jarvisville 250 ....F4	Mallory 1,126 ....C7	Nettie 500 ....E6	Quincy 150 ....C6	Smithers 1,162 ....D6	Washington Lands 400 ....E3	Mud (riv.) B6
Jeffrey 900 ....C7	Mammoth 563 ....D6	New Cumberland▲ 1,363 ....E2	Quinwood 559 ....E6	Smithfield 205 ....E4	Waverly 500 ....D4	New (riv.) E7
Jenkinjones 750 ....D8	Man 914 ....C7	New England 335 ....C4	Rachel 550 ....F4	Smithville 200 ....D4	Wayne▲ 1,128 ....B6	North (riv.) J4
Jesse 400 ....C7	Mannington 2,184 ....F3	New Haven 1,632 ....C5	Racine 725 ....C6	Smoot 300 ....E7	Weirton 24,124 ....E2	Ohio (riv.) B5
Jodie 440 ....D6	Marfrance 225 ....E6	New Manchester 800 ....E1	Radnor 300 ....A6	Sophia 1,182 ....D7	Welch▲ 3,028 ....C8	Patterson (creek) J4
Jumping Branch 700 ....E7	Marlinton▲ 1,148 ....F6	New Martinsville▲ 6,705 ....E3	Rainelle 1,681 ....E7	South Charleston 13,645 ....C6	Wellsburg▲ 3,385 ....E2	Pigeon (creek) B7
Junior 542 ....G5	Marmet 1,879 ....C6	Newburg 378 ....G4	Raleigh 900 ....D7	Spanishburg 550 ....D8	West Columbia 245 ....B5	Pocatalico (riv.) C5
Justice 600 ....C7	Martinsburg▲ 14,073 ....L4	Newell 1,724 ....E1	Ramage 350 ....C7	Spencer▲ 2,279 ....D5	West Hamlin 423 ....B6	Pond Fork (riv.) C6
Kearneysville 250 ....L4	Mason 1,053 ....B4	Newhall 400 ....C8	Ranger 300 ....B6	Spriggs 25 ....D6	West Liberty 1,434 ....E2	Potomac (riv.) L3
Kegley 900 ....D8	Masontown 737 ....G3	Newton 300 ....D5	Ranson 2,890 ....L4	Springfield 250 ....J4	West Logan 524 ....C7	Potts (creek) F7
Keith 175 ....C6	Matewan 619 ....B7	Newville 160 ....C5	Ravencliff 350 ....C7	Spurlockville 250 ....B6	West Milford 519 ....F4	Reedy (creek) D5
Kellysville 165 ....E8	Matoaka 366 ....D8	Nitro 6,851 ....C6	Ravenswood 4,189 ....C5	Squire 900 ....C8	West Union▲ 830 ....E4	Shavers Fork (riv.) G5
Kenna 150 ....C5	Maybeury 300 ....D8	Nolan 250 ....B7	Raymond City 400 ....C6	Star City 1,251 ....F3	Weston▲ 4,994 ....F4	Shenandoah (riv.) K4
Kenova 3,748 ....A6	Maysel 350 ....D5	North Hills 849 ....D4	Reader 950 ....E3	Statts Mills 400 ....C5	Westover 4,201 ....G3	Spruce Knob (mt.) G5
Kentuck 200 ....C5	Maysville 150 ....H4	Northfork 656 ....D8	Red House 600 ....C5	Stickney 150 ....D7	Wharncliffe 900 ....C7	Spruce Knob–Seneca Rocks
Kermit 342 ....B7	McCorkle 150 ....C6	Norton 400 ....G5	Red Jacket 760 ....B7	Stirrat 250 ....C7	Wharton 450 ....C7	Nat'l Rec. Area H5
Keyser▲ 5,870 ....J4	McDowell 500 ....D8	Nutter Fort 1,819 ....F4	Redstar 200 ....D7	Stonewood 1,996 ....F4	Wheeling▲ 34,882 ....E2	Stony (riv.) H4
Keystone 627 ....D8	McMechen 2,130 ....E3	Oak Hill 6,812 ....D6	Reedsville 482 ....G3	Stotesbury 199 ....D7	White Sulphur Springs 2,779 ....F7	Summersville (lake) E6
Kieffer 135 ....C7	McWhorter 150 ....F4	Oakvale 165 ....D8	Reedy 271 ....D5	Strange Creek 175 ....D5	Whites Creek 500 ....A6	Sutton (lake) F5
Kilsyth 200 ....D7	Meador 225 ....B7	Oceana 1,791 ....C7	Renick 200 ....F6	Sullivan 700 ....D7	Whitesville 486 ....C6	Tug Fork (riv.) B7
Kimball 550 ....C8	Meadow Bridge 325 ....E7	Odd 500 ....D7	Replete 200 ....F5	Summersville▲ 2,906 ....E6	Whitmer 400 ....G5	Twelvepole (creek) A6
Kingston 189 ....D7	Meadow Creek 300 ....E7	Ohley 450 ....C6	Rhodell 221 ....D7	Summit Point 455 ....K4	Widen 230 ....E6	Tygart (lake) G4
Kingwood▲ 3,243 ....G4	Meadowbrook 500 ....F4	Omar 900 ....C7	Richwood 2,808 ....F6	Surveyor 300 ....D7	Wiley Ford 1,224 ....J3	Tygart Valley (riv.) F5
Kirk 400 ....B7	Merrimac 140 ....B7	Ona 200 ....B6	Ridgeley 779 ....J3	Sutton▲ 939 ....E5	Wileyville 350 ....E3	West Fork (riv.) E5
Kistler 200 ....C7	Metz 175 ....F3	Onego 400 ....H5	Ridgeway 200 ....K4	Swiss 500 ....E6	Wilkinson 975 ....C7	Williams (riv.) F6
Kopperston 700 ....C7	Middlebourne▲ 922 ....E3	Orgas 500 ....C6	Rio 140 ....J4	Switzer 1,004 ....B7	Williamsburg 350 ....F7	
Lahmansville 200 ....H4	Middleway 350 ....K4	Orlando 700 ....E5	Ripley▲ 3,023 ....C5	Sylvester 191 ....C6	Williamson▲ 4,154 ....B7	▲County seat
Lanark 559 ....D7	Midkiff 650 ....B6	Orleans Cross Roads 150 ....K3	Rippon 500 ....L4	Talcott 800 ....E7		

Wisconsin 315

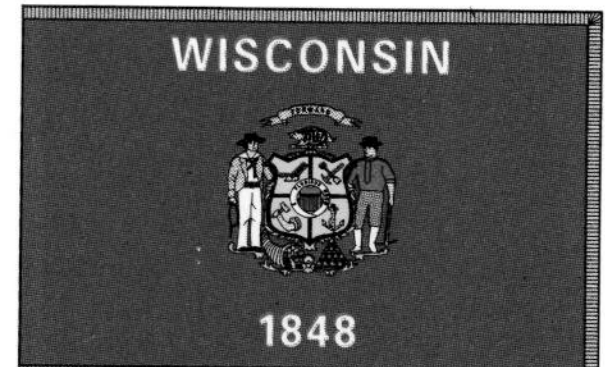
WISCONSIN
1848

AREA 56,153 sq. mi. (145,436 sq. km.)
POPULATION 4,906,745
CAPITAL Madison
LARGEST CITY Milwaukee
HIGHEST POINT Timms Hill 1,951 ft. (595 m.)
SETTLED IN 1670
ADMITTED TO UNION May 29, 1848
POPULAR NAME Badger State
STATE FLOWER Wood Violet
STATE BIRD Robin

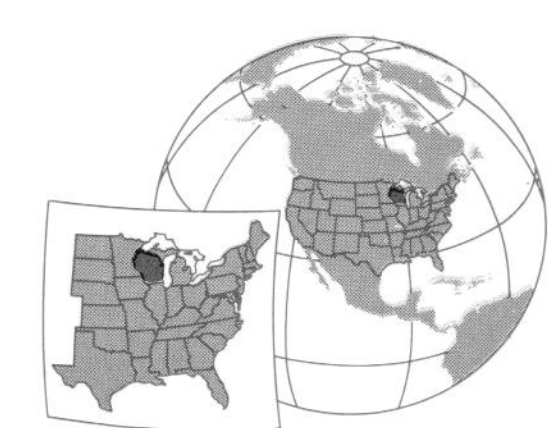

COUNTIES

Adams 15,682 G7
Ashland 16,307 E3
Barron 40,750 C5
Bayfield 14,008 D3
Brown 194,594 L7
Buffalo 13,584 C7
Burnett 13,084 B4
Calumet 34,291 K7
Chippewa 52,360 D5
Clark 31,647 E6
Columbia 45,088 H9
Crawford 15,940 E9
Dane 367,085 H9
Dodge 76,559 J9
Door 25,690 M6
Douglas 41,758 C3
Dunn 35,909 C6
Eau Claire 85,183 D6
Florence 4,590 K4
Fond du Lac 90,083 K8
Forest 8,776 J4
Grant 49,264 E10
Green 30,339 G10
Green Lake 18,651 H8
Iowa 20,150 F9
Iron 6,153 F9
Jackson 16,588 F3
Jefferson 67,783 J9
Juneau 21,650 F8
Kenosha 128,181 K10
Kewaunee 18,878 L6
La Crosse 97,904 D8
Lafayette 16,076 F10
Langlade 19,505 H5
Lincoln 26,993 G5
Manitowoc 80,421 L7
Marathon 115,400 G6
Marinette 40,548 K5
Marquette 12,321 H8
Menominee 3,890 J5
Milwaukee 959,275 L9
Monroe 36,633 E8
Oconto 30,226 K6
Oneida 31,679 G4
Outagamie 140,510 K7
Ozaukee 72,831 L9
Pepin 7,107 C6
Pierce 32,765 B6
Polk 34,773 B5
Portage 61,405 G6
Price 15,600 F4
Racine 175,034 K10
Richland 17,521 F9
Rock 139,510 H10
Rusk 15,079 D5
Saint Croix 43,262 B5
Sauk 46,975 G9
Sawyer 14,181 D4
Shawano 37,157 J6
Sheboygan 103,877 L8
Taylor 18,901 E5
Trempealeau 25,263 D7
Vernon 25,617 E8
Vilas 17,707 G3
Walworth 75,000 J10
Washburn 13,772 C4
Washington 95,328 K9
Waukesha 304,715 K9
Waupaca 46,104 J6
Waushara 19,385 H7
Winnebago 140,320 J8
Wood 73,605 F7

CITIES and TOWNS

Abbotsford 1,916 F6
Abrams 300 L6
Adams 1,715 G8
Adell 510 L8
Afton 225 H10
Albany 1,140 G10
Albion 300 H10
Algoma 3,353 M6
Allenton 915 K9
Allouez 14,431 L7
Alma Center 416 E7
Alma▲ 790 C7
Almena 625 B5
Almond 455 G7
Alto 235 J8
Altoona 5,889 C6
Alvin 160 J4
Amberg 875 K5
Amery 2,657 B5
Amherst 792 H7
Amherst Junction 269 H7
Angelica 200 K6
Angelo 100 E3
Aniwa 249 H6
Antigo▲ 8,276 H5
Appleton▲ 65,695 J7
Arbor Vitae 900 G4
Arcadia 2,166 D7
Arena 525 G9
Argonne 600 G9
Argyle 798 G10
Arkansaw 400 B6
Arlington 440 H9
Armstrong Creek 615 K4
Arpin 312 G6
Ashippun 750 H1
Ashland▲ 8,695 E2
Ashwaubenon 16,376 K7
Athens 951 G5
Auburndale 665 F6
Augusta 1,510 D6
Auroraville 250 H7
Avoca 474 F9
Avon 120 H10
Babcock 250 F7
Bagley 306 D10
Baileys Harbor 250 M5
Baldwin 2,022 B6
Balsam Lake▲ 792 B5
Bancroft 355 G7
Bangor 1,076 E8
Baraboo▲ 9,203 G9
Barnes 225 D3
Barneveld 660 F10
Barron▲ 2,986 C5
Barronett 575 B4
Batavia 125 K8
Bay City 578 B6
Bayfield 686 E2
Bayside 4,789 M1
Bear Creek 418 J6
Beaver 100 K5
Beaver Dam 14,196 J9
Beetown 150 E10
Beldenville 175 A6
Belgium 928 L8
Bell Center 127 E9
Belleville 1,456 G10
Belmont 823 F10
Beloit 35,573 H10
Bennett 350 C3
Benton 898 F10
Berlin 5,371 H8
Bethel 210 F6
Bevent 200 H6
Big Bend 1,299 K2
Birchwood 443 C4
Birnamwood 693 H6
Biron 794 G7
Black Creek 1,152 K7
Black Earth 1,248 G9
Black River Falls▲ 3,490 E7
Blackwell 550 K4
Blair 1,126 D7
Blanchardville 802 G10
Bloom City 167 E8
Bloomer 3,085 D5
Bloomington 776 E10
Blue Mounds 446 G9
Blue River 434 E9
Boardman 100 A5
Boaz 131 E9
Bohners Lake 1,553 K10
Bonduel 1,210 K6
Boscobel 2,706 E9
Boulder Junction 780 G3
Bowler 279 J6
Boyceville 913 C5
Boyd 683 E6
Brackett 150 D6
Bradley 100 G4
Branch 300 L7
Brandon 872 J8
Brantwood 500 F4
Bridgeport 250 D9
Briggsville 250 H8
Brighton 100 K3
Brill 200 C4
Brillion 2,840 L7
Brodhead 3,165 G10
Brokaw 224 G5
Brookfield 35,184 K1
Brooklyn 789 H10
Brooks 103 G8
Brothertown 100 K7
Brown Deer 12,236 L1
Brown's Lake 1,725 K3
Brownsville 415 J8
Browntown 256 G10
Bruce 844 D5
Brule 335 C2
Brussels 500 L6
Buffalo 915 C7
Burlington 8,855 K10
Burnett 260 J9
Butler 2,079 K1
Butte Des Morts J7
Butternut 416 E3
Cable 227 D3
Cadott 1,328 D6
Caldwell 101 J2
Caledonia 100 L2
Cambria 768 H8
Cambridge 963 H9
Cameron 1,273 C5
Camp Douglas 512 F8
Camp Lake 2,291 K10
Campbellsport 1,732 K8
Canton 100 C5
Caroline 450 J6
Carter 100 J5
Cascade 620 K8
Casco 544 L6
Cashton 780 E8
Cassville 1,144 E10
Cataract 200 E7
Catawba 178 E4
Cazenovia 288 F8
Cecil 373 K6
Cedar Grove 1,521 L8
Cedarburg 9,895 L9
Centuria 790 A5
Chaseburg 365 D8
Chelsea 120 F5
Chenequa 601 J1
Chetek 1,953 C5
Chili 185 F6
Chilton▲ 3,240 K7
Chippewa Falls▲ 12,727 D6
City Point 110 F7
Clam Lake 140 E3
Clayton 450 B5
Clear Lake 932 B5
Clearwater Lake 200 H4
Cleveland 1,398 L8
Clinton 1,849 J10
Clintonville 4,351 J6
Clyman 370 J9
Cobb 440 F10
Cochrane 475 C7
Colby 1,532 F6
Coleman 839 L5
Colfax 1,110 C6
Coloma 383 H7
Columbus 4,093 H9
Combined Locks 2,190 K7
Commonwealth 240 K4
Como 1,353 K10
Comstock 160 C5
Concord 200 H1
Conover 480 H3
Conrath 92 E5
Coon Valley 817 E8
Cornell 1,541 D5
Cornucopia 250 D2
Couderay 92 D4
Crandon▲ 1,958 H4
Cream 120 C7
Crivitz 996 L5
Cross Plains 2,098 G9
Cuba City 2,024 F10
Cudahy 18,659 M2
Cumberland 2,163 C4
Curtiss 173 F6
Cushing 150 A4
Cylon 100 B5
Dale 410 J7
Dallas 452 C5
Dalton 300 H8
Danbury 350 B3
Dane 621 G9
Darien 1,158 J10
Darlington▲ 2,235 F10
De Forest 4,882 H9
De Pere 16,569 K7
De Soto 326 D9
Deer Park 237 B5
Deerfield 1,617 H9
Delafield 5,347 J1
Delavan 6,073 J10
Delavan Lake 2,177 J10
Dellwood 120 G7
Denmark 1,612 L7
Dexterville 100 F7
Diamond Bluff 100 A6
Dickeyville 862 E10
Dodge 185 D7
Dodgeville▲ 3,882 F10
Dorchester 697 F5
Dousman 1,277 J1
Downing 250 B5
Downsville 200 C6
Doylestown 316 H9
Draper 125 E4
Dresser 614 A5
Drummond 200 D3
Dunbar 106 K4
Durand▲ 2,003 C6
Dyckesville 300 L6
Eagle 1,182 H2
Eagle River▲ 1,374 H4
East Troy 2,664 J2
Eastman 369 D9
Easton 130 G8
Eau Claire▲ 56,856 D6
Eden 610 K8
Edgar 1,318 G6
Edgerton 4,254 H10
Egg Harbor 183 M5
Eland 247 H6
Elcho 500 H5
Elderon 175 H6
Eldorado 200 J8
Eleva 491 D6
Elk Mound 765 C6
Elkhart Lake 1,019 L8
Elkhorn▲ 5,337 J10
Ellison Bay 112 M5
Ellsworth▲ 2,706 A6
Elm Grove 6,261 K1
Elmwood 775 B6
Elmwood Park 534 M3
Elroy 1,533 F8
Elton 150 J5
Embarrass 461 J6
Emerald 128 B5
Endeavor 316 G8
Ephraim 261 M5
Ettrick 461 D7
Evansville 3,174 H10
Exeland 180 D4
Fair Water 310 J8
Fairchild 504 D6
Fall Creek 1,034 D6
Fall River 842 H9
Fence 200 K4
Fennimore 2,378 E9
Fenwood 214 F6
Ferryville 154 D9
Fifield 310 F4
Fish Creek 119 M5
Florence▲ 780 K4
Fond du Lac▲ 37,757 K8
Fontana 1,635 J10
Footville 764 H10
Forest Junction 140 K7
Forestville 470 L6
Fort Atkinson 10,227 J10
Fountain City 938 C7
Fox Lake 1,269 J8
Fox Point 7,238 M1
Foxboro 360 B2
Francis Creek 562 L7
Franklin 21,855 L2
Franksville 375 M3
Frederic 1,124 B4
Fredonia 1,558 L8
Fremont 632 J7
Friendship▲ 728 G8
Friesland 271 H8
Galesville 1,278 D7
Galloway 200 H6
Gays Mills 578 E9
Genesee 375 J2
Genesee Depot 350 J2
Genoa 266 D8
Genoa City 1,277 K11
Germantown 13,658 K1
Gibbsville 408 L8
Gillett 1,303 K6
Gilman 412 E5
Gilmanton 300 C7
Gleason 200 G5
Glen Flora 108 E4
Glen Haven 160 E10
Glenbeulah 386 L8
Glendale 14,088 M1
Glenwood City 1,026 B5
Glidden 940 E3
Goodman 875 K4
Gordon 600 C3
Gotham 250 F9
Grafton 9,340 L9
Grand Marsh 725 G8
Grand View 447 D3
Granton 379 E6
Grantsburg▲ 1,144 A4
Gratiot 207 F10
Green Bay▲ 96,466 K6
Green Lake▲ 1,064 H8
Green Valley 104 K6
Greendale 15,128 L2
Greenfield 33,403 L2
Greenleaf 300 L7
Greenville 900 J7
Greenwood 969 E6
Gresham 515 J6
Gurney 145 F3
Hager City 110 A6
Hales Corners 7,623 K2
Hallie D6
Hamburg 170 G5
Hammond 1,097 A6
Hancock 382 G7
Hartford 8,188 K9
Hartland 6,906 J1
Hatfield 500 E7

(continued on following page)

Agriculture, Industry and Resources

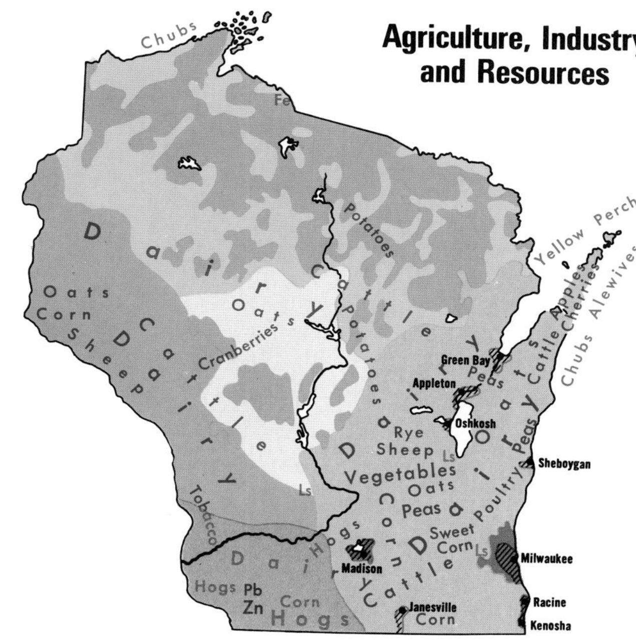
Chubs
Fe
Potatoes
Yellow Perch
Apples
Cherries
Alewives
Chubs
Dairy
Oats
Corn
Sheep
Cattle
Cranberries
Oats
Potatoes
Cattle
Dairy
Green Bay
Appleton
Peas
Oats
Oshkosh
Rye
Sheep
Vegetables
Oats
Peas
Poultry
Sheboygan
Sweet Corn
Milwaukee
Tobacco
Hogs
Madison
Cattle
Racine
Kenosha
Janesville
Corn
Hogs
Pb
Zn
Ls

DOMINANT LAND USE

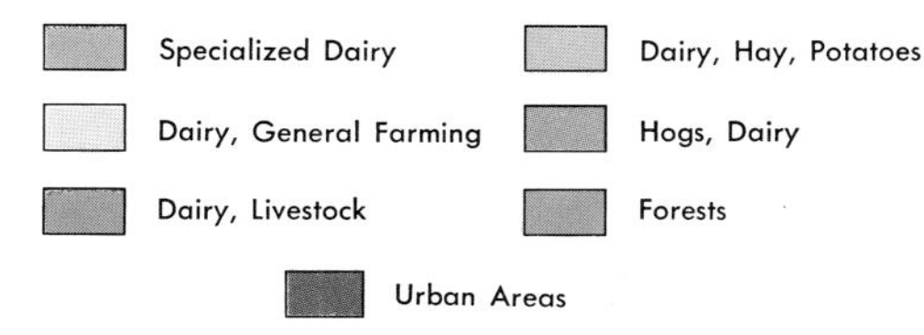
Specialized Dairy
Dairy, Hay, Potatoes
Dairy, General Farming
Hogs, Dairy
Dairy, Livestock
Forests
Urban Areas

MAJOR MINERAL OCCURRENCES

Fe Iron Ore
Pb Lead
Ls Limestone
Zn Zinc

Major Industrial Areas

Hatley 295 ... H6
Haugen 305 ... C4
Hawkins 375 ... E4
Hawthorne 200 ... C3
Hayward▲ 1,897 ... D3
Hazel Green 1,171 ... F11
Hazelhurst 630 ... G4
Heafford Junction 110 ... G4
Hebron 450 ... J10
Helenville 300 ... J10
Hersey 125 ... B6
Hewitt 595 ... F6
High Bridge 525 ... E3
Highland 799 ... F9
Hilbert 1,211 ... K7
Hiles 350 ... J4
Hillsboro 1,288 ... F8
Hillsdale 160 ... C5
Hingham 250 ... K8
Hixton 345 ... E7
Holcombe 200 ... D5
Hollandale 256 ... G10
Holmen 3,220 ... D8
Holy Cross 150 ... L9
Honey Creek 300 ... J3
Horicon 3,873 ... J9
Hortonville 2,029 ... J7
Houlton 915 ... A5
Howard 9,874 ... K6
Howards Grove-Millersville 1,838 ... L8
Hubertus 600 ... K1
Hudson▲ 6,378 ... A6
Humbird 190 ... E6
Hurley▲ 1,782 ... F3
Hustisford 979 ... J9
Hustler 156 ... F8
Independence 1,041 ... D7
Ingram 91 ... E5
Iola 1,125 ... H6
Iron Belt 300 ... F3
Iron Ridge 887 ... K9
Iron River 878 ... D2
Ironton 200 ... F8
Ithaca 160 ... F9
Ixonia 525 ... H1
Jackson 2,486 ... K9
Jacksonport 150 ... M6
Janesville▲ 52,133 ... H10
Jefferson▲ 6,078 ... J10
Johnson Creek 1,259 ... J9
Juda 500 ... H10
Junction City 502 ... G6
Juneau▲ 2,157 ... J9
Kansasville 150 ... L3
Kaukauna 11,982 ... K7
Kekoskee 188 ... J8
Kellnersville 350 ... L7
Kempster 121 ... H5
Kendall 453 ... F8
Kennan 169 ... F5
Kenosha▲ 80,352 ... M3
Keshena▲ 685 ... J6
Kewaskum 2,515 ... K8
Kewaunee▲ 2,750 ... M7
Kiel 2,910 ... L8
Kieler 800 ... E10
Kimberly 5,406 ... K7
King ... H7
Kingston 346 ... H8
Knapp 419 ... B6
Knowlton 127 ... G6
Kohler 1,817 ... L8
Krakow 345 ... K6
La Crosse▲ 51,003 ... D8
La Farge 766 ... E8
La Pointe 300 ... E2
La Valle 446 ... F8
Lac La Belle 258 ... H1
Lac du Flambeau 1,423 ... G4
Ladysmith▲ 3,938 ... D5
Lake Church 175 ... L9
Lake Delton 1,470 ... G8
Lake Geneva 5,979 ... K10
Lake Mills 4,143 ... H9
Lake Nebagamon 900 ... C3
Lake Tomahawk 600 ... H4
Lake Wazeecha 2,278 ... G7
Lake Wissota 2,175 ... D6
Lakewood 425 ... K5
Lamartine 190 ... J8
Lancaster▲ 4,192 ... E10
Land O'Lakes 786 ... H3
Lannon 924 ... K1
Lebanon 250 ... H1
Lena 590 ... K6
Leopolis 200 ... J6
Lewis 200 ... B4
Lily 125 ... J5
Lima Center 175 ... J10
Limeridge 152 ... F9
Linden 429 ... F10
Little Chute 9,207 ... K7
Little Suamico 190 ... L6
Livingston 576 ... E10
Lodi 2,093 ... G9
Loganville 228 ... F9
Lohrville 368 ... H7
Lomira 1,542 ... J8
London 317 ... H9
Lone Rock 641 ... F9
Long Lake 150 ... J4
Loretta 200 ... E4
Lowell 300 ... J9
Loyal 1,244 ... E6
Lublin 129 ... E5
Luck 1,022 ... B4
Luxemburg 1,151 ... L6
Lyndon Station 474 ... F8
Lynn 117 ... F6
Lynxville 153 ... D9
Lyons 550 ... K10
Madison (cap.)▲ 191,262 ... H9
Maiden Rock 146 ... B6
Manawa 1,169 ... J7
Manchester 160 ... J8
Manitowoc▲ 32,520 ... L7
Maple 596 ... C2
Maplewood 200 ... M6
Marathon 1,606 ... G6
Marengo 130 ... E3
Maribel 372 ... L7
Marinette▲ 11,843 ... L5
Marion 1,242 ... J6
Markesan 1,496 ... J8
Marquette 182 ... H8
Marshall 2,329 ... H9
Marshfield 19,291 ... F6
Martell 200 ... B6
Mason 102 ... D3
Mattoon 431 ... J5
Mauston▲ 3,439 ... F8
Mayville 4,374 ... K9
Mazomanie 1,377 ... G9
McFarland 5,232 ... H10
McNaughton 450 ... H4
Medford▲ 4,283 ... F5
Mellen 935 ... E3
Melrose 551 ... E7
Melvina 115 ... E8
Menasha 14,711 ... J7
Menomonee Falls 26,840 ... K1
Menomonie▲ 13,547 ... C6
Mequon 18,885 ... L1
Mercer ... V3
Merrill▲ 9,860 ... G5
Merrillan 553 ... E7
Merrimac 392 ... G9
Merton 1,199 ... K1
Middle Inlet 200 ... K5
Middleton 13,289 ... G9
Mikana 200 ... C4
Milan 153 ... F6
Milladore 314 ... G6
Millston 110 ... E7
Milltown 786 ... J10
Milton 4,434 ... J10
Milwaukee▲ 628,088 ... M1
Mindoro 200 ... D7
Mineral Point 2,428 ... F10
Minocqua 950 ... G4
Minong 521 ... C3
Mishicot 1,296 ... L7
Mondovi 2,491 ... C6
Monico 250 ... H4
Monona 8,637 ... G10
Monroe▲ 10,241 ... G10
Montello▲ 1,329 ... H8
Monterey 150 ... J1
Montfort 676 ... E10
Monticello 1,140 ... G10
Montreal 838 ... F3
Morrisonville 375 ... G9
Mosinee 3,820 ... G6
Mount Calvary 558 ... K8
Mount Hope 173 ... D10
Mount Horeb 4,182 ... G10
Mount Sterling 217 ... D9
Mount Vernon 138 ... G10
Mountain 250 ... K5
Mukwonago 4,457 ... J2
Muscoda 1,287 ... F9
Muskego 16,813 ... K2
Nashotah 567 ... J1
Navarino 140 ... J6
Necedah 743 ... F7
Neenah 23,219 ... J7
Neillsville▲ 2,680 ... E6
Nekoosa 2,557 ... G7
Nelson 388 ... C7
Nelsonville 171 ... H7
Neopit 615 ... J6
Neosho 658 ... J9
Neshkoro 384 ... H8
New Amsterdam 120 ... C8
New Auburn 485 ... D5
New Berlin 33,592 ... K2
New Franken 150 ... L6
New Glarus 1,899 ... G10
New Holstein 3,342 ... K8
New Libson 1,491 ... F8
New London 6,658 ... J7
New Richmond 5,106 ... A5
Newald 375 ... J4
Newburg 875 ... K9
Niagara 1,999 ... K4
Nichols 254 ... K6
North Bay 246 ... M3
North Bend 200 ... D7
North Fond du Lac 4,292 ... J8
North Freedom 591 ... G9
North Hudson 3,101 ... A5
North Lake 400 ... J1
North Prairie 1,322 ... J2
North Shore 14,272 ... M1
Norwalk 564 ... E8
Oak Creek 19,513 ... M2
Oakdale 162 ... F8
Oakfield 1,003 ... J8
Oconomowoc 10,993 ... H1
Oconomowoc Lake 493 ... H1
Oconto Falls 2,584 ... K6
Oconto▲ 4,474 ... L6
Odanah 190 ... E2
Ogdensburg 220 ... J7
Ogema 238 ... F5
Okauchee 3,958 ... J1
Okee 250 ... H9
Oliver 265 ... B2
Omro 2,836 ... J7
Onalaska 11,284 ... D8
Oneida 808 ... K7
Ontario 407 ... E8
Oostburg 1,931 ... L8
Oregon 4,519 ... H10
Orfordville 1,219 ... H10
Osceola 2,075 ... A5
Oshkosh▲ 55,006 ... J8
Osseo 1,551 ... D6
Owen 895 ... F6
Oxford 499 ... H8
Packwaukee 271 ... G8
Paddock Lake 2,662 ... K10
Palmyra 1,539 ... H2
Pardeeville 1,630 ... H8
Park Falls 3,104 ... F4
Park Ridge 546 ... H6
Patch Grove 202 ... D10
Pearson 102 ... H5
Peeksville 250 ... E3
Pell Lake 2,018 ... K10
Pembine 500 ... L4
Pence 234 ... F3
Pensaukee 225 ... L6
Pepin 873 ... B7
Perrygo Place ... J10
Peshtigo 3,154 ... L5
Pewaukee 4,941 ... K1
Phelps 950 ... H3
Phillips▲ 1,592 ... E4
Phlox 150 ... J5
Pickerel 107 ... J5
Pickett 120 ... J8
Pigeon Falls 289 ... D7
Pine River 110 ... H7
Pittsville 838 ... F7
Plain 691 ... F9
Plainfield 839 ... G7
Plat 120 ... K1
Platteville 9,708 ... F10
Pleasant Prairie 11,961 ... L10
Plover 8,176 ... G7
Plum City 534 ... B6
Plymouth 6,769 ... L8
Polonia 200 ... H6
Poplar 516 ... C2
Port Edwards 1,848 ... G7
Port Washington▲ 9,338 ... L9
Port Wing 290 ... D2
Portage▲ 8,640 ... G8
Potosi 654 ... E10
Potter 252 ... K7
Pound 434 ... L5
Poy Sippi 425 ... J7
Poynette 1,662 ... G9
Prairie Farm 494 ... C5
Prairie du Chien▲ 5,659 ... D9
Prairie du Sac 2,380 ... G9
Prentice 571 ... F4
Prescott 3,243 ... A6
Presque Isle 251 ... G3
Princeton 1,458 ... H8
Pulaski 2,200 ... K6
Racine▲ 84,298 ... M3
Radisson 237 ... D4
Randolph 1,729 ... H8
Random Lake 1,439 ... K8
Raymond 300 ... L2
Readfield 200 ... J7
Readstown 420 ... E9
Red Cliff 250 ... E2
Redgranite 1,009 ... H7
Reedsburg 5,834 ... G8
Reedsville 1,182 ... L7
Reeseville 673 ... J9
Reserve 371 ... D4
Rewey 220 ... F10
Rhinelander▲ 7,427 ... H4
Rib Falls 145 ... G6
Rice Lake 7,998 ... F5
Richfield 247 ... K1
Richland Center▲ 5,018 ... F9
Ridgeland 246 ... B5
Ridgeway 577 ... F10
Rio 768 ... H9
Rio Creek 200 ... L6
Ripon 7,241 ... J8
River Falls 10,610 ... A6
River Hills 1,612 ... M1
Roberts 1,043 ... A6
Rochester 978 ... K3
Rock Falls 200 ... C6
Rock Springs 432 ... F8
Rockdale 235 ... J10
Rockfield 200 ... L1
Rockland 509 ... D8
Rome 200 ... H1
Rosendale 777 ... J8
Rosholt 512 ... H6
Rothschild 3,310 ... G6
Roxbury 260 ... G9
Royalton 200 ... J7
Rozellville 150 ... G6
Rubicon 261 ... K9
Rudolph 451 ... G7
Saint Cloud 494 ... K8
Saint Croix Falls 1,640 ... A5
Saint Francis 9,245 ... M2
Saint Joseph Ridge 450 ... D8
Saint Nazianz 693 ... L7
Sand Creek 225 ... C5
Sauk City 3,019 ... G9
Saukville 3,695 ... L9
Saxon 375 ... F3
Sayner 300 ... H4
Scandinavia 298 ... H7
Schofield 2,415 ... H6
School Hill 228 ... L8
Seneca 235 ... E9
Sextonville 225 ... F9
Seymour 1,557 ... K6
Sharon 1,250 ... J11
Shawano▲ 7,598 ... J6
Sheboygan▲ 49,676 ... L8
Sheboygan Falls 5,823 ... L8
Sheldon 268 ... D5
Shell Lake▲ 1,161 ... C4
Sherry 115 ... G6
Sherwood 837 ... K7
Shiocton 805 ... K7
Shopiere 350 ... H10
Shorewood 14,116 ... M1
Shorewood Hills 1,680 ... G9
Shullsburg 1,236 ... F10
Silver Lake 1,801 ... K10
Siren 863 ... B4
Sister Bay 675 ... M5
Slinger 2,340 ... K9
Soldiers Grove 564 ... E9
Solon Springs 575 ... C3
Somers 400 ... M3

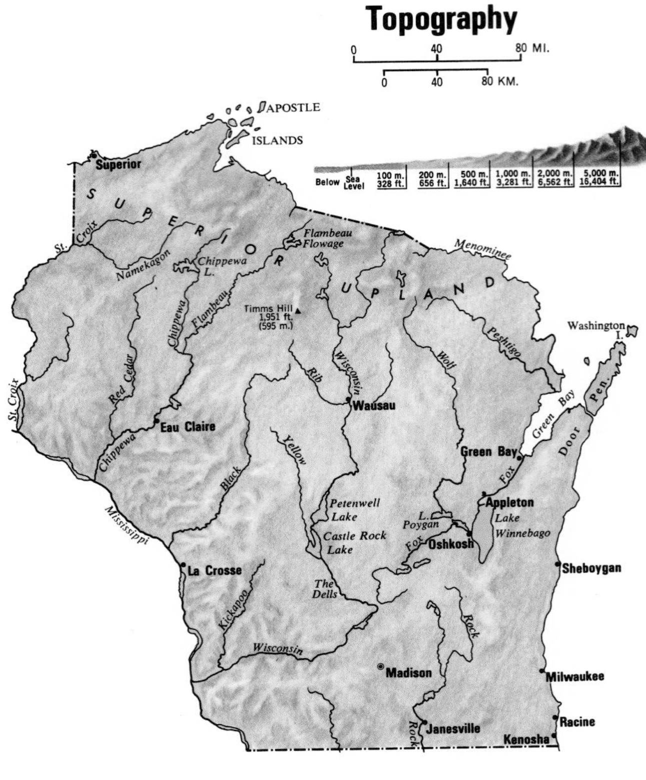
Topography
0
40
80 MI.
0
40
80 KM.
Below Sea Level
100 m. 328 ft.
200 m. 656 ft.
500 m. 1,640 ft.
1,000 m. 3,281 ft.
2,000 m. 6,562 ft.
5,000 m. 16,404 ft.
APOSTLE
ISLANDS
Superior
SUPERIOR UPLAND
St. Croix
Namekagon
Chippewa L.
Flambeau Flowage
Menominee
Timms Hill 1,951 ft. (595 m.)
Flambeau
Chippewa
Red Cedar
Rib
Wisconsin
Wolf
Peshtigo
Washington I.
Wausau
Eau Claire
Yellow
Black
Green Bay
Door Pen.
Fox
Appleton
Lake Winnebago
Petenwell Lake
Castle Rock Lake
L. Poygan
Oshkosh
Mississippi
La Crosse
Sheboygan
The Dells
Kickapoo
Rock
Wisconsin
Madison
Milwaukee
Racine
Janesville
Kenosha

Somerset 1,065 ... A5
South Milwaukee 20,958 ... M2
South Range 149 ... B2
South Wayne 478 ... G10
Sparta▲ 7,788 ... E8
Spencer 1,757 ... F6
Spirit 400 ... F5
Spooner 2,464 ... B4
Spring Green 1,283 ... G9
Spring Valley 1,051 ... B6
Springbrook 150 ... C4
Stangelville 150 ... L7
Stanley 2,011 ... E6
Star Prairie 507 ... A5
Stetsonville 511 ... F5
Steuben 161 ... E9
Stevens Point▲ 23,006 ... G7
Stiles 300 ... L6
Stitzer 190 ... E10
Stockbridge 579 ... K7
Stoddard 775 ... D8
Stone Bank 390 ... J1
Stone Lake 210 ... C4
Stoughton 8,786 ... H10
Stratford 1,515 ... F6
Strum 949 ... D6
Sturgeon Bay▲ 9,176 ... M6
Sturtevant 3,803 ... M3
Suamico 900 ... K6
Sullivan 432 ... H1
Summit Lake 250 ... H5
Sun Prairie 15,333 ... H9
Superior▲ 27,134 ... C2
Superior Village 481 ... B2
Suring 626 ... K5
Sussex 5,039 ... K1
Symco 102 ... J6
Taycheedah 350 ... K8
Taylor 419 ... E7
Tennyson 378 ... E10
Theresa 771 ... K8
Thiensville 3,301 ... L1
Thorp 1,657 ... E6
Three Lakes 950 ... H4
Tichigan Lake 500 ... K2
Tigerton 815 ... H6
Tilleda 102 ... J6
Tisch Mills 315 ... L7
Tomah 7,570 ... E8
Tomahawk 3,328 ... G5
Tony 114 ... E5
Townsend 450 ... K5
Trego 280 ... C4
Trempealeau 1,039 ... C8
Troy Center 250 ... J2
Tunnel City 200 ... E7
Turtle Lake 817 ... B5
Tustin 101 ... J7
Twin Lakes 3,989 ... K11
Two Rivers 13,030 ... M7
Union Center 197 ... F8
Union Grove 3,669 ... L3
Unity 452 ... F6
Upson 115 ... F3
Valders 905 ... L7
Verona 5,374 ... G9
Vesper 598 ... F7
Viola 644 ... E8
Viroqua▲ 3,922 ... D8
Wabeno 800 ... J5
Waldo 442 ... L8
Wales 2,471 ... J1
Walworth 1,614 ... J10
Warrens 343 ... E7
Washburn▲ 2,285 ... D2
Washington Island 550 ... M5
Waterford 2,431 ... K3
Waterloo 2,712 ... J9
Watertown 19,142 ... J9
Waubeka 450 ... L9
Waukesha▲ 56,958 ... K1
Waumandee 115 ... C7
Waunakee 5,897 ... G9
Waupaca▲ 4,957 ... H7
Waupun 8,207 ... J8
Wausau▲ 37,060 ... G6
Wausaukee 656 ... L5
Wautoma▲ 1,784 ... H7
Wauwatosa 49,366 ... L1
Wauzeka 595 ... E9
Wayside 140 ... L7
Webster 623 ... B4
West Allis 63,221 ... L1
West Baraboo 1,021 ... G9
West Bend▲ 23,916 ... K9
West Milwaukee 3,973 ... L1
West Salem 3,611 ... D8
Westboro 750 ... F5
Westby 1,866 ... E8
Westfield 1,125 ... H8
Weston 8,775 ... G6
Weston 9,714 ... C6
Weyauwega 1,665 ... H7
Weyerhaeuser 283 ... D5
Wheeler 348 ... C5
White Lake 304 ... J5
Whitefish Bay 14,272 ... M1
Whitehall▲ 1,494 ... D7
Whitelaw 700 ... L7
Whitewater 12,636 ... J10
Whiting 1,838 ... H7
Wild Rose 676 ... H7
Williams Bay 2,108 ... J10
Wilson 163 ... B6
Wilton 478 ... E8
Winchester 300 ... G3
Wind Lake 3,748 ... L2
Wind Point 1,941 ... M2
Windsor 2,182 ... H9
Winnebago 1,433 ... J7
Winneconne 2,059 ... J7
Winter 383 ... E4
Wiota 125 ... G10
Wisconsin Dells 2,393 ... G8
Wisconsin Rapids▲ 18,245 ... G7
Withee 503 ... E6
Wittenberg 1,145 ... H6
Wonewoc 793 ... F8
Woodford 107 ... G10
Woodman 120 ... E9
Woodruff 850 ... G4
Woodville 942 ... B6
Wrightstown 1,262 ... K7
Wyeville 154 ... F7
Wyocena 620 ... H9
Yuba 77 ... F8

OTHER FEATURES

Apostle (isls.) ... F2
Apostle Islands Nat'l Lakeshore ... E1
Apple (riv.) ... A5
Bad River Ind. Res. ... E2
Bardon (lake) ... E1
Bear (isl.) ... E1
Beaver Dam (lake) ... J9
Beulah (lake) ... J2
Big Eau Pleine (res.) ... G6
Big Muskego (lake) ... L2
Big Rib (riv.) ... G5
Black (riv.) ... E7
Butternut (lake) ... J4
Castle Rock (lake) ... G8
Cat (isl.) ... E1
Chambers (isl.) ... M5
Chequamegon (bay) ... E2
Chetac (lake) ... D4
Chippewa (lake) ... D4
Chippewa (riv.) ... B7
Clam (lake) ... B4
Clam (riv.) ... A4
Dells, The (valley) ... G8
Denoon (lake) ... K2
Door (pen.) ... M6
Du Bay (lake) ... G6
Eagle (lake) ... H2
Eagle (lake) ... K3
Eau Claire (riv.) ... D6
Flambeau (riv.) ... E4
Flambeau Flowage (res.) ... F3
Fox (riv.) ... K2
Fox (riv.) ... K7
General Mitchell Field ... M2
Geneva (lake) ... K10
Golden (lake) ... H1
Green (bay) ... L6
Grindstone (lake) ... C4
Holcombe Flowage (res.) ... D5
Jump (riv.) ... E5
Kegonsa (lake) ... H10
Kickapoo (riv.) ... E9
Koshkonong (lake) ... H10
La Belle (lake) ... H1
Lac Court Oreilles Ind. Res. ... D4
Lac du Flambeau Ind. Res. ... G3
Long (lake) ... C4
Madeline (isl.) ... E2
Mendota (lake) ... H9
Menominee (riv.) ... L5
Menominee Ind. Res. ... J5
Metonga (lake) ... J4
Michigan (isl.) ... F2
Michigan (lake) ... M9
Mississippi (riv.) ... D10
Montreal (riv.) ... F2
Moose (lake) ... E3
Moose (lake) ... F3
Nagawicka (lake) ... J1
Namekagon (lake) ... D3
Namekagon (riv.) ... C3
North (lake) ... J1
Oak (isl.) ... E2
Oconomowoc (lake) ... H1
Oconto (riv.) ... K5
Okauchee (lake) ... J1
Outer (isl.) ... F1
Owen (lake) ... D3
Pecatonica (riv.) ... H11
Pelican (lake) ... H4
Pepin (lake) ... B7
Peshtigo (riv.) ... K5
Petenwell (lake) ... G7
Pewaukee (lake) ... K1
Phantom (lake) ... J2
Pine (lake) ... J1
Porte des Morts (str.) ... N5
Poygan (lake) ... J7
Puckaway (lake) ... H8
Red Cedar (riv.) ... C5
Red Cliff Ind. Res. ... E2
Rock (riv.) ... J9
Round (lake) ... F4
Round (lake) ... D3
Saint Croix (lake) ... A6
Saint Croix (riv.) ... A4
Saint Croix Flowage (res.) ... C3
Saint Louis (riv.) ... A2
Sand (isl.) ... D2
Shawano (lake) ... K6
Shell (lake) ... C4
Spider (lake) ... D3
Stockbridge Ind. Res. ... J6
Stockton (isl.) ... F2
Sugar (riv.) ... H10
Sugarbush Hill (mt.) ... J4
Superior (lake) ... F1
Thunder (lake) ... H4
Tichigan (lake) ... K2
Timms Hill (mt.) ... F5
Trempealeau (riv.) ... C7
Trout (lake) ... G3
Washington (isl.) ... M5
Willow (res.) ... F4
Wind (lake) ... K2
Winnebago (lake) ... K7
Wisconsin (riv.) ... E9
Wolf (riv.) ... J5
Yellow (lake) ... B4
Yellow (riv.) ... F7

▲County seat

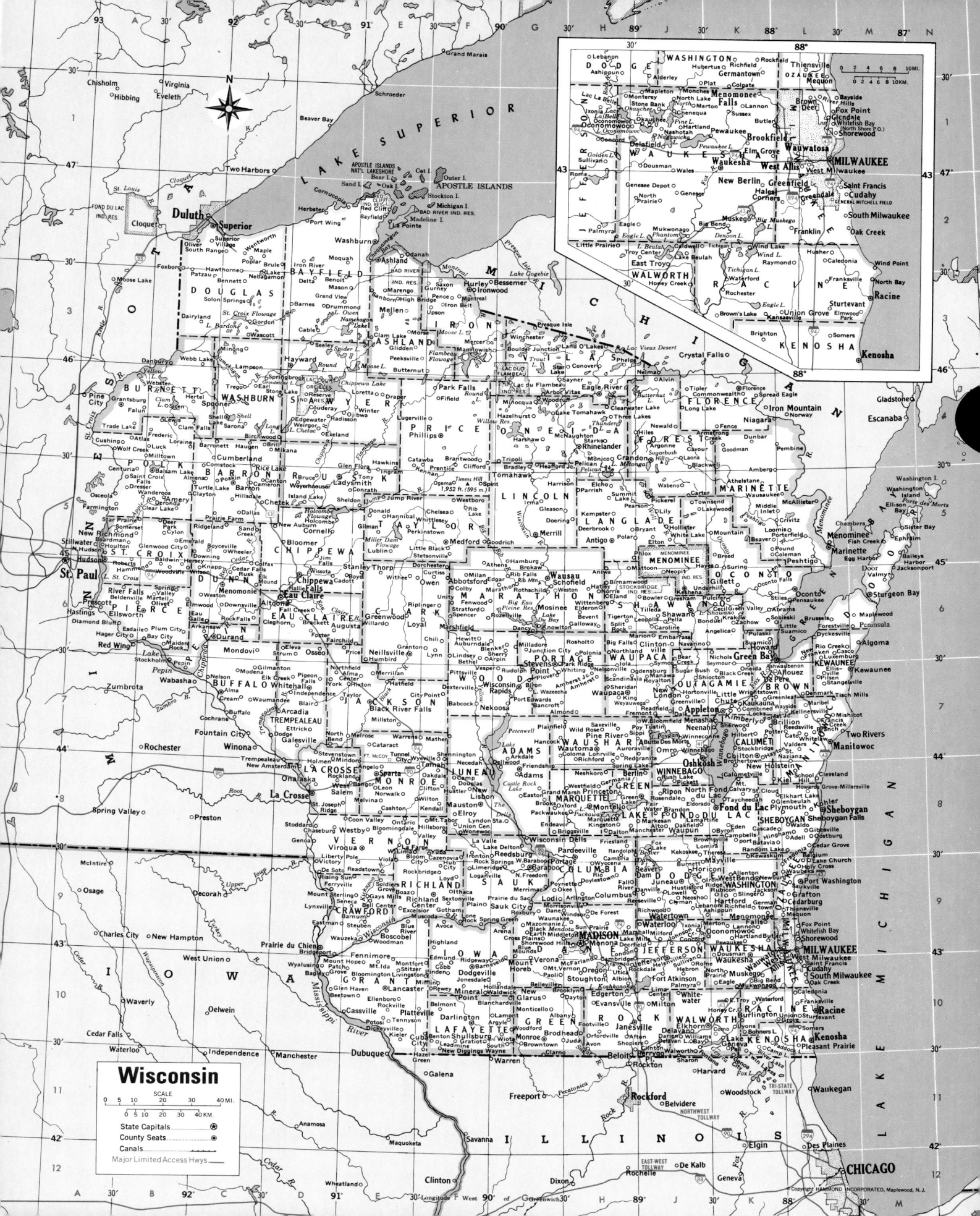

Wisconsin
SCALE
0 5 10 20 30 40 MI.
0 5 10 20 30 40 KM.
State Capitals
County Seats
Canals
Major Limited Access Hwys.
LAKE SUPERIOR
LAKE MICHIGAN
MICHIGAN
MINNESOTA
IOWA
ILLINOIS
APOSTLE ISLANDS
APOSTLE ISLANDS NAT'L LAKESHORE
GREEN BAY
DOUGLAS
BAYFIELD
ASHLAND
IRON
VILAS
BURNETT
WASHBURN
SAWYER
PRICE
ONEIDA
FOREST
FLORENCE
MARINETTE
POLK
BARRON
RUSK
TAYLOR
LINCOLN
LANGLADE
MENOMINEE
OCONTO
DOOR
ST. CROIX
DUNN
CHIPPEWA
EAU CLAIRE
CLARK
MARATHON
SHAWANO
PIERCE
PEPIN
BUFFALO
TREMPEALEAU
JACKSON
WOOD
PORTAGE
WAUPACA
OUTAGAMIE
BROWN
KEWAUNEE
LA CROSSE
MONROE
JUNEAU
ADAMS
WAUSHARA
WINNEBAGO
CALUMET
MANITOWOC
VERNON
MARQUETTE
GREEN LAKE
FOND DU LAC
SHEBOYGAN
RICHLAND
SAUK
COLUMBIA
DODGE
WASHINGTON
OZAUKEE
CRAWFORD
GRANT
IOWA
DANE
JEFFERSON
WAUKESHA
MILWAUKEE
LAFAYETTE
GREEN
ROCK
WALWORTH
RACINE
KENOSHA
MADISON
MILWAUKEE
Duluth
Superior
Ashland
Eau Claire
Wausau
Green Bay
Appleton
Oshkosh
Sheboygan
Manitowoc
La Crosse
Racine
Kenosha
Janesville
Beloit
St. Paul
Dubuque
Rockford
CHICAGO
Longitude West 90° of Greenwich
© Copyright HAMMOND INCORPORATED, Maplewood, N. J.

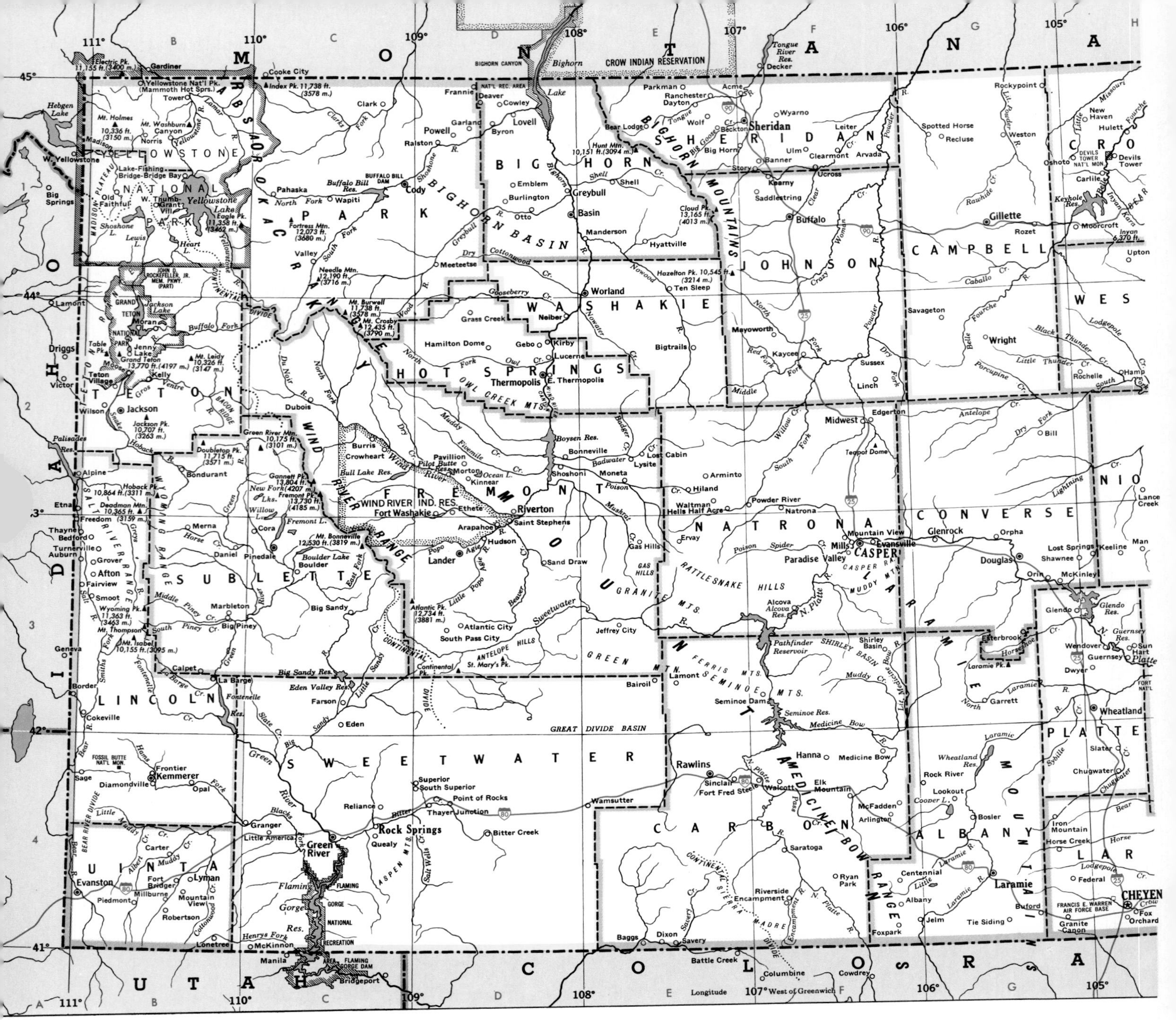

Agriculture, Industry and Resources

DOMINANT LAND USE

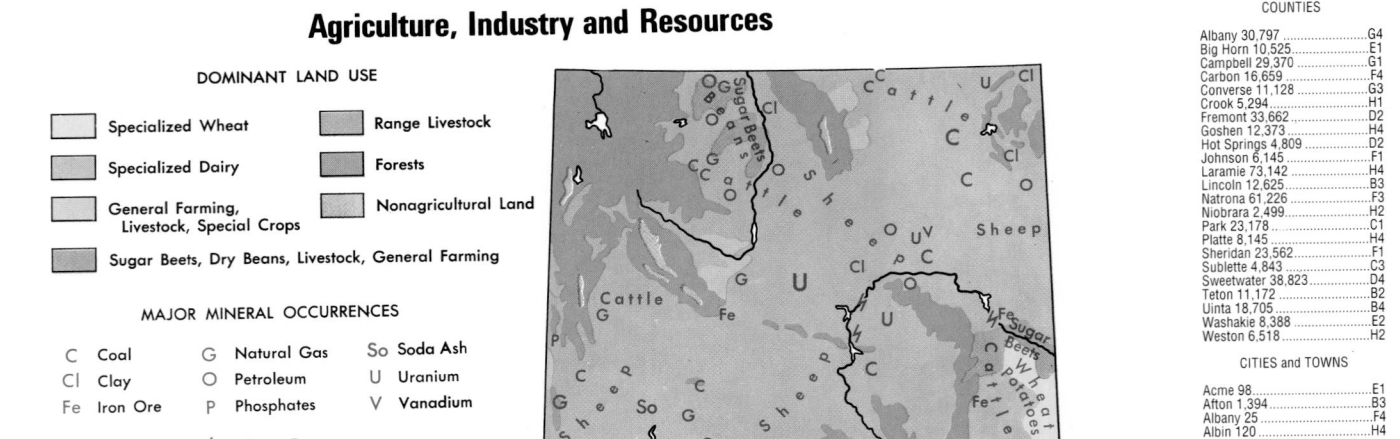

Specialized Wheat

Specialized Dairy

General Farming, Livestock, Special Crops

Sugar Beets, Dry Beans, Livestock, General Farming

Range Livestock

Forests

Nonagricultural Land

MAJOR MINERAL OCCURRENCES

C Coal
Cl Clay
Fe Iron Ore
P Phosphates
G Natural Gas
O Petroleum
So Soda Ash
U Uranium
V Vanadium
⚡ Water Power

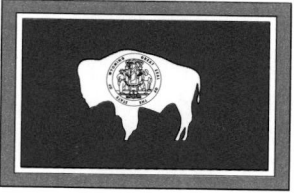

Wyoming

SCALE
0 5 10 20 30 40 MI.
0 5 10 20 30 40 KM.

State Capitals .... ⊛
County Seats .... ⊙
Major Limited Access Hwys.

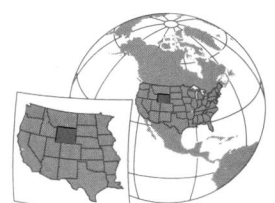

AREA 97,809 sq. mi. (253,325 sq. km.)
POPULATION 455,975
CAPITAL Cheyenne
LARGEST CITY Casper
HIGHEST POINT Gannett Pk. 13,804 ft. (4207 m.)
SETTLED IN 1834
ADMITTED TO UNION July 10, 1890
POPULAR NAME Equality State
STATE FLOWER Indian Paintbrush
STATE BIRD Meadowlark

Topography

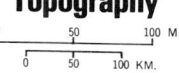

0   50   100 MI.
0   50   100 KM.

5,000 m. | 2,000 m. | 1,000 m. | 500 m. | 200 m. | 100 m. | Sea
16,404 ft. | 6,562 ft. | 3,281 ft. | 1,640 ft. | 656 ft. | 328 ft. | Level | Below

© Copyright HAMMOND INCORPORATED, Maplewood, N.J.

Freedom 400	B3	Midwest 495	F2	Torrington▲ 5,651	H3

Freedom 400 .... B3
Frontier 150 .... B4
Garland 57 .... D1
Gas Hills 150 .... E3
Gillette▲ 17,635 .... G1
Glendo 195 .... G3
Glenrock 2,153 .... G3
Granger 126 .... C4
Granite Canon 80 .... G4
Grass Creek 152 .... D2
Green River▲ 12,711 .... C4
Greybull 1,789 .... E1
Grover 425 .... B3
Guernsey 1,155 .... H3
Hamilton Dome 80 .... D2
Hanna 1,076 .... F4
Hartville 78 .... H3
Hawk Springs 84 .... H4
Hillsdale 160 .... H4
Horse Creek 225 .... G4
Hudson 392 .... D3
Hulett 429 .... H1
Huntley 50 .... H4
Hyattville 110 .... E1
Iron Mountain 45 .... G4
Jackson▲ 4,472 .... B2
Jeffrey City 1,882 .... E3
Jelm 29 .... G4
Kaycee 256 .... F2
Kearny 49 .... F1
Kelly 100 .... B2
Kemmerer▲ 3,020 .... B4
Kinnear 145 .... D2
Kirby 59 .... D2
La Barge 493 .... B3
Lagrange 224 .... H4
Lamont 30 .... E3
Lance Creek 100 .... H2
Lander▲ 7,023 .... D3
Laramie▲ 26,687 .... G4
Leiter 46 .... F1
Linch 187 .... F2
Lingle 473 .... H3
Little America 175 .... C4
Lost Cabin 25 .... E2
Lovell 2,131 .... D1
Lucerne 240 .... D2
Lusk▲ 1,504 .... H3
Lyman 1,896 .... B4
Lysite 175 .... E2
Mammoth Hot Springs
(Yellowstone Nat'l Park)
350 .... B1
Manderson 83 .... E1
Manville 97 .... H3
Marbleton 634 .... B3
Mayoworth F2
McFadden 47 .... F4
McKinnon 135 .... C4
Medicine Bow 389 .... F4
Meeteetse 368 .... D1
Meriden 55 .... H4

Midwest 495 .... F2
Millburne 54 .... B4
Mills 1,574 .... F3
Moorcroft 768 .... H1
Moose 150 .... B2
Moran 200 .... B2
Morrisey 28 .... H2
Morton 35 .... D2
Mountain View 1,345 .... B4
Mountain View 76 .... F3
Neiber D2
New Haven 35 .... H1
Newcastle▲ 3,003 .... H2
Old Faithful 75 .... B1
Opal 95 .... B4
Orchard Valley 3,327 .... H4
Osage 500 .... H2
Otto 50 .... D1
Pahaska 75 .... C1
Paradise Valley F3
Parkman 30 .... E1
Pavillion 126 .... D2
Piedmont 25 .... B4
Pine Bluffs 1,054 .... H4
Pinedale▲ 1,181 .... C3
Point of Rocks 425 .... D4
Powder River 70 .... E2
Powell 5,292 .... D1
Ralston 109 .... D1
Ranchester 676 .... E1
Rawlins▲ 9,380 .... E4
Recluse 225 .... G1
Reliance 325 .... C4
Riverside 85 .... F4
Riverton 9,202 .... D2
Robertson 142 .... B4
Rock River 190 .... G4
Rock Springs 19,050 .... C4
Rozet 30 .... G1
Saddlestring 100 .... F1
Sage 45 .... B4
Saint Stephens 80 .... D3
Sand Draw 40 .... D3
Saratoga 1,969 .... F4
Savageton 30 .... G2
Savery 29 .... E4
Shell 80 .... E1
Sheridan▲ 13,900 .... F1
Shirley Basin 440 .... F3
Shoshoni 497 .... D2
Sinclair 500 .... E4
Smoot 310 .... B4
South Superior 586 .... D4
Story 637 .... F1
Sundance▲ 1,139 .... H1
Sunrise 29 .... H3
Superior 273 .... D4
Sussex 25 .... F2
Ten Sleep 311 .... E1
Teton Village B2
Thayne 267 .... A3
Thermopolis▲ 3,247 .... D2

Torrington▲ 5,651 .... H3
Turnerville 65 .... A3
Ulm 25 .... F1
Upton 980 .... H1
Veteran 60 .... H4
Walcott 200 .... F4
Wamsutter 240 .... D4
Wapiti 130 .... C1
Wheatland▲ 3,271 .... H3
Wilson 480 .... B2
Worland▲ 5,742 .... E1
Wright 1,236 .... G2
Wyarno 101 .... F1
Yellowstone National Park
350 .... B1
Yoder 136 .... H4

OTHER FEATURES

Absaroka (range) C1
Antelope (creek) G2
Antelope (hills) D3
Aspen (mts.) C4
Atlantic (peak) D3
Bear (creek) H4
Bear (riv.) B4
Bear Lodge (mts.) H1
Bear River Divide (mts.) B4
Beaver (creek) D3
Beaver (creek) H2
Belle Fourche (riv.) H1
Big Goose (creek) F1
Bighorn (basin) D1
Bighorn (lake) D1
Bighorn (mts.) E1
Bighorn Canyon Nat'l
Rec. Area D1
Big Sandy (riv.) C3
Bitter (creek) C4
Blacks Fork, Green (riv.) C4
Black Thunder (creek) G2
Bonneville (mt.) C3
Boysen (res.) D2
Buffalo Bill (dam) C1
Buffalo Bill (res.) C1
Buffalo Fork, Snake (riv.) B2
Burwell (mt.) C2
Caballo (creek) G1
Casper (range) F3
Cheyenne (riv.) G2
Chugwater (creek) H4
Clarks Fork (riv.) C1
Clear (creek) F1
Cloud (peak) E1
Cottonwood (creek) B4
Crazy Woman (creek) F1
Crosby (mt.) C1
Crow (riv.) H4
Deadman (mt.) B2
Devils Tower Nat'l Mon. H1
Doubletop (peak) B2

Dry (creek) C2
Dry Cottonwood (creek) D1
Eagle (peak) B1
Fivemile (creek) D2
Flaming Gorge (res.) C4
Flaming Gorge Nat'l
Rec. Area C4
Fontenelle (creek) B3
Fontenelle (res.) B3
Fort Laramie Nat'l Hist. Site H3
Fortress (mt.) C1
Fossil Butte Nat'l Mon. B4
Francis E. Warren
A.F.B. 3,832 .... G4
Fremont (lake) C3
Fremont (peak) C2
Gannett (peak) C2
Gas (hills) E3
Glendo (res.) H3
Gooseberry (creek) D1
Grand Teton (mt.) B2
Grand Teton Nat'l Park B2
Granite (mts.) E3
Great Divide (basin) E3
Green (mt.) C2
Green (riv.) C4
Green, East Fork (riv.) C3
Green River (mt.) C2
Greybull (riv.) D1
Greys (riv.) B3
Gros Ventre (riv.) B2
Guernsey (res.) H3
Hams Fork (riv.) B4
Hazelton (peak) E1
Henrys Fork, Green (riv.) C4
Hoback (peak) B2
Hoback (riv.) B2
Holmes (mt.) B1
Horse (creek) H4
Horseshoe (creek) G3
Hunt (mt.) E1
Index (peak) C1
Inyan Kara (creek) H1
Inyan Kara (mt.) H1
Isabel (mt.) B3
Jackson (lake) B2
Jackson (peak) B2
John D. Rockefeller, Jr.,
Mem. Pkwy. B1
Keyhole (res.) H1
Lamar (riv.) B1
Lance (creek) H2
Laramie (mts.) G3
Laramie (peak) G3
Laramie (riv.) G4
Leidy (mt.) B2
Lewis (lake) B1
Lightning (creek) G2
Little Missouri (riv.) H1
Little Muddy (creek) B4
Little Powder (riv.) G1
Little Sandy (creek) C3

Little Thunder (creek) G2
Lodgepole (creek) H2
Lodgepole (creek) H4
Madison (plat.) B1
Medicine Bow (range) F4
Medicine Bow (riv.) F3
Middle Piney (creek) B3
Muddy (creek) D2
Muskrat (creek) E2
Needle (mt.) C1
Niobrara (riv.) J3
North Laramie (riv.) G3
North Platte (riv.) H3
Nowater (creek) E2
Nowood (riv.) E1
Owl, North Fork (creek) D2
Owl Creek (mts.) D2
Palisades (res.) A2
Pass (creek) F4
Pathfinder (res.) F3
Poison (creek) E2
Poison Spider (creek) F3
Popo Agie (riv.) D3
Powder (riv.) F2
Rattlesnake (hills) E3
Rawhide (creek) G1
Rocky (mts.) C1
Salt (riv.) B3
Salt River (range) B3
Salt Wells (creek) D4
Seminoe (mts.) E3
Seminoe (res.) E3
Shell (creek) E1
Shirley (basin) F3
Shoshone (lake) B1
Shoshone (riv.) D1
Sierra Madre (mts.) E4
Slate (creek) C3
Smiths Fork (riv.) B3
Snake (riv.) B2
South Cheyenne (riv.) H2
South Piney (creek) B3
Sweetwater (riv.) D3
Sybille (creek) G4
Teapot Dome (mt.) F2
Teton (range) B2
Tongue (riv.) E1
Washburn (mt.) B1
Wheatland (res.) G4
Willow (creek) F2
Wind (riv.) C2
Wind River (canyon) D2
Wind River (range) C2
Wind River Ind. Res. C2
Wood (riv.) C1
Wyoming (peak) B3
Wyoming (range) B2
Yellowstone (lake) B1
Yellowstone (riv.) B1
Yellowstone Nat'l Park B1

▲County seat

Alcova 275 .... F3
Alpine 200 .... B2
Alva 50 .... H1
Arapahoe 393 .... D3
Arvada 30 .... F1
Atlantic City 25 .... D3
Auburn 360 .... A3
Baggs 272 .... E4
Bairoil 228 .... E3
Banner 40 .... F1
Basin▲ 1,180 .... E1
Beckton 110 .... E1
Bedford 350 .... A3
Beulah 184 .... H1
Big Horn 350 .... E1
Big Piney 454 .... B3
Bondurant 90 .... B2
Border 25 .... B3
Bosler 195 .... G4
Boulder 50 .... C3
Buffalo▲ 3,302 .... F1
Buford 36 .... G4
Burlington 184 .... D1
Burns 250 .... H4
Burris 30 .... C2
Byron 470 .... D1
Carpenter 75 .... H4
Carter 33 .... B4
Casper▲ 46,742 .... F3
Centennial 140 .... F4
Cheyenne (cap.)▲ 50,008 .... H4
Chugwater 192 .... H4

Clearmont 119 .... F1
Cody▲ 7,897 .... D1
Cokeville 493 .... B3
Colony 50 .... H1
Cowley 477 .... D1
Crowheart 200 .... C2
Daniel 130 .... B3
Dayton 565 .... E1
Deaver 199 .... D1
Devils Tower 28 .... H1
Diamondville 864 .... B4
Dixon 70 .... E4
Douglas▲ 5,076 .... G3
Dubois 895 .... C2
East Thermopolis 221 .... D2
Eden 198 .... C3
Edgerton 247 .... F2
Egbert 75 .... H4
Elk Mountain 174 .... F4
Encampment 611 .... F4
Ethete 1,059 .... D2
Etna 200 .... A2
Evanston▲ 10,903 .... B4
Evansville 1,403 .... F3
Fairview 150 .... A3
Farson 350 .... C3
Fort Bridger 300 .... B4
Fort Laramie 243 .... H3
Fort Washakie 1,334 .... C2
Fox Farm 2,850 .... H4
Foxpark 78 .... F4
Frannie 148 .... D1

Hammond Incorporated, Maplewood, N.J.

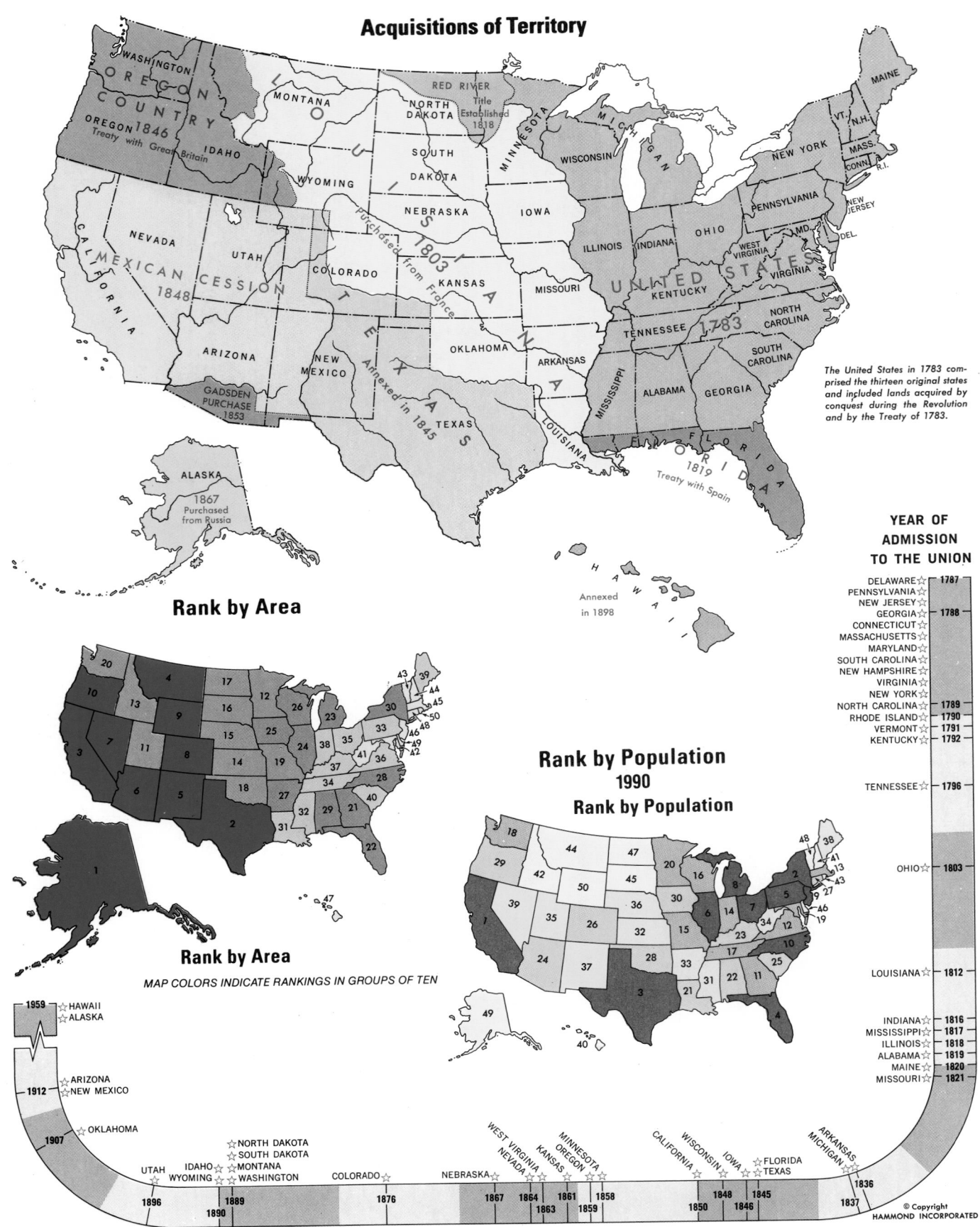

Acquisitions of Territory

WASHINGTON

OREGON COUNTRY

OREGON 1846 Treaty with Great Britain

MONTANA

LOUISIANA

RED RIVER Title Established 1818

NORTH DAKOTA

IDAHO

SOUTH DAKOTA

MINNESOTA

MICHIGAN

WISCONSIN

MAINE

VT. N.H.

NEW YORK

MASS.

CONN. R.I.

WYOMING

NEBRASKA

IOWA

NEW JERSEY

NEVADA

UTAH

CALIFORNIA

MEXICAN CESSION 1848

COLORADO

KANSAS

MISSOURI

ILLINOIS INDIANA OHIO

WEST VIRGINIA

PENNSYLVANIA

MD. DEL.

UNITED STATES

VIRGINIA

KENTUCKY

ARIZONA

NEW MEXICO

GADSDEN PURCHASE 1853

TEXAS

Annexed in 1845

OKLAHOMA

ARKANSAS

TENNESSEE 1783

NORTH CAROLINA

SOUTH CAROLINA

MISSISSIPPI

ALABAMA

GEORGIA

LOUISIANA

Purchased from France 1803

FLORIDA 1819 Treaty with Spain

The United States in 1783 comprised the thirteen original states and included lands acquired by conquest during the Revolution and by the Treaty of 1783.

ALASKA 1867 Purchased from Russia

HAWAII Annexed in 1898

Rank by Area

MAP COLORS INDICATE RANKINGS IN GROUPS OF TEN

Rank by Population 1990
Rank by Population

	YEAR OF ADMISSION TO THE UNION
DELAWARE ☆	1787
PENNSYLVANIA ☆	
NEW JERSEY ☆	
GEORGIA ☆	1788
CONNECTICUT ☆	
MASSACHUSETTS ☆	
MARYLAND ☆	
SOUTH CAROLINA ☆	
NEW HAMPSHIRE ☆	
VIRGINIA ☆	
NEW YORK ☆	
NORTH CAROLINA ☆	1789
RHODE ISLAND ☆	1790
VERMONT ☆	1791
KENTUCKY ☆	1792
TENNESSEE ☆	1796
OHIO ☆	1803
LOUISIANA ☆	1812
INDIANA ☆	1816
MISSISSIPPI ☆	1817
ILLINOIS ☆	1818
ALABAMA ☆	1819
MAINE ☆	1820
MISSOURI ☆	1821

1959 ☆HAWAII ☆ALASKA

1912 ☆ARIZONA ☆NEW MEXICO

1907 ☆OKLAHOMA

☆NORTH DAKOTA
☆SOUTH DAKOTA

UTAH ☆ ☆IDAHO ☆MONTANA
WYOMING ☆ ☆WASHINGTON

COLORADO ☆

WEST VIRGINIA NEVADA

MINNESOTA KANSAS OREGON

CALIFORNIA WISCONSIN IOWA ☆FLORIDA
☆TEXAS

ARKANSAS MICHIGAN

NEBRASKA ☆

1896
1890
1889
1876
1867 1864 1861 1858
1863 1859
1850 1848 1845
1846
1836
1837

© Copyright HAMMOND INCORPORATED

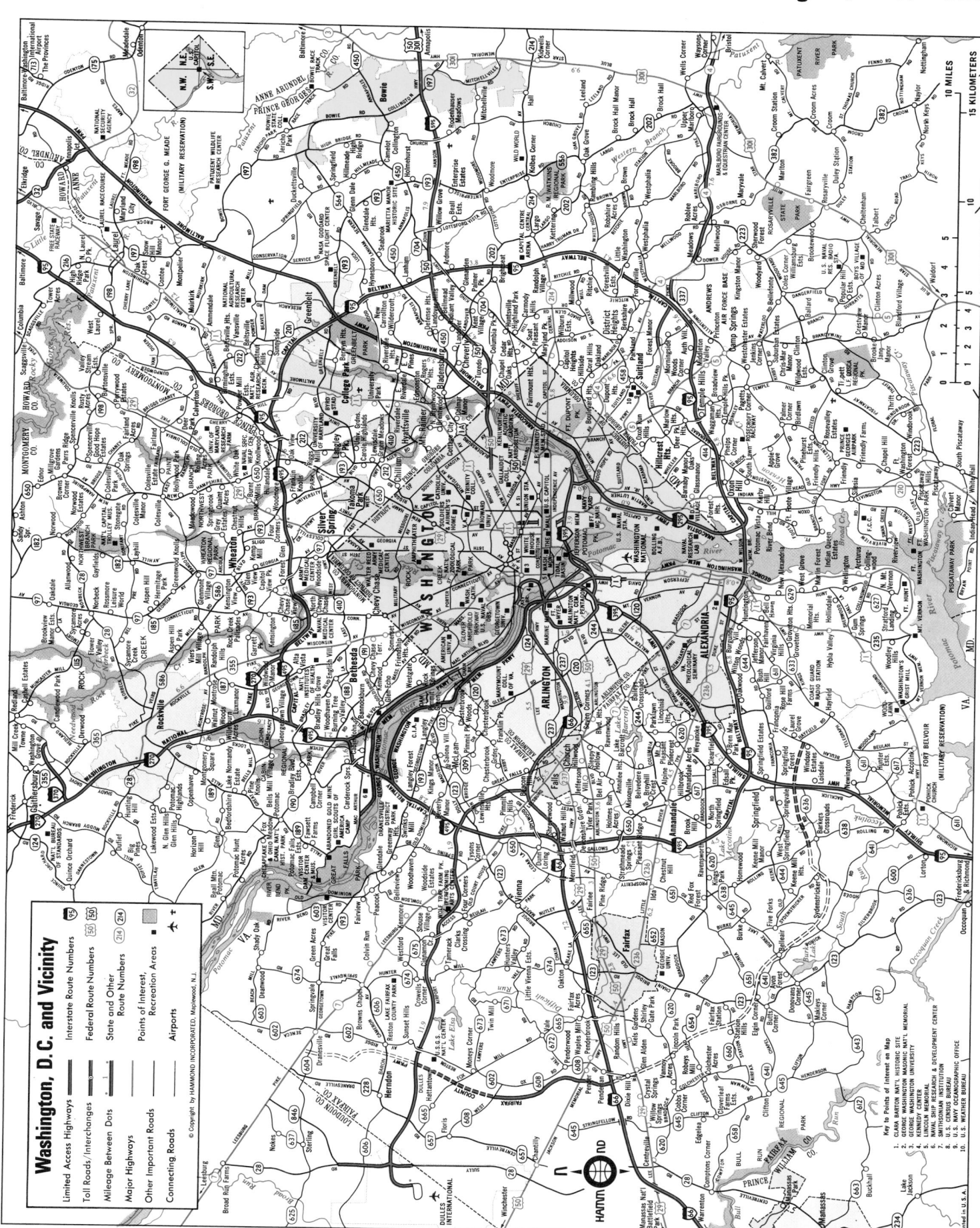
Washington, D.C. and Vicinity
Limited Access Highways
Interstate Route Numbers
Toll Roads/Interchanges
Federal Route Numbers
Mileage Between Dots
State and Other Route Numbers
Major Highways
Points of Interest, Recreation Areas
Other Important Roads
Airports
Connecting Roads
© Copyright by HAMMOND INCORPORATED, Maplewood, N.J.
Key to Points of Interest on Map
1. CLARA BARTON NAT'L HISTORIC SITE
2. GEORGE WASHINGTON MASONIC NAT'L MEMORIAL
3. GEORGE WASHINGTON UNIVERSITY
4. KENNEDY CENTER
5. LINCOLN MEMORIAL
6. NAVAL SHIP RESEARCH & DEVELOPMENT CENTER
7. SMITHSONIAN INSTITUTION
8. U.S. CENSUS BUREAU
9. U.S. NAVY OCEANOGRAPHIC OFFICE
10. U.S. WEATHER BUREAU
10 MILES
15 KILOMETERS
Printed in U.S.A.

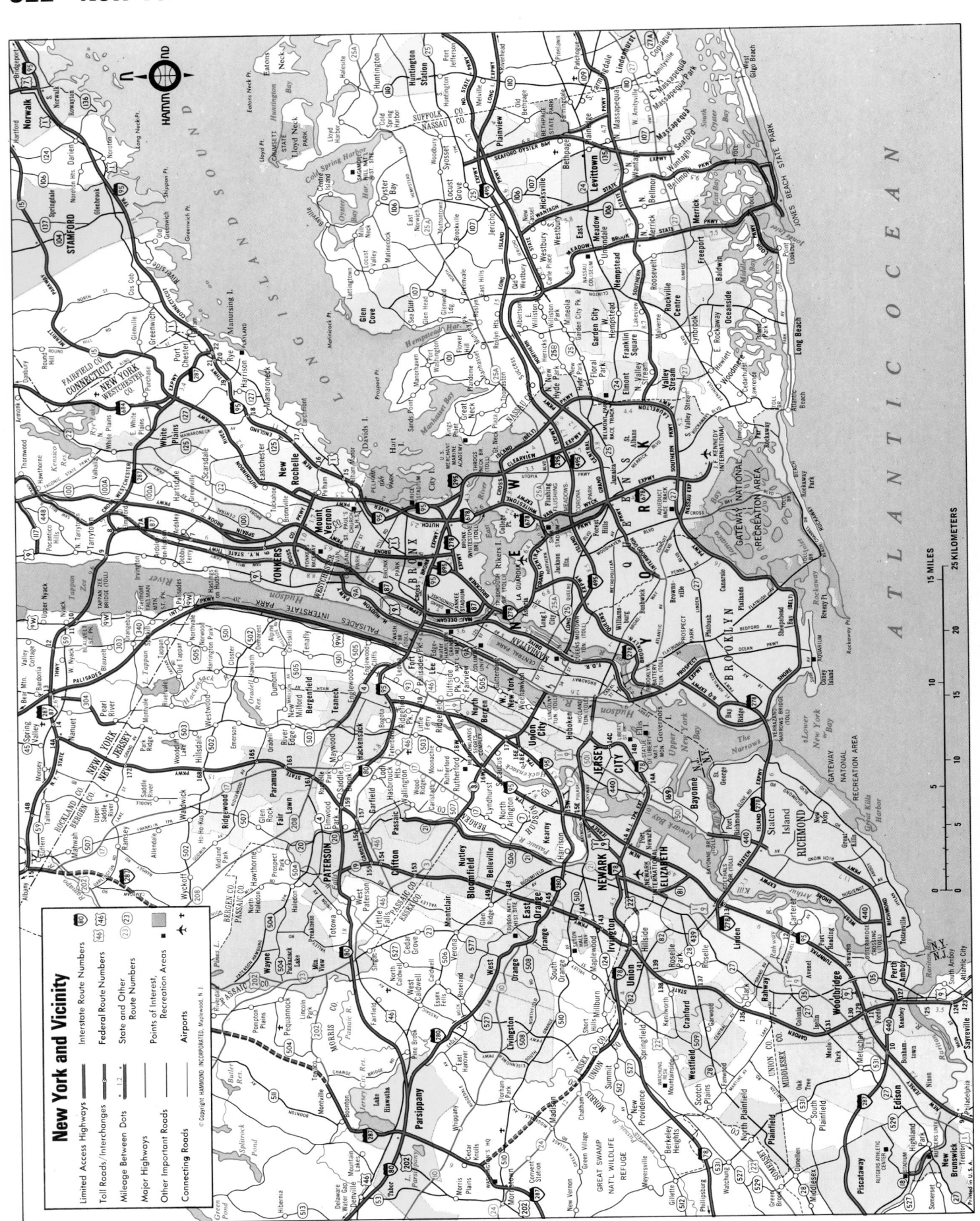

New York and Vicinity
Limited Access Highways
Toll Roads/Interchanges
Mileage Between Dots
Major Highways
Other Important Roads
Connecting Roads
Interstate Route Numbers
Federal Route Numbers
State and Other Route Numbers
Points of Interest, Recreation Areas
Airports
© Copyright HAMMOND INCORPORATED, Maplewood, N.J.
15 MILES
25 KILOMETERS
ATLANTIC OCEAN
LONG ISLAND SOUND
NEW YORK
CONNECTICUT
NEW JERSEY
BRONX
MANHATTAN
BROOKLYN
QUEENS
RICHMOND
YONKERS
NEWARK
JERSEY CITY
ELIZABETH
PATERSON
STAMFORD
Printed in U.S.A.

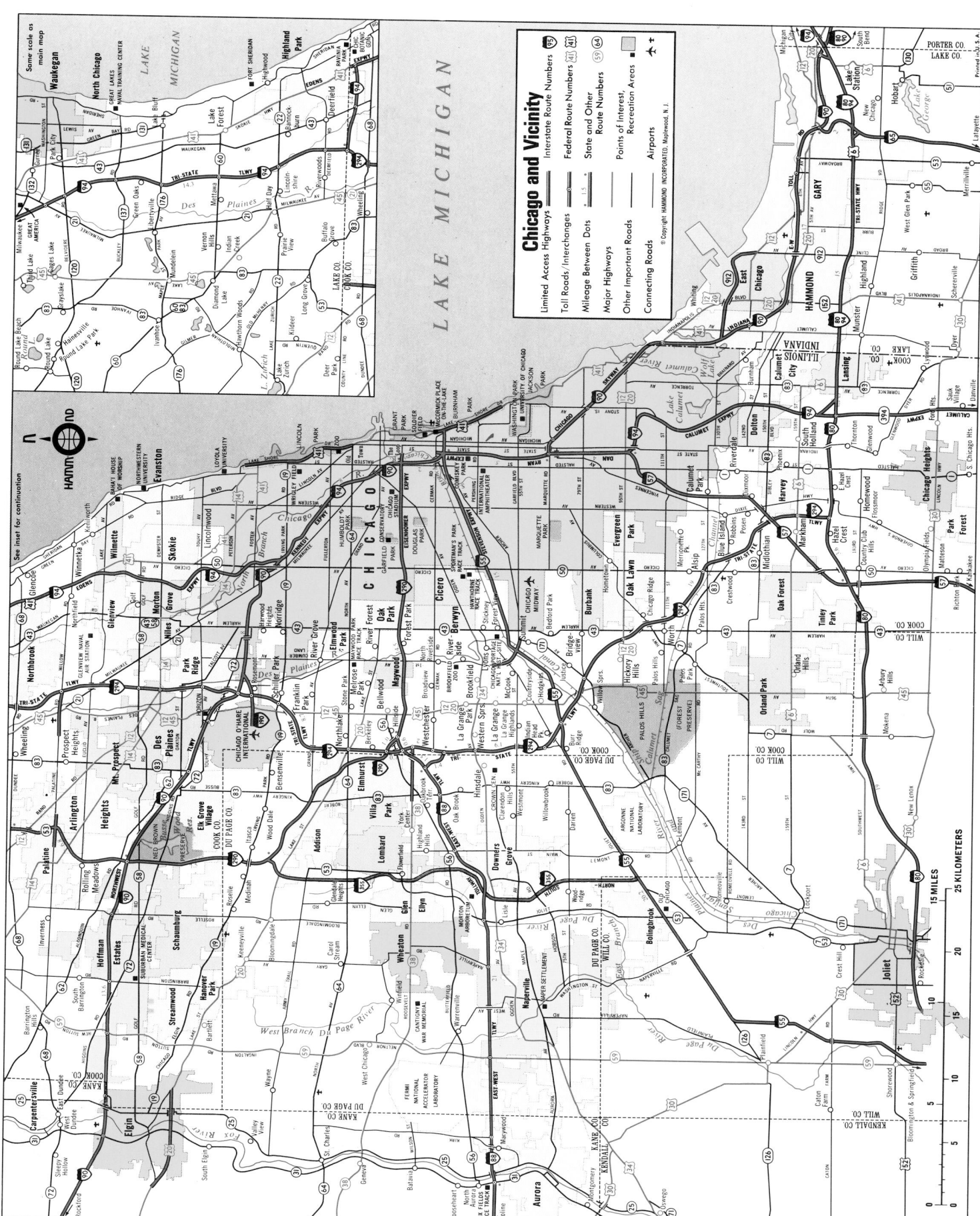
Chicago and Vicinity
Limited Access Highways
Interstate Route Numbers
Toll Roads/Interchanges
Federal Route Numbers
Mileage Between Dots
State and Other Route Numbers
Major Highways
Other Important Roads
Points of Interest, Recreation Areas
Connecting Roads
Airports
© Copyright HAMMOND INCORPORATED, Maplewood, N.J.
LAKE MICHIGAN
See inset for continuation
Same scale as main map
15 MILES
25 KILOMETERS
Printed in U.S.A.

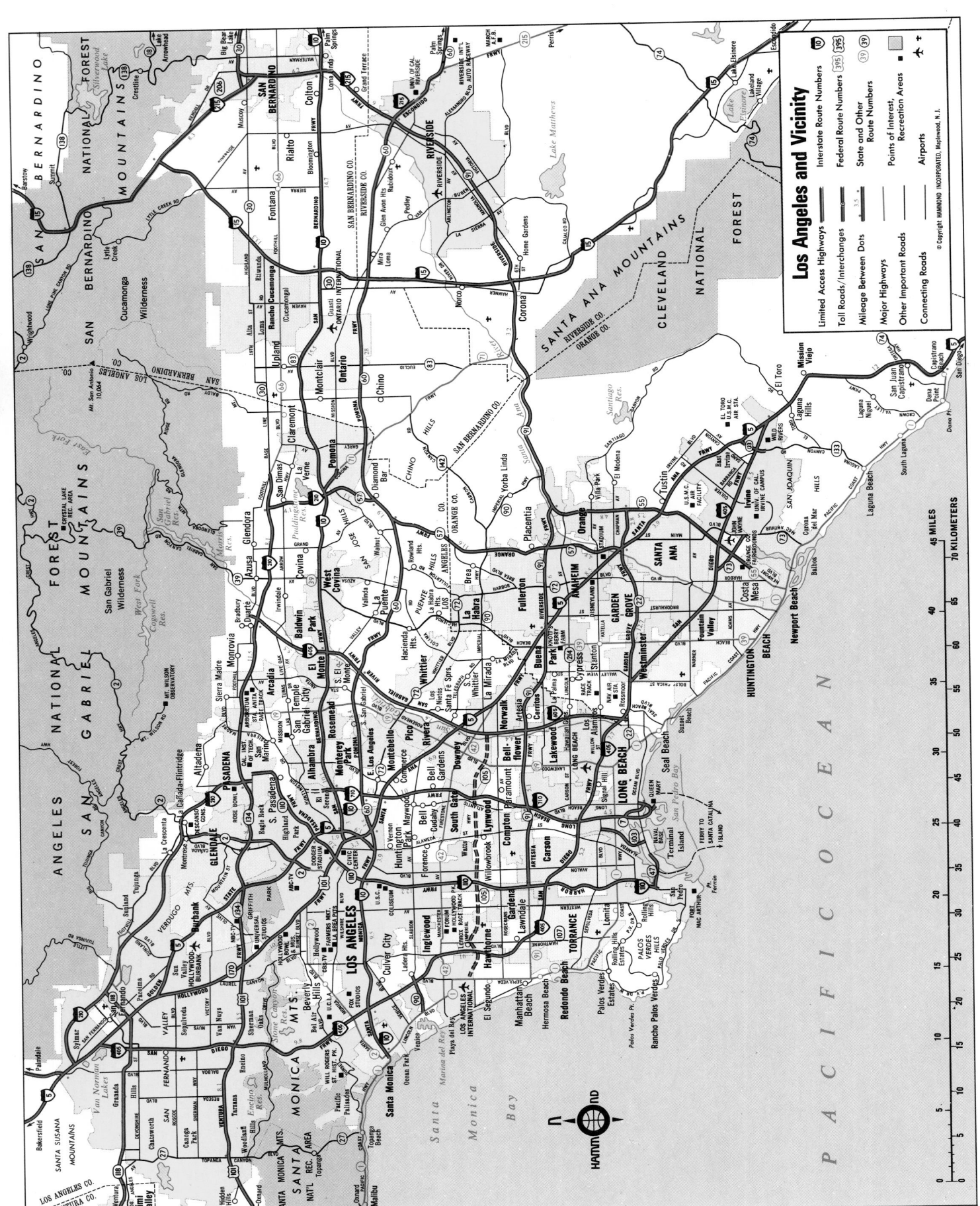

Los Angeles and Vicinity
Limited Access Highways
Toll Roads/Interchanges
Mileage Between Dots
Major Highways
Other Important Roads
Connecting Roads
Interstate Route Numbers
Federal Route Numbers
State and Other Route Numbers
Points of Interest, Recreation Areas
Airports
© Copyright HAMMOND INCORPORATED, Maplewood, N.J.
MILES
KILOMETERS
PACIFIC OCEAN
Santa Monica Bay
SAN GABRIEL MOUNTAINS
ANGELES NATIONAL FOREST
SAN BERNARDINO NATIONAL FOREST
SAN BERNARDINO MOUNTAINS
SANTA ANA MOUNTAINS
CLEVELAND NATIONAL FOREST
SANTA MONICA MTS.
SANTA SUSANA MOUNTAINS
LOS ANGELES
Long Beach
Pasadena
Glendale
Burbank
Santa Monica
Anaheim
Santa Ana
Riverside
San Bernardino
Pomona
Ontario
Torrance
Huntington Beach
Newport Beach
Orange
Fullerton
Garden Grove
Costa Mesa
Irvine
Whittier
Downey
Compton
Inglewood
Malibu
HAMMOND

INDEX OF THE WORLD

Introduction

This index contains a complete alphabetical listing of more than one hundred thousand names shown on all the maps included in this atlas. Names not found in the individual indexes accompanying the maps appear here. The user who is unfamiliar with the location of a country, town, or physical feature, or who is in doubt as to which country, state or province a place belongs will find the answers to his questions in this index. Entries are indexed to all maps or insets showing the place.

The name of the feature sought will be found in its proper alphabetical sequence, followed by the name of the political division in which it is located, the page number of the map on which it will be found, and the key reference necessary for finding its location on the map. After noting the key reference letter-number combination for the place name, turn to the page number indicated. The place name will be found within the square formed by the two lines of latitude and the two lines of longitude which enclose the coordinates–i.e., the marginal letters and numbers. A bullet (●) after the name signifies a township–better known as a town–in the northeastern U.S.

Because of limitations of space on the map, place names do not always appear in their complete form on the map. The complete forms are, however, given in the index. Variant spellings of names and alternate names are also given in this index. The alternate form or spelling of the name appears first, followed in parentheses by the name as it appears on the map. Physical features are usually listed under their proper names and not according to their generic terms; that is to say, Rio Negro will be found under Negro and not under Rio Negro. Exceptions are familiar names such as Rio Grande.

The abbreviations for the political division names and geographical features are explained on page VI of the atlas. In addition, reference can be made to the Gazetteer-Index appearing on pages I through V in which area, population, capital, map reference and type of government may be found for all major political and physical divisions of the world. Population figures for most entries are also included in the comprehensive individual indexes accompanying each map.

A

Aa (riv.), Switzerland 39/F3
Aachen, Germany 22/B3
Aadorf, Switzerland 39/G2
Aalen, Germany 22/D4
Aalsmeer, Netherlands 27/F4
Aalst, Belgium 27/D7
Aalten, Netherlands 27/K5
Aalter, Belgium 27/C6
Äänekoski, Finland 18/O5
Aarau, Switzerland 39/F2
Aarberg, Switzerland 39/D2
Aarburg, Switzerland 39/E2
Aardenburg, Netherlands 27/C6
Aare (riv.), Switzerland 39/E3
Aargau (canton), Switzerland 39/F2
Aarlen (Arlon), Belgium 27/H9
Aarons (creek), Va. 307/L7
Aarschot, Belgium 27/F7
Aat (Ath), Belgium 27/D7
Aba, China 77/F5
Aba, Hungary 41/E3
Aba, Nigeria 106/F7
Aba, Nigeria 102/C4
Aba, Zaire 115/F3
Aba as Sa'ud, Saudi Arabia 59/D6
Abacaxis (riv.), Brazil 132/B4
Abadan, Iran 54/F6
Abadan, Iran 66/F5
Abadan, Iran 59/E3
Abadeh, Iran 66/H5
Abadeh, Iran 59/F3
Abadla, Algeria 106/D2
Abádszalók, Hungary 41/F3
Abaeté, Brazil 132/F6
Abaetetuba, Brazil 132/D3
Abaetetuba, Brazil 120/E3
Abagnar (Silinhot), China 77/J3
Abal, Paraguay 144/E4
Abaiang (atoll), Kiribati 87/H5
'Abaila, Saudi Arabia 59/F5
Abajo (mts.), Utah 304/E6
Abakan, U.S.S.R. 54/L4
Abakan, U.S.S.R. 48/K4
Abala, Congo 115/C4
Abalos (pt.), Cuba 158/A2
Abana, Turkey 63/F2
Abancay, Peru 120/B4
Abancay, Peru 128/F9
Abapó, Bolivia 136/D6
Abaq, China 77/J3
Abarqu, Iran 59/F3
Abarqu, Iran 66/H5
'Abasan, Gaza Strip 65/A5
Abashiri, Japan 81/M1
Abashiri (riv.), Japan 81/M1
Abau, Papua N.G. 85/C7
Abaújszántó, Hungary 41/F2
Abay (riv.), Ethiopia 111/G5

Abay, U.S.S.R. 48/H5
Abaya (lake), Ethiopia 111/G6
Abaza, U.S.S.R. 48/J4
Abbaye (pt.), Mich. 250/B2
Abbe (lake), Djibouti 111/H5
Abbeville, Ala. 195/H7
Abbeville, France 28/D3
Abbeville, Georgia 217/F7
Abbeville, La. 238/F7
Abbeville, Miss. 256/F2
Abbeville (co.), S.C. 296/B3
Abbeville, S.C. 296/C3
Abbey (head), Scotland 15/E6
Abbey, Sask. 181/C5
Abbeydorney, Ireland 17/B7
Abbeyfeale, Ireland 10/B4
Abbeyfeale, Ireland 17/C7
Abbeylara, Ireland 17/F4
Abbeyleix, Ireland 17/G6
Abbotsford, Br. Col. 184/L3
Abbotsford, Wis. 317/F6
Abbott, Ark. 202/B3
Abbott, N. Mex. 274/E2
Abbott, Texas 303/G6
Abbottabad, Pakistan 68/C2
Abbottabad, Pakistan 59/K3
Abbottsburg, N.C. 281/M5
Abbottsford, Georgia 217/B4
Abbottstown, Pa. 294/J6
Abbot Village●, Maine 243/D5
Abbyville, Kansas 232/D4
'Abdul 'Aziz, Jebel (mts.), Syria 63/J4
Abdulino, U.S.S.R. 52/H4
Abéché, Chad 102/D4
Abéché, Chad 111/D5
Abee, Alberta 182/D2
Abell, Md. 245/M8
Abemama (atoll), Kiribati 87/H5
Abengourou, Ivory Coast 106/D7
Abengourou, Ivory Coast 102/B4
Abenrå, Denmark 18/F9
Åbenrå, Denmark 21/C7
Abeokuta, Niger 106/E7
Abeokuta, Nigeria 102/C4
Aberaeron, Wales 13/C5
Aberaeron, Wales 10/D4
Abercarn, Wales 13/B6
Aberchirder, Scotland 15/F3
Abercorn, Québec 172/E4
Abercorn (Mbala), Zambia 115/F5
Abercrombie, N. Dak. 282/S7
Abercrombie, Nova Scotia 168/F3
Abercrombie (mt.), Wash. 310/H2
Aberdare, Wales 13/A6
Aberdare, Wales 10/E5
Aberdaron, Wales 13/C5
Aberdeen, Idaho 220/F7
Aberdeen, Ky. 237/H6
Aberdeen, Md. 245/O2
Aberdeen, Miss. 256/H3
Aberdeen (dam), Miss. 256/H3
Aberdeen●, N.J. 273/E3
Aberdeen, N.S. Wales 97/F3

Aberdeen, N.C. 281/L4
Aberdeen (lake), N.W. Terr. 187/J3
Aberdeen, Ohio 287/C8
Aberdeen, Sask. 181/E3
Aberdeen, Scotland 7/D3
Aberdeen, Scotland 15/F3
Aberdeen, Scotland 10/F2
Aberdeen (trad. co.), Scotland 15/B5
Aberdeen, S. Africa 118/C6
Aberdeen, S. Dak. 146/L5
Aberdeen, S. Dak. 188/G1
Aberdeen, S. Dak. 298/M3
Aberdeen, Wash. 188/B1
Aberdeen, Wash. 310/B3
Aberdeen Proving Ground, Md. 245/N3
Aberdour, Scotland 15/D1
Aberfeldy, Sask. 181/B2
Aberfeldy, Scotland 10/D2
Aberfeldy, Scotland 15/E4
Aberfoyle, Scotland 15/D4
Abergavenny, Wales 13/B6
Abergavenny, Wales 10/E5
Abergele, Wales 13/D4
Aberlady, Scotland 15/F4
Aberlour, Scotland 15/E3
Abernant, Ala. 195/D4
Abernathy, Texas 303/B4
Abernethy, Sask. 181/H5
Abernethy, Scotland 15/E4
Aberporth, Wales 13/C5
Abert (lake), Oreg. 188/C2
Abert (lake), Oreg. 291/G5
Abertillery, Wales 13/B6
Abertillery, Wales 10/E5
Aberystwyth, Wales 13/C5
Aberystwyth, Wales 10/D4
Abez', U.S.S.R. 52/K1
Abha, Saudi Arabia 59/D6
Abha, Saudi Arabia 54/F8
Abhar, Iran 66/F2
Abiad, Ras el (Blanc) (cape), Tunisia 106/G1
Abibe, Serranía de (mts.), Colombia 126/B3
'Abidiya, Sudan 59/B6
Abidjan, Ivory Coast 2/J5
Abidjan, Ivory Coast 102/B4
Abidjan, Ivory Coast 106/D7
Abie, Nebr. 264/H3
Abilene, Kansas 232/E3
Abilene, Texas 146/J6
Abilene, Texas 188/G4
Abilene, Texas 303/E5
Abingdon, England 10/F5
Abingdon, England 13/F6
Abingdon, Ill. 222/C3
Abingdon, Iowa 229/J6
Abingdon, Va. 307/D7
Abington Downs, Queensland 95/B3
Abington, Conn. 210/G1
Abington, Ind. 227/H5
Abington●, Mass. 249/L4

Abington, Pa. 294/M5
Abington, Scotland 15/E5
Abiqua (creek), Oreg. 291/B3
Abiquiu, N. Mex. 274/C2
Abiquiu (res.), N. Mex. 274/C2
Abita Springs, La. 238/L6
Abitibi (lake), Ontario 175/E3
Abitibi (lake), Ontario 175/E3
Abitibi (riv.), Ontario 162/H5
Abitibi (riv.), Ontario 175/D2
Abitibi (riv.), Ontario 177/J5
Abitibi (county), Québec 174/B2
Abitibi (terr.), Québec 174/B3
Abkhaz A.S.S.R., U.S.S.R. 48/E5
Abkhaz A.S.S.R., U.S.S.R. 52/F6
Abminga, S. Australia 94/D2
Abner, N.C. 281/K4
Abnûb, Egypt 111/J4
Åbo (Turku), Finland 18/N6
Aboisso, Ivory Coast 106/D7
Aboite, Ind. 227/G3
Abomey, Benin 106/E7
Abong-Mbang, Cameroon 115/B3
Abony, Hungary 41/E3
Abor (hills), India 68/G3
Aborlan, Philippines 82/B6
Abou Deïa, Chad 111/C5
Aboyne, Scotland 15/F3
Abqaiq, Saudi Arabia 59/E4
Abra (prov.), Philippines 82/C2
Abra (riv.), Philippines 82/C2
Abraham (lake), Alberta 182/B3
Abraham (mt.), Maine 243/C5
Abraham, Utah 304/B4
Abraham●, Vt. 268/B3
Abraham Lincoln Birthplace
   Nat'l Hist. Site, Ky. 237/K5
Abrams, Wis. 317/L6
Abrantes, Portugal 33/B3
Abra Pampa, Argentina 143/C1
Abreus, Cuba 158/D2
'Abri, Sudan 111/F3
Abricots, Haiti 158/A6
Abruzzi (reg.), Italy 34/D3
Absaraka, N. Dak. 282/P6
Absaroka (range), Mont. 262/F5
Absaroka (range), Wyo. 319/C1
Absarokee, Mont. 262/G5
Absecon, N.J. 273/D5
Absecon (inlet), N.J. 273/E5
Abu, India 68/C4
Abu 'Arish, Saudi Arabia 59/D6
Abu Dara, Ras (cape), Sudan 59/C5
Abu Dara, Ras (cape), Sudan 111/G3
Abu Deleiq, Sudan 59/B6
Abu Dhabi (cap.), U.A.E. 54/G7
Abu Dhabi (cap.), U.A.E. 59/F5
Abu ed Duhur, Syria 63/G5
Abu Habl, Wadi (dry riv.), Sudan 111/F5
Abu Hadriya, Saudi Arabia 59/E4
Abu Hamed, Sudan 111/F4
Abu Hamed, Sudan 59/B6
Abuja, Nigeria 106/F7

Abuja, Nigeria 102/C4
Abuja Cap. Terr., Nigeria 106/F7
Abu Kemal, Syria 59/D3
Abu Kemal, Syria 63/J5
Abukuma (riv.), Japan 81/K4
Abu-Mad, Ras (cape), Saudi Arabia 59/C5
Abu Matariq, Sudan 111/E5
Abumombazi, Zaire 115/D3
Abuná, Bolivia 136/B2
Abuná, Brazil 132/H10
Abunã (riv.), Brazil 132/G10
Abu Qir (bay), Egypt 111/J2
Abu Qurqãs, Egypt 111/J4
Abu Road, India 68/C4
Abu Rujmein, Jebel (mts.), Syria 63/H5
Abu Shagara, Ras (cape), Sudan 111/G3
Abu Shagara, Ras (cape), Sudan 59/C5
Abut (head), N. Zealand 100/B5
Abu Tabari (well), Sudan 111/E4
Abuyog, Philippines 82/E5
Abu Zabad, Sudan 59/A7
Abu Zabad, Sudan 111/E5
Abwong, Sudan 111/F6
Aby (lag.), Ivory Coast 106/D8
Åbybro, Denmark 21/C3
Abydos (ruins), Egypt 111/F2
Abydos (ruins), Turkey 63/B6
Abyei, Sudan 111/E6
Acaciás, Colombia 126/D6
Acaciaville, Nova Scotia 168/C4
Academy, Md. 245/M7
Academy●, Maine 243/G7
Acadia (par.), La. 238/F6
Acadia Nat'l Park, Maine 243/G7
Acadia Siding, New Bruns. 170/E2
Acadia Valley, Alberta 182/E4
Acadie Siding, New Bruns. 170/E2
Acadieville, New Bruns. 170/E2
Acahay, Paraguay 144/B5
Acajutla, El Salvador 154/B4
Acala, Mexico 150/N8
Acala, Texas 303/B10
Acámbaro, Mexico 150/J7
Acampo, Calif. 204/C9
Acandí, Colombia 126/B3
Acaponeta, Mexico 150/G5
Acapulco de Juárez, Mexico 146/H8
Acapulco de Juárez, Mexico 150/K8
Acarai, Serra do (range), Brazil 132/B2
Acaraí (mts.), Guyana 131/B5
Acaraú, Brazil 132/F3
Acaray (riv.), Paraguay 144/E4
Acari, Peru 128/E10
Acari (riv.), Peru 128/E10
Acarigua, Venezuela 124/C3
Acatlán de Osorio, Mexico 150/K7
Acatzingo de Hidalgo, Mexico 150/N2
Acayucan, Mexico 150/M8
Accident, Md. 245/A2
Accokeek, Md. 245/L6
Accomac, Va. 307/S5

Accomack (co.), Va. 307/S5
Accord, Mass. 249/E8
Accord, N.Y. 276/M7
Accoville, W. Va. 312/C7
Accra (cap.), Ghana 102/B4
Accra (cap.), Ghana 106/D7
Accra (cap.), Ghana 2/J5
Accrington, England 10/G1
Accrington, England 13/H1
Aceguá, Uruguay 145/E2
Acequia, Idaho 220/E7
Acevedo, Argentina 143/F6
Achacachi, Bolivia 136/A5
Achaguas, Venezuela 124/D4
Achalpur, India 68/D4
Achao, Chile 138/D4
Achar, Uruguay 145/C3
Acharacle, Scotland 15/C4
Achégour (well), Niger 106/G5
Achenwirch, Austria 41/A3
Achill (head), Ireland 10/A4
Achill (head), Ireland 17/A4
Achill (isl.), Ireland 10/A4
Achill (isl.), Ireland 17/A4
Achille, Okla. 288/O7
Achilles, Va. 307/R6
Achill Sound, Ireland 17/B4
Achiltibuie, Scotland 15/C3
Achinsk, U.S.S.R. 48/K4
Achnasheen (butte), Scotland 10/D2
Achnasheen, Scotland 15/C3
Achourat (well), Mali 106/D4
A'Chralaig (mt.), Scotland 15/C3
Acı (lake), Turkey 63/C4
Acıgöl, Turkey 63/F3
Acıpayam, Turkey 63/C4
Acireale, Italy 34/E6
Ackerly, Texas 303/C5
Ackerman, Miss. 256/F4
Ackerville, Ala. 195/D6
Ackley, Iowa 229/G3
Ackworth, Iowa 229/G6
Aclare, Ireland 17/D3
Acle, England 13/J5
Acme, Alberta 182/D4
Acme, La. 238/G4
Acme, Mich. 250/D4
Acme, N.C. 281/N6
Acme, Texas 303/E3
Acme, Wash. 310/C2
Acme, W. Va. 312/D6
Acme, Wyo. 319/E1
Acoaxet, Mass. 249/K7
Acobamba, Peru 128/E9
Acolla, Peru 128/E8
Acoma, N. Mex. 274/B4
Acomayo, Cuzco, Peru 128/G9
Acomayo, Huánuco, Peru 128/E7
Acomita (Pueblo of Acoma), N. Mex. 274/B3
Acona, Miss. 256/D4

Alley 327

Alabama 188/J4
ALABAMA 195
Alabama (riv.), Ala. 188/J4
Alabama (riv.), Ala. 195/C8
Alabama (state), U.S. 146/K6
Alabaster, Ala. 195/E4
Alabaster, Mich. 250/F4
Alabat, Philippines 82/D3
Alabat (isl.), Philippines 82/D3
Alaca, Turkey 63/F2
Alacahan, Turkey 63/G3
Alaçam, Turkey 63/F2
Alachua (co.), Fla. 212/D2
Alachua, Fla. 212/D2
Alacrán (reef), Mexico 150/P5
Alacranes, Cuba 158/D1
Aladağ (mt.), Turkey 63/F4
Aladagh, Kuh-e (mts.), Iran 66/K2
Aladagh, Kuh-i- (mt.), Iran 59/G2
Aladdin, Wyo. 319/H1
Alaejos, Spain 33/D2
Alagir, U.S.S.R. 52/F6
Alagoa Grande, Brazil 132/H4
Alagoas (state), Brazil 132/G5
Alagoinhas, Brazil 120/F4
Alagoinhas, Brazil 132/G6
Alagón, Spain 33/F2
Alagón (riv.), Spain 33/C2
Alah (riv.), Philippines 82/E7
Al Ahqaf (Bahr es Safi) (des.), Saudi Arabia 59/E6
Al 'Ain, Saudi Arabia 59/C4
Alajuela, C. Rica 154/E6
Alakanuk, Alaska 196/E2
Alakol' (lake), U.S.S.R. 48/J5
Al 'Ala, Saudi Arabia 59/C4
Alalakeiki (chan.), Hawaii 218/J3
Alalapadu, Suriname 131/C4
Alamagan (isl.), No. Marianas 87/E4
Alamance (co.), N.C. 281/L3
Alamance, N.C. 281/K2
Alameda (co.), Calif. 204/D6
Alameda, Calif. 204/J2
Alameda (creek), Calif. 204/K3
Alameda, N. Mex. 274/C3
Alameda, Sask. 181/J6
Alamikamba, Nicaragua 154/E4
Alamo (lake), Ariz. 198/B4
Alamo (riv.), Calif. 204/K10
Alamo, Georgia 217/G6
Alamo, Ind. 227/C5
Alamo, Mexico 150/L6
Alamo, Nev. 266/F5
Alamo, N. Dak. 282/D2
Alamo, Tenn. 237/C9
Alamo, Texas 303/F11
Ala Moana, Hawaii 218/C4
Alamo-Danville, Calif. 204/K2
Alamogordo, N. Mex. 188/E4
Alamogordo, N. Mex. 274/C6
Alamo Heights, Texas 303/K10
Álamos, Mexico 150/E3
Alamosa (co.), Colo. 208/H7
Alamosa, Colo. 208/H8
Alamosa (creek), Colo. 208/G8
Alamosa (riv.), N. Mex. 274/B5
Alamota, Kansas 232/B3
Åland (Ahvenanmaa) (prov.), Finland 18/L6
Åland (isls.), Finland 7/F2
Åland (isls.), Finland 18/L6
Alanje, Panama 154/F6
Alanreed, Texas 303/D2
Alanson, Mich. 250/E3
Alanthus Grove, Mo. 261/D2
Alanya, Turkey 59/B2
Alanya, Turkey 63/D4
Alaotra (lake), Madagascar 118/H3
Alapaha (riv.), Fla. 212/C1
Alapaha, Georgia 217/F8
Alapaha (riv.), Georgia 217/F7
Alaqua (creek), Fla. 212/C6
Alarcón (res.), Spain 33/E3
Alarka, N.C. 281/C4
Alas (str.), Indonesia 85/F7
Alaşehir, Turkey 63/C3
Alashtar, Iran 66/E4
Alaska (reg.) 4/C17
Alaska 188/C5
ALASKA 196
Alaska (gulf), Alaska 146/D4
Alaska (gulf), Alaska 188/D6
Alaska (gulf), Alaska 196/K3
Alaska (pen.), Alaska 188/C6
Alaska (pen.), Alaska 146/C4
Alaska (pen.), Alaska 196/G3
Alaska (range), Alaska 188/C6
Alaska (range), Alaska 146/C3
Alaska (range), Alaska 196/H2
Alaska, Mich. 250/D6
Alaska (state), U.S. 2/B2
Alaska (state), U.S. 146/C3
Alaska (gulf), U.S. 4/D17
Alaska (pen.), U.S. 4/D18
Alaska (range), U.S. 4/C17
Alaska Highway, Yukon 187/E3
Alassio, Italy 34/A2
Alatna, Alaska 196/H1
Alatna (riv.), Alaska 196/H1
Alatri, Italy 34/D4
Alatyr', U.S.S.R. 52/G4
Al 'Auda, Saudi Arabia 59/E4
Alausí, Ecuador 128/C4
Álava (prov.), Spain 33/E1
Alava (cape), Wash. 188/A1
Alava (cape), Wash. 310/A2
Alaverdi, U.S.S.R. 52/F6
Alavus, Finland 18/N5
Alayor, Spain 33/J3
Al 'Azair, Iraq 66/E5
Alazeya (riv.), U.S.S.R. 48/Q3
Al 'Aziziya, Iraq 59/E3
Al 'Aziziya, Iraq 66/D4
Alba, Italy 34/B2
Alba, Mich. 250/E4
Alba, Mo. 261/D8
Alba, Pa. 294/J2
Alba, Texas 303/J5
Albacete (prov.), Spain 33/E3
Albacete, Spain 7/D5
Albacete, Spain 33/F3
Alba de Tormes, Spain 33/D2
Albaida, Spain 33/F3
Alba Iulia, Romania 45/F2
Albalate del Arzobispo, Spain 33/F2
Alban, Ontario 177/D1
Albanel, Québec 172/E1
Albanel (lake), Québec 174/C2
Albania 2/K3
Albania 7/G4
ALBANIA 45/E5
Albano (lake), Italy 34/F7
Albano Laziale, Italy 34/F7
Albany, Australia 87/B9
Albany, Calif. 204/J2
Albany, Ga. 146/K6
Albany, Georgia 217/D7
Albany, Ill. 222/C2
Albany, Ind. 227/G4
Albany, Jamaica 158/J6
Albany, Ky. 237/L7
Albany, La. 238/M1
Albany, Minn. 255/D5
Albany, Mo. 261/D2
Albany•, N.H. 268/E4
Albany (cap.), N.Y. 188/M2
Albany (cap.), N.Y. 146/L5
Albany (co.), N.Y. 276/M5
Albany (cap.), N.Y. 276/N5
Albany, N. Zealand 100/B1
Albany, Nova Scotia 168/C4
Albany, Ohio 284/F7
Albany, Okla. 288/O7
Albany (riv.), Ont. 146/K4
Albany (riv.), Ont. 162/H5
Albany (riv.), Ontario 175/C2
Albany, Oreg. 188/B2
Albany, Oreg. 291/D3
Albany, Pr. Edward I. 168/E2
Albany, Texas 303/E5
Albany, Vt. 268/C2
Albany•, Vt. 268/C2
Albany, W. Australia 88/B6
Albany, W. Australia 92/B6
Albany, Wis. 317/G10
Albany (co.), Wyo. 319/G4
Albany, Wyo. 319/F4
Albany Creek, Queensland 88/J2
Albardon, Argentina 143/C3
Albarracín, Spain 33/F2
Albatross (pt.), N. Zealand 100/E3
Albatross (bay), Queensland 88/G2
Albatross (bay), Queensland 95/B2
Albay (prov.), Philippines 82/D4
Albay (gulf), Philippines 82/D4
Albee, S. Dak. 298/S3
Albemarle (pt.), Ecuador 128/B9
Albemarle (sound), N.C. 188/L3
Albemarle, N.C. 281/J4
Albemarle (sound), N.C. 281/S2
Albemarle (co.), Va. 307/L5
Albenga, Italy 34/B3
Albeni Falls (dam), Idaho 220/B1
Alberdi, Paraguay 144/D5
Alberene, Va. 307/L5
Alberga, S. Australia 94/D2
Alberga, The (riv.), S. Australia 94/D2
Alberga, The (riv.), S. Australia 88/E5
Alberhill, Calif. 204/E11
Alberni (inlet), Br. Col. 184/H3
Albers, Ill. 222/D5
Albert (canal), Belgium 27/F6
Albert, France 28/E2
Albert, Kansas 232/C3
Albert (co.), New Bruns. 170/F3
Albert, N. Mex. 274/F3
Albert, N.S. Wales 97/D3
Albert, Okla. 288/K4
Albert (lake), Québec 172/C3
Albert (Mobuto Sese Seko) (lake), Uganda 115/F3
Albert (creek), Wyo. 319/B4
Albert (Mobuto Sese Seko) (lake), Zaire 115/F3
ALBERTA 182
Alberta (prov.) 162/E5
Alberta, Ala. 195/D6
Alberta (mt.), Alberta 182/B3
Alberta (mt.), Alta. 162/E5
Alberta (prov.), Canada 146/G4
Alberta, La. 238/D2
Alberta, Minn. 255/B5
Alberta, Va. 307/N7
Alberta Beach, Alberta 182/C3
Albert City, Iowa 229/C3
Albert Edward (bay), N.W. Terr. 187/H3
Albert Head, Br. Col. 184/J4
Alberti, Argentina 143/G7
Albertirsa, Hungary 41/E3
Albert Lea, Minn. 255/E7
Albert Mines, New Bruns. 170/F3
Alberton, Mont. 262/B3
Alberton, Pr. Edward I. 168/E2
Alberton, S. Africa 118/H6
Albert Town, Jamaica 158/H6
Albertville, Ala. 195/F2
Albertville, France 28/G5
Albertville, Minn. 255/E5
Albertville, Sask. 181/F2
Albeuve, Switzerland 39/D3
Albi, France 28/E6
Albia, Iowa 229/H6
Albin, Wyo. 319/H4
Albina, Suriname 131/D3
Albino, Italy 34/B2
Albion, Calif. 204/B4
Albion, Idaho 220/E7
Albion (mts.), Idaho 220/E7
Albion, Ill. 222/E5
Albion, Ind. 227/G2
Albion, Iowa 229/H4
Albion•, Maine 243/E6
Albion, Mich. 250/E6
Albion, Nebr. 264/F3
Albion, N.Y. 276/D4
Albion, Okla. 288/R5
Albion, Pa. 294/B2
Albion, R.I. 249/H5
Albion, Wash. 310/H4
Albion, Wis. 317/H10
Al Birk, Saudi Arabia 59/D6
Albocácer, Spain 33/F2
Alborán (isl.), Spain 7/D5
Alborán (isl.), Spain 33/E5
Ålborg, Denmark 7/F3
Ålborg, Denmark 18/G8
Ålborg,Ålborg (bay), Denmark 21/D4
Alborn, Minn. 255/F4
Albox, Spain 33/E4
Albreda, Br. Col. 184/H4
Albright, W. Va. 312/G3
Albrightsville, Pa. 294/L3
Albristhorn (mt.), Switzerland 39/D4
Albstadt, Germany 22/C4
Albufeira, Portugal 33/B4
Albuñol, Spain 33/E4
Albuquerque (cays), Colombia 126/A10
Albuquerque, N. Mex. 146/H6
Albuquerque, N. Mex. 188/E3
Albuquerque, N. Mex. 274/C3
Alburg, Vt. 268/A2
Alburg•, Vt. 268/A2
Alburnett, Iowa 229/K4
Alburquerque, Spain 33/C3
Alburtis, Pa. 294/L5
Albury, Australia 87/E9
Albury, N. S. Wales 88/H7
Albury, N.S. Wales 97/D5
Albury, N. Zealand 100/C6
Alca, Peru 128/F10
Alcácer do Sal, Portugal 33/B3
Alcalá, Bolivia 136/C6
Alcalá de Chivert, Spain 33/G2
Alcalá de Guadaira, Spain 33/D4
Alcalá de Henares, Spain 33/G4
Alcalá de los Gazules, Spain 33/D4
Alcalá la Real, Spain 33/E4
Alcalde, N. Mex. 274/C2
Alcamo, Italy 34/D6
Alcanar, Spain 33/G2
Alcañices, Spain 33/C2
Alcañiz, Spain 33/F2
Alcântara, Portugal 33/A1
Alcántara, Spain 33/C3
Alcántara (res.), Spain 33/C3
Alcántaratara (res.), Portugal 33/C3
Alcantarilla, Spain 33/F4
Alcaraz, Argentina 143/G5
Alcaraz, Spain 33/E3
Alcaraz, Sierra de (range), Spain 33/E3
Alcatraz (isl.), Calif. 204/J2
Alcaudete, Spain 33/E4
Alcázar de San Juan, Spain 33/E3
Alcester, S. Dak. 298/R7
Alcida, New Bruns. 170/E1
Alcira, Spain 33/F3
Alco, Ark. 202/F2
Alco, La. 238/D4
Alcoa, Tenn. 237/N9
Alcobaça, Brazil 132/G7
Alcobaça, Portugal 33/B3
Alcolu, S.C. 296/G4
Alcomdale, Alberta 182/C3
Alcona (co.), Mich. 250/F4
Alcona Beach, Ontario 177/E3
Alcones, Chile 138/F5
Alcony, Ohio 284/B5
Alcora, Spain 33/F2
Alcorisa, Spain 33/F2
Alcorn, Ky. 237/O5
Alcorn (co.), Miss. 256/G1
Alcorn State University, Miss. 256/B7
Alcorta, Argentina 143/F6
Alcoutim, Portugal 33/C4
Alcova, Wyo. 319/F3
Alcova (res.), Wyo. 319/F3
Alcoy, Spain 33/F3
Alcudia (bay), Spain 33/H3
Alda, Nebr. 264/F4
Aldabra (isls.), Seychelles 102/G5
Aldabra (isls.), Seychelles 118/H1
Aldama, Chihuahua, Mexico 150/G2
Aldama, Tamaulipas, Mexico 150/L5
Aldan, Pa. 294/M7
Aldan, U.S.S.R. 54/O4
Aldan (riv.), U.S.S.R. 54/P3
Aldan, U.S.S.R. 48/N4
Aldan (plat.), U.S.S.R. 48/N4
Aldan (riv.), U.S.S.R. 48/O3
Aldeburgh, England 13/J5
Aldeburgh, England 10/G4
Aldeia Carajá, Brazil 132/D6
Aldeia Nova de São Bento, Portugal 33/C4
Alden, Ill. 222/E1
Alden, Iowa 229/G4
Alden, Kansas 232/D3
Alden, Mich. 250/D4
Alden, Minn. 255/E7
Alden, N.Y. 276/C5
Alden Bridge, La. 238/C1
Aldenville, Pa. 294/M2
Alder, Mont. 262/D5
Alder, Wash. 310/C4
Alder (lake), Wash. 310/C4
Alder Creek, N.Y. 276/K4
Alder Flats, Alberta 182/C3
Alderley, Wis. 317/J1
Alderney (isl.), Chan. Is. 10/E6
Alderney (isl.), Chan. Is. 13/E8
Alderpoint, Calif. 204/B3
Alder Point, Nova Scotia 168/H2
Aldershot, England 10/F5
Aldershot, England 13/G8
Aldershot, Nova Scotia 168/D3
Alderson, Okla. 288/P5
Alderson, W. Va. 312/E7
Aldersyde, Alberta 182/C4
Aldine, Ind. 227/D2
Aldora, Georgia 217/D4
Aldouane, New Bruns. 170/E2
Aldrich, Ala. 195/E4
Aldrich, Minn. 255/C4
Aldrich, Mo. 261/F7
Aldridge Brownhills, England 10/G3
Aldridge Brownhills, England 13/E5
Aledo, Ill. 222/C2
Aledo, Texas 303/E2
Aleg, Mauritania 106/B5
Alegre, Brazil 135/F2
Alegre, Brazil 132/F8
Alegrete, Brazil 132/B10
Alegrete, Brazil 120/D5
'Aleih, Lebanon 63/F6
Alejandra, Argentina 143/F5
Alejandría, Bolivia 136/C3
Alejandro Selkirk (isl.), Chile 120/A6
Aleknagik, Alaska 196/G3
Aleksandriya, U.S.S.R. 52/D5
Aleksandrov Gay, U.S.S.R. 52/G4
Aleksandrovsk, U.S.S.R. 52/J3
Aleksandrovsk-Sakhalinsky, U.S.S.R. 54/R4
Aleksandrovsk-Sakhalinskiy, U.S.S.R. 48/P5
Aleksandrów Kujawski, Poland 47/D2
Aleksandrów Lodzki, Poland 47/D3
Alekseyevka, U.S.S.R. 48/H4
Alekseyevka, U.S.S.R. 52/E4
Aleksin, U.S.S.R. 52/E4
Aleksinac, Yugoslavia 45/E4
Além Paraíba, Brazil 135/E2
Alençon, France 28/D3
Alenquer, Brazil 132/C3
Alenquer, Brazil 120/D3
Alenuihaha (chan.), Hawaii 218/E7
Aleppo (prov.), Syria 63/G4
Aleppo, Syria 54/E6
Aleppo, Syria 59/C2
Aleppo, Syria 63/G4
Aléria, France 28/B6
Alert, Canada 4/A12
Alert, Ind. 227/F6
Alert, N.C. 281/N2
Alert, N.W.T. 162/N3
Alert, N.W. Terr. 187/M1
Alert (pt.), N.W. Terr. 187/K1
Alert Bay, Br. Col. 184/D5
Alès, France 28/E5
Alessandria (prov.), Italy 34/B2
Alessandria, Italy 34/B2
Ålestrup, Denmark 21/C4
Ålesund, Norway 7/E2
Ålesund, Norway 18/D5
Aletschhorn (mt.), Switzerland 39/F4
Aleutian (isls.), Alaska 188/D6
Aleutian (isls.), Alaska 196/J4
Aleutian (range), Alaska 196/G3
Aleutian (isls.), U.S. 4/D18
Aleutian (isls.), U.S. 2/A3
Alex, Okla. 288/L5
Alexander (arch.), Alaska 146/E4
Alexander (arch.), Alaska 196/L1
Alexander (isl.), Ant. 5/B15
Alexander, Ark. 202/F4
Alexander (lake), Conn. 210/H1
Alexander, Georgia 217/J4
Alexander (co.), Ill. 222/D6
Alexander, Ill. 222/D4
Alexander, Iowa 229/G3
Alexander, Kansas 232/C3
Alexander•, Maine 243/H5
Alexander, Manitoba 179/B5
Alexander, N.Y. 276/D5
Alexander (co.), N.C. 281/G3
Alexander, N. Dak. 282/C4
Alexander (cape), Solomon Is. 86/D2
Alexander (arch.), U.S. 4/D16
Alexander, W. Va. 312/F5
Alexander Bay, S. Africa 102/D7
Alexander Bay, S. Africa 118/B5
Alexander City, Ala. 195/G5
Alexander Mills, N.C. 281/F4
Alexandra, N. Zealand 100/B6
Alexandra, S. Africa 118/H6
Alexandra, Victoria 97/C5
Alexandra Land (isl.), U.S.S.R. 4/A8
Alexandra Land (isl.), U.S.S.R. 48/E1
Alexandretta (Iskenderun), Turkey 63/G4
Alexandretta (gulf), Turkey 63/F4
Alexandria, Ala. 195/G3
Alexandria, Br. Col. 184/F4
Alexandria, Egypt 2/L4
Alexandria, Egypt 102/E1
Alexandria, Egypt 59/A3
Alexandria, Egypt 111/J2
Alexandria, Ind. 227/F4
Alexandria, Jamaica 158/J6
Alexandria, Ky. 237/N3
Alexandria, La. 146/J6
Alexandria, La. 188/H4
Alexandria, La. 238/E4
Alexandria, Minn. 255/C5
Alexandria, Mo. 261/K2
Alexandria, Nebr. 264/G4
Alexandria•, N.H. 268/D4
Alexandria, North. Terr. 93/E5
Alexandria, Ohio 284/E5
Alexandria, Ontario 177/K2
Alexandria, Pa. 294/F4
Alexandria, Romania 45/G3
Alexandria, Scotland 15/A1
Alexandria, Scotland 10/A1
Alexandria, S. Dak. 298/O6
Alexandria, Tenn. 237/J8
Alexandria, Va. 188/L3
Alexandria (I.C.), Va. 307/S3
Alexandria Bay, N.Y. 276/J2
Alexandrina (lake), S. Australia 94/F6
Alexandroúpolis, Greece 45/H5
Alexis, Ill. 222/C2
Alexis (riv.), Newf. 166/C3
Alexis Creek, Br. Col. 184/F4
Aleysk, U.S.S.R. 48/J4
Aleza Lake, Br. Col. 184/G3
Alfalfa (co.), Okla. 288/K1
Alfalfa, Okla. 288/J4
Al Falluja, Iraq 59/D3
Al Falluja, Iraq 66/C4
Alfaro, Spain 33/F1
Alfatar, Bulgaria 45/H4
Al Fatha, Iraq 59/D2
Al Fatha, Iraq 66/C3
Alfeld, Germany 22/C2
Alfenas, Brazil 135/D2
Alférez (riv.), Uruguay 145/E5
Alford, England 13/H4
Alford, Fla. 212/D6
Alford•, Mass. 249/A4
Alford, Scotland 15/F3
Alford, Scotland 10/E2
Alfordsville, Ind. 227/C7
Alfred, Maine 243/B9
Alfred•, Maine 243/B9
Alfred, N.Y. 276/E6
Alfred, N. Dak. 282/N6
Alfred, Ontario 177/K2
Alfredton, N. Zealand 100/F4
Alfreton, England 13/F4
Alga, U.S.S.R. 48/F5
Ålgård, Norway 18/D7
Algarrobo, Chile 138/F3
Algarrobo (pt.), P. Rico 161/A2
Algarrobo del Águila, Argentina 143/C4
Algeciras, Colombia 126/C6
Algeciras, Spain 33/D4
Algemesí, Spain 33/F3
Alger (co.), Mich. 250/C2
Alger, Mich. 250/E4
Alger, Ohio 284/C4
Algeria 2/J4
Algeria 102/C2
ALGERIA 106/D3
Algés, Portugal 33/A1
Algete, Spain 33/G4
Alghero, Italy 34/B4
Algiers (cap.), Algeria 102/C1
Algiers (cap.), Algeria 106/E1
Algiers (cap.), Algeria 2/K4
Algiers, Ind. 227/C7
Algoa, Ark. 202/H3
Algoa (bay), S. Africa 118/D6
Algoa, Texas 303/K3
Algodones, N. Mex. 274/C3
Algoma, Miss. 256/G2
Algoma (terr. dist.), Ontario 177/J5
Algoma (terr. dist.), Ontario 175/D3
Algoma, Oreg. 291/F5
Algoma, W. Va. 312/D8
Algoma, Wis. 317/M6
Algoma Mills, Ontario 177/B1
Algona, Iowa 229/E2
Algona, Wash. 310/C3
Algonac, Mich. 250/G6
Algonquin, Ill. 222/E1
Algonquin (peak), N.Y. 276/M2
Algonquin Park, Ontario 177/F2
Algonquin Prov. Park, Ontario 177/F2
Algonquin Prov. Park, Ontario 175/E3
Algood, Tenn. 237/K8
Algorta, Uruguay 145/B3
Algrove, Sask. 181/H3
Alhama de Granada, Spain 33/E4
Alhama de Murcia, Spain 33/F4
Alhambra, Alberta 182/C3
Alhambra, Calif. 204/C10
Alhambra, Ill. 222/D5
Al Hawtiah, Yemen 59/E6
Al Hilla, Saudi Arabia 59/E5
Al Hoceima, Morocco 106/D1
Alhos Vedros, Portugal 33/B3
Alhué, Estero de (riv.), Chile 138/F4
Alia, Spain 33/D3
'Aliabad, Kuh-e (mt.), Iran 59/F3
'Aliabad, Kuh-e (mt.), Iran 66/G3
Aliağa, Turkey 63/B3
Alibag, India 68/C5
Alibates Flint Quarries Nat'l Mon., Texas 303/C2
Ali-Bayramly, U.S.S.R. 52/G7
Alibeyköyü, Turkey 63/D6
Alicante (prov.), Spain 33/F3
Alicante, Spain 33/F3
Alicante, Spain 7/D5
Alice (lake), Nebr. 264/A2
Alice, N. Dak. 282/P6
Alice (lake), N. Dak. 282/M3
Alice, Ontario 177/G2
Alice (chan.), Philippines 82/B8
Alice (riv.), Queensland 95/C4
Alice, Texas 303/F10
Alice Arm, Br. Col. 184/C2
Alicel, Oreg. 291/J2
Alice Springs, Australia 87/D8
Alice Springs, North. Terr. 88/E4
Alice Springs, North. Terr. 93/D7
Aliceville, Ala. 195/B4
Aliceville (dam), Ala. 195/B4
Aliceville, Kansas 232/G3
Alicia, Ark. 202/H2
Alicia (bank), Colombia 126/B8
Alicudi (isl.), Italy 34/E5
Alida, Minn. 255/C3
Alida, Sask. 181/K6
Aligarh, India 68/D3
'Ali Gharbi, Iraq 66/E4
Alijó, Portugal 33/C2
Alima (riv.), Congo 115/B4
Alimodian, Philippines 82/D5
Alindao, Cent. Afr. Rep. 115/D2
Aline, Georgia 217/H6
Aline, Okla. 288/K1
Alingly, Sask. 181/E2
Alingsås, Sweden 18/H7
Alipore, India 68/F2
Aliquippa, Pa. 294/B4
Ali Sabieh, Djibouti 111/H5
'Ali Sharqi, Iraq 66/E4
Aliskerovo, U.S.S.R. 48/R3
Alivérion, Greece 45/G6
Aliwal North, S. Africa 118/D6
Alix, Alberta 182/D3
Alix, Ark. 202/C3
Aljezur, Portugal 33/B4
Aljojuca, Mexico 150/O1
Aljustrel, Portugal 33/B4
Alkabo, N. Dak. 282/C2
Alkali (lakes), Calif. 204/E2
Alkali (lake), Nev. 266/B1
Alkali (lakes), N. Dak. 282/L3
Alkali Lake, Br. Col. 184/F4
Alkaline (lake), N. Dak. 282/L6
Alken, Belgium 27/G7
Alkmaar, Netherlands 27/F3
Alkmaardermeer (lake), Netherlands 27/F3
Alkol, W. Va. 312/C6
Al Kufa, Iraq 66/D4
Al Kumait, Iraq 66/E4
Al Kuwait (cap.), Kuwait 59/E4
Al Kuwait (cap.), Kuwait 54/F7
Allagash•, Maine 243/F1
Allagash (lake), Maine 243/D3
Allagash (riv.), Maine 243/E2
Allahabad, India 68/E3
Allahabad, India 54/K7
Allaine (riv.), Switzerland 39/D2
Allaire, N.J. 273/E3
Allakaket, Alaska 196/H1
Allakh-Yun', U.S.S.R. 48/O3
Allamakee (co.), Iowa 229/L2
Allaman, Switzerland 39/B4
All American (canal), Calif. 204/K11
Allamoore, Texas 303/C11
Allamuchy, N.J. 273/D2
Allan (mt.), Idaho 220/D4
Allan, Sask. 181/E4
Allan (hills), Sask. 181/E4
Allanmyo, Burma 72/B3
Allanwater, Ontario 175/C2
Allanwater, Ontario 177/G4
'Allaqi, Wadi (dry riv.), Egypt 111/F3
Allard (lake), Québec 174/E2
Allardt, Tenn. 237/M8
Allardville, New Bruns. 170/E1
Allariz, Spain 33/C1
Allatoona (lake), Georgia 217/C2
Alle, Switzerland 39/D2
Alleene, Ark. 202/B6
Allegan (co.), Mich. 250/D6
Allegan, Mich. 250/D6
Allegany (co.), Md. 245/C2
Allegany (co.), N.Y. 276/D6
Allegany, N.Y. 276/C6
Allegany, Oreg. 291/D4
Allegany Ind. Res., N.Y. 276/C6
Alleghany, Calif. 204/E4
Alleghany (co.), N.C. 281/G1
Alleghany (co.), Va. 307/H5
Alleghany, Va. 307/H5
Allegheny (res.), N.Y. 276/C7
Allegheny (riv.), N.Y. 276/C6
Allegheny (co.), Pa. 294/B5
Allegheny (res.), Pa. 294/E2
Allegheny (riv.), Pa. 294/D2
Allegheny (mts.), Va. 307/H5
Allegheny Front (mts.), Md. 245/C2
Allegheny Front (mts.), Pa. 294/E5
Allègre (pt.), Guadeloupe 161/A6
Allegre, Ky. 237/G7
Alleman, Iowa 229/F5
Allemands (lake), La. 238/M4
Allen, Ala. 195/C7
Allen, Argentina 143/C4
Allen (co.), Ind. 227/G2
Allen, Lough (lake), Ireland 10/C3
Allen (lake), Ireland 17/E3
Allen, Bog of (marsh), Ireland 17/H5
Allen (co.), Kansas 232/G4
Allen, Kansas 232/F3
Allen (co.), Ky. 237/J7
Allen, Ky. 237/R5
Allen (par.), La. 238/E5
Allen, La. 238/D3
Allen, Md. 245/R7
Allen, Mich. 250/E7
Allen, Miss. 256/C7
Allen (mt.), Mont. 262/C2
Allen, Nebr. 264/H2
Allen (co.), Ohio 284/B4
Allen, Okla. 288/O5
Allen, Pa. 294/H5
Allen, S. Dak. 298/F7
Allen, Texas 303/H1
Allendale, England 13/E3
Allendale, Ill. 222/F5
Allendale, Mo. 261/D2
Allendale, N.J. 273/B1
Allendale (co.), S.C. 296/E6
Allendale, S.C. 296/E5
Allende, Coahuila, Mexico 150/J2
Allende, Nuevo León, Mexico 150/J4
Allendorf, Iowa 229/B2
Allenford, Ontario 177/C3
Allenhurst, Georgia 217/J7
Allenhurst, N.J. 273/F3
Allen Park, Mich. 250/B7
Allens Mills, Maine 243/C6
Allenspark, Colo. 208/J2
Allen Springs, Ky. 237/J7
Allenstein (Olsztyn), Poland 47/E2
Allenstown•, N.H. 268/E5
Allensville, Ky. 237/G7
Allensville, Ohio 284/E7
Allensville, Pa. 294/G4
Allenton, Mo. 261/M4
Allenton, R.I. 249/H6
Allenton, Wis. 317/K9
Allentown, Georgia 217/F5
Allentown, N.J. 273/D3
Allentown, N.Y. 276/E6
Allentown, Ohio 284/B4
Allentown, Pa. 188/L2
Allentown, Pa. 294/L4
Allentsteig, Austria 41/C2
Allenville, Ill. 222/E4
Allenville, Mo. 261/N8
Allenwood, N.J. 273/E3
Allenwood, Pa. 294/H3
Alleppey-Cochin, India 68/D7
Aller (riv.), Germany 22/C2
Allerton, Ill. 222/F4
Allerton, Iowa 229/G7
Allerton, Mass. 249/E7
Allerton (pt.), Mass. 249/E7
Alley, Jamaica 158/J7

328 Alley Spring

Alley Spring, Mo. 261/J8
Allgäu (reg.), Germany 22/D5
Allgäu Alps (mts.), Austria 41/A3
Allgood, Ala. 195/F3
Alliance, Alberta 182/E3
Alliance, Nebr. 264/A2
Alliance, N.C. 281/R4
Alliance, Ohio 284/H4
Al Lidam, Saudi Arabia 59/D5
Allier (dept.), France 28/E4
Allier (riv.), France 28/E5
Alligator (lake), Fla. 212/E3
Alligator (pt.), La. 238/L6
Alligator, Miss. 256/C2
Alligator (lake), N.C. 281/S3
Alligator (riv.), N.C. 281/S3
Alligator Pond, Jamaica 158/H6
Allingåbro, Denmark 21/D5
Allinge-Sandvig, Denmark 18/J9
Allinge-Sandvig, Denmark 21/F8
Allingham, Alberta 182/D4
Allingtown, Conn. 210/D3
Allison, Iowa 229/H3
Allison, N. Mex. 274/A3
Allison, Texas 303/D2
Allisona, Tenn. 237/H9
Allisonia, Va. 307/G7
Allison Park, Pa. 294/C4
Alliston, Ontario 177/E3
Al Lith, Saudi Arabia 59/C5
Alloa, Scotland 10/B1
Alloa, Scotland 15/C1
Allock, Ky. 237/P6
Allons, Tenn. 237/L8
Allouez, Mich. 250/A1
Allouez, Wis. 317/L7
Allow (riv.), Ireland 17/D7
Alloway, N.J. 273/C4
Alloways (creek), N.J. 273/C4
Allport, Ark. 202/G4
Allred, Tenn. 237/L8
All Saints, Ant. & Bar. 161/E11
All Saints Village, Mo. 261/M2
Allsboro, Ala. 195/B1
Allsbrook, S.C. 296/K3
Allschwil, Switzerland 39/D1
Allyn, Wash. 310/C3
Alma, Ala. 195/C8
Alma, Ark. 202/B3
Alma, Colo. 208/G4
Alma, Georgia 217/G7
Alma, Ill. 222/E5
Alma, Kansas 232/F2
Alma, Mich. 250/E5
Alma, Mo. 261/E4
Alma, Nebr. 264/E4
Alma, New Bruns. 170/F3
Alma, N. Mex. 274/A5
Alma, N.C. 281/L5
Alma, Ontario 177/D4
Alma, Québec 174/C3
Alma, Québec 172/F1
Alma (isl.), Québec 172/F1
Alma, W. Va. 312/E4
Alma, Wis. 317/C7
Alma-Ata, U.S.S.R. 2/N3
Alma-Ata, U.S.S.R. 54/J5
Alma-Ata, U.S.S.R. 48/H5
Alma Center, Wis. 317/E7
Alma City, Minn. 255/E6
Almada, Portugal 33/A1
Almadén, Spain 33/D3
Almagro, Spain 33/E3
Almaguer, Colombia 126/B7
Almanor (lake), Calif. 204/D3
Almansa, Spain 33/F3
Almanza, Spain 33/D1
Almanzor (mt.), Spain 33/D2
Almanzora (riv.), Spain 33/F4
Almartha, Mo. 261/H9
Almazán, Spain 33/E2
Almaznyy, U.S.S.R. 48/M3
Almeida, Sierra (mts.), Chile 138/C4
Almeida, Portugal 33/C2
Almeirim, Portugal 33/B3
Almelo, Netherlands 27/K4
Almelund, Minn. 255/F5
Almena, Kansas 232/C2
Almena, Wis. 317/B5
Almenara, Brazil 120/E4
Almendra (res.), Spain 33/C2
Almendralejo, Spain 33/C3
Almere, Netherlands 27/G4
Almeria, Nebr. 264/E3
Almería (prov.), Spain 33/E4
Almería, Spain 7/D5
Almería, Spain 33/E4
Almería (gulf), Spain 33/E4
Al'met'yevsk, U.S.S.R. 52/H3
Älmhult, Sweden 18/H8
Almira, Wash. 310/G3
Almirantazgo (bay), Chile 138/F11
Almirante, Panama 154/F6
Almirante Montt (gulf), Chile 138/D9
Almirós, Greece 45/F6
Almo, Idaho 220/E7
Almo, Ky. 237/E7
Almodôvar, Portugal 33/B4
Almodóvar del Campo, Spain 33/D3
Almoharín, Spain 33/D3
Almoloya del Río, Mexico 150/K1
Almon, Georgia 217/E3
Almond, N.Y. 276/E6
Almond, N.C. 281/B4
Almond (riv.), Scotland 15/E4
Almond, Wis. 317/G7
Almont, Colo. 208/F5
Almont, Mich. 250/F6
Almont, N. Dak. 282/H6
Almonte, Ontario 177/H2
Almonte, Spain 33/C4
Almora, India 68/D3
Almora, Minn. 255/C4
Almorox, Spain 33/D2
Almota, Wash. 310/H4
Al Muadhdam, Saudi Arabia 59/C4
Almudévar, Spain 33/F1
Almuñécar, Spain 33/E4
Almus, Turkey 63/G2
Al Musaiyib, Iraq 59/D3
Al Musaiyib, Iraq 66/D4
Almyra, Ark. 202/H5
Alna•, Maine 243/D7
Alness, Scotland 15/D3
Alness (riv.), Scotland 15/D3
Alnwick, England 10/F3
Alnwick, England 13/F2
Alofi (cap.), Niue 87/K7
Aloha, Oreg. 291/A2
Aloha, Wash. 310/A3
Alon, Burma 72/B2
Along, India 68/G3
Alonsa, Manitoba 179/C4
Alonso Rojas, Cuba 158/B2
Alor (isl.), Indonesia 85/G7
Álora, Spain 33/D4
Alor Gajah, Malaysia 72/D7
Alor Setar, Malaysia 72/D6
Alorton, Ill. 222/B2
Alost (Aalst), Belgium 27/D7
Alotau, Papua N.G. 87/E7
Aloysius (mt.), W. Australia 92/E4
Alpachiri, Argentina 143/D4
Alpaugh, Calif. 204/F8
Alpena, Ark. 202/D1
Alpena (co.), Mich. 250/F4
Alpena, Mich. 250/F3
Alpena, S. Dak. 298/N5
Alpena, W. Va. 312/G5
Alpen Siding, Alberta 182/D2
Alpera, Spain 33/F3
Alpes-de-Haute-Provence (dept.), France 28/G5
Alpes-Maritimes (dept.), France 28/G6
Alpha, Ill. 222/C2
Alpha, Iowa 229/K3
Alpha, Ky. 237/L7
Alpha, Mich. 250/A2
Alpha, Minn. 255/D7
Alpha, N.J. 273/C2
Alpha, Queensland 88/H4
Alpharetta, Georgia 217/D2
Alphen aan de Rijn, Netherlands 27/F4
Alpiarça, Portugal 33/B3
Alpine, Ala. 195/F4
Alpine, Ariz. 198/F5
Alpine, Ark. 202/D5
Alpine (co.), Calif. 204/F5
Alpine, Calif. 204/J11
Alpine, Ind. 227/G5
Alpine, Ky. 237/M7
Alpine, N.J. 273/C1
Alpine, N.Y. 276/G6
Alpine, Oreg. 291/D3
Alpine, Tenn. 237/L8
Alpine, Texas 303/D12
Alpine, Utah 304/C3
Alpine, Wyo. 319/B2
Alpirsbach, Germany 22/C4
Alpnach, Switzerland 39/F3
Alpoca, W. Va. 312/D7
Alportel, Portugal 33/C4
Alps (mts.) 7/E4
Alpu, Turkey 63/D3
Al Q'aim, Iraq 66/B3
Al Qaiyara, Iraq 66/C3
Al Qosh, Iraq 66/C2
Alquina, Ind. 227/G5
Alquízar, Cuba 158/C1
Al Qurna, Iraq 66/E5
Al Qurna, Iraq 59/E3
Alroy Downs, North. Terr. 93/E5
Als (isl.), Denmark 21/C8
Alsace (trad. prov.), France, 29
Alsager, England 13/E4
Alsager, England 10/G2
Alsask, Sask. 181/B4
Alsatia, La. 238/H1
Alsdorf, Germany 22/B3
Alsea, Oreg. 291/D3
Alsea (riv.), Oreg. 291/D3
Alsek (riv.), Alaska 196/L3
Alsek (riv.), Br. Col. 184/H1
Alsek (riv.), Yukon 187/E3
Alsen, N. Dak. 282/N2
Alsey, Ill. 222/C4
Alsfeld, Germany 22/C3
Alsip, Ill. 222/B6
Alsózsolca, Hungary 41/F2
Alstead•, N.H. 268/C5
Alsten (isl.), Norway 18/H4
Alstfjorden (fjord), Norway 18/G3
Alston, England 13/E3
Alston, Georgia 217/H6
Alston, Mich. 250/G1
Alstonville, N.S. Wales 97/G1
Alta, Iowa 229/C3
Alta, Norway 18/N2
Alta, Utah 304/C3
Altadena, Calif. 204/C10
Altaelv (riv.), Norway 18/N2
Alta Gracia, Argentina 143/D3
Altagracia, Cuba 158/G3
Altagracia, Venezuela 124/C2
Altagracia de Orituco, Venezuela 124/E3
Altai (mts.) 54/K5
Altai (mts.), Mongolia 77/C2
Alta Loma, Calif. 204/E10
Alta Loma, Texas 303/K3
Altamachi (riv.), Bolivia 136/B5
Altamaha (riv.), Ga. 188/K4
Altamaha (riv.), Georgia 217/H7
Altamaha (sound), Georgia 217/K8
Altamahaw, N.C. 281/L2
Altamira, Brazil 132/C3
Altamira, Chile 138/B5
Altamira, Dom. Rep. 158/D5
Altamira, Mexico 150/L5
Altamont, Ill. 222/E4
Altamont, Kansas 232/G4
Altamont, Manitoba 179/D5
Altamont, Mo. 261/D3
Altamont, N.Y. 276/M5
Altamont, Oreg. 291/F5
Altamont, S. Dak. 298/R4
Altamont (canton), Tenn. 237/K10
Altamont, Utah 304/D3
Altamonte Springs, Fla. 212/E3
Altamura, Italy 34/F4
Altar, Mexico 150/D1
Altario, Alberta 182/E4
Altata, Mexico 150/E4
Alt Aussee, Austria 41/B3
Alta Vista, Iowa 229/J2
Alta Vista, Kansas 232/F3
Altavista, Va. 307/K6
Altay, China 77/C2
Altay, Mongolia 77/E2
Altay (mts.), U.S.S.R. 48/J5
Altdorf, Switzerland 39/G3
Altea, Spain 33/G3
Altena, Germany 22/B3
Altenburg, Germany 22/E3
Altenburg, Mo. 261/O7
Altepexi, Mexico 150/L7
Alter do Chão, Portugal 33/C3
Altevatn (lake), Norway 18/L2
Altha, Fla. 212/A1
Altheim, Austria 41/B2
Altheimer, Ark. 202/G5
Althofen, Austria 41/C3
Alticane, Sask. 181/D3
Altındağ, Turkey 63/E2
Altınova, Turkey 63/B3
Altınözü, Turkey 63/G4
Altıntaş, Turkey 63/C3
Altiplano (plat.) 120/C4
Altkirch, France 28/G4
Altmar, N.Y. 276/J3
Altmark (reg.), Germany 22/D2
Altmühl (riv.), Germany 22/D4
Altnaharra, Scotland 15/D2
Alto, Georgia 217/E2
Alto, La. 238/G2
Alto, Mich. 250/D6
Alto, N. Mex. 274/D5
Alto, Tenn. 237/K10
Alto, Texas 303/J6
Alto, Wis. 317/J8
Alto Araguaia, Brazil 132/C7
Alto Chicapa, Angola 115/C6
Alto Cuale, Angola 115/C5
Alto Cuale, Angola 102/D5
Alto de Cantillana (mt.), Chile 138/G4
Alto Lucero, Mexico 150/P1
Alto Molócuè, Mozambique 118/F3
Alton, Ala. 195/E3
Alton, Calif. 204/A3
Alton, England 13/G6
Alton, England 10/F5
Alton, Ill. 188/J3
Alton, Ill. 222/A2
Alton, Ind. 227/E8
Alton, Iowa 229/A3
Alton, Kansas 232/D2
Alton, Ky. 237/M4
Alton, La. 238/L6
Alton•, Maine 243/F5
Alton, Mo. 261/K9
Alton•, N.H. 268/E5
Alton, N.Y. 276/G4
Alton, Nova Scotia 168/E3
Alton, R.I. 249/G7
Alton, Utah 304/B6
Alton, Va. 307/K7
Alton, W. Va. 312/F5
Altona, Ill. 222/C2
Altona, Ind. 227/G2
Altona, Manitoba 179/E5
Altona, Mich. 250/D5
Altona, Mo. 261/D6
Altona, N.Y. 276/N1
Altona, Victoria 97/H5
Altona, Victoria 88/K7
Altona (bay), Victoria 97/H5
Altona (bay), Victoria 88/K7
Altona (lag.), Virgin Is. (U.S.) 161/F4
Altona, Germany 22/C2
Altonah, Utah 304/D3
Alton Bay, N.H. 268/E5
Alton Downs, S. Australia 94/F2
Alto Nevado, Cerro (mt.), Chile 138/E5
Altoona, Ala. 195/F2
Altoona, Fla. 212/E3
Altoona, Iowa 229/G5
Altoona, Kansas 232/G4
Altoona, Pa. 188/L2
Altoona, Pa. 294/F4
Altoona, Wash. 310/B4
Altoona, Wis. 317/C6
Alto Paraguay, Paraguay 144/C2
Alto Paraná, Paraguay 144/E4
Alto Paraná (riv.), Paraguay 144/D5
Alto Park, Georgia 217/B2
Alto Parnaíba, Brazil 132/E5
Alto Pass, Ill. 222/D6
Alto Ritacuva (mt.), Colombia 120/B2
Alto Ritacuva (mt.), Colombia 126/D4
Altos, Brazil 132/F4
Altos, Paraguay 144/B4
Alto Seco, Bolivia 136/D6
Alto Songo, Cuba 158/J4
Altotonga, Mexico 150/P1
Altötting, Germany 22/E4
Alto Velo (chan.), Dom. Rep. 158/C7
Alto Velo (isl.), Dom. Rep. 158/D7
Altrincham, England 13/H2
Altrincham, England 10/G2
Altro, Ky. 237/P6
Altstätten, Switzerland 39/J2
Altun Ha, Belize 154/C2
Altun Shan (range), China 54/K6
Altun Shan (range), China 77/C4
Altura, Minn. 255/G6
Alturas, Calif. 204/E2
Alturas, Fla. 212/E4
Altus, Ark. 202/C3
Altus, Okla. 288/H5
Altus (res.), Okla. 288/H5
Altus A.F.B., Okla. 288/H5
Alubijid, Philippines 82/E6
Alucra, Turkey 63/H2
Alūksne, U.S.S.R. 53/D2
Alula, Somalia 115/K1
Alula, Somalia 102/H3
Alum Bank, Pa. 294/E5
Alum Bridge, W. Va. 312/E4
Alum Creek, W. Va. 312/C6
Aluminé, Argentina 143/B4
Alum Rock, Calif. 204/L3
Alus, Iraq 66/C3
Alushta, U.S.S.R. 52/D6
Alva, Fla. 212/E5
Alva, Ky. 237/P7
Alva (lake), New Bruns. 170/D3
Alva, Okla. 288/J1
Alva, Scotland 10/B1
Alva, Scotland 15/C1
Alva, Wyo. 319/H1
Alva B. Adams (tunnel), Colo. 208/H2
Alvada, Ohio 284/D3
Alvadore, Oreg. 291/D3
Alvalade, Portugal 33/B4
Alvaneu, Switzerland 39/J3
Alvarado, Mexico 150/M7
Alvarado, Minn. 255/B2
Alvarado, Texas 303/G5
Álvaro S. Lima (res.), Brazil 135/B3
Alvaton, Georgia 217/C4
Alvaton, Ky. 237/J7
Ålvdal, Norway 18/G5
Älvdalen, Sweden 18/J6
Alvear, Argentina 143/E2
Alvena, Sask. 181/E3
Alvesta, Sweden 18/J8
Alvin, Br. Col. 184/L2
Alvin, Ill. 222/F3
Alvin, Texas 303/J3
Alvin, Wis. 317/J4
Alvinston, Ontario 177/B5
Alvito, Portugal 33/B3
Älvkarleby, Sweden 18/K6
Alvo, Nebr. 264/H4
Alvon, W. Va. 312/F7
Alvord, Iowa 229/A2
Alvord (lake), Oreg. 291/J5
Alvord, Texas 303/G4
Alvordton, Ohio 284/A2
Älvsborg (co.), Sweden 18/H7
Älvsbyn, Sweden 18/M4
Alvwood, Minn. 255/D3
Alvy, W. Va. 312/E4
Alwar, India 68/D3
Alxa Shamo (des.), China 77/F4
Alxa Youqi, China 77/F4
Alxa Zuoqi, China 77/F4
Aly, Ark. 202/D4
Alyangula, North. Terr. 88/F2
Alyangula, North. Terr. 93/E2
Alyth, Scotland 10/E2
Alyth, Scotland 15/E4
Alytus, U.S.S.R. 53/C3
Alz (riv.), Germany 22/E4
Alzada, Mont. 262/M5
Alzette (riv.), Luxembourg 27/J9
Alzey, Germany 22/C4
Amacuro (riv.), Venezuela 124/H4
Amadeus (lake), Australia 87/D8
Amadeus (lake), North. Terr. 88/E4
Amadeus (lake), North. Terr. 93/B8
Amadi, Sudan 111/F6
'Amadiya, Iraq 59/D2
'Amadiya, Iraq 66/C2
Amadjuak, N.W.T. 162/J3
Amadjuak (lake), N.W.T. 162/K3
Amadjuak, N.W. Terr. 187/L3
Amadjuak (lake), N.W. Terr. 187/L3
Amado, Ariz. 198/D7
Amador (co.), Calif. 204/E5
Amadora, Portugal 33/A1
Amador City, Calif. 204/C9
Amagansett, N.Y. 276/R9
Amagasaki, Japan 81/H8
Amager (isl.), Denmark 21/F6
Amagi, Japan 81/E7
Amagon, Ark. 202/H2
Amahai, Indonesia 85/H6
Amak (isl.), Alaska 196/F3
Amakura (riv.), Guyana 131/A2
Amakusa (isls.), Japan 81/D7
Åmål, Sweden 18/H7
Amalfi, Colombia 126/C4
Amalfi, Italy 34/E4
Amalga, Utah 304/C2
Amalia, N. Mex. 274/D2
Amaliás, Greece 45/E7
Amalner, India 68/C4
Amambaí, Brazil 132/C8
Amambaí, Serra de (range), Brazil 132/C7
Amambay, Paraguay 144/D3
Amambay, Cordillera de (mts.), Paraguay 144/D-E3
Amami (isls.), Japan 54/P7
Amami (isls.), Japan 81/N5
Amami-O-Shima (isl.), Japan 81/N5
Amana, Iowa 229/K5
Amanavén, Colombia 126/G6
Amanda, Ohio 284/E6
Amanda Park, Wash. 310/A3
Amanos (mts.), Turkey 63/G4
Amantea, Italy 34/E5
Amanu (atoll), Fr. Poly. 87/N7
Amapá (terr.), Brazil 132/D2
Amapá, Brazil 120/D2
Amapá, Brazil 132/D2
Amapala, Honduras 154/D4
Amapari (riv.), Brazil 132/C2
'Amara, Iraq 66/E5
'Amara, Iraq 59/E3
Amarante, Brazil 132/F4
Amarante, Portugal 33/B2
Amaranth, Manitoba 179/D4
Amarapura, Burma 72/B2
Amareleja, Portugal 33/C3
Amarete, Bolivia 136/A4
Amargosa, Brazil 132/F6
Amargosa (range), Calif. 204/J7
Amargosa (riv.), Calif. 204/J7
Amarillas, Cuba 158/D2
Amarillo, Texas 188/F3
Amarillo, Texas 146/H6
Amarillo, Texas 303/C2
Amasa, Mich. 250/G2
Amasra, Turkey 63/E2
Amasya (prov.), Turkey 63/F2
Amasya, Turkey 59/C1
Amasya, Turkey 63/G2
Amatignak (isl.), Alaska 196/K4
Amatitlán, Guatemala 154/B3
Amatlán de los Reyes, Mexico 150/P2
Amay, Belgium 27/G7
Amazon (riv.) 2/G6
Amazon (riv.), Brazil 120/D3
Amazon (riv.), Brazil 132/C3
Amazon (riv.), Colombia 126/E9
Amazon (riv.), Peru 128/F4
Amazon, Sask. 181/F4
Amazonas (state), Brazil 132/G9
Amazonas (comm.), Colombia 126/D8
Amazonas, Cuba 158/F2
Amazonas (dept.), Peru 128/C5
Amazonas (terr.), Venezuela 124/E5
Amazonia, Mo. 261/C3
Ambala, India 68/D2
Ambalavao, Madagascar 118/H4
Ambam, Cameroon 115/B3
Ambanja, Madagascar 118/H2
Ambarchik, U.S.S.R. 4/B1
Ambarchik, U.S.S.R. 48/R3
Ambato, Ecuador 120/B3
Ambato, Ecuador 128/C3
Ambato Boeny, Madagascar 118/H3
Ambatofinandrahana, Madagascar 118/H4
Ambatolampy, Madagascar 102/G6
Ambatolampy, Madagascar 118/H3
Ambatomainty, Madagascar 118/H3
Ambatondrazaka, Madagascar 118/H3
Ambatondrazaka, Madagascar 102/G6
Ambelau (isl.), Indonesia 85/H6
Amber, Iowa 229/L4
Amber (Bobaomby) (cape), Madagascar 118/H2
Amber, Okla. 288/L4
Amber, Wash. 310/H3
Amberg, Germany 22/D4
Amberg, Wis. 317/K5
Ambergris (cay), Belize 154/D1
Ambergris (cay), Turks & Caicos 156/D2
Ambérieu-en-Bugey, France 28/F5
Amberley, N. Zealand 100/D5
Amberley, Ohio 284/C9
Amberson, Pa. 294/G5
Ambert, France 28/E5
Ambia, Ind. 227/C4
Ambikapur, India 68/E4
Ambil (isl.), Philippines 82/C4
Ambilobe, Madagascar 118/H2
Amble, England 13/F2
Amble, Mich. 250/D5
Ambler, Alaska 196/G1
Ambler, Pa. 294/M5
Ambo, Peru 128/D8
Amboasary, Madagascar 118/H4
Ambodifototra, Madagascar 118/J3
Ambohimahasoa, Madagascar 118/H4
Amboise, France 28/D4
Ambon (Amboina), Indonesia 85/H6
Ambon, Indonesia 54/O10
Ambositra, Madagascar 102/G7
Ambositra, Madagascar 118/H4
Ambovombe, Madagascar 118/H5
Amboy, Calif. 204/K9
Amboy, Georgia 217/E7
Amboy, Ill. 222/D2
Amboy, Ind. 227/F3
Amboy, Minn. 255/D7
Amboy, Wash. 310/C5
Amboy, W. Va. 312/G4
Amboyna (cay), Philippines 85/E4
Ambridge, Pa. 294/B4
Ambriz, Angola 115/B5
Ambrose, Georgia 217/G7
Ambrose, N. Dak. 282/D2
Ambrym (isl.), Vanuatu 87/G7
Ambunti, Papua N.G. 85/B6
Amburgey, Ky. 237/R6
Amchitka (isl.), Alaska 188/D6
Amchitka (isl.), Alaska 196/K4
Amchitka (passage), Alaska 196/K4
Am-Dam, Chad 111/D5
Amderma, U.S.S.R. 52/K1
Amderma, U.S.S.R. 48/F3
Amdo, China 77/D5
Ameagle, W. Va. 312/D7
Amealco, Mexico 150/K6
Ameca, Mexico 150/H6
Amecameca de Juárez, Mexico 150/L1
Ameghino, Argentina 143/D3
Amel, Belgium 27/J8
Ameland (isl.), Netherlands 27/H2
Amelia (isl.), Fla. 212/E1
Amelia, Italy 34/D3
Amelia, La. 238/H7
Amelia, Nebr. 264/F2
Amelia, Ohio 284/D10
Amelia (co.), Va. 307/M6
Amelia City, Fla. 212/E1
Amelia Court House, Va. 307/N6
Amenia, N.Y. 276/N7
Amenia, N. Dak. 282/R6
America, Ill. 222/D6
American (highlands), Ant. 2/N10
American (riv.), Calif. 204/C8
Americana, Brazil 135/C3
American Corner, Md. 245/P5
American Falls, Idaho 220/E7
American Falls (res.), Idaho 188/D2
American Falls (res.), Idaho 220/F6
American Fork, Utah 304/C3
American Highland, Ant. 5/B4
American Samoa 2/A6
AMERICAN SAMOA 86/N9
American Samoa 87/J7
Americus, Georgia 217/D6
Americus, Ind. 227/D3
Americus, Kansas 232/F3
Americus, Mo. 261/J5
Amersfoort, Netherlands 27/G4
Amersham, England 13/G7
Amery, Man. 162/G4
Amery, Manitoba 179/J2
Amery, Wis. 317/B5
Amery Ice Shelf, Ant. 2/N9
Amery Ice Shelf, Ant. 5/C4
Ames, Iowa 229/F4
Ames, Kansas 232/E2
Ames, N.Y. 276/L5
Ames, Okla. 288/K2
Ames, Texas 303/K7
Amesbury, England 13/F6
Amesbury, Mass. 249/L1
Amesbury•, Mass. 249/L1
Amesville, Conn. 210/B1
Amesville, Ohio 284/F7
Amet (sound), Nova Scotia 168/E3
Amfilokhía, Greece 45/E6
Ámfissa, Greece 45/F6
Amga (riv.), U.S.S.R. 48/O3
Amguid, Algeria 106/F3
Amgun' (riv.), U.S.S.R. 48/O4
Amherst, Burma 72/C3
Amherst, Colo. 208/P1
Amherst•, Maine 243/G6
Amherst, Mass. 249/E3
Amherst•, Mass. 249/E3
Amherst, Nebr. 264/E4
Amherst•, N.H. 268/D6
Amherst, N.Y. 276/C4
Amherst, N.S. 162/K6
Amherst, Nova Scotia 168/D3
Amherst, Ohio 284/F3
Amherst (isl.), Ontario 177/H3
Amherst, S. Dak. 298/O2
Amherst, Texas 303/B4
Amherst (co.), Va. 307/K5
Amherst, Va. 307/K5
Amherst (mt.), W. Australia 92/D2
Amherst, Wis. 317/H7
Amherstburg, Ontario 177/A5
Amherstdale, W. Va. 312/C7
Amherst Junction, Wis. 317/H7
Amherst View, Ontario 177/H3
Amidon, N. Dak. 282/D7
Amiens, France 7/E4
Amiens, France 28/D3
Amindiri (isl.), India 68/C6
Amindivi (isls.), India 68/C6
Aminga, Argentina 143/C2
Amini (Amindiri) (isl.), India 68/C6
'Amir, Ras (cape), Libya 111/D1
Amiret, Minn. 255/C6
Amisk, Alberta 182/E3
Amisk (lake), Sask. 181/M4
Amissville, Va. 307/M3
Amistad (res.) 188/F5
Amistad (res.), Mexico 150/J2
Amistad, N. Mex. 274/F3
Amistad (dam), Texas 303/C8
Amistad (res.), Texas 303/C8
Amistad Nat'l Rec. Area, Texas 303/D8
Amite, La. 238/K5
Amite (riv.), La. 238/L2
Amite (co.), Miss. 256/C8
Amite (riv.), Miss. 256/C9
Amity, Ark. 202/D5
Amity, Georgia 217/G3
Amity, Ind. 227/E6
Amity, Mo. 261/D3
Amity, Oreg. 291/D2
Amity, Pa. 294/B5
Amityville, N.Y. 276/O9
Åmli, Norway 18/F7
Amlia (isl.), Alaska 196/L4
Amlia (passage), Alaska 196/L4
Amlwch, Wales 10/D4
Amlwch, Wales 13/C4
Amma, W. Va. 312/D5
Amman (dist.), Jordan 65/D4
Amman (cap.), Jordan 54/E6
Amman (cap.), Jordan 65/D4
Amman (cap.), Jordan 59/C3
Ammanford, Wales 13/C6
Ammassalik, Greenl. 4/C11
Ammassalik, Greenland 146/Q3
Ammersee (lake), Germany 22/D4
Ammie, Ky. 237/O6
Ammon, Idaho 220/G6
Ammon, Va. 307/N6
Ammonoosuc (riv.), N.H. 268/D3
Amnat, Thailand 72/E4
Amo, Ind. 227/D5
Amol, Iran 59/F2
Amol, Iran 66/H2
Amonate, Va. 307/E6
Amor, Minn. 255/C4
Amora, Portugal 33/A1
Amorbach, Germany 22/C4
Amoret, Mo. 261/C6
Amorgós (isl.), Greece 45/G7
Amorita, Okla. 288/K1
Amory, Miss. 256/H3
Amos, Que. 162/J6
Amos, Québec 174/B3
Åmotfors, Sweden 18/H7
Amoy (Xiamen), China 77/J7
Amozoc de Mota, Mexico 150/N2
Ampana, Indonesia 85/G6
Ampanihy, Madagascar 118/G4
Amparo, Brazil 135/C3
Amper (riv.), Germany 22/D4
Amphitrite (isls.), China 85/E2
Amposta, Spain 33/G2
Ampthill, England 13/G5
Amqui, Québec 172/B2
'Amran, Yemen 59/D6
Amravati, India 68/D4
Amreli, India 68/C4
Amriswil, Switzerland 39/H1
'Amrit (ruins), Syria 63/F5
Amritsar, India 54/J6
Amritsar, India 68/C2
Amrum (isl.), Germany 22/C1
Amsden, Ohio 284/D3
Amstelveen, Netherlands 27/B5

330 Anvil

Anvil (peak), Alaska 196/K4
Anxi, China 77/E3
Anxious (bay), S. Australia 94/D5
Anyang, China 77/H4
A'nyêmaqên Shan (mts.), China 77/E5
Anykščiai, U.S.S.R. 53/C3
Anzá, Colombia 126/C4
'Anza, West Bank 65/C3
Anzac, Alberta 182/E1
Anzaldo, Bolivia 136/C5
Anzhero-Sudzhensk, U.S.S.R. 54/K4
Anzhero-Sudzhensk, U.S.S.R. 48/J4
Anzio, Italy 34/D4
Anzoátegui (state), Venezuela 124/F3
Aoiz, Spain 33/F1
Aoji-ri, N. Korea 81/E2
Aomori (pref.), Japan 81/K3
Aomori, Japan 54/R5
Aomori, Japan 81/K3
Ao Paray (riv.), Paraguay 144/A5
Aosta (prov.), Italy 34/A2
Aosta (reg.), Italy 34/A2
Aosta, Italy 34/A2
Aouara, Fr. Guiana 131/E3
Aouinet Bel Egrâ (well), Algeria 106/C3
Aoulef, Algeria 106/E3
Aozou, Chad 111/C3
Apa (riv.), Paraguay 144/D3
Apache (co.), Ariz. 198/F3
Apache (lake), Ariz. 198/D5
Apache, Okla. 288/K5
Apache (mts.), Texas 303/C11
Apache Creek, N. Mex. 274/A5
Apache Junction, Ariz. 198/D5
Apalachee (bay), Fla. 188/K5
Apalachee (bay), Fla. 212/B2
Apalachee, Georgia 217/E3
Apalachia (res.), N.C. 281/A4
Apalachicola, Fla. 212/A2
Apalachicola (bay), Fla. 212/B2
Apalachicola (riv.), Fla. 212/A1
Apalachin, N.Y. 276/H6
Apalona, Ind. 227/D8
Apan, Mexico 150/M1
Apaporis (riv.), Colombia 126/F8
Aparecida, Brazil 135/D3
Aparri, Philippines 82/C1
Aparri, Philippines 85/G2
Apaturerí, Venezuela 124/G5
Apataki (atoll), Fr. Poly. 87/M7
Apatin, Yugoslavia 45/D3
Apatity, U.S.S.R. 52/D1
Apatzingán de la Constitución, Mexico 150/H7
Ape, U.S.S.R. 53/D2
Apeldoorn, Netherlands 27/H4
Apennines (mts.), Italy 7/F4
Apennines, Central (range), Italy 34/D3
Apennines, Northern (range), Italy 34/B2
Apennines, Southern (range), Italy 34/E4
Apere (riv.), Bolivia 136/C4
Apex, N.C. 281/M3
Apgar, Mont. 262/B2
Apia (cap.), W. Samoa 2/A6
Apia (cap.), W. Samoa 87/J7
Apia (cap.), W. Samoa 86/M8
Apiaí, Brazil 135/B4
Apishapa (riv.), Colo. 208/L8
Apison, Tenn. 237/L10
Ap Iwan, Cerro (mt.), Chile 138/E6
Apizaco, Mexico 150/N1
Aplao, Peru 128/F11
Aplin, Ark. 202/E4
Aplington, Iowa 229/H3
Ap Long Ha, Vietnam 72/F5
Apo (vol.), Philippines 82/E7
Apohaqui, New Bruns. 170/E3
Apolda, Germany 22/D3
Apolima (str.), W. Samoa 86/L8
Apollo, Georgia 217/F4
Apollo, Pa. 294/C4
Apollo Bay, Victoria 97/B6
Apollo Beach, Fla. 212/C3
Apolo, Bolivia 136/A4
Aponguao (riv.), Venezuela 124/H5
Apopka, Fla. 212/E3
Apopka (lake), Fla. 212/E3
Aporé (riv.), Brazil 132/D7
Apostle (isls.), Wis. 317/F2
Apostle Islands Nat'l Lakeshore, Wis. 317/E1
Apóstoles, Argentina 143/E2
Apoteri, Guyana 131/B3
Appalachia, Va. 307/C7
Appalachian (mts.) 188/K3
Appalachian (mts.), N.C. 281/D2
Appalachian (mts.), Pa. 294/H4
Appalachian (mts.), Tenn. 237/M10
Appalachian (mts.), U.S. 146/K6
Appalachian (mts.), Va. 307/J5
Appam, N. Dak. 282/C2
Appanoose (co.), Iowa 229/H7
Appelscha, Netherlands 27/J3
Appenzell, Ausser Rhoden (canton), Switzerland 39/H2
Appenzell, Inner Rhoden (canton), Switzerland 39/H2
Appenzell, Switzerland 39/H2
Apperson, Okla. 288/N1
Appin, Ontario 177/C5
Appin (dist.), Scotland 15/C4
Appingedam, Netherlands 27/K2
Apple (creek), Ill. 222/C4
Apple (riv.), Ill. 222/C1
Apple (creek), N. Dak. 282/J6
Apple (riv.), Wis. 317/A5
Appleby, England 13/E3
Appleby, England 10/E3
Appleby, Texas 303/K6
Apple Creek, Ohio 284/G4
Applecross, Scotland 15/C3
Appledale, Br. Col. 184/J5
Applegate, Calif. 204/E5
Applegate, Mich. 250/G5
Applegate, Oreg. 291/D5
Apple Grove, W. Va. 312/B5
Apple Hill, Ontario 177/K2
Apple River, Ill. 222/C1
Apple River, Nova Scotia 168/D3
Apples, Switzerland 39/B3
Appleton, Ark. 202/E3
Appleton, Maine 243/E7
Appleton•, Maine 243/E7
Appleton, Minn. 255/C5
Appleton (Old Appleton), Mo. 261/N7
Appleton, N.Y. 276/C4
Appleton, Ontario 177/H2
Appleton, S.C. 296/E5
Appleton, Wash. 310/D5
Appleton, Wis. 188/J2
Appleton, Wis. 317/J7
Appleton City, Mo. 261/D6
Apple Valley, Calif. 204/H9
Apple Valley, Minn. 255/G6
Appling (co.), Georgia 217/H7
Appling, Georgia 217/H3
Appomattox (co.), Va. 307/L6
Appomattox, Va. 307/L6
Appomattox (riv.), Va. 307/M6
Appomattox Court House Nat'l Hist. Park, Va. 307/K6
Apponaug, R.I. 249/J6
Approuague (riv.), Fr. Guiana 131/E4
Apra (harb.), Guam 86/K7
Aprilia, Italy 34/D4
Apsheron (pen.), U.S.S.R. 52/H6
Apsheronsk, U.S.S.R. 52/F6
Apsley, Ontario 177/F3
Apsley, Victoria 97/A5
Apt, France 28/F6
Aptos, Calif. 204/K4
Apua (pt.), Hawaii 218/J6
Apulia (Puglia) (reg.), Italy 34/F4
Apulia Station, N.Y. 276/H5
Apure (state), Venezuela 124/D4
Apure (riv.), Venezuela 124/E4
Apurímac (dept.), Peru 128/F10
Apurímac (riv.), Peru 120/B4
Apurímac (riv.), Peru 128/F9
Apurito, Venezuela 124/D4
Ap Vinh Hao, Vietnam 72/F5
Aqaba (gulf) 54/E7
Aqaba (gulf), Egypt 111/G2
Aqaba (gulf), Egypt 59/C4
Aqaba (gulf), Israel 65/D6
'Aqaba, Jordan 65/D6
'Aqaba, Jordan 59/C4
Aqaba (gulf), Jordan 65/D6
Aqaba (gulf), Saudi Arabia 59/C4
Aqcheh, Afghanistan 68/B1
Aqcheh, Afghanistan 59/J2
Aq Darband, Iran 66/M2
'Aqiq, Sudan 111/G4
'Aqqaba, West Bank 65/C3
Aqqikkol Hu (lake), China 77/C4
'Aqra, Iraq 66/D2
'Aqraba, West Bank 65/C3
Aquades Beach, Sask. 181/C2
Aquaforte, Newf. 166/D2
Aqua Park, Okla. 288/R3
Aquarius (range), Ariz. 198/B4
Aquarius (plat.), Utah 304/C5
Aquasco, Md. 245/L6
Aquia, Peru 128/D8
Aquidabán (riv.), Paraguay 144/D3
Aquidauana, Brazil 120/D5
Aquidauana, Brazil 132/C8
Aquila, Mexico 150/H7
Aquila, Switzerland 39/G3
Aquiles Serdán, Mexico 150/G2
Aquilla, Ohio 284/H2
Aquin, Haiti 158/B6
Ara (riv.), Japan 81/O2
Arab, Ala. 195/E2
'Arab, Shatt-al- (riv.), Iran 59/E4
'Arab, Shatt-al- (riv.), Iran 66/F5
'Arab, Shatt-al- (riv.), Iraq 59/E4
'Arab, Shatt-al- (riv.), Iraq 66/F5
Arab, Mo. 261/M8
'Araba, Wadi (valley), Israel 65/D5
'Araba, Wadi (valley), Jordan 65/D5
Arabela, N. Mex. 274/D5
Arabella, Sask. 181/K3
Arabi, Georgia 217/E7
'Arabi (isl.), Iran 66/G7
Arabi, La. 238/P4
Arabia, Ky. 237/M6
Arabia, Ohio 284/F8
Arabian (sea) 54/H8
Arabian (sea) 2/N5
Arabian (des.), Egypt 111/F2
Arabian (des.), Egypt 59/B4
Arabian (sea), India 68/B5
Arabian (sea), Pakistan 68/B5
Arabian (sea), Yemen 59/H5
Arabopó, Venezuela 124/H5
Araç, Turkey 63/E2
Araca, Bolivia 136/B5
Aracaju, Brazil 120/F4
Aracaju, Brazil 132/G5
Aracataca, Colombia 126/D2
Aracati, Brazil 132/G4
Araçatuba, Brazil 132/D8
Araçatuba, Brazil 135/A2
Araceli, Philippines 82/C5
Aracena, Spain 33/C4
Araçuaí, Brazil 132/F7
Arad, Israel 65/C5
Arad, Romania 7/G4
Arad, Romania 45/E2
Arada, Chad 111/D4
'Aradah, U.A.E. 59/F5
Aradan, Iran 66/H3
Arafat, Jebel (mt.), Saudi Arabia 59/D5
Arafura (sea) 87/D6
Arafura (sea) 2/R6
Arafura (sea) 88/E2
Arafura (sea), Indonesia 85/J8
Arafura (sea), North. Terr. 93/D1
Arago, Minn. 255/C3
Arago, Oreg. 291/C4
Arago (cape), Oreg. 291/C4
Aragon, Georgia 217/B2
Aragon, N. Mex. 274/A5
Aragón (reg.), Spain 33/F2
Aragón (riv.), Spain 33/F1
Aragona, Italy 34/D6
Aragua (state), Venezuela 124/E3
Araguacema, Brazil 132/D5
Aragua de Barcelona, Venezuela 124/F3
Aragua de Maturín, Venezuela 124/G3
Araguaia (riv.), Brazil 120/E3
Araguaia (riv.), Brazil 132/D4
Araguaiana, Brazil 132/C6
Araguaina, Brazil 120/E3
Araguarí, Brazil 120/E4
Araguari, Brazil 132/D7
Araguari (riv.), Brazil 132/D2
Araioses, Brazil 132/F3
Arak, Algeria 106/E3
Arak, Iran 54/G6
Arak, Iran 59/E3
Arak, Iran 66/F3
Arakan Yoma (mts.), Burma 72/B3
Araks (riv.) 54/F6
Araks (riv.), Iran 59/E2
Araks (Aras) (riv.), Iran 66/E1
Araks (riv.), Turkey 63/K2
Araks (riv.), U.S.S.R. 7/J5
Araks (riv.), U.S.S.R. 52/G7
Aral (sea), U.S.S.R. 54/G5
Aral (sea), U.S.S.R. 48/F5
Aralık, Turkey 63/L3
Aral Sea (lake), U.S.S.R. 2/M3
Aral'sk, U.S.S.R. 54/H5
Aral'sk, U.S.S.R. 48/G5
Aramac, Queensland 95/C4
Aramberri, Mexico 150/J5
Arampampa, Bolivia 136/B5
Aran (isl.), Ireland 10/B3
Aran (isl.), Ireland 17/D2
Aran (isls.), Ireland 17/B5
Aran (isls.), Ireland 10/B4
Aranda de Duero, Spain 33/E2
Arandas, Mexico 150/H6
Aran Fawddwy (mt.), Wales 13/C5
Arani, Bolivia 136/C5
Aranjuez, Spain 33/E2
Aransas (co.), Texas 303/H10
Aransas (passage), Texas 303/H10
Aransas Pass, Texas 303/G10
Araoua (mts.), Fr. Guiana 131/E4
Araouane, Mali 106/D5
Araouane, Mali 102/B3
Arapaho, Okla. 288/H3
Arapahoe (co.), Colo. 208/L3
Arapahoe, Colo. 208/P5
Arapahoe (peak), Colo. 208/H2
Arapahoe, Nebr. 264/E4
Arapahoe, N.C. 281/R4
Arapahoe, Wyo. 319/D3
Arapaho Nat'l Rec. Area, Colo. 208/G2
Arapey, Uruguay 145/B1
Arapey Chico (riv.), Uruguay 145/B1
Arapey Grande (riv.), Uruguay 145/B2
Arapicos, Ecuador 128/D3
Arapiraca, Brazil 120/F3
Arapkir, Turkey 63/H3
Arapkir, Turkey 59/C2
'Ar'ar, Wadi (dry riv.), Iraq 66/B5
'Ar'ar, Wadi (dry riv.), Iraq 59/D3
'Ar'ar, Wadi (dry riv.), Saudi Arabia 59/D3
Araracuara, Colombia 126/E8
Araracuara, Cerros de (mts.), Colombia 126/E7
Araranguá, Brazil 132/D10
Araraquara, Brazil 132/E8
Araraquara, Brazil 135/B2
Araras, Brazil 135/C3
Ararat, Ala. 195/B7
Ararat, N.C. 281/H2
Ararat (mt.), Pa. 294/M2
Ararat (mt.), Turkey 54/F6
Ararat (mt.), Turkey 63/L3
Ararat (mt.), Turkey 59/D2
Ararat, Victoria 88/G7
Ararat, Victoria 97/B5
Ararat, Va. 307/G7
Arari, Brazil 132/E3
Araruama (lake), Brazil 135/E3
Aras (Araks) (riv.), Iran 66/E1
Aras (Araks) (riv.), Iran 59/E2
Aratürük (Yiwu), China 77/D3
Arauca (riv.) 120/C2
Arauca (inten.), Colombia 126/E4
Arauca, Colombia 120/B2
Arauca, Colombia 126/E4
Arauca (riv.), Colombia 126/E4
Arauca (riv.), Venezuela 124/E4
Arauco, Chile 138/D1
Arauco (gulf), Chile 138/D1
Arauquita, Colombia 126/E4
Araure, Venezuela 124/D3
Aravaca, Spain 33/F4
Aravaipa (creek), Ariz. 198/E6
Arawa, Papua N.G. 86/C2
Arawe, Papua N.G. 86/B2
Arax (Araks) (riv), Asia 59/E2
Araxá, Brazil 132/E7
Araya, Venezuela 124/F2
Arba, Ind. 227/H4
Arba Mench, Ethiopia 111/G6
Arba Mench, Ethiopia 102/F4
Arbeca, Spain 33/G2
Arbedo-Castione, Switzerland 39/G4
Arbela (Erbil), Iraq 59/D2
Arbela (Erbil), Iraq 66/D2
Arbela, Mo. 261/H2
Arboga, Sweden 18/J7
Arbois, France 28/F4
Arbon, Idaho 220/F7
Arbon, Switzerland 39/H1
Arborea, Italy 34/B5
Arborfield, Sask. 181/H2
Arborg, Manitoba 179/E4
Arbor Vitae, Wis. 317/G4
Arbovale, W. Va. 312/G6
Arbrå, Sweden 18/K6
Arbroath, Scotland 15/F4
Arbroath, Scotland 10/E2
Arbroth, La. 238/H5
Arbucias, Spain 33/H2
Arbuckle, Calif. 204/C4
Arbuckle (lake), Fla. 212/E4
Arbuckle, W. Va. 312/C5
Arbuckles, Lake of the (lake), Okla. 288/M6
Arbuthnot, Sask. 181/E6
Arbutus, Md. 245/M4
Arbyrd, Mo. 261/M10
Arcachon, France 28/C5
Arcachon (bay), France 28/C5
Arcade, Georgia 217/E2
Arcade, N.Y. 276/D5
Arcadia, Calif. 204/C10
Arcadia, Fla. 212/E4
Arcadia, Ind. 227/E4
Arcadia, Iowa 229/C4
Arcadia, Kansas 232/H4
Arcadia, La. 238/E1
Arcadia, Mich. 250/C4
Arcadia, Mo. 261/L7
Arcadia, Nebr. 264/F3
Arcadia, Nova Scotia 168/B5
Arcadia, Ohio 284/D3
Arcadia, Okla. 288/M3
Arcadia, Pa. 294/E4
Arcadia, R.I. 249/H6
Arcadia, S.C. 296/C2
Arcadia, Texas 303/K3
Arcadia, Utah 304/D3
Arcadia, Wis. 317/D7
Arcadia Lakes, S.C. 296/F3
Arcahaie, Haiti 158/C6
Arcanum, Ohio 284/A6
Arcas (cay), Mexico 150/N6
Arcata, Calif. 204/A3
Arc Dome (mt.), Nev. 266/D4
Arcelia, Mexico 150/J7
Arch, N. Mex. 274/F4
Archambault (lake), Québec 172/C3
Archangel, U.S.S.R. 4/C7
Archangel, U.S.S.R. 2/M2
Archangel, U.S.S.R. 7/J2
Archangel (Arkhangel'sk), U.S.S.R. 48/E3
Archangel (Arkhangel'sk), U.S.S.R. 52/F2
Archbald, Pa. 294/F6
Archbold, Ohio 284/B2
Arch Cape, Oreg. 291/D2
Archdale, N.C. 281/K3
Archena, Spain 33/F3
Archer, Fla. 212/D2
Archer, Iowa 229/B2
Archer, Nebr. 264/F3
Archer (fiord), N.W. Terr. 187/M1
Archer (riv.), Queensland 95/B2
Archer (co.), Texas 303/F4
Archer City, Texas 303/F4
Archerfield, Queensland 88/K3
Archerfield, Queensland 95/D3
Archerwill, Sask. 181/H3
Arches Nat'l Park, Utah 304/E5
Archibald, La. 238/G2
Archidona, Ecuador 128/D3
Archidona, Spain 33/D4
Archie, La. 238/G3
Archie, Mo. 261/D5
Archiestown, Scotland 15/E3
Archuleta (co.), Colo. 208/E8
Archydal, Sask. 181/F5
Arcis-sur-Aube, France 28/F3
Arckaringa (creek), S. Australia 94/D2
Arco, Georgia 217/J8
Arco, Idaho 220/E6
Arco, Idaho 188/D2
Arco, Minn. 255/B6
Arcola, Ill. 222/E4
Arcola, Ind. 227/G2
Arcola, La. 238/K5
Arcola, Miss. 256/C4
Arcola, Mo. 261/E7
Arcola, N.C. 281/N2
Arcola, Sask. 181/J6
Arcopongo, Bolivia 136/B5
Arcosanti, Ariz. 198/C4
Arcos de Jalón, Spain 33/E2
Arcos de la Frontera, Spain 33/D4
Arcos de Valdevez, Portugal 33/B2
Arcot, India 68/D6
Arcoverde, Brazil 132/G5
Arctic (ocean) 54/C1
Arctic (ocean) 146/B2
Arctic (plain), Alaska 196/G1
Arctic, R.I. 249/J6
Arctic Bay, Canada 4/B14
Arctic Bay, N.W.T. 162/H1
Arctic Bay, N.W. Terr. 187/K2
Arctic Circle 2/J2
Arctic Ocean 2/B2
Arctic Ocean 4/A15
Arctic Ocean, U.S.S.R. 48/K1
Arctic Red (riv.), N.W. Terr. 187/E3
Arctic Red River, N.W.T. 162/C2
Arctic Red River, N.W. Terr. 187/E3
Arctic Village, Alaska 196/K1
Arda (riv.), Greece 45/G5
Ardabil, Iran 54/F6
Ardabil, Iran 59/E2
Ardabil, Iran 66/F1
Ardagh, Limerick, Ireland 17/C7
Ardagh, Longford, Ireland 17/F4
Ardahan, Turkey 59/D1
Ardahan, Turkey 63/K2
Ardal, Iran 66/G4
Årdal, Norway 18/E7
Årdalstangen, Norway 18/F6
Ardanuç, Turkey 63/K2
Ardara, Ireland 17/E2
Ardath, Sask. 181/D4
Ardavasar, Scotland 15/B3
Ardbeg, Ontario 177/D2
Ardèche (dept.), France 28/F5
Ardee, Ireland 17/H4
Ardee, Ireland 10/C4
Arden, Ark. 202/B6
Arden, Del. 245/R1
Arden, Denmark 21/C4
Arden, Manitoba 179/C4
Arden, Ontario 177/G3
Arden, Wash. 310/H2
Arden, W. Va. 312/G4
Arden-Arcade, Calif. 204/B8
Ardencroft, Del. 245/R1
Ardennes (for.), Belgium 27/F9
Ardennes (dept.), France 28/F3
Ardenode, Alberta 182/D4
Ardentown, Del. 245/S1
Ardenvoir, Wash. 310/E3
Ardersier, Scotland 15/E3
Ardeşen, Turkey 63/J2
Ardestan, Iran 59/F3
Ardestan, Iran 66/H4
Ardez, Switzerland 39/K3
Ardfert, Ireland 17/B7
Ardfinnan, Ireland 17/F7
Ardgay, Scotland 15/D3
Ardglass, N. Ireland 17/K3
Ardgour (dist.), Scotland 15/C4
Ardheá, Greece 45/F5
Ardila (riv.), Spain 33/C3
Ardill, Sask. 181/F6
Ardino, Bulgaria 45/G5
Ardivachar (pt.), Scotland 15/A3
Ardle (riv.), Scotland 15/E4
Ardlethan, N.S. Wales 97/D4
Ardmore, Ala. 195/E1
Ardmore, Alberta 182/E2
Ardmore, Ind. 227/E1
Ardmore, Ireland 17/F8
Ardmore, Md. 245/G4
Ardmore, Mo. 261/H3
Ardmore, Okla. 188/G4
Ardmore, Okla. 288/M6
Ardmore, Pa. 294/M6
Ardmore, S. Dak. 298/B7
Ardmore, Tenn. 237/H10
Ardnamurchan (pen.), Scotland 15/B4
Ardnamurchan (pt.), Scotland 15/B4
Ardoch, N. Dak. 282/R3
Ardon, Switzerland 39/D4
Ardooie, Belgium 27/C7
Ardrahan, Ireland 17/D5
Ardrishaig, Scotland 15/C4
Ardrossan, Alberta 182/D3
Ardrossan, Scotland 10/D3
Ardrossan, Scotland 15/D5
Ards (dist.), N. Ireland 17/K2
Ardsley, N.Y. 276/O6
Åre, Sweden 18/H5
Arecibo (dist.), P. Rico 161/C1
Arecibo, P. Rico 156/G1
Arecibo, P. Rico 161/B1
Aredale, Iowa 229/H3
Areguá, Paraguay 144/B4
Areia Branca, Brazil 132/G4
Arelee, Sask. 181/D3
Arena (pt.), Calif. 188/B3
Arena (pt.), Calif. 204/B5
Arena (pt.), Mexico 150/E5
Arena, N. Dak. 282/K5
Arena (isl.), Philippines 82/C6
Arena, Wis. 317/G9
Arenac (co.), Mich. 250/F4
Arenales, Cerro (mt.), Chile 138/D7
Arenas (pt.), Argentina 143/C7
Arenas (cay), Mexico 150/O5
Arenas (pt.), P. Rico 161/F2
Arenas de San Pedro, Spain 33/D2
Arendal, Norway 18/F7
Arendjelovac, Yugoslavia 45/E3
Arendonk, Belgium 27/G6
Arendtsville, Pa. 294/H6
Arenillas, Ecuador 128/B4
Arenys de Mar, Spain 33/H2
Arenzville, Ill. 222/C4
Areópolis, Greece 45/F7
Arequipa (dept.), Peru 128/F10
Arequipa, Peru 128/G11
Arequipa, Peru 120/B4
Arequipa, Peru 2/F6
Arequipa, Peru 128/72
Aresji, Neth. Ant. 161/D9
Areuse (riv.), Switzerland 39/C3
Arévalo, Spain 33/D2
Areyonga, North. Terr. 88/E4
Areyonga, North. Terr. 93/C8
Arezzo (prov.), Italy 34/C3
Arezzo, Italy 34/C3
Arfa Deh, Iran 66/H3
Arga (riv.), Spain 33/F1
Argadargada, North. Terr. 93/E6
Argalant, Mongolia 77/G3
Argalastí, Greece 45/F6
Argamasilla de Alba, Spain 33/E3
Arganda, Spain 33/G4
Argao, Philippines 82/D6
Argenta, Br. Col. 184/J5
Argenta, Ill. 222/E4
Argenta, Italy 34/D2
Argentan, France 28/D3
Argentat, France 28/D5
Argenteuil, France 28/A1
Argenteuil (co.), Québec 172/C4
Argentia, Newf. 166/C2
Argentina 2/F7
Argentina 120/C6
ARGENTINA 143
Argentine, Pa. 294/C3
Argentino (lake), Argentina 143/B7
Argenton-sur-Creusot, France 28/D4
Argeş (riv.), Romania 45/G3
Argo, Ala. 195/E3
Argo, Sudan 111/F4
Argo, Sudan 59/B6
Argo Fay, Ill. 222/C2
Argolis (gulf), Greece 45/F7
Argonia, Kansas 232/E4
Argonne, Wis. 317/J4
Argonne Nat'l Laboratory, Ill. 222/B6
Árgos, Greece 45/F7
Argos, Ind. 227/E2
Argos (cape), Nova Scotia 168/G3
Argostólion, Greece 45/E6
Arguello (pt.), Calif. 204/E9
Arguin (bay), Mauritania 106/A4
Argun (riv.) 54/N4
Argun (Ergun He) (riv.), China 77/K1
Argun (riv.), U.S.S.R. 48/M4
Argungu, Nigeria 106/E6
Argus (range), Calif. 204/H7
Argusville, N. Dak. 282/R5
Arguvan, Turkey 63/H3
Argyle, Fla. 212/C6
Argyle, Georgia 217/G8
Argyle, Iowa 229/K7
Argyle, Maine 243/F5
Argyle, Manitoba 179/E4
Argyle, Mich. 250/G5
Argyle, Minn. 255/B2
Argyle, Mo. 261/J6
Argyle, New Bruns. 170/C2
Argyle, N.Y. 276/O4
Argyle, Texas 303/F1
Argyle (lake), W. Australia 88/D3
Argyle (lake), W. Australia 92/E2
Argyle, Wis. 317/G10
Argyle Downs, W. Australia 92/E2
Argyll (dist.), Scotland 15/C4
Argyll (trad. co.), Scotland 15/B5
Arhangay, Mongolia 77/F2
Arhavi, Turkey 63/J2
Arhli (Arlit), Niger 106/F4
Ar Horqin, China 77/K3
Århus (co.), Denmark 21/D5
Århus, Denmark 7/E3
Århus, Denmark 21/D5
Århus, Denmark 18/F8
Aria, N. Zealand 100/E3
Ariah Park, N.S. Wales 97/D4
Ariail, S.C. 296/B2
Ariamsvlei, Namibia 118/B5
Ariano Irpino, Italy 34/E4
Ariari (riv.), Colombia 126/D6
Aribinda, Burkina Faso 106/D6
Arica, Chile 120/B4
Arica, Chile 138/A1
Arica, Colombia 126/E9
Aricagua, Venezuela 124/C3
Ariccia, Italy 34/F7
Arichat, Nova Scotia 168/H3
Arichuna, Venezuela 124/E4
Arichuna (riv.), Venezuela 124/D4
Arid (cape), W. Australia 88/C6
Arid (cape), W. Australia 92/C6
Ariège (dept.), France 28/D6
Ariel, Wash. 310/C5
Ariguaní (riv.), Colombia 126/D3
Ariha (Jericho), West Bank 65/C4
Arikaree (riv.), Colo. 208/O3
Arima, Trin. & Tob. 156/G5
Arima, Trin. & Tob. 161/B10
Arimo, Idaho 220/F7
Arinagour, Scotland 15/B4
Aringa, Uganda 115/F3
Arinos (riv.), Brazil 132/B5
Ario de Rosales, Mexico 150/J7
Arion, Iowa 229/B5
Aripao, Venezuela 124/F4
Aripeka, Fla. 212/D3
Aripine, Ariz. 198/E4
Aripo, El Cerro del (mt.), Trin. & Tob. 161/B10
Ariporo (riv.), Colombia 126/E4
Aripuanã, Brazil 120/C3
Aripuanã, Brazil 132/A5
Aripuanã (riv.), Brazil 120/D3
Aripuanã (riv.), Brazil 132/A4
Arisaig, Scotland 15/C4
Arisaig (sound), Scotland 15/C4
Arismendi, Venezuela 124/D3
Arispe, Iowa 229/E7
Aristazabal (isl.), Br. Col. 184/C4
Aritao, Philippines 82/C2
Ariton, Ala. 195/G7
Arivaca, Ariz. 198/D7
Arivonimamo, Madagascar 118/H3
Arixang (Wenquan), China 77/B3
Ariza, Spain 33/E2
Arizaro, Salar de (salt dep.), Argentina 143/C2
Arizona 188/D4
ARIZONA 198
Arizona (state), U.S. 146/G6
Arizona City, Ariz. 198/D6
Arizona Sunsites, Ariz. 198/F7
Arizpe, Mexico 150/D1
Årjäng, Sweden 18/H7
Arjay, Ky. 237/O7
Arjeplog, Sweden 18/L3
Arjona, Colombia 126/C2
Arkabutla, Miss. 256/D1
Arkabutla (dam), Miss. 256/D1
Arkabutla (lake), Miss. 256/D1
Arkadelphia, Ala. 195/E3
Arkadelphia, Ark. 202/D5
Arkaig, Loch (lake), Scotland 15/C4
Arkaig, Loch (lake), Scotland 10/D2
Arkalyk, U.S.S.R. 48/G4
Arkansas 188/H3
ARKANSAS 202
Arkansas (riv.) 188/H3
Arkansas (co.), Ark. 202/H5
Arkansas (riv.), Ark. 202/G5
Arkansas (riv.), Colo. 208/P6
Arkansas (riv.), Kansas 232/D3
Arkansas (riv.), Okla. 288/S4
Arkansas (state), U.S. 146/J6
Arkansas (riv.), U.S. 2/E4
Arkansas (riv.), U.S. 146/J6
Arkansas City, Ark. 202/H6
Arkansas City, Kans. 188/G3
Arkansas City, Kansas 232/E4
Arkansas Divide (mts.), Colo. 208/L4
Arkansas Post Nat'l Mem., Ark. 202/H5
Arkansaw, Wis. 317/B6
Arkdale, Wis. 317/G7
Arkhángelos, Greece 45/J7
Arkhipo-Osipovka, U.S.S.R. 52/E6
Arkinda, Ark. 202/B6
Arklow, Ireland 10/C4
Arklow, Ireland 17/J6

Athelstan 331

Arklow (bank), Ireland 17/K6
Arkoe, Mo. 261/C2
Arkoma, Okla. 288/T4
Arkona (cape), Germany 22/E1
Arkona, Ontario 177/C4
Arkport, N.Y. 276/E6
Arkticheskiy Institut (isls.), U.S.S.R. 48/H2
Arkville, N.Y. 276/L6
Arkwright, S.C. 296/C2
Arlee, Mont. 262/B3
Arlee, W. Va. 312/B5
Arles, France 28/F6
Arley, Ala. 195/D2
Arlington, Ala. 195/C6
Arlington, Ariz. 198/C5
Arlington, Colo. 208/N6
Arlington, Georgia 217/C8
Arlington, Ill. 222/D2
Arlington, Ind. 227/F5
Arlington, Iowa 229/K3
Arlington, Kansas 232/D4
Arlington, Ky. 237/D7
Arlington•, Mass. 249/C6
Arlington, Minn. 255/D6
Arlington, Nebr. 264/H3
Arlington, N.Y. 276/N7
Arlington, N.C. 281/H2
Arlington, Ohio 284/C4
Arlington, Oreg. 291/G2
Arlington, S. Dak. 298/P5
Arlington, Tenn. 237/B10
Arlington, Tex. 188/G4
Arlington, Texas 303/F2
Arlington (lake), Texas 303/F2
Arlington, Vt. 268/A5
Arlington•, Vt. 268/A5
Arlington (co.), Va. 307/S2
Arlington, Va. 307/T3
Arlington, Wash. 310/C2
Arlington, Wis. 317/H9
Arlington, Wyo. 319/F4
Arlington Beach, Sask. 181/F4
Arlington Heights, Ill. 222/B5
Arlington Heights, Ohio 284/C9
Arlington Nat'l Cemetery, Va. 307/T3
Arlit (Arhli), Niger 106/F4
Arló, Hungary 41/F2
Arlon, Belgium 27/H9
Arltunga, North. Terr. 93/D7
Arm (riv.), Sask. 181/F5
Arma, Kansas 232/H4
Arma (plat.), Saudi Arabia 59/E4
Armada, Alberta 182/D4
Armada, Mich. 250/G6
Armadale, Scotland 15/C2
Armadale, Scotland 10/B1
Armagh (dist.), N. Ireland 17/H3
Armagh, N. Ireland 10/C3
Armagh, N. Ireland 17/H3
Armagh, Pa. 294/E5
Armagh, Québec 172/G3
Armathwaite, Tenn. 237/M8
Armavir, U.S.S.R. 7/J4
Armavir, U.S.S.R. 48/E5
Armavir, U.S.S.R. 52/F5
Armena, Alberta 182/D3
Armenia, Colombia 120/B2
Armenia, Colombia 126/B5
Armenian S.S.R., U.S.S.R. 7/J4
Armenian S.S.R., U.S.S.R. 52/F6
Armenian S.S.R., U.S.S.R. 48/E6
Armentières, France 28/E2
Armeriá, Mexico 150/G7
Armero, Colombia 126/C5
Armidale, Australia 87/F9
Armidale, N.S. Wales 88/J6
Armidale, N.S. Wales 97/F2
Armington, Ill. 222/D3
Armington, Mont. 262/F3
Arminto, Wyo. 319/E2
Armistead, La. 238/D3
Armit (lake), Manitoba 179/A2
Armley, Sask. 181/G2
Armona, Calif. 204/F7
Armorel, Ark. 202/L2
Armour, S. Dak. 298/N7
Armourdale, N. Dak. 282/M2
Armoy, N. Ireland 17/J1
Armstrong, Br. Col. 184/H5
Armstrong, Ill. 222/F3
Armstrong, Ind. 227/B8
Armstrong, Iowa 229/D2
Armstrong, Mo. 261/G4
Armstrong, Ont. 162/H5
Armstrong, Ontario 175/C2
Armstrong, Ontario 177/H4
Armstrong (co.), Pa. 294/D4
Armstrong (co.), Texas 303/C3
Armstrong, Texas 303/G11
Armstrong Brook, New Bruns. 170/E1
Armstrong Creek, Wis. 317/K4
Armstrongs Mills, Ohio 284/J6
Armuchee, Georgia 217/B2
Army Chemical Center, Md. 245/O3
Army Med. Ctr. Annex (Walter Reed), Md. 245/E4
Arnaiá, Greece 45/F5
Arnaud, Manitoba 179/E5
Arnaud (riv.), Québec 174/F1
Arnaudville, La. 238/G6
Arnauti (cape), Cyprus 59/B2
Arnauti (cape), Cyprus 63/E5
Arnavutköy, Turkey 63/D6
Arnedo, Spain 33/E1
Arnegard, N. Dak. 282/D4
Årnes, Norway 18/G6
Arnett, Okla. 288/G2
Arnett, W. Va. 312/D7
Arney (riv.), N. Ireland 17/F3
Arnheim, Mich. 250/G1
Arnhem (cape), Australia 87/D7
Arnhem, Netherlands 27/H4
Arnhem (cape), North. Terr. 88/F2
Arnhem (cape), North. Terr. 93/E2
Arnhem Land (reg.), Australia 87/D7
Arnhem Land (reg.), North. Terr. 88/E2
Arnhem Land (reg.), North. Terr. 93/D2
Arnhem Land Aboriginal Res., North. Terr. 88/E2
Arnhem Land Aboriginal Res., North. Terr. 93/C2
Arno (riv.), Italy 34/C3
Arno (atoll), Marshall Is. 87/H5
Arnold, Calif. 204/E5
Arnold, England 13/F4
Arnold, Kansas 232/B3
Arnold, Mich. 250/B2
Arnold, Minn. 255/F4
Arnold, Mo. 261/M6
Arnold, Nebr. 264/D3
Arnold (riv.), North. Terr. 93/D3
Arnold, Pa. 294/C4
Arnold Mills, R.I. 249/J5
Arnoldsburg, W. Va. 312/D5
Arnold's Cove, Newf. 166/C2
Arnolds Park, Iowa 229/C2
Arnoldstein, Austria 41/B3
Arnoldsville, Georgia 217/F3
Arnot, Pa. 294/H2
Arnøya (isl.), Norway 18/M1
Arnprior, Ontario 177/H2
Arnsberg, Germany 22/C3
Arnstadt, Germany 22/D3
Årø (isl.), Denmark 21/C7
Aro (riv.), Venezuela 124/F4
Aroa, Venezuela 124/D2
Aroab, Namibia 118/B5
Aroche, Spain 33/C4
Arock, Oreg. 291/K5
Aroland, Ontario 177/H4
Aroland, Ontario 175/C2
Arolla, Switzerland 39/E4
Arolsen, Germany 22/C3
Aroma, Bolivia 136/B6
Aroma, Sudan 111/G4
Aroma Park, Ill. 222/F2
Aromas, Calif. 204/D7
Aroostook (co.), Maine 243/F2
Aroostook (riv.), Maine 243/G2
Aroostook, New Bruns. 170/C2
Arorae (atoll), Kiribati 87/H6
Aroroy, Philippines 82/D4
Arosa, Ria de (est.), Spain 33/B1
Arosa, Switzerland 39/J3
Aroser Rothorn (mt.), Switzerland 39/J3
Årøsund, Denmark 21/C7
Arouca, Trin. & Tob. 161/B10
Arp, Georgia 217/F7
Arp, Texas 303/J5
Arpa (riv.), Turkey 63/K2
Arpaçay, Turkey 63/K2
Arpin, Wis. 317/G6
Arque, Bolivia 136/B5
'Arraba, West Bank 65/C3
'Arrabe, Israel 65/C2
Arrah, India 68/E3
Ar Rahhaliya, Iraq 66/C4
Ar Rahhaliya, Iraq 59/D3
Arraias, Brazil 132/E6
Arran, Fla. 212/B1
Arran, Sask. 181/K4
Arran (isl.), Scotland 15/C5
Arran (isl.), Scotland 10/D3
Arras, Br. Col. 184/G2
Arras, France 28/E2
Arrecifal, Colombia 126/F6
Arrecife, Spain 106/B3
Arrecife, Spain 33/C4
Arrecife de la Media Luna (reefs), Honduras 154/F3
Arrecifes, Argentina 143/F7
Arrecifes (riv.), Argentina 143/G6
Arrey, N. Mex. 274/B6
Arriaga, Mexico 150/N8
Arriba, Colo. 208/N4
Arribeños, Argentina 143/F7
Arrington, Kansas 232/G2
Arrington, Tenn. 237/H9
Arrington, Va. 307/L5
Arriola, Colo. 208/B8
Arrochar, Scotland 15/D4
Arronches, Portugal 33/C3
Arrow (lake), Ireland 17/E3
Arrow (creek), Mont. 262/F3
Arrow Canyon (range), Nev. 266/G6
Arrow Creek, Mont. 262/F3
Arrowhead Mountain (lake), Vt. 268/A2
Arrow River, Manitoba 179/B4
Arrowrock (res.), Idaho 220/C6
Arrow Rock, Mo. 261/F4
Arrowsmith, Ill. 222/E3
Arrowtown, N. Zealand 100/B6
Arrowwood, Alberta 182/D4
Arrowwood (lake), N. Dak. 282/N5
Arroyas, Los (lake), Bolivia 136/C3
Arroyo, P. Rico 161/E3
Arroyo, P. Rico 156/G1
Arroyo Blanco, Cuba 158/F2
Arroyo de la Luz, Spain 33/C3
Arroyo del Valle (dry riv.), Calif. 204/L3
Arroyo Grande, Bolivia 136/A2
Arroyo Grande, Calif. 204/E8
Arroyo Hondo (dry riv.), Calif. 204/L3
Arroyo Hondo, N. Mex. 274/D2
Arroyo Mocho (dry riv.), Calif. 204/L2
Arroyo Seco, Argentina 143/F6
Arroyo Seco (dry riv.), Calif. 204/K10
Arroyo Seco, N. Mex. 274/D2
Arroyos y Esteros, Paraguay 144/B4
Ar Rumaila, Iraq 66/E5
Års, Denmark 21/C4
Ars-en-Ré, France 28/C4
Arsen'yev, U.S.S.R. 48/O5
Arsin, Turkey 63/H2
Arslanköy, Turkey 63/F4
Árta, Greece 45/E6
Artá, Spain 33/H3
Artas, S. Dak. 298/K2
Artawiya, Saudi Arabia 59/E4
Arteaga, Mexico 150/H7
Artem, U.S.S.R. 48/O5
Artemas, Pa. 294/E6
Artemisa, Cuba 158/B1
Artemisa, Cuba 156/A2
Artemovskiy, U.S.S.R. 48/M4
Artemus, Ky. 237/O7
Artena, Italy 34/F7
Artesia, Calif. 204/C11
Artesia, Miss. 256/G4
Artesia, N. Mex. 188/F4
Artesia, N. Mex. 274/E6
Artesian, S. Dak. 298/O6
Artesia Wells, Texas 303/E9
Arth, Switzerland 39/F2
Arthabaska (co.), Québec 172/E4
Arthabaska, Québec 172/F3
Arthur, Ill. 222/E4
Arthur, Ind. 227/C8
Arthur, Iowa 229/C4
Arthur (co.), Nebr. 264/C3
Arthur, Nebr. 264/C3
Arthur (range), N. Zealand 100/D4
Arthur, N. Dak. 282/R5
Arthur, Ontario 177/D4
Arthur (lake), Pa. 294/C4
Arthur (lake), Tasmania 99/D4
Arthur (range), Tasmania 99/C5
Arthur (riv.), Tasmania 99/B3
Arthur, Tenn. 237/O7
Arthur (riv.), W. Australia 92/B2
Arthur, W. Va. 312/H4
Arthurdale, W. Va. 312/G3
Arthuret, England 13/E2
Arthurette, New Bruns. 170/C2
Arthur Kill (str.), N.J. 273/B3
Arthur's (pass), N. Zealand 100/C5
Arthurstown, Ireland 17/H7
Artibonite (dept.), Haiti 158/C5
Artibonite (riv.), Haiti 158/C5
Artigas (dept.), Uruguay 145/B1
Artigas, Uruguay 145/C1
Artillery (lake), N.W. Terr. 187/H3
Artland, Sask. 181/B3
Artois, Calif. 204/C4
Artois (trad. prov.), France 29
Artova, Turkey 63/G2
Artux (Atushi), China 77/A4
Artvin (prov.), Turkey 63/J2
Artvin, Turkey 59/D1
Artvin, Turkey 63/J2
Aru (isls.), Indonesia 85/K7
Aru, Zaire 115/F3
Arua, Uganda 115/F3
Aruba (isl.), Netherlands 161/E9
Aruba (isl.), Netherlands 156/E4
Arucas, Spain 33/B5
Arunachal Pradesh (terr.), India 68/G3
Arundel, England 13/G7
Arundel, England 10/F5
Arundel, Québec 172/C4
Årup, Denmark 21/D7
Aruppukkottai, India 68/D7
'Arura, West Bank 65/C3
Arus, P. Rico 161/C3
Arusha (reg.), Tanzania 115/G4
Arusha, Tanzania 102/F5
Arusha, Tanzania 115/G4
Arusi (prov.), Ethiopia 111/G6
Aruwimi (riv.), Zaire 115/E3
Arva, Ireland 17/F4
Arva, Ontario 177/C4
Arvada, Colo. 208/J3
Arvada, Wyo. 319/F1
Arvayheer, Mongolia 77/F2
Arvel, Ky. 237/O5
Arvi, India 68/D4
Arvida, Québec 172/F1
Arvidsjaur, Sweden 18/L4
Arvika, Sweden 18/H7
Arvilla, N. Dak. 282/P4
Arvin, Calif. 204/G8
Arvonia, Va. 307/M5
Arwad (Ruad) (isl.), Syria 63/F5
Arxan, China 77/K2
Arys', U.S.S.R. 48/G5
Arzamas, U.S.S.R. 48/E4
Arzamas, U.S.S.R. 52/F3
Arzuá, Spain 33/B1
As, Belgium 27/H6
Aš, Czech. 41/B1
Aså, Denmark 21/D3
Asaba, Nigeria 106/F7
Asadabad, Iran 66/F3
Asahan (riv.), Indonesia 85/B5
Asahi, Japan 81/K6
Asahi (mt.), Japan 81/J4
Asahikawa, Japan 81/L2
Asahikawa, Japan 54/P5
Asama (mt.), Japan 81/J5
Asansol, India 68/F4
Åsarna, Sweden 18/J5
Asau, W. Samoa 86/L8
Asbest, U.S.S.R. 48/G4
Asbestos, Québec 172/F4
Asbury, Iowa 229/M4
Asbury, Mo. 261/C8
Asbury, N.J. 273/C2
Asbury, W. Va. 312/E7
Asbury Park, N.J. 273/F3
As Busaiya, Iraq 66/E5
Ascención (Añez), Bolivia 136/D4
Ascensión, Argentina 143/F7
Ascension (par.), La. 238/J6
Ascensión, Mexico 150/E1
Ascension, Neth. Ant. 161/F8
Ascension (isl.), St. Helena 102/A5
Ascension (isl.), St. Helena 2/J6
Aschaffenburg, Germany 22/C4
Aschendorf, Germany 22/B2
Aschersleben, Germany 22/D3
Asco, W. Va. 312/C8
Ascog, Scotland 15/A2
Ascoli Piceno (prov.), Italy 34/D3
Ascoli Piceno, Italy 34/D3
Ascona, Switzerland 39/G4
Ascope, Peru 128/C6
Ascot, Queensland 88/K2
Ascot, Queensland 95/E2
Ascotán, Chile 138/B3
Ascotán, Salar de (salt dep.), Chile 138/B3
Ascot Corner, Québec 172/F4
Ascrib (isls.), Scotland 15/B3
Ascutney, Vt. 268/C5
Ascutney (mt.), Vt. 268/C5
Åseda, Sweden 18/J8
Åsele, Sweden 18/K4
Asenovgrad, Bulgaria 45/G5
Asèr, Ras (cape), Somalia 2/M5
Asèr, Ras (cape), Somalia 115/K1
Ash (riv.), Minn. 255/F2
Ash, N.C. 281/N6
Ash, Oreg. 291/D4
Ash (creek), Utah 304/A6
'Ashaira, Saudi Arabia 59/D5
Ashanti (reg.), Ghana 102/B4
Ashanti (reg.), Ghana 106/D7
Ashaway, R.I. 249/G7
Ashboro, Ind. 227/C6
Ashburn, Georgia 217/E7
Ashburn, Mo. 261/K3
Ashburn, Va. 307/O2
Ashburnham, Mass. 249/G2
Ashburnham•, Mass. 249/G2
Ashburton (riv.), Australia 87/B8
Ashburton, England 13/D7
Ashburton, N. Zealand 100/C5
Ashburton (riv.), W. Australia 88/B4
Ashburton (riv.), W. Australia 92/A3
Ashburton Downs, W. Australia 88/B4
Ashby, Ala. 195/E4
Ashby•, Mass. 249/G2
Ashby, Minn. 255/C4
Ashby, Nebr. 264/C2
Ashbyburg, Ky. 237/G5
Ash Creek, Minn. 255/B7
Ashcroft, Br. Col. 184/G5
Ashdale, Maine 243/D8
Ashdod, Israel 65/B4
Ashdot Ya'aqov, Israel 65/D2
Ashdown, Ark. 202/B6
Ashe (co.), N.C. 281/F2
Ashe (isl.), N.C. 281/P6
Asheboro, N.C. 281/K3
Ashepoo, S.C. 296/G6
Ashepoo (riv.), S.C. 296/F6
Asher, Okla. 288/N5
Ashern, Manitoba 179/D3
Asherton, Texas 303/E9
Asherville, Ind. 227/C6
Asherville, Kansas 232/D2
Asheville, N.C. 188/K3
Asheville, N.C. 281/D3
Asheweig (riv.), Ontario 175/C2
Ashfield•, Mass. 249/C2
Ashfield, N. S. Wales 88/K4
Ashfield, N.S. Wales 97/J3
Ash Flat, Ark. 202/G1
Ashford, Ala. 195/H8
Ashford•, Conn. 210/G1
Ashford, England 10/G5
Ashford, England 13/H6
Ashford, Ireland 17/J5
Ashford, N.S. Wales 97/F1
Ashford, N.C. 281/F3
Ashford, Wash. 310/C4
Ashford, W. Va. 312/C6
Ashford P.O. (Warrenville), Conn. 210/G1
Ash Fork, Ariz. 198/C3
Ash Grove, Kansas 232/D2
Ash Grove, Mo. 261/E8
Ashgrove, Queensland 88/K2
Ashhurst, N. Zealand 100/E4
Ashibetsu, Japan 81/L2
Ashikaga, Japan 81/J5
Ashington, England 13/F2
Ashington, England 10/F3
Ashippun, Wis. 317/H1
Ashiya, Japan 81/H8
Ashizuri (cape), Japan 81/F7
Ashkhabad, U.S.S.R. 54/G6
Ashkhabad, U.S.S.R. 48/F6
Ashkum, Ill. 222/E3
Ash Lake, Minn. 255/F2
Ashland, Ala. 195/G4
Ashland, Calif. 204/K2
Ashland, Georgia 217/F2
Ashland, Ill. 222/C4
Ashland, Kansas 232/C4
Ashland, Ky. 237/R4
Ashland, Ky. 188/K3
Ashland, La. 238/D2
Ashland, Maine 243/G2
Ashland•, Maine 243/G2
Ashland•, Mass. 249/J3
Ashland, Miss. 256/F1
Ashland, Mo. 261/H5
Ashland, Mont. 262/K5
Ashland, Nebr. 264/H3
Ashland, N.H. 268/D4
Ashland•, N.H. 268/D4
Ashland, N.J. 273/B3
Ashland, N.Y. 276/M6
Ashland (co.), Ohio 284/F4
Ashland, Ohio 284/F4
Ashland, Okla. 288/O5
Ashland, Oreg. 291/E5
Ashland, Pa. 294/K4
Ashland, Va. 307/N5
Ashland (co.), Wis. 317/E3
Ashland, Wis. 317/E2
Ashland City, Tenn. 237/G8
Ashley (co.), Ark. 202/G7
Ashley, Ill. 222/D5
Ashley, Ind. 227/G1
Ashley, Mich. 250/E5
Ashley, Mo. 261/K4
Ashley (lake), Mont. 262/B2
Ashley, N.S. Wales 97/E1
Ashley, N. Dak. 282/M7
Ashley, Ohio 284/E5
Ashley, Pa. 294/E7
Ashley (riv.), S.C. 296/G6
Ashley, W. Va. 312/E4
Ashley Falls, Mass. 249/A4
Ashmere (lake), Mass. 249/B3
Ashmont, Alberta 182/E2
Ashmore, Ill. 222/F4
Ashmore, Nova Scotia 168/C4
Ashmore (isls.), Terr. of Ashmore and Cartier Is. 88/C2
Ashmore and Cartier Is., Terr. of, 88/C2
Ashokan, N.Y. 276/M7
Ashokan (res.), N.Y. 276/M7
Ashport, Tenn. 237/B9
Ashqelon, Israel 65/A4
Ash Shabicha, Iraq 66/C5
Ashtabula (lake), N. Dak. 282/P5
Ashtabula (co.), Ohio 284/J2
Ashtabula, Ohio 284/J2
Ashton, Idaho 220/G5
Ashton, Ill. 222/D2
Ashton, Iowa 229/B2
Ashton, Kansas 232/E4
Ashton, Mich. 250/D5
Ashton, Nebr. 264/F3
Ashton, R.I. 249/J5
Ashton, S.C. 296/E5
Ashton, S. Dak. 298/N3
Ashton, W. Va. 312/B5
Ashton Creek, Br. Col. 184/H5
Ashton-under-Lyne, England 13/H2
Ashton-under-Lyne, England 10/G2
Ashuanipi (lake), Newf. 166/A3
Ashuanipi (riv.), Newf. 166/A3
Ashuanpi, Newf. 166/A3
Ashuelot, N.H. 268/C6
Ashuelot (riv.), N.H. 268/C6
Ash Valley, Kansas 232/C3
Ashville, Ala. 195/F3
Ashville, Maine 243/G7
Ashville, Manitoba 179/B3
Ashville, Ohio 284/E6
Ashville, Pa. 294/F4
Ashwaubenon, Wis. 317/K7
Ashwood, Oreg. 291/G3
'Asi (Orontes) (riv.), Syria 63/G5
Asia 2/P3
Asia (isls.), Indonesia 85/J5
Asid (gulf), Philippines 82/D4
Asidonhoppo, Suriname 131/D4
Asilah, Morocco 106/C1
Asinara (gulf), Italy 34/B4
Asinara (isl.), Italy 34/B4
Asino, U.S.S.R. 48/J4
'Asir (reg.), Saudi Arabia 59/D6
Aşkale, Turkey 63/J3
Askeaton, Ireland 17/D6
Askew, Miss. 256/D1
Askewville, N.C. 281/R2
Askim, Norway 18/E4
Askim, Sweden 18/G8
Aski Mosul, Iraq 66/C2
Askival (mt.), Scotland 15/B4
Askov, Denmark 21/C7
Askov, Minn. 255/F4
Askvoll, Norway 18/D6
Asmara, Ethiopia 111/G4
Asmara, Ethiopia 59/C6
Asmara, Ethiopia 102/F3
Asnaes, Denmark 21/E6
Åsnen (lake), Sweden 18/J8
Asnières-sur-Seine, France 28/A1
Aso (mt.), Japan 81/E7
Aso National Park, Japan 81/E7
Asosa, Ethiopia 111/F5
Asoteriba, Jebel (mt.), Sudan 111/G3
Asotin (co.), Wash. 310/H4
Asotin, Wash. 310/H4
Asotin (creek), Wash. 310/H4
Asotin (dam), Wash. 310/J4
Aspang Markt, Austria 41/D3
Aspatria, England 13/D3
Aspe, Spain 33/F3
Aspelund, Minn. 255/F6
Aspen, Colo. 208/F4
Aspen, Nova Scotia 168/F3
Aspen (lake), Oreg. 291/E5
Aspen (mts.), Wyo. 319/C4
Aspen Grove, Br. Col. 184/G5
Aspen Hill, Md. 245/K4
Aspermont, Texas 303/D4
Aspers, Pa. 294/H6
Aspetuck, Conn. 210/B4
Aspetuck (res.), Conn. 210/B4
Aspetuck (riv.), Conn. 210/B3
Aspinwall, Iowa 229/C5
Aspinwall, Pa. 294/C6
Aspiring (mt.), N. Zealand 100/B6
Aspley, Queensland 88/K2
Aspy (bay), Nova Scotia 168/H2
Asquith, Sask. 181/D3
Assab, Ethiopia 59/D7
Assab, Ethiopia 111/H5
Assaba (reg.), Mauritania 106/B5
Assabet (riv.), Mass. 249/H3
Assad, Bahrat (lake), Syria 63/H4
Assakarai (dry riv.), Niger 106/F5
Assal (lake), Djibouti 110/H5
Assal (lake), Djibouti 114/H5
Assale (lake), Ethiopia 111/H5
As Salman, Iraq 59/E3
As Salman, Iraq 66/D5
Assam (state), India 68/G3
Assapan (riv.), Manitoba 179/G2
Assaria, Kansas 232/E3
Assateague Island Nat'l Seashore, Va. 307/T4
Assawompset (pond), Mass. 249/L5
Assay (creek), Utah 304/B6
Asse, Belgium 27/E7
Asselar (well), Mali 106/D5
Asselle, Ethiopia 102/F4
Asselle, Ethiopia 111/G6
Assen, Netherlands 27/K3
Assenede, Belgium 27/D6
Assens, Århus, Denmark 21/D4
Assens, Fyn, Denmark 21/D7
Assesse, Belgium 27/G8
Assigny (lake), Newf. 166/A3
Assiniboia, Sask. 181/E6
Assiniboine (mt.), Alberta 182/C4
Assiniboine (mt.), Br. Col. 184/K5
Assiniboine (riv.), Manitoba 179/C5
Assiniboine (riv.), Sask. 181/J3
Assinica (lake), Québec 174/C3
Assinika (lake), Manitoba 179/G2
Assinika (riv.), Manitoba 179/G2
Assinippi, Mass. 249/E8
Assis, Brazil 132/D8
Assis, Brazil 135/A3
Assisi, Italy 34/D3
Assonet, Mass. 249/K5
Assumption, Ill. 222/E4
Assumption (par.), La. 238/H7
Assumption, Ohio 284/B2
Assumption (isl.), Seychelles 118/H1
Assynt (dist.), Scotland 15/C2
Assynt, Loch (lake), Scotland 15/D2
Assyria, Mich. 250/D6
Astara, U.S.S.R. 52/G7
Astatula, Fla. 212/E3
Asten, Netherlands 27/H6
Asterabad (Gorgan), Iran 59/F2
Asterabad (Gorgan), Iran 66/J2
Asti, Calif. 204/C5
Asti (prov.), Italy 34/B2
Asti, Italy 34/B2
Astillero, Peru 128/H9
Astipálaia, Greece 45/H7
Astipálaia (isl.), Greece 45/H7
Astle, New Bruns. 170/D2
Aston (bay), N.W. Terr. 187/J2
Aston-Jonction, Québec 172/E3
Astor, Fla. 212/E2
Astorga, Spain 33/C1
Astoria, Ill. 222/C3
Astoria, Oreg. 188/B1
Astoria, Oreg. 291/D1
Astoria, S. Dak. 298/S4
Astorville, Ontario 177/E1
Astove (isl.), Seychelles 102/G6
Astove (isl.), Seychelles 118/H2
Astra, Argentina 143/C6
Astrakhan', U.S.S.R. 7/J4
Astrakhan', U.S.S.R. 52/G5
Astrakhan', U.S.S.R. 48/E5
Astray (lake), Newf. 166/A3
Astudillo, Spain 33/D1
Asturias (reg.), Spain 33/C1
Asunción, Bolivia 136/B2
Asuncion (isl.), No. Marianas 87/E4
Asunción, Paraguay 144/A4
Asunción (cap.), Paraguay 2/F7
Asunción (cap.), Paraguay 144/A4
Asunción (cap.), Paraguay 120/D5
Asuncion (passage), Philippines 82/D5
Asunción Mita, Guatemala 154/C3
Asunción Nochixtlán, Mexico 150/L8
Asunta, Bolivia 136/B5
Aswad, Ras al (cape), Saudi Arabia 59/C5
Aswân, Egypt 111/F3
Aswân, Egypt 59/B5
Aswân, Egypt 102/F2
Aswân (dam), Egypt 59/B5
Aswân (dam), Egypt 111/F3
Aswân High (dam), Egypt 102/F2
Aswân High (dam), Egypt 111/F3
Asyût, Egypt 111/J4
Asyût, Egypt 102/F2
Asyût, Egypt 59/B4
Aszód, Hungary 41/E3
Atabapo (riv.), Colombia 126/G6
Atabapo (riv.), Venezuela 124/E6
Atacama, Puna de (reg.), Argentina 143/C2
Atacama (reg.), Chile 138/B6
Atacama (des.), Chile 120/C5
Atacama (des.), Chile 138/B4
Atacama, Salar de (salt dep.), Chile 138/C4
Atafu (atoll), Tokelau Is. 87/J6
Atahona, Uruguay 145/B4
Atakora (mts.), Benin 106/E6
Atakpamé, Togo 106/E7
Atalándi, Greece 45/F6
Atalaya, Peru 128/E8
Atalissa, Iowa 229/L5
Atambua, Indonesia 85/G7
Atami, Japan 81/J6
Atapirire, Venezuela 124/F3
Atar, Mauritania 106/B4
Atar, Mauritania 102/A2
Ataran (riv.), Burma 72/C4
Atascadero, Calif. 204/E8
Atascosa (co.), Texas 303/F9
Atascosa, Texas 303/J11
Atbara (riv.), Ethiopia 111/G4
Atbara, Sudan 111/F4
Atbara, Sudan 59/B7
Atbara, Sudan 102/F3
Atbara (riv.), Sudan 59/C6
Atbara (riv.), Sudan 111/G4
Atbasar, U.S.S.R. 48/G4
Atchafalaya (bay), La. 238/H8
Atchafalaya (riv.), La. 238/G6
Atchison, Kans. 188/G3
Atchison (co.), Kansas 232/G2
Atchison, Kansas 232/G2
Atchison (co.), Mo. 261/B2
Atco, N.J. 273/D4
Ateca, Spain 33/F2
Atén, Bolivia 136/A4
Atenas, C. Rica 154/E6
Atessa, Italy 34/E3
Atglen, Pa. 294/K6
Ath, Belgium 27/D7
Athabasca (lake) 162/F4
Athabasca, Alberta 162/E5
Athabasca, Alberta 182/D2
Athabasca (lake), Alberta 182/C5
Athabasca (riv.), Alberta 182/D1
Athabasca (riv.), Alberta 162/E4
Athabasca (riv.), Alberta 146/G4
Athabasca (lake), Canada 146/H4
Athabasca (lake), Sask. 181/L2
Athalia, Ohio 284/F8
Athalmer, Br. Col. 184/K5
Athboy, Ireland 17/H4
Athea, Ireland 17/C7
Athelstan, Iowa 229/D7

Azerbaidzhan S.S.R., U.S.S.R. 52/G6
Azerbaijan, East (prov.), Iran 66/E1
Azerbaijan, West (prov.), Iran 66/D1
Azerbaijan (reg.), Iran 66/D1
Aziscoos (lake), Maine 243/A5
Azle, Texas 303/E2
Azogues, Ecuador 128/C4
AZORES 33
Azores (isls.), Portugal 2/H4
Azores (isls.), Portugal 33/A2
Azoum, Bahr, Chad 111/D5
Azov (sea), U.S.S.R. 7/H4
Azov, U.S.S.R. 52/E5
Azov (sea), U.S.S.R. 52/E5
Azov (sea), U.S.S.R. 48/D5
Azoyú, Mexico 150/K8
Azpeitia, Spain 33/E1
Azrou, Morocco 106/C2
Aztec, Ariz. 198/B6
Aztec, N. Mex. 274/B2
Aztec Ruins Nat'l Mon., N. Mex. 274/A2
Azua (prov.), Dom. Rep. 158/D6
Azua, Dom. Rep. 156/D3
Azua, Dom. Rep. 158/D6
Azuaga, Spain 33/D3
Azuara, Spain 33/F2
Azuay (prov.), Ecuador 128/C4
Azuero (pen.), Panama 154/G7
Azul, Argentina 143/E4
Azul, Argentina 120/D6
Azul (riv.), Guatemala 154/C2
Azul, Cordillera (mts.), Peru 128/E7
Azurduy, Bolivia 136/C6
Azure (lake), Br. Col. 184/G4
Azusa, Calif. 204/D10
Azwell, Wash. 310/F3
Azzel Mati, Sebkha (lake), Algeria 106/E3
Az Zubair, Iraq 66/E5

B

Ba, Fiji 86/P10
Baa, Indonesia 85/G8
Baaba (isl.), New Caled. 86/G4
Ba'albek, Lebanon 63/G5
Baan Baa, N.S. Wales 97/E2
Baar, Switzerland 39/F2
Baarle-Nassau, Netherlands 27/F6
Baarn, Netherlands 27/G4
Baatsagaan, Mongolia 77/E2
Baba, Ecuador 128/C3
Baba (cape), Turkey 63/D2
Baba (cape), Turkey 63/A3
Babadag, Romania 45/J3
Babadag, Turkey 63/C4
Babaeski, Turkey 63/B2
Babahoyo, Ecuador 128/C3
Babanusa, Sudan 111/E5
Babaomby (cape), Madagascar 102/C6
Babaomby (cape), Madagascar 118/H2
Babar (isl.), Indonesia 85/H7
Babar (isls.), Indonesia 85/H7
Babati, Tanzania 115/G4
Babayevo, U.S.S.R. 52/E3
Babb, Mont. 262/C2
Babbie, Ala. 195/F8
Babbitt, Minn. 255/G3
Babbitt, Nev. 266/C4
Babcock, Wis. 317/F7
Babel (isls.), Tasmania 99/E1
Bab el Mandeb (str.) 102/G3
Bab el Mandeb (str.), Djibouti 111/H5
Babelthuap (isl.), Belau 87/D5
Babia (riv.), Mexico 150/J2
Babil (heads), Iraq 66/D4
Babine (lake), Br. Col. 162/D5
Babine, Br. Col. 184/D2
Babine (lake), Br. Col. 184/E3
Babine (riv.), Br. Col. 184/D2
Babo, Indonesia 85/K7
Babol, Iran 54/G6
Babol, Iran 59/F2
Babol, Iran 66/H2
Babol Sar, Iran 66/H2
Baboquivari (mts.), Ariz. 198/D7
Baboua, Cent. Afr. Rep. 115/C2
Babson Park, Fla. 212/E4
Babuyan (isls.), Philippines 54/O8
Babuyan (chan.), Philippines 82/A3
Babuyan (isl.), Philippines 82/B2
Babuyan (isls.), Philippines 85/G2
Babuyan (isls.), Philippines 82/A2
Babylon (ruins), Iraq 66/D4
Babylon, N.Y. 276/O9
Baca (co.), Colo. 208/O8
Bacabal, Brazil 120/E3
Bacabal, Maranhão, Brazil 132/E4
Bacabal, Pará, Brazil 132/B4
Bacadéhuachi, Mexico 150/E2
Bacalar, Mexico 150/P7
Bacalar (lake), Mexico 150/P7
Bacan (isls.), Indonesia 85/H6
Bacanora, Mexico 150/E2
Bacarra, Philippines 82/C1
Bacău, Romania 7/G4
Bacău, Romania 45/H2
Baccalieu (isl.), Newf. 166/D2
Bac Can, Vietnam 72/E2
Baccaro (pt.), Nova Scotia 168/C5
Bacchus Marsh, Victoria 97/C5
Bacerac, Mexico 150/E1
Bac Giang, Vietnam 72/E2
Bach, Mich. 250/F5
Bachaquero, Venezuela 124/C3
Bache (pen.), N.W. Terr. 187/L2
Bache, Okla. 288/P5
Bachíniva, Mexico 150/F2
Bach Long Vi, Dao (isl.), Vietnam 72/F2
Bachu (Maralwexi), China 77/A4
Back (bay), India 68/B7
Back (riv.), Md. 245/N4
Back (lake), N.H. 268/E1
Back (riv.), N.W.T. 146/H3
Back (riv.), N.W.T. 162/G2
Back (riv.), N.W. Terr. 187/J3
Back (bay), Va. 307/S7
Back (creek), Va. 307/J4
Bačka Topola, Yugoslavia 45/D3
Back Bay, New Bruns. 170/D3
Backbone (mt.), Md. 245/A3
Backnang, Germany 22/C4
Backoo, N. Dak. 282/P2
Backus, Minn. 255/D4
Backway, The (inlet), Newf. 166/C3
Bac Lieu, Vietnam 72/E5
Bacliff, Texas 303/K2
Bac Ninh, Vietnam 72/E2
Baco (mt.), Philippines 82/C4
Bacolod, Philippines 85/G3
Bacolod, Philippines 54/O8
Bacolod, Philippines 82/D5
Bacon (co.), Georgia 217/G7
Bacone, Okla. 288/R3
Bacon Ridge (mts.), Wyo. 319/B2
Bacons, Del. 245/R6
Baconton, Georgia 217/D8
Bácsalmás, Hungary 41/E3
Bács-Kiskun (co.), Hungary 41/E3
Bácum, Mexico 150/D3
Bacuna, Neth. Ant. 161/E8
Bacup, England 13/H1
Bacup, England 10/G1
Bad (riv.), Mich. 250/E5
Bad (hills), Sask. 181/C4
Bad (lake), Sask. 181/C4
Bad (riv.), S. Dak. 298/G5
Badacsonytomaj, Hungary 41/D3
Badagara, India 68/D6
Bad Aibling, Germany 22/D5
Badajoz (prov.), Spain 33/C3
Badajoz, Spain 33/C3
Badalona, Spain 33/H2
Bad Aussee, Austria 41/B3
Bad Axe, Mich. 250/G5
Bad Berleburg, Germany 22/C3
Bad Berneck, Germany 22/D3
Bad Bramstedt, Germany 22/C2
Bad Brückenau, Germany 22/C3
Baddeck, Nova Scotia 168/H2
Baddeck (riv.), Nova Scotia 168/H2
Bad Doberan, Germany 22/D1
Bad Driburg, Germany 22/C3
Bad Dürkheim, Germany 22/C4
Bad Dürrenberg, Germany 22/D3
Bad Ems, Germany 22/B3
Baden, Austria 41/D2
Baden, Manitoba 179/A2
Baden, Md. 245/M6
Baden, Ontario 177/D4
Baden, Pa. 294/B4
Baden, Switzerland 39/F2
Ba Den, Nui (mt.), Vietnam 72/E5
Baden-Baden, Germany 22/C4
Badenoch (dist.), Scotland 15/D4
Badenweiler, Germany 22/B5
Baden-Württemberg (state), Germany 22/C4
Bad Freienwalde, Germany 22/F2
Bad Gandersheim, Germany 22/D3
Badgastein, Austria 41/B3
Badger (peak), Idaho 220/E7
Badger, Iowa 229/E3
Badger, Minn. 255/B2
Badger, Newf. 166/C4
Badger (creek), Oreg. 291/H3
Badger, S. Dak. 298/P5
Badger (creek), Wyo. 319/E2
Badger's Quay, Newf. 166/D4
Bad Goisern, Austria 41/B3
Badham, S.C. 296/F5
Bad Harzburg, Germany 22/D3
Bad Hersfeld, Germany 22/C3
Badhoevedorp, Netherlands 27/B5
Bad Hofgastein, Austria 41/B3
Bad Homburg vor der Höhe, Germany 22/C3
Bad Honnef, Germany 22/B3
Badian, Philippines 82/D6
Badin, N.C. 281/J4
Badin, Pakistan 68/B4
Badiraguato, Mexico 150/F4
Bad Ischl, Austria 41/B3
Bad Kissingen, Germany 22/D3
Bad Kreuznach, Germany 22/B4
Bad Land (cliffs), Utah 304/D4
Bad Lands (reg.), N. Dak. 282/C7
Badlands Nat'l Park, S. Dak. 298/E6
Bad Langensalza, Germany 22/D3
Bad Lauterberg im Harz, Germany 22/D3
Bad Leonfelden, Austria 41/C2
Bad Liebenwerda, Germany 22/E3
Bad Lippspringe, Germany 22/C3
Bad Mergentheim, Germany 22/C4
Bad Münster-Ebernburg, Germany 22/B4
Bad Münstereifel, Germany 22/B3
Bad Muskau, Germany 22/F3
Bad Nauheim, Germany 22/C3
Bad Neuenahr-Ahrweiler, Germany 22/B3
Bad Neustadt an der Saale, Germany 22/D3
Bado, Mo. 261/H8
Bad Oldesloe, Germany 22/D2
Ba Don, Vietnam 72/E3
Bad Orb, Germany 22/C3
Bad Pyrmont, Germany 22/C3
Badr, Saudi Arabia 59/C5
Badra, Iraq 66/D4
Bad Ragaz, Switzerland 39/H2
Bad Reichenhall, Germany 22/E5
Bad River Ind. Res., Wis. 317/E2
Bad Sachsa, Germany 22/D3
Bad Salzschlirf, Germany 22/C3
Bad Salzuflen, Germany 22/C2
Bad Salzungen, Germany 22/C3
Bad Sankt-Leonhard im Lavanttal, Austria 41/C3
Bad Schwartau, Germany 22/D2
Bad Segeberg, Germany 22/D2
Bad Tölz, Germany 22/D5
Baduen, Somalia 115/J2
Badulla, Sri Lanka 68/E7
Bad Vilbel, Germany 22/C3
Bad Waldsee, Germany 22/C5
Badwater (creek), Wyo. 319/E2
Bad Wildungen, Germany 22/C3
Bad Wimpfen, Germany 22/C4
Baelum, Denmark 21/D4
Baena, Spain 33/D4
Baerle-Hertog, Belgium 27/F6
Báez, Cuba 158/E2
Baeza, Ecuador 128/D3
Baeza, Spain 33/E4
Bafa (lake), Turkey 63/B4
Baffin (bay) 4/B13
Baffin (bay) 146/M2
Baffin (bay), Canada 2/F2
Baffin (isl.), Canada 2/F2
Baffin (isl.), Canada 4/C13
Baffin (bay), N.W.T. 162/J1
Baffin (bay), N.W.T. 187/M2
Baffin (isl.), N.W.T. 146/L2
Baffin (isl.), N.W.T. 162/J1
Baffin (isl.), N.W.T. 187/L2
Baffin (reg.), N.W.T. 186/J2
Baffin (bay), Texas 303/G10
Bafia, Cameroon 115/B3
Bafing (riv.), Guinea 106/B6
Bafing (riv.), Mali 106/B6
Bafoulabé, Mali 106/B6
Bafoussam, Cameroon 115/B2
Bafq, Iran 59/G3
Bafq, Iran 66/J5
Bafra, Turkey 59/C1
Bafra, Turkey 63/F2
Bafra (cape), Turkey 59/C1
Bafra (cape), Turkey 63/G2
Baft, Iran 66/K6
Baft, Iran 59/G4
Baga, Nigeria 106/G6
Bagabag, Philippines 82/C2
Bagac, Philippines 82/C3
Bagaces, C. Rica 154/E5
Bagadó, Colombia 126/B5
Bagalkot, India 68/D5
Bagam (well), Niger 106/F5
Bagamoyo, Tanzania 115/G5
Baganga, Philippines 82/F7
Baganian (pen.), Philippines 82/D7
Bagansiapiapi, Indonesia 85/C5
Bagata, Zaire 115/C4
Bagdad, Ariz. 198/B4
Bagdad, Fla. 212/B6
Bagdad, Ky. 237/L4
Bagdad, Tasmania 99/D4
Bagdarin, U.S.S.R. 48/M4
Bagé, Brazil 120/D6
Bagé, Brazil 132/C10
Bagenalstown, Ireland 10/C4
Bagenalstown (Muinebeag), Ireland 17/H6
Bagenkop, Denmark 21/D8
Baggs, Wyo. 319/E4
Baghbaghu, Iran 66/M3
Baghdad (heads), Iraq 66/D4
Baghdad (cap.), Iraq 59/E3
Baghdad (cap.), Iraq 54/F6
Baghdad (cap.), Iraq 2/M4
Baghdad (cap.), Iraq 66/D4
Bagheria, Italy 34/D5
Baghlan, Afghanistan 54/H6
Baghlan, Afghanistan 59/J2
Baghlan, Afghanistan 68/B1
Baghu, Iran 66/K7
Bağirpaşa Daği (mt.), Turkey 59/D2
Bağirpaşa Daği (mt.), Turkey 63/J3
Bagley, Iowa 229/E5
Bagley, Minn. 255/C3
Bagley, N.C. 281/N3
Bagley, Wis. 317/D10
Bagnell, Mo. 261/G6
Bagnell (dam), Mo. 261/G6
Bagnères-de-Bigorre, France 28/D6
Bagnères-de-Luchon, France 28/D6
Bagnolet, France 28/B2
Bagnols-sur-Cèze, France 28/F5
Bågø (isl.), Denmark 21/C7
Bago, Philippines 82/D5
Bagoé (riv.), Ivory Coast 106/C6
Bagoé (riv.), Mali 106/C6
Bagot, Manitoba 179/D5
Bagot (co.), Québec 172/E4
Bagrax (Bosten Hu) (lake), China 77/C3
Bagua, Peru 128/C5
Báguanos, Cuba 158/J3
Baguio, Philippines 54/N8
Baguio, Philippines 85/G2
Baguio, Philippines 82/C2
Baguirmi (reg.), Chad 111/C5
Bagwell, Texas 303/J4
Bahama, N.C. 281/M2
Bahamas 2/F4
Bahamas 146/L7
BAHAMAS 156/C1
Bahariya (oasis), Egypt 111/E2
Bahariya (oasis), Egypt 59/A4
Bahawalnagar, Pakistan 68/C2
Bahawalpur, Pakistan 54/J7
Bahawalpur, Pakistan 68/C3
Bahawalpur, Pakistan 59/K4
Bahçe, Turkey 63/G4
Bahçesaray, Turkey 63/K3
Bahia (state), Brazil 132/F6
Bahia (Salvador), Brazil 132/G6
Bahía (isls.), Honduras 154/D2
Bahía Blanca, Argentina 2/F7
Bahía Blanca, Argentina 143/D4
Bahía Blanca, Argentina 120/C6
Bahía Bustamante, Argentina 143/C6
Bahía de Caráquez, Ecuador 128/B3
Bahía Honda, Cuba 158/B1
Bahía Kino, Mexico 150/C2
Bahía San Blas, Argentina 143/D5
Bahía Thetis, Argentina 143/C7
Bahía Tortugas, Mexico 150/B3
Bahir Dar, Ethiopia 111/G5
Bahomamey, P. Rico 161/A1
Bahoruco (prov.), Dom. Rep. 158/D6
Bahoruco, Sierra de (mts.), Dom. Rep. 158/D6
Bahraich, India 68/E3
Bahrain 54/G7
BAHRAIN 59/F4
Bahramabad (Rafsanjan), Iran 66/K5
Bahr Azoum (riv.), Sudan 111/D5
Bahr el 'Arab (riv.), Sudan 111/E6
Bahr el Ghazal (dry riv.), Chad 111/C5
Bahr El Ghazal (prov.), Sudan 111/E6
Bahr es Safi (des.), Saudi Arabia 59/E6
Bahr ez Zeraf (riv.), Sudan 111/F6
Bahr Yusef (stream), Egypt 111/J4
Baia de Aramă, Romania 45/F3
Baía dos Tigres, Angola 115/B7
Baia Farta, Angola 115/B6
Baia Mare, Romania 45/F2
Baião, Brazil 132/D3
Baibiene, Argentina 143/E2
Baibokoum, Chad 111/C6
Bai Bung, Mui (Ca Mau) (pt.), Vietnam 72/E5
Baicheng (Bay), Xinjiang Uygur, China 7/B3
Baicheng, Jilin, China 77/K2
Baida, Libya 102/E1
Baida, Libya 111/D1
Baidyabati, India 68/F1
Baie-Comeau, Québec 172/A1
Baie-Comeau, Québec 174/D3
Baie de Henne, Haiti 158/B5
Baie-des-Bacons, Québec 172/H1
Baie-des-Moutons, Québec 174/F2
Baie-des-Rochers, Québec 172/H2
Baie-des-Sables, Québec 172/A1
Baie-du-Poste, Québec 174/C2
Baie-d'Urfé, Québec 172/G4
Baie-du-Vieux-Fort, Québec 174/F2
Baie-Johan-Beetz, Québec 174/E2
Baie-Mahault, Guadeloupe 161/A6
Baiersbronn, Germany 22/C4
Baie-Sainte-Anne, New Bruns. 170/F1
Baie-Sainte-Catherine, Québec 172/H1
Baie-Saint-Paul, Que. 162/J6
Baie-Saint-Paul, Québec 174/C3
Baie-Saint-Paul, Québec 172/G2
Baie-Trinité, Québec 172/B1
Baie Verte, Newf. 166/C4
Baie-Verte, New Bruns. 170/F2
Baieville, Québec 172/E3
Baigorrita, Argentina 143/F7
Baiji, Iraq 66/C3
Baildon, Sask. 181/F5
Baile Átha Cliath (Dublin) (cap.), Ireland 17/K5
Baile Átha Cliath (Dublin) (cap.), Ireland 10/C4
Băile Herculane, Romania 45/F3
Bailén, Spain 33/E3
Băileşti, Romania 45/F3
Bailey, Colo. 208/H4
Bailey, Iowa 229/H2
Bailey, Mich. 250/D5
Bailey, Miss. 256/G6
Bailey, N.C. 281/N3
Bailey (co.), Texas 303/B3
Baileyboro, Texas 303/B3
Bailey Island, Maine 243/D8
Bailey Lakes, Ohio 284/F4
Bailey's Crossroads, Va. 307/S3
Baileys Harbor, Wis. 317/M5
Baileyton, Ala. 195/E2
Baileyton, Tenn. 237/R8
Baileyville, Conn. 210/E2
Baileyville, Ill. 222/D1
Baileyville, Kansas 232/F2
Bailieborough, Ireland 17/G4
Bailique (isl.), Brazil 132/D2
Baillivanish, Scotland 15/A3
Baillie (isls.), N.W. Terr. 187/F2
Baillieston, Scotland 15/B2
Baillif, Guadeloupe 161/A7
Bailundo, Angola 115/C6
Baima, China 77/E5
Bainbridge (isl.), Alaska 196/C1
Bainbridge, Georgia 217/C9
Bainbridge, Ind. 227/D5
Bainbridge, N.Y. 276/J6
Bainbridge (dist.), N. Ireland 17/J3
Bainbridge, Ohio 284/D7
Bainbridge, Pa. 294/J5
Bainbridge (isl.), Wash. 310/A2
Bainbridge Island-Winslow (Winslow), Wash. 310/A2
Bainbridge N.T.C., Md. 245/O2
Bainet, Haiti 158/B6
Baingoin, China 77/D5
Bains, La. 238/H5
Bainville, Mont. 262/M2
Baird (inlet), Alaska 196/F2
Baird (mts.), Alaska 196/F1
Baird, Miss. 256/C4
Baird (pen.), N.W. Terr. 187/L3
Baird, Texas 303/E5
Bairdstown, Ohio 284/C3
Bairdsville, New Bruns. 170/C2
Baire, Cuba 158/H4
Bairiki (cap.), Kiribati 87/H5
Bairin Zuoqi, China 77/J3
Bairnsdale, Victoria 88/H7
Bairnsdale, Victoria 97/D5
Bairoil, Wyo. 319/E3
Bais, Philippines 82/D6
Baisden, W. Va. 312/C7
Baïse (riv.), France 28/D6
Baisha, China 77/G8
Baitadi, Nepal 68/E3
Bait al Faqih, Yemen 59/D7
Bai Thuong, Vietnam 72/E3
Baixa da Banheira, Portugal 33/B3
Baixoaixo (isl.), Portugal 33/B2
Baixo Guandu, Brazil 132/F7
Baja, Hungary 41/E3
Baja California (state), Mexico 150/B1
Baja California Sur (state), Mexico 150/C3
Bajadero, P. Rico 161/C1
Bajgiran, Iran 66/L2
Bajo Boquete, Panama 154/F6
Bajo Nuevo (shoal), Colombia 126/C8
Bajos de Haina, Dom. Rep. 158/E6
Bajram Curri, Albania 45/D4
Bakala, Cent. Afr. Rep. 115/D2
Bakar, Yugoslavia 45/B3
Bakel, Senegal 106/B6
Baker (isl.), Alaska 196/M2
Baker, Calif. 204/J8
Baker (riv.), Chile 138/D7
Baker (mt.), Colo. 208/H2
Baker (co.), Fla. 212/D1
Baker, Fla. 212/C5
Baker (co.), Georgia 217/D8
Baker, Idaho 220/E4
Baker, La. 238/K1
Baker (lake), Maine 243/D3
Baker, Minn. 255/B4
Baker, Mo. 261/N9
Baker, Mont. 262/M4
Baker, Nev. 266/G3
Baker (riv.), N.H. 268/D4
Baker, N. Dak. 282/L3
Baker (lake), N.W. Terr. 187/J3
Baker, Okla. 288/D1
Baker, Oreg. 188/C2
Baker (co.), Oreg. 291/K3
Baker, Oreg. 291/K3
Baker (isl.), Pacific 87/J5
Baker (creek), Utah 304/A4
Baker (lake), Wash. 310/D2
Baker (mt.), Wash. 310/D2
Baker (riv.), Wash. 310/D2
Baker, W. Va. 312/J4
Baker Brook, New Bruns. 170/B1
Baker Butte (mt.), Ariz. 198/D4
Baker Hill, Ala. 195/H7
Baker Lake, N.W.T. 162/G3
Baker Lake, N.W. Terr. 187/J3
Bakers (isl.), Mass. 249/F5
Bakersfield, Calif. 146/G6
Bakersfield, Calif. 188/C3
Bakersfield, Calif. 204/G8
Bakersfield, Mo. 261/H9
Bakersfield, Texas 303/B7
Bakersfield •, Vt. 268/B2
Bakers Summit, Pa. 294/F5
Bakersville, Conn. 210/C1
Bakersville, N.C. 281/E2
Bakersville, Ohio 284/G5
Bakersville, Pa. 294/D5
Bakerton, Ky. 237/L7
Bakerton, W. Va. 312/L4
Bakerville, Tenn. 237/F9
Bakewell, England 10/G2
Bakewell, England 13/J2
Bakewell, Tenn. 237/L10
Bakharz, Kuhha-ye (mt.), Iran 66/M3
Bakhchisaray, U.S.S.R. 52/D6
Bakhmach, U.S.S.R. 52/D4
Bakhtaran (prov.), Iran 54/F6
Bakhtaran (prov.), Iran 58/E3
Bakhtaran (prov.), Iran 66/E3
Bakhtaran, Iran 54/F6
Bakhtaran, Iran 58/E3
Bakhtaran, Iran 66/E3
Bakhtegan (lake), Iran 66/J6
Bakhtiari (gov.), Iran 66/F4
Bakhun, Kuh-e (mt.), Iran 66/K6
Bakhuys (mts.), Suriname 131/C3
Bakia, Cent. Afr. Rep. 115/E2
Bakırköy, Turkey 63/D6
Baklan, Turkey 63/C4
Bako, Ethiopia 111/G6
Bakony (mts.), Hungary 41/D3
Bakool (prov.), Somalia 115/H3
Bakouma, Cent. Afr. Rep. 115/D2
Bakoy (riv.), Guinea 106/B6
Bakoy (riv.), Mali 106/B6
Bakraband, Kuh-e (mts.), Iran 66/M7
Baktalórántháza, Hungary 41/G2
Baktu (Paektu) (mt.), N. Korea 81/C3
Baku, U.S.S.R. 2/M3
Baku, U.S.S.R. 7/J4
Baku, U.S.S.R. 48/F5
Baku, U.S.S.R. 52/H6
Bala, Kansas 232/F2
Bala, Ontario 177/E2
Balâ, Turkey 63/E3
Bala, Wales 13/D5
Bala, Wales 10/E4
Balabac, Philippines 82/A7
Balabac (isl.), Philippines 85/F4
Balabac (isl.), Philippines 82/A7
Balabac (str.), Philippines 85/F4
Balabac (str.), Philippines 82/A7
Balabalagan (isls.), Indonesia 85/F6
Balabio (isl.), New Caled. 86/G4
Balaclava, Jamaica 158/H6
Bala-Cynwyd, Pa. 294/N6
Balad, Somalia 115/J3
Balaghat, India 68/E4
Balaguer, Spain 33/G2
Balaïtous (mt.), Spain 33/F1
Balakai (mesa), Ariz. 198/F3
Balakhna, U.S.S.R. 52/F3
Balaklava, S. Australia 94/F6
Balaklava, U.S.S.R. 52/D6
Balakovo, U.S.S.R. 7/J3
Balakovo, U.S.S.R. 48/E4
Balakovo, U.S.S.R. 52/G4
Balallan, Scotland 15/B2
Bal'ama, Jordan 65/E3
Balambangan (isl.), Malaysia 85/F4
Balancán de Domínguez, Mexico 150/O8
Balandra (pt.), Dom. Rep. 158/F5
Balanga, Philippines 82/C3
Balangala, Zaire 115/D3
Ba Lang An, Mui (cape), Vietnam 72/F4
Balangiga, Philippines 82/E5
Balao, Ecuador 128/C4
Balashi, Neth. Ant. 161/E10
Balashov, U.S.S.R. 7/J3
Balashov, U.S.S.R. 52/F4
Balashov, U.S.S.R. 48/E4
Balasore, India 68/F4
Balassagyarmat, Hungary 41/E2
Balaton (lake), Hungary 7/F4
Balaton (lake), Hungary 41/D3
Balaton, Minn. 255/C6
Balatonfüred, Hungary 41/D3
Balatonszentgyörgy, Hungary 41/D3
Balayan (bay), Philippines 82/C4
Balbi (mt.), Papua N.G. 86/C2
Balboa, Panama 154/H6
Balbriggan, Ireland 17/J4
Balbriggan, Ireland 10/C4
Balcarce, Argentina 143/E4
Balcarres, Sask. 181/H5
Balchik, Bulgaria 45/H4
Balch Springs, Texas 303/H2
Balclutha, N. Zealand 100/B7
Balcones Escarpment (plat.), Texas 303/E8
Balcones Heights, Texas 303/J10
Bald (mt.), Colo. 208/H4
Bald (hill), Conn. 210/G1
Bald (mt.), Idaho 220/D5
Bald (mt.), New Bruns. 170/C1
Bald (mts.), N.C. 281/D3
Bald (mts.), Tenn. 237/R9
Bald (mt.), Utah 304/C3
Bald (mt.), Vt. 268/D2
Bald (head), W. Australia 88/B7
Bald (head), W. Australia 92/B6
Bald Eagle (lake), Minn. 255/G3
Baldeggersee (lake), Switzerland 39/F2
Baldhill (Ashtabula) (res.), N. Dak. 282/P5
Bald Hill Branch (riv.), Md. 245/G4
Bald Hills, Queensland 88/K2
Bald Knob, Ark. 202/G3
Bald Knob, W. Va. 312/C7
Baldonnel, Br. Col. 184/G2
Baldur, Manitoba 179/C5
Baldwin (co.), Ala. 195/C9
Baldwin, Fla. 212/E1
Baldwin (co.), Georgia 217/F4
Baldwin, Georgia 217/E2
Baldwin, Ill. 222/D5
Baldwin, Iowa 229/M4
Baldwin, La. 238/H7
Baldwin, Mich. 250/D5
Baldwin, N.Y. 276/R7
Baldwin, N. Dak. 282/J5
Baldwin, Pa. 294/B7
Baldwin, W. Va. 312/E5
Baldwin, Wis. 317/B6
Baldwin City, Kansas 232/G3
Baldwin Park, Calif. 204/D10
Baldwinsville, N.Y. 276/H4
Baldwinton, Sask. 181/B3
Baldwinville, Mass. 249/F2
Baldwyn, Miss. 256/G2
Baldy (peak), Ariz. 198/F5
Baldy (mt.), Manitoba 179/B3
Baldy (peak), N. Mex. 274/D3
Baldy (peak), Utah 304/B5
Bale (prov.), Ethiopia 111/H6
Bale (mt.), Ethiopia 111/G6
Baleares (prov.), Spain 33/H3
Balearic (isls.), Spain 7/E5
Balearic (Baleares) (isls.), Spain 33/H3
Baleine (riv.), Québec 174/D1
Baleine, Grande R. de la (riv.), Que. 162/J4
Baleine, Grand Rivière de la (riv.), Québec 174/B1
Baleine, Petite Rivière de la (riv.), Québec 174/B1
Baleine, R. à la (riv.), Que. 162/K4
Balen, Belgium 27/G6
Baler, Philippines 82/C3
Baler (bay), Philippines 82/C3
Balerna, Switzerland 39/G5
Balerno, Scotland 15/D2
Baleshare (isl.), Scotland 15/A3
Balestrand, Norway 18/E6
Baley, U.S.S.R. 48/M4
Balfate, Honduras 154/D3
Balfour, Br. Col. 184/J5
Balfour, N.C. 281/E4
Balfour, N. Dak. 282/J4
Balfron, Scotland 15/B1
Balgonie, Sask. 181/G5
Balhaf, Yemen 59/E7
Bal Harbour, Fla. 212/C4
Bali, Cameroon 115/A2
Bali (isl.), Indonesia 54/N10
Bali (isl.), Indonesia 85/F7
Bali (sea), Indonesia 85/F7
Bali (str.), Indonesia 85/E7
Baliangao, Philippines 82/D6
Balicuatro (isls.), Philippines 82/E4
Balige, Indonesia 85/B5
Balıkesir (prov.), Turkey 63/B3
Balıkesir, Turkey 63/B3
Balıkesir, Turkey 59/A2
Balikpapan, Indonesia 54/N10
Balikpapan, Indonesia 85/F6
Balık-Uzun (lake), Turkey 63/G2
Balimbing (Bato-Bato), Philippines 82/C8
Baling, Malaysia 72/D6
Balingasag, Philippines 82/E6
Balingen, Germany 22/C4
Balintang (chan.), Philippines 82/A2
Balintang (isls.), Philippines 82/A2
Baljennie, Sask. 181/C3
Balk, Netherlands 27/H3
Balkan (mts.) 7/G4
Balkan (mts.), Bulgaria 45/G4
Balkan, Ky. 237/O7
Balkány, Hungary 41/G3
Balkbrug, Netherlands 27/J3
Balkh, Afghanistan 68/B1
Balkh, Afghanistan 59/J2
Balkhash, U.S.S.R. 48/H5
Balkhash, U.S.S.R. 54/J5
Balkhash (lake), U.S.S.R. 2/N3
Balkhash (lake), U.S.S.R. 48/H5
Balkhash (lake), U.S.S.R. 54/J5
Balko, Okla. 288/E1
Ball (mt.), Conn. 210/C1
Ball (pond), Conn. 210/A3

334 Ball

Ball, La. 238/F4
Ball (bay), Norfolk I. 88/L6
Balla, Ireland 17/C4
Balladonia, W. Australia 92/D6
Ballaghaderreen, Ireland 17/E4
Ballaigues, Switzerland 39/B3
Ballantine, Mont. 262/J5
Ballantrae, Scotland 15/C5
Ballantyne (str.), N.W. Terr. 187/G2
Ballarat, Australia 87/E9
Ballarat, Victoria 88/G7
Ballarat, Victoria 97/C5
Ballard (co.), Ky. 237/C6
Ballard, Mo. 261/D6
Ballard (cape), Newf. 166/D2
Ballard (lake), W. Australia 88/B5
Ballard, W. Va. 312/E8
Ballardsville, Miss. 256/H2
Ballardvale, Mass. 249/K2
Ballater, Scotland 10/E2
Ballater, Scotland 15/F3
Ball Club, Minn. 255/E3
Ballenas (bay), Mexico 150/C3
Ballenero (chan.), Chile 138/E11
Ballengee, W. Va. 312/E7
Ballens, Switzerland 39/B3
Ballenstedt, Germany 22/D3
Ballentine, S.C. 296/E3
Balleny (isls.), Ant. 2/S9
Balleny (isls.), Ant. 5/C9
Ballerup, Denmark 21/F6
Ballesteros, Philippines 82/C1
Balleza, Mexico 150/F3
Ball Ground, Georgia 217/D2
Ballground, Miss. 256/C5
Ballia, India 68/E3
Ballidu, W. Australia 92/B5
Ballina, Mayo, Ireland 17/C3
Ballina, Tipperary, Ireland 17/E6
Ballina, Ireland 10/B3
Ballina, N.S. Wales 97/G1
Ballinagh, Ireland 17/G4
Ballinakill, Ireland 17/G6
Ballinamore, Ireland 17/F3
Ballinasloe, Ireland 10/B4
Ballinasloe, Ireland 17/E5
Ballincollig-Carrigrohane, Ireland 17/D8
Ballindine, Ireland 17/C4
Ballineen, Ireland 17/D8
Ballingarry, Limerick, Ireland 17/D7
Ballingarry, Tipperary, Ireland 17/F6
Ballinger, Texas 303/E6
Ballingry, Scotland 15/D1
Ballinlough, Ireland 17/D4
Ballinluig, Scotland 15/E4
Ballinrobe, Ireland 10/B4
Ballinrobe, Ireland 17/C4
Ballinskelligs (bay), Ireland 17/A8
Ballintober, Ireland 17/E4
Ballintra, Ireland 17/E2
Ballisodare, Ireland 17/E3
Ballivor, Ireland 17/H4
Balloch, Highland, Scotland 15/D3
Balloch, Strathclyde, Scotland 15/B1
Ballouville, Conn. 210/H1
Ballston, Oreg. 291/D2
Ballston Spa, N.Y. 276/N5
Ballsville, Va. 307/M6
Balltown, Iowa 229/M3
Ballville, Ohio 284/D3
Ballwin, Mo. 261/N3
Bally, India 68/F1
Bally, Pa. 294/L5
Ballybay, Ireland 17/G3
Ballybofey-Stranorlar, Ireland 17/F2
Ballybunion, Ireland 10/B4
Ballybunion, Ireland 17/B7
Ballycanew, Ireland 17/J6
Ballycarney, Ireland 17/J6
Ballycarry, N. Ireland 17/K2
Ballycastle, Ireland 17/C3
Ballycastle, N. Ireland 10/C3
Ballycastle, N. Ireland 17/J1
Ballyclare, N. Ireland 17/J2
Ballyconnell, Ireland 17/F3
Ballycotton, Ireland 17/F8
Ballycotton (bay), Ireland 17/F8
Ballydehob, Ireland 17/C8
Ballyduff, Ireland 17/B7
Ballygally, N. Ireland 17/K2
Ballygar, Ireland 17/E4
Ballygawley, N. Ireland 17/G3
Ballygeary, Ireland 17/J7
Ballygrant, Scotland 15/B5
Ballyhaise, Ireland 17/G3
Ballyhaunis, Ireland 17/D4
Ballyheige (bay), Ireland 17/B7
Ballyheigue, Ireland 17/B7
Ballyhoura (hills), Ireland 17/E7
Ballyjamesduff, Ireland 17/G4
Ballykelly, N. Ireland 17/G1
Ballylanders, Ireland 17/E7
Ballylongford, Ireland 17/B6
Ballymahon, Ireland 17/F4
Ballymakeery, Ireland 17/C8
Ballymena (dist.), N. Ireland 17/J2
Ballymena, N. Ireland 17/J2
Ballymena, N. Ireland 10/C3
Ballymoney (dist.), N. Ireland 17/J1
Ballymoney, N. Ireland 10/C3
Ballymoney, N. Ireland 17/J1
Ballymore, Ireland 17/F5
Ballymore Eustace, Ireland 17/J5
Ballymote, Ireland 17/D3
Ballymote, Ireland 10/B3
Ballynahinch, N. Ireland 17/J3
Ballynakill (harb.), Ireland 17/A4
Ballyporeen, Ireland 17/E7
Ballyragget, Ireland 17/G6
Ballyroan, Ireland 17/G6
Ballysadare (bay), Ireland 17/D3
Ballyshannon, Ireland 10/B3
Ballyshannon, Ireland 17/E3
Ballyteige (bay), Ireland 17/H7
Ballytore, Ireland 17/H5
Ballywalter, N. Ireland 17/K2
Balmaceda, Chile 138/E6
Balmat, N.Y. 276/K2
Balmazújváros, Hungary 41/F3
Balmertown, Ontario 175/B2
Balmhorn (mt.), Switzerland 39/E4
Balmoral, Manitoba 179/E4
Balmoral, New Bruns. 170/D1
Balmoral, Queensland 88/K2
Balmoral, Queensland 95/E2
Balmoral, Victoria 97/A5
Balmoral Castle, Scotland 10/E2
Balmoral Castle, Scotland 15/E3
Balmorhea, Texas 303/D11
Balmville, N.Y. 276/M7
Balnearia, Argentina 143/D3
Balneario El Tesoro, Uruguay 145/E5
Balneario La Barra, Uruguay 145/E5
Balneario Solís, Uruguay 145/D5
Balombo, Angola 115/B6
Balonne (riv.), Queensland 88/H5
Balonne (riv.), Queensland 95/D6
Balotra, India 68/C3
Baloy (mt.), Philippines 82/D5
Balpunga, N.S. Wales 97/A3
Balrampur, India 68/E3
Balranald, N. S. Wales 88/G6
Balranald, N.S. Wales 97/B4
Balş, Romania 45/G3
Balsam, N.C. 281/C4
Balsam (lake), Ontario 177/F3
Balsam Creek, Ontario 177/E1
Balsam Lake, Wis. 317/B5
Balsapuerto, Peru 128/D5
Balsas, Brazil 120/E3
Balsas, Brazil 132/E4
Balsas (riv.), Brazil 132/E5
Balsas (riv.), Mexico 146/H8
Balsas (riv.), Mexico 150/J7
Bålsta, Sweden 18/G1
Balsthal, Switzerland 39/E2
Balta, N. Dak. 282/K3
Baltanás, Spain 33/D2
Baltasar Brum, Uruguay 145/B1
Baltasound, Scotland 15/G2
Baltic (sea) 2/K3
Baltic (sea) 7/F3
Baltic, Conn. 210/G2
Baltic (sea), Denmark 21/E9
Baltic (sea), Finland 18/K9
Baltic (sea), Germany 22/E1
Baltic, Mich. 250/G1
Baltic, Ohio 284/G5
Baltic (sea), Poland 47/B1
Baltic, S. Dak. 298/R6
Baltic (sea), Sweden 18/K9
Baltic (sea), U.S.S.R. 52/B3
Baltic (sea), U.S.S.R. 48/B4
Baltimore, Ireland 10/B5
Baltimore, Ireland 17/C9
Baltimore (city county), Md. 245/M3
Baltimore (co.), Md. 245/M3
Baltimore, Md. 245/M3
Baltimore, Md. 188/L3
Baltimore, Md. 146/L6
Baltimore, Ohio 284/E6
Baltimore, Ontario 177/F3
Baltinglass, Ireland 17/H6
Baltistan (reg.), Pakistan 68/D1
Baltit, Pakistan 68/C1
Baltiysk, U.S.S.R. 52/A4
Baltra (isl.), Ecuador 128/B9
Baltray, Ireland 17/J4
Baltrum (isl.), Germany 22/B2
Balty, Va. 307/O5
Baluchistan (reg.), Iran 66/M7
Baluchistan (prov.), Pakistan 68/B3
Baluchistan (reg.), Pakistan 59/J4
Balurghat, India 68/F3
Balvi, U.S.S.R. 53/D2
Balwina Aboriginal Res., W. Australia 88/D4
Balwina Aboriginal Res., W. Australia 92/E3
Balya, Turkey 63/B3
Balykshi, U.S.S.R. 48/F5
Balzac, Alberta 182/C4
Balzar, Ecuador 128/C3
Bam, Iran 54/G7
Bam, Iran 66/L6
Bam, Iran 59/G4
Bam, U.S.S.R. 48/N4
Bama, Nigeria 106/G6
Bamako (cap.), Mali 2/J5
Bamako (cap.), Mali 106/C6
Bamako (cap.), Mali 102/B3
Bamba, Mali 106/D5
Bambamarca, Peru 128/C6
Bamban, Philippines 82/C3
Bambari, Cent. Afr. Rep. 102/E4
Bambari, Cent. Afr. Rep. 115/D2
Bamberg (co.), S.C. 296/E5
Bamberg, S.C. 296/E5
Bamberg, Germany 22/D4
Bambesa, Zaire 115/E3
Bambili, Zaire 115/E3
Bambio, Cent. Afr. Rep. 115/C3
Bamble, Norway 18/F7
Bamboo, Jamaica 158/J6
Bamboo Creek, W. Australia 92/C3
Bambuí, Brazil 132/E8
Bambuí, Brazil 135/C2
Bamenda, Cameroon 115/B2
Bamfield, Br. Col. 184/E6
Bamian, Afghanistan 59/J3
Bamian, Afghanistan 68/B2
Bamingui, Cent. Afr. Rep. 115/D2
Bamingui (riv.), Cent. Afr. Rep. 115/C2
Bamoa, Mexico 150/E4
Bampur, Iran 59/H4
Bampur, Iran 66/M7
Bampur (riv.), Iran 66/M7
Bamyili-Beswick, North. Terr. 93/C3
Banaba (isl.), Kiribati 87/G6
Bañado de Medina, Uruguay 145/E3
Bañado de Rocha, Uruguay 145/C2
Banagher, Ireland 17/F5
Banagüises, Cuba 158/D1
Banahao (mt.), Philippines 82/C3
Banalia, Zaire 115/E3
Banam, Cambodia 72/E5
Banamba, Mali 106/C6
Banamba, Mali 102/B3
Banamichi, Mexico 150/D2
Banana (riv.), Fla. 212/F3
Banana, Zaire 115/B5
Bananal (isl.), Brazil 120/D4
Bananal (isl.), Brazil 132/D5
Bananier, Guadeloupe 161/A7
Banao, Cuba 158/F2
Ban Aranyaprathet, Thailand 72/D4
Bânâs, Ras (cape), Egypt 111/G3
Bânâs, Ras (cape), Egypt 59/C5
Banas (riv.), India 68/D3
Banaz, Turkey 63/C3
Banaz (riv.), Turkey 63/C3
Banbar, China 77/E5
Ban Boun Tai, Laos 72/D2
Banbridge, N. Ireland 17/J3
Banbury, England 10/F4
Banbury, England 13/F5
Bancalan (isl.), Philippines 82/A6
Bancannia (lake), N.S. Wales 97/A2
Banchory, Scotland 10/E2
Banchory, Scotland 15/F3
Bancoran (isl.), Philippines 82/B7
Bancroft, Idaho 220/G7
Bancroft, Iowa 229/E2
Bancroft, Kansas 232/G2
Bancroft, Ky. 237/K4
Bancroft, La. 238/C5
Bancroft, Maine 243/H4
Bancroft•, Maine 243/H4
Bancroft, Mich. 250/E6
Bancroft, Nebr. 264/H2
Bancroft, Ontario 177/G2
Bancroft, Oreg. 291/D5
Bancroft, S. Dak. 298/O4
Bancroft, W. Va. 312/C5
Bancroft, Wis. 317/G7
Bancroft (Chililabombwe), Zambia 115/E6
Banda, Gabon 115/B4
Banda, India 68/D3
Banda (isls.), Indonesia 85/H6
Banda (sea), Indonesia 54/O10
Banda (sea), Indonesia 85/H7
Banda Aceh, Indonesia 85/A4
Banda Aceh, Indonesia 54/L9
Bandai (mt.), Japan 81/K5
Bandai-Asahi National Park, Japan 81/J4
Bandama (riv.), Ivory Coast 106/C7
Bandana, Ky. 237/D6
Bandanaira, Indonesia 85/H6
Bandar (Machilipatnam), India 68/E5
Bandar 'Abbas, Iran 66/J7
Bandar 'Abbas, Iran 54/G7
Bandar 'Abbas, Iran 59/G4
Bandar Behesti (Bahar), Iran 66/M8
Bandar-e Anzali (Enzeli), Iran 66/E2
Bandar-e Bushehr (Bushire), Iran 66/G6
Bandar-e Deylam, Iran 66/G5
Bandar-e Khomeyni, Iran 58/E3
Bandar-e Khomeyni, Iran 66/E3
Bandar-e Lengeh, Iran 66/J7
Bandar-e Lengeh, Iran 59/F4
Bandar-e Ma'shur, Iran 66/F5
Bandar-e Pahlavi (Enzeli), Iran 59/E2
Bandar-e Pahlavi (Enzeli), Iran 66/F2
Bandar-e Rig, Iran 59/F4
Bandar-e Rig, Iran 66/G6
Bandar-e Torkeman, Iran 66/H2
Bandar-e Torkeman, Iran 59/F2
Bandar Khomeini, Iran 66/F5
Bandar Khomeini, Iran 59/E3
Bandar Maharani (Muar), Malaysia 72/D7
Bandar Penggaram (Batu Pahat), Malaysia 72/D7
Bandar Seri Begawan (cap.), Brunei 85/E4
Bandar Seri Begawan (cap.), Brunei 54/N9
Bandar Shahpur, Iran 66/F5
Bandawe, Malawi 115/F6
Bande, Spain 33/B1
Bandeira (mt.), Brazil 120/E5
Bandeira, Pico da (mt.), Brazil 132/F8
Bandeira (mt.), Brazil 135/E2
Bandelier Nat'l Mon., N. Mex. 274/C3
Bandera, Argentina 143/D2
Bandera (co.), Texas 303/E8
Bandera, Texas 303/F8
Banderas (bay), Mexico 150/G6
Banderilla, Mexico 150/P1
Bandholm, Denmark 21/E8
Bandiagara, Mali 106/D6
Bandırma, Turkey 59/A1
Bandırma, Turkey 63/B2
Bandon, Ireland 10/B5
Bandon, Ireland 17/D8
Bandon (riv.), Ireland 17/D8
Bandon, Oreg. 291/C4
Bandra, India 68/B7
Bandundu (prov.), Zaire 115/C4
Bandundu, Zaire 102/D5
Bandundu, Zaire 115/C4
Bandung, Indonesia 54/M10
Bandung, Indonesia 85/H2
Bandy, Va. 307/E6
Bandya, W. Australia 92/C4
Banes, Cuba 156/C2
Banes, Cuba 158/J3
Banff, Alberta 182/C4
Banff, Alta. 162/E5
Banff, Scotland 15/F3
Banff, Scotland 10/E2
Banff (trad. co.), Scotland 15/A5
Banff Nat'l Park, Alberta 182/B4
Banff Nat'l Park, Alta. 162/E5
Banfora, Burkina Faso 106/D6
Bangalore, India 2/N5
Bangalore, India 54/J8
Bangalore, India 68/D6
Bangalow, N.S. Wales 97/G1
Bangar, Philippines 82/C2
Bangassou, Centr. Afr. Rep. 102/E4
Bangassou, Cent. Afr. Rep. 115/D3
Banggai, Indonesia 85/G6
Banggai (arch.), Indonesia 85/G6
Banggi (isl.), Malaysia 85/F4
Bangil, Indonesia 85/K2
Bangka (isl.), Indonesia 54/M10
Bangka (isl.), Indonesia 85/D6
Bangka (str.), Indonesia 85/C6
Bangkalan, Indonesia 85/K2
Bangkok (cap.), Thailand 2/P5
Bangkok (cap.), Thailand 72/D4
Bangkok (cap.), Thailand 54/M8
Bangladesh 2/P4
Bangladesh 54/L7
BANGLADESH 68/G4
Bang Lamung, Thailand 72/D4
Bangong Co (lake), China 77/A5
Bangor, Calif. 204/D4
Bangor, Maine 146/M5
Bangor, Maine 243/F6
Bangor, Maine 188/N2
Bangor, Mich. 250/C6
Bangor, N.Y. 276/M1
Bangor, N. Ireland 17/K2
Bangor, Pa. 294/M4
Bangor, Sask. 181/J5
Bangor, Wales 13/C4
Bangor, Wales 10/D4
Bangor, Wis. 317/E8
Bangs, Texas 303/E6
Bang Saphan, Thailand 72/C5
Bangued, Philippines 85/G2
Bangued, Philippines 82/C2
Banguezane (mt.), Niger 106/F5
Bangui (cap.), Cent. Afr. Rep. 102/D4
Bangui (cap.), Centr. Afr. Rep. 2/K5
Bangui (cap.), Cent. Afr. Rep. 115/C3
Bangui, Philippines 85/G2
Bangui, Philippines 82/C1
Bangui (bay), Philippines 82/C1
Bangweulu (lake), Zambia 115/F6
Ban Houayxay, Laos 72/D2
Baní, Dom. Rep. 158/E6
Baní, Dom. Rep. 156/D3
Bani (riv.), Mali 106/C6
Bani, Jebel (mts.), Morocco 106/C3
Bani, Philippines 82/B2
Bania, Cent. Afr. Rep. 115/C3
Baniara, Papua N.G. 85/C7
Bánica, Dom. Rep. 156/D3
Bánica, Dom. Rep. 158/D5
Banida, Idaho 220/G7
Banister (riv.), Va. 307/K7
Bani Suheila, Gaza Strip 65/A5
Baniyas, Syria 63/F5
Banja Luka, Yugoslavia 7/F4
Banja Luka, Yugoslavia 45/C3
Banjarmasin, Indonesia 54/N10
Banjarmasin, Indonesia 85/E6
Banjul (cap.), Gambia 102/A3
Banjul (cap.), Gambia 106/A6
Banka Banka, North. Terr. 93/C5
Ban Kantang, Thailand 72/C6
Ban Kapong, Thailand 72/C5
Bankass, Mali 106/D6
Bankend, Sask. 181/H4
Ban Kèngkok, Laos 72/E3
Bankfoot, Scotland 15/E4
Bankhead (lake), Ala. 195/D4
Bankhead, Scotland 15/F3
Ban Khlong Yai, Thailand 72/D5
Ban Khon, Laos 72/E4
Banks, Ala. 195/G7
Banks (pt.), Alaska 196/H3
Banks, Ark. 202/F6
Banks (isl.), Br. Col. 184/B3
Banks (isl.), Canada 2/C2
Banks (isl)., Canada 4/B16
Banks (bay), Ecuador 128/B9
Banks (co.), Georgia 217/E2
Banks (lake), Georgia 217/F9
Banks, Idaho 220/B5
Banks, Miss. 256/D1
Banks (cape), N. S. Wales 88/L4
Banks (cape), N.S. Wales 97/K4
Banks (pen.), N. Zealand 100/D5
Banks (isl.), N.W.T. 146/F2
Banks (isl.), N.W.T. 162/D1
Banks (isl.), N.W. Terr. 187/F2
Banks, Oreg. 291/A1
Banks (isl.), Queensland 88/G2
Banks (isl.), Queensland 95/B1
Banks (str.), Tasmania 88/H8
Banks (str.), Tasmania 99/D2
Banks (isls.), Vanuatu 87/G7
Banks (lake), Wash. 310/F3
Bankston, Ala. 195/C3
Bankston, Iowa 229/L3
Bankstown, N.S. Wales 88/K4
Bankstown, N.S. Wales 97/J3
Ban Kui Nua, Thailand 72/D4
Bankura, India 68/F4
Ban Lahanam, Laos 72/E3
Ban Me Thuot, Vietnam 72/F4
Bann (riv.), Ireland 17/J6
Bann (riv.), N. Ireland 17/H2
Bannack, Mont. 262/C5
Banner, Ill. 222/D3
Banner, Ky. 237/R5
Banner, Miss. 256/F2
Banner, Mo. 261/L7
Banner (co.), Nebr. 264/A3
Banner, Va. 307/D7
Banner, Wyo. 319/F1
Banner Elk, N.C. 281/F2
Banner Hill, Tenn. 237/R8
Banner Springs, Tenn. 237/M8
Bannertown, N.C. 281/H1
Ban Ngon, Thailand 72/D3
Banning, Calif. 204/J10
Banning, Georgia 217/C3
Bannister, Mich. 250/E5
Bannock (co.), Idaho 220/F7
Bannock (creek), Idaho 220/F7
Bannock (peak), Idaho 220/F7
Bannock (range), Idaho 220/F7
Bannockburn, Ill. 222/B5
Bannockburn, Ontario 177/G3
Bannockburn, Scotland 15/C1
Bannockburn, Scotland 10/B1
Bannow, Ireland 17/H7
Bannu, Pakistan 59/K3
Bannu, Pakistan 68/C2
Bañolas, Spain 33/H1
Bánovce nad Bebravou, Czech. 41/E2
Ban Pak Phanang, Thailand 72/D5
Banphot Phisai, Thailand 72/C3
Ban Pua, Thailand 72/D3
Banquo, Ind. 227/F3
Ban Sattahip, Thailand 72/D4
Bansberia, India 68/F1
Bansha, Ireland 17/E7
Banská Bystrica, Czech. 41/E2
Banská Štiavnica, Czech. 41/E2
Bansko, Bulgaria 45/F5
Banstead, England 13/H8
Banstead, England 10/B6
Bansud, Philippines 82/C4
Banswara, India 68/C4
Bantam, Conn. 210/B2
Bantam (lake), Conn. 210/C2
Bantam (riv.), Conn. 210/B2
Bantayan, Philippines 82/D5
Bantayan (isl.), Philippines 82/D5
Ban Tha Uthen, Thailand 72/D3
Banton, Philippines 82/D4
Banton (isl.), Philippines 82/D4
Bantry, Ireland 10/B5
Bantry, Ireland 17/C8
Bantry (bay), Ireland 10/A5
Bantry (bay), Ireland 17/B8
Bantry, N. Dak. 282/J3
Bantul, Indonesia 85/J2
Bañuelo (mt.), Spain 33/D3
Banyak (isls.), Indonesia 85/B5
Banyo, Cameroon 115/B2
Banyo, Queensland 88/K2
Banyumas, Indonesia 85/J2
Banyuwangi, Indonesia 85/L2
Banzare Coast (reg.), Ant. 5/C7
Baode, China 77/H4
Baoding (Paoting), China 77/J4
Bao Ha, Vietnam 72/E2
Baoji, China 54/M6
Baoji (Paoki), China 77/G5
Bao Lac, Vietnam 72/E2
Baoshan, China 77/E7
Baoting, China 77/G8
Baotou (Paotow), China 77/G3
Baotou, China 54/M5
Baoulé (riv.), Ivory Coast 106/C6
Baoulé (dry riv.), Mali 106/C6
Baoulé (riv.), Mali 106/C6
Bapaume, Sask. 181/D2
Bapchule, Ariz. 198/D5
Bapsfontein, S. Africa 118/J6
Baptist, La. 238/M1
Baptiste (lake), Ontario 177/G2
Baptistown, N.J. 273/D2
Baqên, China 77/D5
Ba'qūba, Iraq 59/D3
Ba'qūba, Iraq 66/D4
Baquedano, Chile 138/A4
Baquerizo Moreno, Ecuador 128/C9
Baqura, Jordan 65/D2
Bar, Yugoslavia 45/D4
Bara, Sudan 111/F5
Bara, Sudan 59/B7
Barabai, Indonesia 85/F6
Barabinsk, U.S.S.R. 48/H4
Baraboo, Wis. 317/G9
Baracaldo, Spain 33/E1
Barachois, New Bruns. 170/F2
Barachois (pt.), Nova Scotia 168/G4
Barachois, Québec 172/D1
Barachois Pond Prov. Park, Newf. 166/C4
Baracoa, Cuba 158/K4
Baracoa, Cuba 156/C2
Barada, Nebr. 264/J4
Baradères, Haiti 158/B6
Baradères (bay), Haiti 158/B6
Baradero, Argentina 143/G6
Baradine, N.S. Wales 97/E2
Baradine (creek), N.S. Wales 97/E2
Baraga (co.), Mich. 250/A2
Baraga, Mich. 250/G1
Baragoi, Kenya 115/G3
Baraguá, Cuba 158/F2
Baragua, Venezuela 124/D2
Barahona (prov.), Dom. Rep. 158/D6
Barahona, Dom. Rep. 158/D6
Barahona, Dom. Rep. 156/D3
Barajas, Spain 33/F4
Barak, Turkey 63/G4
Baraka (riv.), Ethiopia 111/G4
Baraka (riv.), Sudan 111/G4
Baraka (riv.), Sudan 59/C6
Baraka, Zaire 115/E4
Baraki Barak, Afghanistan 59/J3
Baraki Barak, Afghanistan 68/B2
Baralzon (lake), Manitoba 179/J1
Barama (riv.), Guyana 131/A2
Baramanni, Guyana 131/B2
Baramati, India 68/C5
Baramita, Guyana 131/A2
Baramula, India 68/C2
Baranagar, India 68/F1
Barankwa, Sudan 59/B7
Baranoa, Colombia 126/C2
Baranof (isl.), Alaska 196/M1
Baranovichi, U.S.S.R. 7/G3
Baranovichi, U.S.S.R. 48/C4
Baranovichi, U.S.S.R. 52/C4
Baranya (co.), Hungary 41/E4
Barão de Cocais, Brazil 135/E1
Baras, Philippines 82/E4
Barasat, India 68/F1
Baratang (isl.), India 68/G6
Barataria, La. 238/K7
Barataria (bay), La. 238/L8
Barataria (passage), La. 238/L8
Barawa (Brava), Somalia 115/H3
Baraya, Colombia 126/C6
Barbacena, Brazil 120/E5
Barbacena, Brazil 135/E2
Barbacena, Brazil 132/F8
Barbacoas, Colombia 126/A7
Barbacoas, Venezuela 124/E3
Barbados 2/G5
Barbados 146/N8
BARBADOS 156/G4
BARBADOS 161/B8
Barbar (isls.), Indonesia 85/J7
Barbas (cape), Western Sahara 106/A4
Barbastro, Spain 33/F1
Barbate (riv.), Spain 33/D4
Barbeau, Mich. 250/E2
Barbeau (peak), N.W. Terr. 187/L1
Barber, Ark. 202/B3
Barber (co.), Kansas 232/D4
Barber, Mont. 262/G4
Barber, N.C. 281/H3
Barbers (pt.), Hawaii 218/E2
Barbers Point, Hawaii 218/E2
Barbers Point Nav. Air Sta., Hawaii 218/E2
Barberton, Ohio 284/G4
Barberton, S. Africa 118/E5
Barberville, Fla. 212/E2
Barbezieux-St-Hilaire, France 28/C5
Barbil, India 68/F4
Barbizon, France 28/E3
Barbosa, Colombia 126/D5
Barbour (co.), Ala. 195/H7
Barbour (co.), W. Va. 312/F4
Barbourmeade, Ky. 237/K1
Barboursville, Va. 307/M4
Barboursville, W. Va. 312/B6
Barbourville, Ky. 237/O7
Barbuda (isl.) 146/M8
Barbuda (isl.), Ant. & Bar. 156/G3
Barcaldine, Queensland 88/G4
Barcaldine, Queensland 95/C4
Barcaldine, Scotland 15/C4
Barcarrota, Spain 33/C3
Barce (El Marj), Libya 111/D1
Barcellona Pozzo di Gotto, Italy 34/E5
Barcelona (prov.), Spain 33/G2
Barcelona, Spain 7/E4
Barcelona, Spain 33/H2
Barcelona, Venezuela 124/F2
Barcelona, Venezuela 120/C2
Barceloneta, P. Rico 161/C1
Barcelonnette, France 28/G5
Barcelos, Brazil 120/C3
Barcelos, Brazil 132/H9
Barcelos, Portugal 33/B2
Barclay, Md. 245/P4
Barco, N.C. 281/T2
Barcoo (creek), Queensland 88/G4
Barcoo (creek), Queensland 95/B5
Barcoo (creek), S. Australia 88/F5
Barcoo (creek), S. Australia 94/F3
Barcos (pt.), Cuba 158/B2
Barcs, Hungary 41/D4
Barczewo, Poland 47/E2
Bard, Calif. 204/L11
Bard, N. Mex. 274/F3
Bardai, Chad 111/C3
Bardai, Chad 102/D2
Bardejov, Czech. 41/F2
Bardera, Somalia 115/H3
Bardera, Somalia 102/G4
Bardney, England 13/G4
Bardolph, Ill. 222/C3
Bardon (lake), Wis. 317/C3
Bardonia, N.Y. 276/K8
Bardsey (isl.), Wales 13/C5
Bardstown, Ky. 237/L5
Barduelv (riv.), Norway 18/L2
Bardwell, Ky. 237/D7
Bardwell, Texas 303/H5
Bareilly, India 54/K7
Bareilly, India 68/D3
Barellan, N.S. Wales 97/D4
Bärenhorn (mt.), Switzerland 39/H3
Barents (sea) 2/L2
Barents (sea) 7/J1
Barents (sea) 4/B8
Barents (sea), U.S.S.R. 48/D2
Barents (sea), U.S.S.R. 52/E1
Barentsburg, Norway 18/C2
Barentsøya (isl.), Norway 18/D2
Bäretswil, Switzerland 39/G2
Barfield, Ark. 202/L2
Barfleur, France 28/C3
Barfleur (pt.), France 28/C3
Barga, China 77/B5
Bargal, Somalia 115/K1
Bargamin (creek), Idaho 220/C4
Bargersville, Ind. 227/E5
Bargo, N.S. Wales 97/F4
Bargrax (Bohu), China 77/C3
Barham, N.S. Wales 97/C4
Bar Harbor, Maine 243/G7
Bar Harbor•, Maine 243/G7
Bari (prov.), Italy 34/F4
Bari, Italy 34/F4
Bari, Italy 7/F4
Bari (prov.), Somalia 115/J1
Baria (riv.), Venezuela 124/E7
Barich, Alberta 182/D2
Barichara, Colombia 126/D4
Barida, Ras (cape), Saudi Arabia 59/C5
Barima (riv.), Guyana 131/B2
Barinas (state), Venezuela 124/D3
Barinas, Venezuela 124/C3
Barinas, Venzuela 120/C2
Baring, Maine 243/J5
Baring•, Maine 243/J5
Baring, Mo. 261/H2
Baring (head), N. Zealand 100/B3
Baring (cape), N.W. Terr. 187/G3
Baring, Sask. 181/J5
Baring, Wash. 310/D3
Barinitas, Venezuela 124/C3
Baripada, India 68/F4
Bariri, Brazil 135/B3
Bariri (res.), Brazil 135/B3
Bâris, Egypt 111/F3
Barisal, Bangladesh 68/G4
Barisan (mts.), Indonesia 85/C6
Baritbog (riv.), New Bruns. 170/E1

Bayburt 335

Barito (riv.), Indonesia 85/E6
Bark (lake), Ontario 177/G2
Barkam, China 77/F5
Barker, N.Y. 276/C4
Barker Heights, N.C. 281/D4
Barkeyville, Pa. 294/C3
Barkhamsted•, Conn. 210/D1
Barkhamsted (res.), Conn. 210/D1
Barkhan, Pakistan 68/B3
Barkhan, Pakistan 59/J4
Barking, England 10/C5
Barking, England 13/H8
Barkley (sound), Br. Col. 184/E6
Barkley (dam), Ky. 237/E6
Barkley (lake), Ky. 237/F7
Barkley (lake), Tenn. 237/F7
Barkly Downs, Queensland 95/A4
Barkly East, S. Africa 118/D6
Barkly Tableland (plat.), Australia 87/D7
Barkly Tableland, North. Terr. 88/F3
Barkly Tableland, North. Terr. 93/D4
Barkly Tableland, Queensland 95/A4
Barkmere, Québec 172/C3
Barkol, China 77/D3
Bark River, Mich. 250/B3
Barksdale, Texas 303/D8
Barksdale A.F.B., La. 238/C2
Barlby, England 13/G4
Bar-le-Duc, France 28/F3
Barlee (lake), Australia 87/B8
Barlee (lake), W. Australia 88/B5
Barlee (lake), W. Australia 92/B5
Barletta, Italy 34/F4
Barlinek, Poland 47/B2
Barling, Ark. 202/B3
Barlow, Br. Col. 184/F3
Barlow, Ky. 237/D6
Barlow, Miss. 256/C7
Barlow, N. Dak. 282/M4
Barlow, Ohio 284/G7
Barlow, Oreg. 291/B2
Barlow Bend, Ala. 195/C8
Barmedman, N.S. Wales 97/D4
Barmer, India 68/C3
Barmera, S. Australia 94/G6
Bar Mills, Maine 243/C8
Barmouth, Wales 10/D4
Barmouth, Wales 13/C5
Barna, Ireland 17/C5
Barnabus, W. Va. 312/C7
Barnaby (riv.), New Bruns. 170/E2
Barnaby River, New Bruns. 170/E2
Barnard, Kansas 232/D2
Barnard, Mo. 261/C2
Barnard, N.C. 281/D3
Barnard, S. Dak. 298/N2
Barnard•, Vt. 268/B4
Barnard Castle, England 13/E3
Barnardsville, N.C. 281/E3
Barnaul, U.S.S.R. 54/K4
Barnaul, U.S.S.R. 48/J4
Barn Bluff (mt.), Tasmania 99/B3
Barnegat, Alberta 182/E2
Barnegat, N.J. 273/E4
Barnegat (bay), N.J. 273/E4
Barnegat (inlet), N.J. 273/E4
Barnegat Light, N.J. 273/E4
Barnes (sound), Fla. 212/F6
Barnes, Kansas 232/F2
Barnes (co.), N. Dak. 282/O5
Barnes, Wis. 317/D3
Barnesboro, Pa. 294/E4
Barnes City, Iowa 229/H6
Barnes Corners, N.Y. 276/J3
Barneston, Nebr. 264/H4
Barnesville, Colo. 208/L2
Barnesville, Georgia 217/D4
Barnesville, Md. 245/J4
Barnesville, Minn. 255/B4
Barnesville, N.C. 281/L6
Barnesville, Ohio 284/H6
Barnet, England 13/H7
Barnet, England 10/B5
Barnet•, Vt. 268/C3
Barnett, Georgia 217/G3
Barnett, Miss. 256/G7
Barnett, Mo. 261/G6
Barnettville, New Bruns. 170/E2
Barneveld, Netherlands 27/H4
Barneveld, N.Y. 276/K4
Barneveld, Wis. 317/F10
Barneville-Carteret, France 28/C3
Barney, Georgia 217/E8
Barney, N. Dak. 282/S7
Barnhart, Texas 303/C6
Barnhill, Ohio 284/H5
Barnoldswick, England 13/H1
Barnrock, Ky. 237/R5
Barnsdall, Okla. 288/O1
Barnsley, England 13/J2
Barnsley, England 10/F4
Barnstable (co.), Mass. 249/N6
Barnstable, Mass. 249/N6
Barnstable•, Mass. 249/N6
Barnstaple, England 10/E5
Barnstaple, England 13/D6
Barnstaple (bay), England 10/D5
Barnstaple (bay), England 13/C6
Barnstead•, N.H. 268/E5
Barnum, Iowa 229/E3
Barnum, Minn. 255/F4
Barnum, W. Va. 312/H4
Barnum, Wis. 317/E9
Barnwell, Ala. 195/C10
Barnwell, Alberta 182/D5
Barnwell (co.), S.C. 296/E5
Barnwell, S.C. 296/E5
Baro (riv.), Ethiopia 111/G6
Baro, Nigeria 106/F7
Baroda (Vadodara), India 68/C4
Baroda, India 54/J7
Baroda, Mich. 250/C7
Baroghil (pass), Afghanistan 68/C1
Baroghil (pass), Pakistan 68/C1
Baron, Okla. 288/S3
Baron Bluff (prom.), Virgin Is. (U.S.) 161/E3
Barons, Alberta 182/D4
Barooga, N.S. Wales 97/C4
Barossa (res.), S. Australia 94/C6
Barotseland (reg.), Zambia 115/D7
Barpeta, India 68/G3
Barqa (Cyrenaica) (reg.), Libya 111/D1
Barques (pt.), Mich. 250/C3
Barquisimeto, Venezuela 124/D2
Barquisimeto, Venezuela 120/C2
Barr, Scotland 15/D5
Barr, Tenn. 237/B9
Barra, Brazil 132/F5
Barra (head), Scotland 10/C2
Barra (head), Scotland 15/A4
Barra (isl.), Scotland 15/A4
Barra (isl.), Scotland 10/C2
Barra (isls.), Scotland 10/C2
Barra (sound), Scotland 15/A3
Barraba, N.S. Wales 97/F2
Barra Bonita (res.), Brazil 135/B3
Barrackpore, India 68/F1
Barrackville, W. Va. 312/F3
Barra de Río Grande, Nicaragua 154/F4
Barra do Bugres, Brazil 132/B6
Barra do Corda, Brazil 132/E4
Barra do Piraí, Brazil 132/E8
Barra do Piraí, Brazil 135/E3
Barra Isles (isls.), Scotland 15/A4
Barra Mansa, Brazil 135/D3
Barranca, Lima, Peru 128/C8
Barranca, Loreto, Peru 128/D5
Barrancabermeja, Colombia 126/C4
Barranca de Upía, Colombia 126/D5
Barrancas, Argentina 143/F6
Barrancas (riv.), Argentina 143/G5
Barrancas, Chile 138/G3
Barrancas, Colombia 126/D2
Barrancas, Barinas, Venezuela 124/C3
Barrancas, Monagas, Venezuela 124/G3
Barranco de Loba, Colombia 126/C3
Barrancos, Cerro (mt.), Chile 138/D7
Barrancos, Portugal 33/C3
Barranqueras, Argentina 143/E2
Barranquilla, Colombia 120/B1
Barranquilla, Colombia 126/C2
Barranquitas, P. Rico 161/D2
Barras (riv.), Bolivia 136/B6
Barras, Brazil 132/F4
Barras, Colombia 126/D8
Barraute, Québec 174/B3
Barre, Mass. 249/F3
Barre•, Mass. 249/F3
Barre, Québec 172/G3
Barre, Vt. 268/C3
Barre•, Vt. 268/C3
Barreal, Argentina 143/C3
Barreau (pt.), New Bruns. 170/F1
Barre Center, N.Y. 276/D4
Barreiras, Brazil 120/E4
Barreiras, Brazil 132/E6
Barreirinha, Brazil 132/B3
Barreirinhas, Brazil 132/F3
Barreiro, Portugal 33/B1
Barreiros, Brazil 132/H5
Barren (isls.), Alaska 196/B2
Barren (isl.), India 68/G6
Barren (co.), Ky. 237/K7
Barren (riv.), Ky. 237/H6
Barren (isls.), Madagascar 118/G3
Barren (isl.), Nova Scotia 168/G4
Barren (cape), Tasmania 99/E2
Barren Plains, Tenn. 237/H7
Barren River (lake), Ky. 237/J7
Barren Springs, Va. 307/G7
Barre Plains, Mass. 249/F3
Barrera, Bolivia 136/B3
Barretos, Brazil 132/D8
Barretos, Brazil 135/B2
Barrett, Minn. 255/B5
Barrett, Texas 303/K1
Barrett, W. Va. 312/C7
Barretts, Georgia 217/F8
Barrhead, Alberta 182/C2
Barrhead, Scotland 10/A1
Barrhead, Scotland 15/B2
Barrhill, Scotland 15/D5
Barrie, Ontario 177/E3
Barrie (isl.), Ontario 177/B1
Barrière, Br. Col. 184/H4
Barrineau Park, Fla. 212/B6
Barrington, Ill. 222/A5
Barrington•, N.H. 268/F5
Barrington, N.J. 273/B3
Barrington, Nova Scotia 168/C5
Barrington (bay), Nova Scotia 168/C5
Barrington•, R.I. 249/J6
Barrington, Tasmania 99/C3
Barrington Hills, Ill. 222/A5
Barrington P.O. (East Barrington), N.H. 268/F5
Barrington Passage, Nova Scotia 168/C5
Barrington Tops (mt.), N.S. Wales 97/F2
Barringun, N.S. Wales 97/C1
Barron (co.), Wis. 317/C5
Barron, Wis. 317/C5
Barronett, Wis. 317/B4
Barrouallie, St. Vin. & Grens. 161/A9
Barroui, Dominica 161/E6
Barrow, Alaska 196/G1
Barrow, Alaska 188/C5
Barrow, Alaska 146/C2
Barrow (pt.), Alaska 146/C2
Barrow (pt.), Alaska 196/G1
Barrow (isl.), Australia 87/B8
Barrow (co.), Georgia 217/E2
Barrow (riv.), Ireland 17/H7
Barrow (riv.), Ireland 10/C4
Barrow (str.), N.W.T. 162/G1
Barrow (str.), N.W. Terr. 187/J2
Barrow (bay), Ontario 177/C2
Barrow, U.S. 4/B17
Barrow (pt.), U.S. 2/B2
Barrow (pt.), U.S. 4/B18
Barrow (isl.), W. Australia 88/A4
Barrow (isl.), W. Australia 92/A3
Barrow Creek, North. Terr. 93/D6
Barrow-in-Furness, England 10/E3
Barrow-in-Furness, England 13/D3
Barrows, Manitoba 179/A2
Barrowsville, Mass. 249/K5
Barr Smith (mt.), Ant. 5/C5
Barruelo de Santullán, Spain 33/D1
Barry, Ill. 222/B4
Barry (co.), Mich. 250/D6
Barry, Minn. 255/B5
Barry (co.), Mo. 261/E9
Barry (mts.), Victoria 97/D5
Barry, Wales 13/B7
Barry, Wales 10/E5
Barry's Bay, Ontario 177/G2
Barryton, Mich. 250/D5
Barryville, N.Y. 276/L8
Barsi, India 68/D5
Barsinghausen, Germany 22/C2
Barss Corners, Nova Scotia 168/D4
Barstow, Calif. 204/H9
Barstow, Md. 245/M6
Barstow, Texas 303/A6
Bar-sur-Aube, France 28/F3
Bar-sur-Seine, France 28/F3
Bartelso, Ill. 222/D5
Barterville, Ky. 237/N4
Barth, Germany 22/E1
Barth, Fla. 212/B6
Barthel, Sask. 181/B2
Bartholomew (bayou), Ark. 202/G6
Bartholomew (co.), Ind. 227/F6
Bartibog Bridge, New Bruns. 170/E1
Bartica, Guyana 120/D2
Bartica, Guyana 131/B2
Bartın, Turkey 63/E2
Bartle, Cuba 158/H3
Bartle Frere (mt.), Queensland 88/H3
Bartle Frere (mt.), Queensland 95/C3
Bartlesville, Okla. 288/O1
Bartlett (dam), Ariz. 198/D5
Bartlett (res.), Ariz. 198/D5
Bartlett, Ill. 222/A5
Bartlett, Iowa 229/B7
Bartlett, Kansas 232/G4
Bartlett, Nebr. 264/F3
Bartlett•, N.H. 268/E3
Bartlett, N. Dak. 282/N3
Bartlett, Ohio 284/G7
Bartlett, Tenn. 237/B10
Bartlett, Texas 303/G7
Bartlett Deep, Cayman Is. 156/B3
Bartletts Ferry (dam), Ala. 195/H5
Bartletts Ferry (dam), Georgia 217/B5
Bartley, Nebr. 264/D4
Bartley, W. Va. 312/C8
Barto, Pa. 294/L5
Bartolomeu Dias, Mozambique 118/F4
Barton, Ala. 195/C1
Barton, Ark. 202/J4
Barton (co.), Kansas 232/D3
Barton, Md. 245/B2
Barton (co.), Mo. 261/D7
Barton, N. Dak. 282/K2
Barton, Ohio 284/J5
Barton, Oreg. 291/B2
Barton, Vt. 268/C2
Barton•, Vt. 268/C2
Barton (riv.), Vt. 268/C2
Barton City, Mich. 250/F4
Barton Hills, Mich. 250/F6
Bartonsville, Pa. 294/M4
Bartonsville, Vt. 268/B5
Barton-upon-Humber, England 13/G4
Barton-upon-Humber, England 10/F4
Bartonville, Ill. 222/D3
Bartonville, Texas 303/F1
Bartoszyce, Poland 47/E1
Bartow, Fla. 212/E4
Bartow (co.), Georgia 217/C2
Bartow, Georgia 217/G5
Bartow, W. Va. 312/G5
Bartra Antiguo, Peru 128/E4
Bartra Nuevo, Peru 128/E4
Barú (isl.), Colombia 126/C2
Barú (vol.), Panama 154/F6
Baruipur, India 68/F2
Barus, Indonesia 85/B5
Barut, Tanjong (cape), Malaysia 85/E5
Baruun-Urt, Mongolia 77/H2
Barvas, Scotland 10/C1
Barvas, Scotland 15/B2
Barview, Oreg. 291/C4
Bar View, Oreg. 291/C2
Barville, Québec 174/B3
Barwani, India 68/D4
Barwick, Georgia 217/E9
Barwick, Ontario 175/B3
Barwick, Ontario 177/F5
Barwon (riv.) 88/H5
Barwon (riv.), N.S. Wales 97/D2
Barysh, U.S.S.R. 52/G4
Baryulgil, N.S. Wales 97/G1
Basalt, Colo. 208/E4
Basalt, Idaho 220/F6
Basankusu, Zaire 115/C3
Basavilbaso, Argentina 143/G6
Bas-Caraquet, New Bruns. 170/F1
Bascharage, Luxembourg 27/H9
Basco, Ill. 222/B3
Basco, Philippines 82/A2
Bascom, Fla. 212/A1
Bascom, Ohio 284/D3
Bascuñán (cape), Chile 138/A7
Basehor, Kansas 232/G2
Basel, Switzerland 39/E1
Basel, Switzerland 7/E4
Baselland (canton), Switzerland 39/E2
Baselstadt (canton), Switzerland 39/E1
Basey, Philippines 82/E5
Bashan, Conn. 210/F2
Bashan (lake), Conn. 210/F3
Bashaw, Alberta 182/D3
Bashi, Ala. 195/C7
Bashi (chan.), China 77/K7
Bashi (chan.), Philippines 82/A1
Bashkir A.S.S.R., U.S.S.R. 48/F4
Bashkir A.S.S.R., U.S.S.R. 52/J4
Basht, Iran 66/G5
Basic, Miss. 256/G6
Basilan (prov.), Philippines 82/D7
Basilan (isl.), Philippines 85/G4
Basilan (isl.), Philippines 82/D7
Basilan (str.), Philippines 82/C7
Basildon, England 13/J8
Basildon, England 10/G5
Basile, La. 238/E5
Basilicata (reg.), Italy 34/F4
Basim, India 68/D4
Basin, Mont. 262/D4
Basin (lake), Sask. 181/F3
Basin, Wyo. 319/E1
Basinger, Fla. 212/F4
Basingstoke, England 10/F5
Basingstoke, England 13/F6
Basirhat, India 68/F4
Basit (cape), Syria 63/F5
Baskahegan (lake), Maine 243/H5
Başkale, Turkey 63/K3
Baskatong (res.), Que. 162/J6
Baskatong (res.), Québec 172/B3
Baskerville, Va. 307/M7
Basket (lake), Manitoba 179/C3
Baskett, Ky. 237/F5
Baskil, Turkey 63/H3
Baskin, La. 238/G2
Basking Ridge, N.J. 273/D2
Başmakçı, Turkey 63/C4
Basodino (peak), Switzerland 39/G4
Basoko, Zaire 115/D3
Basom, N.Y. 276/D4
Basongo, Zaire 115/D4
Basora (pt.), Neth. Ant. 161/E10
Basra (gov.), Iraq 66/E5
Basra, Iraq 2/M4
Basra, Iraq 66/E5
Basra, Iraq 59/E3
Basra, Iraq 54/F6
Bas-Rhin (dept.), France 28/G3
Bass (str.) 88/H7
Bass (str.), Australia 87/E9
Bass (isls.), Fr. Poly. 87/M8
Bass (lake), Ind. 227/D2
Bass (str.), Tasmania 99/C1
Bassano, Alberta 182/D4
Bassano del Grappa, Italy 34/C2
Bassas da India (isl.), Réunion 102/F7
Bassas da India (isl.), Réunion 118/F4
Bassecourt, Switzerland 39/D2
Bassein, Burma 54/L8
Bassein, Burma 72/B3
Bassein, India 68/C5
Basse-Pointe, Martinique 161/C5
Basse-Sambre, Belgium 27/F8
Basse Santa Su, Gambia 106/B6
Basse-Terre (cap.), Guadeloupe 161/A7
Basse-Terre (cap.), Guadeloupe 156/F4
Basse-Terre (isl.), Guadeloupe 161/A6
Basseterre (cap.), St. Kitts & Nevis 161/C10
Basseterre (cap.), St. Kitts & Nevis 156/F3
Basse Terre, Trin. & Tob. 161/B11
Bassett, Ark. 202/K2
Bassett, Iowa 229/J2
Bassett, Kansas 232/G4
Bassett, Nebr. 264/E2
Bassett, Va. 307/J7
Bassfield, Miss. 256/E8
Bass Harbor, Maine 243/G7
Bassikounou, Mauritania 106/C5
Bassin Bleu, Haiti 158/B5
Bass River, New Bruns. 170/E2
Bass River, Nova Scotia 168/E3
Bassum, Germany 22/C2
Basswood, Manitoba 179/B4
Basswood (lake), Minn. 255/G2
Basswood (lake), Ontario 175/B3
Båstad, Sweden 18/H8
Bastak, Iran 66/J7
Bastam, Iran 66/J2
Bastar, India 68/E5
Bastelica, France 28/B6
Bastenaken (Bastogne), Belgium 27/H9
Bastia, France 7/E4
Bastia, France 28/B6
Bastian, Va. 307/F6
Bastimentos (isl.), Panama 154/G6
Bastogne, Belgium 27/H9
Bastrop, La. 238/G1
Bastrop (co.), Texas 303/G7
Bastrop, Texas 303/G7
Bastuträsk, Sweden 18/L4
Basye, Va. 307/L3
Bas-Zaïre (prov.), Zaire 115/B4
Bata, Equat. Guinea 102/C4
Bata, Equat. Guinea 115/B3
Bataan (prov.), Philippines 82/C3
Batabanó (gulf), Cuba 158/C2
Batabanó (gulf), Cuba 156/A2
Batag (isl.), Philippines 82/E4
Batagay, U.S.S.R. 48/O3
Batala, India 68/D2
Batalha, Brazil 132/F3
Batalha, Portugal 33/B3
Batan (isls.), Philippines 54/O7
Batan, Albay (isl.), Philippines 82/E4
Batan, Batanes (isl.), Philippines 82/B2
Batan (isls.), Philippines 85/G1
Batan (isls.), Philippines 82/A2
Batanes (prov.), Philippines 82/A2
Batang, China 77/E5
Batang, China 54/L6
Batang, Indonesia 85/J2
Batangafo, Cent. Afr. Rep. 115/C2
Batangas (prov.), Philippines 82/C4
Batangas, Philippines 82/C4
Batangas, Philippines 85/G3
Batas (isl.), Philippines 82/B5
Bátaszék, Hungary 41/E3
Batatais, Brazil 135/C2
Batavia, Ill. 222/E2
Batavia (Jakarta) (cap.), Indonesia 85/H1
Batavia, Iowa 229/J7
Batavia, Mich. 250/D7
Batavia, N.Y. 276/D5
Batavia, Ohio 284/B7
Batavia, Wis. 317/K8
Batawa, Ontario 177/G3
Bataysk, U.S.S.R. 52/E5
Bat Cave, N.C. 281/E4
Batchelor, La. 238/G5
Batchelor (brook), Mass. 248/D3
Batchelor, North. Terr. 93/B2
Batchtown, Ill. 222/C4
Batchwana Bay, Ontario 177/J5
Batdambang, Cambodia 54/M8
Batdambang (Battambang), Cambodia 72/D4
Bateman, Sask. 181/E5
Batemans Bay, N.S. Wales 97/F4
Bates, Ark. 202/B4
Bates, Mich. 250/D4
Bates (co.), Mo. 261/D6
Bates (mt.), Norfolk I. 88/L5
Bates, Oreg. 291/J3
Batesburg, S.C. 296/D4
Bates City, Mo. 261/E5
Batesland, S. Dak. 298/E7
Batesville, Ala. 195/H6
Batesville, Ark. 202/G2
Batesville, Ind. 227/G6
Batesville, Miss. 256/E2
Batesville, Ohio 284/H6
Batesville, Texas 303/E9
Batesville, Va. 307/L5
Bath, England 13/E6
Bath, England 10/E5
Bath, Ill. 222/C3
Bath, Ind. 227/H5
Bath, Jamaica 158/K6
Bath (co.), Ky. 237/O4
Bath, Maine 243/D8
Bath, Mich. 250/E6
Bath, Netherlands 27/E6
Bath, New Bruns. 170/C2
Bath•, N.H. 268/D3
Bath, N.Y. 276/F6
Bath, N.C. 281/R4
Bath, Ontario 177/H3
Bath, Pa. 294/M4
Bath, S.C. 296/D5
Bath, S. Dak. 298/N3
Bath (co.), Va. 307/J4
Batha (riv.), Chad 111/C5
Bathgate, N. Dak. 282/P2
Bathgate, Scotland 15/C2
Bathgate, Scotland 10/C1
Bathsheba, Barbados 161/B8
Bath Springs, Tenn. 237/E10
Bathurst (isl.), Australia 87/C7
Bathurst (isl.), Canada 4/B14
Bathurst (Banjul) (cap.), Gambia 106/A6
Bathurst, N. Br. 162/K6
Bathurst, New Bruns. 170/E1
Bathurst, N.S. Wales 88/H6
Bathurst, N.S. Wales 97/E3
Bathurst (isl.), North. Terr. 88/D2
Bathurst (isl.), North. Terr. 93/A1
Bathurst (cape), N.W.T. 162/D1
Bathurst (cape), N.W.T. 187/F2
Bathurst (inlet), N.W.T. 187/H3
Bathurst (isl.), N.W.T. 162/F1
Bathurst (isl.), N.W.T. 146/H2
Bathurst (isl.), N.W.T. 187/H2
Bathurst (harb.), Tasmania 99/C5
Bathurst Inlet, N.W. Terr. 187/H3
Bathurst Island, North. Terr. 93/B1
Bathurst Island Mission, North. Terr. 88/E2
Bathurst Mines, New Bruns. 170/E1
Batié, Burkina Faso 106/D7
Batı Fırat (riv.), Turkey 63/H3
Batin, Wadi al (dry riv.), Iraq 59/E4
Batin, Wadi al (dry riv.), Iraq 66/E6
Batin, Wadi al (dry riv.), Saudi Arabia 59/E4
Batina (reg.), Oman 59/G5
Batini (mt.), Fiji 86/Q10
Batiscan, Québec 172/E3
Batiscan (lake), Québec 172/E2
Batiscan (riv.), Québec 172/E2
Batley, England 13/J1
Batlow, N.S. Wales 97/E4
Batman, Turkey 63/J4
Batna, Algeria 102/C1
Batna, Algeria 106/F1
Bato, Catanduanes, Philippines 82/E4
Bato, Leyte, Philippines 82/E5
Bato-Bato, Philippines 82/C8
Batobato, Philippines 82/E7
Batoche, Sask. 181/E3
Batoche Nat'l Hist. Site, Sask. 181/E3
Baton Rouge (cap.), La. 146/J6
Baton Rouge (cap.), La. 188/H4
Baton Rouge (cap.), La. 238/K2
Bátonyterenye, Hungary 40/E3
Batopilas, Mexico 150/F3
Batouri, Cameroon 115/B3
Batovi, Uruguay 145/D2
Batrun, Lebanon 63/F5
Bat Shelomo, Israel 65/B2
Batson, Texas 303/K7
Batsto, N.J. 273/D4
Batsto (riv.), N.J. 273/D4
Batten Kill (riv.), N.Y. 276/O4
Batten Kill (riv.), Vt. 268/A5
Batterbee (cape), Ant. 2/N9
Batterbee (cape), Ant. 5/C3
Bätterkinden, Switzerland 39/E2
Battersea, Ontario 177/H3
Batticaloa, Sri Lanka 68/E7
Battiest, Okla. 288/S6
Batti Malv (isl.), India 68/G7
Battle (riv.) 162/E5
Battle (riv.), Alberta 182/D3
Battle, England 13/H7
Battle, England 10/G5
Battle (creek), Idaho 220/B7
Battle (riv.), Minn. 255/D3
Battle (creek), Mont. 262/G1
Battle (creek), Oreg. 291/K5
Battle (creek), Sask. 181/B6
Battle (riv.), Sask. 181/B3
Battle (creek), S. Dak. 298/C6
Battleboro, N.C. 281/O2
Battle Creek, Iowa 229/B4
Battle Creek, Mich. 188/J2
Battle Creek, Mich. 250/D6
Battle Creek, Nebr. 264/G3
Battlefield, Mo. 261/F8
Battleford, Sask. 162/E5
Battleford, Sask. 181/C3
Battle Ground, Ind. 227/D3
Battle Ground, Wash. 310/C5
Battle Harbour, Newf. 166/C3
Battle Harbour, Newf. 162/L5
Battle Lake, Alberta 182/C3
Battle Lake, Minn. 255/C4
Battle Mountain, Nev. 266/E2
Battles Wharf, Ala. 195/C10
Battletown, Ky. 237/J4
Battleview, N. Dak. 282/E2
Battlock (mt.), Scotland 15/F4
Battonya, Hungary 41/F3
Battrum, Sask. 181/C5
Batu (isls.), Indonesia 85/B6
Batuco, Chile 138/G3
Batu Gajah, Malaysia 72/D6
Batulaki, Philippines 82/E8
Batumi, U.S.S.R. 48/E5
Batumi, U.S.S.R. 52/F6
Batu Pahat, Malaysia 72/D7
Baturaja, Indonesia 85/C6
Baturité, Brazil 132/G4
Batusangkar, Indonesia 85/C6
Bat Yam, Israel 65/B3
Bauang, Philippines 82/C2
Baubau, Indonesia 85/G7
Bauchi (state), Nigeria 106/F6
Bauchi, Nigeria 106/F6
Baudette, Minn. 255/D2
Baudette (riv.), Minn. 255/D2
Baudh, India 68/E4
Baudó, Serranía de (mts.), Colombia 126/B5
Baudó (riv.), Colombia 126/B5
Baugé, France 28/D4
Baukau, Indonesia 85/H7
Bauld (cape), Newf. 166/C3
Bauld (cape), Newf. 162/L5
Bauline, Newf. 166/D2
Baulkham Hills, N.S. Wales 88/K4
Baulkham Hills, N.S. Wales 97/H3
Baulmes, Switzerland 39/C3
Bauma, Switzerland 39/G2
Baumann (fjord), N.W. Terr. 187/K2
Baume-les-Dames, France 28/G4
Baures, Bolivia 136/D3
Baures (riv.), Bolivia 136/D3
Bauria, India 68/E2
Baurtregaum (mt.), Ireland 17/A7
Bauru, Brazil 120/E5
Bauru, Brazil 135/B3
Bauru, Brazil 132/D8
Bauska, U.S.S.R. 53/B2
Bauta, Cuba 158/C1
Bauta (riv.), P. Rico 161/C2
Bautzen, Germany 22/F3
Bauxite, Ark. 202/F4
Bavaria, Kansas 232/E3
Bavaria (state), Germany 22/D4
Bavarian (for.), Germany 22/E4
Bavarian Alps (mts.), Austria 41/A3
Bavarian Alps (range), Germany 22/D5
Baviácora, Mexico 150/E2
Bavispe, Mexico 150/E1
Bavispe, Río de (riv.), Mexico 150/E1
Bawean (isl.), Indonesia 85/K1
Bawku, Ghana 106/D6
Bawlf, Alberta 182/D3
Ba Xian, China 77/J4
Baxley, Georgia 217/H7
Baxoi, China 77/E5
Baxter (co.), Ark. 202/F1
Baxter, Iowa 229/G5
Baxter, Minn. 255/D4
Baxter, Miss. 256/F6
Baxter, Pa. 294/D3
Baxter, Tenn. 237/K8
Baxter Springs, Kansas 232/H4
Baxterville, Miss. 256/E8
Bay, Ark. 202/J2
Bay (Baicheng), China 77/B3
Bay (co.), Fla. 212/C6
Bay (co.), Mich. 250/E5
Bay, Mo. 261/J5
Bay, Laguna de (lake), Philippines 82/C3
Bay (prov.), Somalia 115/H3
Bayag (Calanasan), Philippines 82/C1
Bayaguana, Dom. Rep. 158/E6
Bayamhongor, Mongolia 77/E2
Bayamo, Cuba 156/C2
Bayamo, Cuba 158/H4
Bayamón (dist.), P. Rico 161/D1
Bayamón, P. Rico 161/D1
Bayamón, P. Rico 156/G1
Bayamón (riv.), P. Rico 161/D1
Bayanbaraat, Mongolia 77/G2
Bayandalay, Mongolia 77/F3
Bayan Dobo Suma, Mongolia 77/G3
Bayang, Philippines 82/E7
Bayangovĭ, Mongolia 77/F3
Bayan Har Shan (range), China 77/E5
Bayanhongor, Mongolia 77/E2
Bayan Mod, China 77/F3
Bayan Obo, China 77/G3
Bayan-Olgiy, Mongolia 77/C2
Bayan-Ondör, Mongolia 77/E3
Bayan-Uul, Mongolia 77/E2
Bayard, Del. 245/T6
Bayard, Iowa 229/D5
Bayard, Nebr. 264/A3
Bayard, N. Mex. 274/A6
Bayard, Sask. 181/F5
Bayard, W. Va. 312/H4
Bayat, Turkey 63/F2
Baybay, Philippines 82/E5
Baybay, Philippines 85/H3
Bayble, Scotland 15/B2
Bayboro, N.C. 281/R4
Bay Bulls, Newf. 166/D2
Bayburt, Turkey 59/D1

336 Bayburt

Bayburt, Turkey 63/J2
Bay Center, Wash. 310/A4
Bay City, Mich. 188/K2
Bay City, Mich. 250/F5
Bay City, Oreg. 291/D2
Bay City, Texas 303/H9
Bay City, Wash. 310/B4
Bay City, Wis. 317/B6
Baydarata (bay), U.S.S.R. 52/L1
Bay de Verde, Newf. 166/D2
Baydhabo, Somalia 115/H3
Baydhabo, Somalia 102/G4
Baydrag, Mongolia 77/E2
Bay du Vin (riv.), New Bruns. 170/E2
Bayerischer Wald Nat'l Park, Germany 22/E4
Bayeux, France 28/C3
Bayfield, Colo. 208/D8
Bayfield, New Bruns. 170/G2
Bayfield, Ontario 177/C4
Bayfield (sound), Ontario 177/B2
Bayfield (co.), Wis. 317/D3
Bayfield, Wis. 317/E2
Bayham, Ontario 177/D5
Bay Harbor Islands, Fla. 212/B4
Bay Head, N.J. 273/E3
Bayhead, Nova Scotia 168/E3
Bayındır, Turkey 63/B3
Bayırköy, Turkey 63/B6
Baykal (lake), U.S.S.R. 54/N4
Baykal (lake), U.S.S.R. 2/Q3
Baykal (lake), U.S.S.R. 48/L4
Baykal (mts.), U.S.S.R. 48/L4
Baykan, Turkey 63/J3
Baykit, U.S.S.R. 48/K3
Baykonyr, U.S.S.R. 48/G5
Bay Lake, Fla. 212/E3
Bay Lake, Minn. 255/E4
Bay L'Argent, Newf. 166/D4
Baylis, Ill. 222/C4
Baylor (co.), Texas 303/E4
Bay Minette, Ala. 195/C9
Bay Mission, W. Australia 88/C3
Baynes Lake, Br. Col. 184/K5
Bayombong, Philippines 82/C2
Bayombong, Philippines 85/G2
Bayonne, France 28/C6
Bayonne, N.J. 273/B2
Bayonne Military Ocean Terminal, N.J. 273/B2
Bayou, Ky. 237/E6
Bayou Barbary, La. 238/M2
Bayou Bodcau (res.), Ark. 202/C7
Bayou Cane, La. 238/J7
Bayou Chicot, La. 238/F5
Bayou Current, La. 238/G5
Bayou D'Arbonne (lake), La. 238/F1
Bayou Des Arc (riv.), Ark. 202/G3
Bayou Goula, La. 238/J3
Bayou La Batre, Ala. 195/B10
Bayou Meto, Ark. 202/H5
Bayou Vista, La. 238/H7
Bayóvar, Peru 128/B5
Bay Pines, Fla. 212/B3
Bay Point, Maine 243/D8
Bay Point (isl.), S.C. 296/F7
Bayport, Fla. 212/D3
Bay Port, Mich. 250/F5
Bayport, Minn. 255/F5
Bayport, N.Y. 276/O9
Bayram-Ali, U.S.S.R. 48/G6
Bayramiç, Turkey 63/B3
Bayreuth, Germany 22/D4
Bayrischzell, Germany 22/E5
Bay Roberts, Newf. 166/D2
Bays, Ky. 237/P5
Bays (lake), Ontario 177/F2
Bay Saint Lawrence, Nova Scotia 168/H1
Bay Saint Louis, Miss. 256/F10
Bayshore, Fla. 212/E5
Bayshore, Mich. 250/D3
Bay Shore, N.Y. 276/O9
Bayshore Gardens, Fla. 212/D4
Bayside, Calif. 204/B3
Bayside, Maine 243/F7
Bayside, New Bruns. 170/C3
Bayside, Ontario 177/G3
Bayside, Texas 303/G9
Bayside, Wis. 317/M1
Bay Springs, Fla. 212/B6
Bay Springs, Miss. 256/F7
Bay Springs (dam), Miss. 256/H1
Bay Springs (lake), Miss. 256/H1
Bayston Hill, England 13/E5
Baysville, Ontario 177/E2
Baytown, Texas 303/L2
Bay Tree, Alberta 182/A2
Bayuca, Spain 33/B1
Bayview, Calif. 204/A3
Bayview, Idaho 220/B2
Bayview, Md. 245/P2
Bay View, Mich. 250/E3
Bay View, N. Zealand 100/F3
Bay View, Ohio 284/E3
Bay Village, Ohio 284/G9
Bayville, N.J. 273/E4
Bayville, N.Y. 276/R6
Baywood, La. 238/K1
Baywood Park-Los Osos, Calif. 204/E8
Baza, Spain 33/E4
Bazaar, Kansas 232/F3
Bazaruto, Ilha do (isl.), Mozambique 118/F4
Bazas, France 28/C5
Bazhong, China 77/G5
Bazile Mills, Nebr. 264/G2
Bazine, Kansas 232/C3
Bazman, Iran 66/M7
Bazman, Kuh-e (mt.), Iran 66/H4
Bazman, Kuh-e (mt.), Iran 59/H4
Beach (pond), Conn. 210/H2
Beach, Georgia 217/G8
Beach, N. Dak. 282/C6
Beachburg, Ontario 177/H2
Beach City, Ohio 284/G4
Beach City, Texas 303/L2
Beach Haven, N.J. 273/E4
Beach Haven (inlet), N.J. 273/E4
Beach Haven Crest, N.J. 273/E4
Beach Haven Terrace, N.J. 273/E4
Beach Lake, Pa. 294/M2
Beach Meadows, Nova Scotia 168/D4
Beachport, S. Australia 94/F7
Beachton, Georgia 217/D9
Beachville, Ontario 177/D4
Beachwood, N.J. 273/E4
Beachwood, Ohio 284/J9
Beachy (head), England 10/G5
Beachy (head), England 13/H7
Beacon, Iowa 229/H6
Beacon, N.Y. 276/N7
Beacon, Tenn. 237/E9
Beacon Falls•, Conn. 210/C3
Beaconia, Manitoba 179/F4
Beaconsfield, England 13/G8
Beaconsfield, Iowa 229/E7
Beaconsfield, Québec 172/H4
Beaconsfield, Tasmania 99/C3
Beadle, Sask. 181/B4
Beadle (co.), S. Dak. 298/N5
Beagle (chan.), Chile 138/E11
Beagle, Kansas 232/G3
Beagle (gulf), North. Terr. 93/A2
Beagle, W. Australia 88/C3
Beaglebay Aboriginal Res., W. Australia 92/C2
Beagle Bay Mission, W. Australia 92/C2
Beal (range), Queensland 95/B5
Bealanana, Madagascar 118/H2
Beal City, Mich. 250/D5
Beale (cape), Br. Col. 184/E6
Beale A.F.B., Calif. 204/D4
Bealeton, Va. 307/N3
Beallsville, Ohio 284/J6
Beallsville, Pa. 294/C5
Beals, Ky. 237/G5
Beals•, Maine 243/H7
Beals (creek), Texas 303/C5
Beaman, Iowa 229/H4
Beaminster, England 13/E7
Beanblossom, Ind. 227/E6
Beanblossom (creek), Ind. 227/D6
Bean City, Fla. 212/F5
Bean Station, Tenn. 237/P8
Bear (mt.), Alaska 196/K2
Bear (lake), Alberta 182/A2
Bear (lake), Br. Col. 184/D2
Bear (creek), Colo. 208/P8
Bear (hill), Conn. 210/B2
Bear (mt.), Conn. 210/B1
Bear, Del. 245/R2
Bear, Idaho 220/B4
Bear (lake), Idaho 220/G7
Bear (riv.), Idaho 220/G7
Bear (isl.), Ireland 17/B8
Bear (riv.), Maine 243/B6
Bear (riv.), Minn. 255/E3
Bear (creek), N. Dak. 282/O7
Bear (isl.), Norway 4/B9
Bear (creek), Oreg. 291/K2
Bear (creek), Oreg. 291/E5
Bear (creek), Oreg. 291/G4
Bear (hills), Sask. 181/C4
Bear (isls.), U.S.S.R. 4/B1
Bear (lake), Utah 304/C2
Bear (riv.), Utah 304/B2
Bear (isl.), Wis. 317/E1
Bear (creek), Wyo. 319/H4
Bear (riv.), Wyo. 319/B4
Bear Branch, Ind. 227/G7
Bearcamp (riv.), N.H. 268/E4
Bear Canyon, Alberta 182/A1
Bear Creek, Ala. 195/C2
Bearcreek, Mo. 261/E7
Bearcreek, Mont. 262/G5
Bear Creek, N.C. 281/L3
Bear Creek, Pa. 294/F7
Bear Creek, Sask. 181/K5
Bear Creek, Wis. 317/J6
Beard, Ind. 227/E4
Beard, W. Va. 312/F6
Bearden, Ark. 202/E6
Bearden, Okla. 288/O4
Beardmore (glac.), Ant. 5/A8
Beardmore, Ontario 177/H5
Beardmore, Ontario 175/C3
Beards Fork, W. Va. 312/D6
Beardsley, Kansas 232/A2
Beardsley, Minn. 255/B5
Beardstown, Ill. 222/C3
Beardstown, Ind. 227/D2
Beardstown, Tenn. 237/F9
Beargrass, N.C. 281/P3
Bearhat (mt.), Mont. 262/C2
Bear in the Lodge (creek), S. Dak. 298/F6
Bear Island, Ontario 177/K5
Bear Lake, Br. Col. 184/F3
Bear Lake (co.), Idaho 220/G7
Bear Lake, Mich. 250/C4
Bear Lake, Pa. 294/C1
Bear Lodge, Wyo. 319/E1
Bear Lodge (mts.), Wyo. 319/H1
Bearmouth, Mont. 262/C4
Béarn (trad. prov.), France 29
Bear River (range), Idaho 220/G7
Bear River, Minn. 255/E3
Bear River, Nova Scotia 168/C4
Bear River, Pr. Edward I. 168/F2
Bear River (range), Utah 304/C1
Bear River City, Utah 304/B2
Bear River Divide (mts.), Wyo. 319/B4
Bearsden, Scotland 15/B2
Bearskin Lake, Ontario 175/B2
Bears Paw (mts.), Mont. 262/G2
Bear Spring, Tenn. 237/F8
Beartooth (mts.), Mont. 262/G5
Beartown, W. Va. 312/C8
Beas de Segura, Spain 33/E3
Beason, Ill. 222/D3
Beata (cape), Dom. Rep. 158/D7
Beata (cape), Dom. Rep. 156/D3
Beata (chan.), Dom. Rep. 158/C7
Beata (isl.), Dom. Rep. 158/C7
Beata (isl.), Dom. Rep. 156/D3
Beatenberg, Switzerland 39/E3
Beaton, Br. Col. 184/J5
Beatrice, Ala. 195/D7
Beatrice, Nebr. 188/G2
Beatrice, Nebr. 264/H4
Beatrice (cape), North. Terr. 88/F2
Beatrice (cape), North. Terr. 93/E3
Beattie, Kansas 232/F2
Beattock, Scotland 15/E5
Beatton (riv.), Br. Col. 184/G1
Beatton River, Br. Col. 184/G1
Beatty, Nev. 266/E6
Beatty, Oreg. 291/F5
Beatty, Sask. 181/G3
Beattyville, Ky. 237/O5
Beau (lake), Québec 172/H2
Beaubier, Sask. 181/G6
Beaubois, New Bruns. 170/E1
Beaucaire, France 28/F6
Beauce (co.), Québec 172/G3
Beauceville, Québec 172/G3
Beaucoup, Ill. 222/D5
Beaudesert, Queensland 95/E6
Beauford, Minn. 255/D7
Beaufort (sea) 4/B16
Beaufort (sea) 146/D2
Beaufort (sea), Alaska 196/K1
Beaufort, Malaysia 85/F4
Beaufort, Mo. 261/K6
Beaufort (co.), N.C. 281/R4
Beaufort, N.C. 281/R5
Beaufort (sea), N.W.T. 162/C1
Beaufort (sea), N.W. Terr. 187/D2
Beaufort (co.), S.C. 296/F7
Beaufort, S.C. 296/F7
Beaufort, Victoria 97/B5
Beaufort (sea), Yukon 187/E2
Beaufort Marine Air Sta., S.C. 296/F7
Beaufort West, S. Africa 118/C6
Beauharnois (co.), Québec 172/C4
Beauharnois, Québec 172/D4
Beaulac, Québec 172/F4
Beaulieu, Minn. 255/C3
Beauly, Scotland 10/D2
Beauly, Scotland 15/D3
Beauly (riv.), Scotland 15/D3
Beaumaris (bay), Victoria 97/J6
Beaumaris (bay), Victoria 88/L8
Beaumaris, Wales 13/C4
Beaumaris, Wales 10/D4
Beaumont, Alberta 182/D3
Beaumont, Belgium 27/E8
Beaumont, Calif. 204/J10
Beaumont, Kansas 232/F4
Beaumont, Miss. 256/G8
Beaumont, N. Zealand 100/B6
Beaumont, Québec 172/F3
Beaumont (pt.), St. Lucia 161/F6
Beaumont, Texas 146/J6
Beaumont, Texas 188/H4
Beaumont, Texas 303/K7
Beaune, France 28/F4
Beauport, Québec 172/J3
Beaupré, Québec 172/G2
Beauraing, Belgium 27/F8
Beauregard (par.), La. 238/D5
Beauregard, Miss. 256/D7
Beauséjour, Manitoba 179/F4
Beauty, Ky. 237/S5
Beauty Point, Tasmania 99/C3
Beauvais, France 28/E3
Beauval, Sask. 181/L3
Beauvallon, Alberta 182/E3
Beaux Arts Village, Wash. 310/B2
Beaver (riv.) 162/F5
Beaver, Alaska 196/J1
Beaver (creek), Alaska 196/J1
Beaver (riv.), Alberta 182/E2
Beaver, Ark. 202/C1
Beaver (lake), Ark. 202/C1
Beaver (creek), Colo. 208/M3
Beaver (creek), Idaho 220/F5
Beaver, Iowa 229/E4
Beaver, Kansas 232/D3
Beaver (creek), Kansas 232/A2
Beaver, La. 238/E5
Beaver (isl.), Mich. 250/D3
Beaver (lake), Mich. 250/F4
Beaver (creek), Mont. 262/J2
Beaver (creek), Nebr. 264/D5
Beaver (riv.), Newf. 166/B3
Beaver (brook), N.H. 268/E6
Beaver (brook), N.J. 273/C2
Beaver (riv.), N.Y. 276/K3
Beaver (creek), N. Dak. 282/K7
Beaver (creek), N. Dak. 282/B5
Beaver (lake), N. Dak. 282/L7
Beaver, Ohio 284/E7
Beaver (co.), Okla. 288/E1
Beaver, Okla. 288/F1
Beaver (creek), Okla. 288/K6
Beaver (riv.), Okla. 288/F1
Beaver, Oreg. 291/D2
Beaver (co.), Pa. 294/B4
Beaver, Pa. 294/B4
Beaver (riv.), Pa. 294/B4
Beaver (hills), Sask. 181/H4
Beaver (riv.), Sask. 181/L4
Beaver (creek), S. Dak. 298/A6
Beaver (co.), Utah 304/A5
Beaver, Utah 304/B5
Beaver (mts.), Utah 304/A5
Beaver (riv.), Utah 304/A5
Beaver, Wash. 310/A2
Beaver (Glen Hedrick), W. Va. 312/D7
Beaver, Wis. 317/K5
Beaver (creek), Wyo. 319/H2
Beaver (creek), Wyo. 319/D3
Beaverbank, Nova Scotia 168/E4
Beaver Bay, Minn. 255/G3
Beaver Brook Station, New Bruns. 170/E1
Beaver City, Nebr. 264/E4
Beaver Cove, Br. Col. 184/D5
Beaver Creek, Md. 245/H2
Beaver Creek, Minn. 255/B7
Beavercreek, Ohio 284/C6
Beavercreek, Oreg. 291/B2
Beaver Creek, Yukon 187/D3
Beaver Creek Fork, Humboldt (riv.), Nev. 266/F1
Beaver Crossing, Nebr. 264/G4
Beaverdale, Pa. 294/E5
Beaverdam, Alberta 182/E2
Beaver Dam, Ky. 237/H6
Beaverdam, Ohio 284/C4
Beaverdam, Va. 307/N5
Beaver Dam, Wis. 317/J9
Beaver Dam (lake), Wis. 317/J9
Beaver Dams, N.Y. 276/F6
Beaver Dam Wash (creek), Utah 304/A6
Beaverdell, Br. Col. 184/H5
Beaver Falls, N.Y. 276/K3
Beaver Falls, Pa. 294/B4
Beaver Harbour, New Bruns. 170/D3
Beaverhead (mts.), Idaho 220/E4
Beaverhead (co.), Mont. 262/C5
Beaverhead (riv.), Mont. 262/D5
Beaverhill (lake), Alberta 182/D3
Beaverhill (lake), Manitoba 179/J3
Beaver Lake, Alberta 182/E2
Beaver Lake, N.J. 273/D1
Beaverlett, Va. 307/R6
Beaverlodge, Alberta 182/A2
Beaverlodge (lake), Sask. 181/L2
Beaver Meadows, Pa. 294/L4
Beaver Mines, Alberta 182/C5
Beaver Park, Sask. 181/J6
Beaver River, N.Y. 276/L3
Beaver River Flow (lake), N.Y. 276/K3
Beaver Springs, Pa. 294/H4
Beaverton, Ala. 195/B3
Beaverton, Mich. 250/E5
Beaverton, Ontario 177/E3
Beaverton, Oreg. 291/A2
Beavertown, Pa. 294/H4
Beaverville, Ill. 222/F3
Beawar, India 68/C3
Beazer, Alberta 182/D5
Beazley, Argentina 143/C3
Bebedouro, Brazil 132/D8
Bebedouro, Brazil 135/B2
Bebee, W. Va. 312/E3
Bebington, England 10/F2
Bebington, England 13/G2
Bebra, Germany 22/C3
Bécancour, Québec 172/E3
Bécancour (riv.), Québec 172/F3
Beccles, England 13/J5
Beccles, England 10/G4
Bečej, Yugoslavia 45/E3
Becerréa, Spain 33/C1
Béchar, Algeria 102/B1
Béchar, Algeria 106/D2
Bechar (pt.), W. Australia 88/A3
Bechard, Sask. 181/G5
Becharof (lake), Alaska 196/G3
Bechyn, Minn. 255/C6
Bechyně, Czech. 41/C2
Becida, Minn. 255/C3
Beckemeyer, Ill. 222/D5
Becker (co.), Minn. 255/C4
Becker, Minn. 255/E5
Becker, Miss. 256/G3
Becket•, Mass. 249/B3
Becket, Mont. 262/G4
Beckham (co.), Okla. 288/G4
Beckley, W. Va. 312/D7
Beckton, Wyo. 319/E1
Beckville, Texas 303/K5
Beckwourth, Calif. 204/E4
Bečva (riv.), Czech. 41/E2
Bedale, England 13/F3
Bédarieux, France 28/E6
Beddington•, Maine 243/H6
Beddouza, Ras (cape), Morocco 106/C2
Bedele, Ethiopia 111/G6
Bedeque (bay), Pr. Edward I. 168/E2
Bedessa, Ethiopia 111/H6
Bedford, England 10/F4
Bedford, England 13/G5
Bedford (pt.), Grenada 161/D8
Bedford, Ind. 227/E7
Bedford, Iowa 229/D7
Bedford, Ky. 237/L3
Bedford•, Mass. 249/B6
Bedford, Mich. 250/D6
Bedford, Mo. 261/F3
Bedford•, N.H. 268/D6
Bedford (basin), Nova Scotia 168/E4
Bedford, Ohio 284/H9
Bedford (co.), Pa. 294/E6
Bedford, Pa. 294/F5
Bedford, Québec 172/E4
Bedford (co.), Tenn. 237/J9
Bedford, Texas 303/F2
Bedford (co.), Va. 307/J6
Bedford (I.C.), Va. 307/J6
Bedford, Wyo. 319/A3
Bedford Heights, Ohio 284/J9
Bedford Hills, N.Y. 276/N8
Bedford Park, Ill. 222/B6
Bedfordshire (co.), England 13/G5
Bedford Valley, Pa. 294/E6
Bedias, Texas 303/J7
Bedington, W. Va. 312/L3
Bedlington, England 13/F2
Bedlington, England 10/E3
Bedminster•, N.J. 273/D2
Bedminster, Pa. 294/M5
Bedouaram (well), Niger 106/G5
Bedourie, Queensland 95/A5
Bedourie, Queensland 88/F4
Bedretto, Switzerland 39/G4
Bedrock, Colo. 208/B6
Bedsted, Denmark 21/B4
Bedwas and Machen, Wales 13/B6
Bedwellty, Wales 13/B6
Bedworth, England 13/F5
Bedworth, England 10/F4
Będzin, Poland 47/B3
Bee, Nebr. 264/H3
Bee (co.), Texas 303/G9
Beebe, Ark. 202/G3
Beebe Plain, Québec 172/E4
Beebe Plain, Vt. 268/C2
Beebe River, N.H. 268/D4
Bee Branch, Ark. 202/F3
Beech Bluff, Tenn. 237/D9
Beech Bottom, W. Va. 312/E2
Beech Creek, Ky. 237/G6
Beech Creek, Pa. 294/G3
Beecher, Ill. 222/F2
Beecher City, Ill. 222/E4
Beecher Falls, Vt. 268/D2
Beecher Island, Colo. 208/P3
Beech Fork (riv.), Ky. 237/L5
Beech Grove, Ind. 227/E5
Beech Grove, Ky. 237/G5
Beechgrove, Tenn. 237/J9
Beech Island, S.C. 296/D5
Beechwood, Mass. 249/F8
Beechwood, Mich. 250/C6
Beechwood, New Bruns. 170/C2
Beechwood, N.S. Wales 97/G2
Beechwood Village, Ky. 237/K2
Beechworth, Victoria 97/D5
Beechy, Sask. 181/D5
Beechy Point, Alaska 196/H1
Beedeville, Ark. 202/H3
Beekman, La. 238/G1
Beeler, Kansas 232/B3
Bee Log, N.C. 281/E3
Beemer, Nebr. 264/H3
Beenleigh, Queensland 88/J5
Beer Ef'e (well), Israel 65/C5
Be'eri, Israel 65/A5
Bee Ridge, Fla. 212/D4
Be'er Menuha, Israel 65/D5
Beernem, Belgium 27/C6
Be'er Ora, Israel 65/D5
Beersheba (Be'er Sheva'), Israel 65/B5
Beersheba Springs, Tenn. 237/K10
Beer Sheva' (dry riv.), Israel 65/B5
Beersville, New Bruns. 170/E2
Be'er Tuveya, Israel 65/B4
Beeskow, Germany 22/F2
Beesleys Point, N.J. 273/D5
Beeson, W. Va. 312/D8
Bee Spring, Ky. 237/J6
Beeston and Stapleford, England 13/F5
Beeton, Ontario 177/E3
Beetown, Wis. 317/E10
Beeville, Texas 303/G9
Befale, Zaire 115/D3
Befandriana, Madagascar 118/H3
Beg (lake), N. Ireland 17/J2
Bega, N. S. Wales 88/J7
Bega, N.S. Wales 97/E5
Begemdir (prov.), Ethiopia 111/G5
Beger, Mongolia 77/E2
Beggs, Okla. 288/P3
Begnins, Switzerland 39/B4
Béhague (pt.), Fr. Guiana 131/F3
Behan (lake), Alberta 182/E2
Behbehan, Iran 66/G5
Behistun (ruins), Iran 66/E3
Behm Canal (inlet), Alaska 196/N2
Behshahr, Iran 66/H2
Bei'an (Pehan), China 77/L2
Beica, Ethiopia 111/F6
Beihai (Pakhoi), China 77/G7
Beijing (Peking) (cap.), Peoples Rep. of China 54/N5
Beijing (Peking) (cap.), Peoples Rep. of China 77/J3
Beilen, Netherlands 27/K3
Beinn a Ghlo (mt.), Scotland 15/E4
Beinn Bhan (mt.), Scotland 15/C3
Beinn Bheigeir (mt.), Scotland 15/B5
Beinn Dearg (mt.), Scotland 15/D3
Beinn Dearg (mt.), Scotland 15/E4
Beinn Dhorain (mt.), Scotland 15/E2
Beinn Dorain (mt.), Scotland 15/D4
Beinn Eighe (mt.), Scotland 15/C3
Beinwil am See, Switzerland 39/F2
Beira, Mozambique 118/F3
Beira, Mozambique 102/F7
Beira, Somalia 115/J2
Beirne, Ark. 202/D6
Beirut (cap.), Lebanon 54/E6
Beirut (cap.), Lebanon 59/C3
Beirut (cap.), Lebanon 63/F6
Beiseker, Alberta 182/D4
Beishan, China 77/E3
Beitbridge, Zimbabwe 118/E4
Beit Fajjar, West Bank 65/C4
Beit Guvrin, Israel 65/B4
Beith, Scotland 10/A1
Beith, Scotland 15/D5
Beit Hanina, West Bank 65/C4
Beit Hanun, Gaza Strip 65/A4
Beit Jala, West Bank 65/C4
Beit Lahm (Bethlehem), West Bank 65/C4
Beit Sahur, West Bank 65/C4
Beiuș, Romania 45/F2
Beja (dist.), Portugal 33/C3
Beja, Portugal 33/C3
Béja, Tunisia 106/F1
Bejaïa, Algeria 106/F1
Bejaïa, Algeria 102/C1
Béjar, Spain 33/D2
Bejestan, Iran 59/G3
Bejestan, Iran 66/K3
Bejhi (riv.), Pakistan 68/B3
Bejou, Minn. 255/B3
Bejucal, Cuba 158/C1
Bejucal, Cuba 156/A2
Bekasi, Indonesia 85/H2
Békés (co.), Hungary 41/F3
Békés, Hungary 41/F3
Békéscsaba, Hungary 41/F3
Bekily, Madagascar 118/G4
Bekwai, Ghana 106/D7
Bel, La. 238/D6
Bela, Pakistan 68/B3
Bela, Pakistan 59/J4
Bélabo, Cameroon 115/B3
Bela Crkva, Yugoslavia 45/E3
Bélair, Manitoba 179/F4
Bel Air, Md. 245/N2
Bélair, Québec 172/H3
Bel Alton, Md. 245/L7
Belas, Portugal 33/A1
Bela Vista, Brazil 120/D5
Bela Vista, Mato Grosso, Brazil 132/C8
Bela Vista, Rondônia, Brazil 132/H10
Bela Vista, Mozambique 118/E5
Bela Vista de Goiás, Brazil 132/D7
Belawan, Indonesia 85/B5
Belaya (riv.), U.S.S.R. 7/K3
Belaya (riv.), U.S.S.R. 52/H3
Belaya Tserkov', U.S.S.R. 52/C5
Belbeck, Sask. 181/F5
Belbutte, Sask. 181/D2
Bełchatów, Poland 47/D3
Belcher, Ky. 237/S6
Belcher, La. 238/C1
Belcher (isls.), N.W.T. 146/K4
Belcher (isl.), N.W.T. 162/H4
Belcher (chan.), N.W. Terr. 187/J2
Belcheragh, Afghanistan 68/B1
Belcheragh, Afghanistan 59/J2
Belchertown, Mass. 249/E3
Belchertown•, Mass. 249/E3
Belchite, Spain 33/F2
Belcourt, N. Dak. 282/L2
Belcross, N.C. 281/S2
Belden, Calif. 204/D3
Belden, Miss. 256/G2
Belden, Nebr. 264/G2
Belden, N. Dak. 282/F3
Beldenville, Wis. 317/A6
Belding, Mich. 250/D5
Belebey, U.S.S.R. 52/H4
Belém, Brazil 2/G6
Belém, Brazil 120/E3
Belém, Brazil 132/E3
Belém, Portugal 33/A1
Belén, Argentina 143/C2
Belén, Chile 138/B1
Belén, Honduras 154/C3
Belen, Miss. 256/D2
Belen, N. Mex. 274/C4
Belén, Panama 154/G6
Belén, Paraguay 144/D3
Belén, Uruguay 145/B1
Belén (range), Uruguay 145/C1
Belén de los Andaquíes, Colombia 126/C7
Belep (isls.), New Caled. 87/G7
Belet Weyne, Somalia 115/J3
Belet Weyne, Somalia 102/G4
Belev, U.S.S.R. 52/E4
Belfair, Wash. 310/C3
Belfast, Maine 243/E7
Belfast, N.Y. 276/D6
Belfast (dist.), N. Ireland 17/J2
Belfast (cap.), N. Ireland 7/D3
Belfast (cap.), N. Ireland 10/D3
Belfast (cap.), N. Ireland 17/J2
Belfast (inlet), N. Ireland 17/K2
Belfast, Tenn. 237/H10
Belfast Lough (inlet), N. Ireland 10/D3
Belfaux, Switzerland 39/D3
Belfield, N. Dak. 282/D6
Belford, England 13/F2
Belford, N.J. 273/E3
Belfort (terr.), France 28/G4
Belfort, France 28/G4
Belfry, Ky. 237/S5
Belfry, Mont. 262/H5
Belgaum, India 68/C5
Belgique, Mo. 261/N7
Belgium 2/K3
Belgium 7/E3
BELGIUM 27
Belgium, Ill. 222/F3
Belgium, Wis. 317/L8
Belgorod, U.S.S.R. 7/H3
Belgorod, U.S.S.R. 52/E4
Belgorod, U.S.S.R. 48/D4
Belgorod-Dnestrovskiy, U.S.S.R. 52/D5
Belgrade, Maine 243/D7
Belgrade•, Maine 243/D7
Belgrade, Minn. 255/C5
Belgrade, Mo. 261/L7
Belgrade, Mont. 262/E5
Belgrade, Nebr. 264/G3
Belgrade (cap.), Yugoslavia 7/G4
Belgrade (cap.), Yugoslavia 2/K3
Belgrade (cap.), Yugoslavia 45/E3
Belgrade Lakes, Maine 243/D6
Belgrave, Ontario 177/C4
Belgrave Heights, Victoria 97/J5
Belgrave South, Victoria 97/K5
Belgreen, Ala. 195/C2
Belhaven, N.C. 281/R3
Belic, Cuba 158/G4
Belice (riv.), Italy 34/D6
Beli Manastir, Yugoslavia 45/D3
Belington, W. Va. 312/F4
Belitung (Billiton) (isl.), Indonesia 85/D6
Belize 2/E5
Belize 146/K8
BELIZE 154/C2
Belize (riv.), Belize 154/C2
Belize City, Belize 154/C2
Bélizon, Fr. Guiana 131/E3
Belk, Ala. 195/C3
Belknap, Ill. 222/E6
Belknap, Iowa 229/J7
Belknap, Mont. 262/A3
Belknap (co.), N.H. 268/D4
Belknap (mt.), N.H. 268/E5
Belknap (peak), Utah 304/B5
Belkofski, Alaska 196/F3
Bell, Calif. 204/C11
Bell, Fla. 212/D2
Bell (co.), Ky. 237/O7
Bell (isl.), Newf. 166/D2
Bell (isl.), Newf. 166/C3
Bell (isl.), Newf. 162/L5
Bell (pen.), N.W. Terr. 187/K3
Bell (riv.), Que. 162/J6
Bell (riv.), Québec 174/B3
Bell (co.), Texas 303/G6
Bella Bella, Br. Col. 184/D4
Bellac, France 28/D4

Berlin 337

Bellaco, Uruguay 145/B3
Bella Coola, Br. Col. 184/D4
Bella Coola (riv.), Br. Col. 184/D4
Belladère, Haiti 158/C6
Bella Flor, Bolivia 136/A2
Bellaghy, N. Ireland 17/H2
Bellagio, Italy 34/B2
Bellaire, Kansas 232/D2
Bellaire, Mich. 250/D4
Bellaire, Ohio 284/J5
Bellaire, Texas 303/J2
Bellamy, Ala. 195/B6
Bellarmin, Québec 172/G4
Bellarthur, N.C. 281/O3
Bellary, India 68/D5
Bellata, N.S. Wales 97/E1
Bella Unión, Uruguay 145/B1
Bella Villa, Mo. 261/R4
Bella Vista, Corrientes, Argentina 143/E2
Bella Vista, Tucumán, Argentina 143/D2
Bella Vista, Ark. 202/B1
Bella Vista, Bolivia 136/E3
Bella Vista, Salar de (salt dep.), Chile 138/B3
Bella Vista, Paraguay 144/D3
Bella Vista, Paraguay 144/E5
Bellavista, Peru 128/C5
Bell Bay, Tasmania 99/C3
Bellbird-Cessnock, N.S. Wales 97/F3
Bellbrook, Ohio 284/C6
Bell Buckle, Tenn. 237/J9
Bellburns, Newf. 166/C3
Bell Center, Wis. 317/E9
Bell City, La. 238/D6
Bell City, Mo. 261/N8
Belle (riv.), Mich. 250/G6
Belle, Mo. 261/J6
Belle, W. Va. 312/C6
Belleair, Fla. 212/B2
Belleair Beach, Fla. 212/B2
Belleair Bluffs, Fla. 212/B3
Belleair Shore, Fla. 212/B3
Belle-Anse, Haiti 158/C6
Belle Center, Ohio 284/C4
Belle Chasse, La. 238/O4
Bellechasse (co.), Québec 172/G3
Bellechester, Minn. 255/F6
Belle Côte, Nova Scotia 168/G2
Belle D'Eau, La. 238/F4
Belledune, New Bruns. 170/E1
Belleek, N. Ireland 17/E3
Bellefleur, New Bruns. 170/C1
Bellefond, New Bruns. 170/E1
Bellefont, Kansas 232/C4
Bellefontaine, Martinique 161/C6
Bellefontaine, Miss. 256/F3
Bellefontaine, Mo. 261/N2
Bellefontaine, Ohio 284/C5
Bellefontaine Neighbors, Mo. 261/R2
Bellefonte, Ark. 202/D1
Bellefonte, Del. 245/S1
Bellefonte, Pa. 294/G4
Belle Fourche (riv.) 188/F2
Belle Fourche, S. Dak. 298/B4
Belle Fourche (res.), S. Dak. 298/B4
Belle Fourche (riv.), S. Dak. 298/C4
Belle Fourche (riv.), Wyo. 319/H1
Bellegarde, Sask. 181/K6
Belle Glade, Fla. 212/F5
Belle Glade Camp, Fla. 212/F5
Belle Haven, Va. 307/S5
Belle-Île (isl.), France 28/B4
Belle Isle (str.), Canada 146/N5
Belle Isle (str.), Canada 2/G3
Belle Isle, Fla. 212/E3
Belleisle (bay), New Bruns. 170/E3
Belle Isle (isl.), Newf. 166/C3
Belle Isle (str.), Newf. 166/C3
Belle Isle (str.), Newf. 162/L5
Belleisle Creek, New Bruns. 170/E3
Belle-Marche, Nova Scotia 168/H2
Belle Mead, N.J. 273/D3
Bellemeade, Ky. 237/K2
Belle Meade, Tenn. 237/H8
Belle Mina, Ala. 195/E1
Bellemont, Ariz. 198/D3
Belleoram, Newf. 166/C4
Belleplain, N.J. 273/D5
Belleplaine, Barbados 161/B8
Belle Plaine, Iowa 229/J5
Belle Plaine, Kansas 232/E4
Belle Plaine, Minn. 255/E6
Belle Plaine, Sask. 181/F5
Belle Prairie City, Ill. 222/E5
Belle Rive, Ill. 222/E5
Belle River, Minn. 255/C5
Belle River, Ontario 177/B5
Belle Rose, La. 238/K3
Bellerose, N.Y. 276/P7
Belle Terre, N.Y. 276/O9
Belleterre, Québec 174/B3
Belle Union, Ind. 227/D5
Belle Valley, Ohio 284/G6
Belle Vernon, Pa. 294/C5
Belleview, Fla. 212/D2
Belleview, Manitoba 179/B5
Belleview, Mo. 261/L7
Belle View, Va. 307/T3
Belleville, Ark. 202/D3
Belleville, Fla. 212/C1
Belleville, France 28/F4
Belleville, Ill. 188/J3
Belleville, Ill. 222/B3
Belleville, Kansas 232/E2
Belleville, Mich. 250/F6
Belleville, N.J. 273/B2
Belleville, N.Y. 276/H3
Belleville, Ontario 177/G3
Belleville, Pa. 294/G4
Belleville, W. Va. 312/C4
Belleville, Wis. 317/G10
Bellevue, Alberta 182/C5
Bellevue, Idaho 220/D6
Bellevue, Iowa 229/M4
Bellevue, Ky. 237/S1
Bellevue, Md. 245/O6
Bellevue, Mich. 250/E6
Bellevue, Nebr. 264/J3
Bellevue, Newf. 166/D2
Bellevue, Ohio 284/E3
Bellevue, Pa. 294/B6
Bellevue, Sask. 181/F3
Bellevue, Texas 303/F4
Bellevue, Wash. 310/B2
Belley, France 28/F5
Bell Farm, Ky. 237/M7
Bellflower, Calif. 204/C11
Bellflower, Ill. 222/E3
Bellflower, Mo. 261/K4
Bellfountain, Oreg. 291/D3
Bell Gardens, Calif. 204/C11
Bellingen, N.S. Wales 97/G2
Bellingham, England 13/E2
Bellingham, Mass. 249/J4
Bellingham•, Mass. 249/J4
Bellingham, Minn. 255/B5
Bellingham, Wash. 188/B1
Bellingham, Wash. 310/C2
Bellingham, Wash. 310/80
Bellingshausen (sea), Ant. 2/E9
Bellingshausen (sea), Ant. 5/C14
Bellinzona, Switzerland 39/H4
Bell-Irving (riv.), Br. Col. 184/C2
Bellis, Alberta 182/D2
Belliveau Cove, Nova Scotia 168/B4
Bellmawr, N.J. 273/B3
Bellmead, Texas 303/H6
Bellmont, Ill. 222/F5
Bellmore, Ind. 227/C5
Bellmore, N.Y. 276/R7
Bello, Colombia 126/C4
Bello, Colombia 120/B2
Bellona (reefs), New Caled. 87/G8
Bellona (isl.), Solomon Is. 86/D3
Bellot (str.), N.W.T. 162/G1
Bellot (str.), N.W. Terr. 187/J2
Bellows Falls, Vt. 268/C5
Belloy, Alberta 182/A2
Bellport, N.Y. 276/P9
Bell Rock, N.W. Terr. 187/G3
Bell Rock (isl.), Scotland 15/F4
Bells, Tenn. 237/C9
Bells, Texas 303/H4
Bellsbank, Scotland 15/D5
Bellshill, Scotland 15/C2
Bellsite, Manitoba 179/B2
Bellsund, Norway 18/C2
Belluno (prov.), Italy 34/D1
Belluno, Italy 34/D1
Bellview, Ala. 195/D7
Bellview, N. Mex. 274/F4
Bell Ville, Argentina 143/D3
Bell Ville, Argentina 120/C6
Bellville, Georgia 217/H6
Bellville, Ohio 284/E4
Bellville, S. Africa 118/F6
Bellville, Texas 303/H8
Bellvue, Colo. 208/J1
Bellwald, Switzerland 39/F4
Bellwood, Ala. 195/G8
Bellwood, Ill. 222/B5
Bellwood, La. 238/D3
Bellwood, Nebr. 264/G3
Bellwood, Pa. 294/F4
Belly (riv.), Alberta 182/D5
Belmar, N.J. 273/E3
Bélmez, Spain 33/D3
Belmond, Iowa 229/F3
Belmont, Ala. 195/C5
Belmont, Calif. 204/J3
Belmont, Georgia 217/E2
Belmont, Kansas 232/D4
Belmont, Ky. 237/K5
Belmont, La. 238/C3
Belmont•, Maine 243/E7
Belmont, Manitoba 179/C5
Belmont•, Mass. 249/C6
Belmont, Miss. 256/H1
Belmont, Mont. 262/G4
Belmont•, N.H. 268/E5
Belmont, N.Y. 276/E6
Belmont, N. Zealand 100/B2
Belmont, N.C. 281/H4
Belmont, Nova Scotia 168/E3
Belmont (co.), Ohio 284/J5
Belmont, Ohio 284/J5
Belmont, Ontario 177/C5
Belmont, Wash. 310/H3
Belmont, W. Va. 312/D4
Belmont, Wis. 317/F10
Belmonte, Brazil 132/G6
Belmonte, Portugal 33/C2
Belmonte, Spain 33/E3
Belmopan (cap.), Belize 146/K8
Belmopan (cap.), Belize 154/C2
Belmore, N.S. Wales 97/J3
Belmore, Ohio 284/B3
Belmullet, Ireland 17/B3
Bel-Nor, Mo. 261/P2
Belo, W. Va. 312/B7
Beloeil, Belgium 27/D7
Beloeil, Québec 172/D4
Belogorsk, U.S.S.R. 54/O4
Belogorsk, U.S.S.R. 48/N4
Belogradchik, Bulgaria 45/F4
Belo Horizonte, Brazil 2/G6
Belo Horizonte, Brazil 120/E4
Belo Horizonte, Brazil 132/F7
Belo Horizonte, Brazil 135/D1
Beloit, Ala. 195/D6
Beloit, Kansas 232/D2
Beloit, Ohio 284/J4
Beloit, Wis. 188/J2
Beloit, Wis. 317/H10
Belomorsk, U.S.S.R. 48/D3
Belomorsk, U.S.S.R. 52/D2
Belorado, Spain 33/E1
Belorechensk, U.S.S.R. 52/E6
Beloretsk, U.S.S.R. 52/J4
Beloretsk, U.S.S.R. 48/F4
Belorussian S.S.R., U.S.S.R. 7/G3
Belorussian S.S.R., U.S.S.R. 48/C4
Belorussian S.S.R., U.S.S.R. 52/C4
Belo-Tsiribihina, Madagascar 118/G3
Belovo, U.S.S.R. 48/J4
Beloye (lake), U.S.S.R. 48/D3
Beloye (lake), U.S.S.R. 52/E2
Belozersk, U.S.S.R. 52/E3
Belp, Switzerland 39/D3
Belpre, Kansas 232/C4
Belpre, Ohio 284/G7
Bel-Ridge, Mo. 261/P2
Belshaw, Ind. 227/C2
Belt, Mont. 262/E3
Belted (range), Nev. 266/E5
Belterra, Brazil 132/C3
Belton, Ky. 237/H6
Belton, Mo. 261/C5
Belton, S.C. 296/C2
Belton, Texas 303/G7
Beltra (lake), Ireland 17/C4
Beltrami (co.), Minn. 255/C2
Beltrami, Minn. 255/B3
Beltsville, Md. 245/G3
Bel'tsy, U.S.S.R. 7/G4
Bel'tsy, U.S.S.R. 52/C5
Belturbet, Ireland 17/G3
Beluga (lake), Alaska 196/B1
Belumut, Gunong (mt.), Malaysia 72/D7
Belush'ya Guba, U.S.S.R. 4/B7
Belush'ya Guba, U.S.S.R. 52/H1
Belva, W. Va. 312/D6
Belvedere, Calif. 204/H2
Belvedere, Georgia 217/L1
Belvidere, Ill. 222/E1
Belvidere, Kansas 232/C4
Belvidere, Nebr. 264/G4
Belvidere, N.J. 273/C2
Belvidere, N.C. 281/S2
Belvidere, S. Dak. 298/G6
Belvidere, Tenn. 237/J10
Belvidere•, Vt. 268/B2
Belvidere (mt.), Vt. 268/B2
Belvidere Center, Vt. 268/B2
Belvidere Junction, Vt. 268/B2
Belview, Minn. 255/C6
Belville, N.C. 281/N6
Belvue, Kansas 232/F2
Belwood, N.C. 281/F4
Belwood, Ontario 177/D4
Belyando (riv.), Queensland 88/H4
Belyando (riv.), Queensland 95/C4
Belyy (isl.), U.S.S.R. 4/B6
Belyy (isl.), U.S.S.R. 48/G2
Belzoni, Miss. 256/C4
Belzoni, Okla. 288/R6
Bełżyce, Poland 47/F3
Bem, Mo. 261/K6
Bembe, Angola 115/B5
Bemboka, N.S. Wales 97/E5
Bement, Ill. 222/E4
Bemersyde, Sask. 181/J5
Bemidji, Minn. 255/D3
Bemidji (lake), Minn. 255/D3
Bemis, S. Dak. 298/R4
Bemiss, Georgia 217/F9
Bemmel, Netherlands 27/H5
Bemus Point, N.Y. 276/B6
Bena, Minn. 255/D3
Benabarre, Spain 33/G1
Bena-Dibele, Zaire 115/D4
Ben Alder (mt.), Scotland 15/D4
Benalla, Victoria 97/D5
Benalto, Alberta 182/C3
Benanee, N.S. Wales 97/B4
Benares (Varanasi), India 68/E3
Benavente, Spain 33/D1
Benavides, Texas 303/F10
Ben Avon, Pa. 294/B6
Ben Avon (mt.), Scotland 15/E3
Ben Barvas (mt.), Scotland 15/B2
Benbecula (isl.), Scotland 15/A3
Benbecula (isl.), Scotland 10/C2
Benbrook, Texas 303/E2
Benbrook (lake), Texas 303/E3
Benchland, Mont. 262/F3
Ben Cruachan (mt.), Scotland 15/C4
Bencubbin, W. Australia 92/B5
Bend, Oreg. 188/B2
Bend, Oreg. 291/F3
Bend, Texas 303/F7
Ben Dash (hill), Ireland 17/C6
Ben Davis (pt.), N.J. 273/C5
Bendel (state), Nigeria 106/F7
Bendemeer, N.S. Wales 97/F2
Bendena, Kansas 232/G2
Bender Beila, Somalia 115/K2
Bender Beila, Somalia 102/G4
Bender Cassim (Bosaso), Somalia 115/J1
Bendersville, Pa. 294/H6
Bendery, U.S.S.R. 52/C5
Bendigo, Australia 87/E9
Bendigo, Victoria 88/G7
Bendigo, Victoria 97/C5
Bendoc, Victoria 97/E5
Bendon, Mich. 250/D4
Bendorf, Germany 22/B3
Bene Beraq, Israel 65/B3
Benedict (pond), Conn. 210/C1
Benedict, Kansas 232/G4
Benedict, Md. 245/M6
Benedict, Minn. 255/D3
Benedict, Nebr. 264/G3
Benedict (mt.), Newf. 166/C3
Benedict, N. Dak. 282/H4
Benedicta•, Maine 243/G4
Beneditinos, Brazil 132/F4
Benenitra, Madagascar 118/H4
Benešov, Czech. 41/C2
Beneveian, Loch (lake), Scotland 15/D3
Benevento (prov.), Italy 34/E4
Benevento, Italy 34/E4
Benevolence, Georgia 217/C7
Benewah (co.), Idaho 220/B2
Benezett, Pa. 294/F3
Benfica, Portugal 33/A1
Benfleet, England 13/J8
Benga, Mozambique 118/E3
Bengal (bay) 54/K8
Bengal, Bay of (sea) 2/P5
Bengal, Bay of (sea), Bangladesh 68/F5
Bengal, Bay of (sea), Burma 72/B3
Bengal, Bay of (sea), India 68/F5
Bengal, Ind. 227/F6
Bengal, Okla. 288/R5
Ben Gardane, Tunisia 106/G2
Bengbis, Cameroon 115/B3
Bengbu (Pengpu), China 77/J5
Benge, Wash. 310/G4
Benggala (str.), Indonesia 85/A4
Benghazi, Libya 2/L4
Benghazi, Libya 102/D1
Benghazi, Libya 111/C1
Ben Ghnema, Jebel (mts.), Libya 111/C2
Bengkalis, Indonesia 85/C5
Bengkayang, Indonesia 85/E5
Bengkulu, Indonesia 85/C6
Bengo (prov.), Angola 115/B5
Bengough, Sask. 181/F6
Ben Griam More (mt.), Scotland 15/D2
Bengtsfors, Sweden 18/H7
Benguela (prov.), Angola 115/B6
Benguela, Angola 115/B6
Benguela, Angola 102/D6
Ben Guerdane (well), Mauritania 106/B3
Benguet (prov.), Philippines 82/C2
Benha, Egypt 111/J3
Benham, Ky. 237/R7
Benham, N.C. 281/G2
Benhams, Va. 307/D7
Ben Hee (mt.), Scotland 15/D2
Ben Hill (co.), Georgia 217/F7
Ben Hope (mt.), Scotland 15/D2
Ben Horn (mt.), Scotland 15/D2
Ben Hur, Va. 307/B7
Beni, El (dept.), Bolivia 136/C3
Beni (riv.), Bolivia 120/C4
Beni (riv.), Bolivia 136/B2
Beni, Zaire 115/E3
Beni Abbès, Algeria 106/D2
Benicarló, Spain 33/G2
Benicia, Calif. 204/K1
Benicito (riv.), Bolivia 136/C3
Beni Mazar, Egypt 111/J4
Beni Mellal, Morocco 106/C2
Beni Mellal, Morocco 102/B1
Benin 2/K5
Benin 102/C4
BENIN 106/E7
Benin (bight), Benin 106/E8
Benin (bight), Ghana 106/E8
Benin (bight), Nigeria 106/E8
Benin (bight), Togo 106/E8
Benin City, Nigeria 106/F7
Benin City, Nigeria 102/C4
Beni Ounif, Algeria 106/D2
Beni Saf, Algeria 106/D1
Beni Suef, Egypt 111/J3
Beni Suef, Egypt 102/E2
Beni Suef, Egypt 59/B4
Benito, Manitoba 179/A3
Beni Ulid, Libya 111/B1
Benjamín (isl.), Chile 138/D5
Benjamin, New Bruns. 170/D1
Benjamin (lake), Oreg. 291/G4
Benjamin, Texas 303/E4
Benjamin, Utah 304/C3
Benjamín Aceval, Paraguay 144/C4
Benjamin Constant, Brazil 132/G9
Benjamin Constant, Brazil 120/B3
Benjamín Hill, Mexico 150/D1
Benkelman, Nebr. 264/C4
Ben Kilbreck (mt.), Scotland 15/D2
Ben Lawers (mt.), Scotland 15/D4
Benld, Ill. 222/D4
Ben Lomond, Ark. 202/B6
Ben Lomond, Calif. 204/K4
Ben Lomond, New Bruns. 170/E3
Ben Lomond (mt.), Scotland 15/D4
Ben Loyal (mt.), Scotland 15/D2
Ben Lui (mt.), Scotland 15/D4
Ben Macdhui (mt.), Scotland 15/E3
Ben Mhor (mt.), Scotland 15/A3
Ben More (mt.), Scotland 15/D4
Ben More (mt.), Scotland 15/B4
Ben More Assynt (mt.), Scotland 15/D2
Bennan (head), Scotland 15/C5
Bennane (head), Scotland 15/C5
Benndale, Miss. 256/G9
Bennet, Nebr. 264/H4
Bennett, Br. Col. 184/J1
Bennett, W.A.C. (dam), Br. Col. 184/F2
Bennett, Colo. 208/L3
Bennett (peak), Colo. 208/G7
Bennett (creek), Idaho 220/C6
Bennett, Iowa 229/L5
Bennett, N.C. 281/K3
Bennett (lake), North. Terr. 93/B7
Bennett (co.), S. Dak. 298/F7
Bennett, Wis. 317/C3
Bennettsbridge, Ireland 17/G6
Bennetts Point, S.C. 296/G6
Bennetts Switch, Ind. 227/E3
Bennettsville, S.C. 296/H2
Bennettville, Minn. 255/E4
Ben Nevis (mt.), Scotland 7/D3
Ben Nevis (mt.), Scotland 15/D4
Ben Nevis (mt.), Scotland 10/D2
Benning, D.C. 245/F5
Bennington, Idaho 220/G7
Bennington, Ind. 227/G7
Bennington, Kansas 232/E2
Bennington, Nebr. 264/H3
Bennington•, N.H. 268/D5
Bennington, Okla. 288/P7
Bennington (co.), Vt. 268/A6
Bennington, Vt. 268/A6
Bennington•, Vt. 268/A6
Benns Church, Va. 307/P7
Benoit, Miss. 256/C3
Benoit, Wis. 317/D3
Benom, Gunong (mt.), Malaysia 72/D7
Benoni, S. Africa 118/J6
Bensenville, Ill. 222/B5
Bensheim, Germany 22/C4
Benson, Ariz. 198/E7
Benson, Ill. 222/D3
Benson, La. 238/C3
Benson, Minn. 255/C5
Benson, N.C. 281/N4
Benson (co.), N. Dak. 282/M3
Benson (Hollsopple), Pa. 294/E5
Benson, Sask. 181/J6
Benson•, Vt. 268/A4
Benson Landing, Vt. 268/A4
Bens Run, W. Va. 312/D4
Bent (co.), Colo. 208/N7
Bent, N. Mex. 274/D5
Bent Creek, Va. 307/L5
Benteng, Indonesia 85/F7
Bentham, England 13/E3
Bentheim, Germany 22/B2
Bentiaba, Angola 114/B6
Bentinck (isl.), Burma 72/C5
Bentinck (isl.), Queensland 88/F3
Bentinck (isl.), Queensland 95/A3
Bentiu, Sudan 111/E6
Bentley, Alberta 182/C3
Bentley, Ill. 222/B3
Bentley, Iowa 229/B6
Bentley, Kansas 232/E4
Bentley, La. 238/E3
Bentley, Mich. 250/E5
Bentley, N. Dak. 282/F7
Bentley, Okla. 288/O6
Bentley Springs, Md. 245/M2
Bentleyville, Ohio 284/J9
Bentleyville, Pa. 294/B5
Bentley with Arksey, England 13/F4
Bent Mountain, Va. 307/H6
Bento Gonçalves, Brazil 132/C10
Benton, Ala. 195/E6
Benton, Alberta 182/E4
Benton (co.), Ark. 202/B1
Benton, Ark. 202/E4
Benton, Calif. 204/G6
Benton, Ill. 222/E6
Benton (co.), Ind. 227/C3
Benton, Ind. 227/F2
Benton (co.), Iowa 229/J4
Benton, Iowa 229/E7
Benton, Kansas 232/E4
Benton, Ky. 237/E7
Benton, La. 238/C1
Benton•, Maine 243/D6
Benton (co.), Minn. 255/D5
Benton, Minn. 255/F6
Benton (lake), Minn. 255/B6
Benton (co.), Miss. 256/F1
Benton, Miss. 256/D5
Benton (co.), Mo. 261/F6
Benton, Mo. 261/O8
Benton (lake), Mont. 262/E3
Benton, New Bruns. 170/C3
Benton•, N.H. 268/D3
Benton, Ohio 284/G4
Benton (co.), Oreg. 291/D3
Benton, Pa. 294/K3
Benton (co.), Tenn. 237/E8
Benton, Tenn. 237/M10
Benton (co.), Wash. 310/F4
Benton, Wis. 317/F10
Benton City, Mo. 261/J4
Benton City, Wash. 310/F4
Bentong, Malaysia 72/D7
Benton Harbor, Mich. 250/C6
Benton Heights, Mich. 250/C6
Bentonia, Miss. 256/D5
Benton Ridge, Ohio 284/C4
Bentonsport, Iowa 229/K7
Bentonville, Ark. 202/B1
Bentonville, Ind. 227/G5
Bentonville, Ohio 284/C8
Bentonville, Va. 307/M3
Bent's Old Fort Nat'l Hist. Site, Colo. 208/M6
Benué (riv.), Cameroon 115/A2
Benue (state), Nigeria 106/F7
Benue (riv.), Nigeria 102/C4
Benue (riv.), Nigeria 106/F7
Ben Vorlich (mt.), Scotland 15/D4
Ben Vrackie (mt.), Scotland 15/E4
Benwee (head), Ireland 17/B3
Benwood, W. Va. 312/E2
Ben Wyvis (mt.), Scotland 15/D3
Benxi (Penki), China 77/K3
Benxi, China 54/O5
Benzie (co.), Mich. 250/C4
Benzonia, Mich. 250/D4
Beo, Indonesia 85/H5
Beograd (Belgrade) (cap.), Yugoslavia 45/E3
Beowawe, Nev. 266/E2
Beppu, Japan 81/E7
Bequia (isl.), St. Vin. & Grens. 156/G4
Beragh, N. Ireland 17/G2
Berar (reg.), India 68/D4
Berat, Albania 45/D5
Berau (bay), Indonesia 85/J6
Berber, Sudan 111/F4
Berber, Sudan 59/B6
Berber, Sudan 102/F3
Berbera, Somalia 115/J1
Berbera, Somalia 102/G3
Berberati, Cent. Afr. Rep. 102/D4
Berberati, Cent. Afr. Rep. 115/C3
Berbice (riv.), Guyana 131/B3
Berchem, Belgium 27/F6
Berchem-Sainte-Agathe, Belgium 27/B9
Bercher, Switzerland 39/C3
Berchtesgaden, Germany 22/E5
Berck, France 28/D2
Berclair, Texas 303/G9
Berdichev, U.S.S.R. 48/C5
Berdichev, U.S.S.R. 52/C5
Berdsk, U.S.S.R. 48/J4
Berdyansk, U.S.S.R. 7/H4
Berdyansk, U.S.S.R. 52/E5
Berea, Ky. 237/N5
Berea, Nebr. 264/A2
Berea, N.C. 281/M2
Berea, Ohio 284/G10
Berea, S.C. 296/C2
Berea, Spain 33/C1
Berea, W. Va. 312/E4
Bereda, Somalia 115/K1
Bereda, Somalia 102/H3
Beregovo, U.S.S.R. 52/B5
Berekum, Ghana 106/D7
Berenguela, Bolivia 136/A5
Berenice (ruins), Egypt 111/F3
Berens (riv.), Man. 162/G5
Berens (isl.), Manitoba 179/E2
Berens (riv.), Manitoba 179/F2
Berens (riv.), Ontario 175/A2
Berens River, Man. 162/G5
Berens River, Manitoba 179/F2
Beresford (lake), Fla. 212/E3
Beresford, New Bruns. 170/E1
Beresford, S. Dak. 298/R7
Beresford Lake, Manitoba 179/G4
Bereşti Tîrg, Romania 45/H2
Berettyó (riv.), Hungary 41/F3
Berettyóújfalu, Hungary 41/F3
Berezina (riv.), U.S.S.R. 52/C4
Bereznik, U.S.S.R. 52/F2
Berezniki, U.S.S.R. 7/K3
Berezniki, U.S.S.R. 48/F4
Berezniki, U.S.S.R. 52/J3
Berezovo, U.S.S.R. 48/G3
Berg, Norway 18/K2
Berg, Switzerland 39/H1
Berga, Algeria 106/E3
Berga, Spain 33/G1
Bergama, Turkey 63/B3
Bergama, Turkey 59/A2
Bergamo (prov.), Italy 34/B2
Bergamo, Italy 34/B2
Bergeijk, Netherlands 27/G6
Bergen (Mons), Belgium 27/E8
Bergen, Germany 22/E1
Bergen, Minn. 255/D7
Bergen, Netherlands 27/F3
Bergen (co.), N.J. 273/E2
Bergen, N.Y. 276/E4
Bergen, N. Dak. 282/J3
Bergen, Norway 18/D6
Bergen, Norway 7/E2
Berg en Dal, Suriname 131/D3
Bergenfield, N.J. 273/C1
Bergen op Zoom, Netherlands 27/E5
Berger, Mo. 261/K5
Bergerac, France 28/D5
Bergholz, Ohio 284/J4
Bergisch Gladbach, Germany 22/B3
Bergland, Mich. 250/F1
Bergman, Ark. 202/E1
Bergoo, W. Va. 312/F6
Bergos (riv.), Turkey 63/C6
Bergshamra, Sweden 18/L7
Bergsjö, Sweden 18/K5
Bergstrom A.F.B., Texas 303/G7
Bergton, Va. 307/L3
Berguent, Morocco 106/D2
Bergum, Netherlands 27/H2
Bergumermeer (lake), Netherlands 27/J2
Bergün-Bravuogn, Switzerland 39/J3
Berhala (str.), Indonesia 85/C6
Berhampore, India 68/F4
Berhampur, India 68/F5
Berhida, Hungary 41/E3
Bering (sea) 2/A3
Bering (sea) 54/V4
Bering (sea) 146/A3
Bering (str.) 4/C18
Bering (str.) 54/W3
Bering (str.) 146/B3
Bering (glac.), Alaska 196/K2
Bering (sea), Alaska 188/C6
Bering (sea), Alaska 196/D2
Bering (str.), Alaska 188/C5
Bering (str.), Alaska 196/E1
Bering (isl.), U.S.S.R. 48/R4
Bering (sea), U.S.S.R. 48/S4
Bering (str.), U.S.S.R. 48/U3
Beringen, Belgium 27/G6
Bering Land Bridge Nat'l Pres., Alaska 196/F1
Beringovskiy, U.S.S.R. 48/T3
Berino, N. Mex. 274/C6
Berja, Spain 33/E4
Berkåk, Norway 18/G5
Berkel, Netherlands 27/F5
Berkeley, Calif. 188/B3
Berkeley, Calif. 204/J2
Berkeley, Ill. 222/B5
Berkeley, Mo. 261/P2
Berkeley (co.), S.C. 296/G5
Berkeley (co.), W. Va. 312/K4
Berkeley, W. Va. 312/L4
Berkeley Heights•, N.J. 273/E2
Berkeley Lake, Georgia 217/D3
Berkeley Springs, W. Va. 312/K3
Berken, Libya 111/B2
Berkey, Ohio 284/C2
Berkhamsted, England 13/G7
Berkhout, Netherlands 27/F3
Berkley, Iowa 229/E5
Berkley•, Mass. 249/K5
Berkley, Mich. 250/B6
Berkner (isl.), Ant. 2/G10
Berkner (isl.), Ant. 5/B16
Berkovitsa, Bulgaria 45/F4
Berks (co.), Pa. 294/K5
Berkshire, Conn. 210/B3
Berkshire (co.), England 13/F6
Berkshire (co.), Mass. 249/B3
Berkshire (hills), Mass. 249/B4
Berkshire, N.Y. 276/H6
Berkshire•, Vt. 268/B2
Berland (riv.), Alberta 182/A3
Berlanga de Duero, Spain 33/E2
Berleburg (Bad Berleburg), Germany 22/C3
Berlevåg, Norway 18/Q1
Berlin•, Conn. 210/E2
Berlin, Georgia 217/E8
Berlin (cap.), Germany 7/F3
Berlin (cap.), Germany 2/K3
Berlin (cap.), Germany 22/F4
Berlin (state), Germany 22/F4
Berlin, Ill. 222/D4

338 Berlin

Berlin, Md. 245/T7
Berlin•, Mass. 249/H3
Berlin (mt.), Nev. 266/D4
Berlin, N.H. 188/M2
Berlin, N.H. 268/E3
Berlin, N.J. 273/D4
Berlin, N.Y. 276/O5
Berlin, N. Dak. 282/O7
Berlin, Ohio 284/G4
Berlin (lake), Ohio 284/H4
Berlin, Okla. 288/G4
Berlin, Pa. 294/E6
Berlin (pond), Vt. 268/B3
Berlin, W. Va. 312/F4
Berlin, Wis. 317/H8
Berlin Center, Ohio 284/J3
Berlin Heights, Ohio 284/F3
Bermagui, N.S. Wales 97/F5
Bermeja (pt.), Argentina 143/D5
Bermejo (riv.), Argentina 120/C5
Bermejo (riv.), Argentina 143/E2
Bermejo (riv.), Bolivia 136/C8
Bermen (lake), Québec 174/D2
Bermeo, Spain 33/E1
Bermillo de Sayago, Spain 33/D2
Bermuda (isl.) (U.K.) 2/F4
Bermuda (isls.) 146/M6
BERMUDA 156/G3
Bermuda, Ala. 195/D8
Bermuda (isl.), Bermuda 156/H3
Bermuda, La. 238/D3
Bern, Idaho 220/G7
Bern, Kansas 232/F2
Bern (canton), Switzerland 39/D2
Bern (cap.), Switzerland 7/E4
Bern (cap.), Switzerland 39/D3
Bernabé Rivera, Uruguay 145/B1
Bernadotte, Minn. 255/D6
Bernalillo (co.), N. Mex. 274/C4
Bernalillo, N. Mex. 274/C3
Bernard, Iowa 229/M4
Bernardino de Sahagún, Mexico 150/M1
Bernardo, N. Mex. 274/C4
Bernardo de Irigoyen, Argentina 143/F2
Bernardston•, Mass. 249/D2
Bernardsville, N.J. 273/D2
Bernasconi, Argentina 143/D4
Bernau bei Berlin, Germany 22/E2
Bernay, France 28/D3
Bernburg, Germany 22/D3
Berndorf, Austria 41/C3
Berne, Ind. 227/H3
Berne, N.Y. 276/M5
Bernera (isl.), Scotland 15/B2
Berneray (isl.), Scotland 15/A4
Berneray (isl.), Scotland 15/A3
Bernese Oberland (reg.), Switzerland 39/E3
Bernhards Bay, N.Y. 276/J4
Bernic (lake), Manitoba 179/G4
Bernice, La. 238/E1
Bernice, Okla. 288/S1
Bernic Lake, Manitoba 179/G4
Bernie, Mo. 261/M9
Bernier (bay), N.W. Terr. 187/K2
Bernier (isl.), W. Australia 88/A4
Bernier (isl.), W. Australia 92/A4
Bernierville, Québec 172/F3
Bernina (pass), Italy 34/C1
Bernina, Piz (peak), Italy 34/B1
Bernina (mts.), Switzerland 39/J4
Bernina (pass), Switzerland 39/K4
Bernina (peak), Switzerland 39/J4
Bernina (riv.), Switzerland 39/J4
Bernkastel-Kues, Germany 22/B4
Bernstadt, Ky. 237/N6
Bernville, Pa. 294/K5
Bero (riv.), Angola 115/B7
Beromünster, Switzerland 39/F2
Beroroha, Madagascar 118/G4
Beroun, Czech. 41/B2
Beroun, Minn. 255/F5
Berounka (riv.), Czech. 41/C2
Berovo, Yugoslavia 45/F5
Berre (lag.), France 28/F6
Berri, S. Australia 88/G6
Berri, S. Australia 94/G6
Berridale, N.S. Wales 97/E5
Berriedale, Scotland 15/E2
Berrien (co.), Georgia 217/F8
Berrien (co.), Mich. 250/C7
Berrien Springs, Mich. 250/C7
Berrigan, N.S. Wales 97/C4
Berrondo, Uruguay 145/C5
Berry, Ala. 195/C3
Berry (creek), Alberta 182/E4
Berry (isls.), Bahamas 156/B1
Berry (head), England 13/D7
Berry (trad. prov.) France 29
Berry, Ky. 237/N3
Berry, N.S. Wales 97/F4
Berry (head), Nova Scotia 168/G3
Berryessa (lake), Calif. 204/D5
Berry Hill, Tenn. 237/H8
Berry Mills, New Bruns. 170/E2
Berrymoor, Alberta 182/C3
Berrysburg, Pa. 294/J4
Berry's Chapel, Tenn. 237/H9
Berrys Lick, Ky. 237/H6
Berryton, Georgia 217/B2
Berryton, Kansas 232/G3
Berryville, Ark. 202/C1
Berryville, Va. 307/M2
Berseba, Namibia 118/B5
Bertha, Minn. 255/C4
Berthier (co.), Québec 172/C3
Berthier (county), Québec 174/B3
Berthier-en-Bas, Québec 172/G3
Berthierville, Québec 172/D3
Berthold, N. Dak. 282/G3
Berthoud, Colo. 208/J2
Berthoud Pass, Colo. 208/H3
Bertie (co.), N.C. 281/P2
Bertogne, Belgium 27/H8
Bertolinia, Brazil 132/F4
Bertoua, Cameroon 115/B3
Bertraghboy (bay), Ireland 17/A5
Bertram, Iowa 229/K5
Bertram, Texas 303/F7
Bertrand, Cerro (mt.), Chile 138/D8
Bertrand, Mo. 261/O9
Bertrand, Nebr. 264/E4
Bertrand, New Bruns. 170/E1
Bertrandville, La. 238/L7
Bertrix, Belgium 27/G9
Bertwell, Sask. 181/J3
Beru (atoll), Kiribati 87/H6
Beruni, U.S.S.R. 48/G5
Bervie, Ontario 177/C3
Berwick, Ill. 222/C3
Berwick, Iowa 229/G5
Berwick, Kansas 232/G2
Berwick, La. 238/H7
Berwick, Maine 243/B9
Berwick•, Maine 243/B9
Berwick, New Bruns. 170/E3
Berwick, N. Dak. 282/K3
Berwick, Nova Scotia 168/D4
Berwick, Pa. 294/K3
Berwick (trad. co.), Scotland 15/B5
Berwick, Victoria 97/K6
Berwick-upon-Tweed, England 13/F2
Berwick-upon-Tweed, England 10/F3
Berwind, W. Va. 312/C8
Berwyn, Alberta 182/B1
Berwyn, Ill. 222/B6
Berwyn, Nebr. 264/E3
Berwyn, Pa. 294/L5
Berwyn (mts.), Wales 13/D5
Berwyn Heights, Md. 245/G4
Beryl, Utah 304/A6
Beryl, W. Va. 312/H4
Berzence, Hungary 41/D3
Besalampy, Madagascar 118/G3
Besançon, France 28/G4
Besançon, France 7/E4
Beşiktaş, Turkey 63/D6
Beşiri, Turkey 63/J4
Beskids, West (mts.), Czech. 41/E2
Beskids, East (mts.), Czech. 41/F1
Beskids (range), Poland 47/D4
Beslan, U.S.S.R. 52/F6
Besni, Turkey 63/G4
Besor (riv.), Israel 65/B5
Bessbrook, N. Ireland 17/J3
Bessèges, France 28/F5
Bessemer, Ala. 188/J4
Bessemer, Ala. 195/D4
Bessemer, Mich. 250/F2
Bessemer, Pa. 294/B4
Bessemer City, N.C. 281/G4
Bessie, Okla. 288/H4
Best, Texas 303/C6
Beswick, North. Terr. 88/E2
Beswick Aboriginal Res., North. Terr. 88/E2
Beswick Aboriginal Res., North. Terr. 93/C3
Beta, N.C. 281/C4
Betanzos, Bolivia 136/C6
Betanzos, Spain 33/B1
Bétaré-Oya, Cameroon 115/B2
Bete Grise (bay), Mich. 250/B1
Bethalto, Ill. 222/B2
Bethanie, Namibia 118/B5
Bethany (res.), Calif. 204/L2
Bethany•, Conn. 210/C3
Bethany, Ill. 222/E4
Bethany, Ind. 227/E5
Bethany, La. 238/B2
Bethany, Manitoba 179/C4
Bethany, Minn. 255/F6
Bethany, Mo. 261/E2
Bethany, Ohio 284/B7
Bethany, Okla. 288/L3
Bethany, Ontario 177/F3
Bethany, Pa. 294/M2
Bethany, Sask. 181/F3
Bethany, W. Va. 312/E2
Bethany Beach, Del. 245/T6
Bethel, Alaska 188/C6
Bethel, Alaska 196/F2
Bethel, Conn. 210/B3
Bethel•, Conn. 210/B3
Bethel, Del. 245/R6
Bethel, Ky. 237/O4
Bethel, Maine 243/B7
Bethel•, Maine 243/B7
Bethel, Minn. 255/E5
Bethel, Mo. 261/J3
Bethel, N.Y. 276/L7
Bethel, N.C. 281/P3
Bethel, Ohio 284/B8
Bethel, Okla. 288/S6
Bethel, Pa. 294/K5
Bethel, Vt. 268/B4
Bethel•, Vt. 268/B4
Bethel, Wis. 317/F6
Bethel Acres, Okla. 288/M4
Bethel Heights, Ark. 202/B1
Bethel Island, Calif. 204/L1
Bethel Park, Pa. 294/B7
Bethelridge, Ky. 237/M6
Bethel Springs, Tenn. 237/D10
Bethel Town, Jamaica 158/G6
Bethera, S.C. 296/H5
Bethesda, Ark. 202/G2
Bethesda, Md. 245/E4
Bethesda, Ohio 284/H5
Bethesda, Wales 13/D4
Bethlehem, Conn. 210/C2
Bethlehem•, Conn. 210/C2
Bethlehem, Georgia 217/E3
Bethlehem, Ind. 227/G7
Bethlehem, Iowa 229/G7
Bethlehem, Ky. 237/L4
Bethlehem, Md. 245/P6
Bethlehem, Miss. 256/F1
Bethlehem•, N.H. 268/D3
Bethlehem, Pa. 294/M4
Bethlehem, S. Africa 102/E7
Bethlehem, S. Africa 118/D5
Bethlehem, Virgin Is. (U.S.) 161/E4
Bethlehem, West Bank 65/C4
Bethlehem, W. Va. 312/E2
Bethpage, N.Y. 276/R7
Bethpage, Tenn. 237/J7
Bethulie, S. Africa 118/D6
Bethune, Colo. 208/P4
Béthune, France 28/E2
Bethune, Sask. 181/F5
Bethune, S.C. 296/G3
Betijoque, Venezuela 124/C3
Betim, Brazil 135/D2
Betioky, Madagascar 118/G4
Betoota, Queensland 95/B5
Bet-Pak-Dala (des.), U.S.S.R. 48/H5
Bet Qama, Israel 65/B5
Betroka, Madagascar 118/H4
Bet She'an, Israel 65/D3
Bet Shemesh, Israel 65/B4
Betsiamites (riv.), Que. 162/J5
Betsiamites, Québec 174/D3
Betsiamites (riv.), Québec 174/C2
Betsiboka (riv.), Madagascar 118/H3
Betsy Layne, Ky. 237/R5
Bette (peak), Libya 102/D2
Bette (peak), Libya 111/C3
Bettendorf, Iowa 229/N5
Betteravia, Calif. 204/E9
Betterton, Md. 245/O3
Bettiah, India 68/E3
Bettlach, Switzerland 39/D2
Bettles, Alaska 196/H1
Bettles Field, Alaska 196/H1
Bettsville, Ohio 284/D3
Bettyhill, Scotland 15/D2
Betul, India 68/D4
Betula, Pa. 294/F2
Betwa (riv.), India 68/D4
Between, Georgia 217/E3
Betws-y-Coed, Wales 13/D4
Betzdorf, Germany 22/B3
Beulah, Ala. 195/H5
Beulah, Colo. 208/K6
Beulah, Manitoba 179/A4
Beulah, Mich. 250/C4
Beulah, Miss. 256/B3
Beulah, Mo. 261/J7
Beulah, N. Dak. 282/G5
Beulah, Oreg. 291/J4
Beulah (res.), Oreg. 291/J4
Beulah, Victoria 97/B4
Beulah (lake), Wis. 317/J2
Beulah, Wyo. 319/H1
Beulaker Wijde (lake), Netherlands 27/H3
Beulaville, N.C. 281/O5
Beuthen (Bytom), Poland 47/A3
Bevans, N.J. 273/D1
Bevent, Wis. 317/H6
Beveren, Belgium 27/E6
Beverin (peak), Switzerland 39/H3
Beverley, England 10/F4
Beverley, England 13/G4
Beverley, Sask. 181/C5
Beverley, W. Australia 92/B1
Beverly, C. Rica 154/F6
Beverly, Kansas 232/E2
Beverly, Ky. 237/P7
Beverly, Mass. 249/E5
Beverly, Mo. 261/O4
Beverly, N.J. 273/D3
Beverly (lake), N.W. Terr. 187/H3
Beverly, Ohio 284/G6
Beverly, Wash. 310/F4
Beverly, W. Va. 312/G5
Beverly Beach, Fla. 212/E2
Beverly Hills, Calif. 204/B10
Beverly Hills, Mich. 250/B6
Beverly Shores, Ind. 227/C1
Beverwijk, Netherlands 27/F4
Bevier, Mo. 261/G3
Bevington, Iowa 229/F6
Bewdley, England 13/E5
Bewdley, England 10/F3
Bewdley, Ontario 177/F3
Bex, Switzerland 39/D4
Bexar, Ala. 195/B2
Bexar (co.), Texas 303/F8
Bexhill, England 13/H7
Bexhill, England 10/G5
Bexley, England 13/H8
Bexley, England 10/C5
Bexley, Miss. 256/G9
Bexley, Ohio 284/E6
Bey (mts.), Turkey 63/D4
Bey el Kebir, Wadi (dry riv.), Libya 111/B1
Beykoz, Turkey 63/D5
Beyla, Guinea 106/C7
Beylerbeyi, Turkey 63/D6
Beynon, Alberta 182/D4
Beyoğlu, Turkey 63/D6
Beypazarı, Turkey 59/B1
Beypazarı, Turkey 63/D2
Beyşehir, Turkey 59/B2
Beyşehir, Turkey 63/D4
Beyşehir (lake), Turkey 63/D4
Beytüşşebap, Turkey 63/K4
Bezanson, Alberta 182/A2
Bezhetsk, U.S.S.R. 52/E3
Béziers, France 7/E4
Béziers, France 28/E6
Bhadrak, India 68/F4
Bhadravati, India 68/D6
Bhadreswar, India 68/F1
Bhag, Pakistan 68/B3
Bhag, Pakistan 59/J4
Bhagalpur, India 68/F4
Bhaktapur, Nepal 68/F3
Bhaktapur, Nepal 68/F3
Bhamo, Burma 72/C1
Bhandara, India 68/E4
Bhandup, India 68/B7
Bhanjanagar, India 68/E4
Bharatpur, India 68/D3
Bharuch, India 68/C4
Bhatapara, India 68/E4
Bhatinda, India 68/C2
Bhatkal, India 68/C6
Bhatpara, India 68/F1
Bhavnagar, India 68/C4
Bhavnagar, India 54/J7
Bhawanipatna, India 68/E5
Bhera, Pakistan 68/C2
Bheri (riv.), Nepal 68/E3
Bhilai, India 68/E4
Bhilwara, India 68/C3
Bhima (riv.), India 68/D5
Bhimavaram, India 68/E5
Bhimunipatnam, India 68/E5
Bhind, India 68/D3
Bhinmal, India 68/C3
Bhir (Bir), India 68/D5
Bhiwandi, India 68/C5
Bhiwani, India 68/D3
Bhojpur, Nepal 68/F3
Bhopal, India 54/J7
Bhopal, India 68/D4
Bhor, India 68/C5
Bhubaneswar, India 68/F4
Bhuj, India 68/B4
Bhusawal, India 68/D4
Bhutan 2/P4
Bhutan 54/L7
BHUTAN 68/G3
Biafra (bight), Cameroon 115/A3
Biafra (bight), Equat. Guinea 115/A3
Biafra (bight), Nigeria 106/F8
Biak, Indonesia 85/K6
Biak (isl.), Indonesia 85/K6
Biała Podlaska (prov.), Poland 47/F3
Biała Podlaska, Poland 47/F3
Białogard, Poland 47/C1
Białystok (prov.), Poland 47/F2
Białystok, Poland 47/F2
Białystok, Poland 7/G3
Biancavilla, Italy 34/E6
Biarritz, France 28/C6
Bias, W. Va. 312/B7
Biasca, Switzerland 39/H4
Biba, Egypt 111/J4
Bibai, Japan 81/L2
Bibala, Angola 115/B6
Bibb (co.), Ala. 195/D5
Bibb (co.), Georgia 217/E5
Bibb City, Georgia 217/B5
Bibbenluke, N.S. Wales 97/E5
Biberach an der Riss, Germany 22/C4
Biberist, Switzerland 39/D2
Bible Grove, Ill. 222/E5
Bible Hill, Nova Scotia 168/E3
Bic, Québec 172/J1
Bic (isl.), Québec 172/J1
Bicas, Brazil 135/E2
Bicaz, Romania 45/G2
Bicester, England 13/F6
Biche (lake), Alberta 182/E2
Biche, Trin. & Tob. 161/B10
Bicheno, Tasmania 99/E3
Bickerdike, Alberta 182/B3
Bickerton (isl.), North. Terr. 93/E2
Bickerton West, Nova Scotia 168/G3
Bickleigh, Sask. 181/C4
Bickleton, Wash. 310/E5
Bickmore, W. Va. 312/D6
Bicknell, Ind. 227/C7
Bicknell, Utah 304/C5
Bicske, Hungary 41/E3
Bida, Nigeria 106/F7
Bidar, India 68/D5
Biddeford, Maine 243/B9
Biddeford, Maine 188/N2
Biddeford Pool, Maine 243/C9
Biddinghuizen, Netherlands 27/H4
Biddle, Mont. 262/L5
Biddu, West Bank 65/C4
Biddulph, England 13/H2
Bidean nam Bian (mt.), Scotland 15/D4
Bide Arm, Newf. 166/C3
Bideford, England 13/C6
Bideford, England 10/D5
Bidokht, Iran 66/L3
Bidon 5 (Poste Maurice Cordier), Algeria 106/E4
Bidwell, Ohio 284/F8
Bidyadhari (riv.), India 68/F2
Bié (prov.), Angola 115/C6
Bieber, Calif. 204/D2
Biebrza (riv.), Poland 47/F2
Biel, Switzerland 39/D2
Bielawa, Poland 47/C3
Bield, Manitoba 179/A3
Bieldside, Scotland 15/F3
Bielefeld, Germany 22/C2
Bieler (lake), N.W. Terr. 187/L2
Bielersee (lake), Switzerland 39/D2
Biella, Italy 34/B2
Bielsko (prov.), Poland 47/D4
Bielsko-Biała, Poland 47/D4
Bielsk Podlaski, Poland 47/F2
Biencourt, Québec 172/J2
Bienfait, Sask. 181/J6
Bien Hoa, Vietnam 72/E5
Bienvenue, Fr. Guiana 131/E4
Bienville, Lac (lake), Que. 162/J4
Bienville (par.), La. 238/D2
Bienville, La. 238/D2
Bienville (lake), Québec 174/C2
Bière, Switzerland 39/B3
Bietigheim-Bissingen, Germany 22/C4
Bietschhorn (mt.), Switzerland 39/E4
Bièvre, Belgium 27/F9
Bièvres, France 28/A2
Big (isl.), Alberta 182/B5
Big (creek), Idaho 220/C4
Big (creek), Ind. 227/B8
Big (brook), Maine 243/E2
Big (lake), Maine 243/H5
Big (pond), Mass. 249/B4
Big (riv.), Mo. 261/L6
Big (lake), Mont. 262/G5
Big (mt.), Nev. 266/B1
Big (bay), Newf. 166/B2
Big (isl.), Newf. 166/B2
Big (riv.), Newf. 166/C3
Big (isl.), N.W. Terr. 187/L3
Biga, Turkey 63/B2
Bigadiç, Turkey 63/C3
Bigalı, Turkey 63/B6
Big Annemessex (riv.), Md. 245/P8
Big Antelope (creek), Oreg. 290/K5
Big Arm, Mont. 262/B3
Big Bald (mt.), New Bruns. 170/D1
Big Bar, Calif. 204/B3
Big Bar Creek, Br. Col. 184/F4
Big Basin, Calif. 204/J4
Big Bay, Mich. 250/B2
Big Bay (pt.), Mich. 250/B2
Big Bay de Noc (bay), Mich. 250/C3
Big Bear City, Calif. 204/J9
Big Bear Lake, Calif. 204/J9
Big Beaver, Sask. 181/F6
Bigbee, Ala. 195/B7
Bigbee Valley, Miss. 256/H4
Big Bell, W. Australia 92/B4
Big Belt (mts.), Mont. 262/E4
Big Bend (dam), S. Dak. 298/K5
Bigbend, W. Va. 312/D5
Big Bend, Wis. 317/K2
Big Bend City, Minn. 255/C5
Big Bend National Park, Texas 303/A8
Big Bend Nat'l Park, Texas 303/A8
Big Black (riv.), Maine 243/D2
Big Black (riv.), Miss. 256/C6
Big Black (creek), S.C. 296/G2
Big Black River, Manitoba 179/E1
Big Blue (riv.), Ind. 227/F5
Big Blue (riv.), Kansas 232/F1
Big Blue (riv.), Nebr. 264/H4
Big Boulder (creek), Idaho 220/B7
Big Bow, Kansas 232/A4
Big Bras d'Or, Nova Scotia 168/H2
Big Bureau (riv.), Ill. 222/D2
Big Burro (mts.), N. Mex. 274/A6
Bigbury (bay), England 13/C7
Big Cabin, Okla. 288/R1
Big Canoe (creek), Ala. 195/F3
Big Chimney, W. Va. 312/C6
Big Chino Wash (dry riv.), Ariz. 198/C3
Big Clifty, Ky. 237/J5
Big Coulee, Alberta 182/D2
Big Cove Tannery, Pa. 294/F6
Big Creek (lake), Ala. 195/B9
Big Creek, Calif. 204/F6
Big Creek, Idaho 220/C4
Big Creek, Ky. 237/O6
Big Creek, Miss. 256/F3
Big Creek, W. Va. 312/B7
Big Cypress (swamp), Fla. 212/E5
Big Cypress Nat'l Pres., Fla. 212/E5
Big Dry (creek), Mont. 262/K3
Big Eau Pleine (res.), Wis. 317/G6
Big Eddy, Br. Col. 184/H4
Big Elk (peak), Idaho 220/G6
Bigelow, Ark. 202/E3
Bigelow (brook), Conn. 210/G1
Bigelow (bight), Maine 243/C9
Bigelow (mt.), Maine 243/C5
Bigelow (bight), Mass. 249/M1
Bigelow, Minn. 255/C7
Bigelow, Mo. 261/B2
Big Falls, Minn. 255/E2
Big Falls, Wis. 317/H6
Big Flat, Ark. 202/F1
Big Flat (brook), N.J. 273/D1
Big Flats, N.Y. 276/G6
Bigfoot, Texas 303/F9
Big Fork, Ark. 202/B5
Bigfork, Minn. 255/E3
Big Fork (riv.), Minn. 255/E2
Bigfork, Mont. 262/C2
Big Four, W. Va. 312/C8
Bigga, N.S. Wales 97/E4
Biggar, Sask. 162/F5
Biggar, Sask. 181/C3
Biggar, Scotland 10/E3
Biggar, Scotland 15/E5
Bigge (range), Queensland 95/D5
Bigge (isl.), W. Australia 92/D1
Biggers, Ark. 202/J1
Biggleswade, England 10/F4
Biggleswade, England 13/G5
Big Goose (creek), Wyo. 319/E1
Big Grizzly (creek), Colo. 208/G1
Biggs, Calif. 204/D4
Biggs, Oreg. 291/G2
Biggs Field, Texas 303/A10
Biggsville, Ill. 222/C3
Big Hole (mts.), Idaho 220/G6
Big Hole (riv.), Mont. 262/C5
Big Hole Nat'l Battlefield, Mont. 262/C5
Bighorn (riv.) 188/E2
Big Horn (dam), Alberta 182/B3
Bighorn (range), Alberta 182/B3
Big Horn (mts.), Ariz. 198/B5
Big Horn (co.), Mont. 262/J5
Bighorn, Mont. 262/J4
Bighorn (lake), Mont. 262/H5
Bighorn (riv.), Mont. 262/J5
Big Horn (co.), Wyo. 319/E1
Big Horn, Wyo. 319/E1
Bighorn (basin), Wyo. 319/D1
Bighorn (lake), Wyo. 319/D1
Bighorn (mts.), Wyo. 319/E1
Bighorn (riv.), Wyo. 319/D1
Bighorn Canyon Nat'l Rec. Area, Mont. 262/H5
Bighorn Canyon Nat'l Rec. Area, Wyo. 319/D1
Big Indian, N.Y. 276/M6
Big Iron (riv.), Mich. 250/F1
Big Isaac, W. Va. 312/E4
Big Island, Ontario 177/G3
Big Island, Va. 307/K5
Big Lake, Alaska 196/B1
Big Lake, Alaska 196/J1
Big Lake, Minn. 255/E5
Big Lake, Texas 303/C6
Biglake, Wash. 310/C2
Big Lake Ranch, Br. Col. 184/G4
Bigler, Pa. 294/F4
Biglerville, Pa. 294/H6
Big Lick, Tenn. 237/L9
Big Lost (riv.), Idaho 220/E6
Big Moose, N.Y. 276/L3
Big Moose (lake), N.Y. 276/L3
Big Muddy (riv.), Ill. 222/D6
Big Muddy (riv.), Mont. 262/M2
Big Muddy (lake), Sask. 181/G6
Big Muskego (lake), Wis. 317/L2
Bignona, Senegal 106/A6
Big Oak Flat, Calif. 204/E6
Big Otter (riv.), Va. 307/K6
Big Otter, W. Va. 312/D5
Big Pine, Calif. 204/G6
Big Pine (key), Fla. 212/E7
Big Pine (creek), Ind. 227/C3
Big Pine, N.C. 281/D3
Big Piney, Mo. 261/H7
Big Piney, Wyo. 319/B3
Big Pipe (creek), Md. 245/K2
Big Plain, Ohio 284/D6
Bigpoint, Miss. 256/H9
Big Pond, Newf. 166/D2
Big Pond, Nova Scotia 168/H3
Big Pool, Md. 245/F2
Big Porcupine (creek), Mont. 262/J4
Big Prairie, Ohio 284/F4
Big Raccoon (creek), Ind. 227/C5
Big Rapids, Mich. 250/D5
Big Rib (riv.), Wis. 317/G5
Big Rideau (lake), Ontario 177/H3
Big River, Sask. 162/F5
Big River, Sask. 181/D2
Big Rock, Ill. 222/E2
Big Rock, Iowa 229/M5
Big Rock, Tenn. 237/F7
Big Rock, Va. 307/D6
Big Run, Pa. 294/E4
Big Sable (pt.), Mich. 250/C4
Big Sable (riv.), Mich. 250/C4
Big Sage (res.), Calif. 204/E2
Big Salmon (riv.), New Bruns. 170/E3
Big Sand (lake), Manitoba 179/H2
Big Sandy (riv.), Ariz. 198/B4
Big Sandy (creek), Colo. 208/N4
Big Sandy (riv.), Ky. 237/R4
Big Sandy (lake), Minn. 255/E4
Big Sandy, Mont. 262/G2
Big Sandy, Tenn. 237/E8
Big Sandy (riv.), Tenn. 237/E9
Big Sandy, Texas 303/J5
Big Sandy (riv.), W. Va. 312/A6
Big Sandy, Wyo. 319/C3
Big Sandy (res.), Wyo. 319/C3
Big Sandy (riv.), Wyo. 319/C3
Big Sioux (riv.), Iowa 229/A3
Big Sioux (riv.), S. Dak. 188/G2
Big Sioux (riv.), S. Dak. 298/S7
Big Sky, Mont. 262/E5
Big Smoky (valley), Nev. 266/D4
Big Southern (butte), Idaho 220/E6
Big Spencer (mt.), Maine 243/E4
Big Spring, Georgia 217/C5
Big Spring, Ky. 237/J5
Big Spring, Md. 245/G2
Big Spring, Tenn. 237/M10
Big Spring, Texas 188/F4
Big Spring, Texas 303/C5
Big Springs, Nebr. 264/B3
Big Springs, S. Dak. 298/S8
Big Springs, W. Va. 312/D5
Big Star (lake), Mich. 250/C5
Bigstick (lake), Sask. 181/B5
Big Stone, Alberta 182/E4
Bigstone (lake), Manitoba 179/J3
Bigstone (pt.), Manitoba 179/E2
Bigstone (riv.), Manitoba 179/J3
Big Stone (co.), Minn. 255/B5
Big Stone (lake), Minn. 255/B5
Big Stone (lake), S. Dak. 298/R3
Big Stone City, S. Dak. 298/S3
Big Stone Gap, Va. 307/C7
Big Sur, Calif. 204/D7
Big Thicket Nat'l Preserve, Texas 303/K7
Big Thompson (riv.), Colo. 208/H2
Big Timber, Mont. 262/G5
Big Timber (creek), N.J. 273/C4
Big Tracadie (riv.), New Bruns. 170/E1
Bigtrails, Wyo. 319/E2
Big Trout (lake), Ontario 177/F2
Big Trout (lake), Ontario 175/B2
Big Trout Lake, Ontario 175/C2
Big Valley, Alberta 182/D3
Big Walnut (creek), Ind. 227/D5
Big Walnut (creek), Ohio 284/E5
Big Water, Utah 304/C6
Big Wells, Texas 303/E9
Big Whiteshell Lake, Manitoba 179/G4
Big Wood (riv.), Idaho 220/D6
Bihać, Yugoslavia 45/B3
Bihar (state), India 68/F4
Bihar, India 68/F3
Biharamulo, Tanzania 115/F4
Biharkeresztes, Hungary 41/F3
Biharnagybajom, Hungary 41/F3
Bijagós (isls.), Guinea-Biss. 106/A6
Bijagós (isls.), Guinea-Biss. 102/A3
Bijapur, Karnataka, India 68/D5
Bijapur, Madhya Pradesh, India 68/E5
Bijar, Iran 66/E3
Bijeljina, Yugoslavia 45/D3
Bijelo Polje, Yugoslavia 45/D4
Bijiang, China 77/E6
Bijie, China 77/G6
Bijnor, India 68/D3
Bijou (creek), Colo. 208/L3
Bijou Hills, S. Dak. 298/L6
Bikaner, India 54/J7
Bikaner, India 68/C3
Bikar (atoll), Marshall Is. 87/H4
Bikin, U.S.S.R. 48/O5
Bikini (atoll), Marshall Is. 87/G4
Bikoro, Zaire 115/C4
Bikoro, Zaire 102/D5
Bilaspur, India 68/E4
Bilauktaung (range), Burma 72/C4
Bilauktaung (range), Thailand 72/C4
Bilbao, Spain 33/E1
Bilbao, Spain 7/D4
Bileća, Yugoslavia 45/D4
Bilecik (prov.), Turkey 63/D2
Bilecik, Turkey 59/A1
Bilecik, Turkey 63/D2

Block Island 339

Biłgoraj, Poland 47/F3
Bilibino, U.S.S.R. 4/C1
Bilibino, U.S.S.R. 48/R3
Bilin, Burma 72/C3
Bilina, Czech. 41/B1
Biliran (isl.), Philippines 82/E5
Bill, Wyo. 319/G2
Billate (riv.), Ethiopia 111/G6
Billerica•, Mass. 249/J2
Billings (lake), Conn. 210/H2
Billings, Mo. 261/F8
Billings, Mont. 146/H5
Billings, Mont. 188/E1
Billings, Mont. 262/H5
Billings (co.), N. Dak. 282/D5
Billings, Okla. 288/M1
Billingsgate (isl.), Mass. 249/O5
Billingshurst, England 13/G6
Billingsley, Ala. 195/E5
Billiton (isl.), Indonesia 54/M10
Billiton (isl.), Indonesia 85/D6
Bill Williams (riv.), Ariz. 198/B4
Billy Clapp (lake), Wash. 310/F3
Bilma, Niger 102/D3
Bilma, Niger 106/G5
Biloela, Queensland 88/J4
Biloela, Queensland 95/D5
Biloku, Guyana 131/B5
Biloxi, Miss. 146/K6
Biloxi, Miss. 188/J4
Biloxi, Miss. 256/G10
Biltine, Chad 111/D5
Biltine, Chad 102/D3
Biltmore Forest, N.C. 281/E3
Bilwaskarma, Nicaragua 154/F3
Bilzen, Belgium 27/G7
Bim, W. Va. 312/C7
Biminis, The (isls.), Bahamas 156/B1
Bina-Itawa, India 68/D4
Binalbagan, Philippines 82/D5
Binalong, N.S. Wales 97/E4
Binboğa (mts.), Turkey 63/G3
Binbrook, Ontario 177/E4
Binche, Belgium 27/E8
Binda, N.S. Wales 97/E4
Bindloss, Alberta 182/E4
Bindoon, W. Australia 92/B1
Bindura, Zimbabwe 118/E3
Binéfar, Spain 33/G2
Binevenagh (mt.), N. Ireland 17/H1
Binford, N. Dak. 282/O4
Binga (mt.), Mozambique 118/E3
Bingara, N.S. Wales 97/F1
Bingen, Wash. 310/D5
Bingen, Germany 22/B4
Binger, Okla. 288/K4
Bingerville, Ivory Coast 106/D7
Bingham (co.), Idaho 220/F6
Bingham, Ill. 222/D4
Bingham, Maine 243/D5
Bingham•, Maine 243/D5
Bingham, Nebr. 264/B2
Bingham, N. Mex. 274/C5
Bingham, S.C. 296/H3
Bingham (canyon), Utah 304/B3
Bingham Lake, Minn. 255/C7
Binghamton, N.Y. 188/L2
Binghamton, N.Y. 276/J6
Bingöl (prov.), Turkey 63/J3
Bingöl (Çapakçur), Turkey 63/J3
Bingöl Dağları (mts.), Turkey 63/J3
Binhai, China 77/K5
Binh Long (An Loc), Vietnam 72/E5
Binh Son, Vietnam 72/F4
Binjai, Indonesia 85/B5
Binn, Switzerland 39/F4
Binnaway, N.S. Wales 97/E2
Binningen, Switzerland 39/D1
Binongko (isl.), Indonesia 85/G7
Binscarth, Manitoba 179/A4
Bintan (isl.), Indonesia 85/C5
Bintuhan, Indonesia 85/C6
Bintulu, Malaysia 85/E5
Binyamina, Israel 65/B2
Binyang, China 77/G7
Biobío (reg.), Chile 138/E1
Bío-Bío (riv.), Chile 138/E2
Biograd, Yugoslavia 45/B4
Bioko (isl.), Equat. Guinea 102/C4
Bioko (isl.), Equat. Guinea 115/A3
Bioko (terr.), Equat. Guinea 115/A3
Biola, Calif. 204/E7
Bippus, Ind. 227/F3
Bir, India 68/D5
Bira, U.S.S.R. 48/O5
Birag, Kuh-e (mts.), Iran 66/M7
Bir 'Ali, Yemen 59/E7
Birama (pt.), Cuba 158/G4
Birao, Cent. Afr. Rep. 115/D1
Biratnagar, Nepal 68/F3
Biratori, Japan 81/L2
Bir Bala, Iran 66/L8
Bir Bala, Iran 59/G4
Bircao, Somalia 115/H4
Birch (creek), Alaska 196/J1
Birch (hills), Alberta 182/A2
Birch (lake), Alberta 182/E3
Birch (mts.), Alberta 182/B5
Birch (riv.), Alberta 182/B5
Birch (creek), Idaho 220/F5
Birch (isl.), Manitoba 179/C2
Birch (lake), Minn. 255/G3
Birch (creek), Mont. 262/D2
Birch (lake), Sask. 181/C2
Birch (creek), Utah 304/B5
Birch (pt.), Wash. 310/C2
Birch Creek, Alaska 196/J1
Birch Creek (valley), Idaho 220/E5
Birch Creek (res.), Mont. 262/D2
Birchdale, Minn. 255/D2
Birch Harbor, Maine 243/H7
Birch Hills, Sask. 181/F3
Birchip, Victoria 97/B4
Birch Island, Br. Col. 184/H4
Birchleaf, Va. 307/D6
Birch River, Manitoba 179/A2
Birch River, W. Va. 312/E6
Birch Run, Mich. 250/F5
Birchtown, Nova Scotia 168/C5
Birch Tree, Mo. 261/K9
Birchwood, Tenn. 237/M10
Birchwood, Wis. 317/C4
Birchy Bay, Newf. 166/D4
Bird (isl.), La. 238/M8
Bird (creek), Okla. 288/O1
Bird City, Kansas 232/A2
Bird Cove, Newf. 166/C3
Bird Island, Minn. 255/D6
Birds, Ill. 222/F5
Birdsboro, Pa. 294/L5
Birdseye, Ind. 227/D8
Birds Hill, Manitoba 179/F4
Birdsnest, Va. 307/S6
Birdsong, Ark. 202/K3
Birdsville, Ky. 237/D6
Birdsville, Queensland 88/F5
Birdsville, Queensland 95/A5
Birdtail, Manitoba 179/B4
Birdum, North. Terr. 93/C3
Birdwood, S. Australia 94/C7
Birecik, Turkey 63/H4
Bir el Khzaim (well), Mauritania 106/C4
Bireuen, Indonesia 85/B4
Bir Ganduz (well), Western Sahara 106/A4
Birganj, Nepal 68/F3
Bir Hakeim (ruins), Libya 111/D1
Birigui, Brazil 135/A2
Birjand, Iran 66/L4
Birjand, Iran 59/G3
Birjand, Iran 54/G6
Birken, Br. Col. 184/F5
Birkenfeld, Oreg. 291/D1
Birkenfeld, Germany 22/B4
Birkenhead, England 13/G2
Birkenhead, England 10/F2
Birkenhead, N. Zealand 100/B1
Birkenhead Lake Prov. Park, Br. Col. 184/F5
Birkerød, Denmark 21/F6
Birket Qârûn (lake), Egypt 111/J3
Bir Ksaib Ounane (well), Mali 106/C4
Birksgate (range), S. Australia 94/A2
Bîrlad, Romania 45/H2
Bîrlad (riv.), Romania 45/H2
Birmingham, Ala. 146/K6
Birmingham, Ala. 188/J4
Birmingham, Ala. 195/D3
Birmingham, England 7/D3
Birmingham, England 10/G3
Birmingham, England 13/F5
Birmingham, Iowa 229/K7
Birmingham, Mich. 250/B6
Birmingham, Mo. 261/R5
Birmingham, N.J. 273/D4
Birmingham, Ohio 284/F3
Birmingham, Pa. 294/F4
Birmingham, Sask. 181/H5
Birmitrapur, India 68/E4
Bir Mogreïn, Mauritania 106/B3
Birnam, Scotland 15/E4
Birnamwood, Wis. 317/H6
Birney, Mont. 262/K5
Birnie, Manitoba 179/C4
Birnin Kebbi, Nigeria 106/E6
Birni-N'Konni, Niger 106/E6
Birni-N'Konni, Niger 102/C3
Bir Nzaran (well), Western Sahara 106/B4
Birobidzhan, U.S.S.R. 54/O5
Birobidzhan, U.S.S.R. 48/O5
Biron, Wis. 317/G7
Bir Ounane (well), Mali 106/D4
Birqin, West Bank 65/C3
Birr, Ireland 17/F5
Birr, Ireland 10/B4
Birregurra, Victoria 97/B6
Birrie (riv.), N.S. Wales 88/H5
Birrie (riv.), N.S. Wales 97/D1
Birrimbah, North. Terr. 93/C3
Birrindudu, North. Terr. 93/A5
Birriwa, N.S. Wales 97/E3
Birs (riv.), Switzerland 39/D2
Birsay, Sask. 181/D4
Birsk, U.S.S.R. 52/J3
Birta, Ark. 202/D3
Bir Taba, Egypt 59/B4
Bir Taba (well), Egypt 111/F2
Birtle, Manitoba 179/B4
Biru, China 77/D5
Biruaca, Venezuela 124/E4
Biržai, U.S.S.R. 53/C2
Bir Zeit, West Bank 65/C4
Bisbee, Ariz. 188/E4
Bisbee, Ariz. 198/F7
Bisbee, N. Dak. 282/M2
Biscarrosse (lake), France 28/C5
Biscay (bay) 2/J3
Biscay (bay) 7/D4
Biscay (bay), France 28/B5
Biscay, Minn. 255/D6
Biscay (bay), Spain 33/E1
Biscay Bay (riv.), Newf. 166/D2
Biscayne (bay), Fla. 212/F6
Biscayne (key), Fla. 212/B5
Biscayne Nat'l Park, Fla. 212/F6
Biscayne Park, Fla. 212/B4
Bisceglie, Italy 34/F4
Bischofshofen, Austria 41/B3
Bischofswerda, Germany 22/F3
Bischofszell, Switzerland 39/H1
Biscoe (isls.), Ant. 5/C15
Biscoe, Ark. 202/H4
Biscoe, N.C. 281/K4
Biscotasing, Ontario 177/J5
Biscotasing, Ontario 175/D3
Biscucuy, Venezuela 124/D3
Bisha, Saudi Arabia 59/D5
Bisha, Wadi (dry riv.), Saudi Arabia 59/D5
Bishiara (well), Libya 111/D3
Bisho, South Africa 118/D6
Bisho (cap.), Ciskei, S. Africa 102/E8
Bishop, Calif. 204/G6
Bishop, Georgia 217/F3
Bishop, Md. 245/S7
Bishop (creek), Nev. 266/F1
Bishop, Texas 303/G10
Bishop (creek), Utah 304/E3
Bishop, Va. 307/E6
Bishop Auckland, England 10/E3
Bishop Auckland, England 13/E3
Bishopbriggs, Scotland 15/B2
Bishop Hill, Ill. 222/C2
Bishopric, Sask. 181/F5
Bishop's Falls, Newf. 166/C4
Bishops Head, Md. 245/O7
Bishops Mitre (mt.), Newf. 166/B2
Bishop's Stortford, England 10/G5
Bishop's Stortford, England 13/H6
Bishopton, Québec 172/F4
Bishopton, Scotland 15/B2
Bishopville, Md. 245/T7
Bishopville, S.C. 296/G3
Bishri, Jebel el (mts.), Syria 63/H5
Biskra, Algeria 106/F2
Biskra, Algeria 102/C1
Biskupiec, Poland 47/E2
Bislig, Philippines 85/H4
Bislig, Philippines 82/F6
Bismarck, Ark. 202/D5
Bismarck, Ill. 222/F3
Bismarck, Mo. 261/L7
Bismarck (cap.), N. Dak. 146/H5
Bismarck (cap.), N. Dak. 188/G1
Bismarck (cap.), N. Dak. 282/J6
Bismarck (arch.), Papua N.G. 2/S6
Bismarck (arch.), Papua N.G. 87/E6
Bismarck (arch.), Papua N.G. 86/B1
Bismarck (sea), Papua N.G. 86/B1
Bismarck, W. Va. 312/H4
Bismil, Turkey 63/J4
Bison (lake), Alberta 182/B1
Bison, Kansas 232/C3
Bison, Okla. 288/L2
Bison, S. Dak. 298/E2
Bispgården, Sweden 18/K5
Bissau (cap.), Guinea-Biss. 106/A6
Bissau (cap.), Guinea-Biss. 102/A3
Bissett, Manitoba 179/G4
Bistineau (lake), La. 238/D2
Bistrița, Romania 45/G2
Bita (riv.), Colombia 126/F5
Bitagron, Suriname 131/C3
Bitam, Gabon 115/B3
Bitburg, Germany 22/B4
Bitely, Mich. 250/D5
Bithlo, Fla. 212/E3
Bitkine, Chad 111/C5
Bitlis (prov.), Turkey 63/J3
Bitlis, Turkey 63/J3
Bitlis, Turkey 59/D2
Bitola, Yugoslavia 45/E5
Bitola, Yugoslavia 7/G4
Bitonto, Italy 34/F4
Bitter (lakes), Egypt 111/K3
Bitter (lake), Sask. 181/B5
Bitter (creek), Wyo. 319/C4
Bitter Creek, Wyo. 319/D4
Bitterfeld, Germany 22/E3
Bitterfontein, S. Africa 118/B6
Bittern (lake), Alberta 182/D3
Bittern Lake, Alberta 182/D3
Bitterroot (range) 188/D1
Bitterroot (range), Idaho 220/D3
Bitterroot (range), Mont. 262/B4
Bitterroot (riv.), Mont. 262/B4
Bitterroot (range), U.S. 146/G5
Bitti, Italy 34/B4
Bitumount, Alberta 182/E1
Bitung, Indonesia 85/H5
Biu, Nigeria 106/G6
Biu (plat.), Nigeria 106/G6
Bivalve, Md. 245/P7
Bivalve, N.J. 273/C5
Bivolari, Romania 45/H2
Biwa (lake), Japan 81/H6
Biwabik, Minn. 255/F3
Bixby, Minn. 255/E7
Bixby, Mo. 261/K7
Bixby, Okla. 288/P3
Biyang, China 77/H5
Biysk, U.S.S.R. 54/K4
Biysk, U.S.S.R. 48/J4
Bizcocho, Uruguay 145/B4
Bizerte, Tunisia 106/F1
Bizerte, Tunisia 102/C1
Bjargtangar (pt.), Iceland 21/A1
Bjelovar, Yugoslavia 45/C3
Bjerringbro, Denmark 21/C5
Bjorkdale, Sask. 181/H3
Bjørnafjorden (fjord), Norway 18/D6
Bjorne (pen.), N.W. Terr. 187/K2
Bjørnøya (isl.), Norway 18/D3
Blabon, N. Dak. 282/P5
Blachly, Oreg. 291/D3
Black (sea) 2/L3
Black (sea) 54/E5
Black (sea) 7/H4
Black, Ala. 195/G8
Black (riv.), Alaska 196/K1
Black (mesa), Ariz. 198/E2
Black (mts.), Ariz. 198/A3
Black (riv.), Ariz. 198/E5
Black (riv.), Ark. 202/H2
Black (sea), Bulgaria 45/J4
Black (pt.), Conn. 210/G3
Black (pond), Conn. 210/G1
Black (mts.), England 13/D6
Black (creek), Fla. 212/E1
Black (for.), Germany 22/C4
Black (head), Ireland 17/C5
Black (riv.), Jamaica 158/H6
Black (mt.), Ky. 237/R7
Black (lake), La. 238/D3
Black (pond), Maine 243/D3
Black (isl.), Manitoba 179/F3
Black (riv.), Manitoba 179/F4
Black (lake), Mich. 250/E3
Black (riv.), Mich. 250/E3
Black (riv.), Mich. 250/G5
Black (riv.), Minn. 255/D2
Black (creek), Miss. 256/F8
Black, Mo. 261/L7
Black (riv.), Mo. 261/L10
Black (mt.), N. Mex. 274/A6
Black (range), N. Mex. 274/B5
Black (lake), N.Y. 276/J1
Black (riv.), N.Y. 276/K3
Black (riv.), N.C. 281/N5
Black (riv.), Ohio 284/F3
Black (riv.), Ontario 177/E3
Black (sea), Romania 45/J4
Black (lake), Sask. 181/M2
Black (riv.), S.C. 296/H4
Black (sea), Turkey 63/E1
Black (sea), U.S.S.R. 48/D5
Black (sea), U.S.S.R. 52/D6
Black (creek), Vt. 268/B2
Black (riv.), Vt. 268/C2
Black (riv.), Vt. 268/B5
Black (riv.), Vietnam 72/D2
Black (mts.), Wales 13/D6
Black (riv.), Wis. 317/E7
Black (riv.), Yukon 187/D3
Blackall, Australia 87/E8
Blackall, Queensland 88/H4
Blackall, Queensland 95/C5
Black Bear (creek), Okla. 288/M2
Blackberry (riv.), Conn. 210/B1
Blackbird, Del. 245/R3
Blackbourne (pt.), Norfolk I. 88/L6
Black Branch, Nulhegan (riv.), Vt. 268/D2
Blackburn (mt.), Alaska 196/K2
Blackburn, England 13/H1
Blackburn, England 10/G1
Blackburn, La. 238/D1
Blackburn, Mo. 261/F4
Blackburn, Okla. 288/N2
Blackburn, Ontario 177/J2
Blackburn, Scotland 15/C2
Black Butte (lake), Calif. 204/C4
Black Canyon City, Ariz. 198/C4
Black Canyon of the Gunnison Nat'l Mon., Colo. 208/D5
Black Creek, Br. Col. 184/E5
Black Creek, N.C. 281/O3
Black Creek, Wis. 317/K7
Black Diamond, Alberta 182/C4
Black Diamond, Wash. 310/D3
Blackduck, Minn. 255/D3
Black Duck (riv.), Ontario 175/C1
Black Eagle, Mont. 262/E3
Black Earth, Wis. 317/G9
Black Elster (riv.), Germany 22/E3
Blackey, Ky. 237/R6
Blackfalds, Alberta 182/D3
Blackfeet Ind. Res., Mont. 262/D2
Blackfoot, Alberta 182/E3
Blackfoot, Idaho 220/F6
Blackfoot (res.), Idaho 220/G7
Blackfoot (riv.), Idaho 220/G6
Blackfoot, Mont. 262/D2
Blackfoot (riv.), Mont. 262/C4
Blackford (co.), Ind. 227/G4
Blackford, Ky. 237/F6
Blackford, Scotland 15/E4
Black Forest, Colo. 208/K4
Blackfork, Ohio 284/E8
Black Fork, Mohican (riv.), Ohio 284/F4
Blackgum, Okla. 288/S3
Black Hall, Conn. 210/F3
Black Hawk, Colo. 208/J3
Blackhawk, Ind. 227/C6
Black Hawk (co.), Iowa 229/J4
Black Hawk, Miss. 256/E4
Black Hawk, S. Dak. 298/C5
Blackhead (bay), Newf. 166/D2
Blackhead Road, Newf. 166/D2
Black Hills (mts.) 188/F2
Black Hills (mts.), S. Dak. 298/B5
Blackie, Alberta 182/D4
Black Isle (pen.), Scotland 15/D3
Black Jack, Mo. 261/R1
Black Lake (bayou), La. 238/D1
Black Lake, Québec 172/F3
Black Lake, Sask. 181/M2
Blackledge (riv.), Conn. 210/F2
Black Lick, Pa. 294/D4
Blacklock (pt.), Oreg. 291/C5
Black Mesa (mt.), Okla. 288/A1
Blackmore (mt.), Mont. 262/F5
Black Mountain, N.C. 281/E3
Black Oak, Ark. 202/K2
Black Oak, Ind. 227/C1
Black Pine (mts.), Idaho 220/E7
Black Pine (peak), Idaho 220/E7
Black Pine (creek), S. Dak. 298/G6
Black Point, Calif. 204/J1
Black Point, Conn. 210/G3
Black Point, New Bruns. 170/D1
Blackpool, England 13/G1
Blackpool, England 10/F1
Blackridge, Va. 307/M7
Black River, Jamaica 158/H6
Black River, Jamaica 156/B3
Black River (bay), Jamaica 158/G6
Black River, Mich. 250/F4
Black River, New Bruns. 170/E3
Black River (pond), Newf. 166/C2
Black River, N.Y. 276/J3
Black River Bridge, New Bruns. 170/E2
Black River Falls, Wis. 317/E7
Black Rock, Ark. 202/H1
Black Rock (des.), Nev. 266/B2
Black Rock (range), Nev. 266/B1
Black Rock (pt.), R.I. 249/H8
Black Rock, Utah 304/B5
Blacksburg, S.C. 296/D1
Blacksburg, Va. 307/H6
Blacks Fork, Green (riv.), Wyo. 319/C4
Blacks Harbour, New Bruns. 170/D3
Blackshear, Georgia 217/H8
Blackshear (lake), Georgia 217/E7
Blacksher, Ala. 195/C8
Blacksod (bay), Ireland 17/A3
Black Springs, Ark. 202/C5
Black Springs, Nev. 266/B3
Black Squirrel (creek), Colo. 208/L5
Blackstairs (mt.), Ireland 17/H6
Blackstock, Ontario 177/F3
Blackstock, S.C. 296/E2
Blackstone•, Mass. 249/H4
Blackstone (riv.), Mass. 249/G3
Blackstone, Va. 307/N6
Blacksville, W. Va. 312/F3
Black Thunder (creek), Wyo. 319/G2
Black Tickle, Newf. 166/C3
Blackton, Ark. 202/H4
Blacktown, N.S. Wales 88/K4
Blacktown, N.S. Wales 97/H3
Blackville, New Bruns. 170/E2
Blackville, S.C. 296/E5
Black Volta (riv.) 102/B3
Black Volta (Mouhoun) (riv.), Burkina Faso 106/D6
Black Volta (riv.), Ghana 106/D6
Black Volta (riv.), Ivory Coast 106/D6
Black Warrior (riv.), Ala. 195/C5
Blackwater (riv.), England 13/H6
Blackwater (riv.), Fla. 212/B6
Blackwater, Ireland 17/J7
Blackwater (riv.), Ireland 10/B4
Blackwater (riv.), Ireland 17/D7
Blackwater (riv.), Ireland 17/H4
Blackwater, Mo. 261/G5
Blackwater (res.), N.H. 268/D5
Blackwater (riv.), N. Ireland 17/H3
Blackwater, Queensland 95/D4
Blackwater, Queensland 88/H4
Blackwater (res.), Scotland 15/D4
Blackwater, Va. 307/B7
Blackwater (riv.), Va. 307/J6
Blackwater (riv.), Va. 307/O6
Blackwell, Ark. 202/E3
Blackwell (brook), Conn. 210/H1
Blackwell, Okla. 288/M1
Blackwell, Texas 303/D5
Blackwell, Wis. 317/J4
Blackwood (Ngundju) (cape), Indonesia 85/F8
Blackwood, N.J. 273/C4
Blackwood Terrace, N.J. 273/C4
Bladen, Nebr. 264/F4
Bladen (co.), N.C. 281/M5
Bladenboro, N.C. 281/M5
Bladensburg, Md. 245/G4
Bladensburg, Ohio 284/F5
Blades, Del. 245/R6
Bladon Springs, Ala. 195/B7
Bladworth, Sask. 181/E4
Blaeberry, Br. Col. 184/J4
Blaenavon, Wales 13/B6
Blagodarnoye, U.S.S.R. 52/F5
Blagoevgrad, Bulgaria 45/F5
Blagoveshchensk, U.S.S.R. 54/O4
Blagoveshchensk, U.S.S.R. 48/N4
Blagoveshchensk, U.S.S.R. 52/J4
Blain, France 28/C4
Blain, Pa. 294/H5
Blaine, Georgia 217/C1
Blaine (co.), Idaho 220/D6
Blaine, Kansas 232/F2
Blaine, Ky. 237/R4
Blaine•, Maine 243/H2
Blaine, Mich. 250/G5
Blaine, Minn. 255/G5
Blaine, Miss. 256/C3
Blaine (co.), Mont. 262/G2
Blaine (co.), Nebr. 264/E3
Blaine, Ohio 284/J5
Blaine (co.), Okla. 288/K3
Blaine, Oreg. 291/D2
Blaine, Tenn. 237/O8
Blaine, Wash. 310/C2
Blaine Lake, Sask. 181/D3
Blaine-Mars Hill, Maine 243/H2
Blainville, Québec 172/H4
Blair, Kansas 232/H2
Blair, Nebr. 264/H3
Blair, Okla. 288/H5
Blair (co.), Pa. 294/F4
Blair, S.C. 296/E3
Blair, W. Va. 312/C7
Blair, Wis. 317/D7
Blair Athol, Queensland 95/C4
Blair Atholl, Scotland 10/E2
Blair Atholl, Scotland 15/E4
Blairgowrie and Rattray, Scotland 15/E4
Blairgowrie and Rattray, Scotland 10/E2
Blairmore, Alberta 182/C5
Blairs, Va. 307/K7
Blairsburg, Iowa 229/F4
Blairsden, Calif. 204/E4
Blairs Mills, Ky. 237/P4
Blairs Mills, Pa. 294/G5
Blairstown, Iowa 229/J5
Blairstown, Mo. 261/E5
Blairstown•, N.J. 273/C2
Blairsville, Georgia 217/E1
Blairsville, Pa. 294/D5
Blaisdell, N. Dak. 282/F3
Blaj, Romania 45/F2
Blake (pt.), Mich. 250/E1
Blakeley, Minn. 255/E6
Blakeley, W. Va. 312/D6
Blakely, Georgia 217/C8
Blakely, Pa. 294/F6
Blakesburg, Iowa 229/H7
Blakeslee, Ohio 284/A2
Blakeslee, Pa. 294/L3
Blaketown, Newf. 166/D2
Blalock, Ala. 195/D6
Blalock, Georgia 217/E1
Blalock (isl.), Wash. 310/F5
Blanc (cape) 2/J4
Blanc (mt.), France 7/E4
Blanc (mt.), France 28/G5
Blanc (mt.), Italy 34/A2
Blanc (cape), Mauritania 102/A2
Blanc (cape), Mauritania 106/A4
Blanc (cape), Tunisia 106/G1
Blanc (cape), Western Sahara 106/A4
Blanca (bay), Argentina 120/C6
Blanca (bay), Argentina 143/D4
Blanca (lag.), Chile 138/E10
Blanca (peak), Colo. 188/F3
Blanca, Colo. 208/H8
Blanca (peak), Colo. 208/H7
Blanca (pt.), C. Rica 154/F5
Blanca, Cordillera (mts.), Peru 128/D7
Blanch, N.C. 281/L2
Blanchard, Idaho 220/A1
Blanchard, Iowa 229/C7
Blanchard, La. 238/C1
Blanchard•, Maine 243/D5
Blanchard, Mich. 250/D5
Blanchard, N. Dak. 282/R5
Blanchard (riv.), Ohio 284/C4
Blanchard, Okla. 288/L4
Blanchard, Pa. 294/G3
Blanchard, Wash. 310/C2
Blanchardstown, Ireland 17/H5
Blanchardville, Wis. 317/G10
Blanche, Ky. 237/O7
Blanche (riv.), Québec 172/E2
Blanche (lake), S. Australia 88/F5
Blanche (lake), S. Australia 94/F3
Blanche, Tenn. 237/H10
Blanche (lake), W. Australia 88/C4
Blanche Marie (fall), Suriname 131/C3
Blanchester, Ohio 284/B7
Blanchisseuse, Trin. & Tob. 161/B10
Blanco (riv.), Argentina 143/C2
Blanco (riv.), Bolivia 136/D4
Blanco (lake), Chile 138/F10
Blanco (cape), C. Rica 154/E6
Blanco (peak), C. Rica 154/F6
Blanco (riv.), Mexico 150/Q2
Blanco, N. Mex. 274/B2
Blanco (creek), N. Mex. 274/F4
Blanco, Okla. 288/P5
Blanco (cape), Oreg. 188/A2
Blanco (cape), Oreg. 291/C5
Blanco (cape), Peru 128/B5
Blanco (riv.), Peru 128/F6
Blanco (co.), Texas 303/F8
Blanco, Texas 303/F7
Blanc-Sablon, Québec 174/F2
Bland, Mo. 261/J6
Bland (co.), Va. 307/F6
Bland, Va. 307/F6
Blandburg, Pa. 294/F4
Blandford•, Mass. 249/C4
Blandford, Nova Scotia 168/D4
Blandford Forum, England 13/E7
Blandford Forum, England 10/E5
Blanding, Utah 304/E6
Blandinsville, Ill. 222/C3
Blandville, Ky. 237/D7
Blanefield, Scotland 15/B1
Blanes, Spain 33/H2
Blaney Park, Mich. 250/D2
Blanford, Ind. 227/B5
Blankenberge, Belgium 27/C6
Blankenburg am Harz, Germany 22/D3
Blanket, Texas 303/F6
Blanquillo, Uruguay 145/D3
Blansko, Czech. 41/D2
Blanton, Ala. 195/H5
Blanton, Fla. 212/D3
Blantyre, Malawi 115/F7
Blantyre, Malawi 102/F6
Blantyre, Scotland 15/B2
Blarney, Ireland 10/B5
Blarney, Ireland 17/D8
Blas (peak), Switzerland 39/G3
Blasdell, N.Y. 276/C5
Blasket (isls.), Ireland 10/A4
Blasket (isls.), Ireland 17/A7
Blatná, Czech. 41/B2
Blato, Yugoslavia 45/C4
Blatten, Switzerland 39/E4
Blaubeuren, Germany 22/C4
Blauvelt, N.Y. 276/K8
Blåvands Huk (pt.), Denmark 21/A6
Blawenburg, N.J. 273/D3
Blawnox, Pa. 294/C6
Blaydon, England 10/F3
Blaydon, England 13/H3
Blaye, France 28/C5
Blayney, N.S. Wales 97/E3
Blaze (pt.), North. Terr. 88/D2
Blaze (pt.), North. Terr. 93/A2
Bleckley (co.), Georgia 217/F6
Bled, Yugoslavia 45/A2
Bledsoe (co.), Tenn. 237/L9
Bledsoe, Texas 303/A4
Bleecker, Ala. 195/H5
Blekinge (co.), Sweden 18/J8
Blencoe, Iowa 229/A5
Blenheim, N. Zealand 100/D4
Blenheim, Ontario 177/C5
Blenheim, S.C. 296/H2
Blenker, Wis. 317/F6
Blennerhassett (isl.), Ohio 284/G7
Blerick, Netherlands 27/J6
Blesbok (riv.), S. Africa 118/J7
Blessing, Texas 303/H9
Blessington, Ireland 17/J5
Blevins, Ark. 202/C6
Blewett, Texas 303/D8
Blida, Algeria 106/E1
Blida, Algeria 102/C1
Bligh (sound), N. Zealand 100/A6
Bligh Water (bay), Fiji 86/P10
Blind Channel, Br. Col. 184/E5
Blind River, Ont. 162/H6
Blind River, Ontario 177/J5
Blind River, Ontario 175/D3
Blinman, S. Australia 88/F6
Blinman, S. Australia 94/F4
Blinnenhorn (mt.), Switzerland 39/F4
Bliss, Idaho 220/D7
Bliss, N.Y. 276/D5
Blissfield, Mich. 250/F7
Blissfield, New Bruns. 170/D2
Blissfield, Ohio 284/G5
Blitar, Indonesia 85/K2
Blitchton, Georgia 217/J6
Blocher, Ind. 227/F7
Block (isl.), R.I. 249/H8
Blocker, Okla. 288/P4
Block House, Nova Scotia 168/D4
Block Island (sound), N.Y. 276/S8
Block Island, R.I. 249/H8
Block Island (sound), R.I. 249/H8

340 Blockton

Blockton, Iowa 229/D7
Blodgett, Mo. 261/O8
Blodgett, Oreg. 291/D3
Blodgett Landing, N.H. 268/D5
Bloemendaal, Netherlands 27/E4
Bloemfontein, S. Africa 102/E7
Bloemfontein, S. Africa 118/C5
Blois, France 28/D4
Blokzijl, Netherlands 27/H3
Blomkest, Minn. 255/D6
Błonie, Poland 47/E2
Bloodroot (mt.), Vt. 268/B4
Bloodsworth (isl.), Md. 245/O8
Bloodvein (riv.), Manitoba 179/F3
Bloodvein (riv.), Ontario 175/A2
Bloodvein River, Manitoba 179/F3
Bloody Foreland (prom.), Ireland 17/E1
Bloody Foreland (prom.), Ireland 10/B3
Bloom, Kansas 232/C4
Bloom, N. Dak. 282/N6
Bloomburg, Texas 303/L4
Bloom City, Wis. 317/E8
Bloomdale, Ohio 284/D3
Bloomer, Ark. 202/B3
Bloomer, Wis. 317/D5
Bloomery, W. Va. 312/K4
Bloomfield, Sierra (mts.), Bolivia 136/D4
Bloomfield•, Conn. 210/E1
Bloomfield, Ind. 227/D6
Bloomfield, Iowa 229/J7
Bloomfield, Ky. 237/L5
Bloomfield, Mo. 261/M9
Bloomfield, Mont. 262/M3
Bloomfield, Nebr. 264/G2
Bloomfield, Newf. 166/D2
Bloomfield, N.J. 273/B2
Bloomfield, N. Mex. 274/A2
Bloomfield, Ontario 177/G4
Bloomfield (New Bloomfield), Pa. 294/H5
Bloomfield•, Vt. 268/D2
Bloomfield Hills, Mich. 250/B6
Bloomfield Ridge, New Bruns. 170/D2
Bloomfield Station, New Bruns. 170/E3
Bloomingburg, N.Y. 276/L7
Bloomingburg, Ohio 284/D6
Bloomingdale, Georgia 217/K6
Bloomingdale, Ill. 222/A5
Bloomingdale, Ind. 227/C5
Bloomingdale, Mich. 250/C6
Bloomingdale, N.J. 273/E1
Bloomingdale, N.Y. 276/M2
Bloomingdale, Ohio 284/J5
Bloomingdale, Tenn. 237/R7
Bloomingdale, Wis. 317/E8
Blooming Grove, Ind. 227/G5
Blooming Grove, Pa. 294/M3
Blooming Grove, Texas 303/H5
Bloomingport, Ind. 227/G5
Blooming Prairie, Minn. 255/E7
Bloomington, Calif. 204/E10
Bloomington, Idaho 220/G7
Bloomington, Ill. 188/J2
Bloomington, Ill. 222/D3
Bloomington, Ind. 227/D6
Bloomington, Md. 245/B3
Bloomington, Minn. 255/G6
Bloomington, Nebr. 264/F4
Bloomington, Texas 303/H9
Bloomington, Wis. 317/E10
Bloomington Springs, Tenn. 237/K8
Blooming Valley, Pa. 294/B2
Bloomsburg, Pa. 294/J3
Bloomsbury, Alberta 182/C2
Bloomsbury, N.J. 273/C2
Bloomsdale, Mo. 261/M6
Bloomville, N.Y. 276/L6
Bloomville, Ohio 284/D3
Blora, Indonesia 85/K2
Blossburg, Pa. 294/H2
Blossom, Texas 303/J4
Bloubergstrand, S. Africa 118/E6
Blount (co.), Ala. 195/E2
Blount (co.), Tenn. 237/O9
Blounts Creek, N.C. 281/P4
Blount Springs, Ala. 195/E3
Blountstown, Fla. 212/A1
Blountsville, Ala. 195/E2
Blountsville, Ind. 227/G4
Blountville, Tenn. 237/S7
Blowering (res.), N.S. Wales 97/E4
Blowing Rock, N.C. 281/F2
Bloxom, Va. 307/S5
Bludenz, Austria 41/A3
Blue, Ariz. 198/F5
Blue (riv.), Ariz. 198/F5
Blue (mt.), Colo. 208/B2
Blue (riv.), Colo. 208/G3
Blue (riv.), Ind. 227/E8
Blue (mts.), Jamaica 158/J6
Blue (mt.), Maine 243/C6
Blue (hills), Mass. 249/C8
Blue (creek), Nebr. 264/B3
Blue (mt.), New Bruns. 170/D1
Blue (mt.), N.H. 268/E2
Blue (mts.), N.S. Wales 88/H6
Blue (mts.), N.S. Wales 97/F3
Blue, Okla. 288/O7
Blue (riv.), Okla. 288/O6
Blue (mts.), Oreg. 291/J3
Blue (mt.), Pa. 294/G5
Blue (creek), Utah 304/B2
Blue (lake), Utah 304/B4
Blue (lake), Wash. 310/F3
Blue (mts.), Wash. 310/H4
Blue Ash, Ohio 284/C9
Blue Ball, Ark. 202/C4
Blue Bell, S. Dak. 298/C6
Bluebell, Utah 304/D3
Blueberry Creek, Br. Col. 184/J5
Blueberry Mountain, Alberta 182/A2
Blue Creek, Ohio 284/D8
Blue Creek, Utah 304/B2
Bluecreek, Wash. 310/H2
Blue Creek, W. Va. 312/D6
Blue Cypress (lake), Fla. 212/F4
Blue Diamond, Ky. 237/P6
Blue Earth (co.), Minn. 255/D6
Blue Earth, Minn. 255/D7
Blue Earth (riv.), Minn. 255/D7
Blue Eye, Ark. 202/D1
Blue Eye, Mo. 261/F9
Bluefield, Va. 307/F6
Bluefield, W. Va. 188/K3
Bluefield, W. Va. 312/D8
Bluefields, Jamaica 158/G6
Bluefields, Nicaragua 154/F4
Bluegrass, Ind. 227/E3
Blue Grass, Iowa 229/M5
Blue Grass, Minn. 255/C4
Blue Grass, Va. 307/J3
Blue Heron, Sask. 181/E2
Blue Hill, Maine 243/F7
Blue Hill•, Maine 243/F7
Blue Hill (bay), Maine 243/G7
Blue Hill, Nebr. 264/F4
Blue Hill Falls, Maine 243/F7
Blue Hills, Conn. 210/E1
Blue Island, Ill. 222/B6
Bluejacket, Okla. 288/R1
Blue Jay, Calif. 204/H9
Blue Joint (lake), Oreg. 291/H5
Blue Knob (mt.), Pa. 294/E5
Blue Lake, Calif. 204/A3
Blue Mesa (res.), Colo. 208/E5
Bluemont, Va. 307/N2
Blue Mound, Ill. 222/D4
Blue Mound, Kansas 232/H3
Blue Mound, Texas 303/E2
Blue Mounds, Wis. 317/G9
Blue Mountain, Ala. 195/G3
Blue Mountain, Ark. 202/C3
Blue Mountain (lake), Ark. 202/C3
Blue Mountain (peak), Jamaica 158/K6
Blue Mountain (peak), Jamaica 156/C3
Blue Mountain, Miss. 256/G1
Blue Mountain (lake), N.Y. 276/M3
Blue Mountain Lake, N.Y. 276/M3
Blue Mountains, Australia 87/E9
Blue Mountains, N.S. Wales 88/J6
Blue Mountains, N.S. Wales 97/F3
Blue Nile (riv.) 102/F3
Blue Nile (Abay) (riv.), Ethiopia 111/G5
Blue Nile (prov.), Sudan 111/F5
Blue Nile (riv.), Sudan 59/B6
Blue Nile (riv.), Sudan 111/F5
Blue Nose (mt.), Idaho 220/D4
Bluenose (lake), N.W. Terr. 187/G3
Blue Rapids, Kansas 232/F2
Blue Ridge, Alberta 182/C2
Blue Ridge, Georgia 217/D1
Blue Ridge (lake), Georgia 217/D1
Blue Ridge (mts.), Georgia 217/D1
Blue Ridge, Ind. 227/F5
Blue Ridge (mts.), Md. 245/H3
Blue Ridge (mts.), N.C. 281/E3
Blue Ridge (mts.), S.C. 296/B1
Blue Ridge, Va. 307/J6
Blue Ridge (mts.), Va. 307/J6
Blue Ridge Manor, Ky. 237/L2
Blue Ridge Summit, Pa. 294/G6
Blue River, Br. Col. 184/H4
Blue River, Colo. 208/G4
Blue River, Oreg. 291/E3
Blue River, Wis. 317/E9
Blue Rock, Nova Scotia 168/D4
Blue Rock (Gaysport), Ohio 284/G6
Blue Sea Lake, Québec 172/A3
Bluesky, Alberta 182/A1
Blue Spring (hills), Utah 304/B1
Blue Springs, Ala. 195/G7
Blue Springs, Miss. 256/G2
Blue Springs, Mo. 261/R6
Blue Springs, Nebr. 264/H4
Blue Stack (mts.), Ireland 17/E2
Bluestem (lake), Okla. 288/O1
Bluestone (lake), Va. 307/G5
Bluestone (lake), W. Va. 312/E7
Blue Sulphur Springs, W. Va. 312/E7
Blue Summit, Mo. 261/R5
Bluevale, Ontario 177/C4
Bluewater, N. Mex. 274/A3
Bluewater (creek), N. Mex. 274/B4
Bluewater (creek), N. Mex. 274/D6
Bluewater (lake), N. Mex. 274/A3
Bluff (cape), Newf. 166/C3
Bluff, N. Zealand 100/B7
Bluff, N.C. 281/D3
Bluff, Utah 304/E6
Bluff City, Ark. 202/D6
Bluff City, Ill. 222/E5
Bluff City, Kansas 232/E4
Bluff City, Tenn. 237/S8
Bluff Dale, Texas 303/F5
Bluffdale, Utah 304/B3
Bluff Knoll (mt.), W. Australia 92/B6
Bluff Park, Ala. 195/E4
Bluffs, Ill. 222/C4
Bluffsprings, Fla. 212/B5
Bluffton, Alberta 182/C3
Bluffton, Ark. 202/C4
Bluffton, Georgia 217/C7
Bluffton, Ind. 227/G3
Bluffton, Minn. 255/C4
Bluffton, Ohio 284/C4
Bluffton, S.C. 296/F7
Bluford, Ill. 222/E5
Blum, Texas 303/G5
Blumenau, Brazil 132/D9
Blumenau, Brazil 120/E5
Blumenfeld, Manitoba 179/D5
Blumenheim, Sask. 181/E3
Blumenhof, Sask. 181/D5
Blumenort, Manitoba 179/E5
Blumenort, Manitoba 179/F5
Blumenort, Sask. 181/D5
Blumenstein, Switzerland 39/E3
Blumenthal, Sask. 181/E3
Blümlisalp (mt.), Switzerland 39/E3
Blunt, S. Dak. 298/J4
Bly, Oreg. 291/F5
Blying (sound), Alaska 196/C1
Blyn, Wash. 310/B3
Blyth, England 13/F2
Blyth, England 10/F3
Blyth, Ontario 177/C4
Blyth Bridge, Scotland 15/E5
Blythe, Calif. 204/L10
Blythe, Georgia 217/H4
Blythedale, Md. 245/O2
Blythedale, Mo. 261/E2
Blythedale, Pa. 294/C5
Blytheswood, Ontario 177/B5
Blytheville, Ark. 188/H3
Blytheville, Ark. 202/L2
Blytheville A.F.B., Ark. 202/K2
Blythewood, S.C. 296/E3
Bo, S. Leone 102/A4
Bo, S. Leone 106/B7
Boac, Philippines 82/C4
Boaco, Nicaragua 154/E4
Boa Esperança, Brazil 135/D2
Boalsburg, Pa. 294/G4
Boano (isl.), Indonesia 85/H6
Boa Nova, Brazil 132/B5
Board Camp, Ark. 202/B4
Boardman (riv.), Mich. 250/D4
Boardman, N.C. 281/M6
Boardman, Ohio 284/J3
Boardman, Oreg. 291/H2
Boardman, Wis. 317/A5
Boardmans Bridge, Conn. 210/B2
Boas (riv.), N.W. Terr. 187/K3
Boat Basin, Br. Col. 184/D5
Boat Harbour, Tasmania 99/B2
Boat of Garten, Scotland 15/E3
Boa Vista, Brazil 120/C2
Boa Vista, Brazil 132/H8
Boa Vista (isl.), C. Verde 106/B8
Boayan (isl.), Philippines 82/B5
Boaz, Ala. 195/F2
Boaz, Ky. 237/D7
Boaz, Mo. 261/F8
Boaz, W. Va. 312/D4
Boaz, Wis. 317/E9
Bobadah, N.S. Wales 97/D3
Bobai, China 77/H7
Bobaomby (cape), Madagascar 102/G6
Bobaomby (Amber) (cape), Madagascar 118/H2
Bobare, Venezuela 124/D2
Bobbili, India 68/E5
Bobbitt, N.C. 281/N2
Bobcaygeon, Ontario 177/F3
Bobigny, France 28/B1
Böblingen, Germany 22/C4
Bobo, Miss. 256/C2
Bobo Dioulasso, Burkina Faso 106/D6
Bobo Dioulasso, Burkina Faso 102/B3
Bobon, Philippines 82/F7
Bobonaza (riv.), Ecuador 128/D3
Bobonong, Botswana 118/D4
Bobotov Kuk (mt.), Yugoslavia 45/D4
Bobr (riv.), Poland 47/B3
Bobrov, U.S.S.R. 52/F4
Bobruysk, U.S.S.R. 7/G3
Bobruysk, U.S.S.R. 52/C4
Bobruysk, U.S.S.R. 48/C4
Bobs (lake), Ontario 177/H3
Bobtown, Pa. 294/B6
Bobures, Venezuela 124/C3
Boby, Pic (mt.), Madagascar 118/H4
Bocabec, New Bruns. 170/C3
Boca Chica, Dom. Rep. 158/E6
Boca Chica (key), Fla. 212/E7
Boca Ciega (bay), Fla. 212/B3
Boca de Aroa, Venezuela 124/D2
Boca del Mangle, Venezuela 124/D2
Boca del Pao, Venezuela 124/F3
Boca del Pepé, Colombia 126/B5
Boca del Río, Mexico 150/Q2
Boca del Soco, Dom. Rep. 158/F6
Boca do Acre, Brazil 132/G10
Boca Grande, Fla. 212/D5
Boca Grande (key), Fla. 212/D7
Boca Grande (passage), Trin. & Tob. 161/A10
Boca Grande (gulf), Venezuela 124/H3
Bocaiúva, Brazil 132/E7
Bocaranga, Cent. Afr. Rep. 115/C2
Boca Raton, Fla. 212/F5
Bocas del Toro, Panama 154/F6
Bocay, Nicaragua 154/E3
Bochnia, Poland 47/E4
Bocholt, Belgium 27/H6
Bocholt, Germany 22/B3
Bochov, Czech. 41/B1
Bochum, Germany 22/B3
Bock, Minn. 255/E5
Boco, Chile 138/F2
Boconó, Venezuela 124/C3
Boda, Cent. Afr. Rep. 115/C3
Bodalla, N.S. Wales 97/F5
Bodaybo, U.S.S.R. 54/N4
Bodaybo, U.S.S.R. 48/M4
Bodcaw, Ark. 202/D6
Boddam, Scotland 15/G3
Boddington, W. Australia 92/B2
Bode, Iowa 229/E3
Bodega (bay), Calif. 204/B5
Bodega (head), Calif. 204/B5
Bodega Bay, Calif. 204/B5
Bodegraven, Netherlands 27/F4
Bodélé (depr.), Chad 102/D3
Bodélé (depr.), Chad 111/C4
Boden, Sweden 18/M4
Bodensee (Constance) (lake), Austria 41/A3
Bodensee (Constance) (lake), Switzerland 39/H1
Bodensee (Constance) (lake), Germany 22/C5
Boderg (lake), Ireland 17/E4
Bodfish, Calif. 204/G8
Bodhan, India 68/D5
Bodie (isl.), N.C. 281/T2
Bodinayakkanur, India 68/D6
Bodines, Pa. 294/H3
Bodio, Switzerland 39/G4
Bodkin (pt.), Md. 245/N4
Bodmin, England 13/C7
Bodmin, England 10/D5
Bodmin, Sask. 181/D2
Bodo, Alberta 182/E3
Bodø, Norway 18/J3
Bodø, Norway 7/F2
Bodrum, Turkey 63/B4
Bodrum, Turkey 59/A2
Bo Duc, Vietnam 72/E4
Bódvaszilas, Hungary 41/F2
Boelus, Nebr. 264/F3
Boende, Zaire 115/D4
Boerne, Texas 303/J10
Boeuf (lake), La. 238/J7
Boeuf (riv.), La. 238/G1
Boffa, Guinea 106/B6
Bog (lake), Maine 243/H6
Bogalusa, La. 188/H4
Bogalusa, La. 238/L5
Bogan (riv.), N.S. Wales 97/D2
Bogandé, Burkina Faso 106/E6
Bogan Gate, N.S. Wales 97/D3
Bogantungan, Queensland 95/C4
Bogard, Mo. 261/E4
Bogart, Georgia 217/E3
Bogata, Texas 303/J4
Bogatynia, Poland 47/B3
Boğazlıyan, Turkey 63/F3
Bogen, Germany 22/E4
Bogenfels, Namibia 118/B5
Bogense, Denmark 21/D6
Boger City, N.C. 281/G4
Boggabilla, N.S. Wales 97/F1
Boggabri, N.S. Wales 97/F2
Boggeragh (mts.), Ireland 17/D7
Boggs, W. Va. 312/E6
Boggstown, Ind. 227/F5
Boggy (peak), Ant. & Bar. 161/D11
Boggy Creek, Manitoba 179/A3
Boggy Depot, Okla. 288/O6
Bogia, Papua N.G. 85/B6
Bogie (riv.), Scotland 15/F3
Bognor Regis, England 13/G7
Bognor Regis, England 10/F5
Bogny-sur-Meuse, France 28/F3
Bogo, Philippines 82/E5
Bogon (riv.), N.S. Wales 88/H6
Bogong (mt.), Victoria 97/D5
Bogor, Indonesia 54/M10
Bogor, Indonesia 85/H2
Bogoslof (isl.), Alaska 196/E4
Bogotá (cap.), Colombia 126/D5
Bogotá (cap.), Colombia 120/B2
Bogotá (cap.), Colombia 2/F5
Bogota, Ill. 222/E5
Bogota, N.J. 273/B2
Bogota, Tenn. 237/C8
Bogra, Bangladesh 68/F4
Boguchar, U.S.S.R. 52/F5
Bogue, Kansas 232/C2
Bogué, Mauritania 106/B5
Bogue Chitto, Miss. 256/D8
Bogue Chitto (riv.), Miss. 256/D8
Bogue Homo (lake), Miss. 256/F7
Boguszów-Gorce, Poland 47/B3
Bog Walk, Jamaica 158/J6
Bo Hai (gulf), China 77/J4
Boharm, Sask. 181/F5
Bohemian (for.), Czech. 41/B2
Bohemian (for.), Germany 22/E4
Bohemian-Moravian Heights (hills), Czech. 41/C2
Boherbue, Ireland 17/C7
Bohners Lake, Wis. 317/K10
Bohodleh, Somalia 115/J2
Bohol (prov.), Philippines 82/E6
Bohol (isl.), Philippines 85/G4
Bohol (isl.), Philippines 82/E6
Bohol (sea), Philippines 82/E6
Bohol (str.), Philippines 82/D6
Böhönye, Hungary 41/D3
Bohu (Bagrax), China 77/C3
Boicourt, Kansas 232/H3
Boiestown, New Bruns. 170/D2
Boiling Spring Lakes, N.C. 281/N7
Boiling Springs, N.C. 281/F4
Boiling Springs, Pa. 294/H5
Bois Blanc (isl.), Mich. 250/E3
Boischatel, Québec 172/J3
Boisdale, Nova Scotia 168/H2
Boisdale, Loch (inlet), Scotland 15/A3
Bois D'Arc, Mo. 261/F8
Bois-des-Filion, Québec 172/H4
Bois de Sioux (riv.), Minn. 255/B4
Bois de Sioux (riv.), S. Dak. 298/R1
Boise (co.), Idaho 220/C6
Boise (cap.), Idaho 146/G5
Boise (cap.), Idaho 220/B6
Boise (cap.), Idaho 188/C2
Boise (mts.), Idaho 220/B6
Boise (riv.), Idaho 220/B6
Boise City, Okla. 288/B1
Boissevain, Man. 162/G6
Boissevain, Manitoba 179/C5
Boissevain, Va. 307/F6
Boistfort, Wash. 310/B4
Boisvert (pt.), Québec 172/J1
Boizenburg an der Elbe, Germany 22/D2
Bojador (cape), W. Sahara 102/A2
Bojador (cape), Western Sahara 106/B3
Bojeador (cape), Philippines 82/C1
Bojnurd, Iran 66/K2
Bojnurd, Iran 59/G2
Bojonegoro, Indonesia 85/J2
Bokchito, Okla. 288/O6
Boké, Guinea 106/B6
Bokeelia, Fla. 212/D5
Bokel (cay), Belize 154/D2
Bokhara (riv.), N.S. Wales 97/D1
Bokhoma, Okla. 288/S7
Boknafjord (fjord), Norway 18/D7
Boko, Congo 115/B4
Bokoro, Chad 111/C5
Bokoshe, Okla. 288/S4
Bokote, Zaire 115/D4
Bokpyin, Burma 72/C5
Boksburg, S. Africa 118/J6
Bokungu, Zaire 115/D4
Bol, Chad 111/B5
Bol, Chad 102/D3
Bolair, W. Va. 312/F6
Bolama, Guinea-Biss. 106/A6
Bolan (pass), Pakistan 68/B3
Bolangir, India 68/E4
Bolar, Va. 307/J4
Bolatusha, Miss. 256/E5
Bolayır, Turkey 63/C5
Bolbec, France 28/D3
Bolckow, Mo. 261/C2
Boldersley, Denmark 21/C8
Bolding, Ark. 202/F7
Boldman, Ky. 237/R5
Boldon, England 13/J3
Bolduc, Québec 172/G4
Bole, China 77/B3
Bole, Ghana 106/D7
Boles, Ark. 202/B4
Bolesławiec, Poland 47/B3
Boley, Okla. 288/O4
Bolgatanga, Ghana 106/D6
Boli, China 77/M2
Boligee, Ala. 195/C5
Bolinao, Philippines 82/B2
Bolinao (cape), Philippines 82/B2
Bolinas, Calif. 204/H1
Boling, Texas 303/H8
Bolingbroke, Georgia 217/E5
Bolingbrook, Ill. 222/A6
Bolinger, Ala. 195/B7
Bolinger, La. 238/C1
Bolívar, Argentina 143/D4
Bolívar, Bolivia 136/B3
Bolívar (dept.), Colombia 126/C3
Bolívar, Antioquia, Colombia 126/C5
Bolívar, Cauca, Colombia 126/B7
Bolívar (prov.), Ecuador 128/C3
Bolívar, Ecuador 128/C2
Bolivar (co.), Miss. 256/C3
Bolivar, Mo. 261/F7
Bolivar, N.Y. 276/D6
Bolivar, Ohio 284/G4
Bolivar, Pa. 294/C5
Bolívar, Peru 128/D6
Bolivar, Tenn. 237/C10
Bolivar (pen.), Texas 303/K8
Bolívar (state), Venezuela 124/F7
Bolívar, Cerro (mt.), Venezuela 124/G4
Bolívar, Pico (peak), Venezuela 124/C3
Bolivar, W. Va. 312/L4
Bolivia 2/F6
Bolivia 120/C4
BOLIVIA 136
Bolivia, N.C. 281/N6
Bolkar (mts.), Turkey 63/F4
Bolkhov, U.S.S.R. 52/E4
Bolligen, Switzerland 39/E3
Bolling, Ala. 195/E7
Bolling A.F.B., D.C. 245/E5
Bollinger (co.), Mo. 261/M8
Bollington, England 10/G2
Bollington, England 13/H2
Bollnäs, Sweden 18/K6
Bollon, Queensland 95/C6
Bollon, Queensland 88/H5
Bollstabruk, Sweden 18/L5
Bolmen (lake), Sweden 18/H8
Bolobo, Zaire 115/C4
Bologna (prov.), Italy 34/C2
Bologna, Italy 34/C2
Bologna, Italy 7/F4
Bolognesi, Peru 128/F8
Bolognesi, Peru 128/F6
Bologoye, U.S.S.R. 52/D3
Bolomba, Zaire 115/C3
Bolonchén de Rejón, Mexico 150/O7
Bolondrón, Cuba 156/B2
Bolondrón, Cuba 158/D1
Bolovens (plat.), Laos 72/E4
Bolpebra, Bolivia 136/A2
Bolsena (lake), Italy 34/C3
Bol'shevik (isl.) U.S.S.R. 54/N2
Bol'shevik (isl.), U.S.S.R. 4/A4
Bol'shevik (isl.), U.S.S.R. 48/K2
Bol'shoy Lyakhov (isl.), U.S.S.R. 54/R2
Bol'shoy Lyakhovskiy (isl.), U.S.S.R. 48/P2
Bolsover, England 13/J2
Bolsters Mills, Maine 243/B7
Bolsward, Netherlands 27/H2
Boltaña, Spain 33/F1
Boltigen, Switzerland 39/D3
Bolton•, Conn. 210/F1
Bolton, England 10/G2
Bolton, England 13/H2
Bolton•, Mass. 249/H3
Bolton, Miss. 256/D6
Bolton, N.C. 281/N6
Bolton•, Vt. 268/B3
Bolton (mt.), Vt. 268/B3
Bolton Landing, N.Y. 276/N3
Bolu (prov.), Turkey 63/D2
Bolu, Turkey 59/B1
Bolu, Turkey 63/D2
Bolus (head), Ireland 17/A8
Bolvadin, Turkey 63/D3
Bolvanskiy Nos (cape), U.S.S.R. 52/K1
Bolvanskiy Nos (cape), U.S.S.R. 48/G2
Bolzano (Bolzen), Italy 34/C1
Bolzano, Italy 7/F4
Bolzano-Bozen (prov.), Italy 34/C1
Bolzen (Bolzano), Italy 34/C1
Boma, Zaire 102/D5
Boma, Zaire 115/B5
Bomaderry-Nowra, N.S. Wales 97/F4
Bomarton, Texas 303/E4
Bomba (gulf), Libya 111/D1
Bombala, N.S. Wales 97/E5
Bombardopolis, Haiti 158/B5
Bombay, India 2/N5
Bombay, India 54/J8
Bombay, India 68/C5
Bombay (Greater), India 68/B7
Bombay (harb.), India 68/B7
Bombay, Minn. 255/F6
Bombay, N.Y. 276/M1
Bomboma, Zaire 115/C3
Bom Conselho, Brazil 132/G5
Bom Despacho, Brazil 135/D1
Bom Despacho, Brazil 132/E7
Bomdila, India 68/G3
Bom Futuro, Brazil 120/C4
Bom Futuro, Brazil 132/A5
Bomi, China 77/E6
Bom Jesus, Brazil 132/E5
Bom Jesus da Lapa, Brazil 120/E4
Bom Jesus da Lapa, Brazil 132/F6
Bom Jesus do Itabapoana, Brazil 135/F2
Bomongo, Zaire 115/C3
Bomont, W. Va. 312/D6
Bomoseen, Vt. 268/A4
Bomoseen (lake), Vt. 268/A4
Bom Retiro, Brazil 132/D10
Bom Sucesso, Brazil 135/D2
Bomu (riv.), Centr. Afr. Rep. 102/E4
Bomu (riv.), Cent. Afr. Rep. 115/D3
Bomu (riv.), Zaire 115/D3
Bon (cape), Tunisia 102/D1
Bon (cape), Tunisia 106/G1
Bona (mt.), Alaska 196/K2
Bonabéri, Cameroon 115/A3
Bonacca (Guanaja) (isl.), Honduras 154/E2
Bon Accord, Alberta 182/D3
Bonaduz, Switzerland 39/H3
Bon Air, Ala. 195/F4
Bonair, Iowa 229/J2
Bon Air, Tenn. 237/L9
Bon Air, Va. 307/N5
Bonaire (isl.), Neth. Ant. 156/E4
Bonaire (isl.), Neth. Ant. 161/E9
Bonalbo, N.S. Wales 97/G1
Bonanza, Alberta 182/A2
Bonanza, Ark. 202/B3
Bonanza, Colo. 208/G6
Bonanza, Nicaragua 154/E4
Bonanza, Oreg. 291/F5
Bonanza, Utah 304/E3
Bonanza (peak), Wash. 310/E2
Bonao, Dom. Rep. 158/E6
Bonaparte, Iowa 229/K7
Bonaparte (lake), N.Y. 276/K2
Bonaparte (creek), Wash. 310/F2
Bonaparte (mt.), Wash. 310/F2
Bonaparte (arch.), W. Australia 88/C2
Bonaparte (arch.), W. Australia 92/D1
Bon Aqua, Tenn. 237/G9
Bonar Bridge, Scotland 15/D3
Bonaventure (cape), Newf. 166/D2
Bonaventure (co.), Québec 172/C2
Bonaventure (county), Québec 174/D3
Bonaventure, Québec 172/C2
Bonaventure (isl.), Québec 172/D1
Bonaventure (riv.), Québec 172/C1
Bonavista, Newf. 162/L6
Bonavista, Newf. 166/D2
Bonavista (bay), Newf. 166/D1
Bonavista (cape), Newf. 166/D1
Boncarbo, Colo. 208/K8
Bonchester Bridge, Scotland 15/F5
Boncourt, Switzerland 39/C2
Bond, Colo. 208/F3
Bond (co.), Ill. 222/D5
Bond, Ky. 237/N6
Bond, Miss. 256/F9
Bond (mt.), N.H. 268/E3
Bondeno, Italy 34/C2
Bond Falls (res.), Mich. 250/G2
Bondi (beach), N.S. Wales 97/K3
Bondiss, Alberta 182/D2
Bondo, Zaire 115/D3
Bondoukou, Ivory Coast 106/D7
Bondowoso, Indonesia 85/L2
Bondsville, Mass. 249/E4
Bonduel, Wis. 317/K6
Bondurant, Iowa 229/G5
Bondurant, Wyo. 319/B2
Bondville, Ill. 222/E3
Bondville, Ky. 237/M5
Bondville, Vt. 268/B5
Bondy, France 28/B1
Bône (Annaba), Algeria 106/F1
Bone, Idaho 220/G6
Bone (gulf), Indonesia 54/O10
Bone (gulf), Indonesia 85/G7
Bone Cave, Tenn. 237/L9
Bone Gap, Ill. 222/F5
Bo'ness, Scotland 10/C1
Bo'ness, Scotland 15/C1
Bonesteel, S. Dak. 298/M7
Bonet (riv.), Ireland 17/E3
Boneta, Utah 304/D3
Bonete (dam), Uruguay 145/C3
Bonetraill, N. Dak. 282/C3
Boneville, Georgia 217/G4
Bonfield, Ill. 222/E2
Bonfield, Ontario 177/E1
Bonfol, Switzerland 39/D2
Bong (range), Liberia 106/B7
Bongabong, Philippines 82/C4
Bongandanga, Zaire 115/D3
Bonggaw, Philippines 82/B8
Bongo (isl.), Philippines 82/D7
Bongor, Chad 111/C5
Bongor, Chad 102/D3
Bong Son (Hoai Nhon), Vietnam 72/F4
Bonham, Texas 303/H4
Bonhill, Scotland 15/B1
Bonhomme (isl.), Mo. 261/N2
Bon Homme (co.), S. Dak. 298/O7
Bonifacio, France 28/B7
Bonifacio (str.), France 28/B7
Bonifacio (str.), Italy 34/B4
Bonifay, Fla. 212/C5
Bönigen, Switzerland 39/E3
Bonilla, S. Dak. 298/N4
Bonin (isls.), Japan 2/S4
Bonin (isls.), Japan 54/R7
Bonin (isls.), Japan 87/E3
Bonin (isls.), Japan 81/M3
Bonita, Ariz. 198/E6
Bonita (pt.), Calif. 204/H2
Bonita, La. 238/G1
Bonita, Miss. 256/G6
Bonita Springs, Fla. 212/E5

Brady 341

Bonlee, N.C. 281/L3
Bonn (cap.), Germany 7/E3
Bonn (cap.), Germany 22/B3
Bonne (bay), Newf. 166/C4
Bonneau, S.C. 296/H5
Bonner (co.), Idaho 220/B1
Bonners Ferry, Idaho 220/B1
Bonner Springs, Kansas 232/H2
Bonner-West Riverside, Mont. 262/C4
Bonnet (lake), Manitoba 179/G4
Bonnétable, France 28/D3
Bonnet Carré Spillway and Floodway, La. 238/N3
Bonne Terre, Mo. 261/L7
Bonnet Plume (riv.), Yukon 187/E3
Bonneville, France 28/G4
Bonneville (co.), Idaho 220/G6
Bonneville, Oreg. 291/F2
Bonneville (dam), Oreg. 291/E2
Bonneville (salt flats), Utah 304/A3
Bonneville (dam), Wash. 310/D5
Bonneville (lake), Wash. 310/D5
Bonneville, Wyo. 319/E2
Bonneville (mt.), Wyo. 319/C3
Bonney Lake, Wash. 310/C3
Bonnie, Ill. 222/E5
Bonnieville, Ky. 237/K6
Bonnots Mill, Mo. 261/J5
Bonny (res.), Colo. 208/P3
Bonny, Nigeria 106/F8
Bonny (bight), Nigeria 106/F8
Bonnybridge, Scotland 15/C1
Bonnyman, Ky. 237/P6
Bonnyrigg, N.S. Wales 88/K4
Bonnyrigg, N.S. Wales 97/H3
Bonnyrigg and Lasswade, Scotland 10/C1
Bonnyrigg and Lasswade, Scotland 15/D2
Bonny River, New Bruns. 170/D3
Bonnyville, Alberta 182/E2
Bono, Ark. 202/J2
Bono, Ohio 284/D2
Bonorva, Italy 34/B4
Bonpas (creek), Ill. 222/F5
Bonpland (mt.), N. Zealand 100/A6
Bon Secour, Ala. 195/C10
Bon Secour (bay), Ala. 195/C10
Bonsecours, Québec 172/E4
Bonshaw, Pr. Edward I. 168/E2
Bonthain, Indonesia 85/F7
Bonthe, S. Leone 106/B7
Bontoc, Philippines 85/G2
Bontoc, Philippines 82/C2
Bon Wier, Texas 303/L7
Bonyhád, Hungary 41/E3
Boody, Ill. 222/D4
Book (cliffs), Utah 304/E4
Booker, Texas 303/D1
Booker T. Washington Nat'l Mon., Va. 307/J6
Boolaloo, W. Australia 92/B3
Booligal, N.S. Wales 97/C3
Boom, Belgium 27/E6
Boom, Tenn. 237/L7
Boomer, N.C. 281/G2
Boomer, W. Va. 312/D6
Boomi, N.S. Wales 88/H5
Boomi, N.S. Wales 97/E1
Boon (pt.), Ant. & Bar. 161/E11
Boon, Mich. 250/D4
Boondall, Queensland 88/K2
Boone (co.), Ark. 202/D1
Boone, Colo. 208/L6
Boone (co.), Ill. 222/E1
Boone (co.), Ind. 227/E4
Boone (co.), Iowa 229/F5
Boone, Iowa 229/F4
Boone (co.), Ky. 237/M3
Boone, Ky. 237/N5
Boone (co.), Mo. 261/H4
Boone (co.), Nebr. 264/F3
Boone, Nebr. 264/F3
Boone, N.C. 281/F2
Boone (lake), Tenn. 237/S8
Boone (co.), W. Va. 312/C6
Boone Grove, Ind. 227/C2
Boonesboro, Mo. 261/G4
Boones Mill, Va. 307/J6
Boonesville, Va. 307/L4
Booneville, Ark. 202/C3
Booneville, Ky. 237/O6
Booneville, Miss. 256/G1
Boonsboro, Md. 245/H2
Boonton, N.J. 273/E2
Boonton (res.), N.J. 273/E2
Boonville, Calif. 204/B5
Boonville, Ind. 227/C8
Boonville, Mo. 261/G5
Boonville, N.Y. 276/K4
Boonville, N.C. 281/H2
Boopi (riv.), Bolivia 136/B4
Boorooban, N.S. Wales 97/C4
Boorowa, N.S. Wales 97/E4
Boort, Victoria 97/B5
Booth, Ala. 195/E6
Boothbay, Maine 243/D8
Boothbay•, Maine 243/D8
Boothbay Harbor, Maine 243/D8
Boothia (pen.), Canada 4/B14
Boothia (gulf), Canada 4/B14
Boothia (gulf), N.W.T. 146/J2
Boothia (gulf), N.W.T. 162/G1
Boothia (gulf), N.W.T. 187/K3
Boothia (isthmus), N.W.T. 162/G2
Boothia (pen.), N.W.T. 146/J2
Boothia (pen.), N.W.T. 162/G1
Boothia (pen.), N.W.T. 187/J2
Boothville, La. 238/M8
Boothwyn, Pa. 294/L7
Bootle, England 10/F2
Bootle, England 13/G2
Booué, Gabon 115/B3
Bophuthatswana (bantustan), S. Africa 102/E7
Bophuthatswana (rep.), S. Africa 118/D5
Boppard, Germany 22/B3
Boquerón, Cuba 158/K4
Boquerón, Cuba 156/C3
Boquerón, Paraguay 144/B3
Boquerón, El (pass), Peru 128/E7
Boquerón, P. Rico 156/F1
Boquerón, P. Rico 161/A3
Boquerón (bay), P. Rico 161/A3
Boquilla del Carmen, Mexico 150/H2
Bor, Czech. 41/B2
Bor, Sudan 111/F6
Bor, Turkey 63/F4
Bor, U.S.S.R. 52/F3
Bor, Yugoslavia 45/E3
Bora-Bora (isl.), Fr. Poly. 87/L7
Borah (peak), Idaho 188/D2
Borah (peak), Idaho 220/E5
Borama, Somalia 115/H1
Borås, Sweden 7/F3
Borås, Sweden 18/H8
Borazjan, Iran 66/G6
Borazjan, Iran 59/F4
Borba, Brazil 120/D3
Borba, Brazil 132/H9
Borba, Portugal 33/C3
Borbón, Venezuela 124/F4
Borçka, Turkey 63/J2
Borculo, Netherlands 27/J4
Bordeaux, France 28/C5
Bordeaux, France 7/D4
Bordeaux, S.C. 296/C4
Bordeaux (mt.), Virgin Is. (U.S.) 161/C4
Bordelonville, La. 238/G4
Borden (isl.), Canada 4/B15
Borden, Ind. 227/F8
Borden (isl.), N.W. Terr. 187/G2
Borden (pen.), N.W. Terr. 187/K2
Borden, Pr. Edward I. 168/E2
Borden, Sask. 181/D3
Borden, S.C. 296/G3
Borden (co.), Texas 303/C5
Borden, W. Australia 92/B6
Borden Shaft, Md. 245/B2
Borden Springs, Ala. 195/H3
Bordentown, N.J. 273/D3
Border, Minn. 255/D2
Border, Wyo. 319/B3
Borderland, W. Va. 312/B7
Borders (reg.), Scotland 15/E5
Bordertown, S. Australia 88/F7
Bordertown, S. Australia 94/G7
Bordighera, Italy 34/A3
Bordj Bou Arreridj, Algeria 106/E1
Bordj Fly Sainte Marie, Algeria 106/D3
Bordj Omar Driss, Algeria 106/F3
Bordj Omar Driss, Algeria 102/C2
Bordulac, N. Dak. 282/N5
Boreing, Ky. 237/N6
Boreray (isl.), Scotland 15/A2
Boreray (isl.), Scotland 15/A3
Borgå, Finland 18/O6
Borge, Norway 18/H2
Borger, Netherlands 27/K3
Borger, Texas 303/C2
Borger, Texas 188/F3
Borgerhout, Belgium 27/E6
Borgholm, Sweden 18/K8
Borghorst, Germany 22/B2
Borgloon, Belgium 27/G7
Borgne (lake), La. 238/L7
Borgne (riv.), Switzerland 39/D4
Borgo, Italy 34/C1
Borgomanero, Italy 34/B2
Borgo San Lorenzo, Italy 34/C2
Borgworm (Waremme), Belgium 27/G7
Borikan, Laos 72/D3
Boring, Md. 245/L2
Boring, Oreg. 291/E2
Borinquen (pt.), P. Rico 156/F1
Borinquen (pt.), P. Rico 161/A1
Borislav, U.S.S.R. 52/B5
Borisoglebsk, U.S.S.R. 48/E4
Borisoglebsk, U.S.S.R. 52/F4
Borisov, U.S.S.R. 52/C4
Borisovka, U.S.S.R. 52/E4
Bo River Post, Sudan 111/E6
Borja, Peru 128/D5
Borja, Spain 33/F2
Borjas Blancas, Spain 33/G2
Borken, Germany 22/B3
Børkop, Denmark 21/C6
Borku, Chad 111/C4
Borkum, Germany 22/B2
Borkum (isl.), Germany 22/B2
Borlänge, Sweden 18/J6
Borna, Germany 22/E3
Borndiep (chan.), Netherlands 27/H2
Borne, Netherlands 27/K4
Borneo (isl.) 2/Q6
Borneo (isl.) 54/N9
Borneo (isl.), Indonesia 85/E5
Borneo (isl.), Malaysia 85/E5
Bornheim, Germany 22/B3
Bornholm (co.), Denmark 21/F9
Bornholm (isl.), Denmark 7/F3
Bornholm (isl.), Denmark 18/J9
Bornholm (isl.), Denmark 21/F9
Borno (state), Nigeria 106/G6
Bornova, Turkey 63/B3
Borocay (isl.), Philippines 82/D5
Borojó, Venezuela 124/C2
Boron, Calif. 204/H8
Borongan, Philippines 82/E5
Borot Kidod (well), Israel 65/C5
Borovichi, U.S.S.R. 52/D3
Borradaile, Alberta 182/E3
Borre, Norway 18/D4
Borrego Springs, Calif. 204/J10
Borris, Ireland 17/H6
Borris-in-Ossory, Ireland 17/F6
Borrisokane, Ireland 17/E6
Borrisoleigh, Ireland 17/E6
Borroloola, North. Terr. 88/F3
Borroloola, North. Terr. 93/E4
Borşa, Romania 45/G2
Borsod-Abaúj-Zemplén (co.), Hungary 41/F2
Bortala (Bole), China 77/B3
Borth, Wales 13/C5
Bort-les-Orgues, France 28/E5
Boruca, C. Rica 154/F6
Borujerd, Iran 59/E3
Borujerd, Iran 66/F4
Borup, Denmark 21/E7
Borup, Minn. 255/B3
Börzsöny (mts.), Hungary 41/E3
Borzya, U.S.S.R. 48/M4
Bosa, Italy 34/B4
Bosanska Dubica, Yugoslavia 45/C3
Bosanska Gradiška, Yugoslavia 45/C3
Bosanska Kostajnica, Yugoslavia 45/B3
Bosanska Krupa, Yugoslavia 45/C3
Bosanski Brod, Yugoslavia 45/D3
Bosanski Novi, Yugoslavia 45/C3
Bosanski Petrovac, Yugoslavia 45/C3
Bosanski Šamac, Yugoslavia 45/D3
Bosaso, Somalia 115/J1
Bosaso, Somalia 102/G3
Boscawen•, N.H. 268/D5
Bosch, van den (cape), Indonesia 85/J6
Bosco, La. 238/F2
Boscobel, Wis. 317/E9
Bose, China 77/G7
Boshan, China 77/J4
Boskoop, Netherlands 27/F4
Boskovice, Czech. 41/D2
Bosler, Wyo. 319/G4
Bosna (riv.), Yugoslavia 45/D3
Bosnia and Hercegovina (rep.), Yugoslavia 45/C3
Boso (pen.), Japan 81/K6
Bosobolo, Zaire 115/D3
Bosporus (str.), Turkey 7/G4
Bosporus (str.), Turkey 59/A1
Bosporus (str.), Turkey 63/C2
Bosque, N. Mex. 274/C4
Bosque (co.), Texas 303/G6
Boss, Mo. 261/K7
Bossangoa, Centr. Afr. Rep. 102/D4
Bossangoa, Cent. Afr. Rep. 115/C2
Bossburg, Wash. 310/H2
Bossé, New Bruns. 170/B1
Bossembele, Cent. Afr. Rep. 115/C2
Bossier (par.), La. 238/C1
Bossier City, La. 238/C1
Bosso, Niger 106/G6
Bostan, Iran 66/F5
Bostan, Pakistan 68/B2
Bostanabad-e-Bala, Iran 66/E2
Bosten (Bagrax) Hu (lake), China 77/C3
Boston (mts.), Ark. 202/B2
Boston, England 13/G5
Boston, England 10/F4
Boston, Georgia 217/E9
Boston, Ind. 227/H5
Boston, Ky. 237/K5
Boston (cap.), Mass. 146/L5
Boston (cap.), Mass. 188/M2
Boston (cap.), Mass. 249/D7
Boston (bay), Mass. 249/E6
Boston (harb.), Mass. 249/D7
Boston, Mo. 261/D8
Boston, N.Y. 276/C5
Boston (mts.), Okla. 288/S3
Boston, Pa. 294/C7
Boston, Tenn. 237/G9
Boston, Texas 303/K4
Boston, U.S. 2/F3
Boston, Va. 307/M3
Boston Bar, Br. Col. 184/G5
Boston Heights, Ohio 284/J10
Bostonnais (isl.), Québec 172/E2
Bostonnais, Grand Lac (lake), Québec 172/E2
Bostonnais (riv.), Québec 172/E2
Boston Nat'l Hist. Park, Mass. 249/D6
Bostwick, Fla. 212/E2
Bostwick, Georgia 217/E3
Bostwick, Nebr. 264/F4
Boswell, Ark. 202/F1
Boswell, Br. Col. 184/J5
Boswell, Ind. 227/C3
Boswell, Okla. 288/P6
Boswell, Pa. 294/E5
Boswell Bay, Alaska 196/J2
Boswil, Switzerland 39/F2
Bosworth, Mo. 261/F4
Bot (riv.), S. Africa 118/G7
Botany, N.S. Wales 88/L4
Botany (bay), N.S. Wales 88/L4
Botany, N.S. Wales 97/J4
Botany (bay), N.S. Wales 97/J4
Botene, Laos 72/D3
Botetourt (co.), Va. 307/J5
Botevgrad, Bulgaria 45/F4
Botha, Alberta 182/D3
Botha (riv.), Alberta 182/B1
Bothell, Wash. 310/B1
Bothnia (gulf) 7/G2
Bothnia (gulf), Finland 18/M5
Bothnia (gulf), Sweden 18/N4
Bothwell, Ontario 177/C5
Bothwell, Tasmania 99/C4
Bothwell, Utah 304/B2
Botkins, Ohio 284/B5
Botna, Iowa 229/C5
Botoşani, Romania 45/H2
Botrange (mt.), Belgium 27/J8
Botrivier, S. Africa 118/F7
Botsford, Conn. 210/C3
Botswana 2/L7
Botswana 102/E7
BOTSWANA 118/C4
Bottesford, England 13/G4
Bottineau (co.), N. Dak. 282/J2
Bottineau, N. Dak. 282/J2
Bottrel, Alberta 182/C4
Bottrop, Germany 22/B3
Botucatu, Brazil 135/B3
Botucatu, Brazil 132/D8
Botwood, Newf. 166/C4
Bouaflé, Ivory Coast 106/C7
Bouaké, Ivory Coast 102/B4
Bouaké, Ivory Coast 106/D7
Bouali, Cent. Afr. Rep. 115/C3
Bouar, Cent. Afr. Rep. 102/D4
Bouar, Cent. Afr. Rep. 115/C2
Bou Arfa, Morocco 106/D2
Bouca, Cent. Afr. Rep. 115/C2
Boucaut (bay), North. Terr. 93/D1
Boucherville, Québec 172/J4
Boucherville (isl.), Québec 172/J4
Bouches-du-Rhône (dept.), France 28/F6
Bouchette, Québec 172/A3
Bouckville, N.Y. 276/J5
Bou Djebeha, Mali 106/D5
Boudreau (bay), La. 238/M7
Boudreaux, La. 238/J8
Boudreaux (lake), La. 238/J8
Boudry, Switzerland 39/C3
Boufarik, Algeria 106/E1
Bougainville (reef), Coral Sea Is. Terr. 95/C2
Bougainville (reef), Coral Sea Is. Terr. 88/H3
Bougainville (isl.), Papua N.G. 87/F6
Bougainville (isl.), Papua N.G. 86/C2
Bougainville (str.), Papua N.G. 86/D2
Bougainville (str.), Solomon Is. 86/D2
Bougainville (cape), W. Australia 88/D2
Bougainville (cape), W. Australia 92/D1
Bougaroun (cape), Algeria 106/F1
Boughton (isl.), Pr. Edward I. 168/F2
Bougie (Béjaïa), Algeria 106/F1
Bougouni, Mali 106/C6
Bouillante, Guadeloupe 161/A6
Bouillon, Belgium 27/G9
Bou Izakarn, Morocco 106/C3
Boujad, Morocco 106/C2
Boula, Cent. Afr. Rep. 115/C3
Boulanger, Québec 172/E1
Boularderie (isl.), Nova Scotia 168/H2
Boulder, Australia 87/C9
Boulder, Colo. 188/E2
Boulder, Colo. 146/H6
Boulder (co.), Colo. 208/J2
Boulder, Colo. 208/J2
Boulder (mts.), Idaho 220/D6
Boulder, Mont. 262/E4
Boulder (lake), N. Mex. 274/C2
Boulder, Utah 304/C6
Boulder (creek), Utah 304/C6
Boulder, W. Australia 88/C6
Boulder, Wyo. 319/C3
Boulder (lake), Wyo. 319/C3
Boulder City, Nev. 266/G7
Boulder Creek, Calif. 204/J4
Boulder Junction, Wis. 317/G3
Boulder-Kalgoorlie, W. Australia 92/C5
Boulevard, Calif. 204/J11
Boulevard Heights, Md. 245/F5
Boulia, Queensland 95/A4
Boulia, Queensland 88/F4
Boulogne, Fla. 212/E1
Boulogne-Billancourt, France 28/A2
Boulogne-sur-Mer, France 28/D2
Bouna, Ivory Coast 106/D7
Boundary, Alaska 196/K2
Boundary (co.), Idaho 220/B1
Boundary (peak), Nev. 266/C5
Boundary (plat.), Sask. 181/B6
Boundary (bay), Wash. 310/C1
Boundary (dam), Wash. 310/H2
Boundary (lake), Wash. 310/H2
Boundary Bend, Victoria 97/B4
Bound Brook, N.J. 273/D2
Boundiali, Ivory Coast 106/C7
Boundji, Congo 115/C4
Boun Nua, Laos 72/D2
Bountiful, Utah 304/C3
Bounty (isls.), N. Zealand 87/H10
Bounty, Sask. 181/D4
Bourail, New Caled. 87/G8
Bourail, New Caled. 86/G4
Bourbon, Ill. 222/E4
Bourbon, Ind. 227/E2
Bourbon (co.), Kansas 232/H4
Bourbon (co.), Ky. 237/N4
Bourbon, Miss. 256/C4
Bourbon, Mo. 261/K6
Bourbonnais (trad. prov.), France 29
Bourbonnais, Ill. 222/F2
Bourem, Mali 106/E5
Bourg, La. 238/J7
Bourganeuf, France 28/D5
Bourg-des-Saintes, Guadeloupe 161/A7
Bourg-en-Bresse, France 28/F4
Bourgeois, New Bruns. 170/F2
Bourges, France 28/E4
Bourget, Ontario 177/J2
Bourg-Léopold (Leopoldsburg), Belgium 27/G6
Bourgoin-Jallieu, France 28/F5
Bourg Saint-Pierre, Switzerland 39/D5
Bourke, N.S. Wales 88/H6
Bourke, N.S. Wales 97/D2
Bourne, England 13/G5
Bourne, Mass. 249/M6
Bourne•, Mass. 249/M6
Bournedale, Mass. 249/M5
Bournemouth, England 13/F7
Bournemouth, England 10/F5
Bourneville, Ohio 284/D7
Bou Saâda, Algeria 106/E1
Bouse, Ariz. 198/A5
Bouse Wash (dry riv.), Ariz. 198/A4
Boussac, France 28/D4
Bousso, Chad 111/C5
Boussu, Belgium 27/D8
Boutilimit, Mauritania 106/B5
Boutilimit, Mauritania 102/A3
Bouton, Iowa 229/E5
Boutte, La. 238/N4
Bouvard (cape), W. Australia 92/A2
Bouvet (isl.), Ant. 5/D1
Bouvetøya (Bouvet) (isl.), Ant. 5/D1
Boven Bolivia, Neth. Ant. 161/E8
Boves, Italy 34/A2
Bovey, Minn. 255/E3
Bovey Tracey, England 13/D7
Bovill, Idaho 220/B3
Bovina, Miss. 256/C6
Bovina, Texas 303/A3
Bovril, Argentina 143/G5
Bow (riv.), Alberta 182/D4
Bow (riv.), Alta. 162/E5
Bow (lake), N.H. 268/E5
Bow, Wash. 310/C2
Bowbells, N. Dak. 282/F2
Bow City, Alberta 182/D4
Bowden, Alberta 182/C4
Bowden, Jamaica 158/K6
Bowden, W. Va. 312/G5
Bowdens, N.C. 281/N4
Bowdle, S. Dak. 298/K3
Bowdoin (lake), Mont. 262/J2
Bowdoinham•, Maine 243/D7
Bowdon, Georgia 217/B3
Bowdon, N. Dak. 282/L5
Bowdon Junction, Georgia 217/B3
Bowell, Alberta 182/E4
Bowen, Australia 87/E7
Bowen, Ill. 222/B3
Bowen, Ky. 237/O5
Bowen, Queensland 95/D3
Bowen, Queensland 88/H3
Bowen Island, Br. Col. 184/K3
Bowens, Md. 245/M6
Bowerbank•, Maine 243/E5
Bowers, Ind. 227/D4
Bowers Beach, Del. 245/S4
Bowerston, Ohio 284/H5
Bowersville, Georgia 217/G2
Bowersville, Ohio 284/C6
Bowes, England 13/F3
Bowesmont, N. Dak. 282/R2
Bowie, Ariz. 198/F6
Bowie, Colo. 208/D5
Bowie, Md. 245/L4
Bowie (creek), Miss. 256/E7
Bowie (co.), Texas 303/K4
Bowie, Texas 303/G4
Bow Island, Alberta 182/E5
Bowkan, Iran 66/E2
Bowlegs, Okla. 288/N4
Bowler, Wis. 317/J6
Bowling Green, Fla. 212/E4
Bowling Green, Ind. 227/D6
Bowling Green, Ky. 237/H7
Bowling Green, Ky. 188/J3
Bowling Green, Mo. 261/K4
Bowling Green, Ohio 284/C3
Bowling Green (cape), Queensland 88/H3
Bowling Green (cape), Queensland 95/C3
Bowling Green, S.C. 296/E1
Bowling Green, Va. 307/O4
Bowlus, Minn. 255/D5
Bowman, Calif. 204/C8
Bowman, Georgia 217/G2
Bowman (co.), N. Dak. 282/C7
Bowman, N. Dak. 282/D7
Bowman (bay), N.W.T. 162/J2
Bowman (bay), N.W. Terr. 187/L3
Bowman (dam), Oreg. 291/G3
Bowman, S.C. 296/F5
Bowmansdale, Pa. 294/J5
Bowmanstown, Pa. 294/L4
Bowmansville, Pa. 294/L5
Bow Mills, N.H. 268/D5
Bowmont, Idaho 220/B6
Bowmore, Scotland 15/B5
Bowmore, Scotland 10/C3
Bowral, N.S. Wales 97/F4
Bowraville, N.S. Wales 97/G2
Bowring, Okla. 288/O1
Bowron Lake Prov. Park, Br. Col. 184/G3
Bowser, Br. Col. 184/H2
Bowser (lake), Br. Col. 184/C2
Bowsman, Manitoba 179/A2
Bowstring, Minn. 255/E3
Bowstring (lake), Minn. 255/E3
Boxborough•, Mass. 249/H3
Box Butte (co.), Nebr. 264/A2
Box Butte (res.), Nebr. 264/A2
Box Canyon (dam), Wash. 310/H2
Box Elder (creek), Colo. 208/K4
Box Elder, Mont. 262/F2
Boxelder (creek), Mont. 262/M5
Boxelder (creek), Mont. 262/H3
Box Elder, S. Dak. 298/D5
Boxelder (creek), S. Dak. 298/D5
Box Elder (co.), Utah 304/A2
Boxford, Mass. 249/L2
Boxford•, Mass. 249/L2
Box Hill, Victoria 97/J5
Box Hill, Victoria 88/L7
Boxholm, Iowa 229/E4
Bo Xian (Pohsien), China 77/J5
Boxley, Ark. 202/D2
Boxmeer, Netherlands 27/H5
Box Springs, Georgia 217/C5
Boxtel, Netherlands 27/G5
Boyabat, Turkey 63/F2
Boyacá (dept.), Colombia 126/D5
Boyama (Stanley) (falls), Zaire 102/E5
Boyama (Stanley) (falls), Zaire 115/D3
Boyanup, W. Australia 92/A2
Boyce, La. 238/E4
Boyce, Va. 307/M2
Boyceville, Wis. 317/C5
Boyd, Ala. 195/B5
Boyd, Fla. 212/C1
Boyd (co.), Ky. 237/R4
Boyd, Minn. 255/C6
Boyd, Mont. 262/G5
Boyd (co.), Nebr. 264/F2
Boyd, Okla. 288/E1
Boyd, Oreg. 291/F2
Boyd, Texas 303/E1
Boyd, Wis. 317/E6
Boydell, Ark. 202/H7
Boyden, Iowa 229/B2
Boyd Lake, Maine 243/F5
Boyds, Md. 245/J4
Boyds, Wash. 310/G2
Boydton, Va. 307/M7
Boyer (riv.), Alberta 182/A5
Boyer, Iowa 229/C4
Boyer (riv.), Iowa 229/B5
Boyer, W. Va. 312/G5
Boyero, Colo. 208/N5
Boyers, Pa. 294/C3
Boyertown, Pa. 294/L5
Boyes, Mont. 262/M5
Boykin, Georgia 217/C8
Boykin, S.C. 296/F3
Boykins, Va. 307/O7
Boyle, Alberta 182/D2
Boyle, Ireland 17/E4
Boyle, Ireland 10/B3
Boyle (co.), Ky. 237/M5
Boyle, Miss. 256/C3
Boyleston, Ind. 227/E4
Boylston•, Mass. 249/H3
Boylston, Nova Scotia 168/G3
Boyne (riv.), Ireland 17/J4
Boyne City, Mich. 250/E3
Boyne Falls, Mich. 250/E3
Boyne Lake, Alberta 182/E5
Boynton, Okla. 288/P3
Boynton Beach, Fla. 212/F5
Boy River, Minn. 255/D3
Boysen (res.), Wyo. 319/D2
Boysen Bay, N.Y. 276/H4
Boys Ranch, Texas 303/B2
Boys Town, Nebr. 264/H3
Boyuibe, Bolivia 136/D7
Bozcaada (isl.), Turkey 63/A3
Bozdoğan, Turkey 63/C4
Bozeman, Mont. 188/D1
Bozeman, Mont. 262/E5
Bozkır, Turkey 63/E4
Bozkurt, Turkey 63/F2
Bozman, Md. 245/N5
Bozoum, Cent. Afr. Rep. 115/C2
Bozova, Turkey 63/H4
Bozqush, Kuh-e (mts.), Iran 66/E2
Bozüyük, Turkey 59/B2
Bozüyük, Turkey 63/C3
Bra, Italy 34/A2
Brabant (prov.), Belgium 27/F7
Brabant Lake, Sask. 181/M3
Brač (isl.), Yugoslavia 45/C4
Bracadale, Loch (inlet), Scotland 15/B3
Bracciano, Italy 34/C3
Bracciano (lake), Italy 34/D3
Bracebridge, Ontario 177/E2
Braceville, Ill. 222/E2
Bracey, Va. 307/M7
Bräcke, Sweden 18/J5
Bracken (co.), Ky. 237/N3
Bracken, Sask. 181/C6
Brackendale, Br. Col. 184/F5
Brackenridge, Pa. 294/C4
Brackett, Wis. 317/D6
Brackettville, Texas 303/D8
Brackley, England 10/F4
Brackley, England 13/F5
Bracknell, England 13/G8
Bracknell, Tasmania 99/C3
Brackney, Pa. 294/K2
Braço Maior do Araguaia (riv.), Brazil 132/D5
Braço Menor do Araguaia (riv.), Brazil 132/D6
Brad, Romania 45/F2
Bradbury, Calif. 204/D10
Braddock, N. Dak. 282/K6
Braddock, Pa. 294/C7
Braddock, Sask. 181/D5
Braddyville, Iowa 229/D7
Braden, Okla. 288/S4
Braden, Tenn. 237/B10
Bradenton, Fla. 212/D4
Bradenton Beach, Fla. 212/D4
Bradford, Ark. 202/G3
Bradford, England 13/J1
Bradford, England 10/H1
Bradford (co.), Fla. 212/D2
Bradford, Ill. 222/D2
Bradford, Ind. 227/E8
Bradford, Iowa 229/G3
Bradford, Ky. 237/N3
Bradford, Maine 243/F5
Bradford•, Maine 243/F5
Bradford•, N.H. 268/D5
Bradford, Ohio 284/B5
Bradford, Ontario 177/E3
Bradford (co.), Pa. 294/J2
Bradford, Pa. 294/E2
Bradford, R.I. 249/H7
Bradford, Tenn. 237/D8
Bradford, Vt. 268/C3
Bradford•, Vt. 268/C3
Bradford Center, Maine 243/F5
Bradford-on-Avon, England 13/E6
Bradfordsville, Ky. 237/L6
Bradgate, Iowa 229/E3
Bradley (co.), Ark. 202/F7
Bradley, Ark. 202/C7
Bradley, Calif. 204/E8
Bradley, Fla. 212/D4
Bradley, Georgia 217/E4
Bradley, Ill. 222/F2
Bradley•, Maine 243/F6
Bradley, Miss. 256/G4
Bradley, Ohio 284/J5
Bradley, Okla. 288/L5
Bradley, S.C. 296/C3
Bradley, S. Dak. 298/O3
Bradley (co.), Tenn. 237/M10
Bradley, Wis. 317/G4
Bradley Beach, N.J. 273/F3
Bradleyton, Ala. 195/F7
Bradleyville, Mo. 261/F9
Bradner, Ohio 284/C3
Bradshaw, Nebr. 264/G4
Bradshaw, Texas 303/D5
Bradshaw, W. Va. 312/C8
Bradwardine, Manitoba 179/B5
Bradwell, Sask. 181/E4
Brady (glac.), Alaska 196/M1
Brady, Mont. 262/E2
Brady, Nebr. 264/D3
Brady (mt.), S. Australia 94/D3
Brady, Texas 303/E6

342 Brady Lake

Brady Lake, Ohio 284/H3
Bradyville, Tenn. 237/J9
Brae, Scotland 15/G2
Braedstrup, Denmark 21/C6
Braemar, Scotland 15/E3
Braemar, Scotland 10/E2
Braemar (dist.), Scotland 15/E3
Braemar, Tenn. 237/S8
Braeside, Ontario 177/H2
Braeside, W. Australia 92/C3
Braga (dist.), Portugal 33/B2
Braga, Portugal 7/D4
Braga, Portugal 33/B2
Bragado, Argentina 143/F7
Bragança, Brazil 120/E3
Bragança, Brazil 132/E3
Bragança (dist.), Portugal 33/C2
Bragança, Portugal 33/C2
Bragança Paulista, Brazil 135/C3
Bragança Paulista, Brazil 132/E8
Braggadocio, Mo. 261/N10
Bragg City, Mo. 261/N10
Bragg Creek, Alberta 182/C4
Braggs, Ala. 195/E6
Braggs, Okla. 288/R3
Bragman's Bluff (Puerto Cabezas), Nicaragua 154/F3
Braham, Minn. 255/E5
Brahmaputra (riv.) 54/L7
Brahmaputra (riv.), Bangladesh 68/G3
Brahmaputra (riv.), India 68/G3
Braich-y-Pwll (prom.), Wales 10/D4
Braich-y-Pwll (prom.), Wales 13/C5
Braidwood, Ill. 222/E2
Braidwood, N.S. Wales 97/E4
Brăila, Romania 7/G4
Brăila, Romania 45/H3
Brăila (marshes), Romania 45/H3
Brainard, Nebr. 264/G3
Brainards, N.J. 273/C2
Braine-l'Alleud, Belgium 27/E7
Braine-le-Comte, Belgium 27/D7
Brainerd, Minn. 188/H1
Brainerd, Minn. 255/D4
Braintree•, Mass. 249/D8
Braintree (West Braintree), Vt. 268/B4
Braintree•, Vt. 268/B4
Braintree and Bocking, England 13/H6
Braintree and Bocking, England 10/G5
Braithwaite, La. 238/P4
Brak, Libya 102/D2
Brak, Libya 111/B2
Brake, Germany 22/C2
Brakna (reg.), Mauritania 106/B5
Brakpan, S. Africa 118/J6
Bralorne, Br. Col. 184/F5
Braman, Okla. 288/M1
Bramber, Nova Scotia 168/D3
Bramberg am Wildkogel, Austria 41/B3
Bramble (bay), Queensland 95/E2
Bramming, Denmark 21/B7
Bramon, Venezuela 124/B4
Brampton, England 13/E3
Brampton, Mich. 250/B3
Brampton, N. Dak. 282/P7
Brampton, Ontario 177/J4
Bramsche, Germany 22/B2
Bramwell, W. Va. 312/D8
Bran (riv.), Scotland 15/D3
Brancepeth, Sask. 181/F2
Branch, Ark. 202/C3
Branch, La. 238/F6
Branch (co.), Mich. 250/D7
Branch, Mich. 250/D5
Branch, Minn. 255/F5
Branch, Mo. 261/G7
Branch, Newf. 166/D2
Branch (riv.), Newf. 166/C2
Branch, Wis. 317/L7
Branch Dale, Pa. 294/K4
Branchport, N.Y. 276/F5
Branchton, Pa. 294/C3
Branchville, Ala. 195/F3
Branchville, Conn. 210/B3
Branchville, Ind. 227/D8
Branchville, N.J. 273/D1
Branchville, S.C. 296/F5
Branchville, Va. 307/O7
Branco (riv.), Brazil 120/C2
Branco (riv.), Brazil 132/H8
Brandberg (mt.), Namibia 118/A4
Brande, Denmark 21/B6
Brandenburg, Germany 22/E2
Brandenburg (state), Germany 22/E2
Brandenburg, Ky. 237/J4
Brandon, Colo. 208/P6
Brandon, England 13/H5
Brandon, Fla. 212/D4
Brandon, Iowa 229/K4
Brandon (bay), Ireland 17/A7
Brandon (head), Ireland 17/A7
Brandon (mt.), Ireland 17/A7
Brandon, Man. 146/H4
Brandon, Man. 162/F6
Brandon, Manitoba 179/C5
Brandon, Minn. 255/C5
Brandon, Miss. 256/E6
Brandon, Nebr. 264/C4
Brandon, Ohio 284/F5
Brandon, S. Dak. 298/R6
Brandon, Vt. 268/A4
Brandon•, Vt. 268/A4
Brandon, Wis. 317/J8
Brandon Gap (pass), Vt. 268/B4
Brandonville, W. Va. 312/G3
Brandreth (lake), N.Y. 276/L3
Brandsville, Mo. 261/J9
Brandt, Ohio 284/B6
Brandt, S. Dak. 298/R4
Brandvlei, S. Africa 118/B6
Brandýs nad Labem-Stará Boleslavv, Czech. 41/C1
Brandy Station, Va. 307/N4
Brandywine, Md. 245/L6
Brandywine, W. Va. 312/H5
Branford, Conn. 210/D3
Branford•, Conn. 210/D3
Branford (harb.), Conn. 210/D4
Branford (riv.), Conn. 210/D3
Branford, Fla. 212/D2
Braniewo, Poland 47/D1
Brannock (isls.), Ireland 17/A5
Bransfield (str.), Ant. 5/C16
Branson, Colo. 208/M8
Branson, Mo. 261/F9
Brant, Alberta 182/D4
Brant, Mich. 250/E5
Brant, N.Y. 276/B5
Brant (lake), N.Y. 276/N3
Brant (county), Ontario 177/D4
Brant (lake), S. Dak. 298/R6
Brant Beach, N.J. 273/E4
Brantford, Kansas 232/E2
Brantford, N. Dak. 282/N4
Brantford, Ontario 177/D4
Brant Lake, N.Y. 276/N3
Brantley, Ala. 195/F7
Brantley (co.), Georgia 217/J8
Brant Rock-Ocean Bluff, Mass. 249/M4
Brantville, New Bruns. 170/E1
Brantwood, Wis. 317/F4
Branxholm, Tasmania 99/D3
Branxholme, Victoria 97/A5
Branxton-Greta, N.S. Wales 97/F3
Bras d'Or, Nova Scotia 168/H2
Bras d'Or (lake), Nova Scotia 168/H3
Braselton, Georgia 217/E2
Brasfield, Ark. 202/H4
Brashear, Mo. 261/H2
Brasher, Mo. 261/N10
Brasher Falls-Winthrop, N.Y. 276/L1
Brasiléia, Brazil 132/G10
Brasília (cap.), Brazil 2/G6
Brasília (cap.), Brazil 120/E4
Brasília (cap.), Brazil 132/E6
Brasília de Minas, Brazil 132/F7
Brașov, Romania 45/G3
Brașov, Romania 7/G4
Brass, Nigeria 106/F8
Brass (isls.), Virgin Is. (U.S.) 161/A4
Brassey (range), W. Australia 92/C4
Brasstown Bald (mt.), Georgia 217/E1
Brassua (lake), Maine 243/D4
Braswell, Georgia 217/C3
Brate, Norway 18/G7
Bratenahl, Ohio 284/H9
Bratislava, Czech. 7/F4
Bratislava (city), Czech. 41/D2
Bratislava, Czech. 41/D2
Bratsk, U.S.S.R. 54/M4
Bratsk, U.S.S.R. 48/L4
Bratsk (res.), U.S.S.R. 48/L4
Brattleboro, Vt. 268/B6
Brattleboro•, Vt. 268/B6
Bratton, Sask. 181/D4
Braunau am Inn, Austria 41/B2
Braunlage, Germany 22 D3
Braunschweig (Brunswick), Germany 22/D2
Braunton, England 13/C6
Brava (isl.), C. Verde 106/B8
Brava, Somalia 115/H3
Brava, Somalia 102/G4
Brava (pt.), Uruguay 145/B7
Brave, Pa. 294/B6
Bravo (riv.), Chile 138/D7
Bravo (Grande) (riv.), Mexico 150/G2
Brawley, Calif. 188/C4
Brawley, Calif. 204/K11
Braxton, Miss. 256/D6
Braxton (co.), W. Va. 312/E5
Bray, Ireland 17/K5
Bray, Ireland 10/C4
Bray (head), Ireland 17/A8
Bray (isl.), N.W. Terr. 187/L3
Bray, Okla. 288/L5
Braymer, Mo. 261/E3
Brayton, Iowa 229/D5
Brazeau (dam), Alberta 182/C3
Brazeau (mt.), Alberta 182/B3
Brazeau (riv.), Alberta 182/B3
Brazil 2/F6
Brazil 120/D4
BRAZIL 132, 135
Brazil, Ind. 227/C5
Brazil, Miss. 256/D2
Brazil, Tenn. 237/C9
Brazilian Highlands (plat.), Brazil 120/E4
Brazilton, Kansas 232/H4
Brazito, Mo. 261/H6
Brazoria (co.), Texas 303/J8
Brazoria, Texas 303/J9
Brazos (peak), N. Mex. 274/C2
Brazos (co.), Texas 303/H7
Brazos (riv.), Texas 188/G4
Brazos (riv.), Texas 146/J6
Brazos (riv.), Texas 303/H7
Brazo Sur, Pilcomayo (riv.), Argentina 143/E1
Brazzaville (cap.), Congo 115/C4
Brazzaville (cap.), Congo 2/K6
Brazzaville (cap.), Congo 102/D5
Brčko, Yugoslavia 45/D3
Brda (riv.), Poland 47/C2
Brea, Calif. 204/D11
Breadalbane (dist.), Scotland 15/D4
Bread Loaf, Vt. 268/B4
Bread Loaf (mt.), Vt. 268/A3
Breakabeen, N.Y. 276/M5
Breakeyville, Québec 172/J3
Breaks, Va. 307/D6
Breaksea (sound), N. Zealand 100/A6
Bream (bay), N. Zealand 100/E1
Breasclete, Scotland 15/B2
Breathitt (co.), Ky. 237/P5
Breau-Village, New Bruns. 170/F2
Breaux Bridge, La. 238/G6
Brebes, Indonesia 85/H2
Brébeuf, Québec 172/C3
Brébeuf (lake), Québec 172/G1
Brechin, Ontario 177/E3
Brechin, Scotland 10/E2
Brechin, Scotland 15/F4
Brecht, Belgium 27/F6
Breckenridge, Colo. 208/G4
Breckenridge, Mich. 250/E5
Breckenridge, Minn. 255/B4
Breckenridge, Mo. 261/E3
Breckenridge, Texas 303/F5
Breckenridge Hills, Mo. 261/O2
Breckinridge (co.), Ky. 237/H5
Breckinridge, Okla. 288/L2
Brecknock (Brecon), Wales 13/D6
Brecksville, Ohio 284/H10
Břeclav, Czech. 41/D2
Brecon, Wales 13/D6
Brecon, Wales 10/E5
Brecon Beacons (mt.), Wales 13/D6
Brecon Beacons National Park, Wales 13/D6
Breda, Iowa 229/C4
Breda, Netherlands 27/F5
Bredasdorp, S. Africa 118/B6
Bredasdorp Nat'l Park, S. Africa 118/C6
Bredbo, N.S. Wales 97/E4
Bredbyn, Sweden 18/L5
Bredebro, Denmark 21/B7
Bredenbury, Sask. 181/K5
Bredene, Belgium 27/B6
Bredstedt, Germany 22/C1
Bree, Belgium 27/H6
Breed, Wis. 317/K5
Breeden, W. Va. 312/B7
Breeding, Ky. 237/L7
Breedsville, Mich. 250/C6
Breese, Ill. 222/D5
Breesport, N.Y. 276/G6
Breezand, Netherlands 27/F3
Breezy Point, Minn. 255/D4
Bregenz, Austria 41/A3
Bregovo, Bulgaria 45/F3
Breidhafjördhur (fjord), Iceland 7/B2
Breidhafjördhur (fjord), Iceland 21/B1
Breien, N. Dak. 282/H7
Breil-Brigels, Switzerland 39/H3
Breil-sur-Roya, France 28/G6
Breisach am Rhein, Germany 22/B4
Breisgau (reg.), Germany 22/B5
Breitenbach, Switzerland 39/E2
Breitenbush, Oreg. 291/F3
Breithorn (mt.), Switzerland 39/E5
Breithorn (mt.), Switzerland 39/E4
Brejo, Brazil 132/F3
Bremanger (isl.), Norway 18/D6
Bremen, Ala. 195/E3
Bremen, Georgia 217/B3
Bremen, Ill. 222/D6
Bremen, Ind. 227/E2
Bremen, Kansas 232/F2
Bremen, Ky. 237/G6
Bremen, N. Dak. 282/M4
Bremen, Ohio 284/F6
Bremen, Sask. 181/F3
Bremen (state), Germany 22/C2
Bremen, Germany 7/E3
Bremen, Germany 22/C2
Bremer (co.), Iowa 229/J3
Bremer, Iowa 229/J3
Bremerhaven, Germany 22/C2
Bremerton, Wash. 188/B1
Bremerton, Wash. 310/A2
Bremervörde, Germany 22/C2
Bremgarten, Switzerland 39/F2
Bremo Bluff, Va. 307/M5
Bremond, Texas 303/H6
Brenham, Texas 303/H7
Brenner (pass), Austria 41/A3
Brenner (pass), Italy 34/C1
Brent, Ala. 195/D5
Brent, England 13/H8
Brent, England 10/B5
Brent, Ontario 177/F1
Brentford, S. Dak. 298/N3
Brenton (pt.), R.I. 249/J7
Brentwood, Ark. 202/B2
Brentwood, Calif. 204/L2
Brentwood, England 10/C5
Brentwood, England 13/J8
Brentwood, Md. 245/F4
Brentwood, Mo. 261/P3
Brentwood•, N.H. 268/E6
Brentwood, N.Y. 276/O9
Brentwood, Pa. 294/B7
Brentwood, Tenn. 237/H8
Brentwood Park, S. Africa 118/J6
Brereton Lake, Manitoba 179/G5
Bresaylor, Sask. 181/C3
Brescia (prov.), Italy 34/C2
Brescia, Italy 7/E4
Brescia, Italy 34/C2
Breskens, Netherlands 27/C6
Breslau (Wrocław), Poland 47/C3
Bressanone, Italy 34/C1
Bressay (isl.), Scotland 15/G2
Bressay (isl.), Scotland 10/G1
Bressuire, France 28/C4
Brest, France 7/D4
Brest, France 28/A3
Brest, Georgia 217/D8
Brest, New Bruns. 170/E2
Brest, U.S.S.R. 7/G3
Brest, U.S.S.R. 48/C4
Brest, U.S.S.R. 52/B4
Bretaña, Peru 128/E5
Brethren, Mich. 250/D4
Breton, Alberta 182/C3
Breton (isls.), La. 238/M8
Breton (sound), La. 238/M7
Breton (cape), Nova Scotia 168/J3
Breton Cove, Nova Scotia 168/H2
Breton Woods, N.J. 273/E3
Brett (cape), N. Zealand 100/E1
Bretten, Germany 22/C4
Bretton Woods, N.H. 268/E3
Brevard (co.), Fla. 212/F3
Brevard, N.C. 281/D4
Breves, Brazil 132/D3
Brevig Mission, Alaska 196/E1
Brevik, Minn. 255/D3
Brevoort (lake), Mich. 250/D3
Brevoort (isl.), N.W. Terr. 187/M3
Brevort, Mich. 250/E2
Brewarrina, N. S. Wales 88/H5
Brewarrina, N.S. Wales 97/D1
Brewer, Maine 243/F6
Brewer, Mo. 261/N7
Brewers, Ky. 237/E7
Brewers Mills, New Bruns. 170/C2
Brewersville, Ind. 227/F6
Brewerton, N.Y. 276/H4
Brewster (pond), Conn. 210/F2
Brewster, Kansas 232/A2
Brewster, Mass. 249/O5
Brewster•, Mass. 249/O5
Brewster (isls.), Mass. 249/E7
Brewster, Minn. 255/C7
Brewster, Nebr. 264/D3
Brewster (lake), N.S. Wales 97/D3
Brewster, N.Y. 276/N8
Brewster, Ohio 284/G4
Brewster, Cerro (mt.), Panama 154/H6
Brewster (co.), Texas 303/A8
Brewster, Wash. 310/F2
Brewton, Ala. 195/D8
Breynat, Alberta 182/D2
Brežice, Yugoslavia 45/B3
Brezina, Algeria 106/E2
Březnice, Czech. 41/B2
Breznik, Bulgaria 45/F4
Brezno, Czech. 41/E2
Bria, Cent. Afr. Rep. 102/E4
Bria, Cent. Afr. Rep. 115/D2
Briançon, France 28/G5
Brian Head, Utah 304/B6
Briar, Texas 303/E1
Briar Creek, Pa. 294/K3
Briare, France 28/E4
Briartown, Okla. 288/R4
Briarwood, N. Dak. 282/S6
Bribbaree, N.S. Wales 97/D3
Brice, Ohio 284/E6
Bricelyn, Minn. 255/E7
Brices Cross Roads Nat'l Battlefield Site, Miss. 256/G2
Briceville, Tenn. 237/N8
Brí Chualann (Bray), Ireland 17/K5
Brick•, N.J. 273/E3
Brickaville (Vohibinany), Madagascar 118/H3
Brickerville, Pa. 294/K5
Brickeys, Ark. 202/J4
Bricks, N.C. 281/O2
Brickton, Nova Scotia 168/C4
Bridal Veil, Oreg. 291/E2
Bride (riv.), Ireland 17/E7
Bridesville, Br. Col. 184/H6
Bridge, Idaho 220/E7
Bridge, Oreg. 291/D4
Bridgeboro, Georgia 217/E8
Bridge City, Texas 303/L7
Bridgedale, New Bruns. 170/F3
Bridgeford, Sask. 181/E5
Bridgehampton, N.Y. 276/R9
Bridge Lake, Br. Col. 184/G4
Bridgeland, Utah 304/D3
Bridgend, Wales 13/A7
Bridgenorth, Ontario 177/F3
Bridge of Allan, Scotland 10/B1
Bridge of Allan, Scotland 15/C1
Bridge of Don, Scotland 15/F3
Bridge of Weir, Scotland 15/A2
Bridgeport, Ala. 195/G1
Bridgeport, Calif. 204/F5
Bridgeport, Conn. 188/M2
Bridgeport, Conn. 210/C4
Bridgeport, Ill. 222/F5
Bridgeport, Kansas 232/E3
Bridgeport, Mich. 250/F5
Bridgeport, Nebr. 264/A3
Bridgeport, N.J. 273/C4
Bridgeport, N.Y. 276/J4
Bridgeport, Ohio 284/J5
Bridgeport, Okla. 288/K3
Bridgeport, Oreg. 291/K3
Bridgeport, Pa. 294/M5
Bridgeport, Texas 303/G4
Bridgeport, Wash. 310/F3
Bridgeport, W. Va. 312/F4
Bridgeport, Wis. 317/D9
Bridger, Mont. 262/H5
Bridgeton, Ind. 227/C5
Bridgeton, Mich. 250/D5
Bridgeton, Mo. 261/O2
Bridgeton, N.J. 273/C5
Bridgeton, N.C. 281/R4
Bridgeton Terrace, Mo. 261/O2
Bridgetown (cap.), Barbados 156/G4
Bridgetown (cap.), Barbados 161/B9
Bridgetown, Md. 245/P4
Bridgetown, Nova Scotia 168/C4
Bridgetown, Ohio 284/B9
Bridgetown, W. Australia 88/B6
Bridgetown, W. Australia 92/B6
Bridgeview, Ill. 222/B6
Bridgeville, Calif. 204/B3
Bridgeville, Del. 245/R6
Bridgeville, Nova Scotia 168/F3
Bridgeville, Pa. 294/B5
Bridgeville, Québec 172/D1
Bridgewater•, Conn. 210/B2
Bridgewater, Iowa 229/D6
Bridgewater•, Maine 243/H3
Bridgewater, Mass. 249/K5
Bridgewater•, Mass. 249/K5
Bridgewater•, N.H. 268/D4
Bridgewater•, N.J. 273/D2
Bridgewater, N.Y. 276/K5
Bridgewater, N.S. 162/K7
Bridgewater, Nova Scotia 168/D4
Bridgewater, Pa. 294/B4
Bridgewater, S. Dak. 298/P6
Bridgewater, Tasmania 99/D4
Bridgewater•, Vt. 268/B4
Bridgewater (cape), Victoria 97/A6
Bridgewater, Va. 307/K4
Bridgewater Center, Vt. 268/B4
Bridgewater Corners, Vt. 268/B4
Bridgman, Mich. 250/C7
Bridgnorth, England 13/E5
Bridgnorth, England 10/E4
Bridgton, Maine 243/B7
Bridgton•, Maine 243/B7
Bridgwater, England 10/E5
Bridgwater, England 13/E6
Bridlington, England 13/G3
Bridlington, England 10/F3
Bridlington (bay), England 13/G3
Bridport, England 13/E7
Bridport, England 10/E5
Bridport, Tasmania 99/D3
Bridport•, Vt. 268/A4
Brieg (Brzeg), Poland 47/C3
Brielle, Netherlands 27/E5
Brielle, N.J. 273/E3
Briensburg, Ky. 237/E7
Brienz, Switzerland 39/F3
Brienzer Rothorn (mt.), Switzerland 39/F3
Brienzersee (lake), Switzerland 39/F3
Brier (isl.), Nova Scotia 168/B4
Brier, Wash. 310/C3
Briercrest, Sask. 181/F5
Brierfield, Ala. 195/E4
Brier Hill, N.Y. 276/J1
Brig, Switzerland 39/F4
Brigantine, N.J. 273/E5
Brigantine (inlet), N.J. 273/E5
Brigden, Ontario 177/B5
Brigg, England 13/G4
Briggs, Texas 303/F7
Briggs Corner, New Bruns. 170/E2
Briggsdale, Colo. 208/L1
Briggsville, Ark. 202/C4
Briggsville, Wis. 317/H8
Brigham City, Utah 188/D2
Brigham City, Utah 304/C2
Brighowe, England 13/J1
Bright, Ind. 227/H6
Bright, Victoria 97/D5
Brightlingsea, England 13/J6
Brightlingsea, England 10/G5
Brighton, Ala. 195/D4
Brighton, Colo. 208/K3
Brighton, England 10/F5
Brighton, England 13/G7
Brighton, Fla. 212/E4
Brighton, Ill. 222/C4
Brighton, Ind. 227/G1
Brighton, Iowa 229/K6
Brighton•, Maine 243/D5
Brighton, Mich. 250/F6
Brighton, Mo. 261/F8
Brighton, Nova Scotia 168/C4
Brighton, Ohio 284/F3
Brighton, Ontario 177/G3
Brighton, Oreg. 291/C2
Brighton, S. Australia 88/D8
Brighton, S. Australia 94/A8
Brighton, Tasmania 99/D4
Brighton, Tenn. 237/B10
Brighton, Utah 304/C3
Brighton, Victoria 97/J5
Brighton, Victoria 88/L7
Brighton, Wis. 317/K3
Brightons, Scotland 15/C1
Brightsand (lake), Sask. 181/B2
Brights Grove, Ontario 177/B4
Brightshade, Ky. 237/O7
Brightstar, Ark. 202/C7
Brightwood, D.C. 245/F4
Brightwood, Oreg. 291/E2
Brightwood, Va. 307/M4
Brignoles, France 28/G6
Brigus, Newf. 166/D2
Brihuega, Spain 33/E2
Brikama, Gambia 106/A6
Brill, Wis. 317/C4
Brilliant, Ala. 195/C2
Brilliant, Ohio 284/J5
Brillion, Wis. 317/L7
Brilon, Germany 22/C3
Brimfield, Ill. 222/D3
Brimfield, Ind. 227/G2
Brimfield•, Mass. 249/F4
Brimfield, Ohio 284/H3
Brimley, Mich. 250/E2
Brimson, Minn. 255/F3
Brimson, Mo. 261/E2
Brimstone (hill), St. Kitts & Nevis 161/C10
Brinckerhoff, N.Y. 276/N7
Brindakit, U.S.S.R. 48/O4
Brindisi (prov.), Italy 34/G4
Brindisi, Italy 7/F4
Brindisi, Italy 34/G4
Bringhurst, Ind. 227/E3
Brinkhaven, Ohio 284/F5
Brinkley, Ark. 202/H4
Brinkman, Okla. 288/G4
Brinktown, Mo. 261/J6
Brinnon, Wash. 310/B3
Brinsmade, N. Dak. 282/M3
Brinson, Georgia 217/C9
Briny Breezes, Fla. 212/G5
Brione, Switzerland 39/G4
Brioude, France 28/E5
Brisbane, Australia 2/S7
Brisbane, Calif. 204/J2
Brisbane (cap.), Queensland 95/D2
Brisbane (cap.), Queensland 88/K3
Brisbane (riv.), Queensland 88/J3
Brisbane (riv.), Queensland 95/D2
Brisbane Airport, Queensland 95/E2
Brisbane International Airport, Queensland 88/K2
Brisbane Water, N.S. Wales 88/J6
Brisbane Water, N.S. Wales 97/F3
Brisbin, Pa. 294/F4
Brisco, Br. Col. 184/J5
Briscoe (co.), Texas 303/C3
Briscoe, Texas 303/D2
Brisighella, Italy 34/C2
Brissago, Switzerland 39/G4
Bristol (bay), Alaska 188/C6
Bristol (bay), Alaska 146/B4
Bristol (bay), Alaska 196/F3
Bristol (lake), Calif. 204/K9
Bristol, Colo. 208/P6
Bristol, Conn. 210/D2
Bristol, England 13/E6
Bristol, England 7/D3
Bristol, England 10/E5
Bristol (chan.), England 13/C6
Bristol (chan.), England 10/E5
Bristol, Fla. 212/B1
Bristol, Georgia 217/H8
Bristol, Ind. 227/F1
Bristol, Maine 243/D8
Bristol•, Maine 243/D8
Bristol, Md. 245/M5
Bristol (co.), Mass. 249/K5
Bristol, Mich. 250/D4
Bristol, New Bruns. 170/C2
Bristol, N.H. 268/D4
Bristol•, N.H. 268/D4
Bristol, Pa. 294/N5
Bristol•, Pa. 294/N5
Bristol (co.), R.I. 249/J6
Bristol, R.I. 249/J6
Bristol, S. Dak. 298/O3
Bristol, Tenn. 188/K3
Bristol, Tenn. 237/S7
Bristol (bay), U.S. 4/D18
Bristol, Va. 188/K3
Bristol, Vt. 268/A3
Bristol•, Vt. 268/A3
Bristol (I.C.), Va. 307/D7
Bristol (chan.), Wales 13/C6
Bristol (chan.), Wales 10/E5
Bristol, W. Va. 312/F4
Bristolville, Ohio 284/J3
Bristow, Ind. 227/D8
Bristow, Iowa 229/H3
Bristow, Nebr. 264/F2
Bristow, Okla. 288/O3
Bristow, Va. 307/N3
Britannia Beach, Br. Col. 184/K2
British (mts.), Alaska 196/K1
British (mts.), Yukon 187/D3
British Columbia (prov.) 162/D4
BRITISH COLUMBIA 184
British Columbia (prov.), Canada 146/F4
British Empire (range), N.W.T. 186/L1
British Indian Ocean Territory 2/N6
British Indian Ocean Territory 54/J10
British Isles 7/D3
Brits, S. Africa 118/D5
Britstown, S. Africa 118/C6
Britt, Iowa 229/F2
Britt, Minn. 255/F3
Britt, Ontario 177/D2
Brittany (trad. prov.), France 29
Brittany, La. 238/L3
Brittnau, Switzerland 39/E2
Britton, Mich. 250/F6
Britton, S. Dak. 298/O2
Brive-la-Gaillarde, France 28/D5
Briviesca, Spain 33/E1
Brno, Czech. 7/F4
Brno, Czech. 41/D2
Broa (inlet), Cuba 158/C1
Broach (Bharuch), India 68/C4
Broad (brook), Conn. 210/H2
Broad (creek), Del. 245/R6
Broad (riv.), N.C. 281/E4
Broad (sound), Queensland 88/H4
Broad (sound), Queensland 95/D4
Broad (bay), Scotland 15/B2
Broad (riv.), S.C. 296/F7
Broad (riv.), S.C. 296/E2
Broadacres, Oreg. 291/A3
Broadacres, Sask. 181/B3
Broadalbin, N.Y. 276/M4
Broad Arrow, W. Australia 88/C6
Broad Arrow, W. Australia 92/C5
Broadback (riv.), Québec 174/B2
Broadbent, Oreg. 291/C4
Broad Brook, Conn. 210/E1
Broad Cove, Newf. 166/D2
Broad Cove, Nova Scotia 168/D4
Broaddus, Texas 303/K6
Broadfields, Ky. 237/K2
Broadford, Ireland 17/C7
Broadford, Scotland 15/B3
Broadford, Victoria 97/C5
Broadford, Va. 307/E7
Broad Haven (harb.), Ireland 17/B3
Broadhurst, Georgia 217/J8
Broadkill (riv.), Del. 245/S5
Broadland, S. Dak. 298/N4
Broadlands, Ill. 222/E4
Broad Law (mt.), Scotland 15/E5
Broadmeadows, Victoria 88/L6
Broadmeadows, Victoria 97/H4
Broadstairs and Saint Peter's, England 13/J6
Broad Top, Pa. 294/F5
Broadus, Mont. 262/L5
Broad Valley, Manitoba 179/E4
Broadview, Ill. 222/B6
Broadview, Mont. 262/H4
Broadview, N. Mex. 274/F4
Broadview, Sask. 181/J5
Broadview Heights, Ohio 284/H10
Broadview Park, Fla. 212/B4
Broadwater (co.), Mont. 262/E4
Broadwater, Nebr. 264/B3
Broadway, N.J. 273/C2
Broadway, N.C. 281/L4
Broadway, Ohio 284/C5
Broadway, Va. 307/L3
Broadwell, Ill. 222/D3
Broager, Denmark 21/C8
Broc, Switzerland 39/D3
Brochet, Man. 162/F4
Brochet, Manitoba 179/H2
Brock (isl.), N.W.T. 162/M3
Brock, Nebr. 264/H4
Brock (isl.), N.W. Terr. 187/G2
Brock, Sask. 181/C4
Brockdell, Tenn. 237/L10
Brocken (mt.), Germany 22/D3
Brocket, Alberta 182/D5
Brocket, N. Dak. 282/O3
Brockington, Sask. 181/G2
Brockport, N.Y. 276/D4

Buffalo Narrows **343**

Brockport, Pa. 294/E3
Brockton, Mass. 249/K4
Brockton, Mont. 262/M2
Brockville, Ontario 177/J3
Brockway, Mont. 262/L3
Brockway, New Bruns. 170/C3
Brockway, Pa. 294/E3
Brocton, Ill. 222/F4
Brocton, N.Y. 276/B6
Broderick, Sask. 181/E4
Broderick-Bryte, Calif. 204/B8
Brodeur (pen.), Canada 4/B14
Brodeur (pen.), N.W.T. 146/K2
Brodeur (pen.), N.W.T. 162/H1
Brodeur (pen.), N.W. Terr. 187/K2
Brodhead, Ky. 237/N6
Brodhead, Wis. 317/G10
Brodheadsville, Pa. 294/M4
Brodick, Scotland 15/C5
Brodick, Scotland 10/D3
Brodnax, Va. 307/N7
Brodnica, Poland 47/D2
Broek in Waterland, Netherlands 27/C4
Brogan, Oreg. 291/K3
Brohard, W. Va. 312/D4
Brohman, Mich. 250/D5
Brokaw, Wis. 317/G5
Broken (bay), N.S. Wales 97/F3
Broken Arrow, Okla. 288/P2
Broken Bow, Nebr. 264/E3
Broken Bow, Okla. 288/S7
Broken Bow (lake), Okla. 288/S6
Broken Hill, Australia 87/E9
Broken Hill, N.S. Wales 88/G6
Broken Hill, N.S. Wales 97/A3
Broken Hill (Kabwe), Zambia 115/E6
Brokensword, Ohio 284/E4
Brokopondo (dist.), Suriname 131/D4
Brokopondo, Suriname 131/D3
Brome (co.), Québec 172/E4
Brome, Québec 172/E4
Brome (lake), Québec 172/E4
Bromer, Ind. 227/E7
Bromhead, Sask. 181/H6
Bromide, Okla. 288/N6
Bromley, England 13/H8
Bromley, England 10/C5
Bromley, Ky. 237/S2
Bromley (mt.), Vt. 268/B5
Bromont, Québec 172/E4
Brompton (lake), Québec 172/E4
Bromptonville, Québec 172/F4
Bromsgrove, England 13/E5
Bromyard, England 13/E5
Bronaugh, Mo. 261/C7
Bronco, Texas 303/B4
Brønderslev, Denmark 18/F8
Brønderslev, Denmark 21/C3
Brønnøysund, Norway 18/G4
Brøns, Denmark 21/B7
Bronson, Fla. 212/D2
Bronson, Iowa 229/A4
Bronson, Kansas 232/H4
Bronson, Mich. 250/D7
Bronson (lake), Sask. 181/B2
Bronson, Texas 303/L6
Bronston, Ky. 237/M7
Bronte, Italy 34/E6
Bronte, Texas 303/D6
Bronwood, Georgia 217/D7
Bronx (co.), N.Y. 276/N9
Bronx (borough), N.Y. 276/N9
Bronxville, N.Y. 276/O7
Brook, Ind. 227/C3
Brookdale, Calif. 204/J4
Brookdale, Manitoba 179/C4
Brookdale, Nova Scotia 168/D3
Brooke, Va. 307/O4
Brooke (co.), W. Va. 312/E2
Brookeborough, N. Ireland 17/G3
Brookeland, Texas 303/L6
Brooker, Fla. 212/D2
Brooke's Point, Philippines 82/A6
Brookeville, Md. 245/K4
Brookfield•, Conn. 210/B3
Brookfield, Georgia 217/F8
Brookfield, Ill. 222/B6
Brookfield, Mass. 249/F4
Brookfield•, Mass. 249/F4
Brookfield, Mo. 261/F3
Brookfield•, N.H. 268/E4
Brookfield, N.Y. 276/K5
Brookfield, Nova Scotia 168/E3
Brookfield, Ohio 284/J3
Brookfield•, Vt. 268/B3
Brookfield, Wis. 317/K1
Brookfield Center, Conn. 210/B3
Brookford, N.C. 281/G3
Brookhaven, Georgia 217/K1
Brookhaven, Miss. 256/C7
Brookhaven, Pa. 294/M7
Brookhaven Nat'l Lab., N.Y. 276/P9
Brookings, Oreg. 291/C5
Brookings (co.), S. Dak. 298/R5
Brookings, S. Dak. 298/R5
Brookland, Ark. 202/J2
Brookland, D.C. 245/F4
Brooklawn, N.J. 273/B3
Brooklet, Georgia 217/J6
Brooklin•, Maine 243/F7
Brookline•, Mass. 249/C7
Brookline•, N.H. 268/D6
Brookline•, Vt. 268/B5
Brookline Station (Brookline), Mo. 261/F8
Brooklyn, Ala. 195/E8
Brooklyn•, Conn. 210/H1
Brooklyn, Georgia 217/C6
Brooklyn (Lovejoy), Ill. 222/A2
Brooklyn, Ill. 222/C3
Brooklyn, Ind. 227/E5
Brooklyn, Iowa 229/J5
Brooklyn, Ky. 237/H6
Brooklyn, Mich. 250/E6
Brooklyn, Miss. 256/F8
Brooklyn, Newf. 166/D2
Brooklyn (borough), N.Y. 276/N9
Brooklyn, Nova Scotia 168/D4
Brooklyn, Ohio 284/H9
Brooklyn, Pa. 294/L2
Brooklyn, Wash. 310/B4
Brooklyn, Wis. 317/H10
Brooklyn Center, Minn. 255/G5
Brooklyn Heights, Ohio 284/H9
Brooklyn Park, Md. 245/M4
Brooklyn Park, Minn. 255/G5
Brookmere, Br. Col. 184/G5
Brookneal, Va. 307/L6
Brook Park, Minn. 255/F5
Brook Park, Ohio 284/G9
Brookport, Ill. 222/E6
Brooks (range), Alaska 146/C3
Brooks (range), Alaska 188/C5
Brooks (range), Alaska 196/G1
Brooks, Alberta 182/E4
Brooks (pen.), Br. Col. 184/D5
Brooks, Calif. 204/C5
Brooks (co.), Georgia 217/E9
Brooks, Georgia 217/D4
Brooks, Iowa 229/D7
Brooks, Ky. 237/K4
Brooks•, Maine 243/E6
Brooks, Minn. 255/B3
Brooks, Mont. 262/G3
Brooks, Oreg. 291/A3
Brooks (co.), Texas 303/F11
Brooks (range), U.S. 4/C17
Brooks, W. Va. 312/E7
Brooks, Wis. 317/G8
Brooks A.F.B., Texas 303/K11
Brooksburg, Ind. 227/G7
Brooksby, Sask. 181/G2
Brookshire, Texas 303/J8
Brookside, Ala. 195/E3
Brookside, Colo. 208/J6
Brookside, Del. 245/R2
Brookside, N.J. 273/D2
Brookside, Ohio 284/J5
Brookside Village, Texas 303/J2
Brookston, Ind. 227/D3
Brookston, Minn. 255/F4
Brooksville, Ala. 195/F2
Brooksville, Fla. 212/D3
Brooksville, Ky. 237/N3
Brooksville, Maine 243/F7
Brooksville•, Maine 243/F7
Brooksville, Miss. 256/G4
Brooksville, Okla. 288/M4
Brookton, Georgia 217/E2
Brookton, Maine 243/H4
Brookton, W. Australia 92/B2
Brooktondale, N.Y. 276/H6
Brookview, Md. 245/P6
Brook Village, Nova Scotia 168/G2
Brookville, Ind. 227/G6
Brookville (lake), Ind. 227/G6
Brookville, Kansas 232/E3
Brookville, Mass. 249/K4
Brookville, N.Y. 276/R6
Brookville, Ohio 284/B6
Brookville, Pa. 294/D3
Brookwood, Ala. 195/D4
Broom, Loch (inlet), Scotland 15/C3
Broomall, Pa. 294/M6
Broome, Australia 87/C7
Broome (co.), N.Y. 276/J6
Broome, W. Australia 88/C3
Broome, W. Australia 92/C2
Broomfield, Colo. 208/J3
Broomhill, Manitoba 179/B5
Brooten, Minn. 255/C5
Brora, Scotland 15/E2
Brora (riv.), Scotland 15/D2
Brørup, Denmark 21/C7
Broseley, Mo. 261/M9
Brosna, Ireland 17/C7
Brosna (riv.), Ireland 17/F5
Brossard, Québec 172/H4
Brosseau, Alberta 182/E3
Brothers, Oreg. 291/G4
Brotherton, Tenn. 237/L8
Brothertown, Wis. 317/K7
Brou, France 28/D3
Brough (head), Scotland 15/E1
Brough Ness (prom.), Scotland 15/F2
Broughshane, N. Ireland 17/J2
Broughton, Ill. 222/E6
Broughton, Ohio 284/B3
Broughton, Pa. 294/B7
Broughton, Scotland 15/E5
Broughton Island, N.W. Terr. 187/M3
Broumov, Czech. 41/D1
Brounland, W. Va. 312/C6
Brouse, Br. Col. 184/J5
Broussard, La. 238/F6
Brouwershaven, Netherlands 27/D5
Brovst, Denmark 21/C3
Broward (co.), Fla. 212/F5
Browardale, Fla. 212/B4
Browder, Ky. 237/H6
Browerville, Minn. 255/D4
Brown (co.), Ill. 222/C4
Brown (co.), Ind. 227/E6
Brown (co.), Kansas 232/G2
Brown (co.), Minn. 255/D6
Brown (co.), Nebr. 264/E2
Brown (lake), N.W. Terr. 187/J3
Brown (co.), Ohio 284/C8
Brown (reefs), Philippines 85/F3
Brown (co.), S. Dak. 298/N2
Brown (co.), Texas 303/F6
Brown (Roan) (cliffs), Utah 304/E4
Brown (pt.), Wash. 310/A4
Brown, W. Va. 312/F4
Brown (co.), Wis. 317/L7
Brownbranch, Mo. 261/G9
Brown City, Mich. 250/G5
Brown Deer, Wis. 317/L1
Browndell, Texas 303/L7
Browne (bay), N.W. Terr. 187/J2
Brownell, Kansas 232/C3
Browney (riv.), England 13/H3
Brownfield, Alberta 182/E3
Brownfield, Ill. 222/E6
Brownfield, Maine 243/B8
Brownfield•, Maine 243/B8
Brownfield, Miss. 256/G1
Brownfield, Texas 303/B4
Browning, Ill. 222/C3
Browning, Mo. 261/F2
Browning, Mont. 262/C2
Browning, N.S. Wales 97/E4
Browning, Sask. 181/J6
Browning Entrance (str.), Br. Col. 184/B3
Brownington, Mo. 261/E6
Brownington•, Vt. 268/C2
Brownlee (dam), Idaho 220/B5
Brownlee, Nebr. 264/D2
Brownlee, Oreg. 291/L3
Brownlee (dam), Oreg. 291/L3
Brownlee, Sask. 181/F5
Browns, Ala. 195/D6
Browns, Ill. 222/F5
Brown's (riv.), Vt. 268/A2
Brownsboro, Ala. 195/F1
Brownsboro, Oreg. 291/E5
Brownsboro, Texas 303/J5
Brownsboro Farm, Ky. 237/L1
Brownsburg, Ind. 227/E5
Brownsburg, Québec 172/C4
Brownsburg, Va. 307/K5
Brownsdale, Minn. 255/F7
Brownsdale, Newf. 166/D2
Browns Flat, New Bruns. 170/D3
Brown's Lake, Wis. 317/K3
Browns Mills, N.J. 273/D4
Browns Spring, Mo. 261/F9
Browns Summit, N.C. 281/K2
Brownstown, Ill. 222/E5
Brownstown, Ind. 227/F7
Browns Town, Jamaica 158/J6
Brownstown, Pa. 294/K5
Brownstown, Wash. 310/E4
Browns Valley, Ind. 227/C5
Browns Valley, Minn. 255/B5
Browns Village, Fla. 212/B4
Brownsville, Ind. 227/H5
Brownsville, Ky. 237/J6
Brownsville, Md. 245/H3
Brownsville, Minn. 255/G7
Brownsville, Miss. 256/D6
Brownsville, Oreg. 291/E3
Brownsville, Pa. 294/C5
Brownsville, Tenn. 237/C9
Brownsville, Texas 303/G12
Brownsville, Texas 188/G5
Brownsville, Texas 146/J7
Brownsville, Vt. 268/B5
Brownsville, Wash. 310/A2
Brownsville, Wis. 317/J8
Brownton, Minn. 255/D6
Brownton, W. Va. 312/F4
Browntown, Va. 307/M3
Browntown, Wis. 317/G10
Brownvale, Alberta 182/B1
Brownville, Ala. 195/C4
Brownville, Fla. 212/E4
Brownville, Maine 243/E5
Brownville•, Maine 243/E5
Brownville, Nebr. 264/J4
Brownville, N.Y. 276/H3
Brownville Junction, Maine 243/E5
Brown Willy (mt.), England 13/C7
Brownwood, Texas 303/F6
Brownwood (lake), Texas 303/E6
Browse (isl.), W. Australia 88/C2
Browse (isl.), W. Australia 92/C1
Broxburn, Scotland 15/D1
Broxton, Georgia 217/G7
Broye (riv.), Switzerland 39/C3
Broyle (cape), Newf. 166/D2
Brozas, Spain 33/C3
Brozville, Miss. 256/D4
Brtnice, Czech. 41/C2
Bruay-en-Artois, France 28/E2
Bruce, Alberta 182/E3
Bruce (mt.), Australia 87/C8
Bruce, Fla. 212/C6
Bruce, Miss. 256/F3
Bruce (mts.), N.W. Terr. 187/L2
Bruce (county), Ontario 177/C3
Bruce (pen.), Ontario 177/C2
Bruce, S. Dak. 298/R5
Bruce (mt.), W. Australia 88/B4
Bruce (mt.), W. Australia 92/B3
Bruce, Wis. 317/D5
Bruce Crossing, Mich. 250/G2
Brucefield, Ontario 177/C4
Bruce Lake, Ontario 175/B2
Bruce Mines, Ontario 177/J5
Bruce Mines, Ontario 175/D3
Bruce Rock, W. Australia 88/B6
Bruce Rock, W. Australia 92/B5
Bruceton, Tenn. 237/E8
Bruceton Mills, W. Va. 312/G3
Brucetown, Va. 307/M2
Bruceville, Ind. 227/C7
Bruchsal, Germany 22/C4
Bruck an der Leitha, Austria 41/D2
Bruck an der Mur, Austria 41/C3
Bruderheim, Alberta 182/D3
Bruff, Ireland 17/D7
Bruges, Belgium 27/C6
Brugg, Switzerland 39/F2
Brugge (Bruges), Belgium 27/C6
Brühl, Germany 22/B3
Bruin, Ky. 237/P4
Bruin (cape), New Bruns. 170/G2
Bruin, Pa. 294/C3
Bruins, Ark. 202/K4
Brûlé, Alberta 182/B3
Brule (riv.), Mich. 250/A3
Brule, Nebr. 264/C3
Brule, Nova Scotia 168/E3
Brûlé (lake), Québec 172/C3
Brûlé (lake), Québec 172/B2
Brule (co.), S. Dak. 298/L6
Brule (mt.), Switzerland 39/D4
Brule, Wis. 317/C2
Brumado, Brazil 120/E4
Brumado, Brazil 132/F6
Brumley, Mo. 261/H6
Brummen, Netherlands 27/J4
Brundidge, Ala. 195/G7
Bruneau, Idaho 220/C7
Bruneau (riv.), Idaho 220/C7
Brunei 2/Q5
Brunei 54/N9
BRUNEI 85/E4
Bruner, Mo. 261/F8
Brunete, Spain 33/F4
Brunette (isl.), Newf. 166/C4
Brunflo, Sweden 18/J5
Bruni, Texas 303/F10
Brunico, Italy 34/D1
Bruning, Nebr. 264/G4
Brunkild, Manitoba 179/E5
Brunner, N. Zealand 100/C5
Brunner (lake), N. Zealand 100/C5
Bruno, Ark. 202/E1
Bruno, Minn. 255/F4
Bruno, Nebr. 264/G3
Bruno, Sask. 181/F3
Brunot, Mo. 261/M8
Brunsbüttel, Germany 22/C2
Brunson, S.C. 296/E6
Brunssum, Netherlands 27/J7
Brunsville, Iowa 229/A3
Brunswick (pen.), Chile 138/E10
Brunswick, Ga. 188/K4
Brunswick, Georgia 217/K8
Brunswick, Germany 7/E3
Brunswick, Germany 22/D2
Brunswick, Maine 243/C8
Brunswick•, Maine 243/C8
Brunswick, Md. 245/H3
Brunswick, Minn. 255/E5
Brunswick, Miss. 256/C5
Brunswick, Mo. 261/F4
Brunswick, Nebr. 264/G2
Brunswick (co.), N.C. 281/N6
Brunswick, N.C. 281/M6
Brunswick, Ohio 284/G3
Brunswick, Tenn. 237/B10
Brunswick, Victoria 88/K7
Brunswick, Victoria 97/H5
Brunswick (co.), Va. 307/N7
Brunswick (bay), W. Australia 88/C3
Brunswick (bay), W. Australia 92/D1
Brunswick Heads, N.S. Wales 97/G1
Brunswick Junction, W. Australia 92/A2
Bruntál, Czech. 41/D2
Bruree, Ireland 17/D7
Brus (lag.), Honduras 154/E2
Brusett, Mont. 262/J3
Brush, Colo. 208/M2
Brush Creek, Minn. 255/E7
Brush Creek, Mo. 261/G7
Brush Creek, Tenn. 237/J8
Brush Prairie, Wash. 310/C5
Brushton, N.Y. 276/L1
Brushy Prairie, Ind. 227/G1
Brusio, Switzerland 39/K4
Brus Laguna, Honduras 154/E3
Brusly, La. 238/J2
Brusque, Brazil 132/D9
Brussels (cap.), Belgium 7/E3
Brussels, Ill. 222/C5
Brussels, Ontario 177/C4
Brussels, Wis. 317/L6
Bruthen, Victoria 97/D5
Brutus, Mich. 250/E3
Bruxelles, Manitoba 179/C5
Bruzual, Venezuela 124/D3
Bryan (co.), Georgia 217/K6
Bryan, Ohio 284/A3
Bryan (co.), Okla. 288/O7
Bryan, Texas 188/G4
Bryan, Texas 303/H7
Bryan (lake), Wash. 310/H4
Bryansk, U.S.S.R. 7/H3
Bryansk, U.S.S.R. 52/D4
Bryansk, U.S.S.R. 48/D4
Bryanston, Ontario 177/C4
Bryant, Ala. 195/G1
Bryant, Ark. 202/F4
Bryant, Fla. 212/F5
Bryant (lake), Fla. 212/E2
Bryant, Ill. 222/C3
Bryant, Ind. 227/G3
Bryant, Iowa 229/N5
Bryant, Okla. 288/P4
Bryant, S. Dak. 298/P4
Bryant, Wis. 317/J5
Bryant Pond, Maine 243/B7
Bryantsburg, Ind. 227/G7
Bryantsville, Ky. 237/M5
Bryantville, Mass. 249/L4
Bryce (mt.), Br. Col. 184/J4
Bryce, Utah 304/B6
Bryce Canyon, Utah 304/B6
Bryce Canyon Nat'l Park, Utah 304/B6
Bryceland, La. 238/E2
Bryceville, Fla. 212/D1
Bryn Athyn, Pa. 294/M5
Brynica (riv.), Poland 47/B4
Bryn Mawr, Pa. 294/M5
Brynmawr, Wales 10/E5
Brynmawr, Wales 13/B6
Bryn Mawr-Skyway, Wash. 310/B2
Bryrup, Denmark 21/C5
Bryson, Texas 303/F4
Bryson City, N.C. 281/C4
Bryte-Broderick, Calif. 204/B8
Brzeg, Poland 47/C3
Brzeg Dolny, Poland 47/C3
Brzesko, Poland 47/E4
Brzozów, Poland 47/F4
B-Say-Tah, Sask. 181/G5
Bua Chum, Thailand 72/D4
Buad (isl.), Philippines 82/E5
Buba, Guinea-Biss. 106/B6
Bubali, Neth. Ant. 161/D10
Bubaque, Guinea-Biss. 106/A6
Bubendorf, Switzerland 39/E2
Bubikon, Switzerland 39/G2
Bubiyan (isl.), Kuwait 59/E4
Bucak, Turkey 63/D4
Bucaramanga, Colombia 120/B2
Bucaramanga, Colombia 126/D4
Bucareli (bay), Alaska 196/M2
Bucas Grande (isl.), Philippines 82/F6
Bucasia, Queensland 95/D4
Buccaneer (arch.), W. Australia 88/C3
Buccaneer (arch.), W. Australia 92/C2
Buchan (gulf), N.W. Terr. 187/L2
Buchan (dist.), Scotland 15/F3
Buchanan, Georgia 217/B3
Buchanan (co.), Iowa 229/K4
Buchanan, Iowa 229/L5
Buchanan, Ky. 237/R4
Buchanan, Liberia 106/B7
Buchanan, Liberia 102/A4
Buchanan, Mich. 250/C7
Buchanan (co.), Mo. 261/C3
Buchanan, N.Y. 276/N8
Buchanan, N. Dak. 282/N5
Buchanan, Sask. 181/J4
Buchanan, Tenn. 237/E8
Buchanan (lake), Texas 303/F7
Buchanan (co.), Va. 307/D6
Buchanan, Va. 307/J5
Buchan Ness (prom.), Scotland 15/G3
Buchans, Newf. 166/C4
Bucharest (cap.), Romania 7/G4
Bucharest (cap.), Romania 2/L3
Bucharest (Bucureşti) (cap.), Romania 45/G3
Buchegg (mts.), Switzerland 39/D2
Buchholz in der Nordheide, Germany 22/C2
Buchlyvie, Scotland 15/B1
Buchon (pt.), Calif. 204/D8
Buchs, Switzerland 39/H2
Buchtel, Ohio 284/F7
Buck (creek), Ind. 227/E8
Buck (creek), S.C. 296/J3
Buck (creek), Texas 303/D3
Buck (isl.), Virgin Is. (U.S.) 161/G3
Buck, W. Va. 312/E7
Buckatunna, Miss. 256/G7
Buck Creek, Alberta 182/C3
Buck Creek, Ind. 227/D4
Bückeburg, Germany 22/C2
Buckeye, Ariz. 198/C5
Buckeye, Iowa 229/G4
Buckeye, La. 238/F4
Buckeye, N. Mex. 274/F6
Buckeye (lake), Ohio 284/F6
Buckeye, W. Va. 312/F6
Buckeye Lake, Ohio 284/F6
Buckeystown, Md. 245/J3
Buckfastleigh, England 13/C7
Buckfield•, Maine 243/C7
Buck Grove, Iowa 229/C5
Buckhannon, W. Va. 312/F5
Buckhannon (riv.), W. Va. 312/F5
Buckhaven and Methil, Scotland 15/F4
Buckhaven and Methil, Scotland 10/E2
Buckhead, Georgia 217/F3
Buck Hollow (creek), Oreg. 291/G2
Buckholts, Texas 303/H7
Buckhorn (lake), Ky. 237/O6
Buckhorn, Mo. 261/M8
Buckhorn, N. Mex. 274/A5
Buckhorn, Ontario 177/F3
Buckhorn (lake), Ontario 177/F3
Buckie, Scotland 15/E3
Buckie, Scotland 10/E2
Buckingham, Colo. 208/L1
Buckingham, Conn. 210/E2
Buckingham, England 13/G6
Buckingham, England 10/F5
Buckingham, Ill. 222/E2
Buckingham, Iowa 229/J4
Buckingham, Québec 172/B4
Buckingham, Texas 303/H2
Buckingham (co.), Va. 307/L5
Buckingham, Va. 307/L5
Buckinghamshire (co.), England 13/G6
Buck Island (chan.), Virgin Is. (U.S.) 161/F3
Buck Island Reef Nat'l Mon., Virgin Is. (U.S.) 161/G3
Buck Lake, Alberta 182/C3
Buckland, Alaska 196/F1
Buckland, Conn. 210/E1
Buckland•, Mass. 249/C2
Buckland, Ohio 284/B4
Buckland, Québec 172/G3
Buckley, Ill. 222/F3
Buckley, Mich. 250/D4
Buckley, Wales 13/G2
Buckley, Wash. 310/C3
Bucklin, Kansas 232/C4
Bucklin, Mo. 261/G3
Buckman, Minn. 255/D5
Buckner, Ark. 202/D7
Buckner, Ill. 222/E6
Buckner, Ky. 237/L4
Buckner, Mo. 261/R5
Bucks, Ala. 195/B8
Bucks (co.), Pa. 294/M5
Bucksburn, Scotland 15/F3
Bucks Harbor, Maine 243/J6
Buckskin (mts.), Ariz. 198/B4
Buckskin, Ind. 227/C8
Bucksport, Maine 243/F6
Bucksport•, Maine 243/F6
Bucksport, S.C. 296/J4
Buckville, Ark. 202/D4
Bucoda, Mo. 261/M10
Bucoda, Wash. 310/C4
Buco-Zau, Angola 115/B4
Buctouche, New Bruns. 170/F2
Buctouche (harb.), New Bruns. 170/F2
Buctouche (riv.), New Bruns. 170/F2
Bucureşti (Bucharest) (cap.), Romania 45/G3
Bucyrus, Kansas 232/H3
Bucyrus, Mo. 261/H8
Bucyrus, N. Dak. 282/E7
Bucyrus, Ohio 284/E4
Bud, Ind. 227/E6
Bud, W. Va. 312/D7
Buda, Ill. 222/D2
Buda, Texas 303/G7
Budafok, Hungary 41/E3
Budakeszi, Hungary 41/E3
Budaörs, Hungary 41/E3
Budapest (co.), Hungary 41/E3
Budapest (cap.), Hungary 41/E3
Budapest (cap.), Hungary 7/F4
Budaun, India 68/D3
Budd (lake), N.J. 273/D2
Budd Coast (reg.), Ant. 5/C6
Budd Lake, N.J. 273/D2
Buddon Ness (prom.), Scotland 15/F4
Bude (bay), England 13/C7
Bude, Miss. 256/C8
Bude-Stratton, England 13/C7
Budge-Budge, India 68/F2
Budgewoi Lake, N.S. Wales 97/F3
Budia, Spain 33/E2
Büdingen, Germany 22/C3
Budišov, Czech. 41/D2
Budjala, Zaire 115/C3
Budleigh Salterton, England 13/D7
Budrio, Italy 34/C2
Budva, Yugoslavia 45/D4
Buea, Cameroon 115/A3
Buechel, Ky. 237/K2
Buel (lake), Mass. 249/A4
Buellton, Calif. 204/E9
Buena, N.J. 273/D4
Buena, Wash. 310/E4
Buena Esperanza, Argentina 143/C3
Buena Park, Calif. 204/D11
Buenaventura, Colombia 126/B6
Buenaventura, Colombia 120/B2
Buenaventura (bay), Colombia 126/B6
Buenaventura, Cuba 158/H3
Buenaventura, Mexico 150/F2
Buena Vista, Ala. 195/D7
Buena Vista, Ark. 202/D7
Buena Vista, Bolivia 136/D5
Buena Vista (lake), Calif. 204/F8
Buena Vista, Colo. 208/G5
Buenavista, Cuba 158/F2
Buenavista (bay), Cuba 158/F2
Buena Vista, Georgia 217/C6
Buena Vista (co.), Iowa 229/C3
Buena Vista, Miss. 256/G3
Buena Vista, N. Mex. 274/D3
Buena Vista, Ohio 284/D8
Buena Vista, Oreg. 291/D3
Buena Vista, Paraguay 144/D5
Buenavista, Philippines 82/E6
Buena Vista, Sask. 181/F5
Buena Vista, Tenn. 237/E9
Buena Vista, Uruguay 145/E3
Buena Vista, Anzoátegui, Venezuela 124/F3
Buena Vista, Apure, Venezuela 124/D4
Buena Vista, Falcón, Venezuela 124/D2
Buena Vista (I.C.), Va. 307/K5
Buendía (res.), Spain 33/E2
Bueno (riv.), Chile 138/D3
Buenos Aires (lake) 120/B7
Buenos Aires (prov.), Argentina 143/D4
Buenos Aires (cap.), Argentina 120/C6
Buenos Aires (cap.), Argentina 143/H7
Buenos Aires (cap.), Argentina 2/F7
Buenos Aires (lake), Argentina 143/B6
Buenos Aires (lake), Chile 138/E6
Buenos Aires, Amazonas, Colombia 126/F9
Buenos Aires, Caquetá, Colombia 126/D7
Buenos Aires, C. Rica 154/F6
Buesaco, Colombia 126/B7
Buey Arriba, Cuba 158/H4
Bueyeros, N. Mex. 274/F3
Buffalo, Ala. 195/H5
Buffalo, Alberta 182/E4
Buffalo (lake), Alberta 182/D3
Buffalo (riv.), Ark. 202/E2
Buffalo, Ill. 222/D4
Buffalo, Ind. 227/D3
Buffalo, Iowa 229/M6
Buffalo, Kansas 232/G4
Buffalo, Ky. 237/K6
Buffalo (bay), Manitoba 179/G5
Buffalo, Minn. 255/E5
Buffalo (riv.), Minn. 255/B4
Buffalo, Mo. 261/F7
Buffalo, Mont. 262/G4
Buffalo (co.), Nebr. 264/E4
Buffalo (creek), Nev. 266/B2
Buffalo, N.Y. 146/L5
Buffalo, N.Y. 188/L2
Buffalo, N.Y. 276/B5
Buffalo, N. Dak. 282/R6
Buffalo, Ohio 284/G6
Buffalo, Okla. 288/G1
Buffalo, S.C. 296/D2
Buffalo (co.), S. Dak. 298/L5
Buffalo, S. Dak. 298/B2
Buffalo (creek), S. Dak. 298/F6
Buffalo (lake), S. Dak. 298/P2
Buffalo (riv.), Tenn. 237/F9
Buffalo, Texas 303/J6
Buffalo, W. Va. 312/C5
Buffalo (co.), Wis. 317/C7
Buffalo, Wis. 317/C7
Buffalo, Wyo. 319/F1
Buffalo Bill (dam), Wyo. 319/C1
Buffalo Bill (res.), Wyo. 319/C1
Buffalo Center, Iowa 229/F2
Buffalo City, Ark. 202/E1
Buffalo City, N.C. 281/T3
Buffalo Creek, Br. Col. 184/G4
Buffalo Creek, Colo. 208/J4
Buffalo Fork, Snake (riv.), Wyo. 319/B2
Buffalo Gap, Sask. 181/F6
Buffalo Gap, S. Dak. 298/C6
Buffalo Gap, Texas 303/E5
Buffalo Grove, Ill. 222/B5
Buffalo Head (hills), Alberta 182/B5
Buffalo Junction, Va. 307/L7
Buffalo Lake, Minn. 255/D6
Buffalo Lodge (lake), N. Dak. 282/J3
Buffalo Mills, Pa. 294/E6
Buffalo Narrows, Sask. 181/L3

Cascade 347

Capiz (prov.), Philippines 82/D5
Caplan, Québec 172/C2
Capleville, Tenn. 237/B10
Caplin Cove, Newf. 166/D2
Caplinger Mills, Mo. 261/E7
Čapljina, Yugoslavia 45/C4
Cap Lumière, New Bruns. 170/F2
Capon Bridge, W. Va. 312/K4
Capon Springs, W. Va. 312/K4
Capotoan (mt.), Philippines 82/E4
Cappahayden, Newf. 166/D2
Cappamore, Ireland 17/E6
Cappawhite, Ireland 17/E6
Cap-Pelé, New Bruns. 170/F2
Cappoquin, Ireland 17/F7
Capps, Ala. 195/H8
Capraia (isl.), Italy 34/B3
Capreol, Ontario 175/D3
Capreol, Ontario 177/K5
Capri (isl.), Italy 34/E4
Capricorn (chan.), Queensland 95/D4
Capricorn Group (isls.), Queensland 88/J4
Capricorn Group (isls.), Queensland 95/E4
Caprivi Strip (reg.), Namibia 102/E6
Caprivi Strip (reg.), Namibia 118/C3
Caprock, N. Mex. 274/F5
Capron, Ill. 222/E1
Capron, Okla. 288/J1
Capron, Va. 307/O7
Cap-Rouge, Québec 172/H3
Cap-Saint-Ignace, Québec 172/G2
Cap-Santé, Québec 172/F3
Cap-Seize, Québec 172/C1
Capshaw, Ala. 195/E1
Capstan (cape), Nova Scotia 168/D3
Capstick, Nova Scotia 168/H1
Captain Bermúdez, Argentina 143/F6
Captain Cook, Hawaii 218/G5
Captains Flat, N.S. Wales 97/E4
Captieux, France 28/C5
Captina (creek), Ohio 284/J6
Captiva, Fla. 212/D5
Captiva (isl.), Fla. 212/D5
Capua, Italy 34/E4
Capuchin (cape), Dominica 161/E5
Capulhuac de Mirafuentes, Mexico 150/K1
Capulin, Colo. 208/G8
Capulin, N. Mex. 274/F2
Capulin Volcano Nat'l Mon., N. Mex. 274/E2
Caputa, S. Dak. 298/D5
Caquetá (dept.), Colombia 126/C7
Caquetá (riv.), Colombia 120/B2
Caquetá (riv.), Colombia 126/E8
Caquiaviri, Bolivia 136/A5
Carabao (isl.), Philippines 82/D4
Carabelas, Argentina 143/F6
Carabobo (state), Venezuela 124/D2
Carabobo, Bolívar, Venezuela 124/H4
Carabobo, Carabobo, Venezuela 124/D3
Carabuco, Bolivia 136/A4
Caracal, Romania 45/G3
Caracaraí, Brazil 120/C2
Caracas (bay), Neth. Ant. 161/G9
Caracas (cap.), Venezuela 120/C2
Caracas (cap.), Venezuela 124/E2
Caracas (cap.), Venuzuela 2/F5
Carache, Venezuela 124/C3
Caracollo, Bolivia 136/B5
Caraga, Philippines 82/F7
Caragabal, N.S. Wales 97/D3
Caraguatá, Uruguay 145/D3
Caraguatá (riv.), Uruguay 145/D3
Caraguatatuba, Brazil 135/D3
Caraguatay, Paraguay 144/B4
Carahue, Chile 138/D2
Carajás, Serra dos (range), Brazil 132/D4
Caramat, Ontario 177/H5
Caramat, Ontario 175/C3
Caramoan, Philippines 82/D4
Caranavi, Bolivia 136/B4
Carandaí, Brazil 135/E2
Carandaiti, Bolivia 136/D7
Carandotta, Queensland 95/A4
Carangola, Brazil 135/E2
Caransebeş, Romania 45/F3
Carapa (riv.), Paraguay 144/E4
Carapa, Venezuela 124/G3
Caraparaná (riv.), Colombia 126/D8
Carapari, Bolivia 136/D7
Carapeguá, Paraguay 144/B5
Carapichaima, Trin. & Tob. 161/B10
Caraquet, New Bruns. 170/E1
Caraquet (isl.), New Bruns. 170/F1
Carás, Peru 128/D7
Caratasca, Honduras 154/F3
Caratasca (cays), Honduras 154/F2
Caratasca (lag.), Honduras 154/F3
Caratinga, Brazil 132/F7
Caratinga, Brazil 135/E1
Caratunk, Maine 243/C5
Caratunk•, Maine 243/C5
Carauari, Brazil 120/C3
Carauari, Brazil 132/G9
Caraúbas, Brazil 132/G4
Caravaca de le Cruz, Spain 33/E3
Caravaggio, Italy 34/B2
Caravelas, Brazil 132/G7
Caravelí, Peru 128/F10
Caravelle (pen.), Martinique 161/D6
Caraway, Ark. 202/K2
Carayaó, Paraguay 144/C4
Carazinho, Brazil 132/C10
Carballino, Spain 33/B1
Carballo, Spain 33/B1
Carberry, Manitoba 179/C5
Carbo, Mexico 150/D2
Carbon, Alberta 182/D4
Carbon (peak), Colo. 208/E5
Carbon, Ind. 227/C5
Carbon, Iowa 229/D6
Carbon (co.), Mont. 262/G5
Carbon (co.), Pa. 294/L4
Carbon, Texas 303/F5
Carbon (co.), Utah 304/D4
Carbon, W. Va. 312/D6
Carbon (co.), Wyo. 319/F4
Carbonado, Wash. 310/D3
Carbonara (cape), Italy 34/B5
Carbon Cliff, Ill. 222/C2
Carbondale, Alberta 182/D3
Carbondale, Colo. 208/E4
Carbondale, Ill. 222/D6
Carbondale, Kansas 232/G3
Carbondale, Ohio 284/F7
Carbondale, Pa. 294/L2
Carbonear, Newf. 166/D2
Carbon Hill, Ala. 195/D3
Carbon Hill, Ill. 222/E2
Carbon Hill, Ohio 284/F7
Carbonia, Italy 34/B5
Carbonton, N.C. 281/L3
Carbost, Scotland 15/B3
Carbury, Ireland 17/H5
Carbury, N. Dak. 282/J2
Carcagente, Spain 33/F3
Carcans (lake), France 28/C5
Carcarañá, Argentina 143/F6
Carcarañá (riv.), Argentina 143/F6
Carcassonne, France 28/D6
Carchi (prov.), Ecuador 128/C2
Carcoar, N.S. Wales 97/E3
Carcross, Yukon 187/E3
Çardak, Turkey 63/C6
Cardal, Uruguay 145/C5
Cardale, Manitoba 179/B4
Cárdenas, Cuba 158/D1
Cárdenas, Cuba 156/B2
Cárdenas (bay), Cuba 158/D1
Cárdenas, San Luis Potosí, Mexico 150/K6
Cárdenas, Tabasco, Mexico 150/N8
Cardenden, Scotland 15/D1
Cardiel (lake), Argentina 143/B6
Cardiff, Ala. 195/E3
Cardiff, Md. 245/N2
Cardiff, Wales 7/D3
Cardiff, Wales 13/B7
Cardiff, Wales 10/E5
Cardiff-by-the-Sea, Calif. 204/H10
Cardigan (mt.), N.H. 268/D4
Cardigan, Pr. Edward I. 168/F2
Cardigan (bay), Pr. Edward I. 168/F2
Cardigan, Wales 13/C5
Cardigan, Wales 10/D4
Cardigan (bay), Wales 10/D4
Cardigan (bay), Wales 13/C5
Cardin, Okla. 288/S1
Cardinal (lake), Alberta 182/B1
Cardinal, Manitoba 179/D5
Cardinal, Ontario 177/J3
Cardington, Ohio 284/E5
Cardona, Uruguay 145/B4
Cardoso (isl.), Brazil 135/C4
Cardozo, Uruguay 145/C3
Cardross, Sask. 181/F6
Cardston, Alberta 182/D5
Cardston, Alta. 162/E6
Cardville, Maine 243/F5
Cardwell, Mo. 261/M10
Cardwell, Mont. 262/E5
Cardwell, Queensland 95/C3
Cardwell, Va. 307/N5
Carefree, Ariz. 198/C5
Carefree, Ind. 227/E8
Carei, Romania 45/F2
Carén, Chile 138/A8
Carencro, La. 238/G6
Carentan, France 28/C3
Caretta, W. Va. 312/C8
Carey, Idaho 220/E6
Carey, Ohio 284/D4
Carey (lake), W. Australia 88/C5
Carey (lake), W. Australia 92/C5
Careywood, Idaho 220/B1
Cargill, Ontario 177/C3
Carhuás, Peru 128/D7
Cariaco, Venezuela 124/G2
Cariamanga, Ecuador 128/C5
Caribbean (sea) 2/F5
Caribbean (sea) 146/K8
Caribbean (sea), 156/B4
Caribbean (sea), Ant. & Bar. 156/B4
Caribbean (sea), Cayman Is. 156/B4
Caribbean (sea), Cuba 156/B4
Caribbean (sea), Dominica 156/B4
Caribbean (sea), Dom. Rep. 156/B4
Caribbean (sea), Grenada 156/B4
Caribbean (sea), Guadeloupe 156/B4
Caribbean (sea), Haiti 156/B4
Caribbean (sea), Jamaica 156/B4
Caribbean (sea), Martinique 156/B4
Caribbean (sea), Neth. Ant. 156/B4
Caribbean (sea), P. Rico 156/B4
Caribbean (sea), St. Kitts & Nevis 156/B4
Caribbean (sea), St. Lucia 156/B4
Caribbean (sea), St. Vin. & Grens. 156/B4
Caribbean (sea), Virgin Is. (U.S.) 156/B4
Caribbean (sea), Virgin Is. (U.K.) 156/B4
Caribén, Venezuela 124/E4
Cariboo (mts.), Br. Col. 184/G3
Caribou (mts.), Alberta 182/B5
Caribou (co.), Idaho 220/G7
Caribou (mt.), Idaho 220/G6
Caribou (range), Idaho 220/G6
Caribou, Maine 188/N1
Caribou, Maine 243/G2
Caribou (riv.), Manitoba 179/J1
Caribou, Nova Scotia 168/F3
Caribou (isl.), Nova Scotia 168/F3
Caribou (isl.), Ontario 175/C3
Caribou (lake), Ontario 177/H4
Caribou (lake), Québec 172/D3
Caribou River, Nova Scotia 168/F3
Carib Reserve, Dominica 161/F6
Caribrod (Dimitrovgrad), Yugoslavia 45/F4
Carichic, Mexico 150/F2
Carievale, Sask. 181/K6
Carigara, Philippines 82/E5
Carignan, Québec 172/J4
Carignan (lake), Québec 172/E2
Carillon, Québec 172/C4
Carina, Queensland 88/K3
Carinda, N.S. Wales 97/D2
Cariñena, Spain 33/F2
Carinhanha, Brazil 132/E6
Carini, Italy 34/D5
Carinthia (prov.), Austria 41/B3
Caripe, Venezuela 124/G2
Caripito, Venezuela 124/G2
Cariquima, Chile 138/B2
Carirubana, Venezuela 124/C2
Carite (lake), P. Rico 161/E2
Cark (mt.), Ireland 17/F2
Carl, Georgia 217/E3
Carl Blackwell (lake), Okla. 288/M2
Carlea, Sask. 181/H2
Carleton, Mich. 250/F6
Carleton, Nebr. 264/G4
Carleton (co.), New Bruns. 170/C2
Carleton (mt.), New Bruns. 170/D1
Carleton, Nova Scotia 168/C4
Carleton (riv.), Nova Scotia 168/C4
Carleton, Québec 172/C2
Carleton Place, Ontario 177/H2
Carlile, Wyo. 319/H1
Carlin, Nev. 266/E2
Carlingford, Ireland 17/J3
Carlingford (inlet), Ireland 17/J3
Carlingford (mt.), Ireland 17/J3
Carlingford, New Bruns. 170/C2
Carlinville, Ill. 222/D4
Carlisle, Ark. 202/G4
Carlisle (bay), Barbados 161/B9
Carlisle, England 13/D3
Carlisle, England 10/E3
Carlisle, Ind. 227/C7
Carlisle, Iowa 229/G6
Carlisle (co.), Ky. 237/C7
Carlisle, Ky. 237/N4
Carlisle, La. 238/L7
Carlisle•, Mass. 249/J2
Carlisle, Minn. 255/B4
Carlisle, Miss. 256/C7
Carlisle, New Bruns. 170/C2
Carlisle, N.Y. 276/L5
Carlisle, Ohio 284/B6
Carlisle, Ontario 177/D4
Carlisle, Pa. 294/H5
Carlisle, S.C. 296/D2
Carl Junction, Mo. 261/C8
Carlock, Ill. 222/D3
Carlock, S. Dak. 298/L7
Carloforte, Italy 34/B5
Carlos, Ind. 227/G4
Carlos, Minn. 255/C5
Carlos Casares, Argentina 143/F7
Carlos Reyles, Uruguay 145/C4
Carlos Tejedor, Argentina 143/D4
Carlow (co.), Ireland 17/H6
Carlow, Ireland 17/H6
Carlow, Ireland 10/C4
Carloway, Scotland 15/B2
Carlowrie, Manitoba 179/E5
Carlowville, Ala. 195/D6
Carl Sandburg Home Nat'l Hist. Site, N.C. 281/D4
Carlsbad, Ca. 204/H10
Carlsbad, N. Mex. 188/F4
Carlsbad, N. Mexico 146/H6
Carlsbad, N. Mex. 274/E6
Carlsbad, Texas 303/D6
Carlsbad Caverns Nat'l Park, N. Mex. 274/E6
Carlsbad Springs, Ontario 177/J2
Carlsborg, Wash. 310/B2
Carlshend, Mich. 250/B2
Carlstadt, N.J. 273/B2
Carlton, Ala. 195/C8
Carlton, Barbados 161/B8
Carlton, England 13/F5
Carlton, Georgia 217/F2
Carlton, Kansas 232/E3
Carlton (co.), Minn. 255/F4
Carlton, Minn. 255/F4
Carlton, N.Y. 276/D4
Carlton, Oreg. 291/D2
Carlton, Pa. 294/C3
Carlton, Sask. 181/E3
Carlton, Texas 303/F6
Carlton, Wash. 310/F2
Carlton (pass), Wash. 310/D4
Carltonville, S. Africa 118/G7
Carluke, Scotland 15/E5
Carluke, Scotland 10/B1
Carlyle, Ill. 222/D5
Carlyle (lake), Ill. 222/D5
Carlyle, Kansas 232/G4
Carlyle, Mont. 262/M4
Carlyle, Sask. 181/J6
Carlyle Lake Resort, Sask. 181/J6
Carmacks, Yukon 187/E3
Carmagnola, Italy 34/A2
Carman, Ill. 222/B3
Carman, Man. 162/G6
Carman, Manitoba 179/D5
Carmangay, Alberta 182/D4
Carmanville, Newf. 166/D4
Carmarthen, Wales 13/C6
Carmarthen, Wales 10/D5
Carmarthen (bay), Wales 10/D5
Carmarthen (bay), Wales 13/C6
Carmaux, France 28/E5
Carmel, Calif. 204/D7
Carmel, Ind. 227/E5
Carmel (cape), Israel 65/B2
Carmel (mt.), Israel 65/C2
Carmel•, Maine 243/E6
Carmel•, N.Y. 276/N8
Carmel, Sask. 181/F3
Carmel (head), Wales 13/C4
Carmelo, Uruguay 145/A4
Carmelo, Venezuela 124/C2
Carmel Valley, Calif. 204/D7
Carmen, Ariz. 198/D7
Carmen, Bolivia 136/B2
Carmen (riv.), Chile 138/B7
Carmen, C. Rica 154/F5
Carmen, Idaho 220/E4
Carmen (isl.), Mexico 150/D3
Carmen, Okla. 288/J1
Carmen, Bohol, Philippines 82/E6
Carmen, North Cotabato, Philippines 82/E7
Carmen, Uruguay 145/D4
Carmen de Areco, Argentina 143/F7
Carmen del Paraná, Paraguay 144/D5
Carmen de Patagones, Argentina 143/D5
Carmensa, Argentina 143/C4
Carmi, Br. Col. 184/H5
Carmi, Ill. 222/E5
Carmi (lake), Vt. 268/B2
Carmichael, Calif. 204/C8
Carmichael, Miss. 256/G7
Carmichael, Sask. 181/C5
Carmichaels, Pa. 294/B6
Carmiel, Israel 65/C2
Carmila, Queensland 95/D4
Carmine, Texas 303/H7
Carmody Hills-Pepper Mill Village, Md. 245/G5
Carmona, Spain 33/D4
Carnac, France 28/B4
Carnadero (creek), Calif. 204/L4
Carnamah, W. Australia 92/A5
Carnarvon, Australia 87/B8
Carnarvon, Iowa 229/C4
Carnarvon, Ontario 177/F2
Carnarvon (range), Queensland 95/D5
Carnarvon, S. Africa 118/C6
Carnarvon, W. Australia 88/A4
Carnarvon, W. Australia 92/A4
Carnation, Wash. 310/D3
Carnaxide, Portugal 33/A1
Carn Ban (mt.), Scotland 15/D3
Carndonagh, Ireland 17/G1
Carnduff, Sask. 181/K6
Carnegie, Georgia 217/C7
Carnegie, Okla. 288/J4
Carnegie, Pa. 294/B7
Carnegie (lake), W. Australia 88/C5
Carnegie (lake), W. Australia 92/C4
Carn Eige (mt.), Scotland 15/C3
Carneiro, Kansas 232/D3
Carnes, Miss. 256/F8
Carnesville, Georgia 217/F2
Carnew, Ireland 17/H6
Carney, Mich. 250/B3
Carney, Okla. 288/N3
Carneys Point, N.J. 273/C4
Carnic Alps (mts.), Austria 41/B3
Carnic Alps (range), Italy 34/D1
Car Nicobar (isl.), India 68/G7
Carnlough, N. Ireland 17/K2
Carn More (mt.), Scotland 15/E3
Carnot, Cent. Afr. Rep. 115/C3
Carnoustie, Scotland 15/F4
Carnoustie, Scotland 10/E2
Carnsore (pt.), Ireland 10/C4
Carnsore (pt.), Ireland 17/J7
Carnwath (riv.), N.W. Terr. 187/F3
Carnwath, Scotland 15/E5
Carnwood, Alberta 182/C3
Caro, Mich. 250/F5
Caroga Lake, N.Y. 276/L4
Carol City, Fla. 212/B4
Carolina, Ala. 195/E8
Carolina, Brazil 132/E4
Carolina, P. Rico 161/E1
Carolina, R.I. 249/H7
Carolina Beach, N.C. 281/O6
Caroline, Alberta 182/C3
Caroline (isl.), Kiribati 87/M7
Caroline (co.), Md. 245/P5
Caroline, N.Y. 276/H6
Caroline (isls.), Fed. States of Micronesia 87/E5
Caroline (isls.), Fed. States of Micronesia 2/S5
Caroline (co.), Va. 307/O4
Caroline, Wis. 317/J6
Carol Stream, Ill. 222/A5
Caron, Sask. 181/F5
Caron Brook, New Bruns. 170/B1
Carondelet, Ecuador 128/C2
Caroni, Trin. & Tob. 161/B10
Caroní (riv.), Venezuela 120/C2
Caroní (riv.), Venezuela 124/G4
Carora, Venezuela 124/C2
Carouge, Switzerland 39/B4
Carp, Ind. 227/D6
Carp, Minn. 255/D2
Carp, Nev. 266/G5
Carp, Ontario 177/H2
Carpathian (mts.) 7/G4
Carpathian (mts.), Romania 45/G2
Carpentaria (gulf) 88/F2
Carpentaria (gulf), Australia 87/D7
Carpentaria (gulf), North. Terr. 93/E3
Carpentaria (gulf), Queensland 95/A2
Carpenter (lake), Br. Col. 184/F5
Carpenter, Iowa 229/H2
Carpenter, Ky. 237/O7
Carpenter, Miss. 256/C6
Carpenter (lake), N. Dak. 282/L2
Carpenter, Ohio 284/F7
Carpenter, S. Dak. 298/O4
Carpenter, Wyo. 319/H4
Carpentersville, Ill. 222/E1
Carpentersville, N.J. 273/C2
Carpenterville, Oreg. 291/C5
Carpentras, France 28/F5
Carpertee (riv.), N.S. Wales 97/F3
Carpi, Italy 34/C2
Carpinteria, Calif. 204/F9
Carpio, N. Dak. 282/G3
Carp Lake, Mich. 250/E3
Carp Lake Prov. Park, Br. Col. 184/F3
Carr, Colo. 208/K1
Carra (lake), Ireland 17/C4
Carrabassett Valley•, Maine 243/C5
Carrabelle, Fla. 212/B2
Carradale, Scotland 15/C5
Carragana, Sask. 181/J3
Carraguao (pt.), Cuba 158/B2
Carraipía, Colombia 126/D2
Carraízo (lake), P. Rico 161/E1
Carranglan, Philippines 82/C3
Carrantuohill (mt.), Ireland 10/B5
Carrantuohill (mt.), Ireland 17/B7
Carranza, Venustiano (res.), Mexico 150/J3
Carrao (riv.), Venezuela 124/G5
Carrara, Italy 34/C2
Carrasco, Uruguay 145/B7
Carrasquero, Venezuela 124/B2
Carrathool, N. S. Wales 88/G6
Carrathool, N.S. Wales 97/C4
Carrboro, N.C. 281/L3
Carrbridge, Scotland 15/E3
Carrera de Yeguas, Dom. Rep. 158/D6
Carrera Pinto, Chile 138/B6
Carreta (pt.), C. Rica 154/F6
Carreto, Panama 154/J6
Carriacou (isl.), Grenada 156/G4
Carrick, Manitoba 179/F5
Carrick (dist.), Scotland 15/D5
Carrickfergus (dist.), N. Ireland 17/K2
Carrickfergus, N. Ireland 10/D3
Carrickfergus, N. Ireland 17/K2
Carrickmacross, Ireland 10/C3
Carrickmacross, Ireland 17/H4
Carrick-on-Shannon, Ireland 17/F4
Carrick-on-Shannon, Ireland 10/C4
Carrick-on-Suir, Ireland 17/F7
Carrick-on-Suir, Ireland 10/C4
Carrier, Okla. 288/K2
Carriere, Miss. 256/E9
Carrier Mills, Ill. 222/E6
Carrigaholt, Ireland 17/B6
Carrigain (mt.), N.H. 268/E3
Carrigaline, Ireland 17/E8
Carrigallen, Ireland 17/F4
Carrigan (head), Ireland 17/D2
Carrigart, Ireland 17/F1
Carrigtwohill, Ireland 17/E8
Carrington, Mo. 261/H5
Carrington, N. Dak. 282/M5
Carrión de los Condes, Spain 33/D1
Carrizal, Colombia 126/D1
Carrizal Bajo, Chile 138/A7
Carrizo (creek), Ariz. 198/E4
Carrizo (mts.), Ariz. 198/G2
Carrizo (creek), N. Mex. 274/F2
Carrizo (creek), Texas 303/A1
Carrizo Springs, Texas 303/E9
Carrizozo, N. Mex. 274/D5
Carroll (co.), Ark. 202/C1
Carroll (co.), Georgia 217/B3
Carroll (co.), Ill. 222/D1
Carroll (co.), Ind. 227/D3
Carroll (co.), Iowa 229/D4
Carroll, Iowa 229/D4
Carroll (co.), Ky. 237/L3
Carroll•, Maine 243/G5
Carroll, Manitoba 179/B5
Carroll (lake), Manitoba 179/G3
Carroll (co.), Md. 245/K2
Carroll (co.), Miss. 256/E4
Carroll (co.), Mo. 261/F4
Carroll, Nebr. 264/G2
Carroll (co.), N.H. 268/E4
Carroll•, N.H. 268/D3
Carroll, N.S. Wales 97/F2
Carroll (co.), Ohio 284/H4
Carroll, Ohio 284/E6
Carroll (co.), Tenn. 237/E9
Carroll (co.), Va. 307/G7
Carrolls, Wash. 310/C4
Carrolls Crossing, New Bruns. 170/D2
Carrollton, Ala. 195/B4
Carrollton, Georgia 217/C3
Carrollton, Ill. 222/C4
Carrollton, Iowa 229/D5
Carrollton, Ky. 237/L3
Carrollton, Md. 245/L2
Carrollton, Mich. 250/E5
Carrollton, Miss. 256/E4
Carrollton, Mo. 261/E4
Carrollton, Ohio 284/J4
Carrollton, Texas 303/G2
Carrolltown, Pa. 294/E4
Carroll Valley, Pa. 294/H6
Carron, Scotland 15/C1
Carron (riv.), Scotland 15/D3
Carron (riv.), Scotland 15/C3
Carron (riv.), Scotland 15/C1
Carron Valley (res.), Scotland 15/B1
Carrot (riv.), Sask. 181/J2
Carrot Creek, Alberta 182/B3
Carrothers, Ohio 284/D3
Carrot River, Sask. 181/H2
Carrowdore, N. Ireland 17/K2
Carrowkeel, Ireland 17/G1
Carrowmore (lake), Ireland 17/B3
Carrsville, Ky. 237/E6
Carrsville, Va. 307/P7
Carruthers, Sask. 181/B3
Carryduff, N. Ireland 17/K2
Carryville, Ark. 202/K1
Çarşamba, Turkey 63/G2
Carseland, Alberta 182/D4
Carson, Ala. 195/C8
Carson, Calif. 204/C11
Carson, Iowa 229/C6
Carson, Miss. 256/E7
Carson (lake), Nev. 266/C3
Carson (riv.), Nev. 266/B3
Carson (sink), Nev. 266/C3
Carson, N. Mex. 274/D2
Carson, N. Dak. 282/H7
Carson (co.), Texas 303/C2
Carson, Va. 307/O6
Carson, Wash. 310/D5
Carson City, Mich. 250/E5
Carson City (co.), Nev. 266/B3
Carson City (cap.), Nev. 146/G6
Carson City (cap.), Nev. 188/C3
Carson City (cap.), Nev. 266/B3
Carson Lake, Ark. 202/K2
Carson Sink (depr.), Nev. 188/C3
Carsonville, Georgia 217/D5
Carsonville, Mich. 250/G5
Carsphairn, Scotland 15/D5
Carstairs, Alberta 182/D4
Carswell A.F.B., Texas 303/E2
Cartagena, Chile 138/F3
Cartagena, Colombia 120/B1
Cartagena, Colombia 126/C2
Cartagena, Cuba 158/D2
Cartagena, Spain 7/D5
Cartagena, Spain 33/F4
Cartago, Calif. 204/G7
Cartago, Colombia 126/B5
Cartago, C. Rica 154/F6
Carta Valley, Texas 303/D8
Cartaxo, Portugal 33/B3
Cartecay, Georgia 217/D1
Carter (co.), Ky. 237/P4
Carter, Ky. 237/P4
Carter (co.), Mo. 261/L9
Carter (co.), Mont. 262/M5
Carter, Mont. 262/E3
Carter (co.), Okla. 288/M6
Carter, Okla. 288/H4
Carter, S. Dak. 298/J7
Carter (co.), Tenn. 237/S8
Carter, Tenn. 237/S8
Carter, Wis. 317/J5
Carter, Wyo. 319/B4
Carter Dome (mt.), N.H. 268/E3
Carteret, N.J. 273/E2
Carteret (co.), N.C. 281/R5
Carter Lake, Iowa 229/B6
Carter Nine, Okla. 288/N1
Carters, Georgia 217/C1
Carters (lake), Georgia 217/C1
Cartersburg, Ind. 227/E5
Cartersville, Georgia 217/C2
Cartersville, Iowa 229/G2
Cartersville, Mont. 262/K4
Cartersville, Okla. 288/S4
Cartersville, S.C. 296/H3
Cartersville, Va. 307/M5
Carterton, N. Zealand 100/E4
Carterton and Black Bourton, England 13/F6
Carterville, Ill. 222/D6
Carterville, Mo. 261/D8
Carthage, Ark. 202/E5
Carthage, Ill. 222/B3
Carthage, Ind. 227/F5
Carthage, Maine 243/C6
Carthage•, Maine 243/C6
Carthage, Miss. 256/E5
Carthage, Mo. 261/D8
Carthage, N.Y. 276/J3
Carthage, N.C. 281/K4
Carthage, S. Dak. 298/O5
Carthage, Tenn. 237/K8
Carthage, Texas 303/K5
Cartier, Ontario 177/J5
Cartier (isl.), Terr. Ashmore and Cartier Is. 88/C2
Cartwright, Manitoba 179/C5
Cartwright, Newf. 146/N4
Cartwright, Newf. 166/C3
Cartwright, Newf. 162/L5
Cartwright, N. Dak. 282/C4
Caruai (riv.), Venezuela 124/H5
Caruaru, Brazil 132/G5
Carumás, Peru 128/G11
Carúpano, Venezuela 120/C1
Carúpano, Venezuela 124/G2
Carurú, Colombia 126/E7
Carutapera, Brazil 132/E3
Caruth, Mo. 261/N10
Caruthers, Calif. 204/E7
Caruthersville, Mo. 261/N10
Carver•, Mass. 249/M5
Carver (co.), Minn. 255/E6
Carver, Minn. 255/E6
Carville, La. 238/K3
Carvoeiro (cape), Portugal 33/B3
Cary, Ill. 222/E1
Cary•, Maine 243/H4
Cary, Miss. 256/C5
Cary, N.C. 281/M3
Caryapundy (swamp), N.S. Wales 97/B1
Caryapundy (swamp), Queensland 95/B6
Carysbrook, Va. 307/M5
Carytown, Mo. 261/D8
Caryville, Fla. 212/C6
Caryville, Mass. 249/J4
Caryville, Tenn. 237/N8
Casa, Ark. 202/D3
Casa Agapito, Colombia 126/D6
Casablanca, Chile 138/F3
Casablanca, Estero de (riv.), Chile 138/F3
Casablanca, Morocco 102/B1
Casablanca, Morocco 106/C2
Casablanca, Morocco 2/J4
Casa Blanca, N. Mex. 274/B4
Casa Branca, Brazil 135/C2
Casa Cruz (cape), Trin. & Tob. 161/B11
Casa Grande, Ariz. 188/D4
Casa Grande, Ariz. 198/D6
Casa Grande Nat'l Mon., Ariz. 198/D6
Casale Monferrato, Italy 34/B2
Casalmaggiore, Italy 34/C2
Casamance (riv.), Senegal 106/A6
Casanare (inten.), Colombia 126/B3
Casanare (riv.), Colombia 126/E4
Casanay, Venezuela 124/G2
Casa Nova, Brazil 132/F5
Casanova, Va. 307/N3
Casa Piedra, Texas 303/C12
Casar, N.C. 281/F3
Casar de Cáceres, Spain 33/C3
Casas Grandes (riv.), Mexico 150/F1
Casas-Ibáñez, Spain 33/F3
Cascade (range) 188/B1
Cascade (range), Calif. 204/D1
Cascade, Colo. 208/K5

350 Charleville

Charleville, Queensland 95/C5
Charleville, Queensland 88/H5
Charleville-Mézières, France 28/F3
Charlevoix (co.), Mich. 250/D3
Charlevoix, Mich. 250/D3
Charlevoix (lake), Mich. 250/D3
Charlevoix-Est (co.), Québec 172/G2
Charlevoix-Est (county), Québec 174/C3
Charlevoix-Ouest (co.), Québec 172/G2
Charlevoix-Ouest (county), Québec 174/C3
Charley, Ky. 237/R5
Charlie Lake, Br. Col. 184/G2
Charlo, Mont. 262/B3
Charlo, New Bruns. 170/D1
Charlo (riv.), New Bruns. 170/D1
Charlotte, Ark. 202/H2
Charlotte (lake), Br. Col. 184/E4
Charlotte (harb.), Fla. 188/K5
Charlotte (co.), Fla. 212/E5
Charlotte (harb.), Fla. 212/D5
Charlotte, Iowa 229/M5
Charlotte•, Maine 243/J5
Charlotte, Mich. 250/E6
Charlotte (co.), New Bruns. 170/C3
Charlotte, N.C. 281/H4
Charlotte, N.C. 188/L3
Charlotte, N.C. 146/K6
Charlotte (lake), Nova Scotia 168/F4
Charlotte, Tenn. 237/G8
Charlotte, Texas 303/F9
Charlotte•, Vt. 268/A3
Charlotte (co.), Va. 307/L6
Charlotte Amalie (cap.), Virgin Is. (U.S.) 156/H1
Charlotte Amalie (cap.), Virgin Is. (U.S.) 161/B4
Charlotte Court House, Va. 307/L6
Charlotte Hall, Md. 245/M7
Charlotte Harbor, Fla. 212/E5
Charlottenberg, Sweden 18/H6
Charlottenburg, Germany 22/E4
Charlottesville, Ind. 227/F5
Charlottesville, Va. 188/L3
Charlottesville (I.C.), Va. 307/M4
Charlottetown, Newf. 166/D2
Charlottetown, Newf. 166/C3
Charlottetown (cap.), P.E.I. 146/M5
Charlottetown (cap.), P.E.I. 162/K6
Charlottetown (cap.), Pr. Edward I. 168/E2
Charlotteville, N.Y. 276/L5
Charlotte Waters, North. Terr. 93/D8
Charlson, N. Dak. 282/E3
Charlton (co.), Georgia 217/H9
Charlton•, Mass. 249/F4
Charlton (isl.), N.W.T. 162/H5
Charlton, Ontario 177/K5
Charlton, Ontario 175/D3
Charlton, Victoria 97/B5
Charlton City, Mass. 249/F4
Charlton Depot, Mass. 249/F4
Charlton Kings, England 13/F6
Charmco, W. Va. 312/E6
Charmey, Switzerland 39/D3
Charny, Québec 172/J3
Charolles, France 28/F4
Charouine, Algeria 106/D3
Charqueada Aguas de São Pedro, Brazil 135/B3
Charron (lake), Manitoba 179/G2
Charsk, U.S.S.R. 48/J5
Charter Oak, Iowa 229/C4
Charters, Ky. 237/P3
Charters Towers, Australia 87/E7
Charters Towers, Queensland 95/C4
Charters Towers, Queensland 88/H4
Chartierville, Québec 172/F4
Chartley, Mass. 249/K5
Chartres, France 28/D3
Chascomús, Argentina 143/H7
Chase, Ala. 195/E1
Chase, Br. Col. 184/H5
Chase (co.), Kansas 232/F3
Chase, Kansas 232/D3
Chase, La. 238/G2
Chase, Md. 245/N3
Chase, Mich. 250/D5
Chase (co.), Nebr. 264/C4
Chase (lake), N. Dak. 282/M5
Chaseburg, Wis. 317/D8
Chase City, Va. 307/M7
Chaseley, N. Dak. 282/L5
Chase Mills, N.Y. 276/K1
Chase N.A.S., Texas 303/G9
Chaska, Minn. 255/F6
Chaska, Tenn. 237/N7
Chasm, Br. Col. 184/G4
Chasŏng, N. Korea 81/C3
Chasseron (mt.), Switzerland 39/C3
Chastang, Ala. 195/B8
Chastre, Belgium 27/F7
Chaswood, Nova Scotia 168/E3
Chataignier, La. 238/F5
Chatanika, Alaska 196/J1
Chatawa, Miss. 256/D8
Chatcolet, Idaho 220/B2
Chateaubelair, St. Vin. & Grens. 161/A8
Châteaubriant, France 28/C4
Château-Chinon, France 28/E4
Château-d'Oex, Switzerland 39/D4
Château-du-Loir, France 28/D4
Châteaudun, France 28/D3
Chateaugay, N.Y. 276/N1
Chateaugay, Upper (lake), N.Y. 276/M1
Château-Gontier, France 28/C4
Châteauguay (co.), Québec 172/D4
Châteauguay, Québec 172/H4
Châteauguay-Centre, Québec 172/H4
Châteauneuf-sur-Loire, France 28/E4
Château-Renault, France 28/D4
Château-Richer, Québec 172/F3
Châteauroux, France 28/D4
Château-Salins, France 28/G3
Château-Thierry, France 28/E3
Châteaux (pt.), Guadeloupe 161/B6
Chateh, Alberta 182/A5
Châtelet, Belgium 27/F8
Châtellerault, France 28/D4
Châtel-Saint-Denis, Switzerland 39/C3
Chater, Manitoba 179/C5
Chatfield, Ark. 202/K3
Chatfield, Manitoba 179/E4
Chatfield, Minn. 255/F7
Chatfield, Ohio 284/E4
Chatham (str.), Alaska 196/M1
Chatham (sound), Br. Col. 184/B3
Chatham (isl.), Chile 138/D9
Chatham, England 13/J8
Chatham, England 10/G5
Chatham (co.), Georgia 217/K6
Chatham, Ill. 222/D4
Chatham, La. 238/F2
Chatham, Mass. 249/P6
Chatham•, Mass. 249/P6
Chatham, Mich. 250/B2
Chatham, Miss. 256/B4
Chatham, N. Br. 162/K6
Chatham, New Bruns. 170/E1
Chatham•, N.H. 268/E3
Chatham, N.J. 273/E2
Chatham, N.Y. 276/N6
Chatham (isl.), N. Zealand 100/D7
Chatham (isls.), N. Zealand 87/J10
Chatham (isls.), N. Zealand 100/D7
Chatham (co.), N.C. 281/L3
Chatham, Ontario 177/B5
Chatham, Va. 307/K7
Chatham Center, N.Y. 276/N6
Chatham Head, New Bruns. 170/E2
Chatham Port, Mass. 249/P6
Châtillon, France 28/B2
Châtillon-sur-Indre, France 28/D4
Châtillon-sur-Seine, France 28/F4
Chato, Cerro (mt.), Argentina 143/B5
Chato, Cerro (mt.), Chile 138/E4
Chatom, Ala. 195/B8
Chatou, France 28/A1
Chatrapur, India 68/F5
Chatsworth, Calif. 204/B10
Chatsworth, Georgia 217/C1
Chatsworth, Ill. 222/E3
Chatsworth, Iowa 229/A3
Chatsworth, N.J. 273/D4
Chatsworth, Ontario 177/D3
Chattahoochee (riv.) 188/K4
Chattahoochee (riv.), Ala. 195/H8
Chattahoochee, Fla. 212/B1
Chattahoochee (riv.), Fla. 212/B1
Chattahoochee (co.), Georgia 217/C6
Chattahoochee (riv.), Georgia 217/B8
Chattahoochee River Nat'l Rec. Area, Georgia 217/K1
Chattanooga, Ohio 284/A4
Chattanooga, Okla. 288/J6
Chattanooga, Tenn. 188/J3
Chattanooga, Tenn. 146/K6
Chattanooga, Tenn. 237/K10
Chattaroy, Wash. 310/H3
Chattaroy, W. Va. 312/B7
Chatteris, England 13/H5
Chattooga (riv.), Ala. 195/H2
Chattooga (co.), Georgia 217/B1
Chattooga (riv.), Georgia 217/A2
Chattooga (riv.), Georgia 217/F1
Chattooga (riv.), S.C. 296/A2
Chatuge (lake), Georgia 217/E1
Chatuge (lake), N.C. 281/B5
Chatwood, Pa. 294/L6
Chaud (lake), Québec 172/C3
Chaudière (riv.), Québec 172/G4
Chauk, Burma 72/B2
Chauk, Burma 54/L7
Chaukan (pass), Burma 72/C1
Chaumont, France 28/F3
Chaumont, N.Y. 276/H2
Chauncey, Georgia 217/F6
Chauncey, Ohio 284/F7
Chauny, France 28/E3
Chau Phu, Vietnam 72/E5
Chauques (isls.), Chile 138/D4
Chautauqua, Ill. 222/C5
Chautauqua (co.), Kansas 232/F4
Chautauqua, Kansas 232/F4
Chautauqua (co.), N.Y. 276/B6
Chautauqua, N.Y. 276/A6
Chautauqua (lake), N.Y. 276/A6
Chauvin, Alberta 182/E3
Chauvin, La. 238/J8
Chavantes, Serra dos (range), Brazil 132/D5
Chaves, Brazil 132/D3
Chaves (Santa Cruz) (isl.), Ecuador 128/C9
Chaves (co.), N. Mex. 274/E5
Chaves, Portugal 33/C2
Chavies, Ky. 237/P6
Chavornay, Switzerland 39/C3
Chayanta, Bolivia 136/B6
Chaykovskiy, U.S.S.R. 52/H3
Chazelles-sur-Lyon, France 28/F5
Chazy, N.Y. 276/N1
Chazy (lake), N.Y. 276/N1
Cheadle, Alberta 182/D4
Cheadle, England 13/E5
Cheadle and Gatley, England 13/H2
Cheadle and Gatley, England 10/G2
Cheaha (mt.), Ala. 195/G4
Cheam View, Br. Col. 184/M3
Cheap (chan.), Chile 138/D7
Cheat (lake), W. Va. 312/G3
Cheat (riv.), W. Va. 312/G3
Cheatham (co.), Tenn. 237/G8
Cheatham (dam), Tenn. 237/G8
Cheatham (lake), Tenn. 237/H8
Cheb, Czech. 41/B1
Chebanse, Ill. 222/F3
Chebeague Island, Maine 243/C8
Chebogue (harb.), Nova Scotia 168/B5
Cheboksary, U.S.S.R. 7/J3
Cheboksary, U.S.S.R. 52/G3
Cheboksary, U.S.S.R. 48/E4
Cheboygan, Mich. 188/K1
Cheboygan (co.), Mich. 250/E3
Cheboygan, Mich. 250/E3
Chech, Erg (des.), Algeria 106/D3
Chech, Erg (des.) 102/B2
Chech, Erg (des.), Mali 106/D4
Chechaouene, Morocco 106/D1
Chechen-Ingush A.S.S.R., U.S.S.R. 48/E5
Chechen-Ingush A.S.S.R., U.S.S.R. 52/G6
Chech'ŏn, S. Korea 81/D5
Check, Va. 307/H6
Checker Hall, Barbados 161/B8
Checotah, Okla. 288/R4
Chedabucto (bay), Nova Scotia 168/G3
Cheduba (isl.), Burma 72/B3
Cheektowaga, N.Y. 276/C5
Cheekye, Br. Col. 184/F5
Cheesequake, N.J. 273/E3
Cheesman (lake), Colo. 208/J4
Chefoo (Yantai), China 77/K4
Chefornak, Alaska 196/F2
Chegdomyn, U.S.S.R. 48/O4
Chegga (well), Mauritania 106/C3
Chegutu, Zimbabwe 115/F7
Chegutu, Zimbabwe 118/E3
Chehalis (lake), Br. Col. 184/L3
Chehalis, Wash. 310/C4
Chehalis (pt.), Wash. 310/A4
Chehalis (riv.), Wash. 310/B4
Chehalis Ind. Res., Wash. 310/B4
Chehar Deh, Iran 66/K4
Cheju (isl.), S. Korea 54/O6
Cheju, S. Korea 81/C7
Cheju (isl.), S. Korea 81/C7
Cheju (str.), S. Korea 81/C7
Chekiang (Zhejiang), China 77/K6
Chelan, Sask. 181/H3
Chelan (lake), Wash. 188/B1
Chelan (co.), Wash. 310/E3
Chelan, Wash. 310/E3
Chelan (dam), Wash. 310/E3
Chelan (lake), Wash. 310/E2
Chelan (range), Wash. 310/E2
Chelan Falls, Wash. 310/E3
Cheleken, U.S.S.R. 48/F6
Chelia (mt.), Algeria 106/F1
Chelif (riv.), Algeria 106/E1
Chelkar, U.S.S.R. 48/F5
Chelles, France 28/C1
Chełm (prov.), Poland 47/F3
Chełm, Poland 47/F3
Chełmno, Poland 47/D2
Chelmsford, England 13/J7
Chelmsford, England 10/G5
Chelmsford•, Mass. 249/J2
Chełmża, Poland 47/D2
Chelsea, Ala. 195/E4
Chelsea, Ind. 227/F7
Chelsea, Iowa 229/J5
Chelsea•, Maine 243/D7
Chelsea, Mass. 249/D6
Chelsea, Mich. 250/E6
Chelsea, Okla. 288/P1
Chelsea, S. Dak. 298/M3
Chelsea, Vt. 268/C4
Chelsea, Victoria 88/L8
Chelsea, Victoria 97/J6
Chelsea, Wis. 317/F5
Cheltenham, England 13/E6
Cheltenham, England 10/F5
Cheltenham, Md. 245/L6
Cheltenham•, Pa. 294/M5
Chelva, Spain 33/F3
Chelyabinsk, U.S.S.R. 2/N3
Chelyabinsk, U.S.S.R. 54/H4
Chelyabinsk, U.S.S.R. 48/G4
Chelyuskin (cape), U.S.S.R. 54/N2
Chelyuskin (cape), U.S.S.R. 4/B4
Chelyuskin (cape), U.S.S.R. 48/M2
Chemainus, Br. Col. 184/J3
Chemawa, Oreg. 291/A3
Chemba, Mozambique 118/E3
Chembur, India 68/B7
Chemehuevi Valley Ind. Res., Calif. 204/L9
Chemeketa Park-Redwood Estates, Calif. 204/K4
Chemnitz, Germany 22/E3
Chemnitz, Germany 7/E3
Chemquasabamticook (lake), Maine 243/D3
Chemult, Oreg. 291/F4
Chemung, Ill. 222/E1
Chemung (co.), N.Y. 276/G6
Chemung, N.Y. 276/G6
Chenab (riv.), India 68/C2
Chenab (riv.), Pakistan 68/C2
Chenab (riv.), Pakistan 59/K4
Chenachane, Algeria 106/D3
Chena Hot Springs, Alaska 196/J1
Chenango (co.), N.Y. 276/J6
Chenango (riv.), N.Y. 276/J6
Chenango Bridge, N.Y. 276/J6
Chenango Forks, N.Y. 276/J6
Chen Barag, China 77/J2
Chêne-Bougeries, Switzerland 39/B4
Chenequa, Wis. 317/J1
Chénéville, Québec 172/B4
Cheney, Kansas 232/E4
Cheney (res.), Kansas 232/E4
Cheney, Wash. 310/H3
Cheneyville, Ill. 222/F3
Cheneyville, La. 238/F4
Chengchow (Zhengzhou), China 77/H5
Chengde (Chengteh), China 77/J3
Chengdu (Chengtu), China 77/F5
Chengdu, China 54/M6
Chengdu, China 2/P4
Chengkou, China 77/G5
Chengteh (Chengde), China 77/J3
Chengtu (Chengdu), China 77/F5
Chenier (lake), La. 238/F2
Chenoa, Ill. 222/E3
Chenoa, Ky. 237/O7
Chenoweth, Oreg. 291/F2
Chen Xian, China 77/H6
Chepachet, R.I. 249/H5
Chepén, Peru 128/C6
Chépénéhé, New Caled. 86/H4
Chepes, Argentina 143/C3
Chépica, Chile 138/A10
Chepo, Panama 154/H6
Chepo (riv.), Panama 154/H6
Chepstow, Ontario 177/C3
Chepstow, Wales 10/E5
Chepstow, Wales 13/E6
Chequamegon (bay), Wis. 317/E2
Cher (dept.), France 28/E4
Cher (riv.), France 28/D4
Cheraw, Colo. 208/N6
Cheraw, Miss. 256/E8
Cheraw, S.C. 296/H2
Cherbourg, France 28/C3
Cherbourg, France 7/D4
Cherbourg, Queensland 95/D5
Cherchell, Algeria 106/E1
Cherchen (Qiemo), China 77/C4
Cherdyn', U.S.S.R. 52/J2
Cheremkhovo, U.S.S.R. 54/L4
Cheremkhovo, U.S.S.R. 48/L4
Cherepovets, U.S.S.R. 7/H3
Cherepovets, U.S.S.R. 52/E3
Cherepovets, U.S.S.R. 48/D4
Chergui, Chott Ech (salt lake), Algeria 106/E2
Cherhill, Alberta 182/C3
Cherial (riv.), India 68/F2
Cheriton, Va. 307/R6
Cherkassy, U.S.S.R. 7/H4
Cherkassy, U.S.S.R. 52/D5
Cherkessk, U.S.S.R. 48/E5
Cherkessk, U.S.S.R. 52/F6
Chermside, Queensland 88/K2
Chermside, Queensland 95/D2
Chernigov, U.S.S.R. 7/H3
Chernigov, U.S.S.R. 48/D4
Chernigov, U.S.S.R. 52/D4
Chernobyl', U.S.S.R. 52/D4
Chernogorsk, U.S.S.R. 48/K4
Chernorechenskiy, U.S.S.R. 52/H2
Chernovtsy, U.S.S.R. 7/G4
Chernovtsy, U.S.S.R. 52/C5
Chernovtsy, U.S.S.R. 48/C5
Chernushka, U.S.S.R. 52/J3
Chernyshevsk, U.S.S.R. 48/M4
Chernyshevskiy, U.S.S.R. 48/M3
Cherokee (co.), Ala. 195/G2
Cherokee, Ala. 195/C1
Cherokee (co.), Georgia 217/D2
Cherokee (co.), Iowa 229/B3
Cherokee, Iowa 229/B3
Cherokee (co.), Kansas 232/H4
Cherokee, Kansas 232/H4
Cherokee, Ky. 237/R4
Cherokee (co.), N.C. 281/A4
Cherokee, N.C. 281/C4
Cherokee (co.), Okla. 288/R3
Cherokee, Okla. 288/K1
Cherokee (co.), S.C. 296/D1
Cherokee (dam), Tenn. 237/P8
Cherokee (lake), Tenn. 237/P8
Cherokee (co.), Texas 303/J6
Cherokee, Texas 303/F7
Cherokee City, Ark. 202/A1
Cherokee Falls, S.C. 296/D1
Cherokee Ind. Res., N.C. 281/C3
Cherokees, Lake O' The (lake), Okla. 288/S1
Cherokee Village, Ark. 202/G1
Cherrapunji, India 68/G3
Cherry, Ariz. 198/C4
Cherry (creek), Ariz. 198/E4
Cherry (brook), Conn. 210/D1
Cherry, Ill. 222/D2
Cherry (co.), Nebr. 264/C2
Cherry, N.C. 281/R3
Cherry (creek), N. Dak. 282/D4
Cherry (creek), S. Dak. 298/F5
Cherry (creek), S. Dak. 298/F4
Cherry, Tenn. 237/B9
Cherry (creek), Utah 304/B4
Cherry (riv.), W. Va. 312/E6
Cherry Creek, Br. Col. 184/G5
Cherry Creek, Nev. 266/G3
Cherry Creek, N.Y. 276/B6
Cherry Creek, S. Dak. 298/F4
Cherryfield•, Maine 243/H6
Cherry Fork, Ohio 284/C8
Cherry Grove, Alberta 182/E2
Cherry Grove, Minn. 255/F7
Cherry Grove, Ohio 284/C10
Cherry Grove, Oreg. 291/D2
Cherry Hill, Ark. 202/B4
Cherry Hill, Md. 245/P2
Cherry Hill•, N.J. 273/B3
Cherry Lake Farms, Fla. 212/C1
Cherryland, Calif. 204/K2
Cherrylog, Georgia 217/D1
Cherry Point, Alberta 182/A1
Cherry Point Marine Air Sta., N.C. 281/R5
Cherry Run, W. Va. 312/L3
Cherry Tree, Pa. 294/E4
Cherryvale, Kansas 232/G4
Cherry Valley, Ark. 202/J3
Cherry Valley, Ill. 222/D1
Cherry Valley, Mass. 249/G3
Cherry Valley, N.Y. 276/L5
Cherry Valley, Ontario 177/G4
Cherry Valley, Pa. 294/C3
Cherryville, Br. Col. 184/H5
Cherryville, Mo. 261/K7
Cherryville, N.C. 281/G4
Cherryville, Oreg. 291/E2
Cherskiy, U.S.S.R. 54/T3
Cherskiy, U.S.S.R. 4/C1
Cherskiy (range), U.S.S.R. 54/R3
Cherskiy, U.S.S.R. 48/Q3
Cherskiy (range), U.S.S.R. 48/P3
Cherta, Spain 33/G2
Chertsey, England 13/G8
Chertsey, England 10/B6
Chervonograd, U.S.S.R. 52/B4
Chesaning, Mich. 250/E5
Chesapeake (bay) 188/L3
Chesapeake (bay), Md. 245/N7
Chesapeake, Ohio 284/E9
Chesapeake (bay), U.S. 146/L6
Chesapeake (I.C.), Va. 307/R7
Chesapeake (bay), Va. 307/R5
Chesapeake, W. Va. 312/C6
Chesapeake and Delaware (canal), Del. 245/R2
Chesapeake and Delaware (canal), Md. 245/R2
Chesapeake and Ohio Canal Nat'l Hist. Park, Md. 245/J4
Chesapeake and Ohio Canal Nat'l Mon., Va. 307/O2
Chesapeake and Ohio Canal Nat'l Hist. Park, W. Va. 312/J3
Chesapeake Beach, Md. 245/N6
Chesapeake City, Md. 245/P2
Chesaw, Wash. 310/G2
Chésery, Pointe de (mt.), Switzerland 39/C4
Chesham, England 10/F5
Chesham, England 13/G7
Chesham, N.H. 268/C6
Cheshire, Conn. 210/D2
Cheshire•, Conn. 210/D2
Cheshire (co.), England 13/E4
Cheshire•, Mass. 249/B2
Cheshire (res.), Mass. 249/A2
Cheshire (co.), N.H. 268/C6
Cheshire, Ohio 284/F8
Cheshire, Oreg. 291/D3
Cheshskaya (bay), U.S.S.R. 7/J2
Cheshskaya (bay), U.S.S.R. 52/G1
Cheshunt, England 13/H7
Cheshunt, England 10/B5
Chesilhurst, N.J. 273/D4
Cheslatta, Br. Col. 184/E3
Chesley, Ontario 177/C3
Chesnaye, Manitoba 179/K2
Chesnee, S.C. 296/D1
Chester, Ark. 202/B2
Chester, Calif. 204/D3
Chester, Conn. 210/F3
Chester•, Conn. 210/F3
Chester, England 10/F2
Chester, England 13/G2
Chester, Georgia 217/F6
Chester, Idaho 220/G5
Chester, Ill. 222/D6
Chester, Ind. 227/H5
Chester, Iowa 229/J2
Chester•, Maine 243/F5
Chester, Md. 245/N5
Chester (riv.), Md. 245/O4
Chester•, Mass. 249/C3
Chester, Minn. 255/F6
Chester, Miss. 256/F4
Chester, Mont. 262/E2
Chester, Nebr. 264/G4
Chester•, N.H. 268/E6
Chester, N.J. 273/D2
Chester, N.Y. 276/M8
Chester, Nova Scotia 168/D4
Chester, Ohio 284/G7
Chester, Okla. 288/J2
Chester (co.), Pa. 294/L6
Chester, Pa. 294/L7
Chester (creek), Pa. 294/L7
Chester (co.), S.C. 296/E2
Chester, S.C. 296/E2
Chester, S. Dak. 298/R6
Chester (co.), Tenn. 237/D10
Chester, Texas 303/K7
Chester, Utah 304/C4
Chester•, Vt. 268/B5
Chester, Va. 307/O6
Chester, W. Va. 312/E1
Chester Basin, Nova Scotia 168/D4
Chester-Chester Depot, Vt. 268/B5
Chesterfield, Conn. 210/G3
Chesterfield, England 13/J2
Chesterfield, England 10/F4
Chesterfield, Idaho 220/G7
Chesterfield (res.), Idaho 220/F7
Chesterfield, Ill. 222/D4
Chesterfield, Ind. 227/F4
Chesterfield (isl.), Madagascar 118/G3
Chesterfield•, Mass. 249/C3
Chesterfield, Mo. 261/N2
Chesterfield (isls.), New Caled. 87/F7
Chesterfield•, N.H. 268/C6
Chesterfield•, N.J. 273/D3
Chesterfield (inlet), N.W.T. 146/J3
Chesterfield (inlet), N.W.T. 162/G2
Chesterfield (inlet), N.W. Terr. 187/J3
Chesterfield (co.), S.C. 296/G2
Chesterfield, S.C. 296/G2
Chesterfield, Tenn. 237/E9
Chesterfield (co.), Va. 307/N6
Chesterfield, Va. 307/N6
Chesterfield Inlet, N.W.T. 162/G3
Chesterfield Inlet, N.W. Terr. 187/K3
Chester Gap, Va. 307/M3
Chester Heights, Pa. 294/L7
Chesterhill, Ohio 284/G6
Chester Hill, Pa. 294/F4
Chesterland, Ohio 284/H2
Chester-le-Street, England 10/E3
Chester-le-Street, England 13/J3
Chester Morse (lake), Wash. 310/D3
Chesterton, Ind. 227/D1
Chestertown, Md. 245/O4
Chestertown, N.Y. 276/N3
Chesterville, Ill. 222/E4
Chesterville, Maine 243/C6
Chesterville•, Maine 243/C6
Chesterville, Md. 245/P3
Chesterville, Ohio 284/E5
Chesterville, Ontario 177/J2
Chesterville, Québec 172/F4
Chestnut, Ala. 195/D7
Chestnut, Ill. 222/D3
Chestnut, La. 238/D2
Chestnut Hill, Conn. 210/G2
Chestnut Mound, Tenn. 237/K8
Chest Springs, Pa. 294/E4
Chesuncook, Maine 243/D3
Chesuncook (lake), Maine 243/E3
Cheswick, Pa. 294/C6
Cheswold, Del. 245/R4
Chetac (lake), Wis. 317/D4
Chetco (riv.), Oreg. 291/C5
Chetek, Wis. 317/C5
Chéticamp, Nova Scotia 168/G2
Chéticamp (isl.), Nova Scotia 168/G2
Chetlat (isl.), India 68/C6
Chetopa, Kansas 232/G4
Chetumal, Mexico 150/Q7
Chetumal (bay), Mexico 150/P8
Chetwynd, Br. Col. 184/G2
Chevak, Alaska 196/E2
Cheval Blanc (pt.), Haiti 158/B5
Chevelon (creek), Ariz. 198/E4
Cheverly, Md. 245/G4
Cheville (pass), Switzerland 39/D4
Cheviot (hills), England 13/E2
Cheviot, The (mt.), England 13/E2
Cheviot, N. Zealand 100/D5
Cheviot, Ohio 284/B9
Cheviot (hills), Scotland 15/F5
Cheviot, The (mt.), Scotland 15/F5
Chevrolet, Ky. 237/P7
Chevy Chase, Md. 245/E4
Chevy Chase Section Four, Md. 245/E4
Chewuch (riv.), Wash. 310/E2
Chewalla, Tenn. 237/D10
Chewelah, Wash. 310/H2
Chewsville, Md. 245/H2
Chexbres, Switzerland 39/C3
Cheyenne (riv.) 188/F2
Cheyenne (co.), Colo. 208/O5
Cheyenne (co.), Kansas 232/A2
Cheyenne (co.), Nebr. 264/A3
Cheyenne, Okla. 288/G3
Cheyenne (riv.), S. Dak. 298/F4
Cheyenne (riv.), U.S. 146/H5
Cheyenne (cap.), Wyo. 146/H5
Cheyenne (cap.), Wyo. 188/E2
Cheyenne (cap.), Wyo. 319/H4
Cheyenne (riv.), Wyo. 319/H2
Cheyenne Bottoms (lake), Kansas 232/D3
Cheyenne River Ind. Res., S. Dak. 298/F4
Cheyenne Wells, Colo. 208/P5
Cheyne (bay), W. Australia 92/B6
Cheyney, Pa. 294/M6
Cheyres, Switzerland 39/C3
Chezacut, Br. Col. 184/F4
Chhatarpur, India 68/D4
Chhindwara, India 68/D4
Chi, Mae Nam (riv.), Thailand 72/D3
Chiai, China 77/K7
Chiambone, Somalia 115/H4
Chiang Dao, Thailand 72/C3
Chiange, Angola 115/B7
Chiang Khan, Thailand 72/D3
Chiang Mai, Thailand 72/C3
Chiang Mai, Thailand 54/L8
Chiang Rai, Thailand 72/C3
Chiang Saen, Thailand 72/C2
Chiapa de Corzo, Mexico 150/N8
Chiapas (state), Mexico 150/N8
Chiari, Italy 34/C2
Chiasso, Switzerland 39/G5
Chiatura, U.S.S.R. 52/F6
Chiautempan, Mexico 150/N1
Chiavari, Italy 34/B2
Chiba (pref.), Japan 81/P2
Chiba, Japan 81/P2
Chibabava, Mozambique 118/E4
Chibia, Angola 115/B7
Chiblow (lake), Ontario 177/A1
Chibougamau, Québec 174/C3
Chibougamau, Que. 162/J6
Chibukak (cape), Alaska 196/D2
Chibuto, Mozambique 118/E4
Chibwe, Zambia 115/E6
Chicago, Ill. 146/K5
Chicago, Ill. 188/J2
Chicago, Ill. 222/C5
Chicago, North Branch (riv.), Ill. 222/B5
Chicago, U.S. 2/E3
Chicago Heights, Ill. 222/C6
Chicago Portage Nat'l Hist. Site, Ill. 222/B6
Chicago Ridge, Ill. 222/B6
Chicama, Peru 128/C6
Chicamacomico (riv.), Md. 245/P7
Chicamocha (riv.), Colombia 126/D4
Chicanán (riv.), Venezuela 124/H4
Chicapa (riv.), Angola 115/D5
Chicapa (riv.), Zaire 115/D5
Chic-Chocs (mts.), Québec 172/C1
Chichagof (isl.) Alaska 188/D6
Chichagof (isl.), Alaska 196/M1
Chichén-Itzá (ruin), Mexico 150/P6
Chichester, England 13/G7
Chichester, England 10/F5
Chichester•, N.H. 268/E5
Chichester, N.Y. 276/M6
Chichi (isl.), Japan 87/E3
Chichi (isl.), Japan 81/M3
Chichibu, Japan 81/J5
Chichibu-Tama National Park, Japan 81/J6
Chichicaste, Honduras 154/E3
Chichicastenango, Guatemala 154/B3
Chichigalpa, Nicaragua 154/D4
Chichiriviche, Venezuela 124/D2
Chickalah, Ark. 202/D3
Chickaloon, Alaska 196/C1
Chickamauga, Georgia 217/B1
Chickamauga (dam), Tenn. 237/L10
Chickamauga (lake), Tenn. 188/J3
Chickamauga (lake), Tenn. 237/L10
Chickamauga and Chattanooga Nat'l Mil. Park, Georgia 217/B1
Chickamaw Beach, Minn. 255/D4
Chickasaw, Ala. 195/B9
Chickasaw (co.), Iowa 229/J2
Chickasaw (co.), Miss. 256/G3
Chickasaw, Ohio 284/A5
Chickasawhay (riv.), Miss. 256/G7
Chickasaw Village, Natchez Trace Pkwy., Miss. 256/G2
Chickasha, Okla. 188/G4

Circle 351

Chickasha, Okla. 288/L4
Chickasha (lake), Okla. 288/K4
Chicken, Alaska 196/K2
Chiclana de la Frontera, Spain 33/C4
Chiclayo, Peru 128/C6
Chiclayo, Peru 120/B3
Chico (riv.), Argentina 120/C7
Chico (riv.), Argentina 143/C6
Chico (riv.), Argentina 143/C5
Chico, Calif. 204/D4
Chico, Mont. 262/F5
Chico (riv.), Philippines 82/C2
Chico, Texas 303/G4
Chicoana, Argentina 143/C2
Chico Arroyo (creek), N. Mex. 274/B3
Chicopee, Kansas 232/H4
Chicopee, Mass. 249/D4
Chicopee (riv.), Mass. 249/D4
Chicora, Miss. 256/G7
Chicora, Pa. 294/C4
Chicot (co.), Ark. 202/H7
Chicot, Ark. 202/H7
Chicot (pt.), La. 238/M7
Chicoutimi, Que. 162/J6
Chicoutimi, Que. 146/L5
Chicoutimi (county), Québec 174/C2
Chicoutimi (co.), Québec 172/G1
Chicoutimi, Québec 172/G1
Chicoutimi, Québec 174/C3
Chicoutimi (riv.), Québec 172/F2
Chicoutimi-Nord, Québec 172/F1
Chicualacuala, Mozambique 118/E4
Chidambaram, India 68/E6
Chidester, Ark. 202/D6
Chidley (cape), Canada 146/M3
Chidley (cape), Newf. 166/B1
Chidley (cape), Newf. 162/K3
Chidley (cape), N.W. Terr. 187/M3
Chidlow, W. Australia 88/B2
Chief Joseph (dam), Wash. 310/F3
Chiefland, Fla. 212/D2
Chiefs (pt.), Ontario 177/C3
Chiemsee (lake), Germany 22/E5
Chienti (riv.), Italy 34/D3
Chieri, Italy 34/A2
Chieti (prov.), Italy 34/E3
Chieti, Italy 34/E3
Chietla, Mexico 150/M2
Chièvres, Belgium 27/D7
Chifeng, China 77/J3
Chigasaki, Japan 81/O3
Chiginagak (mt.), Alaska 196/G3
Chignahuapan, Mexico 150/N1
Chignecto (bay), New Bruns. 170/F3
Chignecto (bay), Nova Scotia 168/D3
Chignecto (cape), Nova Scotia 168/C3
Chignecto (isth.), Nova Scotia 168/D3
Chignik, Alaska 196/G3
Chignik (bay), Alaska 196/G3
Chignik Lagoon, Alaska 196/G3
Chignik Lake, Alaska 196/G3
Chiguana, Bolivia 136/A7
Chigubo, Mozambique 118/E4
Chigwell, England 13/H8
Chigwell, England 10/C5
Chihuahua (state), Mexico 150/F2
Chihuahua, Mexico 150/F2
Chihuahua, Mexico 146/H7
Chikaskia (riv.), Kansas 232/E4
Chik Ballapur, India 68/D6
Chikmagalur, India 68/D6
Chilanga, Zambia 115/E7
Chilanko Forks, Br. Col. 184/E4
Chilapa de Álvarez, Mexico 150/K8
Chilas, Pakistan 68/C1
Chilas, Pakistan 59/K2
Chilca (Pucusana), Peru 128/D9
Chilcoot, Calif. 204/E4
Chilcotin (riv.), Br. Col. 184/E4
Childers, Queensland 88/J5
Childersburg, Ala. 195/F4
Childress (co.), Texas 303/D3
Childress, Texas 303/D3
Childs (lake), Manitoba 179/A3
Childs, Md. 245/P2
Childwold, N.Y. 276/L2
Chile 2/F7
Chile 120/B5
CHILE 138
Chile Chico, Chile 138/E6
Chilecito, Argentina 143/C2
Chiles, Colombia 126/A7
Chilete, Peru 128/C6
Chilga, Ethiopia 111/G5
Chilhowee, Mo. 261/E5
Chilhowee (mt.), Tenn. 237/O9
Chilhowie, Va. 307/E7
Chili, Ind. 227/F3
Chili, Wis. 317/F6
Chililabombwe, Zambia 115/E6
Chililabombwe, Zambia 102/E6
Chilili, N. Mex. 274/C4
Chilka (lake), India 68/F5
Chilko (lake), Br. Col. 184/F4
Chilko (riv.), Br. Col. 184/E4
Chilkoot (pass), Alaska 196/M1
Chilkoot (pass), Br. Col. 184/J1
Chillán, Chile 120/B6
Chillán, Chile 138/A11
Chillicothe, Ill. 222/D3
Chillicothe, Iowa 229/J6
Chillicothe, Mo. 261/E3
Chillicothe, Ohio 284/E7
Chillicothe, Texas 303/E3
Chilliwack, Br. Col. 162/D6
Chilliwack, Br. Col. 184/M3
Chillum, Md. 245/F4
Chilmark•, Mass. 249/M7
Chilo, Ohio 284/B8
Chilocco, Okla. 288/M1
Chiloé (isl.), Chile 120/B7
Chiloé (isl.), Chile 138/D4
Chiloquin, Oreg. 291/F5
Chilpancingo de los Bravos, Mexico 150/K8
Chiltern (hills), England 13/G6
Chilton (co.), Ala. 195/E5
Chilton, Texas 303/G6
Chilton, Wis. 317/K7
Chiltonville, Mass. 249/M5
Chilumba, Malawi 115/F6
Chilwa (lake), Malawi 115/G7
Chilwa (lake), Mozambique 118/F3
Chimacum, Wash. 310/C3
Chimaltenango, Guatemala 154/B3
Chimán, Panama 154/H6
Chimanimani, Zimbabwe 118/E3
Chimantá-tepuí (mt.), Venezuela 124/G5
Chimay, Belgium 27/E8
Chimayo, N. Mex. 274/D3
Chimbarongo, Chile 138/A10
Chimbay, U.S.S.R. 48/F5
Chimborazo (prov.), Ecuador 128/C3
Chimborazo (mt.), Ecuador 120/B3
Chimborazo (mt.), Ecuador 128/C3
Chimbote, Peru 120/B3
Chimbote, Peru 128/C7
Chimbote (bay), Peru 128/C7
Chimichagua, Colombia 126/D3
Chimkent, U.S.S.R. 54/H5
Chimkent, U.S.S.R. 48/H5
Chimney Point, Vt. 268/A3
Chimney Rock, Colo. 208/E8
Chimney Rock Nat'l Hist. Site, Nebr. 264/A3
Chimoio, Mozambique 118/E3
Chimoio, Mozambique 102/F6
Chin, Alberta 182/D5
Chin (state), Burma 72/B2
Chin (hills), Burma 72/B2
Chin (cape), Ontario 177/C2
China 2/P4
China 54/L6
CHINA 77
CHINA 85
China, Maine 243/E7
China•, Maine 243/E7
China, Campeche, Mexico 150/O7
China, Nuevo León, Mexico 150/K4
Chinácota, Colombia 126/D4
China Gardens (dam), Wash. 310/J4
China Grove, Ala. 195/G7
China Grove, N.C. 281/H3
China Grove, Texas 303/K11
China Lake, Calif. 204/H8
China Lake Naval Weapons Center, Calif. 204/H8
Chinameca, El Salvador 154/C4
Chinandega, Nicaragua 154/D4
Chinati (mts.), Texas 303/C12
Chinati (peak), Texas 303/C12
Chincha (isls.), Peru 128/D9
Chincha Alta, Peru 128/D9
Chincha Alta, Peru 120/B4
Chinchaga (riv.), Alberta 182/A5
Chinchilla, Pa. 294/F6
Chinchilla, Queensland 88/J5
Chinchilla de Monte-Aragón, Spain 33/F3
Chinchiná, Colombia 126/C5
Chinchón, Spain 33/G5
Chinchoua, Gabon 115/A4
Chinchow (Jinzhou), China 77/K3
Chincoteague (bay), Md. 245/S8
Chincoteague, Va. 307/T5
Chincoteague (bay), Va. 307/T4
Chincoteague (inlet), Va. 307/T5
Chinde, Mozambique 118/F3
Chinde, Mozambique 102/F6
Chindu, China 77/E5
Chindwin (riv.), Burma 72/B2
Chinese Camp, Calif. 204/E6
Chingleput, India 68/E6
Chingola, Zambia 115/E6
Chingola, Zambia 102/E6
Chinguar, Angola 115/C6
Chinguetti, Mauritania 106/B4
Chinhae, S. Korea 81/D6
Chiniak (cape), Alaska 196/H3
Chinhoyi, Zimbabwe 115/F7
Chinhoyi, Zimbabwe 118/D3
Chiñijo, Bolivia 136/A4
Chiniot, Pakistan 68/C2
Chinipas, Mexico 150/E3
Chinju, S. Korea 81/D6
Chinkapin Knob (mt.), Ark. 202/E2
Chinkiang (Zhenjiang), China 77/J5
Chinle, Ariz. 198/F2
Chinle (creek), Ariz. 198/F2
Chinle (valley), Ariz. 198/F2
Chinle (creek), Utah 304/E6
Chinle Wash (dry riv.), Ariz. 198/F2
Chino (valley), Ariz. 198/C3
Chino, Calif. 204/D10
Chinon, France 28/D4
Chinook, Alberta 182/E4
Chinook, Mont. 262/G2
Chinook (lake), Oreg. 291/F3
Chinook, Wash. 310/B4
Chinook (pass), Wash. 310/D4
Chinook Valley, Alberta 182/B1
Chino Valley, Ariz. 198/C4
Chinquapin, N.C. 281/O5
Chinsali, Zambia 115/F6
Chinsi (Jinxi), China 77/K3
Chintheche, Malawi 115/F6
Chinú, Colombia 126/C3
Chinwangtao (Qinhuangdao), China 77/K4
Chiny, Belgium 27/G9
Chioggia, Italy 34/D2
Chip (lake), Alberta 182/C3
Chipamanu (riv.), Bolivia 136/A2
Chipata, Zambia 115/F6
Chipata, Zambia 102/F6
Chipewyan (lake), Alberta 182/D1
Chipewyan (riv.), Alberta 182/D1
Chipewyan Lake, Alberta 182/D1
Chipindo, Angola 102/D6
Chipindo, Angola 115/C6
Chipinge, Zimbabwe 118/E4
Chipley, Fla. 212/D6
Chiplun, India 68/C5
Chipman, Alberta 182/D3
Chipman, New Bruns. 170/E2
Chipman (riv.), Sask. 181/M2
Chipoka, Malawi 115/F6
Chipola (riv.), Fla. 212/D6
Chipola, La. 238/J5
Chippenham, England 13/E6
Chippenham, England 10/F5
Chippewa (co.), Mich. 250/E2
Chippewa (riv.), Mich. 250/E5
Chippewa (co.), Minn. 255/C5
Chippewa (riv.), Minn. 255/C5
Chippewa (riv.), Wis. 188/H1
Chippewa (co.), Wis. 317/D5
Chippewa (lake), Wis. 317/D4
Chippewa (riv.), Wis. 317/B7
Chippewa Falls, Wis. 317/D6
Chippewa Lake, Mich. 250/D5
Chipping Norton, England 13/F6
Chippis, Switzerland 39/E4
Chiputneticook (lakes), Maine 243/H4
Chiputneticook (lakes), New Bruns. 170/C3
Chiquián, Peru 128/D8
Chiquimula, Guatemala 154/C3
Chiquinquirá, Colombia 126/C5
Chiquita (lake), Argentina 120/C6
Chir (riv.), U.S.S.R. 52/F5
Chira (riv.) 120/A3
Chira (riv.), Ecuador 128/B5
Chirala, India 68/E5
Chirchik, U.S.S.R. 48/H5
Chireno, Texas 303/K6
Chirfa, Niger 106/G4
Chiri (mt.), S. Korea 81/C6
Chiribiquete, Sierra de (mts.), Colombia 126/D7
Chiricahua (mts.), Ariz. 198/F6
Chiricahua Nat'l Mon., Ariz. 198/F6
Chiriguaná, Colombia 126/D3
Chirikof (isl.), Alaska 196/G3
Chirinos, Peru 128/C5
Chiriquí (gulf), Panama 154/F7
Chiriquí (lag.), Panama 154/G6
Chiriquí Grande, Panama 154/F6
Chirk, Wales 13/D5
Chirnside, Scotland 15/F5
Chiromo, Malawi 115/F7
Chironico, Switzerland 39/G4
Chirpan, Bulgaria 45/G4
Chirripó Grande (mt.), C. Rica 154/F6
Chirundu, Zimbabwe 118/D3
Chisago (co.), Minn. 255/F5
Chisago City, Minn. 255/E5
Chisamba, Zambia 115/E6
Chisana, Alaska 196/K2
Chisasibi, Québec 162/J5
Chisasibi, Québec 174/B2
Chisec, Guatemala 154/B3
Chisholm, Maine 243/C7
Chisholm, Minn. 255/E3
Chisholm Mills, Alberta 182/C2
Chishui, China 77/G6
Chisimayu, Somalia 115/H4
Chisimayu, Somalia 102/G5
Chişineu Criş, Romania 45/E2
Chismville, Ark. 202/C3
Chisos (mts.), Texas 303/A8
Chistochina, Alaska 196/K2
Chistopol', U.S.S.R. 52/H3
Chiswick, Ontario 177/E1
Chita, U.S.S.R. 54/N4
Chita, U.S.S.R. 48/M4
Chitado, Angola 115/B7
Chitado, Namibia 118/A3
Chitato, Angola 114/D5
Chitek (lake), Manitoba 179/C2
Chitek (lake), Sask. 181/D2
Chitek Lake, Sask. 181/D2
Chitembo, Angola 115/C6
Chitina, Alaska 196/K2
Chitina (riv.), Alaska 196/K2
Chitipa, Malawi 115/F5
Chitorgarh, India 68/C4
Chitose, Japan 81/K2
Chitradurga, India 68/D6
Chitral, Pakistan 59/K2
Chitral, Pakistan 68/C1
Chitré, Panama 154/G7
Chittagong, Bangladesh 54/L7
Chittagong, Bangladesh 68/G4
Chittenango, N.Y. 276/J4
Chittenden (co.), Vt. 268/A3
Chittenden•, Vt. 268/B4
Chittenden (res.), Vt. 268/B4
Chittering, W. Australia 88/B6
Chittoor, India 68/D6
Chiumbe (riv.), Angola 115/D5
Chiva, Spain 33/F3
Chivacoa, Venezuela 124/D2
Chivapure (riv.), Venezuela 124/E4
Chivasso, Italy 34/A2
Chivato (mesa), N. Mex. 274/B3
Chivay, Peru 128/G10
Chive, Bolivia 136/A3
Chivho, Zimbabwe 118/E3
Chivilcoy, Argentina 143/F7
Chivilcoy, Argentina 120/C6
Chivington, Colo. 208/O6
Chiwawa (riv.), Wash. 310/E2
Chixoy (riv.), Guatemala 154/B2
Chizha, U.S.S.R. 52/F1
Chloe, W. Va. 312/D5
Chloride, Ariz. 198/A3
Chloride, Mo. 261/L8
Chlumec, Czech. 41/C1
Choam Khsant, Cambodia 72/E4
Choapa, Chile 138/A9
Choapa (riv.), Chile 138/A9
Choate, Br. Col. 184/M3
Chobe (riv.), Botswana 118/C3
Chobe (riv.), Namibia 118/C3
Chobe Nat'l Park, Botswana 118/D3
Choc, St. Lucia 161/G5
Choc (bay), St. Lucia 161/G5
Chocalán, Chile 138/F4
Chocaya, Bolivia 136/B7
Chococolocco, Ala. 195/G3
Choceň, Czech. 41/D1
Choch'iwŏn, S. Korea 81/C5
Chocó (dept.), Colombia 126/B4
Chocó (bay), Colombia 126/B6
Chocolate (mts.), Ariz. 198/A5
Chocolate (mts.), Calif. 204/K10
Chocomán, Mexico 150/P2
Choconut, Pa. 294/K2
Chocorua, N.H. 268/E4
Chocorua (mt.), N.H. 268/E4
Chocowinity, N.C. 281/P4
Choctaw (co.), Ala. 195/B6
Choctaw, Ala. 195/B6
Choctaw, Ark. 202/F2
Choctaw (co.), Miss. 256/F4
Choctaw (co.), Okla. 288/P6
Choctaw, Okla. 288/M3
Choctaw Bluff, Ala. 195/C8
Choctawhatchee (riv.), Ala. 195/H8
Choctawhatchee (bay), Fla. 212/C6
Choctawhatchee (riv.), Fla. 212/C6
Choctaw Ind. Res., Miss. 256/F6
Chodov, Czech. 41/B1
Chodzież, Poland 47/C2
Choele-Choel, Argentina 143/C4
Choele-Choel, Argentina 120/C6
Choestoe, Georgia 217/E1
Chofu, Japan 81/O2
Choiceland, Sask. 181/G2
Choiseul (sound), Falkland Is. 143/E7
Choiseul, St. Lucia 161/F7
Choiseul (isl.), Solomon Is. 87/F6
Choiseul (isl.), Solomon Is. 86/D2
Choisy-le-Roi, France 28/B2
Choix, Mexico 150/E3
Chojna, Poland 47/B2
Chojnice, Poland 47/C2
Chojnów, Poland 47/B3
Chokai (mt.), Japan 81/J4
Chokio, Minn. 255/B5
Chokoloskee, Fla. 212/E6
Chokurdakh, U.S.S.R. 4/B2
Chokurdakh, U.S.S.R. 54/R2
Chokurdakh, U.S.S.R. 48/P2
Cholame, Calif. 204/E8
Cholet, France 28/C4
Choloma, Honduras 154/C3
Cholula de Rivadavia, Mexico 150/M1
Choluteca, Honduras 154/D4
Choluteca (riv.), Honduras 154/D4
Choma, Zambia 115/E7
Choma, Zambia 102/E6
Chomes, C. Rica 154/E5
Chomo Lhari (mt.), Bhutan 68/F3
Chomutov, Czech. 41/B1
Ch'ŏnan, S. Korea 81/C5
Chon Buri, Thailand 72/D4
Chonchi, Chile 138/D4
Ch'ŏnch'ŏn, N. Korea 81/C3
Chone, Ecuador 128/B3
Ch'ŏngjin, N. Korea 54/P5
Ch'ŏngjin, N. Korea 81/E2
Chŏngju, N. Korea 81/B4
Ch'ŏngju, S. Korea 81/C5
Chongqing (Chungking), China 77/G6
Chongqing, China 2/P4
Chongqing, China 54/M7
Chŏngŭp, S. Korea 81/C6
Chongyang, China 77/H6
Chongzuo, China 77/G7
Chŏnju, S. Korea 81/C6
Chon May, Vung (bay), Vietnam 72/F3
Chonos (arch.), Chile 120/B7
Chonos (arch.), Chile 138/D6
Chopin, La. 238/E4
Chopin (lake), Québec 172/B2
Choptank (riv.), Del. 245/P5
Choptank, Md. 245/P6
Choptank (riv.), Md. 245/O6
Choquecota, Bolivia 136/A6
Chorley, England 10/G2
Chorley, England 13/G2
Chorleywood, England 13/G7
Chorleywood, England 10/A5
Choroní, Venezuela 124/E2
Choros (cape), Chile 138/A7
Choros, Los (riv.), Chile 138/A7
Chortitz, Sask. 181/D5
Chortkov, U.S.S.R. 52/B5
Ch'ŏrwŏn, S. Korea 81/C4
Chorzele, Poland 47/E2
Chorzów, Poland 47/B4
Ch'osan, N. Korea 81/C3
Choshi, Japan 81/K6
Chosica, Peru 128/D8
Chos-Malal, Argentina 143/C4
Choszczno, Poland 47/B2
Chota, Peru 128/C6
Choteau, Mont. 262/D3
Choteau (creek), S. Dak. 298/N7
Chotěboř, Czech. 41/C2
Choudrant, La. 238/F1
Chouteau (co.), Mont. 262/F3
Chouteau, Okla. 288/R2
Chovoreca, Cerro (mt.), Bolivia 136/F6
Chovoreca (mt.), Paraguay 144/C1
Chowan (co.), N.C. 281/R2
Chowan (riv.), N.C. 281/R2
Chowchilla, Calif. 204/E6
Choybalsan, Mongolia 54/N5
Choybalsan, Mongolia 77/J2
Chrastava, Czech. 41/C1
Chriesman, Texas 303/H7
Chrisman, Ill. 222/F4
Chrisney, Ind. 227/C8
Christchurch, England 10/F5
Christchurch, England 13/F7
Christchurch, N. Zealand 2/T8
Christchurch, N. Zealand 100/D5
Christian (sound), Alaska 196/M2
Christian (co.), Ill. 222/D4
Christian (co.), Ky. 237/F7
Christian (co.), Mo. 261/F9
Christian (cape), N.W. Terr. 187/M2
Christian (isl.), Ontario 177/D3
Christian, W. Va. 312/C7
Christiana, Del. 245/R2
Christiana, Jamaica 158/H6
Christiana, Pa. 294/K6
Christiana, S. Africa 118/D5
Christiana, Tenn. 237/J9
Christiansburg, Ohio 284/C5
Christiansburg, Va. 307/H6
Christiansfeld, Denmark 21/C7
Christiansted, Virgin Is. (U.S.) 156/H2
Christiansted, Virgin Is. (U.S.) 161/F4
Christiansted Nat'l Hist. Site, Virgin Is. (U.S.) 161/F4
Christie, Okla. 288/S3
Christina (lake), Alberta 182/E2
Christina (riv.), Alberta 182/E1
Christina (lake), Minn. 255/C4
Christina, Mont. 262/G3
Christina Lake, Br. Col. 184/H5
Christine, N. Dak. 282/S6
Christine, Texas 303/F9
Christmas, Ariz. 198/E5
Christmas (isl.), Australia 54/M11
Christmas (isl.), Australia 2/O6
Christmas, Fla. 212/E3
Christmas (Kiritimati) (isl.), Kiribati 87/L5
Christmas, Mich. 250/C2
Christmas (lake), Oreg. 291/G4
Christmas (riv.), W. Australia 88/D3
Christmas Creek, W. Australia 92/D2
Christmas Island, Nova Scotia 168/H3
Christopher, Ill. 222/D6
Christopher Lake, Sask. 181/F2
Christoval, Texas 303/D6
Chromo, Colo. 208/F8
Chrudim, Czech. 41/C2
Chrudimka (riv.), Czech. 41/C2
Chrysler, Ala. 195/C8
Chryston, Scotland 15/C2
Chrzanów, Poland 47/B4
Chu (riv.), U.S.S.R. 48/H5
Chualar, Calif. 204/D7
Chüanchow (Quanzhou), China 77/J7
Chuathbaluk, Alaska 196/G2
Chubbuck, Idaho 220/F7
Chubu-Sangaku Nat'l Park, Japan 81/H5
Chubut (prov.), Argentina 143/C5
Chubut (riv.), Argentina 120/C7
Chubut (riv.), Argentina 143/C5
Chuchi (lake), Br. Col. 184/E2
Chuchow (Zhuzhou), China 77/H6
Chuckey, Tenn. 237/R8
Chucunaque (riv.), Panama 154/J6
Chudleigh, Tasmania 99/C3
Chudovo, U.S.S.R. 52/D3
Chugach (isls.), Alaska 196/B2
Chugash (mts.), Alaska 196/C1
Chugiak, Alaska 196/C1
Chuginadak (isl.), Alaska 196/D4
Chuguchak (Tacheng), China 77/B2
Chugwater, Wyo. 319/H4
Chugwater (creek), Wyo. 319/H4
Chukai, Malaysia 72/D6
Chukchi (sea) 4/C18
Chukchi (sea) 54/W3
Chukchi (sea), Alaska 196/E1
Chukchi (pen.), U.S.S.R. 54/V3
Chukchi (pen.), U.S.S.R. 4/C18
Chukchi (pen.), U.S.S.R. 48/T3
Chukchi (sea), U.S.S.R. 48/U3
Chukchi Aut. Okr., U.S.S.R. 48/R3
Chukhloma, U.S.S.R. 52/F3
Chula, Ark. 202/C4
Chula, Georgia 217/E7
Chula, Mo. 261/F3
Chula, Va. 307/N6
Chu Lai, Vietnam 72/F4
Chula Vista, Calif. 204/J11
Chulucanas, Peru 128/B5
Chulumani, Bolivia 136/B5
Chulym (riv.), U.S.S.R. 48/J4
Chuma, Bolivia 136/A4
Chumatien (Zhumadian), China 77/H5
Chumbicha, Argentina 143/C2
Chumikan, U.S.S.R. 48/O4
Chumphon, Thailand 72/C5
Chuna (riv.), U.S.S.R. 48/K4
Chunchi, Ecuador 128/C4
Ch'unch'ŏn, S. Korea 81/D5
Chunchula, Ala. 195/B9
Ch'ungju, S. Korea 81/C5
Chungking (Chongqing), China 77/G6
Chŭngsan, N. Korea 81/B4
Chungshan (Zhongshan), China 77/H7
Chunky, Miss. 256/G6
Chunya, Tanzania 115/F5
Chunya (riv.), U.S.S.R. 48/K3
Chupaca, Peru 128/E9
Chupadera (mesa), N. Mex. 274/C5
Chupara (pt.), Trin. & Tob. 161/B10
Chuquibamba, Peru 128/F10
Chuquibambilla, Peru 128/F9
Chuquicamata, Chile 138/B3
Chuquichambi, Bolivia 136/B5
Chuquisaca (dept.), Bolivia 136/C6
Chur, Switzerland 39/J3
Churachandpur, India 68/G4
Church, Iowa 229/L2
Churchbridge, Sask. 181/J5
Church Creek, Md. 245/O6
Church Hill, Md. 245/O4
Church Hill, Miss. 256/B7
Church Hill, Tenn. 237/R7
Churchill (riv.) 162/G4
Churchill (pk.), Br. Col. 162/D4
Churchill (peak), Br. Col. 184/L2
Churchill (riv.), Canada 146/J4
Churchill, Man. 146/J4
Churchill, Man. 162/G4
Churchill, Manitoba 179/K2
Churchill (cape), Manitoba 162/G4
Churchill (cape), Manitoba 179/K2
Churchill (riv.), Manitoba 179/J2
Churchill (co.), Nev. 266/C3
Churchill (falls), Newf. 166/B3
Churchill (riv.), Newf. 166/B3
Churchill, Pa. 294/C7
Churchill (riv.), Que. 162/K5
Churchill (riv.), Sask. 181/M3
Churchill, Victoria 97/D6
Churchill Falls, Newf. 166/B3
Churchman (mt.), W. Australia 92/B5
Church Point, La. 238/F6
Church Point, Nova Scotia 168/B4
Church's Ferry, N. Dak. 282/M3
Church Stretton, England 13/E5
Churchton, Md. 245/N5
Churchtown, Pa. 294/L5
Church View, Va. 307/P5
Churchville, Md. 245/N2
Churchville, N.Y. 276/E4
Churchville, Va. 307/K4
Churchville, W. Va. 312/E4
Churdan, Iowa 229/D4
Churfirsten (mt.), Switzerland 39/H2
Churín, Peru 128/D8
Churu, India 68/D3
Churubusco, Ind. 227/G2
Churubusco, N.Y. 276/N1
Churuguara, Venezuela 124/D2
Churwalden, Switzerland 39/J3
Chushul, India 68/D2
Chuska (mts.), N. Mex. 274/A2
Chusovoy, U.S.S.R. 52/J3
Chute-à-Blondeau, Ontario 177/K2
Chute-aux-Outardes, Québec 172/A1
Chute-des-Passes, Québec 174/C3
Chute-Saint-Philippe, Québec 172/B3
Chuvash A.S.S.R., U.S.S.R. 48/E4
Chuvash A.S.S.R., U.S.S.R. 52/G3
Chu Xian, China 77/J5
Chuxiong, China 77/F7
Chuy, Uruguay 145/F4
Chvalšiny, Czech. 41/C2
Ciales, P. Rico 161/C1
Ciamis, Indonesia 85/H2
Ciampino, Italy 34/F7
Cianjur, Indonesia 85/H2
Cibecue, Ariz. 198/E4
Cibola (co.), N. Mex. 274/B3
Cibolo, Texas 303/K10
Cibolo (creek), Texas 303/K11
Çiçekdagı, Turkey 63/F3
Cicero, Ill. 222/B5
Cicero, Ind. 227/E4
Cícero Dantas, Brazil 132/G5
Cicerone, W. Va. 312/D5
Ciconsine (lake), Québec 172/D2
Cid, N.C. 281/J3
Cide, Turkey 63/E2
Cidlina (riv.), Czech. 41/C1
Cidra, Cuba 158/D1
Cidra, P. Rico 161/D2
Ciechanów (prov.), Poland 47/E2
Ciechanów, Poland 47/E2
Ciechocinek, Poland 47/D2
Ciego de Ávila (prov.), Cuba 158/F2
Ciego de Ávila, Cuba 156/B2
Ciego de Ávila, Cuba 158/F2
Ciempozuelos, Spain 33/F5
Ciénaga, Colombia 120/B1
Ciénaga, Colombia 126/C2
Ciénaga de Oro, Colombia 126/C3
Cienfuegos (prov.), Cuba 158/E2
Cienfuegos, Cuba 156/B2
Cienfuegos, Cuba 146/K7
Cienfuegos, Cuba 158/D2
Cienfuegos (bay), Cuba 158/D2
Cieplice Śląskie-Zdrój, Poland 47/B3
Čierny Balog, Czech. 41/E2
Cieszyn, Poland 47/D4
Cieza, Spain 33/F3
Çifteler, Turkey 63/D3
Cifuentes, Spain 33/E2
Cigánd, Hungary 41/F2
Cihanbeyli, Turkey 63/E3
Cihuatlán, Mexico 150/G7
Cijara (res.), Spain 33/D3
Cijulang, Indonesia 85/H2
Cilacap, Indonesia 85/H2
Çıldır, Turkey 63/K2
Çıldır (lake), Turkey 63/K2
Cilleros, Spain 33/C2
Cilo Dağı (mt.), Turkey 63/K4
Cima, Calif. 204/K8
Cimahi, Indonesia 85/H2
Cimarron (riv.) 188/G3
Cimarron, Colo. 208/D6
Cimarron, Kansas 232/B4
Cimarron (riv.), Kansas 232/B4
Cimarron, N. Mex. 274/E2
Cimarron (riv.), N. Mex. 274/E2
Cimarron (co.), Okla. 288/A1
Cimarron, Okla. 288/L3
Cimarron (riv.), Okla. 288/N2
Cimin, Turkey 63/H3
Cimone (mt.), Italy 34/C2
Cîmpeni, Romania 45/F2
Cîmpia Turzii, Romania 45/F2
Cîmpina, Romania 45/H3
Cîmpulung, Romania 45/G3
Cîmpulung Moldovenesc, Romania 45/G2
Cinaruco (riv.), Colombia 126/F4
Cinaruco (riv.), Venezuela 124/D4
Cinca (riv.), Spain 33/G2
Cincinnati, Ark. 202/B1
Cincinnati, Iowa 229/G7
Cincinnati, Ohio 146/K6
Cincinnati, Ohio 284/B9
Cincinnati, Ohio 188/K3
Cincinnatus, N.Y. 276/H5
Cinclare, La. 238/J2
Cinco, W. Va. 312/D6
Cinco Balas (cays), Cuba 158/E3
Cinco Bayou, Fla. 212/B6
Cinco Saltos, Argentina 143/C4
Cinderella, W. Va. 312/B7
Cinderford, England 13/E6
Çine, Turkey 63/B4
Cinebar, Wash. 310/C4
Ciney, Belgium 27/G8
Cinnaminson•, N.J. 273/B3
Cintalapa de Figueroa, Mexico 150/N8
Cinto (mt.), France 28/B6
Cipolletti, Argentina 143/C4
Circeo (cape), Italy 34/D4
Circle, Alaska 196/K1
Circle, Mont. 262/L3
Circle (cliffs), Utah 304/C6

Colombia 353

Cloan, Sask. 181/C3
Cloates (pt.), W. Australia 92/A3
Clode (sound), Newf. 166/D2
Cloe, Pa. 294/E4
Cloghan, Ireland 17/F5
Clogh-Chatsworth, Ireland 17/G6
Clogheen, Ireland 17/F7
Clogher, N. Ireland 17/G3
Clogherhead, Ireland 17/J4
Cloghy, N. Ireland 17/K3
Clonakilty, Ireland 10/B5
Clonakilty, Ireland 17/D8
Clonakilty (bay), Ireland 17/D8
Clonaslee, Ireland 17/F5
Cloncurry, Australia 87/E8
Cloncurry, Queensland 95/B4
Cloncurry, Queensland 88/G4
Cloncurry (riv.), Queensland 95/B4
Clondalkin, Ireland 17/J5
Clonegal, Ireland 17/H6
Clones, Ireland 10/C3
Clones, Ireland 17/G3
Clonfert, Ireland 17/E5
Clonmany, Ireland 17/G1
Clonmel, Ireland 17/F7
Clonmel, Ireland 10/C4
Clonmellon, Ireland 17/H4
Clonroche, Ireland 17/H7
Clontarf, Minn. 255/C5
Clontuskert, Ireland 17/E4
Cloone, Ireland 17/F4
Cloppenburg, Germany 22/B2
Clopton, Ala. 195/G7
Cloquet, Minn. 255/F4
Cloquet (riv.), Minn. 255/F4
Cloridorme, Québec 172/D1
Clorinda, Argentina 143/E2
Closeburn, Scotland 15/E5
Closplint, Ky. 237/P7
Closter, N.J. 273/C1
Clothier, W. Va. 312/C7
Clotho, Minn. 255/C4
Cloud (co.), Kansas 232/E2
Cloud (peak), Wyo. 319/E1
Cloud Chief, Okla. 288/J4
Cloudcroft, N. Mex. 274/D6
Cloudland, Georgia 217/A1
Cloudy (bay), N. Zealand 100/E4
Cloudy, Okla. 288/R6
Cloughjordan, Ireland 17/E6
Cloughmills, N. Ireland 17/J2
Cloutierville, La. 238/E3
Clova, Québec 174/B3
Clover (creek), Oreg. 291/K3
Clover, S.C. 296/E1
Clover, Va. 307/L7
Clover, W. Va. 312/D5
Clover Bar, Alberta 182/D3
Clover Bend, Ark. 202/H2
Clover Bottom, Ky. 237/N5
Cloverdale, Ala. 195/C1
Cloverdale, Calif. 204/B5
Cloverdale, Ind. 227/D5
Cloverdale, Minn. 255/F4
Cloverdale, Ohio 284/B3
Cloverdale, Oreg. 291/D2
Cloverdale, Va. 307/J6
Cloverland, Ind. 227/C6
Cloverland, Wash. 310/H4
Cloverleaf, Manitoba 179/F5
Clover Lick, W. Va. 312/F6
Clover Pass, Alaska 196/N2
Cloverport, Ky. 237/H5
Cloverton, Minn. 255/F4
Clovis, Calif. 204/F7
Clovis, N.Mex. 188/F4
Clovis, N. Mex. 274/F4
Clovulin, Scotland 15/C4
Cloyne, Ireland 17/E8
Cloyne, Ontario 177/G3
Cluanie, Loch (lake), Scotland 15/C3
Club (isl.), Ontario 177/C2
Cluff Lake, Sask. 181/L2
Cluj-Napoca, Romania 45/F2
Cluj-Napoca, Romania 7/G4
Clun, England 10/E4
Clun, England 13/D6
Clune, Pa. 294/D4
Clunes, Victoria 97/B5
Cluny, Alberta 182/D4
Cluny, France 28/F4
Cluses, France 28/G4
Clusone-Fiorine, Italy 34/C2
Cluster Springs, Va. 307/L7
Clute, Texas 303/J9
Clutha (riv.), N. Zealand 100/B6
Clutier, Iowa 229/J4
Clwyd (co.), Wales 13/D4
Clyattville, Georgia 217/F9
Clyde, Alberta 182/D2
Clyde (lake), Alberta 182/E2
Clyde, Canada 4/B13
Clyde (riv.), Dominica 161/F6
Clyde, Kansas 232/E2
Clyde, Mo. 261/C2
Clyde, N.Y. 276/G4
Clyde, N.C. 281/D3
Clyde, N. Dak. 282/N2
Clyde, N.W.T. 162/J1
Clyde (inlet), N.W.T. 162/K1
Clyde (inlet), N.W. Terr. 187/M2
Clyde (riv.), Nova Scotia 168/C5
Clyde, Ohio 284/E3
Clyde (firth), Scotland 15/D5
Clyde (firth), Scotland 10/D3
Clyde (riv.), Scotland 10/E3
Clyde (riv.), Scotland 15/D5
Clyde (riv.), Tasmania 99/D4
Clyde, Texas 303/E5
Clyde (riv.), Vt. 268/C2
Clyde, Wash. 310/G4
Clydebank, Scotland 15/B2
Clydebank, Scotland 10/A1
Clyde Hill, Wash. 310/B2
Clyde Park, Mont. 262/F5
Clyde River, N.W.T. 162/J7
Clyde River, N.W.T. 186/M2
Clyde River, Nova Scotia 168/C5
Clyman, Wis. 317/J9
Clymer, N.Y. 276/A6
Clymer, Pa. 294/E4
Clymers, Ind. 227/E3
Clyo, Georgia 217/K6
Cnoc May (mt.), Scotland 15/C5
Coachella, Calif. 204/J10
Coachella (canal), Calif. 204/K10
Coachford, Ireland 17/D8
Coahoma (co.), Miss. 256/C2
Coahoma, Miss. 256/C2
Coahoma, Texas 303/C5
Coahuila (state), Mexico 150/H3
Coakley, Ky. 237/K6
Coal (creek), Ind. 227/C4
Coal, Mo. 261/E6
Coal (co.), Okla. 288/O5
Coal (pt.), Oreg. 291/C5
Coal (cliffs), Utah 304/C5
Coal (creek), Wash. 310/G3
Coal (riv.), W. Va. 312/C6
Coal Bluff, Ind. 227/C5
Coal Branch, New Bruns. 170/E2
Coalburn, Scotland 15/E5
Coal City, Ill. 222/E2
Coal City, Ind. 227/D6
Coal City, W. Va. 312/D7
Coalcomán de Matamoros, Mexico 150/H7
Coal Creek, Alaska 196/K1
Coal Creek, Colo. 208/J6
Coal Creek, Ind. 227/C4
Coal Creek, New Bruns. 170/E2
Coaldale, Alberta 182/D5
Coaldale, Colo. 208/H6
Coaldale, Nev. 266/D4
Coaldale, Pa. 294/L4
Coaldale (Six Mile Run), Pa. 294/F5
Coalfield, Tenn. 237/N8
Coalfield, Wash. 310/B2
Coal Fork, W. Va. 312/D6
Coalgate, Okla. 288/O5
Coal Grove, Ohio 284/E9
Coal Harbour, Br. Col. 184/D5
Coal Hill, Ark. 202/C3
Coalhurst, Alberta 182/D5
Coaling, Ala. 195/D4
Coalinga, Calif. 204/E7
Coalisland, N. Ireland 17/H2
Coalmont, Br. Col. 184/G5
Coalmont, Colo. 208/F1
Coalmont, Ind. 227/C6
Coalmont, Tenn. 237/K10
Coalport, Pa. 294/E4
Coalridge, Mont. 262/M2
Coal Run, Ky. 237/R5
Coalspur, Alberta 182/B3
Coalton, Ill. 222/D4
Coalton, Ohio 284/E7
Coalton, W. Va. 312/G5
Coal Valley, Alberta 182/B3
Coal Valley, Ill. 222/C2
Coalville, England 13/F5
Coalville, Iowa 229/E4
Coalville, Utah 304/C3
Coalwood, Mont. 262/L5
Coalwood, W. Va. 312/C8
Coambo, Angola 115/C5
Coambo, Angola 102/D5
Coamo, P. Rico 161/D2
Coamo, P. Rico 156/G1
Coamo (res.), P. Rico 161/D3
Coamo (riv.), P. Rico 161/D3
Coari, Brazil 120/C3
Coari, Brazil 132/H9
Coarsegold, Calif. 204/F6
Coast (mts.) 162/C4
Coast (ranges) 188/B2
Coast (mts.), Alaska 196/N1
Coast (mts.), Br. Col. 146/E4
Coast (mts.), Br. Col. 184/D3
Coast (ranges), Calif. 204/D7
Coast (prov.), Kenya 115/G4
Coast (ranges), Oreg. 291/D5
Coast (ranges), U.S. 146/F5
Coast (ranges), Wash. 310/B3
Coast Guard Academy, Conn. 210/G3
Coatbridge, Scotland 10/B1
Coatbridge, Scotland 15/C2
Coatepec, Mexico 150/P1
Coatepeque, Guatemala 154/A3
Coates, Minn. 255/E6
Coatesville, Ind. 227/D5
Coatesville, Pa. 294/L5
Coatetelco, Mexico 150/L2
Coaticook, Québec 172/F4
Coatopa, Ala. 195/B6
Coats, Kansas 232/D4
Coats, N.C. 281/M4
Coats (isl.), N.W.T. 162/H3
Coats (isl.), N.W.T. 146/K3
Coats (isl.), N.W. Terr. 187/K3
Coatsburg, Ill. 222/B3
Coats Land (reg.), Ant. 2/H10
Coats Land (reg.), Ant. 5/B17
Coatsville, Mo. 261/G1
Coatzacoalcos, Mexico 146/J8
Coatzacoalcos, Mexico 150/M7
Coatzingo, Mexico 150/N2
Cobalt, Conn. 210/E2
Cobalt, Idaho 220/D4
Cobalt, Ont. 162/H6
Cobalt, Ontario 177/K5
Cobalt, Ontario 175/D3
Cobalt City, Mo. 261/M7
Cobán, Guatemala 154/B3
Cobar, N. S. Wales 88/H6
Cobar, N.S. Wales 97/C2
Cobargo, N.S. Wales 97/E5
Cobb (co.), Georgia 217/C3
Cobb, Georgia 217/E7
Cobb, Ky. 237/F6
Cobb (riv.), Minn. 255/E7
Cobb (isl.), Va. 307/S6
Cobb, Wis. 317/F10
Cobbadah, N.S. Wales 97/F2
Cobble Hill, Br. Col. 184/K3
Cobble Mountain (res.), Mass. 249/C4
Cobbs Creek, Va. 307/R6
Cobbtown, Georgia 217/H6
Cobden, Ill. 222/D6
Cobden, Minn. 255/D6
Cobden, Ontario 177/H2
Cobden, Victoria 97/B6
Cobequid (bay), Nova Scotia 168/E3
Cóbh, Ireland 10/B5
Cóbh, Ireland 17/E8
Cobham (riv.), Manitoba 179/G1
Cobham (riv.), Ontario 175/A2
Cobija, Bolivia 136/A2
Cobija, Brazil 120/C4
Coble, Tenn. 237/F9
Cobleskill, N.Y. 276/L5
Coboconk, Ontario 177/F3
Cobourg (pen.), North. Terr. 88/E2
Cobourg (pen.), North. Terr. 93/C1
Cobourg, Ontario 177/F4
Cobquecura, Chile 138/D1
Cobram, Victoria 97/C4
Cobre, Nev. 266/G1
Cóbuè, Mozambique 118/F2
Coburg, Germany 22/D3
Coburg, Iowa 229/C7
Coburg (isl.), N.W. Terr. 187/L2
Coburg, Oreg. 291/E3
Coburg, Victoria 88/K7
Coburg, Victoria 97/H5
Coburn, Pa. 294/H4
Coburn, W. Va. 312/F3
Coca, Ecuador 128/D3
Cocachacra, Peru 128/G11
Cocagne, New Bruns. 170/F2
Cocagne (isl.), New Bruns. 170/F2
Cocagne (riv.), New Bruns. 170/F2
Cocagne Cape, New Bruns. 170/F2
Cocama, Peru 128/G8
Cocanada (Kakinada), India 68/E5
Cocani, Bolivia 136/B7
Cocapata, Bolivia 136/B5
Cocentaina, Spain 33/F3
Cochabamba (dept.), Bolivia 136/C5
Cochabamba, Bolivia 120/C4
Cochabamba, Bolivia 136/C5
Cochamó, Chile 138/E3
Coche (isl.), Venezuela 124/F2
Cocheco (riv.), N.H. 268/E5
Cochecton, N.Y. 276/K7
Cochem, Germany 22/B3
Cochenour, Ontario 175/B2
Cochetopa (creek), Colo. 208/F6
Cochimbo, Serra do (mts.), Brazil 132/C5
Cochin, Sask. 181/C2
Cochin-Alleppey, India 68/D6
Cochinos (bay), Cuba 158/D2
Cochise (co.), Ariz. 198/F7
Cochise, Ariz. 198/F6
Cochiti, N. Mex. 274/C3
Cochituate, Mass. 249/A7
Cochituate (lake), Mass. 249/A7
Cochran, Georgia 217/F6
Cochran (co.), Texas 303/B4
Cochrane, Ala. 195/B4
Cochrane, Alberta 182/C4
Cochrane (lake), Chile 138/E7
Cochrane, Cerro (mt.), Chile 138/E7
Cochrane (riv.), Manitoba 179/H2
Cochrane, Ont. 146/K5
Cochrane, Ont. 162/H6
Cochrane (terr. dist.), Ontario 177/J4
Cochrane (terr. dist.), Ontario 175/D2
Cochrane, Ontario 177/K5
Cochrane, Ontario 175/D3
Cochrane (riv.), Sask. 181/N2
Cochrane, Wis. 317/C7
Cochranton, Pa. 294/B2
Cochranville, Pa. 294/L6
Cockburn (chan.), Chile 138/E11
Cockburn (isl.), Ontario 177/A2
Cockburn, S. Australia 94/G5
Cockburn (sound), W. Australia 88/B2
Cockburn Harbour, Turks & Caicos 156/D2
Cockburnspath, Scotland 15/F5
Cocke (co.), Tenn. 237/P9
Cockenoe (isl.), Conn. 210/B4
Cockenzie and Port Seton, Scotland 15/D1
Cockermouth, England 13/D3
Cockermouth, England 10/E3
Cockeysville, Md. 245/M3
Cockrell Hill, Texas 303/G2
Cockrum, Miss. 256/E1
Coclé del Norte, Panama 154/G6
Coco (chan.), Burma 72/B4
Coco (cay), Cuba 158/G1
Coco (riv.), Honduras 154/E3
Coco (chan.), India 68/G6
Coco (riv.), Nicaragua 154/E3
Coco, W. Va. 312/D6
Cocoa, Fla. 212/F3
Cocoa Beach, Fla. 212/F3
Cocobeach, Gabon 115/B3
Cocodrie (lake), La. 238/E5
Cocolamus, Pa. 294/H4
Coconino (co.), Ariz. 198/C3
Coconino (plat.), Ariz. 198/C3
Coconut Creek, Fla. 212/F5
Cocopah Ind. Res., Ariz. 198/A6
Cocorit, Mexico 150/E3
Cocos (isls.), Australia 2/P6
Cocos (isls.), Australia 54/L11
Cocos (isl.), C. Rica 146/K9
Cocos (isl.), Guam 86/K7
Cocos (bay), Trin. & Tob. 161/B10
Cocuy, Sierra Nevada del (mts.), Colombia 126/D4
Cod (cape), Mass. 146/M5
Cod (cape), Mass. 188/N2
Cod (cape), Mass. 249/O4
Cod (isl.), Newf. 166/B2
Codajás, Brazil 120/C3
Codajás, Brazil 132/H9
Coddle (harb.), Nova Scotia 168/G3
Codegua, Chile 138/G4
Codell, Kansas 232/C2
Coden, Ala. 195/B10
Codera (cape), Venezuela 124/F2
Coderre, Sask. 181/E5
Codesa, Alberta 182/B2
Codes Corner, Ontario 177/H3
Codette, Sask. 181/H2
Codfish (isl.), N. Zealand 100/A7
Codigua, Chile 138/F4
Codington (co.), S. Dak. 298/P4
Codó, Brazil 120/E3
Codó, Brazil 132/E4
Codorus, Pa. 294/J6
Codpa, Chile 138/B1
Codrington, Ant. & Bar. 156/G3
Codrington, Barbados 161/B8
Codroipo, Italy 34/D2
Codroy, Newf. 166/C4
Cody, Nebr. 264/C2
Cody, Wyo. 319/D1
Codys, New Bruns. 170/E3
Coe, Ind. 227/C8
Coeburn, Va. 307/D7
Coe Hill, Ontario 177/G3
Coelemu, Chile 138/D1
Coello, Ill. 222/D6
Coen, Queensland 88/G2
Coen, Queensland 95/B2
Coeroeni (riv.), Suriname 131/C4
Coesfeld, Germany 22/B3
Coesse, Ind. 227/G2
Coeur d'Alene, Idaho 220/B2
Coeur d'Alene, Idaho 188/C1
Coeur d'Alene (lake), Idaho 220/B2
Coeur d'Alene (mts.), Idaho 220/C2
Coeur d'Alene (riv.), Idaho 220/B2
Coevorden, Netherlands 27/K3
Coeymans, N.Y. 276/N6
Coffee (co.), Ala. 195/G8
Coffee (co.), Georgia 217/G8
Coffee (co.), Tenn. 237/J9
Coffee Creek, Mont. 262/F3
Coffeen, Ill. 222/D4
Coffee Springs, Ala. 195/G8
Coffeeville, Ala. 195/B7
Coffeeville (dam), Ala. 195/B7
Coffeeville, Miss. 256/E3
Coffey (co.), Kansas 232/G3
Coffey, Mo. 261/E2
Coffeyville, Kans. 188/G3
Coffeyville, Kansas 232/G4
Coffin (bay), S. Australia 94/D6
Coffin Bay (pen.), S. Australia 94/D6
Coffs Harbour, N. S. Wales 88/J6
Coffs Harbour, N.S. Wales 97/G2
Cofield, N.C. 281/R2
Cogan Station, Pa. 294/H3
Cogar, Okla. 288/K4
Cogdell, Georgia 217/G8
Cogealac, Romania 45/J3
Coggon, Iowa 229/L4
Coghinas (riv.), Italy 34/B4
Coglians (Hohe Warte) (mt.), Austria 41/B3
Cognac, France 28/C5
Cogolludo, Spain 33/E2
Cogotí, Chile 138/A8
Cogswell, N. Dak. 282/P7
Cogtong, Philippines 82/E6
Cohagen, Mont. 262/K3
Cohansey (riv.), N.J. 273/C5
Cohasset, Ala. 195/E8
Cohasset•, Mass. 249/F7
Cohasset, Minn. 255/E3
Cohoctah, Mich. 250/F6
Cohocton, N.Y. 276/F5
Cohocton (riv.), N.Y. 276/F6
Cohoe, Alaska 196/B1
Cohoes, N.Y. 276/N5
Cohoni, Bolivia 136/B5
Cohuna, Victoria 97/C4
Cohutta, Georgia 217/C1
Coiba, Isla de (isl.), Panama 154/F7
Coihaique, Chile 138/E6
Coihaique Alto, Chile 138/E6
Coihueco, Chile 138/A11
Coila, Miss. 256/E4
Coill Dubh, Ireland 17/H5
Coimbatore, India 54/J8
Coimbatore, India 68/D6
Coimbra (dist.), Portugal 33/B2
Coimbra, Portugal 7/D4
Coimbra, Portugal 33/B2
Coin, Iowa 229/C7
Coín, Spain 33/D4
Coinco, Chile 138/G5
Coinjock, N.C. 281/S2
Coipasa, Bolivia 136/A6
Coipasa (lake), Bolivia 136/B6
Coipasa (salt dep.), Bolivia 136/A6
Coire, Loch (lake), Scotland 15/D2
Cojata, Peru 128/H10
Cojedes (state), Venezuela 124/D3
Cojedes (riv.), Venezuela 124/D3
Cojimíes, Ecuador 128/B2
Cojoro, Venezuela 124/C2
Cojutepeque, El Salvador 154/C4
Cokato, Minn. 255/D5
Coke (co.), Texas 303/D6
Cokeburg, Pa. 294/B5
Cokedale, Colo. 208/K8
Coker, Ala. 195/C4
Cokercreek, Tenn. 237/N10
Coketon, W. Va. 312/G4
Cokeville, Wyo. 319/B3
Colaba (pt.), India 68/B7
Colac, Victoria 88/G7
Colac, Victoria 97/B6
Colachel, India 68/D7
Colair (lake), India 68/E5
Colamus (riv.), Nebr. 264/E2
Colasay, Peru 128/C5
Colatina, Brazil 120/E4
Colatina, Brazil 132/F7
Colbeck (cape), Ant. 5/B10
Colbert (co.), Ala. 195/C1
Colbert, Georgia 217/F2
Colbert, Okla. 288/O7
Colbert, Wash. 310/H3
Colborne, Ontario 177/G4
Colbún, Chile 138/A11
Colburn, Idaho 220/B1
Colburn, Ind. 227/D3
Colby, Kansas 232/A2
Colby, Wash. 310/A2
Colby, Wis. 317/F6
Colcamar, Peru 128/D6
Colchester, Conn. 210/F2
Colchester•, Conn. 210/F2
Colchester, England 13/H6
Colchester, England 10/G5
Colchester, Ill. 222/C3
Colchester (co.), Nova Scotia 168/E3
Colchester, Ontario 177/B6
Colchester•, Vt. 268/A2
Colcord, Okla. 288/S2
Colcord, W. Va. 312/D7
Cold (bay), Alaska 196/F4
Cold (lake), Alberta 182/E2
Cold (riv.), N.H. 268/C5
Cold Bay, Alaska 196/F3
Cold Brook, N.Y. 276/L4
Coldbrook Station, Nova Scotia 168/D3
Colden, N.Y. 276/C5
Coldingham, Scotland 15/F5
Cold Lake, Alberta 182/E2
Cold Spring, Ky. 237/T2
Cold Spring, Minn. 255/D5
Cold Spring, N.J. 273/D6
Cold Spring, N.Y. 276/N8
Coldspring (head), Nova Scotia 168/E3
Coldspring, Texas 303/J7
Cold Spring Harbor, N.Y. 276/R6
Cold Springs, Okla. 288/J5
Coldstream, Br. Col. 184/H5
Cold Stream (pond), Maine 243/G5
Coldstream, New Bruns. 170/C2
Coldstream, Scotland 10/E3
Coldstream, Scotland 15/F5
Coldstream, Victoria 97/K4
Coldwater, Kansas 232/C4
Coldwater, Mich. 250/D7
Coldwater, Miss. 256/E1
Coldwater (riv.), Miss. 256/D1
Coldwater, Ohio 284/A5
Coldwater, Ontario 177/E3
Coldwater, Tenn. 237/H10
Coldwater (creek), Texas 303/B1
Coldwater, W. Va. 312/E4
Cole (co.), Mo. 261/H6
Cole (harb.), Nova Scotia 168/E4
Cole, Okla. 288/L5
Colebrook•, Conn. 210/C1
Colebrook, N.H. 268/E2
Colebrook•, N.H. 268/E2
Colebrook, Ohio 284/J2
Colebrook, Tasmania 99/D4
Colebrook River (lake), Conn. 210/C1
Cole Camp, Mo. 261/F6
Coleen (riv.), Alaska 196/K1
Colegrove, Pa. 294/F2
Coleharbor, N. Dak. 282/H4
Coleman, Alberta 182/C5
Coleman, Alta. 162/E6
Coleman, Fla. 212/D3
Coleman, Georgia 217/C7
Coleman, Mich. 250/E5
Coleman, Okla. 288/O6
Coleman (riv.), Queensland 95/B2
Coleman (co.), Texas 303/E6
Coleman, Texas 303/E6
Coleman, Wis. 317/L5
Coleman Falls, Va. 307/K6
Colemans Lake, Georgia 217/H5
Çölemerik, Turkey 63/K4
Colerain, N.C. 281/R2
Coleraine, Minn. 255/E3
Coleraine (dist.), N. Ireland 17/H1
Coleraine, N. Ireland 17/H1
Coleraine, N. Ireland 10/C3
Coleraine, Québec 172/F4
Coleraine, Victoria 97/A5
Coleridge, Nebr. 264/G2
Coleridge (lake), N. Zealand 100/C5
Coleridge, N.C. 281/K3
Coles (co.), Ill. 222/E4
Coles, Miss. 256/C8
Coles (pt.), Peru 128/G11
Colesberg, S. Africa 118/D6
Colesburg, Georgia 217/J9
Colesburg, Iowa 229/L3
Colesburg, Ky. 237/K5
Coles Island, New Bruns. 170/E3
Coles Point, Va. 307/P4
Colesville, Md. 245/K4
Colesville, N.J. 273/D1
Coleta, Ill. 222/D2
Coleville, Calif. 204/F5
Coleville, Sask. 181/B4
Colfax, Calif. 204/E4
Colfax, Ill. 222/E3
Colfax, Ind. 227/D4
Colfax, Iowa 229/G5
Colfax, La. 238/E3
Colfax (co.), Nebr. 264/G3
Colfax (co.), N. Mex. 274/E2
Colfax, N. Dak. 282/S7
Colfax, Sask. 181/H6
Colfax, Wash. 310/H4
Colfax, Wis. 317/C6
Colgan, N. Dak. 282/C2
Colgate, N. Dak. 282/P5
Colgate (cape), N.W. Terr. 187/J1
Colgate, Sask. 181/H6
Colgate, Wis. 317/K1
Colhué Huapi (lake), Argentina 143/C6
Co Lieu, Vietnam 72/E3
Colignan, Victoria 97/B4
Colijnsplaat, Netherlands 27/D5
Colima (state), Mexico 150/G7
Colima, Mexico 150/H7
Colina, Chile 138/G3
Colina (riv.), Chile 138/G3
Colinas, Brazil 132/F4
Colinet, Newf. 166/D2
Colington, N.C. 281/T3
Colinton, Alberta 182/D2
Coll, Scotland 15/B2
Coll (isl.), Scotland 15/B4
Coll (isl.), Scotland 10/C2
Collaguasi, Chile 138/B3
Collamer, Ind. 227/F2
Collarenebri, N.S. Wales 97/E1
Collbran, Colo. 208/C4
Colle di Val d'Elsa, Italy 34/C3
College, Alaska 196/J1
College Bridge, New Bruns. 170/F3
College City, Ark. 202/J1
College Corner, Ohio 284/A6
Collegedale, Tenn. 237/M10
College Grove, Tenn. 237/H9
College Heights, Alberta 182/D3
College Hill, Ky. 237/N5
College Hill, Miss. 256/E2
College Mound, Mo. 261/G3
College Park, Georgia 217/K2
College Park, Md. 245/G4
College Place, Wash. 310/G4
College Springs, Iowa 229/C7
College Station, Texas 303/H7
Collegeville, Ind. 227/C3
Collegeville, Minn. 255/D5
Collegeville, Pa. 294/M5
Colle Sestriere, Italy 34/A2
Colleton (co.), S.C. 296/F6
Collett, Ind. 227/H4
Collette, New Bruns. 170/E2
Collettsville, N.C. 281/F3
Colley, Pa. 294/K2
Colleyville, Texas 303/F2
Collie, Australia 87/B9
Collie, N.S. Wales 97/E2
Collie, W. Australia 88/B6
Collie, W. Australia 92/B2
Collier (co.), Fla. 212/E5
Collier (bay), W. Australia 88/C3
Collier (bay), W. Australia 92/C1
Colliers, Newf. 166/D2
Colliers, S.C. 296/C4
Colliers, W. Va. 312/E2
Collierstown, Va. 307/J5
Collierville, Tenn. 237/B10
Colliguay, Chile 138/F3
Collin (co.), Texas 303/H4
Collingdale, Pa. 294/N7
Collingswood, N.J. 273/B3
Collingsworth (co.), Texas 303/D3
Collingwood, N. Zealand 100/D4
Collingwood, Ontario 177/D3
Collingwood, Victoria 97/J5
Collingwood, Victoria 88/L7
Collingwood Corner, Nova Scotia 168/E3
Collins, Ark. 202/G6
Collins, Georgia 217/H6
Collins, Iowa 229/G5
Collins, Miss. 256/E7
Collins, Mo. 261/E7
Collins, Mont. 262/E3
Collins, N.Y. 276/C6
Collins (head), Norfolk I. 88/L6
Collins, Ohio 284/E3
Collins, Ontario 177/G4
Collins (riv.), Tenn. 237/K9
Collins Bay, Ontario 177/H3
Collins Bay, Sask. 181/M2
Collins Center, N.Y. 276/C6
Collinston, La. 238/G1
Collinston, Utah 304/B2
Collinsville, Ala. 195/G2
Collinsville, Calif. 204/L1
Collinsville, Conn. 210/D1
Collinsville, Ill. 222/B2
Collinsville, Mass. 249/J2
Collinsville, Miss. 256/G6
Collinsville, Ohio 284/A6
Collinsville, Okla. 288/P2
Collinsville, Queensland 88/H4
Collinsville, Queensland 95/C4
Collinsville, Va. 307/J7
Collinwood, Tenn. 237/F10
Collipulli, Chile 138/E2
Collirene, Ala. 195/E6
Collis, Minn. 255/B5
Collison, Ill. 222/F3
Collista, Ky. 237/R5
Collombey-Muraz, Switzerland 39/C4
Collon, Ireland 17/J4
Collon (mt.), Switzerland 39/D5
Collonge-Bellerive, Switzerland 39/B4
Collooney, Ireland 17/E3
Collpa, Bolivia 136/C6
Collyer, Kansas 232/B2
Colma, Calif. 204/J2
Colman, S. Dak. 298/R6
Colmar, France 28/G3
Colmar, Pa. 294/M5
Colmar Manor, Md. 245/F4
Colmenar, Spain 33/D4
Colmenar de Oreja, Spain 33/G5
Colmenar Viejo, Spain 33/F4
Colmesneil, Texas 303/K7
Colmonell, Scotland 15/D5
Colne, England 10/G1
Colne, England 13/H1
Colne (riv.), England 10/B5
Colne (riv.), England 13/G8
Colne Valley, England 10/G2
Colne Valley, England 13/J2
Colo, Iowa 229/G4
Colo (riv.), N.S. Wales 97/F3
Cologne, Germany 7/E3
Cologne, Germany 22/B3
Cologne, Minn. 255/E6
Cologne, N.J. 273/D4
Coloma, Calif. 204/D5
Coloma, Mich. 250/C6
Coloma, Wis. 317/H7
Colombes, France 28/A1
Colombia 2/F5
Colombia 120/B2

354 Colombia

COLOMBIA 126
Colombia, Colombia 126/C6
Colombo (cap.), Sri Lanka 54/J9
Colombo (cap.), Sri Lanka 2/N5
Colombo (cap.), Sri Lanka 68/D7
Colome, S. Dak. 298/K7
Colón, Buenos Aires, Argentina 143/F6
Colón, Entre Ríos, Argentina 143/G6
Colón, Colombia 120/B1
Colón, Colombia 126/B7
Colón, Cuba 158/D1
Colón, Cuba 156/B2
Colón, Archipiélago de (terr.), Ecuador 128/C8
Colón (mts.), Honduras 154/E3
Colón, Mexico 150/K6
Colon, Mich. 250/D7
Colon, Nebr. 264/H3
Colón, Pan. 146/K9
Colón, Panama 154/H6
Colón, Isla de (isl.), Panama 154/G6
Colón, Lavalleja, Uruguay 145/E4
Colón, Montevideo, Uruguay 145/B7
Colón, Venezuela 124/E6
Colona, Colo. 208/D6
Colona, Ill. 222/C2
Colonarie, St. Vin. & Grens. 161/A9
Colonarie (pt.), St. Vin. & Grens. 161/A9
Colonel Light Gardens, S. Australia 88/D8
Colonel Light Gardens, S. Australia 94/A8
Colonia, N.J. 273/E2
Colonia (dept.), Uruguay 145/B5
Colonia, Uruguay 145/B5
Colonia Agraciada, Uruguay 145/A4
Colonia Arrué, Uruguay 145/B5
Colonia Artigas, Uruguay 145/B1
Colonia Concordia, Uruguay 145/A4
Colonia Elisa, Argentina 143/E2
Colonia Itacumbú, Uruguay 145/B1
Colonia Josefa, Argentina 143/D4
Colonia Las Heras, Argentina 143/C6
Colonia Lavalleja, Uruguay 145/C2
Colonial Beach, Va. 307/P4
Colonial Heights, Tenn. 237/R8
Colonial Heights (I.C.), Va. 307/O6
Colonial Nat'l Hist. Park, Va. 307/P6
Colonia Neuland, Paraguay 144/B3
Colonia Palma, Uruguay 145/B1
Colonia Pte. Stroessner, Paraguay 144/D3
Colonia Rossel y Rius, Uruguay 145/D4
Colonias, N. Mex. 274/E3
Colonia San Alfredo, Paraguay 144/D3
Colonia Sgto. José E. López, Paraguay 144/D3
Colonia Valdense, Uruguay 145/B5
Colonia Yby Yu, Paraguay 144/E3
Colonie, N.Y. 276/N5
Colonne (cape), Italy 34/F5
Colonsay, Sask. 181/F4
Colonsay (isl.), Scotland 10/C2
Colonsay (isl.), Scotland 15/B4
Colony, Kansas 232/G3
Colony, Mo. 261/H2
Colony, Okla. 288/J4
Colony, Wyo. 319/H1
Colora, Md. 245/O2
Colorada (lag.), Bolivia 136/A8
Colorado 188/E3
COLORADO 208
Colorado (riv.) 188/D4
Colorado (riv.), Argentina 2/F5
Colorado (riv.), Argentina 120/C6
Colorado (riv.), Argentina 143/D4
Colorado (riv.), Ariz. 198/A5
Colorado (riv.), Calif. 204/L8
Colorado (riv.), Colo. 208/A5
Colorado (riv.), Mexico 150/B1
Colorado, Arroyo (riv.), N. Mex. 274/B4
Colorado (co.), Texas 303/H8
Colorado (riv.), Texas 188/G4
Colorado (riv.), Texas 146/H6
Colorado (riv.), Texas 303/F7
Colorado (state), U.S. 146/H6
Colorado (riv.), U.S. 146/G6
Colorado (riv.), U.S. 2/D4
Colorado (riv.), Utah 304/E5
Colorado City, Ariz. 198/B2
Colorado City, Colo. 208/K6
Colorado City, Texas 303/C5
Colorado Nat'l Mon., Colo. 208/B4
Colorado River Aqueduct, Calif. 204/K10
Colorado River Ind. Res., Ariz. 198/A5
Colorado River Ind. Res., Calif. 204/L10
Colorados, Los (arch.), Cuba 158/A1
Colorado Springs, Colo. 146/H6
Colorado Springs, Colo. 188/F3
Colorado Springs, Colo. 208/K5
Colored Hill, W. Va. 312/D8
Colotlán, Mexico 150/H5
Colp, Ill. 222/D6
Colpoy (bay), Ontario 177/C3
Colpoys Bay, Ontario 177/C3
Colquechaca, Bolivia 136/B6
Colquiri, Bolivia 136/B5
Colquitt (co.), Georgia 217/E8
Colquitt, Georgia 217/C8
Colrain•, Mass. 249/D2
Colson, Ky. 237/R6
Colstrip, Mont. 262/K5
Colt, Ark. 202/J3
Coltauco, Chile 138/F5
Colton, Calif. 204/E10
Colton, N.Y. 276/L1
Colton, Ohio 284/C3
Colton, Oreg. 291/B3
Colton, S. Dak. 298/P6
Colton, Utah 304/C4
Colton, Wash. 310/H4
Coltons Point, Md. 245/M8
Colts Neck, N.J. 273/E3
Coluene (riv.), Brazil 120/D4
Columbia (riv.) 188/B1
Columbia, Ala. 195/H8
Columbia (glac.), Alaska 196/C1
Columbia (mt.), Alberta 182/B3
Columbia (co.), Ark. 202/D7
Columbia (lake), Br. Col. 184/K5
Columbia (mt.), Br. Col. 184/J4
Columbia (riv.), Br. Col. 184/H4
Columbia, Calif. 204/E5
Columbia (cape), Canada 4/A13
Columbia•, Conn. 210/F2
Columbia (co.), Fla. 212/D1
Columbia, Fla. 212/D1
Columbia (co.), Georgia 217/H3
Columbia, Ill. 222/C5
Columbia, Iowa 229/G6
Columbia, Ky. 237/L6
Columbia, La. 238/F2
Columbia•, Maine 243/H6
Columbia, Md. 245/L4
Columbia, Miss. 256/E8
Columbia, Mo. 261/H5
Columbia, Mo. 188/H3
Columbia, N.J. 273/C2
Columbia (co.), N.Y. 276/N6
Columbia, N.C. 281/S3
Columbia (cape), N.W.T. 162/N3
Columbia (cape), N.W. Terr. 187/M1
Columbia (co.), Oreg. 291/D2
Columbia (riv.), Oreg. 291/G2
Columbia (co.), Pa. 294/K3
Columbia, Pa. 294/K5
Columbia (cap.), S.C. 146/K6
Columbia (cap.), S.C. 188/K4
Columbia (cap.), S.C. 296/F4
Columbia, S. Dak. 298/N2
Columbia, Tenn. 188/J3
Columbia, Tenn. 237/G9
Columbia (riv.), U.S. 146/F5
Columbia, Utah 304/D4
Columbia, Va. 307/M5
Columbia (co.), Wash. 310/H4
Columbia (riv.), Wash. 310/B4
Columbia (co.), Wis. 317/H9
Columbia City, Ind. 227/G2
Columbia City, Oreg. 291/E2
Columbia Falls•, Maine 243/H6
Columbia Falls, Mont. 262/B2
Columbia Furnace, Va. 307/L3
Columbia Heights, Minn. 255/G5
Columbia Heights, Wash. 310/C4
Columbiana, Ala. 195/E4
Columbiana (co.), Ohio 284/J4
Columbiana, Ohio 284/J4
Columbia Reach (riv.), Br. Col. 184/J4
Columbia Road (res.), S. Dak. 298/N2
Columbia Station, Ohio 284/G10
Columbiaville, Mich. 250/F5
Columbine, Colo. 208/E1
Columbretes (isls.), Spain 33/G3
Columbus (dam), 256/H3
Columbus, Ark. 202/C6
Columbus, Ga. 188/K4
Columbus, Ga. 146/K6
Columbus, Georgia 217/C6
Columbus, Ill. 222/B4
Columbus, Ind. 227/E6
Columbus, Kansas 232/H4
Columbus, Ky. 237/C7
Columbus, Miss. 188/J4
Columbus, Miss. 256/H3
Columbus, Mont. 262/G5
Columbus, Nebr. 264/G3
Columbus, N.J. 273/D3
Columbus, N. Mex. 274/B7
Columbus (co.), N.C. 281/M6
Columbus, N.C. 281/E4
Columbus, N. Dak. 282/E2
Columbus (cap.), Ohio 188/K3
Columbus (cap.), Ohio 146/K6
Columbus (cap.), Ohio 284/E6
Columbus, Pa. 294/C2
Columbus, Texas 303/H8
Columbus, Wis. 317/H9
Columbus A.F.B., Miss. 256/H3
Columbus City, Iowa 229/L6
Columbus Grove, Ohio 284/B4
Columbus Junction, Iowa 229/L6
Columbus Salt (marsh), Nev. 266/C4
Colusa (co.), Calif. 204/C4
Colusa, Calif. 204/C4
Colusa, Ill. 222/B3
Colver, Pa. 294/E4
Colville (riv.), Alaska 188/C5
Colville (riv.), Alaska 196/G1
Colville (cape), N. Zealand 100/E2
Colville (bay), N.W. Terr. 187/K3
Colville (lake), N.W. Terr. 187/F3
Colville, Wash. 310/H2
Colville (riv.), Wash. 310/H2
Colville Ind. Res., Wash. 310/G2
Colville Lake, N.W. Terr. 187/F3
Colwell, Iowa 229/H2
Colwich, Kansas 232/E4
Colwyn, Pa. 294/N7
Colwyn Bay, Wales 10/E4
Colwyn Bay, Wales 13/D4
Comacchio, Italy 34/D2
Comai, China 77/D6
Comal (co.), Texas 303/F8
Comala, Mexico 150/H7
Comalapa, Guatemala 154/B3
Comalapa, Nicaragua 154/E4
Comalcalco, Mexico 150/N7
Comanche (co.), Kansas 232/C4
Comanche, Mont. 262/H4
Comanche (co.), Okla. 288/K5
Comanche, Okla. 288/L6
Comanche (co.), Texas 303/F5
Comanche, Texas 303/F6
Comandante Fontana, Argentina 143/D2
Comandante Luis Piedrabuena, Argentina 143/C6
Comaneşti, Romania 45/H2
Comarapa, Bolivia 136/C5
Comayagua, Honduras 154/D3
Combahee (riv.), S.C. 296/F6
Combarbalá, Chile 138/A8
Comber, N. Ireland 17/K2
Comber, Ontario 177/B5
Combermere (bay), Burma 72/B3
Combermere, Ontario 177/G2
Combine, Texas 303/H3
Combined Locks, Wis. 317/K7
Comblain-au-Pont, Belgium 27/G8
Combourg, France 28/C3
Comboyne, N.S. Wales 97/G2
Combs, Ark. 202/C2
Combs, Ky. 237/P6
Comb Wash (creek), Utah 304/E6
Comeauville, Nova Scotia 168/B4
Come By Chance, Newf. 166/C2
Come-by-Chance, N.S. Wales 97/E2
Comendador, Dom. Rep. 158/C6
Comer, Ala. 195/H6
Comer, Georgia 217/F2
Comeragh (mts.), Ireland 17/F7
Comerford (dam), N.H. 268/D3
Comerford (dam), Vt. 268/D3
Comerío, P. Rico 161/D2
Comet (riv.), Queensland 88/H4
Comet (riv.), Queensland 95/D5
Comfort, N.C. 281/O5
Comfort (cape), N.W. Terr. 187/K3
Comfort, Texas 303/F7
Comfrey, Minn. 255/D6
Comilla, Bangladesh 68/G4
Comines, Belgium 27/B7
Comino (isl.), Malta 34/E7
Comins, Mich. 250/E4
Comiso, Italy 34/E6
Comitán de Domínguez, Mexico 150/O8
Comite, La. 238/K1
Commack, N.Y. 276/O9
Commentry, France 28/E4
Commerce, Calif. 204/C10
Commerce, Georgia 217/E2
Commerce, Mo. 261/O8
Commerce, Okla. 288/R1
Commerce, Texas 303/J4
Commerce City, Colo. 208/K3
Commercial Point, Ohio 284/E6
Commercy, France 28/F3
Commewijne (dist.), Suriname 131/D3
Commewijne (riv.), Suriname 131/D3
Commiskey, Ind. 227/F7
Commissaires (lake), Québec 172/E1
Commissioner (isl.), Manitoba 179/E2
Committee (bay), N.W.T. 162/H2
Committee (bay), N.W. Terr. 187/K3
Commodore, Pa. 294/D4
Commodore (reef), Philippines 85/F4
Commonwealth, Wis. 317/K4
Communism (mt.), U.S.S.R. 54/J6
Communism (peak), U.S.S.R. 48/H6
Como, Colo. 208/H4
Como (prov.), Italy 34/B2
Como, Italy 7/E4
Como, Italy 34/B2
Como (lake), Italy 34/B1
Como, La. 238/G2
Como, Miss. 256/E1
Como, N.C. 281/P1
Como, Tenn. 237/E8
Como, Texas 303/J4
Como, Wis. 317/K10
Comodoro Rivadavia, Argentina 143/C6
Comodoro Rivadavia, Argentina 120/C7
Comoé (riv.), Ivory Coast 106/D7
Comoé (riv.), Burkina Faso 106/D7
Comorin (cape), India 54/J9
Comorin (cape), India 2/N5
Comorin (cape), India 68/D7
Comoros 2/M6
Comoros 102/G6
COMOROS 118/G2
Comox, Br. Col. 184/H2
Compañero, Arroyo (creek), N. Mex. 274/B2
Compass Lake, Fla. 212/D6
Compeer, Alberta 182/E4
Compiègne, France 28/E3
Compostela, Mexico 150/G6
Comprida (isl.), Brazil 135/C4
Comptche, Calif. 204/B4
Compton, Calif. 204/C11
Compton, Ill. 222/D2
Compton, Md. 245/M7
Compton (co.), Québec 172/F4
Compton, Québec 172/F4
Comrie, Scotland 15/E4
Comstock, Mich. 250/D6
Comstock, Minn. 255/B4
Comstock, Nebr. 264/E3
Comstock, N.Y. 276/O4
Comstock, Texas 303/C8
Comstock, Wis. 317/C5
Comstocks Bridge, Conn. 210/F2
Comté (riv.), Fr. Guiana 131/E3
Comunidad, Venezuela 124/E6
Cona, China 77/D6
Conaica, Peru 128/E9
Conakry (cap.), Guinea 102/A4
Conanicut (isl.), R.I. 249/J6
Conara Junction, Tasmania 99/D3
Conargo, N.S. Wales 97/C4
Conasauga, Tenn. 237/M10
Conasauga (riv.), Tenn. 237/M11
Concarneau, France 28/A4
Conceição da Barra, Brazil 132/G7
Conceição do Araguaia, Brazil 132/D5
Conceição do Araguaia, Brazil 120/D3
Concepción, Corrientes, Argentina 143/E2
Concepción, Tucumán, Argentina 143/C2
Concepción, El Beni, Bolivia 136/B2
Concepción, Santa Cruz, Bolivia 136/D5
Concepción (lag.), Bolivia 136/E5
Concepción, Chile 138/D1
Concepción, Chile 120/B6
Concepción (chan.), Chile 138/D9
Concepción (bay), Mexico 150/D3
Concepción, Paraguay 144/D3
Concepción, Paraguay 144/D3
Concepción, Paraguay 120/D5
Concepción, Peru 128/E8
Concepcion, Texas 303/F10
Concepción de la Sierra, Argentina 143/E2
Concepción del Oro, Mexico 150/J4
Concepción del Uruguay, Argentina 143/G6
Concepción de María, Honduras 154/D4
Conception (pt.), Calif. 188/B4
Conception (pt.), Calif. 204/E9
Conception (bay), Newf. 166/D2
Conception Harbour, Newf. 166/D2
Conception Junction, Mo. 261/C2
Conchas (res.), N. Mex. 188/F3
Conchas (dam), N. Mex. 274/E3
Conchas (lake), N. Mex. 274/E3
Conchas (riv.), N. Mex. 274/E3
Conchas Dam, N. Mex. 274/E3
Conche, Newf. 166/C3
Conchi, Chile 138/B3
Conchillas, Uruguay 145/B5
Conchi Viejo, Chile 138/B3
Concho, Ariz. 198/F4
Concho, Okla. 288/L3
Concho (co.), Texas 303/E6
Conchos (riv.), Mexico 146/H7
Conchos (riv.), Mexico 150/G2
Concise, Switzerland 39/C3
Concón, Chile 138/F2
Conconully, Wash. 310/F2
Concord, Ark. 202/G2
Concord, Calif. 204/K1
Concord, Del. 245/R6
Concord, Fla. 212/B1
Concord, Georgia 217/D4
Concord, Ill. 222/C4
Concord, Ky. 237/P3
Concord•, Mass. 249/B6
Concord (riv.), Mass. 249/J2
Concord, Mich. 250/E6
Concord, Mo. 261/P4
Concord, Nebr. 264/H2
Concord (cap.), N.H. 146/L5
Concord (cap.), N.H. 188/M2
Concord (cap.), N.H. 268/D5
Concord, N.S. Wales 88/K4
Concord, N.S. Wales 97/J3
Concord, N.C. 281/H4
Concord, Pa. 294/G5
Concord, Tenn. 237/N9
Concord•, Vt. 268/D3
Concord, Va. 307/K6
Concord, Wis. 317/H1
Concordia, Argentina 143/G5
Concordia, Argentina 120/D6
Concórdia, Brazil 132/D9
Concordia, Honduras 154/D3
Concordia, Kansas 232/E2
Concordia, Ky. 237/J4
Concordia (par.), La. 238/G4
Concordia, Mexico 150/G5
Concordia, Mo. 261/E5
Concordia, Peru 128/E5
Concordville, Pa. 294/M6
Concrete, N. Dak. 282/P2
Concrete, Wash. 310/D2
Con Cuong, Vietnam 72/E3
Conda, Idaho 220/G7
Condado, Cuba 158/E2
Condamine, Queensland 88/H5
Condamine (riv.), Queensland 95/D5
Condar, Colombia 126/D8
Conde, Brazil 132/G5
Conde, S. Dak. 298/N3
Condega, Nicaragua 154/D4
Condit, Ohio 284/E5
Condo, Bolivia 136/B6
Condobolin, N.S. Wales 97/D3
Condobolin, N. S. Wales 88/H6
Condom, France 28/D6
Condon, Mont. 262/C3
Condon, Oreg. 291/G2
Condor, Alberta 182/C3
Cóndor, Cordillera del (range), Ecuador 128/C5
Cóndor, Cordillera del (range), Peru 128/C5
Condoto, Colombia 126/B5
Cone, Texas 303/C4
Conecuh (co.), Ala. 195/E8
Conecuh (riv.), Ala. 195/D8
Conegliano, Italy 34/D2
Conehatta, Miss. 256/F6
Conejos (co.), Colo. 208/G8
Conejos, Colo. 208/G8
Conejos (peak), Colo. 208/G8
Conejos (riv.), Colo. 208/G8
Conemaugh (riv.), Pa. 294/D5
Conemaugh River (lake), Pa. 294/D4
Conestee, S.C. 296/C2
Conestoga, Pa. 294/K6
Conesus, N.Y. 276/E5
Conesus (lake), N.Y. 276/E5
Conesville, Iowa 229/L6
Conesville, Ohio 284/G5
Conetoe, N.C. 281/O3
Conewango, N.Y. 276/C6
Conewango (creek), N.Y. 276/B6
Conewango (creek), Pa. 294/D1
Confidence, Iowa 229/G7
Confluence, Ky. 237/P6
Confluence, Pa. 294/D6
Confolens, France 28/D4
Confusion (range), Utah 304/A4
Confuso (riv.), Paraguay 144/C4
Cong, Ireland 17/C4
Congamond (lakes), Conn. 210/E1
Congamond (lakes), Mass. 249/D4
Congaree (riv.), S.C. 296/F4
Congaree Nat'l Mon., S.C. 296/F4
Conger, Minn. 255/E7
Conger (range), N.W. Terr. 187/K1
Congerville, Ill. 222/D3
Conghua, China 77/H7
Congleton, England 13/H2
Congo 2/K6
Congo 102/D5
CONGO 115/C3
Congo (riv.) 102/D5
Congo (riv.) 2/L5
Congo (riv.), Angola 115/C4
Congo (riv.), Congo 115/C4
Congo, Ohio 284/F6
Congo (riv.), Zaire 115/C4
Congonhas, Brazil 135/E2
Congress, Ariz. 198/C4
Congress, Ohio 284/F4
Congress, Sask. 181/E6
Congress Heights, D.C. 245/F5
Cónico, Cerro (mt.), Argentina 143/B5
Cónico, Cerro (mt.), Chile 138/E4
Conimicut, R.I. 249/J6
Coningsby, England 13/G4
Coniston, North. Terr. 93/C7
Conjuror (bay), N.W. Terr. 187/G3
Conklin, Alberta 182/E2
Conklin, Mich. 250/D5
Conley, Georgia 217/K2
Conn, Lough (lake), Ireland 10/B3
Conn (lake), Ireland 17/C3
Conn (lake), N.W. Terr. 187/L2
Connacht (prov.), Ireland 17/C4
Connacht (trad. prov.), Ireland 17
Connah's Quay, Wales 13/G2
Connaught Heights, Sask. 181/G3
Conneaut, Ohio 284/J2
Conneaut Lake, Pa. 294/B2
Conneaut Lake Park, Pa. 294/B2
Conneautville, Pa. 294/A2
Connecticut 188/M2
CONNECTICUT 210
Connecticut (riv.) 188/M2
Connecticut (riv.), Conn. 210/E2
Connecticut (riv.), Mass. 249/D2
Connecticut (riv.), N.H. 268/B6
Connecticut (state), U.S. 146/L5
Connecticut (riv.), Vt. 268/C4
Connel, Scotland 15/C4
Connell, New Bruns. 170/C2
Connell, Wash. 310/G4
Connell Creek, Sask. 181/H2
Connellsville, Pa. 294/C5
Connellys Springs, N.C. 281/F3
Connelsville, Mo. 261/G2
Connemara (dist.), Ireland 17/B5
Conner, Mont. 262/B5
Conner (mt.), North. Terr. 93/B8
Connersville, Ind. 227/G5
Connerville, Okla. 288/N6
Connétable (isls.), Fr. Guiana 131/F3
Connoquenessing, Pa. 294/B4
Connors, New Bruns. 170/B1
Conoble, N.S. Wales 97/C3
Conococheague (creek), Md. 245/G1
Cononbridge, Scotland 15/D3
Conover, N.C. 281/G3
Conover, Ohio 284/B5
Conover, Wis. 317/H3
Conowingo, Md. 245/O2
Conowingo (dam), Md. 245/O2
Conquerall Bank, Nova Scotia 168/D4
Conquest, Sask. 181/D4
Conquista, Bolivia 136/B2
Conrad, Alberta 182/D5
Conrad, Iowa 229/H4
Conrad, Mont. 262/D2
Conrad, Pa. 294/G2
Conran, Mo. 261/N10
Conrath, Wis. 317/E5
Conroe, Texas 303/J7
Conroy, Iowa 229/J5
Consecon, Ontario 177/G3
Conselheiro Lafaiete, Brazil 135/E2
Conselheiro Lafaiete, Brazil 132/E8
Consett, England 13/H3
Conshohocken, Pa. 294/M5
Consolación del Norte, Cuba 158/B1
Consolación del Sur, Cuba 158/B2
Consolación del Sur, Cuba 156/A2
Consort, Alberta 182/E3
Constable, N.Y. 276/M1
Constableville, N.Y. 276/J3
Constance (lake), Austria 41/A3
Constance (lake), Germany 22/C5
Constance, Ky. 237/R2
Constance, Sask. 181/F6
Constance (lake), Switzerland 39/H1
Constance (mt.), Wash. 310/B3
Constancia, Uruguay 145/B3
Constant, Morne (hill), Guadeloupe 161/B7
Constanţa, Romania 7/G4
Constanţa, Romania 45/J3
Constantia, N.Y. 276/H4
Constantia, S. Africa 118/E6
Constantina, Spain 33/D4
Constantine (cape), Alaska 196/G3
Constantine, Algeria 102/C1
Constantine, Algeria 106/F1
Constantine, Mich. 250/D7
Constanza, Argentina 143/G6
Constanza, Dom. Rep. 158/D6
Constitución, Chile 138/A11
Constitución, Uruguay 145/A2
Constitution, Georgia 217/K2
Constitution, Ohio 284/G7
Consuegra, Spain 33/E3
Consul, Ala. 195/C6
Consul, Sask. 181/B6
Contact, Nev. 266/G1
Contamana, Peru 128/E6
Contas (riv.), Brazil 132/F6
Contentnea (creek), N.C. 281/N3
Conthey, Switzerland 39/D4
Continental, Ariz. 198/D7
Continental, Ohio 284/B3
Continental (peak), Wyo. 319/D3
Contla, Mexico 150/N1
Contoocook, N.H. 268/D5
Contoocook (riv.), N.H. 268/D6
Contra Costa (co.), Calif. 204/D6
Contramaestre, Cuba 158/G3
Contratación, Colombia 126/D4
Contrecoeur, Québec 172/D4
Contreras (isl.), Chile 138/D9
Contreras (isls.), Panama 154/F7
Controller (bay), Alaska 196/J3
Contulmo, Chile 138/D2
Contumazá, Peru 128/C6
Contwoyto (lake), N.W.T. 162/E2
Contwoyto (lake), N.W. Terr. 187/H3
Convención, Colombia 126/D3
Convent, La. 238/L3
Convent Station, N.J. 273/E2
Conversano, Italy 34/F4
Converse (hill), Conn. 210/F1
Converse, Ind. 227/F3
Converse, La. 238/C3
Converse, S.C. 296/D2
Converse, Texas 303/K11
Converse (co.), Wyo. 319/G3
Convoy, Ireland 17/F2
Convoy, Ohio 284/A4
Conway (co.), Ark. 202/E3
Conway, Ark. 202/F3
Conway (lake), Ark. 202/F3
Conway, Iowa 229/D7
Conway, Kansas 232/E3
Conway, Ky. 237/N6
Conway•, Mass. 249/D2
Conway, Mich. 250/E3
Conway, Miss. 256/E5
Conway, Mo. 261/G7
Conway, N.H. 268/E4
Conway•, N.H. 268/E4
Conway (lake), N.H. 268/E4
Conway, N.C. 281/P2
Conway, N. Dak. 282/P3
Conway, Nova Scotia 168/C4
Conway, Pa. 294/B4
Conway, S.C. 296/J4
Conway, Texas 303/C2
Conway, Wash. 310/C2
Conway Springs, Kansas 232/E4
Conwy, Wales 10/E4
Conwy, Wales 13/D4
Conwy (bay), Wales 13/C4
Conyers, Georgia 217/D3
Conyngham, Pa. 294/K3
Coober Pedy, S. Australia 88/E5
Coober Pedy, S. Australia 94/D3
Cooch Behar, India 68/F3
Coogee, N.S. Wales 97/K3
Cook (isls.) 87/K7
Cook (inlet), Alaska 196/B1
Cook (mt.), Alaska 196/K2
Cook (cape), Br. Col. 184/C5
Cook (bay), Chile 138/E11
Cook (co.), Georgia 217/F8
Cook (co.), Ill. 222/F2
Cook (co.), Minn. 255/H3
Cook, Minn. 255/F3
Cook, Nebr. 264/H4
Cook (isls.), N. Zealand 2/B6
Cook (mt.), N. Zealand 87/G10
Cook (mt.), N. Zealand 100/C5
Cook (str.), N. Zealand 87/H10
Cook (str.), N. Zealand 100/E4
Cook, S. Australia 88/E6
Cook, S. Australia 94/B4
Cook (inlet), U.S. 4/D17
Cook (pt.), Victoria 97/H5
Cook (pt.), Victoria 88/K7
Cook, Wash. 310/D5
Cooke (co.), Texas 303/G4
Cooke City, Mont. 262/G5
Cookes (range), N. Mex. 274/B6
Cookeville, Tenn. 237/L8
Cooking Lake, Alberta 182/D3
Cook's (Paopao) (bay), Fr. Poly. 86/S12
Cooks, Mich. 250/C3
Cooksburg, Pa. 294/D3
Cooks Falls, N.Y. 276/K7
Cook's Harbour, Newf. 166/C3
Cookshire, Québec 172/F4
Cooks Mills, Ill. 222/E4
Cook Station, Mo. 261/K7
Cookstown, N.J. 273/D3
Cookstown (dist.), N. Ireland 17/H2
Cookstown, N. Ireland 10/C3
Cookstown, N. Ireland 17/H2
Cookstown, Ontario 177/E3
Cooksville, Ill. 222/E3
Cooksville, Md. 245/K3
Cooksville, Miss. 256/H5
Cooktown, Australia 87/E7
Cooktown, Queensland 95/C2
Cooktown, Queensland 88/H3
Cool, Texas 303/G5
Coolabah, N.S. Wales 97/D2
Cooladdi, Queensland 95/C5
Cooladdi, Queensland 88/H5
Coolah, N.S. Wales 97/E2
Coolamon, N.S. Wales 97/D4
Coolaney, Ireland 17/D3
Coolatai, N.S. Wales 97/F1
Cooleemee, N.C. 281/H3
Coolgardie, W. Australia 88/C6
Coolgardie, W. Australia 92/C5
Coolgreany, Ireland 17/J6
Coolibah, North. Terr. 93/B3
Coolidge, Ariz. 198/D6
Coolidge (dam), Ariz. 198/E5
Coolidge, Georgia 217/E8
Coolidge, Kansas 232/A3
Coolidge, Texas 303/H6
Coolidge Dam, Ariz. 198/E5
Coolin, Idaho 220/B1
Cool Spring, Del. 245/T6
Cool Valley, Mo. 261/P2
Coolville, Ohio 284/G7
Cooma, N.S. Wales 88/H7
Cooma, N.S. Wales 97/E5
Coombs, Br. Col. 184/H3
Coonabarabran, N.S. Wales 97/E2
Coonamble, N.S. Wales 88/H6
Coonamble, N.S. Wales 97/E2
Coondapoor, India 68/C6
Coon Rapids, Iowa 229/D5
Coon Rapids, Minn. 255/G5
Coon Valley, Wis. 317/E8

Coventry 355

Cooper, Ala. 195/E5
Cooper (pt.), Calif. 204/D7
Cooper, Iowa 229/E5
Cooper, Ky. 237/M7
Cooper, Maine 243/H6
Cooper•, Maine 243/H6
Cooper (co.), Mo. 261/G5
Cooper (riv.), N.J. 273/B3
Cooper, S.C. 296/H4
Cooper (riv.), S.C. 296/H6
Cooper, Texas 303/J4
Cooper (lake), Wyo. 319/G4
Co-Operative, Ky. 237/M7
Cooper City, Fla. 212/B4
Cooperdale, Ohio 284/F5
Cooper Landing, Alaska 196/C1
Coopers (Barcoo) (creek), Queensland 95/B5
Coopers (Barcoo) (creek), S. Australia 88/G5
Coopers (Barcoo) (creek), S. Australia 94/F3
Coopersburg, Pa. 294/M5
Coopers Mills, Maine 243/E7
Coopers Plains, N.Y. 276/F6
Coopers Plains, Queensland 95/D3
Coopers Plains, Queensland 88/K3
Cooperstown, N.Y. 276/L5
Cooperstown, N. Dak. 282/O5
Cooperstown, Pa. 294/C2
Coopersville, Ky. 237/M7
Coopersville, Mich. 250/C5
Cooperton, Okla. 288/J5
Coorabie, S. Australia 88/E6
Coorabie, S. Australia 94/B4
Coorong, The (lag.), S. Australia 94/F6
Coorow, W. Australia 92/B5
Coos (co.), N.H. 268/E2
Coos (co.), Oreg. 291/C4
Coos (riv.), Oreg. 291/D4
Coosa (co.), Ala. 195/F5
Coosa (riv.), Ala. 195/F4
Coosa, Georgia 217/B2
Coosa (riv.), Georgia 217/A2
Coosada, Ala. 195/F5
Coosaw (riv.), S.C. 296/G7
Coosawattee (riv.), Georgia 217/C1
Coosawhatchie, S.C. 296/F6
Coosawhatchie (riv.), S.C. 296/E6
Coos Bay, Oreg. 188/A2
Coos Bay, Oreg. 291/C4
Cootamundra, N.S. Wales 88/H6
Cootamundra, N.S. Wales 97/D4
Cootehill, Ireland 17/G3
Cootehill, Ireland 10/C3
Cooter, Mo. 261/N10
Copacabana, Argentina 143/C2
Copacabana, Bolivia 136/A5
Copake, N.Y. 276/N6
Copake Falls, N.Y. 276/N6
Copala, Mexico 150/K8
Copalis Beach, Wash. 310/A3
Copalis Crossing, Wash. 310/B3
Copan, Okla. 288/P1
Copano (bay), Texas 303/G9
Copco (lake), Calif. 204/C2
Cope, Colo. 208/O3
Cope, Ind. 227/E6
Cope, S.C. 296/E5
Cope (cape), Spain 33/F4
Copeland, Ala. 195/B7
Copeland, Fla. 212/E6
Copeland, Idaho 220/B1
Copeland, Kansas 232/B4
Copeland (isl.), N. Ireland 17/K2
Copemish, Mich. 250/D4
Copen, W. Va. 312/E5
Copenhagen (commune), Denmark 21/F6
Copenhagen (cap.), Denmark 7/F3
Copenhagen (cap.), Denmark 21/F6
Copenhagen (cap.), Denmark 18/G9
Copenhagen, N.Y. 276/J3
Copere, Bolivia 136/D6
Copiague, N.Y. 276/O9
Copiah (co.), Miss. 256/D7
Copiapó, Chile 120/B5
Copiapó, Chile 138/B6
Copiapó (bay), Chile 138/A6
Copiapó (riv.), Chile 138/A6
Copinsay (isl.), Scotland 15/F2
Coplay, Pa. 294/L4
Copley, S. Australia 94/F4
Copmanhurst, N.S. Wales 97/G1
Coporito, Venezuela 124/H3
Coporolo (riv.), Angola 115/B6
Coppell, Texas 303/G2
Coppename (riv.), Suriname 131/C3
Copper (riv.), Alaska 196/J2
Copper (mts.), Ariz. 198/B6
Copperas Cove, Texas 303/G6
Copper Canyon, Texas 303/F1
Copper Center, Alaska 196/J2
Copper City, Mich. 250/A1
Copperfield, W. Australia 88/C5
Copperfield, W. Australia 92/B5
Copper Harbor, Mich. 250/B1
Copperhill, Tenn. 237/N10
Copper Hill, Va. 307/H6
Coppermine, Canada 4/C15
Coppermine, N.W.T. 162/E2
Coppermine (riv.), N.W.T. 162/E2
Coppermine (riv.), N.W.T. 187/G3
Coppermine, N.W. Terr. 187/G3
Copper Mountain, Br. Col. 184/G5
Copperton, Utah 304/B3
Copper Valley, Va. 307/G7
Coppet, Switzerland 39/B4
Coppock, Iowa 229/K6
Coqên, China 77/C5
Coquet (riv.), England 13/F2
Coquí, P. Rico 161/D3
Coquille, Oreg. 291/C4
Coquille (pt.), Oreg. 291/C4
Coquimatlán, Mexico 150/G7
Coquimbo (reg.), Chile 138/A8
Coquimbo, Chile 120/B6
Coquimbo, Chile 138/A8
Coquitlam, Br. Col. 184/K3
Cora, Ill. 222/D6
Cora, Wyo. 319/C3
Corabia, Romania 45/G4
Coracora, Peru 128/F10
Corail, Haiti 158/A6
Coraki, N.S. Wales 97/G1
Coral (sea) 87/F7
Coral (sea) 88/H2
Coral (sea) 2/S6
Coral, Mich. 250/D5
Coral (sea), New Caled. 86/G4
Coral (sea), Papua N.G. 85/B7
Coral, Pa. 294/D5
Coral (bay), Philippines 82/A6
Coral (sea), Queensland 95/C1
Coral (bay), Virgin Is. (U.S.) 161/C4
Coral Cove, Fla. 212/D4
Coral Gables, Fla. 212/B5
Coral Harbour, N.W.T. 162/H2
Coral Harbour, N.W. Terr. 187/K3
Coral Hills, Md. 245/G5
Coral Sea Islands (terr.), Australia 87/E7
CORAL SEA ISLANDS TERR. 95/C2
Coral Sea Islands Territory, Australia 88/J3
Coral Springs, Fla. 212/F5
Coralville, Iowa 229/K5
Coralville (lake), Iowa 229/K5
Coram, Mont. 262/C2
Coramba, N.S. Wales 97/G2
Corangamite (lake), Victoria 97/B6
Corantijn (riv.), Suriname 131/C3
Coraopolis, Pa. 294/B4
Corapeake, N.C. 281/R1
Corato, Italy 34/F4
Corbeil, Ontario 177/E1
Corberrie, Nova Scotia 168/C4
Corbigny, France 28/E4
Corbin, Kansas 232/E4
Corbin, Ky. 237/N7
Corbin City, N.J. 273/D5
Corbridge, England 13/E3
Corby, England 13/G5
Corcelles-près-Payerne, Switzerland 39/C3
Corcoran, Calif. 204/F7
Corcoran, Minn. 255/F5
Corcovado (gulf), Chile 120/B7
Corcovado (gulf), Chile 138/D4
Corcovado (vol.), Chile 138/D5
Corcubión, Spain 33/B1
Cord, Ark. 202/H2
Cordaville, Mass. 249/H3
Cordele, Georgia 217/E7
Cordelia, Calif. 204/K1
Cordell, Okla. 288/H4
Cordell Hull (res.), Tenn. 237/K8
Corder, Mo. 261/E4
Cordesville, S.C. 296/H5
Cordillera, Paraguay 144/D4
Cordillo Grounds, S. Australia 94/G2
Córdoba (prov.), Argentina 143/D3
Córdoba, Argentina 2/F7
Córdoba, Argentina 143/D3
Córdoba, Argentina 120/C6
Córdoba (dept.), Colombia 126/C3
Córdoba, Mexico 150/P2
Córdoba (prov.), Spain 33/D3
Córdoba, Spain 33/D4
Córdoba, Spain 7/D5
Cordobés (riv.), Uruguay 145/D3
Cordova, Ala. 195/D3
Cordova, Alaska 196/D1
Cordova, Alaska 188/D6
Cordova, Alaska 146/D3
Cordova (bay), Alaska 196/M2
Cordova, Ill. 222/C2
Cordova, Manitoba 179/C4
Cordova, Md. 245/O5
Cordova, Nebr. 264/G4
Cordova, N. Mex. 274/D2
Córdova, Peru 128/E10
Cordova, S.C. 296/F5
Cordova, Tenn. 237/B10
Cordova, U.S. 4/C17
Cordova Mines, Ontario 177/G3
Core (banks), N.C. 281/S5
Core (sound), N.C. 281/S5
Core, W. Va. 312/F3
Corea, Maine 243/H7
Coredó (Humboldt) (bay), Colombia 126/B4
Coree South, N.S. Wales 97/C4
Corella, Spain 33/F1
Corey, La. 238/F2
Corfield, Queensland 88/G4
Corfield, Queensland 95/B4
Corfu (Kérkira) (isl.), Greece 45/D6
Corfu, N.Y. 276/D5
Corgémont, Switzerland 39/D2
Cori, Italy 34/F7
Coria, Spain 33/C3
Coria del Río, Spain 33/C4
Corigliano Calabro, Italy 34/F5
Corinda, Queensland 88/K3
Corinda, Queensland 95/A3
Corinda, Queensland 95/D3
Coringa (islets), Australia 87/F7
Coringa (isls.), Coral Sea Is. Terr. 88/H3
Corinna•, Maine 243/E6
Corinne, Okla. 288/R6
Corinne, Sask. 181/G5
Corinne, Utah 304/B2
Corinne, W. Va. 312/D7
Corinth, Ark. 202/C3
Corinth, Georgia 217/B4
Corinth, Greece 45/F7
Corinth (gulf), Greece 45/F6
Corinth, Ky. 237/M3
Corinth, Miss. 256/G1
Corinth, N.Y. 276/N4
Corinth, N. Dak. 282/D2
Corinth•, Vt. 268/C3
Corinth, W. Va. 312/H4
Corinto, Brazil 132/E7
Corinto, Colombia 126/B6
Corinto, Nicaragua 154/D4
Coriole, Somalia 115/H3
Coripata, Bolivia 136/B5
Corisco (isl.), Equat. Guinea 115/A3
Cork (co.), Ireland 17/D7
Cork, Ireland 7/D3
Cork, Ireland 10/B5
Cork, Ireland 17/E8
Cork (harb.), Ireland 17/E8
Cork (harb.), Ireland 10/B5
Cork, New Bruns. 170/D3
Corker (cay), Belize 154/D2
Corleone, Italy 34/D6
Corley, W. Va. 312/E5
Çorlu, Turkey 63/B2
Cormorant, Manitoba 179/H3
Cormorant (lake), Manitoba 179/H3
Cormorant, Minn. 255/B4
Corn (creek), Ariz. 198/E3
Corn, Okla. 288/J4
Cornaca, Bolivia 136/C7
Corncake (inlet), N.C. 281/O7
Cornelia, Georgia 217/E1
Cornélio Procópio, Brazil 132/D8
Cornelius, N.C. 281/H4
Cornelius, Oreg. 291/A2
Cornell, Ill. 222/E3
Cornell, Mich. 250/B3
Cornell, Wis. 317/D5
Corner (inlet), Victoria 97/D6
Corner Brook, Newf. 166/C4
Corner Brook, Newf. 162/K6
Cornerstone, Ark. 202/G5
Cornersville, Md. 245/O6
Cornersville, Miss. 256/F1
Cornersville, Tenn. 237/H10
Cornerville, Ark. 202/G6
Cornettes de Bise (mts.), Switzerland 39/C4
Cornfield (pt.), Conn. 210/F3
Cornfields, Ariz. 198/F3
Cornhill, New Bruns. 170/E3
Cornhill, Scotland 15/F3
Corning, Ark. 202/J1
Corning, Calif. 204/C4
Corning, Iowa 229/D7
Corning, Kansas 232/F2
Corning, Mo. 261/B2
Corning, N.Y. 276/F6
Corning, Ohio 284/F6
Corning, Sask. 181/J6
Cornish, Colo. 208/L2
Cornish•, Maine 243/B8
Cornish, Okla. 288/L6
Cornish, Utah 304/B2
Cornish Flat, N.H. 268/C4
Cornishville, Ky. 237/M5
Cornland, Ill. 222/D4
Cornlea, Nebr. 264/G3
Corno (mt.), Italy 34/D3
Cornucopia, Wis. 317/D2
Cornville, Ariz. 198/D4
Cornville•, Maine 243/D6
Cornwall•, Conn. 210/B1
Cornwall (co.), England 13/C7
Cornwall (cape), England 13/B7
Cornwall (isl.), N.W.T. 162/M3
Cornwall (isl.), N.W. Terr. 187/J2
Cornwall, Ont. 162/J7
Cornwall, Ontario 177/K2
Cornwall, Pa. 294/K5
Cornwall, Pr. Edward I. 168/E2
Cornwall, Tasmania 99/E3
Cornwall•, Vt. 268/A4
Cornwall Bridge, Conn. 210/B1
Cornwall Center, Conn. 210/B1
Cornwall Hollow, Conn. 210/B1
Cornwallis (isl.), N.W.T. 162/F1
Cornwallis (isl.), N.W. Terr. 187/J2
Cornwall On Hudson, N.Y. 276/M8
Cornwell, Fla. 212/E4
Coro, Venezuela 124/D2
Coro, Venezuela 120/C1
Coroatá, Brazil 132/F3
Corocoro, Bolivia 120/C4
Corocoro, Bolivia 136/A5
Corofin, Ireland 17/C6
Coroico, Bolivia 136/B5
Corolla, N.C. 281/T2
Coromandel, Brazil 132/E7
Coromandel, N. Zealand 100/E2
Coromandel (pen.), N. Zealand 100/F2
Coromandel (range), N. Zealand 100/E2
Coromandel Coast (reg.), India 68/E6
Coron, Philippines 82/C4
Coron (isl.), Philippines 82/C5
Corona, Ala. 195/C3
Corona, Calif. 204/E11
Corona, N. Mex. 274/D4
Corona, S. Dak. 298/R3
Coronaca, S.C. 296/C3
Coronach, Sask. 181/F6
Coronada (bay), C. Rica 154/F6
Coronado, Calif. 204/H11
Coronado (pt.), Philippines 82/C7
Coronado Nat'l Memorial, Ariz. 198/E7
Coronados (gulf), Chile 138/D4
Coronation (isl.), Alaska 196/M2
Coronation, Alberta 182/E3
Coronation (isl.), Ant. 5/C16
Coronation (gulf), N.W.T. 162/E2
Coronation (gulf), N.W. Terr. 187/G3
Coronda, Argentina 143/F6
Coronel, Chile 138/D1
Coronel, Chile 120/B6
Coronel Bogado, Argentina 143/F6
Coronel Bogado, Paraguay 144/D5
Coronel Brandsen, Argentina 143/H7
Coronel Dorrego, Argentina 143/D4
Coronel F. Cabrera, Bolivia 136/E6
Coronel F. Cabrera (mt.), Paraguay 144/B1
Coronel Martínez, Paraguay 144/B5
Coronel Moldes, Argentina 143/C2
Coronel Oviedo, Paraguay 144/C5
Coronel Pringles, Argentina 143/D4
Coronel Suárez, Argentina 143/D4
Coronel Vidal, Argentina 143/E4
Corongo, Peru 128/D7
Coronie (dist.), Suriname 131/C3
Coropuna, Nudo (mt.), Peru 128/F10
Cororooke, Victoria 97/B6
Çorovodë, Albania 45/E5
Corowa, N.S. Wales 97/D4
Corozal, Colombia 126/C3
Corozal, P. Rico 161/D1
Corozal Town, Belize 154/C1
Corozo Pando, Venezuela 124/E3
Corpach, Scotland 15/C4
Corpus Christi, Texas 188/G5
Corpus Christi, Texas 146/J7
Corpus Christi, Texas 303/G10
Corpus Christi (bay), Texas 188/G5
Corpus Christi (lake), Texas 303/F9
Corpus Christi N.A.S., Texas 303/G10
Corque, Bolivia 136/B6
Corquín, Honduras 154/C3
Corral, Chile 138/D3
Corral, Idaho 220/D6
Corral City, Texas 303/F1
Corral de Almaguer, Spain 33/E3
Corral de Bustos, Argentina 143/D3
Corrales, N. Mex. 274/C3
Corralillo, Cuba 158/D1
Corralitos, Calif. 204/L4
Corral Viejo, P. Rico 161/C2
Correct, Ind. 227/G7
Correctionville, Iowa 229/B4
Correggio, Italy 34/C2
Corregidor (isl.), Philippines 82/C3
Correll, Minn. 255/B5
Corrente, Brazil 132/E5
Corrente (riv.), Brazil 132/E6
Correntina, Brazil 132/E6
Corrèze (dept.), France 28/D5
Corrib (lake), Ireland 17/C5
Corrib, Lough (lake), Ireland 10/B4
Corridon, Mo. 261/L8
Corrie, Scotland 15/C5
Corrientes (prov.), Argentina 143/E2
Corrientes, Argentina 143/E2
Corrientes, Argentina 120/D5
Corrientes (riv.), Argentina 143/E2
Corrientes (cape), Colombia 120/B2
Corrientes (cape), Colombia 126/B5
Corrientes (cape), Cuba 158/A2
Corrientes (inlet), Cuba 158/A2
Corrientes (cape), Mexico 146/H7
Corrientes (cape), Mexico 150/F6
Corrientes (riv.), Peru 128/E4
Corrigan, Texas 303/K7
Corriganville, Md. 245/C2
Corrigin, W. Australia 92/B6
Corriverton, Guyana 131/C3
Corrumpa (creek), N. Mex. 274/F2
Corry, Pa. 294/C2
Corryong, Victoria 97/D5
Corryton, Tenn. 237/O8
Corse (cape), France 28/B6
Corse du Sud (dept.), France 28/B6
Corserine (mt.), Scotland 15/D5
Corsewall (pt.), Scotland 15/C5
Corsham, England 13/E6
Corsica (isl.), France 7/E4
Corsica (isl.), France 28/B6
Corsica, Pa. 294/D3
Corsica, S. Dak. 298/N7
Corsicana, Texas 188/G4
Corsicana, Texas 303/H5
Corso, Mo. 261/K4
Corson (inlet), N.J. 273/D5
Corson (co.), S. Dak. 298/G2
Corson, S. Dak. 298/R6
Cortaro, Ariz. 198/D6
Corte, France 28/B6
Corte Madera, Calif. 204/J2
Cortés, Cuba 158/A2
Cortés (inlet), Cuba 158/B2
Cortez, Colo. 208/B8
Cortez, Fla. 212/D4
Cortez (mts.), Nev. 266/E2
Cortina d'Ampezzo, Italy 34/D1
Cortland, Ill. 222/E2
Cortland, Ind. 227/F7
Cortland, Nebr. 264/H4
Cortland (co.), N.Y. 276/H5
Cortland, N.Y. 276/H5
Cortland, Ohio 284/J3
Cortona, Italy 34/C3
Coruche, Portugal 33/B3
Çoruh (riv.), Turkey 59/D1
Çoruh (riv.), Turkey 63/J2
Çorum (prov.), Turkey 63/F2
Çorum, Turkey 59/B1
Çorum, Turkey 63/F2
Çorum (riv.), Turkey 63/F2
Corumbá, Brazil 120/D4
Corumbá, Brazil 132/B7
Corunna, Ind. 227/G2
Corunna, Mich. 250/E6
Corunna, Ontario 177/B5
Corvallis, Mont. 262/C4
Corvallis, Oreg. 188/B2
Corvallis, Oreg. 291/D3
Corvo (isl.), Portugal 33/A1
Corvuso, Minn. 255/D6
Corwen (delta), Wales 10/E4
Corwen, Wales 13/D5
Corwin, Kansas 232/D4
Corwin, Ohio 284/B6
Corwin Springs, Mont. 262/F5
Corwith, Iowa 229/F3
Cory, Ind. 227/C6
Corydon, Ind. 227/E8
Corydon, Iowa 229/G7
Corydon, Ky. 237/F5
Coryell (co.), Texas 303/G6
Coryville, Pa. 294/F2
Corzoneso, Switzerland 39/G4
Cosalá, Mexico 150/F4
Cosamaloapan de Carpio, Mexico 150/M7
Cosapa, Bolivia 136/A6
Cosautlán de Carvajal, Mexico 150/P1
Cosby, Mo. 261/C3
Cosby, Tenn. 237/P9
Cos Cob, Conn. 210/A4
Coscomatepec de Bravo, Mexico 150/P2
Cosegüina (pt.), Nicaragua 154/D4
Cosenza (prov.), Italy 34/F5
Cosenza, Italy 34/F5
Cosenza, Italy 7/F5
Coshocton (co.), Ohio 284/G5
Coshocton, Ohio 284/G5
Cosine, Sask. 181/A3
Cosío, Mexico 150/H5
Cosmoledo (isls.), Seychelles 102/G5
Cosmoledo (isls.), Seychelles 118/H1
Cosmo Newbery Aboriginal Res., W. Australia 88/C5
Cosmo Newbery Aboriginal Res., W. Australia 92/C5
Cosmopolis, Wash. 310/B4
Cosmos, Minn. 255/D6
Cosne-Cours-sur-Loire, France 28/E4
Cosperville, Ind. 227/F1
Cosquín, Argentina 143/D3
Cossonay, Switzerland 39/B3
Costa, W. Va. 312/C6
Costa Azul, Uruguay 145/E5
Costa Brava (reg.), Spain 33/H2
Costa da Caparica, Portugal 33/A1
Costa de Sola (Costa del Sol) (reg.), Spain 33/D4
Costa Mesa, Calif. 204/D11
Costa Rica 2/E5
Costa Rica 146/K8
COSTA RICA 154/E5
Costa Rica, Bolivia 136/A2
Costa Rica, Mexico 150/F4
Costa Smeralda (reg.), Italy 34/B4
Costa Verde (reg.), Italy 34/B5
Costello, Pa. 294/G2
Costessey, England 13/J5
Costeşti, Romania 45/G3
Costigan, Maine 243/F5
Costilla (co.), Colo. 208/J8
Costilla, N. Mex. 274/D2
Costilla (peak), N. Mex. 274/D2
Cosumnes (riv.), Calif. 204/C9
Coswig, Dresden, Germany 22/E3
Coswig, Halle, Germany 22/E3
Cotabato, Philippines 85/G4
Cotabato, Philippines 82/D7
Cotacajes (riv.), Bolivia 136/B5
Cotagaita, Bolivia 136/C7
Cotahuasi, Peru 128/F10
Cotati, Calif. 204/C5
Coteau, N. Dak. 282/F2
Coteau (hills), Sask. 181/D4
Coteau-du-Lac, Québec 172/C4
Coteau du Missouri (plain), N. Dak. 282/G3
Coteau-Landing, Québec 172/C4
Coteaux, Haiti 158/A6
Côte-d'Or (dept.), France 28/F4
Côte-d'Or (mts.), France 28/F4
Cotentin (pen.), France 28/C3
Côte-Saint-Luc, Québec 172/H4
Côtes de Fer, Haiti 158/B6
Côtes-du-Nord (dept.), France 28/B3
Cotesfield, Nebr. 264/F3
Cotija de la Paz, Mexico 150/H7
Cotile (lake), La. 238/E4
Coto, Argentina 143/D2
Cotoca, Bolivia 136/D5
Coto Laurel, P. Rico 161/C2
Cotonou, Benin 102/C4
Cotonou, Benin 106/E7
Cotopaxi, Colo. 208/H6
Cotopaxi (prov.), Ecuador 128/C3
Cotopaxi (mt.), Ecuador 128/C3
Cotswold (hills), England 13/E6
Cottage City, Md. 245/F4
Cottage Grove, Ala. 195/F5
Cottage Grove, Ind. 227/H5
Cottage Grove, Minn. 255/F6
Cottage Grove, Oreg. 291/D4
Cottage Grove (lake), Oreg. 291/E4
Cottage Grove, Tenn. 237/E8
Cottagehill, Fla. 212/B6
Cottage Hills, Ill. 222/B2
Cottageville, S.C. 296/G6
Cottageville, W. Va. 312/C5
Cottam, Ontario 177/B5
Cottbus, Germany 22/F3
Cotter, Ark. 202/E1
Cotter, Iowa 229/L6
Cottesloe, W. Australia 88/B2
Cottian Alps (range), France 28/G5
Cottian Alps (range), Italy 34/A2
Cottica, Suriname 131/D4
Cottica (riv.), Suriname 131/D3
Cottle, Ky. 237/P5
Cottle (co.), Texas 303/D3
Cottleville, Mo. 261/M2
Cotton, Georgia 217/D8
Cotton, Minn. 255/F3
Cotton (co.), Okla. 288/K6
Cottonburg, Ky. 237/N5
Cotton Center, Texas 303/C4
Cottondale, Ala. 195/D4
Cottondale, Fla. 212/D6
Cotton Ground, St. Kitts & Nevis 161/C11
Cotton Plant, Ark. 202/H3
Cottonport, La. 238/F5
Cottonton, Ala. 195/H6
Cottontown, Tenn. 237/H8
Cotton Valley, La. 238/D1
Cottonwood, Ala. 195/H8
Cottonwood, Ariz. 198/D4
Cottonwood (cliffs), Ariz. 198/B3
Cottonwood, Br. Col. 184/G3
Cottonwood, Calif. 204/C3
Cottonwood (creek), Calif. 204/C3
Cottonwood, Idaho 220/B3
Cottonwood (butte), Idaho 220/C4
Cottonwood (riv.), Kansas 232/F3
Cottonwood (co.), Minn. 255/C6
Cottonwood, Minn. 255/C6
Cottonwood (riv.), Minn. 255/C6
Cottonwood (creek), Mont. 262/E2
Cottonwood (creek), Oreg. 291/K4
Cottonwood, S. Dak. 298/F6
Cottonwood (creek), S. Dak. 298/E5
Cottonwood (lake), S. Dak. 298/M4
Cottonwood, Texas 303/D5
Cottonwood (creek), Utah 304/C4
Cottonwood (creek), Utah 304/E4
Cottonwood (creek), Wyo. 319/B4
Cottonwood Draw (dry riv.), Texas 303/C10
Cottonwood Falls, Kansas 232/F3
Cottonwood Wash (dry riv.), Ariz. 198/E4
Cottonwood Wash (creek), Utah 304/E6
Cotuí, Dom. Rep. 158/E5
Cotuit, Mass. 249/N6
Cotulla, Texas 303/E9
Couch, Mo. 261/K9
Couchiching (lake), Ontario 177/E3
Couchwood, La. 238/D1
Coudekerque-Branche, France 28/E2
Couderay, Wis. 317/D4
Coudersport, Pa. 294/G2
Coudres (isl.), Québec 172/G2
Cougar (res.), Oreg. 291/E3
Cougar, Wash. 310/C4
Coughlan, New Bruns. 170/E2
Coulee, N. Dak. 282/F2
Coulee City, Wash. 310/F3
Coulee Dam, Wash. 310/G3
Coulee Dam Nat'l Rec. Area, Wash. 310/G2
Coulihaut, Dominica 161/E6
Coulommiers, France 28/E3
Coulter, Iowa 229/G3
Coulter, Manitoba 179/B5
Coulterville, Calif. 204/E6
Coulterville, Ill. 222/D5
Counamama, Fr. Guiana 131/E3
Counce, Tenn. 237/E10
Council, Alaska 196/F2
Council, Georgia 217/G9
Council, Idaho 220/B5
Council, N.C. 281/M6
Council Bluffs, Iowa 229/B6
Council Bluffs, Iowa 188/G2
Council Grove, Kansas 232/F3
Council Grove (lake), Kansas 232/F3
Council Hill, Okla. 288/P3
Countess, Alberta 182/D4
Country (harb.), Nova Scotia 168/G3
Country Club Hills, Ill. 222/B6
Country Club Village, Mo. 261/C3
Country Harbour Mines, Nova Scotia 168/G3
Country Life Acres, Mo. 261/N3
Countryside, Ill. 222/B6
County Line, Ala. 195/E3
Countyline, Okla. 288/L6
Coupar Angus, Scotland 10/E2
Coupar Angus, Scotland 15/E4
Coupeville, Wash. 310/C2
Courantyne (riv.) 120/D2
Courantyne (riv.), Guyana 131/C3
Courbevoie, France 28/A1
Courcelles, Belgium 27/E8
Courcelles, Québec 172/G4
Courgenay, Switzerland 39/D2
Courmayeur, Italy 34/A2
Courrendlin, Switzerland 39/D2
Courroux, Switzerland 39/D2
Courtelary, Switzerland 39/C2
Courtenay, Br. Col. 162/D6
Courtenay, Br. Col. 184/E5
Courtenay, N. Dak. 282/N5
Courtételle, Switzerland 39/D2
Courtland, Ala. 195/D1
Courtland, Calif. 204/B9
Courtland, Kansas 232/E2
Courtland, Minn. 255/D6
Courtland, Miss. 256/E2
Courtland, Ontario 177/D5
Courtland, Va. 307/O7
Courtmacsherry, Ireland 17/D8
Courtmacsherry (bay), Ireland 17/D8
Courtney, Mo. 261/R5
Courtney, Okla. 288/L7
Courtois, Mo. 261/K7
Courtown (Este Sudeste) (cays), Colombia 126/A10
Courtown Harbour, Ireland 17/J6
Courtrai (Kortrijk), Belgium 27/C7
Courtright, Ontario 177/B5
Courval, Sask. 181/E5
Courville, Québec 172/J3
Coushatta, La. 238/D2
Coutances, France 28/C3
Coutras, France 28/C5
Coutts, Alberta 182/D5
Coutts (inlet), N.W. Terr. 187/L2
Couva, Trin. & Tob. 161/B10
Couvet, Switzerland 39/C3
Couvin, Belgium 27/F8
Cova da Piedade, Portugal 33/A1
Cove, Ark. 202/B5
Cove (pt.), Md. 245/N7
Cove, Minn. 255/E4
Cove, Ohio 284/E8
Cove (isl.), Ontario 177/C2
Cove, Oreg. 291/K2
Cove, Texas 303/L1
Cove (creek), Utah 304/B5
Cove and Kilcreggan, Scotland 15/A1
Cove Bay, Scotland 15/F3
Cove City, N.C. 281/P4
Cove Creek, N.C. 281/D3
Covedale, Ohio 284/B10
Cove Fort, Utah 304/B5
Cove Gap, W. Va. 312/B6
Covelo, Calif. 204/B4
Covena, Georgia 217/H6
Covendo, Bolivia 136/B4
Cove Neck, N.Y. 276/R6
Coventry•, Conn. 210/F1
Coventry, England 13/F5

356 Coventry

Coventry, England 10/F4
Coventry•, R.I. 249/H6
Coventry•, Vt. 268/C2
Coventry Center, R.I. 249/H6
Cove Orchard, Oreg. 291/D2
Coverdale, Georgia 217/E7
Coverdale, Ontario 177/F4
Covert, Mich. 250/C6
Cove Run (lake), Ky. 237/O4
Covesville, Va. 307/L5
Covilhã, Portugal 33/C2
Covin, Ala. 195/C3
Covina, Calif. 204/D10
Covington (co.), Ala. 195/F8
Covington, Georgia 217/E3
Covington, Ind. 227/C4
Covington, Iowa 229/K5
Covington, Ky. 237/S2
Covington, Ky. 188/J3
Covington, La. 238/K5
Covington, Mich. 250/G2
Covington (co.), Miss. 256/E7
Covington, Ohio 284/B5
Covington, Okla. 288/L2
Covington, Pa. 294/J2
Covington, Tenn. 237/B9
Covington (I.C.), Va. 307/H5
Cow (creek), Mont. 262/G2
Cow (creek), Oreg. 291/K4
Cow (lake), Oreg. 291/K4
Cow (creek), Wash. 310/G3
Cowal (lake), N.S. Wales 97/D3
Cowal (dist.), Scotland 15/C4
Cowan, Ind. 227/G4
Cowan, Ky. 237/O4
Cowan, Manitoba 179/B2
Cowan (lake), Sask. 181/D2
Cowan, Tenn. 237/K10
Cowan (lake), W. Australia 88/C6
Cowan (lake), W. Australia 92/C5
Cowanesque, Pa. 294/H2
Cowangie, Victoria 97/A4
Cowansville, Pa. 294/C4
Cowansville, Québec 172/E4
Cowaramup, W. Australia 92/A6
Coward, S.C. 296/H4
Coward Springs, S. Australia 94/E3
Cowarie, S. Australia 94/F2
Cowarts, Ala. 195/H8
Cow Bay, Nova Scotia 168/E4
Cowbridge, Wales 13/A7
Cowcreek, Ky. 237/O6
Cowden, Ill. 222/E4
Cowdenbeath, Scotland 10/C1
Cowdenbeath, Scotland 15/D1
Cowdrey, Colo. 208/G1
Cowell, S. Australia 88/F6
Cowell, S. Australia 94/E5
Cowen, W. Va. 312/E6
Cowes, England 10/F5
Cowes, England 13/F7
Coweta (co.), Georgia 217/C4
Coweta, Okla. 288/P3
Cowgill, Mo. 261/E3
Cow Head, Newf. 166/C4
Cowichan (lake), Br. Col. 184/J3
Cowiche, Wash. 310/E4
Cowie, Scotland 15/C1
Cowikee, North Fork (creek), Ala. 195/H6
Cow Island, La. 238/F7
Cowles, Nebr. 264/F4
Cowles, N. Mex. 274/D3
Cowlesville, N.Y. 276/D5
Cowley, Alberta 182/D5
Cowley (co.), Kansas 232/F4
Cowley, Wyo. 319/D1
Cowley, Yukon 187/E3
Cowlington, Okla. 288/S4
Cowlitz (co.), Wash. 310/C4
Cowlitz (pass), Wash. 310/D4
Cowlitz (riv.), Wash. 310/C4
Cowpasture (riv.), Va. 307/J4
Cowpens, S.C. 296/D1
Cowpens Nat'l Battlefield, S.C. 296/D1
Cowra, N.S. Wales 88/H6
Cowra, N.S. Wales 97/E3
Cox (bight), Tasmania 99/C5
Coxburg, Miss. 256/D5
Cox City, Okla. 288/L5
Coxim, Brazil 132/C7
Coxsackie, N.Y. 276/N6
Cox's Bazar, Bangladesh 68/G4
Cox's Cove, Newf. 166/C4
Coxs Mills, W. Va. 312/E4
Cox Station (Bel Alton), Md. 245/L7
Coxton, Ky. 237/P7
Coy, Ala. 195/D7
Coy, Ark. 202/G4
Coyame, Mexico 150/G2
Coyle (riv.), Argentina 143/B7
Coyle, Okla. 288/M3
Coyoacán, Mexico 150/L1
Coyote (creek), Calif. 204/L3
Coyote (res.), Calif. 204/L4
Coyote, N. Mex. 274/C2
Coyotepec, Mexico 150/L1
Coyuca (riv.), Mexico 150/O1
Coyuca de Benítez, Mexico 150/J8
Coyuca de Catalán, Mexico 150/J7
Coyutla, Mexico 150/L6
Coyville, Kansas 232/G4
Cozad, Nebr. 264/E4
Cozumel, Mexico 150/Q6
Cozumel (isl.), Mexico 150/Q6
Crab (creek), Wash. 310/F3
Crab Hill, Barbados 161/B8
Crab Orchard (lake), Ill. 222/E6
Crab Orchard, Ky. 237/M6
Crab Orchard, Nebr. 264/H4
Crab Orchard, Tenn. 237/M9
Crabtree, Oreg. 291/E3
Crabtree, Pa. 294/D5
Crabtree, Québec 172/D4
Cracow (city prov.), Poland 47/E4
Cracow (Kraków) (prov.), Poland 47/E4
Cracow, Poland 47/E4
Cracow, Poland 7/F3
Cradle (mt.), Tasmania 99/B3
Cradle Mt. Lake St. Clair Nat'l Park, Tasmania 99/B3
Cradock, S. Africa 102/E8
Cradock, S. Africa 118/D6
Crafters-Bridgewater, S. Australia 88/E8
Crafters-Bridgewater, S. Australia 94/B8
Crafton, Pa. 294/B7
Craftsbury•, Vt. 268/C2
Craftsbury Common, Vt. 268/C2
Cragford, Ala. 195/G4
Craig, Alaska 196/M2
Craig, Colo. 208/D2
Craig (mts.), Idaho 220/B4
Craig, Iowa 229/A3
Craig, Mo. 261/B2
Craig, Mont. 262/D3
Craig, Nebr. 264/H3
Craig (co.), Okla. 288/R1
Craig (co.), Va. 307/H6
Craig (creek), Va. 307/H5
Craigavon (dist.), N. Ireland 17/J3
Craigavon, N. Ireland 10/C3
Craigavon, N. Ireland 17/J3
Craig Beach, Ohio 284/H3
Craigellachie, Scotland 15/E3
Craighead (co.), Ark. 202/J2
Craighouse, Scotland 15/C5
Craigieburn, Victoria 97/C5
Craigleath, Ontario 177/D3
Craigmont, Idaho 220/B3
Craigmyle, Alberta 182/D4
Craignish (hills), Nova Scotia 168/G3
Craignure, Scotland 15/C4
Craigs (Sainte Rita), Manitoba 179/F5
Craig Springs, Va. 307/H6
Craigsville, Va. 307/J4
Craigsville, W. Va. 312/E6
Craigville, Ind. 227/G3
Craigville, Minn. 255/E3
Craik, Sask. 181/F4
Crail, Scotland 15/F4
Crail, Scotland 10/E2
Crailsheim, Germany 22/D4
Craiova, Romania 45/F3
Craiova, Romania 7/G4
Cramerton, N.C. 281/G4
Cramond (isl.), Scotland 15/D1
Cranberry (lake), N.Y. 276/L2
Cranberry (lake), N. Dak. 282/L3
Cranberry, Pa. 294/C3
Cranberry, W. Va. 312/D7
Cranberry Isles, Maine 243/G7
Cranberry Isles•, Maine 243/G7
Cranberry Lake, N.J. 273/D2
Cranberry Lake, N.Y. 276/L2
Cranberry Portage, Manitoba 179/H3
Cranbourne, Victoria 97/C6
Cranbourne, Victoria 88/M8
Cranbrook, Br. Col. 162/E6
Cranbrook, Br. Col. 184/K5
Cranbrook, Tasmania 99/D4
Cranbrook, W. Australia 92/B6
Cranbury, Conn. 210/B4
Cranbury, N.J. 273/E3
Crandall, Georgia 217/C1
Crandall, Ind. 227/E8
Crandall, Manitoba 179/B4
Crandall, S. Dak. 298/O3
Crandall, Texas 303/H5
Crandon, Va. 307/G6
Crandon, Wis. 317/H4
Crane, Barbados 161/C9
Crane, Ind. 227/D7
Crane, Mo. 261/E9
Crane, Mont. 262/M3
Crane, Oreg. 291/J4
Crane (creek), Oreg. 291/J4
Crane (lake), Sask. 181/B5
Crane (co.), Texas 303/B6
Crane, Texas 303/B6
Crane Creek (res.), Idaho 220/B5
Crane Hill, Ala. 195/D2
Crane Lake, Minn. 255/F2
Crane Nest, Ky. 237/O7
Crane Prairie (res.), Oreg. 291/F4
Crane River, Manitoba 179/C3
Cranesville, Pa. 294/B2
Cranesville, W. Va. 312/G3
Crane Valley, Sask. 181/F6
Cranfills Gap, Texas 303/G6
Cranford•, N.J. 273/E2
Cranleigh, England 13/G6
Cransac, France 28/E5
Cranston, Iowa 229/L6
Cranston, R.I. 249/J5
Crapaud, Pr. Edward I. 168/E2
Crapo, Md. 245/O7
Crary, N. Dak. 282/N3
Craster, England 13/F2
Crater (lake), Oreg. 291/E5
Crater Lake, Oreg. 291/E5
Crater Lake Nat'l Park, Oreg. 291/E5
Craters of the Moon Nat'l Mon., Idaho 220/E6
Crateús, Brazil 132/F4
Crateús, Brazil 120/E3
Crati (riv.), Italy 34/F5
Crato, Brazil 132/G4
Crato, Brazil 120/E3
Crato e Mártires, Portugal 33/C3
Crauford (cape), N.W. Terr. 187/K2
Craven (co.), N.C. 281/P4
Craven, Sask. 181/G5
Cravens, La. 238/E5
Cravo Norte, Colombia 126/F4
Cravo Norte (riv.), Colombia 126/E4
Cravo Sur (riv.), Colombia 126/E5
Crawford (co.), Ark. 202/B2
Crawford, Colo. 208/D5
Crawford (co.), Georgia 217/E5
Crawford, Georgia 217/F3
Crawford (co.), Ill. 222/F4
Crawford (co.), Ind. 227/E8
Crawford (co.), Iowa 229/C4
Crawford (co.), Kansas 232/H4
Crawford, Kansas 232/E3
Crawford•, Maine 243/H5
Crawford (lake), Maine 243/H5
Crawford (co.), Mich. 250/E4
Crawford, Miss. 256/G4
Crawford (co.), Mo. 261/K7
Crawford, Nebr. 264/A2
Crawford (co.), Ohio 284/E4
Crawford, Okla. 288/G3
Crawford (co.), Pa. 294/B2
Crawford, Scotland 15/E5
Crawford, Tenn. 237/L8
Crawford, Texas 303/G6
Crawford, W. Va. 312/F5
Crawford (co.), Wis. 317/E9
Crawford Bay, Br. Col. 184/J5
Crawford House, N.H. 268/E3
Crawford Notch (pass), N.H. 268/E3
Crawfordsville, Ark. 202/K3
Crawfordsville, Ind. 227/D4
Crawfordsville, Iowa 229/K6
Crawfordsville, Oreg. 291/E3
Crawfordville, Fla. 212/B1
Crawfordville, Georgia 217/G3
Crawley, England 13/G6
Crawley, W. Va. 312/E7
Crayne, Ky. 237/E6
Crazy (peak), Mont. 262/F4
Crazy Horse Mon., S. Dak. 298/B6
Crazy Woman (creek), Wyo. 319/F1
Creach Bheinn (mt.), Scotland 15/C4
Creagerstown, Md. 245/J2
Creag Meagaidh (mt.), Scotland 15/D4
Creal Springs, Ill. 222/E6
Cream (hill), Conn. 210/B1
Cream, Wis. 317/C7
Creamridge, N.J. 273/E3
Crean (lake), Sask. 181/E1
Creciente (isl.), Mexico 150/D5
Credenhill, England 13/E5
Crediton, England 13/D7
Crediton, England 10/E5
Crediton, Ontario 177/C4
Cree (lake), Sask. 162/F4
Cree (lake), Sask. 181/L3
Cree (riv.), Sask. 181/M2
Cree (riv.), Scotland 15/D5
Creede, Colo. 208/E7
Creedmoor, N.C. 281/M2
Creek (co.), Okla. 288/O3
Creekside, Pa. 294/D4
Creek Stand, Ala. 195/G6
Creekville, Ky. 237/P6
Creel, Mexico 150/E3
Cree Lake, Sask. 181/L3
Creelman, Sask. 181/H6
Creelsboro, Ky. 237/L7
Creemore, Ontario 177/D3
Creeslough, Ireland 17/F1
Creetown, Scotland 15/D6
Creighton, Mo. 261/D6
Creighton, Nebr. 264/G2
Creighton, Pa. 294/C4
Creighton, Sask. 181/N4
Creighton, S. Dak. 298/E5
Creignish, Nova Scotia 168/G3
Creil, France 28/E3
Crellin, Md. 245/A3
Crema, Italy 34/B2
Cremona, Alberta 182/C4
Cremona (prov.), Italy 34/B2
Cremona, Italy 34/B2
Crenshaw (co.), Ala. 195/F7
Crenshaw, Miss. 256/D2
Crenshaw, Pa. 294/E3
Creola, Ala. 195/B9
Creola, Ohio 284/E7
Creole, La. 238/D7
Crépy-en-Valois, France 28/E3
Creran, Loch (inlet), Scotland 15/C4
Cres (isl.), Yugoslavia 45/B3
Cresaptown, Md. 245/C2
Cresbard, S. Dak. 298/M3
Crescent (isls.), China 85/E2
Crescent (lake), Fla. 212/E2
Crescent, Iowa 229/B6
Crescent, La. 238/J2
Crescent, Mo. 261/N4
Crescent (lake), Nebr. 264/B3
Crescent (valley), Nev. 266/E2
Crescent, Okla. 288/L3
Crescent, Oreg. 291/F4
Crescent (lake), Tasmania 99/D4
Crescent (lake), Wash. 310/B2
Crescent Beach, Conn. 210/G3
Crescent City, Calif. 204/A2
Crescent City, Fla. 212/E2
Crescent City, Ill. 222/F3
Crescent Head, N.S. Wales 97/G2
Crescent Lake, Maine 243/C7
Crescent Lake, Oreg. 291/E4
Crescent Lake, Sask. 181/J4
Crescent Mills, Calif. 204/E3
Crescent Springs, Ky. 237/R2
Cresco, Iowa 229/J2
Cresco, Pa. 294/M3
Crespo, Argentina 143/F6
Cresskill, N.J. 273/C1
Cressmont, W. Va. 312/E6
Cresson, Pa. 294/E5
Cresson, Texas 303/G5
Cressona, Pa. 294/K4
Cressy, Tasmania 99/C3
Crest, France 28/F5
Crest, Georgia 217/D5
Crested Butte, Colo. 208/E5
Crest Hill, Ill. 222/E2
Crestline, Calif. 204/H9
Crestline, Kansas 232/H4
Crestline, Ohio 284/E4
Creston, Br. Col. 184/J5
Creston, Calif. 204/E8
Creston, Ill. 222/D2
Creston, Ind. 227/C2
Creston, Iowa 229/E6
Creston, Ky. 237/L6
Creston, La. 238/E3
Creston, Mont. 262/C2
Creston, Nebr. 264/G3
Creston, Newf. 166/C4
Creston, Ohio 284/G3
Creston, S.C. 296/F4
Creston, Wash. 310/G3
Creston, W. Va. 312/D5
Crestone, Colo. 208/H7
Crestone (peak), Colo. 208/H7
Crestview, Fla. 212/C6
Crestview, Ky. 237/S2
Crestview Hills, Ky. 237/R2
Crestwood, Ill. 222/B6
Crestwood, Ky. 237/L4
Crestwood, Mo. 261/O3
Crestwynd, Sask. 181/F5
Creswell, N.C. 281/S3
Creswell (bay), N.W. Terr. 187/J2
Creswell, Oreg. 291/D4
Creswell Downs, North. Terr. 93/E4
Creswick, Victoria 97/B5
Crete (reg.), Greece 45/G8
Crete (isl.), Greece 7/G5
Crete (isl.), Greece 45/G8
Crete (sea), Greece 45/G7
Crete, Ill. 222/F2
Crete, Nebr. 264/G4
Crete, N. Dak. 282/P7
Créteil, France 28/B2
Cretin (cape), Papua N.G. 86/B2
Creus (cape), Spain 33/H1
Creuse (dept.), France 28/D4
Creuse (riv.), France 28/D4
Creve Coeur, Ill. 222/D3
Creve Coeur, Mo. 261/O2
Crevillente, Spain 33/F3
Crewe, Va. 307/M6
Crewe and Nantwich, England 13/E4
Crewe and Nantwich, England 10/F2
Crewkerne, England 13/E7
Crewkerne, England 10/E5
Crews, Ala. 195/B3
Crianlarich, Scotland 15/D4
Criccieth, Wales 13/C5
Criccieth, Wales 10/D4
Crichton, Sask. 181/D6
Criciúma, Brazil 132/D10
Crider, Ky. 237/F6
Cridersville, Ohio 284/B4
Crieff, Scotland 15/E4
Crieff, Scotland 10/E2
Criehaven, Maine 243/F8
Crillon (mt.), Alaska 196/L1
Crimea (pen.), U.S.S.R. 7/H4
Crimea (pen.), U.S.S.R. 48/D5
Crimea (pen.), U.S.S.R. 52/D5
Crimean Oblast, U.S.S.R. 52/D6
Crimmitschau, Germany 22/E3
Crimond, Scotland 15/G3
Crimora, Va. 307/L4
Crinan, Scotland 15/C4
Cripple Creek, Colo. 188/F3
Cripple Creek, Colo. 208/J5
Cripple Creek, Va. 307/F7
Crisfield, Md. 245/P9
Crisp (co.), Georgia 217/E7
Crisp (pt.), Mich. 250/D2
Crisp, N.C. 281/O3
Crissolo, Italy 34/A2
Cristal, Sierra del (mts.), Cuba 158/J3
Cristalina, Brazil 132/E7
Cristóbal (mt.), Colombia 120/B1
Cristóbal (pt.), Ecuador 128/B9
Cristóbal, Panama 154/G6
Cristóbal Colón, Pico (peak), Colombia 126/D2
Crişul Alb (riv.), Romania 45/F2
Crişul Repede (riv.), Romania 45/F2
Crittenden (co.), Ark. 202/K3
Crittenden (co.), Ky. 237/E6
Crittenden, Ky. 237/M3
Critz, Va. 307/H7
Crivitz, Wis. 317/L5
Croagh Patrick (mt.), Ireland 17/C4
Croatan (sound), N.C. 281/T3
Croatia (rep.), Yugoslavia 45/C3
Croche (riv.), Québec 172/E2
Crocheron, Md. 245/O8
Crochu, Grenada 161/D8
Crocker, Mo. 261/H7
Crocker, S. Dak. 298/O3
Crocketford, Scotland 15/E5
Crockett, Calif. 204/J1
Crockett (co.), Tenn. 237/C9
Crockett (co.), Texas 303/C7
Crockett, Texas 303/J6
Crockett, Va. 307/F7
Crockett Mills, Tenn. 237/C9
Crocketts Bluff, Ark. 202/H5
Crocketville, S.C. 296/E6
Crocodile (riv.), S. Africa 118/H6
Croft, Kansas 232/D4
Crofton, Br. Col. 184/J3
Crofton, Ky. 237/G6
Crofton, Md. 245/M4
Crofton, Nebr. 264/G2
Croghan, N.Y. 276/K3
Croix des Bouquets, Haiti 158/C6
Croker (cape), North. Terr. 88/E2
Croker (cape), North. Terr. 93/C1
Croker (bay), N.W. Terr. 187/K2
Croker (cape), Ontario 177/D3
Croker Island Mission, North. Terr. 88/E2
Croker Island Mission, North. Terr. 93/C1
Cromarty, Scotland 15/E3
Cromarty, Scotland 10/D2
Cromarty (firth), Scotland 15/D3
Cromdale, Scotland 15/E3
Cromer, England 13/J5
Cromer, England 10/G4
Cromer, Manitoba 179/A5
Cromwell, Ala. 195/B6
Cromwell•, Conn. 210/E2
Cromwell, Ind. 227/F2
Cromwell, Iowa 229/E6
Cromwell, Ky. 237/H6
Cromwell, Minn. 255/F4
Cromwell, N. Zealand 100/B6
Cromwell, Okla. 288/N4
Cronulla, N.S. Wales 88/L5
Cronulla, N.S. Wales 97/J4
Crook, Colo. 208/O1
Crook (co.), Oreg. 291/G3
Crook (pt.), Oreg. 291/C5
Crook (co.), Wyo. 319/H1
Crook and Willington, England 13/E3
Crooked (isl.), Bahamas 156/D2
Crooked (creek), Ind. 227/D2
Crooked (creek), Kansas 232/B4
Crooked (creek), Minn. 255/F4
Crooked (lake), Minn. 255/G2
Crooked (lake), N. Dak. 282/J4
Crooked (creek), Oreg. 291/K5
Crooked (riv.), Oreg. 291/G3
Crooked (creek), S.C. 296/H2
Crooked Creek, Alaska 196/G2
Crooked Creek, Alberta 182/B2
Crooked Island (passage), Bahamas 156/C2
Crooked River, Sask. 181/H3
Crookhaven, Ireland 17/B9
Crooks, S. Dak. 298/R6
Crookston, Minn. 188/G1
Crookston, Minn. 255/B3
Crookston, Nebr. 264/D2
Crooksville, Ohio 284/F6
Crookwell, N.S. Wales 97/E4
Croom, Ireland 17/D6
Cropper, Ky. 237/L4
Cropsey, Ill. 222/E3
Crosby, Ala. 195/H8
Crosby, England 13/G2
Crosby, England 10/F2
Crosby, Minn. 255/D4
Crosby, Miss. 256/B8
Crosby, N. Dak. 282/D2
Crosby, Pa. 294/F2
Crosby (co.), Texas 303/C4
Crosby, Texas 303/J8
Crosby (mt.), Wyo. 319/C2
Crosbyton, Texas 303/C4
Crosland, Georgia 217/E8
Cross (sound), Alaska 196/L1
Cross (co.), Ark. 202/J3
Cross (riv.), Cameroon 115/A2
Cross (lake), La. 238/C2
Cross (isl.), Maine 243/J6
Cross (lake), Maine 243/G2
Cross (bay), Manitoba 179/C1
Cross (lake), Manitoba 179/J3
Cross (cape), Namibia 118/A4
Cross (riv.), Nigeria 106/F7
Cross (isl.), Nova Scotia 168/D4
Cross, S.C. 296/G5
Cross Anchor, S.C. 296/D2
Crossapoll, Scotland 15/B4
Cross City, Fla. 212/C2
Cross Creek, New Bruns. 170/D2
Crossett, Ark. 202/G7
Crossfarnoge (pt.), Ireland 17/J7
Cross Fell (mt.), England 13/E3
Crossfield, Alberta 182/C4
Cross Fork, Pa. 294/G3
Crossgar, N. Ireland 17/K3
Crosshaven, Ireland 17/E8
Crosshill, Scotland 15/D5
Cross Hill, S.C. 296/D3
Cross Junction, Va. 307/M2
Cross Keys, S.C. 296/D2
Cross Lake, Manitoba 179/J3
Crosslake, Minn. 255/E4
Crossley (mt.), N. Zealand 100/D5
Crossmaglen, N. Ireland 17/H3
Crossmichael, Scotland 15/D6
Crossmolina, Ireland 17/C3
Crossnore, N.C. 281/F2
Cross Plains, Ind. 227/G7
Cross Plains, Tenn. 237/H7
Cross Plains, Texas 303/E5
Cross Plains, Wis. 317/G9
Cross River (state), Nigeria 106/F7
Cross Roads, Calif. 204/L9
Crossroads, N. Mex. 274/F5
Cross Roads, Pa. 294/J6
Cross Timbers, Mo. 261/F6
Crosstown, Mo. 261/N7
Cross Village, Mich. 250/D3
Crossville, Ala. 195/G2
Crossville, Ill. 222/F5
Crossville, Tenn. 237/L9
Crosswicks, N.J. 273/D3
Crosswicks (creek), N.J. 273/D3
Croswell, Mich. 250/G5
Crotch (lake), Ontario 177/H3
Crothersville, Ind. 227/F7
Croton (Hartford), Ohio 284/E5
Crotone, Italy 34/F5
Croton Falls, N.Y. 276/N8
Croton-on-Hudson, N.Y. 276/N8
Crouch, Idaho 220/B5
Crouseville, Maine 243/G2
Crow (creek), Colo. 208/L1
Crow (riv.), Minn. 255/F5
Crow, Oreg. 291/D4
Crow (creek), S. Dak. 298/A4
Crow (creek), Wyo. 319/H4
Crow Agency, Mont. 262/J5
Crowborough, England 13/H6
Crow Creek Ind. Res., S. Dak. 298/L5
Crowder, Miss. 256/D2
Crowder, Okla. 288/P4
Crowduck (lake), Manitoba 179/G4
Crowdy (head), N.S. Wales 97/G2
Crowell, Texas 303/E4
Crowfoot, Alberta 182/D4
Crowheart, Wyo. 319/C2
Crow Ind. Res., Mont. 262/H5
Crowl (creek), N.S. Wales 97/C2
Crow Lake, S. Dak. 298/M6
Crowle, England 13/G4
Crowley (lake), Calif. 204/G6
Crowley (co.), Colo. 208/M6
Crowley, Colo. 208/M6
Crowley, La. 238/F6
Crowley, Texas 303/E3
Crowley Lake, Calif. 204/G6
Crowley's Ridge (mt.), Ark. 202/J2
Crown, Minn. 255/E5
Crown (mt.), Virgin Is. (U.S.) 161/A4
Crown City, Ohio 284/F8
Crown King, Ariz. 198/C4
Crown Point, Ind. 227/C2
Crownpoint, N. Mex. 274/A3
Crown Point, N.Y. 276/N3
Crown Prince Frederik (isl.), N.W. Terr. 187/K3
Crownsville, Md. 245/M4
Crows Landing, Calif. 204/D6
Crowsnest (pass), Alberta 182/C5
Crowsnest, Br. Col. 184/K5
Crowsnest (pass), Br. Col. 184/K5
Crowville, La. 238/G2
Crow Wing (co.), Minn. 255/D4
Crow Wing (riv.), Minn. 255/D4
Croydon, England 13/H8
Croydon, England 10/B6
Croydon•, N.H. 268/C5
Croydon (peak), N.H. 268/C5
Croydon, Queensland 88/G3
Croydon, Queensland 95/B3
Croydon, Utah 304/C2
Croydon, Victoria 88/M7
Croydon, Victoria 97/K5
Croydon Branch, Sugar (riv.), N.H. 268/C5
Crozet (isls.) 2/M8
Crozet, Va. 307/L4
Crozier (chan.), N.W. Terr. 187/G2
Crozier, Va. 307/N5
Cruces, Cuba 158/E2
Cruces, Cuba 156/B2
Cruden Bay, Scotland 15/G3
Cruger, Miss. 256/D4
Cruillas, Mexico 150/K4
Crum (creek), Pa. 294/M7
Crum, W. Va. 312/B7
Crumlin, N. Ireland 17/J2
Crum Lynne, Pa. 294/M7
Crummies, Ky. 237/P7
Crump, Mich. 250/E5
Crump (lake), Oreg. 291/H5
Crump, Tenn. 237/E10
Crumpton (pt.), Dominica 161/F5
Crumpton, Md. 245/P4
Crumrod, Ark. 202/H5
Crumstown, Ind. 227/E1
Crusheen, Ireland 17/D6
Cruso, N.C. 281/D4
Cruta, Honduras 154/F3
Crutchfield, Ky. 237/D7
Crutwell, Sask. 181/E2
Cruz (cape), Cuba 156/C3
Cruz (cape), Cuba 158/G4
Cruz Alta, Brazil 120/D5
Cruz Alta, Brazil 132/C10
Cruz Bay, Virgin Is. (U.S.) 161/C4
Cruz del Eje, Argentina 143/C3
Cruz del Eje, Argentina 120/C6
Cruz de Piedra, Uruguay 145/E3
Cruz de San Pedro, Uruguay 145/E2
Cruzeiro, Brazil 135/D3
Cruzeiro do Sul, Brazil 120/B3
Cruzeiro do Sul, Brazil 132/G10
Cruz Grande, Chile 138/A7
Crysler, Ontario 177/J2
Crystal (mts.), Congo 115/B4
Crystal (lake), Conn. 210/F1
Crystal (pond), Conn. 210/G1
Crystal (bay), Fla. 212/D3
Crystal (mts.), Gabon 115/B4
Crystal, Ind. 227/D8
Crystal•, Maine 243/G4
Crystal, Mich. 250/E5
Crystal (lake), Mich. 250/C4
Crystal, Minn. 255/G5
Crystal, N.H. 268/E2
Crystal (lake), N.H. 268/E5
Crystal, N. Mex. 274/A2
Crystal, N. Dak. 282/P2
Crystal (lake), Vt. 268/C2
Crystal, W. Va. 312/D8
Crystal Bay (Orono), Minn. 255/F5
Crystal Bay, Nev. 266/A3
Crystal Beach, Texas 303/K8
Crystal Brook, S. Australia 94/E5
Crystal City, Manitoba 179/C5
Crystal City, Mo. 261/M6
Crystal City, Texas 303/E9
Crystal Falls, Mich. 250/A2
Crystal Falls, Ontario 177/E1
Crystal Hill, Va. 307/L7
Crystal Lake, Conn. 210/F1
Crystal Lake, Fla. 212/D6
Crystal Lake, Ill. 222/E1
Crystal Lake, Iowa 229/F2
Crystal Lake Park, Mo. 261/O3
Crystal River, Fla. 212/D3
Crystal Springs, Ark. 202/D5
Crystal Springs (res.), Calif. 204/J3
Crystal Springs, Fla. 212/D3
Crystal Springs, Georgia 217/B2
Crystal Springs, Kansas 232/D4
Crystal Springs, Miss. 256/D7
Crystal Springs, N. Dak. 282/L6
Crystal Springs, Sask. 181/F3
Crystal Valley, Mich. 250/C5
Csabrendek, Hungary 41/D3
Csákvár, Hungary 41/E3
Csanádpalota, Hungary 41/F3
Csenger, Hungary 41/G3
Csepel, Hungary 41/E3
Csepelsziget (isl.), Hungary 41/E3
Csepreg, Hungary 41/D3
Csongrád (co.), Hungary 41/F3
Csongrád, Hungary 41/E3
Csorna, Hungary 41/D3
Csorvás, Hungary 41/F3
Csurgó, Hungary 41/D3
Ctesiphon (ruins), Iraq 66/D4
Cúa, Venezuela 124/E2
Cuadro Nacional, Argentina 143/C3
Cuamba, Mozambique 118/F2
Cuando (riv.), Angola 115/C7
Cuando (riv.), Zambia 115/D7

Dalhousie East 357

Cuando Cubango (prov.), Angola 115/C7
Cuangar, Angola 115/C7
Cuango (riv.) 102/D5
Cuango, Angola 115/C5
Cuango (riv.), Angola 115/C5
Cuanza (riv.), Angola 102/D6
Cuanza (riv.), Angola 115/C5
Cuanza-Norte (prov.), Angola 115/B5
Cuanza-Sul (prov.), Angola 115/C6
Cuao (riv.), Venezuela 124/E5
Cua Rao, Vietnam 72/E3
Cuareim (riv.), Uruguay 145/B1
Cuaró, Uruguay 145/D2
Cuatrociénagas de Carranza, Mexico 150/H3
Cuatro Compañeros, Cuba 158/G3
Cuatro Ojos, Bolivia 136/D5
Cuauhtémoc, Mexico 150/F2
Cuautepec de Hinojosa, Mexico 150/K6
Cuautitlán de Romero Rubio, Mexico 150/L1
Cuautla Morelos, Mexico 150/L2
Cub (creek), Utah 304/C1
Cub (creek), Va. 307/L6
Cuba 2/E4
Cuba 146/L7
CUBA 156/B2
CUBA 158
Cuba, Ala. 195/B6
Cuba, Ill. 222/C3
Cuba, Ind. 227/D6
Cuba, Kansas 232/E2
Cuba, Mo. 261/K6
Cuba, N. Mex. 274/B2
Cuba, N.Y. 276/D6
Cuba (chan.), N. Zealand 100/D7
Cuba, Ohio 284/C7
Cuba, Portugal 33/C3
Cuba City, Wis. 317/F10
Cubage, Ky. 237/O7
Cubagua (isl.), Venezuela 124/F2
Cuballing, W. Australia 92/B2
Cubango (riv.), Angola 102/D6
Cubango (riv.), Angola 115/C7
Cubango (riv.), Namibia 118/B3
Cubatão, Brazil 135/C3
Cube (mt.), N.H. 268/D4
Cubero, N. Mex. 274/B3
Cubiro, Venezuela 124/D3
Cub Run, Ky. 237/J6
Çubuk, Turkey 63/E2
Cubulco, Guatemala 154/B3
Cuchara, Colo. 208/J8
Cuchi, Angola 115/C6
Cuchi, Angola 102/D6
Cuchillo, N. Mex. 274/B5
Cuchillo-Có, Argentina 143/D4
Cuchillo Negro (creek), N. Mex. 274/B5
Cuchivero, Venezuela 124/F4
Cuchivero (riv.), Venezuela 124/F4
Cuckfield, England 13/G6
Cuckfield, England 10/F5
Cucumber, W. Va. 312/C8
Cúcuta, Colombia 126/D4
Cúcuta, Colombia 120/B2
Cudahy, Calif. 204/C5
Cudahy, Wis. 317/M2
Cudal, N.S. Wales 97/E3
Cuddalore, India 68/E6
Cuddapah, India 68/D6
Cuddeback (lake), Calif. 204/H8
Cuddy, Pa. 294/B5
Cudgewa, Victoria 97/D5
Cudillero, Spain 33/C1
Cudjoe (key), Fla. 212/E7
Cudrefin, Switzerland 39/D3
Cudworth, Sask. 181/F3
Cue, W. Australia 88/B5
Cue, W. Australia 92/B4
Cuéllar, Spain 33/D2
Cuéllar-Baza, Spain 33/E4
Cuemaní (riv.), Colombia 126/D7
Cuenca, Ecuador 120/B3
Cuenca, Ecuador 128/C4
Cuenca (prov.), Spain 33/E2
Cuenca, Spain 33/E2
Cuenca, Sierra de (range), Spain 33/F3
Cuencamé de Ceniceros, Mexico 150/H4
Cuernavaca, Mexico 150/L2
Cuero, Texas 303/G8
Cuervo, N. Mex. 274/E3
Cuervo (creek), N. Mex. 274/E3
Cueto, Cuba 158/J3
Cuevas, Miss. 256/F10
Cuevas del Almanzora, Spain 33/F4
Cuevas de Vinromá, Spain 33/F2
Cuevo, Bolivia 136/D7
Cufré, Uruguay 145/B5
Cuiabá, Brazil 120/D4
Cuiabá, Brazil 132/C6
Cuiabá (riv.), Brazil 132/B7
Cuicatlán, Mexico 150/L8
Cuicuina, Nicaragua 154/E4
Cuilapa, Guatemala 154/B3
Cuilapa Miravalles (vol.), C. Rica 154/E5
Cuilcagh (mt.), Ireland 17/F3
Cuilco, Guatemala 154/B3
Cuillin (hills), Scotland 15/B3
Cuillin (sound), Scotland 10/C2
Cuillin (sound), Scotland 15/B3
Cuilo, Angola 115/C5
Cuitlahuac, Mexico 150/P2
Cuito (riv.), Angola 115/C7
Cuito-Cuanavale, Angola 115/C7
Cuitzeo (lake), Mexico 150/J7
Cuivre (riv.), Mo. 261/N2
Cujmir, Romania 45/F3
Cukmantl, Czech. 41/D1
Çukur, Turkey 63/F3
Çukurca, Turkey 63/K4
Culaba, Philippines 82/E5
Cu Lao, Hon (isls.), Vietnam 72/F5
Culberson, N.C. 281/A4
Culberson (co.), Texas 303/C11
Culbertson, Mont. 262/M2
Culbertson, Nebr. 264/C4
Culcairn, N.S. Wales 97/D4
Culdaff, Ireland 17/G1
Culdaff (bay), Ireland 17/G1
Culdesac, Idaho 220/B3
Cul-de-Sac du Marin (bay), Martinique 161/D7
Culebra (creek), Colo. 208/H8
Culebra (peak), Colo. 208/J8
Culebra, P. Rico 161/G1
Culebra (isl.), P. Rico 161/G1
Culebra (isl.), P. Rico 156/G1
Culebras, Peru 128/C7
Culebrinas (riv.), P. Rico 161/A1
Culebrita (isl.), P. Rico 161/G2
Culemborg, Netherlands 27/G5
Culgoa (riv.), N.S. Wales 97/D1
Culgoa (riv.), Queensland 95/C6
Culiacán, Mexico 150/F4
Culiacán, Mexico 146/H7
Culion, Philippines 82/C5
Culion (isl.), Philippines 82/B5
Cullasaja, N.C. 281/C4
Cullburra-Orient Point, N.S. Wales 97/F4
Cullen, La. 238/D1
Cullen, Sask. 181/J6
Cullen, Scotland 15/F3
Cullen, Va. 307/L6
Cullen Bullen, N.S. Wales 97/F3
Culleoka, Tenn. 237/G10
Cullera, Spain 33/F3
Cullin (lake), Ireland 17/C4
Cullison, Kansas 232/D4
Cullman (co.), Ala. 195/E2
Cullman, Ala. 195/E2
Culloden, Georgia 217/D5
Culloden, W. Va. 312/B6
Cullom, Ill. 222/E3
Cullomburg, Ala. 195/B7
Cullompton, England 13/D7
Cullowhee, N.C. 281/C4
Cully, Switzerland 39/C4
Cullybackey, N. Ireland 17/J2
Culotte (lake), Québec 172/C2
Culp, Alberta 182/B2
Culp Creek, Oreg. 291/E4
Culpeper (co.), Va. 307/M3
Culpeper, Va. 307/M4
Culpepper (isl.), Ecuador 128/B8
Culpina, Bolivia 136/C7
Culross, Manitoba 179/E5
Culross, Scotland 10/B1
Culross, Scotland 15/C1
Culta, Bolivia 136/B6
Cults, Scotland 15/F3
Cultus (lake), Oreg. 291/F4
Cultus Lake, Br. Col. 184/M3
Culuene (riv.), Brazil 132/C6
Culver, Ind. 227/E2
Culver, Kansas 232/E3
Culver, Minn. 255/F4
Culver, Oreg. 291/F3
Culver (pt.), W. Australia 88/D6
Culver (pt.), W. Australia 92/D6
Culver City, Calif. 204/B10
Culverden, N. Zealand 100/D5
Culvers (lake), N.J. 273/D1
Culverton, Georgia 217/G4
Cuma, Angola 115/B6
Cumaná, Venezuela 120/C2
Cumaná, Venezuela 124/F2
Cumanacoa, Venezuela 124/F2
Cumanayagua, Cuba 158/E2
Cumaria, Peru 128/F7
Cumback, Ind. 227/C7
Cumbal, Colombia 126/B7
Cumberland (riv.) 188/J3
Cumberland (plat.), Ala. 195/F1
Cumberland, Br. Col. 184/E5
Cumberland (sound), Canada 4/C13
Cumberland (isl.), Georgia 217/K9
Cumberland (co.), Ill. 222/E4
Cumberland, Ind. 227/E5
Cumberland, Iowa 229/D6
Cumberland (co.), Ky. 237/L7
Cumberland, Ky. 237/R6
Cumberland (lake), Ky. 237/M7
Cumberland (mt.), Ky. 237/P7
Cumberland (riv.), Ky. 237/K8
Cumberland (co.), Maine 243/C8
Cumberland, Md. 188/L3
Cumberland, Md. 245/D2
Cumberland (basin), New Bruns. 170/F3
Cumberland (co.), N.J. 273/C5
Cumberland (co.), N.C. 281/M4
Cumberland, N.C. 281/M5
Cumberland (pen.), N.W.T. 162/K2
Cumberland (pen.), N.W. Terr. 187/M3
Cumberland (sound), N.W.T. 146/N3
Cumberland (sound), N.W.T. 162/K2
Cumberland (sound), N.W. Terr. 187/M3
Cumberland (co.), Nova Scotia 168/D3
Cumberland (basin), Nova Scotia 168/D3
Cumberland, Ohio 284/G6
Cumberland, Okla. 288/N6
Cumberland, Ontario 177/J2
Cumberland (co.), Pa. 294/H5
Cumberland (isls.), Queensland 88/H4
Cumberland (isls.), Queensland 95/D4
Cumberland (bay), St. Vin. & Grens. 161/A8
Cumberland (lake), Sask. 181/J1
Cumberland (co.), Tenn. 237/L9
Cumberland (plat.), Tenn. 237/L9
Cumberland (riv.), Tenn. 237/K8
Cumberland (co.), Va. 307/M6
Cumberland, Va. 307/M6
Cumberland (mt.), Va. 307/B7
Cumberland, Wash. 310/D3
Cumberland, Wis. 317/C4
Cumberland Bay, New Bruns. 170/E2
Cumberland Beach, Ontario 177/E3
Cumberland Center, Maine 243/C8
Cumberland Center•, Maine 243/C8
Cumberland City, Tenn. 237/F8
Cumberland Furnace, Tenn. 237/G8
Cumberland Gap, Tenn. 237/O8
Cumberland Gap Nat'l Hist. Park, Ky. 237/P7
Cumberland Gap Nat'l Hist. Park, Tenn. 237/O7
Cumberland Gap Nat'l Hist. Park, Va. 307/A7
Cumberland House, Sask. 181/J2
Cumberland Island Nat'l Seashore, Georgia 217/K9
Cumbernauld, Scotland 15/C1
Cumbre del Laudo (mt.), Argentina 143/C2
Cumbre Negra, Cerro (mt.), Argentina 143/C5
Cumbre Negra, Cerro (mt.), Chile 138/E5
Cumbria (co.), England 13/D3
Cumbrian (mts.), England 13/D3
Cumbum, India 68/D5
Cumby, Texas 303/J4
Cuming (co.), Nebr. 264/H3
Cummaquid, Mass. 249/N6
Cumming, Georgia 217/D2
Cumming, Iowa 229/F6
Cummings, Kansas 232/G2
Cummings, N. Dak. 282/S4
Cummings, S.C. 296/E6
Cummingsville, Tenn. 237/L9
Cummington•, Mass. 249/C3
Cummins, S. Australia 94/D6
Cumnock, N.S. Wales 97/E3
Cumnock, N.C. 281/L3
Cumnock and Holmhead, Scotland 10/D3
Cumnock and Holmhead, Scotland 15/D5
Cumpas, Mexico 150/E1
Çumra, Turkey 63/E4
Cuñapirú, Uruguay 145/D2
Cuñapirú, Arroyo (riv.), Uruguay 145/D2
Cunapo, Trin. & Tob. 161/B10
Cuñare, Colombia 126/D7
Cunaviche, Venezuela 124/E4
Cunco, Chile 138/E2
Cuncumén, Coquimbo, Chile 138/A9
Cuncumén, Santiago, Chile 138/F4
Cundeelee Aboriginal Res., W. Australia 88/C6
Cundeelee Aboriginal Res., W. Australia 92/C5
Cunderdin, W. Australia 92/B5
Cundiff, Ky. 237/L7
Cundinamarca (dept.), Colombia 126/C5
Cundiyo, N. Mex. 274/D3
Cunduacán, Mexico 150/N7
Cundys Harbor, Maine 243/D8
Cunene (riv.) 102/D6
Cunene (prov.), Angola 115/C7
Cunene (dam), Angola 115/B7
Cunene (riv.), Angola 115/B7
Cuneo (prov.), Italy 34/A2
Cuneo, Italy 34/A2
Çüngüş, Turkey 63/H3
Cunnamulla, Australia 87/E8
Cunnamulla, Queensland 95/C5
Cunnamulla, Queensland 88/H5
Cunningham, Kansas 232/D4
Cunningham, Ky. 237/D7
Cunningham, N.C. 281/L1
Cunningham, Tenn. 237/G8
Cunningham, Wash. 310/G4
Cuorgnè, Italy 34/A2
Cupar, Sask. 181/G5
Cupar, Scotland 15/E4
Cupar, Scotland 10/E2
Cupertino, Calif. 204/K3
Cupica (gulf), Colombia 126/B4
Cupids, Newf. 166/D2
Cuprija, Yugoslavia 45/E4
Cuprum, Idaho 220/B4
Cupsuptic (riv.), Maine 243/B5
Cuquenán (riv.), Venezuela 124/H5
Cuquiari (riv.), Colombia 126/E7
Curaçá, Brazil 132/G5
Curaçao (isl.), Neth. Ant. 161/G7
Curaçao (isl.), Neth. Ant. 156/E4
Curacautín, Chile 138/E2
Curacaví, Chile 138/G3
Curahuara de Carangas, Bolivia 136/A5
Curahuara de Pacajes, Bolivia 136/A5
Curanilahue, Chile 138/D1
Curaray (riv.), Ecuador 128/D3
Curaumilla (pt.), Chile 138/E2
Curdsville, Ky. 237/G5
Curecanti Nat'l Rec. Area, Colo. 208/F6
Curepipe, Mauritius 118/G5
Curepto, Chile 138/A10
Curiapo, Venezuela 124/H3
Curiche, Bolivia 136/D6
Curicó, Chile 120/B6
Curicó, Chile 138/A10
Curieuse (isl.), Seychelles 118/H5
Curitiba, Brazil 132/D9
Curitiba, Brazil 120/F5
Curitiba, Brazil 135/B4
Curlew, Iowa 229/D3
Curlew (isls.), La. 238/M7
Curlew, Wash. 310/G2
Curlew (lake), Wash. 310/G2
Curlewis, N.S. Wales 97/F2
Curllsville, Pa. 294/D3
Curnamona, S. Australia 94/F4
Curragh, The, Ireland 17/H5
Curragh, The (racecourse), Ireland 10/C4
Currais Novos, Brazil 132/G4
Curran, Ill. 222/D4
Curran, Mich. 250/F4
Currant, Nev. 266/F4
Currawilla, Queensland 95/B5
Current (riv.), Ark. 202/J1
Current (riv.), Mo. 261/K8
Currie, Minn. 255/C6
Currie, Nev. 266/G2
Currie, N.C. 281/N6
Currie, Scotland 15/D2
Currie, Tasmania 99/A1
Currituck (co.), N.C. 281/S2
Currituck, N.C. 281/T2
Currituck (sound), N.C. 281/T2
Curry, Alaska 196/J2
Curry (co.), N. Mex. 274/F4
Curry (co.), Oreg. 291/C5
Curryville, Mo. 261/K4
Curryville, Pa. 294/F5
Curtea de Argeș, Romania 45/G3
Curtice, Ohio 284/D2
Curtin, Oreg. 291/D4
Curtina, Uruguay 145/C3
Curtis, Ark. 202/D6
Curtis, La. 238/C2
Curtis, Mich. 250/D2
Curtis, Nebr. 264/D4
Curtis, Okla. 288/H2
Curtis (isl.), Queensland 88/J4
Curtis (isl.), Queensland 95/D4
Curtis, Wash. 310/B4
Curtis Group (isls.), Tasmania 99/C1
Curtiss, Wis. 317/F6
Curtis Station, Miss. 256/D2
Curtisville, Ind. 227/F4
Curuá (riv.), Brazil 132/C4
Curuçá, Brazil 132/E3
Curuguaty, Paraguay 144/E4
Curup, Indonesia 85/C6
Cururú, Bolivia 136/D4
Cururupu, Brazil 132/E3
Curutú (riv.), Venezuela 124/G5
Curuzú Cuatiá, Argentina 143/G5
Curuzú Cuatiá, Argentina 120/D5
Curve, Tenn. 237/B9
Curvelo, Brazil 132/E7
Curwensville, Pa. 294/E4
Curwood (mt.), Mich. 250/A2
Cusachón (isl.), Colombia 126/D1
Cusco, Peru 120/B4
Cusco (dept.), Peru 128/F9
Cusco (Cuzco), Peru 128/F9
Cushendall, N. Ireland 17/J1
Cushing, Iowa 229/B4
Cushing•, Maine 243/E7
Cushing, Minn. 255/D4
Cushing, Nebr. 264/F3
Cushing, Okla. 288/N3
Cushing, Texas 303/J6
Cushing, Wis. 317/A4
Cushman, Ark. 202/G2
Cushman, Mass. 249/D3
Cushman, Oreg. 291/D4
Cushman (lake), Wash. 310/B3
Cusiana (riv.), Colombia 126/D5
Cusick, Wash. 310/H2
Cuslett, Newf. 166/C2
Cusset, France 28/E4
Cusseta, Ala. 195/H5
Cusseta, Georgia 217/C6
Cusson, Minn. 255/F2
Custar, Ohio 284/C3
Custer (co.), Colo. 208/J6
Custer (co.), Idaho 220/D5
Custer, Ky. 237/J5
Custer, Mich. 250/C5
Custer (co.), Mont. 262/L4
Custer, Mont. 262/J4
Custer (co.), Nebr. 264/E3
Custer (co.), Okla. 288/H3
Custer (co.), S. Dak. 298/B6
Custer, S. Dak. 298/B6
Custer, Wash. 310/C2
Custer City, Okla. 288/J3
Custer City, Pa. 294/E2
Custer Park, Ill. 222/E2
Cut Bank, Mont. 262/D2
Cut Bank (creek), Mont. 262/D2
Cut Bank (creek), N. Dak. 282/H2
Cutbank, Sask. 181/E4
Cutchogue-New Suffolk, N.Y. 276/P8
Cutervo, Peru 128/C6
Cuthbert, Georgia 217/C7
Cut Knife, Sask. 181/B3
Cutler, Calif. 204/F7
Cutler, Ill. 222/D5
Cutler, Ind. 227/D4
Cutler, Maine 243/J6
Cutler•, Maine 243/J6
Cutler, Ohio 284/G7
Cutler Ridge, Fla. 212/F6
Cutlerville, Mich. 250/D6
Cut Off, La. 238/K7
Cutra (lake), Ireland 17/D5
Cutral-Có, Argentina 143/C4
Cutshin, Ky. 237/P6
Cuttaburra (creek), N.S. Wales 97/C1
Cuttack, India 54/K7
Cuttack, India 68/F4
Cutten, Calif. 204/A3
Cuttingsville, Vt. 268/B4
Cuttyhunk, Mass. 249/L7
Cuttyhunk (isl.), Mass. 249/L7
Cuvier (isl.), N. Zealand 100/E2
Cuvier (cape), W. Australia 88/A4
Cuvier (cape), W. Australia 92/A4
Cuvo (riv.), Angola 115/B6
Cuxhaven, Germany 22/C2
Cuya, Chile 138/B2
Cuyabeno, Ecuador 128/E3
Cuyahoga (co.), Ohio 284/G3
Cuyahoga (riv.), Ohio 284/H10
Cuyahoga Falls, Ohio 284/G3
Cuyahoga Heights, Ohio 284/H9
Cuyama, Calif. 204/F9
Cuyama (riv.), Calif. 204/E8
Cuyapaipe Ind. Res., Calif. 204/J11
Cuyk, Netherlands 27/H5
Cuylerville, N.Y. 276/E5
Cuyo, Philippines 82/C5
Cuyo (isl.), Philippines 82/C5
Cuyo (isls.), Philippines 82/C5
Cuyo (isls.), Philippines 85/G3
Cuyocuyo, Peru 128/H10
Cuyo East (passage), Philippines 82/C5
Cuyo West (passage), Philippines 82/C5
Cuyuna, Minn. 255/E4
Cuyuna (range), Minn. 255/D4
Cuyuni (riv.) 120/C2
Cuyuni (riv.), Guyana 131/B2
Cuyuni (riv.), Venezuela 124/H4
Cuyu Tigni, Nicaragua 154/F3
Cuzco, Ind. 227/D8
Cuzzart, W. Va. 312/H3
Čvrsnica (mt.), Yugoslavia 45/C4
Cwmamman, Wales 13/D6
Cwmbran, Wales 13/B6
Cyangugu, Rwanda 115/E4
Cyclades (isls.), Greece 45/G7
Cycle, N.C. 281/H2
Cyclone, Ind. 227/E4
Cyclone, Pa. 294/E2
Cyclone, W. Va. 312/C7
Cygnet, Ohio 284/C3
Cygnet, Tasmania 99/C5
Cylinder, Iowa 229/D2
Cylon, Wis. 317/B5
Cymric, Sask. 181/G4
Cynthia, Alberta 182/C3
Cynthiana, Ind. 227/B8
Cynthiana, Ky. 237/N4
Cynthiana, Ohio 284/D7
Cypert, Ark. 202/J5
Cypress, Ala. 195/C5
Cypress (hills), Alberta 182/E5
Cypress (bayou), Ark. 202/F3
Cypress, Calif. 204/D11
Cypress, Fla. 212/A1
Cypress (lake), Fla. 212/E3
Cypress, Ill. 222/D6
Cypress, Ind. 227/B9
Cypress (pond), Ind. 227/B8
Cypress, La. 238/D3
Cypress (hills), Sask. 181/B6
Cypress (lake), Sask. 181/B6
Cypress Gardens, Fla. 212/E3
Cypress Hills Prov. Park, Alberta 182/E5
Cypress Hills Prov. Park, Sask. 181/B6
Cypress Inn, Tenn. 237/F10
Cypress Prov. Park, Br. Col. 184/K3
Cypress Quarters, Fla. 212/F4
Cypress River, Manitoba 179/D5
Cyprus 2/L4
Cyprus 54/E6
CYPRUS 59/B2
CYPRUS 63/E5
Cyrenaica (reg.), Libya 102/E1
Cyrenaica (reg.), Libya 111/D1
Cyrene (Shahat), Libya 111/D1
Cyrene, Mo. 261/K4
Cyril, Okla. 288/K5
Cyrus, Minn. 255/C5
Czar, Alberta 182/E3
Czar, W. Va. 312/F5
Czarna Białostocka, Poland 47/F2
Czarnków, Poland 47/C2
Czechoslovakia 2/K3
Czechoslovakia 7/F4
CZECHOSLOVAKIA 41
Czechowice-Dziedzice, Poland 47/D4
Czech Republic, Czech. 41/B1
Czeladź, Poland 47/B4
Czersk, Poland 47/D2
Częstochowa (prov.), Poland 47/D3
Częstochowa, Poland 47/D3
Częstochowa, Poland 7/F3
Człuchów, Poland 47/C2

D

Da'an (Talai), China 77/K2
Daaquam, Québec 172/H3
Dabajuro, Venezuela 124/C2
Dabakala, Ivory Coast 106/D7
Dabas, Hungary 41/E3
Daba Shan (range), China 77/G5
Dabeiba, Colombia 126/B4
Dabhoi, India 68/C4
Dabney, Ind. 227/G6
Dabob (bay), Wash. 310/C3
Dabola, Guinea 106/B6
Dabou, Ivory Coast 106/D7
Daboya, Ghana 106/D7
Dąbrowa Górnicza, Poland 47/B3
Dąbrowa Tarnowska, Poland 47/E3
Dăbuleni, Romania 45/F4
Dachau, Germany 22/D4
Dačice, Czech. 41/C2
Dac Lac, Cao Nguyen (plat.), Vietnam 72/F4
Dacoma, Okla. 288/J1
Dacono, Colo. 208/K2
Dacre, Ontario 177/G2
Dacula, Georgia 217/E3
Dacusville, S.C. 296/B2
Dadanawa, Guyana 131/B4
Daday, Turkey 63/E2
Dade (co.), Fla. 212/F6
Dade (co.), Georgia 217/A1
Dade (co.), Mo. 261/E8
Dade City, Fla. 212/D3
Dadeville, Ala. 195/G5
Dadeville, Mo. 261/E8
Dadra and Nagar Haveli (terr.), India 68/C4
Dads (lake), Nebr. 264/D2
Dadu, Pakistan 68/B3
Dadu, Pakistan 59/J4
Dăeni, Romania 45/J3
Daer (res.), Scotland 15/E5
Daet, Philippines 85/G3
Daet, Philippines 82/D3
Dafang, China 77/G6
Dafna, Israel 65/D1
Dafoe, Sask. 181/G4
Dafter, Mich. 250/E2
Dagabur, Ethiopia 111/H6
Dagana, Senegal 106/A5
Dagda, U.S.S.R. 53/D2
Dagelet (Ullŭng) (isl.), S. Korea 81/E5
Dagestan A.S.S.R., U.S.S.R. 48/E5
Dagestan A.S.S.R., U.S.S.R. 52/G6
Dagestanskiye Ogni, U.S.S.R. 52/G6
Daggett, Calif. 204/H9
Daggett, Mich. 250/B3
Daggett (co.), Utah 304/E3
Dagmar, Mont. 262/M2
Dagö (Hiiumaa) (isl.), U.S.S.R. 52/B3
Dagsboro, Del. 245/S6
Dagua, Colombia 126/B6
Daguan, China 77/F6
D'Aguilar (range), Tasmania 99/B4
Dagupan, Philippines 82/C2
Daguscahonda, Pa. 294/E3
Dagus Mines, Pa. 294/E3
Dahab, Egypt 111/F2
Dahana (des.), Saudi Arabia 54/F7
Dahana (des.), Saudi Arabia 59/E4
Dahinda, Ill. 222/C3
Dahinda, Sask. 181/G6
Da Hingan Ling (Great Khingan) (range), China 54/O5
Da Hingan Ling (range), China 77/J3
Dahlak (arch.), Ethiopia 111/H4
Dahlak (arch.), Ethiopia 59/D6
Dahlak (isl.), Ethiopia 59/D6
Dahlak (isl.), Ethiopia 111/H4
Dahlem, Germany 22/E4
Dahlen, N. Dak. 282/P3
Dahlgren, Ill. 222/E5
Dahlgren, Va. 307/O4
Dahlia, N. Mex. 274/D3
Dahlonega, Georgia 217/D1
Dahme, Germany 22/E3
Dai (mt.), Japan 81/F6
Dailekh, Nepal 68/E3
Dailey, Colo. 208/O1
Dailly, Scotland 15/D5
Daimanji (mt.), Japan 81/F5
Daimiel, Spain 33/E3
Daingean, Ireland 17/G5
Daingerfield, Texas 303/K4
Daio (cape), Japan 81/H6
Daiquirí, Cuba 158/J4
Daireaux, Argentina 143/D4
Dairût, Egypt 111/J4
Dairy, Oreg. 291/F5
Dairy Flat-Redvale, N. Zealand 100/B1
Dairyland, Wis. 317/B3
Daisen-Oki Nat'l Park, Japan 81/F6
Daisetsu (mt.), Japan 81/L2
Daisetsu-Zan Nat'l Park, Japan 81/L2
Daisetta, Texas 303/K7
Daisy, Ark. 202/C5
Daisy, Georgia 217/J6
Daisy, Ky. 237/P6
Daisy, Mo. 261/N7
Daisy, Okla. 288/P5
Daisy, Wash. 310/G2
Daito, Japan 81/J8
Daito (isls.), Japan 54/P7
Dajabón (prov.), Dom. Rep. 158/D5
Dajabón, Dom. Rep. 158/D5
Dajarra, Queensland 88/F4
Dajarra, Queensland 95/A4
Dakar (cap.), Senegal 2/J5
Dakar (cap.), Senegal 102/A3
Dakar (cap.), Senegal 106/A6
Dakhla (oasis), Egypt 111/E2
Dakhla (oasis), Egypt 59/A4
Dakhla, W. Sahara 102/A2
Dakhla, Western Sahara 106/A4
Dakoro, Niger 106/F6
Dakota, Georgia 217/E7
Dakota, Ill. 222/D1
Dakota (co.), Minn. 255/E6
Dakota, Minn. 255/G7
Dakota (co.), Nebr. 264/H2
Dakota City, Iowa 229/E3
Dakota City, Nebr. 264/H2
Dal (riv.), Sweden 7/F2
Dala, Angola 115/D6
Dalaba, Guinea 106/B6
Dalälven (riv.), Sweden 18/K6
Dalaman (riv.), Turkey 63/C4
Dalandzadgad, Mongolia 77/G3
Dalanganem (isls.), Philippines 82/C5
Dalark, Ark. 202/E5
Da Lat, Vietnam 72/F5
Dalavich, Scotland 15/C4
Dalbandin, Pakistan 68/A3
Dalbandin, Pakistan 59/H4
Dalbeattie, Scotland 10/E3
Dalbeattie, Scotland 15/E6
Dalbo, Minn. 255/E5
Dalby, Queensland 95/D5
Dalby, Queensland 88/J5
Dalby, Sweden 18/H6
Dalcahue, Chile 138/D4
Dalcour, La. 238/P4
Dale (co.), Ala. 195/G8
Dale, Ill. 222/E6
Dale, Ind. 227/D8
Dale, Minn. 255/B4
Dale, Norway 18/E6
Dale, Okla. 288/M4
Dale, Oreg. 291/J3
Dale, Pa. 294/E5
Dale, S.C. 296/F6
Dale (mt.), W. Australia 88/B2
Dale (mt.), W. Australia 92/B1
Dale, Wis. 317/J7
Dale City, Va. 307/O3
Dale Hollow (lake), Ky. 237/L7
Dale Hollow (lake), Tenn. 237/L7
Dalemead, Alberta 182/D4
Dalen, Netherlands 27/K3
Daleside, S. Africa 118/H7
Daleville, Ala. 195/G8
Daleville, Ind. 227/F4
Daleville, Miss. 256/G5
Daleville, Va. 307/J6
Dale West, W. Australia 92/B2
Dalhart, Texas 303/B1
Dalhousie, New Bruns. 170/D1
Dalhousie (cape), N.W. Terr. 187/E2
Dalhousie (mt.), Nova Scotia 168/E3
Dalhousie East, Nova Scotia 168/D4

358 Dalhousie Junction

Dalhousie Junction, New Bruns. 170/D1
Dalhousie West, Nova Scotia 168/C4
Dali, China 77/E6
Dalian (Lüda), China 77/K4
Dalías, Spain 33/E4
Daliburgh, Scotland 15/A3
Dalizi, China 77/L3
Dalkeith, Ontario 177/K2
Dalkeith, Scotland 10/C1
Dalkeith, Scotland 15/D2
Dalkena, Wash. 310/H2
Dall (isl.), Alaska 196/M2
Dall (mt.), Alaska 196/H2
Dallam (co.), Texas 303/B1
Dallas (co.), Ala. 195/D6
Dallas (co.), Ark. 202/E6
Dallas, Georgia 217/C3
Dallas (co.), Iowa 229/E5
Dallas, Iowa 229/G6
Dallas, Manitoba 179/E3
Dallas (co.), Mo. 261/F7
Dallas, N.C. 281/G4
Dallas, Oreg. 291/D3
Dallas, Pa. 294/E7
Dallas, Scotland 15/E3
Dallas, S. Dak. 298/K7
Dallas (co.), Texas 303/H5
Dallas, Texas 303/G2
Dallas, Texas 188/G4
Dallas, Texas 146/J6
Dallas, U.S. 2/E4
Dallas, W. Va. 312/E2
Dallas, Wis. 317/C5
Dallas Center, Iowa 229/E5
Dallas City, Ill. 222/B3
Dallas Naval Air Sta., Texas 303/G2
Dallastown, Pa. 294/J6
Dalles, The, Oreg. 291/F2
Dalles, The (dam), Oreg. 291/F2
Dalles, The (dam), Wash. 310/D5
Dallesport, Wash. 310/D5
Dallol, Ethiopia 111/G5
Dallol Bosso (dry riv.), Niger 106/E6
Dalmaj, Hor (lake), Iraq 66/D4
Dalmally, Scotland 10/D2
Dalmally, Scotland 15/D4
Dalmatia, Pa. 294/J4
Dalmatia (reg.), Yugoslavia 45/C4
Dalmellington, Scotland 15/D5
Dalmellington, Scotland 10/D3
Dalmeny, Sask. 181/E3
Dal'negorsk, U.S.S.R. 48/O5
Dal'nerechensk, U.S.S.R. 48/O5
Daloa, Ivory Coast 106/C7
Daloa, Ivory Coast 102/B4
Dalroy, Alberta 182/D4
Dalry, Scotland 10/A1
Dalry, Scotland 15/D5
Dalrymple, Scotland 15/D5
Dalton, Ark. 202/H1
Dalton, Georgia 217/C1
Dalton, Ky. 237/F6
Dalton•, Mass. 249/B3
Dalton, Mich. 250/C5
Dalton, Minn. 255/C4
Dalton, Mo. 261/F4
Dalton, Nebr. 264/B3
Dalton•, N.H. 268/D3
Dalton, N.Y. 276/E5
Dalton, N.C. 281/J2
Dalton, Ohio 284/G4
Dalton, Pa. 294/L2
Dalton, Wis. 317/H8
Dalton City, Ill. 222/E4
Daltonganj, India 68/E4
Dalton Gardens, Idaho 220/B2
Dalton-in-Furness, England 13/D3
Dalupiri (isl.), Philippines 82/A3
Dalwallinu, W. Australia 88/B6
Dalwallinu, W. Australia 92/B5
Dalwhinnie, Scotland 15/D4
Dalworthington Gardens, Texas 303/F2
Daly (cape), Ant. 5/C4
Daly (riv.), North. Terr. 88/E2
Daly (riv.), North. Terr. 93/B2
Daly (bay), N.W. Terr. 187/K3
Dalyat al-Karmel, Israel 65/B2
Daly City, Calif. 204/H2
Daly River, North. Terr. 88/E2
Daly River, North. Terr. 93/B2
Daly River Aboriginal Res., North. Terr. 88/D2
Daly River Aboriginal Res., North. Terr. 93/A2
Dalyup, W. Australia 92/C6
Daly Waters, Australia 87/D7
Daly Waters, North. Terr. 88/E3
Daly Waters, North. Terr. 93/C4
Dalzell, Ill. 222/D2
Dalzell, S.C. 296/G3
Dam, Saudi Arabia 59/D5
Daman (dist.), India 68/C4
Daman & Diu (terr.), India 68/C4
Damanhur, Egypt 111/J3
Damanhur, Egypt 59/A3
Damar (isl.), Indonesia 85/H7
Damar (isls.), Indonesia 85/H7
Damar, Kansas 232/C2
Damara, Cent. Afr. Rep. 115/C2
Damaraland (reg.), Namibia 118/B4
Damariscotta•, Maine 243/E7
Damariscotta-Newcastle, Maine 243/E7
Damascus, Ark. 202/F3
Damascus, Georgia 217/C8
Damascus, Md. 245/K3
Damascus, Ohio 284/J4
Damascus, Pa. 294/M2
Damascus (prov.), Syria 63/G6
Damascus (cap.), Syria 59/C3
Damascus (cap.), Syria 54/E6
Damascus (cap.), Syria 63/G6
Damascus, Va. 307/E7
Damavand, Iran 66/H3
Damavand (mt.), Iran 54/G6
Damavand (mt.), Iran 59/F2
Damavend (Demavend) (mt.), Iran 66/G3
Damazin (Ed Damazin), Sudan 111/F5
Damba, Angola 115/B5
Dam Doi, Vietnam 72/E5
Dame Marie, Haiti 158/A6
Dame Marie (cape), Haiti 158/A6
Dame Marie (cape), Haiti 156/C3
Dameron, Md. 245/N8
Dames Ferry, Georgia 217/E4
Dames Quarter, Md. 245/P8
Damghan, Iran 59/F2
Damghan, Iran 66/J2
Damh, Loch (lake), Scotland 15/C3
Damietta, Egypt 102/F1
Damietta, Egypt 111/J3
Damietta, Egypt 59/B3
Damiya, Jordan 65/D3
Dammam, Saudi Arabia 59/F4
Dammastock (mt.), Switzerland 39/F3
Damme, Belgium 27/C6
Damodar (riv.), India 68/F4
Damoh, India 68/D4
Damongo, Ghana 106/D7
Dampier (str.), Indonesia 85/J6
Dampier (str.), Papua N.G. 86/B2
Dampier (str.), Papua N.G. 85/C7
Dampier, W. Australia 88/B4
Dampier, W. Australia 92/B3
Dampier (arch.), W. Australia 88/B4
Dampier (arch.), W. Australia 92/B3
Dampier Downs, W. Australia 92/C2
Dampier Land (reg.), W. Australia 88/C3
Dampier Land (reg.), W. Australia 92/C2
Damqut, Yemen 59/F6
Damvant, Switzerland 39/C2
Dan, Israel 65/D1
Dan (riv.), N.C. 281/L1
Dan (riv.), Va. 307/K7
Dana, Ill. 222/E3
Dana, Ind. 227/C5
Dana, Iowa 229/E4
Dana, Jordan 65/E5
Dana, Sask. 181/F3
Danakil (reg.), Ethiopia 111/H5
Danané, Ivory Coast 106/C7
Da Nang, Vietnam 72/E3
Da Nang, Vietnam 54/M8
Da Nang, Mui (cape), Vietnam 72/F3
Danao, Philippines 82/D5
Dana Point, Calif. 204/H10
Danba, China 77/F5
Danburg, Georgia 217/G3
Danbury, Conn. 210/B3
Danbury, Iowa 229/B4
Danbury, Nebr. 264/D4
Danbury•, N.H. 268/D4
Danbury, N.C. 281/J2
Danbury, Sask. 181/J4
Danbury, Texas 303/J8
Danbury, Wis. 317/B3
Danbury P.O. (South Danbury), N.H. 268/D5
Danby (lake), Calif. 204/K9
Danby•, Vt. 268/A5
Dancing (pt.), Manitoba 179/D2
Dancy, Ala. 195/B4
Dancy, Miss. 256/F3
Dancy, Wis. 317/G6
Dancyville, Tenn. 237/C10
Dand, Manitoba 179/B5
Dandaragan, W. Australia 88/B6
Dandaragan, W. Australia 92/A5
Dandenong, Victoria 97/K5
Dandenong, Victoria 88/M7
Dandenong (creek), Victoria 88/M7
Dandenong (creek), Victoria 97/K5
Dandenong (mt.), Victoria 97/K5
Danderyd, Sweden 18/H1
Dandong (Tantung), China 77/K3
Dandong, China 54/O5
Dandridge, Tenn. 237/O8
Dane (riv.), England 13/H2
Dane (co.), Wis. 317/H9
Dane, Wis. 317/G9
Daneborg, Greenl. 4/B10
Danford Lake, Québec 172/A4
Danforth, Ill. 222/E3
Danforth, Maine 243/H4
Danforth•, Maine 243/H4
Danger (Pukapuka) (atoll), Cook Is. 87/K7
Dangila, Ethiopia 111/G5
Dangrek (mts.), Cambodia 72/D4
Dangrek (Dong Rak) (mts.), Thailand 72/D4
Dangriga (Stann Creek), Belize 154/C2
Dania, Fla. 212/B4
Daniel (mt.), Wash. 310/D3
Daniel, Wyo. 319/B3
Daniel-Johnson (dam), Québec 174/D2
Daniels, Md. 245/L3
Daniels (co.), Mont. 262/L2
Daniels, W. Va. 312/D7
Daniel's Harbour, Newf. 166/C3
Danielson, Conn. 210/H1
Danielson Prov. Park, Sask. 181/E4
Danielstown, Guyana 131/B2
Danielsville, Georgia 217/F2
Danielsville, Pa. 294/M4
Danilov, U.S.S.R. 52/E3
Dankov, U.S.S.R. 52/E4
Danlí, Honduras 154/D3
Danmarks Havn, Greenl. 4/B10
Dannebrog, Nebr. 264/F3
Dannelly (res.), Ala. 195/D6
Dannemora, N.Y. 276/N1
Dannemora, Sweden 18/K6
Dannenberg, Germany 22/D2
Danner, Oreg. 291/K5
Dannevirke, N. Zealand 100/F4
Dan Sai, Thailand 72/D3
Dansville, Mich. 250/E6
Dansville, N.Y. 276/E5
Dante (Hafun), Somalia 115/K1
Dante, S. Dak. 298/N7
Dante, Va. 307/D7
Danube (riv.) 7/G4
Danube (riv.), Austria 41/C2
Danube (riv.), Bulgaria 45/H4
Danube (riv.), Czech. 41/C2
Danube (riv.), Hungary 41/E3
Danube, Minn. 255/C6
Danube (delta), Romania 45/J3
Danube (riv.), Romania 45/H4
Danube (riv.), Germany 22/C4
Danube (riv.), Yugoslavia 45/E3
Danubyu, Burma 72/B3
Danvers, Ill. 222/D3
Danvers•, Mass. 249/D5
Danvers, Minn. 255/C5
Danvers, Mont. 262/G3
Danversport, Mass. 249/E5
Danville, Ala. 195/D2
Danville, Ark. 202/D3
Danville, Calif. 204/K2
Danville, Georgia 217/F5
Danville, Ill. 188/J3
Danville, Ill. 222/F3
Danville, Ind. 227/D5
Danville, Iowa 229/L7
Danville, Kansas 232/E4
Danville, Ky. 237/M5
Danville, La. 238/E2
Danville, Mo. 261/J5
Danville•, N.H. 268/E6
Danville, Ohio 284/F5
Danville, Pa. 294/J4
Danville, Québec 172/E4
Danville•, Vt. 268/C3
Danville, Va. 188/L3
Danville, Va. 146/L6
Danville (I.C.), Va. 307/J7
Danville, Wash. 310/G2
Danville, W. Va. 312/C6
Danville, Wis. 317/J9
Dan Xian, China 77/G8
Danzig (Gdańsk), Poland 47/D1
Danzig (Gdańsk) (gulf), Poland 47/D1
Daocheng, China 77/F6
Dao Xian, China 77/H6
Dapa, Philippines 82/E6
Dapaong, Togo 106/E6
Daphne, Ala. 195/C9
Daphne, Sask. 181/G3
Dapitan, Philippines 82/D6
Dapoli, India 68/C5
Dapp, Alberta 182/C2
Da Qaidam, China 77/E4
Darab, Iran 59/G4
Darab, Iran 66/J6
Darabani, Romania 45/H1
Dar al Hamra, Saudi Arabia 59/C4
Daram (isl.), Philippines 82/E5
Daran, Iran 66/G4
Darbandikhan (dam), Iraq 66/D3
Darbhanga, India 68/F3
Darbun, Miss. 256/D8
Darby (cape), Alaska 196/F2
Darby, Mont. 262/B4
Darby (creek), Ohio 284/D5
Darby, Pa. 294/M7
Darby (creek), Pa. 294/M6
Darby, Victoria 97/D6
Darbydale, Ohio 284/D6
Darbyville, Ohio 284/D6
D'Arcy, Br. Col. 184/F5
D'Arcy, Sask. 181/C4
Dardanelle, Ark. 202/D3
Dardanelle (lake), Ark. 202/D3
Dardanelles (str.), Turkey 7/G5
Dardanelles (str.), Turkey 59/A2
Dardanelles (str.), Turkey 63/B6
Darden, Tenn. 237/E9
Dare (co.), N.C. 281/T3
Dar-el-Beida (Casablanca), Morocco 106/C2
Darende, Turkey 63/G3
Dar es Salaam (cap.), Tanzania 102/F5
Dar es Salaam (cap.), Tanzania 2/M6
Dar es Salaam (cap.), Tanzania 115/G5
Dareton, N.S. Wales 97/B4
Daretown, N.J. 273/C4
Darfur, Minn. 255/D6
Darfur, Northern (prov.), Sudan 111/D5
Darfur, Southern (prov.), Sudan 111/E5
Dargan, Md. 245/H3
Dargaville, N. Zealand 100/D1
Dar Hamid (reg.), Sudan 111/F5
Darham Muminggan Lianheqi, China 77/H3
Darhan (Darkhan), Mongolia 77/G2
Darien•, Conn. 210/B4
Darien, Georgia 217/K8
Darien, Ill. 222/B6
Darien, N.Y. 276/D5
Darién (mts.), Panama 154/J6
Darien, Wis. 317/J10
Darien Center, N.Y. 276/D5
Dariense, Cordillera (range), Nicaragua 154/E4
Darjeeling, India 68/F3
Dark (head), St. Vin. & Grens. 161/A8
Darkan, W. Australia 92/B2
Dark Canyon (creek), N. Mex. 274/E6
Dark Cove, Newf. 166/D4
Darke (co.), Ohio 284/A5
Darkesville, W. Va. 312/L4
Darkin (riv.), W. Australia 88/B2
Darlag, China 77/E5
Darling (river), Australia 87/E9
Darling, Miss. 256/D2
Darling (riv.), N.S. Wales 88/G6
Darling (riv.), N.S. Wales 97/B3
Darling (lake), N. Dak. 282/G2
Darling, Pa. 294/L7
Darling (range), W. Australia 88/B6
Darling (range), W. Australia 92/A1
Darling Downs, Queensland 95/D5
Darlingford, Manitoba 179/D5
Darlington, Ala. 195/D7
Darlington, England 10/F3
Darlington, England 13/F3
Darlington, Fla. 212/C5
Darlington, Idaho 220/E6
Darlington, Ind. 227/D4
Darlington, La. 238/J5
Darlington, Md. 245/N2
Darlington, Mo. 261/D2
Darlington, New Bruns. 170/D1
Darlington, Pa. 294/A4
Darlington (co.), S.C. 296/H3
Darlington, S.C. 296/H3
Darlington, Wis. 317/F10
Darlington Heights, Va. 307/L6
Darlington Point, N.S. Wales 97/C4
Darliston, Jamaica 158/H6
Darłowo, Poland 47/C1
Dar Masalit (reg.), Sudan 111/D5
Darmody, Sask. 181/E5
Darmstadt, Germany 22/C4
Darmstadt, Ill. 222/D5
Darmstadt, Ind. 227/B8
Darnell, La. 238/G1
Darnestown, Md. 245/J4
Darnick, N.S. Wales 97/B3
Darnley (cape), Ant. 5/C4
Darnley (bay), N.W. Terr. 187/F3
Daroca, Spain 33/F2
Darra, Queensland 88/K3
Darreh Gaz, Iran 66/L2
Darrington, Wash. 310/D2
Dar Rounga (reg.), Cent. Afr. Rep. 115/D2
Darrouzett, Texas 303/D1
Darrow, La. 238/K3
Darrtown, Ohio 284/A7
Darsser Ort (pt.), Germany 22/E1
Dart (cape), Ant. 5/B12
Dart (riv.), England 13/D7
D'Artagnan, Québec 172/J3
Dartford, England 13/J8
Dartford, England 10/C5
Dartmoor, Victoria 97/A5
Dartmoor Nat'l Park, England 13/C7
Dartmouth (Clifton Dartmouth Hardness), England 10/E5
Dartmouth (Clifton Dartmouth Hardness), England 13/D7
Dartmouth•, Mass. 249/K6
Dartmouth, Nova Scotia 162/K7
Dartmouth, Nova Scotia 168/E4
Dartmouth (riv.), Québec 172/D1
Darton, England 13/J2
Dartuch (cape), Spain 33/H3
Daru, Papua N.G. 87/E6
Daru, Papua N.G. 85/B7
Daruvar, Yugoslavia 45/C3
Darvel, Scotland 15/D5
Darwell, Alberta 182/C3
Darwen, England 10/G1
Darwen, England 13/H1
Darwin, Australia 2/R6
Darwin, Australia 87/D7
Darwin, Calif. 204/H7
Darwin (bay), Chile 138/D6
Darwin, Cordillera (mts.), Chile 138/D8
Darwin, Cordillera (mts.), Chile 138/E11
Darwin (Culpepper) (isl.), Ecuador 128/B8
Darwin, Ill. 222/F4
Darwin, Minn. 255/D5
Darwin (cap.), North. Terr. 88/E2
Darwin (cap.), North. Terr. 93/B2
Darwin, Okla. 288/P6
Das (isl.), U.A.E. 59/F4
Dash, Ben (hill), Ireland 17/C6
Dashan, Ras (mt.), Ethiopia 59/C7
Dashbalbar, Mongolia 77/H2
Dasher, Georgia 217/F9
Dashinchilen, Mongolia 77/F2
Dasht (riv.), Pakistan 68/A3
Dasht (riv.), Pakistan 59/H4
Dashtiari, Iran 66/M8
Dashtiari, Iran 59/H4
Dashwood, Br. Col. 184/H3
Dashwood, Ontario 177/C4
Dasol (bay), Philippines 82/B3
Dassel, Minn. 255/D5
Datça, Turkey 63/B4
Dateland, Ariz. 198/B6
Datia, India 68/D3
Datil, N. Mex. 274/B4
Datil (mts.), N. Mex. 274/B4
Datong, Qinghai, China 77/F4
Datong (Tatung), Shanxi, China 77/H3
Datto, Ark. 202/J1
Datu Piang, Philippines 82/E7
Daua (riv.), Kenya 115/H3
Daufuskie Island, S.C. 296/F7
Daugava (Western Dvina) (riv.), U.S.S.R. 53/D2
Daugavpils, U.S.S.R. 7/G3
Daugavpils, U.S.S.R. 53/D3
Daugavpils, U.S.S.R. 48/C4
Daugavpils, U.S.S.R. 52/C3
Daule, Ecuador 128/B3
Daulnay, New Bruns. 170/E1
Daun, Germany 22/B3
Daung Kyun (isl.), Burma 72/C4
Dauphin, Man. 162/F5
Dauphin, Manitoba 179/B3
Dauphin (lake), Manitoba 179/C3
Dauphin (riv.), Manitoba 179/D3
Dauphin (cape), Nova Scotia 168/H2
Dauphin (co.), Pa. 294/J5
Dauphin, Pa. 294/J5
Dauphin, St. Lucia 161/G5
Dauphiné (trad. prov.), France 29
Dauphin Island, Ala. 195/B10
Daus, Tenn. 237/L10
Davangere, India 68/D6
Davant, La. 238/L7
Davao, Philippines 85/H4
Davao, Philippines 54/O9
Davao, Philippines 2/R5
Davao, Philippines 82/E7
Davao (gulf), Philippines 82/E7
Davao (gulf), Philippines 85/H4
Davao del Norte (prov.), Philippines 82/E7
Davao del Sur (prov.), Philippines 82/E7
Davao Oriental (prov.), Philippines 82/F7
Daveluyville, Québec 172/E3
Davenport, Calif. 204/K4
Davenport, Fla. 212/E3
Davenport, Iowa 229/M5
Davenport, Iowa 188/H2
Davenport, Nebr. 264/G4
Davenport, N.Y. 276/L6
Davenport, N. Dak. 282/R6
Davenport (mt.), North. Terr. 93/B7
Davenport, Okla. 288/N3
Davenport, Va. 307/D6
Davenport, Wash. 310/G3
Daventry, England 13/F5
Davey, Nebr. 264/H4
Davey (riv.), Tasmania 99/B4
David (pt.), Grenada 161/D8
David, Ky. 237/R5
David, Panama 154/F6
David City, Nebr. 264/G3
Davidson (mts.), Alaska 196/K1
Davidson, Maine 243/F4
Davidson (co.), N.C. 281/J3
Davidson, N.C. 281/H4
Davidson, Okla. 288/J6
Davidson, Sask. 181/E4
Davidson (co.), Tenn. 237/H8
Davidson (mts.), Yukon 187/D3
Davidsonville, Md. 245/M5
Davie, Fla. 212/B4
Davie (co.), N.C. 281/H3
Daviess (co.), Ind. 227/C7
Daviess (co.), Ky. 237/G5
Daviess (co.), Mo. 261/E3
Davik, Norway 18/D6
Davilla, Texas 303/G7
Davin, Sask. 181/H5
Daviot, Scotland 15/D3
Davis (str.) 2/G2
Davis (str.) 146/N3
Davis (str.) 4/C12
Davis (sea), Ant. 5/C5
Davis (dam), Ariz. 198/A3
Davis, Calif. 204/B8
Davis (isl.), Fla. 212/C3
Davis, Ill. 222/D1
Davis (co.), Iowa 229/J7
Davis (dam), Nev. 266/G7
Davis, N.C. 281/R5
Davis (str.), N.W.T. 162/K1
Davis (str.), N.W. Terr. 187/M3
Davis, Okla. 288/M5
Davis (lake), Oreg. 291/F4
Davis (mt.), Pa. 294/D6
Davis, Sask. 181/F2
Davis, S. Dak. 298/P7
Davis (mts.), Texas 303/C11
Davis (co.), Utah 304/B3
Davis, W. Va. 312/H4
Davisboro, Georgia 217/G5
Davis City, Iowa 229/F7
Davis Cove, Newf. 166/D4
Davis Creek, Calif. 204/E2
Davis Dam, Ariz. 198/A3
Davis Inlet, Newf. 166/B2
Davis Junction, Ill. 222/D1
Davis-Monthan A.F.B., Ariz. 198/E6
Davison, Mich. 250/F5
Davison (co.), S. Dak. 298/N6
Davis Station, Ant. 5/C4
Davis Station, S.C. 296/G4
Daviston, Ala. 195/G4
Davisville, Mo. 261/K7
Davisville, R.I. 249/H6
Davisville, W. Va. 312/C4
Davlekanovo, U.S.S.R. 52/H4
Davos, Switzerland 39/J3
Davos (valley), Switzerland 39/J3
Davy, W. Va. 312/C8
Dawa (riv.), Ethiopia 111/G7
Dawasir, Hadhb (range), Saudi Arabia 59/D5
Dawasir, Wadi (dry riv.), Saudi Arabia 59/E5
Dawes (co.), Nebr. 264/A2
Dawes, W. Va. 312/D6
Dawlish, England 13/D7
Dawn, Mo. 261/E3
Dawn, Texas 303/B3
Dawna (range), Burma 72/C3
Dawson, Ala. 195/G2
Dawson, Canada 4/C16
Dawson (isl.), Chile 138/E10
Dawson (co.), Georgia 217/D2
Dawson, Georgia 217/D7
Dawson, Ill. 222/D4
Dawson, Iowa 229/E5
Dawson (bay), Manitoba 179/B2
Dawson, Minn. 255/B6
Dawson, Mo. 261/H8
Dawson (co.), Mont. 262/M3
Dawson (co.), Nebr. 264/E4
Dawson, Nebr. 264/J4
Dawson, N. Dak. 282/L6
Dawson (inlet), N.W. Terr. 187/J3
Dawson (riv.), Queensland 88/H4
Dawson (riv.), Queensland 95/D5
Dawson (co.), Texas 303/C5
Dawson, Texas 303/H6
Dawson, W. Va. 312/E7
Dawson, Yukon 146/E3
Dawson, Yukon 162/C3
Dawson, Yukon 187/E3
Dawson Bay, Manitoba 179/B2
Dawson Creek, Br. Col. 146/F4
Dawson Creek, Br. Col. 162/D4
Dawson Creek, Br. Col. 184/G2
Dawson Springs, Ky. 237/F6
Dawsonville, Georgia 217/D2
Dawsonville, New Bruns. 170/C1
Dawu, China 77/H5
Dawu, China 77/F5
Dax, France 28/C6
Da Xian, China 77/G5
Day, Fla. 212/C1
Day, Minn. 255/E5
Day (co.), S. Dak. 298/O3
Day Book, N.C. 281/E3
Daykin, Nebr. 264/G4
Daylesford, Victoria 97/C5
Daylight, Tenn. 237/K9
Daymán, Uruguay 145/B2
Daymán (range), Uruguay 145/B2
Daymán (riv.), Uruguay 145/B2
Dayong, China 77/H6
Days Creek, Oreg. 291/D5
Daysland, Alberta 182/D3
Daysville, Ky. 237/G7
Dayton, Ala. 195/C6
Dayton, Idaho 220/F7
Dayton, Ill. 222/E2
Dayton, Ind. 227/D4
Dayton, Iowa 229/E4
Dayton, Ky. 237/T1
Dayton, Mich. 250/C7
Dayton, Minn. 255/E5
Dayton, Mont. 262/B3
Dayton, Nev. 266/B3
Dayton, N.J. 273/D3
Dayton, N.Y. 276/C6
Dayton, Ohio 284/B6
Dayton, Ohio 146/K6
Dayton, Ohio 188/K3
Dayton, Oreg. 291/A3
Dayton, Pa. 294/D4
Dayton, Tenn. 237/L9
Dayton, Texas 303/J7
Dayton, Va. 307/L4
Dayton, Wash. 310/H4
Dayton, Wis. 317/H10
Dayton, Wyo. 319/E1
Daytona Beach, Fla. 188/K5
Daytona Beach, Fla. 146/K7
Daytona Beach, Fla. 212/F2
Daytona Beach Shores, Fla. 212/F2
Dayu, China 77/H6
Dayville, Conn. 210/H1
Dayville, Oreg. 291/H3
Dazey, N. Dak. 282/O5
Dazhai, China 77/H4
Dazkırı, Turkey 63/D4
De Aar, S. Africa 118/C6
Dead (lake), Fla. 212/D6
Dead (sea), Israel 65/C4
Dead (sea), Israel 59/C3
Dead (sea), Jordan 59/C3
Dead (sea), Jordan 65/C4
Dead (riv.), Maine 243/C5
Dead (riv.), Mich. 250/B2
Dead (lake), Minn. 255/C4
Dead (sea), West Bank 59/C3
Deadhorse, Alaska 196/J1
Deadman (creek), Wash. 310/H4
Deadman (mt.), Wyo. 319/B2
Deadwood, Alberta 182/B1
Deadwood (res.), Idaho 220/C5
Deadwood (riv.), Idaho 220/C5
Deadwood, S. Dak. 298/B5
Deaf Smith (co.), Texas 303/B3
Deal, England 13/J6
Deal, England 10/G5
Deal, N.J. 273/F3
Deal (isl.), Tasmania 99/D1
Deale, Md. 245/M5
Deal Island, Md. 245/P8
Dean (chan.), Br. Col. 184/D4
Dean (riv.), Br. Col. 184/D4
Dean, Nova Scotia 168/F3
Deán Funes, Argentina 143/D3
Deanville, Texas 303/H7
Dearborn (co.), Ind. 227/H6
Dearborn, Mich. 250/B7
Dearborn, Mo. 261/C3
Dearborn Heights, Mich. 250/B7
Dearing, Georgia 217/H4
Dearing, Kansas 232/G4
De Armanville, Ala. 195/G3
Dearne, England 13/K2
Deary, Idaho 220/B3
Dease (inlet), Alaska 196/H1
Dease (lake), Br. Col. 184/K2
Dease (riv.), Br. Col. 184/K2
Dease (str.), N.W.T. 146/G3
Dease (str.), N.W.T. 162/F2
Dease (str.), N.W. Terr. 187/H3
Dease Arm (inlet), N.W. Terr. 187/F3
Death (valley), Calif. 204/H7
Death Valley, Calif. 204/J7
Death Valley (depr.), Calif. 188/C3
Death Valley Junction, Calif. 204/J7
Death Valley Nat'l Mon., Calif. 204/H7
Death Valley Nat'l Mon., Nev. 266/E6
Deatsville, Ala. 195/F5
Deauville, France 28/C3
Deauville, Québec 172/E4
Deaver, Wyo. 319/D1
Deavertown, Ohio 284/G6
De Baca (co.), N. Mex. 274/E4
Deba Habe, Nigeria 106/G6
Debar, Yugoslavia 45/E5
De Bary, Fla. 212/E3
Debden, Sask. 181/E2
Débé, Trin. & Tob. 161/B11
Debec, New Bruns. 170/C2
De Beque, Colo. 208/C4
De Berry, Texas 303/L5
Debert, Nova Scotia 168/E3
Dębica, Poland 47/E3
De Bilt, Netherlands 27/G4
Dęblin, Poland 47/E3
Deblois•, Maine 243/H6
Dębno, Poland 47/B2
Débo (lake), Mali 106/D5
Debolt, Alberta 182/B2
De Borgia, Mont. 262/A3
Debra Birhan, Ethiopia 111/G6
Debra Markos, Ethiopia 111/G5
Debra Markos, Ethiopia 102/F3
Debra Tabor, Ethiopia 111/G5
Debrecen, Hungary 41/F3
Debrecen, Hungary 7/G4
Decatur, Ala. 195/D1
Decatur, Ark. 202/A1
Decatur (co.), Georgia 217/C9
Decatur, Georgia 217/K1
Decatur, Ill. 188/J3
Decatur, Ill. 146/K6
Decatur, Ill. 222/E4
Decatur (lake), Ill. 222/E4

360 De Soto

De Soto, Miss. 256/G7
De Soto, Mo. 261/L6
De Soto, Texas 303/G3
De Soto, Wis. 317/D9
De Soto Nat'l Mem., Fla. 212/D4
Des Peres, Mo. 261/O3
Des Plaines, Ill. 222/B5
Des Plaines (riv.), Ill. 222/A6
Dessa, Niger 106/E6
Dessalines, Haiti 158/C5
Dessau, Germany 22/E3
Dessel, Belgium 27/G6
Dessye, Ethiopia 102/G3
Dessye, Ethiopia 111/G5
Destelbergen, Belgium 27/D6
Destin, Fla. 212/C6
Destrehan, La. 238/N4
Destruction (isl.), Wash. 310/A3
Destruction Bay, Yukon 187/E3
Deta, Romania 45/E3
Detah, N.W. Terr. 187/G3
Dete, Zimbabwe 118/D3
Detlor, Ontario 177/G2
Detmold, Germany 22/C3
De Tour (passage), Mich. 250/E3
Detour (pt.), Mich. 250/C3
De Tour Village, Mich. 250/E3
Detrital Wash (dry riv.), Ariz. 198/A3
Detroit, Ala. 195/B2
Detroit, Ill. 222/C4
Detroit, Kansas 232/E3
Detroit•, Maine 243/E6
Detroit, Mich. 146/K5
Detroit, Mich. 188/K2
Detroit, Mich. 250/B7
Detroit (riv.), Mich. 250/B7
Detroit, Oreg. 291/E3
Detroit (lake), Oreg. 291/E3
Detroit, Texas 303/J4
Detroit, U.S. 2/E3
Detroit Beach, Mich. 250/F7
Detroit Lakes, Minn. 255/C4
Detva, Czech. 41/E2
De Twente (reg.), Netherlands 27/K4
Deuel (co.), Nebr. 264/B3
Deuel (co.), S. Dak. 298/R4
Deûle (riv.), Belgium 27/B7
Deurne, Belgium 27/F6
Deurne, Netherlands 27/H6
Deustua, Peru 128/G10
Deutsch Feistritz, Austria 41/C3
Deutschkreutz, Austria 41/D3
Deutsch Landsberg, Austria 41/C3
Deutsch Wagram, Austria 41/D2
Deux Frères, Les (isls.), Vietnam 72/E5
Deux-Montagnes (co.), Québec 172/C4
Deux-Montagnes, Québec 172/H4
Deux Montagnes (lake), Québec 172/C4
Deux Rivières, Ontario 177/F1
Deux-Sèvres (dept.), France 28/C4
Deva, Romania 45/F3
De Valls Bluff, Ark. 202/H4
Devault, Pa. 294/L5
Dévaványa, Hungary 41/F3
Devecser, Hungary 41/D3
Develi, Turkey 59/C2
Develi, Turkey 63/F3
Deventer, Netherlands 27/J4
Devenyns (lake), Québec 172/D2
Devereux, Georgia 217/F4
Deveron (riv.), Scotland 15/F3
De View (bayou), Ark. 202/J3
Deville, La. 238/F4
Devil River (peak), N. Zealand 100/D4
Devils (isl.), Fr. Guiana 120/D2
Devil's (isl.), Fr. Guiana 131/E3
Devils (lake), N. Dak. 282/N3
Devils (riv.), Texas 303/D7
Devilsbit (mt.), Ireland 17/F6
Devil's Hole (Death Valley Nat'l Mon.), Nev. 266/E6
Devils Lake, N. Dak. 188/G1
Devils Lake, N. Dak. 282/N3
Devils Paw (mt.), Alaska 196/N1
Devils Postpile Nat'l Mon., Calif. 204/F6
Devils Slide, Utah 304/C2
Devils Thumb (mt.), Br. Col. 184/A1
Devils Tower, Wyo. 319/H1
Devils Tower Nat'l Mon., Wyo. 319/H1
Devin, Bulgaria 45/G5
Devine, Texas 303/E8
Devizes, England 13/F6
Devizes, England 10/F5
Devol, Okla. 288/J6
Devola, Ohio 284/H7
De Volet (pt.), St. Vin. & Grens. 161/A8
Devon, Alberta 182/D3
Devon (isl.), Canada 4/B14
Devon, Conn. 210/C4
Devon (co.), England 13/D7
Devon, Jamaica 158/H6
Devon, Kansas 232/H4
Devon, Mont. 262/E2
Devon (isl.), N.W.T. 162/M3
Devon (isl.), N.W.T. 146/K2
Devon (isl.), N.W. Terr. 187/K2
Devondale, Ky. 237/K2
Devonia, Tenn. 237/N8
Devonport, Australia 87/E10
Devonport, N. Zealand 100/C1
Devonport, Tasmania 88/H8
Devonport, Tasmania 99/C3
Devrek, Turkey 63/D2
Devrekâni, Turkey 63/E2
Devrez (riv.), Turkey 63/E2
Dewar, Iowa 229/J3
Dewar, Okla. 288/P4
Dewart, Pa. 294/J3
Dewas, India 68/D4
Dewberry, Alberta 182/E3
Dewees (isl.), S.C. 296/H6
De Weese (plat.), Colo. 208/J6
Deweese, Nebr. 264/F4
Dewey, Ariz. 198/C4
Dewey, Ill. 222/E3
Dewey (lake), Ky. 237/R5
Dewey (co.), Okla. 288/H2
Dewey, Okla. 288/P1
Dewey (Culebra), P. Rico 161/G1
Dewey (co.), S. Dak. 298/G3
Dewey Park, Ill. 222/B2
Deweyville, Texas 303/L7
Deweyville, Utah 304/B2
De Wijk, Netherlands 27/J3
De Winton, Alberta 182/C4
De Witt, Ark. 202/H5
De Witt (co.), Ill. 222/E3
Dewitt, Ill. 222/E3
De Witt, Iowa 229/N5
Dewitt, Ky. 237/O7
De Witt, Mich. 250/E6
De Witt, Mo. 261/F4
De Witt, Nebr. 264/G4
DeWitt, N.Y. 276/H4
De Witt (co.), Texas 303/G9
Dewitt, Va. 307/N6
Dewittville, Québec 172/C4
Dewsbury, England 10/H2
Dewsbury, England 13/J1
Dewy Rose, Georgia 217/G2
Dexter (lake), Fla. 212/E2
Dexter, Georgia 217/G6
Dexter, Iowa 229/E5
Dexter, Kansas 232/F4
Dexter, Ky. 237/E7
Dexter, Maine 243/E5
Dexter•, Maine 243/E5
Dexter, Mich. 250/F6
Dexter, Minn. 255/F7
Dexter, Mo. 261/N9
Dexter, N. Mex. 274/E5
Dexter, N.Y. 276/H2
Dexter, Oreg. 291/E4
Dexter City, Ohio 284/G6
Dexterville, Wis. 317/F7
Deyang, China 77/F5
Dey Dey (lake), S. Australia 88/E5
Dey Dey (lake), S. Australia 94/B3
DeYoung, Pa. 294/E2
Dez (riv.), Iran 59/E3
Dez (riv.), Iran 66/F4
De Zaan (riv.), Netherlands 27/B4
Dezful, Iran 59/E3
Dezful, Iran 54/F6
Dezful, Iran 66/F4
Dezhnev (cape), U.S.S.R. 4/C18
Dezhnev (cape), U.S.S.R. 48/T3
Dezhou (Tehchow), China 77/J4
Dezh Shahpur, Iran 66/E3
Dezh Shahpur, Iran 59/E2
Dhaba, Saudi Arabia 59/C4
Dhahiriya, West Bank 65/B5
Dhahran, Saudi Arabia 54/F7
Dhahran, Saudi Arabia 59/E4
Dhaka (Dacca) (cap.), Bangladesh 68/G4
Dhaka (Dacca) (cap.), Bangladesh 54/L7
Dhali, Cyprus 63/E5
Dhamar, Yemen 59/D7
Dhamtari, India 68/E4
Dhanbad, India 68/F4
Dhangarhi, Nepal 68/E3
D'Hanis, Texas 303/E8
Dhank, Oman 59/G5
Dhankuta, Nepal 68/F3
Dhar, India 68/C4
Dharma, Saudi Arabia 59/E5
Dharmsala, India 68/D2
Dharwar-Hubli, India 68/C5
Dhaulagiri (mt.), Nepal 68/E3
Dhenkanal, India 68/E4
Dhidhimótikhon, Greece 45/H5
Dhikaia, Greece 45/H5
Dhimitsána, Greece 45/F7
Dhi Qar (heads), Iraq 66/E5
Dhira', Jordan 65/D5
Dhofar (reg.), Oman 59/F6
Dholpur, India 68/D3
Dhomokós, Greece 45/F6
Dhond, India 68/C5
Dhoraji, India 68/C4
Dhubri, India 68/G3
Dhulia, India 68/C4
Día (isl.), Greece 45/G8
Diable (pt.), Martinique 161/D5
Diablerets (mt.), Switzerland 39/D4
Diablo (canyon), Ariz. 198/D4
Diablo, Calif. 204/K2
Diablo, Sierra (mts.), Texas 303/C10
Diablo, Wash. 310/D2
Diablo (dam), Wash. 310/D2
Diablo (lake), Wash. 310/D2
Diablotin, Morne (mt.), Dominica 161/E6
Diadema, Brazil 135/C3
Diagonal, Iowa 229/E7
Dial, Georgia 217/D1
Diamant, Rocher du (isl.), Martinique 161/C7
Diamante, Argentina 143/F6
Diamante (riv.), Argentina 143/C3
Diamantina, Brazil 132/F7
Diamantina (riv.), Queensland 88/G4
Diamantina (riv.), Queensland 95/B4
Diamantina Lakes, Queensland 95/B4
Diamantino, Brazil 132/B6
Diamond (lake), Conn. 210/F2
Diamond (head), Hawaii 218/C5
Diamond (peak), Idaho 220/E5
Diamond, Ind. 227/C5
Diamond, La. 238/L7
Diamond, Mo. 261/D9
Diamond, Ohio 284/H3
Diamond, Oreg. 291/J4
Diamond (lake), Oreg. 291/E4
Diamond (peak), Oreg. 291/E4
Diamond, Pa. 294/C2
Diamond, Virgin Is. (U.S.) 161/F4
Diamond, Wash. 310/H4
Diamond (lake), Wash. 310/H2
Diamond Bluff, Wis. 317/A6
Diamond City, Alberta 182/D5
Diamond City, Ark. 202/E1
Diamond Coast (reg.), Namibia 118/A5
Diamond Lake, Oreg. 291/E4
Diamond Point, N.Y. 276/N4
Diamond Springs, Calif. 204/D8
Diamondville, Wyo. 319/B4
Diana, W. Va. 312/F5
Dian Chi (lake), China 77/F7
Dianjiang, China 77/G5
Diano Marina, Italy 34/B3
Dianópolis, Brazil 132/E5
Diapaga, Burkina Faso 106/E6
Dias Creek, N.J. 273/D5
Díaz, Argentina 143/F6
Diaz, Ark. 202/H2
Dibaya, Zaire 115/D5
Dibaya-Lubue, Zaire 115/C4
Dibble, Okla. 288/L4
Dibeng, S. Africa 118/C5
D'Iberville, Miss. 256/G10
Dibete, Botswana 118/D4
Diboll, Texas 303/K6
Dibrugarh, India 68/G3
Dibulla, Colombia 126/D2
Dickens, Iowa 229/C2
Dickens, Nebr. 264/C4
Dickens (pt.), R.I. 249/H8
Dickens (co.), Texas 303/D4
Dickens, Texas 303/D4
Dickenson (co.), Va. 307/D6
Dickerson, Md. 245/J4
Dickey, Georgia 217/C7
Dickey (co.), N. Dak. 282/N7
Dickey, N. Dak. 282/N6
Dickeyville, Wis. 317/E10
Dickinson, Ala. 195/C7
Dickinson (co.), Iowa 229/C2
Dickinson (co.), Kansas 232/E3
Dickinson (co.), Mich. 250/B2
Dickinson, N. Dak. 188/F1
Dickinson, N. Dak. 282/E6
Dickinson, Pa. 294/H5
Dickinson, Texas 303/K3
Dickinson Center, N.Y. 276/M1
Dickson, Alberta 182/C3
Dickson, Okla. 288/M6
Dickson (lake), Ontario 177/F2
Dickson (co.), Tenn. 237/G8
Dickson, Tenn. 237/G8
Dickson, W. Va. 312/B6
Dickson City, Pa. 294/F7
Dicle, Turkey 63/J3
Dicle (riv.), Turkey 63/J4
Didam, Netherlands 27/J5
Didcot, England 13/F6
Dido, La. 238/E5
Didsbury, Alberta 182/C4
Didsbury, Alta. 162/E5
Didyme, Québec 172/E1
Die, France 28/F5
Diébougou, Burkina Faso 106/D6
Diefenbaker (lake), Sask. 181/E4
Diego de Almagro (isl.), Chile 138/D9
Diego Garcia (isl.), Br. Ind. Ocean Terr. 54/J10
Diego Lamas, Uruguay 145/C1
Diego Pérez (cay), Cuba 158/C2
Diégo-Suarez (Antsiranana), Madagascar 118/H2
Diehlstadt, Mo. 261/N9
Diekirch, Luxembourg 27/J9
Dielsdorf, Switzerland 39/F1
Diemen, Netherlands 27/C5
Diemtigen, Switzerland 39/D3
Dien Bien Phu, Vietnam 72/D2
Diep (riv.), S. Africa 118/F6
Diepholz, Germany 22/C2
Diepoldsau, Switzerland 39/J2
Dieppe, France 28/D3
Dieppe, New Bruns. 170/F2
Dieppe Bay, St. Kitts & Nevis 161/C10
Dieren, Netherlands 27/J4
Dierks, Ark. 202/B5
Diessenhofen, Switzerland 39/G1
Diest, Belgium 27/F7
Dieterich, Ill. 222/E4
Dietikon, Switzerland 39/F2
Dietrich, Idaho 220/D7
Diever, Netherlands 27/J3
Diez y Nueve de Abril, Uruguay 145/E5
Diez y Ocho de Julio, Uruguay 145/F4
Dif, Somalia 115/H3
Diffa, Niger 106/G6
Differdange, Luxembourg 27/H9
Difficult, Tenn. 237/K8
Difficult (mt.), Victoria 97/B5
Digboi, India 68/H3
Digby (co.), Nova Scotia 168/C4
Digby, Nova Scotia 168/C4
Digby Gut (chan.), Nova Scotia 168/C4
Digby Neck (pen.), Nova Scotia 168/B4
Digdeguash (riv.), New Bruns. 170/C3
Digges (isls.), N.W. Terr. 187/L3
Diggins, Mo. 261/G8
Dighton, Kansas 232/B3
Dighton•, Mass. 249/K5
Dighton, Mich. 250/D4
Digne, France 28/G5
Digoin, France 28/F4
Digor, Turkey 63/K2
Digos, Philippines 82/E7
Digul (riv.), Indonesia 85/K7
Dijon, France 28/F4
Dijon, France 7/E4
Dike, Iowa 229/H4
Dikhil, Djibouti 111/H5
Dikili, Turkey 63/B3
Diksmuide, Belgium 27/B6
Dikson, U.S.S.R. 4/B5
Dikson, U.S.S.R. 48/J2
Dikwa, Nigeria 106/G6
Dikwa, Nigeria 102/D3
Dilam, Saudi Arabia 59/E5
Dilbeek, Belgium 27/B9
Dildo, Newf. 166/D2
Dili, Indonesia 54/O10
Dili, Indonesia 85/H7
Dilia, N. Mex. 274/D3
Diligent River, Nova Scotia 168/D3
Di Linh, Vietnam 72/F5
Dilke, Sask. 181/F5
Dilkon, Ariz. 198/E3
Dilla, Ethiopia 111/G6
Dillabough, Sask. 181/J3
Dillard, Georgia 217/F1
Dillard, Mo. 261/K7
Dillard, Oreg. 291/D4
Dill City, Okla. 288/H4
Dille, W. Va. 312/E6
Dillenburg, Germany 22/C3
Diller, Nebr. 264/H4
Dilley, Oreg. 291/A2
Dilley, Texas 303/E9
Dillia (dry riv.), Niger 106/G5
Dilliner, Pa. 294/B6
Dilling, Sudan 111/E5
Dillingen, Germany 22/B4
Dillingen an der Donau, Germany 22/D4
Dillingham, Alaska 188/C6
Dillingham, Alaska 196/G3
Dillon (riv.), Alberta 182/E2
Dillon, Colo. 208/H3
Dillon, Kansas 232/E3
Dillon, Mont. 262/D5
Dillon (lake), Ohio 284/F5
Dillon (co.), S.C. 296/J3
Dillon, S.C. 296/J3
Dillonvale, Ohio 284/J5
Dillsboro, Ind. 227/G6
Dillsboro, N.C. 281/C4
Dillsburg, Pa. 294/J5
Dilltown, Pa. 294/E5
Dillwyn, Va. 307/M5
Dilolo, Zaire 115/D6
Dilsen, Belgium 27/H6
Dilworth, Minn. 255/B4
Dimas, Cuba 158/A2
Dimas, Mexico 150/F5
Dimashq (Damascus) (cap.), Syria 63/G6
Dimashq (Damascus) (cap.), Syria 59/C3
Dimbelenge, Zaire 115/D5
Dimbokro, Ivory Coast 106/D7
Dimboola, Victoria 97/B5
Dime Box, Texas 303/H7
Dimitrovgrad, Bulgaria 45/G4
Dimitrovgrad, U.S.S.R. 52/G4
Dimitrovgrad, U.S.S.R. 48/F4
Dimitrovgrad, Yugoslavia 45/F4
Dimlang (mt.), Nigeria 106/G7
Dimmit (co.), Texas 303/E9
Dimmitt, Texas 303/B3
Dimock, Pa. 294/L2
Dimock, S. Dak. 298/O7
Dimona, Israel 65/D4
Dimona (mt.), Israel 65/C5
Dimondale, Mich. 250/E6
Dimsdale, Alberta 182/A2
Dinagat, Philippines 82/E5
Dinagat (isl.), Philippines 85/H3
Dinagat (isl.), Philippines 82/E5
Dinagat (sound), Philippines 82/E5
Dinajpur, Bangladesh 68/F3
Dinan, France 28/B3
Dinant, Belgium 27/F8
Dinar, Kuh-e (mts.), Iran 66/G5
Dinar, Turkey 63/D3
Dinard, France 28/B3
Dinaric Alps (mts.), Yugoslavia 45/B3
Dinas Powis, Wales 13/B7
Dinder (riv.), Ethiopia 111/F5
Dinder (riv.), Sudan 59/B7
Dinder (riv.), Sudan 111/F5
Dindigul, India 68/D6
Dingalan (bay), Philippines 82/C3
Dingbian, China 77/G4
Dingess, W. Va. 312/B7
Dinggye, China 77/C6
Dinghai, China 77/K5
Dingle, Idaho 220/G7
Dingle, Ireland 10/A4
Dingle, Ireland 17/A7
Dingle (bay), Ireland 10/A4
Dingle (bay), Ireland 17/A7
Dingmans Ferry, Pa. 294/N3
Dingolfing, Germany 22/E4
Dinguiraye, Guinea 106/B6
Dingwall, Nova Scotia 168/H2
Dingwall, Scotland 15/D3
Dingwall, Scotland 10/D2
Dingxi, China 77/F4
Dingxing, China 77/H4
Dinh, Mui (cape), Vietnam 72/F5
Dinkelsbühl, Germany 22/D4
Dinnebito Wash (dry riv.), Ariz. 198/E3
Dinokwe, Botswana 118/D4
Dinorwic, Ontario 177/G5
Dinorwic, Ontario 175/B3
Dinosaur, Colo. 208/B2
Dinosaur Nat'l Mon., Colo. 208/B2
Dinosaur Nat'l Mon., Utah 304/E3
Dinsdale, Iowa 229/H4
Dinsmore, Sask. 181/D4
Dinsor, Somalia 115/H3
Dinuba, Calif. 204/F7
Dinwiddie (co.), Va. 307/N6
Dinwiddie, Va. 307/N6
Dinxperlo, Netherlands 27/K5
Diogo (isl.), Philippines 82/B2
Dioila, Mali 106/C6
Diomede, Alaska 196/E1
Diourbel, Senegal 106/A6
Diphu, India 68/G3
Dipilto, Cordillera (range), Nicaragua 154/D4
Diplo, Pakistan 68/B4
Dipolog, Philippines 82/D6
Dipper Harbour, New Bruns. 170/D3
Dir, Pakistan 68/C1
Dir, Pakistan 59/K2
Dire, Mali 106/D5
Direction (cape), Queensland 88/G2
Direction (cape), Queensland 95/B2
Dire Dawa, Ethiopia 102/G4
Dire Dawa, Ethiopia 111/H6
Diriamba, Nicaragua 154/D5
Dirico, Angola 115/D7
Dirico, Namibia 118/C3
Dirk Hartogs (isl.), Australia 87/B8
Dirk Hartogs (isl.), W. Australia 88/A5
Dirk Hartogs (isl.), W. Australia 92/A4
Dirksland, Netherlands 27/E5
Dirmil, Turkey 63/C4
Dirranbandi, Queensland 88/H5
Dirranbandi, Queensland 95/D6
Dirty Devil (riv.), Utah 304/D5
Disappointment (lake), Australia 87/C8
Disappointment (creek), Colo. 208/B7
Disappointment (isls.), Fr. Poly. 87/N7
Disappointment (lake), Newf. 166/B3
Disappointment (cape), Wash. 188/A1
Disappointment (cape), Wash. 310/A4
Disappointment (lake), W. Australia 88/C4
Disappointment (lake), W. Australia 92/C3
Discovery (bay), Victoria 88/E7
Discovery (bay), Victoria 97/A6
Discovery Bay, Jamaica 158/J5
Disentis-Mustér, Switzerland 39/G3
Dishman, Wash. 310/H3
Disko (isl.), Greenl. 4/C12
Disko (isl.), Greenland 146/N3
Disko, Ind. 227/E2
Disley, Sask. 181/F5
Dismal (riv.), Nebr. 264/C3
Dismal (Great) (swamp), N.C. 281/S1
Disney, Okla. 288/S2
Dison, Belgium 27/H7
Dispur, India 68/G3
Disputanta, Va. 307/O6
Disraeli (fiord), N.W. Terr. 187/L1
Disraëli, Québec 172/F4
Diss, England 13/J5
Diss, England 10/G4
Disston (lake), Fla. 212/E2
Disston, Oreg. 291/E4
District Heights, Md. 245/G5
District of Columbia 146/L6
District of Columbia 188/L3
DISTRICT OF COLUMBIA 245
Distrito Especial, Colombia 126/C5
Distrito Federal, Argentina 143/H7
Distrito Federal, Mexico 150/L1
Distrito Federal, Venezuela 124/E2
Distrito Nacional, Dom. Rep. 158/E6
Disûq, Egypt 111/J3
Dittmer, Mo. 261/L6
Ditton (riv.), Québec 172/F4
Diu (dist.), India 68/C4
Diu, India 68/C4
Diuata (mts.), Philippines 82/E6
Divernon, Ill. 222/D4
Divide, Colo. 208/J5
Divide, Mont. 262/D5
Divide (co.), N. Dak. 282/C2
Dividing (creek), Md. 245/R8
Dividing Creek, N.J. 273/C5
Divino, Brazil 135/E2
Divinópolis, Brazil 132/E8
Divinópolis, Brazil 120/E5
Divinópolis, Brazil 135/D2
Divis (mt.), N. Ireland 17/J2
Divisa Nova, Brazil 135/C2
Division (peak), Nev. 266/B1
Divo, Ivory Coast 106/C7
Divriği, Turkey 63/H3
Divriği, Turkey 59/C2
Dix, Ill. 222/E5
Dix (riv.), Ky. 237/M5
Dix, Nebr. 264/A3
Dixfield, Maine 243/C6
Dixfield•, Maine 243/C6
Dix Hills, N.Y. 276/O9
Dixie, Ala. 195/E8
Dixie (co.), Fla. 212/C2
Dixie, Georgia 217/E9
Dixie, Idaho 220/C4
Dixie, La. 238/C1
Dixie, Wash. 310/G4
Dixie, W. Va. 312/D6
Dixie Inn, La. 238/D1
Dixmont, Maine 243/E6
Dixmont•, Maine 243/E6
Dixmoor, Ill. 222/C6
Dixmude (Diksmuide), Belgium 27/B6
Dixon, Calif. 204/B9
Dixon, Ill. 222/D2
Dixon, Iowa 229/M5
Dixon, Ky. 237/F5
Dixon, Miss. 256/F5
Dixon, Mo. 261/H6
Dixon, Mont. 262/B3
Dixon (co.), Nebr. 264/H2
Dixon, Nebr. 264/H2
Dixon, N. Mex. 274/D2
Dixon, N.C. 281/D5
Dixon, Ohio 284/A4
Dixon, S. Dak. 298/L7
Dixon, Wyo. 319/E4
Dixon Entrance (chan.) 146/E4
Dixon Entrance (chan.), Alaska 196/M2
Dixon Entrance (chan.), Br. Col. 184/A3
Dixons Mills, Ala. 195/C6
Dixon Springs, Ill. 222/E6
Dixon Springs, Tenn. 237/J8
Dixonville, Ala. 195/E8
Dixonville, Alberta 182/B1
Dixonville, Pa. 294/D4
Dixville (peak), N.H. 268/E2
Dixville, Québec 172/F4
Dixville Notch, N.H. 268/E2
Dixville Notch (pass), N.H. 268/E2
Diyadin, Turkey 63/K3
Diyala (heads), Iraq 66/D4
Diyala (riv.), Iraq 66/D4
Diyarbakır (prov.), Turkey 63/H4
Diyarbakır, Turkey 54/F6
Diyarbakır, Turkey 63/H4
Diyarbakır, Turkey 59/C2
Dizful (Dezful), Iran 66/F4
Dja (riv.), Cameroon 115/B3
Dja (riv.), Congo 115/B3
Djado (plat.) 102/D2
Djado, Niger 102/D2
Djado, Niger 106/G4
Djado (plat.), Niger 106/G4
Djakarta (Jakarta) (cap.), Indonesia 85/H1
Djakovica, Yugoslavia 45/E4
Djakovo, Yugoslavia 45/D3
Djambala, Congo 115/B4
Djambi (Jambi), Indonesia 85/C6
Djanet, Algeria 106/F4
Djanet, Algeria 102/C2
Djelfa, Algeria 106/E2
Djema, Cent. Afr. Rep. 115/E2
Djemaa, Algeria 106/F2
Djenné, Mali 102/B3
Djenné, Mali 106/D6
Djerba (isl.), Tunisia 106/G2
Djerid, Shott el (salt lake), Tunisia 106/F2
Djibo, Burkina Faso 106/D6
Djibouti 2/L5
Djibouti 102/G3
DJIBOUTI 111/H5
Djibouti (cap.), Djibouti 111/H5
Djibouti (cap.), Djibouti 102/G3
Djokjakarta (Yogyakarta), Indonesia 85/J2
Djolu, Zaire 115/D3
Djouf, El (des.), Mauritania 106/C4
Djougou, Benin 106/E7
Djoum, Cameroon 115/B3
Djugu, Zaire 115/F3
D'Lo, Miss. 256/E7
Dmitriya Lapteva (str.), U.S.S.R. 4/B2
Dmitriya Lapteva (str.), U.S.S.R. 48/O2
Dneprodzerzhinsk, U.S.S.R. 7/H4
Dneprodzerzhinsk, U.S.S.R. 52/D5
Dnepropetrovsk, U.S.S.R. 7/H4
Dnepropetrovsk, U.S.S.R. 48/D5
Dnepropetrovsk, U.S.S.R. 52/D5
Dnieper (riv.), U.S.S.R. 7/H3
Dnieper (riv.), U.S.S.R. 48/D5
Dnieper (riv.), U.S.S.R. 52/D5
Dniester (riv.), U.S.S.R. 7/G4
Dniester (riv.), U.S.S.R. 52/C5
Dniester (riv.), U.S.S.R. 48/C5
Dno, U.S.S.R. 52/D3
Doaghbeg, Ireland 17/F1
Doaktown, New Bruns. 170/D2
Doans, Ind. 227/D7
Doba, Chad 111/C6
Doba, Chad 102/D4
Dobbie (mt.), North. Terr. 93/E7
Dobbin (bay), N.W. Terr. 187/L2
Dobbins A.F.B., Georgia 217/J1
Dobbs Ferry, N.Y. 276/O6
Dobbyn, Queensland 95/A3
Dobele, U.S.S.R. 53/B2
Döbeln, Germany 22/E3
Doberai (pen.), Indonesia 85/J6
Dobiegniew, Poland 47/B2
Doblas, Argentina 143/D4
Dobo, Indonesia 85/J7
Doboj, Yugoslavia 45/C3
Doboy (sound), Georgia 217/K8
Dobřany, Czech. 41/B2
Dobre Miasto, Poland 47/E2
Dobrich (Tolbukhin), Bulgaria 45/H4
Dobříš, Czech. 41/C2
Dobrush, U.S.S.R. 52/D4
Dobruška, Czech. 41/D1
Dobryanka, U.S.S.R. 52/J3
Dobšiná, Czech. 41/F2
Dobson, N.C. 281/H2
Doce (riv.), Brazil 135/E2
Doce (riv.), Brazil 132/F7
Doce Leguas (cays), Cuba 158/F3
Docker River, North. Terr. 93/A8
Docking, England 13/H5
Dock Junction (Arco), Georgia 217/J8
Doctor Arroyo, Mexico 150/K5
Doctor Cecilio Báez, Paraguay 144/D4
Doctor Juan L. Mallorquín, Paraguay 144/E4
Doctor Juan Manuel Frutos, Paraguay 144/E4
Doctor M. Irala, Paraguay 144/E4
Doctor Pedro P. Peña, Paraguay 144/A3
Doctors Inlet, Fla. 212/E1
Doctortown, Georgia 217/J7
Doddridge, Ark. 202/C7
Doddridge (co.), W. Va. 312/E4
Dodds, Alberta 182/D3
Doddsville, Miss. 256/C3
Dodecanese (isls.), Greece 45/H8
Dodge (co.), Georgia 217/F6
Dodge, Mass. 249/G4
Dodge (co.), Minn. 255/F7
Dodge (co.), Nebr. 264/H3
Dodge, Nebr. 264/H3
Dodge, N. Dak. 282/F5
Dodge, Texas 303/J7
Dodge (co.), Wis. 317/J9
Dodge, Wis. 317/D7
Dodge Center, Minn. 255/F6
Dodge City, Kans. 188/F3
Dodge City, Kansas 232/B4
Dodgeville, Wis. 317/F10
Dodgingtown, Conn. 210/B3
Dodman (pt.), England 13/C7
Dodoma (reg.), Tanzania 115/G5
Dodoma, Tanzania 102/F5
Dodoma, Tanzania 115/G5
Dodsland, Sask. 181/C4
Dodson, La. 238/E2
Dodson, Mont. 262/H2
Dodson, Texas 303/D3
Doe (lake), Ontario 177/E2
Doe (lake), Wash. 310/C2
Doe Bay, Wash. 310/C2
Doe Hill, Va. 307/K4
Doering, Wis. 317/G5
Doerun, Georgia 217/E8
Doe Run, Mo. 261/M7
Doesburg, Netherlands 27/J4
Doetinchem, Netherlands 27/J5

Druzhina 361

Dog (pond), Conn. 210/C1
Dog (isl.), Fla. 212/B2
Dog (lake), Manitoba 179/D3
Dog (isl.), Newf. 166/B2
Dog (lake), Ontario 177/G5
Dogai Coring (lake), China 77/C5
Doğanbey, Turkey 63/D4
Doğanhisar, Turkey 63/D3
Doğanşehir, Turkey 63/G3
Dog Creek, Br. Col. 184/G4
Dog Ear (creek), S. Dak. 298/K6
Döger, Turkey 63/D3
Dogo (isl.), Japan 81/F5
Dogondoutchi, Niger 106/E6
Dogondoutchi, Niger 102/C3
Dogpatch, Ark. 202/D1
Dog Pound, Alberta 182/C4
Dogskin (lake), Manitoba 179/G3
Doğubeyazıt, Turkey 63/K3
Dogwood (pt.), St. Kitts & Nevis 161/D11
Doha (cap.), Qatar 54/G7
Doha (cap.), Qatar 59/F4
Dohad, India 68/C4
Doheny, Québec 172/E2
Dohuk (gov.), Iraq 66/C2
Dohuk, Iraq 66/C2
Doi Inthanon (mt.), Thailand 72/C3
Doilungdêqên, China 77/C6
Doi Pha Hom Pok (mt.), Thailand 72/C2
Doi Pia Fai (mt.), Thailand 72/D4
Doische, Belgium 27/F8
Dois Córregos, Brazil 135/B3
Dois Irmãos, Serra (range), Brazil 132/F5
Dokkum, Netherlands 27/H2
Doksy, Czech. 41/C1
Dokterstuin, Neth. Ant. 161/F8
Dola, Ohio 284/C4
Dola, W. Va. 312/F4
Dolan, Ind. 227/E6
Doland, S. Dak. 298/N4
Dolan Springs, Ariz. 198/A3
Dolavon, Argentina 143/C5
Dolbeau, Québec 174/C3
Dolbeau, Québec 172/E1
Doldenhorn (mt.), Switzerland 39/E4
Dôle, France 28/F4
Dolega, Panama 154/F6
Dolent (mt.), Switzerland 39/C5
Doles, Georgia 217/E7
Dolgellau, Wales 13/D5
Dolgellau, Wales 10/E4
Dolgeville, N.Y. 276/L4
Dolgiy (isl.), U.S.S.R. 52/J1
Dolinsk, U.S.S.R. 48/P5
Dollar, Scotland 10/B1
Dollar, Scotland 15/E4
Dollar Bay, Mich. 250/G1
Dollard (bay), Netherlands 27/L2
Dollard, Sask. 181/C6
Dollard-des-Ormeaux, Québec 172/H4
Dollart (est.), Germany 22/B2
Dollarville, Mich. 250/D2
Dolliver, Iowa 229/D2
Dolny Kubín, Czech. 41/E2
Dolo, Ethiopia 111/H7
Dolomite, Ala. 195/D4
Dolomite Alps (range), Italy 34/C1
Dolores, Argentina 143/E4
Dolores, Argentina 120/D6
Dolores (co.), Colo. 208/C7
Dolores, Colo. 208/C8
Dolores (riv.), Colo. 208/B5
Dolores, Guatemala 154/C2
Dolores, Philippines 82/E4
Dolores, Spain 33/F3
Dolores, Uruguay 145/A4
Dolores (riv.), Utah 304/E5
Dolores, Venezuela 124/D3
Dolores Hidalgo de la Independencia Nacional, Mexico 150/J6
Dolphin and Union (str.), N.W. Terr. 187/G3
Dölsach, Austria 41/B3
Dolton, Ill. 222/C6
Dolton, S. Dak. 298/P7
Dom (mt.), Switzerland 39/E4
Domain, Manitoba 179/E5
Domaniç, Turkey 63/C3
Domar (dry riv.), Chad 111/C4
Domat-Ems, Switzerland 39/H3
Domažlice, Czech. 41/B2
Dombås, Norway 18/F5
Dombe Grande, Angola 115/B6
Dombóvár, Hungary 41/E3
Dombrád, Hungary 41/F2
Dombresson, Switzerland 39/C2
Domburg, Netherlands 27/C5
Domburg, Suriname 131/D3
Dome, Ariz. 198/A6
Dome Creek, Br. Col. 184/G3
Domeiko, Chile 138/A7
Domeyko, Cordillera (mts.), Chile 138/B4
Domínguez, Argentina 143/G6
Dominica 2/F5
Dominica 146/M8
DOMINICA 156/G4
DOMINICA 161/E7
Dominica (passage), Dominica 161/E5
Dominican Republic 2/F4
Dominican Republic 146/L8
DOMINICAN REPUBLIC 156/D3
DOMINICAN REPUBLIC 158
Dominion (lake), Newf. 166/B3
Dominion (cape), N.W. Terr. 187/L3
Dominion, Nova Scotia 168/J2
Dominion City, Manitoba 179/E5
Domino, Newf. 166/C3
Dömitz, Germany 22/D2
Domjor, India 68/F1
Domleschg (valley), Switzerland 39/E2
Dommel (riv.), Netherlands 27/H6
Domo, Ethiopia 111/J6
Domodossola, Italy 34/A1
Dom Pedrito, Brazil 132/C10
Dompu, Indonesia 85/F7
Domremy, Sask. 181/F3
Domrémy-la-Pucelle, France 28/F3
Dom Silvério, Brazil 135/E2
Dömsöd, Hungary 41/E3
Domuyo (vol.), Argentina 143/B4
Don (riv.), England 10/F4
Don (riv.), England 13/F4
Don (riv.), Ontario 177/J4
Don (riv.), Scotland 15/F3
Don (riv.), Scotland 10/E2
Don (riv.), U.S.S.R. 7/J4
Don (riv.), U.S.S.R. 48/E5
Don (riv.), U.S.S.R. 52/F5
Dona Ana (Mutarara), Mozambique 118/F3
Dona Ana (co.), N. Mex. 274/C6
Dona Ana, N. Mex. 274/C6
Donabate, Ireland 17/J5
Donaghadee, N. Ireland 17/K2
Donahue, Iowa 229/M5
Donald, Br. Col. 184/J4
Donald, Oreg. 291/A3
Donald, Victoria 97/B5
Donald, Wash. 310/E4
Donald, Wis. 317/E5
Donalda, Alberta 182/D3
Donalds, S.C. 296/C3
Donaldson, Ark. 202/E5
Donaldson, Ind. 227/E2
Donaldson, Minn. 255/B2
Donaldson A.F.B., S.C. 296/C2
Donaldsonville, La. 238/K3
Donalsonville, Georgia 217/C8
Donansburg, Ky. 237/K6
Donath, Switzerland 39/H3
Donatville, Alberta 182/D2
Donau (Danube) (riv.), Austria 41/D2
Donau (Danube) (riv.), Germany 22/C4
Donaueschingen, Germany 22/C5
Donauwörth, Germany 22/D4
Donavon, Sask. 181/D4
Donbar, Queensland 95/B3
Don Benito, Spain 33/C3
Doncaster, England 13/F4
Doncaster, England 10/F4
Doncaster, Md. 245/K7
Doncaster and Templestowe, Victoria 88/L7
Doncaster and Templestowe, Victoria 97/J5
Dondo, Angola 115/B5
Dondo, Mozambique 118/F3
Dondra (head), Sri Lanka 68/E7
Dondra Head (cape), Sri Lanka 54/K9
Donegal (co.), Ireland 17/K2
Donegal, Ireland 10/B3
Donegal, Ireland 17/F2
Donegal (bay), Ireland 17/D3
Donegal (bay), Ireland 10/B3
Donegal (harb.), Ireland 17/E2
Donegal (pt.), Ireland 17/B6
Donegal, Pa. 294/D5
Donel, Honduras 154/E3
Doneraile, Ireland 17/D7
Doneraile, S.C. 296/H3
Donets (riv.), U.S.S.R. 7/H4
Donets (riv.), U.S.S.R. 48/D5
Donets (riv.), U.S.S.R. 52/E5
Donetsk, U.S.S.R. 7/H4
Donetsk, U.S.S.R. 48/D5
Donetsk, U.S.S.R. 52/E5
Donga (riv.), Cameroon 115/B2
Donga, Nigeria 106/G7
Donga (riv.), Nigeria 106/G7
Dongara, W. Australia 92/A5
Dongchuan, China 77/F6
Dongen, Netherlands 27/F5
Dongfang, China 77/G8
Dongfanghong, China 77/M2
Donggala, Indonesia 85/F6
Dônghén, Laos 72/E3
Dong Hoi, Vietnam 72/E3
Dongio, Switzerland 39/H4
Dongning, China 77/M3
Dongo, Zaire 115/C3
Dongola, Ill. 222/D6
Dongola, Sudan 102/E3
Dongola, Sudan 59/B6
Dongola, Sudan 111/F4
Dongou, Congo 115/C3
Dong Rak (mts.), Thailand 72/D4
Dongsha (isl.), China 77/J7
Dongsheng, China 77/H4
Dongtai, China 77/K5
Dongting (lake), China 54/N7
Dongting Hu (riv.), China 77/H6
Dong Ujimqin, China 77/J2
Dongwe (riv.), Zambia 115/D6
Donie, Texas 303/H6
Doñihue, Chile 138/G5
Doniphan (co.), Kansas 232/G2
Doniphan, Mo. 261/L9
Doniphan, Nebr. 264/F4
Donji Vakuf, Yugoslavia 45/C3
Donkin, Nova Scotia 168/J2
Donley (co.), Texas 303/D2
Dønna (isl.), Norway 18/H3
Donna, Texas 303/F11
Donnacona, Québec 172/F3
Donnellson, Ill. 222/D4
Donnellson, Iowa 229/K7
Donnelly, Alberta 182/B2
Donnelly, Idaho 220/B5
Donnelly, Minn. 255/B5
Donner (pass), Calif. 204/E4
Donner, La. 238/J7
Donner and Blitzen (riv.), Oreg. 291/J4
Donnybrook, N. Dak. 282/G2
Donnybrook, Queensland 95/D5
Donnybrook, W. Australia 92/A2
Donora, Pa. 294/C5
Donovan, Georgia 217/G5
Donovan, Ill. 222/F3
Donsol, Philippines 82/D4
Donwell, Sask. 181/J4
Donzère, France 28/F5
Dooagh-Keel, Ireland 17/A4
Doole, Texas 303/E6
Dooling, Georgia 217/E6
Doolittle (pond), Conn. 210/C1
Doolittle, Mo. 261/J7
Doolittle Mills, Ind. 227/D8
Dooly (co.), Georgia 217/E6
Doon, Iowa 229/A2
Doon, Ireland 17/E6
Doon, Loch (lake), Scotland 15/D5
Doon (riv.), Scotland 15/D5
Doonerak (mt.), Alaska 196/H1
Doonside, Sask. 181/K6
Door (pt.), La. 238/M6
Door (co.), Wis. 317/M6
Door (pen.), Wis. 317/M6
Doorn, Netherlands 27/G4
Doornik (Tournai), Belgium 27/C7
Doqa, Saudi Arabia 59/D6
Dor, Israel 65/B2
Dora, Ala. 195/D3
Dora, Mo. 261/H9
Dora, N. Mex. 274/F5
Dora, Oreg. 291/D4
Dora (lake), W. Australia 88/C4
Dora (lake), W. Australia 92/C3
Dora Baltea (riv.), Italy 34/A2
Dorado, P. Rico 161/D1
Dora Lake, Minn. 255/D3
Doran, Minn. 255/B4
Dora Riparia (riv.), Italy 34/A2
Doraville, Georgia 217/K1
D'Orbigny, Bolivia 136/D7
Dorbiljin (Emin), China 77/B2
Dorbod, China 77/K2
Dorcas, W. Va. 312/H5
Dorchester, England 10/E5
Dorchester, England 13/E7
Dorchester, Georgia 217/K7
Dorchester, Ill. 222/D4
Dorchester, Iowa 229/L2
Dorchester (co.), Md. 245/O7
Dorchester, Mass. 249/D7
Dorchester, Nebr. 264/G4
Dorchester, New Bruns. 170/F3
Dorchester•, N.H. 268/D4
Dorchester, N.J. 273/D5
Dorchester (cape), N.W. Terr. 187/L3
Dorchester, Ontario 177/C5
Dorchester (co.), Québec 172/C3
Dorchester (co.), S.C. 296/G5
Dorchester, S.C. 296/G5
Dorchester, Wis. 317/F5
Dorchester Crossing, New Bruns. 170/F2
Dordogne (dept.), France 28/D5
Dordogne (riv.), France 7/E4
Dordogne (riv.), France 28/D5
Dordrecht, Netherlands 27/F5
Doré (lake), Ontario 177/G2
Doré (lake), Sask. 181/L3
Dore Alps (mts.), France 28/E5
Doré Lake, Sask. 181/L4
Dorena, Mo. 261/O9
Dorena, Oreg. 291/E4
Dorena (lake), Oreg. 291/E4
Dorenlee, Alberta 182/D3
Dores, Scotland 15/D3
Dores do Indaiá, Brazil 132/E7
Dorgali, Italy 34/B4
Dörgön Nuur (lake), Mongolia 77/D2
Dori, Mali 102/B3
Dori, Burkina Faso 106/D6
Doring (riv.), S. Africa 118/B6
Dorintosh, Sask. 181/L4
Dorion, Ontario 177/H5
Dorion, Québec 172/C4
Dorking, England 13/G8
Dorking, England 10/F5
Dormont, Pa. 294/B7
Dornach, Switzerland 39/E2
Dornbirn, Austria 41/A3
Dornie, Scotland 15/C3
Dornoch, Scotland 10/D2
Dornoch, Scotland 15/D3
Dornoch (firth), Scotland 15/E3
Dornoch (firth), Scotland 10/E2
Dornod, Mongolia 77/H2
Dornogovĭ, Mongolia 77/G3
Dorog, Hungary 41/E3
Dorohoi, Romania 45/H2
Dorotea, Sweden 18/K4
Dorothy, Alberta 182/D4
Dorothy, Minn. 255/B3
Dorothy, N.J. 273/D5
Dorothy, W. Va. 312/D7
Dorr (lake), Fla. 212/E2
Dorr, Mich. 250/D6
Dorrance, Kansas 232/D3
Dorre (isl.), W. Australia 88/A5
Dorre (isl.), W. Australia 92/A4
Dorreen, Br. Col. 184/C3
Dorrigo, N.S. Wales 97/G2
Dorris, Calif. 204/D2
Dorset (co.), England 13/E7
Dorset, Minn. 255/D4
Dorset, Ohio 284/J2
Dorset•, Vt. 268/A5
Dorset (peak), Vt. 268/A5
Dorset Heights (hills), England 13/E7
Dorsey, Miss. 256/H2
Dorsten, Germany 22/B3
Dortches, N.C. 281/O2
Dortmund, Germany 7/E3
Dortmund, Germany 22/B3
Dorton, Ky. 237/R6
Dörtyol, Turkey 63/F4
Doruma, Zaire 115/E3
Dorval, Québec 172/H4
Dory Point, N.W. Terr. 187/G3
Dos Bahías (cape), Argentina 143/D5
Dos Cabezas, Ariz. 198/F6
Dos Caminos, Cuba 158/J4
Dos de Mayo, Peru 128/E6
Dos Hermanas, Spain 33/D4
Dos Palos, Calif. 204/E6
Dosquet, Québec 172/F3
Dos Reyes (pt.), Chile 138/A5
Dos Ríos, Cuba 158/J4
Dosso, Niger 106/E6
Dossor, U.S.S.R. 48/F5
Dossville, Miss. 256/F5
Doswell, Va. 307/N5
Dothan, Ala. 188/J4
Dothan, Ala. 195/H8
Doti, Nepal 68/E3
Dot Klish (canyon), Ariz. 198/E2
Dot Lake, Alaska 196/K2
Dott, W. Va. 312/D8
Döttingen, Switzerland 39/F1
Doty, Wash. 310/B4
Douai, France 28/E2
Douala, Cameroon 115/B3
Douala, Cameroon 102/D4
Douarnenez, France 28/A3
Double Branches, Georgia 217/H3
Double Mer (lake), Newf. 166/C3
Double Mountain Fork, Brazos (riv.) Texas 303/C4
Double Oak, Texas 303/F1
Double Springs, Ala. 195/D2
Doubletop (peak), Wyo. 319/B2
Doubs (dept.), France 28/G4
Doubs (riv.), France 28/G4
Doubs, Md. 245/J3
Doubs (riv.), Switzerland 39/C2
Doubtful (sound), N. Zealand 100/A6
Doubtless (bay), N. Zealand 100/D1
Doucette, Texas 303/K7
Douds, Iowa 229/J7
Doué-la-Fontaine, France 28/C4
Douentza, Mali 106/D6
Douentza, Mali 102/B3
Dougherty (co.), Georgia 217/D7
Dougherty, Iowa 229/G3
Dougherty, Okla. 288/M6
Dougherty, Texas 303/C4
Douglas, Ala. 195/F2
Douglas (mt.), Alaska 196/H3
Douglas, Ariz. 146/G6
Douglas, Ariz. 188/E4
Douglas, Ariz. 198/F7
Douglas (chan.), Br. Col. 184/C3
Douglas (co.), Colo. 208/K4
Douglas (creek), Colo. 208/B3
Douglas (bay), Dominica 161/E5
Douglas (co.), Georgia 217/C3
Douglas, Georgia 217/G7
Douglas (co.), Ill. 222/E4
Douglas, Ireland 17/D8
Douglas (cap.), I. of Man 13/C3
Douglas (cap.), I. of Man 10/D3
Douglas (co.), Kansas 232/G3
Douglas, Manitoba 179/C5
Douglas•, Mass. 249/H4
Douglas, Mich. 250/C6
Douglas (co.), Minn. 255/C5
Douglas, Minn. 255/F6
Douglas (co.), Mo. 261/G9
Douglas (mt.), Mont. 262/F5
Douglas (co.), Nebr. 264/H3
Douglas, Nebr. 264/H4
Douglas (co.), Nev. 266/B4
Douglas, N. Dak. 282/G4
Douglas, North. Terr. 93/B2
Douglas, Okla. 288/L2
Douglas, Ontario 177/H2
Douglas (pt.), Ontario 177/C3
Douglas (co.), Oreg. 291/D4
Douglas, Scotland 15/E5
Douglas, S. Africa 118/C5
Douglas (co.), S. Dak. 298/N7
Douglas (lake), Tenn. 237/P9
Douglas (co.), Wash. 310/F3
Douglas, Wash. 310/F3
Douglas (co.), Wis. 317/C3
Douglas, Wyo. 319/G3
Douglas Harbour, New Bruns. 170/D3
Douglas Lake, Br. Col. 184/H5
Douglas Prov. Park, Sask. 181/E4
Douglass, Kansas 232/F4
Douglass, Texas 303/K6
Douglass Hills, Ky. 237/L2
Douglassville, Pa. 294/L5
Douglastown, New Bruns. 170/E1
Douglastown, Québec 172/D1
Douglasville, Georgia 217/C3
Doullens, France 28/E2
Doulus (head), Ireland 17/A8
Doumé, Cameroon 115/B3
Dounby, Scotland 15/E1
Doune, Scotland 15/D4
Dour, Belgium 27/D8
Dourados, Brazil 120/D5
Dourados, Brazil 132/C8
Douro (riv.), Portugal 7/D4
Douro (riv.), Portugal 33/B2
Douro (riv.), Spain 33/C2
Dousman, Wis. 317/J1
Douthat, Okla. 288/S1
Douville, Québec 172/D4
Dove (riv.), England 13/J2
Dove (creek), Utah 304/A2
Dove Creek, Colo. 208/A7
Dover, Ark. 202/D3
Dover (cap.), Del. 146/L6
Dover (cap.), Del. 188/L3
Dover (cap.), Del. 245/R4
Dover, England 7/E3
Dover, England 10/G5
Dover, England 13/J6
Dover (str.), England 13/J7
Dover (str.), England 10/G5
Dover, Fla. 212/D4
Dover, Georgia 217/J5
Dover, Idaho 220/B1
Dover, Ill. 222/D2
Dover, Ind. 227/H6
Dover, Kansas 232/G3
Dover, Ky. 237/O3
Dover, Mass. 249/B7
Dover•, Mass. 249/B7
Dover, Minn. 255/F7
Dover, Mo. 261/E4
Dover, N.H. 268/F5
Dover, N.J. 273/D2
Dover, N.C. 281/P4
Dover, Ohio 284/G4
Dover (lake), Ohio 284/H4
Dover, Okla. 288/L3
Dover, Pa. 294/J6
Dover, Tasmania 99/C5
Dover, Tenn. 237/F8
Dover (pt.), W. Australia 88/D6
Dover (pt.), W. Australia 92/D6
Dover A.F.B., Del. 245/S4
Doverel, Georgia 217/D7
Dover-Foxcroft, Maine 243/E5
Dover-Foxcroft•, Maine 243/E5
Dover Hill, Ind. 227/D7
Dover Plains, N.Y. 276/O7
Dover South Mills, Maine 243/E5
Dovesville, S.C. 296/H3
Dovey (riv.), Wales 10/D4
Dovey (riv.), Wales 13/D5
Dovns Klint (cliff), Denmark 21/D8
Dovray, Minn. 255/C6
Dovre, Norway 18/F6
Dovrefjell (hills), Norway 18/F5
Dow (Xau) (lake), Botswana 118/C4
Dow, Ill. 222/C4
Dow, Okla. 288/P5
Dowa, Malawi 115/F6
Dowagiac, Mich. 250/D6
Dow City, Iowa 229/B5
Dowell, Ill. 222/D6
Dowelltown, Tenn. 237/K8
Dowlatabad, Afghanistan 59/H3
Dowlatabad, Afghanistan 68/A2
Dowlatabad, Kerman, Iran 66/K6
Dowlatabad, Khorasan, Iran 66/M2
Dowlat Yar, Afghanistan 59/J3
Dowlat Yar, Afghanistan 68/B2
Dowling, Alberta 182/E4
Dowling (lake), Alberta 182/D4
Dowling, Mich. 250/D6
Dowling Park, Fla. 212/C1
Down (dist.), N. Ireland 17/K3
Downe, Sask. 181/C4
Downer, Minn. 255/B4
Downers Grove, Ill. 222/A6
Downey, Calif. 204/C11
Downey, Idaho 220/F7
Downey, Iowa 229/L5
Downfall (creek), Queensland 95/D2
Downham Market, England 13/H5
Downham Market, England 10/G4
Downieville, Calif. 204/E4
Downing, Mo. 261/H2
Downing, Wis. 317/B5
Downings, Va. 307/P5
Downingtown, Pa. 294/L5
Downpatrick (head), Ireland 17/C3
Downpatrick, N. Ireland 10/C3
Downpatrick, N. Ireland 17/K3
Downs, Ill. 222/E3
Downs, Kansas 232/D2
Downsville, La. 238/F1
Downsville, Md. 245/G2
Downsville, N.Y. 276/L6
Downsville, Wis. 317/C6
Downton, England 13/F6
Dows, Iowa 229/F3
Dowshi, Afghanistan 59/J2
Dowshi, Afghanistan 68/B1
Doyle, Calif. 204/E3
Doyle, Georgia 217/D6
Doyle, Tenn. 237/K9
Doylestown, Ohio 284/G4
Doylestown, Pa. 294/M5
Doylestown, Wis. 317/H9
Doyleville, Colo. 208/F6
Doyline, La. 238/D1
Doyon, N. Dak. 282/O3
Dozen (isls.), Japan 81/F5
Dozier, Ala. 195/F7
Dozier, Texas 303/D2
Dozois (res.), Québec 174/B3
Dra, Wadi (dry riv.), Morocco 106/C3
Drachten, Netherlands 27/J2
Dracut•, Mass. 249/J2
Drăgăneşti Olt, Romania 45/G3
Drăgăşani, Romania 45/F3
Dragonera (isl.), Spain 33/H3
Dragons Mouth (str.), Trin. & Tob. 156/F5
Dragons Mouth (str.), Trin. & Tob. 161/A10
Dragons Mouth (str.), Venezuela 124/H2
Dragoon, Ariz. 198/F6
Dragoon (mts.), Ariz. 198/F7
Draguignan, France 28/G6
Drain, Oreg. 291/D4
Drake (passage) 2/F8
Drake (passage), Ant. 5/C15
Drake (passage), Chile 138/E11
Drake, Colo. 208/J2
Drake, Mo. 261/K6
Drake, N. Dak. 282/K4
Drake, Sask. 181/G4
Drakensberg (range), Lesotho 118/D6
Drakensberg (range), S. Africa 118/D6
Drakensberg (range), Swaziland 118/D6
Drakes (creek), Ky. 237/J7
Drakesboro, Ky. 237/H6
Drakes Branch, Va. 307/L7
Drakesville, Iowa 229/J7
Draketown, Georgia 217/B3
Dráma, Greece 45/F5
Drammen, Norway 7/E3
Drammen, Norway 18/C4
Drance (riv.), Switzerland 39/D4
Drancy, France 28/B1
Drang, Ia (riv.), Cambodia 72/E4
Draper, S. Dak. 298/J6
Draper, Utah 304/C3
Draper, Va. 307/G7
Draper, Wis. 317/E4
Draperstown, N. Ireland 17/H2
Draperstown, N. Ireland 10/C3
Drasco, Ark. 202/G2
Drau (riv.), Austria 41/C3
Drava (riv.) 7/F4
Dráva (riv.), Hungary 41/D3
Drava (riv.), Yugoslavia 45/C3
Dravosburg, Pa. 294/C7
Drawsko Pomorskie, Poland 47/B2
Drax Hall, Barbados 161/B8
Drayden, Md. 245/N8
Drayton, N. Dak. 282/R2
Drayton, Ontario 177/D4
Drayton Plains, Mich. 250/F6
Drayton Valley, Alberta 182/C3
Drenthe (prov.), Netherlands 27/K3
Dresbach, Minn. 255/G7
Dresden, Germany 7/F3
Dresden, Germany 22/E3
Dresden, Kansas 232/B2
Dresden•, Maine 243/D7
Dresden, Mo. 261/F5
Dresden, N.Y. 276/F5
Dresden, N. Dak. 282/O2
Dresden, Ohio 284/G5
Dresden, Ontario 177/B5
Dresden, Tenn. 237/D8
Dresden Station, N.Y. 276/O3
Dresser, Wis. 317/A5
Dreux, France 28/D3
Drew (co.), Ark. 202/G6
Drew, Miss. 256/C3
Drew, Oreg. 291/E5
Drewry, Ala. 195/D8
Drewryville, Va. 307/O7
Drews (res.), Oreg. 291/G5
Drewsey, Oreg. 291/J4
Drewsville, N.H. 268/C5
Drexel, Mo. 261/C6
Drexel, N.C. 281/F3
Drexel Hill, Pa. 294/M6
Dreyfus, Ky. 237/N5
Drezdenko, Poland 47/B2
Driebergen, Netherlands 27/G4
Driffield, England 13/G3
Driffield, England 10/F4
Drift (creek), Oreg. 291/B3
Drifton, Pa. 294/L3
Driftwood, Okla. 288/K1
Driftwood, Pa. 294/F3
Driggs, Ark. 202/C3
Driggs, Idaho 220/G6
Drill, Va. 307/E6
Drimoleague, Ireland 17/C8
Drin (riv.), Albania 45/E4
Drina (riv.), Yugoslavia 45/D3
Drinkwater, Sask. 181/F5
Dripping Springs, Texas 303/F7
Driscoll, N. Dak. 282/K6
Driscoll, Texas 303/G10
Drishane, Ireland 17/C7
Driskill (mt.), La. 238/E2
Drøbak, Norway 18/D4
Drobeta-Turnu Severin, Romania 45/F3
Drogenbos, Belgium 27/B10
Drogheda, Ireland 17/J4
Drogheda, Ireland 10/C4
Drogobych, U.S.S.R. 52/B5
Drogobych, U.S.S.R. 48/C5
Droichead Nua, Ireland 10/C4
Droichead Nua, Ireland 17/H5
Droitwich, England 13/E5
Dromahair, Ireland 17/E3
Drôme (dept.), France 28/F5
Drôme (riv.), France 28/F5
Dromore, Bainbridge, N. Ireland 17/J3
Dromore, Omagh, N. Ireland 17/G3
Dromore West, Ireland 17/D3
Dronfield, England 13/J2
Drongan, Scotland 15/D5
Dronne (riv.), France 28/D5
Dronninglund, Denmark 21/D3
Dronten, Netherlands 27/H3
Dropmore, Manitoba 179/A3
Drouin, Victoria 97/C6
Druid, Sask. 181/C4
Druif, Neth. Ant. 161/D10
Drum (hills), Ireland 17/F7
Drum (bay), La. 238/M7
Drum (inlet), N.C. 281/S5
Drumaness, N. Ireland 17/K3
Drumbeg, Scotland 15/C2
Drumbo, Ontario 177/D4
Drumcar, Ireland 17/J4
Drumconrath, Ireland 17/H4
Drumheller, Alberta 182/D4
Drumheller, Alta. 162/E5
Drumhill, N.C. 281/R1
Drumkeerin, Ireland 17/E3
Drumlish, Ireland 17/F4
Drummond, Idaho 220/G5
Drummond (isl.), Mich. 250/F2
Drummond, Mont. 262/D4
Drummond, New Bruns. 170/C1
Drummond (mt.), North. Terr. 93/E5
Drummond, Okla. 288/L2
Drummond (co.), Québec 172/E4
Drummond (range), Queensland 88/H4
Drummond (range), Queensland 95/C5
Drummond (lake), Va. 307/P7
Drummond, Wis. 317/D3
Drummond Island, Mich. 250/F3
Drummonds, Tenn. 237/A10
Drummondville, Québec 172/E4
Drummondville-Nord, Québec 172/E4
Drummondville-Sud, Québec 172/E4
Drummore, Scotland 15/D6
Drummoyne, N.S. Wales 88/K4
Drummoyne, N.S. Wales 97/J3
Drumnadrochit, Scotland 15/D3
Drumquin, N. Ireland 17/F2
Drumright, Okla. 288/N3
Drums, Pa. 294/K3
Drumshanbo, Ireland 17/E3
Drury, Mo. 261/H9
Druskininkai, U.S.S.R. 53/C3
Druten, Netherlands 27/H5
Druz, Jebel ed (mts.), Syria 63/G6
Druzhba, U.S.S.R. 48/J5
Druzhina, U.S.S.R. 48/P3

Edenvale 363

Eagle (riv.), Newf. 166/C3
Eagle, Ontario 177/C5
Eagle (lake), Ontario 177/F5
Eagle (lake), Ontario 177/E2
Eagle (creek), Oreg. 291/K3
Eagle (hills), Sask. 181/C3
Eagle (peak), Texas 303/C11
Eagle (mt.), Virgin Is. (U.S.) 161/E4
Eagle, Wis. 317/H2
Eagle (lake), Wis. 317/H2
Eagle (lake), Wis. 317/K3
Eagle (peak), Wyo. 319/B1
Eagle Bay, N.Y. 276/L3
Eagle Bend, Minn. 255/D4
Eagle Bridge, N.Y. 276/O5
Eagle Butte, S. Dak. 298/G4
Eagle City, Okla. 288/J3
Eagle Crags (mt.), Calif. 204/J8
Eagle Creek, Oreg. 291/E2
Eagle Grove, Iowa 229/F3
Eagle Harbor, Md. 245/M6
Eagle Harbor, Mich. 250/A1
Eaglehawk, Victoria 97/C5
Eaglehill (creek), Sask. 181/D4
Eagle Lake, Fla. 212/E4
Eagle Lake, Maine 243/F1
Eagle Lake•, Maine 243/F1
Eagle Lake, Minn. 255/E6
Eagle Lake, Ontario 177/F2
Eagle Lake, Texas 303/H8
Eagle Mills, Ark. 202/E6
Eagle Mountain (lake), Texas 303/E2
Eagle Nest, N. Mex. 274/D2
Eagle Nest (lake), N. Mex. 274/D2
Eagle Pass, Texas 303/D9
Eagle Point, Oreg. 291/E5
Eagle River, Alaska 196/C1
Eagle River, Mich. 250/A1
Eagle River, Wis. 317/H4
Eagle Rock, Mo. 261/E9
Eagle Rock, Va. 307/J5
Eaglesfield, Scotland 15/E5
Eaglesham, Alberta 182/B2
Eaglesham, Scotland 15/D5
Eagles Mere, Pa. 294/J3
Eagle Springs, N.C. 281/K4
Eagleton Village, Tenn. 237/O9
Eagletown, Ind. 227/E4
Eagletown, Okla. 288/S6
Eagleville, Calif. 204/E2
Eagleville, Conn. 210/F1
Eagleville, Mo. 261/D2
Eagleville, Tenn. 237/H9
Eakly, Okla. 288/K4
Ealing, England 13/H8
Ealing, England 10/B5
Ear (lake), Sask. 181/B3
Earby, England 13/H1
Eardley (lake), Manitoba 179/F2
Ear Falls, Ontario 175/B2
Earl (lake), Calif. 204/A2
Earl, N.C. 281/F4
Earl, Wis. 317/C4
Earle, Ark. 202/K3
Earle Naval Weapons Sta., N.J. 273/E3
Earleton, Fla. 212/D2
Earleville, Md. 245/P3
Earl Grey, Sask. 181/G5
Earlham, Iowa 229/E6
Earlimart, Calif. 204/F8
Earling, Iowa 229/C5
Earlington, Ky. 237/F6
Earl Park, Ind. 227/C3
Earlsboro, Okla. 288/N4
Earlston, Scotland 15/F5
Earlton, Kansas 232/G4
Earlton, Ontario 177/K5
Earltown, Nova Scotia 168/E3
Earlville, Ill. 222/E2
Earlville, Iowa 229/L4
Earlville, N.Y. 276/J5
Early (co.), Georgia 217/C8
Early, Iowa 229/C4
Early Branch, S.C. 296/F6
Earlysville, Va. 307/M4
Earn, Loch (lake), Scotland 15/D4
Earn (riv.), Scotland 15/E4
Earnslaw (mt.), N. Zealand 100/B6
Earp, Calif. 204/L9
Earth, Texas 303/B3
Earthquake (lake), Mont. 262/E6
Easby, N. Dak. 282/O2
Easington, England 13/J3
Easingwold, England 13/F3
Eask (lake), Ireland 17/E2
Easky, Ireland 17/D3
Easley, S.C. 296/B2
East (cape), Alaska 196/K4
East (riv.), Conn. 210/E3
East (pt.), Fla. 212/E6
East (bay), La. 238/M8
East (pt.), Mass. 249/E6
East (range), Nev. 266/D2
East (pt.), N.S. Wales 97/J2
East (riv.), N.Y. 276/N9
East (cape), N. Zealand 87/H9
East (cape), N. Zealand 100/G2
East (bay), Nova Scotia 168/H3
East (riv.), Nova Scotia 168/F3
East (lake), Oreg. 291/F4
East (pt.), Pr. Edward I. 168/G2
East (Dezhnev) (cape), U.S.S.R. 4/C18
East (pt.), Virgin Is. (U.S.) 161/G4
Eastaboga, Ala. 195/F3
Eastabuchie, Miss. 256/F8
East Albany, Vt. 268/C2
East Alburg, Vt. 268/A2
East Aldfield, Québec 172/A4
East Alligator (riv.), North. Terr. 93/C2
East Alton, Ill. 222/A2
East Andover, Maine 243/B6
East Andover, N.H. 268/D5
East Angus, Québec 172/F4
Eastanollee, Georgia 217/F1
East Arcadia, N.C. 281/N6
East Arlington, Vt. 268/A5
East Arrow Park, Br. Col. 184/J5
East Aspetuck (riv.), Conn. 210/B2
East Aurora, N.Y. 276/C5
East Baldwin, Maine 243/B8
East Bangor, Pa. 294/M4
East Bank, W. Va. 312/D6
East Barnet, Vt. 268/C3
East Barre-Graniteville, Vt. 268/C3
East Barrington, N.H. 268/F5
East Baton Rouge (par.), La. 238/K1
East Bay, Nova Scotia 168/H2
East Bay (hills), Nova Scotia 168/H3
East Bend, N.C. 281/H2
East Berbice-Corantyne (dist.), Guyana 131/C3
East Berkshire, Vt. 268/B2
East Berlin, Conn. 210/E2
East Berlin, Pa. 294/J6
East Bernard, Texas 303/H8
East Bernstadt, Ky. 237/N6
East Berwick, Pa. 294/K3
East Bethany, N.Y. 276/D5
East Bethel, Minn. 255/E5
East Bethel, Vt. 268/B4
East Bloomfield, N.Y. 276/E5
East Blue Hill, Maine 243/G7
East Blythe, Calif. 204/L10
East Boothbay, Maine 243/D8
Eastborough, Kansas 232/E4
Eastbourne, England 13/H7
Eastbourne, England 10/G5
Eastbourne, N. Zealand 100/B3
East Brady, Pa. 294/C3
East Braintree, Manitoba 179/G5
East Braintree, Mass. 249/D8
East Braintree, Vt. 268/B3
East Branch, N.Y. 276/K7
East Branch, Rocky (riv.), Ohio 284/G10
East Brewster, Mass. 249/O5
East Brewton, Ala. 195/E8
East Bridgewater•, Mass. 249/L4
East Brisbane, Queensland 88/K3
East Brisbane, Queensland 95/E3
East Brookfield, Mass. 249/G4
East Brookfield•, Mass. 249/G4
East Brookfield, Vt. 268/C3
East Brooklyn, Conn. 210/H1
East Broughton, Québec 172/F3
East Broughton Station, Québec 172/F3
East Brownfield, Maine 243/B8
East Brunswick•, N.J. 273/E3
East Burke, Vt. 268/D2
East Butler, Pa. 294/C4
East Calais, Vt. 268/C3
East Calder, Scotland 15/D2
East Camden, Ark. 202/E6
East Canaan, Conn. 210/B1
East Candia, N.H. 268/E5
East Canton, Ohio 284/H4
East Canyon (res.), Utah 304/C3
East Cape Girardeau, Ill. 222/D6
East Carbon, Utah 304/D4
East Carondelet, Ill. 222/A3
East Carroll (par.), La. 238/H1
East Chain, Minn. 255/D7
East Charleston, Vt. 268/D2
Eastchester, N.Y. 276/P6
East Chester, Nova Scotia 168/D4
East Chevington, England 13/F2
East Chezzetcook, Nova Scotia 168/E4
East Chicago, Ind. 227/C1
East China (sea) 54/O7
East China (sea), China 77/L6
East China (sea), Japan 81/C8
East China (sea), S. Korea 81/C8
East Chop (pt.), Mass. 249/M7
East Claridon, Ohio 284/H2
East Cleveland, Ohio 284/H9
East Coast Bays, N. Zealand 100/B1
East Concord, Vt. 268/D3
East Conemaugh, Pa. 294/E5
East Corinth, Maine 243/F5
East Corinth, Vt. 268/C3
East Cote Blanche (bay), La. 238/G7
East Coulée, Alberta 182/D4
East Craftsbury, Vt. 268/C2
East Dedham, Mass. 249/C8
East Demerara-West Coast Berbice (dist.), Guyana 131/C2
East Dennis, Mass. 249/O5
East Dereham, England 13/H5
East Dereham, England 10/G4
East Derry, N.H. 268/E6
East Detroit, Mich. 250/B6
East Devils (lake), N. Dak. 282/N4
East Dixfield, Maine 243/C6
East Dixmont, Maine 243/E6
East Dorset, Vt. 268/A5
East Douglas, Mass. 249/G4
East Dover, Vt. 268/B6
East Dublin, Georgia 217/G5
East Dubuque, Ill. 222/C1
East Dundee (Dundee), Ill. 222/E1
East Durham, N.Y. 276/M6
East Eddington, Maine 243/F6
East Ellijay, Georgia 217/C1
Eastend, Sask. 181/C6
Eastend, Virgin Is. (U.S.) 161/D4
East Enterprise, Ind. 227/H7
Easter (isl.), Chile 87/Q8
Easter (isl.), Chile 2/D7
Eastern (pt.), Conn. 210/G3
Eastern (Arabian) (des.), Egypt 111/F2
Eastern (prov.), Kenya 115/G4
Eastern (bay), Md. 245/N5
Eastern (pt.), Mass. 249/M2
Eastern (creek), N.S. Wales 97/H3
Eastern Channel (str.), Japan 81/D7
Eastern Ghats (mts.), India 68/D6
Eastern Samar (prov.), Philippines 82/E5
Eastern Scheldt (est.), Netherlands 27/D5
Eastern Taurus (mts.), Turkey 63/J3
Eastern Wolf (isl.), New Bruns. 170/D4
Easterville, Manitoba 179/C1
East Fairfield, Vt. 268/B2
East Falkland (isl.), Falk. Is. 143/E7
East Falkland (isl.), Falk. Is. 120/D8
East Falmouth (Teaticket), Mass. 249/M6
East Farnham, Québec 172/E4
East Faxon, Pa. 294/J3
East Feliciana (par.), La. 238/H5
East Ferry, Nova Scotia 168/B4
East Flanders (prov.), Belgium 27/D7
East Flat Rock, N.C. 281/E4
Eastford•, Conn. 210/G1
East Fork, Little Miami (riv.), Ohio 284/C7
East Fork, Green (riv.), Wyo. 319/C3
East Foxboro, Mass. 249/K4
East Franklin, Maine 243/G6
East Franklin, Vt. 268/B2
East Freedom, Pa. 294/E5
East Freetown, Mass. 249/L5
East Friesland (reg.), Germany 22/B2
East Frisian (isls.), Germany 22/B2
East Gaffney, S.C. 296/D1
East Galesburg, Ill. 222/C3
Eastgate, Nev. 266/D3
East Georgia, Vt. 268/A2
East Germantown (Pershing), Ind. 227/G5
East Gillespie, Ill. 222/D4
East Glacier Park, Mont. 262/C2
East Glastonbury, Conn. 210/E2
East Grafton, N.H. 268/D4
East Granby•, Conn. 210/E1
East Grand Forks, Minn. 255/B3
East Grand Rapids, Mich. 250/D6
East Granville, Vt. 268/B3
East Greenbush, N.Y. 276/N5
East Green Harbour, Nova Scotia 168/C5
East Greenville, Ohio 284/G4
East Greenville, Pa. 294/L5
East Greenwich, R.I. 249/H6
East Grinstead, England 10/G5
East Grinstead, England 13/G6
Eastgulf, W. Va. 312/D7
East Gull Lake, Minn. 255/D4
East Haddam•, Conn. 210/F3
Eastham•, Mass. 249/O5
East Hampstead, N.H. 268/E6
East Hampton, Conn. 210/E2
East Hampton•, Conn. 210/E2
Easthampton•, Mass. 249/D3
East Hampton, N.Y. 276/R9
East Hanover•, N.J. 273/E2
East Hardin, Ill. 222/C4
East Hardwick, Vt. 268/C2
East Hartford•, Conn. 210/E1
East Hartland, Conn. 210/D1
East Harwich, Mass. 249/O6
East Haven•, Conn. 210/D3
East Haven•, Vt. 268/D2
East Haverhill, N.H. 268/D3
East Hazelcrest, Ill. 222/C6
East Hebron, N.H. 268/D4
East Helena, Mont. 262/E4
East Hereford, Québec 172/F4
East Hickory, Pa. 294/D2
East Hills, N.Y. 276/R7
East Hiram, Maine 243/B8
East Hodge, La. 238/E2
East Holden, Maine 243/F6
East Hope, Idaho 220/B1
East Jackson, Maine 243/E6
East Jamaica, Vt. 268/B5
East Jordan, Mich. 250/D3
East Juliette, Georgia 217/E4
East Keansburg, N.J. 273/E3
East Kelowna, Br. Col. 184/H5
East Kent, Conn. 210/B2
East Kilbride, Scotland 15/B2
East Killingly, Conn. 210/H1
East Kingsford, Mich. 250/A3
East Kingston•, N.H. 268/F6
East Knox, Maine 243/E7
East Korea (bay), N. Korea 81/D4
East Lake, Mich. 250/C4
East Lake, Minn. 255/E4
East Lake, N.C. 281/S3
Eastlake, Ohio 284/J8
East Lake-Orient Park, Fla. 212/C2
Eastland, Tenn. 237/L9
Eastland (co.), Texas 303/F5
Eastland, Texas 303/F5
East Lansdowne, Pa. 294/M7
East Lansing, Mich. 250/E6
East Laport, N.C. 281/C4
East Las Vegas, Nev. 266/F6
East Laurinburg, N.C. 281/L5
East Lebanon, Maine 243/B9
East Lee, Mass. 249/B3
Eastleigh, England 13/F7
Eastleigh, England 10/F5
East Lempster, N.H. 268/C5
East Limington, Maine 243/B8
East Linton, Scotland 15/F5
East Litchfield, Conn. 210/C1
East Livermore, Maine 243/C7
East Liverpool, Ohio 284/J4
East Loch (inlet), Hawaii 218/B3
East Loch Tarbert (inlet), Scotland 15/B3
East London, S. Africa 102/E8
East London, S. Africa 118/D6
East Longmeadow•, Mass. 249/E4
East Los Angeles, Calif. 204/C10
East Lowell, Maine 243/G5
East Lyme•, Conn. 210/G3
East Lynn, Ill. 222/F3
East Lynn, W. Va. 312/B6
East Lynn (lake), W. Va. 312/B6
East Lynne, Mo. 261/D5
East Machias, Maine 243/J6
East Machias•, Maine 243/J6
East Machias (riv.), Maine 243/H6
East Madison, Maine 243/D6
East Madison, N.H. 268/E4
Eastmain, Que. 162/J5
Eastmain, Québec 174/B2
Eastmain (riv.), Que. 146/L4
Eastmain (riv.), Que. 162/J5
Eastmain (riv.), Que. 174/B2
Eastman, Georgia 217/F6
Eastman, Québec 172/E4
Eastman, Wis. 317/D9
East Marion, N.C. 281/F3
East Meadow, N.Y. 276/R7
East Meredith, N.Y. 276/L6
East Middlebury, Vt. 268/A4
East Millcreek, Utah 304/C3
East Millinocket, Maine 243/F4
East Millinocket•, Maine 243/F4
East Millstone, N.J. 273/D3
East Milton, Mass. 249/D7
East Mines, Nova Scotia 168/E3
East Moline, Ill. 222/C2
East Montpelier•, Vt. 268/B3
East Moriches, N.Y. 276/P9
East Morris, Conn. 210/C2
East Murton, England 13/J3
East Musquash (lake), Maine 243/H5
East Naples, Fla. 212/E5
East Newark, N.J. 273/B2
East New Market, Md. 245/P6
East Newnan, Georgia 217/C4
East New Portland, Maine 243/D6
East Nishnabotna (riv.), Iowa 229/C6
East Northfield, Mass. 249/E2
East Northport, N.Y. 276/O9
East Norton, Mass. 249/K5
East Norwalk, Conn. 210/B4
East Olympia, Wash. 310/B4
Easton, Calif. 204/F7
Easton•, Conn. 210/B4
Easton (res.), Conn. 210/B3
Easton, Ill. 222/D3
Easton, Kansas 232/G2
Easton, La. 238/F5
Easton•, Maine 243/H2
Easton, Md. 245/O5
Easton•, Mass. 249/K4
Easton, Minn. 255/E7
Easton, Mo. 261/C3
Easton•, N.H. 268/D3
Easton, Pa. 294/M4
Easton, Wash. 310/D3
Easton, Wis. 317/G8
Eastondale, Mass. 249/K4
East Orange, N.J. 273/B2
East Orland, Maine 243/F6
East Orleans, Mass. 249/P5
East Otis, Mass. 249/B4
East Otisfield, Maine 243/B7
East Otto, N.Y. 276/C6
Eastover, S.C. 296/F4
East Palatka, Fla. 212/E2
East Palestine, Ohio 284/J4
East Park (res.), Calif. 204/C4
East Parsonfield, Maine 243/B8
East Peacham, Vt. 268/C3
East Pembroke, Mass. 249/M4
East Pembroke, N.Y. 276/D5
East Peoria, Ill. 222/D3
East Pepperell, Mass. 249/H2
East Peru (Peru), Iowa 229/F6
East Peru, Maine 243/C7
East Petersburg, Pa. 294/K5
East Pleasant Plain, Iowa 229/K6
Eastpoint, Fla. 212/B2
East Point, Georgia 217/K2
East Point, Ky. 237/R5
East Point, La. 238/D2
East Poland, Maine 243/C7
East Poplar, Sask. 181/F6
Eastport, Idaho 220/B1
Eastport, Maine 188/N2
Eastport, Maine 243/K6
Eastport, Mich. 250/D3
Eastport, Newf. 166/D1
Eastport, N.Y. 276/P9
East Poultney, Vt. 268/A4
East Prairie, Mo. 261/O9
East Preston, England 13/G7
East Prospect, Pa. 294/J6
East Providence, R.I. 249/J5
East Putnam, Conn. 210/H1
East Randolph, N.Y. 276/C6
East Randolph, Vt. 268/B4
East Retford, England 13/G4
East Retford, England 10/F4
East Richford, Vt. 268/B2
East Ridge, Tenn. 237/L11
Eastriggs, Scotland 15/E5
East Rindge, N.H. 268/D6
East River, Conn. 210/E3
East River Saint Marys, Nova Scotia 168/F3
East Riverside-Kingshurst, New Bruns. 170/E3
East Rochester, N.Y. 276/F4
East Rochester, Ohio 284/H4
East Rockaway, N.Y. 276/R7
East Rutherford, N.J. 273/B2
Eastry, England 13/J6
East Ryegate, Vt. 268/C3
East Saint Louis, Ill. 188/J3
East Saint Louis, Ill. 222/A2
East Sandwich, Mass. 249/N6
East Saugus, Mass. 249/D6
East Sebago, Maine 243/B8
East Selkirk, Manitoba 179/F4
East Shoal (lake), Manitoba 179/E4
East Siberian (sea), U.S.S.R. 4/B1
East Siberian (sea), U.S.S.R. 54/T2
East Siberian (sea), U.S.S.R. 48/S2
East Side, Pa. 294/L3
East Sister (peak), Idaho 220/C2
East Sister (isl.), Tasmania 99/E1
East Smithfield, Pa. 294/J2
Eastsound, Wash. 310/B2
East Sparta, Ohio 284/H4
East Spencer, N.C. 281/J3
East Springfield, N.Y. 276/L5
East Springfield, Pa. 294/A2
East Stone Gap, Va. 307/C7
East Stoneham, Maine 243/B7
East Stroudsburg, Pa. 294/M4
East Sullivan, Maine 243/G6
East Sullivan, N.H. 268/C6
East Sumner, Maine 243/C7
East Sussex (co.), England 13/H7
East Swan (riv.), Minn. 255/F3
East Swanzey, N.H. 268/C6
East Syracuse, N.Y. 276/H4
East Tawas, Mich. 250/F4
East Templeton, Mass. 249/G2
East Thermopolis, Wyo. 319/D2
East Thetford, Vt. 268/C4
East Thompson, Conn. 210/H1
East Tintic (creek), Utah 304/B4
East Tohopekaliga (lake), Fla. 212/E3
East Troy, Wis. 317/J2
East Union, Maine 243/E7
Eastvale, Pa. 294/B4
Eastvale, Texas 303/G1
East Vassalboro, Maine 243/D7
East Verde (riv.), Ariz. 198/D4
Eastview, Tenn. 237/D10
East View, W. Va. 312/F4
East Village, Conn. 210/C3
Eastville, Georgia 217/E3
Eastville, Va. 307/R6
East Wakefield, N.H. 268/E4
East Walker (riv.), Nev. 266/B4
East Wallingford, Vt. 268/B5
East Walpole, Mass. 249/C8
East Wareham, Mass. 249/M5
East Washington, Pa. 294/B5
East Waterboro, Maine 243/B8
East Waterford, Pa. 294/G5
East Wenatchee, Wash. 310/E3
East Weymouth, Mass. 249/E8
East Whately, Mass. 249/D3
East Williamson, N.Y. 276/F4
East Willington, Conn. 210/G1
East Wilton, Maine 243/C6
East Windsor•, Conn. 210/E1
East Windsor Hill, Conn. 210/E1
East Winn, Maine 243/G5
East Wolfeboro, N.H. 268/E4
Eastwood, Mich. 250/D6
Eastwood, N.S. Wales 88/K4
Eastwood, N.S. Wales 97/J3
Eastwood, Ontario 177/D4
East Woodstock, Conn. 210/H1
East Worcester, N.Y. 276/L5
East York, Ontario 177/J4
Eaton, Colo. 208/K1
Eaton, Ill. 222/F4
Eaton, Ind. 227/G4
Eaton, Maine 243/H4
Eaton (co.), Mich. 250/E6
Eaton (Eaton Center)•, N.H. 268/E4
Eaton, N.Y. 276/J5
Eaton, Ohio 284/A6
Eaton, Tenn. 237/C9
Eaton Center, N.H. 268/E4
Eaton Estates, Ohio 284/G3
Eatonia, Sask. 181/B4
Eaton Rapids, Mich. 250/E6
Eatonton, Georgia 217/F4
Eatontown, N.J. 273/E3
Eatonville, Fla. 212/E3
Eatonville, Wash. 310/C4
Eau Claire, Mich. 250/C6
Eau Claire, Pa. 294/C3
Eau Claire (lake), Québec 174/C1
Eau Claire, Lac à l' (lake), Que. 162/J4
Eau Claire (co.), Wis. 317/D6
Eau Claire, Wis. 188/H2
Eau Claire, Wis. 317/D6
Eau Claire (riv.), Wis. 317/D6
Eau Galle, Wis. 317/B6
Eauripik (atoll), Micronesia 87/E5
Ebal (mt.), Jordan 65/C3
Ebano, Mexico 150/K5
Ebb, Fla. 212/C1
Ebb and Flow (lake), Manitoba 179/C3
Ebbw Vale, Wales 13/B6
Ebbw Vale, Wales 10/E5
Ebeltoft, Denmark 21/D5
Ebeltoft, Denmark 18/G8
Ebenezer, Miss. 256/D5
Ebenezer, Sask. 181/J4
Ebenfurth, Austria 41/D3
Eben Junction, Mich. 250/B2
Ebensburg, Pa. 294/E5
Ebensee, Austria 41/B3
Eberbach, Germany 22/C4
Ebersbach, Germany 22/F3
Eberswalde-Finow, Germany 22/E2
Ebetsu, Japan 81/K2
Ebinur Hu (lake), China 77/B2
Ebnat-Kappel, Switzerland 39/H2
Eboli, Italy 34/E4
Ebolowa, Cameroon 102/D4
Ebolowa, Cameroon 115/B3
Ebon (atoll), Marshall Is. 87/G5
Ebony, Va. 307/N7
Ebor, Manitoba 179/A5
Ebrach, Germany 22/D4
Ebrié (lag.), Ivory Coast 106/D8
Ebro, Fla. 212/C6
Ebro, Minn. 255/C3
Ebro (riv.), Spain 7/D4
Ebro (riv.), Spain 33/G2
Ecatepec de Morelos, Mexico 150/L1
Ecaussinnes, Belgium 27/E7
Ecclefechan, Scotland 15/E5
Eccles, W. Va. 312/D7
Ecclesville, Trin. & Tob. 161/B11
Eceabat, Turkey 63/B6
Echallens, Switzerland 39/C3
Echarate, Peru 128/F9
Ech Cheliff (El Asnam), Algeria 106/E1
Echeconnee, Georgia 217/E5
Echmiadzin, U.S.S.R. 52/F6
Echo, Ala. 195/G8
Echo (cliffs), Ariz. 198/D2
Echo, La. 238/F4
Echo, Minn. 255/C6
Echo (lake), N.J. 273/E1
Echo, Oreg. 291/H2
Echo (lake), Tasmania 99/C4
Echo, Utah 304/C3
Echo (res.), Utah 304/C3
Echo (lake), Vt. 268/D2
Echo Bay (Port Radium), Canada 4/C15
Echo Bay (Port Radium), N.W.T. 146/G3
Echo Bay (Port Radium), N.W.T. 162/E3
Echo Bay (Port Radium), N.W.T. 187/G3
Echo Bay, Ontario 177/J5
Echo Bay, Ontario 175/D3
Echola, Ala. 195/C4
Echo Lake, N.J. 273/E1
Echo Lake, Nova Scotia 168/E4
Echols (co.), Georgia 217/G9
Echols, Ky. 237/H6
Echo Valley Prov. Park, Sask. 181/G5
Echt, Netherlands 27/H6
Echternach, Luxembourg 27/J9
Echuca, Victoria 97/C5
Echuca, Victoria 88/G7
Ecija, Spain 33/D4
Eck, Loch (lake), Scotland 15/A1
Eckelson, N. Dak. 282/O6
Eckerman, Mich. 250/E2
Eckernförde, Germany 22/D1
Eckerty, Ind. 227/D8
Eckhart Mines, Md. 245/C2
Eckley, Colo. 208/P2
Eckman, N. Dak. 282/H2
Eckman, W. Va. 312/C8
Eckville, Alberta 182/C3
Eclectic, Ala. 195/F5
Eclipse (harb.), Newf. 166/B2
Eclipse (sound), N.W. Terr. 187/L2
Economy, Ind. 227/G5
Economy, Nova Scotia 168/D3
Economy, Pa. 294/B4
Ecorce (lake), Québec 172/A2
Ecorces (riv.), Québec 172/F1
Ecorse, Mich. 250/B7
Ecrins, Les (mt.), France 28/G5
Ecru, Miss. 256/F2
Ector (co.), Texas 303/B6
Ecuador 2/D6
Ecuador 120/B3
ECUADOR 128
Ecublens, Switzerland 39/B3
Ecum Secum, Nova Scotia 168/F3
Ecum Secum Bridge, Nova Scotia 168/F4
Edam, Sask. 181/C2
Edam-Volendam, Netherlands 27/G4
Eday (isl.), Scotland 10/E1
Eday (isl.), Scotland 15/F1
Edberg, Alberta 182/D3
Edcouch, Texas 303/G11
Edd, Ethiopia 111/H5
Edd, Ethiopia 59/D7
Ed Da'ein, Sudan 111/E5
Ed Damazin, Sudan 111/F5
Ed Damer, Sudan 111/F4
Ed Damer, Sudan 59/B6
Ed Damer, Sudan 102/F3
Ed Debba, Sudan 111/F4
Ed Debba, Sudan 59/B6
Edderton, Scotland 15/D3
Eddiceton, Miss. 256/C8
Eddington, Maine 243/F6
Eddington•, Maine 243/F6
Eddington, Pa. 294/N5
Eddleston, Scotland 15/E5
Eddontenajon, Br. Col. 184/K2
Eddrachillis (bay), Scotland 15/C2
Ed Dueim, Sudan 59/B7
Ed Dueim, Sudan 111/F5
Ed Dueim, Sudan 102/F3
Eddy (co.), N. Mex. 274/E6
Eddy (co.), N. Dak. 282/N4
Eddy, Texas 303/G6
Eddystone (rocks), England 13/C7
Eddystone (rocks), England 10/D5
Eddystone, Manitoba 179/C3
Eddystone, Pa. 294/M7
Eddystone (pt.), Tasmania 88/H8
Eddystone (pt.), Tasmania 99/E2
Eddyville, Ill. 222/E6
Eddyville, Iowa 229/H6
Eddyville, Ky. 237/E6
Eddyville, Nebr. 264/E3
Eddyville, Oreg. 291/D3
Ede, Netherlands 27/H4
Ede, Nigeria 106/E7
Edéa, Cameroon 115/B3
Edelény, Hungary 41/F2
Edelstein, Ill. 222/D3
Eden, Ariz. 198/F6
Edén, Ecuador 128/E3
Eden (riv.), England 13/E3
Eden (riv.), England 10/E3
Eden, Georgia 217/K6
Eden, Idaho 220/D7
Eden, Ind. 227/F5
Eden, Manitoba 179/C4
Eden, Md. 245/R7
Eden, Miss. 256/D5
Eden, Mont. 262/E3
Eden, N.S. Wales 97/E5
Eden, N.Y. 276/C5
Eden, N.C. 281/K1
Eden (riv.), Scotland 15/F4
Eden, S. Dak. 298/P2
Eden, Texas 303/E6
Eden, Utah 304/C2
Eden•, Vt. 268/B2
Eden, Wis. 317/K8
Eden, Wyo. 319/C3
Edenburg, Sask. 181/E3
Edenburg, S. Africa 118/D5
Edendale, S. Africa 118/D5
Edenderry, Ireland 10/C4
Edenderry, Ireland 17/G5
Edenhope, Victoria 97/A5
Eden Mills, Ontario 177/D4
Eden Mills, Vt. 268/C2
Eden Prairie, Minn. 255/G6
Edenton, N.C. 281/R2
Edenton, Ohio 284/C7
Edenvale, S. Africa 118/H6

366 Engelhartszell

Engelhartszell, Austria 41/B2
Engel's, U.S.S.R. 7/J3
Engel's, U.S.S.R. 52/G4
Engel's, U.S.S.R. 48/E4
Engen, Br. Col. 184/E3
Enggano (isl.), Indonesia 85/C7
Enghien, Belgium 27/D7
Engi, Switzerland 39/H3
ENGLAND 10/F5
ENGLAND 13
England, Ark. 202/G4
England, U.K. 7/D3
England A.F.B., La. 238/E4
Engle, N. Mex. 274/B5
Englee, Newf. 166/C3
Englefeld, Sask. 181/G3
Englehart, Ont. 162/H6
Englehart, Ontario 177/K5
Englehart, Ontario 175/E3
Englevale, Kansas 232/H4
Englevale, N. Dak. 282/P7
Englewood, Colo. 208/K3
Englewood, Fla. 212/D5
Englewood, Kansas 232/C4
Englewood, N.J. 273/C2
Englewood, Ohio 284/B6
Englewood, Tenn. 237/M10
Englewood Cliffs, N.J. 273/C2
English (chan.) 7/D4
English (chan.), Chan. Is. 13/D8
English (chan.), England 13/D8
English (chan.), England 10/E6
English (chan.), France 28/B3
English, Ind. 227/E8
English, Ky. 237/L3
English (riv.), Ontario 175/B2
English, W. Va. 312/C8
English Bay, Alaska 196/B2
English Bazar, India 68/F3
English Coast (reg.), Ant. 5/B15
English Creek, N.J. 273/D5
English Harbour, Newf. 166/D2
English Harbour West, Newf. 166/C4
English Lake, Ind. 227/D2
Englishman (bay), Maine 243/J6
English River, Ontario 177/G5
English River, Ontario 175/B3
Englishtown, N.J. 273/E3
Englishtown, Nova Scotia 168/H2
Enguera, Spain 33/F3
Enid, Miss. 256/E2
Enid (lake), Miss. 256/E2
Enid, Mont. 262/M3
Enid, Okla. 188/G3
Enid, Okla. 288/L2
Enid (mt.), W. Australia 92/B3
Enigma, Georgia 217/F8
Enilda, Alberta 182/B2
Eniwa, Japan 81/K2
Enka, N.C. 281/D3
Enkhuizen, Netherlands 27/G3
Enköping, Sweden 18/G1
Enmore, Guyana 131/C2
Enna (prov.), Italy 34/E6
Enna, Italy 34/E6
Ennadai (lake), N.W. Terr. 187/H3
En Nahud, Sudan 111/E5
En Nahud, Sudan 102/E3
En Naqura, Lebanon 63/F6
En Nebk, Syria 59/C3
En Nebk, Syria 63/G5
Ennedi (plat.), Chad 111/D4
Ennell (lake), Ireland 17/G5
Ennenda, Switzerland 39/H2
Ennery, Haiti 158/C5
Enngonia, N.S. Wales 97/C1
Enning, S. Dak. 298/E4
Ennis, Ireland 10/B4
Ennis, Ireland 17/D6
Ennis, Ky. 237/H6
Ennis, Mont. 262/E5
Ennis (lake), Mont. 262/E5
Ennis, Texas 303/H5
Enniscorthy, Ireland 17/J7
Enniscorthy, Ireland 10/C4
Enniskerry, Ireland 17/J5
Enniskillen, New Bruns. 170/D3
Enniskillen, N. Ireland 10/C3
Enniskillen, N. Ireland 17/F3
Ennistymon, Ireland 10/B4
Ennistymon, Ireland 17/C6
Enns, Austria 41/C2
Enns (riv.), Austria 41/C3
Enoch, Utah 304/A6
Enoch, W. Va. 312/E6
Enochs, Texas 303/B4
Enoggera, Queensland 88/K2
Enoggera (creek), Queensland 95/D2
Enola, Ark. 202/F3
Enola, Pa. 294/J5
Enon, Mo. 261/G6
Enon, Ohio 284/C6
Enontekiö, Finland 18/N2
Enon Valley, Pa. 294/B4
Enoree, S.C. 296/D2
Enoree (riv.), S.C. 296/C2
Enos, Ind. 227/C2
Enosburg Falls, Vt. 268/B2
Enrage (cape), New Bruns. 170/F3
Enrile, Philippines 82/C2
Enrique Carbó, Argentina 143/G6
Enriquillo, Dom. Rep. 158/D7
Enriquillo, Dom. Rep. 156/D3
Enriquillo (lake), Dom. Rep. 158/C6
Ens, Sask. 181/F3
Enschede, Netherlands 27/K4
Ensenada, Argentina 143/H7
Ensenada, Mexico 150/A1
Ensenada, P. Rico 161/B3
Enshi, China 77/G5
Ensign, Alberta 182/D4
Ensign, Kansas 232/B4
Ensign, Mich. 250/C3
Ensley, Fla. 212/B6
Ent A.F.B., Colo. 208/K5
Entebbe, Uganda 115/F4
Entebbe, Uganda 102/F5
Enterprise, Ala. 195/G8
Enterprise, Calif. 204/C3
Enterprise, Guyana 131/B2
Enterprise, Kansas 232/E3
Enterprise, La. 238/G3
Enterprise, Miss. 256/G6
Enterprise, N.W. Terr. 187/G3
Enterprise, Ohio 284/F6
Enterprise, Okla. 288/R4
Enterprise, Ontario 177/H3
Enterprise, Oreg. 291/K2
Enterprise, Utah 304/A6
Enterprise, W. Va. 312/F4
Entiat, Wash. 310/E3
Entiat (lake), Wash. 310/E3
Entiat (mts.), Wash. 310/E2
Entiat (riv.), Wash. 310/E3
Entlebuch, Switzerland 39/F3
Entrance, Alberta 182/B3
Entrejo, Neth. Ant. 161/E8
Entrelacs, Québec 172/C3
Entrepeñas (res.), Spain 33/E2
Entre Ríos (prov.), Argentina 143/E3
Entre Ríos, Bolivia 136/C7
Entre Rios, Brazil 132/C4
Entre Rios de Minas, Brazil 135/D2
Entriken, Pa. 294/F5
Entwistle, Alberta 182/C3
Enugu, Nigeria 102/C4
Enugu, Nigeria 106/F7
Enumclaw, Wash. 310/D3
Envigado, Colombia 126/C4
Enville, Tenn. 237/E10
Enwarak (mt.), Guyana 131/B3
Enyellé, Congo 115/C3
Enying, Hungary 41/E3
Eola, La. 238/F5
Eola, Texas 303/E6
Eolia, Ky. 237/R6
Eolia, Mo. 261/L4
Eoline, Ala. 195/D4
Epe, Netherlands 27/H4
Epéna, Congo 115/C3
Epéna, Congo 102/D4
Epenarra, North. Terr. 93/D6
Épernay, France 28/E3
Epes, Ala. 195/B5
Ephesus, Georgia 217/B4
Ephesus (ruins), Turkey 63/B3
Ephraim, Utah 304/C4
Ephraim, Wis. 317/M5
Ephrata, Pa. 294/K5
Ephrata, Wash. 310/F3
Ephratah, N.Y. 276/L4
Épinal, France 28/G3
Épinay-sur-Seine, France 28/B1
Epiphany, S. Dak. 298/O6
Epira, Guyana 131/C3
Epirus (reg.), Greece 45/E6
Episkopi, Cyprus 63/E5
Eport, Loch (inlet), Scotland 15/A3
Epoufette, Mich. 250/D2
Epping, England 13/H7
Epping, England 10/C5
Epping, N.H. 268/E5
Epping•, N.H. 268/E5
Epping, N. Dak. 282/D3
Epps, La. 238/G1
Epsie, Mont. 262/L5
Epsom, Ind. 227/C7
Epsom•, N.H. 268/E5
Epsom and Ewell, England 13/G8
Epsom and Ewell, England 10/B6
Epukiro, Namibia 118/B4
Epworth, Georgia 217/D1
Epworth, Iowa 229/M4
Equality, Ala. 195/F5
Equality, Ill. 222/E6
Equateur (prov.), Zaire 115/D3
Equator 2/H5
Equatoria, Eastern (prov.), Sudan 111/F6
Equatoria, Western (prov.), Sudan 111/E6
Equatorial Guinea 2/K5
Equatorial Guinea 102/C4
EQUATORIAL GUINEA 115/A3
Equinox (mt.), Vt. 268/A5
Equinunk, Pa. 294/M2
Era, Ohio 284/D6
Era, Texas 303/G4
Eran, Philippines 82/A6
Erath, La. 238/F7
Erath (co.), Texas 303/F5
Erbaa, Turkey 63/G2
Erbach, Germany 22/C4
Erbacon, W. Va. 312/E5
Erbil (gov.), Iraq 66/C3
Erbil, Iraq 59/D2
Erbil, Iraq 54/F6
Erbil, Iraq 66/D2
Erçek (lake), Turkey 63/K3
Ercilla, Chile 138/E2
Erciş, Turkey 59/D2
Erciş, Turkey 63/K3
Erciyas Dağı (mt.), Turkey 63/F3
Érd, Hungary 41/E3
Erdahl, Minn. 255/C5
Erdek, Turkey 63/B2
Erdemli, Turkey 63/F4
Erdentsagaan, Mongolia 77/J2
Erdőtelek, Hungary 41/F3
Erebato (riv.), Venezuela 124/F5
Ereen, Mongolia 77/H2
Ereğli, Turkey 63/D2
Ereğli, Turkey 59/B2
Ereğli, Turkey 63/F4
Erenhot, China 77/H3
Erenhot, China 54/N5
Erenköy, Turkey 63/D6
Eresma (riv.), Spain 33/D2
Erexim, Brazil 132/C9
Érezée, Belgium 27/G8
Erfoud, Morocco 106/D2
Erfurt, Germany 7/F3
Erfurt, Germany 22/D3
Ergani, Turkey 63/H3
Ergene (riv.), Turkey 63/B2
Ergli, U.S.S.R. 53/C2
Ergun He (Argun') (riv.), China 77/K1
Ergun Youqi, China 77/K1
Ergun Zuoqi, China 77/K1
Ergun Zuoqi, China 54/O4
Er Hai (lake), China 77/F6
Erhard, Minn. 255/B4
Eriboll, Loch (inlet), Scotland 15/D2
Erica, Netherlands 27/K3
Erica, Victoria 97/D5
Erice, Italy 34/D5
Ericeira, Portugal 33/B3
Erichsen (lake), N.W. Terr. 187/K2
Ericht, Loch (lake), Scotland 15/D4
Erick, Okla. 288/G4
Erickson, Br. Col. 184/J5
Erickson, Manitoba 179/C4
Ericsburg, Minn. 255/E2
Ericson, Nebr. 264/F3
Erie (lake) 146/K5
Erie (lake) 188/K2
Erie (lake) 162/H7
Erie, Colo. 208/K2
Erie, Ill. 222/C2
Erie, Kansas 232/G4
Erie, Mich. 250/F7
Erie (lake), Mich. 250/G7
Erie (co.), N.Y. 276/C5
Erie (lake), N.Y. 276/A5
Erie, N. Dak. 282/R5
Erie (co.), Ohio 284/E3
Erie (lake), Ohio 284/H1
Erie (lake), Ontario 177/E5
Erie (co.), Pa. 294/B2
Erie, Pa. 188/K2
Erie, Pa. 146/L5
Erie, Pa. 294/B1
Erie (lake), Pa. 294/B1
Erie, Tenn. 237/M9
Erieau, Ontario 177/C5
Erie Beach, Ontario 177/B5
Erieville, N.Y. 276/J5
Erigabo, Somalia 115/J1
Eriksdale, Manitoba 179/D4
Erimo (cape), Japan 81/L3
Erin, Ontario 177/D4
Erin, Tenn. 237/F8
Erin (bay), Trin. & Tob. 161/A11
Erin (pt.), Trin. & Tob. 161/A11
Erinferry, Sask. 181/D2
Erinview, Manitoba 179/E4
Eriskay (isl.), Scotland 15/A3
Erisort, Loch (inlet), Scotland 15/B2
Erith, Alberta 182/B3
Eritrea (prov.), Ethiopia 111/G4
Eritrea (reg.), Ethiopia 102/F3
Eritrea (reg.), Ethiopia 59/C6
Erkilet, Turkey 63/F3
Erkina (riv.), Ireland 17/G6
Erkowit, Sudan 59/C6
Erlach, Switzerland 39/D2
Erlands Point, Wash. 310/A2
Erlangen, Germany 22/D4
Erlanger, Ky. 237/R2
Erldunda, North. Terr. 93/C8
Erlenbach im Simmental, Switzerland 39/E3
Erling (lake), Ark. 202/C7
Ermatingen, Switzerland 39/H1
Ermelo, Netherlands 27/H4
Ermelo, S. Africa 118/E5
Ermenak, Turkey 63/E4
Ermeran Station, N.S. Wales 97/D3
Ermoúpolis, Greece 45/G7
Ernabella, S. Australia 94/C2
Ernakulam, India 68/D7
Erne (riv.), Ireland 17/E3
Erne (lake), N. Ireland 17/F3
Erne, Lough (lake), N. Ireland 10/C3
Ernée, France 28/C3
Ernen, Switzerland 39/F4
Ernest, Pa. 294/D4
Ernfold, Sask. 181/D5
Ernul, N.C. 281/P4
Erode, India 68/D6
Eromanga, Queensland 88/G5
Eromanga, Queensland 95/B5
Eros, La. 238/F2
Erquelinnes, Belgium 27/E8
Err (peak), Switzerland 39/J3
Er Rachidia, Morocco 106/D2
Er Rafid, Jordan 65/D2
Er Rahad, Sudan 111/F5
Er Rahad, Sudan 59/B7
Er Ramtha, Jordan 65/E2
Er Ras, Saudi Arabia 59/D4
Errata, Miss. 256/F7
Errego, Mozambique 118/F3
Er Rif (range), Morocco 106/D2
Errigal (mt.), Ireland 17/E1
Er Rihiya, West Bank 65/C5
Errington, Br. Col. 184/J3
Erris (head), Ireland 10/A3
Erris (head), Ireland 17/A3
Errol•, N.H. 268/E2
Errol, Scotland 15/E4
Erromanga (isl.), Vanuatu 87/H7
Er Roseires, Sudan 111/F5
Er Rumman, Jordan 65/D3
Er Ruseifa, Jordan 65/E3
Ersekë, Albania 45/E5
Erskine, Alberta 182/D3
Erskine, Minn. 255/B3
Erstein, France 28/G3
Erstfeld, Switzerland 39/G3
Ertai, China 77/C2
Ertil', U.S.S.R. 52/F4
Eruh, Turkey 63/K4
Erval, Brazil 132/C11
Ervay, Wyo. 319/E3
Erving•, Mass. 249/E2
Erwin, N.C. 281/M4
Erwin, S. Dak. 298/P5
Erwin, Tenn. 237/S8
Erwinna, Pa. 294/N5
Erwinville, La. 238/H5
Erwood, Sask. 181/J3
Eryuan, China 77/F6
Erzgebirge (mts.), Czech. 41/B1
Erzgebirge (mts.), Germany 22/E3
Erzin, Turkey 63/G4
Erzincan (prov.), Turkey 63/H3
Erzincan, Turkey 63/H3
Erzincan, Turkey 59/C2
Erzurum (prov.), Turkey 63/J3
Erzurum, Turkey 59/D2
Erzurum, Turkey 54/E5
Erzurum, Turkey 63/J3
Esan (pt.), Japan 81/K3
Esashi, Iwate, Japan 81/K4
Esashi, Hokkaido, Japan 81/J3
Esashi, Hokkaido, Japan 81/L1
Esbjerg, Denmark 21/B7
Esbjerg, Denmark 7/E3
Esbjerg, Denmark 18/F9
Esbon, Kansas 232/D2
Escabosa, N. Mex. 274/C4
Escalante, Philippines 82/D5
Escalante, Utah 304/C6
Escalante (des.), Utah 304/A6
Escalante (riv.), Utah 304/C6
Escalon, Calif. 204/E6
Escalón, Mexico 150/G3
Escalona, Spain 33/D2
Escambia (co.), Ala. 195/D8
Escambia (creek), Ala. 195/D8
Escambia (riv.), Ala. 195/D8
Escambia (co.), Fla. 212/B6
Escambia (riv.), Fla. 212/B6
Escanaba, Mich. 250/C3
Escanaba (riv.), Mich. 250/B2
Escarcega, Mexico 150/O7
Escatawpa (riv.), 256/H8
Escatawpa, Ala. 195/B8
Escatawpa (riv.), Ala. 195/B9
Escatawpa, Miss. 256/G10
Eschenbach, Switzerland 39/G2
Escholzmatt, Switzerland 39/E3
Esch-sur-Alzette, Luxembourg 27/J9
Esch-sur-Sûre, Luxembourg 27/H9
Eschwege, Germany 22/C3
Eschweiler, Germany 22/B3
Escobar, Argentina 143/G7
Escobar, Paraguay 144/B5
Escocesa (bay), Dom. Rep. 158/E5
Escoma, Bolivia 136/A4
Escondido, Calif. 204/J10
Escondido (riv.), Nicaragua 154/F4
Escoumins, Québec 172/H1
Escudo de Veraguas (isl.), Panama 154/G6
Escuinapa de Hidalgo, Mexico 150/G5
Escuintla, Guatemala 154/B3
Escuintla, Mexico 150/N9
Escuminac, New Bruns. 170/F1
Escuminac (bay), New Bruns. 170/D1
Escuminac (pt.), New Bruns. 170/F1
Esdaile, Wis. 317/A6
Eséka, Cameroon 115/B3
Eşen, Turkey 63/C4
Esfahan (Isfahan) (prov.), Iran 66/H4
Esfahan (Isfahan), Iran 66/G4
Esfandak, Iran 66/N7
Esh, England 13/H3
Esher, England 13/H8
Esher, England 10/B6
Eshowe, S. Africa 118/E5
Esh Shaubak (interm. str.), Jordan 65/D5
Esk (riv.), England 13/D2
Esk, Queensland 95/E5
Esk, Sask. 181/G4
Esk (riv.), Scotland 15/F5
Eska, Alaska 196/B1
Eskdale, W. Va. 312/D6
Esker, Newf. 166/A3
Eskilstuna, Sweden 18/K7
Eskimalatya, Turkey 63/H3
Eskimo (lakes), N.W. Terr. 187/E3
Eskimo Point, N.W.T. 162/G3
Eskimo Point, N.W. Terr. 187/J3
Eskipazar, Turkey 63/E2
Eskişehir (prov.), Turkey 63/D3
Eskişehir, Turkey 54/D6
Eskişehir, Turkey 59/B2
Eskişehir, Turkey 63/D3
Esko, Minn. 255/F4
Eskridge, Kansas 232/F3
Eskutassis (pond), Maine 243/G5
Esla (riv.), Spain 33/D2
Eslamabad, Iran 66/E3
Eslöv, Sweden 18/H9
Esme, Sask. 181/D6
Eşme, Turkey 63/C3
Esmeralda (isl.), Chile 138/C8
Esmeralda, Cuba 158/G1
Esmeralda (co.), Nev. 266/D5
Esmeraldas (prov.), Ecuador 128/C2
Esmeraldas, Ecuador 120/A2
Esmeraldas, Ecuador 128/B2
Esmeraldas (riv.), Ecuador 128/C2
Esmond, Ill. 222/E1
Esmond, N. Dak. 282/L3
Esmond, R.I. 249/H5
Esmond, S. Dak. 298/O5
Esmont, Va. 307/L5
Esmoraca, Bolivia 136/B7
Esneux, Belgium 27/H7
Esom Hill, Georgia 217/B3
Espada (pt.), Colombia 126/E1
Espada (pt.), Dom. Rep. 158/F6
Espagnol (pt.), St. Vin. & Grens. 161/A8
Espaillat (prov.), Dom. Rep. 158/E5
Espalion, France 28/E5
Española (isl.), Ecuador 128/C10
Espanola, Fla. 212/E2
Espanola, N. Mex. 274/C3
Espanola, Ontario 177/J5
Espanola, Ontario 175/D3
Espanola, Wash. 310/H3
Esparta, C. Rica 154/E5
Esparto, Calif. 204/C5
Espejo, Chile 138/G3
Espejo, Spain 33/D4
Espelkamp, Germany 22/C2
Espenberg (cape), Alaska 196/F1
Esperança, Brazil 132/G4
Esperance, Australia 87/C9
Esperance, N.Y. 276/M5
Esperance, W. Australia 88/C6
Esperance, W. Australia 92/C6
Esperance (bay), W. Australia 92/C6
Esperanza, Argentina 143/F5
Esperanza, Br. Col. 184/D5
Esperanza, Cuba 158/E2
Esperanza, Dom. Rep. 158/D5
Esperanza (mts.), Honduras 154/E3
Esperanza, Puebla, Mexico 150/O2
Esperanza, Sonora, Mexico 150/E3
Esperanza, Peru 128/G7
Esperanza, P. Rico 161/G2
Esperanza, Texas 303/B11
Esperanza, Venezuela 124/E6
Espichel (cape), Portugal 33/B3
Espigão Mestre (Geral de Goiás) (range), Brazil 132/E6
Espinal, Colombia 126/C5
Espinar, Peru 128/G10
Espinhaço (mts.), Brazil 120/E4
Espinhaço, Serra do (range), Brazil 132/F7
Espinho, Portugal 33/B2
Espinillo, Argentina 143/E2
Espinillo (pt.), Uruguay 145/A7
Espino, Venezuela 124/F3
Espírito Santo (state), Brazil 132/F7
Espírito Santo (state), Brazil 135/F2
Espiritu Santo (isl.), Mexico 150/D4
Espiritu Santo (cape), Philippines 85/H3
Espiritu Santo (cape), Philippines 82/E4
Espiritu Santo (isl.), Vanuatu 87/G7
Espita, Mexico 150/Q6
Espiye, Turkey 63/H2
Esplanada, Brazil 132/G5
Espluga de Francolí, Spain 33/G2
Espoir (bay), Newf. 166/C4
Espoo, Finland 18/O6
Esposende, Portugal 33/B2
Esprit-Saint, Québec 172/J1
Espungabera, Mozambique 118/E4
Espy, Pa. 294/K4
Espyville Station, Pa. 294/B2
Esqueda, Mexico 150/E1
Esquel, Argentina 143/B5
Esquel, Argentina 120/B7
Esquimalt, Br. Col. 184/K4
Esquina, Argentina 143/G5
Esquipulas, Nicaragua 154/E4
Es Sahab, Jordan 65/E4
Es Salt, Jordan 65/D3
Es Salt, Jordan 59/C3
Essaouira, Morocco 106/B2
Essaouira, Morocco 102/A1
Essé, Cameroon 115/B3
Essen, Belgium 27/F6
Essen, Germany 7/E3
Essen, Germany 22/B3
Essendon, Victoria 88/K7
Essendon, Victoria 97/H5
Essequibo (riv.), Guyana 120/D2
Essequibo (riv.), Guyana 131/B3
Esserville, Va. 307/G2
Essex, Calif. 204/K9
Essex, Conn. 210/F3
Essex•, Conn. 210/F3
Essex (co.), England 13/H6
Essex, Ill. 222/E2
Essex, Iowa 229/C7
Essex, Md. 245/N3
Essex (co.), Mass. 249/L2
Essex, Mass. 249/L2
Essex•, Mass. 249/L2
Essex, Mo. 261/N9
Essex, Mont. 262/C2
Essex (co.), N.J. 273/E2
Essex (co.), N.Y. 276/N2
Essex, N.Y. 276/O2
Essex (county), Ontario 177/B5
Essex, Ontario 177/B5
Essex (co.), Vt. 268/D2
Essex• Vt. 268/A2
Essex (co.), Va. 307/P5
Essex Fells, N.J. 273/B2
Essex Junction, Vt. 268/A3
Essexville, Mich. 250/F5
Es Sidr, Libya 111/C1
Essie, Ky. 237/P6
Essig, Minn. 255/D6
Essington, Pa. 294/M7
Esslingen am Neckar, Germany 22/C4
Essonne (dept.), France 28/E3
Es Sukhna, Jordan 65/E3
Es Sukhne, Syria 59/C3
Es Sukhne, Syria 63/H5
Es Suki, Sudan 59/B7
Es Suweida (prov.), Syria 63/G6
Es Suweida, Syria 59/C3
Es Suweide, Syria 63/G6
Est (pt.), Haiti 158/C4
Est (lake), Québec 172/H2
Estacada, Oreg. 291/E2
Estaca de Vares (pt.), Spain 33/C1
Estación Atlántida, Uruguay 145/B6
Estación Cuaró, Uruguay 145/C1
Estación J.J. Castro, Uruguay 145/C4
Estación José Ignacio, Uruguay 145/E5
Estación La Floresta, Uruguay 145/C7
Estación Lasala, Uruguay 145/C7
Estación Laureles, Uruguay 145/C2
Estación Margat, Uruguay 145/B6
Estación Migues, Uruguay 145/C6
Estación Pampa, Uruguay 145/C3
Estación Puma, Uruguay 145/D5
Estación Rincón, Uruguay 145/F3
Estación Sosa Díaz, Uruguay 145/C6
Estación Tapia, Uruguay 145/C6
Estación Villasboas, Uruguay 145/C4
Estación Yi, Uruguay 145/C4
Estados (isl.), Argentina 120/C8
Estados, Los (isl.), Argentina 143/D7
Estahbanat, Iran 59/F4
Estahbanat, Iran 66/J6
Estaire, Ontario 177/D1
Estampuis, Belgium 27/C7
Estância, Brazil 132/G5
Estância, Brazil 120/F4
Estancia, N. Mex. 274/D4
Estancia Caleta Josefina, Chile 138/F10
Estancia Laguna Blanca, Chile 138/E9
Estancia Morro Chico, Chile 138/E9
Estancia Punta Delgada, Chile 138/E9
Estancia San Gregorio, Chile 138/E9
Estancia Springhill (Cerro Manantiales), Chile 138/F10
Estanzuela, Uruguay 145/B5
Estanzuelas, El Salvador 154/C4
Estarca, Bolivia 136/C7
Estats (peak), Spain 33/G1
Estavayer-le-Lac, Switzerland 39/C3
Estcourt, S. Africa 118/D5
Este (pt.), Cuba 158/C3
Este, Italy 34/C2
Este (pt.), P. Rico 161/G2
Este (pt.), Uruguay 120/D6
Este (pt.), Uruguay 145/D6
Esteban Rams, Argentina 143/F5
Estelí, Nicaragua 154/D4
Estella, Spain 33/E1
Estelline, S. Dak. 298/R4
Estelline, Texas 303/D3
Estell Manor, N.J. 273/D5
Estepa, Spain 33/D4
Estepona, Spain 33/D4
Ester, Alaska 196/J2
Esterbrook, Wyo. 319/G3
Estérel, Québec 172/C3
Esterhazy, Sask. 181/K5
Estero (bay), Calif. 204/D8
Estero (pt.), Calif. 204/D8
Estero, Fla. 212/E5
Estero (isl.), Fla. 212/E5
Estes Park, Colo. 208/J2
Este Sudeste (cays), Colombia 126/A10
Estevan, Sak. 162/F6
Estevan, Sask. 181/J6
Estevan Point, Br. Col. 184/D5
Estey, Mich. 250/E5
Esther (isl.), Alaska 196/C1
Esther, Alberta 182/E4
Esther, La. 238/F7
Esther, Mo. 261/M7
Estherville, Iowa 229/D2
Estherwood, La. 238/F6
Estill (co.), Ky. 237/O5
Estill, Miss. 256/C4
Estill, S.C. 296/E6
Estillfork, Ala. 195/F1
Estill Springs, Tenn. 237/J10
Estlin, Sask. 181/G5
Esto, Fla. 212/C5
Eston, England 13/F3
Eston, Sask. 162/F5
Eston, Sask. 181/C4
ESTONIA 53
Estonian S.S.R., U.S.S.R. 7/G3
Estonian S.S.R., U.S.S.R. 48/C4
Estonian S.S.R., U.S.S.R. 52/C3
Estoril, Portugal 33/B3
Estral Beach, Mich. 250/F7
Estreito (res.), Brazil 135/C2
Estrela, Serra da (mts.), Portugal 33/C2
Estrella (riv.), Calif. 204/E8
Estremadura (reg.), Spain 33/C3
Estremoz, Portugal 33/C3
Estrondo, Serra do (range), Brazil 132/D4
Estuary, Sask. 181/B5
Esztergom, Hungary 41/E3
Etadunna, S. Australia 94/F3
Étalle, Belgium 27/H9
Étampes, France 28/E3
Étaples, France 28/D2
Etawah, India 68/D3
Etawney (lake), Manitoba 179/J2
Etchojoa, Mexico 150/E3
Ethan, S. Dak. 298/N6
Ethel, Ark. 202/H5
Ethel (mt.), Colo. 208/F1
Ethel, La. 238/H5
Ethel, Miss. 256/F4
Ethel, Mo. 261/G3
Ethel, Ontario 177/C4
Ethel, Wash. 310/C4
Ethel, W. Va. 312/C7
Ethelbert, Manitoba 179/B3
Ethel Creek, W. Australia 92/C3
Ethelsville, Ala. 195/B4
Ethelton, Sask. 181/G3
Ether, N.C. 281/K4
Ethete, Wyo. 319/D2
Ethiopia 2/L5
ETHIOPIA 59/C7
Ethiopia 102/F4
ETHIOPIA 111/G5
Ethridge, Mont. 262/D2
Ethridge, Tenn. 237/G10
Etive, Loch (inlet), Scotland 15/C4
Etiwanda, Calif. 204/E10
Etna, Calif. 204/C2
Etna, Ind. 227/F2
Etna (vol.), Italy 7/F5
Etna (vol.), Italy 34/E6
Etna•, Maine 243/E6
Etna, N.H. 268/C4
Etna, Ohio 284/E6
Etna, Pa. 294/B6
Etna, Utah 304/A2
Etna, Wyo. 319/A2
Etna Green, Ind. 227/E2
Etobicoke, Ontario 177/J4
Etoile, Ky. 237/K7
Etoile, Zaire 115/E6
Etolin (isl.), Alaska 196/N2
Etolin (str.), Alaska 196/E2
Etomami (riv.), Manitoba 179/F2
Etomami (riv.), Sask. 181/J3
Eton, England 10/F5
Eton, England 13/G8
Eton, Georgia 217/C1
Etorofu (Iturup) (isl.), Japan 81/N1
Etosha Pan (salt pan), Namibia 118/B3

Gagnon 371

Franklin (co.), Pa. 294/G6
Franklin, Pa. 294/C3
Franklin, S. Dak. 298/P6
Franklin, Tasmania 99/C5
Franklin (riv.), Tasmania 99/B4
Franklin (co.), Tenn. 237/J10
Franklin, Tenn. 237/H9
Franklin (co.), Texas 303/J4
Franklin, Texas 303/H7
Franklin (co.), Vt. 268/B2
Franklin•, Vt. 268/B2
Franklin (co.), Va. 307/J6
Franklin (I.C.), Va. 307/P7
Franklin (co.), Wash. 310/G4
Franklin, W. Va. 312/H5
Franklin, Wis. 317/L2
Franklin D. Roosevelt (lake), Wash. 310/G2
Franklin Falls (res.), N.H. 268/D4
Franklin Furnace, Ohio 284/E8
Franklin Grove, Ill. 222/D2
Franklin Lakes, N.J. 273/B1
Franklin Park, Ill. 222/B5
Franklin Park•, N.J. 273/D3
Franklin River, Br. Col. 184/H3
Franklin Springs, Georgia 217/F2
Franklin Square, N.Y. 276/R7
Franklinton, La. 238/K5
Franklinton, N.C. 281/N2
Franklintown, Pa. 294/H5
Franklinville, N.J. 273/C4
Franklinville, N.Y. 276/D6
Franklinville, N.C. 281/K3
Franks (pond), Newf. 166/D2
Frankslake, Sask. 181/G5
Frankston, Texas 303/J5
Franksville, Wis. 317/M3
Frankton, Ind. 227/F4
Franktown, Colo. 208/K4
Franktown, Ontario 177/H2
Franktown, Va. 307/S6
Frankville, Ala. 195/B7
Frankville, Iowa 229/K2
Frankville, Nova Scotia 168/G3
Frankville, Ontario 177/J2
Frannie, Wyo. 319/D1
Franquelin, Québec 172/B1
Franquia, Uruguay 145/B1
Franschhoek, S. Africa 118/F6
Fransfontein, Namibia 118/A4
Františkovy Lázně, Czech. 41/B1
Franz, Ontario 177/J5
Franz, Ontario 175/D3
Franz Josef Land (isls.), U.S.S.R. 2/L1
Franz Josef Land (isls.), U.S.S.R. 4/A7
Franz Josef Land (isls.), U.S.S.R. 48/F1
Frascati, Italy 34/F7
Fraser (isl.), Australia 87/F8
Fraser (lake), Br. Col. 184/E3
Fraser (riv.), Br. Col. 146/F4
Fraser (riv.), Br. Col. 162/D5
Fraser (riv.), Br. Col. 184/F4
Fraser, Colo. 208/H3
Fraser, Iowa 229/E4
Fraser, Mich. 250/B6
Fraser, Minn. 255/F3
Fraser (riv.), Newf. 166/B2
Fraser (isl.), Queensland 88/J4
Fraser (isl.), Queensland 95/E5
Fraserburgh, Scotland 15/G3
Fraserburgh, Scotland 10/E2
Fraserdale, Ontario 175/D3
Fraserdale, Ontario 177/J5
Fraser Lake, Br. Col. 184/E3
Fraser Mills, Br. Col. 184/K3
Fraser Reach (chan.), Br. Col. 184/C3
Frasertown, N. Zealand 100/F3
Fraserwood, Manitoba 179/E4
Frasnes-lez Anvaing, Belgium 27/D7
Frauenfeld, Switzerland 39/G1
Frauenkirchen, Austria 41/D3
Fray Benito, Cuba 158/J3
Fray Bentos, Uruguay 145/A4
Fray Marcos, Uruguay 145/D5
Frazee, Minn. 255/C4
Frazer, Mont. 262/K2
Frazeysburg, Ohio 284/F5
Frazier Park, Calif. 204/F9
Fraziers Bottom, W. Va. 312/B5
Frechen, Germany 22/B3
Fred, Texas 303/K7
Freda, N. Dak. 282/H7
Fredensborg, Denmark 21/F6
Fredensdal, Virgin Is. (U.S.) 161/F4
Frederic, Mich. 250/E4
Frederic, Wis. 317/B4
Frederica, Del. 245/S4
Fredericia, Denmark 21/C6
Fredericia, Denmark 18/F9
Frederick (sound), Alaska 196/N1
Frederick, Colo. 208/K2
Frederick, Ill. 222/C3
Frederick, Kansas 232/D3
Frederick (co.), Md. 245/J3
Frederick, Md. 245/J3
Frederick, Okla. 288/H6
Frederick, S. Dak. 298/N2
Frederick (co.), Va. 307/M2
Fredericksburg, Ind. 227/E8
Fredericksburg, Iowa 229/J3
Fredericksburg, Ohio 284/G4
Fredericksburg, Pa. 294/J5
Fredericksburg, Pa. 294/B2
Fredericksburg, Texas 303/E7
Fredericksburg (I.C.), Va. 307/N4
Fredericks Hall, Va. 307/N4
Frederickton, N.S. Wales 97/G2
Fredericktown, Mo. 261/M7
Fredericktown, Ohio 284/F5
Fredericktown, Pa. 294/C6
Fredericton (cap.), N. Br. 146/M5
Fredericton, N. Br. 162/K6
Fredericton (cap.), New Bruns. 170/D3
Fredericton Junction, New Bruns. 170/D3
Frederika, Iowa 229/J3
Frederik Hendrik (Kolepom) (isl.), Indonesia 85/K7
Frederiksberg (commune), Denmark 21/F6
Frederiksberg, Denmark 21/F6
Frederiksborg (co.), Denmark 21/E5
Frederikshåb (Paamiut), Greenl. 4/C12
Frederikshåb (Paamiut), Greenl. 146/N3
Frederikshavn, Denmark 18/G8
Frederikshavn, Denmark 21/D3
Frederikssund, Denmark 21/E6
Frederiksted, Virgin Is. (U.S.) 161/E4
Frederiksted, Virgin Is. (U.S.) 156/G2
Frederiksvaerk, Denmark 21/E6
Frederiksvaerk, Denmark 18/G8
Frederik Willem IV (falls), Suriname 131/C4
Fredonia, Ala. 195/H5
Fredonia, Ariz. 198/C2
Fredonia (Biscoe), Ark. 202/H4
Fredonia, Ind. 227/E8
Fredonia, Iowa 229/L6
Fredonia, Kansas 232/G4
Fredonia, Ky. 237/E6
Fredonia, N.Y. 276/B6
Fredonia, N. Dak. 282/M7
Fredonia, Pa. 294/B3
Fredonia, Texas 303/E7
Fredonia, Wis. 317/L8
Fredric, Iowa 229/H6
Fredrika, Sweden 18/L4
Fredrikstad, Norway 18/D4
Freeborn (co.), Minn. 255/E7
Freeborn, Minn. 255/E7
Freeburg, Ill. 222/D5
Freeburg, Minn. 255/G7
Freeburg, Mo. 261/J6
Freeburg, Pa. 294/H4
Freeburn, Ky. 237/S5
Freedhem, Minn. 255/D4
Freedom, Calif. 204/L4
Freedom, Ind. 227/D6
Freedom, Ky. 237/K7
Freedom•, Maine 243/E7
Freedom•, N.H. 268/E4
Freedom, Okla. 288/H1
Freedom, Pa. 294/B4
Freedom, Wyo. 319/B3
Freehold, N.J. 273/E3
Freehold, N.Y. 276/N6
Freel (peak), Calif. 204/F5
Freeland, Md. 245/M2
Freeland, Mich. 250/E5
Freeland, N.C. 281/N6
Freeland, Pa. 294/L3
Freeland, Wash. 310/C2
Freeland Park, Ind. 227/C3
Freelandville, Ind. 227/C7
Freels (cape), Newf. 166/D3
Freelton, Ontario 177/D4
Freeman (riv.), Alberta 182/C2
Freeman, Ind. 227/D6
Freeman (lake), Ind. 227/D3
Freeman, Mo. 261/C5
Freeman, S. Dak. 298/O7
Freeman, Wash. 310/H3
Freemansburg, Pa. 294/M4
Freemanville, Ala. 195/D8
Free Mason (isls.), La. 238/M7
Freemont, Calif. 188/B3
Freemont, Sask. 181/B3
Freeport, Bahamas 156/B1
Freeport, Fla. 212/C6
Freeport, Ill. 188/J2
Freeport, Ill. 222/D1
Freeport, Ind. 227/F5
Freeport, Kansas 232/E4
Freeport, Maine 243/C8
Freeport•, Maine 243/C8
Freeport, Mich. 250/D6
Freeport, Minn. 255/D5
Freeport, N.Y. 276/R7
Freeport, Nova Scotia 168/B4
Freeport, Ohio 284/H5
Freeport, Pa. 294/C4
Freeport, Texas 303/J9
Freer, Texas 303/F10
Free Soil, Mich. 250/C4
Freestone (co.), Texas 303/H6
Freetown, Ant. & Bar. 161/E11
Freetown, Ind. 227/E7
Freetown, N.Y. 276/R9
Freetown (cap.), S. Leone 102/A4
Freetown (cap.), S. Leone 106/B7
Free Union, Va. 307/L4
Freeville, N.Y. 276/H5
Freezeout (lake), Mont. 262/D3
Fregenal de la Sierra, Spain 33/C3
Fregene, Italy 34/F6
Freiberg, Germany 22/E3
Freiburg, Germany 7/E4
Freiburg im Breisgau, Germany 22/B5
Freidberg, Austria 41/D3
Freienbach, Switzerland 39/G2
Freire, Chile 138/E2
Freirina, Chile 138/A7
Freising, Germany 22/D4
Freistadt, Austria 41/C2
Freistatt, Mo. 261/E8
Freital, Germany 22/E3
Freixo de Espada à Cinta, Portugal 33/C2
Fréjus, France 28/G6
Fréjus (pass), France 28/G5
Fréjus (pass), Italy 34/A2
Frelighsburg, Québec 172/E4
Fremantle, Australia 2/Q7
Fremantle, Australia 87/B9
Fremantle, W. Australia 88/B6
Fremantle, W. Australia 92/A1
Fremington, England 13/C6
Fremont, Calif. 204/K3
Fremont (peak), Calif. 204/H8
Fremont (co.), Colo. 208/J5
Fremont (co.), Idaho 220/G5
Fremont, Ind. 227/H1
Fremont (co.), Iowa 229/B7
Fremont, Iowa 229/H6
Fremont, Mich. 250/D5
Fremont, Mo. 261/K9
Fremont, Nebr. 188/G2
Fremont, Nebr. 264/H3
Fremont•, N.H. 268/E6
Fremont, N.C. 281/N3
Fremont, Ohio 284/D3
Fremont, Utah 304/C5
Fremont (isl.), Utah 304/B2
Fremont (riv.), Utah 304/C5
Fremont, Wis. 317/J7
Fremont (co.), Wyo. 319/D2
Fremont (lake), Wyo. 319/C3
Fremont (peak), Wyo. 319/C2
French, Argentina 143/F7
French (riv.), Conn. 210/H1
French (riv.), Ontario 177/D1
French (creek), Pa. 294/C2
French (creek), S. Dak. 298/C6
French (isl.), Victoria 97/C6
Frenchboro•, Maine 243/G7
French Broad (riv.), N.C. 281/D3
French Broad (riv.), Tenn. 237/R9
Frenchburg, Ky. 237/O5
French Camp, Miss. 256/F4
French Creek, W. Va. 312/F5
French Frigate (shoal), Hawaii 188/F6
French Frigate (shoals), Hawaii 87/K3
French Frigate (shoals), Hawaii 218/C6
Frenchglen, Oreg. 291/H5
French Guiana 2/G5
French Guiana 120/D2
FRENCH GUIANA 131/E3
French Lick, Ind. 227/D7
Frenchman (creek), Colo. 208/P1
Frenchman (bay), Maine 243/G7
Frenchman (riv.), Mont. 188/E1
Frenchman (riv.), Mont. 262/J1
Frenchman (creek), Nebr. 264/C4
Frenchman (riv.), Sask. 181/C6
Frenchman (cay), Virgin Is. (U.K.) 161/C4
Frenchman Butte, Sask. 181/B2
Frenchman Flat (basin), Nev. 266/F6
Frenchmans Cap (mt.), Tasmania 99/B4
Frenchmans Island, Newf. 166/C3
Frenchpark, Ireland 17/E4
French Polynesia 87/L8
French River, Minn. 255/G4
French River, Ontario 177/D1
French Settlement, La. 238/L2
Frenchton, W. Va. 312/F5
Frenchtown, Mont. 262/B3
Frenchtown, N.J. 273/C2
Frenchville, Maine 243/G1
Frenchville•, Maine 243/G1
Frenchville, Pa. 294/F3
Frenštát pod Radhoštěm, Czech. 41/E2
Fresco, Ivory Coast 106/C7
Fresh (pond), Mass. 249/C6
Freshford, Ireland 17/G6
Freshwater, Calif. 204/B3
Freshwater (Guffey), Colo. 208/H5
Freshwater, England 13/F7
Freshwater, Newf. 166/D2
Fresia, Chile 138/D3
Fresillo, Mexico 146/H7
Fresnillo de González Echererría, Mexico 150/H5
Fresno (co.), Calif. 204/E7
Fresno, Calif. 146/G6
Fresno, Calif. 188/C3
Fresno, Calif. 204/F7
Fresno (riv.), Calif. 204/E7
Fresno, Colombia 126/C5
Fresno, Mont. 262/G2
Fresno (res.), Mont. 262/F2
Fresno, Texas 303/J2
Freudenstadt, Germany 22/C4
Frew, Ky. 237/P6
Frewena, North. Terr. 93/D5
Frewsburg, N.Y. 276/B6
Freycinet (pen.), Tasmania 99/E4
Fria, Guinea 106/B6
Fria (cape), Namibia 102/D6
Fria (cape), Namibia 118/A3
Friant, Calif. 204/F7
Friant-Kern (canal), Calif. 204/F8
Friars Point, Miss. 256/C2
Frías, Argentina 143/D2
Fribourg (canton), Switzerland 39/D3
Fribourg, Switzerland 39/D3
Frick, Switzerland 39/E1
Friday Harbor, Wash. 310/B2
Fridley, Minn. 255/G5
Fried, N. Dak. 282/N5
Friedberg, Germany 22/C3
Friedland, Germany 22/E2
Friedrichshafen, Germany 22/C5
Friedrichstadt, Germany 22/C1
Friend, Kansas 232/B3
Friend, Nebr. 264/G4
Friend, Oreg. 291/F2
Friendly, W. Va. 312/D3
Friendship, Ark. 202/E5
Friendship, Ind. 227/G7
Friendship, Maine 243/E7
Friendship•, Maine 243/E7
Friendship, Md. 245/M6
Friendship, N.Y. 276/D6
Friendship, Ohio 284/D8
Friendship, Tenn. 237/C9
Friendship, Wis. 317/G8
Friendship Hill Nat'l Hist. Site, Pa. 294/C6
Friendsville, Ill. 222/F5
Friendsville, Md. 245/A2
Friendsville, Pa. 294/L2
Friendsville, Tenn. 237/N9
Friendswood, Texas 303/J2
Frienisberg (mt.), Switzerland 39/D2
Frierson, La. 238/C2
Fries, Va. 307/F7
Friesach, Austria 41/C3
Friesche Gat (chan.), Netherlands 27/J2
Friesland, Minn. 255/E4
Friesland (prov.), Netherlands 27/H2
Friesland, Wis. 317/H8
Frigate (isl.), Seychelles 118/J5
Frigate Bay, St. Kitts & Nevis 161/C10
Frimley and Camberley, England 13/G8
Frink, Fla. 212/D6
Frinton and Walton, England 10/G5
Frinton and Walton, England 13/J6
Frio (cape), Brazil 120/E5
Frio (cape), Brazil 135/F3
Frio (co.), Texas 303/E9
Frio (riv.), Texas 303/E8
Friockheim, Scotland 15/F4
Friol, Spain 33/C1
Friona, Texas 303/B3
Fripp (isl.), S.C. 296/G7
Frisches Haff (lag.), Poland 47/D1
Frisco, Colo. 208/G3
Frisco, N.C. 281/T4
Frisco, Pa. 294/B4
Frisco, Texas 303/H4
Frisco City, Ala. 195/D8
Frisian (isls.) 7/E3
Frisian, North (isls.), Denmark 21/B7
Frisian, East (isls.), Germany 22/B2
Frisian, North (isls.), Germany 22/B1
Frisian, West (isls.), Netherlands 27/G2
Frissell (mt.), Conn. 210/B1
Fristoe, Mo. 261/F6
Fritch, Texas 303/C2
Fritchton, Ind. 227/C7
Fritz Creek, Alaska 196/B2
Fritzlar, Germany 22/C3
Friuli-Venezia Giulia (reg.), Italy 34/D1
Frizzellburg, Md. 245/K2
Frobisher (bay), N.W.T. 162/K3
Frobisher (bay), N.W. Terr. 187/M3
Frobisher, Sask. 181/J6
Frobisher (lake), Sask. 181/L3
Froelich, Iowa 229/L2
Frog (lake), Alberta 182/E3
Frog Lake, Alberta 182/E3
Frogue, Ky. 237/L7
Frohavet (bay), Norway 18/F5
Frohna, Mo. 261/N7
Frohnleiten, Austria 41/C3
Froid, Mont. 262/M2
Froidchapelle, Belgium 27/E8
Frolovo, U.S.S.R. 48/E5
Frolovo, U.S.S.R. 52/F5
Fromberg, Mont. 262/H5
Frome (lake), Australia 87/E9
Frome, England 10/E5
Frome, England 13/E6
Frome, Jamaica 158/G6
Frome (lake), S. Australia 88/G6
Frome (lake), S. Australia 94/G4
Front (range), Colo. 208/H1
Fronteira, Portugal 33/C3
Fronteiras, Brazil 132/F4
Frontenac, Kansas 232/H4
Frontenac, Minn. 255/F6
Frontenac, Mo. 261/O3
Frontenac (county), Ontario 177/H3
Frontenac (co.), Québec 172/G4
Frontera, Mexico 150/N7
Frontier, Mich. 250/E7
Frontier (co.), Nebr. 264/D4
Frontier, N. Dak. 282/S6
Frontier, Sask. 181/C6
Frontier, Wyo. 319/B4
Front Royal, Va. 307/M3
Frosinone (prov.), Italy 34/D4
Frosinone, Italy 34/D4
Frösö, Sweden 18/J5
Frost, La. 238/L2
Frost, Minn. 255/D7
Frost, Texas 303/H5
Frost, W. Va. 312/G6
Frostburg, Md. 245/C2
Frostproof, Fla. 212/E4
Froude, Sask. 181/H6
Frövi, Sweden 18/J7
Frøya (isl.), Norway 18/F5
Frozen (str.), N.W.T. 162/H2
Frozen (str.), N.W. Terr. 187/K3
Fruita, Colo. 208/B4
Fruita, Utah 304/C5
Fruitdale, Ala. 195/B8
Fruitdale, S. Dak. 298/B4
Fruitdale-Harbeck, Oreg. 291/D5
Fruitgrove, Queensland 88/K3
Fruit Heights, Utah 304/C2
Fruithurst, Ala. 195/G3
Fruitland, Idaho 220/B6
Fruitland, Iowa 229/L6
Fruitland, Md. 245/R7
Fruitland, Mo. 261/N8
Fruitland, N. Mex. 274/A2
Fruitland, Tenn. 237/D9
Fruitland, Utah 304/D3
Fruitland, Wash. 310/G2
Fruitland Park, Fla. 212/D3
Fruitland Park, Miss. 256/F9
Fruitport, Mich. 250/C5
Fruitvale, Br. Col. 184/J5
Fruitvale, Idaho 220/B5
Fruitvale, Tenn. 237/C9
Fruitvale, Wash. 310/E4
Fruitville, Fla. 212/D4
Frunze, U.S.S.R. 54/J5
Frunze, U.S.S.R. 48/H5
Frutal, Brazil 135/B2
Frutigen, Switzerland 39/E3
Frutillar, Chile 138/D3
Fry, Georgia 217/D1
Fryburg, N. Dak. 282/D6
Fryburg, Ohio 284/B4
Fryburg, Pa. 294/D3
Fry Canyon, Utah 304/D6
Frýdek-Místek, Czech. 41/E2
Frýdlant nad Ostravicí, Czech. 41/E2
Frýdlant v. Čechách, Czech. 41/C1
Frye, Maine 243/B6
Fryeburg, La. 238/D2
Fryeburg, Maine 243/A7
Fryeburg•, Maine 243/A7
Fu'an, China 77/K6
Fuchu, Hiroshima, Japan 81/F6
Fuchu, Tokyo, Japan 81/O2
Fuding, China 77/K6
Fuengirola, Spain 33/D4
Fuensalida, Spain 33/D2
Fuente-Álamo, Spain 33/F4
Fuente de Cantos, Spain 33/C3
Fuentelapeña, Spain 33/D2
Fuente Obejuna, Spain 33/D3
Fuenterrabía, Spain 33/E1
Fuentesaúco, Spain 33/D2
Fuentes de Andalucía, Spain 33/D4
Fuentes de Oñoro, Spain 33/C2
Fuerte (isl.), Colombia 126/B3
Fuerte (riv.), Mexico 150/E3
Fuerte Bulnes, Chile 138/E10
Fuerte Olimpo, Argentina 120/D5
Fuerte Olimpo, Paraguay 144/C2
Fuerteventura (isl.), Spain 102/A2
Fuerteventura (isl.), Spain 106/B3
Fuerteventura (isl.), Spain 33/C4
Fuga (isl.), Philippines 82/A3
Fuglebjerg, Denmark 21/E7
Fugu, China 77/H4
Fuhai (Burultokay), China 77/C2
Fuik, Neth. Ant. 161/G9
Fujairah, U.A.E. 59/G4
Fuji, Japan 81/J6
Fuji (mt.), Japan 81/J6
Fuji (riv.), Japan 81/J6
Fujian (Fukien), China 77/J6
Fujieda, Japan 81/J6
Fuji-Hakone-Izu Nat'l Park, Japan 81/H6
Fujin, China 77/M2
Fujisawa, Japan 81/O3
Fukagawa, Japan 81/L2
Fukang, China 77/C3
Fukuchiyama, Japan 81/G6
Fukue, Japan 81/D7
Fukui (pref.), Japan 81/G5
Fukui, Japan 81/G5
Fukuoka (pref.), Japan 81/D7
Fukuoka, Japan 54/O6
Fukuoka, Japan 81/D7
Fukushima (pref.), Japan 81/K5
Fukushima, Japan 81/K5
Fukuyama, Japan 81/F6
Fulbourn, England 13/H5
Fulbright, Texas 303/J4
Fulda, Germany 22/C3
Fulda, Ind. 227/D8
Fulda, Minn. 255/C7
Fulda, Sask. 181/F3
Fulda (riv.), Germany 22/C3
Fulford, England 13/F4
Fulford Harbour, Br. Col. 184/K3
Fuling, China 77/G6
Fulks Run, Va. 307/L3
Fullarton, Trin. & Tob. 161/A11
Fullerton, Calif. 204/D11
Fullerton, Ky. 237/P3
Fullerton, La. 238/D4
Fullerton, Nebr. 264/F3
Fullerton, N. Dak. 282/O7
Fully, Switzerland 39/D4
Fulnek, Czech. 41/D2
Fulpmes, Austria 41/A3
Fulton, Ala. 195/C7
Fulton (co.), Ark. 202/G1
Fulton, Ark. 202/C6
Fulton (co.), Georgia 217/D3
Fulton (co.), Ill. 222/C3
Fulton, Ill. 222/C2
Fulton (co.), Ind. 227/E2
Fulton, Ind. 227/E3
Fulton, Iowa 229/M4
Fulton, Kansas 232/H4
Fulton (co.), Ky. 237/C7
Fulton, Ky. 237/D7
Fulton, Mich. 250/D6
Fulton, Miss. 256/H2
Fulton, Mo. 261/J5
Fulton (co.), N.Y. 276/M4
Fulton, N.Y. 276/H4
Fulton (co.), Ohio 284/B2
Fulton, Ohio 284/E5
Fulton (co.), Pa. 294/F6
Fulton, S. Dak. 298/O6
Fulton, Tenn. 237/B9
Fulton, Texas 303/H9
Fulton Chain (lakes), N.Y. 276/K3
Fultondale, Ala. 195/E3
Fultonham, Ohio 284/F6
Fultonville, N.Y. 276/M5
Fults, Ill. 222/C5
Fulwood, England 10/G1
Fulwood, England 13/G1
Funabashi, Japan 81/P2
Funafuti (atoll), Tuvalu 87/H6
Funchal, Portugal 33/A2
Funchal (cap.), Madeira, Port. 102/A1
Funchal (cap.), Madeira, Portugal 106/A2
Fundación, Colombia 126/C2
Fundão, Portugal 33/C2
Fundy (bay) 162/K7
Fundy (bay), New Bruns. 170/E3
Fundy (bay), Nova Scotia 168/C3
Fundy Nat'l Park, New Bruns. 170/E3
Funhalouro, Mozambique 118/E4
Funing, China 77/K5
Funk, Nebr. 264/E4
Funk (isl.), Newf. 166/D4
Funkley, Minn. 255/D3
Funkstown, Md. 245/H2
Funston, Georgia 217/E8
Funter, Alaska 196/M1
Funtua, Nigeria 106/F6
Fuping, China 77/H4
Fuquay-Varina, N.C. 281/M3
Furancungo, Mozambique 118/E2
Furka (pass), Switzerland 39/F3
Furman, Ala. 195/E6
Furman, S.C. 296/E6
Furmanov, U.S.S.R. 52/F3
Furnace, Ky. 237/O5
Furnace, Mass. 249/F3
Furnace, Scotland 15/C4
Furnas (res.), Brazil 120/E5
Furnas (dam), Brazil 135/C2
Furnas (co.), Nebr. 264/E4
Furneaux Group (isls.), Australia 87/E9
Furneaux Group (isls.), Tasmania 88/H8
Furneaux Group (isls.), Tasmania 99/E1
Furnes (Veurne), Belgium 27/B6
Furness, Sask. 181/B2
Furry Creek, Br. Col. 184/K2
Fürstenberg, Germany 22/E2
Fürstenfeld, Austria 41/C3
Fürstenfeldbruck, Germany 22/D4
Fürstenwalde, Germany 22/F2
Fürth, Germany 22/D4
Furth im Wald, Germany 22/E4
Furukawa, Japan 81/K4
Fury and Hecla (str.), N.W.T. 162/H2
Fury and Hecla (str.), N.W. Terr. 187/K3
Fusagasugá, Colombia 126/C5
Fushun, China 77/K3
Fushun, China 54/O5
Fusilier, Sask. 181/B4
Fusin (Fuxin), China 77/K3
Fusingchen (Simao), China 77/F7
Fusio, Switzerland 39/G4
Fusong, China 77/L3
Füssen, Germany 22/D5
Futa Jallon (lag.), Guinea 106/B6
Futaleufú, Chile 138/E4
Futrono, Chile 138/E3
Futuna (Hoorn) (isls.), Wallis and Futuna 87/J7
Fu Xian, Liaoning, China 77/K4
Fu Xian, Shaanxi, China 77/G4
Fuxin (Fusin), China 77/K3
Fuxin, China 54/O5
Fuyang (Fowyang), China 77/J5
Fuyu, Heilongjiang, China 77/K2
Fuyu, Jilin, China 77/L2
Fuyuan, Heilongjiang, China 77/M2
Fuyuan, Yunnan, China 77/F6
Fuyun, China 77/C2
Füzesabony, Hungary 41/F3
Füzesgyarmat, Hungary 41/F3
Fuzhou, Jiangxi, China 77/J6
Fuzhou, China 2/R4
Fuzhou, China 54/N7
Fuzhou (Foochow), Fujian, China 77/J6
Fyffe, Ala. 195/G2
Fylingdales, England 13/G3
Fyn (co.), Denmark 21/D7
Fyn (isl.), Denmark 21/D7
Fyn (isl.), Denmark 18/G9
Fyne, Loch (inlet), Scotland 10/D2
Fyne, Loch (inlet), Scotland 15/C5
Fyns Hoved (pt.), Denmark 21/D6
Fyvie, Scotland 15/F3
Fyzabad, Trin. & Tob. 161/A11

G

Gaastra, Mich. 250/G2
Gabarus, Nova Scotia 168/H3
Gabarus (bay), Nova Scotia 168/H3
Gabarus (cape), Nova Scotia 168/J3
Gabbettville, Georgia 217/B5
Gabbs, Nev. 266/D4
Gabela, Angola 115/B6
Gabès, Tunisia 106/F2
Gabès, Tunisia 102/D1
Gabès (gulf), Tunisia 106/G2
Gabgaba, Wadi (dry riv.), Sudan 111/F3
Gable, S.C. 296/G4
Gabon 2/K6
Gabon 102/D4
GABON 115/B4
Gaborone (cap.), Botswana 2/L7
Gaborone (cap.), Botswana 118/D4
Gaborone (cap.), Botswana 102/E7
Gabras, Sudan 111/E5
Gabredarre, Ethiopia 111/H6
Gabriel (str.), N.W. Terr. 187/M3
Gabrik (riv.), Iran 66/L7
Gabriola, Br. Col. 184/J3
Gabrovo, Bulgaria 45/G4
Gachalá, Colombia 126/D5
Gach Saran, Iran 59/F3
Gach Saran, Iran 66/F5
Gackle, N. Dak. 282/M6
Gacko, Yugoslavia 45/D4
Gadag-Betgeri, India 68/D5
Gäddede, Sweden 18/J4
Gadê, China 77/E5
Gadebusch, Germany 22/D2
Gadmen, Switzerland 39/F3
Gadsby, Alberta 182/D3
Gadsden, Ala. 188/J4
Gadsden, Ala. 195/G2
Gadsden, Ariz. 198/A6
Gadsden (co.), Fla. 212/B1
Gadsden, S.C. 296/F4
Gadsden, Tenn. 237/D9
Gads Hill, Mo. 261/L8
Gadston (pt.), Fla. 212/C3
Gadwal, India 68/D5
Gadyach, U.S.S.R. 52/D4
Găeşti, Romania 45/G3
Gaeta, Italy 34/D4
Gaeta (gulf), Italy 34/D4
Gaferut (isl.), Micronesia 87/E5
Gaffney, S.C. 296/D1
Gafsa, Tunisia 106/F2
Gagarin, U.S.S.R. 52/D3
Gage, Alberta 182/A1
Gage (co.), Nebr. 264/H4
Gage, N. Mex. 274/A6
Gage, Okla. 288/G2
Gagetown, Mich. 250/F5
Gagetown, New Bruns. 170/D3
Gaggenau, Germany 22/C4
Gagnoa, Ivory Coast 102/B4
Gagnoa, Ivory Coast 106/C7
Gagnon, Que. 162/K5
Gagnon, Québec 174/D2

Glacier 373

Geertruidenberg, Netherlands 27/F5
Geesthacht, Germany 22/D2
Geetingsville, Ind. 227/D4
Geeveston, Tasmania 99/C5
Geff, Ill. 222/E5
Gê'gyai, China 77/B5
Geh, Iran 59/H4
Geh, Iran 66/L7
Gehua, Papua N.G. 85/C8
Geidam, Nigeria 106/G6
Geiger, Ala. 195/B5
Geiger Heights, Wash. 310/H3
Geikie (riv.), Sask. 181/M3
Geilo, Norway 18/F6
Geiranger, Norway 18/E5
Geislingen an der Steige, Germany 22/C4
Geismar, La. 238/K3
Geist (res.), Ind. 227/F5
Geistown, Pa. 294/E5
Geita, Tanzania 115/F4
Gejiu (Kokiu), China 77/F7
Gejiu, China 54/M7
Gela, Italy 34/E6
Gelang, Tanjong (pt.), Malaysia 72/D6
Geldenaken (Jodoigne), Belgium 27/F7
Gelderland (prov.), Netherlands 27/H4
Geldermalsen, Netherlands 27/G5
Geldern, Germany 22/B3
Geldrop, Netherlands 27/H6
Geleen, Netherlands 27/H7
Gelendzhik, U.S.S.R. 52/E6
Gelgia (riv.), Switzerland 39/J3
Gelibolu (Gallipoli), Turkey 63/C5
Gelidonya (cape), Turkey 59/B2
Gelidonya (cape), Turkey 63/D4
Gelligaer, Wales 13/A6
Gelnhausen, Germany 22/C3
Gelnica, Czech. 41/F2
Gelså (riv.), Denmark 21/C7
Gelsenkirchen, Germany 22/B3
Gelsted, Denmark 21/C7
Gelterkinden, Switzerland 39/E2
Gem, Alberta 182/D4
Gem (co.), Idaho 220/B6
Gem, Idaho 220/C2
Gem, Ind. 227/F5
Gem, Kansas 232/B2
Gem (lake), Manitoba 179/G4
Gem, W. Va. 312/E5
Gemas, Malaysia 72/D7
Gembloux-sur-Orneau, Belgium 27/F7
Gemena, Zaire 115/D3
Gemena, Zaire 102/E4
Gemerek, Turkey 63/G3
Gemert, Netherlands 27/H5
Gemlik, Turkey 63/C2
Gemmell, Minn. 255/D3
Gemona, Italy 34/D1
Gemsa, Egypt 111/F2
Genç, Turkey 63/J3
Gendringen, Netherlands 27/J5
Gene Autry, Okla. 288/N6
Genemuiden, Netherlands 27/H3
General Acha, Argentina 143/C4
General Alvear, Buenos Aires, Argentina 143/F7
General Alvear, Mendoza, Argentina 143/C3
General Arenales, Argentina 143/F7
General Artigas, Paraguay 144/D5
General Belgrano, Argentina 143/G7
General Bravo, Mexico 150/K4
General Campos, Argentina 143/G5
General Cepeda, Mexico 150/J4
General Conesa, Argentina 143/C5
General Elizardo Aquino, Paraguay 144/D4
General Enrique Martínez, Uruguay 145/F4
General Eugenio A. Garay, Paraguay 144/A2
General Galarza, Argentina 143/C6
General Grant Grove Section (King's Canyon), Calif. 204/G7
General Güemes, Argentina 143/D1
General Guido, Argentina 143/E4
General José de San Martín, Argentina 143/E2
General Juan Madariaga, Argentina 143/E4
General Lagos, Chile 138/B1
General La Madrid, Argentina 143/D4
General Las Heras, Argentina 143/G7
General Lavalle, Argentina 143/E4
General Manuel Belgrano, Cerro (mt.), Argentina 143/C2
General Mitchell Field, Wis. 317/M2
General O'Brien, Argentina 143/F7
General Paz, Argentina 143/E2
General Paz, Argentina 143/H7
General Paz (lake), Chile 138/E5
General Pico, Argentina 143/D4
General Ramírez, Argentina 143/F6
General Roca, Argentina 143/C4
General Saavedra, Bolivia 136/D5
General San Martín, Buenos Aires, Argentina 143/G4
General San Martín, La Pampa, Argentina 143/D4
General Santos, Philippines 82/E7
General Terán, Mexico 150/K4
General Tinio, Philippines 82/C3
General-Toshevo, Bulgaria 45/H4
General Viamonte, Argentina 143/F7
General Villegas, Argentina 143/D4
Generoso (mt.), Switzerland 39/H5
Genesee, Idaho 220/B3
Genesee (co.), Mich. 250/F5
Genesee (co.), N.Y. 276/D4
Genesee (riv.), N.Y. 276/E5
Genesee, Pa. 294/G2
Genesee, Wis. 317/J2
Genesee Depot, Wis. 317/J2
Geneseo, Ill. 222/C2
Geneseo, Kansas 232/D3
Geneseo, N.Y. 276/E5
Geneseo, N. Dak. 282/R7
Geneva (lake) 7/E4
Geneva (co.), Ala. 195/G8
Geneva, Ala. 195/G8
Geneva, Fla. 212/E3
Geneva (lake), France 28/G4
Geneva, Georgia 217/C5
Geneva, Idaho 220/G7
Geneva, Ill. 222/E2
Geneva, Ind. 227/H3
Geneva, Iowa 229/G3
Geneva, Ky. 237/F5
Geneva, Minn. 255/E7
Geneva, Nebr. 264/G4
Geneva, N.Y. 276/G5
Geneva, Ohio 284/J2
Geneva, Pa. 294/B2
Geneva (Genève) (canton), Switzerland 39/B4
Geneva (Genève), Switzerland 39/B4
Geneva, Switzerland 7/E4
Geneva (lake), Switzerland 39/C4
Geneva, Texas 303/L6
Geneva (lake), Wis. 317/K10
Geneva-on-the-Lake, Ohio 284/H2
Genezin, Turkey 63/F3
Genichesk, U.S.S.R. 52/E5
Genil (riv.), Spain 33/D4
Genk, Belgium 27/H7
Gennargentu, Monti del (mt.), Italy 34/B5
Gennep, Netherlands 27/H5
Gennevilliers, France 28/B1
Genoa, Ark. 202/C7
Genoa, Colo. 208/N4
Genoa, Ill. 222/E1
Genoa (prov.), Italy 34/B2
Genoa, Italy 7/E4
Genoa, Italy 34/B2
Genoa (gulf), Italy 34/B2
Genoa, Nebr. 264/G3
Genoa, Nev. 266/B4
Genoa, N.Y. 276/G5
Genoa, Ohio 284/D2
Genoa, W. Va. 312/A6
Genoa, Wis. 317/D8
Genoa City, Wis. 317/K11
Genola, Minn. 255/D5
Genola, Utah 304/C4
Genova (Genoa), Italy 34/B2
Genovesa (isl.), Ecuador 128/C9
Gent (Ghent), Belgium 27/D6
Genthin, Germany 22/E2
Gentilly, France 28/B2
Gentilly, Minn. 255/B3
Genting, Indonesia 85/D5
Gentofte, Denmark 21/F6
Gentry, Ark. 202/A1
Gentry (co.), Mo. 261/D2
Gentry, Mo. 261/D2
Gentryville, Ind. 227/C8
Gentryville, Mo. 261/D2
Genzano di Roma, Italy 34/F7
Geographe (bay), W. Australia 92/A6
Geographe (chan.), W. Australia 88/A4
Geographe (chan.), W. Australia 92/A4
Geographical Center of North America, N. Dak. 282/K3
Geographical Center of U.S., S. Dak. 298/B4
George (isl.), Falk. Is. 143/E7
George (lake), Fla. 212/E2
George, Iowa 229/B2
George (isl.), Manitoba 179/E2
George (lake), Manitoba 179/G4
George (co.), Miss. 256/G9
George (isl.), Newf. 166/C3
George (lake), N.S. Wales 97/E4
George (lake), N.Y. 276/N4
George (sound), N. Zealand 100/A6
George (lake), N. Dak. 282/L6
George (cape), Nova Scotia 168/G3
George (lake), Nova Scotia 168/B5
George (riv.), Que. 162/K4
George (riv.), Que. 146/M4
George (riv.), Québec 174/F2
George, S. Africa 118/C6
George (lake), Uganda 115/F4
George, Wash. 310/F3
George A.F.B., Calif. 204/H9
George B. Stevenson (dam), Pa. 294/G3
George Land (isl.), U.S.S.R. 4/B7
George Land (isl.), U.S.S.R. 48/E1
George Rogers Clark Nat'l Hist. Park, Ind. 227/B7
Georges (isls.), Maine 243/E8
Georges (riv.), N.S. Wales 88/K4
Georges (riv.), N.S. Wales 97/H4
Georges Brook, Newf. 166/D2
George's Cove, Newf. 166/C3
Georges Fork, Va. 307/C6
Georges Mills, N.H. 268/C5
Georgetown, Ark. 202/G3
Georgetown, Calif. 204/E5
George Town (cap.), Cayman Is. 156/B3
Georgetown, Colo. 208/H3
Georgetown, Conn. 210/B4
Georgetown, Del. 245/S6
Georgetown, D.C. 245/E5
Georgetown, Fla. 212/E2
Georgetown, Gambia 106/A6
Georgetown, Georgia 217/B7
Georgetown (cap.), Guyana 2/G5
Georgetown (cap.), Guyana 131/C2
Georgetown (cap.), Guyana 120/D2
Georgetown, Idaho 220/G7
Georgetown, Ill. 222/F4
Georgetown, Ind. 227/F8
Georgetown, Ky. 237/M4
Georgetown, La. 238/F3
Georgetown, Maine 243/D8
Georgetown•, Maine 243/D8
George Town (Pinang), Malaysia 72/C6
George Town, Malaysia 54/M9
Georgetown, Mass. 249/L2
Georgetown•, Mass. 249/L2
Georgetown, Minn. 255/B3
Georgetown, Miss. 256/D7
Georgetown (lake), Mont. 262/C4
Georgetown, Ohio 284/C8
Georgetown, Pa. 294/A4
Georgetown, Pr. Edward I. 168/F2
Georgetown, Queensland 88/G3
Georgetown, Queensland 95/B3
Georgetown, St. Vin. & Grens. 161/A8
Georgetown, St. Vin. & Grens. 156/G4
Georgetown, S.C. 188/L4
Georgetown (co.), S.C. 296/J5
Georgetown, S.C. 296/J5
George Town, Tasmania 99/C3
George Town, Tasmania 88/H8
Georgetown, Tenn. 237/L10
Georgetown, Texas 303/G7
George V Coast (reg.), Ant. 5/C8
Georgeville, Minn. 255/C5
Georgeville, Nova Scotia 168/F3
George Washington Carver Nat'l Mon., Mo. 261/D9
George Washington Birthplace Nat'l Mon., Va. 307/P4
George West, Texas 303/F9
Georgia 188/K4
GEORGIA 217
Georgia (str.), Br. Col. 184/J3
Georgia (state), U.S. 146/K6
Georgia•, Vt. 268/A2
Georgia (str.), Wash. 310/B2
Georgia Center, Vt. 268/A2
Georgian (bay), Ont. 162/H6
Georgian (bay), Ontario 177/D2
Georgian (bay), Ontario 175/D3
Georgiana, Ala. 195/E7
Georgian Bay Is. Nat'l Park, Ontario 177/C2,D3
Georgian S.S.R., U.S.S.R. 7/J4
Georgian S.S.R., U.S.S.R. 52/F6
Georgian S.S.R., U.S.S.R. 48/D5
Georgiaville, R.I. 249/H5
Georgina (riv.), North. Terr. 93/E6
Georgina (isl.), Ontario 177/E3
Georgina (riv.), Queensland 88/F4
Georgina (riv.), Queensland 95/A4
Georgiu-Dezh, U.S.S.R. 52/E4
Georgsmarienhütte, Germany 22/B2
Gera, Germany 22/E3
Geraardsbergen, Belgium 27/D7
Gerald, Mo. 261/K6
Gerald, Sask. 181/K5
Geral de Goiás, Serra (range), Brazil 132/E6
Geraldine, Ala. 195/G2
Geraldine, Mont. 262/F3
Geraldine, N. Zealand 100/C6
Geraldton, Australia 87/B8
Geraldton, Ont. 162/H6
Geraldton, Ontario 177/H5
Geraldton, Ontario 175/C3
Geraldton, W. Australia 88/A5
Geraldton, W. Australia 92/A5
Gerar (dry riv.), Israel 65/B5
Gerber, Calif. 204/C3
Gerber (res.), Oreg. 291/F5
Gercüş, Turkey 63/J4
Gerdine (mt.), Alaska 196/A1
Gerede, Turkey 63/E2
Gereshk, Afghanistan 59/H3
Gereshk, Afghanistan 68/A2
Geretsried, Germany 22/D5
Gérgal, Spain 33/E4
Gerger, Turkey 63/H3
Gerik, Malaysia 72/D6
Gering, Nebr. 264/A3
Gerlach, Nev. 266/B2
Gerlachovka (mt.), Czech. 41/E2
Gerlogubi, Ethiopia 111/H6
Germania, Miss. 256/C5
Germania, Pa. 294/G2
Germania, Wis. 317/H8
Germano, Ohio 284/J5
Germansen (lake), Br. Col. 184/E2
Germansen Landing, Br. Col. 184/E2
Germanton, N.C. 281/J2
Germantown, Ill. 222/D5
Germantown, Ky. 237/O3
Germantown, Md. 245/J4
Germantown, New Bruns. 170/F3
Germantown, N.Y. 276/N6
Germantown, Ohio 284/B6
Germantown, Tenn. 237/B10
Germantown, Wis. 317/K1
German Valley, Ill. 222/D1
Germany 2/K3
Germany 7/F3
GERMANY 22
Germencik, Turkey 63/B4
Germersheim, Germany 22/C4
Germfask, Mich. 250/C2
Germiston, S. Africa 102/E7
Germiston, S. Africa 118/H6
Gerofit, Israel 65/D5
Gerolstein, Germany 22/B3
Gerona (Girona) (prov.), Spain 33/H1
Gerona (Girona), Spain 33/H2
Geronimo, Ariz. 198/F5
Geronimo, Okla. 288/K6
Gerpinnes, Belgium 27/F8
Gerpir (cape), Iceland 21/D1
Gerra, Switzerland 39/G4
Gerrardstown, W. Va. 312/K4
Gerringong, N.S. Wales 97/F4
Gerrish, N.H. 268/D5
Gerry, N.Y. 276/B6
Gers (dept.), France 28/D6
Gers (riv.), France 28/D6
Gersau, Switzerland 39/G2
Gersfeld, Germany 22/C3
Gerster, Mo. 261/E7
Gerty, Okla. 288/O5
Gervais, Oreg. 291/A3
Gervasio, Uruguay 145/F4
Gêrzê, China 77/B5
Gerze, Turkey 63/F2
Geser, Indonesia 85/J6
Gesher, Israel 65/C2
Gesher Haziv, Israel 65/C1
Gessie, Ind. 227/C4
Getafe, Spain 33/F4
Getaway, Ohio 284/F9
Gettysburg, Ohio 284/A5
Gettysburg, Pa. 294/H6
Gettysburg, S. Dak. 298/K3
Gettysburg Nat'l Mil. Park, Pa. 294/H6
Getulio Vargas, Uruguay 145/F3
Getz Ice Shelf, Ant. 5/B12
Geuda Springs, Kansas 232/E4
Geurie, N.S. Wales 97/E3
Gevar'am, Israel 65/B4
Gevaş, Turkey 63/K3
Gevgelija, Yugoslavia 45/F5
Gex, France 28/G4
Geyser, Mont. 262/F3
Geyserville, Calif. 204/B5
Geyve, Turkey 63/D2
Gezira, El (reg.), Sudan 111/F5
Ghabaghib, Syria 63/H5
Ghadames, Libya 102/D2
Ghadames, Libya 111/A2
Ghaemshar, Iran 66/H2
Ghaghra (riv.), India 68/E3
Ghaida, Yemen 59/F6
Ghalla, Wadi el (dry riv.), Sudan 111/E5
Ghana 2/J5
Ghana 102/B4
GHANA 106/D7
Ghanzi, Botswana 118/C4
Ghard Abu Muharik (des.), Egypt 111/J4
Ghardaïa, Algeria 106/E2
Ghardaïa, Algeria 102/C1
Gharian, Libya 102/D1
Gharian, Libya 111/B1
Gharib, Jebel (mt.), Egypt 59/B4
Ghat, Libya 102/D2
Ghat, Libya 111/B3
Ghat Kopar, India 68/B7
Ghazaouet, Algeria 106/D2
Ghaziabad, India 68/D3
Ghazipur, India 68/E3
Ghazni, Afghanistan 68/B2
Ghazni, Afghanistan 59/J3
Ghea (riv.), India 68/F1
Gheen, Minn. 255/F3
Gheens, La. 238/K7
Ghemines, Libya 111/C1
Ghenghis Khan Wall (ruin), China 77/H2
Ghenghis Khan Wall (ruins), Mongolia 77/H2
Ghent, Belgium 27/D6
Ghent, Ky. 237/L3
Ghent, Minn. 255/C6
Ghent, N.Y. 276/N6
Ghent, W. Va. 312/D7
Gheorghe Gheorghiu-Dej, Romania 45/H2
Gheorghieni, Romania 45/G2
Gherla, Romania 45/G2
Ghimbi, Ethiopia 111/G6
Ghio, N.C. 281/K5
Ghisonaccia, France 28/B7
Ghizar, Pakistan 68/C1
Gholson, Miss. 256/G5
Ghost Dam, Alberta 182/C4
Ghost Lake, Alberta 182/C4
Ghurian, Afghanistan 68/A2
Ghurian, Afghanistan 59/H3
Giacomo (pass), Switzerland 39/G4
Gia Dinh, Vietnam 72/E5
Giannutri (isl.), Italy 34/C3
Giant's Causeway, N. Ireland 17/H1
Giarre, Italy 34/E6
Giatto, W. Va. 312/D8
Gibara, Cuba 156/C2
Gibara, Cuba 158/J3
Gibbon, Minn. 255/D6
Gibbon, Nebr. 264/F4
Gibbon, Oreg. 291/J2
Gibbons, Alberta 182/D3
Gibbonsville, Idaho 220/E4
Gibb River, W. Australia 92/D2
Gibbs, Mo. 261/H2
Gibbs, Sask. 181/G5
Gibbsboro, N.J. 273/B4
Gibbs City, Mich. 250/G2
Gibbstown, N.J. 273/C4
Gibbsville, Wis. 317/L8
Gibeon, Namibia 118/B5
Gibloux (mt.), Switzerland 39/D3
Gibraltar 7/D5
Gibraltar (str.) 2/J4
Gibraltar (str.) 102/B1
Gibraltar (str.) 7/D5
Gibraltar 2/J4
GIBRALTAR 33
Gibraltar, Gibraltar 33/D4
Gibraltar (pt.), England 13/H4
Gibraltar, Mich. 250/F6
Gibraltar (str.), Morocco 106/C1
Gibraltar (str.), Spain 33/D5
Gibsland, La. 238/E1
Gibson (desert), Australia 87/C8
Gibson, Georgia 217/G4
Gibson (co.), Ind. 227/B8
Gibson, Iowa 229/J6
Gibson, La. 238/J7
Gibson, Miss. 256/G3
Gibson, Mo. 261/M10
Gibson (res.), Mont. 262/D3
Gibson, N.C. 281/K5
Gibson, Pa. 294/L2
Gibson (co.), Tenn. 237/D9
Gibson, Tenn. 237/D9
Gibson, W. Australia 88/C6
Gibson, W. Australia 92/C6
Gibson (des.), W. Australia 88/C4
Gibson (des.), W. Australia 92/D3
Gibsonburg, Ohio 284/D3
Gibson City, Ill. 222/E3
Gibsonia, Pa. 294/B4
Gibsons, Br. Col. 184/K3
Gibson Station, Va. 307/A7
Gibsonton, Fla. 212/C3
Gibsonville, N.C. 281/K2
Giddings, Texas 303/H7
Gideälv (riv.), Sweden 18/L5
Gideon, Mo. 261/N10
Gideon, Okla. 288/R2
Gien, France 28/E4
Giese, Minn. 255/E4
Giessendam-Hardinxveld, Netherlands 27/F5
Giethoorn, Netherlands 27/J3
Gif, France 28/E3
Gifan, Iran 66/K2
Giffard, Québec 172/J3
Giffnock, Scotland 15/B2
Gifford, Fla. 212/F4
Gifford, Ill. 222/E3
Gifford, Iowa 229/G4
Gifford (riv.), N.W. Terr. 187/K2
Gifford, Scotland 15/F5
Gifford, S.C. 296/E6
Gifford, Wash. 310/G2
Gifhorn, Germany 22/D2
Gift Lake, Alberta 182/C2
Gifu (pref.), Japan 81/H6
Gifu, Japan 81/H6
Giganta, Sierra de la (mts.), Mexico 150/D4
Gigante, Colombia 126/C6
Gigha (isl.), Scotland 15/C5
Gigha (sound), Scotland 15/C5
Gig Harbor, Wash. 310/C3
Giglio (isl.), Italy 34/C3
Gijón, Spain 7/D4
Gijón, Spain 33/D1
Gil (isl.), Br. Col. 184/C3
Gila (riv.) 188/D4
Gila (co.), Ariz. 198/E5
Gila (mts.), Ariz. 198/A6
Gila (mts.), Ariz. 198/F5
Gila (riv.), Ariz. 198/B6
Gila, N. Mex. 274/A6
Gila (riv.), N. Mex. 274/A6
Gila (riv.), U.S. 146/G6
Gila Bend, Ariz. 198/C6
Gila Bend (mts.), Ariz. 198/B5
Gila Bend Ind. Res., Ariz. 198/C6
Gila Cliff Dwellings Nat'l Mon., N. Mex. 274/A5
Gila Hot Springs, N. Mex. 274/A5
Gilan (prov.), Iran 66/F2
Gilan (reg.), Iran 66/F2
Gila River Ind. Res., Ariz. 198/C5
Gilat, Israel 65/B5
Gilbert, Ariz. 198/D5
Gilbert, Ark. 202/E2
Gilbert, Iowa 229/F4
Gilbert (isls.), Kiribati 2/T5
Gilbert (isls.), Kiribati 87/H6
Gilbert, La. 238/G2
Gilbert, Minn. 255/F3
Gilbert (riv.), Newf. 166/C3
Gilbert (riv.), Queensland 88/G3
Gilbert (riv.), Queensland 95/B3
Gilbert, S.C. 296/E4
Gilbert (peak), Utah 304/D3
Gilbert, W. Va. 312/C7
Gilberton, Pa. 294/K4
Gilbertown, Ala. 195/B7
Gilbert Plains, Manitoba 179/B3
Gilberts, Ill. 222/E1
Gilbertsville, Ky. 237/E7
Gilbertsville, N.Y. 276/K6
Gilbertville, Iowa 229/J4
Gilbertville, Mass. 249/F3
Gilbjerg Hoved (pt.), Denmark 21/F5
Gilboa, N.Y. 276/M6
Gilboa, Ohio 284/C3
Gilboa, W. Va. 312/E6
Gilbués, Brazil 132/E5
Gilby, N. Dak. 282/R3
Gilchrist (co.), Fla. 212/D2
Gilchrist (creek), Manitoba 179/F2
Gilchrist (lake), Manitoba 179/G2
Gilcrest, Colo. 208/K2
Gildford, Mont. 262/F2
Gilé, Mozambique 118/F3
Gilead, Conn. 210/F2
Gilead, Ind. 227/E3
Gilead•, Maine 243/B7
Gilead, Nebr. 264/G4
Giles (co.), Tenn. 237/G10
Giles (co.), Va. 307/G6
Gilf Kebir (plat.), Egypt 111/E3
Gilford, Mich. 250/F5
Gilford•, N.H. 268/E4
Gilford, N. Ireland 17/J3
Gilford Park, N.J. 273/E4
Gilgai, N.S. Wales 97/F1
Gilgandra, N. S. Wales 88/H6
Gilgandra, N.S. Wales 97/E2
Gilgil, Kenya 115/G4
Gilgit, Pakistan 68/C1
Gilgit, Pakistan 59/K2
Gilgunnia, N.S. Wales 97/C3
Gill, Colo. 208/L2
Gill (lake), Ireland 17/E3
Gill•, Mass. 249/D2
Gillam, Manitoba 179/K2
Gilleleje, Denmark 21/F5
Gilles (lake), S. Australia 94/E5
Gillespie, Ill. 222/D4
Gillespie, New Bruns. 170/C2
Gillespie (co.), Texas 303/F7
Gillett, Ark. 202/H5
Gillett, Pa. 294/J2
Gillett, Texas 303/G8
Gillett, Wis. 317/K6
Gillette, N.J. 273/E2
Gillette, Wyo. 319/G1
Gillett Grove, Iowa 229/C2
Gilleyville, La. 238/G2
Gillham, Ark. 202/B5
Gilliam, La. 238/C1
Gilliam, Mo. 261/F4
Gilliam (co.), Oreg. 291/G2
Gillies Bay, Br. Col. 184/H2
Gillingham, Dorset, England 13/E6
Gillingham, Kent, England 13/J8
Gillis (range), Nev. 266/C4
Gillisonville, S.C. 296/E6
Gillsburg, Miss. 256/C8
Gillsville, Georgia 217/E2
Gilly, Switzerland 39/B4
Gilman, Colo. 208/G3
Gilman, Conn. 210/G2
Gilman, Ill. 222/E3
Gilman, Ind. 227/F4
Gilman, Iowa 229/H5
Gilman, Minn. 255/E5
Gilman, Vt. 268/D3
Gilman, Wis. 317/E5
Gilman City, Mo. 261/D2
Gilmanton•, N.H. 268/E5
Gilmanton, Wis. 317/C7
Gilmanton Iron Works, N.H. 268/E5
Gilmer (co.), Georgia 217/D1
Gilmer, Texas 303/J5
Gilmer (co.), W. Va. 312/E5
Gilmer, W. Va. 312/E5
Gilmore, Ark. 202/K3
Gilmore, Georgia 217/J1
Gilmore City, Iowa 229/D3
Gilpin (co.), Colo. 208/H3
Gilroy, Calif. 204/D6
Gilson, Ill. 222/C3
Gilsum•, N.H. 268/C5
Gilt Edge, Tenn. 237/B9
Giltner, Nebr. 264/F4
Gilze, Netherlands 27/F5
Gimel, Switzerland 39/B3
Gimie (mt.), St. Lucia 161/G6
Gimlet, Ky. 237/P4
Gimli, Manitoba 179/F4
Gimo, Sweden 18/K6
Gingerland, St. Kitts and Nevis 161/D11
Gingin, W. Australia 92/A1
Gingoog, Philippines 82/E6
Gingoog (bay), Philippines 82/E6
Gings, Ind. 227/G5
Ginir, Ethiopia 111/H6
Ginnosar, Israel 65/D2
Ginzo de Limia, Spain 33/C1
Gio, Hon (isl.), Vietnam 72/E3
Giohar, Somalia 102/G4
Giohar, Somalia 115/J3
Gioia del Colle, Italy 34/F4
Gioiosa Ionica, Italy 34/F5
Giornico, Switzerland 39/G4
Giovinazzo, Italy 34/F4
Gi-Paraná (riv.), Brazil 132/H10
Gippsland (reg.), Victoria 97/D6
Gipsy (lake), Alberta 182/E1
Gipsy, Mo. 261/M8
Gipsy, Pa. 294/E4
Giraltovce, Czech. 41/F2
Girard, Ill. 222/D4
Girard, Georgia 217/J4
Girard, Kansas 232/H4
Girard, La. 238/G2
Girard, Mich. 250/E6
Girard, Ohio 284/J3
Girard, Pa. 294/B2
Girard, Texas 303/D4
Girardot, Colombia 126/C5
Girardville, Pa. 294/K4
Girardville, Québec 172/E1
Girdle Ness (prom.), Scotland 15/G3
Girdler, Ky. 237/O7
Girdletree, Md. 245/S8
Giresun (prov.), Turkey 63/H2
Giresun, Turkey 59/C1
Giresun, Turkey 63/H2
Girga, Egypt 59/B4
Girga, Egypt 111/F2
Girga, Egypt 102/F2
Giri (riv.), Zaire 115/C3
Girilambone, N.S. Wales 97/D2
Girón, Ecuador 128/C4
Girona (prov.), Spain 33/H1
Girona, Spain 33/H2
Gironde (dept.), France 28/C5
Gironde (riv.), France 28/C5
Giroux, Manitoba 179/F5
Girouxville, Alberta 182/B2
Girvan, Scotland 15/D5
Girvan, Scotland 10/D3
Girvin, Sask. 181/F4
Girvin, Texas 303/B6
Gisborne, N. Zealand 100/G3
Giscome, Br. Col. 184/F3
Gisenyi, Rwanda 115/E4
Gislaved, Sweden 18/H8
Gisors, France 28/D3
Gistel, Belgium 27/B6
Giswil, Switzerland 39/F3
Gitega, Burundi 115/F4
Giuba (riv.), Somalia 115/H3
Giubiasco, Switzerland 39/H4
Giulianova, Italy 34/E3
Giurgiu, Romania 45/G3
Giv'atayim, Israel 65/B3
Giv'at Brenner, Israel 65/B4
Giv'at Hayyim, Israel 65/B3
Give, Denmark 21/C6
Given, W. Va. 312/C5
Givet, France 28/F2
Givhans, S.C. 296/G5
Givors, France 28/F5
Giza, Egypt 111/J3
Giza, Egypt 59/B4
Gizab, Afghanistan 59/J3
Gizab, Afghanistan 68/B2
Gizhiga (bay), U.S.S.R. 48/Q3
Gizo, Solomon Is. 86/D3
Giżycko, Poland 47/E1
Gjerlev, Denmark 21/D4
Gjerrild Klint (cliff), Denmark 21/D5
Gjirokastër, Albania 45/D5
Gjoa Haven, N.W.T. 162/G2
Gjoa Haven, N.W. Terr. 187/J3
Gjøvik, Norway 18/G6
Gjøvik, Norway 7/E2
Glace Bay, Nova Scotia 162/L6
Glace Bay, Nova Scotia 168/J2
Glacier (bay), Alaska 196/M1
Glacier, Br. Col. 184/J4
Glacier (co.), Mont. 262/C2

374 Glacier

Glacier, Wash. 310/D2
Glacier (peak), Wash. 310/D2
Glacier Bay Nat'l Park, Alaska 196/M1
Glacier Bay Nat'l Pres., Alaska 196/L1
Glacier Nat'l Pk., Br. Col. 162/D5
Glacier Nat'l Park, Br. Col. 184/J4
Glacier Nat'l Park, Mont. 188/D1
Glacier Nat'l Park, Mont. 262/C2
Gladbrook, Iowa 229/H4
Glade, Kansas 232/C2
Glade, La. 238/G4
Gladehill, Va. 307/J7
Glade Park, Colo. 208/B5
Glades (co.), Fla. 212/E5
Glade Spring, Va. 307/E7
Glade Valley, N.C. 281/G2
Gladeville, Tenn. 237/J8
Gladewater, Texas 303/K5
Gladmar, Sask. 181/G6
Gladstone, Ill. 222/B3
Gladstone, Manitoba 179/D4
Gladstone, Mich. 250/C3
Gladstone, Mo. 261/P5
Gladstone, Nebr. 264/G4
Gladstone, N. Mex. 274/F2
Gladstone, N. Dak. 282/F6
Gladstone, Oreg. 291/B2
Gladstone, Queensland 88/J4
Gladstone, Queensland 95/D4
Gladstone, S. Australia 94/F5
Gladstone, Tasmania 99/D2
Gladstone, Va. 307/L5
Glad Valley, S. Dak. 298/F3
Gladwin (co.), Mich. 250/E4
Gladwin, Mich. 250/E5
Glady, W. Va. 312/G5
Gladys, Va. 307/K6
Glåma (riv.), Norway 7/F2
Glåma (riv.), Norway 18/G6
Glamis, Calif. 204/K11
Glamis, Sask. 181/D4
Glamis, Scotland 15/F4
Glamoč, Yugoslavia 45/C3
Glamsbjerg, Denmark 21/D7
Glan, Philippines 85/G4
Glan, Philippines 82/E8
Glancy, Miss. 256/C7
Gland, Switzerland 39/B4
Glandore, Ireland 17/C8
Glandore (harb.), Ireland 17/C9
Glandorf, Ohio 284/B3
Glâne (riv.), Switzerland 39/C3
Glanmire-Riverstown, Ireland 17/E8
Glanworth, Ireland 17/E7
Glärnisch (mt.), Switzerland 39/H2
Glarus (canton), Switzerland 39/H3
Glarus, Switzerland 39/H2
Glarus Alps (mts.), Switzerland 39/H3
Glasco, Kansas 232/E2
Glasco, N.Y. 276/M6
Glascock (co.), Georgia 217/G4
Glasford, Ill. 222/D3
Glasgo, Conn. 210/H2
Glasgow, Del. 245/R2
Glasgow, Ill. 222/C4
Glasgow, Ky. 237/J7
Glasgow, Mo. 261/G4
Glasgow, Mont. 262/K2
Glasgow, Pa. 294/E4
Glasgow, Scotland 7/D3
Glasgow, Scotland 10/B1
Glasgow, Scotland 15/B2
Glasgow, Va. 307/K5
Glasgow, W. Va. 312/D6
Glasier (lake), New Bruns. 170/A1
Glaslyn, Sask. 181/C2
Glas Maol (mt.), Scotland 15/E4
Glasnevin, Sask. 181/F6
Glass, Manitoba 179/F5
Glass (riv.), Scotland 15/D3
Glass (mts.), Texas 303/A7
Glassboro, N.J. 273/C4
Glasscock (co.), Texas 303/C6
Glasser, N.J. 273/D2
Glassport, Pa. 294/C7
Glasston, N. Dak. 282/R2
Glassville, New Bruns. 170/C2
Glastenbury (mt.), Vt. 268/A6
Glastonbury, Conn. 210/E2
Glastonbury•, Conn. 210/E2
Glastonbury, England 13/E6
Glastonbury, England 10/E5
Glatt (riv.), Switzerland 39/G2
Glattfelden, Switzerland 39/F1
Glauchau, Germany 22/E3
Glazier, Texas 303/D2
Glazov, U.S.S.R. 7/K3
Glazov, U.S.S.R. 52/H3
Gleason, Tenn. 237/D8
Gleason, Wis. 317/G5
Gleasondale, Mass. 249/J3
Gleeson, Ariz. 198/F7
Gleichen, Alberta 182/D4
Gleisdorf, Austria 41/C3
Gleiwitz (Gliwice), Poland 47/A4
Glen (lake), Ireland 17/F1
Glen (lake), Mich. 250/C4
Glen, Minn. 255/E4
Glen, Miss. 256/H1
Glen, Mont. 262/D5
Glen, N.H. 268/E3
Glen (canyon), Utah 304/D6
Glen, W. Va. 312/D6
Glenada, Oreg. 291/C4
Glenaire, Mo. 261/R5
Glen Alice, Tenn. 237/M9
Glen Allan, Miss. 256/B4
Glen Allen, Ala. 195/C3
Glenallen, Mo. 261/M8
Glen Allen, Va. 307/N5
Glen Almond, Québec 172/B4
Glen Alpine, N.C. 281/F3
Glenamaddy, Ireland 17/D4
Glen Arbor, Mich. 250/C4
Glenarden, Md. 245/G4
Glen Arm, Md. 245/N3
Glenarm, N. Ireland 17/J2
Glenavon, Sask. 181/J5
Glen Avon Heights, Calif. 204/E10
Glenavy, N. Zealand 100/C6
Glenavy, N. Ireland 17/J2
Glen Bain, Sask. 181/E6
Glenbarr, Scotland 15/C5
Glenbeigh, Ireland 17/B7
Glenbeulah, Wis. 317/L8
Glenboro, Manitoba 179/C5
Glenbrook, Nev. 266/B3
Glenburn•, Maine 243/F6
Glenburn, N. Dak. 282/H2
Glen Burnie, Md. 245/M4
Glenbush, Sask. 181/D2
Glen Campbell, Pa. 294/E4
Glen Canyon (dam), Ariz. 198/D2
Glen Canyon Nat'l Rec. Area, Ariz. 198/D1
Glen Canyon Nat'l Rec. Area, Utah 304/D6
Glencaple, Scotland 15/E5
Glen Carbon, Ill. 222/B2
Glencliff, N.H. 268/D4
Glencoe, Ala. 195/G3
Glencoe, Ill. 222/B5
Glencoe, Ky. 237/M3
Glencoe, La. 238/G7
Glencoe, Minn. 255/D6
Glencoe, Mo. 261/M3
Glencoe, New Bruns. 170/D1
Glencoe, N. Mex. 274/D5
Glencoe, Ohio 284/J6
Glencoe, Okla. 288/M2
Glencoe, Ontario 177/C5
Glencoe, Pa. 294/E6
Glencoe, Scotland 15/C4
Glencoe, S. Africa 118/E5
Glencolumbkille, Ireland 17/D2
Glen Cove, Maine 243/E7
Glen Cove, N.Y. 276/R6
Glencross, S. Dak. 298/H3
Glendale, Ariz. 198/C5
Glendale, Calif. 188/C4
Glendale, Calif. 204/C10
Glendale, Fla. 212/C5
Glendale, Ind. 227/C7
Glendale, Kansas 232/E3
Glendale, Ky. 237/K5
Glendale, Mass. 249/A3
Glendale, Mo. 261/P3
Glendale, Nev. 266/G6
Glendale, N.H. 268/E4
Glendale, Nova Scotia 168/G3
Glendale, Ohio 284/C9
Glendale, Oreg. 291/D5
Glendale (lake), Pa. 294/F4
Glendale, R.I. 249/H5
Glendale, S.C. 296/D2
Glendale, Utah 304/B6
Glen Dale, W. Va. 312/E3
Glendale, Wis. 317/M1
Glendale Heights, Ill. 222/A5
Glen Daniel, W. Va. 312/D7
Glen Dean, Ky. 237/J5
Glendevey, Colo. 208/H1
Glendive, Mont. 262/M3
Glendo, Wyo. 319/G3
Glendo (res.), Wyo. 319/H3
Glendon, Alberta 182/E2
Glendon, N.C. 281/L4
Glendora, Calif. 204/D10
Glendora, Miss. 256/D3
Glendora, N.J. 273/B4
Glen Easton, W. Va. 312/E3
Glen Echo, Md. 245/E4
Glen Eden, N. Zealand 100/B1
Gleneden Beach, Oreg. 291/C3
Glen Elder, Kansas 232/D2
Glenelg, Md. 245/L3
Glenelg (cay), Scotland 10/D2
Glenelg, Scotland 15/C3
Glenelg, S. Australia 88/D8
Glenelg, S. Australia 94/A8
Glenelg (riv.), Victoria 97/A5
Glenella, Manitoba 179/C4
Glen Ellyn, Ill. 222/A5
Glenevis, Alberta 182/C3
Glen Ewen, Sask. 181/K6
Glen Ferris, W. Va. 312/D6
Glenfield, N.Y. 276/K3
Glenfield, N. Zealand 100/B1
Glenfield, N. Dak. 282/N5
Glenfield, Pa. 294/B6
Glen Flora, Texas 303/H8
Glen Flora, Wis. 317/E4
Glenford, Ohio 284/F6
Glen Gardner, N.J. 273/D2
Glengarriff, Ireland 17/C8
Glengarry, Mont. 262/G3
Glengarry (county), Ontario 177/K2
Glengary, W. Va. 312/K4
Glenham, S. Dak. 298/J2
Glen Harbour, Sask. 181/G5
Glen Haven, Colo. 208/H2
Glen Haven, Mich. 250/C4
Glen Haven, Wis. 317/E10
Glenhayes, W. Va. 312/A6
Glen Hedrick (Beaver), W. Va. 312/D7
Glen Hope, Pa. 294/F4
Glen Innes, N. S. Wales 88/J5
Glen Innes, N.S. Wales 97/F1
Glen Jean, W. Va. 312/D7
Glen Kerr, Sask. 181/D5
Glenlea, Manitoba 179/E5
Glenlivet, New Bruns. 170/D1
Glenluce, Scotland 15/D6
Glen Lyn, Va. 307/G6
Glen Lyon, Pa. 294/E7
Glenmary, Tenn. 237/M8
Glenmere, Sask. 181/J5
Glen Miller, Ontario 177/G3
Glenmont, Ohio 284/F4
Glenmora, La. 238/E5
Glen More (dist.), Scotland 15/D3
Glenmorgan, Queensland 95/D5
Glenn (co.), Calif. 204/C4
Glenn, Georgia 217/B4
Glenn, Mich. 250/C6
Glennallen, Alaska 196/D1
Glenn Heights, Texas 303/G3
Glennie, Mich. 250/F4
Glenns Ferry, Idaho 220/C7
Glenn Springs, S.C. 296/D2
Glennville, Calif. 204/G8
Glennville, Georgia 217/J7
Glenolden, Pa. 294/M7
Glenoma, Wash. 310/C4
Glenora, Br. Col. 184/K2
Glenorchy, Tasmania 88/H8
Glenorchy, Tasmania 99/D4
Glenormiston, Queensland 95/A4
Glen Park, N.Y. 276/J3
Glenpool, Okla. 288/P3
Glen Raven, N.C. 281/L2
Glenreagh, N.S. Wales 97/G2
Glen Riddle, Pa. 294/L7
Glen Ridge, N.J. 273/B2
Glenrio, N. Mex. 274/F3
Glen Robertson, Ontario 177/K2
Glen Rock, N.J. 273/B1
Glen Rock, Pa. 294/J6
Glenrock, Wyo. 319/G3
Glen Rogers, W. Va. 312/D7
Glen Rose, Texas 303/G5
Glenrothes, Scotland 15/E4
Glen Roy, Ohio 284/E7
Glen Saint Mary, Fla. 212/D1
Glens Falls, N.Y. 276/N4
Glens Fork, Ky. 237/L6
Glenshaw, Pa. 294/C6
Glenside, Pa. 294/M5
Glenside, Sask. 181/E4
Glenside-Churton Park, N. Zealand 100/B2
Glensted, Mo. 261/G5
Glentana, Mont. 262/K2
Glenties, Ireland 10/B3
Glenties, Ireland 17/E2
Glentrool, Scotland 15/D5
Glentworth, Sask. 181/E6
Glen Ullin, N. Dak. 282/G6
Glenview, Ill. 222/B5
Glenview, Ky. 237/K1
Glenview Nav. Air. Sta., Ill. 222/B5
Glenvil, Nebr. 264/F4
Glenville, Conn. 210/A4
Glenville, Ireland 17/D7
Glenville, Minn. 255/E7
Glenville, N.C. 281/C4
Glenville, W. Va. 312/E5
Glen Walter, Ontario 177/K2
Glen White, W. Va. 312/D7
Glenwillow, Ohio 284/J10
Glen Wilton, Va. 307/J5
Glenwood, Ala. 195/F7
Glenwood, Alberta 182/D5
Glenwood, Ark. 202/C5
Glenwood, Fla. 212/E2
Glenwood, Georgia 217/L1
Glenwood, Ill. 222/C6
Glenwood, Ind. 227/G5
Glenwood, Iowa 229/B6
Glenwood, Mich. 250/C6
Glenwood, Minn. 255/C5
Glenwood, Mo. 261/G1
Glenwood, Newf. 166/D4
Glenwood, N.J. 273/D1
Glenwood, N. Mex. 274/A5
Glenwood, N.C. 281/F3
Glenwood, Oreg. 291/D2
Glenwood, Utah 304/C5
Glenwood, Va. 307/K7
Glenwood, Wash. 310/D4
Glenwood, W. Va. 312/B5
Glenwood City, Wis. 317/B5
Glenwood Springs, Colo. 208/E4
Glezen, Ind. 227/C8
Glidden, Iowa 229/D4
Glidden, Sask. 181/B4
Glidden, Wis. 317/E3
Glide, Oreg. 291/D4
Glin, Ireland 17/C6
Glis, Switzerland 39/E4
Glittertinden (mt.), Norway 7/E2
Glittertinden (mt.), Norway 18/F6
Gliwice, Poland 47/A4
Globe, Ariz. 188/D4
Globe, Ariz. 198/E5
Gloggnitz, Austria 41/D3
Głogów (Glogau), Poland 47/C3
Glomawr, Ky. 237/P6
Glomfjord, Norway 18/J3
Gloria (bay), Cuba 158/G2
Glorieta, N. Mex. 274/D3
Glorioso (isls.), Réunion 118/H2
Glory, Minn. 255/E4
Glory of Russia (cape), Alaska 196/D2
Glossop, England 13/J2
Glossop, England 10/G2
Gloster, La. 238/C2
Gloster, Miss. 256/B8
Glostrup, Denmark 21/F6
Gloucester, England 13/E6
Gloucester, England 10/E5
Gloucester, Mass. 249/M2
Gloucester (co.), New Bruns. 170/E1
Gloucester (co.), N.J. 273/C4
Gloucester, N.S. Wales 97/F2
Gloucester, N.C. 281/S5
Gloucester (cape), Papua N.G. 86/B2
Gloucester (co.), Va. 307/P6
Gloucester, Va. 307/P6
Gloucester City, N.J. 273/B3
Gloucester Junction, New Bruns. 170/E1
Gloucester Point, Va. 307/R6
Gloucestershire (co.), England 13/E6
Glouster, Ohio 284/F6
Glover (reef), Belize 154/D2
Glover, Mo. 261/L8
Glover (isl.), Newf. 166/C4
Glover, N. Dak. 282/O7
Glover, Okla. 288/S6
Glover•, Vt. 268/C2
Glovergap, W. Va. 312/F3
Gloversville, N.Y. 276/M4
Glovertown, Newf. 166/C1
Gloverville, S.C. 296/D4
Głowno, Poland 47/D2
Głubczyce, Poland 47/C3
Glubokoye, U.S.S.R. 52/C3
Głuchołazy, Poland 47/C3
Glücksburg, Germany 22/C1
Gluckstadt, Miss. 256/D5
Glückstadt, Germany 22/C2
Glukhov, U.S.S.R. 52/D4
Glumsø, Denmark 21/E7
Glyde (riv.), Ireland 17/H4
Glynco, Georgia 217/J8
Glyncorrwg, Wales 13/D6
Glyndon, Md. 245/L3
Glyndon, Minn. 255/B4
Glyngøre, Denmark 21/C4
Glynn (co.), Georgia 217/J8
Glynn, La. 238/H5
Glynn, N. Ireland 17/K2
Gmünd, Carinthia, Austria 41/B3
Gmünd, Lower Austria, Austria 41/C2
Gmunden, Austria 41/B3
Gnadenhutten, Ohio 284/G5
Gnaw Bone, Ind. 227/E6
Gnesta, Sweden 18/G2
Gniew, Poland 47/D2
Gniewkowo, Poland 47/D2
Gniezno, Poland 47/C2
Gnjilane, Yugoslavia 45/E4
Gnowangerup, W. Australia 88/B6
Gnowangerup, W. Australia 92/B6
Goa (state), India 68/C5
Goalpara, India 68/G3
Goascorán, Honduras 154/D4
Goat Fell (mt.), Scotland 15/C5
Goat River, Br. Col. 184/G3
Goat Rock (dam), Ala. 195/H5
Goat Rock (lake), Ala. 195/H5
Goat Rock (dam), Georgia 217/B5
Goat Rock (lake), Georgia 217/B5
Goat Rocks (mt.), Wash. 310/D4
Goba, Ethiopia 111/H6
Goba, Ethiopia 102/G4
Goba, Mozambique 118/E5
Gobabis, Namibia 118/B4
Gobabis, Namibia 102/D7
Gobernador Crespo, Argentina 143/F5
Gobernador Gregores, Argentina 143/C6
Gobernador Mansilla, Argentina 143/G6
Gobi (des.) 54/M5
Gobi (des.), China 77/G3
Gobi (des.), Mongolia 77/G3
Goble, Oreg. 291/E1
Gobler, Mo. 261/N10
Gobles, Mich. 250/D6
Gobo, Japan 81/G7
Gobwen, Somalia 115/H4
Goch, Germany 22/B3
Go Cong, Vietnam 72/E5
Godahl, Minn. 255/D6
Godalming, England 13/G8
Godalming, England 10/F5
Godavari (riv.), India 54/J8
Godavari (riv.), India 68/D5
Godbout, Québec 174/D3
Godbout, Québec 172/B1
Goddard, Kansas 232/E4
Godech, Bulgaria 45/F4
Goderich, Ontario 177/C4
Godfrey, Georgia 217/F4
Godfrey, Ill. 222/A2
Godhavn (Qeqertarsauq), Greenland 4/C12
Godhavn (Qeqertarsauq), Greenland 146/N3
Godhra, India 68/C4
Gödöllő, Hungary 41/E3
Godoy Cruz, Argentina 143/C3
Gods (lake), Man. 162/G5
Gods (lake), Manitoba 179/K3
Gods (riv.), Man. 162/G4
Gods (riv.), Manitoba 179/K3
Gods Mercy (bay), N.W. Terr. 187/K3
Gods River, Manitoba 179/K3
Godthåb (Nuuk) (cap.), Greenl. 4/C12
Godthåb (Nuuk) (cap.), Greenland 2/G2
Godthåb (Nuuk) (cap.), Greenland 146/N3
Godwin, N.C. 281/M4
Godwin Austen (mt.), Pakistan 68/D1
Godwinsville, Georgia 217/F6
Goehner, Nebr. 264/G4
Goéland (lake), Québec 174/B3
Goélands (lake), Québec 174/E1
Goeree (isl.), Netherlands 27/D5
Goes, Netherlands 27/D6
Goessel, Kansas 232/E3
Goetzville, Mich. 250/E2
Goff, Kansas 232/G2
Goff (creek), Okla. 288/C1
Goffstown•, N.H. 268/D5
Gogama, Ontario 175/D3
Gogama, Ontario 177/J5
Gogebic (co.), Mich. 250/F2
Gogebic (lake), Mich. 250/F2
Gogrial, Sudan 111/E6
Goi, Ben (bay), Vietnam 72/F4
Goiana, Brazil 132/H4
Goiandira, Brazil 132/E7
Goiânia, Brazil 132/D7
Goiânia, Brazil 120/D4
Goiás (state), Brazil 132/D6
Goiás, Brazil 132/D6
Goiás, Brazil 120/D4
Goil, Loch (lake), Scotland 15/A1
Goin, Tenn. 237/O8
Goirle, Netherlands 27/G5
Góis, Portugal 33/B2
Gojjam (prov.), Ethiopia 111/G5
Gökçe, Turkey 63/B2
Gökçeada (isl.), Turkey 59/A1
Gökçeada (isl.), Turkey 63/A2
Gökırmak (riv.), Turkey 63/F2
Göksu (riv.), Turkey 63/E4
Göksun, Turkey 63/G3
Gokteik, Burma 72/C2
Gol, Norway 18/F6
Gola (isl.), Ireland 17/E1
Golan Heights, West Bank 65/D1
Gölbaşı, Turkey 63/G4
Golborne, England 13/G2
Gol'chikha, U.S.S.R. 48/J2
Golconda, Ill. 222/E6
Golconda (ruins), India 68/D5
Golconda, Nev. 266/D2
Gölcük, Turkey 63/C2
Golčův Jeníkov, Czech. 41/C2
Gold (riv.), Nova Scotia 168/D4
Gołdap, Poland 47/F1
Gold Bar, Wash. 310/D3
Gold Beach, Oreg. 291/C5
Goldbond, Va. 307/G6
Goldboro, Nova Scotia 168/G3
Gold Bridge, Br. Col. 184/F5
Gold Coast (reg.), Ghana 106/D8
Gold Coast, Queensland 95/E6
Gold Coast, Queensland 88/J5
Goldcreek, Mont. 262/D4
Golden, Br. Col. 184/J4
Golden, Colo. 208/J3
Golden, Idaho 220/C4
Golden, Ill. 222/B3
Golden, Ireland 17/F7
Golden, Miss. 256/H2
Golden, Mo. 261/E9
Golden, N. Mex. 274/C3
Golden (bay), N. Zealand 100/D4
Golden, Okla. 288/S6
Golden (lake), Ontario 177/G2
Golden (lake), Wis. 317/H1
Golden Beach, Fla. 212/C4
Golden City, Mo. 261/D8
Goldendale, Wash. 310/E5
Golden Ears Prov. Park, Br. Col. 184/L2
Golden Gate (chan.), Calif. 188/B3
Golden Gate (chan.), Calif. 204/H2
Golden Gate, Fla. 212/E5
Golden Gate, Ill. 222/E5
Golden Gate (range), Nev. 266/F5
Golden Gate Nat'l Rec. Area, Calif. 204/H2
Golden Grove, Jamaica 158/K6
Golden Hill, Md. 245/O7
Golden Lake, Ontario 177/G2
Golden Meadow, La. 238/K8
Golden Prairie, Sask. 181/B5
Golden Rock, St. Kitts & Nevis 161/C10
Golden's Bridge, N.Y. 276/N8
Golden Shores, Ariz. 198/A4
Golden Spike Nat'l Hist. Site, Utah 304/B2
Golden Vale (plain), Ireland 17/E7
Golden Valley, Minn. 255/G5
Golden Valley (co.), Mont. 262/G4
Golden Valley (co.), N. Dak. 282/C5
Goldenvalley, N. Dak. 282/F5
Golden Valley, Ontario 177/E2
Goldfield, Iowa 229/F3
Goldfield, Nev. 188/C3
Goldfield, Nev. 266/D5
Gold Hill, Ala. 195/G5
Gold Hill, Nev. 266/B3
Gold Hill, N.C. 281/J3
Gold Hill, Oreg. 291/D5
Goldonna, La. 238/D2
Gold Point, Nev. 266/D6
Gold River, Br. Col. 184/D5
Goldsberry, Mo. 261/G3
Goldsboro, Md. 245/P4
Goldsboro, N.C. 188/L3
Goldsboro, N.C. 281/O4
Goldsboro (Etters), Pa. 294/J5
Goldsby, Okla. 288/L4
Goldsmith, Ind. 227/E4
Goldsmith, Texas 303/B5
Goldston, N.C. 281/L3
Goldstone (mt.), Idaho 220/E4
Goldsworthy, W. Australia 88/C4
Goldsworthy, W. Australia 92/B3
Goldthwaite, Texas 303/F6
Goldvein, Va. 307/N4
Goldville, Ala. 195/G4
Göle, Turkey 63/K2
Goleniów, Poland 47/B2
Goleta, Calif. 204/F9
Golf, Fla. 212/F5
Golf, Ill. 222/B5
Golfito, C. Rica 154/F6
Golf Manor, Ohio 284/C9
Golfo Santa Clara, Mexico 150/B1
Gölhisar, Turkey 63/C4
Goliad (co.), Texas 303/G9
Goliad, Texas 303/G9
Gölköy, Turkey 63/G2
Golling an der Salzach, Austria 41/B3
Gölmarmara, Turkey 63/C3
Golmud (Golmo), China 77/D4
Golmud, China 54/L6
Golo (riv.), France 28/B6
Golo (isl.), Philippines 82/C4
Golovin, Alaska 196/F2
Golpayegan, Iran 59/F3
Golpayegan, Iran 66/G4
Gölpazarı, Turkey 63/D2
Golshan (Tabas), Iran 66/K4
Golspie, Scotland 15/E3
Goltry, Okla. 288/K1
Golts, Md. 245/P3
Golub-Dobrzyn, Poland 47/D2
Golungo Alto, Angola 115/B5
Golva, N. Dak. 282/C6
Goma, Zaire 115/E4
Goma, Zaire 102/E5
Gombari, Zaire 115/E3
Gombe, Nigeria 106/G6
Gomel', U.S.S.R. 7/H3
Gomel', U.S.S.R. 48/D4
Gomel', U.S.S.R. 52/D4
Gomer, Ohio 284/B4
Gomera (isl.), Spain 106/A3
Gomera (isl.), Spain 33/B5
Gometra (isl.), Scotland 15/B4
Gomez, Fla. 212/F4
Gómez Farías, Mexico 150/F2
Gómez Palacio, Mexico 150/G4
Gomishan, Iran 66/J2
Goms (valley), Switzerland 39/F4
Gona, Papua N.G. 85/C7
Gonabad, Iran 59/G3
Gonabad, Iran 66/L3
Gonaïves, Haiti 158/B5
Gonaïves, Haiti 156/D3
Gonâve (gulf), Haiti 158/B5
Gonâve (isl.), Haiti 158/B6
Gonâve (isl.), Haiti 156/D3
Gonbad-e Kavus, Iran 66/J2
Gonbadli, Iran 66/M2
Gönc, Hungary 41/F2
Gonda, India 68/E3
Gondal, India 68/C4
Gondar, Ethiopia 102/F3
Gondar, Ethiopia 59/C7
Gondar, Ethiopia 111/G5
Gondia, India 68/E4
Gondola Point, New Bruns. 170/D3
Gondomar, Portugal 33/B2
Gönen, Turkey 63/B2
Gonggar, China 77/D6
Gongga Shan (mt.), China 77/F6
Gonghe, China 77/F4
Gongliu, China 77/B3
Gongola (state), Nigeria 106/G7
Gongola (riv.), Nigeria 106/G6
Gongolgan, N.S. Wales 97/D2
Góngora (mt.), C. Rica 154/E5
Goñi, Uruguay 145/C4
Gonjo, China 77/E5
Gonvick, Minn. 255/C3
Gonzaga, Philippines 82/D1
Gonzales, Calif. 204/D7
Gonzales, La. 238/L2
Gonzales (co.), Texas 303/G8
Gonzales, Texas 303/G8
Gonzalez, Fla. 212/B6
González, Mexico 150/K5
González, Riacho (riv.), Paraguay 144/C3
Goobies, Newf. 166/D2
Goochland (co.), Va. 307/N5
Goochland, Va. 307/N5
Goodbee, La. 238/K6
Goode (mt.), Alaska 196/C1
Goode, Va. 307/K6
Goodell, Iowa 229/F3
Goodenough (cape), Ant. 5/C7
Gooderham, Ontario 177/F3
Goodeve, Sask. 181/H4
Goodfare, Alberta 182/A2
Goodfellow A.F.B., Texas 303/D6
Goodfield, Ill. 222/D3
Good Harbor (bay), Mich. 250/D3
Good Hart, Mich. 250/D3
Good Hope, Ala. 195/E2
Goodhope (bay), Alaska 196/F1
Good Hope, Georgia 217/E3
Good Hope, Ill. 222/C3
Good Hope, La. 238/N3
Good Hope, Miss. 256/E5
Good Hope, Ohio 284/D7
Good Hope (cape), S. Africa 102/D8
Good Hope (cape), S. Africa 2/K7
Good Hope (cape), S. Africa 118/E7
Goodhue (co.), Minn. 255/F6
Goodhue, Minn. 255/F6
Gooding (co.), Idaho 220/D6
Gooding, Idaho 220/D7
Goodland, Fla. 212/E6
Goodland, Ind. 227/C3
Goodland, Kansas 232/A2
Goodland, Minn. 255/E3
Goodlands, Manitoba 179/B5
Goodlettsville, Tenn. 237/H8
Goodlow, Br. Col. 184/G2
Good Luck, Md. 245/G4
Goodman, Miss. 256/E5
Goodman, Mo. 261/C9
Goodman, Wis. 317/K4
Goodnews Bay, Alaska 196/F3
Goodnight, Texas 303/C3
Goodnoe Hills, Wash. 310/E5
Goodooga, N.S. Wales 97/D1
Good Pine, La. 238/F3
Goodrich, Colo. 208/M2
Goodrich, Mich. 250/F6
Goodrich, N. Dak. 282/K5
Goodrich, Texas 303/K7
Goodrich, Wis. 317/G5
Goodridge, Alberta 182/E2
Goodridge, Minn. 255/C2
Goodsoil, Sask. 181/L4
Goodson, Mo. 261/F7
Good Spirit (lake), Sask. 181/J4
Goodspirit Lake Prov. Park, Sask. 181/J4
Goodspring, Tenn. 237/G10
Goodsprings, Ala. 195/D3
Goodsprings, Nev. 266/F7
Good Thunder, Minn. 255/D6
Goodview, Minn. 255/G6
Goodwater, Ala. 195/F4
Goodwater, Okla. 288/S7
Goodwater, Sask. 181/H6
Goodway, Ala. 195/D8
Goodwell, Okla. 288/C1
Goodwin, Ark. 202/J4
Goodwin, S. Dak. 298/R4
Goodwins Mills, Maine 243/B8
Goodwood, Ontario 177/E3
Goodwood, S. Africa 118/F6
Goodyear, Ariz. 198/C5
Gooik, Belgium 27/E7
Goole, England 10/F4
Goole, England 13/G4
Goolgowi, N.S. Wales 97/C3
Gooloogong, N.S. Wales 97/E3
Goomalling, W. Australia 88/B6
Goomalling, W. Australia 92/B1
Goombalie, N.S. Wales 97/C1
Goondiwindi, Queensland 88/H5
Goondiwindi, Queensland 95/D6
Goor, Netherlands 27/K4
Goose (lake) 188/B2
Goose (lake), Calif. 204/E1

Granite 375

Goose (creek), Idaho 220/E7
Goose (riv.), Newf. 166/B3
Goose (riv.), N. Dak. 282/P4
Goose (isl.), Nova Scotia 168/F4
Goose (isl.), Nova Scotia 168/G3
Goose (lake), Oreg. 291/G5
Goose (creek), Va. 307/J6
Goose (creek), Va. 307/N3
Goose Airport P.O. (Goose Bay), Newf. 162/K5
Goose Bay, Newf. 162/K5
Goose Bay, Newf. 146/M4
Goose Bay-Happy Valley, Newf. 166/B3
Gooseberry (creek), Wyo. 319/D1
Gooseberry Cove, Newf. 166/C2
Goose Cove, Newf. 166/C2
Goose Cove, Newf. 166/C3
Goose Cove, Nova Scotia 168/H2
Goose Creek (mts.), Idaho 220/E7
Goose Creek, Ky. 237/L1
Goose Creek, S.C. 296/H6
Goose Lake, Iowa 229/N5
Goose Prairie, Wash. 310/D4
Goose Rock, Ky. 237/O6
Goose Rocks Beach, Maine 243/C9
Göppingen, Germany 22/C4
Góra, Poland 47/C3
Gorakhpur, India 68/E3
Gorchs, Argentina 143/G7
Gorda (pt.), Cuba 158/C2
Gorda (bank), Honduras 154/F3
Gorda (cay), Honduras 154/F3
Gorda (pt.), Nicaragua 154/F5
Gorda (pt.), Panama 154/H6
Gördes, Turkey 63/C3
Gordevio, Switzerland 39/G4
Gørding, Denmark 21/B7
Gordo, Ala. 195/C4
Gordola, Switzerland 39/G4
Gordon, Ala. 195/H8
Gordon (lake), Alberta 182/E1
Gordon (riv.), Br. Col. 184/H3
Gordon (isl.), Chile 138/E11
Gordon (co.), Georgia 217/C2
Gordon, Georgia 217/F5
Gordon, Kansas 232/F4
Gordon, Nebr. 264/B2
Gordon, Ohio 284/B6
Gordon, Scotland 15/F5
Gordon, Tasmania 99/G5
Gordon (lake), Tasmania 99/C4
Gordon (riv.), Tasmania 99/B4
Gordon, Texas 303/F5
Gordon, W. Va. 312/C7
Gordon, Wis. 317/C3
Gordondale, Alberta 182/A2
Gordon Downs, W. Australia 92/E2
Gordon's Bay, S. Africa 118/F7
Gordonsburg, Tenn. 237/F9
Gordonsville, Ala. 195/E6
Gordonsville, Minn. 255/E7
Gordonsville, Tenn. 237/K8
Gordonsville, Va. 307/M4
Gordonvale, Queensland 88/H3
Gordonvale, Queensland 95/C3
Gordonville, Mo. 261/N8
Gore (pt.), Alaska 196/C2
Goré, Chad 111/C6
Gore (range), Colo. 208/G3
Gore, Ethiopia 111/G6
Gore, Ethiopia 102/F4
Gore, N. Zealand 100/B7
Gore, Ohio 284/F6
Gore, Okla. 288/R3
Gore (mt.), Vt. 268/D2
Gore, Va. 307/M2
Gore Bay, Ontario 177/B2
Gorebridge, Scotland 10/C1
Gorebridge, Scotland 15/D2
Goree, Texas 303/E4
Goregaon, India 68/B7
Görele, Turkey 63/H2
Gore Springs, Miss. 256/E3
Goreville, Ill. 222/E6
Gorey, Chan. Is. 13/F8
Gorey, Ireland 17/J6
Gorey, Ireland 10/C4
Gorgan, Iran 54/G6
Gorgan, Iran 59/F2
Gorgan (Gurgan), Iran 66/J2
Gorgan (riv.), Iran 66/J2
Gorgan (riv.), Iran 59/F2
Gorgas, Ala. 195/D3
Gorgol (reg.), Mauritania 106/B5
Gorgona (isl.), Colombia 126/A6
Gorgona (isl.), Italy 34/B3
Gorham, Ill. 222/D6
Gorham, Kansas 232/D3
Gorham, Maine 243/C8
Gorham•, Maine 243/C8
Gorham, N.H. 268/E3
Gorham•, N.H. 268/E3
Gorham, N.Y. 276/F5
Gorham, N. Dak. 282/D5
Gori, U.S.S.R. 52/F6
Gorin, Mo. 261/H2
Gorinchem, Netherlands 27/G5
Gorizia (prov.), Italy 34/D2
Gorizia, Italy 34/D2
Gorki, U.S.S.R. 52/D4
Gørlev, Denmark 21/E7
Gorlice, Poland 47/E4
Görlitz, Germany 22/F3
Görlitz, Germany 7/F3
Gorlitz, Sask. 181/J4
Gorlovka, U.S.S.R. 7/H4
Gorlovka, U.S.S.R. 52/E5
Gorman, Calif. 204/G9
Gorman, Tenn. 237/F8
Gorman, Texas 303/F5
Gormania, W. Va. 312/H4
Gormanston, Ireland 17/J4
Gormanston, Tasmania 99/B4
Gorna Oryakhovitsa, Bulgaria 45/G4
Gornji Milanovac, Yugoslavia 45/D3
Gornji Vakuf, Yugoslavia 45/C4
Gorno-Altay Aut. Obl., U.S.S.R. 48/J4
Gorno-Altaysk, U.S.S.R. 48/J4
Gorno-Badakhshan Aut. Obl., U.S.S.R. 48/H6
Gornyak, U.S.S.R. 48/J4
Gorodets, U.S.S.R. 52/F3
Gorodok, U.S.S.R. 52/D3
Goroka, Papua N.G. 85/B7
Goroke, Victoria 97/A5
Gorong (isl.), Indonesia 85/J6
Gorong (isls.), Indonesia 85/J6
Gorongosa Nat'l Park, Mozambique 118/E3
Gorongoza, Mozambique 118/E3
Gorontalo, Indonesia 85/G5
Gorrahei, Ethiopia 111/H6
Gorredijk, Netherlands 27/J2
Gorrie, Ontario 177/C4
Gorst, Wash. 310/C3
Gort, Ireland 10/B4
Gort, Ireland 17/D5
Gortin, N. Ireland 17/G2
Gorum, La. 238/E4
Gorumna (isl.), Ireland 17/B5
Goryn' (riv.), U.S.S.R. 52/C4
Gorzów (prov.), Poland 47/B2
Gorzów Wielkopolski, Poland 47/B2
Gorzów Wielkopolski, Poland 7/F3
Göschenen, Switzerland 39/G3
Gose, Japan 81/J8
Gosen, Japan 81/J5
Goshen, Ala. 195/F7
Goshen, Ark. 202/C1
Goshen, Calif. 204/F7
Goshen•, Conn. 210/C1
Goshen (pt.), Conn. 210/G3
Goshen, Ind. 227/F1
Goshen, Ky. 237/K4
Goshen•, Mass. 249/C3
Goshen•, N.H. 268/C5
Goshen, N.J. 273/D5
Goshen, N.Y. 276/M8
Goshen, Nova Scotia 168/G3
Goshen, Ohio 284/B7
Goshen, Oreg. 291/D4
Goshen, Utah 304/C4
Goshen, Va. 307/K5
Goshen (co.), Wyo. 319/H4
Goshen Springs, Miss. 256/E6
Goshogawara, Japan 81/K3
Goshute (mts.), Nev. 266/G2
Goshute Ind. Res., Nev. 266/G3
Goshute Ind. Res., Utah 304/A4
Gosier, Guadeloupe 161/B6
Goslar, Germany 22/D3
Gosnell, Ark. 202/K2
Gosper (co.), Nebr. 264/E4
Gospić, Yugoslavia 45/B3
Gosport, Ala. 195/C7
Gosport, England 13/F7
Gosport, England 10/F5
Gosport, Ind. 227/D6
Goss, Miss. 256/E8
Gossau, Switzerland 39/H2
Gossville, N.H. 268/E5
Gostivar, Yugoslavia 45/E5
Gostyń, Poland 47/C3
Gostynin, Poland 47/D2
Göta (canal), Sweden 18/J7
Göta (riv.), Sweden 18/H7
Gotebo, Okla. 288/J4
Göteborg, Sweden 7/F3
Göteborg, Sweden 18/G8
Göteborg och Bohus (co.), Sweden 18/G7
Gotha, Germany 22/D3
Gotham, Wis. 317/F9
Gothenburg, Nebr. 264/D4
Gothic (mesa), Ariz. 198/F2
Gotland (co.), Sweden 18/L8
Gotland (isl.), Sweden 7/F3
Gotland (isl.), Sweden 18/L8
Goto (isls.), Japan 81/D7
Goto (lake), Neth. Ant. 161/D8
Gotse Delchev, Bulgaria 45/F5
Gotska Sandön (isl.), Sweden 18/L7
Gotsu, Japan 81/F6
Göttingen, Germany 22/D3
Gottwaldov, Czech. 41/D2
Götzis, Austria 41/A3
Goubere, Cent. Afr. Rep. 115/E2
Gouda, Netherlands 27/F4
Goudeau, La. 238/G5
Gough (lake), Alberta 182/D3
Gough, Georgia 217/H4
Gough (isl.), St. Helena 2/J8
Gouin (res.), Que. 162/J6
Gouin (res.), Québec 174/C3
Goulburn, N.S. Wales 88/J6
Goulburn, N.S. Wales 97/E4
Goulburn (isls.), North. Terr. 88/E2
Goulburn (isls.), North. Terr. 93/C1
Goulburn (riv.), Victoria 97/C5
Goulburn Island, North. Terr. 93/C1
Gould, Ark. 202/G6
Gould, Colo. 208/G2
Gould, Okla. 288/G5
Gould, Québec 172/F4
Gould City, Mich. 250/D2
Goulding, Fla. 212/B6
Goulds, Fla. 212/F6
Goulds, Newf. 166/D2
Gouldsboro, Maine 243/H7
Gouldsboro•, Maine 243/H7
Gouldsboro, Pa. 294/L3
Gouldtown, Sask. 181/D5
Goulmima, Morocco 106/C2
Goumbou, Mali 106/C6
Gounamitz (riv.), New Bruns. 170/C1
Goundam, Mali 106/D5
Goundam, Mali 102/B3
Gourara (oasis), Algeria 106/E3
Gourbeyre, Guadeloupe 161/A7
Gourdon, France 28/D5
Gouré, Niger 106/G6
Gourma-Rharous, Mali 106/D5
Gournay-en-Bray, France 28/D3
Gouro, Chad 111/C4
Gourock, Scotland 10/A1
Gourock, Scotland 15/A1
Gouveia, Portugal 33/C2
Gouverneur, N.Y. 276/K2
Gouvy, Belgium 27/H8
Gouyave, Grenada 161/C8
Gouyave, Grenada 156/F4
Govan, Sask. 181/G4
Govan, S.C. 296/E5
Gove (co.), Kansas 232/B3
Gove, Kansas 232/B3
Gove (Nhulunbuy), North. Terr. 93/E2
Govena (cape), U.S.S.R. 48/R4
Govenlock, Sask. 181/B6
Governador Valadares, Brazil 132/F7
Governador Valadares, Brazil 120/E4
Government (mt.), Ariz. 198/C3
Government (peak), Mich. 250/F1
Government (creek), Utah 304/B3
Government Camp, Oreg. 291/F2
Governor (lake), Nova Scotia 168/F3
Govĭ-Altay, Mongolia 77/E3
Gowan, Minn. 255/F4
Gowanda, N.Y. 276/B6
Gowd-e Zerreh (depr.), Afghanistan 59/H4
Gowen, Mich. 250/D5
Gowen, Okla. 288/R5
Gowensville, S.C. 296/C1
Gower, Mo. 261/C3
Gower (isl.), N.S. Wales 97/J2
Gower (mt.), N.S. Wales 97/J2
Gower (pen.), Wales 13/C6
Gowna (lake), Ireland 17/G4
Gowran, Ireland 17/G6
Gowrie, Iowa 229/E4
Gowrie Park, Tasmania 99/C3
Goya, Argentina 120/D5
Goya, Argentina 143/G4
Goyave, Guadeloupe 161/A6
Goyder (riv.), North. Terr. 93/D2
Goyders (lag.), S. Australia 94/F2
Göynücek, Turkey 63/F2
Göynük, Turkey 63/D2
Goz Beïda, Chad 111/D5
Gozo (isl.), Malta 34/E6
Goz Regeb, Sudan 111/G4
Graaff-Reinet, S. Africa 118/C6
Graal-Müritz, Germany 22/E1
Graauw, Netherlands 27/E6
Grabill, Ind. 227/H2
Grabouw, S. Africa 118/F7
Grabs, Switzerland 39/H2
Gračac, Yugoslavia 45/B3
Gračanica, Yugoslavia 45/D3
Grace, Idaho 220/G7
Grace (mt.), Mass. 249/E2
Grace, Miss. 256/C5
Grace (pt.), R.I. 249/H8
Grace City, N. Dak. 282/N4
Gracefield, Québec 172/A3
Graceham, Md. 245/J2
Gracemont, Okla. 288/K4
Graceton, Minn. 255/D2
Graceton, Pa. 294/D4
Graceville, Fla. 212/D5
Graceville, Minn. 255/B5
Graceville, Queensland 88/K3
Gracewood, Georgia 217/H4
Gracey, Ky. 237/F7
Grächen, Switzerland 39/E4
Gracias, Honduras 154/C3
Gracias a Dios (cape), Nic. 146/K8
Gracias a Dios (cape), Nicaragua 154/F3
Graciosa (isl.), Portugal 33/C1
Gradačac, Yugoslavia 45/D3
Gradaús, Brazil 120/D3
Gradaús, Brazil 132/D4
Gradaús, Serra dos (range), Brazil 132/D4
Grado, Spain 33/D1
Grady, Ala. 195/F7
Grady, Ark. 202/G5
Grady (co.), Georgia 217/D9
Grady (isl.), Newf. 166/C3
Grady, N. Mex. 274/F4
Grady (co.), Okla. 288/L5
Grady, Okla. 288/L6
Gradyville, Ky. 237/L6
Graeagle, Calif. 204/E4
Graested, Denmark 21/F5
Graettinger, Iowa 229/D2
Graf, Iowa 229/M3
Grafenau, Germany 22/E4
Grafenwöhr, Germany 22/D4
Graff, Mo. 261/H8
Graff-Reinet, S. Africa 102/E8
Graford, Texas 303/F5
Grafton, Australia 87/F8
Grafton (isls.), Chile 138/D10
Grafton, Ill. 222/C5
Grafton, Ind. 227/B9
Grafton, Iowa 229/G2
Grafton•, Mass. 249/H4
Grafton, Nebr. 264/G4
Grafton, New Bruns. 170/C2
Grafton (co.), N.H. 268/D4
Grafton•, N.H. 268/D4
Grafton, N.S. Wales 88/J5
Grafton, N.S. Wales 97/G1
Grafton, N.Y. 276/N5
Grafton, N. Dak. 282/R3
Grafton, Ohio 284/F3
Grafton, Ontario 177/G4
Grafton•, Vt. 268/B5
Grafton, Va. 307/P6
Grafton, W. Va. 312/G4
Grafton, Wis. 317/L9
Grafton Center, N.H. 268/D4
Graham, Ala. 195/H4
Graham (lake), Alberta 182/C1
Graham (co.), Ariz. 198/E6
Graham (mt.), Ariz. 198/F6
Graham (isl.), Br. Col. 184/A3
Graham (peak), Colo. 208/E8
Graham, Fla. 212/D2
Graham, Georgia 217/H7
Graham (creek), Ind. 227/F7
Graham (co.), Kansas 232/C2
Graham, Ky. 237/G6
Graham (lake), Maine 243/G6
Graham, Mo. 261/C2
Graham (co.), N.C. 281/B4
Graham, N.C. 281/L2
Graham (isl.), N.W.T. 162/M3
Graham (isl.), N.W. Terr. 187/J2
Graham, Okla. 288/M6
Graham, Ontario 175/B3
Graham, Ontario 177/G5
Graham, Texas 303/F4
Graham Bell (isl.), U.S.S.R. 4/A6
Graham Bell (isl.), U.S.S.R. 48/G1
Grahamdale, Manitoba 179/D3
Graham Land (reg.), Ant. 2/G9
Graham Land (reg.), Ant. 5/C15
Graham Reach (chan.), Br. Col. 184/C3
Grahamstown, S. Africa 102/E8
Grahamstown, S. Africa 118/D6
Grahamsville, N.Y. 276/L7
Grahn, Ky. 237/P4
Graian Alps (range), France 28/G5
Graian Alps (range), Italy 34/A2
Graiguenamanagh-Tinnahinch, Ireland 17/H6
Grain Coast (reg.), Liberia 106/B8
Grainfield, Kansas 232/B2
Grainger (co.), Tenn. 237/O8
Graingers, N.C. 281/O4
Grainola, Okla. 288/N1
Grainton, Nebr. 264/C4
Grain Valley, Mo. 261/S6
Grajaú, Brazil 132/E4
Grajaú (riv.), Brazil 132/E4
Grajewo, Poland 47/F2
Gram, Denmark 21/C7
Gramalote, Colombia 126/D4
Gramat, France 28/D5
Grambling, La. 238/E1
Gramercy, La. 238/M3
Gramling, S.C. 296/C1
Grammer, Ind. 227/F6
Grammont (Geraardsbergen), Belgium 27/D7
Grampian, Pa. 294/E4
Grampian (reg.), Scotland 15/F3
Grampian (mts.), Scotland 15/D4
Gramsbergen, Netherlands 27/K3
Gran, Norway 18/G6
Granada, Colo. 208/P6
Granada, Minn. 255/D7
Granada, Nicaragua 154/E5
Granada (prov.), Spain 33/E4
Granada, Spain 33/E4
Granada, Spain 7/D5
Granada Hills, Calif. 204/B10
Granados, Mexico 150/E2
Granard, Ireland 17/F4
Granbury, Texas 303/G5
Granby, Colo. 208/H2
Granby (lake), Colo. 208/G2
Granby, Conn. 210/D1
Granby•, Conn. 210/D1
Granby, Mass. 249/E3
Granby•, Mass. 249/E3
Granby, Mo. 261/D9
Granby, Québec 172/E4
Granby•, Vt. 268/D2
Gran Canaria (isl.), Spain 33/B5
Gran Chaco (reg.) 120/C5
Gran Chaco (reg.), Argentina 143/D1
Gran Chaco (reg.), Paraguay 144/B2-3
Gran Couva, Trin. & Tob. 161/B11
Grand (canal), China 54/N6
Grand (canal), China 77/J4
Grand (co.), Colo. 208/G2
Grand (bay), Dominica 161/F7
Grand (canal), Ireland 17/G5
Grand (lake), La. 188/H4
Grand (lake), La. 238/H8
Grand (lake), La. 238/E7
Grand (lake), Maine 243/H4
Grand (isl.), Mich. 250/C2
Grand (lake), Mich. 250/F3
Grand (riv.), Mich. 250/D6
Grand (riv.), Mo. 261/F3
Grand (bay), New Bruns. 170/D3
Grand (lake), New Bruns. 170/D3
Grand (lake), New Bruns. 170/C3
Grand (lake), Newf. 166/B3
Grand (lake), Newf. 166/C4
Grand (isl.), N.Y. 276/B5
Grand (riv.), Ohio 284/H2
Grand (riv.), Ontario 177/D4
Grand (riv.), S. Dak. 298/F2
Grand (co.), Utah 304/E5
Grand Anse, Grenada 161/C9
Grand Bahama (isl.), Bahamas 146/L7
Grand Bahama (isl.), Bahamas 156/B1
Grand Bank, Newf. 166/C4
Grand-Bassam, Ivory Coast 106/D7
Grand Bay, Ala. 195/B10
Grand Bay, Dominica 161/F7
Grand Bay, New Bruns. 170/D3
Grand Bayou, La. 238/C2
Grand Beach, Manitoba 179/F4
Grand Beach, Mich. 250/C7
Grand Bend, Ontario 177/C4
Grand Blanc, Mich. 250/F6
Grand-Bourg, Guadeloupe 161/B7
Grand Bruit, Newf. 166/C4
Grand Caicos (isl.), Turks & Caicos 156/D2
Grand Caille (pt.), St. Lucia 161/F6
Grand Canary (isl.), Spain 102/A2
Grand Canary (isl.), Spain 106/A3
Grand Cane, La. 238/C2
Grand Canyon, Ariz. 188/D3
Grand Canyon, Ariz. 198/C2
Grand Canyon, Snake R. (canyon), Oreg. 291/L2
Grand Canyon Nat'l Mon., Ariz. 198/C2
Grand Canyon Nat'l Park, Ariz. 188/D3
Grand Canyon Nat'l Park, Ariz. 198/C2
Grand Canyon of the Snake River (canyon), Idaho 220/B4
Grand Cayman (isl.), Cayman Is. 156/B3
Grand Centre, Alberta 182/E2
Grand Cess, Liberia 106/C8
Grand Chain, Ill. 222/E6
Grand Chenier, La. 238/E7
Grand Combin (mt.), Switzerland 39/D5
Grand Comoro (Njazidja) (isl.), Comoros 102/G6
Grand Comoro (Njazidja) (isl.), Comoros 118/G2
Grand Coteau, La. 238/G6
Grand Coulee, Sask. 181/G5
Grand Coulee, Wash. 310/G3
Grand Coulee (canyon), Wash. 310/F3
Grand Coulee (dam), Wash. 310/F3
Grandcour, Switzerland 39/C3
Grand Cul de Sac (riv.), St. Lucia 161/G6
Grand Cul-de-Sac Marin (bay), Guadeloupe 161/A6
Grand Desert, Nova Scotia 168/E4
Grand Detour, Ill. 222/D2
Grande (bay), Argentina 120/C8
Grande (bay), Argentina 143/C7
Grande (falls), Argentina 143/E3
Grande (riv.), Argentina 143/C4
Grande (marsh), Bolivia 136/F5
Grande (riv.), Bolivia 136/C6
Grande (riv.), Bolivia 136/C4
Grande (isl.), Brazil 132/C8
Grande (isl.), Brazil 135/D3
Grande (riv.), Brazil 120/E5
Grande (riv.), Brazil 132/D8
Grande (riv.), Brazil 132/E5
Grande (riv.), Brazil 135/B2
Grande (isl.), Chile 138/A6
Grande (riv.), Chile 138/F10
Grande, Salar (salt dep.), Chile 138/B3
Grande, Salto (falls), Colombia 126/D8
Grande (isl.), Colombia 126/B4
Grande (riv.), Guatemala 154/A3
Grande (riv.), Jamaica 158/K6
Grande (riv.), Mexico 150/G2
Grande (riv.), Mexico 150/N8
Grande (riv.), New Bruns. 170/C1
Grande (riv.), Nicaragua 154/E4
Grande (riv.), Peru 128/E10
Grande (range), Uruguay 145/D4
Grande, Arroyo (riv.), Uruguay 145/B4
Grande-Anse, New Bruns. 170/E1
Grande-Anse, Québec 172/E2
Grande Cache, Alberta 182/A3
Grande-Cascapédia, Québec 172/C2
Grande Cayemite (isl.), Haiti 158/B6
Grande-Clairière, Manitoba 179/B5
Grande de Añasco (riv.), P. Rico 161/B2
Grande de Arecibo (riv.), P. Rico 161/C1
Grande de Lípez (riv.), Bolivia 136/B7
Grande de Loíza (riv.), P. Rico 161/E1
Grande de Manatí (riv.), P. Rico 161/C1
Grande de Santiago (riv.), Mexico 150/G6
Grande de Tierra del Fuego (isl.), Argentina 143/C7
Grande de Tierra del Fuego (isl.), Chile 138/E11
Grande Dixence (dam), Switzerland 39/D4
Grande-Grève, Québec 172/D1
Grande Inferior (range), Uruguay 145/C4
Grande Pointe, Manitoba 179/F5
Grande Prairie, Alberta 182/A2
Grande Prairie, Alta. 162/E4
Grande-Prairie, Alta. 146/G4
Grande Prairie, Texas 303/G2
Grand Erg Occidental (des.), Algeria 102/C1
Grand Erg Occidental (des.), Algeria 106/E2
Grand Erg Oriental (des.), Algeria 102/C1
Grand Erg Oriental (des.), Algeria 106/F2
Grand Erg Oriental (des.), Tunisia 106/F2
Grande' Rivière, Martinique 161/C5
Grande-Rivière, Québec 172/D2
Grande-Rivière, La (riv.), Que. 146/L4
Grande Rivière, La (riv.), Québec 174/B2
Grande Rivière, Trin. & Tob. 161/B10
Grande Rivière du Nord, Haiti 158/C5
Grande Ronde (riv.), Oreg. 291/K2
Grande Ronde (riv.), Wash. 310/H5
Grande Saline, Haiti 158/B5
Grandes-Bergeronnes, Québec 172/H1
Grandes-Piles, Québec 172/E3
Grand-Étang, Nova Scotia 168/G2
Grande-Terre, Guadeloupe 161/B6
Grande-Vallée, Québec 172/D1
Grande Vigie, Guadeloupe 161/B5
Grand Falls (lake), Maine 243/H5
Grand Falls, New Bruns. 170/C1
Grand Falls, Newf. 166/C4
Grand Falls, Newf. 146/N5
Grand Falls, Newf. 162/L6
Grandfalls, Texas 303/B6
Grand Falls Hill, New Bruns. 170/C1
Grandfield, Okla. 288/J6
Grand Forks, Br. Col. 184/H6
Grand Forks, N. Dak. 146/J5
Grand Forks, N. Dak. 188/G1
Grand Forks (co.), N. Dak. 282/P3
Grand Forks, N. Dak. 282/R4
Grand Forks A.F.B., N. Dak. 282/R4
Grand Glaise, Ark. 202/G3
Grand Goâve, Haiti 158/B6
Grand Gorge, N.Y. 276/L6
Grand Gosier, Haiti 158/C6
Grand Gulf, Miss. 256/B6
Grand Harbour, New Bruns. 170/D4
Grand Haven, Mich. 250/C5
Grand-Îlet (isl.), Guadeloupe 161/A7
Grandin, Fla. 212/E2
Grandin, Mo. 261/L9
Grandin, N. Dak. 282/R5
Grand Island, Nebr. 146/J5
Grand Island, Nebr. 188/G2
Grand Island, Nebr. 264/F4
Grand Island, N.Y. 276/B5
Grand Isle, La. 238/L8
Grand Isle, Maine 243/G1
Grand Isle (co.), Vt. 268/A2
Grand Isle•, Vt. 268/A2
Grand Junction, Colo. 146/H6
Grand Junction, Colo. 188/E3
Grand Junction, Colo. 208/B4
Grand Junction, Iowa 229/E4
Grand Junction, Mich. 250/C6
Grand Junction, Tenn. 237/C10
Grand-Lahou, Ivory Coast 106/C8
Grand Lake, Ark. 202/H7
Grand Lake, Colo. 208/H2
Grand Lake, La. 238/D6
Grand Lake, Nova Scotia 168/E4
Grand Lake Seboeis (lake), Maine 243/F3
Grand Lake Stream•, Maine 243/H5
Grand Lake Towne, Okla. 288/S1
Grand Ledge, Mich. 250/E6
Grand-Lieu (lake), France 28/C4
Grand Manan (chan.), Maine 243/K6
Grand Manan (chan.), New Bruns. 170/C4
Grand Manan (isl.), New Bruns. 170/D4
Grand Marais, Manitoba 179/F4
Grand Marais, Mich. 250/D2
Grand Marais, Minn. 255/G2
Grand Marsh, Wis. 317/G8
Grand Meadow, Minn. 255/F7
Grand'Mère, Québec 172/E3
Grand Mound, Iowa 229/M5
Grand Mound, Wash. 310/C4
Grand Muveran (mt.), Switzerland 39/D4
Grand Narrows, Nova Scotia 168/H3
Grândola, Portugal 33/B3
Grandora, Sask. 181/E3
Grand Pass, Mo. 261/F4
Grand-Popo, Benin 106/E7
Grand Portage, Minn. 255/G2
Grand Portage Ind. Res., Minn. 255/G2
Grand Portage Nat'l Mon., Minn. 255/G2
Grand Pré, Nova Scotia 168/D3
Grand Rapids, Manitoba 179/C1
Grand Rapids, Mich. 146/K5
Grand Rapids, Mich. 188/K2
Grand Rapids, Mich. 250/D5
Grand Rapids, Minn. 255/E3
Grand Rapids, N. Dak. 282/N7
Grand Rapids, Ohio 284/C3
Grand-Remous, Québec 172/B3
Grand Ridge, Fla. 212/A1
Grand Ridge, Ill. 222/E2
Grand River, Iowa 229/F7
Grand River, Nova Scotia 168/H3
Grand River, Ohio 284/H2
Grand River (valley), Utah 304/E4
Grand Rivers, Ky. 237/E7
Grand Ronde, Oreg. 291/D2
Grand Roy, Grenada 161/C8
Grand Saline, Texas 303/J5
Grand Santi, Fr. Guiana 131/D3
Grandson, Switzerland 39/C3
Grand Terrace, Calif. 204/E10
Grand Terre (isls.), La. 238/L8
Grand Teton (mt.), Wyo. 319/B2
Grand Teton Nat'l Park, Wyo. 319/B2
Grand Tower, Ill. 222/D6
Grand Traverse (co.), Mich. 250/D4
Grand Traverse (bay), Mich. 250/D3
Grand Turk (isl.), Turks & Caicos 156/D2
Grand Valley, Ontario 177/D4
Grand Valley, Pa. 294/C2
Grandview, Ark. 202/C1
Grand View, Idaho 220/B7
Grandview, Ill. 222/D4
Grand View, Ill. 222/F4
Grandview, Ind. 227/C9
Grandview, Iowa 229/L6
Grandview, Manitoba 179/B3
Grandview, Mo. 261/P6
Grandview, Ohio 284/H7
Grandview, Tenn. 237/M9
Grandview, Texas 303/G5
Grandview, Wash. 310/F4
Grand View, Wis. 317/D3
Grandview Heights, Ohio 284/D6
Grand-View-on-Hudson, N.Y. 276/K8
Grandview Plaza, Kansas 232/F2
Grandville, Mich. 250/D6
Grand Wash (butte), Ariz. 198/B2
Grand Wash (riv.), Ariz. 198/B2
Grandy, Minn. 255/E5
Grandy, N.C. 281/T2
Graneros, Chile 138/G5
Grange, England 13/E3
Grange, N.H. 268/E3
Grangeburg, Ala. 195/H8
Grange City, Ky. 237/O4
Grangemouth, Scotland 10/B1
Grangemouth, Scotland 15/C1
Granger, Ind. 227/E1
Granger, Iowa 229/F5
Granger, Minn. 255/F7
Granger, Mo. 261/H2
Granger, Texas 303/G7
Granger, Wash. 310/E4
Granger, Wyo. 188/D2
Granger, Wyo. 319/C4
Grangeville, Idaho 220/B4
Grangeville, La. 238/J5
Granisle, Br. Col. 184/D3
Granite, Colo. 208/G4
Granite, Md. 245/L3
Granite (pt.), Mich. 250/B2
Granite (co.), Mont. 262/C4
Granite (peak), Mont. 262/F5
Granite (peak), Nev. 266/B4
Granite (range), Nev. 266/B2
Granite, Okla. 288/H5

Hartsville 379

Hamilton, Ontario 177/E4
Hamilton, Oreg. 291/H3
Hamilton, Pa. 294/D4
Hamilton (riv.), Queensland 95/B4
Hamilton, R.I. 249/J6
Hamilton, Scotland 15/C2
Hamilton, Scotland 10/B1
Hamilton, The (riv.), S. Australia 94/D2
Hamilton, The (riv.), S. Australia 88/E5
Hamilton, Tasmania 99/C4
Hamilton (co.), Tenn. 237/L10
Hamilton (co.), Texas 303/F6
Hamilton, Texas 303/G6
Hamilton, Victoria 88/G7
Hamilton, Victoria 97/B5
Hamilton, Va. 307/N2
Hamilton, Wash. 310/D2
Hamilton City, Calif. 204/C4
Hamilton Dome, Wyo. 319/D2
Hamilton Square-Mercerville, N.J. 273/D3
Hamilton-Wentworth (reg. munic.), Ontario 177/D4
Hamina, Finland 18/P6
Hamiota, Manitoba 179/B4
Ham Lake, Minn. 255/E5
Hamler, Ohio 284/B3
Hamlet, Ind. 227/D2
Hamlet, Nebr. 264/C4
Hamlet, N.Y. 276/B6
Hamlet, N.C. 281/K5
Hamlet, N. Dak. 282/E2
Hamlet, Ohio 284/B8
Hamletsburg, Ill. 222/E6
Hamlin, Alberta 182/D2
Hamlin, Iowa 229/D5
Hamlin, Kansas 232/G2
Hamlin, Ky. 237/E7
Hamlin•, Maine 243/H1
Hamlin (lake), Mich. 250/C4
Hamlin, N.Y. 276/E4
Hamlin, Pa. 294/M3
Hamlin, Sask. 181/C3
Hamlin (co.), S. Dak. 298/P4
Hamlin, Texas 303/E5
Hamlin, W. Va. 312/B6
Hamm, Germany 22/B3
Hammamet (gulf), Tunisia 106/G1
Hammar, Hor al (lake), Iraq 66/E5
Hammarstrand, Sweden 18/J5
Hamme, Belgium 27/E6
Hammel, Denmark 21/C5
Hammelburg, Germany 22/C3
Hammer, S. Dak. 298/R2
Hammerdal, Sweden 18/J5
Hammerfest, Norway 4/B9
Hammerfest, Norway 18/N1
Hammerfest, Norway 7/G1
Hammersmith, England 10/B5
Hammersmith, England 13/H8
Hammerum, Denmark 21/C5
Hammett, Idaho 220/C7
Hammon, Okla. 288/H3
Hammonasset (pt.), Conn. 210/E3
Hammonasset (res.), Conn. 210/E3
Hammonasset (riv.), Conn. 210/E3
Hammond, Ill. 222/E4
Hammond, Ind. 227/B1
Hammond, Ky. 237/O7
Hammond, La. 238/N1
Hammond, Minn. 255/F6
Hammond, Mo. 261/G9
Hammond, Mont. 262/M5
Hammond (riv.), New Bruns. 170/E3
Hammond, N.Y. 276/J2
Hammond, Oreg. 291/C1
Hammond, Wis. 317/A6
Hammondsport, N.Y. 276/F6
Hammondsville, Ohio 284/J4
Hammondvale, New Bruns. 170/E3
Hammondville, Ala. 195/G1
Hammonton, N.J. 273/D4
Hamnavoe, Scotland 15/G2
Ham-Nord, Québec 172/F4
Hamoa, Hawaii 218/K2
Hamois, Belgium 27/G8
Hamont-Achel, Belgium 27/H6
Hampden, Maine 243/F6
Hampden•, Maine 243/F6
Hampden (co.), Mass. 249/D4
Hampden•, Mass. 249/E4
Hampden, Newf. 166/C4
Hampden, N. Zealand 100/C6
Hampden, N. Dak. 282/N2
Hampden, W. Va. 312/C7
Hampden Highlands, Maine 243/F6
Hampden-Sydney, Va. 307/L6
Hampshire (co.), England 13/F6
Hampshire, Ill. 222/E1
Hampshire (co.), Mass. 249/D3
Hampshire, Tenn. 237/G9
Hampshire (co.), W. Va. 312/J4
Hampshire, Wyo. 319/H2
Hampstead, Dominica 161/E5
Hampstead, Md. 245/L2
Hampstead, New Bruns. 170/D3
Hampstead•, N.H. 268/E6
Hampstead, N.C. 281/O6
Hampstead, Québec 172/H4
Hampton, Ark. 202/F6
Hampton•, Conn. 210/G1
Hampton, Fla. 212/D2
Hampton, Georgia 217/D4
Hampton, Ill. 222/C2
Hampton, Iowa 229/G3
Hampton, Ky. 237/E6
Hampton, Minn. 255/E6
Hampton, Miss. 256/B4
Hampton, Nebr. 264/G4
Hampton, New Bruns. 170/E3
Hampton, N.H. 268/F6
Hampton•, N.H. 268/F6
Hampton, N.J. 273/D2
Hampton, N.Y. 276/O3
Hampton, Nova Scotia 168/C4
Hampton, Oreg. 291/G4
Hampton, Pa. 294/H6
Hampton (co.), S.C. 296/E6
Hampton, S.C. 296/E6
Hampton, Tenn. 237/S8
Hampton (I.C.), Va. 307/R6
Hampton Bays, N.Y. 276/R9
Hampton Beach, N.H. 268/F6
Hampton Falls•, N.H. 268/F6
Hampton Nat'l Hist. Site, Md. 245/M3
Hampton Park, Victoria 97/K6
Hampton Park, Victoria 88/M8
Hampton Roads (est.), Va. 307/R7
Hampton Springs, Fla. 212/C1
Hamptonville, N.C. 281/H2
Hamrat esh Sheikh, Sudan 111/E5
Hamrin, Jabal (mts.), Iraq 66/D3
Hams Bluff (prom.), Virgin Is. (U.S.) 161/E3
Hams Fork (riv.), Wyo. 319/B4
Ham-Sud, Québec 172/F4
Hamton, Sask. 181/J4
Hamtramck, Mich. 250/B6
Hamur, Turkey 63/K3
Han (riv.), China 54/N6
Han (riv.), S. Korea 81/C5
Hana, Hawaii 188/F5
Hana, Hawaii 218/K2
Hanac, Turkey 63/K2
Hanaford (Logan), Ill. 222/E6
Hanagita (peak), Alaska 196/K2
Hanahan, S.C. 296/H6
Hanakiya, Saudi Arabia 59/D5
Hanalei, Hawaii 218/C1
Hanalei (bay), Hawaii 218/C1
Hanalei (riv.), Hawaii 218/C1
Hanamaki, Japan 81/K4
Hanamalo (pt.), Hawaii 218/F7
Hanamaulu, Hawaii 218/C1
Hanapepe, Hawaii 218/C2
Hanapepe (bay), Hawaii 218/C2
Hanau, Germany 22/C3
Hanbogd, Mongolia 77/G3
Hanceville, Ala. 195/E2
Hancheng, China 77/H4
Hanchung (Hanzhong), China 77/G5
Hancock, Conn. 210/C2
Hancock (co.), Georgia 217/G4
Hancock (co.), Ill. 222/B3
Hancock (co.), Ind. 227/F5
Hancock (co.), Iowa 229/F2
Hancock, Iowa 229/C6
Hancock (co.), Ky. 237/H5
Hancock (co.), Maine 243/G6
Hancock•, Maine 243/G6
Hancock, Md. 245/F2
Hancock•, Mass. 249/A2
Hancock, Mich. 250/G1
Hancock, Minn. 255/C5
Hancock (co.), Miss. 256/E10
Hancock, Mo. 261/H7
Hancock•, N.H. 268/C6
Hancock (mt.), N.H. 268/D3
Hancock, N.Y. 276/K7
Hancock (co.), Ohio 284/C3
Hancock (co.), Tenn. 237/P7
Hancock•, Vt. 268/B4
Hancock (co.), W. Va. 312/E2
Hancock, W. Va. 312/K3
Hancock, Wis. 317/G7
Hancocks Bridge, N.J. 273/C4
Hand (co.), S. Dak. 298/L4
Handa (isl.), Scotland 15/C2
Handan (Hantan), China 77/H4
Handan, China 54/N6
Handel, Sask. 181/C3
Handeni, Tanzania 115/G5
Handies (peak), Colo. 208/E7
Handley, W. Va. 312/D6
Handlová, Czech. 41/E2
Handsom, Va. 307/O7
Handsworth, Sask. 181/J6
Haney, Br. Col. 184/L3
Hanford, Calif. 204/F7
Hanford Reservation, Wash. 310/F4
Hangayn Nuruu (mts.), Mongolia 77/E2
Hangchow (Hangzhou), China 77/J5
Hanggin, China 77/G4
Hanging Rock, Ohio 284/E8
Hangklip (cape), S. Africa 118/F7
Hangman (creek), Wash. 310/H3
Hangö, Finland 18/N7
Hangöudd (prom.), Finland 18/N7
Hangzhou (Hangchow), China 77/J5
Hangzhou, China 54/N6
Hangzhou Wan (bay), China 77/K5
Hanh, Mongolia 77/F1
Hani, Turkey 63/J3
Haniqra, Rosh (cape), Israel 65/C1
Hanish (isls.), Yemen 59/D7
Hankinson, N. Dak. 282/S7
Hanko (Hangö), Finland 18/N7
Hanks, N. Dak. 282/C2
Hanksville, Utah 304/D5
Hanle, India 68/D2
Hanley, Sask. 181/E4
Hanley Falls, Minn. 255/C6
Hanley Hills, Mo. 261/P2
Hanlontown, Iowa 229/G2
Hanmer, N. Zealand 100/D5
Hann (mt.), W. Australia 92/D1
Hanna, Alberta 182/E4
Hanna, Alta. 162/E5
Hanna, Ind. 227/D2
Hanna, La. 238/D3
Hanna, Okla. 288/P4
Hanna, Utah 304/D3
Hanna, Wyo. 319/F4
Hanna City, Ill. 222/D3
Hannaford, N. Dak. 282/O5
Hannah, N. Dak. 282/N2
Hannah (bay), Ontario 175/D2
Hannawa Falls, N.Y. 276/L1
Hannibal, Mo. 261/K3
Hannibal, Mo. 188/H3
Hannibal, N.Y. 276/G4
Hannibal, Ohio 284/J6
Hannibal, Wis. 317/E5
Hanno, Japan 81/O2
Hannover, Germany 7/E3
Hannover, Germany 22/C2
Hannover, N. Dak. 282/H5
Hannuit (Hannut), Belgium 27/G7
Hannut, Belgium 27/G7
Hanöbukten (bay), Sweden 18/J9
Hanoi (cap.), Vietnam 2/Q4
Hanoi (cap.), Vietnam 54/M7
Hanoi (cap.), Vietnam 72/E2
Hanover (isl.), Chile 120/B8
Hanover (isl.), Chile 138/D9
Hanover, Conn. 210/G2
Hanover, Ill. 222/C1
Hanover, Ind. 227/F7
Hanover, Kansas 232/F2
Hanover•, Maine 243/B7
Hanover, Md. 245/M4
Hanover•, Mass. 249/L4
Hanover, Mich. 250/E6
Hanover, Minn. 255/E5
Hanover, N.H. 268/C4
Hanover•, N.H. 268/C4
Hanover, N. Mex. 274/A6
Hanover, Ohio 284/F5
Hanover, Ontario 177/C3
Hanover, Pa. 294/J6
Hanover (co.), Va. 307/N5
Hanover, Va. 307/O5
Hanover, W. Va. 312/C7
Hanover Park, Ill. 222/A5
Hanoverton, Ohio 284/J4
Hansboro, N. Dak. 282/M2
Hansell, Iowa 229/G3
Hansen, Idaho 220/D7
Hansford (co.), Texas 303/C1
Han Shui (riv.), China 77/H5
Hanska, Minn. 255/D6
Hans Lollik (isls.), Virgin Is. (U.S.) 161/B4
Hanson, Ky. 237/G6
Hanson, Mass. 249/L4
Hanson•, Mass. 249/L4
Hanson (bay), N. Zealand 100/E7
Hanson (riv.), North. Terr. 93/C6
Hanson, Okla. 288/S4
Hanson (co.), S. Dak. 298/O6
Hansonville, Va. 307/D7
Hanstholm, Denmark 21/B3
Hanston, Kansas 232/C3
Hansville, Wash. 310/C3
Hantan (Handan), China 77/H4
Hants (co.), Nova Scotia 168/D4
Hant's Harbour, Newf. 166/D2
Hantsport, Nova Scotia 168/D3
Hantzsch (riv.), N.W. Terr. 187/L3
Hanumangarh, India 68/C3
Hanwood, N.S. Wales 97/C4
Hanyuan, China 77/F6
Hanzhong (Hanchung), China 77/G5
Hao (atoll), Fr. Poly. 87/N7
Haouach, Wadi (dry riv.), Chad 111/C4
Haparanda, Sweden 18/N4
Hapeville, Georgia 217/K2
Happy, Ky. 237/P6
Happy, Texas 303/C3
Happy Adventure, Newf. 166/D2
Happy Camp, Calif. 204/B2
Happy Jack, Ariz. 198/D4
Happy Jack, La. 238/L7
Happy Valley, Oreg. 291/B2
Happy Valley-Goose Bay, Newf. 166/B3
Haql, Saudi Arabia 59/C4
Harad, Saudi Arabia 59/E5
Harads, Sweden 18/M3
Harahan, La. 238/O4
Haraja, Saudi Arabia 59/D6
Haralson (co.), Georgia 217/B3
Haralson, Georgia 217/C4
Haramachi, Japan 81/K5
Harar (prov.), Ethiopia 111/H6
Harar, Ethiopia 111/H6
Harar, Ethiopia 102/G4
Harardera, Somalia 115/J3
Harare (Salisbury) (cap.), Zimbabwe 102/E6
Harare (cap.), Zimbabwe 118/E3
Haraz, Chad 111/C5
Harbel, Liberia 106/B7
Harbeson, Del. 245/S6
Harbin, China 77/L2
Harbin, China 2/R3
Harbin, China 54/O5
Harbine, Nebr. 264/G4
Harbinger, N.C. 281/T2
Harboør, Denmark 21/B4
Harbor, Oreg. 291/C5
Harbor Beach, Mich. 250/G5
Harbor City, Calif. 204/C11
Harborcreek, Pa. 294/C1
Harbor Springs, Mich. 250/D3
Harborton, Va. 307/S5
Harbor View, Ohio 284/C2
Harbour (isl.), Bahamas 156/C1
Harbour Breton, Newf. 166/C4
Harbour Deep, Newf. 166/C3
Harbour Grace, Newf. 166/D2
Harbour Grace, Newf. 162/L6
Harbour Main, Newf. 166/D2
Harbourton, N.J. 273/D3
Harbourville, Nova Scotia 168/D3
Harburg-Wilhelmsburg, Germany 22/C2
Hårby, Denmark 21/D7
Harco, Ill. 222/E6
Harcourt, Iowa 229/E4
Harcourt, New Bruns. 170/E2
Harcourt, Ontario 177/F2
Harcuvar (mts.), Ariz. 198/B5
Harda, India 68/D4
Hardangerfjord (fjord), Norway 18/D7
Hardangerfjorden (fjord), Norway 7/E3
Hardangervidda (plat.), Norway 18/E6
Hardaway, Ala. 195/G6
Hardburly, Ky. 237/P6
Hardee (co.), Fla. 212/E4
Hardee, Miss. 256/C5
Hardeeville, S.C. 296/E7
Hardeman (co.), Tenn. 237/C10
Hardeman (co.), Texas 303/E3
Hardenberg, Netherlands 27/J3
Harden City, Okla. 288/N5
Harderwijk, Netherlands 27/H4
Hardesty, Okla. 288/D1
Hardieville, Alberta 182/D5
Hardin (co.), Ill. 222/E6
Hardin, Ill. 222/C4
Hardin (co.), Iowa 229/G4
Hardin (co.), Ky. 237/K5
Hardin, Ky. 237/E7
Hardin, Mo. 261/E4
Hardin, Mont. 262/J5
Hardin (co.), Ohio 284/C4
Hardin (co.), Tenn. 237/E10
Hardin (co.), Texas 303/K7
Harding (lake), Ala. 195/H5
Harding (lake), Georgia 217/B5
Harding, Manitoba 179/B5
Harding, Minn. 255/E4
Harding (co.), N. Mex. 274/F3
Harding (pt.), Nova Scotia 168/D5
Harding (co.), S. Dak. 298/B2
Harding, W. Va. 312/G5
Harding Icefield, Alaska 196/C2
Hardingville, N.J. 273/C4
Hardinsburg, Ind. 227/E8
Hardinsburg, Ky. 237/H5
Hardin Springs, Ky. 237/J5
Hardinville, Ill. 222/F5
Hardinxveld-Giessendam, Netherlands 27/G5
Hardisty, Alberta 182/E3
Hardisty (lake), N.W. Terr. 187/G3
Hardman, Oreg. 291/H2
Hardoi, India 68/E3
Hardshell, Ky. 237/P6
Hardt (mts.), Germany 22/C4
Hardtner, Kansas 232/D4
Hardwar, India 68/D2
Hardwick (Midway-Hardwick), Georgia 217/F4
Hardwick•, Mass. 249/F3
Hardwick, Minn. 255/B7
Hardwick, Vt. 268/C2
Hardwick•, Vt. 268/C2
Hardwick (lake), Vt. 268/C2
Hardwicke, New Bruns. 170/E1
Hardwicke Island, Br. Col. 184/E5
Hardwood Ridge, New Bruns. 170/D2
Hardy, Ark. 202/H1
Hardy (pen.), Chile 138/F11
Hardy, Iowa 229/E3
Hardy, Ky. 237/S5
Hardy, Miss. 256/E3
Hardy, Nebr. 264/G4
Hardy, Okla. 288/N1
Hardy, Sask. 181/G6
Hardy, Va. 307/J6
Hardy (co.), W. Va. 312/J4
Hardyville, Ky. 237/K6
Hare (bay), Newf. 166/C3
Hare (fjord), N.W. Terr. 187/K1
Hare Bay, Newf. 166/D4
Harelbeke, Belgium 27/C7
Harfleur, France 28/D3
Harford (co.), Md. 245/N2
Harford, N.Y. 276/H6
Harford, Pa. 294/L2
Hargeysa, Somalia 115/H2
Hargeysa, Somalia 102/G4
Hargill, Texas 303/F11
Hargrave, Manitoba 179/A5
Hargwen, Alberta 182/B3
Har Hu (lake), China 77/E4
Hari (riv.), Indonesia 85/C6
Harib, Yemen 59/E7
Haricha Hamada (des.), Mali 106/D4
Harim, Syria 63/G4
Harima (sea), Japan 81/G6
Harima, Jordan 65/D2
Haringey, England 10/B5
Haringey, England 13/H8
Haringvliet (str.), Netherlands 27/E5
Hariq, Saudi Arabia 59/E5
Harirud (riv.), Afghanistan 68/A1
Harirud (riv.), Afghanistan 59/H3
Hari Rud (riv.), Iran 66/M3
Haris, West Bank 65/C3
Harjavalta, Finland 18/M6
Harjo, Okla. 288/N4
Harkaway, Victoria 97/K5
Harkers Island, N.C. 281/R5
Harkiko, Ethiopia 111/G4
Harlan, Ind. 227/H2
Harlan, Iowa 229/C5
Harlan, Kansas 232/D2
Harlan (co.), Ky. 237/P7
Harlan, Ky. 237/P7
Harlan (co.), Nebr. 264/E4
Harlan, Oreg. 291/D3
Harlan County (lake), Nebr. 264/E5
Harlech (comm.), Wales 10/E4
Harlech, Wales 13/C5
Harlem, Fla. 212/F5
Harlem, Georgia 217/H4
Harlem, Mont. 262/H2
Harlem Springs, Ohio 284/J4
Harleston, England 13/J5
Harleton, Texas 303/K5
Hårlev, Denmark 21/F7
Harleyville, S.C. 296/G5
Harlingen, Netherlands 27/G2
Harlingen, N.J. 273/D3
Harlingen, Texas 303/G11
Harlingen, Texas 188/G5
Harlow, England 13/H7
Harlow, N. Dak. 282/M3
Harlowton, Mont. 262/F4
Harman, W. Va. 312/G5
Harman-Maxie, Va. 307/D6
Harmans, Md. 245/M4
Harmattan, Alberta 182/C4
Harmon, Ill. 222/D2
Harmon (co.), Okla. 288/G5
Harmon, Okla. 288/G2
Harmonsburg, Pa. 294/B2
Harmony, Ark. 202/D2
Harmony, Ind. 227/C5
Harmony, Maine 243/D6
Harmony•, Maine 243/D6
Harmony, Minn. 255/F7
Harmony, N.C. 281/H3
Harmony, Pa. 294/B4
Harmony, R.I. 249/H5
Harmony, W. Va. 312/D5
Harms, Tenn. 237/H10
Harned, Ky. 237/J5
Harnett (co.), N.C. 281/M4
Harney (lake), Fla. 212/F3
Harney, Md. 245/K2
Harney (co.), Oreg. 291/H4
Harney, Oreg. 291/J4
Harney (lake), Oreg. 291/H4
Harney (peak), S. Dak. 298/B6
Härnösand, Sweden 18/L5
Haro, Spain 33/E1
Haro (str.), Wash. 310/B2
Harold, Fla. 212/B6
Harold, Ky. 237/R5
Harp (lake), Newf. 166/B2
Harper, Ill. 222/D1
Harper, Iowa 229/J6
Harper (co.), Kansas 232/D4
Harper, Kansas 232/D4
Harper, Liberia 106/C8
Harper, Liberia 102/B4
Harper (co.), Okla. 288/G1
Harper, Oreg. 291/K4
Harper, Texas 303/E7
Harper, Wash. 310/A2
Harper, W. Va. 312/D7
Harpers Ferry, Iowa 229/L2
Harpers Ferry, W. Va. 312/L4
Harpers Ferry Nat'l Hist. Park, Md. 245/G3
Harpers Ferry Nat'l Hist. Park, W. Va. 312/L4
Harpersville, Ala. 195/F4
Harperville, Miss. 256/E6
Harper Woods, Mich. 250/B6
Harpeth (riv.), Tenn. 237/G8
Harpster, Idaho 220/C4
Harpster, Ohio 284/D4
Harpswell•, Maine 243/D8
Harpswell Center, Maine 243/D8
Harpursville, N.Y. 276/J6
Harput, Turkey 63/H3
Harquahala (mts.), Ariz. 198/B5
Harrah, Okla. 288/M4
Harrah, Wash. 310/E4
Harran, Turkey 63/H4
Harrell, Ark. 202/F7
Harrells, N.C. 281/N5
Harrellsville, N.C. 281/R2
Harricana (riv.), Québec 174/B3
Harriet, Ark. 202/E2
Harrietsfield, Nova Scotia 168/E4
Harrietta, Mich. 250/D4
Harriettsville, Ohio 284/H6
Harrigan Cove, Nova Scotia 168/F4
Harriman, N.Y. 276/M8
Harriman, Oreg. 291/E5
Harriman, Tenn. 237/M9
Harriman (res.), Vt. 268/B6
Harrington (sound), Bermuda 156/G3
Harrington, Del. 245/R5
Harrington•, Maine 243/H6
Harrington (lake), Maine 243/E4
Harrington, N.S. Wales 97/G2
Harrington, S. Dak. 298/G7
Harrington, Wash. 310/G3
Harrington Harbour, Québec 174/F2
Harrington Park, N.J. 273/C1
Harris, Calif. 204/B3
Harris (co.), Georgia 217/C5
Harris, Iowa 229/C2
Harris, Kansas 232/G3
Harris, Mich. 250/B3
Harris, Minn. 255/F5
Harris, Mo. 261/F2
Harris, Okla. 288/S7
Harris, Sask. 181/D4
Harris (dist.), Scotland 15/B3
Harris (dist.), Scotland 10/C2
Harris (sound), Scotland 15/A3
Harris (sound), Scotland 10/C2
Harris (lake), S. Australia 94/D4
Harris, Tenn. 237/C8
Harris (co.), Texas 303/J8
Harrisburg, Ark. 202/J2
Harrisburg, Ill. 222/E6
Harrisburg, Ind. 227/G5
Harrisburg, Mo. 261/H4
Harrisburg, Nebr. 264/A3
Harrisburg, N.C. 281/H4
Harrisburg, Ohio 284/D6
Harrisburg, Oreg. 291/D3
Harrisburg (cap.), Pa. 188/L2
Harrisburg (cap.), Pa. 146/L5
Harrisburg (cap.), Pa. 294/H5
Harrisburg, S. Dak. 298/R7
Harrismith, S. Africa 118/D5
Harrison (bay), Alaska 196/H1
Harrison, Ark. 202/D1
Harrison (lake), Br. Col. 184/M2
Harrison, Georgia 217/G5
Harrison, Idaho 220/B2
Harrison, Ill. 222/D1
Harrison (co.), Ind. 227/E8
Harrison (co.), Iowa 229/B5
Harrison (co.), Ky. 237/N4
Harrison•, Maine 243/B7
Harrison, Mich. 250/E4
Harrison (co.), Miss. 256/F10
Harrison (co.), Mo. 261/E2
Harrison, Mont. 262/E5
Harrison, Nebr. 264/A2
Harrison (cape), Newf. 166/C3
Harrison, N.J. 273/B2
Harrison, N.Y. 276/P6
Harrison (co.), Ohio 284/H5
Harrison, Ohio 284/A9
Harrison, S. Dak. 298/M7
Harrison, Tenn. 237/L10
Harrison (co.), Texas 303/K5
Harrison (co.), W. Va. 312/F4
Harrison, Wis. 317/G5
Harrisonburg, La. 238/G3
Harrisonburg (I.C.), Va. 307/K4
Harrison Hot Springs, Br. Col. 184/M3
Harrison Valley, Pa. 294/G2
Harrisonville, Ill. 222/C5
Harrisonville, Mo. 261/D5
Harrisonville, N.J. 273/C4
Harrisonville, Ohio 284/F7
Harrisonville, Pa. 294/F6
Harriston, Miss. 256/C7
Harriston, Ontario 177/D4
Harristown, Ill. 222/D4
Harrisville, Ind. 227/H4
Harrisville, Mich. 250/F4
Harrisville, Miss. 256/D7
Harrisville•, N.H. 268/C6
Harrisville, N.Y. 276/K2
Harrisville, Ohio 284/J5
Harrisville, Pa. 294/B3
Harrisville, R.I. 249/H5
Harrisville, Utah 304/C2
Harrisville, W. Va. 312/E4
Harris Wash (creek), Utah 304/C6
Harrod, Ohio 284/C4
Harrodsburg, Ind. 227/D6
Harrodsburg, Ky. 237/M5
Harrods Creek, Ky. 237/K4
Harrogate, Br. Col. 184/J5
Harrogate, England 13/J1
Harrogate, England 10/F4
Harrogate-Shawanee, Tenn. 237/O8
Harrold, S. Dak. 298/K4
Harrold, Texas 303/F3
Harrop (lake), Manitoba 179/G2
Harrow, England 13/G8
Harrow, England 10/B5
Harrow, Ontario 177/B5
Harrow, Victoria 97/A5
Harrowby, Manitoba 179/A4
Harrowsmith, Ontario 177/H3
Harry S. Truman Nat'l Hist. Site, Mo. 261/R5
Harry Strunk (lake), Nebr. 264/D4
Harsens Island, Mich. 250/G6
Harshaw, Wis. 317/G4
Harstad, Norway 18/K2
Hart (lake), Fla. 212/E3
Hart (co.), Georgia 217/G2
Hart (co.), Ky. 237/K6
Hart, Mich. 250/C5
Hart (lake), Oreg. 291/H5
Hart (mt.), Oreg. 291/H5
Hart, Texas 303/B3
Hart (riv.), Yukon 187/E3
Hartbees (riv.), S. Africa 118/C5
Hartberg, Austria 41/C3
Harte, Manitoba 179/C4
Harte (mt.), Manitoba 179/A2
Hartell, Alberta 182/C4
Hartfield, Va. 307/R5
Hartford, Ala. 195/G8
Harrison (cape), Newf. 162/L5
Hartford, Ark. 202/B3
Hartford (co.), Conn. 210/D1
Hartford (cap.), Conn. 146/L5
Hartford (cap.), Conn. 188/M2
Hartford (cap.), Conn. 210/E1
Hartford, Ill. 222/A2
Hartford, Iowa 229/G6
Hartford, Kansas 232/F3
Hartford, Ky. 237/H6
Hartford•, Maine 243/C7
Hartford, Mich. 250/C6
Hartford, N.J. 273/D4
Hartford, N.Y. 276/O4
Hartford, Ohio 284/E5
Hartford, Ohio 284/J3
Hartford, S. Dak. 298/P6
Hartford, Tenn. 237/P9
Hartford•, Vt. 268/C4
Hartford, W. Va. 312/C4
Hartford, Wis. 317/K9
Hartford City, Ind. 227/G4
Harthill, Scotland 15/C2
Hartington, Nebr. 264/G2
Hartington, Ontario 177/H3
Hartland•, Conn. 210/D1
Hartland, England 13/C7
Hartland (pt.), England 13/C6
Hartland (pt.), England 10/D5
Hartland, Maine 243/D6
Hartland•, Maine 243/D6
Hartland, Mich. 250/F6
Hartland, Minn. 255/E7
Hartland, New Bruns. 170/C2
Hartland•, Vt. 269/C4
Hartland, W. Va. 312/D6
Hartland, Wis. 317/J1
Hartland Four Corners, Vt. 268/C4
Hartlepool, England 10/F3
Hartlepool, England 13/F3
Hartleton, Pa. 294/H4
Hartley, Iowa 229/C2
Hartley (co.), Texas 303/B2
Hartley, Texas 303/B2
Hartleyville, Alberta 182/D5
Hartline, Wash. 310/F3
Hartly, Del. 245/R4
Hartman, Ark. 202/C3
Hartman, Colo. 208/P6
Hartney, Manitoba 179/B5
Harts (pass), Wash. 310/E2
Harts, W. Va. 312/B6
Hartsburg, Ill. 222/D3
Hartsburg, Mo. 261/H5
Hartsdale, N.Y. 276/P6
Hartsel, Colo. 208/H4
Hartselle, Ala. 195/E2
Hartsfield, Georgia 217/E8
Hartsgrove, Ohio 284/J2
Hartshorn, Mo. 261/J8
Hartshorne, Okla. 288/R5
Harts Range, North. Terr. 88/F4
Harts Range, North. Terr. 93/D7
Hartstown, Pa. 294/B2
Hartsville, Ind. 227/F6
Hartsville, Mass. 249/B4
Hartsville, S.C. 296/G3
Hartsville, Tenn. 237/J8

380 Hartville

Hartville, Mo. 261/G8
Hartville, Ohio 284/H4
Hartville, Wyo. 319/H3
Hartwell, Georgia 217/G2
Hartwell (dam), Georgia 217/G2
Hartwell (lake), Georgia 217/G2
Hartwell, Mo. 261/E6
Hartwell (dam), S.C. 296/B3
Hartwell (lake), S.C. 296/A3
Hartwick, Iowa 229/J5
Hartwick, N.Y. 276/K5
Hartz (mt.), Tasmania 99/C5
Harug el Asued, El (mts.), Libya 111/C2
Haruniye, Turkey 63/G4
Har Us Nuur (lake), Mongolia 77/D2
Harvard (mt.), Colo. 208/G5
Harvard, Idaho 220/B3
Harvard, Ill. 222/E1
Harvard, Iowa 229/G7
Harvard•, Mass. 249/H2
Harvard, Nebr. 264/F4
Harvel, Ill. 222/D4
Harvest, Ala. 195/E1
Harvester, Mo. 261/N2
Harvey, Ill. 222/B6
Harvey, Iowa 229/H6
Harvey (co.), Kansas 232/E3
Harvey, La. 238/O4
Harvey, Albert, New Bruns. 170/F3
Harvey, York, New Bruns. 170/D3
Harvey (lake), New Bruns. 170/C3
Harvey (mt.), New Bruns. 170/D3
Harvey, N. Dak. 282/L4
Harvey, W. Australia 88/B6
Harvey, W. Australia 92/A2
Harvey, W. Va. 312/D7
Harvey Cedars, N.J. 273/E4
Harveys (lake), Vt. 268/C3
Harveysburg, Ohio 284/C7
Harveys Lake, Pa. 294/E7
Harveyton, Ky. 237/P6
Harveyville, Kansas 232/F3
Harviell, Mo. 261/M9
Harwich, England 13/J6
Harwich, England 10/G5
Harwich, Mass. 249/O6
Harwich•, Mass. 249/O6
Harwich Port, Mass. 249/O6
Harwinton, Conn. 210/C1
Harwinton•, Conn. 210/C1
Harwood, Mo. 261/D7
Harwood, N. Dak. 282/S6
Harwood, Ontario 177/F3
Harwood, Texas 303/G8
Harwood Heights, Ill. 222/B5
Harwood Island, N.S. Wales 97/G1
Harworth, England 13/F4
Haryana (state), India 68/D3
Harz (mts.), Germany 22/D3
Harzgerode, Germany 22/D3
Hasa, Wadi el (dry riv.), Jordan 65/E5
Hasan Dağı, Büyük (mt.), Turkey 63/E3
Hasbrouck Heights, N.J. 273/B2
Hase (riv.), Germany 22/B2
Haseke (prov.), Syria 63/J4
Haselünne, Germany 22/B2
Hasenkamp, Argentina 143/F5
Hashtpar, Iran 66/F2
Haskeir (isl.), Scotland 15/A3
Haskell, Ark. 202/E4
Haskell (co.), Kansas 232/B4
Haskell, N.J. 273/A1
Haskell (co.), Okla. 288/R4
Haskell, Okla. 288/P3
Haskell (co.), Texas 303/E4
Haskell, Texas 303/E4
Haskett, Manitoba 179/D5
Haskins, Iowa 229/K6
Haskins, Ohio 284/C3
Haslach an der Mühl, Austria 41/C2
Hasle, Denmark 21/F8
Haslemere, England 13/G6
Haslemere, England 10/F5
Haslet, Texas 303/E2
Haslett, Mich. 250/E6
Haslev, Denmark 21/E7
Haslingden, England 13/H1
Hassa, Turkey 63/G4
Hassan, India 68/D6
Hassayampa (riv.), Ariz. 198/C5
Hasse, Texas 303/F6
Hassel (sound), N.W. Terr. 187/J2
Hassel (isl.), Virgin Is. (U.S.) 161/B4
Hassell, N.C. 281/P3
Hasselt, Belgium 27/G7
Hasselt, Netherlands 27/J3
Hassfurt, Germany 22/D3
Hassi Messaoud, Algeria 106/F2
Hassi R'Mel, Algeria 106/E2
Hässleholm, Sweden 18/H8
Hassloch, Germany 22/C4
Haster, Scotland 15/E2
Hastière, Belgium 27/F8
Hastings, England 10/G5
Hastings, England 13/H7
Hastings, Fla. 212/E2
Hastings, Iowa 229/C6
Hastings, Mich. 250/D6
Hastings, Minn. 255/F6
Hastings, Nebr. 188/G2
Hastings, Nebr. 264/F4
Hastings, N. Zealand 100/F3
Hastings, N. Dak. 282/O6
Hastings, Okla. 288/K6
Hastings (county), Ontario 177/G3
Hastings, Ontario 177/G3
Hastings, Pa. 294/E4
Hastings On Hudson, N.Y. 276/O6
Hasty, Ark. 202/D1
Hasty, Colo. 208/O6
Hasvik, Norway 18/M1
Haswell, Colo. 208/N6
Hat (peak), Calif. 204/E2
Hat (creek), S. Dak. 298/B7
Hatay (prov.), Turkey 63/G4
Hatay (Antakya), Turkey 63/G4
Hatboro, Pa. 294/M5
Hatch, N. Mex. 274/B6
Hatch, Utah 304/B6
Hatchechubbee, Ala. 195/H6
Hatcher, Georgia 217/B7
Hatches Creek, North. Terr. 88/F4
Hatches Creek, North. Terr. 93/D6
Hatchet (mts.), N. Mex. 274/A7
Hatchett (pt.), Conn. 210/G3
Hatchie (riv.), Tenn. 237/B9
Hatchineha (lake), Fla. 212/E3
Hațeg, Romania 45/F3
Hatfield, Ark. 202/B5
Hatfield, England 13/H7
Hatfield, Ind. 227/C9
Hatfield, Ky. 237/S5
Hatfield, Mass. 249/D3
Hatfield•, Mass. 249/D3
Hatfield, Minn. 255/B7
Hatfield, Mo. 261/D1
Hatfield, N.S. Wales 97/B3
Hatfield, Pa. 294/M5
Hatfield, Sask. 181/F4
Hatfield, Wis. 317/E7
Hatfield Point, New Bruns. 170/E3
Hatgal, Mongolia 77/E1
Hathaway, Mont. 262/K4
Hatherleigh, Sask. 181/C2
Hathras, India 68/D3
Hatiba, Ras (cape), Saudi Arabia 59/C5
Ha Tien, Vietnam 72/E5
Hatillo, P. Rico 161/B1
Ha Tinh, Vietnam 72/E3
Hatira (mt.), Israel 65/B6
Hatley, Miss. 256/H3
Hatley, Québec 172/F4
Hatley, Wis. 317/H6
Hato, Neth. Ant. 161/G8
Hato del Volcán, Panama 154/F6
Hato Mayor, Dom. Rep. 158/F6
Hato Rey, P. Rico 161/E1
Hatseva, Israel 65/D5
Hattem, Netherlands 27/H4
Hatteras (cape), N.C. 146/L6
Hatteras (cape), N.C. 188/M3
Hatteras, N.C. 281/T4
Hatteras (cape), N.C. 281/U4
Hatteras (inlet), N.C. 281/T4
Hatteras (isl.), N.C. 281/U4
Hatteras (cape), U.S. 2/F4
Hattiesburg, Miss. 188/H4
Hattiesburg, Miss. 256/F8
Hattieville, Ark. 202/E3
Hattieville, Belize 154/C2
Hatton, Ala. 195/D1
Hatton, N. Dak. 282/R4
Hatton, Sask. 181/B5
Hatton, Scotland 15/G3
Hatton, Utah 304/B5
Hatton, Wash. 310/G4
Hatuey, Cuba 158/G3
Hatvan, Hungary 41/E3
Hat Yai, Thailand 72/C6
Hatzic, Br. Col. 184/L3
Hau Bon, Vietnam 72/E4
Haubstadt, Ind. 227/B8
Haud (reg.), Ethiopia 111/J6
Haud (plat.), Somalia 115/J2
Haugan, Mont. 262/A3
Hauge, Norway 18/E7
Haugen, Wis. 317/C4
Haugesund, Norway 7/E3
Haugesund, Norway 18/D7
Haughton, La. 238/C1
Hauhungaroa (range), N. Zealand 100/E3
Haukivesi (lake), Finland 18/Q5
Haultain (riv.), Sask. 181/L3
Hauppauge, N.Y. 276/O9
Haura, Yemen 59/E7
Hauraki (gulf), N. Zealand 100/C1
Hauran, Wadi (dry riv.), Iraq 59/D3
Hauran, Wadi (dry riv.), Iraq 66/B4
Hauroko (lake), N. Zealand 100/A6
Hauru (pt.), Fr. Poly. 86/S12
Hauser, Idaho 220/A2
Hauser (lake), Mont. 262/E4
Hauser, Oreg. 291/C4
Hausstock (mt.), Switzerland 39/H3
Haut (isl.), Maine 243/G7
Haute (isl.), Nova Scotia 168/C3
Haute-Corse (dept.), France 28/B6
Haute-Garonne (dept.), France 28/D6
Haute-Loire (dept.), France 28/E5
Haute-Marne (dept.), France 28/F3
Hauterive, Québec 172/A1
Hauterive, Québec 174/D3
Hautes-Alpes (dept.), France 28/G5
Haute-Saône (dept.), France 28/G4
Haute-Savoie (dept.), France 28/G5
Hautes-Pyrénées (dept.), France 28/D6
Haute-Vienne (dept.), France 28/D5
Hautmont, France 28/F2
Haut-Rhin (dept.), France 28/G4
Hauts-de-Seine (dept.), France 28/A2
Haut-Zaïre (prov.), Zaire 115/E3
Hauula, Hawaii 218/E1
Havaco, W. Va. 312/C8
Havana, Ala. 195/C5
Havana, Ark. 202/D3
Havana (prov.), Cuba 158/C1
Havana (cap.), Cuba 2/E4
Havana (cap.), Cuba 146/K7
Havana (cap.), Cuba 156/A2
Havana (cap.), Cuba 158/C1
Havana, Fla. 212/B1
Havana, Ill. 222/D3
Havana, Kansas 232/G4
Havana, Minn. 255/E6
Havana, N. Dak. 282/P8
Havana, Ohio 284/E3
Havannah (chan.), New Caled. 86/H5
Havant and Waterloo, England 13/G7
Havasu (lake) 188/D4
Havasu (lake), Ariz. 198/A4
Havasu (lake), Calif. 204/L9
Havasu (lake), U.S. 146/G6
Havasupai Ind. Res., Ariz. 198/C2
Havdrup, Denmark 21/F6
Havel (riv.), Germany 22/E2
Havelange, Belgium 27/G8
Havelberg, Germany 22/D2
Havelock, Iowa 229/D3
Havelock, New Bruns. 170/E3
Havelock, N. Zealand 100/D4
Havelock, N.C. 281/P5
Havelock, N. Dak. 282/E7
Havelock, Ontario 177/G3
Havelock North, N. Zealand 100/F3
Haven, Kansas 232/E4
Havensville, Kansas 232/F2
Haverford•, Pa. 294/M6
Haverfordwest, Wales 10/D5
Haverfordwest, Wales 13/B6
Haverhill, England 13/H5
Haverhill, Iowa 229/H5
Haverhill, Mass. 249/K1
Haverhill•, N.H. 268/C3
Haverhill, Ohio 284/E8
Havering, England 10/C5
Havering, England 13/J8
Haverstraw, N.Y. 276/M6
Havertown, Pa. 294/M6
Haviland, Kansas 232/C4
Haviland, Ohio 284/A3
Havillah, Wash. 310/F2
Havířov, Czech. 41/E2
Havlíčkův Brod, Czech. 41/C2
Havran, Turkey 63/B3
Havre, Mont. 146/G5
Havre, Mont. 188/E1
Havre, Mont. 262/G2
Havre Boucher, Nova Scotia 168/G3
Havre de Grace, Md. 245/O2
Havre-Saint-Pierre, Québec 174/E2
Havre-St-Pierre, Que. 162/K5
Havsa, Turkey 63/B2
Havza, Turkey 63/F2
Haw (riv.), N.C. 281/K2
HAWAII 218
Hawaii 188/F5
Hawaii (co.), Hawaii 218/K7
Hawaii (isl.), Hawaii 87/L4
Hawaii (isl.), Hawaii 188/F6
Hawaii (isl.), Hawaii 218/H5
Hawaii (state), U.S. 188/F5
Hawaii (state), U.S. 87/K4
Hawaiian (isls.) 87/J3
Hawaii Kai, Hawaii 218/F2
Hawaii Nat'l Park, Hawaii 218/J6
Hawaii Volcanoes Nat'l Park, Hawaii 218/H6
Hawara, Jordan 65/D2
Hawarden, Iowa 229/A2
Hawarden, N. Zealand 100/D5
Hawarden, Sask. 181/E4
Hawarden, Wales 13/G2
Hawea (lake), N. Zealand 100/B6
Hawera, N. Zealand 100/E3
Hawes, England 13/E3
Hawesville, Ky. 237/H5
Hawi, Hawaii 218/G3
Hawick, Minn. 255/D5
Hawick, Scotland 10/E3
Hawick, Scotland 15/F5
Hawk (hills), Alberta 182/B1
Hawke (hills), Newf. 166/D2
Hawke (isl.), Newf. 166/C3
Hawke (riv.), Newf. 166/C3
Hawke (bay), N. Zealand 100/F3
Hawker, S. Australia 88/F6
Hawker, S. Australia 94/F4
Hawke's Bay, Newf. 166/C3
Hawkesbury (isl.), Br. Col. 184/C3
Hawkesbury, Ontario 177/K2
Hawkestone, Ontario 177/E3
Hawkeye, Iowa 229/J3
Hawkins, Mich. 250/D5
Hawkins (co.), Tenn. 237/P8
Hawkins, Texas 303/J5
Hawkins, Wis. 317/E4
Hawkinsville, Georgia 217/E6
Hawk Junction, Ontario 175/D3
Hawk Junction, Ontario 177/J5
Hawk Point, Mo. 261/K5
Hawk Run, Pa. 294/F4
Hawks, Mich. 250/F3
Hawk Springs, Wyo. 319/H4
Hawley, Minn. 255/B4
Hawley, Pa. 294/M3
Hawley, Texas 303/E5
Hawleyville, Conn. 210/B3
Haworth, N.J. 273/C1
Haworth, Okla. 288/S7
Hawston, S. Africa 118/G7
Hawthorn, La. 238/D4
Hawthorn, Pa. 294/D3
Hawthorn, Victoria 97/J5
Hawthorne, Calif. 204/C11
Hawthorne, Fla. 212/D2
Hawthorne, Nev. 266/C4
Hawthorne, N.J. 273/B2
Hawthorne, N.Y. 276/O6
Hawthorne, Victoria 88/L7
Hawthorne, Wis. 317/C3
Hawthorn Woods, Ill. 222/B5
Haxby, England 13/F3
Haxtun, Colo. 208/O1
Hay (riv.) 162/E4
Hay (lake), Alberta 182/A5
Hay (riv.), Alberta 182/A5
Hay (riv.), Canada 146/G4
Hay, N.S. Wales 88/H6
Hay, N.S. Wales 97/C4
Hay (dry riv.), North. Terr. 88/F4
Hay (cape), North. Terr. 93/A3
Hay (dry riv.), North. Terr. 93/E7
Hay (lake), Ontario 177/F2
Hay, Wales 10/E4
Hay, Wales 13/D5
Hay, Wash. 310/H4
Hayama, Japan 81/O3
Hayange, France 28/F3
Haycock, Alaska 196/F1
Hayden, Ala. 195/E3
Hayden, Ariz. 198/E5
Hayden, Colo. 208/E2
Hayden, Idaho 220/B2
Hayden (lake), Idaho 220/B2
Hayden, Ind. 227/F7
Hayden, Mo. 261/H6
Hayden, N. Mex. 274/F3
Hayden (peak), Utah 304/C3
Haydenburg, Tenn. 237/K8
Hayden Lake, Idaho 220/B2
Haydenville, Mass. 249/C3
Haydenville, Ohio 284/F7
Hayes (mt.), Alaska 196/J2
Hayes (pen.), Greenl. 4/B13
Hayes, Jamaica 158/J6
Hayes, La. 238/E6
Hayes (riv.), Man. 162/G4
Hayes (riv.), Manitoba 179/K3
Hayes (co.), Nebr. 264/C4
Hayes (riv.), N.W. Terr. 187/J3
Hayes, S. Dak. 298/H5
Hayes, Wis. 317/J5
Hayes Center, Nebr. 264/C4
Hayesville, Iowa 229/J6
Hayesville, New Bruns. 170/D2
Hayesville, N.C. 281/B4
Hayesville, Ohio 284/F4
Hayesville, Oreg. 291/A3
Hayfield, Iowa 229/F2
Hayfield, Minn. 255/F7
Hayfork, Calif. 204/B3
Hay Fork, Trinity (riv.), Calif. 204/B3
Hay Lakes, Alberta 182/D3
Hayle, England 13/B7
Haylow, Georgia 217/G9
Haymana, Turkey 63/E3
Haymarket, Va. 307/N3
Hayne, N.C. 281/M5
Haynes, Alberta 182/D3
Haynes, Ark. 202/J4
Haynes, N. Dak. 282/F8
Haynesville, La. 238/D1
Haynesville•, Maine 243/G4
Haynesville, Va. 307/P5
Hayneville, Ala. 195/E6
Hayrabolu, Turkey 63/B2
Hay River, N.W.T. 162/E3
Hay River, N.W.T. 146/G3
Hay River, N.W. Terr. 187/G3
Hays, Alberta 182/E4
Hays, Kansas 232/C3
Hays, Mont. 262/H2
Hays, N.C. 281/G2
Hays (co.), Texas 303/F7
Haysi, Va. 307/D6
Hay Springs, Nebr. 264/B2
Haystack (mt.), Conn. 210/C1
Haystack (peak), Mont. 262/A3
Haystack (mt.), N.Y. 276/N2
Haystack (mt.), Vt. 268/B6
Haysville, Ind. 227/D8
Haysville, Kansas 232/E4
Haysville, Pa. 294/B4
Hayter, Alberta 182/E3
Hayti, Mo. 261/N10
Hayti, S. Dak. 298/P4
Hayti Heights, Mo. 261/N10
Hayton, Wis. 317/K7
Hayward, Calif. 204/K2
Hayward (lake), Conn. 210/F2
Hayward, Minn. 255/E7
Hayward, Mo. 261/N10
Hayward, Wis. 317/D3
Haywards-Manor Park, N. Zealand 100/B2
Haywood, Manitoba 179/D5
Haywood (co.), N.C. 281/C3
Haywood, N.C. 281/L3
Haywood, Okla. 288/P5
Haywood (co.), Tenn. 237/C9
Haywood City, Mo. 261/N9
Hazar (lake), Turkey 63/H3
Hazaran, Kuh-e (mt.), Iran 66/K6
Hazard, Ky. 237/P6
Hazard, Nebr. 264/F3
Hazardville, Conn. 210/E1
Hazaribagh, India 68/F4
Hazar Qadam, Afghanistan 59/J3
Hazar Qadam, Afghanistan 68/B2
Hazebrouck, France 28/E2
Hazel, Ky. 237/E7
Hazel, S. Dak. 298/P4
Hazel Cliffe, Sask. 181/J5
Hazel Crest, Ill. 222/B6
Hazeldean, New Bruns. 170/C2
Hazel Dell, Ill. 222/E4
Hazel Dell, Sask. 181/H4
Hazeldine, Alberta 182/E3
Hazel Green, Ala. 195/E1
Hazel Green, Ky. 237/O5
Hazelgreen, Mo. 261/H7
Hazel Green, Wis. 317/F11
Hazel Grove and Bramhall, England 13/H2
Hazel Hill, Nova Scotia 168/G3
Hazelhurst, Ill. 222/D2
Hazel Hurst, Pa. 294/E2
Hazelhurst, Wis. 317/G4
Hazel Park, Mich. 250/B6
Hazel Patch, Ky. 237/N6
Hazelridge, Manitoba 179/F5
Hazelrigg, Ind. 227/D4
Hazel Run, Minn. 255/C6
Hazelton, Br. Col. 162/D5
Hazelton, Br. Col. 184/D2
Hazelton (mts.), Br. Col. 184/C2
Hazelton, Idaho 220/E7
Hazelton, Kansas 232/D4
Hazelton, N. Dak. 282/K7
Hazelton, W. Va. 312/G3
Hazelton (peak), Wyo. 319/E1
Hazelwood, Ind. 227/D5
Hazelwood, Mo. 261/P2
Hazelwood, N.C. 281/C4
Hazen (bay), Alaska 196/E2
Hazen, Ark. 202/G4
Hazen, Nev. 266/C3
Hazen, N. Dak. 282/G5
Hazen (lake), N.W. Terr. 187/L1
Hazen (str.), N.W. Terr. 187/G2
Hazenmore, Sask. 181/D6
Hazerim, Israel 65/B5
Hazlehurst, Georgia 217/G7
Hazlehurst, Miss. 256/D7
Hazlet, N.J. 273/E3
Hazlet, Sask. 181/C5
Hazleton, Ind. 227/B8
Hazleton, Iowa 229/K3
Hazleton, Pa. 294/L4
Hazlett (lake), W. Australia 88/D4
Hazlettville, Del. 245/R4
Hazor Hagelilit, Israel 65/D2
Hazro, Turkey 63/J3
Heacham, England 13/H5
Headford, Ireland 17/C5
Headland, Ala. 195/H8
Headlee, Ind. 227/D3
Head of Amherst, Nova Scotia 168/E3
Head of Bay d'Espoir, Newf. 166/C4
Head of Bight (bay), S. Australia 94/B4
Head of Grassy, Ky. 237/P4
Head of Island, La. 238/L2
Head of Jeddore, Nova Scotia 168/E4
Head of Millstream, New Bruns. 170/E3
Head of Saint Margarets Bay, Nova Scotia 168/E4
Headquarters, Idaho 220/C3
Headrick, Okla. 288/H5
Heads, The (prom.), Oreg. 291/C5
Heads of Ayr (cape), Scotland 15/D5
Head Waters, Va. 307/K4
Heafford Junction, Wis. 317/G4
Healdsburg, Calif. 204/B5
Healdton, Okla. 288/M6
Healdville, Vt. 268/B5
Healesville, Victoria 97/C5
Healing Springs, Ala. 195/B7
Healing Springs, Va. 307/J5
Healy, Alaska 196/J2
Healy, Kansas 232/B3
Healys, Va. 307/R5
Heanor, England 13/F4
Heard (isl.), Australia 2/N8
Heard (co.), Georgia 217/B4
Hearne, Sask. 181/F5
Hearne, Texas 303/H7
Hearst (isl.), Ant. 5/B16
Hearst, Ont. 162/H6
Hearst, Ontario 177/J5
Hearst, Ontario 175/D3
Heart (lake), Alberta 182/E2
Heart (butte), N. Dak. 282/G6
Heart (riv.), N. Dak. 282/F6
Heart (lake), Wyo. 319/B1
Heart Butte, Mont. 262/C2
Heart River Settlement, Alberta 182/B2
Heart's Content, Newf. 166/D2
Heart's Delight, Newf. 166/D2
Heart's Desire, Newf. 166/D2
Hearts Hill, Sask. 181/B3
Heartwell, Nebr. 264/F4
Heartwellville, Vt. 268/A6
Heaters, W. Va. 312/E5
Heath, Ala. 195/F8
Heath, Alberta 182/E3
Heath (riv.), Bolivia 136/A3
Heath•, Mass. 249/C2
Heath, Mont. 262/G3
Heath, Ohio 284/F5
Heath (riv.), Peru 128/H9
Heath (pt.), Québec 174/E3
Heathcote, Victoria 97/C5
Heatherton, Newf. 166/C4
Heatherton, Nova Scotia 168/G3
Heathhall, Scotland 15/E5
Heath Springs, S.C. 296/F2
Heath Steele, New Bruns. 170/D1
Heathsville, Va. 307/P5
Heaton, N. Dak. 282/L5
Heavener, Okla. 288/S5
Hebbardsville, Ky. 237/G5
Hebbronville, Texas 303/F10
Hebbs Cross, Nova Scotia 168/D4
Hebburn, England 13/J3
Hebei (Hopei), China 77/J4
Hebel, Queensland 95/C6
Heber, Ariz. 198/E4
Heber, Calif. 204/K11
Heber City, Utah 304/C3
Heber Springs, Ark. 202/G2
Hebert, La. 238/G2
Hébert (riv.), Nova Scotia 168/D3
Hébertville, Québec 172/F1
Hébertville-Station, Québec 172/F1
Hebgen (dam), Mont. 262/E6
Hebgen (lake), Mont. 262/E6
Hebi, China 77/H4
Hebo, Oreg. 291/D2
Hebrides, Inner (isls.), Scotland 10/C2
Hebrides, Inner (isls.), Scotland 15/B4
Hebrides, Outer (isls.), Scotland 10/C2
Hebrides, Outer (isls.), Scotland 15/A3
Hebrides (sea), Scotland 15/B3
Hebrides (sea), Scotland 10/C2
Hebron•, Conn. 210/F2
Hebron, Ill. 222/E1
Hebron, Ind. 227/C2
Hebron, Ky. 237/R2
Hebron•, Maine 243/C7
Hebron, Md. 245/R7
Hebron, Nebr. 264/G4
Hebron (fjord), Newf. 166/B2
Hebron•, N.H. 268/D4
Hebron, N. Dak. 282/G6
Hebron, Nova Scotia 168/B5
Hebron, Ohio 284/E6
Hebron, Texas 303/G1
Hebron, West Bank 65/C4
Hebron, West Bank 59/C3
Hebron, W. Va. 312/D4
Hebron, Wis. 317/J10
Hecate (str.), Br. Col. 162/C5
Hecate (str.), Br. Col. 146/E4
Hecate (str.), Br. Col. 184/B3
Hecelchakán, Mexico 150/O6
Heceta (isl.), Alaska 196/M2
Heceta (head), Oreg. 291/C3
Hechi, China 77/G7
Hechingen, Germany 22/C4
Hechuan (Hochwan), China 77/G5
Hecker, Ill. 222/D5
Hecla, Manitoba 179/F3
Hecla (isl.), Manitoba 179/F3
Hecla, S. Dak. 298/N2
Hecla Prov. Park, Manitoba 179/F3
Hector, Ark. 202/E3
Hector, Minn. 255/D6
Hector, N.Y. 276/G5
Hede, Sweden 18/H5
Hedemora, Sweden 18/K6
Hedenäset, Sweden 18/N3
Hedensted, Denmark 21/C6
Hedgesville, Mont. 262/G4
Hedgesville, W. Va. 312/K3
Hedley, Br. Col. 184/G5
Hedley, Texas 303/D3
Hedmark (co.), Norway 18/G6
Hedon, England 13/G4
Hedrick, Iowa 229/J6
Hedville, Kansas 232/E3
Hedwig Village, Texas 303/H1
Heemskerk, Netherlands 27/F3
Heemstede, Netherlands 27/F4
Heer, Netherlands 27/H7
Heerde, Netherlands 27/H4
Heerenveen, Netherlands 27/H3
Heerhugowaard, Netherlands 27/F3
Heerlen, Netherlands 27/J7
Heesch, Netherlands 27/G5
Hefei (Hofei), China 77/J5
Hefei, China 54/N6
Heffley Creek, Br. Col. 184/G5
Heflin, Ala. 195/G3
Heflin, La. 238/D2
Hegang (Hokang), China 77/L2
Hegang, China 54/O5
Hegau (reg.), Germany 22/C5
Hegeler, Ill. 222/F3
Hegins, Pa. 294/K4
Heiban, Sudan 111/F5
Heiberger, Ala. 195/D5
Heide, Germany 22/C1
Heidelberg, Germany 22/C4
Heidelberg, Ky. 237/O5
Heidelberg, Minn. 255/E6
Heidelberg, Miss. 256/F7
Heidelberg, Pa. 294/B7
Heidelberg, S. Africa 118/J7
Heidelberg, Victoria 97/J5
Heidelberg, Victoria 88/L7
Heiden, Switzerland 39/H2
Heidenau, Germany 22/E3
Heidenheim an der Brenz, Germany 22/D4
Heidenreichstein, Austria 41/C2
Heidrick, Ky. 237/O7
Heihe (Aihui) (Aigun), China 77/L1
Heijo (P'yŏngyang) (cap.), N. Korea 81/C4
Heil, N. Dak. 282/G7
Heilbron, S. Africa 118/D5
Heilbronn, Germany 22/C4
Heiligenblut, Austria 41/B3
Heiligenhafen, Germany 22/D1
Heiligenstadt, Germany 22/D3
Heilman, Ind. 227/C8
Heilongjiang (Heilungkiang), China 77/K2
Heilong Jiang (Amur) (riv.), China 77/L2
Heiloo, Netherlands 27/F3
Heilwood, Pa. 294/E4
Heimberg, Switzerland 39/E3
Heimdal, N. Dak. 282/L4
Heinola, Finland 18/P6
Heinola, Minn. 255/C4
Heinsburg, Alberta 182/E3
Heinze Chaung (bay), Burma 72/C4
Heise, Idaho 220/G6
Heiskell, Tenn. 237/O8
Heisler, Alberta 182/D3
Heislerville, N.J. 273/D5
Heisson, Wash. 310/C5
Heist-Knokke, Belgium 27/C6
Heist-op-den-Berg, Belgium 27/F6
Heizer, Kansas 232/D3
Hejaz (reg.), Saudi Arabia 59/C4
Hejian, China 77/J4
Hejing, China 77/C3
Hekimhan, Turkey 63/G3
Hekla (mt.), Iceland 4/C11
Hekla (mt.), Iceland 7/C2
Hekla (vol.), Iceland 21/B1
Hekou, China 77/F7
Hel, Poland 47/D1
Hel (pen.), Poland 47/D1
Helan, China 77/G4
Heldens (pt.), St. Kitts & Nevis 161/C10
Helechawa, Ky. 237/P5
Helen, Georgia 217/E1
Helen, Md. 245/M7
Helen (lake), N. Dak. 282/K5
Helena, Ala. 195/E4
Helena, Ark. 202/J4
Helena, Calif. 204/B3
Helena, Georgia 217/G6
Helena, Mo. 261/C3
Helena (cap.), Mont. 146/G5
Helena (cap.), Mont. 188/D1
Helena (cap.), Mont. 262/E4
Helena (lake), Mont. 262/E4
Helena, N.Y. 276/L1
Helena, Ohio 284/D3
Helena, Okla. 288/K1
Helena, S.C. 296/D3
Helensburgh, N.S. Wales 97/F4
Helensburgh, Scotland 10/A1
Helensburgh, Scotland 15/A1
Helen Springs, North. Terr. 93/C5
Helensville, N. Zealand 100/B1
Helenville, Wis. 317/J10
Helenwood, Tenn. 237/M8
Helez, Israel 65/B4

Hillsborough 381

Helgoland (bay), Germany 22/C1
Helgoland (isl.), Germany 22/B1
Heliopolis, Egypt 111/J3
Helix, Oreg. 291/J2
Hellam, Pa. 294/J6
Hell Canyon (creek), S. Dak. 298/B6
Hellebaek, Denmark 21/F5
Hellendoorn, Netherlands 27/J4
Hellertown, Pa. 294/M4
Helles (cape), Turkey 63/B6
Hellevoetsluis, Netherlands 27/E5
Hellier, Ky. 237/S6
Hellín, Spain 33/F3
Hells (canyon), Idaho 220/B4
Hells Canyon (dam), Idaho 220/B4
Hells Canyon (dam), Oreg. 291/L2
Hells Canyon Nat'l Rec. Area, Idaho 220/B4
Hells Canyon Nat'l Rec. Area, Oreg. 291/K2
Hells Canyon Nat'l Rec. Area, Wash. 310/H5
Hells Half Acre, Wyo. 319/E2
Hell-Ville, Madagascar 102/G6
Hell-Ville, Madagascar 118/H2
Helm, Miss. 256/C4
Helmand (riv.), Afghanistan 54/H6
Helmand (riv.), Afghanistan 59/J3
Helmand (riv.), Afghanistan 68/B2
Helmand (Sistan, Daryacheh-ye) (lake), Iran 66/M5
Helmer, Ind. 227/G1
Helmetta, N.J. 273/E3
Helmond, Netherlands 27/H6
Helmsburg, Ind. 227/E6
Helmsdale, Scotland 10/E1
Helmsdale, Scotland 15/E2
Helmsdale (riv.), Scotland 15/E2
Helmsley, England 13/G3
Helmstedt, Germany 22/D2
Helmville, Mont. 262/C4
Helotes, Texas 303/J10
Helper, Utah 304/D4
Helsenhorn (mt.), Switzerland 39/F4
Helsingborg, Sweden 18/H8
Helsingborg, Sweden 7/F3
Helsinge, Denmark 21/F6
Helsingør, Denmark 21/F6
Helsingør, Denmark 18/H8
Helsinki (cap.), Finland 18/O6
Helsinki (cap.), Finland 7/G2
Helsinki (cap.), Finland 2/L2
Helston, England 13/B7
Helston, England 10/D5
Helston, Manitoba 179/C4
Helton, Ky. 237/P7
Helton, N.C. 281/G1
Heltonville, Ind. 227/E7
Helvecia, Argentina 143/F5
Helvetia, Pa. 294/E3
Helvetia, W. Va. 312/F5
Helvick (head), Ireland 17/G7
Helwân, Egypt 59/B4
Helwân, Egypt 111/J3
Hemar (dry riv.), Israel 65/C5
Hemaruka, Alberta 182/E4
Hematite, Mo. 261/L6
Hemel Hempstead, England 10/F5
Hemel Hempstead, England 13/G7
Hemet, Calif. 204/H10
Hemford, Nova Scotia 168/D4
Hemingford, Nebr. 264/A2
Hemingway, S.C. 296/J4
Hemlock, Ind. 227/F4
Hemlock, Mich. 250/E5
Hemlock, N.Y. 276/E5
Hemlock (lake), N.Y. 276/E5
Hemlock, Ohio 284/F6
Hemlock (Eureka), S.C. 296/E2
Hemlock Grove, Ohio 284/F7
Hemmingford, Québec 172/D4
Hemnes, Norway 18/J3
Hemphill (co.), Texas 303/D2
Hemphill, Texas 303/L6
Hemphill, W. Va. 312/C8
Hemple, Mo. 261/D3
Hempstead (co.), Ark. 202/C6
Hempstead, N.Y. 276/R7
Hempstead, Texas 303/J7
Hemse, Sweden 18/L8
Henagar, Ala. 195/G1
Henan (Honan), China 77/H5
Henan, China 77/F5
Hen and Chickens (isls.), N. Zealand 100/E1
Henares (riv.), Spain 33/G4
Henbury, North. Terr. 93/C8
Hendaye, France 28/C6
Hendek, Turkey 63/D2
Henderson, Ala. 195/F7
Henderson (co.), Ill. 222/C3
Henderson, Ill. 222/C2
Henderson (riv.), Ill. 222/C2
Henderson, Ind. 227/F5
Henderson, Iowa 229/B6
Henderson (co.), Ky. 237/F5
Henderson, Ky. 237/F5
Henderson, La. 238/G6
Henderson, Md. 245/P4
Henderson, Minn. 255/E6
Henderson, Nebr. 264/G4
Henderson, Nev. 266/G6
Henderson, N.Y. 276/H3
Henderson, N. Zealand 100/B1
Henderson (co.), N.C. 281/D4
Henderson, N.C. 281/N2
Henderson (isl.), Pitcairn Is. 87/O8
Henderson (co.), Tenn. 237/E9
Henderson, Tenn. 237/D10
Henderson (co.), Texas 303/J5
Henderson, Texas 303/K5
Henderson, W. Va. 312/B5
Hendersonville, N.C. 281/E4
Hendersonville, Pa. 294/B5
Hendersonville, S.C. 296/F6
Hendersonville, Tenn. 237/H8
Hendley, Nebr. 264/D4
Hendon, Sask. 181/H3
Hendorabi (isl.), Iran 66/H7
Hendra, Queensland 88/K2
Hendricks (co.), Ind. 227/D5
Hendricks, Ky. 237/P5
Hendricks, Minn. 255/B6
Hendricks, W. Va. 312/G4
Hendrickson, Mo. 261/M9
Hendrix, Okla. 288/O7
Hendrix Lake, Br. Col. 184/G4
Hendrum, Minn. 255/B3
Hendry (co.), Fla. 212/E5
Hendrysburg, Ohio 284/H5
Henefer, Utah 304/C2
Hengchun, China 77/K7
Hengduan Shan (mts.), China 77/E6
Hengelo, Gelderland, Netherlands 27/J4
Hengelo, Overijssel, Netherlands 27/K4
Hengshan, China 77/G4
Hengshui, China 77/J4
Heng Xian, China 77/G7
Hengyang, China 77/H6
Hengyang, China 54/N7
Henik (lakes), N.W. Terr. 187/J3
Hénin-Beaumont, France 28/E2
Henjam (isl.), Iran 66/J7
Henlawson, W. Va. 312/B7
Henley, Mo. 261/H6
Henley and Grange, S. Australia 88/D8
Henley Harbour, Newf. 166/C3
Henley on Klip, S. Africa 118/H7
Henley-on-Thames, England 13/G8
Henlopen (cape), Del. 245/T5
Henlopen Acres, Del. 245/T6
Henne, Denmark 21/B6
Hennebont, France 28/B4
Hennef, Germany 22/B3
Hennepin, Ill. 222/D2
Hennepin (co.), Minn. 255/E5
Hennepin, Okla. 288/M5
Hennessey, Okla. 288/L2
Hennigsdorf bei Berlin, Germany 22/E3
Henniker, N.H. 268/D5
Henniker•, N.H. 268/D5
Henning, Ill. 222/F3
Henning, Minn. 255/C4
Henning, Tenn. 237/B9
Henribourg, Sask. 181/F2
Henrico (co.), Va. 307/O6
Henrietta, Mo. 261/E4
Henrietta, N.Y. 276/E4
Henrietta, N.C. 281/F4
Henrietta, Texas 303/F4
Henrietta Maria (cape), Ont. 162/H4
Henrietta Maria (cape), Ontario 175/D1
Henriette, Minn. 255/E5
Henrieville, Utah 304/C6
Henry (co.), Ala. 195/H7
Henry (co.), Georgia 217/D4
Henry, Idaho 220/G7
Henry (co.), Ill. 222/C2
Henry, Ill. 222/D2
Henry (co.), Ind. 227/G5
Henry (co.), Iowa 229/K6
Henry (co.), Ky. 237/L4
Henry (co.), Mo. 261/E6
Henry, Nebr. 264/A2
Henry (isl.), Nova Scotia 168/G3
Henry (co.), Ohio 284/B3
Henry, S.C. 296/J4
Henry, S. Dak. 298/P4
Henry (co.), Tenn. 237/E8
Henry, Tenn. 237/E8
Henry (mts.), Utah 304/D6
Henry (co.), Va. 307/J7
Henry, Va. 307/J7
Henry (cape), Va. 307/R7
Henryetta, Okla. 288/O4
Henry House, Alberta 182/B3
Henry Kater (cape), N.W. Terr. 187/M3
Henrys (lake), Idaho 220/G5
Henrys Fork, Snake (riv.), Idaho 220/G5
Henrys Fork, Green (riv.), Wyo. 319/C4
Henryton, Md. 245/L3
Henryville, Ind. 227/F7
Henryville, Pa. 294/M3
Henryville, Québec 172/D4
Henryville, Tenn. 237/G10
Hensall, Ontario 177/C4
Hensel, N. Dak. 282/P2
Henshaw, Ky. 237/F5
Hensies, Belgium 27/D8
Hensler, N. Dak. 282/H5
Hensley, Ark. 202/F4
Henson (creek), Md. 245/F6
Hentiy, Mongolia 77/H2
Henty, N.S. Wales 97/D4
Henzada, Burma 72/B3
Henzada, Burma 54/L8
Hepburn, Iowa 229/C7
Hepburn, Ohio 284/D4
Hepburn, Sask. 181/E3
Hephzibah, Georgia 217/H4
Hepler, Kansas 232/H4
Heppner, Oreg. 291/H2
Hepu (Hoppo), China 77/G7
Hepworth, Ontario 177/C3
Hepzibah, W. Va. 312/F4
Hequ, China 77/H4
Herald, Calif. 204/C9
Heralds (cays), Australia 95/D3
Herat, Afghanistan 54/H6
Herat, Afghanistan 59/H3
Herat, Afghanistan 68/A2
Hérault (dept.), France 28/E6
Hérault (riv.), France 28/E6
Herbert, Ala. 195/E8
Herbert (riv.), Queensland 88/H3
Herbert, Sask. 181/D5
Herbert Hoover Nat'l Hist. Site, Iowa 229/L5
Herbes (isl.), Ala. 195/B10
Herbeumont, Belgium 27/G9
Herb Lake, Manitoba 179/H3
Herborn, Germany 22/C3
Herbst, Ind. 227/F3
Herbster, Wis. 317/D2
Herceg Novi, Yugoslavia 45/D4
Herchmer, Man. 162/G4
Herchmer, Manitoba 179/K2
Herculaneum, Mo. 261/M6
Hercules, Calif. 204/J1
Herd, Okla. 288/O1
Heredia, C. Rica 154/E5
Hereford, Ariz. 198/E7
Hereford, Colo. 208/L1
Hereford, England 13/E5
Hereford, England 10/E4
Hereford, Md. 245/M2
Hereford (inlet), N.J. 273/D5
Hereford, Oreg. 291/K3
Hereford, Pa. 294/L5
Hereford, S. Dak. 298/D5
Hereford, Texas 303/B3
Hereford and Worcester (co.), England 13/E5
Hérémence, Switzerland 39/D4
Herencia, Spain 33/E3
Herentals, Belgium 27/F6
Heretaunga-Pinehaven, N. Zealand 100/C2
Herford, Germany 22/C2
Hergiswil, Switzerland 39/F3
Héricourt, France 28/G4
Heringsdorf, Germany 22/F1
Herington, Kansas 232/E3
Heriot Bay, Br. Col. 184/E5
Herisau, Switzerland 39/H2
Herkimer, Kansas 232/F2
Herkimer (co.), N.Y. 276/L4
Herkimer, N.Y. 276/L4
Herlen Gol (Kerulen) (riv.), Mongolia 77/H2
Herlong, Calif. 204/E3
Herm (isl.), Chan. Is. 13/E8
Hermagor-Preseggersee, Austria 41/B3
Herman, Mich. 250/A2
Herman, Minn. 255/B5
Herman, Nebr. 264/H3
Herman, Pa. 294/C4
Herman (lake), S. Dak. 298/P5
Herma Ness (prom.), Scotland 15/G2
Hermann, Mo. 261/K5
Hermannsburg, North. Terr. 88/E4
Hermannsburg, North. Terr. 93/C7
Hermansverk, Norway 18/E6
Hermansville, Mich. 250/B3
Hermantown, Minn. 255/F4
Hermanus, S. Africa 118/G7
Hermanville, Miss. 256/C7
Hermidale, N.S. Wales 97/D2
Hermil, Lebanon 63/G5
Herminie, Pa. 294/C5
Hermiston, Oreg. 291/H2
Hermitage, Ark. 202/F7
Hermitage, Grenada 161/D8
Hermitage, Mo. 261/F7
Hermitage, Newf. 166/C4
Hermitage (bay), Newf. 166/C4
Hermitage Springs, Tenn. 237/K7
Hermite (isls.), Chile 138/F11
Hermleigh, Texas 303/D5
Hermon, Ill. 222/C3
Hermon•, Maine 243/F6
Hermon, N.Y. 276/K2
Hermon (mt.), Syria 63/F6
Hermosa (peak), Colo. 208/D7
Hermosa, S. Dak. 298/C6
Hermosa Beach, Calif. 204/B11
Hermosillo, Mexico 146/G7
Hermosillo, Mexico 150/D2
Hermsdorf, Germany 22/E3
Hernád (riv.), Hungary 41/F2
Hernandarias, Argentina 143/F5
Hernandarias, Paraguay 144/E4
Hernández, Argentina 143/F6
Hernandez, N. Mex. 274/C2
Hernando, Argentina 143/D3
Hernando (co.), Fla. 212/D3
Hernando, Fla. 212/D3
Hernando, Miss. 256/E1
Herndon, Georgia 217/H5
Herndon, Iowa 229/E5
Herndon, Kansas 232/B2
Herndon, Ky. 237/G7
Herndon, Pa. 294/J4
Herndon, Va. 307/O3
Herndon, W. Va. 312/D7
Herne, Belgium 27/E7
Herne, Germany 22/B3
Herning, Denmark 18/F8
Herning, Denmark 21/B5
Herod, Georgia 217/D7
Herod, Ill. 222/E6
Heroica Caborca, Mexico 150/C1
Heroica Nogales, Mexico 150/D1
Heron (lake), Minn. 255/C7
Heron, Mont. 262/A2
Heron (isl.), New Bruns. 170/D1
Heron Bay, Ontario 177/H5
Heron Bay, Ontario 175/C3
Heron Lake, Minn. 255/C7
Hérouxville, Québec 172/E3
Herradura, Argentina 143/E2
Herradura, Cuba 158/B1
Herreid, S. Dak. 298/K2
Herrera, Argentina 143/D2
Herrera del Duque, Spain 33/D3
Herrera de Pisuerga, Spain 33/D1
Herrero (pt.), Mexico 150/Q7
Herrick, Ill. 222/D4
Herrick, S. Dak. 298/L7
Herrick, Tasmania 99/D3
Herrick Center, Pa. 294/L2
Herrin, Ill. 222/E6
Herring Cove, Nova Scotia 168/E4
Herrings, N.Y. 276/J2
Herrington (lake), Ky. 237/M5
Herron, Mich. 250/F3
Herronton, Alberta 182/D4
Hersbruck, Germany 22/D4
Herschel, Sask. 181/C4
Herschel (isl.), Yukon 187/E3
Herscher, Ill. 222/E2
Herselt, Belgium 27/F6
Hersey, Mich. 250/D5
Hersey, Wis. 317/B6
Hershey, Nebr. 264/D3
Hershey, Pa. 294/J5
Hersman, Ill. 222/C4
Herstal, Belgium 27/H7
Hertel, Wis. 317/B4
Hertford, England 13/H7
Hertford, England 10/G5
Hertford (co.), N.C. 281/P2
Hertford, N.C. 281/S2
Hertfordshire (co.), England 13/G6
Hervás, Spain 33/D2
Herve, Belgium 27/H7
Hervey (bay), Queensland 88/J4
Hervey (bay), Queensland 95/E5
Hervey Bay, Queensland 88/J5
Hervey Bay, Queensland 95/E5
Herzberg, Germany 22/E3
Herzeliyya, Israel 65/B3
Herzogenbuchsee, Switzerland 39/E2
Herzogenburg, Austria 41/C2
Heshui, China 77/G4
Hesketh, Alberta 182/D4
Hesper, Iowa 229/K2
Hesper, N. Dak. 282/L4
Hesperange, Luxembourg 27/J9
Hesperia, Calif. 204/H9
Hesperia, Mich. 250/D5
Hespero, Alberta 182/C3
Hesperus, Colo. 208/C8
Hesperus (mt.), Colo. 208/C8
Hess, Okla. 288/H6
Hess (riv.), Yukon 187/E3
Hesse (state), Germany 22/C3
Hessel, Mich. 250/E2
Hessmer, La. 238/F4
Hesston, Kansas 232/E3
Hesston, Pa. 294/F5
Hester, La. 238/L3
Hester, Okla. 288/H5
Hesterville, Miss. 256/E4
Hetch Hetchy (res.), Calif. 204/F6
Heth, Ark. 202/K3
Het IJ (est.), Netherlands 27/C4
Hetland, S. Dak. 298/P5
Hettick, Ill. 222/C4
Hettinger (co.), N. Dak. 282/E7
Hettinger, N. Dak. 282/E8
Hetton, England 13/J3
Hettstedt, Germany 22/D3
Heusden, Netherlands 27/G5
Heuvelland, Belgium 27/B7
Heuvelton, N.Y. 276/K1
Heves (co.), Hungary 41/F3
Heves, Hungary 41/F3
Heward, Sask. 181/H6
Hewins, Kansas 232/F4
Hewitt, Minn. 255/C4
Hewitt, N.J. 273/E1
Hewitt, Wis. 317/F6
Hewlett, N.Y. 276/P7
Hewlett Harbor, N.Y. 276/P7
Hexham, England 13/E3
Hexham, England 10/E3
He Xian, China 77/M7
Hexigten, China 77/J3
Hext, Texas 303/E7
Heybeli (isl.), Turkey 63/D6
Heybridge, Tasmania 99/C3
Heyburn, Idaho 220/E7
Heyburn (res.), Okla. 288/O3
Heyden, Ontario 177/J5
Heyfield, Victoria 97/D6
Heyuan, China 77/H7
Heywood (chan.), Burma 72/B3
Heywood, England 13/H2
Heywood, Victoria 97/A6
Heyworth, Ill. 222/E3
Heze, China 77/J4
Hezuo, China 77/F5
Hialeah, Fla. 188/K5
Hialeah, Fla. 212/B4
Hialeah Gardens, Fla. 212/B4
Hiattville, Kansas 232/H4
Hiawassee, Georgia 217/E1
Hiawatha, Iowa 229/K4
Hiawatha, Kansas 232/G2
Hiawatha, Mich. 250/C2
Hiawatha, Utah 304/D4
Hibbard, Ind. 227/E2
Hibbing, Minn. 188/H1
Hibbing, Minn. 255/F3
Hibbs (pt.), Tasmania 99/B4
Hibernia, N.J. 273/E2
Hibuson (isl.), Philippines 82/E5
Hicacos (pen.), Cuba 158/D1
Hicacos (pt.), Cuba 158/D1
Hickam A.F.B., Hawaii 218/B4
Hickam Housing, Hawaii 218/B4
Hickman, Ark. 202/L2
Hickman, Del. 245/R5
Hickman (co.), Ky. 237/C7
Hickman, Ky. 237/C7
Hickman, Nebr. 264/H4
Hickman (co.), Tenn. 237/G9
Hickman, Tenn. 237/K8
Hickman's Harbour, Newf. 166/D2
Hickok, Kansas 232/A4
Hickory, Ky. 237/D7
Hickory, Miss. 256/F6
Hickory (co.), Mo. 261/F7
Hickory, N.C. 281/G3
Hickory, Okla. 288/N5
Hickory Corners, Mich. 250/D6
Hickory Creek, Texas 303/F1
Hickory Flat, Ala. 195/H4
Hickory Flat, Miss. 256/F1
Hickory Grove, S.C. 296/E2
Hickory Hills, Ill. 222/B6
Hickory Plains, Ark. 202/G3
Hickory Ridge, Ark. 202/J3
Hickory Valley, Tenn. 237/C10
Hickory Withe, Tenn. 237/B10
Hickox, Georgia 217/H8
Hicks, La. 238/E4
Hickson, N. Dak. 282/S6
Hickson, Ontario 177/D4
Hicksville, N.Y. 276/R7
Hicksville, Ohio 284/A3
Hico, La. 238/E1
Hico, Texas 303/F6
Hico, W. Va. 312/D6
Hida (riv.), Japan 81/H6
Hidalgo, Ill. 222/E4
Hidalgo, Ky. 237/M7
Hidalgo (state), Mexico 150/K6
Hidalgo, Coahuila, Mexico 150/K3
Hidalgo, Tamaulipas, Mexico 150/K4
Hidalgo (co.), N. Mex. 274/A7
Hidalgo (co.), Texas 303/F11
Hidalgo, Texas 303/F11
Hidalgo del Parral (Parral), Mexico 150/G3
Hidden Hills, Calif. 204/B10
Hiddenite, N.C. 281/G3
Hiddensee (isl.), Germany 22/E1
Hieflau, Austria 41/C3
Hienghene, New Caled. 86/G4
Hierro (isl.), Spain 106/A3
Hierro (isl.), Spain 33/A5
Higashiosaka, Japan 81/J8
Higbee, Mo. 261/H4
Higden, Ark. 202/F2
Higdon, Ala. 195/G1
Higganum, Conn. 210/E2
Higgins (lake), Mich. 250/E4
Higgins, Texas 303/D1
Higgins Lake, Mich. 250/E4
Higginson, Ark. 202/G3
Higginsport, Ohio 284/C8
Higginsville, Mo. 261/E4
Higgston, Georgia 217/G6
High, Iowa 229/K5
High (isl.), Ireland 17/A4
High (isl.), Mich. 250/D3
High Atlas (ranges), Morocco 106/C2
High Bluff, Manitoba 179/D4
High Bridge, Ky. 237/M5
High Bridge, N.J. 273/D2
High Bridge, Wis. 317/E3
Highbury, W. Australia 92/B2
High Falls, N.Y. 276/M7
Highfalls, N.C. 281/K4
Highfield-Cascade, Md. 245/J2
Highfill, Ark. 202/B1
Highgate, Jamaica 158/J6
Highgate, Ontario 177/C5
Highgate•, Vt. 268/B2
Highgate Center, Vt. 268/B2
Highgate Falls, Vt. 268/A2
Highgate Springs, Vt. 268/A2
Highgrove, Calif. 204/E10
High Hill, Mo. 261/K5
High Island, Texas 303/K8
Highland, Calif. 204/H9
Highland (lake), Conn. 210/C1
Highland (pt.), Fla. 212/E6
Highland, Ill. 222/D5
Highland, Ind. 227/B1
Highland, Kansas 232/G2
Highland (peak), Nev. 266/G5
Highland (lake), N.H. 268/C5
Highland, N.Y. 276/M7
Highland (co.), Ohio 284/C7
Highland, Ohio 284/C7
Highland (reg.), Scotland 15/D3
Highland, Utah 304/C3
Highland (co.), Va. 307/J4
Highland, W. Va. 312/D4
Highland, Wis. 317/F9
Highland Beach, Fla. 212/F5
Highland Beach, Md. 245/M5
Highland Center, Iowa 229/J6
Highland City, Fla. 212/E4
Highland Falls, N.Y. 276/M8
Highland Heights, Ky. 237/T2
Highland Heights, Ohio 284/J9
Highland Home, Ala. 195/F7
Highland Lake, Ala. 195/F3
Highland Lake, Maine 243/C8
Highland Lakes, N.J. 273/E1
Highland Park, Conn. 210/F1
Highland Park, Fla. 212/E4
Highland Park, Ill. 222/B5
Highland Park, Mich. 250/B6
Highland Park, N.J. 273/D2
Highland Park, Pa. 294/H4
Highland Park, Texas 303/G2
Highlands (co.), Fla. 212/E4
Highlands, N.J. 273/F3
Highlands, N.C. 281/C4
Highlands, Texas 303/K1
Highland Springs, Va. 307/O5
Highland Village, Texas 303/F1
Highlandville, Iowa 229/K2
Highlandville, Mo. 261/F9
High Level, Alberta 182/A5
Highmore, S. Dak. 298/L4
Highpine, Maine 243/B9
High Plateaus (ranges), Algeria 106/D2
High Point, Fla. 212/B3
Highpoint, Miss. 256/F4
High Point, Mo. 261/G5
High Point (mt.), N.J. 273/D1
High Point, N.C. 188/K3
High Point, N.C. 281/J3
High Prairie, Alberta 182/B2
Highridge, Alberta 182/D2
High Ridge, Mo. 261/M6
High River, Alberta 182/D4
High River, Alta. 162/E5
High Rock (creek), Nev. 266/B1
High Rock, N.C. 281/J3
High Rock (lake), N.C. 281/J3
High Rocky (pt.), Tasmania 99/B4
High Rolls-Mountain Park, N. Mex. 274/D5
High Shoals, N.C. 281/G4
Highspire, Pa. 294/J5
Highsplint, Ky. 237/P7
High Springs, Fla. 212/D2
High Tatra (range), Poland 47/D4
Hightower, Ala. 195/H3
Hightown, Va. 307/J4
Hightstown, N.J. 273/D3
Highway, Ky. 237/L7
High Willhays (mt.), England 13/C7
Highwood (riv.), Alberta 182/C4
Highwood, Ill. 222/B5
Highwood, Mont. 262/F3
Highworth, England 13/F6
High Wycombe, England 13/G8
High Wycombe, England 10/F5
Higley, Ariz. 198/D5
Higuerote, Venezuela 124/F2
Higüey, Dom. Rep. 158/F6
Hiiraan (prov.), Somalia 115/J3
Hiiumaa (isl.), U.S.S.R. 7/G3
Hiiumaa (isl.), U.S.S.R. 52/B3
Hiiumaa (isl.), U.S.S.R. 53/B1
Hiiumaa (isl.), U.S.S.R. 48/C4
Híjar, Spain 33/F2
Hijuelas, Chile 138/F2
Hiko, Nev. 266/F5
Hikone, Japan 81/H6
Hikueru (atoll), Fr. Poly. 87/M7
Hikurangi, N. Zealand 100/E1
Hikurangi (mt.), N. Zealand 100/G2
Hiland, Wyo. 319/E2
Hiland Park, Fla. 212/C6
Hilbert, Wis. 317/K7
Hilbre, Manitoba 179/D3
Hilda, Alberta 182/E4
Hilda, S.C. 296/E5
Hildale, Utah 304/A6
Hildburghausen, Germany 22/D3
Hildebran, N.C. 281/F3
Hildebrand, Oreg. 291/F5
Hilden, Nova Scotia 168/E3
Hildesheim, Germany 22/D2
Hildreth, Nebr. 264/E4
Hiles, Wis. 317/J4
Hilgard (mt.), Utah 304/C5
Hilger, Mont. 262/G3
Hilham, Tenn. 237/L8
Hill (riv.), Minn. 255/C3
Hill (co.), Mont. 262/F2
Hill•, N.H. 268/D4
Hill (co.), Texas 303/G5
Hill (creek), Utah 304/E4
Hilla, Iraq 66/D4
Hilla, Iraq 59/D3
Hill A.F.B., Utah 304/C2
Hillaby (mt.), Barbados 161/B8
Hillahdale, Md. 245/F4
Hill Bank, Belize 154/C2
Hillburn, N.Y. 276/M8
Hill City, Idaho 220/D6
Hill City, Kansas 232/C2
Hill City, Minn. 255/E4
Hill City, S. Dak. 298/B6
Hill Country Village, Texas 303/K10
Hill Creek Ext., Uintah and Ouray Ind. Res., Utah 304/E4
Hillcrest, Alberta 182/C5
Hillcrest, Ill. 222/D2
Hillcrest, N.Y. 276/K8
Hillcrest, Texas 303/J3
Hillcrest Heights, Fla. 212/E4
Hillcrest Heights, Md. 245/F5
Hillegom, Netherlands 27/E4
Hillemann, Ark. 202/H3
Hill End, N.S. Wales 97/E3
Hillerød, Denmark 18/H9
Hillerød, Denmark 21/F6
Hillers (mt.), Utah 304/D6
Hillham, Ind. 227/D7
Hillhead, S. Dak. 298/O2
Hillhouse, Miss. 256/C2
Hilliard, Alberta 182/D3
Hilliard, Fla. 212/E1
Hilliard, Ohio 284/D5
Hilliards, Pa. 294/C3
Hilliardville, Fla. 212/B1
Hillingdon, England 10/B5
Hillingdon, England 13/G8
Hillisburg, Ind. 227/E4
Hill Island (lake), N.W. Terr. 187/H3
Hillman, Mich. 250/F3
Hillman, Minn. 255/E4
Hillman, New Bruns. 170/C2
Hillmond, Sask. 181/B2
Hill of Fearn, Scotland 15/D3
Hillridge, Manitoba 179/C3
Hillrose, Colo. 208/N2
Hills, Iowa 229/K5
Hills, Minn. 255/B7
Hillsboro, Ala. 195/D1
Hillsboro, Georgia 217/E4
Hillsboro, Ill. 222/D4
Hillsboro, Ind. 227/C4
Hillsboro, Iowa 229/K7
Hillsboro, Kansas 232/E3
Hillsboro, Ky. 237/O4
Hillsboro, Md. 245/P5
Hillsboro, Miss. 256/E6
Hillsboro, Mo. 261/L6
Hillsboro, N.H. 268/D5
Hillsboro•, N.H. 268/D5
Hillsboro, N. Mex. 274/B6
Hillsboro, N. Dak. 282/S5
Hillsboro, Ohio 284/C7
Hillsboro, Oreg. 291/A2
Hillsboro, Tenn. 237/K10
Hillsboro, Texas 303/G5
Hillsboro, Va. 307/N2
Hillsboro, W. Va. 312/F6
Hillsboro, Wis. 317/F8
Hillsboro Beach, Fla. 212/F5
Hillsboro Lower Village, N.H. 268/D5
Hillsborough, Calif. 204/J2
Hillsborough (co.), Fla. 212/D4
Hillsborough (bay), Fla. 212/C3
Hillsborough (canal), Fla. 212/F5
Hillsborough (riv.), Fla. 212/C2
Hillsborough, New Bruns. 170/F3
Hillsborough (co.), N.H. 268/D6
Hillsborough, N.C. 281/L2
Hillsborough, N. Ireland 17/J3

382 Hillsborough

Hillsborough (bay), Pr. Edward I. 168/E2
Hillsboro Upper Village, N.H. 268/D5
Hillsburgh, Ontario 177/D4
Hillsburn, Nova Scotia 168/C4
Hills Creek (lake), Oreg. 291/E4
Hillsdale, Ill. 222/C2
Hillsdale, Ind. 227/C5
Hillsdale, Kansas 232/H3
Hillsdale (co.), Mich. 250/E7
Hillsdale, Mich. 250/E7
Hillsdale, Mo. 261/R2
Hillsdale, N.J. 273/B1
Hillsdale, N.Y. 276/O6
Hillsdale, Okla. 288/K1
Hillsdale, Ontario 177/E3
Hillsdale, Pa. 294/E4
Hillsdale, Wis. 317/C5
Hillsdale, Wyo. 319/H4
Hillsgrove, Pa. 294/J3
Hillsgrove, R.I. 249/J6
Hillside, Ariz. 198/B4
Hillside, Colo. 208/H6
Hillside, Ill. 222/B5
Hillside•, N.J. 273/B2
Hillside, Scotland 15/F4
Hillside, S. Dak. 298/N7
Hillside Beach, Manitoba 179/F4
Hillsport, Ontario 175/C3
Hillsport, Ontario 177/H5
Hill Spring, Alberta 182/D5
Hillston, N.S. Wales 88/G6
Hillston, N.S. Wales 97/C3
Hillsview, S. Dak. 298/L2
Hillsville, Pa. 294/A4
Hillsville, Va. 307/G7
Hillswick, Scotland 15/G2
Hilltonia, Georgia 217/J5
Hilltop, Ariz. 198/F6
Hilltown, N. Ireland 17/J3
Hillview, Ill. 222/C4
Hillview, Minn. 255/C4
Hillview, Newf. 166/D2
Hilmar-Irwin, Calif. 204/E6
Hilo, Hawaii 87/L4
Hilo, Hawaii 218/J5
Hilo, Hawaii 188/G6
Hilo (bay), Hawaii 218/J5
Hilongos, Philippines 82/E5
Hilshire Village, Texas 303/J1
Hilt, Calif. 204/C2
Hilterfingen, Switzerland 39/E3
Hilton (inlet), Ant. 5/B16
Hilton, Georgia 217/C8
Hilton, Manitoba 179/C5
Hilton, N.Y. 276/E4
Hilton Beach, Ontario 177/J5
Hilton Head (isl.), S.C. 296/F7
Hilton Head Island, S.C. 296/F7
Hiltons, Va. 307/D7
Hilvan, Turkey 63/H4
Hilvarenbeek, Netherlands 27/G6
Hilversum, Netherlands 27/G4
Hima, Ky. 237/O6
Himachal Pradesh (state), India 68/D2
Himalaya (mts.) 54/L7
Himalaya (mts.), Bhutan 68/E2
Himalaya (mts.), China 77/C6
Himalaya (mts.), India 68/D2
Himalaya (mts.), Nepal 68/D2
Himanka, Finland 18/N5
Himeji, Japan 81/G6
Himi, Japan 81/H5
Himlerville (Beauty), Ky. 237/S5
Himrod, N.Y. 276/F5
Himyar, Ky. 237/O7
Hinatuan, Philippines 82/F6
Hinchcliff, Miss. 256/D2
Hinche, Haiti 158/C5
Hinche, Haiti 156/D3
Hinchinbrook (isl.), Alaska 196/D1
Hinchinbrook (isl.), Queensland 88/H3
Hinchinbrook (isl.), Queensland 95/C3
Hinchinbrook Entrance (chan.), Alaska 196/J3
Hinchliffe, Sask. 181/J3
Hinckley, England 10/F4
Hinckley, England 13/F5
Hinckley, Ill. 222/E2
Hinckley, Maine 243/D6
Hinckley, Minn. 255/E4
Hinckley, N.Y. 276/K4
Hinckley (res.), N.Y. 276/K4
Hinckley, Ohio 284/G3
Hinckley, Utah 304/B4
Hindeloopen, Netherlands 27/G3
Hindenburg (Zabrze), Poland 47/A4
Hinderwell, England 13/G3
Hindiya, Iraq 66/C4
Hindman, Ky. 237/R6
Hindmarsh, S. Australia 88/D8
Hindmarsh, S. Australia 94/A7
Hindmarsh (lake), Victoria 97/A5
Hinds (co.), Miss. 256/D6
Hinds, N. Zealand 100/C6
Hindsboro, Ill. 222/E4
Hindsville, Ark. 202/C1
Hindubagh, Pakistan 68/B2
Hindu Kush (mts.) 54/J6
Hindu Kush (mts.), Afghanistan 68/B1
Hindu Kush (mts.), Afghanistan 59/J2
Hindu Kush (mts.), India 68/C1
Hindu Kush (mts.), Pakistan 68/B1
Hindupur, India 68/D6
Hi-Nella, N.J. 273/B4
Hines, Minn. 255/D3
Hines, Oreg. 291/H4
Hinesburg•, Vt. 268/A3
Hines Creek, Alberta 182/A1
Hines Creek, Alta. 162/E4
Hineston, La. 238/E4
Hinesville, Georgia 217/J7
Hinganghat, India 68/D4
Hingham, Mass. 249/E8
Hingham•, Mass. 249/E8
Hingham (bay), Mass. 249/E7
Hingham, Mont. 262/F2
Hingham, Wis. 317/K8
Hingoli, India 68/D5
Hinigaran, Philippines 82/D5
Hınıs, Turkey 63/J3
Hinkley, Calif. 204/H9
Hinkston (creek), Ky. 237/N4
Hinlopenstreten (str.), Norway 18/C1
Hinnerup, Denmark 21/D5
Hinnøya (isl.), Norway 18/K2
Hino, Japan 81/O2
Hinojosa del Duque, Spain 33/D3
Hinsdale (co.), Colo. 208/E7
Hinsdale, Ill. 222/B6
Hinsdale•, Mass. 249/B3
Hinsdale, Mont. 262/K2
Hinsdale, N.H. 268/C6
Hinsdale•, N.H. 268/C6
Hinsdale, N.Y. 276/D6
Hinson, Fla. 212/B1
Hinsonton, Georgia 217/D8
Hinterrhein (riv.), Switzerland 39/H3
Hinton, Alberta 182/B3
Hinton, Iowa 229/A3
Hinton, Mo. 261/H4
Hinton, Okla. 288/K4
Hinton, W. Va. 312/E7
Hintonville, Miss. 256/F8
Hinwil, Switzerland 39/G2
Hinze, Miss. 256/F4
Hippolytushoef, Netherlands 27/G3
Hipswell, England 13/F3
Hirakata, Japan 81/J7
Hiram, Georgia 217/C3
Hiram, Ky. 237/P7
Hiram, Maine 243/B8
Hiram•, Maine 243/B8
Hiram, Mo. 261/M8
Hiram, Ohio 284/H3
Hirara, Japan 81/L7
Hirata, Japan 81/F6
Hiratsuka, Japan 81/O3
Hîrlău, Romania 45/H2
Hiroo, Japan 81/L2
Hirosaki, Japan 81/K3
Hiroshima (pref.), Japan 81/E6
Hiroshima, Japan 54/P6
Hiroshima, Japan 81/E6
Hirsch, Sask. 181/J6
Hirschberg (Jelenia Góra), Poland 47/B3
Hirson, France 28/F3
Hîrşova, Romania 45/J3
Hirtshals, Denmark 21/C2
Hisarönü, Turkey 63/E2
Hisban, Jordan 65/D4
Hisega, S. Dak. 298/C5
Hiseville, Ky. 237/K6
Hisle, S. Dak. 298/F7
Hispaniola (isl.) 146/L7
Hispaniola (isl.), Dom. Rep. 156/D2
Hispaniola (isl.), Haiti 156/D2
Hispaniola (isl.), W. Indies 156/D2
Hissar, India 68/D3
Hissop, Ala. 195/F5
Hit, Iraq 59/D3
Hit, Iraq 66/C4
Hitachi, Japan 81/K5
Hitachiota, Japan 81/K5
Hitchcock (lakes), Conn. 210/D2
Hitchcock (co.), Nebr. 264/C4
Hitchcock, Okla. 288/K3
Hitchcock, Sask. 181/J6
Hitchcock, S. Dak. 298/M4
Hitchcock, Texas 303/K3
Hitchin, England 13/G6
Hitchin, England 10/F5
Hitchins, Ky. 237/R4
Hitchita, Okla. 288/P3
Hiteman, Iowa 229/H6
Hitoyoshi, Japan 81/E7
Hitra (isl.), Norway 18/F5
Hitt, Mo. 261/H1
Hitterdal, Minn. 255/B4
Hitzacker, Germany 22/D2
Hitzkirch, Switzerland 39/F2
Hivaoa (isl.), Fr. Poly. 87/N6
Hiwannee, Miss. 256/G7
Hiwasse, Ark. 202/B1
Hiwassee (lake), N.C. 281/A4
Hiwassee (riv.), N.C. 281/A4
Hiwassee (riv.), Tenn. 237/O10
Hiwassee, Va. 307/G7
Hixon, Br. Col. 184/F3
Hixson, Tenn. 237/L10
Hixton, Wis. 317/E7
Hizan, Turkey 63/K3
Hjallerup, Denmark 21/C3
Hjälmaren (lake), Sweden 18/J7
Hjerm, Denmark 21/B5
Hjerting, Denmark 21/B6
Hjo, Sweden 18/J7
Hjørring, Denmark 18/F8
Hjørring, Denmark 21/C3
Hka, Nam (riv.), Burma 72/C2
Hkakabo Razi (mt.), Burma 72/C1
Hlinsko, Czech. 41/D2
Hlohovec, Czech. 41/D2
Hlučín, Czech. 41/E2
Hmawbi, Burma 72/C3
Hnúšť'a-Likier, Czech. 41/E2
Ho, Ghana 106/E7
Hoa Binh, Vietnam 72/E2
Hoa Da, Vietnam 72/F5
Hoadley, Alberta 182/C3
Hoadly, Va. 307/O3
Hoagland, Ind. 227/H3
Hoai Nhon, Vietnam 72/F4
Hoaksbergen, Netherlands 27/K4
Hoare (bay), N.W. Terr. 187/M3
Hoback (peak), Wyo. 319/B2
Hoback (riv.), Wyo. 319/B2
Hobart, Australia 2/S8
Hobart, Ind. 227/C1
Hobart, N.Y. 276/L6
Hobart, Okla. 288/J5
Hobart (cap.), Tasmania 88/H8
Hobart (cap.), Tasmania 99/D4
Hobart, Wash. 310/D3
Hobbema, Alberta 182/D3
Hobbs, Ind. 227/F4
Hobbs (lake), Manitoba 179/G3
Hobbs, Md. 245/P5
Hobbs, N. Mex. 188/F4
Hobbs, N. Mex. 274/F6
Hobbs Coast (reg.), Ant. 5/B12
Hobbs Island, Ala. 195/F1
Hobbsville, N.C. 281/R2
Hoberg, Mo. 261/E8
Hobe Sound, Fla. 212/F4
Hobgood, N.C. 281/P2
Hoboken, Belgium 27/E6
Hoboken, Georgia 217/H8
Hoboken, N.J. 273/C2
Hoboksar, China 77/C2
Hobro, Denmark 21/C4
Hobro, Denmark 18/F8
Hobson (lake), Br. Col. 184/H4
Hobson, Mont. 262/G4
Hobson City, Ala. 195/G3
Hobsons (bay), Victoria 97/H5
Hobsons (bay), Victoria 88/L7
Hobucken, N.C. 281/S4
Hoburgen (cliff), Sweden 18/L8
Hochdorf, Switzerland 39/F2
Hochfeld, Manitoba 179/E5
Hochgolling (mt.), Austria 41/B3
Ho Chi Minh City, Vietnam 2/Q5
Ho Chi Minh City, Vietnam 54/M8
Ho Chi Minh City, Vietnam 72/E5
Hochwan (Hechuan), China 77/G5
Hochwang (mt.), Switzerland 39/J3
Hockaday, Mich. 250/E4
Hockanum, Conn. 210/E2
Hockanum (riv.), Conn. 210/E1
Hockenheim, Germany 22/C4
Hockerville, Okla. 288/S1
Hockessin, Del. 245/R1
Hocking (co.), Ohio 284/F6
Hocking (riv.), Ohio 284/F7
Hockingport, Ohio 284/G7
Hockley (co.), Texas 303/B4
Hodaka (mt.), Japan 81/H5
Hodder (riv.), England 13/H1
Hoddesdon, England 13/H7
Hodeida, Yemen 54/F8
Hodeida, Yemen 59/D7
Hodgdon•, Maine 243/H3
Hodge, La. 238/E2
Hodge, Mo. 261/E4
Hodgeman (co.), Kansas 232/C3
Hodgen, Okla. 288/S5
Hodgenville, Ky. 237/K5
Hodges, Ala. 195/C2
Hodges, Mont. 262/M4
Hodges, S.C. 296/C3
Hodge's Cove, Newf. 166/D2
Hodgesville, W. Va. 312/F4
Hodgeville, Sask. 181/E5
Hodgkins, Ill. 222/B6
Hodgson, Manitoba 179/E3
Hodh (reg.), Mauritania 106/C5
Hod Hasharon, Israel 65/B3
Hodiyya, Israel 65/B4
Hódmezővásárhely, Hungary 41/F3
Hodonín, Czech. 41/D2
Hoehne, Colo. 208/L8
Hoei (Huy), Belgium 27/G8
Hoek, Netherlands 27/D6
Hoek van Holland (Hook of Holland), Netherlands 27/D4
Hoek van Holland (cape), Netherlands 27/D5
Hoensbroek, Netherlands 27/H7
Hoeryŏng, N. Korea 81/D2
Hoeselt, Belgium 27/G7
Hoey, Sask. 181/F3
Hof, Germany 22/D3
Hofei (Hefei), China 77/J5
Hoffman (mt.), Calif. 204/D2
Hoffman, Ill. 222/D5
Hoffman, Minn. 255/C5
Hoffman, N.C. 281/K4
Hoffman, Okla. 288/P4
Hoffman Estates, Ill. 222/A5
Hofgeismar, Germany 22/C3
Hofors, Sweden 18/K6
Hofs (glac.), Iceland 21/C1
Hofu, Japan 81/E6
Hofuf, Saudi Arabia 59/E4
Hofuf, Saudi Arabia 54/F7
Hog (isl.), Mich. 250/D3
Hog (isl.), Pr. Edward I. 168/E2
Hog (isl.), Va. 307/S6
Hogan, Mo. 261/L7
Hogan (lake), Ontario 177/F2
Höganäs, Sweden 18/H8
Hogan Group (isls.), Tasmania 99/D1
Hogansburg, N.Y. 276/L1
Hogansville, Georgia 217/C4
Hogarth (mt.), North. Terr. 93/E6
Hogatza, Alaska 196/G1
Hogeland, Mont. 262/H2
Hog Island (bay), Va. 307/S6
Hog River (Hogatza), Alaska 196/G1
Hogshead (pt.), Conn. 210/E3
Högyész, Hungary 41/E3
Hoh (head), Wash. 310/A3
Hoh (riv.), Wash. 310/A3
Hohenau, Paraguay 144/E5
Hohenau an der March, Austria 41/D2
Hohenberg, Austria 41/C3
Hohenems, Austria 41/A3
Hohenlinden, Miss. 256/F3
Hohen Neuendorf, Germany 22/E2
Hohen Solms, La. 238/K3
Hohenstollen (mt.), Switzerland 39/F3
Hohenwald, Tenn. 237/F9
Hohe Tauern (range), Austria 41/B3
Hohe Venn (plat.), Belgium 27/H8
Hohe Warte (mt.), Austria 41/B3
Hohhot (Huhehot), China 77/H3
Hohhot, China 54/N5
Hoh Ind. Res., Wash. 310/A3
Hohokam Pima Nat'l Mon., Ariz. 198/D5
Ho Ho Kus, N.J. 273/B1
Hoholitna (riv.), Alaska 196/G2
Hoh Xil Shan (mts.), China 77/C4
Hoi An, Vietnam 72/F4
Hoihow (Haikou), China 77/H7
Hoima, Uganda 115/F3
Hoisington, Kansas 232/D3
Hoi Xuan, Vietnam 72/E2
Højer, Denmark 21/B8
Højslev, Denmark 21/C4
Hokah, Minn. 255/G7
Hokang (Hegang), China 77/L2
Hoke (co.), N.C. 281/L4
Hokes Bluff, Ala. 195/G3
Hokianga (harb.), N. Zealand 100/D1
Hokitika, N. Zealand 100/C5
Hokkaido (pref.), Japan 81/K2
Hokkaido (isl.), Japan 2/S3
Hokkaido (isl.), Japan 54/R5
Hokkaido (isl.), Japan 81/L2
Holabird, S. Dak. 298/K4
Holbaek, Denmark 21/E6
Holbaek, Denmark 18/G9
Holbeach, England 10/F4
Holbeach, England 13/H5
Holbein, Sask. 181/E2
Holberg, Br. Col. 184/C5
Holbrook, Ariz. 198/E4
Holbrook, Idaho 220/F7
Holbrook, Iowa 229/K5
Holbrook•, Mass. 249/D8
Holbrook, Nebr. 264/D4
Holbrook, N.S. Wales 97/D4
Holbrook, Oreg. 291/A1
Holcomb, Ill. 222/D1
Holcomb, Kansas 232/B3
Holcomb, Miss. 256/D3
Holcomb, Mo. 261/N10
Holcomb, N.Y. 276/F5
Holcomb, W. Va. 312/E6
Holcombe, Wis. 317/D5
Holcombe Flowage (res.), Wis. 317/D5
Holden, Alberta 182/D3
Holden, La. 238/M1
Holden•, Mass. 249/G3
Holden, Mo. 261/E5
Holden, Utah 304/B4
Holden, W. Va. 312/B7
Holden Beach, N.C. 281/N7
Holdenville, Okla. 288/O4
Holder, Fla. 212/D3
Holderness (dist.), England 13/G4
Holderness•, N.H. 268/D4
Holdfast, Sask. 181/F5
Holdingford, Minn. 255/D5
Holdrege, Nebr. 264/E4
Holeby, Denmark 21/E8
Holen, Norway 18/D4
Holešov, Czech. 41/D2
Holetown, Barbados 161/B8
Holgate, Ohio 284/B3
Holguín (prov.), Cuba 158/J3
Holguín, Cuba 146/L7
Holguín, Cuba 158/J3
Holguín, Cuba 156/C2
Holič, Czech. 41/D2
Holice, Czech. 41/C1
Holiday Hills, Ill. 222/A4
Holijsloot, Netherlands 27/C4
Holitna (riv.), Alaska 196/G2
Hollabrunn, Austria 41/D2
Holladay, Tenn. 237/E9
Holladay, Utah 304/C3
Hollam's Bird (isl.), Namibia 118/A4
Holland, Georgia 217/B2
Holland, Ind. 227/C8
Holland, Iowa 229/H4
Holland, Ky. 237/J7
Holland, Manitoba 179/D5
Holland•, Mass. 249/F4
Holland, Mich. 250/C6
Holland, Minn. 255/B6
Holland, Mo. 261/N10
Holland, N.Y. 276/C5
Holland, Ohio 284/C2
Holland, Texas 303/G7
Holland•, Vt. 268/D2
Hollandale, Minn. 255/E7
Hollandale, Miss. 256/C4
Hollandale, Wis. 317/G10
Holland Centre, Ontario 177/D3
Hollandia (Jayapura), Indonesia 85/K6
Holland Landing, Ontario 177/E3
Holland Park, Queensland 88/K3
Holland Park, Queensland 95/E3
Holland Patent, N.Y. 276/K4
Hollandsburg, Ind. 227/C5
Hollandstoun, Scotland 15/F1
Hollansburg, Ohio 284/A5
Hollenbeck (riv.), Conn. 210/B1
Hollenberg, Kansas 232/F2
Holley, N.Y. 276/D4
Holley, Oreg. 291/E3
Hollick-Kenyon (plat.), Ant. 5/B13
Holliday, Mo. 261/H3
Holliday, Texas 303/F4
Hollidaysburg, Pa. 294/F5
Hollins, Ala. 195/F4
Hollins College, Va. 307/H6
Hollis, Ark. 202/D4
Hollis, Kansas 232/E2
Hollis•, N.H. 268/D6
Hollis, N.C. 281/F4
Hollis, Okla. 288/G5
Hollis Center•, Maine 243/B8
Hollister, Calif. 204/D7
Hollister, Fla. 212/E2
Hollister, Idaho 220/D7
Hollister, Mo. 261/F9
Hollister, N.C. 281/O2
Hollister, Okla. 288/J6
Hollister, Wis. 317/J5
Holliston•, Mass. 249/A8
Holloman A.F.B., N. Mex. 274/C6
Holloway, Minn. 255/C5
Holloway, Ohio 284/H5
Hollowayville, Ill. 222/D2
Hollow Creek, Ky. 237/K4
Hollow Rock, Tenn. 237/E8
Hollsopple, Pa. 294/E5
Hollum, Netherlands 27/H2
Holly, Colo. 208/P6
Holly, Mich. 250/F6
Holly, Wash. 310/C3
Holly Bluff, Miss. 256/C5
Holly Grove, Ark. 202/H4
Holly Hill, Fla. 212/E2
Holly Hill, S.C. 296/G5
Holly Oak, Del. 245/S1
Holly Pond, Ala. 195/E2
Holly Ridge, La. 238/G2
Holly Ridge, Miss. 256/C4
Holly Ridge, N.C. 281/O6
Holly Shelter (swamp), N.C. 281/O6
Holly Springs, Ark. 202/E6
Holly Springs, Georgia 217/D2
Holly Springs, Miss. 256/E1
Holly Springs, N.C. 281/M3
Hollytree, Ala. 195/F1
Hollyville, Del. 245/T6
Hollywood, Ala. 195/G1
Hollywood, Ark. 202/D5
Hollywood, Calif. 204/C10
Hollywood, Fla. 188/K5
Hollywood, Fla. 212/B4
Hollywood, Georgia 217/E1
Hollywood, La. 238/D6
Hollywood, Md. 245/M7
Hollywood, Miss. 256/D1
Hollywood, S.C. 296/G6
Hollywood, W. Va. 312/F7
Hollywood Park, Texas 303/K10
Holman, N. Mex. 274/D2
Holman (isl.), N.W.T. 187/G2
Holman (isl.), N.W.T. 162/D1
Holman, Canada 4/B15
Holman, N.W. Terr. 187/G2
Holmdel•, N.J. 273/E3
Holmen, Wis. 317/D8
Holmes (reef), Australia 95/C3
Holmes (reef), Coral Sea Is. Terr. 88/H3
Holmes (co.), Fla. 212/C5
Holmes (creek), Fla. 212/D5
Holmes, Iowa 229/F3
Holmes (co.), Miss. 256/D4
Holmes (co.), Ohio 284/G4
Holmes (mt.), Wyo. 319/B1
Holmes Beach, Fla. 212/D4
Holmes City, Minn. 255/C5
Holmeson, N.J. 273/E3
Holmestrand, Norway 18/C4
Holmesville, Miss. 256/D8
Holmesville, Nebr. 264/H4
Holmesville, New Bruns. 170/C2
Holmesville, Ohio 284/G4
Holmesville, Ontario 177/C4
Holmfield, Manitoba 179/C5
Holmfirth, England 13/J2
Holmquist, S. Dak. 298/O3
Holmsbu, Norway 18/D4
Holmsund, Sweden 18/M5
Holmwood, La. 238/D6
Holon, Israel 65/B3
Holopaw, Fla. 212/E3
Holroyd, N.S. Wales 97/H3
Holroyd (riv.), Queensland 95/B2
Holstebro, Denmark 18/F8
Holstebro, Denmark 21/B5
Holsted, Denmark 21/B6
Holstein, Iowa 229/B4
Holstein, Mo. 261/K5
Holstein, Nebr. 264/F4
Holstein, Ontario 177/D3
Holsteinsborg (Sisimiut), Greenl. 4/C12
Holston (riv.), Tenn. 237/O8
Holston, Va. 307/D7
Holston, North Fork (riv.), Va. 307/D7
Holston Valley, Tenn. 237/S7
Holsworthy, England 10/D5
Holsworthy, England 13/C7
Holt, Ala. 195/D4
Holt (dam), Ala. 195/D4
Holt, Calif. 204/D6
Holt, England 13/J5
Holt, Fla. 212/C6
Holt, Mich. 250/E6
Holt, Minn. 255/B2
Holt (co.), Mo. 261/B2
Holt, Mo. 261/D4
Holt (co.), Nebr. 264/F2
Holte, Denmark 21/F6
Holter (lake), Mont. 262/D4
Holtland, Tenn. 237/H9
Holton, Ind. 227/G6
Holton, Kansas 232/G2
Holton, La. 238/K5
Holton, Mich. 250/C5
Holton, Newf. 166/C3
Holts Summit, Mo. 261/H5
Holtville, Ala. 195/F5
Holtville, Calif. 204/K11
Holtville, New Bruns. 170/D2
Holtwood, Pa. 294/K6
Holualoa, Hawaii 218/G5
Holualoa, Hawaii 188/F6
Holwerd, Netherlands 27/H2
Holy (isl.), England 13/F2
Holy (isl.), England 10/F3
Holy (isl.), Scotland 15/C5
Holy (isl.), Wales 10/D4
Holy (isl.), Wales 13/C4
Holy City, Calif. 204/K4
Holy Cross, Alaska 196/G2
Holy Cross (mt.), Colo. 208/F4
Holy Cross, Iowa 229/L3
Holycross, Ireland 17/F6
Holy Cross, Wis. 317/L9
Holyhead, Wales 10/D4
Holyhead, Wales 13/C4
Holy Loch (inlet), Scotland 15/A1
Holyoke, Colo. 208/P1
Holyoke, Mass. 249/D4
Holyoke (range), Mass. 249/D3
Holyoke, Minn. 255/F4
Holyrood, Kansas 232/D3
Holyrood, Newf. 166/D2
Holyrood (bay), Newf. 166/D2
Holyrood (pond), Newf. 166/D2
Holyroyd, N. S. Wales 88/K4
Holy Trinity, Ala. 195/H6
Holywell, Wales 13/G2
Holywood, N. Ireland 17/K2
Holzminden, Germany 22/C3
Homalin, Burma 72/B1
Homathko (riv.), Br. Col. 184/E4
Hombori, Mali 106/D5
Hombori (mts.), Mali 106/D5
Homburg, Germany 22/B4
Home (bay) 162/K2
Home, Kansas 232/F2
Home (isl.), Newf. 166/B1
Home (bay), N.W. Terr. 187/M3
Home, Pa. 294/D4
Homedale, Idaho 220/A6
Home Gardens, Calif. 204/E11
Home Hill, Queensland 88/H3
Home Hill, Queensland 95/C3
Homeland, Calif. 204/H10
Homeland, Georgia 217/H9
Home Place, La. 238/L8
Homer, Alaska 196/B2
Homer, Georgia 217/F2
Homer, Ill. 222/F3
Homer, Ind. 227/F5
Homer, Ky. 237/H7
Homer, La. 238/D1
Homer, Mich. 250/E6
Homer, Minn. 255/G6
Homer, Nebr. 264/H2
Homer, N.Y. 276/H5
Homer, Ohio 284/E5
Homer City, Pa. 294/D4
Homerville, Georgia 217/G8
Homerville, Ohio 284/F3
Homestead, Fla. 212/F6
Homestead, Iowa 229/K5
Homestead, Mont. 262/M2
Homestead, Okla. 288/K2
Homestead, Pa. 294/B7
Homestead, Queensland 95/C4
Homestead A.F.B., Fla. 212/F6
Homestead Nat'l Mon., Nebr. 264/H4
Homestown, Mo. 261/N10
Hometown, Ill. 222/B6
Home Valley, Wash. 310/D5
Homewood, Ala. 195/E4
Homewood, Calif. 204/E4
Homewood, Ill. 222/B6
Homewood, Kansas 232/G3
Homewood, Manitoba 179/E5
Homewood, Miss. 256/E6
Homewood, Pa. 294/B4
Homeworth, Ohio 284/J4
Hominy, Okla. 288/O2
Hominy Falls, W. Va. 312/E6
Homochitto (riv.), Miss. 256/B8
Homoine, Mozambique 118/E4
Homonhon (isl.), Philippines 82/E5
Homosassa, Fla. 212/D3
Homosassa (isls.), Fla. 212/D3
Homosassa Springs, Fla. 212/D3
Homra, Hamada el (des.), Libya 111/B2
Homs, Libya 102/D1
Homs, Libya 111/B1
Homs (prov.), Syria 63/G5
Homs, Syria 59/C3
Homs, Syria 63/G5
Homs, Syria 54/E6
Hon, Ark. 202/B4
Hon, Libya 102/D2
Hon, Libya 111/C2
Honaker, Va. 307/D6
Honan (Henan), China 77/H5
Honaunau, Hawaii 218/G6
Honavar, India 68/C6
Honaz Dağı (mt.), Turkey 63/C4
Hon Chong, Vietnam 72/E5
Honda, Colombia 126/C5
Honda (bay), Cuba 158/B1
Honda (bay), Philippines 82/B6
Honda (bay), P. Rico 161/F2
Hondo (riv.), Belize 154/C1
Hondo, Japan 81/E7
Hondo (riv.), Mexico 150/P7
Hondo, N. Mex. 274/D5
Hondo, Texas 303/E8
Hondsrug (hills), Netherlands 27/K3
Honduras 2/E5
Honduras 146/K8
Honduras 154/D3
Honduras (gulf) 146/K8
Honduras (gulf), Belize 154/D2
Honduras (gulf), Guatemala 154/D2
Honduras (cape), Honduras 154/E2
Honduras (gulf), Honduras 154/D2
Honea Path, S.C. 296/C3
Honegg (mt.), Switzerland 39/E3
Honeoye, N.Y. 276/F5
Honeoye (lake), N.Y. 276/F5
Honeoye Falls, N.Y. 276/F5
Honesdale, Pa. 294/M2
Honey (lake), Calif. 204/E3
Honey (creek), Ind. 227/C6
Honey (creek), Oreg. 291/G5
Honey Brook, Pa. 294/L5
Honey Creek, Ind. 227/F4
Honey Creek, Iowa 229/B6
Honey Creek, Wis. 317/J3
Honeydale, New Bruns. 170/C3
Honeyford, N. Dak. 282/R3
Honey Grove, Texas 303/J4
Honey Harbour, Ontario 177/E3
Honey Hill, S.C. 296/H5
Honey Island, Texas 303/K7
Honeymoon Bay, Br. Col. 184/J3
Honeyville, Utah 304/B2
Honeywood, Ontario 177/D3
Honfleur, France 28/D3
Honfleur, Québec 172/G3
Høng, Denmark 21/E7
Honga (riv.), Md. 245/O7
Hon Gai, Vietnam 72/E2
Hongch'ŏn, S. Korea 81/D5
Hong Kong 54/N7
Hong Kong 2/Q4
HONG KONG 77

Jiayuguan 387

Jackson Springs, N.C. 281/K4
Jacksontown, Ohio 284/F6
Jacksonville, Ala. 195/G3
Jacksonville, Ark. 202/F4
Jacksonville, Fla. 146/K6
Jacksonville, Fla. 188/K4
Jacksonville, Fla. 212/E1
Jacksonville, Georgia 217/G7
Jacksonville, Ill. 222/C4
Jacksonville, Maine 243/J6
Jacksonville, Md. 245/M2
Jacksonville, Mo. 261/G3
Jacksonville, New Bruns. 170/C2
Jacksonville, N.C. 281/O5
Jacksonville, Ohio 284/F7
Jacksonville, Oreg. 291/D5
Jacksonville (Kent), Pa. 294/D4
Jacksonville, Texas 303/J5
Jacksonville, Vt. 268/B6
Jacksonville Beach, Fla. 212/E1
Jacksonville Naval Air Sta., Fla. 212/E1
Jacmel, Haiti 158/C6
Jacmel, Haiti 156/D3
Jacobabad, Pakistan 59/J4
Jacobabad, Pakistan 68/B3
Jacobina, Brazil 120/E4
Jacobina, Brazil 132/F5
Jacob Lake, Ariz. 198/C2
Jacobson, Minn. 255/E4
Jacobstown, N.J. 273/D3
Jacobsville, Mich. 250/A1
Jacobus, Pa. 294/J6
Jacques-Cartier (lake), Québec 172/F2
Jacques-Cartier (mt.), Québec 172/C1
Jacques-Cartier (passage), Québec 174/E3
Jacques-Cartier (riv.), Québec 172/F2
Jacquet (riv.), New Bruns. 170/D1
Jacquet River, New Bruns. 170/E1
Jacquinot (bay), Papua N.G. 86/B2
Jacuípe (riv.), Brazil 132/F5
Jacumba, Calif. 204/J11
Jacupiranga, Brazil 135/B4
Jaddi, Ras (cape), Pakistan 59/H4
Jaddi, Ras (pt.), Pakistan 68/A4
Jade (bay), Germany 22/C2
Jadwin, Mo. 261/K8
Jaén, Peru 128/C5
Jaén (prov.), Spain 33/E4
Jaén, Spain 7/D5
Jaén, Spain 33/E4
Jaffa (cape), S. Australia 94/F7
Jaffna, Sri Lanka 68/E7
Jaffna, Sri Lanka 54/K9
Jaffray, Br. Col. 184/K5
Jaffrey, N.H. 268/C6
Jaffrey•, N.H. 268/C6
Jaffrey Center, N.H. 268/C6
Jafura (des.), Saudi Arabia 59/F5
Jagdalpur, India 68/E5
Jagdaqi, China 77/K1
Jagersfontein, S. Africa 118/D5
Jagfontein, S. Africa 118/G7
Jaghbub (Jarabub), Libya 111/D2
Jagin (riv.), Iran 66/L8
Jagna, Philippines 82/E6
Jagtial, India 68/D5
Jagua, Cuba 158/D2
Jaguaquara, Brazil 132/F6
Jaguara (res.), Brazil 135/C2
Jaguarão, Brazil 132/C11
Jaguariaíva, Brazil 132/D9
Jaguariaíva, Brazil 135/B4
Jaguaribe (riv.), Brazil 132/G4
Jagüey Grande, Cuba 158/D2
Jagüey Grande, Cuba 156/B2
Jahrom, Iran 59/F4
Jahrom, Iran 66/H6
Jaicoa, Cordillera (mts.), P. Rico 161/B1
Jaicós, Brazil 132/F4
Jailolo, Indonesia 85/H5
Jainca, China 77/F4
Jaipur, India 54/J7
Jaipur, India 68/D3
Jaisalmer, India 68/C3
Jajarm, Iran 66/K2
Jajce, Yugoslavia 45/C3
Jajpur, India 68/F4
Jakarta (cap.), Indonesia 2/Q6
Jakarta (cap.), Indonesia 54/M10
Jakarta (cap.), Indonesia 85/H1
Jakin, Georgia 217/C8
Jakobstad, Finland 18/N5
Jakubany, Czech. 41/F2
Jal, N. Mex. 274/F6
Jala, Mexico 150/G6
Jalacingo, Mexico 150/P1
Jalaid, China 77/K2
Jalalabad, Afghanistan 68/B2
Jalalabad, Afghanistan 59/K3
Jalama, West Bank 65/C3
Jalapa, Guatemala 154/B3
Jalapa, Ind. 227/F3
Jalapa, Nicaragua 154/E4
Jalapa, S.C. 296/D3
Jalapa Enríquez, Mexico 146/J8
Jalapa Enríquez, Mexico 150/P1
Jalbun, West Bank 65/C3
Jaleswar, Nepal 68/F3
Jalgaon, India 68/D4
Jalingo, Nigeria 106/G7
Jalisco (state), Mexico 150/H6
Jalkot, Pakistan 59/K2
Jalna, India 68/D4
Jalo, Libya 111/D2
Jalo (oasis), Libya 111/D2
Jalón (riv.), Spain 33/E2
Jalor, India 68/C3
Jalpa, Mexico 150/H6
Jalpa de Méndez, Mexico 150/N7
Jalpaiguri, India 68/F3
Jalpan, Mexico 150/K6
Jalq, Iran 66/N7
Jáltipan de Morelos, Mexico 150/M8
Jalud, West Bank 65/C3
Jaluit (atoll), Marshall Is. 87/G5
Jam, Iran 66/H7
Jama, Ecuador 128/B3
Jamaica 2/F5
Jamaica 146/L8
JAMAICA 158
JAMAICA 156/C3
Jamaica, Cuba 158/K4
Jamaica (chan.), Haiti 156/C3
Jamaica, Iowa 229/E5
Jamaica (chan.), Jamaica 156/C3
Jamaica, N.Y. 276/N9
Jamaica•, Vt. 268/B5
Jamaica Plain, Mass. 249/C7
Jamaiké, Suriname 131/D4
Jamalpur, Bangladesh 68/F4
Jamalpur, India 68/F3
Jamama, Somalia 115/H3
Jamanota (mt.), Neth. Ant. 161/E10
Jamanxim (riv.), Brazil 132/C4
Jambi, Indonesia 85/C6
Jambi, Indonesia 54/M10
Jambuair (cape), Indonesia 85/B4
James (bay) 162/H5
James (riv.) 188/G2
James (bay), Canada 146/K4
James (isl.), Chile 138/D5
James (peak), Colo. 208/H3
James, Georgia 217/E5
James, Iowa 229/A3
James (pt.), Md. 245/N6
James, Miss. 256/B4
James (lake), N.C. 281/E3
James (riv.), N. Dak. 282/N6
James (bay), Ontario 175/D2
James (bay), Québec 174/A2
James (isl.), S.C. 296/H6
James (riv.), S. Dak. 298/N5
James (riv.), Va. 307/O6
James A. Garfield Nat'l Hist. Site, Ohio 284/G2
James Bay, Ontario 177/E2
Jamesburg, N.J. 273/E3
James City, N.C. 281/R4
James City, Pa. 294/E2
James City (co.), Va. 307/P6
James Creek, Pa. 294/F5
Jameson, Mo. 261/E2
Jameson Park, S. Africa 118/J7
Jamesport, Mo. 261/E3
James Ross (isl.), Ant. 5/C16
James Ross (str.), N.W.T. 162/G1
James Ross (str.), N.W. Terrs. 187/J3
Jamestown, Ala. 195/G2
Jamestown, Ark. 202/G2
Jamestown, Calif. 204/E6
Jamestown, Colo. 208/J2
Jamestown, Ill. 222/D5
Jamestown, Ind. 227/D5
Jamestown, Kansas 232/E2
Jamestown, Ky. 237/L7
Jamestown, La. 238/D2
Jamestown, Miss. 256/E8
Jamestown, Mo. 261/G5
Jamestown, N.Y. 188/L2
Jamestown, N.Y. 276/B6
Jamestown, N.C. 281/K3
Jamestown, N. Dak. 188/G1
Jamestown, N. Dak. 282/N6
Jamestown (dam), N. Dak. 282/N6
Jamestown (res.), N. Dak. 282/N6
Jamestown, Ohio 284/C6
Jamestown, Pa. 294/A3
Jamestown, R.I. 249/J6
Jamestown•, R.I. 249/J6
Jamestown, S. Australia 88/F6
Jamestown, S. Australia 94/F5
Jamestown, S.C. 296/H5
Jamestown, Tenn. 237/M8
Jamestown, Va. 307/P6
Jamestown Nat'l Hist. Site, Va. 307/P6
Jamesville, N.Y. 276/H5
Jamesville, N.C. 281/R3
Jamesville, Va. 307/S5
Jamieson, Fla. 212/B1
Jamieson, Oreg. 291/K3
Jamison, Nebr. 264/E2
Jamison, S.C. 296/F4
Jamma, Somalia 102/G4
Jammerbugt (bay), Denmark 21/C3
Jammu, India 54/J6
Jammu, India 68/D2
Jammu and Kashmir (state), India 68/D2
Jamnagar, India 68/B4
Jamnagar, India 54/H7
Jampur, Pakistan 59/K4
Jämsä, Finland 18/O6
Jamshedpur, India 54/K7
Jamshedpur, India 68/F4
Jämtland (co.), Sweden 18/J5
Jamursba (cape), Indonesia 85/J5
Janakpur, Nepal 68/F3
Jandaq, Iran 66/J3
Jandowae, Queensland 95/D5
Jane, Mo. 261/D9
Jane Lew, W. Va. 312/F4
Janesville, Calif. 204/E3
Janesville, Ill. 222/E4
Janesville, Iowa 229/J3
Janesville, Minn. 255/E6
Janesville (Smithmill), Pa. 294/F4
Janesville, Wis. 188/J2
Janesville, Wis. 317/H10
Janesville-Beloit, Wis. 317/H10
Janetstown, Scotland 15/E2
Janeville, New Bruns. 170/E1
Jánico, Dom. Rep. 158/D5
Janikowo, Poland 47/C2
Janiuay, Philippines 82/D5
Jan Mayen (isl.), Norway 4/B10
Jan Mayen (isl.), Norway 7/D1
Janos, Mexico 150/F1
Jánoshalma, Hungary 41/E3
Jánosháza, Hungary 41/D3
Janów Lubelski, Poland 47/F3
Jansen, Colo. 208/K8
Jansen, Nebr. 264/G4
Jansen, Sask. 181/G4
Jantetelco, Mexico 150/L2
Januária, Brazil 120/E4
Januária, Brazil 132/E6
Janvrin (isl.), Nova Scotia 168/G3
Jaora, India 68/D4
Japan 2/S4
Japan 54/R6
JAPAN 81
Japan (sea) 2/R4
Japan (sea) 54/P6
Japan (sea), Japan 81/G4
Japan (sea), N. Korea 81/G4
Japan (sea), S. Korea 81/G4
Japan (sea), U.S.S.R. 48/O6
Japurá, Brazil 132/G9
Japurá (riv.), Brazil 120/C3
Japurá (riv.), Brazil 132/G9
Jaquet (pt.), Dominica 161/E5
Jara, Cerrito (mt.), Bolivia 136/F6
Jara (hill), Paraguay 144/C1
Jarabacoa, Dom. Rep. 158/E5
Jarabub, Libya 102/E2
Jarabub, Libya 111/D2
Jaragua, Dom. Rep. 158/D6
Jaraíz de la Vera, Spain 33/D2
Jarales, N. Mex. 274/C4
Jarama (riv.), Spain 33/E2
Jaramillo, Argentina 143/C6
Jarandilla de la Vera, Spain 33/D2
Jarash, Jordan 65/D3
Jarbalo, Kansas 232/G2
Jarbidge (riv.), Idaho 220/C7
Jarbidge, Nev. 266/F1
Jardim, Brazil 132/G4
Jardine, Mont. 262/F5
Jardines de la Reina (arch.), Cuba 158/F3
Jardines de la Reina (arch.), Cuba 156/B2
Jargalant, Mongolia 77/J2
Jari (riv.), Brazil 120/D2
Jari (riv.), Brazil 132/C3
Järna, Sweden 18/G2
Jarnac, France 28/C5
Jaro, Philippines 82/E5
Jarocin, Poland 47/C3
Jaroměř, Czech. 41/C1
Jarosław, Poland 47/F4
Jaroso, Colo. 208/H8
Järpen, Sweden 18/H5
Jarrahdale, W. Australia 88/B3
Jarrahdale, W. Australia 92/B2
Jarratt, Va. 307/O7
Jarrettsville, Md. 245/M2
Jarrow, Alberta 182/E3
Jarrow, England 13/J3
Jarrow, England 10/F3
Jars (plain), Laos 72/D3
Jartai, China 77/G4
Jaruco, Cuba 158/C1
Jarud, China 77/K3
Järvenpää, Finland 18/O6
Jarvie, Alberta 182/D2
Jarvis (isl.), Pacific 87/K6
Jarvisburg, N.C. 281/T2
Jarvisville, W. Va. 312/F4
Järvsö, Sweden 18/K6
Jask, Iran 59/G4
Jask, Iran 54/G7
Jask, Iran 66/K8
Jasło, Poland 47/E4
Jasmin, Sask. 181/H4
Jasmine Estates, Fla. 212/D3
Jason (isls.), Falkland Is. 143/D7
Jason, Ky. 237/O6
Jason, N.C. 281/O4
Jasonville, Ind. 227/C6
Jasper, Ala. 195/D3
Jasper, Alberta 182/B3
Jasper, Alta. 162/E5
Jasper, Ark. 202/D1
Jasper, Fla. 212/D1
Jasper (co.), Georgia 217/E4
Jasper, Georgia 217/D2
Jasper (co.), Ill. 222/E4
Jasper (co.), Ind. 227/C2
Jasper, Ind. 227/D8
Jasper (co.), Iowa 229/G5
Jasper, Mich. 250/E7
Jasper, Minn. 255/B7
Jasper (co.), Miss. 256/F6
Jasper (co.), Mo. 261/D8
Jasper, Mo. 261/D8
Jasper, N.Y. 276/F6
Jasper, Ohio 284/D7
Jasper, Ontario 177/H3
Jasper, Oreg. 291/E3
Jasper (co.), S.C. 296/E6
Jasper, Tenn. 237/K10
Jasper (co.), Texas 303/K7
Jasper, Texas 303/L7
Jasper Nat'l Park, Alberta 182/A3
Jasper Nat'l Park, Alta. 162/E5
Jastrowie, Poland 47/C2
Jastrzębie Zdroj, Poland 47/D3
Jászapáti, Hungary 41/E3
Jászárokszállás, Hungary 41/E3
Jászberény, Hungary 41/E3
Jászfényszaru, Hungary 41/E3
Jászkarajenő, Hungary 41/E3
Jászkisér, Hungary 41/F3
Jászladány, Hungary 41/F3
Jataí, Brazil 120/D4
Jataí, Brazil 132/D7
Jatibonico, Cuba 158/F2
Jatibonico del Sur (riv.), Cuba 158/F3
Játiva, Spain 33/F3
Jaú, Brazil 132/D8
Jaú, Brazil 135/B3
Jauaperi (riv.), Brazil 132/A2
Jauari, Serra (mts.), Brazil 132/C3
Jauco, Cuba 158/K4
Jauf, Saudi Arabia 54/F7
Jauf, Saudi Arabia 59/C4
Jauja, Peru 128/E8
Jaumave, Mexico 150/K5
Jaun, Switzerland 39/D3
Jaunjelgava, U.S.S.R. 53/C2
Jaunpur, India 68/E3
Jauri, Iran 66/M6
Java (head), Indonesia 85/C7
Java (isl.), Indonesia 2/Q6
Java (isl.), Indonesia 54/M10
Java (isl.), Indonesia 85/J2
Java (sea), Indonesia 2/Q6
Java (sea), Indonesia 54/M10
Java (sea), Indonesia 85/D6
Java, S. Dak. 298/K3
Java, Va. 307/K7
Javari (riv.), Brazil 132/F9
Jávea, Spain 33/G3
Javier de Viana, Uruguay 145/C1
Jaworzno, Poland 47/B4
Jay, Fla. 212/B5
Jay (co.), Ind. 227/G4
Jay, Maine 243/C7
Jay•, Maine 243/C7
Jay, N.Y. 276/N2
Jay, Okla. 288/S2
Jay•, Vt. 268/C2
Jay (peak), Vt. 268/B2
Jaya, Puncak (mt.), Indonesia 85/K6
Jayanca, Peru 128/B6
Jayapura, Indonesia 85/L6
Jayawijaya (range), Indonesia 85/K6
Jay Creek, North. Terr. 88/E4
Jay Em, Wyo. 319/H3
Jayess, Miss. 256/D8
Jayton, Texas 303/D4
Jayuya, P. Rico 156/G1
Jayuya, P. Rico 161/C2
Jaz Murian, Hamun-e (marsh), Iran 66/L7
Jaz Murian, Hamun-e (marsh), Iran 59/G4
Jean, Nev. 266/F7
Jean, Texas 303/F4
Jean Côté, Alberta 182/B2
Jeanerette, La. 238/G7
Jeanette (bay), Newf. 166/C3
Jean Lafitte, La. 238/K7
Jean Lafitte Nat'l Hist. Park, La. 238/P4
Jean-Marie River, N.W. Terrs. 187/F3
Jeanne Mance, New Bruns. 170/E1
Jeannette, Pa. 294/C5
Jean-Rabel, Haiti 158/B5
Jean-Rabel (pt.), Haiti 158/B5
Jebba, Nigeria 106/E7
Jebel Abyad (plat.), Sudan 111/E4
Jebel Aulia (dam), Sudan 102/F3
Jebel Aulia (dam), Sudan 111/F4
Jebel Dhanna, U.A.E. 59/F5
Jeberos, Peru 128/D5
Jeble, Syria 63/F5
Jedburg, S.C. 296/G5
Jedburgh, Sask. 181/J4
Jedburgh, Scotland 10/E3
Jedburgh, Scotland 15/F5
Jeddah (Jidda), Saudi Arabia 59/C5
Jeddito, Ariz. 198/E3
Jeddo, Mich. 250/G5
Jeddo, Pa. 294/L3
Jeddore (cape), Nova Scotia 168/E4
Jeddore (harb.), Nova Scotia 168/F4
Jędrzejów, Poland 47/E3
Jefara (reg.), Libya 111/B1
Jefara (reg.), Tunisia 106/G2
Jeff, Ala. 195/E1
Jeff, Ky. 237/P6
Jeff Davis (co.), Georgia 217/G7
Jeff Davis (co.), Texas 303/C11
Jeffers, Minn. 255/C6
Jeffers, Mont. 262/E5
Jefferson (co.), Ala. 195/E3
Jefferson, Ala. 195/C6
Jefferson (co.), Ark. 202/G5
Jefferson, Ark. 202/F5
Jefferson (co.), Colo. 208/J3
Jefferson, Colo. 208/H4
Jefferson (co.), Fla. 212/C1
Jefferson (co.), Georgia 217/H4
Jefferson, Georgia 217/F2
Jefferson (co.), Idaho 220/F6
Jefferson (co.), Ill. 222/E5
Jefferson (co.), Ind. 227/G7
Jefferson, Ind. 227/D4
Jefferson (co.), Iowa 229/K6
Jefferson, Iowa 229/E4
Jefferson (co.), Kansas 232/G2
Jefferson (co.), Ky. 237/K4
Jefferson (par.), La. 238/K7
Jefferson•, Maine 243/D7
Jefferson, Md. 245/J3
Jefferson, Mass. 249/G3
Jefferson (co.), Miss. 256/B7
Jefferson (co.), Mo. 261/L6
Jefferson (co.), Mont. 262/E4
Jefferson (riv.), Mont. 262/D5
Jefferson (co.), Nebr. 264/G4
Jefferson•, N.H. 268/D3
Jefferson (mt.), N.H. 268/E3
Jefferson (co.), N.Y. 276/J2
Jefferson, N.Y. 276/L6
Jefferson, N.C. 281/G2
Jefferson (co.), Ohio 284/J5
Jefferson (West Jefferson), Ohio 284/D6
Jefferson, Ohio 284/J2
Jefferson (co.), Okla. 288/L6
Jefferson, Okla. 288/L1
Jefferson (co.), Oreg. 291/F3
Jefferson, Oreg. 291/D3
Jefferson (mt.), Oreg. 291/F3
Jefferson (co.), Pa. 294/D3
Jefferson, Pa. 294/B7
Jefferson, Pa. 294/B6
Jefferson (Codorus), Pa. 294/J6
Jefferson, S.C. 296/G2
Jefferson, S. Dak. 298/S8
Jefferson (co.), Tenn. 237/P8
Jefferson (co.), Texas 303/K8
Jefferson, Texas 303/K5
Jefferson, Va. 307/N5
Jefferson (co.), Wash. 310/B3
Jefferson (co.), W. Va. 312/L4
Jefferson (co.), Wis. 317/J9
Jefferson, Wis. 317/J10
Jefferson City (cap.), Mo. 261/H5
Jefferson City (cap.), Mo. 146/J6
Jefferson City (cap.), Mo. 188/H3
Jefferson City, Mont. 262/E4
Jefferson City, Tenn. 237/P8
Jefferson Davis (par.), La. 238/E6
Jefferson Davis (co.), Miss. 256/E7
Jefferson Heights, La. 238/O4
Jefferson Island, Mont. 262/E5
Jefferson Manor, Va. 307/S3
Jefferson Nat'l Expansion Mem. Nat'l Hist. Site, Mo. 261/R3
Jefferson Proving Ground, Ind. 227/G7
Jeffersonton, Va. 307/N3
Jeffersontown, Ky. 237/L2
Jeffersonville, Georgia 217/F5
Jeffersonville, Ind. 227/F8
Jeffersonville, Ky. 237/O5
Jeffersonville, N.Y. 276/L7
Jeffersonville, Ohio 284/C6
Jeffersonville, Vt. 268/B2
Jeffrey (res.), Nebr. 264/D4
Jeffrey, W. Va. 312/C7
Jeffrey City, Wyo. 319/E3
Jeffrey's, Newf. 166/C4
Jef Jef es Seghin (plat.), Chad 111/D3
Jef Jef es Seghin (plat.), Libya 111/D3
Jega, Nigeria 106/E6
Jegenstorf, Switzerland 39/D2
Jeinemeni, Cerro (mt.), Chile 138/E6
Jeiseyville, Ill. 222/D4
Jejuí-Guazú (riv.), Paraguay 144/D4
Jēkabpils, U.S.S.R. 53/C2
Jēkabpils, U.S.S.R. 52/C3
Jekyll (isl.), Georgia 217/K8
Jeleń, Poland 47/B4
Jelenia Góra (prov.), Poland 47/B3
Jelenia Góra, Poland 47/B3
Jelgava, U.S.S.R. 7/G3
Jelgava, U.S.S.R. 53/B2
Jelgava, U.S.S.R. 52/B3
Jellico, Tenn. 237/N7
Jellico Creek, Ky. 237/N7
Jellicoe, Ontario 177/H5
Jelling, Denmark 21/C6
Jelloway, Ohio 284/F4
Jelm, Wyo. 319/G4
Jelšava, Czech. 41/F2
Jemaja (isl.), Indonesia 85/D5
Jemappes, Belgium 27/D8
Jember, Indonesia 85/K2
Jemez (riv.), N. Mex. 274/C3
Jemez Canyon (res.), N. Mex. 274/C3
Jemez Pueblo, N. Mex. 274/C3
Jemez Springs, N. Mex. 274/C3
Jeminay, China 77/C2
Jemison, Ala. 195/E5
Jemnice, Czech. 41/C2
Jemseg, New Bruns. 170/D3
Jemtland, Maine 243/G1
Jena, Germany 22/D3
Jena, La. 238/F3
Jenaz, Switzerland 39/J3
Jenbach, Austria 41/A3
Jendouba, Tunisia 106/F1
Jeneponto, Indonesia 85/F7
Jenera, Ohio 284/C4
Jenifer, Ala. 195/G3
Jenin, West Bank 65/C3
Jenison, Mich. 250/D6
Jenkinjones, W. Va. 312/D8
Jenkins (co.), Georgia 217/J5
Jenkins, Ky. 237/R6
Jenkins, Minn. 255/D4
Jenkins, Mo. 261/E9
Jenkinsburg, Georgia 217/E4
Jenkinsville, S.C. 296/E3
Jenkintown, Pa. 294/M5
Jenks, Okla. 288/P2
Jenner, Alberta 182/E4
Jennersdorf, Austria 41/C3
Jennerstown, Pa. 294/D5
Jennie, Ark. 202/H7
Jennie, Suriname 131/C3
Jennings, Ant. & Bar. 161/D11
Jennings, Fla. 212/C1
Jennings (co.), Ind. 227/F7
Jennings, Kansas 232/B2
Jennings, La. 238/E6
Jennings, Md. 245/B2
Jennings, Mich. 250/D4
Jennings, Mo. 261/R2
Jennings, N.S. Wales 97/F1
Jennings, Okla. 288/N2
Jennings Lodge, Oreg. 291/B2
Jenny (creek), Oreg. 291/E5
Jenny Lake, Wyo. 319/B2
Jenny Lind, Calif. 204/C9
Jenny Lind (isl.), N.W. Terr. 187/H3
Jenolan Caves, N.S. Wales 97/E3
Jenpeg, Manitoba 179/J2
Jensen, Utah 304/E3
Jensen Beach, Fla. 212/F4
Jens Munk (isl.), N.W.T. 162/H2
Jens Munk (isl.), N.W. Terr. 187/K3
Jepara, Indonesia 85/J2
Jequié, Brazil 120/E4
Jequié, Brazil 132/F6
Jequitinhonha, Brazil 132/F7
Jequitinhonha (riv.), Brazil 120/E4
Jequitinhonha (riv.), Brazil 132/F7
Jerablus, Syria 63/G4
Jerada, Morocco 106/D2
Jerauld (co.), S. Dak. 298/M5
Jérémie, Haiti 156/C3
Jérémie, Haiti 158/A6
Jeremoabo, Brazil 132/G5
Jeremy (riv.), Conn. 210/F2
Jerez, Spain 7/D5
Jerez de García Salinas, Mexico 150/H5
Jerez de la Frontera, Spain 33/C4
Jerez de los Caballeros, Spain 33/C3
Jericho, Ark. 202/K3
Jericho, N.Y. 276/R6
Jericho, Queensland 95/C4
Jericho, Vt. 268/A2
Jericho•, Vt. 268/A2
Jericho, West Bank 65/C4
Jericho Center, Vt. 268/B3
Jerico Springs, Mo. 261/E7
Jeriel, Ky. 237/R4
Jerilderie, N.S. Wales 97/C4
Jerimoth (hill), R.I. 249/G5
Jermyn, Pa. 294/L2
Jermyn, Texas 303/F4
Jerome, Ariz. 198/C4
Jerome, Ark. 202/G7
Jerome (co.), Idaho 220/D7
Jerome, Idaho 220/D7
Jerome, Ill. 222/D4
Jerome, Mo. 261/J7
Jerome, Pa. 294/D5
Jeromesville, Ohio 284/F4
Jerry City, Ohio 284/C3
Jersey, Ark. 202/F7
Jersey (isl.), Chan. Is. 13/E8
Jersey (isl.), Chan. Is. 10/E6
Jersey, Georgia 217/E3
Jersey (co.), Ill. 222/C4
Jersey, Ohio 284/E5
Jersey (bay), Virgin Is. (U.S.) 161/B4
Jersey City, N.J. 188/M2
Jersey City, N.J. 273/B2
Jersey Mills, Pa. 294/H3
Jersey Shore, Pa. 294/H3
Jerseyside, Newf. 166/B3
Jerseytown, Pa. 294/J3
Jersey Village, Texas 303/J1
Jerseyville, Ill. 222/C4
Jerslev, Denmark 21/D3
Jerumenha, Brazil 132/F4
Jerusalem, Ark. 202/E3
Jerusalem (dist.), Israel 65/B4
Jerusalem (cap.), Israel 54/E6
Jerusalem (cap.), Israel 65/C4
Jerusalem (cap.), Israel 59/C3
Jerusalem, Ohio 284/H6
Jervis (inlet), Br. Col. 184/E5
Jervis (mt.), Chile 138/D8
Jervis Bay, Aust. Cap. Terr. 97/F4
Jervois Range, North. Terr. 88/F4
Jesenice, Yugoslavia 45/A2
Jeseník, Czech. 41/D1
Jeseníky (mts.), Czech. 41/D1
Jesenské, Czech. 41/F2
Jesi, Italy 34/D3
Jessamine (co.), Ky. 237/M5
Jesse, W. Va. 312/C7
Jessie, N. Dak. 282/O4
Jessieville, Ark. 202/D4
Jessnitz, Germany 22/E3
Jessore, Bangladesh 68/F4
Jessup, Pa. 294/F6
Jesterville, Md. 245/P7
Jesuit Bend, La. 238/K7
Jesup, Georgia 217/J7
Jesup, Iowa 229/J4
Jesús, Paraguay 144/E5
Jesús de Machaca, Bolivia 136/A5
Jesús de Otoro, Honduras 154/C3
Jesús María, Argentina 143/D3
Jesús María (reef), Mexico 150/L4
Jet, Okla. 288/K1
Jetersville, Va. 307/M6
Jetmore, Kansas 232/B3
Jett, Ky. 237/M4
Jette, Belgium 27/B9
Jetts Creek, Ky. 237/O6
Jever, Germany 22/B2
Jevíčko, Czech. 41/D2
Jewel Cave Nat'l Mon., S. Dak. 298/B6
Jewell, Georgia 217/G4
Jewell, Iowa 229/F4
Jewell (co.), Kansas 232/D2
Jewell, Kansas 232/D2
Jewell, Ohio 284/B3
Jewell, Oreg. 291/D2
Jewell Ridge, Va. 307/E6
Jewett, Ill. 222/E4
Jewett, Ohio 284/H5
Jewett, Texas 303/H6
Jewett City, Conn. 210/H2
Jewish Aut. Obl., U.S.S.R. 48/O5
Jeypore, India 68/E5
Jhalawar, India 68/D4
Jhal Jhao, Pakistan 59/H4
Jhal Jhao, Pakistan 68/B3
Jhang Sadar, Pakistan 59/K3
Jhang Sadar, Pakistan 68/C2
Jhansi, India 68/D3
Jharsuguda, India 68/E4
Jhelum (riv.), India 68/C2
Jhelum, Pakistan 68/C2
Jhelum, Pakistan 59/K3
Jhelum (riv.), Pakistan 68/C2
Jhudo, Pakistan 68/B3
Jhunjhunu, India 68/D3
Jialing (riv.), China 54/M6
Jiamusi (Kiamusze), China 77/M2
Ji'an (Kian), China 77/J6
Jiande, China 77/J6
Jiangcheng, China 77/F7
Jiangmen (Kongmoon), China 77/H7
Jiangsu (Kiangsu), China 77/K5
Jiangxi (Kiangsi), China 77/J6
Jiangyou, China 77/G5
Jian'ou, China 77/J6
Jianshi, China 77/H5
Jianshui, China 77/F7
Jianyang, China 77/J6
Jiaohe, China 77/L3
Jiao Xian, China 77/K4
Jiaozuo (Tsiaotso), China 77/H4
Jiashan, China 77/J5
Jia Xian, China 77/H4
Jiaxing (Kashing), China 77/K5
Jiayin, China 77/M2
Jiayu, China 77/H6
Jiayuguan, China 77/E4

Karlstad 389

Kaduna (riv.), Nigeria 106/F7
Kadzherom, U.S.S.R. 52/J2
Kaech'ŏn, N. Korea 81/B4
Kaédi, Mauritania 106/B5
Kaédi, Mauritania 102/A3
Kaélé, Cameroon 115/B1
Kaena (pt.), Hawaii 218/D1
Kaeo, N. Zealand 100/D1
Kaesŏng, N. Korea 81/C4
Kaf, Saudi Arabia 59/C3
Kafan, U.S.S.R. 52/G7
Kafar Kanna, Israel 65/C2
Kaffa (prov.), Ethiopia 111/G6
Kaffrine, Senegal 106/A6
Kafia Kingi, Sudan 111/D6
Kafirévs (cape), Greece 45/G6
Kafr Yasif, Israel 65/C2
Kafue, Zambia 115/E7
Kafue (riv.), Zambia 115/E7
Kafue Nat'l Park, Zambia 115/E6
Kaga, Japan 81/H5
Kaga Bandoro, Cent. Afr. Rep. 115/C2
Kagalaska (isl.), Alaska 196/L4
Kagan, U.S.S.R. 48/G6
Kagawa (pref.), Japan 81/G6
Kagawong, Ontario 177/B2
Kagawong (lake), Ontario 177/B2
Kagera (reg.), Tanzania 114/F4
Kagera Nat'l Park, Rwanda 115/F4
Kağıthane, Turkey 63/D6
Kağızman, Turkey 63/K2
Kagoshima (pref.), Japan 81/E8
Kagoshima, Japan 81/E8
Kagoshima, Japan 54/O6
Kagoshima (bay), Japan 81/E8
Kagul, U.S.S.R. 52/C5
Kaguyak, Alaska 196/H3
Kahakuloa, Hawaii 218/J1
Kahala, Hawaii 218/D5
Kahala (pt.), Hawaii 218/D1
Kahaluu, Hawaii 218/E2
Kahama, Tanzania 115/F4
Kahana, Hawaii 218/F1
Kahana (bay), Hawaii 218/F1
Kahayan (riv.), Indonesia 85/E6
Kahemba, Zaire 115/C5
Kahiltna (riv.), Alaska 196/B1
Kahlotus, Wash. 310/G4
Kah-Nee-Ta, Oreg. 291/F3
Kahoka, Mo. 261/J2
Kahoolawe (isl.), Hawaii 188/F5
Kahoolawe (isl.), Hawaii 87/L4
Kahoolawe (isl.), Hawaii 218/H3
Kahouanne (isl.), Guadeloupe 161/A6
Kahramanmaraş (prov.), Turkey 63/G4
Kâhta, Turkey 63/H4
Kahuku, Hawaii 218/E1
Kahuku, Hawaii 188/F5
Kahuku (pt.), Hawaii 218/E1
Kahului, Hawaii 218/J2
Kahului, Hawaii 188/F5
Kahului (harb.), Hawaii 218/J1
Kai (isls.), Indonesia 85/J7
Kaiama, Nigeria 106/E7
Kaiapit, Papua N.G. 85/B7
Kaiapoi, N. Zealand 100/D5
Kaibab (plat.), Ariz. 198/C2
Kaibab Ind. Res., Ariz. 198/C2
Kaibito, Ariz. 198/D2
Kaibito (plat.), Ariz. 198/D2
Kaieteur (fall), Guyana 131/B3
Kaifeng, China 77/H5
Kaifeng, China 54/N6
Kaikohe, N. Zealand 100/D1
Kaikoura, N. Zealand 100/D5
Kaikoura (pen.), N. Zealand 100/E5
Kaikoura (range), N. Zealand 100/D5
Kaili, China 77/G6
Kailu, China 77/K3
Kailua (Kailua Kona), Hawaii, Hawaii 218/F5
Kailua, Oahu, Hawaii 218/F2
Kailua (bay), Hawaii 218/F2
Kailua (bay), Hawaii 218/F5
Kailua Kona, Hawaii 218/F5
Kaimana, Indonesia 85/J6
Kaimanawa (range), N. Zealand 100/E3
Kaimu, Hawaii 218/J6
Kaimuki, Hawaii 218/D4
Kainaliu, Hawaii 218/G5
Kainaliu, Hawaii 188/F6
Kainan (bay), Ant. 5/B10
Kaingaroa, N. Zealand 100/E7
Kainji (res.), Nigeria 106/E6
Kaipara (harb.), N. Zealand 100/D2
Kaipara (riv.), N. Zealand 100/A1
Kaiparowits (plat.), Utah 304/C6
Kaipokok (bay), Newf. 166/B2
Kaipokok (riv.), Newf. 166/B3
Kairouan, Tunisia 106/F1
Kairuku, Papua N.G. 85/B7
Kaiser, Mo. 261/G6
Kaiseregg (mt.), Switzerland 39/D3
Kaiserslautern, Germany 22/B4
Kaiserstuhl (mt.), Germany 22/B4
Kaitaia, N. Zealand 100/D1
Kaitangata, N. Zealand 100/C7
Kaitumälv (riv.), Sweden 18/M3
Kaiwi (chan.), Hawaii 218/E6
Kaiyuan, Liaoning, China 77/K3
Kaiyuan, Yunnan, China 77/F7
Kaiyuh (mts.), Alaska 196/G2
Kaizuka, Japan 81/H8
Kajaani, Finland 7/G2
Kajaani, Finland 18/P4
Kajabbi, Queensland 88/G3
Kajabbi, Queensland 95/A4
Kajiado, Kenya 115/G4
Kajok, Sudan 111/E6
Kaka, Cent. Afr. Rep. 115/E2
Kaka, Sudan 111/F5
Kakabeka Falls, Ontario 177/G5
Kakabeka Falls, Ontario 175/B3
Kakamega, Kenya 115/F3
Kake, Alaska 196/M1
Kakhk, Iran 66/L3
Kakhovka, U.S.S.R. 52/D5
Kakhovka (res.), U.S.S.R. 48/D5
Kakhovka (res.), U.S.S.R. 52/D5
Kakinada, India 54/K8
Kakinada, India 68/E5
Kakisa, N.W. Terr. 187/G3
Kakkiviak (cape), Newf. 166/B1
Kakogawa, Japan 81/G6
Kaktovik, Alaska 196/K1
Kakwa (riv.), Alberta 182/A2
Kalaa-Kebira, Tunisia 106/F1
Kalaallit-Nunaat (Greenland) 2/G2
Kalaallit-Nunaat (Greenland) 4/B12
Kalaallit-Nunaat (Greenland) 146/P2
Kalabahi, Indonesia 85/G7
Kalabo, Zambia 115/D6
Kalach, U.S.S.R. 52/F4
Kalachinsk, U.S.S.R. 48/H4
Kalach-na-Donu, U.S.S.R. 52/F5
Kaladan (riv.), Burma 72/B2
Kaladar, Ontario 177/H3
Kalae, Hawaii 218/G1
Ka Lae (cape), Hawaii 218/G7
Kalahari (des.) 102/E7
Kalahari (des.), Botswana 118/C4
Kalahari (des.), Namibia 118/C4
Kalahari Gemsbok Nat'l Park, S. Africa 118/C5
Kalaheo, Hawaii 218/C2
Kalajoki, Finland 18/N4
Kalajoki (riv.), Finland 18/O4
Kalakan, U.S.S.R. 48/M4
Kalaloch, Wash. 310/A3
Kalam, Pakistan 68/C1
Kalama, Wash. 310/C4
Kalama (riv.), Wash. 310/C4
Kalámai, Greece 7/G5
Kalámai, Greece 45/F7
Kalamazoo, Mich. 188/J2
Kalamazoo (co.), Mich. 250/D6
Kalamazoo, Mich. 250/D6
Kalamazoo (riv.), Mich. 250/C6
Kalambo (falls), Tanzania 115/F5
Kalambo (falls), Zambia 115/F5
Kalamo, Mich. 250/D6
Kalampáka, Greece 45/E6
Kalamunda, W. Australia 88/B2
Kalan, Turkey 63/H3
Kalao (isl.), Indonesia 85/G7
Kalaoa, Hawaii 218/G5
Kalaotoa (isl.), Indonesia 85/G5
Kalapana, Hawaii 218/J6
Kalasin, Thailand 72/D3
Kalat (Qalat), Afghanistan 68/B2
Kalat (Qalat), Afghanistan 59/J3
Kalat, Pakistan 54/H7
Kalat, Pakistan 59/J4
Kalat, Pakistan 68/B3
Kalaupapa, Hawaii 218/G1
Kalaupapa (pen.), Hawaii 218/H1
Kalaupapa Nat'l Hist. Park, Hawaii 218/H1
Kalávrita, Greece 45/F6
Kalawao (co.), Hawaii 218/G1
Kalbarri, W. Australia 92/A4
Kale, Turkey 63/C4
Kalecik, Turkey 63/E2
Kaleden, Br. Col. 184/H5
Kalegauk (isl.), Burma 72/C4
Kalehe, Zaire 115/E4
Kaleida, Manitoba 179/D5
Kalemie, Zaire 115/E5
Kalemie, Zaire 102/E5
Kalemyo, Burma 72/B2
Kaleva, Mich. 250/C4
Kalevala, U.S.S.R. 52/D1
Kalewa, Burma 72/B2
Kalgan (Zhangjiakou), China 77/J3
Kalgin (isl.), Alaska 196/B1
Kalgoorlie, Australia 2/R7
Kalgoorlie, W. Australia 88/C6
Kalgoorlie, W. Australia 92/C5
Kalgoorlie-Boulder, W. Australia 92/C5
Kaliakra (cape), Bulgaria 45/J4
Kalianda, Indonesia 85/D7
Kalibo, Philippines 82/D5
Kalida, Ohio 284/B4
Kalihi, Hawaii 218/C4
Kalihi (channel), Hawaii 218/B4
Kalihi (stream), Hawaii 218/C3
Kalihiwai, Hawaii 218/C1
Kalima, Zaire 115/E4
Kalimantan (reg.), Indonesia 85/E5
Kálimnos, Greece 45/H7
Kálimnos (isl.), Greece 45/H7
Kalinga, Queensland 88/K2
Kalinga-Apayao (prov.), Philippines 82/C1
Kalinin (Tver'), U.S.S.R. 7/H3
Kalinin (Tver'), U.S.S.R. 48/D4
Kalinin (Tver'), U.S.S.R. 52/E3
Kaliningrad, U.S.S.R. 7/G3
Kaliningrad, U.S.S.R. 48/B4
Kaliningrad, Kaliningrad, U.S.S.R. 52/B4
Kaliningrad, Moscow Oblast, U.S.S.R. 52/E3
Kalininsk, U.S.S.R. 52/F4
Kalinkovichi, U.S.S.R. 52/C4
Kalispel Ind. Res., Wash. 310/H2
Kalispell, Mont. 188/C1
Kalispell, Mont. 262/B2
Kalisz (prov.), Poland 47/D3
Kalisz, Poland 7/F3
Kalisz, Poland 47/D3
Kaliua, Tanzania 115/F5
Kalix, Sweden 18/N4
Kalixälv (riv.), Sweden 18/N3
Kalkaska (co.), Mich. 250/D4
Kalkaska, Mich. 250/D4
Kalkfeld, Namibia 118/B4
Kalkfontein, Botswana 118/C4
Kallaste, U.S.S.R. 53/D1
Kallavesi (lake), Finland 18/P5
Kallsjö (lake), Sweden 18/H5
Kalmalo, Nigeria 106/F6
Kalmar (co.), Sweden 18/K8
Kalmar, Sweden 7/F3
Kalmar, Sweden 18/K8
Kalmarsund (sound), Sweden 18/K8
Kalmthout, Belgium 27/F6
Kalmuck A.S.S.R., U.S.S.R. 52/F5
Kalmuck A.S.S.R., U.S.S.R. 48/E5
Kalmunai, Sri Lanka 68/E7
Kalmykovo, U.S.S.R. 48/F5
Kalo, Iowa 229/E4
Kalocsa, Hungary 41/E3
Kalohi (chan.), Hawaii 218/G1
Kaloko-Honokohau Nat'l Hist. Park, Hawaii 218/F6
Kaloli (pt.), Hawaii 218/K5
Kalomo, Zambia 115/E7
Kalona, Iowa 229/K6
Kalpeni (isl.), India 68/C7
Kalpin, China 77/A3
Kalskag, Alaska 196/F2
Kaltag, Alaska 196/G2
Kaltbrunn, Switzerland 39/H2
Kaluaaha, Hawaii 218/H1
Kaluga, U.S.S.R. 7/H3
Kaluga, U.S.S.R. 48/D4
Kaluga, U.S.S.R. 52/E4
Kalumburu Mission, W. Australia 88/D2
Kalumburu Mission, W. Australia 92/D1
Kalundborg, Denmark 21/D6
Kalundborg, Denmark 18/G9
Kalush, U.S.S.R. 52/B5
Kalutara, Sri Lanka 68/D7
Kalvarija, U.S.S.R. 53/B3
Kalvesta, Kansas 232/B3
Kalyan, India 68/C5
Kama, Burma 72/B3
Kama (res.), U.S.S.R. 52/J3
Kama (riv.), U.S.S.R. 7/K3
Kama (riv.), U.S.S.R. 52/H2
Kama, Zaire 115/E4
Kamaiki (pt.), Hawaii 218/H2
Kamaing, Burma 72/C1
Kamaishi, Japan 81/L4
Kamakou (peak), Hawaii 218/H1
Kamakura, Japan 81/O3
Kamakusa, Guyana 131/A3
Kamalino, Hawaii 218/A2
Kamalo, Hawaii 218/H1
Kaman, Turkey 63/E3
Kamanisкeg (lake), Ontario 177/G2
Kamanjab, Namibia 118/A3
Kamaran (isl.), Yemen 59/D6
Kamarang, Guyana 131/A3
Kamarhati, India 68/F1
Kamaria (falls), Guyana 131/B2
Kamas, Utah 304/C3
Kamay, Texas 303/F4
Kambalda, W. Australia 88/C6
Kambalda, W. Australia 92/C5
Kambia, S. Leone 106/B7
Kambove, Zaire 115/E6
Kambove, Zaire 102/E6
Kamchatka (pen.), U.S.S.R. 54/S4
Kamchatka (pen.), U.S.S.R. 2/T3
Kamchatka (pen.), U.S.S.R. 48/Q4
Kamela, Oreg. 291/J2
Kamenets-Podol'skiy, U.S.S.R. 52/C5
Kamenice, Czech. 41/C2
Kamenjak (cape), Yugoslavia 45/A3
Kamenka, Archangel, U.S.S.R. 52/F1
Kamenka, Penza, U.S.S.R. 52/F4
Kamen'-na-Obi, U.S.S.R. 48/H4
Kamenskoye, U.S.S.R. 48/R3
Kamensk-Shakhtinskiy, U.S.S.R. 52/F5
Kamensk-Ural'skiy, U.S.S.R. 48/G4
Kamenz, Germany 22/F3
Kameoka, Japan 81/J7
Kames, Scotland 15/C5
Kamet (mt.), India 68/D2
Kamiah, Idaho 220/B3
Kamienna Góra, Poland 47/B3
Kamień Pomorski, Poland 47/B2
Kamiisco, Japan 81/K3
Kamil, Oman 59/G5
Kamilo (pt.), Hawaii 218/H7
Kamilukuak (lake), N.W. Terr. 187/H3
Kamina, Zaire 102/E5
Kamina, Zaire 115/D5
Kaminak (lake), N.W. Terr. 187/J3
Kaminoyama, Japan 81/J4
Kaminuriak (lake), N.W. Terr. 187/J3
Kamishak (bay), Alaska 196/H3
Kamiyaku, Japan 81/E8
Kamloops, Br. Col. 162/D5
Kamloops, Br. Col. 146/G4
Kamloops, Br. Col. 184/G5
Kamo, Japan 81/J7
Kamoa (riv.), Guyana 131/B5
Kamouraska (co.), Québec 172/H2
Kamouraska, Québec 172/H2
Kamp (riv.), Austria 41/C2
Kampala (cap.), Uganda 2/L5
Kampala (cap.), Uganda 102/F4
Kampala (cap.), Uganda 115/F3
Kampar (riv.), Indonesia 85/C5
Kampar, Malaysia 72/D6
Kampen, Netherlands 27/H3
Kampen, Germany 22/C1
Kampene, Zaire 115/E4
Kampeska (lake), S. Dak. 298/P4
Kamphaeng Phet, Thailand 72/C3
Kampong Cham, Cambodia 54/M8
Kampong Cham, Cambodia 72/E4
Kampong Chhnang, Cambodia 72/D4
Kampong Khleang, Cambodia 72/E4
Kampong Kuala Besut, Malaysia 72/D6
Kampong Saom, Cambodia 72/D5
Kampong Sedenak, Malaysia 72/E5
Kampong Sibuti, Malaysia 85/E5
Kampong Spoe, Cambodia 72/E5
Kampong Thum, Cambodia 72/E4
Kampong Trabek, Cambodia 72/E5
Kampot, Cambodia 72/E5
Kampsville, Ill. 222/C4
Kamptee, India 68/D4
KAMPUCHEA (CAMBODIA) 72
Kampung Baru (Tolitoli), Indonesia 85/G5
Kamrar, Iowa 229/F4
Kamsack, Sask. 162/F5
Kamsack, Sask. 181/K4
Kamsack Beach, Sask. 181/K4
Kamsar, Guinea 106/B6
Kamuela, Hawaii 218/G3
Kamui (cape), Japan 81/K2
Kamyshin, U.S.S.R. 7/J3
Kamyshin, U.S.S.R. 52/F4
Kamyshin, U.S.S.R. 48/E4
Kanaaupscow (riv.), Québec 174/B2
Kanab (creek), Ariz. 198/C2
Kanab (plat.), Ariz. 198/C2
Kanab, Utah 304/B6
Kanab (creek), Utah 304/B7
Kanabec (co.), Minn. 255/E5
Kanaga (isl.), Alaska 196/L4
Kanagawa (pref.), Japan 81/O2
Kanaio, Hawaii 218/J3
Kanairiktok (riv.), Newf. 166/B3
Kanakanak, Alaska 196/G3
Kananaskis, Alberta 182/C4
Kananga, Zaire 115/D5
Kananga, Zaire 102/E5
Kanapou (bay), Hawaii 218/J3
Kanaranzi, Minn. 255/B7
Kanaranzi (creek), Minn. 255/C7
Kanarraville, Utah 304/A6
Kanash, U.S.S.R. 52/G3
Kanata, Ontario 177/J2
Kanauga, Ohio 284/F8
Kanawha, Iowa 229/F3
Kanawha (co.), W. Va. 312/C6
Kanawha (riv.), W. Va. 312/C5
Kanawha Falls, W. Va. 312/D6
Kanawha Head, W. Va. 312/F5
Kanazawa, Japan 81/H5
Kanazawa, Japan 54/P6
Kanbalu, Burma 72/B2
Kanchanaburi, Thailand 72/C4
Kanchenjunga (mt.), India 68/F3
Kanchenjunga (mt.), Nepal 68/F3
Kanchipuram, India 68/E6
Kanchow (Ganzhou), China 77/H6
Kanchrapara, India 68/F1
Kandahar (Qandahar), Afghanistan 59/J3
Kandahar (Qandahar), Afghanistan 68/B2
Kandahar, Sask. 181/G4
Kanda-Kanda, Zaire 115/D5
Kandalaksha, U.S.S.R. 7/H2
Kandalaksha, U.S.S.R. 52/D1
Kandalaksha, U.S.S.R. 48/C3
Kandalaksha (gulf), U.S.S.R. 52/D1
Kandangan, Indonesia 85/F6
Kándanos, Greece 45/F8
Kandava, U.S.S.R. 53/B2
Kandavu (Kadavu) (isl.), Fiji 87/H7
Kandavu (isl.), Fiji 86/Q11
Kandavu (passage), Fiji 86/Q11
Kander (riv.), Switzerland 39/C2
Kandersteg, Switzerland 39/E4
Kandi, Benin 106/E6
Kandıra, Turkey 63/D2
Kandiyohi (co.), Minn. 255/C5
Kandiyohi, Minn. 255/D5
Kandla, India 68/C4
Kandos, N.S. Wales 97/F3
Kandrach, Pakistan 68/A3
Kandrach, Pakistan 59/H4
Kandukur, India 68/E5
Kandy, Sri Lanka 54/K9
Kandy, Sri Lanka 68/E7
Kane (basin) 4/B13
Kane (co.), Ill. 222/E2
Kane, Ill. 222/C4
Kane, Manitoba 179/E5
Kane (basin), N.W.T. 162/N3
Kane (basin), N.W. Terr. 187/L2
Kane, Pa. 294/E2
Kane (co.), Utah 304/B6
Kanem (reg.), Chad 111/C5
Kaneohe, Hawaii 218/F2
Kaneohe (bay), Hawaii 218/F2
Kaneohe Bay U.S.M.C. Air Station, Hawaii 218/F2
Kaneville, Ill. 222/E2
Kang, Botswana 118/C4
Kanga, Tanzania 115/G5
Kangaba, Mali 106/C6
Kangal, Turkey 63/G3
Kangan, Iran 59/F4
Kangan, Iran 66/G7
Kangar, Malaysia 72/D6
Kangarilla, S. Australia 94/B8
Kangaroo (isl.), Australia 87/D9
Kangaroo (isl.), S. Australia 88/F7
Kangaroo (isl.), S. Australia 94/E7
Kangaroo Ground, Victoria 97/J4
Kangaruma, Guyana 131/B3
Kangavar, Iran 59/E3
Kangavar, Iran 66/F3
Kangding, China 77/F5
Kangean (isl.), Indonesia 85/F7
Kangean (isls.), Indonesia 85/F7
Kanggye, N. Korea 81/C3
Kanghwa (bay), N. Korea 81/B5
Kanghwa (bay), S. Korea 81/B5
Kangiqsualujjuaq, Québec 162/K4
Kangiqsualujjuaq, Québec 174/F2
Kangiqsujuaq, Québec 162/J3
Kangiqsujuaq, Québec 174/F1
Kangirsuk, Québec 162/J3
Kangsiruk, Québec 174/F1
Kangley, Ill. 222/E2
Kangnŭng, S. Korea 81/D5
Kango, Gabon 115/B3
Kangrinboqê Feng (mt.), China 77/B5
Kani, Burma 72/B2
Kaniama, Zaire 115/D5
Kanin (pen.), U.S.S.R. 7/J2
Kanin (pen.), U.S.S.R. 4/C7
Kanin (pen.), U.S.S.R. 48/E3
Kanin (pen.), U.S.S.R. 52/G1
Kaningo, Kenya 115/G4
Kanin Nos (cape), U.S.S.R. 48/E3
Kanin Nos (cape), U.S.S.R. 52/F1
Kaniva, Victoria 97/A5
Kanjiža, Yugoslavia 45/D2
Kankaanpää, Finland 18/M6
Kankakee, Ill. 188/J2
Kankakee (co.), Ill. 222/F2
Kankakee, Ill. 222/F2
Kankakee (riv.), Ill. 222/F2
Kankakee (riv.), Ind. 227/C2
Kankan, Guinea 106/C6
Kankan, Guinea 102/B3
Kanker, India 68/E4
Kankossa, Mauritania 102/A3
Kankossa, Mauritania 106/B5
Kannapolis, N.C. 281/H4
Kannata Valley, Sask. 181/G5
Kannauj, India 68/D3
Kano (state), Nigeria 106/F6
Kano, Nigeria 106/F6
Kano, Nigeria 102/C3
Kanon (pt.), Neth. Ant. 161/G9
Kanona, N.Y. 276/F6
Kanonji, Japan 81/F6
Kanopolis, Kansas 232/D3
Kanopolis (lake), Kansas 232/D3
Kanorado, Kansas 232/A2
Kanosh, Utah 304/B5
Kanosh Ind. Res., Utah 304/B5
Kanoya, Japan 81/E8
Kanpur, India 54/K7
Kanpur, India 68/E3
Kanrach, Pakistan 59/H4
Kansas 188/G3
KANSAS 232
Kansas, Ala. 195/C3
Kansas, Ill. 222/F4
Kansas (riv.), Kans. 188/G3
Kansas (riv.), Kansas 232/F2
Kansas, Ohio 284/D3
Kansas, Okla. 288/S2
Kansas (state), U.S. 146/J6
Kansas City, Kans. 188/G3
Kansas City, Kansas 232/H2
Kansas City, Mo. 261/P5
Kansas City, Mo. 188/H3
Kansas City, Mo. 146/J6
Kansasville, Wis. 317/L3
Kansk, U.S.S.R. 54/L4
Kansk, U.S.S.R. 48/K4
Kansu (Gansu), China 77/E3
Kantishna (riv.), Alaska 196/H2
Kanton (isl.), Kiribati 87/J6
Kantunilkin, Mexico 150/Q6
Kanturk, Ireland 10/B4
Kanturk, Ireland 17/D7
Kanuku (mts.), Guyana 131/B4
Kanuma, Japan 81/J5
Kanye, Botswana 102/E7
Kanye, Botswana 118/C5
Kanzi (cape), Tanzania 115/G5
Kaohsiung, China 77/J7
Kaohsiung, Taiwan 54/N7
Kaokoveld (reg.), Namibia 118/A3
Kaolack, Senegal 106/A6
Kaolack, Senegal 102/A3
Kaoma, Zambia 115/D6
Kao Prawa (mt.), Thailand 72/C3
Kapaa, Hawaii 218/D1
Kapaa, Hawaii 188/E5
Kapaahu, Hawaii 218/J6
Kapaau, Hawaii 218/G3
Kapalama, Hawaii 218/C4
Kapalong, Philippines 82/E7
Kapanga, Zaire 115/D5
Kapchagay, U.S.S.R. 48/H5
Kapellen, Belgium 27/E6
Kapenguria, Kenya 115/G3
Kapfenberg, Austria 41/C3
Kapingamarangi (atoll), Micronesia 87/F5
Kapiri Mposhi, Zambia 115/E6
Kapiskau (riv.), Ontario 175/D2
Kapit, Malaysia 85/E5
Kapiti (isl.), N. Zealand 100/E4
Kaplan, La. 238/F6
Kaplice, Czech. 41/C2
Kapoeta, Sudan 111/F7
Kapoho, Hawaii 218/K5
Kapos (riv.), Hungary 41/D3
Kaposvár, Hungary 41/D3
Kapowsin, Wash. 310/C4
Kappa, Ill. 222/D3
Kappl, Austria 41/A3
Kaprun, Austria 41/B3
Kapsan, N. Korea 81/C3
Kapsukas, U.S.S.R. 53/B3
Kapsukas, U.S.S.R. 52/B4
Kapuas (riv.), Indonesia 85/D6
Kapulena, Hawaii 218/H4
Kapunda, S. Australia 94/F6
Kapuskasing, Ont. 162/H6
Kapuskasing, Ontario 175/D3
Kapuskasing, Ontario 177/J5
Kapuskasing (riv.), Ontario 177/J5
Kapuskasing (riv.), Ontario 175/D3
Kapuvár, Hungary 41/D3
Kapydzhik (mt.), U.S.S.R. 52/G7
Kara, U.S.S.R. 48/G3
Kara, U.S.S.R. 52/L1
Kara (sea), U.S.S.R. 4/B6
Kara (sea), U.S.S.R. 54/H2
Kara (sea), U.S.S.R. 52/K1
Kara (sea), U.S.S.R. 48/G2
Kara-Bogaz-Gol (gulf), U.S.S.R. 48/F5
Karabük, Turkey 63/E2
Karaburun, Turkey 63/B3
Karacabey, Turkey 63/C2
Karaca Dağ (mt.), Turkey 63/H4
Karachay-Cherkess Aut. Obl., U.S.S.R. 48/E5
Karachay-Cherkess Aut. Obl., U.S.S.R. 52/F6
Karachayevsk, U.S.S.R. 52/F6
Karachev, U.S.S.R. 52/E4
Karachi, Pakistan 2/N4
Karachi, Pakistan 59/J5
Karachi, Pakistan 68/B4
Karachi, Pakistan 54/H7
Karád, Hungary 41/D3
Karad, India 68/C5
Karadağ (mt.), Turkey 59/B2
Karadağ (mt.), Turkey 63/E4
Karadeniz Boğazı (Bosporus) (str.), Turkey 63/C2
Karadeniz Boğazı (Bosporus) (str.), Turkey 59/A1
Karaganda, U.S.S.R. 2/N3
Karaganda, U.S.S.R. 54/J5
Karaganda, U.S.S.R. 48/H5
Karaginskiy (isl.), U.S.S.R. 54/T4
Karaginskiy (isl.), U.S.S.R. 48/R4
Karahallı, Turkey 63/C3
Karaikudi, India 68/D7
Karaisalı, Turkey 63/F4
Karaj, Iran 66/G3
Karakalpak A.S.S.R., U.S.S.R. 48/G5
Karakax (Kara Kash) (Moyu), China 77/A4
Karakax He (riv.), China 77/A4
Karakelong (isl.), Indonesia 85/H5
Karakhoto (ruins), China 77/F3
Karakoçan, Turkey 63/H3
Karakoram (mts.), India 68/D1
Karakoram (mts.), Pakistan 68/D1
Karakorum (ruins), Mongolia 54/M5
Karakorum (ruins), Mongolia 77/F2
Karaköse, Turkey 59/D2
Karaköse (Ağrı), Turkey 63/K3
Kara-Kum (canal), U.S.S.R. 48/F6
Kara-Kum (des.), U.S.S.R. 48/F5
Karakuwisa, Namibia 118/B3
Karaman, Turkey 59/B2
Karaman, Turkey 63/E4
Karamanlı, Turkey 63/C4
Karamay, China 77/B2
Karamay, China 54/K5
Karamea, N. Zealand 100/C4
Karamea (bight), N. Zealand 100/C4
Karamiran Shankou (pass), China 77/C4
Karan (state), Burma 72/C3
Karangasem, Indonesia 85/F7
Karanja, India 68/D4
Karapelit, Bulgaria 45/H4
Karapınar, Turkey 63/E4
Karas, Namibia 118/B5
Karasabai, Guyana 131/B4
Karasavey (cape), U.S.S.R. 4/B6
Karasburg, Namibia 118/B5
Karasjok, Norway 18/O2
Karasu, Turkey 63/D2
Karasu (riv.), Turkey 63/J3
Karasu-Aras (mts.), Turkey 63/J3
Karasuk, U.S.S.R. 48/H4
Karat, Iran 66/M3
Karataş, Turkey 63/F4
Karataş (cape), Turkey 63/F4
Karatau, U.S.S.R. 48/H5
Karathuri, Burma 72/C5
Karatsu, Japan 81/D7
Karawanken (range), Austria 41/C3
Karayaka, Turkey 63/G2
Karayazı, Turkey 63/J3
Karazhal, U.S.S.R. 48/H5
Karbala (gov.), Iraq 66/B4
Karbal'a, Iraq 59/D3
Karbala, Iraq 54/F6
Karbal'a, Iraq 66/C4
Karbers Ridge, Ill. 222/E6
Karby, Denmark 21/B4
Karcag, Hungary 41/F3
Kardhítsa, Greece 45/E6
Kärdla, U.S.S.R. 53/B1
Karelian A.S.S.R., U.S.S.R. 48/D3
Karelian A.S.S.R., U.S.S.R. 52/D2
Karema, Tanzania 115/F5
Karesuando, Sweden 18/M2
Kargasok, U.S.S.R. 48/J4
Kargı, Turkey 63/F2
Kargil, India 68/D2
Kargopol', U.S.S.R. 52/E2
Karhula, Finland 18/P6
Kariá, Greece 45/E6
Kariaí, Greece 45/G5
Kariba (lake) 102/E6
Kariba (mt.), Japan 81/K2
Kariba (dam), Zambia 115/E7
Kariba (lake), Zambia 115/E7
Kariba, Zimbabwe 118/D3
Kariba (dam), Zimbabwe 118/D3
Kariba (lake), Zimbabwe 118/D3
Karibib, Namibia 118/B4
Karikal, India 68/E6
Karikari (cape), N. Zealand 100/D1
Karima, Sudan 59/B6
Karima, Sudan 111/F4
Karimata (arch.), Indonesia 85/D6
Karimata (isl.), Indonesia 85/D6
Karimata (str.), Indonesia 85/D6
Karimunjawa (isls.), Indonesia 85/J1
Karin, Somalia 115/J1
Karis, Finland 18/N6
Karise, Denmark 21/F7
Karisimbi (mt.), Rwanda 115/E4
Karisimbi (mt.), Zaire 115/E4
Káristos, Greece 45/G6
Kariz, Iran 66/M3
Karjaa (Karis), Finland 18/N6
Karkabat, Ethiopia 111/G4
Karkal, India 68/C6
Karkar (isl.), Papua N.G. 85/B6
Karkas, Kuh-e (mt.), Iran 66/G4
Karkheh (riv.), Iran 66/E4
Karkkila, Finland 18/N6
Karkur-Pardes Hanna, Israel 65/C3
Karlıova, Turkey 63/J3
Karlö (Hailuoto) (isl.), Finland 18/O4
Karlovac, Yugoslavia 45/B3
Karlovo, Bulgaria 45/G4
Karlovy Vary, Czech. 41/B1
Karlshamn, Sweden 18/J8
Karlskoga, Sweden 18/J7
Karlskrona, Sweden 18/J8
Karlsruhe, N. Dak. 282/J3
Karlsruhe, Germany 7/E4
Karlsruhe, Germany 22/C4
Karlstad, Germany 22/C4
Karlstad, Minn. 255/B2
Karlstad, Sweden 7/F3
Karlstad, Sweden 18/H7

390 Karluk

Karluk, Alaska 196/H3
Karnak (El Karnak), Egypt 111/F2
Karnak, Ill. 222/E6
Karnak, N. Dak. 282/O5
Karnal, India 68/D3
Karnataka (state), India 68/D6
Karnes (co.), Texas 303/G9
Karnes City, Texas 303/G9
Karnobat, Bulgaria 45/H4
Karns, Tenn. 237/N9
Karns City, Pa. 294/C4
Karonga, Malawi 115/F5
Karora, Sudan 111/G4
Karoro, N. Zealand 100/C5
Karosa, Indonesia 85/F6
Karpakora, N.S. Wales 97/B3
Kárpathos, Greece 45/H8
Kárpathos (isl.), Greece 45/H8
Karpenísion, Greece 45/E6
Karpinsk, U.S.S.R. 48/F4
Karratha, W. Australia 88/B4
Karratha, W. Australia 92/B3
Kars, Ontario 177/J2
Kars (prov.), Turkey 63/K2
Kars, Turkey 59/D1
Kars, Turkey 63/K2
Kärsava, U.S.S.R. 53/D2
Karshi, U.S.S.R. 48/G6
Karşıyaka, Turkey 63/B3
Karskiye Vorota (str.), U.S.S.R. 4/B7
Karskiye Vorota (str.), U.S.S.R. 52/J1
Karskiye Vorota (str.), U.S.S.R. 48/F2
Kartal, Turkey 63/D6
Kartaly, U.S.S.R. 48/G4
Karthaus, Pa. 294/F3
Kartuzy, Poland 47/C1
Karumba, Queensland 88/G3
Karumba, Queensland 95/B3
Karun (riv.), Iran 59/E3
Karun (riv.), Iran 66/F5
Karunjie, W. Australia 92/D2
Karunki, Finland 18/O4
Karup, Denmark 21/C5
Karval, Colo. 208/N5
Karviná, Czech. 41/E2
Karwar, India 68/C6
Kaş, Turkey 63/C4
Kasaan, Alaska 196/N2
Kasabonika, Ontario 175/C2
Kasai (riv.) 102/E5
Kasai (riv.), Angola 115/D5
Kasai (riv.), Zaire 115/C4
Kasai-Occidental (prov.), Zaire 115/D4
Kasai-Oriental (prov.), Zaire 115/D5
Kasaji, Zaire 115/D6
Kasama, Zambia 102/F6
Kasama, Zambia 115/F6
Kasane, Botswana 118/D3
Kasanga, Tanzania 115/F5
Kasanga, Tanzania 102/F5
Kasangulu, Zaire 115/C4
Kasar, Ras (cape), Ethiopia 111/G4
Kasar, Ras (cape), Sudan 111/G4
Kasar, Ras (cape), Sudan 59/C6
Kasaragod, India 68/C6
Kasba (lake), N.W.T. 162/F3
Kasba (lake), N.W. Terr. 187/H3
Kasbeer, Ill. 222/D2
Kaseda, Japan 81/D8
Kasempa, Zambia 115/E6
Kasenga, Zaire 115/E6
Kasenyi, Zaire 115/E3
Kasese, Uganda 115/F3
Kasese, Zaire 115/E4
Kasganj, India 68/D3
Kashabowie, Ontario 177/G5
Kashaf Rud (riv.), Iran 66/M2
Kashan, Iran 59/F3
Kashan, Iran 66/G3
Kashechewan, Ontario 175/D2
Kashegelok, Alaska 196/G2
Kashi, China 77/A4
Kashi, China 54/J6
Kashihara, Japan 81/J8
Kashin, U.S.S.R. 52/E3
Kashing (Jiaxing), China 77/K5
Kashiwa, Japan 81/P2
Kashiwara, Japan 81/J8
Kashiwazaki, Japan 81/J5
Kashmar, Iran 66/L3
Kashmar, Iran 59/G2
Kashmor, Pakistan 68/C3
Kashunuk (riv.), Alaska 196/F2
Kasigluk, Alaska 196/F2
Kasilof, Alaska 196/B1
Kasimov, U.S.S.R. 52/F4
Kaskaskia, Ill. 222/C6
Kaskaskia (riv.), Ill. 222/E4
Kaskinen (Kaskö), Finland 18/M5
Kaskö, Finland 18/M5
Kaslo, Br. Col. 162/E6
Kaslo, Br. Col. 184/J5
Kasongo, Zaire 115/E4
Kasongo-Lunda, Zaire 115/C5
Kásos (isl.), Greece 45/H8
Kasota, Minn. 255/D6
Kasper Creek, Sask. 181/F6
Kaspiysk, U.S.S.R. 52/G6
Kaspiyskiy, U.S.S.R. 52/G5
Kassala (prov.), Sudan 111/F4
Kassala, Sudan 111/G4
Kassala, Sudan 59/C6
Kassala, Sudan 102/F3
Kassándra (pen.), Greece 45/F6
Kassel, Germany 7/E3
Kassel, Germany 22/C3
Kasserine, Tunisia 106/F1
Kasson, Minn. 255/F6
Kasson, W. Va. 312/G4
Kastamonu (prov.), Turkey 63/E2
Kastamonu, Turkey 59/B1
Kastamonu, Turkey 63/F2
Kastéllion, Greece 45/G8
Kastéllion (Kíssamos), Greece 45/F8
Kasterlee, Belgium 27/F6
Kastoría, Greece 45/E5
Kastrup, Denmark 21/F6
Kastrup, Denmark 18/H9
Kasugai, Japan 81/H6
Kasukabe, Japan 81/O2
Kasulu, Tanzania 115/F4
Kasumiga (lag.), Japan 81/K5
Kasungu, Malawi 115/F6
Kasur, Pakistan 68/C2
Kasur, Pakistan 59/K3
Kataba, Zambia 115/D7
Katahdin (mt.), Maine 243/F4
Katako-Kombe, Zaire 115/D4
Katákolon, Greece 45/E7
Katanga (reg.), Zaire 102/E5
Katangli, U.S.S.R. 48/P4
Katanning, W. Australia 88/B6
Katanning, W. Australia 92/B6
Katarnian Ghat, India 68/E3
Kata Tjuta (Mt. Olga) (mt.), North. Terr. 93/B8
Katchall (isl.), India 68/G7
Katchiungo, Angola 115/C6
Katemcy, Texas 303/E7
Katenga, Zaire 115/E5
Katepwa Beach, Sask. 181/H5
Katepwa Prov. Park, Sask. 181/H5
Kateríni, Greece 45/F5
Kates Needle (mt.), Alaska 196/N1
Kates Needle (mt.), Br. Col. 184/A1
Katha, Burma 72/C1
Katherina, Jebel (mt.), Egypt 111/F2
Katherina, Jebel (mt.), Egypt 59/B4
Katherine, Ariz. 198/A3
Katherine, Australia 87/D7
Katherine, North. Terr. 88/E2
Katherine, North. Terr. 93/B3
Katherine (riv.), North. Terr. 93/C3
Kathiawar (pen.), India 68/B4
Kathleen, Alberta 182/B2
Kathleen, Fla. 212/D3
Kathleen, Georgia 217/E6
Kathmandu (cap.), Nepal 54/K7
Kathmandu (cap.), Nepal 68/E3
Kathryn, Alberta 182/D4
Kathryn, N. Dak. 282/P6
Kati, Mali 106/C6
Katihar, India 68/F3
Katima Mulilo, Namibia 118/C3
Katimik (lake), Manitoba 179/C2
Katiola, Ivory Coast 106/C7
Katipunan, Philippines 82/D6
Katmai (vol.), Alaska 196/H3
Katmai Nat'l Park, Alaska 196/H3
Katmai Nat'l Pres., Alaska 196/H3
Katni (Murwara), India 68/E4
Katonah, N.Y. 276/N8
Katoomba-Wentworth Falls, N.S. Wales 97/F3
Katowice (prov.), Poland 47/D3
Katowice, Poland 7/F3
Katowice, Poland 47/B4
Katrime, Manitoba 179/D4
Katrine, Ontario 177/E2
Katrine, Loch (lake), Scotland 15/D4
Katrineholm, Sweden 18/K7
Katsina, Nigeria 102/C3
Katsina, Nigeria 106/F6
Katsina Ala, Nigeria 106/F7
Katsuta, Japan 81/K5
Katsuura, Japan 81/K6
Kattakurgan, U.S.S.R. 48/G5
Kattegat (str.) 7/F3
Kattegat (str.), Denmark 21/E4
Kattegat (str.), Denmark 18/G8
Kattegat (str.), Sweden 18/G8
Katwe, Uganda 115/F4
Katwijk aan Zee, Netherlands 27/E4
Katy, Texas 303/J8
Kau (des.), Hawaii 218/J6
Kau, Indonesia 85/H5
Kauai (co.), Hawaii 218/A1
Kauai (isl.), Hawaii 87/L3
Kauai (isl.), Hawaii 188/E5
Kauai (chan.), Hawaii 218/E6
Kauai (isl.), Hawaii 218/C1
Kaufbeuren, Germany 22/D5
Kaufman (co.), Texas 303/H5
Kaufman, Texas 303/H5
Kauhola (pt.), Hawaii 218/G3
Kauiki (head), Hawaii 218/K2
Kaukauna, Wis. 317/K7
Kaukauveld (mts.), Botswana 118/C3
Kaukauveld (mts.), Namibia 118/C3
Kaukonahua (stream), Hawaii 218/E1
Kaula (isl.), Hawaii 188/F6
Kaula (isl.), Hawaii 218/D6
Kaulakahi (chan.), Hawaii 218/B2
Kauliranta, Finland 18/O3
Kaumajet (mts.), Newf. 166/B2
Kaumakani, Hawaii 218/C2
Kaumalapau (harb.), Hawaii 218/G2
Kaumalapau Harbor, Hawaii 218/G2
Kauna (pt.), Hawaii 218/G7
Kaunakakai, Hawaii 218/G1
Kaunakakai (harb.), Hawaii 218/G1
Kaunas, U.S.S.R. 7/G3
Kaunas, U.S.S.R. 53/C3
Kaunas, U.S.S.R. 48/C4
Kaunas, U.S.S.R. 52/B4
Kauniainien, Finland 18/O6
Kaunuopou (pt.), Hawaii 218/B2
Kaupakulua, Hawaii 218/K2
Kaupo, Hawaii 218/K2
Kaura Namoda, Nigeria 106/F6
Kauswagan, Philippines 82/E6
Kautokeino, Norway 18/N2
Kauttua, Finland 18/M6
Kavadarci, Yugoslavia 45/E5
Kavajë, Albania 45/D5
Kavak, Çanakkale, Turkey 63/C5
Kavak, Samsun, Turkey 63/F2
Kavalerovo, U.S.S.R. 48/O5
Kavalga (isl.), Alaska 196/K4
Kavali, India 68/E6
Kavála, Greece 7/G4
Kavála, Greece 45/G5
Kavanagh, Alberta 182/D3
Kavanayen, Venezuela 124/H5
Kavaratti, India 68/C6
Kavarna, Bulgaria 45/J4
Kaveri (riv.), India 68/D6
Kavieng, Papua N.G. 87/E6
Kavieng, Papua N.G. 86/B1
Kavir, Dasht-e (salt des.), Iran 59/G3
Kavir, Dasht-e (salt des.), Iran 66/J3
Kavir-e Namak (salt des.), Iran 59/G3
Kavirondo (gulf), Kenya 115/F4
Kavungo, Angola 114/D6
Kaw, Fr. Guiana 131/E3
Kaw (lake), Okla. 288/N1
Kawachinagano, Japan 81/J8
Kawagama (lake), Ontario 177/F2
Kawagoe, Japan 81/O2
Kawaguchi, Japan 81/J6
Kawaihae, Hawaii 218/G4
Kawaihae (bay), Hawaii 218/G4
Kawaihoa (cape), Hawaii 218/A2
Kawaikini (peak), Hawaii 218/C1
Kawailoa, Hawaii 218/E1
Kawakawa, N. Zealand 100/E1
Kawambwa, Zambia 115/E5
Kawanishi, Japan 81/H7
Kawardha, India 68/E4
Kawasaki, Japan 81/O2
Kawau (isl.), N. Zealand 100/E2
Kaw City, Okla. 288/N1
Kawerau, N. Zealand 100/F3
Kawhia, N. Zealand 100/E3
Kawhia (harb.), N. Zealand 100/E3
Kawi (mt.), Indonesia 85/K2
Kawich (peak), Nev. 266/E5
Kawich (range), Nev. 266/E5
Kawinaw (lake), Manitoba 179/C2
Kawio (isls.), Indonesia 85/G5
Kawkawlin, Mich. 250/F5
Kawlin, Burma 72/B2
Kawludo, Burma 72/C3
Kawthaung, Burma 72/C5
Kay (co.), Okla. 288/M1
Kaya, Burkina Faso 106/D6
Kayah (state), Burma 72/C3
Kayak (isl.), Alaska 196/K3
Kayan (riv.), Indonesia 54/N9
Kayan (riv.), Indonesia 85/F5
Kaycee, Wyo. 319/F2
Kayenta, Ariz. 198/E2
Kayes, Mali 106/B6
Kayes, Mali 102/A3
Kayjay, Ky. 237/O7
Kaylor, Pa. 294/C4
Kaylor, S. Dak. 298/O7
Kayser (mts.), Suriname 131/C4
Kayseri (prov.), Turkey 63/F3
Kayseri, Turkey 63/F3
Kayseri, Turkey 59/C2
Kayseri, Turkey 54/E6
Kaysville, Utah 304/B2
Kayuagung, Indonesia 85/D6
Kayville, Sask. 181/F6
Kazabazua, Québec 172/A4
Kazakh, S.S.R., U.S.S.R. 54/H5
Kazakh, S.S.R., U.S.S.R. 48/G5
Kazan (riv.), N.W.T. 162/F3
Kazan (riv.), N.W. Terr. 187/H3
Kazan', U.S.S.R. 7/J3
Kazan', U.S.S.R. 48/F4
Kazan', U.S.S.R. 52/G3
Kazanlı, Turkey 63/F4
Kazanlŭk, Bulgaria 45/G4
Kazan-retto (Volcano) (isls.), Japan 81/M4
Kazatin, U.S.S.R. 52/C5
Kazbek (mt.), U.S.S.R. 52/F6
Kazerun, Iran 66/G6
Kazerun, Iran 59/F4
Kazhim, U.S.S.R. 52/H2
Kazimierza Wielka, Poland 47/E3
Kazımkarabekir, Turkey 63/E4
Kazincbarcika, Hungary 41/F2
Kazlu-Rūda, U.S.S.R. 53/B3
Kazumba, Zaire 115/D5
Kazvin (Qazvin), Iran 66/F2
Kdyně, Czech. 41/B2
Kéa, Greece 45/G7
Kéa (isl.), Greece 45/G7
Keaau, Hawaii 188/G6
Keaau, Hawaii 218/J5
Keady, N. Ireland 17/H3
Keahi (pt.), Hawaii 218/A4
Keahole (pt.), Hawaii 218/F5
Kealaikahiki (chan.), Hawaii 218/H3
Kealakekua, Hawaii 218/G5
Kealakekua (bay), Hawaii 218/F6
Kealia, Hawaii, 218/G6
Kealia, Kauai, Hawaii 218/D1
Keams Canyon, Ariz. 198/E3
Keanae, Hawaii 218/K2
Keanapapa (pt.), Hawaii 218/G2
Keansburg, N.J. 273/E3
Kearney, Mo. 261/D4
Kearney, Nebr. 188/G2
Kearney (co.), Nebr. 264/F4
Kearney, Nebr. 264/E4
Kearney, Ontario 177/E2
Kearneysville, W. Va. 312/L4
Kearns, Utah 304/B3
Kearny, Ariz. 198/E5
Kearny (co.), Kansas 232/A3
Kearny, N.J. 273/B2
Kearny, Wyo. 319/F1
Kearsarge, N.H. 268/E3
Kearsarge (mt.), N.H. 268/D5
Kearsarge, Pa. 294/B1
Keasbey, N.J. 273/E2
Keatchie, La. 238/C2
Keating, Oreg. 291/K3
Keating Summit, Pa. 294/F2
Keatley, Sask. 181/D3
Keaton, Ky. 237/P5
Keats, Kansas 232/F2
Keats (mt.), W. Australia 92/A2
Keauhou, Hawaii 218/F5
Keavy, Ky. 237/N6
Keawekaheka (pt.), Hawaii 218/F5
Keban, Turkey 63/H3
Kebang (mt.), S. Korea 81/D5
Ke Bao, Vietnam 72/E2
Kebbi (riv.), Nigeria 106/E6
Kebnekaise (mt.), Sweden 7/F2
Kebnekaise (mt.), Sweden 18/L3
Kebock (head), Scotland 15/B2
Kebumen, Indonesia 85/J2
Kecel, Hungary 41/E3
Kechi, Kansas 232/E4
Kechika (riv.), Br. Col. 184/L2
Keçiborlu, Turkey 63/D4
Kecskemét, Hungary 7/F4
Kecskemét, Hungary 41/E3
Kedah (state), Malaysia 72/D6
Kedainiai, U.S.S.R. 53/C3
Keddie, Calif. 204/E3
Kedges (strs), Md. 245/O8
Kedgwick, New Bruns. 170/C1
Kedgwick (riv.), New Bruns. 170/C1
Kedgwick Ouest, New Bruns. 170/C1
Kedgwick River, New Bruns. 170/C1
Kediri, Indonesia 85/K2
Kédougou, Senegal 106/B6
Kedron (brook), Queensland 95/D2
Kędzierzyn-Koźle, Poland 47/C3
Keechelus (lake), Wash. 310/D3
Keedysville, Md. 245/H3
Keefers, Br. Col. 184/G5
Keefton, Okla. 288/R3
Keegan, Maine 243/G1
Keego Harbor, Mich. 250/F6
Keehi (lag.), Hawaii 218/B4
Keel-Dooagh, Ireland 17/A4
Keele (riv.), N.W. Terr. 187/F3
Keele (peak), Yukon 187/E3
Keeler, Calif. 204/H7
Keeler, Sask. 181/F5
Keeline, Wyo. 319/H3
Keeling (Cocos) (isls.), Australia 2/P6
Keeling, Va. 307/K7
Keels, Newf. 166/D1
Keelung, China 77/K6
Keenan, W. Va. 312/F7
Keenan Siding, New Bruns. 170/E2
Keene, Calif. 204/G8
Keene, Ky. 237/M5
Keene, N.H. 268/C6
Keene, N.Y. 276/N2
Keene, N. Dak. 282/E4
Keene, Ohio 284/G5
Keene, Ontario 177/F3
Keene, Texas 303/G5
Keener, Ala. 195/G2
Keenes, Ill. 222/E5
Keenesburg, Colo. 208/L2
Keene Valley, N.Y. 276/N2
Keensburg, Ill. 222/F5
Keeny (creek), Oreg. 291/K4
Keeper (hill), Ireland 17/E6
Keerweer (cape), Queensland 88/G2
Keerweer (cape), Queensland 95/B2
Keeseville, N.Y. 276/O2
Keesler A.F.B., Miss. 256/G10
Keetley, Utah 304/C3
Keetmanshoop, Namibia 118/B5
Keetmanshoop, Namibia 102/D7
Keewatin, Minn. 255/E3
Keewatin (reg.), N.W.T. 162/G3
Keewatin (reg.), N.W.T. 187/J3
Keewatin, Ontario 177/F5
Keewatin, Ontario 175/A3
Keewong, N.S. Wales 97/C3
Keezletown, Va. 307/L4
Kefallinia (isl.), Greece 45/E6
Kefar Blum, Israel 65/D1
Kefar Gil'adi, Israel 65/C1
Kefar Ruppin, Israel 65/D3
Kefar Sava, Israel 65/B3
Kefar Vitkin, Israel 65/B3
Kefar Zekhariya, Israel 65/B4
Keffi, Nigeria 106/F7
Keflavík, Iceland 21/B1
Kégashka, Québec 174/E2
Kegley, W. Va. 312/D8
Kegonsa (lake), Wis. 317/H10
Keg River, Alberta 182/A5
Kehl, Germany 22/B4
Kehoe, Ky. 237/P4
Kehra, U.S.S.R. 53/C1
Keila, U.S.S.R. 53/C1
Keilor, Victoria 88/K7
Keilor, Victoria 97/H5
Keimoes, S. Africa 118/C5
Keirn, Miss. 256/D4
Keiser, Ark. 202/K2
Keiss, Scotland 15/E2
Keitele (lake), Finland 18/O5
Keith (co.), Nebr. 264/C3
Keith, Scotland 10/E2
Keith, Scotland 15/F3
Keith, S. Australia 94/G7
Keith, W. Va. 312/C6
Keith Arm (inlet), N.W. Terr. 187/F3
Keithley Creek, Br. Col. 184/G4
Keithsburg, Ill. 222/B2
Keith Sebelius (res.), Kansas 232/C2
Keithville, La. 238/C2
Keizer, Oreg. 291/A3
Kejimkujik (lake), Nova Scotia 168/C4
Kejimkujik Nat'l Park, Nova Scotia 168/C4
Kekaa (pt.), Hawaii 218/H2
Kekaha, Hawaii 218/C2
Kekaha, Hawaii 188/E5
Kekertaluk (isl.), N.W. Terr. 187/M3
Kékes (mt.), Hungary 41/E3
Kekoskee, Wis. 317/J8
Kelang, Malaysia 72/D7
Kelantan (state), Malaysia 72/D6
Kelantan, Sungai (riv.), Malaysia 72/D6
Kelasa (str.), Indonesia 85/D6
Keldron, S. Dak. 298/F2
Keles, Turkey 63/C3
Kelfield, Sask. 181/C4
Kelford, N.C. 281/P2
Kelheim, Germany 22/D4
Kelkit, Turkey 63/H2
Kelkit (riv.), Turkey 59/C1
Kelkit (riv.), Turkey 63/G2
Kell, Ill. 222/E5
Kellé, Congo 115/B4
Keller (lake), N.W. Terr. 187/F3
Keller, Texas 303/F2
Keller, Va. 307/S5
Keller, Wash. 310/G2
Kellerberrin, W. Australia 88/B6
Kellerberrin, W. Australia 92/B5
Kellerman, Ala. 195/D4
Kellerton, Iowa 229/E7
Kellerville, Texas 303/D2
Kellett (cape), N.W.T. 162/D1
Kellett (cape), N.W. Terr. 187/F2
Kellett (str.), N.W. Terr. 187/G2
Kellettville, Pa. 294/D2
Kelley, Iowa 229/F5
Kelley (creek), Nev. 266/D1
Kelleys (isl.), Ohio 284/E2
Kelleys Island, Ohio 284/E2
Kelligrews, Newf. 166/D2
Kelliher, Minn. 255/D3
Kelliher, Sask. 181/H4
Kellnersville, Wis. 317/L7
Kellogg (mt.), Ariz. 198/E6
Kellogg, Idaho 220/B2
Kellogg, Iowa 229/H5
Kellogg, Minn. 255/G6
Kelloggsville, Ohio 284/J2
Kelloselkä, Finland 18/Q3
Kells (Ceanannus Mór), Ireland 17/G4
Kells, Ireland 17/G6
Kells, N. Ireland 17/J2
Kelly, Georgia 217/E4
Kelly (creek), Idaho 220/C3
Kelly, Kansas 232/G2
Kelly, Ky. 237/G7
Kelly, La. 238/F3
Kelly, N.C. 281/N6
Kelly, Wyo. 319/B2
Kelly A.F.B., Texas 303/J11
Kelly Lake, Br. Col. 184/G4
Kelly Lake, Minn. 255/F3
Kellys, N. Dak. 282/R4
Kellysville, W. Va. 312/E8
Kellyton, Ala. 195/F5
Kellyville, Okla. 288/O3
Kelmė, U.S.S.R. 53/B3
Kélo, Chad 111/C6
Kélo, Chad 102/D4
Kelowna, Br. Col. 146/G4
Kelowna, Br. Col. 162/E6
Kelowna, Br. Col. 184/H5
Kelsey, Alberta 182/D3
Kelsey, Minn. 255/F3
Kelsey Bay, Br. Col. 184/D5
Kelseyville, Calif. 204/C5
Kelso, Ark. 202/H6
Kelso, Calif. 204/K8
Kelso, Mo. 261/O8
Kelso, Sask. 181/K6
Kelso, Scotland 10/E3
Kelso, Scotland 15/F5
Kelso, Tenn. 237/J10
Kelso, Wash. 310/C4
Kelstern, Sask. 181/E5
Kelston West, N. Zealand 100/B1
Keltie (cape), Ant. 5/C7
Keltner, Ky. 237/K6
Kelton, S.C. 296/D2
Kelty, Scotland 10/C1
Kelty, Scotland 15/D1
Keluang, Malaysia 72/D7
Kelvington, Sask. 181/H3
Kelwood, Manitoba 179/C4
Kem', U.S.S.R. 7/H2
Kem', U.S.S.R. 4/C8
Kem', U.S.S.R. 52/D2
Kem', U.S.S.R. 48/D3
Ké-Macina, Mali 106/C6
Kemah, Texas 303/K2
Kemah, Turkey 63/H3
Kemaliye, Turkey 63/H3
Kemalpaşa, Turkey 63/J2
Kemano, Br. Col. 184/D3
Kemasik, Malaysia 72/D6
Kembe, Cent. Afr. Rep. 115/D3
Kemble, Ontario 177/D3
Kemboma, Gabon 115/B3
Kemecse, Hungary 41/F2
Kemer, Turkey 63/D4
Kemerburgaz, Turkey 63/D5
Kemerovo, U.S.S.R. 54/K4
Kemerovo, U.S.S.R. 48/J4
Kemi, Finland 7/G2
Kemi, Finland 18/O4
Kemi (riv.), Finland 7/G2
Kemijärvi, Finland 18/P3
Kemijärvi (lake), Finland 18/Q3
Kemijoki (riv.), Finland 18/O3
Kemikli, Büyük (cape), Turkey 63/B6
Kemirhisar, Turkey 63/F4
Kemmerer, Wyo. 319/B4
Kemnay, Manitoba 179/B5
Kemnay, Scotland 15/F3
Kemp, Ill. 222/E4
Kemp, Okla. 288/O7
Kemp, Texas 303/H5
Kemp (lake), Texas 303/E4
Kemp City (Hendrix), Okla. 288/O7
Kemp Coast (reg.), Ant. 5/C3
Kemper (co.), Miss. 256/G5
Kemp Mill, Md. 245/F3
Kempsey, N. S. Wales 88/J6
Kempsey, N.S. Wales 97/G2
Kempster, Wis. 317/H5
Kempston, England 13/G5
Kempt, Nova Scotia 168/C4
Kempt (lake), Québec 172/C2
Kempten, Germany 22/D5
Kempton, Ill. 222/E3
Kempton, Ind. 227/E4
Kempton, Md. 245/A4
Kempton, N. Dak. 282/P4
Kempton, Pa. 294/L4
Kempton, Tasmania 99/D4
Kempton Park, S. Africa 118/J6
Kemptown, Md. 245/J3
Kemptown, Nova Scotia 168/E3
Kemptville, Nova Scotia 168/C4
Kemptville, Ontario 177/J2
Ken, Afghanistan 68/A2
Ken, Afghanistan 59/H3
Kenadsa, Algeria 106/D2
Kenai, Alaska 196/B1
Kenai (lake), Alaska 196/C1
Kenai (mt.), Alaska 196/C2
Kenai (pen.), Alaska 196/C2
Kenai Fjords Nat'l Park, Alaska 196/C3
Kenamu (riv.), Newf. 166/B3
Kenansville, Fla. 212/F4
Kenansville, N.C. 281/O5
Kenaston, N. Dak. 282/F2
Kenaston, Sask. 181/E4
Kenbridge, Va. 307/M7
Kendal, Barbados 161/B8
Kendal, England 13/E3
Kendal, England 10/E3
Kendal, Indonesia 85/J2
Kendal, Sask. 181/H5
Kendall, Fla. 212/B5
Kendall (co.), Ill. 222/E2
Kendall, Kansas 232/A4
Kendall, N.S. Wales 97/G2
Kendall, N.Y. 276/E4
Kendall (cape), N.W. Terr. 187/K3
Kendall (co.), Texas 303/F8
Kendall, Wash. 310/C2
Kendall, Wis. 317/F8
Kendall Park, N.J. 273/D3
Kendallville, Ind. 227/G2
Kendallville, Iowa 229/K2
Kendari, Indonesia 85/G6
Kendawangan, Indonesia 85/D6
Kendrapara, India 68/F4
Kendrick (peak), Ariz. 198/D3
Kendrick, Fla. 212/D2
Kendrick, Idaho 220/B3
Kendrick, Okla. 288/N3
Kenduskeag•, Maine 243/E6
Kenedy (co.), Texas 303/G11
Kenedy, Texas 303/G9
Kenefic, Okla. 288/O6
Kenel, S. Dak. 298/H2
Kenema, S. Leone 102/A4
Kenema, S. Leone 106/B7
Kenesaw, Nebr. 264/F4
Kengah (isls.), Indonesia 85/F7
Kenge, Zaire 115/C4
Keng Hkam, Burma 72/C2
Keng Tung, Burma 72/C2
Kenhardt, S. Africa 118/C5
Kenhorst, Pa. 294/L5
Kéniéba, Mali 106/B6
Kenilworth, England 13/F5
Kenilworth, Ill. 222/B5
Kenilworth, N.J. 273/E2
Kenilworth, Ontario 177/D4
Kenilworth, Utah 304/D4
Keningau, Malaysia 85/F4
Kenitra, Morocco 102/B1
Kenitra, Morocco 106/C2
Kenli, China 77/J4
Kenly, N.C. 281/N3
Kenmare, Ireland 10/B5
Kenmare, Ireland 17/B8
Kenmare (riv.), Ireland 17/A8
Kenmare, N. Dak. 282/G2
Kenmore, N.Y. 276/C5
Kenmore, Queensland 88/J3
Kenmore, Scotland 15/E4
Kenmore, Wash. 310/B1
Kenna, N. Mex. 274/F5
Kenna, W. Va. 312/C5
Kennan, Wis. 317/F5
Kennard, Ind. 227/G5
Kennard, Nebr. 264/H3
Kennard, Pa. 294/B3
Kennard, Texas 303/J6
Kennebago Lake, Maine 243/B5
Kennebec (co.), Maine 243/D7
Kennebec (riv.), Maine 243/D7
Kennebec, S. Dak. 298/K6
Kennebecasis (bay), New Bruns. 170/E3
Kennebecasis (riv.), New Bruns. 170/E3
Kennebunk, Maine 243/B9
Kennebunk•, Maine 243/B9
Kennebunk Beach, Maine 243/C9
Kennebunkport, Maine 243/C9
Kennebunkport•, Maine 243/C9
Kennedale, Texas 303/F3
Kennedy, Ala. 195/B3
Kennedy (Canaveral) (cape), Fla. 212/F3
Kennedy, Minn. 255/B2
Kennedy, N.Y. 276/B6
Kennedy (chan.), N.W.T. 162/N3
Kennedy (chan.), N.W. Terr. 187/M1
Kennedy, Sask. 181/J5
Kennedy Center, D.C. 245/A5
Kennedy Entrance (str.), Alaska 196/H3
Kennedyville, Md. 245/P3
Kenner, La. 238/N4
Kennesaw, Georgia 217/C2
Kennesaw Mtn. Nat'l Battlefield Park, Georgia 217/J1
Kennet (riv.), England 13/F6
Kennetcook, Nova Scotia 168/E3
Kennetcook (riv.), Nova Scotia 168/E3
Kenneth, Ind. 227/E3
Kenneth, Minn. 255/B7
Kenneth City, Fla. 212/B3
Kennett, Mo. 261/M10
Kennett Square, Pa. 294/L6
Kennewick, Wash. 310/F4
Kenney (dam), Br. Col. 184/E3
Kenney, Ill. 222/D3
Kennisis (lake), Ontario 177/F2
Keno, Oreg. 291/F5
Kenogami (riv.), Ont. 162/H6
Kenogami (riv.), Ontario 177/H4
Kenogami (riv.), Ontario 175/C2
Kénogami (lake), Québec 172/F1

Kimhae 391

Keno Hill, Yukon 187/E3
Kenoma, Mo. 261/D8
Kenora, Ont. 146/J4
Kenora, Ont. 162/G5
Kenora (terr. dist.), Ontario 177/G5
Kenora (terr. dist.), Ontario 175/C2
Kenora, Ontario 175/B3
Kenora, Ontario 177/F4
Kenosee Park, Sask. 181/J6
Kenosha (co.), Wis. 317/K10
Kenosha, Wis. 317/M3
Kenova, W. Va. 312/A6
Kensal, N. Dak. 282/N5
Kenscoff, Haiti 158/C6
Kensett, Ark. 202/G3
Kensett, Iowa 229/G2
Kensington, Calif. 204/J2
Kensington, Conn. 210/D2
Kensington, Kansas 232/C2
Kensington, Md. 245/E4
Kensington, Minn. 255/C5
Kensington, N.S. Wales 97/J4
Kensington, Ohio 284/J4
Kensington, Pr. Edward I. 168/E2
Kensington and Chelsea, England 13/G8
Kensington and Chelsea, England 10/B5
Kensington and Norwood, S. Australia 88/E8
Kensington and Norwood, S. Australia 94/B8
Kent, Ala. 195/G5
Kent, Br. Col. 184/M3
Kent•, Conn. 210/B2
Kent (co.), Del. 245/R4
Kent (co.), England 13/H6
Kent, Ill. 222/D1
Kent, Ind. 227/F7
Kent, Iowa 229/E7
Kent (co.), Md. 245/O3
Kent (isl.), Md. 245/N5
Kent (pt.), Md. 245/N5
Kent (co.), Mich. 250/D5
Kent, Minn. 255/B4
Kent (co.), New Bruns. 170/E2
Kent (pen.), N.W. Terr. 187/H3
Kent, Ohio 284/H3
Kent (county), Ontario 177/B5
Kent, Oreg. 291/G2
Kent, Pa. 294/D4
Kent (co.), R.I. 249/H6
Kent (co.), Texas 303/D4
Kent, Texas 303/C11
Kent, Wash. 310/C3
Kentau, U.S.S.R. 48/G5
Kent Bridge, Ontario 177/B5
Kent City, Mich. 250/D5
Kent Furnace, Conn. 210/B2
Kent Group (isls.), Tasmania 99/D1
Kent Junction, New Bruns. 170/E2
Kent Lake, New Bruns. 170/E2
Kentland, Ind. 227/C3
Kenton, Del. 245/R4
Kenton (co.), Ky. 237/M3
Kenton, Ky. 237/N3
Kenton, Manitoba 179/B5
Kenton, Mich. 250/G2
Kenton, Ohio 284/C4
Kenton, Okla. 288/A1
Kenton, Tenn. 237/C8
Kenton Vale, Ky. 237/S2
Kents Hill, Maine 243/D7
Kents Store, Va. 307/M5
Kentuck, W. Va. 312/C5
Kentucky 188/J3
KENTUCKY 237
Kentucky (lake) 188/J3
Kentucky (dam), Ky. 237/E7
Kentucky (lake), Ky. 237/E8
Kentucky (riv.), Ky. 237/M3
Kentucky (lake), Tenn. 237/E8
Kentucky (state), U.S. 146/K6
Kentville, Nova Scotia 168/D3
Kentwood, La. 238/J5
Kentwood, Mich. 250/D6
Kenville, Manitoba 179/A3
Kenvir, Ky. 237/P7
Kenwood, Georgia 217/D3
Kenwood, Okla. 288/S2
Kenya 2/L5
Kenya 102/F4
KENYA 115/G3
Kenya (mt.), Kenya 102/F4
Kenya (mt.), Kenya 115/G4
Kenyon, Minn. 255/E6
Kenyon, R.I. 249/H7
Kenyonville, Conn. 210/G1
Keo, Ark. 202/G4
Keokea, Hawaii, Hawaii 218/G6
Keokea, Maui, Hawaii 218/J2
Keokee, Va. 307/C7
Keokuk (co.), Iowa 229/J6
Keokuk, Iowa 188/H2
Keokuk, Iowa 229/L8
Keoma, Alberta 182/D4
Keomah, Iowa 229/J6
Keomuku, Hawaii 218/H2
Keonjhar, India 68/F4
Keosauqua, Iowa 229/J7
Keota, Colo. 208/L1
Keota, Iowa 229/K6
Keota, Okla. 288/S4
Keowee (lake), S.C. 296/B2
Keowee (riv.), S.C. 296/B2
Kepez, Turkey 63/B6
Kepi, Indonesia 85/K7
Kępno, Poland 47/C3
Keppel (harb.), Singapore 72/F6
Kepsut, Turkey 63/C3
Kerala (state), India 68/D6
Kerama (isls.), Japan 81/M6
Kerang, Victoria 97/B4
Kerava, Finland 18/O6
Kerby, Oreg. 291/D5
Kerch', U.S.S.R. 7/H4
Kerch', U.S.S.R. 52/E5
Kerchoual, Mali 106/E5
Kerema, Papua N.G. 85/B7
Keremeos, Br. Col. 184/G5
Kerempe (cape), Turkey 63/E1
Keren, Ethiopia 59/C6
Keren, Ethiopia 111/G4
Kerens, Texas 303/H5
Kerens, W. Va. 312/G4
Keret', U.S.S.R. 52/D1
Kerguélen (isl.), (Fr.) 2/N8
Kerhonkson, N.Y. 276/M7
Kericho, Kenya 115/F4
Kerinci (mt.), Indonesia 85/C6
Keriya (Yutian), China 77/B4
Keriya He (riv.), China 77/B4
Keriya Shankou (pass), China 77/B4
Kerkdriel, Netherlands 27/G5
Kerkennah (isls.), Tunisia 106/G2
Kerkhoven, Minn. 255/C5
Kerki, U.S.S.R. 48/G6
Kérkira, Greece 45/D6
Kérkira (isl.), Greece 7/F5
Kérkira (isl.), Greece 45/D6
Kerkrade, Netherlands 27/J7
Kerlin, Ark. 202/D7
Kerma, Sudan 111/F4
Kerma, Sudan 59/B6
Kermadec (isls.), N. Zealand 2/T7
Kermadec (isls.), N. Zealand 87/J9
Kerman, Calif. 204/E7
Kerman (prov.), Iran 66/K6
Kerman, Iran 54/G6
Kerman, Iran 59/G3
Kerman, Iran 66/K5
Kerme (gulf), Turkey 63/B4
Kermit, Texas 303/B6
Kermit, W. Va. 312/B7
Kern (co.), Calif. 204/G8
Kern (riv.), Calif. 204/G8
Kernan, Ill. 222/E2
Kernersville, N.C. 281/J2
Kerns, Switzerland 39/F3
Kernville, Calif. 204/G8
Kernville, Oreg. 291/D3
Kérouané, Guinea 106/C7
Kerr (lake), Fla. 212/E2
Kerr, N.C. 281/N5
Kerr, W. Scott (res.), N.C. 281/G2
Kerr, Robert S. (res.), Okla. 288/S4
Kerr (co.), Texas 303/E7
Kerrera (isl.), Scotland 15/C4
Kerrick, Minn. 255/F4
Kerrick, Texas 303/B1
Kerrobert, Sask. 181/C4
Kerrville, Tenn. 237/B10
Kerrville, Texas 303/E7
Kerry (co.), Ireland 17/B7
Kerry (head), Ireland 17/A7
Kerry, Wales 13/D5
Kersey, Colo. 208/L2
Kersey, Ind. 227/C2
Kersey, Pa. 294/E3
Kershaw (co.), S.C. 296/F3
Kershaw, S.C. 296/G2
Kersley, Br. Col. 184/F4
Kerteminde, Denmark 21/D7
Kerulen (riv.) 54/N5
Kerulen (riv.), Mongolia 77/H2
Kerwood, Ontario 177/C5
Kerzaz, Algeria 106/D3
Kerzers, Switzerland 39/D3
Kesagami (lake), Ontario 175/E2
Keşan, Turkey 63/B2
Keşap, Turkey 63/H2
Kesch (peak), Switzerland 39/J3
Kesennuma, Japan 81/K4
Kesgrave, England 13/J5
Kesh, N. Ireland 17/F3
Keshena, Wis. 317/J6
Keşiş Tepesi (mt.), Turkey 63/H3
Keskin, Turkey 63/E3
Keski-Suomi (prov.), Finland 18/O5
Kesley, Iowa 229/H3
Kessel, W. Va. 312/H4
Kesten'ga, U.S.S.R. 52/D1
Kesteren, Netherlands 27/G5
Keswick, England 13/D3
Keswick, England 10/E3
Keswick, Iowa 229/J6
Keswick, New Bruns. 170/D3
Keswick (riv.), New Bruns. 170/C2
Keswick, Ontario 177/E3
Keswick, Va. 307/M4
Keswick Grove, N.J. 273/E4
Keszthely, Hungary 41/D3
Keta, Ghana 106/E7
Ketapang, Indonesia 85/E6
Ketchen, Sask. 181/J3
Ketch Harbour, Nova Scotia 168/E4
Ketchikan, Alaska 146/E4
Ketchikan, Alaska 188/E6
Ketchikan, Alaska 196/N2
Ketchum, Idaho 220/D6
Ketchum, Okla. 288/R1
Kétegyháza, Hungary 41/F3
Kete Krachi, Ghana 106/E7
Kętrzyn, Poland 47/E1
Kettering, England 13/G5
Kettering, England 10/F4
Kettering, Ohio 284/B6
Kettering, Tasmania 99/D5
Kettle (riv.), Br. Col. 184/H5
Kettle (riv.), Minn. 255/F4
Kettle (pt.), Ontario 177/B4
Kettle (riv.), Wash. 310/G2
Kettle Falls, Wash. 310/H2
Kettleman City, Calif. 204/E7
Kettle River, Minn. 255/E4
Kettle River (range), Wash. 310/G2
Kettlersville, Ohio 284/B5
Kettle Valley, Br. Col. 184/H5
Keuka (lake), N.Y. 276/F5
Keuka Park, N.Y. 276/F5
Keuterville, Idaho 220/B3
Kevelaer, Germany 22/B3
Kevil, Ky. 237/D6
Kevin, Mont. 262/D2
Kevisville, Alberta 182/C4
Kew, Victoria 88/L7
Kew, Victoria 97/J5
Kewa, Wash. 310/G2
Kewanee, Ill. 222/C2
Kewanee, Miss. 256/H6
Kewanee, Mo. 261/N9
Kewanna, Ind. 227/E2
Kewaskum, Wis. 317/K8
Kewaunee (co.), Wis. 317/L6
Kewaunee, Wis. 317/M7
Keweenaw (co.), Mich. 250/A1
Keweenaw (bay), Mich. 250/A1
Keweenaw (pt.), Mich. 250/B1
Keweenaw Bay, Mich. 250/G1
Key, Ala. 195/G2
Key (lake), Ireland 17/E3
Keya Paha (co.), Nebr. 264/E2
Keya Paha (riv.), Nebr. 264/D1
Keyapaha, S. Dak. 298/J7
Keya Paha (riv.), S. Dak. 298/K7
Key Biscayne, Fla. 212/B5
Key Colony Beach, Fla. 212/F7
Keyes, Calif. 204/E6
Keyes, Manitoba 179/C4
Keyes, Okla. 288/B1
Keyesport, Ill. 222/D5
Keyhole (res.), Wyo. 319/H1
Key Largo, Fla. 212/F6
Key Largo (key), Fla. 212/F6
Keymar, Md. 245/K2
Keynsham, England 13/E6
Keyport, N.J. 273/E3
Keyport, Wash. 310/A2
Keysbrook, W. Australia 88/B3
Keyser, W. Va. 312/J4
Keystone, Ind. 227/G3
Keystone, Iowa 229/J5
Keystone, Nebr. 264/C3
Keystone (res.), Ohio 284/K2
Keystone (lake), Okla. 288/O2
Keystone, S. Dak. 298/C6
Keystone, W. Va. 312/D8
Keystone Heights, Fla. 212/E2
Keystown, Sask. 181/F5
Keysville, Georgia 217/H4
Keysville, Va. 307/M6
Keytesville, Mo. 261/G4
Key Vaca (key), Fla. 212/E7
Key West, Fla. 146/K7
Key West, Fla. 188/K6
Key West, Fla. 212/E7
Key West Naval Air Sta., Fla. 212/E7
Kezar (lake), Maine 243/B7
Kezar (pond), Maine 243/B7
Kezar Falls, Maine 243/B8
Kežmarok, Czech. 41/F2
Khabake (Habahe), China 77/C2
Khabarovsk, U.S.S.R. 54/P5
Khabarovsk, U.S.S.R. 2/R3
Khabarovsk, U.S.S.R. 48/O5
Khabur (riv.), Syria 63/J5
Khabur (riv.), Syria 59/D2
Khachmas, U.S.S.R. 52/G6
Khadyzhensk, U.S.S.R. 52/E6
Khaf, Iran 66/L3
Khaibar, 'Asir, Saudi Arabia 59/D6
Khaibar, Hejaz, Saudi Arabia 59/C4
Khairpur, Pakistan 68/B3
Khairpur, Pakistan 59/J4
Khakass Aut. Obl., U.S.S.R. 48/J4
Khalkhal, Iran 66/F2
Khálki (isl.), Greece 45/H7
Khalkis, Greece 45/F6
Khal'mer-Yu, U.S.S.R. 52/K1
Khaluf, Oman 59/G5
Khamgaon, India 68/D4
Khamis Mushait, Saudi Arabia 59/D6
Khamkeut, Laos 72/E3
Khamman, India 68/D5
Khanabad, Afghanistan 59/J2
Khanabad, Afghanistan 68/B1
Khanaqin, Iraq 59/D3
Khanaqin, Iraq 66/D3
Khancoban, N.S. Wales 97/E5
Khandwa, India 68/D4
Khandyga, U.S.S.R. 48/O3
Khan esh Shamat, Syria 63/G6
Khanewal, Pakistan 68/C2
Khanh Hoa, Vietnam 72/F4
Khanh Hung, Vietnam 72/E5
Khaniá, Greece 45/G8
Khaniá, Greece 7/G5
Khaniá (gulf), Greece 45/G8
Khanka (lake) 54/P5
Khanka (lake), China 77/M3
Khanka (lake), U.S.S.R. 48/O5
Khanpur, Pakistan 68/C3
Khanpur, Pakistan 59/K4
Khan Sheikhun, Syria 63/G5
Khanty-Mansi Aut. Okr., U.S.S.R. 48/H3
Khanty-Mansiysk, U.S.S.R. 54/J3
Khanty-Mansiysk, U.S.S.R. 48/H3
Khanu, Thailand 72/C3
Khan Yunis, Gaza Strip 65/A5
Khao Luang (mt.), Burma 72/C5
Khao Luang (mt.), Thailand 72/C5
Khapcheranga, U.S.S.R. 48/M5
Kharagpur, India 68/F4
Kharan, Pakistan 59/J4
Kharan Kalat, Pakistan 68/A3
Kharas, West Bank 65/C4
Kharasavey (cape), U.S.S.R. 48/G2
Khardah, India 68/F1
Khârga (oasis), Egypt 111/F2
Khârga (oasis), Egypt 59/B4
Khark (Kharg) (isl.), Iran 59/F4
Khark (Kharg) (isl.), Iran 66/G6
Khar'kov, U.S.S.R. 7/H4
Khar'kov, U.S.S.R. 2/L3
Khar'kov, U.S.S.R. 52/E5
Khar'kov, U.S.S.R. 48/D4
Kharmanli, Bulgaria 45/H5
Kharovsk, U.S.S.R. 48/D3
Kharovsk, U.S.S.R. 52/F3
Khartoum (prov.), Sudan 111/F4
Khartoum (cap.), Sudan 2/L5
Khartoum (cap.), Sudan 59/B6
Khartoum (cap.), Sudan 111/F4
Khartoum (cap.), Sudan 102/F3
Khartoum North, Sudan 102/F3
Khartoum North, Sudan 59/B6
Khartoum North, Sudan 111/F4
Khasab, Oman 59/G4
Khasavyurt, U.S.S.R. 52/G6
Khash, Afghanistan 68/A2
Khash, Afghanistan 59/H3
Khash, Iran 59/H4
Khash, Iran 66/M6
Khashm el Girba, Sudan 111/G5
Khashuri, U.S.S.R. 52/F6
Khasi (hills), India 68/G3
Khaskovo, Bulgaria 45/G5
Khatanga, U.S.S.R. 4/B4
Khatanga, U.S.S.R. 54/M2
Khatanga, U.S.S.R. 48/L2
Khatuniye, Syria 63/J4
Khay, Saudi Arabia 59/D6
Khedive, Sask. 181/G6
Khemis Miliana, Algeria 106/E1
Khemmarat, Thailand 72/E4
Khenifra, Morocco 106/C2
Kherson, U.S.S.R. 7/H4
Kherson, U.S.S.R. 48/D5
Kherson, U.S.S.R. 52/D5
Khe Sanh, Vietnam 72/E3
Kheta (riv.), U.S.S.R. 48/K2
Khilok, U.S.S.R. 48/M4
Khíos, Greece 45/G6
Khíos (isl.), Greece 45/G6
Khirbet Qumran (site), Jordan 65/D4
Khiva, U.S.S.R. 48/F5
Khiyav, Iran 66/E1
Khmel'nitskiy, U.S.S.R. 7/G4
Khmel'nitskiy, U.S.S.R. 52/C5
Khoai, Hon (isl.), Vietnam 72/E5
Khodzheyli, U.S.S.R. 48/F5
Kholm, Afghanistan 68/B1
Kholm, Afghanistan 59/J2
Kholm, U.S.S.R. 52/D3
Kholmsk, U.S.S.R. 48/P5
Khoman, Iran 66/F2
Khomeinshar, Iran 66/G4
Khon Kaen, Thailand 72/D3
Khoper (riv.), U.S.S.R. 52/F4
Khorasan (prov.), Iran 66/K3
Khóra Sfakíon, Greece 45/G8
Khorat (Nakhon Ratchasima), Thailand 72/D4
Khoreyver, U.S.S.R. 52/J1
Khorixas, Namibia 118/A4
Khorog, U.S.S.R. 48/H6
Khorol, U.S.S.R. 52/D5
Khorramabad, Iran 59/E3
Khorramabad, Iran 66/F4
Khorramshahr, Iran 59/E3
Khorramshahr, Iran 66/F5
Khotan (Hotan), China 77/B4
Khotin, U.S.S.R. 52/C5
Khouribga, Morocco 106/C2
Khowst, Afghanistan 68/B2
Khromtau, U.S.S.R. 48/F4
Khuaf, Iran 59/H3
Khugiani, Afghanistan 68/B2
Khugiani, Afghanistan 59/J3
Khuis, Botswana 118/C5
Khu Khan, Thailand 72/E4
Khulna, Bangladesh 68/F4
Khurda, India 68/F4
Khurma, Saudi Arabia 59/D5
Khusf Rud (riv.), Iran 66/L4
Khushab, Pakistan 68/C2
Khust, U.S.S.R. 52/B5
Khuzdar, Pakistan 59/J4
Khuzestan (prov.), Iran 66/F5
Khvaf, Iran 66/L3
Khvalynsk, U.S.S.R. 52/G4
Khvojeh Lak, Kuh-e (mt.), Iran 66/E3
Khvonsar, Iran 66/F4
Khvor, Iran 59/G3
Khvor, Iran 66/J4
Khvoy, Iran 59/E2
Khvoy (Khoi), Iran 66/D1
Khwae Noi, Mae Nam (riv.), Thailand 72/C4
Khyber (pass) 54/J6
Khyber (pass), Pakistan 59/K3
Khyber (pass), Pakistan 68/C2
Kia, Solomon Is. 86/D2
Kiahsville, W. Va. 312/B6
Kiama, N.S. Wales 97/F4
Kiamba, Philippines 82/E8
Kiambi, Zaire 115/E5
Kiambu, Kenya 115/G4
Kiamichi, Okla. 288/R5
Kiamichi (mts.), Okla. 288/R5
Kiamichi (riv.), Okla. 288/R6
Kiamika, Québec 172/B3
Kiamika (lake), Québec 172/B3
Kiamika (riv.), Québec 172/B3
Kiamusze (Jiamusi), China 77/M2
Kian (Ji'an), China 77/J6
Kiana, Alaska 196/F1
Kiangsi (Jiangxi), China 77/J6
Kiangsu (Jiangsu), China 77/K5
Kiantajärvi (lake), Finland 18/Q4
Kiáton, Greece 45/F6
Kiawah (isl.), S.C. 296/G6
Kibaek, Denmark 21/B5
Kibangou, Congo 115/B4
Kibara, Tanzania 115/F4
Kibaya, Tanzania 115/G5
Kibbee, Georgia 217/H6
Kibler, Ark. 202/B3
Kibombo, Zaire 115/E4
Kibondo, Tanzania 115/F4
Kibre Mengist, Ethiopia 111/G6
Kibwezi, Kenya 115/G4
Kičevo, Yugoslavia 45/E5
Kickapoo (riv.), Wis. 317/E9
Kickapoo Ind. Res., Kansas 232/G2
Kickinghorse (pass), Alberta 182/B4
Kicking Horse (pass), Br. Col. 184/J4
Kidal, Mali 102/C3
Kidal, Mali 106/E5
Kidapawan, Philippines 82/E7
Kidder, Mo. 261/D3
Kidder (co.), N. Dak. 282/L6
Kidder, S. Dak. 298/O2
Kidderminster, England 10/G3
Kidderminster, England 13/E5
Kidepo Nat'l Park, Uganda 115/F3
Kidnappers (cape), N. Zealand 100/F3
Kidron, Ohio 284/G4
Kidsgrove, England 13/E4
Kidwelly, Wales 13/C6
Kidwelly, Wales 10/D5
Kief, N. Dak. 282/J4
Kiefer, Okla. 288/O3
Kieffer, W. Va. 312/E7
Kiel, Germany 7/E3
Kiel, Germany 22/D1
Kiel (bay), Germany 22/D1
Kiel (Nord-Ostsee) (canal), Germany 22/C1
Kiel, Wis. 317/L8
Kielce (prov.), Poland 47/E3
Kielce, Poland 47/E3
Kielce, Poland 7/G3
Kieler, Wis. 317/E10
Kien Hung, Vietnam 72/E5
Kienyang (Qianyang), China 77/H6
Kiester, Minn. 255/E7
Kieta, Papua N.G. 86/C2
Kieta, Papua N.G. 87/F6
Kiev, U.S.S.R. 2/L3
Kiev, U.S.S.R. 7/H3
Kiev, U.S.S.R. 48/D4
Kiev, U.S.S.R. 52/D4
Kiev (res.), U.S.S.R. 52/C4
Kiffa, Mauritania 106/B5
Kifri, Iraq 66/D3
Kigali (cap.), Rwanda 115/F4
Kigali (cap.), Rwanda 102/F5
Kiger (creek), Oreg. 291/J5
Kiği, Turkey 63/J3
Kiglapait (cape), Newf. 166/B2
Kiglapait (mts.), Newf. 166/B2
Kigoma (reg.), Tanzania 115/F4
Kigoma-Ujiji, Tanzania 115/E4
Kigoma-Ujiji, Tanzania 102/F5
Kihei, Hawaii 218/J2
Kihnu (isl.), U.S.S.R. 53/B1
Kiholo, Hawaii 218/G4
Kiholo (bay), Hawaii 218/F4
Kii (chan.), Japan 81/G7
Kiiminki, Finland 18/P4
Kikai (isl.), Japan 81/O5
Kikiktaksoak (isl.), Newf. 166/B2
Kikinda, Yugoslavia 45/E3
Kikino, Alberta 182/D2
Kikkertavak (isl.), Newf. 166/B2
Kikoira, N.S. Wales 97/D3
Kikonai, Japan 81/K3
Kikori, Papua N.G. 85/B7
Kikwit, Zaire 115/C5
Kikwit, Zaire 102/D5
Kila, Mont. 262/B2
Kilafors, Sweden 18/K6
Kilauea, Hawaii 188/E5
Kilauea, Hawaii 218/C1
Kilauea (crater), Hawaii 218/H6
Kilauea (pt.), Hawaii 218/C1
Kilbaha, Ireland 17/B6
Kilbarchan, Scotland 15/A2
Kilbeggan, Ireland 17/G5
Kilbirnie, Scotland 15/A2
Kilbourne, Ill. 222/D3
Kilbourne, La. 238/H1
Kilbrannan (sound), Scotland 15/C5
Kilbride, Newf. 166/D2
Kilbuck (mts.), Alaska 196/G2
Kilburn, New Bruns. 170/C2
Kilcar, Ireland 17/D2
Kilchoan, Scotland 15/B4
Kilchu, N. Korea 81/D3
Kilcock, Ireland 17/H5
Kilconnell, Ireland 17/E5
Kilcoole, Ireland 17/K5
Kilcormac, Ireland 17/F5
Kilcoy, Queensland 95/E5
Kilcullen, Ireland 17/H5
Kildare, Georgia 217/K5
Kildare (co.), Ireland 17/H5
Kildare, Ireland 10/C4
Kildare, Ireland 17/H5
Kildare, Okla. 288/M1
Kildare (cape), Pr. Edward I. 168/E2
Kildare, Texas 303/K5
Kildeer, Ill. 222/A5
Kil'din (isl.), U.S.S.R. 52/D1
Kildonan, Br. Col. 184/E5
Kildonan, Scotland 15/E2
Kildonan, Zimbabwe 118/E3
Kildurk, North. Terr. 93/A4
Kildysart, Ireland 17/C6
Kilembe, Uganda 115/F3
Kilembe, Zaire 115/C5
Kilfenora, Ireland 17/C6
Kilfinane, Ireland 17/D7
Kilgarvan, Ireland 17/B8
Kilgore, Idaho 220/G5
Kilgore, Nebr. 264/D2
Kilgore, Ohio 284/H5
Kilgore, Texas 303/K5
Kili (isl.), Marshall Is. 87/G5
Kilifi, Kenya 115/G4
Kilimanjaro (reg.), Tanzania 115/G4
Kilimanjaro (mt.), Tanzania 102/F5
Kilimanjaro (mt.), Tanzania 115/G4
Kilimli, Turkey 63/D2
Kilinailau (isls.), Papua N.G. 86/C2
Kilingi-Nõmme, U.S.S.R. 53/C1
Kilis, Turkey 63/G4
Kilitbahir, Turkey 63/B6
Kiliya, U.S.S.R. 52/C5
Kilkee, Ireland 10/B4
Kilkee, Ireland 17/B6
Kilkeel, N. Ireland 17/K3
Kilkelly, Ireland 17/D4
Kilkenny (co.), Ireland 17/G6
Kilkenny, Ireland 10/C4
Kilkenny, Ireland 17/G6
Kilkenny, Minn. 255/E6
Kilkieran (bay), Ireland 17/B5
Kilkis, Greece 45/F5
Killala, Ireland 17/C3
Killala (bay), Ireland 17/C3
Killaloe, Ireland 10/B4
Killaloe, Ireland 17/D6
Killaloe Station, Ontario 177/G2
Killaly, Sask. 181/J5
Killam, Alberta 182/E3
Killam, New Bruns. 170/E2
Killarney, Ireland 10/B4
Killarney, Ireland 17/C7
Killarney (lakes), Ireland 10/B4
Killarney, Man. 162/G6
Killarney, Manitoba 179/C5
Killarney, North. Terr. 93/B4
Killarney, Ontario 177/C2
Killarney Prov. Park, Ontario 177/C1
Killary (harb.), Ireland 17/A4
Killavullen, Ireland 17/D7
Killbear Point Prov. Park, Ontario 177/D2
Kill Buck, N.Y. 276/C6
Killbuck, Ohio 284/G5
Killbuck (creek), Ohio 284/G4
Killdeer, N. Dak. 282/E5
Killdeer, Sask. 181/E6
Kill Devil Hills, N.C. 281/T3
Killduff, Iowa 229/H5
Killearn, Scotland 15/B1
Killeen, Texas 303/G6
Killen, Ala. 195/D1
Killenaule, Ireland 17/F6
Killeshandra, Ireland 17/F3
Killian, La. 238/M2
Killimor, Ireland 17/E5
Killin, Scotland 15/D4
Killinaboy, Ireland 17/C6
Killingly•, Conn. 210/H1
Killington, Vt. 268/B4
Killington (peak), Vt. 268/B4
Killingworth•, Conn. 210/E3
Killona, La. 238/M3
Killorglin, Ireland 17/B7
Killough, N. Ireland 17/K3
Killucan-Rathwire, Ireland 17/G4
Kill Van Kull (str.), N.J. 273/B2
Killybegs, Ireland 17/E2
Killyclogher, N. Ireland 17/G2
Killyleagh, N. Ireland 17/K3
Kilmacolm, Scotland 15/A2
Kilmacrennan, Ireland 17/F1
Kilmacthomas, Ireland 17/G7
Kilmallock, Ireland 17/D7
Kilmarnock, Scotland 15/D5
Kilmarnock, Scotland 10/D3
Kilmarnock, Va. 307/R5
Kilmaurs, Scotland 15/D5
Kilmeadan, Ireland 17/G7
Kilmichael, Miss. 256/E4
Kilmihill, Ireland 17/C6
Kilmoganny, Ireland 17/G7
Kilmore, Victoria 97/C5
Kilmore Quay, Ireland 17/H7
Kilmurry, Ireland 17/C6
Kiln, Miss. 256/F10
Kilnaleck, Ireland 17/G4
Kilninver, Scotland 15/C4
Kilo, Zaire 115/E3
Kilombero (riv.), Tanzania 115/G5
Kilosa, Tanzania 115/G5
Kilpisjärvi (lake), Finland 18/M2
Kilpisjärvi (lake), Sweden 18/M2
Kilrea, N. Ireland 17/H2
Kilrenny and Anstruther, Scotland 15/F4
Kilrenny and Anstruther, Scotland 10/E2
Kilronan, Ireland 17/B5
Kilrush, Ireland 10/B4
Kilrush, Ireland 17/C6
Kilsheelan, Ireland 17/F7
Kilsyth, Scotland 15/B1
Kilsyth, Scotland 10/B1
Kilsyth, W. Va. 312/D7
Kiltan (isl.), India 68/C6
Kiltimagh, Ireland 17/C4
Kilwa, Zaire 115/E5
Kilwa Kivinje, Tanzania 115/G5
Kilwa Masoko, Tanzania 115/G5
Kilwinning, Sask. 181/E2
Kilwinning, Scotland 15/D5
Kilworth, Ireland 17/E7
Kilyos, Turkey 63/D5
Kim, Colo. 208/N8
Kimba, S. Australia 88/F6
Kimba, S. Australia 94/E5
Kimball (mt.), Alaska 196/K2
Kimball, Alberta 182/D5
Kimball, Kansas 232/G4
Kimball, Minn. 255/D5
Kimball (co.), Nebr. 264/A3
Kimball, Nebr. 264/A3
Kimball, S. Dak. 298/M6
Kimball, Tenn. 237/K10
Kimball, W. Va. 312/C8
Kimballton, Iowa 229/D5
Kimballton, Va. 307/G6
Kimbe, Papua N.G. 86/B2
Kimbe, Papua N.G. 87/F6
Kimberley, Br. Col. 184/K5
Kimberley, S. Africa 102/E7
Kimberley, S. Africa 118/C5
Kimberley (plat.), W. Australia 88/D3
Kimberley (plat.), W. Australia 92/D2
Kimberley Research Station, W. Australia 88/D3
Kimberling City, Mo. 261/F9
Kimberlin Heights, Tenn. 237/O9
Kimberly, Ala. 195/E3
Kimberly, Idaho 220/D7
Kimberly, Minn. 255/E4
Kimberly, Oreg. 291/H3
Kimberly, Wis. 317/K7
Kimble (co.), Texas 303/E7
Kimbolton, Ohio 284/G5
Kimbrough, Ala. 195/C6
Kimch'aek, N. Korea 81/D3
Kimch'ŏn, S. Korea 81/D5
Kimesville, N.C. 281/L3
Kimhae, Pakistan 81/D6

Krotoszyn 393

Knockboy (mt.), Ireland 17/B8
Knocklayd (mt.), N. Ireland 17/J1
Knocklong, Ireland 17/D7
Knockmealdown (mts.), Ireland 17/F7
Knocknagashel, Ireland 17/C7
Knoke, Iowa 229/D3
Knokke-Heist, Belgium 27/C6
Knøsen (mt.), Denmark 21/D3
Knott (co.), Ky. 237/R6
Knott, Texas 303/C5
Knotts Island, N.C. 281/T2
Knottsville, Ky. 237/H5
Knowles, Okla. 288/F1
Knowlesville, New Bruns. 170/C2
Knowlesville, N.Y. 276/D4
Knowlton, Mont. 262/L4
Knowlton, Québec 172/E4
Knowlton, Wis. 317/G6
Knox (cape), Br. Col. 162/C5
Knox (cape), Br. Col. 184/A3
Knox (co.), Ill. 222/C3
Knox (co.), Ind. 227/C7
Knox, Ind. 227/D2
Knox (co.), Ky. 237/O7
Knox (co.), Maine 243/E7
Knox•, Maine 243/E6
Knox (co.), Mo. 261/H2
Knox (co.), Nebr. 264/G2
Knox (lake), Newf. 166/A3
Knox, N. Dak. 282/L3
Knox (co.), Ohio 284/F5
Knox, Pa. 294/C3
Knox (co.), Tenn. 237/O9
Knox (co.), Texas 303/E4
Knox, Victoria 97/K5
Knox, Victoria 88/M7
Knoxboro, N.Y. 276/J5
Knox Center, Maine 243/E6
Knox City, Mo. 261/H2
Knox City, Texas 303/E4
Knox Coast (reg.), Ant. 5/C6
Knoxville, Ala. 195/C4
Knoxville, Ark. 202/D3
Knoxville, Georgia 217/E5
Knoxville, Ill. 222/C3
Knoxville, Iowa 229/G6
Knoxville, Md. 245/H3
Knoxville, Miss. 256/B8
Knoxville, Mo. 261/E4
Knoxville, Pa. 294/H2
Knoxville, Tenn. 146/K6
Knoxville, Tenn. 188/K3
Knoxville, Tenn. 237/O9
Knud Rasmussen Land (reg.), Greenl. 4/B12
Knudshoved (pt.), Denmark 21/D7
Knurów, Poland 47/A4
Knutsford, Br. Col. 184/G5
Knutsford, England 13/H2
Knutsford, England 10/G2
Knutsford, Pr. Edward I. 168/D2
Knysna, S. Africa 118/C6
Koah Kong (isl.), Cambodia 72/D5
Koah Nhek, Cambodia 72/E4
Koah Rung (isl.), Cambodia 72/D5
Koah Tang (isl.), Cambodia 72/D5
Koali, Hawaii 218/K2
Koa Mill, Hawaii 218/G6
Koani, Tanzania 115/G5
Kobayashi, Japan 81/E8
Kobbfjorden (fjord), Norway 18/O1
Kobdo (Hovd), Mongolia 77/D2
Kobe, Japan 81/H7
Kobe, Japan 54/P6
København (Copenhagen) (cap.), Denmark 21/F6
København (Copenhagen) (commune), Denmark 21/F6
København (co.), Denmark 21/F6
Koblenz, Germany 22/B3
Koblenz, Switzerland 39/F1
Kobrin, U.S.S.R. 52/B4
Kobroor (isl.), Indonesia 85/K7
Kobuk, Alaska 196/G1
Kobuk (riv.), Alaska 188/C5
Kobuk (riv.), Alaska 196/G1
Kobuk Valley Nat'l Park, Alaska 196/F1
Kobuleti, U.S.S.R. 52/F6
Koca (riv.), Turkey 63/C3
Koca (riv.), Turkey 63/C6
Koca (riv.), Turkey 63/E2
Kocaeli (prov.), Turkey 63/C2
Kocaeli (İzmit), Turkey 63/D2
Kočani, Yugoslavia 45/F5
Koçarlı, Turkey 63/B4
Kočevje, Yugoslavia 45/B3
Koch (isl.), N.W. Terr. 187/L3
Koch'ang, S. Korea 81/C6
Kochevo, U.S.S.R. 52/J3
Kochi (pref.), Japan 81/F7
Kochi, Japan 81/F7
Kodaira, Japan 81/O2
Kodak, Tenn. 237/O9
Kodiak, Alaska 188/D6
Kodiak, Alaska 196/H3
Kodiak (isl.), Alaska 146/C4
Kodiak (isl.), Alaska 196/H3
Kodiak, U.S. 4/D17
Kodiak (isl.), U.S. 4/D17
Kodok, Sudan 111/F6
Kodok, Sudan 102/F4
Koekelare, Belgium 27/B6
Koekelberg, Belgium 27/B9
Koenig, Mo. 261/J6
Koenton, Ala. 195/B7
Koes, Namibia 118/B5
Kofa (mts.), Ariz. 198/B5
Kofçaz, Turkey 63/B2
Koffiefontein, S. Africa 118/D5
Köflach, Austria 41/C3
Koforidua, Ghana 106/D7
Kofu, Japan 81/J6
Koga, Japan 81/J5
Kogaluc (riv.), Québec 174/E1
Kogaluk (riv.), Newf. 166/B2
Koganei, Japan 81/O2
Kogarah, N. S. Wales 88/K4
Kogarah, N.S. Wales 97/J4
Køge, Denmark 21/F7
Køge (bay), Denmark 21/F7
Koggiung, Alaska 196/G3
Kogo, Equat. Guinea 106/F8
Kogo, Equat. Guinea 115/A3
Kohala (Kapaau), Hawaii 218/G3
Kohala (mts.), Hawaii 218/G4
Kohala (peak), Hawaii 218/G4
Kohat, Pakistan 59/K3
Kohat, Pakistan 68/C2
Kohila, U.S.S.R. 53/C1
Kohima, India 68/G3
Kohkiluyeh and Boyer Ahmediyeh (gov.), Iran 66/G5
Kohler, Wis. 317/L8
Kohls Ranch, Ariz. 198/D4
Kohtla-Järve, U.S.S.R. 52/C3
Kohtla-Järve, U.S.S.R. 53/D1
Kohŭng, S. Korea 81/C6
Koidern, Yukon 187/D3
Koitere (lake), Finland 18/R5
Kŏje (isl.), S. Korea 81/D6
Kojetín, Czech. 41/D2
Kojonup, W. Australia 88/B6
Kojonup, W. Australia 92/B6
Kokadjo, Maine 243/E4
Kokand, U.S.S.R. 48/H5
Kokanee Glacier Prov. Park, Br. Col. 184/J5
Kokava nad Rimavicou, Czech. 41/E2
Kokchetav, U.S.S.R. 54/J4
Kokchetav, U.S.S.R. 48/H4
Kokemäki, Finland 18/N6
Kokish, Br. Col. 184/D5
Kokiu (Gejiu), China 77/F7
Kokkola, Finland 18/N5
Koknanok, Alaska 196/H3
Koko (head), Hawaii 218/F2
Koko, Nigeria 106/F7
Kokoda, Papua N.G. 85/C7
Kokole (pt.), Hawaii 218/B2
Kokolik (riv.), Alaska 196/F1
Kokomo, Hawaii 218/K2
Kokomo, Ind. 188/J2
Kokomo, Ind. 227/E4
Kokomo, Miss. 256/E8
Kokonau, Indonesia 85/K6
Kokopo, Papua N.G. 86/B2
Kokosing (riv.), Ohio 284/E5
Kokrines, Alaska 196/G1
Kokrines (hills), Alaska 196/H1
Koksan, N. Korea 81/C4
Koksijde, Belgium 27/B6
Koksilah, Br. Col. 184/J3
Koksoak (riv.), Que. 162/K4
Koksoak (riv.), Québec 174/D1
Kokstad, S. Africa 118/D6
Kokubu, Japan 81/E8
Kola, Manitoba 179/A5
Kola (pen.), U.S.S.R. 7/H2
Kola (pen.), U.S.S.R. 4/C8
Kola (pen.), U.S.S.R. 52/E1
Kola (pen.), U.S.S.R. 48/D3
Kolahun, Liberia 106/C7
Kolaka, Indonesia 85/G6
Kolar, India 68/D6
Kolar Gold Fields, India 68/D6
Kolari, Finland 18/O3
Kolárovo, Czech. 41/D3
Kolašin, Yugoslavia 45/D4
Kolberg (Kołobrzeg), Poland 47/B1
Kolbio, Kenya 115/H4
Kolbuszowa, Poland 47/E3
Kolda, Senegal 106/B6
Kolding, Denmark 18/F9
Kolding, Denmark 21/C7
Kole, Haut-Zaïre, Zaire 115/E3
Kole, Kasai-Oriental, Zaire 115/D4
Koleen, Ind. 227/D7
Kolekole (stream), Hawaii 218/J4
Kölen (mts.), Sweden 18/K3
Kolepom (isl.), Indonesia 85/K7
Kolguyev (isl.), U.S.S.R. 7/J2
Kolguyev (isl.), U.S.S.R. 4/B7
Kolguyev (isl.), U.S.S.R. 52/G1
Kolguyev (isl.), U.S.S.R. 48/E3
Kolhapur, India 68/C5
Kolhapur, India 54/J8
Koliganek, Alaska 196/G3
Kolín, Czech. 41/C1
Kolin, Mont. 262/G3
Kolind, Denmark 21/D5
Kölliken, Switzerland 39/F2
Kollum, Netherlands 27/J2
Kolmanskop, Namibia 118/B5
Köln (Cologne), Germany 22/B3
Kolno, Poland 47/F2
Koło, Poland 47/D2
Koloa, Hawaii 188/E5
Koloa, Hawaii 218/C2
Koloa Landing, Hawaii 218/C2
Kołobrzeg, Poland 47/B1
Kologriv, U.S.S.R. 52/F3
Kolokani, Mali 106/C6
Kolola Springs, Miss. 256/H3
Kolombangara (isl.), Solomon Is. 86/D2
Kolomiya, U.S.S.R. 52/B5
Kolomna, U.S.S.R. 7/H3
Kolomna, U.S.S.R. 48/D4
Kolomna, U.S.S.R. 52/E4
Kolondiéba, Mali 106/C6
Kolonia (cap.), Micronesia 87/F5
Kolonodale, Indonesia 85/G6
Kolovrat (mt.), Solomon Is. 86/E3
Kolpashevo, U.S.S.R. 54/K4
Kolpashevo, U.S.S.R. 48/J4
Kolpino, U.S.S.R. 52/D3
Kolva (riv.), U.S.S.R. 52/J1
Kolwezi, Zaire 102/E6
Kolwezi, Zaire 115/E6
Kolyma (range), U.S.S.R. 4/C1
Kolyma (riv.), U.S.S.R. 4/C2
Kolyma (range), U.S.S.R. 48/Q3
Kolyma (range), U.S.S.R. 54/S3
Kolyma (riv.), U.S.S.R. 54/S3
Kolyma (riv.), U.S.S.R. 48/Q3
Koma, Burma 72/C4
Komádi, Hungary 41/F3
Komadugu Yobe (riv.), Niger 106/G6
Komadugu Yobe (riv.), Nigeria 106/G6
Komaga (mt.), Japan 81/K2
Komagane, Japan 81/H6
Komandorskiye (isls.), U.S.S.R. 54/T4
Komandorskiye (isls.), U.S.S.R. 2/T3
Komandorskiye (isls.), U.S.S.R. 48/R4
Komárno, Czech. 41/D3
Komarno, Manitoba 179/E4
Komárom (co.), Hungary 41/E3
Komárom, Hungary 41/E3
Komatke, Ariz. 198/C5
Komatsu, Japan 81/H5
Komba, Zaire 115/D3
Kŏmdŏk (mt.), N. Korea 81/D3
Komi A.S.S.R., U.S.S.R. 48/F3
Komi A.S.S.R., U.S.S.R. 52/H2
Komi-Permyak Aut. Okr., U.S.S.R. 52/H3
Komi-Permyak Aut. Okr., U.S.S.R. 48/F4
Komló, Hungary 41/E3
Kommetjie, S. Africa 118/E7
Kommunarsk, U.S.S.R. 52/E5
Komodo (isl.), Indonesia 85/F7
Komoka, Ontario 177/C5
Kôm Ombo, Egypt 111/F3
Kôm Ombo, Egypt 59/B5
Komono, Congo 115/B4
Komoran (isl.), Indonesia 85/K7
Komotiní, Greece 45/G5
Komrat, U.S.S.R. 52/C5
Komsomolets (isl.), U.S.S.R. 4/A5
Komsomolets (isl.), U.S.S.R. 54/M1
Komsomolets (isl.), U.S.S.R. 48/L1
Komsomol'sk, U.S.S.R. 54/P4
Komsomol'sk, U.S.S.R. 48/G4
Komsomol'skiy, U.S.S.R. 52/K1
Komsomol'sk-na-Amure, U.S.S.R. 48/O4
Kona, Ky. 237/R6
Konahuanui (peaks), Hawaii 218/C3
Konar (riv.), Afghanistan 68/C1
Konar (riv.), Afghanistan 59/K2
Konar (riv.), Pakistan 68/C1
Konawa, Okla. 288/N5
Kondoa, Tanzania 115/G4
Kondopoga, U.S.S.R. 52/D2
Kondopoga, U.S.S.R. 48/D3
Kondoros, Hungary 41/F3
Konduz, Afghan. 58/J2
Konduz, Afghan. 68/B1
Konduz (riv.), Afghan. 58/J2
Konduz (riv.), Afghan. 68/B1
Koné, New Caled. 86/G4
Kong, Koh (isl.), Cambodia 72/D5
Kong, Ivory Coast 106/D7
Kongiganak, Alaska 196/F3
Kongju, S. Korea 81/C5
Kong Karls Land (isl.), Norway 18/E1
Kongmoon (Jiangmen), China 77/H7
Kongolo, Zaire 115/E5
Kongolo, Zaire 102/E5
Kongor, Sudan 111/F6
Kongsberg, N. Dak. 282/J4
Kongsberg, Norway 18/F7
Kongsfjorden (fjord), Norway 18/B2
Kongsvinger, Norway 18/H6
Kongur Shan (mt.), China 77/A4
Kongwa, Tanzania 115/G5
Koni (pen.), U.S.S.R. 48/Q4
Koniecpol, Poland 47/D3
Königsberg (Kaliningrad), U.S.S.R. 52/B4
Königssee (lake), Germany 22/E5
Königswiesen, Austria 41/C2
Königswinter, Germany 22/B3
Königs Wusterhausen, Germany 22/E2
Konin (prov.), Poland 47/D2
Konin, Poland 47/D2
Kónitsa, Greece 45/E5
Koniuji (isls.), Alaska 196/G3
Köniz, Switzerland 39/D3
Konjic, Yugoslavia 45/D4
Konkiep, Namibia 118/B5
Konnagar, India 68/F1
Konolfingen, Switzerland 39/E3
Konomoc (lake), Conn. 210/G3
Konosha, U.S.S.R. 52/F2
Konotop, U.S.S.R. 52/D4
Konqi He (riv.), China 77/C3
Końskie, Poland 47/E3
Konstantinovka, U.S.S.R. 52/E5
Konstantynów Łódzki, Poland 47/D3
Konstanz, Germany 22/C5
Kontagora, Nigeria 106/F6
Kontcha, Cameroon 115/B2
Kontich, Belgium 27/E6
Kontiomäki, Finland 18/Q4
Kon Tum, Vietnam 72/E4
Kon Tum (plat.), Vietnam 72/E4
Konya (prov.), Turkey 63/E4
Konya, Turkey 63/E4
Konya, Turkey 59/B2
Konya, Turkey 54/E6
Konza, Kenya 115/G4
Koocanusa (lake), Br. Col. 184/K6
Koocanusa (lake), Mont. 262/A2
Koochiching (co.), Minn. 255/E2
Koog aan de Zaan, Netherlands 27/A4
Koolan (isl.), W. Australia 88/C3
Koolan (isl.), W. Australia 92/C1
Koolau (range), Hawaii 218/E2
Kooline Station, W. Australia 92/B3
Koolpinyah, North. Terr. 93/B2
Koolyanobbing, W. Australia 88/B6
Koolyanobbing, W. Australia 92/B5
Koondrook, Victoria 97/B4
Koonibba, S. Australia 88/E6
Koonibba, S. Australia 94/C4
Koontz Lake, Ind. 227/D2
Koorawatha, N.S. Wales 97/E4
Koosharem, Utah 304/C5
Koosharem Ind. Res., Utah 304/C5
Kooskia, Idaho 220/C3
Koostatak, Manitoba 179/E3
Kootenai (co.), Idaho 220/B2
Kootenai, Idaho 220/B1
Kootenai (riv.), Idaho 220/C1
Kootenai (riv.), Mont. 262/A2
Kootenay (lake), Br. Col. 162/E5
Kootenay (lake), Br. Col. 184/J5
Kootenay (riv.), Br. Col. 184/K5
Kootenay Nat'l Park, Br. Col. 184/J4
Kootenay Nat'l Pk., Br. Col. 162/E5
Kootingal, N.S. Wales 97/F2
Kópavogur, Iceland 21/B1
Köpenick, Germany 22/F4
Koper, Yugoslavia 45/A3
Kopervik, Norway 18/D7
Kopeysk, U.S.S.R. 48/G4
Köping, Sweden 18/J7
Koppal, India 68/D5
Koppang, Norway 18/G6
Kopparberg (co.), Sweden 18/J6
Kopparberg, Sweden 18/J7
Koppel, Pa. 294/B4
Kopperston, W. Va. 312/C7
Koprivnica, Yugoslavia 45/C2
Köprü (riv.), Turkey 63/D4
Kor (riv.), Iran 66/H6
Korab (mt.), Albania 45/E5
Korab (mt.), Yugoslavia 45/E5
Koraka (cape), Turkey 63/B3
Koran, La. 238/D2
Koraput, India 68/E5
Korba, India 68/E4
Korbach, Germany 22/C3
Korbel, Calif. 204/B3
Korçë, Albania 45/E5
Korčula (isl.), Yugoslavia 45/C4
Kordestan (Kurdistan) (prov.), Iran 66/E3
Kord Kuy, Iran 66/J2
Kordofan, Southern (prov.), Sudan 111/E5
Kordofan, Northern (prov.), Sudan 111/E5
Korea (North) 2/R4
Korea (South) 2/R4
KOREA (NORTH) 81
KOREA (SOUTH) 81
Korea (bay), N. Korea 81/B4
Korea (str.), S. Korea 81/D6
Korenovsk, U.S.S.R. 52/E5
Korf, U.S.S.R. 54/T3
Korf, U.S.S.R. 4/C1
Korf, U.S.S.R. 48/R3
Korhogo, Ivory Coast 106/C7
Korhogo, Ivory Coast 102/B4
Kőrishegy (mt.), Hungary 41/D3
Koriyama, Japan 81/K5
Korkuteli, Turkey 63/D4
Korla, China 77/C3
Kormakiti (cape), Cyprus 59/B2
Kormakiti (cape), Cyprus 63/E5
Körmend, Hungary 41/D3
Kornat (isl.), Yugoslavia 45/B4
Korneuburg, Austria 41/D2
Kornsjø, Norway 18/G7
Kornwestheim, Germany 22/C4
Koro (isl.), Fiji 86/Q10
Koro (sea), Fiji 86/Q10
Köroğlu (mts.), Turkey 63/E2
Köroğlu Dağı (mt.), Turkey 63/E2
Korogwe, Tanzania 115/G5
Koroit, Victoria 97/B6
Korona, Fla. 212/E2
Koronadal, Philippines 82/E7
Koronowo, Poland 47/C2
Koropí, Greece 45/G7
Koror (cap.), Belau 87/D5
Kororoit (creek), Victoria 97/H5
Kororoit (creek), Victoria 88/K7
Körös (riv.), Hungary 41/F3
Körösladány, Hungary 41/F3
Korosten', U.S.S.R. 52/C4
Korostyshev, U.S.S.R. 52/C4
Koro Toro, Chad 111/C4
Korpilombolo, Sweden 18/N3
Korsakov, U.S.S.R. 48/P5
Korsnäs, Finland 18/M5
Korsør, Denmark 21/E7
Korsør, Denmark 18/G9
Kortemark, Belgium 27/C6
Korti, Sudan 111/F4
Korti, Sudan 59/B6
Kortrijk, Belgium 27/C7
Korumburra, Victoria 97/D6
Koryak (range), U.S.S.R. 54/U3
Koryak (range), U.S.S.R. 48/S3
Koryak Aut. Okr., U.S.S.R. 48/R3
Koryazhma, U.S.S.R. 52/G2
Kos, Greece 45/H7
Kos (isl.), Greece 45/H7
Kościan, Poland 47/C2
Kościerzyna, Poland 47/C1
Kosciusko (mt.), Australia 87/F9
Kosciusko (co.), Ind. 227/F2
Kosciusko, Miss. 256/E4
Kosciusko (mt.), N. S. Wales 88/H7
Kosciusko (mt.), N.S. Wales 97/E5
Koshigaya, Japan 81/P2
Koshiki (isls.), Japan 81/D8
Koshke-e Kohneh, Afghanistan 68/A2
Koshkonong, Mo. 261/J9
Koshkonong (lake), Wis. 317/H10
Košice, Czech. 7/G4
Košice, Czech. 41/F2
Koslan, U.S.S.R. 48/E3
Koslan, U.S.S.R. 52/G2
Köslin (Koszalin), Poland 47/C1
Kosoma, Okla. 288/P6
Kosŏng, N. Korea 81/D4
Kosovo (aut. reg.), Yugoslavia 45/E4
Kosovska Mitrovica, Yugoslavia 45/E4
Kosrae (isl.), Micronesia 87/G5
Kosse, Texas 303/H6
Kössen, Austria 41/B3
Kossou, Lac de (lake), Ivory Coast 106/C7
Kossuth, Ind. 227/E7
Kossuth (co.), Iowa 229/E2
Kossuth, Miss. 256/G1
Kostajnica, Yugoslavia 45/C3
Kostelec nad černými Lesy, Czech. 41/C2
Kostelec nad Orlicí, Czech. 41/D1
Kosti, Sudan 59/B7
Kosti, Sudan 111/F5
Kosti, Sudan 102/F3
Kostopol', U.S.S.R. 52/C4
Kostroma, U.S.S.R. 7/J3
Kostroma, U.S.S.R. 52/F3
Kostroma, U.S.S.R. 48/E4
Kostrzyń, Poland 47/B2
Koszalin (prov.), Poland 47/C1
Koszalin, Poland 7/F3
Koszalin, Poland 47/C1
Kőszeg, Hungary 41/D3
Koszta, Iowa 229/J5
Kota, India 68/D3
Kota, India 54/J7
Kotaagung, Indonesia 85/C7
Kotabaharu, Indonesia 85/E6
Kota Baharu, Malaysia 54/M9
Kota Baharu, Malaysia 72/D6
Kotabaru, Indonesia 85/F6
Kotabumi, Indonesia 85/C7
Kota Kinabalu, Malaysia 54/N9
Kota Kinabalu, Malaysia 85/F4
Kotamobagu, Indonesia 85/G5
Kota Tinggi, Malaysia 72/F5
Kotawaringin, Indonesia 85/E6
Kotcho (lake), Br. Col. 184/M2
Kotcho (riv.), Br. Col. 184/M2
Kotel, Bulgaria 45/H4
Kotel'nich, U.S.S.R. 52/G3
Kotel'nikovo, U.S.S.R. 52/F5
Kotel'nyy (isl.), U.S.S.R. 4/B2
Kotel'nyy (isl.), U.S.S.R. 48/O2
Köthen, Germany 22/E3
Kotido, Uganda 115/F3
Kotka, Finland 7/G2
Kotka, Finland 18/P6
Kotlas, U.S.S.R. 7/J2
Kotlas, U.S.S.R. 48/E3
Kotlas, U.S.S.R. 52/G2
Kotlik, Alaska 196/F2
Kotor, Yugoslavia 45/D4
Kotovo, U.S.S.R. 52/G4
Kotovsk, Odessa, U.S.S.R. 52/C5
Kotovsk, Tambov, U.S.S.R. 52/F4
Kotri, Pakistan 68/B3
Kötschach-Mauthen, Austria 41/B3
Kottaguden, India 68/E5
Kottayam, India 68/D7
Kotto (riv.), Cent. Afr. Rep. 115/D2
Kotturu, India 68/D6
Kotuy (riv.), U.S.S.R. 4/B4
Kotuy (riv.), U.S.S.R. 54/M2
Kotuy (riv.), U.S.S.R. 48/L3
Kotzebue, Alaska 196/F1
Kotzebue, Alaska 146/B3
Kotzebue, Alaska 188/C5
Kotzebue (sound), Alaska 196/F1
Kotzebue, U.S. 4/C18
Kouango, Cent. Afr. Rep. 115/D2
Kouchibouguac, New Bruns. 170/F2
Kouchibouguac (bay), New Bruns. 170/F2
Kouchibouguacis (riv.), New Bruns. 170/E2
Kouchobouguac Nat'l Park, New Bruns. 170/F2
Koudougou, Burkina Faso 106/D6
Kouilou (riv.), Congo 115/B4
Koukdjuak (riv.), N.W. Terr. 187/L3
Kouki, Cent. Afr. Rep. 115/C2
Koula-Moutou, Gabon 115/B4
Koula-Moutou, Gabon 102/D5
Koulikoro, Mali 106/C6
Koulikoro, Mali 102/B3
Koumala, Queensland 95/D4
Koumbi Saleh (ruins), Mauritania 106/C5
Koumra, Chad 102/D4
Koumra, Chad 111/C6
Koundara, Guinea 106/B6
Kounde, Cent. Afr. Rep. 115/B2
Kouno, Chad 111/C6
Kounradskiy, U.S.S.R. 48/H5
Kountze, Texas 303/K7
Koupela, Burkina Faso 106/D6
Kourou, Fr. Guiana 131/E3
Kourouba, Mali 106/B6
Kouroussa, Guinea 106/C6
Kousseri, Cameroon 115/B1
Koutiala, Mali 106/C6
Koutiala, Mali 102/B3
Kouts, Ind. 227/C2
Kouvola, Finland 18/P6
Kovdor, U.S.S.R. 52/D1
Kovel', U.S.S.R. 52/C4
Kovel', U.S.S.R. 48/C4
Kovrov, U.S.S.R. 52/F3
Kovrov, U.S.S.R. 48/E4
Kovur, India 68/E6
Kovylkino, U.S.S.R. 52/F4
Kowary, Poland 47/B3
Kowst, Afghanistan 59/J3
Kowt-e 'Ashrow, Afghanistan 68/B2
Koyama, Japan 81/E8
Köyceğiz, Turkey 63/C4
Köyceğiz (lake), Turkey 63/C4
Koyuk, Alaska 196/F1
Koyukuk, Alaska 196/G1
Koyukuk (riv.), Alaska 188/C5
Koyukuk (riv.), Alaska 196/G1
Koyulhisar, Turkey 63/G2
Kozaklı, Turkey 63/F3
Kozan, Turkey 63/F4
Kozáni, Greece 45/F5
Kozhevnikovo, U.S.S.R. 48/L2
Kozhikode, India 68/D6
Kozhikode, India 54/J8
Kozhva, U.S.S.R. 52/J1
Kozienice, Poland 47/E3
Kozlu, Turkey 63/D2
Kozluk, Turkey 63/J3
Kozmin, Poland 47/C3
Kożuchów, Poland 47/B3
Kpalimé, Togo 106/E7
Kpandu, Ghana 106/D7
Kpémé, Togo 106/E7
Kra (isth.), Thailand 72/C5
Kraaifontein, S. Africa 118/F6
Kraainem, Belgium 27/C9
Krabi, Thailand 72/C5
Kra Buri, Thailand 72/C5
Kracheh, Cambodia 72/E4
Kraemer, La. 238/M4
Kragan, Indonesia 85/K2
Kragerø, Norway 18/F7
Kragujevac, Yugoslavia 45/E3
Kragujevac, Yugoslavia 7/G4
Krakatau (Rakata) (isl.), Indonesia 85/C7
Krakow, Mo. 261/K6
Kraków (Cracow), Poland 47/E4
Krakow, Wis. 317/K6
Kralendijk (cap.), Bonaire, Neth. Ant. 161/E8
Kralendijk, Neth. Ant. 156/E4
Králíky, Czech. 41/D1
Kraljevo, Yugoslavia 45/E4
Kralovice, Czech. 41/B2
Kráľovský Chlmec, Czech. 41/G2
Kralupy nad Vltavou, Czech. 41/C1
Kramatorsk, U.S.S.R. 52/E5
Kramer, Ind. 227/C4
Kramer, Nebr. 264/H4
Kramer, N. Dak. 282/J2
Kramfors, Sweden 18/L5
Kranidhion, Greece 45/F7
Kranj, Yugoslavia 45/B2
Kranzburg, S. Dak. 298/R4
Krapkowice, Poland 47/D3
Krasino, U.S.S.R. 52/H1
Krasino, U.S.S.R. 48/F2
Krāslava, U.S.S.R. 53/D3
Kraslice, Czech. 41/B1
Krásná Lípa, Czech. 41/C1
Kraśnik Fabryczny, Poland 47/F3
Krasnoarmeysk, U.S.S.R. 52/G4
Krasnoborsk, U.S.S.R. 52/G2
Krasnodar, U.S.S.R. 7/H4
Krasnodar, U.S.S.R. 48/E5
Krasnodar, U.S.S.R. 52/E6
Krasnograd, U.S.S.R. 52/E5
Krasnokamensk, U.S.S.R. 48/M4
Krasnokamsk, U.S.S.R. 52/H3
Krasnokamsk, U.S.S.R. 48/F4
Krasnoperekopsk, U.S.S.R. 52/D5
Krasnoslobodsk, U.S.S.R. 52/G5
Krasnotur'insk, U.S.S.R. 48/G3
Krasnoural'sk, U.S.S.R. 48/G4
Krasnovishersk, U.S.S.R. 52/J2
Krasnovodsk, U.S.S.R. 54/G5
Krasnovodsk, U.S.S.R. 48/F5
Krasnoyarsk, U.S.S.R. 54/L4
Krasnoyarsk, U.S.S.R. 2/P3
Krasnoyarsk, U.S.S.R. 48/K4
Krasnystaw, Poland 47/F3
Krasnyy Kut, U.S.S.R. 52/G4
Krasnyy Luch, U.S.S.R. 52/E5
Krasnyy Sulin, U.S.S.R. 52/F5
Krasnyy Yar, U.S.S.R. 52/G5
Kraulshavn (Nussaq), Greenl. 4/B13
Krause Lagoon (chan.), Virgin Is. (U.S.) 161/F4
Krawang, Indonesia 85/H2
Krebs, Okla. 288/P5
Krefeld, Germany 22/B3
Kremenchug, U.S.S.R. 7/H4
Kremenchug, U.S.S.R. 48/D5
Kremenchug, U.S.S.R. 52/D5
Kremlin, Mont. 262/F2
Kremlin, Okla. 288/L1
Kremmling, Colo. 208/G2
Kremnica, Czech. 41/E2
Krems an der Donau, Austria 41/C2
Krenitzin (isls.), Alaska 196/E4
Kresgeville, Pa. 294/L4
Kress, Texas 303/C3
Kretinga, U.S.S.R. 53/A3
Kreuztal, Germany 22/C3
Kreuzlingen, Switzerland 39/H1
Kribi, Cameroon 115/B3
Krichev, U.S.S.R. 52/D4
Kriens, Switzerland 39/F2
Krimml, Austria 41/B3
Krimpen aan den IJssel, Netherlands 27/F5
Kriós (cape), Greece 45/F8
Krishna (Kistna) (riv.), India 68/D5
Krishnanagar, India 68/F4
Kristiansand, Norway 18/F8
Kristiansand, Norway 7/E3
Kristianstad (co.), Sweden 18/J8
Kristianstad, Sweden 18/J9
Kristiansund, Norway 7/E2
Kristiansund, Norway 18/E5
Kristiinankaupunki (Kristinestad), Finland 18/N5
Kristinehamn, Sweden 18/H7
Kristinestad, Finland 18/N5
Kriti (Crete) (isl.), Greece 45/G8
Krivoy Rog, U.S.S.R. 7/H4
Krivoy Rog, U.S.S.R. 48/D5
Krivoy Rog, U.S.S.R. 52/D5
Križevci, Yugoslavia 45/C2
Krk, Yugoslavia 45/B3
Krk (isl.), Yugoslavia 45/B3
Krnov, Czech. 41/D1
Krolevets, U.S.S.R. 52/D4
Kroměříž, Czech. 41/D2
Krompachy, Czech. 41/F2
Kronach, Germany 22/D3
Kronau, Sask. 181/G5
Krong Kaoh Kong, Cambodia 72/D4
Krong Keb, Cambodia 72/E5
Kronoberg (co.), Sweden 18/J8
Kronshtadt, U.S.S.R. 52/C3
Kroonstad, S. Africa 118/D5
Kropotkin, U.S.S.R. 52/F5
Kroschel, Minn. 255/E4
Krosno (prov.), Poland 47/E4
Krosno, Poland 47/E4
Krosno Odrzanskie, Poland 47/B2
Krotoszyn, Poland 47/C3

394 Krotz Springs

Krotz Springs, La. 238/G5
Krško, Yugoslavia 45/B3
Kru Coast (reg.), Liberia 106/C8
Kruger Nat'l Park, S. Africa 118/E4
Krugersdorp, S. Africa 118/H6
Krugloi (pt.), Alaska 196/J3
Kruis (riv.), S. Africa 118/F6
Krujë, Albania 45/D5
Krum, Texas 303/G4
Krumbach, Germany 22/D4
Krummenau, Switzerland 39/H2
Krumovgrad, Bulgaria 45/G5
Krung Thep (Bangkok) (cap.), Thailand 72/D4
Krupina, Czech. 41/E2
Krupka, Czech. 41/B1
Krupp (Marlin), Wash. 310/F3
Krusenstern (cape), Alaska 196/F1
Krusenstern (cape), N.W. Terr. 187/G3
Kruševac, Yugoslavia 45/E4
Krušné Hory (Erzgebirge) (mts.), Czech. 41/B1
Kruszwica, Poland 47/D2
Kruzof (isl.), Alaska 196/M1
Krydor, Sask. 181/D3
Krymsk, U.S.S.R. 52/E5
Krynica, Poland 47/E4
Krypton, Ky. 237/P6
Krzyż, Poland 47/C2
Ksar el Boukhari, Algeria 106/E1
Ksar el Kebir, Morocco 106/C2
Ktima, Cyprus 63/E5
Kuala Dungun, Malaysia 72/D6
Kualakapuas, Indonesia 85/E6
Kuala Kerai, Malaysia 72/D6
Kualakurun, Indonesia 85/E6
Kuala Lipis, Malaysia 72/D6
Kuala Lumpur (cap.), Malaysia 72/D7
Kuala Lumpur (cap.), Malaysia 54/M9
Kuala Lumpur (cap.), Malaysia 2/P5
Kuala Pilah, Malaysia 72/D7
Kualapuu, Hawaii 218/G1
Kuala Rompin, Malaysia 72/D7
Kuala Selangor, Malaysia 72/D7
Kuala Terengganu, Malaysia 72/D6
Kuancheng, China 77/J3
Kuantan, Malaysia 72/D7
Kuba, U.S.S.R. 52/G6
Kubachi, U.S.S.R. 52/G6
Kubaisa, Iraq 66/C4
Kuban (riv.), U.S.S.R. 7/J4
Kuban' (riv.), U.S.S.R. 52/E5
Kubbum, Sudan 111/D5
Kubeno (lake), U.S.S.R. 52/E3
Küblis, Switzerland 39/J3
Kubohama, Japan 81/F7
Kubrat, Bulgaria 45/H4
Kuching, Malaysia 54/N9
Kuching, Malaysia 85/E5
Kuchino (isl.), Japan 81/O4
Kuçovë (Stalin), Albania 45/D5
Küçükköy, Turkey 63/B3
Kudarebe (pt.), Neth. Ant. 161/D9
Kudat, Malaysia 85/F4
Kudowa Zdroj, Poland 47/B3
Kudus, Indonesia 85/J2
Kudymkar, U.S.S.R. 48/F4
Kudymkar, U.S.S.R. 52/H3
Kufra (oasis), Libya 102/E2
Kufra (oasis), Libya 111/D3
Kufrinja, Jordan 65/D3
Kufstein, Austria 41/A3
Kuh (cape), Iran 66/K8
Kuhak, Iran 66/N7
Kuhestan, Afghanistan 59/H3
Kuhestan, Afghanistan 68/A2
Kühlungsborn, Germany 22/D1
Kuhmo, Finland 18/Q4
Kuhpayeh, Iran 66/H4
Kuilsrivier, S. Africa 118/F6
Kuiseb (riv.), Namibia 118/B4
Kuito, Angola 115/C6
Kuiu (isl.), Alaska 196/M2
Kuivaniemi, Finland 18/O4
Kuji, Japan 81/K3
Kuju (mt.), Japan 81/E7
Kuk (riv.), Alaska 196/G1
Kukaiau, Hawaii 218/H4
Kukaklek (lake), Alaska 196/G3
Kukalar, Kuh-e (mt.), Iran 59/F3
Kukalar, Kuh-e (mt.), Iran 66/G5
Kukalaya (riv.), Nicaragua 154/F4
Kukawa, Nigeria 106/G6
Kukës, Albania 45/E4
Kuki, Japan 81/O2
Kukpowruk (riv.), Alaska 196/F1
Kukui (riv.), Guyana 131/A3
Kukuihaele, Hawaii 218/H3
Kula, Bulgaria 45/F4
Kula, Hawaii 218/J2
Kula, Turkey 63/C3
Kulai, Malaysia 72/F5
Kula Kangri (mt.), Bhutan 68/G3
Kuldīga, U.S.S.R. 53/A2
Kuldja (Yining), China 77/B3
Kulebaki, U.S.S.R. 52/F3
Kulen, Cambodia 72/E4
Kulen Vakuf, Yugoslavia 45/B3
Kulgera, North. Terr. 88/E5
Kulgera, North. Terr. 93/C8
Kulkyne (creek), N.S. Wales 97/C1
Kulm, N. Dak. 282/N7
Kulmbach, Germany 22/D3
Kuloy, U.S.S.R. 52/F2
Kulp, Turkey 63/J3
Kulpmont, Pa. 294/J4
Kulpsville, Pa. 294/M5
Kul'sary, U.S.S.R. 48/F5
Kulu, India 68/D2
Kulu, Turkey 63/E3
Kulunda, U.S.S.R. 48/H4
Kulyab, U.S.S.R. 48/H6
Kŭm (riv.), S. Korea 81/C5
Kuma (riv.), U.S.S.R. 7/J4
Kuma (riv.), U.S.S.R. 48/E5
Kuma (riv.), U.S.S.R. 52/G5
Kumagaya, Japan 81/J5
Kumai, Indonesia 85/E6
Kumai, Indonesia 85/E6
Kumaka, Guyana 131/B4
Kumamoto (pref.), Japan 81/E7
Kumamoto, Japan 54/P6
Kumamoto, Japan 81/E7
Kumano, Japan 81/G7
Kumanovo, Yugoslavia 45/E4
Kumara, N. Zealand 100/C5
Kumasi, Ghana 106/D7
Kumasi, Ghana 102/B4
Kumba, Cameroon 115/A3
Kumbakonam, India 68/D6
Kumbo, Cameroon 115/B2
Kum-Dag, U.S.S.R. 48/F6
Kume (isl.), Japan 81/M6
Kumertau, U.S.S.R. 52/J4
Kumeu, N. Zealand 100/B1
Kŭmgang (mt.), N. Korea 81/D4
Kumiyama, Japan 81/J7
Kumkale, Turkey 63/B6
Kumköy, Turkey 63/B6
Kumla, Sweden 18/J7
Kumluca, Turkey 63/D4
Kummerowersee (lake), Germany 22/E2
Kumo (riv.), Finland 7/G2
Kumo, Nigeria 106/G7
Kumphawapi, Thailand 72/D3
Kumta, India 68/C6
Kumukahi (cape), Hawaii 218/K5
Kumul (Hami), China 77/D3
Kuna, Idaho 220/B6
Kunágota, Hungary 41/F3
Kunashiri (isl.), Japan 81/N1
Kunda, U.S.S.R. 52/C3
Kunda, U.S.S.R. 53/D1
Kundiawa, Papua N.G. 85/B7
Kundl, Austria 41/A3
Künes (Xinyuan), China 77/B3
Künes He (riv.), China 77/B3
Kungälv, Sweden 18/G8
Kunghit (isl.), Br. Col. 184/B4
Kungsbacka, Sweden 18/G8
Kungu, Zaire 102/D4
Kungu, Zaire 115/C3
Kungur, U.S.S.R. 7/K3
Kungur, U.S.S.R. 48/F4
Kungur, U.S.S.R. 52/J3
Kunhegyes, Hungary 41/F3
Kunia, Hawaii 218/E2
Kuningan, Indonesia 85/H2
Kunkle, Ohio 284/A2
Kunkletown, Pa. 294/M4
Kunlong, Burma 72/C2
Kunlun (range), China 54/K6
Kunlun (range), India 68/D1
Kunlun Shan (range), China 77/B4
Kunmadaras, Hungary 41/F3
Kunming, China 77/F6
Kunming, China 2/O4
Kunming, China 54/M7
Kunsan, S. Korea 81/C6
Kunszentmárton, Hungary 41/F3
Kunszentmiklós, Hungary 41/E3
Kununurra, W. Australia 88/D3
Kununurra, W. Australia 92/E2
Kuolayarvi, U.S.S.R. 52/D1
Kuopio (prov.), Finland 18/P5
Kuopio, Finland 7/G2
Kuopio, Finland 18/Q5
Kupa (riv.), Yugoslavia 45/B3
Kupang, Indonesia 54/O11
Kupang, Indonesia 85/G8
Kuparuk (riv.), Alaska 196/H1
Kupino, U.S.S.R. 48/H4
Kupiškis, U.S.S.R. 53/C3
Kupreanof (isl.), Alaska 196/N1
Kupreanov, Alaska 196/M2
Kupyansk, U.S.S.R. 52/E5
Kuqa, China 77/B3
Kur (isl.), Indonesia 85/J7
Kura (riv.), U.S.S.R. 48/E6
Kura (riv.), U.S.S.R. 52/G6
Kuraiyima, Jordan 65/D3
Kurang (riv.), Iran 66/G4
Kurashiki, Japan 81/F6
Kurayoshi, Japan 81/F6
Kurdistan (Kordestan) (prov.), Iran 66/E3
Kurdistan (reg.), Iran 59/D2
Kurdistan (reg.), Iran 66/D2
Kurdistan (reg.), Iraq 59/D2
Kurdistan (reg.), Iraq 66/C2
Kurdistan (reg.), Turkey 59/D2
Kŭrdzhali, Bulgaria 45/G5
Kure (atoll), Hawaii 87/J3
Kure (atoll), Hawaii 218/A5
Kure, Japan 81/F6
Küre, Turkey 63/E2
Küre (mts.), Turkey 63/E2
Kure Beach, N.C. 281/O7
Kuressaare, U.S.S.R. 53/B1
Kuressaare, U.S.S.R. 52/B3
Kurgan, U.S.S.R. 54/H4
Kurgan, U.S.S.R. 48/G4
Kurgan-Tyube, U.S.S.R. 48/G6
Kuria Muria (isls.), Oman 54/G8
Kuria Muria (isls.), Oman 59/G6
Kurikka, Finland 18/M5
Kuril (isls.), U.S.S.R. 2/S3
Kuril (isls.), U.S.S.R. 54/R5
Kuril (isls.), U.S.S.R. 48/P5
Kuril'sk, U.S.S.R. 48/P5
Ku-ring-gai, N. S. Wales 88/K4
Kurla, India 68/B7
Kurmuk, Sudan 111/F5
Kurnell (pen.), N.S. Wales 97/J4
Kurnool, India 54/J8
Kurnool, India 68/D5
Kuroiso, Japan 81/K5
Kuroki, Sask. 181/H4
Kurow, N. Zealand 100/C6
Kurri Kurri-Weston, N.S. Wales 97/F3
Kuršėnai, U.S.S.R. 53/B2
Kursk, U.S.S.R. 7/H3
Kursk, U.S.S.R. 48/D4
Kursk, U.S.S.R. 52/E4
Kurşunlu, Turkey 63/E2
Kurtalan, Turkey 63/J3
Kurthwood, La. 238/D4
Kurtistown, Hawaii 218/J5
Kurtz, Ind. 227/E7
Kuruçaşile, Turkey 63/E2
Kuruçay (riv.), Turkey 63/K2
Kuruktag Shan (range), China 77/C3
Kuruman, S. Africa 118/C5
Kurume, Japan 81/E7
Kurundi, North. Terr. 93/D6
Kurunegala, Sri Lanka 68/E7
Kurungiku (mts.), Guyana 131/B3
Kurupukari, Guyana 131/B3
Kuş (lake), Turkey 63/B2
Kuşada (gulf), Turkey 63/B4
Kuşadası, Turkey 63/B4
Kushchevskaya, U.S.S.R. 52/E5
Kushequa, Pa. 294/E2
Kushikino, Japan 81/E8
Kushima, Japan 81/E8
Kushimoto, Japan 81/G7
Kushiro, Japan 54/R5
Kushiro, Japan 81/M2
Kushka, U.S.S.R. 48/G6
Kushog (lake), Ontario 177/F2
Kuskokwim (bay), Alaska 196/F3
Kuskokwim (mts.), Alaska 196/G2
Kuskokwim (riv.), Alaska 146/C3
Kuskokwim (riv.), Alaska 188/C6
Kuskokwim (riv.), Alaska 196/G2
Kuskokwim, North Fork (riv.), Alaska 196/H2
Kuskokwim, South Fork (riv.), Alaska 196/H2
Kuskokwim (riv.), U.S. 4/C17
Küsnacht, Switzerland 39/G2
Kusŏng, N. Korea 81/B4
Küssnacht am Rigi, Switzerland 39/F2
Kustanay, U.S.S.R. 54/H4
Kustanay, U.S.S.R. 48/G4
Kustatan, Alaska 196/B1
Küstrin, Poland 47/B2
Kut, Iraq 59/E3
Kut, Iraq 66/D4
Kut, Ko (isl.), Thailand 72/D5
Kuta, Nigeria 106/F7
Kütahya (prov.), Turkey 63/C3
Kütahya, Turkey 59/B2
Kütahya, Turkey 63/C3
Kutaisi, U.S.S.R. 7/J4
Kutaisi, U.S.S.R. 48/E5
Kutaisi, U.S.S.R. 52/F6
Kutaraja (Banda Aceh), Indonesia 85/A4
Kutari (riv.), Guyana 131/C4
Kutari (riv.), Suriname 131/C4
Kutch, Colo. 208/M5
Kutch (Kachchh), Rann of (salt marsh) 54/H7
Kutch (Kachchh) (gulf), India 68/B4
Kutch (Kachchh) (reg.), India 68/B4
Kutch (Kachchh), Rann of (salt marsh), India 68/B4
Kutch (Kachchh), Rann of (salt lake), Pakistan 59/K5
Kutch (Kachchh), Rann of (salt marsh), Pakistan 68/B4
Kutcharo (lake), Japan 81/M2
Kutina, Yugoslavia 45/C3
Kutná Hora, Czech. 41/C2
Kutno, Poland 47/D2
Kutoarjo, Indonesia 85/J2
Kuttawa, Ky. 237/E6
Küttigen, Switzerland 39/F2
Kutu, Zaire 115/C4
Kutum, Sudan 111/D5
Kúty, Czech. 41/D2
Kutztown, Pa. 294/L4
Kuujjuac (Fort-Chimo), Québec 162/K4
Kuujjuac (Fort-Chimo), Québec 174/F2
Kuujjuarapik, Québec 162/J4
Kuujjuarapik, Québec 174/B1
Kuusamo, Finland 18/Q4
Kuusamojärvi (lake), Finland 18/Q4
Kuusankoski, Finland 18/P6
Kuvandyk, U.S.S.R. 52/J4
Kuwait 2/M4
Kuwait 54/F7
KUWAIT 59/E4
Kuvango, Angola 115/C6
Kuybyshev (Samara), U.S.S.R. 2/M3
Kuybyshev (Samara), U.S.S.R. 7/K3
Kuybyshev (Samara), U.S.S.R. 48/F4
Kuybyshev (Samara), U.S.S.R. 52/H4
Kuybyshev (Samara), U.S.S.R. 48/H4
Kuybyshev (res.), U.S.S.R. 48/F4
Kuybyshev (res.), U.S.S.R. 52/G4
Kuybyshev (res.), U.S.S.R. 7/K3
Kuyto (lake), U.S.S.R. 52/D2
Kuytun, China 77/C3
Kuyucak, Turkey 63/C4
Kuyuwini (riv.), Guyana 131/B4
Kuznetsk, U.S.S.R. 52/G4
Kuzomen', U.S.S.R. 52/E1
Kvaenangen (fjord), Norway 18/N2
Kvaerndrup, Denmark 21/D7
Kvaløya (isl.), Norway 18/O1
Kvaløya (isl.), Norway 18/K2
Kvarner (gulf), Yugoslavia 45/B3
Kvichak, Alaska 196/G3
Kvichak (bay), Alaska 196/G3
Kvikkjokk, Sweden 18/K3
Kvinnherad, Norway 18/E6
Kvissleby, Sweden 18/K5
Kviteseid, Norway 18/F7
Kwa (riv.), Zaire 115/C4
Kwai (Mae Nam Khwae Noi) (riv.), Thailand 72/C4
Kwajalein (atoll), Marshall Is. 87/G5
Kwakoegron, Suriname 131/D3
Kwakwani, Guyana 131/C3
Kwale, Kenya 102/F5
Kwale, Kenya 115/G4
Kwamouth, Zaire 115/C4
Kwangchow (Canton), China 77/H7
Kwangju, S. Korea 54/O6
Kwangju, S. Korea 81/C6
Kwango (riv.), Zaire 115/C5
Kwangsi Chuang Aut. Reg. (Guangxi Zhuangzu), China 77/G7
Kwangtung (Guangdong), China 77/H7
Kwanmo (mt.), N. Korea 81/D3
Kwara (state), Nigeria 106/E7
Kwekwe, Zimbabwe 118/D3
Kwekwe, Zimbabwe 102/E6
Kweichow (Guizhou), China 77/G6
Kweilin (Guilin), China 77/G6
Kweisui (Hohhot), China 77/H3
Kweiyang (Guiyang), China 77/G6
Kwethluk, Alaska 196/F2
Kwidzin, Poland 47/D2
Kwigillingok, Alaska 196/F3
Kwilu (riv.), Angola 115/C5
Kwilu (riv.), Zaire 115/C5
Kwinana-Newtown, W. Australia 88/B2
Kwinana New Town, W. Australia 92/A1
Kwinitsa, Br. Col. 184/C3
Kwitaro (riv.), Guyana 131/B4
Kyabé, Chad 111/C6
Kyabram, Victoria 97/C5
Kyaikto, Burma 72/C3
Kya-in Seikkyi, Burma 72/C3
Kyakhta, U.S.S.R. 54/M4
Kyakhta, U.S.S.R. 48/L4
Kyalite, N.S. Wales 97/B4
Kyana, Ind. 227/D8
Kyancutta, S. Australia 94/D5
Kyangin, Burma 72/B3
Kyaukme, Burma 72/C2
Kyaukpadaung, Burma 72/B2
Kyaukpyu, Burma 72/B3
Kyaukse, Burma 72/C2
Kybartai, U.S.S.R. 53/B3
Kyeburn, N. Zealand 100/C6
Kyger, Ohio 284/F8
Kyger, W. Va. 312/D5
Kyjov, Czech. 41/D2
Kykosmovi, Ariz. 198/E3
Kyle, Sask. 181/C5
Kyle, S. Dak. 298/E7
Kyle, Texas 303/G8
Kyleakin, Scotland 15/C3
Kylemore, Sask. 181/H4
Kyle of Lochalsh, Scotland 15/C3
Kyle of Tongue (inlet), Scotland 15/D2
Kyles Ford, Tenn. 237/R7
Kylestrome, Scotland 15/D2
Kymi (prov.), Finland 18/Q6
Kyneton, Victoria 97/C5
Kynšperk, Czech. 41/B1
Kynuna, Queensland 95/B4
Kyogle, N.S. Wales 97/G1
Kyonan, Japan 81/O3
Kyŏnghŭng, N. Korea 81/E2
Kyŏngju, S. Korea 81/D6
Kyoto (pref.), Japan 81/J7
Kyoto, Japan 54/P6
Kyoto, Japan 81/J7
Kyrenia, Cyprus 63/E5
Kyritz, Germany 22/E2
Kysucké Nové Mesto, Czech. 41/E2
Kythréa, Cyprus 63/E5
Kyuquot, Br. Col. 184/D5
Kyuquot (sound), Br. Col. 184/D5
Kyushu (isl.), Japan 2/R4
Kyushu (isl.), Japan 54/P6
Kyushu (isl.), Japan 81/E7
Kyustendil, Bulgaria 45/F4
Kyusyur, U.S.S.R. 48/N2
Kywebwe, Burma 72/C3
Kyzyl (riv.), U.S.S.R. 54/L4
Kyzyl, U.S.S.R. 48/K4
Kyzyl-Kum (des.), U.S.S.R. 48/G5
Kzyl-Orda, U.S.S.R. 54/H5
Kzyl-Orda, U.S.S.R. 48/G5

L

Laa an der Thaya, Austria 41/D2
La Aduana, Venezuela 124/D3
Laager, Tenn. 237/K10
La Aguja (cape), Colombia 126/C2
Laakirchen, Austria 41/B3
La Almunia de Doña Godina, Spain 33/F2
La Altagracia (prov.), Dom. Rep. 158/F6
La Anna, Pa. 294/M3
La Antigua Veracruz, Mexico 150/Q1
La Araucanía (reg.), Chile 138/E2
La Asunción, Venezuela 124/G2
Laau (pt.), Hawaii 218/G1
Laax, Switzerland 39/H3
Laayoune, W. Sahara 102/A2
Laayoune, Western Sahara 106/B3
Labadie, Mo. 261/L5
Labadieville, La. 238/K4
La Baie, Québec 172/G1
La Baie-de-Shawinigan, Québec 172/E3
La Banda, Argentina 143/D2
La Bandera (pt.), P. Rico 161/F1
La Bañeza, Spain 33/C1
La Barca, Mexico 150/H6
La Barge, Wyo. 319/B3
La Barge (creek), Wyo. 319/B3
La Barra de Navidad, Mexico 150/G7
Labasheeda, Ireland 17/C6
La Baule-Escoublac, France 28/B4
L'Abbaye, Switzerland 39/B3
Labe (riv.), Czech. 41/C1
Labé, Guinea 106/B6
La Bella (lag.), Paraguay 144/B4
La Belle, Fla. 212/E5
La Belle, Mo. 261/J2
Labelle (co.), Québec 172/B3
Labelle, Québec 172/C3
Labelle (lake), Québec 172/C3
La Belle (lake), Wis. 317/H1
Laberge (lake), Yukon 162/C3
Laberinto de las Doce Leguas (cays), Cuba 158/F3
La Berra (mt.), Switzerland 39/D3
Labette (co.), Kansas 232/G4
Labette, Kansas 232/G4
Labinsk, U.S.S.R. 52/F6
La Bisbal, Spain 33/H1
La Blanquilla (isl.), Venezuela 124/F2
Labo, Philippines 82/D3
Labo (mt.), Philippines 82/D3
La Bolsa, Uruguay 145/C1
La Bolt, S. Dak. 298/R3
La Bonita, Ecuador 128/D2
La Boquilla (res.), Mexico 150/G3
Laborec (riv.), Czech. 41/F2
Laborie, St. Lucia 161/G7
La Bostonnais, Québec 172/E2
Labougle, Argentina 143/G5
Laboulaye, Argentina 143/D3
Labrador (sea) 146/N4
Labrador (sea) 162/L4
Labrador (reg.), Canada 2/G3
Labrador (reg.), Newf. 166/B2
Labrador (sea), Newf. 166/C2
Labrador (reg.), Newf. 146/M4
Labrador (reg.), Newf. 162/K4
Labrador City, Newf. 166/A3
La Branche, Mich. 250/B3
Lábrea, Brazil 132/G10
La Brea, Trin. & Tob. 161/A11
Labrieville, Québec 174/C3
La Broquerie, Manitoba 179/F5
Labuan, Malaysia 85/E4
Labuan (isl.), Malaysia 85/E4
Labuan (state), Malaysia 85/F4
Labuha, Indonesia 85/H6
Labuhan, Indonesia 85/G2
Labuk (bay), Malaysia 85/F4
Labutta, Burma 72/B3
Labyrinth (canyon), Utah 304/D5
Labytnangi, U.S.S.R. 48/G3
Lac (bay), Neth. Ant. 161/D9
Lac-à-Beauce, Québec 172/E2
Lacadena, Sask. 181/C5
Lacadie, Québec 172/J4
La Cahouane, Haiti 158/A6
Lac-à-la-Croix, Québec 172/F1
La Calera, Chile 138/F2
Lac-Alouette, Québec 172/D4
Lacamp, La. 238/E4
La Canada Flintridge, Calif. 204/C10
Lacanau (lake), France 28/C5
La Canoa, Venezuela 124/G3
Lacantum (riv.), Mexico 150/O8
La Capilla, 136/C8
La Carlota, Argentina 143/D3
La Carlota, Philippines 82/D5
La Carlota, Spain 33/D4
La Carolina, Spain 33/E3
Lacassine, La. 238/E6
Lac-au-Saumon, Québec 172/B2
Lac-aux-Sables, Québec 172/E3
Lac Baker, New Bruns. 170/B1
Lac-Beauport, Québec 172/F3
Lac-Bouchette, Québec 172/E1
Lac-Carré, Québec 172/C3
Lac-Cayamant, Québec 172/A3
Lac-Chat, Québec 172/E2
Lac Court Oreilles Ind. Res., Wis. 317/D4
Lac de Gras (lake), N.W. Terr. 187/G3
Lac-Delage, Québec 172/H3
Lac-des-Aigles, Québec 172/J2
Lac des Arcs, Alberta 182/C4
Lac-des-Écorces, Québec 172/B3
Lac-des-Îles, Québec 172/B3
Lac-Drolet, Québec 172/G4
Lac du Bonnet, Manitoba 179/G4
Lac-du-Cerf, Québec 172/B3
Lac du Flambeau, Wis. 317/G4
Lac du Flambeau Ind. Res., Wis. 317/G3
Lac-Édouard, Québec 172/E2
La Ceiba, Hond. 146/K8
La Ceiba, Honduras 154/D3
La Ceiba, Apure, Venezuela 124/C4
La Ceiba, Trujillo, Venezuela 124/C3
La Center, Ky. 237/C6
La Center, Wash. 310/C5
Lacepede (bay), S. Australia 88/F7
Lacepede (bay), S. Australia 94/F7
Lacepede (range), W. Australia 88/D3
Lacepede (isls.), W. Australia 92/C2
La Cerbatana, Serranía de (mts.), Venezuela 124/E4
Lac-Etchemin, Québec 172/G3
Lacey, Ark. 202/G7
Lacey, Wash. 310/C3
Lacey Spring, Va. 307/L3
Laceys Spring, Ala. 195/E1
Laceyville, Pa. 294/K2
Lac-Frontière, Québec 172/H3
Lac Giao (Ban Me Thuot), Vietnam 72/E4
Lacha (lake), U.S.S.R. 52/E2
La Chapelle, Haiti 158/C5
La Charité-sur-Loire, France 28/E4
La Châtre, France 28/D4
La Chaux-de-Fonds, Switzerland 39/C2
Lachay (pt.), Peru 128/D8
Lachen, Switzerland 39/G2
Lachenaie, Québec 172/D4
Lachine, Mich. 250/F3
Lachine, Québec 172/H4
Lachlan (riv.), N.S. Wales 88/G6
Lachlan (range), N.S. Wales 97/C3
Lachlan (riv.), N.S. Wales 97/C3
La Chorrera, Colombia 126/D8
La Chorrera, Panama 154/H6
Lac-Humqui, Québec 172/B2
Lachute, Québec 172/C4
La Ciénaga, Dom. Rep. 158/D6
La Ciotat, France 28/F6
Lackawanna, N.Y. 276/B5
Lackawanna (co.), Pa. 294/L3
Lackawaxen, Pa. 294/N3
Lackey, Ky. 237/R6
Lackland A.F.B., Texas 303/J11
Lac La Belle, Wis. 317/H1
Lac La Biche, Alberta 182/E2
Lac La Biche, Alta. 162/E5
Lac La Hache, Br. Col. 184/G4
Lac la Martre, N.W. Terr. 187/G3
La Clarita, Argentina 143/G5
Lac La Ronge Prov. Park, Sask. 181/M3
Laclede, Idaho 220/B1
La Clede, Ill. 222/E5
Laclede (co.), Mo. 261/G7
Laclede, Mo. 261/F3
Lac-Mégantic, Québec 172/G4
Lacolle, Québec 172/D4
La Colmena, Paraguay 144/B5
La Coloma, Cuba 158/B2
La Colonia, Chile 138/D7
Lacomb, Oreg. 291/E3
Lacombe, Alberta 182/D3
Lacombe, Alta. 162/E5
Lacombe, La. 238/L6
Lacon, Ill. 222/D2
Lacona, Iowa 229/G6
Lacona, N.Y. 276/J3
La Concepción, Honduras 154/E3
La Concepción, Panama 154/F6
La Concepción, Venezuela 124/C2
La Concepción, Venezuela 124/B2
La Conception, Québec 172/C3
La Concordia, Mexico 150/N9
Laconia, Ind. 227/E8
Laconia, N.H. 268/E4
Laconia, Tenn. 237/C10
La Conner, Wash. 310/C2
La Conquista, Nicaragua 154/D5
Lacoochee, Fla. 212/D3
La Corey, Alberta 182/E2
La Coronilla, Uruguay 145/F4
La Coruña (prov.), Spain 33/B1
La Coruña, Spain 33/B1
La Coruña, Spain 7/D4
La Coste, Texas 303/J11
La Courneuve, France 28/B1
Lacovia, Jamaica 158/H6
Lac Pelletier, Sask. 181/C6
Lac-Poulin, Québec 172/G3
Lac qui Parle (co.), Minn. 255/B6
Lac qui Parle, Minn. 255/B5
Lac qui Parle (lake), Minn. 255/C5
Lac qui Parle (riv.), Minn. 255/B6
Lacre (pt.), Neth. Ant. 161/E9
La Crescent, Minn. 255/G7
La Crescenta-Montrose, Calif. 204/C10
La Crete, Alberta 182/B5
La Croche, Québec 172/E2
La Croix (lake), Minn. 255/F2
La Crosse, Fla. 212/D2
La Crosse, Georgia 217/D6
La Crosse, Ind. 227/D2
La Crosse, Kansas 232/C3
La Crosse, Va. 307/M7
Lacrosse, Wash. 310/H4
La Crosse, Wis. 146/J5
La Crosse, Wis. 188/H2
La Crosse (co.), Wis. 317/D8
La Crosse, Wis. 317/D8
La Cruz, Argentina 143/E2
La Cruz, Chile 138/F2
La Cruz, Colombia 126/B7
La Cruz, Chihuahua, Mexico 150/G3
La Cruz, Sinaloa, Mexico 150/F5
La Cruz, Nicaragua 154/E4
La Cruz, Uruguay 145/C4
Lac-Saguay, Québec 172/B3
Lac-Saint-Charles, Québec 172/H3
Lac-Sainte-Marie, Québec 172/A4
Lac-Saint-Jean-Est (co.), Québec 172/F1
Lac-Saint-Jean-Est (county), Québec 174/C3
Lac-Saint-Jean-Ouest (co.), Québec 172/E1
Lac-Saint-Jean-Ouest (county), Québec 174/C2
Lac-Saint-Joseph, Québec 172/F3
Lac-Saint-Paul, Québec 172/B3
Lac-Sergent, Québec 172/F3
Lac Seul, Ontario 175/B2
La Cuchilla, Uruguay 145/F3
La Cueva, N. Mex. 274/D3
La Cumbre, Argentina 143/C3
La Cure, Switzerland 39/B4
Lacuy (pen.), Chile 138/D4
Lac Vert, Sask. 181/G3
La Cygne, Kansas 232/H3
Ladakh (reg.), India 68/D2
Ladd, Ill. 222/D2
Ladder (creek), Kansas 232/A3
Ladder (hills), Scotland 15/E3
Laddonia, Mo. 261/J4
La Decharge, Québec 172/F1
Ladelle, Ark. 202/G7
Ladgasht (Qila Ladgasht), Pakistan 68/A3
Ladhar Bheinn (mt.), Scotland 15/C3
Ladiesburg, Md. 245/J2
La Digue (isl.), Seychelles 118/J5
Lâdik, Turkey 63/G2
Ladispoli, Italy 34/E6
Ladiz, Iran 66/M6
Ladner, S. Dak. 298/B2
Lado, Sudan 111/F6
Ladoga, Ind. 227/D5
Ladoga (lake), U.S.S.R. 7/H2
Ladoga (lake), U.S.S.R. 48/D3
Ladoga (lake), U.S.S.R. 52/D2
La Dôle (mt.), Switzerland 39/B4
Ladonia, Texas 303/J4
Ladora, Iowa 229/J5
La Dorada, Colombia 126/C5
Ladrillero (gulf), Chile 138/C8
Ladrillero (mt.), Chile 138/E10
Ladrillo (pt.), Cuba 158/E3
Ladron (mts.), N. Mex. 274/B4
Ladrones (isls.), Panama 154/F7
Ladson, S.C. 296/G6
La Due, Mo. 261/E6
Ladue, Mo. 261/P3
La Durantaye, Québec 172/G3
Lady (pond), Newf. 166/D2
Lady Ann (str.), N.W. Terr. 187/K2
Ladybank, Scotland 15/E4
Lady Barron, Tasmania 99/E2
Ladybrand, S. Africa 118/D5
Lady Franklin (bay), N.W. Terr. 187/M1

Lanai 395

Lady Franklin (isl.), N.W. Terr. 187/M3
Lady Lake, Fla. 212/E3
Lady Lake, Sask. 181/J3
Lady's Island Lake (inlet), Ireland 17/J7
Ladysmith, Br. Col. 184/J3
Ladysmith, S. Africa 102/F7
Ladysmith, S. Africa 118/D5
Ladysmith, Va. 307/N4
Ladysmith, Wis. 317/D5
Ladywood, Manitoba 179/F4
Lae, Papua N.G. 85/B7
Lae, Papua N.G. 86/A2
Lae, Papua N.G. 87/E6
Lae, Thailand 72/D3
Laem Chong Phra (cape), Thailand 72/C5
Laem Pho (cape), Thailand 72/D6
Laem Talumphuk (cape), Thailand 72/D5
Lae o Kealaikahiki (pt.), Hawaii 218/H3
Laerdal, Norway 18/E6
La Esmeralda, Argentina 143/G5
La Esmeralda, Bolivia 136/D8
La Esmeralda, Venezuela 124/F6
Laesø (isl.), Denmark 18/G8
Laesø (isl.), Denmark 21/D3
La Esperanza, Argentina 143/B7
La Esperanza, Bolivia 136/D4
La Esperanza, Honduras 154/C3
La Esperanza, Venezuela 124/H3
La Estrada, Spain 33/B1
La Estrella, Chile 138/F5
La Estrelleta (prov.), Dom. Rep. 158/C5
La Falda, Argentina 143/D3
La Farge, Wis. 317/E8
La Fargeville, N.Y. 276/J2
Lafayette, Ala. 195/H5
Lafayette (co.), Ark. 202/C7
Lafayette, Calif. 204/K2
Lafayette, Colo. 208/K3
Lafayette (co.), Fla. 212/C2
La Fayette, Georgia 217/B1
La Fayette, Ill. 222/C2
Lafayette, Ind. 188/J2
Lafayette, Ind. 227/D4
La Fayette, Ky. 237/F7
Lafayette (par.), La. 238/F6
Lafayette, La. 238/F6
Lafayette, Minn. 255/D6
Lafayette (co.), Miss. 256/E2
Lafayette (co.), Mo. 261/E4
Lafayette (mt.), N.H. 268/D3
Lafayette, N.J. 273/D1
La Fayette, N.Y. 276/H5
Lafayette, Ohio 284/C4
Lafayette, Oreg. 291/A2
La Fayette, R.I. 249/H6
Lafayette, Tenn. 237/J7
Lafayette (co.), Wis. 317/F10
Lafayette-Elliston, Va. 307/H6
Lafayette Springs, Miss. 256/F2
Lafe, Ark. 202/J1
La Fe, Cuba 158/A2
La Feria, Texas 303/G11
La Ferté-Macé, France 28/C3
Lafferty, Ohio 284/H5
Lafia, Nigeria 106/F7
Lafiagi, Nigeria 106/F7
Lafitte, La. 238/K7
La Flèche, France 28/C4
Lafleche, Sask. 181/E6
La Floresta, Uruguay 145/C7
Lafnitz (riv.), Austria 41/D3
La Follette, Tenn. 237/N8
La Fontaine, Ind. 227/F3
Lafontaine, Kansas 232/G4
Lafontaine, Québec 172/C4
Lafourche (par.), La. 238/K7
Lafourche, La. 238/J7
Lafourche (bayou), La. 238/K8
La France, S.C. 296/B2
La Fría, Venezuela 124/B3
Laful, India 68/G7
Lagacéville, New Bruns. 170/E1
La Gallareta, Argentina 143/F5
Lagan (riv.), N. Ireland 17/K2
Lagarfljót (stream), Iceland 21/C1
La Garita, Colo. 208/G7
La Garita (mts.), Colo. 208/F7
Lagawe, Philippines 82/C2
Lagayan, Philippines 82/C2
Lage, Germany 22/C3
Lågen (riv.), Norway 18/G6
Lages, Brazil 132/D9
Lages, Brazil 120/D5
Laggan, Scotland 15/D3
Laggan, Scotland 10/D2
Laggan (bay), Scotland 15/B5
Laggan, Loch (lake), Scotland 15/D4
Laghouat, Algeria 106/E2
Laghouat, Algeria 102/C1
Laghy, Ireland 17/E2
La Gineta, Spain 33/E3
Lagkadia, Greece 45/E7
La Glace, Alberta 182/A2
La Gloria, Colombia 126/D3
La Gloria, Cuba 158/G2
Lago, Neth. Ant. 161/E10
Lagoa, Portugal 33/B4
Lagoa da Prata, Brazil 135/D2
Lagoa Dourada, Brazil 135/D2
Lago Blanco, Argentina 143/B6
Lagoen, Neth. Ant. 161/F8
La Goleta, Colombia 126/B3
La Gomera, Guatemala 154/B3
Lagonegro, Italy 34/E4
Lagonoy (gulf), Philippines 82/E4
Lagoon (lake), S. Australia 88/F6
Lago Ranco, Chile 138/E3
Lagos (state), Nigeria 106/E7
Lagos (cap.), Nigeria 2/K5
Lagos (cap.), Nigeria 102/C4
Lagos (cap.), Nigeria 106/E7
Lagos, Portugal 33/B4
Lago Salto Grande (res.), Brazil 132/B10
Lagos de Moreno, Mexico 150/J6
Lagosta (Lastovo) (isl.), Yugoslavia 45/C4
La Goulette (Halq el Oued), Tunisia 106/G1
Lago Verde, Chile 138/E5
La Grand-Combe, France 28/E5
La Grande, Oreg. 188/C1
La Grande, Oreg. 291/J2
La Grande, Wash. 310/C4
La Grand Rivière (riv.), Que. 162/J5
La Grange, Ark. 202/J4
La Grange, Australia 87/C7
La Grange, Calif. 204/E6
La Grange, Ga. 188/K4
La Grange, Georgia 217/B4
La Grange, Ill. 222/B6
Lagrange (co.), Ind. 227/G1
Lagrange, Ind. 227/F1
La Grange, Ky. 237/L4
Lagrange, Maine 243/F5
Lagrange•, Maine 243/F5
La Grange, Mo. 261/K2
La Grange, N.C. 281/O4
Lagrange, Ohio 284/F3
La Grange, Tenn. 237/C10
La Grange, Texas 303/G8
La Grange, W. Australia 92/C2
Lagrange, Wyo. 319/H4
La Grange Park, Ill. 222/B5
La Granja (San Ildefonso), Spain 33/E2
La Gran Sabana (plain), Venezuela 124/G5
La Grita, Venezuela 124/C3
Lagro, Ind. 227/F3
La Grue (bayou), Ark. 202/H5
La Guadeloupe, Québec 172/F4
La Guaira, Venezuela 124/E2
La Guaira, Venezuela 120/C1
La Guajira (dept.), Colombia 126/D2
La Guardia, Bolivia 136/D5
La Guardia, Spain 33/B2
Laguardia, Spain 33/E1
La Guata, Honduras 154/D3
Laguna (creek), Ariz. 198/E2
Laguna (dam), Ariz. 198/A6
Laguna (res.), Ariz. 198/A6
Laguna, Brazil 132/D10
Laguna (res.), Calif. 204/L11
Laguna, N. Mex. 274/B3
Laguna (prov.), Philippines 82/C3
Laguna Beach, Calif. 204/G10
Laguna de Perlas, Nicaragua 154/F4
Laguna Hills, Calif. 204/D11
Laguna Niguel, Calif. 204/H10
Laguna Paiva, Argentina 143/F5
Lagunas, Chile 138/B3
Lagunas, Peru 128/E5
Laguna Yema, Argentina 143/D1
Lagunetas, Venezuela 124/C3
Lagunillas, Bolivia 136/D6
Lagunillas, Chile 138/F3
Lagunillas, Venezuela 124/C2
Lagunitas, Calif. 204/H1
La Habana (Havana) (prov.), Cuba 158/C1
La Habana, Ciudad de (prov.), Cuba 158/C1
La Habra, Calif. 204/D11
Lahad Datu, Malaysia 85/F5
Lahaina, Hawaii 218/H2
Lahaina, Hawaii 188/F5
Laham, Indonesia 85/F5
Lahan, Nong (lake), Thailand 72/D3
La Harpe, Ill. 222/C3
La Harpe, Kansas 232/G4
Lahat, Indonesia 85/C6
La Have, Nova Scotia 168/D4
La Have (isl.), Nova Scotia 168/D4
La Have (riv.), Nova Scotia 168/D4
Lahej, Yemen 59/E7
La Higuera, Chile 138/A7
Lahijan, Iran 66/G2
Lahinch, Ireland 17/C6
Lahmansville, W. Va. 312/H4
Lahn, Germany 22/C3
Lahn (riv.), Germany 22/C3
Lahnstein, Germany 22/B3
Laholm, Sweden 18/H8
Lahoma, Okla. 288/K2
La Honda, Calif. 204/J3
Lahontan (res.), Nev. 266/B3
Lahore, Pakistan 59/K3
Lahore, Pakistan 68/C2
Lahore, Pakistan 54/J6
Lahore, Va. 307/N4
La Horqueta, Venezuela 124/G3
Lahr, Germany 22/B4
Lahri, Pakistan 68/B3
Lahti, Finland 7/G2
Lahti, Finland 18/O6
La Huaca, Peru 128/B5
La Huerta, Mexico 150/G7
Laï, Chad 111/C6
Laï, Chad 102/D4
Lai Chau, Vietnam 72/D2
Laidlaw, Br. Col. 184/M3
Laidon, Loch (lake), Scotland 15/D4
Laie, Hawaii 218/E1
Laie (pt.), Hawaii 218/E1
L'Aigle, France 28/D3
Lai-hka, Burma 72/C2
Laila, Saudi Arabia 59/E5
Lailan, Iraq 66/D3
La Inglesa, Venezuela 124/G3
Laings, Ohio 284/J6
Laingsburg, Mich. 250/E6
Lainioälv (riv.), Sweden 18/N3
Lair, Ky. 237/N4
Laird, Colo. 208/P2
Laird, Sask. 181/E3
Lairdsville, Pa. 294/J3
Lairg, Scotland 10/D1
Lairg, Scotland 15/D2
Lais, Philippines 82/E7
Laisamis, Kenya 115/G3
La Isla, Texas 303/A10
Laiwui, Indonesia 85/H6
Laiyang, China 77/K4
Laja (riv.), Chile 138/E1
La Jalca, Peru 128/D6
La Jara, Colo. 208/H8
La Jara, N. Mex. 274/B2
Lajas, P. Rico 161/A2
Lajes do Pico, Portugal 33/B1
Lajinha, Brazil 135/F2
La Jolla, Calif. 204/H11
La Jolla Ind. Res., Calif. 204/J10
Lajord, Sask. 181/G5
La Jose, Pa. 294/E4
Lajosmizse, Hungary 41/E3
La Joya, Bolivia 136/B5
Lajoya, N. Mex. 274/C4
La Joya, Peru 128/G11
La Joya, Texas 303/F11
La Junta, Colo. 188/F3
La Junta, Colo. 208/M7
Lak Dera (dry riv.), Kenya 115/H3
Lak Dera (dry riv.), Somalia 115/H3
Lake (co.), Calif. 204/C4
Lake (co.), Colo. 208/G4
Lake (co.), Fla. 212/E3
Lake (co.), Ill. 222/E1
Lake (co.), Ind. 227/C2
Lake, Ky. 237/O6
Lake (co.), Mich. 250/D5
Lake, Mich. 250/E5
Lake (co.), Minn. 255/G3
Lake, Miss. 256/F6
Lake (co.), Mont. 262/B3
Lake (co.), Ohio 284/H2
Lake (co.), Oreg. 291/G5
Lake (creek), Oreg. 291/J3
Lake (co.), S. Dak. 298/P5
Lake (riv.), Tasmania 99/D3
Lake (co.), Tenn. 237/B8
Lake (creek), Utah 304/A5
Lake (creek), Wash. 310/G3
Lake Alfred, Fla. 212/E3
Lake Alma, Sask. 181/G6
Lake Alpine, Calif. 204/F5
Lake Andes, S. Dak. 298/M7
Lake Ann, Mich. 250/D4
Lake Ariel, Pa. 294/M3
Lake Arrowhead, Calif. 204/H9
Lake Arthur, La. 238/E6
Lake Arthur, N. Mex. 274/E5
Lake Arthur, N.S. Wales 97/D4
Lake Barcroft, Va. 307/S3
Lake Barrington, Ill. 222/A5
Lake Benton, Minn. 255/B6
Lake Beulah, Wis. 317/J2
Lake Bluff, Ill. 222/B4
Lake Boga, Victoria 97/B4
Lake Bolac, Victoria 97/B5
Lake Bronson, Minn. 255/B2
Lake Bruce, Ind. 227/E2
Lake Buena Vista, Fla. 212/E3
Lake Butler, Fla. 212/D1
Lake Butte Des Morts (Butte Des Morts), Wis. 317/J7
Lake Cargelligo, N.S. Wales 97/D3
Lake Carmel, N.Y. 276/N8
Lake Carroll, Fla. 212/C2
Lake Catherine, Ill. 222/E1
Lake Charles, La. 188/H4
Lake Charles, La. 238/D6
Lake Chelan Nat'l Rec. Area, Wash. 310/E2
Lake Church, Wis. 317/L9
Lake Cicott, Ind. 227/D3
Lake City, Ark. 202/K2
Lake City, Calif. 204/E2
Lake City, Colo. 208/E6
Lake City, Fla. 212/D1
Lake City, Georgia 217/K2
Lake City, Ill. 222/E4
Lake City, Iowa 229/D4
Lake City, Kansas 232/D4
Lake City, Mich. 250/D4
Lake City, Minn. 255/F6
Lake City, Pa. 294/B1
Lake City, S.C. 296/H4
Lake City, S. Dak. 298/O2
Lake City, Tenn. 237/N8
Lake City Arsenal, Mo. 261/R5
Lake Clark Nat'l Park, Alaska 196/H2
Lake Clark Nat'l Pres., Alaska 196/H2
Lake Clear, N.Y. 276/M2
Lake Como, Fla. 212/E2
Lake Como, Miss. 256/F7
Lake Como, Pa. 294/M2
Lake Cormorant, Miss. 256/D1
Lake Cowichan, Br. Col. 184/J3
Lakecreek, Oreg. 291/E5
Lake Crystal, Minn. 255/D6
Lake Dallas, Texas 303/G1
Lake Delton, Wis. 317/G8
Lake District Nat'l Park, England 13/D3
Lake Dunmore, Vt. 268/A4
Lake Elmo, Minn. 255/F6
Lake Elmore, Vt. 268/B2
Lake Elsinore, Calif. 204/F11
Lake End, La. 238/D3
Lake Erie Beach, N.Y. 276/B5
Lakefield, Minn. 255/C7
Lakefield, Ontario 177/F3
Lake-Fishing Bridge—Bridge Bay, Wyo. 319/B1
Lake Forest, Fla. 212/B4
Lake Forest, Ill. 222/B4
Lake Forest Park, Wash. 310/B1
Lake Fork, Gunnison (riv.), Colo. 208/E6
Lake Fork, Idaho 220/B5
Lake Fork, Ill. 222/D4
Lake Frances, Ark. 202/B1
Lake Francis, Manitoba 179/E4
Lake Fremont (Zimmerman), Minn. 255/E5
Lake Geneva, Wis. 317/K10
Lake George, Colo. 208/J5
Lake George, Mich. 250/E5
Lake George, Minn. 255/D3
Lake George, New Bruns. 170/C3
Lake George, N.Y. 276/N4
Lake Grace, W. Australia 88/B6
Lake Grace, W. Australia 92/B6
Lake Harbor, Fla. 212/F5
Lake Harbour, N.W.T. 162/J3
Lake Harbour, N.W. Terr. 187/L3
Lake Hart, Ind. 227/E5
Lake Havasu City, Ariz. 188/D4
Lake Havasu City, Ariz. 198/A4
Lakehead, Calif. 204/C3
Lake Helen, Fla. 212/E3
Lake Henry, Minn. 255/D5
Lake Hiawatha, N.J. 273/E2
Lake Hopatcong, N.J. 273/D2
Lake Hubert, Minn. 255/D4
Lake Hughes, Calif. 204/G9
Lake Huntington, N.Y. 276/L7
Lakehurst, N.J. 273/E3
Lakehurst Naval Air Engineering Center, N.J. 273/E3
Lake in the Hills, Ill. 222/E1
Lake Isabella, Calif. 204/G8
Lake Itasca, Minn. 255/C3
Lake Jackson, Texas 303/J8
Lake James, Ind. 227/H1
Lake Jem, Fla. 212/E3
Lake Katrine, N.Y. 276/M7
Lake King, W. Australia 88/C6
Lakeland, Fla. 188/K5
Lakeland, Fla. 212/D3
Lakeland, Georgia 217/F8
Lakeland, La. 238/H5
Lakeland, Manitoba 179/D4
Lakeland, Mich. 250/F6
Lakeland, Minn. 255/F6
Lakeland, Tenn. 237/B10
Lake Landing, N.C. 281/T4
Lakeland Village, Calif. 204/E11
Lake Leelanau, Mich. 250/D4
Lake Lenore, Sask. 181/G3
Lake Lillian, Minn. 255/C6
Lake Linden, Mich. 250/A1
Lakeline, Ohio 284/J8
Lake Lotawana, Mo. 261/R6
Lake Louise, Alberta 182/B4
Lake Louise, Alta. 162/E5
Lakelse Lake, Br. Col. 184/C3
Lake Lure, N.C. 281/E4
Lake Luzerne-Hadley, N.Y. 276/N4
Lake Mackay Aboriginal Reserve, North. Terr. 88/D4
Lake MacKay Aboriginal Res., North. Terr. 93/A6
Lake Macleod, W. Australia 92/A4
Lake Magdalene, Fla. 212/D3
Lake Mary, Fla. 212/E3
Lake McDonald, Mont. 262/B2
Lake Mead Nat'l Rec. Area, Ariz. 198/A2
Lake Mead Nat'l Rec. Area, Nev. 266/G6
Lake Meredith Nat'l Rec. Area, Texas 303/C2
Lake Michigan Beach, Mich. 250/C6
Lake Mills, Iowa 229/F2
Lake Mills, Wis. 317/H9
Lake Minchumina, Alaska 196/H2
Lake Minnewanka, Alberta 182/C4
Lake Mohawk, N.J. 273/D1
Lake Monroe, Fla. 212/E3
Lakemont, Georgia 217/F1
Lakemont, Pa. 294/F5
Lake Montezuma, Ariz. 198/D4
Lakemoor, Ill. 222/A4
Lakemore, Ohio 284/H3
Lake Moxie, Maine 243/D5
Lake Nash, North. Terr. 88/F4
Lake Nash, North. Terr. 93/E6
Lake Nebagamon, Wis. 317/C3
Lakenheath, Sask. 181/E6
Lake Norden, S. Dak. 298/P4
Lake Odessa, Mich. 250/D6
Lake of the Woods (lake), Manitoba 179/H5
Lake of the Woods (co.), Minn. 255/D2
Lake of the Woods (lake), Minn. 255/D1
Lake of the Woods (lake), Ontario 177/F5
Lake of the Woods (lake), Ontario 175/B3
Lake Orion, Mich. 250/F6
Lake Oswego, Oreg. 291/B2
Lake Ozark, Mo. 261/G6
Lake Park, Fla. 212/F5
Lake Park, Georgia 217/F9
Lake Park, Iowa 229/C2
Lake Park, Minn. 255/B4
Lake Placid, Fla. 212/E4
Lake Placid, N.Y. 276/N2
Lake Pleasant, N.Y. 276/M4
Lake Pocotopaug, Conn. 210/F2
Lakeport, Calif. 204/C4
Lakeport, Fla. 212/E5
Lakeport, Ontario 177/G4
Lake Preston, S. Dak. 298/P5
Lake Providence, La. 238/H1
Lakes, England 13/E3
Lakes, England 10/E3
Lake Saint Croix Beach, Minn. 255/F6
Lake Saint Louis, Mo. 261/N2
Lake Saint Peter, Ontario 177/F2
Lakes Entrance, Victoria 97/E5
Lakeshire, Mo. 261/P4
Lake Shore, Minn. 255/D4
Lakeshore, Miss. 256/F10
Lakeside, Ariz. 198/E4
Lakeside, Conn. 210/B2
Lakeside, Iowa 229/C3
Lakeside, Mont. 262/B2
Lakeside, Nebr. 264/B2
Lakeside, Nova Scotia 168/E4
Lakeside, Ohio 284/E2
Lakeside, Oreg. 291/C4
Lakeside, Texas 303/E2
Lakeside, Utah 304/B2
Lakeside, Va. 307/N5
Lakeside Park, Ky. 237/R2
Lakesite, Tenn. 237/L10
Lake Spring, Mo. 261/J7
Lake Station, Ind. 227/C1
Lake Stevens, Wash. 310/D3
Lake Success, N.Y. 276/P7
Lake Superior Prov. Park, Ontario 175/D3
Lake Superior Prov. Park, Ontario 177/J5
Lakesville, Md. 245/O7
Lake Tapawingo, Mo. 261/R6
Lake Tomahawk, Wis. 317/H4
Laketon, Ind. 227/F3
Laketon, New Bruns. 170/E2
Laketown, Utah 304/C2
Lake Toxaway, N.C. 281/D4
Lakevale, Nova Scotia 168/G3
Lake Valley, Sask. 181/E5
Lakeview, Ala. 195/G2
Lake View, Ark. 202/J5
Lakeview, Ark. 202/E1
Lake View, Iowa 229/C4
Lake View•, Maine 243/F5
Lakeview, Mich. 250/D5
Lake View, Miss. 256/D1
Lakeview, Mont. 262/E6
Lake View, N.Y. 276/B5
Lakeview, N.C. 281/L4
Lakeview, Ohio 284/C4
Lakeview, Oreg. 291/G5
Lake View, S.C. 296/J3
Lakeview, Texas 303/D3
Lakeview Heights, Mo. 261/F6
Lake Villa, Ill. 222/A4
Lake Village, Ark. 202/H7
Lake Village, Ind. 227/C2
Lakeville, Conn. 210/B1
Lakeville, Ind. 227/E1
Lakeville, Mass. 249/L5
Lakeville•, Mass. 249/L5
Lakeville, Minn. 255/E6
Lakeville, New Bruns. 170/C2
Lakeville, N.Y. 276/E5
Lakeville, Ohio 284/F4
Lake Waccamaw, N.C. 281/M6
Lake Wales, Fla. 212/E4
Lake Waukomis, Mo. 261/P5
Lake Way, W. Australia 88/C5
Lake Way, W. Australia 92/C4
Lake Wazeecha, Wis. 317/G7
Lake Williams, N. Dak. 282/L5
Lake Wilson, Minn. 255/B7
Lake Winnebago, Mo. 261/R6
Lake Wissota, Wis. 317/D6
Lakewood, Calif. 204/C11
Lakewood, Colo. 188/E3
Lakewood, Colo. 208/J3
Lakewood, Fla. 212/C5
Lakewood, Ill. 222/E4
Lakewood, N.J. 273/E3
Lakewood, N. Mex. 274/E6
Lakewood, N.Y. 276/B6
Lakewood, Ohio 284/G9
Lakewood, Pa. 294/M2
Lakewood, Tenn. 237/H8
Lakewood, Wash. 310/C2
Lakewood, Wis. 317/K5
Lakewood Club, Mich. 250/C5
Lake Worth, Fla. 212/G5
Lake Worth, Texas 303/E2
Lake Zurich, Ill. 222/A5
Lakhdenpokh'ya, U.S.S.R. 52/C2
Lakhish (dry riv.), Israel 65/B4
Lakin, Kansas 232/A4
Lakonía (gulf), Greece 45/F7
Lakor (isl.), Indonesia 85/H7
Lakota, Iowa 229/E2
Lakota, N. Dak. 282/O3
Laksefjorden (fjord), Norway 18/P1
Lakselv, Norway 18/O2
Lakshadweep (terr.), India 68/C6
Lakshadweep (sea), India 68/C6
La Laguna, Chile 138/F2
La Laguna, Spain 106/A3
La Laja (lag.), Chile 138/E1
La Lande, N. Mex. 274/E4
Lalapaşa, Turkey 63/B2
Lalara, Gabon 115/B3
La Lata, Uruguay 145/E2
Laleh Zar, Kuh-e (mt.), Iran 59/G4
Laleh Zar, Kuh-e (mt.), Iran 66/K6
La Leona, Venezuela 124/G3
Lalibela, Ethiopia 111/G5
La Libertad, Ecuador 128/B4
La Libertad, El Salvador 154/C4
La Libertad, Guatemala 154/B2
La Libertad, Nicaragua 154/E4
La Libertad (dept.), Peru 128/C6
La Ligua, Chile 138/A9
La Ligua (riv.), Chile 138/A9
Lalín, Spain 33/C1
La Línea de la Concepción, Spain 33/D4
Lalitpur, Nepal 68/E3
Lalitpur, Nepal 68/E3
La Loche, Sask. 181/L3
La Louvière, Belgium 27/E8
La Lune, Trin. & Tob. 161/B11
La Luz, N. Mex. 274/C6
La Luz, Venezuela 124/D3
La Macarena, Serranía de (mts.), Colombia 126/D6
La Macaza, Québec 172/C3
La Maddalena, Italy 34/B4
La Madera, N. Mex. 274/C2
Lamag, Malaysia 85/F4
Lama-Kara, Togo 106/E7
La Malbaie, Québec 172/G2
Lamaline, Newf. 166/C4
La Manche Valley Prov. Park, Newf. 166/D2
Lamar (co.), Ala. 195/B3
Lamar, Ark. 202/D3
Lamar, Colo. 208/O6
Lamar (co.), Georgia 217/D4
Lamar, Ind. 227/D8
Lamar, La. 238/G2
Lamar (co.), Miss. 256/E8
Lamar, Miss. 256/F1
Lamar, Mo. 261/D8
Lamar, Nebr. 264/C4
Lamar, Okla. 288/O4
Lamar, Pa. 294/H4
Lamar, S.C. 296/G3
Lamar (co.), Texas 303/J4
Lamar (riv.), Wyo. 319/B1
La Margarita, Venezuela 124/H3
Lamar Heights, Mo. 261/D8
La Marque, Texas 303/K3
Lamartine, Pa. 294/C3
Lamartine, Québec 172/G2
Lamartine, Wis. 317/J8
La Martre (lake), N.W. Terr. 187/G3
Lamas, Peru 128/D6
Lamasco, Ky. 237/F7
La Maurice Nat'l Park, Québec 172/D3
La Maya, Cuba 158/J4
Lamb, Ind. 227/G7
Lamb (co.), Texas 303/B3
Lambach, Austria 41/C2
Lamballe, France 28/B3
Lambaré, Paraguay 144/A4
Lambaréné, Gabon 115/B4
Lambaréné, Gabon 102/D5
Lambari, Brazil 135/D2
Lambasa, Fiji 86/Q10
Lambay (isl.), Ireland 17/K4
Lambayeque (dept.), Peru 128/B6
Lambayeque, Peru 128/B6
Lambeg, N. Ireland 17/J2
Lambert, Ark. 202/D5
Lambert, Miss. 256/D2
Lambert, Mo. 261/O8
Lambert, Mont. 262/M3
Lambert, Okla. 288/J1
Lambert Lake, Maine 243/H4
Lamberton, Minn. 255/C6
Lambert's Bay, S. Africa 118/B6
Lambertville, Mich. 250/F7
Lambertville, New Bruns. 170/C3
Lambertville, N.J. 273/D3
Lambeth, England 13/H8
Lambeth, England 10/B5
Lambeth, Ontario 177/C5
Lambric, Ky. 237/P5
Lamb's (head), Ireland 17/A8
Lambsburg, Va. 307/G7
Lambs Grove, Iowa 229/G5
Lambton (cape), N.W. Terr. 187/F2
Lambton (county), Ontario 177/B5
Lambton, Québec 172/F4
Lame Deer, Mont. 262/K5
Lamego, Portugal 33/C2
Lame Johnny (creek), S. Dak. 298/C6
Lamentin, Guadeloupe 161/A6
Lamèque, New Bruns. 170/F1
Lamèque (isl.), New Bruns. 170/F1
La Merced, Argentina 143/C2
La Merced, Bolivia 136/C8
Lameroo, S. Australia 94/G6
La Mesa, Calif. 204/H11
La Mesa, N. Mex. 274/C6
Lamesa, Texas 303/C5
Lamía, Greece 45/F6
La Minerve, Québec 172/C3
Lamington, N.J. 273/D2
Lamington (riv.), N.J. 273/D2
La Mirada, Calif. 204/D11
Lamison, Ala. 195/C6
Lamitan, Philippines 82/D7
Lamkin, Texas 303/F6
Lamlam (mt.), Guam 86/K7
Lamlash, Scotland 15/C5
Lammermuir (hills), Scotland 15/F5
Lamming Mills, Br. Col. 184/G3
La Moille, Ill. 222/D2
La Moille, Iowa 229/G4
Lamoille, Minn. 255/G6
Lamoille, Nev. 266/F2
Lamoille (co.), Vt. 268/B2
Lamoille (riv.), Vt. 268/A2
La Moine (riv.), Ill. 222/C3
Lamoine•, Maine 243/G7
Lamon (bay), Philippines 82/C3
Lamona, Wash. 310/G3
Lamongan, Indonesia 85/K2
Lamoni, Iowa 229/E7
Lamont, Alberta 182/D3
Lamont, Calif. 204/G8
Lamont, Fla. 212/C1
Lamont, Idaho 220/G6
Lamont, Iowa 229/K3
Lamont, Kansas 232/F3
Lamont, Miss. 256/B3
Lamont, Okla. 288/L1
Lamont, Wash. 310/H3
Lamont, Wis. 317/G10
Lamont, Wyo. 319/E3
La Monte, Mo. 261/F5
Lamotrek (atoll), Micronesia 87/E5
La Motte, Iowa 229/M4
Lamotte (peak), Utah 304/D3
LaMoure (co.), N. Dak. 282/N7
LaMoure, N. Dak. 282/O7
Lampa, Chile 138/G3
Lampa, Peru 128/G10
Lampang, Thailand 72/C3
Lampard, Sask. 181/G4
Lampasas (co.), Texas 303/F6
Lampasas, Texas 303/F6
Lampasas (riv.), Texas 303/G6
Lampe, Mo. 261/F9
Lampedusa (isl.), Italy 34/D7
Lampertheim, Germany 22/C4
Lampeter, Pa. 294/K6
Lampeter, Wales 13/D5
Lampeter, Wales 10/D4
Lamphun, Thailand 72/C3
Lampman, Sask. 181/J6
Lamprey (riv.), N.H. 268/E5
Lampson, Wis. 317/C3
Lamu, Burma 72/B3
Lamu, Kenya 115/H4
Lamu, Kenya 102/G5
Lamud, Peru 128/C6
Lamy, N. Mex. 274/D3
Lamy, Québec 172/H2
Lanagan, Mo. 261/C9
Lanai (isl.), Hawaii 87/L3
Lanai (isl.), Hawaii 188/F5

396 Lanai

Lanai (isl.), Hawaii 218/H2
Lanai City, Hawaii 188/F5
Lanai City, Hawaii 218/H2
Lanaihale (mt.), Hawaii 218/H2
Lanaken, Belgium 27/H7
Lanao (lake), Philippines 82/E7
Lanao del Norte (prov.), Philippines 82/E6
Lanao del Sur (prov.), Philippines 82/E7
Lanark, Ill. 222/D1
Lanark (county), Ontario 177/H3
Lanark, Ontario 177/H2
Lanark, Scotland 15/E5
Lanark, Scotland 10/E3
Lanark (trad. co.), Scotland 15/A5
Lanark, W. Va. 312/D7
Lanbi Kyun (isl.), Burma 72/C5
Lancang, China 77/E7
Lancang Jiang (riv.), China 77/F7
Lancashire (co.), England 13/E4
Lancaster, Calif. 204/G9
Lancaster (sound), Canada 4/B14
Lancaster, England 13/E3
Lancaster, England 10/E3
Lancaster, Ill. 222/F5
Lancaster, Ind. 227/F7
Lancaster, Kansas 232/G2
Lancaster, Ky. 237/M5
Lancaster•, Mass. 249/H3
Lancaster, Minn. 255/B2
Lancaster, Mo. 261/H1
Lancaster (co.), Nebr. 264/H4
Lancaster, N.H. 268/D3
Lancaster•, N.H. 268/D3
Lancaster, N.Y. 276/C5
Lancaster (sound), N.W.T. 162/H1
Lancaster (sound), N.W.T. 146/K2
Lancaster (sound), N.W. Terr. 187/K2
Lancaster, Ohio 284/E6
Lancaster, Ontario 177/K2
Lancaster, Pa. 188/L2
Lancaster (co.), Pa. 294/K5
Lancaster, Pa. 294/K5
Lancaster (co.), S.C. 296/F2
Lancaster, S.C. 296/F2
Lancaster, Texas 303/G3
Lancaster (co.), Va. 307/R5
Lancaster, Va. 307/R5
Lancaster, Wis. 317/E10
Lancaster Mills, S.C. 296/F2
Lance (creek), Wyo. 319/H2
Lance Creek, Wyo. 319/H2
Lancer, Sask. 181/C5
Lanchester, England 13/H3
Lanchow (Lanzhou), China 77/F4
Lanciano, Italy 34/E3
Lancing, Tenn. 237/M8
Lanco, Chile 138/D2
Lancret, Cuba 158/D1
Łancut, Poland 47/F3
Lancy, Switzerland 39/B4
Land, Ala. 195/B6
Landa, N. Dak. 282/J2
Landaff•, N.H. 268/D3
Landaff Center, N.H. 268/D3
Landau an der Isar, Germany 22/E4
Landau in der Pfalz, Germany 22/C4
Landay, Afghanistan 68/A2
Landay, Afghanistan 59/H3
Land Between The Lakes Rec. Area, Ky. 237/E7
Land Between The Lakes Rec. Area, Tenn. 237/E7
Landeck, Austria 41/A3
Landeck, Ohio 284/B4
Landen, Belgium 27/G7
Landenberg, Pa. 294/L6
Lander (co.), Nev. 266/D3
Lander (dry riv.), North. Terr. 88/E4
Lander (riv.), North. Terr. 93/C6
Lander, Pa. 294/D2
Lander, Wyo. 188/E2
Lander, Wyo. 319/D3
Landerneau, France 28/B3
Landersville, Ala. 195/D2
Landes (dept.), France 28/C5
Landes, W. Va. 312/H5
Landess, Ind. 227/F3
Landfall (isl.), India 68/G6
Landhi, Pakistan 59/J4
Landing, N.J. 273/D2
Landing (creek), N.J. 273/D4
Landis, N.C. 281/H3
Landis, Sask. 181/C3
Landisburg, Pa. 294/H5
Landisburg, W. Va. 312/E7
Landisville, N.J. 273/D4
Landisville, Pa. 294/K5
Landmark, Manitoba 179/F5
Lando, S.C. 296/E2
Land O'Lakes, Fla. 212/D3
Land O'Lakes, Wis. 317/H3
Landover, Md. 245/G4
Landover Hills, Md. 245/G4
Landquart (riv.), Switzerland 39/J3
Landrum, S.C. 296/C1
Landry, New Bruns. 170/E1
Landsberg (Gorzów Wielkopolski), Poland 47/B2
Landsberg am Lech, Germany 22/D4
Land's End (prom.), England 7/D3
Land's End (prom.), England 13/B7
Land's End (prom.), England 10/D5
Lands End (cape), N.W. Terr. 187/F2
Landshut, Germany 22/E4
Landskrona, Sweden 18/H9
Landsman (creek), Colo. 208/P4
Landsmeer, Netherlands 27/C4
Landstuhl, Germany 22/B4
Landusky, Mont. 262/H3
Landville, W. Va. 312/C7
Lane, Ill. 222/E3
Lane (co.), Kansas 232/B3
Lane, Kansas 232/G3
Lane, Okla. 288/O6
Lane (co.), Oreg. 291/E4
Lane, S.C. 296/H5
Lane, S. Dak. 298/N5
Lane, Tenn. 237/C8
Laneburg, Ark. 202/D6
Lane Cove, N.S. Wales 88/L4
Lane Cove (riv.), N.S. Wales 88/K4
Lane Cove, N.S. Wales 97/J3
Lane Cove (riv.), N.S. Wales 97/J3
Lanes (creek), N.C. 281/J5
Lanesboro, Iowa 229/D4
Lanesboro•, Mass. 249/A2
Lanesboro, Minn. 255/G7
Lanesboro, Pa. 294/L2
Lanesborough-Ballyleague, Ireland 17/E4
Lanes Prairie, Mo. 261/J6
Lanesville, Ind. 227/E8
Lanesville, Va. 307/P5
Lanett, Ala. 195/H5
La Neuveville, Switzerland 39/D2
Lanfine, Alberta 182/E4
Lanford, S.C. 296/C2
Lang, Ontario 177/F3
Lang, Sask. 181/G6
Langå, Denmark 21/C5
Langadhás, Greece 45/F5
Langádhia, Greece 45/F7
Langara (isl.), Br. Col. 184/A3
Langavat (lake), Scotland 15/B2
Langbank, Sask. 181/J5
Lang Bay, Br. Col. 184/E5
Lang Bian, Nui (mts.), Vietnam 72/E4
Langdon, Alberta 182/D4
Langdon, Iowa 229/C2
Langdon, Kansas 232/D4
Langdon, Mo. 261/A2
Langdon•, N.H. 268/C5
Langdon, N. Dak. 282/O2
Langdondale, Pa. 294/F5
Langeac, France 28/E5
L'Ange-Gardien, Québec 172/F3
Langeland (isl.), Denmark 21/D8
Langelands Baelt (chan.), Denmark 21/D8
Längelmävesi (lake), Finland 18/O6
Langeloth, Pa. 294/A5
Langemark-Poelkapelle, Belgium 27/B7
Langen, Germany 22/C4
Langenburg, Sask. 181/K5
Längenfeld, Austria 41/A3
Langenhagen, Germany 22/C2
Langenlois, Austria 41/C2
Langenthal, Switzerland 39/E2
Langenwang, Austria 41/C3
Langeoog (isl.), Germany 22/B2
Langford, Miss. 256/E6
Langford, S. Dak. 298/O2
Langham, Sask. 181/E3
Langholm, Scotland 15/E5
Langholm, Scotland 10/E3
Langhorne, Pa. 294/N5
Langjökull (glac.), Iceland 21/B1
Langkawi, Pulau (isl.), Malaysia 72/C6
Langlade (co.), Wis. 317/H5
Langlais, Québec 172/F1
Langley, Ark. 202/C5
Langley, Br. Col. 184/L3
Langley, Okla. 288/R2
Langley, S.C. 296/D4
Langley, Wash. 310/C2
Langley A.F.B., Va. 307/R6
Langley Park, Md. 245/F4
Langleyville, Ill. 222/D4
Langlois, Oreg. 291/C5
Langnau am Albis, Switzerland 39/G2
Langnau in Emmental, Switzerland 39/E3
Langness (prom.), I. of Man 13/C3
Langogne, France 28/E5
Langon, France 28/C5
Langøy (isl.), Norway 18/J2
Langres, France 28/F4
Langres (plat.), France 28/F4
Langruth, Manitoba 179/D4
Langsa, Indonesia 85/B5
Långsele, Sweden 18/K5
Långshyttan, Sweden 18/K6
Lang Son, Vietnam 72/E2
Langston, Ala. 195/G1
Langston, Okla. 288/M3
Lang Suan, Thailand 72/C5
Langsville, Ohio 284/F7
Langton, Ontario 177/D5
Langtry, Texas 303/C8
Languedoc (trad. prov.), France 29
L'Anguille (riv.), Ark. 202/J3
Langwies, Switzerland 39/J3
Langworthy, Iowa 229/L4
Lanham, Nebr. 264/H4
Lanham-Seabrook, Md. 245/G4
Lanier (co.), Georgia 217/F8
Lanigan, Sask. 181/F4
Lanigan (creek), Sask. 181/F4
Lanín (vol.), Argentina 143/B4
Lanín (vol.), Chile 138/E2
Lanín Nat'l Park, Argentina 143/B4
Lankin, N. Dak. 282/P3
Lanlacuni Bajo, Peru 128/G9
Lannion, France 28/B3
Lannon, Wis. 317/K1
L'Annonciation, Québec 172/C3
Lanoka Harbor, N.J. 273/E4
Lanoraie, Québec 172/D4
Lansdale, Pa. 294/M5
Lansdowne, India 68/D3
Lansdowne, Ontario 177/H3
Lansdowne, Pa. 294/M7
Lansdowne-Baltimore Highlands, Md. 245/M3
Lansdowne House, Ontario 175/C2
L'Anse, Mich. 250/G1
Lanse, Pa. 294/F4
L'Anse-Amour, Newf. 166/C3
L'Anse-au-Clair, Newf. 166/C3
L'Anse-au-Loup, Newf. 166/C3
L'Anse au Meadow, Newf. 166/C3
L'Anse Ind. Res., Mich. 250/A2
Lansford, N. Dak. 282/H2
Lansford, Pa. 294/L4
Lansing, Ill. 222/C6
Lansing, Iowa 229/L2
Lansing, Kansas 232/H2
Lansing (cap.), Mich. 146/K5
Lansing (cap.), Mich. 188/K2
Lansing (cap.), Mich. 250/E6
Lansing, Minn. 255/F7
Lansing, N.Y. 276/H5
Lansing, N.C. 281/F1
Lansing, Ohio 284/J5
Lanškroun, Czech. 41/D2
Lanta, Ko (isl.), Thailand 72/C6
Lantana, Fla. 212/F5
Lanton, Mo. 261/J9
Lantry, S. Dak. 298/G3
Lantsch-Lenz, Switzerland 39/J3
Lantz, Md. 245/J2
Lantz, Nova Scotia 168/E4
Lantzville, Br. Col. 184/J3
Lanus, Argentina 143/H7
Lanus, Argentina 120/D6
Lanusei, Italy 34/B5
Lanuvio, Italy 34/F7
Lanuza, Philippines 82/F6
Lanuza (bay), Philippines 82/F6
Lanyon, Iowa 229/E4
Lanza, Bolivia 136/B5
Lanzarote (isl.), Spain 102/A2
Lanzarote (isl.), Spain 106/B3
Lanzarote (isl.), Spain 33/C4
Lanzhou (Lanchow), China 77/F4
Lanzhou, China 54/M6
Lanzhou, China 2/P4
Laoag, Philippines 82/C1
Laoag, Philippines 54/N8
Laoag, Philippines 85/F2
Laoang, Philippines 82/E4
Lao Cai, Vietnam 54/M7
Lao Cai, Vietnam 72/E2
Laoha He (riv.), China 77/J3
Laois (co.), Ireland 17/G6
Laon, France 28/E3
Laona, Wis. 317/J4
La Orchila (isl.), Venezuela 124/F2
La Orotava, Spain 33/B4
La Oroya, Peru 120/B4
La Oroya, Peru 128/D8
Laos 2/Q5
Laos 54/M8
LAOS 72
Laotto, Ind. 227/G2
Lapa, Brazil 132/D9
Lapa, Philippines 82/C8
Lapalisse, France 28/E4
La Pallice, France 28/C4
La Palma, Colombia 126/C5
La Palma, El Salvador 154/C3
La Palma, Panama 154/H6
La Palma (isl.), Spain 102/A2
La Palma (isl.), Spain 106/A3
La Palma (isl.), Spain 33/A4
La Palma del Condado, Spain 33/C4
La Paloma, Uruguay 145/F5
La Pampa (prov.), Argentina 143/C4
La Paragua, Venezuela 124/G4
Laparan (isl.), Philippines 82/B8
Laparan (isls.), Philippines 82/B8
La Passe, Ontario 177/H2
La Patrie, Québec 172/F4
La Paz, Entre Ríos, Argentina 143/G5
La Paz, Mendoza, Argentina 143/C3
La Paz (co.), Ariz. 198/A5
La Paz (dept.), Bolivia 136/A4
La Paz (cap.), Bolivia 136/B5
La Paz (cap.), Bolivia 2/F6
La Paz (cap.), Bolivia 120/C4
La Paz, Honduras 154/D3
Lapaz, Ind. 227/E2
La Paz, Mexico 146/G7
La Paz, Baja California Sur, Mexico 150/D5
La Paz, San Luis Potosí, Mexico 150/J5
La Paz (bay), Mexico 150/D4
La Paz, Philippines 82/E6
La Paz, Canelones, Uruguay 145/B6
La Paz, Colonia, Uruguay 145/B5
La Paz Central, Nicaragua 154/D4
La Paz de Oriente, Nicaragua 154/E5
La Pêche, Québec 172/B4
La Pedrera, Colombia 126/F8
La Pedrera, Uruguay 145/F5
Lapeer (co.), Mich. 250/F5
Lapeer, Mich. 250/F5
Lapel, Ind. 227/F4
La Pelada, Argentina 143/F5
La Pérade, Québec 172/E3
La Pérouse (str.) 54/R5
La Perouse, N.S. Wales 88/L4
La Perouse, N.S. Wales 97/J4
La Pérouse (str.), U.S.S.R. 48/P5
La Pesca, Mexico 150/L4
Lapeyrère (lake), Québec 172/E2
La Piedad Cavadas, Mexico 150/H6
Lapine, Ala. 195/F7
La Pine, Oreg. 291/F4
Lapinin (isl.), Philippines 82/E5
La Pintada, Panama 154/G6
Lapithos, Cyprus 63/E5
La Place, Ill. 222/E4
La Place, La. 238/N3
La Plaine, Dominica 161/F6
Lapland (reg.) 7/G2
Lapland (reg.), Finland 18/O2
Lapland (reg.), Norway 18/K2
Lapland (reg.), Sweden 18/M2
Lapland (reg.), U.S.S.R. 52/D1
La Plant, S. Dak. 298/H3
Laplante, New Bruns. 170/E1
La Plata (est.) 120/D6
La Plata, Argentina 143/H7
La Plata, Argentina 120/D6
La Plata, Río de (est.), Argentina 143/E4
La Plata, Colombia 126/C6
La Plata (co.), Colo. 208/D8
La Plata (peak), Colo. 208/G4
La Plata (riv.), Colo. 208/C8
La Plata, Md. 245/L6
La Plata, Mo. 261/H2
La Plata, N. Mex. 274/A2
La Plata (riv.), N. Mex. 274/A1
La Plume, Pa. 294/L2
La Pobla de Lillet, Spain 33/G1
La Pocatière, Québec 172/H2
La Poile, Newf. 166/C4
La Poile (bay), Newf. 166/C4
Lapoint, Utah 304/E3
La Pointe, Wis. 317/E2
La Porte, Calif. 204/E4
Laporte, Colo. 208/J1
LaPorte (co.), Ind. 227/D1
LaPorte, Ind. 227/D1
Laporte, Mich. 250/E5
Laporte, Minn. 255/D3
Laporte, Pa. 294/K3
Laporte, Sask. 181/B4
La Porte, Texas 303/K2
La Porte City, Iowa 229/J4
Lappajärvi, Finland 18/O5
Lappajärvi (lake), Finland 18/O5
Lappeenranta, Finland 7/G2
Lappeenranta, Finland 18/P6
Lappi (prov.), Finland 18/P3
La Prairie, Ill. 222/B3
La Prairie, Minn. 255/E3
Laprairie (co.), Québec 172/H4
La Prairie, Québec 172/J4
Laprida, Argentina 143/D4
La Protección, Honduras 154/D3
La Providence, Québec 172/E4
La Pryor, Texas 303/E9
Lâpseki, Turkey 63/C6
Laptev (sea), U.S.S.R. 4/B3
Laptev (sea), U.S.S.R. 54/O2
Laptev (sea), U.S.S.R. 48/N2
Lapua, Finland 18/N5
Lapuanjoki (riv.), Finland 18/N5
La Puebla, Spain 33/H3
La Puebla de Montalbán, Spain 33/D3
La Puente, Calif. 204/D10
La Puerto, Cuba 158/H3
Lapu-Lapu, Philippines 82/E5
La Puntilla (cape), Ecuador 128/B4
La Purísima, Mexico 150/D3
La Push, Wash. 310/A3
Lapwai, Idaho 220/B3
Łapy, Poland 47/F2
Laqiya 'Umran (well), Sudan 111/E3
Laquey, Mo. 261/H7
La Quiaca, Argentina 143/C1
L'Aquila (prov.), Italy 34/D3
L'Aquila, Italy 34/D3
Lar, Iran 59/F4
Lar, Iran 66/J7
Lara (state), Venezuela 124/C2
Lara, Victoria 97/C6
Larabee, Pa. 294/F2
Larache, Morocco 106/C1
Laracor, Ireland 17/H4
Larak (isl.), Iran 66/K7
La Rambla, Spain 33/D4
Laramie (co.), Wyo. 319/H4
Laramie (mts.), Colo. 208/H1
Laramie (riv.), Colo. 208/H1
Laramie, Wyo. 146/H5
Laramie, Wyo. 188/E2
Laramie, Wyo. 319/G4
Laramie (mts.), Wyo. 319/G3
Laramie (peak), Wyo. 319/G3
Laramie (riv.), Wyo. 319/G4
Laranjeiras do Sul, Brazil 132/C9
Larantuka, Indonesia 85/G7
Larat (isl.), Indonesia 85/J7
Larbert, Scotland 10/B1
Larbert, Scotland 15/C1
Lärbro, Sweden 18/L8
Larchmont, N.Y. 276/P7
Larchwood, Iowa 229/A2
Lardeau, Br. Col. 184/J5
Larder Lake, Ontario 175/E3
Larder Lake, Ontario 177/K5
L'Ardoise West, Nova Scotia 168/H3
La Rédemption, Québec 172/B2
Laredo (sound), Br. Col. 184/C4
Laredo, Mo. 261/E2
Laredo, Mont. 262/G2
Laredo, Spain 33/E1
Laredo, Texas 303/E10
Laredo, Texas 188/G5
Laredo, Texas 146/J7
La Reine, Québec 174/B3
Laren, Netherlands 27/G4
Larena, Philippines 82/D6
La Réole, France 28/C5
Lares, P. Rico 161/B2
Lares, P. Rico 156/F1
La Retuca, Chile 138/F3
Larew, W. Va. 312/G4
Largentière, France 28/F5
Largo (cay), Cuba 158/D2
Largo (cay), Cuba 156/B2
Largo, Fla. 212/B3
Largo (key), Fla. 212/F6
Largo, Md. 245/G5
Largo, Cañon (creek), N. Mex. 274/B2
Largs, Scotland 15/A2
Largs, Scotland 10/A1
Lariat, Texas 303/B3
Larimer (co.), Colo. 208/H1
Larimer, Pa. 294/C5
Larimore, N. Dak. 282/P4
Larino, Italy 34/E4
La Rioja (prov.), Argentina 143/G2
La Rioja, Argentina 120/C5
La Rioja, Argentina 143/C2
La Rioja, Cuba 158/H3
Lárisa, Greece 45/F6
Lárisa, Greece 7/G5
Laristan (reg.), Iran 66/J7
La Rivière, Manitoba 179/D5
Lark, N. Dak. 282/H7
Larkana, Pakistan 59/J4
Larkana, Pakistan 68/B3
Larkhall, Scotland 10/B1
Larkhall, Scotland 15/E5
Lark Harbour, Newf. 166/C4
Larkinburg, Kansas 232/G2
Larkinsville, Ala. 195/F1
Larkspur, Calif. 204/H1
Larkspur, Colo. 208/K4
Larksville, Pa. 294/E7
Larnaca, Cyprus 59/B3
Larnaca, Cyprus 63/E5
Larnaca (bay), Cyprus 63/E5
Larne (dist.), N. Ireland 17/K2
Larne, N. Ireland 17/K2
Larne, N. Ireland 10/D3
Larne (inlet), N. Ireland 17/K2
Larned, Kansas 232/C3
La Robla, Spain 33/D1
La Roche, Switzerland 39/D3
La Roche-en-Ardenne, Belgium 27/G8
La Rochelle, France 7/D4
La Rochelle, France 28/C4
La Rochelle, Manitoba 179/F5
La Roche-sur-Yon, France 28/C4
La Roda, Spain 33/E3
La Romana (prov.), Dom. Rep. 158/F6
La Romana, Dom. Rep. 158/F6
La Romana, Dom. Rep. 156/E3
La Ronge, Sask. 181/L3
La Rose, Ill. 222/D3
Larose, La. 238/K7
Larouche, Québec 172/F1
Larrabee, Iowa 229/B3
Larrimah, North. Terr. 88/E3
Larrimah, North. Terr. 93/C3
Larroque, Argentina 143/F5
Larry's River, Nova Scotia 168/G3
Larsen (sound), N.W. Terr. 187/J2
Larsen Bay, Alaska 196/H3
Larsen Ice Shelf, Ant. 2/F9
Larsen Ice Shelf, Ant. 5/C16
Larslan, Mont. 262/K2
Larsmont, Minn. 255/G4
Larson, N. Dak. 282/E2
Larto, La. 238/G4
Larue (co.), Ky. 237/K5
La Rue, Ohio 284/D4
Laruns, France 28/C6
La Russell, Mo. 261/D8
Larvik, Norway 18/C4
Larwill, Ind. 227/F2
La Sal, Utah 304/E5
La Salle, Colo. 208/K2
La Salle (co.), Ill. 222/E2
La Salle, Ill. 222/E2
La Salle (par.), La. 238/F3
La Salle, Manitoba 179/E5
La Salle (riv.), Manitoba 179/E5
La Salle, Mich. 250/F7
La Salle, Minn. 255/D6
La Salle, Québec 172/H4
Lasalle (lake), Québec 172/E2
La Salle (co.), Texas 303/E9
Las Animas (co.), Colo. 208/L8
Las Animas, Colo. 208/N6
Las Animas (creek), N. Mex. 274/B5
Las Anod, Somalia 115/J2
La Sarraz, Switzerland 39/C3
La Sarre, Que. 162/J6
La Sarre, Québec 174/B3
Lasauces, Colo. 208/H8
Las Aves (isls.), Venezuela 124/E2
Las Bonitas, Venezuela 124/F4
Las Breas, Chile 138/B7
Lasca, Ala. 195/C6
Las Cabras, Chile 138/F5
Lascahobas, Haiti 156/D3
Lascahobas, Haiti 158/C6
Lascano, Uruguay 145/E4
Las Carreras, Bolivia 136/C7
Lascassas, Tenn. 237/J9
L'Ascension, Labelle, Québec 172/C3
L'Ascension, Lac-St-Jean-E., Québec 172/F1
L'Ascension-de-Patapédia, Québec 172/B2
Las Choapas, Mexico 150/M7
La Scie, Newf. 166/C4
Las Cruces, Chile 138/F3
Las Cruces, N. Mex. 146/H6
Las Cruces, N. Mex. 188/E4
Las Cruces, N. Mex. 274/C6
Las Dureh, Somalia 115/J1
La Selva Beach, Calif. 204/K4
La Serena, Chile 120/B5
La Serena, Chile 138/A8
La Seyne-sur-Mer, France 28/F6
Las Flores, Argentina 143/E4
Las Flores, Uruguay 145/D5
Las Hadas, Mexico 150/G7
Lashburn, Sask. 181/B2
Lash-e Joveyn, Afghanistan 68/A2
Lash-e Joveyn, Afghanistan 59/H3
Lashio, Burma 72/C2
Lashkar Gah, Afghanistan 68/A2
Lashkar Gah, Afghanistan 59/H3
La Sierra, Uruguay 145/D5
L'Asile, Haiti 158/B6
Las Juntas, Colombia 126/E6
Las Juntas, C. Rica 154/E5
Łask, Poland 47/D3
Lasker, N.C. 281/P2
La Skhirra, Tunisia 106/G2
Las Khoreh, Somalia 115/J1
Las Lajas, Argentina 143/B4
Las Lajitas, Venezuela 124/F4
Las Lomitas, Argentina 143/D1
Las Marias, P. Rico 161/B2
Las Martinas, Cuba 158/A2
Las Matas de Farfán, Dom. Rep. 158/D6
Las Matas de Farfán, Dom. Rep. 156/D3
Las Mercedes, Venezuela 124/E3
Las Navas del Marqués, Spain 33/D2
Lasne, Belgium 27/F7
Las Nieves, Mexico 150/G3
La Solana, Spain 33/E3
La Sorcière (mt.), St. Lucia 161/G6
La Souterraine, France 28/D4
Las Palmas, Argentina 143/E2
Las Palmas, Panama 154/G6
Las Palmas (prov.), Spain 33/C4
Las Palmas (cap.), Canary Is., Spain 102/A2
Las Palmas de Gran Canaria, Spain 33/B4
Las Palmas de Gran Canaria, Spain 106/B3
Las Pampitas, Bolivia 136/C3
Las Parejas, Argentina 143/F6
Las Pedroñeras, Spain 33/E3
Las Petas, Bolivia 136/F5
La Spezia (prov.), Italy 34/B2
La Spezia, Italy 34/B2
La Spezia, Italy 7/E4
Las Piedras, Peru 128/H9
Las Piedras, P. Rico 161/E2
Las Piedras, Uruguay 145/B6
Las Piedras, Falcón, Venezuela 124/C2
Las Piedras, Zulia, Venezuela 124/B2
Las Plumas, Argentina 143/C5
Lasqueti Island, Br. Col. 184/J2
Las Rosas, Argentina 143/F6
Las Rosas, Mexico 150/N8
Lassen (co.), Calif. 204/E3
Lassen (peak), Calif. 204/D3
Lassen Volcanic Nat'l Park, Calif. 204/D3
L'Assomption (co.), Québec 172/D4
L'Assomption, Québec 172/D4
L'Assomption (riv.), Québec 172/D3
Las Tablas, N. Mex. 274/C2
Las Tablas, Panama 154/G7
Lastarria (vol.), Chile 138/B5
La Station-du-Coteau, Québec 172/C4
Last Chance (creek), Utah 304/C6
Las Termas, Argentina 143/D2
Last Mountain (lake), Sask. 181/F4
Las Toscas, Uruguay 145/E3
Lastoursville, Gabon 115/B4
Lastovo (Lagosta) (isl.), Yugoslavia 45/C4
Las Trincheras, Venezuela 124/F4
Las Truchas, Mexico 150/H7
Lastrup, Minn. 255/D4
Las Tunas (prov.), Cuba 158/H3
Las Varillas, Argentina 143/D3
Las Vegas, Nev. 146/G6
Las Vegas, Nev. 188/C3
Las Vegas, Nev. 266/F6
Las Vegas (range), Nev. 266/F6
Las Vegas, N. Mex. 188/E3
Las Vegas, N. Mex. 274/D3
Las Vegas, Venezuela 124/D3
Las Yaras, Peru 128/G11
Las Yungas (reg.), Bolivia 136/B5
La Tabatière, Québec 174/F2
Latacunga, Ecuador 128/C3
La Tagua, Colombia 126/C8
Latah (co.), Idaho 220/B3
Latah, Wash. 310/H3
Latakia (prov.), Syria 63/G5
Latakia, Syria 54/E6
Latakia, Syria 63/F5
Latakia, Syria 59/C2
La Taste, Grenada 161/D8
Latchford, Ontario 177/K5
Laterrière, Québec 172/F1
Latexo, Texas 303/J6
Latham, Ala. 195/C8
Latham, Ill. 222/D4
Latham, Kansas 232/F4
Latham, Mo. 261/G5
Latham, N.Y. 276/N5
Latham, Ohio 284/D7
Latham, Tenn. 237/D8
Lathrop, Calif. 204/D6
Lathrop, Mich. 250/B2
Lathrop, Mo. 261/D3
La Tigra, Venezuela 124/H4
Latimer, Iowa 229/G3
Latimer, Kansas 232/F3
Latimer (co.), Okla. 288/R5
Latimers (brook), Conn. 210/G3
Latina (prov.), Italy 34/D4
Latina, Italy 34/D4
La Tina, Peru 128/B5
Latium (Lazio) (reg.), Italy 34/D3
La Tola, Ecuador 128/C2
La Toma, Argentina 143/C3
Laton, Calif. 204/F7
Latorica (riv.), Czech. 41/F2
La Tortuga (isl.), Venezuela 124/F2
Latouche Treville (cape), W. Australia 88/C3
Latouche Treville (cape), W. Australia 92/C2
Latour, Mo. 261/D5
La Tour-de-Peilz, Switzerland 39/C4
La Tour-du-Pin, France 28/F5
Latourell Falls, Oreg. 291/E2
La Trinidad, Nicaragua 154/D4
La Trinidad, Philippines 82/C2
La Trinidad, Venezuela 124/D3
La Trinidad de Arauca, Venezuela 124/D4
La Trinidad de Orichuna, Venezuela 124/D4
La Trinité, Martinique 161/D6
La Trinité-des-Monts, Québec 172/J1
Latrobe, Pa. 294/D5
Latrobe, Tasmania 99/C3
Latta, S.C. 296/J3
Lattimore, N.C. 281/F4
Lattingtown, N.Y. 276/R6
Latty, Ohio 284/A3
La Tuque, Que. 162/J6
La Tuque, Québec 172/E2
La Tuque, Québec 174/C3
Latur, India 68/D5
LATVIA 53/B2
Latvian S.S.R., U.S.S.R. 7/G3
Latvian S.S.R., U.S.S.R. 52/B3
Latvian S.S.R., U.S.S.R. 48/C4
Lauca (riv.), Bolivia 136/A6
Lauca (riv.), Chile 138/B1
Lauchhammer, Germany 22/E3
Laud, Ind. 227/G2
Laudat, Dominica 161/E6
Lauder, Manitoba 179/B5

Lauder, Scotland 10/E3
Lauder, Scotland 15/F5
Lauderdale (co.), Ala. 195/C1
Lauderdale, Minn. 255/G5
Lauderdale (co.), Miss. 256/G6
Lauderdale, Miss. 256/G5
Lauderdale, Tasmania 99/D4
Lauderdale (co.), Tenn. 237/B9
Lauderdale-by-the-Sea, Fla. 212/C3
Lauderdale Lakes, Fla. 212/B3
Lauderhill, Fla. 212/B3
Lauenburg an der Elbe, Germany 22/D2
Lauenen, Switzerland 39/D4
Lauf an der Pegnitz, Germany 22/D4
Läufelfingen, Switzerland 39/E2
Laufen, Switzerland 39/D2
Laufen, Germany 22/E5
Laufenburg, Switzerland 39/F1
Laughery (creek), Ind. 227/G6
Laughing Fish (pt.), Mich. 250/B2
Laughlin A.F.B., Texas 303/D8
Lau Group (isls.), Fiji 87/J7
Lauingen, Germany 22/D4
Launceston, England 13/C7
Launceston, England 10/D5
Launceston, Tasmania 99/C3
Launceston, Tasmania 88/H8
Laune (riv.), Ireland 17/B7
Launglon Bok (isls.), Burma 72/C4
La Unión, Chile 138/D3
La Unión, Colombia 126/B7
La Unión, El Salvador 154/D4
La Unión, Mexico 150/J8
La Union, N. Mex. 274/C7
La Unión, Peru 128/D7
La Union (prov.), Philippines 82/C2
La Unión, Spain 33/F4
La Unión, Venezuela 124/E3
Laupahoehoe, Hawaii 218/J4
Laupen, Switzerland 39/D3
Lauperswil, Switzerland 39/E3
Laura, Ill. 222/D3
Laura, Ohio 284/B6
Laura, Queensland 88/G3
Laura, Queensland 95/C2
Laura, Sask. 181/D4
Laura, S. Australia 94/F5
La Urbana, Venezuela 124/E4
Laurel, Del. 245/R6
Laurel, Fla. 212/D4
Laurel, Ind. 227/G6
Laurel, Iowa 229/H5
Laurel (co.), Ky. 237/N6
Laurel, Md. 245/L4
Laurel, Miss. 188/J4
Laurel, Miss. 256/F7
Laurel, Mont. 262/H5
Laurel, Nebr. 264/G2
Laurel, Oreg. 291/A2
Laurel, Pa. 294/K6
Laurel, Wash. 310/D5
Laurel (mt.), W. Va. 312/G4
Laurel Bay, S.C. 296/F7
Laurel Bloomery, Tenn. 237/T7
Laureldale, Pa. 294/L5
Laurel Dale, W. Va. 312/H4
Laureles, Paraguay 144/D5
Laurel Fork, Va. 307/G7
Laurel Hill, Fla. 212/C5
Laurel Hill, N.C. 281/K5
Laurel Hill (mt.), Pa. 294/D5
Laurel Park, N.C. 281/D4
Laurel River (lake), Ky. 237/N6
Laurel Run, Pa. 294/F7
Laurel Springs, N.J. 273/B4
Laurelton, Pa. 294/H4
Laurelville, Ohio 284/E7
Laurence G. Hanscom Field, Mass. 249/B6
Laurence Harbor, N.J. 273/E3
Laurencekirk, Scotland 10/E2
Laurencekirk, Scotland 15/F4
Laurens (co.), Georgia 217/G6
Laurens, Iowa 229/D3
Laurens, N.Y. 276/K5
Laurens (co.), S.C. 296/D2
Laurens, S.C. 296/C3
Laurentides, Québec 172/D4
Laurentides Prov. Park, Québec 174/C3
Laurentides Prov. Park, Québec 172/F2
Lauria, Italy 34/E4
Laurie (lake), Manitoba 179/A3
Laurie, Mo. 261/G6
Laurier, Manitoba 179/C4
Laurier, Wash. 310/G2
Laurier-Station, Québec 172/F3
Laurierville, Québec 172/F3
Laurieston, Scotland 15/D6
Laurin, Mont. 262/D5
Laurinburg, N.C. 281/K5
Lauritsala, Finland 18/Q6
Laurium, Mich. 250/A1
Laurot (Laut Kecil) (isls.), Indonesia 85/E7
Lausanne, Switzerland 39/C3
Lauscha, Germany 22/D3
Laut (isl.), Indonesia 85/F6
Laut (North Natuna) (isl.), Indonesia 85/D5
Lautaro, Chile 138/E2
Lauterbach, Germany 22/C3
Lauterbrunnen, Switzerland 39/E3
Lauterique, Honduras 154/D4
Laut Kecil (isls.), Indonesia 85/E7
Lautoka, Fiji 86/P10
Lauwers (chan.), Netherlands 27/J1
Lauwers Zee (bay), Netherlands 27/J2
Lauzon, Québec 172/J3
Lava (lake), Oreg. 291/F4
Lava Beds Nat'l Mon., Calif. 204/D2
Lavaca, Ala. 195/B6
Lavaca, Ark. 202/B3
Lavaca (co.), Texas 303/H8
Lavaca (bay), Texas 303/H9
Lava Hot Springs, Idaho 220/F7
Laval, France 28/C3
Laval, Québec 172/H4
Laval (bay), Québec 172/J1
La Vale-Narrows Park, Md. 245/C2
Lavalette, W. Va. 312/B6
Lavalle, Argentina 143/G4
La Valle, Wis. 317/F8
Lavalleja (dept.), Uruguay 145/D5
Lavallette, N.J. 273/E4
Lavalley, Colo. 208/J8
Lavaltrie, Québec 172/D4
Lavamünd, Austria 41/C3
Lavapié (pt.), Chile 138/D1
Lavaur, France 28/D6
La Vecilla de Curueño, Spain 33/D1
Laveen, Ariz. 198/C5
La Vega (prov.), Dom. Rep. 158/D6
La Vega, Dom. Rep. 158/E5
La Vega, Dom. Rep. 156/D3
La Vega, Spain 33/C1
La Vela (cape), Colombia 126/D1
La Vela de Coro, Venezuela 124/D2
Lavelanet, France 28/E6
Lavello, Italy 34/E4
Lavenham, Manitoba 179/D5
L'Avenir, Québec 172/E4
La Vergne, Tenn. 237/H9
La Verkin, Utah 304/A6
La Verne, Calif. 204/D10
Laverne, Okla. 288/G1
La Vernia, Texas 303/K11
Laverton, Australia 87/C8
Laverton, W. Australia 88/C5
Laverton, W. Australia 92/C5
La Veta, Colo. 208/J8
Lavey-Morcles, Switzerland 39/D4
Lavezares, Philippines 82/E4
La Victoria, Colombia 126/A7
La Victoria, Apure, Venezuela 124/D4
La Victoria, Aragua, Venezuela 124/E2
Lavieille (lake), Ontario 177/F2
La Vieja (pt.), Chile 138/A11
Lavik, Norway 18/D6
Lavillette, New Bruns. 170/E1
Lavina, Mont. 262/H4
Lavinia, Manitoba 179/B4
Lavinia, Tenn. 237/D9
La Vista, Nebr. 264/J3
Lavon (lake), Texas 303/H1
Lavongai (isl.), Papua N.G. 87/F6
Lavongai (isls.), Papua N.G. 86/B1
Lavonia, Georgia 217/F2
Lavos, Portugal 33/B2
Lavoy, Alberta 182/E3
Lavras, Brazil 132/E8
Lavras, Brazil 135/D2
Lávrion, Greece 45/G7
Lawa (riv.), Fr. Guiana 131/D4
Lawa (riv.), Suriname 131/D4
Lawai, Hawaii 218/C2
Lawang, Indonesia 85/K2
Lawen, Oreg. 291/J4
Lawler, Iowa 229/J2
Lawler, Minn. 255/E4
Lawlers, W. Australia 92/C5
Lawley, Ala. 195/E5
Lawn, Newf. 166/C4
Lawn, Pa. 294/J5
Lawn, Texas 303/E5
Lawndale, Calif. 204/B11
Lawndale, Ill. 222/D3
Lawndale, Minn. 255/B4
Lawndale, N.C. 281/F4
Lawnhill, Br. Col. 184/A3
Lawn Hill, Queensland 95/A3
Lawnside, N.J. 273/B3
Lawra, Ghana 106/D6
Lawrence (co.), Ala. 195/D1
Lawrence (co.), Ark. 202/H1
Lawrence (co.), Ill. 222/F5
Lawrence (co.), Ind. 227/E7
Lawrence, Ind. 227/E5
Lawrence, Kans. 188/G3
Lawrence, Kansas 232/G3
Lawrence (co.), Ky. 237/R4
Lawrence, Mass. 188/M2
Lawrence, Mass. 249/K2
Lawrence, Mich. 250/C6
Lawrence (co.), Miss. 256/D7
Lawrence, Miss. 256/F6
Lawrence (co.), Mo. 261/E8
Lawrence, Nebr. 264/F4
Lawrence, N.Y. 276/P7
Lawrence, N. Zealand 100/B6
Lawrence, N.C. 281/O2
Lawrence (co.), Ohio 284/E8
Lawrence (co.), Pa. 294/B4
Lawrence (co.), S. Dak. 298/B5
Lawrence (co.), Tenn. 237/G10
Lawrenceburg, Ind. 227/H6
Lawrenceburg, Ky. 237/M4
Lawrenceburg, Tenn. 237/G10
Lawrence Park•, Pa. 294/C1
Lawrenceport, Ind. 227/D7
Lawrence Station, New Bruns. 170/C3
Lawrencetown, Nova Scotia 168/C4
Lawrenceville, Georgia 217/D3
Lawrenceville, Ill. 222/F5
Lawrenceville, Ind. 227/H6
Lawrenceville•, N.J. 273/D3
Lawrenceville, N.Y. 276/L1
Lawrenceville, Ohio 284/C6
Lawrenceville, Pa. 294/H2
Lawrenceville, Québec 172/E4
Lawrenceville, Va. 307/N7
Lawson, Ark. 202/F7
Lawson, Colo. 208/H3
Lawson, Mo. 261/D4
Lawson, Sask. 181/E5
Lawsonville, N.C. 281/J2
Lawtell, La. 238/F5
Lawtey, Fla. 212/D1
Lawton, Ind. 227/D2
Lawton, Iowa 229/A4
Lawton, Kansas 232/H4
Lawton, Ky. 237/P4
Lawton, Mich. 250/D6
Lawton, N. Dak. 282/O3
Lawton, Okla. 146/J6
Lawton, Okla. 188/G4
Lawton, Okla. 288/K5
Lawton, Pa. 294/K2
Lawton, W. Va. 312/E7
Lawtonka (lake), Okla. 288/K5
Lawu (mt.), Indonesia 85/J2
Lax, Georgia 217/F8
Lax, Switzerland 39/F4
Laxå, Sweden 18/J7
Laxey, I. of Man 13/C3
Laxford, Loch (inlet), Scotland 15/C2
Lay (dam), Ala. 195/E5
Lay (lake), Ala. 195/F4
Lay (pt.), Alaska 196/F1
Lay, Colo. 208/D2
Lay, Mui (cape), Vietnam 72/E3
Layang Layang, Malaysia 72/E5
Layland, W. Va. 312/E7
Layopolis (Sand Fork), W. Va. 312/E5
Layou (riv.), Dominica 161/E6
Layou, St. Vin. & Grens. 161/A9
Laysan (isl.), Hawaii 87/J3
Laysan (isl.), Hawaii 188/E6
Laysan (isl.), Hawaii 218/B5
Laysville, Conn. 210/F3
Layton, Fla. 212/F7
Layton, N.J. 273/D1
Layton, Utah 304/C2
Laytonsville, Md. 245/K4
Laytonville, Calif. 204/B4
Laytown-Bettystown-Mornington, Ireland 17/J4
Lazarev Station 5/C1
Lazdijai, U.S.S.R. 53/B3
Lazear, Colo. 208/D5
Lazi, Philippines 82/D6
Łaziska Górne, Poland 47/A4
Lazy Lake, Fla. 212/B3
Lea (riv.), England 13/G6
Lea (co.), N. Mex. 274/F6
Leaburg, Oreg. 291/E3
Leach, Okla. 288/S2
Leach, Tenn. 237/E9
Leachville, Ark. 202/K2
Leacross, Sask. 181/H2
Lead, S. Dak. 188/F2
Lead, S. Dak. 298/B5
Leadbetter (pt.), Wash. 310/A4
Leader, Minn. 255/D4
Leader, Sask. 181/B5
Lead Hill, Ark. 202/D1
Leadington, Mo. 261/M7
Leadmine (brook), Conn. 210/C1
Lead Mine, W. Va. 312/G4
Leadmine, Wis. 317/F10
Leadore, Idaho 220/E5
Leadpoint, Wash. 310/H2
Leadville, Colo. 188/E3
Leadville, Colo. 208/G4
Leadwood, Mo. 261/L7
Leaf, Georgia 217/E1
Leaf (riv.), Manitoba 179/F2
Leaf (riv.), Minn. 255/C4
Leaf, Miss. 256/G8
Leaf (riv.), Miss. 256/F8
Leaf (lake), Sask. 181/J2
Leaf River, Ill. 222/D1
Leaf Valley, Minn. 255/C4
League City, Texas 303/K2
Leah, Georgia 217/H3
Leake (co.), Miss. 256/E5
Leakesville, Miss. 256/G8
Leakey, Texas 303/E8
Leal, N. Dak. 282/O5
Lealui, Zambia 115/D6
Leamington, Ontario 177/B5
Leamington, Utah 304/B4
Leamington Spa, England 10/F4
Leander, La. 238/E4
Leane (lake), Ireland 17/G4
Leane (lake), Ireland 17/B7
Leapwood, Tenn. 237/E10
Learmonth, W. Australia 88/A4
Learmonth, W. Australia 92/A3
Learned, Miss. 256/C6
Leary, Georgia 217/C8
Leasburg, Mo. 261/K6
Leasburg, N.C. 281/L2
Leask, Sask. 181/E2
Leatherhead, England 13/G8
Leatherhead, England 10/B6
Leathersville, Georgia 217/G3
Leatherwood, Ky. 237/P6
Leavenworth, Ind. 227/E8
Leavenworth, Kans. 188/G3
Leavenworth (co.), Kansas 232/G2
Leavenworth, Kansas 232/H2
Leavenworth, Wash. 310/E3
Leavitt, Alberta 182/D5
Leavittsburg, Ohio 284/J3
Leawood, Kansas 232/H3
Łeba, Poland 47/C1
Lebak, Philippines 82/D7
Lebam, Wash. 310/B4
Lebanon 2/L4
Lebanon 54/E6
LEBANON 59/C3
LEBANON 63/F6
Lebanon, Colo. 208/B8
Lebanon•, Conn. 210/G2
Lebanon, Georgia 217/D2
Lebanon, Ill. 222/D5
Lebanon, Ind. 227/D4
Lebanon, Kansas 232/D2
Lebanon, Ky. 237/L5
Lebanon (mts.), Lebanon 63/F6
Lebanon, Mo. 261/G7
Lebanon, Nebr. 264/D4
Lebanon, N.H. 268/C4
Lebanon, N.J. 273/D2
Lebanon, Ohio 284/B7
Lebanon, Okla. 288/N7
Lebanon, Oreg. 291/E3
Lebanon (co.), Pa. 294/K5
Lebanon, Pa. 294/K5
Lebanon, S. Dak. 298/K3
Lebanon, Tenn. 237/J8
Lebanon, Va. 307/D7
Lebanon, Wis. 317/H1
Lebanon Church, Va. 307/L2
Lebanon Junction, Ky. 237/K5
Lebanon Springs, N.Y. 276/O6
Lebeau, La. 238/F5
Lebec, Calif. 204/G9
Lebedin, U.S.S.R. 52/D4
Lebedinyy, U.S.S.R. 48/N4
Lebel-sur-Quévillon, Québec 174/B3
Lébénymiklós, Hungary 41/D3
Lebesby, Norway 18/P1
Le Blanc, France 28/D4
Le Blanc, La. 238/E5
Le Blanc-Mesnil, France 28/B1
Lebo, Kansas 232/G3
Le Borgne, Haiti 158/C5
Lębork, Poland 47/C1
Le Bourget, France 28/B1
Le Brassus, Switzerland 39/B3
Lebret, Sask. 181/H5
Lebrija (riv.), Colombia 126/D4
Lebrija, Spain 33/D4
Lebu, Chile 138/D1
Lecanto, Fla. 212/D3
Le Carbet, Martinique 161/C6
Le Cateau, France 28/E2
Lecce (prov.), Italy 34/G4
Lecce, Italy 34/G4
Lecce, Italy 7/F4
Lecco, Italy 34/B2
Le Center, Minn. 255/E6
Lech (riv.), Germany 22/D4
Le Châble, Switzerland 39/D4
Le Chasseral (mt.), Switzerland 39/D2
Leche (lag.), Cuba 158/F2
Le Chenit (Le Brassus), Switzerland 39/B3
Le Chesnay, France 28/A2
Lechiguanas (isls.), Argentina 143/G6
Lechuguilla (des.), Ariz. 198/A6
Le Claire, Iowa 229/N5
Leclercville, Québec 172/F3
Lecointre (lake), Québec 172/B2
Lecoma, Mo. 261/J7
Lecompte, La. 238/F4
Lecompton, Kansas 232/G2
Lecontes Mills, Pa. 294/F3
Le Creusot, France 28/F4
Le Croisic, France 28/B4
Lecta, Ky. 237/K6
Łęczyca, Poland 47/D2
Ledang, Gunong (mt.), Malaysia 72/D7
Ledbury (cays), England 10/E5
Ledbury, England 13/E5
Lede, Belgium 27/D7
Ledeč, Czech. 41/C2
Ledesma, Spain 33/C2
Ledford, Ill. 222/E6
Ledge, Bermuda 156/G2
Ledger, Mont. 262/E2
Ledgewood, N.J. 273/D2
Le Diamant, Martinique 161/D7
Ledoux, N. Mex. 274/D3
Leduc, Alberta 182/D3
Leduc, Alta. 162/E5
Ledyard•, Conn. 210/G3
Ledyard, Iowa 229/E2
Lee (co.), Ala. 195/H5
Lee (co.), Ark. 202/J4
Lee (co.), Fla. 212/E5
Lee, Fla. 212/C1
Lee (co.), Georgia 217/D7
Lee (co.), Ill. 222/D2
Lee, Ill. 222/E2
Lee, Ind. 227/D3
Lee (co.), Iowa 229/L7
Lee (riv.), Ireland 17/D8
Lee (riv.), Ireland 10/B5
Lee (co.), Ky. 237/O5
Lee•, Maine 243/G5
Lee, Mass. 249/B3
Lee•, Mass. 249/B3
Lee (co.), Miss. 256/G2
Lee, Nev. 266/F2
Lee•, N.H. 268/F5
Lee (co.), N.C. 281/L4
Lee (co.), S.C. 296/G3
Lee (co.), Texas 303/H7
Lee (co.), Va. 307/B7
Lee Bayou, La. 238/G3
Lee Center, Ill. 222/D2
Lee Center, N.Y. 276/K4
Leech (lake), Minn. 188/G1
Leech (lake), Minn. 255/D3
Leech, New Bruns. 170/E1
Leech (lake), Sask. 181/J4
Leechburg, Pa. 294/C4
Leech Lake Ind. Res., Minn. 255/D3
Leechville, N.C. 281/R3
Lee City, Ky. 237/P5
Leeco, Ky. 237/O5
Leecreek, Ark. 202/B2
Leedale, Alberta 182/C3
Leedey, Okla. 288/H3
Leeds, Ala. 195/E3
Leeds, England 13/J1
Leeds, England 7/D3
Leeds, England 10/F4
Leeds, Maine 243/C7
Leeds•, Maine 243/C7
Leeds, Md. 245/P2
Leeds, N.Y. 276/N6
Leeds, N. Dak. 282/M3
Leeds (county), Ontario 177/H3
Leeds, Québec 172/F3
Leeds, S.C. 296/E2
Leeds, Utah 304/A6
Leeds Junction, Maine 243/C7
Leeds Point, N.J. 273/E4
Leek, England 13/H2
Leek, England 10/E4
Leek, Netherlands 27/J2
Leelanau (co.), Mich. 250/D4
Leelanau (lake), Mich. 250/D4
Leenane, Ireland 17/B4
Leeper, Mo. 261/L8
Leeper, Pa. 294/D3
Leer, Germany 22/B2
Leerdam, Netherlands 27/F5
Leesburg, Ala. 195/G2
Leesburg, Fla. 212/E3
Leesburg, Georgia 217/D7
Leesburg, Ind. 227/F2
Leesburg, Miss. 256/E6
Leesburg, N.J. 273/D5
Leesburg, Ohio 284/D7
Leesburg, Pa. 294/B3
Leesburg, Va. 307/N2
Lees Creek, Ohio 284/C7
Leesdale, Miss. 256/B7
Lees Ferry, Ariz. 198/D2
Leesport, Pa. 294/K5
Lee's Summit, Mo. 261/R6
Leeston, N. Zealand 100/D5
Leesville, Conn. 210/F2
Leesville, Ind. 227/E7
Leesville, La. 238/D4
Leesville, Ohio 284/H5
Leesville (lake), Ohio 284/H5
Leesville, S.C. 296/E4
Leesville, Va. 307/K6
Leesville (lake), Va. 307/K6
Leet, W. Va. 312/B6
Leetes Island, Conn. 210/E3
Leeton, Mo. 261/E5
Leeton, N. S. Wales 88/H6
Leeton, N.S. Wales 97/D4
Leeton, Utah 304/E3
Leetonia, Ohio 284/J4
Leetsdale, Pa. 294/B4
Leetsville, Mich. 250/D4
Leeuwarden, Netherlands 27/H2
Leeuwin (cape), Australia 87/B9
Leeuwin (cape), Australia 2/Q7
Leeuwin (cape), W. Australia 88/A6
Leeuwin (cape), W. Australia 92/A6
Lee Vining, Calif. 204/F6
Leeward (passage), Virgin Is. (U.S.) 161/B4
Leeward (isls.), W. Indies 156/F3
Lefaivre, Ontario 177/K2
Lefka, Cyprus 63/E5
Lefkara, Cyprus 63/E5
Leflore (co.), Miss. 256/D3
Le Flore, Miss. 256/D3
Le Flore (co.), Okla. 288/S5
Leflore, Okla. 288/S5
Lefor, N. Dak. 282/F6
Lefors, Texas 303/D2
Le François, Martinique 161/D6
Lefroy, Ontario 177/E3
Lefroy (lake), W. Australia 88/C6
Lefroy (lake), W. Australia 92/C5
Left Hand, W. Va. 312/D5
Legal, Alberta 182/D3
Legana, Tasmania 99/C3
Leganés, Spain 33/F4
Legazpi, Philippines 82/D4
Legazpi, Philippines 85/G3
Legend, Alberta 182/E5
Legend (lake), Alberta 182/D1
Léger Brook, New Bruns. 170/F2
Légerville, New Bruns. 170/F2
Legerwood, Tasmania 99/D3
Legges Tor (mt.), Tasmania 99/D3
Leggett, N.C. 281/O3
Leghorn (Livorno) (prov.), Italy 34/C3
Leghorn (Livorno), Italy 7/E4
Leghorn (Livorno), Italy 34/C3
Legionowo, Poland 47/E2
Léglise, Belgium 27/H9
Legnago, Italy 34/C2
Legnica (prov.), Poland 47/C4
Legnica, Poland 47/C3
Le Gore, Md. 245/J2
Le Goulet, New Bruns. 170/F1
Le Grand, Calif. 204/E6
Le Grand, Iowa 229/H5
Le Grand (cape), W. Australia 88/C6
Le Grand (cape), W. Australia 92/C6
Le Gros Crêt (mt.), Switzerland 39/B3
Leguan (isl.), Guyana 131/B2
Legune, North. Terr. 93/A3
Leh, India 68/D2
Le Havre, France 7/E4
Le Havre, France 28/C3
Lehew, W. Va. 312/K4
Lehi, Utah 304/C3
Lehigh, Alberta 182/D4
Lehigh, Iowa 229/E4
Lehigh, Kansas 232/E3
Lehigh, N. Dak. 282/E6
Lehigh, Okla. 288/O6
Lehigh (co.), Pa. 294/L4
Lehigh (riv.), Pa. 294/L3
Lehigh Acres, Fla. 212/E5
Lehighton, Pa. 294/L4
Lehman, Pa. 294/E7
Lehr, N. Dak. 282/M7
Lehrte, Germany 22/D2
Lehua (isl.), Hawaii 218/A2
Lehututu, Botswana 118/C4
Leiah, Pakistan 68/C2
Leibnitz, Austria 41/C3
Leicester, England 13/F5
Leicester, England 10/F4
Leicester•, Mass. 249/G4
Leicester, N.Y. 276/D5
Leicester•, Vt. 268/A4
Leicester Junction, Vt. 268/A4
Leicestershire (co.), England 13/F5
Leichhardt, N.S. Wales 88/L4
Leichhardt, N.S. Wales 97/J3
Leichhardt (range), Queensland 95/C4
Leichhardt (riv.), Queensland 88/F3
Leichhardt (riv.), Queensland 95/A3
Leiden, Netherlands 27/E4
Leidy (mt.), Wyo. 319/B2
Leigh, England 10/G2
Leigh, England 13/H2
Leigh, Nebr. 264/G3
Leigh Creek, S. Australia 88/F6
Leigh Creek, S. Australia 94/F4
Leighlindridge, Ireland 17/H6
Leighton, Ala. 195/D1
Leighton, Iowa 229/H6
Leighton-Linslade, England 13/F7
Leijun, Yemen 59/E6
Leimebamba, Peru 128/D6
Leinan, Sask. 181/D5
Leine (riv.), Germany 22/C2
Leinster (prov.), Ireland 17/G5
Leinster (trad. co.), Ireland 17
Leinster (mt.), Ireland 17/H6
Leipers Fork, Tenn. 237/G9
Leipsic, Del. 245/S4
Leipsic (riv.), Del. 245/R4
Leipsic, Ind. 227/E7
Leipsic, Ohio 284/C3
Leipzig, Germany 7/F3
Leipzig, Germany 22/E3
Leipzig, Sask. 181/C3
Leiria (dist.), Portugal 33/B3
Leiria, Portugal 33/B3
Leisler (mt.), North. Terr. 93/A7
Leiston-cum-Sizewell, England 13/J5
Leisure, Ind. 227/F4
Leisure City, Fla. 212/F6
Leitchfield, Ky. 237/J6
Leiter, Wyo. 319/F1
Leitersburg, Md. 245/H2
Leiters Ford, Ind. 227/E2
Leith, N. Dak. 282/G7
Leith, Ontario 177/D3
Leitrim (co.), Ireland 17/E3
Leitrim, Ireland 17/F3
Leivasy, W. Va. 312/E6
Leix (Laoighis) (co.), Ireland 17/G6
Leixlip, Ireland 17/H5
Leiyang, China 77/H6
Leizhou Bandao (pen.), China 77/G7
Lejunior, Ky. 237/P7
Lek (riv.), Netherlands 27/F5
Leka (isl.), Norway 18/G4
Le Kef (El Kef), Tunisia 106/F1
Lekitobi, Indonesia 85/G6
Lekoni, Gabon 102/D5
Lekoni, Gabon 115/B4
Leksand, Sweden 18/J6
Leksula, Indonesia 85/H6
Lela, Okla. 288/N2
Lela, Texas 303/D2
Le Lamentin, Martinique 161/D6
Leland, Georgia 217/J1
Leland, Ill. 222/E2
Leland, Iowa 229/F2
Leland, Mich. 250/D3
Leland, Miss. 256/C4
Leland, N.C. 281/N6
Leland, Oreg. 291/D5
Le Landeron, Switzerland 39/C2
Leleiwi (pt.), Hawaii 218/K5
Leleque, Argentina 143/B5
Lelia Lake, Texas 303/D3
Le Lieu, Switzerland 39/B3
Le Locle, Switzerland 39/C2
Le Lorrain, Martinique 161/D6
Le Loup, Kansas 232/G3
Lely (mts.), Suriname 131/D3
Lelydorp, Suriname 131/D3
Lelystad, Netherlands 27/H3
Lem, Denmark 21/B5
Léman (Geneva) (lake), Switzerland 39/C4
Le Mans, France 28/C3
Le Mans, France 7/E4
Le Marin, Martinique 161/D7
Le Mars, Iowa 229/A3
Lemasters, Pa. 294/G6
Lemay, Mo. 261/R4
Lemberg, Sask. 181/H5
Leme, Brazil 135/C3
Lemelerberg (hill), Netherlands 27/J4
Lemery, Philippines 82/C4
Lemesurier (isl.), Alaska 196/M1
Lemgo, Germany 22/C2
Lemhi (co.), Idaho 220/D4
Lemhi, Idaho 220/E5
Lemhi (pass), Idaho 220/E5
Lemhi (range), Idaho 220/E5
Lemhi (riv.), Idaho 220/E5
Lemhi (pass), Mont. 262/C6
Lemieux (isls.), N.W. Terr. 187/M3
Lemington•, Vt. 268/D2
Lemitar, N. Mex. 274/B4
Lemmer, Netherlands 27/H3
Lemmon (mt.), Ariz. 198/E6
Lemmon, S. Dak. 298/E2
Lemon (lake), Ind. 227/E6
Lemon, Miss. 256/E6
Lemoncove, Calif. 204/G7
Lemon Grove, Calif. 204/J11
Lemons, Mo. 261/F2
Lemon Springs, N.C. 281/L4
Lemont, Ill. 222/B6
Lemont, Pa. 294/G4
Lemont Furnace, Pa. 294/C6
Le Mont-sur-Lausanne, Switzerland 39/C3
Lemoore, Calif. 204/F7
Lemoore N.A.S., Calif. 204/F7
Le Morne-Rouge, Martinique 161/C5
Le Morne-Vert, Martinique 161/C6
Lemoyne, Nebr. 264/C3
Lemoyne, Ohio 284/D3
Lemoyne, Pa. 294/J5
Le Moyne, Québec 172/J4
Le Moyne (lake), Québec 174/D1
Lempa (riv.), El Salvador 154/C4
Lempster•, N.H. 268/C5
Lemreway, Scotland 15/B2
Lemsford, Sask. 181/B5
Lemvig, Denmark 18/F8
Lemvig, Denmark 21/B4
Lena, Ill. 222/D1
Lena, La. 238/E4
Lena, Manitoba 179/C5
Lena, Miss. 256/E5
Lena, Ohio 284/B5
Lena, S.C. 296/E6
Lena (riv.), U.S.S.R. 4/C3
Lena (riv.), U.S.S.R. 2/R2
Lena (riv.), U.S.S.R. 54/O3

Lena (riv.), U.S.S.R. 48/N3
Lena, Wis. 317/K6
Lenapah, Okla. 288/P1
Lenawee (co.), Mich. 250/E7
Lençóis, Brazil 132/F6
Lendery, U.S.S.R. 52/D2
Lendinara, Italy 34/C2
Lenexa, Kansas 232/H2
Leney, Sask. 181/D3
Lengau, Switzerland 39/D2
Lengby, Minn. 255/C3
Lengerich, Germany 22/B2
Lenghu, China 77/D4
Lengshuijiang, China 77/H6
Lengua de Vaca (pt.), Chile 138/A8
Lengyeltóti, Hungary 41/D3
Lenhartsville, Pa. 294/L4
Leninabad, U.S.S.R. 48/G5
Leninakan, U.S.S.R. 7/J4
Leninakan, U.S.S.R. 48/E5
Leninakan, U.S.S.R. 52/F6
Leningrad, U.S.S.R. 7/H3
Leningrad, U.S.S.R. 2/L3
Leningrad, U.S.S.R. 48/D4
Leningrad, U.S.S.R. 52/C3
Leninogorsk, U.S.S.R. 48/J5
Leninogorsk, U.S.S.R. 52/H4
Leninsk, U.S.S.R. 54/H5
Leninsk, U.S.S.R. 48/G5
Leninsk-Kuznetskiy, U.S.S.R. 54/K4
Leninsk-Kuznetskiy, U.S.S.R. 48/J4
Leninskoye, U.S.S.R. 48/O5
Leninváros, Hungary 41/F3
Lenk, Switzerland 39/D4
Lenkoran', U.S.S.R. 48/E6
Lenkoran', U.S.S.R. 52/G7
Lennard, Manitoba 179/A4
Lennep, Mont. 262/F4
Lenni, Pa. 294/L7
Lennig, Va. 307/L7
Lennon, Mich. 250/E5
Lennox (isl.), Argentina 143/C8
Lennox (isl.), Chile 138/F11
Lennox (isl.), Pr. Edward I. 168/E2
Lennox (hills), Scotland 15/B1
Lennox, S. Dak. 298/R7
Lennox and Addington (county), Ontario 177/G3
Lennoxtown, Scotland 15/B1
Lennoxville, Québec 172/F4
Lenoir (co.), N.C. 281/O4
Lenoir, N.C. 281/G3
Lenoir City, Tenn. 237/N9
Le Noirmont, Switzerland 39/C2
Lenora, Kansas 232/C2
Lenora, Minn. 255/G7
Lenorah, Texas 303/B5
Lenore, Manitoba 179/B5
Lenore (lake), Sask. 181/G3
Lenore (lake), Wash. 310/F3
Lenore, W. Va. 312/B7
Lenox, Ala. 195/D8
Lenox, Georgia 217/F8
Lenox, Iowa 229/D7
Lenox, Mass. 249/A3
Lenox•, Mass. 249/A3
Lenox, Mo. 261/J7
Lenox, Tenn. 237/C8
Lenox Dale, Mass. 249/B3
Lens, Belgium 27/D7
Lens, France 28/E2
Lens, Switzerland 39/D4
Lensk, U.S.S.R. 54/N3
Lensk, U.S.S.R. 48/M3
Lenswood, Manitoba 179/B2
Lenswood, S. Australia 94/C8
Lent, Netherlands 27/H5
Lenti, Hungary 41/D3
Lentini, Italy 34/E6
Lentner, Mo. 261/H3
Lenvik, Norway 18/L2
Lenwood, Calif. 204/H9
Lenya, Burma 72/C5
Lenzburg, Ill. 222/D5
Lenzburg, Switzerland 39/F2
Lenzing, Austria 41/B3
Leo, Ind. 227/G2
Leo, S.C. 296/H4
Léo, Burkina Faso 106/D6
Leoben, Austria 41/C3
Léogâne, Haiti 156/D3
Léogâne, Haiti 158/C6
Leola, Ark. 202/E5
Leola, S. Dak. 298/M2
Leoma, Tenn. 237/G10
Leominster, England 13/E5
Leominster, England 10/E4
Leominster, Mass. 249/G2
Leon (co.), Fla. 212/B1
Leon, Iowa 229/F7
Leon, Kansas 232/F4
León, Mexico 146/H7
León, Mexico 150/J6
Leon, N.Y. 276/C6
León, Nic. 146/K8
León, Nicaragua 154/D4
Leon, Okla. 288/M7
León (mt.), Paraguay 144/B2
León (prov.), Spain 33/C1
León, Spain 7/D4
León, Spain 33/D1
León (reg.), Spain 33/C1
Leon (co.), Texas 303/J6
Leon (riv.), Texas 303/F6
Leon, W. Va. 312/C5
Leon, Wis. 317/E8
Leona, Kansas 232/G2
Leona, Texas 303/H6
Leonard, Mich. 250/F6
Leonard, Minn. 255/C3
Leonard, Mo. 261/H3
Leonard, N. Dak. 282/R6
Leonard, Okla. 288/P3
Leonard, Texas 303/H4
Leonardo, N.J. 273/E3
Leonardsburg, Ohio 284/D5
Leonardsville, N.Y. 276/K5
Leonardtown, Md. 245/M7
Leonardville, Kansas 232/F2
Leonardville, New Bruns. 170/C4
Leone (mt.), Switzerland 39/F4
Leonforte, Italy 34/E6
Leongatha, Victoria 97/C6
Leonia, Fla. 212/C5
Leonia, N.J. 273/C2
Leonidas, Mich. 250/D6
Leonidas, Minn. 255/F3
Leonídhion, Greece 45/F7
Leonora, W. Australia 88/C5
Leonora, W. Australia 92/C5
Leonore, Ill. 222/E2
Leon Springs, Texas 303/J10
Leontes (Litani) (riv.), Lebanon 63/F6
Leon Valley, Texas 303/J10
Leonville, La. 238/G6
Leopold, Ind. 227/D8
Leopold, Mo. 261/N8
Leopold, W. Va. 312/E4
Leopoldina, Brazil 135/E2
Leopoldsburg, Belgium 27/G6
Leopolis, Wis. 317/J6
Leora, Mo. 261/M9
Leota, Minn. 255/C7
Leota, Utah 304/E3
Leoti, Kansas 232/A3
Leoville, Kansas 232/B2
Leoville, Sask. 181/D2
Lepanto, Ark. 202/K2
Lepel', U.S.S.R. 52/C4
Lephepe, Botswana 118/D4
Leping, China 77/J6
L'Épiphanie, Québec 172/D4
Lepontine Alps (range), Italy 34/B1
Lepontine Alps (range), Switzerland 39/G4
Le Port, Réunion 118/F5
Lepreau, New Bruns. 170/D3
Lepreau (pt.), New Bruns. 170/D3
Lepreau (riv.), New Bruns. 170/D3
Le Prêcheur, Martinique 161/C5
Leptis Magna (ruins), Libya 111/B1
Le Puy, France 28/F5
Lequille, Nova Scotia 168/C4
Lequire, Okla. 288/R4
Le Raimeux (mt.), Switzerland 39/D2
Le Raysville, Pa. 294/K2
Lerdal, Minn. 255/E7
Lerdo de Tejada, Mexico 150/M8
Léré, Chad 111/B6
Lere, Nigeria 106/F7
Leribe, Lesotho 118/D5
Lerici, Italy 34/B2
Lérida, Colombia 126/E7
Lérida (Lleida) (prov.), Spain 33/G2
Lérida (Lleida), Spain 7/D4
Lérida (Lleida), Spain 33/G2
Lerín, Spain 33/F1
Lerma, Mexico 150/O7
Lerma, Spain 33/E2
Lerna, Ill. 222/E4
Le Robert, Martinique 161/D6
Le Roeulx, Belgium 27/E8
Lerona, W. Va. 312/D8
Léros (isl.), Greece 45/H7
Leross, Sask. 181/H4
Leroy, Ala. 195/B8
Le Roy, Ill. 222/E3
Leroy, Ind. 227/C2
Le Roy, Iowa 229/F7
Le Roy, Kansas 232/G3
Leroy, La. 238/F6
Le Roy, Mich. 250/D4
Le Roy, Minn. 255/F7
Le Roy, N.Y. 276/E5
Leroy, N. Dak. 282/P2
Le Roy, Pa. 294/J2
Leroy, Sask. 181/G4
Leroy, Texas 303/G6
Le Roy, W. Va. 312/C5
Leroy Anderson (res.), Calif. 204/L4
Lerwick, Scotland 10/G1
Lerwick, Scotland 15/G2
Léry, Québec 172/H4
Les Abymes, Guadeloupe 161/B6
Lesage, W. Va. 312/B5
Le Saint-Esprit, Martinique 161/D6
Les Andelys, France 28/D3
Les Anglais, Haiti 158/A6
Les Anse-d'Arlets, Martinique 161/C7
Les Becquets, Québec 172/E3
Les Bois, Switzerland 39/C2
Les Cayes, Haiti 158/B6
Les Cayes, Haiti 156/C3
Les Éboulements, Québec 172/G2
Les Epey, Switzerland 39/D4
Les Étroits, Québec 172/J2
Leshan (Loshan), China 77/F6
Leshan, China 54/M6
Leshara, Nebr. 264/H3
Les Haudères, Switzerland 39/E4
Les Hauteurs-de-Rimouski, Québec 172/J1
Leshukonskoye, U.S.S.R. 52/G2
Lesina (lake), Italy 34/E3
Les Irois, Haiti 158/A6
Lesja, Norway 18/F5
Leskovac, Yugoslavia 45/E4
Leskovik, Albania 45/E5
Leslie, Ark. 202/E2
Leslie, Georgia 217/D7
Leslie, Idaho 220/E6
Leslie (co.), Ky. 237/P6
Leslie, Mich. 250/E6
Leslie, Mo. 261/K6
Leslie, Sask. 181/H4
Leslie, Scotland 15/E4
Leslie, W. Va. 312/E6
Leslieville, Alberta 182/C3
Lesmahagow, Scotland 15/E5
Les Méchins, Québec 172/B1
Lesnoy, U.S.S.R. 52/H3
Lesosibirsk, U.S.S.R. 48/K4
Lesotho 2/L7
Lesotho 102/E7
LESOTHO 118/D5
Lesozavodsk, U.S.S.R. 48/O5
Lesparre-Médoc, France 28/C5
Les Ponts-de-Martel, Switzerland 39/C2
Les Sables-d'Olonne, France 28/B4
Lesse (riv.), Belgium 27/F8
Lessebo, Sweden 18/J8
Lessen (Lessines), Belgium 27/D7
Lesser Antilles (isls.) 146/M8
Lesser Slave (lake), Alberta 182/C2
Lesser Slave (lake), Alta. 162/E4
Lessines, Belgium 27/D7
Lessley, Miss. 256/B8
Lesslie, S.C. 296/E2
Les Tantes (isls.), Grenada 161/D7
Lester, Ala. 195/D1
Lester, Iowa 229/A2
Lester, Pa. 294/M7
Lester, Wash. 310/D3
Lester, W. Va. 312/D7
Lester Prairie, Minn. 255/D6
Lesterville, Mo. 261/L8
Lesterville, S. Dak. 298/O7
Lestijärvi (lake), Finland 18/O5
Lestock, Sask. 181/G4
Les Trois-Îlets, Martinique 161/D6
Le Sueur (co.), Minn. 255/E6
Le Sueur, Minn. 255/E6
Les Verrières, Switzerland 39/B3
Lésvos (isl.), Greece 7/G5
Lésvos (isl.), Greece 45/G6
Leswalt, Scotland 15/C6
Leszcyny, Poland 47/A4
Leszno (prov.), Poland 47/C3
Leszno, Poland 47/C3
L'Étape, Québec 172/F2
Letart, W. Va. 312/C5
Letart Falls, Ohio 284/F8
Létavértes, Hungary 41/G3
Letcher (co.), Ky. 237/R6
Letcher, S. Dak. 298/N6
Letchworth, England 13/G6
Le Teil, France 28/F5
Letellier, Manitoba 179/E5
Letenye, Hungary 41/D3
Letha, Idaho 220/B6
Letham, Scotland 15/F4
Lethbridge, Alberta 182/D5
Lethbridge, Alta. 146/G4
Lethbridge, Alta. 162/E6
Lethbridge, Newf. 166/D2
Lethem, Guyana 120/D2
Lethem, Guyana 131/B4
Leti (isls.), Indonesia 85/H7
Leticia, Colombia 126/F10
Leticia, Colombia 120/B3
L'Etivaz, Switzerland 39/D4
Letka, U.S.S.R. 52/H3
Leto, Fla. 212/C2
Letohatchee, Ala. 195/E6
Leton, La. 238/D1
Letona, Ark. 202/G3
Letong, Indonesia 85/D5
Le Touquet-Paris-Plage, France 28/D2
Letpadan, Burma 72/C3
Le Tréport, France 28/D2
Letsôk-aw Kyun (isl.), Burma 72/C5
Lette, N.S. Wales 97/B4
Letterkenny, Ireland 10/B3
Letterkenny, Ireland 17/F2
Letterkenny Army Depot, Pa. 294/G6
Lettermullan (isl.), Ireland 17/B5
Letts, Ind. 227/F6
Letts, Iowa 229/L6
Lettsworth, La. 238/G5
Leucadia, Calif. 204/H10
Leucate (mts.), France 28/E6
Leuchars, Scotland 15/F4
Leuk, Switzerland 39/E4
Leukerbad, Switzerland 39/E4
Leupp, Ariz. 198/E3
Leurbost, Scotland 15/B2
Leuser (mt.), Indonesia 85/B5
Leuven, Belgium 27/F7
Leuze-en-Hainaut, Belgium 27/D7
Levádhia, Greece 45/F6
Levallois-Perret, France 28/A1
Levan, Utah 304/C4
Levanger, Norway 18/G5
Levant, Kansas 232/A2
Levant•, Maine 243/F6
Levanzo (isl.), Italy 34/D5
Levasy, Mo. 261/S5
Le Vauclin, Martinique 161/D6
Levee, Ky. 237/O5
Level, Md. 245/O2
Level Green, Ky. 237/N6
Level Land, S.C. 296/C3
Levelland, Texas 303/B4
Levelock, Alaska 196/G3
Level Plains, Ala. 195/G8
Levels, W. Va. 312/J4
Leven, Scotland 10/E2
Leven, Scotland 15/F4
Leven, Loch (inlet), Scotland 15/D4
Leven (lake), Scotland 15/E4
Leven (riv.), Tasmania 99/B3
Leveque (cape), Australia 87/C7
L'Eveque (cape), N. Zealand 100/D7
Lévêque (cape), W. Australia 88/C3
Lévêque (cape), W. Australia 92/C2
Leverburgh, Scotland 15/B3
Le Verdon-sur-Mer, France 28/C5
Leverett•, Mass. 249/E3
Levering, Mich. 250/E3
Leverkusen, Germany 22/B3
Levesque, New Bruns. 170/C1
Levice, Czech. 41/E2
Levick (mt.) 5/B8
Levie, France 28/B7
Le Vigan, France 28/E5
Levin, N. Zealand 100/E4
Lévis (co.), Québec 172/J3
Lévis, Québec 172/J3
Lévis, Québec 174/C3
Levisa Fork (riv.), Va. 307/C5
Levitha (isl.), Greece 45/H7
Levittown, N.Y. 276/R7
Levittown, Pa. 294/N5
Levittown, P. Rico 161/D1
Levkás, Greece 45/E6
Levkás (isl.), Greece 45/E6
Levoča, Czech. 41/F2
Lévrier (bay), Mauritania 106/A4
Levuka, Fiji 87/H7
Levukaa, Fiji 86/Q10
Levy (co.), Fla. 212/D2
Levy (lake), Fla. 212/D2
Levy, N. Mex. 274/E2
Lewe, Burma 72/B3
Lewellen, Nebr. 264/B3
Lewes, Del. 245/T5
Lewes, England 13/H7
Lewes, England 10/G5
Lewis, Colo. 208/B8
Lewis (isl.), Fla. 212/B3
Lewis (co.), Idaho 220/B3
Lewis, Ind. 227/C6
Lewis, Iowa 229/C6
Lewis, Kansas 232/C4
Lewis (co.), Ky. 237/P3
Lewis, Manitoba 179/F5
Lewis (lake), Manitoba 179/G2
Lewis (co.), Mo. 261/J2
Lewis, Mo. 261/E6
Lewis (co.), N.Y. 276/K3
Lewis, N.Y. 276/N2
Lewis (dist.), Scotland 15/B2
Lewis (dist.), Scotland 10/C1
Lewis, Butt of (prom.), Scotland 15/B2
Lewis, Butt of (prom.), Scotland 10/C1
Lewis, S.C. 296/E2
Lewis (co.), Tenn. 237/F9
Lewis (creek), Vt. 268/A3
Lewis (co.), Wash. 310/C4
Lewis (riv.), Wash. 310/C5
Lewis (co.), W. Va. 312/F4
Lewis, Wis. 317/B4
Lewis (lake), Wyo. 319/B1
Lewis and Clark (co.), Mont. 262/D3
Lewis and Clark (range), Mont. 262/C2
Lewis and Clark (lake), Nebr. 264/G2
Lewis and Clark (lake), S. Dak. 298/O8
Lewis and Clark Village, Mo. 261/C3
Lewisberry, Pa. 294/J5
Lewisburg, Ky. 237/G6
Lewisburg, La. 238/F6
Lewisburg, Ohio 284/A6
Lewisburg, Pa. 294/J4
Lewisburg, Tenn. 237/H10
Lewisburg, W. Va. 312/E7
Lewis Center, Ohio 284/D5
Lewis Creek, Ind. 227/F6
Lewisetta, Va. 307/R4
Lewisham, England 10/B5
Lewisham, England 13/H8
Lewis Hill (mt.), Newf. 166/C4
Lewisport, Ky. 237/H5
Lewisporte, Newf. 166/C4
Lewis Run, Pa. 294/E2
Lewis Smith (dam), Ala. 195/D3
Lewis Smith (lake), Ala. 195/D2
Lewiston, Calif. 204/C3
Lewiston, Idaho 188/C1
Lewiston, Idaho 220/A3
Lewiston, Maine 188/N2
Lewiston, Maine 243/C7
Lewiston, Mich. 250/E4
Lewiston, Minn. 255/G7
Lewiston, Nebr. 264/H4
Lewiston, N.Y. 276/B4
Lewiston, Utah 304/C2
Lewiston, Vt. 268/C4
Lewiston Woodville, N.C. 281/P2
Lewistown, Ill. 222/C3
Lewistown, Md. 245/J2
Lewistown, Mo. 261/J2
Lewistown, Mont. 262/G3
Lewistown, Ohio 284/C5
Lewistown, Pa. 294/G4
Lewisville, Ark. 202/C7
Lewisville, Idaho 220/F6
Lewisville, Ind. 227/G5
Lewisville, Minn. 255/D7
Lewisville, Ohio 284/H6
Lewisville (Ulysses), Pa. 294/G2
Lewisville, Pa. 294/L6
Lewisville, Texas 303/G1
Lewisville (lake), Texas 303/G1
Lewvan, Sask. 181/H5
Lexa, Ark. 202/J4
Lexie, Miss. 256/D8
Lexington, Ala. 195/D1
Lexington, Ark. 202/F2
Lexington, Georgia 217/F3
Lexington, Ill. 222/E3
Lexington, Ind. 227/F7
Lexington, Ky. 237/N4
Lexington, Ky. 146/K6
Lexington, Ky. 188/K3
Lexington•, Mass. 249/B6
Lexington, Mich. 250/G5
Lexington, Minn. 255/G5
Lexington, Miss. 256/D4
Lexington, Mo. 261/E4
Lexington, Nebr. 264/E4
Lexington, N.Y. 276/M6
Lexington, N.C. 281/J3
Lexington, Ohio 284/F4
Lexington, Okla. 288/M4
Lexington, Oreg. 291/H2
Lexington (co.), S.C. 296/E4
Lexington, S.C. 296/E4
Lexington, Tenn. 237/E9
Lexington, Texas 303/G7
Lexington (I.C.), Va. 307/J5
Lexington Blue Grass Army Depot, Ky. 237/N5
Lexington Park, Md. 245/M7
Lexsy, Georgia 217/H6
Leyba, N. Mex. 274/D3
Leyburn, England 13/F3
Leyden•, Mass. 249/D2
Leye, China 77/G7
Leyland, England 13/G1
Leyland, England 10/F1
Leyond (riv.), Manitoba 179/F3
Leysin, Switzerland 39/C4
Leyte (prov.), Philippines 82/E5
Leyte (isl.), Philippines 54/O8
Leyte (gulf), Philippines 82/E5
Leyte (isl.), Philippines 85/H3
Leyte (isl.), Philippines 82/E5
Leżajsk, Poland 47/F3
Lezama, Argentina 143/H7
Lézarde (riv.), Martinique 161/D6
Lezhë, Albania 45/D5
Lézignan-Corbières, France 28/E6
Lezuza, Spain 33/E3
L'gov, U.S.S.R. 52/E4
Lhanbryde, Scotland 15/E3
Lhari, China 77/D5
Lhasa, China 77/D6
Lhasa, China 2/P4
Lhasa, China 54/L7
Lhazê (Lhatse), China 77/C6
Lhazhong, China 77/C5
L'Hirondelle (Little Buffalo) (lake), Alta. 182/B1
Lhokseumawe, Indonesia 85/B4
Lhorong, China 77/E5
Lhozhag, China 77/D6
Lhünzê, China 77/D6
Lhünzhub, China 77/D5
Liancheng, China 77/J6
Lianga, Philippines 82/E6
Lianga (bay), Philippines 82/F6
Lianping, China 77/H7
Lian Xian, China 77/H7
Lianyungang (Lienyünkang), China 77/J5
Lianyunggang, China 54/N6
Liao (riv.), China 54/O5
Liaodong Bandao (pen.), China 77/K3
Liao He (riv.), China 77/K3
Liaoning (prov.), China 77/K3
Liaoyang, China 77/K3
Liaoyuan, China 77/K3
Liard (riv.) 162/D3
Liard (riv.), Br. Col. 184/L2
Liard (riv.), Canada 146/F3
Liard (riv.), N.W. Terr. 187/F4
Liard (riv.), Yukon 187/E3
Liard River, Br. Col. 184/L2
Libáň, Czech. 41/C1
Líbano, Colombia 126/C5
Libau, Manitoba 179/F4
Libby, Minn. 255/E4
Libby, Mont. 262/A2
Libenge, Zaire 115/C3
Liberal, Kansas 232/B4
Liberal, Mo. 261/D7
Liberal, Oreg. 291/B3
Liberdade, Brazil 135/D3
Liberec, Czech. 41/C1
Liberia 2/J5
Liberia 102/B4
LIBERIA 106/C7
Liberia, C. Rica 154/E5
Liberta, Ant. & Bar. 161/E11
Libertad, Belize 154/C1
Libertad, Uruguay 145/C5
Libertad, Barinas, Venezuela 124/D3
Libertad, Cojedes, Venezuela 124/D3
Liberty, Ariz. 198/C5
Liberty (co.), Fla. 212/B1
Liberty (co.), Georgia 217/J7
Liberty, Ill. 222/B4
Liberty, Ind. 227/H5
Liberty, Kansas 232/G4
Liberty, Ky. 237/M6
Liberty, Maine 243/E7
Liberty•, Maine 243/E7
Liberty (lake), Md. 245/L3
Liberty, Miss. 256/C8
Liberty, Mo. 261/R5
Liberty (co.), Mont. 262/E2
Liberty, Nebr. 264/H4
Liberty (mt.), N.H. 268/D3
Liberty, N.Y. 276/L7
Liberty, N.C. 281/K3
Liberty, Pa. 294/H2
Liberty, Pa. 294/C7
Liberty, Sask. 181/F4
Liberty, S.C. 296/B2
Liberty, Tenn. 237/K8
Liberty (co.), Texas 303/K7
Liberty, Texas 303/K7
Liberty, Wash. 310/E3
Liberty, W. Va. 312/C5
Liberty Center, Ind. 227/G3
Liberty Center, Iowa 229/F6
Liberty Center, Ohio 284/B3
Liberty Corner, N.J. 273/D2
Liberty Grove, Md. 245/O2
Liberty Hill, Conn. 210/G2
Liberty Hill, La. 238/E2
Liberty Hill, S.C. 296/F3
Liberty Lake, Wash. 310/J3
Liberty Mills, Ind. 227/F2
Liberty Pole, Wis. 317/D8
Libertytown, Md. 245/J3
Libertyville, Ala. 195/F8
Libertyville, Ill. 222/B4
Libertyville, Iowa 229/K7
Libiaz, Poland 47/D3
Libin, Belgium 27/G9
Libochovice, Czech. 41/B1
Libon, Philippines 82/D4
Libong, Ko (isl.), Thailand 72/C6
Libourne, France 28/C5
Libramont-Chevigny, Belgium 27/G9
Library, Pa. 294/B7
Libres, Mexico 150/O1
Libreville (cap.), Gabon 2/K6
Libreville (cap.), Gabon 115/A3
Libreville (cap.), Gabon 102/C4
Libuse, La. 238/F4
Libya 2/K4
Libya 102/D2
LIBYA 111/B2
Libyan (des.) 102/E2
Libyan (des.), Egypt 111/E2
Libyan (plat.), Egypt 111/E1
Libyan (des.), Libya 111/D2
Libyan (plat.), Libya 111/D1
Libyan (des.), Sudan 111/E3
Licancábur, Cerro (mt.), Chile 138/B4
Licantén, Chile 138/A10
Licata, Italy 34/D6
Lice, Turkey 63/J3
Lichfield, England 13/F5
Lichfield, England 10/G2
Lichinga, Mozambique 102/F6
Lichinga, Mozambique 118/F2
Lichtenberg, Germany 22/F4
Lichtenfels, Germany 22/D3
Lichtenrade, Germany 22/F4
Lichterfelde, Germany 22/E4
Lichtervelde, Belgium 27/C6
Lick (creek), Tenn. 237/R8
Lick Creek, Ill. 222/D6
Licking, South Fork (riv.), Ky. 237/N3
Licking, North Fork (riv.), Ky. 237/O3
Licking (riv.), Ky. 237/N3
Licking, Mo. 261/J8
Licking (co.), Ohio 284/F5
Licking (riv.), Ohio 284/F5
Licking (creek), Pa. 294/F6
Licosa (cape), Italy 34/E4
Lida, Ky. 237/O6
Lida (lake), Minn. 255/C4
Lida, U.S.S.R. 52/C4
Lidcombe, N.S. Wales 97/J3
Liddel Water (riv.), Scotland 15/F5
Lidderdale, Iowa 229/D4
Liddes, Switzerland 39/D5
Liddon (gulf), N.W. Terr. 187/G4
Lidgerwood, N. Dak. 282/R7
Lidice, Czech. 41/C1
Lidingö, Sweden 18/H1
Lidköping, Sweden 18/H7
Lido di Ostia, Italy 34/F7
Lido di Venezia, Italy 34/D2
Lidzbark, Poland 47/D2
Lidzbark Warmiński, Poland 47/E1
Liebenthal, Kansas 232/C3
Liebenthal, Sask. 181/B5
Liechtensteig, Switzerland 39/H2
Liechtenstein 7/F4
LIECHTENSTEIN 39/J2
Liedekerke, Belgium 27/D7
Liège (riv.), Alberta 182/D1
Liège (prov.), Belgium 27/H7
Liège, Belgium 7/E3
Liège, Belgium 27/H7
Liegnitz (Legnica), Poland 47/C3
Lieksa, Finland 18/R5
Lienyünkang (Lianyungang), China 77/J5
Lienz, Austria 41/B3
Liepāja, U.S.S.R. 7/F3
Liepāja, U.S.S.R. 53/A2
Liepāja, U.S.S.R. 48/B4
Liepāja, U.S.S.R. 52/B3
Lier, Belgium 27/F6
Lierneux, Belgium 27/H8
Lierre (Lier), Belgium 27/F6
Liestal, Switzerland 39/E2
Liévin, France 28/E2
Lièvre (riv.), Québec 172/B4
Lièvres (isl.), Québec 172/H2
Liezen, Austria 41/C3
Liffey (riv.), Ireland 17/H5
Liffey (riv.), Ireland 10/C4
Lifford, Ireland 10/C3
Lifford, Ireland 17/F2
Lifu (isl.), New Caled. 87/G8
Lifu (isl.), New Caled. 86/H4
Ligao, Philippines 82/D4
Līgatne, U.S.S.R. 53/C2
Liggett, Ky. 237/P7
Lightfoot, Va. 307/P6
Lighthouse (pt.), Fla. 212/B2
Light House (pt.), Mich. 250/D3
Lighthouse Point, Fla. 212/F5
Lightning (creek), Oreg. 291/L2
Lightning (creek), Wyo. 319/G2
Lightning Ridge, N.S. Wales 97/E1
Lightsville, Ohio 284/A5
Lignite, N. Dak. 282/F2
Ligon, Ky. 237/R6
Ligonha (riv.), Mozambique 118/F3
Ligonier, Ind. 227/F2
Ligonier, Pa. 294/D5
Liguria (reg.), Italy 34/B2

400 Little Sevogle

Little Sevogle (riv.), New Bruns. 170/D1
Little Sheep (creek), Oreg. 291/K2
Little Shippegan, New Bruns. 170/F1
Little Silver, N.J. 273/F3
Little Sioux, Iowa 229/B5
Little Sioux (riv.), Iowa 229/B3
Little Sitkin (isl.), Alaska 196/K4
Little Smoky, Alberta 182/B2
Little Smoky (riv.), Alberta 182/B2
Little Smoky (valley), Nev. 266/E4
Little Southwest Miramichi (riv.), New Bruns. 170/D2
Little Spokane (riv.), Wash. 310/H3
Littlestown, Pa. 294/H6
Little Suamico, Wis. 317/L6
Little Summer (isl.), Mich. 250/C3
Little Tallahatchie (riv.), Miss. 256/D2
Little Tennessee (riv.), N.C. 281/B4
Little Tennessee (riv.), Tenn. 237/N10
Little Thunder (creek), Wyo. 319/G2
Little Tinicum (isl.), Pa. 294/M7
Little Tobago (isl.), Virgin Is. (U.K.) 161/B3
Little Tobique (riv.), New Bruns. 170/C1
Littleton, Colo. 208/K3
Littleton, Ill. 222/C3
Littleton, Iowa 229/K3
Littleton, Ireland 17/F6
Littleton•, Maine 243/H3
Littleton•, Mass. 249/H2
Littleton, N.H. 268/D3
Littleton•, N.H. 268/D3
Littleton, N.C. 281/O2
Littleton, Va. 307/O7
Littleton, W. Va. 312/F3
Littleton Common, Mass. 249/J2
Little Traverse (bay), Mich. 250/D3
Little Trout River (pond), Newf. 166/C4
Little Tupper (lake), N.Y. 276/L2
Little Valley, N.Y. 276/C6
Little Vermilion (riv.), Ind. 227/B5
Littleville, Ala. 195/C1
Little Wabash (riv.), Ill. 222/E5
Little Weiser (riv.), Idaho 220/B5
Little White (riv.), S. Dak. 298/H7
Little Wood (riv.), Idaho 220/D6
Little Yenisey (riv.), U.S.S.R. 48/K4
Little York, Ill. 222/C2
Little York, Ind. 227/F7
Little York, N.J. 273/C2
Little Zab (riv.), Iraq 66/C3
Lituya (bay), Alaska 196/L1
Litvinov, Czech. 41/B1
Liuba, China 77/G5
Liukang Tenggaja (isls.), Indonesia 85/F7
Liuli, Tanzania 115/F6
Liuzhou (Liuchow), China 77/G7
Liuzhou, China 54/M7
Līvāni, U.S.S.R. 53/D2
Livelong, Sask. 181/C2
Lively (isl.), Falkland Is. 143/E7
Lively, Va. 307/P5
Livengood, Alaska 196/J1
Live Oak, Calif. 204/K4
Live Oak, Calif. 204/D4
Live Oak, Fla. 212/D1
Live Oak (co.), Texas 303/F9
Live Oak, Texas 303/K10
Liveringa, W. Australia 88/C3
Liveringa, W. Australia 92/D2
Livermore, Calif. 204/L2
Livermore, Colo. 208/J1
Livermore, Iowa 229/E3
Livermore, Ky. 237/G5
Livermore, Maine 243/C7
Livermore•, Maine 243/C7
Livermore (mt.), Texas 303/C11
Livermore Falls, Maine 243/C7
Livermore Falls•, Maine 243/C7
Livermore Falls, N.H. 268/D4
Liverpool (swamp), Bolivia 136/D4
Liverpool, England 10/F2
Liverpool, England 13/G2
Liverpool, England 7/D3
Liverpool (bay), England 13/D4
Liverpool, Ill. 222/C3
Liverpool, N. S. Wales 88/K4
Liverpool, N.S. Wales 97/H4
Liverpool (range), N.S. Wales 97/F2
Liverpool, N.Y. 276/H4
Liverpool (bay), N.W. Terr. 187/E2
Liverpool (cape), N.W. Terr. 187/L2
Liverpool, Nova Scotia 168/D4
Liverpool (bay), Nova Scotia 168/D5
Liverpool, Pa. 294/H4
Liverpool, Texas 303/J3
Liverpool, W. Va. 312/C5
Livia, Ky. 237/G5
Livigno, Italy 34/C1
Livingston, Ala. 195/B5
Livingston, Calif. 204/E6
Livingston, Guatemala 154/C3
Livingston (co.), Ill. 222/E3
Livingston, Ill. 222/D5
Livingston (co.), Ky. 237/E6
Livingston, Ky. 237/N6
Livingston (par.), La. 238/L2
Livingston, La. 238/L1
Livingston (co.), Mich. 250/F6
Livingston (co.), Mo. 261/E3
Livingston, Mont. 188/D1
Livingston, Mont. 262/F5
Livingston•, N.J. 273/E2
Livingston (co.), N.Y. 276/E5
Livingston, Scotland 15/C2
Livingston, Scotland 10/C1
Livingston, S.C. 296/E4
Livingston, Tenn. 237/L8
Livingston, Texas 303/K7
Livingston (lake), Texas 303/K7
Livingston, Wis. 317/E10
Livingstone (range), Alberta 182/C4
Livingstone (falls), Zaire 115/B5
Livingstone, Zambia 115/E7
Livingstone, Zambia 102/E6
Livingstonia, Malawi 115/F6
Livingston Manor, N.Y. 276/L7
Livingstonville, N.Y. 276/M6
Livno, Yugoslavia 45/C4
Livny, U.S.S.R. 52/E4
Livona, N. Dak. 282/K6
Livonia, Ind. 227/E7
Livonia, La. 238/G5
Livonia, Mich. 250/F6
Livonia, Mo. 261/G1
Livonia, N.Y. 276/E5
Livonia, Pa. 294/H4
Livorno (prov.), Italy 34/C3
Livorno, Italy 7/E4
Livorno, Italy 34/C3
Livry-Gargan, France 28/C1
Liwale, Tanzania 115/G5
Li Xian, China 77/H6
Lixoúrion, Greece 45/E6
Lizard, The (dist.), England 13/B8
Lizard (pt.), England 10/D6
Lizard (pt.), England 13/B8
Lizella, Georgia 217/E5
Lizemores, W. Va. 312/D6
Lizton, Ind. 227/D5
Ljubinje, Yugoslavia 45/D4
Ljubljana, Yugoslavia 45/B3
Ljubljana, Yugoslavia 7/F4
Ljubuški, Yugoslavia 45/C4
Ljugarn, Sweden 18/L8
Ljungan (riv.), Sweden 18/K5
Ljungby, Sweden 18/H8
Ljusdal, Sweden 18/J6
Ljusna (riv.), Sweden 7/F2
Ljusnan (riv.), Sweden 18/H5
Ljusne, Sweden 18/K6
Llagostera, Spain 33/H2
Llaima (vol.), Chile 138/E2
Llallagua, Bolivia 136/B6
Llallagua, Bolivia 120/C4
Llamara, Salar de (salt dep.), Chile 138/B3
Llanarth, Wales 13/C5
Llancanelo (lag.), Argentina 143/C4
Llancanelo, Salina y Laguna (salt dep.), Argentina 143/C4
Llandeilo, Wales 13/C6
Llandovery, Wales 13/D5
Llandovery, Wales 10/D5
Llandrindod Wells, Wales 10/E4
Llandrindod Wells, Wales 13/D5
Llandudno, Wales 13/D4
Llandudno, Wales 10/E4
Llandybie, Wales 13/C6
Llandyssul, Wales 13/C5
Llanelli, Wales 13/C6
Llanelli, Wales 10/D5
Llanes, Spain 33/D1
Llanfair Caereinion, Wales 13/D5
Llanfairfechan, Wales 13/D4
Llanfyllin, Wales 10/E4
Llanfyllin, Wales 13/D5
Llangefni, Wales 13/C4
Llangollen, Wales 13/D5
Llangollen, Wales 10/E4
Llanguicke, Wales 13/D6
Llanidloes, Wales 13/D5
Llanidloes, Wales 10/E4
Llanllyfni, Wales 13/C4
LLannon, Wales 13/C6
Llano, N. Mex. 274/D2
Llano (co.), Texas 303/F7
Llano, Texas 303/F7
Llano (riv.), Texas 303/D7
Llano Estacado (Staked) (plain), N. Mex. 274/F5
Llano Estacado (plain), Texas 303/B4
Llanon, Wales 13/C5
Llanos (plain) 120/B2
Llanos (plains), Colombia 126/D5
Llanquera, Bolivia 136/A6
Llanquihue (lake), Chile 138/E3
Llanrhaeadr, Wales 13/D5
Llanrhystyd, Wales 13/C5
Llanrian, Wales 13/B6
Llanrwst, Wales 13/D4
Llanrwst, Wales 10/E4
Llantrisant, Wales 13/A7
Llantwit Major, Wales 13/A7
Llanwnog, Wales 13/D5
Llanwrtyd Wells, Wales 13/D5
Llata, Peru 128/D7
Llay-Llay, Chile 138/G2
Lleida (prov.), Spain 33/G2
Lleida, Spain 33/G2
Lleida, Spain 7/D4
Llera de Canales, Mexico 150/K5
Llerena (pt.), C. Rica 154/F6
Llerena, Spain 33/C3
Lleyn (pen.), Wales 13/C5
Llica, Bolivia 136/A6
Llico, Chile 138/A10
Llivia, Spain 33/G1
Llobregat (riv.), Spain 33/H2
Llodio, Spain 33/E1
Llolleo, Chile 138/F4
Llorente, Philippines 82/E5
Lloyd, Fla. 212/C1
Lloyd (res.), Ga. 188/K4
Lloyd, Ky. 237/R3
Lloyd, Mont. 262/G2
Lloyd Harbor, N.Y. 276/R6
Lloydminster, Alberta 182/E3
Lloydminster, Alta.-Sask. 162/E5
Lloydminster, Sask. 181/A2
Lluchmayor, Spain 33/H3
Lluidas Vale, Jamaica 158/J6
Llullaillaco (mt.) 120/C5
Llullaillaco (vol.), Argentina 143/C1
Llullaillaco (vol.), Chile 138/B5
Lluta (riv.), Chile 138/B1
Llwchwr, Wales 13/D6
Loa (riv.), Chile 120/C5
Loa (riv.), Chile 138/B3
Loa, Utah 304/C5
Loachapoka, Ala. 195/G5
Loami, Ill. 222/D4
Loange (riv.), Angola 115/C5
Loange (riv.), Zaire 115/C5
Loanhead, Scotland 10/C1
Loanhead, Scotland 15/D2
Lobatse, Botswana 118/D5
Löbau, Germany 22/F3
Lobaye (riv.), Cent. Afr. Rep. 115/C2
Lobdell, La. 238/J1
Lobeco, S.C. 296/F6
Lobelia, W. Va. 312/F6
Lobelville, Tenn. 237/F9
Lobenstein, Germany 22/D3
Lobería, Argentina 143/E4
Lobethal, S. Australia 94/C7
Łobez, Poland 47/B2
Lobito, Angola 115/B6
Lobito, Angola 102/D6
Lobitos, Peru 128/B5
Lobo, Philippines 82/C4
Lobo (cay), P. Rico 161/G1
Lobos, Argentina 143/G7
Lobos (pt.), Chile 138/A3
Lobos (cape), Mexico 150/C2
Lobos (pt.), Mexico 150/D3
Lobos (isl.), Uruguay 145/E6
Lobos de Afuera (isls.), Peru 128/B6
Lobos de Tierra (isl.), Peru 128/B6
Lobster (lake), Maine 243/E4
Locarno, Switzerland 39/G4
Locate, Mont. 262/L4
Lochaber, Nova Scotia 168/F3
Lochaber (dist.), Scotland 15/D4
Lochailort, Scotland 15/C4
Lochaline, Scotland 15/C4
Lochans, Scotland 15/D6
Locharbriggs, Scotland 15/E5
Lochawe, Scotland 15/C4
Lochboisdale, Scotland 15/A3
Lochbuie, Colo. 208/K2
Lochcarron, Scotland 10/D2
Lochcarron, Scotland 15/C3
Lochearnhead, Scotland 15/D4
Lochem, Netherlands 27/J4
Lochend, Scotland 15/D3
Loches, France 28/D4
Lochgelly, Scotland 10/C1
Lochgelly, Scotland 15/D1
Lochgelly, W. Va. 312/D6
Lochgilphead, Scotland 10/D2
Lochgilphead, Scotland 15/C4
Lochgoilhead, Scotland 15/D4
Lochindorb (lake), Scotland 15/E3
Lochinver, Scotland 10/D1
Lochinver, Scotland 15/C2
Lochloosa, Fla. 212/E2
Lochloosa (lake), Fla. 212/D2
Loch Lynn Heights, Md. 245/A3
Lochmaben, Scotland 10/E3
Lochmaben, Scotland 15/E5
Lochmaddy, Scotland 15/A3
Lochmere, N.H. 268/D5
Lochnagar (mt.), Scotland 15/E4
Lochore, Scotland 15/D1
Lochranza, Scotland 15/C5
Loch Raven (res.), Md. 245/M3
Lochristi, Belgium 27/D6
Lochsa (riv.), Idaho 220/C3
Lochwinnoch, Scotland 15/A2
Lochy, Loch (lake), Scotland 15/D3
Lochy, Loch (lake), Scotland 10/D2
Lock, S. Australia 94/D5
Lockatong (creek), N.J. 273/C3
Lockbourne, Ohio 284/E6
Locke, Calif. 204/B9
Locke, N.Y. 276/H5
Locke (mt.), Texas 303/D11
Lockeford, Calif. 204/C9
Locke Mills, Maine 243/B7
Lockeport, Nova Scotia 168/C5
Lockerbie, Scotland 10/E3
Lockerbie, Scotland 15/E5
Lockesburg, Ark. 202/B6
Lockhart, Ala. 195/F8
Lockhart, Minn. 255/B3
Lockhart (mt.), Mont. 262/D3
Lockhart, N.S. Wales 97/D4
Lockhart (riv.), N.W. Terr. 187/H3
Lockhart, S.C. 296/E2
Lockhart, Texas 303/G8
Lock Haven, Pa. 294/H3
Lockington, Ohio 284/B5
Lockland, Ohio 284/C9
Lockney, Texas 303/C3
Lockney, W. Va. 312/E5
Lockport, Ill. 222/B6
Lockport, Ky. 237/M4
Lockport, La. 238/K7
Lockport, Manitoba 179/F4
Lockport, N.Y. 276/C4
Lockridge, Iowa 229/K7
Lock Springs, Mo. 261/E3
Lockwood, Mo. 261/E8
Lockwood, Sask. 181/G4
Lockwood, W. Va. 312/D6
Loc Ninh, Vietnam 72/E5
Loco, Okla. 288/L6
Loco Hills, N. Mex. 274/F6
Locumba, Peru 128/G11
Locumba (riv.), Peru 128/G11
Locust, N.C. 281/J4
Locust Bayou, Ark. 202/E6
Locust Fork, Ala. 195/E3
Locust Fork (riv.), Ala. 195/E3
Locust Grove, Ark. 202/G2
Locust Grove, Georgia 217/D4
Locust Grove, N.Y. 276/R6
Locust Grove, Ohio 284/D8
Locust Grove, Okla. 288/R2
Locust Hill, Ky. 237/J5
Locustville, Va. 307/S5
Lod (Lydda), Israel 65/B4
Loda, Ill. 222/E3
Lodar, Yemen 59/E7
Loddon, England 13/J5
Loddon (riv.), Victoria 97/B5
Loddon (riv.), Victoria 88/G7
Lodève, France 28/E6
Lodeynoye Pole, U.S.S.R. 52/D2
Lodge (creek), Mont. 262/G1
Lodge (creek), Sask. 181/B6
Lodge, S.C. 296/F5
Lodge Bay, Newf. 166/C3
Lodge Grass, Mont. 262/J5
Lodge Hill, Barbados 161/B8
Lodgepole, Alberta 182/C3
Lodge Pole, Mont. 262/H2
Lodgepole, Nebr. 264/B3
Lodgepole (creek), Nebr. 264/A3
Lodgepole, S. Dak. 298/D2
Lodgepole (creek), Wyo. 319/H2
Lodgepole (creek), Wyo. 319/H4
Lodi, Calif. 188/B3
Lodi, Calif. 204/C9
Lodi, Italy 34/B2
Lodi, Miss. 256/E3
Lodi, Mo. 261/M8
Lodi, N.J. 273/B2
Lodi, N.Y. 276/G5
Lodi, Ohio 284/F3
Lodi (cape), Tasmania 99/E3
Lodi, Texas 303/K5
Lodi, Wis. 317/G9
Lødingen, Norway 18/J2
Lodja, Zaire 102/E5
Lodja, Zaire 115/D4
Lodosa, Spain 33/E1
Lodrino, Switzerland 39/G4
Lodwar, Kenya 115/G3
Łódź (prov.), Poland 47/D3
Łódź (city prov.), Poland 47/D3
Łódź, Poland 7/F3
Łódź, Poland 47/D3
Loei, Thailand 72/D3
Loen, Norway 18/E6
Lofer, Austria 41/B3
Lofoten (isls.), Norway 4/C9
Lofoten (isls.), Norway 7/F2
Lofoten (isls.), Norway 18/H2
Loftus, England 13/G3
Loftus, England 10/F3
Lofty (mt.), S. Australia 88/E8
Lofty (mt.), S. Australia 94/B8
Lofty (range), Tasmania 99/B3
Logan, Ala. 195/E2
Logan (lake), Alberta 182/E2
Logan (co.), Ark. 202/C3
Logan (mt.), Canada 4/C17
Logan (co.), Colo. 208/N1
Logan (co.), Ill. 222/D3
Logan, Ill. 222/E6
Logan, Ind. 227/H6
Logan, Iowa 229/B5
Logan (co.), Kansas 232/A3
Logan, Kansas 232/C2
Logan (co.), Ky. 237/H7
Logan, Mont. 262/E5
Logan (co.), Nebr. 264/D3
Logan (creek), Nebr. 264/H2
Logan, N. Mex. 274/F3
Logan (co.), N. Dak. 282/L7
Logan, N. Dak. 282/H3
Logan (co.), Ohio 284/C5
Logan, Ohio 284/F6
Logan (co.), Okla. 288/M3
Logan, Okla. 288/F1
Logan, Oreg. 291/B2
Logan, Utah 304/C2
Logan, Utah 188/D2
Logan (mt.), Wash. 310/E2
Logan (co.), W. Va. 312/C7
Logan, W. Va. 312/B7
Logan (mt.), Yukon 162/B3
Logan (mt.), Yukon 187/D3
Logan (mts.), Yukon 187/F3
Logandale, Nev. 266/G6
Logan Internat'l Airport, Mass. 249/D7
Logan Lake, Br. Col. 184/G5
Logan Martin (lake), Ala. 195/F4
Logansport, Ind. 227/E3
Logansport, Ky. 237/H6
Logansport, La. 238/C3
Loganton, Pa. 294/H3
Loganville, Georgia 217/E3
Loganville, Pa. 294/J6
Loganville, Wis. 317/F9
Loge (riv.), Angola 115/B5
Loggieville, New Bruns. 170/E1
Log Lane Village, Colo. 208/M2
Logone (riv.) 102/D3
Logone (riv.), Cameroon 115/C2
Logone (riv.), Chad 111/C5
Logroño (prov.), Spain 33/E1
Logroño, Spain 7/D4
Logroño, Spain 33/E1
Logrosán, Spain 33/D3
Logsden, Oreg. 291/D3
Løgstør, Denmark 21/C4
Løgstør, Denmark 18/F8
Løgstør Bredning (fjord), Denmark 21/C4
Løgumkloster, Denmark 21/B7
Lohals, Denmark 21/D7
Lohardaga, India 68/E4
Lohatlha, S. Africa 118/C5
Lohman, Mo. 261/H5
Lohman, Mont. 262/G2
Lohn, Texas 303/E6
Löhne, Germany 22/C2
Loho (Luohe), China 77/H5
Lohr am Main, Germany 22/C4
Lohrville, Iowa 229/D4
Lohrville, Wis. 317/H7
Loica, Chile 138/F4
Loi-kaw, Burma 72/C3
Loi Leng (mt.), Burma 72/C2
Loimaa, Finland 18/N6
Loir (riv.), France 28/D4
Loire (dept.), France 28/F5
Loire (riv.), France 7/E4
Loire (riv.), France 28/C4
Loire-Atlantique (dept.), France 28/C4
Loiret (dept.), France 28/E4
Loir-et-Cher (dept.), France 28/D4
Loíza, P. Rico 161/E1
Loíza Aldea, P. Rico 161/E1
Loja (prov.), Ecuador 128/C4
Loja, Ecuador 128/C4
Loja, Ecuador 120/B3
Loja, Spain 33/D4
Løjt Kirkeby, Denmark 21/C7
Loka, Sudan 111/F7
Lokeren, Belgium 27/D6
Lokitaung, Kenya 115/G3
Lokka (res.), Finland 18/Q3
Løkken, Denmark 21/C3
Løkken, Norway 18/F5
Lokoja, Nigeria 106/F7
Lokolama, Zaire 115/D4
Lokoro (riv.), Zaire 115/C4
Lökösháza, Hungary 41/F3
Lokossa, Benin 106/E7
Loksa, U.S.S.R. 53/C1
Loks Land (isl.), N.W.T. 187/M3
Lol (dry riv.), Sudan 111/E6
Lola, Ky. 237/E6
Loleta, Calif. 204/A3
Lolgorien, Kenya 115/G4
Lolita, Texas 303/H9
Lolland (isl.), Denmark 18/G9
Lolland (isl.), Denmark 21/E8
Lollie, Georgia 217/G6
Lolo (creek), Idaho 220/C3
Lolo (pass), Idaho 220/D3
Lolo, Mont. 262/B4
Lolo (pass), Mont. 262/B4
Lolo Hot Springs, Mont. 262/B4
Lom, Bulgaria 45/F4
Lom (riv.), Cameroon 115/B2
Lom, Norway 18/F6
Loma, Colo. 208/B4
Loma, Mont. 262/F3
Loma, N. Dak. 282/O2
Loma, Mansa (lag.), S. Leone 106/B7
Loma Alta, Bolivia 136/B2
Loma Bonita, Mexico 150/M7
Loma Linda, Calif. 204/F10
Loma Mar, Calif. 204/J3
Lomami (riv.), Zaire 115/D4
Loman, Minn. 255/E2
Loma Plata, Paraguay 144/C3
Lomas, Peru 128/E10
Lomas de Zamora, Argentina 143/G7
Lomax, Ala. 195/E5
Lomax, Ill. 222/B3
Lomax, Texas 303/K2
Lombard, Ill. 222/B5
Lombarda, Serra (mts.), Brazil 132/D2
Lombardville, Ill. 222/D2
Lombardy (reg.), Italy 34/B2
Lombardy, S. Africa 118/H6
Lombez, France 28/D6
Lomblen (isl.), Indonesia 85/G7
Lombok (isl.), Indonesia 54/N10
Lombok (isl.), Indonesia 85/F7
Lombok (str.), Indonesia 85/E7
Lomé (cap.), Togo 102/C4
Lomé (cap.), Togo 106/E7
Lomela, Zaire 115/D4
Lomela (riv.), Zaire 115/D4
Lometa, Texas 303/F6
Lomié, Cameroon 115/B3
Lomira, Wis. 317/J8
Lo Miranda, Chile 138/G5
Lomita, Calif. 204/C11
Lommel, Belgium 27/G6
Lomnice, Czech. 41/C2
Lomond, Alberta 182/D4
Lomond, Loch (lake), Nova Scotia 168/H3
Lomond, Loch (lake), Scotland 15/D4
Lomond, Loch (lake), Scotland 10/A1
Lompoc, Calif. 204/E9
Lom Sak, Thailand 72/D3
Łomża (prov.), Poland 47/F2
Łomża, Poland 47/F2
Lonaconing, Md. 245/C2
Loncoche, Chile 138/D2
Loncopué, Argentina 143/B4
London, Ark. 202/D3
London, Greater, England 13/H8
London (cap.), England 7/D3
London (cap.), England 10/B5
London (cap.), England 13/H8
London, Ind. 227/F5
London, Ky. 237/N6
London, Minn. 255/E7
London, Ohio 284/C6
London, Ont. 146/K5
London, Ont. 162/H7
London, Ontario 177/C5
London, Texas 303/E7
London (cap.), U.K. 2/J3
London, Wis. 317/H9
Londonderry (isl.), Chile 138/E11
Londonderry•, N.H. 268/E6
Londonderry, N. Ireland 7/D3
Londonderry (dist.), N. Ireland 17/G2
Londonderry (Derry), N. Ireland 10/C3
Londonderry (Derry), N. Ireland 17/G2
Londonderry, Nova Scotia 168/E3
Londonderry, Ohio 284/E7
Londonderry•, Vt. 268/B5
Londonderry (cape), W. Australia 88/D2
Londonderry (cape), W. Australia 92/D1
Londonderry Station, Nova Scotia 168/E3
London Mills, Ill. 222/C3
Londontowne, Md. 245/M4
Londrina, Brazil 132/D8
Londrina, Brazil 120/D5
Lone (mt.), Mont. 262/E5
Lone (mt.), Nev. 266/D4
Lone Butte, Br. Col. 184/G4
Lone Cedar, W. Va. 312/C4
Lone Cone (mt.), Colo. 208/C7
Lone Elm, Kansas 232/G3
Lone Grove, Okla. 288/M6
Lone Jack, Mo. 261/S6
Lonely (lake), Manitoba 179/C3
Lonely (isl.), Ontario 177/C2
Lone Mountain, Tenn. 237/O8
Lone Oak, Georgia 217/C4
Lone Oak, Ky. 237/D6
Lone Oak, Texas 303/H5
Lone Pine, Alberta 182/C2
Lone Pine, Calif. 204/H7
Lone Pine (peak), Idaho 220/D5
Lonepine, La. 238/F5
Lonepine, Mont. 262/B3
Lone Prairie, Br. Col. 184/G2
Lone Rock, Iowa 229/E2
Lonerock, Oreg. 291/H2
Lone Rock, Sask. 181/A2
Lone Rock, Wis. 317/F9
Lone Star, S.C. 296/F4
Lone Tree (creek), Colo. 208/K1
Lone Tree, Iowa 229/L6
Lonetree, N. Dak. 282/G3
Lonetree, Wyo. 319/B4
Lone Wolf, Okla. 288/H5
Long, Alaska 196/G2
Long (isl.), Alaska 196/M2
Long (isl.), Ant. & Bar. 161/E11
Long (isl.), Bahamas 146/L7
Long (cay), Bahamas 156/C2
Long (isl.), Bahamas 156/C2
Long (bay), Barbados 161/B9
Long (mt.), Conn. 210/B2
Long (pond), Conn. 210/H3
Long (key), Fla. 212/F7
Long (key), Fla. 212/B3
Long (pond), Fla. 212/D2
Long (co.), Georgia 217/J7
Long (bay), Jamaica 158/H7
Long (lake), Maine 243/E2
Long (lake), Maine 243/G1
Long (lake), Maine 243/B7
Long (pond), Maine 243/E5
Long (pond), Maine 243/D6
Long (pond), Maine 243/C4
Long (lake), Manitoba 179/G4
Long (pt.), Manitoba 179/D1
Long (pt.), Manitoba 179/D4
Long (isl.), Martinique 161/D6
Long (isl.), Mass. 249/E7
Long (pond), Mass. 249/L5
Long (pt.), Mass. 249/O4
Long (lake), Mich. 250/F3
Long (lake), Minn. 255/D4
Long (lake), Minn. 255/F3
Long, Miss. 256/C4
Long (valley), Nev. 266/B1
Long (isl.), New Bruns. 170/D3
Long (lake), New Bruns. 170/D1
Long (isl.), Newf. 166/C2
Long (isl.), Newf. 166/D2
Long (lake), Newf. 166/A3
Long (lake), Newf. 166/B3
Long (pt.), Newf. 166/C4
Long (mt.), N.H. 268/E2
Long (beach), N.J. 273/E4
Long (isl.), N.Y. 188/M2
Long (isl.), N.Y. 276/P9
Long (lake), N.Y. 276/M2
Long (isl.), N. Zealand 100/A7
Long (lake), N.C. 281/P5
Long (lake), N. Dak. 282/K6
Long (lake), N. Dak. 282/J4
Long (lake), N. Dak. 282/L2
Long (isl.), Nova Scotia 168/B4
Long (lake), Ontario 177/H5
Long (lake), Ontario 175/C3
Long (pt.), Ontario 177/D5
Long (isl.), Papua N.G. 85/B7
Long (isl.), Papua N.G. 86/A2
Long (creek), Sask. 181/H6
Long, Loch (inlet), Scotland 10/A1
Long, Loch (inlet), Scotland 15/D4
Long (lake), S. Dak. 298/L2
Long (pt.), Tasmania 99/E3
Long (str.), U.S.S.R. 48/S2
Long (pt.), Virgin Is. (U.S.) 161/B4
Long (pt.), Virgin Is. (U.S.) 161/E4
Long (isl.), Wash. 310/A4
Long (lake), Wash. 310/H3
Long (reef), W. Australia 92/D1
Long (lake), Wis. 317/C4
Longa, Angola 115/C6
Longa (isl.), Scotland 15/C3
Longaví, Chile 138/A11
Long Bay, Jamaica 158/K6
Long Beach, Br. Col. 184/E5
Long Beach, Calif. 146/F6
Long Beach, Calif. 188/C4
Long Beach, Calif. 204/C11
Long Beach (pen.), Conn. 210/C4
Long Beach, Ind. 227/D1
Long Beach, Minn. 255/C5
Long Beach, Miss. 256/F10
Long Beach (isl.), N.J. 273/E4
Long Beach, N.Y. 276/R7
Long Beach, N.C. 281/N7

402 Lozovaya

Lozovaya, U.S.S.R. 52/E5
Lua (riv.), Zaire 115/C3
Luacano, Angola 115/D6
Lualaba (riv.), Zaire 102/E5
Lualaba (riv.), Zaire 115/E4
Lu'an, China 77/J5
Luana, Iowa 229/K2
Luana (pt.), Jamaica 158/G6
Luanchuan, China 77/H5
Luanda (prov.), Angola 115/B5
Luanda (cap.), Angola 2/K6
Luanda (cap.), Angola 115/B5
Luanda (cap.), Angola 102/D5
Luang, Thale (lag.), Thailand 72/D6
Luang (mt.), Thailand 72/C5
Luang Prabang (Louangphrabang), Laos 72/D3
Luangwa, Zambia 115/E7
Luangwa, Zambia 118/D3
Luangwa (Feira), Zambia 115/E7
Luangwa (riv.), Zambia 115/F6
Luanshya, Zambia 115/E6
Luanshya, Zambia 102/E6
Luapula (riv.), Zaire 115/E6
Luapula (riv.), Zambia 115/E6
Luarca, Spain 33/C1
Luashi, Zaire 115/D6
Luau, Angola 115/D6
Luba, Equat. Guinea 115/A3
Lubaczów, Poland 47/F3
Lubań, Poland 47/B3
Lubāna (lake), U.S.S.R. 53/D2
Lubang, Philippines 82/C4
Lubang (isls.), Philippines 85/F3
Lubang (isls.), Philippines 82/B4
Lubango, Angola 115/B6
Lubango, Angola 102/D6
Lubartów, Poland 47/F3
Lubawa, Poland 47/D2
Lübben, Germany 22/E3
Lübbenau, Germany 22/F3
Lubbock (co.), Texas 303/C4
Lubbock, Texas 146/H6
Lubbock, Texas 303/C4
Lubbock, Texas 188/F4
Lubec, Maine 243/K6
Lubec•, Maine 243/K6
Lübeck, Germany 7/E3
Lübeck, Germany 22/D2
Lubeck, W. Va. 312/C4
Lubefu, Zaire 115/D4
Lubero, Zaire 115/E4
L'ubica, Czech. 41/F2
Lubicon (lake), Alberta 182/C1
Lubien Kujawski, Poland 47/D2
Lubilash (riv.), Zaire 115/D5
Lublin (prov.), Poland 47/F3
Lubin, Poland 47/C3
Lublin, Poland 47/F3
Lublin, Poland 7/G3
Lublin, Wis. 317/E5
Lubliniec, Poland 47/D3
Lubny, U.S.S.R. 52/D4
Luboń, Poland 47/C2
Lubrín, Spain 33/F4
Lubsko, Poland 47/B3
Lubuagan, Philippines 82/C2
Lubudi, Zaire 115/E5
Lubuklinggau, Indonesia 85/C6
Lubuksikaping, Indonesia 85/B5
Lubumbashi, Zaire 2/L6
Lubumbashi, Zaire 115/E6
Lubumbashi, Zaire 102/E6
Lubutu, Zaire 115/E4
Lübz, Germany 22/D2
Lucama, N.C. 281/N3
Lucan, Minn. 255/C6
Lucan, Ontario 177/C4
Luc An Chau, Vietnam 72/E2
Lucan-Doddsborough, Ireland 17/J5
Lucapa, Angola 114/D5
Lucas (co.), Iowa 229/G6
Lucas, Iowa 229/G6
Lucas, Kansas 232/D2
Lucas, Ky. 237/K7
Lucas, Mich. 250/D4
Lucas (co.), Ohio 284/C2
Lucas, Ohio 284/F4
Lucas, S. Dak. 298/L7
Lucas, Texas 303/H1
Lucas E. de Peña, Dom. Rep. 158/D5
Lucas González, Argentina 143/G6
Lucasville, Ohio 284/E8
Lucban, Philippines 82/C3
Lucca (prov.), Italy 34/C3
Lucca, Italy 34/C3
Lucca, N. Dak. 282/P6
Luce (co.), Mich. 250/D2
Luce, Minn. 255/C4
Luce (bay), Scotland 10/D3
Luce (bay), Scotland 15/D6
Lucea, Jamaica 158/G5
Lucedale, Miss. 256/G9
Lucena, Philippines 85/G3
Lucena, Philippines 82/C4
Lucena, Spain 33/D4
Lucena del Cid, Spain 33/F2
Lučenec, Czech. 41/E2
Lucens, Switzerland 39/C3
Lucera, Italy 34/E4
Lucerna, Peru 128/H9
Lucerne, Calif. 204/C4
Lucerne, Colo. 208/K2
Lucerne, Ind. 227/E3
Lucerne, Mo. 261/F2
Lucerne, Québec 172/B4
Lucerne (Luzern) (canton), Switzerland 39/F2
Lucerne, Switzerland 39/F2
Lucerne (lake), Switzerland 39/F3
Lucerne, Wash. 310/E2
Lucerne, Wyo. 319/D2
Lucernemines, Pa. 294/D4
Lucerne Valley, Calif. 204/J9
Lucero (lake), N. Mex. 274/C6
Luceville, Québec 172/J1
Luchow (Luzhou), China 77/G6
Lüchow, Germany 22/D2
Lucia, Calif. 204/D7
Lucie (riv.), Suriname 131/C4
Lucien, Miss. 256/C7
Lucien, Okla. 288/M2
Lucile, Georgia 217/C8
Lucile, Idaho 220/B4
Lucile, Ky. 237/P4
Lucinda, Pa. 294/D3
Lucira, Angola 115/B6
Luck, Wis. 317/B4
Luckau, Germany 22/E3
Luckenwalde, Germany 22/E2
Lucketts, Va. 307/N2
Luckey, Ohio 284/D3
Lucknow, India 68/E3
Lucknow, India 54/K7
Lucknow, Ontario 177/C4
Lucky, La. 238/E2
Lucky Lake, Sask. 181/D5
Lucky Peak (lake), Idaho 220/B6
Luçon, France 28/C4
Lucrecia (cape), Cuba 158/J3
Lucy, La. 238/M3
Lucy, Tenn. 237/B10
Lucy Creek, North. Terr. 93/E7
Ludden, N. Dak. 282/O7
Ludell, Kansas 232/B2
Lüdenscheid, Germany 22/B3
Lüderitz, Namibia 118/A5
Lüderitz, Namibia 102/D7
Lüderitz (bay), Namibia 118/A5
Ludhiana, India 54/J6
Ludhiana, India 68/D2
Ludington, Mich. 250/C5
Ludlow, Calif. 204/J9
Ludlow (ridge), England 10/E4
Ludlow, England 13/E5
Ludlow, Ill. 222/E3
Ludlow, Ky. 237/S2
Ludlow•, Maine 243/G3
Ludlow•, Mass. 249/E4
Ludlow, Miss. 256/E5
Ludlow, Mo. 261/E3
Ludlow, New Bruns. 170/D2
Ludlow, Pa. 294/E2
Ludlow, S. Dak. 298/C2
Ludlow, Vt. 268/B5
Ludlow•, Vt. 268/B5
Ludlow (mt.), Vt. 268/B5
Ludlow Center, Mass. 249/E4
Ludlow Falls, Ohio 284/B6
Ludowici, Georgia 217/J7
Luduș, Romania 45/G2
Ludvika, Sweden 18/J6
Ludville, Georgia 217/C2
Ludwigsburg, Germany 22/C4
Ludwigshafen am Rhein, Germany 22/C4
Ludwigslust, Germany 22/D2
Ludza, U.S.S.R. 53/D2
Lue, N.S. Wales 97/E3
Luebbering, Mo. 261/L6
Luebo, Zaire 115/D5
Lueders, Texas 303/E5
Luella, Georgia 217/D4
Luena, Angola 102/D6
Luena, Angola 115/C6
Luepa, Venezuela 124/H5
Lüeyang, China 77/G5
Lufeng, China 77/J7
Lufira (riv.), Zaire 115/E5
Lufkin, Texas 303/K6
Luga, U.S.S.R. 52/C3
Luga, U.S.S.R. 48/D4
Lugano, Switzerland 39/G4
Lugano (lake), Switzerland 39/H5
Lugansk, U.S.S.R. 48/E5
Lugansk, U.S.S.R. 52/E5
Luganville, Vanuatu 87/G7
Lugareño, Cuba 158/G3
Lugenda (riv.), Mozambique 118/F2
Lugerville, Wis. 317/E4
Lugnaquillia (mt.), Ireland 17/J5
Lugo, Italy 34/D2
Lugo (prov.), Spain 33/C1
Lugo, Spain 33/C1
Lugoff, S.C. 296/F3
Lugoj, Romania 45/F3
Luhaiya, Yemen 59/D6
Luiana, Angola 115/D7
Luiana, Angola 102/E6
Luik (Liège), Belgium 27/H7
Luilaka (riv.), Zaire 115/C4
Luimneach (Limerick), Ireland 10/B4
Luimneach (Limerick), Ireland 17/D6
Luina, Tasmania 99/B3
Luing (isl.), Scotland 15/C4
Luís Correia, Brazil 132/F3
Luis de Saboya, Cerro (mt.), Chile 138/F11
Luishia, Zaire 115/E6
Luitpold Coast (reg.) 5/B17
Luiza, Zaire 115/D5
Luján, Argentina 143/G7
Lujiang, China 77/J5
Lukachukai, Ariz. 198/F2
Lukachukai (mts.), Ariz. 198/F2
Luke, Md. 245/B3
Luke A.F.B., Ariz. 198/C5
Lukenie (riv.), Zaire 115/D4
Lukeville, Ariz. 198/C7
Lukolela, Equateur, Zaire 115/C4
Lukolela, Kasai-Oriental, Zaire 115/D5
Lukovit, Bulgaria 45/G4
Łuków, Poland 47/F3
Lukuga (riv.), Zaire 115/E5
Lukula, Zaire 115/B5
Lukulu, Zambia 115/D6
Lula, Georgia 217/E2
Lula, Miss. 256/C2
Lula, Okla. 288/O5
Lule (riv.), Sweden 7/G2
Luleå, Sweden 7/G2
Luleå, Sweden 18/N4
Luleälv (riv.), Sweden 18/M4
Lüleburgaz, Turkey 63/B2
Lules, Argentina 143/C2
Luling, La. 238/N4
Luling, Texas 303/G8
Lulu, Fla. 212/D1
Lulua (riv.), Zaire 115/D5
Lum, Mich. 250/F5
Lumajang, Indonesia 85/K2
Lumajangdong Co (lake), China 77/B5
Lumbala N'guimbo, Angola 115/D6
Lumber (riv.), N.C. 281/L6
Lumber (riv.), S.C. 296/J3
Lumber Bridge, N.C. 281/L5
Lumber City, Georgia 217/G7
Lumber City, Pa. 294/E4
Lumberport, W. Va. 312/F4
Lumberton, Miss. 256/E8
Lumberton, N.J. 273/D4
Lumberton, N. Mex. 274/C2
Lumberton, N.C. 281/L5
Lumberton, Texas 303/K7
Lumberville, Pa. 294/N5
Lumbo, Mozambique 118/G3
Lumbrales, Spain 33/C2
Lumbrein, Switzerland 39/H3
Lumby, Br. Col. 184/H5
Lumding, India 68/G3
Lummen, Belgium 27/G7
Lummi (isl.), Wash. 310/C2
Lummi Ind. Res., Wash. 310/C2
Lummi Island, Wash. 310/C2
Lumphat, Cambodia 72/E4
Lumpkin (co.), Georgia 217/D1
Lumpkin, Georgia 217/C6
Lumsden, Newf. 166/D4
Lumsden, N. Zealand 100/B6
Lumsden, Sask. 181/G5
Lumsden, Scotland 15/F3
Lumsden Beach, Sask. 181/F5
Lumut, Malaysia 72/D6
Luna, Ark. 202/H7
Luna (co.), N. Mex. 274/B6
Luna, N. Mex. 274/A5
Luna Pier, Mich. 250/F7
Luncarty, Scotland 15/E4
Lund, Br. Col. 184/E5
Lund, Idaho 220/G7
Lund, Nev. 266/F4
Lund, Sweden 18/H9
Lund, Utah 304/A5
Lundale, W. Va. 312/C7
Lunda Norte (prov.), Angola 115/C5
Lundar, Manitoba 179/D4
Lunda Sul (prov.), Angola 115/D5
Lundazi, Zambia 115/F6
Lundbreck, Alberta 182/C5
Lundby, Denmark 21/E7
Lundell, Ark. 202/H5
Lunderskov, Denmark 21/C7
Lundi (riv.), Zimbabwe 118/E4
Lunds Corner, Mass. 249/L6
Lundsvalley, N. Dak. 282/E3
Lundy, England 13/C6
Lundy (isl.), England 10/D5
Lune (riv.), England 13/E3
Lüneburg, Germany 22/D2
Lüneburger Heide (dist.), Germany 22/C2
Lunel, France 28/E6
Lünen, Germany 22/B3
Lunenburg, Mass. 249/H2
Lunenburg•, Mass. 249/H2
Lunenburg, N.S. 162/K7
Lunenburg (co.), Nova Scotia 168/D4
Lunenburg, Nova Scotia 168/D4
Lunenburg (bay), Nova Scotia 168/D4
Lunenburg•, Vt. 268/D3
Lunenburg (co.), Va. 307/M7
Lunenburg, Va. 307/M7
Lunéville, France 28/G3
Lung (riv.), Ireland 17/D4
Lungchen (Longzhen), China 77/L2
Lungdo, China 77/B5
Lungern, Switzerland 39/F3
Lungi, S. Leone 106/B7
Lungleh, India 68/G4
Lungwebungu (riv.), Angola 115/D6
Lungwebungu (riv.), Zambia 115/D6
Luni (riv.), India 68/C3
Luninets, U.S.S.R. 52/C4
Luning, Nev. 266/C4
Lunita, La. 238/C6
Lunsford, Ark. 202/K2
Luocheng, China 77/G7
Luodian, China 77/G6
Luoding, China 77/H7
Luohe, China 77/H5
Luoyang (Loyang), China 77/H5
Luoyang, China 54/N6
Luozi, Zaire 115/B5
Lupeni, Romania 45/F3
Luperón, Dom. Rep. 158/D5
Lupon, Philippines 82/E7
Lupton, Ariz. 198/F3
Lupton, Mich. 250/F4
Lupus, Mo. 261/H5
Luputa, Zaire 115/D5
Luqu, China 77/F5
Luque, Paraguay 144/B4
Luquillo, P. Rico 161/F1
Luquillo, Sierra de (mts.), P. Rico 161/E2
Lurah (riv.), Afghanistan 68/B2
Lurah (riv.), Afghanistan 59/J3
Luray, Kansas 232/D2
Luray, Mo. 261/J2
Luray, S.C. 296/E6
Luray, Tenn. 237/D9
Luray, Va. 307/M3
Lure, France 28/G4
Lurgan, N. Ireland 17/J3
Luribay, Bolivia 136/B5
Lúrio, Mozambique 118/G2
Lúrio (riv.), Mozambique 118/F2
Luristan (Lorestan) (governorate), Iran 66/F4
Lurton, Ark. 202/D2
Lusaka (cap.), Zambia 115/E7
Lusaka (cap.), Zambia 102/E6
Lusaka (cap.), Zambia 2/L6
Lusambo, Zaire 102/E5
Lusambo, Zaire 115/D4
Lusatia (reg.), Germany 22/F3
Lusby, Md. 245/N7
Luseland, Sask. 181/B3
Lushi, China 77/H5
Lushnjë, Albania 45/D5
Lushoto, Tanzania 115/G4
Lushton, Nebr. 264/G4
Lushui, China 77/E6
Lüshun, China 77/K4
Lusk, Ireland 17/J4
Lusk, Wyo. 319/H3
Luss, Scotland 15/A1
Lustenau, Austria 41/A3
Lustre, Mont. 262/K2
Lut, Dasht-e (des.), Iran 59/G3
Lut, Dasht-e (des.), Iran 66/L5
Lüta (Lüda), China 77/K4
Lutcher, La. 238/L3
Lutesville, Mo. 261/M8
Luther, Iowa 229/F5
Luther, Mich. 250/D4
Luther, Mont. 262/G5
Luther, Okla. 288/M3
Luther, Tenn. 237/P8
Luthern, Switzerland 39/E2
Luthersburg, Pa. 294/E3
Luthersville, Georgia 217/C4
Lutherville-Timonium, Md. 245/M3
Lutie, Okla. 288/R6
Luton, England 13/G6
Luton, England 10/F5
Luton, Iowa 229/A4
Lutry, Switzerland 39/C3
Lutsen, Minn. 255/F2
Lutsk, U.S.S.R. 7/G3
Lutsk, U.S.S.R. 52/B4
Lutsk, U.S.S.R. 48/C4
Luttrell, Tenn. 237/O8
Lutts, Tenn. 237/F10
Lutz, Fla. 212/D3
Lützelflüh, Switzerland 39/E3
Lützow-Holm (bay) 5/C3
Luuq, Somalia 115/H3
Luverne, Ala. 195/F7
Lu Verne, Iowa 229/E3
Luverne, Minn. 255/B7
Luverne, N. Dak. 282/P5
Luvua (riv.), Zaire 115/E5
Luwingu, Zambia 115/E6
Luwuk, Indonesia 85/G6
Lux, Miss. 256/F8
Luxembourg 7/E4
Luxembourg (prov.), Belgium 27/G9
LUXEMBOURG 27/J9
Luxembourg (cap.), Luxembourg 27/J9
Luxemburg, Iowa 229/L3
Luxemburg, Minn. 255/D5
Luxemburg, Wis. 317/L6
Luxeuil-les-Bains, France 28/G4
Luxi, China 77/E7
Luxi, China 77/F7
Luxor, Egypt 102/F2
Luxor, Egypt 59/B4
Luxor, Egypt 111/F2
Luxora, Ark. 202/K2
Luz, Brazil 135/D1
Luz (isl.), Chile 138/D6
Luza, U.S.S.R. 52/G2
Luzein, Switzerland 39/J3
Luzern (canton), Switzerland 39/F2
Luzern (Lucerne), Switzerland 39/F2
Luzerne, Iowa 229/J5
Luzerne, Mich. 250/E4
Luzerne (co.), Pa. 294/L3
Luzerne, Pa. 294/E7
Luzhai, China 77/G7
Luzhi, China 77/G6
Luzhou (Luchow), China 77/G6
Luziânia, Brazil 132/E7
Luzilândia, Brazil 132/F3
Lužnice (riv.), Czech. 41/C2
Luzon (isl.), Philippines 2/R5
Luzon (isl.), Philippines 54/O8
Luzon (isl.), Philippines 82/C3
Luzon (isl.), Philippines 85/G2
Luzon (sea), Philippines 82/B4
Luzon (str.), Philippines 82/A2
Luz-Saint-Sauveur, France 28/C6
L'vov, U.S.S.R. 7/G4
L'vov, U.S.S.R. 48/C4
L'vov (Lwów), U.S.S.R. 52/B5
Lyakhov (isls.), U.S.S.R. 4/B3
Lyal (isl.), Ontario 177/C3
Lyallpur (Faisalabad), Pakistan 68/C2
Lyallpur (Faisalabad), Pakistan 59/K3
Lyalta, Alberta 182/D4
Lyatkhovskiye (isls.), U.S.S.R. 48/O2
Lybster, Scotland 10/E1
Lybster, Scotland 15/E2
Lycan, Colo. 208/P7
Lycksele, Sweden 18/L4
Lycoming, N.Y. 276/H3
Lycoming (co.), Pa. 294/H3
Lycoming (creek), Pa. 294/H3
Lydallville, Conn. 210/F1
Lydd, England 13/H7
Lydda, Israel 65/B4
Lydenburg, S. Africa 118/E4
Lydia, Minn. 255/E6
Lydia, S.C. 296/G3
Lydia Mills, S.C. 296/D3
Lydick, Ind. 227/E1
Lyell (mt.), Alberta 182/B4
Lyell (isl.), Br. Col. 184/B4
Lyell (mt.), Br. Col. 184/J4
Lyell (mt.), Tasmania 99/B4
Lyerly, Georgia 217/B2
Lyford, Ind. 227/C5
Lyford, Texas 303/G11
Lykens, Pa. 294/J4
Lyle, Minn. 255/F7
Lyle, Wash. 310/D5
Lyles, Tenn. 237/G9
Lyleton, Manitoba 179/A5
Lyman, Miss. 256/F10
Lyman, Nebr. 264/A3
Lyman•, N.H. 268/D3
Lyman, S.C. 296/C2
Lyman (co.), S. Dak. 298/J6
Lyman, Utah 304/C5
Lyman, Wash. 310/D2
Lyman, Wyo. 319/B4
Lyme (bay), England 13/D7
Lyme (bay), England 10/E5
Lyme•, N.H. 268/C4
Lyme Center, N.H. 268/C4
Lyme Regis, England 13/E7
Lyme Regis, England 10/E5
Lymington, England 10/F5
Lymington, England 13/F7
Lymm, England 13/H2
Lymm, England 10/G2
Lyn, Ontario 177/J3
Łyna (riv.), Poland 47/E1
Lynbrook, N.Y. 276/P7
Lynch, Ky. 237/R7
Lynch, Md. 245/O3
Lynch, Nebr. 264/F2
Lynchburg, Mo. 261/H7
Lynchburg, N. Dak. 282/R6
Lynchburg, Ohio 284/C7
Lynchburg, S.C. 296/G3
Lynchburg, Tenn. 237/J10
Lynchburg, Va. 188/L3
Lynchburg, Va. 146/K6
Lynchburg (I.C.), Va. 307/K6
Lynches (riv.), S.C. 296/H3
Lynch Station, Va. 307/K6
Lynd, Minn. 255/C6
Lynd, Queensland 95/C3
Lyndeborough•, N.H. 268/D6
Lynden, Ontario 177/D4
Lynden, Wash. 310/C2
Lyndhurst•, N.J. 273/B2
Lyndhurst, N.S. Wales 97/E3
Lyndhurst, Ohio 284/J9
Lyndhurst, Ontario 177/H3
Lyndhurst, S. Australia 88/F6
Lyndhurst, S. Australia 94/E4
Lyndoch, S. Australia 94/C6
Lyndon, Ill. 222/D2
Lyndon, Kansas 232/G3
Lyndon, Ohio 284/D7
Lyndon•, Vt. 268/C2
Lyndon, W. Australia 92/A3
Lyndon B. Johnson Nat'l Hist. Site, Texas 303/F7
Lyndon B. Johnson Space Ctr., Texas 303/K2
Lyndon Center, Vt. 268/C2
Lyndon Station, Wis. 317/F8
Lyndonville, N.Y. 276/D4
Lyndonville, Vt. 268/D2
Lyndora, Pa. 294/B4
Lynedoch, Ontario 177/D5
Lyness, Scotland 15/E2
Lyngby, Denmark 21/F6
Lynhurst, Ontario 177/C5
Lynn, Ala. 195/C2
Lynn, Ark. 202/H2
Lynn, Ind. 227/H4
Lynn, Mass. 249/D6
Lynn, N.C. 281/E4
Lynn (co.), Texas 303/C4
Lynn, Wis. 317/F6
Lynn Canal (inlet), Alaska 196/M1
Lynn Center, Ill. 222/C2
Lynn Creek, Miss. 256/G4
Lynndyl, Utah 304/B4
Lynnfield•, Mass. 249/D5
Lynnfield Center (Lynnfield P.O.), Mass. 249/C5
Lynn Grove, Ky. 237/E7
Lynn Haven, Fla. 212/C6
Lynn Lake, Man. 162/G4
Lynn Lake, Man. 146/H4
Lynn Lake, Manitoba 179/H2
Lynnview, Ky. 237/K4
Lynnville, Ill. 222/C4
Lynnville, Ind. 227/C8
Lynnville, Iowa 229/H5
Lynnville, Ky. 237/D7
Lynnville, Tenn. 237/G10
Lynnwood, Wash. 310/C3
Lynton, England 10/E5
Lynton, England 13/D6
Lynwood, Calif. 204/C11
Lynwood, Ill. 222/C6
Lynx (lake), N.W. Terr. 187/H3
Lynxville, Wis. 317/D9
Lyon, France 7/E4
Lyon, France 28/F5
Lyon (co.), Iowa 229/A2
Lyon (co.), Kansas 232/F3
Lyon (co.), Ky. 237/E6
Lyon (co.), Minn. 255/C6
Lyon, Miss. 256/D2
Lyon (co.), Nev. 266/B3
Lyon (inlet), N.W. Terr. 187/K3
Lyon, Loch (lake), Scotland 15/D4
Lyon (riv.), Scotland 15/D4
Lyon Mountain, N.Y. 276/N1
Lyonnais (trad. prov.), France 29
Lyons, Colo. 208/J2
Lyons, Georgia 217/H6
Lyons, Ill. 222/B6
Lyons, Ind. 227/C7
Lyons, Kansas 232/D3
Lyons, Ky. 237/K5
Lyons, Mich. 250/E6
Lyons, Nebr. 264/H3
Lyons, N.J. 273/D2
Lyons, N.Y. 276/F4
Lyons, Ohio 284/B2
Lyons, Oreg. 291/E3
Lyons (Lyon Station), Pa. 294/L5
Lyons, S. Dak. 298/R6
Lyons (riv.), W. Australia 88/B4
Lyons (riv.), W. Australia 92/A4
Lyons, Wis. 317/K10
Lyons Brook, Nova Scotia 168/F3
Lyons Falls, N.Y. 276/K3
Lyons Plain, Conn. 210/B4
Lyon Station, Pa. 294/L5
Lyra (reef), Papua N.G. 86/C1
Lys (riv.), Belgium 27/B7
Lys (riv.), France 28/E2
Lysaker, Norway 18/D3
Lysá nad Labem, Czech. 41/C1
Lysander, N.Y. 276/H4
Lysekil, Sweden 18/G7
Lysite, Wyo. 319/E2
Lyss, Switzerland 39/D2
Lyster, Québec 172/F3
Lys'va, U.S.S.R. 7/K3
Lys'va, U.S.S.R. 48/F4
Lys'va, U.S.S.R. 52/J3
Lytham Saint Anne's, England 13/G1
Lytham Saint Anne's, England 10/F1
Lytle, Texas 303/J11
Lyttelton, N. Zealand 100/D5
Lytton, Br. Col. 184/G5
Lytton, Iowa 229/D4
Lyubertsy, U.S.S.R. 52/E3
Lyubotin, U.S.S.R. 52/E4
Lyudinovo, U.S.S.R. 52/D4

M

Ma'ad, Jordan 65/D2
Maalaea, Hawaii 218/J2
Maalaea (bay), Hawaii 218/J2
Ma'alot-Tarshiha, Israel 65/C1
Ma'an (dist.), Jordan 65/D5
Ma'an, Jordan 65/E5
Ma'an, Jordan 59/C3
Ma'anshan, China 77/J5
Maarianhamina (Mariehamn), Finland 18/M7
Maarssen, Netherlands 27/F4
Maas (riv.), Netherlands 27/G5
Maasbree, Netherlands 27/H6
Maaseik, Belgium 27/H6
Maasin, Philippines 82/E5
Maasmechelen, Belgium 27/H7
Maassluis, Netherlands 27/E5
Maastricht, Netherlands 27/H7
Maatsuyker (isls.), Tasmania 99/C5
Mababe (depr.), Botswana 118/C3
Mabalane, Mozambique 118/E4
Mabank, Texas 303/H5
Mabaruma, Guyana 131/B1
Mabay, Cuba 158/H4
Mabel (lake), Br. Col. 184/H5
Mabel, Minn. 255/G7
Mabelvale, Ark. 202/F4
Maben, Miss. 256/F3
Maben, W. Va. 312/D7
Maberly, Ontario 177/H3
Mabie, W. Va. 312/F5
Mabille (lake), Newf. 166/B3
Mabini, Philippines 82/E6
Mablethorpe and Sutton, England 13/H4
Mablethorpe and Sutton, England 10/G4
Mableton, Georgia 217/J1
Mabote, Mozambique 118/E4
Mabou, Nova Scotia 168/G2
Mabou (harb.), Nova Scotia 168/G2
Mabou Highlands (hills), Nova Scotia 168/G2
Mabrouk, Mali 106/D5
Mabscott, W. Va. 312/D7
Mabton, Wash. 310/E4
Macá (mt.), Chile 138/D5
Macachín, Argentina 143/D4
Macaé, Brazil 135/F3
Macaé, Brazil 132/F8
Macaíba, Brazil 132/H4
Macajalar (bay), Philippines 82/E6
Macalister, Br. Col. 184/F4
Macaloge, Mozambique 118/F2
MacAlpine (lake), N.W. Terr. 187/H3
Macamic, Québec 174/B3
Macan (isls.), Indonesia 85/G7
Macanao (pen.), Venezuela 124/F2
Mação, Portugal 33/B3
Macapá, Brazil 120/D2
Macapá, Brazil 132/D2
Macará, Ecuador 128/C5
Macaranaima, Colombia 126/E7
Macarena, Serranía de La (mts.), Colombia 126/D6
Macareo Santo Niño, Venezuela 124/H3
Macarthur, Victoria 97/A6
Macas, Ecuador 128/D4
Macassar, S. Africa 118/F6
Macau 54/N7
MACAU (MACAO) 77
Macau, Brazil 120/F3
Macau, Brazil 132/G4
Macau (Macao) (cap.), Macau 77/H7

404 Major

Major, Sask. 181/B4
Majorca (isl.), Spain 7/E5
Majorca (isl.), Spain 33/H3
Majorsville, W. Va. 312/F3
Majunga, Madagascar 118/H3
Majuro (atoll) (cap.), Marshall Is. 87/H5
Makaha, Hawaii 218/D2
Makaha (pt.), Hawaii 218/B1
Makah Ind. Res., Wash. 310/A2
Makahuena (pt.), Hawaii 218/C2
Makaiwa, Hawaii 218/H2
Makakilo, Hawaii 218/E2
Makale, Ethiopia 102/F3
Makale, Ethiopia 111/G5
Makallé, Argentina 143/E2
Makanda, Ill. 222/D6
Makanza, Zaire 115/C3
Makapala, Hawaii 218/G3
Makapuu (pt.), Hawaii 218/F2
Makara Beach, N. Zealand 100/A2
Makara-Ohariu, N. Zealand 100/A3
Makari, Cameroon 115/B1
Makaroff, Manitoba 179/A3
Makarov, U.S.S.R. 48/P5
Makarska, Yugoslavia 45/C4
Makar'yev, U.S.S.R. 52/F3
Makassar (Ujung Pandang), Indonesia 85/F7
Makassar (str.), Indonesia 54/N10
Makassar (str.), Indonesia 85/F6
Makatea (isl.), Fr. Poly. 87/L7
Makawao, Hawaii 218/K2
Makaweli, Hawaii 218/B2
Makena, Hawaii 218/J2
Makeni, S. Leone 102/A4
Makeni, S. Leone 106/B7
Makepeace, Alberta 182/D4
Makeyevka, U.S.S.R. 7/H4
Makeyevka, U.S.S.R. 52/E5
Makgadikgadi (salt pan), Botswana 102/E7
Makgadikgadi (salt pan), Botswana 118/D3
Makhachkala, U.S.S.R. 7/J4
Makhachkala, U.S.S.R. 48/E5
Makhachkala, U.S.S.R. 52/G6
Makharadze, U.S.S.R. 52/F6
Makhmur, Iraq 66/C3
Makiki, Hawaii 218/C4
Makin (Butaritari) (atoll), Kiribati 87/H5
Makinak, Manitoba 179/C4
Makinen, Minn. 255/F3
Makinsk, U.S.S.R. 48/H4
Makinson (inlet), N.W. Terr. 187/L2
Makkovik, Newf. 166/C2
Makkovik (cape), Newf. 166/C2
Makkum, Netherlands 27/G2
Makó, Hungary 41/F3
Makokou, Gabon 115/B3
Makoti, N. Dak. 282/G4
Makoua, Congo 115/C3
Maków Mazowiecki, Poland 47/E2
Makran (reg.), Iran 66/M8
Makteir (des.), Mauritania 106/B4
Maku, Iran 66/D1
Makubetsu, Japan 81/L2
Makumbako, Tanzania 115/G5
Makurazaki, Japan 81/O3
Makurdi, Nigeria 102/C4
Makurdi, Nigeria 106/F7
Makushin (vol.), Alaska 196/E4
Makwa, Sask. 181/C2
Makwa (lake), Sask. 181/B1
Makwa (riv.), Sask. 181/B1
Mal, Mauritania 106/B5
Mala, Punta (cape), Panama 154/H7
Malå, Sweden 18/L4
Malabang, Philippines 82/D7
Malabar, Fla. 212/F3
Malabar (hill), India 68/B7
Malabar (pt.), India 68/B7
Malabar Coast (reg.), India 68/C6
Malabo (cap.), Equat. Guinea 102/C4
Malabo (cap.), Equat. Guinea 115/A3
Malabrigo, Argentina 143/F4
Mal Abrigo, Uruguay 145/C5
Malabungan, Philippines 82/A6
Malacca (str.) 54/M9
Malacca (str.), Indonesia 85/C5
Malacca (Melaka), Malaysia 72/D7
Malacca (str.), Malaysia 72/D7
Malacky, Czech. 41/D2
Malad (riv.), Idaho 220/F7
Malad, India 68/B6
Malad (creek), India 68/B7
Malad (riv.), Utah 304/B1
Malad City, Idaho 220/F7
Maladers, Switzerland 39/J3
Málaga, Colombia 126/D4
Malaga, N.J. 273/C4
Malaga, N. Mex. 274/E6
Malaga, Ohio 284/H6
Málaga (prov.), Spain 33/D4
Málaga, Spain 7/D5
Málaga, Spain 33/D4
Malaga, Wash. 310/E3
Malagash, Nova Scotia 168/E3
Malagash (pt.), Nova Scotia 168/E3
Malagón, Spain 33/E3
Malagueta (bay), Cuba 158/H3
Malahide, Ireland 17/J5
Malaita (isl.), Solomon Is. 86/E3
Malaita (isl.), Solomon Is. 87/G6
Malakal, Sudan 111/F6
Malakal, Sudan 102/F4
Malakanagiri, India 68/E5
Malakand, Pakistan 68/C2
Malakand, Pakistan 59/K3
Malakoff, France 28/A2
Malakoff, Texas 303/H5
Malakwa, Br. Col. 184/H5
Malalag, Philippines 82/E7
Malamir (Izeh), Iran 66/F5
Malang, Indonesia 54/N10
Malang, Indonesia 85/K2
Malangka (cape), Indonesia 85/G5
Malanje (prov.), Angola 115/C6
Malanje, Angola 102/D5
Malanje, Angola 115/C5
Malans, Switzerland 39/J3
Malanville, Benin 106/E6
Mälaren (lake), Sweden 18/G1
Malargüe, Argentina 120/C6
Malargüe, Argentina 143/C4
Malartic, Québec 174/B3
Malaspina (glac.), Alaska 196/K3
Malaspina (str.), Br. Col. 184/J2
Malatya (prov.), Turkey 63/H3
Malatya, Turkey 59/C2
Malatya, Turkey 54/E6
Malatya, Turkey 63/H3
Malawi 2/L6
Malawi 102/F6
MALAWI 115/F6
Malawi (Nyasa) (lake), Malawi 115/F6
Malay (pen.), Malaysia 72/D6
Malay (pen.), Malaysia 85/B4
Malay (pen.), Thailand 72/D6
MALAYA, MALAYSIA 72
Malaya (reg.), Malaysia 54/M9
Malaya (West Malaysia) (reg.), Malaysia 72/E6
Malaya Vishera, U.S.S.R. 52/D3
Malaybalay, Philippines 82/E6
Malayer, Iran 66/F3
Malaysia 2/Q5
Malaysia 54/M9
MALAYSIA 85/D4
Malazgirt, Turkey 63/K3
Malbaie (riv.), Québec 172/G2
Malbon, Queensland 95/B4
Malbork (Marienburg), Poland 47/D1
Malchinersee (lake), Germany 22/E2
Malchow, Germany 22/E2
Malcolm, Ala. 195/B8
Malcolm, Nebr. 264/H4
Malcom, Iowa 229/H5
Maldegem, Belgium 27/C6
Malden, Ill. 222/D2
Malden, Ind. 227/C2
Malden (isl.), Kiribati 87/L6
Malden, Mass. 249/D6
Malden, Mo. 261/M9
Malden, New Bruns. 170/G2
Malden, Wash. 310/H3
Malden, W. Va. 312/C6
Maldives 2/N5
MALDIVES 68
Maldives 54/J9
Maldives (isls.) 68/C7
Maldon, England 10/G5
Maldon, England 13/H6
Maldon, Victoria 97/C5
Maldonado (pt.), Mexico 150/K8
Maldonado (dept.), Uruguay 145/E5
Maldonado, Uruguay 145/D6
Male (cap.), Maldives 54/J9
Male (cap.), Maldives 2/N5
Maléa (cape), Greece 45/F7
Malebo (Stanley Pool) (lake), Zaire 115/C4
Malegaon, India 54/J7
Malegaon, India 68/C4
Malekula (isl.), Vanuatu 87/G7
Malema, Mozambique 118/F2
Malemba-Nkulu, Zaire 115/E5
Malente, Germany 22/D1
Maler Kotla, India 68/D2
Malesus, Tenn. 237/D9
Malgobek, U.S.S.R. 52/F6
Malhão da Estrela (mt.), Portugal 33/C2
Malheur (co.), Oreg. 291/K4
Malheur (lake), Oreg. 188/C2
Malheur (lake), Oreg. 291/J4
Malheur (riv.), Oreg. 291/J4
Mali 2/J5
Mali 102/B2
MALI 106/D5
Mali (riv.), Burma 72/C1
Mali, Guinea 106/B6
Malibu, Calif. 204/B10
Malignant Cove, Nova Scotia 168/F3
Maligne (lake), Alberta 182/B3
Mali Kyun (isl.), Burma 72/C4
Malili, Indonesia 85/G6
Malin, Ireland 17/G1
Malin (head), Ireland 17/F1
Malin (head), Ireland 10/C3
Malin, Oreg. 291/T2
Malin, U.S.S.R. 52/C4
Malinau, Indonesia 85/F5
Malindang (mt.), Philippines 82/D6
Malindi, Kenya 102/B2
Malindi, Kenya 115/H4
Malines (Mechelen), Belgium 27/F6
Malinta, Ohio 284/B3
Malita, Philippines 82/E7
Maliwun, Burma 72/C5
Malkapur, India 68/D4
Malkara, Turkey 63/B2
Malkiya, Israel 65/D1
Malko Tŭrnovo, Bulgaria 45/H4
Mallacoota, Victoria 97/E5
Mallaig, Alberta 182/E2
Mallaig, Scotland 10/D2
Mallaig, Scotland 15/C4
Mallanganee, N.S. Wales 97/G1
Mallard, Iowa 229/D3
Mallawi, Egypt 111/J4
Mallawi, Egypt 59/B4
Mallén, Spain 33/F2
Malleray, Switzerland 39/D2
Mallet Creek, Ohio 284/G3
Malling, Denmark 21/D5
Mallnitz, Austria 41/B3
Malloa, Chile 138/G5
Malloch (cape), N.W. Terr. 187/H2
Mallorca (Majorca) (isl.), Spain 33/H3
Mallory, N.Y. 276/H4
Mallory, W. Va. 312/C7
Mallorytown, Ontario 177/J3
Mallow, Ireland 17/D7
Mallow, Ireland 10/B4
Malmanoury, Fr. Guiana 131/E3
Malmberget, Sweden 18/M3
Malmédy, Belgium 27/J8
Malmesbury, England 13/E6
Malmesbury, S. Africa 118/B6
Malmköping, Sweden 18/F1
Malmo, Minn. 255/E4
Malmo, Nebr. 264/H3
Malmö, Sweden 18/H9
Malmöhus (co.), Sweden 18/H9
Malmok (mt.), Neth. Ant. 161/E8
Malmstrom A.F.B., Mont. 262/E3
Malo, Wash. 310/G2
Maloca, Brazil 132/C4
Maloca, Brazil 120/D3
Maloelap (atoll), Marshall Is. 87/H5
Malolos, Philippines 82/C3
Malone, Fla. 212/A1
Malone, Ky. 237/P5
Malone, N.Y. 276/M1
Malone, Texas 303/H6
Malone, Wash. 310/B4
Maloneton, Ky. 237/R3
Maloney (res.), Nebr. 264/D3
Malonton, Manitoba 179/E4
Malott, Wash. 310/F2
Maloy, Iowa 229/E7
Malpartida de Cáceres, Spain 33/C3
Malpartida de Plasencia, Spain 33/C2
Malpelo (isl.), Colombia 120/A2
Malpeque (bay), Pr. Edward I. 168/E2
Malta 2/K4
Malta 7/F5
MALTA 34
Malta, Colo. 208/G4
Malta, Idaho 220/E7
Malta, Ill. 222/E2
Malta (chan.), Italy 34/E6
Malta (isl.), Malta 34/E7
Malta, Mont. 262/J2
Malta, Ohio 284/G6
Malta Bend, Mo. 261/F4
Maltahöhe, Namibia 118/B4
Maltepe, Turkey 63/D6
Malters, Switzerland 39/F2
Malton, England 13/G3
Malton, England 10/F3
Maltrata, Mexico 150/O2
Malung, Sweden 18/H6
Malvaglia, Switzerland 39/H4
Malvan, India 68/C5
Malvern, Ala. 195/G8
Malvern, Ark. 202/E5
Malvern, England 13/E5
Malvern, England 10/E4
Malvern, Iowa 229/B7
Malvern, Jamaica 158/H6
Malvern, Ohio 284/H4
Malvern, Pa. 294/L5
Malvern, Victoria 88/L7
Malvern, Victoria 97/J5
Malverne, N.Y. 276/R7
Malvina, Miss. 256/C3
Malvinas (Falkland) (isls.), 143/D7
Malyye Karmakuly, U.S.S.R. 52/H1
Mama, U.S.S.R. 48/M4
Mamala (bay), Hawaii 218/B4
Mamalu (bay), Hawaii 218/K3
Mamanguape, Brazil 132/H4
Mamaroneck, N.Y. 276/P7
Mambahenauhan (isl.), Philippines 82/B7
Mambajao, Philippines 82/E6
Mambasa, Zaire 115/E3
Mamberamo (riv.), Indonesia 85/K6
Mambrui, Kenya 115/H4
Mamburao, Philippines 82/C4
Ma-Me-O Beach, Alberta 182/D3
Mamer, Luxembourg 27/H9
Mamers, France 28/D3
Mamers, N.C. 281/L4
Mamfé, Cameroon 115/A2
Mamie, N.C. 281/T2
Mamiña, Chile 138/B2
Mammoth, Ariz. 198/E6
Mammoth, Utah 304/B4
Mammoth (creek), Utah 304/B6
Mammoth, W. Va. 312/D6
Mammoth Cave Nat'l Park, Ky. 237/J6
Mammoth Hot Springs (Yellowstone Nat'l Park), Wyo. 319/B1
Mammoth Lakes, Calif. 204/G6
Mammoth Spring, Ark. 202/G1
Mamoré (riv.), Bolivia 120/C4
Mamoré (riv.), Bolivia 136/C2
Mamou, Guinea 106/B6
Mamou, La. 238/F5
Mampong, Ghana 106/D7
Mamry, Jezioro (lake), Poland 47/E1
Mamuju, Indonesia 85/F6
Man (isl.), I. of Man 13/C3
Man, Ivory Coast 106/C7
Man, Ivory Coast 102/B4
Man, W. Va. 312/C7
Mana, Fr. Guiana 131/E3
Mana (riv.), Fr. Guiana 131/E3
Mana (isl.), N. Zealand 100/B2
Manabí (prov.), Ecuador 128/B3
Manacacias (riv.), Colombia 126/D6
Manacapuru, Brazil 120/C3
Manacapuru, Brazil 132/H9
Manacas, Cuba 158/E1
Manacle (pt.), England 13/C7
Manacor, Spain 33/H3
Manado, Indonesia 54/O9
Manado, Indonesia 85/G5
Manage, Belgium 27/E7
Managua (cap.), Nic. 146/K8
Managua (cap.), Nicaragua 154/D4
Managua (lake), Nicaragua 154/E4
Manah, Oman 59/G5
Manahawkin, N.J. 273/E4
Manaia, N. Zealand 100/E3
Manakara, Madagascar 118/H4
Manakara, Madagascar 102/G7
Manakha, Yemen 59/D6
Manakin-Sabot, Va. 307/N5
Manalapan, N.J. 273/E3
Manama (cap.), Bahrain 59/F4
Manana (isl.), Hawaii 218/F2
Mananara, Madagascar 118/J3
Mananara (riv.), Madagascar 118/H4
Mananbao (riv.), Madagascar 118/G3
Mananjary, Madagascar 118/H4
Mananjary, Madagascar 102/G7
Manannah, Minn. 255/D5
Manapire (riv.), Venezuela 124/E3
Manapouri (lake), N. Zealand 100/A6
Manaqil, Sudan 59/B7
Manar, Jebel (mt.), Yemen 59/D7
Manare, Colombia 126/E4
Manas, China 77/C3
Manas He (riv.), China 77/C3
Manas Hu (lake), China 77/C2
Manasquan, N.J. 273/E3
Manasquan (riv.), N.J. 273/E3
Manassa, Colo. 208/H8
Manassas, Georgia 217/H6
Manassas (I.C.), Va. 307/O3
Manassas Nat'l Battlefield Park, Va. 307/O3
Manassas Park (I.C.), Va. 307/O3
Manatee (co.), Fla. 212/D4
Manatee (riv.), Fla. 212/D4
Manatí, Cuba 158/H3
Manatí, P. Rico 156/G1
Manatí, P. Rico 161/C1
Manaus, Brazil 2/F6
Manaus, Brazil 120/D3
Manaus, Brazil 132/H9
Manavgat, Turkey 63/D4
Manawa, Wis. 317/J7
Manay, Philippines 82/F7
Mancelona, Mich. 250/E4
Mancha, La (reg.), Spain 33/E3
Manchac (passage), La. 238/N2
Manchaca, Texas 303/G7
Mancha Real, Spain 33/E4
Manchaug, Mass. 249/G4
Manche (dept.), France 28/C3
Manche, La (English) (chan.), France 28/B3
Manchester, Ala. 195/D3
Manchester, Calif. 204/B5
Manchester, Conn. 210/E1
Manchester•, Conn. 210/E1
Manchester, Greater (co.), England 13/H2
Manchester, England 7/D3
Manchester, England 10/G2
Manchester, England 13/H2
Manchester, Georgia 217/C5
Manchester, Ill. 222/C4
Manchester, Ind. 227/H6
Manchester, Iowa 229/L3
Manchester, Kansas 232/E2
Manchester, Ky. 237/O6
Manchester•, Maine 243/D7
Manchester, Md. 245/L2
Manchester, Mich. 250/E6
Manchester, Minn. 255/E7
Manchester, Mo. 261/O3
Manchester, N.H. 188/M2
Manchester, N.H. 268/E6
Manchester, N.Y. 276/F5
Manchester, Ohio 284/C8
Manchester, Okla. 288/L1
Manchester, Pa. 294/J5
Manchester, S. Dak. 298/O5
Manchester, Tenn. 237/J10
Manchester, Vt. 268/A5
Manchester•, Vt. 268/A5
Manchester, Wash. 310/A2
Manchester, Wis. 317/J8
Manchester-by-the-Sea•, Mass. 249/F5
Manchester Center, Vt. 268/A5
Manchioneal, Jamaica 158/K6
Manchouli (Manzhouli), China 77/J2
Máncora, Peru 128/B5
Mancos, Colo. 208/C8
Mancos (riv.), Colo. 208/B8
Manda, Tanzania 115/F6
Mandabe, Madagascar 118/G4
Mandah, Mongolia 77/G3
Mandal, Norway 18/E7
Mandalay (div.), Burma 72/B2
Mandalay, Burma 54/L7
Mandalay, Burma 72/C2
Mandalgovĭ, Mongolia 77/G2
Mandali, Iraq 66/D4
Mandal-Ovoo, Mongolia 77/F3
Mandalya (gulf), Turkey 63/B4
Mandan, N. Dak. 188/F1
Mandan, N. Dak. 282/J6
Mandaon, Philippines 82/D4
Mandar (cape), Indonesia 85/F6
Mandaree, N. Dak. 282/E4
Mandaue, Philippines 82/E5
Mandeb, Bab el (str.), Saudi Arabia 59/D7
Mandeb, Bab el (str.), Yemen 59/D7
Mandera, Kenya 115/H3
Manderson, S. Dak. 298/D7
Manderson, Wyo. 319/E1
Mandeville, Ark. 202/C7
Mandeville, Jamaica 158/H6
Mandeville, La. 238/L6
Mandi, India 68/D2
Mandié, Mozambique 118/E3
Mandimba, Mozambique 118/F2
Mandinga, Panama 154/H6
Mandioré (lag.), Bolivia 136/F6
Mandla, India 68/E4
Mándok, Hungary 41/G2
Mandritsara, Madagascar 118/H3
Mand Rud (riv.), Iran 59/F4
Mand Rud (riv.), Iran 66/G6
Mandsaur, India 68/C4
Mandurah, W. Australia 88/B3
Mandurah, W. Australia 92/A2
Manduria, Italy 34/F4
Mandvi, India 68/B4
Manele (bay), Hawaii 218/H2
Manele Bay, Hawaii 218/H2
Manendragarh, India 68/E4
Manes, Mo. 261/H8
Manfalût, Egypt 111/J4
Manfalût, Egypt 59/B4
Manfred, N. Dak. 282/L4
Manfredonia, Italy 34/F4
Manfredonia (gulf), Italy 34/F4
Manga, Brazil 132/E6
Manga, Uruguay 145/B7
Mangai, Zaire 115/C4
Mangaia (isl.), Cook Is. 87/L8
Mangakino, N. Zealand 100/E3
Mangalia, Romania 45/J4
Mangalore, India 54/J8
Mangalore, India 68/C6
Mangareva (isl.), Fr. Poly. 87/N8
Mangaweka, N. Zealand 100/E3
Mangere (isl.), N. Zealand 100/E7
Mangerton (mt.), Ireland 17/C8
Mangham, La. 238/G2
Mangkalihat (cape), Indonesia 85/F5
Manglaralto, Ecuador 128/B3
Mangle (pt.), Cuba 158/J3
Manglillo (pt.), P. Rico 161/B3
Mangnai, China 77/D4
Mango, Fla. 212/D4
Mango, Togo 106/E6
Mangochi, Malawi 115/G6
Mangoky (riv.), Madagascar 102/G7
Mangoky (riv.), Madagascar 118/G4
Mangole (isl.), Indonesia 85/H6
Mangonui, N. Zealand 100/D1
Mangoro (riv.), Madagascar 118/H3
Mangotsfield, England 10/E5
Mangotsfield, England 13/E6
Mangrol, India 68/B4
Mangsee (isls.), Philippines 82/A7
Mangualde, Portugal 33/C2
Mangueigne, Chad 111/D5
Mangueira (lag.), Brazil 132/D11
Manguera Azul, Uruguay 145/D4
Mangui, China 77/K1
Manguito, Cuba 158/D1
Mangum, Okla. 288/G5
Mangyshlak (pen.), U.S.S.R. 48/F5
Manhan (riv.), Mass. 249/D4
Manhasset, N.Y. 276/P7
Manhattan, Ill. 222/F2
Manhattan, Ind. 227/D5
Manhattan, Kansas 232/F2
Manhattan, Mont. 262/E5
Manhattan, Nev. 266/E4
Manhattan (borough), N.Y. 276/M9
Manhattan (isl.), N.Y. 276/M9
Manhattan Beach, Calif. 204/B11
Manhattan Beach, Minn. 255/E4
Manhay, Belgium 27/H8
Manheim, Pa. 294/K5
Manheim, W. Va. 312/G4
Manhiça, Mozambique 118/E5
Man Hpang, Burma 72/C2
Manhuaçu, Brazil 132/F8
Manhuaçu, Brazil 135/E2
Manhumirim, Brazil 135/E2
Maní, Colombia 126/D5
Maniamba, Mozambique 102/F6
Maniamba, Mozambique 118/F2
Manibridge, Manitoba 179/J2
Manica (prov.), Mozambique 118/E4
Mánica, Mozambique 118/E3
Manicani (isl.), Philippines 82/E5
Manicaragua, Cuba 158/E2
Manicoré, Brazil 120/C3
Manicoré, Brazil 132/H9
Manicouagan (riv.), Que. 162/K5
Manicouagan, Québec 174/D2
Manicouagan (pt.), Québec 172/B1
Manicouagan (res.), Québec 174/D2
Manicouagan (riv.), Québec 174/D2
Manifest, La. 238/G3
Manifold (cape), Queensland 88/J4
Manifold (cape), Queensland 95/D4
Manigotagan, Manitoba 179/F3
Manigotagan (lake), Manitoba 179/G4
Manigotagan (riv.), Manitoba 179/G3
Manigouche, Québec 174/C3
Manihiki (atoll), Cook Is. 87/K7
Maniitsoq, Greenland 4/C12
Manila, Ala. 195/C7
Manila, Ark. 202/K2
Manila (prov.), Philippines 82/C3
Manila (cap.), Philippines 2/R5
Manila (cap.), Philippines 85/G3
Manila (cap.), Philippines 82/C3
Manila (cap.), Philippines 54/N8
Manila (bay), Philippines 82/C3
Manila, Utah 304/E3
Manildra, N.S. Wales 97/E3
Manilla, Ind. 227/F5
Manilla, Iowa 229/C5
Manilla, N.S. Wales 97/F2
Maningrida, North. Terr. 93/C2
Manipa (str.), Indonesia 85/H6
Manipur (riv.), Burma 72/B2
Manipur (state), India 68/G4
Manisa (prov.), Turkey 63/B3
Manisa, Turkey 63/B3
Manisa, Turkey 59/A2
Manistee (co.), Mich. 250/C4
Manistee, Mich. 188/J2
Manistee, Mich. 250/C4
Manistee (riv.), Mich. 250/C4
Manistique, Mich. 250/C3
Manistique (lake), Mich. 250/D2
Manistique (riv.), Mich. 250/C2
Manito, Ill. 222/D3
Manito (lake), Sask. 181/B3
MANITOBA 179
Manitoba (prov.) 162/G5
Manitoba (prov.), Canada 146/J4
Manitoba (lake), Man. 146/H4
Manitoba (lake), Man. 162/G5
Manitoba (lake), Manitoba 179/D4
Manitou, Ky. 237/F6
Manitou, Manitoba 179/D5
Manitou (isl.), Mich. 250/B1
Manitou, N. Dak. 282/E3
Manitou, Okla. 288/J5
Manitou (lake), Ontario 177/C2
Manitou (lake), Québec 172/C3
Manitou Beach, Sask. 181/F4
Manitoulin (terr. dist.), Ontario 175/D3
Manitoulin (terr. dist.), Ontario 177/B2
Manitoulin (isl.), Ontario 162/H6
Manitoulin (isl.), Ontario 175/D3
Manitoulin (isl.), Ontario 177/B2
Manitou Springs, Colo. 208/J5
Manitouwadge, Ontario 177/H5
Manitouwadge, Ontario 175/C3
Manitowaning, Ontario 177/C2
Manitowish, Wis. 317/F3
Manitowoc (co.), Wis. 317/L7
Manitowoc, Wis. 317/L7
Maniwaki, Québec 174/B3
Maniwaki, Québec 172/B3
Manizales, Colombia 126/C5
Manizales, Colombia 120/B2
Manja, Jordan 65/D4
Manja, Madagascar 118/G4
Manjacaze, Mozambique 118/E5
Manjimup, W. Australia 88/B6
Manjimup, W. Australia 92/B6
Mankato, Kansas 232/D2
Mankato, Minn. 188/H2
Mankato, Minn. 255/E6
Mankono, Ivory Coast 106/C7
Mankota, Sask. 181/D6
Manley, Nebr. 264/H4
Manley Hot Springs, Alaska 196/H2
Manlius, Ill. 222/D2
Manlius, N.Y. 276/J5
Manlleu, Spain 33/H1
Manly, Iowa 229/G2
Manly, N.S. Wales 88/L4
Manly, N.S. Wales 97/K3
Manly, N.C. 281/L4
Manly, Queensland 88/L2
Manmad, India 68/C4
Manmanoc (mt.), Philippines 82/C2
Mann (riv.), North. Terr. 93/D2
Manna, Indonesia 85/C6
Mannahill, S. Australia 94/F5
Mannar (gulf) 54/J9
Mannar (gulf), India 68/D7
Mannar, Sri Lanka 68/E7
Mannar (gulf), Sri Lanka 68/D7
Mannargudi, India 68/E6
Mannboro, Va. 307/N6
Männedorf, Switzerland 39/G2
Mannersdorf am Leithagebirge, Austria 41/D3
Manners Sutton, New Bruns. 170/D3
Mannford, Okla. 288/O2
Mannheim, Germany 7/E4
Mannheim, Germany 22/C4
Manning, Alberta 182/B1
Manning, Ark. 202/E5
Manning, Iowa 229/C5
Manning, Kansas 232/B3
Manning (riv.), N.S. Wales 97/F2
Manning, N. Dak. 282/E5
Manning (cape), N.W. Terr. 187/F2
Manning (str.), Solomon Is. 86/D2
Manning, S.C. 296/G4
Manning Prov. Park, Br. Col. 184/G5
Mannington, Ky. 237/G6
Mannington, W. Va. 312/F3
Männlifluh (mt.), Switzerland 39/E3
Manns Choice, Pa. 294/E6
Manns Harbor, N.C. 281/T3
Mannsville, Ky. 237/L6
Mannsville, N.Y. 276/H3
Mannsville, Okla. 288/N6
Mannu (riv.), Italy 34/B5
Mannum, S. Australia 94/F6
Mannville, Alberta 182/E3
Mano (riv.), Liberia 106/B7
Mano (riv.), S. Leone 106/B7
Manoa, Bolivia 136/C1

Markleville 405

Manokin, Md. 245/P8
Manokin (riv.), Md. 245/P8
Manokotak, Alaska 196/G3
Manokwari, Indonesia 85/J6
Manola, Alberta 182/C2
Manombo, Madagascar 118/G4
Manomet, Mass. 249/M5
Manomet (pt.), Mass. 249/N5
Manono, Zaire 115/E5
Manono, Zaire 102/E5
Manor, Georgia 217/G8
Manor, Pa. 294/C5
Manor, Sask. 181/K6
Manor, Texas 303/G7
Manorhamilton, Ireland 17/E3
Manori, India 68/B6
Manori (creek), India 68/B7
Manorville, N.Y. 276/P9
Manorville, Pa. 294/C4
Manosque, France 28/G6
Manotick, Ontario 177/J2
Manouane, Québec 172/C2
Manouane (lake), Québec 174/C2
Manp'o, N. Korea 81/B3
Manquin, Va. 307/O5
Manra (Sydney) (isl.), Kiribati 87/K6
Manresa, Spain 33/G2
Mansa, Zambia 115/E6
Mansa, Zambia 102/E6
Mansalay, Philippines 82/C4
Mansavillagra, Uruguay 145/D4
Manseau, Québec 172/E3
Mansel (isl.), N.W.T. 162/H3
Mansel (isl.), N.W.T. 146/K3
Mansel (isl.), N.W.T. 187/K3
Mansel'ka (mts.), U.S.S.R. 52/C1
Mansfield, Ark. 202/B3
Mansfield•, Conn. 210/F1
Mansfield, England 13/K2
Mansfield, England 10/F4
Mansfield, Georgia 217/E4
Mansfield, Ill. 222/E3
Mansfield, Ind. 227/C5
Mansfield, La. 238/C2
Mansfield, Mass. 249/J4
Mansfield•, Mass. 249/J4
Mansfield, Minn. 255/E7
Mansfield, Mo. 261/G8
Mansfield, Ohio 188/K2
Mansfield, Ohio 284/F4
Mansfield, Pa. 294/H2
Mansfield, S. Dak. 298/N3
Mansfield, Tenn. 237/E8
Mansfield, Texas 303/F3
Mansfield (mt.), Vt. 268/B2
Mansfield, Victoria 97/D5
Mansfield, Wash. 310/F3
Mansfield Center, Conn. 210/G1
Mansfield Depot, Conn. 210/F1
Mansfield Woodhouse, England 13/F4
Mansilla de las Mulas, Spain 33/D1
Manso (riv.), Brazil 132/C6
Manso (riv.), Chile 138/E4
Manson, Ind. 227/D4
Manson, Iowa 229/D3
Manson, Manitoba 179/A4
Manson, N.C. 281/N2
Manson, Wash. 310/E3
Manson Creek, Br. Col. 184/E2
Mansonville, Québec 172/E4
Mansura, La. 238/G4
Manta, Ecuador 128/B3
Manta, Ecuador 120/A3
Manta (bay), Ecuador 128/B3
Mantachie, Miss. 256/H2
Mantador, N. Dak. 282/R7
Mantagao (lake), Manitoba 179/E3
Mantagao (riv.), Manitoba 179/E3
Mantalingajan (mt.), Philippines 82/A6
Mantario, Sask. 181/B4
Mantaro (riv.), Peru 128/E8
Mantas (well), Niger 106/E5
Manteca, Calif. 204/D6
Mantecal, Apure, Venezuela 124/D4
Mantecal, Bolívar, Venezuela 124/F4
Mantee, Miss. 256/F3
Manteigas, Portugal 33/C2
Manteno, Ill. 222/F2
Manteo, N.C. 281/T3
Manter, Kansas 232/A4
Mantes-la-Jolie, France 28/D3
Manti, Utah 304/C4
Mantiqueira (range), Brazil 135/D3
Manto, Honduras 154/D3
Mantoloking, N.J. 273/E3
Manton, Calif. 204/D3
Manton, Mich. 250/D4
Manton, R.I. 249/J5
Mantorville, Minn. 255/F6
Mänttä, Finland 18/O6
Mantua, Ala. 195/C4
Mantua, Cuba 158/A2
Mantua (prov.), Italy 34/C2
Mantua, Italy 34/C2
Mantua•, N.J. 273/C4
Mantua, Ohio 284/H3
Mantua, Utah 304/C2
Mantua, Va. 307/S3
Manturovo, U.S.S.R. 52/F3
Manú, Peru 128/G9
Manú (riv.), Peru 128/G8
Manua (isls.), Amer. Samoa 87/K7
Manuae (atoll), Cook Is. 87/K7
Manuel Benavides, Mexico 150/H2
Manuelito, N. Mex. 274/A3
Manuel Rodríguez (isl.), Chile 138/D10
Manuels, New Bruns. 170/F1
Manuels, Newf. 166/D2
Manui (isl.), Indonesia 85/G6
Manukan, Philippines 82/D6
Manukau, N. Zealand 100/C1
Manukau (harb.), N. Zealand 100/B1
Manulla, Ireland 17/C4
Manumuskin (riv.), N.J. 273/D5
Manunui, N. Zealand 100/E3
Manuripi (riv.), Bolivia 136/B2
Manus (isl.), Papua N.G. 87/E6
Manus (isl.), Papua N.G. 86/A1
Manutuke, N. Zealand 100/F3
Manvel, N. Dak. 282/R3
Manvel, Texas 303/J3
Manville, N.J. 273/D2
Manville, R.I. 249/H5
Manville, Wyo. 319/H3
Many, La. 238/C3
Manyara (lake), Tanzania 115/G4
Manyas, Turkey 63/B3
Manyberries, Alberta 182/E5
Manych-Gudilo (lake), U.S.S.R. 52/F5
Many Farms, Ariz. 198/F2
Manyoni, Tanzania 115/G5
Manzai, Pakistan 59/K3
Manzanar, Chile 138/F2
Manzanares, Spain 33/E3
Manzanares (riv.), Spain 33/F4
Manzanillo, Cuba 158/H4
Manzanillo, Cuba 156/C2
Manzanillo (bay), Dom. Rep. 158/C5
Manzanillo (bay), Haiti 158/C5
Manzanillo, Mexico 150/G7
Manzanillo, Mexico 146/H8
Manzanillo (pt.), Panama 154/H6
Manzanita, Oreg. 291/C2
Manzanita Ind. Res., Calif. 204/J11
Manzano, N. Mex. 274/C4
Manzano (mts.), N. Mex. 274/C4
Manzano (peak), N. Mex. 274/C4
Manzanola, Colo. 208/M6
Manzhouli (Manchouli), China 77/J2
Manzini, Swaziland 118/E5
Mao, Chad 111/C5
Mao, Dom. Rep. 158/D5
Maoke (mts.), Indonesia 85/K6
Maoming (Mowming), China 77/H7
Mapai, Mozambique 118/E4
Mapararí, Venezuela 124/D2
Mapastepec, Mexico 150/N9
Mapes, N. Dak. 282/O3
Mapia (isls.), Indonesia 85/J5
Mapimí, Mexico 150/G4
Mapimí (depr.), Mexico 150/G3
Mapire, Venezuela 124/F4
Mapiri, Bolivia 136/B4
Mapiripán, Laguna (lake), Colombia 126/E6
Maple (peak), Ariz. 198/F5
Maple (riv.), Mich. 250/E5
Maple (lake), Minn. 255/B3
Maple (riv.), Minn. 255/E7
Maple (riv.), N. Dak. 282/O8
Maple (riv.), N. Dak. 282/R6
Maple (creek), Sask. 181/B5
Maple (riv.), S. Dak. 298/M1
Maple, Wis. 317/C2
Maple Bay, Br. Col. 184/K3
Maple Bay, Minn. 255/B3
Maple City, Kansas 232/F4
Maple City, Mich. 250/D4
Maple Creek, Sask. 162/F6
Maple Creek, Sask. 181/B6
Maple Falls, Wash. 310/D2
Maple Grove, Minn. 255/G5
Maple Grove, Ontario 177/F4
Maple Grove, Québec 172/H4
Maple Heights, Ohio 284/H9
Maple Hill, Iowa 229/D2
Maple Hill, Kansas 232/F2
Maple Hill, N.C. 281/O5
Maple Island, Minn. 255/E7
Maple Lake, Minn. 255/D5
Maple Park, Ill. 222/E2
Maple Plain, Minn. 255/F5
Maple Rapids, Mich. 250/E5
Maple Ridge, Br. Col. 184/L3
Maple River, Iowa 229/D4
Maples, Ind. 227/H2
Maples, Mo. 261/J7
Maple Shade•, N.J. 273/B3
Maplesville, Ala. 195/E5
Mapleton, Iowa 229/B4
Mapleton, Kansas 232/H3
Mapleton•, Maine 243/G2
Mapleton, Mich. 250/D4
Mapleton, Minn. 255/E7
Mapleton, N.C. 281/P2
Mapleton, N. Dak. 282/R6
Mapleton, Oreg. 291/C3
Mapleton (Mapleton Depot), Pa. 294/F5
Mapleton, Utah 304/C3
Mapleton, Wis. 317/J1
Mapleton Depot, Pa. 294/F5
Maple Valley, Wash. 310/C3
Mapleview, Minn. 255/E7
Mapleview, New Bruns. 170/C2
Mapleville, Md. 245/H2
Mapleville, R.I. 249/H5
Maplewood, La. 238/D6
Maplewood, Minn. 255/G5
Maplewood, Mo. 261/P3
Maplewood, N.H. 268/D3
Maplewood•, N.J. 273/E2
Maplewood, Ohio 284/B5
Maplewood, Wis. 317/M6
Mapocho (riv.), Chile 138/G3
Mapoon Mission Station, Queensland 88/G2
Mapoon Mission Station, Queensland 95/B1
Maporal, Venezuela 124/C4
Mapos (Amazones), Cuba 158/F2
Mappsville, Va. 307/T5
Mapuera (riv.), Brazil 132/B3
Maputo (city) (prov.), Mozambique 118/E5
Maputo (prov.), Mozambique 118/E5
Maputo (cap.), Mozambique 2/L7
Maputo (cap.), Mozambique 118/E5
Maputo (cap.), Mozambique 102/F7
Maqatin (ruins), Yemen 59/E7
Maqên, China 77/F5
Maqna, Saudi Arabia 59/C4
Ma Qu (Huang He) (riv.), China 77/F5
Maquapit (lake), New Bruns. 170/D3
Maqueda (chan.), Philippines 82/D3
Maquela do Zombo, Angola 102/D5
Maquela do Zombo, Angola 115/C5
Maquereau (pt.), Québec 172/D2
Maquinchao, Argentina 143/C5
Maquoketa, Iowa 229/M4
Maquon, Ill. 222/C3
Mar (mts.), Brazil 120/E5
Mar (range), Brazil 135/C4
Mar, Serra do (range), Brazil 132/E9
Mar (dist.), Scotland 15/F3
Mara, Guyana 131/C3
Mara (reg.), Tanzania 115/F4
Marabá, Brazil 132/D4
Marabá, Brazil 120/E3
Marabahan, Indonesia 85/E6
Marabella, Trin. & Tob. 161/All
Maracá (isl.), Brazil 120/E2
Maracá (isl.), Brazil 132/D2
Maracaibo, Venezuela 124/C2
Maracaibo, Venezuela 120/B1
Maracaibo (lake), Venezuela 120/B2
Maracaibo (lake), Venezuela 124/C3
Maracaju, Brazil 132/C8
Maracas (bay), Trin & Tob. 161/C10
Maracay, Venezuela 124/E2
Marada, Libya 111/C2
Maradi, Niger 106/F6
Maradi, Niger 102/C3
Maragheh, Iran 59/E2
Maragheh, Iran 66/E2
Maragogipe, Brazil 132/G6
Maraira (pt.), Philippines 82/C1
Marajó (bay), Brazil 132/E2
Marajó (est.), Brazil 120/E2
Marajó (isl.), Brazil 120/E3
Marajó (isl.), Brazil 132/D3
Maralal, Kenya 115/G3
Maralinga, S. Australia 88/E6
Maralwexi (Bachu), China 77/A4
Maramag, Philippines 82/E7
Maramec, Okla. 288/N2
Marampa, S. Leone 106/B7
Marana, Ariz. 198/D6
Marand, Iran 59/E2
Marand, Iran 66/D1
Marang, Malaysia 72/D6
Maranguape, Brazil 132/G3
Maranhão (state), Brazil 132/E4
Maranoa (riv.), Queensland 95/C5
Marañón (riv.), Peru 120/B3
Marañón (riv.), Peru 128/E5
Marapanim, Brazil 132/E3
Maras (mt.), Indonesia 85/D6
Maraş, Turkey 59/C2
Maraş (Kahramanmaraş), Turkey 63/G4
Marathon, Fla. 212/E7
Marathón, Greece 45/G6
Marathon, Iowa 229/C3
Marathon, N.Y. 276/J6
Marathon, Ohio 284/C7
Marathon, Ont. 162/H6
Marathon, Ontario 177/H5
Marathon, Ontario 175/C3
Marathon, Texas 303/A7
Marathon (co.), Wis. 317/G6
Marathon, Wis. 317/G6
Maratua (isl.), Indonesia 85/F5
Maravillas, Bolivia 136/B2
Maravillas (creek), Texas 303/A7
Marawi, Philippines 85/G4
Marawi, Philippines 82/E6
Marbach, Switzerland 39/E3
Marbach am Neckar, Germany 22/C4
Marbella, Spain 33/D4
Marble, Ark. 202/C1
Marble, Colo. 208/E4
Marble, Minn. 255/E3
Marble, N.C. 281/B4
Marble (isl.), N.W.T. 162/G3
Marble (isl.), N.W.T. 187/J3
Marble Bar, Australia 87/C8
Marble Bar, W. Australia 88/B4
Marble Bar, W. Australia 92/C3
Marble Canyon, Ariz. 198/D2
Marble Canyon Nat'l Mon., Ariz. 198/D2
Marble City, Okla. 288/S3
Marble Dale, Conn. 210/B2
Marble Falls, Texas 303/F7
Marblehead, Ill. 222/B4
Marblehead•, Mass. 249/E7
Marblehead (neck), Mass. 249/F6
Marblehead, Ohio 284/E2
Marble Hill, Georgia 217/D2
Marble Hill, Mo. 261/N8
Marblemount, Wash. 310/D2
Marble Rock, Iowa 229/H3
Marbleton, Québec 172/F4
Marbleton, Wyo. 319/B3
Marble Valley, Ala. 195/F4
Marburg an der Lahn, Germany 22/C3
Marbury, Ala. 195/E5
Marbury, Md. 245/K6
Marcala, Honduras 154/C3
Marcali, Hungary 41/D3
Marcapata, Peru 128/G9
Marcelin, Sask. 181/E3
Marceline, Mo. 261/F3
Marcell, Minn. 255/E3
Marcella, Ark. 202/G2
Marcella, N.J. 273/E2
Marcelline, Ill. 222/B3
Marcellus, Mich. 250/D6
Marcellus, N.Y. 276/H5
Marcelville, New Bruns. 170/E2
March (riv.), Austria 41/D2
March, England 10/G4
March, England 13/H5
March A.F.B., Calif. 204/E11
Marchand, Manitoba 179/F5
Marche, Ark. 202/F4
Marche (trad. prov.) France 29
Marche (reg.), Italy 34/D3
Marche-en-Famenne, Belgium 27/G8
Marchegg, Austria 41/D2
Marchena (isl.), Ecuador 128/B9
Marchena, Spain 33/D4
Marchfield, Barbados 161/B9
Marchigüe, Chile 138/F5
Marchin, Belgium 27/G8
Mar Chiquita (lake), Argentina 143/D3
Marchwell, Sask. 181/K5
Marco (Marco Island), Fla. 212/E6
Marco (isl.), Fla. 212/E6
Marco, Ind. 227/C7
Marco, La. 238/E3
Marcola, Oreg. 291/E3
Marcona, Peru 128/E10
Marcos Juárez, Argentina 143/D3
Marcus, Iowa 229/B3
Marcus (isl.), Japan 87/F3
Marcus, S. Dak. 298/E4
Marcus, Wash. 310/H2
Marcus Baker (mt.), Alaska 196/C1
Marcus Hook, Pa. 294/L7
Marcy, N.Y. 276/K4
Marcy (mt.), N.Y. 276/N2
Mardan, Pakistan 68/C2
Mardan, Pakistan 59/K3
Mardela Springs, Md. 245/P7
Mar del Plata, Argentina 143/E4
Mar del Plata, Argentina 120/D6
Mardin (prov.), Turkey 63/J4
Mardin, Turkey 59/D2
Maré (isl.), New Caled. 87/G8
Maré (isl.), New Caled. 86/J4
Mareb (riv.), Ethiopia 59/C7
Marechal Deodoro, Brazil 132/H5
Maree, Loch (lake), Scotland 10/D2
Maree, Loch (lake), Scotland 15/C3
Mareeba, Queensland 95/C3
Mareeba, Queensland 88/G3
Mare Island Navy Yard, Calif. 204/J1
Marengo (co.), Ala. 195/C6
Marengo, Ala. 195/C6
Marengo, Ill. 222/E1
Marengo, Ind. 227/E8
Marengo, Iowa 229/J5
Marengo, Ohio 284/E5
Marengo, Sask. 181/B4
Marengo, Wash. 310/G3
Marengo, Wis. 317/E3
Marenisco, Mich. 250/F2
Marennes, France 28/C5
Mareth, Tunisia 106/F2
Marettimo (isl.), Italy 34/C6
Marfa, Texas 303/C12
Marfield, N.S. Wales 97/C3
Marfrance, W. Va. 312/E6
Margai Caka (lake), China 77/C4
Marganets, U.S.S.R. 52/E5
Margao, India 68/C5
Margaree, Nova Scotia 168/G2
Margaree (isl.), Nova Scotia 168/F4
Margaree Centre, Nova Scotia 168/H2
Margaree Forks, Nova Scotia 168/G2
Margaree Harbour, Nova Scotia 168/G2
Margaree Valley, Nova Scotia 168/H2
Margaret, Ala. 195/F3
Margaret (lake), Alberta 182/B5
Margaret, Manitoba 179/C5
Margaret, Texas 303/E3
Margaret (riv.), W. Australia 88/D3
Margaret River, W. Australia 88/A6
Margaret River, W. Australia 92/A6
Margaret River Station, W. Australia 92/D2
Margaretsville, Nova Scotia 168/C3
Margaretville, N.Y. 276/L6
Margarita, Argentina 143/F5
Margarita (isl.), Venezuela 120/C1
Margarita (isl.), Venezuela 124/F2
Margate, England 13/J6
Margate, England 10/G5
Margate, Fla. 212/F5
Margate, S. Africa 118/E6
Margate, Tasmania 99/D4
Margate City, N.J. 273/E5
Margento, Colombia 126/C4
Margerum, Ala. 195/B1
Margherita (Jamama), Somalia 115/H3
Margherita (mt.), Uganda 115/E3
Margherita (mt.), Zaire 102/E4
Margherita (mt.), Zaire 115/E3
Margie, Minn. 255/E2
Margo, Sask. 181/H4
Margos, Peru 128/D8
Margosatubig, Philippines 82/D7
Margow, Dasht-e (des.), Afghanistan 59/H3
Margow, Dasht-e (des.), Afghanistan 68/A2
Margraten, Netherlands 27/H7
Margret, Georgia 217/D1
Margrethe (lake), Mich. 250/E4
Marguerite (bay) 5/C15
Maria (isl.), Fr. Poly. 87/L8
Maria (creek), Ind. 227/C7
Maria, Québec 172/C2
Maria (isls.), St. Lucia 161/G7
Maria (isl.), Tasmania 99/E4
Mari A.S.S.R., U.S.S.R. 52/G3
Mari A.S.S.R., U.S.S.R. 48/E4
María Albina, Uruguay 145/E4
María Cleófas (isl.), Mexico 150/F6
María Elena, Chile 138/B3
Mariager, Denmark 21/D4
Mariager, Denmark 18/G8
Mariager (fjord), Denmark 21/D4
Mariah Hill, Ind. 227/D8
María Madre (isl.), Mexico 150/F6
María Magdalena (isl.), Mexico 150/F6
Marian (lake), Fla. 212/E4
Marian (lake), N.W. Terr. 187/G3
Marian, Queensland 88/H4
Marian, Queensland 95/D4
Mariana, Brazil 135/E2
Mariana Lake, Alberta 182/D2
Marianao, Cuba 158/C1
Marianao, Cuba 156/A2
Marianas, Northern 87/E4
Mariana Trench, Pacific 87/E4
Marianna, Ark. 202/J4
Marianna, Fla. 212/A1
Marianna, Pa. 294/B5
Mariano I. Loza, Argentina 143/G4
Mariano Roque Alonso, Paraguay 144/A4
Mariánské Lázně, Czech. 41/B2
María Pinto, Chile 138/G3
Mariapolis, Manitoba 179/C5
Marias, Islas (isls.), Mexico 150/F6
Marias (riv.), Mont. 188/D1
Marias (riv.), Mont. 262/D2
Maria Stein, Ohio 284/A5
Mariato, Punta (cape), Panama 154/G7
María Trinidad Sánchez (prov.), Dom. Rep. 158/E5
Maria van Diemen (cape), N. Zealand 100/D1
Mariazell, Austria 41/C3
Marib, Saudi Arabia 59/E6
Marib, Yemen 59/E6
Mariba, Ky. 237/O5
Maribel, Wis. 317/L7
Maribo, Denmark 21/E8
Maribor, Yugoslavia 7/F4
Maribor, Yugoslavia 45/B2
Maribyrnong (riv.), Victoria 97/H5
Maribyrnong (riv.), Victoria 88/K7
Maricao, P. Rico 161/B2
Maricopa (co.), Ariz. 198/C5
Maricopa, Ariz. 198/C5
Maricopa (mts.), Ariz. 198/C5
Maricopa, Calif. 204/F8
Maricopa Ind. Res., Ariz. 198/C6
Maricunga, Salar de (salt dep.), Chile 138/B6
Maridi, Sudan 111/E7
Marie (lake), Alberta 182/E2
Marie, Ark. 202/K2
Marie, W. Va. 312/E7
Marie Byrd Land (reg.), Ant. 2/D10
Marie Byrd Land (reg.) 5/B13
Mariefred, Sweden 18/F1
Marie-Galante (isl.), Guadeloupe 161/B7
Marie-Galante (isl.), Guadeloupe 156/G4
Mariehamn, Finland 18/M7
Mariel, Cuba 158/B1
Mariemont, Ohio 284/C9
Marienberg, Papua N.G. 85/B6
Marienburg (Malbork), Poland 47/D1
Mariënburg, Suriname 131/D2
Mariental, Namibia 118/B4
Mariental, Namibia 102/D7
Marienthal, Kansas 232/A3
Marienville, Pa. 294/D3
Marie-Reine, Alberta 182/B1
Maries (co.), Mo. 261/J6
Mariestad, Sweden 18/H7
Marietta, Georgia 217/J1
Marietta, Ill. 222/C3
Marietta, Ind. 227/F6
Marietta, Minn. 255/B5
Marietta, Miss. 256/H2
Marietta, N.C. 281/L6
Marietta, Ohio 284/G7
Marietta, Okla. 288/M7
Marietta, Pa. 294/J5
Marietta-Alderwood, Wash. 310/C2
Marietta-Slater, S.C. 296/C1
Marieval, Sask. 181/J5
Marieville, Québec 172/D4
Marigot, Dominica 161/F6
Marigot, Haiti 158/C6
Marigot, Martinique 161/D5
Marigot, St. Lucia 161/G6
Marigüitar, Venezuela 124/G2
Marihatag, Philippines 82/F6
Marília, Brazil 120/D5
Marília, Brazil 135/A3
Marília, Brazil 132/D8
Marilla, N.Y. 276/C5
Marin (co.), Calif. 204/C5
Marín, Spain 33/B1
Marina, Calif. 204/D7
Marinduque (prov.), Philippines 82/C4
Marinaduque (isl.), Philippines 82/C4
Marine, Ill. 222/D5
Marine City, Mich. 250/G6
Marineland, Fla. 212/E2
Marine on Saint Croix, Minn. 255/F5
Marinette (co.), Wis. 317/K5
Marinette, Wis. 317/L5
Maringá, Brazil 120/D5
Maringá, Brazil 132/D8
Maringouin, La. 238/G6
Marinha Grande, Portugal 33/B3
Marinhas, Portugal 33/B2
Marino, Italy 34/F7
Marion (reef) 95/E3
Marion (co.), Ala. 195/C2
Marion, Ala. 195/D5
Marion (lake), Alberta 182/D3
Marion (co.), Ark. 202/E1
Marion, Ark. 202/K3
Marion, Conn. 210/D2
Marion (co.), Fla. 212/D2
Marion (co.), Georgia 217/C6
Marion (co.), Ill. 222/E5
Marion, Ill. 222/E6
Marion (co.), Ind. 227/E5
Marion, Ind. 188/J2
Marion, Ind. 227/F3
Marion (co.), Iowa 229/G8
Marion, Iowa 229/K4
Marion (co.), Kansas 232/E3
Marion, Kansas 232/F3
Marion (lake), Kansas 232/E3
Marion (co.), Ky. 237/L5
Marion, Ky. 237/E6
Marion, La. 238/F1
Marion, Mass. 249/L6
Marion•, Mass. 249/L6
Marion, Mich. 250/D4
Marion (co.), Miss. 256/E8
Marion, Miss. 256/G6
Marion (co.), Mo. 261/J3
Marion, Mont. 262/B2
Marion, N.Y. 276/F4
Marion, N.C. 281/E3
Marion, N. Dak. 282/O6
Marion (co.), Ohio 284/D4
Marion, Ohio 188/K2
Marion, Ohio 284/D4
Marion (co.), Oreg. 291/E3
Marion, Oreg. 291/D3
Marion, Pa. 294/G6
Marion (res.), Queensland 88/J3
Marion, S. Australia 88/D8
Marion, S. Australia 94/A8
Marion (lake), S.C. 188/K4
Marion (co.), S.C. 296/J3
Marion, S.C. 296/J3
Marion (lake), S.C. 296/G5
Marion, S. Dak. 298/P7
Marion (bay), Tasmania 99/E4
Marion (co.), Tenn. 237/K10
Marion (co.), Texas 303/K5
Marion, Va. 307/E7
Marion (co.), W. Va. 312/F4
Marion, Wis. 317/J6
Marion Bridge, Nova Scotia 168/H3
Marion Center, Pa. 294/D4
Marion Junction, Ala. 195/D6
Marion Station, Md. 245/R8
Marionville, Mo 261/E8
Maripa, Fr. Guiana 131/E4
Maripa, Venezuela 124/F4
Maripasoula, Fr. Guiana 131/D4
Mariposa (co.), Calif. 204/E6
Mariposa, Calif. 204/E6
Mariscala, Uruguay 145/E5
Mariscal Estigarribia, Paraguay 120/C5
Mariscal Estigarribia, Paraguay 144/B3
Marismas, Las (marsh), Spain 33/C4
Marissa, Ill. 222/D5
Maritime Alps (range), France 28/G5
Maritime Alps (range), Italy 34/A2
Maritsa, Bulgaria 45/H4
Maritsa (riv.), Bulgaria 45/G4
Mariupol', U.S.S.R. 52/E5
Mariupol', U.S.S.R. 48/D5
Marivan (Dezh Shahpur), Iran 66/E3
Mariveles, Philippines 82/C3
Märjamaa, U.S.S.R. 53/C1
Mark (riv.), Belgium 27/F6
Mark, Ill. 222/D2
Mark (riv.), Netherlands 27/F6
Marka (Merka), Somalia 116/H3
Marka, Somalia 102/G4
Markam, China 77/E6
Markaryd, Sweden 18/H8
Mark Center, Ohio 284/A3
Markdale, Ontario 177/D3
Marked Tree, Ark. 202/K2
Marken (isl.), Netherlands 27/G4
Markerwaard Polder, Netherlands 27/G3
Markesan, Wis. 317/J8
Market Drayton, England 10/E4
Market Drayton, England 13/E5
Market Harborough, England 13/G5
Markethill, N. Ireland 17/H3
Market Rasen, England 13/G4
Market Weighton, England 13/G4
Markha (riv.), U.S.S.R. 48/M3
Markham (mt.) 5/A8
Markham, Ill. 222/B6
Markham (bay), N.W. Terr. 187/L3
Markham (inlet), N.W. Terr. 187/L1
Markham, Ontario 177/K4
Markham, Va. 307/N3
Markham, Wash. 310/B4
Markinch, Sask. 181/G5
Markinch, Scotland 15/E4
Markit, China 77/A4
Markkleeberg, Germany 22/E3
Markland, Ind. 227/G3
Markland, Newf. 166/D2
Markle, Ind. 227/G3
Markleeville, Calif. 204/F5
Marklesburg (James Creek), Pa. 294/F5
Markleton, Pa. 294/D6
Markleville, Ind. 227/F5

406 Markleysburg

Markleysburg, Pa. 294/C6
Markounda, Cent. Afr. Rep. 115/C2
Markovo, U.S.S.R. 4/C1
Markovo, U.S.S.R. 48/S3
Marks, Miss. 256/D2
Marks, U.S.S.R. 52/G4
Markstay, Ontario 177/D1
Marksville, La. 238/G4
Marktredwitz, Germany 22/E4
Markville, Minn. 255/F4
Marl, Germany 22/B3
Marland, Okla. 288/M1
Marlbank, Ontario 177/G3
Marlboro, Alberta 182/B3
Marlboro•, N.J. 273/E3
Marlboro, N.Y. 276/M7
Marlboro (co.), S.C. 296/H2
Marlboro•, Vt. 268/B6
Marlborough, Conn. 210/F2
Marlborough•, Conn. 210/F2
Marlborough, England 13/F6
Marlborough, England 10/F5
Marlborough, Mass. 249/H3
Marlborough, Mo. 261/P3
Marlborough, N.H. 268/C6
Marlborough•, N.H. 268/C6
Marlborough, Queensland 95/D4
Marlette, Mich. 250/G5
Marlin, Texas 303/H6
Marlin, Wash. 310/F3
Marlinton, W. Va. 312/F6
Marlow, Ala. 195/C10
Marlow, England 13/G8
Marlow, Georgia 217/K6
Marlow•, N.H. 268/C5
Marlow, Okla. 288/K5
Marlton, N.J. 273/D4
Marmaduke, Ark. 202/K1
Marmagao, India 68/C5
Marmande, France 28/C5
Marmara (sea), Turkey 7/G4
Marmara (isl.), Turkey 63/B2
Marmara (sea), Turkey 63/C2
Marmara (sea), Turkey 59/A1
Marmaris, Turkey 63/C4
Marmarth, N. Dak. 282/B7
Mar Menor (lag.), Spain 33/F4
Marmet, W. Va. 312/C6
Marmolada (mt.), Italy 34/C1
Marmontana (mt.), Switzerland 39/H4
Marmora, N.J. 273/D5
Marmora, Ontario 177/G3
Marmot (bay), Alaska 196/H3
Marmot (isl.), Alaska 196/H3
Mar Muerto (lag.), Mexico 150/N9
Marne (dept.), France 28/F3
Marne (riv.), France 28/C2
Marne, Germany 22/C2
Marne, Iowa 229/C6
Marne, Mich. 250/D5
Maro (dry riv.), Chad 111/C4
Maro (reef), Hawaii 188/F6
Maro (reef), Hawaii 218/C6
Maroa, Ill. 222/E3
Maroa, Venezuela 124/E6
Maroantsetra, Madagascar 118/J3
Marolambo, Madagascar 118/H4
Maromokotro (mt.), Madagascar 102/G6
Maromokotro (mt.), Madagascar 118/H2
Marondera, Zimbabwe 118/E3
Maroni (riv.) 120/D2
Maroni (riv.), Fr. Guiana 131/D3
Maroochydore-Mooloolaba, Queensland 88/J5
Maroochydore-Mooloolaba, Queensland 95/E5
Maroon (peak), Colo. 208/F4
Maroon Town, Jamaica 158/H6
Maros (riv.), Hungary 41/F3
Maros, Indonesia 85/F6
Maroua, Cameroon 102/D3
Maroua, Cameroon 115/B1
Maroubra, N.S. Wales 97/K3
Marouini (riv.), Fr. Guiana 131/D4
Marovoay, Madagascar 102/G6
Marovoay, Madagascar 118/H3
Marowijne (dist.), Suriname 131/D4
Marowijne (riv.), Suriname 131/D3
Marquam, Oreg. 291/B3
Marquand, Mo. 261/M8
Marquesas (keys), Fla. 212/D7
Marquesas (isls.), Fr. Polynesia 2/B6
Marquesas (isls.), Fr. Poly. 87/N6
Marquette, Iowa 229/L2
Marquette, Kansas 232/E3
Marquette, Manitoba 179/E4
Marquette, Mich. 146/K5
Marquette, Mich. 188/J1
Marquette (co.), Mich. 250/B2
Marquette, Mich. 250/B2
Marquette (isl.), Mich. 250/E3
Marquette, Nebr. 264/G4
Marquette (co.), Wis. 317/H8
Marquette, Wis. 317/H8
Marquette Heights, Ill. 222/D3
Marquez, Texas 303/H6
Marquis, Grenada 161/D8
Marquis, St. Lucia 161/G6
Marquis, Sask. 181/F5
Marra, Jebel (mt.), Sudan 102/E3
Marra (creek), N.S. Wales 97/D2
Marra, Jebel (mt.), Sudan 111/D5
Marracuene, Mozambique 118/E5
Marrakech, Morocco 102/B1
Marrakech, Morocco 106/C2
Marrawah, Tasmania 99/A2
Marree, S. Australia 88/F5
Marree, S. Australia 94/E3
Marrero, La. 238/O4
Marrickville, N.S. Wales 88/L4
Marrickville, N.S. Wales 97/J3
Marriott, Sask. 181/D4
Marromeu, Mozambique 118/F3
Marrowbone, Ky. 237/K7
Marrowie (creek), N.S. Wales 97/C3
Marrupa, Mozambique 118/F2
Mars, Pa. 294/C4
Mars (riv.), Québec 172/G1
Marsabit, Kenya 115/G3
Marsabit, Kenya 102/F4
Marsa el Brega, Libya 111/D1
Marsa el Hariga, Libya 111/D1
Marsala, Italy 34/D6
Marsa Oseif, Sudan 111/G3
Mars Bluff, S.C. 296/H3
Marsciano, Italy 34/D3
Marsden, N.S. Wales 97/D3
Marsden, Sask. 181/B3
Marsden Park, N.S. Wales 97/H3
Marsdiep (chan.), Netherlands 27/F3
Marseille, France 7/E4
Marseille, France 28/F6
Marseilles, Ill. 222/E2
Marseilles, Ohio 284/D4
Marsh (creek), Idaho 220/F7
Marsh (isl.), La. 238/G7
Marsh (lake), Minn. 255/B5
Marsh, Mont. 262/M4
Marsh (peak), Utah 304/E3
Marshall (co.), Ala. 195/F2
Marshall, Ark. 202/E2
Marshall (co.), Ill. 222/D2
Marshall, Ill. 222/F4
Marshall (co.), Ind. 227/E2
Marshall, Ind. 227/C5
Marshall (co.), Iowa 229/G4
Marshall (co.), Kansas 232/F2
Marshall (co.), Ky. 237/E7
Marshall, Liberia 106/B7
Marshall (isl.), Maine 243/G7
Marshall, Mich. 250/E6
Marshall (co.), Minn. 255/B2
Marshall, Minn. 255/C6
Marshall (co.), Miss. 256/E1
Marshall, Mo. 261/F4
Marshall, N.C. 281/D3
Marshall, N. Dak. 282/F5
Marshall (riv.), North. Terr. 88/F4
Marshall (riv.), North. Terr. 93/D7
Marshall, Ohio 284/C7
Marshall (co.), Okla. 288/N6
Marshall, Okla. 288/L2
Marshall, Sask. 181/B2
Marshall (co.), S. Dak. 298/O2
Marshall (co.), Tenn. 237/H10
Marshall, Texas 188/H4
Marshall, Texas 303/K5
Marshall, Va. 307/N3
Marshall (isls.), U.S. 2/T5
Marshall (co.), W. Va. 312/E3
Marshall, Wis. 317/H9
Marshallberg, N.C. 281/S5
Marshall Hall, Md. 245/K6
Marshall Islands 87/G4
Marshalls Creeks, Pa. 294/M3
Marshallton, Del. 245/R2
Marshalltown, Iowa 229/G4
Marshalltown, Iowa 188/H2
Marshallville, Georgia 217/D6
Marshallville, Ohio 284/G4
Marshes Siding, Ky. 237/M7
Marshfield, Ind. 227/C4
Marshfield, Mass. 249/M4
Marshfield•, Mass. 249/M4
Marshfield, Mo. 261/G8
Marshfield, Vt. 268/C3
Marshfield•, Vt. 268/C3
Marshfield, Wis. 317/F6
Marshfield Hills, Mass. 249/M4
Marsh Hill, Pa. 294/H3
Mars Hill•, Maine 243/H2
Mars Hill, N.C. 281/D3
Mars Hill-Blaine, Maine 243/H2
Marshland, Oreg. 291/D1
Marshville, N.C. 281/J4
Marshy (lake), Manitoba 179/B5
Marshyhope (creek), Md. 245/P6
Marsing, Idaho 220/B6
Marsland, Nebr. 264/A2
Marsoui, Québec 172/C1
Märsta, Sweden 18/K7
Marstal, Denmark 21/D8
Marston, Mo. 261/N9
Marston, N.C. 281/K5
Marstons Mills, Mass. 249/N6
Marstrand, Sweden 18/G8
Mart, Texas 303/H6
Martaban, Burma 72/C3
Martaban (gulf), Burma 54/L8
Martaban (gulf), Burma 72/C4
Martapura, Indonesia 85/F6
Martel, Ohio 284/E4
Martel, Tenn. 237/N9
Martelange, Belgium 27/H9
Martell, Calif. 204/C9
Martell, Wis. 317/B6
Martelle, Iowa 229/L4
Marten (mt.), Alberta 182/C2
Martensdale, Iowa 229/F6
Martensville, Sask. 181/E3
Martha, Ky. 237/R4
Martha, Okla. 288/H5
Martha, Tenn. 237/J8
Marthaguy (creek), N.S. Wales 97/D2
Marthasville, Mo. 261/L5
Martha's Vineyard (isl.), Mass. 188/N2
Martha's Vineyard (isl.), Mass. 249/M7
Marthaville, La. 238/D3
Martí, Camagüey, Cuba 158/G3
Martí, Matanzas, Cuba 158/D1
Martí, Cuba 156/C2
Martigny, Switzerland 39/C4
Martigues, France 28/F6
Martin (dam), Ala. 195/G5
Martin (lake), Ala. 195/G5
Martin, Czech. 41/E2
Martin (co.), Fla. 212/F4
Martin•, Georgia 217/F2
Martin (co.), Ind. 227/D7
Martin (co.), Ky. 237/R5
Martin, Ky. 237/R5
Martin, La. 238/D2
Martin, Mich. 250/D6
Martin (co.), Minn. 255/D7
Martin, New Bruns. 170/E3
Martin (head), New Bruns. 170/E3
Martin (co.), N.C. 281/P3
Martin, N. Dak. 282/K4
Martin, Ohio 284/D2
Martin, S.C. 296/D5
Martin, S. Dak. 298/F7
Martin, Tenn. 237/D8
Martin (co.), Texas 303/C5
Martin, W. Va. 312/H4
Martina Franca, Italy 34/F4
Martinborough, N. Zealand 100/E4
Martín Chico, Uruguay 145/A5
Martinez, Calif. 204/K1
Martinez, Georgia 217/H3
Martínez de la Torre, Mexico 150/L6
Martín García (isl.), Argentina 143/H6
Martinique (isl.) 146/M8
MARTINIQUE 161/D5
MARTINIQUE 156/G4
Martinique (passage), Dominica 161/E7
Martinique (passage), Martinique 161/C5
Martin Luther King, Jr., Nat'l Hist. Site, Georgia 217/K1
Martinsburg, Ind. 227/E8
Martinsburg, Iowa 229/J6
Martinsburg, Mo. 261/J4
Martinsburg, Nebr. 264/H2
Martinsburg, N.Y. 276/J3
Martinsburg, Ohio 284/F5
Martinsburg, Pa. 294/F5
Martinsburg, W. Va. 312/K4
Martins Creek, Pa. 294/M4
Martinsdale, Mont. 262/F4
Martinsdale (res.), Mont. 262/F4
Martins Ferry, Ohio 284/J5
Martins Mills, Tenn. 237/F10
Martins River, Nova Scotia 168/D4
Martinsville, Ill. 222/F4
Martinsville, Ind. 227/D6
Martinsville, Miss. 256/D7
Martinsville, Mo. 261/D2
Martinsville, N.J. 273/D2
Martinsville, Ohio 284/C7
Martinsville (I.C.), Va. 307/J7
Martinton, Ill. 222/F3
Martintown, Ontario 177/K2
Martin Van Buren Nat'l Hist. Site, N.Y. 276/N6
Martinville, Ark. 202/F3
Martinville, Québec 172/F4
Martock, England 13/E7
Martofte, Denmark 21/D6
Marton, N. Zealand 100/E4
Martos, Spain 33/E4
Martre, Lac la (lake), N.W.T. 162/E3
Martwick, Ky. 237/H6
Marty, S. Dak. 298/N8
Marudi (mts.), Guyana 131/B5
Marudi, Malaysia 85/E5
Ma'ruf, Afghanistan 68/B2
Ma'ruf, Afghanistan 59/J3
Maruim, Brazil 132/G5
Marulan, N.S. Wales 97/E4
Marungu (mts.), Zaire 115/E5
Marutea (atoll), Fr. Poly. 87/N8
Marv Dasht, Iran 66/H6
Marvejols, France 28/E5
Marvel, Ala. 195/D4
Marvel, Colo. 208/C8
Marvell, Ark. 202/J4
Marvin, S. Dak. 298/R3
Marvindale, Pa. 294/E2
Marvine (mt.), Utah 304/C5
Marvyn, Ala. 195/H6
Marwayne, Alberta 182/E3
Marwood, Pa. 294/C4
Mary, Ky. 237/O5
Mary (lake), Minn. 255/C5
Mary (riv.), Queensland 95/E5
Mary, U.S.S.R. 54/H6
Mary (Merv), U.S.S.R. 48/G6
Maryborough, Australia 87/F8
Maryborough (Portlaoise), Ireland 17/G5
Maryborough (Portlaoise), Ireland 10/C4
Maryborough, Queensland 95/E5
Maryborough, Queensland 88/J5
Maryborough, Victoria 97/B5
Maryborough, Victoria 88/G7
Marydel, Md. 245/P4
Marydell, Miss. 256/F5
Mary Esther, Fla. 212/B6
Maryfield, Sask. 181/K6
Maryhill, Wash. 310/E5
Mary Kathleen, Queensland 88/G4
Mary Kathleen, Queensland 95/A4
Marykirk, Scotland 15/F4
Maryland 188/L3
MARYLAND 245
Maryland, N.Y. 276/L5
Maryland (state), U.S. 146/L6
Maryland City, Md. 245/L4
Maryland Heights, Mo. 261/O2
Maryland Line, Md. 245/M2
Maryneal, Texas 303/D5
Maryport, England 10/E3
Maryport, England 13/D3
Mary Ronan (lake), Mont. 262/B3
Marys (creek), Idaho 220/C7
Marys (riv.), Nev. 266/F1
Mary's Harbour, Newf. 166/C3
Marystown, Newf. 166/D4
Marysvale, Utah 304/B5
Marysvale (peak), Utah 304/B5
Marysville, Calif. 188/B3
Marysville, Calif. 204/D4
Marysville, Ind. 227/F7
Marysville, Iowa 229/G6
Marysville, Kansas 232/F2
Marysville, Mich. 250/G6
Marysville, Mont. 262/D4
Marysville, Ohio 284/D5
Marysville, Pa. 294/H5
Marysville, Wash. 310/C2
Marytown, W. Va. 312/C8
Maryvale, Queensland 95/C3
Maryvale, Queensland 88/H3
Maryville, Ill. 222/B2
Maryville, Mo. 261/C2
Maryville, Tenn. 237/O9
Marzo (pt.), Colombia 126/B4
Masagua, Guatemala 154/B3
Masahim, Kuh-e (mt.), Iran 66/J5
Masai (steppe), Tanzania 115/G4
Masaka, Uganda 115/F4
Masamba, Indonesia 85/G6
Masan, S. Korea 81/D6
Masardis•, Maine 243/G3
Masaryktown, Fla. 212/D3
Masasi, Tanzania 115/G6
Masatepe, Nicaragua 154/D5
Masaya, Nicaragua 154/D5
Masbate (prov.), Philippines 82/D4
Masbate, Philippines 82/D4
Masbate (isl.), Philippines 82/D4
Masbate (isl.), Philippines 85/G3
Mascara, Algeria 106/D1
Mascarene (isls.), Mauritius 118/F5
Mascarene (isls.), Réunion 118/F5
Mascoma, N.H. 268/C4
Mascoma (lake), N.H. 268/C4
Mascot, Tenn. 237/O8
Mascota, Mexico 150/G6
Mascotte, Fla. 212/E3
Mascouche, Québec 172/H4
Mascoutah, Ill. 222/D5
Masefield, Sask. 181/D6
Masela (isl.), Indonesia 85/H7
Maseru (cap.), Lesotho 102/E8
Maseru (cap.), Lesotho 118/D5
Mash'Abbe Sade, Israel 65/B6
Mashabi (isl.), Saudi Arabia 59/C4
Masham, England 13/F3
Mashapaug, Conn. 210/G1
Mashapaug (lake), Conn. 210/G1
Mashash, Wadi (dry riv.), Jordan 65/C4
Mashhad (Meshed), Iran 66/L2
Mashike, Japan 81/K2
Mashkel, Hamun-i- (swamp), Pakistan 68/A3
Mashkel, Hamun-i- (swamp), Pakistan 59/H4
Mashkid (riv.), Iran 66/N7
Mashkid (riv.), Iran 59/H4
Mashkid (riv.), Pakistan 59/H4
Mashkid (riv.), Pakistan 68/A3
Mashonaland (reg.), Zimbabwe 118/E3
Mashpee•, Mass. 249/M6
Mashulaville, Miss. 256/G4
Masi-Manimba, Zaire 115/C4
Masindi, Uganda 115/F3
Masinloc, Philippines 82/B3
Masío (cay), Cuba 158/C2
Masira (isl.), Oman 54/G7
Masira (gulf), Oman 59/G6
Masira (isl.), Oman 59/G5
Masisea, Peru 128/E7
Masisi, Zaire 115/E4
Masjed Soleyman, Iran 66/F5
Mask (lake), Ireland 17/C4
Mask, Lough (lake), Ireland 10/B4
Maskell, Nebr. 264/H2
Maskinongé (co.), Québec 172/D3
Maskinongé (county), Québec 174/C3
Maskinongé, Québec 172/E3
Maskinongé (riv.), Québec 172/D3
Masoala (pen.), Madagascar 118/J3
Masoller, Uruguay 145/C2
Mason (isl.), Conn. 210/H3
Mason (co.), Ill. 222/D3
Mason, Ill. 222/E5
Mason (co.), Ky. 237/O3
Mason, Ky. 237/M3
Mason (co.), Mich. 250/C4
Mason, Mich. 250/E6
Mason, Nev. 266/B4
Mason (peak), Nev. 266/F1
Mason (bay), N. Zealand 100/A7
Mason, Ohio 284/B7
Mason, Okla. 288/O3
Mason, Tenn. 237/B10
Mason (co.), Texas 303/E7
Mason, Texas 303/E7
Mason (co.), Wash. 310/B3
Mason (co.), W. Va. 312/B5
Mason, W. Va. 312/B4
Mason, Wis. 317/D3
Mason City, Ill. 222/D3
Mason City, Iowa 229/G2
Mason City, Iowa 188/H2
Mason City, Nebr. 264/E3
Mason Hall, Tenn.237/C8
Mason Springs, Md. 245/K6
Masontown, Pa. 294/C6
Masontown, W. Va. 312/G3
Masonville, Colo. 208/J2
Masonville, Iowa 229/K4
Masonville, N.Y. 276/K6
Masqat (Muscat) (cap.), Oman 59/G5
Massa, Italy 34/C2
Massabesic (lake), N.H. 268/E6
Massac (co.), Ill. 222/E6
Massa-Carrara (prov.), Italy 34/C2
Massachusetts 188/M2
MASSACHUSETTS 249
Massachusetts (bay), Mass. 249/M4
Massachusetts (state), U.S. 146/L5
Massacre (bay), Amer. Samoa 86/N9
Massacre (lake), Nev. 266/B1
Massafra, Italy 34/F4
Massakory, Chad 111/C5
Massa Marittima, Italy 34/C3
Massamgo (Forte República), Angola 115/C5
Massangena, Mozambique 118/E4
Massanutten (mt.), Va. 307/L3
Massapê, Brazil 132/G3
Massapeag, Conn. 210/G3
Massapequa, N.Y. 276/R7
Massapequa Park, N.Y. 276/R7
Massaponax, Va. 307/O4
Massawa, Ethiopia 59/C6
Massawa, Ethiopia 111/G4
Massawa, Ethiopia 102/F3
Massbach, Ill. 222/C1
Mass City, Mich. 250/G1
Massena, Iowa 229/D6
Massena, N.Y. 276/L1
Massénya, Chad 111/C5
Masset, Br. Col. 184/B3
Masset (inlet), Br. Col. 184/A3
Massey, Md. 245/P3
Massey, N. Zealand 100/B1
Massey, Ontario 177/C1
Massies Mill, Va. 307/K5
Massillon, Ala. 195/D6
Massillon, Iowa 229/L5
Massillon, Ohio 284/H4
Massinga, Mozambique 118/F4
Massingir, Mozambique 118/E4
Massive (mt.), Colo. 208/F4
Masson, Québec 172/B4
Massueville, Québec 172/E4
Mastaba, Saudi Arabia 59/C5
Mastens Corners, Del. 245/R5
Masters, Colo. 208/L2
Masterton, N. Zealand 100/E4
Mastic Beach, N.Y. 276/P9
Mastuj, Pakistan 59/K2
Mastung, Pakistan 59/J4
Mastung, Pakistan 68/B3
Mastura, Saudi Arabia 59/C5
Masuda, Japan 81/E6
Masurian (lakes), Poland 47/E2
Masury, Ohio 284/J3
Masvingo, Zimbabwe 118/E4
Masyaf, Syria 63/G5
Matabeleland (reg.), Zimbabwe 118/D3
Matachewan, Ontario 177/J5
Matachewan, Ontario 175/D3
Mata de São João, Brazil 132/G6
Matadi, Zaire 115/B5
Matadi, Zaire 102/D5
Matador, Sask. 181/D5
Matador, Texas 303/D3
Matagalpa, Nicaragua 154/E4
Matagami, Québec 174/B3
Matagami (lake), Québec 174/B3
Matagorda (co.), Texas 303/H9
Matagorda, Texas 303/J9
Matagorda (bay), Texas 188/G5
Matagorda (bay), Texas 303/H9
Matagorda (isl.), Texas 303/H9
Matagorda (pen.), Texas 303/J9
Matagorda Isl. Bombing and Gunnery Range, Texas 303/H9
Matakana (isl.), N. Zealand 100/F2
Matala (dam), Angola 115/B6
Matam, Senegal 106/B5
Matamoras, Pa. 294/N3
Matamoros, Mexico 146/J7
Matamoros, Coahuila, Mexico 150/H4
Matamoros, Tamaulipas, Mexico 150/L4
Matane (co.), Québec 172/B1
Matane (county), Québec 174/D3
Matane, Québec 172/B1
Matane, Québec 174/D3
Matane (riv.), Québec 172/B1
Matane Prov. Park, Québec 172/B1
Matanuska (riv.), Alaska 196/C1
Matanza, Colombia 126/D4
Matanzas (prov.), Cuba 158/D1
Matanzas, Cuba 146/K7
Matanzas, Cuba 158/D1
Matanzas, Cuba 156/B2
Matanzas (bay), Cuba 158/C1
Matanzas (inlet), Fla. 212/E2
Mata Palacio, Dom. Rep. 158/F6
Matapalo (cape), C. Rica 154/F6
Matapan (Taínaron) (cape), Greece 45/F7
Matapédia (county), Québec 174/D3
Matapédia (co.), Québec 172/B2
Matapédia, Québec 172/B2
Matapédia (lake), Québec 172/B1
Matapédia (riv.), Québec 172/B2
Mataquito (riv.), Chile 138/A10
Matara, Sri Lanka 68/E7
Mataram, Indonesia 85/F7
Matarani, Peru 120/B4
Matarani, Peru 128/F11
Mataranka, North. Terr. 93/C3
Matarinao (bay), Philippines 82/E5
Mataró, Spain 33/H2
Matatiele, S. Africa 118/D6
Matatindoc (pt.), Philippines 82/D6
Mataura, N. Zealand 100/B7
Mataura (riv.), N. Zealand 100/B6
Mata Utu (cap.), Wallis and Futuna 87/J7
Matawai, N. Zealand 100/F3
Matawan, Minn. 255/E7
Matawan, N.J. 273/E3
Matawin (lake), Québec 172/D3
Matawin (riv.), Québec 172/C3
Mateare, Nicaragua 154/D4
Mateguá, Bolivia 136/D3
Matehuala, Mexico 150/J5
Matelot, Trin. & Tob. 161/B10
Matera (prov.), Italy 34/F4
Matera, Italy 34/F4
Maternillos (pt.), Cuba 158/H2
Mátészalka, Hungary 41/G3
Matetsi, Zimbabwe 118/D3
Mateur, Tunisia 106/F1
Matewan, W. Va. 312/B7
Matfield Green, Kansas 232/F3
Mather, Manitoba 179/C5
Mather, Wis. 317/F7
Mather A.F.B., Calif. 204/C8
Matherville, Ill. 222/C2
Matherville, Miss. 256/G7
Matheson, Colo. 208/M4
Matheson, Ontario 177/K5
Matheson Island, Manitoba 179/E3
Mathews, Ala. 195/F6
Mathews (lake), Calif. 204/E11
Mathews, La. 238/J7
Mathews (co.), Va. 307/R6
Mathews, Va. 307/R6
Mathias, W. Va. 312/J5
Mathinna, Tasmania 99/E3
Mathis, Texas 303/G9
Mathis, Texas 303/G9
Mathiston, Miss. 256/F3
Mathoura, N.S. Wales 97/C4
Mathura, India 68/D3
Mati, Philippines 85/H4
Mati, Philippines 82/F7
Matías Romero, Mexico 150/M8
Matinenda (lake), Ontario 177/B1
Matinicus, Maine 243/F8
Matinicus Rock (isl.), Maine 243/F8
Matlock, England 10/F4
Matlock, England 13/J2
Matlock, Iowa 229/A2
Matlock, Wash. 310/B3
Matoaca, Va. 307/N6
Matoaka, W. Va. 312/D8
Matochkin Shar (str.), U.S.S.R. 48/F2
Mato Grosso (state), Brazil 132/B6
Mato Grosso, Brazil 120/D4
Mato Grosso, Brazil 132/B6
Mato Grosso (plat.), Brazil 120/D4
Mato Grosso, Planalto de (plat.), Brazil 132/B6
Mato Grosso do Sul (state), Brazil 132/C7
Matopos, Zimbabwe 118/D4
Matosinhos, Portugal 33/B2
Matoury, Fr. Guiana 131/E3
Mátra (mts.), Hungary 41/E3
Matrah, Oman 54/G7
Matrah, Oman 59/G5
Matrei in Osttirol, Austria 41/B3
Matruh, Egypt 59/A3
Matsqui, Br. Col. 184/L3
Matsu (Mazu) (isl.), China 77/K6
Matsubara, Japan 81/H8
Matsue, Japan 81/F6
Matsumae, Japan 81/J3
Matsumoto, Japan 81/H5
Matsusaka, Japan 81/H6
Matsuto, Japan 81/H5
Matsuyama, Japan 81/F7
Matsuyama, Japan 54/P6
Matt, Switzerland 39/H3
Mattabesset (riv.), Conn. 210/E2
Mattagami (riv.), Ontario 175/D3
Mattagami (riv.), Ontario 177/J5
Mattamiscontis (lake), Maine 243/F4
Mattamuskeet (lake), N.C. 281/S3
Mattapan, Mass. 249/C7
Mattapoisett, Mass. 249/L6
Mattapoisett•, Mass. 249/L6
Mattaponi, Va. 307/P5
Mattaponi (riv.), Va. 307/O5
Mattaponi Ind. Res., Va. 307/P5
Mattawa, Ont. 162/J6
Mattawa, Ontario 177/F1
Mattawa, Ontario 175/E3
Mattawa, Wash. 310/F4
Mattawamkeag•, Maine 243/G5
Mattawamkeag (lake), Maine 243/G4
Mattawamkeag (riv.), Maine 243/G4
Mattawan, Mich. 250/D6
Mattawana, Pa. 294/G5
Mattawoman (creek), Md. 245/K6
Matterhorn (mt.), Switzerland 39/E4
Mattersburg, Austria 41/D3
Matteson, Ill. 222/B6
Matthew, Ky. 237/P5
Matthews, Georgia 217/H4
Matthews, Ind. 227/F4
Matthews, Mo. 261/N9
Matthews, N.C. 281/H4
Matthews Ridge, Guyana 131/B2
Mattice, Ontario 175/D3
Mattice, Ontario 177/J5
Mattighofen, Austria 41/B2
Mattituck, N.Y. 276/P9
Mattoon, Ill. 222/E4
Mattoon, Wis. 317/J5
Mattson, Miss. 256/C2
Matu, Venezuela 124/F4
Matucana, Peru 128/D8
Matuku (isl.), Fiji 86/Q11
Matún, Cuba 158/D2
Matura, Trin. & Tob. 161/B10
Matura (bay), Trin. & Tob. 161/B10
Maturín, Venezuela 120/C2
Maturín, Venezuela 124/G3
Matutum (mt.), Philippines 82/E7
Matutum (mt.), Philippines 85/G4
Matveyev (isl.), U.S.S.R. 52/J1
Mau, India 68/E3
Maúa, Brazil 135/C3
Mauá, Mozambique 118/F2
Maubeuge, France 28/F2

Meadow Vale 407

Ma-ubin, Burma 72/B3
Mauch Chunk (Jim Thorpe), Pa. 294/L4
Mauchline, Scotland 15/D5
Mauckport, Ind. 227/E8
Maud, Ala. 195/B1
Maud, Ky. 237/L5
Maud, Miss. 256/D1
Maud, Ohio 284/B7
Maud, Okla. 288/N4
Maud, Scotland 15/F3
Maud, Texas 303/K4
Maude, N.S. Wales 97/C4
Maudlow, Mont. 262/E4
Mauerkirchen, Austria 41/B2
Maués, Brazil 132/B3
Maués, Brazil 120/D3
Maués-Açu (riv.), Brazil 132/B4
Maugansville, Md. 245/H2
Mauger (cay), Belize 154/D2
Maugerville, New Bruns. 170/D3
Maui (co.), Hawaii 218/J1
Maui (isl.), Hawaii 87/L3
Maui (isl.), Hawaii 188/F5
Maui (isl.), Hawaii 218/J2
Mauk, Georgia 217/D6
Mauke (isl.), Cook Is. 87/L8
Mauldin, S.C. 296/C2
Maule (reg.), Chile 138/A11
Maule (riv.), Chile 138/A11
Mauléon-Licharre, France 28/C6
Maullín, Chile 138/D4
Maullín (riv.), Chile 138/D3
Maumakeogh (mt.), Ireland 17/C3
Maumee (riv.), Ind. 227/H2
Maumee (bay), Mich. 250/F7
Maumee, Ohio 284/C2
Maumee (bay), Ohio 284/D2
Maumee (riv.), Ohio 284/A3
Maumelle (lake), Ark. 202/E4
Maumere, Indonesia 85/G7
Maumturk (mts.), Ireland 17/85
Maun, Botswana 118/C4
Maunabo, P. Rico 161/ E3
Mauna Kea (mt.), Hawaii 87/L4
Mauna Kea (mt.), Hawaii 188/G6
Mauna Kea (mt.), Hawaii 218/H4
Maunaloa, Hawaii 218/G1
Mauna Loa (mt.), Hawaii 188/G6
Mauna Loa (mt.), Hawaii 188/G6
Mauna Loa (mt.), Hawaii 218/G6
Maunalua, Hawaii 218/F2
Maunawill, Hawaii 218/F2
Maungaturoto, N. Zealand 100/E1
Maungdaw, Burma 72/B2
Maunie, Ill. 222/E5
Maupin, Oreg. 291/F2
Maurepas, La. 238/M2
Maurepas (lake), La. 238/M2
Maurertown, Va. 307/L3
Mauriac, France 28/E5
Maurice, Iowa 229/A3
Maurice, La. 238/F6
Maurice (riv.), N.J. 273/C4
Maurice (lake), S. Australia 88/E5
Maurice (lake), S. Australia 94/B3
Mauricetown, N.J. 273/D5
Mauricio Hirsch, Argentina 143/F7
Maurine, S. Dak. 298/E3
Mauritania 2/J4
Mauritania 102/A3
MAURITANIA 106/B5
Mauritius 2/M6
MAURITIUS 118/G5
Maury, N.C. 281/O4
Maury (co.), Tenn. 237/G9
Maury (riv.), Va. 307/K5
Maury City, Tenn. 237/C9
Mauston, Wis. 317/F8
Mautern in Steiermark, Austria 41/C3
Mauthausen, Austria 41/C2
Mauthen-Kötschach, Austria 41/B3
Mauvoisin (dam), Switzerland 39/D4
Mavaca (riv.), Venezuela 124/F6
Maverick, Ariz. 198/F5
Maverick (co.), Texas 303/D9
Mavila, Peru 128/H8
Mavillette, Nova Scotia 168/B4
Mavinga, Angola 115/ D7
Mavora (mt.), N. Zealand 100/B6
Mavqi'im, Israel 65/B4
Mawai, Malaysia 72/F5
Mawbanna, Tasmania 99/B2
Mawer, Sask. 181/E5
Mawkmai, Burma 72/C2
Mawlaik, Burma 72/B2
Mawlu, Burma 72/C1
Mawson Station, Ant. 5/C4
Max, Minn. 255/D3
Max, Nebr. 264/C4
Max, N. Dak. 282/H4
Maxbass, N. Dak. 282/H2
Maxcanú, Mexico 150/O6
Maxeys, Georgia 217/F3
Maxie, La. 238/F6
Maxie, Miss. 256/F9
Máximo Gómez, Ciego de Ávila, Cuba 158/F2
Máximo Gómez, Matanzas, Cuba 158/D1
Máximo Paz, Argentina 143/F6
Maxinkuckee, Ind. 227/E2
Maxinkuckee (lake), Ind. 227/E2
Maxixe, Mozambique 118/F4
Max Meadows, Va. 307/G6
Maxstone, Sask. 181/F6
Maxton, N.C. 281/L5
Maxville, Mont. 262/C4
Maxville, Ontario 177/K2
Maxwell, Calif. 204/C4
Maxwell, Ind. 227/F5
Maxwell, Iowa 229/G5
Maxwell, Nebr. 264/D3
Maxwell, New Bruns. 170/C3
Maxwell, N. Mex. 274/E2
Maxwell (bay), N.W. Terr. 187/K2
Maxwell, Tenn. 237/J10
Maxwell Air Force Base, Ala. 195/F6
Maxwelton, Queensland 88/G4
May, Idaho 220/E5
May (cape), N.J. 188/M3
May (cape), N.J. 273/C6
May, Okla. 288/G1
May, Isle of (isl.), Scotland 15/F4
May, Texas 303/F5
Maya (mts.), Belize 154/C2
Maya (riv.), U.S.S.R. 54/P4
Maya (riv.), U.S.S.R. 48/O4
Maya Beach, Belize 154/C2
Mayaguana (isl.), Bahamas 146/L7
Mayaguana (isl.), Bahamas 156/D2
Mayaguana (passage), Bahamas 156/D2
Mayagüez (dist.), P. Rico 161/B2
Mayagüez, P. Rico 161/A2
Mayagüez, P. Rico 156/F1
Mayagüez (bay), P. Rico 161/A2
Mayajigua, Cuba 158/F2
Mayáis, Spain 33/G2
Mayarí, Cuba 158/J3
Mayarí Arriba, Cuba 158/J4
Mayaro, Trin. & Tob. 161/B11
Mayaro (bay), Trin. & Tob. 161/B11
Maybee, Mich. 250/F6
Maybell, Colo. 208/C2
Mayberry, Md. 245/K2
Maybeury, W. Va. 312/D8
Maybole, Scotland 10/D3
Maybole, Scotland 15/D5
Maybrook, N.Y. 276/M8
Mayburg, Pa. 294/D2
Maydena, Tasmania 99/C4
Mayen, Germany 22/B3
Mayenne (dept.), France 28/C3
Mayenne, France 28/C3
Mayenne (riv.), France 28/C4
Mayer, Ariz. 198/C4
Mayer, Chile 138/E7
Mayer, Minn. 255/E6
Mayersville, Miss. 256/B5
Mayerthorpe, Alberta 182/C3
Mayes (co.), Okla. 288/R2
Mayesville, S.C. 296/G4
Mayetta, Kansas 232/G2
Mayetta, N.J. 273/E4
Mayfair, Sask. 181/D2
Mayfield, Georgia 217/G4
Mayfield, Kansas 232/E4
Mayfield, Ky. 237/D7
Mayfield (creek), Ky. 237/C7
Mayfield, N.Y. 276/M4
Mayfield, Ohio 284/J9
Mayfield, Okla. 288/G4
Mayfield, Pa. 294/L2
Mayfield, Scotland 15/D2
Mayfield, Utah 304/C4
Mayfield (lake), Wash. 310/C4
Mayfield Heights, Ohio 284/J9
Mayflower, Ark. 202/F4
Mayger, Oreg. 291/D1
Mayhew, Miss. 256/G4
Mayhill, N. Mex. 274/D6
Maykop, U.S.S.R. 7/H4
Maykop, U.S.S.R. 48/D5
Maykop, U.S.S.R. 52/F6
Mayland, Tenn. 237/L8
Maylene, Ala. 195/E4
Maymont, Sask. 181/D3
Maymyo, Burma 72/C2
Mayna, La. 238/G4
Maynard, Ark. 202/J1
Maynard, Iowa 229/K3
Maynard•, Mass. 249/J3
Maynard, Minn. 255/C6
Maynardville, Tenn. 237/O8
Mayne, Br. Col. 184/K3
Maynooth, Ireland 17/H5
Maynooth, Ontario 177/G2
Mayo, Canada 4/C16
Mayo, Fla. 212/C1
Mayo (co.), Ireland 17/C4
Mayo, Md. 245/M5
Mayo (riv.), Peru 128/D6
Mayo (bay), Philippines 82/F7
Mayo, S.C. 296/D1
Mayo, Yukon 187/E3
Mayo, Yukon 162/C3
Mayo (lake), Yukon 187/E3
Mayodan, N.C. 281/K2
Mayon (vol.), Philippines 82/D4
Mayor (isl.), N. Zealand 100/F2
Mayor (cape), Spain 33/E1
Mayor Martínez, Paraguay 144/C5
Mayor Pablo Lagerenza, Paraguay 144/B1
MAYOTTE 118/G2
Mayotte (isl.), France 102/G6
Mayoworth, Wyo. 319/F2
May Park, Oreg. 291/J2
May Pen, Jamaica 158/J6
Mayport Naval Air Sta., Fla. 212/E1
Mayrhofen, Austria 41/A3
Mays, Ind. 227/G5
Maysan (gov.), Iraq 66/E5
Maysel, W. Va. 312/D5
Mays Landing, N.J. 273/D5
Mays Lick, Ky. 237/O3
Maysville, Ark. 202/A1
Maysville, Georgia 217/E2
Maysville, Iowa 229/M5
Maysville, Ky. 237/O3
Maysville, Mo. 261/D3
Maysville, N.C. 281/P5
Maysville, Okla. 288/M5
Maysville, W. Va. 312/H4
Maytiguid (isl.), Philippines 82/B5
Maytown, Ky. 237/O5
Mayumba, Gabon 115/A4
Mayuram, India 68/D6
Mayview, Mo. 261/E4
Mayville, Mich. 250/F5
Mayville, N.Y. 276/A6
Mayville, N. Dak. 282/R4
Mayville, Oreg. 291/G2
Mayville, Wis. 317/K9
Maywood, Calif. 204/C10
Maywood, Ill. 222/B5
Maywood, Mo. 261/J3
Maywood, Nebr. 264/D4
Maywood, N.J. 273/B2
Maywood Park, Oreg. 291/B2
Maza, N. Dak. 282/M3
Mazabuka, Zambia 115/E7
Mazabuka, Zambia 102/E6
Mazagan (El Jadida), Morocco 106/C2
Mazama, Wash. 310/E2
Mazamet, France 28/E6
Mazán, Peru 128/F4
Mazana (lake), Québec 172/C2
Mazana (riv.), Québec 172/C2
Mazandaran (prov.), Iran 66/H2
Mazangano, Uruguay 145/E3
Mazapil, Mexico 150/J4
Mazapil, Mexico 150/J4
Mazara del Vallo, Italy 34/D6
Mazar-e Sharif, Afghanistan 59/J2
Mazar-e Sharif, Afghanistan 68/B1
Mazarrón, Spain 33/F4
Mazaruni (riv.), Guyana 131/A2
Mazaruni-Potaro (dist.), Guyana 131/A2
Mazatán, Mexico 150/E2
Mazatenango, Guatemala 154/B3
Mazatlán, Mexico 146/H7
Mazatlán, Mexico 150/F5
Mazatzal (peak), Ariz. 198/D4
Mažeikiai, U.S.S.R. 53/A2
Mazenod, Sask. 181/E6
Mazeppa, Alberta 182/D4
Mazeppa, Minn. 255/F6
Mazgirt, Turkey 63/H3
Mazıdağı, Turkey 63/J4
Mazie, Okla. 288/R2
Mazinaw (lake), Ontario 177/G3
Mazirbe, U.S.S.R. 53/B2
Mazocruz, Peru 128/H11
Mazomanie, Wis. 317/G9
Mazon, Ill. 222/E2
Mazowe (riv.), Mozambique 118/E3
Mazowe, Zimbabwe 118/E3
Mazowe (riv.), Zimbabwe 118/E3
Mazra', Israel 65/C5
Mazu (Matsu) (isl.), China 77/K6
Mazzarino, Italy 34/E6
Mbabane (cap.), Swaziland 118/E5
Mbabane (cap.), Swaziland 102/F7
Mbai'ki, Centr. Afr. Rep. 115/C3
Mbakou (res.), Cameroon 115/B2
Mbala, Zambia 102/F5
Mbala, Zambia 115/F5
Mbale, Uganda 115/F3
Mbale, Uganda 102/F4
Mbalmayo, Cameroon 115/B3
Mbamba Bay, Tanzania 115/G6
Mbandaka, Zaire 115/C3
Mbandaka, Zaire 102/D5
M'banza Congo, Angola 115/B5
Mbanza-Ngungu, Zaire 102/D5
Mbanza-Ngungu, Zaire 115/C5
Mbaracayú, Cordillera de (mts.), Paraguay 144/E3
Mbarangandu (riv.), Tanzania 115/G5
Mbarara, Uganda 115/F4
Mbemkuru (riv.), Tanzania 115/G5
Mbengga (isl.), Fiji 86/Q11
Mbéré (riv.), Cameroon 115/B2
Mbéré (riv.), Cent. Afr. Rep. 115/B2
Mbéré (riv.), Chad 111/C6
Mbeya (reg.), Tanzania 115/F5
Mbeya, Tanzania 102/F5
Mbeya, Tanzania 115/F5
M'Bigou, Gabon 115/B4
Mbinda, Congo 115/B4
Mbini, Equat. Guinea 115/A3
Mbocayaty, Paraguay 144/C5
M'Bour, Senegal 106/A6
M'Bout, Mauritania 106/B5
Mbres, Cent. Afr. Rep. 115/D2
M'Bridge (riv.), Angola 115/B5
Mbuji-Mayi, Zaire 102/E5
Mbuji-Mayi, Zaire 115/D5
Mbulu, Tanzania 115/G4
Mburucuyá, Argentina 143/E2
Mbuyapey, Paraguay 144/D5
McAdam, New Bruns. 170/C3
McAdams, Miss. 256/E4
McAdoo, Pa. 294/L4
McAdoo, Texas 303/D4
McAfee, N.J. 273/D1
McAlester, Okla. 188/G4
McAlester, Okla. 288/P5
McAlester (lake), Okla. 288/P4
McAlister, N. Mex. 274/F4
McAlisterville, Pa. 294/H4
McAllaster, Kansas 232/A3
McAllen, Texas 188/G5
McAllen, Texas 303/F11
McAllister, Mont. 262/E5
McAllister, Wis. 317/L5
McAlpin, Fla. 212/D1
McAndrews, Ky. 237/S5
McArthur, Calif. 204/D2
McArthur, Ohio 284/F7
McArthur River, North. Terr. 88/F3
McAuley, Manitoba 179/A4
McBain, Mich. 250/D4
McBaine, Mo. 261/H5
McBean, Georgia 217/J4
McBee, S.C. 296/G3
McBride, Br. Col. 184/G3
McBride, Miss. 256/C7
McBride, Mo. 261/N7
McBride, Okla. 288/N7
McBride Lake, Sask. 181/J3
McBrides, Mich 250/D5
McCabe, Mont. 262/M2
McCain, N.C. 281/L4
McCall, Idaho 220/C5
McCall, La. 238/K3
McCalla, Ala. 195/E4
McCall Creek, Miss. 256/C7
McCallsburg, Iowa 229/G4
McCallum, Newf. 166/C4
McCamey, Texas 303/B6
McCammon, Idaho 220/F7
McCanna, N. Dak. 282/P3
McCarley, Miss. 256/E3
McCarr, Ky. 237/S5
McCarthy, Alaska 196/K2
McCaskill, Ark. 202/C6
McCauley (isl.), Br. Col. 184/B3
McCaulley, Texas 303/E5
McCausland, Iowa 229/M5
McCaysville, Georgia 217/D1
McChord A.F.B., Wash. 310/C3
McClain (co.), Okla. 288/L5
McClave, Colo. 208/O6
McCleary, Wash. 310/B3
McClellan A.F.B., Calif. 204/B8
McClelland (lake), Alberta 182/E1
McClelland, Ark. 202/H3
McClelland, Iowa 229/B6
McClellanville, S.C. 296/H5
McCloud, Calif. 204/C2
McCloud, Tenn. 237/R8
McClure (lake), Calif. 204/E6
McClure, Ill. 222/D6
McClure, Ohio 284/C3
McClure, Pa. 294/H4
McClure, Va. 307/D6
McClusky, N. Dak. 282/K4
McColl, S.C. 296/H2
McComb, Miss. 256/D8
McComb, Ohio 284/C3
McConaughy, C.W. (lake), Nebr. 264/C3
McCondy, Miss. 256/G3
McCone (co.), Mont. 262/L3
McConnell, Ill. 222/D1
McConnell, Manitoba 179/B4
McConnell, Tenn. 237/D8
McConnell A.F.B., Kansas 232/E4
McConnells, S.C. 296/F2
McConnellsburg, Pa. 294/F6
McConnellsville, N.Y. 276/J4
McConnelsville, Ohio 284/G6
McCook, Nebr. 264/D4
McCook (co.), S. Dak. 298/P6
McCool, Miss. 256/F4
McCool Junction, Nebr. 264/G4
McCord, Sask. 181/E6
McCordsville, Ind. 227/F5
McCorkle, W. Va. 312/C6
McCormick (co.), S.C. 296/C4
McCormick, S.C. 296/C4
McCoy, Colo. 208/F3
McCoy (head), New Bruns. 170/E3
McCoy, Oreg. 291/D2
McCoy (creek), Oreg. 291/J5
McCoy, Va. 307/G6
McCoy A.F.B., Fla. 212/E3
McCoysburg, Ind. 227/C3
McCracken, Kansas 232/C3
McCracken (co.), Ky. 237/D6
McCrea, Pa. 294/H5
McCreary (co.), Ky. 237/N7
McCreary, Manitoba 179/C4
McCrory, Ark. 202/H3
McCulloch (co.), Texas 303/E6
McCullom Lake, Ill. 222/E1
McCullough, Ala. 195/D8
McCune, Kansas 232/G4
McCurtain (co.), Okla. 288/S6
McCurtain, Okla. 288/R4
McCutchenville, Ohio 284/D4
McDade, Texas 303/G7
McDaniel, Md. 245/N5
McDaniels, Ky. 237/J5
McDavid, Fla. 212/B5
McDermitt, Nev. 266/D1
McDermott, Ohio 284/D8
McDonald (isls.), Australia 2/N8
McDonald, Kansas 232/A2
McDonald (co.), Mo. 261/D9
McDonald (lake), Mont. 262/B2
McDonald, N. Mex. 274/F5
McDonald, N.C. 281/L5
McDonald, Ohio 284/J3
McDonald, Pa. 294/B5
McDonald, Tenn. 237/M10
McDonalds Corners, Ontario 177/H3
McDonnell, Queensland 95/B1
McDonough (lake), Conn. 210/D1
McDonough, Del. 245/R3
McDonough, Georgia 217/D4
McDonough (co.), Ill. 222/C3
McDonough, N.Y. 276/J5
McDougal, Ark. 202/K1
McDougall (lake), New Bruns. 170/D3
McDowell, Ala. 195/C5
McDowell, Ky. 237/R6
McDowell (co.), N.C. 281/E3
McDowell, Va. 307/J4
McDowell (co.), W. Va. 312/C8
McDowell, W. Va. 312/D8
McDuffie (co.), Georgia 217/H4
McElhattan, Pa. 294/H3
McElmo (creek), Colo. 208/B8
McElmo (creek), Utah 304/E6
McEwen, Tenn. 237/F8
McFadden, Wyo. 319/F4
McFall, Mo. 261/D2
McFarlan, N.C. 281/J5
McFarland, Calif. 204/F8
McFarland, Kansas 232/F2
McFarland, Mich. 250/B2
McFarland, Wis. 317/H10
McFarlane (riv.), Sask. 181/L2
McGaffey, N. Mex. 274/A3
McGaheysville, Va. 307/L4
McGee, Sask. 181/C4
McGees Mills, Pa. 294/E4
McGehee, Ark. 202/H6
McGill, Nev. 266/G3
McGivney, New Bruns. 170/D2
McGloughlin (peak), Mont. 262/C4
McGrath, Alaska 188/C5
McGrath, Alaska 196/H2
McGrath, Minn. 255/E4
McGraw, N.Y. 276/H5
McGraw Brook, New Bruns. 170/D2
McGrawsville, Ind. 227/E3
McGregor (lake), Alberta 182/D4
McGregor, Br. Col. 184/G3
McGregor (riv.), Br. Col. 184/G3
McGregor, Iowa 229/L2
McGregor, Minn. 255/E4
McGregor (lake), Mont. 262/B3
McGregor, N. Dak. 282/D2
McGregor, Ontario 177/B5
McGregor, Texas 303/G6
McGrew, Nebr. 264/A3
McGuffey, Ohio 284/C4
McGuire (mt.), Idaho 220/D4
McGuire A.F.B., N.J. 273/D3
McHenry (co.), Ill. 222/E1
McHenry, Ill. 222/E1
McHenry, Ky. 237/H6
McHenry, Miss. 256/F9
McHenry (co.), N. Dak. 282/J3
McHenry, N. Dak. 282/N4
McHenry Shores, Ill. 222/E1
Mchinga, Tanzania 115/H5
Mchinji, Malawi 115/F6
McIlwraith (range), Queensland 95/B2
McIndoe Falls, Vt. 268/C3
McIntire, Iowa 229/H2
McIntosh, Ala. 195/B8
McIntosh, Fla. 212/D2
McIntosh (co.), Georgia 217/K7
McIntosh, Georgia 217/K7
McIntosh, Minn. 255/C3
McIntosh, N. Mex. 274/D4
McIntosh (co.), N. Dak. 282/L7
McIntosh (co.), Okla. 288/P4
McIntosh, Ontario 177/F4
McIntosh, Ontario 175/B3
McIntosh, S. Dak. 298/G2
McIntyre, Georgia 217/F5
McIvor, Mich 250/F4
McKague, Sask. 181/G3
McKamie, Ark. 202/C7
McKay (lake), Manitoba 179/C2
McKay (res.), Oreg. 291/J2
McKean (co.), Pa. 294/E2
McKean, Pa. 294/B2
McKeand (riv.), N.W. Terr. 187/M3
McKee (creek), Ill. 222/C4
McKee, Ky. 237/O6
McKee City, N.J. 273/D5
McKeesport, Pa. 188/L2
McKeesport, Pa. 294/C7
McKees Rocks, Pa. 294/B7
McKellar, Ontario 177/D2
McKendrick, New Bruns. 170/D1
McKenna, Wash. 310/C4
McKenney, Va. 307/N7
McKenzie, Ala. 195/E7
McKenzie (co.), N. Dak. 282/D4
McKenzie, N. Dak. 282/K6
McKenzie, South Fork (riv.), Oreg. 291/E3
McKenzie, Tenn. (38201 237/E8
McKenzie Bridge, Oreg. 291/E3
McKerrow, Ontario 177/C1
McKinlay, Queensland 95/B4
McKinlay, Queensland 88/G4
McKinley, Ala. 195/C6
McKinley (mt.), Alaska 146/C3
McKinley (mt.), Alaska 188/D5
McKinley (mt.), Alaska 196/H2
McKinley, Cuba 158/B2
McKinley, Minn. 255/F3
McKinley (co.), N. Mex. 274/A3
McKinley (mt.), U.S. 4/C17
McKinley, Wyo. 319/G3
McKinley Park, Alaska 196/J2
McKinleyville, Calif. 204/A3
McKinney (lake), Kansas 232/A3
McKinney, Ky. 237/M6
McKinney, Texas 303/H4
McKinnon, Georgia 217/J8
McKinnon, Tenn. 237/F8
McKinnon, Wyo. 319/C4
McKittrick, Calif. 204/F8
McKittrick, Mo. 261/J5
McLain, Miss. 256/G8
McLane, Pa. 294/B2
McLaughlin, Alberta 182/E3
McLaughlin, S. Dak. 298/H2
McLaurin, Miss. 256/F8
McLean (co.), Ill. 222/E3
McLean, Ill. 222/D3
McLean (co.), Ky. 237/G5
McLean, Nebr. 264/G2
McLean, N.Y. 276/H5
McLean (co.), N. Dak. 282/G4
McLean, Sask. 181/G5
McLean, Texas 303/D2
McLean, Va. 307/S2
McLeansboro, Ill. 222/E5
McLelan (str.), Newf. 166/B1
McLemoresville, Tenn. 237/D9
McLennan, Alberta 182/B2
McLennan (co.), Texas 303/G6
McLeod (riv.), Alberta 182/B3
McLeod (co.), Minn. 255/D6
McLeod, Mont. 262/G5
McLeod, N. Dak. 282/R7
McLeod (bay), N.W. Terr. 187/G3
McLeod (lake), W. Australia 88/A4
McLeod (lake), W. Australia 92/A4
McLeod Lake, Br. Col. 184/F2
McLeod River, Alberta 182/B3
M'Clintock, Manitoba 179/K2
M'Clintock (chan.), N.W.T. 146/H2
M'Clintock (chan.), N.W.T. 162/F1
M'Clintock (chan.), N.W. Terr. 187/H2
M'Clintock (inlet), N.W. Terr. 187/K1
McLoud, Okla. 288/M4
McLoughlin (mt.), Oreg. 291/E5
McLoughlin House Nat'l Hist. Site, Oreg. 291/B2
McLouth, Kansas 232/G2
McLure, Br. Col. 184/H4
M'Clure (str.), Canada 4/B15
M'Clure (cape), N.W.T. 162/D1
M'Clure (cape), N.W.T. 187/F2
M'Clure (str.), N.W.T. 146/F2
M'Clure (str.), N.W.T. 162/E1
M'Clure (str.), N.W.T. 187/G2
McMahon, Sask. 181/D5
McMechen, W. Va. 312/E3
McMillan, Mich. 250/D2
McMillan (lake), N. Mex. 274/E6
McMillan (lake), N. Mex. 188/F4
McMillan, Okla. 288/M6
McMinn (co.), Tenn. 237/M10
McMinnville, Oreg. 291/D2
McMinnville, Tenn. 237/K9
McMorran, Sask. 181/C4
McMullen (co.), Texas 303/F9
McMunn, Manitoba 179/G5
McMurdo (sound), Ant. 2/A10
McMurdo (sound) 5/B9
McMurdo, Br. Col. 184/J4
McMurray, Wash. 310/C2
McNab, Alberta 182/D5
McNab, Ark. 202/C6
McNabb, Ill. 222/D2
McNair, Texas 303/K1
McNairy (co.), Tenn. 237/D10
McNairy, Tenn. 237/D10
McNamee, New Bruns. 170/D2
McNary, Ariz. 198/F4
McNary, La. 238/E5
McNary, Oreg. 291/H2
McNary (dam), Oreg. 291/H2
McNary, Texas 303/B11
McNary (dam), Wash. 310/F5
McNaughton, Wis. 317/H4
McNeal, Ariz. 198/F7
McNeil, Ark. 202/D7
McNeill, Miss. 256/E9
McNulty, Oreg. 291/E2
McNutt (isl.), Nova Scotia 168/C5
McPhadyen (riv.), Newf. 166/A3
McPhail (riv.), Manitoba 179/F2
McPherson (co.), Kansas 232/E3
McPherson, Kansas 232/E3
McPherson (co.), Nebr. 264/C3
McPherson (range), N.S. Wales 97/G1
McPherson (co.), S. Dak. 298/L2
McQuady, Ky. 237/H5
McRae, Alberta 182/E2
McRae, Ark. 202/G3
McRae, Georgia 217/G6
McRoberts, Ky. 237/R6
McShan, Ala. 195/B4
McSherrystown, Pa. 294/H6
McTaggart, Sask. 181/H6
McTavish, Manitoba 179/E5
McTavish Arm (inlet), N.W. Terr. 187/G3
McVeigh, Ky. 237/S5
McVeytown, Pa. 294/G4
McVicar Arm (inlet), N.W. Terr. 187/F3
McVille, N. Dak 282/O4
McWhorter, W. Va. 312/F4
McWilliams, Ala. 195/D7
Meacham (lake), N.Y. 276/M1
Meacham, Oreg. 291/J2
Meacham, Sask. 181/F3
Mead (lake) 188/D3
Mead (lake), Ariz. 198/A2
Mead, Colo. 208/K2
Mead, Nebr. 264/H3
Mead (lake), Nev. 266/G6
Mead, Okla. 288/O7
Mead (lake), U.S. 146/G6
Mead, Wash. 310/H3
Meade (riv.), Alaska 196/G1
Meade (peak), Idaho 220/G7
Meade (co.), Kansas 232/B4
Meade, Kansas 232/B4
Meade (co.), Ky. 237/J5
Meade (co.), S. Dak. 298/D5
Meador, W. Va. 312/B7
Meadow (creek), Idaho 220/C4
Meadow (mt.), Md. 245/B2
Meadow (lake), Sask. 181/C1
Meadow, S. Dak. 298/E2
Meadow, Texas 303/B4
Meadow, Utah 304/B5
Meadow (riv.), W. Va. 312/E6
Meadow Bluff, W. Va. 312/E7
Meadow Bridge, W. Va. 312/E7
Meadowbrook, Ill. 222/B2
Meadowbrook, W. Va. 312/F4
Meadow Creek, W. Va. 312/E7
Meadow Grove, Nebr. 264/G2
Meadow Lake, Sask. 181/C1
Meadow Lake Prov. Park, Sask. 181/K4
Meadowlands, Minn. 255/F3
Meadow Lands, Pa. 294/B5
Meadow Portage, Manitoba 179/C3
Meadows, Idaho 220/B5
Meadows, Ill. 222/E3
Meadows, Md. 245/G5
Meadows, N.H. 268/E3
Meadows, S. Australia 94/B8
Meadows of Dan, Va. 307/H7
Meadow Vale, Ky. 237/L1

408 Meadow Valley

Meadow Valley, Calif. 204/D4
Meadow Valley Wash (riv.), Nev. 266/G5
Meadowview-Emory, Va. 307/D7
Meadow Vista, N. Mex. 274/C7
Meadville, Miss. 256/C8
Meadville, Mo. 261/F3
Meadville, Pa. 188/L2
Meadville, Pa. 294/B2
Meaford, Ontario 177/D3
Meagher (co.), Mont. 262/F4
Meaghers Grant, Nova Scotia 168/E4
Meakan (mt.), Japan 81/L2
Mealhada, Portugal 33/B2
Meally, Ky. 237/R5
Mealy (lake), Newf. 166/C3
Meander, Tasmania 99/C3
Meander River, Alberta 182/A5
Meanook, Alberta 182/D2
Means, Ky. 237/O5
Meansville, Georgia 217/D4
Meares (cape), Oreg. 291/C2
Mearim (riv.), Brazil 132/E4
Mearns, Alberta 182/D3
Mears, Mich. 250/C5
Meath (co.), Ireland 17/H4
Meathas Truim, Ireland 17/G4
Meath Park, Sask. 181/F2
Meaux, France 28/E3
Mebane, N.C. 281/L2
Mecca, Calif. 204/K10
Mecca, Ind. 227/C5
Mecca, Saudi Arabia 2/M4
Mecca, Saudi Arabia 59/C5
Mecca, Saudi Arabia 54/F7
Mechanic Falls, Maine 243/C7
Mechanic Falls•, Maine 243/C7
Mechanicsburg, Ill. 222/D4
Mechanicsburg, Ind. 227/G5
Mechanicsburg, Ohio 284/D5
Mechanicsburg, Pa. 294/H5
Mechanicsburg, Va. 307/G6
Mechanicstown, Ohio 284/H4
Mechanicsville, Conn. 210/H1
Mechanicsville, Georgia 217/L1
Mechanicsville, Iowa 229/L5
Mechanicsville, Md. 245/M7
Mechanicsville, Va. 307/O5
Mechanicville, N.Y. 276/N5
Mechelen, Belgium 27/F6
Mecheria, Algeria 106/D2
Mechernich, Germany 22/B3
Mecidiye, Turkey 63/B5
Mecitözü, Turkey 63/F2
Mecklenburg (bay), Germany 22/D1
Mecklenburg, N.Y. 276/G6
Mecklenburg (co.), N.C. 281/H4
Mecklenburg (co.), Va. 307/M7
Mecklenburg-West Pomerania (state), Germany 22/E2
Meckling, S. Dak. 298/R8
Meconta, Mozambique 118/F3
Mecosta (co.), Mich. 250/D5
Mecosta, Mich. 250/D5
Mecoya, Bolivia 136/C8
Mecsek (mts.), Hungary 41/D3
Mecúfi, Mozambique 118/G2
Mecula, Mozambique 118/G2
Medain Salih, Saudi Arabia 59/C4
Medan, Indonesia 54/L9
Medan, Indonesia 85/B5
Médanos, Buenos Aires, Argentina 143/D4
Médanos, Entre Ríos, Argentina 143/G6
Médanos (isth.), Venezuela 124/D2
Medanosa (pt.), Argentina 143/D6
Medaryville, Ind. 227/D2
Meddybemps•, Maine 243/J5
Meddybemps (lake), Maine 243/J5
Médéa, Algeria 106/E1
Medel (mt.), Switzerland 39/D2
Medellín, Colombia 120/B2
Medellín, Colombia 126/C4
Medellín de Bravo, Mexico 150/Q2
Medemblik, Netherlands 27/G3
Médenine, Tunisia 106/F2
Méderdra, Mauritania 106/A5
Mederville, Iowa 229/K3
Medetsiz Tepe (mt.), Turkey 63/F4
Medfield, Mass. 249/B8
Medfield•, Mass. 249/B8
Medford, Maine 243/F5
Medford•, Maine 243/F5
Medford, Mass. 249/C6
Medford, Minn. 255/E6
Medford, N.J. 273/D4
Medford, Okla. 288/L1
Medford, Oreg. 188/D2
Medford, Oreg. 146/F5
Medford, Oreg. 291/E5
Medford, Wis. 317/F5
Medford Center, Maine 243/F5
Medford Lakes, N.J. 273/D4
Medgidia, Romania 45/J3
Medgun (creek), N.S. Wales 97/E1
Medhishar, Iran 66/H3
Media, Ill. 222/C3
Media, Pa. 294/L7
Media Agua, Argentina 143/C3
Media Luna, Cuba 158/G4
Mediapolis, Iowa 229/L6
Mediaş, Romania 45/G2
Medical Lake, Wash. 310/H3
Medical Springs, Oreg. 291/K2
Medicine (lake), Mont. 262/M2
Medicine (creek), Nebr. 264/D4
Medicine (creek), S. Dak. 298/J6
Medicine Bow (range), Colo. 208/G1
Medicine Bow, Wyo. 319/F4
Medicine Bow (range), Wyo. 319/F4
Medicine Bow (riv.), Wyo. 319/F3
Medicine Creek (dam), Nebr. 264/D4
Medicine Hat, Alberta 182/E4
Medicine Hat, Alta. 146/H4
Medicine Hat, Alta. 162/E5
Medicine Knoll (creek), S. Dak. 298/J5
Medicine Lake, Minn. 255/G5
Medicine Lake, Mont. 262/M2
Medicine Lodge (creek), Idaho 220/F5
Medicine Lodge, Kansas 232/D4
Medicine Lodge (riv.), Kansas 232/D4
Medicine Mound, Texas 303/E3
Medicine Park, Okla. 288/J5
Medill, Mo. 261/J2
Medina, Colombia 126/D5
Medina (Hamel), Minn. 255/F5
Medina, N.Y. 276/D4
Medina, N. Dak. 282/M6
Medina (co.), Ohio 284/G3
Medina, Ohio 284/G3
Medina, Saudi Arabia 54/F7
Medina, Saudi Arabia 59/D5
Medina, Tenn. 237/D9
Medina (co.), Texas 303/E8
Medina, Texas 303/E8
Medina (lake), Texas 303/E8
Medina (riv.), Texas 303/J11
Medina, Wash. 310/B2
Medinaceli, Spain 33/E2
Medina del Campo, Spain 33/D2
Medina de Rioseco, Spain 33/D2
Medina-Sidonia, Spain 33/D4
Mediodía, Colombia 126/D8
Mediterranean (sea) 2/K4
Mediterranean (sea) 7/E5
Mediterranean (sea), Algeria 106/E1
Mediterranean (sea), Egypt 111/E1
Mediterranean (sea), France 28/E7
Mediterranean (sea), Italy 34/B6
Mediterranean (sea), Libya 111/C1
Mediterranean (sea), Morocco 106/D1
Mediterranean (sea), Tunisia 106/F1
Medix Run, Pa. 294/F3
Medjerda (riv.), Algeria 106/F1
Medjerda (riv.), Tunisia 106/F1
Medley, Fla. 212/B4
Medley, W. Va. 312/H4
Mednogorsk, U.S.S.R. 52/J4
Mednogorsk, U.S.S.R. 48/F4
Médoc (reg.), France 28/C5
Mêdog, China 77/E6
Medon, Tenn. 237/D10
Medora, Ill. 222/C4
Medora, Ind. 227/E7
Medora, Kansas 232/E3
Medora, Manitoba 179/B5
Medora, N. Dak. 282/C6
Médouneu, Gabon 115/B3
Medstead, Sask. 181/C2
Meductic, New Bruns. 170/C3
Medveditsa (riv.), U.S.S.R. 52/F4
Medvezh'yegorsk, U.S.S.R. 48/D3
Medvezh'yegorsk, U.S.S.R. 52/D2
Medway (riv.), England 13/H6
Medway•, Maine 243/G4
Medway•, Mass. 249/J4
Medway (harb.), Nova Scotia 168/D4
Medway (riv.), Nova Scotia 168/C4
Medzilaborce, Czech. 41/F2
Meeandah, Queensland 88/K2
Meehan, Miss. 256/G6
Meekatharra, Australia 87/B8
Meekatharra, W. Australia 88/B5
Meekatharra, W. Australia 92/B4
Meeker, Colo. 208/D2
Meeker, La. 238/F4
Meeker (co.), Minn. 255/D5
Meeker, Ohio 284/D4
Meeker, Okla. 288/N4
Meeks, Georgia 217/G5
Meeks Bay, Calif. 204/E5
Meelpaeg (lake), Newf. 166/C4
Meerane, Germany 22/E3
Meerhout, Belgium 27/G6
Meers, Okla. 288/J5
Meersburg, Germany 22/C5
Meerssen, Netherlands 27/H7
Meerut, India 54/J7
Meerut, India 68/D3
Meeteetse, Wyo. 319/D1
Meeting (lake), Sask. 181/D2
Meeting Creek, Alberta 182/D3
Mega, Ethiopia 111/G7
Mega (isl.), Indonesia 85/C6
Megalópolis, Greece 45/E7
Mégantic (co.), Québec 172/F3
Mégantic (lake), Québec 172/G4
Mégara, Greece 45/F6
Megargel, Ala. 195/D8
Megargel, Texas 303/F4
Meggett, S.C. 296/G6
Meghalaya (state), India 68/G3
Megiddo, Israel 65/C2
Mehama, Oreg. 291/E3
Mehan, Okla. 288/M2
Meherrin (riv.), N.C. 281/P1
Meherrin, Va. 307/M6
Meherrin (riv.), Va. 307/M7
Mehetia (isl.), Fr. Poly. 87/M7
Mehlville, Mo. 261/P4
Mehoopany, Pa. 294/K2
Mehran, Iran 66/E4
Mehran (riv.), Iran 59/F4
Mehran (riv.), Iran 66/J7
Mehsana, India 68/C4
Mehun-sur-Yèvre, France 28/E4
Meifa, Yemen 59/E7
Meiganga, Cameroon 115/B2
Meighen (isl.), N.W.T. 162/M3
Meighen (isl.), N.W.T. 187/H1
Meigle, Scotland 15/E4
Meigs, Georgia 217/D8
Meigs (co.), Ohio 284/F7
Meigs (co.), Tenn. 237/M9
Meikle (riv.), Alberta 182/A1
Meiktila, Burma 72/B2
Meilen, Switzerland 39/G2
Meiners Oaks-Mira Monte, Calif. 204/F9
Meiningen, Germany 22/D3
Meire Grove, Minn. 255/C5
Meiringen, Switzerland 39/F3
Meiron (mt.), Israel 65/C1
Meise, Belgium 27/E7
Meissen, Germany 22/E3
Mei Xian, China 77/J7
Mejillones, Chile 120/B5
Mejillones, Chile 138/A4
Mejillones del Sur (bay), Chile 138/A4
Mekambo, Gabon 115/B3
Mekerrhane, Sebkha (salt lake), Algeria 106/E3
Mekili, Libya 111/D1
Mékinac (lake), Québec 172/E2
Mekinock, N. Dak. 282/R4
Meknès, Morocco 102/B1
Meknès, Morocco 106/C2
Mekong (riv.) 2/Q4
Mekong (riv.), Asia 54/M8
Mekong (riv.), Burma 72/D2
Mekong (riv.), Cambodia 72/E4
Mekong (Lancang Jiang) (riv.), China 77/F7
Mekong (riv.), Laos 72/D3
Mekong (riv.), Thailand 72/E3
Mekong, Mouths of the (delta), Vietnam 72/E5
Mekoryuk, Alaska 196/E2
Melaka (state), Malaysia 72/D7
Melaka, Malaysia 54/M9
Melaka, Malaysia 72/D7
Melanesia (reg.), Pacific 87/E5
Melaval, Sask. 181/E6
Melba, Idaho 220/B6
Melber, Ky. 237/D7
Melbern, Ohio 284/A3
Melbeta, Nebr. 264/A3
Melbourne, Ark. 202/G1
Melbourne, Australia 2/R7
Melbourne, Australia 87/E9
Melbourne, Fla. 188/F5
Melbourne, Fla. 212/F3
Melbourne, Iowa 229/G5
Melbourne, Ky. 237/T2
Melbourne, Mo. 261/E2
Melbourne (isl.), N.W. Terr. 187/H3
Melbourne, Ontario 177/C5
Melbourne, Québec 172/E4
Melbourne (cap.), Victoria 88/H7
Melbourne (cap.), Victoria 97/H5
Melbourne, Wash. 310/B4
Melbourne Airport, Victoria 88/K7
Melbourne Beach, Fla. 212/F3
Melby, Minn. 255/C4
Melcher, Honduras 154/D3
Melcher, Iowa 229/G6
Melchor (isl.), Chile 138/D6
Melchor Múzquiz, Mexico 150/H3
Melchor Ocampo, Mexico 150/H4
Melchor Ocampo del Balsas, Mexico 150/H8
Melder, La. 238/E4
Meldorf, Germany 22/C1
Meldrim, Georgia 217/K6
Meldrum Bay, Ontario 177/A2
Meldrum Creek, Br. Col. 184/F4
Meleb, Manitoba 179/E4
Melenki, U.S.S.R. 52/F3
Meleuz, U.S.S.R. 52/J4
Mélèzes (riv.), Québec 174/C1
Melfa, Va. 307/S5
Melfi, Chad 111/C5
Melfi, Italy 34/E4
Melfort, Sask. 162/F5
Melfort, Sask. 181/G3
Melfort, Loch (inlet), Scotland 15/C4
Melgaço, Portugal 33/B1
Melgar de Fernamental, Spain 33/D1
Melide, Switzerland 39/G5
Meligalá, Greece 45/F7
Melilla, Spain 106/D1
Melilla, Spain 106/B1
Melilla, Spain 7/D5
Melimoyu (mt.), Chile 138/D5
Melinca, Chile 138/D5
Melincué, Argentina 143/F6
Melipilla, Chile 138/F4
Melita, Manitoba 179/A5
Melitopol', U.S.S.R. 7/H4
Melitopol', U.S.S.R. 52/D5
Melitota, Md. 245/O4
Melk, Austria 41/C2
Melkbosstrand, S. Africa 118/E6
Melksham, England 13/E6
Melksham, England 10/E5
Mellansel, Sweden 18/L5
Melle, Germany 22/C2
Mellen, Wis. 317/E3
Mellerud, Sweden 18/H7
Mellette (co.), S. Dak. 298/H6
Mellette, S. Dak. 298/N3
Mellingen, Switzerland 39/F2
Mellott, Ind. 227/C4
Mellwood, Ark. 202/H5
Melmore, Ohio 284/D3
Mělník, Czech. 41/C1
Melo, Uruguay 120/D6
Melo, Uruguay 145/E3
Melocheville, Québec 172/C4
Melozitna (riv.), Alaska 196/H1
Melrhir, Chott (salt lake), Algeria 106/F2
Melrose, Conn. 210/E1
Melrose, Fla. 212/D2
Melrose, Iowa 229/G7
Melrose, La. 238/E3
Melrose, Md. 245/L2
Melrose, Mass. 249/D6
Melrose, Minn. 255/D5
Melrose, Mont. 262/D5
Melrose, New Bruns. 170/F2
Melrose, Newf. 166/D2
Melrose, N. Mex. 274/F4
Melrose, N.S. Wales 97/D3
Melrose, Ohio 284/B3
Melrose, Oreg. 291/D4
Melrose, Scotland 15/F5
Melrose, Scotland 10/E3
Melrose, Wis. 317/E7
Melrose Park, Fla. 212/B4
Melrose Park, Ill. 222/B5
Melrose Park, N.Y. 276/G5
Melrude, Minn. 255/F3
Mels, Switzerland 39/H2
Melstone, Mont. 262/H4
Melsungen, Germany 22/C3
Melton, Victoria 97/C5
Melton Hill (lake), Tenn. 237/N9
Melton Mowbray, England 10/F4
Melton Mowbray, England 13/G5
Meltonville, Iowa 229/G2
Melun, France 28/E3
Melut, Sudan 111/F5
Melvaig, Scotland 15/C3
Melvern, Kansas 232/G3
Melvern (lake), Kansas 232/G3
Melvern Square, Nova Scotia 168/C3
Melvich, Scotland 15/E2
Melville (isl.), Australia 87/D7
Melville (isl.), Canada 4/B15
Melville (pen.), Canada 4/C14
Melville (bay), Greenl. 4/B13
Melville, La. 238/G5
Melville, Mont. 262/F4
Melville (lake), Newf. 166/C3
Melville, N.Y. 276/O9
Melville, N. Dak. 282/M5
Melville (bay), North. Terr. 88/F2
Melville (bay), North. Terr. 93/E2
Melville (isl.), North. Terr. 88/E2
Melville (isl.), North. Terr. 93/B1
Melville (isl.), N.W.T. 146/G2
Melville (isl.), N.W.T. 162/E1
Melville (isl.), N.W.T. 187/G2
Melville (lake), N.W.T. 162/L5
Melville (pen.), N.W.T. 146/K3
Melville (pen.), N.W.T. 162/H2
Melville (pen.), N.W.T. 187/K3
Melville (cape), Queensland 88/G2
Melville (cape), Queensland 95/C2
Melville, Sask. 162/F5
Melville, Sask. 181/J5
Melville, W. Australia 92/A1
Melvin, Ala. 195/B7
Melvin, Ill. 222/E3
Melvin, Iowa 229/B2
Melvin, Lough (lake), Ireland 10/B3
Melvin (lake), Ireland 17/E3
Melvin, Mich. 250/G5
Melvin, Minn. 255/B3
Melvin, Lough (lake), N. Ireland 10/B3
Melvin, Texas 303/E6
Melvina, Wis. 317/E8
Melvindale, Mich. 250/B7
Melvin Mills, N.H. 268/D5
Melvin Village, N.H. 268/E4
Mélykút, Hungary 41/E3
Memaliaj, Albania 45/D5
Memba, Mozambique 118/G2
Membij, Syria 63/G4
Memel (Klaipeda), U.S.S.R. 52/B3
Memel (Klaipeda), U.S.S.R. 53/A3
Memmingen, Germany 22/D5
Mempawah, Indonesia 85/D5
Memphis, Ala. 195/B4
Memphis (ruins), Egypt 111/J3
Memphis, Fla. 212/D4
Memphis, Ind. 227/F8
Memphis, Mich. 250/G6
Memphis, Miss. 256/D1
Memphis, Mo. 261/H2
Memphis, Nebr. 264/H3
Memphis, Tenn. 146/K6
Memphis, Tenn. 188/J3
Memphis, Tenn. 237/B10
Memphis, Texas 303/D3
Memphis Naval Air Sta., Tenn. 237/B10
Memphremagog (lake), Québec 172/E4
Memphremagog (lake), Vt. 268/C1
Memramcook, New Bruns. 170/F2
Mena, Ark. 202/B4
Menafra, Uruguay 145/B3
Menahga, Minn. 255/C4
Menai (str.), Wales 13/C4
Menai Bridge, Wales 13/C4
Menaik, Alberta 182/D3
Ménaka, Mali 106/E5
Menan, Idaho 220/F6
Menands, N.Y. 276/N5
Menarandra (riv.), Madagascar 118/H4
Menard (co.), Ill. 222/D3
Menard (co.), Texas 303/E7
Menard, Texas 303/E7
Menasalbas, Spain 33/D3
Menasha, Wis. 317/J7
Mencué, Argentina 143/C5
Mendak, Saudi Arabia 59/D5
Mende, France 28/E5
Mendenhall (cape), Alaska 196/E3
Mendenhall, Miss. 256/E7
Menderes, Büyük (riv.), Turkey 59/A2
Menderes, Büyük (riv.), Turkey 63/C4
Mendes, Georgia 217/H7
Méndez, Ecuador 128/C4
Mendham, N.J. 273/D2
Mendham, Sask. 181/B5
Mendi, Ethiopia 111/G6
Mendi, Papua N.G. 85/B7
Mendip (hills), England 13/E6
Mendocino (cape), Calif. 146/F5
Mendocino (cape), Calif. 188/A2
Mendocino (co.), Calif. 204/B4
Mendocino, Calif. 204/B4
Mendocino (cape), Calif. 204/A3
Mendon, Ill. 222/B3
Mendon•, Mass. 249/H4
Mendon, Mich. 250/D7
Mendon, Mo. 261/F3
Mendon, N.Y. 276/E4
Mendon, Ohio 284/A4
Mendon, Utah 304/B2
Mendon•, Vt. 268/B4
Mendooran, N.S. Wales 97/E2
Mendota, Calif. 204/E7
Mendota, Ill. 222/D2
Mendota, Minn. 255/G5
Mendota, Va. 307/D7
Mendota (lake), Wis. 317/H9
Mendota Heights, Minn. 255/G6
Mendoza (prov.), Argentina 143/C4
Mendoza, Argentina 120/C6
Mendoza, Argentina 143/C3
Mendoza (riv.), Argentina 143/C3
Mendoza, Cuba 158/A2
Mendoza, Peru 128/D6
Mendoza, Uruguay 145/C5
Mendrisio, Switzerland 39/G5
Mene de Mauroa, Venezuela 124/C2
Mene Grande, Venezuela 124/C3
Menemen, Turkey 63/B3
Menemsha, Mass. 249/L7
Menen, Belgium 27/C7
Meneses, Cuba 158/F2
Menfi, Italy 34/D6
Menfro, Mo. 261/N7
Mengcheng, China 77/J5
Mengen, Turkey 63/D2
Menggala, Indonesia 85/D6
Menghai, China 77/E7
Mengla, China 77/F7
Mengshan, China 77/H7
Mengzi, China 77/F7
Menifee, Ark. 202/E3
Menifee (co.), Ky. 237/O5
Menihek, Newf. 166/A3
Menihek (lake), Newf. 166/A3
Menin (Menen), Belgium 27/C7
Menindee, N.S. Wales 97/B3
Menindee (lake), N.S. Wales 97/B3
Meningie, S. Australia 94/F6
Menisino, Manitoba 179/F5
Menistouc (lake), Newf. 166/A3
Menlo, Georgia 217/B2
Menlo, Iowa 229/E5
Menlo, Kansas 232/B2
Menlo, Wash. 310/B4
Menlo Park, Calif. 204/J3
Menlo Park, N.J. 273/E2
Menneval, New Bruns. 170/C1
Menno, S. Dak. 298/P7
Meno, Okla. 288/K2
Menoken, N. Dak 282/J6
Menominee, Ill. 222/C1
Menominee (co.), Mich. 250/B3
Menominee, Mich. 250/B3
Menominee (riv.), Mich. 250/B3
Menominee (co.), Wis. 317/J5
Menominee (riv.), Wis. 317/L5
Menominee Ind. Res., Wis. 317/J5
Menomonee Falls, Wis. 317/K1
Menomonie, Wis. 317/C6
Menongue, Angola 102/D6
Menongue, Angola 115/C6
Menorca (Minorca) (isl.), Spain 33/J2
Mentasta (pass), Alaska 196/K2
Mentasta Lake, Alaska 196/K2
Mentawai (isls.), Indonesia 54/L10
Mentawai (isls.), Indonesia 85/B6
Mentmore, N. Mex. 274/A3
Menton, France 28/G6
Mentone, Ala. 195/G1
Mentone, Calif. 204/H9
Mentone, Ind. 227/E2
Mentone, Texas 303/D10
Mentor, Kansas 232/E3
Mentor, Ky. 237/N3
Mentor, Minn. 255/B3
Mentor, Ohio 284/H2
Mentor-on-the-Lake, Ohio 284/G2
Menunketesuck (riv.), Conn. 210/E3
Menye, Turkey 63/C3
Menyuan, China 77/F4
Menzel Bourguiba, Tunisia 106/F1
Menzel Temime, Tunisia 106/G1
Menzie, Manitoba 179/B4
Menzies, W. Australia 88/C5
Menzies, W. Australia 92/C5
Menzingen, Switzerland 39/G2
Menznau, Switzerland 39/E2
Meoqui, Mexico 150/G2
Meota, Sask. 181/C2
Meppel, Netherlands 27/J3
Meppen, Germany 22/B2
Mequinenza (res.), Spain 33/F2
Mequon, Wis. 317/L1
Mera, Ecuador 128/C3
Mera (riv.), Switzerland 39/E2
Merabéllou (gulf), Greece 45/H8
Meraia (reg.), Mauritania 106/C5
Meråker, Norway 18/G5
Meramangye (lake), S. Australia 94/C3
Meramec (riv.), Mo. 261/N3
Merano, Italy 34/C1
Merasheen (isl.), Newf. 166/C2
Merauke, Indonesia 85/K7
Merbein, Victoria 97/A4
Mercaderes, Colombia 126/B7
Mercara, India 68/D6
Merced (co.), Calif. 204/E6
Merced, Calif. 204/E6
Merced, Calif. 204/E6
Merced (riv.), Calif. 204/E6
Mercedario, Cerro (mt.), Argentina 143/B3
Mercedes, Buenos Aires, Argentina 143/G7
Mercedes, San Luis, Argentina 143/C3
Mercedes, Argentina 120/C6
Mercedes, Corrientes, Argentina 143/G4
Mercedes, Texas 303/F12
Mercedes, Uruguay 120/D6
Mercedes, Uruguay 145/B4
Merceditas, Chile 138/B7
Mercer (co.), Ill. 222/C2
Mercer (co.), Ky. 237/M5
Mercer•, Maine 243/D6
Mercer (co.), Mo. 261/E2
Mercer, Mo. 261/F2
Mercer (co.), N.J. 273/D3
Mercer, N. Zealand 100/E2
Mercer (co.), N. Dak. 282/G5
Mercer, N. Dak. 282/J5
Mercer (co.), Ohio 284/A4
Mercer, Ohio 284/A4
Mercer (co.), Pa. 294/B3
Mercer, Pa. 294/B3
Mercer, Tenn. 237/D10
Mercer (co.), W. Va. 312/D8
Mercer, Wis. 317/F3
Mercer Island (city), Wash. 310/B2
Mercersburg, Pa. 294/G6
Mercerville-Hamilton Square, N.J. 273/D3
Merchantville, N.J. 273/B3
Merchtem, Belgium 27/E7
Mercier, Bolivia 136/B2
Mercier, Kansas 232/G2
Mercier, Québec 172/H4
Mercier (dam), Québec 172/A3
Mercoal, Alberta 182/B3
Mercury, Nev. 266/E6
Mercury (bay), N. Zealand 100/F2
Mercury (isls.), N. Zealand 100/F2
Mercury, Texas 303/E6
Mercy (bay), N.W. Terr. 187/G2
Mercy (cape), N.W. Terr. 187/M3
Mere, England 13/E6
Meredith, Colo. 208/F4
Meredith (lake), Colo. 208/M6
Meredith, N.H. 268/D4
Meredith•, N.H. 268/D4
Meredith Center, N.H. 268/D4
Meredosia, Ill. 222/C4
Merefa, U.S.S.R. 52/E5
Meregh, Somalia 115/J3
Merelbeke, Belgium 27/D7
Merevari (riv.), Venezuela 124/F5
Mergui, Burma 54/L8
Mergui, Burma 72/C4
Mergui (arch.), Burma 72/C5
Meriç, Turkey 63/B2
Meriç, Turkey 63/B2
Merid, Sask. 181/B4
Mérida, Mexico 146/J7
Mérida, Mexico 150/P6
Mérida, Spain 7/D5
Mérida, Spain 33/C3
Mérida (state), Venezuela 124/C3
Mérida, Venezuela 120/B2
Mérida, Venezuela 124/C3
Mérida, Cordillera de (range), Venezuela 124/C3
Meriden, Conn. 210/D2
Meriden, Iowa 229/B3
Meriden, Kansas 232/G2
Meriden, Minn. 255/E6
Meriden, N.H. 268/C4
Meriden, Wyo. 319/H4
Meridian, Georgia 217/K8
Meridian, Idaho 220/B6
Meridian, Miss. 146/K6
Meridian, Miss. 188/J4
Meridian, Miss. 256/G6
Meridian, N.Y. 276/G4
Meridian, Okla. 288/M3
Meridian, Texas 303/G6
Meridian Naval Air Sta., Miss. 256/G5
Meridianville, Ala. 195/F1
Merigold, Miss. 256/C3
Merigomish, Nova Scotia 168/F3
Merigomish (harb.), Nova Scotia 168/F3
Merimbula, N.S. Wales 97/F5
Merín (lag.), Uruguay 145/F4
Merino, Colo. 208/N2
Merino, Victoria 97/A5
Merino Jarpa (isl.), Chile 138/D7
Merinos, Uruguay 145/C3
Merino Village, Mass. 249/G4

Mildenhall 409

Merion Station, Pa. 294/M6
Merir (isl.), Belau 87/D5
Meriwether (co.), Georgia 217/C4
Meriwether Lewis Park, Natchez Trace Pkwy., Tenn. 237/G10
Merj 'Uyun, Lebanon 63/F6
Mérk, Hungary 41/G3
Merkel, Texas 303/E5
Merksem, Belgium 27/E6
Merksplas, Belgium 27/F6
Merlin, Ontario 177/B5
Merlin, Oreg. 291/D5
Merlo, Argentina 143/G7
Mermentau, La. 238/E6
Mermentau (riv.), La. 238/E7
Merna, Nebr. 264/E3
Merna, Wyo. 319/B3
Meroe (ruins), Sudan 111/F4
Merom, Ind. 227/B6
Merowe, Sudan 111/F4
Merowe, Sudan 59/B6
Merredin, W. Australia 88/B6
Merredin, W. Australia 92/B5
Merri (riv.), Victoria 88/L7
Merriam, Ind. 227/G2
Merriam, Kansas 232/H3
Merrick (co.), Nebr. 264/F3
Merrick, N.Y. 276/R7
Merrick (mt.), Scotland 15/D5
Merrickville, Ontario 177/J3
Merricourt, N. Dak. 282/N7
Merrifield, Minn. 255/D4
Merrifield (bay), Newf. 166/B2
Merrifield, N. Dak. 282/R4
Merrifield, Va. 307/S3
Merrill (pass), Alaska 196/H2
Merrill, Iowa 229/A3
Merrill, Mich. 250/E5
Merrill, Miss. 256/G9
Merrill, N.Y. 276/N1
Merrill, Oreg. 291/F5
Merrill, Wis. 317/G5
Merrillan, Wis. 317/E7
Merrillville, Georgia 217/E9
Merrillville, Ind. 227/C2
Merrimac, Ky. 237/L6
Merrimac•, Mass. 249/L1
Merrimac, W. Va. 312/B7
Merrimac, Wis. 317/G9
Merrimack (riv.), Mass. 249/K1
Merrimack (co.), N.H. 268/D5
Merrimack•, N.H. 268/D6
Merrimack (riv.), N.H. 268/D5
Merrimacport, Mass. 249/L1
Merriman, Nebr. 264/C2
Merrimon, N.C. 281/R5
Merrionette Park, Ill. 222/B6
Merritt, Br. Col. 162/D5
Merritt, Br. Col. 184/G5
Merritt (isl.), Fla. 212/F3
Merritt, Ill. 222/C4
Merritt, Mich. 250/D4
Merritt (res.), Nebr. 264/D2
Merritt, Wash. 310/E3
Merritt Island, Fla. 212/F3
Merriwa, N.S. Wales 97/F3
Merriwagga, N.S. Wales 97/C3
Merriweather, Mich. 250/F1
Mer Rouge, La. 238/G1
Merrow, Conn. 210/F1
Merry Hill, N.C. 281/R2
Merrymeeting (lake), N.H. 268/E5
Merry Oaks, N.C. 281/L3
Merryville, La. 238/D5
Mersa Fatma, Ethiopia 111/H5
Mersá Matrûh, Egypt 111/E1
Mersá Matrûh, Egypt 102/E1
Mersch, Luxembourg 27/J9
Mersea (dist.), England 13/J6
Merseburg, Germany 22/D3
Mersey (riv.), England 10/F2
Mersey (riv.), England 13/G2
Mersey (riv.), Nova Scotia 168/C4
Mersey (riv.), Tasmania 99/C3
Merseyside (co.), England 13/G2
Mershon, Georgia 217/H8
Mersin, Turkey 63/F4
Mersin, Turkey 59/B2
Mersin, Turkey 54/E6
Mersing, Malaysia 72/E7
Mērsrags, U.S.S.R. 53/B2
Mertert, Luxembourg 27/J9
Merthyr Tydfil, Wales 13/A6
Merthyr Tydfil, Wales 10/E5
Mértola, Portugal 33/C4
Merton, England 10/B5
Merton, England 13/H8
Merton, Wis. 317/K1
Mertz Glacier Tongue, Ant. 5/C8
Mertzon, Texas 303/C6
Mertztown, Pa. 294/L4
Mèru, Kenya 115/G3
Meru (mt.), Tanzania 115/G4
Merv (Mary), U.S.S.R. 48/F8
Merville, Br. Col 184/E5
Mervin, Sask. 181/C2
Merwin, Mo. 261/C6
Merwin (lake), Wash. 310/C5
Merzifon, Turkey 63/F2
Merzig, Germany 22/B4
Mesa, Ariz. 146/G6
Mesa, Ariz. 188/D4
Mesa, Ariz. 198/D5
Mesa (co.), Colo. 208/B5
Mesa, Colo. 208/C4
Mesa, Idaho 220/B5
Mesa, Miss. 256/D8
Mesa, Wash. 310/G4
Mesabi (range), Minn. 255/E3
Mesa Bolívar, Venezuela 124/C3
Mesachie Lake, Br. Col. 184/J3
Mesa del Seri, Mexico 150/D2
Mesagne, Italy 34/G4
Mesai (riv.), Colombia 126/D7
Mesará (gulf), Greece 45/G8
Mesa Verde National Park, Colo. 208/C8
Mesa Verde Nat'l Park, Colo. 208/C8
Mescalero, N. Mex. 274/D5
Mescalero (ridge), N. Mex. 274/F6
Mescalero (valley), N. Mex. 274/F5
Mescalero Apache Ind. Res., N. Mex. 274/D5
Meschede, Germany 22/C3
Mesena, Georgia 217/G4
Meservey, Iowa 229/G3
Meshed, Iran 54/G6
Meshed, Iran 66/L2
Meshed, Iran 59/H2
Meshed-i-Sar (Babol Sar), Iran 66/H2
Meshik, Alaska 196/G3
Meshoppen, Pa. 294/L2
Meshra er Req, Sudan 111/E6
Mesic, N.C. 281/R4
Mesick, Mich. 250/D4
Mesilla, N. Mex. 274/C6
Mesilla Park, N. Mex. 274/C6
Mesita, Colo. 208/H8
Meskanaw, Sask. 181/F3
Meskene, Syria 59/C2
Meskene, Syria 63/H5
Mesocco, Switzerland 39/H4
Mesolóngion, Greece 45/E6
Mesopotamia (reg.), Iraq 66/B3
Mesopotamia (reg.), Iraq 59/D3
Mesopotamia, Ohio 284/J3
Mesquite, Nev. 266/G6
Mesquite, N. Mex. 274/C6
Mesquite, Texas 303/H2
Messancy, Belgium 27/H9
Messina (prov.), Italy 34/E5
Messina, Italy 34/E5
Messina, Italy 7/F5
Messina (str.), Italy 34/E6
Messina, S. Africa 118/D4
Messines, Québec 172/B3
Messíni, Greece 45/E7
Messíni (gulf), Greece 45/E7
Mesta (riv.), Bulgaria 45/F5
Mestre, Italy 34/D2
Mesudiye, Turkey 63/F4
Meta (riv.) 120/B2
Meta (dept.), Colombia 126/D6
Meta (riv.), Colombia 126/D6
Meta, Ky. 237/S5
Meta, Mo. 261/H6
Meta (riv.), Venezuela 124/E4
Metabetchouan, Québec 172/F1
Métabetchouane (riv.), Québec 172/F1
Metairie, La. 238/O4
Metaine, Wash. 310/H2
Metaline Falls, Wash. 310/H2
Metamma, Ethiopia 111/G5
Metamora, Ill. 222/D3
Metamora, Ind. 227/G6
Metamora, Mich. 250/F6
Metamora, Ohio 284/C2
Metán, Argentina 143/D2
Metangula, Mozambique 118/F2
Metapán, El Salvador 154/C3
Métascouac (lake), Québec 172/F2
Metasville, Georgia 217/G3
Metauro (riv.), Italy 34/D3
Metcalf, Georgia 217/E9
Metcalf, Ill. 222/F4
Metcalfe (co.), Ky. 237/K7
Metcalfe, Miss. 256/B4
Metcalfe, Ontario 177/J2
Metchin (riv.), Newf. 166/B3
Metchosin, Br. Col. 184/K4
Metea, Ind. 227/E3
Metedeconk (riv.), N.J. 273/E3
Meteghan, Nova Scotia 168/B4
Meteghan Centre, Nova Scotia 168/B4
Meteghan River, Nova Scotia 168/B4
Meteor (crater), Ariz. 198/E3
Metepec, Mexico 150/M2
Methlick, Scotland 15/F3
Methow, Wash. 310/E2
Methow (riv.), Wash. 310/E2
Methuen•, Mass. 249/K2
Methven, N. Zealand 100/C5
Methven, Scotland 15/E4
Metica (riv.), Colombia 126/D6
Metigoshe (lake), N. Dak. 282/K2
Metinic (isl.), Maine 243/E8
Metinota, Sask. 181/C2
Metiskow, Alberta 182/E3
Métis-sur-Mer, Québec 172/A1
Metlakatla, Alaska 196/N2
Metlakatla, Br. Col. 184/B3
Metlatonoc, Mexico 150/K8
Metlili Chaamba, Algeria 106/E2
Meto (bayou), Ark. 202/H5
Metolius, Oreg. 291/F3
Metolius (riv.), Oreg. 291/F3
Metompkin (inlet), Va. 307/T5
Metompkin (isl.), Va. 307/T5
Metonga (lake), Wis. 317/J4
Metropolis, Ill. 222/E6
Metropolitan, Mich. 250/A3
Métsovon, Greece 45/E6
Mettawa, Ill. 222/B4
Mettawee (riv.), Vt. 268/A5
Metter, Georgia 217/H6
Mettet, Belgium 27/F8
Mettler, Calif. 204/G8
Metu, Ethiopia 111/G6
Metu, Ethiopia 115/G2
Metuchen, N.J. 273/E2
Metula, Israel 65/D1
Metz, France 7/E4
Metz, France 28/G3
Metz, Ind. 227/H1
Metz, Mo. 261/C6
Metz, W. Va. 312/F3
Metzger, Oreg. 291/A2
Metzingen, Germany 22/C4
Meudon, France 28/A2
Meulaboh, Indonesia 85/B5
Meulebeke, Belgium 27/C7
Meung-sur-Loire, France 28/D4
Meurthe-et-Moselle (dept.), France 28/G3
Meuse (riv.), Belgium 27/F8
Meuse (dept.), France 28/F3
Meuse (riv.), France 28/F3
Meuselwitz, Germany 22/E3
Mexia, Ala. 195/D8
Mexia, Texas 303/H6
Mexiana (isl.), Brazil 132/D2
Mexicali, Mexico 150/B1
Mexicali, Mexico 146/G6
Mexican Hat, Utah 304/E6
Mexican Springs, N. Mex. 274/A3
Mexico 2/D4
Mexico 146/H7
MEXICO 150
Mexico (gulf) 188/J5
Mexico (gulf) 2/E4
Mexico (gulf) 146/K7
Mexico (gulf), Ala. 195/E10
Mexico (gulf), Cuba 158/A1
Mexico (gulf), Fla. 212/C4
Mexico, Ind. 227/E3
Mexico, Ky. 237/E6
Mexico (gulf), La. 238/F8
Mexico, Maine 243/B6
Mexico•, Maine 243/B6
México (state), Mexico 150/K7
Mexico (gulf), Mexico 150/N4
Mexico, Mo. 261/J4
Mexico, N.Y. 276/H4
Mexico, Pa. 294/H4
Mexico (gulf), Texas 303/K9
Mexico Beach, Fla. 212/D6
Mexico City (cap.), Mexico 150/L1
Mexico City (cap.), Mexico 146/J7
Mexico City (cap.), Mexico 2/E5
Meyadin, Syria 59/C3
Meyadin, Syria 63/J5
Meybod, Iran 66/J4
Meydani, Ras-e (cape), Iran 59/G4
Meydani, Ras-e (cape), Iran 66/L8
Meyer, Iowa 229/H2
Meyers Chuck, Alaska 196/N2
Meyersdale, Pa. 294/E6
Meyers Lake, Ohio 284/H4
Meyerton, S. Africa 118/H7
Meymaneh, Afghanistan 68/A1
Meymaneh, Afghanistan 54/H6
Meymaneh, Afghanistan 59/H2
Meyrin, Switzerland 39/B4
Meyronne, Sask. 181/E6
Mezcala (riv.), Mexico 150/J8
Mezen', U.S.S.R. 4/C7
Mezen', U.S.S.R. 7/J2
Mezen', U.S.S.R. 48/E3
Mezen', U.S.S.R. 52/F1
Mezen' (bay), U.S.S.R. 52/F1
Mezen' (riv.), U.S.S.R. 48/E3
Mezen' (riv.), U.S.S.R. 52/G1
Mézenc (mt.), France 28/E5
Mezhdurechenskiy, U.S.S.R. 48/G4
Mezhdusharskiy (isl.), U.S.S.R. 52/G1
Meziadin (lake), Br. Col. 184/C2
Mézin, France 28/D5
Mezőberény, Hungary 41/F3
Mezőcsát, Hungary 41/F3
Mezőfalva, Hungary 41/E3
Mezőhegyes, Hungary 41/F3
Mezőkovácsháza, Hungary 41/F3
Mezőkövesd, Hungary 41/F3
Mezőszilas, Hungary 41/E3
Mezőtúr, Hungary 41/F3
Mezquital, Mexico 150/G5
Mezquital (riv.), Mexico 150/G5
Mhor, Loch (lake), Scotland 15/D3
Mhow, India 68/D4
Miacatlán, Mexico 150/K2
Miahuatlán de Porfirio Diaz, Mexico 150/L8
Miajadas, Spain 33/D3
Miami, Ariz. 198/E5
Miami, Fla. 188/K5
Miami, Fla. 146/K7
Miami, Fla. 212/B5
Miami (canal), Fla. 212/F5
Miami (riv.), Fla. 212/B5
Miami (co.), Ind. 227/E3
Miami, Ind. 227/E3
Miami (co.), Kansas 232/H3
Miami, Manitoba 179/D5
Miami, Mo. 261/F4
Miami, N. Mex. 274/E2
Miami (co.), Ohio 284/B5
Miami, Okla. 288/S1
Miami, Texas 303/D2
Miami, U.S. 2/F4
Miami Beach, Fla. 188/L5
Miami Beach, Fla. 212/C5
Miami Lakes, Fla. 212/B4
Miamisburg, Ohio 284/B6
Miami Shores, Fla. 212/B4
Miami Springs, Fla. 212/B5
Miamitown, Ohio 284/A9
Miamiville, Ohio 284/D9
Miandowab, Iran 66/E2
Miandrivazo, Madagascar 118/G3
Mianeh, Iran 59/E2
Mianeh, Iran 66/E2
Mianus, Conn. 210/A4
Mianus (riv.), Conn. 210/A4
Mianwali, Pakistan 68/C2
Mianwali, Pakistan 59/K3
Mianyang, Hubei, China 77/H5
Mianyang, Sichuan, China 77/G5
Mianzhu, China 77/F5
Miass, U.S.S.R. 48/G4
Miastko, Poland 47/C2
Miazal, Ecuador 128/D4
Mica (dam), Br. Col. 184/H4
Mica, Wash. 310/H3
Mica Creek, Br. Col. 184/H4
Micanopy, Fla. 212/D2
Micawber, Okla. 288/N3
Micay, Colombia 126/B6
Micco, Fla. 212/F4
Miccosukee, Fla. 212/B1
Miccosukee (lake), Fla. 212/B1
Michael, I. of Man 13/C3
Michael (lake), Newf. 166/C3
Michalovce, Czech. 41/G2
Michaud (pt.), Nova Scotia 168/H3
Michelago, N.S. Wales 97/E4
Michelson (mt.), Alaska 196/K1
Michelstadt, Germany 22/C4
Miches, Dom. Rep. 158/F6
Michiana, Mich. 250/C7
Michiana Shores, Ind. 227/D1
Michichi, Alberta 182/D4
Michie, Tenn. 237/E10
Michigamme, Mich. 250/B2
Michigamme (lake), Mich. 250/A2
Michigamme (res.), Mich. 250/B2
Michigamme (riv.), Mich. 250/A2
Michigan 188/J1
MICHIGAN 250/80
Michigan (lake) 188/J2
Michigan (lake), Ill. 222/F1
Michigan (lake), Ind. 227/C1
Michigan (lake), Mich. 250/B5
Michigan, N. Dak. 282/O3
Michigan (state), U.S. 146/K5
Michigan (lake), U.S. 146/K5
Michigan (isl.), Wis. 317/F2
Michigan (lake), Wis. 317/M9
Michigan Bar, Calif. 204/C8
Michigan Center, Mich. 250/E6
Michigan City, Ind. 227/C1
Michigan City, Miss. 256/F1
Michigantown, Ind. 227/E4
Michigan Valley, Kansas 232/G3
Michipicoten (isl.), Ontario 177/H5
Michipicoten (isl.), Ontario 175/C3
Michipicoten River, Ontario 177/H5
Michipicoten River, Ontario 177/C3
Michoacán (state), Mexico 150/H7
Michurin, Bulgaria 45/H4
Michurinsk, U.S.S.R. 52/F4
Michurinsk, U.S.S.R. 48/E4
Mickelton, N.J. 273/C4
Micotrin (mt.), Dominica 161/F6
Micoua, Québec 174/D3
Micoud, St. Lucia 161/G6
Micro, N.C. 281/N3
Micronesia, Federated States of 2/S5
Micronesia, Federated States of 87/F5
Micronesia (reg.), Pacific 87/E4
Midale, Sask. 181/H6
Midas, Nev. 266/E1
Middelburg, Netherlands 27/C6
Middelburg, Cape Prov., S. Africa 118/D6
Middelburg, Transvaal, S. Africa 118/D5
Middelfart, Denmark 21/C7
Middelfart, Denmark 18/G9
Middelharnis, Netherlands 27/E5
Middelkerke, Belgium 27/B6
Middelvlei, S. Africa 118/G7
Middenmeer, Netherlands 27/F3
Middle (riv.), Conn. 210/F1
Middle (pt.), Fla. 212/E6
Middle, Iowa 229/K5
Middle (riv.), Minn. 255/B2
Middle Alkali (lake), Calif. 204/E2
Middle Andaman (isl.), India 68/G6
Middle Arm, Newf. 166/C4
Middle Atlas (ranges), Morocco 106/C2
Middle Bass, Ohio 284/E2
Middle Bass (isl.), Ohio 284/E2
Middle Beaver (creek), Colo. 208/P4
Middleboro, Mass. 249/L5
Middleboro•, Mass. 249/L5
Middleboro (McKean), Pa. 294/B2
Middlebourne, W. Va. 312/E3
Middlebranch, Ohio 284/H4
Middlebro, Manitoba 179/G5
Middlebrook, Va. 307/K4
Middleburg, Fla. 212/E1
Middleburg, Ky. 237/M6
Middleburg, Md. 245/K2
Middleburg, N.C. 281/N2
Middleburg, Ohio 284/C5
Middleburg, Pa. 294/H4
Middleburg, Va. 307/N3
Middleburgh, N.Y. 276/M5
Middleburg Heights, Ohio 284/G10
Middlebury•, Conn. 210/C2
Middlebury, Ind. 227/F1
Middlebury, Vt. 268/A3
Middlebury•, Vt. 268/A3
Middlebury Center, Pa. 294/H2
Middlebury Gap (pass), Vt. 268/B4
Middlebush, N.J. 273/D3
Middlechurch, Manitoba 179/E4
Middle Concho (riv.), Texas 303/C6
Middledam, Maine 243/B6
Middle Falls, N.Y. 276/O4
Middlefield•, Conn. 210/E2
Middlefield•, Mass. 249/B3
Middlefield, Ohio 284/H3
Middle Fork (peak), Idaho 220/D5
Middlefork, Ind. 227/E4
Middle Fork, Powder (riv.), Wyo. 319/F2
Middlegate, Norfolk Is. 88/L6
Middle Granville, N.Y. 276/O4
Middlegrove, Ill. 222/C3
Middle Grove, Mo. 261/H4
Middle Haddam, Conn. 210/E2
Middle Harbour (creek), N.S. Wales 88/K3
Middle Harbour (creek), N.S. Wales 97/J3
Middle Hope, N.Y. 276/M7
Middle Inlet, Wis. 317/K5
Middle Lake, Sask. 181/F3
Middle Loch (inlet), Hawaii 218/A3
Middle Loup (riv.), Nebr. 264/D3
Middlemarch, N. Zealand 100/B6
Middle Musquodoboit, Nova Scotia 168/E3
Middle Patuxent (riv.), Md. 245/L3
Middle Piney (creek), Wyo. 319/B3
Middle Point, Ohio 284/B4
Middleport, N.Y. 276/C4
Middleport, Ohio 284/F7
Middleport, Pa. 294/K4
Middle River, Md. 245/N3
Middle River, Minn. 255/B2
Middle River, Nova Scotia 168/G2
Middle Saranac (lake), N.Y. 276/M2
Middlesboro, Ky. 237/O7
Middlesboro, Ky. 188/K3
Middlesbrough, England 7/D3
Middlesbrough, England 13/F3
Middlesbrough, England 10/F3
Middlesex (co.), Conn. 210/E3
Middlesex (co.), Mass. 249/J3
Middlesex (co.), N.J. 273/E3
Middlesex, N.J. 273/E2
Middlesex, N.Y. 276/F5
Middlesex, N.C. 281/N3
Middlesex (county), Ontario 177/C4
Middlesex•, Vt. 268/B3
Middlesex (co.), Va. 307/R5
Middle Stewiacke, Nova Scotia 168/E3
Middleton (isl.), Alaska 196/J3
Middleton, England 13/H2
Middleton, England 10/G2
Middleton, Georgia 217/G2
Middleton, Idaho 220/B6
Middleton•, Mass. 249/K2
Middleton, Mich. 250/E5
Middleton•, N.H. 268/E5
Middleton, Nova Scotia 168/C4
Middleton, Tenn. 237/D10
Middleton, Wis. 317/G9
Middletown, Calif. 204/C5
Middletown, Conn. 210/E2
Middletown, Del. 245/R3
Middletown, Ill. 222/D3
Middletown, Ind. 227/F4
Middletown, Iowa 229/L7
Middletown, Ky. 237/L2
Middletown, Md. 245/J3
Middletown, Mo. 261/J4
Middletown•, N.J. 273/E3
Middletown, N.Y. 276/L8
Middletown, N.C. 281/T4
Middletown, N. Ireland 17/H3
Middletown, Ohio 284/A6
Middletown, Pa. 294/J5
Middletown•, R.I. 249/J6
Middletown, Va. 307/M2
Middletown Springs•, Vt. 268/A5
Middle Valley, N.J. 273/D2
Middleville, Mich. 250/D6
Middleville, N.J. 273/D1
Middleville, N.Y. 276/K4
Middleville, Ontario 177/H2
Middle Water, Texas 303/B2
Middleway, W. Va. 312/K4
Middlewich, England 13/H2
Middlewich, England 10/G2
Middlewood, Nova Scotia 168/D4
Midfield, Ala. 195/E4
Midgic Station, New Bruns. 170/F3
Mid Glamorgan, Wales 13/D6
Midhurst, Ontario 177/E3
Midian (dist.), Saudi Arabia 59/C4
Midkiff, W. Va. 312/B6
Midland, Ark. 202/B3
Midland, Ind. 227/C6
Midland, La. 238/F6
Midland, Md. 245/C2
Midland (co.), Mich. 250/E5
Midland, Mich. 250/E5
Midland, N.C. 281/J4
Midland, Ohio 284/C7
Midland, Ontario 177/D3
Midland, Oreg. 291/F5
Midland, Pa. 294/A4
Midland, S. Dak. 298/G5
Midland, Tex. 188/F4
Midland (co.), Texas 303/B6
Midland, Texas 303/C6
Midland, Va. 307/N3
Midland City, Ala. 195/H8
Midland Park, N.J. 273/B1
Midlandvale, Alberta 182/D4
Midleton, Ireland 17/E8
Midleton, Ireland 10/B5
Midlothian, Ill. 222/B6
Midlothian (trad. co.), Scotland 15/B5
Midlothian, Texas 303/G5
Midlothian, Va. 307/N6
Midnapore, India 68/F4
Midnight, Miss. 256/C4
Midnight (lake), Sask. 181/C2
Midongy Atsimo, Madagascar 118/H4
Midvale, Idaho 220/B5
Midvale, Ohio 284/H5
Midvale, Utah 304/B3
Midville, Georgia 217/H5
Midway (isls.) 188/E6
Midway, Ala. 195/H6
Midway, Br. Col. 184/H6
Midway, Del. 245/T6
Midway, Fla. 212/B1
Midway, Georgia 217/K7
Midway, Ind. 227/C8
Midway, Ky. 237/M4
Midway (Sedalia), Ohio 284/D6
Midway, Pa. 294/B5
Midway, Tenn. 237/P8
Midway (isls.), U.S. 87/J3
Midway, Utah 304/C3
Midway City, Calif. 204/D11
Midway Park, N.C. 281/O5
Midwest, Wyo. 319/F2
Midwest City, Okla. 288/M4
Midyat, Turkey 63/J4
Midye, Turkey 63/C2
Mid Yell, Scotland 15/G2
Midzhur (mt.), Bulgaria 45/F4
Midzhur (mt.), Yugoslavia 45/F4
Mie (pref.), Japan 81/H6
Miechów, Poland 47/E3
Międzychód, Poland 47/B2
Międzylesie, Poland 47/C3
Międzyrzec Podlaski, Poland 47/F3
Międzyrzecz, Poland 47/B2
Mielec, Poland 47/E3
Mier, Ind. 227/F3
Mier, Mexico 150/K3
Miercurea Ciuc, Romania 45/G2
Mieres, Spain 33/D1
Miesso, Ethiopia 111/H6
Miesso, Ethiopia 102/G4
Miesville, Minn. 255/F6
Miette, Alberta 182/B3
Mifflin, Ohio 284/F4
Mifflin (co.), Pa. 294/G4
Mifflin, Pa. 294/H4
Mifflin, Wis. 317/F10
Mifflinburg, Pa. 294/H4
Mifflintown, Pa. 294/H4
Miflin, Ala. 195/C10
Migdal, Israel 65/C2
Migdal Ha 'Emeq, Israel 65/C2
Mignon, Ala. 195/F4
Migori, Kenya 115/F4
Miguel Alves, Brazil 132/F4
Miguel Auza, Mexico 150/H4
Miguel de la Borda, Panama 154/G6
Miguelete, Uruguay 145/B5
Miguel Riglos, Argentina 143/D4
Migues, Uruguay 145/C6
Mihalıççık, Turkey 63/D3
Mihara, Japan 81/F6
Mikado, Mich. 250/F4
Mikado, Sask. 181/J4
Mikana, Wis. 317/C4
Mikhaylovgrad, Bulgaria 45/F4
Mikhaylovka, U.S.S.R. 52/F4
Mikhmoret, Israel 65/B3
Miki, Japan 81/H7
Mikinai, Greece 45/F7
Mikkalo, Oreg. 291/G2
Mikkeli (prov.), Finland 18/P6
Mikkeli, Finland 18/P6
Mikkwa (riv.), Alberta 182/B5
Miklów, Poland 47/B4
Mikonos (isl.), Greece 45/G7
Mikulov, Czech. 41/D2
Mikumi Nat'l Park, Tanzania 115/G5
Mikun', U.S.S.R. 52/H2
Mikuni, Japan 81/G5
Milaca, Minn. 255/E5
Milagro, Ecuador 120/A3
Milagro, Ecuador 128/C4
Milagros, Philippines 82/D4
Milam (co.), Texas 303/H7
Milam, Texas 303/L6
Milam, W. Va. 312/H5
Milan, Georgia 217/G6
Milan, Ill. 222/C2
Milan, Ind. 227/G6
Milan (prov.), Italy 34/B2
Milan, Italy 2/K3
Milan, Italy 7/E4
Milan, Italy 34/B2
Milan, Kansas 232/E4
Milan, Mich. 250/F6
Milan, Minn. 255/C5
Milan, Mo. 261/F2
Milan•, N.H. 268/E2
Milan, N. Mex. 274/B3
Milan, Ohio 284/E3
Milan, Québec 172/F4
Milan, Tenn. 237/D9
Milan, Wash. 310/H3
Milan, Wis. 317/F6
Milanje, Mozambique 118/F3
Milano, Texas 303/H7
Milanville, Pa. 294/M2
Milâs, Turkey 63/B4
Milazzo, Italy 34/E5
Milbank, S. Dak. 298/R3
Milbanke (sound), Br. Col. 184/C4
Milberger, Kansas 232/D3
Milbridge•, Maine 243/H6
Milburn, Ky. 237/D7
Milburn, Nebr. 264/E3
Milburn, Okla. 288/O6
Milden, Sask. 181/D4
Mildenhall, England 13/H5

410 Mildmay

Mildmay, Ontario 177/C3
Mildred, Kansas 232/G3
Mildred, Mont. 262/M4
Mildred, Pa. 294/K3
Mildred, Sask. 181/D2
Mildred Lake, Alberta 182/E1
Mildura, Victoria 88/G6
Mildura, Victoria 97/A4
Mile, China 77/F7
Miles, Iowa 229/N4
Miles, Queensland 88/H5
Miles, Texas 303/D6
Milesburg, Pa. 294/G4
Miles City, Mont. 188/E1
Miles City, Mont. 262/L4
Milestone, Sask. 181/G5
Milesville, S. Dak 298/F5
Milevsko, Czech. 41/C2
Miley, S.C. 296/E6
Milfay, Okla. 288/N3
Milford, Calif. 204/E3
Milford, Conn. 210/C4
Milford (pt.), Conn. 210/C4
Milford, Del. 245/S5
Milford, Georgia 217/C8
Milford, Ill. 222/F3
Milford, Ind. 227/F2
Milford, Ind. 227/F6
Milford, Iowa 229/C2
Milford, Ireland 17/F1
Milford, Kansas 232/F2
Milford (lake), Kansas 232/E2
Milford, Ky. 237/N3
Milford, Maine 243/F6
Milford•, Maine 243/F6
Milford, Mass. 249/H4
Milford•, Mass. 249/H4
Milford, Mich. 250/F6
Milford, Mo. 261/D7
Milford, Nebr. 264/H4
Milford, N.H. 268/D6
Milford•, N.H. 268/D6
Milford, N.J. 273/C2
Milford (sound), N. Zealand 100/A6
Milford, Ohio 284/D9
Milford, Pa. 294/N3
Milford, Texas 303/H5
Milford, Utah 304/A5
Milford, Va. 307/O4
Milford, Wis. 317/J9
Milford Bay, Ontario 177/E2
Milford Center, Ohio 284/D5
Milford Haven, Wales 13/B6
Milford Haven, Wales 10/D5
Milford Haven (inlet), Wales 13/B6
Milford Haven (inlet), Wales 10/D5
Milford Station, Nova Scotia 168/E3
Milh, Bahr al (lake), Iraq 66/C4
Mili (atoll), Marshall Is. 87/H5
Miliana, Algeria 106/E1
Milicz, Poland 47/C3
Milieu (riv.), Québec 172/C3
Mililani Town, Hawaii 218/E2
Milingimbi, North. Terr. 93/D2
Milk (riv.) 146/H5
Milk (riv.), Alberta 182/D5
Milk (riv.), Mont. 188/D1
Milk (riv.), Mont. 262/J2
Milk, Wadi el (dry riv.), Sudan 59/A6
Milk, Wadi el (dry riv.), Sudan 111/E4
Milk River, Alberta 182/D5
Mill (creek), Calif. 204/D3
Mill (riv.), Conn. 210/D3
Mill (riv.), Conn. 210/B4
Mill (creek), Ind. 227/D5
Mill (riv.), Mass. 249/D3
Mill (riv.), Mass. 249/C3
Mill (creek), Mich. 250/G5
Mill (creek), N.J. 273/E4
Mill (isl.), N.W. Terr. 187/L3
Mill (riv.), Vt. 268/B4
Mill (creek), W. Va. 312/C5
Milladore, Wis. 317/G6
Millard, Ky. 237/S6
Millard, Mo. 261/G2
Millard (co.), Utah 304/A4
Millarton, N. Dak. 282/N6
Millarville, Alberta 182/C4
Millau, France 28/E5
Millbank, Ontario 177/D4
Mill Bay, Br. Col 184/K3
Millboro, S. Dak. 298/K7
Millboro, Va. 307/J5
Millboro Springs, Va. 307/J4
Millbourne, Pa. 294/M6
Millbrae, Calif. 204/J2
Millbridge, Ontario 177/G3
Millbrook, Ala. 195/F6
Millbrook, Ill. 222/E2
Millbrook, Mich. 250/D5
Millbrook, N.Y. 276/N7
Millbrook, N.C. 281/M3
Millbrook, Ontario 177/F3
Millburn•, N.J. 273/E2
Millburne, Wyo. 319/B4
Millbury•, Mass. 249/H4
Millbury, Ohio 284/D2
Mill City, Nev. 266/D2
Mill City, Oreg. 291/E3
Mill Cove, New Bruns. 170/D3
Mill Cove, Nova Scotia 168/D4
Millcreek, Ill. 222/D6
Mill Creek, Ind. 227/D1
Millcreek, Mo. 261/M7
Mill Creek, Okla. 288/N6
Mill Creek, Pa. 294/G5
Mill Creek, W. Va. 312/G5
Milldale, Conn. 210/D2
Millecoquins (lake), Mich. 250/D2
Milledgeville, Georgia 217/F4
Milledgeville, Ill. 222/D1
Milledgeville, Ohio 284/C6
Milledgeville, Tenn. 237/E10
Mille Iles (riv.), Québec 172/H4
Mille Lac Ind. Res., Minn. 255/E4
Mille Lacs (co.), Minn. 255/E5
Mille Lacs (lake), Minn. 188/H1
Mille Lacs (lake), Minn. 255/E4
Mille Lacs (lake), Ontario 177/G5
Mille Lacs (lake), Ontario 175/B3
Millen, Georgia 217/J5
Miller (peak), Ariz. 198/E7
Miller (co.), Ark. 202/C7
Miller (co.), Georgia 217/C8
Miller, Iowa 229/F2
Miller, Kansas 232/F3
Miller, Miss. 256/E1
Miller (co.), Mo. 261/H6
Miller, Mo. 261/E8
Miller, Nebr. 264/E4
Miller, Ohio 284/F8
Miller (creek), Oreg. 291/F5
Miller, S. Dak. 298/L4
Miller City, Ohio 284/B3
Miller Dam Flowage (res.), Wis. 317/E5
Miller House, Alaska 196/J1
Millerovo, U.S.S.R. 48/E5
Millerovo, U.S.S.R. 52/F5
Millers, Md. 245/L2
Millers (riv.), Mass. 249/E2
Millersburg, Ind. 227/F1
Millersburg, Iowa 229/J5
Millerburg, Ky. 237/N4
Millersburg, Mich. 250/F3
Millersburg, Ohio 284/F4
Millersburg, Oreg. 291/E3
Millersburg, Pa. 294/J4
Millers Falls, Mass. 249/E2
Millers Ferry, Ala. 195/D6
Millers Ferry, Fla. 212/C6
Millersport, Ohio 284/E6
Millerstown, Ky. 237/J6
Millerstown, Pa. 294/H4
Millersview, Texas 303/E6
Millersville, Md. 245/M4
Millersville, Ohio 284/D3
Millersville, Pa. 294/K6
Millerton (lake), Calif. 204/F6
Millerton, Iowa 229/G7
Millerton, New Bruns. 170/E2
Millerton, N.Y. 276/O7
Millerton, Okla. 288/S7
Millerton, Pa. 294/J2
Millertown, Newf. 166/C4
Millerville, Ala. 195/G4
Millerville, Minn. 255/C4
Millet, Alberta 182/D3
Millet, S.C. 296/D5
Millet, Texas 303/E9
Millgrove, Ind. 227/G4
Mill Grove, Mo. 261/E2
Mill Hall, Pa. 294/G3
Millhaven, Georgia 217/J5
Millheim, Pa. 294/G4
Millhousen, Ind. 227/G6
Millican, Oreg. 291/F4
Millicent, Alberta 182/E4
Millicent, S. Australia 88/F7
Millicent, S. Australia 94/F7
Milligan, Fla. 212/C6
Milligan, Ind. 227/C5
Milligan, Nebr. 264/G4
Milligan College, Tenn. 237/S8
Milliken, Colo. 208/K2
Millikin, La. 238/H1
Millingen aan den Rijn, Netherlands 27/J5
Millington, Conn. 210/F3
Millington, Ill. 222/E2
Millington, Md. 245/P3
Millington, Mich. 250/F5
Millington, N.J. 273/D2
Millington, Tenn. 237/B10
Millinocket•, Maine 243/F4
Millinocket (lake), Maine 243/F3
Millinocket (lake), Maine 243/F4
Mill Iron, Mont. 262/M5
Millis•, Mass. 249/A8
Millis-Clicquot, Mass. 249/A8
Millisle, N. Ireland 17/K2
Millmerran, Queensland 95/D5
Millmont, Pa. 294/H4
Mill Neck, N.Y. 276/R6
Millom, England 13/D3
Mill Plain, Conn. 210/A3
Mill Point, W. Va. 312/F6
Millport, Ala. 195/B3
Millport, N.Y. 276/G6
Millport, Pa. 294/F2
Millport, Scotland 15/A2
Millport, Scotland 10/A1
Millrift, Pa. 294/N3
Mill River, Mass. 249/A4
Mill Road, Nova Scotia 168/D4
Millrose, W. Australia 92/C4
Mill Run, Pa. 294/C6
Millry, Ala. 195/B7
Mills (co.), Iowa 229/B6
Mills, Ky. 237/O7
Mills, Nebr. 264/E2
Mills, N. Mex. 274/E2
Mills (lake), N.W. Terr. 187/G3
Mills, Pa. 294/G2
Mills (co.), Texas 303/F6
Mills, Utah 304/B4
Mills, Wyo. 319/F3
Millsap, Texas 303/G5
Millsboro, Del. 245/S6
Millsboro, Pa. 294/B6
Mill Shoals, Ill. 222/E5
Mill Spring, Mo. 261/L8
Mill Springs, Ky. 237/M7
Millstadt, Ill. 222/B3
Millston, Wis. 317/E7
Millstone, Ky. 237/R6
Millstone, N.J. 273/D2
Millstone (riv.), N.J. 273/D3
Millstone, W. Va. 312/D5
Millstream Station, W. Australia 92/B3
Millstreet, Ireland 17/D7
Millthorpe, N.S. Wales 97/E5
Milltown, Ala. 195/H4
Milltown, Ind. 227/E8
Milltown, Ireland 17/A7
Milltown, Ky. 237/L6
Milltown, Mont. 262/C4
Milltown, Newf. 166/C4
Milltown, N.J. 273/E3
Milltown, S. Dak. 298/O7
Milltown, Wis. 317/B4
Millungera, Queensland 95/B3
Millvale, Pa. 294/B7
Mill Valley, Calif. 204/H2
Mill Village, Nova Scotia 168/D4
Mill Village, Pa. 294/C2
Millville, Del. 245/T6
Millville, Ind. 227/G5
Millville, Iowa 229/L3
Millville•, Mass. 249/H4
Millville, Minn. 255/F6
Millville, New Bruns. 170/C2
Millville, N.J. 273/C5
Millville, Ohio 284/A7
Millville, Pa. 294/J3
Millville, Utah 304/C2
Millwood (lake), Ark. 202/C6
Millwood, Georgia 217/G8
Millwood, Ky. 237/J6
Millwood, Manitoba 179/A4
Millwood, Ohio 284/F5
Millwood, Va. 307/N2
Millwood, Wash. 310/H3
Millwood, W. Va. 312/C5
Milly Milly, W. Australia 92/B4
Milmay, N.J. 273/D5
Milmine, Ill. 222/E4
Milmont Park, Pa. 294/M7
Milnathort, Scotland 15/E4
Milne (inlet), N.W. Terr. 187/K2
Milne (bay), Papua N.G. 85/C8
Milner, Colo. 208/F2
Milner, Georgia 217/D4
Milner Ridge, Manitoba 179/F4
Milnerton, S. Africa 118/F6
Milnesand, N. Mex. 274/F5
Milnes Landing, Br. Col. 184/J4
Milngavie, Scotland 10/B1
Milngavie, Scotland 15/B1
Milnor, N. Dak. 282/R7
Milo, Alberta 182/D4
Milo (riv.), Guinea 106/C7
Milo, Iowa 229/G6
Milo, Ky. 237/R5
Milo, Maine 243/F5
Milo•, Maine 243/F5
Milo, Mo. 261/D7
Milo, Okla. 288/M6
Milo, Oreg. 291/E5
Milo, Tenn. 237/L9
Milolii, Hawaii 218/G6
Milos, Greece 45/G7
Milos (isl.), Greece 45/G7
Milot, Québec 172/F1
Milpa, N.S. Wales 97/B2
Milparinka, N.S. Wales 97/A1
Milperra, N.S. Wales 97/H4
Milpitas, Calif. 204/L3
Milroy, Ind. 227/G6
Milroy, Minn. 255/C6
Milroy, Pa. 294/G4
Milstead, Ala. 195/G6
Milstead, Georgia 217/D3
Milton (res.), Colo. 208/K2
Milton, Conn. 210/C1
Milton, Del. 245/S5
Milton, Fla. 212/B6
Milton, Ill. 222/C4
Milton, Ind. 227/G5
Milton, Iowa 229/J7
Milton, Kansas 232/E4
Milton, Ky. 237/L3
Milton, La. 238/F6
Milton•, Mass. 249/D7
Milton, Newf. 166/C2
Milton•, N.H. 268/F5
Milton, N.J. 273/D1
Milton, N.S. Wales 97/F4
Milton, N.Y. 276/M7
Milton, N.Y. 276/N4
Milton, N. Zealand 100/B7
Milton, N.C. 281/L1
Milton, N. Dak. 282/O2
Milton, Nova Scotia 168/D4
Milton, Okla. 288/S4
Milton, Ontario 177/E4
Milton, Pa. 294/J3
Milton, Tenn. 237/J9
Milton, Vt. 268/A2
Milton•, Vt. 268/A2
Milton, Wash. 310/C3
Milton, W. Va. 312/B6
Milton, Wis. 317/J10
Miltona, Minn. 255/C4
Miltona (lake), Minn. 255/C4
Milton Center, Ohio 284/C3
Milton-Freewater, Oreg. 291/J2
Milton Keynes, England 13/F5
Milton Mills, N.H. 268/F4
Miltonsburg, Ohio 284/H6
Miltonvale, Kansas 232/E2
Miltownmalbay, Ireland 17/C6
Milverton, Ontario 177/D4
Milwaukee, N.C. 281/P2
Milwaukee, Wis. 146/K5
Milwaukee, Wis. 188/J2
Milwaukee (co.), Wis. 317/L9
Milwaukee, Wis. 317/M1
Milwaukie, Oreg. 291/B2
Mima, Ky. 237/P5
Mimbres, N. Mex. 274/B6
Mimbres (mts.), N. Mex. 274/B6
Mimbres (riv.), N. Mex. 274/B6
Miminegash, Pr. Edward I. 168/D2
Mimizan, France 28/C5
Mimon, Czech. 41/C1
Mimongo, Gabon 115/B4
Mimosa Park, La. 238/N4
Mimoso do Sul, Brazil 135/F2
Mims, Fla. 212/F3
Mina, Nev. 266/C4
Mina, S. Dak. 298/M3
Mina al Ahmadi, Kuwait 59/E4
Mina al Fahal, Oman 59/G5
Minab, Iran 59/G2
Minab, Iran 66/K7
Minaki, Ontario 177/F4
Minaki, Ontario 175/A3
Minam, Oreg. 291/K2
Minamata, Japan 81/E7
Minami Iwo (isl.), Japan 87/D3
Minami Iwo (isl.), Japan 81/M5
Minapasuk, Philippines 82/D5
Minard, Ireland 17/A7
Minas, Cuba 158/G2
Minas (mts.), Guatemala 154/C3
Minas (basin), Nova Scotia 168/D3
Minas (chan.), Nova Scotia 168/D3
Minas, Uruguay 145/D5
Mina Saud, Kuwait 59/E4
Mina Sa'ud, Saudi Arabia 59/E4
Minas-Cué, Paraguay 144/C3
Minas de Corrales, Uruguay 145/D2
Minas de Matahambre, Cuba 158/A1
Minas de Ríotinto, Spain 33/C4
Minas Gerais (state), Brazil 135/D2
Minas Gerais (state), Brazil 132/E7
Minas Novas, Brazil 132/F7
Minatare, Nebr. 264/A3
Minatare (lake), Nebr. 264/A3
Minatitlán, Mexico 150/M8
Minbu, Burma 72/B2
Minburn, Alberta 182/E3
Minburn, Iowa 229/E5
Minbay, Burma 72/B2
Mincha, Chile 138/A8
Minchinmávida (vol.), Chile 138/E4
Mincio (riv.), Italy 34/C2
Minco, Okla. 288/L4
Mindanao (isl.), Philippines 54/O9
Mindanao (isl.), Philippines 2/R5
Mindanao (isl.), Philippines 85/H4
Mindanao (isl.), Philippines 82/D7
Mindanao (riv.), Philippines 82/E7
Mindanao (sea), Philippines 85/G4
Mindanao (sea), Philippines 82/D7
Mindelheim, Germany 22/D4
Mindelo, C. Verde 106/A7
Mindemoya, Ontario 177/B2
Mindemoya (lake), Ontario 177/B2
Minden, Germany 22/C2
Minden, Iowa 229/C6
Minden, La. 238/D1
Minden, Nebr. 264/F4
Minden, Nev. 266/B4
Minden, Ontario 177/F3
Minden, Texas 303/K5
Minden City, Mich. 250/G5
Mindenmines, Mo. 261/C8
Mindiptana, Indonesia 85/L7
Mindoro (isl.), Philippines 54/N8
Mindoro (isl.), Philippines 85/G3
Mindoro (isl.), Philippines 82/C4
Mindoro (isl.), Philippines 85/F3
Mindoro (str.), Philippines 82/C4
Mindoro, Wis. 317/D7
Mindouli, Congo 115/B4
Mindszent, Hungary 41/F3
Mine (head), Ireland 17/F8
Mine Centre, Ontario 177/G5
Mine Centre, Ontario 175/B3
Minehead, England 13/D6
Minehead, England 10/E5
Mine Hill•, N.J. 273/D2
Mineiros, Brazil 132/C7
Mineiros, Brazil 120/D4
Mine La Motte, Mo. 261/M7
Mineola, Iowa 229/B6
Mineola, Mo. 261/J5
Mineola, N.Y. 276/R7
Mineola, Texas 303/J5
Miner, Mo. 261/N9
Miner, Mont. 262/E5
Miner (co.), S. Dak. 298/O5
Mineral, Calif. 204/D3
Mineral (co.), Colo. 208/F7
Mineral, Ill. 222/E2
Mineral (co.), Mont. 262/B3
Mineral (co.), Nev. 266/C4
Mineral, Ohio 284/F7
Mineral, Texas 303/G9
Mineral (mts.), Utah 304/B5
Mineral, Va. 307/N4
Mineral, Wash. 310/C4
Mineral (co.), W. Va. 312/J4
Mineral Bluff, Georgia 217/D1
Mineral Center, Minn. 255/G2
Mineral City, Ohio 284/H4
Mineral del Monte, Mexico 150/K6
Mineral Hills, Mich. 250/G2
Mineral'nye Vody, U.S.S.R. 52/F6
Mineral Point, Mo. 261/L7
Mineral Point, Wis. 317/F10
Mineral Springs, Ark. 202/C6
Mineral Springs, N.C. 281/H5
Mineral Wells, Miss. 256/E1
Mineral Wells, Texas 303/F5
Mineralwells, W. Va. 312/C4
Minersville, Ohio 284/G7
Minersville, Pa. 294/K4
Minersville, Utah 304/A5
Mine Run, Va. 307/N4
Minerva, Ky. 237/O3
Minerva, N.Y. 276/N3
Minerva, Ohio 284/H4
Minerva (reefs), Tonga 87/H8
Minerva Park, Ohio 284/E5
Minetto, N.Y. 276/H4
Mineville-Witherbee, N.Y. 276/O2
Minfeng (Niya), China 77/B4
Minford, Ohio 284/E8
Mingan, Que. 162/K5
Mingan, Québec 174/E2
Mingechaur, U.S.S.R. 52/G6
Mingenew, W. Australia 88/B5
Mingenew, W. Australia 92/A5
Minginish (dist.), Scotland 15/B3
Minglanilla, Spain 33/F3
Mingo, Iowa 229/G5
Mingo, Kansas 232/B2
Mingo (lake), N.W. Terr. 187/L3
Mingo, Ohio 284/C5
Mingo (co.), W. Va. 312/B7
Mingo, W. Va. 312/F5
Mingo Junction, Ohio 284/J5
Mingshui, Gansu, China 77/E3
Mingshui, Heilongjiang, China 77/L2
Mingulay (isl.), Scotland 15/A4
Mingus, Texas 303/F5
Minhla, Burma 72/B3
Minho (riv.), Jamaica 158/J6
Minho (riv.), Portugal 33/B2
Minicoy (isl.), India 68/C7
Minidoka (co.), Idaho 220/E7
Minidoka, Idaho 220/E7
Minier, Ill. 222/D3
Minigwal (lake), W. Australia 88/C5
Minigwal (lake), W. Australia 92/C5
Minilya, W. Australia 92/A4
Miniota, Manitoba 179/B4
Minipi (lake), Newf. 166/B3
Minipi (riv.), Newf. 166/B3
Ministikwan (lake), Sask. 181/B1
Ministre (pt.), St. Lucia 161/G7
Minitonas, Manitoba 179/B2
Min Jiang (riv.), China 77/J6
Minlaton, S. Australia 94/E6
Minle, China 77/F4
Minna, Nigeria 106/F7
Minneapolis, Kansas 232/E2
Minneapolis, Minn. 146/J5
Minneapolis, Minn. 188/H1
Minneapolis, Minn. 255/G5
Minneapolis, U.S. 2/E3
Minneapolis-St. Paul Airport, Minn. 255/G5
Minnechaduza (creek), S. Dak. 298/H7
Minnedosa, Manitoba 179/B4
Minnedosa (riv.), Manitoba 179/B4
Minnehaha (co.), S. Dak. 298/R6
Minnehaha Springs, W. Va. 312/G6
Minneiska, Minn. 255/G6
Minneola, Fla. 212/E3
Minneola, Kansas 232/C4
Minneota, Minn. 255/C6
Minnesota 188/H1
MINNESOTA 255
Minnesota (riv.), Minn. 188/G2
Minnesota (riv.), Minn. 255/E6
Minnesota (riv.), S. Dak. 298/S3
Minnesota (state), U.S. 146/J5
Minnesota City, Minn. 255/G6
Minnesota Lake, Minn. 255/E7
Minnesott Beach, N.C. 281/R5
Minnetonka, Minn. 255/G5
Minnetonka (lake), Minn. 255/F5
Minnetrista, Minn. 255/F5
Minnewaska (lake), Minn. 255/C5
Minnewaukan, N. Dak. 282/M3
Minnigaff, Scotland 15/D6
Minnipa, S. Australia 88/F6
Minnipa, S. Australia 94/D5
Minnitaki (lake), Ontario 177/G4
Minnith, Mo. 261/M7
Minnora, W. Va. 312/D5
Miño (riv.), Spain 7/D4
Miño (riv.), Spain 33/B1
Minoa, N.Y. 276/J4
Minobu, Japan 81/J6
Minocqua, Wis. 317/G4
Minong, Wis. 317/C3
Minonk, Ill. 222/D3
Minoo, Japan 81/J7
Minooka, Ill. 222/E2
Minorca (isl.), Spain 7/E4
Minorca (isl.), Spain 33/J2
Minor Hill, Tenn. 237/G10
Minor Lane Heights, Ky. 237/K4
Minortown, Conn. 210/C2
Minot, Maine 243/C7
Minot•, Maine 243/C7
Minot, Mass. 249/F8
Minot, N. Dak. 188/F1
Minot, N. Dak. 146/H5
Minot, N. Dak. 282/H3
Minot A.F.B., N. Dak. 282/H3
Minotola, N.J. 273/D4
Minqin, China 77/F4
Minsk, U.S.S.R. 7/G3
Minsk, U.S.S.R. 2/L3
Minsk, U.S.S.R. 48/C4
Minsk, U.S.S.R. 52/C4
Mińsk Mazowiecki, Poland 47/E2
Minster, Ohio 284/B5
Minstrel Island, Br. Col. 184/D5
Minter, Ala. 195/D6
Minter City, Miss. 256/D3
Mint Hill, N.C. 281/H4
Mintlaw, Scotland 15/F3
Minto, Alaska 196/J2
Minto, Manitoba 179/B5
Minto, New Bruns. 170/D2
Minto, N. Dak. 282/R3
Minto (inlet), N.W. Terr. 187/G2
Minto (lake), Que. 162/J4
Minto (lake), Québec 174/E2
Minto, Yukon 187/E3
Minton, Sask. 181/G6
Minturn, Ark. 202/H2
Minturn, Colo. 208/G3
Minturn, Maine 243/G7
Minturn, S.C. 296/J2
Minturno, Italy 34/D4
Minûf, Egypt 111/J3
Minusinsk, U.S.S.R. 48/K4
Minusio, Switzerland 39/G4
Minute Man Nat'l Hist. Park, Mass. 249/B6
Minvoul, Gabon 115/B3
Min Xian, China 77/F5
Minyip, Victoria 97/B5
Mio, Mich. 250/E4
Miocene, Br. Col. 184/G4
Miquan, China 77/C3
Miquelon (isl.), 166/C4
Miquihuana, Mexico 150/J5
Miquillo (pt.), P. Rico 161/F1
Mira (riv.), Colombia 126/A7
Mira (riv.), Ecuador 128/C2
Mira, La. 238/C1
Mira (bay), Nova Scotia 168/J2
Mira (riv.), Nova Scotia 168/H3
Mira, Portugal 33/B2
Mira (riv.), Portugal 33/B4
Mirabad, Afghanistan 68/A2
Mirabad, Afghanistan 59/H3
Mirabel, Québec 172/H4
Mirabile, Mo. 261/D3
Miracema, Brazil 135/E2
Miracema, Brazil 132/F8
Miraema do Norte, Brazil 132/D5
Mirador, Brazil 132/E4
Mirador Nacional (mt.), Uruguay 145/D5
Miraflores, Boyacá, Colombia 126/D5
Miraflores, Vaupés, Colombia 126/D7
Miragoâne, Haiti 158/B6
Miragoâne, Haiti 156/D3
Miraj, India 68/D5
Miraje, Salar del (salt dep.), Chile 138/B3
Mira Loma, Calif. 204/E10
Miramar, Argentina 143/E4
Miramar, C. Rica 154/E5
Miramar, Fla. 212/B4
Miramar, Panama 154/H6
Miramichi (bay), New Bruns. 170/E1
Miram Shah, Pakistan 68/C2
Miranda, Brazil 132/C8
Miranda (riv.), Brazil 132/B8
Miranda, Colombia 126/B6
Miranda, S. Dak. 298/M4
Miranda (state), Venezuela 124/E2
Miranda de Ebro, Spain 33/E1
Miranda do Corvo, Portugal 33/B2
Miranda do Douro, Portugal 33/C2
Mirande, France 28/D6
Mirandela, Portugal 33/C2
Mirando City, Texas 303/E10
Mirandola, Italy 34/C2
Mira Por Vos (cays), Bahamas 156/C2
Mira Road, Nova Scotia 168/H2
Mirassol, Brazil 135/B2
Mira Taglio, Italy 34/D2
Mirebalais, Haiti 156/D3
Mirebalais, Haiti 158/C6
Mirecourt, France 28/G3
Mirgorod, U.S.S.R. 52/D5
Miri (hills), India 68/G3
Miri, Malaysia 85/E5
Mirik (Timiris) (cape), Mauritania 106/A5
Mirim (lake), Brazil 120/D6
Mirim (lag.), Brazil 132/C11
Mirirmire, Venezuela 124/D2
Mirína, Greece 45/G6
Miritiparaná (riv.), Colombia 126/E8
Mirjaveh, Iran 59/H4
Mirjaveh, Iran 66/M6
Mirjaveh, Pakistan 59/H4
Mirnyy Station, Ant. 5/C5
Mirnyy, U.S.S.R. 54/N3
Mirnyy, U.S.S.R. 48/M3
Mirpur, Pakistan 68/C2
Mirpur Khas, Pakistan 68/B3
Mirror, Alberta 182/D3
Mirror Lake, N.H. 268/E4
Mirtóön (sea), Greece 45/F7
Miryang, S. Korea 81/D6
Mirzapur-cum-Vindhyachal, India 68/E4
Misamis Occidental (prov.), Philippines 82/D6
Misamis Oriental (prov.), Philippines 82/E6
Misantia, Mexico 150/P1
Misawa, Japan 81/K3
Miscou (isl.), New Bruns. 170/F1
Miscou (pt.), New Bruns. 170/F1
Miscou Centre, New Bruns. 170/F1
Miscouche, Pr. Edward I. 168/D2

Mount Olive 413

Morea, Victoria 97/A5
Moreau (riv.), S. Dak. 298/G3
Moreauville, La. 238/G4
Morebattle, Scotland 15/F5
Morecambe, Alberta 182/E3
Morecambe (bay), England 10/E3
Morecambe (bay), England 13/D3
Moree, N.S. Wales 88/H5
Moree, N.S. Wales 97/E1
Morehead, Kansas 232/G4
Morehead, Ky. 237/P4
Morehead City, N.C. 281/R5
Morehouse (par.), La. 238/G1
Morehouse, Mo. 261/N9
Moreland, Ark. 202/E3
Moreland, Georgia 217/C4
Moreland, Idaho 220/F6
Moreland Hills, Ohio 284/J9
Morelia, Mexico 150/J7
Morelia, Mexico 146/H8
Morelia, Queensland 95/B4
Morell, Pr. Edward I. 168/F2
Morella, Queensland 88/G4
Morella, Spain 33/F2
Morelos (state), Mexico 150/K7
Morelos, Mexico 150/J2
Morelos Cañada, Mexico 150/O2
Morena, India 68/D3
Morena, Sierra (mts.), Spain 7/D5
Morena, Sierra (range), Spain 33/E3
Morenci, Ariz. 198/F5
Morenci, Mich. 250/E7
Moreni, Romania 45/G3
Moreno, Bolivia 136/B2
Moreno, Calif. 204/H10
Moreno (bay) Chile 138/A4
Møre og Romsdal (co.), Norway 18/E5
Mores (creek), Idaho 220/C6
Moresby, Br. Col. 184/B3
Moresby (isl.), Br. Col. 184/B4
Moreton (bay), Queensland 88/K2
Moreton (bay), Queensland 95/E5
Moreton (isl.), Queensland 88/J5
Moreton (isl.), Queensland 95/E5
Moretonhampstead, England 13/C7
Moreton-in-Marsh, England 13/F6
Moretown•, Vt. 268/B3
Morewood, Ontario 177/J2
Morgan (co.), Ala. 195/E2
Morgan (co.), Colo. 208/M2
Morgan (pt.), Conn. 210/D4
Morgan (co.), Georgia 217/F3
Morgan, Georgia 217/C7
Morgan (co.), Ill. 222/C4
Morgan (co.), Ind. 227/E6
Morgan (co.), Ky. 237/P5
Morgan, Ky. 237/N3
Morgan, Minn. 255/D6
Morgan (co.), Mo. 261/G6
Morgan, Mo. 261/G7
Morgan (co.), Ohio 284/G6
Morgan (co.), Tenn. 237/M8
Morgan, Texas 303/G5
Morgan (co.), Utah 304/C2
Morgan, Utah 304/C2
Morgan•, Vt. 268/D2
Morgan (co.), W. Va. 312/K3
Morgan Center, Vt. 268/D2
Morgan City, La. 238/H7
Morgan City, Miss. 256/D4
Morgan Falls (dam), Georgia 217/K1
Morganfield, Ky. 237/E5
Morgan Hill, Calif. 204/L4
Morganito, Venezuela 124/E5
Morgans Point, Texas 303/K2
Morgansville, W. Va. 312/E4
Morganton, Ark. 202/F3
Morganton, Georgia 217/D1
Morganton, N.C. 281/F3
Morgantown, Ind. 227/E6
Morgantown, Ky. 237/H6
Morgantown, Miss. 256/E8
Morgantown, Miss. 256/B7
Morgantown, Ohio 284/D7
Morgantown, Pa. 294/L5
Morgantown, W. Va. 312/G3
Morganville, Kansas 232/E2
Morganville, N.J. 273/E3
Morganza, La. 238/G5
Morges, Switzerland 39/B3
Morguilla (pt.), Chile 138/D1
Mori, China 77/D3
Mori, Japan 81/K2
Moriah, N.Y. 276/N2
Moriah Center, N.Y. 276/N2
Moriarty, N. Mex. 274/D4
Morice (lake), Br. Col. 184/D3
Morice (riv.), Br. Col. 184/D3
Morichal, Colombia 126/E6
Morichal Largo (riv.), Venezuela 124/G3
Morien (cape), Nova Scotia 168/J2
Moriguchi, Japan 81/J7
Morin Creek, Sask. 181/C1
Morin Dawa Daurzu, China 77/K2
Morin Heights, Québec 172/C4
Morinville, Alberta 182/D3
Morioka, Japan 81/K4
Morisset, N.S. Wales 97/F3
Morisset, Québec 172/G3
Moriston (riv.), Scotland 15/D3
Morjärv, Sweden 18/N3
Morlaix, France 28/B3
Morland, Kansas 232/B2
Morley, Alberta 182/C4
Morley, Iowa 229/L4
Morley, Mich. 250/D5
Morley, Mo. 261/N8
Morley, N.Y. 276/K1
Morley, Tenn. 237/O7
Mormon (lake), Ariz. 198/D4
Mormon (mt.), Idaho 220/D4
Mormon (mts.), Nev. 266/G5
Mormon Lake, Ariz. 198/D4
Morne-à-l'Eau, Guadeloupe 161/A6
Morne Seychellois (mt.), Seychelles 118/H5
Morningside, Alberta 182/D3
Morningside, Md. 245/G5
Morningside, Queensland 88/K2
Morningside Park, Conn. 210/G3
Morning Sun, Iowa 229/L6
Mornington (isl.), Chile 138/D8
Mornington (isl.), Queensland 88/F3
Mornington (isl.), Queensland 95/A3
Mornington, Victoria 97/C6
Mornington (pen.), Victoria 97/C6
Morning View, Ky. 237/N3
Moro, Ark. 202/H4
Moro (creek), Ark. 202/F7
Moro, Oreg. 291/G2
Moro (gulf), Philippines 82/D7
Moro (gulf), Philippines 85/G4
Moro (mt.), Switzerland 39/E5
Moro Bay, Ark. 202/F7
Morobe, Papua N.G. 85/C7
Morocco 2/J4
Morocco 102/B1
MOROCCO 106/C2
Morocco, Ind. 227/C3
Morocelí, Honduras 154/D3
Morochata, Bolivia 136/B5
Morococha, Peru 128/D8
Morogoro (reg.), Tanzania 115/G5
Morogoro, Tanzania 115/G5
Morogoro, Tanzania 102/F5
Moroleón, Mexico 150/J6
Morombe, Madagascar 118/G4
Moromoro, Bolivia 136/C6
Morón, Argentina 143/G7
Morón, Cuba 158/F2
Morón, Cuba 156/B2
Moron, Haiti 158/A6
Mörön (Muren), Mongolia 77/F2
Moron (mt.), Switzerland 39/D2
Morón, Venezuela 124/D2
Morona, Ecuador 128/D4
Morona (riv.), Peru 128/D5
Morona-Santiago (prov.), Ecuador 128/C4
Morondava, Madagascar 118/G3
Morondava, Madagascar 102/G7
Morón de la Frontera, Spain 33/D4
Morongo Ind. Res., Calif. 204/J10
Moroni (cap.), Comoros 118/G2
Moroni (cap.), Comoros 102/G6
Moroni, Utah 304/C4
Moron Us He (riv.), China 77/D5
Morotai (isl.), Indonesia 54/O9
Morotai (isl.), Indonesia 85/H5
Moroto, Uganda 115/F3
Morovis, P. Rico 161/D1
Morpeth, England 13/F2
Morpeth, England 10/F3
Morpeth, Ontario 177/C5
Morphou, Cyprus 63/E5
Morphou (bay), Cyprus 63/E5
Morral, Ohio 284/D4
Morrice, Mich. 250/E6
Morrill, Kansas 232/G2
Morrill•, Maine 243/E7
Morrill, Minn. 255/E5
Morrill (co.), Nebr. 264/A3
Morrill, Nebr. 264/A3
Morrilton, Ark. 202/E3
Morrin, Alberta 182/D4
Morrinhos, Brazil 132/D7
Morrinsville, N. Zealand 100/E2
Morris, Ala. 195/E3
Morris (res.), Calif. 204/D10
Morris•, Conn. 210/C2
Morris, Georgia 217/C7
Morris, Ill. 222/E2
Morris, Ind. 227/G6
Morris (co.), Kansas 232/F3
Morris, Manitoba 179/E5
Morris, Minn. 255/C5
Morris (co.), N.J. 273/D2
Morris, N.Y. 276/K5
Morris, Okla. 288/P3
Morris, Pa. 294/H2
Morris (mt.), S. Australia 94/B2
Morris (isl.), S.C. 296/H6
Morris (co.), Texas 303/K4
Morris, W. Va. 312/E5
Morrisburg, Ontario 177/J3
Morris Chapel, Tenn. 237/E10
Morrisdale, New Bruns. 170/D3
Morrisdale, Pa. 294/F4
Morrissey, Wyo. 319/H2
Morris Fork, Ky. 237/O6
Morris Jessup (cape), Greenl. 4/A11
Morrison, Colo. 208/J3
Morrison, Ill. 222/C2
Morrison, Iowa 229/H4
Morrison (lake), Manitoba 179/C1
Morrison (co.), Minn. 255/D4
Morrison, Mo. 261/J5
Morrison, Okla. 288/M2
Morrison, Tenn. 237/K9
Morrison Bluff, Ark. 202/D3
Morrison City, Tenn. 237/R7
Morrisonville, Ill. 222/D4
Morrisonville, N.Y. 276/N1
Morrisonville, Wis. 317/G9
Morris Plains, N.J. 273/D2
Morris Run, Pa. 294/J2
Morriston, Ark. 202/G1
Morriston, Fla. 212/D2
Morriston, Ontario 177/D4
Morristown, Ariz. 198/C5
Morristown, Ill. 222/D1
Morristown, Ind. 227/F5
Morristown, Minn. 255/E6
Morristown, N.J. 273/D2
Morristown, N.Y. 276/J1
Morristown, Ohio 284/H5
Morristown, S. Dak. 298/F2
Morristown, Tenn. 237/P8
Morristown•, Vt. 268/B2
Morristown Nat'l Hist. Park., N.J. 273/D2
Morrisvale, W. Va. 312/C6
Morrisville, Mo. 261/F8
Morrisville, N.Y. 276/J5
Morrisville, N.C. 281/M3
Morrisville, Pa. 294/N5
Morrisville, Vt. 268/B2
Murrito, Nicaragua 154/E5
Morro (pt.), Chile 138/A6
Morro Bay, Calif. 204/D8
Morro do Chapéu, Brazil 132/F5
Morropón, Peru 128/C5
Morros, Brazil 132/F3
Morrosquillo (gulf), Colombia 126/C3
Morrow, Ark. 202/B2
Morrow, Georgia 217/K2
Morrow, La. 238/F5
Morrow (co.), Ohio 284/E4
Morrow, Ohio 284/B7
Morrow (co.), Oreg. 291/H2
Morrow Point (res.), Colo. 208/E6
Morrowville, Kansas 232/E2
Morrumbala, Mozambique 118/F3
Morrumbene, Mozambique 118/F4
Mors (isl.), Denmark 21/B4
Morse (res.), Ind. 227/E4
Morse, La. 238/F6
Morse, Sask. 181/D5
Morse, Texas 303/C1
Morse, Wis. 317/E3
Morse Bluff, Nebr. 264/H3
Morse Mill, Mo. 261/L6
Morses Line, Vt. 268/A2
Morshank, U.S.S.R. 52/F4
Mortagne-au-Perche, France 28/D3
Mortara, Italy 34/B2
Morte (pt.), England 13/C6
Morteau, France 28/G4
Morteros, Argentina 143/D3
Mortes (Manso) (riv.), Brazil 132/D6
Mortlach, Sask. 181/E5
Mortlake, Victoria 97/B6
Morton, Ill. 222/D3
Morton (co.), Kansas 232/A4
Morton, Minn. 255/C6
Morton, Miss. 256/E6
Morton (co.), N. Dak. 282/H6
Morton, Ontario 177/H3
Morton, Pa. 294/M7
Morton, Texas 303/B4
Morton, Wash. 310/C4
Morton, Wyo. 319/D2
Morton Grove, Ill. 222/B5
Morton Mills, Iowa 229/C6
Mortons Gap, Ky. 237/F6
Mortsel, Belgium 27/E6
Moruga, Trin. & Tob. 161/B11
Moruka (riv.), Guyana 131/B2
Morundah, N.S. Wales 97/D4
Moruya, N.S. Wales 97/D4
Morvan (plat.), France 28/F4
Morven, Georgia 217/E9
Morven, N. Zealand 100/C6
Morven, N.C. 281/J5
Morven, Queensland 95/C5
Morven (dist.), Scotland 15/C4
Morven (mt.), Scotland 15/E2
Morvi, India 68/C4
Morvin, Ala. 195/C7
Morwell, Victoria 97/D5
Morwell, Victoria 88/H7
Mosbach, Germany 22/C4
Mosby, Mo. 261/R4
Mosby, Mont. 262/J4
Mosca, Colo. 208/H7
Moscavide, Portugal 33/A1
Moscow, Ark. 202/G5
Moscow, Idaho 220/B3
Moscow, Idaho 188/C1
Moscow, Ind. 227/F6
Moscow, Iowa 229/L5
Moscow, Kansas 232/A4
Moscow, Ky. 237/D7
Moscow, Miss. 256/G5
Moscow, Ohio 284/B8
Moscow, Pa. 294/F7
Moscow, Tenn. 237/C10
Moscow (cap.), U.S.S.R. 2/L3
Moscow (cap.), U.S.S.R. 7/H3
Moscow (cap.), U.S.S.R. 48/D4
Moscow (Moskva) (cap.), U.S.S.R. 52/E3
Moscow, Vt. 268/B3
Moscow Mills, Md. 245/B2
Moscow Mills, Mo. 261/K5
Mosel (riv.), Germany 22/B3
Mosel (riv.), Luxembourg 27/J9
Moseley, Sask. 181/G3
Moseley, Va. 307/N6
Moselle (dept.), France 28/G3
Moselle (riv.), France 28/G3
Moselle, Miss. 256/F8
Moselle, Mo. 261/L6
Moser River, Nova Scotia 168/F4
Moses (lake), Wash. 310/F3
Moses Coulee (canyon), Wash. 310/F3
Moses Lake, Wash. 310/F3
Moses Point, Alaska 196/F2
Mosetenes, Cordillera de (range), Bolivi 136/B5
Mosgiel, N. Zealand 100/C6
Mosgrove, Pa. 294/D4
Moshannon, Pa. 294/F3
Mosheim, Tenn. 237/R8
Mosher, S. Dak. 298/J7
Moshi, Tanzania 115/G4
Moshi, Tanzania 102/F5
Mosier, Oreg. 291/F2
Mosina, Poland 47/C2
Mosinee, Wis. 317/G6
Mosi-Oa-Tunya (Victoria) (falls), Africa 102/E6
Mosi-Oa-Tunya (Victoria) (falls), Zambia 115/E7
Mosi-Oa-Tunya (Victoria) (falls), Zimbabwe 118/C3
Mosjøen, Norway 18/H4
Moskenesøya (isl.), Norway 18/H3
Moskva (Moscow) (cap.), U.S.S.R 52/E3
Moskva (riv.), U.S.S.R. 52/E3
Mosler, Oreg. 291/C2
Mosman, N.S. Wales 88/L4
Mosman, N.S. Wales 97/J3
Mosonmagyaróvár, Hungary 41/D3
Mosquera, Colombia 126/A6
Mosquero, N. Mex. 274/F3
Mosquic (lake), Québec 172/C3
Mosquito (lag.), Fla. 212/F3
Mosquito, Riacho (riv.), Paraguay 144/C3
Mosquito Creek (lake), Ohio 284/J3
Mosquitos, Costa de (reg.), Nicaragua 154/E4
Mosquitos, Golfo de los (gulf), Panama 154/G6
Moss, Miss. 256/F7
Moss, Norway 18/D4
Moss, Tenn. 237/K7
Mossaka, Congo 115/C4
Mossbank, Sask. 181/E6
Moss Beach, Calif. 204/H3
Mossel Bay, S. Africa 102/E8
Mossel Bay, S. Africa 118/C6
Mossendjo, Congo 115/B4
Mossgiel, N.S. Wales 97/C4
Moss Landing, Calif. 204/C7
Mossleigh, Alberta 182/D4
Mossman, Queensland 88/G3
Mossman, Queensland 95/C3
Mossoró, Brazil 120/F3
Mossoró, Brazil 132/G4
Moss Point, Miss. 256/G10
Mossuril, Mozambique 118/G2
Moss Vale, N.S. Wales 97/F4
Mossville, Ill. 222/D3
Mossy (riv.), Manitoba 179/C3
Mossy (riv.), Sask. 181/H1
Mossy Head, Fla. 212/C6
Mossyrock, Wash. 310/C4
Most, Czech. 41/B1
Mostaganem, Algeria 102/C1
Mostaganem, Algeria 106/D1
Mostar, Yugoslavia 7/F4
Mostar, Yugoslavia 45/D4
Mosty, U.S.S.R. 52/B4
Mosul, Iraq 66/C2
Mosul, Iraq 59/D2
Mosul, Iraq 54/F6
Motacucito, Bolivia 136/E5
Mota del Cuervo, Spain 33/E3
Motagua (riv.), Guatemala 154/C3
Motala, Sweden 18/J7
Motherwell and Wishaw, Scotland 10/B1
Motherwell and Wishaw, Scotland 15/C2
Motilla del Palancar, Spain 33/E3
Motiti (isl.), N. Zealand 100/F2
Motley, Minn. 255/D4
Motley (co.), Texas 303/D3
Motobu, Japan 81/N6
Motozintla de Mendoza, Mexico 150/N9
Motril, Spain 33/E4
Motsuta (cape), Japan 81/J2
Mott, N. Dak. 282/F7
Motu (riv.), N. Zealand 100/F3
Motueka, N. Zealand 100/D4
Motuhora (isl.), N. Zealand 100/F2
Motuihe (isl.), N. Zealand 100/C1
Motul de Fielipe Carillo Puerto, Mexico 150/P6
Motupe, Peru 128/C6
Motutapu (isl.), N. Zealand 100/C1
Motygino, U.S.S.R. 48/K4
Mouchoir (passage), Turks & Caicos 156/D2
Moúdros, Greece 45/G6
Moudjéria, Mauritania 106/B5
Moudon, Switzerland 39/C3
Mouhoun (riv.), Burkina Faso 106/D6
Mouila, Gabon 115/B4
Mouka, Cent. Afr. Rep. 115/D2
Moulamein, N.S. Wales 97/C4
Moulamein (creek), N.S. Wales 97/C4
Mould Bay, Canada 4/B16
Mould Bay, N.W. Terr. 187/F2
Moule, Guadeloupe 161/B6
Moule à Chique (cape), St. Lucia 161/G7
Moulin-Morneault, New Bruns. 170/B1
Moulins, France 28/E4
Moulmein, Burma 72/C3
Moulmein, Burma 54/L8
Moulouya (riv.), Morocco 106/D2
Moulton, Ala. 195/D2
Moulton, Iowa 229/H7
Moulton, Mont. 262/G3
Moulton, Texas 303/H8
Moultonboro•, N.H. 268/E4
Moultrie, Fla. 212/E2
Moultrie, Georgia 217/E8
Moultrie (co.), Ill. 222/E4
Moultrie (lake), S.C. 188/K4
Moultrie (lake), S.C. 296/G5
Mounana, Gabon 115/B4
Mound, La. 238/H2
Mound, Minn. 255/E6
Mound Bayou, Miss. 256/C3
Mound City, Ill. 222/D6
Mound City, Kansas 232/H3
Mound City, Mo. 261/B2
Mound City, S. Dak. 298/K2
Mound City Group Nat'l Mon., Ohio 284/E7
Moundou, Chad 111/C6
Moundou, Chad 102/D4
Moundridge, Kansas 232/E3
Mounds, Ill. 222/D6
Mounds, Okla. 288/O3
Mound Station (Timewell), Ill. 222/C3
Mounds View, Minn. 255/G5
Moundsville, W. Va. 312/E3
Mound Valley, Kansas 232/G4
Moundville, Ala. 195/C5
Moundville, Mo. 261/C7
Moung Roussei, Cambodia 72/D4
Mouniapamôk, Laos 72/E4
Mount (cape), Liberia 106/B7
Mountain, N. Dak. 282/P2
Mountain (riv.), N.W. Terr. 187/F3
Mountain, Ontario 177/J2
Mountain (prov.), Philippines 82/C2
Mountain, W. Va. 312/E4
Mountain, Wis. 317/K5
Mountainair, N. Mex. 274/C4
Mountain Ash, Ky. 237/N7
Mountain Ash, Wales 13/A6
Mountain Ash, Wales 10/E5
Mountainboro, Ala. 195/F2
Mountain Brook, Ala. 195/E4
Mountainburg, Ark. 202/B2
Mountain City, Georgia 217/F1
Mountain City, Nev. 266/F1
Mountain City, Tenn. 237/T8
Mountain Creek, Ala. 195/E5
Mountain Creek (lake), Texas 303/G2
Mountaindale, Md. 245/J2
Mountain Dale, N.Y. 276/L7
Mountaindale, Oreg. 291/A1
Mountain Fork (riv.), Ark. 202/A5
Mountain Fork (riv.), Okla. 288/S6
Mountain Grove, Mo. 261/H8
Mountain Grove, Ontario 177/H3
Mountain Home, Ark. 202/F1
Mountain Home, Idaho 220/C6
Mountain Home (res.), Idaho 220/C6
Mountainhome, Pa. 294/M3
Mountain Home, Utah 304/D3
Mountain Home A.F.B., Idaho 220/C6
Mountain Iron, Minn. 255/F3
Mountain Lake, Minn. 255/D7
Mountain Lake Park, Md. 245/A3
Mountain Lakes, N.J. 273/E2
Mountain Meadows (res.), Calif. 204/E3
Mountain Park, Georgia 217/D2
Mountain Park, Okla. 288/J5
Mountain Pine, Ark. 202/D4
Mountain Point, Alaska 196/N2
Mountain Rest, S.C. 296/A2
Mountain Road, Manitoba 179/C4
Mountainside, N.J. 273/E2
Mountain Valley, Ark. 202/D4
Mountain View, Alberta 182/D5
Mountain View, Ark. 202/F2
Mountain View, Calif. 204/K3
Mountain View, Georgia 217/K2
Mountainview, Hawaii 218/J5
Mountain View, Mo. 261/J8
Mountain View, N.J. 273/B2
Mountain View, Okla. 288/J4
Mountain View, Wyo. 319/B4
Mountain View, Wyo. 319/F3
Mountain Village, Alaska 196/E2
Mountain Zebra Nat'l Park, S. Africa 118/C6
Mount Airy, Georgia 217/F1
Mount Airy, La. 238/M3
Mount Airy, Md. 245/K3
Mount Airy, N.C. 281/H1
Mount Airy, Tenn. 237/L10
Mount Albert, N. Zealand 100/B1
Mount Albert, Ontario 177/E3
Mount Alto, W. Va. 312/C5
Mount Alton, Pa. 294/E2
Mount Andrew, Ala. 195/H7
Mount Angel, Oreg. 291/B3
Mount Apo National Park, Philippine 82/E7
Mount Arlington, N.J. 273/D2
Mount Arrowsmith, N.S. Wales 97/A2
Mount Assiniboine Prov. Park, Br. Col. 184/K5
Mount Auburn, Ill. 222/D4
Mount Auburn, Ind. 227/G5
Mount Auburn, Iowa 229/J4
Mount Aukum, Calif. 204/E5
Mount Ayr, Ind. 227/C3
Mount Ayr, Iowa 299/E7
Mount Barker, S. Australia 94/C8
Mount Barker, W. Australia 88/B6
Mount Barker, W. Australia 92/B6
Mount Beauty, Victoria 97/D5
Mount Bellew, Ireland 17/D5
Mount Berry, Georgia 217/B2
Mount Bethel, Georgia 217/K1
Mount Blanchard, Ohio 284/D4
Mount Bold (res.), S. Australia 94/B8
Mount Brydges, Ontario 177/C5
Mount Calm, Texas 303/H6
Mount Calvary, Wis. 317/K8
Mount Carbon, W. Va. 312/D7
Mount Carleton Prov. Park, New Bruns. 170/D1
Mount Carmel, Ala. 195/F6
Mount Carmel, Ill. 222/F5
Mount Carmel, Ind. 227/H6
Mount Carmel, Miss. 256/E7
Mount Carmel, Newf. 166/D2
Mount Carmel, N. Dak. 282/O2
Mount Carmel, Ohio 284/C10
Mount Carmel, Pa. 294/K4
Mount Carmel, Pr. Edward I. 168/D2
Mount Carmel, S.C. 296/C3
Mount Carmel, Tenn. 237/R8
Mount Carmel, Utah 304/B6
Mount Carroll, Ill. 222/D1
Mount Cavenagh, North. Terr. 93/C8
Mountcharles, Ireland 17/E2
Mount Clare, W. Va. 312/F4
Mount Clemens, Mich. 250/G6
Mount Cory, Ohio 284/C4
Mount Crawford, Va. 307/L4
Mount Croghan, S.C. 296/G2
Mount Currie, Br. Col. 184/F5
Mount Darwin, Zimbabwe 118/E3
Mount Desert, Maine 243/G7
Mount Desert•, Maine 243/G7
Mount Desert (isl.), Maine 243/G7
Mount Desert Rock (isl.), Maine 243/G8
Mount Dora, Fla. 212/E3
Mount Dora, N. Mex. 274/F2
Mount Doreen, North. Terr. 93/B7
Mount Douglas, Queensland 95/C4
Mount Drysdale, N.S. Wales 97/C2
Mount Eaton, Ohio 284/G4
Mount Eba, S. Australia 94/D4
Mount Eden, Ky. 237/L4
Mount Eden, N. Zealand 100/B1
Mount Edziza Prov. Park and Rec. Area Br. Col. 184/B1
Mount Elgin, Ontario 177/D5
Mount Emu (creek), Victoria 97/B5
Mount Enterprise, Texas 303/K6
Mount Ephraim, N.J. 273/B3
Mount Erie, Ill. 222/E5
Mount Etna, Ind. 227/F3
Mount Etna, Iowa 229/D6
Mount Everard, Guyana 131/B2
Mount Forest, Mich. 250/F5
Mount Forest, Ontario 177/D4
Mount Freedom, N.J. 273/D2
Mount Gambier, Australia 87/D9
Mount Gambier, S. Australia 88/G7
Mount Gambier, S. Australia 94/G7
Mount Gay, W. Va. 312/C7
Mount Gilead, N.C. 281/K4
Mount Gilead, Ohio 284/E4
Mount Gravatt, Queensland 88/K3
Mount Hagen, Papua N.G. 85/B7
Mount Hamill, Iowa 229/K7
Mount Healthy, Ohio 284/B9
Mount Hermon, Calif. 204/K4
Mount Hermon, La. 238/K5
Mount Hermon, Mass. 249/D2
Mount Holly, Ark. 202/E7
Mount Holly•, N.J. 273/D4
Mount Holly, N.C. 281/H4
Mount Holly, S.C. 296/H5
Mount Holly•, Vt. 268/B5
Mount Holly, Va. 307/P4
Mount Holly Springs, Pa. 294/H5
Mount Hood, Oreg. 291/F2
Mount Hope, Ala. 195/D2
Mount Hope (riv.), Conn. 210/G1
Mount Hope, Kansas 232/E4
Mount Hope (bay), Mass. 249/K6
Mount Hope, N.J. 273/D2
Mount Hope, N.S. Wales 97/C3
Mount Hope, Ohio 284/G4
Mount Hope, Ontario 177/E4
Mount Hope (bay), R.I. 249/K6
Mount Hope, W. Va. 312/D7
Mount Hope, Wis. 317/D10
Mount Horeb, Wis. 317/G10
Mount Ida, Ark. 202/C4
Mount Ida, Wis. 317/E10
Mount Isa, Queensland 95/A4
Mount Isa, Queensland 88/F4
Mount Jackson, Va. 307/L3
Mount Jewett, Pa. 294/E2
Mount Joy, Pa. 294/K5
Mount Judea, Ark. 202/D2
Mount Juliet, Tenn. 237/H8
Mount Kisco, N.Y. 276/N8
Mount Kuring-gai, N.S. Wales 97/J3
Mountlake Terrace, Wash. 310/B1
Mount Laurel•, N.J. 273/D4
Mount Lebanon, La. 238/D2
Mount Lebanon•, Pa. 294/B7
Mount Lemmon, Ariz. 198/E6
Mount Leonard, Mo. 261/F4
Mount Liberty, Ohio 284/E5
Mount Lofty (range), S. Australia 88/F6
Mount Lookout, W. Va. 312/E6
Mount Magnet, W. Australia 88/B5
Mount Magnet, W. Australia 92/B5
Mount Margaret, Queensland 95/A3
Mount Margaret, W. Australia 88/C5
Mount Margaret, W. Australia 92/C5
Mount Maunganui, N. Zealand 100/E2
Mount Meigs, Ala. 195/F6
Mountmellick, Ireland 10/C4
Mountmellick, Ireland 17/G5
Mount Meridian, Ind. 227/D5
Mount Molloy, Queensland 95/C3
Mount Montgomery, Nev. 266/C5
Mount Morgan, Queensland 88/J4
Mount Morgan, Queensland 95/D4
Mount Moriah, Mo. 261/E2
Mount Morris, Ill. 222/D1
Mount Morris, Mich. 250/F5
Mount Morris, N.Y. 276/E5
Mount Morris, Pa. 294/B6
Mount Mourne, N.C. 281/H3
Mount Nebo, W. Va. 312/E6
Mount Olive, Ill. 222/D4

414 Mount Olive

Mount Olive, Miss. 256/E7
Mount Olive•, N.J. 273/D2
Mount Olive, N.C. 281/O4
Mount Oliver, Pa. 294/B7
Mount Olivet, Ky. 237/N3
Mount Orab, Ohio 284/C7
Mount Pearl, Newf. 166/D2
Mount Penn, Pa. 294/L5
Mount Pleasant, Ark. 202/G2
Mount Pleasant, Del. 245/R2
Mount Pleasant, Fla. 212/B1
Mount Pleasant, Ind. 227/D8
Mount Pleasant, Iowa 229/L7
Mount Pleasant, Md. 245/J3
Mount Pleasant, Mich. 250/E5
Mount Pleasant, Miss. 256/E1
Mount Pleasant, N.C. 281/J4
Mount Pleasant, Nova Scotia 168/C4
Mount Pleasant, Ohio 284/J5
Mount Pleasant, Ontario 177/D4
Mount Pleasant, Pa. 294/D5
Mount Pleasant, S.C. 296/H6
Mount Pleasant, Tenn. 237/G9
Mount Pleasant, Texas 303/K4
Mount Pleasant, Utah 304/C4
Mount Pocono, Pa. 294/M3
Mount Prospect, Ill. 222/B5
Mount Pulaski, Ill. 222/D3
Mountrail (co.), N. Dak. 282/E3
Mount Rainier, Md. 245/F4
Mount Rainier Nat'l Park, Wash. 310/D4
Mountrath, Ireland 17/F5
Mount Revelstoke Nat'l Park, Br. Col. 184/H4
Mount Robson, Br. Col. 184/H3
Mount Robson Prov. Park, Br. Col. 184/H3
Mount Rogers Nat'l Rec. Area, Va. 307/F7
Mount Roskill, N. Zealand 100/B1
Mount Royal, N.J. 273/C4
Mount Royal (range), N.S. Wales 97/F2
Mount Rushmore Nat'l Mem., S. Dak. 298/B6
Mounts (bay), England 10/D6
Mounts (bay), England 13/B7
Mount Saint Helens Nat'l Volcanic Mon., Wash. 310/C4
Mount Salem, Ky. 237/M6
Mount Savage, Md. 245/C2
Mount Shasta, Calif. 204/C5
Mount Sherman, Ark. 202/D1
Mount Sherman, Ky. 237/K6
Mount Sidney, Va. 307/K4
Mount Solon, Va. 307/K4
Mount Standfast, Barbados 161/B8
Mount Sterling, Ala. 195/B6
Mount Sterling, Ill. 222/C4
Mount Sterling, Ind. 227/G7
Mount Sterling, Iowa 229/J7
Mount Sterling, Ky. 237/N4
Mount Sterling, Ohio 284/D6
Mount Sterling, Wis. 317/D9
Mount Stewart, Pr. Edward I. 168/F2
Mount Storm, W. Va. 312/H4
Mount Storm (lake), W. Va. 312/H4
Mount Summit, Ind. 227/G4
Mount Sunapee, N.H. 268/C5
Mount Surprise, Queensland 95/C3
Mount Tabor, N.J. 273/E2
Mount Tabor•, Vt. 268/B5
Mount Tabor, Wis. 317/F8
Mount Tivoli, Grenada 161/D8
Mount Tom, Mass. 249/D3
Mount Trumbull, Ariz. 198/B2
Mount Uniacke, Nova Scotia 168/E4
Mount Union, Iowa 229/L6
Mount Union, Pa. 294/G5
Mount Upton, N.Y. 276/K6
Mount Vernon, Ala. 195/B8
Mount Vernon, Ark. 202/F3
Mount Vernon, Georgia 217/G6
Mount Vernon, Ill. 222/E5
Mount Vernon, Ind. 227/B9
Mount Vernon, Iowa 229/K5
Mount Vernon, Ky. 237/N6
Mount Vernon•, Maine 243/D7
Mount Vernon, Md. 245/P8
Mount Vernon, Mo. 261/E8
Mount Vernon, N.Y. 276/O7
Mount Vernon, Ohio 284/E5
Mount Vernon, Oreg. 291/H3
Mount Vernon, S. Dak. 298/N6
Mount Vernon, Tenn. 237/N10
Mount Vernon, Texas 303/J4
Mount Vernon, Va. 307/O3
Mount Vernon, Wash. 310/C2
Mount Vernon, W. Australia 92/B4
Mount Vernon, Wis. 317/G10
Mount Vernon Springs, N.C 281/L3
Mount Victory, Ohio 284/D4
Mountview, W. Va. 312/D7
Mountville, Georgia 217/C4
Mountville, Pa. 294/K5
Mountville, S.C. 296/C3
Mount Washington, Ky. 237/K4
Mount Washington•, Mass. 249/A4
Mount Wellington, N. Zealand 100/C1
Mount Willing, Ala. 195/E6
Mount Wolf, Pa. 294/J5
Mount Zion, Georgia 217/B3
Mount Zion, Ill. 222/E4
Mount Zion, Ind. 227/G3
Mount Zion, Iowa 229/K7
Mount Zion, W. Va. 312/D5
Moura, Portugal 33/C3
Moura, Queensland 95/D5
Moura, Queensland 88/J4
Mourão, Portugal 33/C3
Mourdi (depr.), Chad 111/D4
Mourne (Newry and Mourne) (dist.), N. Ireland 17/J3
Mourne (mts.), N. Ireland 17/J3
Mourne (riv.), N. Ireland 17/G2
Mouscron, Belgium 27/C7
Moussoro, Chad 111/C5
Mouthcard, Ky. 237/S6
Mouth of Wilson, Va. 307/F7
Moutier, Switzerland 39/D2
Moûtiers, France 28/G5
Mouton (isl.), Nova Scotia 168/D5
Mouydir (mts.), Algeria 106/E3
Moville, Iowa 229/A4
Moville, Ireland 17/G1
Mowbray, Manitoba 179/D5
Mowdok Mual (mt.), Bangladesh 68/G4
Moweaqua, Ill. 222/E4
Mower (co.), Minn. 255/F7
Mowming (Maoming), China 77/H7
Mowrystown, Ohio 284/C7
Moxahala, Ohio 284/F6
Moxee City, Wash. 310/E4
Moxico (prov.), Angola 115/D6
Moxie (lake), Maine 243/D5
Moxley, Georgia 217/H5
Moy (riv.), Ireland 17/C3
Moy, N. Ireland 17/H3
Moyale, Ethiopia 111/G7
Moyale, Kenya 115/G3
Moyamba, S. Leone 106/B7
Moycullen, Ireland 17/C5
Moyers, Okla. 288/P6
Moyers, W. Va. 312/H6
Moyeuvre-Grande, France 28/G3
Moygashel, N. Ireland 17/H3
Moyie, Br. Col. 184/K5
Moyie (riv.), Idaho 220/B1
Moyie Springs, Idaho 220/B1
Moyle (dist.), N. Ireland 17/J1
Moynalty, Ireland 17/H4
Moyo, Uganda 115/F3
Moyobamba, Peru 120/B3
Moyobamba, Peru 128/D6
Moyock, N.C. 281/S1
Moyogalpa, Nicaragua 154/E5
Moyu (Karakax), China 77/A4
Moza Illit, Israel 65/C4
Mozambique 2/L6
Mozambique 102/F6
MOZAMBIQUE 118/E4
Mozambique (chan.), Africa 2/L7
Mozambique (chan.), Africa 102/G6
Mozambique (pt.), La. 238/M7
Mozambique (chan.), Madagascar 118/G3
Mozambique (chan.), Mozambique 118/G3
Mozart, Sask. 181/G4
Mozer, W. Va. 312/H5
Mozhaysk, U.S.S.R. 52/E3
Mozhga, U.S.S.R. 52/H3
Mozier, Ill. 222/C4
Mozyr', U.S.S.R. 48/C4
Mozyr', U.S.S.R. 52/C4
Mpanda, Tanzania 115/F5
Mpika, Zambia 115/F6
Mporokoso, Zambia 115/F5
M'Pouya, Congo 115/C4
Mpraeso, Ghana 106/D7
Mpulungu, Zambia 115/F5
Mpwapwa, Tanzania 115/G5
Mrągowo, Poland 47/E2
Msaken, Tunisia 106/G1
M'Sila, Algeria 106/E1
Msta (riv.), U.S.S.R. 52/D3
Mtakuja, Tanzania 115/F5
Mtsensk, U.S.S.R. 52/E4
Mtwara (reg.), Tanzania 115/G5
Mtwara-Mikindani, Tanzania 102/G6
Mtwara-Mikindani, Tanzania 115/H6
Mu (riv.), Burma 72/B2
Mualama, Mozambique 118/F3
Muang Hinboun, Laos 72/E3
Muang Kènthao, Laos 72/D3
Muang Khammouan, Laos 72/E3
Muang Không, Laos 72/E4
Muang Khôngxédôn, Laos 72/E4
Muang Khoua, Laos 72/D2
Muang May, Laos 72/E4
Muang Ou Tai, Laos 72/D2
Muang Pak-Lay, Laos 72/D3
Muang Paktha, Laos 72/D2
Muang Pakxan, Laos 72/D2
Muang Phin, Laos 72/E3
Muang Sing, Laos 72/D2
Muang Tahoi, Laos 72/E3
Muang Vangviang, Laos 72/D3
Muang Vapi, Laos 72/E4
Muang Xaignabouri (Sayaboury), Laos 72/D3
Muang Xay, Laos 72/D3
Muang Xépôn, Laos 72/E3
Muang Xon, Laos 72/D2
Muar, Malaysia 72/D7
Muarabungo, Indonesia 85/C6
Muarasiberut, Indonesia 85/B6
Muaratewe, Indonesia 85/F6
Muari, Ras (cape), Pakistan 68/B4
Muari, Ras (cape), Pakistan 59/J5
Mubarraz, Saudi Arabia 59/E4
Mubende, Uganda 115/F3
Mubi, Nigeria 106/G6
Muchanes, Bolivia 136/B4
Müchein, Germany 22/D3
Muck (isl.), Scotland 10/C2
Muck (isl.), Scotland 15/B4
Muckamore, N. Ireland 17/J2
Muckle Flugga (isl.), Scotland 15/G2
Muckleshoot Ind. Res., Wash. 310/C3
Muckno (lake), Ireland 17/H3
Muco (riv.), Colombia 126/E5
Mucojo, Mozambique 118/G2
Mucondá, Angola 115/D6
Mucondá, Angola 118/C2
Mucope, Angola 115/B7
Mucuchachi, Venezuela 124/C3
Mucuchies, Venezuela 124/C3
Mucugê, Brazil 132/F6
Mucur, Turkey 63/F3
Mucurapo, Trin. & Tob. 161/A10
Mucuri, Brazil 132/G7
Mucuripe (pt.), Brazil 132/G3
Mucusso, Angola 115/D7
Mud (lake), Idaho 220/F6
Mud (riv.), Ky. 237/H7
Mud (lake), La. 238/D7
Mud (lake), Minn. 255/C2
Mud (lake), Minn. 255/B5
Mud (riv.), Minn. 255/C2
Mud (isl.), Nova Scotia 168/B5
Mud (creek), Okla. 288/L6
Mud (creek), Oreg. 291/K2
Mud (creek), S. Dak. 298/N3
Mud (lake), S. Dak. 298/R2
Mud, W. Va. 312/C6
Mud (riv.), W. Va. 312/B6
Mudanjiang (Mutankiang), China 77/M3
Mudanjiang, China 54/O5
Mudan Jiang (riv.), China 77/L3
Mudanya, Turkey 63/C2
Mudauwara, Jordan 59/C4
Mud Bay, Br. Col. 184/H2
Mud Butte, S. Dak 298/D4
Muddy (creek), Colo. 208/E4
Muddy (brook), Conn. 210/H1
Muddy (pond), Conn. 210/G1
Muddy (riv.), Conn. 210/D3
Muddy, Ill. 222/E6
Muddy (mts.), Nev. 266/G6
Muddy (creek), N. Dak. 282/G6
Muddy (pt.), St. Kitts & Nevis 161/C10
Muddy (lake), Sask. 181/B3
Muddy (creek), Utah 304/A2
Muddy (creek), Utah 304/C4
Muddy (creek), Wyo. 319/F3
Muddy (creek), Wyo. 319/D2
Muddy (mt.), Wyo. 319/F3
Muddy Boggy (creek), Okla. 288/O5
Mudge (pond), Conn. 210/B1
Mudgee, N.S. Wales 88/J6
Mudgee, N.S. Wales 97/E3
Mudhnib, Saudi Arabia 59/D4
Mudjatik (riv.), Sask. 181/L3
Mud Lake, Idaho 220/F6
Mud Lake, Newf. 166/B3
Mud Lake (res.), S. Dak. 298/N2
Mud Mountain (lake), Wash. 310/D3
Mudon, Burma 72/C3
Mudug (prov.), Somalia 115/J2
Mudurnu, Turkey 63/D2
Muecate, Mozambique 118/F2
Mueda, Mozambique 118/F2
Muenster, Sask. 181/F3
Muenster, Texas 303/G4
Muerto, Mar (lag.), Mexico 150/N9
Muezerskiy, U.S.S.R. 52/D2
Muff, Ireland 17/G1
Mufulira, Zambia 102/E6
Mufulira, Zambia 115/E6
Muge, Portugal 33/B3
Mugford (cape), Newf. 166/B2
Mughar, Israel 65/C2
Muğla (prov.), Turkey 63/C4
Muğla, Turkey 59/A2
Muğla, Turkey 63/C4
Muglad, Sudan 111/E5
Muhammad, Ras (cape), Egypt 59/B4
Muhammad, Ras (cape), Egypt 111/F2
Muhammad Qol, Sudan 59/C5
Muhammad Qol, Sudan 111/G3
Muharraq, Bahrain 59/F4
Mühldorf am Inn, Germany 22/E4
Muhlenberg (co.), Ky. 237/G6
Mühlhausen, Germany 22/D3
Mühlviertel (reg.), Austria 41/C2
Muhu (isl.), U.S.S.R. 53/B1
Mui Bai Bung (pt.), Vietnam 54/M9
Muiden, Netherlands 27/G4
Muinebeag, Ireland 17/H6
Muir (glac.), Alaska 196/M1
Muir, Mich. 250/D5
Muir, Pa. 294/J4
Muirkirk, Md. 245/L4
Muirkirk, Scotland 15/E5
Muir of Ord, Scotland 15/D3
Muiron (isls.), W. Australia 88/A4
Muiron (isls.), W. Australia 92/A3
Muir Woods Nat'l Mon., Calif. 204/H2
Muizenberg, S. Africa 118/E7
Muju, S. Korea 81/C6
Mukachevo, U.S.S.R. 52/B5
Mukah, Malaysia 85/E5
Mukalla, Yemen 54/F8
Mukalla, Yemen 59/E7
Mukdahan, Thailand 72/E3
Mukden, Bolivia 136/A2
Mukden (Shenyang), China 77/K3
Mukilteo, Wash. 310/C3
Mukinbudin, W. Australia 92/B5
Muko, Japan 81/J7
Muko (isl.), Japan 81/M3
Muko (riv.), Japan 81/H7
Mukutawa (lake), Manitoba 179/G2
Mukutawa (riv.), Manitoba 179/E1
Mukwonago, Wis. 317/J2
Mula, Spain 33/F3
Mulaló, Ecuador 128/C3
Mulanje (mt.), Malawi 102/F6
Mulanje (mts.), Malawi 115/G7
Mulatos, Colombia 126/B3
Mulberry (creek), Ala. 195/E5
Mulberry, Ark. 202/B2
Mulberry (riv.), Ark. 202/C2
Mulberry, Calif. 204/D4
Mulberry, Fla. 212/E4
Mulberry, Ind. 227/D4
Mulberry, Kansas 232/H4
Mulberry, Ohio 284/B7
Mulberry, Tenn. 237/H10
Mulberry Fork (riv.), Ala. 195/E3
Mulberry Grove, Ill. 222/D5
Mulchatna (riv.), Alaska 196/G2
Mulchén, Chile 138/E1
Mulde (riv.), Germany 22/E3
Muldon, Miss. 256/G3
Muldoon, Texas 303/G8
Muldraugh, Ky. 237/J5
Muldrow, Okla. 288/S4
Mule (mts.), Ariz. 198/E7
Mule (creek), Kansas 232/C4
Mule Creek, N. Mex. 274/A5
Mule Creek, Wyo. 319/H2
Muleculus, Nicaragua 154/E4
Mulegé, Mexico 150/C3
Mulegns, Switzerland 39/J3
Muleshoe, Texas 303/B3
Mulgrave, Nova Scotia 168/G3
Mulgrave (lake), Nova Scotia 168/F3
Mulhacén (mt.), Spain 33/E4
Mulhall, Okla. 288/M2
Mülheim an der Ruhr, Germany 22/B3
Mulhouse, France 7/E4
Mulhouse, France 28/G4
Mulhurst, Alberta 182/D3
Muli, China 77/F6
Muli (str.), Indonesia 85/K7
Mulino, Oreg. 291/B2
Mulinu'u (cape), W. Samoa 86/L8
Mulkear (riv.), Ireland 17/E6
Mull (head), Scotland 15/F2
Mull (head), Scotland 15/F1
Mull (isl.), Scotland 10/D2
Mull (isl.), Scotland 15/C4
Mull (sound), Scotland 15/C4
Mullagh, Ireland 17/H4
Mullaghareirk (mts.), Ireland 17/C7
Mullaghearn (mt.), N. Ireland 17/G2
Mullaghmore, Ireland 17/D3
Mullaittivu, Sri Lanka 68/E7
Mullaley, N.S. Wales 97/E2
Mullan, Idaho 220/C2
Mullardoch, Loch (lake), Scotland 15/C3
Mullen, Nebr. 264/C2
Mullens, W. Va. 312/D7
Müller (mts.), Indonesia 85/E5
Mullet (key), Fla. 212/D4
Mullett (lake), Mich. 250/E3
Mullett Lake, Mich. 250/E3
Mullewa, W. Australia 88/B5
Mullewa, W. Australia 92/A5
Müllheim, Germany 22/B5
Müllheim, Switzerland 39/G1
Mullica (riv.), N.J. 273/D4
Mullica Hill, N.J. 273/C4
Mulliken, Mich. 250/E6
Mullin, Texas 303/F6
Mullinahone, Ireland 17/F7
Mullinavat, Ireland 17/G7
Mullingar, Ireland 10/C4
Mullingar, Ireland 17/G4
Mullingar, Sask. 181/D2
Mullins, S.C. 296/J3
Mullinville, Kansas 232/C4
Mullion, England 13/B7
Mull of Galloway (prom.), Scotland 15/D6
Mull of Kintyre (prom.), Scotland 15/C5
Mull of Oa (prom.), Scotland 15/B5
Mullumbimby, N.S. Wales 97/G1
Mulobezi, Zambia 115/E7
Mulongo, Zaire 115/E5
Mulroy (bay), Ireland 17/F1
Multan, Pakistan 54/J6
Multan, Pakistan 68/C2
Multan, Pakistan 59/K3
Multnomah (co.), Oreg. 291/E2
Mulund, India 68/B6
Mulungushi (dam), Zambia 115/E6
Mulvane, Kansas 232/E4
Mulvihill, Manitoba 179/D4
Mulwala, N.S. Wales 97/D4
Mumbwa, Zambia 115/E6
Mumford, N.Y. 276/E4
Mümliswil-Ramiswil, Switzerland 39/E2
Mumra, U.S.S.R. 52/G5
Mun, Mae Nam (riv.), Thailand 72/D4
Muna (isl.), Indonesia 85/G7
Muna, Mexico 150/P6
Munbura, Queensland 95/C2
Munbura, Queensland 88/G2
Müncheberg, Germany 22/F2
München (Munich), Germany 22/D4
Münchenbuchsee, Switzerland 39/E2
Muncho Lake, Br. Col. 184/L2
Muncho Lake Prov. Park, Br. Col. 184/L2
Muncie, Ill. 222/F3
Muncie, Ind. 188/J2
Muncie, Ind. 227/G4
Muncy, Pa. 294/J3
Muncy Valley, Pa. 294/J3
Munda, Solomon Is. 86/D3
Mundabullangana, W. Australia 92/B3
Mundare, Alberta 182/D3
Mundaring (res.), W. Australia 88/B2
Munday, Texas 303/E4
Mundelein, Ill. 222/A4
Munden, Kansas 232/E2
Münden, Germany 22/C3
Mundesley, England 13/J5
Mundijong, W. Australia 88/B3
Mundijong, W. Australia 92/A2
Mundiwindi, W. Australia 92/B3
Mundo Novo, Brazil 132/F5
Mundrabilla, W. Australia 92/E5
Mundubbera, Queensland 88/J5
Munera, Spain 33/E3
Munford, Ala. 195/F3
Munford, Tenn. 237/B10
Munfordville, Ky. 237/J6
Mungbere, Zaire 115/E3
Munger, Mich. 250/F5
Mungindi, N.S. Wales 97/E1
Mungindi, Queensland 95/D6
Munguba, Brazil 132/C2
Munhall, Pa. 294/C7
Munhango, Angola 115/C6
Munich, Germany 7/F4
Munich, Germany 22/D4
Munich, N. Dak. 282/N2
Munising, Mich. 250/C2
Munith, Mich. 250/E6
Munjor, Kansas 232/C3
Munku-Sardyk (mt.), Mongolia 77/F1
Munnerlyn, Georgia 217/H5
Munning (pt.), N. Zealand 100/E7
Munnsville, N.Y. 276/J4
Muñoz Gamero (pen.), Chile 138/D10
Munro (mt.), Tasmania 99/E2
Munroe Falls, Ohio 284/H3
Münsingen, Switzerland 39/E3
Munson, Alberta 182/D4
Munson, Fla. 212/B5
Munson, Pa. 294/F4
Munsonville, N.H. 268/C5
Munster, Ind. 227/B1
Munster (prov.), Ireland 17/D7
Munster (trad. prov.), Ireland 17
Munster, Ontario 177/J2
Münster, Germany 22/B3
Münster, Switzerland 39/F4
Munsungan (lake), Maine 243/E3
Muntendam, Netherlands 27/K2
Muntok, Indonesia 85/D6
Munuscong (lake), Mich. 250/E2
Muojärvi (lake), Finland 18/R4
Muong Khoung, Vietnam 72/E2
Muonio (riv.) 7/G2
Muonio, Finland 18/O3
Muonio (riv.), Finland 18/M2
Muonioälven (riv.), Sweden 18/M2
Muota (riv.), Switzerland 39/G3
Muotathal, Switzerland 39/G3
Muqaddam, Wadi (dry riv.), Sudan 111/F4
Muqdadiyah, Iraq 66/D4
Muqdisho (Mogadishu) (cap.), Somalia 115/J3
Muqdisho (Mogadishu) (cap.), Somalia 102/G4
Muqeible, Israel 65/C2
Muqui, Brazil 132/F8
Mur (riv.), Austria 41/C3
Mur (riv.), Yugoslavia 45/B2
Mura (riv.), Hungary 41/D3
Muradiye, Turkey 63/K3
Murakami, Japan 81/J4
Murallón, Cerro (mt.), Argentina 143/B6
Murallón, Cerro (mt.), Chile 138/D8
Murarrie, Queensland 88/K2
Murashi, U.S.S.R. 52/G3
Murat, France 28/E5
Murat (riv.), Turkey 59/C2
Murat (riv.), Turkey 63/H3
Murat Dağı (mt.), Turkey 63/C3
Murau, Austria 41/C3
Murbat, Oman 59/G6
Murchison, N. Zealand 100/D4
Murchison (range), North. Terr. 93/D6
Murchison (Kabalega) (falls), Uganda 115/F3
Murchison (mt.), W. Australia 92/B4
Murchison (riv.), W. Australia 88/B5
Murchison (riv.), W. Australia 92/B4
Murchison Downs, W. Australia 88/B5
Murcia (prov.), Spain 33/F4
Murcia, Spain 7/D5
Murcia, Spain 33/F4
Murcia (reg.), Spain 33/F3
Murderers (creek), Oreg. 291/H3
Murderkill (riv.), Del. 245/R5
Murdo, S. Dak. 298/H6
Murdochville, Québec 172/C1
Murdock, Fla. 212/D4
Murdock, Ill. 222/E4
Murdock, Kansas 232/E4
Murdock, Minn. 255/C5
Murdock, Nebr. 264/H4
Muren (Mörön), Mongolia 77/F2
Mureş (riv.), Romania 45/E2
Muret, France 28/D6
Muretto (pass), Switzerland 39/J4
Murfreesboro, Ark. 202/C5
Murfreesboro, N.C. 281/R2
Murfreesboro, Tenn. 237/J9
Murg (riv.), Switzerland 39/G1
Murgab, U.S.S.R. 48/H6
Murgab (riv.), U.S.S.R. 48/G6
Murghab (riv.), Afghanistan 59/H2
Murgon, Queensland 88/J5
Murgon, Queensland 95/D5
Murgoo, W. Australia 92/B4
Muri, Switzerland 39/F2
Muriaé, Brazil 135/E2
Muriaé, Brazil 132/F8
Murias de Paredes, Spain 33/C1
Muri bei Bern, Switzerland 39/E3
Muriel (lake), Alberta 182/E2
Murindó, Colombia 126/B4
Müritzsee (lake), Germany 22/E2
Murjek, Sweden 18/M3
Murl, Ky. 237/M7
Murle, Ethiopia 111/G6
Murmansk, U.S.S.R. 2/L2
Murmansk, U.S.S.R. 4/C8
Murmansk, U.S.S.R. 7/H2
Murmansk, U.S.S.R. 48/D3
Murmansk, U.S.S.R. 52/D1
Murnau, Germany 22/D5
Murnpeowie, S. Australia 94/F3
Murom, U.S.S.R. 52/F3
Murongo, Tanzania 115/F4
Muroran, Japan 81/K2
Muros, Spain 33/B1
Muroto, Japan 81/G7
Muroto (pt.), Japan 81/G7
Murphy, Idaho 220/B6
Murphy, Miss. 256/C4
Murphy, Mo. 261/O4
Murphy, N.C. 281/B4
Murphy, Oreg. 291/D5
Murphy (isl.), S.C. 296/J5
Murphy, Texas 303/H1
Murphys, Calif. 204/E5
Murphysboro, Ill. 222/D6
Murphytown, W. Va. 312/D4
Murra Murra, Queensland 95/C6
Murray (riv.), Australia 88/G6
Murray (riv.), Australia 87/E9
Murray (riv.), Br. Col. 184/G3
Murray (co.), Georgia 217/C1
Murray, Idaho 220/C2
Murray, Ind. 227/G3
Murray, Iowa 229/F6
Murray, Ky. 237/E7
Murray (co.), Minn. 255/C6
Murray, Nebr. 264/J4
Murray (riv.), N.S. Wales 97/A4
Murray (co.), Okla. 288/M6
Murray (lake), Okla. 288/M6
Murray (lake), Papua N.G. 85/B7
Murray (riv.), S. Australia 94/F6
Murray (lake), S.C. 188/K4
Murray (lake), S.C. 296/D4
Murray, Utah 304/C3
Murray, Utah 188/D2
Murray (bay), Victoria 88/H7
Murray (riv.), Victoria 97/A4
Murray (riv.), W. Australia 92/A2
Murray Bridge, S. Australia 88/F7
Murray Bridge, S. Australia 94/F6
Murray City, Ohio 284/F6
Murray Corner, New Bruns. 170/G2
Murray Downs, North. Terr. 93/D6
Murray Harbour, Pr. Edward I. 168/F2
Murray Lake Hills, Tenn. 237/L10
Murray River, Pr. Edward I. 168/F2
Murraysville, W. Va. 312/C4
Murrayville, Georgia 217/E2
Murrayville, Ill. 222/C4
Murrayville, Victoria 97/A4
Murree, Pakistan 68/C2
Murrells Inlet, S.C. 296/K4
Mürren, Switzerland 39/E3
Murrieta, Calif. 204/H10
Murringo, N.S. Wales 97/E4
Murrumbidgee (riv.), N.S. Wales 88/H6
Murrumbidgee (riv.), N.S. Wales 97/C4
Murrumburrah, N.S. Wales 97/E4
Murrupula, Mozambique 118/F3
Murrurundi, N.S. Wales 97/F2
Murrysville, Pa. 294/C5
Murska Sobota, Yugoslavia 45/C2
Murtaröl (peak), Switzerland 39/K3
Murtaugh, Idaho 220/D7
Murten, Switzerland 39/D3
Murtle (lake), Br. Col. 184/H4
Murtoa, Victoria 97/B5
Murud, India 68/C5
Murupara, N. Zealand 100/F3
Mururoa (isl.), Fr. Poly. 87/M8
Murwara, India 68/E4
Murwillumbah, N.S. Wales 88/J5
Murwillumbah, N.S. Wales 97/G1
Muryo (mt.), Indonesia 85/J2
Mürz (riv.), Austria 41/C3
Murzuk, Libya 102/D2
Murzuk, Libya 111/B2
Mürzzuschlag, Austria 41/C3
Muş (prov.), Turkey 63/J3
Muş, Turkey 63/J3
Muş, Turkey 59/D2
Musa Khel Bazar, Pakistan 59/K3
Musa Khel Bazar, Pakistan 68/B2
Musala (mt.), Bulgaria 45/F4
Musan, N. Korea 81/D2
Musandam, Ras (cape), Oman 59/G4
Musashino, Japan 81/O2
Muscadine, Ala. 195/H3
Muscat (cap.), Oman 54/G7
Muscat (cap.), Oman 2/M4
Muscat (cap.), Oman 59/G5
Muscatatuck (riv.), Ind. 227/E7
Muscatine (co.), Iowa 229/L5
Muscatine, Iowa 188/H2
Muscatine, Iowa 229/L6
Muscle Shoals, Ala. 195/C1
Muscoda, Wis. 317/F9
Muscogee (co.), Georgia 217/C6
Musconetcong (riv.), N.J. 273/C2
Muscongus (bay), Maine 243/E8
Muscotah, Kansas 232/G2
Muscoy, Calif. 204/E10
Muse, Okla. 288/S5
Musella, Georgia 217/E5
Musgrave (ranges), Australia 87/D8
Musgrave, Queensland 95/B2
Musgrave (range), S. Australia 88/E5
Musgrave (ranges), S. Australia 94/B2
Musgrave Harbour, Newf. 166/D4
Musgravetown, Newf. 166/C2

Narrandera 415

Mushaboom, Nova Scotia 168/F4
Mushandike Nat'l Park, Zimbabwe 118/D4
Mushie, Zaire 102/D5
Mushie, Zaire 115/C4
Musi (riv.), Indonesia 85/C6
Musidora, Alberta 182/E3
Muskeg (bay), Manitoba 179/G6
Muskeg (bay), Minn. 255/C2
Muskeget (chan.), Mass. 249/N7
Muskeget (isl.), Mass. 249/N7
Muskego, Wis. 317/K2
Muskegon (co.), Mich. 250/C5
Muskegon, Mich. 188/J2
Muskegon, Mich. 250/C5
Muskegon (riv.), Mich. 250/C5
Muskegon Heights, Mich. 250/C5
Muskeg River, Alberta 182/A3
Muskingum (co.), Ohio 284/G5
Muskingum (riv.), Ohio 284/G6
Muskogee, Okla. 188/H3
Muskogee (co.), Okla. 288/R3
Muskogee, Okla. 288/R3
Muskoka (dist. munic.), Ontario 177/E3
Muskoka (lake), Ontario 177/E2
Muskrat (creek), Wyo. 319/E2
Muskwa (lake), Alberta 182/C1
Muskwa (riv.), Alberta 182/C1
Muskwa (riv.), Br. Col. 184/M2
Muslimiya, Syria 63/G4
Musmar, Sudan 111/G4
Musoma, Tanzania 115/F4
Musoma, Tanzania 102/F5
Musquacook (lakes), Maine 243/E2
Musquash (harb.), New Bruns. 170/D3
Musquodoboit (riv.), Nova Scotia 168/E4
Musquodoboit Harbour, Nova Scotia 168/E4
Mussau (isl.), Papua N.G. 86/B1
Musselburgh, Scotland 15/D2
Musselburgh, Scotland 10/C1
Musselshell (riv.) 188/E1
Musselshell (co.), Mont. 262/H4
Musselshell, Mont. 262/H4
Musselshell (riv.), Mont. 262/J3
Mustafakemalpaşa, Turkey 63/C3
Mustahil, Ethiopia 111/H6
Müstair, Switzerland 39/K3
Mustang, Nepal 68/E3
Mustang, Okla. 288/L4
Mustang (creek), Texas 303/A1
Mustang (isl.), Texas 303/G10
Mustang Draw (dry riv.), Texas 303/B5
Musters (lake), Argentina 143/C6
Mustinka (riv.), Minn. 255/B5
Mustoe, Va. 307/J4
Mustvee, U.S.S.R. 53/D1
Muswellbrook, N.S. Wales 88/J6
Muswellbrook, N.S. Wales 97/F3
Mût, Egypt 111/E2
Mût, Egypt 59/A4
Mût, Egypt 102/E2
Mut, Turkey 63/E4
Mutankiang (Mudanjiang), China 77/M3
Mutarara (Dona Ana), Mozambique 118/F3
Mutare (Umtali), Zimbabwe 118/E3
Muthanna (gov.), Iraq 66/D5
Muthill, Scotland 15/E4
Muting, Indonesia 85/K7
Mutki, Turkey 63/J3
Mutrie, Sask. 181/H5
Mutsamudu, Comoros 118/G2
Mutshatsha, Zaire 115/D6
Mutsu, Japan 81/K3
Mutsu (bay), Japan 81/K3
Muttaburra, Queensland 95/C4
Muttalip, Turkey 63/D3
Muttenz, Switzerland 39/E1
Muttler (mt.), Switzerland 39/K3
Mutton (isl.), Ireland 17/B6
Mutton Bird (isl.), N.S. Wales 97/J2
Muttonville, Mich. 250/G6
Mutual, Ohio 284/C5
Mutual, Okla. 288/H2
Mutum, Brazil 135/F1
Mu Us Shamo (des.), China 77/G4
Muwailih, Saudi Arabia 59/C4
Muwale, Tanzania 115/F5
Muxima, Angola 115/B5
Muy Muy, Nicaragua 154/E4
Muy Muy Viejo, Nicaragua 154/E4
Muynak, U.S.S.R. 48/F5
Muyumba, Zaire 115/E5
Muzaffarabad, Pakistan 68/C2
Muzaffarnagar, India 68/D3
Muzaffarpur, India 68/E3
Muzambinho, Brazil 135/C2
Muzo, Colombia 126/D5
Muzon (cape), Alaska 196/M2
Muztag (mt.), China 77/B4
Muztagata (mt.), China 77/A4
Mvadhi-Ousyé, Gabon 115/B3
M'Vouti, Congo 115/B4
Mvuma, Zimbabwe 118/D3
Mwadingusha, Zaire 115/E6
Mwadui, Tanzania 115/F4
Mwali (isl.), Comoros 102/G6
Mwali (isl.), Comoros 118/D3
Mwanza, Malawi 115/F7
Mwanza (reg.), Tanzania 115/F4
Mwanza, Tanzania 115/F4
Mwanza, Tanzania 102/F5
Mwanza, Zaire 115/E5
Mwaya, Tanzania 115/F5
Mweelrea (mt.), Ireland 17/B4
Mweenish (isl.), Ireland 17/B5
Mweka, Zaire 115/D4
Mwene-Ditu, Zaire 115/D5
Mwenezi, Zimbabwe 118/E4
Mwenga, Zaire 115/E4
Mweru (lake), 102/E5
Mweru (lake), Zaire 115/E5
Mweru (lake), Zambia 115/E5
Mwesi, Tanzania 115/F5
Mwinilunga, Zambia 115/D6
Mya, Wadi (dry riv.), Algeria 106/E2
Myakka (riv.), Fla. 212/D4
Myakka City, Fla. 212/D4
Myall (lake), N.S. Wales 97/G3
Myanaung, Burma 72/B3
Myaungmya, Burma 72/B3
Myebon, Burma 72/B2
Myers, Ky. 237/O4
Myers, Mont. 262/J4
Myerstown, Pa. 294/K5
Myersville, Md. 245/H3
Myingyan, Burma 72/B2
Myitkyina, Burma 54/L7
Myitkyina, Burma 72/C1
Myitnge, Burma 72/C2
Myitnge (riv.), Burma 72/C2
Myjava, Czech. 41/D2
Mylo, N. Dak. 282/L2
Mymensingh (Nasirabad), Bangladesh 68/G4
Mynyddislwyn, Wales 13/B6
Myohaung, Burma 72/B6
Myohyang (mt.), N. Korea 81/C3
Myŏngch'ŏn, N. Korea 81/D3
Myra, Texas 303/G4
Myra, W. Va. 312/B6
Myricks, Mass. 249/K5
Myrnam, Alberta 182/E3
Myrtle, Idaho 220/B3
Myrtle, Manitoba 179/E5
Myrtle, Minn. 255/E7
Myrtle, Miss. 256/F1
Myrtle, Mo. 261/K9
Myrtle (lake), N. Dak. 282/L5
Myrtle Beach, S.C. 296/K4
Myrtle Beach A.F.B., S.C. 296/K4
Myrtle Creek, Oreg. 291/D4
Myrtleford, Victoria 97/D5
Myrtle Grove, Fla. 212/B6
Myrtle Grove, La. 238/K7
Myrtle Point, Oreg. 291/C4
Myrtlewood, Ala. 195/C6
Mysen, Norway 18/G7
Myślenice, Poland 47/E4
Myślibórz, Poland 47/B2
Mysłowice, Poland 47/C4
Mysore, India 68/D6
Mysore, India 54/J8
Mys Shmidta, U.S.S.R. 4/C1
Mys Shmidta, U.S.S.R. 48/T3
Mystery Lake, Manitoba 179/J2
Mystic, Conn. 210/H3
Mystic (riv.), Conn. 210/H3
Mystic, Georgia 217/F7
Mystic, Iowa 229/H7
Mystic (lake), Mass. 249/C6
Mystic (riv.), Mass. 249/C6
Mystic, S. Dak. 298/B5
Mystic Islands, N.J. 273/E4
Myszków, Poland 47/D3
My Tho, Vietnam 72/E5
Mytishchi, U.S.S.R. 52/E3
Myton, Utah 304/D3
M'zab (oasis), Algeria 106/E2
Mže (riv.), Czech. 41/B2
Mzimba, Malawi 115/F6
Mzimba, Malawi 102/F6

N

Naab (riv.), Germany 22/E4
Naafkopf (mt.), Switzerland 39/J2
Naaldwijk, Netherlands 27/E4
Naalehu, Hawaii 218/H7
Naalehu, Hawaii 188/G6
Naantali, Finland 18/M6
Naarden, Netherlands 27/G4
Naas, Ireland 10/C4
Naas, Ireland 17/H5
Naba, Burma 72/B1
Nababeep, S. Africa 118/B5
Nabari, Kiribati 87/J6
Nabb, Ind. 227/F7
Nabburg, Germany 22/E4
Naberezhnye Chelny, U.S.S.R. 52/H3
Nabesna, Alaska 196/K2
Nabeul, Tunisia 106/G1
Nabiac, N.S. Wales 97/G3
Nabire, Indonesia 85/K6
Nablus (Nabulus), West Bank 65/C3
Nabnasset, Mass. 249/J2
Nabua, Philippines 82/D4
Nacala, Mozambique 118/G2
Nacala, Mozambique 102/G6
Nacaome, Honduras 154/D4
Naches, Wash. 310/E4
Naches (pass), Wash. 310/D3
Naches (riv.), Wash. 310/E4
Nachikatsuura, Japan 81/H7
Nachingwea, Tanzania 115/G6
Náchod, Czech. 41/D1
Nachusa, Ill. 222/D2
Nachvak (fjord), Newf. 166/B2
Nacimiento (riv.), Calif. 204/D8
Nacimiento, Chile 138/D1
Nacimiento (mts.), N. Mex. 274/C3
Nacimiento (peak), N. Mex. 274/C2
Nacka, Sweden 18/H1
Nackawic, New Bruns. 170/C2
Nacmine, Alberta 182/D4
Naco, Ariz. 198/E7
Naco, Mexico 150/D1
Nacogdoches (co.), Texas 303/K6
Nacogdoches, Texas 303/J6
Nacozari, Mexico 150/E1
Ñacunday, Paraguay 144/E5
Nadadores, Mexico 150/H3
Nadawah, Ala. 195/D7
Nadeau, Mich. 250/B3
Nadi, Fiji 86/P10
Nadi, Fiji 87/H7
Nadiad, India 68/C4
Nădlac, Romania 45/E2
Nador, Morocco 106/D1
Nádudvar, Hungary 41/F3
Nadvoitsy, U.S.S.R. 52/D2
Nadym, U.S.S.R. 48/H3
Nadym (riv.), U.S.S.R. 48/H3
Naestved, Denmark 21/E7
Naestved, Denmark 18/G9
Naf, Idaho 220/E7
Näfels, Switzerland 39/H2
Nafenen, Switzerland 39/H3
Naft-e Shah, Iran 66/D4
Naft Kaneh, Iraq 66/D3
Naga, Philippines 85/G3
Naga, Philippines 54/O8
Naga, Philippines 82/D4
Nagahama, Ehime, Japan 81/F7
Nagahama, Shiga, Japan 81/H6
Nagai (isl.), Alaska 196/F4
Nagaland (state), India 68/G3
Nagambie, Victoria 97/C5
Nagano (pref.), Japan 81/J5
Nagano, Japan 81/J5
Nagaoka, Kyoto, Japan 81/J7
Nagaoka, Niigata, Japan 81/J5
Nagaokakyo, Japan 81/J7
Nagapattinam, India 68/E6
Nagar, Pakistan 68/D1
Nagarote, Nicaragua 154/D4
Nagar Parkar, Pakistan 68/C4
Nagarzê, China 77/C6
Nagasaki (pref.), Japan 81/D7
Nagasaki, Japan 54/O6
Nagasaki, Japan 81/D7
Nagato, Japan 81/E6
Nagaur, India 68/C3
Nagawicka (lake), Wis. 317/J1
Nagele, Netherlands 27/H3
Nagercoil, India 68/D7
Nagina, India 68/D3
Nagishot, Sudan 111/F7
Nagles (mts.), Ireland 17/E7
Nago, Japan 81/N6
Nagold, Germany 22/C4
Nagorno-Karabakh Aut. Obl., U.S.S.R. 48/E5
Nagorno-Karabakh Aut. Obl., U.S.S.R. 52/G7
Nagornyy, U.S.S.R. 48/N4
Nagoya, Japan 81/H6
Nagoya, Japan 2/R4
Nagoya, Japan 54/P6
Nagpur, India 54/J7
Nagpur, India 68/D4
Nagqu, China 77/D5
Nags Head, N.C. 281/T3
Nagua, Dom. Rep. 158/E5
Naguabo, P. Rico 161/F2
Naguabo, P. Rico 156/G1
Nagyatád, Hungary 41/D3
Nagybajom, Hungary 41/D3
Nagyecsed, Hungary 41/G3
Nagyhalász, Hungary 41/F2
Nagykálló, Hungary 41/F3
Nagykanizsa, Hungary 41/D3
Nagykáta, Hungary 41/E3
Nagykőrös, Hungary 41/E3
Nagyszénás, Hungary 41/F3
Naha, Japan 54/O7
Naha, Japan 81/N6
Nahan, India 68/D2
Nahang (riv.), Iran 66/N7
Nahanni Butte, N.W.T. 187/F3
Nahanni Nat'l Park, N.W.T. 162/D3
Nahanni Nat'l Park, N.W.T. 187/F3
Nahant•, Mass. 249/E6
Nahant (bay), Mass. 249/E6
Nahariyya, Israel 65/C1
Nahavand, Iran 59/E3
Nahavand, Iran 66/F3
Nahcotta, Wash. 310/A4
Nahhalin, West Bank 65/C4
Nahiku, Hawaii 218/K2
Nahma, Mich. 250/C3
Nahmakanta (lake), Maine 243/E4
Nahuel Huapi (lake), Argentina 120/B7
Nahuel Huapi (lake), Argentina 143/B5
Nahuel Huapi Nat'l Park, Argentina 143/B5
Nahunta, Georgia 217/H8
Naica, Mexico 150/G2
Naicam, Sask. 181/G3
Naihati, India 68/F1
Nailsworth, England 13/E6
Naiman, China 77/K3
Na'in, Iran 66/H4
Na'in, Iran 59/F3
Nain, Jamaica 158/H6
Nain, Newf. 166/B2
Nain, Newf. 162/K4
Naini Tal, India 68/D3
Nainpur, India 68/E4
Naipo (isl.), Colombia 126/F6
Nairn, La. 238/L8
Nairn, Ontario 177/C1
Nairn, Scotland 15/E3
Nairn, Scotland 10/E2
Nairn (trad. co.), Scotland 15/B5
Nairn (riv.), Scotland 15/D3
Nairne, S. Australia 94/C8
Nairobi (cap.), Kenya 2/L6
Nairobi (cap.), Kenya 115/G4
Nairobi (cap.), Kenya 102/F5
Naivasha, Kenya 115/G4
Najafabad, Iran 59/F3
Najafabad, Iran 66/G4
Najayo Abajo, Dom. Rep. 158/E6
Najin, N. Korea 81/E2
Najran (Aba as Sa'ud), Saudi Arabia 59/D6
Naka (riv.), Japan 81/K5
Nakalele (pt.), Hawaii 218/J1
Nakaminato, Japan 81/K5
Nakamti, Ethiopia 102/F4
Nakamti, Ethiopia 111/G6
Nakamura, Japan 81/F7
Nakanbe (riv.), Burkina Faso 106/D6
Nakasato, Japan 81/K3
Nakatane (cape), Japan 81/E8
Nakatsu, Japan 81/E7
Na Keal, Loch (inlet), Scotland 15/B4
Naked (isl.), Alaska 196/D1
Nakfa, Ethiopia 111/G4
Nakhichevan', U.S.S.R. 7/J5
Nakhichevan', U.S.S.R. 48/E6
Nakhichevan', U.S.S.R. 52/F7
Nakhichevan' A.S.S.R., U.S.S.R. 52/F7
Nakhichevan' A.S.S.R., U.S.S.R. 48/E6
Nakhodka, U.S.S.R. 54/P5
Nakhodka, U.S.S.R. 48/O5
Nakhon Nayok, Thailand 72/D4
Nakhon Pathom, Thailand 72/C4
Nakhon Phanom, Thailand 72/D3
Nakhon Ratchasima, Thailand 72/D4
Nakhon Ratchasima, Thailand 54/M8
Nakhon Sawan, Thailand 72/D4
Nakhon Si Thammarat, Thailand 54/M9
Nakhon Si Thammarat, Thailand 72/D5
Nakina, N.C. 281/M6
Nakina, Ont. 162/H5
Nakina, Ontario 177/H4
Nakina, Ontario 175/C2
Nakło nad Notecia, Poland 47/C2
Naknek, Alaska 196/G3
Naknek (lake), Alaska 196/G3
Nakonde, Zambia 115/F5
Nakskov, Denmark 21/E8
Nakskov, Denmark 18/G9
Naktong (riv.), S. Korea 81/D6
Nakuru, Kenya 102/F5
Nakuru, Kenya 115/G4
Nakusp, Br. Col. 184/J5
Nal, Pakistan 59/J4
Nal, Pakistan 68/B3
Nal (riv.), Pakistan 59/J4
Nal (riv.), Pakistan 68/B3
Nalate, Turkey 63/G4
Nalayh (Nalaikha), Mongolia 77/G2
Nalcayec (isl.), Chile 138/D6
Nal'chik, U.S.S.R. 7/J4
Nal'chik, U.S.S.R. 48/E5
Nal'chik, U.S.S.R. 52/F6
Nalgonda, India 68/D5
Nallen, W. Va. 312/E6
Nallıhan, Turkey 63/D2
Nalut, Libya 111/B1
Namacurra, Mozambique 118/F3
Namak, Daryacheh-ye (salt lake), Iran 59/F3
Namak, Daryacheh-ye (salt lake), Iran 66/G3
Namaka, Alberta 182/D4
Namaksar (salt lake), Afghanistan 59/H3
Namaksar (salt lake), Afghanistan 68/A2
Namaksar (lake), Iran 66/M4
Namaksar (salt lake), Iran 59/H3
Namakzar-e Shahdad (salt lake), Iran 59/G3
Namakzar-e Shahdad (salt lake), Iran 66/L5
Namanga, Kenya 115/G4
Namangan, U.S.S.R. 48/H5
N'amaniya, Iraq 66/D4
Namapa, Mozambique 118/F2
Namaqualand (reg.), S. Africa 118/B5
Namarrói, Mozambique 118/F3
Namasagali, Uganda 115/F3
Namasigüe, Honduras 154/D4
Namatanai, Papua N.G. 87/F6
Namatanai, Papua N.G. 86/C1
Nambe, N. Mex. 274/D3
Nambour, Queensland 88/J5
Nambour, Queensland 95/E5
Nambucca Heads, N.S. Wales 97/G2
Nam Co (lake), China 77/D5
Nam Dinh (cliff), Vietnam 72/E2
Namekagon (lake), Wis. 317/D3
Namekagon (riv.), Wis. 317/C3
Namen (Namur), Belgium 27/F8
Námestovo, Czech. 41/E2
Nametil, Mozambique 118/F3
Namhkam, Burma 72/C2
Namib (des.), Namibia 118/A3
Namibe (prov.), Angola 115/B7
Namibe (Moçâmedes), Angola 115/B7
Namibe, Angola 102/D6
Namibia 2/K7
Namibia 102/D7
NAMIBIA 118/D3
Namibia (des.) 102/D6
Naminga, U.S.S.R. 48/M4
Namiquipa, Mexico 150/F2
Namlan, Burma 72/C2
Namlea, Indonesia 85/H6
Namoi (riv.), N.S. Wales 88/H6
Namoi (riv.), N.S. Wales 97/E2
Namonuito (atoll), Micronesia 87/E5
Namorik (atoll), Marshall Is. 87/G5
Nampa, Alberta 182/B1
Nampa, Idaho 146/G5
Nampa, Idaho 220/B6
Nampa, Idaho 188/C2
Nampala, Mali 106/C5
Namp'o, N. Korea 81/B4
Nampo-Shoto (isls.), Japan 81/M3
Nampula (prov.), Mozambique 118/F2
Nampula, Mozambique 118/F3
Nampula, Mozambique 102/F6
Namsen (riv.), Norway 18/H4
Namsos, Norway 7/F2
Namsos, Norway 18/G4
Nam Tram, Mui (cape), Vietnam 72/F4
Namtu, Burma 72/C2
Namu, Br. Col. 184/D4
Namuac, Philippines 82/C1
Namuli, Serra (mt.), Mozambique 118/F3
Namuno, Mozambique 118/F2
Namur (lake), Alberta 182/D1
Namur (prov.), Belgium 27/F8
Namur, Belgium 27/F8
Namur, Québec 172/C4
Namutoni, Namibia 118/B3
Namwala, Zambia 115/E7
Namwŏn, S. Korea 81/C6
Namysłów, Poland 47/C3
Namzha Parwa (mt.), China 77/E6
Nan, Thailand 72/D3
Nan, Mae Nam (riv.), Thailand 72/D3
Nanacamilpa, Mexico 150/M1
Nanafalia, Ala. 195/B6
Nanaimo, Br. Col. 146/F5
Nanaimo, Br. Col. 162/D6
Nanaimo, Br. Col. 184/J3
Nanakuli, Hawaii 218/D2
Nanao, Japan 81/H5
Nanay (riv.), Peru 128/E4
Nancagua, Chile 138/F6
Nance (co.), Nebr. 264/F3
Nanchang, China 77/J6
Nanchang, China 54/N7
Nancheng, China 77/J6
Nanchong (Nanchung), China 77/G5
Nanchong, China 54/M6
nan Clar, Loch (lake), Scotland 15/D2
Nancowry (isl.), India 68/G7
Nancy, France 28/G3
Nancy, France 7/E4
Nancy, Ky. 237/M6
Nanda Devi (mt.), India 68/D2
Nandaime, Nicaragua 154/E5
Nander, India 68/D5
Nandi (Nadi), Fiji 87/H7
Nando, Uruguay 145/F3
Nandurbar, India 68/C4
Nandyal, India 68/D5
Nanga-Eboko, Cameroon 115/B3
Nanga Parbat (mt.), Pakistan 68/D1
Nangapinoh, Indonesia 85/E6
Nangatayap, Indonesia 85/E6
Nangnim-sanmaek (range), N. Korea 81/C3
Nangong, China 77/H4
Nangqên, China 77/E5
Nang Rong, Thailand 72/D4
Nangwarry, S. Australia 94/G7
Nang Xian, China 77/D6
Nanika (dam), Br. Col. 184/D3
Nanika (lake), Br. Col. 184/D3
Nanisivik, N.W. Terr. 187/K2
Nanjemoy, Md. 245/K7
Nanjing (Nanking), China 77/J5
Nanjing, China 2/O4
Nanjing, China 54/N6
Nanking (Nanjing), China 77/J5
Nankoku, Japan 81/F7
Nan Ling (mts.), China 77/H6
Nannine, W. Australia 92/B4
Nanning, China 77/G7
Nanning, China 54/M7
Nannup, W. Australia 92/B6
Nanoose Bay, Br. Col. 184/J3
Nanortalik, Greenl. 4/D12
Nanpan Jiang (riv.), China 77/F7
Nanping, China 77/J6
Nansei Shoto (Ryukyu) (isls.), Japan 81/M6
Nansen (sound), N.W. Terr. 187/J1
Nanson, N. Dak. 282/L2
Nantahala, N.C. 281/B4
Nantahala (lake), N.C. 281/B4
Nantai (mt.), Japan 81/J5
Nantasket Beach, Mass. 249/E7
Nanterre, France 28/A1
Nantes, France 28/C4
Nantes, France 7/D4
Nantes, Québec 172/F4
Nanticoke (riv.), Del. 245/R6
Nanticoke, Md. 245/P7
Nanticoke (riv.), Md. 245/P7
Nanticoke, Ontario 177/E5
Nanticoke, Pa. 294/E7
Nanton, Alberta 182/D4
Nantong, China 77/K5
Nantua, France 28/F4
Nantucket (co.), Mass. 249/O7
Nantucket, Mass. 249/O7
Nantucket•, Mass. 249/O7
Nantucket (isl.), Mass. 188/N2
Nantucket (isl.), Mass. 249/O8
Nantucket (sound), Mass. 249/N6
Nanty Glo, Pa. 294/E5
Nantyglo and Blaina, Wales 13/B6
Nanuet, N.Y. 276/K8
Nanuktok (isls.), Newf. 166/C2
Nanuku (passage), Fiji 86/R10
Nanumea (atoll), Tuvalu 87/H6
Nanuque, Brazil 132/F7
Nanuque, Brazil 120/E4
Nanxiong, China 77/H6
Nanyang, China 77/H5
Nanyuki, Kenya 115/G3
Nanzhang, China 77/H5
Nanzhao, China 77/H5
Nao (cape), Spain 33/G3
Naococane (lake), Québec 174/C2
Naolinco de Victoria, Mexico 150/P1
Naomi, Ky. 237/M6
Náousa, Greece 45/F5
Napa (co.), Calif. 204/C5
Napa, Calif. 188/B3
Napa, Calif. 204/C5
Napadogan, New Bruns. 170/D2
Napa Junction, Calif. 204/J1
Napakiak, Alaska 196/F2
Napaktok (bay), Newf. 166/B2
Napanee, Ontario 177/G3
Napanoch, N.Y. 276/M7
Napaskiak, Alaska 196/F2
Napata (ruins), Sudan 111/F4
Napavine, Wash. 310/C4
Napè, Laos 72/E3
Naper, Nebr. 264/E2
Naperville, Ill. 222/A6
Napf (mt.), Switzerland 39/E3
Napier, Ky. 237/P7
Napier, N. Zealand 100/F3
Napier, N. Zealand 87/H9
Napier (mt.), North. Terr. 93/A4
Napier, W. Va. 312/E5
Napier Field, Ala. 195/H8
Napierville (co.), Québec 172/D4
Napierville, Québec 172/D4
Napili-Honokowai, Hawaii 218/H1
Napinka, Manitoba 179/B5
Naplate, Ill. 222/E2
Naples, Fla. 212/E5
Naples, Idaho 220/B1
Naples, Ill. 222/C4
Naples (prov.), Italy 34/E4
Naples, Italy 7/F4
Naples, Italy 34/E4
Naples•, Maine 243/B8
Naples, N.Y. 276/F5
Naples, S. Dak. 298/O4
Naples, Texas 303/K4
Naples Park, Fla. 212/E5
Napo (riv.) 120/B3
Napo, China 77/G7
Napo (prov.), Ecuador 128/D3
Napo (riv.), Ecuador 128/D3
Napo (riv.), Peru 128/F4
Napoleon, Ind. 227/G6
Napoleon, Mich. 250/E6
Napoleon, Mo. 261/E4
Napoleon, N. Dak. 282/L6
Napoleon, Ohio 284/B3
Naponee, Nebr. 264/E4
Nappa Merri, Queensland 95/B5
Nappan, Nova Scotia 168/D3
Nappanee, Ind. 227/F2
Napperby, North. Terr. 93/C7
Napton, Mo. 261/F4
Naqa (ruins), Sudan 111/F4
Nara (pref.), Japan 81/J8
Nara, Japan 81/J8
Nara, Mali 106/C5
Naracoopa, Tasmania 99/B1
Naracoorte, S. Australia 88/F7
Naracoorte, S. Australia 94/G7
Naradhan, N.S. Wales 97/D3
Naramata, Br. Col. 184/H5
Naranja, Fla. 212/F6
Naranjal (riv.), Ecuador 128/C4
Naranjito, Honduras 154/C3
Naranjito, P. Rico 161/D1
Naranjos, Mexico 150/L6
Naraq, Iran 66/G3
Narashino, Japan 81/P2
Narathiwat, Thailand 72/D6
Nara Visa, N. Mex. 274/F3
Narayanganj, Bangladesh 68/G4
Narayanpet, India 68/D5
Narberth, Pa. 294/M6
Narberth, Wales 13/C6
Narbonne, France 28/E6
Narcissa, Okla. 288/S1
Narcisse, Manitoba 179/E4
Narcondam (isl.), India 68/G6
Narcoossee, Fla. 212/E3
Nardin, Okla. 288/M1
Nardò, Italy 34/F4
Naré, Argentina 143/F5
Nare, Colombia 126/C4
Narellan, N.S. Wales 97/F3
Nares (str.) 146/L2
Nares (str.), N.W.T. 162/N3
Nares (str.), N.W. Terr. 187/L2
Narew (riv.), Poland 47/E2
Naricual, Venezuela 124/F2
Narinda, Madagascar 118/H3
Nariño (dept.), Colombia 126/B7
Nariva (swamp), Trin. & Tob. 161/B10
Narka, Kansas 232/E2
Narmada (riv.), India 54/J7
Narmada (riv.), India 68/D4
Narman, Turkey 63/J2
Narnaul, India 68/D3
Narni, Italy 34/D3
Naro, Italy 34/D6
Narodnaya (mt.), U.S.S.R. 7/K2
Narodnaya (mt.), U.S.S.R. 48/G3
Narodnaya (mt.), U.S.S.R. 52/J1
Narok, Kenya 115/G4
Narooma, N.S. Wales 97/F5
Narrabeen, N.S. Wales 88/L3
Narrabeen, N.S. Wales 97/K3
Narrabri, N. S. Wales 88/J6
Narrabri, N.S. Wales 97/E2
Narragansett, R.I. 249/J7
Narragansett•, R.I. 249/J7
Narragansett (bay), R.I. 249/J6
Narran (lake), N.S. Wales 97/D1
Narran (riv.), N.S. Wales 97/D1
Narrandera, N.S. Wales 88/H6
Narrandera, N.S. Wales 97/D4

North Randall 419

Nonamesset (isl.), Mass. 249/M6
Nondalton, Alaska 196/G2
Nong Het, Laos 72/E3
Nong Khai, Thailand 72/D3
Nong Lahan (lake), Thailand 72/D3
Nonoava, Mexico 150/F3
Nonouti (atoll), Kiribati 87/H6
Nonquitt, Mass. 249/L6
Nonsan, S. Korea 81/C5
Nontron, France 28/D5
Nooksack, Wash. 310/C2
Nooksack (riv.), Wash. 310/C2
Noonan, N. Dak. 282/D2
Noord (pt.), Neth. Ant. 161/F8
Noord (pt.), Neth. Ant. 161/D8
Noord di Salinja, Neth. Ant. 161/E8
Noordwijk, Netherlands 27/E4
Noorvik, Alaska 196/F1
Nootka, Br. Col. 184/D5
Nootka (isl.), Br. Col. 184/D5
Nootka (sound), Br. Col. 184/D5
Nopalucan de la Granja, Mexico 150/O1
Nopeming, Minn. 255/F4
Nopiming Prov. Park, Manitoba 179/G4
Nóqui, Angola 115/B5
Noquochoke P.O. (Westport), Mass. 249/K6
Nora, Ill. 222/D1
Nora, Nebr. 264/G4
Nora, Sask. 181/H3
Nora, S. Dak. 298/R8
Nora, Sweden 18/J7
Nora, Va. 307/D6
Noranda, Québec 162/J6
Noranda, Québec 174/B3
Noranside, Queensland 95/A4
Nora Springs, Iowa 229/H2
Norbeck, S. Dak. 298/L3
Norberg, Sweden 18/K6
Norberto de la Riestra, Argentina 143/G7
Norbertville, Québec 172/F3
Norborne, Mo. 261/E4
Norcatur, Kansas 232/B2
Norco, Calif. 204/E11
Norco, La. 238/N3
Norcross, Georgia 217/D3
Norcross, Maine 243/F4
Norcross, Minn. 255/B5
Nord (dept.), France 28/E2
Nord (pt.), Guadeloupe 161/B7
Nord (dept.), Haiti 158/C5
Nord (riv.), Québec 172/C4
Nordaustlandet (isl.), Norway 18/D1
Nordborg, Denmark 21/C7
Nordby, Arhus, Denmark 21/D5
Nordby, Ribe, Denmark 21/B7
Norddeich, Germany 22/B2
Nordegg, Alberta 182/B3
Nordegg (riv.), Alberta 182/C3
Norden, Nebr. 264/D2
Norden, Germany 22/B2
Nordenham, Germany 22/C2
Norderney, Germany 22/B2
Norderney (isl.), Germany 22/B2
Norderstedt, Germany 22/D2
Nord-Est (bay), Guadeloupe 161/B6
Nordfjord (fjord), Norway 18/E6
Nordhausen, Germany 22/D3
Nordheim, Texas 303/G9
Nordhorn, Germany 22/B2
Nordin, New Bruns. 170/E1
Nordjylland (co.), Denmark 21/D4
Nordkapp (cape), Norway 7/G1
Nordkapp (pt.), Norway 18/C1
Nordkinn (headland), Norway 18/Q1
Nordkinn (pen.), Norway 18/P1
Nordland (co.), Norway 18/J3
Nordland, Wash. 310/C2
Nordli, Norway 18/H4
Nördlingen, Germany 22/D4
Nordmaling, Sweden 18/L5
Nordman, Idaho 220/B1
Nord-Ostsee (canal), Germany 22/C1
Nord-Ouest (dept.), Haiti 158/B5
Nordstrand (isl.), Germany 22/C1
Nord-Trøndelag (co.), Norway 18/H4
Nordvik-Ugol'naya, U.S.S.R. 4/B4
Nordvik-Ugol'naya, U.S.S.R. 48/M2
Nore (riv.), Ireland 10/C4
Nore (riv.), Ireland 17/G7
Norene, Tenn. 237/J8
Norfield, Miss. 256/C8
Norfolk (isl.), Australia 2/T7
Norfolk•, Conn. 210/C1
Norfolk (co.), England 13/H5
Norfolk (co.), Mass. 249/K4
Norfolk•, Mass. 249/J4
Norfolk, Nebr. 188/G2
Norfolk, Nebr. 264/G2
Norfolk, N.Y. 276/K1
Norfolk (bay), Tasmania 99/D4
Norfolk, Va. 188/L3
Norfolk, Va. 146/L6
Norfolk (I.C.), Va. 307/R7
Norfolk Island (terr.), Australia 88/L5
Norfolk Island (terr.), Australia 87/G8
Norfork, Ark. 202/F1
Norfork (lake), Ark. 202/F1
Norfork (lake), Mo. 261/H10
Norg, Netherlands 27/J2
Norge, Okla. 288/K4
Norge, Va. 307/P6
Norglenwold, Alberta 182/C3
Noril'sk, U.S.S.R. 2/P2
Noril'sk, U.S.S.R. 54/L3
Noril'sk, U.S.S.R. 4/B5
Noril'sk, U.S.S.R. 48/J3
Norland, Fla. 212/B4
Norland, Ontario 177/F3
Norlina, N.C. 281/N2
Norma, N.J. 273/C4
Norma, N. Dak. 282/G2
Norma, Tenn. 237/N8
Normal, Ill. 222/E3
Normalville, Pa. 294/D5
Norman, Ark. 202/C5
Norman, Ind. 227/E7
Norman (co.), Minn. 255/B3
Norman, Nebr. 264/F4
Norman (cape), Newf. 166/C3
Norman, N.C. 281/K4
Norman (lake), N.C. 281/H3
Norman, Okla. 288/M4
Norman (riv.), Queensland 88/G3
Norman (creek), Queensland 95/D3
Norman (riv.), Queensland 95/B3
Norman (isl.), Virgin Is. (U.K.) 161/D4
Normanby, Queensland 88/K2
Normand (lake), Québec 172/D2
Normandale, Ontario 177/D5
Normandin, Québec 172/E1
Normandy (trad. prov.), France 29
Normandy, Mo. 261/R2
Normandy (riv.), Queensland 95/C2
Normandy, Tenn. 237/J10
Normandy, Texas 303/D9
Normandy Beach, N.J. 273/E3
Normandy Park, Wash. 310/A2
Normangee, Texas 303/H6
Norman Park, Georgia 217/E8
Norman's Cove, Newf. 166/D2
Normanton, Australia 87/E7
Normanton, Queensland 95/B3
Normanton, Queensland 88/G3
Normantown, Georgia 217/H6
Normantown, W. Va. 312/E5
Norman Wells, Canada 4/C16
Norman Wells, N.W.T. 146/F3
Norman Wells, N.W.T. 162/D2
Norman Wells, N.W. Terr. 187/F3
Normétal, Québec 174/B3
Noroton, Conn. 210/B4
Noroton Heights, Conn. 210/B4
Norphlet, Ark. 202/E7
Norquay, Sask. 181/J4
Ñorquincó, Argentina 143/B5
Norrbotten (co.), Sweden 18/L3
Nørre Åby, Denmark 21/C7
Nørre Alslev, Denmark 21/E8
Nørre Broby, Denmark 21/D7
Nørre Nebel, Denmark 21/B6
Nørre Snede, Denmark 21/C6
Nørre Vorupør, Denmark 21/B4
Norridge, Ill. 222/B5
Norridgewock, Maine 243/D6
Norridgewock•, Maine 243/D6
Norrie, Wis. 317/H6
Norris, Ill. 222/C3
Norris, Miss. 256/F6
Norris, Mont. 262/E5
Norris, S.C. 296/B2
Norris, S. Dak. 298/G7
Norris, Tenn. 237/N8
Norris (dam), Tenn. 237/N8
Norris (lake), Tenn. 188/K3
Norris (lake), Tenn. 237/O8
Norris, Wyo. 319/B1
Norris Arm, Newf. 166/C4
Norris City, Ill. 222/E6
Norris Point, Newf. 166/C4
Norristown, Georgia 217/H5
Norristown, Ind. 227/F6
Norristown, Pa. 294/M5
Norrisville, Md. 245/N2
Norrköping, Sweden 7/F3
Norrköping, Sweden 18/K7
Norrsundet, Sweden 18/K6
Norrtälje, Sweden 18/L7
Norseland, Minn. 255/D6
Norseman, W. Australia 88/C6
Norseman, W. Australia 92/C6
Norsjö, Sweden 18/L4
Norte (pt.), Argentina 143/D5
Norte (chan.), Brazil 120/E2
Norte (chan.), Brazil 132/D2
Norte, Serra do (range), Brazil 132/B5
Norte del Cabo San Antonio (pt.), Argentina 143/E4
Norte de Santander (dept.), Colombia 126/D3
North (sea) 2/K3
North (sea) 7/E3
North (cape), Alaska 196/L4
North (pt.), Barbados 161/B8
North (sea), Belgium 27/D4
North (rocks), Bermuda 156/H2
North (sea), Denmark 21/B9
North (sea), England 13/J4
North (sea), France 28/E1
North (sea), Germany 22/B2
North (cape), Ice. 4/C11
North (Horn) (cape), Iceland 21/B1
North (sound), Ireland 17/B5
North (isls.), La. 238/M7
North (pass), La. 238/N8
North (pt.), La. 238/M7
North (pt.), Md. 245/N4
North (riv.), Mass. 249/D2
North (riv.), Mass. 249/L4
North (chan.), Mich. 250/F2
North (pt.), Mich. 250/F3
North (lake), Minn. 255/F1
North (sea), Netherlands 27/E3
North (lake), New Bruns. 170/C3
North (riv.), Newf. 166/C3
North (riv.), Newf. 166/B2
North (isl.), N. Zealand 87/H9
North (cape), N. Zealand 87/H9
North (cape), N. Zealand 100/D1
North (isl.), N. Zealand 100/F1
North (lake), N. Dak. 282/J3
North (chan.), N. Ireland 10/D3
North (chan.), N. Ireland 17/K1
North (Nordkapp) (cape), Norway 7/G1
North (cape), Norway 4/B8
North (cape), Nova Scotia 162/K6
North (cape), Nova Scotia 168/H1
North (mt.), Nova Scotia 168/D3
North (chan.), Ontario 177/A1
North (chan.), Ontario 175/D3
North (mt.), Pa. 294/K3
North (pt.), Pr. Edward I. 168/E1
North (chan.), Scotland 10/D3
North (chan.), Scotland 15/C5
North (sound), Scotland 15/G4
North (sound), Scotland 15/F1
North (isl.), Seychelles 118/H5
North, S.C. 296/E4
North (inlet), S.C. 296/J5
North (isl.), S.C. 296/J5
North (pt.), Tasmania 99/E1
North (creek), Utah 304/C6
North (lake), Utah 304/B2
North (riv.), Wash. 310/B4
North (riv.), W. Va. 312/J4
North (lake), Wis. 317/J1
North Abington, Mass. 249/L4
North Acton, Mass. 249/J2
North Adams, Mass. 249/B2
North Adams, Mich. 250/E7
Northallerton, England 10/F3
Northallerton, England 13/F3
Northam, England 13/C6
Northam, W. Australia 88/B6
Northam, W. Australia 92/B1
NORTH AMERICA 146
North America 2/C4
North Amherst, Mass. 249/E3
North Amity, Maine 243/H4
Northampton, England 13/F5
Northampton, England 10/F4
Northampton, Mass. 249/D3
Northampton (co.), N.C. 281/P2
Northampton (co.), Pa. 294/M4
Northampton, Pa. 294/M4
Northampton (co.), Va. 307/S6
Northampton, W. Australia 88/A5
Northampton, W. Australia 92/A5
Northamptonshire (co.), England 13/G5
North Andaman (isl.), India 68/G6
North Andover•, Mass. 249/K2
North Anna (riv.), Va. 307/M4
North Anson, Maine 243/D6
North Apollo, Pa. 294/D4
North Arlington, N.J. 273/B2
North Arm (inlet), N.W. Terr. 187/G3
North Ashford, Conn. 210/G1
North Aspy (riv.), Nova Scotia 168/H2
North Atlantic Ocean 2/H3
North Attleboro•, Mass. 249/J5
North Augusta, Ontario 177/J3
North Augusta, S.C. 296/C5
North Aulatsivik (isl.), Newf. 166/B2
North Aurora, Ill. 222/E2
North Avondale, Colo. 208/L6
North Ballachulish, Scotland 15/C4
North Baltimore, Ohio 284/C3
North Bangor, N.Y. 276/M1
North Barrington, Ill. 222/A5
North Bass (isl.), Ohio 284/E2
North Battleford, Sask. 146/H4
North Battleford, Sask. 162/F5
North Battleford, Sask. 181/C3
North Bay, N.Y. 276/J4
North Bay, Ont. 146/L5
North Bay, Ont. 162/J6
North Bay, Ontario 177/E1
North Bay, Ontario 175/E3
North Bay, Wis. 317/M3
North Bay Ingonish (bay), Nova Scotia 168/H2
North Bay Village, Fla. 212/B4
North Beach, Md. 245/N6
North Belgrade, Maine 243/D7
North Bellingham, Mass. 249/J4
North Bend, Br. Col. 184/G5
North Bend, Nebr. 264/H3
North Bend, Ohio 284/B9
North Bend, Oreg. 291/C4
North Bend, Pa. 294/G3
North Bend, Wash. 310/D3
North Bend, Wis. 317/D7
North Bennington, Vt. 268/A6
North Bergen•, N.J. 273/B2
North Berwick, Maine 243/B9
North Berwick•, Maine 243/B9
North Berwick, Scotland 15/F4
North Berwick, Scotland 10/E2
North Beveland (isl.), Netherlands 27/D5
North Billerica, Mass. 249/J2
North Bloomfield, Conn. 210/E1
North Bloomfield, Ohio 284/J3
North Bonneville, Wash. 310/C5
North Borneo (Sabah) (state), Malaysia 85/F3
Northboro, Iowa 229/C7
Northborough, Mass. 249/H3
Northborough•, Mass. 249/H3
North Boston, N.Y. 276/C5
North Bourke, N.S. Wales 97/C2
North Brabant (prov.), Netherlands 27/F5
North Braddock, Pa. 294/C7
North Bradford, Maine 243/F5
North Bradley, Mich. 250/E5
Northbranch, Kansas 232/D2
North Branch, Md. 245/D2
North Branch, Mich. 250/F5
North Branch, Minn. 255/F5
North Branch, N.H. 268/D5
North Branch, N.J. 273/D2
North Branch Oromocto (riv.), New Bruns. 170/D3
North Branford•, Conn. 210/E3
North Brentwood, Md. 245/F4
Northbridge•, Mass. 249/H4
North Bridgton, Maine 243/B7
Northbrook, Ill. 222/B5
North Brook, Ontario 177/G3
North Brookfield, Mass. 249/F3
North Brookfield•, Mass. 249/F3
North Brooksville, Maine 243/F7
North Brunswick•, N.J. 273/D3
North Bruny (isl.), Tasmania 99/D5
North Buena Vista, Iowa 229/L3
North Calais, Vt. 268/C3
North Caldwell, N.J. 273/B2
North Calling Lake, Alberta 182/D2
North Canadian (riv.) 188/G3
North Canadian (riv.), Okla. 288/K3
North Canton, Conn. 210/D1
North Canton, Georgia 217/C2
North Canton, Ohio 284/H4
North Cape (Nordkapp) (pt.), Norway 18/P1
North Cape May, N.J. 273/C6
North Caribou (lake), Ontario 175/B2
North Carolina 188/L3
NORTH CAROLINA 281
North Carolina (state), U.S. 146/K6
North Carrizo (creek), Colo. 208/N8
North Carrizo (riv.), Okla. 288/A1
North Carrollton, Miss. 256/E3
North Carter (mt.), N.H. 268/E3
North Carver, Mass. 249/L5
North Cascades Nat'l Park, Wash. 310/D2
North Catasauqua, Pa. 294/L4
North Charleston, S.C. 296/G6
North Charlestown, N.H. 268/C5
North Chatham, Mass. 249/O6
North Chatham, N.H. 268/E3
North Chelmsford, Mass. 249/J2
North Chesterville, Maine 243/C6
North Chicago, Ill. 222/B4
North Chichester, N.H. 268/E5
North Chili, N.Y. 276/E4
North City (Coello), Ill. 222/E5
North Clarendon, Vt. 268/B4
Northcliffe, W. Australia 92/B6
North Cohasset, Mass. 249/F7
North Colebrook, Conn. 210/C1
North College Hill, Ohio 284/B9
North Collins, N.Y. 276/C5
North Concho (riv.), Texas 303/C6
North Concord, Vt. 268/D3
North Conway, N.H. 268/E3
North Cooking Lake, Alberta 182/D3
North Cotabato (prov.), Philippines 82/E7
Northcote, Minn. 255/A2
Northcote, N. Zealand 100/B1
Northcote, Victoria 88/L7
Northcote, Victoria 97/J5
North Cove, N.C. 281/F3
North Cove, Wash. 310/A4
North Cowichan, Br. Col. 184/J3
North Creek, N.Y. 276/M3
North Crossett, Ark. 202/G7
North Cutler, Maine 243/J6
North Dakota 188/F1
NORTH DAKOTA 282
North Dakota (state), U.S. 146/H5
North Dandalup, W. Australia 88/B3
North Danger (reef), Philippines 85/E3
North Danville, Vt. 268/C3
North Dartmouth, Mass. 249/K6
North Dexter, Maine 243/E5
North Dighton, Mass. 249/K5
North Dixmont, Maine 243/E6
North Down (dist.), N. Ireland 17/K2
North Downs (hills), England 13/G6
North Eagle Butte, S. Dak. 298/G3
Northeast (cape), Alaska 196/E2
North East (pt.), Jamaica 158/K6
Northeast (pass), La. 238/M8
North East, Md. 245/P2
North East, Pa. 294/C1
North East Breakers, Bermuda 156/H2
North East Cape Fear (riv.), N.C. 281/O4
North East Carry, Maine 243/D4
North-Eastern (prov.), Kenya 115/G3
Northeast Foreland (pen.), Greenl. 4/A10
North Eastham, Mass. 249/O5
Northeast Harbor, Maine 243/G7
Northeast Land (isl.), Norway 4/B8
North East Margaree (riv.), Nova Scotia 168/H2
North Easton, Mass. 249/K4
North East Providence (chan.), Bahamas 156/C1
North Edisto (riv.), S.C. 296/G6
North Edwards, Calif. 204/H8
North Egremont, Mass. 249/A4
Northeim, Germany 22/C3
North English, Iowa 229/J5
North Enid, Okla. 288/L2
Northern (dist.), Israel 65/C2
Northern (head), New Bruns. 170/D4
Northern (prov.), Sudan 111/E3
Northern Cheyenne Ind. Res., Mont. 262/K5
Northern Dvina (riv.), U.S.S.R. 52/F2
Northern Dvina (riv.), U.S.S.R. 48/E3
Northern Indian (lake), Manitoba 179/J2
NORTHERN IRELAND 17
NORTHERN IRELAND, 10/C3
Northern Ireland, U.K. 7/D3
Northern Marianas 87/E4
Northern Marianas, U.S. 2/S5
Northern Peninsula Aboriginal Reserve, Queensland 88/G2
Northern Peninsula Aboriginal Res., Queensland 95/B1
Northern Samar (prov.), Philippines 82/E4
Northern Sporades (isls.), Greece 45/F6
Northern Territory, 88/E3
NORTHERN TERRITORY 93
Northern Territory (terr.), Australia 87/D7
Northern Yukon Nat'l Park, Yukon 162/B2
Northern Yukon Nat'l Park, Yukon 187/D3
North Esk (riv.), Scotland 15/F4
North Esk (riv.), Tasmania 99/D3
North Fairfield, Ohio 284/E3
North Falmouth, Mass. 249/M6
North Ferrisburg, Vt. 268/A3
Northfield, Conn. 210/C2
Northfield, Ill. 222/B5
Northfield, Ky. 237/K1
Northfield•, Maine 243/H6
Northfield, Mass. 249/E2
Northfield•, Mass. 249/E2
Northfield, Minn. 255/E6
Northfield•, N.H. 268/D5
Northfield, N.J. 273/D5
Northfield, Ohio 284/J10
Northfield, Texas 303/D3
Northfield, Vt. 268/B3
Northfield•, Vt. 268/B3
Northfield, Wis. 317/D7
Northfield Falls, Vt. 268/B3
Northfield Farms, Mass. 249/E2
Northfield-Tilton, N.H. 268/D5
Northfleet, England 10/C5
Northfleet, England 13/J8
North Fond du Lac, Wis. 317/J8
Northford, Conn. 210/D3
North Foreland (prom.), England 10/G5
North Foreland (prom.), England 13/J6
North Fork, Calif. 204/F6
North Fork, Frenchman (creek), Colo. 208/O1
Forth Fork, Gunnison (riv.), Colo. 208/D5
North Fork, Smoky Hill (riv.), Colo. 208/P4
North Fork, Idaho 220/D4
North Fork (riv.), Idaho 220/B7
North Fork, Flathead (riv.), Mont. 262/B2
North Fork, Little Humboldt (riv.), Nev. 266/D1
North Fork, Grand (riv.), N. Dak. 282/E8
Northfork, W. Va. 312/D8
North Fork, Powder (riv.), Wyo. 319/F2
North Fork, Wind (riv.), Wyo. 319/C2
North Fork, Shoshone (riv.), Wyo. 319/C1
North Fort Myers, Fla. 212/E5
North Foster, R.I. 249/H5
North Fourchu, Nova Scotia 168/H3
North Fox (isl.), Mich. 250/D3
North Franklin, Conn. 210/G2
North Freedom, Wis. 317/G9
North Friars (bay), St. Kitts and Nevis 161/D10
North Friesland (reg.), German 22/C1
North Frisian (isls.), Denmark 21/B7
North Frisian (isls.), Germany 22/B1
North Fryeburg, Maine 243/B7
North Galiano, Br. Col. 184/K3
North Garden, Va. 307/L5
Northgate, N. Dak. 282/F2
Northgate, Sask. 181/J6
Northglenn, Colo. 208/K3
North Gorham, Maine 243/B8
North Gosforth, England 13/J3
North Gower, Ontario 177/J2
North Grafton, Mass. 249/H4
North Granby, Conn. 210/D1
North Grant, Nova Scotia 168/G3
North Grosvenor Dale, Conn. 210/H1
North Groton, N.H. 268/D4
North Grove, Ind. 227/F3
North Guilford, Conn. 210/E3
North Gulfport, Miss. 256/F10
North Hadley, Mass. 249/D3
North Haledon, N.J. 273/B1
North Hampton•, N.H. 268/F6
North Hampton, Ohio 284/C5
North Hanover, Mass. 249/L4
North Hansel (mts.), Utah 304/B2
North Harbour, Newf. 166/D2
North Harlowe, N.C. 281/R5
North Hartland, Vt. 268/C4
North Hartsville, S.C. 296/G3
North Harwich, Mass. 249/O6
North Hatfield, Mass. 249/D3
North Hatley, Québec 172/F4
North Haven•, Conn. 210/D3
North Haven, Maine 243/F7
North Haven•, Maine 243/F7
North Haverhill, N.H. 268/D3
North Havre, Mont. 262/G2
North Hayden, Ind. 227/B2
North Head, New Bruns. 170/D4
North Henderson, Ill. 222/C2
North Hero, Vt. 268/A2
North Highlands, Calif. 204/B8
North High Shoals, Georgia 217/F3
North Hills, W. Va. 312/D4
North Hodge, La. 238/E2
North Holland (prov.), Netherlands 27/F3
North Holland (canal), Netherlands 27/C4
North Hollywood, Calif. 204/B10
North Hornell, N.Y. 276/E6
North Horr, Kenya 115/G3
North Hudson, N.Y. 276/N3
North Hudson, Wis. 317/A5
North Hyde Park, Vt. 268/B2
North Hykeham, England 13/G4
North Industry, Ohio 284/H4
North Inishkea (isl.), Ireland 17/A3
North Java, N.Y. 276/D5
North Jay, Maine 243/C6
North Johns, Ala. 195/D4
North Judson, Ind. 227/D2
North Kansas City, Mo. 261/P5
North Kedgwick (riv.), New Bruns. 170/C1
North Kent, Conn. 210/B1
North Kent (isl.), N.W. Terr. 187/J2
North Kingstown•, R.I. 249/J6
North Kingsville, Ohio 284/J2
North Knife (lake), Manitoba 179/J2
North Knife Lake, Manitoba 179/J2
North Korea 54/O5
North La Junta, Colo. 208/N7
Northlake, Ill. 222/B5
Northlake, Texas 303/F1
North Lake, Wis. 317/J1
North Lakhimpur, India 68/G3
Northland, Mich. 250/B2
Northland, Wis. 317/H6
North Landgrove, Vt. 268/B5
North Laramie (riv.), Wyo. 319/G3
North Las Vegas, Nev. 266/F6
North Lauderdale, Fla. 212/B3
North Lawrence, N.Y. 276/L1
North Lawrence, Ohio 284/G4
North Leeds, Maine 243/C7
North Lewisburg, Ohio 284/C5
North Liberty, Ind. 227/E1
North Liberty, Iowa 229/K5
North Lima, Ohio 284/J4
North Limington, Maine 243/B8
North Little Rock, Ark. 202/F4
North Livermore, Maine 243/C7
North Loup, Nebr. 264/F3
North Loup (riv.), Nebr. 264/E3
North Lovell, Maine 243/B7
North Lubec, Maine 243/J6
North Luconia (shoals), Philippines 85/E4
North Madison, Conn. 210/E3
North Madison, Ohio 284/H2
North Magnetic Pole (dist.) 162/F1
North Magnetic Pole, Canada 4/B15
North Magnetic Pole, N.W. Terr. 187/H2
North Manchester, Ind. 227/F3
North Manitou (isl.), Mich. 250/C3
North Mankato, Minn. 255/D6
North Marshfield, Mass. 249/M4
North Merritt (isl.), Fla. 212/F3
North Miami, Fla. 212/B4
North Miami, Okla. 288/R1
North Miami Beach, Fla. 212/C4
North Middleboro, Mass. 249/L5
North Middletown, Ky. 237/N4
North Minch (sound), Scotland 10/D1
North Minch (sound), Scotland 15/B3
North Montpelier, Vt. 268/C3
Northmoor, Mo. 261/P5
North Motton, Tasmania 99/C3
North Mountain, W. Va. 312/K3
North Muskegon, Mich. 250/C5
North Myrtle Beach, S.C. 296/K4
North Naples, Fla. 212/E5
North Natuna (isl.), Indonesia 85/D4
North Negril (pt.), Jamaica 158/G6
North Newport, N.H. 268/C5
North New Portland, Maine 243/C6
North New River (canal), Fla. 212/F5
North Newry, Maine 243/B6
North Newton, Kansas 232/E3
North Oaks, Minn. 255/G5
North Ogden, Utah 304/C2
North Olmsted, Ohio 284/G9
Northome, Minn. 255/D3
North Ossetian A.S.S.R., U.S.S.R. 48/E5
North Ossetian A.S.S.R., U.S.S.R. 52/F6
North Oxford, Mass. 249/G4
North Pacific (ocean) 87/F4
North Pacific Ocean 2/B5
North Pacific Ocean 2/T4
North Pagai (isl.), Indonesia 85/C6
North Palm Beach, Fla. 212/F5
North Parsonfield, Maine 243/A8
North Pease (riv.), Texas 303/D3
North Pekin, Ill. 222/D3
North Pembroke, Mass. 249/M4
North Pender Island, Br. Col. 184/K3
North Penobscot, Maine 243/F7
North Perry, Maine 243/J5
North Perry, Ohio 284/H2
North Petherton, England 13/D6
North Pine, Br. Col. 184/G2
North Plain, Conn. 210/F3
North Plainfield, N.J. 273/E2
North Plains, Oreg. 291/A2
North Platte (riv.) 188/F2
North Platte (riv.), Colo. 208/G1
North Platte, Nebr. 188/F2
North Platte, Nebr. 264/D3
North Platte (riv.), Nebr. 264/B3
North Platte (riv.), U.S. 146/H5
North Platte (riv.), Wyo. 319/H3
North Plymouth, Mass. 249/L5
North Pole 4/A1
North Pole 2/F1
North Pole, Alaska 196/J2
North Pole (brook), New Bruns. 170/D1
North Pomfret, Vt. 268/B4
Northport, Ala. 195/C4
North Port, Fla. 212/D4
Northport•, Maine 243/E7
Northport, Mich. 250/D3
Northport, Nebr. 264/B3
Northport, N.Y. 276/O9
Northport, Nova Scotia 168/E3
Northport, Wash. 310/H2
North Portal, Sask. 181/J6
North Potomac, Md. 245/K4
North Powder, Oreg. 291/K2
North Pownal, Vt. 268/A6
North Prairie, Wis. 317/J2
North Providence•, R.I. 249/J5
North Pulaski, Va. 307/G6
North Randall, Ohio 284/H9

422 Okaloacoochee Slough

Okaloacoochee Slough (swamp), Fla. 212/E5
Okaloosa (co.), Fla. 212/C6
Okamanpeedan (lake), Iowa 229/D2
Okanagan (lake), Br. Col. 162/D6
Okanagan (lake), Br. Col. 184/H5
Okanagan Centre, Br. Col. 184/H5
Okanagan Falls, Br. Col. 184/H5
Okanagan Landing, Br. Col. 184/H5
Okanagan Mission, Br. Col. 184/H5
Okanagan Mtn. Prov. Park, Br. Col. 184/G5
Okanogan (riv.), Br. Col. 184/H6
Okanogan (co.), Wash. 310/F2
Okanogan, Wash. 310/F2
Okanogan (riv.), Wash. 310/F2
Okarche, Okla. 288/L3
Okatibbee (creek), Miss. 256/G5
Okatibbee (lake), Miss. 256/G5
Okato, N. Zealand 100/D3
Okaton, S. Dak. 298/H6
Okauchee, Wis. 317/J1
Okauchee (lake), Wis. 317/J1
Okaukuejo, Namibia 118/B3
Okawa, Japan 81/E7
Okawville, Ill. 222/D5
Okay, Okla. 288/R3
Okaya, Japan 81/H5
Okayama (pref.), Japan 81/F6
Okayama, Japan 81/F6
Okazaki, Japan 81/H6
O'Kean, Ark. 202/J1
Okeana, Ohio 284/A7
Okee, Wis. 317/H9
Okeechobee (co.), Fla. 212/F4
Okeechobee, Fla. 212/F4
Okeechobee (lake), Fla. 188/K5
Okeechobee (lake), Fla. 212/F5
O'Keeffe Nat'l Hist. Site, N. Mex. 274/C2
Okeene, Okla. 288/K2
Okefenokee (swamp), Fla. 212/D1
Okefenokee (swamp), Georgia 217/H9
Okehampton, England 13/D7
Okehampton, England 10/D5
Okemah, Okla. 288/O4
Okemo (Ludlow) (mt.), Vt. 268/B5
Okemos, Mich. 250/E6
Okene, Nigeria 106/F7
Oker (riv.), Germany 22/D2
Okesa, Okla. 288/O1
Oketo, Kansas 232/F2
Okfuskee (co.), Okla. 288/O3
Okha, U.S.S.R. 54/R4
Okha, U.S.S.R. 48/P4
Okha Port, India 68/B4
Okhotsk (sea) 2/S3
Okhotsk (sea), Japan 81/M1
Okhotsk, U.S.S.R. 48/P4
Okhotsk, U.S.S.R. 54/R4
Okhotsk (sea), U.S.S.R. 48/P4
Okhotsk (sea), U.S.S.R. 54/R4
Oki (isls.), Japan 81/F5
Okiep, S. Africa 118/B5
Okinawa (pref.), Japan 81/N6
Okinawa (isls.), Japan 54/O7
Okinawa (isl.), Japan 81/N6
Okinawa (isls.), Japan 81/N6
Okinoerabu (isl.), Japan 81/N5
Okino-Tori-Shima (Parace Vela) (isls.), Japan 85/D3
Okkan, Burma 72/B3
Okla, Sask. 181/H3
Oklahoma 188/G3
OKLAHOMA 288
Oklahoma (co.), Okla. 288/M3
Oklahoma (state), U.S. 146/J6
Oklahoma City (cap.), Okla. 146/J6
Oklahoma City (cap.), Okla. 188/G3
Oklahoma City (cap.), Okla. 288/L4
Oklaunion, Texas 303/F3
Oklawaha, Fla. 212/E2
Oklawaha (riv.), Fla. 212/E2
Oklee, Minn. 255/C3
Okmulgee, Okla. 188/G3
Okmulgee (co.), Okla. 288/P3
Okmulgee, Okla. 288/O3
Okoboji, Iowa 229/C2
Okobojo (creek), S. Dak. 298/J4
Okolona, Ark. 202/D5
Okolona, Ky. 237/K4
Okolona, Miss. 256/G2
Okolona, Ohio 284/B3
Okondja, Gabon 115/B4
Okotoks, Alberta 182/C4
Okovango (riv.) 102/D6
Okovango (riv.), Botswana 118/C3
Okovango (swamps), Botswana 118/C3
Okovango (riv.), Namibia 118/C3
Okoyo, Congo 115/C4
Okpo, Burma 72/C3
Okreek, S. Dak. 298/J7
Oksino, U.S.S.R. 52/H1
Oktaha, Okla. 288/R3
Oktibbeha (co.), Miss. 256/G4
Oktyabr'sk, U.S.S.R. 52/G4
Oktyabr'skiy, U.S.S.R. 52/H4
Okulovka, U.S.S.R. 52/D3
Okushiri (isl.), Japan 81/J2
Ola, Ark. 202/D3
Ola, Georgia 217/E4
Ola, Idaho 220/B5
Olá, Panama 154/G6
Olafsfjördhur, Iceland 21/C1
Ola Grande (pt.), P. Rico 161/D3
Olalla, Br. Col. 184/H5
Olalla, Wash. 310/A2
Olamon, Maine 243/F5
Olancha, Calif. 204/H7
Olanchito, Honduras 154/D3
Öland (isl.), Sweden 7/F3
Öland (isl.), Sweden 18/K8
Olanta, Pa. 294/F4
Olanta, S.C. 296/H4
Olar, S.C. 296/E5
Olary, S. Australia 94/G5
Olathe, Colo. 208/D5
Olathe, Kansas 232/H3
Olathe Nav. Air Sta., Kansas 232/H3
Olavarría, Argentina 143/D4
Olavarría, Argentina 120/C6
Oława, Poland 47/C3
Olberg, Ariz. 198/D5
Olbernhau, Germany 22/E3
Olbia, Italy 34/B4
Olcott, N.Y. 276/C4
Old (riv.), Calif. 204/L1
Old (riv.), La. 238/G5
Old (stream), Maine 243/H6
Oldany (isl.), Scotland 15/C2
Old Appleton, Mo. 261/N7
Old Bahama (chan.), Bahamas 156/B2
Old Bahama (chan.), Cuba 158/G1
Old Bahama (chan.), Cuba 156/B2
Old Bar, N.S. Wales 97/G2
Old Barkerville, Br. Col. 184/G3
Old Bennington, Vt. 268/A6
Old Bonaventure, Newf. 166/D2
Old Bridge, N.J. 273/E3
Old Castile (reg.), Spain 33/D2
Oldcastle, Ireland 10/C4
Oldcastle, Ireland 17/G4
Old Crow, Yukon 187/E3
Oldemarkt, Netherlands 27/J3
Olden, Mo. 261/J9
Olden, Norway 18/E6
Olden, Texas 303/F5
Oldenburg, Germany 22/C2
Oldenburg, Ind. 227/G6
Oldenburg, Miss. 256/C7
Oldenburg in Holstein, Germany 22/D1
Old England, Jamaica 158/H6
Old Entrance, Alberta 182/B3
Oldenzaal, Netherlands 27/K4
Old Faithful, Wyo. 319/B1
Oldfield, La. 238/L1
Old Fields, W. Va. 312/J4
Old Forge, N.Y. 276/L3
Old Forge, Pa. 294/F7
Old Fort, N.C. 281/E3
Old Fort, Ohio 284/D3
Oldfort, Tenn. 237/M10
Old Glory, Texas 303/D4
Old Greenwich, Conn. 210/A4
Oldham, England 13/H2
Oldham, England 10/G2
Oldham (co.), Ky. 237/L4
Oldham, S. Dak. 298/P5
Oldham (co.), Texas 303/B2
Old Harbor, Alaska 196/H3
Old Harbour, Jamaica 158/J6
Old Harbour (bay), Jamaica 158/J6
Old Harbour Bay, Jamaica 158/J6
Old Hickory (dam), Tenn. 237/H8
Old Hickory (lake), Tenn. 237/J8
Old Kilpatrick, Scotland 15/B2
Old Landing, Ky. 237/O5
Old Leighlin, Ireland 17/G6
Old Lyme•, Conn. 210/F3
Old Main Centre, Sask. 181/D5
Oldman (riv.), Alberta 182/D5
Oldman (riv.), Sask. 181/L2
Oldmans (creek), N.J. 273/C4
Old Marsh Bed, North. Terr. 93/B6
Oldmeldrum, Scotland 15/F3
Oldmeldrum, Scotland 10/E2
Old Mill Creek, Ill. 222/B4
Old Mission, Mich. 250/D4
Old Monroe, Mo. 261/L5
Old Mystic, Conn. 210/H3
Old Orchard Beach, Maine 243/C9
Old Orchard Beach•, Maine 243/C9
Old Perlican, Newf. 166/D2
Old Rhine (riv.), Netherlands 27/E4
Old Rhodes (key), Fla. 212/F6
Old Ripley, Ill. 222/D5
Old Road, Ant. & Bar. 161/D11
Old Road Town, St. Kitts & Nevis 161/C10
Olds, Alberta 182/D4
Olds, Iowa 229/K6
Old Saybrook, Conn. 210/F3
Old Saybrook•, Conn. 210/F3
Old Shawneetown, Ill. 222/E6
Oldsmar, Fla. 212/B2
Old Spring Hill, Ala. 195/C6
Old Sturbridge Village, Mass. 249/F4
Old Tampa (bay), Fla. 212/B3
Old Tappan, N.J. 273/C1
Old Town, Fla. 212/C2
Oldtown, Idaho 220/A1
Oldtown, Ky. 237/R4
Old Town, Maine 243/F6
Oldtown, Md. 245/D2
Old Trap, N.C. 281/T2
Olduvai Gorge (canyon), Tanzania 115/G4
Old Washington, Ohio 284/H5
Oldwick, N.J. 273/D2
Old Wives, Sask. 181/E5
Old Wives (lake), Sask. 181/E5
Old Woman (creek), Wyo. 319/H3
Olean, Mo. 261/G6
Olean, N.Y. 276/D6
O'Leary (peak), Ariz. 198/D3
O'Leary, Pr. Edward I. 168/D2
Olecko, Poland 47/F1
Oleiros, Portugal 33/B3
Olëkma (riv.), U.S.S.R. 48/N4
Olëkminsk, U.S.S.R. 48/N3
Olema, Calif. 204/H1
Olenegorsk, U.S.S.R. 52/D1
Olenek, U.S.S.R. 4/C4
Olenëk (riv.), U.S.S.R. 54/N3
Olenëk, U.S.S.R. 48/M3
Olënek (bay), U.S.S.R. 48/N2
Olënek (riv.), U.S.S.R. 48/M3
Olentangy (riv.), Ohio 284/D4
Oléron (isl.), France 28/C5
Oleśnica, Poland 47/C3
Olesno, Poland 47/D3
Oleta, Okla. 288/R6
Olex, Oreg. 291/G2
Oley, Pa. 294/L5
Olga, N. Dak. 282/O2
Olga (Kata Tjuta) (mt.), North. Terr. 93/B8
Olga, Wash. 310/C2
Olgiy (Ulegei), Mongolia 77/C2
Ølgod, Denmark 21/B6
Olha, Manitoba 179/B4
Olhão, Portugal 33/C4
Oliena, Italy 34/B4
Olifants (riv.), Mozambique 118/D4
Olifants (riv.), S. Africa 118/D4
Olimar, Uruguay 145/E3
Olimar Grande (riv.), Uruguay 145/E4
Olímpia, Brazil 135/B2
Olin, Iowa 229/L5
Olin, Ky. 237/N6
Olin, N.C. 281/H3
Olinda, Brazil 120/F3
Olinda, Brazil 132/H4
Olinda, Calif. 204/C3
Olinda, Victoria 97/K5
Oliva, Argentina 143/D3
Oliva, Spain 33/F3
Oliva de la Frontera, Spain 33/C3
Olivais, Portugal 33/A1
Olivar Alto, Chile 138/G5
Olivares, Cerro de (mt.), Argentina 143/B3
Olivares, Cerro de (mt.), Chile 138/B8
Olive, Mont. 262/L5
Olive, Okla. 288/O2
Olive Branch, Ill. 222/D6
Olive Branch, Miss. 256/E1
Olive Branch, Ohio 284/D10
Olive Hill, Ky. 237/P4
Olivehill, Tenn. 237/E10
Oliveira, Brazil 135/D2
Olivenza, Spain 33/C3
Oliver (dam), Ala. 195/J5
Oliver, Br. Col. 184/H5
Oliver, Georgia 217/J5
Oliver (dam), Georgia 217/B6
Oliver (lake), Georgia 217/B5
Oliver, Ind. 227/B8
Oliver (co.), N. Dak. 282/H5
Oliver, Pa. 294/C6
Oliver, Wis. 317/B2
Oliver Springs, Tenn. 237/N8
Olivet, Ill. 222/F4
Olivet, Kansas 232/G3
Olivet, Md. 245/N7
Olivet, Mich. 250/E6
Olivet, S. Dak. 298/O7
Olivet, Wis. 317/B6
Olivette, Mo. 261/O2
Olivia, Minn. 255/C6
Olivia, N.C. 281/L4
Olivier, La. 238/G7
Olivone, Switzerland 39/G3
Olkusz, Poland 47/D3
Olla, La. 238/F3
Ollachea, Peru 128/G9
Ollagüe (vol.), Bolivia 136/B7
Ollagüe, Chile 120/C5
Ollagüe, Chile 138/B3
Ollantaytambo, Peru 128/F9
Ollie, Iowa 229/J6
Ollon, Switzerland 39/D4
Olmedo, Spain 33/D2
Olmitz, Kansas 232/D3
Olmos, Peru 128/C5
Olmos Park, Texas 303/F8
Olmstead, Ky. 237/H7
Olmsted, Ill. 222/D6
Olmsted (co.), Minn. 255/F7
Olmsted Falls, Ohio 284/G9
Olmstedville, N.Y. 276/N3
Olmué, Chile 138/F2
Olney, Ill. 222/E5
Olney, Md. 245/K4
Olney, Mo. 261/K4
Olney, Mont. 262/B2
Olney, Okla. 288/O6
Olney, Oreg. 291/D1
Olney, Texas 303/F4
Olney Springs, Colo. 208/M6
Olofström, Sweden 18/J8
Oloh, Miss. 256/E8
Olomouc, Czech. 7/F4
Olomouc, Czech. 41/D2
Olonets, U.S.S.R. 52/D2
Olongapo, Philippines 82/C3
Oloron-Sainte-Marie, France 28/C6
Olot, Spain 33/H1
Olowalu, Hawaii 218/H2
Oloy (range), U.S.S.R. 48/R3
Olpe, Kansas 232/F3
Olsa (riv.), Austria 41/C3
Olsburg, Kansas 232/F2
Olst, Netherlands 27/J4
Olsztyn (prov.), Poland 47/E2
Olsztyn, Poland 7/G3
Olsztyn, Poland 47/E2
Olsztynek, Poland 47/E2
Olt (riv.), Romania 7/G4
Olt (riv.), Romania 45/G3
Olta, Argentina 143/C3
Olten, Switzerland 39/E2
Oltenița, Romania 45/H3
Olton, Texas 303/B3
Oltu, Turkey 63/J2
Olur, Turkey 63/K2
Olustee, Fla. 212/D1
Olustee (riv.), Fla. 212/D1
Olustee, Okla. 288/H5
Olutanga (isl.), Philippines 82/D7
Olutanga (isl.), Philippines 85/G4
Olvera, Spain 33/D4
Olvey, Ark. 202/E1
Olwampi (cape), China 77/K7
Olympia (isls.), Greece 45/E7
Olympia, Ky. 237/O4
Olympia (cap.), Wash. 146/F5
Olympia (cap.), Wash. 188/B1
Olympia (cap.), Wash. 310/C3
Olympia Fields, Ill. 222/B6
Olympian Village, Mo. 261/M6
Olympic (mts.), Wash. 310/B3
Olympic Nat'l Park, Wash. 188/A1
Olympic Nat'l Park, Wash. 310/B3
Olympic Valley, Calif. 204/E4
Olympus (mt.), Greece 45/F5
Olympus (mt.), Wash. 310/B3
Olyphant, Ark. 202/H3
Olyphant, Pa. 294/F7
Olyphic, N.C. 281/M7
Olyutorskiy (cape), U.S.S.R. 54/U4
Olyutorskiy (cape), U.S.S.R. 48/S4
Oma (cape), Japan 81/K3
Oma, Miss. 256/D7
Omagari, Japan 81/K4
Omagh (dist.), N. Ireland 17/G2
Omagh, N. Ireland 10/C3
Omagh, N. Ireland 17/G2
Omaguas, Peru 128/F5
Omaha, Ala. 195/H4
Omaha, Ark. 202/D1
Omaha (beach), France 28/C3
Omaha, Georgia 217/C6
Omaha, Ill. 222/E6
Omaha, Nebr. 188/G2
Omaha, Nebr. 146/J5
Omaha, Nebr. 264/J3
Omaha Ind. Res., Nebr. 264/H2
Omak, Wash. 310/F2
Omak (lake), Wash. 310/F2
Oman 2/M5
Oman 54/G8
OMAN 59/G6
Oman (gulf) 54/G7
Oman (gulf), Iran 59/G5
Oman (gulf), Iran 66/M8
Oman (gulf), Oman 59/G5
Oman (reg.), Oman 59/G5
Oman (gulf), U.A.E. 59/G5
Omar, W. Va. 312/C7
Omaruru, Namibia 118/B4
Omas, Peru 128/D9
Omatako (riv.), Namibia 118/B3
Omate, Peru 128/G11
Ombai (str.), Indonesia 85/H7
Omboué, Gabon 115/A4
Ombrone (riv.), Italy 34/C3
Ombúes de Lavalle, Uruguay 145/B4
Ombúes de Oribe, Uruguay 145/C4
Omdurman, Sudan 102/F3
Omdurman, Sudan 59/B6
Omdurman, Sudan 111/F4
Omega, Georgia 217/E8
Omega, Ind. 227/F4
Omega, Ohio 284/E7
Omega, Okla. 288/K3
Omemee, N. Dak. 282/K2
Omemee, Ontario 177/F3
Omena, Mich. 250/D3
Omeo, Victoria 97/D5
'Omer, Israel 65/B5
Omer, Mich. 250/F4
Ömerli, Turkey 63/J4
Omerville, Québec 172/E4
Ometepe (isl.), Nicaragua 154/E5
Ometepec, Mexico 150/K8
Omey (isl.), Ireland 17/A5
Omineca (mts.), Br. Col. 184/E2
Omineca (riv.), Br. Col. 184/E2
Omiš, Yugoslavia 45/C4
Omiya, Japan 81/O2
Ommaney (cape), Alaska 196/M2
Ommanney (bay), N.W. Terr. 187/H2
Omme (riv.), Denmark 21/B6
Ommen, Netherlands 27/J3
Ömnögovĭ, Mongolia 77/F3
Omø (isl.), Denmark 21/E7
Omo (riv.), Ethiopia 111/G6
Omoa, Honduras 154/C3
Omolon (riv.), U.S.S.R. 54/S3
Omolon (riv.), U.S.S.R. 4/C1
Omolon (riv.), U.S.S.R. 48/Q3
Omoloy (riv.), U.S.S.R. 48/O3
Omono (riv.), Japan 81/J4
Ompah, Ontario 177/H2
Omps, W. Va. 312/K4
Omro, Wis. 317/J7
Omsk, U.S.S.R. 54/J4
Omsk, U.S.S.R. 2/N3
Omsk, U.S.S.R. 48/H4
Omsukchan, U.S.S.R. 48/Q3
Omu, Japan 81/L1
Omura, Bonin Is., Japan 81/M3
Omura, Nagasaki, Japan 81/E7
Omurtag, Bulgaria 45/H4
Omuta, Japan 81/E7
Omutninsk, U.S.S.R. 48/F4
Omutninsk, U.S.S.R. 52/H3
Ona, Fla. 212/E4
Ona, W. Va. 312/B6
Onaga, Kansas 232/F2
Onagawa, Japan 81/K4
Onaka, S. Dak. 298/L3
Onalaska, Texas 303/J7
Onalaska, Wash. 310/C4
Onalaska, Wis. 317/D8
Onaman (lake), Ontario 177/H4
Onamia, Minn. 255/E4
Onancock, Va. 307/S5
Onangué (lake), Gabon 115/A4
Onanole, Manitoba 179/C4
Onaping Falls, Ontario 177/J5
Onaping Falls, Ontario 175/D3
Onaqui, Utah 304/B3
Onarga, Ill. 222/F3
Onawa, Iowa 229/A4
Onawa, Maine 243/E5
Onawa (lake), Maine 243/E5
Onaway, Idaho 220/B3
Onaway, Mich. 250/E3
Onchan, I. of Man 13/C3
Onchiota, N.Y. 276/M2
Oncócua, Angola 115/B7
Onda, Spain 33/F3
Ondangwa, Namibia 118/B3
Ondava (riv.), Czech. 41/F2
Ondjiva, Angola 102/D6
Ondjiva, Angola 114/C7
Ondo (state), Nigeria 106/F7
Ondo, Nigeria 106/F7
Öndörhaan (Undur Khan), Mongolia 77/G2
Öndörhaan, Mongolia 54/N5
Ondverdharnes (mt.), Iceland 21/A1
O'Neals, Calif. 204/F6
Oneco, Conn. 210/H2
Oneco, Fla. 212/D4
Onefour, Alberta 182/E5
Onega, U.S.S.R. 7/H2
Onega (lake), U.S.S.R. 7/H2
Onega (riv.), U.S.S.R. 7/H2
Onega, U.S.S.R. 52/E2
Onega, U.S.S.R. 48/D3
Onega (bay), U.S.S.R. 52/E2
Onega (lake), U.S.S.R. 48/D3
Onega (lake), U.S.S.R. 52/E2
Onega (riv.), U.S.S.R. 48/D3
Onega (riv.), U.S.S.R. 52/E2
Onego, W. Va. 312/H5
One Hundred and Fifty Mile House, Br. Col. 184/G4
One Hundred Mile House, Br. Col. 184/G4
Onehunga, N. Zealand 100/B1
Oneida, Ark. 202/J5
Oneida (co.), Idaho 220/F7
Oneida, Ill. 222/C2
Oneida, Iowa 229/L3
Oneida, Kansas 232/G2
Oneida, Ky. 237/O6
Oneida (co.), N.Y. 276/J4
Oneida, N.Y. 276/J4
Oneida (lake), N.Y. 276/J4
Oneida, Pa. 294/K4
Oneida, Tenn. 237/N7
Oneida (co.), Wis. 317/G4
Oneida, Wis. 317/K7
O'Neill, Nebr. 264/F2
Onekama, Mich. 250/C4
Oneonta, Ala. 195/E3
Oneonta, N.Y. 276/K6
One Tree Hill, N. Zealand 100/B1
Ong, Nebr. 264/G4
Ongjin, N. Korea 81/B5
Ongniud, China 77/J3
Ongole, India 68/E5
Onhaye, Belgium 27/F8
Oni, U.S.S.R. 52/F6
Onida, S. Dak. 298/K4
Onilahy (riv.), Madagascar 118/G4
Onima, Neth. Ant. 161/E8
Onion Lake, Sask. 181/B2
Onitsha, Nigeria 106/F7
Onitsha, Nigeria 102/C4
Onkaparinga (riv.), S. Australia 88/D8
Onkaparinga (riv.), S. Australia 94/B8
Onkivesi (lake), Finland 18/P5
Onley, Va. 307/S5
Only, Tenn. 237/F9
Ono, Calif. 204/C3
Ono, Japan 81/H6
Ono (riv.), Japan 81/E7
Ono, Pa. 294/J5
Onoda, Japan 81/E6
Onomea, Hawaii 218/J4
Onomichi, Japan 81/F6
Onon, Mongolia 77/H2
Onondaga, Mich. 250/E6
Onondaga (co.), N.Y. 276/H5
Onondaga Ind. Res., N.Y. 276/H5
Onota (lake), Mass. 249/A3
Onoto, Venezuela 124/F3
Onotoa (atoll), Kiribati 87/H6
Onoway, Alberta 182/C3
Onrusrivier, S. Africa 118/G7
Onset, Mass. 249/M6
Onslow, Australia 87/B8
Onslow, Iowa 229/M4
Onslow (co.), N.C. 281/P5
Onslow (bay), N.C. 281/P6
Onslow, W. Australia 88/B4
Onslow, W. Australia 92/A3
Onsŏng, N. Korea 81/E2
Onsted, Mich. 250/E6
Onstwedde, Netherlands 27/K2
Ontake (mt.), Japan 81/H6
ONTARIO 177
ONTARIO, NORTHERN 175
Ontario (prov.) 162/H5
Ontario (lake) 146/L5
Ontario (lake) 162/J7
Ontario, Calif. 204/D10
Ontario (prov.), Canada 146/K4
Ontario, Ind. 227/G1
Ontario, Iowa 229/F4
Ontario (lake), N.Y. 188/L2
Ontario (co.), N.Y. 276/F5
Ontario, N.Y. 276/F4
Ontario (lake), N.Y. 276/F3
Ontario, Ohio 284/E4
Ontario (lake), Ontario 177/G4
Ontario, Oreg. 291/K3
Ontario, Wis. 317/E8
Onteniente, Spain 33/F3
Onton, Ky. 237/G5
Ontonagon (co.), Mich. 250/F1
Ontonagon, Mich. 250/F1
Ontonagon (riv.), Mich. 250/G1
Ontonagon Ind. Res., Mich. 250/F1
Ontong Java (isl.), Solomon Is. 87/G6
Ontong Java (isls.), Solomon Is. 86/D2
Onverwacht, Suriname 131/D3
Onward, Ind. 227/E3
Onward, Miss. 256/C5
Onycha, Ala. 195/F8
Onyx, Ark. 202/D4
Onyx, Calif. 204/G8
Oobagooma, W. Australia 92/D2
Oodnadatta, Australia 87/D8
Oodnadatta, S. Australia 88/E5
Oodnadatta, S. Australia 94/D2
Ookala, Hawaii 218/J4
Oola, Ireland 17/E6
Ooldea, S. Australia 94/B4
Oolitic, Ind. 227/E7
Oologah, Okla. 288/P2
Oologah (lake), Okla. 288/P1
Ooltewah, Tenn. 237/M10
Oona River, Br. Col. 184/C3
Oosterwolde, Netherlands 27/J2
Oostanaula, Georgia 217/B1
Oostanaula (riv.), Georgia 217/B2
Oostburg, Netherlands 27/C6
Oostburg, Wis. 317/L8
Oostende (Ostend), Belgium 27/B6
Oosterend, Netherlands 27/G2
Oosterhout, Netherlands 27/F5
Oostkamp, Belgium 27/C6
Oostmahorn, Netherlands 27/J2
Oost-Vlieland, Netherlands 27/F2
Oostzaan, Netherlands 27/C4
Oostzaan Polder, Netherlands 27/B4
Ootacamund, India 68/D6
Ootmarsum, Netherlands 27/K4
Ootsa (lake), Br. Col. 184/D3
Ootsa Lake, Br. Col. 184/E3
Oozewekwun, Manitoba 179/B5
Opal, Alberta 182/D3
Opal, S. Dak. 298/D4
Opal, Wyo. 319/B4
Opala, Zaire 115/D4
Opal Cliffs, Calif. 204/K4
Opa Locka, Fla. 212/B4
Opalton, Queensland 95/B4
Opari, Sudan 111/F7
Oparino, U.S.S.R. 52/G3
Opasatika, Ontario 177/J5
Opasatika, Ontario 175/D3
Opasatika (riv.), Ontario 175/D3
Opatija, Yugoslavia 45/A3
Opatów, Poland 47/E3
Opava, Czech. 41/E2
Opdyke, Ill. 222/E5
Opelika, Ala. 195/H5
Opelousas, La. 238/G5
Opeongo (lake), Ontario 177/F2
Opfikon, Switzerland 39/G2
Opheim, Ill. 222/C2
Opheim, Mont. 262/K2
Ophir, Alaska 196/G2
Ophir, Colo. 208/D7
Ophir, Oreg. 291/C5
Ophir, Utah 304/B3
Opihikao, Hawaii 218/K6
Opinaca (riv.), Que. 162/J5
Opinaca (riv.), Québec 174/B2
Opine, Ala. 195/C7
Opinnagau (riv.), Ontario 175/D2
Opiscotéo (lake), Québec 174/D2
Opochka, U.S.S.R. 52/C3
Opoco, Bolivia 136/B6
Opoczno, Poland 47/E3
Opole, Minn. 255/D5
Opole (prov.), Poland 47/C3
Opole, Poland 47/C3
Opolis, Kansas 232/H4
Oporto (Porto) (dist.), Portugal 33/B2
Oporto (Porto), Portugal 33/B2
Opotiki, N. Zealand 100/F3
Opp, Ala. 195/F8
Oppdal, Norway 18/F5
Oppeln, Poland 47/C3
Oppelo, Ark. 202/E3
Oppenheim, Germany 22/C4
Oppland (co.), Norway 18/F6
Opportunity, Wash. 310/H3
Oppy, Ky. 237/S5
Optima, Okla. 288/D1
Optima (lake), Okla. 288/D1
Opua, N. Zealand 100/D1
Opunake, N. Zealand 100/D3
Opuntia (lake), Sask. 181/C4
Opwijk, Belgium 27/E7
Opuwo, Namibia 118/A3
'Oqair, Saudi Arabia 59/E4
Oquawka, Ill. 222/C3
Oquossoc, Maine 243/B6
Ora, Ind. 227/D2
Ora, Miss. 256/E7
Ora, S.C. 296/D2
Oracabessa, Jamaica 158/J5
Oracle, Ariz. 198/E6
Oradea, Romania 7/G4
Oradea, Romania 45/E2
Oradell, N.J. 273/B1
Oradell (res.), N.J. 273/B1
Orai, India 68/D3
Oraibi Wash (dry riv.), Ariz. 198/E3
Oral, S. Dak. 298/C7
Oran, Algeria 106/D1
Oran, Algeria 102/B1
Oran, Iowa 229/J3
Oran, Mo. 261/N8
Orange (riv.) 2/K7
Orange (riv.) 102/D7
Orange, Australia 87/E9
Orange (riv.), Botswana 118/B5
Orange (cape), Brazil 132/D1
Orange (co.), Calif. 204/H10
Orange, Calif. 204/D11
Orange•, Conn. 210/C3
Orange (co.), Fla. 212/E3
Orange, Fla. 212/B1
Orange (lake), Fla. 212/D2
Orange, France 28/F5
Orange, Georgia 217/D2
Orange (co.), Ind. 227/E7
Orange, Ind. 227/F5
Orange, Mass. 249/E2
Orange•, Mass. 249/E2
Orange (canal), Netherlands 27/K3
Orange•, N.H. 268/D4
Orange, N.J. 273/B2
Orange, N.S. Wales 88/H6

424 Ouachita

Ouachita, Ark. 202/E6
Ouachita (lake), Ark. 202/C4
Ouachita (mts.), Ark. 202/B4
Ouachita (riv.), Ark. 202/E7
Ouachita (par.), La. 238/F2
Ouachita (riv.), La. 238/F1
Ouachita (mts.), Okla. 288/R5
Ouadane, Mauritania 106/B4
Ouadda, Cent. Afr. Rep. 115/D2
Ouagadougou (cap.), Burkina Faso 106/D6
Ouagadougou (cap.), Burkina Faso 102/B3
Ouahigouya, Burkina Faso 106/D6
Ouahigouya, Burkina Faso 102/B3
Oualata, Mauritania 106/C5
Ouallene, Algeria 106/E4
Ouanaminthe, Haiti 158/C5
Ouanary, Fr. Guiana 131/F3
Ouanda Djallé, Cent. Afr. Rep. 115/D2
Ouango, Cent. Afr. Rep. 115/D3
Ouaqui, Fr. Guiana 131/D4
Ouarane (reg.), Mauritania 106/B4
Ouareau (lake), Québec 172/D3
Ouareau (riv.), Québec 172/D3
Ouargla, Algeria 106/F2
Ouargla, Algeria 102/C1
Ouarzazate, Morocco 106/C2
Ouchy, Switzerland 39/C4
Oud-Beijerland, Netherlands 27/E5
Ouddorp, Netherlands 27/D5
Oudenaarde, Belgium 27/D7
Oudenbosch, Netherlands 27/E5
Oudenburg, Belgium 27/B6
Oude-Pekela, Netherlands 27/K2
Oudeschild, Netherlands 27/F2
Oude-Tonge, Netherlands 27/E5
Oudewater, Netherlands 27/F4
Oudtshoorn, S. Africa 102/E8
Oudtshoorn, S. Africa 118/C6
Oud-Turnhout, Belgium 27/F6
Oued Zem, Morocco 106/C2
Ouelle (riv.), Québec 172/H2
Ouellette, Maine 243/G1
Ouémé (riv.), Benin 106/E7
Ouessant (isl.), France 28/A3
Ouesso, Congo 115/C3
Ouest (dept.), Haiti 158/C6
Ouest (pt.), Haiti 158/B4
Ouest (pt.), Haiti 158/B6
Ouezzane, Morocco 106/C2
Oughter (lake), Ireland 17/G3
Oughterard, Ireland 17/C5
Ouham (riv.), Cent. Afr. Rep. 115/C2
Ouham (riv.), Chad 111/C6
Ouidah, Benin 106/E7
Oujaf, Mauritania 106/C5
Oujda, Morocco 106/D2
Oujda, Morocco 102/B1
Oujeft, Mauritania 106/B4
Oulainen, Finland 18/O4
Ouled Djellal, Algeria 106/F2
Oullins, France 28/F5
Oulu (prov.), Finland 18/P4
Oulu, Finland 7/G2
Oulu, Finland 18/O4
Oulu (lake), Finland 7/G2
Oulujärvi (lake), Finland 18/P4
Oulujoki (riv.), Finland 18/O4
Oum Chalouba, Chad 111/D4
Oum el Asel (well), Mali 106/D4
Oum Hadjer, Chad 102/E3
Oum Hadjer, Chad 111/D5
Ounas (riv.), Finland 7/G2
Ounasjoki (riv.), Finland 18/O3
Oundle, England 13/G5
Oungre, Sask. 181/H6
Ounianga-Kébir, Chad 111/D4
Oupeye, Belgium 27/H7
Oupu, China 77/L1
Our (riv.), Germany 22/B3
Our (riv.), Luxembourg 27/J9
Ouray (co.), Colo. 208/D6
Ouray, Colo. 208/D6
Ouray (peak), Colo. 208/G6
Ouray, Utah 304/E3
Ourinhos, Brazil 132/D8
Ourinhos, Brazil 135/B3
Ourique, Portugal 33/B4
Ouro Fino, Brazil 132/E8
Ouro Fino, Brazil 135/C3
Ouro Prêto, Brazil 132/F8
Ouro Prêto, Brazil 135/E2
Ourthe (riv.), Belgium 27/G8
Ouse (riv.), England 13/G6
Ouse (riv.), England 13/G4
Ouse, Tasmania 99/C4
Ouse (riv.), Tasmania 99/C4
Ousley, Georgia 217/F9
Outagamie (co.), Wis. 317/K7
Outardes (riv.), Québec 174/D2
Outer (isl.), Wis. 317/F1
Outer Harbor, S. Australia 94/A7
Outer Hebrides (isls.), Scotland 15/A3
Outer Santa Barbara (passage), Calif. 204/G10
Outing, Minn. 255/E4
Outjo, Namibia 118/B4
Outjo, Namibia 102/D7
Outlook, Mont. 262/M2
Outlook, Sask. 181/E4
Outlook, Wash. 310/E4
Outokumpu, Finland 18/Q5
Outram, Sask. 181/H6
Outremont, Québec 172/H4
Ouyen, Victoria 88/G7
Ouyen, Victoria 97/B4
Ouzinkie, Alaska 196/H3
Ovacık, Çankırı, Turkey 63/E2
Ovacık, İçel, Turkey 63/E4
Ovacık, Tunceli, Turkey 63/H3
Ovalau (isl.), Fiji 86/Q10
Ovalle, Chile 120/B6
Ovalle, Chile 138/A8
Ovamboland (reg.), Namibia 118/B3
Ovando, Mont. 262/C3
Ovar, Portugal 33/B2
Ovens (riv.), Victoria 97/D5
Overall, Tenn. 237/J9
Overbrook, Kansas 232/G3
Overbrook, Okla. 288/M6
Overflakkee (isl.), Netherlands 27/E5
Overflow (bay), Manitoba 179/A1
Overflowing (riv.), Manitoba 179/A1
Overflowing (riv.), Sask. 181/K2
Overflowing River, Manitoba 179/A1
Overgaard, Ariz. 198/E4
Overhills, N.C. 281/L4
Overijse, Belgium 27/F7
Overijssel (prov.), Netherlands 27/J4
Overisel, Mich. 250/C6
Överkalix, Sweden 18/N3
Overland, Mo. 261/O2
Overland Park, Kansas 232/H3
Overlea, Md. 245/N3
Overloon, Netherlands 27/H5
Overly, N. Dak. 282/K2
Overpelt, Belgium 27/G6
Overstreet, Fla. 212/D6
Overton, Nebr. 264/E4
Overton, Nev. 266/G6
Overton, Pa. 294/K2
Overton (co.), Tenn. 237/L8
Overton, Texas 303/K5
Övertorneå, Sweden 18/N3
Överum, Sweden 18/K7
Ovett, Miss. 256/F8
Ovid, Colo. 208/P1
Ovid, Idaho 220/G7
Ovid, Mich. 250/E5
Ovid, N.Y. 276/G5
Oviedo, Dom. Rep. 158/D7
Oviedo, Fla. 212/E3
Oviedo (prov.), Spain 33/C1
Oviedo, Spain 33/C1
Oviedo, Spain 7/D4
Ovilla, Texas 303/G2
Ovoca (riv.), Ireland 17/J6
Övörhangay, Mongolia 77/F2
Øvre-Sirdal, Norway 18/E7
Ovruch, U.S.S.R. 52/C4
Ovtrup, Denmark 21/B6
Owaka, N. Zealand 100/B7
Owando, Congo 115/C3
Owando, Congo 102/D5
Owaneco, Ill. 222/D4
Owanka, S. Dak. 298/D5
Owasa, Iowa 229/G4
Owasco, N.Y. 276/G5
Owasco (lake), N.Y. 276/G5
Owase, Japan 81/H6
Owassa, Ala. 195/E8
Owassa (lake), N.J. 273/D1
Owasso, Okla. 288/P2
Owatonna, Minn. 255/E6
Owbeh, Afghanistan 68/A2
Owbeh, Afghanistan 59/H3
Owego, N.Y. 276/H6
Owell (lake), Ireland 17/G4
Owen (co.), Ind. 227/D6
Owen (co.), Ky. 237/M3
Owen (mt.), N. Zealand 100/D4
Owen (chan.), Ontario 177/C2
Owen (sound), Ontario 177/D3
Owen, Wis. 317/F6
Owen (lake), Wis. 317/D3
Owendale, Alberta 182/D5
Owendale, Mich. 250/F5
Owendo, Gabon 115/A3
Owen Falls (dam), Uganda 115/F3
Owenga, N. Zealand 100/E7
Owenkillew (riv.), N. Ireland 17/G2
Owenmore (riv.), Ireland 17/D3
Owenmore (riv.), Ireland 17/B3
Owens (lake), Calif. 188/C3
Owens (lake), Calif. 204/H7
Owens (peak), Calif. 204/H8
Owens (riv.), Calif. 204/G6
Owensboro, Ky. 237/G5
Owensboro, Ky. 188/J3
Owensburg, Ind. 227/D7
Owens Cross Roads, Ala. 195/E1
Owen Sound, Ont. 162/H7
Owen Sound, Ontario 177/D3
Owensville, Ark. 202/E4
Owensville, Ind. 227/B8
Owensville, Mo. 261/K6
Owensville, Ohio 284/B7
Owenton, Ky. 237/M3
Owenton, Va. 307/O5
Owerri, Nigeria 106/F7
Owey (isl.), Ireland 17/D1
Owia (bay), St. Vin. & Grens. 161/A8
Owikeno (lake), Br. Col. 184/D4
Owings, Md. 245/M6
Owings, S.C. 296/C2
Owings Mills, Md. 245/L3
Owingsville, Ky. 237/O4
Owl (creek), Colo. 208/K1
Owl (riv.), Manitoba 179/K2
Owl (creek), S. Dak. 298/B4
Owl, North Fork (creek), Wyo. 319/D2
Owl Creek (mts.), Wyo. 319/D2
Owl River, Alberta 182/E2
Owlseye, Alberta 182/E2
Owls Head•, Maine 243/F7
Owo, Nigeria 106/F7
Owosso, Mich. 250/E5
Owraman, Iran 66/E3
Owsley (co.), Ky. 237/O6
Owyhee (riv.) 188/C2
Owyhee (co.), Idaho 220/B7
Owyhee (mts.), Idaho 220/B6
Owyhee, East Fork (riv.), Idaho 220/B7
Owyhee, Nev. 266/F1
Owyhee (riv.), Nev. 266/E1
Owyhee (dam), Oreg. 291/K4
Owyhee (lake), Oreg. 291/K4
Owyhee (mts.), Oreg. 291/K4
Owyhee, North Fork (riv.), Oreg. 291/K5
Owyhee (riv.), Oreg. 291/K5
Ox (Slieve Gamph) (mts.), Ireland 17/D3
Oxapampa, Peru 128/E8
Oxbow (dam), Idaho 220/B5
Oxbow•, Maine 243/G3
Oxbow, Oreg. 291/L2
Oxbow (dam), Oreg. 291/L3
Oxbow, Sask. 181/J6
Oxelösund, Sweden 18/K7
Oxford, Ala. 195/G3
Oxford, Ark. 202/G1
Oxford•, Conn. 210/C3
Oxford, England 13/F6
Oxford, England 10/F5
Oxford, Fla. 212/D3
Oxford, Georgia 217/E3
Oxford, Idaho 220/F7
Oxford, Ind. 227/C3
Oxford, Iowa 229/K5
Oxford, Kansas 232/E4
Oxford, La. 238/C3
Oxford (co.), Maine 243/B7
Oxford, Maine 243/B7
Oxford•, Maine 243/B7
Oxford (lake), Manitoba 179/J3
Oxford, Md. 245/O6
Oxford, Mass. 249/G4
Oxford•, Mass. 249/G4
Oxford, Mich. 250/F6
Oxford, Miss. 256/F2
Oxford, Nebr. 264/E4
Oxford, N.J. 273/C2
Oxford, N.Y. 276/J6
Oxford, N. Zealand 100/D5
Oxford, N.C. 281/M2
Oxford, Nova Scotia 168/E3
Oxford, Ohio 284/A6
Oxford, Pa. 294/K6
Oxford, W. Va. 312/E4
Oxford, Wis. 317/H8
Oxford House, Manitoba 179/J3
Oxford Junction, Iowa 229/M4
Oxford Junction, Nova Scotia 168/E3
Oxford Mills, Iowa 229/L5
Oxford Mills, Ontario 177/J3
Oxfordshire (co.), England 13/F6
Oxkutzcab, Mexico 150/P6
Oxley, N.S. Wales 97/C4
Oxley (creek), Queensland 95/D3
Oxly, Mo. 261/L9
Oxnard, Calif. 204/F9
Oxnard A.F.B., Calif. 204/F9
Oxon Hill, Md. 245/F6
Oxon Run (riv.), Md. 245/F5
Oxton, Scotland 15/F5
Oxtongue Lake, Ontario 177/E2
Oyabe, Japan 81/H5
Oyahue (vol.), Chile 138/C3
Oyama, Br. Col. 184/H5
Oyama, Japan 81/J5
Oyapock (riv.) 120/D2
Oyapock (riv.), Brazil 132/C2
Oyapock (riv.), Fr. Guiana 131/E4
Oyem, Gabon 102/D4
Oyem, Gabon 115/B3
Oyen, Alberta 182/E4
Oyens, Iowa 229/A3
Oykel (riv.), Scotland 15/D3
Oykel Bridge, Scotland 15/D3
Oylen, Minn. 255/D4
Oymyakon, U.S.S.R. 4/C2
Oymyakon, U.S.S.R. 48/O3
Oyo, Congo 115/C4
Oyo (state), Nigeria 106/E7
Oyo, Nigeria 106/E7
Oyón, Peru 128/D8
Oyonnax, France 28/F4
Oyster (bay), Tasmania 88/H8
Oyster (bay), Tasmania 99/E4
Oyster, Va. 307/S6
Oyster Bay, N.Y. 276/R6
Oyster River (pt.), Conn. 210/D4
Oysterville, Wash. 310/A4
Ozalp, Turkey 63/K3
Ozamis, Philippines 82/D6
Ozan, Ark. 202/C6
Ozark (mts.) 188/H3
Ozark, Ala. 195/G8
Ozark, Ark. 202/C3
Ozark (lake), Ark. 202/C3
Ozark (plat.), Ark. 202/C1
Ozark (res.), Ark. 202/C3
Ozark, Ill. 222/E6
Ozark (co.), Mo. 261/H9
Ozark, Mo. 261/F8
Ozark (plat.), Mo. 261/F9
Ozark Nat'l Scenic Riverways, Mo. 261/K8
Ozarks, Lake of the (lake), Mo. 261/F6
Ozaukee (co.), Wis. 317/L9
Ozawkie, Kansas 232/G2
Ózd, Hungary 41/F2
Ozernovskiy, U.S.S.R. 48/Q4
Ozernoy (cape), U.S.S.R. 48/R4
Ozette, Wash. 310/A2
Ozette (lake), Wash. 310/A2
Ozette Ind. Res., Wash. 310/A2
Ozieri, Italy 34/B4
Ozona, Fla. 212/D3
Ozona, Texas 303/C7
Ozone, Ark. 202/D2
Ozone, Tenn. 237/M9
Ozorków, Poland 47/D3
Ozu, Japan 81/F7
Ozuluama, Mexico 150/L6
Ozumba de Alzate, Mexico 150/M1

P

Paamiut, Greenland 4/C12
Pa-an, Burma 72/C3
Paarden (bay), Neth. Ant. 161/D10
Paarl, S. Africa 102/D8
Paarl, S. Africa 118/F6
Paauhau, Hawaii 218/H4
Paauilo, Hawaii 218/H4
Paavola, Finland 18/O4
Pabbay (isl.), Scotland 15/A4
Pabbay (isl.), Scotland 15/A3
Pabianice, Poland 47/D3
Pablo, Mont. 262/B3
Pabna, Bangladesh 68/F4
Pabos, Québec 172/D2
Pabos-Mills, Québec 172/D2
Pabradė, U.S.S.R. 53/C3
Pacajá Grande (riv.), Brazil 132/D4
Pacaraimã, Serra da (mts.), Brazil 132/H8
Pacaraima, Sierra (mts.), Venezuela 124/G5
Pacasmayo, Peru 128/C6
Pace, Fla. 212/B6
Pace, Miss. 256/C3
Pachaug, Conn. 210/H2
Pachaug (pond), Conn. 210/H2
Pachaug (riv.), Conn. 210/H2
Pacheco, Calif. 204/K1
Pachino, Italy 34/E6
Pachitea (riv.), Peru 128/E7
Pachiza, Peru 128/D6
Pachmarhi, India 68/D4
Pacho, Colombia 126/C5
Pachuca de Soto, Mexico 150/K6
Pachuta, Miss. 256/G6
Pacific (ocean) 54/T5
Pacific (ocean) 146/E6
Pacific, Mo. 261/L5
Pacific (co.), Wash. 310/B4
Pacific, Wash. 310/C3
Pacifica, Calif. 204/H2
Pacific Beach, Calif. 204/H11
Pacific Beach, Wash. 310/A3
Pacific City, Oreg. 291/C2
Pacific Grove, Calif. 204/C7
Pacific Heights, Hawaii 218/C4
Pacific Junction, Iowa 229/B6
Pacific Palisades, Hawaii 218/E2
Pacific Rim Nat'l Park, Br. Col. 184/E6
Pacitan, Indonesia 85/J2
Pack (riv.), Idaho 220/B1
Pack (creek), Utah 304/E5
Packanack Lake, N.J. 273/B1
Packertown, Ind. 227/F2
Packerville, Conn. 210/H2
Packington, Québec 172/J2
Packsville, W. Va. 312/C7
Packwaukee, Wis. 317/G8
Packwood, Iowa 229/J6
Packwood, Wash. 310/D4
Paco, Philippines 82/C2
Pacoa, Colombia 126/E7
Paço de Arcos, Portugal 33/A1
Pacoima, Calif. 204/B10
Pacolet, S.C. 296/D2
Pacolet (riv.), S.C. 296/D1
Pacolet Mills, S.C. 296/D2
Pacov, Czech. 41/C2
Pacsa, Hungary 41/D3
Pacsan (mt.), Philippines 82/C2
Pactolus, N.C. 281/P3
Padada, Philippines 82/E7
Padang, Indonesia 54/L10
Padang, Indonesia 85/B6
Padangpanjang, Indonesia 85/B6
Padangsidempuan, Indonesia 85/B5
Padany, U.S.S.R. 52/D2
Padborg, Denmark 21/C8
Padcaya, Bolivia 136/C7
Paddle Prairie, Alberta 182/A5
Paddock Lake, Wis. 317/K10
Paddockwood, Sask. 181/F2
Paden, Miss. 256/H1
Paden, Okla. 288/N3
Paden City, W. Va. 312/D3
Paderborn, Germany 22/C3
Padgett, S.C. 296/F5
Padiham, England 13/H1
Padilla, Bolivia 136/C6
Padilla, Mexico 150/K5
Padilla (creek), N. Mex. 274/D5
Padilla (bay), Wash. 310/C2
Padloping (isl.), N.W.T. 162/K2
Padloping (isl.), N.W.T. 187/M3
Padre (isl.), Texas 188/G5
Padre (isl.), Texas 303/G10
Padre Island Nat'l Seashore, Texas 303/G11
Padre Las Casas, Dom. Rep. 158/D6
Padrón, Spain 33/B1
Padroni, Colo. 208/N1
Padstow, England 10/D5
Padstow, England 13/B7
Padua (prov.), Italy 34/C2
Padua, Italy 7/F4
Padua, Italy 34/C2
Padua, Minn. 255/C5
Paducah, Ky. 237/D6
Paducah, Ky. 146/K6
Paducah, Ky. 188/J3
Paducah, Texas 303/D4
Padul, Spain 33/E4
Paekam, N. Korea 81/D3
Paektu (mt.), N. Korea 81/C3
Paeroa, N. Zealand 100/E2
Páez, Colombia 126/C6
Pafúri, Mozambique 118/E4
Pag, Yugoslavia 45/B3
Pag (isl.), Yugoslavia 45/B3
Pagadian, Philippines 82/D7
Pagalungan, Philippines 82/E7
Pagan, Burma 72/B2
Pagan (isl.), No. Marianas 87/E4
Page, Ariz. 198/D2
Page (co.), Iowa 229/C7
Page, Nebr. 264/F2
Page, N. Dak. 282/P5
Page, Okla. 288/S5
Page (co.), Va. 307/M3
Page, W. Va. 312/D6
Page City, Kansas 232/A2
Pagedale, Mo. 261/P2
Pageland, S.C. 296/G2
Pago (bay), Guam 86/K7
Pagoda (peak), Colo. 208/E2
Pago Pago (cap.), Amer. Samoa 86/N9
Pago Pago (cap.), Amer. Samoa 87/J7
Pagosa Junction, Colo. 208/E8
Pagosa Springs, Colo. 208/E8
Pagoua (bay), Dominica 161/F6
Paguate, N. Mex. 274/B3
Pagwa River, Ontario 177/J5
Pagwa River, Ontario 175/D3
Pahala, Hawaii 188/G6
Pahala, Hawaii 218/H6
Pahang (state), Malaysia 72/D7
Pahang, Sungai (riv.), Malaysia 72/D7
Pahaska, Wyo. 319/C1
Pahiatua, N. Zealand 100/F4
Pahlevi (Enzeli), Iran 59/E2
Pahlevi (Enzeli), Iran 66/F2
Pahoa, Hawaii 218/J5
Pahokee, Fla. 212/F5
Pahranagat (range), Nev. 266/F5
Pahrock (range), Nev. 266/F5
Pah-rum (peak), Nev. 266/B2
Pahrump, Nev. 266/E6
Pahrump (valley), Nev. 266/F6
Pahsimeroi (riv.), Idaho 220/E5
Pahute (mesa), Nev. 266/E5
Pahvant (range), Utah 304/B5
Paia, Hawaii 218/J2
Paicheng (Baicheng), China 77/K2
Paicines, Calif. 204/D7
Paide, U.S.S.R. 53/C1
Paige, Texas 303/G7
Paihia, N. Zealand 100/D1
Paihuano, Chile 138/B8
Paiján, Peru 128/C6
Päijänne (lake), Finland 18/O6
Pailin, Cambodia 72/D4
Paillaco, Chile 138/D3
Pailolo (chan.), Hawaii 218/H1
Paimboeuf, France 28/C4
Paimpol, France 28/B3
Painan, Indonesia 85/B6
Paincourt, Ontario 177/B5
Paincourtville, La. 238/K3
Paine, Chile 138/G4
Paine, Cerro (mt.), Chile 138/D9
Painesdale, Mich. 250/G1
Painesville, Ohio 284/H2
Painswick, Ontario 177/E3
Paint (lake), Manitoba 179/J2
Paint (riv.), Mich. 250/A2
Paint (creek), Ohio 284/D7
Paint, Pa. 294/E5
Paint Bank, Va. 307/H5
Paint Branch (riv.), Md. 245/F4
Painted (des.), Ariz. 198/D2
Painted Desert Section (Petrified Forest), Ariz. 198/F3
Painted Post, N.Y. 276/F6
Painted Rock (dam), Ariz. 198/C5
Painter, Ala. 195/F2
Painter, Va. 307/S5
Painter Ridge (hills), Conn. 210/B2
Paintersville, Ohio 284/C6
Paint Lick, Ky. 237/N5
Paint Lick (riv.), Ky. 237/M5
Paint Rock, Ala. 195/F1
Paint Rock (riv.), Ala. 195/F1
Paint Rock, Texas 303/E6
Paintsville, Ky. 237/R5
Paipa, Colombia 126/D5
Paipote, Chile 138/B6
Paipote, Quebrada de (riv.), Chile 138/B6
Paisley, Ontario 177/C3
Paisley, Oreg. 291/G5
Paisley, Scotland 10/A1
Paisley, Scotland 15/B2
Paita, Peru 128/B5
Paita (bay), Peru 128/B5
Paiute Ind. Res., Calif. 204/G6
Pajala, Sweden 18/N3
Paján, Ecuador 128/B3
Pajarito (creek), N. Mex. 274/A2
Pajaro, Calif. 204/D7
Pájaros (isls.), Chile 138/A7
Pakanbaru, Indonesia 54/M9
Pakanbaru, Indonesia 85/C5
Pakaraima (mts.), Guyana 131/A3
Pakawau, N. Zealand 100/D4
Pakchan (riv.), Burma 72/C5
Pakchan (riv.), Thailand 72/C5
Pakch'ŏn, N. Korea 81/B4
Pakenham, Ontario 177/H2
Pakhoi (Beihai), China 77/G7
Pakistan 2/N4
Pakistan 54/H7
PAKISTAN 59/J4
PAKISTAN 68/B3
Pakokku, Burma 72/B2
Pakowki (lake), Alberta 182/E5
Paks, Hungary 41/E3
Pakwach, Uganda 115/F3
Pakxé, Laos 72/E4
Pala, Chad 111/B6
Palacios, Texas 303/H9
Palafrugell, Spain 33/H2
Palagruža (Pelagosa) (isl.), Yugoslavia 45/C4
Pala Ind. Res., Calif. 204/H10
Palamós, Spain 33/H2
Palana, U.S.S.R. 54/S4
Palana, U.S.S.R. 48/R4
Palanan, Philippines 82/D2
Palanan, Philippines 85/G2
Palanan (bay), Philippines 82/D2
Palanda, Ecuador 128/C5
Palanga, U.S.S.R. 53/A3
Palangkaraya, Indonesia 85/E6
Palanpur, India 68/C4
Palaoa (pt.), Hawaii 218/G2
Palapag, Philippines 82/E4
Palapye, Botswana 118/D4
Palas de Rey, Spain 33/C1
Palatine, Ill. 222/B5
Palatka, Ark. 202/J1
Palatka, Fla. 212/E2
Palau 87/D5
Palauli (bay), W. Samoa 86/L8
Palaumerak, Indonesia 85/G1
Palaw, Burma 72/C4
Palawan (prov.), Philippines 82/B6
Palawan (isl.), Philippines 2/Q5
Palawan (isl.), Philippines 54/N8
Palawan (isl.), Philippines 85/F4
Palawan (isl.), Philippines 82/B6
Palawan (passage), Philippines 85/F4
Palawan (passage), Philippines 82/A6
Palaya, Bolivia 136/A6
Palayan, Philippines 82/C3
Palayankottai, India 68/D7
Palazzolo Acreide, Italy 34/E6
Palca, Bolivia 136/A5
Palco, Kansas 232/C2
Paldiski, U.S.S.R. 53/B1
Paldiski, U.S.S.R. 52/B3
Paleleh, Indonesia 85/G5
Palembang, Indonesia 54/M10
Palembang, Indonesia 85/D6
Palena, Chile 138/E5
Palena (lake), Chile 138/E5
Palena (riv.), Chile 138/D5
Palencia (prov.), Spain 33/D1
Palencia, Spain 33/D2
Palenque (pt.), Dom. Rep. 158/E6
Palenque, Mexico 150/O8
Palenque (ruin), Mexico 150/O8
Palenville, N.Y. 276/M6
Palermo, Calif. 204/D4
Palermo (prov.), Italy 34/D5
Palermo, Italy 7/F5
Palermo, Italy 34/D5
Palermo•, Maine 243/E7
Palermo, N.J. 273/D5
Palermo, N. Dak. 282/F3
Palermo, Uruguay 145/D4
Palestina, Chile 138/B4
Palestine, Ala. 195/H3
Palestine, Ark. 202/J4
Palestine, Ill. 222/F4
Palestine, Ind. 227/F2
Palestine, Ohio 284/A5
Palestine, Texas 188/H4
Palestine, Texas 303/J6
Palestine, W. Va. 312/D4
Palestrina, Italy 34/F7
Paletwa, Burma 72/B2
Palghat, India 68/D6
Palha, Mar da (bay), Portugal 33/A1
Pali, India 68/C3
Palidoro, Italy 34/F6
Paliocabe (Payocabe), Chile 138/F4
Palisade, Colo. 208/C4
Palisade, Minn. 255/E4
Palisade, Nebr. 264/C4
Palisade, Nev. 266/E2
Palisades, Idaho 220/G6
Palisades (res.), Idaho 220/G6
Palisades, N.J. 273/C1
Palisades, N.Y. 276/K8
Palisades, Wash. 310/E3
Palisades (res.), Wyo. 319/A2
Palisades Park, N.J. 273/C2
Paliseul, Belgium 27/G9
Palizada, Mexico 150/O7
Palk (str.), India 68/D7
Palk (str.), Sri Lanka 68/D7
Pallamallawa, N.S. Wales 97/F1
Palling, Br. Col. 184/D3
Palliser (bay), N. Zealand 100/C3
Palliser (cape), N. Zealand 100/E4
Pall Mall, Tenn. 237/M7
Palm (beach), Neth. Ant. 161/D10
Palma (bay), Alaska 196/L1
Palma, Mozambique 118/G2
Palma, Spain 7/E5
Palma, Spain 33/H3
Palma (bay), Spain 33/H3
Palma del Río, Spain 33/D4
Palma di Montechiaro, Italy 34/D6
Palmarejo, Venezuela 124/C2
Palmares, Brazil 132/H5
Palmares, C. Rica 154/F6
Palmarito, Apure, Venezuela 124/D4
Palmarito, Guárico, Venezuela 124/F3
Palmarito, Mérida, Venezuela 124/C3
Palmarola (isl.), Italy 34/D4
Palmas (cape) 102/B4
Palmas, Brazil 132/C9
Palmas (cape), Liberia 106/C8
Palmas Altas (pt.), P. Rico 161/C1
Palma Soriano, Cuba 158/J4
Palm Bay, Fla. 212/F3
Palm Beach, Fla. 188/L5
Palm Beach (co.), Fla. 212/F5
Palm Beach, Fla. 212/G4
Palm Beach Gardens, Fla. 212/F5
Palm Beach Shores, Fla. 212/G5
Palm City, Fla. 212/F4
Palm Coast, Fla. 212/E2
Palmdale, Calif. 204/G9
Palmdale, Fla. 212/E5
Palm Desert, Calif. 204/J10
Palmeira, Brazil 132/D9
Palmeira, Brazil 135/B4
Palmeira das Missões, Brazil 132/C9
Palmeiras, Brazil 132/F6
Palmeirinhas (pt.), Angola 115/B5
Palmer, Alaska 196/C1
Palmer, Alaska 188/D5
Palmer (arch.) Ant. 5/C15

426 Parry Sound

Parry Sound (terr. dist.), Ontario 175/E3
Parry Sound, Ontario 175/D3
Parry Sound, Ontario 177/E2
Parseierspitze (mt.), Austria 41/A3
Parshall, Colo. 208/G2
Parshall, N. Dak. 282/F4
Parsippany-Troy Hills•, N.J. 273/E2
Parsnip (riv.), Br. Col. 184/F3
Parson, Br. Col. 184/J4
Parsons, Kans. 188/G3
Parsons, Kansas 232/G4
Parsons, Tenn. 237/E9
Parsons, W. Va. 312/G4
Parsonsburg, Md. 245/R7
Parson's Pond, Newf. 166/C3
Partanna, Italy 34/D6
Partapgarh, India 68/C4
Parthenay, France 28/C4
Partinico, Italy 34/D6
Partizansk, U.S.S.R. 48/O5
Partizánske, Czech. 41/E2
Partlow, Va. 307/N4
Partridge, Kansas 232/D4
Partridge (riv.), Minn. 255/G3
Partridge (bay), Newf. 166/C3
Partridge (pt.), Newf. 166/C3
Partry (mts.), Ireland 17/C4
Paru (riv.), Brazil 132/C3
Paru de Oeste (riv.), Brazil 120/D3
Paru de Oeste (riv.), Brazil 132/B3
Paruro, Peru 128/F9
Parvatipuram, India 68/E5
Parys, S. Africa 118/D5
Pas, De (riv.), Québec 174/D1
Pasadena, Calif. 188/C4
Pasadena, Calif. 204/C10
Pasadena, Md. 245/M4
Pasadena, Newf. 166/C4
Pasadena, Texas 303/J2
Pasado (cape), Ecuador 128/B3
Pasaje, Ecuador 128/C4
Pa Sak, Mae Nam (riv.), Thailand 72/D4
Pasangkayu, Indonesia 85/F6
Pasargadae (ruins), Iran 66/H5
Pasatiempo, Calif. 204/K4
Pasawng, Burma 72/C3
Pasayten (riv.), Wash. 310/E2
Pascagoula, Miss. 256/G10
Pascagoula (riv.), Miss. 256/G9
Pascalis, Québec 174/B3
Paşcani, Romania 45/H2
Paschall, N.C. 281/N1
Pasco (co.), Fla. 212/D3
Pasco (dept.), Peru 128/E8
Pasco, Wash. 310/F4
Pascoag, R.I. 249/H5
Pascola, Mo. 261/N10
Pascua (riv.), Chile 138/D7
Pas-de-Calais (dept.), France 28/E2
Pasewalk, Germany 22/F2
Pasighat, India 68/G3
Pasinler, Turkey 63/J3
Pasión (riv.), Guatemala 154/B2
Paskenta, Calif. 204/C4
Pasłek, Poland 47/D1
Pasley (bay), N.W.T. 187/J2
Pasni, Pakistan 68/A3
Pasni, Pakistan 54/H7
Pasni, Pakistan 59/H4
Paso Ataques, Uruguay 145/D2
Paso Barreto, Paraguay 144/D3
Paso de Andrés Pérez, Uruguay 145/B3
Paso de Indios, Argentina 143/C5
Paso de la Laguna, Salto, Uruguay 145/B2
Paso de la Laguna, Tacuarembó, Uruguay 145/D3
Paso de las Piedras, Uruguay 145/C2
Paso del Borracho, Uruguay 145/D2
Paso del Cerro, Uruguay 145/C2
Paso de León, Uruguay 145/B1
Paso del Horno, Uruguay 145/C2
Paso de Los Libres, Argentina 143/E2
Paso de los Toros, Uruguay 145/C3
Paso del Parque, Uruguay 145/B2
Paso de Ovejas, Mexico 150/Q2
Paso de Patria, Paraguay 144/C5
Paso de Ramos, Uruguay 145/C1
Paso de Uleste, Uruguay 145/B3
Paso Flores, Argentina 143/C5
Paso Hondo, Uruguay 145/B4
Paso Potrero, Uruguay 145/C2
Pasorapa, Bolivia 136/C6
Paso Real, Honduras 154/E3
Paso Robles, Calif. 204/E8
Paspébiac, Québec 172/D2
Pasqua, Sask. 181/F5
Pasque (isl.), Mass. 249/L7
Pasquia (hills), Sask. 181/J2
Pasquia (riv.), Sask. 181/K2
Pasquotank (co.), N.C. 281/S2
Pass (creek), Wyo. 319/F4
Passaconaway (mt.), N.H. 268/E4
Passadumkeag•, Maine 243/F5
Passage (isl.), Mich. 250/E1
Passage East, Ireland 17/G7
Passagem Franca, Brazil 132/E4
Passage West, Ireland 17/E8
Passage West, Ireland 10/B5
Passaic, Mo. 261/D6
Passaic (co.), N.J. 273/E1
Passaic, N.J. 273/E2
Passaic (riv.), N.J. 273/E2
Passamaquoddy (bay), Maine 243/J5
Passamaquoddy (bay), New Bruns. 170/C3
Passamaquoddy Ind. Res., Maine 243/J6
Passau, Germany 22/E4
Pass Christian, Miss. 256/F10
Passero (cape), Italy 7/F5
Passero (cape), Italy 34/E6
Passes (lake), Québec 172/F2
Passi, Philippines 82/D5
Passo Fundo, Brazil 120/D5
Passo Fundo, Brazil 132/D10
Passos, Brazil 132/E8
Passos, Brazil 135/C2
Passumpsic, Vt. 268/D3
Passumpsic (riv.), Vt. 268/D2
Pastaza (riv.) 120/B3
Pastaza (prov.), Ecuador 128/D3
Pastaza (riv.), Ecuador 128/D4
Pastaza (riv.), Peru 128/D5
Pasto, Colombia 120/B2
Pasto, Colombia 126/B7
Pastol (bay), Alaska 196/F2
Pastora (peak), Ariz. 198/F2
Pastos Bons, Brazil 132/E4
Pastrana, Spain 33/E2
Pastura, N. Mex. 274/E4
Pasuquin, Philippines 82/C1
Pasuruan, Indonesia 85/K2
Pasvalys, U.S.S.R. 53/C2
Pasvikelv (riv.), Norway 18/Q2
Paswegin, Sask. 181/H4
Pásztó, Hungary 41/E3
Pata, Bolivia 136/A4
Patacamaya, Bolivia 136/B5
Patagonia (reg.), Argentina 120/C7
Patagonia (reg.), Argentina 143/C5
Patagonia, Ariz. 198/E7
Pataguanset (lake), Conn. 210/G3
Pataha, Wash. 310/H4
Pataha (creek), Wash. 310/H4
Patan, India 68/C4
Patapédia (riv.), New Bruns. 170/C1
Patapédia (riv.), Québec 172/B2
Patapsco, Md. 245/L2
Patapsco (riv.), Md. 245/M4
Pataskala, Ohio 284/E5
Pataz, Peru 128/D6
Patchewollock, Victoria 97/A4
Patch Grove, Wis. 317/D10
Patchogue, N.Y. 276/P9
Patea, N. Zealand 100/E3
Paternion, Austria 41/B3
Paterno, Italy 34/E6
Pateros, Wash. 310/E2
Pateros (lake), Wash. 310/F2
Paterson, N.J. 188/M2
Paterson, N.J. 273/B2
Paterson, Wash. 310/F5
Patesville, Ky. 237/H5
Pathankot, India 68/D2
Pathfinder (res.), Wyo. 188/E2
Pathfinder (res.), Wyo. 319/F3
Pathiu, Thailand 72/C5
Pathlow, Sask. 181/G3
Pati (pt.), Guam 86/K6
Pati, Indonesia 85/J2
Patía, Colombia 126/B6
Patía (riv.), Colombia 126/B6
Patiala, India 68/D2
Patillas, P. Rico 161/E2
Patillas (lake), P. Rico 161/E2
Pativilca (riv.), Peru 128/D8
Patmos, Ark. 202/C7
Pátmos (isl.), Greece 45/H7
Patna, India 54/K7
Patna, India 68/F3
Patna, Scotland 15/D5
Patnanongan (isl.), Philippines 82/D3
Patnos, Turkey 63/K3
Patoka, Ill. 222/D5
Patoka, Ind. 227/B8
Patoka (riv.), Ind. 227/C8
Paton, Iowa 229/E4
Patos, Brazil 120/F3
Patos, Brazil 132/G4
Patos (lake), Brazil 120/D6
Patos (lag.), Brazil 132/D10
Patos de Minas, Brazil 120/E4
Patos de Minas, Brazil 132/E7
Patoutville, La. 238/G7
Patquía, Argentina 143/C3
Pátrai, Greece 7/G5
Pátrai, Greece 45/E6
Patricia, Alberta 182/E4
Patricia, S. Dak. 298/G7
Patricia, Texas 303/B5
Patricio Lynch (isl.), Chile 138/D7
Patrick, Neth. Ant. 161/F8
Patrick, S.C. 296/G2
Patrick (co.), Va. 307/H7
Patrick A.F.B., Fla. 212/F3
Patricksburg, Ind. 227/D6
Patrick's Cove, Newf. 166/C2
Patrick Springs, Va. 307/H7
Patrickswell, Ireland 17/D6
Patriot, Ind. 227/H7
Patriot, Ohio 284/F8
Patrocínio, Brazil 132/E7
Patronville, Ind. 227/C9
Patroon, Texas 303/L6
Patsaliga (creek), Ala. 195/F7
Patsburg, Ala. 195/F7
Patta (isl.), Kenya 115/H4
Pattani, Thailand 72/D6
Patten, Maine 243/F4
Patten•, Maine 243/F4
Pattenburg, N.J. 273/C2
Patterson, Ark. 202/H3
Patterson, Calif. 204/D6
Patterson, Georgia 217/H8
Patterson, Ill. 222/C4
Patterson, Iowa 229/F6
Patterson, La. 238/H7
Patterson (pt.), Mich. 250/D3
Patterson, Mo. 261/L8
Patterson, N.Y. 276/N7
Patterson, N.C. 281/F3
Patterson, Edward A. (lake), N. Dak. 282/E6
Patterson, Ohio 284/C4
Patterson, Va. 307/D6
Patterson (creek), W. Va. 312/J4
Patterson Creek, W. Va. 312/J3
Pattersonville, N.Y. 276/M5
Patti, Italy 34/E5
Pattison, Miss. 256/C7
Patton, Mo. 261/M8
Patton, Pa. 294/E4
Pattonsburg, Mo. 261/D2
Patuanak, Sask. 181/L3
Patuca, Honduras 154/E3
Patuca (pt.), Honduras 154/E3
Patuca (riv.), Honduras 154/E3
Patuha (mt.), Indonesia 85/H2
Pătulele, Romania 45/F3
Patutahi, N. Zealand 100/F3
Patuxent (riv.), Md. 245/M7
Patuxent River Nav. Air Test Ctr., Md. 245/N7
Patzau, Wis. 317/B3
Pátzcuaro, Mexico 150/J7
Pátzcuaro (lake), Mexico 150/J7
Pau, France 28/C6
Pau, France 7/D4
Paucarbamba, Peru 128/E9
Paucartambo, Cuzco, Peru 128/G9
Paucartambo, Pasco, Peru 128/E8
Paudash (lake), Ontario 177/F3
Pau dos Ferros, Brazil 132/G4
Pauillac, France 28/C5
Paukaa, Hawaii 218/J5
Paul, Ala. 195/E8
Paul, Idaho 220/E7
Paul (isl.), Newf. 166/B2
Paul (stream), Vt. 268/D2
Paulatuk, N.W.T. 162/D2
Paulatuk, N.W.T. 187/F3
Paulaya (riv.), Honduras 154/E3
Paulden, Ariz. 198/C4
Paulding (co.), Georgia 217/C3
Paulding, Miss. 256/F6
Paulding (co.), Ohio 284/A3
Paulding, Ohio 284/A3
Paulette, Miss. 256/H4
Paulina, La. 238/L3
Paulina, Oreg. 291/G3
Paulina (lake), Oreg. 291/F4
Pauline, Kansas 232/G3
Pauline, Nebr. 264/F4
Pauline, S.C. 296/D2
Paulins Kill (riv.), N.J. 273/D1
Paul Isnard, Fr. Guiana 131/D3
Paulistana, Brazil 132/F4
Paullina, Iowa 229/B3
Paulo Afonso, Brazil 120/F3
Paulo Afonso, Brazil 132/G5
Paulo Afonso (falls), Brazil 120/F3
Paulo de Faria, Brazil 135/B2
Paulsboro, N.J. 273/C4
Paul Smiths, N.Y. 276/M2
Paul Spur, Ariz. 198/F7
Pauls Valley, Okla. 288/M5
Paungassi, Manitoba 179/G2
Paungde, Burma 72/B3
Pauni, India 68/E4
Paunsaugunt (plat.), Utah 304/B6
Paupack, Pa. 294/M3
Paute, Ecuador 128/C4
Pauto (riv.), Colombia 126/E5
Pauwalu (pt.), Hawaii 218/K2
Pauwela, Hawaii 218/K2
Pavia (prov.), Italy 34/B2
Pavia, Italy 34/B2
Pavilion (key), Fla. 212/E6
Pavilion, N.Y. 276/D5
Pavillion, Wyo. 319/D2
Pavilosta, U.S.S.R. 53/A2
Pavilosta, U.S.S.R. 52/B3
Pavlodar, U.S.S.R. 54/J4
Pavlodar, U.S.S.R. 48/H4
Pavlof (bay), Alaska 196/F3
Pavlof (vol.), Alaska 196/F3
Pavlograd, U.S.S.R. 52/E5
Pavlovo, U.S.S.R. 52/F3
Pavo, Georgia 217/E9
Pavón, Colombia 126/D6
Pavullo nel Frignano, Italy 34/C2
Pawcatuck, Conn. 210/H3
Pawcatuck (riv.), Conn. 210/H3
Pawcatuck (riv.), R.I. 249/G7
Pawhuska, Okla. 288/O1
Pawlet•, Vt. 268/A5
Pawleys Island, S.C. 296/J5
Pawling, N.Y. 276/N7
Pawn, Nam (riv.), Burma 72/C2
Pawnee (creek), Colo. 208/M1
Pawnee, Ill. 222/D4
Pawnee (co.), Kansas 232/C3
Pawnee (riv.), Kansas 232/B3
Pawnee (co.), Nebr. 264/H4
Pawnee (co.), Okla. 288/N2
Pawnee, Okla. 288/N2
Pawnee City, Nebr. 264/H4
Pawnee Rock, Kansas 232/D3
Pawpaw, Ill. 222/E2
Paw Paw, Mich. 250/D6
Paw Paw (riv.), Mich. 250/C6
Paw Paw, W. Va. 312/K3
Paw Paw Lake, Mich. 250/C6
Pawtuckaway (pond), N.H. 268/E5
Pawtucket, R.I. 249/J5
Pax, W. Va. 312/D7
Paxico, Kansas 232/F2
Paxoí (isl.), Greece 45/D6
Paxson, Alaska 196/J2
Paxton, Fla. 212/C5
Paxton, Ill. 222/E3
Paxton, Ind. 227/C6
Paxton•, Mass. 249/G3
Paxton, Nebr. 264/C3
Paxville, S.C. 296/G4
Payakumbuh, Indonesia 85/C6
Paya Lebar, Singapore 72/F6
Payerne, Switzerland 39/C3
Payette (co.), Idaho 220/B5
Payette, Idaho 220/B5
Payette (lake), Idaho 220/C4
Payette (mts.), Idaho 220/B5
Payette (riv.), Idaho 220/B6
Payne, Georgia 217/E5
Payne, Minn. 255/F3
Payne, Ohio 284/A3
Payne (co.), Okla. 288/N2
Payne (lake), Que. 162/J4
Payne (lake), Québec 174/E1
Payneham, S. Australia 88/E8
Payneham, S. Australia 94/B7
Paynes, Miss. 256/D3
Paynes Creek, Calif. 204/D3
Payne's Find, W. Australia 92/B5
Paynesville, Ind. 227/F7
Paynesville, Mich. 250/G2
Paynesville, Minn. 255/D5
Paynesville, Mo. 261/L4
Payneville, Ky. 237/J5
Paynton, Sask. 181/B2
Paysandú (dept.), Uruguay 145/B3
Paysandú, Uruguay 145/A3
Paysandú, Uruguay 120/D6
Payson, Ariz. 198/D4
Payson, Ill. 222/B4
Payson, Utah 304/C3
Pay-Yer (mt.), U.S.S.R. 52/K1
Pazanan, Iran 66/F5
Pazar, Rize, Turkey 63/J2
Pazar, Tokat, Turkey 63/G2
Pazarcık, Turkey 63/G4
Pazardzhik, Bulgaria 45/G4
Pazaryeri, Turkey 63/C3
Paz de Ariporo, Colombia 126/E5
Paz de Río, Colombia 126/D4
Pazña, Bolivia 136/B6
Pea (riv.), Ala. 195/F8
Peabody, Kansas 232/E3
Peabody, Ky. 237/O6
Peabody, Mass. 249/E5
Peace (riv.), Alberta 182/B1
Peace (riv.), Alta. 162/E4
Peace (riv.), Br. Col. 162/D4
Peace (riv.), Br. Col. 184/G2
Peace (riv.), Canada 146/G4
Peace (riv.), Fla. 212/E4
Peace Dale-Wakefield, R.I. 249/J7
Peace Garden, Manitoba 179/C5
Peace River, Alberta 182/B1
Peace River, Alta. 146/G4
Peace River, Alta. 162/E4
Peace Valley, Mo. 261/J9
Peach (co.), Georgia 217/E5
Peacham•, Vt. 268/C3
Peach Bottom, Pa. 294/K6
Peachland, Br. Col. 184/G5
Peachland, N.C. 281/J5
Peach Orchard, Ark. 202/J1
Peach Springs, Ariz. 198/B3
Peachtree (creek), Georgia 217/K1
Peachtree, North Fork (creek), Georgia 217/L1
Peachtree City, Georgia 217/C4
Peacock, Alberta 182/D4
Peacock, Mich. 250/D4
Peacock, Texas 303/D4
Peahi, Hawaii 218/K4
Peak, The (mt.), England 13/J2
Peak (range), Queensland 95/C4
Peak, S.C. 296/E3
Peak District National Park, England 13/F4
Peak Hill, N.S. Wales 97/E3
Peak Hill, W. Australia 92/B4
Peaks, Va. 307/O5
Peale (mts.), Idaho 220/G7
Peale (mt.), Utah 304/E5
Peapack-Gladstone, N.J. 273/D2
Pear, W. Va. 312/E7
Pearblossom, Calif. 204/H9
Pearce, Alberta 182/D5
Pearce, Ariz. 198/F7
Pearcy, Ark. 202/D5
Peard (bay), Alaska 196/G1
Pea Ridge, Ark. 202/B1
Pea Ridge Nat'l Mil. Park, Ark. 202/B1
Pearisburg, Va. 307/G6
Pearl (harb.), Hawaii 188/F5
Pearl (harb.), Hawaii 218/A3
Pearl, Ill. 222/C4
Pearl (riv.), La. 238/L5
Pearl, Miss. 256/D6
Pearl (riv.), Miss. 256/D8
Pearl (cays), Nicaragua 154/F4
Pearl (creek), S. Dak. 298/N5
Pearl, Texas 303/F6
Pearl (riv.), U.S. 188/J4
Pearland, Texas 303/J2
Pearl and Hermes (reef), Hawaii 188/E5
Pearl and Hermes (atoll), Hawaii 218/B5
Pearl Beach, Mich. 250/G6
Pearl City, Hawaii 218/B3
Pearl City, Ill. 222/D1
Pearl Harbor Naval Station, Hawaii 218/B3
Pearlington, Miss. 256/E10
Pearl Lake, Québec 172/E2
Pearl River, La. 238/L6
Pearl River (co.), Miss. 256/E9
Pearl River, N.Y. 276/K8
Pearsall, Texas 303/E9
Pearse (canal), Alaska 196/N2
Pearson, Ark. 202/F3
Pearson, Georgia 217/G8
Pearson, Okla. 288/N4
Pearson, Wis. 317/H5
Peary (chan.), N.W.T. 162/M3
Peary (chan.), N.W.T. 187/H2
Peary Land (reg.), Greenl. 4/A11
Peary Land (reg.), Greenland 146/Q1
Pease, Minn. 255/E5
Pease (riv.), Texas 303/D3
Pease A.F.B., N.H. 268/F5
Peasleeville, N.Y. 276/N1
Peason, La. 238/D4
Pebane, Mozambique 118/F3
Pebble (isl.), 143/E7
Pebble Beach, Calif. 204/C7
Pebworth, Ky. 237/O5
Peć, Yugoslavia 45/E4
Peçanha, Brazil 132/F7
Pecan Island, La. 238/F7
Pecan Point, Ark. 202/L3
Pecatonica, Ill. 222/D1
Pecatonica (riv.), Wis. 317/H11
Peccia, Switzerland 39/G4
Pechea, Romania 45/H3
Pechenga, U.S.S.R. 48/C3
Pechenga, U.S.S.R. 48/D2
Pechenga, U.S.S.R. 52/D1
Pechora, U.S.S.R. 7/K2
Pechora (riv.), U.S.S.R. 4/C7
Pechora (riv.), U.S.S.R. 7/K2
Pechora, U.S.S.R. 48/F3
Pechora, U.S.S.R. 52/J1
Pechora (bay), U.S.S.R. 52/H1
Pechora (riv.), U.S.S.R. 52/H1
Pechora (riv.), U.S.S.R. 48/F3
Pechora (sea), U.S.S.R. 52/H1
Pecica, Romania 45/E2
Peck, Idaho 220/B3
Peck, Kansas 232/E4
Peck, La. 238/G3
Peck, Mich. 250/G5
Peckerwood (lake), Ark. 202/G4
Peckham, Okla. 288/M1
Pecks Mill, W. Va. 312/B7
Peconic, N.Y. 276/P8
Peconic (bay), N.Y. 276/R9
Pecos (riv.) 188/F4
Pecos, N. Mex. 274/D3
Pecos (riv.), N. Mex. 274/E5
Pecos (co.), Texas 303/B7
Pecos, Texas 303/D10
Pecos (riv.), Texas 303/C7
Pecos (riv.), U.S. 146/H6
Pecos Nat'l Mon., N. Mex. 274/D3
Pécs, Hungary 7/F4
Pécs, Hungary 41/E3
Pécsvárad, Hungary 41/E3
Peculiar, Mo. 261/D5
Pedasí, Panama 154/G7
Pedder (lake), Tasmania 99/B4
Pedee, Oreg. 291/D3
Pedernal, Argentina 143/G5
Pedernales, Salar de (salt dep.), Chile 138/B5
Pedernales (prov.), Dom. Rep. 158/D7
Pedernales, Dom. Rep. 158/C7
Pedernales, Ecuador 128/B2
Pedernales (riv.), Texas 303/F7
Pedernales, Venezuela 124/G3
Pederneiras, Brazil 135/B3
Pedlar Mills, Va. 307/K5
Pedley, Alberta 182/B3
Pedley, Calif. 204/E10
Pedra Azul, Brazil 132/F6
Pedraza, Colombia 126/C2
Pedregal, Venezuela 124/C2
Pedreiras, Brazil 132/E4
Pedrera, Uruguay 145/C6
Pedricktown, N.J. 273/C4
Pedrika, S. Australia 94/D2
Pedro (bank), Jamaica 156/B3
Pedro (cays), Jamaica 156/C3
Pedro, Ohio 284/E8
Pedro, S. Dak. 298/E5
Pedro (pt.), Sri Lanka 68/E6
Pedro Afonso, Brazil 132/E5
Pedro Antonio de los Santos, Mexico 150/Q7
Pedro Bay, Alaska 196/H3
Pedro Betancourt, Cuba 158/D1
Pedro Chico, Colombia 126/E7
Pedro de Valdivia, Chile 138/B4
Pedro Díaz Colodrero, Argentina 143/G5
Pedro Juan Caballero, Argentina 120/D5
Pedro Juan Cabellero, Paraguay 144/E3
Pedro Luro, Argentina 143/D4
Pedro Montoya, Mexico 150/K6
Pedro Segundo, Brazil 132/F4
Peduyim, Israel 65/B5
Peebles, Ohio 284/D8
Peebles, Sask. 181/J5
Peebles (trad. co.), Scotland 15/B5
Peebles, Scotland 10/E3
Peebles, Scotland 15/E5
Peebles, Texas 303/G7
Pee Dee, N.C. 281/K5
Pee Dee (riv.), N.C. 281/J4
Peedee, S.C. 296/H3
Pee Dee (riv.), S.C. 296/H2
Peekskill, N.Y. 276/N8
Peeksville, Wis. 317/E3
Peel (riv.) 162/C2
Peel, I. of Man 10/D3
Peel, I. of Man 13/C3
Peel, New Bruns. 170/C2
Peel (sound), N.W.T. 162/G1
Peel (sound), N.W.T. 187/J2
Peel (reg. munic.), Ontario 177/E4
Peel (inlet), W. Australia 92/A2
Peel (riv.), Yukon 187/E3
Peel Fell (mt.), England 13/E2
Peel Fell (mt.), Scotland 15/F5
Pe Ell, Wash. 310/B4
Peene (riv.), Germany 22/E2
Peenemünde, Germany 22/E1
Peer, Belgium 27/G6
Peera Peera Poolanna (lake), S. Australia 94/F2
Peerless (lake), Alberta 182/C1
Peerless, Mont. 262/L2
Peerless, Sask. 181/L4
Peerless Lake, Alberta 182/C1
Peerless Park, Mo. 261/N4
Peers, Alberta 182/B3
Peers, Mo. 261/K5
Peery (lake), N.S. Wales 97/B2
Peesane, Sask. 181/H3
Peetz, Colo. 208/N1
Peever, S. Dak. 298/R2
Pefferlaw, Ontario 177/E3
Pegarah, Tasmania 99/B1
Pegasus (bay), N. Zealand 100/D5
Pegasus, Port (inlet), N. Zealand 100/B7
Peggs, Okla. 288/R2
Pegnitz, Germany 22/D4
Pego, Spain 33/F3
Pegram, Tenn. 237/H8
Pegu (div.), Burma 72/C3
Pegu, Burma 54/L8
Pegu, Burma 72/C3
Pegun (isl.), Indonesia 85/J5
Pegu Yoma (mts.), Burma 72/B3
Pehan (Bei'an), China 77/L2
Pehuajó, Argentina 143/D4
Pehuajó, Argentina 120/C6
Peine, Germany 22/D2
Peiplin, Poland 47/D2
Peipus (lake), U.S.S.R. 7/G3
Peipus (lake), U.S.S.R. 53/D1
Peipus (lake), U.S.S.R. 48/C4
Peipus (lake), U.S.S.R. 52/C3
Peixe, Brazil 132/D6
Pei Xian, China 77/J5
Pejepscot, Maine 243/D8
Pejivalle, C. Rica 154/F6
Pekalongan, Indonesia 85/J2
Pekan, Malaysia 72/D7
Pekan Nanas, Malaysia 72/E5
Pekelmeer (lake), Neth. Ant. 161/E9
Pekin, Ill. 222/D3
Pekin, Ind. 227/E7
Pekin, N. Dak. 282/O4
Peking (Beijing) (cap.), China 54/N5
Peking (Beijing) (cap.), China 2/Q3
Peking (Beijing) (cap.), China 77/J3
Pekisko, Alberta 182/C4
Pelabuhan Ratu (bay), Indonesia 85/G2
Pelagie (isls.), Italy 34/D7
Pelagosa (Palagruža) (isl.), Yugoslavia 45/C4
Pelahatchie, Miss. 256/E6
Peleaga (mt.), Romania 45/F3
Pelechuco, Bolivia 136/A4
Peleduy, U.S.S.R. 48/M4
Pelée (vol.), Martinique 161/C5
Pelée (vol.), Martinique 156/G4
Pelee (pt.), Ontario 177/B6
Pelaihari, Indonesia 85/E6
Peleliu (isl.), Belau 87/D5
Peleng (isl.), Indonesia 85/G6
Pelequén, Chile 138/G5
Pelham, Ala. 195/E4
Pelham, Georgia 217/D8
Pelham•, Mass. 249/E3
Pelham•, N.H. 268/E6
Pelham, N.Y. 276/O7
Pelham, N.C. 281/L1
Pelham, Ontario 177/E4
Pelham, Queensland 95/B3
Pelham, Tenn. 237/K10
Pelham Manor, N.Y. 276/O7
Pelhřimov, Czech. 41/C2
Pelican, Alaska 196/M1
Pelican (lake), Alberta 182/D2
Pelican (mt.), Alberta 182/D2
Pelican (mts.), Alberta 182/D2
Pelican (isl.), Barbados 161/B9
Pelican, La. 238/C3
Pelican (bay), Manitoba 179/B2
Pelican (lake), Manitoba 179/C5
Pelican (lake), Manitoba 179/B2
Pelican (lake), Minn. 255/C4
Pelican (lake), Minn. 255/D4
Pelican (lake), Minn. 255/F2
Pelican (riv.), Minn. 255/B4
Pelican (riv.), Minn. 255/F2
Pelican (lake), Nebr. 264/D2
Pelican (lake), Sask. 181/E5
Pelican (lake), Wis. 317/H4
Pelican Lake, Wis. 317/H4
Pelican Lakes (Breezy Point), Minn. 255/D4
Pelican Narrows, Sask. 181/N3
Pelican Portage, Alberta 182/D2
Pelican Rapids, Manitoba 179/B2
Pelican Rapids, Minn. 255/B4
Pelileo, Ecuador 128/C3
Pelion, S.C. 296/E4
Pelkie, Mich. 250/G1
Pelkosenniemi, Finland 18/P3
Pella, Iowa 229/H6
Pella, Wis. 317/J6
Pell City, Ala. 195/F3
Pellegrini, Argentina 143/D4
Pelletier Mills, New Bruns. 170/B1
Pell Lake, Wis. 317/K10
Pello, Finland 18/O3
Pellston, Mich. 250/E3
Pellville, Ky. 237/H5
Pellworm (isl.), Germany 22/C1
Pelly (bay), N.W. Terr. 187/J3
Pelly (lake), N.W. Terr. 187/H3
Pelly, Sask. 181/K4
Pelly (riv.), Yukon 162/C3
Pelly (mts.), Yukon 187/E3
Pelly (riv.), Yukon 187/E3
Pelly Bay, N.W.T. 162/G2
Pelly Bay, N.W.T. 187/K3
Pelly Crossing, Yukon 187/E3
Peloncillo (mts.), Ariz. 198/F6
Peloncillo (mts.), N. Mex. 274/A6
Pelopónnisos (reg.), Greece 45/F7
Pelotas, Brazil 120/D6
Pelotas, Brazil 132/C10
Pelsor, Ark. 202/D2
Pelzer, Ind. 227/C8
Pelzer, S.C. 296/B2
Pemadumcook (lake), Maine 243/E4
Pemalang, Indonesia 85/J2
Pemaquid, Maine 243/E8
Pematangsiantar, Indonesia 54/L9
Pematangsiantar, Indonesia 85/B5
Pemba, Mozambique 118/G2
Pemba, Mozambique 102/F6
Pemba (reg.), Tanzania 115/H5
Pemba (isl.), Tanzania 102/G5
Pemba (isl.), Tanzania 115/H5
Pemberton, Br. Col. 184/F5

Princess Harbour 431

Port O'Connor, Texas 303/H9
Porto de Mós, Portugal 33/B3
Porto de Moz, Brazil 132/D3
Porto Empedocle, Italy 34/D6
Porto Esperança, Brazil 132/B7
Porto Feliz, Brazil 135/C3
Portoferraio, Italy 34/C3
Portofino, Italy 34/B2
Porto Franco, Brazil 132/E4
Port-of-Spain (cap.), Trin. & Tob. 161/A10
Port-of-Spain (cap.), Trin. & Tob. 156/G5
Portogruaro, Italy 34/D2
Portola, Calif. 204/E4
Pôrto La Cruz, Venezuela 120/C1
Portola Valley, Calif. 204/J3
Portomaggiore, Italy 34/C2
Porto Moniz, Portugal 33/A2
Porto Moroco, Brazil 132/C6
Porto Murtinho do Sul, Brazil 132/B8
Porto Nacional, Brazil 120/E4
Porto Nacional, Brazil 132/E5
Porto-Novo (cap.), Benin 106/E7
Porto-Novo (cap.), Benin 102/C4
Porto Novo, India 68/E6
Porto Poet, Brazil 132/C2
Port Orange, Fla. 212/F2
Port Orchard, Wash. 310/A2
Porto Recanati, Italy 34/D3
Port Orford, Oreg. 291/C5
Porto Santo, Portugal 33/A2
Porto Santo (isl.), Portugal 102/A1
Pôrto Santo (isl.), Portugal 106/A2
Porto Santo (isl.), Portugal 33/B2
Porto Seguro, Brazil 132/G7
Porto Tolle, Italy 34/D2
Porto Torres, Italy 34/B4
Porto União, Brazil 132/D9
Porto-Vecchio, France 28/B7
Porto Velho, Brazil 132/H10
Porto Velho, Brazil 120/C3
Portoviejo, Ecuador 120/A3
Portoviejo, Ecuador 128/B3
Portpatrick, Scotland 15/C6
Portpatrick, Scotland 10/D3
Port Pegasus (inlet), N. Zealand 100/B7
Port Penn, Del. 245/R2
Port Perry, Ontario 177/E3
Port Phaeton (bay), Fr. Poly. 86/T13
Port Phillip (bay), Victoria 97/C6
Port Phillip (bay), Victoria 88/K7
Port Pirie, Australia 87/D9
Port Pirie, S. Australia 88/F6
Port Pirie, S. Australia 94/E5
Port Praslin (bay), St. Lucia 161/G6
Port Reading, N.J. 273/E2
Portree, Scotland 10/C2
Portree, Scotland 15/B3
Portreeve, Sask. 181/B5
Port Renfrew, Br. Col. 184/J3
Port Republic, Md. 245/N6
Port Republic, N.J. 273/D4
Port Republic, Va. 307/L4
Port Rexton, Newf. 166/D2
Port Rhoades, Jamaica 158/H5
Port Richey, Fla. 212/D3
Port Rowan, Ontario 177/D5
Port Royal, Jamaica 158/J6
Port Royal, Ky. 237/L3
Port Royal, Nova Scotia 168/H3
Port Royal, Pa. 294/H4
Port Royal, S.C. 296/F7
Port Royal (sound), S.C. 296/F7
Port Royal, Va. 307/O4
Portrush, N. Ireland 10/C3
Portrush, N. Ireland 17/H1
Port Safâga, Egypt 59/B4
Port Safâga, Egypt 111/F2
Port Said, Egypt 102/F1
Port Said, Egypt 59/B3
Port Said, Egypt 111/K2
Port Saint Joe, Fla. 212/D6
Port Saint Johns (Umzimbuvu), S. Africa 118/D6
Port-Saint-Louis-du-Rhône, France 28/F6
Port Saint Lucie, Fla. 212/F4
Port Saint Mary, I. of Man 13/C3
Port Salerno, Fla. 212/F4
Port-Salut, Haiti 158/A6
Port Sanilac, Mich. 250/G5
Port Saunders, Newf. 166/C3
Pörtschach am Wörthersee, Austria 41/C3
Port Severn, Ontario 177/E3
Port Severn, Ontario 175/C1
Port Shepstone, S. Africa 102/F8
Port Shepstone, S. Africa 118/E6
Port Simpson, Br. Col. 184/B3
Portslade-by-Sea, England 13/G7
Portsmouth, Dominica 156/G4
Portsmouth, Dominica 161/E5
Portsmouth, England 10/F5
Portsmouth, England 7/D3
Portsmouth, England 13/F7
Portsmouth, Iowa 229/C5
Portsmouth, N.H. 188/N2
Portsmouth, N.H. 268/F5
Portsmouth, N.C. 281/S4
Portsmouth (isl.), N.C. 281/T5
Portsmouth, Ohio 188/K3
Portsmouth, Ohio 284/D8
Portsmouth•, R.I. 249/J6
Portsmouth, Va. 188/L3
Portsmouth (I.C.), Va. 307/R7
Port Sorell, Tasmania 99/C3
Portsoy, Scotland 15/F3
Port Stanley, Ontario 177/C5
Port Stephens (inlet), N.S. Wales 97/G3
Portstewart, N. Ireland 17/H1
Port Sudan, Sudan 111/G4
Port Sudan, Sudan 102/F3
Port Sudan, Sudan 59/C6
Port Sulphur, La. 238/L8
Port Talbot, Wales 10/E5
Port Talbot, Wales 13/D6
Port Tampa (harb.), Fla. 212/B3
Port Taufiq, Egypt 111/K3
Port Tobacco, Md. 245/K6
Port Townsend, Wash. 310/C2
Port Trevorton, Pa. 294/J4
Portugal 2/J3
Portugal 7/D5
PORTUGAL 33/B3
Portugal Cove, Newf. 166/D2
Portugal Cove South, Newf. 166/D2
Portugalete, Bolivia 136/B7
Portugalete, Spain 33/E1
Portuguesa (state), Venezuela 124/D3
Portuguesa (riv.), Venezuela 124/D3
Portuguese Cove, Nova Scotia 168/E4
Portumna, Ireland 17/E5
Port Union, Newf. 166/D2
Port-Valais, Switzerland 39/C4
Port-Vendres, France 28/E6
Portville, N.Y. 276/D6
Port Vincent, La. 238/L2
Port Vue, Pa. 294/C7
Port Washington, N.Y. 276/R6
Port Washington, Ohio 284/G5
Port Washington, Wis. 317/L9
Port Weld, Malaysia 72/D6
Port Wells (inlet), Alaska 196/C1
Port Wentworth, Georgia 217/K6
Port William, Ohio 284/C6
Port William, Scotland 15/D6
Port Williams, Nova Scotia 168/D3
Port Wing, Wis. 317/D2
Porum, Okla. 288/R4
Porus, Jamaica 158/H6
Porvenir, Santa Cruz, Bolivia 136/E4
Porvenir, Pando, Bolivia 136/A2
Porvenir, Chile 138/E10
Porvenir, Peru 128/E5
Porvenir, Uruguay 145/B3
Porz am Rhein, Germany 22/B3
Posadas, Argentina 143/E2
Posadas, Argentina 120/D5
Posadas, Paraguay 144/E5
Posadas, Spain 33/D4
Poschiavo, Switzerland 39/J4
Poschiavo (riv.), Switzerland 39/K4
Poschiavo (valley), Switzerland 39/K4
Posen, Ill. 222/B6
Posen, Mich. 250/F3
Posey (co.), Ind. 227/B8
Poseyville, Ind. 227/B8
Posio, Finland 18/Q3
Poskin, Wis. 317/C5
Poso, Indonesia 85/G6
Posof, Turkey 63/K2
Posŏng, S. Korea 81/C6
Posorja, Ecuador 128/B4
Posse, Brazil 132/E6
Possel, Cent. Afr. Rep. 115/C2
Pössneck, Germany 22/D3
Possum Kingdom (lake), Texas 303/F5
Post, Oreg. 291/G3
Post, Texas 303/C4
Postavy, U.S.S.R. 52/C3
Poste (riv.), Québec 172/D3
Postelle, Ark. 202/J4
Postelle, Tenn. 237/N10
Poste Maurice Cortier, Algeria 106/E4
Poste Weygand, Algeria 106/D4
Post Falls, Idaho 220/A2
Postmasburg, S. Africa 118/C5
Post Mills, Vt. 268/C4
Postoak, Mo. 261/E5
Postoak, Texas 303/F4
Postojna, Yugoslavia 45/B3
Poston, Ariz. 198/A4
Poston, S.C. 296/J4
Postrervalle, Bolivia 136/D6
Postville, Iowa 229/K2
Postville, Newf. 166/B3
Pot (creek), Colo. 208/A1
Pot (mt.), Idaho 220/C3
Pot (creek), Utah 304/E3
Potagannissing (bay), Mich. 250/F2
Potam, Mexico 150/D3
Potaro (riv.), Guyana 131/B3
Potato Creek, S. Dak. 298/F6
Potawatomi Ind. Res., Kansas 232/G2
Potchefstroom, S. Africa 118/D5
Poteau (mt.), Ark. 202/B4
Poteau, Okla. 288/S4
Poteau (riv.), Okla. 288/S5
Poteca, Nicaragua 154/E4
Poteet, Texas 303/F8
Potenza (prov.), Italy 34/E4
Potenza, Italy 34/E4
Potes, Spain 33/D1
Potgietersrus, S. Africa 118/D4
Poth, Texas 303/F8
Potholes (res.), Wash. 310/F3
Poti, U.S.S.R. 52/F6
Potlatch, Idaho 220/A3
Potlatch (riv.), Idaho 220/B3
Potlatch, Wash. 310/B3
Potomac (riv.) 188/L3
Potomac, Ill. 222/F3
Potomac (riv.), Md. 245/M8
Potomac, Mont. 262/C4
Potomac (riv.), Va. 307/O4
Potomac, South Branch (riv.), W. Va. 312/J4
Potomac (riv.), W. Va. 312/L3
Potomac, North Branch (riv.), W. Va. 312/J4
Potomac Beach, Va. 307/P4
Potomac Heights, Md. 245/K6
Potomac Park-Bowling Green, Md. 245/C2
Potomac Valley, Md. 245/E4
Potosí (dept.), Bolivia 136/B7
Potosí, Bolivia 136/C6
Potosí, Bolivia 120/C4
Potosí, Colombia 126/C7
Potosi, Mo. 261/L7
Potosi (mt.), Nev. 266/F7
Potosi, Wis. 317/E10
Potrerillo (peak), Cuba 158/E2
Potrerillos, Chile 138/B6
Potrero, Calif. 204/J11
Potrillo (mts.), N. Mex. 274/B7
Potro, Cerro del (mt.), Argentina 143/C2
Potro, Cerro del (mt.), Chile 138/B7
Potsdam, Germany 22/E2
Potsdam, Minn. 255/F6
Potsdam, N.Y. 276/K1
Potsdam, Ohio 284/B6
Pottageville, Ontario 177/J3
Pottawatomie (co.), Kansas 232/F2
Pottawatomie (co.), Okla. 288/N4
Pottawattamie (co.), Iowa 229/B6
Pottawattomie Park, Ind. 227/C1
Potter, Kansas 232/G2
Potter, Nebr. 264/A3
Potter (co.), Pa. 294/G2
Potter (co.), S. Dak. 298/J3
Potter (co.), Texas 303/C2
Potter, Wis. 317/K7
Potter Hill, R.I. 249/H7
Potters Bar, England 13/H7
Potters Bar, England 10/B5
Pottersdale, Pa. 294/F3
Pottersville, Mo. 261/H9
Pottersville, N.J. 273/D2
Pottersville, N.Y. 276/N3
Potterville, Mich. 250/E6
Potts (creek), W. Va. 312/F7
Pottsboro, Texas 303/H4
Potts Camp, Miss. 256/F1
Pottstown, Pa. 294/L5
Pottsville, Ark. 202/D3
Pottsville, Pa. 294/K4
Pottsville, Texas 303/F6
Potwin, Kansas 232/F4
Pouce-Coupé, Br. Col. 184/G2
Pouch Cove, Newf. 166/D2
Poudre d'Or, Mauritius 118/G5
Poughkeepsie, Ark. 202/H1
Poughkeepsie, N.Y. 276/N7
Pouillon, France 28/C6
Poulan, Georgia 217/E8
Poulet Cove (bay), Nova Scotia 168/H2
Poulin-de-Courval (lake), Québec 172/G1
Poulo Wai (isls.), Cambodia 72/D5
Poulsbo, Wash. 310/A1
Poultney, Vt. 268/A4
Poultney•, Vt. 268/A4
Poultney (riv.), Vt. 268/A4
Poulton le Fylde, England 10/F1
Poulton-le-Fylde, England 13/G1
Pound, Va. 307/C6
Pound, Wis. 317/L5
Pounding Mill, Va. 307/E6
Pouso Alegre, Brazil 135/D3
Pouthisat, Cambodia 72/D4
Považská Bystrica, Czech. 41/E2
Povenets, U.S.S.R. 52/E2
Poverty Point Nat'l Monument, La. 238/L1
Poverty (isl.), Mich. 250/C3
Poverty (bay), N. Zealand 100/G3
Póvoa de Varzim, Portugal 33/B2
Povorino, U.S.S.R. 52/F4
Povungnituk, Que. 162/J3
Povungnituk, Québec 174/E1
Powassan, Ontario 177/E1
Poway, Calif. 204/J11
Powder (riv.) 188/E2
Powder (riv.), Mont. 262/L4
Powder (riv.), Oreg. 291/K3
Powder (riv.), Wyo. 319/F2
Powderhorn, Colo. 208/E6
Powderly, Ky. 237/G6
Powderly, Texas 303/J4
Powder River (co.), Mont. 262/L5
Powder River, Wyo. 319/F2
Powder Springs, Georgia 217/C3
Powder Springs, Tenn. 237/O8
Powderville, Mont. 262/L5
Powe, Mo. 261/M9
Powell (lake) 188/D3
Powell (lake), Ariz. 198/E1
Powell (co.), Ky. 237/O5
Powell, Manitoba 179/A2
Powell (co.), Mont. 262/D4
Powell, Nebr. 264/G4
Powell, Ohio 284/D5
Powell, Pa. 294/J2
Powell, Tenn. 237/N8
Powell (riv.), Tenn. 237/P8
Powell (lake), U.S. 146/G6
Powell (lake), Utah 304/D6
Powell (riv.), Va. 307/B7
Powell, Wyo. 319/D1
Powell Butte, Oreg. 291/G3
Powell Creek, North. Terr. 93/C5
Powell River, Br. Col. 184/E5
Powell's Crossroads, Ala. 195/G1
Powells Crossroads, Tenn. 237/L10
Powells Point, N.C. 281/T2
Powellsville, N.C. 281/R2
Powellton, W. Va. 312/D6
Powellville, Md. 245/S7
Powelton, Georgia 217/G4
Power (co.), Idaho 220/F7
Power, Mont. 262/E3
Powers (lake), Conn. 210/G3
Powers, Mich. 250/B3
Powers, Oreg. 291/D5
Powers Lake, N. Dak. 282/E2
Powersville, Georgia 217/E5
Powersville, Iowa 229/H3
Powersville, Mo. 261/F1
Powerview, Manitoba 179/F4
Poweshiek (co.), Iowa 229/H5
Powhatan, Ark. 202/H1
Powhatan, La. 238/D3
Powhatan (co.), Va. 307/N5
Powhatan, Va. 307/N5
Powhatan, W. Va. 312/D8
Powhatan Point, Ohio 284/J6
Powhattan, Kansas 232/G2
Pownal•, Maine 243/C8
Pownal•, Vt. 268/A6
Pownal Center, Vt. 268/A6
Powys (co.), Wales 13/D5
Poxoréo, Brazil 132/C6
Poyang (lake), China 54/N7
Poyang Hu (lake), China 77/J6
Poyen, Ark. 202/E5
Poygan (lake), Wis. 317/J7
Poynette, Wis. 317/G9
Poynor, Mo. 261/L9
Poynor, Texas 303/J5
Poysdorf, Austria 41/D2
Poy Sippi, Wis. 317/J7
Pozantı, Turkey 63/F4
Požarevac, Yugoslavia 45/E3
Poza Rica de Hidalgo, Mexico 150/L6
Poznań (prov.), Poland 47/C2
Poznań, Poland 47/C2
Poznań, Poland 7/F3
Pozo Almonte, Chile 138/B2
Pozoblanco, Spain 33/D3
Pozo Colorado, Paraguay 144/C3
Pozo Hondo, Argentina 143/D2
Pozohondo, Spain 33/F3
Pozuelo de Alarcón, Spain 33/D2
Pozuelos, Venezuela 124/F2
Pozuzo, Peru 128/E8
Pozzallo, Italy 34/E6
Pozzuoli, Italy 34/D4
Prabuty, Poland 47/D2
Prachatice, Czech. 41/B2
Prachin Buri, Thailand 72/D4
Prachuap Khiri Khan, Thailand 72/D5
Pradera, Colombia 126/B6
Prades, France 28/E6
Prado (dam), Calif. 204/E11
Praestø, Denmark 21/F7
Pragel (pass), Switzerland 39/G2
Prague (cap.), Czech. 7/F3
Prague (Praha) (cap.), Czech. 41/C1
Prague, Nebr. 264/H3
Prague, Okla. 288/N4
Praha (city) (reg.), Czech. 41/C1
Prahan, Victoria 88/L7
Prahran, Victoria 97/J5
Praia (cap.), C. Verde 106/B8
Prainha, Amazonas, Brazil 132/A4
Prainha, Pará, Brazil 132/C3
Prairie, Ala. 195/D6
Prairie (co.), Ark. 202/G4
Prairie (creek), Ind. 227/C7
Prairie (riv.), Mich. 250/D7
Prairie (riv.), Minn. 255/E3
Prairie, Miss. 256/G3
Prairie (co.), Mont. 262/L4
Prairie, Queensland 95/C4
Prairie (lake), S. Dak. 298/P3
Prairieburg, Iowa 229/L4
Prairie City, Ill. 222/C3
Prairie City, Iowa 229/G5
Prairie City, Oreg. 291/J3
Prairie City, S. Dak. 298/D2
Prairie Creek, Ind. 227/C6
Prairie Dog Town Fork, Red (riv.), Okla. 288/F5
Prairie Dog Town Fork, Red (riv.), Texas 303/C3
Prairie du Chien, Wis. 317/D9
Prairie du Rocher, Ill. 222/C5
Prairie du Sac, Wis. 317/G9
Prairie Farm, Wis. 317/C5
Prairie Grove, Ark. 202/B2
Prairie Grove, Ill. 222/E1
Prairie Home, Mo. 261/G5
Prairie Point, Miss. 256/H4
Prairie River, Sask. 181/J3
Prairies (riv.), Québec 172/H4
Prairieton, Ind. 227/B6
Prairietown, Ill. 222/B2
Prairie View, Ark. 202/C3
Prairie View, Kansas 232/C2
Prairie View, Texas 303/J7
Prairie Village, Kansas 232/H2
Prairieville, La. 238/K2
Pran Buri, Thailand 72/D4
Prangins, Switzerland 39/B4
Prapat, Indonesia 85/B5
Praslin, St. Lucia 161/G6
Praslin (isl.), Seychelles 118/H5
Prat (isl.), Chile 138/D7
Pratas (Dongsha) (isl.), China 77/J7
Prathersville, Mo. 261/R4
Prato, Italy 34/C3
Prato-Sornico, Switzerland 39/G4
Pratt (co.), Kansas 232/D4
Pratt, Kansas 232/D4
Pratt, Manitoba 179/D5
Pratt, Minn. 255/E6
Pratt, W. Va. 312/D6
Pratteln, Switzerland 39/E1
Prattsburg, Georgia 217/D5
Prattsburg•, N.Y. 276/F5
Prattsville, Ark. 202/F5
Prattsville, N.Y. 276/M6
Prattville, Ala. 195/E6
Pratum, Oreg. 291/A3
Pravia, Spain 33/C1
Prawda, Manitoba 179/G5
Prawle (pt.), England 13/D7
Prawle (pt.), England 10/E5
Praxedis G. Guerrero, Mexico 150/G1
Pray, Mont. 262/F5
Praya, Indonesia 85/F7
Preble, Ind. 227/H3
Preble, N.Y. 276/H5
Preble (co.), Ohio 284/A6
Preeceville, Sask. 181/J4
Preemption, Ill. 222/C2
Preesall, England 13/E4
Preetz, Germany 22/D1
Pregarten, Austria 41/C2
Pregnall, S.C. 296/G5
Pregonero, Venezuela 124/C3
Preiji, U.S.S.R. 53/D2
Prek Po, Cambodia 72/E5
Prelate, Sask. 181/B5
Přelouč, Czech. 41/C1
Premier, W. Va. 312/C8
Premium, Ky. 237/R6
Premont, Texas 303/F10
Prentice, Ill. 222/C4
Prentice, Wis. 317/F4
Prentiss•, Maine 243/G5
Prentiss (co.), Miss. 256/G1
Prentiss, Miss. 256/E7
Prentiss, N.C. 281/C4
Prenzlau, Germany 22/E2
Preparis (isl.), Burma 72/B4
Preparis North (chan.), Burma 72/B4
Preparis South (chan.), Burma 72/B4
Přerov, Czech. 41/D2
Presanella (mt.), Italy 34/C1
Prescott, Ariz. 188/D4
Prescott, Ariz. 198/C4
Prescott, Ark. 202/D6
Prescott, Ind. 227/F6
Prescott, Iowa 229/D6
Prescott, Kansas 232/H3
Prescott, Mich. 250/F4
Prescott (county), Ontario 177/K2
Prescott, Ontario 177/J3
Prescott, Oreg. 291/D1
Prescott, Wash. 310/G4
Prescott, Wis. 317/A6
Prescott Valley, Ariz. 198/C4
Preseli (mts.), Wales 13/C6
Preševo, Yugoslavia 45/E4
Presho, S. Dak. 298/J6
Presidencia de la Plaza, Argentina 143/D2
Presidencia R. Sáenz Peña, Argentina 120/C5
Presidencia Roque Sáenz Peña, Argentina 143/D2
President, Pa. 294/C3
Presidente Dutra, Brazil 132/E4
Presidente Hayes, Paraguay 144/C3
Presidente Prudente, Brazil 132/D8
Presidente Prudente, Brazil 120/D5
Presidente Ríos (lake), Chile 138/D6
Presidente Venceslau, Brazil 132/D8
Presidential (range), N.H. 268/E3
Presidio, Calif. 204/J2
Presidio (co.), Texas 303/C12
Presidio, Texas 303/C12
Presidio Modelo, Cuba 158/C2
Prešov, Czech. 41/F2
Prespa (lake), Albania 45/E5
Prespa (lake), Greece 45/E5
Prespa (lake), Yugoslavia 45/E5
Presque Isle, Maine 243/H2
Presque Isle (co.), Mich. 250/F3
Presque Isle, Mich. 250/F3
Presque Isle (riv.), Mich. 250/F1
Presque Isle, Wis. 317/G3
Presque Isle A.F.B., Maine 243/G2
Presqu'île Prov. Park, Ontario 177/G4
Prestatyn, Wales 13/D4
Prestea, Ghana 106/D7
Presteigne, Wales 10/E4
Presteigne, Wales 13/D5
Přeštice, Czech. 41/B2
Presto, Bolivia 136/C6
Preston•, Conn. 210/H2
Preston, England 10/F1
Preston, England 13/G1
Preston, Georgia 217/C6
Preston, Idaho 220/G7
Preston, Ill. 222/D5
Preston, Iowa 229/N4
Preston, Kansas 232/D4
Preston, Ky. 237/O4
Preston, Md. 245/P6
Preston, Minn. 255/F7
Preston, Miss. 256/G5
Preston, Mo. 261/F7
Preston, Nebr. 264/J4
Preston, Nev. 266/G4
Preston, Okla. 288/P3
Preston, Scotland 15/F5
Preston, Victoria 88/L7
Preston, Victoria 97/J4
Preston, Wash. 310/D3
Preston (co.), W. Va. 312/G4
Preston City, Conn. 210/H2
Preston Hollow, N.Y. 276/M6
Prestonpans, Scotland 15/D1
Prestonsburg, Ky. 237/R5
Prestonville, Ky. 237/L3
Prestwich, England 13/H2
Prestwick, Scotland 10/D3
Prestwick, Scotland 15/D5
Prêto (riv.), Brazil 132/E5
Preto (riv.), Brazil 135/E3
Prêto (riv.), Brazil 132/A4
Pretoria (cap.), S. Africa 2/L7
Pretoria (cap.), S. Africa 102/E7
Pretoria (cap.), S. Africa 118/D5
Prettyboy (res.), Md. 245/M2
Pretty Prairie, Kansas 232/D4
Préveza, Greece 45/E6
Prévost, Québec 172/C4
Prevost, Wash. 310/B2
Prewitt (res.), Colo. 208/N2
Prewitt, N. Mex. 274/B3
Prey Veng, Cambodia 72/E5
Pribilof (isls.), Alaska 188/C6
Pribilof (isls.), Alaska 196/D3
Pribilof (isls.), U.S. 4/D18
Priboj, Yugoslavia 45/D4
Příbor, Czech. 41/E2
Příbram, Czech. 41/B2
Price (isl.), Br. Col. 184/C4
Price, Md. 245/P4
Price, N. Dak. 282/H5
Price, Québec 172/A1
Price, Utah 304/D4
Price, Utah 188/D3
Price (riv.), Utah 304/E4
Price (co.), Wis. 317/F4
Price, Wis. 317/E6
Pricedale, Miss. 256/D8
Priceville, Ala. 195/E1
Priceville, Ky. 237/K6
Priceville, Ontario 177/D3
Prichard, Ala. 195/B9
Prichard, Miss. 256/D1
Prichard, W. Va. 312/A6
Prickly (pt.), Grenada 161/C9
Priddis, Alberta 182/C4
Priddy, Texas 303/F6
Pride, Ky. 237/F5
Pride, La. 238/K1
Pridgen, Georgia 217/G7
Priego, Spain 33/E2
Priego de Córdoba, Spain 33/D4
Priekule, U.S.S.R. 53/A2
Priekulė, U.S.S.R. 53/A3
Prien am Chiemsee, Germany 22/E5
Prieska, S. Africa 118/C5
Priest (lake), Idaho 220/B1
Priest (riv.), Idaho 220/B1
Priest, J. Percy (lake), Tenn. 237/J8
Priestly (lake), Maine 243/E2
Priest Rapids (dam), Wash. 310/F4
Priest Rapids (lake), Wash. 310/E4
Priest River, Idaho 220/A1
Prievidza, Czech. 41/E2
Prijedor, Yugoslavia 45/C3
Prijepolje, Yugoslavia 45/D4
Prikumsk, U.S.S.R. 52/F6
Prikumsk, U.S.S.R. 48/E5
Prilep, Yugoslavia 45/E5
Priluki, U.S.S.R. 52/D4
Prim (pt.), Nova Scotia 168/C4
Prim (pt.), Pr. Edward I. 168/E2
Prima Porta, Italy 34/F6
Primate, Sask. 181/B3
Prime, New Bruns. 170/B1
Primero de Marzo, Paraguay 144/B4
Primero Enero, Cuba 158/F2
Primghar, Iowa 229/B2
Primm Springs, Tenn. 237/G9
Primorsk, U.S.S.R. 52/C2
Primorsko-Akhtarsk, U.S.S.R. 52/E5
Primos, Pa. 294/M7
Primrose (lake), Alberta 182/E2
Primrose, Georgia 217/C4
Primrose, Iowa 229/K7
Primrose, Nebr. 264/F3
Primrose (lake), Sask. 181/L3
Primrose Lake Air Weapons Range, Sask. 181/L3
Prince (co.), Pr. Edward I. 168/D2
Prince, Sask. 181/C3
Prince Albert (pen.), N.W.T. 162/E1
Prince Albert (pen.), N.W.T. 187/G2
Prince Albert (sound), N.W.T. 162/E1
Prince Albert (sound), N.W.T. 187/G2
Prince Albert, Sask. 162/F5
Prince Albert, Sask. 146/H4
Prince Albert, Sask. 181/F2
Prince Albert, S. Africa 118/C6
Prince Albert Nat'l Park, Sask. 162/F5
Prince Albert Nat'l Park, Sask. 181/E1
Prince Alfred (cape), N.W.T. 187/F2
Prince Charles (isl.), Canada 4/C13
Prince Charles (isl.), N.W.T. 162/J2
Prince Charles (isl.), N.W.T. 187/L3
Prince Edward (isls.) Ant. 5/E2
Prince Edward (county), Ontario 177/G3
Prince Edward (isls.), S. Africa 2/L8
Prince Edward (co.), Va. 307/M6
Prince Edward Island (prov.) 162/K6
PRINCE EDWARD ISLAND 168
Prince Edward Island (prov.), Canada 146/M5
Prince Edward Island Nat'l Park, Pr. Edward I. 168/E2
Prince Frederick, Md. 245/M6
Prince George, Br. Col. 146/F4
Prince George, Br. Col. 162/D5
Prince George, Br. Col. 184/F3
Prince George (co.), Va. 307/O6
Prince George, Va. 307/O6
Prince Georges (co.), Md. 245/L5
Prince Gustav Adolf (sea), N.W.T. 187/H2
Prince of Wales (cape), Alaska 196/E1
Prince of Wales (isl.), Alaska 196/N2
Prince of Wales (isl.), Canada 4/B14
Prince of Wales, New Bruns. 170/D3
Prince of Wales (str.), N.W.T. 162/D1
Prince of Wales (isl.), N.W.T. 146/J2
Prince of Wales (isl.), N.W.T. 162/F1
Prince of Wales (isl.), N.W.T. 187/J2
Prince of Wales (str.), N.W.T. 187/G2
Prince of Wales (isl.), Queensland 88/G2
Prince of Wales (isl.), Queensland 95/B1
Prince of Wales (cape), U.S. 4/C18
Prince Olav Coast (reg.) 5/C3
Prince Patrick (isl.), Canada 4/B16
Prince Patrick (isl.), N.W.T. 146/F2
Prince Patrick (isl.), N.W.T. 162/M3
Prince Patrick (isl.), N.W.T. 187/F2
Prince Regent (inlet), N.W.T. 162/G1
Prince Regent (inlet), N.W.T. 187/J2
Prince Rupert, Br. Col. 162/C5
Prince Rupert, Br. Col. 146/F4
Prince Rupert, Br. Col. 184/B3
Prince Rupert (bay), Dominica 161/E5
Princes Lakes, Ind. 227/E6
Princess Anne, Md. 245/P8
Princess Astrid Coast (reg.) 5/B1
Princess Charlotte (bay), Queensland 88/G2
Princess Charlotte (bay), Queensland 95/C2
Princess Harbour, Manitoba 179/F3

432 Princess Martha Coast

Princess Martha Coast (reg.) 5/B18
Princess Ragnhild Coast (reg.) 5/B2
Princess Royal (isl.), Br. Col. 184/C3
Princes Town, Trin. & Tob. 161/B11
Princeton, Ala. 195/F1
Princeton, Ark. 202/E6
Princeton, Br. Col. 184/G5
Princeton, Calif. 204/C4
Princeton (mt.), Colo. 208/G5
Princeton, Fla. 212/F6
Princeton, Idaho 220/B3
Princeton, Ill. 222/D2
Princeton, Ind. 227/B8
Princeton, Iowa 229/N5
Princeton, Kansas 232/G3
Princeton, Ky. 237/F6
Princeton, La. 238/C1
Princeton•, Maine 243/H5
Princeton•, Mass. 249/G3
Princeton, Mich. 250/B2
Princeton, Minn. 255/E5
Princeton, Mo. 261/E2
Princeton, Newf. 166/D2
Princeton, N.J. 273/D3
Princeton, N.C. 281/N4
Princeton, Ontario 177/D4
Princeton, Oreg. 291/J4
Princeton, S.C. 296/C2
Princeton, W. Va. 312/D8
Princeton, Wis. 317/H8
Princeton Junction, N.J. 273/D3
Princeville, Hawaii 218/C1
Princeville, Ill. 222/D3
Princeville, N.C. 281/P3
Princeville, Québec 172/F3
Prince William (sound), Alaska 196/D1
Prince William, New Bruns. 170/C3
Prince William (co.), Va. 307/O3
Principe (chan.), Br. Col. 184/C3
Príncipe (isl.), S. Tomé & Pr. 106/F8
Principio Furnace, Md. 245/P2
Prineville, Oreg. 291/G3
Prineville (res.), Oreg. 291/G3
Pringle, S. Dak. 298/B6
Prinkipo (Adalar) (isl.), Turkey 63/D6
Prinsburg, Minn. 255/C6
Prins Karls Forland (isl.), Norway 18/B2
Prinzapolca (riv.), Nicaragua 154/F4
Prinzapolka, Nicaragua 154/F4
Prior (cape), Spain 33/B1
Prior Lake, Minn. 255/E6
Priozersk, U.S.S.R. 52/D2
Pripet (marshes), U.S.S.R. 52/C4
Pripyat' (riv.), U.S.S.R. 7/G3
Pripyat' (riv.), U.S.S.R. 52/C4
Priština, Yugoslavia 45/E4
Pritchards (isl.), S.C. 296/G7
Pritchardville, S.C. 296/E7
Pritchett, Colo. 208/O8
Pritzwalk, Germany 22/E2
Privas, France 28/F5
Privateer (pt.), Virgin Is. (U.S.) 161/D4
Priverno, Italy 34/D4
Privolzhskiy, U.S.S.R. 52/G4
Priyutnoye, U.S.S.R. 52/F5
Priyutovo, U.S.S.R. 52/H4
Prizren, Yugoslavia 45/E4
Probolinggo, Indonesia 85/K2
Procious, W. Va. 312/D5
Procter, Br. Col. 184/J5
Proctor, Ark. 202/K3
Proctor, Colo. 208/N1
Proctor, Minn. 255/F4
Proctor, Mont. 262/B3
Proctor, Okla. 288/S3
Proctor, Pa. 294/J3
Proctor, Texas 303/F5
Proctor•, Vt. 268/A4
Proctor, W. Va. 312/E3
Proctorsville, Vt. 268/B5
Proctorville, N.C. 281/M6
Proctorville, Ohio 284/F9
Proddatur, India 68/D6
Proença-a-Nova, Portugal 33/B3
Profesor Rafael Ramírez, Mexico 150/O1
Profondeville, Belgium 27/F8
Progreso, Mexico 150/P6
Progreso, Uruguay 145/B6
Progress, Br. Col. 184/G2
Progress, Oreg. 291/A2
Progress, U.S.S.R. 48/O5
Progress Village, Fla. 212/C3
Project City, Calif. 204/C3
Prokhladnyy, U.S.S.R. 52/F6
Prokop'yevsk, U.S.S.R. 54/K4
Prokop'yevsk, U.S.S.R. 48/J4
Prokuplje, Yugoslavia 45/E4
Prole, Iowa 229/F6
Prome (Pye), Burma 72/B3
Promise City, Iowa 229/G7
Promissão, Brazil 135/B2
Promontory, Utah 304/B2
Prompton, Pa. 294/M2
Prongua, Sask. 181/C3
Prony (bay), New Caled. 86/H5
Prophet (riv.), Br. Col. 184/M2
Prophetstown, Ill. 222/D2
Propriá, Brazil 132/G5
Proserpine, Queensland 88/H4
Proserpine, Queensland 95/D4
Prosit, Minn. 255/F4
Prosna (riv.), Poland 47/C3
Prospect, Ala. 195/D3
Prospect•, Conn. 210/D2
Prospect, Ky. 237/K4
Prospect•, Maine 243/F6
Prospect (res.), N. S. Wales 88/K4
Prospect (res.), N.S. Wales 97/H3
Prospect, N.Y. 276/K4
Prospect, Nova Scotia 168/E4
Prospect, Ohio 284/D5
Prospect, Oreg. 291/E5
Prospect, Pa. 294/B4
Prospect, S. Australia 88/D8
Prospect, S. Australia 94/B7
Prospect, Tenn. 237/G10
Prospect, Va. 307/L6
Prospect Harbor, Maine 243/H7
Prospect Heights, Ill. 222/B5
Prospect Hill, N.C. 281/L2
Prospect Park, N.J. 273/B1
Prospect Park, Pa. 294/M7
Prosper, Mich. 250/E4
Prosper, Minn. 255/G7
Prosper, N. Dak. 282/R6
Prosper, Oreg. 291/C4
Prosperidad, Philippines 82/F6
Prosperity, Pa. 294/B5
Prosperity, S.C. 296/D3
Prosser, Nebr. 264/F4
Prosser, Wash. 310/F4
Prostějov, Czech. 41/D2
Protection, Kansas 232/C4
Protem, Mo. 261/G9
Protivín, Czech. 41/C2
Protivin, Iowa 229/J2
Proulxville, Québec 172/E3
Prouts Neck, Maine 243/C8
Provadiya, Bulgaria 45/H4
Provencal, La. 238/D3
Provence (trad. prov.), France 29
Providence, Ala. 195/C6
Providence (mts.), Calif. 204/K8
Providence, Fla. 212/D2
Providence, Grenada 161/D9
Providence, Ind. 227/E6
Providence, Ky. 237/F6
Providence (cape), N. Zealand 100/A7
Providence (cap.), R.I. 188/M2
Providence (cap.), R.I. 146/L5
Providence (co.), R.I. 249/H5
Providence (cap.), R.I. 249/H5
Providence, Utah 304/C2
Providence Bay, Ontario 177/B2
Providence Forge, Va. 307/P6
Providencia (isl.), Colombia 126/B9
Providenciales (isl.), Turks & Caicos 156/D2
Provideniya, U.S.S.R. 4/C18
Provideniya, U.S.S.R. 48/T3
Province Lake, N.H. 268/E4
Provincetown, Mass. 249/O4
Provincetown•, Mass. 249/O4
Provins, France 28/E3
Provo, Ark. 202/B5
Provo, S. Dak. 298/B7
Provo, Utah 146/G6
Provo, Utah 304/C3
Provo, Utah 188/D2
Provo (peak), Utah 304/C3
Provo (riv.), Utah 304/C3
Provost, Alberta 182/E3
Prowers (co.), Colo. 208/P7
Prozor, Yugoslavia 45/C4
Pruden, Tenn. 237/O7
Prudence (isl.), R.I. 249/J6
Prudence Island, R.I. 249/J6
Prudentópolis, Brazil 132/D9
Prudenville, Mich. 250/E4
Prudhoe (bay), Alaska 146/D2
Prudhoe (bay), Alaska 196/J1
Prudhoe, England 13/H3
Prudhoe Bay, Alaska 196/J1
Prud'homme, Sask. 181/F3
Prudnik, Poland 47/C3
Prue, Okla. 288/O2
Pruitt, Ark. 202/D1
Prüm, Germany 22/B3
Pruntytown, W. Va. 312/F4
Pruszcz Gdanski, Poland 47/D1
Pruszków, Poland 47/E2
Prut (riv.) 7/G4
Prut (riv.), Romania 45/J2
Prut (riv.), U.S.S.R. 52/C5
Prydz (bay) 5/C4
Pryor, Colo. 208/K8
Pryor, Mont. 262/H5
Pryor, Okla. 288/R2
Pryorsburg, Ky. 237/D7
Pryse, Ky. 237/O5
Przasnysz, Poland 47/E2
Przemkow, Poland 47/B2
Przemsza (riv.), Poland 47/B4
Przemyśl (prov.), Poland 47/F4
Przemyśl, Poland 47/F4
Przemyśl, Poland 7/G4
Przeworsk, Poland 47/F3
Przheval'sk, U.S.S.R. 48/H5
Psakhná, Greece 45/F6
Psará (isl.), Greece 45/G6
Psári, Greece 45/E7
Psel (riv.), U.S.S.R. 52/D4
Psevdhókavos (cape), Greece 45/G6
Pskov, U.S.S.R. 7/G3
Pskov, U.S.S.R. 48/C4
Pskov, U.S.S.R. 52/C3
Pskov (lake), U.S.S.R. 53/D1
Ptolemaís, Greece 45/E5
Ptuj, Yugoslavia 45/C2
Puako, Hawaii 218/G4
Puán, Argentina 143/D4
Puangue, Chile 138/F4
Puangue, Estero de (riv.), Chile 138/F3
Pubnico, Nova Scotia 168/C5
Pubnico (harb.), Nova Scotia 168/C5
Puca Barranca, Peru 128/E4
Pucallpa, Peru 128/E7
Pucallpa, Peru 120/B3
Pucara, Bolivia 136/C6
Pucará, Peru 128/G10
Pucarani, Bolivia 136/A5
Pucatrihue, Chile 138/D3
Pucaurco, Peru 128/G4
Puce, Ontario 177/B5
Pucheng, China 77/J6
Púchov, Czech. 41/E2
Puchuncaví, Chile 138/F2
Pucio (pt.), Philippines 82/C5
Pucioasa, Romania 45/G3
Puck, Poland 47/D1
Puckaway (lake), Wis. 317/H8
Puckett, Miss. 256/E6
Pucón, Chile 138/E2
Pucusana, Peru 128/D9
Pudahuel, Chile 138/G3
Pudasjärvi, Finland 18/P4
Pudding (riv.), Oreg. 291/A3
Pudozh, U.S.S.R. 52/E2
Puduchcheri (Pondicherry), India 68/E6
Pudukkottai, India 68/D6
Puebla (state), Mexico 150/L7
Puebla, Mexico 146/J8
Puebla de Alcocer, Spain 33/D3
Puebla de Don Fadrique, Spain 33/E4
Puebla del Caramiñal, Spain 33/B1
Puebla de Sanabria, Spain 33/C1
Puebla de Trives, Spain 33/C1
Puebla de Zaragoza, Mexico 150/N2
Pueblo, Colo. 146/H6
Pueblo, Colo. 188/F3
Pueblo (co.), Colo. 208/K6
Pueblo, Colo. 208/K6
Pueblo (res.), Colo. 208/K6
Pueblo (mts.), Oreg. 291/J5
Pueblo Army Depot, Colo. 208/L6
Pueblo Colorado Wash (dry riv.), Ariz. 198/F3
Pueblo del Sauce, Uruguay 145/E4
Pueblo Hondo, Venezuela 124/B3
Pueblo Hundido, Chile 138/B6
Pueblo Ind. Res., N. Mex. 274/B4
Pueblo Ind. Res., N. Mex. 274/D2
Pueblo Ind. Res., N. Mex. 274/C4
Pueblo Ind. Res., N. Mex. 274/D3
Pueblo La Paloma, Uruguay 145/D3
Pueblo Nuevo, Uruguay 145/B2
Pueblo Nuevo, Venezuela 124/D1
Pueblo of Acoma, N. Mex. 274/B3
Puebloviejo, Colombia 126/D5
Puelches, Argentina 143/C4
Puelén, Argentina 143/C4
Puelo (riv.), Chile 138/E4
Puente Alto, Chile 138/B10
Puenteareas, Spain 33/B1
Puente de Ixtla, Mexico 150/K2
Puente del Inca, Argentina 143/B3
Puentedeume, Spain 33/C1
Puente-Genil, Spain 33/D4
Puente Nacional, Colombia 126/D5
Pueo (pt.), Hawaii 218/A2
Pu'er, China 77/F7
Puerca (pt.), P. Rico 161/F2
Puerco (riv.), Ariz. 198/F3
Puerco (riv.), N. Mex. 274/A3
Puercos, Morro de (head), Panama 154/H7
Puerto Acosta, Bolivia 136/A4
Puerto Aisén, Chile 138/E6
Puerto Aisén, Chile 120/B7
Puerto Alegre, Bolivia 136/E3
Puerto Alianza, Peru 128/D5
Puerto Almacen, Bolivia 136/C4
Puerto Amaro, Uruguay 145/F3
Puerto América, Peru 128/D5
Puerto Ángel, Mexico 150/L9
Puerto Antioquia, Colombia 126/C4
Puerto Arazatí, Uruguay 145/C5
Puerto Argentina, Colombia 126/C7
Puerto Armuelles, Panama 154/F6
Puerto Arturo, Peru 128/F3
Puerto Asís, Colombia 126/B7
Puerto Ayacucho, Venezuela 120/C2
Puerto Ayacucho, Venezuela 124/E5
Puerto Ayora, Ecuador 128/B9
Puerto Bahía Negra, Paraguay 144/C2
Puerto Ballivián, Bolivia 136/C4
Puerto Barrios, Guatemala 154/C3
Puerto Bermúdez, Peru 128/E8
Puerto Berrío, Colombia 126/C4
Puerto Bertrand, Chile 138/E7
Puerto Boy, Colombia 126/C7
Puerto Caballas, Peru 128/E10
Puerto Caballo, Paraguay 144/C2
Puerto Cabello, Venezuela 124/E2
Puerto Cabello, Venezuela 120/C1
Puerto Cabezas, Nicaragua 154/F3
Puerto Calvimonte, Bolivia 136/C4
Puerto Carlos Pfannl, Paraguay 144/D4
Puerto Carranza, Colombia 126/F9
Puerto Carreño, Colombia 120/C2
Puerto Carreño, Colombia 126/G4
Puerto Casado, Paraguay 144/C3
Puerto Castilla, Honduras 154/D3
Puerto Chacabuco, Chile 138/D6
Puerto Chicama, Peru 128/C6
Puerto Cisnes, Chile 138/E5
Puerto Coig, Argentina 143/C7
Puerto Colombia, Colombia 126/C2
Puerto Colón, Paraguay 144/C3
Puerto Cooper, Paraguay 144/C3
Puerto Córdoba, Colombia 126/E8
Puerto Cortés, C. Rica 154/F6
Puerto Cortés, Honduras 154/D2
Puerto Cortés, Mexico 150/D4
Puerto Crevaux, Colombia 126/C6
Puerto Cristal, Chile 138/E6
Puerto Cumarebo, Venezuela 124/D2
Puerto de Cayo, Ecuador 128/B3
Puerto de la Concordia, El Salvador 154/C4
Puerto de Luna, N. Mex. 274/E4
Puerto de Nutrias, Venezuela 124/D3
Puerto Deseado, Argentina 143/D6
Puerto Deseado, Argentina 120/C7
Puerto El Carmen, Ecuador 128/E3
Puerto Escondido, Colombia 126/B3
Puerto Escondido, Mexico 150/L9
Puerto Esperanza, Cuba 158/A1
Puerto Esperanza, Paraguay 144/C2
Puerto Estrella, Colombia 126/E1
Puerto Eten, Peru 128/B6
Puerto Fonciere, Paraguay 144/D3
Puerto Frey, Bolivia 136/E4
Puerto Galileo, Paraguay 144/C4
Puerto General Busch, Bolivia 136/G7
Puerto General Ovando, Bolivia 136/50
Puerto Grether, Bolivia 136/C5
Puerto Guachalla, Bolivia 136/F6
Puerto Guaraní, Paraguay 144/C2
Puerto Harberton, Argentina 143/C7
Puerto Heath, Bolivia 136/A3
Puerto Hierro, Venezuela 124/H2
Puerto Huitoto, Colombia 126/D7
Puerto Iguazú, Argentina 143/F2
Puerto Inca, Peru 128/E7
Puerto Ingeniero Ibáñez, Chile 138/E6
Puerto Inírida, Colombia 126/G6
Puerto Irigoyen, Argentina 143/D1
Puerto Isabel, Bolivia 136/F6
Puerto Izozog, Bolivia 136/D6
Puerto José Pardo, Peru 128/D4
Puerto Juárez, Mexico 150/Q6
Puerto La Concordia, Colombia 126/D6
Puerto La Cruz, Venezuela 124/F2
Puerto Leguía, Loreto, Peru 128/D4
Puerto Leguía, Puno, Peru 128/G9
Puerto Leguízamo, Colombia 126/C8
Puerto Lempira, Honduras 154/F3
Puerto Libertador General San Martín, Argentina 143/E2
Puerto Limón, Colombia 126/B7
Puertollano, Spain 33/D3
Puerto López, La Guajira, Colombia 126/E2
Puerto López, Meta, Colombia 126/D5
Puerto Madero, Mexico 150/N9
Puerto Madryn, Argentina 143/C5
Puerto Madryn, Argentina 120/C7
Puerto Maldonado, Peru 128/H9
Puerto Maldonado, Peru 120/C4
Puerto Mamoré, Bolivia 136/C5
Puerto Manglares, Colombia 126/B5
Puerto María, Paraguay 144/C2
Puerto Max, Paraguay 144/D3
Puerto Mayor Otaño, Paraguay 144/E5
Puerto Medio Mundo (bay), P. Rico 161/F2
Puerto Mercedes, Colombia 126/D7
Puerto Mihanovich, Paraguay 144/C2
Puerto Miranda, Venezuela 124/E4
Puerto Montt, Chile 120/B7
Puerto Montt, Chile 138/E4
Puerto Morelos, Mexico 150/Q6
Puerto Morín, Peru 128/C7
Puerto Mosquito, Colombia 126/C3
Puerto Murillo, Colombia 126/G4
Puerto Mutis, Colombia 126/B4
Puerto Napo, Ecuador 128/D3
Puerto Nare, Colombia 126/D7
Puerto Nariño, Colombia 126/F5
Puerto Natales, Chile 120/B8
Puerto Natales, Chile 138/E9
Puerto Niño, Colombia 126/C5
Puerto Nuevo, Colombia 126/F5
Puerto Nuevo, Paraguay 144/C2
Puerto Nuevo, P. Rico 161/D1
Puerto Nuevo (pt.), P. Rico 161/C1
Puerto Obaldía, Panama 154/J6
Puerto Ocopa, Peru 128/E8
Puerto Olaya, Colombia 126/C4
Puerto Ospina, Colombia 126/C7
Puerto Padre, Cuba 158/H3
Puerto Padre, Cuba 156/C2
Puerto Páez, Venezuela 124/E4
Puerto Palena, Chile 138/D5
Puerto Pando, Bolivia 136/B4
Puerto Paraíso, Paraguay 144/A5
Puerto Pardo, Peru 128/F7
Puerto Patiño, Bolivia 136/C5
Puerto Paulina, Colombia 126/D7
Puerto Peñasco, Mexico 150/C1
Puerto Pinasco, Paraguay 144/C3
Puerto Pirámides, Argentina 143/D5
Puerto Píritu, Venezuela 124/F2
Puerto Pizarro, Colombia 126/D8
Puerto Pizarro, Peru 128/B4
Puerto Plata (prov.), Dom. Rep. 158/D5
Puerto Plata, Dom. Rep. 156/D3
Puerto Plata, Dom. Rep. 158/D5
Puerto Portillo, Peru 128/F7
Puerto Prado, Peru 128/E8
Puerto Presidente Franco, Paraguay 144/E4
Puerto Princesa, Philippines 85/F4
Puerto Princesa, Philippines 82/B6
Puerto Quellón, Chile 138/D4
Puerto Quijarro, Bolivia 136/G5
Puerto Ramírez, Chile 138/E5
Puerto Real, P. Rico 161/A2
Puerto Real (Playa de Fajardo), P. Rico 161/F1
Puerto Real, Spain 33/D4
Puerto Reyes, Colombia 126/B5
Puerto Rico 2/F5
Puerto Rico 146/M8
PUERTO RICO 161
PUERTO RICO 156/G1
Puerto Rico, Argentina 143/D1
Puerto Rico, Bolivia 136/B2
Puerto Rico, Caquetá, Colombia 126/C7
Puerto Rico, Meta, Colombia 126/C6
Puerto Rondón, Colombia 126/E4
Puerto Rosario, Paraguay 144/D4
Puerto Ruiz, Argentina 143/G6
Puerto Saavedra, Chile 138/D2
Puerto Salgar, Colombia 126/C5
Puerto Samanco, Peru 128/C7
Puerto San Francisco, Bolivia 136/C5
Puerto San José, Paraguay 144/C3
Puerto San Rafael, Paraguay 144/E5
Puerto Sastre, Paraguay 144/C3
Puerto Saucedo, Bolivia 136/D3
Puerto Siles, Bolivia 136/C3
Puerto Suárez, Bolivia 136/F6
Puerto Tacurú Pytá, Paraguay 144/D3
Puerto Tahuantinsuyo, Peru 128/G9
Puerto Tarafa, Cuba 158/H3
Puerto Tejada, Colombia 126/B6
Puerto Toledo, Colombia 126/C8
Puerto Torno, Bolivia 136/C5
Puerto Tres Palmas, Paraguay 144/C2
Puerto Vallarta, Mexico 150/G6
Puerto Varas, Chile 138/E3
Puerto Velarde, Bolivia 136/D5
Puerto Victoria, Peru 128/E7
Puerto Villarroel, Bolivia 136/C5
Puerto Villazón, Bolivia 136/D3
Puerto Wilches, Colombia 126/D4
Puerto Williams, Chile 138/F11
Puerto Yartou, Chile 138/E10
Puerto Ybapobó, Paraguay 144/D3
Pueyrredón (lake), Argentina 143/B6
Puffin (isl.), Ireland 17/A8
Pugachev, U.S.S.R. 52/G4
Puget (isl.), Wash. 310/B4
Puget (sound), Wash. 310/C3
Puget Sound Navy Yard, Wash. 310/A2
Pugwash, Nova Scotia 168/E3
Pugwash (harb.), Nova Scotia 168/E3
Puha, N. Zealand 100/F3
Puhi, Hawaii 218/C2
Puigcerdá, Spain 33/G1
Puina, Bolivia 136/A4
Puinagua, Canal de (riv.), Peru 128/E5
Pujada (bay), Philippines 82/F7
Pujehun, S. Leone 106/B7
Pujilí, Ecuador 128/C3
Pujut (pt.), Indonesia 85/G1
Pukaki (lake), N. Zealand 100/B6
Pukalani, Hawaii 218/J2
Pukapuka (atoll), Cook Is. 87/K7
Puka-Puka (atoll), Fr. Poly. 87/N7
Pukaskwa Nat'l Park, Ont. 162/H6
Pukaskwa Prov. Park, Ontario 175/C3
Pukaskwa Prov. Park, Ontario 177/H5
Pukch'ŏng, N. Korea 81/C3
Pukë, Albania 45/E4
Pukekohe, N. Zealand 100/E2
Pukoo, Hawaii 218/H1
Puksubaek (mt.), N. Korea 81/C3
Pukwana, S. Dak. 298/L6
Pula, Yugoslavia 45/A3
Pulacayo, Bolivia 120/C5
Pulacayo, Bolivia 136/B7
Pulai, Sungai (riv.), Malaysia 72/E5
Pulanduta (pt.), Philippines 82/D5
Pulangi (riv.), Philippines 82/E7
Pulap (atoll), Micronesia 87/E5
Pülar, Cerro (mt.), Chile 138/B4
Pulaski (co.), Ark. 202/F4
Pulaski (co.), Georgia 217/E6
Pulaski, Georgia 217/J6
Pulaski (co.), Ill. 222/D6
Pulaski, Ill. 222/D6
Pulaski (co.), Ind. 227/D2
Pulaski, Ind. 227/D3
Pulaski, Iowa 229/J7
Pulaski (co.), Ky. 237/M6
Pulaski, Ky. 237/M6
Pulaski, Miss. 256/E6
Pulaski (co.), Mo. 261/H7
Pulaski, N.Y. 276/H3
Pulaski, Ohio 284/A2
Pulaski, Pa. 294/B3
Pulaski, Tenn. 237/G10
Pulaski (co.), Va. 307/G6
Pulaski, Va. 307/G6
Pulaski, Wis. 317/K6
Puławy, Poland 47/F3
Pulcifer, Wis. 317/K6
Pulehu, Hawaii 218/J2
Pulicat (lake), India 68/E6
Pull (pt.), Virgin Is. (U.S.) 161/F3
Pullman, Mich. 250/C6
Pullman, Wash. 310/H4
Pullman, W. Va. 312/D4
Pully, Switzerland 39/C4
Pulo Anna (isl.), Belau 87/D5
Pulog (mt.), Philippines 82/C2
Pulpit Harbor, Maine 243/F7
Pulteney, Alberta 182/D4
Pulteney, N.Y. 276/F5
Pulteneyville, N.Y. 276/F4
Pułtusk, Poland 47/E2
Pülümür, Turkey 63/H3
Pulusuk (atoll), Micronesia 87/F5
Puluwat (atoll), Micronesia 87/E5
Pumanque, Chile 138/F6
Pumphrey, Md. 245/M4
Pumpkin (creek), Nebr. 264/A3
Pumpville, Texas 303/C8
Puna, Bolivia 136/C6
Puná (isl.), Ecuador 128/B4
Punaauia, Fr. Poly. 86/S13
Puna de Atacama (reg.), Argentina 143/C2
Punakha, Bhutan 68/G3
Punaluu, Hawaii 218/H7
Punaluu (harb.), Hawaii 218/H7
Punata, Bolivia 136/C5
Punchaw, Br. Col. 184/F3
Punchbowl (hill), Hawaii 218/C4
Punchestown, Ireland 17/H5
Pune, India 68/C5
Pungo, N.C. 281/R3
Pungo (lake), N.C. 281/S3
Pungo (riv.), N.C. 281/R4
Pungoteague, Va. 307/S5
P'ungsan, N. Korea 81/D3
Punia, Zaire 115/E4
Punitaqui, Chile 138/A8
Punjab (state), India 68/D2
Punjab (prov.), Pakistan 68/C2
Punk (isl.), Manitoba 179/F3
Punnichy, Sask. 181/G4
Puno (dept.), Peru 128/G10
Puno, Peru 128/G10
Puno, Peru 120/B4
Punta, Cerro de (mt.), P. Rico 161/C2
Punta Abreojos, Mexico 150/C3
Punta Alta, Argentina 143/D4
Punta Alta, Argentina 120/C6
Punta Arenas, Chile 120/B8
Punta Arenas, Chile 138/E10
Punta Cardón, Venezuela 124/C2
Punta de Bombón, Peru 128/F11
Punta de Díaz, Chile 138/B7
Punta del Este, Uruguay 145/E6
Punta de Mata, Venezuela 124/G3
Punta de Piedras, Venezuela 124/F2
Punta Gorda, Belize 154/C2
Punta Gorda (pt.), Calif. 204/A3
Punta Gorda, Fla. 212/E5
Punta Medanosa, Argentina 143/C6
Punta Moreno, Peru 128/C6
Punta Negra, Salar de (salt dep.), Chile 138/B5
Puntarenas, C. Rica 154/E6
Punta Santiago (Playa de Humacao), P. Rico 161/F2
Puntas de Maciel, Uruguay 145/C4
Punto Fijo, Venezuela 120/C1
Punto Fijo, Venezuela 124/D2
Punxsutawney, Pa. 294/E4
Puolanka, Finland 18/P4
Puolo (pt.), Hawaii 218/C2
Pupiales, Colombia 126/B7
Puposky, Minn. 255/C3
Pupuke (lake), N. Zealand 100/B1
Pupuya, Nevada (mt.), Bolivia 136/A4
Puqi, China 77/H6
Puquina, Peru 128/G11
Puquintica, Nevado (mt.), Bolivia 136/A6
Puquintica, Cerro (mt.), Chile 138/B1
Puquio, Peru 128/F10
Puquios, Chile 138/B1
Pur (riv.), U.S.S.R. 48/H3
Puracé (vol.), Colombia 126/B6
Purbeck, Isle of (pen.), England 13/F7
Purbolinggo, Indonesia 85/J2
Purcell (mts.), Br. Col. 184/J5
Purcell (mts.), Idaho 220/B1
Purcell, Kansas 232/G2
Purcell, Mo. 261/D8
Purcell (mts.), Mont. 262/A2
Purcell, Okla. 288/M4
Purcellville, Va. 307/N2
Purchase, N.Y. 276/P6
Purdin, Mo. 261/F3
Purdum, Nebr. 264/D2
Purdy, Mo. 261/E9
Purdy, Va. 307/N7
Pure Air, Mo. 261/G2
Purén, Chile 138/D2
Purgatoire (riv.), Colo. 208/M8
Purgitsville, W. Va. 312/J4
Puri, India 68/F5
Purial, Sierra de (mts.), Cuba 158/K4
Purificación, Colombia 126/C6
Purificación, Mexico 150/G7
Purli, India 68/D5
Purmerend, Netherlands 27/F4
Purnea, India 68/F3
Purple Springs, Alberta 182/E5
Purple Valley, Ontario 177/C3
Purranque, Chile 138/D3
Pursat (Pouthisat), Cambodia 72/D4
Puruándiro, Mexico 150/J7
Puruey, Venezuela 124/F4
Purukcahu, Indonesia 85/E6
Purulia, India 68/F4
Puruname, Venezuela 124/E6
Puruni (riv.), Guyana 131/B2
Purus (riv.), Brazil 120/C3
Purus (riv.), Brazil 132/H9
Purús (riv.), Peru 128/G8
Puruvesi (lake), Finland 18/Q6
Purves, Manitoba 179/D5
Purvis, Miss. 256/F8
Purwakarta, Indonesia 85/H2
Purwodadi, Indonesia 85/J2
Purwokerto, Indonesia 85/H2
Purworejo, Indonesia 85/J2
Puryear, Tenn. 237/E8
Pusan, S. Korea 54/O6
Pusan, S. Korea 81/D6
Pushaw (lake), Maine 243/F6
Pushkin, U.S.S.R. 48/C4
Pushkin, U.S.S.R. 52/C3
Pushmataha, Ala. 195/B6
Pushmataha (co.), Okla. 288/R6
Püspökladány, Hungary 41/F3
Pustunich, Mexico 150/O7
Pusztaszabolcs, Hungary 41/E3
Putaendo, Chile 138/A9
Putao, Burma 72/C1
Putaruru, N. Zealand 100/E3
Putbus, Germany 22/E1
Puteau, France 28/A2
Putian, China 77/J6
Putignano, Italy 34/F4
Putina, Peru 128/H10
Put-in-Bay, Ohio 284/E2
Puting, Borneo (cape), Indonesia 85/E6
Puting, Sumatra (cape), Indonesia 85/C7
Putla de Guerrero, Mexico 150/L8
Putnam, Ala. 195/B6
Putnam, Conn. 210/H1
Putnam•, Conn. 210/H1
Putnam (co.), Fla. 212/E2
Putnam (co.), Georgia 217/F4
Putnam, Georgia 217/D6
Putnam (co.), Ill. 222/D2
Putnam, Ill. 222/D2
Putnam (co.), Ind. 227/D5
Putnam (co.), Mo. 261/F2
Putnam (co.), N.Y. 276/N8
Putnam (co.), Ohio 284/B3
Putnam, Okla. 288/J3

Putnam (co.), Tenn. 237/K8
Putnam, Texas 303/E5
Putnam (co.), W. Va. 312/C6
Putnam Heights, Conn. 210/H1
Putnam Valley•, N.Y. 276/N8
Putnamville, Ind. 227/D5
Putney, Georgia 217/D8
Putney, S. Dak. 298/N2
Putney•, Vt. 268/B6
Putnok, Hungary 41/F2
Putre, Chile 138/B1
Puttalam, Sri Lanka 68/D7
Putte, Belgium 27/F6
Putten, Netherlands 27/H4
Puttgarden, Germany 22/D1
Puttur, India 68/D6
Putumayo (riv.) 120/B3
Putumayo (inten.), Colombia 126/C7
Putumayo (riv.), Colombia 126/E9
Putumayo, Ecuador 128/E3
Putumayo (riv.), Ecuador 128/E2
Putumayo (riv.), Peru 128/G4
Pütürge, Turkey 63/H3
Putussibau, Indonesia 85/E5
Puuanahulu, Hawaii 218/G4
Puuhonua O Honaunau Nat'l Hist. Park, Hawaii 218/F6
Puuiki, Hawaii 218/K2
Puu Keahiakahoe (mt.), Hawaii 218/D3
Puukohola Heiau Nat'l Hist. Site, Hawaii 218/G4
Puu Kukui (mt.), Hawaii 218/J2
Puu Lanihuli (mt.), Hawaii 218/D3
Puulavesi (lake), Finland 18/P5
Puu Moaulanui (mt.), Hawaii 218/H3
Puunene, Hawaii 218/J2
Puunui, Hawaii 218/C4
Puuwaawaa, Hawaii 218/G5
Puuwai, Hawaii 218/A2
Pu Xian, China 77/H4
Puxico, Mo. 261/M9
Puyallup, Wash. 188/B1
Puyallup, Wash. 310/C3
Puyallup (riv.), Wash. 310/C4
Puy-de-Dôme (dept.), France 28/E5
Puy-de-Dôme (mt.), France 28/E5
Puyehue, Chile 138/E3
Puyehue (lake), Chile 138/E3
Puyo, Ecuador 128/D3
Puysegur (pt.), N. Zealand 100/A7
Pwani (Coast) (reg.), Tanzania 115/G5
Pweto, Zaire 115/E5
Pwllheli, Wales 10/D4
Pwllheli, Wales 13/C5
Pyapon, Burma 72/B3
Pyasina (riv.), U.S.S.R. 48/J2
Pyatigorsk, U.S.S.R. 52/F6
Pyatt, Ark. 202/E1
Pye (isls.), Alaska 196/C2
Pye, Burma 72/B3
Pye, Burma 54/L8
Pyengana, Tasmania 99/E3
Pygmalion (Indira) (pt.), India 68/G7
Pyhäjärvi (lake), Finland 18/M6
Pyhäjärvi (lake), Finland 18/O5
Pyinmana, Burma 72/C3
Pyland, Miss. 256/F3
Pymatuning (res.), Ohio 284/J2
Pymatuning (res.), Pa. 294/A2
P'yŏnggang, N. Korea 81/C4
P'yŏngsan, N. Korea 81/C4
P'yŏngyang (cap.), N. Korea 54/O6
P'yŏngyang (cap.), N. Korea 81/C4
Pyote, Texas 303/A6
Pyramid (peak), Idaho 220/E4
Pyramid, Ky. 237/R5
Pyramid (lake), Nev. 266/B2
Pyramid (isl.), N. Zealand 100/E7
Pyramid Lake Ind. Res., Nev. 266/B2
Pyramids (ruins), Egypt 111/J3
Pyrenees (mts.) 7/D4
Pyrenees (range), France 28/C6
Pyrenees (range), Spain 33/F1
Pyrénées-Atlantiques (dept.), France 28/C6
Pyrénées-Orientales (dept.), France 28/E6
Pyrites, N.Y. 276/K1
Pyriton, Ala. 195/G4
Pyrzyce, Poland 47/B2
Pytalovo, U.S.S.R. 52/C3
Pyu, Burma 72/C3
Pyuthan, Nepal 68/E3

Q

Qaanaq, Greenland 4/B13
Qabalan, West Bank 65/C3
Qabatiya, West Bank 65/C3
Qabr Hud, Yemen 59/E6
Qadhima, Saudi Arabia 59/C5
Qadima, Israel 65/B3
Qadisiya (heads), Iraq 66/D4
Qafar, Saudi Arabia 59/D4
Qaffin, West Bank 65/C3
Qagan Nur, China 77/H3
Qâhira, El (Cairo) (cap.), Egypt 111/J3
Qaidam (basin), China 54/L6
Qaidam Pendi (basin) (swamp), China 77/D4
Qala'en Nahl, Sudan 59/C7
Qala'en Nahl, Sudan 111/F5
Qalansuwa, Israel 65/B3
Qal'a Sharqat, Iraq 59/D2
Qal'a Sharqat, Iraq 66/C3
Qalat, Afghanistan 68/B2
Qalat, Afghanistan 59/J3
Qal'at Diza, Iraq 66/D2
Qal'at es Salihiye, Syria 63/J5
Qal'eh Mureh (riv.), Iran 66/J3
Qal'eh-ye Now, Afghanistan 68/A1
Qal'eh-ye Now, Afghanistan 59/H3
Qal'eh-ye Panjeh, Afghanistan 59/K2
Qal'eh-ye Panjeh, Afghanistan 68/C1
Qalqiliya, West Bank 65/C3
Qalyub, Egypt 111/J3
Qamdo, China 77/E5
Qamdo, China 54/L6
Qamishliye, Syria 63/J4
Qamr (bay), Yemen 59/F6
Qandahar, Afghanistan 54/H6
Qandahar, Afghanistan 68/B2
Qandahar, Afghanistan 59/J3
Qantara, El, Egypt 111/K3
Qaqortoq, Greenland 4/D12
Qaranqu (riv.), Iran 66/E2
Qareh Dagh (mts.), Iran 66/E1
Qareh Su (riv.), Iran 66/E1
Qareh Su (riv.), Iran 66/G3
Qarkilik (Ruoqiang), China 77/C4
Qarn (riv.), Israel 65/C1
Qarqan (Qiemo), China 77/C4
Qarqan He (riv.), China 77/C4
Qasr al Haiyanya, Saudi Arabia 59/D4
Qasr al Khubbaz, Iraq 66/B4
Qasr-e Qand, Iran 59/H4
Qasr-e Qand, Iran 66/M7
Qasr-e-Shirin, Iran 66/E3
Qasr Farâfra, Egypt 111/E2
Qasr Farâfra, Egypt 102/E2
Qasr Farâfra, Egypt 59/A4
Qatar 2/M4
Qatar 54/G7
QATAR 59/F4
Qatif, Saudi Arabia 59/E4
Qattara (depr.), Egypt 59/A4
Qattara (depr.), Egypt 111/E2
Qayen, Iran 66/L4
Qayen, Iran 59/G3
Qazvin, Iran 54/F6
Qazvin, Iran 59/E2
Qazvin, Iran 66/F2
Qedma, Israel 65/B4
Qena, Egypt 111/F2
Qena, Egypt 102/F2
Qena, Egypt 59/B4
Qeqertarsuaq, Greenland 4/C12
Qeshm (isl.), Iran 59/G4
Qeshm (isl.), Iran 66/J7
Qeys (isl.), Iran 59/F4
Qeys (isl.), Iran 66/J7
Qezel Owzan (riv.), Iran 66/F2
Qezel Owzan (riv.), Iran 59/E2
Qianyang (Kienyang), China 77/H6
Qiaowan, China 77/E3
Qibya, West Bank 65/C4
Qiebei, China 77/F7
Qiema, China 54/K6
Qiemo (Qarqan), China 77/C4
Qijiang, China 77/G6
Qila Ladgasht, Pakistan 68/A3
Qila Ladgasht, Pakistan 59/H4
Qilian, China 77/E4
Qilian Shan (range), China 54/L6
Qilian Shan (range), China 77/E4
Qimen, China 77/J5
Qina (Qena), Egypt 59/B4
Qingdao (Tsingtao), China 77/K4
Qingdao, China 54/O6
Qinghai (Tsinghai) (prov.), China 77/E4
Qinghai (lake), China 54/L6
Qinghai Hu (lake), China 77/E4
Qinghe (Qinggil), China 77/D2
Qingjiang, Jiangxi, China 77/J6
Qingjiang, Anhui, China 77/J5
Qingtongxia, China 77/F4
Qingyuan, China 77/H7
Qinhuangdao (Chinwangtao), China 77/K4
Qinzhou, China 77/G7
Qionghai, China 77/H8
Qiongshan, China 77/H8
Qiongzhou Haixia (str.), China 77/G7
Qiqihar (Tsitsihar), China 77/K2
Qiqihar, China 54/O5
Qira, China 77/B4
Qiryat Atta, Israel 65/C2
Qiryat Bialik, Israel 65/C2
Qiryat Gat, Israel 65/B4
Qiryat Mal'akhi, Israel 65/B4
Qiryat Motzkin, Israel 65/C2
Qiryat Shemona, Israel 65/C1
Qiryat Tiv'on, Israel 65/C2
Qiryat Yam, Israel 65/C2
Qishn, Yemen 59/F6
Qishon (riv.), Israel 65/C2
Qitai, China 77/C3
Qitaihe, China 77/M2
Qizan, Saudi Arabia 59/D6
Qog, China 77/G3
Qom (Qum), Iran 54/G6
Qom, Iran 59/F3
Qom, Iran 66/G3
Qonduz (Konduz), Afghanistan 68/B1
Qonduz (Konduz), Afghanistan 59/J2
Qonduz (Konduz) (riv.), Afghanistan 68/B1
Qonduz (Konduz) (riv.), Afghanistan 59/J2
Qorveh, Iran 66/E3
Qotur, Iran 66/D1
Quabbin (res.), Mass. 249/E3
Quaboag (riv.), Mass. 249/F4
Quaco (head), New Bruns. 170/E3
Quaddick, Conn. 210/H1
Quaddick (res.), Conn. 210/H1
Quadeville, Ontario 177/G2
Quail, Texas 303/D3
Quairading, W. Australia 92/B1
Quajote Wash (dry riv.), Ariz. 198/D6
Quakenbrück, Germany 22/C2
Quaker City, Ohio 284/H6
Quaker Farms, Conn. 210/C3
Quaker Hill, Conn. 210/G3
Quakertown, N.J. 273/D2
Quakertown, Pa. 294/M5
Qualicum Beach, Br. Col. 184/J3
Quality, Ky. 237/H6
Quallam, Niger 106/E6
Quamba, Minn. 255/E5
Quambatook, Victoria 97/B4
Quambone, N.S. Wales 97/E2
Quanah, Texas 303/E3
Quan Dao Nam Du (isls.), Vietnam 72/D5
Quandary (peak), Colo. 208/G4
Quandialla, N.S. Wales 97/D4
Quanduck (brook), Conn. 210/H1
Quang Nam, Vietnam 72/E4
Quang Ngai, Vietnam 72/F4
Quang Tri, Vietnam 72/E3
Quang Yen, Vietnam 72/E2
Quan Long, Vietnam 72/E5
Quantico, Md. 245/R7
Quantico, Va. 307/O3
Quantico Marine Corps Air Sta., Va. 307/O4
Quanzhou, China 77/H6
Quanzhou (Chüanchow), China 77/J7
Quapaw, Okla. 288/S1
Qu'Appelle, Sask. 181/H5
Qu'Appelle (riv.), Sask. 181/J5
Quaqtaq, Québec 174/F1
Quaraí, Brazil 132/C10
Quaregnon, Belgium 27/D8
Quarryville, New Bruns. 170/E2
Quarryville, Pa. 294/K6
Quartu Sant'Elena, Italy 34/B5
Quartz (peak), Calif. 204/L11
Quartz Hill, Calif. 204/G9
Quartz Mountain, Oreg. 291/G5
Quartzsite, Ariz. 198/A5
Quasqueton, Iowa 229/K4
Quassapaug (pond), Conn. 210/C2
Quatervals (peak), Switzerland 39/K3
Quathiaski Cove, Br. Col. 184/E5
Quatre Bornes, Mauritius 118/G5
Quatsino (sound), Br. Col. 184/C5
Quay (co.), N. Mex. 274/F3
Quay, N. Mex. 274/F4
Quay, Okla. 288/N2
Quchan, Iran 66/L2
Quchan, Iran 59/G2
Quealy, Wyo. 319/C4
Queanbeyan, N. S. Wales 88/H7
Queanbeyan, N.S. Wales 97/E4
QUÉBEC 172
QUÉBEC, NORTHERN 174
Québec (prov.) 162/J5
Québec, Canada 2/F3
Québec (prov.), Canada 146/L4
Québec (co.), Québec 172/F3
Québec (county), Québec 174/C3
Québec (cap.), Que. 146/L5
Québec (cap.), Que. 162/J6
Québec (cap.), Québec 172/H3
Québec (cap.), Québec 174/C3
Quebeck, Tenn. 237/K9
Quebracho, Uruguay 145/B2
Quebracho Coto, Argentina 143/D2
Quebrada de Alvarado, Chile 138/F2
Quebradillas, P. Rico 161/B1
Quechee, Vt. 268/C4
Quechisla, Bolivia 136/C7
Quecholac, Mexico 150/O2
Quecreek, Pa. 294/D5
Quedlinburg, Germany 22/D3
Queen (cape), N.W. Terr. 187/L3
Queen, Pa. 294/E5
Queen Anne, Md. 245/O5
Queen Annes (co.), Md. 245/P4
Queenborough, England 13/H6
Queenborough, England 10/G5
Queen Charlotte (isls.), Br. Col. 146/E4
Queen Charlotte (isls.), Br. Col. 162/C5
Queen Charlotte, Br. Col. 184/A3
Queen Charlotte (isls.), Br. Col. 184/B3
Queen Charlotte (sound), Br. Col. 184/C4
Queen Charlotte (str.), Br. Col. 184/D5
Queen Charlotte (sound), N.W.T. 162/D5
Queen City, Mo. 261/H2
Queen City, Texas 303/L4
Queen Creek, Ariz. 198/D5
Queen Elizabeth (isls.), Canada 2/C2
Queen Elizabeth (isls.), Canada 4/B15
Queen Elizabeth (isls.), N.W.T. 146/G2
Queen Elizabeth (isls.), N.W.T. 162/M3
Queen Elizabeth (isls.), N.W.T. 187/H1
Queen Mary Coast (reg.) 5/C5
Queen Maud (mts.) 5/A12
Queen Maud (gulf), N.W.T. 162/F2
Queen Maud (gulf), N.W.T. 187/H3
Queen Maud Land (reg.), Ant. 2/K10
Queen Maud Land (reg.) 5/B1
Queens (sound), Br. Col. 184/C4
Queen's (co.), New Bruns. 170/D3
Queens (co.), N.Y. 276/N9
Queens (borough), N.Y. 276/N9
Queens (chan.), N.W.T. 187/J2
Queens (co.), Nova Scotia 168/C4
Queens (co.), Pr. Edward I. 168/E2
Queens, W. Va. 312/F5
Queensberry (mt.), Scotland 15/E5
Queenscliff, Victoria 97/C6
Queensferry, Scotland 10/C1
Queensferry, Scotland 15/D1
Queen Shoals, W. Va. 312/D6
QUEENSLAND 95
Queensland (state), Australia 88/G4
Queensland (state), Australia 87/E8
Queensport, Nova Scotia 168/G3
Queenstown, Alberta 182/D4
Queenstown, Guyana 131/B2
Queenstown (Cóbh), Ireland 10/B5
Queenstown (Cóbh), Ireland 17/E8
Queenstown, Md. 245/O5
Queenstown, New Bruns. 170/D3
Queenstown, N. Zealand 100/B6
Queenstown, S. Africa 102/E8
Queenstown, S. Africa 118/D6
Queenstown, Tasmania 99/B4
Queenstown, Tasmania 88/H8
Queensville, Ind. 227/F6
Queets, Wash. 310/A3
Queets (riv.), Wash. 310/A3
Queilén, Chile 138/D4
Queimadas, Brazil 132/F5
Quela, Angola 115/C5
Quelimane, Mozambique 118/F3
Quelimane, Mozambique 102/F6
Quelpart (Cheju) (isl.), S. Korea 81/C7
Queluz, Portugal 33/A1
Quemado (pt.), Cuba 158/K4
Quemado, N. Mex. 274/A4
Quemado, Texas 303/D9
Quemado de Güines, Cuba 158/E1
Quemchi, Chile 138/D4
Quemoy (Jinmen) (isl.), China 77/J7
Quemú-Quemú, Argentina 143/D4
Quenemo, Kansas 232/G3
Quentin, Miss. 256/C8
Quepos, C. Rica 154/E6
Quequay Chico (riv.), Uruguay 145/B3
Quequay Grande (riv.), Uruguay 145/B3
Que Que (Kwekwe), Zimbabwe 118/D3
Que Que (Kwekwe), Zimbabwe 102/E6
Quequén, Argentina 143/E4
Querecotillo, Peru 128/B5
Querétaro (state), Mexico 150/J6
Querétaro, Mexico 146/J7
Querétaro, Mexico 150/J6
Quesada, Spain 33/E4
Queshan, China 77/H5
Quesnel, Br. Col. 162/D5
Quesnel (lake), Br. Col. 162/D5
Quesnel, Br. Col. 184/F4
Quesnel (lake), Br. Col. 184/G4
Quesnel (riv.), Br. Col. 184/F4
Quesnel (lake), Manitoba 179/G4
Questa, N. Mex. 274/D2
Queteña, Bolivia 136/B8
Quetico Prov. Park, Ontario 175/B3
Quetico Prov. Park, Ontario 177/G5
Quetta, Pakistan 54/H6
Quetta, Pakistan 59/J3
Quetta, Pakistan 68/B2
Queule, Chile 138/D2
Quevedo, Ecuador 128/C3
Quévy, Belgium 27/D8
Quezaltenango, Guatemala 154/B3
Quezaltepeque, Guatemala 154/C3
Quezon (prov.), Philippines 82/C3
Quezon City, Philippines 82/C3
Quibala, Angola 115/C6
Quibaxe, Angola 115/B5
Quibdó, Colombia 126/B5
Quiberon, France 28/B4
Quibor, Venezuela 124/D3
Quicacha, Peru 128/F10
Quick, Br. Col. 184/D3
Quick, W. Va. 312/D6
Quicksand, Ky. 237/P5
Quicksburg, Va. 307/L3
Quiebra Hacha, Cuba 158/B1
Quiévrain, Belgium 27/D8
Quigley, Alberta 182/E1
Quiindy, Paraguay 144/B5
Quijotoa, Ariz. 198/C6
Quilalí, Nicaragua 154/E4
Quilán (cape), Chile 138/D4
Quilán (isl.), Chile 138/D5
Quilca, Peru 128/F11
Quilcene, Wash. 310/B3
Quilchena, Br. Col. 184/G5
Quilengues, Angola 115/B6
Quilicura, Chile 138/G3
Quill (lakes), Sask. 181/G4
Quillabamba, Peru 128/F9
Quillacas, Bolivia 136/B6
Quillacollo, Bolivia 136/B5
Quillacollo, Bolivia 120/C4
Quillagua, Chile 138/B3
Quillaicillo, Chile 138/A8
Quillan, France 28/E6
Quillayute Ind. Res., Wash. 310/A3
Quilleco, Chile 138/E1
Quill Lake, Sask. 181/G3
Quillota, Chile 138/F2
Quilon, India 68/D7
Quilpie, Queensland 88/G5
Quilpie, Queensland 95/C5
Quilpué, Chile 138/F2
Quimby, Iowa 229/B3
Quimby, Maine 243/F2
Quime, Bolivia 136/B5
Quimili, Argentina 143/D2
Quimper, France 28/A4
Quimperlé, France 28/B4
Quinault, Wash. 310/B3
Quinault (lake), Wash. 310/B3
Quinault (riv.), Wash. 310/A3
Quinault Ind. Res., Wash. 310/A3
Quinby, S.C. 296/H3
Quinby, Va. 307/S5
Quinby (inlet), Va. 307/S6
Quince Mil, Peru 128/G9
Quincy, Calif. 204/E4
Quincy, Fla. 212/B1
Quincy, Ill. 188/H3
Quincy, Ill. 222/B4
Quincy, Ind. 227/D6
Quincy, Kansas 232/F4
Quincy, Ky. 237/P3
Quincy, Mass. 249/D7
Quincy (bay), Mass. 249/D7
Quincy, Mich. 250/E7
Quincy, Miss. 256/H3
Quincy, Mo. 261/F6
Quincy, N.H. 268/D4
Quincy, Ohio 284/C5
Quincy, Wash. 310/F3
Quincy, W. Va. 312/C6
Quindío (dept.), Colombia 126/C5
Quinebaug, Conn. 210/H1
Quinebaug (riv.), Conn. 210/H2
Quinebaug (riv.), Mass. 249/F4
Quines, Argentina 143/C3
Quinhagak, Alaska 196/F3
Qui Nhon, Vietnam 72/F4
Qui Nhon, Vietnam 54/M8
Quiniluban (isls.), Philippines 82/C5
Quinlan, Okla. 288/J2
Quinlan, Texas 303/H5
Quinn (riv.), Nev. 266/D1
Quinn, S. Dak. 298/E5
Quinn Canyon (range), Nev. 266/F4
Quinnesec, Mich. 250/A3
Quinnimont, W. Va. 312/D7
Quinnipiac, Conn. 210/D3
Quinnipiac (riv.), Conn. 210/D3
Quinta de Tilcoco, Chile 138/G5
Quintana de la Serena, Spain 33/D3
Quintanar de la Orden, Spain 33/E3
Quintana Roo (state), Mexico 150/P7
Quintay, Chile 138/F3
Quinter, Kansas 232/B2
Quintero, Chile 138/F2
Quinto (riv.), Argentina 143/D3
Quinto, Spain 33/F2
Quinto, Switzerland 39/G3
Quinton, Ky. 237/M7
Quinton, N.J. 273/C4
Quinton, Okla. 288/R4
Quinton, Sask. 181/G4
Quinton, Va. 307/O5
Quinwood, W. Va. 312/E6
Quinzau, Angola 115/B5
Quionga, Mozambique 118/G2
Quipapá, Brazil 132/G5
Quipungo, Angola 115/B6
Quirey, Colombia 126/F5
Quirihue, Chile 138/E1
Quirindi, N.S. Wales 97/F2
Quirino (prov.), Philippines 82/C2
Quirino, Philippines 82/C2
Quiriquire, Venezuela 124/G3
Quirke (lake), Ontario 177/B1
Quiroga, Argentina 143/F7
Quiroga, Bolivia 136/C6
Quiroga, Spain 33/C1
Quirusillas, Bolivia 136/D6
Quisiro, Venezuela 124/C2
Quispamsis, New Bruns. 170/E3
Quissanga, Mozambique 118/G2
Quissett, Mass. 249/M6
Quissico, Mozambique 118/F4
Quitaque, Texas 303/C3
Quitasueño (bank), Colombia 126/A8
Quitilipi, Argentina 143/D2
Quitman, Ark. 202/F3
Quitman (co.), Georgia 217/B7
Quitman, Georgia 217/E9
Quitman, La. 238/E2
Quitman (co.), Miss. 256/D2
Quitman, Miss. 256/G6
Quitman, Mo. 261/C2
Quitman, Texas 303/J5
Quitman (mts.), Texas 303/B11
Quito (cap.), Ecuador 2/F6
Quito (cap.), Ecuador 128/C3
Quito (cap.), Ecuador 120/B2
Quixadá, Brazil 120/F3
Quixadá, Brazil 132/G4
Quixeramobim, Brazil 132/F4
Qujing, China 77/F6
Qulin, Mo. 261/M9
Qum, Iran 54/G6
Qum (Qom), Iran 59/F3
Qum (Qom), Iran 66/G3
Qumar He (riv.), China 77/D4
Qumarlêb, China 77/D5
Qumeim, Jordan 65/D2
Qunfidha, Saudi Arabia 59/D6
Quogue, N.Y. 276/P9
Quoich (riv.), N.W. Terr. 187/J3
Quoich, Loch (lake), Scotland 15/C3
Quonnipaug (lake), Conn. 210/E3
Quorn, S. Australia 88/F6
Quorn, S. Australia 94/F5
Quryat, Oman 59/G5
Qusaiba, Saudi Arabia 59/D4
Quteife, Syria 63/G6
Qu Xian, Sichuan, China 77/G5
Qüxü, China 77/D6
Quyon, Québec 172/A4
Quyquyó, Paraguay 144/D5
Quzhou, China 77/J6

R

Raab (riv.), Austria 41/C3
Raabs an der Thaya, Austria 41/C2
Raahe, Finland 18/O4
Raalte, Netherlands 27/J4
Ra'anana, Israel 65/B3
Raanes (pen.), N.W. Terr. 187/K2
Raasay (isl.), Scotland 15/C3
Raasay (sound), Scotland 15/B3
Rab, Yugoslavia 45/B3
Rab (isl.), Yugoslavia 45/B3
Rába (riv.), Hungary 41/D3
Raba, Indonesia 85/F7
Rabat (cap.), Morocco 2/J4
Rabat (cap.), Morocco 106/C2
Rabat (cap.), Morocco 102/B1
Rabaul, Papua N.G. 87/F6
Rabaul, Papua N.G. 86/B2
Rabbit (riv.), Mich. 250/D6
Rabbit (isl.), N.S. Wales 97/J2
Rabbit (creek), S. Dak. 298/E3
Rabbit Ears (peak), Colo. 208/G2
Rabbit Ears (range), Colo. 208/F2
Rabbithash, Ky. 237/M3
Rabbit Lake, Sask. 181/D2
Rabbit Lake, Sask. 181/M2
Rabigh, Saudi Arabia 59/C5
Rabinal, Guatemala 154/B3
Rabka, Poland 47/D4
Rabocheostrovsk, U.S.S.R. 52/D1
Rabun, Ala. 195/C8
Rabun (co.), Georgia 217/F1
Rabun (lake), Georgia 217/E1
Rabun Gap, Georgia 217/F1
Raccoon (pt.), Fla. 212/D3
Raccoon, Ind. 227/D5
Raccoon (riv.), Iowa 229/D4
Raccoon (pt.), La. 238/H8
Raccoon (creek), N.J. 273/C4
Raccoon (creek), Ohio 284/F8
Race (pt.), Mass. 249/N4
Race (cape), Newf. 166/D2
Race (cape.), Newf. 146/N5
Race (cape), Newf. 162/L6
Raceland, Ky. 237/R3
Raceland, La. 238/J7
Racepond, Georgia 217/H8
Rachel, W. Va. 312/F3
Rach Gia, Vietnam 72/E5
Racibórz, Poland 47/C3
Racine, Minn. 255/F7
Racine, Mo. 261/C9
Racine, Ohio 284/G8
Racine, Québec 172/E4
Racine, W. Va. 312/C6
Racine (co.), Wis. 317/K10
Racine, Wis. 188/J2
Racine, Wis. 317/M3
Ráckeve, Hungary 41/E3
Rackham, Manitoba 179/B4
Raco, Mich. 250/E2
Racola, Mo. 261/L6
Radama (isls.), Madagascar 118/H2
Rădăuţi, Romania 45/G2
Radbuza (riv.), Czech. 41/B2
Radcliff, Ky. 237/K5
Radcliff, Ohio 284/F7
Radcliffe, England 13/H2
Radcliffe, Iowa 229/G4
Radeberg, Germany 22/E3
Radebeul, Germany 22/E3
Radenthein, Austria 41/B3
Rader, Tenn. 237/R8
Radersburg, Mont. 262/E4
Radford (I.C.), Va. 307/G6
Radhanpur, India 68/C4
Radiant, Va. 307/M4
Radisson, Québec 174/B2
Radisson, Sask. 181/D3
Radisson, Wis. 317/D4
Radium, Colo. 208/G3
Radium, Kansas 232/D3
Radium, Minn. 255/B2
Radium Hill, S. Australia 88/G6
Radium Hill, S. Australia 94/G5
Radium Hot Springs, Br. Col. 184/J5
Radium Springs, N. Mex. 274/B6
Radkersburg, Austria 41/C3
Radley, Ind. 227/F4
Radnice, Czech. 41/B2
Radnor, Ind. 227/D3
Radnor, Ohio 284/D5
Radnor (for.), Wales 13/D5
Radnor, W. Va. 312/A6
Radolfzell, Germany 22/C5
Radom, Ill. 222/D5
Radom (prov.), Poland 47/E3
Radom, Poland 7/G3
Radom, Poland 47/E3
Radomir, Bulgaria 45/F4
Radomsko, Poland 47/D3
Radoviš, Yugoslavia 45/F5
Radstadt, Austria 41/B3
Radviliškis, U.S.S.R. 53/B3
Radville, Sask. 162/F6
Radville, Sask. 181/G6
Radway, Alberta 182/D2
Radziejów, Poland 47/D2
Radzyń Podlaski, Poland 47/F3
Rae (isth.), N.W.T. 162/H2
Rae (isth.), N.W.T. 187/K3
Rae (riv.), N.W.T. 187/G3
Rae (str.), N.W.T. 187/J3
Rae-Edzo, N.W.T. 162/E3
Rae-Edzo, N.W.T. 187/G3
Raeford, N.C. 281/L5
Rae Lake, N.W.T. 187/G3
Raeren, Belgium 27/J7
Raeside (lake), W. Australia 88/C5
Raeside (lake), W. Australia 92/C5
Raetihi, N. Zealand 100/E3
Raeville, Nebr. 264/F3
Rafaela, Argentina 143/F5
Rafaela, Argentina 120/C6
Rafah, Gaza Strip 65/A5
Rafai, Cent. Afr. Rep. 115/D2
Rafidiya, West Bank 65/C3
Rafsanjan, Iran 59/G3
Rafsanjan, Iran 66/K5
Raft (riv.), Idaho 220/E7
Raft (riv.), Utah 304/A1
Raft River (mts.), Utah 304/A2
Rafz, Switzerland 39/G1
Raga, Sudan 111/E6
Ragan, Nebr. 264/E4
Ragang (vol.), Philippines 82/E7
Ragay (gulf), Philippines 82/D4
Ragged (isl.), Bahamas 156/C2
Ragged (pt.), Barbados 161/C8
Ragged (isl.), Maine 243/F8
Ragged (lake), Maine 243/E4
Ragged (isls.), Newf. 166/C2
Raglan, N. Zealand 100/E2
Raglan (harb.), N. Zealand 100/E2
Ragland, Ala. 195/F3
Ragley, La. 238/D5
Rago, Kansas 232/D4
Ragsdale, Ind. 227/C7
Ragusa (prov.), Italy 34/E6
Ragusa, Italy 34/E6
Ragusa (Dubrovnik), Yugoslavia 45/C4
Raha, Indonesia 85/G6

Roseau 437

Riverton, Nova Scotia 168/F3
Riverton, Oreg. 291/C4
Riverton, Utah 304/B3
Riverton, Vt. 268/B3
Riverton, Va. 307/M3
Riverton, Wash. 310/B2
Riverton, W. Va. 312/H5
Riverton, Wyo. 319/D2
Riverton Heights, Wash. 310/B2
Rivervale, Ark. 202/K2
River Vale•, N.J. 273/B1
River Valley, Ontario 177/D1
Riverview, Ala. 195/D8
Riverview, Fla. 212/D4
Riverview, Mich. 250/B7
Riverview, Mo. 261/R2
Riverview, New Bruns. 170/F2
Riverville, Va. 307/L5
Riverwood, Ky. 237/K1
Riverwoods, Ill. 222/B5
Rives, Mo. 261/M10
Rives, Tenn. 237/C8
Rives Junction, Mich. 250/E6
Rivesville, W. Va. 312/F3
Riviera (reg.), France 28/G6
Riviera, Texas 303/G10
Riviera Beach, Fla. 212/G5
Riviera Beach, Md. 245/N4
Riviera-Bullhead, Ariz. 198/A3
Rivière-à-Claude, Québec 172/C1
Rivière-à-Pierre, Québec 172/E3
Rivière-au-Renard, Québec 172/D1
Rivière-au-Tonnerre, Québec 174/D2
Rivière-Bleue, Québec 172/J2
Rivière-Bois-Clair, Québec 172/F3
Rivière-du-Loup (co.), Québec 172/H2
Rivière-du-Loup, Québec 172/H2
Rivière-du-Loup, Québec 174/D3
Rivière-du-Loup, Québec 172/H2
Rivière-du-Moulin, Québec 172/G1
Rivière-du-Portage, New Bruns. 170/F1
Rivière-Éternité, Québec 172/G1
Rivière-la-Madeleine, Québec 172/C1
Rivière-Matawin, Québec 172/E3
Rivière-Ouelle, Québec 172/G2
Rivière-Pentecôte, Québec 174/D3
Rivière-Pilote, Martinique 161/D7
Rivière-Port-Daniel, Québec 172/D2
Rivière-Portneuf, Québec 172/H1
Rivière-Saint-Paul, Québec 174/F2
Rivière-Salée, Martinique 161/D7
Rivière-Trois-Pistoles, Québec 172/J1
Rivière Verte, New Bruns. 170/B1
Rivière-Verte, Québec 172/H2
Riwaka, N. Zealand 100/D4
Riwoqê, China 77/E5
Rixeyville, Va. 307/M3
Rixford, Pa. 294/F2
Riyadh (cap.), Saudi Arabia 2/M4
Riyadh (cap.), Saudi Arabia 54/F7
Riyadh (cap.), Saudi Arabia 59/E5
Riyan, Yemen 59/E7
Rizal (prov.), Philippines 82/C3
Rize (prov.), Turkey 63/J2
Rize, Turkey 59/D1
Rize, Turkey 63/J2
Rizokarpasso, Cyprus 63/F5
Rjukan, Norway 18/F7
Roa, Norway 18/G6
Roa, Spain 33/E2
Roachdale, Ind. 227/D5
Road (bay), Virgin Is. (U.K.) 161/D3
Roadside, Scotland 15/F4
Roadstown, N.J. 273/C5
Road Town (cap.), Virgin Is. (U.K.) 161/D3
Road Town (cap.), Virgin Is. (U.K.) 156/H1
Roag, Loch (inlet), Scotland 15/B2
Roan (creek), Colo. 208/C4
Roan (plat.), Colo. 208/B3
Roan, Norway 18/G4
Roan (isl.), Scotland 15/D2
Roan (cliffs), Utah 304/E4
Roane (co.), Tenn. 237/M9
Roane (co.), W. Va. 312/D5
Roan Mountain, Tenn. 237/S8
Roann, Ind. 227/F3
Roanne, France 28/E4
Roanoke (riv.) 188/L3
Roanoke, Ala. 195/H4
Roanoke, Ill. 222/D3
Roanoke, Ind. 227/G3
Roanoke, La. 238/E6
Roanoke, Mo. 261/G4
Roanoke (isl.), N.C. 281/T3
Roanoke (riv.), N.C. 281/P2
Roanoke, Texas 303/F1
Roanoke, Va. 146/L6
Roanoke, Va. 188/K3
Roanoke (co.), Va. 307/H6
Roanoke (I.C.), Va. 307/H6
Roanoke (riv.), Va. 307/N8
Roanoke, W. Va. 312/F5
Roanoke Rapids, N.C. 281/O2
Roaring (brook), Conn. 210/F1
Roaring (brook), Conn. 210/E2
Roaring Branch, Pa. 294/J2
Roaring Fork, Colorado (riv.), Colo. 208/E4
Roaring Gap, N.C. 281/H2
Roaring River, N.C. 281/G2
Roaring Spring, Pa. 294/F5
Roaring Springs, Texas 303/D4
Roaringwater (bay), Ireland 17/B9
Roark, Ky. 237/P6
Roatán, Honduras 154/D2
Roatán (isl.), Honduras 154/D2
Roba, Ala. 195/G6
Robards, Ky. 237/F5
Robat Karim, Iran 66/G3
Robb, Alberta 182/B3
Robben (isl.), S. Africa 118/E6
Robbins, Calif. 204/B8
Robbins, Ill. 222/B6
Robbins, N.C. 281/K4
Robbins (isl.), Tasmania 99/B2
Robbins, Tenn. 237/M8
Robbinsdale, Minn. 255/G5
Robbinston, Maine 243/J5
Robbinston•, Maine 243/J5
Robbinsville, N.J. 273/D3
Robbinsville, N.C. 281/B4
Robe (mt.), N.S. Wales 97/A2
Robe, S. Australia 94/F7
Robe, Wash. 310/D2
Robeline, La. 238/D3
Roberdel, N.C. 281/K5
Robersonville, N.C. 281/P3
Robert (isl.), China 85/E2
Robert, La. 238/N1
Robert (harb.), Martinique 161/D6
Roberta, Georgia 217/D5
Roberta, Okla. 288/K7
Robert Lee, Texas 303/D6
Roberto Payán, Colombia 126/A7
Roberts, Idaho 220/F6
Roberts, Ill. 222/E3
Roberts, Mont. 262/G5
Roberts (co.), S. Dak. 298/P2
Roberts (co.), Texas 303/D2
Roberts, Wis. 317/A6
Robert's Arm, Newf. 166/C4
Robertsburg, W. Va. 312/C5
Roberts Creek, Br. Col. 184/J3
Robertsdale, Ala. 195/C9
Robertsdale, Pa. 294/F5
Roberts Field Int'l Airport, Liberia 106/C7
Robertsfors, Sweden 18/M4
Robertsganj, India 68/E4
Robertson (co.), Ky. 237/N3
Robertson, S. Africa 118/C6
Robertson (co.), Tenn. 237/H7
Robertson (co.), Texas 303/H6
Robertson, Wyo. 319/B4
Robertsonville, Québec 172/F3
Robertsport, Liberia 102/A4
Robertsport, Liberia 106/B7
Robertstown, Georgia 217/E1
Robertsville, Conn. 210/C1
Robertsville, Ohio 284/H4
Robertville, New Bruns. 170/E1
Roberval, Québec 162/J6
Roberval, Québec 174/C3
Roberval, Québec 172/E1
Robeson (co.), N.C. 281/L5
Robeson (chan.), N.W. Terr. 187/M1
Robesonia, Pa. 294/K5
Robichaud, New Bruns. 170/F2
Robinhood, Sask. 181/C2
Robins, Iowa 229/K4
Robins, Ohio 284/H6
Robins A.F.B., Georgia 217/F5
Robinson, Ill. 222/F5
Robinson, Iowa 229/K4
Robinson, Kansas 232/G2
Robinson, Ky. 237/N4
Robinson, N. Dak. 282/L5
Robinson (riv.), North. Terr. 93/E4
Robinson, Pa. 294/D5
Robinson (lake), S.C. 296/G3
Robinson (ranges), W. Australia 92/B4
Robinson Creek, Ky. 237/S6
Robinson Crusoe (isl.), Chile 120/B6
Robinson River, North. Terr. 93/E4
Robinsons, Maine 243/H3
Robinsonville, Miss. 256/D1
Robinsonville, New Bruns. 170/C1
Robinvale, Victoria 97/B4
Robles, Colombia 126/D2
Roblin, Manitoba 179/A3
Roblin, Ontario 177/G3
Roboré, Bolivia 136/F6
Roboré, Bolivia 120/D4
Rob Roy, Ind. 227/C4
Robsart, Sask. 181/B6
Robson, Br. Col. 184/J5
Robson (mt.), Br. Col. 162/D5
Robson (mt.), Br. Col. 184/H3
Robstown, Texas 303/G10
Roby, Mo. 261/H7
Roby, Texas 303/D5
Roca, Nebr. 264/H4
Roca (cape), Portugal 33/B3
Rocafuerte, Ecuador 128/B3
Rocanville, Sask. 181/K5
Roca Partida (isl.), Mexico 150/C7
Roca que Vela (cay), Colombia 126/B8
Rocas (isl.), Brazil 120/F3
Rocas de Santo Domingo, Chile 138/F4
Roccastrada, Italy 34/C3
Rocha (dept.), Uruguay 145/E4
Rocha, Uruguay 145/E5
Rocha (lag.), Uruguay 145/E5
Rochdale, England 13/H2
Rochdale, England 10/G2
Rochdale, Mass. 249/G4
Roche, Switzerland 39/C4
Rochechouart, France 28/D5
Rochefort, Belgium 27/G8
Rochefort, France 28/C4
Roche Harbor, Wash. 310/B2
Rochelle, Georgia 217/F7
Rochelle, Ill. 222/D2
Rochelle, Texas 303/E6
Rochelle, Wyo. 319/H2
Rochelle Park•, N.J. 273/B2
Roche Percé, Sask. 181/J6
Rocheport, Mo. 261/H5
Rocher River, N.W.T. 162/E3
Rocher River, N.W.T. 187/G3
Rochert, Minn. 255/C4
Rochester, Alberta 182/D2
Rochester, England 13/J8
Rochester, England 10/G5
Rochester, Ill. 222/D4
Rochester, Ind. 227/E2
Rochester, Iowa 229/L5
Rochester, Ky. 237/H6
Rochester•, Mass. 249/L6
Rochester, Mich. 250/F6
Rochester, Minn. 188/H2
Rochester, Minn. 255/F6
Rochester, N.H. 268/E5
Rochester, N.Y. 188/L2
Rochester, N.Y. 146/L5
Rochester, N.Y. 276/E4
Rochester, Ohio 284/F3
Rochester, Pa. 294/B4
Rochester, Texas 303/E4
Rochester•, Vt. 268/B4
Rochester, Victoria 97/C5
Rochester, Wash. 310/C4
Rochester, Wis. 317/K3
Rochester Mills, Pa. 294/D4
Rochford, S. Dak. 298/B5
Rochfort Bridge, Alberta 182/C3
Rochon Sands, Alberta 182/D3
Rociada, N. Mex. 274/D3
Rock (creek), Idaho 220/F7
Rock (creek), Ill. 222/D2
Rock (riv.), Ill. 222/C2
Rock (riv.), Iowa 229/A2
Rock, Kansas 232/F4
Rock (lake), Manitoba 179/C5
Rock (creek), Md. 245/K4
Rock, Mass. 249/L5
Rock, Mich. 250/B2
Rock (co.), Minn. 255/B7
Rock (riv.), Minn. 255/B7
Rock (creek), Mont. 262/C4
Rock (co.), Nebr. 264/E2
Rock (creek), Nev. 266/E2
Rock (creek), Oreg. 291/E4
Rock (creek), Oreg. 291/G2
Rock (creek), Oreg. 291/H3
Rock (creek), S. Dak. 298/O6
Rock (creek), Wash. 310/H3
Rock (lake), Wash. 310/H3
Rock (co.), Wis. 317/H10
Rock (riv.), Wis. 317/J9
Rockall (isl.), Scotland 7/C3
Rockaway, N.J. 273/D2
Rockaway, Oreg. 291/C2
Rockaway Beach, Mo. 261/F9
Rock Bluff, Fla. 212/B1
Rockbridge, Ill. 222/C4
Rockbridge, Mo. 261/H9
Rockbridge, Ohio 284/E6
Rockbridge (co.), Va. 307/K5
Rockbridge, Wis. 317/F9
Rockcastle (co.), Ky. 237/N6
Rockcastle (riv.), Ky. 237/N6
Rock Castle, W. Va. 312/C5
Rock Cave, W. Va. 312/F5
Rock City, Ill. 222/D1
Rockcliffe Park, Ontario 177/J2
Rockcorry, Ireland 17/H3
Rock Creek, Br. Col. 184/H6
Rock Creek, Kansas 232/G2
Rock Creek, Minn. 255/F5
Rock Creek, Ohio 284/J2
Rock Creek, Yukon 187/E3
Rockdale (co.), Georgia 217/D3
Rockdale, Ill. 222/E2
Rockdale, N. S. Wales 88/K4
Rockdale, N.S. Wales 97/J4
Rockdale, Texas 303/G7
Rockdale, Wis. 317/J10
Rock Dell, Minn. 255/F7
Rockerville, S. Dak. 298/C6
Rockfall, Conn. 210/E2
Rock Falls, Ill. 222/D2
Rock Falls, Iowa 229/G2
Rock Falls, Wis. 317/C6
Rockfield, Ind. 227/D3
Rockfield, Ky. 237/J7
Rockfield, Wis. 317/L1
Rockfish, N.C. 281/L5
Rockford, Ala. 195/F5
Rockford, Idaho 220/F6
Rockford, Ill. 146/K5
Rockford, Ill. 188/J2
Rockford, Ill. 222/D1
Rockford, Iowa 229/H2
Rockford, Mich. 250/D5
Rockford, Minn. 255/F5
Rockford, N.C. 281/H2
Rockford, Ohio 284/A4
Rockford, Sask. 181/J3
Rockford, Tenn. 237/O9
Rockford, Wash. 310/H3
Rock Forest, Québec 172/F4
Rock Glen, Pa. 294/K4
Rockglen, Sask. 181/F6
Rock Grove, Ill. 222/D1
Rock Hall, Md. 245/O4
Rockham, S. Dak. 298/M4
Rockhampton, Australia 2/S7
Rockhampton, Australia 87/F8
Rockhampton, Queensland 88/H4
Rockhampton, Queensland 95/D4
Rockhampton Downs, North. Terr. 93/D5
Rockhaven, Sask. 181/B3
Rock Hill, Mo. 261/P3
Rock Hill, S.C. 188/K4
Rock Hill, S.C. 296/E2
Rockholds, Ky. 237/N7
Rockingham, Georgia 217/H7
Rockingham (co.), N.H. 268/E5
Rockingham (co.), N.C. 281 208/H2
Rocky Point, N.C. 281/O6
Rocky Point, Wash. 310/A2
Rockypoint, Wyo. 319/G1
Rocky Rapids, Alberta 182/C3
Rocky Reach (dam), Wash. 310/E3
Rocky Ridge (mt.), Idaho 220/C3
Rocky Ridge, Ohio 284/D2
Rocky River, Ohio 284/G9
Rodanthe, N.C. 281/U3
Rodarte, N. Mex. 274/D2
Rodas, Cuba 158/E2
Rødby, Denmark 21/E8
Rødby, Denmark 18/G9
Roddickton, Newf. 166/C3
Rødding, Denmark 21/B7
Roddy, Tenn. 237/M9
Rødekro, Denmark 21/C7
Roden, Netherlands 27/J2
Rodeo, Calif. 204/J1
Rodeo, Mexico 150/G4
Rodeo, N. Mex. 274/A7
Roderfield, W. Va. 312/C8
Roderick (isl.), Br. Col. 184/C4
Rodessa, La. 238/B1
Rodez, France 28/E5
Ródhos, Greece 45/J7
Roding (riv.), England 13/J7
Rodinga, North. Terr. 93/D8
Rødkaersbro, Denmark 21/C5
Rodman, Iowa 229/D2
Rodman, N.Y. 276/J3
Rodman, S.C. 296/E2
Rodney, Iowa 229/A4
Rodney, Mich. 250/D5
Rodney, Miss. 256/B7
Rodney, Ontario 177/C5
Rodney Village, Del. 245/R4
Rodrigues, Brazil 132/F10
Rodríguez, Uruguay 145/C5
Rødvig, Denmark 21/F7
Roe, Ark. 202/H4
Roe (riv.), N. Ireland 17/H1
Roebling-Florence, N.J. 273/D3
Roebourne, W. Australia 88/B4
Roebourne, W. Australia 92/B3
Roebuck (bay), W. Australia 88/C3
Roebuck (bay), W. Australia 92/C2
Roebuck Plains, W. Australia 92/C2
Roeland Park, Kansas 232/H2
Roer (riv.), Netherlands 27/J6
Roermond, Netherlands 27/J6
Roeselare, Belgium 27/C7
Roes Welcome (sound), N.W.T. 162/H2
Roes Welcome (sound), N.W.T. 187/K3
Roff, Okla. 288/N5
Rogachev, U.S.S.R. 52/D4
Rogagua (lake), Bolivia 136/B3
Rogaguado (lake), Bolivia 136/C3
Rogaland (co.), Norway 18/E7
Rogatica, Yugoslavia 45/D4
Roger Mills (co.), Okla. 288/G3
Rogers, Ark. 202/B1
Rogers, Br. Col. 184/J4
Rogers (lake), Calif. 204/H9
Rogers, Conn. 210/H1
Rogers (lake), Conn. 210/F3
Rogers, La. 238/F3
Rogers, Minn. 255/E5
Rogers, Nebr. 264/H3
Rogers, N. Mex. 274/F5
Rogers, N. Dak. 282/O5
Rogers, Ohio 284/J4
Rogers (co.), Okla. 288/P2
Rogers, Texas 303/G7
Rogers (mt.), Va. 307/E7
Rogers City, Mich. 250/F3
Rogerson, Idaho 220/D7
Rogers Springs, Tenn. 237/D10
Rogersville, Ala. 195/D1
Rogersville, Mo. 261/G8
Rogersville, New Bruns. 170/E2
Rogersville, Pa. 294/B6
Rogersville, Tenn. 237/P8
Roger Williams Nat'l Mem., R.I. 249/J5
Roggen, Colo. 208/L2
Roggwil, Switzerland 39/E2
Rogliano, France 28/B6
Rogozno, Poland 47/C2
Rogue (riv.), Oreg. 291/C5
Rogue River, Oreg. 291/D5
Roha, India 68/C5
Rohnert Park, Calif. 204/C5
Rohnerville, Calif. 204/B3
Rohrbach in Oberösterreich, Austria 41/B2
Rohrersville, Md. 245/H3
Rohri, Pakistan 68/B3
Rohtak, India 68/C5
Rohwer, Ark. 202/H6
Roi Et, Thailand 72/D4
Roja, U.S.S.R. 53/B2
Rojas, Argentina 143/F7
Rojo (cape), Mexico 150/L6
Rojo (cape), P. Rico 161/A3
Rojo (cape), P. Rico 156/F1
Rokan (riv.), Indonesia 85/C5
Rokeby, Sask. 181/J4
Rokiškis, U.S.S.R. 53/C2
Rokycany, Czech. 41/B2
Rokytnice nad Jizerou, Czech. 41/C1
Rola Co (lake), China 77/C4
Roland, Ark. 202/E4
Roland, Iowa 229/F4
Roland, Manitoba 179/D5
Roland, Okla. 288/S4
Røldal, Norway 18/E7
Roldán, Argentina 143/F6
Rolecha, Chile 138/D4
Rolesville, N.C. 281/N3
Rolette (co.), N. Dak. 282/L2
Rolette, N. Dak. 282/L2
Roleystone, W. Australia 88/B2
Rolfe, Iowa 229/D3
Roll, Ariz. 198/A6
Rolla, Ark. 202/E5
Rolla, Br. Col. 184/G2
Rolla, Kansas 232/A4
Rolla, Mo. 261/J7
Rolla, N. Dak. 282/L2
Rollag, Minn. 255/B4
Rolle, Switzerland 39/B4
Rollingbay, Wash. 310/A2
Rollingdam, New Bruns. 170/C3
Rolling Fields, Ky. 237/K2
Rolling Fork (riv.), Ky. 237/L5
Rolling Fork, Miss. 256/C5
Rolling Hills, Alberta 182/E4
Rolling Hills, Calif. 204/B11
Rolling Hills, Ky. 237/L1
Rolling Hills Estates, Calif. 204/B11
Rolling Meadows, Ill. 222/A5
Rolling Prairie, Ind. 227/D1
Rollingstone, Minn. 255/G6
Rollins, Mont. 262/B3
Rollo (bay), Pr. Edward I. 168/F2
Rolphton, Ontario 177/G1
Roma, Australia 87/E8
Roma (Rome) (cap.), Italy 34/F6
Roma, Queensland 88/H5
Roma, Queensland 95/D5
Roma, Sweden 18/L8
Romain (cape), S.C. 296/J6
Romaine (riv.), Newf. 166/B3
Romaine (riv.), Que. 162/K5
Romaine, Québec 174/E2
Romaine (riv.), Québec 174/E2
Roma-Los Saenz, Texas 303/E11
Roman, Romania 45/H2
Romance, Ark. 202/F3
Romance, Sask. 181/G3
Romance, W. Va. 312/C5
Romang, Argentina 143/F4
Romang (isl.), Indonesia 85/H7
Romania 2/L3
Romania 7/G4
ROMANIA 45/F3
Romano (cay), Cuba 158/G2
Romano (cay), Cuba 156/C2
Romano (cape), Fla. 212/E6
Romanshorn, Switzerland 39/H1
Romans-sur-Isère, France 28/F5
Romanzof (cape), Alaska 196/E2
Rombauer, Mo. 261/M9
Romblon (prov.), Philippines 82/D4
Romblon, Philippines 82/D4
Romblon (isl.), Philippines 82/D4
Rome, Ga. 188/K4
Rome, Georgia 217/B2
Rome, Ill. 222/D3
Rome, Ind. 227/D9
Rome, Iowa 229/K7
Rome (prov.), Italy 34/F6
Rome (cap.), Italy 7/F4
Rome (cap.), Italy 34/F6
Rome (cap.), Italy 2/K3
Rome•, Maine 243/D6
Rome, Miss. 256/C3
Rome, N.Y. 188/M2
Rome, N.Y. 276/J4
Rome (Stout), Ohio 284/D8
Rome, Ohio 284/J2
Rome, Oreg. 291/K5
Rome, Pa. 294/K2
Rome, Wis. 317/H1
Rome City, Ind. 227/G1
Romeo, Colo. 208/G8
Romeo, Mich. 250/F6
Romeoville, Ill. 222/B6
Romeroville, N. Mex. 274/D3
Romeville, La. 238/L3
Romilly-sur-Seine, France 28/F3
Romney, Ind. 227/D4
Romney, W. Va. 312/J4
Romny, U.S.S.R. 52/D4
Rømø, Denmark 21/B7
Rømø (isl.), Denmark 21/B7
Rømø (isl.), Denmark 18/F9
Romont, Switzerland 39/C3
Romorantin-Lanthenay, France 28/D4
Romsdalsfjorden (fjord), Norway 18/E5
Romsey, England 10/F5
Romsey, England 13/F6
Romulus, Mich. 250/F6
Romulus, N.Y. 276/G5
Ron, Vietnam 72/E3
Ron, Mui (cape), Vietnam 72/E3
Rona (isl.), Scotland 15/B3
Ronald, Wash. 310/E3
Ronan, Mont. 262/C3
Ronay (isl.), Scotland 15/A3
Roncador, Serra do (range), Brazil 132/D5
Roncador (cays), Colombia 126/B9
Ronceverte, W. Va. 312/F7
Ronciglione, Italy 34/C3
Ronda, N.C. 281/H2
Ronda, Spain 33/D4
Rønde, Denmark 21/D5
Ronde (isl.), Grenada 161/D7
Rondeau Prov. Park, Ontario 177/C5
Rondo, Ark. 202/J4
Rondônia (state), Brazil 132/H10
Rondônia, Brazil 132/H10
Rondonópolis, Brazil 120/D4
Rondout (res.), N.Y. 276/M7
Rondu, Pakistan 68/D1
Rong, Koh (isl.), Cambodia 72/D5
Rong'an, China 77/G6
Ronge, Lac La (lake), Sask. 162/F4
Ronge, La (lake), Sask. 181/M3
Rongelap (atoll), Marshall Is. 87/G4
Rongjiang, China 77/G6
Rong Kwang, Thailand 72/D3
Rong Xian, China 77/H7
Ronju (mt.), Fr. Poly. 86/T13
Ronkonkoma, N.Y. 276/O9
Rønne, Denmark 21/F9
Rønne, Denmark 18/J9
Ronneby, Minn. 255/E5
Ronneby, Sweden 18/J8
Ronne Entrance (inlet), Ant. 5/B15
Ronne Ice Shelf, Ant. 2/F10
Ronne Ice Shelf, Ant. 5/B15
Ronse, Belgium 27/D7
Ronuro (riv.), Brazil 132/C6
Roodeport, S. Africa 118/H6
Roodhouse, Ill. 222/C4
Roof Butte (mt.), Ariz. 198/F2
Rooi, Neth. Ant. 161/E8
Rooks (co.), Kansas 232/C2
Roopville, Georgia 217/B4
Roosendaal, Netherlands 27/F5
Roosevelt (isl.), Ant. 2/A10
Roosevelt (isl.), Ant. 5/A10
Roosevelt (res.), Ariz. 188/D4
Roosevelt, Ariz. 198/D5
Roosevelt (riv.), Brazil 120/C3
Roosevelt (riv.), Brazil 132/A5
Roosevelt, La. 238/H1
Roosevelt, Minn. 255/C2
Roosevelt (co.), Mont. 262/L2
Roosevelt, N.J. 273/E3
Roosevelt (co.), N. Mex. 274/F4
Roosevelt, N.Y. 276/R7
Roosevelt, Okla. 288/J5
Roosevelt, Texas 303/D7
Roosevelt, Utah 304/D3
Roosevelt, Wash. 310/E5
Roosevelt Campobello Int'l Park, New Bruns. 170/D4
Roosevelt City, Ala. 195/E4
Roosevelt Park, Mich. 250/C5
Roosevelt Road Naval Res., P. Rico 161/F2
Roosville, Br. Col. 184/K5
Root (riv.), Minn. 255/G7
Rootstown, Ohio 284/H3
Roper, N.C. 281/R3
Roper (riv.), North. Terr. 88/E3
Roper (riv.), North. Terr. 93/C3
Roper River, North. Terr. 93/D3
Roper River Mission, North. Terr. 88/E2
Roper Valley, North. Terr. 93/D3
Ropesville, Texas 303/B4
Roque Bluffs•, Maine 243/H6
Roque González de Santa Cruz, Paraguay 144/B5
Roque Pérez, Argentina 143/G7
Roquetas, Spain 33/G2
Rora (head), Scotland 15/E2
Roraima (mt.) 120/C2
Roraima (terr.), Brazil 132/H8
Roraima (mt.), Guyana 131/A3
Roraima (mt.), Venezuela 124/H5
Rørby, Denmark 21/E6
Rorketon, Manitoba 179/C3
Røros, Norway 18/G5
Rorschach, Switzerland 39/H2
Rosa, Ala. 195/E3
Rosa (cape), Ecuador 128/B10
Rosa (mt.), Italy 34/A1
Rosa, La. 238/G5
Rosa, Manitoba 179/F5
Rosa (mt.), Switzerland 39/E5
Rosaire, Québec 172/G3
Rosaireville, New Bruns. 170/E2
Rosalia, Kansas 232/F4
Rosalia, Wash. 310/H3
Rosalie, Dominica 161/F6
Rosalie, Nebr. 264/H2
Rosalina, Paraguay 144/D3
Rosalind, Alberta 182/D3
Rosamond, Calif. 204/G9
Rosamond (lake), Calif. 204/G9
Rosamond, Ill. 222/D4
Rosamorada, Mexico 150/G5
Rosapenna, Ireland 17/F1
Rosario, Argentina 143/F6
Rosario, Argentina 120/C6
Rosário, Brazil 132/F3
Rosario, Chile 138/F5
Rosario (cay), Cuba 158/C2
Rosario, Sinaloa, Mexico 150/G5
Rosario, Sonora, Mexico 150/E3
Rosario, Paraguay 144/D4
Rosario, P. Rico 161/A2
Rosario, Uruguay 145/B5
Rosario, Venezuela 124/B2
Rosario (str.), Wash. 310/C2
Rosario de la Frontera, Argentina 143/D2
Rosario de Lerma, Argentina 143/C1
Rosario del Tala, Argentina 143/G6
Rosário do Sul, Brazil 132/C10
Rosário Oeste, Brazil 132/C6
Rosas, Spain 33/H1
Rosas (gulf), Spain 33/H1
Rosati, Mo. 261/J6
Rosa Zárate, Ecuador 128/C2
Rosburg, Wash. 310/B4
Rosbys Rock, W. Va. 312/E3
Roscoe, Ill. 222/D1
Roscoe, Minn. 255/D5
Roscoe, Mo. 261/E7
Roscoe, Mont. 262/G5
Roscoe, Nebr. 264/C3
Roscoe, N.Y. 276/L7
Roscoe, Pa. 294/C5
Roscoe, S. Dak. 298/L3
Roscoe, Texas 303/D5
Roscoff, France 28/A3
Roscommon (co.), Ireland 17/E4
Roscommon, Ireland 10/B4
Roscommon, Ireland 17/E4
Roscommon (co.), Mich. 250/E4
Roscommon, Mich. 250/E4
Roscrea, Ireland 10/B4
Roscrea, Ireland 17/F6
Rose (peak), Ariz. 198/F5
Rose (pt.), Br. Col. 184/B3
Rose (pt.), Martinique 161/D6
Rose, Nebr. 264/E2
Rose, N.Y. 276/G4
Rose (riv.), North. Terr. 93/D2
Rose, Okla. 288/R2
Roseau (cap.), Dominica 156/G4
Roseau (cap.), Dominica 161/E7
Roseau (riv.), Dominica 161/E7
Roseau (co.), Minn. 255/C2
Roseau, Minn. 255/C2
Roseau (riv.), Minn. 255/B2

440 Saint Charles

Saint Charles, Va. 307/B7
Saint-Charles-de-Mandeville, Québec 172/D3
Saint-Charles-Garnier, Québec 172/J1
Saint-Charles-sur-Richelieu, Québec 172/D4
Saint Christopher (Saint Kitts) (isl.), St. Kitts & Nevis 156/F3
Saint Christopher (Saint Kitts) (isl.), St. Kitts & Nevis 161/D10
Saint Chrysostom, Pr. Edward I. 168/E2
Saint-Chrysostome, Québec 172/D4
Saint Clair (co.), Ala. 195/F3
Saint Clair, Ala. 195/E6
Saint Clair, Georgia 217/H4
Saint Clair (co.), Ill. 222/D5
Saint Clair (lake), Mich. 188/K2
Saint Clair (co.), Mich. 250/G6
Saint Clair, Mich. 250/G6
Saint Clair (lake), Mich. 250/G6
Saint Clair (riv.), Mich. 250/G6
Saint Clair, Minn. 255/E6
Saint Clair (co.), Mo. 261/E6
Saint Clair, Mo. 261/K6
Saint Clair (lake), Ontario 177/B5
Saint Clair (riv.), Ontario 177/B5
Saint Clair, Pa. 294/K4
Saint Clair (lake), Tasmania 99/C4
Saint Clair Beach, Ontario 177/B5
Saint Clair Shores, Mich. 250/B6
Saint Clair Springs, Ala. 195/F3
Saint Clairsville, Ohio 284/J5
Saint Clairsville, Pa. 294/F5
Saint-Claude, France 28/F4
Saint-Claude, Guadeloupe 161/A7
Saint Claude, Manitoba 179/D5
Saint-Claude, Québec 172/F4
Saint Clears, Wales 13/C6
Saint-Clément, Québec 172/H2
Saint Clements, Ontario 177/D4
Saint-Cléophas, Québec 172/D3
Saint-Clet, Québec 172/C4
Saint Cloud, Fla. 212/E3
Saint-Cloud, France 28/A2
Saint Cloud, Minn. 188/H1
Saint Cloud, Minn. 255/D5
Saint Cloud, Wis. 317/K8
Saint Columb Major, England 13/B7
Saint Combs, Scotland 15/G3
Saint-Côme, Québec 172/D3
Saint-Constant, Québec 172/H4
Saint Croix (riv.) 188/H1
Saint Croix, Ind. 227/D8
Saint Croix (riv.), Maine 243/J5
Saint Croix (riv.), Minn. 255/F5
Saint Croix, New Bruns. 170/C3
Saint Croix (riv.), New Bruns. 170/C3
Saint Croix, Nova Scotia 168/E4
Saint Croix (isl.), Virgin Is. (U.S.) 156/H2
Saint Croix (isl.), Virgin Is. (U.S.) 161/G4
Saint Croix (co.), Wis. 317/B5
Saint Croix (lake), Wis. 317/A6
Saint Croix (riv.), Wis. 317/A4
Saint Croix Falls, Wis. 317/A5
Saint Croix Flowage (res.), Wis. 317/C3
Saint Croix Isl. Nat'l Mon., Maine 243/J5
Saint-Cuthbert, Québec 172/D3
Saint-Cyprien, Québec 172/H2
Saint-Cyrille, Québec 172/E4
Saint-Cyrille-de-L'Islet, Québec 172/G3
Saint Cyrus, Scotland 15/F4
Saint-Damase, Québec 172/B1
Saint-Damase-des-Aulnaies, Québec 172/C2
Saint-Damien-de-Brandon, Québec 172/D3
Saint-Damien-de-Buckland, Québec 172/G3
Saint David, Ariz. 198/E7
Saint David, Ill. 222/C3
Saint David, Maine 243/G1
Saint-David, Québec 172/J3
Saint-David-de-Falardeau, Québec 172/F1
Saint-David-d'Yamaska, Québec 172/E4
Saint Davids (isl.), Bermuda 156/H2
Saint David's, Wales 13/B6
Saint David's (head), Wales 10/D5
Saint David's (head), Wales 13/B6
Saint-Denis, France 28/B1
Saint-Denis, Québec 172/D4
Saint-Denis (cap.), Réunion 118/F5
Saint Denis, Sask. 181/F3
Saint-Denis-de-la-Bouteillerie, Québec 172/G2
Saint-Didace, Québec 172/D3
Saint-Dié, France 28/G3
Saint-Dizier, France 28/F3
Saint-Dominique, Québec 172/E4
Saint-Donat-de-Montcalm, Québec 172/C3
Saint-Donat-de-Rimouski, Québec 172/J1
Saint Donatus, Iowa 229/M4
Sainte-Adèle, Québec 172/C4
Sainte Agathe, Manitoba 179/E5
Sainte-Agathe, Québec 172/F3
Sainte-Agathe-des-Monts, Québec 172/C3
Sainte-Agnès-de-Charlevoix, Québec 172/G2
Sainte Amélie, Manitoba 179/C4
Sainte-Anastasie, Québec 172/F3
Sainte-Angèle-de-Mérici, Québec 172/J1
Sainte Anne (lake), Alberta 182/C3
Sainte-Anne, Guadeloupe 161/B6
Sainte Anne, Manitoba 179/F5
Sainte-Anne, Martinique 161/D7
Sainte-Anne, New Bruns. 170/E1
Sainte-Anne (lake), Québec 172/H2
Sainte-Anne (riv.), Québec 172/C1
Sainte-Anne (riv.), Québec 172/G2
Sainte-Anne (riv.), Québec 172/F3
Sainte Anne (isl.), Seychelles 118/H5
Sainte-Anne-de-Beaupré, Québec 172/F2
Sainte-Anne-de-Bellevue, Québec 172/H4
Sainte-Anne-de-Kent, New Bruns. 170/F2
Sainte-Anne-de-Madawaska, New Bruns. 170/B1
Sainte-Anne-des-Monts, Québec 172/C1
Sainte-Anne-des-Plaines, Québec 172/H4
Sainte-Anne-du-Lac, Québec 172/B3
Sainte-Apolline, Québec 172/G3
Sainte-Aurélie, Québec 172/G3
Sainte-Béatrix, Québec 172/D3
Sainte-Bernadette, Québec 172/G1
Sainte-Blandine, Québec 172/J1
Sainte-Brigide, Québec 172/D4
Sainte-Catherine, Québec 172/F3
Sainte-Cécile-de-Frontenac, Québec 172/G4
Sainte-Cécile-de-Masham, Québec 172/A4
Sainte-Claire, Québec 172/G3
Sainte-Clothilde-de-Horton, Québec 172/E4
Sainte-Croix, Québec 172/F3
Sainte-Croix, Switzerland 39/B3
Saint-Édouard-de-Kent, New Bruns. 170/F2
Saint-Édouard-de-Maskinongé, Québec 172/D3
Saint-Édouard-de-Napierville, Québec 172/D4
Saint Edward, Nebr. 264/G3
Saint Edward, Pr. Edward I. 168/D2
Sainte-Edwidge, Québec 172/F4
Sainte-Élisabeth, Québec 172/D3
Sainte-Émélie-de-l'Énergie, Québec 172/D3
Sainte-Eulalie, Québec 172/E3
Sainte-Euphémie, Québec 172/G3
Sainte-Famille-d'Aumond, Québec 172/B3
Sainte-Famille-d'Orléans, Québec 172/G3
Sainte-Félicité, Québec 172/B1
Sainte-Flavie, Québec 172/J1
Sainte-Florence, Québec 172/B2
Sainte-Foy, Québec 172/H3
Sainte-Françoise, Québec 172/H1
Sainte-Geneviève, Manitoba 179/F5
Sainte Genevieve (co.), Mo. 261/M7
Sainte Genevieve, Mo. 261/M6
Sainte-Geneviève, Québec 172/H4
Sainte-Geneviève-de-Batiscan, Québec 172/E3
Sainte-Hedwidge-de-Roberval, Québec 172/E1
Sainte-Hélène-de-Bagot, Québec 172/E4
Sainte-Hélène-de-Kamouraska, Québec 172/H2
Sainte-Hénédine, Québec 172/F3
Sainte-Julie-de-Verchères, Québec 172/J4
Sainte-Julienne, Québec 172/D4
Sainte-Julie-Station, Québec 172/F3
Sainte-Justine, Québec 172/G3
Sainte-Justine-de-Newton, Québec 172/C4
Saint Eleanors, Pr. Edward I. 168/E2
Saint-Éleuthère, Québec 172/H2
Saint Elias (cape), Alaska 196/K3
Saint Elias (mt.), Alaska 188/D5
Saint Elias (mt.), Alaska 196/K2
Saint Elias (mts.), Alaska 196/L2
Saint Elias (mt.), Yukon 162/B3
Saint Elias (mt.), Yukon 187/D3
Saint Elias (mts.), Yukon 187/E3
Saint-Élie, Fr. Guiana 131/E3
Saint-Élie, Québec 172/E3
Saint Elizabeth, Mo. 261/H6
Saint Elmo, Ala. 195/B10
Saint Elmo, Colo. 208/G5
Saint Elmo, Ill. 222/E4
Saint-Éloi, Québec 172/H1
Sainte-Louise, Québec 172/G2
Sainte-Luce, Martinique 161/D7
Sainte-Luce, Québec 172/J1
Sainte-Lucie-de-Beauregard, Québec 172/H3
Sainte-Lucie-de-Doncaster, Québec 172/C3
Saint-Elzéar, Québec 172/F3
Saint-Elzéar-de-Bonaventure, Québec 172/C2
Sainte-Marguerite, Guadeloupe 161/B6
Sainte-Marguerite-de-Dorchester, Québec 172/G3
Sainte-Marguerite-Marie, Québec 172/B2
Sainte-Marguerite (riv.), Québec 172/G1
Sainte-Marguerite (riv.), Québec 174/D2
Sainte-Marguerite Nord-Est (riv.), Québec 172/H1
Sainte-Marie, Guadeloupe 161/A6
Sainte Marie, Ill. 222/E5
Sainte-Marie (cape), Madagascar 2/M4
Sainte-Marie (Vohimena) (cape), Madagascar 118/G5
Sainte-Marie (Nosy Boraha) (isl.), Madagascar 118/J3
Sainte-Marie, Martinique 161/D5
Sainte-Marie, Beauce, Québec 172/G3
Sainte-Marie, Nicolet, Québec 172/E3
Sainte-Marie (lake), Québec 172/B4
Sainte-Marie-de-Kent, New Bruns. 170/F2
Sainte-Marie-sur-Mer, New Bruns. 170/F1
Sainte-Marthe-de-Gaspé, Québec 172/C1
Sainte-Martine, Québec 172/D4
Sainte-Menehould, France 28/F3
Sainte-Mère-Église, France 28/C3
Saint-Émile, Québec 172/H3
Saint-Émile-de-Suffolk, Québec 172/B4
Sainte-Monique, Nicolet, Québec 172/E3
Sainte-Monique, Lac-St-Jean-E., Québec 172/F1
Sainte-Ode, Belgium 27/H8
Sainte-Perpétue, Québec 172/E3
Sainte-Perpétue-de-L'Islet, Québec 172/H2
Saint-Éphrem-de-Tring, Québec 172/G3
Saint-Épiphane, Québec 172/H2
Sainte-Pudentienne, Québec 172/E4
Sainte Rita, Manitoba 179/F5
Sainte-Rosalie, Québec 172/E4
Sainte-Rose, Guadeloupe 161/A6
Sainte-Rose-de-Watford, Québec 172/G3
Sainte Rose du Lac, Manitoba 179/C3
Sainte-Rose-du-Nord, Québec 172/G1
Sainte-Rose-Gloucester, New Bruns. 170/F1
Saintes, France 28/C5
Saintes (chan.), Guadeloupe 161/A7
Saintes (isls.), Guadeloupe 161/A7
Sainte-Sabine-de-Bellechasse, Québec 172/G3
Sainte-Savine, France 28/E3
Sainte-Sophie-de-Lévrard, Québec 172/E3
Sainte-Sophie-de-Mégantic, Québec 172/F3
Saint-Esprit, Québec 172/D4
Sainte-Thècle, Québec 172/E3
Sainte-Thérèse, Québec 172/H4
Sainte-Thérèse (isl.), Québec 172/J4
Sainte-Thérèse-de-L'Enfant-Jésus, Québec 172/D2
Sainte-Thérèse-Ouest, Québec 172/H4
Saint-Étienne, France 7/E4
Saint-Étienne, France 28/F5
Saint-Étienne-de-Grès, Québec 172/E3
Saint-Étienne-de-Lauzon, Québec 172/J3
Saint-Eugène, Ontario 177/K2
Saint-Eugène-de-Grantham, Québec 172/E4
Sainte-Ursule, Québec 172/D3
Saint-Eusèbe, Québec 172/J2
Saint Eustache, Manitoba 179/E5
Saint-Eustache, Québec 172/H4
Saint Eustatius (isl.), Neth. Ant. 156/F3
Saint-Évariste-de-Forsyth, Québec 172/F4
Sainte-Véronique, Québec 172/C3
Sainte-Victoire, Québec 172/D4
Saint-Fabien, Québec 172/J1
Saint-Fabien-de-Panet, Québec 172/G3
Saint-Félicien, Québec 172/E1
Saint-Félicien, Québec 174/C3
Saint-Félix-de-Valois, Québec 172/D3
Saint Fergus, Scotland 15/G3
Saint-Fidèle, Québec 172/H2
Saintfield, N. Ireland 17/K3
Saint Finan's (bay), Ireland 17/A8
Saint-Flavien, Québec 172/F3
Saint-Florent (gulf), France 28/B6
Saint-Florent-sur-Cher, France 28/E4
Saint Florian, Ala. 195/C1
Saint-Flour, France 28/E5
Saint-Fortunat, Québec 172/F4
Saint Francis (co.), Ark. 202/J3
Saint Francis, Ark. 202/K1
Saint Francis (riv.), Ark. 202/J4
Saint Francis, Kansas 232/A2
Saint Francis, Ky. 237/L5
Saint Francis•, Maine 243/E1
Saint Francis (riv.), Maine 243/E1
Saint Francis, Minn. 255/E5
Saint Francis (riv.), Mo. 261/M9
Saint Francis (riv.), New Bruns. 170/A1
Saint Francis (cape), Newf. 166/D2
Saint Francis (bay), S. Africa 118/D6
Saint Francis, S. Dak. 298/H7
Saint Francis, Wis. 317/M2
Saint Francis Harbour, Nova Scotia 168/G3
Saint Francisville, Ill. 222/F5
Saint Francisville, La. 238/H5
Saint Francisville, Mo. 261/J2
Saint-François, Guadeloupe 161/B6
Saint François (co.), Mo. 261/M7
Saint François (mts.), Mo. 261/L7
Saint-François (lake), Québec 172/F4
Saint-François (riv.), Québec 172/E4
Saint-François-d'Assise, Québec 172/G1
Saint François de Madawaska, New Bruns. 170/B1
Saint-François-de-Montmagny, Québec 172/G3
Saint-François-de-Sales, Québec 172/E1
Saint-François-du-Lac, Québec 172/E3
Saint-Frédéric, Québec 172/G3
Saint Froid (lake), Maine 243/F2
Saint Front, Sask. 181/G3
Saint-Fulgence, Québec 172/G1
Saint Gabriel, La. 238/K2
Saint-Gabriel, Québec 172/D3
Saint-Gabriel-de-Rimouski, Québec 172/J1
Saint Gall (Sankt Gallen), Switzerland 39/H2
Saint-Gaudens, France 28/D6
Saint-Gaudens Nat'l Hist. Site, N.H. 268/B4
Saint-Gédéon, Frontenac, Québec 172/G4
Saint-Gédéon, Lac-St-Jean-E., Québec 172/F1
Saint George, Alaska 196/E3
Saint George (isl.), Alaska 196/D3
Saint George (head), Aust. Cap. Terr. 97/F4
Saint George, Bermuda 156/H2
Saint George (pt.), Calif. 204/A2
Saint George (cape), Fla. 212/A2
Saint George (isl.), Fla. 212/B2
Saint George (sound), Fla. 212/B2
Saint George, Georgia 217/H9
Saint George, Kansas 232/F2
Saint George, Maine 243/E7
Saint George•, Maine 243/E7
Saint George, Manitoba 179/F4
Saint George (lake), Manitoba 179/E3
Saint George (isl.), Md. 245/M8
Saint George, Minn. 255/D6
Saint George, Mo. 261/P4
Saint George, New Bruns. 170/D3
Saint George (cape), Newf. 166/C4
Saint George, N.Y. 276/M9
Saint George, Ontario 177/D4
Saint George (cape), Papua N.G. 86/C2
Saint George, Queensland 95/D5
Saint George, Queensland 88/H5
Saint George, S.C. 296/F5
Saint George, Utah 304/A6
Saint George, Utah 188/D3
Saint George•, Vt. 268/A2
Saint George (ranges), W. Australia 92/D2
Saint George, W. Va. 312/G4
Saint George's (chan.) 7/D3
Saint Georges (cay), Belize 154/D2
Saint George's (isl.), Bermuda 156/H2
Saint Georges, Del. 245/R2
Saint-Georges, Fr. Guiana 131/F4
Saint George's (cap.), Grenada 156/F5
Saint George's (cap.), Grenada 161/C9
Saint George's (chan.), Ireland 10/D4
Saint George's (chan.), Ireland 17/K7
Saint George's, Newf. 166/C4
Saint George's (bay), Newf. 166/C4
Saint Georges (bay), Nova Scotia 168/G3
Saint George's (chan.), Papua N.G. 86/C2
Saint-Georges, Beauce, Québec 172/G3
Saint-Georges, Champlain, Québec 172/E3
Saint George's (chan.), Wales 13/B5
Saint George's (chan.), Wales 10/D4
Saint-Georges-de-Malbaie, Québec 172/D1
Saint-Georges-de-Windsor, Québec 172/F4
Saint-Georges-Ouest, Québec 172/G3
Saint-Georges-sur-Meuse, Belgium 27/G7
Saint-Gérard, Québec 172/F4
Saint-Germain-de-Grantham, Québec 172/E4
Saint-Germain-de-Kamouraska, Québec 172/H2
Saint-Germain-en-Laye, France 28/D3
Saint-Gervais, Québec 172/G3
Saint-Gilles, Belgium 27/B9
Saint-Gilles, Québec 172/F3
Saint-Gilles-Croix-de-Vie, France 28/B4
Saint-Gingolph, Switzerland 39/C4
Saint-Girons, France 28/D6
Saint-Godefroi, Québec 172/D2
Saint Gotthard (pass), Switzerland 39/G3
Saint Gotthard (tunnel), Switzerland 39/G3
Saint Gowans (head), Wales 13/C6
Saint-Grégoire, Québec 172/D4
Saint-Grégoire-de-Greenlay, Québec 172/E4
Saint Gregor, Sask. 181/G3
Saint Gregory (cape), Newf. 166/C4
Saint-Guillaume-Nord, Québec 172/D3
Saint Hedwig, Texas 303/K11
Saint Helen, Mich. 250/E4
Saint Helena (isl.) (U.K.) 2/J6
Saint Helena, Calif. 204/C5
Saint Helena (par.), La. 238/J5
Saint Helena, Nebr. 264/G2
Saint Helena (bay), S. Africa 118/B6
Saint Helena (isl.), S.C. 296/F7
Saint Helena (sound), S.C. 296/G7
Saint Helena (isl.), U.K. 102/B6
Saint Helenas Island, S.C. 296/F7
Saint Helens, England 10/F2
Saint Helens, England 13/G2
Saint Helens, Ky. 237/O5
Saint Helens, Oreg. 291/E2
Saint Helens, Tasmania 99/E3
Saint Helens (pt.), Tasmania 99/E3
Saint Helens (mt.), Wash. 188/B1
Saint Helens (mt.), Wash. 310/C4
Saint Helier (cap.), Jersey, Chan. Is. 13/E8
Saint Helier (cap.), Jersey, Chan. Is. 10/E6
Saint-Henri, Québec 172/J3
Saint Henry, Ind. 227/D8
Saint Henry, Ohio 284/A5
Saint-Herménégilde, Québec 172/F4
Saint Hilaire, Minn. 255/B2
Saint Hilaire, New Bruns. 170/B1
Saint-Hilarion, Québec 172/G2
Saint Hippolyte, Sask. 181/C2
Saint-Honoré, Beauce, Québec 172/G4
Saint-Honoré, Chicoutimi, Québec 172/F1
Saint-Honoré-de-Témiscouata, Québec 172/H2
Saint-Hubert, Belgium 27/G8
Saint-Hubert, Québec 172/J4
Saint-Hubert-de-Témiscouata, Québec 172/J2
Saint Hubert Mission, Sask. 181/J5
Saint-Hugues, Québec 172/E4
Saint-Hyacinthe (co.), Québec 172/D4
Saint-Hyacinthe, Québec 172/D4
Saint Ignace, Mich. 250/E3
Saint-Ignace, New Bruns. 170/F2
Saint Ignace (isl.), Ontario 177/H5
Saint Ignace (isl.), Ontario 175/C3
Saint Ignatius, Mont. 262/C3
Saint-Imier, Switzerland 39/D2
Saint Inigoes, Md. 245/N8
Saint-Irénée, Québec 172/G2
Saint Isidore, Alberta 182/B1
Saint-Isidore, New Bruns. 170/E1
Saint-Isidore, Québec 172/F3
Saint-Isidore-d'Auckland, Québec 172/F4
Saint-Isidore-de-Gaspé, Québec 172/D1
Saint-Isidore-de-Laprairie, Québec 172/D4
Saint Isidore de Prescott, Ontario 177/K2
Saint Issells, Wales 13/C6
Saint Ives, Cornwall, England 13/B7
Saint Ives, England 10/G4
Saint Ives, England 10/D5
Saint Ives, Cambs., England 13/G5
Saint Ives (bay), England 13/B7
Saint Jacob, Ill. 222/D5
Saint Jacobs, Ontario 177/D4
Saint-Jacques, New Bruns. 170/B1
Saint-Jacques, Québec 172/D4
Saint-Jacques-le-Mineur, Québec 172/H4
Saint James, Ark. 202/F2
Saint James (cape), Br. Col. 184/B4
Saint James, Ill. 222/E5
Saint James (par.), La. 238/L3
Saint James, La. 238/L3
Saint James, Md. 245/G2
Saint James, Mich. 250/D3
Saint James, Minn. 255/D7
Saint James, Mo. 261/J6
Saint James, N.Y. 276/O9
Saint James (isls.), Virgin Is. (U.S.) 161/B4
Saint James City, Fla. 212/D5
Saint-Jean, Fr. Guiana 131/D3
Saint-Jean (lake), Que. 162/J6
Saint-Jean (co.), Québec 172/D4
Saint-Jean, Québec 172/D4
Saint-Jean (lake), Québec 172/E1
Saint-Jean (lake), Québec 174/C3
Saint-Jean (riv.), Québec 172/D1
Saint Jean Baptiste, Manitoba 179/E5
Saint-Jean-Baptiste-de-Restigouche, New Bruns. 170/C1
Saint-Jean-Chrysostome, Québec 172/J3
Saint-Jean-d'Angély, France 28/C4
Saint-Jean-de-Dieu, Québec 172/J1
Saint-Jean-de-Luz, France 28/C6
Saint-Jean-de-Matha, Québec 172/D3
Saint-Jean-de-Maurienne, France 28/G5
Saint-Jean-de-Monts, France 28/B4
Saint-Jean-des-Piles, Québec 172/E3
Saint-Jean-d'Orléans, Québec 172/G3
Saint-Jean du Sud, Haiti 158/B6
Saint-Jean-Pied-de-Port, France 28/C6
Saint-Jean-Port-Joli, Québec 172/G2
Saint-Jean-sur-le-Lac, Québec 172/B3
Saint-Jérôme, Terrebonne, Québec 172/H4
Saint Jo, Texas 303/G4
Saint-Joachim, Québec 172/G2
Saint Joe, Ark. 202/E1
Saint Joe, Idaho 220/B2
Saint Joe (riv.), Idaho 220/B2
Saint Joe, Ind. 227/H2
Saint John, Ind. 227/C2
Saint John, Kansas 232/D3
Saint John•, Maine 243/F1
Saint John (pond), Maine 243/D3
Saint John (riv.), Maine 188/N1
Saint John (riv.), Maine 243/G1
Saint John, Mo. 261/P2
Saint John (co.), New Bruns. 170/E3
Saint John (cap.), New Bruns. 170/E3
Saint John (cap.), N. Br. 146/M5
Saint John, N. Br. 162/K6
Saint John (harb.), New Bruns. 170/E3
Saint John (riv.), New Bruns. 170/C2
Saint John (bay), Newf. 166/C3
Saint John (cape), Newf. 166/C3
Saint John (isl.), Newf. 166/C3
Saint John, N. Dak. 282/L2
Saint John, Utah 304/B3
Saint John (isl.), Virgin Is. (U.S.) 161/C4
Saint John (isl.), Virgin Is. (U.S.) 156/H1
Saint John, Wash. 310/H3
Saint John's (cap.), Ant. & Bar. 161/E11
Saint John's, Ant. & Bar. 156/G3
Saint John's (harb.), Ant. & Bar. 161/C11
Saint Johns, Ariz. 198/F4
Saint John's, Canada 2/G3
Saint Johns (co.), Fla. 212/E2
Saint Johns (riv.), Fla. 212/E2
Saint Johns, Ill. 222/D5
Saint John's (pt.), Ireland 17/D2
Saint Johns, Mich. 250/E6
Saint John's (cap.), Newf. 166/D2
Saint John's (cap.), Newf. 146/N5
Saint John's (cap.), Newf. 162/L6
Saint John's (pt.), N. Ireland 17/K3
Saint Johns, Ohio 284/B4
Saint John's (head), Scotland 15/E2
Saint Johns Branch, Nanticoke (riv.), Del. 245/R6
Saint Johnsbury, Vt. 268/D3
Saint Johnsbury•, Vt. 268/D3
Saint Johnsbury Center, Vt. 268/D3
Saint Johnston, Ireland 17/F2
Saint Johnsville, N.Y. 276/L5
Saint John the Baptist (par.), La. 238/M3
Saint Jones (riv.), Del. 245/R4
Saint Joseph, Dominica 161/E6
Saint Joseph (bay), Fla. 212/D6
Saint Joseph (pen.), Fla. 212/D7
Saint Joseph (pt.), Fla. 212/D6
Saint Joseph, Ill. 222/E3
Saint Joseph (co.), Ind. 227/E1
Saint Joseph (riv.), Ind. 227/H2
Saint Joseph (riv.), Ind. 227/E1
Saint Joseph, Kansas 232/E2
Saint Joseph, Ky. 237/G5
Saint Joseph, La. 238/H3
Saint Joseph, Manitoba 179/E5
Saint-Joseph, Martinique 161/D6
Saint Joseph (co.), Mich. 250/D7
Saint Joseph, Mich. 250/C6
Saint Joseph (riv.), Mich. 250/C7
Saint Joseph, Minn. 255/D5
Saint Joseph, Mo. 261/C3
Saint Joseph, Mo. 188/H3
Saint Joseph, Mo. 146/J6
Saint-Joseph, New Bruns. 170/F3
Saint Joseph (riv.), Ohio 284/A3
Saint Joseph (lake), Ont. 162/G5
Saint Joseph (lake), Ontario 175/B2
Saint-Joseph, Réunion 118/G6
Saint Joseph, Tenn. 237/G10
Saint Joseph, Trin. & Tob. 161/B10
Saint Joseph, Trin. & Tob. 161/B11
Saint-Joseph-de-Beauce, Québec 172/G3
Saint-Joseph-de-Kamouraska, Québec 172/H2
Saint-Joseph-de-la-Rive, Québec 172/G2
Saint-Joseph-de-Madawaska, New Bruns. 170/B1
Saint-Joseph-de-Mékinac, Québec 172/E3
Saint-Joseph-de-Sorel, Québec 172/D3
Saint-Joseph-du-Lac, Québec 172/C4
Saint-Joseph-du-Moine, Nova Scotia 168/G2
Saint Joseph Ridge, Wis. 317/D8
Saint Joseph's, Newf. 166/D2
Saint-Josse-ten-Noode, Belgium 27/C9
Saint-Jovite, Québec 172/C3
Saint-Jude, Québec 172/E4
Saint-Junien, France 28/D5
Saint Just, England 13/B7
Saint-Justin, Québec 172/D3
Saint Kilda, N. Zealand 100/C7
Saint Kilda (isl.), Scotland 15/A2
Saint Kilda, Victoria 88/L7
Saint Kilda, Victoria 97/J5
Saint Kilian, Minn. 255/C7
Saint Kitts (isl.), St. Kitts & Nevis 156/F3
Saint Kitts (isl.), St. Kitts & Nevis 161/D10
SAINT KITTS AND NEVIS 156/F3
SAINT KITTS AND NEVIS 161/D11
Saint-Lambert, Québec 172/J4
Saint Landry (par.), La. 238/F5
Saint Landry, La. 238/F5
Saint Laurent, Manitoba 179/D4
Saint-Laurent, Québec 172/H4
Saint-Laurent-de-la-Salanque, France 28/E6
Saint-Laurent-d'Orléans, Québec 172/G3
Saint-Laurent-du-Maroni, Fr. Guiana 120/D2
Saint-Laurent du Maroni (dist.), Fr. Guiana 131/E4
Saint-Laurent du Maroni, Fr. Guiana 131/E3
Saint Lawrence (gulf) 146/M5
Saint Lawrence (riv.) 162/K6
Saint Lawrence (riv.) 146/L5
Saint Lawrence (isl.), Alaska 146/A3
Saint Lawrence (isl.), Alaska 196/D2
Saint Lawrence, Barbados 161/B9
Saint Lawrence (gulf), Canada 2/G3
Saint Lawrence (riv.), N.Y. 188/N1
Saint Lawrence (gulf), New Bruns. 170/F1
Saint Lawrence, Newf. 166/C4
Saint Lawrence (gulf), Newf. 166/B4
Saint Lawrence (co.), N.Y. 276/K2
Saint Lawrence (lake), N.Y. 276/K1
Saint Lawrence (riv.), N.Y. 276/J2
Saint Lawrence (bay), Nova Scotia 168/H1
Saint Lawrence (cape), Nova Scotia 168/H1
Saint Lawrence (lake), Ontario 177/K3
Saint Lawrence (riv.), Ontario 177/J3
Saint Lawrence (gulf), Pr. Edward I. 168/F2
Saint Lawrence (gulf), Que. 162/K6
Saint Lawrence (gulf), Québec 172/D2
Saint Lawrence (gulf), Québec 174/E3
Saint Lawrence (riv.), Québec 174/D3
Saint Lawrence (riv.), Québec 172/H1

Saint Lawrence, Queensland 95/D4
Saint Lawrence, S. Dak. 298/M4
Saint Lawrence (isl.), U.S. 4/C18
Saint Lawrence Is. Nat'l Park, Ontario 177/J3
Saint Lazare, Manitoba 179/A4
Saint-Lazare, Québec 172/B1
Saint-Léandre, Québec 172/B1
Saint-Léger, Belgium 27/H9
Saint-Léger-La Chiésaz, Switzerland 39/C4
Saint Leo, Fla. 212/D3
Saint Leo, Minn. 255/C6
Saint Leon, Ind. 227/H6
Saint Leon, Manitoba 179/D5
Saint-Léon, Québec 172/D3
Saint Leonard, Md. 245/N7
Saint Leonard, New Bruns. 170/C1
Saint-Léonard, Québec 172/H4
Saint-Léonard-d'Aston, Québec 172/E3
Saint-Léonard-de-Noblat, France 28/D5
Saint-Léonard-de-Portneuf, Québec 172/E3
Saint-Léon-de-Chicoutimi, Québec 172/F1
Saint-Léon-de-Standon, Québec 172/G3
Saint-Léon-le-Grand, Québec 172/B2
Saint Lewis (cape), Newf. 166/C3
Saint Lewis (riv.), Newf. 166/C3
Saint-Liboire, Québec 172/E4
Saint Libory, Ill. 222/D5
Saint Libory, Nebr. 264/F3
Saint Lina, Alberta 182/E2
Saint-Lô, France 28/C3
Saint-Louis, Guadeloupe 161/B7
Saint Louis, Minn. 250/E5
Saint Louis (co.), Minn. 255/F3
Saint Louis (riv.), Minn. 255/F4
Saint Louis (bay), Miss. 256/F10
Saint Louis, Mo. 261/O3
Saint Louis (city county), Mo. 261/P3
Saint Louis, Mo. 261/R3
Saint Louis, Mo. 146/K6
Saint Louis, Mo. 188/H3
Saint Louis, Okla. 288/N4
Saint Louis, Oreg. 291/A3
Saint Louis, Pr. Edward I. 168/D2
Saint-Louis (lake), Québec 172/H4
Saint-Louis, Réunion 118/D5
Saint Louis, Sask. 181/F3
Saint-Louis, Senegal 102/A3
Saint-Louis, Senegal 106/A5
Saint Louis, U.S. 2/E4
Saint Louis (riv.), Wis. 317/A2
Saint Louis Crossing, Ind. 227/F6
Saint-Louis-de-Gonzague, Québec 172/D4
Saint-Louis-de-Kent, New Bruns. 170/F2
Saint-Louis-de-Terrebonne, Québec 172/H4
Saint-Louis-du-Ha! Ha!, Québec 172/H2
Saint-Louis du Nord, Haiti 158/B5
Saint-Louis du Sud, Haiti 158/B6
Saint Louis Park, Minn. 255/G5
Saint Louisville, Ohio 284/F6
Saint-Luc, Québec 172/D4
Saint-Luc-de-Matane, Québec 172/B1
Saint Lucia 2/G5
Saint Lucia 146/M8
SAINT LUCIA 161/G5
SAINT LUCIA 156/G4
Saint Lucia, Queensland 88/K3
Saint Lucia, Queensland 95/D3
Saint Lucia (chan.), St. Lucia 156/G4
Saint Lucia (chan.), St. Lucia 161/G5
Saint Lucia (cape), S. Africa 118/E5
Saint Lucia (lake), S. Africa 118/E5
Saint Lucie (co.), Fla. 212/F4
Saint Lucie, Fla. 212/F4
Saint Lucie (canal), Fla. 212/F4
Saint Lucie (inlet), Fla. 212/F4
Saint-Ludger, Québec 172/G4
Saint Lunaire-Griquet, Newf. 166/C3
Saint-Magloire, Québec 172/G3
Saint Magnus (bay), Scotland 10/G1
Saint Magnus (bay), Scotland 15/F2
Saint-Malachie, Québec 172/G3
Saint-Malo, France 28/B3
Saint Malo, Manitoba 179/F5
Saint-Malo, Québec 172/F4
Saint-Mandé, France 28/B2
Saint-Marc, Haiti 158/B5
Saint-Marc (chan.), Haiti 158/B6
Saint-Marc (pt.), Haiti 158/B5
Saint-Marc, Québec 172/D4
Saint-Marc-des-Carrières, Québec 172/E3
Saint-Marcel (mt.), Fr. Guiana 131/E4
Saint-Marcel-de-L'Islet, Québec 172/G3
Saint-Marcellin, France 28/F5
Saint Margarets, New Bruns. 170/E2
Saint Margarets (bay), Nova Scotia 168/G4
Saint Margaret's Bay, Jamaica 158/K6
Saint Margaret's Hope, Scotland 15/F2
Saint Margaret Village, Nova Scotia 168/H2
Saint Maries, Idaho 220/B2
Saint Maries (riv.), Idaho 220/B2
Saint Marks, Fla. 212/B1
Saint Marks, Georgia 217/C4
Saint Marks, Manitoba 179/E4
Saint-Martin (isl.), Guadeloupe 156/F3
Saint Martin (par.), La. 238/G6
Saint Martin (lake), Manitoba 179/D3
Saint-Martin (cape), Martinique 161/C5

Saint Martin, Md. 245/T7
Saint Martin (bay), Mich. 250/E3
Saint Martin (isl.), Mich. 250/E3
Saint Martin, Minn. 255/D5
Saint Martin (Sint Maarten) (isl.), Neth. Ant. 156/F3
Saint Martin, Ohio 284/C7
Saint-Martin, Switzerland 39/E4
Saint Martin de Restigouche, New Bruns. 170/C1
Saint Martins, Barbados 161/C9
Saint Martin's (isl.), England 13/A8
Saint Martins, Mo. 261/H5
Saint Martins, New Bruns. 170/E3
Saint Martin Station, Manitoba 179/D3
Saint Martinville, La. 238/G6
Saint Mary (res.), Alberta 182/E5
Saint Mary (riv.), Alberta 182/D5
Saint Mary, Ky. 237/L5
Saint Mary (par.), La. 238/H7
Saint Mary (lake), Mont. 262/C2
Saint Mary (riv.), Mont. 262/C1
Saint Mary, Nebr. 264/H4
Saint Mary (cape), Nova Scotia 168/B4
Saint Mary (peak), S. Australia 94/F4
Saint Mary-of-the-Woods, Ind. 227/B6
Saint Marys, Alaska 196/F2
Saint Mary's (isl.), England 13/A8
Saint Marys, Georgia 217/J9
Saint Marys (riv.), Georgia 217/J9
Saint Marys, Ind. 227/E1
Saint Marys (lake), Ind. 227/H3
Saint Marys (riv.), Ind. 227/H3
Saint Marys, Iowa 229/F6
Saint Marys, Kansas 232/G2
Saint Marys (co.), Md. 245/M7
Saint Marys, Md. 245/N8
Saint Marys (riv.), Mich. 250/E2
Saint Marys, Mo. 261/M7
Saint Mary's (bay), Newf. 166/C2
Saint Mary's (cape), Newf. 166/C2
Saint Marys (bay), Nova Scotia 168/B4
Saint Marys (riv.), Nova Scotia 168/F3
Saint Marys, Ohio 284/B4
Saint Marys (lake), Ohio 284/A4
Saint Mary's, Ontario 177/C4
Saint Marys, Pa. 294/A3
Saint Mary's, Scotland 15/F2
Saint Marys, Tasmania 99/E3
Saint Marys, W. Va. 294/E1
Saint Marys (peak), Wyo. 319/D3
Saint Marys City, Md. 245/N8
Saint Marvs Entrance (inlet), Fla. 212/F1
Saint-Mathieu, Québec 172/J1
Saint-Mathieu (lake), Québec 172/J1
Saint Matthew (isl.), Alaska 188/C5
Saint Matthew (isl.), Alaska 196/B2
Saint Matthew (isl.), Alaska 196/D2
Saint Matthew (isl.), U.S. 4/C18
Saint Matthews, Ky. 237/K2
Saint Matthews, S.C. 296/F4
Saint Matthias Group (isls.), Papua N.G. 86/B1
Saint-Maur-des-Fossés, France 28/B2
Saint Maurice, Ind. 227/G6
Saint Maurice, La. 238/E3
Saint-Maurice (co.), Québec 172/D3
Saint-Maurice (county), Québec 174/C3
Saint-Maurice (riv.), Québec 172/E2
Saint-Médard, Québec 172/J1
Saint Meinrad, Ind. 227/D8
Saint-Méthode, Québec 172/E1
Saint-Méthode-de-Frontenac, Québec 172/F3
Saint Michael, Alaska 196/F2
Saint Michael, Alberta 182/D3
Saint Michael, Minn. 255/E5
Saint Michael, N. Dak. 282/N4
Saint Michael, Pa. 294/E5
Saint Michaels, Ariz. 198/F3
Saint Michaels, Md. 245/N6
Saint Michaels (bay), Newf. 166/C3
Saint-Michel-de-Bellechasse, Québec 172/G3
Saint-Michel de l'Atalaye, Haiti 158/C5
Saint-Michel-des-Saints, Québec 172/D3
Saint-Michel du Sud, Haiti 158/B6
Saint-Mihiel, France 28/F3
Saint-Modeste, Québec 172/H2
Saint-Moïse, Québec 172/B1
Saint Monance, Scotland 15/F4
Saint Moritz, Switzerland 39/J3
Saint-Narcisse-de-Rimouski, Québec 172/J1
Saint-Nazaire, France 28/B4
Saint-Nazaire, France 28/B4
Saint-Nazaire, Fr. Guiana 131/E3
Saint-Nazaire, Québec 172/E4
Saint-Nazaire-de-Buckland, Québec 172/G3
Saint-Nazaire-de-Chicoutimi, Québec 172/F1
Saint Nazianz, Wis. 317/L7
Saint Neots, England 13/G5
Saint-Nérée, Québec 172/G3
Saint-Nicolas, Belgium 27/G7
Saint Niklaus, Switzerland 39/E4
Saint-Noël, Québec 172/B1
Saint-Octave, Québec 172/B1
Saint-Odilon, Québec 172/G3
Saint Olaf, Iowa 229/L5
Saint-Omer, France 28/E2
Saint Omer, Ind. 227/F6
Saint-Omer, Québec 172/C2

Saint-Onésime, Québec 172/H2
Saintonge (trad. prov.), France 29
Saint Onge, S. Dak. 298/B4
Saint-Ouen, France 28/B1
Saint-Ours, Québec 172/D4
Saint-Pacôme, Québec 172/G2
Saint-Pamphile, Québec 172/H3
Saint Paris, Ohio 284/C5
Saint-Pascal, Québec 174/D3
Saint-Pascal, Québec 172/H2
Saint-Patrice-de-Beaurivage, Québec 172/F3
Saint Patrick (lake), Manitoba 179/E3
Saint Patrick (chan.), Nova Scotia 168/G3
Saint Paul (isl.), (Fr.) 2/P7
Saint Paul (isl.), Alaska 196/D3
Saint Paul, Alberta 182/E3
Saint Paul, Alta. 162/E5
Saint Paul, Ark. 202/C2
Saint Paul (cape), Ghana 106/E7
Saint Paul, Ind. 227/F6
Saint Paul, Iowa 229/L7
Saint Paul, Kansas 232/G4
Saint Paul (cap.), Minn. 188/H1
Saint Paul (cap.), Minn. 146/J3
Saint Paul (cap.), Minn. 255/G6
Saint Paul, Mo. 261/L5
Saint Paul, Nebr. 264/F3
Saint-Paul, New Bruns. 170/E2
Saint Paul (isl.), Newf. 166/D2
Saint Paul (isl.), Nova Scotia 168/H1
Saint-Paul, Oreg. 291/A3
Saint-Paul, Québec 172/E4
Saint Paul (cap.), Québec 174/F2
Saint Paul, S.C. 296/G4
Saint Paul, Texas 303/H1
Saint Paul, Va. 307/D2
Saint-Paul-de-Montminy, Québec 172/G3
Saint-Paul-du-Nord, Québec 172/H1
Saint-Paulin, Québec 172/D3
Saint Paul Island, Alaska 196/D3
Saint-Paul-l'Ermite, Québec 172/J4
Saint Paul Park, Minn. 255/G6
Saint Paul's, Newf. 166/C3
Saint Pauls, N.C. 281/M5
Saint Peter, Ill. 222/E5
Saint Peter, Ind. 227/B6
Saint Peter, Kansas 232/C2
Saint Peter, Minn. 255/E6
Saint Peter Port (cap.), Guernsey, Chan. Is. 13/E8
Saint Peter Port (cap.), Guernsey, Chan. Is. 10/E6
Saint Peters, Mo. 261/M1
Saint Peters Church, Nova Scotia 168/H3
Saint Peters (bay), Nova Scotia 168/H3
Saint Peters, Pr. Edward I. 168/F2
Saint Peters (bay), Pr. Edward I. 168/F2
Saint Peters (isl.), Pr. Edward I. 168/E2
Saint Peters, S. Australia 88/E8
Saint Petersburg, Fla. 188/K5
Saint Petersburg, Fla. 146/K7
Saint Petersburg, Fla. 212/B3
Saint Petersburg, Pa. 294/C3
Saint Petersburg Beach, Fla. 212/B3
Saint-Petronille, Québec 172/J3
Saint-Philémon, Québec 172/G3
Saint Philip, Ind. 227/B9
Saint-Philippe-de-Laprairie, Québec 172/J4
Saint-Philippe-de-Néri, Québec 172/H2
Saint Philips, Sask. 181/K4
Saint Phillips, Mont. 262/M4
Saint Phillips, Newf. 166/D2
Saint-Pie, Québec 172/E4
Saint-Pierre, Martinique 161/C6
Saint-Pierre, Martinique 156/C4
Saint-Pierre (bay), Martinique 161/C6
Saint-Pierre, Ile-de-Mont., Québec 172/H4
Saint-Pierre, Joliette, Québec 172/D3
Saint-Pierre (lake), Québec 172/E3
Saint-Pierre, Québec 172/D1
Saint-Pierre, Réunion 118/F6
Saint-Pierre (cap.), Saint Pierre & Miquelon 166/C4
Saint-Pierre (isl.), Saint Pierre & Miquelon 166/C4
SAINT PIERRE AND MIQUELON 166/C4
Saint Pierre & Miquelon (isls.) (Fr.) 162/L6
Saint Pierre and Miquelon (isls.) (Fr.) 146/N5
Saint-Pierre-Baptiste, Québec 172/F3
Saint-Pierre-de-Broughton, Québec 172/F3
Saint-Pierre-d'Orléans, Québec 172/G3
Saint Pierre-Jolys, Manitoba 179/F5
Saint-Pierre-Montmagny, Québec 172/G3
Saint-Placide, Québec 172/C4
Saint-Pol-de-Léon, France 28/A3
Saint-Pol-sur-Ternoise, France 28/E2
Saint-Polycarpe, Québec 172/C4
Saint-Pons, France 28/E6
Saint-Prex, Switzerland 39/B4
Saint-Prime, Québec 172/E1
Saint-Prosper-de-Dorchester, Québec 172/G3
Saint-Quentin, France 28/E3
Saint Quentin, New Bruns. 170/C1
Saint-Raphaël, France 28/G6
Saint-Raphaël, Haiti 158/C5
Saint-Raphaël, Québec 172/G3
Saint-Raphaël-sur-Mer, New Bruns. 170/F1
Saint-Raymond, Québec 172/F3
Saint-Rédempteur, Québec 172/J3
Saint Regis, Mont. 262/A3

Saint Regis (riv.), N.Y. 276/L1
Saint-Régis, Québec 172/C4
Saint Regis Falls, N.Y. 276/M1
Saint Regis Ind. Res., N.Y. 276/M1
Saint Regis Park, Ky. 237/K2
Saint-Rémi, Québec 172/D4
Saint-Rémi-d'Amherst, Québec 172/C3
Saint-Rémi-de-Tingwick, Québec 172/F4
Saint-René-de-Matane, Québec 172/B1
Saint Robert, Mo. 261/H7
Saint-Roch-de-l'Achigan, Québec 172/D4
Saint-Roch-de-Mékinac, Québec 172/E3
Saint-Roch-de-Richelieu, Québec 172/D4
Saint-Romain, Québec 172/F4
Saint-Romuald-d'Etchemin, Québec 172/J3
Saint Rosa, Minn. 255/D5
Saint Rose, Ill. 222/D5
Saint Rose, La. 238/N4
Saint Sampson's, Chan. Is. 13/E8
Saints-Anges, Québec 172/F3
Saint Sauveur, New Bruns. 170/E1
Saint-Sauveur-des-Monts, Québec 172/C4
Saint-Sébastien (cape), Madagascar 118/H2
Saint-Sébastien, Frontenac, Québec 172/G4
Saint-Sébastien, Iberville, Québec 172/D4
Saint-Sever, France 28/C6
Saint-Séverin-de-Beaurivage, Québec 172/F3
Saint Shotts, Newf. 166/D2
Saint-Siméon, Québec 172/G2
Saint-Siméon-de-Bonaventure, Québec 172/C2
Saint-Simon, Québec 172/H1
Saint-Simon-le-Bagot, Québec 172/E4
Saint Simons, Georgia 217/K8
Saint Simons Island, Georgia 217/K8
Saint-Stanislas, Québec 172/E3
Saint Stephan, Switzerland 39/D3
Saint Stephen, Minn. 255/D5
Saint Stephen, N. Bruns. 162/K6
Saint Stephen, New Bruns. 170/C3
Saint Stephen, S.C. 296/H5
Saint Stephen-in-Brannel, England 13/B7
Saint Stephens, Ala. 195/B7
Saint Stephens, Wyo. 319/D3
Šakiai, U.S.S.R. 53/B3
Sakishima (isls.) Japan 54/O7
Sakishima (isls.), Japan 81/K7
Sakon Nakhon, Thailand 72/E3
Sakonnet (pt.), R.I. 249/K7
Sakonnet (riv.), R.I. 249/K7
Sakrivier, S. Africa 118/C6
Sakskøbing, Denmark 21/E8
Saku, Japan 81/J5
Sakurai, Japan 81/J8
Sakwatamau (riv.), Alberta 182/C2
Sal (isl.), C. Verde 106/B7
Šal'a, Czech. 41/D2
Sala, Sweden 18/K7
Salabangka (isls.), Indonesia 85/G6
Salacgrīva, U.S.S.R. 53/C2
Sala Consilina, Italy 34/F4
Saladas, Argentina 143/E2
Saladillo, Argentina 143/E3
Saladillo (riv.), Argentina 143/D2
Saladillo, Bolivia 136/D7
Salado (riv.), Argentina 120/C6
Salado (riv.), Argentina 143/H7
Salado (riv.), Argentina 143/C3
Salado, Ark. 202/E2
Salado, Chile 138/A6
Salado, Quebrado del (riv.), Chile 138/B6
Salado, Cuba 158/H3
Salado, Honduras 154/D3
Salado del Norte (riv.), Argentina 120/C5
Salado del Norte (riv.), Argentina 143/D2
Salaga, Ghana 106/D7
Salahuddin (gov.), Iraq 66/C3
Sala'ilua, W. Samoa 86/L8
Salala, Oman 59/F6
Salala, Oman 54/G8
Salamá, Guatemala 154/B3
Salamanca, Mexico 150/J6
Salamanca, N.Y. 276/C6
Salamanca (prov.), Spain 33/C2
Salamanca, Spain 33/D2
Salamanca, Spain 7/D4
Salamat, Bahr (riv.), Chad 111/C6
Salamina, Colombia 126/C5
Salamis, Greece 45/F6
Salamonia, Ind. 227/H4
Salamonie (lake), Ind. 227/F3
Salamonie (riv.), Ind. 227/G4
Salas, Spain 33/C1
Salas de los Infantes, Spain 33/E2
Salatiga, Indonesia 85/J2
Salavat, U.S.S.R. 7/K3
Salavat, U.S.S.R. 52/H4
Salaverry, Peru 128/C7
Salawati (isl.), Indonesia 85/J6
Salay, Philippines 82/E6
Sala y Gómez (isl.), Chile 2/D7
Sala y Gómez (isl.), Chile 87/P8
Salazar, Colombia 126/D2
Salcantay (mt.), Peru 128/F9
Salcedo (prov.), Dom. Rep. 158/E5
Salcedo, Dom. Rep. 158/E5
Salcombe, England 13/D7
Salcombe, England 10/D5
Saldaña (riv.), Colombia 126/C6
Saldaña, Spain 33/D1

Saldanha, S. Africa 118/B6
Saldee, Ky. 237/P6
Saldus, U.S.S.R. 53/B2
Sale, England 13/H4
Salé, Morocco 106/C2
Sale (riv.), Manitoba 179/E5
Salé, Victoria 88/H7
Sale, Victoria 97/C6
Sale City, Georgia 217/G8
Sale Creek, Tenn. 237/L10
Salée (riv.), Guadeloupe 161/A6
Salekhard, U.S.S.R. 53/P6
Salekhard, U.S.S.R. 4/C6
Salekhard, U.S.S.R. 2/N2
Salekhard, U.S.S.R. 48/G3
Salem, Ala. 195/H5
Salem, Ark. 202/G1
Salem•, Conn. 210/F3
Salem•, Fla. 212/C2
Salem, Ill. 222/E5
Salem, India 54/J8
Salem, India 68/D6
Salem, Ind. 227/E7
Salem, Ind. 227/H3
Salem, Iowa 229/K7
Salem, Ky. 237/F6
Salem, Maine 243/C6
Salem, Mass. 249/E5
Salem, Md. 245/P7
Salem, Mich. 250/F6
Salem, Mo. 261/J7
Salem•, N.H. 268/E6
Salem (co.), N.J. 273/C4
Salem, N.J. 273/C4
Salem, N. Mex. 274/B6
Salem, N.Y. 276/O4
Salem, Ohio 284/J4
Salem, Ontario 177/D4
Salem (cap.), Oreg. 146/F5
Salem (cap.), Oreg. 188/B1
Salem (cap.), Oreg. 291/A3
Salem, S.C. 296/A2
Salem, S. Dak. 298/P6
Salem, Utah 304/D3
Salem (riv.), Vt. 268/C2
Salem (I.C.), Va. 307/H6
Salem, W. Va. 312/E4
Salemburg, N.C. 281/N4
Salem Center, Ind. 227/G1
Salem Depot, N.H. 268/E6
Salemi, Italy 34/D6
Salem Maritime Nat'l Hist. Site, Mass. 249/E5
Salen, Scotland 15/C4
Saleratus Wash (creek), Utah 304/D4
Salernes, France 28/G6
Salerno (prov.), Italy 34/E4
Salerno, Italy 7/F4
Salerno, Italy 34/E4
Salerno (gulf), Italy 34/E4
Salesville, Ark. 202/F1
Salesville, Ohio 284/H6
Salfit, West Bank 65/C3
Salford, England 13/H2
Salford, England 10/G2
Salgótarján, Hungary 41/E2
Salgueiro, Brazil 132/G5
Salí (riv.), Argentina 143/C2
Salida, Colo. 208/H6
Salies-de-Béarn, France 28/C6
Salihli, Turkey 63/C3
Salima, Malawi 115/F6
Salina (isl.), Italy 34/E5
Salina, Kans. 188/G3
Salina, Kansas 232/E3
Salina, Kansas 146/J6
Salina, Okla. 288/N2
Salina, Utah 304/C5
Salina (creek), Utah 304/C5
Salina Cruz, Mexico 150/M9
Salinas, Brazil 132/F7
Salinas, Calif. 188/B3
Salinas, Calif. 204/D7
Salinas (riv.), Calif. 204/D7
Salinas, Chile 138/B4
Salinas (bay), C. Rica 154/D5
Salinas (pt.), Dom. Rep. 158/E6
Salinas, Ecuador 128/B4
Salinas (riv.), Guatemala 154/B2
Salinas, Mexico 150/J5
Salinas (riv.), Mexico 150/O8
Salinas (bay), Nicaragua 154/D5
Salinas, P. Rico 156/G1
Salinas, P. Rico 161/F1
Salinas (pt.), P. Rico 161/D1
Salinas de Garci Mendoza, Bolivia 136/D6
Salinas de Santiago, Bolivia 136/E6
Salinas Grandes (salt dep.), Argentina 143/D2
Salinas Pueblo Missions Nat'l Mon., N. Mex. 274/C4
Saline (co.), Ark. 202/E4
Saline (co.), Ark. 202/E5
Saline (pt.), Grenada 161/C9
Saline (co.), Ill. 222/E6
Saline (riv.), Ill. 222/E6
Saline (co.), Kansas 232/E3
Saline (riv.), Kansas 232/D3
Saline, La. 238/E2
Saline (lake), La. 238/E3
Saline, Mich. 250/F6
Saline (co.), Mo. 261/F4
Saline, Mo. 261/E1
Saline (co.), Nebr. 264/G4
Saline, Scotland 15/E1
Saline City, Ind. 227/C6
Salineño, Texas 303/E11
Salines (pt.), Martinique 161/D7
Salines (pt.), Martinique 161/D7
Salineville, Ohio 284/J4
Salinópolis, Brazil 132/E3
Salins-les-Bains, France 28/F4
Salisbury (sound), Alaska 196/M1

Santa Cruz 443

San Félix, Panama 154/G6
San Félix, Venezuela 124/C2
San Fernando, Argentina 143/G7
San Fernando (riv.), Bolivia 136/F5
San Fernando, Calif. 204/C10
San Fernando, Chile 138/G6
San Fernando, Tamaulipas, Mexico 150/L4
San Fernando, La Union, Philippines 82/C2
San Fernando, Masbate, Philippines 82/D4
San Fernando, Pampanga, Philippines 82/C3
San Fernando, Spain 33/C4
San Fernando, Trin. & Tob. 161/A11
San Fernando, Trin. & Tob. 156/G5
San Fernando, Venezuela 120/C2
San Fernando de Apure, Venezuela 124/E4
San Fernando de Atabapo, Venezuela 124/E5
San Fidel, N. Mex. 274/B3
Sanford, Ala. 195/F8
Sanford (mt.), Alaska 196/K2
Sanford, Colo. 208/H8
Sanford, Fla. 188/K5
Sanford, Fla. 212/E3
Sanford, Maine 243/B9
Sanford•, Maine 243/B9
Sanford, Manitoba 179/E5
Sanford, Mich. 250/E5
Sanford, Miss. 256/F8
Sanford, N.C. 281/L4
Sanford, Nova Scotia 168/B5
San Francique, Trin. & Tob. 161/A11
San Francisco, Argentina 120/C6
San Francisco, San Luis, Argentina 143/C3
San Francisco, Córdoba, Argentina 143/D3
San Francisco (riv.), Ariz. 198/F5
San Francisco, Bolivia 136/C4
San Francisco (city county), Calif. 204/J2
San Francisco, Calif. 146/F6
San Francisco, Calif. 188/B3
San Francisco, Calif. 204/H2
San Francisco (bay), Calif. 204/J2
San Francisco, Colombia 126/B7
San Francisco (cape), Ecuador 128/B2
San Francisco, Honduras 154/D3
San Francisco (riv.), N. Mex. 274/A5
San Francisco, Nicaragua 154/E5
San Francisco, Panama 154/G6
San Francisco (creek), Texas 303/B8
San Francisco, U.S. 2/C4
San Francisco, Lara, Venezuela 124/C2
San Francisco de la Paz, Honduras 154/D3
San Francisco del Chañar, Argentina 143/C2
San Francisco del Oro, Mexico 150/F3
San Francisco del Rincón, Mexico 150/H6
San Francisco de Macorís, Dom. Rep. 158/E5
San Francisco de Macorís, Dom. Rep. 156/E3
San Francisco de Mostazal, Chile 138/G4
San Francisco Gotera, El Salvador 154/C4
Sanga (riv.), Cameroon 115/C3
Sanga (riv.), Cent. Afr. Rep. 115/C3
San Gabriel, Calif. 204/C10
San Gabriel (res.), Calif. 204/D10
San Gabriel, Ecuador 128/D2
San Gabriel Chilac, Mexico 150/K7
San Gallán (isl.), Peru 128/D9
Sangamner, India 68/C5
Sangamon (co.), Ill. 222/D4
Sangamon (riv.), Ill. 222/C3
Sangan, Iran /M3
Sangar, U.S.S.R. 54/O3
Sangar, U.S.S.R. 48/N3
Sangaredyi, Guinea 106/B6
Sangay (mt.), Ecuador 128/C4
Sangeang (isl.), Indonesia 85/F7
San Genaro, Argentina 143/F6
Sanger, Calif. 204/F7
Sanger, N. Dak. 282/H5
Sanger, Texas 303/G4
Sangerhausen, Germany 22/D3
San Germán, Cuba 158/J3
San Germán, P. Rico 161/A2
San Germán, P. Rico 156/F1
Sangerville•, Maine 243/E5
Sangestan, Kuh-e (mt.), Iran 66/H5
Sanggabuwana (mt.), Indonesia 85/G2
Sanggau, Indonesia 85/E5
Sangha (riv.), Congo 115/C3
Sangihe (isls.), Indonesia 54/O9
Sangihe (isl.), Indonesia 85/H5
Sangihe (isls.), Indonesia 85/G5
San Gil, Colombia 126/D4
San Giovanni in Fiore, Italy 34/F5
San Giovanni in Persiceto, Italy 34/C2
San Giuliano Terme, Italy 34/C3
Sangju, S. Korea 81/D5
Sangkulirang, Indonesia 85/F5
Sangli, India 68/C5
Sangmélima, Cameroon 115/B3
Sangolquí, Ecuador 128/C3
Sangre de Cristo (mts.), Colo. 208/H6
Sangre de Cristo (mts.), N. Mex. 274/D3
San Gregorio, Calif. 204/J3
San Gregorio, San José, Uruguay 145/C4
San Gregorio, Tacuarembó, Uruguay 145/D3
Sangre Grande, Trin. & Tob. 161/B10
Sangre Grande, Trin. & Tob. 156/G5
Sangri, China 77/D6
Sangro (riv.), Italy 34/E4
Sangudo, Alberta 182/C3
Sangue (riv.), Brazil 132/B6
Sangüesa, Spain 33/F1
Sanhe, China 77/K1
Sanibel, Fla. 212/D5
Sanibel (isl.), Fla. 212/D5
San Ignacio, Argentina 143/E2
San Ignacio, Belize 154/C2
San Ignacio, El Beni, Bolivia 136/C4
San Ignacio, Santa Cruz, Bolivia 136/E5
San Ignacio, Chile 138/E1
San Ignacio, C. Rica 154/E6
San Ignacio, Baja California Sur, Mexico 150/C3
San Ignacio, Sinaloa, Mexico 150/F5
San Ignacio, Paraguay 144/D5
San Ignacio, Venezuela 124/B2
Sanilac (co.), Mich. 250/G5
San Ildefonso, N. Mex. 274/C3
San Ildefonso (cape), Philippines 82/D2
San Ildefonso, Spain 33/E2
San'in Kaigan National Park, Japan 81/G6
San Isabel, Colo. 208/K7
Sanish, N. Dak. 282/E4
San Isidro, Argentina 143/C2
San Isidro, Philippines 82/E5
Saniya, Hor (lake), Iraq 66/E5
San Jacinto, Calif. 204/H10
San Jacinto, Colombia 126/C3
San Jacinto, Nev. 266/G1
San Jacinto, Philippines 82/D4
San Jacinto (co.), Texas 303/J7
San Jacinto, Uruguay 145/C6
San Jaime de la frontera, Argentina 143/G5
San Javier, Río Negro, Argentina 143/D5
San Javier, Santa Fe, Argentina 143/F5
San Javier, Santa Cruz, Bolivia 136/D5
San Javier, El Beni, Bolivia 136/C4
San Javier, Chile 138/A11
San Javier, Uruguay 145/A3
San Jerónimo de Juárez, Mexico 150/J8
Sanjo, Japan 81/J5
San Joaquin, Bolivia 136/C3
San Joaquin (riv.), Calif. 188/C3
San Joaquin (co.), Calif. 204/D6
San Joaquin, Calif. 204/E7
San Joaquin (riv.), Calif. 204/E6
San Joaquin (valley), Calif. 204/D6
San Joaquin, Paraguay 144/E4
San Jon, N. Mex. 274/F3
San Jorge (gulf), Argentina 120/C7
San Jorge (gulf), Argentina 143/C6
San Jorge (riv.), Colombia 126/C3
San Jorge (bay), Mexico 150/C1
San Jorge, Nicaragua 154/E5
San Jorge (gulf), Spain 33/G2
San José, Belize 154/C2
San Jose, Calif. 146/F6
San Jose, Calif. 188/B3
San Jose, Calif. 204/L3
San José, Colombia 126/F6
San José (cap.), C. Rica 146/K9
San José (cap.), C. Rica 154/F5
San José, Guatemala 154/B4
San Jose, Ill. 222/D3
San José (isl.), Mexico 150/D4
San Jose, N. Mex. 274/D3
San Jose (riv.), N. Mex. 274/B3
San José (isl.), Panama 154/H6
San José, Paraguay 144/B5
San José, Peru 128/B6
San Jose, Philippines 85/G3
San Jose, Nueva Ecija, Philippines 82/C3
San Jose, Occ. Mindoro, Philippines 82/C4
San José (lag.), P. Rico 161/E1
San Jose (isl.), Texas 303/H9
San José (dept.), Uruguay 145/C5
San José (riv.), Uruguay 145/C4
San José, Amazonas, Venezuela 124/E5
San José, Zulia, Venezuela 124/B3
San José de Amacuro, Venezuela 124/H3
San José de Areocuar, Venezuela 124/G2
San Jose de Buenavista, Philippines 82/C5
San José de Chiquitos, Bolivia 136/E5
San José de Feliciano, Argentina 143/G5
San José de Guanipa, Venezuela 124/G3
San José de la Costa, Venezuela 124/D2
San José de la Mariquina, Chile 138/D2
San José de las Lajas, Cuba 158/C1
San José de las Matas, Dom. Rep. 158/D5
San José del Cabo, Mexico 150/D5
San José del Guaviare, Colombia 126/D6
San José del Monte, Philippines 82/C3
San José del Ocune, Colombia 126/E5
San José de los Ramos, Cuba 158/D1
San José de Maipo, Chile 138/B10
San José de Mayo, Uruguay 145/C5
San José de Ocoa, Dom. Rep. 158/E6
San José de Río Chico, Venezuela 124/F2
San José de Sisa, Peru 128/D6
San José de Tiznados, Venezuela 124/E3
San José de Uchupiamonas, Bolivia 136/A4
San Juan (riv.) 188/E3
San Juan (prov.), Argentina 143/C3
San Juan, Argentina 143/C3
San Juan, Argentina 120/C6
San Juan (riv.), Argentina 143/C3
San Juan, Potosí, Bolivia 136/B7
San Juan, Santa Cruz, Bolivia 136/F5
San Juan (riv.), Bolivia 136/C7
San Juan (riv.), Br. Col. 184/J3
San Juan (creek), Calif. 204/E8
San Juan (riv.), Colombia 126/B5
San Juan (co.), Colo. 208/D7
San Juan (mts.), Colo. 208/F7
San Juan (riv.), Colo. 208/E8
San Juan (riv.), C. Rica 154/E5
San Juan (prov.), Dom. Rep. 158/D6
San Juan, Dom. Rep. 158/D6
San Juan, Mexico 150/K6
San Juan (co.), N. Mex. 274/A2
San Juan (riv.), N. Mex. 274/B2
San Juan (riv.), Nicaragua 154/E5
San Juan, Peru 128/E10
San Juan, Philippines 82/E5
San Juan (dist.), P. Rico 161/D1
San Juan (cap.), P. Rico 146/M8
San Juan (cap.), P. Rico 161/E1
San Juan (cap.), P. Rico 156/G1
San Juan (cape), P. Rico 156/G1
San Juan, Cabezas de (prom.), P. Rico 161/F1
San Juan, Texas 303/F11
San Juan, Trin. & Tob. 161/A10
San Juan (co.), Utah 304/E6
San Juan (riv.), Utah 304/D6
San Juan (co.), Wash. 310/C2
San Juan (isl.), Wash. 310/B2
San Juan Bautista, Calif. 204/D7
San Juan Bautista, Paraguay 144/D5
San Juan Bautista de Neembucú, Paraguay 144/D5
San Juan Capistrano, Calif. 204/H10
San Juan de Colón, Venezuela 124/B3
San Juan de Flores, Honduras 154/D3
San Juan de las Galdonas, Venezuela 124/G2
San Juan del César, Colombia 126/D2
San Juan del Norte, Nicaragua 154/F5
San Juan del Norte (bay), Nicaragua 154/F5
San Juan de los Cayos, Venezuela 124/D2
San Juan de los Lagos, Mexico 150/H6
San Juan de los Morros, Venezuela 124/E3
San Juan de los Planes, Mexico 150/D4
San Juan del Piray, Bolivia 136/C7
San Juan del Potrero, Bolivia 136/C5
San Juan del Sur, Nicaragua 154/D5
San Juan de Manapiare, Venezuela 124/E5
San Juan de Payara, Venezuela 124/E4
San Juan Island Nat'l Hist. Park, Wash. 310/B2
San Juan Nat'l Hist. Site, P. Rico 161/D1
San Juan Nepomuceno, Paraguay 144/E5
San Juan Pueblo, N. Mex. 274/C2
San Juan Xiutetelco, Mexico 150/O1
San Juan y Martínez, Cuba 158/B2
San Julián, Argentina 143/C6
San Julián, Argentina 120/C7
San Justo, Argentina 143/F5
Sankrail, India 68/E2
Sankt Aegyd am Neuwalde, Austria 41/C3
Sankt Anton am Arlberg, Austria 41/A3
Sankt Blasien, Germany 22/C5
Sankt Gallen (canton), Switzerland 39/H2
Sankt Gallen, Switzerland 39/H2
Sankt Goar, Germany 22/B3
Sankt Ingbert, Germany 22/B4
Sankt Johann in Tirol, Austria 41/B3
Sankt Margrethen, Switzerland 39/J2
Sankt Michael im Lungau, Austria 41/B3
Sankt Michael in Obersteiermark, Austria 41/C3
Sankt Paul im Lavanttal, Austria 41/C3
Sankt Peter-Ording, Germany 22/C1
Sankt Pölten, Austria 41/C2
Sankt Valentin, Austria 41/C2
Sankt Veit an der Glan, Austria 41/C3
Sankt Vith, Belgium 27/J8
Sankt Wendel, Germany 22/B4
Sankt Wolfgang im Dalzkammergut, Austria 41/B3
Sankuru (riv.), Zaire 102/E5
Sankuru (riv.), Zaire 115/D4
San Lázaro (cape), Mexico 150/C4
San Lázaro, Paraguay 144/D3
San Leandro, Calif. 204/J2
San Leon, Texas 303/L2
San Lorenzo, Argentina 143/F6
San Lorenzo, Cerro (mt.), Argentina 143/B6
San Lorenzo, El Beni, Bolivia 136/C4
San Lorenzo, Pando, Bolivia 136/B2
San Lorenzo, Tarija, Bolivia 136/C7
San Lorenzo, Serranía (mts.), Bolivia 136/E5
San Lorenzo, Calif. 204/K2
San Lorenzo (riv.), Calif. 204/K4
San Lorenzo, Cerro (Cochrane) (mt.), Chile 138/E7
San Lorenzo, Ecuador 128/C2
San Lorenzo (cape), Ecuador 128/B3
San Lorenzo, N. Mex. 274/B6
San Lorenzo, Paraguay 144/B4
San Lorenzo, Peru 128/H8
San Lorenzo (isl.), Peru 128/D9
San Lorenzo, P. Rico 161/E2
San Lorenzo, P. Rico 156/G1
San Lorenzo, Falcón, Venezuela 124/D2
San Lorenzo, Zulia, Venezuela 124/C3
San Lorenzo de El Escorial, Spain 33/E2
Sanlúcar de Barrameda, Spain 33/C4
Sanlúcar la Mayor, Spain 33/C4
San Lucas, Bolivia 136/C7
San Lucas, Calif. 204/E7
San Lucas (cape), Mexico 146/G7
San Lucas (cape), Mexico 2/D4
San Lucas (cape), Mexico 150/E5
San Luis (prov.), Argentina 143/C3
San Luis, Argentina 143/C3
San Luis, Argentina 120/C6
San Luis, Ariz. 198/A6
San Luis (lake), Bolivia 136/C3
San Luis (res.), Calif. 204/E7
San Luis, Colo. 208/J8
San Luis (creek), Colo. 208/H6
San Luis (lake), Colo. 208/H7
San Luis (peak), Colo. 208/F6
San Luis, Cuba 156/C2
San Luis, Pinar del Río, Cuba 158/B2
San Luis, Santiago de Cuba, Cuba 158/J4
San Luis, Guatemala 154/C2
San Luis, Honduras 154/C3
San Luis, Philippines 82/E6
San Luis (passage), Texas 303/K8
San Luis, Venezuela 124/D2
San Luis de la Paz, Mexico 150/J6
San Luis del Cordero, Mexico 150/H4
San Luis Jilotepeque, Guatemala 154/C3
San Luis Obispo, Calif. 188/B3
San Luis Obispo, Calif. 146/F6
San Luis Obispo (co.), Calif. 204/E8
San Luis Obispo, Calif. 204/E8
San Luis Potosí (state), Mexico 150/J5
San Luis Potosí, Mexico 150/J5
San Luis Potosí, Mexico 146/H7
San Luis Río Colorado, Mexico 150/B1
San Manuel, Ariz. 198/E6
San Marcelino, Philippines 82/B3
San Marco in Lamis, Italy 34/E4
San Marcos, Calif. 204/H10
San Marcos, Colombia 126/C3
San Marcos, C. Rica 154/E6
San Marcos, Guatemala 154/B3
San Marcos, Honduras 154/C3
San Marcos, Mexico 150/K8
San Marcos (isl.), Mexico 150/D3
San Marcos, Texas 303/F8
San Mariano, Philippines 82/D2
San Marino 7/F4
SAN MARINO 34
San Marino, Calif. 204/D10
San Marino (cap.), San Marino 34/D3
San Martín (lake) 120/B7
San Martín, Argentina 143/C3
San Martín (lake), Argentina 143/B6
San Martín (riv.), Bolivia 136/D3
San Martin, Calif. 204/L4
San Martin (cape), Calif. 204/D8
San Martín (lake), Chile 138/E7
San Martín, Colombia 126/D6
San Martín (dept.), Peru 128/D6
San Martín, Peru 128/E3
San Martín de las Pirámides, Mexico 150/M1
San Martín de los Andes, Argentina 143/C5
San Martín de Valdeiglesias, Spain 33/D2
San Martine Draw (dry riv.), Texas 303/C11
San Martín Jilotepeque, Guatemala 154/B3
San Martín Texmelucan, Mexico 150/M1
San Mateo (co.), Calif. 204/C3
San Mateo, Calif. 204/J3
San Mateo, Fla. 212/E2
San Mateo, N. Mex. 274/B3
San Mateo (mts.), N. Mex. 274/B5
San Mateo, Spain 33/F2
San Mateo, Venezuela 124/F3
San Mateo Ixtatán, Guatemala 154/B3
San Matías (gulf), Argentina 120/C7
San Matías (gulf), Argentina 143/D5
San Matías, Bolivia 136/F5
Sanmaur, Québec 174/C3
San Mauricio, Venezuela 124/E3
Sanmenxia, China 77/H5
San Miguel, Argentina 143/E2
San Miguel, Bolivia 136/E5
San Miguel (riv.), Bolivia 136/D4
San Miguel, Calif. 204/E8
San Miguel (isl.), Calif. 204/E9
San Miguel (riv.), Colombia 126/B7
San Miguel (co.), Colo. 208/C6
San Miguel (mts.), Colo. 208/C7
San Miguel (riv.), Colo. 208/B6
San Miguel, Cuba 158/H3
San Miguel, Ecuador 128/C3
San Miguel (riv.), Ecuador 128/D2
San Miguel, El Salvador 154/D4
San Miguel (co.), N. Mex. 274/D3
San Miguel, N. Mex. 274/C6
San Miguel, Golfo de (gulf), Panama 154/H6
San Miguel, Paraguay 144/D5
San Miguel, Ayacucho, Peru 128/F9
San Miguel, Cajamarca, Peru 128/C6
San Miguel (bay), Philippines 82/D3
San Miguel (isls.), Philippines 85/F4
San Miguel (isls.), Philippines 82/B7
San Miguel (swamp), Uruguay 145/F4
San Miguel de Allende, Mexico 150/J6
San Miguel de Huachi, Bolivia 136/B4
San Miguel del Monte, Argentina 143/G7
San Miguel de Salcedo, Ecuador 128/C3
San Miguel de Tucumán, Argentina 143/D2
San Miguel de Tucumán, Argentina 120/C5
San Miguelito, Bolivia 136/A2
San Miguelito, Nicaragua 154/E5
San Miguel Nuevo, Colombia 126/B7
Sanming, China 77/J6
San Miniato, Italy 34/C3
San Narciso, Philippines 82/D4
Sannicandro Garganico, Italy 34/E4
San Nicolás, Argentina 143/F6
San Nicolás, Argentina 120/D6
San Nicolas (isl.), Calif. 204/F10
San Nicolás, Cuba 158/C1
San Nicolás (bay), Peru 128/E10
San Nicolás de los Garza, Mexico 150/J3
Sannikova (str.), U.S.S.R. 48/O2
San Nua (Sam Neua), Laos 72/E2
Sano, Ky. 237/L6
Sanok, Poland 47/F4
San Onofre, Colombia 126/C3
San Pablo, Potosí, Bolivia 136/B7
San Pablo, Santa Cruz, Bolivia 136/D4
San Pablo, Calif. 204/J1
San Pablo (bay), Calif. 204/J1
San Pablo, Chile 138/D3
San Pablo, Colombia 126/B7
San Pablo, Colo. 208/J8
San Pablo, Sierra (mts.), Honduras 154/E3
San Pablo, Laguna, Philippines 82/C3
San Pablo, Negros Occ., Philippines 82/D5
San Pascual, Philippines 82/D4
San Patricio, N. Mex. 274/D5
San Patricio, Paraguay 144/D5
San Patricio (co.), Texas 303/G10
San Pedro, Buenos Aires, Argentina 143/F6
San Pedro, Jujuy, Argentina 143/D1
San Pedro (riv.), Ariz. 188/D4
San Pedro (riv.), Ariz. 198/E6
San Pedro, Belize 154/D2
San Pedro, Chuquisaca, Bolivia 136/C6
San Pedro, El Beni, Bolivia 136/C4
San Pedro, Pando, Bolivia 136/B2
San Pedro, Santa Cruz, Bolivia 136/D5
San Pedro, Calif. 204/C11
San Pedro (bay), Calif. 204/C11
San Pedro (chan.), Calif. 204/G10
San Pedro, Santiago, Chile 138/F4
San Pedro, Valparaíso, Chile 138/F2
San Pedro (pt.), Chile 138/A5
San Pedro, Colombia 126/E5
San Pedro, Cuba 158/B2
San Pedro (riv.), Cuba 158/G3
San Pedro (riv.), Guatemala 154/B2
San Pedro, Ivory Coast 106/C8
San Pedro, Nicaragua 154/E4
San Pedro, Paraguay 144/D4-5
San Pedro, Paraguay 144/D3
San Pedro (bay), Philippines 82/E5
San Pedro, Sierra de (range), Spain 33/C3
San Pedro Carchá, Guatemala 154/B3
San Pedro de Arimena, Colombia 126/E5
San Pedro de Atacama, Chile 138/C4
San Pedro de Buena Vista, Bolivia 136/C6
San Pedro de las Bocas, Venezuela 124/G4
San Pedro de las Colonias, Mexico 150/H4
San Pedro del Gallo, Mexico 150/G4
San Pedro de Lloc, Peru 128/C6
San Pedro del Paraná, Paraguay 144/D5
San Pedro de Macorís (prov.), Dom. Rep. 158/F6
San Pedro de Macorís, Dom. Rep. 156/E3
San Pedro de Macorís, Dom. Rep. 158/F6
San Pedro de Quemes, Bolivia 136/A7
San Pedro Pochutla, Mexico 150/L9
San Pedro Sula, Honduras 154/C3
San Pedro Zacapa, Honduras 154/D3
San Perlita, Texas 303/G11
Sanpete (co.), Utah 304/C4
San Pierre, Ind. 227/D2
San Pietro (isl.), Italy 34/B5
San Pitch (riv.), Utah 304/C4
Sanpoil (riv.), Wash. 310/G2
San Quentin, Calif. 204/H1
Sanquhar, Scotland 15/D5
San Quintin, Philippines 82/C3
San Rafael, Argentina 143/C3
San Rafael, Argentina 120/C6
San Rafael, Bolivia 136/E5
San Rafael, Calif. 204/J1
San Rafael (cape), Dom. Rep. 158/F5
San Rafael, Mexico 150/M1
San Rafael (reef), Mexico 150/L4
San Rafael, N. Mex. 274/A3
San Rafael (riv.), Utah 304/D4
San Rafael, Venezuela 124/C2
San Rafael de Atamaica, Venezuela 124/E4
San Rafael del Norte, Nicaragua 154/E4
San Rafael del Sur, Nicaragua 154/D5
San Rafael del Yuma, Dom. Rep. 158/F6
San Rafael de Orituco, Venezuela 124/E3
San Rafael Swell (mts.), Utah 304/D5
San Ramón, El Beni, Bolivia 136/C3
San Ramón, Santa Cruz, Bolivia 136/D5
San Ramon, Calif. 204/K2
San Ramón, C. Rica 154/E5
San Ramón, Cuba 158/H4
San Ramón, Nicaragua 154/E4
San Ramón, Peru 128/E8
San Ramón, Uruguay 145/D5
San Ramon de la Nva. Orán, Argentina 143/D1
San Remo, Italy 34/A3
San Roque, Colombia 126/C4
San Roque, Spain 33/D4
San Rosendo, Chile 138/E1
San Saba (co.), Texas 303/F6
San Saba, Texas 303/F6
San Saba (riv.), Texas 303/D7
San Salvador, Argentina 143/G5
San Salvador (isl.), Bahamas 156/D1
San Salvador (isl.), Ecuador 128/B9
San Salvador (cap.), El Salvador 154/C4
San Salvador (cap.), El Salvador 146/J8
San Salvador, Paraguay 144/C5
San Salvador (riv.), Uruguay 145/B4
San Salvador el Seco, Mexico 150/O1
Sans Bois (mts.), Okla. 288/R4
San Sebastián, Argentina 143/C7
San Sebastián, Chile 138/F3
San Sebastián, P. Rico 161/B1
San Sebastián, Spain 7/D4
San Sebastián, Spain 33/E1
San Sebastián, Venezuela 124/E2
Sansepolcro, Italy 34/C3
San Servando, Uruguay 145/F3
San Severino Marche, Italy 34/D3
San Severo, Italy 34/E4
San Simeon, Calif. 204/D8
San Simon, Ariz. 198/F6
San Simon (riv.), Ariz. 198/F6
San Simón, Serranía (mts.), Bolivia 136/D4
San Simón del Cocuy, Venezuela 124/E3
Sanski Most, Yugoslavia 45/C3
Sansom Park Village, Texas 303/E2
Sans Souci, Trin. & Tob. 161/B10
Sans Toucher (mt.), Guadeloupe 161/A6
Santa, Idaho 220/B2
Santa, Peru 128/C7
Santa (riv.), Peru 128/C7
Santa Ana, El Beni, Bolivia 136/C3
Santa Ana, La Paz, Bolivia 136/B4
Santa Ana, Santa Cruz, Bolivia 136/E5
Santa Ana, Santa Cruz, Bolivia 136/F6
Santa Ana, Calif. 188/C4
Santa Ana, Calif. 204/D11
Santa Ana (riv.), Calif. 204/E11
Santa Ana, Colombia 126/F6
Santa Ana, Ecuador 128/B3
Santa Ana, El Salvador 154/C4
Santa Ana (mt.), El Salvador 154/C4
Santa Ana, Guatemala 154/C2
Santa Ana, Mexico 150/D1
Santa Ana (reef), Mexico 150/N7
Santa Ana, Uruguay 145/B1
Santa Ana (range), Uruguay 145/D2
Santa Ana, Anzoátegui, Venezuela 124/F3
Santa Ana, Táchira, Venezuela 124/B4
Santa Ana Chiautempan (Chiautempan), Mexico 150/N1
Santa Anna, Texas 303/E6
Santa Barbara (co.), Calif. 204/E9
Santa Barbara, Calif. 204/F9
Santa Barbara, Calif. 146/F6
Santa Barbara, Calif. 188/C4
Santa Barbara (chan.), Calif. 204/E9
Santa Barbara (isls.), Calif. 146/F6
Santa Barbara (isls.), Calif. 188/C4
Santa Barbara (isl.), Calif. 204/G10
Santa Barbara (isls.), Calif. 204/F10
Santa Bárbara, Chile 138/E1
Santa Bárbara, Colombia 126/C5
Santa Bárbara, Cuba 158/B2
Santa Bárbara, Honduras 154/C3
Santa Bárbara, Mexico 150/F3
Santa Barbara, Neth. Ant. 161/G9
Santa Bárbara, Amazonas, Venezuela 124/E6
Santa Bárbara, Barinas, Venezuela 124/C4
Santa Bárbara, Monagas, Venezuela 124/G3
Santa Bárbara, Zulia, Venezuela 124/C3
Santa Catalina, Argentina 143/C1
Santa Catalina (mts.), Ariz. 198/E6
Santa Catalina (gulf), Calif. 204/G11
Santa Catalina (isl.), Calif. 204/G10
Santa Catalina (isl.), Colombia 126/A9
Santa Catalina (isl.), Mexico 150/D4
Santa Catalina, Philippines 82/D6
Santa Catalina, Uruguay 145/B4
Santa Catalina, Delta Amacuro, Venezuela 124/H3
Santa Catalina, Barinas, Venezuela 124/D4
Santa Catarina (state), Brazil 132/D9
Santa Catarina (isl.), Brazil 120/E5
Santa Catarina (isl.), Brazil 132/E9
Santa Catharina, Neth. Ant. 161/G9
Santa Clara (co.), Calif. 204/D6
Santa Clara, Calif. 204/K3
Santa Clara, Colombia 126/F9
Santa Clara, Cuba 158/E2
Santa Clara, Cuba 146/K7
Santa Clara, Cuba 156/B2
Santa Clara (bay), Cuba 158/D1
Santa Clara, Mexico 150/H4
Santa Clara, Utah 304/A6
Santa Clara (riv.), Utah 304/A6
Santa Clara de Olimar, Uruguay 145/D3
Santa Clarita, Calif. 204/G9
Santa Claus, Georgia 217/H6
Santa Claus, Ind. 227/D8
Santa Clotilde, Peru 128/E4
Santa Cruz (prov.), Argentina 143/C6
Santa Cruz, Argentina 120/C8
Santa Cruz, Argentina 143/C7
Santa Cruz (riv.), Argentina 120/B7
Santa Cruz (riv.), Argentina 143/B7
Santa Cruz (co.), Ariz. 198/E7
Santa Cruz (riv.), Ariz. 198/D6
Santa Cruz (dept.), Bolivia 136/E5
Santa Cruz, Bolivia 120/C4
Santa Cruz, Santa Cruz, Bolivia 136/D5
Santa Cruz, Brazil 132/G4
Santa Cruz, Calif. 188/B3
Santa Cruz (co.), Calif. 204/C6
Santa Cruz, Calif. 204/K4
Santa Cruz (chan.), Calif. 204/F10
Santa Cruz (isl.), Calif. 204/F10
Santa Cruz (cap.), Canary Is., Spain 102/A2
Santa Cruz, Chile 138/F6
Santa Cruz, C. Rica 154/E5
Santa Cruz (isl.), Ecuador 128/C9

444 Santa Cruz

Santa Cruz, India 68/B7
Santa Cruz, Jamaica 158/H6
Santa Cruz, Mexico 150/D1
Santa Cruz (isl.), Mexico 150/D4
Santa Cruz, N. Mex. 274/D2
Santa Cruz, Nicaragua 154/E4
Santa Cruz, Cajamarca, Peru 128/C6
Santa Cruz, Loreto, Peru 128/E5
Santa Cruz, Davao del Sur, Philippines 82/E7
Santa Cruz, Laguna, Philippines 82/C3
Santa Cruz, Marinduque, Philippines 82/D4
Santa Cruz, Zambales, Philippines 82/B3
Santa Cruz, Portugal 33/A2
Santa Cruz (isls.), Solomon Is. 87/G6
Santa Cruz, Venezuela 124/C3
Santa Cruz das Flores, Portugal 33/A1
Santa Cruz de Bucaral, Venezuela 124/D2
Santa Cruz de la Palma, Spain 33/B4
Santa Cruz de la Palma, Spain 106/A3
Santa Cruz de la Zarza, Spain 33/E3
Santa Cruz del Norte, Cuba 158/C1
Santa Cruz de los Pinos, Cuba 158/B1
Santa Cruz del Quiché, Guatemala 154/B3
Santa Cruz del Sur, Cuba 158/G3
Santa Cruz del Sur, Cuba 156/B2
Santa Cruz del Valle Ameno, Bolivia 136/A4
Santa Cruz del Zulia, Venezuela 124/B3
Santa Cruz de Mara, Venezuela 124/C2
Santa Cruz de Mudela, Spain 33/E3
Santa Cruz de Orinoco, Venezuela 124/F3
Santa Cruz de Tenerife (prov.), Spain 33/B5
Santa Cruz de Tenerife, Spain 33/B4
Santa Cruz de Tenerife, Spain 106/A3
Santa Cruz de Yojoa, Honduras 154/D3
Santa Cruz do Rio Pardo, Brazil 135/B3
Santa Cruz do Sul, Brazil 132/C10
Santa Elena, Argentina 143/F5
Santa Elena, Bolivia 136/C7
Santa Elena (cape), C. Rica 154/D5
Santa Elena, Ecuador 128/B4
Santa Elena (bay), Ecuador 128/B3
Santa Elena, Paraguay 144/B5
Santa Elena, Peru 128/F5
Santa Elena, Venezuela 124/H5
Santa Eugenia (pt.), Mexico 146/G7
Santa Eugenia (pt.), Mexico 150/B3
Santa Eugenia, Spain 33/B1
Santa Fe (prov.), Argentina 143/D3
Santa Fe, Argentina 120/C6
Santa Fe, Argentina 143/F5
Santa Fe, Bolivia 136/D6
Santa Fe (peak), Colo. 208/H4
Santa Fe, Cuba 158/B2
Santa Fe, Cuba 156/A2
Santa Fe (isl.), Ecuador 128/C9
Santa Fe, Fla. 212/D2
Santa Fe (lake), Fla. 212/D2
Santa Fe (riv.), Fla. 212/D2
Santa Fe, Ind. 227/E3
Santa Fe, Mo. 261/J4
Santa Fe (co.), N. Mex. 274/C3
Santa Fe (cap.), N. Mex. 146/H6
Santa Fe (cap.), N. Mex. 188/E3
Santa Fe (cap.), N. Mex. 274/C3
Santa Fe, Panama 154/G6
Santa Fe, Philippines 82/C2
Santa Fé, Spain 33/E4
Santa Fe, Tenn. 237/G9
Santa Fe, Texas 303/K3
Santa Fe Springs, Calif. 204/C11
Santa Filomena, Brazil 132/E5
Santa Helena de Goiás, Brazil 132/D7
Santai, China 77/G5
Santa Inés (isl.), Chile 120/B8
Santa Inés (isl.), Chile 138/D10
Santa Inés, Anzoátegui, Venezuela 124/F3
Santa Inés, Barinas, Venezuela 124/C3
Santa Isabel, Bolivia 136/B7
Santa Isabel, Brazil 132/B5
Santa Isabel, Colombia 126/B9
Santa Isabel, Ecuador 128/C4
Santa Isabel, P. Rico 161/C3
Santa Isabel (isl.), Solomon Is. 87/G6
Santa Isabel (isl.), Solomon Is. 86/D2
Santa Isabel (creek), Texas 303/E10
Santa Isabel, Venezuela 124/F7
Santa Isabel de las Lajas, Cuba 158/E2
Santa Isabel de Sihuas, Peru 128/F11
Santa Leopoldina, Brazil 132/G7
Santa Lucía, Buenos Aires, Argentina 143/F6
Santa Lucía, Corrientes, Argentina 143/E2
Santa Lucía, Camagüey, Cuba 158/H3
Santa Lucía, Holguín, Cuba 158/J3
Santa Lucía, Pinar del Río, Cuba 158/A1
Santa Lucía, Uruguay 145/B6
Santa Lucía (riv.), Uruguay 145/D5
Santa Lucía, Venezuela 124/D3
Santa Lucía Chico (riv.), Uruguay 145/D4
Santa Luzia, Brazil 135/E1
Santa Luzia (isl.), C. Verde 106/B8
Santa Margarita, Calif. 204/E8
Santa Margarita (isl.), Mexico 150/C4
Santa Maria (cape), Angola 115/B6
Santa María, Argentina 143/C2
Santa Maria (riv.), Ariz. 198/B4
Santa Maria, Brazil 132/C10
Santa Maria, Brazil 120/D5
Santa Maria, Calif. 204/E9
Santa Maria (riv.), Calif. 204/E9
Santa Maria, C. Verde 106/B8
Santa María, Chile 138/G2
Santa María (isl.), Chile 138/D1
Santa María (cay), Cuba 158/F1
Santa María (isl.), Ecuador 128/B10
Santa María (lake), Mexico 150/F1
Santa María (riv.), Mexico 150/F1
Santa María, Paraguay 144/D5
Santa Maria, Philippines 82/C7
Santa Maria (cape), Portugal 33/C4
Santa Maria (isl.), Portugal 33/D2
Santa Maria, Texas 303/F12
Santa María (cape), Uruguay 145/F5
Santa María, Bolívar, Venezuela 124/G3
Santa Maria Capua Vetere, Italy 34/E4
Santa Maria da Vitória, Brazil 132/F6
Santa María de Erebató, Venezuela 124/F5
Santa María de Ipire, Venezuela 124/F3
Santa María del Orinoco, Venezuela 124/E4
Santa María del Oro, Mexico 150/G3
Santa María del Río, Mexico 150/J6
Santa María del Tule, Mexico 150/L8
Santa María de Nanay, Peru 128/F4
Santa Maria di Leuca (cape), Italy 34/G5
Santa Maria im Münstertal, Switzerland 39/K3
Santa Marta, Colombia 126/D2
Santa Marta, Colombia 120/B1
Santa Marta, Sierra Nevada de (range), Colombia 126/D2
Santa Monica, Calif. 204/B10
Santa Monica (bay), Calif. 204/B11
Santana, Brazil 132/E6
Santana, Portugal 33/A2
Santana do Ipanema, Brazil 132/G5
Santana do Jacaré, Brazil 135/D2
Santana do Livramento, Brazil 132/C10
Santana do Livramento, Brazil 120/D6
Santander (dept.), Colombia 126/D4
Santander, Colombia 126/B6
Santander, Philippines 82/D6
Santander (prov.), Spain 33/D1
Santander, Spain 33/D1
Santander, Spain 7/D4
Santander Jiménez, Mexico 150/K4
Santanilla (isls.), Honduras 154/F2
Sant'Antioco (pen.), Italy 34/B5
Santañy, Spain 33/H3
Santa Olalla del Cala, Spain 33/C4
Santa Paula, Calif. 204/F9
Santaquin, Utah 304/C4
Santarém, Brazil 132/C3
Santarém, Brazil 120/D3
Santarém (dist.), Portugal 33/B3
Santarém, Portugal 33/B3
Santarén (chan.), Bahamas 156/B1
Santarén (chan.), Cuba 156/B1
Santa Rita, Cuba 158/H4
Santa Rita, Guam 86/K7
Santa Rita, Honduras 154/D3
Santa Rita, Mont. 262/D2
Santa Rita, N. Mex. 274/B6
Santa Rita, Philippines 82/E5
Santa Rita, Guárico, Venezuela 124/E3
Santa Rita, Zulia, Venezuela 124/C2
Santa Rita do Sapucaí, Brazil 135/D3
Santa Rosa, Argentina 120/C6
Santa Rosa, Córdoba, Argentina 143/D3
Santa Rosa, La Pampa, Argentina 143/D4
Santa Rosa, San Luis, Argentina 143/C3
Santa Rosa, Cochabamba, Bolivia 136/B5
Santa Rosa, Cochabamba, Bolivia 136/C5
Santa Rosa, El Beni, Bolivia 136/B4
Santa Rosa, Pando, Bolivia 136/B2
Santa Rosa, Santa Cruz, Bolivia 136/D5
Santa Rosa, Brazil 132/C4
Santa Rosa, Calif. 188/B3
Santa Rosa, Calif. 204/C5
Santa Rosa (isl.), Calif. 204/E10
Santa Rosa, C. Rica 154/E5
Santa Rosa, Ecuador 128/C4
Santa Rosa (co.), Fla. 212/B6
Santa Rosa (isl.), Fla. 212/B6
Santa Rosa (sound), Fla. 212/B6
Santa Rosa, Mo. 261/D3
Santa Rosa (range), Nev. 266/D1
Santa Rosa, N. Mex. 274/E4
Santa Rosa, Paraguay 144/D5
Santa Rosa, Uruguay 145/B6
Santa Rosa, Anzoátegui, Venezuela 124/F3
Santa Rosa, Apure, Venezuela 124/D4
Santa Rosa, Barinas, Venezuela 124/D3
Santa Rosa Beach, Fla. 212/C6
Santa Rosa de Aguán, Honduras 154/E2
Santa Rosa de Amanadona, Venezuela 124/E7
Santa Rosa de Cabal, Colombia 126/C5
Santa Rosa de Copán, Honduras 154/C3
Santa Rosa de la Mina, Bolivia 136/D5
Santa Rosa de la Roca, Bolivia 136/E5
Santa Rosa de Lima, El Salvador 154/D4
Santa Rosa de Lima, Guatemala 154/B3
Santa Rosa del Palmar, Bolivia 136/E5
Santa Rosa de Osos, Colombia 126/C4
Santa Rosa Ind. Res., Calif. 204/J10
Santa Rosalía, Mexico 150/C3
Santa Rosalía, Venezuela 124/F4
Santa Rosa Wash (dry riv.), Ariz. 198/D6
Santa Teresa, North. Terr. 93/D8
Santa Teresa, Venezuela 124/E2
Santa Venetia, Calif. 204/J1
Santa Victoria, Argentina 143/D1
Santa Vitória do Palmar, Brazil 132/C11
Santa Ynez (riv.), Calif. 204/E9
Santa Ysabel Ind. Res., Calif. 204/J10
Santee, Calif. 204/J11
Santee, Nebr. 264/G2
Santee (riv.), S.C. 188/L4
Santee, S.C. 296/F5
Santee (dam), S.C. 296/G4
Santee (riv.), S.C. 296/H5
Santee Ind. Res., Nebr. 264/G2
Santeetlah (lake), N.C. 281/B4
Sant'Elpidio a Mare, Italy 34/E3
Santeramo in Colle, Italy 34/F4
Sant'Eufemia (gulf), Italy 34/F5
Santiago, Potosí, Bolivia 136/A7
Santiago, Santa Cruz, Bolivia 136/F6
Santiago, Serranía de (mts.), Bolivia 136/F6
Santiago, Brazil 132/C10
Santiago, Región Metropolitana de (Santiago Metropolitan Region) (reg.), Chile 138/A9
Santiago (cap.), Chile 2/F7
Santiago (cap.), Chile 120/B6
Santiago (cap.), Chile 138/G3
Santiago (prov.), Dom. Rep. 158/D5
Santiago, Dom. Rep. 158/D5
Santiago, Dom. Rep. 156/D3
Santiago (San Salvador) (isl.), Ecuador 128/B9
Santiago, Mexico 150/E5
Santiago (riv.), Mexico 146/H7
Santiago, Minn. 255/E5
Santiago, Panama 154/G6
Santiago, Cerro (mt.), Panama 154/G6
Santiago, Paraguay 144/D5
Santiago, Peru 128/E10
Santiago (riv.), Peru 128/D4
Santiago, Philippines 82/C2
Santiago, Spain 33/B1
Santiago (mts.), Texas 303/A8
Santiago (peak), Texas 303/D12
Santiago de Cao, Peru 128/C6
Santiago de Chocorvos, Peru 128/E9
Santiago de Chuco, Peru 128/C7
Santiago de Cuba (prov.), Cuba 158/H4
Santiago de Cuba, Cuba 146/L8
Santiago de Cuba, Cuba 156/C3
Santiago de Cuba, Cuba 158/J4
Santiago de Huata, Bolivia 136/A5
Santiago de las Vegas, Cuba 158/C1
Santiago del Estero (prov.), Argentina 143/D2
Santiago del Estero, Argentina 120/C5
Santiago del Estero, Argentina 143/D2
Santiago de Machaca, Bolivia 136/A5
Santiago de Pacaguaras, Bolivia 136/A3
Santiago do Cacem, Portugal 33/B3
Santiago Ixcuintla, Mexico 150/G6
Santiago Jamiltepec, Mexico 150/K8
Santiago Juxtlahuaca, Mexico 150/K8
Santiago Miahuatlán, Mexico 150/O2
Santiago Papasquiaro, Mexico 150/F4
Santiago Pinotepa Nacional, Mexico 150/K8
Santiago Rodríguez (prov.), Dom. Rep. 158/D5
Santiago Tuxtla, Mexico 150/M7
Santiago Vázquez, Uruguay 145/A7
Santiaguillo (lake), Mexico 150/G4
San Timoteo, Venezuela 124/C3
Santipur, India 68/F4
Säntis (mt.), Switzerland 39/H2
Santo, Texas 303/F5
Santo Amaro, Brazil 132/G6
Santo André, Brazil 135/C3
Santo Ângelo, Brazil 132/C10
Santo Antão (isl.), C. Verde 106/A7
Santo António, São T. & Pr. 106/F8
Santo Antônio da Platina, Brazil 132/D8
Santo Antônio da Platina, Brazil 135/A3
Santo Antônio do Leverger, Brazil 132/C6
Santo Corazón, Bolivia 136/F5
Santo Domingo, C. Rica 154/F6
Santo Domingo, Cuba 158/E1
Santo Domingo (cap.), Dom. Rep. 146/L8
Santo Domingo (cap.), Dom. Rep. 156/E3
Santo Domingo (cap.), Dom. Rep. 158/E6
Santo Domingo, Nicaragua 154/E4
Santo Domingo de la Calzada, Spain 33/E1
Santo Domingo de los Colorados, Ecuador 128/C3
Santo Domingo Pueblo, N. Mex. 274/C3
San Tomé, Venezuela 124/F3
Santoña, Spain 33/E1
Santos, Brazil 2/G7
Santos, Brazil 132/E9
Santos, Brazil 120/E5
Santos, Brazil 135/C3
Santos, Fla. 212/D2
Santos Dumont, Brazil 132/F8
Santos Dumont, Brazil 135/E2
Santos Mercado, Bolivia 136/B1
Santo Tomás, Mexico 150/A1
Santo Tomás, Nicaragua 154/E5
Santo Tomás, Amazonas, Peru 128/C6
Santo Tomás, Cuzco, Peru 128/G10
Santo Tomas, Davao, Philippines 82/E7
Santo Tomas, La Union, Philippines 82/C2
Santo Tomas (mt.), Philippines 82/C2
Santo Tomás de Andoas, Peru 128/D4
Santo Tomás de Castilla, Guatemala 154/C3
Santo Tomé, Corrientes, Argentina 143/E2
Santo Tomé, Santa Fe, Argentina 143/F5
Santuck, S.C. 296/D2
Santuit, Mass. 249/N6
Santurce, P. Rico 161/E1
San Urbano, Argentina 143/F6
San Valentín, Cerro (mt.), Chile 138/D6
San Vicente, Chile 138/F4
San Vicente (San Vicente de Tagua Tagua), Chile 138/F5
San Vicente, El Salvador 154/C4
San Vicente, Mexico 150/B1
San Vicente, Apure, Venezuela 124/D4
San Vicente, Amazonas, Venezuela 124/E5
San Vicente de Alcántara, Spain 33/C3
San Vicente de Cañete, Peru 128/D9
San Vicente del Caguán, Colombia 126/C6
San Vito, Italy 34/B5
San Vito (cape), Italy 34/D5
San Vito al Tagliamento, Italy 34/D2
San Vito dei Normanni, Italy 34/F4
San Vito Romano, Italy 34/F6
San Xavier Ind. Res., Ariz. 198/D6
Sanyati (riv.), Zimbabwe 118/D3
San Ygnacio, Texas 303/E10
San Ysidro, N. Mex. 274/C3
Sanyuan, China 77/G5
Sanza Pombo, Angola 115/C5
São Bento, Brazil 132/E3
São Bernardo do Campo, Brazil 135/C3
São Borja, Brazil 132/C10
São Brás de Alportel (Alportel), Portugal 33/C4
São Carlos, Brazil 135/C3
São Cristóvão, Brazil 132/G5
São Domingos, Brazil 132/E6
São Félix, Brazil 132/G6
São Fidélis, Brazil 132/F8
São Fidélis, Brazil 135/F2
São Francisco, Brazil 132/E6
São Francisco (riv.), Brazil 120/E4
São Francisco (riv.), Brazil 2/G6
São Francisco (riv.), Brazil 132/F5
São Francisco (riv.), Brazil 135/D2
São Francisco do Sul, Brazil 132/E9
São Gabriel, Brazil 132/C10
São Gonçalo, Brazil 132/F8
São Gonçalo, Brazil 135/E3
São Gonçalo do Sapucaí, Brazil 135/D2
São João da Boa Vista, Brazil 132/E8
São João da Boa Vista, Brazil 135/C2
São João da Madeira, Portugal 33/B2
São João da Pesqueira, Portugal 33/C2
São João del Rei, Brazil 132/E8
São João del Rei, Brazil 135/D2
São João de Meriti, Brazil 135/E3
São João do Piauí, Brazil 132/F5
São João dos Patos, Brazil 132/F4
São João Nepomuceno, Brazil 135/E2
São Joaquim da Barra, Brazil 135/C2
São Jorge (isl.), Portugal 33/B1
São José, Brazil 132/D9
São José da Laje, Brazil 132/H5
São José do Gurupi, Brazil 132/E3
São José do Rio Pardo, Brazil 135/C2
São José do Rio Preto, Brazil 120/E5
São José do Rio Preto, Brazil 132/D8
São José do Rio Preto, Brazil 135/B2
São José dos Campos, Brazil 135/D3
São José dos Pinhais, Brazil 132/D9
São Leopoldo, Brazil 132/D10
São Lourenço, Brazil 135/D3
São Lourenço (riv.), Brazil 132/C7
São Lourenço do Sul, Brazil 132/C10
São Luís, Brazil 132/F3
São Luís, Brazil 120/E3
São Luís Gonzaga, Brazil 132/C10
São Manuel, Brazil 135/B3
São Marcos (bay), Brazil 120/E3
São Marcos (bay), Brazil 132/F3
São Martinho do Porto, Portugal 33/B3
São Mateus, Brazil 132/G7
São Miguel (isl.), Portugal 33/D2
São Miguel Arcanjo, Brazil 135/C3
São Miguel do Guamá, Brazil 132/E3
São Miguel dos Campos, Brazil 132/G5
Saona (isl.), Dom. Rep. 156/E3
Saona (isl.), Dom. Rep. 158/F6
Saône (riv.), France 28/F4
Saône-et-Loire (dept.), France 28/F4
Saonek, Indonesia 85/J6
São Nicolau (isl.), C. Verde 106/B8
São Paulo (state), Brazil 135/B3
São Paulo (state), Brazil 132/D8
São Paulo, Brazil 120/E5
São Paulo, Brazil 2/G6
São Paulo, Brazil 132/E8
São Paulo, Brazil 135/C3
São Paulo de Olivença, Brazil 132/G9
São Pedro do Piauí, Brazil 132/F4
São Pedro do Sul, Portugal 33/B2
São Raimundo das Mangabeiras, Brazil 132/E4
São Raimundo Nonato, Brazil 132/F5
São Romão, Brazil 132/E7
São Roque, Brazil 135/C3
São Roque (cape), Brazil 2/H6
São Roque (cape), Brazil 120/F3
São Roque (cape), Brazil 132/H4
São Sebastião, Brazil 135/D3
São Sebastião (isl.), Brazil 120/E5
São Sebastião (isl.), Brazil 135/D3
São Sebastião (isl.), Brazil 132/E8
São Sebastião (pt.), Mozambique 118/F4
São Sebastião do Paraíso, Brazil 135/C2
São Sebastião do Paraíso, Brazil 132/E8
São Simão, Brazil 135/C2
São Teotónio, Portugal 33/B4
São Tiago (isl.), C. Verde 106/B8
São Tomé (cape), Brazil 120/F5
São Tomé (cape), Brazil 132/F8
São Tomé (cap.), São T. & Pr. 106/F8
São Tomé (isl.), São T. & Pr. 106/F8
São Tomé & Príncipe 102/C4
SÃO TOMÉ AND PRÍNCIPE 106/F8
Saoura, Wadi (dry riv.), Algeria 106/D3
São Vicente, Brazil 135/C4
São Vicente (isl.), C. Verde 106/B7
São Vicente, Portugal 33/A2
São Vicente (cape), Portugal 7/C5
São Vicente Ferrer, Brazil 132/E3
São Vincent (cape), Portugal 33/B4
Sapahaqui, Bolivia 136/B5
Sápai, Greece 45/G5
Sapanca, Turkey 63/D2
Saparua, Indonesia 85/H6
Sapawe, Ontario 177/G5
Sapawe, Ontario 175/B3
Sapele, Nigeria 106/F7
Sapello, N. Mex. 274/D3
Sapelo (isl.), Georgia 217/K8
Sapelo (sound), Georgia 217/K7
Sapelo Island, Georgia 217/K8
Şaphane, Turkey 63/C3
Saponac, Maine 243/G5
Saposoa, Peru 128/D6
Sappa (creek), Kansas 232/B2
Sappemeer-Hoogezand, Netherlands 27/K2
Sapphire, N.C. 281/D4
Sappho, Wash. 310/A2
Sappington, Mo. 261/O4
Sapporo, Japan 2/S3
Sapporo, Japan 54/P5
Sapporo, Japan 81/K2
Sapse, Bolivia 136/C6
Sapucaí (riv.), Brazil 135/D2
Sapucaí, Paraguay 144/B5
Sapulpa, Okla. 288/O3
Saqqez, Iran 59/E2
Saqqez, Iran 66/E2
Saquena, Peru 128/F5
Sara (riv.), Cent. Afr. Rep. 115/C2
Sara (riv.), Chad 111/C6
Sara, Philippines 82/D5
Sarab, Iran 66/E2
Sara Buri, Thailand 72/D4
Saragosa, Texas 303/D11
Saragossa, Ala. 195/D3
Saragossa, Spain 7/D4
Saragossa, Spain 33/F2
Saraguro, Ecuador 128/C4
Sarah (lake), Minn. 255/F5
Sarah, Miss. 256/D1
Sarahsville, Ohio 284/H6
Sarajevo, Yugoslavia 7/F4
Sarajevo, Yugoslavia 45/D4
Sarakhs, Iran 66/M2
Saraland, Ala. 195/B9
Saramacca (dist.), Suriname 131/C3
Saramacca (riv.), Suriname 131/D3
Sarampiuni, Bolivia 136/A4
Saran', U.S.S.R. 48/H5
Saranac, Mich. 250/D6
Saranac, N.Y. 276/N1
Saranac (lkes), N.Y. 276/M2
Saranac (riv.), N.Y. 276/N1
Saranac Lake, N.Y. 276/M2
Sarandë, Albania 45/E6
Sarandí del Yi, Uruguay 145/D4
Sarandí de Navarro, Uruguay 145/C3
Sarandí Grande, Uruguay 145/C4
Sarangani (bay), Philippines 82/E8
Sarangani (isls.), Philippines 82/E8
Sarangani (isls.), Philippines 85/G4
Sarangani (str.), Philippines 82/E8
Saransk, U.S.S.R. 7/J3
Saransk, U.S.S.R. 48/E4
Saransk, U.S.S.R. 52/G4
Sarapul, U.S.S.R. 7/K3
Sarapul, U.S.S.R. 48/F4
Sarapul, U.S.S.R. 52/H3
Sarare, Venezuela 124/D3
Sarare (riv.), Venezuela 124/C4
Sarasota, Fla. 188/K5
Sarasota (co.), Fla. 212/D4
Sarasota, Fla. 212/D4
Sarasota (pt.), Fla. 212/D4
Sarasota Springs, Fla. 212/D4
Saraswati (riv.), India 68/F1
Saratoga, Ark. 202/C6
Saratoga, Calif. 204/K4
Saratoga, Ind. 227/H4
Saratoga, Iowa 229/J2
Saratoga, Miss. 256/E7
Saratoga (co.), N.Y. 276/N4
Saratoga (lake), N.Y. 276/N4
Saratoga, Texas 303/K7
Saratoga, Wyo. 319/F4
Saratoga Nat'l Hist. Park, N.Y. 276/N4
Saratoga Springs, N.Y. 276/N4
Saratov, U.S.S.R. 7/J3
Saratov, U.S.S.R. 48/E4
Saratov, U.S.S.R. 52/G4
Saravan, Iran 59/H4
Saravan, Iran 66/N7
Saravan, Laos 72/E4
Sarawak (state), Malaysia 2/Q5
Sarawak (state), Malaysia 85/E5
Sarawak (reg.), Malaysia 54/N9
Sarayacu, Ecuador 128/D3
Sarayköy, Turkey 63/C4
Sarayönü, Turkey 63/E3
Sarbaz, Iran 66/M7
Sarbaz, Iran 59/H4
Sarben, Nebr. 264/C3
Sárbogárd, Hungary 41/E3
Sarco (bay), Chile 138/A7
Sarcoxie, Mo. 261/D8
Sardarshahr, India 68/C3
Sar Dasht, Iran 66/D2
Sardina (pt.), P. Rico 161/A1
Sardinata, Colombia 126/D3
Sardinia, Ind. 227/F6
Sardinia (reg.), Italy 34/B4
Sardinia (isl.), Italy 7/E4
Sardinia (isl.), Italy 34/B4
Sardinia, N.Y. 276/C5
Sardinia, Ohio 284/C7
Sardinia, S.C. 296/G4
Sardis, Ala. 195/E6
Sardis, Ala. 195/F2
Sardis, Br. Col. 184/M3
Sardis, Georgia 217/J5
Sardis, Ky. 237/O3
Sardis (lake), Miss. 188/J4
Sardis, Miss. 256/E2
Sardis (dam), Miss. 256/E2
Sardis (lake), Miss. 256/E2
Sardis, Ohio 284/J6
Sardis, Okla. 288/R5
Sardis, Tenn. 237/E10
Sardis, W. Va. 312/F4
Sar-e Pol, Afghanistan 68/B1
Sar-e Pol, Afghanistan 59/J2
Sarepta, La. 238/D1
Sarepta, Miss. 256/F2
Sargans, Switzerland 39/H2
Sargeant, Minn. 255/F7
Sargent, Georgia 217/C4
Sargent, Nebr. 264/E3
Sargent (co.), N. Dak. 282/P7
Sargents, Colo. 208/F6
Sargodha, Pakistan 59/K3
Sargodha, Pakistan 68/C2
Sarh, Chad 111/C6
Sarh, Chad 102/D4
Sarhro, Jebel (mts.), Morocco 106/C2
Sari, Iran 59/F2
Sari, Iran 66/H2
Saría (isl.), Greece 45/H8
Sarigan (isl.), No. Marianas 87/E4
Sarıgöl, Turkey 63/C3
Sarih, Jordan 65/D2
Sarıkamış, Turkey 63/K2
Sarıkamış, Turkey 59/D1
Sarıkaya, Turkey 63/F3
Sarıköy, Turkey 63/B2
Sarina, Queensland 88/H4
Sarina, Queensland 95/D4
Sarine (Saane) (riv.), Switzerland 39/D3
Sariñena, Spain 33/F2
Sarıoğlan, Turkey 63/G3
Sarita, Texas 303/G10
Sariwŏn, N. Korea 81/B4
Sarıyer, Turkey 63/D5
Sarız, Turkey 63/G3
Sark (isl.), Chan. Is. 13/E8
Sark (isl.), Chan. Is. 10/E6
Sarkad, Hungary 41/F3
Sarkand, U.S.S.R. 48/J5
Şarkikaraağaç, Turkey 63/D3
Şarkışla, Turkey 63/G3
Şarköy, Turkey 63/B2
Sarlat-La-Canéda, France 28/D5
Sarles, N. Dak. 282/N2
Sarmi, Indonesia 85/K6
Sarmiento, Argentina 143/B6
Sarmiento, Argentina 120/C7
Sarmiento, Cerro (mt.), Chile 138/E11
Särna, Sweden 18/H6
Sarnath, India 68/E3
Sarnen, Switzerland 39/F3
Sarnen (lake), Switzerland 39/F3
Sarnia, Ont. 162/H7
Sarnia, Ontario 177/B5
Sarny, U.S.S.R. 52/C4
Sarona, Wis. 317/C4
Saronic (gulf), Greece 45/F7
Saronno, Italy 34/B2
Saronville, Nebr. 264/G4
Saros (gulf), Turkey 63/B2
Sárospatak, Hungary 41/F2
Sarpsborg, Norway 18/D4
Sarpy (co.), Nebr. 264/H3
Sarra (well), Libya 111/D3
Sarralbe, France 28/G3
Sarrebourg, France 28/G3
Sarreguemines, France 28/G3
Sarria, Spain 33/C1
Sarroch, Italy 34/B5
Sarsati (riv.), India 68/F1
Sarstún (riv.), Belize 154/C3
Sarstún (riv.), Guatemala 154/C3
Sartell, Minn. 255/D5
Sartène, France 28/B7
Sarthe (dept.), France 28/D3
Sarthe (riv.), France 28/D4
Sartrouville, France 28/A1
Sarufutsu, Japan 81/L1
Sarur, Oman 59/G5
Sárvár, Hungary 41/D3
Sarver, Pa. 294/C4
Sárviz csatorna (canal), Hungary 41/E3
Saryshagan, U.S.S.R. 48/H5
Sary Su (riv.), U.S.S.R. 48/H5
Sasabe, Ariz. 198/D7
Sasabe, Mexico 150/C1
Sasaginnigak (lake), Manitoba 179/G3
Sasakwa, Okla. 288/N5
Sasaram, India 68/E4
Sasebo, Japan 81/D7
Saseenos, Br. Col. 184/J3
SASKATCHEWAN 181
Saskatchewan (prov.) 162/F5
Saskatchewan (riv.) 162/F5
Saskatchewan (prov.), Canada 146/H4
Saskatchewan (riv.), Canada 2/D3
Saskatchewan (riv.), Sask. 181/H2
Saskatchewan Beach, Sask. 181/G5
Saskatchewan Landing Prov. Park, Sask. 181/C5
Saskatoon, Sask. 162/F5
Saskatoon, Sask. 146/H4
Saskatoon, Sask. 181/E3
Saskeram (riv.), Sask. 181/K2
Sason, Turkey 63/J3
Sasovo, U.S.S.R. 52/F4
Saspamco, Texas 303/K11
Sassafras, Md. 245/P3
Sassafras (riv.), Md. 245/P3
Sassafras (mt.), S.C. 296/B1
Sassafras, Tasmania 99/C3
Sassandra, Ivory Coast 106/C8
Sassandra (riv.), Ivory Coast 106/C7
Sassari (prov.), Italy 34/B4
Sassari, Italy 34/B4
Sassari, Italy 7/E4
Sasseneire (mt.), Switzerland 39/E4
Sasser, Georgia 217/D7

446 Sebastian

Sebastian (co.), Ark. 202/B3
Sebastian, Fla. 212/F4
Sebastian (cape), Oreg. 291/C5
Sebastián Vizcaíno (bay), Mexico 150/B2
Sebasticook (lake), Maine 243/E6
Sebastopol, Calif. 204/C5
Sebastopol, Miss. 256/F5
Sebastopol, Victoria 97/B5
Sebatik (isl.), Indonesia 85/F5
Sebatik (isl.), Malaysia 85/F5
Sebec, Maine 243/E5
Sebec•, Maine 243/E5
Sebec Lake, Maine 243/E5
Sebec Station, Maine 243/E5
Sebeka, Minn. 255/C4
Seben, Turkey 63/D2
Sebeş, Romania 45/F3
Sebes Kürüs (riv.), Hungary 41/F3
Sebewaing, Mich. 250/F5
Sebha, Libya 102/D2
Sebha, Libya 111/B2
Şebinkarahisar, Turkey 63/H2
Sebiş, Romania 45/F2
Sebnitz, Germany 22/F3
Seboeis•, Maine 243/F5
Seboeis (lake), Maine 243/F5
Seboeis (riv.), Maine 243/F3
Seboomook, Maine 243/D4
Seboomook (lake), Maine 243/D4
Seboruco, Venezuela 124/B3
Sebou (riv.), Morocco 106/C2
Seboyeta, N. Mex. 274/B3
Sebree, Ky. 237/F5
Sebrell, Va. 307/O7
Sebring, Fla. 212/E4
Sebring, Ohio 284/H4
Sebringville, Ontario 177/C4
Sebuku (bay), Indonesia 85/F5
Secane, Pa. 294/M7
Secas (isls.), Panama 154/G7
Secaucus, N.J. 273/B2
Secesh (riv.), Idaho 220/C4
Sechelt, Br. Col. 184/J2
Sechura, Peru 128/B5
Sechura (bay), Peru 128/B5
Seco, Ky. 237/R6
Second (lake), N.H. 268/E1
Second Cataract, Sudan 59/B5
Second Cataract, Sudan 111/F3
Secondcreek, W. Va. 312/F7
Second Mesa, Ariz. 198/E3
Secor, Ill. 222/D3
Sečovce, Czech. 41/F2
Secretan, Sask. 181/E5
Secretary, Md. 245/P6
Secretary (isl.), N. Zealand 100/A6
Section, Ala. 195/G1
Secunderabad, India 68/D5
Sécure (riv.), Bolivia 136/C4
Security-Widefield, Colo. 208/K5
Sedalia, Alberta 182/E4
Sedalia, Colo. 208/K4
Sedalia, Ind. 227/E4
Sedalia, Ky. 237/D7
Sedalia, Mo. 261/F5
Sedalia, Mo. 188/H3
Sedalia, Ohio 284/D6
Sedalia, S.C. 296/D2
Sedan, France 28/F3
Sedan, Ind. 227/G2
Sedan, Kansas 232/F4
Sedan, Minn. 255/C5
Sedan, N. Mex. 274/F2
Sedano, Spain 33/E1
Sedbergh (co.), England 10/E3
Sedbergh, England 13/E3
Seddon, N. Zealand 100/E4
Seddonville, N. Zealand 100/C4
Seddülbahir, Turkey 63/B6
Sede Boqer, Israel 65/D5
Sederot, Israel 65/B4
Sedgewick, Alberta 182/E3
Sedgewickville, Mo. 261/N7
Sedgwick, Ark. 202/J2
Sedgwick (co.), Colo. 208/P1
Sedgwick, Colo. 208/O1
Sedgwick (co.), Kansas 232/E4
Sedgwick, Kansas 232/E4
Sedgwick•, Maine 243/F7
Sedhiou, Senegal 106/A6
Sedili Kechil, Tanjong (pt.), Malaysia 72/F5
Sedlčany, Czech. 41/C2
Sedley, Sask. 181/H5
Sedley, Va. 307/P7
Sedom, Israel 65/D5
Sedona, Ariz. 198/D4
Sedot Yam, Israel 65/B3
Sedro-Woolley, Wash. 310/C2
Šeduva, U.S.S.R. 53/B3
Seebe, Alberta 182/C4
Seebert, W. Va. 312/F6
Seechelt (inlet), Br. Col. 184/J2
Seechelt (pen.), Br. Col. 184/J2
Seeheim, Namibia 118/B5
Seeis, Namibia 118/B4
Seekonk•, Mass. 249/J5
Seeley, Calif. 204/K11
Seeley, Wis. 317/D3
Seeley Lake, Mont. 262/C3
Seeleys Bay, Ontario 177/H3
Seelyville, Ind. 227/C6
Seelyville, Pa. 294/M2
Seesen, Germany 22/D3
Seewis im Prättigau, Switzerland 39/J2
Seez (riv.), Switzerland 39/H2
Şefaatli, Turkey 63/F3
Seferihisar, Turkey 63/B3
Seffner, Fla. 212/D4
Sefrou, Morocco 106/D2
Sefton, N. Zealand 100/D5
Seg (lake), U.S.S.R. 52/D2
Segamat, Malaysia 72/D7
Segarcea, Romania 45/F3
Segezha, U.S.S.R. 52/D2
Segezha, U.S.S.R. 48/D3
Segnes (pass), Switzerland 39/H3
Segni, Italy 34/F7
Segorbe, Spain 33/F3
Ségou, Mali 106/C6
Ségou, Mali 102/B3
Segovia, Colombia 126/C4
Segovia (Coco) (riv.), Honduras 154/E3
Segovia (Coco) (riv.), Nicaragua 154/E3
Segovia (prov.), Spain 33/D2
Segovia, Spain 33/D2
Segré, France 28/C4
Segre (riv.), Spain 33/G2
Segreganset, Mass. 249/K5
Seguam (isl.), Alaska 196/D4
Seguam (passage), Alaska 196/D4
Séguéla, Ivory Coast 106/C7
Seguí, Argentina 143/F6
Seguin, Kansas 232/B2
Séguin (lake), Québec 172/B2
Seguin, Texas 303/G8
Segula (isl.), Alaska 196/K4
Segundo, Colo. 208/K8
Segura (riv.), Spain 33/F3
Sehore, India 68/D4
Sehwan, Pakistan 59/J4
Sehwan, Pakistan 68/B3
Seiad Valley, Calif. 204/B2
Seibert (lake), Alberta 182/E2
Seibert, Colo. 208/O4
Seibo, Dom. Rep. 156/E3
Seil (isl.), Scotland 15/C4
Seiland (isl.), Norway 18/N1
Seiling, Okla. 288/J2
Sein (isl.), France 28/A3
Seinäjoki, Finland 18/N5
Seine (riv.), France 7/E4
Seine (bay), France 28/C3
Seine (riv.), France 28/D3
Seine (riv.), Ontario 175/B3
Seine-et-Marne (dept.), France 28/E3
Seine-Saint-Denis (dept.), France 28/C1
Seistan (reg.), Iran 66/M5
Seixal, Portugal 33/A1
Seiyun, Yemen 59/E6
Sejerø (isl.), Denmark 21/E6
Sejny, Poland 47/F1
Seke-Banza, Zaire 115/B5
Sekenke, Tanzania 115/F4
Se Khong (riv.), Cambodia 72/E4
Se Khong (riv.), Laos 72/E4
Sekiu, Wash. 310/A2
Sekkane, Erg (des.), Mali 106/D4
Sekondi, Ghana 106/D8
Selah, Wash. 310/E4
Selama, Malaysia 72/D6
Selangor (state), Malaysia 72/D7
Selaphum, Thailand 72/E3
Selaru (isl.), Indonesia 85/J7
Selatan (cape), Indonesia 85/E6
Selawik, Alaska 196/G1
Selawik (lake), Alaska 196/F1
Selayar (isl.), Indonesia 85/G7
Selb, Germany 22/E3
Selby, England 13/F4
Selby, S. Dak. 298/J3
Selby, Victoria 97/K5
Selby-on-the-Bay, Md. 245/N5
Selbyville, Del. 245/S7
Selbyville, W. Va. 312/F5
Selçuk, Turkey 63/B3
Selden, Kansas 232/B2
Seldom, Newf. 166/D4
Seldovia, Alaska 196/B2
Sele (riv.), Italy 34/E4
Selebi-Pikwe, Botswana 118/D4
Selemdzha (riv.), U.S.S.R. 48/O4
Selemiya, Syria 63/G5
Selendi, Turkey 63/C3
Selenga (riv.) 54/M5
Selenge, Mongolia 77/G2
Selenge, Mongolia 77/F2
Selenge Mörün (Selenga) (riv.), Mongolia 77/G2
Sélestat, France 28/G3
Selfridge, N. Dak. 282/J7
Sélibaby, Mauritania 106/B5
Seligman, Ariz. 198/B3
Seligman, Mo. 261/D9
Selim, Turkey 63/K2
Selima (oasis), Sudan 111/E3
Selima (oasis), Sudan 59/A5
Selimiye, Turkey 63/B4
Selinsgrove, Pa. 294/J4
Selje, Norway 18/D5
Selkirk (mts.), Br. Col. 184/J4
Selkirk (mts.), Idaho 220/B1
Selkirk, Kansas 232/A3
Selkirk, Man. 162/G5
Selkirk, Manitoba 179/F4
Selkirk (isl.), Manitoba 179/C1
Selkirk, Mich. 250/E4
Selkirk (trad. co.), Scotland 15/B5
Selkirk, Scotland 10/E3
Selkirk, Scotland 15/F5
Sella, Bolivia 136/C7
Selle (peak), Haiti 158/C6
Selleck, Wash. 310/D3
Sellers, Ala. 195/F6
Sellers, S.C. 296/H3
Sellersburg, Ind. 227/F8
Sellersville, Pa. 294/M5
Sells, Ariz. 198/D7
Sells, Georgia 217/E2
Sellye, Hungary 41/D4
Selma, Ala. 188/J4
Selma, Ala. 195/E6
Selma, Ark. 202/G6
Selma, Calif. 204/F7
Selma, Ind. 227/G4
Selma, Iowa 229/J7
Selma, Miss. 256/B7
Selma, N.C. 281/N3
Selma, Ohio 284/C6
Selma, Oreg. 291/D5
Selma, Texas 303/K10
Selma, Va. 307/J5
Selmah, Nova Scotia 168/E3
Selman, Okla. 288/H1
Selmer, Tenn. 237/D10
Selmont, Ala. 195/E6
Selous (mt.), Yukon 187/E3
Selsey, England 13/G7
Selsey Bill (prom.), England 13/G7
Selva, Argentina 143/D2
Selvas (for.), Brazil 120/C3
Selvin, Ind. 227/C8
Selway (riv.), Idaho 220/C3
Selwyn (lake), N.W. Terr. 187/H4
Selwyn, Queensland 95/B4
Selwyn (range), Queensland 95/B4
Selwyn (lake), Sask. 181/M2
Selwyn, W. Va. 312/B7
Selwyn (mts.), Yukon 187/E3
Selz, N. Dak. 282/L4
Seman, Ala. 195/F5
Semans, Sask. 181/G4
Semara, W. Sahara 102/A2
Semara, W. Sahara 106/B3
Semarang, Indonesia 54/N10
Semarang, Indonesia 85/J2
Sematan, Malaysia 85/D5
Sembé, Congo 115/B3
Sembrancher, Switzerland 39/D4
Şemdinli, Turkey 63/L4
Semenov, U.S.S.R. 52/F3
Semeru (mt.), Indonesia 85/K2
Semichi (isls.), Alaska 196/J3
Semidi (isls.), Alaska 196/G3
Semiluki, U.S.S.R. 52/E4
Semily, Czech. 41/C1
Seminary, Miss. 256/E7
Seminoe (res.), Wyo. 188/E2
Seminoe (mts.), Wyo. 319/E3
Seminoe (res.), Wyo. 319/F3
Seminoe Dam, Wyo. 319/E3
Seminole, Ala. 195/D10
Seminole (co.), Fla. 212/E3
Seminole, Fla. 212/B3
Seminole (lake), Fla. 212/B1
Seminole (co.), Georgia 217/C9
Seminole (lake), Georgia 217/B9
Seminole (co.), Okla. 288/N4
Seminole, Okla. 288/N4
Seminole, Pa. 294/D4
Seminole, Texas 303/B5
Seminole Ind. Res., Fla. 212/F5
Seminole Ind. Res., Fla. 212/E4
Semipalatinsk, U.S.S.R. 54/K4
Semipalatinsk, U.S.S.R. 48/H4
Semirara (isls.), Philippines 82/C5
Semisopochnoi (isl.), Alaska 196/K4
Semitau, Indonesia 85/E5
Semmering (pass), Austria 41/C3
Semmes, Ala. 195/B9
Semnan (governorate), Iran 66/J3
Semnan, Iran 59/F2
Semnan, Iran 66/H3
Semois (riv.), Belgium 27/G9
Semora, N.C. 281/L2
Sempach, Switzerland 39/F2
Sempach (lake), Switzerland 39/F2
Semporna, Malaysia 85/F5
Semsales, Switzerland 39/C3
Semur-en-Auxois, France 28/F4
Sen, Stoeng (riv.), Cambodia 72/E4
Sena, Bolivia 136/B2
Sena, N. Mex. 274/D3
Senador Pompeu, Brazil 132/G4
Senai, Malaysia 72/F5
Sena Madureira, Brazil 132/G10
Senanga, Zambia 115/D7
Senate, Sask. 181/B6
Senath, Mo. 261/M10
Senatobia, Miss. 256/E1
Sendai, Japan 54/R6
Sendai, Kagoshima, Japan 81/E8
Sendai, Miyagi, Japan 81/K4
Senec, Czech. 41/D2
Seneca, Ill. 222/E2
Seneca, Kansas 232/F2
Seneca, Miss. 256/F8
Seneca, Mo. 261/C9
Seneca, Nebr. 264/D2
Seneca, N. Mex. 274/F2
Seneca (co.), N.Y. 276/G5
Seneca (lake), N.Y. 276/G5
Seneca (riv.), N.Y. 276/G5
Seneca (co.), Ohio 284/D3
Seneca, Oreg. 291/J3
Seneca, S.C. 296/A2
Seneca (riv.), S.C. 296/B2
Seneca, S. Dak. 298/L3
Seneca, Wis. 317/E9
Seneca Falls, N.Y. 276/G5
Seneca Gardens, Ky. 237/K2
Senécal (lake), Newf. 166/B3
Senecaville, Ohio 284/H6
Senecaville (lake), Ohio 284/H6
Senegal 2/J5
Senegal 102/A3
SENEGAL 106/A5
Senegal (riv.) 102/A3
Senegal (riv.), Mali 106/B5
Senegal (riv.), Mauritania 106/B5
Senegal (riv.), Senegal 106/B5
Senekal, S. Africa 118/D5
Seney, Iowa 229/H3
Seney, Mich. 250/C2
Senftenberg, Germany 22/F3
Sengiley, U.S.S.R. 52/G4
Senguerr (riv.), Argentina 143/B6
Senhor do Bonfim, Brazil 120/F4
Senhor do Bonfim, Brazil 132/F5
Senica, Czech. 41/D2
Senigallia, Italy 34/D3
Senirkent, Turkey 63/D3
Senj, Yugoslavia 45/B3
Senja (isl.), Norway 7/F2
Senja (isl.), Norway 18/K2
Şenkaya, Turkey 63/K2
Senlac, Sask. 181/B3
Senlis, France 28/E3
Senmonoron, Cambodia 72/E4
Sennar, Sudan 59/B7
Sennar, Sudan 111/F5
Sennar, Sudan 102/F3
Sennar (dam), Sudan 59/B7
Sennar (dam), Sudan 111/F5
Senne (riv.), Belgium 27/E7
Senneterre, Québec 174/B3
Senneville, Québec 172/G4
Senoia, Georgia 217/C4
Sens, France 28/E3
Sense (riv.), Switzerland 39/D3
Sensuntepeque, El Salvador 154/C4
Sent, Switzerland 39/K3
Senta, Yugoslavia 45/D3
Sentery, Zaire 115/E5
Sentinel, Alberta 182/C5
Sentinel, Ariz. 198/B6
Sentinel (butte), N. Dak. 282/C6
Sentinel, Okla. 288/H4
Sentinel Butte, N. Dak. 282/C6
Senyavin (isls.), Micronesia 87/F5
Seo de Urgel, Spain 33/G1
Seon, Switzerland 39/F2
Seoni, India 68/D4
Seoul (cap.), S. Korea 2/R4
Seoul (cap.), S. Korea 54/O6
Seoul (cap.), S. Korea 81/C5
Separ, N. Mex. 274/A6
Sepetiba (bay), Brazil 135/D3
Sepik (riv.), Papua N.G. 85/B6
Sępólno Krajeńskie, Poland 47/C2
Septentrional, Cordillera (range), Dom. Rep. 158/D5
Sept-Îles, Québec 146/M4
Sept-Îles, Québec 162/K5
Sept-Îles, Québec 174/D2
Septimer (pass), Switzerland 39/J4
Sepulga (riv.), Ala. 195/E7
Sepulveda, Calif. 204/B10
Sequatchie (co.), Tenn. 237/L10
Sequatchie, Tenn. 237/K10
Sequatchie (riv.), Tenn. 237/L10
Sequeira, Uruguay 145/C1
Sequeros, Spain 33/C2
Sequim, Wash. 310/B2
Sequoia Nat'l Park, Calif. 204/G7
Sequoyah (co.), Okla. 288/S3
Sera (isl.), Indonesia 85/J7
Serafimovich, U.S.S.R. 52/F5
Serafina, N. Mex. 274/D3
Seraing, Belgium 27/G7
Serakhs, U.S.S.R. 48/G6
Serampore, India 68/F1
Serang, Indonesia 85/G1
Serangoon, Singapore 72/F6
Serasan (isl.), Indonesia 85/D5
Serbia (rep.), Yugoslavia 45/E3
Serçiler, Turkey 63/C6
Serdobol (Sortavala), U.S.S.R. 52/D2
Serdobsk, U.S.S.R. 52/F4
Sered', Czech. 41/D2
Şereflikoçhisar, Turkey 63/E3
Seremban, Malaysia 72/D7
Serena, Ill. 222/E2
Serengeti Nat'l Park, Tanzania 115/F4
Serenje, Zambia 115/F6
Sergach, U.S.S.R. 52/F3
Sergeant, Pa. 294/E2
Sergeant Bluff, Iowa 229/A4
Sergeantsville, N.J. 273/D3
Sergeya Kirova (isls.), U.S.S.R. 48/J2
Sergipe (state), Brazil 132/G5
Seria, Brunei 85/E5
Serian, Malaysia 85/E5
Sérifos (isl.), Greece 45/G7
Sérigny (riv.), Québec 174/D1
Serik, Turkey 63/D4
Seringapatam, India 68/D6
Sermata (isl.), Indonesia 85/H7
Serón, Spain 33/E4
Serós, Spain 33/G2
Serov, U.S.S.R. 54/H4
Serov, U.S.S.R. 48/G4
Serowe, Botswana 118/D4
Serowe, Botswana 102/E7
Serpa, Portugal 33/C4
Serpentine (lake), New Bruns. 170/D1
Serpentine (lakes), S. Australia 88/D5
Serpentine (lakes), S. Australia 94/A3
Serpentine (riv.), W. Australia 88/B3
Serpents Mouth (passage), Trin. & Tob. 156/G5
Serpents Mouth (passage), Trin. & Tob. 161/A11
Serpents Mouth (passage), Venezuela 124/H3
Serpukhov, U.S.S.R. 7/H3
Serpukhov, U.S.S.R. 48/D4
Serpukhov, U.S.S.R. 52/E4
Serra do Navio, Brazil 132/C2
Sérrai, Greece 7/G4
Sérrai, Greece 45/F5
Serrana (bank), Colombia 126/B9
Serra Namuli (mt.), Mozambique 102/F6
Serranilla (bank), Colombia 126/B8
Serra Talhada, Brazil 132/G4
Serres, France 28/F5
Serrinha, Brazil 120/F4
Serrinha, Brazil 132/G5
Sertã, Portugal 33/B3
Sertânia, Brazil 132/G5
Sertãozinho, Brazil 135/B2
Serua (isl.), Indonesia 85/H7
Serui, Indonesia 85/K6
Serule, Botswana 118/D4
Sérvia, Greece 45/F5
Servia, Ind. 227/F3
Servia, W. Va. 312/E5
Service Creek, Oreg. 291/G3
Serviceton, Victoria 97/A5
Sêrxü, China 77/E5
Se San (riv.), Vietnam 72/E4
Sese (isls.), Uganda 115/F4
Sesegenaga (lake), Ontario 177/G4
Sesfontein, Namibia 118/A3
Sesfontein, S. Africa 118/J6
Sesheke, Zambia 115/D7
Sesimbra, Portugal 33/B3
Sesser, Ill. 222/D5
Sessums, Miss. 256/G4
Sesto Fiorentino, Italy 34/C3
Sestri Levante, Italy 34/B2
Sesvenna (peak), Switzerland 39/K3
Sète, France 28/E6
Sete Lagoas, Brazil 120/E4
Sete Lagoas, Brazil 132/E7
Sete Quedas, (Grande) (isl.), Brazil 132/C8
Seth, W. Va. 312/C6
Sétif, Algeria 106/F1
Sétif, Algeria 102/C1
Setit (riv.), Sudan 111/G5
Seto, Japan 81/H6
Setonaikai National Park, Japan 81/H7
Seton Portage, Br. Col. 184/F5
Setouchi, Japan 81/O5
Settat, Morocco 106/C2
Settebagni, Italy 34/F6
Setté-Cama, Gabon 115/A4
Settecamini, Italy 34/F6
Setting (lake), Manitoba 179/H3
Settle, England 13/E3
Settsu, Japan 81/J8
Sétubal (dist.), Portugal 33/B3
Setúbal, Portugal 7/D5
Setúbal, Portugal 33/B3
Setúbal (bay), Portugal 33/B3
Seul (lake), Ontario 177/G4
Seul (lake), Ontario 175/B2
Seul Choix (pt.), Mich. 250/D3
Seuzach, Switzerland 39/G1
Sevan (lake), U.S.S.R. 7/J4
Sevan (lake), U.S.S.R. 52/G6
Sevaruyo, Bolivia 136/B6
Sevastopol', U.S.S.R. 7/H4
Sevastopol', U.S.S.R. 48/D5
Sevastopol', U.S.S.R. 52/D6
Sevelen, Switzerland 39/H2
Seven (heads), Ireland 17/D8
Seven Corners, Va. 307/S3
Seven Devils (res.), Ark. 202/G6
Seven Devils (mts.), Idaho 220/B4
Seven Hills, Ohio 284/H9
Seven Hogs, The (isls.), Ireland 17/A7
Seven Islands (bay), Newf. 166/B2
Seven Mile, Ohio 284/A7
Sevenmile (creek), Ohio 284/A6
Seven Mile Ford, Va. 307/E7
Sevenoaks, England 13/J8
Sevenoaks, England 10/C6
Seven Persons, Alberta 182/E5
Seven Rivers (riv.), N. Mex. 274/E6
Seven Sisters, Texas 303/F9
Seven Sisters Falls, Manitoba 179/G4
Seven Springs, N.C. 281/O4
Seven Springs, Pa. 294/D6
Seventy Mile House, Br. Col. 184/G4
Seven Valleys, Pa. 294/J6
Severance, Colo. 208/K1
Severance, Kansas 232/G2
Severn (riv.), England 13/E6
Severn (riv.), England 10/E5
Severn, Md. 245/M4
Severn (riv.), Md. 245/N4
Severn (riv.), N.S. Wales 97/F1
Severn, N.C. 281/P2
Severn (riv.), Ont. 146/J4
Severn (riv.), Ont. 162/G5
Severn (lake), Ontario 175/B2
Severn (riv.), Ontario 177/E3
Severn (riv.), Ontario 175/B2
Severn, Mouth of the (est.), Wales 13/B7
Severn (riv.), Wales 13/E5
Severna Park, Md. 245/M4
Severnaya Zemlya (isls.), U.S.S.R. 4/A4
Severnaya Zemlya (isls.), U.S.S.R. 54/M1
Severnaya Zemlya (isls.), U.S.S.R. 2/P1
Severnaya Zemlya (isls.), U.S.S.R. 48/L1
Severnyy, U.S.S.R. 52/K1
Severobaykal'sk, U.S.S.R. 48/M4
Severočeský (reg.), Czech. 41/C1
Severodonetsk, U.S.S.R. 52/E5
Severodvinsk, U.S.S.R. 7/H2
Severodvinsk, U.S.S.R. 48/E3
Severodvinsk, U.S.S.R. 52/E2
Severo-Kuril'sk, U.S.S.R. 48/Q4
Severomoravský (reg.), Czech. 41/D2
Severomorsk, U.S.S.R. 52/D1
Severoural'sk, U.S.S.R. 48/G3
Severo-Yeniseysk, U.S.S.R. 48/K3
Severy, Kansas 232/F4
Sevier (co.), Ark. 202/B6
Sevier, N.C. 281/E3
Sevier (co.), Tenn. 237/O9
Sevier (co.), Utah 304/C5
Sevier, Utah 304/B5
Sevier (des.), Utah 304/B4
Sevier (lake), Utah 188/D3
Sevier (lake), Utah 304/A5
Sevier (riv.), Utah 188/D3
Sevier (riv.), Utah 304/B4
Sevier, East Fork (riv.), Utah 304/B6
Sevier Bridge (res.), Utah 304/C4
Sevierville, Tenn. 237/P9
Sevilla, Colombia 126/C5
Sevilla (prov.), Spain 33/D4
Seville, Fla. 212/E2
Seville, Georgia 217/E7
Seville, Ohio 284/G3
Seville, Spain 7/D5
Seville, Spain 33/D4
Sevlievo, Bulgaria 45/G4
Sèvres, France 28/A2
Sewal, Iowa 229/G7
Sewalls Point, Fla. 212/F4
Sewanee, Tenn. 237/K10
Seward, Alaska 146/C3
Seward, Alaska 188/D6
Seward, Alaska 196/C1
Seward (pen.), Alaska 146/B3
Seward (pen.), Alaska 196/E1
Seward (co.), Kansas 232/B4
Seward, Kansas 232/D3
Seward (co.), Nebr. 264/G4
Seward, Nebr. 264/H4
Seward, Okla. 288/M3
Seward, Pa. 294/E5
Seward, U.S. 4/D17
Seward (pen.), U.S. 4/C18
Sewaren, N.J. 273/E2
Sewart A.F.B., Tenn. 237/J8
Sewell, Br. Col. 184/A3
Sewell, Ky. 237/P5
Sewell, N.J. 273/C4
Sewickley, Pa. 294/B4
Sexsmith, Alberta 182/A2
Sexton, Ind. 227/G5
Sexton, Iowa 229/E2
Sextons Creek, Ky. 237/O6
Sextonville, Wis. 317/F9
Seybaplaya, Mexico 150/O7
Seychelles 2/M6
SEYCHELLES 118/H5
Seydhisfjördhur, Iceland 21/D1
Seydişehir, Turkey 63/D4
Seyfe (lake), Turkey 63/F3
Seyhan (riv.), Turkey 63/F4
Seyhan (riv.), Turkey 59/C2
Seyitgazi, Turkey 63/D3
Seym (riv.), U.S.S.R. 52/D4
Seymour (canal), Alaska 196/N1
Seymour (inlet), Br. Col. 184/D4
Seymour•, Conn. 210/C3
Seymour, Ill. 222/E3
Seymour, Ind. 227/F7
Seymour, Iowa 229/G7
Seymour, Mo. 261/G8
Seymour, Tenn. 237/O9
Seymour, Texas 303/E4
Seymour (lake), Vt. 268/D2
Seymour, Victoria 88/H7
Seymour, Victoria 97/C5
Seymour, Wis. 317/K6
Seymour Johnson A.F.B., N.C. 281/O4
Seymourville, La. 238/J2
Seymourville, Manitoba 179/F3
Seyppel, Ark. 202/K4
Sézanne, France 28/E3
Sezze, Italy 34/D4
Sfax, Tunisia 106/G2
Sfax, Tunisia 102/D1
Sfîntu Gheorghe, Romania 45/G3
Sfîntu Gheorghe, Romania 45/J3
's-Gravenbrakel (Braine-le-Comte), Belgium 27/D7
's Gravendeel, Netherlands 27/E5
's Gravenhage (The Hague) (cap.), Netherlands 27/E4
's Gravenzande, Netherlands 27/E4
Sgurr a Choire Ghlais (mt.), Scotland 15/D3
Sgurr Alasdair (mt.), Scotland 15/B3
Sgurr Mor (mt.), Scotland 15/C3
Sgurr na Ciche (mt.), Scotland 15/C3
Sgurr na Lapaich (mt.), Scotland 15/C3
Shaanxi (Shensi), China 77/G5
Shaba (prov.), Zaire 115/E5
Shabasha, Sudan 59/B7
Shabbona, Ill. 222/E2
Shabeellaha Dhexe (prov.), Somalia 115/J3
Shabeellaha Hoose (prov.), Somalia 115/H3
Shabla, Bulgaria 45/J4
Shabo, Newf. 166/A3
Shabogamo (lake), Newf. 166/A3
Shabunda, Zaire 115/E4
Shabwa, Yemen 59/E6
Shache (Yarkand), China 77/A4
Shache, China 54/J6
Shackelford (co.), Texas 303/E5
Shackleton, Sask. 181/C5
Shackleton Ice Shelf, Ant. 2/P9
Shackleton Ice Shelf, Ant. 5/C5
Shade, Ohio 284/G7
Shadegan, Iran 66/F5
Shade Gap, Pa. 294/G5
Shadehill, S. Dak. 298/E2
Shadehill (res.), S. Dak. 298/E2
Shadeland, Ind. 227/C4
Shader, Scotland 15/B2
Shadrinsk, U.S.S.R. 48/G4
Shady Bend, Kansas 232/D2
Shady Cove, Oreg. 291/E5
Shady Dale, Georgia 217/E4
Shady Grove, Ala. 195/F7
Shady Grove, Fla. 212/C1
Shady Grove, Ky. 237/F6
Shady Grove, Pa. 294/G6
Shady Point, Okla. 288/S4
Shady Side, Md. 245/M5
Shadyside, Ohio 284/J6
Shady Valley, Tenn. 237/T7
Shafer (lake), Ind. 227/D3
Shafer, Minn. 255/F5
Shafter, Calif. 204/F8
Shafter, Nev. 266/G2
Shafter, Texas 303/C12
Shaftesbury, England 13/E7
Shaftesbury, England 10/E5
Shaftsbury•, Vt. 268/A6
Shageluk, Alaska 196/G2
Shag Harbour, Nova Scotia 168/C5
Shahat, Libya 102/E1
Shahat, Libya 111/D1
Shahbandar, Pakistan 68/B4
Shahdad, Iran 59/G3
Shahdad, Iran 66/K5
Shahdol, India 68/E4
Shahistan (Saravan), Iran 66/M5
Shah Jahan, Kuh-e (mts.), Iran 66/L2
Shahjahanpur, India 68/E3
Shah Juy, Afghanistan 59/J3

Shoalwater 447

Shahrakht, Iran 66/M4
Shahreza, Iran 59/F3
Shahreza, Iran 66/H4
Shahr Kord, Iran 66/G4
Shahrud, Iran 59/G2
Shahrud, Iran 66/J2
Shaibara (isl.), Saudi Arabia 59/C4
Sha'ib Hisb, Wadi (dry riv.), Iraq 66/C5
Shaikh Sa'ad, Iraq 66/E4
Shaikh Shu'aib (isl.), Iran 66/H7
Shaikh Shu'aib (isl.), Iran 59/F4
Shailerville, Conn. 210/E3
Shajapur, India 68/D4
Shakawe, Botswana 118/C3
Shaker Heights, Ohio 284/H9
Shakespeare, Ontario 177/D4
Shakhtinsk, U.S.S.R. 48/H5
Shakhty, U.S.S.R. 7/J4
Shakhty, U.S.S.R. 48/E5
Shakhty, U.S.S.R. 52/F5
Shakhun'ya, U.S.S.R. 52/G3
Shaki, Nigeria 106/E7
Shâkir (isl.), Egypt 59/B4
Shakopee, Minn. 255/F6
Shakopee (creek), Minn. 255/C5
Shaktoolik, Alaska 196/F2
Shalath, Br. Col. 184/F5
Shaler (mts.), N.W. Terr. 187/G2
Shalimar, Fla. 212/C6
Shallala, Wadi esh (dry riv.), Jordan 65/D2
Shallotte, N.C. 281/N7
Shallow (lake), Maine 243/E3
Shallowater, Texas 303/B4
Shallow Lake, Ontario 177/C3
Shallow Water, Kansas 232/B3
Sham, Jebel (mt.), Oman 59/G5
Shamattawa, Manitoba 179/K2
Shamattawa (riv.), Ontario 175/C2
Shambaugh, Iowa 229/D7
Shambe, Sudan 111/F6
Shamil, Iran 66/K7
Shammar, Jebel (plat.), Saudi Arabia 59/D4
Shamokin, Pa. 294/J4
Shamokin Dam, Pa. 294/J4
Shamrock, Okla. 288/N3
Shamrock, Sask. 181/E5
Shamrock, Texas 303/D2
Shamrock Lakes, Ind. 227/G4
Shamva, Zimbabwe 118/E3
Shan (state), Burma 72/C2
Shan (plat.), Burma 72/C2
Shanagolden, Ireland 17/C6
Shandan, China 77/F4
Shandon, Calif. 204/E8
Shandong (Shantung) (prov.), China 77/J4
Shangani (riv.), Zimbabwe 118/D3
Shangdu, China 77/H3
Shanghai, China 2/R4
Shanghai, China 54/O6
Shanghai, China 77/K5
Shanghai, Va. 307/P5
Shanghai, W. Va. 312/K4
Shanghang, China 77/J6
Shangnan, China 77/H5
Shangqui (Shangkiu), China 77/J5
Shangrao (Shangjao), China 77/J6
Shangshui, China 77/J5
Shang Xian, China 77/H5
Shangzhi, China 77/L2
Shaniko, Oreg. 291/G3
Shanks, W. Va. 312/J4
Shanksville, Pa. 294/E5
Shannock, R.I. 249/H7
Shannon, Georgia 217/B2
Shannon (isl.), Greenl. 4/B10
Shannon, Ill. 222/D1
Shannon, Mouth of the (est.), Ireland 17/B6
Shannon (riv.), Ireland 10/B4
Shannon (riv.), Ireland 17/E6
Shannon, Miss. 256/G2
Shannon (co.), Mo. 261/K8
Shannon, New Bruns. 170/E3
Shannon, N. Zealand 100/E4
Shannon, N.C. 281/L5
Shannon, Québec 172/F3
Shannon (co.), S. Dak. 298/D7
Shannon (lake), Wash. 310/D2
Shannon Airport, Ireland 17/D6
Shannon Bridge, Ireland 17/F5
Shannon City, Iowa 229/E7
Shannondale, Ind. 227/D4
Shannon Hills, Ark. 202/F4
Shannontown, S.C. 296/G4
Shannonville, Ontario 177/G3
Shanshan (Piqan), China 77/D3
Shansi (Shanxi) (prov.), China 77/H4
Shantar (isls.), U.S.S.R. 54/P4
Shantar (isls.), U.S.S.R. 48/O4
Shantou (Swatou), China 77/J7
Shantou, China 54/N7
Shantung (Shandong) (prov.), China 77/J4
Shanty Bay, Ontario 177/E3
Shanxi (Shansi) (prov.), China 77/H4
Shanyang, China 77/G5
Shanyin, China 77/H4
Shaoguan (Shiukwan), China 77/H7
Shaowu, China 77/J6
Shaoxing (Shaohing), China 77/K5
Shaoyang, China 77/H6
Shap, England 13/E3
Shapinsay (isl.), Scotland 15/F1
Shapio (lake), Newf. 166/B3
Shapleigh, Maine 243/B8
Shapleigh•, Maine 243/B8
Shaqlawa, Iraq 66/D2
Shaqra, Saudi Arabia 54/F7
Shaqra, Saudi Arabia 59/D4
Sharafkhaneh, Iran 66/D1
Sharbatat, Ras (cape), Oman 59/G6
Sharbot Lake, Ontario 177/H3
Shari (riv.) 102/D4
Shari (riv.), Cent. Afr. Rep. 115/C2
Shari (riv.), Chad 111/C5
Shari, Japan 81/M2
Sharifabad, Iran 66/L2
Sharjah, U.A.E. 59/F4
Shark (pt.), Fla. 212/E6
Shark (bay), W. Australia 88/A5
Shark (bay), W. Australia 92/A4
Shark Bay, W. Australia 88/A5
Sharkey (co.), Miss. 256/C5
Sharlyk, U.S.S.R. 52/H4
Sharon•, Conn. 210/B1
Sharon, Georgia 217/G3
Sharon, Kansas 232/D4
Sharon, Mass. 249/K4
Sharon•, Mass. 249/K4
Sharon, Miss. 256/E5
Sharon•, N.H. 268/D6
Sharon, N. Dak. 282/P4
Sharon, Ohio 284/G6
Sharon, Okla. 288/H2
Sharon, Pa. 294/B3
Sharon, S.C. 296/E2
Sharon, Tenn. 237/D8
Sharon•, Vt. 268/C4
Sharon, W. Va. 312/D6
Sharon, Wis. 317/J11
Sharon Center, Ohio 284/G3
Sharon Grove, Ky. 237/G7
Sharon Hill, Pa. 294/N7
Sharon Springs, Kansas 232/A3
Sharon Springs, N.Y. 276/L5
Sharon Valley, Conn. 210/B1
Sharonville, Ohio 284/C9
Sharp (co.), Ark. 202/G1
Sharpe, Kansas 232/G3
Sharpe (lake), S. Dak. 298/J5
Sharpe Army Depot, Calif. 204/D6
Sharpes, Fla. 212/F3
Sharples, W. Va. 312/C7
Sharps (isl.), Md. 245/N6
Sharps, Va. 307/P5
Sharpsburg, Georgia 217/C4
Sharpsburg, Iowa 229/D7
Sharpsburg, Ky. 237/O4
Sharpsburg, Md. 245/G3
Sharpsburg, N.C. 281/O3
Sharpsburg, Pa. 294/B6
Sharps Chapel, Tenn. 237/O8
Sharpsville, Ind. 227/E4
Sharpsville, Pa. 294/A3
Sharptown, Md. 245/R6
Sharptown, N.J. 273/C4
Shar'ya, U.S.S.R. 48/E4
Shar'ya, U.S.S.R. 52/G3
Shashe, Botswana 118/D4
Shashe (riv.), Botswana 118/D4
Shashe (riv.), Zimbabwe 118/D4
Shashi (Shasi), China 77/H5
Shasta, Calif. 204/C3
Shasta (co.), Calif. 204/C3
Shasta (dam), Calif. 204/C3
Shasta (lake), Calif. 204/C3
Shasta (mt.), Calif. 188/B2
Shasta (mt.), Calif. 204/C2
Shasta (res.), Calif. 188/B2
Shasta (riv.), Calif. 204/C2
Shati, Wadi esh (dry riv.), Libya 111/B2
Shatra, Iraq 66/E5
Shattuc, Ill. 222/D5
Shattuck, Okla. 288/G2
Shattuckville, Mass. 249/D2
Shauck, Ohio 284/E4
Shaughnessy, Alberta 182/D5
Shaunavon, Sask. 162/F6
Shaunavon, Sask. 181/C6
Shavano Park, Texas 303/J10
Shaver Lake, Calif. 204/F6
Shavers Fork (riv.), W. Va. 312/G5
Shave Ziyyon, Israel 65/B2
Shaw, Kansas 232/G4
Shaw, La. 238/G4
Shaw, Minn. 255/F3
Shaw, Miss. 256/C3
Shaw (mt.), N.H. 268/E4
Shaw, Oreg. 291/A3
Shaw A.F.B., S.C. 296/F4
Shawan, China 77/B3
Shawanese, Pa. 294/E7
Shawano (co.), Wis. 317/J6
Shawano, Wis. 317/J6
Shawano (lake), Wis. 317/K6
Shawboro, N.C. 281/S2
Shawbost, Scotland 15/B2
Shawbridge, Québec 172/C4
Shawinigan, Que. 162/J6
Shawinigan, Québec 174/C3
Shawinigan, Québec 172/E3
Shawinigan (riv.), Québec 172/E3
Shawinigan-Sud, Québec 172/E3
Shaw Island, Wash. 310/B2
Shawmut, Maine 243/D6
Shawmut, Mont. 262/G4
Shawmut, Pa. 294/E3
Shawnee, Colo. 208/H4
Shawnee (co.), Kansas 232/G2
Shawnee, Kansas 232/H2
Shawnee, Ohio 284/F6
Shawnee, Okla. 188/G3
Shawnee, Okla. 288/N4
Shawnee, Wyo. 319/G3
Shawnee Hills, Ohio 284/D5
Shawnee on Delaware, Pa. 294/N3
Shawneetown, Ill. 222/E6
Shawnigan Lake, Br. Col. 184/J3
Shawomet, R.I. 249/J6
Shawsheen Village, Mass. 249/K2
Shawshine (riv.), Mass. 249/K2
Shawsville, Md. 245/M2
Shawsville, Va. 307/H6
Shawville, Québec 172/A4
Shay Gap, W. Australia 92/C3
Shayib, Jebel (mt.), Egypt 59/B4
Shay Juy, Afghanistan 68/B2
Shchekino, U.S.S.R. 52/E4
Shchel'yayur, U.S.S.R. 52/H1
Shchigry, U.S.S.R. 52/E4
Shchuchinsk, U.S.S.R. 48/H4
Sheakleyville, Pa. 294/B3
Sheaville, Oreg. 291/K4
Shebandowan, Ontario 177/G5
Sheberghan, Afghanistan 54/H6
Sheberghan, Afghanistan 68/B1
Sheberghan, Afghanistan 59/H2
Sheboygan, Wis. 188/J2
Sheboygan (co.), Wis. 317/L8
Sheboygan, Wis. 317/L8
Sheboygan Falls, Wis. 317/L8
Shedd, Oreg. 291/D3
Shedden, Ontario 177/C5
Shediac, New Bruns. 170/F2
Shediac (isl.), New Bruns. 170/F2
Shediac Bridge, New Bruns. 170/F2
Sheeffry (hills), Ireland 17/B4
Sheelin (lake), Ireland 17/G4
Sheenjek (riv.), Alaska 196/K1
Sheep (mt.), Colo. 208/E6
Sheep (mt.), Mont. 262/C2
Sheep (range), Nev. 266/F6
Sheep (creek), Oreg. 291/L2
Sheep (creek), Utah 304/E3
Sheep Creek, Alberta 182/A2
Sheep Haven (harb.), Ireland 17/F1
Sheeps (head), Ireland 17/B8
Sheepscott, Maine 243/D7
's Heerenberg, Netherlands 27/J5
Sheerness, Alberta 182/E4
Sheet (harb.), Nova Scotia 168/F4
Sheet Harbour, Nova Scotia 168/F4
Shefar'am, Israel 65/C2
Shefayim, Israel 65/B3
Sheffield, Ala. 195/C1
Sheffield, England 7/D3
Sheffield, England 10/F4
Sheffield, England 13/J2
Sheffield, Ill. 222/D2
Sheffield, Iowa 229/G3
Sheffield•, Mass. 249/A4
Sheffield, Mont. 262/K4
Sheffield, New Bruns. 170/D3
Sheffield, Ohio 284/F3
Sheffield, Pa. 294/D2
Sheffield, Tasmania 99/C3
Sheffield, Texas 303/B7
Sheffield•, Vt. 268/C2
Sheffield Lake, Ohio 284/F3
Shefford (co.), Québec 172/E4
Sheguiandah, Ontario 177/C2
Sheho, Sask. 181/H4
Shehy (mts.), Ireland 17/C8
Sheikh Sa'id, Yemen 59/D7
Sheila, New Bruns. 170/F1
Sheki, U.S.S.R. 52/G6
Shelagh (riv.), Iran 66/M5
Shelagskiy (cape), U.S.S.R. 48/R2
Shelbiana, Ky. 237/R6
Shelbina, Mo. 261/H3
Shelburn, Ind. 227/C6
Shelburne, N.H. 268/E3
Shelburne•, N.H. 268/E3
Shelburne (co.), Nova Scotia 168/C5
Shelburne, Nova Scotia 168/C5
Shelburne, Ontario 177/D3
Shelburne•, Vt. 268/A3
Shelburne (pond), Vt. 268/A3
Shelburne Falls, Mass. 249/D2
Shelby (co.), Ala. 195/E4
Shelby, Ala. 195/E4
Shelby (co.), Ill. 222/E4
Shelby (co.), Ind. 227/F5
Shelby, Ind. 227/C2
Shelby (co.), Iowa 229/C5
Shelby, Iowa 229/C5
Shelby (co.), Ky. 237/L4
Shelby, Mich. 250/C5
Shelby, Miss. 256/C3
Shelby (co.), Mo. 261/H3
Shelby, Mont. 262/E2
Shelby, Nebr. 264/G3
Shelby, N.C. 281/G4
Shelby (co.), Ohio 284/B5
Shelby, Ohio 284/E4
Shelby (co.), Tenn. 237/B10
Shelby (co.), Texas 303/K6
Shelby Center, N.Y. 276/D4
Shelbyville, Ill. 222/E4
Shelbyville (lake), Ill. 222/E4
Shelbyville, Ind. 227/F6
Shelbyville, Ky. 237/L4
Shelbyville, Mo. 261/H3
Shelbyville, Tenn. 237/H10
Shelbyville, Texas 303/L6
Sheldahl, Iowa 229/F5
Sheldon, Ill. 222/F3
Sheldon, Iowa 229/B2
Sheldon, Minn. 255/G7
Sheldon, Mo. 261/D7
Sheldon, N. Dak. 282/P6
Sheldon, S.C. 296/F6
Sheldon, Texas 303/K1
Sheldon•, Vt. 268/B2
Sheldon, Wis. 317/D5
Sheldon Junction, Vt. 268/B2
Sheldon Point, Alaska 196/E2
Sheldon Springs, Vt. 268/A2
Sheldonville, Mass. 249/J4
Shelekhov (gulf), U.S.S.R. 54/S3
Shelekhov (gulf), U.S.S.R. 48/Q4
Shelikof (str.), Alaska 196/H3
Shell (pt.), Fla. 212/B1
Shell (riv.), Minn. 255/C4
Shell (creek), N. Dak. 282/F3
Shell, Loch (inlet), Scotland 15/B3
Shell (lake), Wis. 317/C4
Shell, Wyo. 319/E1
Shell (creek), Wyo. 319/E1
Shellbrook, Sask. 162/F5
Shellbrook, Sask. 181/E2
Shelldrake (riv.), Mich. 250/D2
Shelley, Br. Col. 184/F3
Shelley, Idaho 220/F6
Shellharbour, N.S. Wales 97/F4
Shell Knob, Mo. 261/E9
Shell Lake, Sask. 181/D2
Shell Lake, Wis. 317/C4
Shellman, Georgia 217/C7
Shellmouth, Manitoba 179/A4
Shell Rock, Iowa 229/H3
Shellsburg, Iowa 229/K4
Shelltown, Md. 245/R9
Shelly, Minn. 255/B3
Shelmerdine, N.C. 281/P4
Shelocta, Pa. 294/D4
Shelter (isl.), N.Y. 276/R8
Shelton, Conn. 210/C3
Shelton, Nebr. 264/F4
Shelton, S.C. 296/E3
Shelton, Wash. 310/B3
Shemakha, U.S.S.R. 52/G6
Shemogue, New Bruns. 170/F2
Shemya (isl.), Alaska 196/J3
Shemya Air Force Base, Alaska 196/J3
Shenandoah, Iowa 229/C7
Shenandoah, Pa. 294/K4
Shenandoah (co.), Va. 307/L3
Shenandoah, Va. 307/L4
Shenandoah (mt.), Va. 307/K3
Shenandoah (riv.), Va. 307/N2
Shenandoah (riv.), W. Va. 312/K4
Shenandoah Junction, W. Va. 312/L4
Shenandoah Nat'l Park, Va. 307/L3
Shenango, Pa. 294/A3
Shenango River (lake), Pa. 294/B3
Shendam, Nigeria 106/F7
Shendi, Sudan 59/B6
Shendi, Sudan 102/F3
Shendi, Sudan 111/F4
Shëngjin, Albania 45/D5
Sheng Xian, China 77/K6
Shenipsit (lake), Conn. 210/F1
Shenkursk, U.S.S.R. 52/F2
Shenkursk, U.S.S.R. 48/E3
Shenmu, China 77/G4
Shennington, Wis. 317/F7
Shennongjia, China 77/H5
Shensi (Shaanxi) (prov.), China 77/G5
Shenyang (Mukden), China 77/K3
Shenyang, China 54/O5
Shenyang, China 2/R3
Sheopur, India 68/D3
Shepard, Alberta 182/D4
Shepardsville, Ind. 227/B5
Shepaug (dam), Conn. 210/B3
Shepaug (riv.), Conn. 210/B2
Shepetovka, U.S.S.R. 52/C4
Shepherd, Mich. 250/E5
Shepherd, Mont. 262/H5
Shepherd (bay), N.W. Terr. 187/J3
Shepherd, Texas 303/K7
Shepherdstown, W. Va. 312/L4
Shepherdsville, Ky. 237/K4
Shepody, New Bruns. 170/F3
Shepody (bay), New Bruns. 170/F3
Sheppard A.F.B., Texas 303/F3
Shepparton, Victoria 88/G7
Shepparton, Victoria 97/C5
Sheppey (isl.), England 13/J6
Sheppton, Pa. 294/K4
Shepshed, England 13/F5
Shepton Mallet, England 13/E6
Shepton Mallet, England 10/E5
Sheqi, China 77/H5
Sherack, Minn. 255/B2
Sherard, Miss. 256/C2
Sherard (cape), N.W. Terr. 187/L2
Sherborn•, Mass. 249/A8
Sherborne, England 10/E5
Sherborne, England 13/E7
Sherbro (isl.), S. Leone 106/B7
Sherbrooke, Nova Scotia 168/G3
Sherbrooke (lake), Nova Scotia 168/D4
Sherbrooke (riv.), Nova Scotia 168/D4
Sherbrooke, Que. 162/J7
Sherbrooke (co.), Québec 172/E4
Sherbrooke, Québec 172/E4
Sherburn, Minn. 255/D7
Sherburne (co.), Minn. 255/E5
Sherburne, N.Y. 276/K5
Shercock, Ireland 17/G4
Shereik, Sudan 111/F4
Sheridan, Ark. 202/F5
Sheridan, Calif. 204/D5
Sheridan, Colo. 208/J3
Sheridan, Ill. 222/E2
Sheridan, Ind. 227/E4
Sheridan (co.), Kansas 232/B2
Sheridan, Maine 243/F2
Sheridan, Mich. 250/D5
Sheridan, Mo. 261/C1
Sheridan (co.), Mont. 262/M2
Sheridan, Mont. 262/D5
Sheridan (co.), Nebr. 264/B2
Sheridan, N.Y. 276/B5
Sheridan (co.), N. Dak. 282/K4
Sheridan, Oreg. 291/D2
Sheridan, W. Va. 312/B6
Sheridan, Wis. 317/H7
Sheridan, Wyo. 188/E2
Sheridan, Wyo. 146/H5
Sheridan (co.), Wyo. 319/F1
Sheridan, Wyo. 319/F1
Sheridan Lake, Colo. 208/P6
Sheringham, England 13/J5
Sheringham, England 10/G4
Sherkin (isl.), Ireland 17/C9
Sherman (mt.), Colo. 208/G4
Sherman•, Conn. 210/B2
Sherman, Ill. 222/D4
Sherman (co.), Kansas 232/A2
Sherman, Kansas 232/H4
Sherman, Ky. 237/M3
Sherman, Maine 243/G4
Sherman•, Maine 243/G4
Sherman, Mich. 250/D4
Sherman, Miss. 256/G2
Sherman, Mo. 261/N3
Sherman (co.), Nebr. 264/F3
Sherman (res.), Nebr. 264/E3
Sherman, N. Mex. 274/B6
Sherman, N.Y. 276/A6
Sherman (inlet), N.W. Terr. 187/J3
Sherman (co.), Oreg. 291/G2
Sherman, S. Dak. 298/S6
Sherman (co.), Texas 303/C1
Sherman, Texas 303/H4
Sherman, Texas 188/G4
Sherman, W. Va. 312/C5
Sherman City, Mich. 250/D5
Sherman Mills, Maine 243/G4
Shermans Dale, Pa. 294/H5
Sherman Station, Maine 243/F4
Sherrard, Ill. 222/C2
Sherrard, W. Va. 312/E3
Sherridon, Man. 162/G4
Sherridon, Manitoba 179/H3
Sherrill, Ark. 202/F5
Sherrill, Iowa 229/M3
Sherrill, N.Y. 276/J4
Sherrington, Québec 172/D4
Sherrodsville, Ohio 284/H4
Sherry, Wis. 317/G6
's Hertogenbosch, Netherlands 27/G5
Sherwood, Ark. 202/F4
Sherwood (pt.), Conn. 210/B4
Sherwood (for.), England 13/F4
Sherwood, Mich. 250/D6
Sherwood, N. Dak. 282/G2
Sherwood, Ohio 284/A3
Sherwood, Okla. 288/S6
Sherwood, Oreg. 291/A2
Sherwood, Pr. Edward I. 168/E2
Sherwood, Tenn. 237/K10
Sherwood, Texas 303/D6
Sherwood, Wis. 317/K7
Sherwood Park, Alberta 182/D3
Sheslay (riv.), Br. Col. 184/J2
Shetek (lake), Minn. 255/C6
Shetland (islands area), Scotland 15/F2
Shetland (isls.), Scotland 7/D2
Shetland (isls.), Scotland 10/G1
Shetland (isls.), Scotland 15/G2
Shetucket (riv.), Conn. 210/G2
Shevchenko, U.S.S.R. 54/G5
Shevchenko, U.S.S.R. 48/F5
Shevlin, Manitoba 179/A3
Shevlin, Minn. 255/C3
Sheyenne, N. Dak. 282/M4
Sheyenne (riv.), N. Dak. 188/G1
Sheyenne (riv.), N. Dak. 282/O6
Sheykh Sho'eyb (isl.), Iran 66/H7
Shiant (isls.), Scotland 15/B3
Shiant (sound), Scotland 15/B3
Shiawassee (co.), Mich. 250/E6
Shiawassee (riv.), Mich. 250/E5
Shibam, Yemen 59/E6
Shibata, Japan 81/J5
Shibetsu, Japan 81/M2
Shibin el Kom, Egypt 111/J3
Shibogama (lake), Ontario 175/C2
Shickley, Nebr. 264/G4
Shickshinny, Pa. 294/K3
Shideler, Ind. 227/G4
Shidler, Okla. 288/N1
Shiel, Loch (lake), Scotland 10/D2
Shiel, Loch (lake), Scotland 15/C4
Shieldaig, Scotland 15/C3
Shields, Kansas 232/B3
Shields (riv.), Mont. 262/F4
Shields, N. Dak. 282/H7
Shieldsville, Minn. 255/E6
Shifnal, England 13/E5
Shiga (pref.), Japan 81/J7
Shigatse (Xigazê), China 77/C6
Shigawake, Québec 172/D2
Shihezi (Shihhotzu), China 77/C3
Shihr, Yemen 59/E7
Shijak, Albania 45/D5
Shijiazhuang (Shihkiachwang), China 77/J4
Shijiazhuang, China 54/N6
Shikarpur, Pakistan 68/B3
Shikarpur, Pakistan 59/J4
Shikoku, Japan 54/P6
Shikoku (isl.), Japan 2/R4
Shikoku (isl.), Japan 81/F7
Shikotan (isl.), Japan 81/N2
Shikotsu (lake), Japan 81/K2
Shikotsu-Toya Nat'l Park, Japan 81/K2
Shilbottle, England 13/F2
Shildon, England 13/F3
Shilka (riv.), U.S.S.R. 54/N4
Shilka, U.S.S.R. 48/M4
Shillelagh, Ireland 17/J6
Shillelagh, Ireland 10/C4
Shillington, Pa. 294/K5
Shillong, India 68/G3
Shilo, Manitoba 179/C5
Shiloh, Ala. 195/G2
Shiloh, Ala. 195/C6
Shiloh, Georgia 217/C5
Shiloh, Ill. 222/B3
Shiloh, N.J. 273/C5
Shiloh, Ohio 284/E4
Shiloh, S.C. 296/G4
Shiloh, Tenn. 237/E10
Shiloh, Va. 307/O4
Shiloh Nat'l Mil. Park, Tenn. 237/E10
Shilovo, U.S.S.R. 52/F4
Shimabara, Japan 81/E7
Shimamoto, Japan 81/J7
Shimane (pref.), Japan 81/F6
Shimane (pen.), Japan 81/F6
Shimanovsk, U.S.S.R. 48/N4
Shimbir Berris (mt.), Somalia 115/J1
Shimizu, Japan 81/J6
Shimoda, Japan 81/J6
Shimoga, India 68/D6
Shimokita (pen.), Japan 81/K3
Shimonoseki, Japan 81/E6
Shin (falls), Scotland 15/D3
Shin, Loch (lake), Scotland 15/D2
Shin, Loch (lake), Scotland 10/D1
Shin (riv.), Scotland 15/D3
Shinano (riv.), Japan 81/J5
Shinas, Oman 59/G5
Shindand, Afghanistan 59/H3
Shindand, Afghanistan 68/A2
Shindler, S. Dak. 298/R7
Shiner, Texas 303/G8
Shingbwiyang, Burma 72/B1
Shinglehouse, Pa. 294/F2
Shingler, Georgia 217/E7
Shingle Springs, Calif. 204/C8
Shingleton, Mich. 250/C2
Shingu, Japan 81/H7
Shining Tree, Ontario 177/J5
Shinjo, Japan 81/K4
Shinko (riv.), Cent. Afr. Rep. 115/D2
Shinnecock Ind. Res., N.Y. 276/R9
Shinnston, W. Va. 312/F4
Shin Pond, Maine 243/F3
Shinrone, Ireland 17/F5
Shinyanga (reg.), Tanzania 115/F4
Shinyanga, Tanzania 115/F4
Shinyanga, Tanzania 102/F5
Shiocton, Wis. 317/K7
Shiogama, Japan 81/K4
Shiono (cape), Japan 81/H7
Ship (isl.), Miss. 256/G10
Ship Bottom, N.J. 273/E4
Ship Harbour, Newf. 166/D2
Ship Harbour, Nova Scotia 168/F4
Shiping, China 77/F7
Shipki (pass), India 68/D2
Shipman, Ill. 222/C4
Shipman, Sask. 181/F2
Shipman, Va. 307/L5
Shippan (pt.), Conn. 210/A4
Shippegan, New Bruns. 170/F1
Shippegan (bay), New Bruns. 170/E1
Shippegan (gully), New Bruns. 170/F1
Shippensburg, Pa. 294/H5
Shippenville, Pa. 294/D3
Shiprock, N. Mex. 274/A2
Ship Rock (peak), N. Mex. 274/A2
Shipshaw (riv.), Québec 172/F1
Shipshewana, Ind. 227/F1
Ship Shoal (isl.), Va. 307/S6
Shipston on Stour, England 13/F5
Shiqian, China 77/G6
Shiqma (riv.), Israel 65/B4
Shiquan, China 77/G5
Shiquanhe, China 77/A5
Shiragami (cape), Japan 81/J3
Shirakawa, Japan 81/K5
Shirane (mt.), Japan 81/H6
Shirane (mt.), Japan 81/J5
Shiranuka, Japan 81/M2
Shiraz, Iran 54/G7
Shiraz, Iran 66/H6
Shiraz, Iran 59/F4
Shire (riv.), Malawi 115/G7
Shire (riv.), Mozambique 118/E3
Shiretoko (cape), Japan 81/M1
Shiriya (cape), Japan 81/K3
Shir Kuh (mt.), Iran 59/F3
Shir Kuh (mt.), Iran 66/J5
Shirland, Ill. 222/D1
Shirley, Ark. 202/F2
Shirley, Ill. 222/E3
Shirley, Ind. 227/F5
Shirley, Mass. 249/H2
Shirley•, Mass. 249/H2
Shirley, Mo. 261/L7
Shirley, W. Va. 312/E4
Shirley (basin), Wyo. 319/F3
Shirley Basin, Wyo. 319/F3
Shirley Center, Mass. 249/H2
Shirley City (Woodburn), Ind. 227/H2
Shirley Mills, Maine 243/D5
Shirley Mills•, Maine 243/D5
Shirleysburg, Pa. 294/G5
Shiro, Texas 303/J7
Shiroishi, Japan 81/K4
Shirvan, Iran 59/G2
Shirvan, Iran 66/K2
Shirvan (riv.), Iran 66/E3
Shishaldin (vol.), Alaska 196/E4
Shishmaref, Alaska 196/E1
Shithatha, Iraq 59/D3
Shithatha, Iraq 66/C4
Shitike (creek), Oreg. 291/F3
Shiukwan (Shaoyuan), China 77/H7
Shively, Calif. 204/B3
Shively, Ky. 237/K4
Shivers, Miss. 256/E7
Shivpuri, India 68/D3
Shivwits (plat.), Ariz. 198/B2
Shivwits Ind. Res., Utah 304/A6
Shiyan, China 77/H5
Shizuishan (Shihsuishan), China 77/G4
Shizunai, Japan 81/L2
Shizuoka (pref.), Japan 81/H6
Shizuoka, Japan 54/P6
Shizuoka, Japan 81/H6
Shkodër, Albania 7/F4
Shkodër, Albania 45/D5
Shoa (prov.), Ethiopia 111/G6
Shoal (riv.), Fla. 212/C6
Shoal (creek), Ill. 222/D5
Shoal (lake), Manitoba 179/B4
Shoal (lake), Manitoba 179/G5
Shoal (riv.), Manitoba 179/B2
Shoal (bay), Newf. 166/D2
Shoal (bay), Nova Scotia 168/F4
Shoal (creek), Tenn. 237/F10
Shoal (creek), Utah 304/A6
Shoal Branch, Wading (riv.), N.J. 273/D4
Shoal Cove, Newf. 166/C3
Shoal Harbour, Newf. 166/C2
Shoalhaven (riv.), N.S. Wales 97/E4
Shoal Lake, Manitoba 179/B4
Shoals, Ind. 227/D7
Shoals (isls.), N.H. 268/F6
Shoals, N.C. 281/J2
Shoals, W. Va. 312/B6
Shoals Junction, S.C. 296/C3
Shoalwater (bay), Queensland 88/J4
Shoalwater (cape), Wash. 310/A4

Sobral 449

Sipacate, Guatemala 154/B4
Sipalay, Philippines 82/D6
Sipaliwini (riv.), Suriname 131/C4
Sipapo (riv.), Venezuela 124/E5
Siparia, Trin. & Tob. 156/G5
Siparia, Trin. & Tob. 161/B11
Sipí, Colombia 126/B5
Siping (Szeping), China 77/K3
Sipiwesk (lake), Manitoba 179/J3
Siple (mt.), Ant. 5/B12
Sipocot, Philippines 82/D4
Sipsey, Ala. 195/D3
Sipsey (riv.), Ala. 195/B4
Sipsey Fork (riv.), Ala. 195/D2
Sip Song Chau Thai (mts.), Vietnam 72/D2
Sipura (isl.), Indonesia 85/B6
Siquijor (prov.), Philippines 82/D6
Siquijor, Philippines 82/D6
Siquijor (isl.), Philippines 82/D6
Siquirres, C. Rica 154/F5
Siquisique, Venezuela 124/D2
Siracusa (Syracuse), Italy 34/E6
Sirajganj, Bangladesh 68/F4
Şiran, Turkey 63/H2
Sirdar, Br. Col. 184/J5
Sir Edward Pellew Group (isls.), North. Terr. 88/F3
Sir Edward Pellew Group (isls.), North. Terr. 93/E3
Siren, Wis. 317/B4
Siret (riv.) 7/G4
Siret, Romania 45/G1
Siret (riv.), Romania 45/H2
Sir Francis Drake (chan.), Virgin Is. (U.K.) 161/D4
Sirhan, Wadi (dry riv.), Saudi Arabia 59/C3
Sirik, Iran 66/K7
Sirik (cape), Malaysia 85/E5
Siris, West Bank 65/C3
Sirius (pt.), Alaska 196/J4
Sir James MacBrien (mt.), N.W. Terr. 187/F3
Sirjan (Sa'idabad), Iran 66/J6
Sirjan (Sa'idabad), Iran 59/G4
Sir John's (peak), Jamaica 158/K6
Sir Johns Run, W. Va. 312/K3
Sir Joseph Banks Group (isls.), S. Australia 94/E6
Sirnach, Switzerland 39/G2
Şirnak, Turkey 63/K4
Sirohi, India 68/C4
Sironj, India 68/D4
Síros (isl.), Greece 45/G7
Sirri (isl.), Iran 66/J8
Sirsa, India 68/D3
Sir Sandford (mt.), Br. Col. 184/H4
Sirsi, India 68/D6
Siruma, Philippines 82/D3
Şirvan, Turkey 63/K3
Širvintos, U.S.S.R. 53/C3
Sisak, Yugoslavia 45/C3
Sisaket, Thailand 72/E4
Sisal, Mexico 150/O6
Sishen, S. Africa 118/C5
Sisi (cape), Indonesia 85/F6
Sisib (lake), Manitoba 179/C2
Sisikon, Switzerland 39/G3
Sisimiut, Greenland 4/C12
Siskiwit (bay), Mich. 250/E1
Siskiyou (co.), Calif. 204/C2
Siskiyou (mts.), Calif. 204/C2
Siskiyou (mts.), Oreg. 291/D6
Sisophon, Cambodia 72/D4
Sissach, Switzerland 39/E2
Sisseton, S. Dak. 298/R2
Sissiboo (riv.), Nova Scotia 168/C4
Sisson Branch, Tobique (riv.), New Bruns. 170/C1
Sisson Ridge, New Bruns. 170/C2
Sissonville, W. Va. 312/C5
Sistan and Baluchestan (prov.), Iran 66/M6
Sister Bay, Wis. 317/M5
Sister Lakes, Mich. 250/C6
Sisteron, France 28/G5
Sisters, The (isls.), N. Zealand 100/D6
Sisters, Oreg. 291/F3
Sistersville, W. Va. 312/D3
Sitapur, India 68/E3
Siteki, Swaziland 118/E5
Sites, Calif. 204/C4
Sitges, Spain 33/G2
Sithoniá (pen.), Greece 45/F5
Sitia, Greece 45/H8
Sitio d'Abadia, Brazil 132/E6
Sitionuevo, Colombia 126/C2
Sitka, Alaska 146/E4
Sitka, Alaska 188/D6
Sitka, Alaska 196/M1
Sitka (sound), Alaska 196/M1
Sitka, Ark. 202/H1
Sitka, Kansas 232/C4
Sitka, U.S. 4/D16
Sitkalidak (isl.), Alaska 196/H3
Sitka Nat'l Hist. Park, Alaska 196/M1
Sitkinak (isl.), Alaska 196/H3
Sitkinak (str.), Alaska 196/H3
Sitkum, Oreg. 291/D4
Sittang (riv.), Burma 72/C3
Sittard, Netherlands 27/H6
Sittingbourne and Milton, England 13/H6
Sittwe, Burma 54/L7
Sittwe, Burma 72/B2
Situbondo, Indonesia 85/L2
Siuna, Nicaragua 154/E4
Siuslaw (riv.), Oreg. 291/D4
Sivand, Iran 66/H5
Sivas (prov.), Turkey 63/G3
Sivas, Turkey 54/E5
Sivas, Turkey 63/G3
Sivas, Turkey 59/C1
Sivasli, Turkey 63/C3
Siverek, Turkey 63/H4
Siviriez, Switzerland 39/C3
Sivrihisar, Turkey 63/D3
Sivry-Rance, Belgium 27/E8
Siwa, Egypt 111/E2
Siwa, Egypt 102/E2
Siwa (oasis), Egypt 111/E2
Sixes, Oreg. 291/C5
Sixes (riv.), Oreg. 291/C5
Six Flags Over Georgia, Georgia 217/J1
Six Flags Over Mid America, Mo. 261/M4
Six Lakes, Mich. 250/D5
Six Mens, Barbados 161/B8
Six Mile, S.C. 296/B2
Sixmilebridge, Ireland 17/D6
Sixmilecross, N. Ireland 17/G2
Six Mile Run, Pa. 294/F5
Six Roads, New Bruns. 170/F1
Six Run (creek), N.C. 281/N4
Sixteen, Mont. 262/F4
Sixteen Island Lake, Québec 172/C4
Sixth Cataract, Sudan 111/F4
Sixth Cataract (dam), Sudan 102/F3
Sixth Cataract, Sudan 59/B6
Siyah Kuh (mt.), Iraq 66/D2
Siyeh (mt.), Mont. 262/C2
Sizerock, Ky. 237/P6
Siziwang, China 77/H3
Sjaelland (isl.), Denmark 21/E6
Sjaelland (isl.), Denmark 18/H9
Sjaellands Odde (pen.), Denmark 21/E5
Sjenica, Yugoslavia 45/E4
Skadovsk, U.S.S.R. 52/D5
Skaelskør, Denmark 21/E7
Skaerbaek, Denmark 21/B7
Skagata (cape), Iceland 21/B1
Skagen, Denmark 21/D2
Skagen, Denmark 18/G8
Skagens Odde (cape), Denmark 21/D2
Skagens Odde (cape), Denmark 18/G8
Skagerrak (str.) 7/E3
Skagerrak (str.), Denmark 21/C2
Skagerrak (str.), Denmark 18/F8
Skagerrak (str.), Norway 18/F8
Skagerrak (str.), Sweden 18/F8
Skagit (riv.), Br. Col. 184/G6
Skagit (co.), Wash. 310/D2
Skagit (riv.), Wash. 310/C2
Skagway, Alaska 146/E4
Skagway, Alaska 196/M1
Skalica, Czech. 41/D2
Skals, Denmark 21/C4
Skamania (co.), Wash. 310/D5
Skamania, Wash. 310/C5
Skamokawa, Wash. 310/B4
Skanderborg, Denmark 21/D5
Skanderborg, Denmark 18/F8
Skaneateles, N.Y. 276/H5
Skaneateles (lake), N.Y. 276/H5
Skanee, Mich. 250/A2
Skåneviksjøen, Norway 18/E7
Skanür med Falsterbo, Sweden 18/H9
Skara, Sweden 18/H7
Skaraborg (co.), Sweden 18/H7
Skardu, Pakistan 68/D1
Skårup, Denmark 21/D7
Skarzysko-Kamienna, Poland 47/E3
Skateraw, Scotland 15/F3
Skaudvilė, U.S.S.R. 53/B3
Skaw, The (Skagens Odde) (cape), Denmark 18/G8
Skaw, The (Skagens Odde) (cape), Denmark 21/D2
Skawina, Poland 47/D4
Skedee, Okla. 288/N2
Skeena (mts.), Br. Col. 184/C2
Skeena (riv.), Br. Col. 162/D5
Skeena (riv.), Br. Col. 184/C3
Skegness, England 13/H4
Skegness, England 10/G4
Skeleton (lake), Ontario 177/E2
Skeleton Coast (reg.), Namibia 118/A3
Skellefte (riv.), Sweden 7/F2
Skellefteå, Sweden 7/F2
Skellefteå, Sweden 18/M4
Skellefteälv (riv.), Sweden 18/L4
Skellytown, Texas 303/C2
Skelmersdale, England 10/F2
Skelmersdale, England 13/G2
Skelmorlie, Scotland 15/A2
Skelton, Ind. 227/B8
Skelton and Brotton, England 13/G3
Skene, Miss. 256/C3
Skerries, Ireland 17/J4
Skerries, Ireland 10/D4
Skerries, The (isls.), Wales 13/C4
Ski, Norway 18/D4
Skiathos, Greece 45/F6
Skiatook, Okla. 288/O2
Skibbereen, Ireland 10/B5
Skibbereen, Ireland 17/C8
Skibby, Denmark 21/E6
Skidaway (isl.), Georgia 217/L7
Skiddaw (mt.), England 13/D3
Skiddy, Kansas 232/F3
Skidegate, Br. Col. 184/B3
Skidegate (inlet), Br. Col. 184/B3
Skidmore, Mo. 261/B2
Skidmore, Texas 303/G9
Skien, Norway 7/E3
Skien, Norway 18/F7
Skierniewice (prov.), Poland 47/E3
Skierniewice, Poland 47/E2
Skiff, Alberta 182/E5
Skiff (lake), New Bruns. 170/C3
Skikda, Algeria 102/C1
Skikda, Algeria 106/F1
Skilak (lake), Alaska 196/C1
Skillet Fork (riv.), Ill. 222/E5
Skillman, N.J. 273/D3
Skinners Eddy, Pa. 294/K2
Skipness, Scotland 15/C5
Skippack, Pa. 294/M5
Skippers, Va. 307/O7
Skipperville, Ala. 195/G7
Skipsea, England 13/G4
Skipton, England 13/H1
Skipton, England 10/E4
Skipwith, Va. 307/L7
Skir Dhu, Nova Scotia 168/H2
Skíros, Greece 45/G6
Skíros (isl.), Greece 45/G6
Skive, Denmark 18/F8
Skive, Denmark 21/B4
Skive (riv.), Denmark 21/C5
Skjåk, Norway 18/F6
Skjálfandafljót (stream), Iceland 21/C1
Skjern, Denmark 21/B6
Skodborg, Denmark 21/C7
Škofja Loka, Yugoslavia 45/A2
Skokie, Ill. 222/B5
Skokomish (mt.), Wash. 310/B3
Skokomish Ind. Res., Wash. 310/B3
Skomer (isl.), Wales 13/B6
Skookumchuck, Br. Col. 184/K5
Skootamatta (lake), Ontario 177/G3
Skópelos, Greece 45/F6
Skopin, U.S.S.R. 52/F4
Skopje, Yugoslavia 7/G4
Skopje, Yugoslavia 45/E5
Skørping, Denmark 21/C4
Skövde, Sweden 18/H7
Skovorodino, U.S.S.R. 54/O4
Skovorodino, U.S.S.R. 48/N4
Skowhegan, Maine 243/D6
Skowhegan•, Maine 243/D6
Skownan, Manitoba 179/C3
Skradin, Yugoslavia 45/B4
Skreia, Norway 18/G6
Skudeneshavn, Norway 18/D7
Skull Valley, Ariz. 198/C4
Skull Valley Ind. Res., Utah 304/B3
Skuna (riv.), Miss. 256/F2
Skungamaug (riv.), Conn. 210/F1
Skunk (riv.), Iowa 229/K6
Skuteč, Czech. 41/D2
Skutskär, Sweden 18/K6
Skwentna, Alaska 196/B1
Skwentna (riv.), Alaska 196/A1
Skwierzyna, Poland 47/B2
Skye, Isle of (isl.), Scotland 15/B3
Skye (isl.), Scotland 10/C2
Skykomish, Wash. 310/D3
Skykomish (riv.), Wash. 310/D3
Skyland, N.C. 281/D4
Skylight (mt.), N.Y. 276/M2
Skyline, Minn. 255/D6
Skyring (bay), Chile 138/E10
Skytop, Pa. 294/M3
Sky Valley, Georgia 217/F1
Slab Fork, W. Va. 312/D7
Slade, Ky. 237/O5
Sládečkovce, Czech. 41/D2
Slag (bay), Neth. Ant. 161/D8
Slagelse, Denmark 21/E7
Slagelse, Denmark 18/G9
Slagle, La. 238/D4
Sławkow, Poland 47/B4
Slamannan, Scotland 15/C2
Slamet (mt.), Indonesia 85/J2
Slana, Alaska 196/K2
Slaná (riv.), Czech. 41/F2
Slane, Ireland 17/H4
Slanesville, W. Va. 312/K4
Slaney (riv.), Ireland 17/H7
Slangerup, Denmark 21/E6
Slangkop (pt.), S. Africa 118/E7
Slănic, Romania 45/G3
Slantsy, U.S.S.R. 52/C3
Slany, Czech. 41/C1
Slate (mt.), Ariz. 198/D3
Slate (riv.), Colo. 208/E5
Slate (creek), Idaho 220/B4
Slate (isls.), Ontario 175/C3
Slate (riv.), Va. 307/L5
Slate, W. Va. 312/D4
Slate (creek), Wyo. 319/C3
Slatedale, Pa. 294/L4
Slater, Colo. 208/E1
Slater, Iowa 229/F5
Slater, Mo. 261/G4
Slater, Wyo. 319/H4
Slater-Marietta, S.C. 296/C1
Slatersville, R.I. 249/H4
Slate Run, Pa. 294/H3
Slaterville Springs, N.Y. 276/H6
Slate Spring, Miss. 256/F3
Slatina, Romania 45/G3
Slatington, Pa. 294/L4
Slaton, Texas 303/C4
Slaughter, La. 238/H5
Slaughter Beach, Del. 245/S5
Slaughters, Ky. 237/F6
Slaughterville, Okla. 288/M4
Slave (riv.) 162/E3
Slave (riv.), Alberta 182/C5
Slave (riv.), Canada 146/G3
Slave (riv.), N.W. Terr. 187/G3
Slave Coast (reg.), Benin 106/E7
Slave Coast (reg.), Nigeria 106/E7
Slave Coast (reg.), Togo 106/E7
Slave Lake, Alberta 182/C2
Slavgorod, U.S.S.R. 48/H4
Slavkov, Czech. 41/D2
Slavonia (reg.), Yugoslavia 45/C3
Slavonska Požega, Yugoslavia 45/C3
Slavonski Brod, Yugoslavia 45/D3
Slavuta, U.S.S.R. 52/C4
Slavyansk, U.S.S.R. 52/E5
Slavyansk-na-Kubani, U.S.S.R. 52/E5
Sławno, Poland 47/C1
Slayden, Miss. 256/F1
Slayden, Tenn. 237/G8
Slayton, Minn. 255/C7
Sleaford, England 13/G5
Sleaford, England 10/F4
Sleat (dist.), Scotland 15/C3
Sleat (pt.), Scotland 15/B4
Sleat (sound), Scotland 15/C3
Sledge, Miss. 256/D2
Sleeper, Mo. 261/G7
Sleeping Bear Dunes Nat'l Lakeshore, Mich. 250/C4
Sleeping Deer (mt.), Idaho 220/D5
Sleepy Creek, W. Va. 312/K3
Sleepy Eye, Minn. 255/D6
Sleepy Eye (creek), Minn. 255/C6
Sleepy Hollow, Ill. 222/E1
Sleetmute, Alaska 196/G2
Sleeve (lake), Manitoba 179/E3
Slemish (mt.), N. Ireland 17/J2
Slemon (lake), Manitoba 179/G1
Slemp, Ky. 237/P6
Slick, Okla. 288/O3
Slickford, Ky. 237/M7
Slickville, Pa. 294/C5
Slide (mt.), N.Y. 276/L6
Slidell, La. 238/L6
Sliedrecht, Netherlands 27/F5
Sliema, Malta 34/E7
Slieve Anierin (mt.), Ireland 17/F3
Slieve Aughty (mts.), Ireland 17/D5
Slieve Beagh (mt.), N. Ireland 17/G3
Slieve Bernagh (mt.), Ireland 17/D6
Slieve Bloom (mts.), Ireland 17/F5
Slieve Callan (mt.), Ireland 17/C6
Slieve Car (mt.), Ireland 17/B3
Slieve Donard (mt.), N. Ireland 10/D3
Slieve Donard (mt.), N. Ireland 17/K3
Slieve Elva (mt.), Ireland 17/C5
Slievefelim (mts.), Ireland 17/E6
Slieve Gamph (mts.), Ireland 17/D3
Slieve Gullion (mt.), N. Ireland 17/J3
Slieve League (mt.), Ireland 17/D2
Slieve Mishkish (mts.), Ireland 17/B8
Slievenaman (mt.), Ireland 17/F7
Sligo (co.), Ireland 17/D3
Sligo, Ireland 17/E3
Sligo, Ireland 10/B3
Sligo (bay), Ireland 10/B3
Sligo (bay), Ireland 17/D3
Sligo, La. 238/C2
Sligo, Pa. 294/C3
Slinger, Wis. 317/K9
Slipper (isl.), N. Zealand 100/F2
Slippery Rock, Pa. 294/B3
Slite, Sweden 18/L8
Sliven, Bulgaria 45/H4
Sliven, Bulgaria 7/G4
Sloan, Iowa 229/A4
Sloan, Nev. 266/F7
Sloan, N.Y. 276/C5
Sloans Valley, Ky. 237/N7
Sloat, Calif. 204/E4
Sloatsburg, N.Y. 276/M8
Slobodskoy, U.S.S.R. 48/E4
Slobodskoy, U.S.S.R. 52/H3
Slobozia, Romania 45/H3
Slocan, Br. Col. 184/J5
Slocan (lake), Br. Col. 184/J5
Slocan Park, Br. Col. 184/J5
Slochteren, Netherlands 27/K2
Slocomb, Ala. 195/G8
Slocum, R.I. 249/H6
Slocum, Texas 303/J6
Slonim, U.S.S.R. 52/B4
Slope (co.), N. Dak. 282/C7
Slot, The (chan.), Solomon Is. 86/D3
Sloten, Friesland, Netherlands 27/H3
Sloten, North Holland, Netherlands 27/B5
Sloterdijk, Netherlands 27/B4
Slotermeer (lake), Netherlands 27/H3
Slough, England 13/G8
Sloughhouse, Calif. 204/C8
Slovak Rep., Czech. 41/E2
Slovenia (rep.), Yugoslavia 45/B2
Slovenské Rudohorie (mts.), Czech. 41/E2
Słubice, Poland 47/B2
Sluis, Netherlands 27/C6
Słupca, Poland 47/D2
Słupia (riv.), Poland 47/C1
Słupsk (prov.), Poland 47/C1
Słupsk, Poland 47/C1
Słupsk, Poland 7/F3
Slutsk, U.S.S.R. 52/C4
Slyne (head), Ireland 10/A4
Slyne (head), Ireland 17/A5
Slyudyanka, U.S.S.R. 48/L4
Smackover, Ark. 202/E7
Smale, Ark. 202/H4
Small, Idaho 220/F5
Small (cape), Maine 243/D8
Small Isles (isls.), Scotland 15/B4
Small Point, Maine 243/D8
Smallwood (res.), Newf. 166/B3
Smallwood (res.), Newf. 146/M4
Smallwood (res.), Newf. 162/K5
Smarr, Georgia 217/E5
Smarts (mt.), N.H. 268/C4
Smartt, Tenn. 237/K9
Smartville, Calif. 204/D4
Smeaton, Sask. 181/G2
Smederevo, Yugoslavia 45/E3
Smederevska Palanka, Yugoslavia 45/E3
Smedjebacken, Sweden 18/J6
Smela, U.S.S.R. 52/D5
Smelterville, Idaho 220/B2
Smerwick (harb.), Ireland 17/A7
Smethport, Pa. 294/F2
Smicksburg, Pa. 294/D4
Smilax, Ky. 237/P6
Smilde, Netherlands 27/K3
Smiley, Sask. 181/B4
Smiley, Texas 303/G8
Smiltene, U.S.S.R. 53/C2
Smith (bay), Alaska 196/H1
Smith, Alberta 182/D2
Smith (sound), Br. Col. 184/C4
Smith (riv.), Calif. 204/A2
Smith (creek), Idaho 220/B1
Smith (co.), Kansas 232/D2
Smith (isl.), Md. 245/O8
Smith (co.), Miss. 256/E6
Smith (riv.), Mont. 262/E3
Smith, Nev. 266/B4
Smith (sound), Newf. 166/D2
Smith (isl.), N.C. 281/O7
Smith (basin), N.W.T. 162/N3
Smith (bay), N.W.T. 187/L2
Smith (cape), N.W.T. 162/H3
Smith (cape), N.W.T. 187/L3
Smith (sound), N.W.T. 187/L2
Smith (cape), Ontario 177/C2
Smith (riv.), Oreg. 291/D4
Smith (creek), S. Dak. 298/L6
Smith (co.), Tenn. 237/J8
Smith (co.), Texas 303/J5
Smith (isl.), Va. 307/S6
Smith (riv.), Va. 307/J7
Smith Arm (inlet), N.W. Terr. 187/F3
Smithboro, Ill. 222/D5
Smithburg, N.J. 273/E3
Smithburg, W. Va. 312/E4
Smith Center, Kansas 232/D2
Smith Creek (valley), Nev. 266/D3
Smith Creek, W. Va. 312/H5
Smithdale, Miss. 256/C8
Smithers, Br. Col. 146/F4
Smithers, Br. Col. 162/D5
Smithers, Br. Col. 184/D3
Smithers, W. Va. 312/D6
Smithfield, Ill. 222/C3
Smithfield, Ky. 237/L4
Smithfield•, Maine 243/D6
Smithfield, Nebr. 264/E4
Smithfield, N.C. 281/N3
Smithfield, Ohio 284/J5
Smithfield, Ontario 177/G3
Smithfield, Pa. 294/C6
Smithfield, Texas 303/F2
Smithfield, Utah 304/C2
Smithfield, Va. 307/P7
Smithfield, W. Va. 312/E4
Smith Hill, Manitoba 179/C5
Smithland, Iowa 229/B4
Smithland, Ky. 237/E6
Smithmill, Pa. 294/F4
Smith Mills, Ky. 237/F5
Smith Mountain (lake), Va. 307/J6
Smithonia, Georgia 217/F2
Smithport (lake), La. 238/C2
Smith River, Calif. 204/A2
Smiths, Ala. 195/H5
Smithsburg, Md. 245/H2
Smiths Cove, Nova Scotia 168/C4
Smiths Creek, Mich. 250/G6
Smiths Creek, New Bruns. 170/E3
Smiths Falls, Ontario 177/H3
Smiths Ferry, Idaho 220/C5
Smiths Fork (riv.), Wyo. 319/B3
Smiths Grove, Ky. 237/J6
Smithshire, Ill. 222/C3
Smiths Station, Miss. 256/C6
Smithton, Ark. 202/D6
Smithton, Ill. 222/C5
Smithton, Mo. 261/F5
Smithton, Pa. 294/C5
Smithton, Tasmania 99/A2
Smithton, Tasmania 88/H8
Smith Town, Ky. 237/M7
Smithtown, N.H. 268/F6
Smithtown, N.Y. 276/O9
Smithtown-Gladstone, N.S. Wales 97/G2
Smith Valley, Ind. 227/E5
Smithville, Ark. 202/H1
Smithville, Georgia 217/D7
Smithville, Ind. 227/D6
Smithville, Miss. 256/H2
Smithville, Mo. 261/D4
Smithville, N.J. 273/D4
Smithville, N.J. 273/E5
Smithville, Ohio 284/G4
Smithville, Okla. 288/S6
Smithville, Ontario 177/E4
Smithville, Tenn. 237/K9
Smithville, Texas 303/G7
Smithville, W. Va. 312/D4
Smithville Flats, N.Y. 276/J6
Smithwick, S. Dak. 298/C7
Smoaks, S.C. 296/F5
Smoke Bend, La. 238/K3
Smoke Creek (des.), Nev. 266/B2
Smoke Hole, W. Va. 312/H5
Smokey Burn, Sask. 181/H2
Smoky (riv.), Alberta 182/A2
Smoky (riv.), Alta. 162/E5
Smoky (mts.), Idaho 220/D6
Smoky (cape), N.S. Wales 97/G2
Smoky (lake), N. Dak. 282/K3
Smoky (cape), Nova Scotia 168/H2
Smoky Bay, S. Australia 88/E6
Smoky Bay, S. Australia 94/D5
Smoky Hill (riv.) 188/G3
Smoky Hill (riv.), Colo. 208/P5
Smoky Hill, North Fork (riv.), Kansas 232/A2
Smoky Hill (riv.), Kansas 232/C3
Smoky Junction, Tenn. 237/N8
Smoky Lake, Alberta 182/D2
Smøla (isl.), Norway 18/E5
Smolan, Kansas 232/E3
Smolensk, U.S.S.R. 7/H3
Smolensk, U.S.S.R. 48/D4
Smolensk, U.S.S.R. 52/D4
Smolyan, Bulgaria 45/G5
Smoot, W. Va. 312/E7
Smoot, Wyo. 319/B3
Smooth Rock Falls, Ontario 177/J5
Smooth Rock Falls, Ontario 175/D3
Smugglers Notch (pass), Vt. 268/B2
Smuts, Sask. 181/F3
Smyadovo, Bulgaria 45/H4
Smyer, Ala. 195/B7
Smyrna, Del. 245/R3
Smyrna (res.), Del. 245/R3
Smyrna, Georgia 217/K1
Smyrna, Mich. 250/D5
Smyrna, N.Y. 276/J5
Smyrna, N.C. 281/R5
Smyrna, S.C. 296/E1
Smyrna, Tenn. 237/H9
Smyrna (İzmir), Turkey 63/B3
Smyrna, Wash. 310/F4
Smyrna Mills, Maine 243/G3
Smyrna Mills•, Maine 243/G3
Smyth (co.), Va. 307/E7
Snaefell (mt.), I. of Man 13/C3
Snaefell (mt.), I. of Man 10/D3
Snake (riv.) 188/C1
Snake (riv.), Idaho 220/A3
Snake (riv.), Minn. 255/A2
Snake (riv.), Minn. 255/E4
Snake (riv.), Nebr. 264/C2
Snake (mts.), Nev. 266/F1
Snake (range), Nev. 266/G3
Snake (riv.), Oreg. 291/K3
Snake (creek), S. Dak. 298/F4
Snake (creek), S. Dak. 298/F5
Snake (creek), S. Dak. 298/M3
Snake (riv.), U.S. 146/G5
Snake (isl.), Victoria 97/D6
Snake (riv.), Wash. 310/G4
Snake (riv.), Wyo. 319/B2
Snake Creek (canal), Fla. 212/B4
Snake Indian (riv.), Alberta 182/A3
Snake River (plain), Idaho 220/D7
Snake River (range), Idaho 220/G6
Snake River, Wash. 310/G4
Snare (riv.), N.W. Terr. 187/G3
Snare Lake, N.W. Terr. 187/G3
Snares, The (isls.), N. Zealand 100/A7
Snåsa, Norway 18/H4
Snåsavatn (lake), Norway 18/H4
Snead, Ala. 195/F2
Sneads, Fla. 212/B1
Sneads Ferry, N.C. 281/P5
Snedsted, Denmark 21/B4
Sneedville, Tenn. 237/P7
Sneek, Netherlands 27/H2
Sneekermeer (lake), Netherlands 27/H2
Sneem, Ireland 17/B8
Sneeuwkop (mt.), S. Africa 118/F6
Sneffels (mt.), Colo. 208/D7
Snegamook (lake), Newf. 166/B3
Snell, Va. 307/N4
Snelling, Calif. 204/E6
Snelling, S.C. 296/E5
Snellville, Georgia 217/D3
Snezhnogorsk, U.S.S.R. 48/J3
Śniardwy, Jezioro (lake), Poland 47/E2
Sniečkus, U.S.S.R. 53/D3
Snina, Czech. 41/G2
Snipe (lake), Alberta 182/B2
Snipe Lake, Sask. 181/B4
Snizort, Loch (inlet), Scotland 15/B3
Snohomish (co.), Wash. 310/D2
Snohomish, Wash. 310/D3
Snohomish (riv.), Wash. 310/C3
Snoqualmie, Wash. 310/D3
Snoqualmie (pass), Wash. 310/D3
Snoqualmie (riv.), Wash. 310/D3
Snoqualmie Falls, Wash. 310/D3
Snover, Mich. 250/G5
Snow, Okla. 288/R6
Snow (mt.), Vt. 268/B6
Snow (peak), Wash. 310/G2
Snowball, Ark. 202/E2
Snowbird (lake), N.W. Terr. 187/H3
Snow Camp, N.C. 281/L3
Snowden, N.C. 281/S2
Snowden, Sask. 181/G2
Snowdon (mt.), Wales 13/D4
Snowdon (mt.), Wales 10/D4
Snowdonia Nat'l Park, Wales 13/D4
Snowdoun, Ala. 195/F6
Snowdrift, N.W.T. 162/E3
Snowdrift, N.W. Terr. 187/G3
Snowfield (peak), Wash. 310/D2
Snowflake, Ariz. 198/E4
Snowflake, Manitoba 179/D5
Snow Hill, Ala. 195/E7
Snow Hill, Ark. 202/E7
Snow Hill, Md. 245/S8
Snow Hill, N.C. 281/O4
Snow Lake, Ark. 202/H5
Snow Lake, Man. 162/G5
Snow Lake, Manitoba 179/H3
Snowmass, Colo. 208/E4
Snowshoe (lake), Manitoba 179/G4
Snow Shoe, Pa. 294/G3
Snowtown, S. Australia 94/E5
Snowville, N.H. 268/E4
Snowville, Utah 304/B2
Snow Water (lake), Nev. 266/G2
Snowy (mts.), N.S. Wales 97/E5
Snowy (riv.), N.S. Wales 97/E5
Snowy (riv.), Victoria 88/H7
Snug, Tasmania 99/D5
Snyder, Ark. 202/G7
Snyder, Colo. 208/M2
Snyder, Mo. 261/F3
Snyder, Nebr. 264/H3
Snyder, Okla. 288/J5
Snyder (co.), Pa. 294/H4
Snyder, Texas 303/D5
Snydertown, Pa. 294/J4
So (isl.), S. Korea 81/C6
Soalala, Madagascar 118/H3
Soalara, Madagascar 118/G4
Soanierana-Ivongo, Madagascar 118/H3
Soap (lake), Wash. 310/F3
Soap Lake, Wash. 310/F3
Soasiu, Indonesia 85/H5
Soatá, Colombia 126/D4
Soay (isl.), Scotland 15/A2
Soay (isl.), Scotland 15/B3
Sobat (riv.), Sudan 111/F6
Sober (isl.), Nova Scotia 168/F4
Soběslav, Czech. 41/C2
Sobieski, Minn. 255/D5
Sobieski, Wis. 317/L6
Sobotka, Czech. 41/C1
Sobradinho (res.), Brazil 120/E3
Sobradinho (res.), Brazil 132/F5
Sobral, Brazil 120/E3
Sobral, Brazil 132/G3

450 Sobrance

Sobrance, Czech. 41/G2
Soca, Uruguay 145/C6
Sochaczew, Poland 47/E2
Soche (Shache), China 77/A4
Sochi, U.S.S.R. 7/H4
Sochi, U.S.S.R. 48/D5
Sochi, U.S.S.R. 52/E6
Social Circle, Georgia 217/E3
Society (isls.), Fr. Poly. 87/L7
Society Hill, Ala. 195/H6
Society Hill, S.C. 296/H2
Socompa (vol.), Chile 138/B4
Socorro, Brazil 135/C3
Socorro, Colombia 126/D4
Socorro (isl.), Mexico 150/D7
Socorro, N. Mex. 188/E4
Socorro (co.), N. Mex. 274/C5
Socorro, N. Mex. 274/C4
Socotra (isl.), Yemen 54/G8
Socotra (isl.), Yemen 2/M5
Socotra (isl.), Yemen 59/F7
Socuéllamos, Spain 33/E3
Soda (lake), Calif. 204/K8
Soda (plains), India 68/D1
Soda, Jebel es (mts.), Libya 111/C2
Soda Creek, Br. Col. 184/F4
Sodankylä, Finland 18/P3
Soda Plains, Pakistan 68/D1
Soda Springs, Calif. 204/E4
Soda Springs, Idaho 220/G7
Sodaville, Oreg. 291/E3
Soddu, Ethiopia 111/G6
Soddy-Daisy, Tenn. 237/L10
Söderhamn, Sweden 18/K6
Söderköping, Sweden 18/K7
Södermanland (co.), Sweden 18/K7
Södertälje, Sweden 18/G1
Sodiri, Sudan 111/E5
Sodus, Mich. 250/C6
Sodus, N.Y. 276/G4
Sodus Point, N.Y. 276/G4
Soe, Indonesia 85/G7
Soest, Netherlands 27/G4
Soest, Germany 22/C3
Soesterberg, Netherlands 27/G4
Soeurs (isl.), Québec 172/H4
Sofala (prov.), Mozambique 118/E3
Sofia (cap.), Bulgaria 7/G4
Sofia (cap.), Bulgaria 45/F4
Sofia (riv.), Madagascar 118/H3
Sofkee, Georgia 217/E5
Soft Shell, Ky. 237/P6
Sogamoso, Colombia 126/D5
Sogamoso (riv.), Colombia 126/D4
Soğanlı (mts.), Turkey 63/H2
Soğanlı (riv.), Turkey 63/E2
Sognafjorden (fjord), Norway 18/D6
Sognefjorden (fjord), Norway 7/E2
Sogn og Fjordane (co.), Norway 18/E6
Sogod, Philippines 82/E5
Sogod (bay), Philippines 82/E5
Söğüt, Turkey 63/D3
Söğüt (lake), Turkey 63/D4
Sog Xian, China 77/D5
Soh, Iran 66/G4
Sohâg, Egypt 111/F2
Sohâg, Egypt 59/B4
Sohâg, Egypt 102/F2
Soham, N. Mex. 274/D3
Sohar, Oman 59/G5
Sŏhŭng, N. Korea 81/C4
Soignies, Belgium 27/D7
Sointula, Br. Col. 184/D5
Soissons, France 28/E3
Soka, Japan 81/O2
Sokch'o, S. Korea 81/D4
Söke, Turkey 63/B4
Söke, Turkey 59/A2
Sokna, Libya 111/C2
Sokodé, Togo 106/E7
Sokol, U.S.S.R. 52/F3
Sokol, U.S.S.R. 48/E4
Sokółka, Poland 47/F2
Sokolo, Mali 106/C6
Sokolov, Czech. 41/B1
Sokołów Podlaski, Poland 47/F2
Sokota, Ethiopia 111/G5
Sokoto (state), Nigeria 106/F6
Sokoto, Nigeria 102/C3
Sokoto, Nigeria 106/F6
Sokoto (riv.), Nigeria 106/F6
Sola, Cuba 158/G2
Solana Beach, Calif. 204/H11
Solander (isl.), N. Zealand 100/A7
Solano (co.), Calif. 204/D5
Solano (pt.), Colombia 126/B4
Solano, N. Mex. 274/E3
Solano, Philippines 82/C2
Solano, Venezuela 124/E6
Solbad Hall in Tirol, Austria 41/A3
Solca, Romania 45/G2
Soldado (pt.), P. Rico 161/G2
Soldier, Iowa 229/B5
Soldier, Kansas 232/G2
Soldier, Ky. 237/P4
Soldier Pond, Maine 243/F1
Soldiers Cove, Nova Scotia 168/H3
Soldiers Grove, Wis. 317/E9
Soldier Summit, Utah 304/C4
Soldotna, Alaska 196/B1
Soledad, Argentina 143/F5
Soledad, Calif. 204/D7
Soledad, Colombia 126/C2
Soledad, Venezuela 124/G3
Soledad de Doblado, Mexico 150/Q2
Soledad Díez Gutiérrez, Mexico 150/J5
Soleduck (riv.), Wash. 310/A3
Solen, N. Dak. 282/J7
Solent (chan.), England 13/F7
Solentiname (isls.), Nicaragua 154/E5
Soleure (Solothurn) (canton), Switzerland 39/E2
Solgohachia, Ark. 202/E3
Solhan, Turkey 63/J3
Soligalich, U.S.S.R. 52/F3
Soligorsk, U.S.S.R. 52/C4
Solihull, England 13/F5
Solihull, England 10/G3
Solikamsk, U.S.S.R. 7/K3
Solikamsk, U.S.S.R. 48/F3
Solikamsk, U.S.S.R. 52/J3
Sol'-Iletsk, U.S.S.R. 52/J4
Solingen, Germany 22/B3
Solís, Uruguay 145/D5
Solís de Mataojo, Uruguay 145/D5
Solitary (isl.), N.S. Wales 97/G1
Sollefteå, Sweden 18/K5
Sollentuna, Sweden 18/H1
Sóller, Spain 33/H3
Søllested, Denmark 21/E8
Solna, Sweden 18/H1
Solo (Surakarta), Indonesia 85/J2
Solo, Mo. 261/J8
Sologne (reg.), France 28/E4
Solok, Indonesia 85/C6
Sololá, Guatemala 154/B3
Solomon (sea) 87/F6
Solomon, Alaska 196/F2
Solomon, Ariz. 198/F6
Solomon, Kansas 232/E3
Solomon (riv.), Kansas 232/E2
Solomon (isls.), Pacific 87/F6
Solomon (isls.), Papua N.G. 86/C3
Solomon (sea), Papua N.G. 85/C7
Solomon (isls.), Solomon Is. 86/C3
Solomon (sea), Solomon Is. 86/D3
Solomon Islands 2/T6
SOLOMON ISLANDS 86/D2
Solomon Islands 87/G6
Solomons, Md. 245/N7
Solon, China 77/K2
Solon, Ind. 227/F7
Solon, Iowa 229/L5
Solon•, Maine 243/D6
Solon, Ohio 284/J9
Solon Springs, Wis. 317/C3
Solor (isl.), Indonesia 85/G7
Solothurn (elec. div.), Switzerland 39/E2
Solothurn (Soleure), Switzerland 39/E2
Solovetskiye (isls.), U.S.S.R. 52/E1
Solsberry, Ind. 227/D6
Solsgirth, Manitoba 179/B4
Solsona, Philippines 82/C1
Solsona, Spain 33/G2
Solt, Hungary 41/E3
Šolta (isl.), Yugoslavia 45/C4
Soltau, Germany 22/C2
Soltvadkert, Hungary 41/E3
Soluk, Libya 111/D1
Solund, Norway 18/D6
Solvang, Calif. 204/E9
Solvay, N.Y. 276/H4
Sölvesborg, Sweden 18/J9
Solway (firth), England 13/D3
Solway, Minn. 255/C3
Solway (firth), Scotland 10/D3
Solway (firth), Scotland 15/E6
Solwezi, Zambia 115/E6
Soma, Japan 81/K5
Soma, Turkey 63/B3
Somabhula, Zimbabwe 118/D3
Somalia 2/M5
Somalia 102/G4
SOMALIA 115/J2
Sombor, Yugoslavia 45/D3
Sombra, Ontario 177/B5
Sombrerete, Mexico 150/H5
Sombrero (chan.), India 68/G7
Sombrero (isl.), St. Kitts & Nevis 156/F3
Somerdale, N.J. 273/B4
Somers, Conn. 210/F1
Somers•, Conn. 210/F1
Somers, Iowa 229/E4
Somers, Mont. 262/B2
Somers, Wis. 317/M3
Somerset, Va. 307/M4
Somerset (isl.), Bermuda 156/G3
Somerset (isl.), Canada 4/B14
Somerset, Colo. 208/E5
Somerset (co.), England 13/E6
Somerset, Ind. 227/F3
Somerset, Ky. 237/M6
Somerset, La. 238/H2
Somerset (co.), Maine 243/C4
Somerset, Manitoba 179/D5
Somerset (co.), Md. 245/R8
Somerset, Md. 245/E4
Somerset•, Mass. 249/K5
Somerset (co.), N.J. 273/D2
Somerset, N.Y. 276/C4
Somerset (isl.), N.W.T. 146/J2
Somerset (isl.), N.W.T. 162/G1
Somerset (isl.), N.W.T. 187/J2
Somerset, Nova Scotia 168/D3
Somerset, Ohio 284/F6
Somerset (co.), Pa. 294/D6
Somerset, Pa. 294/D6
Somerset, Texas 303/J11
Somerset (res.), Vt. 268/A5
Somerset, Wis. 317/A5
Somerset East, S. Africa 118/D6
Somerset West, S. Africa 118/F6
Somers Point, N.J. 273/D5
Somersville, Conn. 210/F1
Somersworth, N.H. 268/F5
Somerton, Ariz. 198/A6
Somerton, England 13/E6
Somerton, Ohio 284/H6
Somervell (co.), Texas 303/G5
Somerville, Ala. 195/E2
Somerville, Ind. 227/C8
Somerville•, Maine 243/D7
Somerville, Mass. 249/C6
Somerville, New Bruns. 170/C2
Somerville, N.J. 273/D2
Somerville, Ohio 284/A6
Somerville, Tenn. 237/C10
Somerville, Texas 303/H7
Somes (isl.), N. Zealand 100/B2
Someş (riv.), Romania 45/F2
Somesbar, Calif. 204/B2
Somesville (Mount Desert), Maine 243/G7
Somme (dept.), France 28/E3
Somme (riv.), France 28/D2
Somme, Sask. 181/J3
Somme-Leuze, Belgium 27/G8
Sommen (lake), Sweden 18/J8
Sömmerda, Germany 22/D3
Somogy (co.), Hungary 41/D3
Somonauk, Ill. 222/E2
Somotillo, Nicaragua 154/D4
Somoto, Nicaragua 154/D4
Somvix, Switzerland 39/G3
Son (riv.), India 68/E3
Son, Norway 18/D4
Son, Con (isls.), Vietnam 72/E5
Soná, Panama 154/G6
Sonaguera, Honduras 154/D3
Sŏnch'ŏn, N. Korea 81/B4
Sønderborg, Denmark 21/C8
Sønderborg, Denmark 18/G9
Sønderho, Denmark 21/B7
Sønderjylland (co.), Denmark 21/C7
Sønder Nissum, Denmark 21/A5
Sønder Omme, Denmark 21/B6
Sondershausen, Germany 22/D3
Sønderså, Denmark 21/D7
Sondheimer, La. 238/H1
Søndre Strømfjord, Greenl. 4/C12
Sondrio (prov.), Italy 34/B1
Sondrio, Italy 34/B1
Sonepur, India 68/E4
Sonestown, Pa. 294/K3
Song Ba (riv.), Vietnam 72/F4
Song Ca (riv.), Vietnam 72/E3
Song Cai (riv.), Vietnam 72/E4
Song Cau, Vietnam 72/F4
Song Da (Black) (riv.), Vietnam 72/E2
Songea, Tanzania 115/G6
Songea, Tanzania 102/F6
Song Hong (Red) (riv.), Vietnam 72/E2
Songhua (riv.), China 54/P5
Songhua Hu (lake), China 77/L3
Songhua Jiang (Sungari) (riv.), China 77/M2
Songkhla, Thailand 54/L9
Songkhla, Thailand 72/D6
Songling, China 77/K2
Songnim, N. Korea 81/B4
Songo, Angola 115/C5
Songo, Angola 102/D5
Songo, Mozambique 118/E3
Songololo, Zaire 115/B5
Songololo, Zaire 102/D5
Songpan, China 77/F5
Songxi, China 77/J6
Son Ha, Vietnam 72/F4
Sonid Youqi, China 77/H3
Sonid Zuoqi, China 77/H3
Son La, Vietnam 72/D2
Sonmiani, Pakistan 68/B3
Sonmiani, Pakistan 59/J4
Sonneberg, Germany 22/D3
Sonnenhorn (mt.), Switzerland 39/F4
Sonnette, Mont. 262/L5
Sonningdale, Sask. 181/D3
Sono (riv.), Brazil 132/E5
Sonobe, Japan 81/J7
Sonoita, Ariz. 198/E7
Sonoma (co.), Calif. 204/C5
Sonoma, Calif. 204/C5
Sonoma (range), Nev. 266/D2
Sonora, Calif. 204/E6
Sonora, Ky. 237/K5
Sonora (state), Mexico 150/D2
Sonora (riv.), Mexico 150/D2
Sonora, Nova Scotia 168/G3
Sonora, Texas 303/D7
Sonoyta, Mexico 150/C1
Songor, Iran 66/E3
Sonseca, Spain 33/D3
Sonsón, Colombia 126/C5
Sonsonate, El Salvador 154/C4
Sonsorol (isl.), Belau 87/D5
Sontag, Miss. 256/D7
Son Tay, Vietnam 72/E2
Sonthofen, Germany 22/D5
Sonvico, Switzerland 39/G4
Soochow (Suzhou), China 77/K5
Sooke, Br. Col. 184/J4
Sopachuy, Bolivia 136/C6
Sopas, Arroyo (riv.), Uruguay 145/C2
Sopchoppy, Fla. 212/B1
Soper, Okla. 288/P6
Soperton, Georgia 217/G6
Sopetrán, Colombia 126/C4
Sophia, N.C. 281/K3
Sophia, W. Va. 312/D7
Sophie, Fr. Guiana 131/E4
Sopi (cape), Indonesia 85/H5
Sopot, Poland 47/D1
Sopron, Hungary 41/D3
Soquel, Calif. 204/K4
Sora, Italy 34/D4
Sorah, Pakistan 68/B3
Sorata, Bolivia 136/A4
Sorbas, Spain 33/E4
Sorcière, La (mt.), St. Lucia 161/G6
Sorel, Québec 172/D4
Sorell (cape), Tasmania 99/B4
Sorell (lake), Tasmania 99/D4
Sorell-Midway Point, Tasmania 99/D4
Sorento, Ill. 222/D5
Soresina, Italy 34/C2
Sorgun, Turkey 63/F3
Soria (prov.), Spain 33/E2
Soria, Spain 33/E2
Soriano (dept.), Uruguay 145/B4
Soriano, Uruguay 145/A4
Sorikmerapi (mt.), Indonesia 85/B5
Sørkapp (pt.), Norway 18/C2
Sorø, Denmark 21/E7
Sorocaba, Brazil 132/D8
Sorocaba, Brazil 120/E5
Sorocaba, Brazil 135/C3
Sorochinsk, U.S.S.R. 52/H4
Soroki, U.S.S.R. 52/C5
Sorol (atoll), Micronesia 87/D5
Sorong, Indonesia 54/P10
Sorong, Indonesia 85/J6
Sororieng (mt.), Guyana 131/B2
Soroti, Uganda 115/F3
Sörüya (isl.), Norway 7/G1
Sørøya (isl.), Norway 18/N1
Sorrento, Br. Col. 184/H5
Sorrento, Fla. 212/E3
Sorrento, Italy 34/E4
Sorrento, La. 238/L3
Sorrento•, Maine 243/G7
Sorsele, Sweden 18/K4
Sorso, Italy 34/B4
Sorsogon (prov.), Philippines 82/E4
Sorsogon, Philippines 82/E4
Sorsogon, Philippines 85/G3
Sort, Spain 33/G1
Sortavala, U.S.S.R. 48/C3
Sortavala, U.S.S.R. 52/D2
Sør-Trøndelag (co.), Norway 18/G5
Sorum, S. Dak. 298/D3
Sŏsan, S. Korea 81/C5
Sos del Rey Católico, Spain 33/F1
Sosnogorsk, U.S.S.R. 7/K2
Sosnogorsk, U.S.S.R. 48/F3
Sosnogorsk, U.S.S.R. 52/H2
Sosnovka, U.S.S.R. 52/F4
Sosnovo-Ozerskoye, U.S.S.R. 48/M4
Sosnowiec, Poland 47/B4
Soso, Miss. 256/F7
Sosúa, Dom. Rep. 158/E5
Sosumav, Madagascar 118/H2
Sotkamo, Finland 18/Q4
Soto la Marina, Mexico 150/L4
Sotomayor, Bolivia 136/C6
Sotrondio, Spain 33/D1
Sotteville-lès-Rouen, France 28/D3
Sotuta, Mexico 150/P6
Souanké, Congo 115/B3
Soubey, Switzerland 39/D2
Soudan, Ark. 202/J4
Soudan, Minn. 255/F3
Soudan, North. Terr. 93/E6
Souderton, Pa. 294/M5
Souf (oasis), Algeria 106/F2
Souflion, Greece 45/H5
Soufrière, Dominica 161/E7
Soufrière (bay), Dominica 161/E7
Soufrière (mt.), Guadeloupe 161/A7
Soufrière, St. Lucia 161/F6
Soufrière, St. Lucia 156/G4
Soufrière (bay), St. Lucia 161/F6
Soufrière (mt.), St. Vin. & Grens. 161/A8
Souhegan (riv.), N.H. 268/D6
Souillac, Mauritius 118/G5
Souk Ahras, Algeria 106/F1
Soul (lake), Manitoba 179/C2
Soulanges (co.), Québec 172/C4
Soul City, N.C. 281/N2
Sounding (creek), Alberta 182/E4
Sound View, Conn. 210/F3
Sourdnahunk (lake), Maine 243/F3
Sourdough, Alaska 196/J2
Soure, Brazil 132/D3
Soure, Portugal 33/B2
Souris, Man. 162/F6
Souris, Manitoba 179/B5
Souris (riv.), Manitoba 179/B5
Souris (riv.), N. Dak. 188/F1
Souris, N. Dak. 282/J2
Souris (riv.), N. Dak. 282/J2
Souris, P.E.I. 162/K6
Souris, Pr. Edward I. 168/F2
Souris (riv.), Sask. 181/H6
Sour Lake, Texas 303/K7
Sousa, Brazil 120/F3
Sousel, Portugal 33/C3
Sousse, Tunisia 102/D1
Sousse, Tunisia 106/G1
Soustons, France 28/C6
South, Ala. 195/E8
South (pt.), Barbados 161/B9
South (riv.), Georgia 217/K2
South (Ka Lae) (cape), Hawaii 218/G7
South (sound), Ireland 17/C5
South, Ky. 237/J6
South (pass), La. 238/M8
South (pt.), La. 238/G8
South (riv.), Mass. 249/D2
South (bay), Mich. 250/C2
South (chan.), Mich. 250/E3
South (pt.), Mich. 250/F4
South (isl.), N. Zealand 87/G10
South (cape), N. Zealand 100/A7
South (isl.), N. Zealand 100/B5
South (riv.), N.C. 281/M5
South (bay), N.W. Terr. 187/K3
South (bay), Ontario 177/C2
South (mt.), Pa. 294/H6
South (isl.), S.C. 296/J5
South (cape), Tasmania 99/C5
South Acton, Maine 243/B8
South Acton, Mass. 249/J3
South Acworth, N.H. 268/C5
South Addison, Maine 243/H6
South Africa 2/L7
South Africa 102/E7
SOUTH AFRICA 118/C5
South Alexandria, N.H. 268/D4
South Allan, Sask. 181/E4
South Alligator (riv.), North. Terr. 88/E2
South Alligator (riv.), North. Terr. 93/C2
Southam, N. Dak. 282/N3
South Amana, Iowa 229/J5
South Amboy, N.J. 273/E3
South America 2/D6
South Amherst, Mass. 249/E3
South Amherst, Ohio 284/F3
Southampton, England 7/D3
Southampton, England 10/F5
Southampton, England 13/F7
Southampton•, Mass. 249/C4
Southampton, N.Y. 276/R9
Southampton (cape), N.W.T. 187/K3
Southampton (isl.), N.W.T. 162/H2
Southampton (isl.), N.W.T. 187/K3
Southampton, Nova Scotia 168/D3
Southampton, Ontario 177/C3
Southampton (co.), Va. 307/O7
South Andaman (isl.), India 68/G6
South Anna (riv.), Va. 307/N5
Southard, Okla. 288/K2
South Ashburnham, Mass. 249/G2
South Athol, Mass. 249/F2
South Atlantic Ocean 2/J6
South Aulatsivik (isl.), Newf. 166/B2
South Australia 88/F6
SOUTH AUSTRALIA 94
South Australia (state), Australia 87/D8
Southaven, Miss. 256/E1
South Bancroft, Maine 243/G4
Southbank, Br. Col. 184/E3
South Barre, Mass. 249/F3
South Barre, Vt. 268/B3
South Barrington, Ill. 222/A5
South Barwon, Victoria 97/C6
South Bass (isl.), Ohio 284/E2
South Bay, Fla. 212/F5
South Bay Aqueduct, Calif. 204/L2
South Baymouth, Ontario 177/B2
South Beach, Oreg. 291/C3
South Belmar, N.J. 273/E3
South Beloit, Ill. 222/E1
South Bend, Ind. 188/J2
South Bend, Ind. 227/E1
South Bend, Nebr. 264/H4
South Bend, Texas 303/F5
South Bend, Wash. 310/B4
South Bennettsville, S.C. 296/H2
South Bentinck Arm (inlet), Br. Col. 184/D4
South Berlin, Mass. 249/H3
South Berwick, Maine 243/B9
South Berwick•, Maine 243/B9
South Bethany, Del. 245/T6
South Bethlehem, N.Y. 276/N5
South Bethlehem, Pa. 294/D4
South Beveland (isl.), Netherlands 27/D6
South Bloomfield, Ohio 284/D6
South Bloomingville, Ohio 284/E7
South Boardman, Mich. 250/D4
South Bolton, Québec 172/E4
Southborough, England 13/J8
Southborough•, Mass. 249/H3
South Boston (I.C.), Va. 307/L7
South Boston, Ind. 227/F7
South Bound Brook, N.J. 273/E2
South Braintree, Mass. 249/D8
South Branch, Mich. 250/E4
South Branch, Minn. 255/D7
South Branch, New Bruns. 170/F2
South Branch, Newf. 166/C4
South Branch, N.J. 273/D2
South Branch Oromocto (riv.), New Bruns. 170/D3
Southbridge, Mass. 249/G4
Southbridge•, Mass. 249/G4
Southbridge, N. Zealand 100/D5
South Bridgton, Maine 243/B8
South Bristol•, Maine 243/D8
South Britain, Conn. 210/B3
South Broadway, Wash. 310/E4
South Brook, Green Bay Dist., Newf. 166/C4
South Brook, Humber Dist., Newf. 166/C4
South Brookfield, Nova Scotia 168/D4
South Brooksville, Maine 243/F7
South Brunswick•, N.J. 273/E3
South Bruny (isl.), Tasmania 99/D5
South Burlington, Vt. 268/A3
South Burro (mt.), Utah 304/D3
Southbury•, Conn. 210/C3
South Calling Lake, Alberta 182/D2
South Canaan, Conn. 210/B1
South Carolina 188/K4
SOUTH CAROLINA 296
South Carolina (state), U.S. 146/K6
South Carrollton, Ky. 237/G6
South Carthage, Tenn. 237/K8
South Carver, Mass. 249/M5
South Casco, Maine 243/B8
South Charleston, Ohio 284/C6
South Charleston, W. Va. 312/C6
South Chatham, Mass. 249/O6
South Chatham, N.H. 268/E3
South Cheyenne (riv.), Wyo. 319/H2
South Chicago Heights, Ill. 222/C6
South China (sea) 54/N8
South China (sea) 2/Q5
South China (sea), China 77/J7
South China (sea), Indonesia 85/D4
South China, Maine 243/D7
South China (sea), Malaysia 85/D4
South China (sea), Philippines 85/D4
South China (sea), Philippines 82/B3
South China (sea), Vietnam 72/F4
South Cle Elum, Wash. 310/D3
South Cleveland, Tenn. 237/M10
South Clinton, Tenn. 237/N8
South Coffeyville, Okla. 288/P1
South Colby, Wash. 310/A2
South Colton, N.Y. 276/L1
South Congaree, S.C. 296/E4
South Connellsville, Pa. 294/C6
South Corning, N.Y. 276/F6
South Cotabato (prov.), Philippines 82/E7
South Coventry (Coventry), Conn. 210/F1
South Cow (creek), Calif. 204/C3
South Dakota 188/F2
SOUTH DAKOTA 298
South Dakota (state), U.S. 146/H5
South Danbury, N.H. 268/D5
South Danville, N.H. 268/E6
South Dartmouth, Mass. 249/L6
South Dayton, N.Y. 276/C6
South Daytona, Fla. 212/F2
South Deerfield, Mass. 249/D3
South Deerfield, N.H. 268/E5
South Dennis, Mass. 249/O6
South Dennis, N.J. 273/D5
South Dorset, Vt. 268/A5
South Dos Palos, Calif. 204/E7
South Downs (hills), England 13/G7
South Dum Dum, India 68/F2
South Duxbury, Mass. 249/M4
Southeast (cape), Alaska 196/E2
South East (cape), Australia 87/E10
South East (pt.), Jamaica 158/K6
Southeast (pass), La. 238/M8
South East (cape), Tasmania 88/H8
South East (cape), Tasmania 99/C5
South East (pt.), Victoria 97/D6
SOUTHEAST ASIA 85
Southeast Loch (inlet), Hawaii 218/B3
South Easton, Mass. 249/K4
Southeast Upsalquitch (riv.), New Bruns. 170/D1
South Effingham, N.H. 268/E4
South Egremont, Mass. 249/A4
South Elgin, Ill. 222/E2
South Eliot, Maine 243/B9
South El Monte, Calif. 204/C10
Southend, Scotland 15/C5
Southend-on-Sea, England 10/G5
Southend-on-Sea, England 13/H6
South English, Iowa 229/J6
Southern (dist.), Israel 65/B5
Southern Alps (range), N. Zealand 100/C5
Southern Cross, Mont. 262/C4
Southern Cross, W. Australia 88/E6
Southern Cross, W. Australia 92/B5
Southern Harbour, Newf. 166/C2
Southern Indian (lake), Man. 162/G4
Southern Indian (lake), Man. 146/J4
Southern Indian (lake), Manitoba 179/H2
Southern Leyte (prov.), Philippines 82/E5
Southern Pines, N.C. 281/L4
Southern Ute Ind. Res., Colo. 208/D8
South Esk (riv.), Scotland 15/F4
South Esk (riv.), Tasmania 99/D3
Southesk Tablelands, W. Australia 92/D3
South Euclid, Ohio 284/H9
South Exeter, Maine 243/E6
Southey, Sask. 181/G5
South Fallsburg, N.Y. 276/L7
Southfield, Mass. 249/B4
Southfield, Mich. 250/F6
Southfields, N.Y. 276/M8
Southford, Conn. 210/C3
South Foreland (prom.), England 13/J6
South Fork, Colo. 208/F7
South Fork, Frenchman, Colo. 208/O1
South Fork, Mo. 261/J9
South Fork, Flathead (riv.), Mont. 262/C3
South Fork, Humboldt (riv.), Nev. 266/F2
South Fork, Owyhee (riv.), Nev. 266/E1
South Fork, Pa. 294/E5
South Fork, Sask. 181/C6
South Fork, Shoshone (riv.), Wyo. 319/C1
South Fork, Powder (riv.), Wyo. 319/F2
South Foster, R.I. 249/H5
South Fowl (lake), Minn. 255/G1
South Fox (isl.), Mich. 250/D3
South Friars (bay), St. Kitts & Nevis 161/C10
South Fulton, Tenn. 237/D8
South Gate, Calif. 204/C11
Southgate, Ky. 237/T2
South Gate, Md. 245/M4
Southgate, Mich. 250/F6
South Georgia (isl.), Ant. (U.K.) 2/H8
South Georgia (isl.), Ant. 5/D17
South Gifford, Mo. 261/G2
South Glamorgan, Wales 13/A7
South Glastonbury, Conn. 210/E2
South Glens Falls, N.Y. 276/N4
South Goldsboro, N.C. 281/N4
South Grafton, Mass. 249/H4
South Greenfield, Mo. 261/E8
South Groveland, Mass. 249/L2
South Hadley•, Mass. 249/D4
South Hadley Falls, Mass. 249/D4
Southhampton (isl.), N.W.T. 146/K3
South Hampton•, N.H. 268/F6
South Hanover, Mass. 249/L4
South Harbour, Nova Scotia 168/H2
South Harpswell, Maine 243/C8
South Harwich, Mass. 249/O6
South Haven, Kansas 232/E4
South Haven, Mich. 250/C6
South Haven, Minn. 255/D5
South Haven, Nova Scotia 168/H2
South Hazelton, Br. Col. 184/D2
South Heart, N. Dak. 282/D6
South Heights, Pa. 294/B4
South Hero•, Vt. 268/A2
South Hill, Va. 307/M7
South Hiram, Maine 243/B8
South Holland, Ill. 222/C6
South Holland (prov.), Netherlands 27/E5
South Holston (lake), Tenn. 237/S7
South Holston (lake), Va. 307/E7
South Hope, Maine 243/E7
South Horr, Kenya 115/G3
South Houston, Texas 303/J2
South Hutchinson, Kansas 232/D3
South Indian Lake, Manitoba 179/H2
Southington•, Conn. 210/D2
South International Falls, Minn. 255/E2
South Irvine, Ky. 237/N5
South Jacksonville, Ill. 222/C4
South Jordan, Utah 304/B3
South Junction, Manitoba 179/G5
South Junction, Oreg. 291/F3
South Kedgwick (riv.), New Bruns. 170/B1

Squibnocket 451

South Kensington, Md. 245/E4
South Kent, Conn. 210/B2
South Killingly, Conn. 210/H1
South Knife (riv.), Manitoba 179/J2
South Knife Lake, Manitoba 179/J2
South Korea 54/O6
South La Grange, Maine 243/F5
Southlake, Texas 303/F2
South Lake Tahoe, Calif. 204/F5
South Lancaster, Mass. 249/H3
Southland, Texas 303/C4
South Laurel, Md. 245/L4
South Lead Hill, Ark. 202/D1
South Lebanon, Maine 243/A9
South Lebanon, Ohio 284/B7
South Lee, Mass. 249/A3
South Lee, N.H. 268/E5
South Liberty, Maine 243/E7
South Lincoln, Maine 243/F5
South Lincoln, Vt. 268/B3
South Lineville, Mo. 261/E1
South Londonderry, Vt. 268/B5
South Loup (riv.), Nebr. 264/E3
South Luconia (shoal), Philippines 85/E4
South Lunenburg, Vt. 268/D3
South Lyme, Conn. 210/F3
South Lyndeboro, N.H. 268/D6
South Lynnfield, Mass. 249/D5
South Lyon, Mich. 250/F6
South Magnetic Pole, Ant. 2/R9
South Magnetic Pole, Ant. 5/C8
South Maitland, Nova Scotia 168/E3
South Manitou, Mich. 250/C3
South Manitou (isl.), Mich. 250/C3
South Mansfield, La. 238/C3
South Marsh (isl.), Md. 245/O8
South Mayo (riv.), Va. 307/H7
South Medford, Oreg. 291/E5
South Melbourne, Victoria 97/J5
South Melbourne, Victoria 88/K7
South Merrimack, N.H. 268/D6
South Miami, Fla. 212/B5
South Miami Heights, Fla. 212/F6
South Middleboro, Mass. 249/L5
South Milford, Ind. 227/G1
South Mills, N.C. 281/S2
South Milwaukee, Wis. 317/M2
South Molton, England 10/E5
South Molton, England 13/D6
South Monmouth, Maine 243/D7
South Monroe, Mich. 250/F7
Southmont, N.C. 281/J3
South Mound, Kansas 232/G4
South Mountain, Ontario 177/J3
South Mountain, Pa. 294/H6
South Nahanni (riv.), N.W. Terr. 187/F3
South Naknek, Alaska 196/G3
South Natick, Mass. 249/A7
South Natuna (isls.), Indonesia 85/D5
South Negril (pt.), Jamaica 158/G6
South Negril (pt.), Jamaica 156/B3
South New Berlin, N.Y. 276/K5
South Newbury, N.H. 268/D5
South Newbury, Vt. 268/C3
South Newfane, Vt. 268/B6
South Newport, Georgia 217/K7
South New River (canal), Fla. 212/F5
South Norfolk, Conn. 210/C1
South Norwalk, Conn. 210/B4
South Nyack, N.Y. 276/K8
South Ogden, Utah 304/C2
South Ohio, Nova Scotia 168/B5
Southold, N.Y. 276/P8
South Olive, Ohio 284/G6
South Orange•, N.J. 273/A2
South Orkney (isls.), Ant. (U.K.) 2/G9
South Orkney (isls.), Ant. 5/C16
South Orleans, Mass. 249/O5
South Oromocto (lake), New Bruns. 170/D3
South Oroville, Calif. 204/D4
South Orrington, Maine 243/F6
South Ossetian Aut. Obl., U.S.S.R. 48/E5
South Ossetian Aut. Obl., U.S.S.R. 52/F6
South Otselic, N.Y. 276/J5
South Pacific (ocean) 87/H8
South Pacific Ocean 2/C8
South Padre Island, Texas 303/G11
South Pagai (isl.), Indonesia 85/C6
South Para (riv.), S. Australia 94/C7
South Paris, Maine 243/C7
South Pasadena, Calif. 204/C10
South Pasadena, Fla. 212/B3
South Pass City, Wyo. 319/D3
South Patrick Shores, Fla. 212/F3
South Pekin, Ill. 222/D3
South Pender Island, Br. Col. 184/K3
South Penobscot, Maine 243/F7
South Perry, Ohio 284/E6
South Perth, W. Australia 88/B2
South Perth, W. Australia 92/A1
South Philipsburg, Pa. 294/F4
South Piney (creek), Wyo. 319/B3
South Pittsburg, Tenn. 237/K10
South Pittsfield, N.H. 268/E5
South Plainfield, N.J. 273/E2
South Plains, Texas 303/C3
South Platte (riv.) 188/F2
South Platte (riv.), Colo. 208/N1
South Platte (riv.), Nebr. 264/C3
South Platte (riv.), U.S. 146/H6
South Point, Ohio 284/E9
South Polar (plat.), Ant. 5/A1
South Pole 2/E11
South Pole, Ant. 5/A4
South Pomfret, Vt. 268/B4
South Porcupine, Ontario 175/D3
Southport, Conn. 210/B4
Southport, England 10/F2
Southport, England 13/G1
Southport, Fla. 212/C6
Southport, Ind. 227/E5
Southport, Maine 243/D8
Southport•, Maine 243/D8
Southport, N.Y. 276/G6
Southport, N.C. 281/N7
South Portland, Maine 243/C8
South Portsmouth, Ky. 237/P3
South Prairie, Wash. 310/D3
South Pugwash, Nova Scotia 168/E3
South Range, Mich. 250/G1
South Range, Wis. 317/B2
South Renous (riv.), New Bruns. 170/D2
South Renovo, Pa. 294/G3
South River (peak), Colo. 208/F7
South River, Newf. 166/D2
South River, N.J. 273/E3
South River, Ontario 177/E2
South Rockwood, Mich. 250/F7
South Ronaldsay (isl.), Scotland 10/E1
South Ronaldsay (isl.), Scotland 15/F2
South Roxana, Ill. 222/B2
South Royalston, Mass. 249/F2
South Royalton, Vt. 268/C4
South Russell, Ohio 284/H3
South Ryegate, Vt. 268/C3
South Sacramento, Calif. 204/B8
South Saint Paul, Minn. 255/G6
South Salem, Ohio 284/D7
South Salt Lake, Utah 304/C3
South Sandisfield, Mass. 249/B4
South Sandwich (isls.), Ant. (U.K.) 2/H8
South Sandwich (isls.), Ant. 5/D17
South Sanford, Maine 243/B9
South San Francisco, Calif. 204/J2
South Santiam (riv.), Oreg. 291/E3
South Saskatchewan (riv.), Alberta 182/E4
South Saskatchewan (riv.), Canada 146/G4
South Saskatchewan (riv.), Sask. 181/C5
South Seabrook, N.H. 268/F6
South Seal (riv.), Manitoba 179/J2
South Seaville, N.J. 273/D5
South Sevogle (riv.), New Bruns. 170/D1
South Shaftsbury, Vt. 268/A6
South Shetland (isls.) 2/F9
South Shetland (isls.) 5/C15
South Shields, England 13/J3
South Shields, England 10/F3
South Shore, Ky. 237/R3
South Shore, S. Dak. 298/P3
Southside, Ala. 195/F3
Southside, Tenn. 237/G8
Southside Place, Texas 303/J2
South Sioux City, Nebr. 264/H2
South Skunk (riv.), Iowa 229/H6
South Slocan, Br. Col. 184/J5
South Solon, Ohio 284/C6
South Spectacle (lake), Conn. 210/B2
South Stoddard, N.H. 268/C5
South Strafford, Vt. 268/C4
South Suburban, India 68/F2
South Sudbury, Mass. 249/J3
South Superior, Wyo. 319/D4
South Sutton, N.H. 268/D5
South Sydney, N. S. Wales 88/L4
South Sydney, N.S. Wales 97/J3
South Taft, Calif. 204/F8
South Tamworth, N.H. 268/E4
South Taranaki (bight), N. Zealand 100/D3
South Thomaston•, Maine 243/E7
South Toms River, N.J. 273/E4
South Trap (isl.), N. Zealand 100/B7
South Tucson, Ariz. 198/D6
South Tunnel, Tenn. 237/H7
South Twin (mt.), N.H. 268/D3
South Tyne (riv.), England 13/E3
South Uist (isl.), Scotland 10/C2
South Uist (isl.), Scotland 15/A3
South Umpqua (riv.), Oreg. 291/E4
South Union, Ky. 237/H7
South Union, Maine 243/E7
South Ural (mts.), U.S.S.R. 52/J4
South Venice, Fla. 212/D4
South Vienna, Ohio 284/C6
Southville, Mass. 249/H3
South Wabasca (lake), Alberta 182/D2
South Wadesboro, N.C. 281/J5
South Waldoboro, Maine 243/E7
South Wallingford, Vt. 268/A5
South Walpole, Mass. 249/K4
South Wanatah, Ind. 227/D2
Southwark, England 13/H8
Southwark, England 10/B5
South Warren, Maine 243/E7
South Waterford, Maine 243/B7
South Waverly, Pa. 294/J2
South Wayne, Wis. 317/G10
South Weare, N.H. 268/D5
South Webster, Ohio 284/E8
South Weldon, N.C. 281/O2
South Wellfleet, Mass. 249/P5
South Wellington, Br. Col. 184/J3
Southwest (pass), La. 238/L8
Southwest (head), New Bruns. 170/D4
South West (brook), Newf. 166/C2
South West (cape), Tasmania 88/G7
South West (cape), Tasmania 99/B5
Southwest (cape), Virgin Is. (U.S.) 161/E4
South West Arm (inlet), Newf. 166/D2
South West City, Mo. 261/D9
South West Gander (riv.), Newf. 166/C4
Southwest Harbor, Maine 243/G7
Southwest Harbor•, Maine 243/G7
South West Margaree (riv.), Nova Scotia 168/G2
Southwest Miramichi (riv.), New Bruns. 170/D2
South Westport, Mass. 249/K6
South West Port Mouton, Nova Scotia 168/D5
South West Rocks, N.S. Wales 97/G2
South Weymouth, Mass. 249/E8
South Whitley, Ind. 227/F2
Southwick, England 13/G7
Southwick, Idaho 220/B3
Southwick•, Mass. 249/C4
South Williamson, Ky. 237/S5
South Williamsport, Pa. 294/J3
South Willington, Conn. 210/F1
South Wilmington, Ill. 222/E2
South Wilton, Conn. 210/B4
South Windham, Conn. 210/G2
South Windham (Little Falls-South Windham), Maine 243/C8
South Windham, Vt. 268/B5
South Windsor•, Conn. 210/E1
Southwold, England 13/J5
Southwold, England 10/G4
South Wolf (isl.), Newf. 166/C3
South Wolfeboro, N.H. 268/E4
South Woodbury, Vt. 268/C3
South Woodstock, Conn. 210/G1
South Woodstock, Vt. 268/B4
Southworth, Wash. 310/A2
South Worthington, Mass. 249/C3
South Yadkin (riv.), N.C. 281/H3
South Yarmouth, Mass. 249/O6
South Yorkshire (co.), England 13/F4
South Zanesville, Ohio 284/F6
Sovata, Romania 45/G2
Sovereign, Sask. 181/D4
Sovetsk, U.S.S.R. 7/J3
Sovetsk, U.S.S.R. 52/G3
Sovetsk (Tilsit), U.S.S.R. 52/B4
Sovetskaya Gavan', U.S.S.R. 54/R5
Sovetskaya Gavan', U.S.S.R. 48/P5
SOVIET UNION (U.S.S.R.) 48
Sowerby Bridge, England 13/H1
Sowerby Bridge, England 10/G2
Soweto, S. Africa 118/H6
Soya (pt.), Japan 81/L1
Soyhières, Switzerland 39/D2
Soyo, Angola 115/B5
Soyo, Angola 102/D5
Sozopol, Bulgaria 45/H4
Spa, Belgium 27/H8
Spades, Ind. 227/G6
Spain 2/J3
Spain 7/D4
SPAIN 33
SPAIN-Canary Islands, Ceuta and Melilla 106
Spalding, England 13/G5
Spalding, England 10/F4
Spalding (co.), Georgia 217/D4
Spalding, Mich. 250/B3
Spalding, Mo. 261/J3
Spalding, Nebr. 264/F3
Spalding, Sask. 181/G3
Spaldings, Jamaica 158/H6
Spallumcheen, Br. Col. 184/H5
Spanaway, Wash. 310/C3
Spandau, Germany 22/E3
Spangle, Wash. 310/H3
Spangler, Pa. 294/E4
Spaniard's Bay, Newf. 166/D2
Spanish (head), I. of Man 13/C3
Spanish, Ontario 177/J5
Spanish (riv.), Ontario 177/C1
Spanishburg, W. Va. 312/D8
Spanish Fork, Utah 304/C3
Spanish Fork (riv.), Utah 304/C3
Spanish Fort, Ala. 195/C9
Spanish Fort, Texas 303/G4
Spanish Lake, Mo. 261/R1
Spanish Ship Bay, Nova Scotia 168/G4
Spanish Town, Jamaica 158/J6
Spanish Town, Jamaica 156/C3
Sparkill, N.Y. 276/K8
Sparkman, Ark. 202/E6
Sparks, Georgia 217/F8
Sparks, Kansas 232/G2
Sparks, Nebr. 264/D2
Sparks, Nev. 188/C3
Sparks, Nev. 266/B3
Sparks, Okla. 288/N3
Sparks (lake), Oreg. 291/F3
Sparksville, Ky. 237/L6
Sparland, Ill. 222/D2
Sparlingville, Mich. 250/G6
Sparr, Fla. 212/D2
Sparrow Bush, N.Y. 276/L8
Sparrows Point, Md. 245/N4
Sparta, Georgia 217/F4
Sparta, Greece 45/F7
Sparta, Ill. 222/D5
Sparta, Ky. 237/M3
Sparta, Mich. 250/D5
Sparta, Mo. 261/F9
Sparta•, N.J. 273/D1
Sparta, N.C. 281/G1
Sparta, Ohio 284/E5
Sparta, Ontario 177/C5
Sparta, Oreg. 291/K3
Sparta, Tenn. 237/K9
Sparta, Va. 307/O4
Sparta, Wis. 317/E8
Spartanburg, Ind. 227/H4
Spartanburg, S.C. 188/K4
Spartanburg (co.), S.C. 296/D2
Spartanburg, S.C. 296/C1
Spartansburg, Pa. 294/C2
Spartivento (cape), Italy 34/B5
Spartivento (cape), Italy 34/F6
Sparwood, Br. Col. 184/K5
Spassk-Dal'niy, U.S.S.R. 48/O5
Spátha (cape), Greece 45/F8
Spaulding, Ill. 222/D4
Spavinaw, Okla. 288/R2
Spavinaw (lake), Okla. 288/S2
Spean (riv.), Scotland 15/D4
Spean Bridge, Scotland 15/D4
Spear (cape), New Bruns. 170/G2
Spear (cape), Newf. 166/D2
Spearfish, S. Dak. 298/B5
Spearman, Texas 303/C1
Spearsville, Ind. 227/E6
Spearsville, La. 238/E1
Spearville, Kansas 232/C4
Spectacle (lakes), Conn. 210/B2
Specter (range), Nev. 266/E6
Speculator, N.Y. 276/M3
Spedden, Alberta 182/E2
Spednik (lake), New Bruns. 170/C3
Speed, Ind. 227/F8
Speed, Kansas 232/C2
Speed, N.C. 281/P3
Speedway, Ind. 227/E5
Speedwell, Tenn. 237/O8
Speedwell, Va. 307/F8
Speer (mt.), Switzerland 39/H2
Speers, Sask. 181/D3
Speightstown, Barbados 161/B8
Speightstown, Barbados 156/G4
Speigner, Ala. 195/F5
Spelterville, Ind. 227/C5
Spelve, Loch (inlet), Scotland 15/C4
Spenard, Alaska 196/C1
Spenborough, England 13/J1
Spence Bay, N.W. Terr. 187/J3
Spencer (cape), Alaska 196/L1
Spencer (pt.), Alaska 196/E1
Spencer (lake), Alberta 182/E2
Spencer (gulf), Australia 87/D9
Spencer, Idaho 220/F5
Spencer (co.), Ind. 227/C9
Spencer, Ind. 227/D6
Spencer, Iowa 229/C2
Spencer (co.), Ky. 237/L4
Spencer, La. 238/F1
Spencer (pond), Maine 243/D4
Spencer (stream), Maine 243/C5
Spencer, Mass. 249/F3
Spencer•, Mass. 249/F3
Spencer, Nebr. 264/F2
Spencer (cape), New Bruns. 170/E3
Spencer, N.Y. 276/H6
Spencer, N.C. 281/H3
Spencer, Ohio 284/F3
Spencer, Okla. 288/M3
Spencer (creek), Oreg. 291/E5
Spencer (gulf), S. Australia 88/F6
Spencer (cape), S. Australia 88/F7
Spencer (cape), S. Australia 94/E6
Spencer (gulf), S. Australia 94/E6
Spencer, S. Dak. 298/O6
Spencer, Tenn. 237/L9
Spencer, Va. 307/J7
Spencer, W. Va. 312/D5
Spencer, Wis. 317/F6
Spencerburg, Mo. 261/K4
Spencerport, N.Y. 276/E4
Spencers Island, Nova Scotia 168/D3
Spencerville, Ind. 227/G2
Spencerville, Ohio 284/B4
Spencerville, Okla. 288/R6
Spencerville, Ontario 177/J3
Spences Bridge, Br. Col. 184/G5
Spennymoor, England 13/F3
Spennymoor, England 10/F3
Spenser (mts.), N. Zealand 100/D5
Sperling, Manitoba 179/E5
Sperrin (mts.), N. Ireland 17/G2
Sperry, Iowa 229/L7
Sperry, Okla. 288/P2
Sperryville, Va. 307/M3
Spessart (range), Germany 22/C4
Spétsai, Greece 45/F7
Spey (riv.), Scotland 10/E2
Spey (riv.), Scotland 15/E3
Speyer, Germany 22/C4
Sphinx (mt.), Mont. 262/E5
Spiceland, Ind. 227/F5
Spicer, Minn. 255/C5
Spicer (isls.), N.W. Terr. 187/L3
Spicewood, Texas 303/F7
Spickard, Mo. 261/F2
Spiddal, Ireland 17/C5
Spider (lake), Maine 243/E3
Spider (lake), Wis. 317/D3
Spiekeroog (isl.), Germany 22/B2
Spies, N.C. 281/K4
Spiez, Switzerland 39/E3
Spili, Greece 45/G8
Spillimacheen, Br. Col. 184/J5
Spillville, Iowa 229/J2
Spilsby, England 13/H4
Spin Buldak, Afghanistan 68/B2
Spin Buldak, Afghanistan 59/J3
Spindale, N.C. 281/F4
Spink (co.), S. Dak. 298/N4
Spink, S. Dak. 298/R8
Spinnerstown, Pa. 294/M5
Spirit (lake), Idaho 220/B2
Spirit (lake), Iowa 229/C2
Spirit (lake), S. Dak. 298/O4
Spirit (lake), Wash. 310/C4
Spirit, Wis. 317/F5
Spirit Lake, Idaho 220/A2
Spirit Lake, Iowa 229/C2
Spirit River, Alberta 182/A2
Spirit River, Alta. 162/E4
Spiritwood, N. Dak. 282/N6
Spiritwood, Sask. 181/D3
Spiro, Okla. 288/S4
Spišská Belá, Czech. 41/F2
Spišská Nová Ves, Czech. 41/F2
Spital am Pyhrn, Austria 41/C3
Spithead (chan.), England 13/F7
Spitsbergen (isl.), Norway 4/B9
Spitsbergen (isl.), Norway 18/C2
Spittal an der Drau, Austria 41/B3
Spitz, Austria 41/C2
Spivey, Kansas 232/D4
Splendora, Texas 303/J7
Split (lake), Manitoba 179/J2
Split (cape), Nova Scotia 168/D3
Split, Yugoslavia 7/F4
Split, Yugoslavia 45/C4
Split Lake, Manitoba 179/J2
Split Rock, Wis. 317/H6
Splügen (pass), Italy 34/B1
Splügen, Switzerland 39/H3
Splügen (pass), Switzerland 39/H3
Spofford, N.H. 268/C6
Spofford, Texas 303/D8
Spokane, Mo. 261/F9
Spokane (co.), Wash. 310/H3
Spokane, Wash. 146/G5
Spokane, Wash. 188/C1
Spokane, Wash. 310/H3
Spokane (mt.), Wash. 310/H3
Spokane (riv.), Wash. 310/H3
Spokane Ind. Res., Wash. 310/G3
Spöl (riv.), Switzerland 39/F2
Spoleto, Italy 34/D3
Spoon (riv.), Ill. 222/C3
Spooner, Wis. 317/B4
Spot (pond), Mass. 249/C6
Spotswood, N.J. 273/E3
Spotsylvania (co.), Va. 307/N4
Spotsylvania, Va. 307/N4
Spotted (range), Nev. 266/F6
Spotted Horse, Wyo. 319/G1
Spottsville, Ky. 237/G5
Spottswood, Va. 307/K5
Spotville, Ark. 202/D7
Spragge, Ontario 177/J5
Sprague, Ala. 195/F6
Sprague, Manitoba 179/G5
Sprague, Nebr. 264/H4
Sprague (riv.), Oreg. 291/F5
Sprague, Wash. 310/G3
Sprague (lake), Wash. 310/G3
Sprague River, Oreg. 291/F5
Sprageville, Iowa 229/N4
Spratly (isl.), Philippines 85/E4
Spratt, Mich. 250/F3
Spray (mts.), Alberta 182/C4
Spray, Oreg. 291/H3
Spray Lakes, Alberta 182/C4
Spraytown, Ind. 227/E6
Spread Eagle, Wis. 317/K4
Spreckelsville, Hawaii 218/J1
Spree (riv.), Germany 22/F3
Spreewald (for.), Germany 22/F3
Spremberg, Germany 22/F3
Sprent, Tasmania 99/C3
Sprigg, W. Va. 312/B7
Sprimont, Belgium 27/H8
Spring (riv.), Ark. 202/H1
Spring (creek), Nev. 266/D2
Spring (mts.), Nev. 266/F6
Spring (valley), Nev. 266/G3
Spring (creek), N. Dak. 282/E5
Spring (creek), S. Dak. 298/J2
Spring (creek), S. Dak. 298/C6
Spring, Texas 303/J7
Spring Arbor, Mich. 250/E6
Spring Bay, Ill. 222/D3
Spring Bay, Ontario 177/B2
Springbok, S. Africa 118/B5
Springboro, Ohio 284/B6
Springboro, Pa. 294/B2
Springbrook, Iowa 229/N4
Spring Brook, N. Dak. 282/D3
Springbrook, Ontario 177/G3
Springbrook, Oreg. 291/A2
Springbrook, Wis. 317/C4
Spring City, Mo. 261/C9
Spring City, Pa. 294/L5
Spring City, Tenn. 237/M9
Spring City, Utah 304/C4
Spring Coulée, Alberta 182/D5
Spring Creek, Pa. 294/D2
Spring Creek, Tenn. 237/D9
Spring Creek, W. Va. 312/F7
Springdale, Ark. 202/B1
Springdale, Iowa 229/L5
Springdale, Mont. 262/F5
Springdale, Newf. 166/C4
Springdale, Ohio 284/B9
Springdale, Pa. 294/C6
Springdale, S.C. 296/F2
Springdale, S.C. 296/E4
Springdale, Utah 304/B6
Springdale, Wash. 310/H2
Springe, Germany 22/C2
Springer (mt.), Georgia 217/D1
Springer, N. Mex. 274/E2
Springer, Okla. 288/M6
Springerton, Ill. 222/E5
Springerville, Ariz. 198/F4
Springfield, Ark. 202/E3
Springfield, Colo. 208/O8
Springfield, Fla. 212/D6
Springfield, Georgia 217/K6
Springfield, Idaho 220/F6
Springfield (cap.), Ill. 146/J6
Springfield (cap.), Ill. 188/H3
Springfield (cap.), Ill. 222/D4
Springfield (lake), Ill. 222/D4
Springfield, Ind. 227/B8
Springfield, Ky. 237/L5
Springfield, La. 238/M2
Springfield•, Maine 243/G5
Springfield, Mass. 188/M2
Springfield, Mass. 249/D4
Springfield, Mich. 250/D6
Springfield, Minn. 255/C6
Springfield, Mo. 261/F8
Springfield, Mo. 146/J6
Springfield, Nebr. 264/H3
Springfield, King's, New Bruns. 170/E3
Springfield, York, New Bruns. 170/C2
Springfield•, N.H. 268/C4
Springfield•, N.J. 273/E2
Springfield, Nova Scotia 168/D4
Springfield, Ohio 188/K2
Springfield, Ohio 284/C6
Springfield, Ontario 177/C5
Springfield, Oreg. 291/E3
Springfield•, Pa. 294/M7
Springfield, Queensland 88/G5
Springfield, Queensland 95/B5
Springfield, S.C. 296/E4
Springfield, S. Dak. 298/N8
Springfield, Tenn. 237/H8
Springfield, Vt. 268/B5
Springfield•, Vt. 268/B5
Springfield, Va. 307/S3
Springfield, W. Va. 312/J4
Springfield Armory Nat'l Hist. Site, Mass. 249/D4
Springford, Ontario 177/D5
Spring Garden, Ala. 195/G3
Spring Garden, Calif. 204/D4
Spring Garden, Ill. 222/E5
Spring Green, Wis. 317/G9
Spring Grove, Ill. 222/E1
Spring Grove, Ind. 227/H5
Spring Grove, Minn. 255/G7
Spring Grove, Pa. 294/J6
Spring Grove, Va. 307/P6
Spring Hall, Barbados 161/B8
Springhaven, Nova Scotia 168/C5
Spring Hill, Ark. 202/C6
Spring Hill, Iowa 229/F6
Spring Hill, Kansas 232/H3
Springhill, La. 238/D1
Spring Hill, Minn. 255/D5
Springhill, Nova Scotia 168/E3
Spring Hill, Tenn. 237/H9
Springhill Junction, Nova Scotia 168/D3
Springhills, Ohio 284/C5
Springholm, Scotland 15/E5
Spring Hope, N.C. 281/N3
Springhouse, Br. Col. 184/G4
Spring Lake, Ind. 227/F5
Spring Lake, Mich. 250/C5
Spring Lake, Minn. 255/E5
Spring Lake, Minn. 255/E3
Spring Lake, N.J. 273/F3
Spring Lake, N.C. 281/M4
Springlake, Texas 303/B3
Spring Lake, Wis. 317/H8
Spring Lake Heights, N.J. 273/E3
Spring Lake Park, Minn. 255/E5
Springlee, Ky. 237/K2
Spring Lick, Ky. 237/H6
Spring Mills, Pa. 294/G4
Spring Mills, S.C. 296/F2
Spring Park, Minn. 255/F5
Spring Place, Georgia 217/C1
Springport, Ind. 227/G4
Springport, Mich. 250/E6
Spring Ridge, La. 238/B2
Springs, S. Africa 118/J6
Springside, Sask. 181/J4
Springstein, Manitoba 179/E5
Springsure, Queensland 95/D5
Springton (res.), Pa. 294/L6
Springtown, Ark. 202/B1
Springtown, Texas 303/G5
Springvale, Georgia 217/C7
Springvale, Maine 243/B9
Springvale, Victoria 88/L7
Springvale, Victoria 97/J5
Spring Valley, Ala. 195/C1
Spring Valley, Ill. 222/D2
Spring Valley, Minn. 255/F7
Spring Valley, N.Y. 276/K8
Spring Valley, Ohio 284/C6
Spring Valley, Sask. 181/F6
Spring Valley, Texas 303/J1
Spring Valley, Wis. 317/B6
Springview, Nebr. 264/E2
Springville, Ala. 195/E3
Springville, Calif. 204/G7
Springville, Ind. 227/D7
Springville, Iowa 229/L4
Springville, La. 238/L2
Springville, Miss. 256/F2
Springville, N.Y. 276/C5
Springville, Pa. 294/L2
Springville, Tenn. 237/E8
Springville, Utah 304/C3
Springwater, N.Y. 276/E5
Springwater, Sask. 181/C4
Springwood, Va. 307/J5
Sproat Lake, Br. Col. 184/H3
Sprott, Ala. 195/D5
Sprowston, England 13/J5
Spruce (isl.), Manitoba 179/B1
Spruce, Mich. 250/F4
Spruce (mt.), Vt. 268/C3
Spruce Creek, Pa. 294/F4
Sprucedale, Ontario 177/E2
Spruce Grove, Alberta 182/D3
Spruce Home, Sask. 181/F2
Spruce Knob (mt.), W. Va. 312/G5
Spruce Knob-Seneca Rocks Nat'l Rec. Area, W. Va. 312/H5
Spruce Lake, Sask. 181/B2
Spruce Pine, Ala. 195/C2
Spruce Pine, N.C. 281/E3
Spruce Run (res.), N.J. 273/D2
Spruce View, Alberta 182/C3
Spruce Woods, Manitoba 179/C5
Spruce Woods Prov. Park, Manitoba 179/C5
Sprule, Ky. 237/O7
Spry (harb.), Nova Scotia 168/F4
Spry Harbour, Nova Scotia 168/F4
Spur, Texas 303/D4
Spurgeon, Ind. 227/C8
Spurlockville, W. Va. 312/B6
Spurn (head), England 13/H4
Spurn (head), England 10/G4
Spurr (mt.), Alaska 196/B1
Spur Tree, Jamaica 158/H6
Spuzzum, Br. Col. 184/G5
Spy (pond), Mass. 249/C6
Spy Hill, Sask. 181/K5
Squam (lake), N.H. 268/E4
Squamish, Br. Col. 184/F5
Squa Pan, Maine 243/G2
Squa Pan (lake), Maine 243/G2
Square (lake), Maine 243/G1
Square Butte, Mont. 262/F3
Square Islands, Newf. 166/C3
Squatec, Québec 172/J2
Squatec (lake), Québec 172/J2
Squaw (creek), Idaho 220/B5
Squaw (peak), Idaho 220/D4
Squaw (creek), Oreg. 291/F3
Squaw (creek), S. Dak. 298/B3
Squaw Harbor, Alaska 196/F3
Squaw Lake, Minn. 255/D3
Squaw Rapids, Sask. 181/H2
Squibnocket (pt.), Mass. 249/M7

452 Squillace

Squillace (gulf), Italy 34/F5
Squinzano, Italy 34/G4
Squire, W. Va. 312/C8
Squires, Mo. 261/G9
Squires Mem. Park, Newf. 166/C4
Squirrel, Idaho 220/G5
Sragen, Indonesia 85/J2
Sre Ambel, Cambodia 72/D5
Srebrenica, Yugoslavia 45/D3
Srednekolymsk, U.S.S.R. 4/C2
Srednekolymsk, U.S.S.R. 48/Q3
Sre Khtum, Cambodia 72/E4
Śrem, Poland 47/C2
Sremska Mitrovica, Yugoslavia 45/D3
Srepok (riv.), Cambodia 72/E4
Sretensk, U.S.S.R. 54/N4
Sretensk, U.S.S.R. 48/M4
Srikakulam, India 68/E5
Sri Lanka 54/K9
SRI LANKA (CEYLON) 68/E7
Srinagar, India 68/D2
Srinagar, India 54/J6
Srivardhan, India 68/C5
Środa Śląska, Poland 47/C3
Środa Wielkopolska, Poland 47/C2
Staaten (riv.), Queensland 88/G3
Staaten (riv.), Queensland 95/B3
Staatsburg, N.Y. 276/N7
Stab, Ky. 237/N6
Stacks (mts.), Ireland 17/B7
Stacy, Minn. 255/E5
Stacy, N.C. 281/S5
Stacy, Va. 307/E6
Stacyville, Iowa 229/H2
Stacyville, Maine 243/F4
Stacyville•, Maine 243/F4
Stade, Germany 22/C2
Staden, Belgium 27/B7
Stadskanaal, Netherlands 27/L3
Stadthagen, Germany 22/C2
Stäfa, Switzerland 39/G2
Staffa (isl.), Scotland 15/B4
Staffelstein, Germany 22/D3
Staffhorst, Germany 22/C2
Stafford•, Conn. 210/F1
Stafford, England 10/G2
Stafford, England 13/E5
Stafford (lake), Fla. 212/D2
Stafford (co.), Kansas 232/D3
Stafford, Kansas 232/D4
Stafford, N.Y. 276/D5
Stafford, Ohio 284/H6
Stafford, Okla. 288/H3
Stafford, Queensland 88/K2
Stafford, Queensland 95/D2
Stafford, Texas 303/J2
Stafford (co.), Va. 307/O4
Stafford, Va. 307/O4
Staffordshire (co.), England 13/E5
Stafford Springs, Conn. 210/F1
Staffordsville, Ky. 237/R5
Staffordville, Conn. 210/G1
Staffordville, N.J. 273/E4
Staines (pen.), Chile 138/D9
Staines, England 10/B5
Staines, England 13/G8
Stainville, Tenn. 237/N8
Staked (Llano Estacado) (plain), N. Mex. 274/F5
Staked (Llano Estacado) (plain), Texas 303/B4
Stakhanov, U.S.S.R. 52/E5
Stalden, Switzerland 39/E4
Staley, N.C. 281/K3
Stalham, England 13/J5
Stalheim, Norway 18/E6
Stalin, Albania 45/D5
Stalingrad (Volgograd), U.S.S.R. 7/J4
Stalingrad (Volgograd), U.S.S.R. 48/E5
Stalingrad (Volgograd), U.S.S.R. 52/F5
Stallings, N.C. 281/H4
Stallo, Miss. 256/F5
Stallworthy (cape), N.W. Terr. 187/J1
Stalowa Wola, Poland 47/F3
Stalwart, Mich. 250/E2
Stalwart, Sask. 181/F4
Stambaugh, Mich. 250/G2
Stamford, Conn. 210/A4
Stamford, England 13/G5
Stamford, England 10/F4
Stamford, Nebr. 264/E4
Stamford, N.Y. 276/L6
Stamford, Queensland 88/G4
Stamford, Texas 303/E5
Stamford (lake), Texas 303/E4
Stamford•, Vt. 268/A6
Stampa, Switzerland 39/J4
Stamping Ground, Ky. 237/M4
Stampriet, Namibia 118/B4
Stamps, Ark. 202/D7
Stanardsville, Va. 307/L4
Stanberry, Mo. 261/C2
Stanbridge-Est, Québec 172/D4
Stanchfield, Minn. 255/E5
Standard, Alberta 182/D4
Standard, Calif. 204/E6
Standard, Ill. 222/D2
Standard, La. 238/F3
Standard City, Ill. 222/D4
Standerton, S. Africa 118/D5
Standfast (pt.), Ant. & Bar. 161/E11
Standing Rock, Ala. 195/H4
Standing Rock Ind. Res., N. Dak. 282/J7
Standish, Calif. 204/E3
Standish, Maine 243/B8
Standish•, Maine 243/B8
Standish, Mich. 250/F5
Standish-with-Langtree, England 13/G2
Stand Off, Alberta 182/D5
Stanfield, Ariz. 198/C6
Stanfield, N.C. 281/J4
Stanfield, Oreg. 291/H2
Stanford, Calif. 204/J3
Stanford, Ill. 222/D3
Stanford, Ind. 227/D6
Stanford, Ky. 237/M5
Stanford, Mont. 262/F3
Stanfordville, N.Y. 276/N7
Stangelville, Wis. 317/L7
Stanger, S. Africa 118/E5
Stanhope, England 13/E3
Stanhope, Iowa 229/F4
Stanhope, N.J. 273/D2
Stanhope, Pr. Edward I. 168/E2
Stanhope, Québec 172/F4
Stanislaus (co.), Calif. 204/D6
Stanke Dimitrov, Bulgaria 45/F4
Stanley, England 13/H3
Stanley (cap.), Falk. Is. 143/E7
Stanley (cap.), Falk. Is. 120/D8
Stanley, Idaho 220/D5
Stanley, Iowa 229/K3
Stanley, Kansas 232/H3
Stanley, Ky. 237/G5
Stanley, La. 238/C3
Stanley, New Bruns. 170/D2
Stanley, N. Mex. 274/D3
Stanley, N.Y. 276/F5
Stanley, N.C. 281/G4
Stanley, N. Dak. 282/F3
Stanley (mt.), North. Terr. 93/B7
Stanley, Nova Scotia 168/E3
Stanley, Okla. 288/R5
Stanley, Scotland 15/E4
Stanley (co.), S. Dak. 298/H5
Stanley, Tasmania 99/B2
Stanley (mt.), Tasmania 99/A1
Stanley, Va. 307/L3
Stanley, Wis. 317/E6
Stanley (Boyoma) (falls), Zaire 102/E5
Stanley (Boyoma) (falls), Zaire 115/D3
Stanley Pool (lake), Zaire 115/C4
Stanleytown, Va. 307/H7
Stanleyville, N.C. 281/J2
Stanly (co.), N.C. 281/J4
Stanmore, Alberta 182/E4
Stannards, N.Y. 276/E6
Stann Creek Town, Belize 154/C2
Stanovoy (range), U.S.S.R. 54/O4
Stanovoy (range), U.S.S.R. 48/N4
Stans, Switzerland 39/F3
Stanstead (co.), Québec 172/F4
Stanstead Plain, Québec 172/F4
Stanthorpe, Queensland 88/J5
Stanthorpe, Queensland 95/D6
Stanton, Ala. 195/E5
Stanton, Calif. 204/D11
Stanton, England 13/H5
Stanton, Iowa 229/C7
Stanton (co.), Kansas 232/A4
Stanton, Ky. 237/O5
Stanton, Mich. 250/D5
Stanton, Miss. 256/B7
Stanton, Mo. 261/K6
Stanton (co.), Nebr. 264/G3
Stanton, Nebr. 264/G3
Stanton, N.J. 273/D2
Stanton, N. Dak. 282/H5
Stanton, Tenn. 237/C10
Stanton, Texas 303/C5
Stantonsburg, N.C. 281/O3
Stantonville, Tenn. 237/E10
Stanwood, Iowa 229/L5
Stanwood, Mich. 250/D5
Stanwood, Wash. 310/C2
Stanzel, Iowa 229/E6
Staphorst, Netherlands 27/J3
Staplehurst, Nebr. 264/G4
Staples, Minn. 255/D4
Staples, Ontario 177/B5
Stapleton, Ala. 195/C9
Stapleton, Georgia 217/H4
Stapleton, Nebr. 264/D3
Stapylton (bay), N.W. Terr. 187/G3
Star, Alberta 182/D3
Star, Idaho 220/B6
Star (lake), Minn. 255/C4
Star, Miss. 256/D6
Star, N.C. 281/K4
Star, Texas 303/F6
Starachowice, Poland 47/E3
Stará L'ubovňa, Czech. 41/F2
Staraya Russa, U.S.S.R. 52/D3
Stara Zagora, Bulgaria 7/G4
Stara Zagora, Bulgaria 45/G4
Starbuck (isl.), Kiribati 87/L6
Starbuck, Manitoba 179/E5
Starbuck, Minn. 255/C5
Starbuck, Wash. 310/G4
Star City, Ark. 202/G6
Star City, Ind. 227/D3
Star City, Sask. 181/G3
Star City, W. Va. 312/F3
Staré Město, Czech. 41/D2
Stargard Szczeciński, Poland 47/B2
Stargo, Ariz. 198/F5
Starhill, La. 238/H5
Stark (co.), Ill. 222/D2
Stark, Kansas 232/G4
Stark, Minn. 255/E5
Stark, Mont. 262/B3
Stark•, N.H. 268/E2
Stark (co.), N. Dak. 282/E6
Stark (co.), Ohio 284/H4
Stark City, Mo. 261/D9
Starke, Fla. 212/D2
Starke (co.), Ind. 227/D2
Starkey, Oreg. 291/J2
Star Keys (isls.), N. Zealand 100/E7
Starks, La. 238/C6
Starks•, Maine 243/D6
Starks, Wis. 317/H4
Starksboro•, Vt. 268/A3
Starkville, Colo. 208/L8
Starkville, Miss. 256/G4
Starkweather, N. Dak. 282/N3
Star Lake, N.Y. 276/K2
Star Lake, Wis. 317/G3
Starlight, Ind. 227/F8
Starnberg, Germany 22/D4
Starnbergersee (lake), Germany 22/D5
Starodub, U.S.S.R. 52/D4
Starogard Gdański, Poland 47/D2
Star Prairie, Wis. 317/A5
Starr, S.C. 296/B3
Starr (co.), Texas 303/F11
Starr King (mt.), N.H. 268/E3
Starrucca, Pa. 294/M2
Start, La. 238/G2
Start (pt.), Scotland 15/F1
Star Tannery, Va. 307/L2
Startex, S.C. 296/C2
Startup, Wash. 310/D3
Starvation (res.), Utah 304/D3
Stary Sacz, Poland 47/E4
Staryy Oskol, U.S.S.R. 52/E4
Staser, Ind. 227/B8
Stassfurt, Germany 22/D3
Staszów, Poland 47/E3
State Center, Iowa 229/G5
State College, Pa. 294/G4
State Line, Idaho 220/A2
State Line, Ind. 227/C4
State Line, Mass. 249/A3
State Line, Miss. 256/G8
State Line, Pa. 294/G6
Staten (Los Estados) (isl.), Argentina 143/D7
Staten (isl.), N.Y. 276/M9
Staten Island (borough), N.Y. 276/M9
Statenville, Georgia 217/G9
State Road, N.C. 281/H2
Statesboro, Georgia 217/J6
Statesville, N.C. 281/H3
Statesville, Tenn. 237/J8
Statham, Georgia 217/E3
Static, Tenn. 237/L7
Station Camp, Ky. 237/N5
Statts Mills, W. Va. 312/C5
Statue of Liberty Nat'l Mon., N.J. 273/B2
Statue of Liberty Nat'l Mon., N.Y. 276/M9
Staunton, Ill. 222/D5
Staunton, Ind. 227/C6
Staunton (I.C.), Va. 307/K4
Staunton (Roanoke) (riv.), Va. 307/K6
Stavanger, Norway 18/D7
Stavanger, Norway 7/E3
Stave (lake), Br. Col. 184/L3
Staveley, England 13/K2
Stavelot, Belgium 27/H8
Stavely, Alberta 182/D4
Staveren, Netherlands 27/G3
Stavern, Norway 18/D4
Stavropol', U.S.S.R. 7/J4
Stavropol', U.S.S.R. 52/F5
Stavropol', U.S.S.R. 48/E5
Stavrós, Greece 45/F5
Stawell, Victoria 97/B5
Stayner, Ontario 177/E3
Stayton, Oreg. 291/E3
Stead, Manitoba 179/F4
Stead, N. Mex. 274/F2
Steamboat, Ariz. 198/F3
Steamboat (mt.), Idaho 220/C4
Steamboat Rock, Iowa 229/G4
Steamboat Springs, Colo. 208/F2
Steamburg, N.Y. 276/C6
Steamtown Nat'l Historic Site, Pa. 294/F7
Stearns, Ky. 237/N7
Stearns (co.), Minn. 255/D5
Stebbins, Alaska 196/F2
Steckborn, Switzerland 39/G1
Stecoah, N.C. 281/B4
Stedman, N.C. 281/M4
Steedman, S.C. 296/E4
Steeds, N.C. 281/K4
Steel (mt.), Idaho 220/C6
Steele, Ala. 195/F3
Steele (co.), Minn. 255/E7
Steele, Mo. 261/N10
Steele (co.), N. Dak. 282/P4
Steele, N. Dak. 282/L6
Steele City, Nebr. 264/G4
Steele Narrows Hist. Park, Sask. 181/B2
Steeles (pt.), Norfolk I. 88/L5
Steeles Tavern, Va. 307/K5
Steeleville, Ill. 222/D6
Steelman, Sask. 181/J6
Steelmanville, N.J. 273/D5
Steelton, Pa. 294/J5
Steelville, Mo. 261/K7
Steen, Minn. 255/B7
Steen, Sask. 181/H3
Steenbergen, Netherlands 27/E5
Steenkool, Indonesia 85/J6
Steenokkerzeel, Belgium 27/C9
Steen River, Alberta 182/B4
Steens, Miss. 256/H3
Steens (mt.), Oreg. 291/J5
Steensby (inlet), N.W. Terr. 187/L2
Steenwijk, Netherlands 27/J3
Steep (pt.), W. Australia 88/A5
Steep (pt.), W. Australia 92/A4
Steep Falls, Maine 243/B8
Steep Rock, Manitoba 179/D3
Ştefăneşti, Romania 45/H2
Stefanie (lake), Ethiopia 111/G7
Stefansson (isl.), N.W.T. 162/F1
Stefansson (isl.), N.W.T. 187/H2
Steffenville, Mo. 261/J3
Steffisburg, Switzerland 39/E3
Stege, Denmark 21/F8
Stege, Denmark 18/H9
Steger, Ill. 222/F2
Stehekin, Wash. 310/E2
Steigerwald (for.), Germany 22/D4
Steilacoom, Wash. 310/C3
Stein, Switzerland 39/E1
Steinach, Austria 41/A3
Steinach, Germany 22/D3
Stein am Rhein, Switzerland 39/G1
Steinauer, Nebr. 264/H4
Steinbach, Manitoba 179/F5
Steinhatchee, Fla. 212/C2
Steinhausen, Namibia 118/B4
Steinhuder Meer (lake), Germany 22/C2
Steinkjer, Norway 18/G4
Steinneset (cape), Norway 18/E2
Stekene, Belgium 27/E6
Stella, Mo. 261/D9
Stella, Nebr. 264/J4
Stella, N.C. 281/P5
Stella, Wash. 310/B4
Stellarton, Nova Scotia 168/F3
Stellenbosch, S. Africa 118/F6
Steller (mt.), Alaska 196/K2
Stelvio (pass), Switzerland 39/K3
Stem, N.C. 281/M2
Stendal, Germany 22/D2
Stendal, Ind. 227/C8
Stenen, Sask. 181/J4
Stenhousemuir, Scotland 15/C1
Stenlille, Denmark 21/E6
Stennett, Iowa 229/C6
Stenstrup, Denmark 21/D7
Stenungsund, Sweden 18/G7
Stepanakert, U.S.S.R. 48/E6
Stepanakert, U.S.S.R. 52/G7
Stepaside, Ireland 17/J5
Stephan, S. Dak. 298/K5
Stephen, Minn. 255/A2
Stephenfield, Manitoba 179/D5
Stephens (passage), Alaska 196/N1
Stephens, Ark. 202/E7
Stephens (isl.), Br. Col. 184/B3
Stephens (co.), Georgia 217/F1
Stephens, Georgia 217/F3
Stephens (isl.), N. Zealand 100/D4
Stephens (co.), Okla. 288/L6
Stephens (co.), Texas 303/F5
Stephensburg, Ky. 237/J5
Stephensburg, N.J. 273/D2
Stephens City, Va. 307/M2
Stephen's Creek, N.S. Wales 97/A2
Stephenson (co.), Ill. 222/D1
Stephenson, Mich. 250/B3
Stephensport, Ky. 237/H5
Stephentown, N.Y. 276/O5
Stephenville, Newf. 166/C4
Stephenville, Newf. 162/L6
Stephenville, Texas 303/F5
Stephenville Crossing, Newf. 166/C4
Stepney, Conn. 210/B3
Stepovak (bay), Alaska 196/G3
Steprock, Ark. 202/G3
Steptoe, Wash. 310/H3
Sterling, Alaska 196/B1
Sterling, Colo. 188/F2
Sterling, Colo. 208/N1
Sterling (res.), Colo. 208/N1
Sterling•, Conn. 210/H2
Sterling, Georgia 217/K8
Sterling, Idaho 220/F6
Sterling, Ill. 222/D2
Sterling, Kansas 232/D3
Sterling•, Mass. 249/G3
Sterling, Mich. 250/E4
Sterling, Nebr. 264/H4
Sterling, N. Dak. 282/K6
Sterling, Ohio 284/G4
Sterling, Okla. 288/K5
Sterling, Pa. 294/M3
Sterling (co.), Texas 303/C6
Sterling, Utah 304/C4
Sterling, Va. 307/O2
Sterling City, Texas 303/D6
Sterling Heights, Mich. 250/B6
Sterling Run, Pa. 294/F3
Sterlington, La. 238/F1
Sterlitamak, U.S.S.R. 7/K3
Sterlitamak, U.S.S.R. 48/F4
Sterlitamak, U.S.S.R. 52/J4
Sternberg, Germany 22/D2
Šternberk, Czech. 41/D2
Sterrett, Ala. 195/F4
Stet, Mo. 261/E4
Stetson•, Maine 243/E6
Stetsonville, Wis. 317/F5
Stettin (Szczecin), Poland 47/B2
Stettler, Alberta 182/D3
Stettler, Alta. 162/E5
Stettyn (mt.), S. Africa 118/G6
Steuben (co.), Ind. 227/G1
Steuben, Maine 243/H6
Steuben•, Maine 243/H6
Steuben, Mich. 250/C2
Steuben (co.), N.Y. 276/F6
Steuben, Wis. 317/E9
Steubenville, Ohio 188/K2
Steubenville, Ohio 284/J5
Steve, Ark. 202/D4
Stevenage, England 13/G6
Stevenage, England 10/F5
Stevens (co.), Kansas 232/A4
Stevens (co.), Minn. 255/B5
Stevens (creek), S.C. 296/C4
Stevens (co.), Wash. 310/H2
Stevens (pass), Wash. 310/D3
Stevensburg, Va. 307/N4
Stevenson, Ala. 195/G1
Stevenson, Conn. 210/C3
Stevenson (lake), Manitoba 179/J3
Stevenson, The (riv.), S. Australia 94/D2
Stevenson, Wash. 310/C5
Stevenson Entrance (str.), Alaska 196/H3
Stevens Point, Wis. 317/G7
Stevens Pottery, Georgia 217/F5
Stevenston, Scotland 15/D5
Stevenstown, Wis. 317/D7
Stevens Village, Alaska 196/J1
Stevensville, Md. 245/N5
Stevensville, Mich. 250/C6
Stevensville, Mont. 262/C4
Stevns Klint (cliff), Denmark 21/F7
Steward, Ill. 222/D2
Stewardson, Ill. 222/E4
Stewart, Ala. 195/C5
Stewart, Br. Col. 162/D4
Stewart, Br. Col. 184/C2
Stewart (isl.), Chile 138/E11
Stewart (co.), Georgia 217/C6
Stewart, Minn. 255/D6
Stewart, Miss. 256/F4
Stewart (isl.), N. Zealand 87/G10
Stewart (isl.), N. Zealand 100/A7
Stewart (cape), North. Terr. 93/D1
Stewart, Ohio 284/G7
Stewart (co.), Tenn. 237/F7
Stewart, Tenn. 237/F8
Stewart (riv.), Yukon 162/C3
Stewart (riv.), Yukon 187/E3
Stewart Crossing, Yukon 187/E3
Stewarton, Scotland 15/D5
Stewart River, Yukon 187/D3
Stewart River, Yukon 162/B3
Stewarts Point, Calif. 204/B5
Stewartstown•, N.H. 268/E2
Stewartstown, N. Ireland 17/H2
Stewartstown, Pa. 294/K6
Stewartsville, Ind. 227/B8
Stewartsville, Mo. 261/C3
Stewartsville, N.J. 273/C2
Stewartsville, Ohio 284/J6
Stewart Town, Jamaica 158/H6
Stewart Valley, Sask. 181/D5
Stewartville, Ala. 195/F4
Stewartville, Minn. 255/F7
Stewiacke, Nova Scotia 168/E3
Stewiacke (riv.), Nova Scotia 168/E3
Steyer, Md. 245/A3
Steyr, Austria 41/C2
Stia, Italy 34/C3
Stickney, Ill. 222/B6
Stickney, New Bruns. 170/C2
Stickney, S. Dak. 298/M6
Stickney, W. Va. 312/D7
Stidham, Okla. 288/P4
Stiens, Netherlands 27/H2
Stigler, Okla. 288/R4
Stikine (riv.), Alaska 196/N2
Stikine (str.), Alaska 196/N2
Stikine (riv.), Br. Col. 162/C4
Stikine (riv.), Br. Col. 184/B1
Stiles, Iowa 229/J7
Stiles, Wis. 317/L6
Stilesville, Ind. 227/D5
Stilis, Greece 45/F6
Still (riv.), Conn. 210/B3
Still (riv.), Conn. 210/C1
Still (riv.), Conn. 210/G1
Stillman Valley, Ill. 222/D1
Stillmore, Georgia 217/H6
Still Pond, Md. 245/O3
Still River, Mass. 249/H3
Stillwater, Ky. 237/O5
Stillwater, Maine 243/F6
Stillwater (riv.), Mass. 249/G3
Stillwater, Minn. 255/F5
Stillwater (co.), Mont. 262/G5
Stillwater (riv.), Mont. 262/G5
Stillwater, Nev. 266/C3
Stillwater (range), Nev. 266/C3
Stillwater, N.J. 273/D1
Stillwater, N.Y. 276/N5
Stillwater, Ohio 284/H5
Stillwater (riv.), Ohio 284/B5
Stillwater, Okla. 288/N2
Stillwater, Pa. 294/K3
Stillwater (res.), R.I. 249/C2
Stillwell, Ill. 222/B3
Stillwell, Ind. 227/D1
Stilson, Georgia 217/J6
Stilwell, Kansas 232/H3
Stilwell, Okla. 288/S3
Stimson (mt.), Mont. 262/C2
Stinchar (riv.), Scotland 15/D5
Stinesville, Ind. 227/D6
Stinnett, Texas 303/C2
Stinson Beach, Calif. 204/H2
Stinson Lake, N.H. 268/D4
Stintino, Italy 34/B4
Štip, Yugoslavia 45/F5
Stiring-Wendel, France 28/G3
Stirling, Alberta 182/D5
Stirling, N.J. 273/E2
Stirling (creek), North. Terr. 88/D3
Stirling (creek), North. Terr. 93/A4
Stirling, Ontario 177/G3
Stirling, Scotland 10/B1
Stirling, Scotland 15/C1
Stirling (trad. co.), Scotland 15/A5
Stirling, W. Australia 88/B2
Stirling, W. Australia 92/A1
Stirling City, Calif. 204/D4
Stirling North, S. Australia 94/E5
Stirling Station, North. Terr. 93/C6
Stirrat, W. Va. 312/C7
Stirum, N. Dak. 282/P7
Stites, Idaho 220/C3
Stittsville, Ontario 177/J2
Stittville, N.Y. 276/K4
Stitzer, Wis. 317/E10
Stockbridge, Georgia 217/D3
Stockbridge, Mass. 249/A3
Stockbridge•, Mass. 249/A3
Stockbridge, Mich. 250/E6
Stockbridge•, Vt. 268/B4
Stockbridge, Wis. 317/K7
Stockbridge Ind. Res., Wis. 317/J6
Stockdale, Ohio 284/E8
Stockdale, Texas 303/G8
Stockerau, Austria 41/D2
Stockertown, Pa. 294/M4
Stockett, Mont. 262/E3
Stockham, Nebr. 264/F4
Stockholm•, Maine 243/G1
Stockholm, N.J. 273/D1
Stockholm, Sask. 181/J5
Stockholm, S. Dak. 298/R3
Stockholm (co.), Sweden 18/L7
Stockholm (cap.), Sweden 2/K3
Stockholm (cap.), Sweden 7/F3
Stockholm (cap.), Sweden 18/G1
Stockholm, Wis. 317/B7
Stockhorn (mt.), Switzerland 39/E3
Stockland, Ill. 222/F3
Stockley, Del. 245/S6
Stockport, England 13/H2
Stockport, England 10/G2
Stockport, Iowa 229/K7
Stockport, Ohio 284/G6
Stocksbridge, England 13/J2
Stockton, Ala. 195/C9
Stockton, Calif. 188/B3
Stockton, Calif. 204/D6
Stockton, Georgia 217/G9
Stockton, Ill. 222/C1
Stockton, Iowa 229/M5
Stockton, Kansas 232/C2
Stockton, Manitoba 179/C5
Stockton, Md. 245/S8
Stockton, Minn. 255/G6
Stockton, Mo. 261/E7
Stockton (lake), Mo. 261/E7
Stockton, N.J. 273/D3
Stockton, N.Y. 276/B6
Stockton (plat.), Texas 303/B7
Stockton, Utah 304/B3
Stockton (isl.), Wis. 317/F2
Stockton-on-Tees, England 13/F3
Stockton-on-Tees, England 10/F3
Stockton Springs, Maine 243/F7
Stockton Springs•, Maine 243/F7
Stockville, Nebr. 264/D4
Stockwell, Ind. 227/D4
Stoco, Ontario 177/G3
Stod, Czech. 41/B2
Stoddard (co.), Mo. 261/N9
Stoddard•, N.H. 268/C5
Stoddard, Wis. 317/D8
Stoeng Treng, Cambodia 72/E4
Stoer (pt.), Scotland 15/C2
Stoholm, Denmark 21/C5
Stoke-on-Trent, England 13/E4
Stoke-on-Trent, England 10/E4
Stokes (bay), Chile 138/D10
Stokes (co.), N.C. 281/J2
Stokes, N.C. 281/P3
Stokes (pt.), Tasmania 99/A1
Stokes Bay, Ontario 177/C2
Stokesdale, N.C. 281/K2
Stolac, Yugoslavia 45/D4
Stolberg, Germany 22/B3
Stolp (Słupsk), Poland 47/C1
Ston, Yugoslavia 45/C4
Stone (co.), Ark. 202/F2
Stone, England 10/E4
Stone, England 13/E5
Stone, Idaho 220/F7
Stone, Ky. 237/S5
Stone (co.), Miss. 256/F9
Stone (co.), Mo. 261/F9
Stone (mts.), N.C. 281/F2
Stone (mts.), Tenn. 237/T8
Stone Bank, Wis. 317/J1
Stonebluff, Ind. 227/C4
Stonebluff, Okla. 288/P3
Stoneboro, Pa. 294/B3
Stoneboro, S.C. 296/F2
Stone City, Iowa 229/L4
Stonecliffe, Ontario 177/G1
Stone Creek, Ohio 284/G5
Stonefort, Ill. 222/E6
Stonega, Va. 307/C7
Stoneham, Colo. 208/M1
Stoneham•, Mass. 249/C6
Stoneham, Québec 172/F2
Stone Harbor, N.J. 273/D5
Stonehaven, Scotland 10/E2
Stonehaven, Scotland 15/F4
Stonehenge (ruins), England 13/F6
Stonehenge, Queensland 95/B5
Stonehenge, Queensland 88/G4
Stonehenge, Sask. 181/F6
Stonehouse, Scotland 15/D5
Stone Lake, Wis. 317/C4
Stone Mountain, Georgia 217/D3
Stone Mountain Prov. Park, Br. Col. 184/L2
Stone Park, Ill. 222/B5
Stoner, Br. Col. 184/F3
Stones (riv.), Tenn. 237/H9
Stones River Nat'l Battlefield, Tenn. 237/H9
Stoneville, Miss. 256/C4
Stoneville, N.C. 281/K2
Stoneville, S. Dak. 298/D4
Stonewall, Ark. 202/J1
Stonewall, Georgia 217/J2
Stonewall, La. 238/C2
Stonewall, Manitoba 179/E4
Stonewall, Miss. 256/G6
Stonewall, N.C. 281/R4
Stonewall, Okla. 288/O5
Stonewall (co.), Texas 303/D4
Stonewall, Texas 303/F7
Stonewood, W. Va. 312/F4
Stoney Creek, Ontario 177/E4
Stoney Point, Ontario 177/B5
Stonington, Colo. 208/P8
Stonington, Conn. 210/H3
Stonington•, Conn. 210/H3
Stonington, Ill. 222/D4
Stonington•, Maine 243/F7
Stonington, Mich. 250/C3
Stono (inlet), S.C. 296/H6
Stony (riv.), Alaska 196/G2
Stony (isl.), Newf. 166/C3
Stony (brook), N.J. 273/D3
Stony (ranges), N.S. Wales 97/B2
Stony (isl.), N.Y. 276/H3
Stony (pt.), N.Y. 276/H3
Stony (lake), Ontario 177/E2
Stony (lake), Ontario 177/G3
Stony (head), Tasmania 99/C2
Stony (creek), Va. 307/N6
Stony (riv.), W. Va. 312/H4
Stony Beach, Sask. 181/F5
Stony Bottom, W. Va. 312/F6
Stony Brook, N.Y. 276/O9
Stony Creek, Conn. 210/E3
Stony Creek, N.Y. 276/M4
Stony Creek, Va. 307/N7
Stonyford, Calif. 204/C4
Stony Gorge (res.), Calif. 204/C4
Stony Island, Nova Scotia 168/C5
Stony Lake, Mich. 250/C5
Stony Mountain, Manitoba 179/E4

Tarabulus 455

Szechwan (Sichuan) (prov.), China 77/F5
Szécsény, Hungary 41/E2
Szeged, Hungary 41/E3
Szeged, Hungary 7/F4
Szeghalom, Hungary 41/F3
Szegvár, Hungary 41/F3
Székesfehérvár, Hungary 41/E3
Szekszárd, Hungary 41/E3
Szendrö, Hungary 41/F2
Szentendre, Hungary 41/E3
Szentendreisziget (isl.), Hungary 41/E3
Szentes, Hungary 41/F3
Szentgotthárd, Hungary 41/D3
Szentlörinc, Hungary 41/E3
Szeping (Siping), China 77/K3
Szerencs, Hungary 41/F2
Szigetvár, Hungary 41/D3
Szikszó, Hungary 41/F2
Szil, Hungary 41/D3
Szirák, Hungary 41/E3
Szolnok (co.), Hungary 41/F3
Szolnok, Hungary 41/F3
Szombathely, Hungary 41/D3
Szprotawa, Poland 47/B3
Sztum, Poland 47/D2
Szubin, Poland 47/C2
Szydłowiec, Poland 47/E3

T

Taal (lake), Philippines 82/C4
Tab, Hungary 41/E3
Tab, Ind. 227/C4
Taba, Bir, Egypt 59/B4
Tabacal (pt.), Cuba 158/H4
Tabacundo, Ecuador 128/C2
Tabaquite, Trin. & Tob. 161/B11
Tabar (isls.), Papua N.G. 86/C1
Tabarka, Tunisia 106/F1
Tabas, Iran 59/G3
Tabas, Iran 66/L4
Tabas, Iran 66/K4
Tabasará (mts.), Panama 154/G6
Tabasco (state), Mexico 150/N7
Tabasco, Mexico 150/H6
Tabask, Kuh-e (mt.), Iran 66/G6
Tabas-Masina (Tabas), Iran 59/H3
Tabb, Va. 307/R6
Tabelbala, Algeria 106/D3
Taber, Alberta 182/E5
Taberg, N.Y. 276/J4
Tabernacle, St. Kitts & Nevis 161/C10
Tabernash, Colo. 208/H3
Tabernes de Valldigna, Spain 33/G3
Taberville, Mo. 261/E6
Tabiang, Kiribati 87/G6
Tabiona, Utah 304/D3
Tabiteuea (atoll), Kiribati 87/H6
Tablas (cape), Chile 138/A9
Tablas (isl.), Philippines 82/D4
Tablas (str.), Philippines 82/C4
Table (mt.), Nev. 266/C3
Table (bay), Newf. 166/C3
Table (bay), S. Africa 118/E6
Table (mt.), S. Africa 118/E6
Table (peak), Wyo. 319/B2
Table Grove, Ill. 222/C3
Tableland, Trin. & Tob. 161/B11
Tableland Station, W. Australia 92/D2
Tabler, Okla. 288/L4
Table Rock (riv.), Ark. 202/D1
Table Rock (res.), Mo. 261/E9
Table Rock, Nebr. 264/H4
Tablers Station, W. Va. 312/K4
Taboada, Spain 33/C1
Taboga (isl.), Panama 154/H6
Tábor, Czech. 41/C2
Tabor, Iowa 229/B7
Tabor (mt.), Israel 65/C2
Tabor, Minn. 255/B2
Tabor, S. Dak. 298/O8
Tabor (mt.), Vt. 268/B5
Tabora (reg.), Tanzania 115/F5
Tabora, Tanzania 115/F5
Tabora, Tanzania 102/F5
Tabor City, N.C. 281/M6
Tabou, Ivory Coast 106/C8
Tabriz, Iran 54/F6
Tabriz, Iran 66/D2
Tabriz, Iran 59/E2
Tabuaeran (isl.), Kiribati 87/L5
Tabuk, Philippines 82/C2
Tabusintac, New Bruns. 170/E1
Tabusintac (gully), New Bruns. 170/F1
Tabusintac (riv.), New Bruns. 170/E1
Täby, Sweden 18/H1
Tacajó, Cuba 158/J3
Tacámbaro de Codallos, Mexico 150/J7
Tacaná, Guatemala 154/A3
Tacaná (vol.), Guatemala 154/A3
Tacarigua, Trin. & Tob. 161/B10
Taché (lake), Québec 172/J1
Tachen (Taizhou) (isls.), China 77/K6
Tacheng, China 77/B2
Tachikawa, Japan 81/O2
Tachina, Ecuador 128/C2
Táchira (state), Venezuela 124/C4
Tachov, Czech. 41/B2
Tacloban, Philippines 82/E5
Tacloban, Philippines 85/H3
Tacna, Ariz. 198/B6
Tacna (dept.), Peru 128/G11
Tacna, Peru 128/G11
Tacna, Peru 120/B4
Tacobamba, Bolivia 136/C6
Tacoma, Va. 307/C7
Tacoma, Wash. 146/F5
Tacoma, Wash. 188/B1
Tacoma, Wash. 310/C3
Tacoma Park, S. Dak. 298/N2
Taconic, Conn. 210/B1
Taconic (mts.), Mass. 249/A2
Taconite, Minn. 255/E3
Taconite Harbor, Minn. 255/H3
Tacopaya, Bolivia 136/B5
Tacora (vol.), Chile 138/B1
Tacotalpa, Mexico 150/N8
Tacuaras, Paraguay 144/C5
Tacuarembó (dept.), Uruguay 145/D3
Tacuarembó, Uruguay 145/D2
Tacuarembó (riv.), Uruguay 145/D2
Tacuarí (riv.), Uruguay 145/E3
Tacuatí, Paraguay 144/D3
Tacutu (riv.), Brazil 132/B2
Tadcaster, England 13/K1
Tademaït (plat.), Algeria 102/C2
Tademaït, Plateau du (plat.), Algeria 106/E3
Tadine, New Caled. 86/H4
Tadjnout Hagguerete (well), Mali 106/D4
Tadjoura, Djibouti 111/H5
Tadley, England 13/F6
Tadmor (Palmyra) (ruin), Syria 59/C3
Tadmore, Sask. 181/J4
Tadmur, Syria 59/C3
Tadmur, Syria 63/H5
Tadó, Colombia 126/B5
Tadoule (lake), Manitoba 179/J2
Tadoussac, Que. 162/J6
Tadoussac, Québec 174/C3
Tadoussac, Québec 172/H1
Tadzhik S.S.R., U.S.S.R. 54/H6
Tadzhik S.S.R., U.S.S.R. 48/H6
Taebaek (mt.), S. Korea 81/D5
Taedong (riv.), N. Korea 81/C4
Taegu, S. Korea 54/O6
Taegu, S. Korea 81/D6
Taejŏn, S. Korea 54/O6
Taejŏn, S. Korea 81/C5
Tafalla, Spain 33/F1
Tafassasset, Wadi (dry riv.), Algeria 106/F4
Tafassasset, Wadi (dry riv.), Niger 106/F4
Tafers, Switzerland 39/D3
Taff (riv.), Wales 13/B7
Tafí Viejo, Argentina 120/C5
Tafí Viejo, Argentina 143/C2
Taft, Calif. 204/F8
Taft, Fla. 212/E3
Taft, Iran 66/J5
Taft, La. 238/N4
Taft, Okla. 288/R3
Taft, Philippines 82/E5
Taft, Tenn. 237/H10
Taft, Texas 303/G9
Taftan, Kuh-e (mt.), Iran 66/M6
Taftan, Kuh-e (mt.), Iran 59/H4
Taftsville, Vt. 268/C4
Taftville, Conn. 210/G2
Tagab, Afghanistan 59/J3
Tagab, Afghanistan 68/B2
Taga Dzong, Bhutan 68/G3
Taganrog, U.S.S.R. 7/H4
Taganrog, U.S.S.R. 52/E5
Taganrog, U.S.S.R. 48/D5
Tagant (reg.), Mauritania 106/B5
Tagapula (isl.), Philippines 82/E4
Tagawa, Japan 81/E7
Tagaytay, Philippines 82/C3
Tagbilaran, Philippines 82/E6
Taghit, Algeria 106/D2
Taghmon, Ireland 17/H7
Tagish (lake), Br. Col. 184/J1
Tagish, Yukon 187/E3
Tagliamento (riv.), Italy 34/D1
Tagolo (pt.), Philippines 82/D6
Tagolo (pt.), Philippines 85/G4
Tagoloan, Philippines 82/E6
Tagomago (isl.), Spain 33/G3
Tagounite, Morocco 106/C3
Tagua, Bolivia 136/B6
Taguatinga, Brazil 120/E4
Taguatinga, Goiás, Brazil 132/E6
Taguatinga, Fed. Dist., Brazil 132/D6
Tague (bay), Virgin Is. (U.S.) 161/G4
Tagula (isl.), Papua N.G. 85/C8
Tagum, Philippines 82/E7
Tagus (riv.) 7/D5
Tagus, N. Dak. 282/G3
Tagus (riv.), Portugal 33/B3
Tagus (riv.), Spain 33/D3
Tahaa (isl.), Fr. Poly. 87/L7
Tahakopa, N. Zealand 100/B7
Tahan, Gunong (mt.), Malaysia 72/D6
Tahat (mt.), Algeria 102/C2
Tahat (mt.), Algeria 106/F4
Tahawus, N.Y. 276/M2
Tahiryuak (lake), N.W. Terr. 187/G2
Tahiti (isl.), Fr. Polynesia 2/B6
TAHITI, Fr. Poly. 86/S13
Tahiti (isl.), Fr. Poly. 87/L7
Tahiti (isl.), Fr. Poly. 86/S13
Tahlequah, Okla. 288/R3
Tahma (riv.), Turkey 63/G3
Tahoe (lake) 188/C3
Tahoe (lake), Calif. 204/F4
Tahoe (lake), Nev. 266/B3
Tahoe City, Calif. 204/E4
Tahoka, Texas 303/C4
Taholah, Wash. 310/A3
Tahoma, Calif. 204/E4
Tahoua, Niger 102/C3
Tahoua, Niger 106/F6
Tahquamenon (falls), Mich. 250/D2
Tahquamenon (riv.), Mich. 250/D2
Tahsis, Br. Col. 184/D5
Tahta, Egypt 59/B4
Tahta, Egypt 111/F2
Tahtsa (lake), Br. Col. 184/D3
Tahua, Bolivia 136/B3
Tahuamanu (riv.), Bolivia 136/A2
Tahuamanu, Peru 128/H8
Tahuamanu (riv.), Peru 128/H8
Tahulandang (isl.), Indonesia 85/H5
Tahuna, Indonesia 85/G5
Tahuya, Wash. 310/B3
Tai'an, China 77/J4
Taiarapu (pen.), Fr. Poly. 86/T13
Taiban, N. Mex. 274/F4
Taibus, China 77/J3
Taichow (Taizhou), China 77/K5
Taichung, China 77/K7
Taichung, Taiwan 54/O7
Taieri (riv.), N. Zealand 100/C7
Taif, Saudi Arabia 54/F7
Taif, Saudi Arabia 59/D5
Taigu, China 77/H4
Taihape, N. Zealand 100/E3
Taihe, China 77/J6
Tai Hu (lake), China 77/J5
Tailem Bend, S. Australia 88/F7
Tailem Bend, S. Australia 94/F6
Taima, Saudi Arabia 59/C4
Tain, Scotland 15/D3
Tain, Scotland 10/D2
Tainan, China 77/J7
Taínaron (cape), Greece 7/G5
Taínaron (cape), Greece 45/F7
Taintor, Iowa 229/H6
Taipei, China 77/K7
Taipei (cap.), Taiwan 54/O7
Taipei (cap.), Taiwan 2/R4
Taiping, Malaysia 72/D6
Taitao (pen.), Chile 120/B7
Taitao (cape), Chile 138/D6
Taitao (pen.), Chile 138/D6
Taits Gap, Ala. 195/F3
Taitung, China 77/K7
Taivalkoski, Finland 18/P4
Taiwan 54/N7
Taiwan 2/R4
Taiwan (str.) 54/N7
Taiwan (isl.) 54/N7
TAIWAN, CHINA 77/K7
Taiwan, China 77/K7
Taiwan (Formosa) (isl.), China 77/K7
Taiwan (Formosa) (str.), China 77/J7
Taiyuan, China 77/H4
Taiyuan, China 54/N6
Taizhou (Taichow), China 77/K5
Taizhou (Tachen) (isls.), China 77/K6
Ta'izz, Yemen 54/F8
Ta'izz, Yemen 59/D7
Tajimi, Japan 81/H6
Tajique, N. Mex. 274/C4
Tajo (Tagus) (riv.), Spain 33/D3
Tajrish, Iran 66/G3
Tajumulco (vol.), Guatemala 154/B3
Tak, Thailand 72/C3
Takaishi, Japan 81/H8
Takaka, N. Zealand 100/D4
Takalar, Indonesia 85/F7
Takama, Guyana 131/C3
Takamatsu, Japan 81/F6
Takaoka, Japan 81/H5
Takapau, N. Zealand 100/F4
Takapuna, N. Zealand 100/B1
Takarazuka, Japan 81/H7
Takaroa (atoll), Fr. Poly. 87/M7
Takasaki, Japan 81/J5
Takatsuki, Japan 81/J7
Takayama, Japan 81/H5
Takefu, Japan 81/G6
Takeshima (isls.), Japan 81/F5
Takestan, Iran 66/F2
Takev, Cambodia 72/E5
Takhiatash, U.S.S.R. 48/F5
Takhta-Bazar, U.S.S.R. 48/G6
Takijuq (lake), N.W.T. 186/G3
Takikawa, Japan 81/K2
Takingeun, Indonesia 85/B5
Takitimu (mts.), N. Zealand 100/A6
Takkaze (riv.), Ethiopia 111/G5
Takla (lake), Br. Col. 184/D2
Takla Makan (des.), China 54/K6
Takla Makan (Taklimakan Shamo) (des.), China 77/B4
Taklimakan Shamo (des.), China 77/B4
Tako, Sask. 181/B3
Takoma Park, Md. 245/F4
Takoradi, Ghana 106/D8
Takoradi-Sekondi, Ghana 102/B4
Taksimo, U.S.S.R. 48/M4
Taku (glac.), Alaska 196/N1
Taku (riv.), Alaska 196/N1
Taku (riv.), Br. Col. 184/J2
Takua Pa, Thailand 72/C5
Takutu (riv.), Guyana 131/B4
Tala, Mexico 150/H6
Tala, Uruguay 145/D5
Talab (riv.), Iran 59/H4
Talab (riv.), Iran 66/N6
Talab (riv.), Pakistan 68/A3
Talagante, Chile 138/G4
Talai (Da'an, Dalai), China 77/K2
Talak (reg.), Niger 106/E5
Talala, Okla. 288/P1
Talamanca (range), C. Rica 154/F6
Talangbetutu, Indonesia 85/C6
Talara, Peru 128/B5
Talara, Peru 120/A3.
Talaud (isls.), Indonesia 54/O9
Talaud (isls.), Indonesia 85/H5
Talavera de la Reina, Spain 33/D2
Talawe (mt.), Papua N.G. 86/B2
Talbert, Ky. 237/P6
Talbingo, N.S. Wales 97/E4
Talbot, Alberta 182/E3
Talbot (isl.), Fla. 212/E1
Talbot (co.), Georgia 217/C5
Talbot, Ind. 227/C3
Talbot (co.), Md. 245/O5
Talbot (inlet), N.W. Terr. 187/L2
Talbot (cape), W. Australia 88/D2
Talbot (cape), W. Australia 92/D1
Talbott, Tenn. 237/P8
Talbotton, Georgia 217/C5
Talca, Chile 138/A11
Talca, Chile 120/B6
Talca (pt.), Chile 138/E3
Talcahuano, Chile 138/D1
Talcahuano, Chile 120/B6
Talcán (isl.), Chile 138/D4
Talco, Texas 303/K4
Talcott (range), Conn. 210/D1
Talcott, W. Va. 312/E7
Talcottville, Conn. 210/F1
Taldy-Kurgan, U.S.S.R. 54/J5
Taldy-Kurgan, U.S.S.R. 48/H5
Taleh, Somalia 115/J2
Talent, Oreg. 291/E5
Talgar, U.S.S.R. 48/H5
Talgarth, Wales 13/D5
Tali (Dali), China 77/E6
Taliabu (isl.), Indonesia 85/G6
Taliaferro (co.), Georgia 217/G3
Talibon, Philippines 82/E5
Talihina, Okla. 288/S5
Talina, Bolivia 136/B7
Tali Post, Sudan 111/F6
Talisayan, Philippines 82/E6
Talisheek, La. 238/L5
Talita, Uruguay 145/D4
Tal Kaif, Iraq 66/C2
Talkeetna, Alaska 196/B1
Talkeetna (mts.), Alaska 196/J2
Talkheh (riv.), Iran 66/E1
Talking Rock, Georgia 217/D1
Tallaboa, P. Rico 161/B3
Talladega (co.), Ala. 195/F4
Talladega, Ala. 195/F4
Talladega Springs, Ala. 195/F4
Tallaght, Ireland 17/J5
Tallahaga (creek), Miss. 256/F4
Tallahala (creek), Miss. 256/F7
Tallahassee (cap.), Fla. 146/K6
Tallahassee (cap.), Fla. 188/K4
Tallahassee (cap.), Fla. 212/B1
Tallahatchie (co.), Miss. 256/D3
Tallahatchie (riv.), Miss. 256/D3
Tallahatta Springs, Ala. 195/C7
Tallangatta, Victoria 97/D5
Tallant, Okla. 288/O1
Tallapoosa (co.), Ala. 195/G5
Tallapoosa (riv.), Ala. 195/G4
Tallapoosa, Georgia 217/B3
Tallapoosa, Mo. 261/N9
Tallassee, Ala. 195/G5
Tallinn, U.S.S.R. 7/G3
Tallinn (cap.), Estonian S.S.R., U.S.S.R. 53/C1
Tallinn, U.S.S.R. 48/C4
Tallinn, U.S.S.R. 52/B3
Tallmadge, Ohio 284/H3
Tallman, N.Y. 276/J8
Tallman, Sask. 181/E3
Tallmansville, W. Va. 312/F5
Tallow, Ireland 17/F7
Tallula, Ill. 222/D4
Tallulah, La. 238/H2
Tallulah Falls, Georgia 217/F1
Talma, Ind. 227/E2
Talmage, Kansas 232/E2
Talmage, Nebr. 264/H4
Talmage, Sask. 181/H6
Talmage, Utah 304/D3
Talmo, Georgia 217/E2
Talmo, Kansas 232/E2
Talmoon, Minn. 255/E3
Talodi, Sudan 111/F5
Talofofo (bay), Guam 86/K7
Taloga, Okla. 288/J2
Talon (lake), Ontario 177/E1
Taloqan, Afghanistan 68/B1
Taloqan, Afghanistan 59/J2
Talpa, Texas 303/E6
Talpa de Allende, Mexico 150/G6
Talparo, Trin. & Tob. 161/B10
Talquin (lake), Fla. 212/B1
Talsi, U.S.S.R. 53/B2
Taltal, Chile 138/A5
Taltal, Chile 120/B5
Taltal, Quebrada de (riv.), Chile 138/B5
Taltson (riv.), N.W. Terr. 187/G3
Talvik, Norway 18/N2
Talyawalka (creek), N.S. Wales 97/B2
Talyawalka Ana Branch, Darling (riv.), N.S. Wales 97/B3
Tama (co.), Iowa 229/H4
Tama, Iowa 229/H5
Tama (riv.), Japan 81/O2
Tamaha, Okla. 288/S4
Tamaki (str.), N. Zealand 100/C1
Tamale, Ghana 102/B4
Tamale, Ghana 106/D7
Tamalpais (mt.), Calif. 204/H1
Tamana (mt.), Trin. & Tob. 161/B10
Tamanrasset, Algeria 106/F4
Tamanrasset, Algeria 102/C2
Tamanrasset, Wadi (dry riv.), Algeria 106/E4
Tamaqua, Pa. 294/L4
Tamar (riv.), England 13/C7
Tamar (riv.), England 10/D5
Tamar (riv.), Tasmania 99/D3
Támara, Colombia 126/D5
Tamarac, Fla. 212/B3
Tamarac (riv.), Minn. 255/A2
Tamarack, Idaho 220/B5
Tamarack (isl.), Manitoba 179/F3
Tamarack, Minn. 255/E4
Tamarack (riv.), Minn. 255/D2
Tamarack, Pa. 294/G3
Tamarite de Litera, Spain 33/G2
Tamaro (mt.), Switzerland 39/G4
Tamaroa, Ill. 222/D5
Tamarugal, Pampa del (plain), Chile 138/B3
Tamási, Hungary 41/E3
Tamassee, S.C. 296/A2
Tamatama, Venezuela 124/F6
Tamatave (Toamasina), Madagascar 118/H3
Tamaulipas (state), Mexico 150/K4
Tamaya, Chile 138/A8
Tamayo, Dom. Rep. 158/D6
Tamazula, Mexico 150/F4
Tamazulapan del Progreso, Mexico 150/L8
Tamazunchale, Mexico 150/K6
Tambacounda, Senegal 106/B6
Tambar Springs, N.S. Wales 97/E2
Tambelan (isls.), Indonesia 85/D5
Tamberías, Argentina 143/C3
Tambey, U.S.S.R. 48/G2
Tambo (riv.), Peru 128/G11
Tambo, Queensland 88/H4
Tambo, Queensland 95/C5
Tambo de Mora, Peru 128/D9
Tambo Grande, Peru 128/B5
Tambohorano, Madagascar 118/G3
Tambopata (riv.), Peru 128/H9
Tambores, Uruguay 145/C2
Tamboril, Dom. Rep. 158/D5
Tamboritha (mt.), Victoria 97/D5
Tambov, U.S.S.R. 7/J3
Tambov, U.S.S.R. 52/F4
Tambov, U.S.S.R. 48/E4
Tambura, Sudan 111/E6
Tamchakett, Mauritania 106/B5
Tame, Colombia 126/E4
Tame (riv.), England 10/G3
Tâmega (riv.), Portugal 33/C2
Tamentit, Algeria 106/D3
Tamiahua, Mexico 150/L6
Tamiami (canal), Fla. 212/E6
Tamil Nadu (state), India 68/D6
Tamin (gov.), Iraq 66/D3
Tamina (riv.), Switzerland 39/H3
Tamins, Switzerland 39/H3
Tamise (Temse), Belgium 27/E6
Tam Ky, Vietnam 72/F4
Tammisaari (Ekenäs), Finland 18/N6
Tamms, Ill. 222/D6
Tammun, West Bank 65/C3
Tamo, Ark. 202/G5
Tamora, Nebr. 264/G4
Tampa, Fla. 188/K5
Tampa, Fla. 146/K7
Tampa, Fla. 212/C2
Tampa (bay), Fla. 188/K5
Tampa (bay), Fla. 212/D4
Tampa, Kansas 232/E3
Tampere, Finland 7/G2
Tampere, Finland 18/N6
Tampico, Ill. 222/D2
Tampico, Ind. 227/F7
Tampico, Mexico 146/J7
Tampico, Mexico 150/L5
Tampico, Mont. 262/K2
Tampico, Wash. 310/E4
Tampoc (riv.), Fr. Guiana 131/E4
Tam Quan, Vietnam 72/F4
Tamra, Saudi Arabia 59/E5
Tams, W. Va. 312/D7
Tamsagbulag, Mongolia 77/J2
Tamsagout, Mauritania 106/C4
Tamshiyacu, Peru 128/F5
Tamsweg, Austria 41/B3
Tamuín, Mexico 150/K6
Tamuning, Guam 86/K7
Tamworth, Australia 87/E9
Tamworth, England 13/F5
Tamworth, England 10/G3
Tamworth•, N.H. 268/E4
Tamworth, N.S. Wales 88/J6
Tamworth, N.S. Wales 97/F2
Tamworth, Ontario 177/H3
Tamyang, S. Korea 81/C6
Tana (lake), Ethiopia 102/F3
Tana (lake), Ethiopia 111/G5
Tana (riv.), Finland 18/P2
Tana (riv.), Kenya 102/G5
Tana (riv.), Kenya 115/G4
Tana, Norway 18/Q1
Tana (riv.), Norway 18/P1
Tanabe, Kyoto, Japan 81/J7
Tanabe, Wakayama, Japan 81/G7
Tanacross, Alaska 196/K2
Tanafjord (fjord), Norway 18/Q1
Tanaga (isl.), Alaska 196/K4
Tanaga (vol.), Alaska 196/K4
Tanahgrogot, Indonesia 85/F6
Tanahmerah, Indonesia 85/K7
Tanah Merah, Malaysia 72/D6
Tanamá (riv.), P. Rico 161/B1
Tanami (des.), North. Terr. 88/E3
Tanami, North. Terr. 93/A5
Tanami (des.), North. Terr. 93/C5
Tánamo, Cuba 158/J3
Tan An, Vietnam 72/E5
Tanana, Alaska 188/D5
Tanana, Alaska 196/H1
Tanana (riv.), Alaska 146/D3
Tanana (riv.), Alaska 188/D5
Tanana (riv.), Alaska 196/J2
Tananarive (Antananarivo) (cap.), Madagascar 118/H3
Tanaro (riv.), Italy 34/B2
Tanch'ŏn, N. Korea 81/D3
Tancook Island, Nova Scotia 168/D4
Tanda, India 68/E3
Tandag, Philippines 82/F6
Tandil, Argentina 143/E4
Tandil, Argentina 120/D6
Tando Adam, Pakistan 68/B3
Tando Allahyar, Pakistan 68/B3
Tandou (lake), N.S. Wales 97/A3
Tandragee, N. Ireland 17/J3
Tanega (isl.), Japan 81/E8
Taney (co.), Mo. 261/F9
Taneycomo (lake), Mo. 261/F9
Taneytown, Md. 245/K2
Taneyville, Mo. 261/F9
Tanezrouft (des.), Algeria 102/C2
Tanezrouft (des.), Algeria 106/E4
Tang, Kas (isl.), Cambodia 72/D5
Tanga (isls.), Papua N.G. 86/C1
Tanga (reg.), Tanzania 115/G5
Tanga, Tanzania 115/G4
Tanga, Tanzania 102/F5
Tangainony, Madagascar 118/H4
Tangalla, Sri Lanka 68/E7
Tanganyika (lake) 102/F5
Tanganyika (lake), Burundi 115/E5
Tanganyika (lake), Tanzania 115/E5
Tanganyika (lake), Zaire 115/E5
Tanganyika (lake), Zambia 115/E5
Tangent (pt.), Alaska 196/H1
Tangent, Alberta 182/B2
Tangent, Oreg. 291/D3
Tangerang, Indonesia 85/G1
Tangermünde, Germany 22/D2
Tanggula Shan (range), China 77/D5
Tangier, Ind. 227/C5
Tangier (sound), Md. 245/P8
Tangier (Tanger), Morocco 106/C1
Tangier, Morocco 102/B1
Tangier, Nova Scotia 168/F4
Tangier (riv.), Nova Scotia 168/F4
Tangier, Okla. 288/G2
Tangier, Va. 307/R5
Tangier (isl.), Va. 307/R5
Tangier (sound), Va. 307/S5
Tangipahoa (par.), La. 238/K5
Tangipahoa, La. 238/J5
Tangipahoa (riv.), La. 238/N1
Tangra Yumco (lake), China 77/C5
Tangshan, China 77/J4
Tangshan, China 54/N5
Tangub, Philippines 82/D6
Tangyanika (lake) 2/L6
Tangyuan, China 77/L2
Tanimbar (isls.), Indonesia 54/P10
Tanimbar (isls.), Indonesia 85/J7
Tanjay, Philippines 82/D6
Tanjore (Thanjovur), India 68/D6
Tanjungbalai, Indonesia 85/C5
Tanjungkarang, Indonesia 54/M10
Tanjungkarang, Indonesia 85/C7
Tanjungpandan, Indonesia 85/D6
Tanjungpinang, Indonesia 85/C5
Tanjungpriok, Indonesia 85/H1
Tanjungpura, Indonesia 85/B5
Tanjungredeb, Indonesia 85/F5
Tanjungselor, Indonesia 85/F5
Tanna (isl.), Vanuatu 87/H7
Tanner, Ala. 195/E1
Tanner, W. Va. 312/E5
Tannersville, N.Y. 276/M6
Tannersville, Pa. 294/M3
Tannis (bay), Denmark 21/D2
Tannu-Ola (range), Mongolia 77/D1
Tannu-Ola (range), U.S.S.R. 48/K5
Tanon (str.), Philippines 82/D6
Tanout, Niger 106/F6
Tanque Verde, Ariz. 198/E6
Tanta, Egypt 111/J3
Tanta, Egypt 59/B3
Tantallon, Sask. 181/K5
Tantalus (mt.), Hawaii 218/D4
Tan-Tan, Morocco 106/B3
Tantoyuca, Mexico 150/L6
Tantung (Dandong), China 77/K3
Tanumshede, Sweden 18/G7
Tanunda, S. Australia 94/C6
Tanzania 2/L6
Tanzania 102/F5
TANZANIA 115/F5
Tao, Ko (isl.), Thailand 72/C5
Tao'an, China 77/K2
Taole, China 77/G4
Taongi (atoll), Marshall Is. 87/G4
Taopi, Minn. 255/F7
Taormina, Italy 34/E6
Taos, Mo. 261/H5
Taos (co.), N. Mex. 274/D2
Taos, N. Mex. 274/D2
Taos Pueblo, N. Mex. 274/D2
Taoudenni, Mali 106/D4
Taoudenni, Mali 102/B2
Taourirt, Algeria 106/E3
Taourirt, Morocco 106/D2
Taouz, Morocco 106/D2
Taoyuan, China 77/K6
Tapa, U.S.S.R. 53/C1
Tapacarí, Bolivia 136/B5
Tapachula, Mexico 150/N9
Tapajós (riv.), Brazil 2/G6
Tapajós (riv.), Brazil 120/D3
Tapajós (riv.), Brazil 132/B4
Tapaktuan, Indonesia 85/B5
Tapalquén, Argentina 143/E4
Tapanahoni (riv.), Suriname 131/D4
Tapani (lake), Québec 172/B3
Tapanui, N. Zealand 100/B6
Tapaz, Philippines 82/D5
Tapera do Jeronimo, Brazil 132/C2
Tapeta, Liberia 106/C7
Tapi, Mae Nam (riv.), Thailand 72/C5
Tapiantana Group (isls.), Philippines 82/D7
Tapiche (riv.), Peru 128/E6
Taping (riv.), Burma 72/C1
Tápiószele, Hungary 41/E3
Tapirapecó, Sierra (mts.), Venezuela 124/F7
Tapiutan (isl.), Philippines 82/B5
Tapoco, N.C. 281/A4
Tapolca, Hungary 41/D3
Tappahannock, Va. 307/O5
Tappan (lake), N.J. 273/C1
Tappan, N.Y. 276/K8
Tappan (lake), Ohio 284/H5
Tappen, N. Dak. 282/L6
Tappi (cape), Japan 81/K3
Tapti (riv.), India 68/D4
Tapul (isl.), Philippines 82/C8
Tapul Group (isls.), Philippines 85/G4
Tapul Group (isls.), Philippines 82/C8
Taputapu (cape), Amer. Samoa 86/N9
Taquari (riv.), Brazil 132/C7
Taquaritinga, Brazil 132/D8
Taquaritinga, Brazil 135/B2
Tar (riv.), N.C. 281/O3
Tara (hill), Ireland 17/H4
Tara, Ontario 177/C3
Tara (isl.), Philippines 82/C4
Tara, Queensland 95/D5
Tara, Queensland 88/J5
Tara, U.S.S.R. 48/H4
Tara (riv.), Yugoslavia 45/D4
Tarabuco, Bolivia 136/C6
Tarabulus, Lebanon 63/F5
Tarabulus, Lebanon 59/C3

Tichlá 457

Tepatitlán de Morelos, Mexico 150/H6
Tepeaca, Mexico 150/N2
Tepeapulco, Mexico 150/M1
Tepehuanes, Mexico 150/G4
Tepeji del Río, Mexico 150/L1
Tepelenë, Albania 45/D5
Tepetlán, Mexico 150/P1
Tepexi de Rodríguez, Mexico 150/N2
Tepeyahualco, Mexico 150/O1
Tepic, Mexico 150/G6
Teplá u Toužimě, Czech. 41/B1
Teplice, Czech. 41/B1
Tepoztlán, Mexico 150/L1
Te Puke, N. Zealand 100/F2
Tequeje (riv.), Bolivia 136/B3
Tequendama (falls), Colombia 126/C5
Tequesquite (creek), N. Mex. 274/E2
Tequesta, Fla. 212/F5
Tequixquitla, Mexico 150/O1
Ter (riv.), Spain 33/H1
Téra, Niger 106/E6
Teraina (isl.), Kiribati 87/L5
Teramo (prov.), Italy 34/D3
Teramo, Italy 34/D3
Terán, Mexico 150/N8
Terang, Victoria 97/B6
Ter Apel, Netherlands 27/L3
Terawhiti (cape), N. Zealand 100/A3
Tercan, Turkey 63/J3
Terceira (isl.), Portugal 33/C1
Tercero (riv.), Argentina 143/D3
Terchová, Czech. 41/E2
Terempa, Indonesia 85/D5
Terence Bay, Nova Scotia 168/E4
Terengganu (state), Malaysia 72/D6
Teresina, Brazil 120/E3
Teresina, Brazil 132/F4
Teresita, Mo. 261/J9
Teresópolis, Brazil 135/E3
Terespol, Poland 47/F2
Teressa (isl.), India 68/G7
Terevinto, Bolivia 136/D5
Terhazza (ruins), Mali 106/C4
Terhune, Ind. 227/E4
Teriberka, U.S.S.R. 52/E1
Terlingua, Texas 303/D12
Terlingua (creek), Texas 303/D12
Terlton, Okla. 288/O2
Termas de Cauquenes, Chile 138/B10
Terme, Turkey 63/G2
Termez, U.S.S.R. 48/G6
Termini Imerese, Italy 34/D6
Términos (lag.), Mexico 150/O7
Termo, Calif. 204/E3
Termoli, Italy 34/E3
Termonde (Dendermonde), Belgium 27/E6
Termonfeckin, Ireland 17/J4
Termunten, Netherlands 27/K2
Ternate, Indonesia 54/O9
Ternate, Indonesia 85/H5
Terneuzen, Netherlands 27/D6
Terni (prov.), Italy 34/D3
Terni, Italy 34/D3
Terni, Italy 7/F4
Ternitz, Austria 41/D3
Ternopol', U.S.S.R. 48/C5
Ternopol', U.S.S.R. 52/C5
Te Roto, N. Zealand 100/D7
Terowie, S. Australia 94/F5
Terpeniye (cape), U.S.S.R. 48/P5
Terra Alta, W. Va. 312/H4
Terra Bella, Calif. 204/G8
Terrabona, Nicaragua 154/E4
Terrace, Br. Col. 162/D5
Terrace, Br. Col. 184/C3
Terrace, Br. Col. 184/C3
Terrace, Minn. 255/C5
Terrace Bay, Ontario 177/H5
Terrace Bay, Ontario 175/C3
Terrace Heights, Wash. 310/E4
Terra Ceia, Fla. 212/D4
Terrace Park, Ohio 284/D9
Terracina, Italy 34/D4
Terra Corra, Neth. Ant. 161/E8
Terråk, Norway 18/H4
Terral, Okla. 288/L7
Terralba, Italy 34/B5
Terra Nova, Newf. 166/C2
Terra Nova (riv.), Newf. 166/C2
Terra Nova Nat'l Park, Newf. 166/D2
Terrebonne (par.), La. 238/J8
Terrebonne (bay), La. 238/J8
Terrebonne, Minn. 255/B3
Terrebonne, Oreg. 291/F3
Terrebonne (co.), Québec 172/H4
Terrebonne, Québec 172/H4
Terre-de-Bas (isl.), Guadeloupe 161/A7
Terre-de-Haut (isl.), Guadeloupe 161/A7
Terre Haute, Ill. 222/C3
Terre Haute, Ind. 188/J3
Terre Haute, Ind. 227/C6
Terre Hill, Pa. 294/L5
Terrell (co.), Georgia 217/D7
Terrell, N.C. 281/G3
Terrell (co.), Texas 303/B7
Terrell, Texas 188/G4
Terrell, Texas 303/H5
Terrell Hills, Texas 303/K11
Terrenate, Mexico 150/N1
Terrenceville, Newf. 166/D4
Terre Neuve, Haiti 158/B5
Terreton, Idaho 220/F6
Terrey Hills, N. S. Wales 88/L3
Terrey Hills, N.S. Wales 97/J3
Terri (mt.), Switzerland 39/D2
Terri (peak), Switzerland 39/H3
Terrigal-Wamberal, N.S. Wales 97/F3
Terril, Iowa 229/C2
Terrill (mt.), Utah 304/C5
Territok (cape), Newf. 166/B2
Terry, La. 238/H1
Terry, Miss. 256/D6
Terry, Mont. 262/L4
Terry (co.), Texas 303/B4
Terry Town, La. 238/O4
Terrytown, Nebr. 264/A3
Terryville, Conn. 210/C2
Terschelling (isl.), Netherlands 27/G2
Teruel (prov.), Spain 33/F2
Teruel, Spain 33/F2
Terutao, Ko (isl.), Thailand 72/C6
Tervola, Finland 18/O3
Tesawa, Libya 111/B2
Tescott, Kansas 232/E2
Teshekpuk (lake), Alaska 196/H1
Teshio, Japan 81/K1
Teshio (mt.), Japan 81/L1
Teshio (riv.), Japan 81/L1
Tesla, W. Va. 312/E5
Teslić, Yugoslavia 45/C3
Teslin (lake) 162/C3
Teslin (lake), Br. Col. 184/K1
Teslin, Yukon 187/E3
Teslin (lake), Yukon 187/E4
Teslin (riv.), Yukon 187/E3
Tessalit, Mali 106/E4
Tessaoua, Niger 106/F6
Tessenderlo, Belgium 27/G6
Tessenei, Ethiopia 59/C6
Tessenei, Ethiopia 111/G4
Tessier, Sask. 181/D4
Test (riv.), England 13/F6
Testa (cape), Italy 34/B4
Testa del Gargano (cape), Italy 34/F4
Tesuque, N. Mex. 274/C3
Tét, Hungary 41/D3
Tetachuck (lake), Br. Col. 184/E3
Tetagouche (riv.), New Bruns. 170/D1
Tetas (pt.), Chile 138/A4
Tete (prov.), Mozambique 118/E3
Tete, Mozambique 102/F6
Tete, Mozambique 118/E3
Tête-à-la-Baleine, Québec 174/E2
Tete Jaune Cache, Br. Col. 184/H4
Te Teko, N. Zealand 100/F3
Teterboro, N.J. 273/B2
Teterow, Germany 22/E2
Teterton, W. Va. 312/H5
Teteven, Bulgaria 45/G4
Tetiaroa (atoll), Fr. Poly. 87/M7
Tetlin, Alaska 196/K2
Teton (co.), Idaho 220/G6
Teton, Idaho 220/G6
Teton (riv.), Idaho 220/G6
Teton (co.), Mont. 262/D3
Teton (riv.), Mont. 262/E3
Teton (co.), Wyo. 319/B2
Teton (range), Wyo. 319/B2
Tetonia, Idaho 220/G6
Teton Village, Wyo. 319/B2
Tetotum, Va. 307/P4
Tétouan, Morocco 106/C1
Tétouan, Morocco 102/B1
Tetovo, Yugoslavia 45/E5
Teuco (riv.), Argentina 143/D1
Teufen, Switzerland 39/H2
Teulada (cape), Italy 7/E5
Teulada (cape), Italy 34/B5
Teulon, Manitoba 179/E4
Teupasenti, Honduras 154/D3
Teustepe, Nicaragua 154/E4
Teutoburger Wald (for.), Germany 22/C2
Teutopolis, Ill. 222/E4
Teuva, Finland 18/M5
Teviot (riv.), Scotland 15/F5
Teviot (riv.), Scotland 10/E3
Te Waewae (bay), N. Zealand 100/A7
Tewantin-Noosa, Queensland 95/E5
Te Whanga (mts.), N. Zealand 100/E7
Tewkesbury, England 10/F5
Tewkesbury, England 13/E6
Tewksbury, Mass. 249/K2
Texa (isl.), Scotland 15/B5
Texada (isl.), Br. Col. 184/J2
Texarkana, Ark. 188/H4
Texarkana, Ark. 202/C7
Texarkana, Texas 188/H4
Texarkana, Texas 146/J6
Texarkana, Texas 303/L4
Texas 188/G4
TEXAS 303
Texas, Georgia 217/B4
Texas, Ky. 237/L5
Texas, Md. 245/M3
Texas (co.), Mo. 261/J8
Texas (co.), Okla. 288/C1
Texas (state), U.S. 146/J6
Texas City, Texas 303/K3
Texas Creek, Colo. 208/H6
Texcoco de Mora, Mexico 150/M1
Texel (isl.), Netherlands 27/F2
Texhoma, Okla. 288/C1
Texhoma, Texas 303/C1
Texico, N. Mex. 274/F4
Texistepeque, El Salvador 154/C3
Texline, Texas 303/B1
Texola, Okla. 288/G4
Texoma (lake) 188/G4
Texoma (lake), Okla. 288/N7
Texoma (lake), Texas 303/H3
Texon, Texas 303/C6
Teykovo, U.S.S.R. 52/E3
Teyvareh, Afghanistan 68/A2
Teyvareh, Afghanistan 59/H3
Teziutlán, Mexico 150/O1
Tezonapa, Mexico 150/P2
Tezontepec, Mexico 150/M1
Tezpur, India 68/G3
Tezu, India 68/H3
Tezzeron (lake), Br. Col. 184/E3
Tha, Nam (riv.), Laos 72/D2
Tha-anne (riv.), N.W. Terr. 187/J3
Thabazimbi, S. Africa 118/D4
Thacher (isl.), Mass. 249/M2
Tha Chin, Mae Nam (riv.), Thailand 72/C4
Thacker, W. Va. 312/B7
Thackeray, Ill. 222/E5
Thackeray, Ohio 284/C5
Thackerville, Okla. 288/M7
Thai Binh, Vietnam 72/E2
Thailand 2/Q5
Thailand 54/M8
THAILAND (SIAM) 72
Thailand (gulf) 2/Q5
Thailand (gulf) 54/M9
Thailand (gulf), Cambodia 72/D5
Thailand (gulf), Thailand 72/D5
Thai Nguyen (cliff), Vietnam 72/E2
Thakhek (Muang Khammouan), Laos 72/E3
Thal, Pakistan 59/K3
Thal, Switzerland 39/J2
Thalberg, Manitoba 179/F4
Thale, Germany 22/D3
Thale Luang (lag.), Thailand 72/D6
Thalia, Texas 303/E4
Thalmann, Georgia 217/J8
Thalu, Ko (isls.), Thailand 72/C5
Thalwil, Switzerland 39/G2
Thame, England 13/G6
Thame (riv.), England 13/G7
Thames (riv.), Conn. 210/G3
Thames (riv.), England 10/F5
Thames (riv.), England 13/H6
Thames, N. Zealand 100/E2
Thames (firth), N. Zealand 100/E2
Thames (riv.), Ontario 177/B5
Thamesford, Ontario 177/C4
Thamesville, Conn. 210/G2
Thamesville, Ontario 177/C5
Thana, India 68/B6
Thana (creek), India 68/B7
Thane, Alaska 196/N1
Thangool, Queensland 95/D5
Thanh Hoa, Vietnam 72/E3
Thanh Tri, Vietnam 72/E5
Thanjavur, India 68/D6
Thann, France 28/G4
Thar (des.), Pakistan 68/C3
Thargomindah, Queensland 88/G5
Thargomindah, Queensland 95/C5
Tharrawaddy, Burma 72/C3
Tharthar, Wadi (dry riv.), Iraq 66/C3
Tharthar (res.), Iraq 66/C3
Thásos, Greece 45/G5
Thásos (isl.), Greece 45/G5
Thatch (cay), Virgin Is. (U.S.) 161/B4
Thatcham, England 13/F6
Thatcher, Ariz. 198/F6
Thatcher, Colo. 208/L7
Thatcher, Idaho 220/G7
That Khe, Vietnam 72/E2
Thaton, Burma 72/C3
Thau (mts.), France 28/F6
Thaungdut, Burma 72/B1
Thawville, Ill. 222/E3
Thaxton, Miss. 256/F2
Thaxton, Va. 307/K6
Thaya (riv.), Austria 41/C2
Thayawthadangyi Kyun (isl.), Burma 72/C4
Thayer, Ill. 222/D4
Thayer, Ind. 227/C2
Thayer, Iowa 229/E6
Thayer, Kansas 232/G4
Thayer, Mo. 261/J9
Thayer (co.), Nebr. 264/G4
Thayer, Nebr. 264/G4
Thayer, W. Va. 312/E7
Thayer Junction, Wyo. 319/D4
Thayetmyo, Burma 72/B3
Thayne, Wyo. 319/A3
Thayngen, Switzerland 39/G1
Thazi, Burma 72/C2
The Alberga (riv.), S. Australia 94/D2
Thealka, Ky. 237/R5
Theano (pt.), Ontario 177/J5
THE ANTILLES 156
Thebarton, S. Australia 88/D8
Thebarton, S. Australia 94/A7
The Battlefords Prov. Park, Sask. 181/C2
Thebes, Ill. 222/D6
The Colony, Texas 303/G1
The Coorong (lag.), S. Australia 94/F6
The Dalles, Oreg. 188/B1
The Dalles, Oreg. 291/F2
The Dalles (dam), Oreg. 291/F2
The Dalles (dam), Wash. 310/D5
Thedford, Nebr. 264/D3
Thedford, Ontario 177/C4
The Entrance, N.S. Wales 88/J6
The Entrance, N.S. Wales 97/F3
The Gap, N.S. Wales 97/A2
The Gap, Queensland 88/J2
The Glen, N.Y. 276/N3
The Granites, North. Terr. 93/B6
The Hamilton (riv.), S. Australia 94/D2
The Hawk, Nova Scotia 168/C5
The Heads (prom.), Oreg. 291/C5
The Hermitage, N. Zealand 100/C5
Theilman, Minn. 255/F6
Thelon (riv.), N.W.T. 146/H3
Thelon (riv.), N.W.T. 162/F3
Thelon (riv.), N.W. Terr. 187/H3
Them, Denmark 21/C5
The Macumba (riv.), S. Australia 94/E2
The Narrows (str.), N.J. 273/E2
Thendara, N.Y. 276/K3
The Neales (riv.), S. Australia 94/E3
Theodore, Ala. 195/B9
Theodore, Queensland 95/D5
Theodore, Sask. 181/J4
Theodore Roosevelt (dam), Ariz. 198/D5
Theodore Roosevelt (lake), Ariz. 198/D5
Theodore Roosevelt Nat'l Mem. Park, N. Dak. 282/D4
Theodore Roosevelt Nat'l Mem. Park, N. Dak. 282/C5
Theodore Roosevelt Nat'l Mem. Park, N. Dak. 282/D6
Theodosia, Mo. 261/G9
The Pas, Man. 162/F5
The Pas, Manitoba 179/H3
The Plains, Ohio 284/F7
The Plains, Va. 307/N3
The Range, New Bruns. 170/E2
Theresa, N.Y. 276/J2
Theresa, Wis. 317/K8
Therien, Alberta 182/E2
Theriot, La. 238/J8
Thermaic (gulf), Greece 45/F6
Thermal, Calif. 204/J10
Thermalito, Calif. 204/D4
Thermopolis, Wyo. 319/D2
The Rock, Georgia 217/D5
The Rock, N.S. Wales 97/D4
The Round (mt.), N.S. Wales 97/G2
Therwil, Switzerland 39/E1
The Salt (lake), N.S. Wales 97/B2
Thesiger (bay), N.W. Terr. 187/F2
The Skaw (Skagens Odde) (cape), Denmark 21/D2
Thessalon, Ont. 162/H6
Thessalon, Ontario 177/J5
Thessalon, Ontario 175/D3
Thessaloníki, Greece 7/G4
Thessaloníki, Greece 45/F5
Thessaly (reg.), Greece 45/F6
The Stevenson (riv.), S. Australia 94/D2
Thetford, England 13/H5
Thetford, England 10/G4
Thetford•, Vt. 268/C4
Thetford Center, Vt. 268/C4
Thetford Mines, Québec 172/F3
Thetis Island, Br. Col. 184/J3
The Twins (mt.), Alberta 182/B3
Theux, Belgium 27/H8
The Village, Okla. 288/L3
The Warburton (riv.), S. Australia 94/F2
Thibault, New Bruns. 170/C1
Thibodaux, La. 238/J7
Thicket Portage, Manitoba 179/J3
Thickwood (hills), Alberta 182/D1
Thickwood (hills), Sask. 181/D2
Thida, Ark. 202/H2
Thief (lake), Minn. 255/C2
Thief (riv.), Minn. 255/B2
Thief River Falls, Minn. 255/B2
Thielsen (mt.), Oreg. 291/F4
Thiensville, Wis. 317/L1
Thiers, France 28/E5
Thiès, Senegal 106/A5
Thiès, Senegal 102/A3
Thika, Kenya 102/F5
Thika, Kenya 115/G4
Thimphu (cap.), Bhutan 54/L7
Thimphu (cap.), Bhutan 68/G3
Thio, Ethiopia 111/H5
Thio, New Caled. 86/H4
Thionville, France 28/G3
Thira, Greece 45/G7
Thira (isl.), Greece 45/G7
Third (lake), Maine 243/H5
Third (lake), N.H. 268/E1
Third Cataract, Sudan 111/E4
Third Cataract (dam), Sudan 102/E3
Third Cataract, Sudan 59/B6
Third Lake, Ill. 222/B4
Thirsk, England 13/F3
Thirty Mile (creek), N. Dak. 282/F6
Thirtymile (creek), Oreg. 291/G2
Thisted, Denmark 21/B4
Thisted, Denmark 18/F8
Thistle (isl.), S. Australia 94/E6
Thistle, Utah 304/C4
Thithia (isl.), Fiji 86/R10
Thívai, Greece 45/F6
Thiviers, France 28/D5
Thjórsá (riv.), Iceland 21/C1
Thlewiaza (riv.), N.W. Terr. 187/J3
Thoa (riv.), N.W. Terr. 187/H3
Tho Chau, Hon (isl.), Vietnam 72/D5
Thoen, Thailand 72/C3
Thohoyandou, S. Africa 118/E4
Thohoyandou (cap.), Venda, S. Africa 102/F7
Tholen, Netherlands 27/E5
Thomas (co.), Georgia 217/E9
Thomas (co.), Kansas 232/A2
Thomas, Md. 245/N6
Thomas (co.), Nebr. 264/D3
Thomas, Okla. 288/J3
Thomas (creek), Oreg. 291/G5
Thomas, S. Dak. 298/P4
Thomas (lake), Texas 303/C5
Thomas (range), Utah 304/A4
Thomas, W. Va. 312/H4
Thomasboro, Ill. 222/E3
Thomas Stone Nat'l Hist. Site, Md. 245/K6
Thomaston, Ala. 195/C6
Thomaston•, Conn. 210/C2
Thomaston (res.), Conn. 210/C2
Thomaston, Georgia 217/D5
Thomaston, Maine 243/E7
Thomaston•, Maine 243/E7
Thomaston, N.Y. 276/P7
Thomastown, Ireland 10/C4
Thomastown, Ireland 17/G7
Thomastown, La. 238/H2
Thomastown, Miss. 256/E5
Thomastown, Victoria 97/J4
Thomasville, Ala. 195/C7
Thomasville, Ga. 188/K4
Thomasville, Georgia 217/E9
Thomasville, Miss. 256/E6
Thomasville, Mo. 261/J9
Thomasville, N.C. 281/J3
Thomasville, Pa. 294/J6
Thomonde, Haiti 158/C6
Thompson, Ala. 195/G6
Thompson (riv.), Br. Col. 184/G5
Thompson•, Conn. 210/H1
Thompson (peak), Idaho 220/C5
Thompson, Iowa 229/F2
Thompson (riv.), Iowa 229/E7
Thompson, Man. 162/G4
Thompson, Man. 146/J4
Thompson, Manitoba 179/J2
Thompson (isl.), Mass. 249/D7
Thompson, Mich. 250/C3
Thompson (creek), Miss. 256/G8
Thompson, Mo. 261/J4
Thompson (peak), N. Mex. 274/D3
Thompson, N. Dak. 282/R4
Thompson, Ohio 284/H2
Thompson, Pa. 294/L2
Thompson (riv.), Queensland 95/B5
Thompson (lake), S. Dak. 298/O5
Thompson (mt.), Wyo. 319/B3
Thompson Falls, Mont. 262/A3
Thompsons (creek), S.C. 296/G2
Thompson Springs, Utah 304/E5
Thompsons Station, Tenn. 237/H9
Thompsontown, Pa. 294/H4
Thompson Valley (res.), Oreg. 291/F5
Thompsonville, Conn. 210/E1
Thompsonville, Ill. 222/E6
Thompsonville, Mich. 250/C4
Thomsen (riv.), N.W. Terr. 187/G2
Thomson, Georgia 217/H4
Thomson, Ill. 222/C2
Thomson, Minn. 255/F4
Thomson (riv.), Queensland 88/G4
Thomson's Falls, Kenya 115/G3
Thon Buri, Thailand 72/D4
Thongwa, Burma 72/C3
Thonon-les-Bains, France 28/G4
Thonotosassa, Fla. 212/D3
Thor, Iowa 229/E3
Thorburn, Nova Scotia 168/F3
Thoreau, N. Mex. 274/A3
Thoresby (mt.), Newf. 166/B2
Thorhild, Alberta 182/D2
Thorn, Miss. 256/F3
Thornaby-on-Tees (hill), England 10/F3
Thornaby-on-Tees, England 13/F3
Thornburg, Iowa 229/J6
Thornburg, Va. 307/N4
Thornbury, England 13/E6
Thornbury, Ontario 177/D3
Thorndale, Ontario 177/C4
Thorndale, Texas 303/G7
Thorndike•, Maine 243/E6
Thorndike, Mass. 249/E4
Thorne, England 13/F4
Thorne, N. Dak. 282/L2
Thorne, Ontario 175/E3
Thorne Bay, Alaska 196/M2
Thornfield, Mo. 261/G9
Thornhill, Br. Col. 184/C3
Thornhill, Ky. 237/K1
Thornhill, Manitoba 179/D5
Thornhill, Central, Scotland 15/D4
Thornhill, Dumf. & Gall., Scotland 15/E5
Thorn Hill, Tenn. 237/P8
Thornhurst, Pa. 294/L3
Thornley, England 13/J4
Thornloe, Ontario 175/E3
Thornloe, Ontario 177/K5
Thornton, Ark. 202/F6
Thornton, Calif. 204/B9
Thornton, Colo. 208/K3
Thornton, Idaho 220/G6
Thornton, Ill. 222/C6
Thornton, Iowa 229/G3
Thornton, Miss. 256/D4
Thornton•, N.H. 268/D4
Thornton, Ontario 177/E3
Thornton, Texas 303/H6
Thornton, Wash. 310/H3
Thornton, W. Va. 312/G4
Thornton Cleveleys, England 13/G1
Thornton Cleveleys, England 10/F1
Thorntown, Ind. 227/D4
Thornville, Ohio 284/F6
Thornwell, La. 238/E6
Thornwood, W. Va. 312/G5
Thorofare, N.J. 273/B4
Thorold, Ontario 177/E4
Thorp, Wash. 310/E3
Thorp, Wis. 317/E6
Thorpe (lake), N.C. 281/C4
Thorpe, W. Va. 312/D8
Thorp Spring, Texas 303/F5
Thorsby, Ala. 195/E5
Thorsby, Alberta 182/C3
Thouars, France 28/C4
Thouin (pt.), W. Australia 88/B4
Thouin (pt.), W. Australia 92/B3
Thousand (isls.), N.Y. 276/H2
Thousand (isls.), Ontario 177/H3
Thousand Island Park, N.Y. 276/J2
Thousand Lake (mt.), Utah 304/C5
Thousand Oaks, Calif. 204/G9
Thousand Palms, Calif. 204/J10
Thousand Spring (creek), Nev. 266/G1
Thousand Springs, Nev. 266/G1
Thrace (reg.), Greece 45/G5
Thrall, Kansas 232/F3
Thrasher, Miss. 256/G1
Three (isls.), New Bruns. 170/D4
Three Bridges, N.J. 273/D2
Three Churches, W. Va. 312/J4
Three Creek, Idaho 220/C7
Three Creeks, Alberta 182/B1
Three Creeks, Ark. 202/E7
Three Forks, Mont. 262/E5
Three Guardsmen (mt.), Br. Col. 184/H1
Three Hills, Alberta 182/D4
Three Hummock (isl.), Tasmania 99/B2
Three Kings (isls.), N. Zealand 100/D1
Three Lakes, Wis. 317/H4
Three Mile Bay, N.Y. 276/H2
Three Mile Plains, Nova Scotia 168/D4
Three Notch, Ala. 195/G6
Three Oaks, Mich. 250/C7
Three Pagodas (pass), Burma 72/C4
Three Pagodas (pass), Thailand 72/C4
Three Points (cape), Ghana 106/D8
Three Rivers, Mass. 249/E4
Three Rivers, Mich. 250/D7
Three Rivers, N. Mex. 274/C5
Three Rivers (Trois-Rivières), Québec 172/E3
Three Rivers, Texas 303/F9
Three Rivers, W. Australia 92/B4
Three Sisters (mt.), Oreg. 291/F3
Three Springs, Pa. 294/G5
Three Springs, W. Australia 88/B5
Three Springs, W. Australia 92/A5
Throckmorton (co.), Texas 303/E4
Throckmorton, Texas 303/F4
Throne, Alberta 182/E3
Throop, Pa. 294/F7
Thrums, Br. Col. 184/J5
Thrumster, Scotland 15/E2
Thuin, Belgium 27/E8
Thule Air Base, Greenland 2/F2
Thule Air Base, Greenland 4/B13
Thule Air Base, Greenland 146/M2
Thumail, Iraq 66/C4
Thun, Switzerland 39/E3
Thunder (bay), Mich. 250/F4
Thunder (hills), Sask. 181/L4
Thunder (creek), S. Dak. 298/N4
Thunder (creek), S. Dak. 298/K6
Thunder (lake), Wis. 317/H4
Thunder Bay (riv.), Mich. 250/F3
Thunder Bay, Ont. 162/H6
Thunder Bay, Ont. 146/K5
Thunder Bay (terr. dist.), Ontario 175/C3
Thunder Bay (terr. dist.), Ontario 177/H5
Thunder Bay, Ontario 175/C3
Thunder Bay, Ontario 177/H5
Thunderbird (lake), Okla. 288/M4
Thunderbolt, Georgia 217/K6
Thunder Butte (creek), S. Dak. 298/E3
Thunder Hawk, S. Dak. 298/F2
Thunder Lake, Alberta 182/C2
Thunersee (lake), Switzerland 39/E3
Thunstetten, Switzerland 39/E2
Thur (riv.), Switzerland 39/G1
Thurgau (canton), Switzerland 39/H1
Thüringer Wald (for.), Germany 22/D3
Thuringia (state), Germany 22/D3
Thurles, Ireland 10/B4
Thurles, Ireland 17/F6
Thurloo Downs, N.S. Wales 97/B1
Thurlow (dam), Ala. 195/G6
Thurlow, Mont. 262/K4
Thurman, Iowa 229/B7
Thurman, N.Y. 276/M3
Thurman, Ohio 284/F8
Thurmond, W. Va. 312/D7
Thurmont, Md. 245/J2
Thurrock, England 13/J8
Thurrock, England 10/C5
Thursday Island, Queensland 88/G2
Thursday Island, Queensland 95/B1
Thurso, Québec 172/B4
Thurso, Scotland 10/E1
Thurso, Scotland 15/E2
Thurso (riv.), Scotland 15/E2
Thurston (isl.) 5/C14
Thurston (co.), Nebr. 264/H2
Thurston, Nebr. 264/H2
Thurston, Ohio 284/E6
Thurston (co.), Wash. 310/C4
Thusis, Switzerland 39/H3
Thutade (lake), Br. Col. 184/D2
Thyatira, Miss. 256/E1
Thyborøn, Denmark 21/A4
Thyolo, Malawi 115/F7
Thyregod, Denmark 21/C6
Tia, N.S. Wales 97/F2
Tiahuanacu, Bolivia 136/A5
Tia Juana, Venezuela 124/C2
Tiandong, China 77/G7
Tianjin, China 2/Q4
Tianjin, China 54/N6
Tianjin (Tientsin), China 77/J4
Tianjun, China 77/E4
Tianlin, China 77/G7
Tian Shan (range), China 77/C3
Tianshui, China 77/F5
Tianzhu, China 77/F4
Tiaret, Algeria 106/E1
Tiatucurá, Uruguay 145/C3
Tiavea, W. Samoa 86/M8
Tiawah, Okla. 288/P2
Tib, Ras el (Bon) (cape), Tunisia 106/G1
Tibagi, Brazil 135/A4
Tibagi (riv.), Brazil 135/A4
Tibaná, Colombia 126/D5
Tibati, Cameroon 115/B2
Tibbie, Ala. 195/B8
Tibbita, N.S. Wales 97/C4
Tiber (riv.), Italy 7/F4
Tiber (riv.), Italy 34/D3
Tiberias, Israel 65/C2
Tiberias (lake), Israel 65/D2
Tibesti (mts.) 102/D2
Tibesti, Serir (des.), Chad 111/C3
Tibesti (mts.), Chad 111/C3
Tibesti, Serir (des.), Libya 111/C3
Tibet (reg.), China 2/P4
Tibet (reg.), China 54/K6
Tibet (reg.), China 77/B5
Tibet Aut. Reg. (Xizang), China 77/B5
Tibooburra, N.S. Wales 88/G5
Tibooburra, N.S. Wales 97/B1
Tibro, Sweden 18/J7
Tibugá (gulf), Colombia 126/B5
Tiburon, Calif. 204/J2
Tiburon, Haiti 158/A6
Tiburon (cape), Haiti 156/C3
Tiburon (cape), Haiti 158/A6
Tiburón (isl.), Mexico 150/C2
Tiburón (pt.), Panama 154/J6
Ticaco, Peru 128/H11
Ticao (isl.), Philippines 82/D4
Tice, Fla. 212/E5
Ticehurst, England 13/H6
Tichfield, Sask. 181/D4
Tichigan (lake), Wis. 317/K2
Tichigan Lake, Wis. 317/K2
Tichitt, Mauritania 106/C5
Tichlá (well), Western Sahara 106/B4

Tres Palmas 459

Tomaszów Mazowiecki, Poland 47/E3
Tomatin, Scotland 15/D3
Tomatlán, Mexico 150/G6
Tomave, Bolivia 136/B7
Tombador, Serra do (range), Brazil 132/B6
Tomball, Texas 303/J7
Tombe, Sudan 111/F6
Tombigbee (riv.) 188/J4
Tombigbee (riv.), Ala. 195/B7
Tombigbee (riv.), Miss. 256/H4
Tombstone, Ariz. 198/F7
Tombua, Angola 115/B7
Tomé, Chile 138/D1
Tome, N. Mex. 274/C4
Tomelilla, Sweden 18/J9
Tomelloso, Spain 33/E3
Tom Green (co.), Texas 303/D6
Tomhannock (res.), N.Y. 276/O5
Tomichi (creek), Colo. 208/F5
Tomifobia, Québec 172/E4
Tomina, Bolivia 136/C6
Tomingley, N.S. Wales 97/E3
Tomini (gulf), Indonesia 54/O10
Tomini (gulf), Indonesia 85/G6
Tomintoul, Scotland 15/E3
Tomiyama, Japan 81/O3
Tomkinson (ranges), W. Australia 92/E4
Tommerup, Denmark 21/D7
Tommot, U.S.S.R. 48/N4
Tomnolen, Miss. 256/F4
Tomo (riv.), Colombia 126/F5
To Mo, Thailand 72/D6
Tompa, Hungary 41/E3
Tompkins (co.), N.Y. 276/H6
Tompkins, Sask. 181/C5
Tompkinsville, Ky. 237/K7
Tompkinsville, Md. 245/L7
Tom Price, W. Australia 88/B4
Tom Price, W. Australia 92/B3
Toms (riv.), N.J. 273/E3
Toms Brook, Va. 307/L3
Toms Creek, Va. 307/D7
Tomsk, U.S.S.R. 54/K4
Tomsk, U.S.S.R. 48/J4
Tomslake, Br. Col. 184/H2
Toms River, N.J. 273/E4
Tom Steed (res.), Okla. 288/J5
Tümük, Turkey 63/F4
Tonalá, Mexico 150/N8
Tonalea, Ariz. 198/E2
Tonasket, Wash. 310/F2
Tonate, Fr. Guiana 131/E3
Tonawanda, N.Y. 276/B4
Tonawanda Ind. Res., N.Y. 276/D4
Tonbridge, England 13/H8
Tonckens (falls), Suriname 131/C3
Tondabayashi, Japan 81/J8
Tondano, Indonesia 85/H5
Tønder, Denmark 21/B8
Tønder, Denmark 18/F9
Tone (riv.), Japan 81/K6
Tonegrama, Peru 128/D4
Tonekabon, Iran 59/F2
Tonekabon, Iran 66/G2
Toney, Ala. 195/E1
Toney River, Nova Scotia 168/F3
Tonga 2/A6
Tonga 87/J8
Tonga, Sudan 111/F6
Tongala, Victoria 97/C5
Tonganoxie, Kansas 232/G2
Tongareva (atoll), Cook Is. 87/L6
Tongatapu (isls.), Tonga 87/J8
Tongcheng, China 77/J5
T'ongch'ŏn, N. Korea 81/D4
Tongchuan (Tungchwan), China 77/G5
Tongde, China 77/F4
Tongeren, Belgium 27/G7
Tonghai, China 77/F7
Tonghe, China 77/L2
Tonghua (Tunghwa), China 77/L3
Tongjiang (Tungkiang), China 77/M2
Tongliao, China 77/K3
Tongling, China 77/J5
Tongo, N.S. Wales 97/B2
Tongo (lake), N.S. Wales 97/B2
Tongoy, Chile 138/A8
Tongoy (bay), Chile 138/A8
Tongquil (isl.), Philippines 82/D8
Tongren, Qinghai, China 77/F4
Tongren, Guizhou, China 77/G6
Tongres (Tongeren), Belgium 27/G7
Tongs, Ky. 237/R3
Tongsa Dzong, Bhutan 68/G3
Tongtian He (Zhi Qu) (riv.), China 77/E5
Tongue (riv.), Mont. 262/K5
Tongue (pt.), N. Zealand 100/A3
Tongue (riv.), N. Dak. 282/P2
Tongue, Scotland 15/D2
Tongue (riv.), Wyo. 319/E1
Tongue of the Ocean (chan.), Bahamas 156/C1
Tongxin, China 77/G4
Tongyu, China 77/K3
Tongzi, China 77/G6
Tonica, Ill. 222/E2
Tonj, Sudan 111/E6
Tonk, India 68/D3
Tonka Bay, Minn. 255/F5
Tonkawa, Okla. 288/M1
Tonkin (gulf) 54/M8
Tonkin (gulf), China 77/G7
Tonkin, Sask. 181/J4
Tonkin (gulf), Vietnam 72/E3
Tonle Sap (lake), Cambodia 72/D4
Ton Mhor (pt.), Scotland 15/B5
Tonneins, France 28/D5
Tonnerre, France 28/E4
Tünning, Germany 22/C1
Tonopah, Ariz. 198/B5
Tonopah, Nev. 188/C3
Tonopah, Nev. 266/D4
Tonosí, Panama 154/G7
Tonota, Botswana 118/D4
Tonota, Botswana 102/E7
Tønsberg, Norway 18/D4
Tonsina, Alaska 196/J2
Tontitown, Ark. 202/B1
Tonto (basin), Ariz. 198/D4
Tonto (creek), Ariz. 198/D4
Tonto Basin, Ariz. 198/D5
Tontogany, Ohio 284/C3
Tonto Nat'l Mon., Ariz. 198/D5
Tony, Wis. 317/E5
Tonya, Turkey 63/H2
Toodyay, W. Australia 88/B2
Toodyay, W. Australia 92/B1
Tooele (co.), Utah 304/A3
Tooele, Utah 304/B3
Tooele, Utah 188/D2
Tooele Army Depot, Utah 304/B3
Toole (co.), Mont. 262/E2
Tooleybuc, N.S. Wales 97/B4
Toombs (co.), Georgia 217/H6
Toomevara, Ireland 17/E6
Tooms (lake), Tasmania 99/D4
Toomsboro, Georgia 217/F5
Toomsuba, Miss. 256/G6
Toone, Tenn. 237/D10
Tooraweenah, N.S. Wales 97/E2
Toowoomba, Australia 87/F8
Toowoomba, Queensland 88/J5
Toowoomba, Queensland 95/D5
Top (lake), U.S.S.R. 52/D1
Topador, Uruguay 145/C1
Topanga, Calif. 204/B10
Topanga Beach, Calif. 204/B10
Topawa, Ariz. 198/D7
Topaz (lake), Nev. 266/B4
Topeka, Ill. 222/D3
Topeka, Ind. 227/F1
Topeka (cap.), Kans. 188/G3
Topeka (cap.), Kansas 146/J6
Topeka (cap.), Kansas 232/G2
Topia, Mexico 150/F4
Topinabee, Mich. 250/E3
Topl'a (riv.), Czech. 41/F2
Topley, Br. Col. 184/D3
Toplița, Romania 45/G2
Topocalma (pt.), Chile 138/A10
Topock, Ariz. 198/A4
Top Of The World Prov. Park, Br. Col. 184/K5
Topographic Center, Md. 245/E4
Topol'čany, Czech. 41/D2
Topolobampo, Mexico 150/E4
Topolovgrad, Bulgaria 45/H4
Toponas, Colo. 208/F2
Toppenish, Wash. 310/E4
Toppenish (creek), Wash. 310/E4
Topsail Beach, N.C. 281/O6
Topsfield•, Maine 243/H5
Topsfield, Mass. 249/L2
Topsfield•, Mass. 249/L2
Topsham, Maine 243/D8
Topsham•, Maine 243/D8
Topsham•, Vt. 268/C3
Top Springs, North. Terr. 93/C4
Topton, N.C. 281/B4
Topton, Pa. 294/L5
Toquepala, Peru 128/G11
Toquerville, Utah 304/A6
Toquima (range), Nev. 266/E4
Tor (bay), Nova Scotia 168/G3
Torata, Peru 128/G11
Torawitan (cape), Indonesia 85/G5
Torbali, Turkey 63/B3
Torbat-e-Heydariyeh, Iran 66/L3
Torbat-e Heydariyeh, Iran 59/G2
Torbat-e Jam, Iran 66/M3
Torbat-e Jam, Iran 59/H2
Torbay, England 10/E5
Torbay, England 13/D7
Torbay, Newf. 166/D2
Torbay (pt.), Newf. 166/D2
Torbeck, Haiti 158/A6
Torch (key), Fla. 212/E7
Torch (lake), Mich. 250/D3
Torch, Ohio 284/G7
Torch (riv.), Sask. 181/H2
Torch River, Sask. 181/G2
Tordesillas, Spain 33/D2
Torgau, Germany 22/E3
Torgelow, Germany 22/F2
Torhout, Belgium 27/C6
Tori, Ethiopia 111/F6
Torino (Turin), Italy 34/A2
Torit, Sudan 111/F7
Torne (riv.) 7/G2
Torneälv (riv.), Sweden 18/M3
Tor Ness (prom.), Scotland 15/E2
Torneträsk (lake), Sweden 18/L2
Torngat (mts.), Newf. 166/B2
Tornillo, Texas 303/A10
Tornio, Finland 18/O4
Tornionjoki (riv.), Finland 18/O3
Tornquist, Argentina 143/D4
Toro, Cerro del (mt.), Argentina 143/B2
Toro (lake), Chile 138/D9
Toro, Cerro del (mt.), Chile 138/B7
Toro (pt.), Chile 138/A10
Toro, La. 238/C4
Toro, El (mt.), P. Rico 161/F2
Toro, Spain 33/D2
Törökszentmiklós, Hungary 41/F3
Toronaic (gulf), Greece 45/F5
Toronto, Canada 2/F3
Toronto, Iowa 229/M5
Toronto, Kansas 232/G4
Toronto (lake), Kansas 232/F4
Toronto (res.), N.Y. 276/L7
Toronto, Ohio 284/J5
Toronto (cap.), Ont. 146/K5
Toronto (cap.), Ont. 162/H7
Toronto (metro. munic.), Ontario 177/K4
Toronto (cap.), Ontario 177/K4
Toronto, S. Dak. 298/R4
Toropalca, Bolivia 136/B7
Toropets, U.S.S.R. 52/D3
Tororo, Uganda 115/F3
Torote (riv.), Spain 33/G4
Torotoro, Bolivia 136/C6
Torpedo, Pa. 294/D2
Torphins, Scotland 15/F3
Torpoint, England 13/C7
Torquay, Sask. 181/H6
Torquemada, Spain 33/D1
Torr (head), N. Ireland 17/K1
Torrance, Calif. 188/C4
Torrance, Calif. 204/C11
Torrance (co.), N. Mex. 274/D4
Torrance, Ontario 177/E3
Torrance, Pa. 294/D5
Torre, Cerro de la (mt.), Chile 138/E4
Torre Annunziata, Italy 34/E4
Torreblanca, Spain 33/G2
Torrecilla (lag.), P. Rico 161/E1
Torre del Greco, Italy 34/E4
Torre de Moncorvo, Portugal 33/C2
Torredonjimeno, Spain 33/D4
Torre Gaia, Italy 34/F6
Torrejón (res.), Spain 33/D3
Torrejoncillo, Spain 33/C3
Torrejón de Ardoz, Spain 33/G4
Torrelaguna, Spain 33/E2
Torrelavega, Spain 33/D1
Torremaggiore, Italy 34/E4
Torremolinos, Spain 33/D4
Torrens (riv.) 88/E7
Torrens (lake), Australia 87/D9
Torrens (isl.), S. Australia 88/D7
Torrens (lake), S. Australia 88/F6
Torrens (lake), S. Australia 94/E4
Torrens (riv.), S. Australia 94/C7
Torrente, Spain 33/F3
Torreón, Mexico 146/H7
Torreón, Mexico 150/H4
Torreon, N. Mex. 274/C4
Torre-Pacheco, Spain 33/F4
Torres (strait) 87/E7
Torres (str.), Papua N.G. 85/A7
Torres (str.), Queensland 88/G2
Torres (str.), Queensland 95/B1
Torres (isls.), Vanuatu 87/G7
Torres Martinez Ind. Res., Calif. 204/J10
Torres Novas, Portugal 33/B3
Torres Vedras, Portugal 33/B3
Torrevieja, Spain 33/F4
Torrey, Utah 304/C5
Torridge (riv.), England 13/C7
Torridon, Loch (inlet), Scotland 15/C3
Torriente, Cuba 158/D1
Torrijos, Philippines 82/D4
Torrijos, Spain 33/D2
Tørring, Denmark 21/C6
Torringford, Conn. 210/C1
Torrington, Alberta 182/D4
Torrington, Conn. 210/C1
Torrington, Wyo. 319/H3
Torroella de Montgrí, Spain 33/H1
Torrowangee, N.S. Wales 97/A2
Torrox, Spain 33/E4
Torsby, Sweden 18/H6
Tors Cove, Newf. 166/D2
Torshälla, Sweden 18/K7
Tórshavn, Denmark 7/D2
Tórshavn (cap.), Faroe Is., Denmark 21/A3
Tortilla Flat, Ariz. 198/D5
Tortola (isl.), Virgin Is. (U.K.) 161/D3
Tortola (isl.), Virgin Is. (U.K.) 156/H1
Tórtolas, Cerro de las (mt.), Chile 138/B8
Tortona, Italy 34/B2
Tortorici, Italy 34/E6
Tortosa, Spain 33/G2
Tortosa (cape), Spain 33/G2
Tortue (chan.), Haiti 158/C5
Tortue (Tortuga) (isl.), Haiti 156/D2
Tortue (Tortuga) (isl.), Haiti 158/C4
Tortuga (isl.), Haiti 158/C4
Tortuga (isl.), Haiti 156/D2
Tortugas (gulf), Colombia 126/B6
Tortuguero (lag.), P. Rico 161/D1
Tortuguilla (pt.), Cuba 158/K4
Tortum, Turkey 63/J2
Torud, Iran 59/F2
Torud, Iran 66/J3
Torul, Turkey 63/H2
Toruń (prov.), Poland 47/D2
Toruń, Poland 7/F3
Toruń, Poland 47/D2
Torunos, Venezuela 124/C3
Türva, U.S.S.R. 53/C1
Tory (isl.), Ireland 17/E1
Tory (isl.), Ireland 10/B3
Tory (sound), Ireland 17/E1
Torysa (riv.), Czech. 41/F2
Torzhok, U.S.S.R. 52/D3
Tosa, Japan 81/F7
Tosa (bay), Japan 81/F7
Tosashimizu, Japan 81/F7
Toson Hu (lake), China 77/E4
Tüss (riv.), Switzerland 39/G1
Tostado, Argentina 143/D2
Toston, Mont. 262/E4
Tosu, Japan 81/E7
Tosya, Turkey 63/F2
Tota, Laguna de (lake), Colombia 126/D5
Totana, Spain 33/F4
Tótkomlós, Hungary 41/F3
Tot'ma, U.S.S.R. 48/E4
Tot'ma, U.S.S.R. 52/F3
Totnes, England 13/D7
Totnes, England 10/E5
Totnes, Sask. 181/C4
Totness, Suriname 131/C3
Toto, Ind. 227/D2
Totoket, Conn. 210/D3
Totonicapán, Guatemala 154/B3
Totora, Cochabamba, Bolivia 136/C5
Totora, Oruro, Bolivia 136/A5
Totoral, Chile 138/A6
Totoral, Quebrada (riv.), Chile 138/A6
Totoral, Uruguay 145/C3
Totowa, N.J. 273/B1
Totoya (isl.), Fiji 86/R11
Tottenham, N.S. Wales 97/D3
Tottenham, Ontario 177/E3
Tottori (pref.), Japan 81/G6
Tottori, Japan 81/G6
Touat (oasis), Algeria 106/E3
Touba, Ivory Coast 106/C7
Touba, Senegal 106/A6
Toubkal, Jebel (mt.), Morocco 102/B1
Toubkal, Jebel (mt.), Morocco 106/C2
Touchet, Wash. 310/G4
Touchet (riv.), Wash. 310/G4
Touchwood (lake), Alberta 182/E2
Touchwood (hills), Sask. 181/G4
Toufourine (well), Mali 106/C4
Tougaloo, Miss. 256/D6
Tougan, Burkina Faso 106/D6
Touggourt, Algeria 106/F2
Touggourt, Algeria 102/C1
Toughkenamon, Pa. 294/L6
Tougué, Guinea 106/B6
Touila (well), Algeria 106/C3
Touila (well), Mauritania 106/C3
Toukoto, Mali 106/C6
Toul, France 28/F3
Touladi, Grand Lac (lake), Québec 172/J1
Toulnustouc (riv.), Québec 174/D2
Toulon, France 7/E4
Toulon, France 28/F6
Toulon, Ill. 222/D2
Toulouse, France 7/E4
Toulouse, France 28/D6
Toumodi, Ivory Coast 106/D7
Toungo, Nigeria 106/G7
Toungoo, Burma 72/C3
Touraine (trad. prov.), France 29
Tourakom, Laos 72/D3
Tourbis (lake), Québec 172/C2
Tourcoing, France 28/E2
Tour d'Ai (mt.), Switzerland 39/C4
Tourelle, Québec 172/C1
Tournai, Belgium 27/C7
Tournavista, Peru 128/E7
Tournon, France 28/F5
Tournus, France 28/F4
Touros, Brazil 132/H4
Touro Synagogue Nat'l Hist. Site, R.I. 249/J7
Tours, France 28/D4
Tours, France 7/E4
Tourville, Québec 172/H2
Toutes Aides, Manitoba 179/C3
Toutle, Wash. 310/C4
Toutle, South Fork (riv.), Wash. 310/C4
Toutle, North Fork (riv.), Wash. 310/C4
Toužim, Czech. 41/B1
Tüv, Mongolia 77/G2
Tovar, Venezuela 124/C3
Tovey, Ill. 222/D4
Towaco, N.J. 273/E2
Towada, Japan 81/K3
Towada (lake), Japan 81/K3
Towada-Hachimantai National Park, Japan 81/K3
Towakaima, Guyana 131/B2
Towanda, Ill. 222/E3
Towanda, Kansas 232/E4
Towanda, Pa. 294/J2
Towanda (creek), Pa. 294/J2
Towaoc, Colo. 208/B8
Towcester, England 13/F5
Tower, Mich. 250/E3
Tower, Minn. 255/F3
Tower, Wyo. 319/B1
Tower City, N. Dak. 282/P6
Tower City, Pa. 294/J4
Tower Hamlets, England 13/H8
Tower Hill, Ill. 222/E4
Tower Lakes, Ill. 222/A4
Towers of Silence, India 68/B7
Tow Law, England 13/H4
Town (creek), Ala. 195/C1
Town (creek), Md. 245/E2
Town and Country, Mo. 261/O3
Town and Country, Wash. 310/H3
Town Creek, Ala. 195/D1
Towner, Colo. 208/P6
Towner (co.), N. Dak. 282/M2
Towner, N. Dak. 282/K3
Townley, Ala. 195/D3
Town 'n Country, Fla. 212/C2
Town of Pines, Ind. 227/D1
Town Point, Md. 245/P3
Towns (co.), Georgia 217/E1
Towns, Georgia 217/G7
Townsend, Del. 245/R3
Townsend, Georgia 217/J7
Townsend, Mass. 249/H2
Townsend•, Mass. 249/H2
Townsend, Mont. 262/E4
Townsend (inlet), N.J. 273/D5
Townsend, Tenn. 237/O9
Townsend, Va. 307/R6
Townsend, Wis. 317/K5
Townsend Harbor, Mass. 249/G2
Townsends Inlet, N.J. 273/D5
Townshend•, Vt. 268/B5
Townsville, Australia 2/S6
Townsville, Australia 87/E7
Townsville, N.C. 281/N1
Townsville, Queensland 88/H3
Townsville, Queensland 95/C3
Townville, Pa. 294/C2
Townville, S.C. 296/B2
Towot, Sudan 111/F6
Towraghondi, Afghanistan 68/A1
Towson, Md. 245/M3
Towuti (lake), Indonesia 85/G6
Towy (riv.), Wales 13/D6
Towy (riv.), Wales 10/E5
Toxey, Ala. 195/B7
Toya (lake), Japan 81/K2
Toyah, Texas 303/D11
Toyah (creek), Texas 303/D11
Toyah (lake), Texas 303/A6
Toyahvale, Texas 303/D11
Toyama (pref.), Japan 81/H5
Toyama, Japan 81/H5
Toyama (bay), Japan 81/H5
Toyohashi, Japan 81/H6
Toyonaka, Japan 81/J7
Toyooka, Japan 81/G6
Toyota, Japan 81/H6
Tozeur, Tunisia 106/F2
Trabzon (prov.), Turkey 63/H2
Trabzon, Turkey 54/E5
Trabzon, Turkey 63/H2
Trabzon, Turkey 59/C1
Tracadie, New Bruns. 170/F1
Tracadie, Nova Scotia 168/G3
Tracadie (bay), Pr. Edward I. 168/F2
Trachselwald, Switzerland 39/E2
Tracy, Calif. 204/D6
Tracy, Conn. 210/D2
Tracy, Iowa 229/H6
Tracy, Ky. 237/K7
Tracy, Minn. 255/C6
Tracy, Mo. 261/C4
Tracy, New Bruns. 170/D3
Tracy, Québec 172/D3
Tracy Arm (inlet), Alaska 196/N1
Tracy City, Tenn. 237/K10
Tracyton, Wash. 310/A2
Trade, Tenn. 237/T8
Trade Lake, Wis. 317/A4
Tradespark, Scotland 15/E3
Tradesville, S.C. 296/F2
Tradewater (riv.), Ky. 237/F6
Trading (bay), Alaska 196/B1
Trading Post, Kansas 232/H3
Traer, Iowa 229/J4
Traer, Kansas 232/B2
Trafalgar, Ind. 227/E6
Trafalgar, Nova Scotia 168/F3
Trafalgar (cape), Spain 33/C4
Trafaria, Portugal 33/A1
Trafford, Ala. 195/E3
Trafford, Pa. 294/C5
Traghen, Libya 111/B2
Traiguén, Chile 138/D2
Traiguén (isl.), Chile 138/D6
Trail, Br. Col. 162/E6
Trail, Br. Col. 146/G4
Trail, Br. Col. 184/J6
Trail, Minn. 255/C3
Trail, Oreg. 291/E5
Trail City, S. Dak. 298/H3
Trail Creek, Ind. 227/D1
Traill (isl.), Greenl. 4/B10
Traill (co.), N. Dak. 282/R5
Traîne (lake), Québec 172/D2
Trainer, Pa. 294/L7
Traiskirchen, Austria 41/D2
Trakai, U.S.S.R. 53/C3
Tralake, Miss. 256/C4
Tralee, Ireland 10/B4
Tralee, Ireland 17/B7
Tralee (bay), Ireland 17/B7
Tramán-tepuí (mt.), Venezuela 124/G5
Tramelan, Switzerland 39/D2
Trammel, Va. 307/D6
Tramore, Ireland 10/C4
Tramore, Ireland 17/G7
Tramore (bay), Ireland 17/G7
Trampas, N. Mex. 274/D2
Tramperos (creek), N. Mex. 274/F2
Tramping (lake), Sask. 181/C3
Tramping Lake, Sask. 181/B3
Tranås, Sweden 18/J7
Trancoso, Portugal 33/C2
Tranebjerg, Denmark 21/D6
Tranebjerg (mt.), Denmark 21/C6
Tranent, Scotland 15/F5
Trang, Thailand 72/C6
Trangan (isl.), Indonesia 85/J7
Trangie, N.S. Wales 97/D3
Trani, Italy 34/F4
Tranquebar, India 68/E6
Tranqueras, Uruguay 145/D2
Tranqui (isl.), Chile 138/D4
Tranquility, N.J. 273/D2
Tranquillity, Calif. 204/E7
Transantarctic (mts.) 5/B17
Trans-Carpathian Oblast, U.S.S.R. 52/B5
Transfer, Pa. 294/A3
Transkei (bantustan), S. Africa 102/E8
Transkei (rep.), S. Africa 118/D6
Transquaking (riv.), Md. 245/P7
Transvaal (prov.), S. Africa 102/E7
Transvaal (prov.), S. Africa 118/D4
Transylvania, La. 238/H1
Transylvania (co.), N.C. 281/D4
Transylvanian Alps (mts.), Romania 45/G3
Trapani (prov.), Italy 34/D5
Trapani, Italy 7/F5
Trapani, Italy 34/D5
Trap Falls (res.), Conn. 210/C3
Traphill, N.C. 281/H2
Trappe, Md. 245/O6
Trappers (lake), Colo. 208/E3
Traralgon, Victoria 97/D6
Traralgon, Victoria 88/H7
Trarza (reg.), Mauritania 106/A5
Trasimeno (lake), Italy 34/D3
Traskwood, Ark. 202/E5
Trat, Thailand 72/D4
Traun, Austria 41/C2
Traun (riv.), Austria 41/C2
Traun See (lake), Austria 41/B3
Traunstein, Germany 22/E5
Travancore (reg.), India 68/D7
Travelers Rest, S.C. 296/C2
Travellers (lake), N.S. Wales 97/B3
Travellers Rest, Ky. 237/O6
Travemünde, Germany 22/D2
Travers, Alberta 182/D4
Travers (res.), Alberta 182/D4
Traverse (bay), Manitoba 179/F4
Traverse (isl.), Mich. 250/A1
Traverse (pt.), Mich. 250/A1
Traverse (co.), Minn. 255/B5
Traverse, Minn. 255/D6
Traverse (lake), Minn. 255/B5
Traverse (lake), S. Dak. 298/R2
Traverse City, Mich. 188/K2
Traverse City, Mich. 250/D4
Tra Vinh (Phu Vinh), Vietnam 72/E5
Travis (co.), Texas 303/G7
Travis (lake), Texas 303/G7
Travis A.F.B., Calif. 204/L1
Travnik, Yugoslavia 45/C3
Trawbreaga (bay), Ireland 17/F1
Traynor, Sask. 181/C3
Traytown, Newf. 166/D1
Trbovlje, Yugoslavia 45/B2
Treadway, Tenn. 237/P8
Treasure (isl.), Fla. 212/B3
Treasure (co.), Mont. 262/J4
Treasure Island, Fla. 212/B3
Treasury (isls.), Solomon Is. 86/C2
Treaty, Ind. 227/F3
Trebbia (riv.), Italy 34/B2
Třebíč, Czech. 41/C2
Trebinje, Yugoslavia 45/D4
Trebišov, Czech. 41/F2
Trebizond (Trabzon), Turkey 63/H2
Trebloc, Miss. 256/G3
Třeboň, Czech. 41/C2
Trece Martires, Philippines 82/C3
Tredegar, Wales 13/B6
Treece, Kansas 232/H4
Treelon, Sask. 181/C6
Trees, La. 238/B1
Treesbank, Manitoba 179/C5
Tregaron, Wales 13/D5
Tregaron, Wales 10/E4
Tregarva, Sask. 181/G5
Trego (co.), Kansas 232/C3
Trego, Mont. 262/B2
Trego, Wis. 317/C4
Treherne, Manitoba 179/D5
Treig, Loch (lake), Scotland 15/D4
Treinta y Tres (dept.), Uruguay 145/E4
Treinta y Tres, Uruguay 145/E4
Trelew, Argentina 143/C5
Trelleborg, Sweden 18/H9
Tremadoc (bay), Wales 10/D4
Tremadoc (prom.), Wales 13/C5
Tremblant (lake), Québec 172/C3
Trembleur (lake), Br. Col. 184/E3
Trementina, N. Mex. 274/E3
Tremiti (isls.), Italy 34/E3
Tremont, Ill. 222/D3
Tremont, Maine 243/G7
Tremont•, Maine 243/G7
Tremont, Miss. 256/H2
Tremont, Pa. 294/K4
Tremont City, Ohio 284/C5
Tremonton, Utah 304/B2
Tremp, Spain 33/G1
Trempealeau (co.), Wis. 317/D7
Trempealeau, Wis. 317/C8
Trempealeau (riv.), Wis. 317/C7
Trenary, Mich. 250/C2
Trenčín, Czech. 41/E2
Trenel, Argentina 143/D4
Trenggalek, Indonesia 85/K2
Trenque Lauquen, Argentina 143/D4
Trent (riv.), England 13/G4
Trent (riv.), England 10/F4
Trent (riv.), N.C. 281/P4
Trent, Oreg. 291/E4
Trent, S. Dak. 298/R6
Trent, Texas 303/D5
Trente et un Milles (lake), Québec 172/B3
Trentham, Manitoba 179/F5
Trentham Cliffs, N.S. Wales 97/B4
Trentino-Alto Adige (reg.), Italy 34/C1
Trento (prov.), Italy 34/C1
Trento, Italy 34/C1
Trenton, Ala. 195/F1
Trenton, Ark. 202/J5
Trenton, Fla. 212/D2
Trenton, Georgia 217/A1
Trenton, Ill. 222/D5
Trenton, Iowa 229/K6
Trenton, Ky. 237/G7
Trenton, Maine 243/G7
Trenton•, Maine 243/G7
Trenton, Md. 245/L2
Trenton, Mich. 250/B7
Trenton, Miss. 256/E6
Trenton, Mo. 261/E2
Trenton, Nebr. 264/D4
Trenton (cap.), N.J. 146/L5
Trenton (cap.), N.J. 188/M2
Trenton (cap.), N.J. 273/D3
Trenton, N.C. 281/P4
Trenton, N. Dak. 282/C3
Trenton, Nova Scotia 168/F3
Trenton, Ohio 284/B7
Trenton, Ontario 177/G3
Trenton, S.C. 296/D4
Trenton, Tenn. 237/D9
Trenton, Texas 303/H4
Trenton, Utah 304/B2
Trent Woods, N.C. 281/P4
Trepassey, Newf. 166/D2
Treptow, Germany 22/F4
Tres Árboles, Uruguay 145/C3
Tres Arroyos, Argentina 143/D4
Tres Arroyos, Argentina 120/C6
Tres Bocas, Uruguay 145/B2
Tresckow, Pa. 294/K4
Tresco (isl.), England 13/A8
Três Corações, Brazil 132/E8
Três Corações, Brazil 135/D2
Tres Cruces, Nevada (mt.), Chile 138/B6
Tres Esquinas, Colombia 126/C7
Treshnish (isls.), Scotland 15/B4
Tres Islas, Uruguay 145/E3
Três Lagoas, Brazil 120/D5
Três Lagoas, Brazil 132/C8
Três Marias (res.), Brazil 120/E4
Tres Montes (cape), Chile 120/B7
Tres Montes (cape), Chile 138/C7
Tres Montes (gulf), Chile 138/D6
Tres Montes (pen.), Chile 138/C6
Tres Palmas, Colombia 126/B3

Verona 463

Valera, Texas 303/E6
Valera, Venezuela 124/C3
Valera, Venezuela 120/B2
Valeria, Iowa 229/G5
Vale Summit, Md. 245/C2
Valga, U.S.S.R. 52/C3
Valga, U.S.S.R. 53/D2
Valhalla, Alberta 182/A2
Valhalla, N.Y. 276/P6
Valhalla Centre, Alberta 182/A2
Valhermoso Springs, Ala. 195/E2
Valiente (pen.), Panama 154/G6
Valier, Ill. 222/D5
Valier, Mont. 262/D2
Valier, Pa. 294/D4
Valjean, Sask. 181/E5
Valjevo, Yugoslavia 45/D3
Valka, U.S.S.R. 53/C2
Valkeakoski, Finland 18/N6
Valkenswaard, Netherlands 27/H6
Valladolid, Mexico 146/K7
Valladolid, Mexico 150/P6
Valladolid (prov.), Spain 33/D2
Valladolid, Spain 33/D2
Valladolid, Spain 7/E4
Vallay (isl.), Scotland 15/A3
Vall de Uxó, Spain 33/F3
Valle, Norway 18/E7
Valle Alegre, Chile 138/F2
Vallecas, Spain 33/G4
Vallecito (res.), Colo. 208/D8
Vallecitos, N. Mex. 274/C2
Valle de Allende, Mexico 150/G3
Valle de Bravo, Mexico 150/J7
Valle de Guanape, Venezuela 124/F3
Valle de la Pascua, Venezuela 124/F3
Valle del Cauca (dept.), Colombia 126/B6
Valledupar, Colombia 120/B1
Valledupar, Colombia 126/D2
Vallée-Jonction, Québec 172/G3
Vallegrande, Bolivia 120/C4
Vallegrande, Bolivia 136/C6
Valle Hermoso, Mexico 150/L4
Vallehermoso, Spain 33/A5
Vallejo, Calif. 188/B3
Vallejo, Calif. 204/J1
Valle Mí, Paraguay 144/D3
Vallenar, Chile 138/A7
Vallentuna, Sweden 18/H1
Valle San Telmo, Mexico 150/A1
Valles Mines, Mo. 261/L6
Valletta (cap.), Malta 7/F5
Valletta (cap.), Malta 34/E7
Valley, Ala. 195/H5
Valley (co.), Idaho 220/C5
Valley (riv.), Manitoba 179/B3
Valley (co.), Mont. 262/K2
Valley (co.), Nebr. 264/E3
Valley, Nebr. 264/H3
Valley, Nova Scotia 168/E3
Valley, Wash. 310/H2
Valley, Wis. 317/F8
Valley, Wyo. 319/C1
Valley Bend, W. Va. 312/F5
Valley Brook, Okla. 288/M4
Valley Center, Kansas 232/E4
Valley Centre, Sask. 181/D4
Valley City, Ill. 222/C4
Valley City, N. Dak. 282/P6
Valley City, Ohio 284/G3
Valley Cottage, N.Y. 276/K8
Valley East, Ontario 177/J5
Valley East, Ontario 175/D3
Valley Falls, Kansas 232/G2
Valley Falls, N.Y. 276/N5
Valley Falls, Oreg. 291/G5
Valley Falls, R.I. 249/J5
Valley Farms, Ariz. 198/D6
Valleyfield, Québec 172/C4
Valleyford, Wash. 310/H3
Valley Forge, Pa. 294/L5
Valley Grove, W. Va. 312/E2
Valley Head, Ala. 195/G1
Valley Head, W. Va. 312/G5
Valley Hi, Ohio 284/C5
Valley Lee, Md. 245/M8
Valley Mills, Texas 303/G6
Valley Park, Miss. 256/C5
Valley Park, Mo. 261/O3
Valley Point, W. Va. 312/G3
Valley River, Manitoba 179/B3
Valley Spring, Texas 303/F7
Valley Springs, Ark. 202/D1
Valley Springs, Calif. 204/C9
Valley Springs, S. Dak. 298/S6
Valley Station, Ky. 237/K4
Valley Stream, N.Y. 276/P7
Valleyview, Alberta 182/B2
Valley View, Ky. 237/N5
Valley View, Ohio 284/D6
Valley View, Ohio 284/H9
Valley View, Pa. 294/J4
Valley View, Texas 303/H4
Vallgrund (isl.), Finland 18/M5
Valliant, Okla. 288/R6
Vallières, Haiti 158/C5
Vallimanca (riv.), Argentina 143/F7
Vallonia, Ind. 227/E7
Vallon-Pont-d'Arc, France 28/F5
Vallorbe, Switzerland 39/B3
Valls, Spain 33/G2
Val Marie, Sask. 181/D6
Valmeyer, Ill. 222/C5
Valmiera, U.S.S.R. 53/C2
Valmiera, U.S.S.R. 52/C3
Valmont, Québec 172/E3
Valmontone, Italy 34/F7
Valmora, N. Mex. 274/D3
Valmy, Nev. 266/D2
Valmy, Wis. 317/M6
Valognes, France 28/C3
Valona, Georgia 217/K8
Valor, Sask. 181/E6
Valpaços, Portugal 33/C2
Valparaíso (reg.), Chile 138/A9
Valparaíso, Chile 2/F7
Valparaíso, Chile 120/B6
Valparaíso, Chile 138/E2
Valparaiso, Fla. 212/C6
Valparaiso, Ind. 227/C2
Valparaiso, Nebr. 264/H3
Valparaiso, Sask. 181/G3
Val-Racine, Québec 172/G4
Vals (cape), Indonesia 85/K7
Vals, Switzerland 39/H3
Valsad, India 68/C4
Valsequillo (res.), Mexico 150/N2
Valserrhein (riv.), Switzerland 39/H3
Valsetz, Oreg. 291/D3
Value, Miss. 256/D6
Valuyki, U.S.S.R. 52/E4
Valverda, La. 238/G5
Valverde (prov.), Dom. Rep. 158/D5
Valverde, Dom. Rep. 158/D5
Val Verde (co.), Texas 303/C8
Valverde del Camino, Spain 33/C4
Vamdrup, Denmark 21/C7
Vammala, Finland 18/N6
Vámos, Greece 45/F8
Vámospércs, Hungary 41/F3
Van, Ky. 237/R6
Van (lake), N. Dak. 282/L5
Van, Oreg. 291/J4
Van, Pa. 294/C3
Van, Texas 303/J5
Van (prov.), Turkey 63/K3
Van, Turkey 59/D2
Van, Turkey 63/K3
Van (lake), Turkey 54/F6
Van (lake), Turkey 59/D2
Van (lake), Turkey 63/K3
Van, W. Va. 312/C7
Vanadium, N. Mex. 274/A6
Van Alstyne, Texas 303/H4
Vananda, Br. Col. 184/E5
Vananda, Mont. 262/K4
Vanatta, Ohio 284/E5
Vanavara, U.S.S.R. 48/L3
Van Blommenstein (lake), Suriname 120/D2
Van Blommestein (lake), Suriname 131/D3
Van Bruyssel, Québec 172/E2
Van Buren (co.), Ark. 202/E2
Van Buren, Ark. 202/B3
Van Buren, Ind. 227/F3
Van Buren (co.), Iowa 229/K7
Van Buren, Maine 243/G1
Van Buren•, Maine 243/G1
Van Buren (co.), Mich. 250/C6
Van Buren, Mo. 261/L8
Van Buren, Ohio 284/C3
Van Buren (co.), Tenn. 237/L9
Vance, Ala. 195/D4
Vance, Miss. 256/D2
Vance (co.), N.C. 281/N2
Vance, S.C. 296/G5
Vance A.F.B., Okla. 288/K2
Vanceboro•, Maine 243/J4
Vanceboro, N.C. 281/P4
Vanceburg, Ky. 237/P3
Vancleave, Miss. 256/G9
Van Cleve, Iowa 229/G5
Vancourt, Texas 303/D6
Vancouver (mt.), Alaska 196/L2
Vancouver, Br. Col. 146/F4
Vancouver, Br. Col. 162/D6
Vancouver (Greater), Br. Col. 184/K3
Vancouver (isl.), Br. Col. 146/F5
Vancouver (isl.), Br. Col. 162/D6
Vancouver, Br. Col. 184/K3
Vancouver (isl.), Br. Col. 184/D5
Vancouver, Canada 2/C3
Vancouver (isl.), Canada 2/C3
Vancouver, Wash. 188/B1
Vancouver, Wash. 310/C5
Vancouver (lake), Wash. 310/C5
Vandalia, Ill. 222/D5
Vandalia, Mich. 250/D7
Vandalia, Mo. 261/J4
Vandalia, Mont. 262/J2
Vandalia, Ohio 284/B6
Vandalia, W. Va. 312/F5
Vandemere, N.C. 281/R4
Vandenberg A.F.B., Calif. 204/E9
Vanderbijl Park, S. Africa 118/D5
Vanderbilt, Mich. 250/E3
Vanderbilt, Pa. 294/C5
Vanderbilt, Texas 303/H9
Vanderburgh (co.), Ind. 227/B8
Vandergrift, Pa. 294/D4
Vanderhoof, Br. Col. 162/D5
Vanderhoof, Br. Col. 184/E3
Vanderlin (isl.), North. Terr. 88/F3
Vanderlin (isl.), North. Terr. 93/E3
Vanderpool, Texas 303/E8
Vanderpool, Va. 307/J4
Vandervoort, Ark. 202/B5
Van Diemen (cape), North. Terr 88/D2
Van Diemen (cape), North. Terr 93/A1
Van Diemen (gulf), North. Terr 88/E2
Van Diemen (gulf), North. Terr 93/B1
Vandiver, Ala. 195/F4
Vandiver, Mo. 261/J4
Vandling, Pa. 294/M2
Vändra, U.S.S.R. 53/C1
Vandura, Sask. 181/K5
Vanduser, Mo. 261/N9
Vanegas, Mexico 150/J5
Vänern (lake), Sweden 7/F3
Vänern (lake), Sweden 18/H7
Vänersborg, Sweden 18/G7
Van Etten, N.Y. 276/G6
Vanga, Kenya 115/G4
Vangaindrano, Madagascar 118/H4
Vanguard, Sask. 181/D6
Vangunu (isl.), Solomon Is. 86/D3
Van Hoa, Vietnam 72/E2
Van Horn, Texas 303/C11
Van Horne, Iowa 229/J4
Van Hornesville, N.Y. 276/L5
Vanier, Ontario 177/J2
Vanier, Québec 172/J3
Vanikoro (isl.), Solomon Is. 87/G7
Vanil Noir (mt.), Switzerland 39/D3
Vanimo, Papua N.G. 87/E6
Vanimo, Papua N.G. 85/B6
Vanino, U.S.S.R. 48/P5
Vaniyambadi, India 68/D6
Vankleek Hill, Ontario 177/K2
Van Lear, Ky. 237/R5
Vanleer, Tenn. 237/G8
Vanlue, Ohio 284/C4
Van Meter, Iowa 229/E5
Vanna, Georgia 217/F2
Vännäs, Sweden 18/L5
Vanndale, Ark. 202/J3
Vannes, France 28/B4
Van Ninh, Vietnam 72/F4
Vannøy (isl.), Norway 18/L1
Van Nuys, Calif. 204/B10
Van Orin, Ill. 222/D2
Vanoss, Okla. 288/N5
Vanrhynsdorp, S. Africa 118/B6
Van Rook, Queensland 95/B3
Vansant, Va. 307/D6
Vansbro, Sweden 18/H6
Vanscoy, Sask. 181/D4
Vansittart (isl.), N.W. Terr. 187/K3
Vansittart (isl.), Tasmania 99/E2
Vantaa, Finland 18/O6
Vantage, Sask. 181/F6
Vantage, Wash. 310/E4
Van Tassell, Wyo. 319/H3
Vanua Levu (isl.), Fiji 87/H7
Vanua Levu (isl.), Fiji 86/Q10
Vanuatu 2/T6
Vanuatu 87/G7
VANUATU 87/G7
Van Vleet, Miss. 256/G3
Vanvoorhis, W. Va. 312/G3
Van Wert, Georgia 217/B3
Van Wert, Iowa 229/F7
Van Wert (co.), Ohio 284/A4
Van Wert, Ohio 284/A4
Van Wyck, S.C. 296/F2
Van Yen, Vietnam 72/E2
Vanylven, Norway 18/E5
Van Zandt (co.), Texas 303/J5
Van Zandt, Wash. 310/C2
Vanzant, Mo. 261/H9
Var (dept.), France 28/G6
Vara, Sweden 18/H7
Vara de María, Venezuela 124/C4
Varadero, Cuba 158/D1
Varakļāni, U.S.S.R. 53/D2
Varallo Pombia, Italy 34/B2
Varamin, Iran 66/G3
Varanasi, India 54/K7
Varanasi, India 68/E3
Varangerfjord (fjord), Norway 18/Q2
Varangerfjorden (fjord), Norway 7/H1
Varangerhalvøya (pen.), Norway 18/Q1
Varano (lake), Italy 34/F3
Varaždin, Yugoslavia 45/B2
Varazze, Italy 34/B2
Varberg, Sweden 18/G8
Vardaman, Miss. 256/F3
Vardar (riv.), Greece 45/E5
Vardar (riv.), Yugoslavia 45/E5
Varde, Denmark 18/F9
Varde, Denmark 21/B6
Varde (riv.), Denmark 21/B6
Vardø, Norway 18/R1
Varel, Germany 22/C2
Varella, Mui (cape), Vietnam 72/F4
Varėna, U.S.S.R. 53/C3
Varennes, Québec 172/J4
Vareš, Yugoslavia 45/D3
Varese (prov.), Italy 34/B2
Varese, Italy 34/B2
Vargem Bonita, Brazil 135/E3
Varginha, Brazil 135/D2
Varginha, Brazil 132/E8
Varina, Iowa 229/D3
Varkaus, Finland 18/Q5
Värmland (co.), Sweden 18/H7
Varna, Bulgaria 7/G4
Varna, Bulgaria 45/J4
Varna, Ill. 222/D2
Varnado, La. 238/L5
Värnamo, Sweden 18/J8
Varnek, U.S.S.R. 52/J1
Varnell, Georgia 217/C1
Varner, Kansas 232/D4
Varney, Ontario 177/D3
Varney, W. Va. 312/B7
Varnsdorf, Czech. 41/C1
Varnville, S.C. 296/E6
Várpalota, Hungary 41/E3
Vars, Ontario 177/J2
Vartholomión, Greece 45/E7
Varto, Turkey 63/J3
Varysburg, N.Y. 276/D5
Varzarin, Kuh-e (mt.), Iran 59/E3
Varzarin, Kuh-e (mt.), Iran 66/E4
Vas (co.), Hungary 41/D3
Vasa (Vaasa), Finland 18/M5
Vasa, Minn. 255/F6
Vasa Barris (riv.), Brazil 132/G5
Vásárosnamény, Hungary 41/G2
Vascongadas (reg.), Spain 33/E1
Vashi, India 68/B7
Vashka (riv.), U.S.S.R. 52/G2
Vashon, Wash. 310/A2
Vasile Roaită, Romania 45/J3
Vasil'kov, U.S.S.R. 52/D4
Vaslui, Romania 45/H2
Vass, N.C. 281/L4
Vassalboro, Maine 243/D7
Vassalboro•, Maine 243/D7
Vassar, Kansas 232/G3
Vassar, Manitoba 179/G5
Vassar, Mich. 250/F5
Vassouras, Brazil 135/E3
Vastenjaure (lake), Sweden 18/K3
Västerås, Sweden 7/F3
Västerås, Sweden 18/K7
Västerbotten (co.), Sweden 18/K4
Västerdalälven (riv.), Sweden 18/H6
Västerhaninge, Sweden 18/H1
Västernorrland (co.), Sweden 18/K5
Västervik, Sweden 18/K8
Västmanland (co.), Sweden 18/K7
Vasto, Italy 34/E3
Vasvár, Hungary 41/D3
Vaternish (dist.), Scotland 15/B3
Vaternish (pt.), Scotland 15/B3
Vatersay (isl.), Scotland 15/A4
Vathí, Greece 45/H7
Vatican City 7/F4
VATICAN CITY 34
Vatican City, Vatican City 34/B6
Vaticano (cape), Italy 34/E5
Vatnajökull (glac.), Iceland 21/C1
Vatomandry, Madagascar 118/H3
Vatra Dornei, Romania 45/G2
Vättern (lake), Sweden 7/F3
Vättern (lake), Sweden 18/J7
Vatukoula, Fiji 86/P10
Vatulele (isl.), Fiji 86/P11
Vauclin (mt.), Martinique 161/D6
Vaucluse (dept.), France 28/F6
Vaucluse, S.C. 296/D7
Vaud (canton), Switzerland 39/B3
Vaudreuil (co.), Québec 172/C4
Vaudreuil, Québec 172/C4
Vaughan, Miss. 256/D5
Vaughan, N.C. 281/N2
Vaughan, Ontario 177/J4
Vaughan, W. Va. 312/D6
Vaughn, Mont. 262/E3
Vaughn, N. Mex. 274/D4
Vaughn, Wash. 310/C3
Vaughnsville, Ohio 284/B4
Vaupés (comm.), Colombia 126/E7
Vaupés (riv.), Colombia 120/B2
Vaupés (riv.), Colombia 126/E7
Vauxhall, Alberta 182/D4
Vauxhall, N.J. 273/A2
Vaux-sur-Sûre, Belgium 27/H9
Vava'u Group (isls.), Tonga 87/J7
Vavenby, Br. Col. 184/H4
Vavuniya, Sri Lanka 68/E7
Vawn, Sask. 181/C2
Vaxholm, Sweden 18/J1
Växjö, Sweden 7/F3
Växjö, Sweden 18/J8
Vaygach (isl.), U.S.S.R. 4/C6
Vaygach (isl.), U.S.S.R. 52/K1
Vayland, S. Dak. 298/M5
Važec, Czech. 41/E2
Vazhgort, U.S.S.R. 52/G2
Vaz-Obervaz, Switzerland 39/J3
Vázquez, Cuba 158/H3
Veagh (lake), Ireland 17/F1
Vealmoor, Texas 303/C5
Veazie•, Maine 243/F6
Veblen, S. Dak. 298/P2
Vechigen, Switzerland 39/E3
Vecht (riv.), Netherlands 27/F4
Vechta, Germany 22/C2
Vechte (riv.), Germany 22/B2
Vechte (riv.), Netherlands 27/J3
Vecsés, Hungary 41/E3
Vedaranniyam, India 68/E6
Vedia, Argentina 143/F7
Veedersburg, Ind. 227/C4
Veendam, Netherlands 27/K2
Veenendaal, Netherlands 27/G4
Veenhuizen, Netherlands 27/J2
Veere, Netherlands 27/D5
Veersche Meer (lake), Netherlands 27/D5
Vega (pt.), Alaska 196/J4
Vega, Alberta 182/C2
Vega (isl.), Norway 18/G4
Vega, Texas 303/B2
Vega Alta, P. Rico 161/D1
Vega Baja, P. Rico 161/D1
Vegafjorden (fjord), Norway 18/G4
Vegas Creek, Nev. 266/G6
Veghel, Netherlands 27/H5
Vegreville, Alberta 182/E3
Vègreville, Alta. 162/E5
Veguita, N. Mex. 274/C4
Vehar (lake), India 68/B7
Veinticinco de Agosto, Uruguay 145/A6
Veinticinco de Diciembre, Paraguay 144/D4
Veinticinco de Mayo, Argentina 143/F7
Veinticinco de Mayo, Ecuador 128/C4
Veinticinco de Mayo, Uruguay 145/C5
Veintiocho de Noviembre, Argentina 143/B7
Vejen, Denmark 21/C7
Vejer de la Frontera, Spain 33/C4
Vejle (co.), Denmark 21/C6
Vejle, Denmark 21/C6
Vejle, Denmark 18/F9
Vejle (fjord), Denmark 21/C6
Vejprty, Czech. 41/B1
Vela, La (cape), Colombia 126/D1
Vela, Roca que (cay), Colombia 126/B8
Vélan (mt.), Switzerland 39/D5
Velarde, N. Mex. 274/C2
Velas (cape), C. Rica 154/D5
Velasco, Ciego de Ávila, Cuba 158/G2
Velasco, Holguín, Cuba 158/H3
Velázquez, Uruguay 145/E5
Velda, Mo. 261/P2
Velden am Würthersee, Austria 41/C3
Veldhoven, Netherlands 27/G6
Veldrif, S. Africa 118/B6
Velence, Hungary 41/E3
Velenje, Yugoslavia 45/B2
Vélez, Colombia 126/D4
Vélez-Blanco, Spain 33/E4
Vélez-Málaga, Spain 33/E4
Vélez-Rubio, Spain 33/E4
Velhas (riv.), Brazil 132/F7
Velika Plana, Yugoslavia 45/E3
Velikaya (riv.), U.S.S.R. 48/S3
Velikaya (riv.), U.S.S.R. 52/C3
Veliki Bečkerek (Zrenjanin), Yugoslavia 45/E3
Velikiye Luki, U.S.S.R. 7/H3
Velikiye Luki, U.S.S.R. 52/D3
Velikiye Luki, U.S.S.R. 48/D4
Velikiy Ustyug, U.S.S.R. 7/J2
Velikiy Ustyug, U.S.S.R. 48/E3
Velikiy Ustyug, U.S.S.R. 52/F2
Veliko Tŭrnovo, Bulgaria 45/G4
Velikovisochnoye, U.S.S.R. 52/H1
Velizh, U.S.S.R. 52/D3
Velká Bíteš, Czech. 41/D2
Velká Bystřice, Czech. 41/D2
Veľké Kapušany, Czech. 41/G2
Velké Meziříčí, Czech. 41/D2
Veľké Rovné, Czech. 41/E2
Vella Lavella (isl.), Solomon Is. 86/D2
Velletri, Italy 34/F7
Vellore, India 68/D6
Velluda, Sierra (mt.), Chile 138/E1
Velma, Okla. 288/L6
Velp, Netherlands 27/J5
Velpen, Ind. 227/C8
Velsen, Netherlands 27/F4
Vel'sk, U.S.S.R. 52/F2
Vel'sk, U.S.S.R. 48/E3
Velten, Germany 22/E2
Veluwe (reg.), Netherlands 27/H4
Velva, N. Dak. 282/J3
Velvendós, Greece 45/F5
Vemb, Denmark 21/B5
Véménd, Hungary 41/E3
Venadillo, Colombia 126/C5
Venado, Mexico 150/J5
Venado Tuerto, Argentina 143/D3
Venafro, Italy 34/E4
Venaissin (trad. prov.), France 29
Venamo (mt.), Guyana 131/A3
Venamo, Cerro (mt.), Venezuela 124/H4
Venamo (riv.), Venezuela 124/H4
Venango, Nebr. 264/C4
Venango (co.), Pa. 294/C3
Venango, Pa. 294/B2
Vena Park, Queensland 95/B3
Vence, France 28/G6
Venda (bantustan), S. Africa 102/F7
Venda (rep.), S. Africa 118/E4
Vendas Novas, Portugal 33/B3
Vendée (dept.), France 28/C4
Vendôme, France 28/D4
Vendrell, Spain 33/G2
Venedocia, Ohio 284/B4
Venedy, Ill. 222/D5
Veneta, Oreg. 291/D3
Venetie, Alaska 196/J1
Veneto (reg.), Italy 34/D3
Venezia (Venice), Italy 34/D2
Venezuela 2/F5
Venezuela 120/C2
VENEZUELA 124
Venezuela, Cuba 158/F2
Venezuela (gulf), Venezuela 120/B1
Venezuela (gulf), Venezuela 124/C2
Vengurla, India 68/C5
Veniaminof (crater), Alaska 196/F3
Venice, Alberta 182/E2
Venice, Calif. 204/B11
Venice, Fla. 212/D4
Venice, Ill. 222/A2
Venice (prov.), Italy 34/D2
Venice, Italy 7/F4
Venice, Italy 34/D2
Venice (gulf), Italy 34/D2
Venice, La. 238/M8
Venice, Utah 304/C5
Vénissieux, France 28/F5
Venkatagiri, India 68/D6
Venlo, Netherlands 27/J6
Venn, Sask. 181/F4
Venosa, Italy 34/E4
Venraij, Netherlands 27/H6
Venta (riv.), U.S.S.R. 53/B2
Venterspos, S. Africa 118/G6
Ventimiglia, Italy 34/A3
Ventnor, England 10/F5
Ventnor, England 13/F7
Ventnor City, N.J. 273/E5
Ventotene (isl.), Italy 34/D4
Ventspils, U.S.S.R. 48/B4
Ventspils, U.S.S.R. 53/A2
Ventspils, U.S.S.R. 52/B3
Ventuari (riv.), Venezuela 124/E5
Ventura (co.), Calif. 204/F9
Ventura, Calif. 204/F9
Ventura, Iowa 229/F2
Venturia, N. Dak. 282/L7
Venus, Fla. 212/E4
Venus (pt.), Fr. Poly. 86/T12
Venus, Pa. 294/C3
Venus (bay), Victoria 97/C6
Venustiano Carranza, Mexico 150/N8
Venustiano Carranza (res.), Mexico 150/J3
Ver (riv.), England 13/H7
Vera, Argentina 143/F5
Vera, Ill. 222/D4
Vera, Okla. 288/P2
Vera (lag.), Paraguay 144/D5
Vera, Spain 33/F4
Vera, Texas 303/E4
Vera, Va. 307/L6
Vera Cruz, Brazil 135/B3
Vera Cruz, Ind. 227/G3
Veracruz (state), Mexico 150/L7
Veracruz, Mexico 150/Q1
Veracruz, Mexico 2/E5
Veracruz, Mexico 146/J8
Veradale, Wash. 310/H3
Veragua Abajo, Dom. Rep. 158/E5
Veras, Uruguay 145/C2
Veraval, India 68/C4
Verbania, Italy 34/B2
Verbena, Ala. 195/E5
Verboort, Oreg. 291/A2
Vercelli (prov.), Italy 34/B2
Vercelli, Italy 34/B2
Verchères (co.), Québec 172/J4
Verchères, Québec 172/J4
Verçinin Tepesi (mt.), Turkey 63/J2
Verda, Ky. 237/P7
Verda, La. 238/E3
Verde (riv.), Ariz. 188/D4
Verde (riv.), Ariz. 198/D5
Verde (cay), Bahamas 156/C2
Verde (riv.), Brazil 132/C7
Verde (riv.), Mexico 150/F3
Verde (riv.), Mexico 150/L8
Verde (riv.), Paraguay 144/C3
Verde (cape), Senegal 102/A3
Verde (cape), Senegal 106/A6
Verde Island (passage), Philippines 82/C4
Verdel, Nebr. 264/F2
Verden, Okla. 288/K4
Verden, Germany 22/C2
Verdery, S.C. 296/C3
Verdi, Minn. 255/B6
Verdi, Nev. 266/B3
Verdigre, Nebr. 264/F2
Verdigris (riv.), Kansas 232/G5
Verdigris, Okla. 288/P2
Verdigris (riv.), Okla. 288/P2
Verdinho (riv.), Brazil 132/D7
Verdon, Nebr. 264/J4
Verdon, S. Dak. 298/N3
Verdun, Québec 172/H4
Verdún, Uruguay 145/D5
Verdun-sur-Meuse, France 28/F3
Verdunville, W. Va. 312/B7
Vereeniging, S. Africa 102/E7
Vereeniging, S. Africa 118/D5
Veregin, Sask. 181/K4
Verendrye, N. Dak. 282/J3
Vereshchagino, U.S.S.R. 52/H3
Verga (cape), Guinea 106/B6
Vergara, Argentina 143/H7
Vergara, Spain 33/E1
Vergara, Uruguay 145/E3
Vergas, Minn. 255/C4
Vergeletto, Switzerland 39/G4
Vergennes, Ill. 222/D6
Vergennes, Vt. 268/A3
Veribest, Texas 303/D6
Verín, Spain 33/C2
Veríssimo, Brazil 135/B1
Verkhnevilyuysk, U.S.S.R. 48/N3
Verkhnyaya Toyma, U.S.S.R. 52/G2
Verkhoyansk, U.S.S.R. 2/R2
Verkhoyansk, U.S.S.R. 4/C3
Verkhoyansk, U.S.S.R. 48/N3
Verkhoyansk, U.S.S.R. 54/P3
Verkhoyansk (range), U.S.S.R. 4/C3
Verkhoyansk (range), U.S.S.R. 48/N3
Verkhoyansk (range), U.S.S.R. 54/O3
Verkniy At-Uryakh, U.S.S.R. 48/Q3
Verlo, Sask. 181/C5
Vermejo (riv.), N. Mex. 274/E2
Vermejo Park, N. Mex. 274/D2
Vermilion, Alberta 182/E3
Vermilion (riv.), Alberta 182/E3
Vermilion (cliffs), Ariz. 198/D2
Vermilion (co.), Ill. 222/F3
Vermilion, Ill. 222/F4
Vermilion (riv.), Ind. 227/B4
Vermilion (par.), La. 238/F7
Vermilion (bay), La. 238/F7
Vermilion (lake), Minn. 188/H1
Vermilion (lake), Minn. 255/F3
Vermilion (range), Minn. 255/F3
Vermilion (riv.), Minn. 255/F2
Vermilion, Ohio 284/F3
Vermilion (riv.), Ohio 284/F3
Vermilion (hills), Sask. 181/E5
Vermilion (cliffs), Utah 304/B6
Vermilion Bay, Ontario 177/G4
Vermilion Bay, Ontario 175/B3
Vermilion Grove, Ill. 222/F4
Vermillion (co.), Ind. 227/C5
Vermillion, Kansas 232/F2
Vermillion, Minn. 255/F6
Vermillion, S. Dak. 298/R8
Vermillion (riv.), S. Dak. 298/P6
Vermillion (riv.), Québec 172/D2
Vermont 188/M2
VERMONT 268
Vermont, Ill. 222/C3
Vermont (state), U.S. 146/L5
Vermontville, Mich. 250/E6
Vernal, Utah 304/E3
Vernayaz, Switzerland 39/D4
Verndale, Minn. 255/C4
Verndon, Minn. 255/E4
Verner, Ontario 177/D1
Verneuil-sur-Avre, France 28/D3
Vernon, Ala. 195/B3
Vernon, Ariz. 198/F4
Vernon, Br. Col. 162/E5
Vernon, Br. Col. 184/H5
Vernon, Colo. 208/P3
Vernon•, Conn. 210/F1
Vernon, Fla. 212/C6
Vernon, France 28/D3
Vernon, Ill. 222/D5
Vernon, Ind. 227/F7
Vernon, Ky. 237/L7
Vernon (par.), La. 238/D4
Vernon, La. 238/E2
Vernon (lake), La. 238/D4
Vernon, Mich. 250/F6
Vernon (co.), Mo. 261/D7
Vernon, N.J. 273/E1
Vernon, Okla. 288/P4
Vernon, Ontario 177/J2
Vernon (lake), Ontario 177/E2
Vernon, Pr. Edward I. 168/E2
Vernon, Texas 303/E3
Vernon, Utah 304/B3
Vernon•, Vt. 268/B6
Vernon (co.), Wis. 317/E8
Vernonburg, Georgia 217/K7
Vernon Center, Conn. 210/F1
Vernon Center, Minn. 255/D7
Vernon Fork (creek), Ind. 227/F7
Vernon Hill, Va. 307/K7
Vernon Hills, Ill. 222/B4
Vernonia, Oreg. 291/D2
Vero Beach, Fla. 212/F4
Veroli, Italy 34/D4
Verona, Ill. 222/E2
Verona (prov.), Italy 34/C2
Verona, Italy 34/C2

Wallace 465

Visp, Switzerland 39/E4
Visp (riv.), Switzerland 39/E4
Vissoie, Switzerland 39/E4
Vista, Calif. 204/H10
Vista, Manitoba 179/B4
Vista, Mo. 261/E7
Vista Hermosa, Cuba 158/G3
Vistula, Ind. 227/F1
Vistula (riv.), Poland 7/F3
Vistula (riv.), Poland 47/D2
Vistula (spit), Poland 47/D1
Vit (riv.), Bulgaria 45/G4
Vita, Manitoba 179/F5
Vitali (isl.), Philippines 82/D7
Vitebsk, U.S.S.R. 7/H3
Vitebsk, U.S.S.R. 52/C3
Vitebsk, U.S.S.R. 48/D4
Viterbo (prov.), Italy 34/C3
Viterbo, Italy 34/C3
Vitiaz (str.), Papua N.G. 85/B7
Vitiaz (str.), Papua N.G. 86/A2
Vitichi, Bolivia 136/C7
Vitigudino, Spain 33/C2
Viti Levu (isl.), Fiji 87/H7
Viti Levu (isl.), Fiji 86/P11
Vitim (riv.), U.S.S.R. 54/N4
Vitim (riv.), U.S.S.R. 48/M4
Vitimskiy, U.S.S.R. 48/M4
Vitkov, Czech. 41/D2
Vitor, Quebrado (riv.), Chile 138/A1
Vitor, Peru 128/G11
Vitor (riv.), Peru 128/F11
Vitória, Brazil 120/F5
Vitória, Brazil 132/G8
Vitoria, Spain 33/E1
Vitoria, Spain 7/D4
Vitória da Conquista, Brazil 120/E4
Vitória da Conquista, Brazil 132/F6
Vitória de Santo Antão, Brazil 132/G4
Vitória de Santo Antão, Brazil 120/F3
Vitré, France 28/C3
Vitry-le-François, France 28/F3
Vitry-sur-Seine, France 28/B2
Vittangi, Sweden 18/M3
Vittel, France 28/F3
Vittoria, Italy 34/E6
Vittoria, Ontario 177/D5
Vittorio Veneto, Italy 34/D1
Vitu (isls.), Papua N.G. 86/B2
Vivero, Spain 33/C1
Vivian, La. 238/B1
Vivian, S. Dak. 298/J6
Vivian, W. Va. 312/D8
Vivorillo (cays), Honduras 154/F3
Vixen, La. 238/F2
Vizagapatam (Visakhapatnam), India 68/E5
Vizcaino (cape), Calif. 204/B4
Vizcaya (prov.), Spain 33/E1
Vize, Turkey 63/B2
Vizianagaram, India 68/E5
Vizille, France 28/F5
Vizinga, U.S.S.R. 52/G2
Viziru, Romania 45/H3
Vizovice, Czech. 41/D2
Vizzini, Italy 34/E6
Vlaardingen, Netherlands 27/E5
Vladimir, U.S.S.R. 7/J3
Vladimir, U.S.S.R. 48/D4
Vladimir, U.S.S.R. 52/F3
Vladimir-Volynskiy, U.S.S.R. 52/B4
Vladivostok, U.S.S.R. 54/P5
Vladivostok, U.S.S.R. 2/R3
Vladivostok, U.S.S.R. 48/O5
Vlagtwedde, Netherlands 27/L3
Vlasenica, Yugoslavia 45/D3
Vlašim, Czech. 41/C2
Vleteren, Belgium 27/B7
Vlieland (isl.), Netherlands 27/F2
Vliestroom (str.), Netherlands 27/G2
Vliets, Kansas 232/F2
Vlijmen, Netherlands 27/G5
Vlissingen (Flushing), Netherlands 27/C6
Vlorë, Albania 45/D5
Vltava (riv.), Czech. 41/C2
Voca, Texas 303/E7
Vöcklabruck, Austria 41/B2
Voda, Kansas 232/C2
Vodl (lake), U.S.S.R. 52/E2
Vodňany, Czech. 41/C2
Vogar, Manitoba 179/D4
Vogel Center, Mich. 250/E4
Vogelkop (Doberai) (pen.), Indonesia 85/J6
Vogelsberg (mts.), Germany 22/C3
Voghera, Italy 34/B2
Voglers Cove, Nova Scotia 168/D4
Voh, New Caled. 86/G4
Vohibinany, Madagascar 118/H3
Vohimarina (Vohémar), Madagascar 118/J2
Vohimena (cape), Madagascar 102/G7
Vohimena (cape), Madagascar 118/G5
Vohipeno, Madagascar 118/H4
Voi, Kenya 115/G4
Voi, Kenya 102/F5
Voil, Loch (lake), Scotland 15/D4
Voiron, France 28/F5
Voisey (bay), Newf. 166/B2
Voitsberg, Austria 41/C3
Voïviïs (lake), Greece 45/F6
Vojens, Denmark 21/C7
Vojmsjön (lake), Sweden 18/J4
Vojnice, Czech. 41/E3
Vojvodina (aut. prov.), Yugoslavia 45/D3
Volador, Colombia 126/C3
Volant, Pa. 294/B3
Volary, Czech. 41/B2
Volborg, Mont. 262/L5
Volcano, Calif. 204/E5
Volcano, Hawaii 218/J6
Volcano (isls.), Japan 87/E3
Volcano (isls.), Japan 81/M4
Volda, Norway 18/E5
Volendam-Edam, Netherlands 27/G4
Volga, Iowa 229/L3
Volga, S. Dak. 298/R5
Volga (riv.), U.S.S.R. 7/J4
Volga (riv.), U.S.S.R. 2/M3
Volga (riv.), U.S.S.R. 48/E5
Volga (riv.), U.S.S.R. 52/G5
Volga, W. Va. 312/F4
Volga-Don (canal), U.S.S.R. 52/F5
Volgodonsk, U.S.S.R. 52/F5
Volgograd, U.S.S.R. 2/M3
Volgograd, U.S.S.R. 7/J4
Volgograd, U.S.S.R. 48/E5
Volgograd, U.S.S.R. 52/F5
Volgograd (res.), U.S.S.R. 52/G5
Volin, S. Dak. 298/P8
Völkermarkt, Austria 41/C3
Volkhov, U.S.S.R. 52/D3
Volkhov (riv.), U.S.S.R. 52/D3
Völklingen, Germany 22/B4
Volkovysk, U.S.S.R. 52/B4
Volksrust, S. Africa 118/D5
Volney, Mich. 250/D5
Volney, Va. 307/F7
Volochanka, U.S.S.R. 48/K2
Vologda, U.S.S.R. 7/J3
Vologda, U.S.S.R. 48/E4
Vologda, U.S.S.R. 52/F3
Vólos, Greece 7/G5
Vólos, Greece 45/F6
Vol'sk, U.S.S.R. 7/J3
Vol'sk, U.S.S.R. 52/G4
Volta (lake), Ghana 102/B4
Volta (riv.), Ghana 102/C4
Volta (lake), Ghana 106/D7
Volta (riv.), Ghana 106/E7
Volta Grande (res.), Brazil 135/B1
Voltaire, N. Dak. 282/J3
Volta Redonda, Brazil 120/E5
Volta Redonda, Brazil 132/E8
Volta Redonda, Brazil 135/D3
Volterra, Italy 34/C3
Volturno (riv.), Italy 34/E4
Voluntown•, Conn. 210/H2
Volusia (co.), Fla. 212/E2
Vólvi (lake), Greece 45/F5
Volyně, Czech. 41/B2
Volyn Oblast, U.S.S.R. 52/C4
Volzhsk, U.S.S.R. 52/G3
Volzhskiy, U.S.S.R. 7/J4
Volzhskiy, U.S.S.R. 52/G5
Vom, Nigeria 106/F7
Vona, Colo. 208/O4
Vonda, Sask. 181/F3
Vónitsa, Greece 45/E6
Vonore, Tenn. 237/N9
Von Ormy, Texas 303/J11
Voorburg, Netherlands 27/E4
Voorhees•, N.J. 273/B3
Voorheesville, N.Y. 276/M5
Voorhies, Iowa 229/J4
Voorne (isl.), Netherlands 27/D5
Voorst, Netherlands 27/J4
Vopnafjürdhur (fjord), Iceland 21/D1
Vorab (mt.), Switzerland 39/H3
Vorarlberg (prov.), Austria 41/A3
Vorbasse, Denmark 21/B6
Vorden, Netherlands 27/J4
Vordernberg, Austria 41/C3
Vorderrhein (riv.), Switzerland 39/G3
Vordingborg, Denmark 21/E7
Vordingborg, Denmark 18/G9
Vorgod (riv.), Denmark 21/B6
Vorkuta, U.S.S.R. 4/C6
Vorkuta, U.S.S.R. 7/L2
Vorkuta, U.S.S.R. 52/K1
Vorkuta, U.S.S.R. 48/G3
Vormsi (isl.), U.S.S.R. 53/B1
Vorona (riv.), U.S.S.R. 52/F4
Voronezh, U.S.S.R. 7/H3
Voronezh, U.S.S.R. 52/E4
Voronezh, U.S.S.R. 48/E4
Voroshilovgrad (Lugansk), U.S.S.R. 7/H4
Voroshilovgrad (Lugansk), U.S.S.R. 52/E5
Voroshilovgrad (Lugansk), U.S.S.R. 48/E5
Vorskla (riv.), U.S.S.R. 52/E4
Vorst (Forest), Belgium 27/B9
Võrtsjärv (lake), U.S.S.R. 53/D1
Võru, U.S.S.R. 52/C2
Võru, U.S.S.R. 53/D2
Vosges (dept.), France 28/G3
Vosges (mts.), France 28/G3
Voskresensk, U.S.S.R. 52/E3
Voss, N. Dak. 282/R3
Voss, Norway 18/E6
Vossburg, Miss. 256/F7
Vostochnyy, U.S.S.R. 48/O5
Vostok (isl.), Kiribati 2/B6
Vostok (isl.), Kiribati 87/L7
Votamo (riv.), Venezuela 124/F6
Votice, Czech. 41/C2
Votkinsk, U.S.S.R. 48/F4
Votkinsk, U.S.S.R. 52/H3
Votuporanga, Brazil 135/B2
Vouvry, Switzerland 39/C4
Voúxa (cape), Greece 45/F8
Vouziers, France 28/F3
Voyageurs Nat'l Park, Minn. 255/F2
Voy-Vozh, U.S.S.R. 48/F3
Voy-Vozh, U.S.S.R. 52/H2
Vozhe (lake), U.S.S.R. 52/F2
Vozhega, U.S.S.R. 52/F2
Vozhma, U.S.S.R. 52/G3
Voznesensk, U.S.S.R. 52/D5
Vrå, Denmark 21/C3
Vrable, Czech. 41/E2
Vracov, Czech. 41/D2
Vrangelya (isl.), U.S.S.R. 54/U2
Vranje, Yugoslavia 45/F4
Vranov nad Teplou, Czech. 41/F2
Vratsa, Bulgaria 45/F4
Vrbas, Yugoslavia 45/D3
Vrbas (riv.), Yugoslavia 45/C3
Vrbno pod Pradědem, Czech. 41/D1
Vrbovce, Czech. 41/D1
Vrbové, Czech. 41/D2
Vrchlabí, Czech. 41/C1
Vrede, S. Africa 118/D5
Vredenburg, S. Africa 118/B6
Vredenburgh, Ala. 195/D7
Vredendal, S. Africa 118/B6
Vreed-en-Hoop, Guyana 131/B2
Vresse-sur-Semois, Belgium 27/F9
Vriezenveen, Netherlands 27/K4
Vrondádhes, Greece 45/G6
Vršac, Yugoslavia 45/E3
Vrútky, Czech. 41/E2
Vryburg, S. Africa 118/C5
Vryheid, S. Africa 118/E5
Vsetin, Czech. 41/D2
Vsevidof (mt.), Alaska 196/E4
Vuadens, Switzerland 39/C3
Vučitrn, Yugoslavia 45/E4
Vught, Netherlands 27/G5
Vukovar, Yugoslavia 45/D3
Vulcan, Alberta 182/D4
Vulcan, Mich. 250/B3
Vulcan, Mo. 261/L8
Vulcan, W. Va. 312/B7
Vulcano (isl.), Italy 34/E5
Vu Liet, Vietnam 72/E3
Vung Tau, Vietnam 72/E5
Vuollerim, Sweden 18/M3
Vuolvojaure (lake), Sweden 18/L3
Vuotso, Finland 18/P2
Vya, Nev. 266/B1
Vyatka (riv.), U.S.S.R. 52/H3
Vyatskiye Polyany, U.S.S.R. 52/H3
Vyazemskiy, U.S.S.R. 48/O5
Vyaz'ma, U.S.S.R. 52/D3
Vyborg, U.S.S.R. 7/G2
Vyborg, U.S.S.R. 52/C2
Vyborg, U.S.S.R. 48/C3
Vychegda (riv.), U.S.S.R. 52/G2
Východočeský (reg.), Czech. 41/C1
Východoslovenský (reg.), Czech. 41/F2
Vyg (lake), U.S.S.R. 52/E2
Vyksa, U.S.S.R. 52/F3
Vym' (riv.), U.S.S.R. 52/H2
Vyshniy Volochek, U.S.S.R. 7/H2
Vyshniy Volochek, U.S.S.R. 52/D3
Vyshniy Volochek, U.S.S.R. 48/D4
Vyškov, Czech. 41/D2
Vysoké Mýto, Czech. 41/D2
Vysoké Tatry, Czech. 41/F2
Vyšší Brod, Czech. 41/C2
Vytegra, U.S.S.R. 52/E2

W

Wa, Ghana 106/D6
Waal (riv.), Netherlands 27/G5
Waalre, Netherlands 27/G6
Waalwijk, Netherlands 27/F5
Waarschoot, Belgium 27/D6
Waas (mt.), Utah 304/E5
Waasis, New Bruns. 170/D3
Wabamun, Alberta 182/C3
Waban, Mass. 249/B7
Wabana, Newf. 166/D2
Wabaningo, Mich. 250/C5
Wabasca, Alberta 182/D2
Wabasca (riv.), Alberta 182/C1
Wabasca (riv.), Alta. 162/E4
Wabash (riv.) 188/J3
Wabash, Ark. 202/J5
Wabash (co.), Ill. 222/F5
Wabash (riv.), Ill. 222/F5
Wabash (co.), Ind. 227/F3
Wabash, Ind. 227/F3
Wabash (riv.), Ind. 227/B7
Wabash, Ohio 284/A4
Wabash (riv.), Ohio 284/A5
Wabasha (co.), Minn. 255/F6
Wabasha, Minn. 255/G6
Wabasso, Fla. 212/F4
Wabasso, Minn. 255/C6
Wabatawangang (lake), Minn. 255/D3
Wabaunsee (co.), Kansas 232/F3
Wabaunsee, Kansas 232/F2
Wabbaseka, Ark. 202/G5
Wabeno, Wis. 317/J5
Wabi (riv.), Ethiopia 111/H6
Wabigoon, Ontario 175/B3
Wabigoon, Ontario 177/G5
Wabi Shebelle (riv.) 102/G4
Wabi Shebelle (riv.), Ethiopia 111/H6
Wabowden, Manitoba 179/J3
Wąbrzeźno, Poland 47/D2
Wabuk (pt.), Ontario 175/D1
Wabush, Newf. 166/A3
Wabush, Newf. 162/K5
Wabuska, Nev. 266/B3
Waccamaw (lake), N.C. 281/N6
Waccamaw (riv.), N.C. 281/M7
Waccamaw (riv.), S.C. 296/J5
Waccasassa (bay), Fla. 212/D2
Waccasassa (riv.), Fla. 212/D2
Wachapreague, Va. 307/S5
Wachapreague (inlet), Va. 307/T6
Wachtebeke, Belgium 27/D6
Wachusett (mt.), Mass. 249/G3
Wachusett (res.), Mass. 249/G3
Wacissa, Fla. 212/B1
Waco, Georgia 217/B3
Waco, Ky. 237/N5
Waco, Mo. 261/C8
Waco, Nebr. 264/G4
Waco, N.C. 281/G4
Waco, Texas 188/G4
Waco, Texas 146/J6
Waco, Texas 303/G6
Waconda (lake), Kansas 232/D2
Waconia, Minn. 255/E6
Wadai (reg.), Chad 111/D5
Waddamana, Tasmania 99/C4
Waddan, Libya 102/D2
Waddan, Libya 111/C2
Waddell, Ariz. 198/C5
Waddenzee (sound), Netherlands 27/G2
Waddington (mt.), Br. Col. 162/D5
Waddington (mt.), Br. Col. 184/E4
Waddington, N.Y. 276/K1
Waddy, Ky. 237/L4
Wade, Miss. 256/G9
Wade (lake), Newf. 166/A3
Wade, N.C. 281/M4
Wade, Okla. 288/O7
Wadebridge, England 13/C7
Wade-Hampton, S.C. 296/C2
Wadena, Ind. 227/C3
Wadena, Iowa 229/K3
Wadena (co.), Minn. 255/D4
Wadena, Minn. 255/C4
Wadena, Sask. 181/H4
Wädenswil, Switzerland 39/G2
Wadesboro, La. 238/M2
Wadesboro, N.C. 281/J5
Wadestown, W. Va. 312/F3
Wadesville, Ind. 227/B8
Wadeville, N.C. 281/J4
Wadhams, N.Y. 276/N2
Wadi Dra, Morocco 102/B2
Wadi es Sir, Jordan 65/D4
Wadi Halfa, Sudan 111/F3
Wadi Musa, Jordan 65/E5
Wading (riv.), N.J. 273/D4
Wading River, N.Y. 276/P9
Wadley, Ala. 195/G4
Wadley, Georgia 217/H5
Wadmalaw (isl.), S.C. 296/G6
Wad Medani, Sudan 111/F5
Wad Medani, Sudan 59/B7
Wad Medani, Sudan 102/F3
Wadowice, Poland 47/D4
Wadsworth, Ala. 195/E5
Wadsworth, Ill. 222/B4
Wadsworth, Nev. 266/B3
Wadsworth, Ohio 284/G3
Wadsworth, Texas 303/J9
Waelder, Texas 303/G8
Wagait Aboriginal Res., North. Terr. 93/B2
Wagarville, Ala. 195/B8
Wagener, S.C. 296/E4
Wageningen, Netherlands 27/H5
Wageningen, Suriname 131/C3
Wager (bay), N.W.T. 146/J3
Wager (bay), N.W.T. 162/G2
Wager (bay), N.W.T. 187/K3
Wagga Wagga, Australia 87/E9
Wagga Wagga, N.S. Wales 88/H7
Wagga Wagga, N.S. Wales 97/D4
Waggoner, Ill. 222/D4
Waggrakine, W. Australia 92/A5
Wagin, W. Australia 88/B6
Wagin, W. Australia 92/B2
Wagner, Alberta 182/C2
Wagner, Mont. 262/H2
Wagner, S. Dak. 298/N7
Wagoner (co.), Okla. 288/P3
Wagoner, Okla. 288/R3
Wagon Mound, N. Mex. 274/E2
Wagontire, Oreg. 291/H4
Wagon Wheel Gap, Colo. 208/F7
Wagram, N.C. 281/L5
Wągrowiec, Poland 47/C2
Wah, Pakistan 68/C2
Wahai, Indonesia 85/H6
Wahalak, Miss. 256/G5
Wahiawa, Hawaii 218/E2
Wahiawa, Hawaii 188/F5
Wahkiacus, Wash. 310/D5
Wahkiakum (co.), Wash. 310/B4
Wahkon, Minn. 255/E4
Wahlern, Switzerland 39/D3
Wahoo, Nebr. 264/H3
Wahpeton, Iowa 229/C2
Wahpeton, N. Dak. 188/G1
Wahpeton, N. Dak. 282/S7
Wahsatch, Utah 304/C2
Wah Wah (mts.), Utah 304/A5
Wahwashkesh (lake), Ontario 177/D2
Wahweap (creek), Utah 304/C6
Wai, Poulo (isls.), Vietnam 72/E4
Waiakoa, Hawaii 218/J2
Waialae, Hawaii 218/D4
Waialeale (mt.), Hawaii 218/C1
Waialee, Hawaii 218/E1
Waialua, Hawaii 188/F5
Waialua, Molokai, Hawaii 218/H1
Waialua, Oahu, Hawaii 218/E1
Waianae, Hawaii 218/D2
Waiau, N. Zealand 100/D5
Waiau (riv.), N. Zealand 100/A6
Waidhofen an der Thaya, Austria 41/C2
Waidhofen an der Ybbs, Austria 41/C3
Waidsboro, Va. 307/J7
Waigama, Indonesia 85/H6
Waigeo (isl.), Indonesia 85/J5
Waihee, Hawaii 218/J2
Waiheke (isl.), N. Zealand 100/E2
Waihi, N. Zealand 100/E2
Waikabubak, Indonesia 85/F7
Waikanae, N. Zealand 100/E4
Waikane, Hawaii 218/F2
Waikapu, Hawaii 218/J2
Waikaremoana (lake), N. Zealand 100/F3
Waikari, N. Zealand 100/D5
Waikato (riv.), N. Zealand 100/E2
Waikawa, N. Zealand 100/B7
Waikerie, S. Australia 94/F6
Waikii, Hawaii 218/H4
Waikiki, Hawaii 218/C4
Waikiki (beach), Hawaii 218/C4
Waikouaiti, N. Zealand 100/C6
Wailau, Hawaii 218/H1
Wailea, Hawaii 218/J4
Wailea, Maui, Hawaii 218/J2
Wailua, Hawaii 218/D2
Wailuku, Hawaii 218/J2
Wailuku, Hawaii 188/F5
Wailuku (riv.), Hawaii 218/J5
Waimakariri (riv.), N. Zealand 100/D5
Waimalu, Hawaii 218/B3
Waimanalo, Hawaii 218/F2
Waimanalo Beach., Hawaii 218/F2
Waimangaroa, N. Zealand 100/C4
Waimate, N. Zealand 100/C6
Waimea (Kamuela), Hawaii 218/G3
Waimea, Kauai, Hawaii 218/B2
Waimea, Oahu, Hawaii 218/E1
Waimea (bay), Hawaii 218/B2
Waimea (riv.), Hawaii 218/C2
Waimes, Belgium 27/J8
Wainaku, Hawaii 218/J5
Wainfleet, Ontario 177/E4
Wainfleet All Saints, England 13/H4
Waingapu, Indonesia 85/G7
Waini (riv.), Guyana 131/B2
Wainiha, Hawaii 218/C1
Wainiha (riv.), Hawaii 218/C1
Wainuiomata, N. Zealand 100/B3
Wainui-o-mata (riv.), N. Zealand 100/B3
Wainwright, Alaska 196/F1
Wainwright, Alberta 182/E3
Wainwright, Ohio 284/G5
Wainwright, Okla. 288/R3
Wainwright, U.S. 4/B18
Waiohinu, Hawaii 218/G7
Waipa (riv.), N. Zealand 100/E2
Waipahu, Hawaii 188/F5
Waipahu, Hawaii 218/A3
Waipara, N. Zealand 100/D5
Waipawa, N. Zealand 100/F3
Waipio, Hawaii 218/H3
Waipio (bay), Hawaii 218/H3
Waipio (pen.), Hawaii 218/A3
Waipio (pt.), Hawaii 218/A4
Waipio Acres, Hawaii 218/E2
Waipiro Bay, N. Zealand 100/G3
Waipukurau, N. Zealand 100/F4
Wairau (riv.), N. Zealand 100/D4
Wairoa, N. Zealand 100/F3
Wairoa (riv.), N. Zealand 100/E1
Waitakere, N. Zealand 100/B1
Waitakere (range), N. Zealand 100/A1
Waitaki (riv.), N. Zealand 100/C6
Waitangi, N. Zealand 100/D7
Waitara, N. Zealand 100/E3
Waite•, Maine 243/H5
Waite Hill, Ohio 284/H2
Waitemata, N. Zealand 100/B1
Waitemata (harb.), N. Zealand 100/B1
Waite Park, Minn. 255/D5
Waiteville, W. Va. 312/F8
Waitotara, N. Zealand 100/E3
Waits (riv.), Vt. 268/C3
Waitsburg, Wash. 310/G4
Waitsfield•, Vt. 268/B3
Waits River, Vt. 268/C3
Waitville, Sask. 181/F3
Waiuku, N. Zealand 100/E2
Waiyevu, Fiji 86/R10
Wajabula, Indonesia 85/H5
Wajima, Japan 81/H5
Wajir, Kenya 115/H3
Wajir, Kenya 102/F4
Waka, Ethiopia 111/G6
Waka, Texas 303/D1
Waka, Zaire 115/D3
Wakarusa, Ind. 227/F1
Wakarusa, Kansas 232/G3
Wakasa, Japan 81/G6
Wakasa (bay), Japan 81/G6
Wakatipu (lake), N. Zealand 100/B6
Wakaw, Sask. 181/F3
Wakaw Lake, Sask. 181/F3
Wakayama (pref.), Japan 81/G6
Wakayama, Japan 54/P6
Wakayama, Japan 81/G6
Wakde (isl.), Indonesia 85/K6
Wake (co.), N.C. 281/M3
Wake (isl.), Pacific 87/G4
WaKeeney, Kansas 232/C2
Wakefield, England 10/F4
Wakefield, England 13/J2
Wakefield, Kansas 232/E2
Wakefield, La. 238/H5
Wakefield•, Mass. 249/C5
Wakefield, Mich. 250/F2
Wakefield, Nebr. 264/H2
Wakefield•, N.H. 268/F4
Wakefield, Ohio 284/E8
Wakefield, Va. 307/O7
Wakefield-Peace Dale, R.I. 249/J7
Wake Forest, N.C. 281/M3
Wakema, Burma 72/B3
Wakeman, Ohio 284/F3
Wakenda, Mo. 261/F4
Wake Village, Texas 303/K4
Wakita, Okla. 288/L1
Wakkanai, Japan 81/K1
Wakonda, S. Dak. 298/P7
Wakool, N.S. Wales 97/C4
Wakopa, Manitoba 179/C5
Wakpala, S. Dak. 298/H2
Waku Kungo, Angola 115/C6
Wakulla (co.), Fla. 212/B1
Wakulla, Fla. 212/B1
Wakwekobi (lake), Ontario 177/A1
Wala, Kuh-i- (mt.), Afghanistan 59/H3
Walbridge, Ohio 284/C2
Wałbrzych (prov.), Poland 47/C3
Wałbrzych, Poland 47/C3
Walcha, N.S. Wales 97/F2
Walchensee (lake), Germany 22/D5
Walcheren (isl.), Netherlands 27/C5
Walcott, Ark. 202/J1
Walcott, Br. Col. 184/D3
Walcott (lake), Idaho 220/E7
Walcott, Iowa 229/M5
Walcott, N. Dak. 282/R6
Walcott, Wyo. 319/F4
Walcourt, Belgium 27/F8
Wałcz, Poland 47/C2
Wald, Switzerland 39/G2
Waldeck, Sask. 181/D5
Walden, Colo. 208/G1
Walden, Georgia 217/E5
Walden, Ky. 237/N7
Walden (pond), Mass. 249/A6
Walden, N.Y. 276/M7
Walden, Ontario 175/D3
Walden, Ontario 177/J5
Walden, Tenn. 237/L10
Walden•, Vt. 268/C3
Waldenburg, Ark. 202/J2
Waldenburg (Wałbrzych), Poland 47/C3
Waldenburg, Switzerland 39/E2
Walden Heights, Vt. 268/C3
Waldersee, Manitoba 179/D4
Waldheim, Germany 22/E3
Waldheim, La. 238/L5
Waldheim, Sask. 181/E3
Waldia, Ethiopia 111/G5
Waldkirch, Switzerland 39/H2
Waldkirch, Germany 22/B4
Waldkraiburg, Germany 22/E4
Waldo, Ala. 195/F4
Waldo, Ark. 202/D7
Waldo, Br. Col. 184/K5
Waldo, Fla. 212/D2
Waldo, Kansas 232/D2
Waldo (co.), Maine 243/E6
Waldo•, Maine 243/E7
Waldo, Ohio 284/D5
Waldo (lake), Oreg. 291/E4
Waldo, Wis. 317/L8
Waldoboro, Maine 243/E7
Waldoboro•, Maine 243/E7
Waldorf, Md. 245/L6
Waldorf, Minn. 255/E7
Waldport, Oreg. 291/C3
Waldron, Ark. 202/B4
Waldron, Ind. 227/F6
Waldron, Kansas 232/D4
Waldron, Mich. 250/E7
Waldron, Mo. 261/O5
Waldron, Sask. 181/J5
Waldron, Wash. 310/B2
Waldrup, Miss. 256/F7
Waldsassen, Germany 22/E3
Waldshut-Tiengen, Germany 22/C5
Waldwick, N.J. 273/B1
Waldwick, Wis. 317/G10
Walensee (lake), Switzerland 39/H2
Walenstadt, Switzerland 39/H2
Wales, Alaska 196/E1
Wales, Alaska 188/C5
Wales•, Mass. 249/F4
Wales, Minn. 255/G3
Wales, N. Dak. 282/N2
Wales (isl.), N.W. Terr. 187/K3
Wales, Tenn. 237/G10
Wales, U.K. 7/D3
Wales, Utah 304/C4
WALES 13
WALES 10/E4
Wales, Wis. 317/J1
Walesboro, Ind. 227/F6
Waleska, Georgia 217/D2
Walford, Iowa 229/K5
Walford, Ontario 177/B1
Walgett, N.S. Wales 88/H6
Walgett, N.S. Wales 97/E2
Walgreen Coast (reg.) 5/B13
Walhachin, Br. Col. 184/G5
Walhalla, Mich. 250/C5
Walhalla, N. Dak. 282/P2
Walhalla, S.C. 296/A2
Walhonding, Ohio 284/F5
Walikale, Zaire 115/E4
Walker (co.), Ala. 195/D3
Walker (creek), Ariz. 198/F2
Walker (mt.), Ark. 202/E2
Walker (co.), Georgia 217/B1
Walker, Iowa 229/K4
Walker, Kansas 232/C3
Walker, Ky. 237/O7
Walker, La. 238/L1
Walker, Mich. 250/D6
Walker, Minn. 255/D3
Walker, Mo. 261/D7
Walker (lake), Nev. 188/C3
Walker (lake), Nev. 266/C4
Walker (riv.), Nev. 266/C3
Walker, N.Y. 276/E4
Walker (bay), N.W. Terr. 187/G2
Walker, Oreg. 291/D4
Walker, S. Dak. 298/G2
Walker (isl.), Tasmania 99/B2
Walker (co.), Texas 303/J7
Walker (creek), Va. 307/F6
Walker, W. Va. 312/D4
Walkerburn, Scotland 15/F5
Walker Mill, Md. 245/F5
Walker River Ind. Res., Nev. 266/C3
Walker Springs, Ala. 195/C7
Walkerston, Queensland 88/H4
Walkerston, Queensland 95/D4
Walkersville, Md. 245/J3
Walkersville, W. Va. 312/F5
Walkerton, Ind. 227/E2
Walkerton, Ontario 177/C3
Walkerton, Va. 307/O5
Walkertown, N.C. 281/J2
Walkerville, Mich. 250/C5
Walkerville, Mont. 262/D4
Walkerville, S. Australia 88/E8
Wall•, N.J. 273/E3
Wall, Pa. 294/C5
Wall, S. Dak. 298/E6
Wall, Texas 303/D6
Wallace, Ala. 195/D8
Wallace (mt.), Alberta 182/C2
Wallace, Calif. 204/C9
Wallace, Idaho 220/C2
Wallace, Ind. 227/C5
Wallace (co.), Kansas 232/A3
Wallace, Kansas 232/A3
Wallace, La. 238/M3
Wallace (lake), La. 238/C2
Wallace, Mich. 250/B3
Wallace, Nebr. 264/C4
Wallace, N.Y. 276/E6
Wallace, N.C. 281/N5

470 Williams Harbour

Williams Harbour, Newf. 166/C3
Williams Lake, Br. Col. 162/D5
Williams Lake, Br. Col. 184/F4
Williamson, Georgia 217/D4
Williamson (co.), Ill. 222/E6
Williamson, Ill. 222/D5
Williamson, Iowa 229/G6
Williamson, N.Y. 276/F4
Williamson (riv.), Oreg. 291/F5
Williamson (co.), Tenn. 237/H9
Williamson (co.), Texas 303/G7
Williamson, W. Va. 312/B7
Williamsport, Ind. 227/C4
Williamsport, Ky. 237/R5
Williamsport, Md. 245/G2
Williamsport, Newf. 166/C3
Williamsport, Ohio 284/D6
Williamsport, Pa. 188/L2
Williamsport, Pa. 294/H3
Williamsport, Tenn. 237/G9
Williamston, Mich. 250/E6
Williamston, N.C. 281/R3
Williamston, S.C. 296/B2
Williamstown, Kansas 232/G2
Williamstown, Ky. 237/M3
Williamstown, Mass. 249/B2
Williamstown•, Mass. 249/B2
Williamstown, Mo. 261/J2
Williamstown, New Bruns. 170/C2
Williamstown, N.J. 273/D4
Williamstown, N.Y. 276/J4
Williamstown, Ontario 177/K2
Williamstown, Pa. 294/J4
Williamstown, S. Australia 94/C7
Williamstown•, Vt. 268/B3
Williamstown, Victoria 97/H5
Williamstown, Victoria 88/K7
Williamstown, W. Va. 312/C4
Williamsville, Ill. 222/D4
Williamsville, Miss. 256/F4
Williamsville, Mo. 261/L9
Williamsville, N.Y. 276/C5
Williamsville, Vt. 268/B6
Williamsville, Va. 307/J4
Willies (range), Queensland 95/C6
Williford, Ark. 202/H1
Willimantic, Conn. 210/G2
Willimantic (riv.), Conn. 210/F1
Willimantic, Maine 243/E5
Willimantic•, Maine 243/E5
Willingboro•, N.J. 273/D3
Willingdon, Alberta 182/E3
Willington•, Conn. 210/F1
Willington, S.C. 296/C4
Willis (islets), Australia 87/F7
Willis (isls.), Coral Sea Is. Terr. 88/J3
Willis, Kansas 232/G2
Willis, Mich. 250/F6
Willis, Okla. 288/N7
Willis, Texas 303/J7
Willis, Va. 307/H7
Willis (riv.), Va. 307/M5
Willisau, Switzerland 39/F2
Willisburg, Ky. 237/L5
Williston (lake), Br. Col. 162/D4
Williston (lake), Br. Col. 184/F2
Williston, Fla. 212/D2
Williston, N. Dak. 188/F1
Williston, N. Dak. 282/C3
Williston, S.C. 296/E5
Williston, Tenn. 237/C10
Williston•, Vt. 268/A3
Williston Park, N.Y. 276/R7
Willisville, Ark. 202/D6
Willisville, Ill. 222/D6
Willisville, Ontario 177/C1
Willis Wharf, Va. 307/S5
Williton, England 13/D6
Willits, Calif. 204/B4
Willmar, Minn. 255/C5
Willmar, Sask. 181/J6
Willmathsville, Mo. 261/G2
Willmore Wilderness Prov. Park, Alberta 182/A3
Willoughby (bay), Ant. & Bar. 161/E11
Willoughby, N.S. Wales 88/K3
Willoughby, N.S. Wales 97/J3
Willoughby, Ohio 284/J8
Willoughby, Vt. 268/C2
Willoughby (lake), Vt. 268/D2
Willoughby Hills, Ohio 284/J9
Willow, Alaska 196/B1
Willow, Ark. 202/E5
Willow (creek), Calif. 204/E3
Willow (creek), Idaho 220/G6
Willow (riv.), Minn. 255/E4
Willow (creek), Mont. 262/E2
Willow, Okla. 288/G4
Willow (creek), Oreg. 291/H2
Willow (creek), Oreg. 291/K3
Willow (creek), S. Dak. 298/C4
Willow (creek), Utah 304/E4
Willow (res.), Wis. 317/F4
Willow (creek), Wyo. 319/F2
Willow (lake), Wyo. 319/C2
Willow Bend, W. Va. 312/F7
Willow Branch, Ind. 227/F5
Willowbrook, Ill. 222/B6
Willowbrook, Kansas 232/D3
Willowbrook, Sask. 181/J4
Willow Bunch, Sask. 181/F6
Willow Bunch (lake), Sask. 181/F6
Willow City, N. Dak. 282/K2
Willow City, Texas 303/F7
Willow Creek, Calif. 204/B3
Willow Creek, Mont. 262/E5
Willow Creek (res.), Mont. 262/D3
Willowcreek, Oreg. 291/K3
Willow Creek, Sask. 181/B6
Willowdale, Oreg. 291/G3
Willow Grove, Del. 245/R4
Willow Grove, New Bruns. 170/E3
Willow Grove, Pa. 294/M5
Willow Hill, Ill. 222/E5
Willow Hill, Pa. 294/G5
Willowick, Ohio 284/J8
Willow Island, Nebr. 264/D4
Willowlake (riv.), N.W. Terr. 187/F3
Willow Lake, S. Dak. 298/O4
Willowmore, S. Africa 118/C6
Willowra, North. Terr. 93/C6
Willow Ranch, Calif. 204/E2
Willow River, Br. Col. 184/F3
Willow River, Minn. 255/F4
Willows, Calif. 204/C4
Willows, Md. 245/M6
Willows, Sask. 181/F6
Willow Springs, Ill. 222/B6
Willow Springs, Mo. 261/H9
Willowton, W. Va. 312/E8
Willow Tree, N.S. Wales 97/F2
Wills (creek), Ohio 284/G5
Wills (lake), W. Australia 88/D4
Willsboro, N.Y. 276/N2
Wills Creek (lake), Ohio 284/G5
Willshire, Ohio 284/A4
Wills Point, La. 238/L7
Wills Point, Texas 303/J5
Willunga, S. Australia 94/F6
Wilma, Fla. 212/B1
Wilmar, Ark. 202/G6
Wilmer, Ala. 195/B9
Wilmer, Br. Col. 184/J5
Wilmer, La. 238/K5
Wilmer, Texas 303/H3
Wilmerding, Pa. 294/C5
Wilmette, Ill. 222/B5
Wilmington, Calif. 204/C11
Wilmington, Del. 188/M3
Wilmington, Del. 245/R2
Wilmington, Ill. 222/E2
Wilmington (Patterson), Ill. 222/C4
Wilmington, Ind. 227/H6
Wilmington•, Mass. 249/C5
Wilmington, N.Y. 276/N2
Wilmington, N.C. 188/L4
Wilmington, N.C. 146/L6
Wilmington, N.C. 281/N6
Wilmington, Ohio 284/C7
Wilmington, S. Australia 94/F6
Wilmington•, Vt. 268/B6
Wilmington Island, Georgia 217/L7
Wilmont, Minn. 255/C7
Wilmore, Kansas 232/C4
Wilmore, Ky. 237/M5
Wilmore, Pa. 294/E5
Wilmot, Ark. 202/G7
Wilmot, Ind. 227/F2
Wilmot, Kansas 232/F4
Wilmot, New Bruns. 170/C3
Wilmot•, N.H. 268/D5
Wilmot, Ohio 284/G4
Wilmot, Pr. Edward I. 168/E2
Wilmot, S. Dak. 298/R3
Wilmot, Tasmania 99/C3
Wilmot Flat, N.H. 268/D5
Wilmot Station, Nova Scotia 168/D4
Wilmslow, England 10/G2
Wilmslow, England 13/H2
Wilno, Ontario 177/G2
Wilpen, Pa. 294/D5
Wilrijk, Belgium 27/E6
Wilsall, Mont. 262/F5
Wilsey, Kansas 232/F3
Wilson (dam), Ala. 195/C1
Wilson, Ark. 202/K2
Wilson (mt.), Calif. 204/D10
Wilson (mt.), Colo. 188/E3
Wilson (mt.), Colo. 208/C7
Wilson, Conn. 210/E1
Wilson (co.), Kansas 232/G4
Wilson, Kansas 232/D3
Wilson (lake), Kansas 232/D3
Wilson, La. 238/H5
Wilson, Maine 243/E5
Wilson, Mich. 250/B3
Wilson, Minn. 255/G7
Wilson, N.Y. 276/C4
Wilson (co.), N.C. 281/O3
Wilson, N.C. 281/O3
Wilson (cape), N.W. Terr. 187/K3
Wilson, Ohio 284/H6
Wilson, Okla. 288/M6
Wilson (riv.), Oreg. 291/D2
Wilson, Pa. 294/M4
Wilson (riv.), Queensland 95/B5
Wilson, S.C. 296/G4
Wilson (co.), Tenn. 237/J8
Wilson (co.), Texas 303/F8
Wilson, Texas 303/C4
Wilson (creek), Wash. 310/F3
Wilson, W. Va. 312/H4
Wilson, Wis. 317/B6
Wilson, Wyo. 319/B2
Wilson Bluff (prom.), S. Australia 94/A4
Wilsonburg, W. Va. 312/F4
Wilson City, Mo. 261/O9
Wilson Creek, Br. Col. 184/J2
Wilson Creek, Wash. 310/F3
Wilsondale, W. Va. 312/B7
Wilson Lake (res.), Idaho 220/D7
Wilson Landing, Br. Col. 184/H5
Wilson Point, New Bruns. 170/F1
Wilsons (prom.), Victoria 88/H7
Wilsons (prom.), Victoria 97/D6
Wilsons, Va. 307/N6
Wilsons Beach, New Bruns. 170/D4
Wilson's Creek Nat'l Battlefield, Mo. 261/F8
Wilsons Mills, Maine 243/B6
Wilsons Mills, N.C. 281/M3
Wilsonville, Ala. 195/E4
Wilsonville, Conn. 210/H1
Wilsonville, Ill. 222/D4
Wilsonville, Nebr. 264/D4
Wilsonville, Oreg. 291/A2
Wilton, Ala. 195/E4
Wilton, Ark. 202/B6
Wilton, Calif. 204/C9
Wilton•, Conn. 210/B4
Wilton, England 13/F6
Wilton, Iowa 229/M6
Wilton, Maine 243/C6
Wilton•, Maine 243/C6
Wilton, Minn. 255/C3
Wilton, N.H. 268/D6
Wilton•, N.H. 268/D6
Wilton, N.Y. 276/N4
Wilton, N. Dak. 282/J5
Wilton, Wis. 317/F8
Wilton Manors, Fla. 212/B3
Wiltshire (co.), England 13/E6
Wiltz, Luxembourg 27/H9
Wiluna, Australia 87/C8
Wiluna, W. Australia 88/C5
Wiluna, W. Australia 92/C4
Wimauma, Fla. 212/D4
Wimbledon, N. Dak. 282/O5
Wimborne, Alberta 182/D4
Wimborne Minster, England 13/E7
Wimico (lake), Fla. 212/A2
Wimmer, Sask. 181/G3
Wimmera (riv.), Victoria 97/A5
Wimmis, Switzerland 39/E3
Winagami (lake), Alberta 182/B2
Winam (bay), Kenya 115/F4
Winamac, Ind. 227/D2
Winborn, Miss. 256/F1
Winburg, S. Africa 118/D5
Winburne, Pa. 294/F4
Wincanton, England 13/E6
Winchburgh, Scotland 15/D1
Winchelsea, Victoria 97/B6
Winchendon, Mass. 249/F2
Winchendon•, Mass. 249/F2
Winchendon Springs, Mass. 249/G2
Winchester, Ark. 202/G6
Winchester•, Conn. 210/C1
Winchester, England 13/F6
Winchester, England 10/F5
Winchester, Idaho 220/B3
Winchester, Ill. 222/C4
Winchester, Ind. 227/G4
Winchester, Kansas 232/G2
Winchester, Ky. 237/N5
Winchester•, Mass. 249/C6
Winchester, Mo. 261/N3
Winchester, Nev. 266/F6
Winchester, N.H. 268/C6
Winchester•, N.H. 268/C6
Winchester, N. Zealand 100/C6
Winchester, Ohio 284/C8
Winchester, Ontario 177/J2
Winchester, Oreg. 291/D4
Winchester (bay), Oreg. 291/C4
Winchester, Tenn. 237/J10
Winchester (I.C.), Va. 307/M2
Winchester, Wash. 310/F3
Winchester, Wis. 317/G3
Winchester Bay, Oreg. 291/C4
Winchester Center, Conn. 210/C1
Wind (riv.), Wash. 310/D5
Wind (lake), Wis. 317/K2
Wind (riv.), Wyo. 319/C2
Windber, Pa. 294/E5
Wind Cave Nat'l Park, S. Dak. 298/B6
Windcrest, Texas 303/K11
Windemere, Conn. 210/F1
Winder (lake), Fla. 212/F3
Winder, Georgia 217/E3
Windermere, Br. Col. 184/K5
Windermere, England 13/E3
Windermere, England 10/E3
Windermere, Fla. 212/E3
Windermere, Ontario 177/E2
Windfall, Ind. 227/F4
Windgap, Pa. 294/M4
Windham (co.), Conn. 210/H1
Windham•, Conn. 210/G2
Windham, Mont. 262/F3
Windham•, N.H. 268/E6
Windham, N.Y. 276/M6
Windham, Ohio 284/H3
Windham (co.), Vt. 268/B5
Windham•, Vt. 268/B5
Windham Depot, N.H. 268/E6
Windhoek (cap.), Namibia 102/D7
Windhoek (cap.), Namibia 118/B4
Windhoek (cap.), Namibia 2/K7
Winding Gulf, W. Va. 312/D7
Windisch, Switzerland 39/F1
Windischgarsten, Austria 41/C3
Wind Lake, Wis. 317/K2
Windom (peak), Colo. 208/D7
Windom, Ind. 227/D7
Windom, Kansas 232/E3
Windom, Minn. 255/C7
Windorah, Queensland 88/G5
Windorah, Queensland 95/B5
Window Rock, Ariz. 198/F3
Wind Point, Wis. 317/M2
Wind River (canyon), Wyo. 319/D2
Wind River (range), Wyo. 319/C2
Wind River Ind. Res., Wyo. 319/C2
Windsor, Calif. 204/C5
Windsor, Colo. 208/J2
Windsor, Conn. 210/E1
Windsor•, Conn. 210/E1
Windsor (New Windsor), Ill. 222/C2
Windsor, Ill. 222/E4
Windsor, Ind. 227/G4
Windsor•, Maine 243/D7
Windsor•, Mass. 249/B2
Windsor, Mo. 261/E5
Windsor, New Bruns. 170/C2
Windsor, Newf. 166/C4
Windsor, N.J. 273/D3
Windsor, N.Y. 276/J6
Windsor, N.C. 281/P2
Windsor, N. Dak. 282/N6
Windsor, Nova Scotia 162/K7
Windsor, Nova Scotia 168/D3
Windsor, Ohio 284/J2
Windsor, Ont. 162/H7
Windsor, Ontario 177/B5
Windsor, Pa. 294/J6
Windsor, Québec 172/F4
Windsor, Queensland 88/K2
Windsor, Queensland 95/D2
Windsor, S.C. 296/E5
Windsor (co.), Vt. 268/B4
Windsor, Vt. 268/C5
Windsor•, Vt. 268/C5
Windsor, Va. 307/P7
Windsor, Wis. 317/H9
Windsor Heights, Iowa 229/F5
Windsor Heights, W. Va. 312/E2
Windsor Locks•, Conn. 210/E1
Windsorville, Conn. 210/E1
Windthorst, Sask. 181/J5
Windthorst, Texas 303/F4
Windward (passg.) 146/L8
Windward (passage), Cuba 156/C3
Windward (passage), Grenada 156/C3
Windward (passage), Haiti 158/A5
Windward (isls.), W. Indies 156/G4
Windy, W. Va. 312/C4
Windy Hill, S.C. 296/H3
Windy Hills, Ky. 237/K1
Windyville, Mo. 261/F7
Winefred (lake), Alberta 182/E2
Winefred (riv.), Alberta 182/E2
Winesburg, Ohio 284/G4
Winfall, N.C. 281/S2
Winfield, Ala. 195/C3
Winfield, Alberta 182/C3
Winfield, Ark. 202/B4
Winfield, Br. Col. 184/H5
Winfield, Ill. 222/A5
Winfield, Iowa 229/L6
Winfield, Kansas 232/F4
Winfield, Md. 245/K3
Winfield, Mo. 261/L5
Winfield•, N.J. 273/B2
Winfield, Pa. 294/J4
Winfield, Tenn. 237/M7
Winfield, Texas 303/K4
Winfield, W. Va. 312/C5
Winfred, S. Dak. 298/P6
Wing, Ala. 195/E8
Wing, Ill. 222/E3
Wing, N. Dak. 282/K5
Wingard, Sask. 181/E3
Wingate, England 13/J4
Wingate, Ind. 227/C4
Wingate, Md. 245/O7
Wingate, N.C. 281/J5
Wingate, Pa. 294/G4
Wingate, Texas 303/D5
Wingate Army Depot, N. Mex. 274/A3
Wingdale, N.Y. 276/N7
Wingene, Belgium 27/C6
Winger, Minn. 255/B3
Winger, Ontario 177/E5
Wingham, N.S. Wales 97/G2
Wingham, Ontario 177/C4
Wingo, Ky. 237/D7
Winifred, Kansas 232/F2
Winifred, Ky. 237/R5
Winifred, Mont. 262/G3
Winifreda, Argentina 143/D4
Winifrede, W. Va. 312/C6
Winigan, Mo. 261/G2
Winisk, Ontario 175/C1
Winisk (lake), Ontario 175/C2
Winisk (riv.), Ontario 162/H5
Winisk (riv.), Ontario 175/C2
Wink, Texas 303/A6
Winkel, Netherlands 27/F3
Winkelman, Ariz. 198/E6
Winkle, Ill. 222/D5
Winkler, Manitoba 179/E5
Winkler (co.), Texas 303/A6
Winlaw, Br. Col. 184/J5
Winlock, Oreg. 291/H3
Winlock, Wash. 310/C4
Winn, Ala. 195/C7
Winn (par.), La. 238/E3
Winn, Maine 243/G5
Winn•, Maine 243/G5
Winn, Mich. 250/E5
Winnabow, N.C. 281/N6
Winnaleah, Tasmania 99/D3
Winneba, Ghana 106/D7
Winnebago (co.), Ill. 222/D1
Winnebago, Ill. 222/D1
Winnebago (co.), Iowa 229/F2
Winnebago, Minn. 255/D7
Winnebago, Nebr. 264/H2
Winnebago (co.), Wis. 317/J8
Winnebago, Wis. 317/J8
Winnebago (lake), Wis. 317/K7
Winnebago Ind. Res., Nebr. 264/H2
Winnecke (creek), North. Terr. 93/B5
Winneconne, Wis. 317/J7
Winnecook (lake), Maine 243/E6
Winnemaug (lake), Conn. 210/C2
Winnemucca, Nev. 188/C2
Winnemucca (lake), Nev. 188/C2
Winnemucca, Nev. 266/D2
Winnemucca (lake), Nev. 266/B2
Winnemucca Ind. Res., Nev. 266/D2
Winner, S. Dak. 298/K7
Winneshiek (co.), Iowa 229/K2
Winnetka, Ill. 222/B5
Winnetoon, Nebr. 264/F2
Winnett, Mont. 262/H4
Winnfield, La. 238/E3
Winnibigoshish (lake), Minn. 255/D3
Winnie, Texas 303/K8
Winnifred, Alberta 182/E5
Winning Pool, W. Australia 92/A3
Winnipauk, Conn. 210/B4
Winnipeg, Canada 2/E3
Winnipeg (cap.), Manitoba 146/J5
Winnipeg (cap.), Manitoba 162/G6
Winnipeg (cap.), Manitoba 179/E5
Winnipeg (lake), Manitoba 162/G5
Winnipeg (lake), Manitoba 146/J4
Winnipeg (lake), Manitoba 179/E2
Winnipeg (riv.), Manitoba 179/G4
Winnipeg (riv.), Ontario 175/A2
Winnipeg Beach, Manitoba 179/F4
Winnipegosis, Man. 162/F5
Winnipegosis (lake), Man. 146/H4
Winnipegosis (lake), Man. 162/F5
Winnipegosis, Manitoba 179/B3
Winnipegosis (lake), Manitoba 179/C2
Winnipesaukee, N.H. 268/E4
Winnipesaukee (lake), N.H. 268/E4
Winnipesaukee (riv.), N.H. 268/D5
Winnisquam, N.H. 268/E5
Winnisquam (lake), N.H. 268/D4
Winnsboro, La. 238/G2
Winnsboro, S.C. 296/E3
Winnsboro, Texas 303/J5
Winnsboro Mills, S.C. 296/E3
Winokapau (lake), Newf. 166/B3
Winokur, Georgia 217/H8
Winona, Ariz. 198/D3
Winona (lake), Ark. 202/E4
Winona, Kansas 232/A2
Winona, Mich. 250/G1
Winona, Minn. 188/H2
Winona (co.), Minn. 255/G6
Winona, Minn. 255/G6
Winona, Miss. 256/E4
Winona, Mo. 261/K9
Winona, Ohio 284/J4
Winona, Tenn. 237/N8
Winona, Texas 303/J5
Winona, Wash. 310/H4
Winona, W. Va. 312/E6
Winona Lake, Ind. 227/F2
Winooski, Vt. 268/A2
Winooski (riv.), Vt. 268/B3
Winschoten, Netherlands 27/L2
Winscombe, England 13/D6
Winsen, Germany 22/D2
Winsford, England 13/G2
Winsford, England 10/G2
Winside, Nebr. 264/G2
Winslow, Ariz. 198/E3
Winslow, Ark. 202/B2
Winslow, Ill. 222/D1
Winslow, Ind. 227/C8
Winslow, Maine 243/D6
Winslow•, Maine 243/D6
Winslow, Nebr. 264/H3
Winslow, N.J. 273/D4
Winslow (Bainbridge Island-Winslow), Wash. 310/A2
Winslows Mills, Maine 243/E7
Winsted, Conn. 210/C1
Winsted, Minn. 255/E6
Winston (co.), Ala. 195/D2
Winston, Georgia 217/C3
Winston, Ky. 237/N5
Winston (co.), Miss. 256/F4
Winston, Mo. 261/D3
Winston, Mont. 262/E4
Winston, N. Mex. 274/B5
Winston, Oreg. 291/D4
Winston Park, Ky. 237/S2
Winston-Salem, N.C. 188/K3
Winston-Salem, N.C. 281/J2
Winstonville, Miss. 256/C3
Winsum, Netherlands 27/K2
Winter (harb.), N.W. Terr. 187/H2
Winter (isl.), N.W. Terr. 187/K3
Winter, Sask. 181/B3
Winter, Wis. 317/E4
Winter Beach, Fla. 212/F4
Winterdale, Pa. 294/M2
Winter Garden, Fla. 212/E3
Winter Harbor•, Maine 243/G7
Winter Harbour, Br. Col. 184/C5
Winterhaven, Calif. 204/L11
Winter Haven, Fla. 212/E3
Winter I. Coast Guard Air Sta., Mass. 249/E5
Winter Park, Colo. 208/H3
Winter Park, Fla. 212/E3
Winterpock, Va. 307/N6
Winterport, Maine 243/F6
Winterport•, Maine 243/F6
Winters, Calif. 204/D5
Winters, Texas 303/E6
Wintersburg, Ariz. 198/B5
Winterset, Iowa 229/E6
Winterset, Ohio 284/H5
Winter Springs, Fla. 212/E3
Winters Run (creek), Md. 245/N2
Wintersville, Ohio 284/J5
Winterswijk, Netherlands 27/K5
Winterthur, Switzerland 39/G1
Winterton, Newf. 166/D2
Winterville, Georgia 217/F3
Winterville, Maine 243/F2
Winterville•, Maine 243/F2
Winterville, Miss. 256/B4
Winterville, N.C. 281/P3
Winthrop, Ark. 202/B6
Winthrop, Conn. 210/E3
Winthrop, Iowa 229/K4
Winthrop, Maine 243/C7
Winthrop•, Maine 243/C7
Winthrop•, Mass. 249/D6
Winthrop, Minn. 255/D6
Winthrop, Wash. 310/E2
Winthrop-Brasher Falls, N.Y. 276/L1
Winthrop Harbor, Ill. 222/F1
Winton, Calif. 204/E6
Winton, Minn. 255/G3
Winton, N. Zealand 100/B7
Winton, N.C. 281/P2
Winton, Queensland 88/G4
Winton, Queensland 95/B4
Winton, Wash. 310/E3
Winyah (bay), S.C. 296/J5
Wiota, Iowa 229/D6
Wiota, Wis. 317/G10
Wirksworth, England 13/F4
Wirral, England 13/G2
Wirral, England 10/F2
Wirral (pen.), England 13/G2
Wirral, New Bruns. 170/D3
Wirrulla, S. Australia 94/D5
Wirt, Ind. 227/G7
Wirt, Minn. 255/E3
Wirt, Okla. 288/L6
Wirt (co.), W. Va. 312/D4
Wirth, Ark. 202/H1
Wirtz, Va. 307/J6
Wirulla, S. Australia 88/E6
Wisacky, S.C. 296/G3
Wisbech, England 10/G4
Wisbech, England 13/H5
Wiscasset, Maine 243/D7
Wiscasset•, Maine 243/D7
Wisconsin 188/J2
WISCONSIN 317
Wisconsin (state), U.S. 146/K5
Wisconsin (riv.), Wis. 188/H2
Wisconsin (riv.), Wis. 317/E9
Wisconsin Dells, Wis. 317/G8
Wisconsin Rapids, Wis. 317/G7
Wisdom, Ky. 237/K7
Wisdom, Mont. 262/C5
Wise, N.C. 281/N2
Wise (co.), Texas 303/G4
Wise (co.), Va. 307/C6
Wise, Va. 307/C7
Wiseman, Alaska 196/H1
Wiseman, Ark. 202/G1
Wise River, Mont. 262/C5
Wiseton, Sask. 181/D4
Wishart, Mo. 261/F7
Wishart, Sask. 181/H4
Wishek, N. Dak. 282/L7
Wishram, Wash. 310/D5
Wisła, Poland 47/D4
Wisła (Vistula) (riv.), Poland 47/D2
Wismar, Germany 22/D2
Wisner, La. 238/G3
Wisner, Mich. 250/F5
Wisner, Nebr. 264/H3
Wissembourg, France 28/G3
Wistaria, Br. Col. 184/D3
Wister, Okla. 288/S5
Wister (lake), Okla. 288/S5
Witbank, S. Africa 118/D5
Witchekan (lake), Sask. 181/D2
Witham, England 13/H6
Witham (riv.), England 10/F4
Witham (riv.), England 13/G4
Withamsville, Ohio 284/C10
Withee, Wis. 317/E6
Witherbee-Mineville, N.Y. 276/N2
Withernsea, England 13/H4
Withernsea, England 10/G4
Witherspoon (mt.), Alaska 196/C1
Withlacoochee (riv.), Fla. 212/C1
Withlacoochee (riv.), Fla. 212/D2
Withrow, Wash. 310/F3
Witkowo, Poland 47/C2
Witless Bay, Newf. 166/D2
Witney, England 13/F6
Witnica, Poland 47/B2
Witoka, Minn. 255/G7
Witt, Ill. 222/D4
Witten, Germany 22/B3
Witten, S. Dak. 298/J7
Wittenberg, Germany 22/E3
Wittenberg, Mo. 261/O7
Wittenberg, Wis. 317/H6
Wittenberge, Germany 22/D2
Wittenoom, W. Australia 88/B4
Wittenoom, W. Australia 92/B3
Witter, Ark. 202/C2
Wittingen, Germany 22/D2
Wittlich, Germany 22/B4
Wittman, Md. 245/N5
Wittmann, Ariz. 198/C5
Witts Springs, Ark. 202/E2
Wittstock, Germany 22/E2
Witu, Kenya 115/H4
Witvlei, Namibia 118/B4
Witwatersberg (range), S. Africa 118/G6
Witwatersrand (reg.), S. Africa 118/H7
Witzenhausen, Germany 22/C3
Wivenhoe, England 13/J6
Wivenhoe, Manitoba 179/K2
Wiville, Ark. 202/H3
Wixom, Mich. 250/F6
Wkra (riv.), Poland 47/E2
Władysławowo, Poland 47/D1
Włocławek (prov.), Poland 47/D2
Włocławek, Poland 47/D2
Włocławskie (lake), Poland 47/D2
Włodawa, Poland 47/F3
Włoszczowa, Poland 47/D3
Woburn, Grenada 161/C9
Woburn, Mass. 249/C6
Woburn, Québec 172/G4
Woden, Iowa 229/F2
Wodonga, Victoria 88/H7
Wodonga, Victoria 97/D5
Wodzisław Śląski, Poland 47/D4
Woensdrecht, Netherlands 27/E6
Woerden, Netherlands 27/F4
Wohlen, Switzerland 39/F2
Wohlen bei Bern, Switzerland 39/D3
Wojkowice, Poland 47/B3
Wokam (isl.), Indonesia 85/K7
Woking, Alberta 182/A2
Woking, England 13/G8
Woking, England 10/B6
Wokingham, England 13/G8
Wokingham, England 10/F5
Wolbach, Nebr. 264/F3
Wolbrom, Poland 47/D3
Wolco, Okla. 288/O1
Wolcott, Colo. 208/F3
Wolcott•, Conn. 210/D2
Wolcott, Ind. 227/C3
Wolcott, N.Y. 276/G4
Wolcott•, Vt. 268/C2
Wolcottsville, N.Y. 276/C4
Wolcottville, Ind. 227/G1
Wolds, The (hills), England 13/G4
Woleai (atoll), Micronesia 87/E5
Wolf (lake), Alberta 182/E2
Wolf (Wenman) (isl.), Ecuador 128/E
Wolf (lake), Ill. 222/C6
Wolf (riv.), Miss. 256/F9
Wolf, Okla. 288/N4
Wolf (creek), Okla. 288/G2
Wolf (creek), S. Dak. 298/L4
Wolf (riv.), Tenn. 237/B10
Wolf (creek), Texas 303/D1
Wolf (creek), Va. 307/F6
Wolf (riv.), Wis. 317/J5
Wolf, Wyo. 319/E1
Wolf Creek, Alberta 182/B3
Wolf Creek, Ky. 237/J4

X

Y

472 Yabis

Yabis, Wadi el (dry riv.), Jordan 65/D3
Yablis, Nicaragua 154/F4
Yablonovyy (range), U.S.S.R. 54/N4
Yablonovyy (range), U.S.S.R. 48/M4
Yabrud, West Bank 65/C4
Yabucoa, P. Rico 161/E2
Yachats, Oreg. 291/C3
Yacimientos de Río Turbio, Argentina 120/B8
Yaco, Bolivia 136/B5
Yacolt, Wash. 310/C5
Yacuiba, Bolivia 120/C5
Yacuiba, Bolivia 136/D7
Yacuma (riv.), Bolivia 136/B3
Yadgir, India 68/D5
Yadkin (co.), N.C. 281/H2
Yadkin (riv.), N.C. 281/J3
Yadkinville, N.C. 281/H2
Yad Mordekhai, Israel 65/A4
Yadong, China 77/C6
Yaeyama (isls.), Japan 81/K7
Yagoua, Cameroon 115/B1
Yagra, China 77/B5
Yagradagzê Shan (mt.), China 77/D4
Yaguachi Nuevo, Ecuador 128/B4
Yaguajay, Cuba 158/F2
Yaguaraparo, Venezuela 124/G2
Yaguarí, Uruguay 145/E2
Yaguarón, Paraguay 144/B5
Yaguarón (riv.), Uruguay 145/F3
Yaguarú, Bolivia 136/D4
Yaguas (riv.), Peru 128/G4
Yaguate, Dom. Rep. 158/E6
Yagüez (riv.), P. Rico 161/A2
Yagur, Israel 65/C2
Yahav, Israel 65/D5
Yahk, Br. Col. 184/J5
Yahuma, Zaire 115/D3
Yahyalî, Turkey 63/F3
Yaizu, Japan 81/J6
Yajalón, Mexico 150/N8
Yakima (co.), Wash. 310/E4
Yakima, Wash. 146/F5
Yakima, Wash. 188/B1
Yakima, Wash. 310/E4
Yakima (ridge), Wash. 310/E4
Yakima (riv.), Wash. 310/F4
Yakima Ind. Res., Wash. 310/E4
Yako, Burkina Faso 106/D6
Yakobi (isl.), Alaska 196/M1
Yakoma, Zaire 115/D3
Yaku (isl.), Japan 81/E8
Yakumo, Japan 81/J2
Yakut A.S.S.R., U.S.S.R. 48/N3
Yakutat, Alaska 188/D6
Yakutat, Alaska 196/L3
Yakutat (bay), Alaska 196/K3
Yakutsk, U.S.S.R. 54/O3
Yakutsk, U.S.S.R. 2/R2
Yakutsk, U.S.S.R. 48/N3
Yala, Thailand 72/D6
Yalaha, Fla. 212/E3
Yalata Aboriginal Res., S. Australia 88/E6
Yalata Aboriginal Res., S. Australia 94/B4
Yale, Br. Col. 184/M2
Yale (mt.), Colo. 208/G5
Yale (lake), Fla. 212/E3
Yale, Ill. 222/E4
Yale, Iowa 229/E5
Yale, Mich. 250/G5
Yale, Okla. 288/N2
Yale, S. Dak. 298/O5
Yale, Va. 307/O7
Yale (lake), Wash. 310/C4
Yalesville, Conn. 210/D3
Yalgoo, W. Australia 92/B5
Yali, Estero (riv.), Chile 138/F4
Yalinga, Cent. Afr. Rep. 115/D2
Yallahs, Jamaica 158/K6
Yallock, N.S. Wales 97/C3
Yallourn, Victoria 97/D6
Yalmer, Mich. 250/B2
Yalobusha (co.), Miss. 256/E2
Yalobusha (riv.), Miss. 256/E3
Yalong (riv.), China 54/M7
Yalong Jiang (riv.), China 77/F6
Yalova, Çanakkale, Turkey 63/B6
Yalova, İstanbul, Turkey 63/C2
Yalpunga, N.S. Wales 97/A1
Yalta, U.S.S.R. 7/H4
Yalta, U.S.S.R. 52/D6
Yalu (riv.) 54/O5
Yalu (riv.), China 77/L3
Yalu (riv.), N. Korea 81/C3
Yalutorsk, U.S.S.R. 48/G4
Yalvaç, Turkey 63/D3
Yalvaç, Turkey 59/B2
Yamachiche, Québec 172/E3
Yamagata (pref.), Japan 81/K4
Yamagata, Japan 81/K4
Yamaguchi (pref.), Japan 81/E6
Yamaguchi, Japan 81/E6
Yamal (pen.), U.S.S.R. 54/H2
Yamal (pen.), U.S.S.R. 4/B6
Yamal (pen.), U.S.S.R. 48/G2
Yamal-Nenets Aut. Okr., U.S.S.R. 48/H3
Yamama, Saudi Arabia 59/E5
Yamanashi (pref.), Japan 81/J6
Yamantau (mt.), U.S.S.R. 52/J4
Yamarna Aboriginal Reserve, W. Australia 88/C5
Yamarna Aboriginal Res., W. Australia 92/D4
Yamasá, Dom. Rep. 158/E6
Yamaska (co.), Québec 172/E3
Yamaska, Québec 172/E4
Yamaska (riv.), Québec 172/E4
Yamaska-Est, Québec 172/E4
Yamato, Japan 81/O2
Yamatokoriyama, Japan 81/J8
Yamatotakada, Japan 81/J8
Yamba, N.S. Wales 97/G1
Yambah, North. Terr. 93/C7
Yambio, Sudan 111/E7
Yambio, Sudan 102/E4
Yambol, Bulgaria 45/H4
Yambou (head), St. Vin. & Grens. 161/A9
Yambrasbamba, Peru 128/D5
Yamdena (isl.), Indonesia 85/J7
Yamethin, Burma 72/C2
Yamhill (co.), Oreg. 291/D2
Yamhill, Oreg. 291/D2
Y'Ami (isl.), Philippines 82/B2
Yamma Yamma (lake), Queensland 88/G5
Yamma Yamma (lake), Queensland 95/B5
Yamoussoukro (cap.), Ivory Coast 102/B4
Yamoussoukro (cap.), Ivory Coast 106/C7
Yampa, Colo. 208/F2
Yampa (riv.), Colo. 208/B2
Yamparaéz, Bolivia 136/C6
Yampi Sound, W. Australia 88/C3
Yampi Sound, W. Australia 92/C2
Yamsk, U.S.S.R. 48/Q4
Yamun, West Bank 65/C3
Yamuna (Jumna) (riv.), Pakistan 68/E3
Yamzho Yumco (lake), China 77/C6
Yan, Nigeria 106/G7
Yana, U.S.S.R. 54/P3
Yana (riv.), U.S.S.R. 4/C3
Yana (riv.), U.S.S.R. 48/O3
Yanac, Victoria 97/A5
Yanacachi, Bolivia 136/B5
Yanahuanca, Peru 128/D8
Yanam, India 68/E5
Yan'an (Yenan), China 77/G4
Yanaoca, Peru 128/G10
Yanaul, U.S.S.R. 52/J3
Yancannia, N.S. Wales 97/B2
Yancey, Ky. 237/P7
Yancey (co.), N.C. 281/E3
Yanceyville, N.C. 281/L2
Yancheng, China 77/K5
Yanchi, China 77/G4
Yanco, N.S. Wales 97/D4
Yandé (isl.), New Caled. 86/F4
Yandeyarra Aboriginal Reserve, W. Australia 88/B4
Yandina, Solomon Is. 86/D3
Yandoon, Burma 72/B3
Yanfolila, Mali 106/C6
Yanga, Mexico 150/P2
Yangambi, Zaire 115/D3
Yangambi, Zaire 102/E4
Yangcheng, China 77/H4
Yangchow (Yangzhou), China 77/J5
Yangchüan (Yangquan), China 77/H4
Yangchun, China 77/H7
Yangdŏk, N. Korea 81/C4
Yanggao, China 77/H3
Yanggu, S. Korea 81/C4
Yangjiang, China 77/H7
Yangquan (Yangchüan), China 77/H4
Yangshan, China 77/H7
Yang Sin, Chu (mt.), Vietnam 72/F4
Yangtze (riv.), China 54/N6
Yangtze (riv.), China 2/O4
Yangtze (Chang Jiang) (riv.), China 77/K5
Yangyang, S. Korea 81/D4
Yangzhou (Yangchow), China 77/J5
Yanhuqu, China 77/B5
Yanji (Yenki), China 77/L3
Yankee Fork, Salmon (riv.), Idaho 220/D5
Yankee Lake, Ohio 284/J3
Yankeetown, Fla. 212/D2
Yankeetown, Ind. 227/C9
Yanko (creek), N.S. Wales 97/C4
Yankton, S. Dak. 188/G2
Yankton (co.), S. Dak. 298/P7
Yankton, S. Dak. 298/P8
Yanqi, China 77/C3
Yanrey, W. Australia 92/A3
Yantabulla, N.S. Wales 97/C1
Yantai (Chefoo), China 77/K4
Yantai, China 54/O6
Yantara, N.S. Wales 97/B1
Yantara (lake), N.S. Wales 97/B1
Yantic, Conn. 210/G2
Yantic (riv.), Conn. 210/G2
Yantis, Texas 303/J5
Yantley, Ala. 195/B6
Yanush, Okla. 288/R5
Yao, Japan 81/J8
Yaoundé (cap.), Cameroon 2/K5
Yaoundé (cap.), Cameroon 102/D4
Yaoundé (cap.), Cameroon 115/B3
Yap (isl), Micronesia 87/D5
Yapacani (riv.), Bolivia 136/C5
Yapei, Ghana 106/D7
Yapen (isl.), Indonesia 85/K6
Yapen (str.), Indonesia 85/K6
Yapraklî, Turkey 63/E2
Yaque del Norte (riv.), Dom. Rep. 158/D5
Yaque del Sur (riv.), Dom. Rep. 158/D6
Yaqui, Mexico 150/D3
Yaqui (riv.), Mexico 146/H7
Yaqui (riv.), Mexico 150/E2
Yaquina, Oreg. 291/C3
Yara, Cuba 158/H4
Yaracuy (state), Venezuela 124/D2
Yaraka, Queensland 95/C5
Yaralîgüz Dağı (mt.), Turkey 59/B1
Yaralîgüz Dağı (mt.), Turkey 63/F2
Yaransk, U.S.S.R. 52/G3
Yarbo, Ala. 195/B7
Yarbo, Sask. 181/K5
Yarda, Chad 111/C4
Yardley, Pa. 294/N5
Yardville, N.J. 273/D3
Yare (riv.), England 13/J5
Yare (riv.), England 10/G4
Yarega, U.S.S.R. 52/H2
Yaretas de Vizcachas, Cerro (mt.), Chile 138/G3
Yarí, Colombia 126/D7
Yarí (riv.), Colombia 126/D8
Yarim, Yemen 59/D7
Yaritagua, Venezuela 124/D2
Yarkand (Shache), China 77/A4
Yarkant (riv.), China 54/K6
Yarkant He (riv.), China 77/A4
Yarker, Ontario 177/H3
Yarle (lkes), S. Australia 94/B4
Yarmouth, Iowa 229/L6
Yarmouth, Maine 243/C8
Yarmouth•, Maine 243/C8
Yarmouth•, Mass. 249/O6
Yarmouth (co.), Nova Scotia 168/C5
Yarmouth, Nova Scotia 162/K7
Yarmouth, Nova Scotia 168/B5
Yarmouth (sound), Nova Scotia 168/B5
Yarmouth Port, Mass. 249/N6
Yarmuk (riv.), Israel 65/D2
Yarnell, Ariz. 198/C4
Yaroslavl', U.S.S.R. 7/H3
Yaroslavl', U.S.S.R. 48/D4
Yaroslavl', U.S.S.R. 52/E3
Yarqon (riv.), Israel 65/B3
Yarra (riv.), Victoria 97/C5
Yarra (riv.), Victoria 88/L6
Yarram, Victoria 97/D6
Yarrawonga, Victoria 97/C5
Yarrow, Br. Col. 184/M3
Yarrow, Mo. 261/G2
Yarrow (riv.), Scotland 15/E5
Yarrowitch, N.S. Wales 97/F2
Yarrow Point, Wash. 310/B2
Yartsevo, U.S.S.R. 48/J4
Yartsevo, U.S.S.R. 52/D3
Yarumal, Colombia 126/C4
Yaruu, Mongolia 77/E2
Yas (isl.), U.A.E. 59/F5
Yasawa Group (isls.), Fiji 86/P10
Yásica Abajo, Dom. Rep. 158/E5
Yasin, Pakistan 59/K2
Yasin, Pakistan 68/C1
Yasnyy, U.S.S.R. 52/J4
Yasothon, Thailand 72/D4
Yass, N.S. Wales 97/E4
Yasuj, Iran 66/G5
Yasun (cape), Turkey 63/G2
Yata (riv.), Bolivia 136/C3
Yatabe, Japan 81/P2
Yatağan, Turkey 63/C4
Yataity, Paraguay 144/C5
Yateley, England 13/G8
Yates (dam), Ala. 195/G5
Yates (co.), N.Y. 276/F5
Yates Center, Kansas 232/G4
Yates City, Ill. 222/C3
Yatesville, Georgia 217/D5
Yathkyed (lake), N.W.T. 162/F3
Yathkyed (lake), N.W.T. 187/J3
Yatina, Bolivia 136/C7
Yatsushiro, Japan 81/E7
Yatta, West Bank 65/C5
Yatton, England 13/E6
Yatua (riv.), Venezuela 124/E7
Yauca, Peru 128/E10
Yauco, P. Rico 161/B2
Yauco, P. Rico 156/F1
Yauco (lake), P. Rico 161/B2
Yauli, Peru 128/D8
Yaúna Moloca, Colombia 126/E8
Yaupi, Ecuador 128/D4
Yaupon Beach, N.C. 281/N7
Yauri (Espinar), Peru 128/G10
Yautepec, Mexico 150/L2
Yauyos, Peru 128/E9
Yava, Ariz. 198/C4
Yavapai (co.), Ariz. 198/C4
Yavapai Ind. Res., Ariz. 198/C4
Yavaraté, Colombia 126/F7
Yavari (riv.) 120/B3
Yavari (riv.), Peru 128/G5
Yavaros, Mexico 150/E3
Yavero (riv.), Peru 128/F9
Yavita, Venezuela 124/E6
Yavne, Israel 65/B4
Yavne'el, Israel 65/D2
Yawata, Japan 81/J7
Yawatahama, Japan 81/F7
Yawkey, W. Va. 312/C6
Yawri (bay), S. Leone 106/B7
Ya Xian, China 77/G8
Yaxley, England 13/G5
Yayladağı, Turkey 63/F5
Yazd (governorate), Iran 66/J5
Yazd (Yezd), Iran 66/J5
Yazd, Iran 59/F3
Yazd, Iran 54/G6
Yazdan, Iran 66/M4
Yazdan, Iran 59/H3
Yazd-e Khvasat, Iran 66/H5
Yazoo (co.), Miss. 256/D5
Yazoo (riv.), Miss. 188/H4
Yazoo (riv.), Miss. 256/C5
Yazoo City, Miss. 256/D5
Ybbs an der Donau, Austria 41/C2
Ybycuí, Paraguay 144/B5
Ybytymí, Paraguay 144/B5
Yding Skovhøj (mt.), Denmark 21/C6
Ye, Burma 72/C4
Yea, Victoria 97/C5
Yeaddiss, Ky. 237/P6
Yeadon, Pa. 294/N7
Yeager, Okla. 288/O4
Yeagertown, Pa. 294/G4
Yebbi-Bou, Chad 111/C3
Yecheng, China 77/A4
Yecla, Spain 33/F3
Yécora, Mexico 150/E2
Yecuatla, Mexico 150/P1
Yeddo, Ind. 227/C4
Yeeda River, W. Australia 92/C2
Yeelirrie, W. Australia 92/C4
Yefremov, U.S.S.R. 52/E4
Yegros, Paraguay 144/D5
Yeguas (pt.), P. Rico 161/F3
Yehualtepec, Mexico 150/O2
Yehud, Israel 65/B3
Yei, Sudan 111/F7
Yelabuga, U.S.S.R. 52/H3
Yelan', U.S.S.R. 52/F4
Yelcho (lake), Chile 138/E4
Yelets, U.S.S.R. 7/H3
Yelets, U.S.S.R. 48/D4
Yelets, U.S.S.R. 52/E4
Yelimané, Mali 106/B5
Yelizavety (cape), U.S.S.R. 54/R4
Yelizavety (cape), U.S.S.R. 48/P4
Yelizovo, U.S.S.R. 48/Q4
Yell (co.), Ark. 202/D3
Yell (isl.), Scotland 15/G2
Yell (isl.), Scotland 10/G1
Yell (sound), Scotland 15/G2
Yellamanchili, India 68/E5
Yelleq, Jebel (mt.), Egypt 59/B3
Yellow (sea) 54/O6
Yellow (Huang He) (riv.), China 77/J4
Yellow (sea), China 77/K4
Yellow (creek), Colo. 208/C3
Yellow (riv.), Fla. 212/B6
Yellow (riv.), Ind. 227/D2
Yellow (brook), N.J. 273/E3
Yellow (sea), N. Korea 81/B6
Yellow (creek), Ohio 284/J4
Yellow (sea), S. Korea 81/B6
Yellow (creek), Tenn. 237/F8
Yellow (creek), W. Va. 312/E1
Yellow (lake), Wis. 317/B4
Yellow (riv.), Wis. 317/F7
Yellow Bluff, Ala. 195/C7
Yellowbud, Ohio 284/D7
Yellowcreek, N.C. 281/A4
Yellow Creek, Sask. 181/F3
Yellow Dog (riv.), Mich. 250/B2
Yellow Grass, Sask. 181/H6
Yellowhead (pass), Alberta 182/A3
Yellowhead (pass), Br. Col. 184/H4
Yellow Jacket, Colo. 208/B7
Yellowknife, Canada 4/C15
Yellowknife, Canada 2/D2
Yellowknife, N.W.T. 146/G3
Yellowknife (cap.), N.W.T. 162/E3
Yellowknife (cap.), N.W.T. 187/G3
Yellowknife (riv.), N.W.T. 187/G3
Yellow Medicine (co.), Minn. 255/B6
Yellow Pine, Ala. 195/B8
Yellow Pine, Idaho 220/C4
Yellow Pine, La. 238/D2
Yellow Spring, W. Va. 312/J4
Yellow Springs, Md. 245/H3
Yellow Springs, Ohio 284/C6
Yellowstone (riv.) 188/E1
Yellowstone (co.), Mont. 262/H4
Yellowstone (riv.), Mont. 262/M3
Yellowstone (riv.), N. Dak. 282/B4
Yellowstone (riv.), U.S. 146/H5
Yellowstone (lake), Wyo. 188/E2
Yellowstone (lake), Wyo. 319/B1
Yellowstone (riv.), Wyo. 319/B1
Yellowstone Nat'l Park, Idaho 220/G5
Yellowstone Nat'l Park, Mont. 262/F6
Yellowstone Nat'l Park, Wyo. 188/E2
Yellowstone Nat'l Park, Wyo. 319/B1
Yellville, Ark. 202/E1
Yelm, Wash. 310/C4
Yelverton (bay), N.W.T. 187/K1
Yelwa, Nigeria 106/F6
Yemassee, S.C. 296/F6
Yemen 2/M5
Yemen 54/F8
YEMEN 59/D-E7
Yemetsk, U.S.S.R. 52/F2
Yenakiyevo, U.S.S.R. 52/E5
Yenan (Yan'an), China 77/G4
Yenangyaung, Burma 72/B2
Yen Bai, Vietnam 72/E2
Yenbo, Saudi Arabia 54/E7
Yenbo, Saudi Arabia 59/C5
Yenda, N.S. Wales 97/D4
Yendi, Ghana 106/D7
Yengisar, China 77/A4
Yenice, Çanakkale, Turkey 63/B3
Yenice, İçel, Turkey 63/F4
Yenice, Zonguldak, Turkey 63/E2
Yeniceoba, Turkey 63/E3
Yeniköy, Çanakkale, Turkey 63/B6
Yeniköy, Çanakkale, Turkey 63/C5
Yeniköy, İstanbul, Turkey 63/D6
Yenimahalle, Turkey 63/E3
Yenişehir, Turkey 63/C2
Yenisey (riv.), U.S.S.R. 4/C5
Yenisey (riv.), U.S.S.R. 2/P2
Yenisey (riv.), U.S.S.R. 54/K3
Yenisey (riv.), U.S.S.R. 48/J3
Yeniseysk, U.S.S.R. 54/L4
Yeniseysk, U.S.S.R. 48/K4
Yenki (Yanji), China 77/L3
Yen Minh, Vietnam 72/E2
Yentai (Yantai) China 77/K4
Yentna (riv.), Alaska 196/A1
Yeo (lake), W. Australia 88/D5
Yeo (lake), W. Australia 92/D5
Yeola, India 68/C4
Yeoman, Ind. 227/D3
Yeotmal, India 68/D4
Yeoval, N.S. Wales 97/E3
Yeovil, England 10/E5
Yeovil, England 13/E7
Yeppoon, Queensland 95/D4
Yeppoon, Queensland 88/J4
Yerevan, U.S.S.R. 48/E6
Yerevan, U.S.S.R. 52/F6
Yerichaña, Venezuela 124/F5
Yerington, Nev. 266/B4
Yerington Ind. Res., Nev. 266/B3
Yerkesik, Turkey 63/C4
Yerküy, Turkey 63/F3
Yerlisu, Turkey 63/C5
Yermak, U.S.S.R. 48/H4
Yermentau, U.S.S.R. 48/H4
Yermo, Calif. 204/J9
Yeroham, Israel 65/B6
Yerolimín, Greece 45/F7
Yeronga, Queensland 95/D3
Yeronga, Queensland 88/K3
Yerseke, Netherlands 27/E6
Yershov, U.S.S.R. 52/G4
Yesagyo, Burma 72/B2
Yeshbum, Yemen 59/E7
Yesil', U.S.S.R. 48/G4
Yeşilhisar, Turkey 63/F3
Yeşilırmak (riv.), Turkey 63/G2
Yeşilköy, Turkey 63/D6
Yeşilova, Niğde, Turkey 63/E3
Yeşilova, Burdur, Turkey 63/C4
Yeşilyurt, Turkey 63/H3
Yeso, N. Mex. 274/E4
Yeso (creek), N. Mex. 274/E4
Yesodot, Israel 65/B4
Yessentuki, U.S.S.R. 52/F6
Yessey, U.S.S.R. 48/L3
Yeste Spain 33/E3
Yesud Hama'ala, Israel 65/D1
Yetholm, Scotland 15/F5
Yetman, N.S. Wales 97/F1
Yettem, Calif. 204/F7
Yetter, Iowa 229/D4
Ye-u, Burma 72/B2
Yeu (isl.), France 28/B4
Yevlakh, U.S.S.R. 52/G6
Yevpatoria, U.S.S.R. 52/D5
Ye Xian, China 77/K4
Yeysk, U.S.S.R. 52/E5
Ygatimí, Paraguay 144/E4
Yhú, Paraguay 144/E4
Yi (riv.), Uruguay 145/B4
Yialousa, Cyprus 63/E5
Yiannitsá, Greece 45/F5
Yibin (Ipin), China 77/F6
Yibin, China 54/M7
Yibug Caka (lake), China 77/C5
Yichang (Ichang), China 77/H5
Yichun, Heilongjiang, China 77/L2
Yichun, Jiangxi, China 77/H6
Yidu, Huei, China 77/H5
Yidu, Shandong, China 77/J4
Yiftah, Israel 65/D1
Yığılca, Turkey 63/D2
Yıldızeli, Turkey 63/G3
Yiliang, China 77/F7
Yinchuan (Ningsia, Yinchwan), China 77/G4
Yinchuan, China 54/M6
Yingjiang, China 77/E7
Yingkou (Yinkow), China 77/K3
Yingshan, Hubei, China 77/H5
Yingshan, Sichuan, China 77/G5
Yining, China 77/B3
Yining, China 54/K5
Yinjiang, China 77/G6
Yin Shan (mts.), China 77/G3
Yirka, Israel 65/C2
Yirol, Sudan 111/F6
Yirrkala, North. Terr. 93/E2
Yishan, China 77/G7
Yíthion, Greece 45/F7
Yiwu (Aratürük), China 77/D3
Yiyang, China 77/H6
Yli-kitka (lake), Finland 18/Q3
Ylitornio, Finland 18/O3
Ylivieska, Finland 18/O4
Ymir, Br. Col. 184/J5
Ynys Môn (Anglesey) (isl.), Wales 10/D4
Ynys Môn (Anglesey) (isl.), Wales 13/C4
Yoakum (co.), Texas 303/B4
Yoakum, Texas 303/G8
Yocalla, Bolivia 136/B6
Yocemento, Kansas 232/C3
Yockanookany (riv.), Miss. 256/E5
Yoco, Venezuela 124/G2
Yocón, Honduras 154/D3
Yocum, Ky. 237/P5
Yoder, Colo. 208/L5
Yoder, Ind. 227/G3
Yoder, Kansas 232/E4
Yoder, Wyo. 319/H4
Yodo (riv.), Japan 81/J7
Yog (pt.), Philippines 82/E3
Yogyakarta, Indonesia 54/M10
Yogyakarta, Indonesia 85/J2
Yoho Nat'l Park, Br. Col. 162/E5
Yoho Nat'l Park, Br. Col. 184/J4
Yoichi, Japan 81/K2
Yojoa (lake), Honduras 154/D3
Yokadouma, Cameroon 115/B3
Yokawa, Japan 81/H7
Yokena, Miss. 256/C6
Yokkaichi, Japan 81/H6
Yoko, Cameroon 115/B2
Yokohama, Japan 2/R4
Yokohama, Japan 81/O3
Yokohama, Japan 54/R6
Yokosuka, Japan 81/O3
Yokote, Japan 81/K4
Yola, Nigeria 106/G7
Yola, Nigeria 102/D4
Yolla, Tasmania 99/B3
Yolo (co.), Calif. 204/D5
Yolo, Calif. 204/B8
Yolyn, W. Va. 312/C7
Yona, Guam 86/K7
Yonago, Japan 81/F6
Yonaguni (isl.), Japan 81/K7
Yoncalla, Oreg. 291/D4
Yonezawa, Japan 81/K5
Yongamp'o, N. Korea 81/B4
Yongchang, China 77/F4
Yŏngch'ŏn, S. Korea 81/D6
Yongchuan, China 77/G6
Yongdeng, China 77/F4
Yŏngdŏk, S. Korea 81/D5
Yonges Island, S.C. 296/G6
Yonghe, China 77/H4
Yŏnghŭng, N. Korea 81/C4
Yŏngju, S. Korea 81/D5
Yongning, China 77/G4
Yongren, China 77/F6
Yongxin, China 77/H6
Yongxing, China 77/H6
Yonkers, Georgia 217/F6
Yonkers, N.Y. 276/O6
Yonne (dept.), France 28/E4
Yonne (riv.), France 28/E3
Yono, Japan 81/O2
Yopal, Colombia 126/D5
Yorba Linda, Calif. 204/D11
Yorito, Honduras 154/D3
York, Ala. 195/B6
York (cape), Australia 2/S6
York (cape), Australia 87/E7
York, England 13/F4
York, England 10/F4
York (cape), Greenl. 4/B13
York, Ky. 237/P3
York (co.), Maine 243/B9
York, Maine 243/B9
York•, Maine 243/B9
York (co.), Nebr. 264/G4
York, Nebr. 264/G4
York (co.), New Bruns. 170/C3
York, N.Y. 276/E5
York, N. Dak. 282/L3
York (reg. munic.), Ontario 177/E4
York, Ontario 177/J4
York (co.), Pa. 294/J6
York, Pa. 188/L3
York, Pa. 294/J6
York (riv.), Québec 172/D1
York (cape), Queensland 88/G2
York (cape), Queensland 95/B1
York (co.), S.C. 296/E2
York, S.C. 296/E1
York (co.), Va. 307/P6
York (riv.), Va. 307/P6
York, W. Australia 88/B6
York, W. Australia 92/B1
York (sound), W. Australia 88/C2
York (sound), W. Australia 92/D1
York, Wis. 317/D7
York Beach, Maine 243/B9
Yorke (pen.), S. Australia 88/F7
Yorke (pen.), S. Australia 94/E6
Yorketown, S. Australia 88/F6
Yorketown, S. Australia 94/E6
York Factory, Man. 162/G4
York Factory, Manitoba 179/K2
York Harbor, Maine 243/B9
York Haven, Pa. 294/J5
York Landing, Man. 146/J4
York Landing, Manitoba 179/J2
Yorklyn, Del. 245/R1
Yorkshire, North (co.), England 13/F3
Yorkshire, South (co.), England 13/F4
Yorkshire, West (co.), England 13/J1
Yorkshire, N.Y. 276/D5
Yorkshire, Ohio 284/B5
Yorkshire Dales Nat'l Park, England 13/E3
York Springs, Pa. 294/H6
Yorkton, Sask. 146/H4
Yorkton, Sask. 162/F5
Yorkton, Sask. 181/J4
Yorktown, Ark. 202/G5
Yorktown, Ind. 227/G4
Yorktown, Iowa 229/C7
Yorktown, N.J. 273/C4
Yorktown, Texas 303/G9
Yorktown, Va. 307/R6
Yorktown Heights, N.Y. 276/N8
Yorkville, Ill. 222/E2
Yorkville, Ind. 227/H6
Yorkville, N.Y. 276/K4
Yorkville, Ohio 284/J5
Yorkville, Tenn. 237/C8
Yoro, Honduras 154/D3
Yoron (isl.), Japan 81/N6
Yorosso, Mali 106/C6
Yosemite, Ky. 237/M6
Yosemite National Park, Calif. 204/F6
Yosemite Nat'l Park, Calif. 188/C3
Yosemite Nat'l Park, Calif. 204/F6
Yoshino (riv.), Japan 81/G6
Yoshino-Kumano Nat'l Park, Japan 81/H7
Yoshkar-Ola, U.S.S.R. 7/J3
Yoshkar-Ola, U.S.S.R. 52/G3
Yoshkar-Ola, U.S.S.R. 48/E4
Yost, Utah 304/A2
Yŏsu, S. Korea 81/C6
Yotala, Bolivia 136/C6
Yotaú, Bolivia 136/D5
Yotvata, Israel 65/D5
Youanmi, W. Australia 92/B5
Youbou, Br. Col. 184/J3
Youghal, Ireland 10/B5
Youghal, Ireland 17/F8
Youghal (bay), Ireland 10/C5
Youghal (bay), Ireland 17/F8
Youghiogheny (riv.), Md. 245/A3
Youghiogheny (dam), Pa. 294/D6
Youghiogheny River (lake), Md. 245/A2
Youghiogheny River (lake), Pa. 294/D6
Young, Ariz. 198/D4
Young, N.S. Wales 88/H6
Young, N.S. Wales 97/E4
Young (cape), N. Zealand 100/D7
Young (mt.), North. Terr. 93/D3
Young, Sask. 181/F4
Young (co.), Texas 303/F4
Young, Uruguay 145/B3
Young America, Ind. 227/E3
Young America, Minn. 255/E6
Youngcane, Georgia 217/D1
Young Cove, Nova Scotia 168/C4
Young Harris, Georgia 217/E1
Youngs Cove, New Bruns. 170/E3
Youngs Creek, Ind. 227/D8
Youngs Creek, Ky. 237/N7
Youngstown, Alberta 182/E4
Youngstown, Fla. 212/D6
Youngstown, Ind. 227/C6
Youngstown, N.Y. 276/C4
Youngstown, Ohio 284/J3
Youngstown, Ohio 188/K2
Youngsville, La. 238/G6
Youngsville, N. Mex. 274/C2
Youngsville, N.Y. 276/L7
Youngsville, N.C. 281/N2
Youngsville, Pa. 294/D2
Youngtown, Ariz. 198/C5
Youngwood, Pa. 294/D5
Yountville, Calif. 204/C5

GEOGRAPHICAL TERMS

A. = Arabic Burm. = Burmese Camb. = Cambodian Ch. = Chinese Czech. = Czechoslovakian Dan. = Danish Du. = Dutch Finn. = Finnish Fr. = French Ger. = German Ice. = Icelandic

It. = Italian Jap. = Japanese Mong. = Mongol Nor. = Norwegian Per. = Persian Port. = Portuguese Russ. = Russian Sp. = Spanish Sw. = Swedish Turk. = Turkish

Term	Language	Meaning
A	Nor., Sw	Stream
Aas	Dan., Nor	Hills
Abajo	Sp	Lower
Ada, Adasi	Turk	Island
Altipiano	It	Plateau
Altiplano	Sp	Plateau
Alv, Alf, Elf	Sw	River
Arrecife	Sp	Reef
Asa	Nor., Sw	Hill
Asaga	Turk	Lower
Austral	Sp	Southern
Baai	Du	Bay
Bab	Arabic	Gate or Strait
Bahia	Sp	Bay
Bahr	Arabic	Marsh, Lake, Sea, River
Baia	Port	Bay
Baie	Fr	Bay, Gulf
Baizo	Port	Low
Bakke	Dan	Hill
Bana	Jap	Cape
Bañados	Sp	Marshes
Band	Per	Mt. Range
Bandao	Ch	Peninsula
Bandar	Per	Harbor
Barra	Sp	Reef
Bel	Turk	Pass
Belt	Ger	Strait
Ben	Gaelic	Mountain
Bera	Du	Mountain
Berg	Ger., Du	Mountain
Bir	Arabic	Well
Boca	Sp	Gulf, Inlet
Boğhaz	Turk	Strait
Bolshoi, Bolshaya	Russ	Big
Bolson	Sp	Depression
Bong	Korean	Mountain
Boreal	Sp	Northern
Breen	Nor	Glacier
Bro	Dan., Nor., Sw	Bridge
Bucht	Ger	Bay
Bugt	Dan	Bay
Bukhta	Russ	Bay
Bukit	Malay	Hill, Mountain
Bukt	Nor., Sw	Bay, Gulf
Burnu, Burun	Turk	Cape, Point
By	Dan., Nor., Sw	Town
Cabo	Port., Sp	Cape
Campos	Port	Plains
Canal	Port., Sp	Channel
Cap, Capo	Fr., It	Cape
Cataratas	Sp	Falls
Catena	It	Mt. Range
Catingas	Port	Open Woodlands
Cayos	Sp	Islands
Central, Centrale	Fr., It	Middle
Cerrito, Cerro	Sp	Hill
Cerros	Sp	Hills, Mountains
Chai	Turk	River
Chott	Arabic	Salt Lake
Ciénaga	Sp	Swamp
Ciudad	Sp	City
Col	Fr	Pass
Cordillera	Sp	Mt. Range, Mts.
Côte	Fr	Coast
Csatoria	Magyar	Canal
Cuchilla	Sp	Mt. Range
Curiche	Sp	Swamp
Dağ, Dağı	Turk	Mountain, Peak
Dağlari	Turk	Mt. Range
Dal	Nor., Sw	Valley
Dar	Arabic	Land
Dar'ya	Russ	River
Daryacheh	Per	Marshy Lake
Dasht	Per	Desert, Plain
Deniz, Denizi	Turk	Sea, Lake
Desierto	Sp	Desert
Détroit	Fr	Strait
Djeziret	Arabic, Turk	Island
Do	Korean	Island
Doi	Thai	Mountain
Eiland	Du	Island
Elv	Dan., Nor	River
Embalse	Sp	Reservoir
Emi	Berber	Mountain
Erg	Arabic	Dune, Desert
Eski	Turk	Old
Est, Este	Fr., Port., Sp	East
Estero	Sp	Estuary, Creek
Estrecho, Estreito	Sp., Port	Strait
Etang	Fr	Pond, Lagoon, Lake
Feng	Ch	Mountain
Fiume	It	River
Fjäll	Sw	Mountain
Fjeld, Fjell	Nor	Hills, Mountain
Fjord	Dan., Nor., Sw	Fiord
Fleuve	Fr	River
Fljót	Ice	Stream
Fluss	Ger	River
Fors	Sw	Waterfall
Fos, Foss	Dan., Nor	Waterfall
Gamla	Nor	Old
Gamle	Dan	Old
Gata	Jap	Lake
Gawa	Jap	River
Gebel	Arabic	Mountain
Gebergte	Du	Mt. Range
Gebirge	Ger	Mt. Range
Gobi	Mongol	Desert
Goe	Jap	Pass
Gol	Mongol, Turk	Lake, Stream
Golf	Ger., Du	Gulf
Golfe	Fr	Gulf
Golfo	Sp., It., Port	Gulf
Gölü	Turk	Lake
Gora	Russ	Mountain
Grand, Grande	Fr., Sp	Big
Groot	Du	Big
Gross	Ger	Big
Grosso	It., Port	Big
Guba	Russ	Bay, Gulf
Gunto	Jap	Archipelago
Gunung	Malay	Mountain
Hai	Ch	Sea
Haixia	Ch	Strait
Halbinsel	Ger	Peninsula
Hamáda, Hammada	Arabic	Rocky Plateau
Hamn	Sw	Harbor
Hamún	Per	Marsh
Hanto	Jap	Peninsula
Has, Hassi	Arabic	Well
Hav	Dan., Nor., Sw	Sea, Ocean
Havet	Nor	Bay
Havn	Dan., Nor	Harbor
Havre	Fr	Harbor
He	Ch	River, Stream
Higashi, Higasi	Jap	East
Hochebene	Ger	Plateau
Hoek	Du	Cape
Hoku	Jap	North
Holm	Dan., Nor., Sw	Island
Hory	Czech	Mountains
Hoved	Dan., Nor	Cape, Promontory
Hu	Ch	Lake
Huang	Ch	Yellow
Huk	Dan., Nor., Sw	Point
Hus, Huus	Dan., Nor., Sw	House
Idehan	Arabic	Desert
Ile	Fr	Island
Ilet	Fr	Islet
Ilot	Fr	Islet
Indre	Dan., Nor	Inner
Inferieur, Inferiore	Fr., It	Lower
Inner, Inre	Sw	Inner
Insel	Ger	Island
Irmak	Turk	River
Isla	Sp	Island
Isola	It	Island
Jabal, Jebel	Arabic	Mountains
Järvi	Finn	Lake
Jaure	Sw	Lake
Jiang	Ch	River, Stream
Jima	Jap	Island
Joki	Finn	River
Kaap	Du	Cape
Kabir, Kebir	Arabic	Big
Kai	Jap	Sea
Kaikyo	Jap	Strait
Kami	Turk	Upper
Kanaal	Du	Canal
Kanal	Russ., Ger	Canal, Channel
Kao	Thai	Mountain
Kap, Kapp	Nor., Sw., Ice	Cape
Kaupunki	Finn	Town
Kawa	Jap	River
Khao	Thai	Mountain
Khrebet	Russ	Mt. Range
Kita	Jap	North
Klein	Du., Ger	Small
Klint	Dan	Promontory
Kô	Jap	Lake
Koh	Camb., Khmer	Island
Kop	Du	Peak, Head
Köping	Sw	Market, Borough
Körfez, Körfezi	Turk	Gulf
Kosa	Russ	Spit
Kosui	Jap	Lake
Kraal	Du	Native Village
Kuchuk	Turk	Small
Kuh, Kuhha	Per	Mt. Range, Mts.
Kul	Sinkiang Turki	Lake
Kum	Turk	Desert
Kuro	Jap	Black
Laag	Du	Low
Lac	Fr	Lake
Lago	Port., Sp., It	Lake
Lagoa	Port	Lagoon
Laguna	Sp	Lagoon
Lagune	Fr	Lagoon
Lahti	Finn	Bay, Bight
Län	Sw	County
Liedao	Ch	Islands, Archipelago
Lilla	Sw	Small
Lille	Dan., Nor	Small
Ling	Ch	Mountain
Llanos	Sp	Plains
Mae Nam	Thai	River
Mali, Malaya	Russ	Small
Man	Korean	Bay
Mar	Sp., Port	Sea
Mare	It	Sea
Medio	Sp	Middle
Meer	Du	Lake
Meer	Ger	Sea
Mer	Fr	Sea
Meridionale	It	Southern
Meseta	Sp	Plateau
Middelst, Midden	Du	Middle
Minami	Jap	Southern
Mis	Russ	Cape
Misaki	Jap	Cape
Mittel	Ger	Middle
Mont	Fr	Mountain
Montagne	Fr	Mountain
Montaña	Sp	Mountains
Monte	Sp., It., Port	Mountain
More	Russ	Sea
Mörön	Mong	Stream
Morro	Port., Sp	Mountain, Promontory
Morue	Fr	Hill
Moyen	Fr	Middle
Muang	Siamese	Town
Mui	Vietnamese	Cape, Point
Mys	Russ	Cape
Nada	Jap	Sea
Naka	Jap	Middle
Nam	Burm., Lao	River
Namakzar	Per	Salt Waste
Nan	Jap	South
Nes	Nor	Cape, Point
Nevado	Sp	Snow-covered Peak
Nieder	Ger	Lower
Nishi, Nisi	Jap	West
Nizhni, Nizhnyaya	Russ	Lower
Njarga	Finn	Peninsula, Promontory
Nong	Thai	Lake
Noord	Du	North
Nord	Fr., Ger	North
Norte	Sp., It., Port	North
Nos	Russ	Cape
Novi, Novaya	Russ	New
Nur, Nuur	Ch., Mong	Lake
Nuruu	Mong	Mountains
Nusa	Malay	Island
Ny, Nya	Nor., Sw	New
O	Jap	Big
Ö	Nor., Sw	Island
Ober	Ger	Upper
Occidental, Occidentale	Sp., It	Western
Odde	Dan	Point
Oeste	Port	West
Ooster	Du	Eastern
Opper, Over	Du	Upper
Oriental	Sp., Fr	Eastern
Orientale	It	Eastern
Orta	Turk	Middle
Ost	Ger	East
Ostrov	Russ	Island
Ouest	Fr	West
Öy	Nor	Island
Ozero	Russ	Lake
Pampa	Sp	Plain
Pas	Fr	Channel, Strait
Paso	Sp	Pass
Passo	It., Port	Pass
Peña	Sp	Rock, Mountain
Pendi	Ch	Basin
Penisola	It	Peninsula
Pequeño	Sp	Small
Pereval	Russ	Pass
Peski	Russ	Desert
Petit, Petite	Fr	Small
Phu	Lao, Annamese	Mtn.
Pic	Fr	Mountain
Piccolo	It	Small
Pico	Port., Sp	Mountain, Peak
Pik	Russ	Mountain, Peak
Piton	Fr	Mountain, Peak
Planalto	Port	Plateau
Plato	Russ	Plateau
Pointe	Fr	Point
Poluostrov	Russ	Peninsula
Ponta	Port	Point
Presa	Sp	Reservoir
Presqu'île	Fr	Peninsula
Proliv	Russ	Strait
Pulou, Pulo	Malay	Island
Punt	Du	Point
Punta	Sp., It., Port	Point
Qiryat	Hebrew	City, Settlement
Qum	Turk	Desert
Qundao	Ch	Islands
Rada	Sp	Inlet
Rade	Fr	Bay, Inlet
Ras	Arabic	Cape
Reka	Russ	River
Retto	Jap	Archipelago
Ria	Sp	Estuary
Río	Sp	River
Rivier, Rivière	Du., Fr	River
Rud	Per	River
Sai	Jap	West
Saki	Jap	Cape
Salar, Salina	Sp	Salt Deposit
Salto	Sp	Falls
San	Jap., Korean	Hill
Sanmaek	Korean	Mt. Range
Schiereiland	Du	Peninsula
Se	Camb., Khmer	River
See	Ger	Sea, Lake
Selvas	Sp., Port	Woods, Forest
Seno	Sp	Bay, Gulf
Serra	Port	Mts.
Serranía	Sp	Mts.
Seto	Jap	Strait
Settentrionale	It	Northern
Severni, Severnaya	Russ	North
Shamo	Ch	Desert
Shan	Ch., Jap	Hill, Mts.
Shankou	Ch	Pass
Shatt	Arabic	River
Shima	Jap	Island
Shimo	Jap	Lower
Shin	Jap	Land
Shiro	Jap	White
Shoto	Jap	Islands
Si	Ch	West
Sierra	Sp	Mt. Range, Mts.
Sjö	Nor., Sw	Lake, Sea
Sok, Suk, Souk	Arabic	Market
Song	Annamese	River
Sopka	Russ	Volcano
Spitze	Ger	Mt. Peak
Sredni, Srednyaya	Russ	Middle
Stad	Dan., Nor., Sw	City
Stari, Staraya	Russ	Old
Step	Russ	Treeless Plain
Straat	Du	Strait
Strasse	Ger	Strait
Stretto	It	Strait
Ström	Dan., Nor., Sw	Sound
Stung	Camb., Khmer	River
Su	Turk	River
Sud, Süd	Sp., Fr., Ger	South
Suido	Jap	Strait, Channel
Sul	Port	South
Sund	Dan., Nor., Sw	Sound
Sungei	Malay	River
Supérieur	Fr	Upper
Superior, Superiore	Sp., It	Upper
Sur	Sp	South
Suyu	Turk	River
Ta	Ch	Big
Tafelland	Du	Plateau
Tagh	Turk	Mt. Range
Take	Jap	Peak, Ridge
Takht	Arabic	Lower
Tal	Ger	Valley
Tanjung	Malay	Cape, Point
Tell	Arabic	Hill
Thale	Thai	Sea, Lake
Tind	Nor	Peak
Tô	Jap	East
To	Jap	Island
Toge	Jap	Pass
Trask	Finn	Lake
Tugh	Somali	Dry Valley
Ujung	Malay	Point
Umi	Jap	Bay
Unter	Ger	Lower
Ura	Jap	Inlet
Uul	Mong	Mountain
Val	Fr	Valley
Vatn	Nor	Lake
Vecchio	It	Old
Veld	Du	Plain, Field
Velho	Port	Old
Verkhni	Russ	Upper
Vesi	Finn	Lake
Viejo	Sp	Old
Vik	Nor., Sw	Bay
Vishni, Vishnyaya	Russ	High
Vodokhranilishche	Russ	Reservoir
Volcán	Sp	Volcano
Vostochni, Vostochnaya	Russ	East, Eastern
Wadi	Arabic	Dry River
Wald	Ger	Forest
Wan	Jap	Bay
Westersch	Du	Western
Wüste	Ger	Desert
Yama	Jap	Mountain
Yug, Yuzhni, Yuzhnaya	Russ	South, Southern
Zaki	Jap	Cape
Zaliv	Russ	Bay, Gulf
Zangbo	Tibetan	River, Stream
Zapadni, Zapadnaya	Russ	Western
Zee	Du	Sea
Zemlya	Russ	Land
Zizhiqu	Ch	Autonomous Region
Zuid	Du	South

MAP PROJECTIONS

by Erwin Raisz

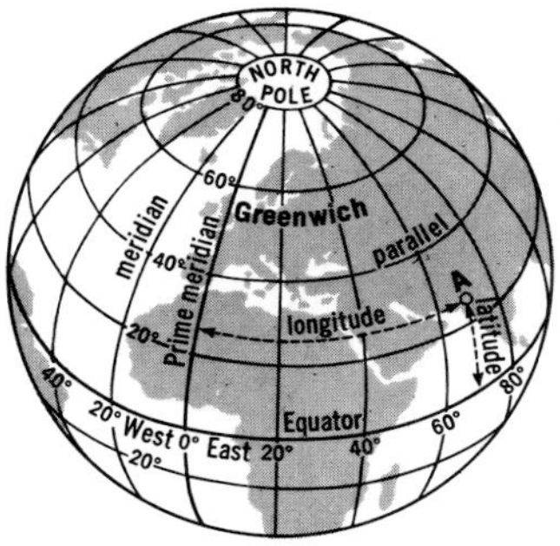

Our earth is rotating around its *axis* once a day. The two end points of its axis are the *poles;* the line circling the earth midway between the poles is the *equator.* The arc from either of the poles to the equator is divided into 90 *degrees.* The distance, expressed in degrees, from the equator to any point is its *latitude* and circles of equal latitude are the *parallels.* On maps it is customary to show parallels of evenly-spaced degrees such as every fifth or every tenth.

The equator is divided into 360 degrees. Lines circling from pole to pole through the degree points on the equator are called *meridians.* They are all equal in length but by international agreement the meridian passing through the Greenwich Observatory in London has been chosen as *prime meridian.* The distance, expressed in degrees, from the prime meridian to any point is its *longitude.* While meridians are all equal in length, parallels become shorter and shorter as they approach the poles. Whereas one degree of latitude represents everywhere approximately 69 miles, one degree of longitude varies from 69 miles at the equator to nothing at the poles.

Each degree is divided into 60 minutes and each minute into 60 seconds. One minute of latitude equals a nautical mile.

The map is flat but the earth is nearly spherical. Neither a rubber ball nor any part of a rubber ball may be flattened without stretching or tearing unless the part is very small. To present the curved surface of the earth on a flat map is not difficult as long as the areas under consideration are small, but the mapping of countries, continents, or the whole earth requires some kind of *projection.* Any regular set of parallels and meridians upon which a map can be drawn makes a map projection. Many systems are used.

In any projection only the parallels or the meridians or some other set of lines can be *true* (the same length as on the globe of corresponding scale); all other lines are too long or too short. Only on a globe is it possible to have both the parallels and the meridians true. The scale given on a flat map cannot be true everywhere. The construction of the various projections begins usually with laying out the parallels or meridians which have true lengths.

Rectangular Projection

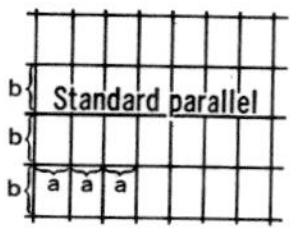

RECTANGULAR PROJECTION — This is a set of evenly-placed meridians and horizontal parallels. The central or *standard parallel* and all meridians are true. All other parallels are either too long or too short. The projection is used for simple maps of small areas, as city plans, etc.

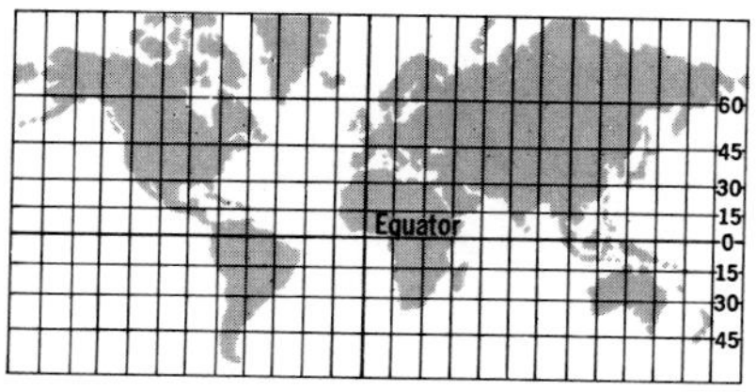

Mercator Projection

MERCATOR PROJECTION — In this projection the meridians are evenly-spaced vertical lines. The parallels are horizontal, spaced so that their length has the same relation to the meridians as on a globe. As the meridians converge at higher latitudes on the globe, while on the map they do not, the parallels have to be drawn also farther and farther apart to maintain the correct relationship. When every very small area has the same shape as on a globe we call the projection *conformal.* The most interesting quality of this projection is that all *compass directions* appear as straight lines. For this reason it is generally used for marine charts. It is also frequently used for world maps in spite of the fact that the high latitudes are very much exaggerated in size. Only the equator is true to scale; all other parallels and meridians are too long. The Mercator projection did *not* derive from projecting a globe upon a cylinder.

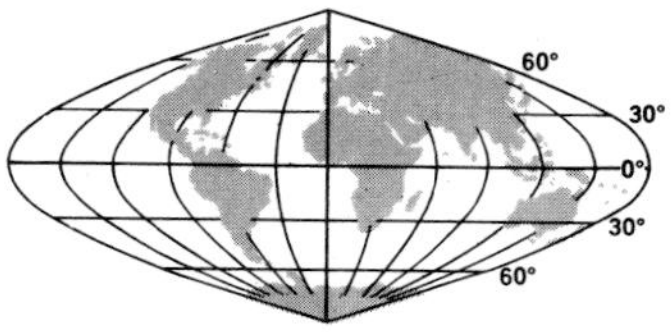

Sinusoidal Projection

SINUSOIDAL PROJECTION — The parallels are truly-spaced horizontal lines. They are divided truly and the connecting curves make the meridians. It does not make a good world map because the outer regions are distorted, but the central portion is good and this part is often used for maps of Africa and South America. Every part of the map has the same area as the corresponding area on the globe. It is an *equal-area* projection.

MOLLWEIDE PROJECTION — The meridians are equally-spaced ellipses; the parallels are horizontal lines spaced so that every belt of latitude should have the same area as on a globe. This projection is popular for world maps, especially in European atlases.

GOODE'S INTERRUPTED PROJECTIONS—Only the good central part of the Mollweide or sinusoidal (or both) projection is used and the oceans are cut. This makes an equal-area map with little distortion of shape. It is commonly used for world maps.

ECKERT PROJECTIONS — These are similar to the sinusoidal or the Mollweide projections, but the poles are shown as lines half the length of the equator. There are several variants; the meridians are either sine curves or ellipses; the parallels are horizontal and spaced either evenly or so as to make the projection equal area. Their use for world maps is increasing. The figure shows the elliptical equal-area variant.

CONIC PROJECTION — The original idea of the conic projection is that of capping the globe by a cone upon which both the parallels and meridians are projected from the center of the globe. The cone is then cut open and laid flat. A cone can be made tangent to any chosen *standard parallel*.

The actually-used conic projection is a modification of this idea. The radius of the standard parallel is obtained as above. The meridians are straight radiating lines spaced truly on the standard parallel. The parallels are concentric circles spaced at true distances. All parallels except the standard are too long. The projection is used for maps of countries in middle latitudes, as it presents good shapes with small scale error.

There are several variants: The use of two *standard parallels*, one near the top, the other near the bottom of the map, reduces the scale error. In the *Albers projection* the parallels are spaced unevenly, to make the projection equal-area. This is a good projection for the United States. In the *Lambert conformal conic projection* the parallels are spaced so that any small quadrangle of the grid should have the same shape as on the globe. This is the best projection for air-navigation charts as it has relatively straight azimuths.

An *azimuth* is a great-circle direction reckoned clockwise from north. A *great-circle direction* points to a place along the shortest line on the earth's surface. This is not the same as compass direction. The center of a great circle is the center of the globe.

BONNE PROJECTION — The parallels are laid out exactly as in the conic projection. All parallels are divided truly and the connecting curves make the meridians. It is an equal-area projection. It is used for maps of the northern continents, as Asia, Europe, and North America.

POLYCONIC PROJECTION — The central meridian is divided truly. The parallels are non-concentric circles, the radii of which are obtained by drawing tangents to the globe as though the globe were covered by several cones rather than by only one. Each parallel is divided truly and the connecting curves make the meridians. All meridians except the central one are too long. This projection is used for large-scale topographic sheets — less often for countries or continents.

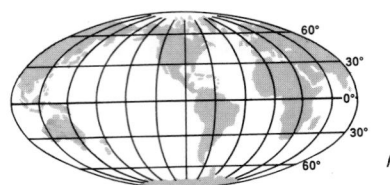

Mollweide Projection

Goode's Interrupted Projection

Eckert Projection

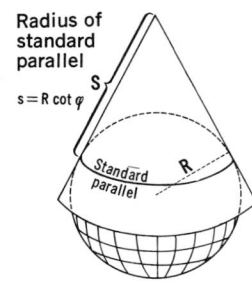

Radius of standard parallel

$s = R \cot \varphi$

Conic Projection

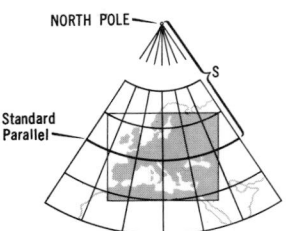

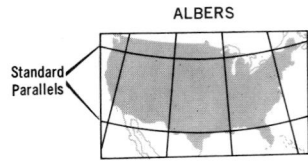

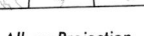

Albers Projection

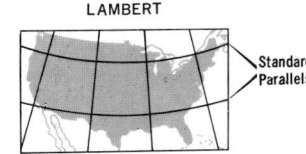

Lambert Conformal Conic Projection

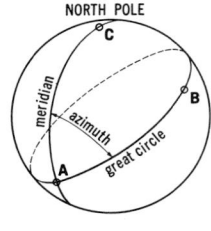

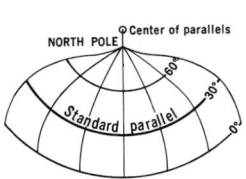

Bonne Projection

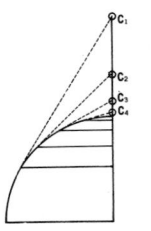

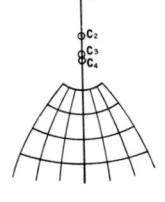

Polyconic Projection

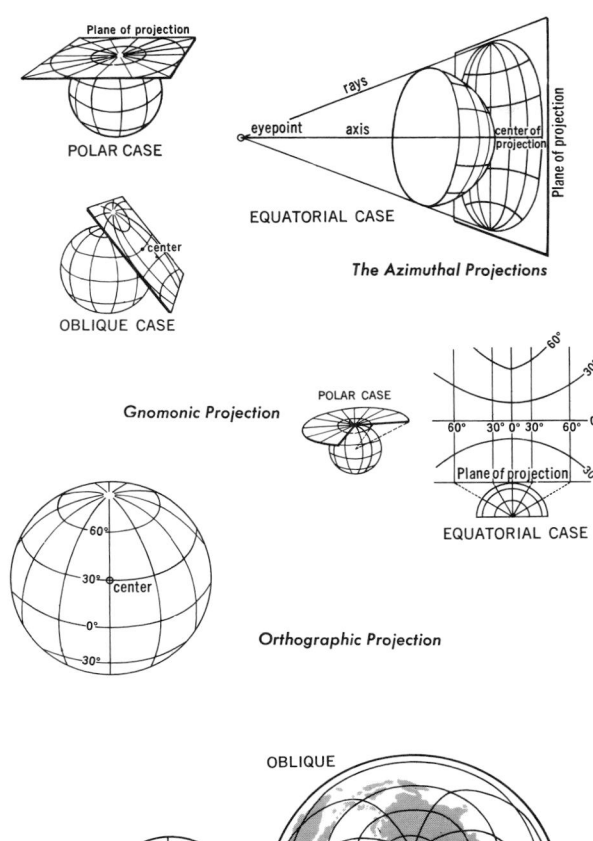

POLAR CASE

EQUATORIAL CASE

The Azimuthal Projections

OBLIQUE CASE

Gnomonic Projection

POLAR CASE

EQUATORIAL CASE

Orthographic Projection

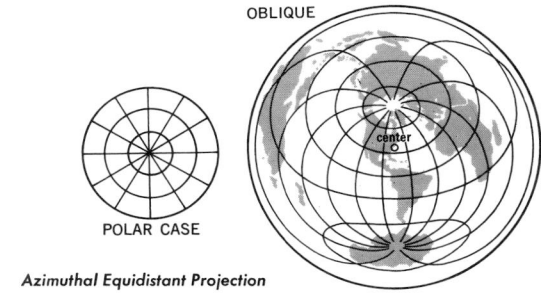

OBLIQUE

POLAR CASE

Azimuthal Equidistant Projection

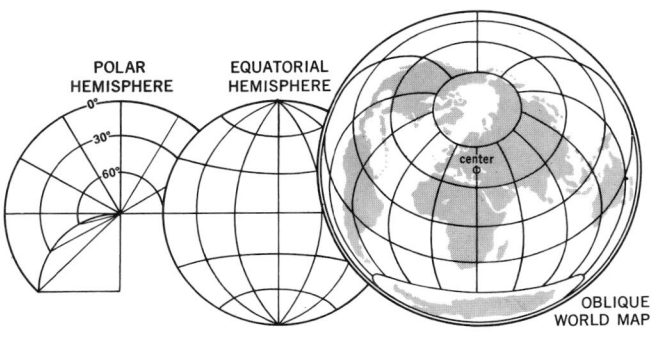

POLAR HEMISPHERE   EQUATORIAL HEMISPHERE

OBLIQUE WORLD MAP

Lambert Azimuthal Equal-Area Projection

THE AZIMUTHAL PROJECTIONS — In this group a part of the globe is projected from an eyepoint onto a plane. The eyepoint can be at different distances, making different projections. The plane of projection can be tangent at the equator, at a pole, or at any other point on which we want to focus attention. The most important quality of all azimuthal projections is that they show every point at its true direction (azimuth) from the center point, and all points equally distant from the center point will be equally distant on the map also.

GNOMONIC PROJECTION — This projection has the eyepoint at the center of the globe Only the central part is good; the outer regions are badly distorted. Yet the projection has one important quality, all great circles being shown as straight lines. For this reason it is used for laying out the routes for long range flying or trans-oceanic navigation.

ORTHOGRAPHIC PROJECTION — This projection has the eyepoint at infinite distance and the projecting rays are parallel. The polar or equatorial varieties are rare but the oblique case became very popular on account of its visual quality. It looks like a picture of a globe. Although the distortion on the peripheries is extreme, we see it correctly because the eye perceives it not as a map but as a picture of a three-dimensional globe. Obviously only a hemisphere (half globe) can be shown.

Some azimuthal projections do not derive from the actual process of projecting from an eyepoint, but are arrived at by other means:

AZIMUTHAL EQUIDISTANT PROJECTION — This is the only projection in which every point is shown both at true great-circle direction and at true distance from the center point, but all other directions and distances are distorted. The principle of the projection can best be understood from the polar case. Most polar maps are in this projection. The oblique case is used for radio direction finding, for earthquake research, and in long-distance flying. A separate map has to be constructed for each central point selected.

LAMBERT AZIMUTHAL EQUAL-AREA PROJECTION—The construction of this projection can best be understood from the polar case. All three cases are widely used. It makes a good polar map and it is often extended to include the southern continents. It is the most common projection used for maps of the Eastern and Western Hemispheres, and it is a good projection for continents as it shows correct areas with relatively little distortion of shape. Most of the continent maps in this atlas are in this projection.

IN THIS ATLAS, on almost all maps, parallels and meridians have been marked because they are useful for the following:

(a) They show the north-south and east-west directions which appear on many maps at oblique angles especially near the margins.

(b) With the help of parallels and meridians every place can be exactly located; for instance, New York City is at 41° N and 74° W on any map.

(c) They help to measure distances even in the distorted parts of the map. The scale given on each map is true only along certain lines which are specified in the foregoing discussion for each projection. One degree of latitude equals nearly 69 statute miles or 60 nautical miles. The length of one degree of longitude varies (1° long. $= 1°$ lat. $\times$ cos lat.).

WORLD STATISTICAL TABLES

Elements of the Solar System

	Mean Distance from Sun: in Miles	in Kilometers	Period of Revolution around Sun	Period of Rotation on Axis	Equatorial Diameter: in Miles	in Kilometers	Surface Gravity (Earth = 1)	Mass (Earth = 1)	Mean Density (Water = 1)	Number of Satellites
MERCURY	35,990,000	57,900,000	87.97 days	59 days	3,032	4,880	0.38	0.055	5.5	0
VENUS	67,240,000	108,200,000	224.70 days	243 days†	7,523	12,106	0.90	0.815	5.25	0
EARTH	93,000,000	149,700,000	365.26 days	23h 56m	7,926	12,755	1.00	1.00	5.5	1
MARS	141,730,000	228,100,000	687.00 days	24h 37m	4,220	6,790	0.38	0.107	4.0	2
JUPITER	483,880,000	778,700,000	11.86 years	9h 50m	88,750	142,800	2.87	317.9	1.3	16
SATURN	887,130,000	1,427,700,000	29.46 years	10h 14m	74,580	120,020	1.32	95.2	0.7	17
URANUS	1,783,700,000	2,870,500,000	84.01 years	10h 49m†	31,600	50,900	0.93	14.6·	1.3	5
NEPTUNE	2,795,500,000	4,498,800,000	164.79 years	15h 48m	30,200	48,600	1.23	17.2	1.8	3
PLUTO	3,667,900,000	5,902,800,000	247.70 years	6.39 days (?)	1,500	2,400	0.03 (?)	0.01(?)	0.7(?)	1

†Retrograde motion

Facts About the Sun

Equatorial diameter	865,000 miles	1,392,000 kilometers
Period of rotation on axis	25-35 days*	
Orbit of galaxy	every 225 million years	
Surface gravity (Earth = 1)	27.8	
Mass (Earth = 1)	333,000	
Density (Water = 1)	1.4	
Mean distance from Earth	93,000,000 miles	149,700,000 kilometers

*Rotation of 25 days at Equator, decreasing to about 35 days at the poles.

Facts About the Moon

Equatorial diameter	2,160 miles	3,476 kilometers
Period of rotation on axis	27 days, 7 hours, 43 minutes	
Period of revolution around Earth (sidereal month)	27 days, 7 hours, 43 minutes	
Phase period between new moons (synodic month)	29 days, 12 hours, 44 minutes	
Surface gravity (Earth = 1)	0.16	
Mass (Earth = 1)	0.0123	
Density (Water = 1)	3.34	
Maximum distance from Earth	252,710 miles	406,690 kilometers
Minimum distance from Earth	221,460 miles	356,400 kilometers
Mean distance from Earth	238,860 miles	384,400 kilometers

Dimensions of the Earth

	Area in Sq. Miles	Sq. Kilometers
Superficial area	196,939,000	510,073,000
Land surface	57,506,000	148,941,000
Water surface	139,433,000	361,132,000

	Miles	Kilometers
Equatorial circumference	24,902	40,075
Polar circumference	24,860	40,008
Equatorial diameter	7,926.4	12,756.4
Polar diameter	7,899.8	12,713.6
Equatorial radius	3,963.2	6,378.2
Polar radius	3,949.9	6,356.8
Volume of the Earth	2.6×10^{11} cubic miles	10.84×10^{11} cubic kilometers
Mass or weight	6.6×10^{21} short tons	6.0×10^{21} metric tons
Maximum distance from Sun	94,600,000 miles	152,000,000 kilometers
Minimum distance from Sun	91,300,000 miles	147,000,000 kilometers

The Continents

	Area in: Sq. Miles	Sq. Km.	Percent of World's Land
Asia	17,128,500	44,362,815	29.5
Africa	11,707,000	30,321,130	20.2
North America	9,363,000	24,250,170	16.2
South America	6,875,000	17,806,250	11.8
Antarctica	5,500,000	14,245,000	9.5
Europe	4,057,000	10,507,630	7.0
Australia	2,966,136	7,682,300	5.1

Oceans and Major Seas

	Area in: Sq. Miles	Sq. Km.	Greatest Depth in: Feet	Meters
Pacific Ocean	64,186,000	166,241,700	36,198	11,033
Atlantic Ocean	31,862,000	82,522,600	28,374	8,648
Indian Ocean	28,350,000	73,426,500	25,344	7,725
Arctic Ocean	5,427,000	14,056,000	17,880	5,450
Caribbean Sea	970,000	2,512,300	24,720	7,535
Mediterranean Sea	969,000	2,509,700	16,896	5,150
Bering Sea	875,000	2,266,250	15,800	4,800
Gulf of Mexico	600,000	1,554,000	12,300	3,750
Sea of Okhotsk	590,000	1,528,100	11,070	3,370
East China Sea	482,000	1,248,400	9,500	2,900
Sea of Japan	389,000	1,007,500	12,280	3,740
Hudson Bay	317,500	822,300	846	258
North Sea	222,000	575,000	2,200	670
Black Sea	185,000	479,150	7,365	2,245
Red Sea	169,000	437,700	7,200	2,195
Baltic Sea	163,000	422,170	1,506	459

Major Ship Canals

	Length in: Miles	Kms.	Minimum Feet	Depth in: Meters
Volga-Baltic, U.S.S.R.	225	362	—	—
Baltic-White Sea, U.S.S.R.	140	225	16	5
Suez, Egypt	100.76	162	42	13
Albert, Belgium	80	129	16.5	5
Moscow-Volga, U.S.S.R.	80	129	18	6
Volga-Don, U.S.S.R.	62	100	—	—
Göta, Sweden	54	87	10	3
Kiel (Nord-Ostsee), Ger.	53.2	86	38	12
Panama Canal, Panama	50.72	82	41.6	13
Houston Ship, U.S.A.	50	81	36	11

Largest Islands

	Area in: Sq. Mi.	Sq. Km.		Area in: Sq. Mi.	Sq. Km.		Area in: Sq. Mi.	Sq. Km.
Greenland	840,000	2,175,600	South I., New Zealand	58,393	151,238	Hokkaido, Japan	28,983	75,066
New Guinea	305,000	789,950	Java, Indonesia	48,842	126,501	Banks, Canada	27,038	70,028
Borneo	290,000	751,100	North I., New Zealand	44,187	114,444	Ceylon, Sri Lanka	25,332	65,610
Madagascar	226,400	586,376	Newfoundland, Canada	42,031	108,860	Tasmania, Australia	24,600	63,710
Baffin, Canada	195,928	507,454	Cuba	40,533	104,981	Svalbard, Norway	23,957	62,049
Sumatra, Indonesia	164,000	424,760	Luzon, Philippines	40,420	104,688	Devon, Canada	21,331	55,247
Honshu, Japan	88,000	227,920	Iceland	39,768	103,000	Novaya Zemlya (north isl.), U.S.S.R.	18,600	48,200
Great Britain	84,400	218,896	Mindanao, Philippines	36,537	94,631	Marajó, Brazil	17,991	46,597
Victoria, Canada	83,896	217,290	Ireland	31,743	82,214	Tierra del Fuego, Chile & Argentina	17,900	46,360
Ellesmere, Canada	75,767	196,236	Sakhalin, U.S.S.R.	29,500	76,405	Alexander, Antarctica	16,700	43,250
Celebes, Indonesia	72,986	189,034	Hispaniola, Haiti & Dom. Rep.	29,399	76,143			

Principal Mountains of the World

Mountain	Feet	Meters
Everest, Nepal-China	29,028	8,848
Godwin Austen (K2), Pakistan-China	28,250	8,611
Kanchenjunga, Nepal-India	28,208	8,598
Lhotse, Nepal-China	27,923	8,511
Makalu, Nepal-China	27,824	8,481
Dhaulagiri, Nepal	26,810	8,172
Nanga Parbat, Pakistan	26,660	8,126
Annapurna, Nepal	26,504	8,078
Gasherbrum, Pakistan-China	26,740	8,068
Nanda Devi, India	25,645	7,817
Rakaposhi, Pakistan	25,550	7,788
Kamet, India	25,447	7,756
Gurla Mandhada, China	25,355	7,728
Kongur Shan, China	25,325	7,719
Tirich Mir, Pakistan	25,230	7,690
Gongga Shan, China	24,790	7,556
Muztagata, China	24,757	7,546
Communism Peak, U.S.S.R.	24,599	7,498
Pobeda Peak, U.S.S.R.	24,406	7,439
Chomo Lhari, Bhutan-China	23,997	7,314
Muztag, China	23,891	7,282
Cerro Aconcagua, Argentina	22,831	6,959
Ojos del Salado, Chile-Argentina	22,572	6,880
Bonete, Chile-Argentina	22,541	6,870
Tupungato, Chile-Argentina	22,310	6,800
Pissis, Argentina	22,241	6,779
Mercedario, Argentina	22,211	6,770
Huascarán, Peru	22,205	6,768
Llullaillaco, Chile-Argentina	22,057	6,723
Nevada Ancohuma, Bolivia	21,489	6,550
Illampu, Bolivia	21,276	6,485
Chimborazo, Ecuador	20,561	6,267
McKinley, Alaska	20,320	6,194
Logan, Canada (Yukon)	19,524	5,951
Cotopaxi, Ecuador	19,347	5,897
Kilimanjaro, Tanzania	19,340	5,895
El Misti, Peru	19,101	5,822
Pico Cristóbal Colón, Colombia	19,029	5,800
Huila, Colombia	18,865	5,750
Citlaltépetl (Orizaba), Mexico	18,855	5,747
El'brus, U.S.S.R.	18,510	5,642
Damavand, Iran	18,376	5,601
St. Elias, Alaska-Canada (Yukon)	18,008	5,489
Vilcanota, Peru	17,999	5,486
Popocatépetl, Mexico	17,887	5,452
Dykhtau, U.S.S.R.	17,070	5,203
Kenya, Kenya	17,058	5,199
Ararat, Turkey	16,946	5,165
Vinson Massif, Antarctica	16,864	5,140
Margherita (Ruwenzori), Africa	16,795	5,119
Kazbek, U.S.S.R.	16,512	5,033
Puncak Jaya, Indonesia	16,503	5,030
Tyree, Antarctica	16,289	4,965
Blanc, France	15,771	4,807
Klyuchevskaya Sopka, U.S.S.R.	15,584	4,750
Fairweather (Br. Col., Canada)	15,300	4,663
Dufourspitze (Mte. Rosa), Italy-Switzerland	15,203	4,634
Ras Dashan, Ethiopia	15,157	4,620
Matterhorn, Switzerland	14,691	4,478
Whitney, California, U.S.A.	14,494	4,418
Elbert, Colorado, U.S.A.	14,433	4,399
Rainier, Washington, U.S.A.	14,410	4,392
Shasta, California, U.S.A.	14,162	4,350
Pikes Peak, Colorado, U.S.A.	14,110	4,301
Finsteraarhorn, Switzerland	14,022	4,274
Mauna Kea, Hawaii, U.S.A.	13,796	4,205
Mauna Loa, Hawaii, U.S.A.	13,677	4,169
Jungfrau, Switzerland	13,642	4,158
Cameroon, Cameroon	13,350	4,069
Grossglockner, Austria	12,457	3,797
Fuji, Japan	12,389	3,776
Cook, New Zealand	12,349	3,764
Etna, Italy	11,053	3,369
Kosciusko, Australia	7,310	2,228
Mitchell, North Carolina, U.S.A.	6,684	2,037

Longest Rivers of the World

River	Miles	Kms.
Nile, Africa	4,145	6,671
Amazon, S. Amer.	3,915	6,300
Chang Jiang (Yangtze), China	3,900	6,276
Mississippi-Missouri-Red Rock, U.S.A.	3,741	6,019
Ob'-Irtysh-Black Irtysh, U.S.S.R.	3,362	5,411
Yenisey-Angara, U.S.S.R.	3,100	4,989
Huang He (Yellow), China	2,877	4,630
Amur-Shilka-Onon, Asia	2,744	4,416
Lena, U.S.S.R.	2,734	4,400
Congo (Zaire), Africa	2,718	4,374
Mackenzie-Peace-Finlay, Canada	2,635	4,241
Mekong, Asia	2,610	4,200
Missouri-Red Rock, U.S.A.	2,564	4,125
Niger, Africa	2,548	4,101
Paraná-La Plata, S. Amer.	2,450	3,943
Mississippi, U.S.A.	2,348	3,778
Murray-Darling, Australia	2,310	3,718
Volga, U.S.S.R.	2,194	3,531
Madeira, S. Amer.	2,013	3,240
Purus, S. Amer.	1,995	3,211
Yukon, Alaska-Canada	1,979	3,185
St. Lawrence, Canada-U.S.A.	1,900	3,058
Rio Grande, Mexico-U.S.A.	1,885	3,034
Syrdar'ya-Naryn, U.S.S.R.	1,859	2,992
São Francisco, Brazil	1,811	2,914
Indus, Asia	1,800	2,897
Danube, Europe	1,775	2,857
Salween, Asia	1,770	2,849
Brahmaputra, Asia	1,700	2,736
Euphrates, Asia	1,700	2,736
Tocantins, Brazil	1,677	2,699
Xi (Si), China	1,650	2,655
Amudar'ya, Asia	1,616	2,601
Nelson-Saskatchewan, Canada	1,600	2,575
Orinoco, S. Amer.	1,600	2,575
Zambezi, Africa	1,600	2,575
Paraguay, S. Amer.	1,584	2,549
Kolyma, U.S.S.R.	1,562	2,514
Ganges, Asia	1,550	2,494
Ural, U.S.S.R.	1,509	2,428
Japurá, S. Amer.	1,500	2,414
Arkansas, U.S.A.	1,450	2,334
Colorado, U.S.A.-Mexico	1,450	2,334
Negro, S. Amer.	1,400	2,253
Dnieper, U.S.S.R.	1,368	2,202
Orange, Africa	1,350	2,173
Irrawaddy, Burma	1,325	2,132
Brazos, U.S.A.	1,309	2,107
Ohio-Allegheny, U.S.A.	1,306	2,102
Kama, U.S.S.R.	1,262	2,031
Red, U.S.A.	1,222	1,966
Don, U.S.S.R.	1,222	1,967
Columbia, U.S.A.-Canada	1,214	1,953
Saskatchewan, Canada	1,205	1,939
Peace-Finlay, Canada	1,195	1,923
Tigris, Asia	1,181	1,901
Darling, Australia	1,160	1,867
Angara, U.S.S.R.	1,135	1,827
Sungari, Asia	1,130	1,819
Pechora, U.S.S.R.	1,124	1,809
Snake, U.S.A.	1,000	1,609
Churchill, Canada	1,000	1,609
Pilcomayo, S. Amer.	1,000	1,609
Magdalena, Colombia	1,000	1,609
Uruguay, S. Amer.	994	1,600
Platte-N. Platte, U.S.A.	990	1,593
Ohio, U.S.A.	981	1,578
Pecos, U.S.A.	926	1,490
Oka, U.S.S.R.	918	1,477
Canadian, U.S.A.	906	1,458
Colorado, Texas, U.S.A.	894	1,439
Dniester, U.S.S.R.	876	1,410

Principal Natural Lakes

Lake	Area Sq. Miles	Area Sq. Km.	Max. Depth Feet	Max. Depth Meters
Caspian Sea, U.S.S.R.-Iran	143,243	370,999	3,264	995
Lake Superior, U.S.A.-Canada	31,820	82,414	1,329	405
Lake Victoria, Africa	26,724	69,215	270	82
Lake Huron, U.S.A.-Canada	23,010	59,596	748	228
Lake Michigan, U.S.A.	22,400	58,016	923	281
Aral Sea, U.S.S.R.	15,830	41,000	213	65
Lake Tanganyika, Africa	12,650	32,764	4,700	1,433
Lake Baykal, U.S.S.R.	12,162	31,500	5,316	1,620
Great Bear Lake, Canada	12,096	31,328	1,356	413
Lake Nyasa (Malawi), Africa	11,555	29,928	2,320	707
Great Slave Lake, Canada	11,031	28,570	2,015	614
Lake Erie, U.S.A.-Canada	9,940	25,745	210	64
Lake Winnipeg, Canada	9,417	24,390	60	18
Lake Ontario, U.S.A.-Canada	7,540	19,529	775	244
Lake Ladoga, U.S.S.R.	7,104	18,399	738	225
Lake Balkhash, U.S.S.R.	7,027	18,200	87	27
Lake Maracaibo, Venezuela	5,120	13,261	100	31
Lake Chad, Africa	4,000-10,000	10,360-25,900	25	8
Lake Onega, U.S.S.R.	3,710	9,609	377	115
Lake Eyre, Australia	3,500-0	9,000-0	—	—
Lake Titicaca, Peru-Bolivia	3,200	8,288	1,000	305
Lake Nicaragua, Nicaragua	3,100	8,029	230	70
Lake Athabasca, Canada	3,064	7,936	400	122
Reindeer Lake, Canada	2,568	6,651	—	—
Lake Turkana (Rudolf), Africa	2,463	6,379	240	73
Issyk-Kul', U.S.S.R.	2,425	6,281	2,303	702
Lake Torrens, Australia	2,230	5,776	—	—
Vänern, Sweden	2,156	5,584	328	100
Nettiling Lake, Canada	2,140	5,543	—	—
Lake Winnipegosis, Canada	2,075	5,374	38	12
Lake Mobutu Sese Seko (Albert), Africa	2,075	5,374	160	49
Kariba Lake, Zambia-Zimbabwe	2,050	5,310	295	90
Lake Nipigon, Canada	1,872	4,848	540	165
Lake Mweru, Zaire-Zambia	1,800	4,662	60	18
Lake Manitoba, Canada	1,799	4,659	12	4
Lake Taymyr, U.S.S.R.	1,737	4,499	85	26
Lake Khanka, China-U.S.S.R.	1,700	4,403	33	10
Lake Kioga, Uganda	1,700	4,403	25	8

Foreign City Weather

Two figures are given for each of the months, thus 88/73. The first figure is the average daily high temperature (°F) and the second is the average daily low temperature (°F) for the month. The boldface figures indicate the average number of days with rain for each month.

	January	February	March	April	May	June	July	August	September	October	November	December
ABIDJAN, Ivory Coast	88/73 3	90/75 4	90/75 6	90/75 9	88/75 16	85/73 18	83/73 8	82/71 7	83/73 8	85/74 13	87/74 13	88/74 6
ACAPULCO, Mexico	85/70 0	87/70 0	87/70 0	87/71 1	89/74 4	89/76 15	89/75 11	89/75 14	88/75 18	88/74 12	88/72 4	87/70 1
ACCRA, Ghana	87/73 1	88/75 2	88/76 4	88/76 6	87/75 9	84/74 10	81/73 4	80/71 3	81/73 4	85/74 8	87/75 3	88/75 2
ADDIS ABABA, Ethiopia	75/43 2	76/47 5	77/49 8	77/50 10	77/50 10	74/49 20	69/50 28	69/50 27	72/49 21	75/45 3	73/43 2	73/41 2
ALGIERS, Algeria	59/49 11	61/49 9	63/52 9	68/55 5	73/59 5	78/65 2	83/70 1	85/71 1	81/69 4	74/63 7	66/56 11	60/51 12
AMSTERDAM, Netherlands	40/34 19	41/34 15	46/37 13	52/43 14	60/50 12	65/55 12	69/59 14	68/59 14	64/56 15	56/48 18	47/41 19	41/35 19
ANKARA, Turkey	39/24 8	42/26 8	51/31 7	63/40 7	73/49 7	78/53 5	86/59 2	87/59 1	78/52 3	69/44 5	57/37 6	43/29 9
APIA, Western Samoa	86/75 22	85/76 19	86/74 19	86/75 14	85/74 12	85/74 7	85/74 9	84/75 9	84/74 11	85/75 14	86/74 16	85/74 19
ATHENS, Greece	54/42 7	55/43 6	60/46 5	67/52 3	77/60 3	85/67 2	90/72 1	90/72 1	83/66 2	74/60 4	64/52 5	57/46 7
BAGHDAD, Iraq	60/39 4	64/42 3	71/48 4	85/57 3	97/67 1	105/73 0	110/76 0	110/76 0	104/70 0	92/61 1	77/51 3	64/42 5
BALI, Indonesia	88/74 19	88/74 14	88/74 13	88/74 13	87/74 9	87/71 3	87/70 1	87/70 1	89/71 1	90/73 2	90/75 6	88/74 14
BANGKOK, Thailand	89/68 1	91/72 1	93/75 3	95/77 7	93/77 9	91/76 10	90/76 13	90/76 13	89/76 15	88/75 14	88/72 5	87/68 1
BARCELONA, Spain	56/42 5	57/44 7	61/47 7	64/51 8	71/57 8	77/63 5	81/69 4	82/69 5	78/65 7	71/58 8	62/50 7	57/44 6
BEIRUT, Lebanon	62/51 15	63/51 12	66/54 9	72/58 5	78/64 2	84/74 1	83/73 11	84/74 11	84/74 9	85/74 4	73/57 6	62/50 7
BELFAST, Northern Ireland	45/34 20	47/34 18	49/35 20	53/39 18	59/43 17	64/49 10	66/51 18	65/51 20	62/48 17	55/42 19	50/37 21	46/35 25
BELGRADE, Yugoslavia	37/27 8	41/27 8	53/35 7	64/45 9	74/53 9	79/58 11	84/61 6	83/60 7	76/55 6	65/47 8	52/39 8	40/30 9
BERLIN, Germany	35/26 10	38/27 8	46/32 9	55/38 9	65/46 9	72/56 10	74/55 10	72/54 10	66/48 8	55/41 8	43/33 8	37/29 11
BIARRITZ, France	54/40 10	52/38 11	52/38 11	63/44 11	69/53 11	72/56 10	76/58 9	77/61 7	77/58 9	74/55 11	58/44 12	53/41 14
BOGOTA, Colombia	67/48 6	68/49 7	67/50 13	67/51 20	66/51 17	65/51 16	64/50 18	65/50 16	66/49 13	66/50 20	66/50 20	66/49 15
BOMBAY, India	83/67 1	83/67 1	86/72 1	89/76 1	91/80 1	89/79 16	85/77 21	85/76 13	85/76 13	89/76 3	89/73 1	87/69 1
BONN, Germany	39/30 7	37/26 6	50/35 7	58/39 14	67/44 13	69/52 19	73/56 16	72/55 15	67/50 16	58/45 16	47/37 15	44/36 15
BRASILIA, Brazil	80/65 17	81/64 20	82/64 17	82/62 10	79/56 5	77/52 2	78/51 2	82/55 3	82/55 4	82/64 16	82/66 17	78/64 16
BRINDISI, Italy	55/43 10	57/43 6	60/45 5	65/50 5	73/57 4	80/64 2	84/68 1	84/69 3	80/65 4	70/58 8	64/52 10	58/46 8
BUCHAREST, Romania	33/20 6	38/24 5	51/33 6	63/41 6	74/51 8	81/58 9	86/61 7	86/60 5	82/61 5	65/44 5	49/35 6	37/26 6
BUDAPEST, Hungary	35/26 7	40/28 6	51/36 7	62/44 8	72/52 9	78/57 7	82/61 7	81/59 6	74/53 7	61/45 8	47/37 8	38/31 9
BUENOS AIRES, Argentina	85/63 7	83/63 7	79/60 7	72/53 8	64/47 7	57/41 7	57/42 8	60/43 9	64/46 8	69/50 9	76/56 9	82/61 8
CAIRO, Egypt	65/47 1	69/48 1	75/52 1	83/57 1	91/63 1	95/68 0	96/70 0	95/71 0	90/68 0	86/65 1	78/58 1	68/50 1
CALCUTTA, India	80/55 1	84/59 2	93/69 2	97/75 3	96/77 7	92/79 13	89/79 18	89/78 18	90/78 13	89/74 6	84/64 1	79/55 1
CAPE TOWN, South Africa	78/60 3	79/60 2	77/58 3	72/53 6	67/49 9	65/46 9	63/45 10	64/46 9	65/49 7	70/52 5	73/55 5	76/58 10
CARACAS, Venezuela	75/56 6	77/56 2	79/58 3	81/60 4	80/62 9	78/62 14	78/61 15	79/61 13	80/61 13	79/61 12	77/60 13	78/58 18
CHARLOTTE AMALIE, Virgin Islands	82/73 18	81/72 13	82/73 12	83/74 13	85/76 15	86/77 15	87/77 18	88/78 18	87/78 17	87/77 18	85/76 19	83/74 18
COLOMBO, Sri Lanka	86/72 7	87/72 7	88/74 8	88/76 14	87/78 19	85/77 18	85/77 11	85/77 11	85/77 13	85/75 19	85/73 16	85/72 11
COPENHAGEN, Denmark	36/29 9	36/28 7	41/31 8	50/37 9	61/44 8	67/51 8	72/55 9	69/54 12	63/49 8	53/42 9	43/35 10	38/32 11
DARWIN, Australia	90/77 20	90/77 18	91/77 18	92/76 6	91/73 1	88/69 1	87/67 0	89/70 0	91/74 2	93/77 5	94/78 10	92/78 15
DJAKARTA, Indonesia	84/74 18	84/74 18	86/74 15	87/75 11	87/75 11	87/74 7	87/73 5	87/73 4	88/74 5	87/74 8	86/74 12	85/74 14
DUBLIN, Ireland	47/35 13	47/35 11	51/36 10	54/38 11	59/42 11	65/48 11	67/51 13	67/51 13	63/47 12	57/43 12	51/38 12	47/36 13
EDINBURGH, Scotland	43/35 18	43/35 15	47/36 15	50/39 16	55/43 15	62/48 15	65/52 17	64/52 17	60/48 16	53/44 18	47/39 18	44/36 17
FLORENCE, Italy	49/35 9	53/36 9	60/40 7	68/46 7	75/53 9	84/58 5	89/63 4	88/62 4	81/58 6	69/51 9	58/42 10	50/37 9
GENEVA, Switzerland	39/29 10	43/30 9	51/35 10	58/41 11	66/48 12	73/55 11	77/58 9	76/57 10	69/52 10	58/44 11	47/37 11	40/31 10
GUAYAQUIL, Ecuador	88/70 20	88/70 20	88/72 24	89/71 14	88/68 4	87/68 4	84/67 2	86/65 0	87/66 2	86/68 3	88/68 4	88/70 10
HAMBURG, Germany	35/28 12	37/30 10	42/33 10	51/39 11	60/47 9	67/53 10	69/56 12	67/55 13	63/51 10	53/44 11	44/36 11	38/31 12
HAMILTON, Bermuda	68/58 14	68/57 13	68/57 12	71/59 9	76/64 7	81/69 11	85/73 10	86/74 11	84/72 10	79/69 12	74/63 13	70/60 15
HAVANA, Cuba	79/65 6	81/67 6	81/67 4	84/69 4	86/72 7	88/74 10	89/75 9	89/75 10	88/75 11	85/73 11	81/69 7	79/67 6
HELSINKI, Finland	27/17 11	26/15 8	32/22 8	43/31 8	55/41 8	63/49 9	71/57 8	66/55 12	57/46 11	45/37 12	37/30 11	31/22 11
HONG KONG	64/56 4	63/55 5	67/60 7	75/67 7	82/74 13	85/78 18	87/78 17	87/78 15	85/77 12	81/73 6	74/65 2	68/59 3
JERUSALEM, Israel	55/41 9	56/42 11	65/46 3	73/50 4	81/57 1	85/60 1	87/63 0	87/64 0	85/62 0	81/59 1	70/53 4	59/45 7
JOHANNESBURG, South Africa	78/58 12	77/58 9	75/55 5	72/50 7	66/43 3	62/39 1	63/39 1	68/43 1	73/48 2	77/53 7	77/55 10	78/57 11
KARACHI, Pakistan	77/55 1	79/58 3	85/67 1	90/73 0	93/79 1	93/82 1	91/81 2	88/79 2	88/77 1	91/72 1	87/64 1	80/57 1
KINGSTON, Jamaica	86/67 3	86/67 3	86/68 2	87/70 3	87/72 4	89/74 4	90/73 4	90/73 7	89/73 6	88/73 8	87/71 5	87/69 4
LAGOS, Nigeria	88/74 2	89/77 3	89/78 3	89/77 10	87/76 16	85/74 20	83/74 16	82/73 16	83/74 14	85/74 16	88/75 7	88/75 2
LA PAZ, Bolivia	63/43 21	63/43 18	64/42 18	65/40 9	64/37 5	62/34 2	62/33 2	63/35 4	64/38 9	66/40 9	67/42 11	65/42 18

Foreign City Weather

City	January	February	March	April	May	June	July	August	September	October	November	December
LAS PALMAS, Canary Is.	70/58 8	71/58 5	71/59 5	71/61 3	73/62 1	75/65 1	77/67 1	79/70 1	79/69 1	79/67 5	76/64 7	72/60 8
LENINGRAD, USSR	23/12 17	24/12 15	33/18 13	45/31 11	58/42 12	66/51 12	71/57 13	66/53 15	57/45 14	45/37 15	34/27 17	26/18 18
LIMA, Peru	82/66 1	83/67 1	83/66 10	80/63 7	74/60 4	68/58 1	67/57 1	66/56 2	68/57 1	71/58 7	74/60 1	78/62 1
LISBON, Portugal	56/46 9	58/47 8	61/49 10	64/52 7	69/56 6	75/60 2	79/63 1	80/64 1	76/62 4	69/57 7	62/52 10	57/47 10
LIVERPOOL, England	44/36 18	44/36 13	48/38 13	52/41 14	58/46 14	63/51 13	66/55 15	65/55 16	61/51 15	55/46 17	48/41 17	45/37 18
LONDON, England	44/35 17	45/35 13	51/47 11	56/40 14	63/45 13	69/51 11	69/51 13	72/54 13	67/51 13	58/44 14	49/39 16	45/36 16
MADRID, Spain	47/33 9	51/35 9	57/40 11	64/44 9	71/50 9	80/57 6	87/62 3	86/62 2	77/56 6	66/48 8	54/40 10	48/35 9
MANILA, Philippines	86/69 6	88/69 3	91/71 4	93/73 4	93/75 12	91/75 17	88/75 24	87/75 23	88/75 22	88/74 19	87/72 14	86/70 11
MARACAIBO, Venezuela	90/73 1	90/73 1	91/74 1	92/76 1	92/77 6	93/77 6	94/76 5	94/77 7	94/77 6	92/76 9	91/76 8	91/75 2
MARSEILLE, France	53/38 10	52/37 9	55/38 8	59/41 10	65/46 10	72/52 9	78/58 6	83/61 4	82/61 5	67/48 14	67/50 10	59/43 11
MELBOURNE, Australia	78/57 9	78/57 8	75/55 9	68/51 13	62/47 14	57/44 16	56/42 17	59/43 17	63/46 15	70/50 13	71/51 13	75/54 11
MEXICO CITY, Mexico	66/42 4	69/43 5	75/47 5	77/51 14	78/54 17	74/55 21	73/53 27	73/54 27	74/53 23	70/50 13	68/46 6	66/43 4
MILAN, Italy	40/29 7	47/33 6	56/38 6	66/46 8	72/54 9	80/61 6	84/64 6	82/63 6	76/58 6	64/49 7	51/39 7	42/33 7
MONTEVIDEO, Uruguay	83/62 6	82/61 5	78/59 5	71/53 6	64/48 6	59/43 5	58/43 6	59/43 7	63/46 6	68/49 6	74/54 7	79/59 7
MOSCOW, USSR	21/9 11	23/10 9	32/17 9	47/31 9	65/44 9	73/51 10	76/55 12	72/52 12	61/43 9	46/34 11	31/23 10	23/13 9
MUNICH, Germany	33/23 10	37/25 9	45/31 10	54/37 13	63/45 13	69/51 14	71/53 13	71/53 13	64/48 11	53/40 10	42/31 9	36/26 11
NAIROBI, Kenya	77/54 5	79/55 6	77/57 11	75/58 16	72/56 17	70/53 9	69/51 6	70/52 6	75/52 6	76/55 8	74/56 15	74/55 11
NAPLES, Italy	54/42 11	55/43 11	60/46 6	67/50 6	73/56 6	81/62 3	86/67 1	86/67 3	81/63 6	72/56 9	63/49 11	57/45 11
NASSAU, Bahamas	77/65 6	77/64 5	79/66 6	81/69 6	84/71 7	87/74 12	88/75 14	89/76 14	88/75 15	85/73 13	81/70 9	79/67 6
NEW DELHI, India	70/44 2	75/49 2	87/58 1	97/68 1	105/79 2	102/83 4	96/81 8	96/81 8	93/75 4	93/65 1	84/52 1	73/46 1
NICE, France	56/40 8	56/41 8	59/45 8	64/49 7	69/56 8	76/62 5	81/66 2	81/66 12	77/62 7	70/55 9	62/48 7	58/43 8
NOUMEA, New Caledonia	86/72 10	86/73 12	85/72 16	83/70 13	79/66 15	77/64 13	76/62 13	76/61 12	78/63 8	80/65 7	83/68 7	86/70 6
ODESSA, USSR	28/22 7	31/26 4	39/32 5	52/41 6	67/55 6	74/62 7	79/65 3	78/65 5	68/56 4	57/47 5	43/35 5	33/27 6
OSLO, Norway	30/20 8	32/20 7	40/25 7	50/34 7	62/43 7	69/51 8	73/56 10	69/53 11	60/45 8	49/37 10	37/29 9	31/24 10
PALERMO, Sicily, Italy	58/47 14	60/47 10	62/49 7	67/53 5	83/59 5	82/66 1	86/71 1	87/72 1	83/69 4	75/62 10	67/55 9	61/50 11
PALMA, Majorca, Spain	57/42 8	59/43 8	62/45 8	66/49 8	73/55 9	80/61 8	84/66 1	86/67 4	81/64 6	74/57 8	65/50 9	59/44 11
PAPEETE, Tahiti	89/72 16	89/72 16	89/72 17	89/72 10	87/70 10	86/69 8	86/69 5	86/68 6	86/69 6	87/70 9	88/71 13	88/72 14
PARIS, France	42/32 15	45/33 13	52/36 15	60/41 14	67/47 13	73/52 11	76/55 12	75/55 12	69/50 11	59/44 14	49/38 14	43/33 17
PHNOM PENH, Cambodia	87/68 1	90/72 1	93/74 3	94/76 6	92/76 14	91/76 15	89/71 13	87/69 11	88/75 19	87/76 17	88/71 7	86/71 4
PEKING, China	35/15 3	41/20 3	53/30 3	70/42 6	80/56 6	88/65 9	89/75 16	89/76 17	80/58 7	69/44 4	50/30 2	37/19 2
PORT-AU-PRINCE, Haiti	87/68 3	88/68 5	89/69 7	89/71 11	92/76 14	92/73 8	94/74 7	93/73 11	91/73 12	90/72 12	86/74 9	86/71 4
PORT OF SPAIN, Trinidad	85/67 14	88/67 8	87/67 8	88/69 7	90/72 13	87/71 17	87/70 20	87/71 21	88/71 18	88/71 16	88/71 7	86/69 16
PRAGUE, Czechoslovakia	34/25 12	38/28 11	45/33 13	55/40 12	89/70 10	72/55 14	74/58 14	73/57 12	65/52 11	54/44 11	41/35 12	34/29 13
RANGOON, Burma	89/65 1	92/67 1	96/71 1	97/76 1	92/77 14	86/76 23	85/76 26	85/76 25	85/76 20	88/76 10	88/73 3	88/67 1
RIO DE JANEIRO, Brazil	84/73 13	85/73 11	83/72 12	80/69 10	77/66 10	76/64 7	75/63 7	76/64 3	75/65 11	77/66 13	79/68 13	82/71 14
ROME, Italy	54/39 8	56/39 11	62/42 5	68/46 6	74/55 6	82/60 3	88/64 2	88/64 3	83/61 6	73/53 9	63/46 8	56/41 9
SAIGON (HO CHI MINH CITY), Vietnam	89/70 2	91/71 1	93/74 2	95/76 4	92/76 16	89/75 21	88/75 23	88/75 21	88/74 21	88/74 20	87/73 11	87/71 7
SAN JUAN, Puerto Rico	80/70 20	80/70 15	81/70 15	82/72 14	84/74 16	85/75 19	85/75 19	85/76 20	86/76 18	85/75 18	84/73 19	81/72 21
SANTIAGO, Chile	85/53 0	84/52 0	80/49 1	74/45 1	65/41 5	58/37 6	59/37 6	62/39 5	66/42 3	72/45 3	78/48 1	83/51 0
SAO PAULO, Brazil	81/63 19	82/64 17	81/62 15	78/58 10	73/54 10	71/51 8	71/49 6	73/51 8	74/54 11	76/57 13	79/59 14	80/61 13
SEOUL, South Korea	32/15 8	37/20 6	47/29 7	62/41 8	72/51 10	80/61 10	84/70 16	87/71 13	78/59 9	67/45 7	51/32 9	37/20 9
SEVILLE, Spain	59/41 8	62/44 9	67/48 9	73/51 8	80/57 5	89/63 4	96/67 1	97/68 1	89/64 2	78/57 4	67/49 9	60/44 8
SHANGHAI, China	46/33 6	46/33 6	55/40 9	66/50 9	77/59 9	82/67 11	90/74 9	87/70 9	82/66 11	74/57 4	63/45 6	53/36 6
SINGAPORE, Singapore	86/73 17	88/73 11	88/75 14	88/75 15	89/75 13	88/75 13	88/75 13	86/72 9	86/72 14	87/74 16	87/74 18	87/74 19
SOFIA, Bulgaria	34/22 6	39/25 6	51/32 8	62/41 6	70/49 11	76/54 9	82/57 7	82/56 5	74/50 6	63/42 7	50/35 7	37/26 9
STOCKHOLM, Sweden	31/23 8	31/22 7	37/26 7	45/32 6	57/41 8	65/49 7	70/55 9	68/53 10	58/46 8	48/39 9	38/31 9	33/26 9
SYDNEY, Australia	78/65 14	78/65 13	76/63 14	71/58 14	66/52 13	61/48 12	60/46 12	66/53 10	67/51 12	74/60 12	74/60 12	77/63 13
TAIPEI, Taiwan, China	66/54 9	65/53 13	70/57 12	77/63 14	83/69 12	89/73 13	92/76 10	91/75 12	88/73 10	81/67 9	75/62 7	69/57 8
TEHRAN, Iran	45/27 4	50/32 4	59/39 5	71/49 3	82/58 2	93/66 0	99/72 1	97/71 1	90/64 1	76/53 1	63/43 3	51/33 4
TEL AVIV, Israel	63/48 10	65/48 6	67/50 9	74/54 2	81/60 1	84/65 0	87/69 0	87/70 0	86/68 1	84/64 2	77/59 7	66/52 11
TOKYO, Japan	47/29 5	48/31 6	54/36 10	63/46 10	71/54 10	76/63 12	83/70 10	86/72 9	79/66 12	69/55 11	60/43 7	52/33 5
VALPARAISO, Chile	72/56 1	72/56 1	70/54 1	67/52 1	63/50 5	60/48 7	60/47 7	61/47 5	62/48 2	65/50 2	69/52 2	71/54 1
VENICE, Italy	43/33 6	46/35 5	54/41 6	63/49 5	71/57 8	78/64 8	82/67 4	82/67 5	78/62 5	65/52 7	54/43 7	46/37 7
VIENNA, Austria	34/26 8	38/28 7	47/34 7	57/41 9	66/50 9	71/56 9	75/59 9	73/58 10	66/52 7	55/44 8	44/36 8	37/30 9
WELLINGTON, New Zealand	69/56 10	69/56 9	67/54 11	63/51 13	58/47 16	55/44 17	53/42 18	54/43 17	57/46 15	60/48 14	63/50 13	67/54 12
ZURICH, Switzerland	36/26 11	52/15 11	62/22 14	70/32 14	77/39 14	83/47 15	86/51 15	84/49 14	78/42 11	68/32 14	57/25 12	49/16 13

U.S. City Weather

City	Record Temperature High (F°)	Record Temperature Low (F°)	Annual Average: Precip. (Water equiv.) (in.)	Annual Average: Snow and Sleet (in.)	Annual Average: Wind Speed (mph)	First Freeze Date 32 F° or less Average	First Freeze Date 32 F° or less Earliest on record	Last Freeze Date 32 F° or less Average	Last Freeze Date 32 F° or less Latest on record	Elevation of Station (feet)
Albany	104	—28	36.46	65.7	8.8	Oct. 13	Sept. 23	Apr. 27	May 20	292
Albuquerque	105	—17	8.33	10.7	9.0	Oct. 29	Oct. 11	Apr. 16	May 18	5,314
Atlanta	103	— 9	48.66	1.5	9.1	Nov. 12	Oct. 24	Mar. 24	Apr. 15	1,034
Baltimore	107	— 7	41.62	21.9	9.5	Oct. 26	Oct. 8	Apr. 15	May 11	155
Birmingham	107	—10	53.46	1.2	7.4	Nov. 10	Oct. 17	Mar. 17	Apr. 21	630
Bismarck	114	—45	16.15	38.4	10.6	Sept. 22	Sept. 6	May 11	May 30	1,660
Boise	111	—23	11.97	21.7	9.0	Oct. 12	Sept. 9	May 6	May 31	2,868
Boston	104	—18	41.55	41.9	12.6	Nov. 7	Oct. 5	Apr. 8	May 3	29
Buffalo	99	—21	35.19	88.6	12.3	Oct. 25	Sept. 23	Apr. 30	May 24	706
Burlington, Vt.	101	—30	32.54	78.4	8.8	Oct. 3	Sept. 13	May 10	May 24	340
Charleston, W. Va.	108	—24	43.66	28.8	6.5	Oct. 28	Sept. 29	Apr. 18	May 11	951
Charlotte	104	— 5	45.00	5.6	7.6	Nov. 4	Oct. 15	Apr. 2	Apr. 16	769
Cheyenne	100	—38	14.48	52.0	13.3	Sept. 27	Aug. 25	May 18	June 18	6,141
Chicago	105	—23	33.47	40.7	10.3	Oct. 26	Sept. 25	Apr. 20	May 14	623
Cincinnati	102	—19	40.40	23.2	9.1	Oct. 25	Sept. 28	Apr. 15	May 25	877
Cleveland	103	—19	34.15	51.5	10.8	Nov. 2	Sept. 29	Apr. 21	May 14	805
Columbia, S.C.	107	— 2	45.23	1.8	6.9	Nov. 3	Oct. 4	Mar. 30	Apr. 21	225
Columbus, Ohio	106	—20	36.98	27.7	8.7	Oct. 31	Oct. 7	Apr. 16	May 9	833
Concord, N.H.	102	—37	38.13	64.1	6.7	Sept. 24	Sept. 13	May 17	June 6	346
Dallas-Ft. Worth, Tex.	112	— 8	32.11	2.7	11.1	Nov. 21	Oct. 27	Mar. 16	Apr. 13	596
Denver	105	—30	14.60	60.1	9.0	Oct. 14	Sept. 16	May 2	May 28	5,332
Des Moines	110	—30	31.49	33.2	11.1	Oct. 10	Sept. 28	Apr. 20	May 11	963
Detroit	105	—24	31.49	31.7	10.2	Oct. 21	Sept. 23	Apr. 23	May 12	626
El Paso	109	— 8	8.47	4.4	9.6	Nov. 11	Oct. 31	Mar. 13	Apr. 11	3,916
Great Falls	107	—49	14.83	57.7	13.1	Sept. 26	Sept. 7	May 14	June 8	3,657
Hartford	102	—26	43.00	53.1	9.0	Oct. 15	Sept. 27	Apr. 22	May 10	179
Houston	108	5	47.07	0.4	7.6	Dec. 11	Oct. 25	Feb. 5	Mar. 27	108
Indianapolis	107	—25	39.98	21.3	9.7	Oct. 22	Sept. 27	Apr. 23	May 27	808
Jackson	107	— 5	50.96	0.8	7.7	Nov. 8	Oct. 9	Mar. 18	Apr. 25	331
Jacksonville	105	10	51.75	Trace	8.6	Dec. 16	Nov. 3	Feb. 6	Mar. 31	31
Juneau	90	—22	53.95	109.1	8.5	Oct. 21	Sept. 9	Apr. 22	June 8	24
Kansas City, Mo.	113	—22	36.66	19.7	10.2	Oct. 26	Sept. 30	Apr. 7	May 6	1,025
Little Rock	110	—13	48.17	5.3	8.2	Nov. 15	Oct. 23	Mar. 16	Apr. 13	265
Los Angeles	110	23	11.94	Trace	7.4	—	Dec. 9	—	Jan. 21	104
Louisville	107	—20	42.94	17.3	8.4	Oct. 25	Oct. 15	Apr. 10	Apr. 19	488
Memphis	106	—13	48.74	5.7	9.2	Nov. 5	Oct. 17	Mar. 20	Apr. 15	284
Miami	100	26	59.21	—	9.1	—	—	—	Feb. 6	12
Milwaukee	105	—25	30.18	45.2	11.8	Oct. 23	Sept. 20	Apr. 25	May 27	693
Minneapolis-St. Paul	108	—34	26.62	45.8	10.6	Oct. 13	Sept. 3	Apr. 29	May 24	838
Mobile	104	— 1	63.26	0.4	9.3	Dec. 12	Nov. 15	Feb. 17	Mar. 20	221
Nashville	107	—15	46.61	10.9	7.9	Oct. 31	Oct. 7	Apr. 3	Apr. 24	605
New Orleans	102	7	58.93	0.2	8.4	Dec. 3	Nov. 11	Feb. 15	Apr. 8	30
New York City	106	—15	43.56	29.1	9.4	Nov. 12	Oct. 19	Apr. 7	Apr. 24	87
Norfolk	105	2	45.22	7.2	10.6	Nov. 21	Nov. 7	Mar. 22	Apr. 14	30
Oklahoma City	113	—17	31.71	9.2	12.9	Nov. 7	Oct. 7	Apr. 1	May 3	1,304
Omaha	114	—32	28.48	32.5	10.9	Oct. 20	Sept. 24	Apr. 14	May 11	982
Philadelphia	106	—11	41.18	20.3	9.6	Nov. 17	Oct. 19	Mar. 30	Apr. 20	28
Phoenix	118	16	7.41	Trace	6.1	Dec. 11	Nov. 4	Jan. 27	Mar. 3	1,107
Pittsburgh	103	—20	36.21	45.5	9.4	Oct. 20	Oct. 10	Apr. 21	May 4	1,225
Portland, Me.	103	—39	42.15	74.3	8.8	Sept. 27	Sept. 17	May 12	May 31	63
Portland, Ore.	107	— 3	37.98	7.5	7.8	Dec. 1	Oct. 26	Feb. 25	May 4	39
Providence	104	—17	40.90	37.8	10.8	Oct. 26	Oct. 3	Apr. 14	Apr. 24	62
Reno	106	—19	7.65	26.8	6.4	Oct. 2	Aug. 30	May 14	June 25	4,400
Richmond	107	—12	43.77	14.3	7.6	Nov. 8	Oct. 5	Apr. 2	May 11	177
Sacramento	115	17	17.33	Trace	8.3	Dec. 11	Nov. 4	Jan. 24	Mar. 14	25
St. Louis	115	—23	36.70	17.8	9.5	Oct. 20	Sept. 28	Apr. 15	May 10	564
Salt Lake City	107	—30	15.63	58.1	8.7	Nov. 1	Sept. 25	Apr. 12	Apr. 30	4,227
San Francisco	106	20	18.88	Trace	10.5	—	Dec. 11	—	Jan. 21	18
Seattle	100	0	40.30	15.2	9.3	Dec. 1	Oct. 19	Feb. 23	Apr. 3	450
Spokane	108	—30	16.19	54.0	8.7	Oct. 12	Sept. 13	Apr. 20	May 16	2,365
Washington, D.C.	106	—15	40.00	16.8	9.2	Nov. 10	Oct. 2	Mar. 29	May 12	65
Wichita	114	—22	30.06	16.3	12.6	Nov. 1	Sept. 27	Apr. 5	Apr. 21	1,340
Wilmington, Del.	107	—15	43.63	20.1	9.1	Oct. 26	Sept. 27	Apr. 18	May 9	80

SOURCE: National Climatic Center

U.S. City Weather

City	Jan.	Feb.	Mar.	April	May	June	July	Aug.	Sept.	Oct.	Nov.	Dec.	ANNUAL
Albany	23.0°	23.7°	33.5°	46.5°	58.4°	67.7°	72.5°	70.2°	62.7°	51.4°	39.7°	27.7°	48.1°
Albuquerque	34.5	39.5	46.3	54.8	63.8	73.3	77.1	75.1	68.4	56.8	43.9	35.1	55.7
Atlanta	43.5	45.6	52.6	61.3	69.6	76.4	78.5	77.8	73.1	62.9	52.0	44.7	61.5
Baltimore	33.2	35.0	42.6	53.6	63.1	72.1	76.8	75.3	68.5	57.3	46.0	36.4	55.0
Birmingham	45.6	47.1	55.0	62.9	70.7	77.8	79.9	79.6	75.2	64.6	53.4	46.3	63.2
Bismarck	8.1	12.2	25.3	42.9	54.6	64.1	70.6	68.5	57.9	45.7	28.6	15.4	41.1
Boise	29.9	35.5	42.3	49.6	57.8	65.4	74.5	72.5	62.7	52.3	40.6	32.1	51.3
Boston	28.9	29.1	36.9	46.9	57.7	67.0	72.6	70.7	64.0	54.2	43.5	32.6	50.3
Buffalo	25.1	24.5	32.3	43.3	54.6	64.7	70.3	68.9	62.6	51.8	40.0	29.5	47.3
Burlington, Vt.	18.0	18.4	29.3	42.6	55.2	64.8	69.7	67.3	59.6	48.8	36.6	23.3	44.5
Charleston, W. Va.	36.6	38.0	46.0	56.0	64.8	72.3	76.0	74.8	69.3	58.0	46.7	38.2	56.4
Charlotte	42.0	43.9	51.0	60.0	68.9	76.0	78.7	77.4	72.2	61.6	50.9	43.1	60.5
Cheyenne	26.1	27.7	32.4	41.4	51.0	61.0	67.7	66.4	57.3	46.4	35.2	28.6	45.1
Chicago	24.7	27.1	36.4	47.8	58.2	68.4	73.8	72.5	65.6	54.5	40.4	29.4	49.9
Cincinnati	30.8	33.6	41.7	53.5	63.3	71.9	75.5	74.2	67.3	56.3	43.6	34.4	53.9
Cleveland	27.5	27.8	35.9	47.0	58.3	67.9	72.2	70.6	64.6	53.8	41.6	31.3	49.9
Columbia, S.C.	46.6	48.1	55.1	63.5	71.9	78.5	80.8	79.9	75.1	64.5	54.4	47.2	63.8
Columbus, Ohio	29.4	30.8	40.0	51.1	61.9	70.9	74.8	72.9	66.6	55.0	42.3	32.4	52.3
Concord, N.H.	21.3	22.8	31.9	44.4	56.2	64.9	70.0	67.3	59.7	49.2	37.5	25.6	45.9
Dallas-Ft. Worth, Tex.	45.6	48.8	56.9	65.2	72.7	80.9	84.5	84.6	77.8	67.8	56.1	47.7	65.7
Denver	30.1	32.8	38.7	47.4	56.7	66.6	72.6	71.3	62.6	51.6	39.6	32.3	50.2
Des Moines	20.8	24.7	36.3	50.4	61.5	71.1	76.1	73.7	65.3	54.2	38.5	26.1	49.9
Detroit	25.3	25.8	34.5	46.7	58.1	68.2	73.0	71.1	64.2	53.1	40.1	29.5	49.2
El Paso	44.7	49.3	55.6	63.8	72.2	80.8	81.9	80.2	74.8	64.7	52.5	45.2	63.8
Great Falls	21.2	26.1	31.4	43.3	53.3	60.9	69.7	67.9	57.6	48.3	34.8	27.1	45.1
Hartford	27.1	27.7	36.9	47.9	59.0	67.9	73.1	70.9	63.7	53.3	42.1	30.4	50.0
Houston	53.2	54.6	62.0	67.9	74.3	79.8	82.4	81.3	77.5	70.2	59.6	55.5	68.2
Indianapolis	28.5	30.8	40.1	52.0	62.5	71.8	75.7	73.7	66.9	55.5	42.0	31.9	52.6
Jackson	48.4	50.9	57.3	65.3	72.6	79.6	81.8	81.5	76.9	66.5	55.7	49.5	65.5
Jacksonville	55.0	56.6	61.8	67.5	73.7	78.5	80.4	80.1	77.1	68.9	60.6	54.9	67.9
Juneau	22.2	27.3	31.2	38.4	46.4	52.8	55.5	54.1	49.0	41.5	32.0	26.9	39.8
Kansas City, Mo.	29.7	33.1	43.2	55.5	65.3	74.7	79.5	78.0	70.0	59.1	44.7	33.6	55.6
Little Rock	41.7	44.8	52.9	62.5	70.1	78.2	81.3	80.5	74.1	63.8	51.9	43.8	62.1
Los Angeles	54.6	55.9	56.9	59.3	62.1	64.9	68.3	69.5	68.5	65.2	60.4	56.4	61.8
Louisville	34.7	36.8	45.6	56.3	66.0	74.6	78.3	76.8	70.4	58.9	46.4	37.2	56.9
Memphis	41.3	44.1	52.2	62.1	70.5	78.2	81.2	80.0	74.1	63.5	51.6	43.6	61.9
Miami	67.5	68.0	71.3	74.9	78.0	80.9	82.2	82.7	81.6	77.8	72.3	68.5	75.5
Milwaukee	20.9	23.2	32.6	44.3	54.3	64.5	70.7	69.7	62.5	51.5	37.7	26.1	46.5
Minneapolis-St. Paul	13.2	16.7	29.6	45.7	57.9	67.8	73.1	70.7	61.5	50.0	33.0	19.5	44.9
Mobile	51.9	54.4	60.1	67.1	74.3	80.3	81.8	81.5	78.1	68.9	58.9	53.1	67.6
Nashville	39.1	41.0	49.5	59.5	68.2	76.3	79.4	78.3	72.2	61.1	48.9	41.1	59.6
New Orleans	54.3	56.5	61.7	68.9	75.4	80.8	82.2	82.0	78.8	70.7	60.7	55.6	69.0
New York City	32.3	32.7	40.6	51.1	61.9	70.9	76.1	74.6	68.0	58.0	46.7	35.7	54.1
Norfolk	41.6	42.3	48.8	57.4	66.7	74.7	78.6	77.5	72.4	62.2	52.1	43.6	59.8
Oklahoma City	37.2	40.8	49.8	60.2	68.2	77.0	81.4	81.1	73.7	62.7	49.4	39.9	60.1
Omaha	22.0	26.5	37.5	51.7	62.7	72.3	77.4	75.1	66.3	55.0	39.3	27.5	51.1
Philadelphia	33.1	33.8	41.6	52.2	63.0	71.8	76.6	74.7	68.4	57.5	46.2	36.2	54.6
Phoenix	51.6	55.4	60.5	67.7	76.0	85.2	90.8	89.0	83.6	71.7	59.8	52.4	70.3
Pittsburgh	30.7	31.3	39.9	51.1	62.0	70.6	74.6	72.8	66.6	55.2	43.2	33.6	52.7
Portland, Me.	22.4	23.4	32.3	42.8	53.2	62.4	68.2	66.6	59.6	49.6	38.6	26.9	45.5
Portland, Ore.	38.5	43.0	45.9	50.6	57.0	60.2	65.8	65.3	62.7	54.0	45.7	41.1	52.5
Providence	29.4	29.3	37.6	47.5	57.8	66.9	72.7	71.0	63.9	54.0	43.4	32.6	50.5
Reno	31.8	36.6	41.2	47.4	54.9	62.5	70.2	68.5	60.7	50.9	41.0	33.4	49.9
Richmond	38.0	39.4	46.9	56.9	66.1	74.0	77.6	76.1	69.9	58.9	48.7	39.7	57.7
Sacramento	44.9	49.8	53.1	58.1	64.5	70.8	75.4	74.3	71.6	63.4	52.9	45.7	60.4
St. Louis	31.7	34.8	44.3	56.1	65.9	75.1	79.3	77.5	70.1	59.0	45.3	35.3	56.2
Salt Lake City	28.0	33.2	40.7	49.0	58.3	68.1	77.2	75.4	65.1	53.1	40.5	31.4	51.7
San Francisco	48.0	50.9	52.9	54.6	57.3	60.3	61.5	62.0	62.9	60.0	54.3	49.3	56.2
Seattle	38.2	42.2	43.9	48.1	55.0	59.9	64.4	63.8	59.6	51.8	44.6	40.5	51.0
Spokane	26.8	31.7	39.4	47.6	55.8	62.5	70.2	68.7	59.5	48.7	37.0	30.4	48.2
Washington, D.C.	36.1	37.7	45.7	56.1	66.0	74.3	78.4	76.9	70.3	59.6	48.4	38.4	57.3
Wichita	31.6	35.2	44.7	56.3	65.4	75.3	80.3	79.3	70.9	59.6	45.2	35.0	56.5
Wilmington, Del.	32.6	33.1	41.9	52.2	62.7	71.4	76.0	74.1	67.9	56.8	45.7	35.2	54.2

SOURCE: National Climatic Center (data based on normals for 1936-1975)

TABLES OF AIRLINE DISTANCES

All Distances in Statute Miles

Between Principal Cities of the World

FROM/TO	Azores	Bagdad	Berlin	Bombay	Buenos Aires	Callao	Cairo	Cape Town	Chicago	Istanbul	Guam	Honolulu	Juneau	London	Los Angeles
Azores	....	3906	2148	5930	5385	4825	3325	5670	3305	2880	8985	7421	4715	1562	5034
Bagdad	3906	....	2040	2022	8215	8618	785	4923	6490	1085	6380	8445	6180	2568	7695
Berlin	2148	2040	....	3947	7411	6937	1823	5949	4458	1068	7158	7384	4638	575	5849
Bombay	5930	2022	3947	....	9380	10530	2698	5133	8144	3043	4831	8172	6992	4526	8810
Buenos Aires	5385	8215	7411	9380	....	1982	7428	4332	5598	7638	10516	7653	7964	6919	6148
Callao	4825	8618	6937	10530	1982	....	7870	6195	3765	7666	9760	5993	5806	6376	4155
Cairo	3325	785	1823	2698	7428	7870	....	4476	6231	780	7175	8925	6352	2218	7675
Cape Town	5670	4923	5949	5133	4332	6195	4476	....	8551	5210	8918	11655	10382	5975	10165
Chicago	3305	6490	4458	8144	5598	3765	6231	8551	....	5530	7510	4315	2310	4015	1741
Istanbul	2880	1085	1068	3043	7638	7666	780	5210	5530	....	7015	8200	5665	1540	6895
Guam	8985	6380	7158	4831	10516	9760	7175	8918	7510	7015	....	3896	5225	7605	6255
Honolulu	7421	8445	7384	8172	7653	5993	8925	11655	4315	8200	3896	....	2825	7320	2620
Juneau	4715	6180	4638	6992	7964	5806	6352	10382	2310	5665	5225	2825	....	4496	1835
London	1562	2568	575	4526	6919	6376	2218	5975	4015	1540	7605	7320	4496	....	5496
Los Angeles	5034	7695	5849	8810	6148	4155	7675	10165	1741	6895	6255	2620	1835	5496	....
Melbourne	12190	8150	9992	6140	7336	8196	8720	6510	9837	9189	3497	5581	8162	10590	8098
Mexico City	4584	8155	6119	9818	4609	2619	7807	8620	1690	7160	7690	3846	3210	5605	1445
Montreal	2548	5814	3776	7582	5619	3954	5502	7975	750	4825	7840	4992	2647	3370	2468
New Orleans	3718	7212	5182	8952	4902	2990	6862	8390	827	6220	7895	4305	2860	4656	1695
New York	2604	6066	4025	7875	5295	3633	5701	7845	727	5060	8115	5051	2874	3500	2466
Panama	3918	7807	5902	9832	3319	1450	7230	7090	2320	6797	9220	5347	4456	5310	3025
Paris	1617	2385	540	4391	6891	6455	2020	5762	4219	1390	7675	7525	4700	210	5711
Rio de Janeiro	4312	7012	6246	8438	1230	2400	6242	3850	5320	6420	11710	8400	7611	5747	6330
San Francisco	5114	7521	5744	8523	6487	4500	7554	10340	1875	6770	5952	2407	1530	5440	345
Santiago	5718	8876	7842	10127	731	1548	8100	5080	5325	8230	9946	6935	7320	7275	5595
Seattle	4720	6848	5121	7830	6956	4964	6915	10305	1753	6124	5785	2707	870	4850	961
Shanghai	7324	4468	5323	3219	12295	10760	5290	8179	7155	5084	1945	5009	4968	5841	6598
Singapore	8338	4443	6226	2425	9940	11700	5152	6025	9475	5440	2990	6874	7375	6818	8955
Tokyo	7370	5242	5623	4247	11601	9740	6005	9234	6410	5649	1596	3940	4117	6050	5600
Wellington	11475	9782	11384	7752	6341	6696	10360	7149	8465	10790	4206	4676	7501	11790	6806

FROM/TO	Melbourne	Mexico City	Montreal	New Orleans	New York	Panama	Paris	Rio de Janeiro	San Francisco	Santiago	Seattle	Shanghai	Singapore	Tokyo	Wellington
Azores	12190	4584	2548	3718	2604	3918	1617	4312	5114	5718	4720	7324	8338	7370	11475
Bagdad	8150	8155	5814	7212	6066	7807	2385	7012	7521	8876	6848	4468	4443	5242	9782
Berlin	9992	6119	3776	5182	4026	5902	540	6246	5744	7842	5121	5323	6226	5623	11384
Bombay	6140	9818	7582	8952	7875	9832	4391	8438	8523	10127	7830	3219	2425	4247	7752
Buenos Aires	7336	4609	5619	4902	5295	3319	6891	1230	6487	731	6956	12295	9940	11601	6341
Callao	8196	2619	3954	2990	3633	1450	6455	2400	4500	1548	4964	10760	11700	9740	6696
Cairo	8720	7807	5502	6862	5701	7230	2020	6242	7554	8100	6915	5290	5152	6005	10360
Cape Town	6510	8620	7975	8390	7845	7090	5732	3850	10340	5080	10305	8179	6025	9234	7149
Chicago	9837	1690	750	827	727	2320	4219	5320	1875	5325	1753	7155	9475	6410	8465
Istanbul	9189	7160	4825	6220	5060	6797	1390	6420	6770	8230	6124	5084	5440	5649	10790
Guam	3497	7690	7840	7895	8115	9220	7675	11710	5952	9946	5785	1945	2990	1596	4206
Honolulu	5581	3846	4992	4305	5051	5347	7525	8400	2407	6935	2707	5009	6874	3940	4676
Juneau	8162	3210	2647	2860	2874	4456	4700	7611	1530	7320	870	4968	7375	4117	7501
London	10590	5605	3370	4656	3500	5310	210	5747	5440	7275	4850	5841	6818	6050	11790
Los Angeles	8098	1445	2468	1695	2466	3025	5711	6330	345	5595	961	6598	8955	5600	6806
Melbourne	....	8599	10553	9455	10541	9211	10500	8340	7970	7130	8330	4967	3768	5172	1655
Mexico City	8599	....	2247	940	2110	1532	5800	4810	1870	4122	2339	8120	10495	7190	7003
Montreal	10553	2247	....	1390	340	2545	3490	5110	2557	5461	2309	7141	9280	6546	9206
New Orleans	9455	940	1390	....	1161	1600	4846	4798	1960	4553	2137	7830	10255	6993	7950
New York	10541	2110	340	1161	....	2211	3600	4810	2606	5134	2440	7460	9617	6846	9067
Panama	9211	1532	2545	1600	2211	....	5440	3311	3349	3000	3680	9430	11800	8560	7580
Paris	10500	5800	3490	4846	3600	5440	....	5710	5680	7300	5080	5855	6730	6132	11865
Rio de Janeiro	8340	4810	5110	4798	4810	3311	5710	....	6655	1852	6945	11510	9875	11600	7510
San Francisco	7970	1870	2557	1960	2606	3349	5680	6655	....	5960	692	6245	8440	5250	6800
Santiago	7130	4122	5461	4553	5134	3000	7300	1852	5960	....	6466	11850	10270	10850	5925
Seattle	8330	2339	2309	2137	2440	3680	5080	6945	692	6466	....	5780	8200	4863	7310
Shanghai	4967	8120	7141	7830	7460	9430	5855	11510	6245	11850	5780	....	2395	1095	6080
Singapore	3768	10495	9280	10255	9617	11800	6730	9875	8440	10270	8200	2395	....	3350	5360
Tokyo	5172	7190	6546	6993	6846	8560	6132	11600	5250	10850	4863	1095	3350	....	5730
Wellington	1655	7003	9206	7950	9067	7580	11865	7510	6800	5925	7310	6080	5360	5730	......

Between Principal Cities of Europe

	Amsterdam	Athens	Baku	Barcelona	Belgrade	Berlin	Brussels	Bucharest	Budapest	Cologne	Copenhagen	Istanbul	Dresden	Dublin	Frankfort
Amsterdam	....	1340	2218	770	875	365	105	1100	710	128	381	1360	385	468	228
Athens	1340	....	1395	1160	500	1112	1292	460	698	1200	1320	350	1022	1765	1113
Baku	2218	1395	....	2427	1487	1867	2240	1220	1562	2127	1980	1070	1837	2490	2055
Barcelona	770	1160	2427	....	998	925	658	1210	924	692	1085	1380	860	919	665
Belgrade	875	500	1487	998	....	618	850	295	205	750	840	502	530	1327	652
Berlin	365	1112	1867	925	618	....	401	798	425	300	225	1068	95	815	268
Brussels	105	1292	2240	658	850	401	....	1110	700	110	475	1345	407	480	198
Bucharest	1100	460	1220	1210	295	798	1110	....	295	982	970	272	725	1560	890
Budapest	710	698	1562	924	205	425	700	295	....	590	629	650	345	1176	504
Cologne	128	1200	2127	692	750	300	110	982	590	....	400	1240	292	585	93
Copenhagen	381	1320	1960	1085	840	225	475	970	629	400	....	1240	315	768	412
Istanbul	1360	350	1070	1380	502	1068	1345	272	650	1240	1240	....	995	1830	1150
Dresden	385	1022	1837	860	530	95	407	725	345	292	315	995	....	852	236
Dublin	468	1765	2490	919	1327	815	480	1560	1176	585	768	1830	852	....	671
Frankfort	228	1113	2055	665	652	268	198	890	504	93	412	1150	236	671	....
Hamburg	232	1250	2020	910	760	165	301	950	572	228	180	1222	238	668	250
St. Petersburg	1090	1535	1570	1740	1165	815	1175	1080	965	1090	708	1292	885	1440	1075
Lisbon	1140	1770	3050	610	1555	1410	998	1842	1515	1126	1520	2005	1380	1015	1160
London	220	1476	2435	707	1040	575	202	1285	900	308	590	1540	592	300	392
Lyon	458	1100	2238	327	752	601	352	1025	680	370	760	1238	540	720	350
Madrid	912	1463	2742	316	1235	1149	807	1518	1214	875	1272	1690	1100	902	888
Marseilles	627	1025	2238	211	750	730	521	1020	718	528	906	1205	655	875	492
Milan	517	900	2028	450	540	570	435	819	476	390	720	1030	435	880	323
Moscow	1325	1388	1175	1852	1160	995	1392	920	965	1285	970	1180	1200	1728	1240
Munich	415	925	1912	648	475	310	372	725	350	282	520	975	227	855	193
Oslo	568	1610	2118	1330	1112	520	672	1245	920	635	303	1505	620	786	675
Paris	257	1300	2335	518	890	540	170	1152	770	250	634	1390	523	480	295
Riga	820	1310	1590	1440	855	520	900	870	685	805	453	1115	585	1210	780
Rome	808	650	1900	530	440	730	730	700	500	675	948	840	630	1175	698
Sofia	1073	335	1360	1072	231	810	945	194	395	945	1010	315	730	1525	860
Stockholm	695	1495	1862	1410	1005	503	793	1080	820	722	330	1340	598	1010	730
Toulouse	625	1215	2425	156	930	815	515	1210	883	875	962	1400	762	761	560
Warsaw	673	990	1555	1150	510	320	720	580	342	602	415	852	325	1130	550
Vienna	580	795	1700	830	300	322	568	520	128	460	538	790	235	1040	370
Zurich	375	1000	2050	513	590	410	312	855	498	259	595	1090	342	768	193

	Hamburg	St. Petersburg	Lisbon	London	Lyon	Madrid	Marseilles	Milan	Moscow	Munich	Oslo	Paris	Riga	Rome	Sofia	Stockholm	Toulouse	Warsaw	Vienna	Zurich
Amsterdam	232	1090	1140	220	458	912	627	517	1325	415	568	257	820	808	1073	695	625	673	580	375
Athens	1250	1535	1770	1476	1100	1463	1025	900	1388	925	1610	1300	1310	650	335	1495	1215	990	795	1000
Baku	2020	1570	3050	2435	2238	2742	2238	2028	1175	1912	2118	2335	1590	1900	1360	1862	2425	1555	1700	2050
Barcelona	910	1740	610	707	327	316	211	450	1852	648	1330	518	1440	530	1072	1410	156	1150	830	513
Belgrade	760	1165	1555	1040	752	1235	750	540	1160	475	1112	890	855	440	231	1005	930	510	300	590
Berlin	165	815	1410	575	601	1149	730	570	995	310	520	540	520	730	810	503	815	320	322	410
Brussels	301	1175	998	202	352	807	521	435	1392	372	672	170	900	730	945	793	515	720	568	312
Bucharest	950	1080	1842	1285	1025	1518	1020	819	920	725	1245	1152	870	700	194	1080	1210	580	520	855
Budapest	572	965	1515	900	680	1214	718	476	965	350	920	770	685	500	395	820	883	342	128	498
Cologne	228	1090	1126	308	370	875	528	390	1285	282	635	250	805	675	945	722	875	602	460	259
Copenhagen	180	708	1520	590	760	1272	906	720	970	520	303	634	453	948	1010	330	962	415	538	595
Istanbul	1222	1292	2005	1540	1238	1690	1205	1030	1180	975	1505	1390	1115	840	315	1340	1400	852	790	1090
Dresden	238	885	1380	592	540	1100	655	435	1200	227	620	523	585	630	730	598	762	325	235	342
Dublin	668	1440	1015	300	720	902	875	880	1728	855	786	480	1210	1175	1525	1010	761	1130	1040	768
Frankfort	250	1075	1160	392	350	888	492	323	1240	193	675	295	780	698	860	730	560	550	370	193
Hamburg	....	880	1301	448	580	1098	730	570	1100	378	445	459	600	810	954	502	780	462	460	432
St. Petersburg	880	....	2235	1300	1420	1980	1540	1315	391	1100	670	1335	300	1440	1218	435	1635	640	975	1225
Lisbon	1301	2235	....	975	850	313	810	1350	430	1208	1690	890	1940	1150	1685	1848	640	1700	1415	1058
London	448	1300	975	....	455	777	620	595	1540	526	720	210	1035	890	1235	885	550	890	762	480
Lyon	580	1420	850	455	....	577	170	210	1560	352	1005	248	1122	462	928	1080	228	850	562	206
Madrid	1098	1980	313	777	557	....	394	728	2120	910	1474	645	1670	840	1385	1598	344	1410	1110	765
Marseilles	730	1540	810	620	170	394	....	238	1642	445	1165	410	1238	372	895	1225	196	950	620	318
Milan	570	1315	1350	595	210	728	238	....	1408	215	1000	400	1010	295	715	1020	400	705	385	137
Moscow	1100	391	430	1540	1560	2120	1642	1408	....	1220	1030	1538	520	1462	1100	770	1770	710	1028	1350
Munich	378	1100	1208	526	352	910	445	215	1220	....	810	425	800	430	672	811	570	500	222	158
Oslo	445	670	1690	720	1005	1474	1165	1000	1030	810	....	830	531	1242	1295	267	1140	653	835	869
Paris	459	1335	890	210	248	645	410	400	1538	425	830	....	1050	690	1080	950	431	845	770	295
Riga	600	300	1940	1035	1122	1670	1238	1010	520	800	531	1050	....	1155	985	276	1335	350	685	930
Rome	810	1440	1150	890	462	840	372	295	1462	430	1242	690	1155	....	545	1220	569	810	470	421
Sofia	954	1218	1685	1235	928	1385	895	715	1100	672	1295	1080	985	545	....	1170	1080	662	500	780
Stockholm	502	435	1848	885	1080	1598	1225	1020	770	811	267	950	276	1220	1170	....	1281	500	770	908
Toulouse	780	1635	640	550	228	344	196	400	1770	570	1140	431	1335	569	1080	1281	....	1062	725	425
Warsaw	462	640	1700	890	850	1410	950	705	710	500	653	845	350	810	662	500	1062	....	345	640
Vienna	460	975	1415	762	562	1110	620	385	1028	222	835	770	685	470	500	770	725	345	....	365
Zurich	432	1225	1058	480	206	765	318	137	1350	158	869	295	930	421	780	908	425	640	365	....

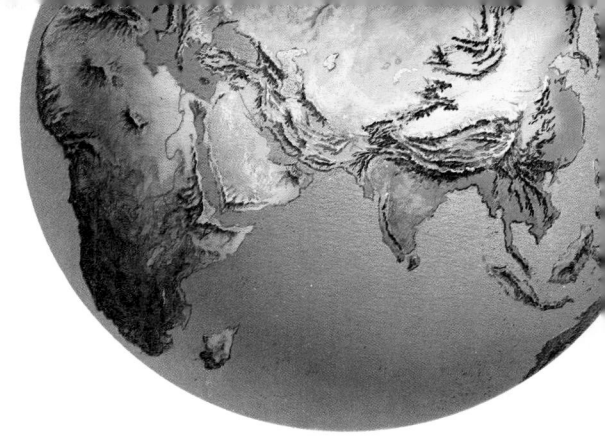

WORLD HISTORY ATLAS

A collection of maps illustrating geographically the most significant periods and events in the history of civilization.

CONTENTS

Published by **HAMMOND**® INCORPORATED **MAPLEWOOD, NEW JERSEY**

Printed in U.S.A.

PREHISTORIC MAN

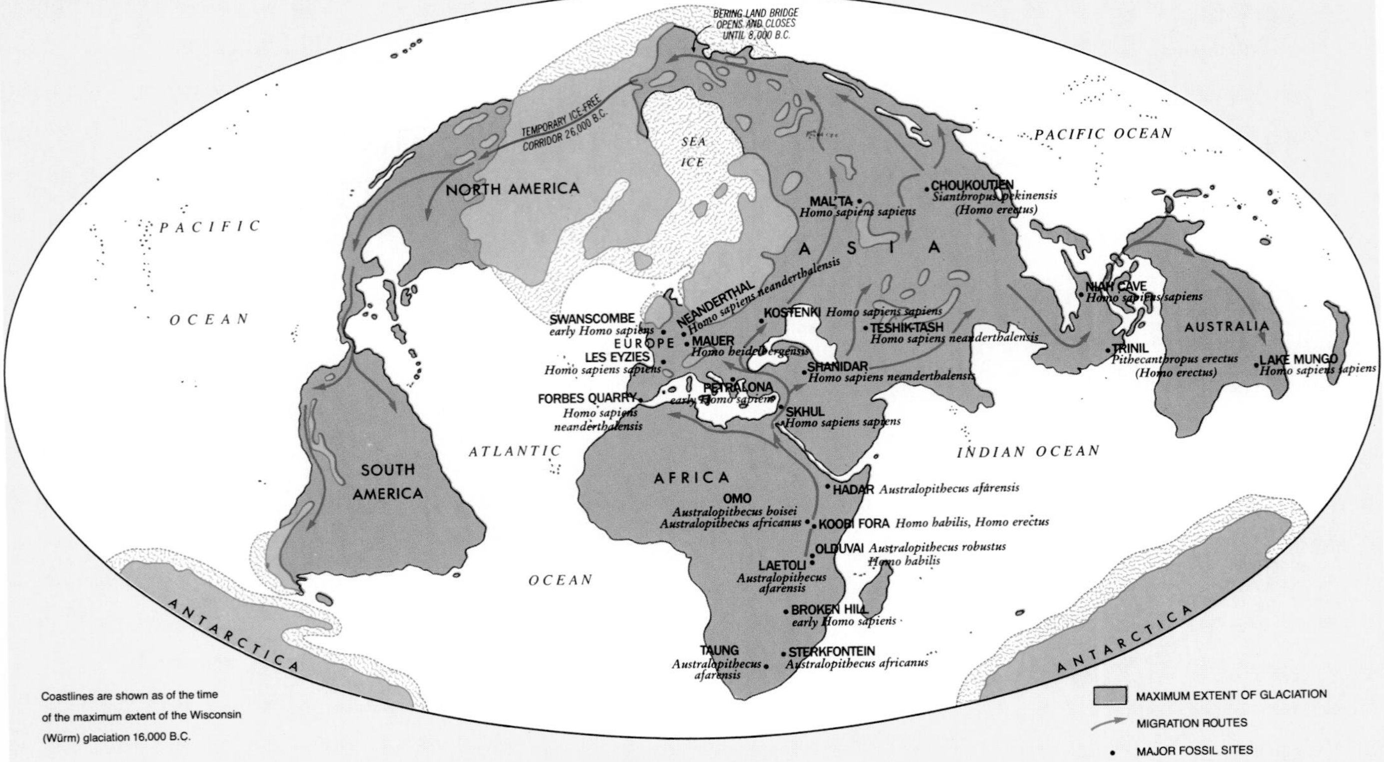

BERING LAND BRIDGE
OPENS AND CLOSES
UNTIL 8,000 B.C.

PACIFIC OCEAN

TEMPORARY ICE-FREE
CORRIDOR 26,000 B.C.

SEA ICE

NORTH AMERICA

PACIFIC

OCEAN

ASIA

MAL'TA
Homo sapiens sapiens

CHOUKOUTIEN
Sianthropus pekinensis
(Homo erectus)

NIAH CAVE
Homo sapiens sapiens

SWANSCOMBE
early *Homo sapiens*

NEANDERTHAL
Homo sapiens neanderthalensis

KOSTENKI *Homo sapiens sapiens*

TESHIK-TASH
Homo sapiens neanderthalensis

EUROPE
LES EYZIES
Homo sapiens sapiens

MAUER
Homo heidelbergensis

SHANIDAR
Homo sapiens neanderthalensis

TRINIL
Pithecanthropus erectus
(Homo erectus)

AUSTRALIA

LAKE MUNGO
Homo sapiens sapiens

FORBES QUARRY
*Homo sapiens
neanderthalensis*

PETRALONA
early *Homo sapiens*

SKHUL
Homo sapiens sapiens

ATLANTIC

SOUTH
AMERICA

OCEAN

AFRICA

HADAR *Australopithecus afarensis*

INDIAN OCEAN

OMO
*Australopithecus boisei
Australopithecus africanus*

KOOBI FORA *Homo habilis, Homo erectus*

OLDUVAI *Australopithecus robustus
Homo habilis*

LAETOLI
*Australopithecus
afarensis*

BROKEN HILL
early *Homo sapiens*

TAUNG
*Australopithecus
afarensis*

STERKFONTEIN
Australopithecus africanus

ANTARCTICA

ANTARCTICA

Coastlines are shown as of the time
of the maximum extent of the Wisconsin
(Würm) glaciation 16,000 B.C.

■ MAXIMUM EXTENT OF GLACIATION

→ MIGRATION ROUTES

• MAJOR FOSSIL SITES

© Copyright 1987 by HAMMOND INCORPORATED, Maplewood, N.J.

THE SPREAD OF FARMING
AND EARLY DOMESTICATION
OF CROPS AND ANIMALS

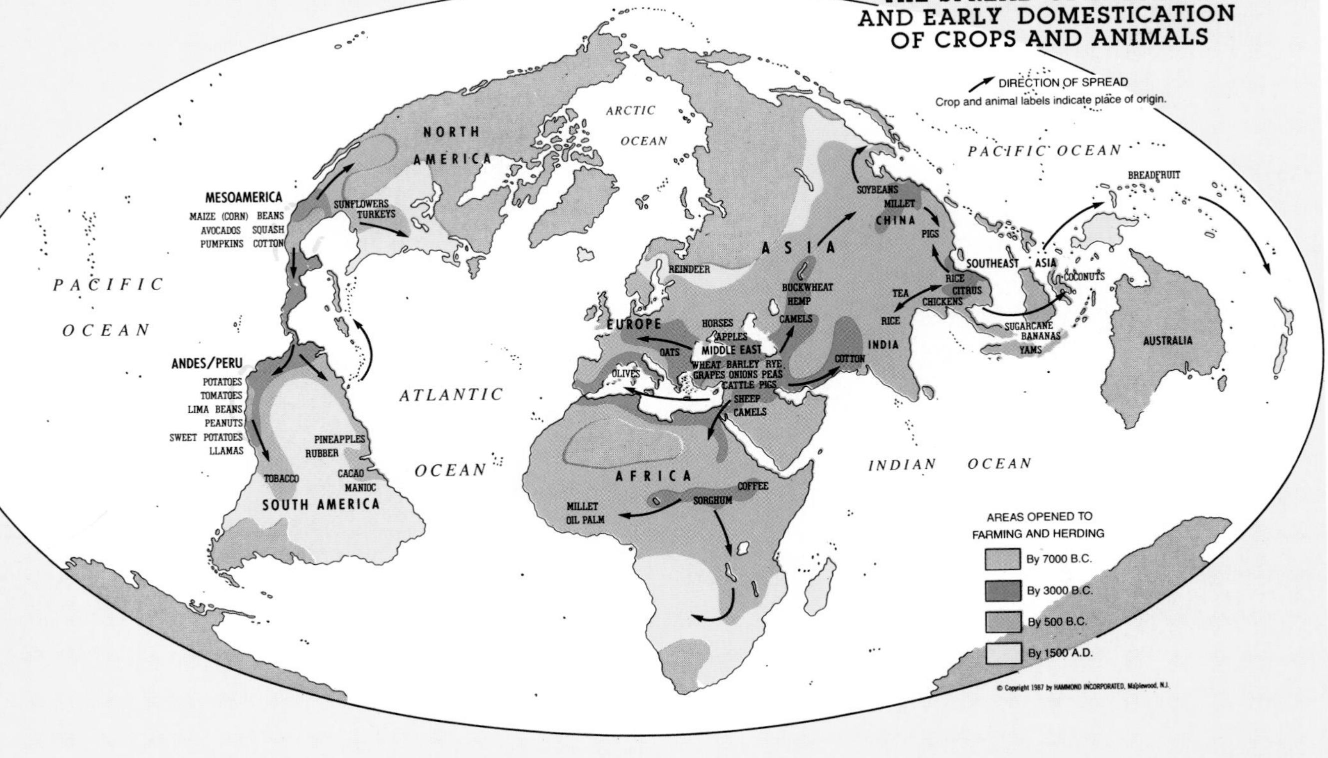

→ DIRECTION OF SPREAD
Crop and animal labels indicate place of origin.

ARCTIC OCEAN

NORTH
AMERICA

PACIFIC OCEAN

BREADFRUIT

MESOAMERICA
MAIZE (CORN) BEANS
AVOCADOS SQUASH
PUMPKINS COTTON

SUNFLOWERS
TURKEYS

SOYBEANS
MILLET
CHINA
PIGS

ASIA

SOUTHEAST ASIA
COCONUTS

PACIFIC

OCEAN

REINDEER

BUCKWHEAT
HEMP
CAMELS

TEA
CHICKENS

RICE
CITRUS

RICE

AUSTRALIA

ANDES/PERU
POTATOES
TOMATOES
LIMA BEANS
PEANUTS
SWEET POTATOES
LLAMAS

EUROPE

HORSES
APPLES
MIDDLE EAST
WHEAT BARLEY RYE
GRAPES ONIONS PEAS
CATTLE PIGS
SHEEP
CAMELS

OATS

OLIVES

INDIA

COTTON

SUGARCANE
BANANAS
YAMS

ATLANTIC

PINEAPPLES
RUBBER

TOBACCO

CACAO
MANIOC

OCEAN

AFRICA

COFFEE

INDIAN OCEAN

SOUTH AMERICA

MILLET
OIL PALM

SORGHUM

AREAS OPENED TO
FARMING AND HERDING

By 7000 B.C.
By 3000 B.C.
By 500 B.C.
By 1500 A.D.

© Copyright 1987 by HAMMOND INCORPORATED, Maplewood, N.J.

MAP A

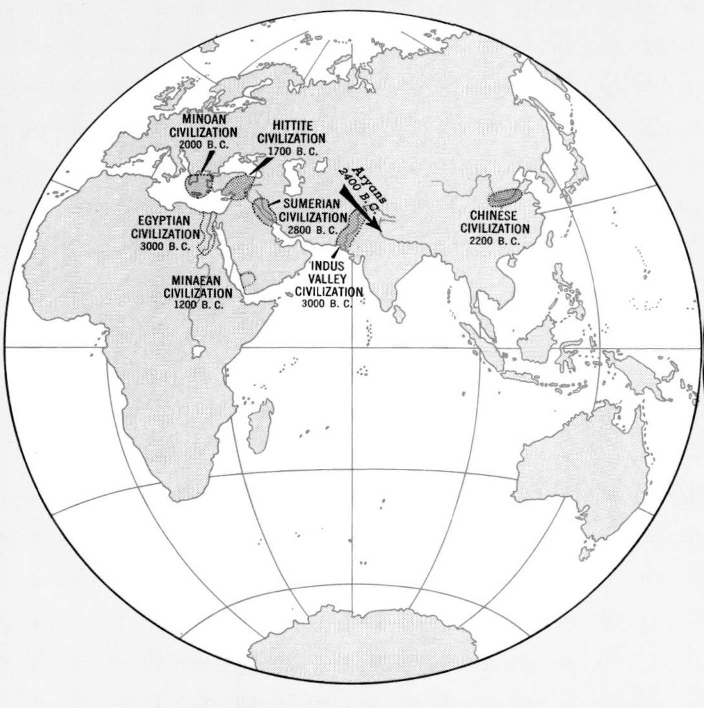

MINOAN
CIVILIZATION
2000 B.C.

HITTITE
CIVILIZATION
1700 B.C.

EGYPTIAN
CIVILIZATION
3000 B.C.

SUMERIAN
CIVILIZATION
2800 B.C.

*Aryans
2000 B.C.*

CHINESE
CIVILIZATION
2200 B.C.

MINAEAN
CIVILIZATION
1200 B.C.

INDUS
VALLEY
CIVILIZATION
3000 B.C.

*The Cradles of Civilization
3000-1000 B.C.*

MAP B

Celts

Scythians

Sakas

Hiung-Nu

Jwen-Jwen

CARTHAGE

GREEK
STATES

PERSIAN EMPIRE

CHINESE
STATES

SABAEAN
KINGDOM

INDIAN
STATES

*Major States and Empires
in 500 B.C.*

MAP C

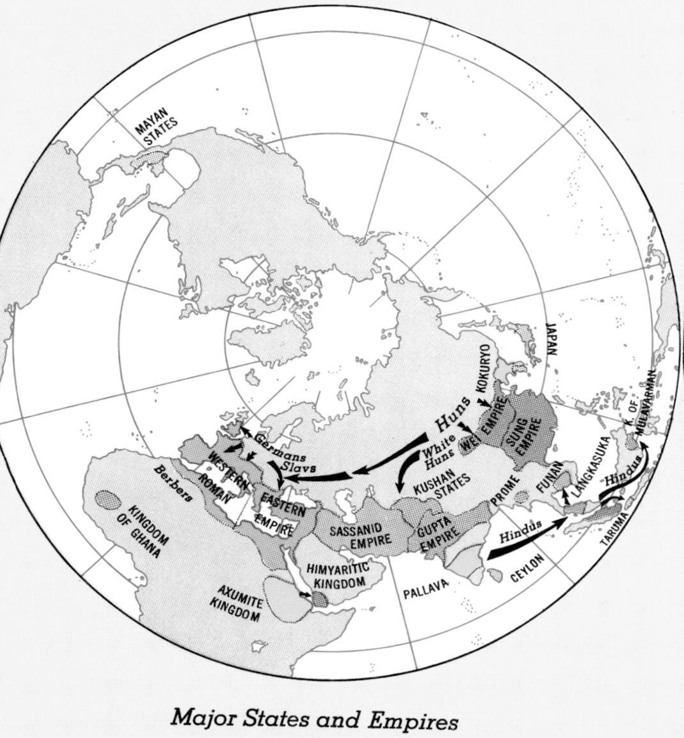

MAYAN
STATES

Huns

KOKURYO

JAPAN

WEI EMPIRE

SUING
EMPIRE

Germans

Slavs

*White
Huns*

Berbers

WESTERN
ROMAN
EMPIRE

EASTERN
EMPIRE

KUSHAN
STATES

PROME

FUNAN

LANGKASUKA

OF
MIDDLE-KINGDOM

Hindus

KINGDOM
OF GHANA

SASSANID
EMPIRE

GUPTA
EMPIRE

Hindus

TARUMA

AXUMITE
KINGDOM

HIMYARITIC
KINGDOM

PALLAVA

CEYLON

*Major States and Empires
in 400 A.D.*

MAP D

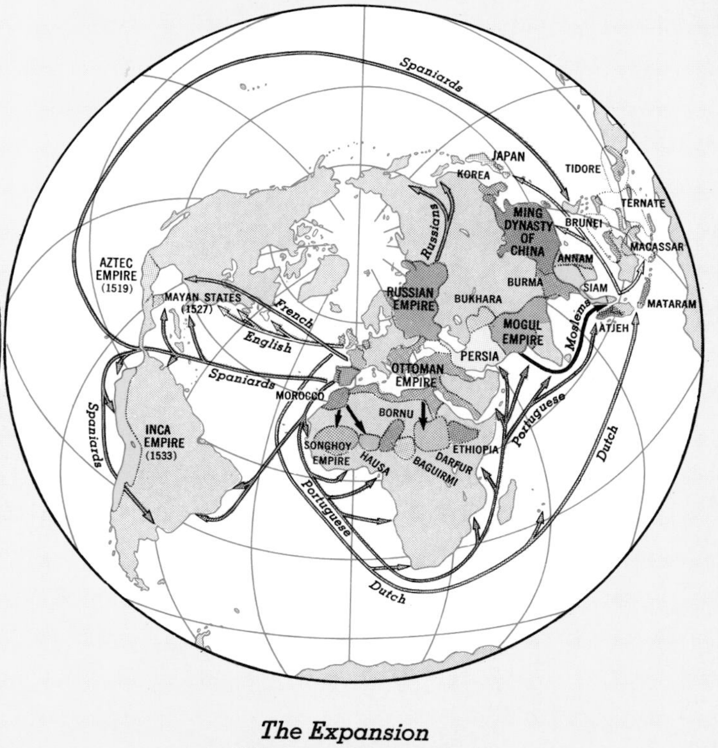

Spaniards

JAPAN

KOREA

TIDORE

TERNATE

MING
DYNASTY
OF
CHINA

BRUNEI

MACASSAR

AZTEC
EMPIRE
(1519)

MAYAN STATES
(1527)

French

English

RUSSIAN
EMPIRE

BUKHARA

ANNAM

BURMA

SIAM

MATARAM

Russians

MOGUL
EMPIRE

Spaniards

MOROCCO

PERSIA

OTTOMAN
EMPIRE

AATJEH

Moslems

Portuguese

Dutch

Spaniards

INCA
EMPIRE
(1533)

SONGHOY
EMPIRE

HAUSA

BORNU

DARFUR

BAGUIRMI

ETHIOPIA

Portuguese

Dutch

*The Expansion
of Western Civilization
1600 A.D.*

488

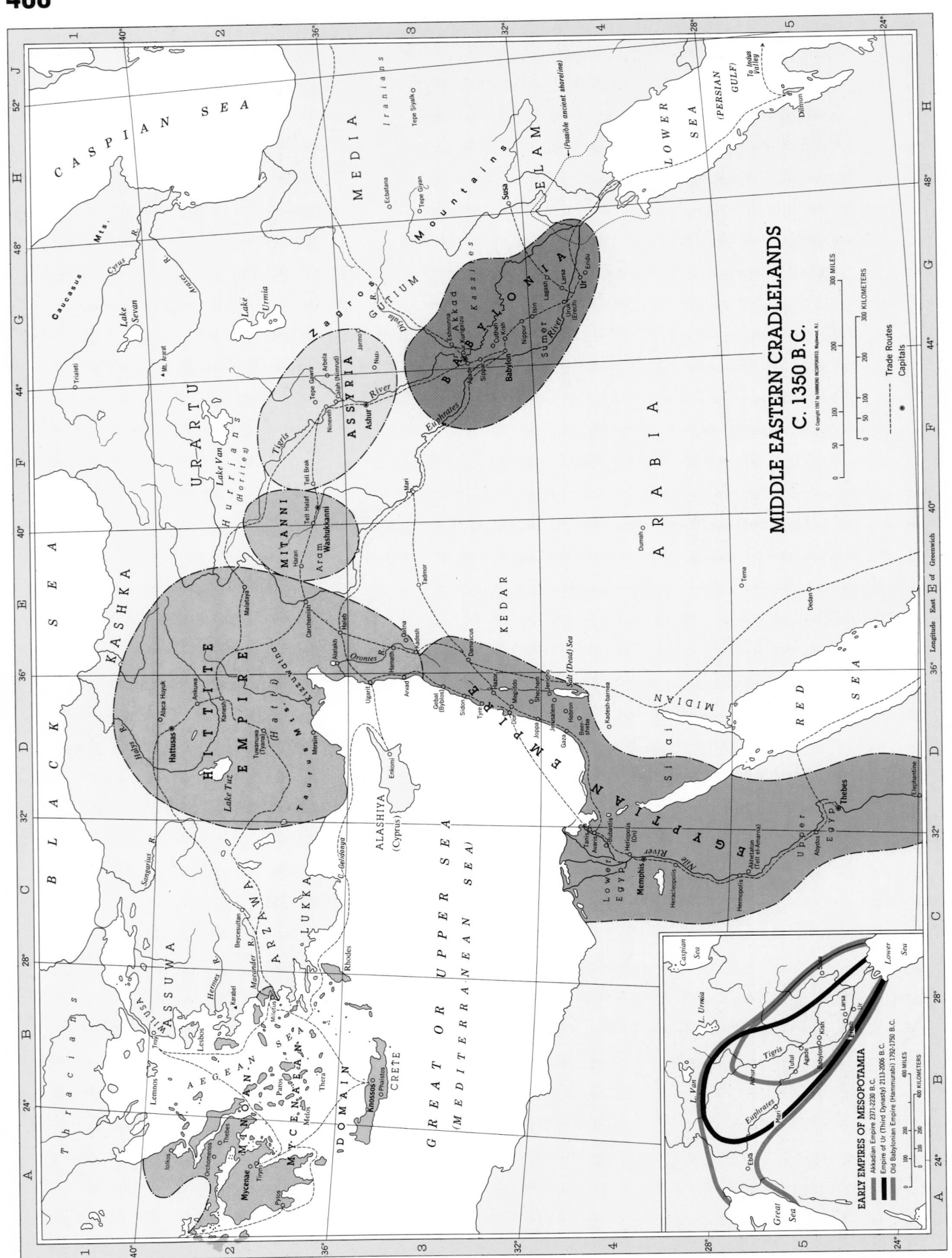

MIDDLE EASTERN CRADLELANDS
C. 1350 B.C.

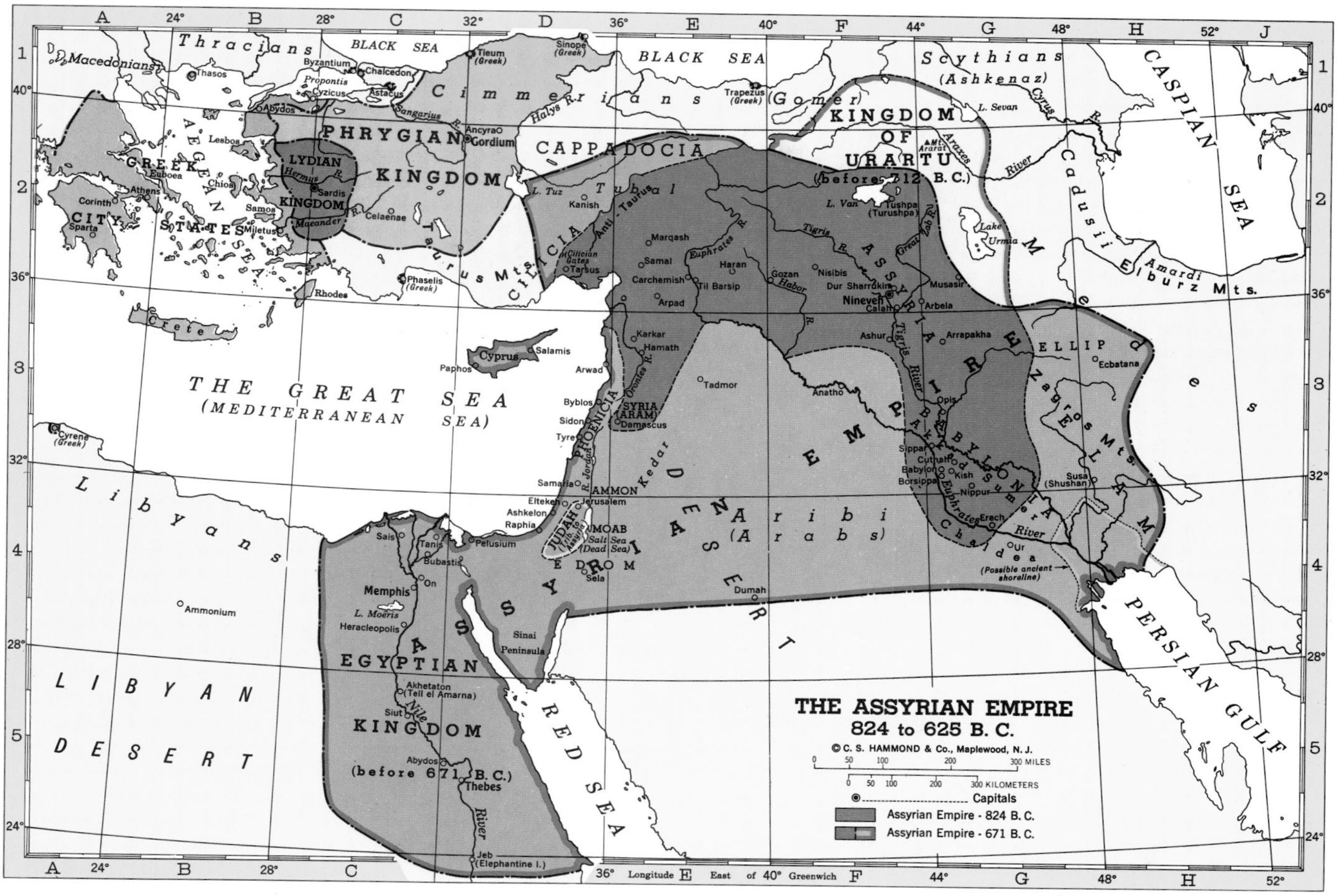

Map 1: THE ASSYRIAN EMPIRE 824 to 625 B.C.

Thracians · Macedonians · BLACK SEA · Cimmerians · Scythians (Ashkenaz) · CASPIAN SEA

PHRYGIAN KINGDOM · LYDIAN KINGDOM · CAPPADOCIA · KINGDOM OF URARTU (before 712 B.C.) · Gomer

GREEK CITY STATES · Sparta · Corinth · Athens · CILICIA

THE GREAT SEA (MEDITERRANEAN SEA)

Cyprus · PHOENICIA · SYRIA (ARAM) · Damascus · Nineveh · Calah · Arbela · Ashur · BABYLONIA · ELLIPI · Ecbatana

Libyans · JUDAH · MOAB · AMMON · EDOM · Jerusalem · ASSYRIAN DESERT · Aribi (Arabs) · Susa (Shushan)

LIBYAN DESERT · EGYPTIAN KINGDOM (before 671 B.C.) · Memphis · Thebes · RED SEA · PERSIAN GULF

THE ASSYRIAN EMPIRE
824 to 625 B.C.
© C. S. HAMMOND & Co., Maplewood, N.J.
Capitals
Assyrian Empire - 824 B.C.
Assyrian Empire - 671 B.C.

Longitude East of 40° Greenwich

Map 2: GREAT EMPIRES OF THE SIXTH CENTURY B.C.

ILLYRIA · Scythians · MACEDONIA · THRACE · BLACK SEA (Pontus Euxinus) · CASPIAN SEA (Mare Hyrcanium) · ARAL SEA · Massagetae (Sakae Scythians)

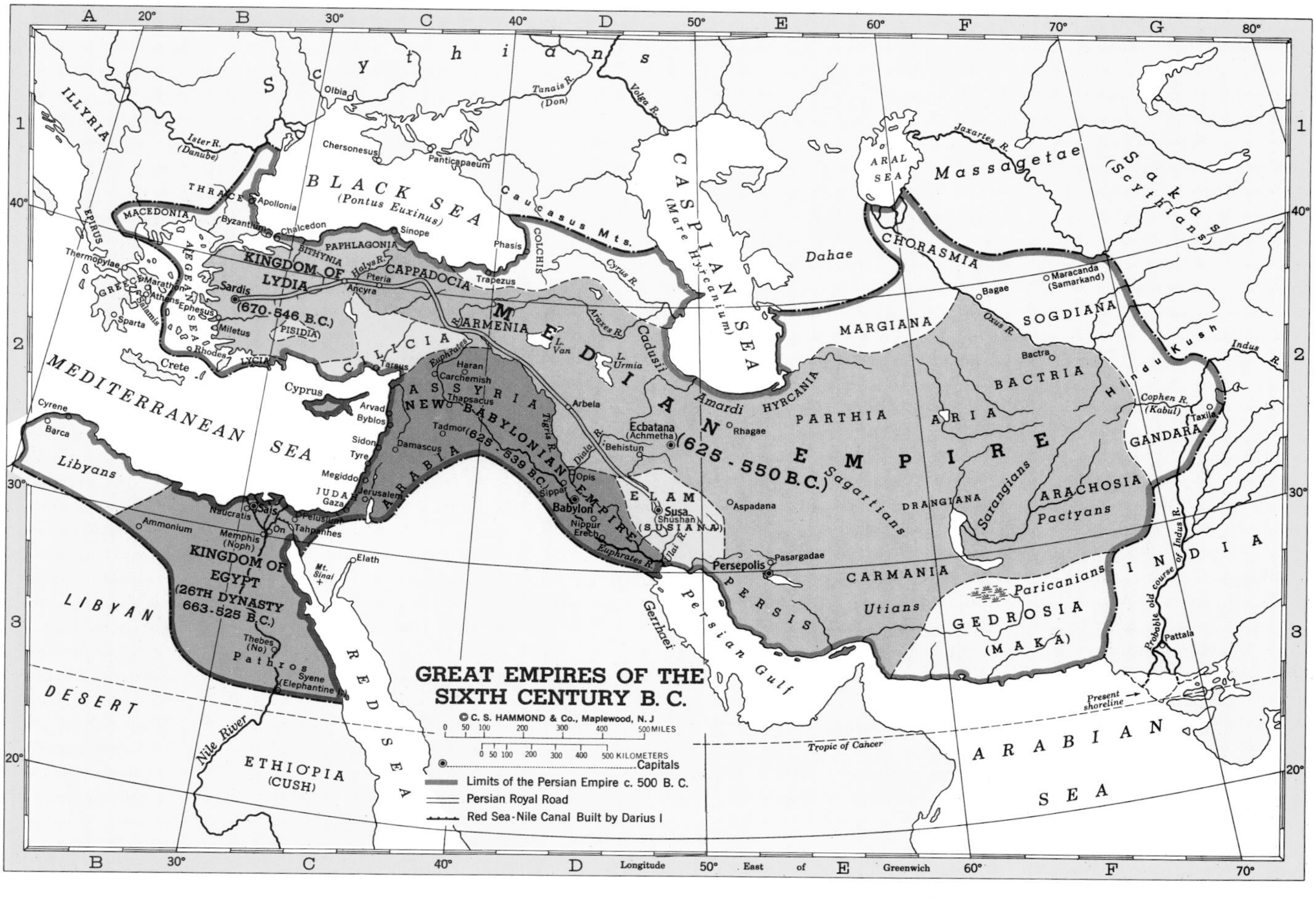

KINGDOM OF LYDIA (670-546 B.C.) · CAPPADOCIA · COLCHIS · Caucasus Mts. · CHORASMIA · SOGDIANA

GREECE · Sparta · Athens · CILICIA · ARMENIA · MEDIAN EMPIRE · HYRCANIA · PARTHIA · MARGIANA · ARIA · BACTRIA · GANDARA · Hindu Kush

MEDITERRANEAN SEA · Cyprus · ASSYRIA · NEW BABYLONIAN EMPIRE (625-539 B.C.) · Ecbatana (Achmetha) (625-550 B.C.) · SAGARTIANS · DRANGIANA · ARACHOSIA · INDIA

Libyans · JUDAEA · Jerusalem · ARABIA · ELAM · Susa (Shushan) (SUSIANA) · PERSIS · Persepolis · CARMANIA · GEDROSIA (MAKA) · Paricanians

KINGDOM OF EGYPT (26TH DYNASTY 663-525 B.C.) · Memphis (Noph) · Thebes (No) · Pathros · Syene · Elephantine

LIBYAN DESERT · RED SEA · ETHIOPIA (CUSH) · ARABIAN SEA · Tropic of Cancer

GREAT EMPIRES OF THE SIXTH CENTURY B.C.
© C. S. HAMMOND & Co., Maplewood, N.J.
Capitals
Limits of the Persian Empire c. 500 B.C.
Persian Royal Road
Red Sea-Nile Canal Built by Darius I

Longitude East of Greenwich

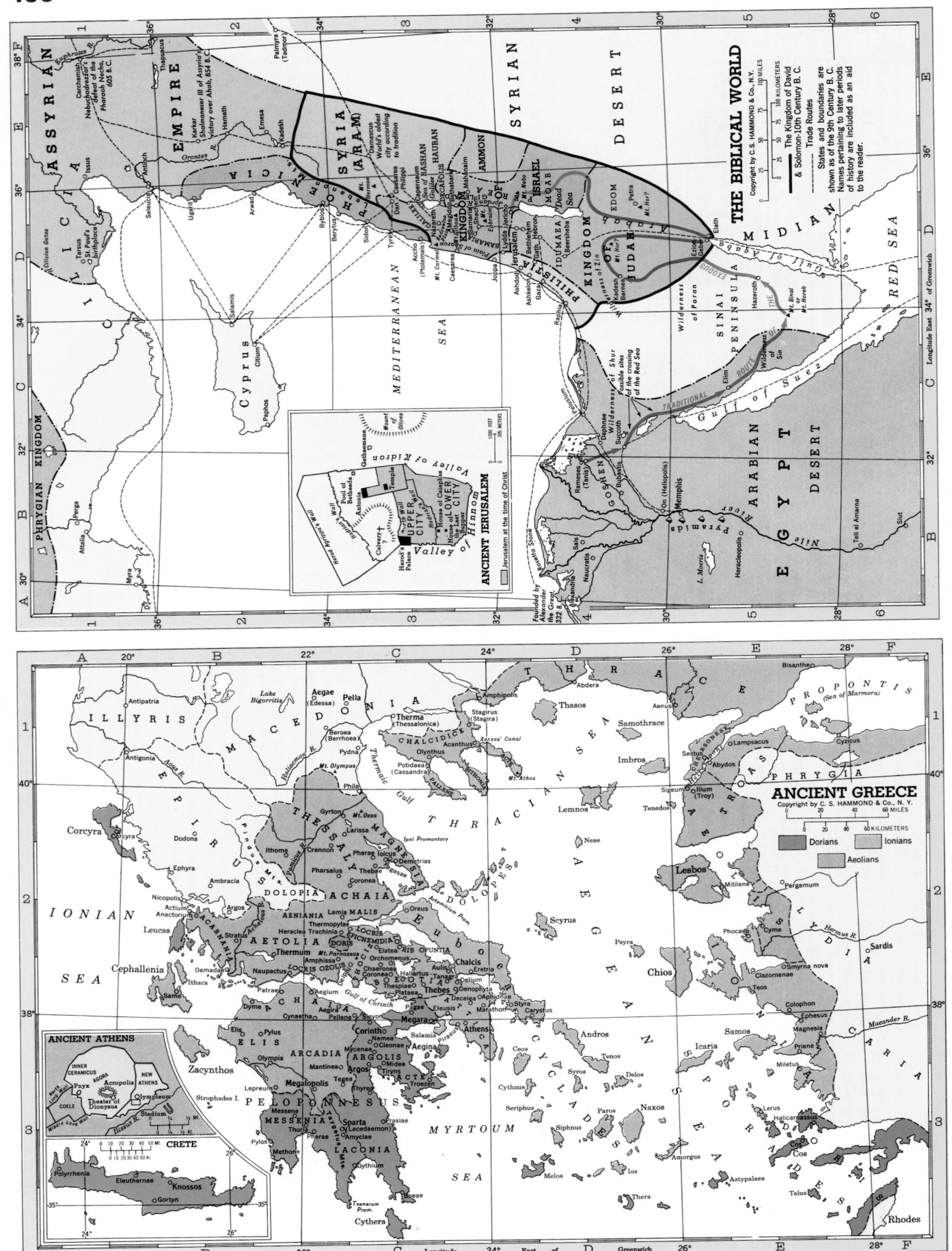

THE BIBLICAL WORLD

Copyright by C. S. HAMMOND & Co., N.Y.

The Kingdom of David & Solomon-10th Century B.C.

Trade Routes

States and boundaries are shown as of the 9th Century B.C. Names pertaining to later periods of history are included as an aid to the reader.

ANCIENT JERUSALEM
Jerusalem at the time of Christ

ANCIENT GREECE
Copyright by C. S. HAMMOND & Co., N.Y.

Dorians   Ionians
Aeolians

ANCIENT ATHENS

CRETE

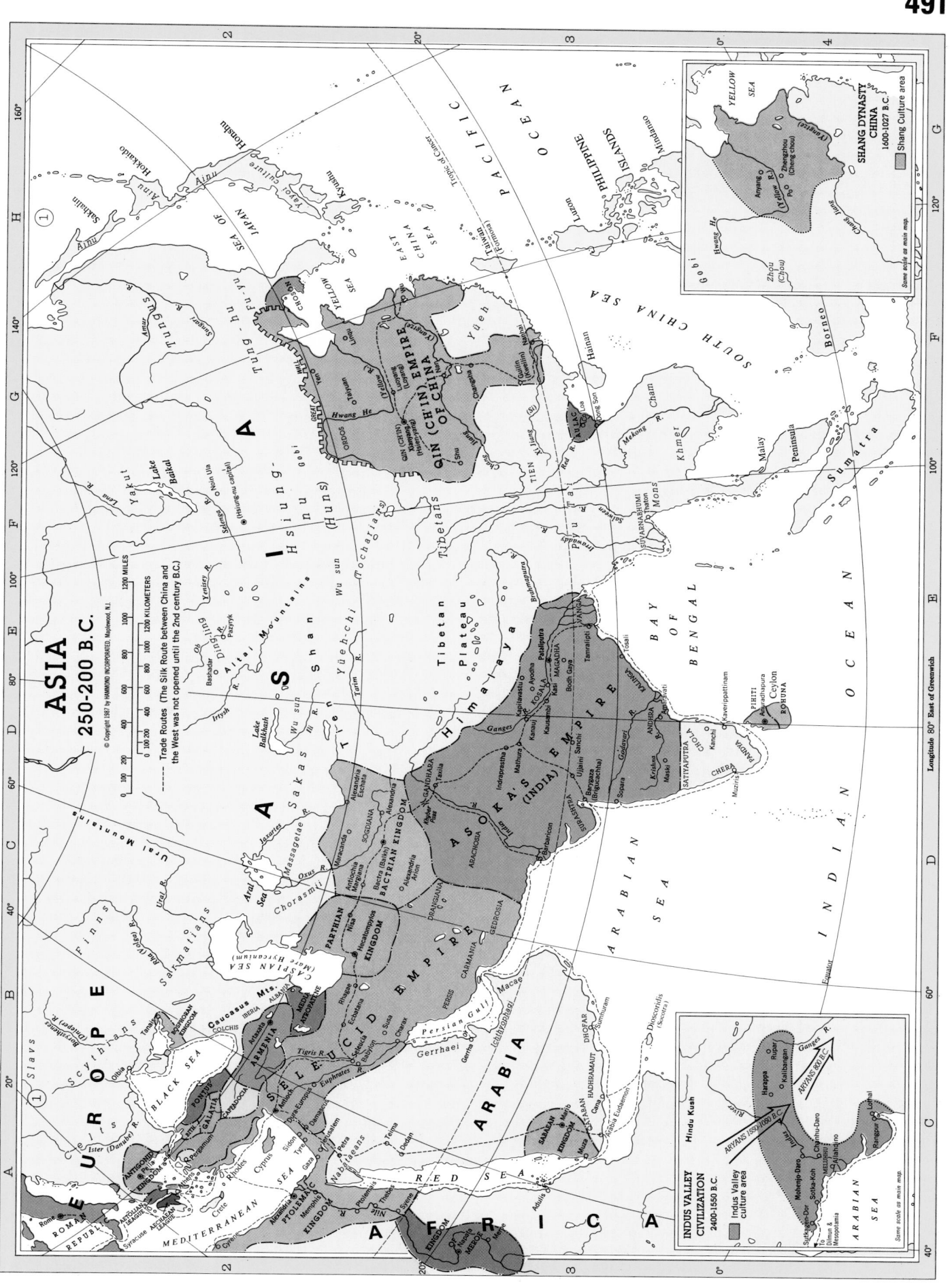
ASIA
250-200 B.C.
© Copyright 1987 by HAMMOND INCORPORATED, Maplewood, N.J.
0 100 200 400 600 800 1000 1200 MILES
0 100 200 400 600 800 1000 1200 KILOMETERS
Trade Routes (The Silk Route between China and the West was not opened until the 2nd century B.C.)
EUROPE
ASIA
AFRICA
ARABIA
ROMAN REPUBLIC
ANTIGONID KINGDOM
AETOLIAN LEAGUE
ACHAEAN LEAGUE
PTOLEMAIC KINGDOM
KINGDOM OF NAPATA MEROE
SELEUCID EMPIRE
PARTHIAN KINGDOM
BACTRIAN KINGDOM
ASOKA'S EMPIRE (INDIA)
QIN (CH'IN) EMPIRE OF CHINA
SABAEAN KINGDOM
ARMENIA
MEDIA ATROPATENE
PONTUS
GALATIA
CAPPADOCIA
BOSPHORAN KINGDOM
AU LAC
CHOSON
GREAT WALL
Slavs
Scythians
Finns
Sarmatians
Celts
Massagetae
Chorasmii
Sakas
Wu sun
Yüeh-chi
Tocharians
Hsiung-nu (Huns)
Tung-hu
Fu-yu
Tungus
Yakut
Ainu
Yayoi culture
Tibetans
Yüeh
Nabataeans
Gerrhaei
Ichthyophagi
Macae
Mons
Khmer
Cham
Malay Peninsula
Pyu
Tai
Ural Mountains
Caucasus Mts.
Altai Mountains
Tien Shan
Himalaya
Tibetan Plateau
Hindu Kush
Ding-ling
BLACK SEA
CASPIAN SEA (Mare Hyrcanium)
Aral Sea
Lake Balkhash
Lake Baikal
MEDITERRANEAN SEA
RED SEA
Persian Gulf
ARABIAN SEA
BAY OF BENGAL
INDIAN OCEAN
SOUTH CHINA SEA
EAST CHINA SEA
YELLOW SEA
SEA OF JAPAN
PACIFIC OCEAN
Tropic of Cancer
Equator
Ister (Danube) R.
Borysthenes (Dnieper) R.
Rha (Volga) R.
Ural R.
Jaxartes R.
Oxus R.
Tigris R.
Euphrates R.
Nile R.
Indus R.
Ganges R.
Brahmaputra R.
Godavari R.
Krishna R.
Irtysh R.
Ob R.
Yenisey R.
Selenga R.
Lena R.
Amur R.
Sungari R.
Tarim R.
Ili R.
Hwang He
Yellow R.
Yangtze
Chang Jiang
Xi Jiang (Si)
Red R.
Mekong R.
Salween
Irrawaddy R.
Rome
Syracuse
Pella
Athens
Crete
Rhodes
Cyprus
Pergamum
Cyrene
Alexandria
Memphis
Ptolemais
Thebes
Syene
Napata
Meroe
Adulis
Sidon
Tyre
Gaza
Jerusalem
Petra
Damascus
Antioch
Dura-Europus
Seleucia
Babylon
Charax
Susa
Ecbatana
Rhagae
Artaxata
Colchis
Iberia
Albania
Olbia
Tanais
Teima
Dedan
Gerrha
Marib
Muza
QATABAN
HADHRAMAUT
DHOFAR
Sumhuram
Cana
Arabia Eudaemon
Dioscoridis (Socotra)
Persis
Carmania
Gedrosia
Drangiana
Arachosia
Sogdiana
Nisa
Hecatompylos
Antiochia Margiana
Maracanda
Alexandria Eschata
Bactra (Balkh)
Alexandria
Alexandria Arion
Khyber Pass
GANDHARA
Taxila
Barbaricon
SURASHTRA
Barygaza (Brigucachha)
Ujjaini
Sanchi
Indraprastha
Mathura
Kanauj
Kausambi
Kapilavastu
KOSALA
Ayodha
Kasi
Pataliputra
MAGADHA
Bodh Gaya
Tamralipti
VANGA
KALINGA
Tosali
Sopara
ANDHRA
Maski
Amaravati
SATIYAPUTRA
CHOLA
Kanchi
CHERA
Muziris
PANDYA
Kaverippattinam
Ceylon
PIHITI
Anuradhapura
ROHUNA
SUVARNABHUMI
Thaton
Loa
Dong Son
Hainan
Bashadar
Pazyryk
Noin Ula
(Hsiung-nu capital)
ORDOS
Yen
Taiyuan
Linqu
Wu
Xianyang (Hsien-yang)
Luoyang (Loyang)
Nan
Shu
Changsha
Guilin (Kweilin)
Nanhai
Taiwan (Formosa)
Luzon
PHILIPPINE ISLANDS
Mindanao
Borneo
Sumatra
Kyushu
Honshu
Hokkaido
Sakhalin
TIEN
INDUS VALLEY CIVILIZATION 2400-1550 B.C.
Indus Valley culture area
ARYANS 1550-1050 B.C.
ARYANS 800 B.C.
Harappa
Rupar
Kalibangan
Mohenjo-Daro
Sutkagen-Dor
Sotka-Koh
Chanhu-Daro
MELUHHU
Allahdino
Rangpur
Lothal
To Dilmun & Mesopotamia
River
Same scale as main map.
SHANG DYNASTY CHINA 1600-1027 B.C.
Shang Culture area
Gobi
Zhou (Chou)
Anyang
Po
Zhengzhou (Cheng-chou)
Longitude 80° East of Greenwich
20° 40° 60° 80° 100° 120° 140° 160°
A B C D E F G H
1 2 3 4

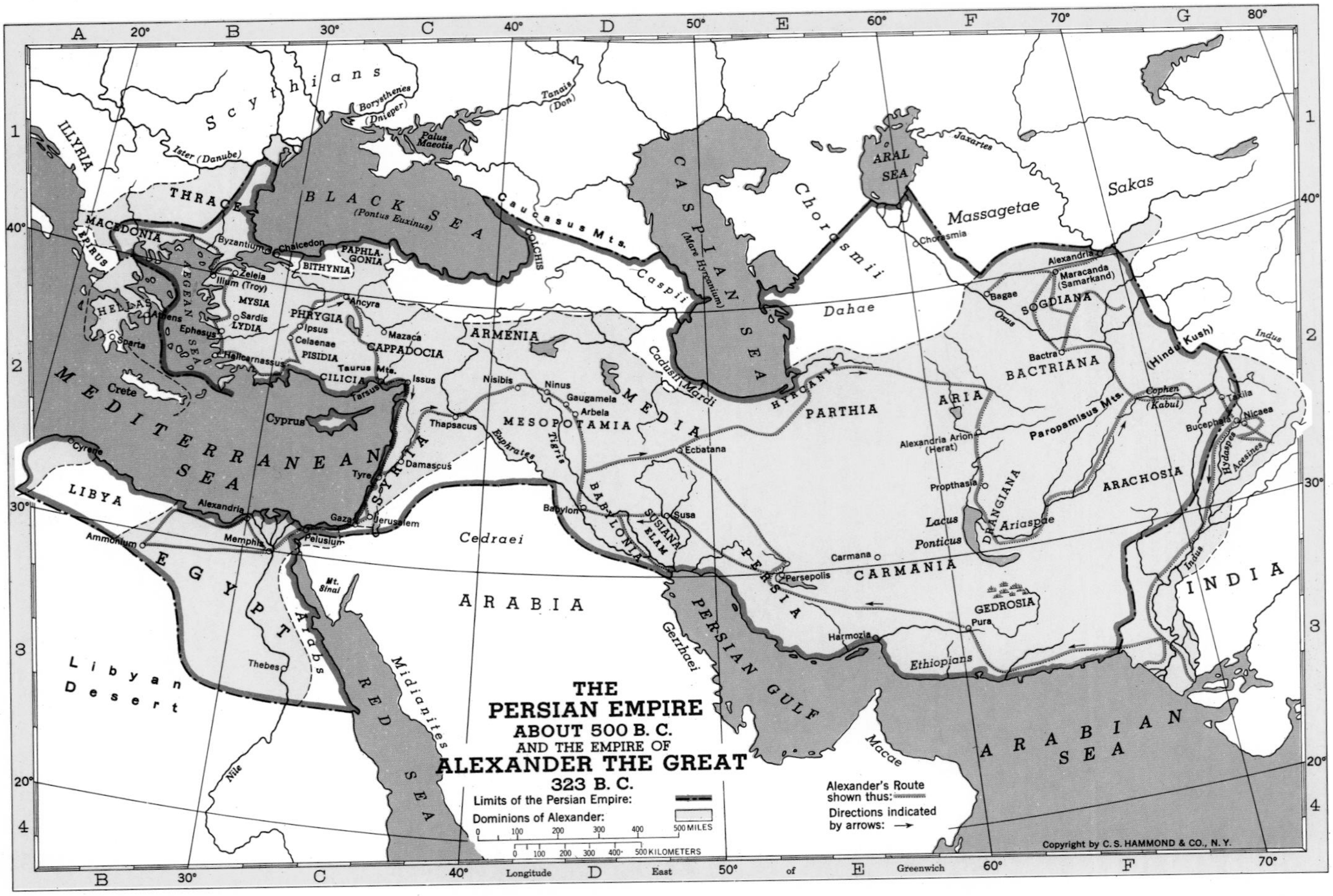

THE PERSIAN EMPIRE
ABOUT 500 B. C.
AND THE EMPIRE OF
ALEXANDER THE GREAT
323 B. C.

Limits of the Persian Empire:
Dominions of Alexander:

500 MILES
100 200 300 400 500 KILOMETERS

Alexander's Route shown thus:
Directions indicated by arrows: →

Copyright by C. S. HAMMOND & CO., N.Y.

Longitude East of Greenwich

Scythians

ILLYRIA THRACE MACEDONIA BLACK SEA (Pontus Euxinus) CASPIAN SEA (Mare Hyrcanium) ARAL SEA Massagetae Sakas Chorasmii Dahae

Ister (Danube) *Borysthenes (Dnieper)* *Palus Maeotis* Byzantium Chalcedon PAPHLAGONIA BITHYNIA Caucasus Mts. COLCHIS *Caspii Mardi* Chorasmia SOGDIANA Alexandria Maracanda (Samarkand) Jaxartes

HELLAS MYSIA PHRYGIA LYDIA Sardis Ephesus PISIDIA CILICIA CAPPADOCIA ARMENIA MEDIA PARTHIA ARIA BACTRIANA Bactra Bagae *Oxus* (Hindu Kush) *Indus*

MEDITERRANEAN SEA Crete Cyprus SYRIA Damascus Tyre Gaza Jerusalem MESOPOTAMIA Nisibis Ninus Arbela Gaugamela Euphrates Tigris Ecbatana Alexandria Ariana (Herat) Propthasia DRANGIANA Ariaspe PAROPAMISUS Mts. Cophen (Kabul) Bucephala Nicaea ARACHOSIA

LIBYA Cyrene Alexandria Memphis Pelusium Mt. Sinai ARABIA BABYLONIA Babylon SUSIANA ELAM Susa PERSIA Persepolis Carmana *Lacus Ponticus* CARMANIA INDIA

Libyan Desert Thebes *Nile* RED SEA Midianites Gerrhaei PERSIAN GULF Harmozia Pura GEDROSIA

EGYPT *Arabs* Ammonium *Cedraei* *Ethiopians* Macae ARABIAN SEA

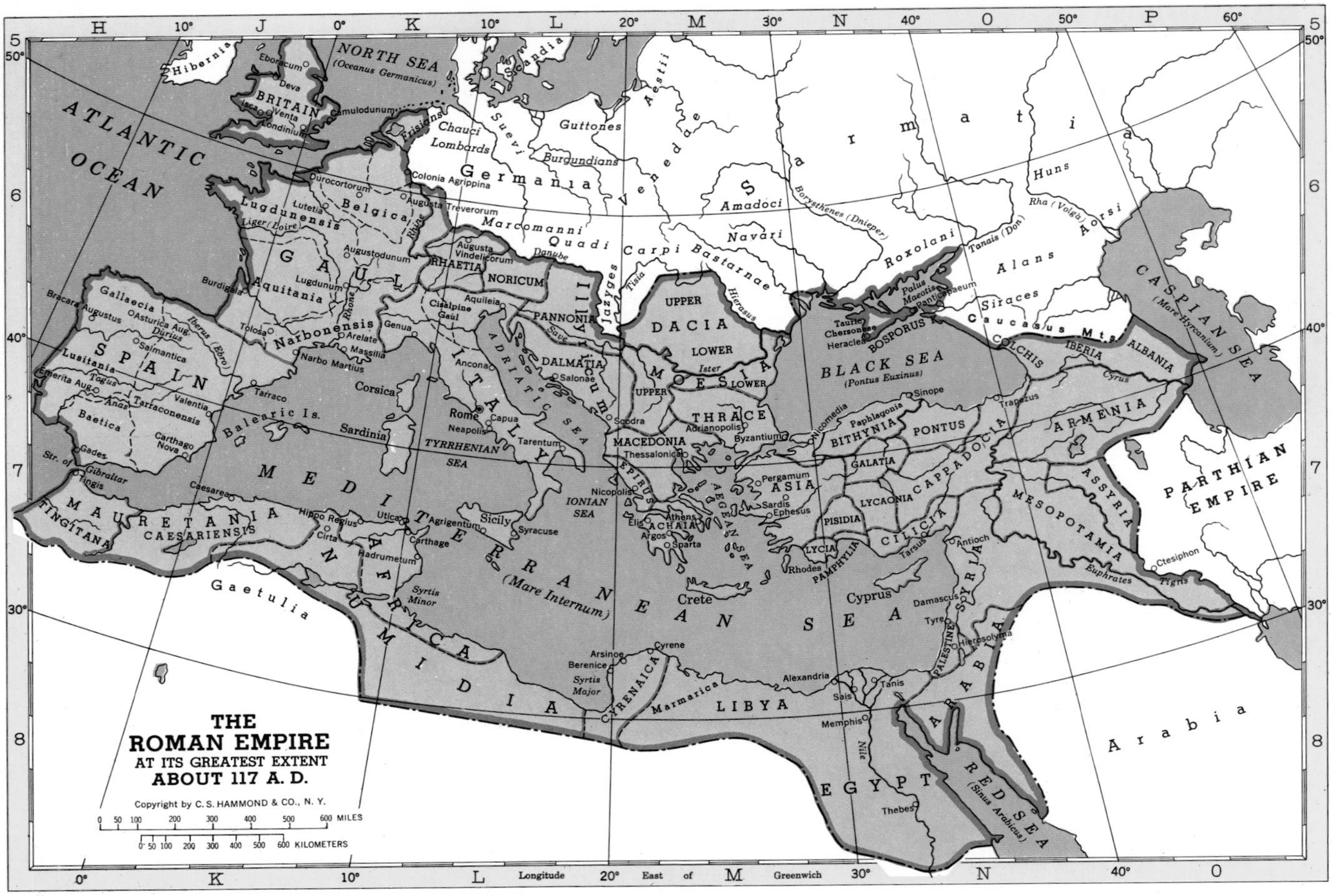

THE
ROMAN EMPIRE
AT ITS GREATEST EXTENT
ABOUT 117 A.D.

Copyright by C. S. HAMMOND & CO., N.Y.

600 MILES
0 50 100 200 300 400 500 600 KILOMETERS

Longitude East of Greenwich

Hibernia NORTH SEA (Oceanus Germanicus) BRITAIN Eboracum Deva Camulodunum Londinium ATLANTIC OCEAN

GAUL BELGICA Lugdunensis Germania Chauci Lombards Suevi Guttones Aestii Sarmatia Huns

Lutetia Durocortorum Augusta Treverorum Colonia Agrippina Marcomanni Quadi Burgundians Venedae Amadoci *Borysthenes (Dnieper)* Roxolani Aorsi *Rha (Volga)*

AQUITANIA Burdigala Lugdunum RHAETIA NORICUM Augusta Vindelicorum PANNONIA Iazyges Carpi Bastarnae Navari Alans *Tanais (Don)* Siraces

Gallaecia Bracara Augusta Asturica Aug. NARBONENSIS Tolosa Arelate Massilia Aquileia DALMATIA UPPER DACIA LOWER Taurica Chersonesus Heraclea BOSPORUS CASPIAN SEA (Mare Hyrcanium)

SPAIN Salmantica Tarraco Tarraconensis Narbo Martius Genua CISALPINE GAUL Ancona DALMATIA Salonae MOESIA UPPER LOWER BLACK SEA (Pontus Euxinus) Sinope COLCHIS IBERIA ALBANIA ARMENIA

Lusitania Emerita Aug. Corduba Baetica Corsica Rome Capua ADRIATIC SEA Scodra THRACE Adrianopolis Byzantium BITHYNIA Nicomedia Paphlagonia PONTUS *Cyrus*

Gades Str. of Gibraltar Tingis Balearic Is. Sardinia Neapolis Tarentum MACEDONIA Thessalonica ASIA Pergamum GALATIA CAPPADOCIA ASSYRIA MESOPOTAMIA PARTHIAN EMPIRE

MAURETANIA TINGITANA CAESARIENSIS Caesarea TYRRHENIAN SEA Sicily Syracuse IONIAN SEA ACHAIA Athens Sparta LYCAONIA LYCIA CILICIA Tarsus Antioch SYRIA Chesiphon *Euphrates* *Tigris*

Gaetulia Nippo Regius Utica Carthage Hadrumetum Agrigentum *Syrtis Minor* MEDITERRANEAN SEA (Mare Internum) Crete PISIDIA PAMPHYLIA Rhodes Cyprus Damascus Tyre PALESTINE ARABIA

NUMIDIA Cirta *Syrtis Major* Arsinoe Cyrene CYRENAICA Berenice *Marmarica* LIBYA Alexandria Sais Tanis Memphis *Nile* RED SEA (Sinus Arabicus) *Arabia*

EGYPT Thebes

THE FORUM
CAPITOLIUM and PALATIUM

1. Templum Saturni
2. Templum Concordiae
3. Scalae Gemoniae
4. Carcer (Tullianum)
5. Senaculum
6. Graecostasis
7. Rostra
8. Templum Jani

IMPERIAL FORA

1. Scalae Gemoniae
2. Templum Vespasiani
3. Porticus Deorum Consentium
4. Equus Caesaris
5. T. Castoris et Pollucis
6. Templum Divi Julii
7. Arcus Augusti
8. Arcus Titi
9. Templum Antonini et Faustinae

ANCIENT ITALY
ITALIA, LIGURIA, VENETIA, GALLIA-CISALPINA, HISTRIA, SICILIA & CORSICA
Before the time of Augustus

Copyright by C.S. HAMMOND & CO., N.Y.

0   20   40   60   80   100 MILES

0   20   40   60   80   100 KILOMETERS

Roman Colonies, thus; ——— **Ostia**
Greek Colonies, thus; --------- SYRACUSAE (G)
Carthaginian Colonies, thus; -·-·-· Eryx (C)
Dotted lines show the Modern shore line

ROME
Under the Emperors

1. Templum Jovis Capitolini
2. Arx
3. Forum Romanum
4. Templum Aesculapii
5. Forum Trajani
6. Forum Augusti
7. Porta Carmentalis
8. Arcus Septimii Severi
9. Arcus Constantini
10. Arcus Titi
11. Arcus Claudii
12. Arcus Tiberii
13. Arcus Gallieni
14. Arcus Marci Aurelii
15. Arcus Diocletiani
16. Porta Flumentara
17. Templum Mercurii
18. Theatrum Marcelli

REGIONES AUGUSTI

I. Porta Capena
II. Caelimontium
III. Isis et Serapis
IV. Templum Pacis
V. Esquiliae
VI. Alta Semita
VII. Via Lata
VIII. Forum Romanum
IX. Circus Flaminius
X. Palatium
XI. Circus Maximus
XII. Piscina Publica
XIII. Aventinus
XIV. Trans Tiberim

ROME
In the time of the Republic

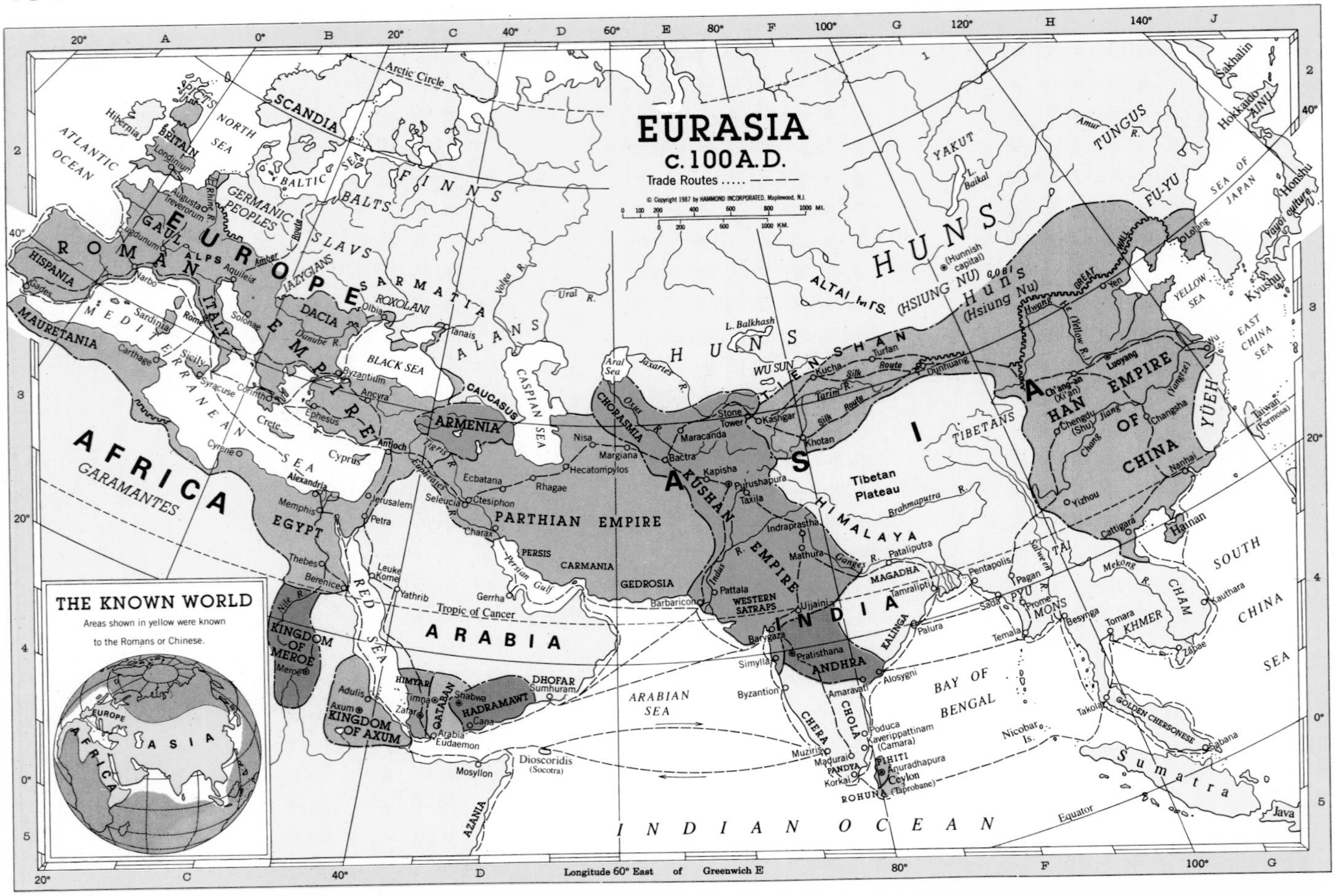

EURASIA
c. 100 A.D.
Trade Routes .....
© Copyright 1987 by HAMMOND INCORPORATED, Maplewood, N.J.

THE KNOWN WORLD
Areas shown in yellow were known to the Romans or Chinese.

EUROPE · AFRICA · ASIA

Major labels: ATLANTIC OCEAN, Hibernia, BRITAIN, SCANDIA, NORTH SEA, BALTIC, FINNS, BALTS, SLAVS, GERMANIC PEOPLES, GAUL, ALPS, ITALY, HISPANIA, ROMAN EMPIRE, MEDITERRANEAN, MAURETANIA, AFRICA, GARAMANTES, EGYPT, Alexandria, Memphis, Thebes, Cyrene, Carthage, Rome, Sicily, Sardinia, Crete, Cyprus, Byzantium, Ancyra, Ephesus, Antioch, Jerusalem, Petra, ARMENIA, CAUCASUS, BLACK SEA, CASPIAN SEA, SARMATIA, DACIA, JAZYGES, ROXOLANI, ALANS, Volga R., Ural R., Tanais, ARABIA, RED SEA, Tropic of Cancer, ARABIAN SEA, KINGDOM OF MEROE, Meroe, KINGDOM OF AXUM, Axum, Adulis, HIMYAR, QATABAN, HADRAMAWT, DHOFAR, Sumhuram, AZANIA, Dioscoridis (Socotra), INDIAN OCEAN, Equator

Central/East: CHORASMIA, Aral Sea, Oxus R., Jaxartes R., Bactra, Maracanda, Stone Tower, KUSHAN EMPIRE, PARTHIAN EMPIRE, PERSIS, CARMANIA, GEDROSIA, Ecbatana, Ctesiphon, Seleucia, Charax, WESTERN SATRAPS, INDIA, ANDHRA, CHOLA, PANDYA, Ceylon (Taprobane), ROHUNA, HUNS, HUNS (HSIUNG NU), ALTAI Mts., TIEN SHAN, WU SUN, Turfan, Kucha, Kashgar, Khotan, Silk Route, TIBETANS, Tibetan Plateau, HIMALAYA, Brahmaputra, Ganges, MAGADHA, Pataliputra, Mathura, Taxila, Kapisha, KALINGA, PYU, MONS, KHMER, CHAM, TAI, Hainan, HAN EMPIRE OF CHINA, Ch'ang-an, Loyang, Chengtu, Changsha, YELLOW SEA, EAST CHINA SEA, SOUTH CHINA SEA, BAY OF BENGAL, YUEH, FU-YU, TUNGUS, YAKUT, L. Baikal, Amur R., SEA OF JAPAN, Sakhalin, Hokkaido, AINU, Kyushu, Sumatra, Java, Nicobar Is., GOLDEN CHERSONESE

Longitude 60° East of Greenwich

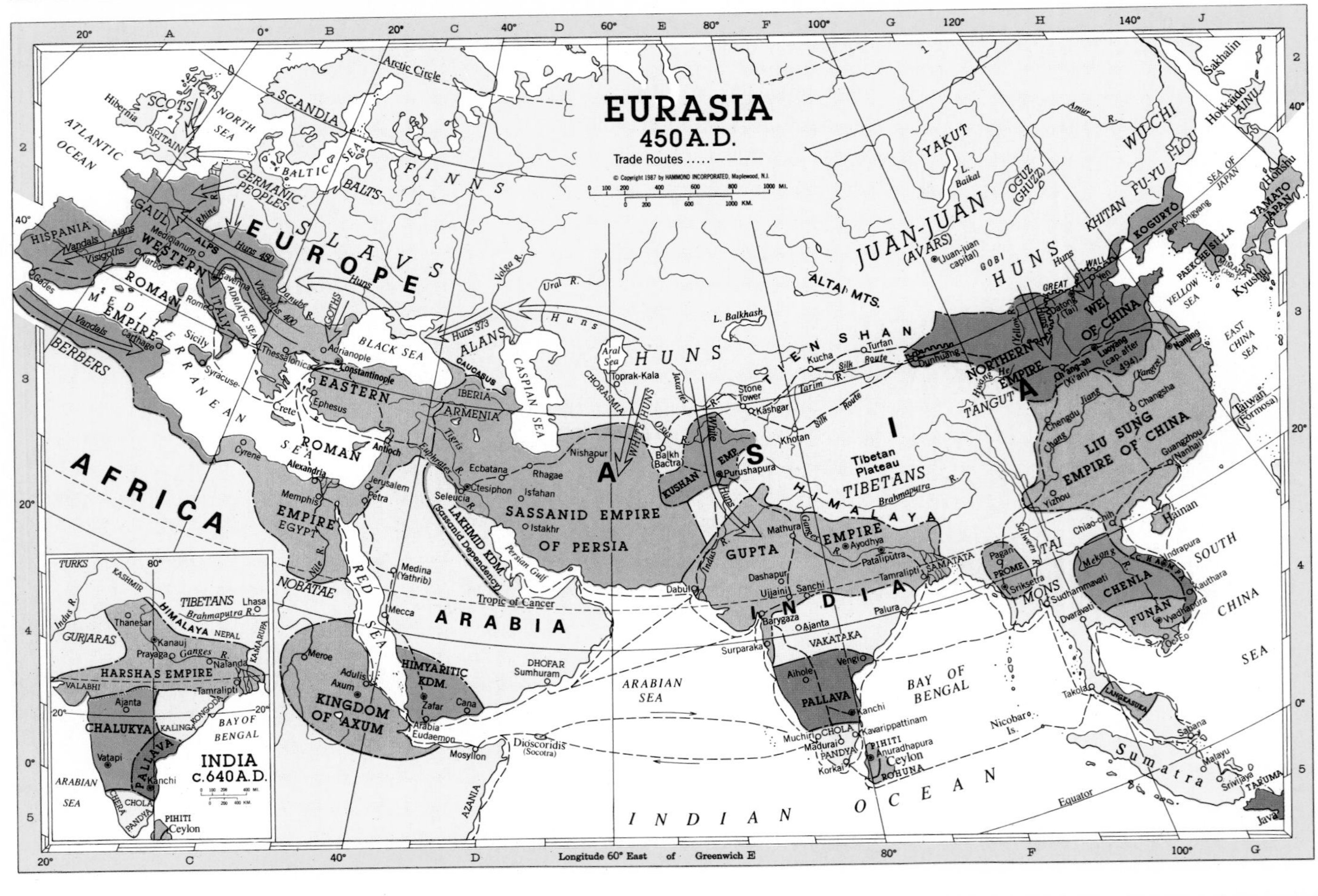

EURASIA
450 A.D.
Trade Routes .....
© Copyright 1987 by HAMMOND INCORPORATED, Maplewood, N.J.

EUROPE · AFRICA · ASIA

Major labels: ATLANTIC OCEAN, Hibernia, BRITAIN, SCOTS, SCANDIA, NORTH SEA, BALTIC, FINNS, BALTS, SLAVS, GERMANIC PEOPLES, GAUL, ALPS, HISPANIA, Vandals, Visigoths, WESTERN ROMAN EMPIRE, EASTERN ROMAN EMPIRE, Huns 451, Huns 450, Huns 373, Huns, Constantinople, Adrianople, Thessalonica, Ravenna, Rome, Sicily, Crete, Ephesus, Antioch, Alexandria, Memphis, Jerusalem, Petra, Cyrene, Carthage, BERBERS, AFRICA, EGYPT, MEDITERRANEAN SEA, ADRIATIC SEA, BLACK SEA, CASPIAN SEA, ARMENIA, IBERIA, CAUCASUS, ALANS, Volga R., Ural R., GOTHS, Danube, Rhine, Loire, Vistula, Dnieper, Don

Central/East: CHORASMIA, Aral Sea, Oxus, Jaxartes, Toprak-Kala, Balkh (Bactra), Nishapur, Ecbatana, Rhagae, Ctesiphon, Seleucia, Isfahan, Istakhr, SASSANID EMPIRE OF PERSIA, LAKHMID KDM., Persian Gulf, Medina (Yathrib), Mecca, ARABIA, RED SEA, Tropic of Cancer, DHOFAR, Sumhuram, Cana, HIMYARITIC KDM., Zafar, KINGDOM OF AXUM, Axum, Adulis, Meroe, Dioscoridis (Socotra), AZANIA, Mosyllon, ARABIAN SEA, INDIAN OCEAN, Equator

HUNS, JUAN-JUAN (AVARS), OGUZ (GHUZ), ALTAI MTS., GOBI, TIEN SHAN, Turfan, Kucha, Kashgar, Khotan, Silk Route, Stone Tower, TANGUT, TIBETANS, Tibetan Plateau, HIMALAYA, GUPTA EMPIRE, Pataliputra, Mathura, Ayodhya, Ujjain, Sanchi, Ajanta, VAKATAKA, PALLAVA, Kanchi, CHOLA, PANDYA, Madurai, Ceylon, ROHUNA, KALINGA, Tamralipti, NORTHERN WEI EMPIRE OF CHINA, Great Wall, LIU SUNG EMPIRE OF CHINA, Ch'ang-an, Loyang, Chengtu, Changsha, Hainan, YELLOW SEA, EAST CHINA SEA, SOUTH CHINA SEA, BAY OF BENGAL, PYU, PROME, MONS, TAI, CHENLA, FUNAN, CHAM, KHITAN, FU-YU, WUCHI, YAKUT, L. Baikal, Amur R., KOGURYO, PAEKCHE, SILLA, YAMATO JAPAN, SEA OF JAPAN, Sakhalin, Hokkaido, AINU, Kyushu, Sumatra, Java, TARUMA, Nicobar Is.

INDIA c. 640 A.D.
TURKS, TIBETANS, Lhasa, HIMALAYA, NEPAL, KASHMIR, GURJARAS, HARSHAS EMPIRE, Thanesar, Kanauj, Prayaga, Nalanda, VALABHI, CHALUKYA, Vatapi, KALINGA, Ajanta, PALLAVA, Kanchi, CHOLA, PANDYA, PIHITI, Ceylon, Indus, Ganges, Brahmaputra R., ARABIAN SEA, BAY OF BENGAL

Longitude 60° East of Greenwich

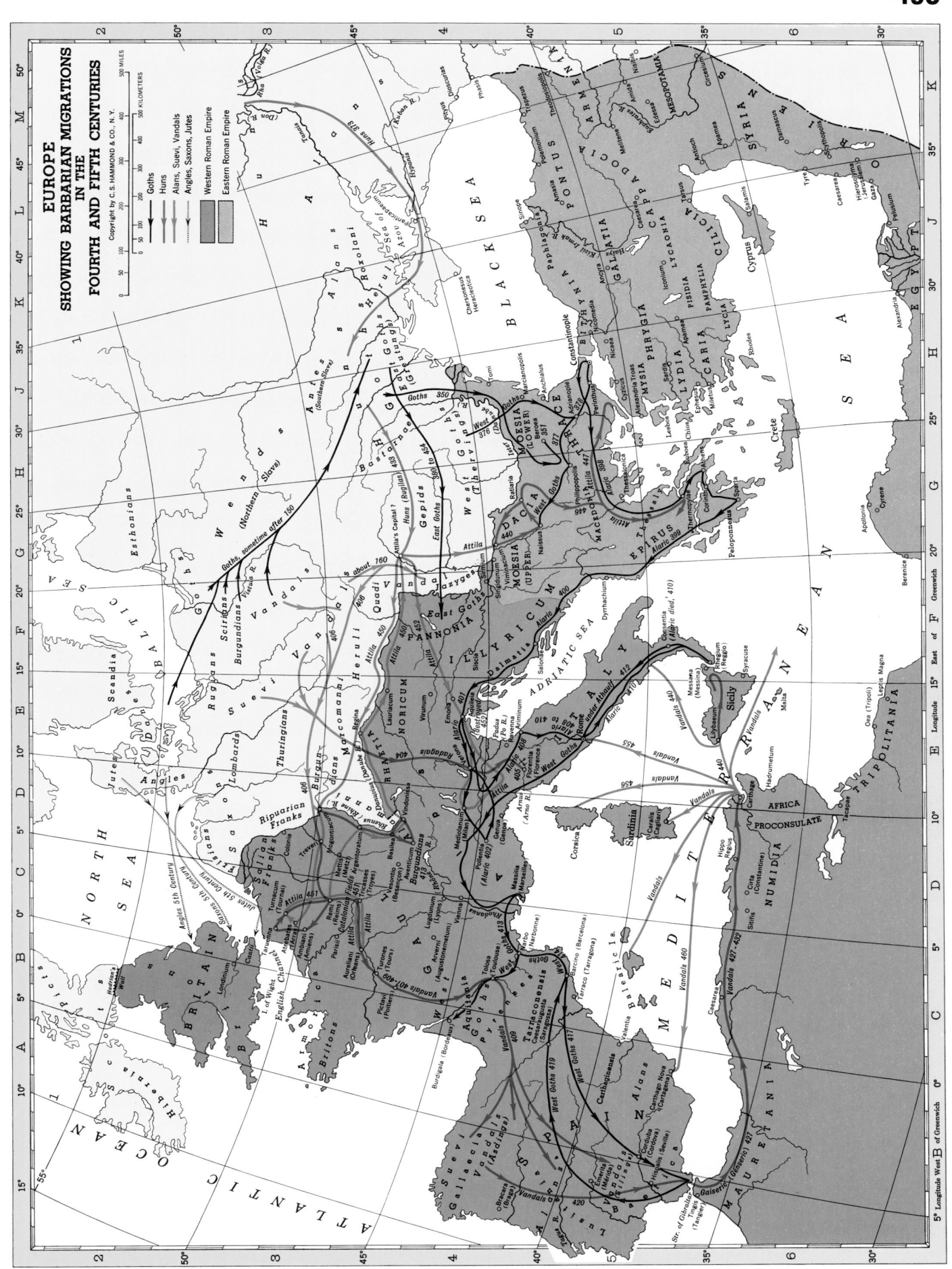

EUROPE
SHOWING BARBARIAN MIGRATIONS
IN THE
FOURTH AND FIFTH CENTURIES

Copyright by C.S. HAMMOND & CO., N.Y.

Goths
Huns
Alans, Suevi, Vandals
Angles, Saxons, Jutes
Western Roman Empire
Eastern Roman Empire

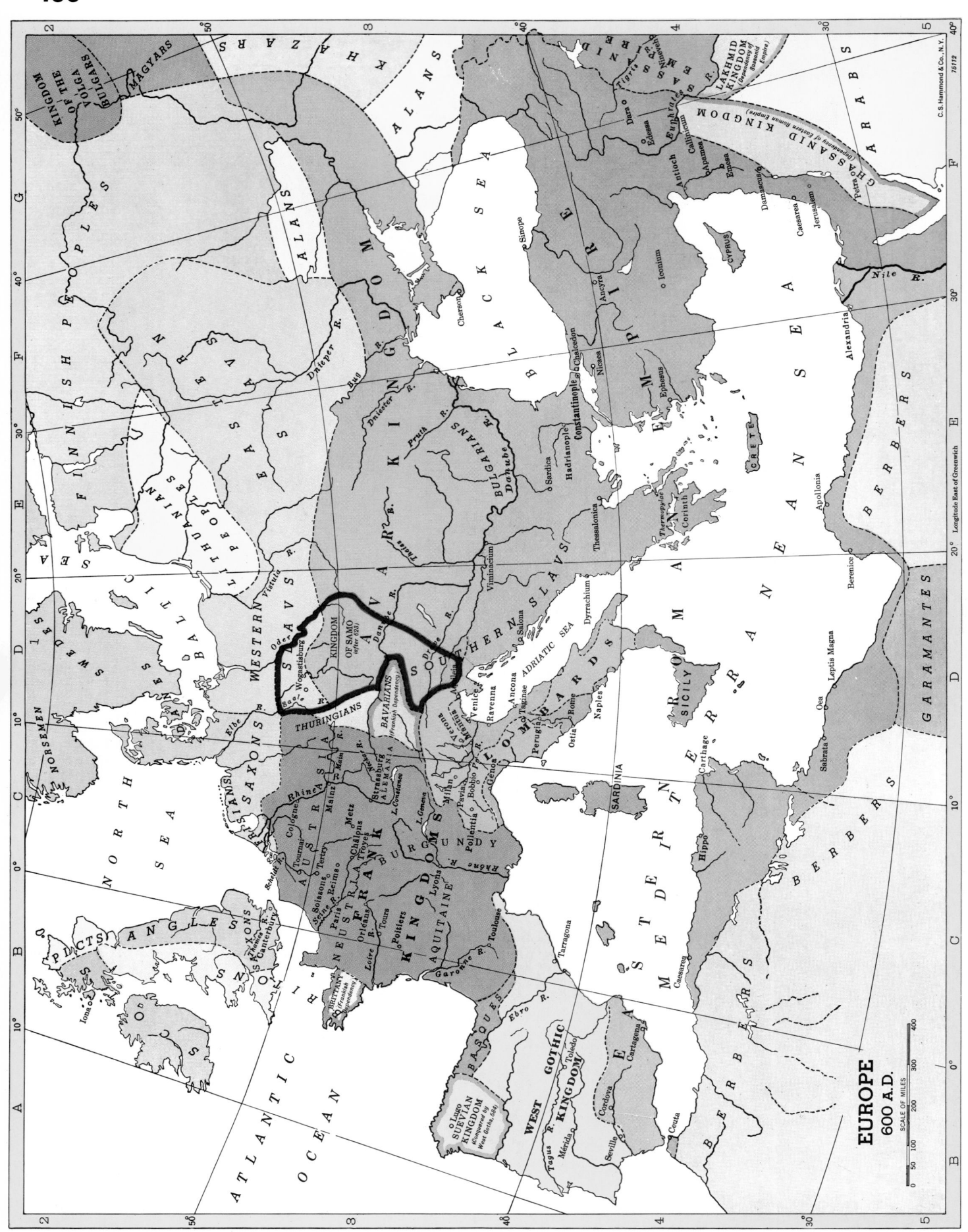

EUROPE
600 A.D.

SCALE OF MILES

0 50 100 200 300 400

C.S. Hammond & Co., N.Y.

76172

KINGDOM OF THE VOLGA BULGARS

MAGYARS

K H A Z A R S

FINNISH PEOPLES

A L A N S

A L A N S

LITHUANIANS

S L A V S

WESTERN

Oder R.

Vistula R.

Bug R.

Dnieper R.

Dniester R.

Pruth R.

A V A R S   K I N G D O M

KINGDOM OF SAMO (after 623)

Elbe

Saale R.

Wogastisburg

Danube R.

Theiss R.

Drave R.

Save R.

SOUTHERN SLAVS

BULGARIANS

Danube

CHERSONESE

B L A C K   S E A

Sinope

Darn

Edessa

Euphrates R.

Tigris R.

Nineveh

Callinicum

Antioch

Apamea

Emesa

Damascus

LAKHMID KINGDOM (Dependency of Sassanid Empire)

GHASSANID KINGDOM (Dependency of Eastern Roman Empire)

Petra

Caesarea

Jerusalem

A R A B S

NORSEMEN

SWEDES

NORTH SEA

BALTIC SEA

DANES

SAXONS

FRISIANS

Rhine R.

Cologne

THURINGIANS

BAVARIANS (Frankish dependency)

ALEMANIA

Mainz

Main R.

Strasburg

Neckar R.

L. Constance

Verona

Mantua

Venice

Aquileia

Salona

Ravenna

Adige R.

Po R.

Pavia

Bobbio

Milan

Genoa

L. Geneva

Pollentia

Perugia

Ancona

Taginae

Rome

Ostia

Naples

A D R I A T I C   S E A

Dyrrachium

Apollonia

Thessalonica

Thermopylae

Corinth

Hadrianople

Sardica

Viminacium

Naissus

SICILY

SARDINIA

CRETE

CYPRUS

M E D I T E R R A N E A N   S E A

Carthage

Hippo

Oea

Sabrata

Leptis Magna

Berenice

B E R B E R S

G A R A M A N T E S

D E S E R T

E   M   P   I   R   E

Nicaea

Chalcedon

Constantinople

Ancyra

Iconium

Ephesus

Alexandria

Nile R.

PICTS

SCOTS

Iona

ANGLES

SAXONS

Canterbury

S. SAXONS

BRITTANY (Frankish dependency)

A U S T R A S I A

AUSTRASIA

Tournai

Soissons

Reims

Metz

Treves

Chalons

Troyes

Scheldt R.

Somme R.

Seine R.

Paris

Orleans

Tours

Loire R.

Poitiers

N E U S T R I A

F R A N K   K I N G D O M

B U R G U N D Y

Rhône R.

Lyons

AQUITAINE

Garonne R.

Toulouse

BASQUES

Ebro R.

Tarragona

Cartagena

Cordova

Sevilla

Merida

Toledo

Tagus R.

SUEVIAN KINGDOM (Conquered by West Goths 584)

L. Lugo

W E S T   G O T H I C   K I N G D O M

Ceuta

Caesarea

B E R B E R S

A T L A N T I C   O C E A N

CARPATHIANS

LOMBARDS

E A S T E R N   R O M A N

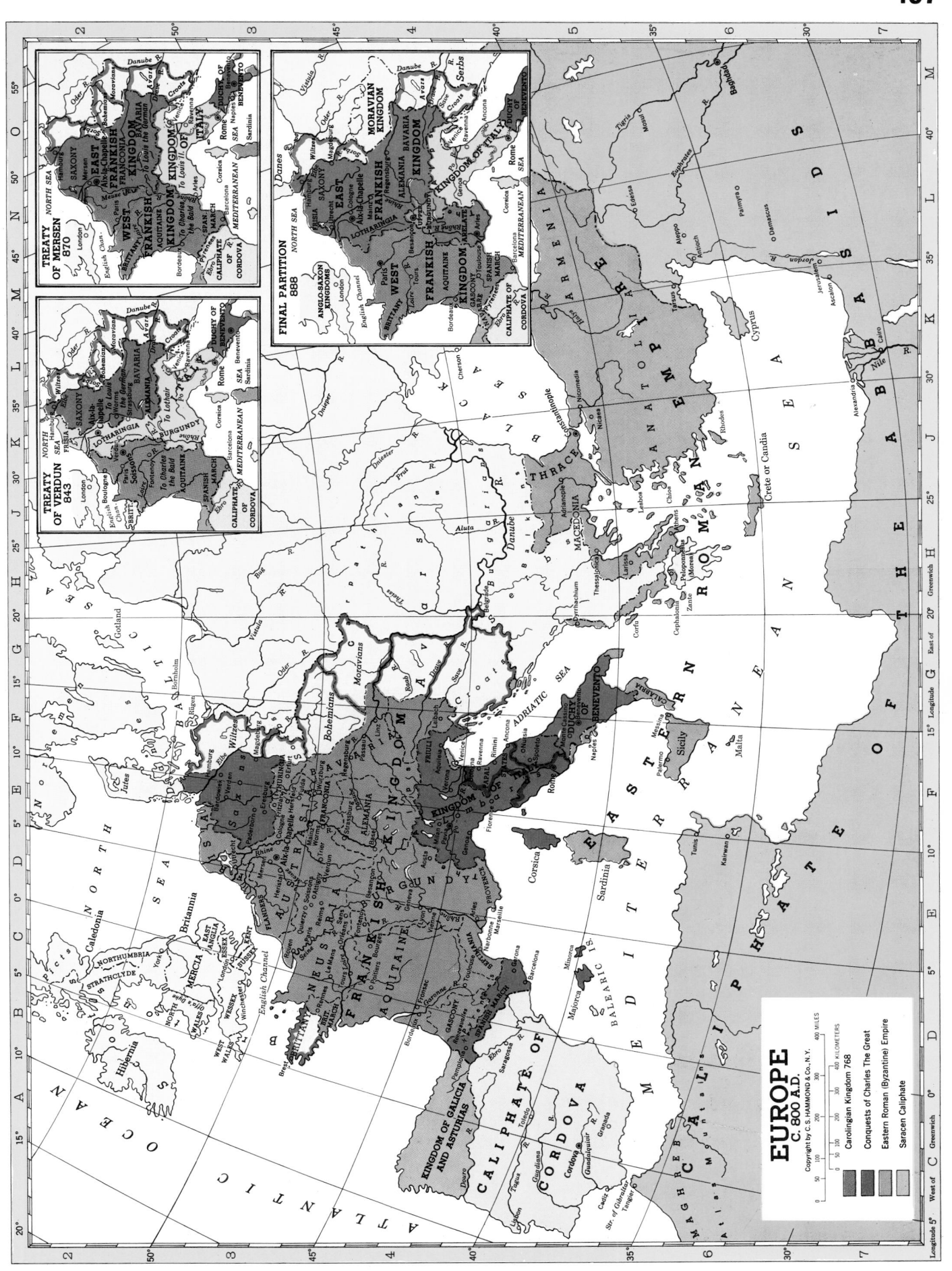
EUROPE
C. 800 A.D.
Copyright by C. S. HAMMOND & Co., N.Y.
Carolingian Kingdom 768
Conquests of Charles The Great
Eastern Roman (Byzantine) Empire
Saracen Caliphate
TREATY OF VERDUN 843
TREATY OF MERSEN 870
FINAL PARTITION 888
ATLANTIC OCEAN
NORTH SEA
BALTIC SEA
BLACK SEA
ADRIATIC SEA
MEDITERRANEAN SEA
FRANKISH KINGDOM
CALIPHATE OF CORDOVA
KINGDOM OF GALICIA AND ASTURIAS
EASTERN ROMAN EMPIRE
EMPIRE OF THE ABBASIDS
DUCHY OF BENEVENTO
PAPAL STATES
KINGDOM OF ITALY
WEST FRANKISH KINGDOM
EAST FRANKISH KINGDOM
LOTHARINGIA
BURGUNDY
SPANISH MARCH
BRITTANY
AQUITAINE
NEUSTRIA
AUSTRASIA
ALEMANIA
BAVARIA
SAXONY
FRISIA
FRANCONIA
THURINGIA
GASCONY
SEPTIMANIA
PROVENCE
ARMENIA
ANATOLIA
THRACE
MACEDONIA
MAGHREB
Caledonia
Britannia
Hibernia
NORTHUMBRIA
MERCIA
EAST ANGLIA
ESSEX
KENT
SUSSEX
WESSEX
STRATHCLYDE
NORTH WALES
WEST WALES
Corsica
Sardinia
Sicily
Crete or Candia
Cyprus
Rhodes
Malta
Majorca
Minorca
BALEARIC IS.
Moravians
Bohemians
Wiltzes
Avars
Croats
Serbs
Danes
Bulgarians
Gotland
Bornholm
Rügen
Jutes
Paris
Rome
Constantinople
Aix-la-Chapelle
Cordova
Toledo
Barcelona
Bordeaux
Jerusalem
Damascus
Baghdad
Alexandria
Cairo
Antioch
Aleppo
Athens
Naples
Venice
Ravenna
Milan
Pavia
Verona
Genoa
Florence
Regensburg
Hamburg
Magdeburg
Cologne
Mainz
Worms
Strassburg
Lyon
Marseille
Arles
Narbonne
Toulouse
Tours
Orléans
Rouen
London
York
Winchester
Tunis
Kairwan
Tangier
Cadiz
Str. of Gibraltar
Danube R.
Rhine R.
Elbe R.
Oder R.
Vistula R.
Dnieper R.
Dniester R.
Ebro R.
Tagus R.
Douro R.
Guadiana R.
Guadalquivir R.
Nile R.
Tigris R.
Euphrates R.
English Channel
Atlas Mountains
Longitude West of Greenwich
Longitude East of Greenwich

BRITANNIA
about 350 A. D.
Showing the
CELTIC TRIBES
and approximately
The 4 Divisions of DIOCLETIAN
MILES
KILOMETERS
CALEDONIA
ANTONINE WALL
HADRIAN'S WALL
OTADINI
SELGOVAE
NOVANTAE
DAMNII
BRIGANTES
MAXIMA
CAESARIENSIS
SETANTII
PARISI
Eburacum (York)
Abus (R. Humber)
Mona
DRUIDS
ORDOVICES
CORNAVII
CORITANI
BRITANNIA PRIMA
CATUVELLAUNI
ICENI
Venta Icenorum (Caistor)
Metaris Aest. (The Wash)
Branodunum
BRITANNIA SECUNDA
DEMETAE
SILURES
DOBUNI
FLAVIA CAESARIENSIS
TRINOBANTES
Camulodunum (Colchester)
Londinium
ATREBATII
BELGAE
CANTII
REGNI
DUROTRIGES
DUMNONII
Isca Dumnoniorum (Exeter)
Vectis I.
Rutupiae
Dubris (Dover)
Fretum Gallicum
GALLIA
HIBERNIA
Monapia (Mona)
OCEANUS HIBERNICUS
OCEANUS GERMANICUS
OCEANUS VERGIONIUS
OCEANUS BRITANNICUS
Longitude West of Greenwich

ENGLISH CONQUEST
From 450 to the End of the 6th Century
Showing the Settlements of the Jutes, Saxons and Angles. Also the Sections of the Country which were retained by the Britons (Celtic Tribes).
MILES
KILOMETERS
Iona
SCOTS
PICTS
Alcluyd
STRATHCLYDE
BERNICIA
Lindisfarne (Holy I.)
Bamborough (Bebbanburh)
DEIRA
ANGLES
CUMBRIA
York (Eoforwic)
Humbra (Humber)
SOUTH-UMBRIANS
LINDISWARAS
Lindum (Lincoln)
MERCIANS
Chester
Uriconium (Wroxeter)
MIDDLE ANGLES
Venta Icenorum (Caistor)
Branodunum (Brancaster)
Northfolc
EAST ANGLES
Suthfolc
CAMBRIA
NORTH WEALAS
Menevia (St. David)
Gleawanceaster (Gloucester)
Cirenceaster
Deorham
Bathanceaster (Bath)
SAXONS
EAST SAXONS
London
Camulodunum (Colchester)
Thanet I.
Aegelesford
Andredsweald
JUTES
Cantwarabyrig (Canterbury)
Lynme
WEST SAXONS
SOUTH SAXONS
Wintanceaster (Winchester)
Cissanceaster (Chichester)
Anderida (Pevensey)
Cerdicesford (Charford)
Wihtgara Burh (Wight)
WESTWEALAS
DAMNONIA
BRITONS
OCEANUS HIBERNICUS (Irish Sea)
OCEANUS GERMANICUS (German Ocean)
OCEANUS BRITANNICUS (English Channel)
GALLIA
Longitude West of Greenwich

ENGLAND
in the Eighth Century
(The "HEPTARCHY")
Kingdoms of the Angles
Kingdoms of the Saxons
Kingdoms of the Jutes
Kingdoms of the Britons
MILES
KILOMETERS
SCOTS
PICTS
Forth
Alcluyd
Eadwinsburh
Lindisfarne (Holy I.)
Bernicia
STRATHCLYDE (CUMBRIA)
NORTHUMBRIA
Galwidia
Hwiterne (Whithorn)
Hagustaldesae (Hexham)
Streanaeshalch (Whitby)
Deira
Eoforwic (York)
Humbra
Eubonia (Man)
Mona (Anglesey)
Lindesse
Lincoln
Benchor
Caernarvon
Gwynedh
Caerleon
Notingaham
Stamford
Medeshamstede (Peterborough)
Northwic (Norwich)
Lichefelda (Lichfield)
Powys
MERCIA
Leagacester (Leicester)
EAST ANGLIA
Domuc
Sutton Hoo
CAMBRIA (NORTH WEALAS)
Dyfed
Demetica
St. David (Menevia)
Llandawa
Benesingtun
EAST SAXONIA (ESSEX)
Londinium
Hrofesceaster
CANTIA (KENT)
Cantuaria
WEST SAXONIA (WESSEX)
Wintanceaster (Winchester)
SUTHSAXONA (SUSSEX)
Cissanceaster (Chichester)
Wiht
Exanceaster
DAMNONIA (WEST WEALAS)
Cornubia
Hafren, Sabrina or Saefern
GERMAN OCEAN (North Sea)
WEST MERE (Irish Sea)
IRELAND
English Channel
GAUL
Longitude West of Greenwich

ENGLAND
after the Peace of Wedmore
(878 A.D.)
Showing the Divisions between
ALFRED and GUTHRUM
MILES
KILOMETERS
SCOTS
Forth
Alcluyd
Eadwinsburh (Edinburgh)
Tweed
BERNICIA (To Alfred)
STRATHCLYDE
BRITONS
Cumberland
Tyne
Tees
Whitby
NORTHUMBRIA
York
Man
THE DANELAW
Manchester
Humber R.
Brunanburh
Lincoln
Chester
Nottingham
Derby
Repton
Anglesey
NORTH WALES
Wroxeter
Stafford
Tamworth
MERCIA
Leicester
Stamford
Crowland
Norwich
East Anglia
Ely
Warwick
Northampton
Peterborough
Huntingdon
Bedford
KINGDOM OF GUTHRUM
London
I. of Sheppey
Gloucester
Ashdown
Chippenham
Ethandun
Reading
Kennet
POSSESSIONS OF ALFRED THE GREAT
WESSEX
Wilton
Ellundun
Rochester
KENT
Winchester
Wedmore
Athelney
Sherborne
Exeter
Wareham
Rocks of Swanage
Isle of Wight
WEST WALES
Hengestdun
IRISH SEA
IRELAND
GERMAN OCEAN or NORTH SEA
English Channel
Longitude West of Greenwich

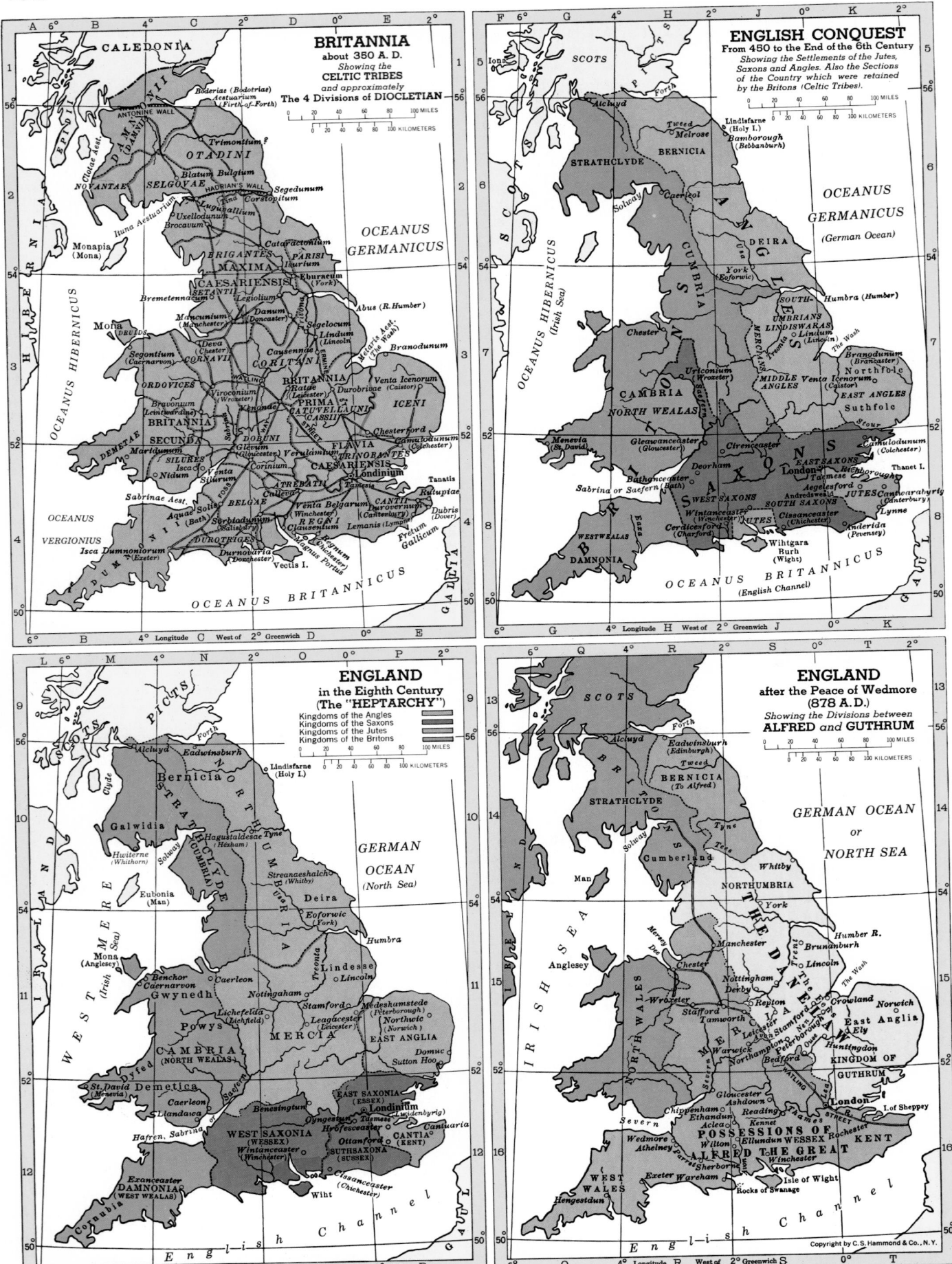

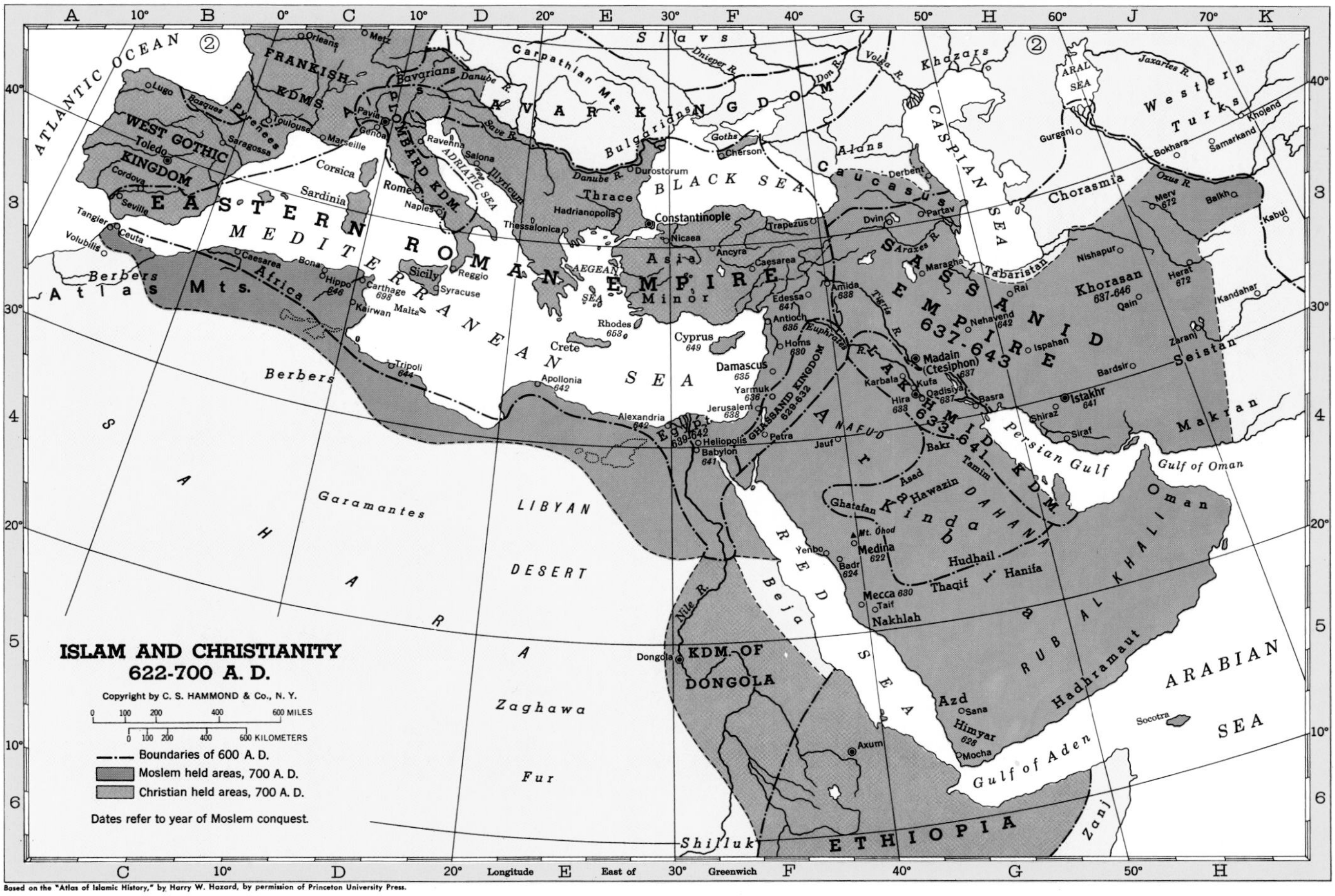

Map 1 (top)

ATLANTIC OCEAN

FRANKISH KDMS.

WEST GOTHIC KINGDOM — Toledo, Cordova, Seville, Tangier, Ceuta, Volubilis

LOMBARD KDM.

BAVARIANS

AVAR KINGDOM

Slavs

Bulgarians

Carpathian Mt.

Corsica, Sardinia, Rome, Naples, Ravenna, Salona

EASTERN ROMAN EMPIRE

Thrace — Constantinople, Nicaea, Hadrianopolis, Thessalonica

BLACK SEA

Goths, Alans, Caucasus, Derbent, Dvin, Partav

CASPIAN SEA

Chorasmia

Western Turks — Gurganj, Bokhara, Samarkand, Khojend

Merv 672, Balkh, Kabul

Sicily, Malta, Syracuse 695, Reggio

MEDITERRANEAN SEA

AEGEAN SEA

Asia Minor — Ancyra, Caesarea, Trapezus, Amida 638, Edessa 641

SASSANID EMPIRE 637–643

Khorasan 637–646 — Nishapur, Rai, Ispahan, Herat 672, Qain, Kandahar

Crete, Rhodes 653, Cyprus 649

Antioch 636, Homs 636, Damascus 635, Yarmuk 636, Jerusalem 638

Madain (Ctesiphon), Kufa 637, Basra, Istakhr 641, Shiraz, Siraf, Bardsir

Seistan

Makran

Berbers

Atlas Mts.

Africa — Caesarea, Carthage 698, Hippo, Kairwan, Tripoli, Apollonia 642

Alexandria 642, Heliopolis 640, Babylon 641, Petra, Jauf

EGYPT

Berbers

Garamantes

LIBYAN DESERT

Zaghawa

Fur

Nile R.

Dongola — KDM. OF DONGOLA

RED SEA

Beja

Yenbo, Medina 622, Badr 624, Mecca 630, Taif, Nakhlah, Mt. Ohod

Hudhail, Thaqif, Hanifa

RUB AL KHALI

DAHANA

Azd, Sana, Himyar 628, Mocha

Socotra

Hadramaut

Oman

Persian Gulf, Gulf of Oman

ARABIAN SEA

Axum

Shilluk

ETHIOPIA

ISLAM AND CHRISTIANITY
622–700 A.D.

Copyright by C. S. HAMMOND & Co., N.Y.

0 100 200 400 600 MILES
0 100 200 400 600 KILOMETERS

— Boundaries of 600 A.D.
■ Moslem held areas, 700 A.D.
■ Christian held areas, 700 A.D.

Dates refer to year of Moslem conquest.

Based on the "Atlas of Islamic History," by Harry W. Hazard, by permission of Princeton University Press.

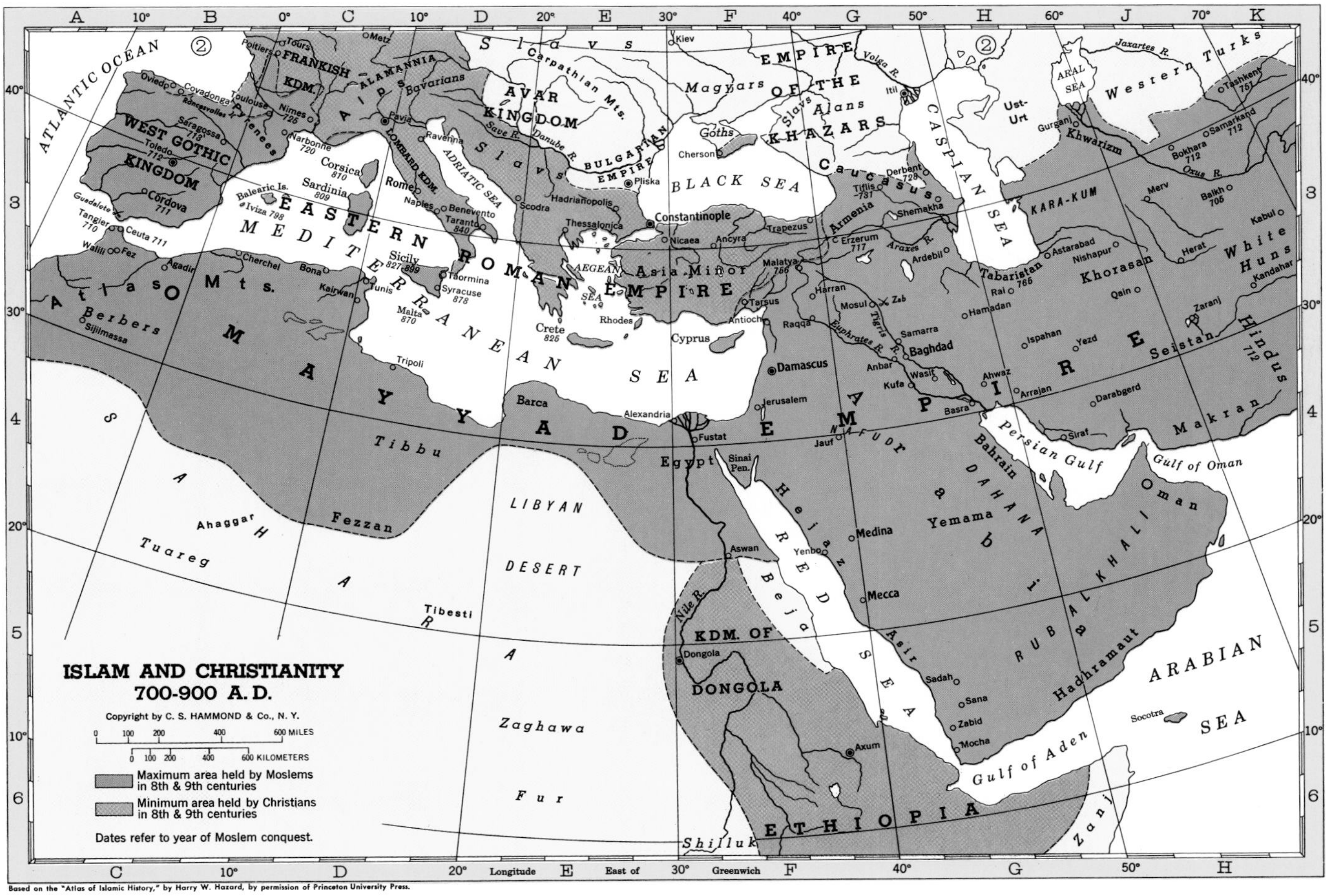

Longitude East of Greenwich

Map 2 (bottom)

ATLANTIC OCEAN

FRANKISH KDM. — Poitiers 732, Tours 732, Toulouse, Narbonne 720, Nimes

ALAMANNIA, Bavarians

AVAR KINGDOM

Slavs

Carpathian Mt.

Kiev

EMPIRE OF THE KHAZARS — Magyars, Slavs, Alans, Itil, Volga R.

BULGARIAN EMPIRE — Pliska

Goths, Cherson

WEST GOTHIC KINGDOM — Oviedo, Covadonga, Toledo 712, Cordova 711, Guadalete 711, Tangier 710, Ceuta 711, Walili, Fez, Qadir

Balearic Is. 798, Iviza 798, Corsica 810, Sardinia 809

LOMBARD KDM., Rome, Naples, Benevento, Ravenna

EASTERN ROMAN EMPIRE

Hadrianopolis, Scodra, Thessalonica, Constantinople, Nicaea, Ancyra

BLACK SEA

Caucasus, Derbent, Tiflis 724, Shemakha, Armenia, Erzerum 717, Araxes R., Ardebil

CASPIAN SEA — Ust-Urt, Gurgani, Khwarizm, KARA-KUM

Western Turks — Tashkend 751, Samarkand 712, Bokhara 712, Balkh 705, Kabul

WHITE HUNS — Merv, Khorasan, Nishapur, Rai 765, Qain, Herat, Kandahar

Sicily 827–859, Taormina, Syracuse 878, Malta 870

MEDITERRANEAN SEA

AEGEAN, Asia Minor, Malatya 766, Tarsus, Harran, Raqqa, Antioch, Mosul, Tigris, Zab

Crete 826, Rhodes, Cyprus

Berbers, Sijilmassa, Cherchel, Bona, Tunis, Kairwan, Tripoli, Barca

Atlas Mts.

UMAYYAD EMPIRE

Samarra, Baghdad, Anbar, Kufa, Wasit, Basra, Ahwaz, Arrajan, Darabgerd, Ispahan, Yezd, Zaranj, Seistan 712

Hamadan

Damascus, Jerusalem, Euphrates R.

Fustat, Egypt, Sinai Pen., Jauf

Makran

Persian Gulf, Bahrain, Siraf, Gulf of Oman, Oman

Tibbu, Tuareg, Ahaggar, Fezzan

LIBYAN DESERT

Tibesti

Zaghawa

Fur

Nile R.

KDM. OF DONGOLA — Dongola

RED SEA, Beja

Aswan, Yenbo, Medina, Mecca, Hejaz

Yemama, DAHANA, Nafud

RUB AL KHALI

Hadramaut

ARABIAN SEA

Asir, Sadah, Sana, Zabid, Mocha, Axum

Socotra

Gulf of Aden

Zanj

Shilluk

ETHIOPIA

Hindus 712

ISLAM AND CHRISTIANITY
700–900 A.D.

Copyright by C. S. HAMMOND & Co., N.Y.

0 100 200 400 600 MILES
0 100 200 400 600 KILOMETERS

■ Maximum area held by Moslems in 8th & 9th centuries
■ Minimum area held by Christians in 8th & 9th centuries

Dates refer to year of Moslem conquest.

Based on the "Atlas of Islamic History," by Harry W. Hazard, by permission of Princeton University Press.

Longitude East of Greenwich

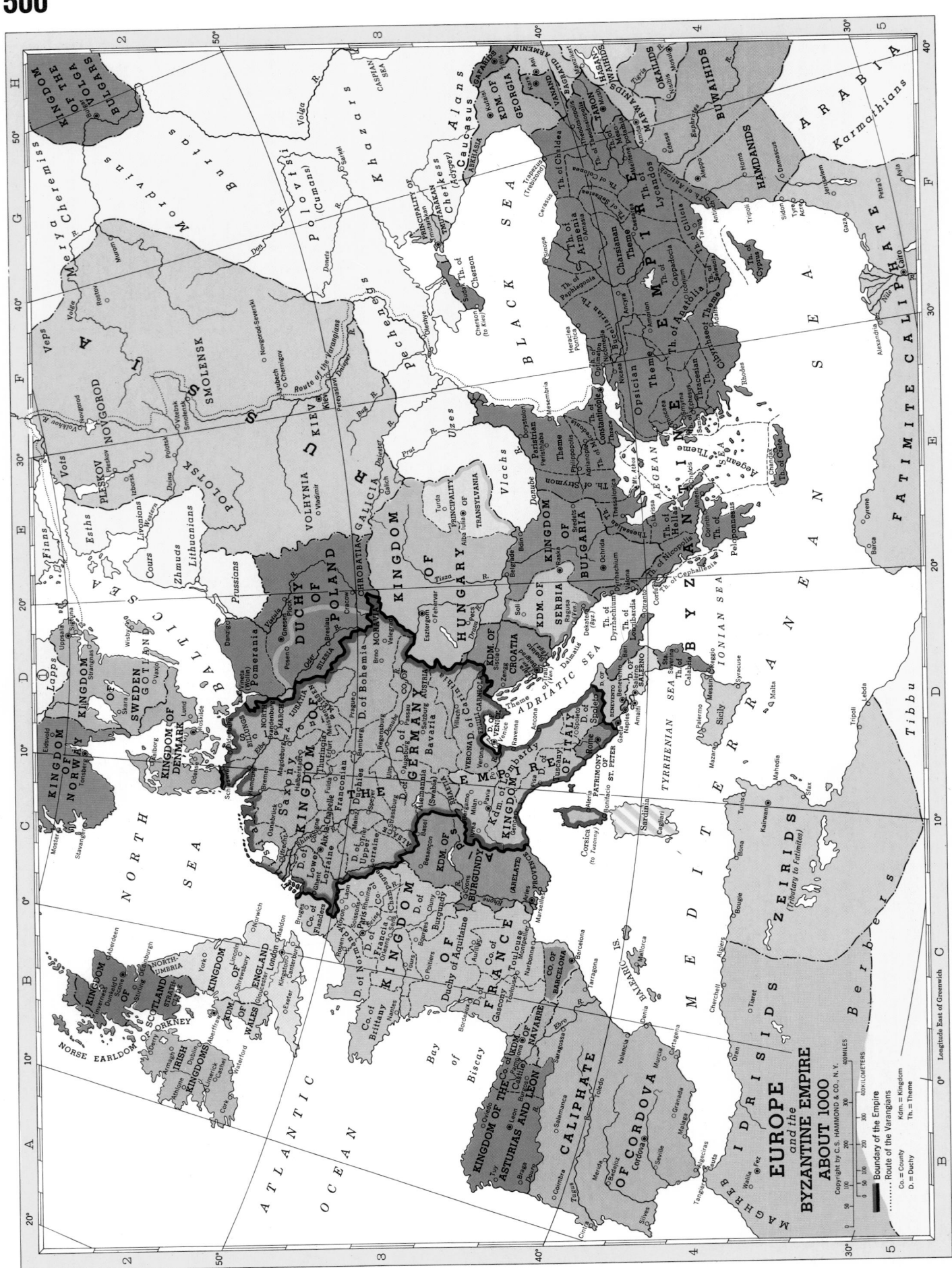

EUROPE
and the
BYZANTINE EMPIRE
ABOUT 1000

Copyright by C.S. HAMMOND & CO., N.Y.

Co. = County
D. = Duchy
Kdm. = Kingdom
Th. = Theme

──── Boundary of the Empire
········· Route of the Varangians

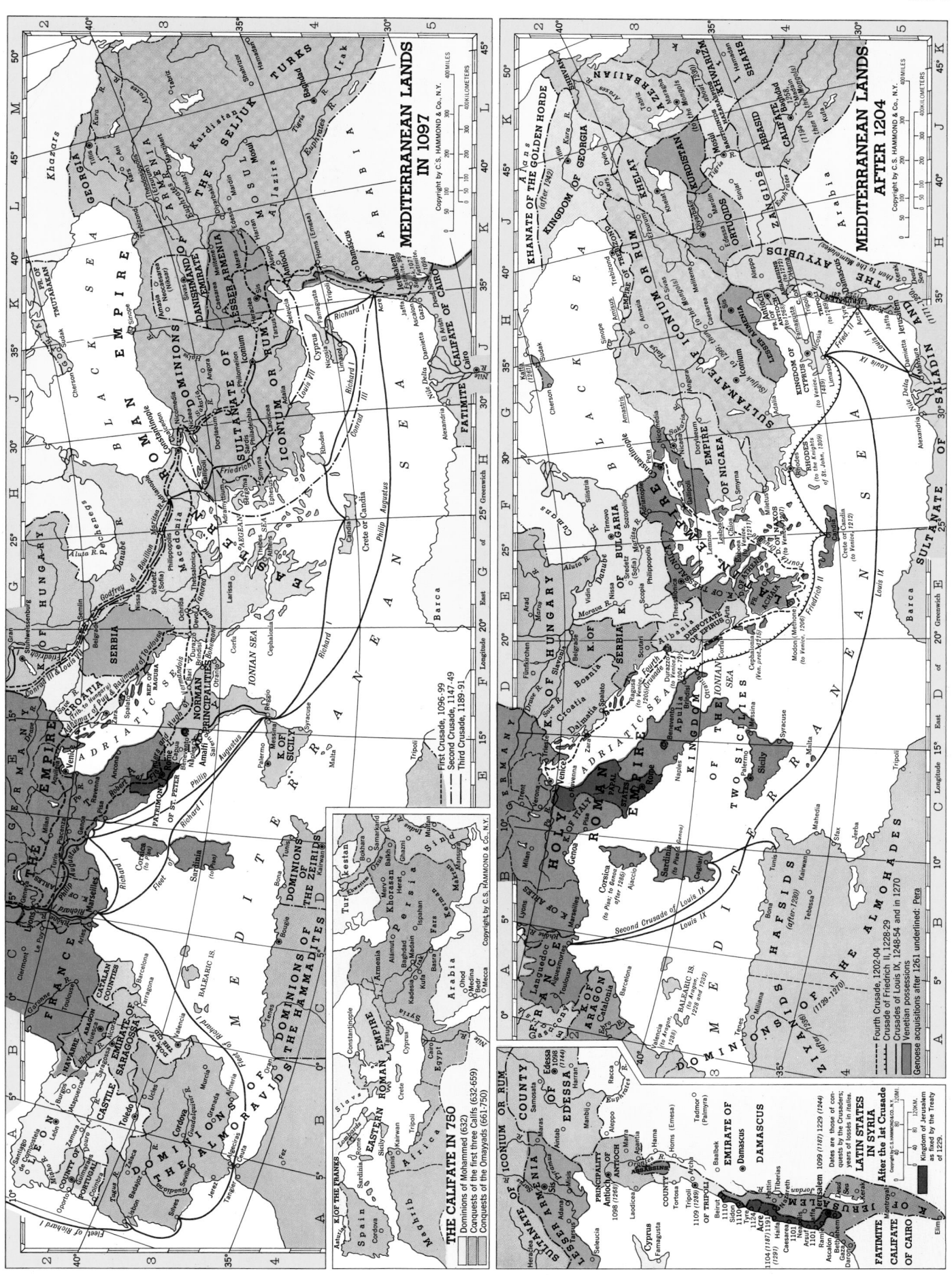

MEDITERRANEAN LANDS IN 1097

MEDITERRANEAN LANDS AFTER 1204

THE CALIFATE IN 750

LATIN STATES IN SYRIA After the 1st Crusade

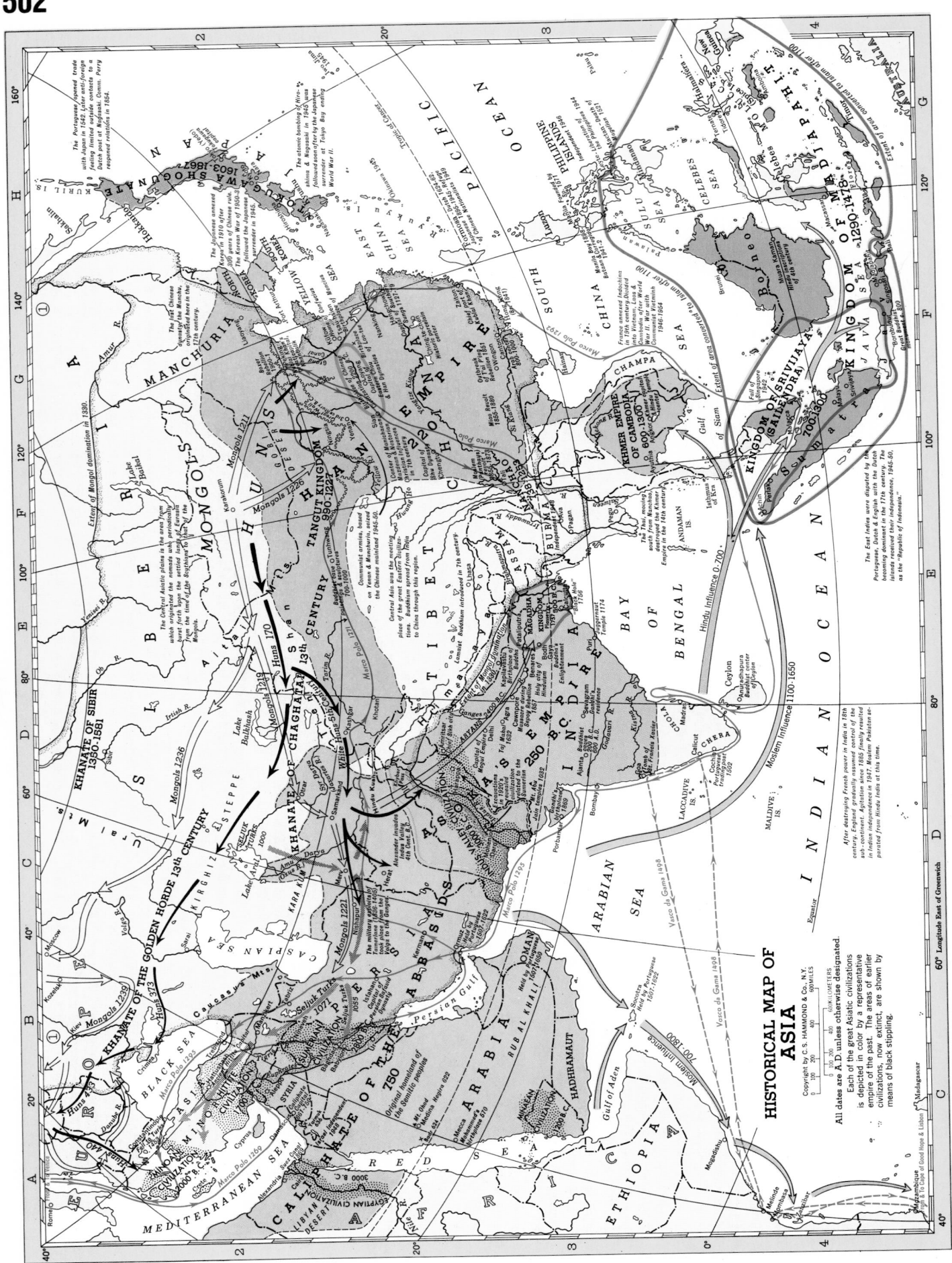

HISTORICAL MAP OF ASIA
Copyright by C.S. HAMMOND & Co., N.Y.
All dates are A.D. unless otherwise designated.
Each of the great Asiatic civilizations is depicted in color by a representative empire of the past. The areas of earlier civilizations, now extinct, are shown by means of black stippling.
60° Longitude East of Greenwich
KHANATE OF SIBIR 1350-1581
KHANATE OF THE GOLDEN HORDE 13th CENTURY
KHANATE OF CHAGHATAI 13th CENTURY
TANGUT KINGDOM 990-1227
HAN EMPIRE
ASOKA'S EMPIRE 250 B.C.
CALIPHATE OF THE ABBASSIDS 750
TOKUGAWA SHOGUNATE 1603-1867
KINGDOM OF MADJAPAHIT 1290-1478
KINGDOM OF SRIVIJAYA (SAILENDRA) 700-1300
KHMER EMPIRE OF CAMBODIA 600-1300
MAGADHA KINGDOM
NANCHAO 738-1253
BURMA
TIBET
MANCHURIA
MONGOLS
HUNS
SIBERIA
STEPPE
KIRGHIZ
ARABIA
PERSIA
INDIA
CHINA
JAPAN
ETHIOPIA
AFRICA
EUROPE
MINOAN CIVILIZATION 2000 B.C.
HITTITE CIVILIZATION
SUMERIAN CIVILIZATION
EGYPTIAN CIVILIZATION 3000 B.C.
INDUS VALLEY CIVILIZATION 3000 B.C.
MINAEAN CIVILIZATION 1200 B.C.
CHAMPA
MEDITERRANEAN SEA
BLACK SEA
CASPIAN SEA
RED SEA
ARABIAN SEA
BAY OF BENGAL
SOUTH CHINA SEA
EAST CHINA SEA
YELLOW SEA
SULU SEA
CELEBES SEA
JAVA SEA
INDIAN OCEAN
PACIFIC OCEAN
Marco Polo 1271
Marco Polo 1292
Marco Polo 1295
Vasco da Gama 1498
Hindu Influence 0-700
Moslem Influence 1100-1650
Moslem Influence 700-1800
Extent of Mongol domination in 1330.
Extent of area converted to Islam after 1100
The Portuguese opened trade with Japan in 1542. Later anti-foreign feeling limited outside contacts to a Dutch post at Nagasaki. Comm. Perry reopened relations in 1854.
The atomic bombing of Hiroshima & Nagasaki in 1945 was followed soon after by the Japanese surrender at Tokyo Bay ending World War II.
The Japanese annexed Korea in 1910 after 300 years of Chinese rule. The Korean War of 1950-3 followed the Japanese surrender in 1945.
The last Chinese dynasty the Manchu, originated here in the 17th century.
The Central Asiatic plains is the area from which originated the nomads who periodically burst forth upon the settled lands of Eurasia from the time of the Scythians to that of the Mongols.
Communist armies, based on Yenan & Manchuria, seized the Chinese mainland 1945-50.
Central Asia was the meeting place of the great Eastern civilizations. Buddhism spread from India to China through this region.
The Thai, moving south from Nanchao, destroyed the Khmer Empire in the 14th century.
France annexed Indochina in 19th century. Divided into Vietnam, Laos & Cambodia after World War II. War with Communist Vietminh 1946-1954.
The military exploits of Tamerlane (1336-1405) took place from the Volga to the Ganges.
After destroying French power in India in 18th century, England gradually assumed control of the sub-continent. Agitation since 1885 finally resulted in Indian independence in 1947. Moslem Pakistan separated from Hindu India at this time.
The East Indies were disputed by the Portuguese, Dutch & English with the Dutch becoming dominant in the 17th century. The islands received their independence, 1945-50, as the "Republic of Indonesia."

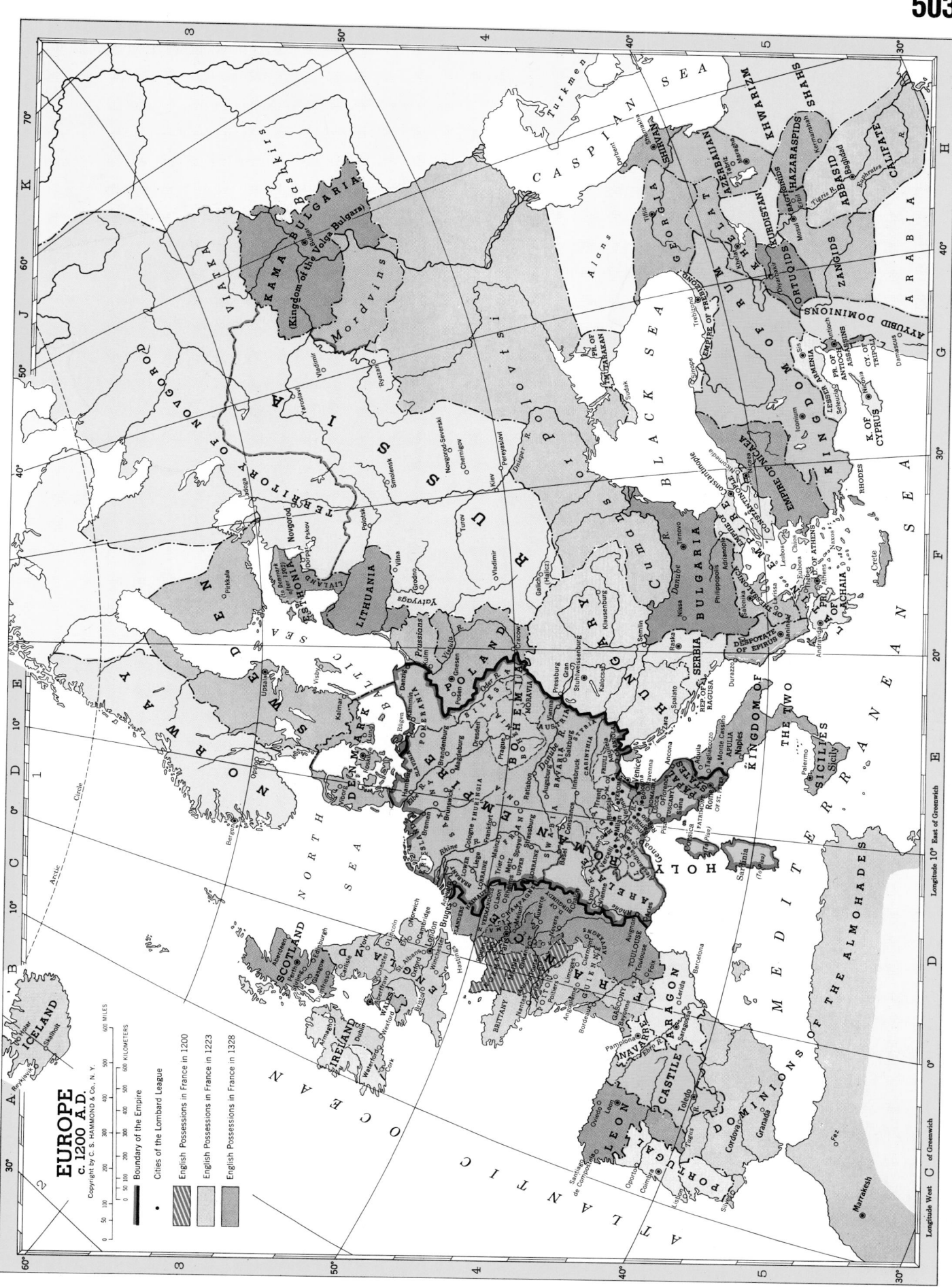

503

EUROPE
c. 1200 A.D.

Copyright by C. S. HAMMOND & Co., N.Y.

Boundary of the Empire

• Cities of the Lombard League

English Possessions in France in 1200

English Possessions in France in 1223

English Possessions in France in 1328

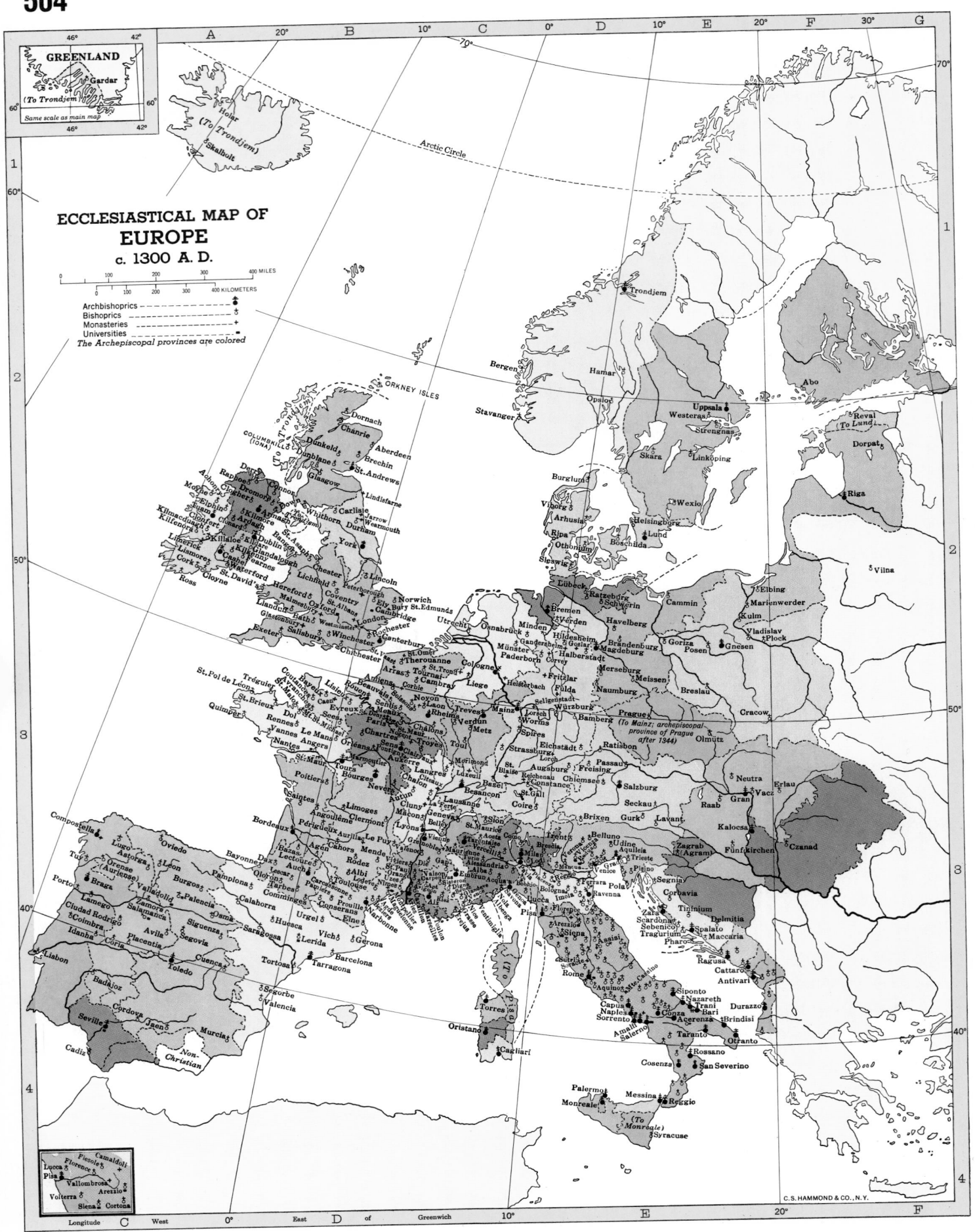

504

ECCLESIASTICAL MAP OF
EUROPE
c. 1300 A. D.

Archbishoprics ----------
Bishoprics ----------
Monasteries ----------
Universities ----------
The Archepiscopal provinces are colored

GREENLAND
Gardar
(To Trondjem)
Same scale as main map

C. S. HAMMOND & CO., N.Y.

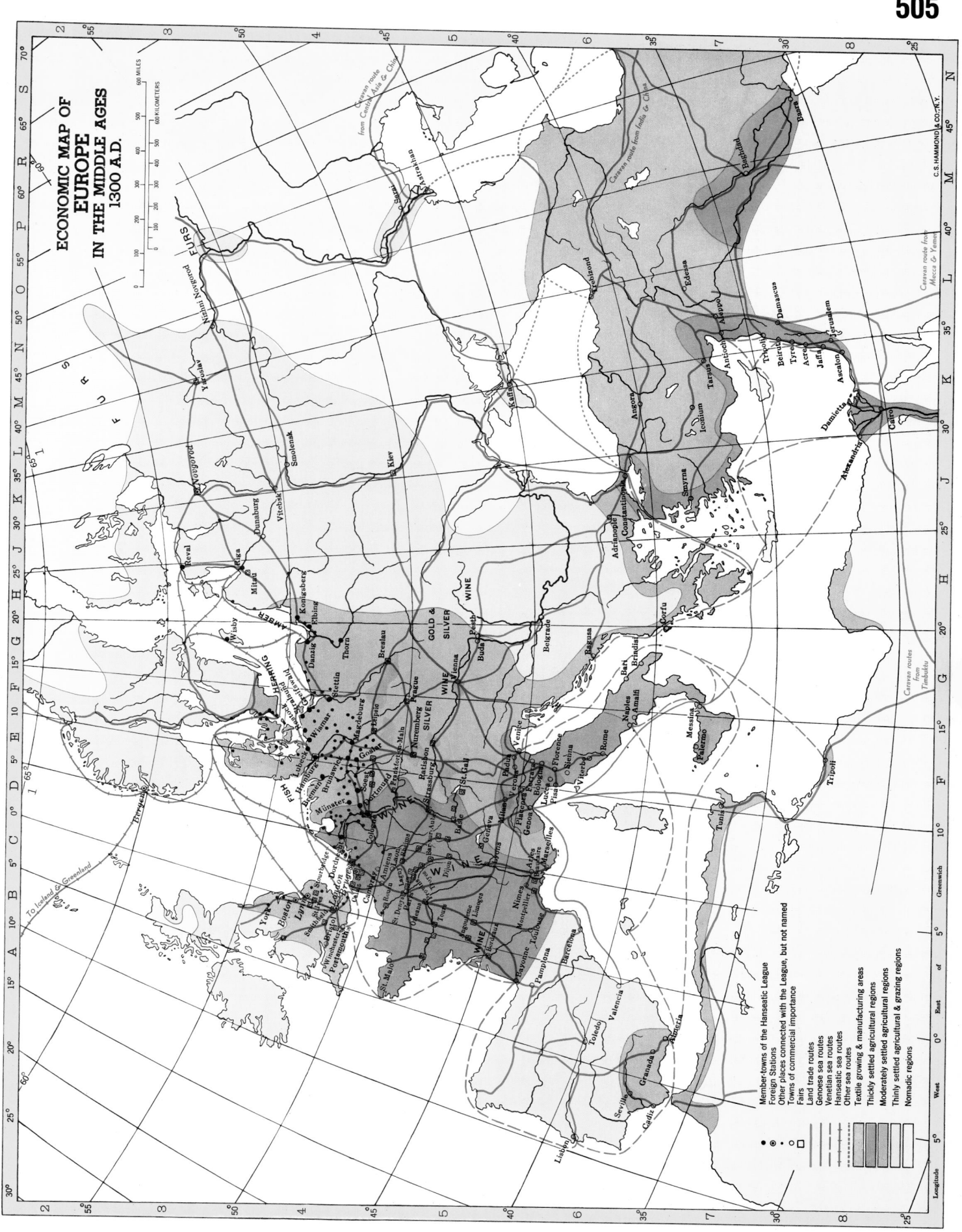

ECONOMIC MAP OF
EUROPE
IN THE MIDDLE AGES
1300 A.D.

C.S. HAMMOND & CO., N.Y.

Member-towns of the Hanseatic League
Foreign Stations
Other places connected with the League, but not named
Towns of commercial importance
Fairs
Land trade routes
Genoese sea routes
Venetian sea routes
Hanseatic sea routes
Other sea routes
Textile growing & manufacturing areas
Thickly settled agricultural regions
Moderately settled agricultural regions
Thinly settled agricultural & grazing regions
Nomadic regions

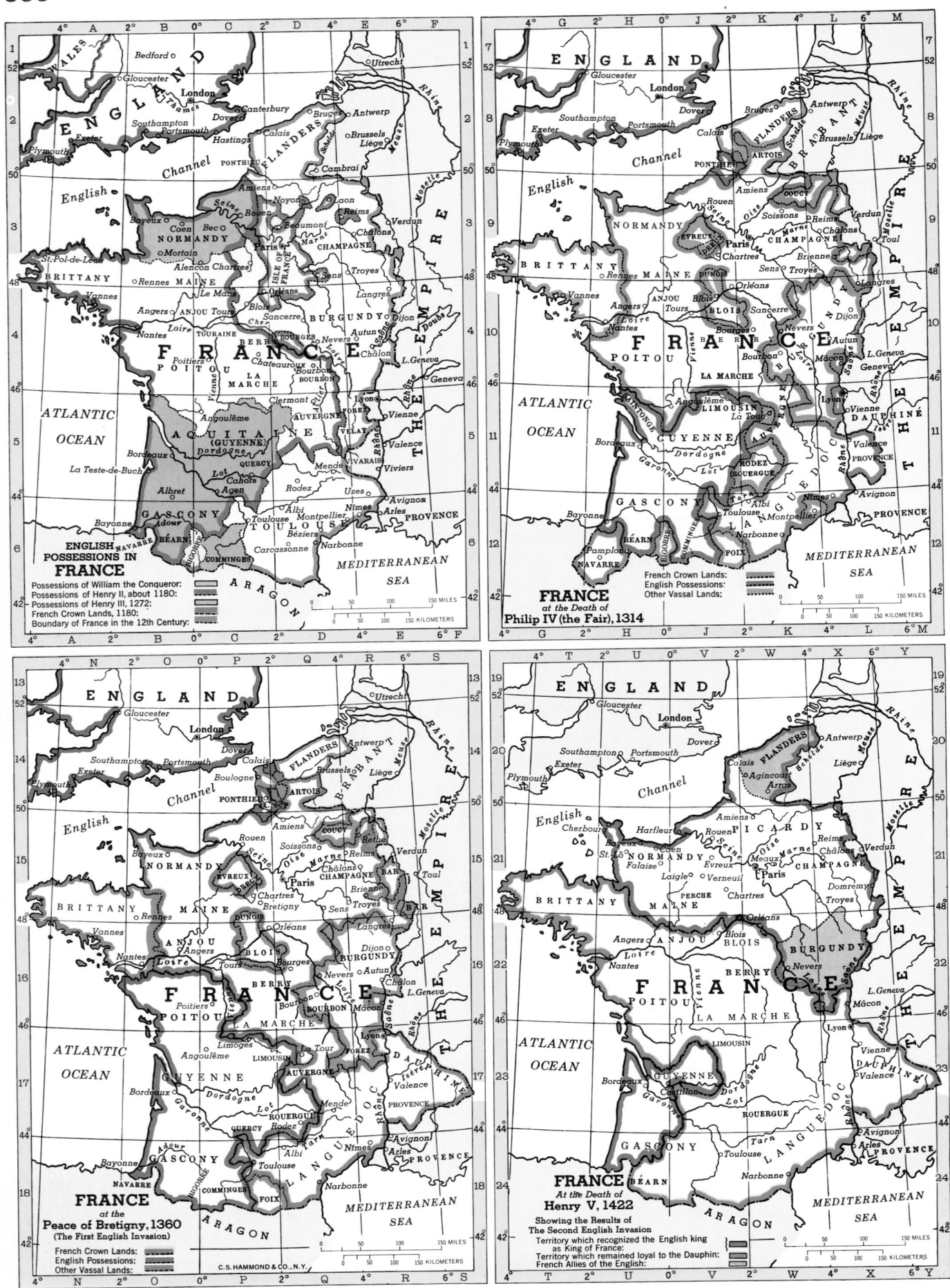

ENGLISH POSSESSIONS IN FRANCE

Possessions of William the Conqueror:
Possessions of Henry II, about 1180:
Possessions of Henry III, 1272:
French Crown Lands, 1180:
Boundary of France in the 12th Century:

FRANCE
at the Death of
Philip IV (the Fair), 1314

French Crown Lands:
English Possessions:
Other Vassal Lands:

FRANCE
at the
Peace of Bretigny, 1360
(The First English Invasion)

French Crown Lands:
English Possessions:
Other Vassal Lands:

C. S. HAMMOND & CO., N.Y.

FRANCE
At the Death of
Henry V, 1422

Showing the Results of
The Second English Invasion

Territory which recognized the English king
as King of France:
Territory which remained loyal to the Dauphin:
French Allies of the English:

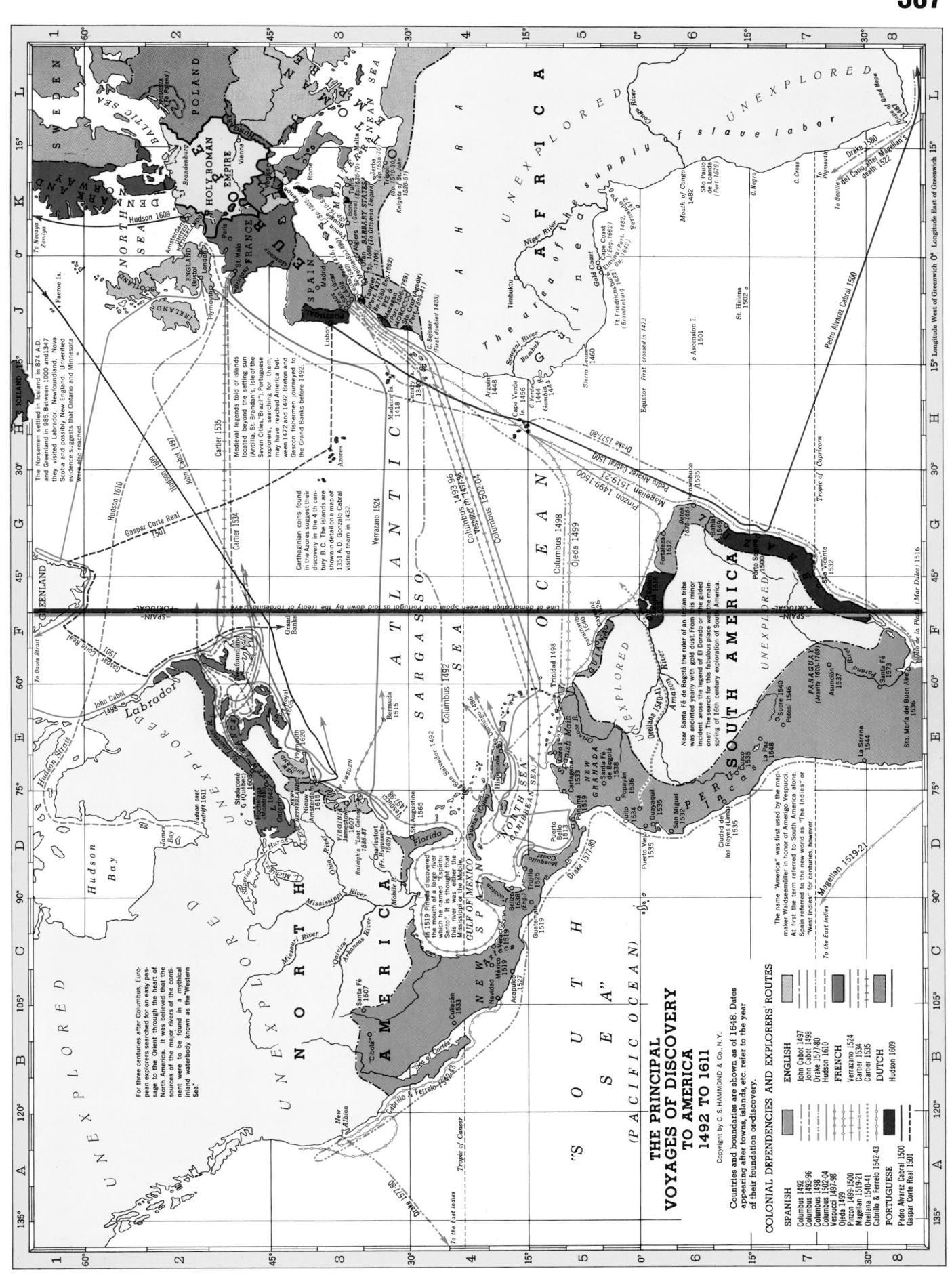

THE PRINCIPAL
VOYAGES OF DISCOVERY
TO AMERICA
1492 TO 1611

Copyright by C. S. HAMMOND & Co., N. Y.

Countries and boundaries are shown as of 1648. Dates
appearing after towns, islands, etc. refer to the year
of their foundation or discovery.

COLONIAL DEPENDENCIES AND EXPLORERS' ROUTES

SPANISH
Columbus 1492
Columbus 1493-96
Columbus 1498
Columbus 1502-04
Vespucci 1497-98
Ojeda 1499
Pinzon 1499-1500
Magellan 1519-21
Orellana 1540-41
Cabrillo & Ferrelo 1542-43

PORTUGUESE
Pedro Alvarez Cabral 1500
Gaspar Corte Real 1501

ENGLISH
John Cabot 1497
John Cabot 1498
Drake 1577-80
Hudson 1610

FRENCH
Verrazano 1524
Cartier 1534
Cartier 1535

DUTCH
Hudson 1609

508

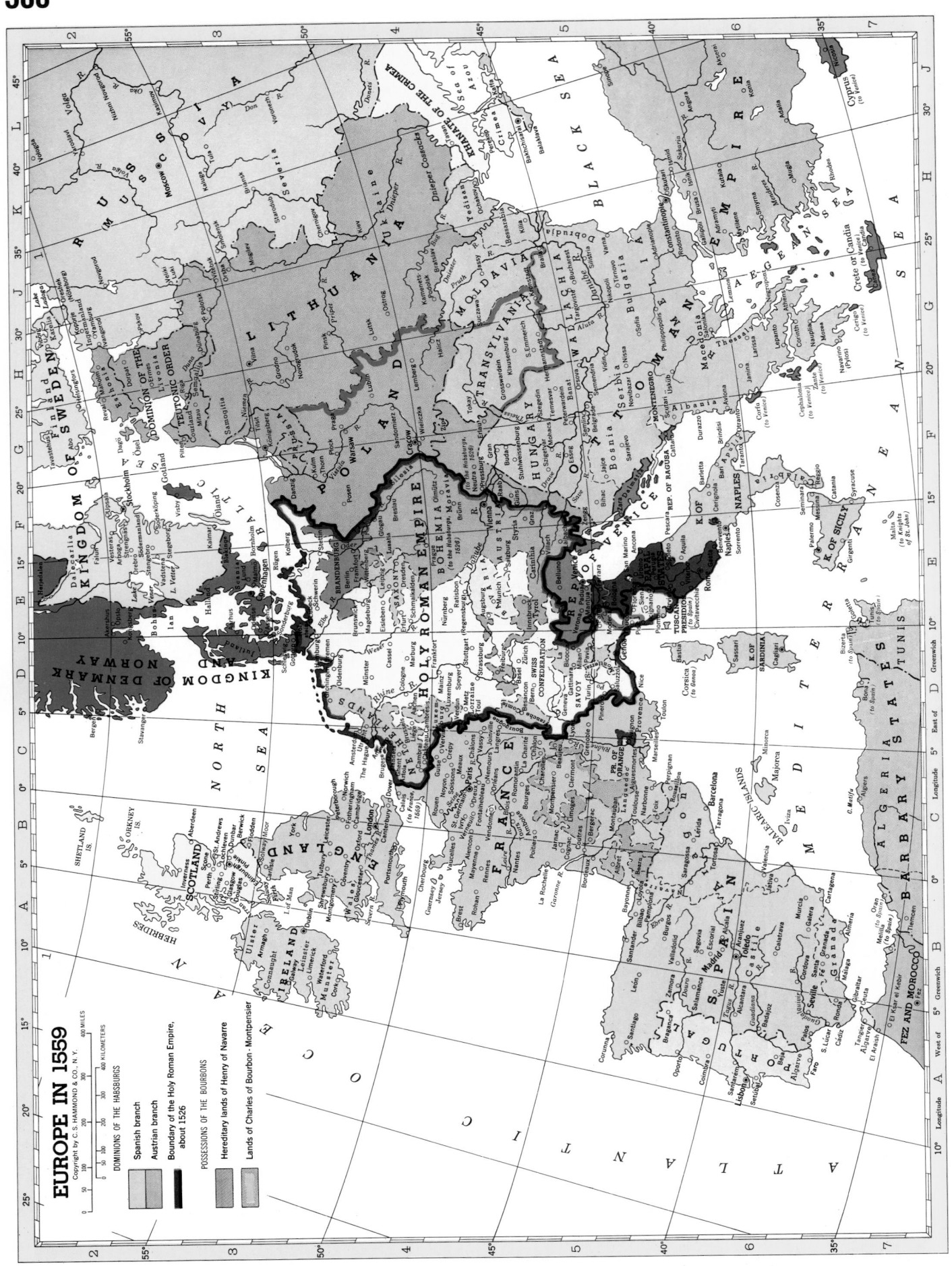

EUROPE IN 1559

Copyright by C. S. HAMMOND & CO., N.Y.

DOMINIONS OF THE HABSBURGS

Spanish branch

Austrian branch

Boundary of the Holy Roman Empire, about 1526

POSSESSIONS OF THE BOURBONS

Hereditary lands of Henry of Navarre

Lands of Charles of Bourbon-Montpensier

EUROPE IN 1648
AT THE PEACE OF WESTPHALIA

Copyright by C. S. HAMMOND & CO., N.Y.

Boundary of the Empire

Church Lands

Transylvania, independent of
Hungarian Kingdom with Turkish
Backing.

DOMINIONS OF THE HABSBURGS

Spanish Branch

Austrian Branch

MILES
0 50 100 200 300 400 MILES
0 50 100 200 300 400 KILOMETERS

ATLANTIC OCEAN

NORTH SEA

BALTIC SEA

MUSCOVITE DOMINIONS

KINGDOM OF SWEDEN

KINGDOM OF NORWAY

KINGDOM OF DENMARK

FINLAND OF SWEDEN

KINGDOM OF POLAND

LITHUANIA

UKRAINE

GREAT POLAND

LITTLE POLAND

VOLHYNIA

PODOLIA

MOLDAVIA

TRANSYLVANIA

HUNGARY

WALLACHIA

BESSARABIA

DOBRUDJA

OTTOMAN EMPIRE

BULGARIA

SERVIA

BOSNIA

RUMELIA

MACEDONIA

ALBANIA

MOREA

ANATOLIA

BLACK SEA

CRIMEA

AEGEAN SEA

MEDITERRANEAN SEA

CRETE or CANDIA (to Venice)

CYPRUS

BOHEMIA

MORAVIA

SILESIA

BRANDENBURG

AUSTRIA

STYRIA

CARINTHIA

CARNIOLA

TIROL

BAVARIA

THE EMPIRE

SWITZERLAND

REP. OF VENICE

KINGDOM OF THE TWO SICILIES

SICILY

SARDINIA (to Spain)

CORSICA (to Genoa)

SAVOY

PIEDMONT

D. OF MILAN

GRD. D. OF TUSCANY

TUSCAN PRESIDIOS (to Spain)

PAPAL STATES

KINGDOM OF NAPLES

CALABRIA

KINGDOM OF FRANCE

BRITTANY

LANGUEDOC

PROVENCE

FRANCHE COMTÉ

KINGDOM OF SPAIN

KINGDOM OF ARAGON

KINGDOM OF CASTILE

GRANADA

NAVARRE

BÉARN

BALEARIC IS.

KINGDOM OF PORTUGAL

ALGERIA

BARBARY STATES

TUNIS

FEZ AND MOROCCO

ALGIERS

ENGLAND

SCOTLAND

IRELAND

WALES

UNITED NETHERLANDS

SPANISH NETH.

SHETLAND IS.

ORKNEY IS.

HEBRIDES

510

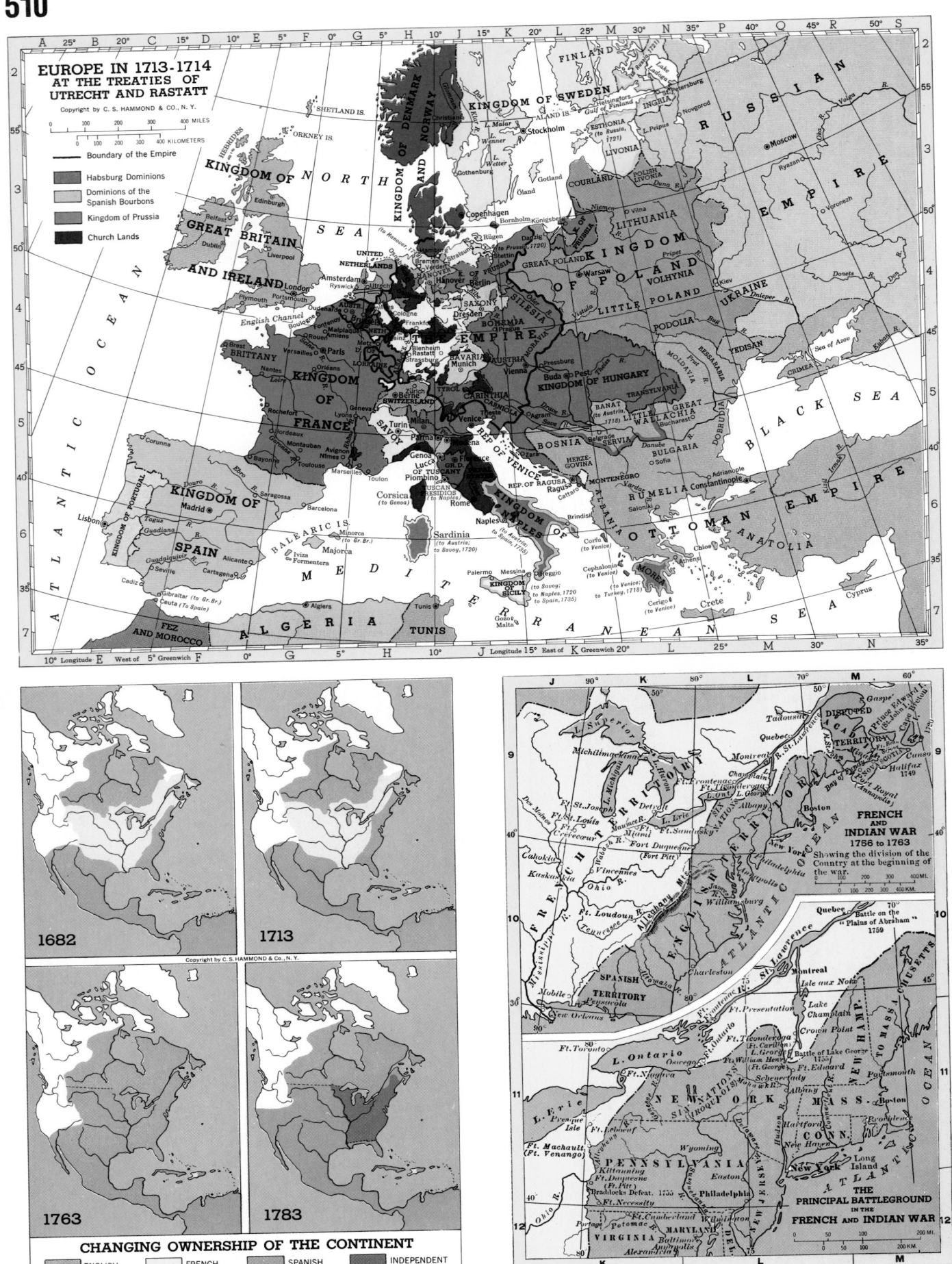

EUROPE IN 1713-1714 AT THE TREATIES OF UTRECHT AND RASTATT

Copyright by C. S. HAMMOND & CO., N.Y.

0   100   200   300   400 MILES
0   100   200   300   400 KILOMETERS

— Boundary of the Empire

Habsburg Dominions
Dominions of the Spanish Bourbons
Kingdom of Prussia
Church Lands

CHANGING OWNERSHIP OF THE CONTINENT

1682   1713   1763   1783

Copyright by C.S. HAMMOND & CO., N.Y.

ENGLISH   FRENCH   SPANISH   INDEPENDENT

FRENCH AND INDIAN WAR 1756 to 1763

Showing the division of the Country at the beginning of the war.

0   100   200   300   400 MI.
0   100   200   300   400 KM.

THE PRINCIPAL BATTLEGROUND IN THE FRENCH AND INDIAN WAR

0   50   100   200 MI.
0   50   100   200 KM.

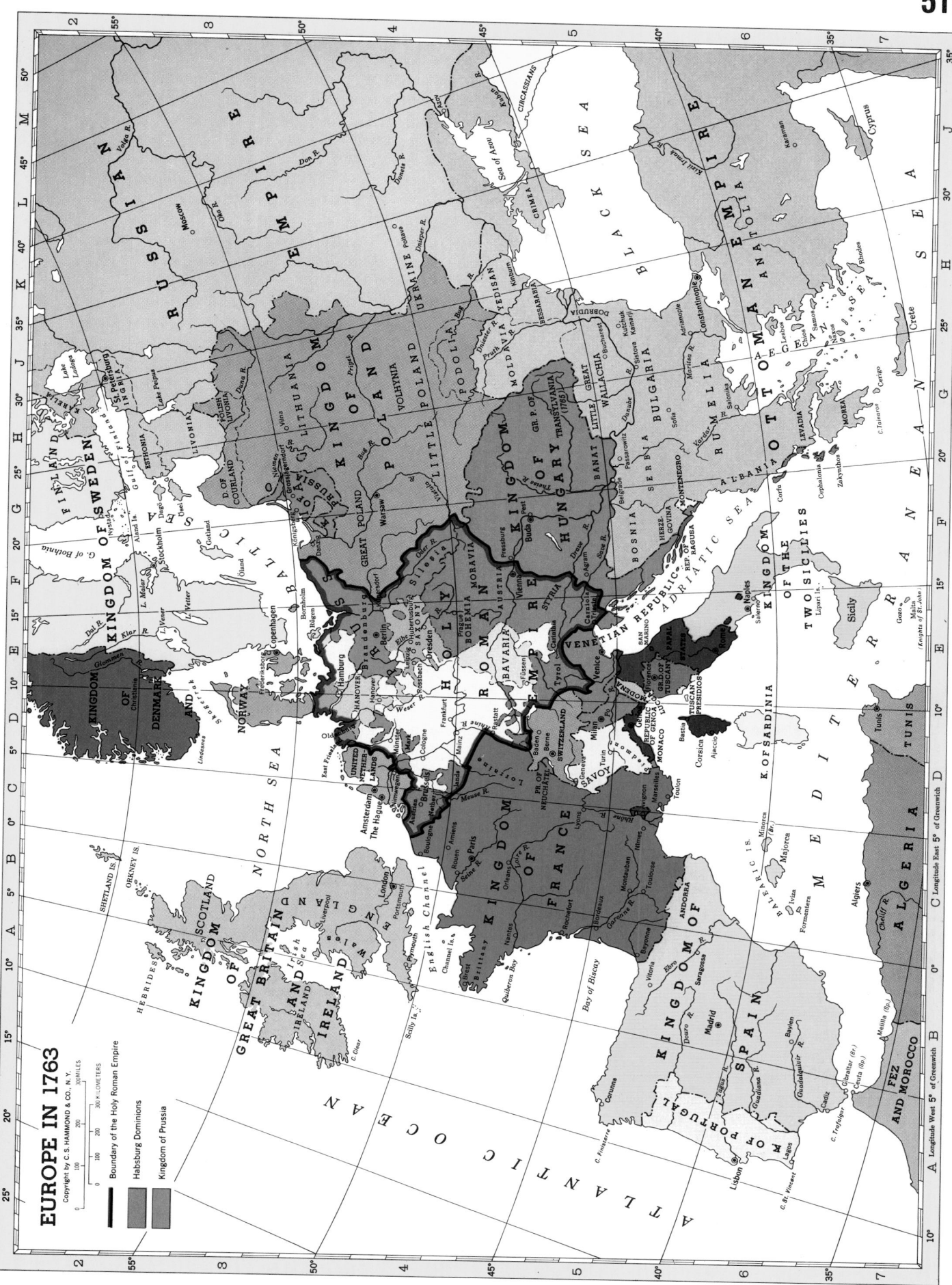

EUROPE IN 1763

Copyright by C. S. HAMMOND & CO., N.Y.

Boundary of the Holy Roman Empire
Habsburg Dominions
Kingdom of Prussia

512

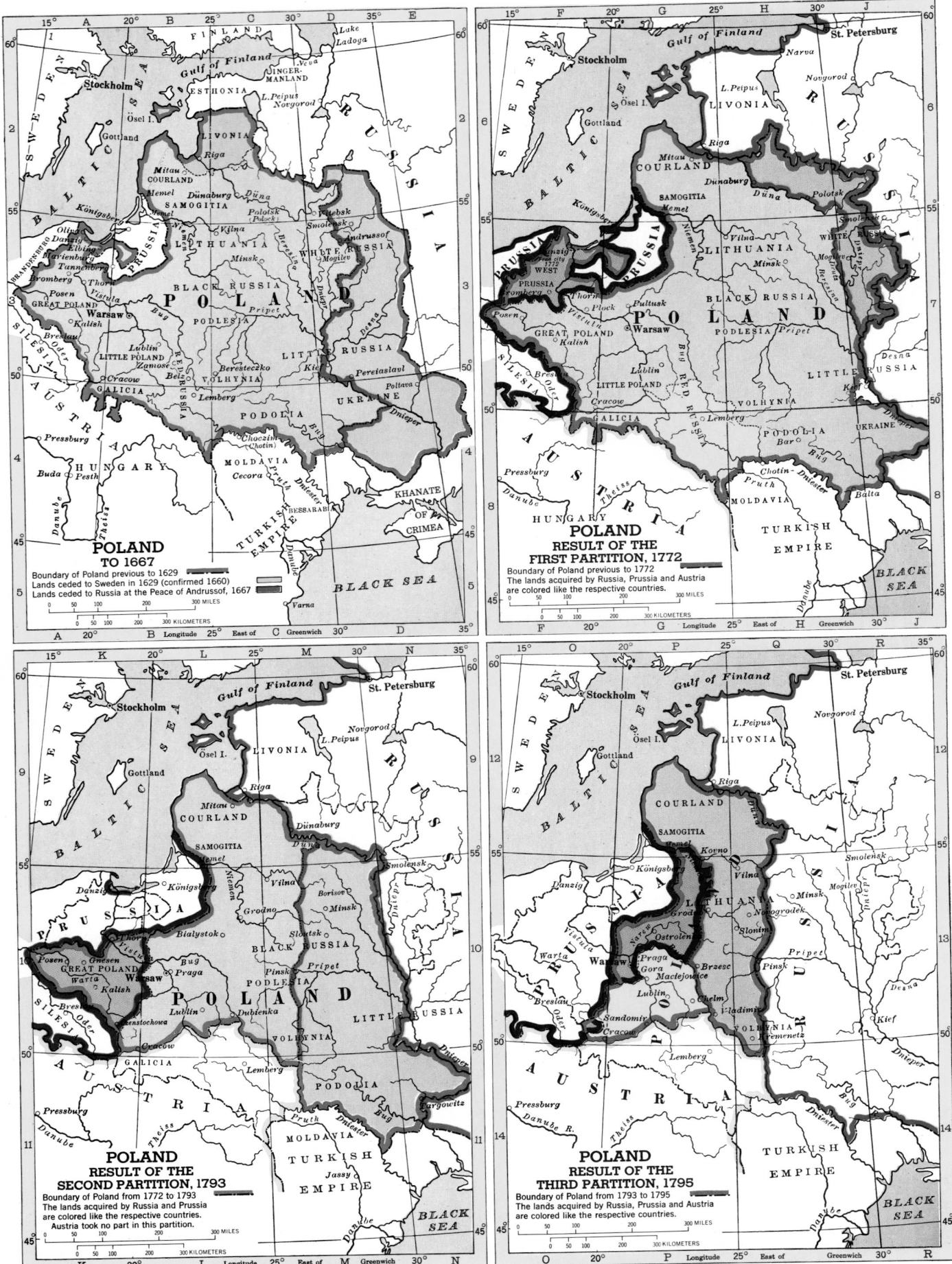

POLAND
TO 1667

Boundary of Poland previous to 1629
Lands ceded to Sweden in 1629 (confirmed 1660)
Lands ceded to Russia at the Peace of Andrussof, 1667

0   50   100   200   300 MILES
0 50 100   200   300 KILOMETERS

POLAND
RESULT OF THE
FIRST PARTITION, 1772

Boundary of Poland previous to 1772
The lands acquired by Russia, Prussia and Austria
are colored like the respective countries.

0   50   100   200   300 MILES
0 50 100   200   300 KILOMETERS

POLAND
RESULT OF THE
SECOND PARTITION, 1793

Boundary of Poland from 1772 to 1793
The lands acquired by Russia and Prussia
are colored like the respective countries.
Austria took no part in this partition.

0   50   100   200   300 MILES
0 50 100   200   300 KILOMETERS

POLAND
RESULT OF THE
THIRD PARTITION, 1795

Boundary of Poland from 1793 to 1795
The lands acquired by Russia, Prussia and Austria
are colored like the respective countries.

0   50   100   200   300 MILES
0 50 100   200   300 KILOMETERS

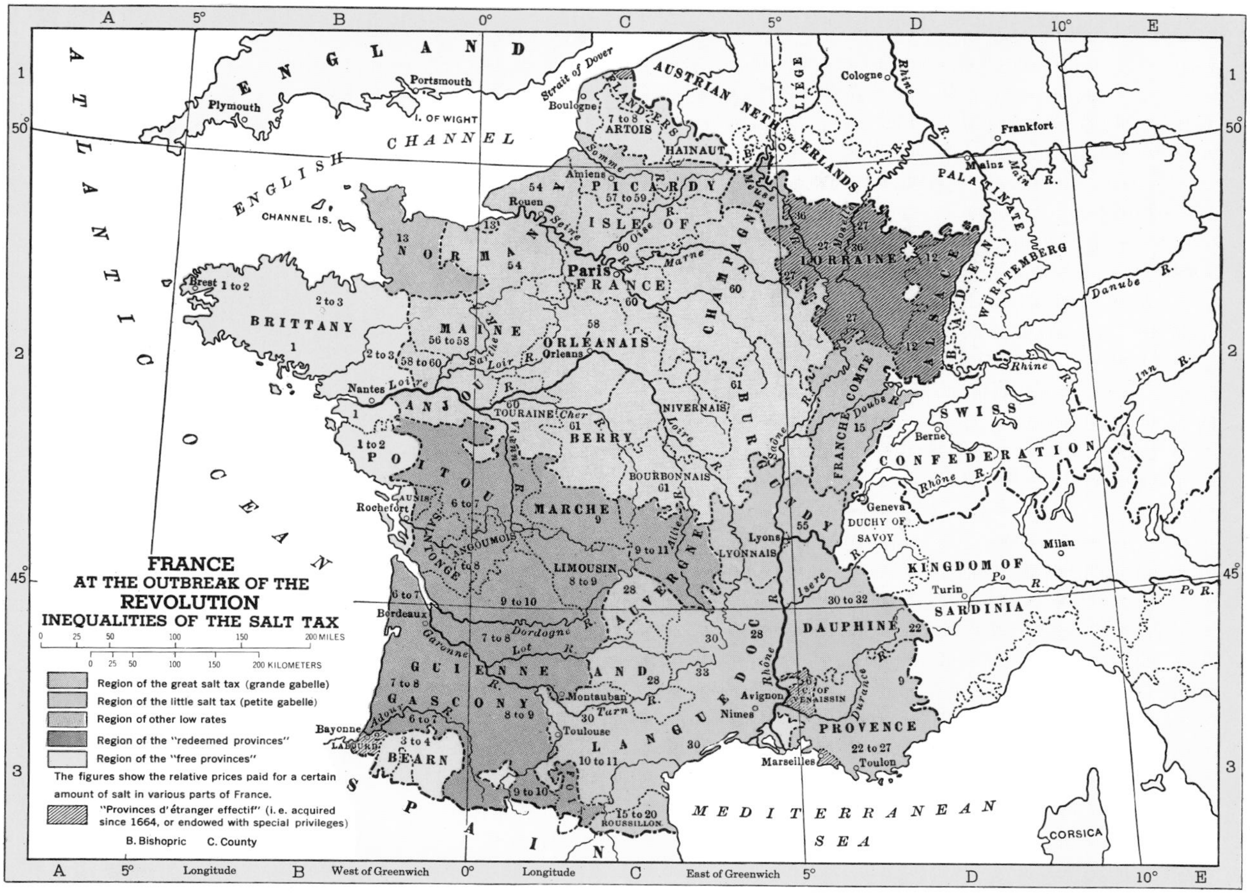

Map 1: France at the Outbreak of the Revolution

ENGLAND

ATLANTIC OCEAN

ENGLISH CHANNEL

Plymouth
Portsmouth
I. OF WIGHT
CHANNEL IS.
Strait of Dover
Boulogne
AUSTRIAN NETHERLANDS
LIÈGE
Cologne
Rhine R.
Frankfort
Mainz Main R.
PALATINATE

ARTOIS
7 to 8
HAINAUT
Amiens
Somme R.
54
PICARDY
57 to 59
Rouen
Seine R.
ISLE OF
Oise R.
60
Paris
FRANCE
60
Marne R.
LORRAINE
27 to 36
12
WÜRTTEMBERG
27
Danube R.
Rhine R.
Inn R.

13
NORMANDY
13
54
BRITTANY
2 to 3
1
Brest 1 to 2
Nantes Loire R.
2 to 3
58 to 60

MAINE
56 to 58
Sarthe R.
ORLÉANAIS
Orleans
Loir R.
58
TOURAINE
Cher R.
61
BERRY
NIVERNAIS
Loire R.
61
BOURBONNAIS
61

ANJOU
POITOU
1 to 2
AUNIS
6 to 7
Rochefort
ANGOUMOIS
6 to 8
SAINTONGE
MARCHE
7 to 9
9 to 11
LIMOUSIN
8 to 9
AUVERGNE
9 to 10
9 to 10
Dordogne R.
7 to 8

BURGUNDY
Saône R.
Doubs R.
15
FRANCHE COMTÉ
15
Berne
SWISS CONFEDERATION

Lyons
LYONNAIS
55
Rhône R.
Geneva
DUCHY OF SAVOY
Milan
Isère R.
30 to 32
KINGDOM OF SARDINIA
Turin
Po R.

Bordeaux
Garonne R.
7 to 8
GUIENNE AND GASCONY
8 to 9
9 to 10
Bayonne
LABOURD
6 to 7
BÉARN
3 to 4
Adour R.
SPAIN

Montauban
Tarn R.
30
Toulouse
10 to 11
LANGUEDOC
28
28
33
33
30
Garonne R.
15 to 20
ROUSSILLON
Nimes
Avignon
CO. OF VENAISSIN
28
DAUPHINÉ
22
Durance R.
9
PROVENCE
22 to 27
Toulon
Marseilles

MEDITERRANEAN SEA

CORSICA

Legend

FRANCE
AT THE OUTBREAK OF THE
REVOLUTION
INEQUALITIES OF THE SALT TAX

0 25 50 100 150 200 MILES
0 25 50 100 150 200 KILOMETERS

- Region of the great salt tax (grande gabelle)
- Region of the little salt tax (petite gabelle)
- Region of other low rates
- Region of the "redeemed provinces"
- Region of the "free provinces"

The figures show the relative prices paid for a certain amount of salt in various parts of France.

"Provinces d'étranger effectif" (i.e. acquired since 1664, or endowed with special privileges)

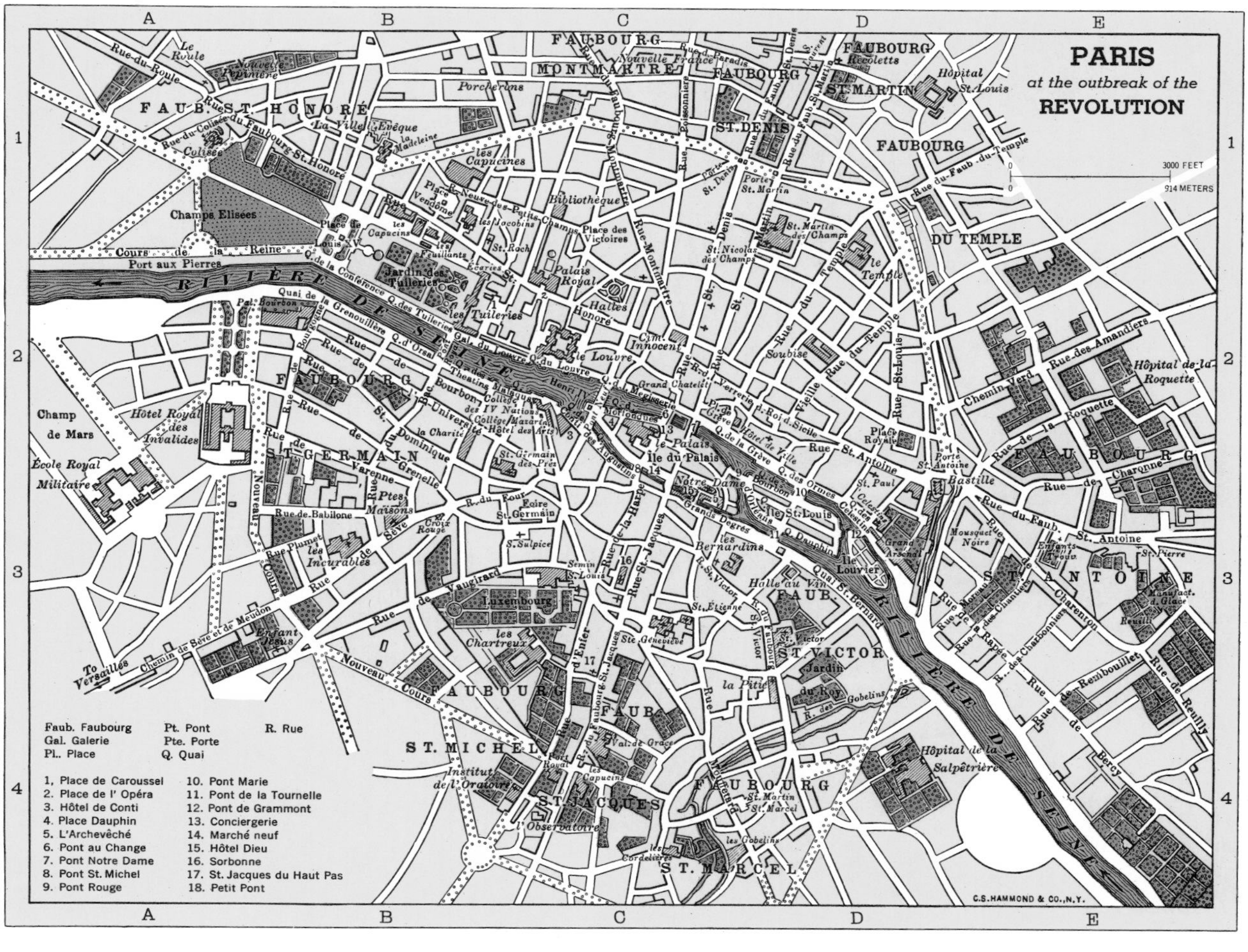

B. Bishopric   C. County

Longitude West of Greenwich   Longitude East of Greenwich

Map 2: Paris at the Outbreak of the Revolution

PARIS
at the outbreak of the
REVOLUTION

FAUBOURG MONTMARTRE
FAUBOURG ST. DENIS
FAUBOURG ST. MARTIN
Hôpital St. Louis
FAUBOURG DU TEMPLE
Le Roule
FAUB. ST. HONORÉ
Champs Elisées
Cours de la Reine
Port aux Pierres
RIVIÈRE DE SEINE
Hôtel Royal des Invalides
Champ de Mars
École Royal Militaire
To Versailles
FAUBOURG ST. GERMAIN
Luxembourg
les Chartreux
FAUBOURG ST. MICHEL
Institut de l'Oratoire
Observatoire
FAUBOURG ST. JACQUES
FAUBOURG ST. MARCEL
FAUBOURG ST. VICTOR
Hôpital de la Salpêtrière
Hôpital de la Roquette
FAUBOURG ST. ANTOINE
Bastille
Tuileries
Palais Royal
Louvre
Notre Dame
Île du Palais
Île St. Louis
Sorbonne
St. Sulpice
St. Geneviève
les Gobelins
3000 FEET
914 METERS

Faub. Faubourg   Pt. Pont   R. Rue
Gal. Galerie   Pte. Porte
Pl. Place   Q. Quai

1. Place de Caroussel
2. Place de l' Opéra
3. Hôtel de Conti
4. Place Dauphin
5. L'Archevêché
6. Pont au Change
7. Pont Notre Dame
8. Pont St. Michel
9. Pont Rouge
10. Pont Marie
11. Pont de la Tournelle
12. Pont de Grammont
13. Conciergerie
14. Marché neuf
15. Hôtel Dieu
16. Sorbonne
17. St. Jacques du Haut Pas
18. Petit Pont

C.S. HAMMOND & CO., N.Y.

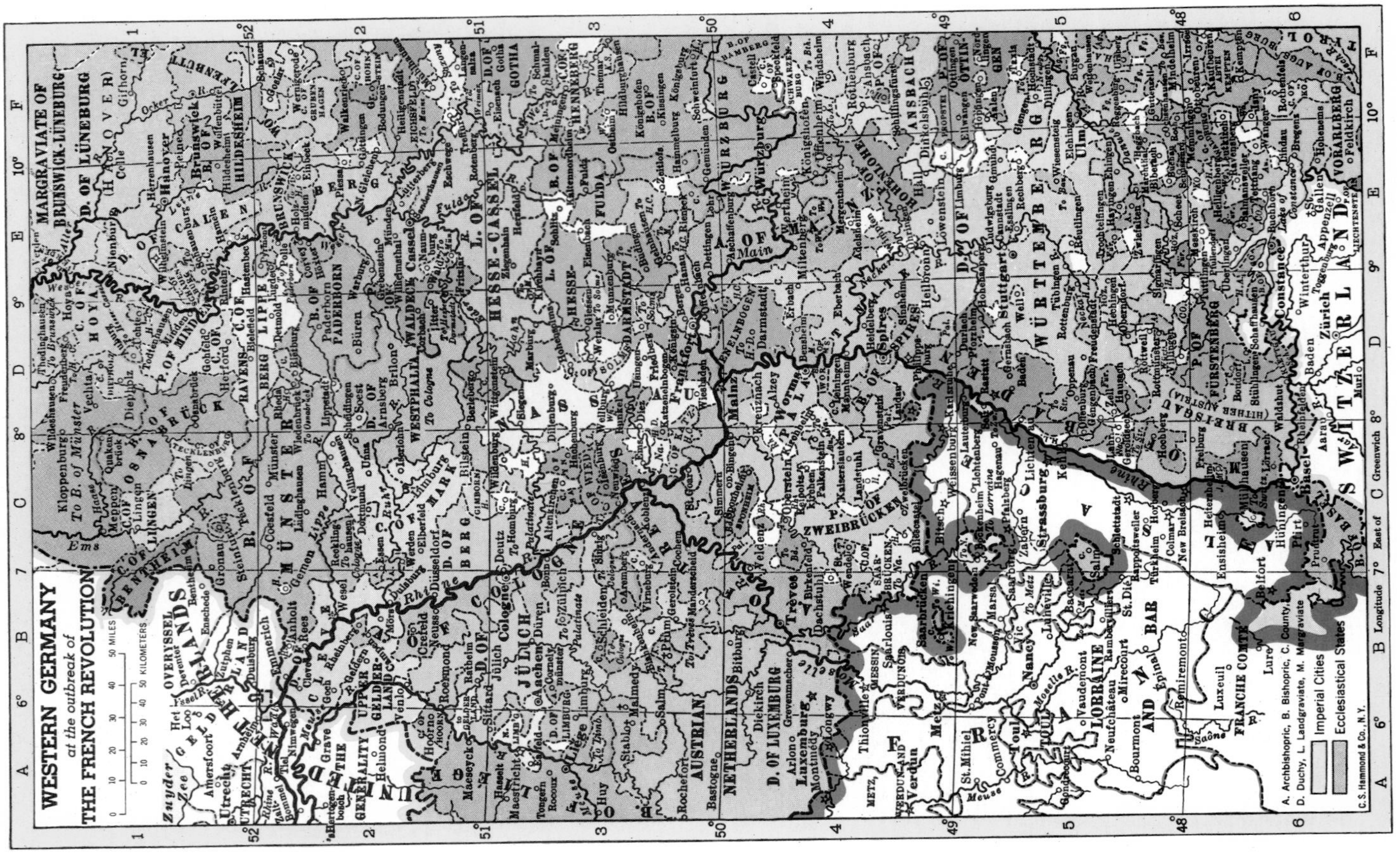

WESTERN GERMANY
at the outbreak of
THE FRENCH REVOLUTION

MARGRAVIATE OF BRUNSWICK-LÜNEBURG

D. OF LÜNEBURG

HESSE-CASSEL

WÜRTEMBERG

FÜRSTENBERG

SWITZERLAND

UNITED NETHERLANDS

AUSTRIAN NETHERLANDS

D. OF LUXEMBURG

LORRAINE AND BAR

FRANCHE COMTÉ

A. Archbishopric, B. Bishopric, C. County,
D. Duchy, L. Landgraviate, M. Margraviate

Imperial Cities
Ecclesiastical States

C. S. Hammond & Co., N.Y.

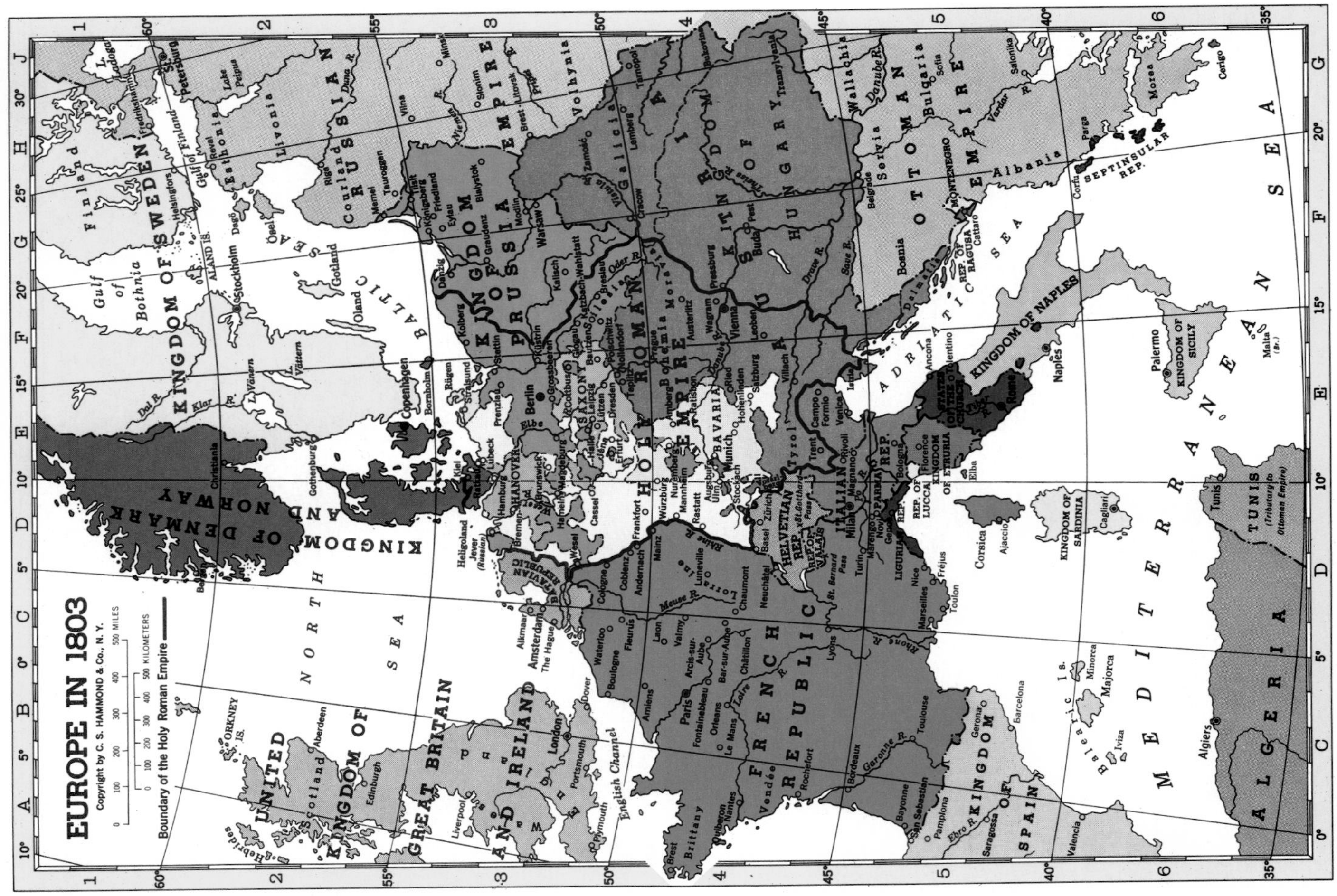

EUROPE IN 1803
Copyright by C. S. HAMMOND & CO., N.Y.
Boundary of the Holy Roman Empire

UNITED KINGDOM OF GREAT BRITAIN AND IRELAND

KINGDOM OF DENMARK AND NORWAY

KINGDOM OF SWEDEN

RUSSIAN EMPIRE

KINGDOM OF PRUSSIA

HOLY ROMAN EMPIRE

KINGDOM OF HUNGARY

OTTOMAN EMPIRE

FRENCH REPUBLIC

HELVETIAN REPUBLIC

ITALIAN REP.

LIGURIAN REP.

KINGDOM OF NAPLES

KINGDOM OF SICILY

KINGDOM OF SARDINIA

KINGDOM OF SPAIN

ALGERIA

TUNIS (Tributary to Ottoman Empire)

SEPTINSULAR REP.

NORTH SEA

BALTIC SEA

MEDITERRANEAN SEA

ADRIATIC SEA

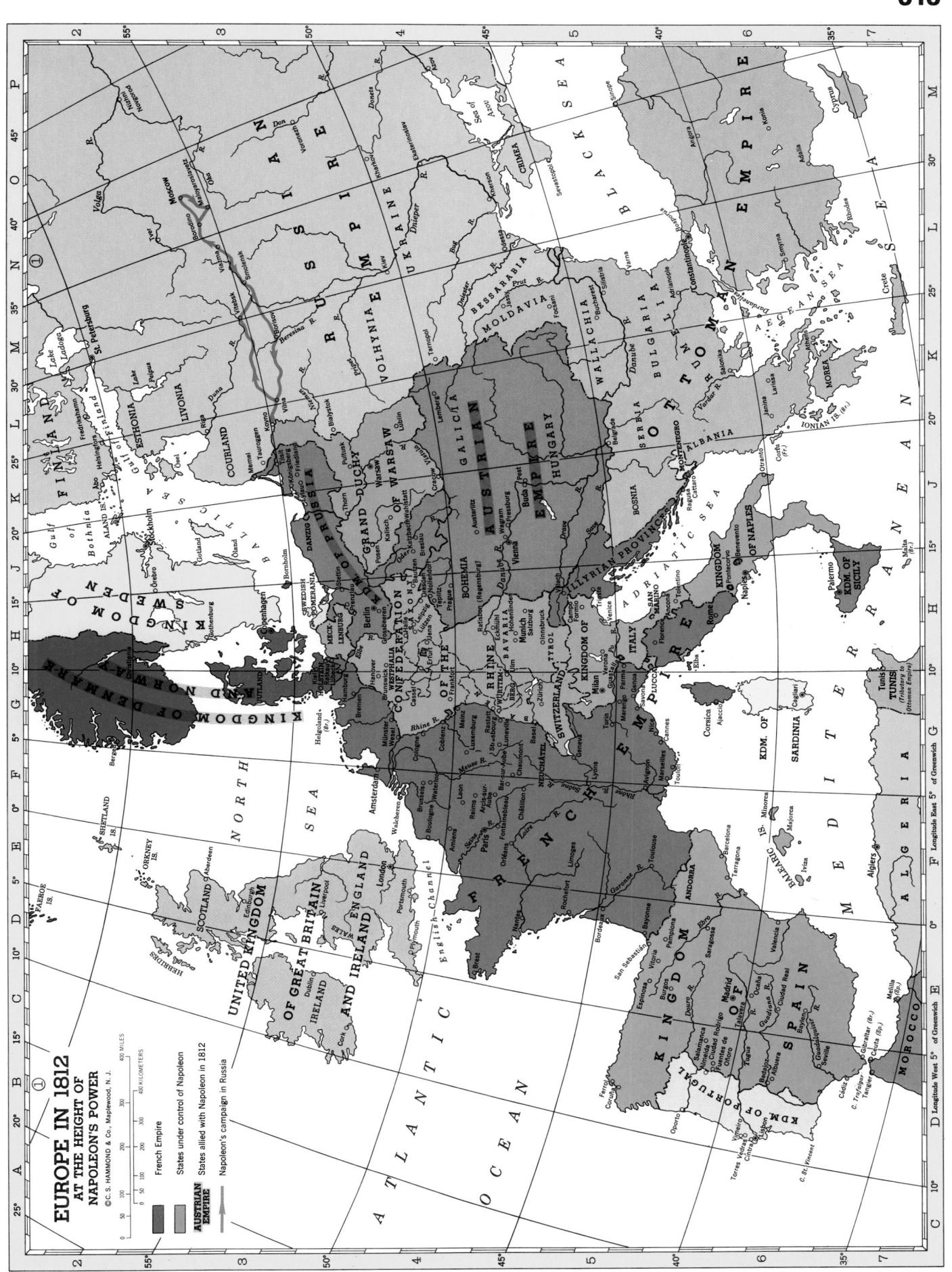

EUROPE IN 1812
AT THE HEIGHT OF NAPOLEON'S POWER

©C. S. HAMMOND & Co., Maplewood, N.J.

0 50 100   200   300   400 MILES
0 50 100 200 300   400 KILOMETERS

French Empire

States under control of Napoleon

States allied with Napoleon in 1812

Napoleon's campaign in Russia

AUSTRIAN EMPIRE

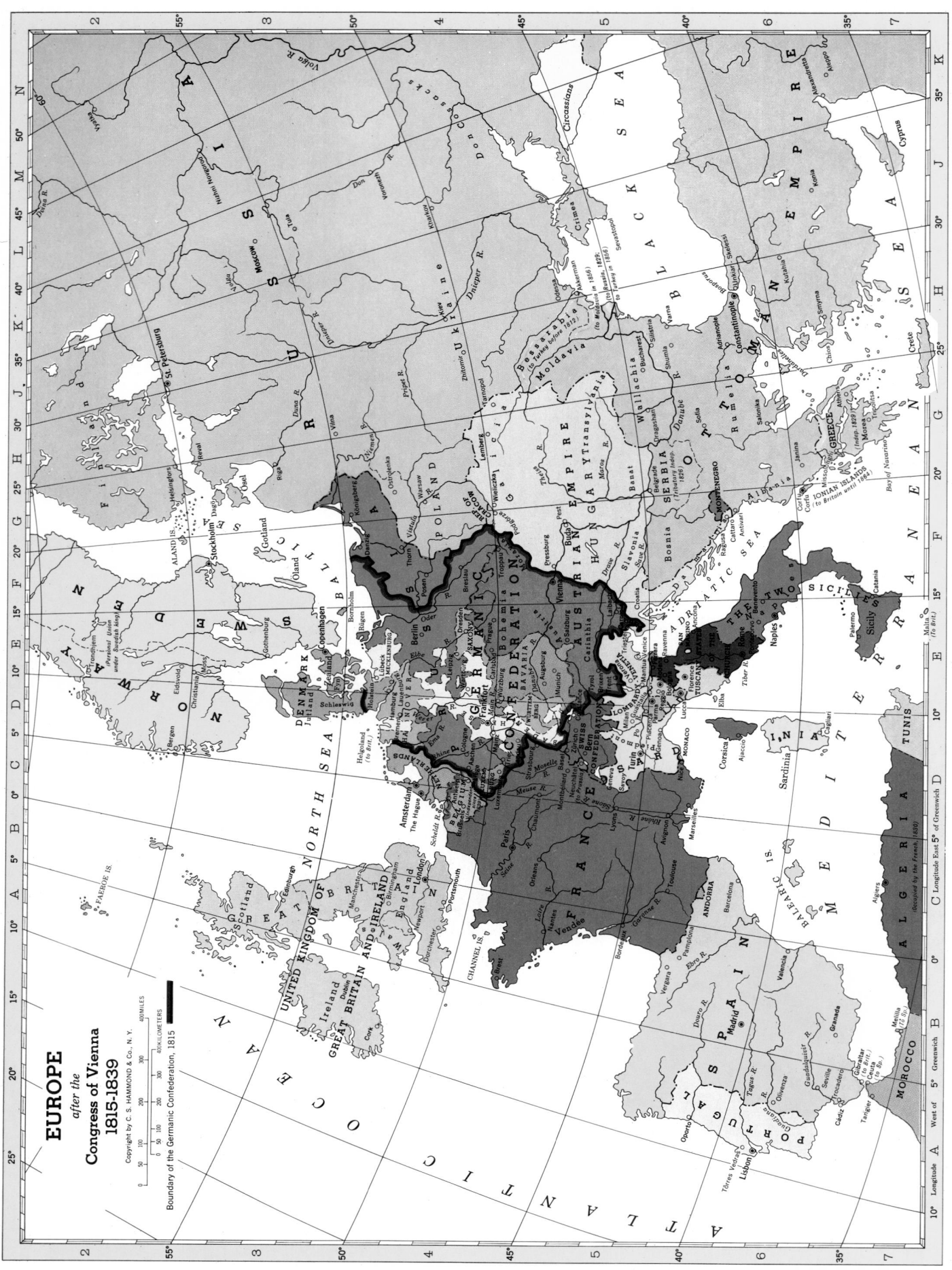

EUROPE
after the
Congress of Vienna
1815-1839

Copyright by C. S. HAMMOND & Co., N.Y.

Boundary of the Germanic Confederation, 1815

THE COLONIZATION OF LATIN AMERICA
Copyright by C.S. HAMMOND & Co., N.Y.
Capitals of Colonies
Seats of Governments
1626 Year of Foundation or Discovery
(1763) Years of Territorial Changes
Explorers Routes
Spanish Trade Routes
Indian Civilizations
Buccaneer Retreats
SOUTH SEA
ATLANTIC OCEAN
BRAZIL
VICEROYALTY OF NEW SPAIN
VICEROYALTY OF NEW CASTILIA OR PERU
VICEROYALTY OF RIO DE LA PLATA
VICEROYALTY OF NEW GRANADA

LATIN AMERICAN COUNTRIES
Showing political & territorial changes since the Colonial period
Copyright by C.S. HAMMOND & Co., N.Y.
Capitals of Nations
Seats of Governments
(1794) Years of Territorial Changes
International Boundaries
Boundaries of Former Claims and Controlled Areas
Names of former Countries in Red
Battles
PACIFIC OCEAN
ATLANTIC OCEAN
UNITED STATES
MEXICO
BRAZIL EMPIRE 1822-1889 REPUBLIC 1889
ARGENTINA
CHILE INDEP. 1818

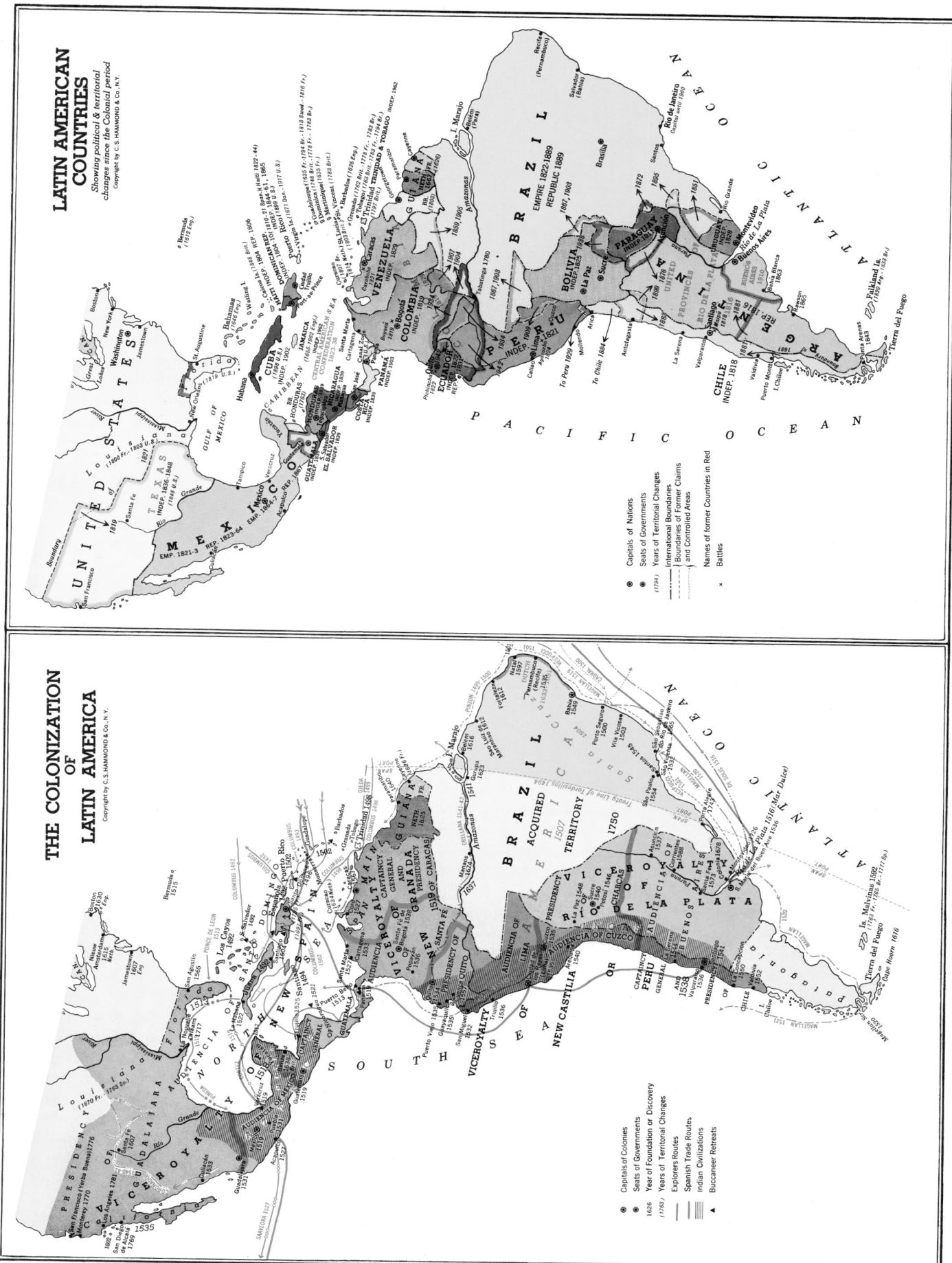

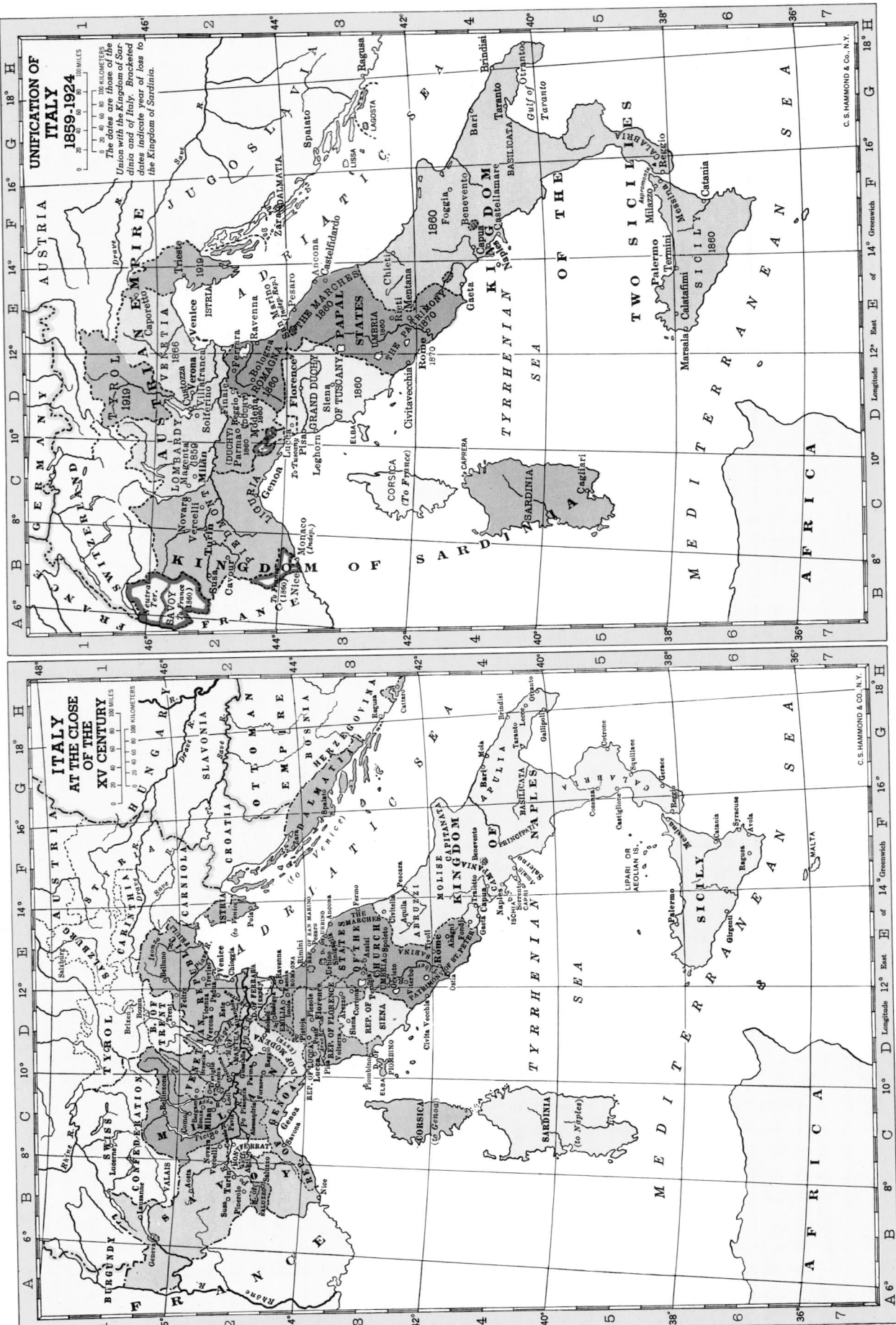
ITALY AT THE CLOSE OF THE XV CENTURY
C. S. HAMMOND & CO., N.Y.
UNIFICATION OF ITALY 1859-1924
The dates are those of the Union with the Kingdom of Sardinia and of Italy. Bracketed dates indicate year of loss to the Kingdom of Sardinia.
C. S. HAMMOND & Co., N.Y.

CENTRAL EUROPE
1815-1871
Boundary of German Confederation 1815-1866
Boundary of North German Confederation 1860-1871
Boundary of German Empire in 1871
0 25 50 100 150 200 MILES
0 25 50 100 150 200 KILOMETERS
Kingdom until 1848
Republic 1848-1852
Empire 1852-1870
Republic since 1870
Longitude 12° East of Greenwich
© The Century Co.

PEOPLES OF
EUROPE
1910
Copyright by C. S. HAMMOND & Co., N. Y.
Longitude 10° East of Greenwich

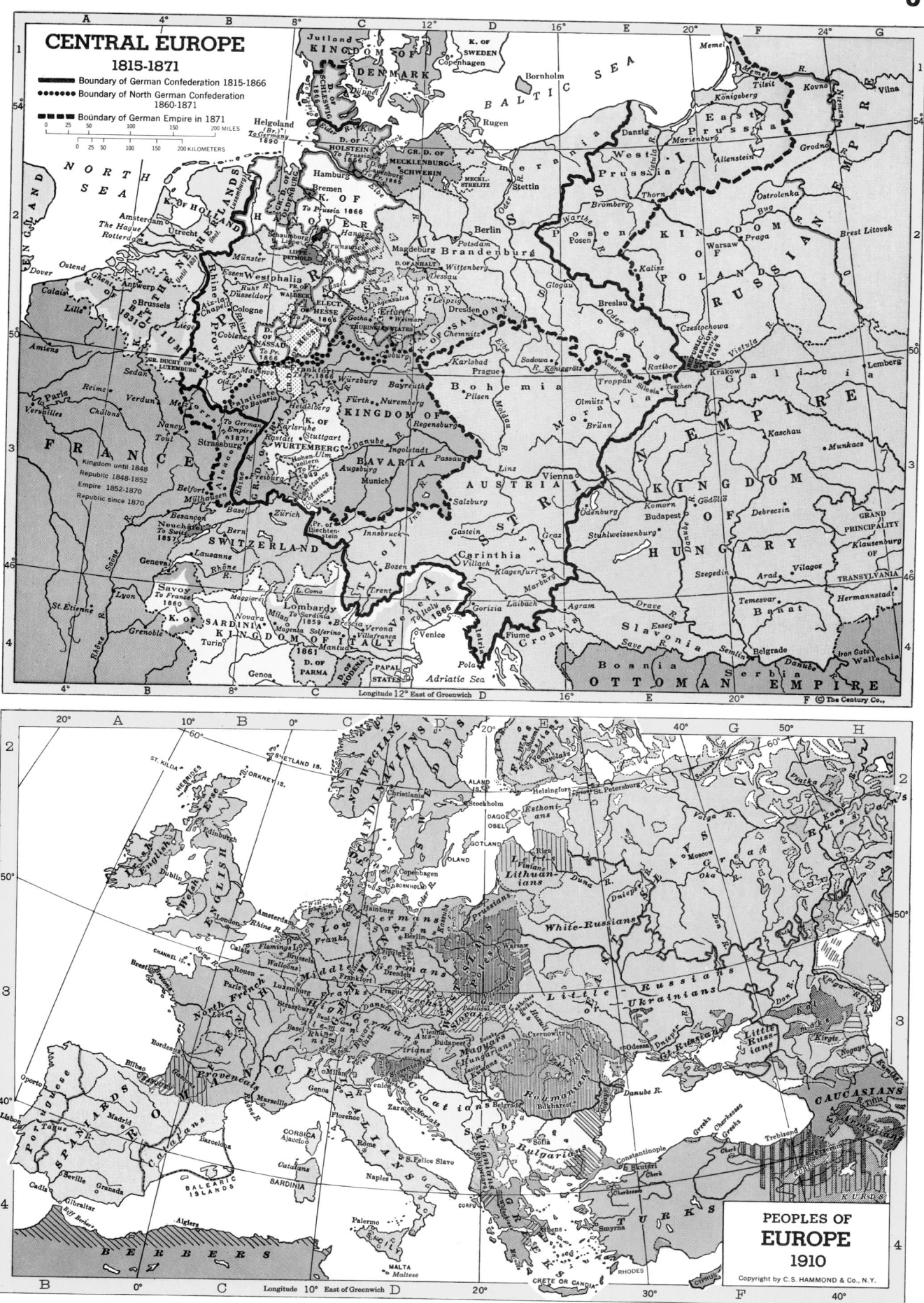

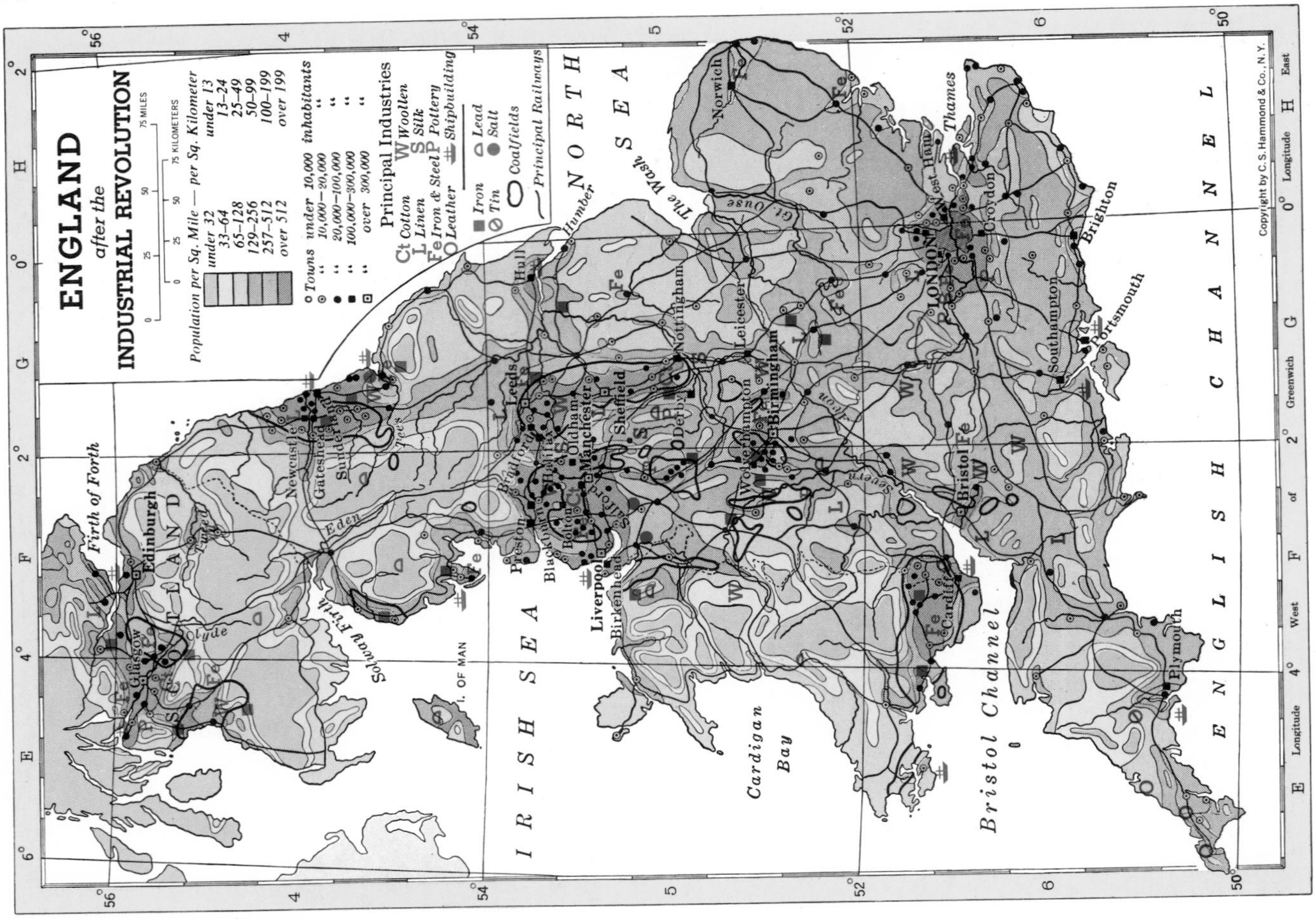

ENGLAND after the INDUSTRIAL REVOLUTION

Population per Sq. Mile — per Sq. Kilometer

under 32	under 13
33–64	13–24
65–128	25–49
129–256	50–99
257–512	100–199
over 512	over 199

75 MILES
75 KILOMETERS
0 25 50 75

Towns under 10,000 inhabitants
10,000–20,000
20,000–100,000
100,000–300,000
over 300,000

Principal Industries
Ct Cotton   W Woollen   S Silk
L Linen   P Pottery
Fe Iron & Steel   Shipbuilding
Leather
Iron   Lead
Tin   Salt   Coalfields
Principal Railways

Copyright by C.S. Hammond & Co., N.Y.

SCOTLAND

Firth of Forth
Edinburgh
Glasgow
Clyde
Solway Firth
Eden
I. OF MAN

NORTH SEA
The Wash
West Ham
Humber
Gt. Ouse
Hull
Norwich
LONDON
Thames
Croydon
Brighton
Southampton
Portsmouth

Newcastle
Gateshead
Sunderland
Leeds
Bradford
Preston
Blackburn
Bolton
Liverpool
Birkenhead
Manchester
Oldham
Sheffield
Derby
Nottingham
Leicester
Birmingham
Wolverhampton
Bristol
Cardiff
Plymouth

IRISH SEA
Cardigan Bay
Bristol Channel
ENGLISH CHANNEL
WOOL

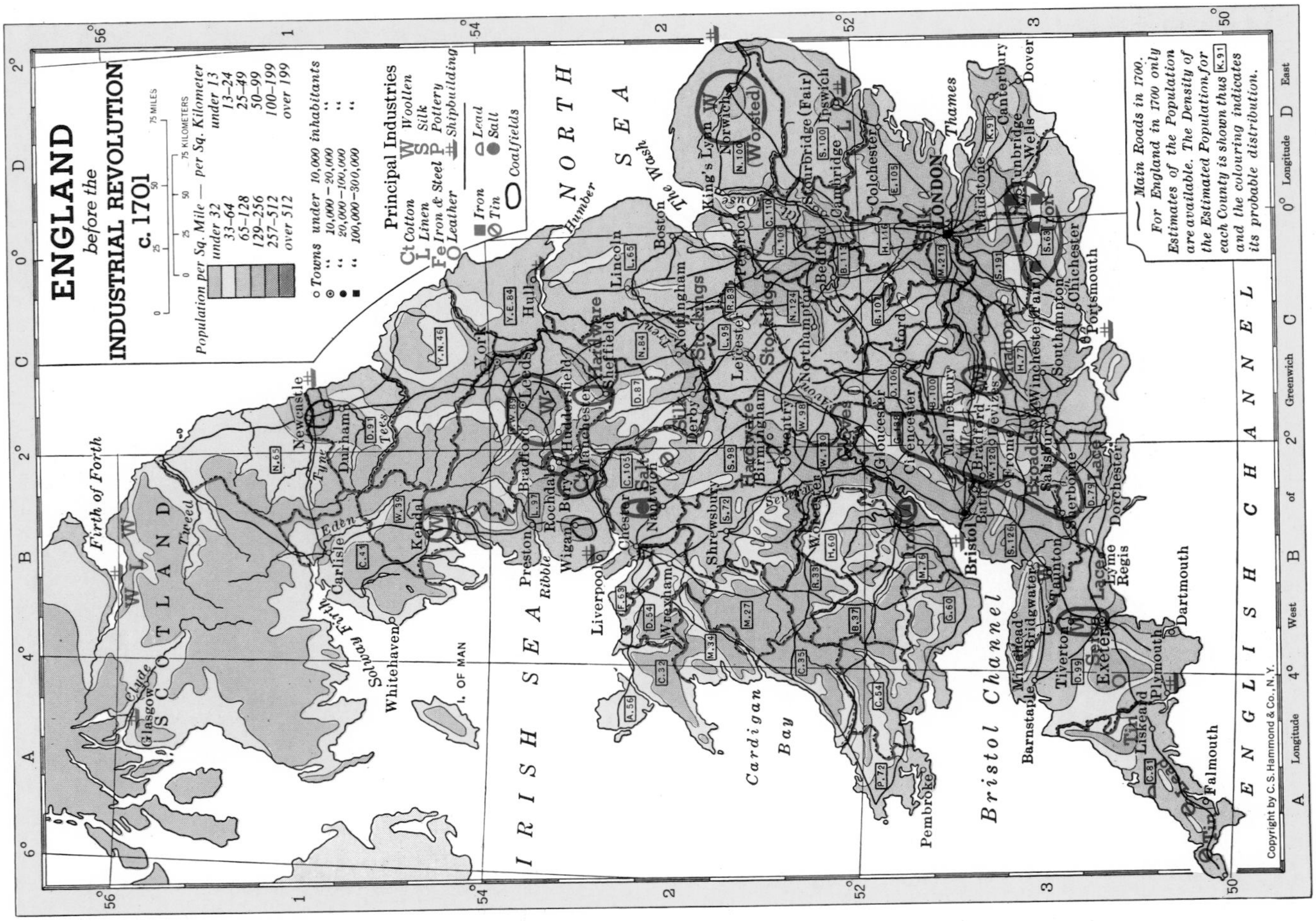

ENGLAND before the INDUSTRIAL REVOLUTION c. 1701

Population per Sq. Mile — per Sq. Kilometer

under 32	under 13
33–64	13–24
65–128	25–49
129–256	50–99
257–512	100–199
over 512	over 199

75 MILES
75 KILOMETERS
0 25 50 75

Towns under 10,000 inhabitants
10,000–20,000
20,000–100,000
100,000–300,000

Principal Industries
Ct Cotton   W Woollen   S Silk
L Linen   P Pottery
Fe Iron & Steel   Shipbuilding
Leather
Iron   Lead
Tin   Salt   Coalfields

Copyright by C.S. Hammond & Co., N.Y.

— Main Roads in 1700 only
For England in 1700 only Estimates of the Population are available. The Density of the Estimated Population for each County is shown thus and the colouring indicates its probable distribution.

SCOTLAND

Firth of Forth
Tweed
Glasgow
Clyde
Solway Firth
Carlisle
Eden
Whitehaven
I. OF MAN

Newcastle
Tyne
Durham
Kendal
Preston
Ribble
Wigan
Liverpool
Wrexham
Chester
Manchester
Rochdale
Bradford
Leeds
Sheffield
York
Hull
Lincoln
Boston
Nottingham
Derby
Leicester
Shrewsbury
Birmingham
Coventry
Northampton
Cambridge
King's Lynn
Norwich
Ipswich
Colchester
LONDON
Thames
Canterbury
Dover
Maidstone
Chichester
Portsmouth
Southampton
Salisbury
Winchester
Dorchester
Exeter
Tiverton
Taunton
Minehead
Bridgwater
Barnstaple
Plymouth
Falmouth
Pembroke

NORTH SEA
The Wash
Humber
IRISH SEA
Cardigan Bay
Bristol Channel
ENGLISH CHANNEL

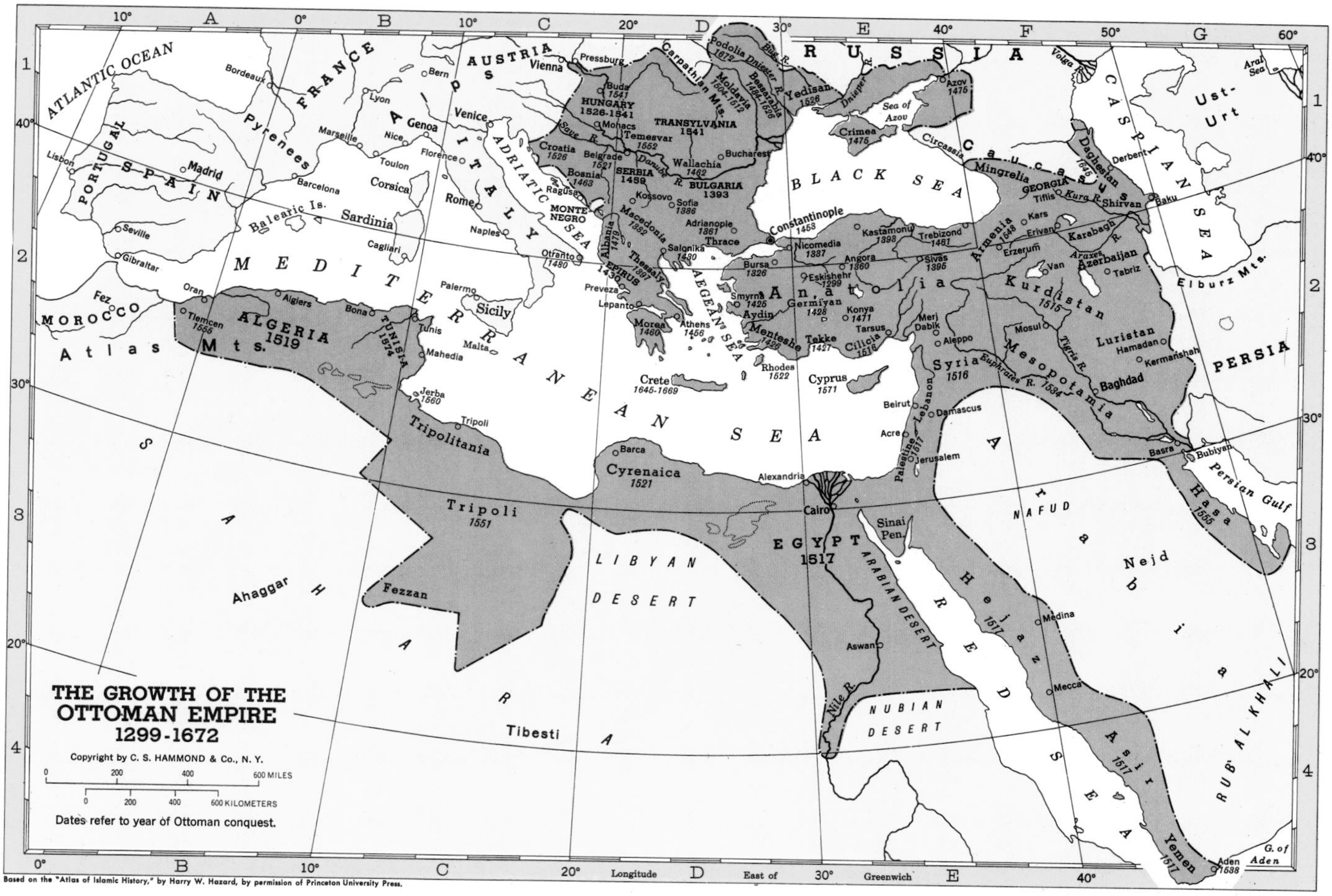

THE GROWTH OF THE OTTOMAN EMPIRE 1299-1672

Copyright by C. S. HAMMOND & Co., N. Y.

200 400 600 MILES
200 400 600 KILOMETERS

Dates refer to year of Ottoman conquest.

Based on the "Atlas of Islamic History," by Harry W. Hazard, by permission of Princeton University Press.

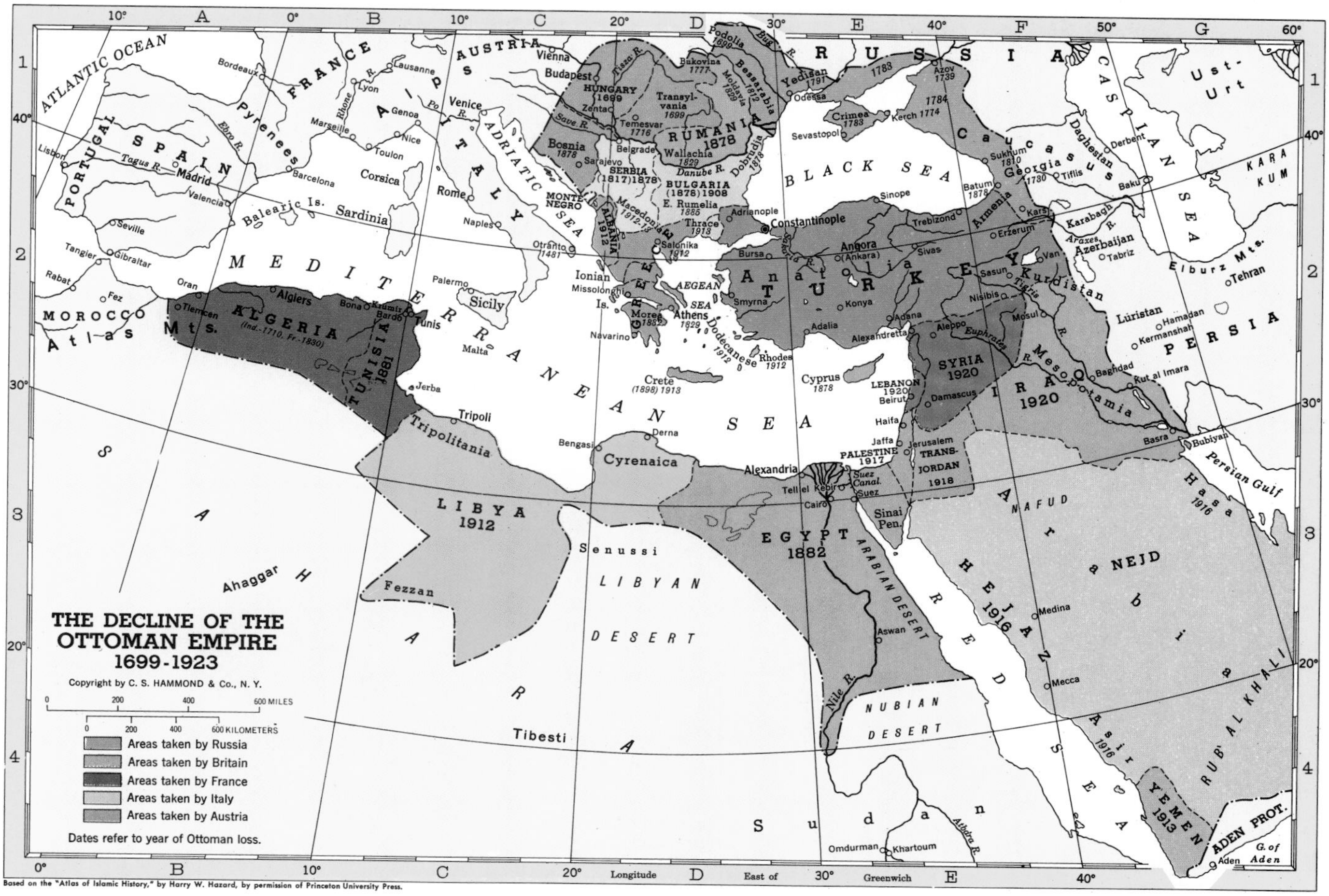

THE DECLINE OF THE OTTOMAN EMPIRE 1699-1923

Copyright by C. S. HAMMOND & Co., N. Y.

200 400 600 MILES
200 400 600 KILOMETERS

Areas taken by Russia
Areas taken by Britain
Areas taken by France
Areas taken by Italy
Areas taken by Austria

Dates refer to year of Ottoman loss.

Based on the "Atlas of Islamic History," by Harry W. Hazard, by permission of Princeton University Press.

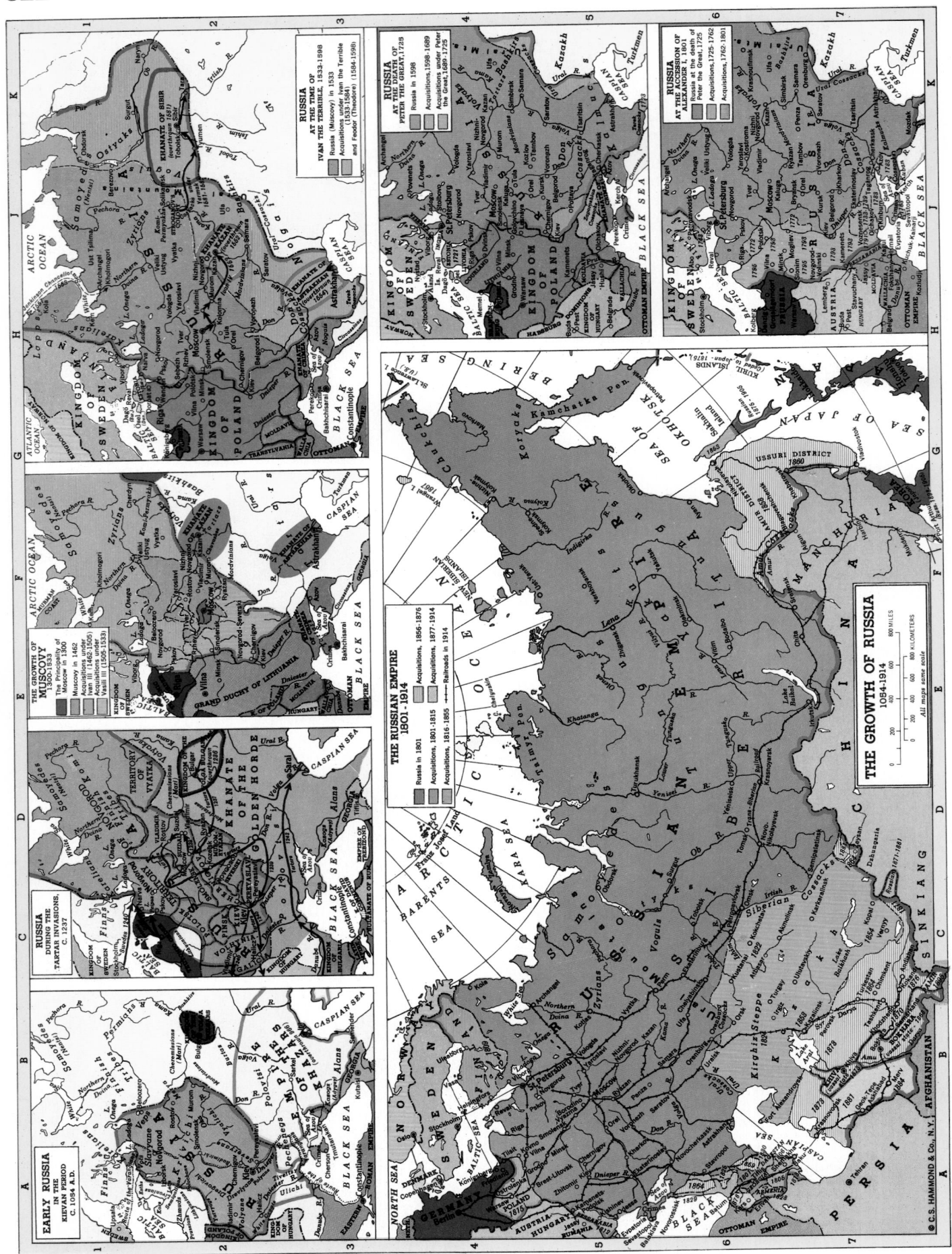

EARLY RUSSIA IN THE KIEVAN PERIOD C. 1054 A.D.

RUSSIA DURING THE TARTAR INVASIONS, C. 1237

THE GROWTH OF MUSCOVY 1300-1533
The Principality of Moscow in 1300
Acquisitions under Ivan III (1462-1505)
Acquisition under Vasili III (1505-1533)

RUSSIA AT THE TIME OF IVAN THE TERRIBLE, 1533-1598
Russia (Muscovy) in 1533
Acquisitions under Ivan the Terrible (1533-1584) and Feodor (Theodore) (1584-1598)

RUSSIA AT THE DEATH OF PETER THE GREAT, 1725
Russia in 1598
Acquisitions, 1598-1689
Acquisitions under Peter the Great, 1689-1725

RUSSIA AT THE ACCESSION OF ALEXANDER I, 1801
Russia at the death of Peter the Great, 1725
Acquisitions, 1725-1762
Acquisitions, 1762-1801

THE RUSSIAN EMPIRE 1801-1914
Russia in 1801
Acquisitions, 1801-1815
Acquisitions, 1816-1855
Acquisitions, 1856-1876
Acquisitions, 1877-1914
Railroads in 1914

THE GROWTH OF RUSSIA 1054-1914

© C.S. Hammond & Co., N.Y. U.S.A.

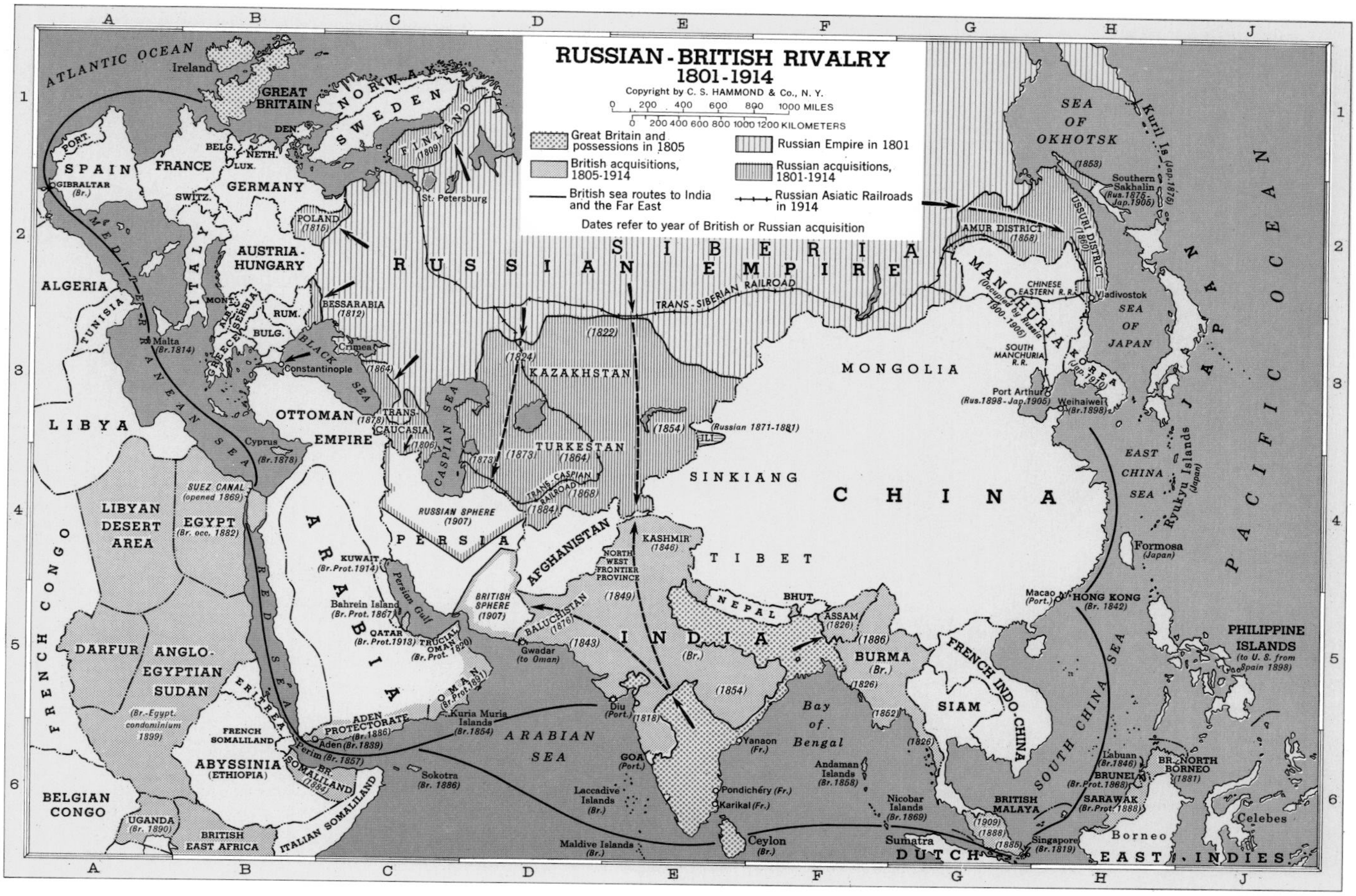

RUSSIAN-BRITISH RIVALRY
1801-1914
Copyright by C. S. Hammond & Co., N. Y.

Great Britain and possessions in 1805
British acquisitions, 1805-1914
British sea routes to India and the Far East
Russian Empire in 1801
Russian acquisitions, 1801-1914
Russian Asiatic Railroads in 1914
Dates refer to year of British or Russian acquisition

ATLANTIC OCEAN — Ireland — GREAT BRITAIN — NORWAY — SWEDEN — FINLAND (1809) — St. Petersburg — DEN. — BELG. NETH. LUX. — FRANCE — GERMANY — POLAND (1815) — SWITZ. — SPAIN — GIBRALTAR (Br.) — PORT. — ITALY — AUSTRIA-HUNGARY — SERBIA — MONT. — RUM. — BULG. — BESSARABIA (1812) — RUSSIAN EMPIRE — SIBERIA — TRANS-SIBERIAN RAILROAD — SEA OF OKHOTSK — Kurile Is. (Jap.1875) — Southern Sakhalin (Rus.1875 Jap.1905)

ALGERIA — TUNISIA — Malta (Br.1814) — GREECE — BLACK SEA — Constantinople — Crimea (1864) — CAUCASIA — CASPIAN SEA — KAZAKHSTAN — (1822) — (1824) — ILI (Russian 1871-1881) — MONGOLIA — AMUR DISTRICT (1858) — MANCHURIA — CHINESE EASTERN R.R. — Vladivostok — SOUTH MANCHURIA R.R. — SEA OF JAPAN — KOREA — JAPAN

LIBYA — OTTOMAN EMPIRE — Cyprus (Br.1878) — TRANS-CAUCASIA (1806) — PERSIA — (1873) — TURKESTAN (1864) — TRANS-CASPIAN RAILROAD (1884) — SINKIANG — CHINA — Port Arthur (Rus.1898-Jap.1905) — Weihaiwei (Br.1898) — EAST CHINA SEA — Ryukyu Islands (Japan) — Formosa (Japan) — PACIFIC OCEAN

LIBYAN DESERT AREA — EGYPT (Br. occ. 1882) — SUEZ CANAL (opened 1869) — ARABIA — KUWAIT (Br. Prot. 1914) — RUSSIAN SPHERE (1907) — AFGHANISTAN — BRITISH SPHERE (1907) — NORTH WEST FRONTIER PROVINCE — KASHMIR (1846) — TIBET — NEPAL — BHUT. — ASSAM (1826) — Macao (Port.) — HONG KONG (Br.1842) — PHILIPPINE ISLANDS (to U.S. from Spain 1898)

FRENCH CONGO — DARFUR — ANGLO-EGYPTIAN SUDAN (Br.-Egypt condominium 1899) — Bahrein Island (Br. Prot. 1867) — QATAR — TRUCIAL OMAN (Br. Prot. 1913) — OMAN (Br.) — Gwadar (to Oman) — BALUCHISTAN (1876) — (1849) — (1843) — Diu (Port.) — INDIA (Br.) — (1854) — BURMA (Br.) 1826 — SIAM — FRENCH INDO-CHINA — Labuan (Br.1846) — BRUNEI (Br. Prot. 1888) — BR. NORTH BORNEO 1881

BELGIAN CONGO — UGANDA (Br.1890) — BRITISH EAST AFRICA — ERITREA — FRENCH SOMALILAND — Aden (Br.1839) — ADEN PROTECTORATE — Perim (Br.1857) — Kuria Muria Islands (Br.1854) — ARABIAN SEA — Diu (Port.) 1818 — GOA (Port.) — Laccadive Islands (Br.) — Pondichéry (Fr.) — Karikal (Fr.) — Andaman Islands 1858 — Nicobar Islands (Br.1869) — FRENCH MALAYA — SARAWAK (Br. Prot. 1888) — Celebes

ABYSSINIA (ETHIOPIA) — ITALIAN SOMALILAND — Sokotra (Br.1886) — Maldive Islands (Br.) — Ceylon (Br.) — Singapore (Br.1819) — Sumatra — DUTCH EAST INDIES — Borneo

---

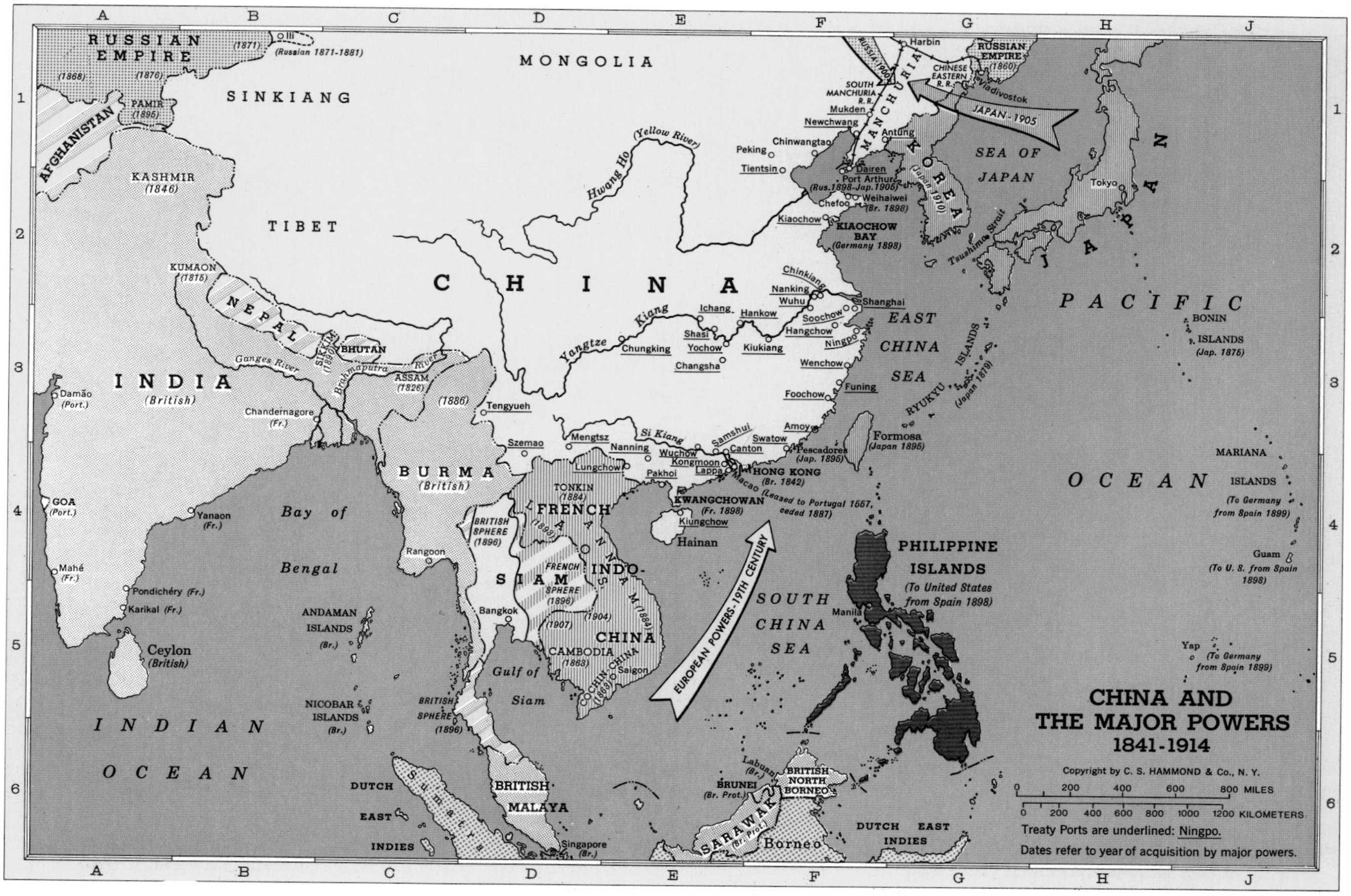

CHINA AND THE MAJOR POWERS
1841-1914
Copyright by C. S. Hammond & Co., N. Y.

RUSSIAN EMPIRE — ILI (Russian 1871-1881) — (1871) — (1868) — (1876) — PAMIR (1895) — AFGHANISTAN — SINKIANG — MONGOLIA — Harbin — SOUTH MANCHURIA R.R. — CHINESE EASTERN R.R. — Mukden — Antung — Vladivostok — RUSSIAN EMPIRE (1860) — JAPAN-1905

KASHMIR (1846) — KUMAON (1815) — TIBET — NEPAL — BHUTAN — KUCH BEHAR — CHINA — Huang Ho (Yellow River) — Peking — Chinwangtao — Tientsin — Newchwang — Port Arthur (Rus.1898-Jap.1905) — Dairen — Weihaiwei (Br.1898) — Chefoo — Kiaochow — KIAOCHOW BAY (Germany 1898) — KOREA — SEA OF JAPAN — Tokyo — PACIFIC OCEAN

INDIA (British) — Damão (Port.) — Chandernagore (Fr.) — ASSAM (1826) — (1886) — Tengyueh — Szemao — Mengtsz — Chungking — Yangtze — Kiang — Ichang — Shasi — Yochow — Changsha — Hankow — Hangchow — Soochow — Wuhu — Nanking — Chinkiang — Kiukiang — Wenchow — Funing — Shanghai — Foochow — EAST CHINA SEA — BONIN ISLANDS (Jap.1876)

GOA (Port.) — Yanaon (Fr.) — Rangoon — BURMA (British) — BRITISH SPHERE (1896) — Si Kiang — Nanning — Lungchow — Pakhoi — Wuchow — Samshui — Canton — Kongmoon — Lappa — Macao — HONG KONG (Br.1842) — KWANGCHOWAN (Fr.1898) — Kiungchow — Hainan — Swatow — Amoy — Pescadores (Jap.1895) — Formosa (Jap.1895) — MARIANA ISLANDS (To Germany from Spain 1899)

Mahé (Fr.) — Pondichéry (Fr.) — Karikal (Fr.) — Bay of Bengal — TONKIN (1884) — ANNAM (1884) — FRENCH INDO-CHINA — SIAM — FRENCH SPHERE (1904) — BRITISH SPHERE (1896) — Bangkok — CAMBODIA (1863) — COCHIN CHINA (1862-1867) — Saigon — SOUTH CHINA SEA — PHILIPPINE ISLANDS (To United States from Spain 1898) — Manila — Guam (To U.S. from Spain 1898) — Yap (To Germany from Spain 1899)

Ceylon (British) — ANDAMAN ISLANDS (Br.) — NICOBAR ISLANDS (Br.) — INDIAN OCEAN — Gulf of Siam — EUROPEAN POWERS-19TH CENTURY — Labuan (Br.) — BRUNEI (Br. Prot.) — BRITISH NORTH BORNEO — SARAWAK (Br. Prot.) — Borneo — DUTCH EAST INDIES — BRITISH MALAYA — Singapore — SUMATRA

Treaty Ports are underlined: Ningpo.
Dates refer to year of acquisition by major powers.

EARLY AFRICA
4500 B.C. TO 1000 A.D.
0 200 400 600 800 MILES
0 200 400 600 800 KILOMETERS
VEGETATION
Desert and Desert Shrub
River Valley and Oasis
Grassland, Shrub and Open Woodland
Rain Forest
Southern boundary of the Carthaginian Empire 500 B.C.
Southern boundary of the Roman Empire 100 A.D.
Spread of domesticated cattle
Spread of ironworking
Expansion of the Bantu c. 500 B.C. to 1000 A.D.
Important archaeological sites
ATLANTIC OCEAN
EUROPE
MEDITERRANEAN SEA
ASIA
SAHARA
SAHEL
ARABIA
RED SEA
Tropic of Cancer
Equator
Tropic of Capricorn
INDIAN OCEAN
Rome
Carthage
Alexandria
EGYPT
NUBIA
MEROE
AXUM
Tassili
Jenne-Jeno
Nok
Ife
Igbo-Ukwu
L. Chad
Gulf of Guinea
Original Bantu dispersal area
Urewe
Katuruka
L. Victoria
Kalumba
Sanga
Lydenburg
Kalahari Desert
Cape of Good Hope
Madagascar
Mozambique Channel
Colonization of Madagascar by Indonesian migrants c. 800 A.D.
Bushman refuge area following Bantu expansion
4500 B.C.
2000 B.C.
450 B.C.
580-450 B.C.
3000 B.C.
500 B.C.
300 B.C.
200 A.D.
500 A.D.
400 A.D.
1000 A.D.
© Copyright 1987 by HAMMOND INCORPORATED, Maplewood, N.J.

AFRICAN KINGDOMS AND EMPIRES
750 B.C.–1901 A.D.
0 200 400 600 800 MILES
0 200 400 600 800 KILOMETERS
European trading posts after 1400
All dates A.D. except where noted.
GHANA 300 – 1076
SONGHAY 1464 – 1591
KANEM – BORNU 1570 – 1610
MEROE (NUBIA) 750 B.C. – 350 A.D.
AXUM 1 – 800
MALI 1234 – 1468
BENIN 1170 – 1900
ASANTE 1695 – 1901
OYO 1200 – 1800
DAHOMEY 1600 – 1894
LAKE KINGDOMS 1200 – 1900
ZANJ CITY – STATES 1000 – 1505
KONGO 1400 – 1709
MONOMOTAPA 1500 – 1620
HOVA 1787 – 1897
Southern limit of Islam 1800
Madeira
Canary Islands
MOROCCO
Arguin
Gorée I.
Timbuktu
Gao
Cape Coast
Elmina
Whydah
Ife
Fernando Po
São Tomé
Luanda
Benguela
Mombasa
Kilwa
Mozambique
Sofala
Zimbabwe
Cape Town
Cape of Good Hope
ATLANTIC OCEAN
INDIAN OCEAN
© Copyright 1987 by HAMMOND INCORPORATED, Maplewood, N.J.

EUROPEAN EXPLORATION OF AFRICA
1455-1900
0 200 400 600 800 MILES
0 200 400 600 800 KILOMETERS
LEGEND
Cadamosto 1455-57
Cão (Cam) 1482-84,85-86
Dias (Diaz) 1487-88
da Gama 1497-99
Hornemann 1797-1801
Park 1805-06
Caillé 1827-28
Lander 1830
Livingstone 1841-56
Barth 1850-55
Burton and Speke 1857-59
Livingstone 1858-64
Speke and Grant 1860-63
Baker 1863-65
Livingstone 1866-73
Nachtigal 1869-74
Stanley 1874-77
von Wissman 1880-85
Foureau-Lamy mission 1898-1900
PORTUGAL
SPAIN
FRANCE
Lisbon
Sagres
ALGERIA
MOROCCO
Madeira
Canary Is.
C. Bojador
Tripoli
Siwa
Cairo
EGYPT
Libyan Desert
Ghat
Murzuk
Timbuktu
C. Verde
Bathurst
Kukawa
Kano
Bussa
Chad
Khartoum
L. Tana
Gondokoro
Murchison Falls
L. Albert
L. Edward
Stanley Falls
L. Victoria
Ujiji
Tabora
Zanzibar
L. Tanganyika
L. Nyasa
Boma
Luanda
Dilolo
Chitambo
Comoro Is.
Quelimane
Victoria Falls
Walvis Bay
Kalahari Desert
C. of Good Hope
To India
© Copyright 1987 by HAMMOND INCORPORATED, Maplewood, N.J.

AFRICA 1885
0 200 400 600 800 MILES
0 200 400 600 800 KILOMETERS
British
French
German
Italian
Portuguese
Spanish
Ottoman
Non-European regimes (including Boer republics)
Boundary of the Congo Free State in 1885
Boundary between German and British spheres of interest in East Africa 1886
OTTOMAN EMPIRE
MOROCCO
ALGERIA (French)
TUNISIA (Fr.)
TRIPOLITANIA (Ottoman)
EGYPT (nominally Ottoman, British occupied)
RIO DE ORO (Sp.)
IFNI (Sp.)
Madeira (Port.)
Canary Is. (Sp.)
SENEGAL (Fr.)
GAMBIA (Br.)
TUKULOR EMPIRE
SAMORI'S EMPIRE
GUINEA (Fr.)
SIERRA LEONE (Br.)
LIBERIA
ASANTE
DAHOMEY
YORUBA
BENIN
GOLD COAST (Br.)
Lagos (Br.)
Grand Bassam (Fr.)
BORNU
SOKOTO SULTANATE
WADAI
RABIH
MAHDIST STATE
ETHIOPIA
BR. SOMALIL'D
KAMERUN (Ger.)
GABON (Fr.)
Fernando Po (Sp.)
São Tomé (Port.)
EQUATORIA (Ottoman)
BUGANDA
British Sphere
German Sphere
WITU (Ger.)
SULTANATE OF ZANZIBAR
TIPPU TIB'S DOMAIN
CHOKWE DOMAIN
MSIRI'S KDM.
CABINDA (Port.)
ANGOLA (Port.)
GERMAN SOUTH-WEST AFRICA
WALVIS BAY (Br.)
Angra Pequena (Lüderitz Bay)
BRIT. BECHUANAL'D
SOUTH AFRICAN REPUBLIC (TRANSVAAL)
ORANGE FREE STATE
BASUTOLAND (Br.)
NATAL (Br.)
ZULUL'D
CAPE COLONY (Br.)
PORTUGUESE EAST AFRICA (MOZAMBIQUE)
MERINA (HOVA) KINGDOM
Comoro Is. (Fr.)
Massawa (It.)
Assab (It.)
Obock (Fr.)
© Copyright 1987 by HAMMOND INCORPORATED, Maplewood, N.J.

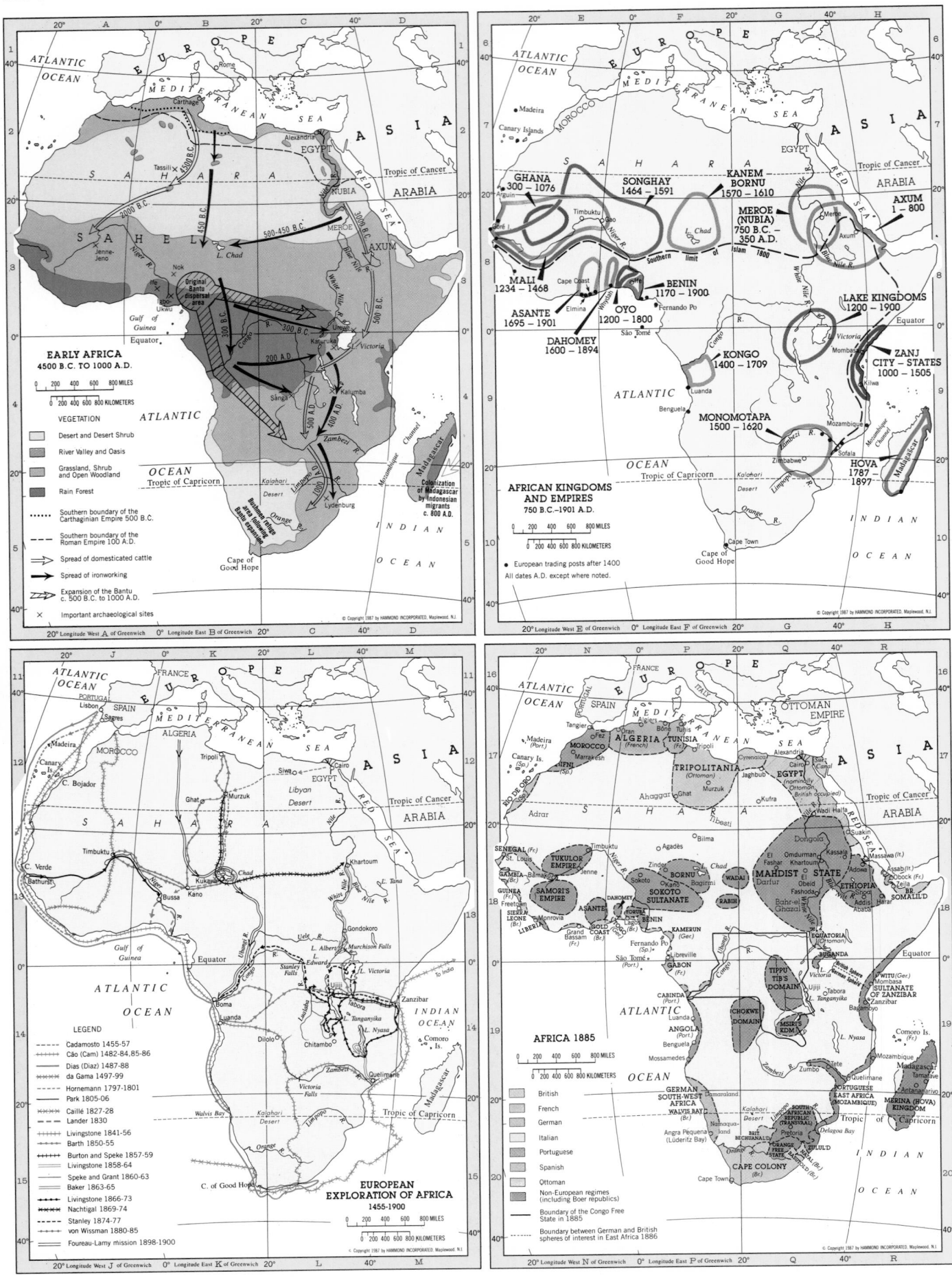

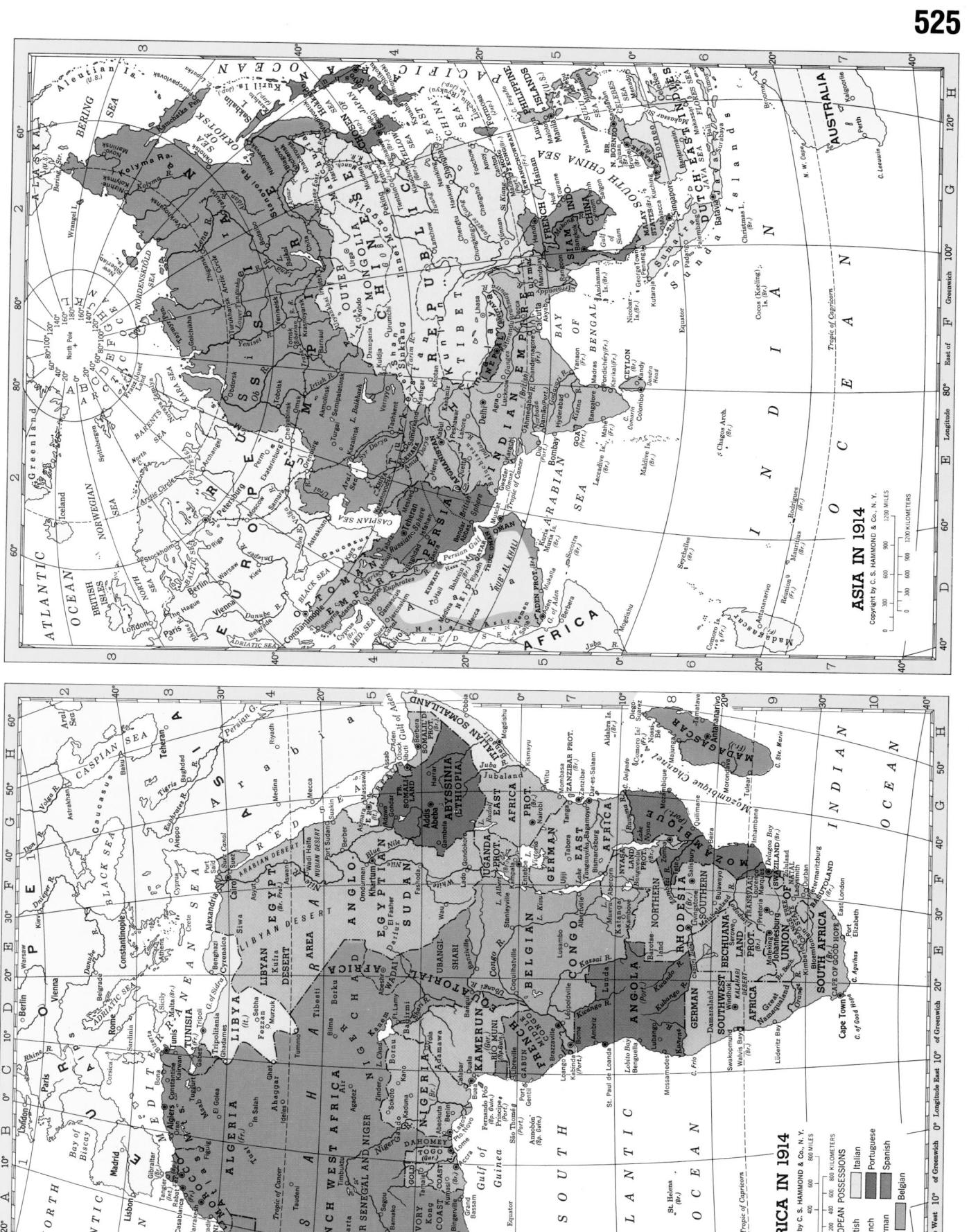

ASIA IN 1914

Copyright by C. S. HAMMOND & Co., N.Y.

AFRICA IN 1914

Copyright by C. S. HAMMOND & Co., N.Y.

EUROPEAN POSSESSIONS
British
French
German
Italian
Portuguese
Spanish
Belgian

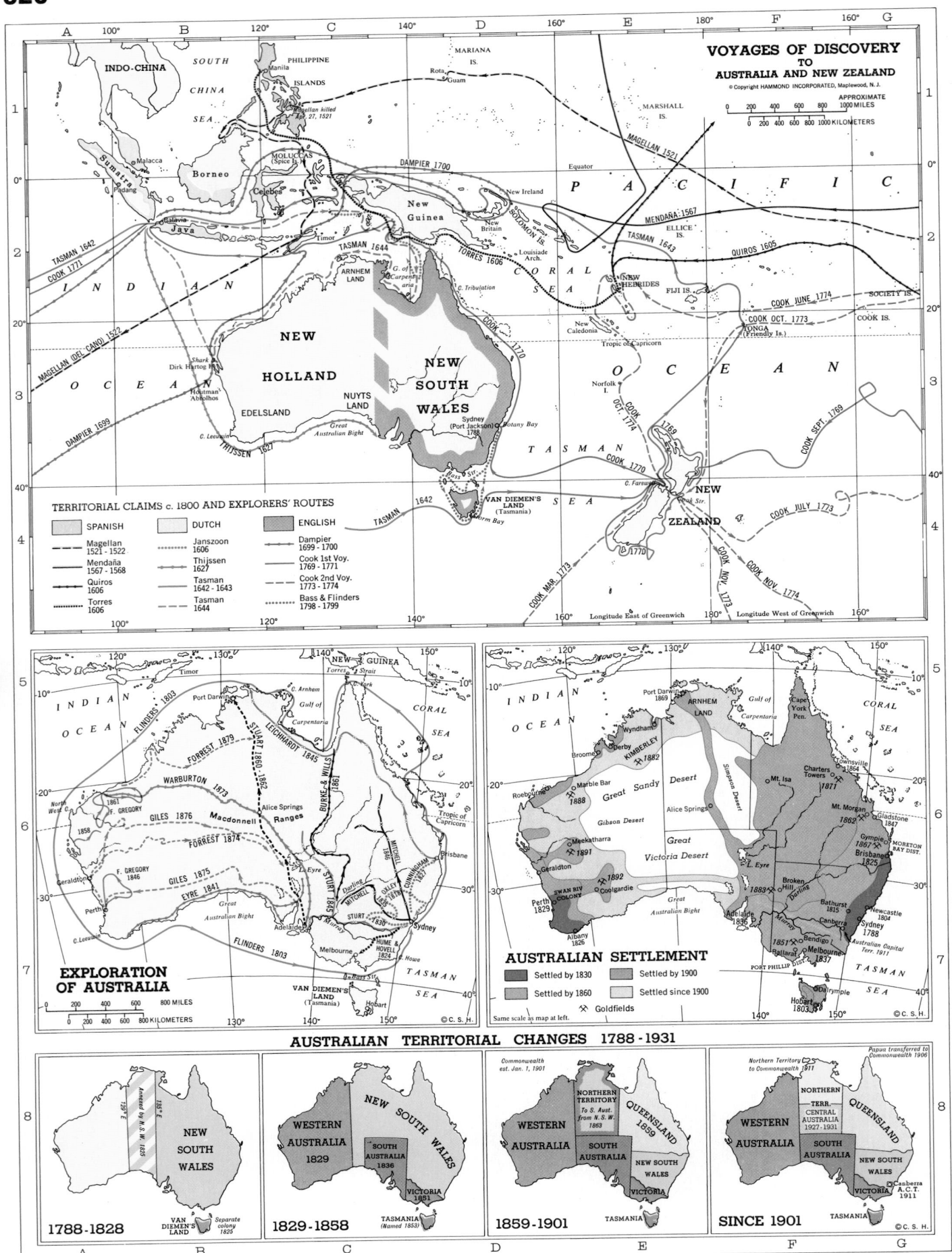

VOYAGES OF DISCOVERY
TO
AUSTRALIA AND NEW ZEALAND
© Copyright HAMMOND INCORPORATED, Maplewood, N.J.

APPROXIMATE

0   200   400   600   800   1000 MILES

0   200   400   600   800   1000 KILOMETERS

INDO-CHINA

SOUTH CHINA SEA

PHILIPPINE ISLANDS

Manila

MARIANA IS.

Rota

Guam

Magellan killed Apr. 27, 1521

Sumatra

Malacca

Padang

Borneo

Java

Batavia

MOLUCCAS (Spice Is.)

Celebes

Timor

DAMPIER 1700

New Ireland

New Britain

New Guinea

TASMAN 1644

TORRES 1606

ARNHEM LAND

G. of Carpentaria

C. Tribulation

Equator

PACIFIC

MARSHALL IS.

MAGELLAN 1521

MENDAÑA 1567

ELLICE IS.

TASMAN 1643

SOLOMON IS.

Louisiade Arch.

CORAL

QUIROS 1605

COOK JUNE 1774

SOCIETY IS.

TASMAN 1642

COOK 1771

MAGELLAN (DEL CANO) 1522

MAGELLAN (DEL CANO) 1522

Dirk Hartog I.

Shark B.

Houtman Abrolhos

Dampier 1699

C. Leeuwin

THIJSSEN 1627

NEW HOLLAND

EDELSLAND

NUYTS LAND

Great Australian Bight

NEW SOUTH WALES

Sydney (Port Jackson) 1788

Botany Bay

COOK 1770

NEW HEBRIDES

New Caledonia

Tropic of Capricorn

COOK OCT. 1773

TONGA (Friendly Is.)

COOK IS.

Norfolk I.

OCEAN

INDIAN OCEAN

SEA

TASMAN

SEA

Bass Str.

C. Farewell

Cook Str.

COOK 1770

OCT. 1774

1769

COOK SEPT. 1769

NEW ZEALAND

VAN DIEMEN'S LAND (Tasmania)

TASMAN 1642

Storm Bay

1642

1770

COOK MAR. 1773

COOK JULY 1773

COOK NOV. 1774

COOK NOV. 1773

Longitude East of Greenwich   Longitude West of Greenwich

TERRITORIAL CLAIMS c. 1800 AND EXPLORERS' ROUTES

▦ SPANISH	▢ DUTCH	▨ ENGLISH
Magellan 1521 - 1522	Janszoon 1606	Dampier 1699 - 1700
Mendaña 1567 - 1568	Thijssen 1627	Cook 1st Voy. 1769 - 1771
Quiros 1606	Tasman 1642 - 1643	Cook 2nd Voy. 1773 - 1774
Torres 1606	Tasman 1644	Bass & Flinders 1798 - 1799

EXPLORATION OF AUSTRALIA

Timor

NEW GUINEA

Torres Strait

C. York

C. Arnhem

Gulf of Carpentaria

CORAL SEA

INDIAN OCEAN

FLINDERS 1803

Port Darwin

LEICHHARDT 1845

STUART 1860-1862

FORREST 1879

WARBURTON 1873

GILES 1876

North West C.

F. GREGORY 1861

Alice Springs

Macdonnell Ranges

BURKE & WILLS 1861

MITCHELL 1846

1858

FORREST 1874

GILES 1875

F. GREGORY 1846

Geraldton

EYRE 1841

L. Eyre

STURT 1845

MITCHELL 1836

Tropic of Capricorn

Brisbane

CUNNINGHAM 1827

OXLEY 1817

Darling

Perth

Great Australian Bight

Adelaide

STURT 1830

Murray

HUME & HOVELL 1824

Sydney

C. Howe

Melbourne

FLINDERS 1803

Bass Str.

VAN DIEMEN'S LAND (Tasmania)

Hobart

C. Leeuwin

TASMAN SEA

0   200   400   600   800 MILES

0   200   400   600   800 KILOMETERS

AUSTRALIAN SETTLEMENT

INDIAN OCEAN

Port Darwin 1869

ARNHEM LAND

Gulf of Carpentaria

Cape York Pen.

CORAL SEA

Wyndham

Broome

KIMBERLEY 1882

Derby

Great Sandy Desert

Simpson Desert

Townsville 1864

Charters Towers 1871

Roebourne

Marble Bar 1888

Mt. Isa

Gibson Desert

Alice Springs

Mt. Morgan 1862

Gladstone 1847

Meekatharra

Great Victoria Desert

L. Eyre

Gympie 1867-52

Brisbane 1825

MORETON BAY DIST.

Geraldton

1891

1892

Coolgardie

SWAN RIV. COLONY 1829

Perth 1829

1883

Broken Hill 1815

Bathurst 1815

Newcastle 1804

Albany 1826

Great Australian Bight

Adelaide 1836

Murray

Darling

Canberra

Sydney 1788

Australian Capital Terr. 1911

1851

Bendigo

Ballarat 1837

Melbourne

PORT PHILLIP DIST.

TASMAN SEA

Hobart 1803

Dalrymple

Same scale as map at left.

▦ Settled by 1830	▨ Settled by 1900
▩ Settled by 1860	▢ Settled since 1900
⚒ Goldfields	

AUSTRALIAN TERRITORIAL CHANGES 1788 - 1931

1788 - 1828

Annexed by N.S.W. 1825

129° E

135° E

NEW SOUTH WALES

VAN DIEMEN'S LAND

Separate colony 1825

1829 - 1858

WESTERN AUSTRALIA 1829

NEW SOUTH WALES

SOUTH AUSTRALIA 1836

VICTORIA 1851

TASMANIA (Named 1853)

1859 - 1901

Commonwealth est. Jan. 1, 1901

WESTERN AUSTRALIA

NORTHERN TERRITORY To S. Aust. from N.S.W. 1863

QUEENSLAND 1859

SOUTH AUSTRALIA

NEW SOUTH WALES

VICTORIA

TASMANIA

SINCE 1901

Northern Territory to Commonwealth 1911

Papua transferred to Commonwealth 1906

NORTHERN TERR.

CENTRAL AUSTRALIA 1927-1931

QUEENSLAND

WESTERN AUSTRALIA

SOUTH AUSTRALIA

NEW SOUTH WALES

Canberra A.C.T. 1911

VICTORIA

TASMANIA

EXPLORATION OF CANADA

© Copyright HAMMOND INCORPORATED, Maplewood, N.J.

0 50 100 200 300 400 MILES

0 100 200 300 400 KILOMETERS

Forts & fur traders posts _____ Battles ✕

The various Indian tribes are shown where they were located during the period of their greatest significance in Canadian history.

1791

1873

THE GROWTH OF CANADA

FROM 1791 TO 1949

Copyright by C.S. HAMMOND & Co., N.Y.

The dates within the provinces, territories or districts indicate the years of their creation as political divisions.

1898 — Boundary of Northwest Territories 1894

1949 — Boundary of Northwest Territories 1949

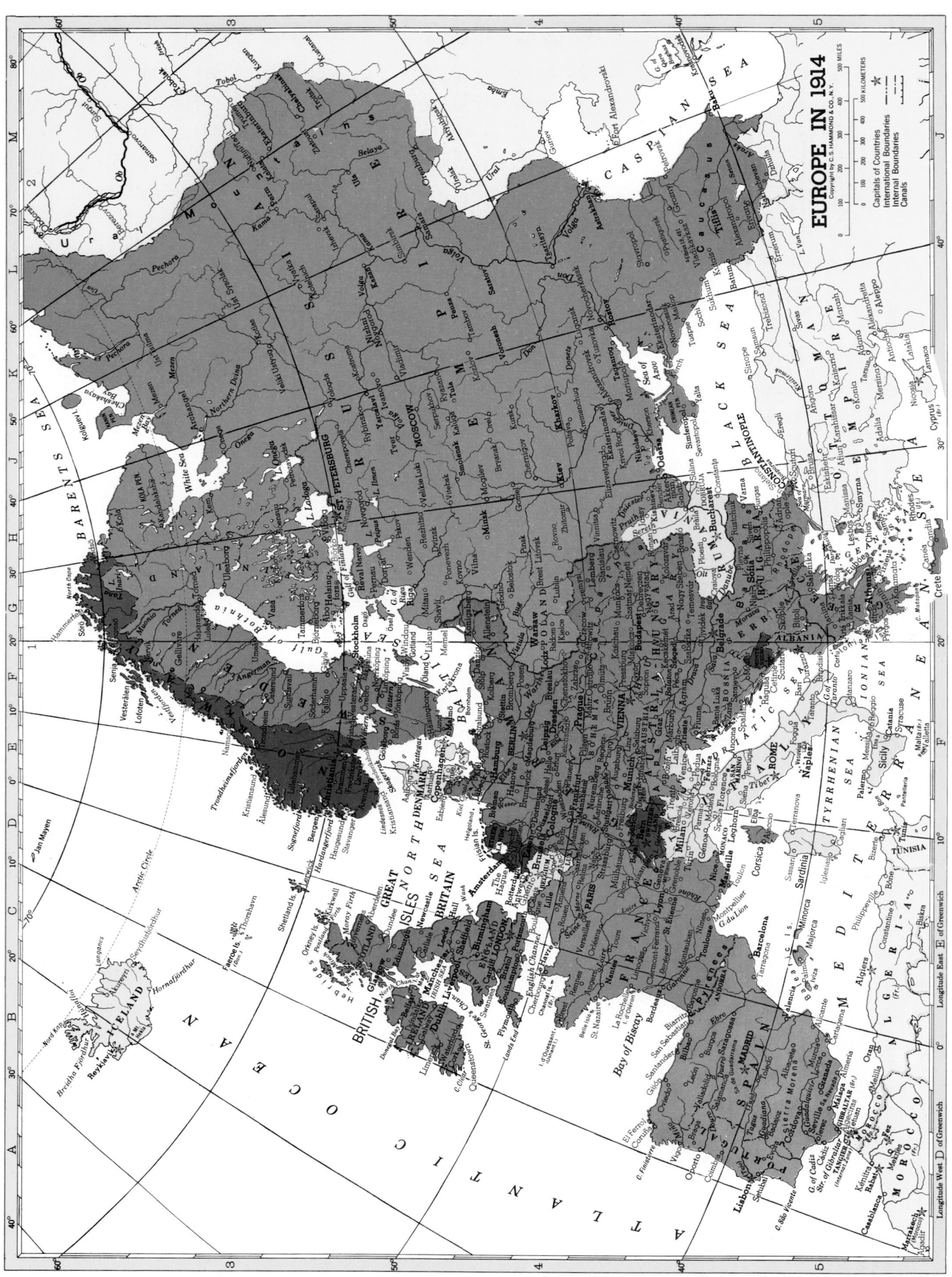

EUROPE IN 1914

Copyright by C. S. HAMMOND & CO., N.Y.

Capitals of Countries
International Boundaries
Internal Boundaries
Canals

EUROPE AND THE
NEAR EAST

Stabilized Line on the
Western Front, 1914-1917

Eastern Front on the Eve of the
Russian Revolution, Oct. 1917

Limit of Allied Advances
in the East

Area Occupied by the Central
Powers after Brest Litovsk
Treaty, 1918

THE FIRST WORLD WAR
1914-1918

© C. S. HAMMOND & Co., Maplewood, N.J.

The Allies

Neutral States

Advances of the Allies

The Central Powers

Areas Occupied by
the Central Powers

Advances of the Central Powers

THE WESTERN FRONT

0   20   40   60   80 MILES

0   20   40   60   80 KILOMETERS

Limit of German Advance, 1914

Limit of Trench Warfare, 1914-1917

Hindenburg Line, 1917

Limit of Final German Advance, 1918

Armistice Line, November 11, 1918

Limit of Allied Occupation Zone

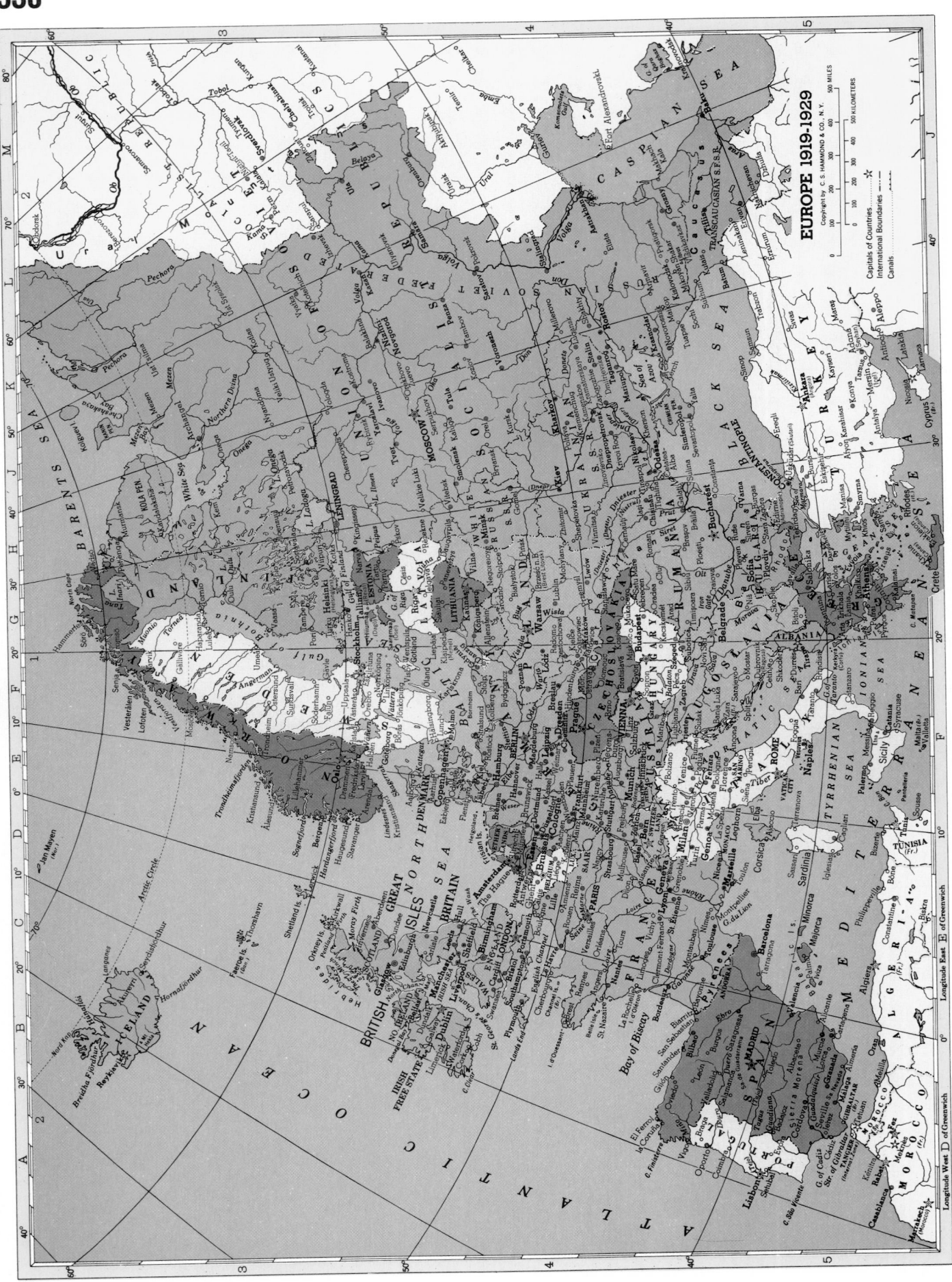

EUROPE 1919-1929

Copyright by C. S. HAMMOND & CO., N.Y.

Capitals of Countries..........☆
International Boundaries..........
Canals..........

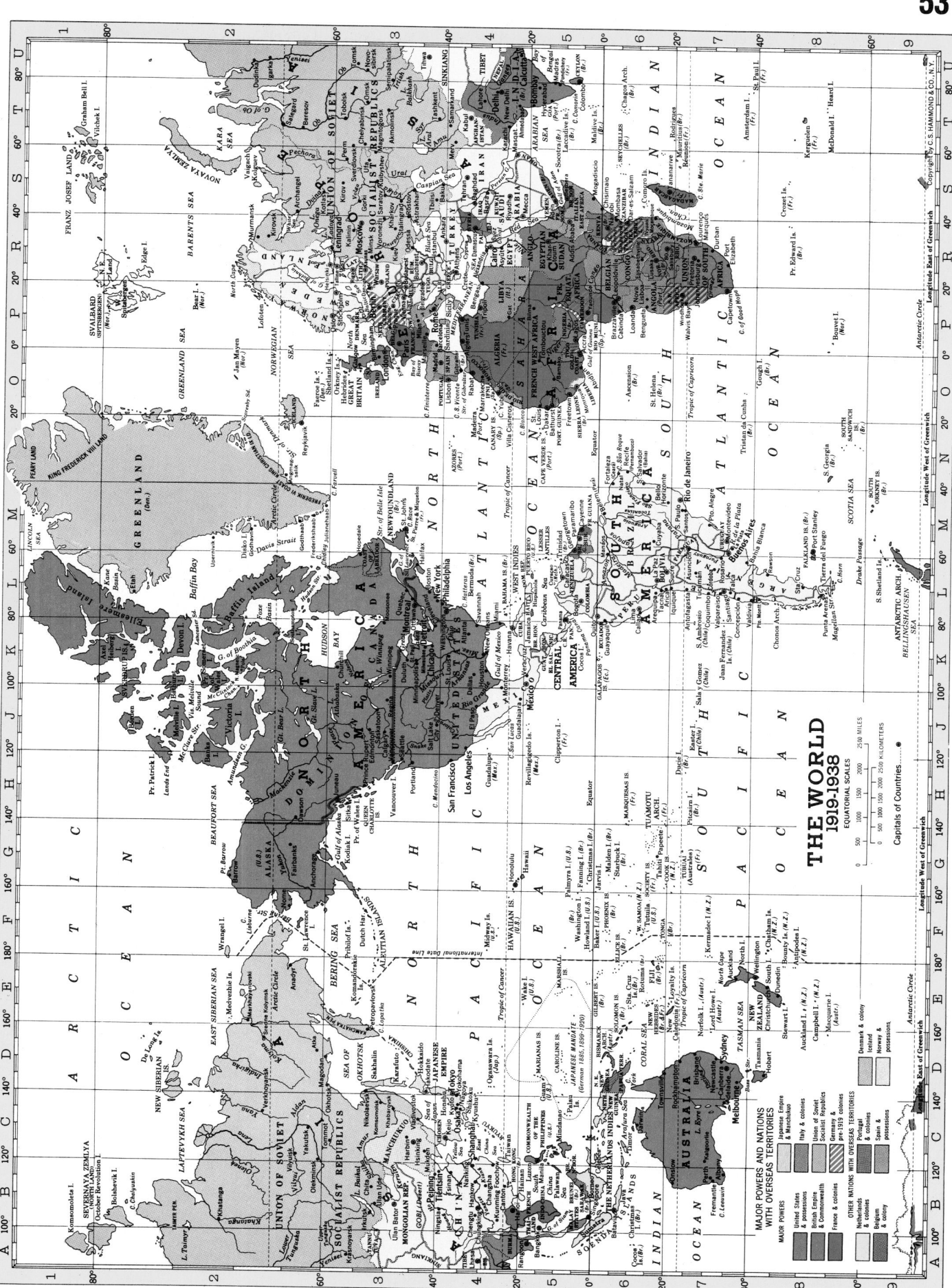

THE WORLD
1919-1938

EQUATORIAL SCALES

```
0      500    1000   1500   2000        2500 MILES
0   500  1000  1500  2000  2500 KILOMETERS
```

● Capitals of Countries

MAJOR POWERS AND NATIONS WITH OVERSEAS TERRITORIES

MAJOR POWERS

- United States & possessions
- British Empire & Commonwealth
- France & colonies
- Japanese Empire & colonies
- Italy & colonies
- Union of Soviet Socialist Republics
- Germany & pre-1919 colonies

OTHER NATIONS WITH OVERSEAS TERRITORIES

- Netherlands & colonies
- Portugal & colonies
- Belgium & colony
- Spain & possessions
- Denmark & possessions
- Iceland
- Norway & possessions

Copyright by C. S. HAMMOND & CO., N.Y.

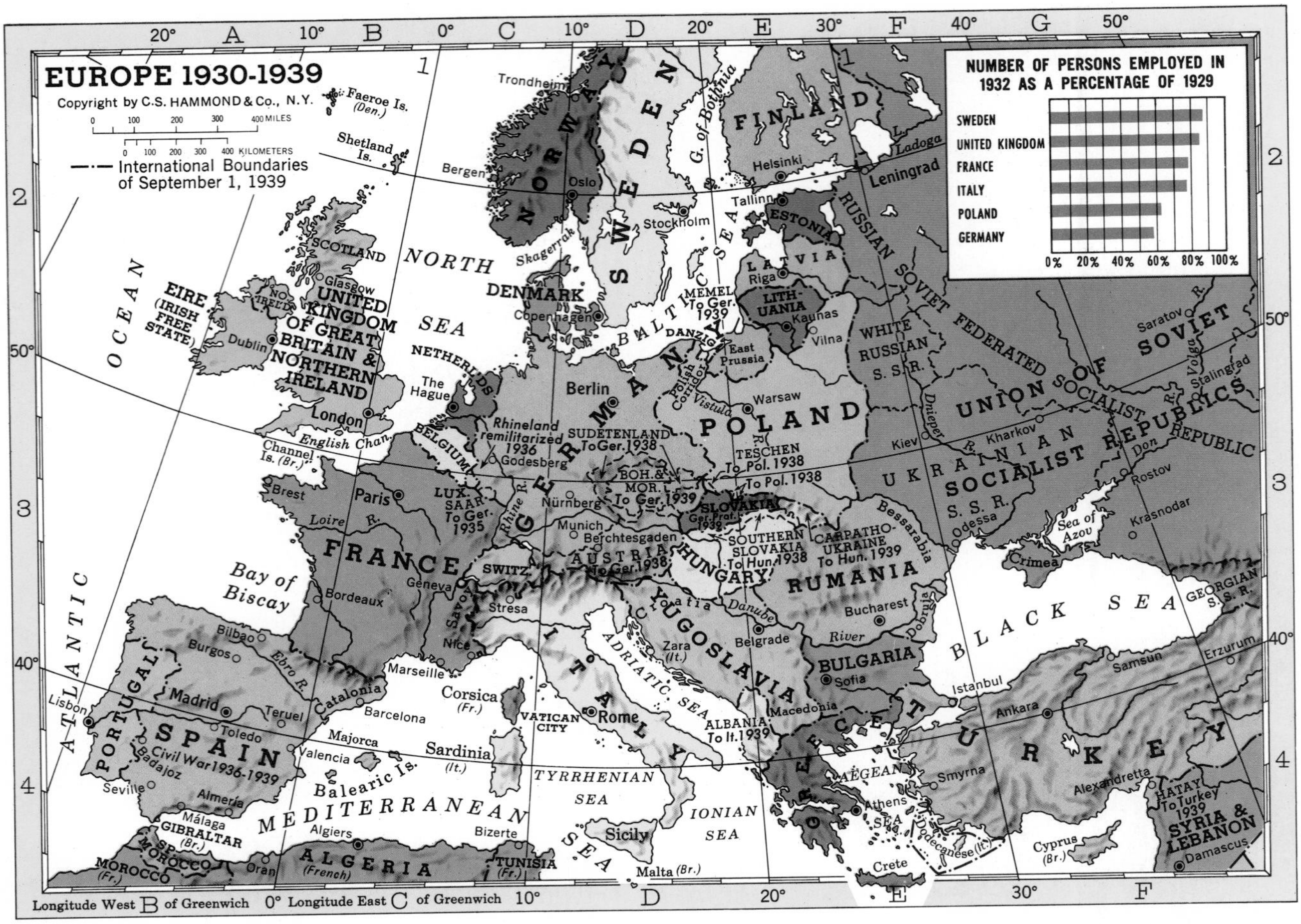

EUROPE 1930-1939

Copyright by C.S. HAMMOND & Co., N.Y.

0 100 200 300 400 MILES
0 100 200 300 400 KILOMETERS

International Boundaries
of September 1, 1939

**NUMBER OF PERSONS EMPLOYED IN
1932 AS A PERCENTAGE OF 1929**

SWEDEN
UNITED KINGDOM
FRANCE
ITALY
POLAND
GERMANY

0% 20% 40% 60% 80% 100%

Faeroe Is. (Den.)
Shetland Is.
Trondheim
NORWAY
SWEDEN
FINLAND
G. of Bothnia
Helsinki
Leningrad
L. Ladoga
Bergen
Oslo
Stockholm
Tallinn
ESTONIA
RUSSIAN SOVIET FEDERATED
SOCIALIST REPUBLIC
Riga
LATVIA
MEMEL To Ger. 1939
LITHUANIA
Kaunas
Vilna
WHITE RUSSIAN S.S.R.
Saratov
UNION OF SOVIET
SOCIALIST REPUBLICS
Stalingrad
NORTH SEA
Skagerrak
DENMARK
Copenhagen
BALTIC SEA
DANZIG
East Prussia
Vistula
Warsaw
POLAND
Kiev
UKRAINIAN S.S.R.
Kharkov
Don
Rostov
SCOTLAND
Glasgow
NO. IRELAND
EIRE (IRISH FREE STATE)
Dublin
UNITED KINGDOM OF GREAT BRITAIN & NORTHERN IRELAND
London
NETHERLANDS
The Hague
Berlin
GERMANY
SUDETENLAND 1938 To Ger.
TESCHEN To Pol. 1938
BOH. & MOR. To Ger. 1939
SLOVAKIA
SOUTHERN SLOVAKIA To Hun. 1938
CARPATHO-UKRAINE To Hun. 1939
Dnieper
Odessa
Crimea
Sea of Azov
Krasnodar
GEORGIAN S.S.R.
Channel Is. (Br.)
English Chan.
Brest
Paris
LUX.
SAAR To Ger. 1935
Rhine R.
Rhineland remilitarized 1936
Godesberg
Nürnberg
Munich
Berchtesgaden
AUSTRIA To Ger. 1938
HUNGARY
Bessarabia
RUMANIA
Bucharest
Danube River
BLACK SEA
Krasnodar
Loire
FRANCE
Bay of Biscay
Bordeaux
Geneva
SWITZ.
Stresa
Nice
Croatia
YUGOSLAVIA
Belgrade
Sofia
BULGARIA
Istanbul
Ankara
TURKEY
Erzurum
Samsun
ATLANTIC OCEAN
Bilbao
Burgos
PORTUGAL
Lisbon
SPAIN Civil War 1936-1939
Madrid
Toledo
Teruel
Catalonia
Barcelona
Valencia
Majorca
Balearic Is.
Corsica (Fr.)
VATICAN CITY
Rome
ITALY
Sardinia (It.)
ADRIATIC SEA
Zara (It.)
ALBANIA To It. 1939
Macedonia
GREECE
Athens
AEGEAN SEA
Smyrna
Alexandretta
HATAY To Turkey 1939
SYRIA & LEBANON
Damascus
Seville
Málaga
Almería
GIBRALTAR (Br.)
MOROCCO (Sp.)
MOROCCO (Fr.)
Oran
Algiers
ALGERIA (French)
Bizerte
TUNISIA (Fr.)
TYRRHENIAN SEA
Sicily
IONIAN SEA
Malta (Br.)
Crete
Dodecanese (It.)
Cyprus (Br.)
MEDITERRANEAN SEA

Longitude West of Greenwich   0° Longitude East of Greenwich

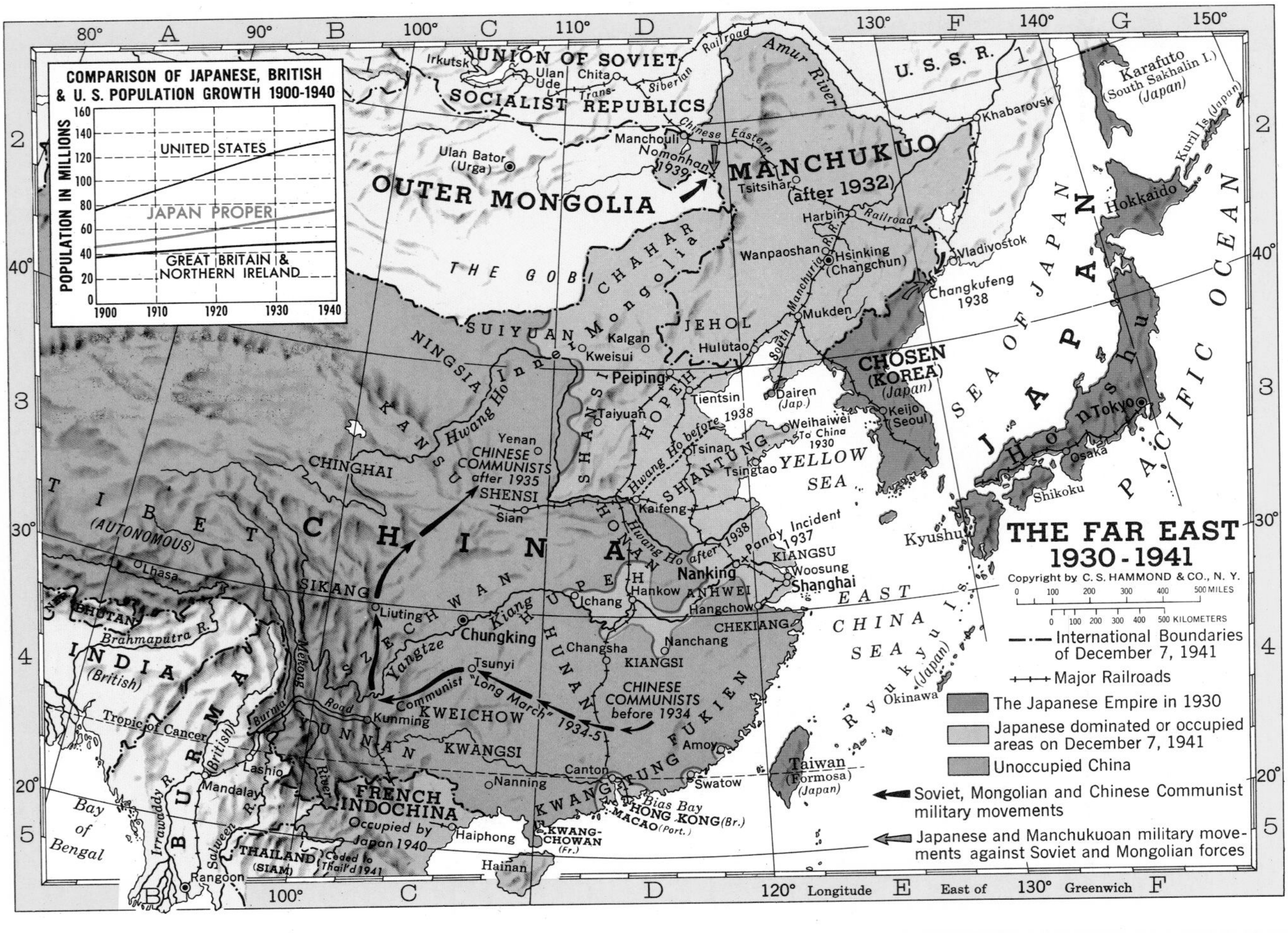

THE FAR EAST 1930-1941

Copyright by C.S. HAMMOND & CO., N.Y.

0 100 200 300 400 500 MILES
0 100 200 300 400 500 KILOMETERS

International Boundaries of December 7, 1941
Major Railroads
The Japanese Empire in 1930
Japanese dominated or occupied areas on December 7, 1941
Unoccupied China
Soviet, Mongolian and Chinese Communist military movements
Japanese and Manchukuoan military movements against Soviet and Mongolian forces

COMPARISON OF JAPANESE, BRITISH & U.S. POPULATION GROWTH 1900-1940

POPULATION IN MILLIONS
160
140
120
100
80
60
40
20

UNITED STATES
JAPAN PROPER
GREAT BRITAIN & NORTHERN IRELAND

1900 1910 1920 1930 1940

UNION OF SOVIET SOCIALIST REPUBLICS
Irkutsk
Ulan Ude
Chita
Siberian Railroad
Trans-Siberian
Chinese Eastern Railroad
Amur River
U.S.S.R.
Karafuto (South Sakhalin I.) (Japan)
Khabarovsk
Ulan Bator (Urga)
OUTER MONGOLIA
Manchouli
Nomonhan 1939
Tsitsihar
MANCHUKUO (after 1932)
Harbin
Railroad
Kurils Is. (Japan)
THE GOBI
CHAHAR
Inner Mongolia
SUIYUAN
NINGSIA
KANSU
Huang Ho
Kalgan
Kweisui
JEHOL
Hulutao
Wanpaoshan
Hsinking (Changchun)
South Manchurian Railroad
Mukden
Vladivostok
Changkufeng 1938
SEA OF JAPAN
Hokkaido
JAPAN
HONSHU
TIBET (AUTONOMOUS)
Lhasa
CHINGHAI
Yenan
CHINESE COMMUNISTS after 1935
SHENSI
SHANSI
Taiyuan
HOPEIH
Peiping
Tientsin
Dairen (Jap.)
Weihaiwei To China 1930
SHANTUNG
Tsingtao
YELLOW SEA
CHOSEN (KOREA) (Japan)
Keijo Seoul
Tokyo
Osaka
BHUTAN
Brahmaputra R.
INDIA (British)
Tropic of Cancer
SIKANG
SZECHWAN
Liuting
Chungking
Tsunyi
Long March 1934-5
KWEICHOW
Communist Road
Kunming
YUNNAN
BURMA (British)
Lashio
Mandalay
Irrawaddy R.
Salween R.
Mekong R.
Yangtze
Sian
HONAN
Huang Ho before 1938
Huang Ho after 1938
Kaifeng
HUPEH
Ichang
Hankow
Hangchow
ANHWEI
CHEKIANG
Nanking
KIANGSU
Woosung
Shanghai
Panay Incident 1937
EAST CHINA SEA
Ryukyu Is. (Japan)
Okinawa
Shikoku
Kyushu
PACIFIC OCEAN
CHINA
Changsha
Nanchang
KIANGSI
HUNAN
CHINESE COMMUNISTS before 1934
FUKIEN
Amoy
KWANGSI
KWANGTUNG
Canton
Nanning
HONG KONG (Br.)
MACAO (Port.)
Bias Bay
KWANG-CHOWAN (Fr.)
Swatow
Taiwan (Formosa) (Japan)
FRENCH INDOCHINA Occupied by Japan 1940
Haiphong
Hainan
THAILAND (SIAM) Ceded to Thai'd 1941
Rangoon
Bay of Bengal

Longitude   East of Greenwich

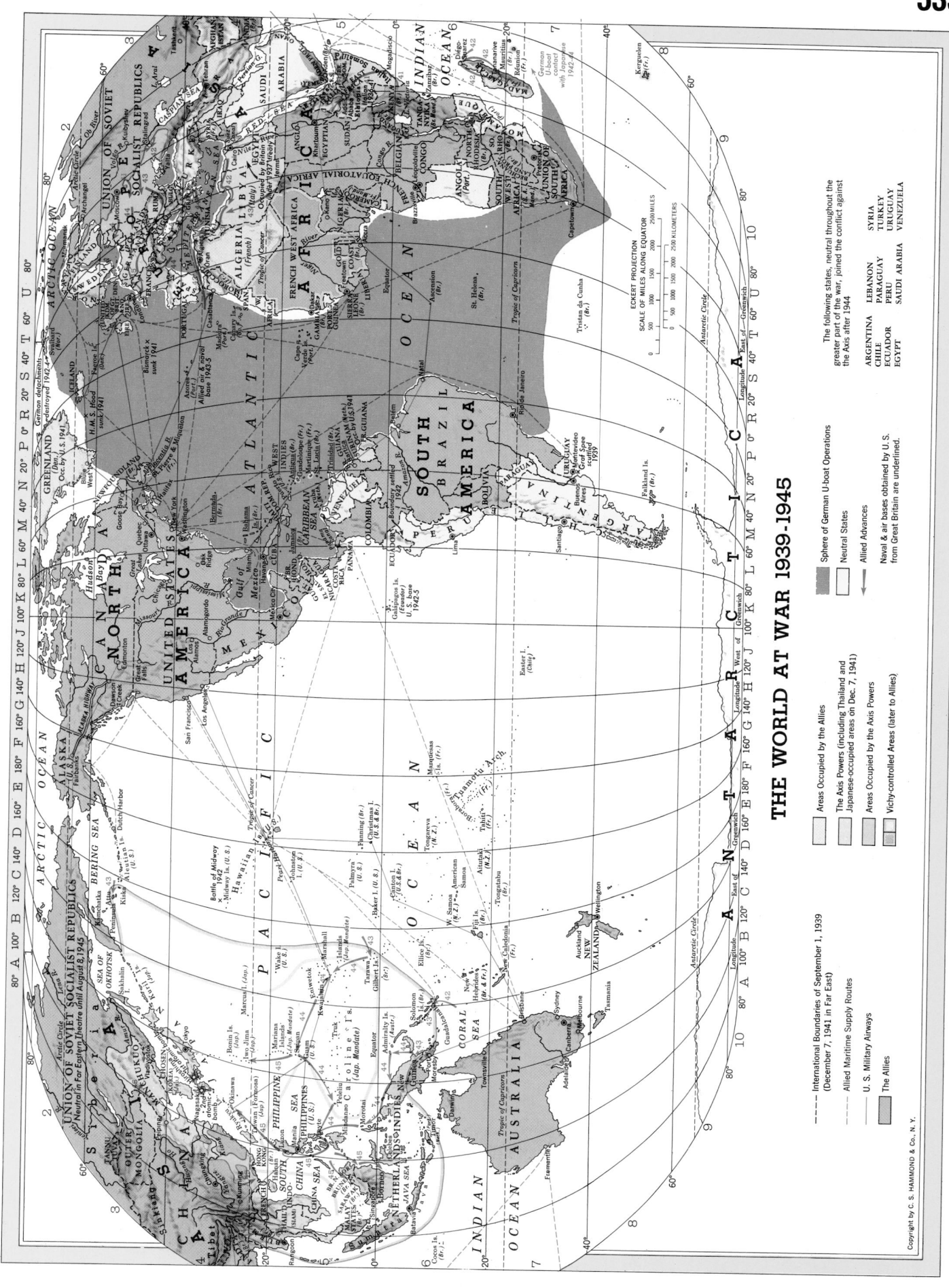

THE WORLD AT WAR 1939-1945

The following states, neutral throughout the war or throughout the greater part of the war, joined the conflict against the Axis after 1944

ARGENTINA   LEBANON   SYRIA
CHILE   PARAGUAY   TURKEY
ECUADOR   PERU   URUGUAY
EGYPT   SAUDI ARABIA   VENEZUELA

Sphere of German U-boat Operations
Neutral States
Allied Advances
Naval & air bases obtained by U.S. from Great Britain are underlined.

Areas Occupied by the Allies
The Axis Powers (including Thailand and Japanese-occupied areas on Dec. 7, 1941)
Areas Occupied by the Axis Powers
Vichy-controlled Areas (later to Allies)

International Boundaries of September 1, 1939 (December 7, 1941 in Far East)
Allied Maritime Supply Routes
U.S. Military Airways
The Allies

Copyright by C. S. HAMMOND & Co., N.Y.

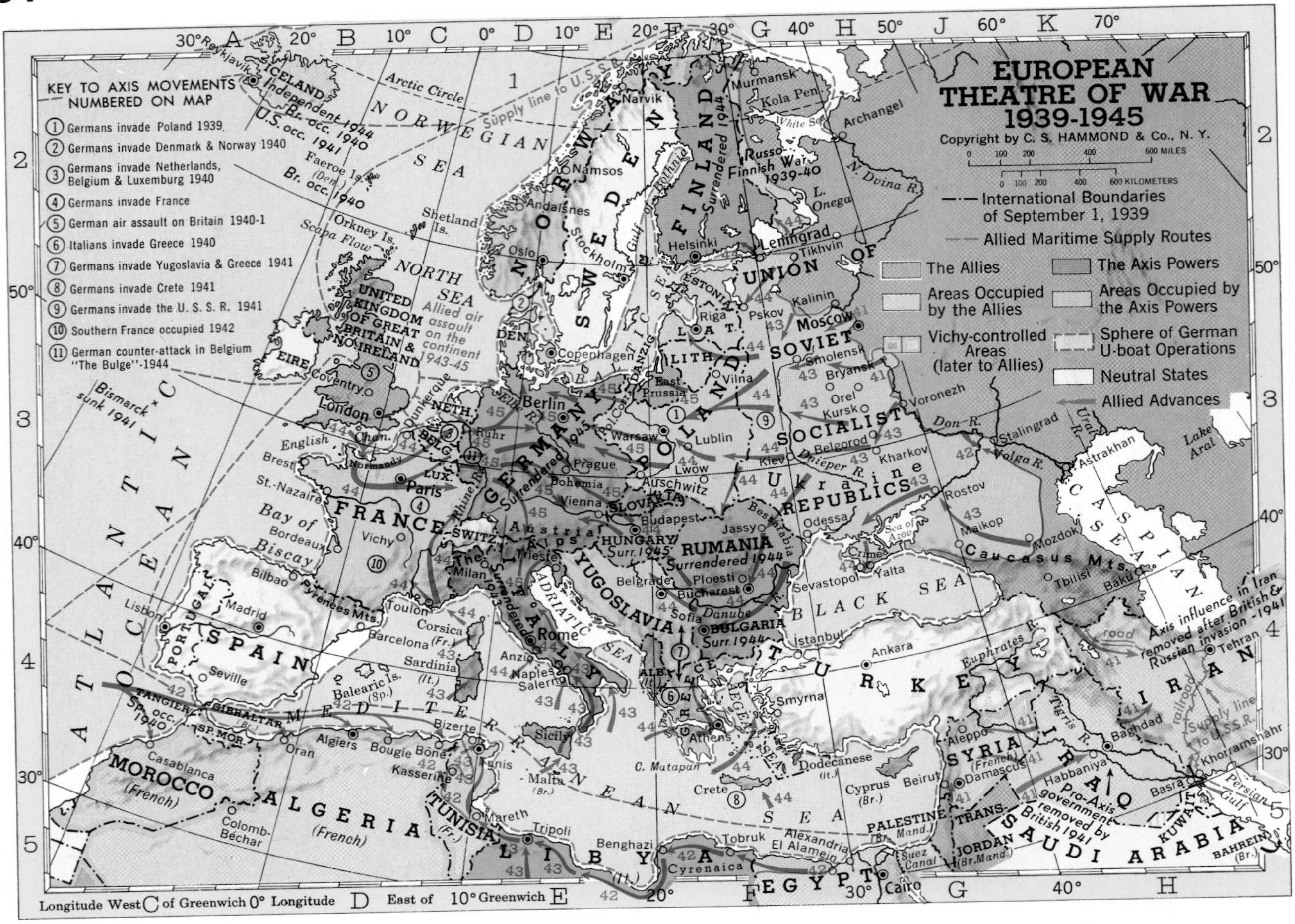

534

EUROPEAN THEATRE OF WAR 1939-1945

Copyright by C. S. Hammond & Co., N.Y.

KEY TO AXIS MOVEMENTS NUMBERED ON MAP

① Germans invade Poland 1939
② Germans invade Denmark & Norway 1940
③ Germans invade Netherlands, Belgium & Luxemburg 1940
④ Germans invade France
⑤ German air assault on Britain 1940-1
⑥ Italians invade Greece 1940
⑦ Germans invade Yugoslavia & Greece 1941
⑧ Germans invade Crete 1941
⑨ Germans invade the U.S.S.R. 1941
⑩ Southern France occupied 1942
⑪ Germans counter-attack in Belgium "The Bulge"-1944

0 100 200 400 600 MILES
0 100 200 400 600 KILOMETERS

International Boundaries of September 1, 1939
Allied Maritime Supply Routes
The Allies — The Axis Powers
Areas Occupied by the Allies — Areas Occupied by the Axis Powers
Vichy-controlled Areas (later to Allies) — Sphere of German U-boat Operations
Neutral States
Allied Advances

ARCTIC CIRCLE
NORWEGIAN SEA
NORTH SEA
ATLANTIC OCEAN
UNITED KINGDOM OF GREAT BRITAIN & NORTHERN IRELAND
EIRE
ICELAND Independent 1944 Br. occ. 1940 U.S. occ. 1941
Faeroe Is. Br. occ. 1940
Orkney Is.
Shetland Is.
Scapa Flow
SWEDEN
NORWAY Surrendered 1940
FINLAND Surrendered 1944
Russo-Finnish War 1939-40
Murmansk
Kola Pen.
White Sea
Archangel
N. Dvina R.
L. Onega
Leningrad
Tikhvin
UNION OF SOVIET SOCIALIST REPUBLICS
Helsinki
Kalinin
Moscow
Smolensk 43
Bryansk 43
Orel 43
Kursk 43
Voronezh
Stalingrad 42
Volga R.
Ural R.
Lake Aral
CASPIAN SEA
Astrakhan
Maikop
Mozdok
Caucasus Mts.
Tbilisi
Baku
Axis influence in Iran removed after British & Russian invasion 1941
IRAN
Supply line to U.S.S.R.
Tehran
Khorramshahr
Persian Gulf
BAHREIN (Br.)
KUWAIT
SAUDI ARABIA
Basra
Baghdad
IRAQ Pro-Axis government removed by British 1941
Habbaniya
Aleppo
Damascus
SYRIA (French)
Beirut
TRANS. JORDAN (Br. Mand.)
PALESTINE (Br. Mand.)
CYPRUS (Br.)
Suez Canal
Alexandria
El Alamein 42
Cairo
EGYPT
Tobruk 41
Benghazi 42
Cyrenaica
LIBYA (It.)
Tripoli
Mareth
TUNISIA (French)
Kasserine 43
Bône 43
Bizerte 43
Tunis 43
SICILY 43
C. Matapan
Crete
AEGEAN SEA
Dodecanese (It.)
Smyrna
TURKEY
Ankara
Istanbul
BLACK SEA
Sevastopol
Yalta
Crimea
Sea of Azov
Rostov
Don R.
Kharkov 43
Belgorod 43
Kiev 43
Dnieper R.
Odessa
RUMANIA Surrendered 1944
Bucharest
Danube
Ploesti
Sofia
BULGARIA Surr. 1944
ALBANIA (It.)
Athens
Salonika
GREECE
Belgrade
YUGOSLAVIA
Jassy
Lwow
Lublin
Warsaw
POLAND
Auschwitz
Cracow
SLOVAKIA
HUNGARY Surr. 1945
Budapest
Vienna
AUSTRIA
Trieste
ADRIATIC SEA
Anzio 44
Rome
Naples 43
Salerno 43
Sardinia (It.)
Corsica (Fr.)
Balearic Is. (Sp.)
Barcelona
MEDITERRANEAN SEA
Algiers
Bougie 42
Oran
TANGIER It. occ. 1942
GIBRALTAR (Br.)
SP. MOR.
Colomb-Bechar
ALGERIA (French)
MOROCCO (French)
Casablanca
Colomb
SPAIN
Madrid
Seville
Bilbao
PORTUGAL
Lisbon
Bay of Biscay
Bordeaux
FRANCE
Pyrenees Mts.
Vichy
SWITZ.
Milan
ITALY
Genoa
Alps
Munich
Prague
BOHEMIA
Berlin
GERMANY
Hamburg
Bremen
NETH.
BELG.
LUX.
Paris
St. Nazaire
Brest
English Channel
Cherbourg
Normandy
London
Coventry
Plymouth
DENMARK
Copenhagen
BALTIC SEA
Danzig
East Prussia
Königsberg
LITH.
LATVIA
ESTONIA
Riga
Pskov
Vilna
Kiel
Oslo
Stockholm
Gulf of Bothnia
Narvik
Namsos
Andalsnes
Gulf of Finland
Bismarck sunk 1941
Allied air assault on the continent 1943-45
Supply line to U.S.S.R.

Longitude West of Greenwich 0° Longitude East of 10° Greenwich

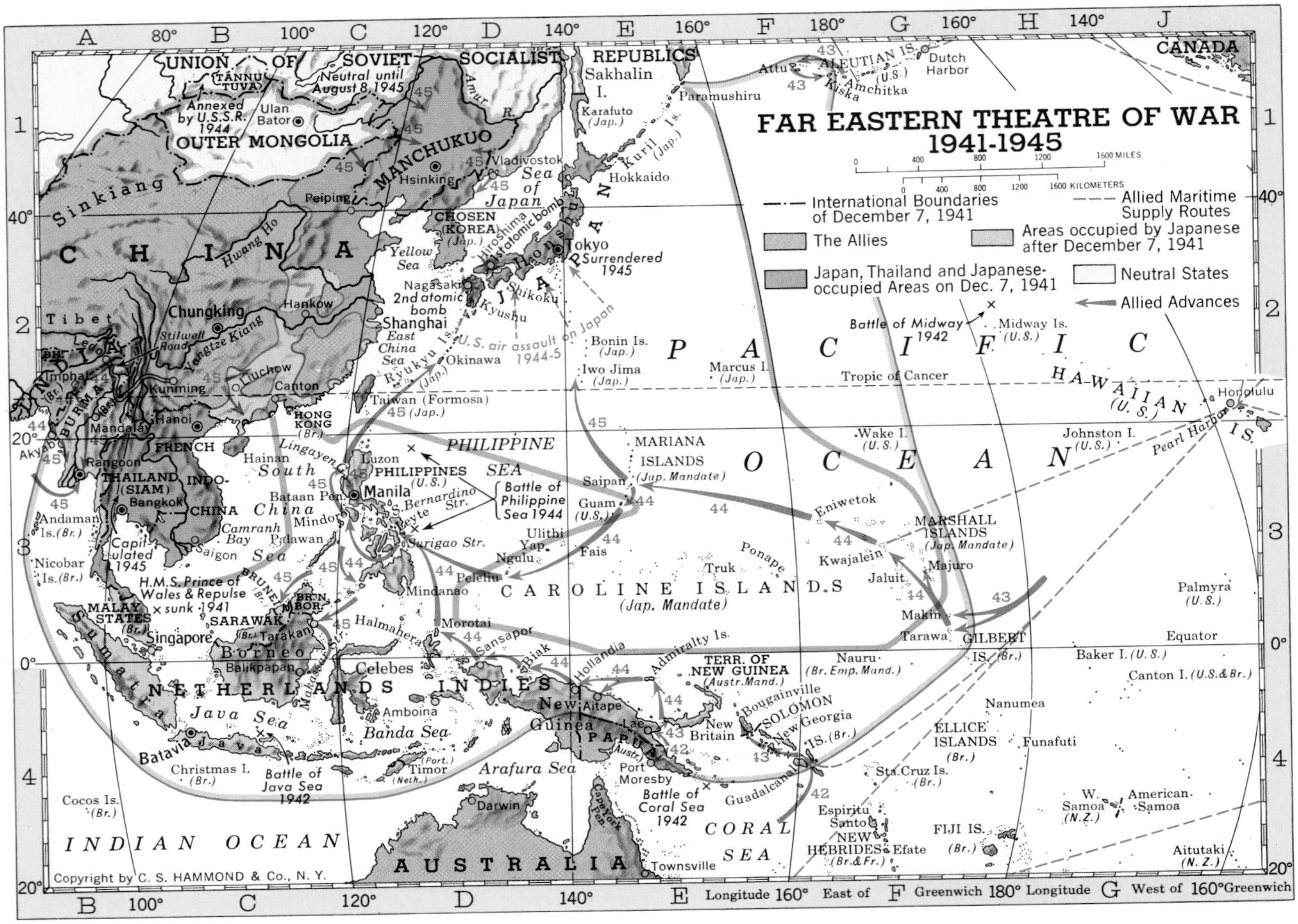

FAR EASTERN THEATRE OF WAR 1941-1945

Copyright by C. S. Hammond & Co., N.Y.

0 400 800 1600 MILES
0 400 800 1600 KILOMETERS

International Boundaries of December 7, 1941
Allied Maritime Supply Routes
The Allies — Areas occupied by Japanese after December 7, 1941
Japan, Thailand and Japanese-occupied Areas on Dec. 7, 1941
Neutral States
Allied Advances

UNION OF SOVIET SOCIALIST REPUBLICS
TANNU TUVA Annexed by U.S.S.R. 1944
OUTER MONGOLIA Neutral until August 8, 1945
Ulan Bator
Sinkiang
CHINA
Tibet
Chungking
Hankow
Hwang Ho
Yangtze Kiang
Peiping
Hsinking
MANCHUKUO
Vladivostok 45
Amur R.
Sea of Japan
Sakhalin I.
Karafuto (Jap.)
Paramushiru
Kuril Is. (Jap.)
Hokkaido
CHOSEN (KOREA)
Yellow Sea
Hiroshima 1st atomic bomb
Tokyo Surrendered 1945
JAPAN
Honshu
Shikoku
Kyushu
Nagasaki 2nd atomic bomb
Shanghai
East China Sea
Ryukyu
Okinawa 1944-5
U.S. air assault on Japan
CANADA
ALEUTIAN IS. (U.S.)
Attu 43
Kiska 43
Amchitka
Dutch Harbor
Battle of Midway 1942
Midway Is. (U.S.)
Marcus I. (Jap.)
Bonin Is. (Jap.)
Iwo Jima (Jap.)
Tropic of Cancer
HAWAIIAN IS. (U.S.)
Honolulu
Pearl Harbor
Taiwan (Formosa) 45 (Jap.)
HONG KONG (Br.)
Canton
Luchow
Hanoi
Mandalay
Rangoon
BURMA
Akyab 45
Imphal
Stilwell Road
Kunming
FRENCH INDO-CHINA
THAILAND (SIAM)
Bangkok
Hainan
Saigon
South China Sea
Lingayen 45
Luzon
Manila
Bataan Pen.
Bernardino Str.
Leyte
Mindoro
Surigao Str.
PHILIPPINES (U.S.)
PHILIPPINE SEA
Battle of Philippine Sea 1944
Yap
Ulithi
Ngulu
Fais
Mindanao
Palelieu
CAROLINE ISLANDS (Jap. Mandate)
Truk
Ponape
Kwajalein
Eniwetok
MARSHALL ISLANDS (Jap. Mandate)
Majuro
Jaluit
Makin
Tarawa
GILBERT IS. (Br.)
MARIANA ISLANDS (Jap. Mandate)
Saipan 44
Guam (U.S.) 44
Wake I. (U.S.)
Johnston I. (U.S.)
Palmyra (U.S.)
Baker I. (U.S.)
Canton I. (U.S. & Br.)
Nanumea
Funafuti
ELLICE ISLANDS (Br.)
Equator
Nauru (Br. Emp. Mand.)
Ocean I.
TERR. OF NEW GUINEA (Austr. Mand.)
Hollandia
Biak
Sansapor
Halmahera
Morotai
Celebes
Banda Sea
Amboina
Timor (Port.)
NETHERLANDS INDIES
Borneo
Balikpapan
Tarakan
BR. N. BORNEO
SARAWAK
BRUNEI
MALAY STATES (Br.)
Singapore
Andaman Is. (Br.) Capitulated 1945
Nicobar Is. (Br.)
H.M.S. Prince of Wales & Repulse sunk 1941
Camranh Bay
Saigon
Java Sea
Batavia
Java
Christmas I. (Br.)
Cocos Is. (Br.)
Battle of Java Sea 1942
INDIAN OCEAN
AUSTRALIA
Darwin
Townsville
Arafura Sea
Port Moresby
PAPUA (Austr.)
Lae
Aitape
Altape
New Britain
Rabaul
Bougainville
New Georgia
SOLOMON IS. (Br.)
Guadalcanal 42
Battle of Coral Sea 1942
CORAL SEA
Sta. Cruz Is. (Br.)
Espiritu Santo
NEW HEBRIDES (Br. & Fr.)
Efate
FIJI IS. (Br.)
W. Samoa (N.Z.)
American Samoa (U.S.)
Aitutaki (N.Z.)
PACIFIC OCEAN
Admiralty Is.
Numea

Copyright by C. S. Hammond & Co., N.Y.

Longitude East of Greenwich 180° Longitude West of 160° Greenwich

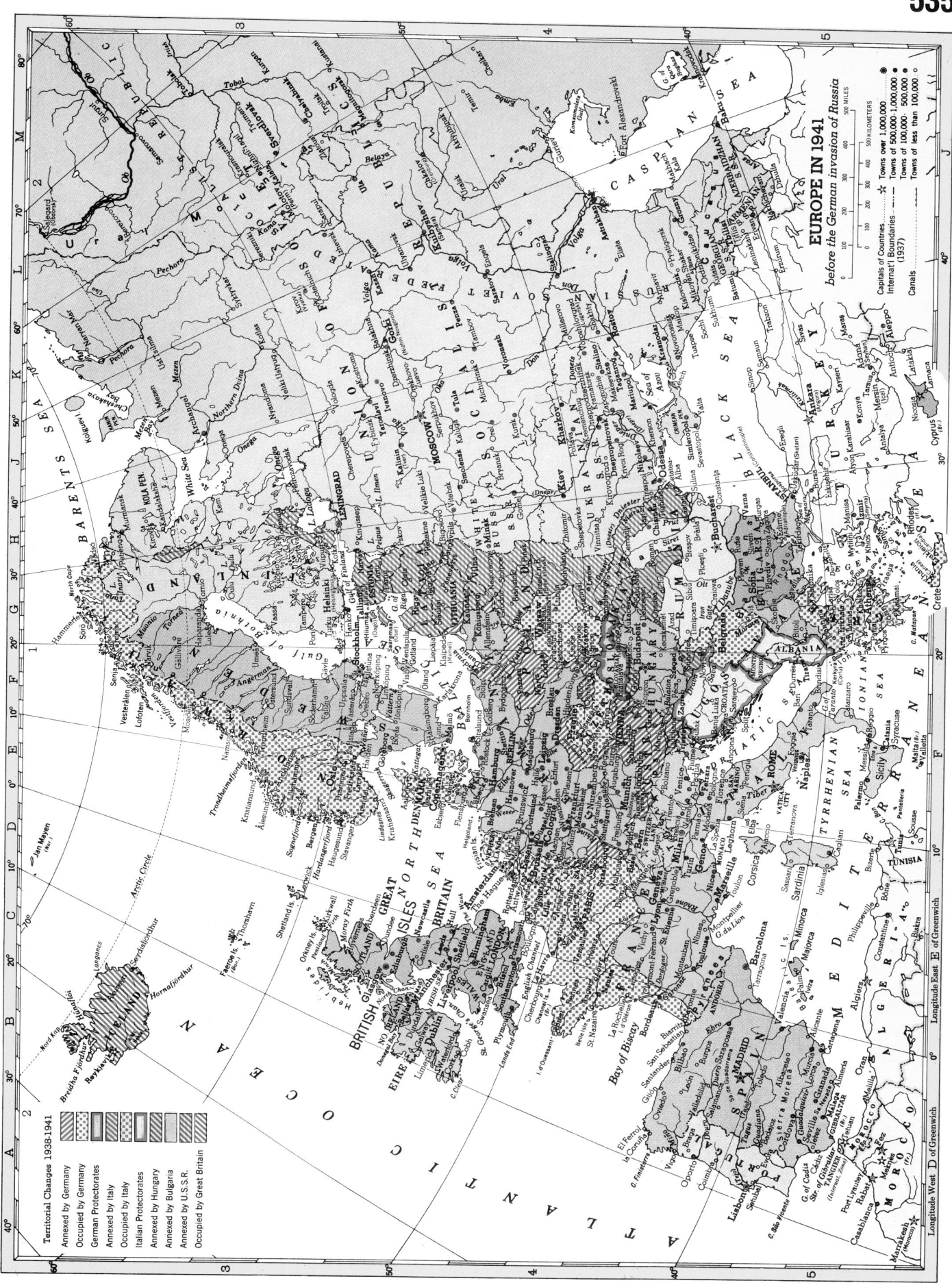

EUROPE IN 1941
before the German invasion of Russia

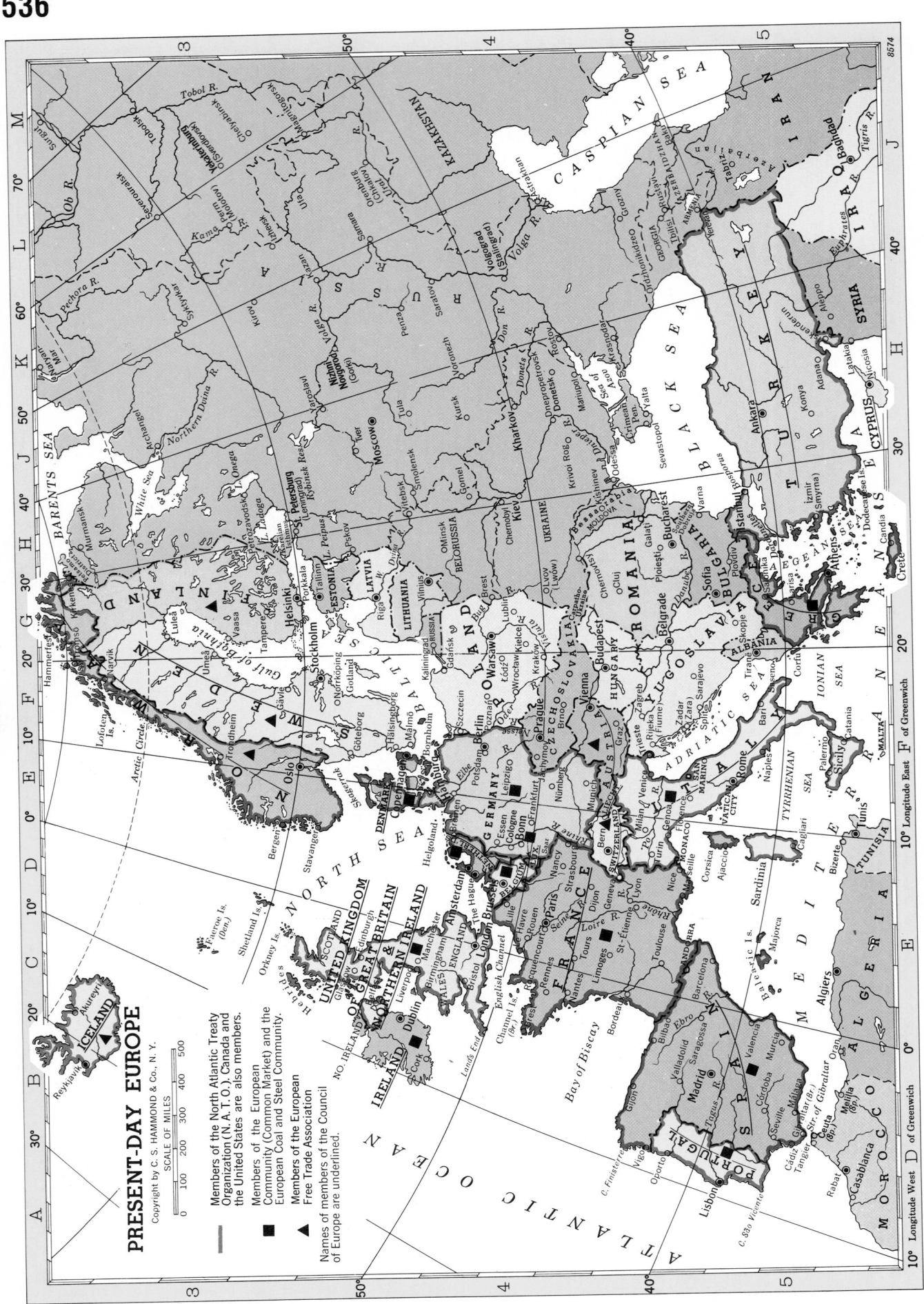
PRESENT-DAY EUROPE
Copyright by C. S. HAMMOND & Co., N. Y.
SCALE OF MILES
0 100 200 300 400 500
Members of the North Atlantic Treaty Organization (N. A. T. O.). Canada and the United States are also members.
Members of the European Community (Common Market) and the European Coal and Steel Community.
Members of the European Free Trade Association
Names of members of the Council of Europe are underlined.
10° Longitude West D of Greenwich
10° Longitude East F of Greenwich
8574

EUROPE
PHYSICAL

Copyright by C. S. HAMMOND & CO. N.Y.

Mountain Altitudes in Feet

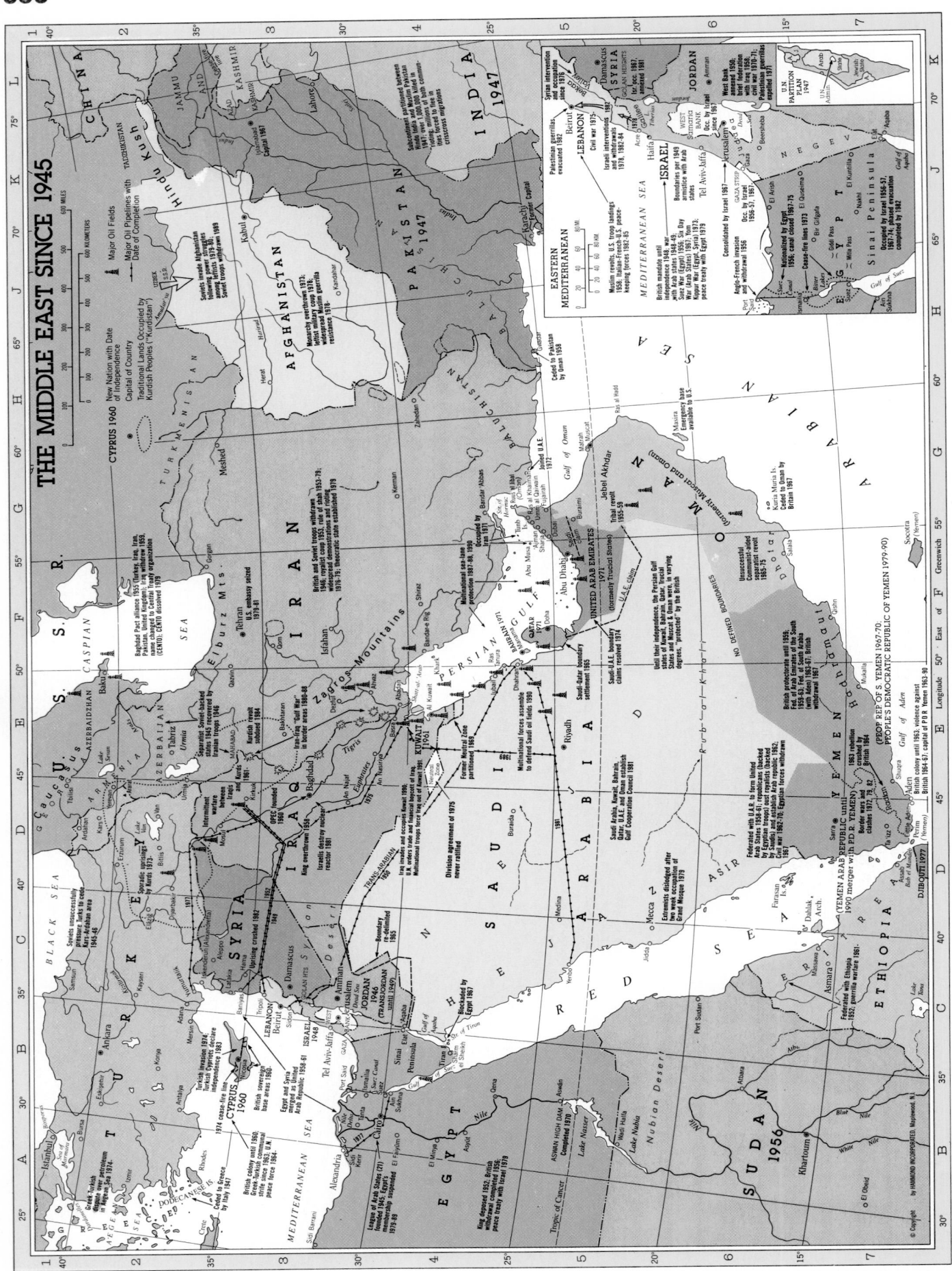

THE MIDDLE EAST SINCE 1945

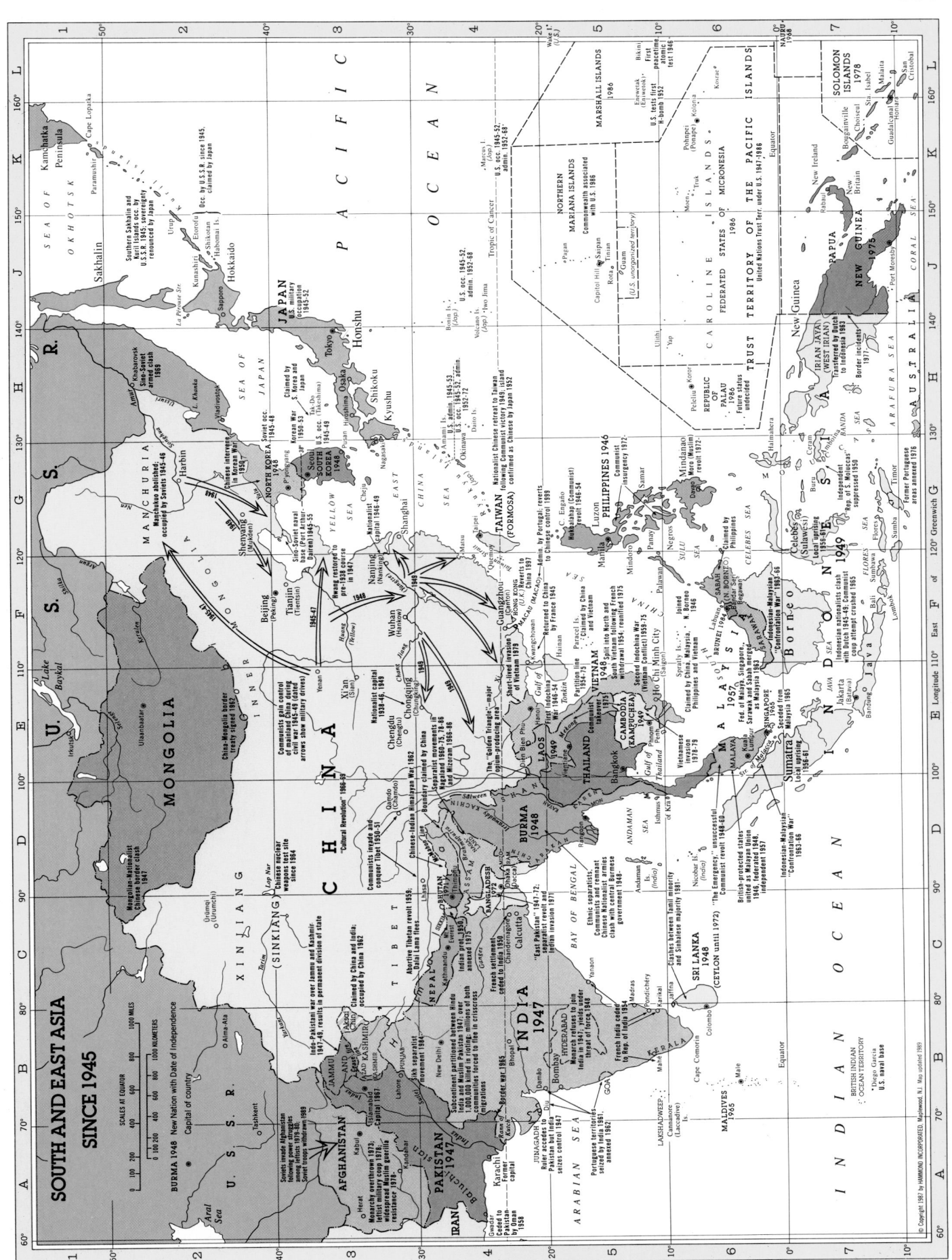

SOUTH AND EAST ASIA SINCE 1945

BURMA 1948 New Nation with Date of Independence
● Capital of country

SCALES AT EQUATOR

0 200 400 600 800 1000 MILES
0 100 200 400 600 800 1000 KILOMETERS

© Copyright 1987 by HAMMOND INCORPORATED, Maplewood, N.J. Map updated 1989

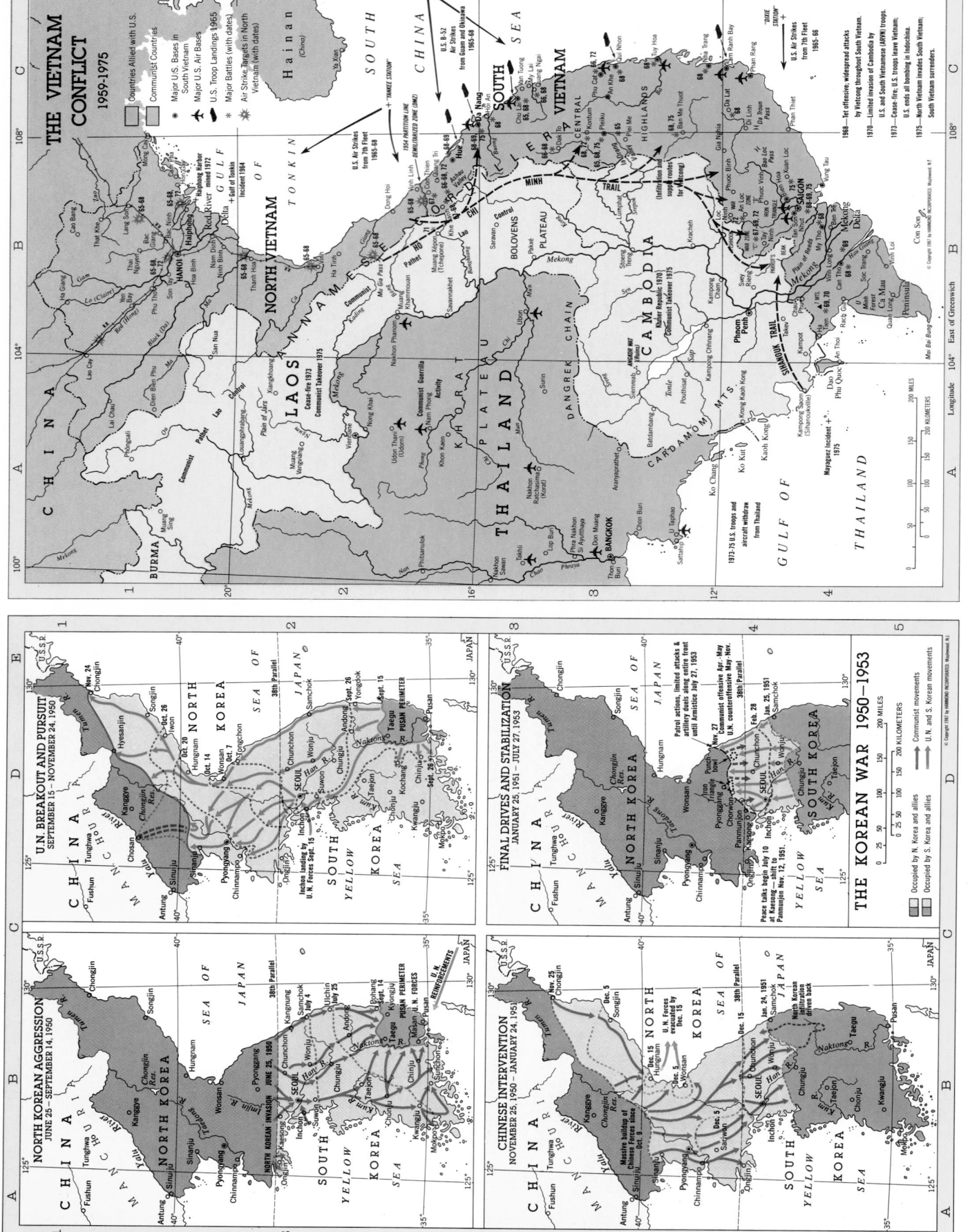

THE VIETNAM CONFLICT
1959-1975

Countries Allied with U.S.

Communist Countries

● Major U.S. Bases in South Vietnam

✈ Major U.S. Air Bases

↘ U.S. Troop Landings 1965 (with dates)

✳ Major Battles (with dates)

✴ Air Strike Targets in North Vietnam (with dates)

1968 —Tet offensive, widespread attacks by Vietcong throughout South Vietnam.

1970 —Limited invasion of Cambodia by U.S. and South Vietnamese (ARVN) troops.

1973 —Cease-fire; U.S. troops leave Vietnam; U.S. ends all bombing in Indochina.

1975 —North Vietnam invades South Vietnam; South Vietnam surrenders.

© Copyright 1987 by HAMMOND INCORPORATED, Maplewood, N.J.

THE KOREAN WAR 1950–1953

NORTH KOREAN AGGRESSION
JUNE 25 – SEPTEMBER 14, 1950

UN BREAKOUT AND PURSUIT
SEPTEMBER 15 – NOVEMBER 24, 1950

CHINESE INTERVENTION
NOVEMBER 25, 1950 – JANUARY 24, 1951

FINAL DRIVES AND STABILIZATION
JANUARY 25, 1951 – JULY 27, 1953

Occupied by N. Korea and allies

Occupied by S. Korea and allies

→ Communist movements

→ U.N. and S. Korean movements

© Copyright 1987 by HAMMOND INCORPORATED, Maplewood, N.J.

AFRICA SINCE 1945
0 200 400 600 800 MILES
0 200 400 600 800 KILOMETERS
SUDAN 1956 New Nation with Date of Independence
Capital of Country
VENDA 1979 Bantu homeland with date of grant of independence by South Africa; Independent status recognized only by South Africa
EDEA 1966 Major Dam and Date of Completion
ATLANTIC OCEAN
MEDITERRANEAN SEA
BLACK SEA
RED SEA
Persian Gulf
Gulf of Aden
INDIAN OCEAN
FRANCE
GERMANY
CZECH.
U. S. S. R.
Vienna
AUSTRIA
SWITZ.
HUNGARY
ROMANIA
YUGOSLAVIA
BULGARIA
ITALY
ALBANIA
GREECE
Athens
Istanbul
TURKEY
PORTUGAL
Madrid
SPAIN
Lisbon
Rome
French withdraw from naval base 1963
Trans-Medit. gas pipeline completed 1983
Str. of Gibraltar
Gibraltar (U.K.)
Tangier
Ceuta (Sp.)
Melilla (Sp.)
Int'l Zone to 1912, 1923-56
Algiers
Kabylia
Annaba (Bône)
Bizerte
Tunis
Sicily
Malta
Crete
CYPRUS
SYRIA
LEBANON
IRAQ
IRAN
Tehran
Madeira (Port.)
Casablanca
Rabat
Safi
MOROCCO 1956
Marrakech
Oran
Sétif Massacre May 1945
Aurès
Nat'l Liberation Front war against French 1954-62
TUNISIA 1956
Gabès
U.S. air raid 1986
U.S. airbase closed 1970
Air battle with U.S. 1985
Tripoli
Misurata
Gulf of Sidra
Benghazi
Tobruk
British bases closed 1970
Egypt and Syria merged as United Arab Republic 1958-61
ISRAEL
JORDAN
Port Said
Nationalized 1956; Anglo-French intervention 1956; canal closed 1967-75
KUWAIT
GAS
Béchar
Border in dispute
Canary Islands (Sp.)
Las Palmas
Ifni
To Morocco 1969
Tarfaya
To Morocco 1958
Laayoune
Tindouf
Saharan guerrilla activity 1976-
WESTERN SAHARA Occupied by Morocco 1976-
Dakhla (Villa Cisneros)
Occ. by Mauritania 1976-79; Morocco 1979-
Fdérik (Ft-Gouraud)
El Goléa
ALGERIA 1962
In Salah
Trans-Sahara Highway completed 1984
Tamanrasset
Tripolitania
Cyrenaica
LIBYA 1951
Monarchy overthrown 1969
Major oil discovery 1959
Sebha
Fezzan
Libyan Desert
Alexandria
Cairo
EGYPT
King deposed 1952; British withdrawal completed 1956; peace treaty with Israel 1979
Suez Canal
Sinai Pen.
Occupied by Israel 1956-57, 1967-82
SAUDI ARABIA
BAHRAIN
QATAR
U.A.E.
Riyadh
Tropic of Cancer
Qena
Nile
ASWAN HIGH 1970
Lake Nasser
Mecca
SAHARA
Occupied by Libya 1973-
Aozou
L. Nubia
Nubian Desert
Nouadhibou (Port-Étienne)
Saharan guerrilla activity 1976-77
MAURITANIA 1960
Nouakchott
(OFF MAP) CAPE VERDE 1975
Senegal
Confederation of Senegambia 1982
Cape Verde
Dakar
SENEGAL 1960
GAMBIA 1965
Banjul (Bathurst)
Bissau
GUINEA-BISSAU 1974
War against Portuguese 1962-74
Kamsar
GUINEA 1958
Conakry
SIERRA LEONE 1961
Freetown
Monrovia
LIBERIA
Cape Palmas
MALI 1960
Mali Federation (with Senegal) 1959-60
Timbuktu
Gao
Major uranium discovery 1966
Agadès
NIGER 1960
SAHEL
Severe drought and famine in Sahel region 1968-74
Bamako
Niamey
Niger
BURKINA FASO 1960 (UPPER VOLTA until 1984)
Ouagadougou
IVORY COAST (CÔTE D'IVOIRE) 1960
KOSSOU 1973
Yamoussoukro
San Pedro
Abidjan
Capital until 1985
GHANA 1957
L. Volta
AKOSOMBO 1965
Takoradi
Accra
Lomé
TOGO 1960
BENIN 1960 (DAHOMEY until 1975)
Porto Novo
Cotonou
Lagos
Ibadan
KAINJI 1968
NIGERIA 1960
Abuja (future capital)
Civil war 1967-70
Benue
Biafra
Port Harcourt
Major oil discovery in Niger Delta 1956
Kano
Maiduguri
Lake Chad
CHAD 1960
Civil war 1965-
Libyan intervention 1980-81, 83
Faya-Largeau
Abéché
N'Djamena (Ft-Lamy)
French support of gov't 1983-
Sarh (Ft-Archambault)
Shari
Logone
CENTRAL AFRICAN REPUBLIC 1960 (CENTRAL AFRICAN EMPIRE 1976-79)
Bangui
Bomu
Uele
Ubangi
SUDAN 1956
El Fasher
El Obeid
Khartoum
KHASHM EL GIRBA 1964
Blue Nile
White Nile
ROSEIRES 1966
Bahr el 'Arab
Sudd
Jonglei Canal Completed 1985
Rebellion against northern rule 1965-
Juba
Port Sudan
Atbara
Federated with Ethiopia 1952; guerrilla warfare 1961-
ERITREA
Massawa
Asmara
YEMEN
Bab el Mandeb
Aden
DJIBOUTI 1977
L. Tana
French Terr. of Afars & Issas 1967-77
Djibouti
Berbera
Hargeysa
Ras Aser (Cape Guardafui)
O.A.U. founded 1963; monarchy overthrown 1974-75
Addis Ababa
Harar
ETHIOPIA
Ogaden
Cuban troop support 1977-; severe drought and famine 1982-
War with Somalia 1964, 1975-78
HORN OF AFRICA
SOMALIA 1960
Admin. by Italy 1950-60
Webi Shabelle
Mogadishu
Border clashes 1964
L. Turkana (L. Rudolf)
KENYA 1963
Mau Mau terrorism 1952-56
Nairobi
Tana
Chisimayu
Equator
CAMEROON 1960
Douala
EDEA 1966
Yaoundé
Sanaga
Bioko (Fernando Po)
Malabo
EQUATORIAL GUINEA 1968
Bata
Rio Muni
Príncipe
SÃO TOMÉ AND PRINCIPE 1975
São Tomé
Libreville
GABON 1960
Port-Gentil
Annobón (Equat. Guinea)
French forces prevent military coup 1964
Ogooué
CONGO 1960
Sangha
Congo (Zaire)
Mbandaka (Coquilhatville)
Kisangani (Stanleyville)
Eastern rebellion 1963-64
ZAIRE 1960 (DEM. REP. OF THE CONGO 1960-71)
Reign of terror 1971-78; guerrilla activity 1981-
L. Mobutu Sese Seko (L. Albert)
L. Edward
UGANDA 1962
Kampala
Entebbe
OWEN FALLS 1959
L. Kioga
Lake Victoria
Tanzanian invasion and occupation 1978-81
Kivu
Kigali
RWANDA 1962
Tribal wars 1959, 1963-65
BURUNDI 1962
Bujumbura
Mwanza
Arusha
Tribal war 1972-73
TANZANIA 1961
Tabora
Lake Tanganyika
Dodoma (future capital)
KIDATU 1975
Tanga
Mombasa
Pemba
Zanzibar
Dar es Salaam
Mafia
Rufiji
L. Rukwa
Groundnuts Scheme—unsuccessful British agricultural development project 1947-51
Tanganyika (1961) and Zanzibar (1963) merged as TANZANIA in 1964
(OFF MAP) SEYCHELLES 1976
Brazzaville
Kinshasa (Léopoldville)
Pointe-Noire
Cabinda (Angola)
INGA 1977
Matadi
Kasai
Kwilu rebellion 1964
South Kasai
Mbuji-Mayi (Bakwanga)
Lomami
Lualaba
Kalemie (Albertville)
Katanga (Shaba)
Secessionist movement 1960-63; U.N. intervention 1961-64
L. Mweru
Tanzam Railway completed 1975
Rebel activity 1975-84
Luanda
Cuanza
ANGOLA 1975
Rebel invasions repulsed 1977-78
Guerrilla wars against Portuguese 1961-74; Cuban troop support against rebels 1975-
Rebel activity 1975-
South African raids against Namibian guerrilla bases 1975-84
Lobito
Benguela
Namibe (Moçâmedes)
CUNENE
RUACANA FALLS 1977
Okavango
Ovamboland
Caprivi Strip
Lubumbashi (Elisabethville)
COPPERBELT
ZAMBIA 1964
Fed. of Rhodesia and Nyasaland 1953-63
Zambezi
Kapiri Mposhi
Lusaka
KAFUE 1972
KARIBA 1960
L. Kariba
MALAWI 1964
Lilongwe
Lake Nyasa
Rovuma
CABORA BASSA 1974
Blantyre
MOZAMBIQUE 1975
Guerrilla wars against Portuguese 1964-74
Quelimane
Beira
Harare (Salisbury)
ZIMBABWE 1980 (ZIM.-RHO. 1979-80)
Unilateral declaration of independence as Rhodesia 1965; U.N. economic sanctions 1965-79; guerrilla war against white rule 1966-79
Bulawayo
Limpopo
VENDA 1979
Resistance movement 1979-
Guerrilla attacks against South African rule 1966-88
NAMIBIA 1990
Windhoek
Walvis Bay (South Africa)
U.N. revokes South African mandate 1966 (Admin. by S. Africa 1966-90)
Lüderitz
BOTSWANA 1966
Kalahari Desert
Gaborone
BOPHUTHATSWANA 1977
Pretoria
Soweto riots 1976
Rand
Johannesburg
Vaal
Sharpeville massacre 1960
Maputo (Lourenço Marques)
Mbabane
SWAZILAND 1968
Zululand
Kimberley
Orange
Bloemfontein
LESOTHO 1966
Maseru
Durban
LE ROUX 1977
VERWOERD 1971
SOUTH AFRICA (UNION OF SOUTH AFRICA UNTIL 1961)
TRANSKEI 1976
Umtata
CISKEI 1981
East London
Port Elizabeth
Cape Town
Cape of Good Hope
Cape Agulhas
Apartheid becomes official state policy 1948; creation of black homelands 1959; withdrawal from Br. Commonwealth 1961; U.N. arms embargo 1977-
Aldabra Is.
Cosmoledo Is. (Seychelles)
Mtwara-Mikindani
COMOROS 1975
Njazidja
Moroni
Nzwani
Mwali
Mayotte (Fr.-claimed by Comoros)
Nacala
Antsiranana (Diégo-Suarez)
Mozambique Channel
Mahajanga (Majunga)
Nationalist uprising 1947-48
Juan de Nova (Réunion)
Antananarivo (Tananarive)
Toamasina (Tamatave)
MADAGASCAR 1960 (MALAGASY REPUBLIC 1958-75)
Bassas da India (Réunion)
Europa (Réunion)
(OFF MAP) MAURITIUS 1968
Réunion (Fr.)
Tropic of Capricorn
Cape Vohimena (C. Ste-Marie)
Faradofay (Ft-Dauphin)
Ascension (St. Helena)
St. Helena (United Kingdom)
AFRICA 1945
TANGIER
MOROCCO
TUNISIA
IFNI
ALGERIA
SPANISH SAHARA
LIBYA
Adm.
EGYPT
MAURITANIA
FRENCH SUDAN
NIGER
FRENCH WEST AFRICA
CHAD
ANGLO-EGYPTIAN SUDAN
ERITREA
FR. SOMALILAND
SOMALILAND PROT.
ETHIOPIA
SENEGAL
GAMBIA
PORT. GUINEA
FR. GUINEA
UPPER VOLTA
DAHOMEY
NIGERIA
SIERRA LEONE
LIBERIA
IVORY COAST
GOLD COAST
TOGO
CAMEROONS
FRENCH EQUATORIAL AFRICA
UBANGI-SHARI
SPANISH GUINEA
SÃO TOMÉ E PRÍNCIPE
GABON
MIDDLE CONGO
BELGIAN CONGO
RUANDA-URUNDI
UGANDA
KENYA
SOMALIA
TANGANYIKA
ZANZIBAR
ANGOLA
NORTHERN RHODESIA
NYASALAND
COMORO IS.
SOUTHERN RHODESIA
MOZAMBIQUE
MADAGASCAR
SOUTH-WEST AFRICA
BECHUANALAND PROT.
UNION OF SOUTH AFRICA
SWAZILAND
BASUTOLAND
BRITISH
FRENCH
SPANISH
PORTUGUESE
BELGIAN
Mandates
Adm. Administration
Longitude West A of Greenwich
Longitude East B of Greenwich

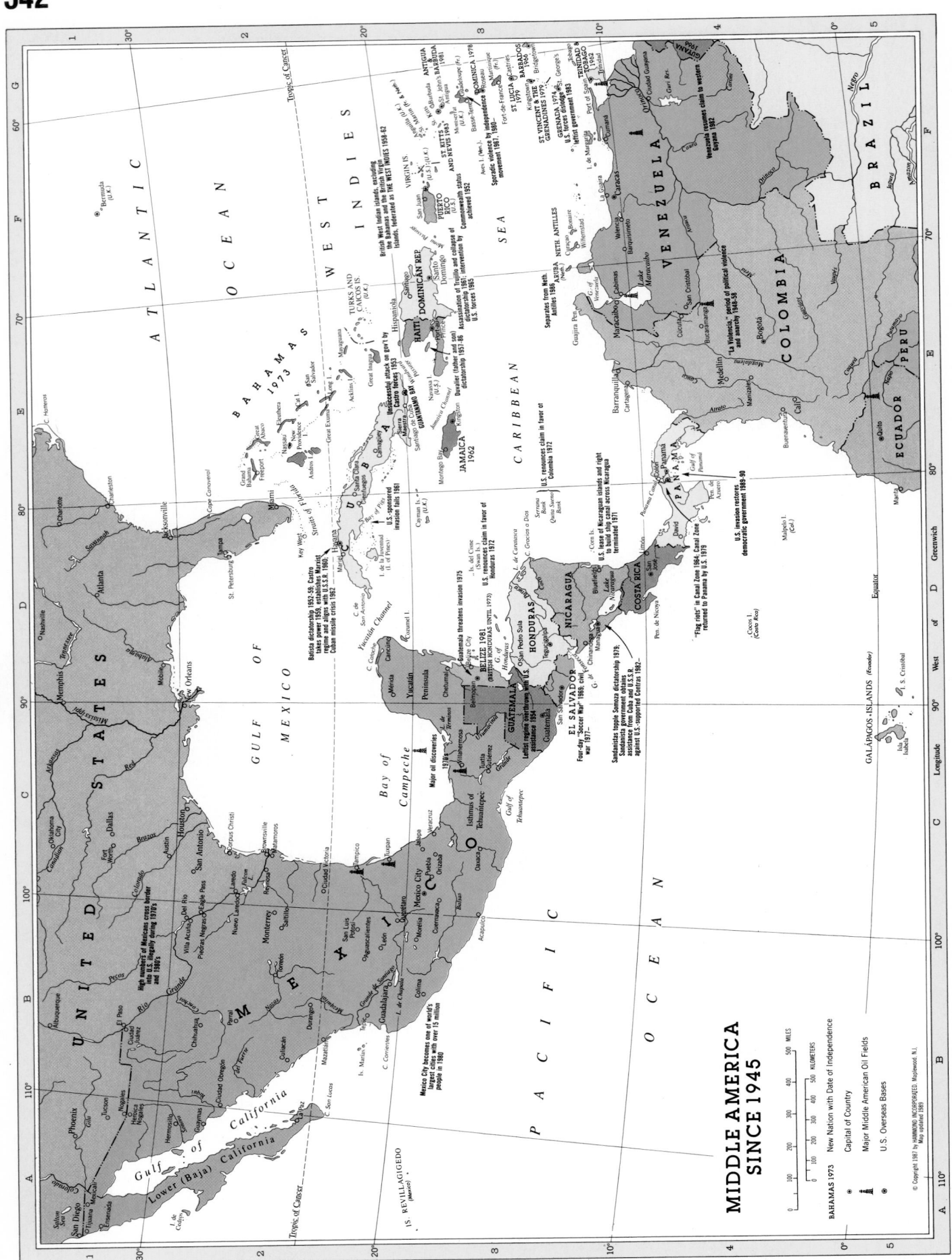

MIDDLE AMERICA
SINCE 1945

BAHAMAS 1973   New Nation with Date of Independence
⊛   Capital of Country
⛟   Major Middle American Oil Fields
⚓   U.S. Overseas Bases

© Copyright 1987 by HAMMOND INCORPORATED, Maplewood, N.J.
Map updated 1989

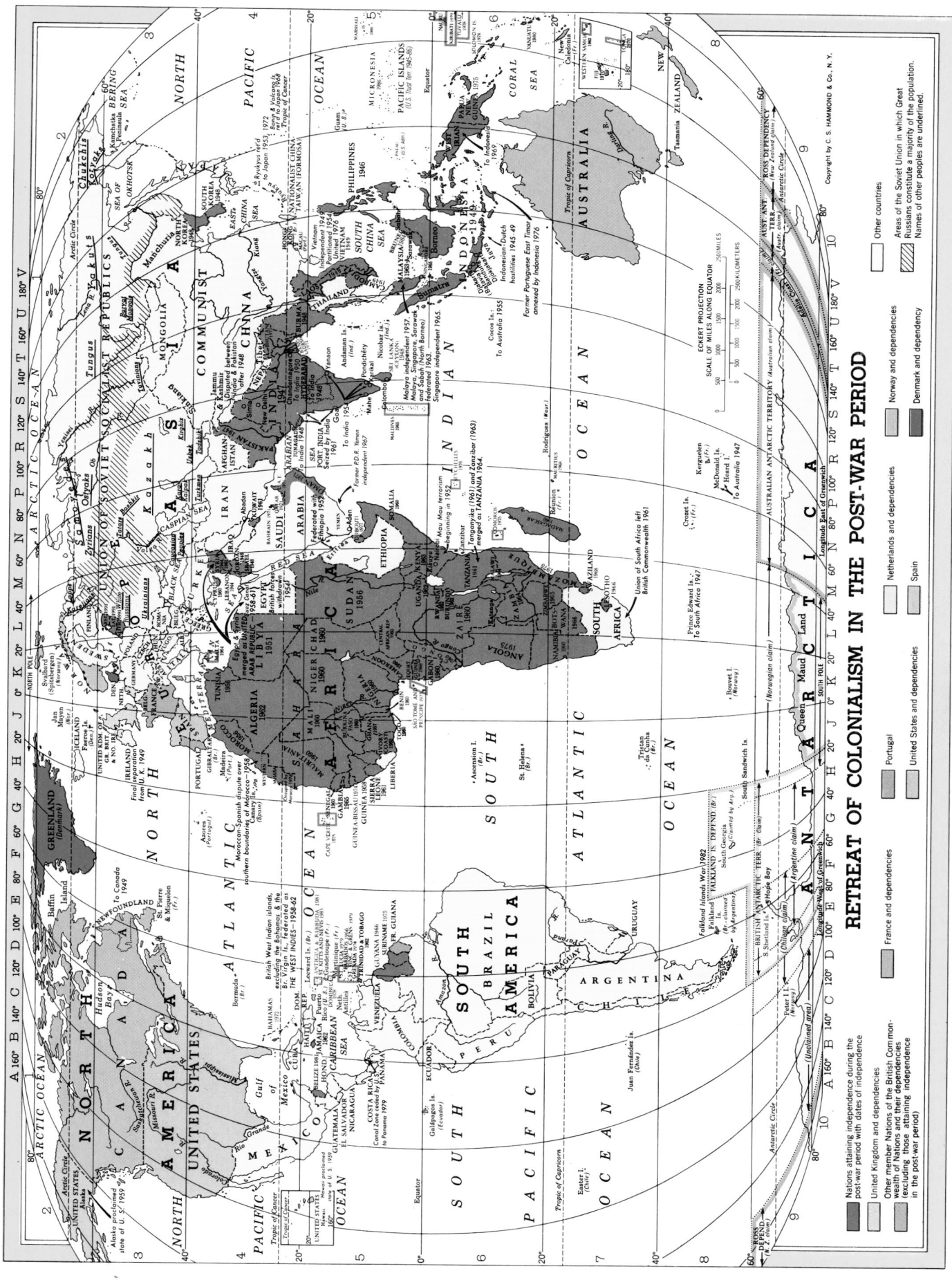

RETREAT OF COLONIALISM IN THE POST-WAR PERIOD

- Nations attaining independence during the post-war period with dates of independence
- United Kingdom and dependencies
- Other member Nations of the British Commonwealth of Nations and their dependencies (excluding those attaining independence in the post-war period)
- France and dependencies
- Portugal
- United States and dependencies
- Netherlands and dependencies
- Spain
- Norway and dependencies
- Denmark and dependency
- Other countries
- Areas of the Soviet Union in which Great Russians constitute a majority of the population. Names of other peoples are underlined.

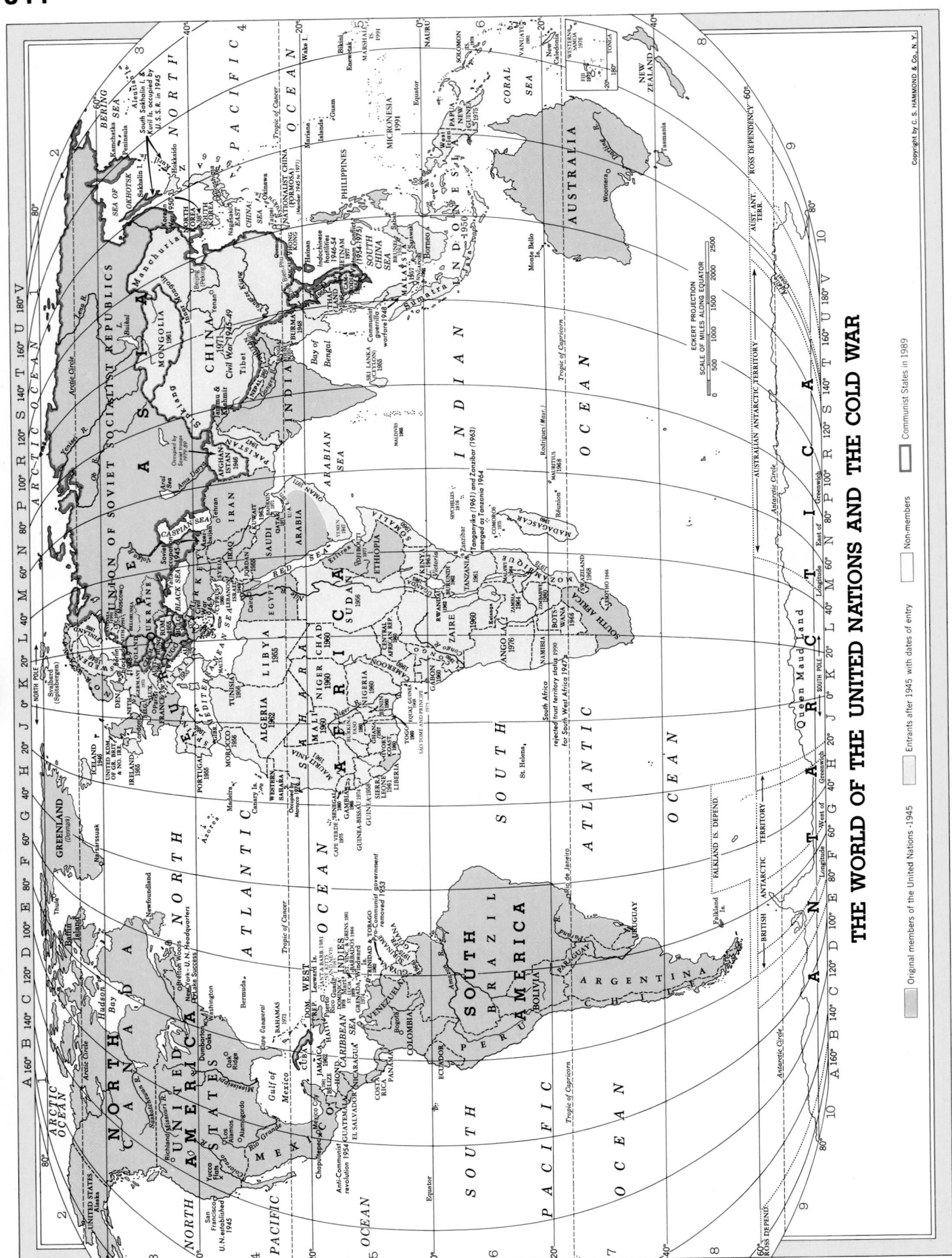

THE WORLD OF THE UNITED NATIONS AND THE COLD WAR

Original members of the United Nations -1945

Entrants after 1945 with dates of entry

Non-members

Communist States in 1989

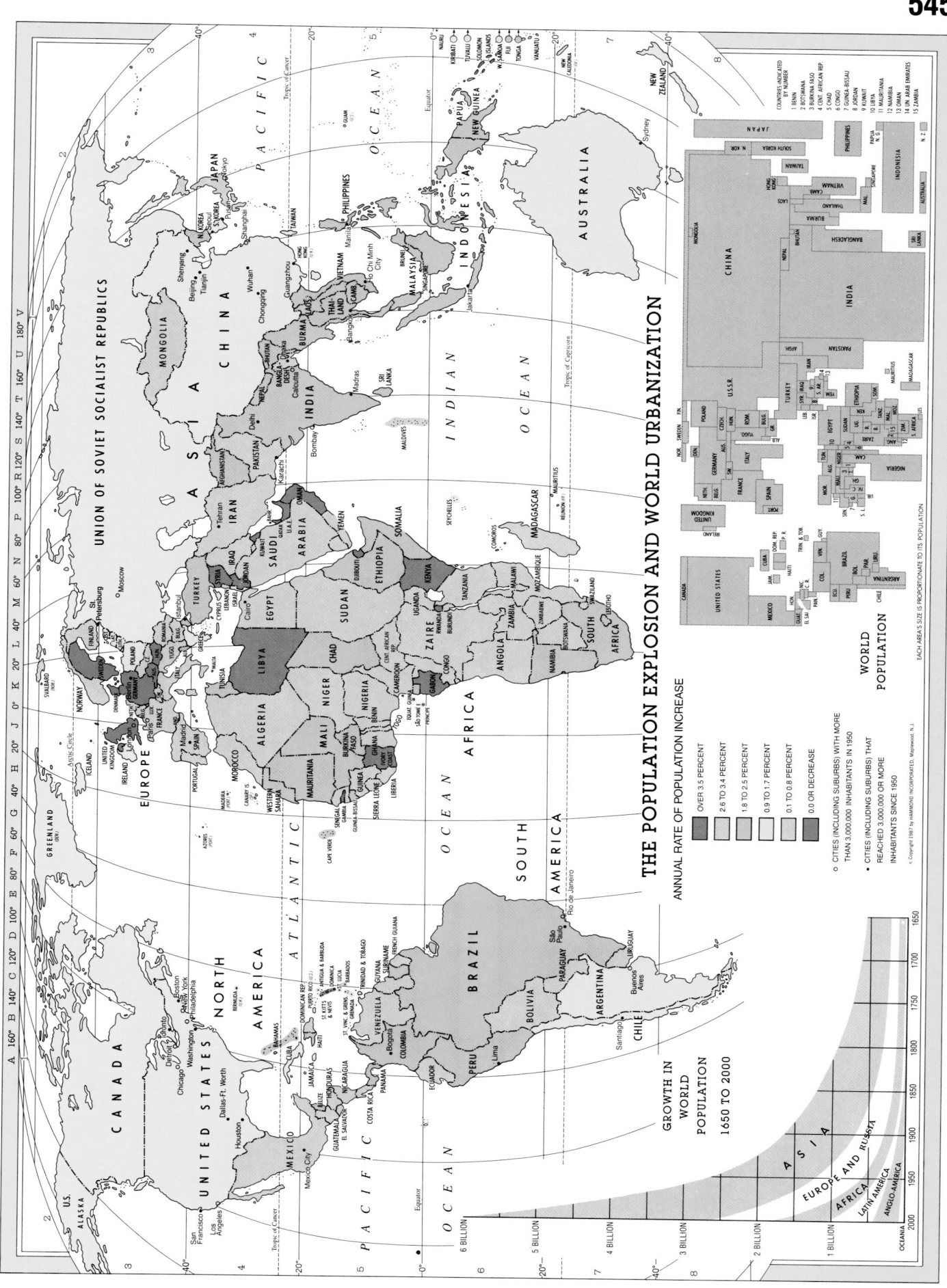

THE POPULATION EXPLOSION AND WORLD URBANIZATION

ANNUAL RATE OF POPULATION INCREASE

OVER 3.5 PERCENT
2.6 TO 3.4 PERCENT
1.8 TO 2.5 PERCENT
0.9 TO 1.7 PERCENT
0.1 TO 0.8 PERCENT
0.0 OR DECREASE

○ CITIES (INCLUDING SUBURBS) WITH MORE THAN 3,000,000 INHABITANTS IN 1950
● CITIES (INCLUDING SUBURBS) THAT REACHED 3,000,000 OR MORE INHABITANTS SINCE 1950

WORLD POPULATION

EACH AREA'S SIZE IS PROPORTIONATE TO ITS POPULATION

COUNTRIES INDICATED BY NUMBER
1 BENIN
2 BOTSWANA
3 BURKINA FASO
4 CENT. AFRICAN REP.
5 CHAD
6 CONGO
7 GUINEA-BISSAU
8 JORDAN
9 KUWAIT
10 LIBYA
11 MAURITANIA
12 NAMIBIA
13 OMAN
14 UN. ARAB EMIRATES
15 ZAMBIA

GROWTH IN WORLD POPULATION 1650 TO 2000

© Copyright 1987 by HAMMOND INCORPORATED, Maplewood, N.J.

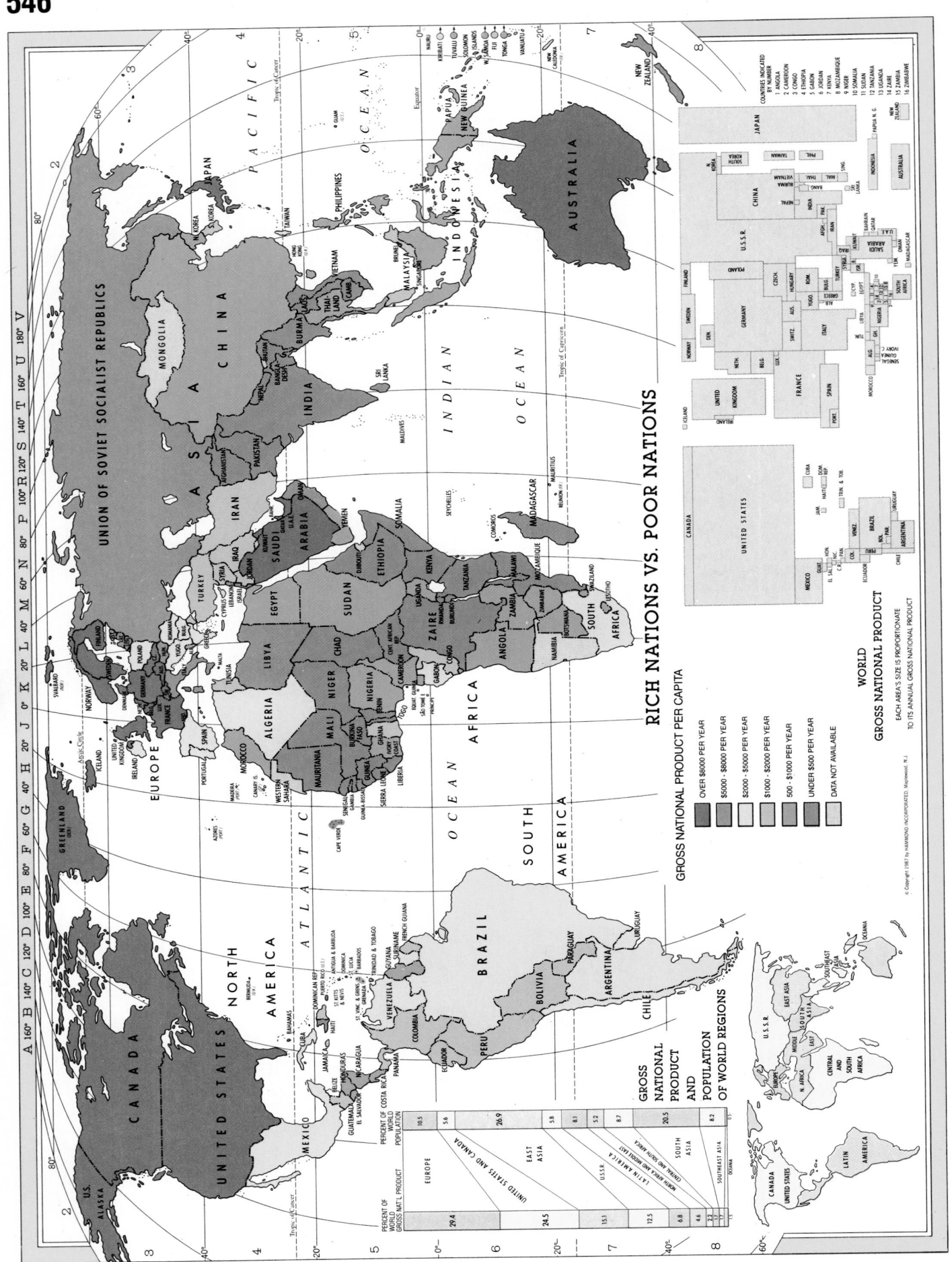

RICH NATIONS vs. POOR NATIONS

GROSS NATIONAL PRODUCT PER CAPITA

- OVER $8000 PER YEAR
- $5000 - $8000 PER YEAR
- $2000 - $5000 PER YEAR
- $1000 - $2000 PER YEAR
- 500 - $1000 PER YEAR
- UNDER $500 PER YEAR
- DATA NOT AVAILABLE

© Copyright 1987 by HAMMOND INCORPORATED, Maplewood, N.J.

WORLD
GROSS NATIONAL PRODUCT
EACH AREA'S SIZE IS PROPORTIONATE
TO ITS ANNUAL GROSS NATIONAL PRODUCT

COUNTRIES INDICATED
BY NUMBER
1 Angola
2 Cameroon
3 Congo
4 Ethiopia
5 Gabon
6 Jordan
7 Kenya
8 Mozambique
9 Niger
10 Somalia
11 Sudan
12 Tanzania
13 Uganda
14 Zaire
15 Zambia
16 Zimbabwe

GROSS NATIONAL PRODUCT AND POPULATION OF WORLD REGIONS

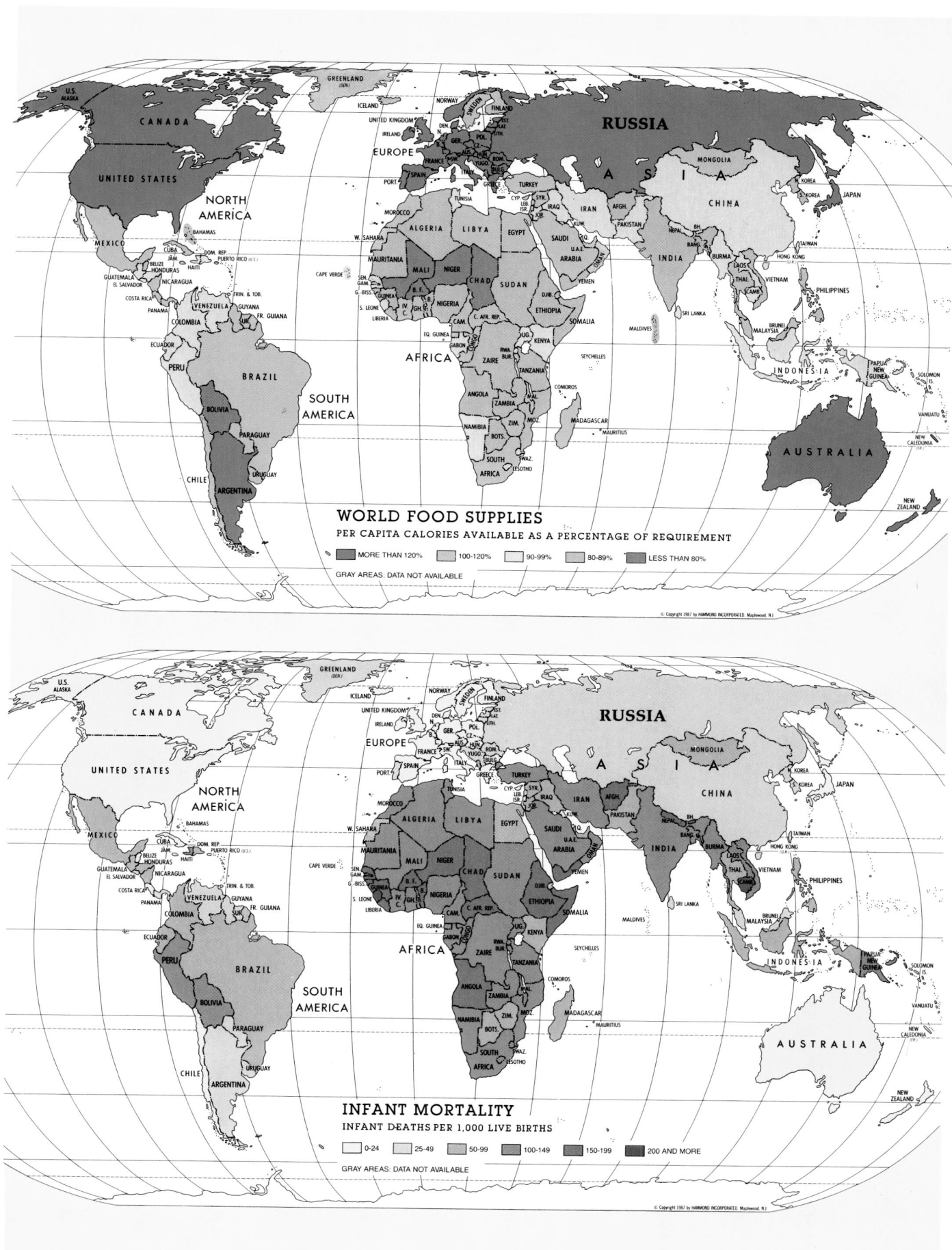

WORLD FOOD SUPPLIES

PER CAPITA CALORIES AVAILABLE AS A PERCENTAGE OF REQUIREMENT

MORE THAN 120% 100-120% 90-99% 80-89% LESS THAN 80%

GRAY AREAS: DATA NOT AVAILABLE

© Copyright 1987 by HAMMOND INCORPORATED, Maplewood, N.J.

INFANT MORTALITY

INFANT DEATHS PER 1,000 LIVE BIRTHS

0-24 25-49 50-99 100-149 150-199 200 AND MORE

GRAY AREAS: DATA NOT AVAILABLE

© Copyright 1987 by HAMMOND INCORPORATED, Maplewood, N.J.

TIME CHART

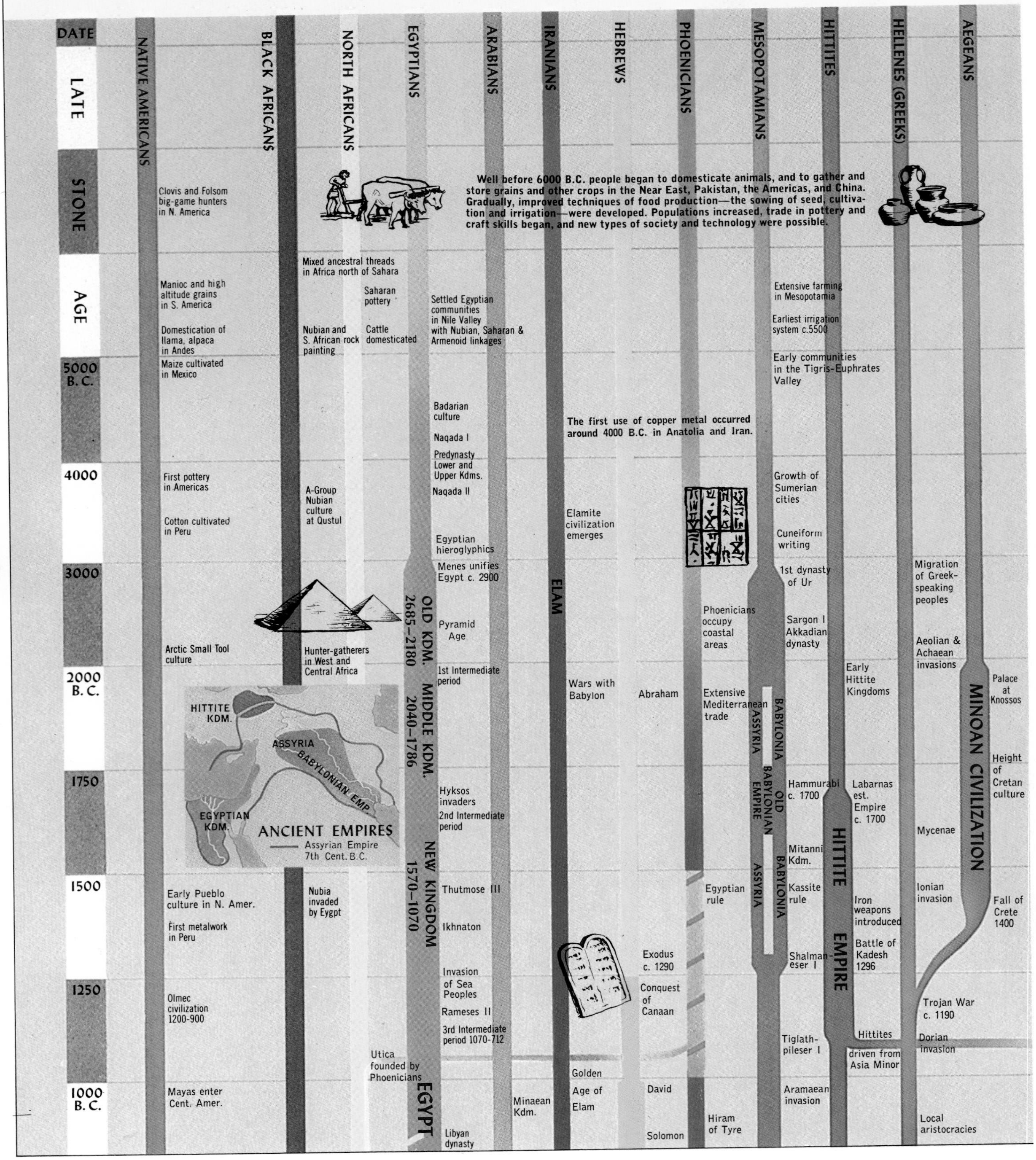

DATE: LATE · STONE · AGE · 5000 B.C. · 4000 · 3000 · 2000 B.C. · 1750 · 1500 · 1250 · 1000 B.C.

Well before 6000 B.C. people began to domesticate animals, and to gather and store grains and other crops in the Near East, Pakistan, the Americas, and China. Gradually, improved techniques of food production—the sowing of seed, cultivation and irrigation—were developed. Populations increased, trade in pottery and craft skills began, and new types of society and technology were possible.

The first use of copper metal occurred around 4000 B.C. in Anatolia and Iran.

NATIVE AMERICANS
- Clovis and Folsom big-game hunters in N. America
- Manioc and high altitude grains in S. America
- Domestication of llama, alpaca in Andes
- Maize cultivated in Mexico
- First pottery in Americas
- Cotton cultivated in Peru
- Arctic Small Tool culture
- Early Pueblo culture in N. Amer.
- First metalwork in Peru
- Olmec civilization 1200-900
- Mayas enter Cent. Amer.

BLACK AFRICANS
- Mixed ancestral threads in Africa north of Sahara
- Nubian and S. African rock painting
- A-Group Nubian culture at Qustul
- Hunter-gatherers in West and Central Africa

NORTH AFRICANS
- Saharan pottery
- Cattle domesticated
- Nubia invaded by Eygpt

EGYPTIANS
- Settled Egyptian communities in Nile Valley with Nubian, Saharan & Armenoid linkages
- Badarian culture
- Naqada I
- Predynasty Lower and Upper Kdms.
- Naqada II
- Egyptian hieroglyphics
- Menes unifies Egypt c. 2900
- Pyramid Age
- OLD KDM. 2685-2180
- 1st Intermediate period
- MIDDLE KDM. 2040-1786
- Hyksos invaders
- 2nd Intermediate period
- NEW KINGDOM 1570-1070
- Thutmose III
- Ikhnaton
- Invasion of Sea Peoples
- Rameses II
- 3rd Intermediate period 1070-712
- Utica founded by Phoenicians
- EGYPT
- Libyan dynasty

IRANIANS
- Elamite civilization emerges
- ELAM
- Wars with Babylon
- Minaean Kdm.
- Golden Age of Elam

HEBREWS
- Abraham
- Exodus c. 1290
- Conquest of Canaan
- David
- Solomon

PHOENICIANS
- Phoenicians occupy coastal areas
- Extensive Mediterranean trade
- Egyptian rule
- Hiram of Tyre

MESOPOTAMIANS
- Extensive farming in Mesopotamia
- Earliest irrigation system c.5500
- Early communities in the Tigris-Euphrates Valley
- Growth of Sumerian cities
- Cuneiform writing
- 1st dynasty of Ur
- Sargon I Akkadian dynasty
- BABYLONIA / ASSYRIA
- OLD BABYLONIAN EMPIRE
- Hammurabi c. 1700
- Mitanni Kdm.
- Kassite rule
- Shalmaneser I
- Tiglath-pileser I
- Aramaean invasion

HITTITES
- Early Hittite Kingdoms
- Labarnas est. Empire c. 1700
- HITTITE EMPIRE
- Iron weapons introduced
- Battle of Kadesh 1296
- Hittites driven from Asia Minor

HELLENES (GREEKS)
- Migration of Greek-speaking peoples
- Aeolian & Achaean invasions
- Mycenae
- Ionian invasion
- Trojan War c. 1190
- Dorian invasion

AEGEANS
- Palace at Knossos
- MINOAN CIVILIZATION
- Height of Cretan culture
- Fall of Crete 1400
- Local aristocracies

Map inset
ANCIENT EMPIRES — Assyrian Empire 7th Cent. B.C.
HITTITE KDM. · ASSYRIA · BABYLONIAN EMP. · EGYPTIAN KDM.

A Graphic History of Mankind

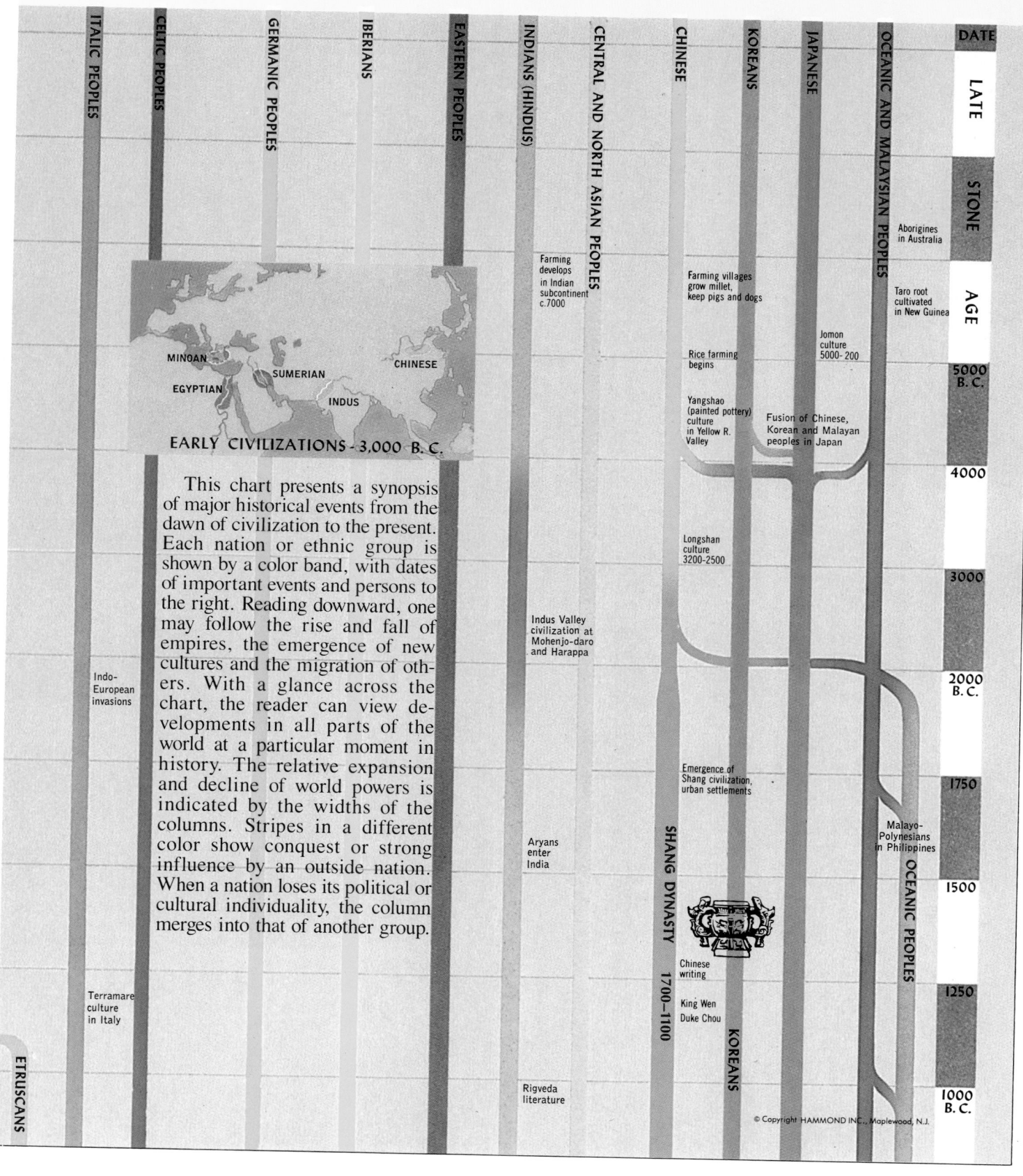

ITALIC PEOPLES

CELTIC PEOPLES

GERMANIC PEOPLES

IBERIANS

EASTERN PEOPLES

INDIANS (HINDUS)

CENTRAL AND NORTH ASIAN PEOPLES

CHINESE

KOREANS

JAPANESE

OCEANIC AND MALAYSIAN PEOPLES

DATE

LATE

STONE

AGE

5000 B.C.

4000

3000

2000 B.C.

1750

1500

1250

1000 B.C.

MINOAN

EGYPTIAN

SUMERIAN

INDUS

CHINESE

EARLY CIVILIZATIONS - 3,000 B.C.

This chart presents a synopsis of major historical events from the dawn of civilization to the present. Each nation or ethnic group is shown by a color band, with dates of important events and persons to the right. Reading downward, one may follow the rise and fall of empires, the emergence of new cultures and the migration of others. With a glance across the chart, the reader can view developments in all parts of the world at a particular moment in history. The relative expansion and decline of world powers is indicated by the widths of the columns. Stripes in a different color show conquest or strong influence by an outside nation. When a nation loses its political or cultural individuality, the column merges into that of another group.

Farming develops in Indian subcontinent c.7000

Farming villages grow millet, keep pigs and dogs

Taro root cultivated in New Guinea

Aborigines in Australia

Rice farming begins

Jomon culture 5000- 200

Yangshao (painted pottery) culture in Yellow R. Valley

Fusion of Chinese, Korean and Malayan peoples in Japan

Longshan culture 3200-2500

Indus Valley civilization at Mohenjo-daro and Harappa

Indo-European invasions

Emergence of Shang civilization, urban settlements

Malayo-Polynesians in Philippines

OCEANIC PEOPLES

Aryans enter India

SHANG DYNASTY 1700–1100

Chinese writing

King Wen Duke Chou

Terramare culture in Italy

KOREANS

ETRUSCANS

Rigveda literature

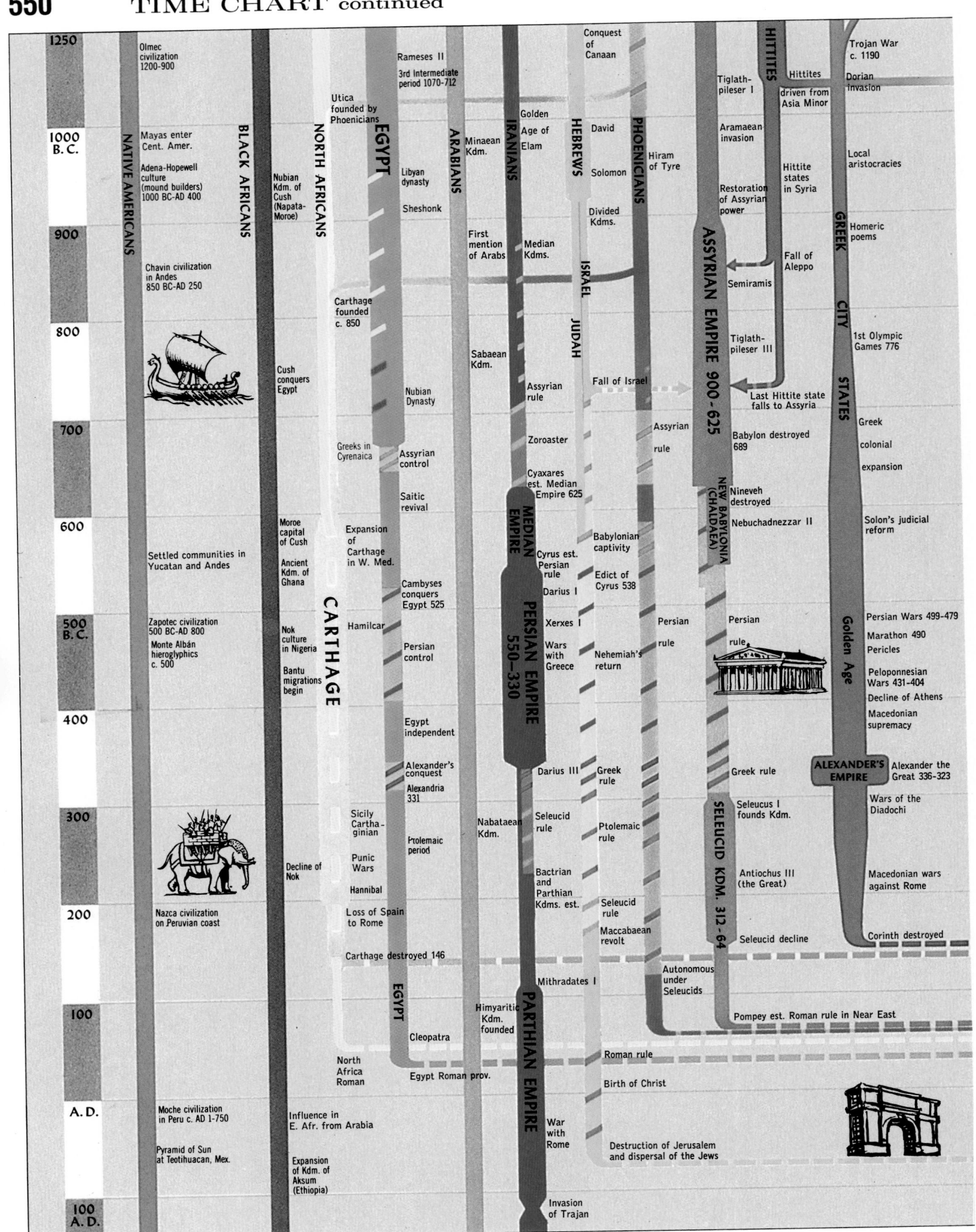

1250	Olmec civilization 1200-900				Utica founded by Phoenicians	Rameses II 3rd Intermediate period 1070-712				Conquest of Canaan				HITTITES	Hittites driven from Asia Minor	Tiglath-pileser I	Trojan War c. 1190	Dorian invasion

NATIVE AMERICANS · BLACK AFRICANS · NORTH AFRICANS · EGYPT · ARABIANS · IRANIANS · HEBREWS · PHOENICIANS · ASSYRIAN EMPIRE 900-625 · GREEK CITY STATES

1000 B.C.	Mayas enter Cent. Amer.					Libyan dynasty	Minaean Kdm.	Golden Age of Elam	David · Solomon	Hiram of Tyre		Aramaean invasion	Hittite states in Syria	Restoration of Assyrian power	Local aristocracies
	Adena-Hopewell culture (mound builders) 1000 BC-AD 400		Nubian Kdm. of Cush (Napata-Moroe)			Sheshonk								
900							First mention of Arabs	Median Kdms.	Divided Kdms.		Semiramis	Fall of Aleppo	Homeric poems
	Chavin civilization in Andes 850 BC-AD 250				Carthage founded c. 850				ISRAEL · JUDAH				
800			Cush conquers Egypt				Sabaean Kdm.				Tiglath-pileser III		1st Olympic Games 776
700			Greeks in Cyrenaica		Nubian Dynasty		Assyrian rule	Fall of Israel	Assyrian rule	Babylon destroyed 689	Last Hittite state falls to Assyria	Greek colonial expansion
				Assyrian control		Zoroaster				NEW BABYLONIA (CHALDAEA)	Nineveh destroyed
600		Moroe capital of Cush · Ancient Kdm. of Ghana	Saitic revival		Cyaxares est. Median Empire 625			Babylonian captivity	Assyrian rule	Nebuchadnezzar II	Solon's judicial reform
	Settled communities in Yucatan and Andes		Expansion of Carthage in W. Med.		MEDIAN EMPIRE · Cyrus est. Persian rule · Darius I		Edict of Cyrus 538			
500 B.C.	Zapotec civilization 500 BC-AD 800 · Monte Albán hieroglyphics c. 500	Nok culture in Nigeria	Hamilcar · Persian control		PERSIAN EMPIRE 550-330 · Xerxes I · Wars with Greece		Nehemiah's return	Persian rule	Persian rule · Golden Age	Persian Wars 499-479 · Marathon 490 · Pericles
		Bantu migrations begin							Peloponnesian Wars 431-404 · Decline of Athens · Macedonian supremacy
400			Egypt independent						
			Alexander's conquest · Alexandria 331		Darius III	Greek rule		Greek rule · ALEXANDER'S EMPIRE · Alexander the Great 336-323	Wars of the Diadochi
300		Sicily Carthaginian	Ptolemaic period	Nabataean Kdm.	Seleucid rule	Ptolemaic rule		Seleucus I founds Kdm. · SELEUCID KDM. 312-64	
		CARTHAGE · Punic Wars · Hannibal			Bactrian and Parthian Kdms. est.	Seleucid rule		Antiochus III (the Great)	Macedonian wars against Rome
200	Nazca civilization on Peruvian coast · Decline of Nok	Loss of Spain to Rome				Maccabaean revolt		Seleucid decline	Corinth destroyed
		Carthage destroyed 146						Autonomous under Seleucids	
100		EGYPT · Cleopatra	Himyaritic Kdm. founded	Mithradates I · PARTHIAN EMPIRE			Pompey est. Roman rule in Near East
		North Africa Roman · Egypt Roman prov.			Roman rule		
A.D.	Moche civilization in Peru c. AD 1-750 · Pyramid of Sun at Teotihuacan, Mex.	Influence in E. Afr. from Arabia				Birth of Christ	
		Expansion of Kdm. of Aksum (Ethiopia)		War with Rome	Destruction of Jerusalem and dispersal of the Jews	
100 A.D.				Invasion of Trajan		

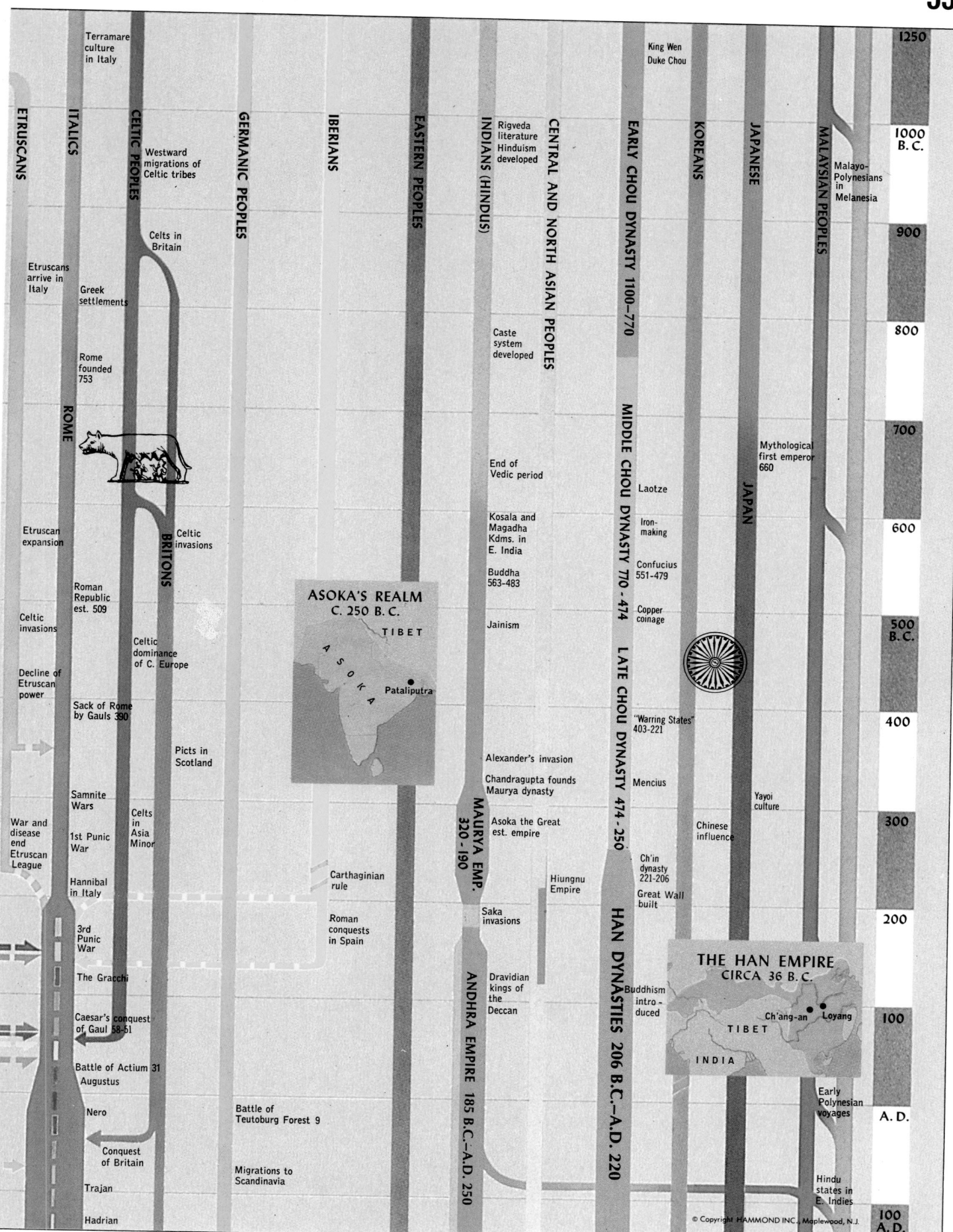

1250

1000 B.C.

900

800

700

600

500 B.C.

400

300

200

100

A.D.

100 A.D.

ETRUSCANS

ITALICS

CELTIC PEOPLES

GERMANIC PEOPLES

IBERIANS

EASTERN PEOPLES

INDIANS (HINDUS)

CENTRAL AND NORTH ASIAN PEOPLES

EARLY CHOU DYNASTY 1100–770

KOREANS

JAPANESE

MALAYSIAN PEOPLES

Terramare culture in Italy

Westward migrations of Celtic tribes

Celts in Britain

Etruscans arrive in Italy

Greek settlements

ROME

Rome founded 753

Etruscan expansion

BRITONS

Celtic invasions

Roman Republic est. 509

Celtic invasions

Celtic dominance of C. Europe

Decline of Etruscan power

Sack of Rome by Gauls 390

Picts in Scotland

War and disease end Etruscan League

Samnite Wars

1st Punic War

Celts in Asia Minor

Hannibal in Italy

3rd Punic War

The Gracchi

Caesar's conquest of Gaul 58-51

Battle of Actium 31 Augustus

Nero

Battle of Teutoburg Forest 9

Conquest of Britain

Trajan

Migrations to Scandinavia

Hadrian

Rigveda literature Hinduism developed

Caste system developed

End of Vedic period

Kosala and Magadha Kdms. in E. India

Buddha 563-483

Jainism

Alexander's invasion

Chandragupta founds Maurya dynasty

MAURYA EMP. 320 - 190

Asoka the Great est. empire

Saka invasions

Dravidian kings of the Deccan

ANDHRA EMPIRE 185 B.C.-A.D. 250

ASOKA'S REALM C. 250 B.C.

TIBET

ASOKA

Pataliputra

Hiungnu Empire

MIDDLE CHOU DYNASTY 770 - 474

LATE CHOU DYNASTY 474 - 250

Laotze

Iron-making

Confucius 551-479

Copper coinage

"Warring States" 403-221

Mencius

HAN DYNASTIES 206 B.C.-A.D. 220

Ch'in dynasty 221-206

Great Wall built

Buddhism intro-duced

THE HAN EMPIRE CIRCA 36 B.C.

TIBET

Ch'ang-an   Loyang

INDIA

King Wen Duke Chou

JAPAN

Mythological first emperor 660

Yayoi culture

Chinese influence

Malayo-Polynesians in Melanesia

Early Polynesian voyages

Hindu states in E. Indies

© Copyright HAMMOND INC., Maplewood, N.J.

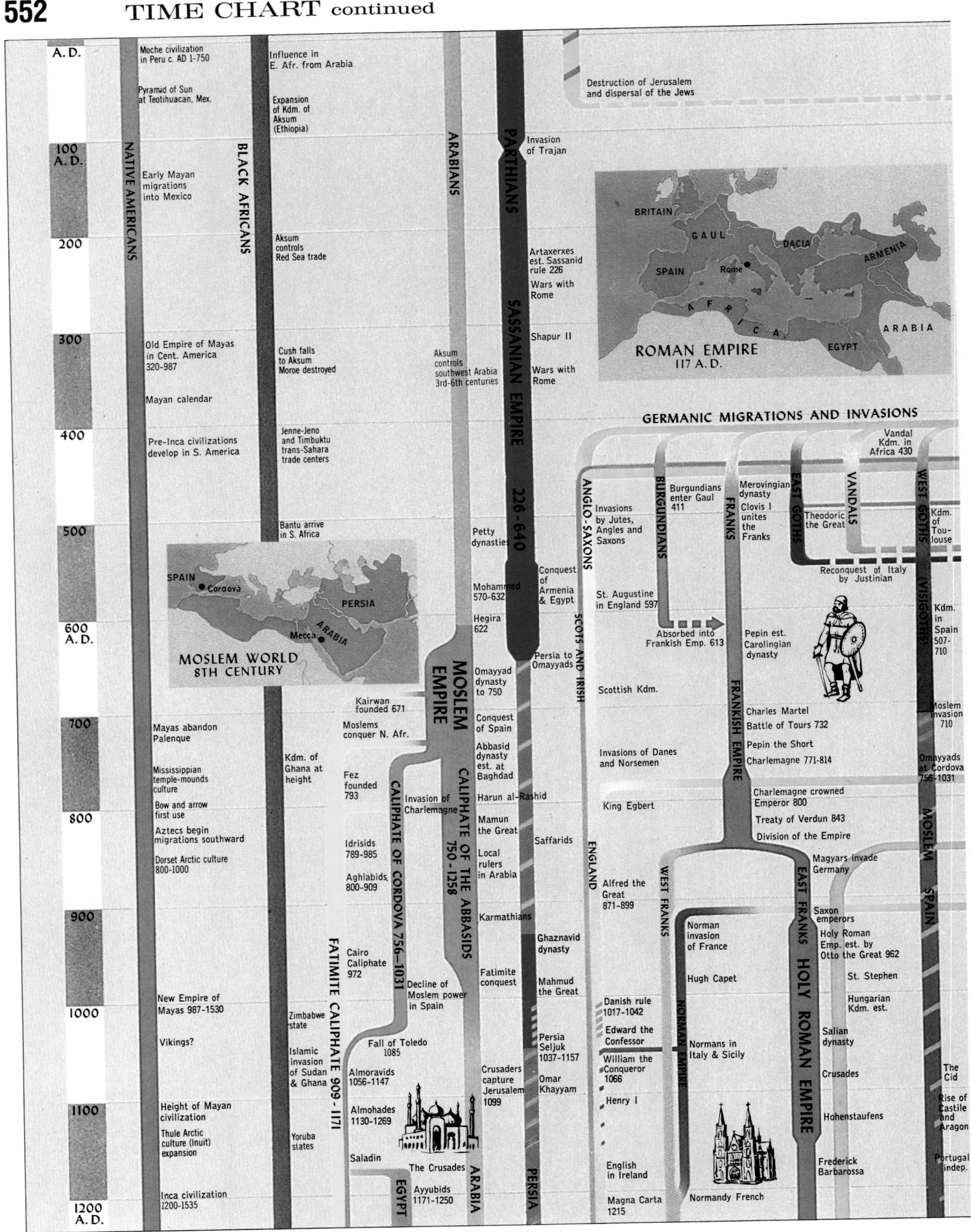

A.D.

Moche civilization in Peru c. AD 1-750

Pyramid of Sun at Teotihuacan, Mex.

Influence in E. Afr. from Arabia

Expansion of Kdm. of Aksum (Ethiopia)

Destruction of Jerusalem and dispersal of the Jews

100 A.D.

Early Mayan migrations into Mexico

Invasion of Trajan

200

Aksum controls Red Sea trade

Artaxerxes est. Sassanid rule 226

Wars with Rome

BRITAIN

GAUL   DACIA   ARMENIA

SPAIN   Rome

A F R I C A   ARABIA

ROMAN EMPIRE 117 A.D.   EGYPT

300

Old Empire of Mayas in Cent. America 320-987

Mayan calendar

Cush falls to Aksum Meroe destroyed

Aksum controls southwest Arabia 3rd-6th centuries

Shapur II

Wars with Rome

400

Pre-Inca civilizations develop in S. America

Jenne-Jeno and Timbuktu trans-Sahara trade centers

GERMANIC MIGRATIONS AND INVASIONS

Vandal Kdm. in Africa 430

500

Bantu arrive in S. Africa

Petty dynasties

Invasions by Jutes, Angles and Saxons

Burgundians enter Gaul 411

Merovingian dynasty

Clovis I unites the Franks

Theodoric the Great

Kdm. of Toulouse

SPAIN   Cordova

PERSIA

ARABIA

Mecca

MOSLEM WORLD 8TH CENTURY

Mohammed 570-632

Hegira 622

Conquest of Armenia & Egypt

St. Augustine in England 597

Reconquest of Italy by Justinian

Kdm. in Spain 507-710

600 A.D.

Persia to Omayyads

Absorbed into Frankish Emp. 613

Pepin est. Carolingian dynasty

Moslem invasion 710

Omayyad dynasty to 750

Scottish Kdm.

700

Mayas abandon Palenque

Mississippian temple-mounds culture

Bow and arrow first use

Kairwan founded 671

Moslems conquer N. Afr.

Kdm. of Ghana at height

Fez founded 793

Conquest of Spain

Abbasid dynasty est. at Baghdad

Harun al-Rashid

Invasions of Danes and Norsemen

Charles Martel Battle of Tours 732

Pepin the Short

Charlemagne 771-814

Omayyads at Cordova 756-1031

800

Aztecs begin migrations southward

Dorset Arctic culture 800-1000

Idrisids 789-985

Aghlabids 800-909

Mamun the Great

Saffarids

King Egbert

Charlemagne crowned Emperor 800

Treaty of Verdun 843

Division of the Empire

Local rulers in Arabia

900

Cairo Caliphate 972

Karmathians

Ghaznavid dynasty

Alfred the Great 871-899

Magyars invade Germany

Saxon emperors

Holy Roman Emp. est. by Otto the Great 962

St. Stephen

Norman invasion of France

1000

New Empire of Mayas 987-1530

Vikings?

Zimbabwe state

Islamic invasion of Sudan & Ghana

Decline of Moslem power in Spain

Fatimite conquest

Mahmud the Great

Danish rule 1017-1042

Edward the Confessor

Hugh Capet

Hungarian Kdm. est.

Salian dynasty

1100

Height of Mayan civilization

Thule Arctic culture (Inuit) expansion

Fall of Toledo 1085

Almoravids 1056-1147

Almohades 1130-1269

Yoruba states

Saladin

Persia Seljuk 1037-1157

Omar Khayyam

Crusaders capture Jerusalem 1099

William the Conqueror 1066

Henry I

Normans in Italy & Sicily

The Crusades

Crusades

Hohenstaufens

Frederick Barbarossa

The Cid

Rise of Castile and Aragon

Portugal indep.

1200 A.D.

Inca civilization 1200-1535

Ayyubids 1171-1250

English in Ireland

Magna Carta 1215

Normandy French

Vertical labels: NATIVE AMERICANS · BLACK AFRICANS · ARABIANS · PARTHIANS · SASSANIAN EMPIRE 226-640 · MOSLEM EMPIRE · CALIPHATE OF CORDOVA 756-1031 · FATIMITE CALIPHATE 909-1171 · CALIPHATE OF THE ABBASIDS 750-1258 · EGYPT · ARABIA · PERSIA · ANGLO-SAXONS · SCOTS AND IRISH · BURGUNDIANS · FRANKS · ENGLAND · WEST FRANKS · NORMAN EMPIRE · FRANKISH EMPIRE · EAST FRANKS · HOLY ROMAN EMPIRE · EAST GOTHS · VANDALS · WEST GOTHS (VISIGOTHS) · MOSLEM SPAIN

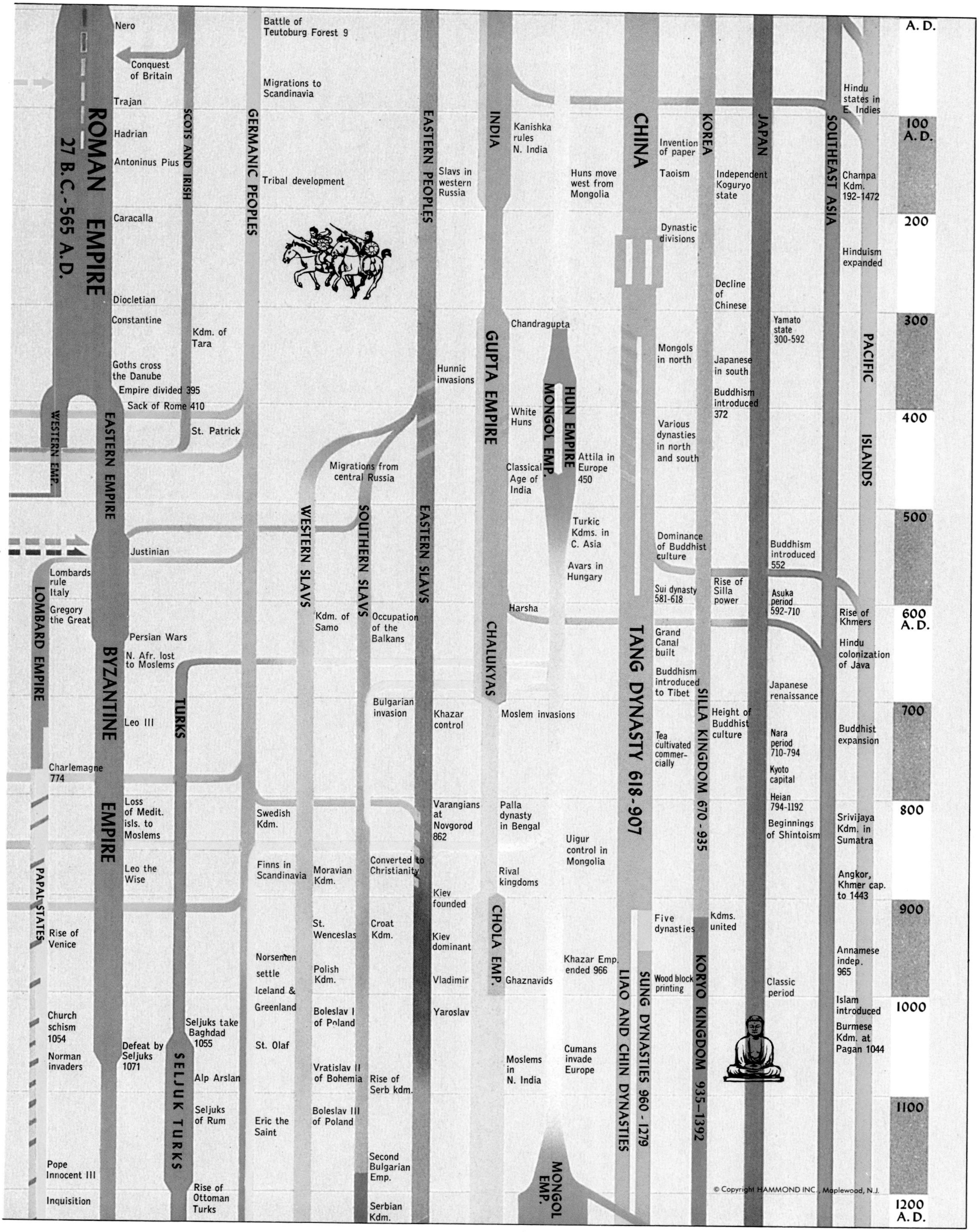

A.D.

ROMAN EMPIRE 27 B.C.-565 A.D.

Nero

Conquest of Britain

Trajan

Hadrian

Antoninus Pius

Caracalla

Diocletian

Constantine

WESTERN EMP.

Goths cross the Danube
Empire divided 395
Sack of Rome 410

EASTERN EMPIRE

BYZANTINE EMPIRE

Justinian

LOMBARD EMPIRE

Lombards rule Italy

Gregory the Great

Persian Wars

N. Afr. lost to Moslems

Leo III

Charlemagne 774

Loss of Medit. isls. to Moslems

Leo the Wise

PAPAL STATES

Rise of Venice

Church schism 1054

Norman invaders

Pope Innocent III

Inquisition

SCOTS AND IRISH

Kdm. of Tara

St. Patrick

GERMANIC PEOPLES

Battle of Teutoburg Forest 9

Migrations to Scandinavia

Tribal development

TURKS

SELJUK TURKS

Defeat by Seljuks 1071

Alp Arslan

Seljuks of Rum

Rise of Ottoman Turks

Seljuks take Baghdad 1055

EASTERN PEOPLES

Slavs in western Russia

Hunnic invasions

Migrations from central Russia

WESTERN SLAVS

Kdm. of Samo

Swedish Kdm.

Finns in Scandinavia

Norsemen settle Iceland & Greenland

SOUTHERN SLAVS

Occupation of the Balkans

Bulgarian invasion

Moravian Kdm.

St. Wenceslas

Polish Kdm.

Boleslav I of Poland

Vratislav II of Bohemia

Boleslav III of Poland

Eric the Saint

Second Bulgarian Emp.

Serbian Kdm.

EASTERN SLAVS

Khazar control

Varangians at Novgorod 862

Converted to Christianity

Kiev founded

Croat Kdm.

Kiev dominant

Vladimir

Yaroslav

Rise of Serb kdm.

INDIA

Kanishka rules N. India

Chandragupta

GUPTA EMPIRE

White Huns

Classical Age of India

CHALUKYAS

Harsha

Moslem invasions

Palla dynasty in Bengal

Rival kingdoms

CHOLA EMP.

Ghaznavids

Moslems in N. India

HUN EMPIRE MONGOL EMP.

Attila in Europe 450

Turkic Kdms. in C. Asia

Avars in Hungary

Uigur control in Mongolia

Khazar Emp. ended 966

Cumans invade Europe

MONGOL EMP.

CHINA

Invention of paper

Taoism

Dynastic divisions

Decline of Chinese

Mongols in north

Japanese in south

Buddhism introduced 372

Various dynasties in north and south

Dominance of Buddhist culture

Sui dynasty 581-618

TANG DYNASTY 618-907

Grand Canal built

Buddhism introduced to Tibet

Tea cultivated commercially

Five dynasties

Wood block printing

SUNG DYNASTIES 960-1279

LIAO AND CHIN DYNASTIES

KOREA

Independent Koguryo state

Rise of Silla power

Buddhism introduced 552

Height of Buddhist culture

SILLA KINGDOM 670-935

Kdms. united

KORYO KINGDOM 935-1392

JAPAN

Yamato state 300-592

Asuka period 592-710

Japanese renaissance

Nara period 710-794

Kyoto capital

Heian 794-1192

Beginnings of Shintoism

Classic period

SOUTHEAST ASIA

Hindu states in E. Indies

Champa Kdm. 192-1472

Hinduism expanded

PACIFIC ISLANDS

Rise of Khmers

Hindu colonization of Java

Buddhist expansion

Srivijaya Kdm. in Sumatra

Angkor, Khmer cap. to 1443

Annamese indep. 965

Islam introduced

Burmese Kdm. at Pagan 1044

100 A.D.

200

300

400

500

600 A.D.

700

800

900

1000

1100

1200 A.D.

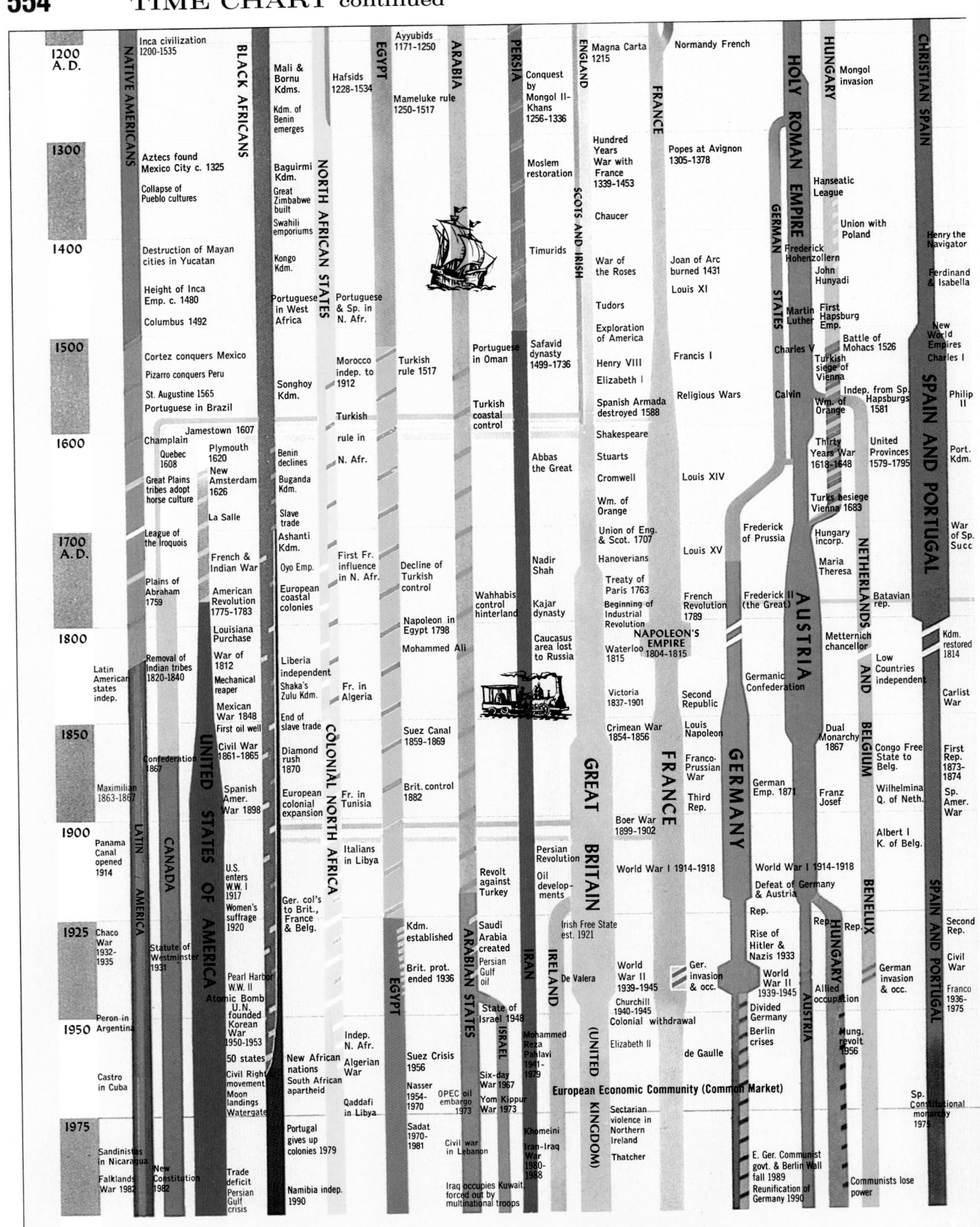

Time axis (left): 1200 A.D., 1300, 1400, 1500, 1600, 1700 A.D., 1800, 1850, 1900, 1925, 1950, 1975

NATIVE AMERICANS
- Inca civilization 1200-1535
- Aztecs found Mexico City c. 1325
- Collapse of Pueblo cultures
- Destruction of Mayan cities in Yucatan
- Height of Inca Emp. c. 1480
- Columbus 1492
- Cortez conquers Mexico
- Pizarro conquers Peru
- St. Augustine 1565
- Portuguese in Brazil
- Champlain
- Quebec 1608
- Great Plains tribes adopt horse culture
- League of the Iroquois
- Plains of Abraham 1759
- Removal of Indian tribes 1820-1840
- Latin American states indep.
- Maximilian 1863-1867

LATIN AMERICA
- Panama Canal opened 1914
- Chaco War 1932-1935
- Peron in Argentina
- Castro in Cuba
- Sandinistas in Nicaragua
- Falklands War 1982

CANADA
- Confederation 1867
- Statute of Westminster 1931
- New Constitution 1982

UNITED STATES OF AMERICA
- Jamestown 1607
- Plymouth 1620
- New Amsterdam 1626
- La Salle
- French & Indian War
- American Revolution 1775-1783
- Louisiana Purchase
- War of 1812
- Mechanical reaper
- Mexican War 1848
- First oil well
- Civil War 1861-1865
- Spanish Amer. War 1898
- U.S. enters W.W. I 1917
- Women's suffrage 1920
- Pearl Harbor W.W. II
- Atomic Bomb
- U.N. founded
- Korean War 1950-1953
- 50 states
- Civil Rights movement
- Moon landings
- Watergate
- Trade deficit
- Persian Gulf crisis

BLACK AFRICANS
- Mali & Bornu Kdms.
- Kdm. of Benin emerges
- Baguirmi Kdm.
- Great Zimbabwe built
- Swahili emporiums
- Kongo Kdm.
- Portuguese in West Africa
- Songhoy Kdm.
- Benin declines
- Buganda Kdm.
- Slave trade
- Ashanti Kdm.
- Oyo Emp.
- European coastal colonies
- Liberia independent
- Shaka's Zulu Kdm.
- End of slave trade
- Diamond rush 1870
- European colonial expansion
- Ger. col's to Brit., France & Belg.
- Kdm. established
- Brit. prot. ended 1936
- New African nations
- South African apartheid
- Portugal gives up colonies 1979
- Namibia indep. 1990

NORTH AFRICAN STATES
- Hafsids 1228-1534
- Portuguese & Sp. in N. Afr.
- Morocco indep. to 1912
- Turkish rule in N. Afr.
- First Fr. influence in N. Afr.
- European coastal colonies
- Fr. in Algeria
- Fr. in Tunisia

COLONIAL NORTH AFRICA
- Italians in Libya
- Indep. N. Afr.
- Algerian War
- Qaddafi in Libya

EGYPT
- Ayyubids 1171-1250
- Mameluke rule 1250-1517
- Portuguese in West Africa
- Turkish rule 1517
- Suez Canal 1859-1869
- Brit. control 1882
- Brit. prot. ended 1936
- Suez Crisis 1956
- Nasser 1954-1970
- Sadat 1970-1981

ARABIA
- Portuguese in Oman
- Wahhabis control hinterland
- Saudi Arabia created
- Persian Gulf oil

ARABIAN STATES
- State of Israel 1948
- OPEC oil embargo 1973
- Civil war in Lebanon
- Iraq occupies Kuwait; forced out by multinational troops

ISRAEL
- Six-day War 1967
- Yom Kippur War 1973

PERSIA
- Conquest by Mongol Il-Khans 1256-1336
- Moslem restoration
- Timurids
- Safavid dynasty 1499-1736
- Turkish coastal control
- Abbas the Great
- Decline of Turkish control
- Nadir Shah
- Kajar dynasty
- Caucasus area lost to Russia
- Persian Revolution
- Oil developments
- Revolt against Turkey

IRAN
- Mohammed Reza Pahlavi 1941-1979
- Khomeini
- Iran-Iraq War 1980-1988

ENGLAND
- Magna Carta 1215
- Hundred Years War with France 1339-1453
- Chaucer

SCOTS AND IRISH
- War of the Roses
- Tudors
- Exploration of America
- Henry VIII
- Elizabeth I
- Spanish Armada destroyed 1588
- Shakespeare
- Stuarts
- Cromwell
- Wm. of Orange
- Union of Eng. & Scot. 1707
- Hanoverians
- Treaty of Paris 1763
- Beginning of Industrial Revolution

GREAT BRITAIN (UNITED KINGDOM)
- Victoria 1837-1901
- Crimean War 1854-1856
- Boer War 1899-1902
- World War I 1914-1918
- Irish Free State est. 1921
- World War II 1939-1945
- Churchill 1940-1945
- Colonial withdrawal
- Elizabeth II
- Sectarian violence in Northern Ireland
- Thatcher

IRELAND
- De Valera

FRANCE
- Normandy French
- Popes at Avignon 1305-1378
- Joan of Arc burned 1431
- Louis XI
- Francis I
- Religious Wars
- Louis XIV
- Louis XV
- French Revolution 1789
- Napoleon in Egypt 1798
- Waterloo 1815
- Second Republic
- Louis Napoleon
- Franco-Prussian War
- Third Rep.
- World War I 1914-1918
- Ger. invasion & occ.
- de Gaulle

NAPOLEON'S EMPIRE 1804-1815

European Economic Community (Common Market)

HOLY ROMAN EMPIRE (GERMAN STATES)
- Frederick Hohenzollern
- Martin Luther
- Charles V
- Calvin
- Thirty Years War 1618-1648
- Frederick of Prussia
- Frederick II (the Great)
- Germanic Confederation

GERMANY
- Germanic Confederation
- German Emp. 1871
- World War I 1914-1918
- Defeat of Germany & Austria
- Rep.
- Rise of Hitler & Nazis 1933
- World War II 1939-1945
- Divided Germany
- Berlin crises
- E. Ger. Communist govt. & Berlin Wall fall 1989
- Reunification of Germany 1990

HUNGARY
- Mongol invasion
- Hanseatic League
- Union with Poland
- John Hunyadi
- First Hapsburg Emp.
- Battle of Mohacs 1526
- Turkish siege of Vienna
- Wm. of Orange
- Turks besiege Vienna 1683
- Hungary incorp.
- Maria Theresa
- Metternich chancellor
- Dual Monarchy 1867
- Franz Josef
- Rep.
- German invasion & occ.
- Allied occupation
- Hung. revolt 1956
- Communists lose power

AUSTRIA

NETHERLANDS AND BELGIUM (BENELUX)
- Indep. from Sp. Hapsburgs 1581
- United Provinces 1579-1795
- Batavian rep.
- Low Countries independent
- Congo Free State to Belg.
- Wilhelmina Q. of Neth.
- Albert I K. of Belg.
- Rep.
- German invasion & occ.

CHRISTIAN SPAIN
- Henry the Navigator
- Ferdinand & Isabella
- New World Empires
- Charles I

SPAIN AND PORTUGAL
- Philip II
- War of Sp. Succ.
- Batavian rep.
- Kdm. restored 1814
- Port. Kdm.
- Carlist War
- First Rep. 1873-1874
- Sp. Amer. War
- Second Rep.
- Civil War
- Franco 1936-1975
- Sp. Constitutional monarchy 1975

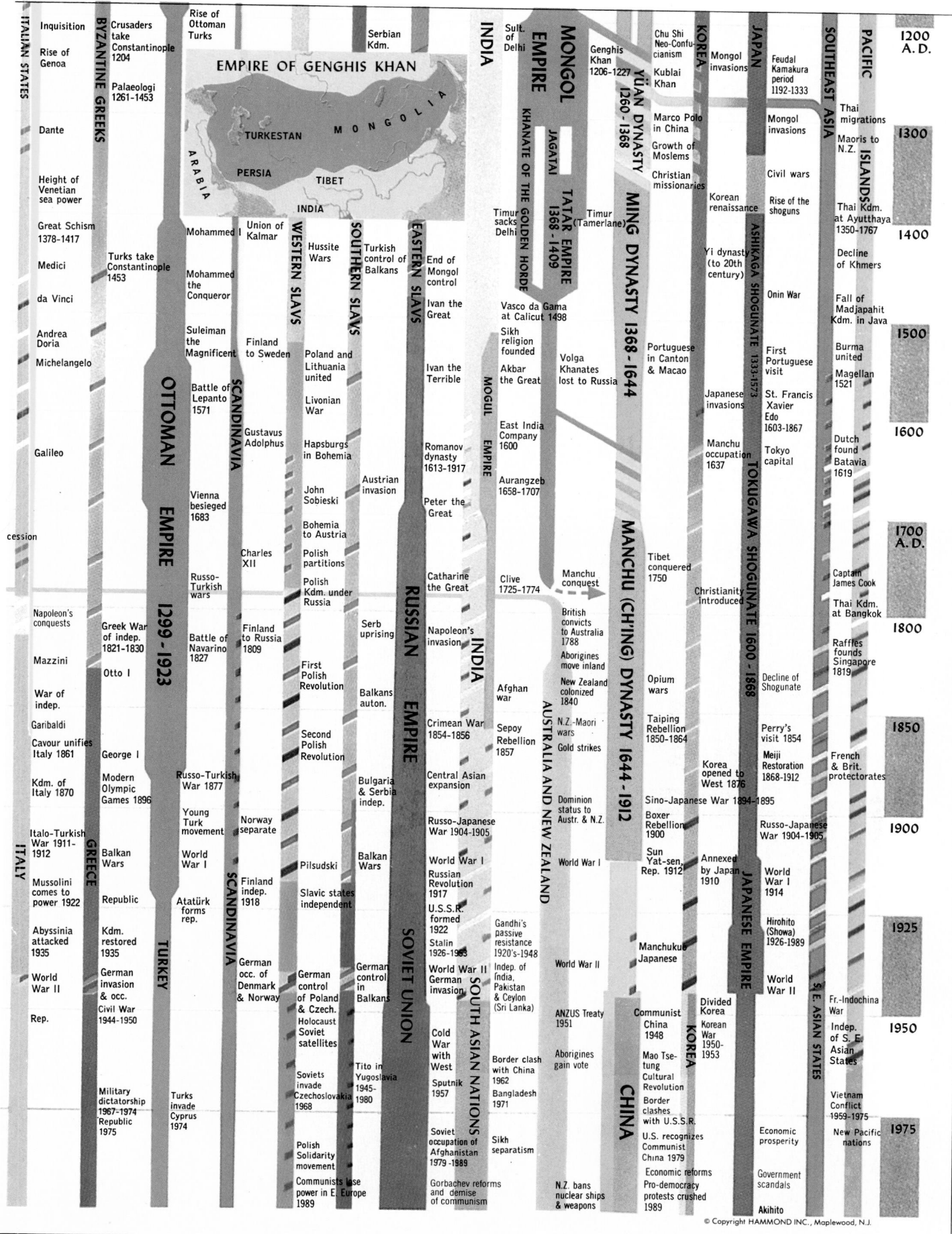

555

Time scale (right margin): 1200 A.D. · 1300 · 1400 · 1500 · 1600 · 1700 A.D. · 1800 · 1850 · 1900 · 1925 · 1950 · 1975

EMPIRE OF GENGHIS KHAN — ARABIA · TURKESTAN · MONGOLIA · PERSIA · TIBET · INDIA

ITALIAN STATES / ITALY
- Inquisition
- Rise of Genoa
- Dante
- Height of Venetian sea power
- Great Schism 1378-1417
- Medici
- da Vinci
- Andrea Doria
- Michelangelo
- Galileo
- cession
- Napoleon's conquests
- Mazzini
- War of indep.
- Garibaldi
- Cavour unifies Italy 1861
- Kdm. of Italy 1870
- Italo-Turkish War 1911-1912
- Mussolini comes to power 1922
- Abyssinia attacked 1935
- World War II
- Rep.

BYZANTINE GREEKS / GREECE / TURKEY
- Crusaders take Constantinople 1204
- Palaeologi 1261-1453
- Turks take Constantinople 1453
- Greek War of indep. 1821-1830
- Otto I
- George I
- Modern Olympic Games 1896
- Young Turk movement
- Balkan Wars
- Republic
- Kdm. restored 1935
- German invasion & occ.
- Civil War 1944-1950
- Military dictatorship 1967-1974
- Republic 1975

OTTOMAN EMPIRE 1299-1923
- Rise of Ottoman Turks
- Mohammed I
- Mohammed the Conqueror
- Suleiman the Magnificent
- Battle of Lepanto 1571
- Vienna besieged 1683
- Russo-Turkish wars
- Balkan Wars
- Atatürk forms rep.
- Turks invade Cyprus 1974

SCANDINAVIA
- Union of Kalmar
- Finland to Sweden
- Gustavus Adolphus
- Charles XII
- Battle of Navarino 1827
- Finland to Russia 1809
- Russo-Turkish War 1877
- Norway separate
- World War I
- Finland indep. 1918
- German occ. of Denmark & Norway
- Turks invade Cyprus 1974

WESTERN SLAVS
- Hussite Wars
- Poland and Lithuania united
- Livonian War
- Hapsburgs in Bohemia
- John Sobieski
- Bohemia to Austria
- Polish partitions
- Polish Kdm. under Russia
- First Polish Revolution
- Second Polish Revolution
- Pilsudski
- Slavic states independent
- German control of Poland & Czech.
- Holocaust
- Soviet satellites
- Soviets invade Czechoslovakia 1968
- Polish Solidarity movement
- Communists lose power in E. Europe 1989

SOUTHERN SLAVS
- Serbian Kdm.
- Turkish control of Balkans
- Austrian invasion
- Serb uprising
- Balkans auton.
- Bulgaria & Serbia indep.
- Balkan Wars
- German control in Balkans
- Tito in Yugoslavia 1945-1980

EASTERN SLAVS / RUSSIAN EMPIRE / SOVIET UNION
- End of Mongol control
- Ivan the Great
- Ivan the Terrible
- Romanov dynasty 1613-1917
- Peter the Great
- Catharine the Great
- Napoleon's invasion
- Crimean War 1854-1856
- Central Asian expansion
- Russo-Japanese War 1904-1905
- World War I
- Russian Revolution 1917
- U.S.S.R. formed 1922
- Stalin 1926-1953
- World War II German invasion
- Cold War with West
- Sputnik 1957
- Soviet occupation of Afghanistan 1979-1989
- Gorbachev reforms and demise of communism

INDIA / MOGUL EMPIRE
- Sult. of Delhi
- Vasco da Gama at Calicut 1498
- Sikh religion founded
- Akbar the Great
- East India Company 1600
- Aurangzeb 1658-1707
- Clive 1725-1774
- Afghan war
- Sepoy Rebellion 1857
- Gandhi's passive resistance 1920's-1948
- Indep. of India, Pakistan & Ceylon (Sri Lanka)
- Border clash with China 1962
- Bangladesh 1971
- Sikh separatism

MONGOL EMPIRE / KHANATE OF THE GOLDEN HORDE / TATAR EMPIRE 1368-1409
- Genghis Khan 1206-1227
- JAGATAI
- Timur sacks Delhi
- Timur (Tamerlane)
- Volga Khanates lost to Russia
- Manchu conquest

MING DYNASTY 1368-1644 / MANCHU (CH'ING) DYNASTY 1644-1912 / CHINA
- Chu Shi Neo-Confucianism
- Kublai Khan
- Marco Polo in China
- Growth of Moslems
- Christian missionaries
- Portuguese in Canton & Macao
- Manchu occupation 1637
- Tibet conquered 1750
- Opium wars
- Taiping Rebellion 1850-1864
- Sino-Japanese War 1894-1895
- Boxer Rebellion 1900
- Sun Yat-sen, Rep. 1912
- Manchukuo Japanese
- Communist China 1948
- Mao Tse-tung
- Cultural Revolution
- Border clashes with U.S.S.R.
- U.S. recognizes Communist China 1979
- Economic reforms
- Pro-democracy protests crushed 1989

YÜAN DYNASTY 1260-1368

KOREA
- Mongol invasions
- Korean renaissance
- Yi dynasty (to 20th century)
- Japanese invasions
- Christianity introduced
- Korea opened to West 1876
- Annexed by Japan 1910
- Divided Korea
- Korean War 1950-1953

JAPAN / ASHIKAGA SHOGUNATE 1333-1573 / TOKUGAWA SHOGUNATE 1600-1868 / JAPANESE EMPIRE
- Feudal Kamakura period 1192-1333
- Mongol invasions
- Civil wars
- Rise of the shoguns
- Onin War
- First Portuguese visit
- St. Francis Xavier
- Edo 1603-1867
- Tokyo capital
- Decline of Shogunate
- Perry's visit 1854
- Meiji Restoration 1868-1912
- Russo-Japanese War 1904-1905
- World War I 1914
- Hirohito (Showa) 1926-1989
- World War II
- Akihito

SOUTHEAST ASIA / S.E. ASIAN STATES
- Thai migrations
- Thai Kdm. at Ayutthaya 1350-1767
- Decline of Khmers
- Fall of Madjapahit Kdm. in Java
- Burma united
- Dutch found Batavia 1619
- French & Brit. protectorates
- Fr.-Indochina War
- Indep. of S. E. Asian States
- Vietnam Conflict 1959-1975

PACIFIC ISLANDS
- Maoris to N.Z.
- Magellan 1521
- Captain James Cook
- Thai Kdm. at Bangkok
- Raffles founds Singapore 1819
- Economic prosperity
- Government scandals
- New Pacific nations

AUSTRALIA AND NEW ZEALAND
- British convicts to Australia 1788
- Aborigines move inland
- New Zealand colonized 1840
- N.Z.-Maori wars
- Gold strikes
- Dominion status to Austr. & N.Z.
- World War I
- World War II
- ANZUS Treaty 1951
- Aborigines gain vote
- N.Z. bans nuclear ships & weapons

© Copyright HAMMOND INC., Maplewood, N.J.

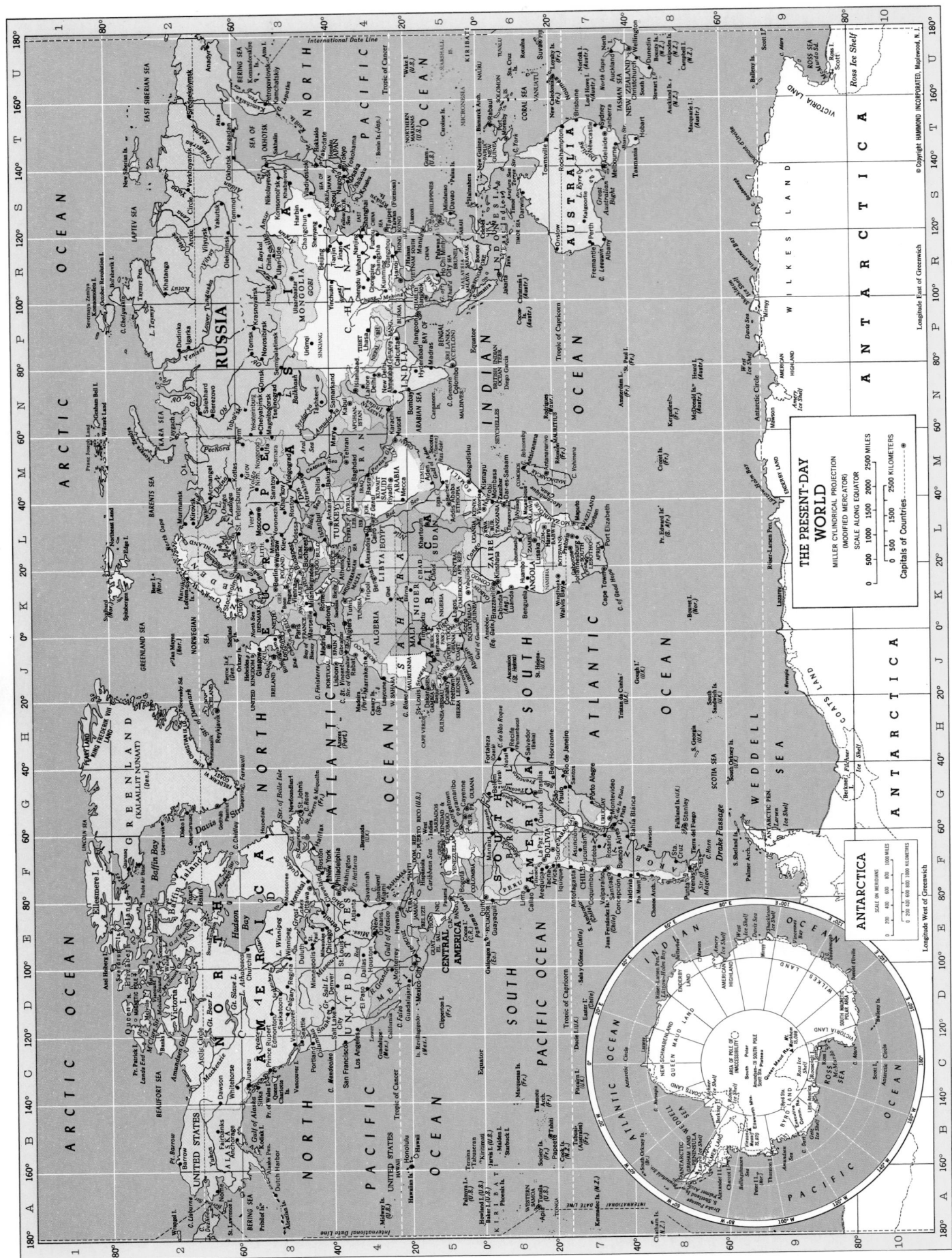

THE PRESENT-DAY
WORLD
MILLER CYLINDRICAL PROJECTION
(MODIFIED MERCATOR)
SCALE ALONG EQUATOR

Capitals of Countries

ANTARCTICA
SCALE ON MERIDIANS

HOMEWORK MAPS
Alphabetical Index

HOMEWORK MAPS

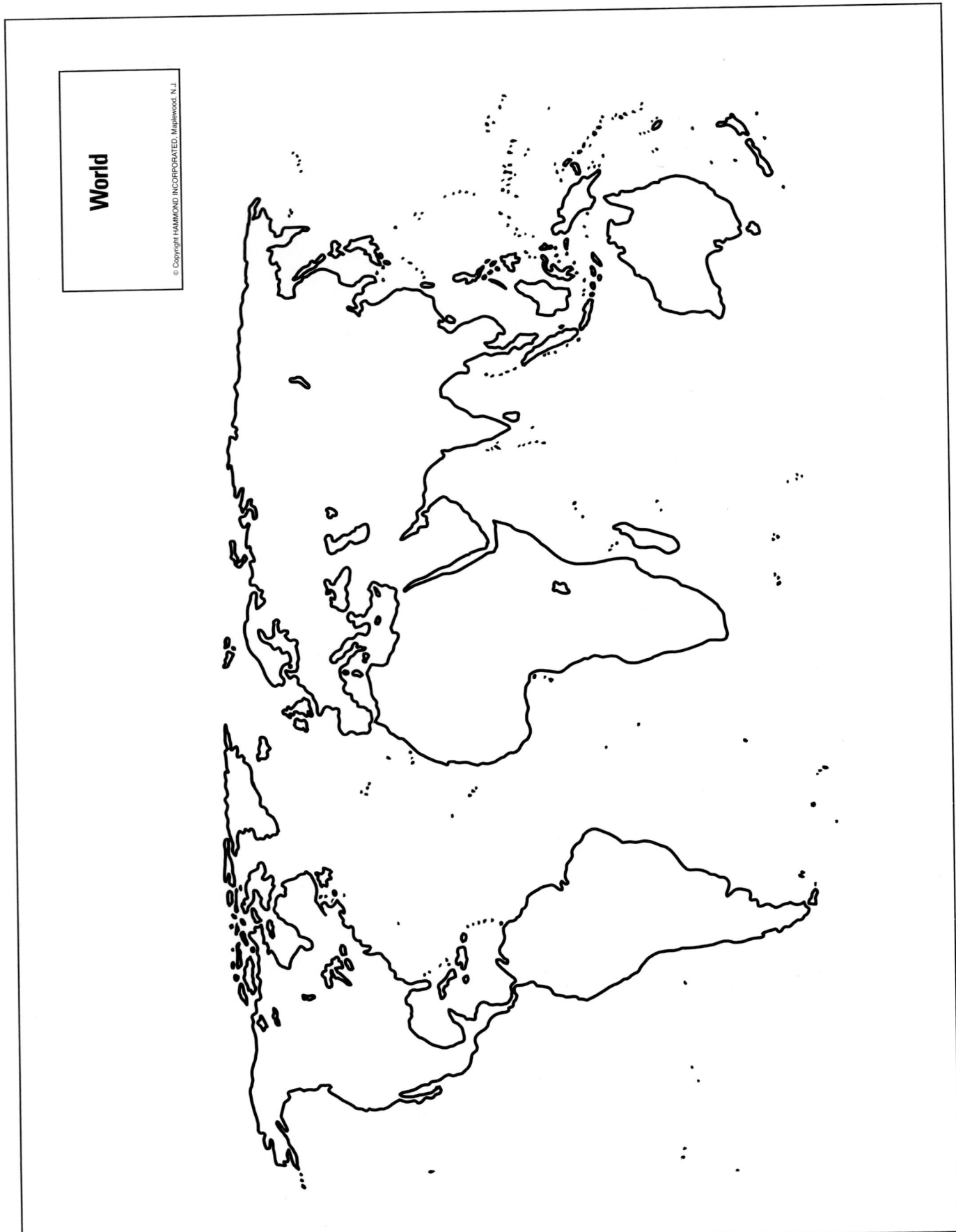

World

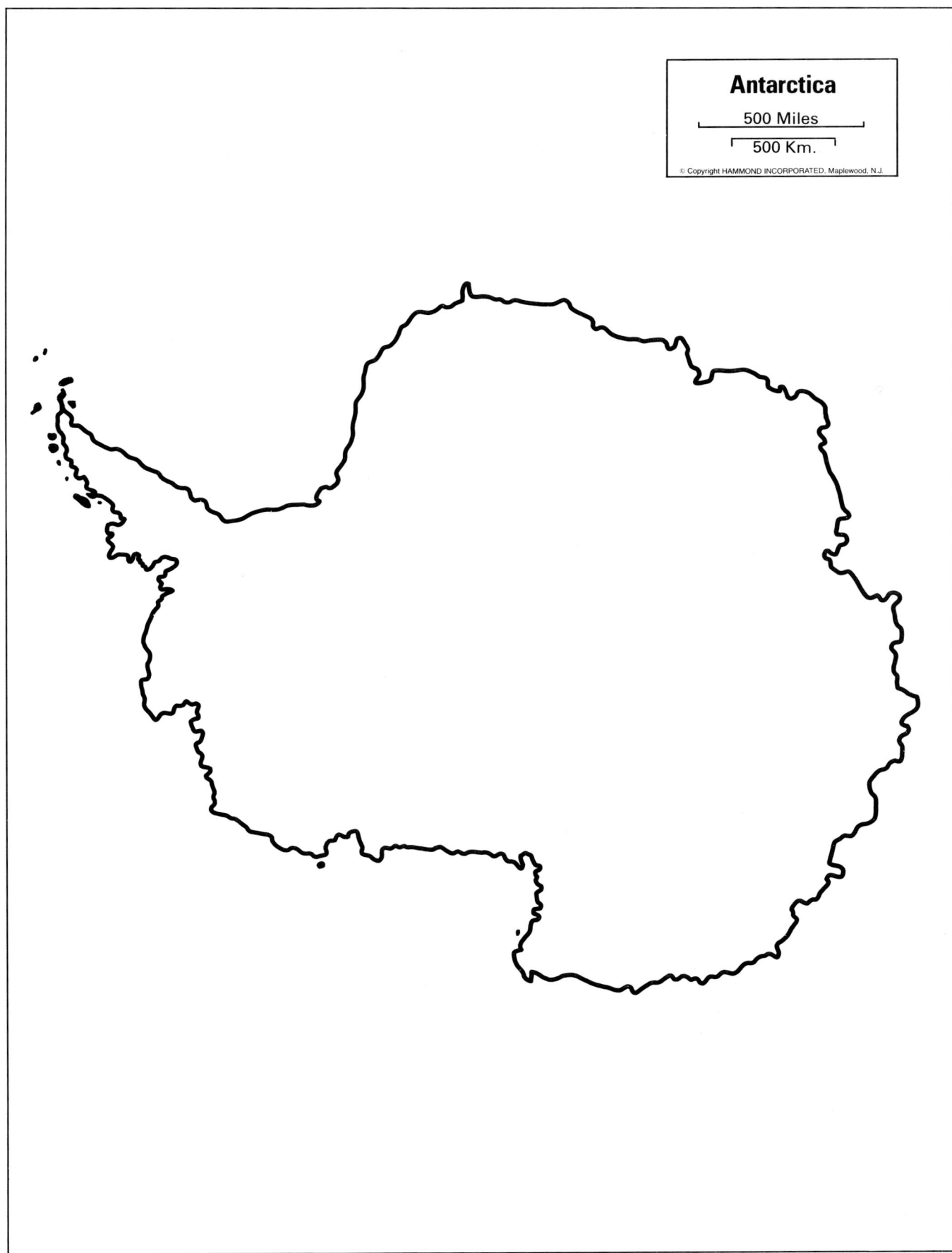

Antarctica

500 Miles

500 Km.

© Copyright HAMMOND INCORPORATED, Maplewood, N.J.

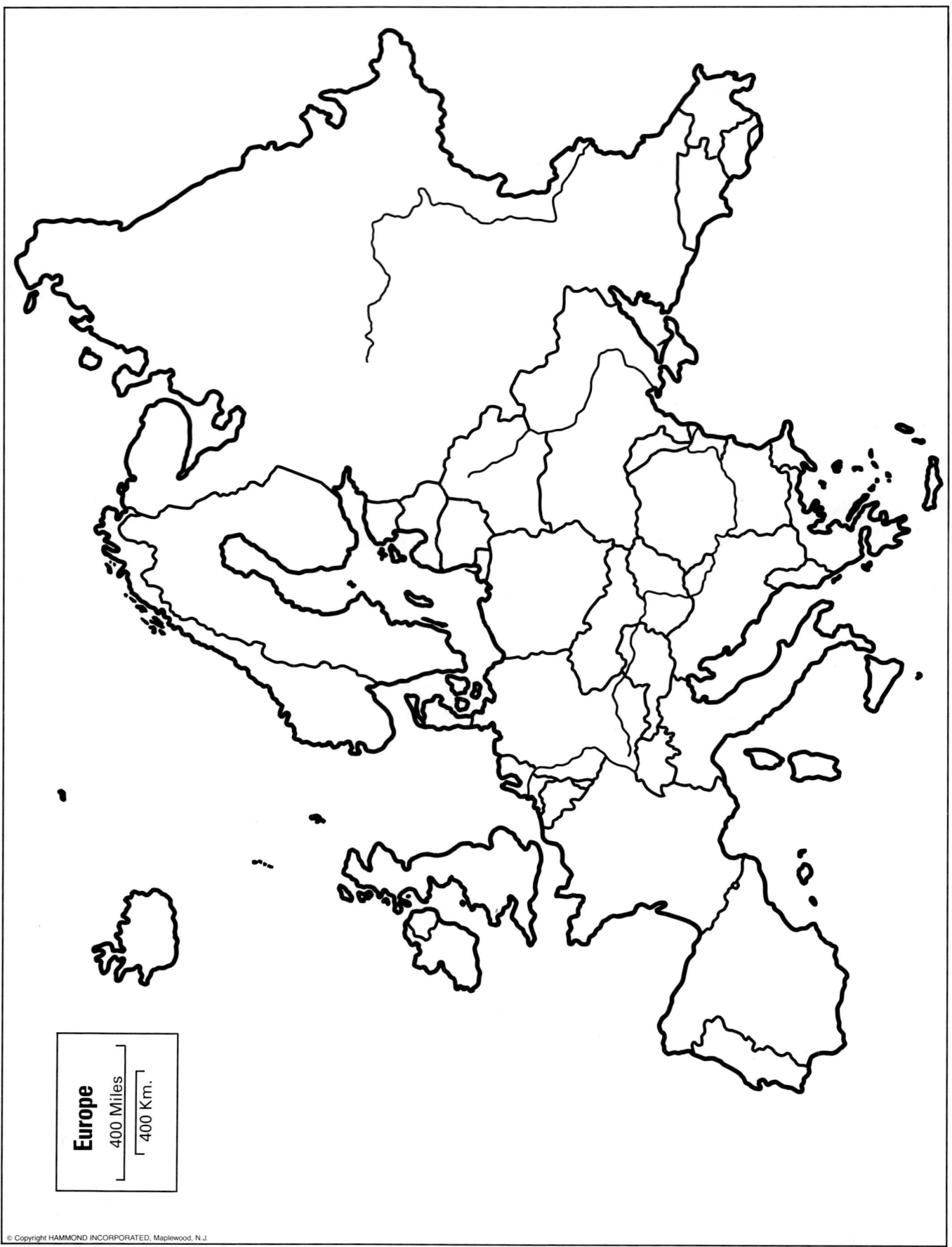

Europe

400 Miles
400 Km.

United Kingdom
and Ireland

100 Miles

100 Km.

© Copyright HAMMOND INCORPORATED, Maplewood, N.J.

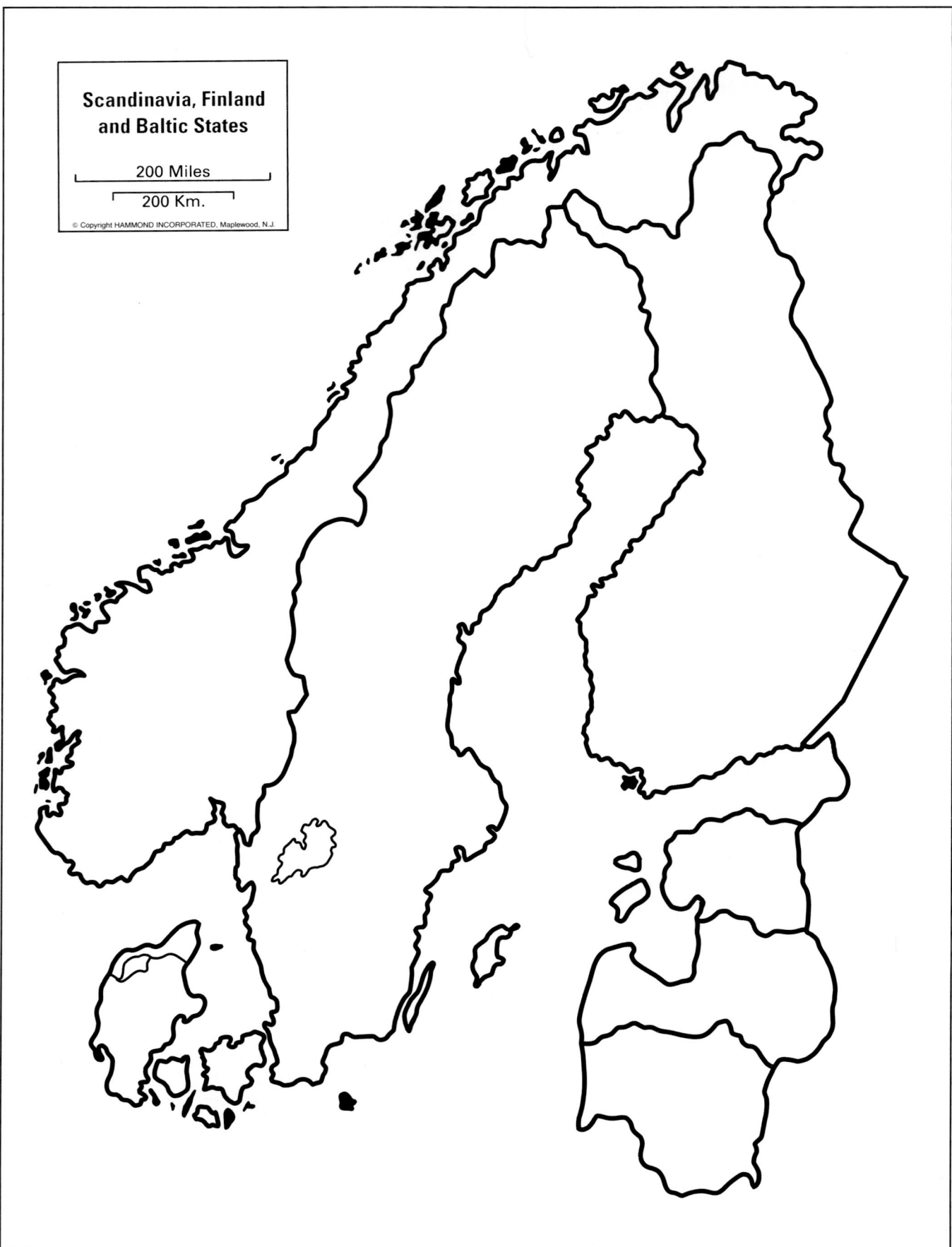
Scandinavia, Finland and Baltic States
200 Miles
200 Km.
© Copyright HAMMOND INCORPORATED, Maplewood, N.J.

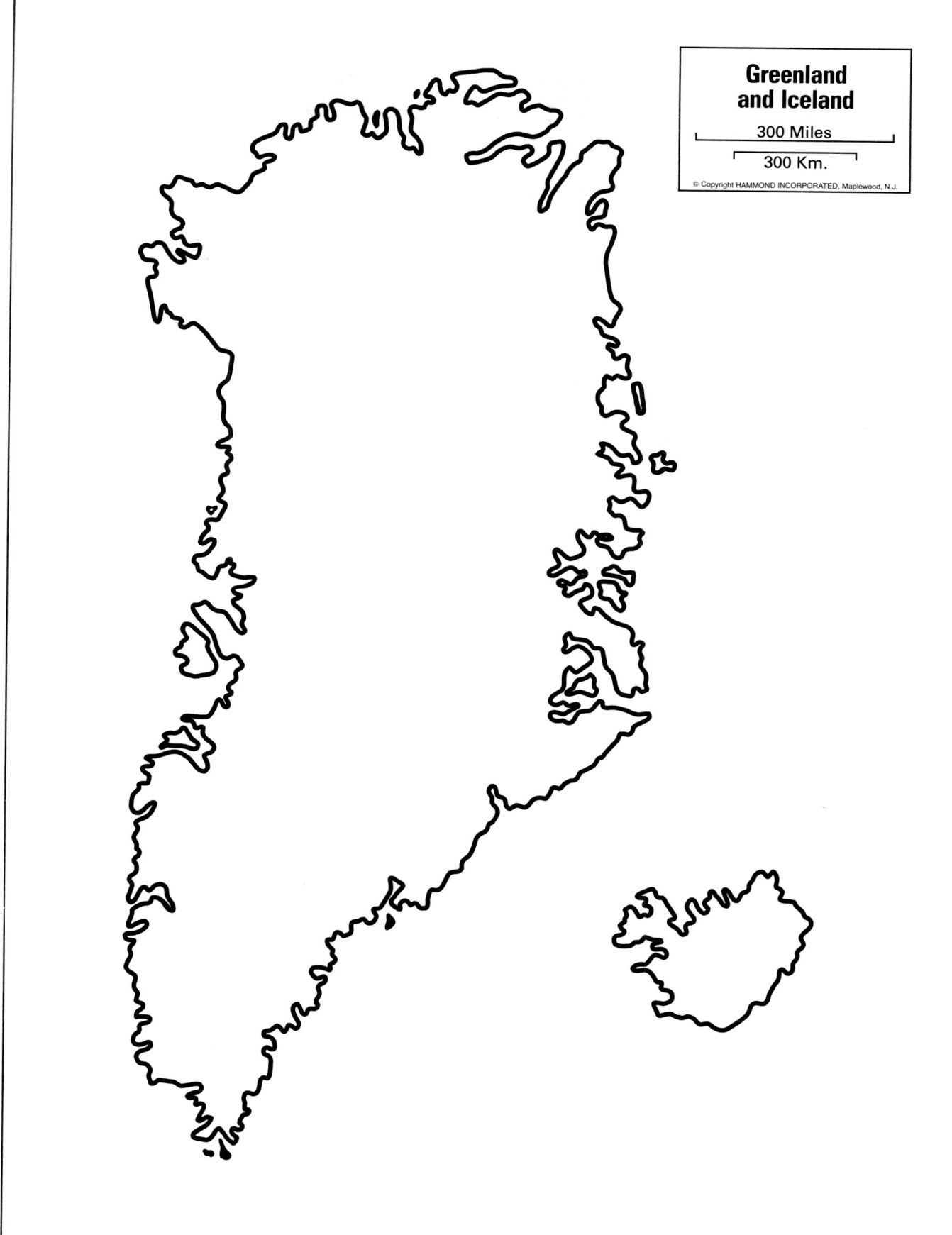

**Greenland
and Iceland**

300 Miles

300 Km.

Germany

80 Miles

80 Km.

© Copyright HAMMOND INCORPORATED, Maplewood, N J

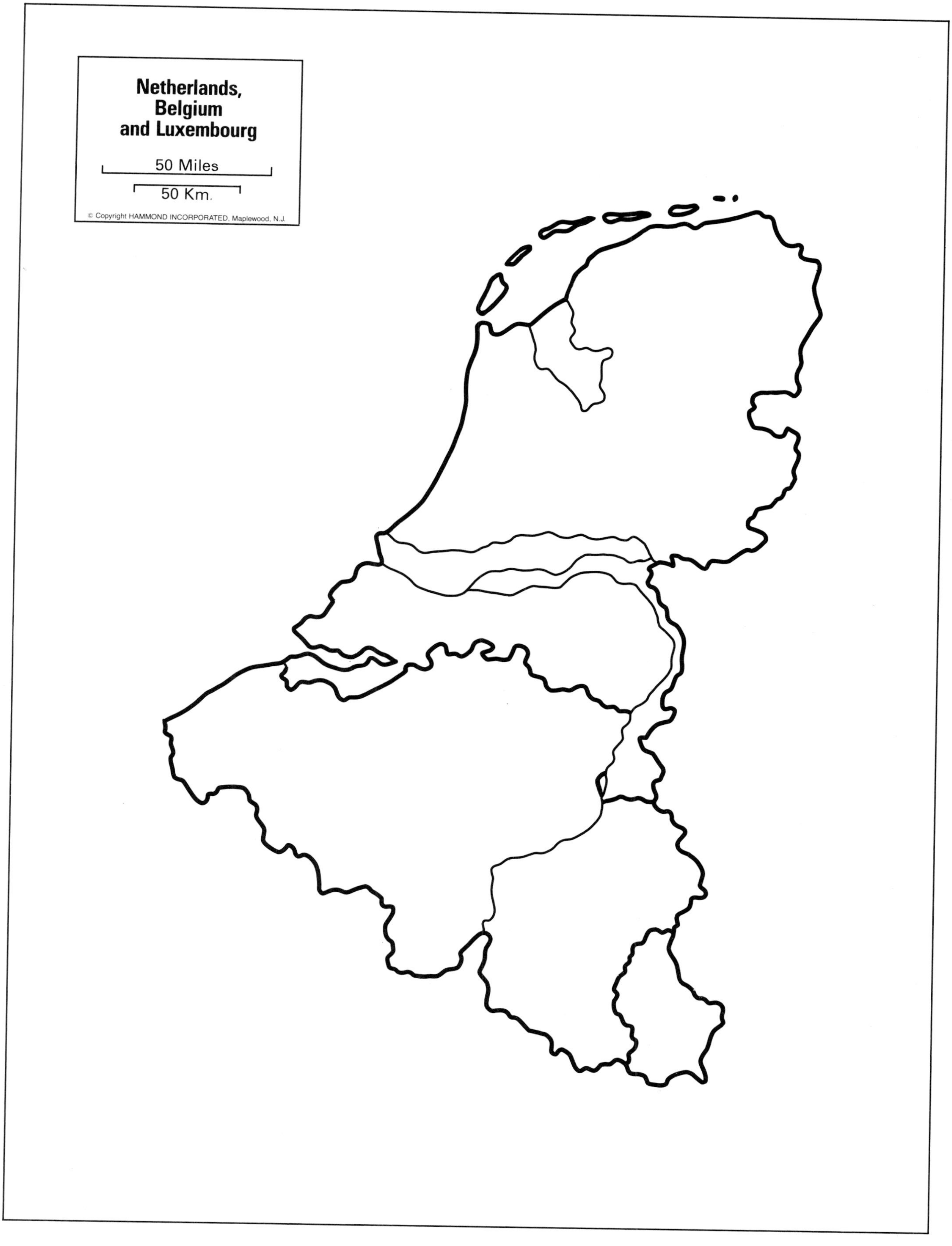

France and Monaco

120 Miles

120 Km.

© Copyright HAMMOND INCORPORATED, Maplewood, N.J.

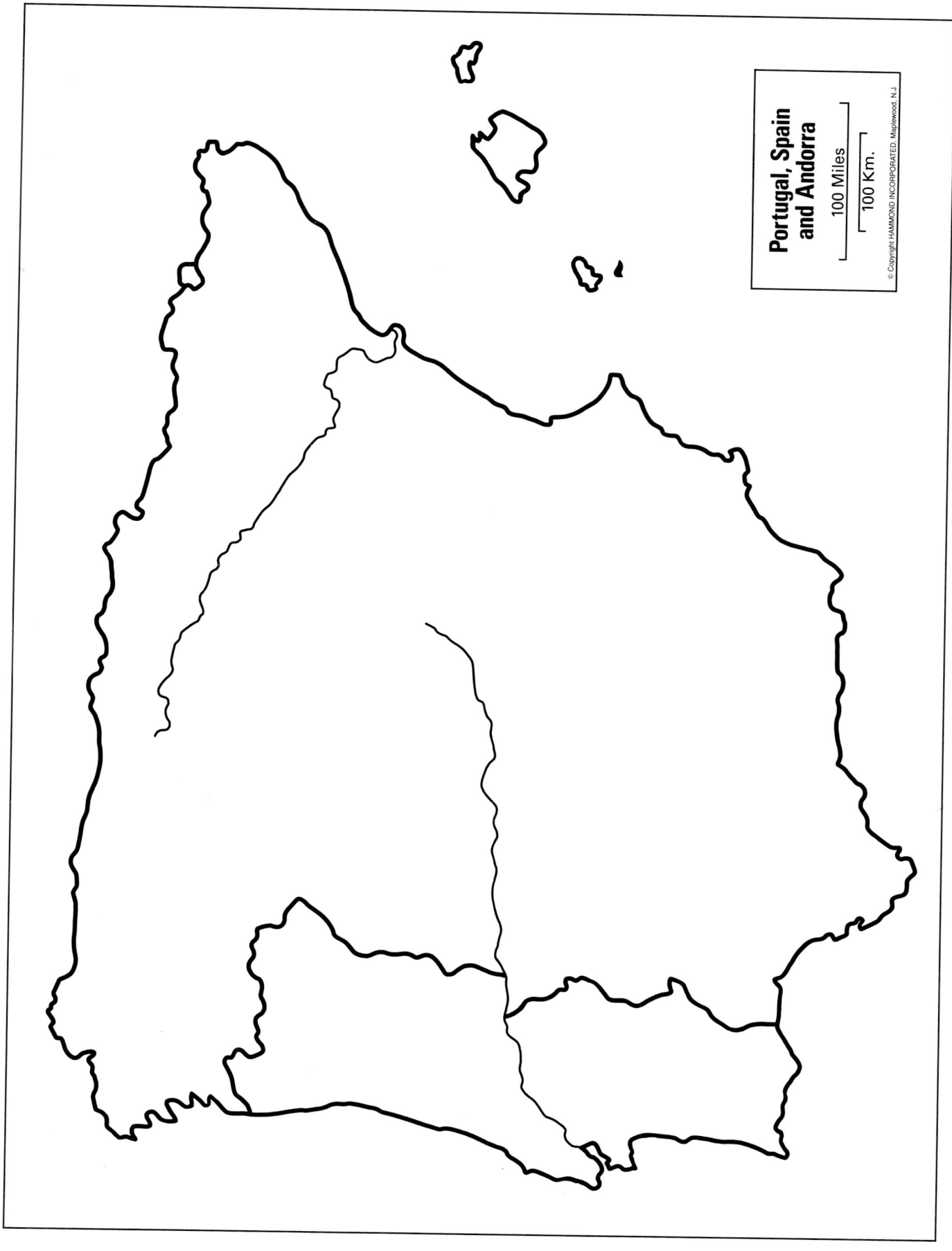

Portugal, Spain and Andorra

100 Miles

100 Km.

© Copyright HAMMOND INCORPORATED, Maplewood, N.J.

568

**Austria,
Switzerland,
Italy and Malta**

200 Miles

200 Km.

© Copyright HAMMOND INCORPORATED, Maplewood, N.J.

**Poland,
Czechoslovakia
and Hungary**

100 Miles

100 Km.

570

**The
Balkans**

150 Miles

150 Km.

© Copyright HAMMOND INCORPORATED, Maplewood, N.J.

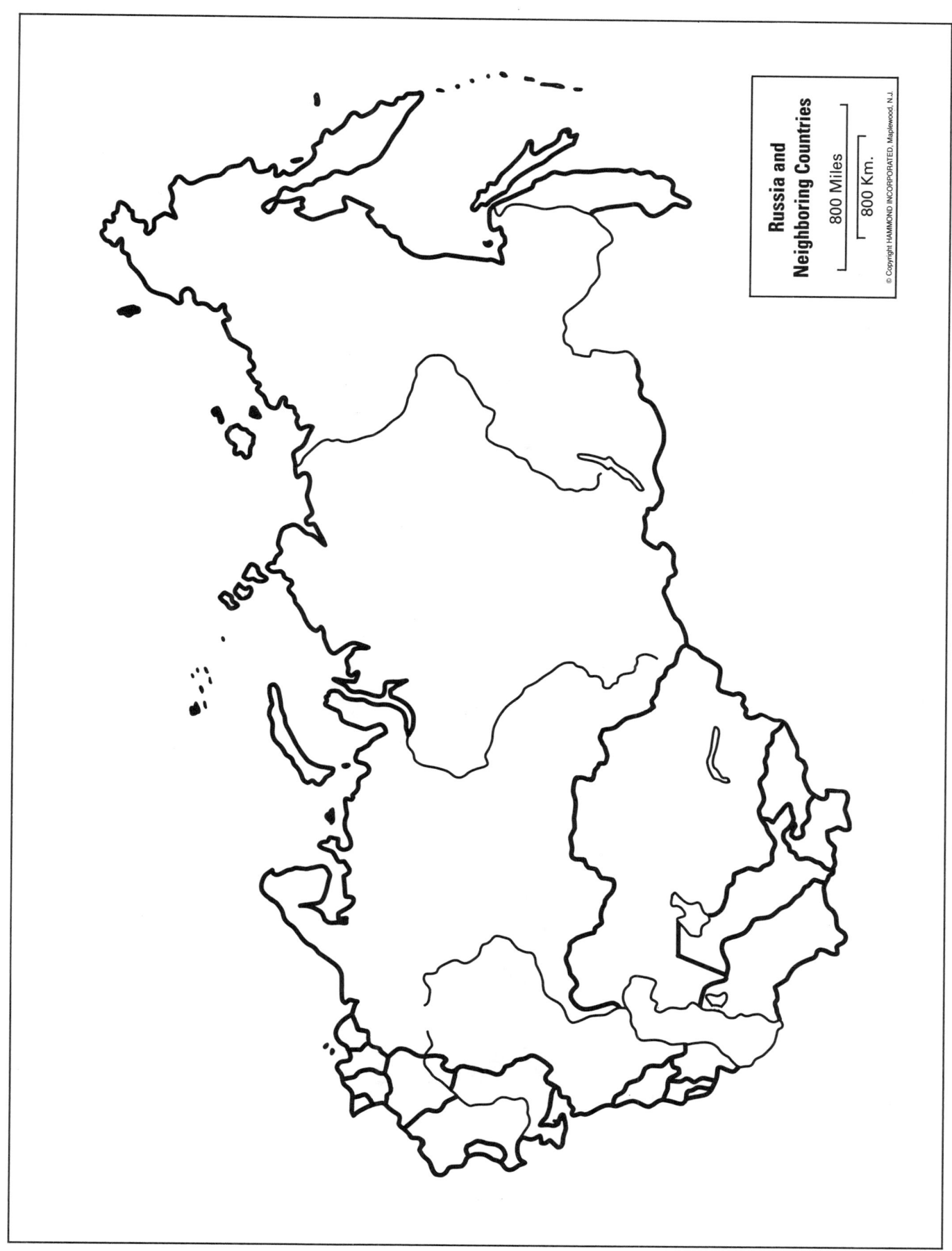

Russia and
Neighboring Countries

800 Miles

800 Km.

© Copyright HAMMOND INCORPORATED, Maplewood, N.J.

572

Asia

1500 Miles

1500 Km.

© Copyright HAMMOND INCORPORATED, Maplewood, N.J.

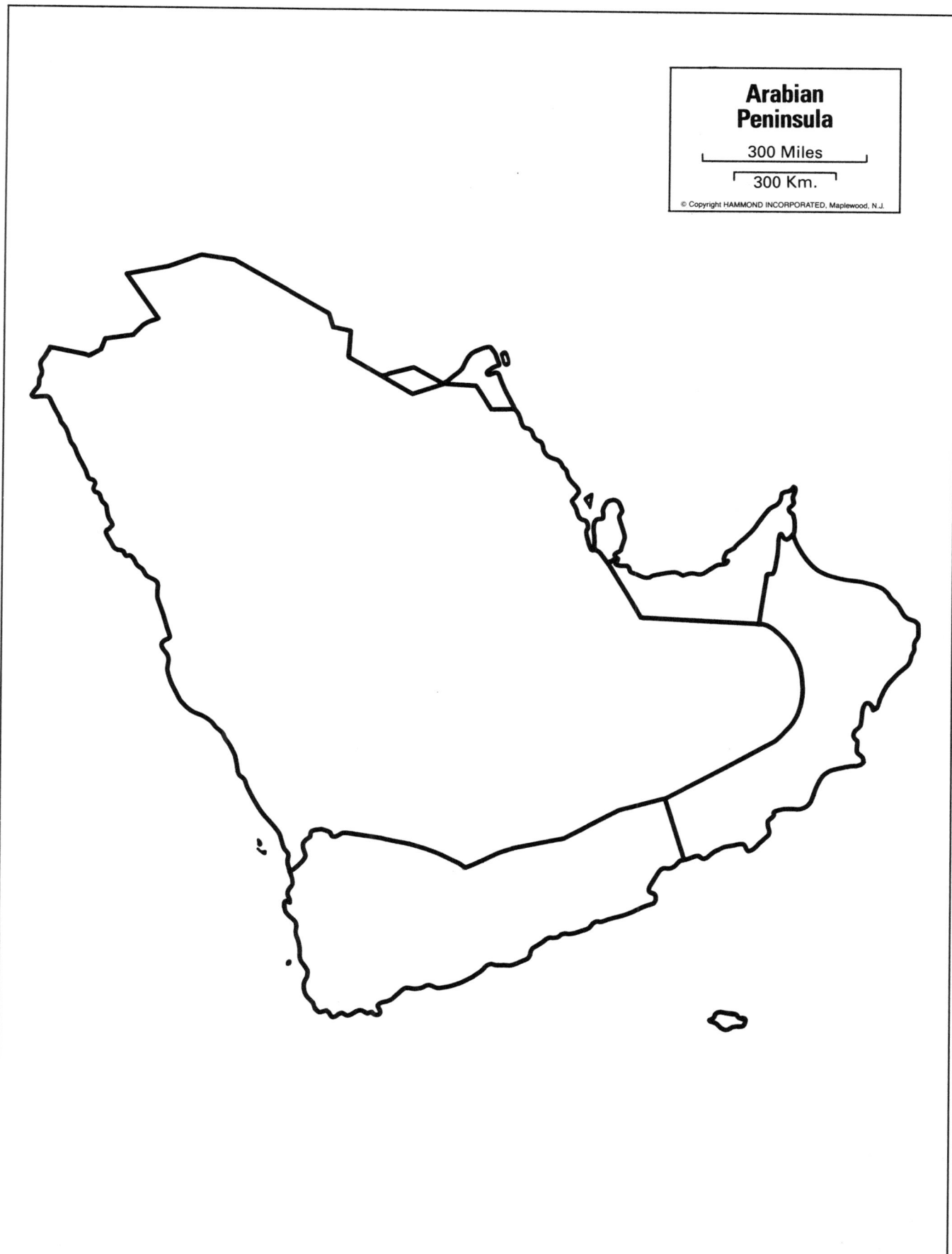

**Arabian
Peninsula**

300 Miles

300 Km.

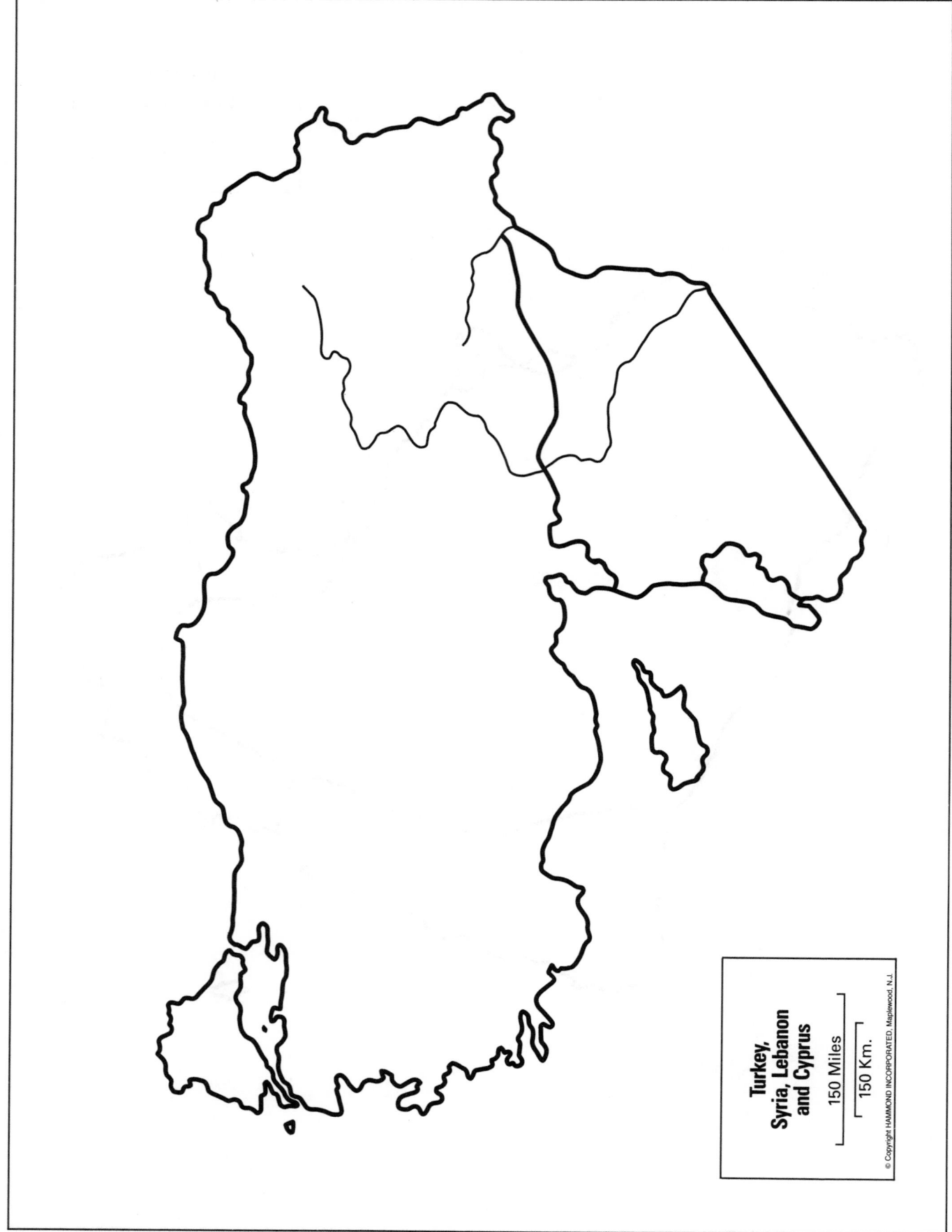

**Turkey,
Syria, Lebanon
and Cyprus**

150 Miles
150 Km.

© Copyright HAMMOND INCORPORATED, Maplewood, N.J.

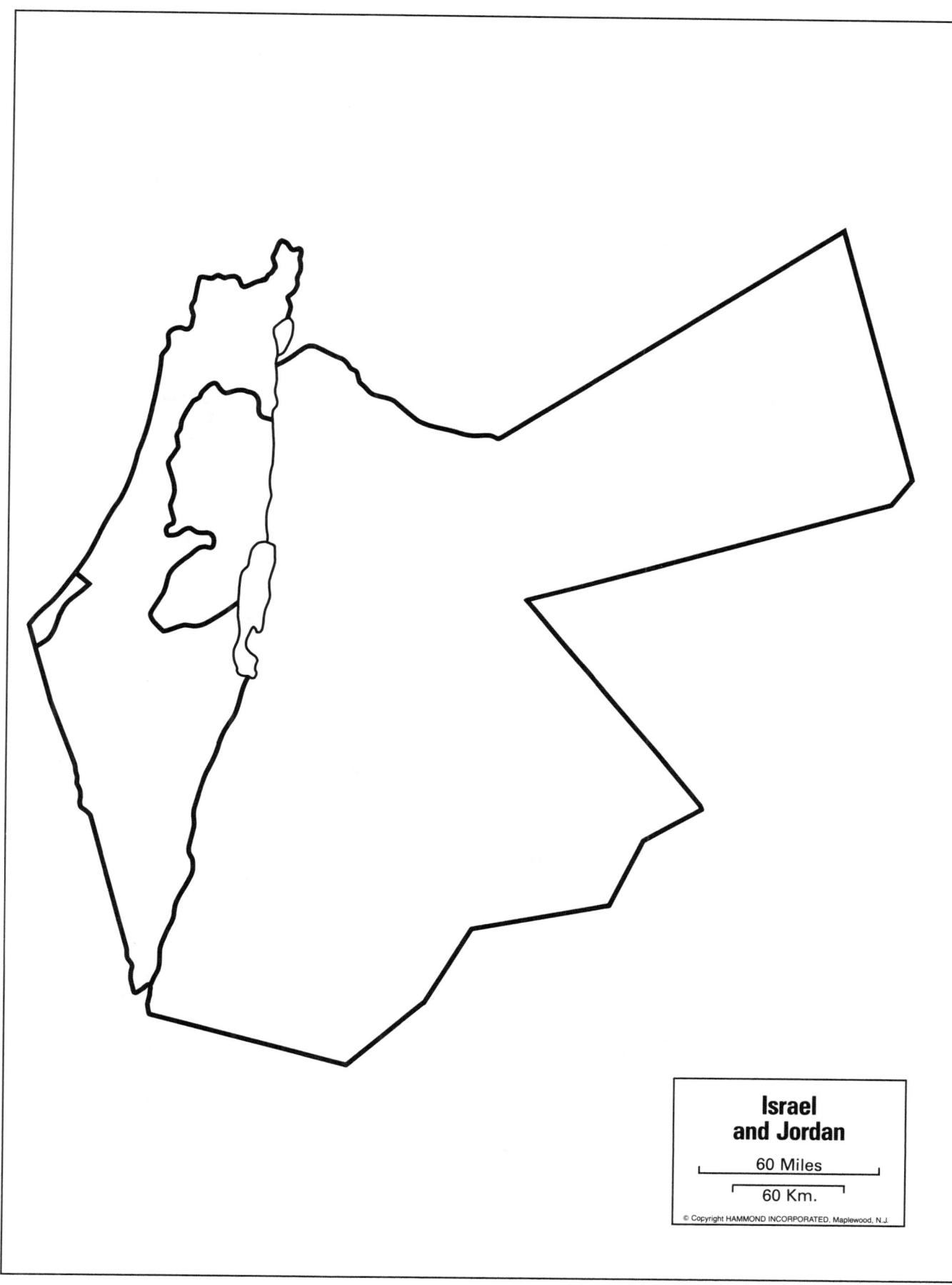

**Israel
and Jordan**

60 Miles

60 Km.

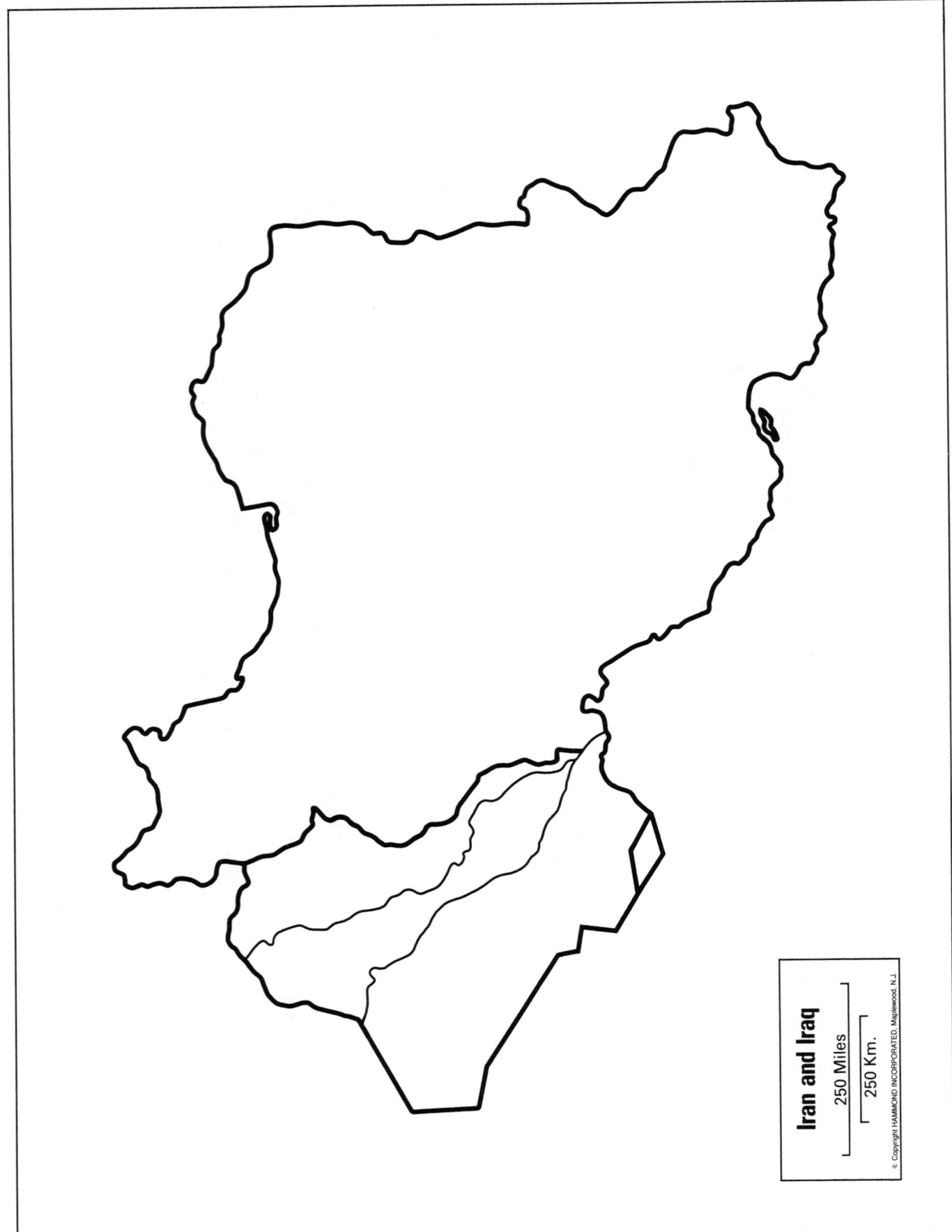

Iran and Iraq

250 Miles

250 Km.

© Copyright HAMMOND INCORPORATED, Maplewood, N.J.

Afghanistan
and Pakistan

200 Miles

200 Km.

© Copyright HAMMOND INCORPORATED, Maplewood, N.J.

India, Nepal,
Bangladesh, Bhutan
and Sri Lanka

300 Miles

300 Km.

© Copyright HAMMOND INCORPORATED, Maplewood, N.J.

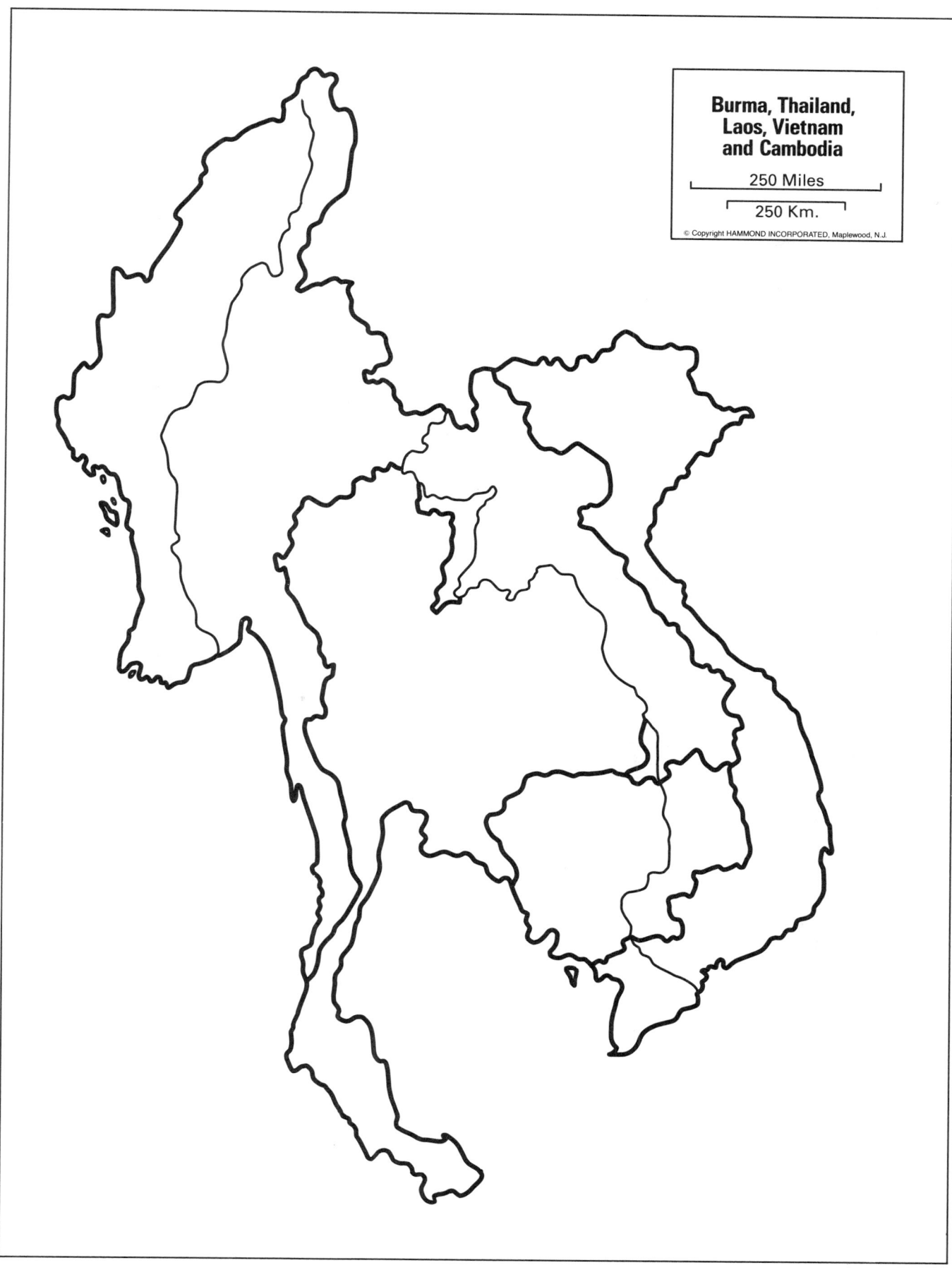

Burma, Thailand, Laos, Vietnam and Cambodia

250 Miles

250 Km.

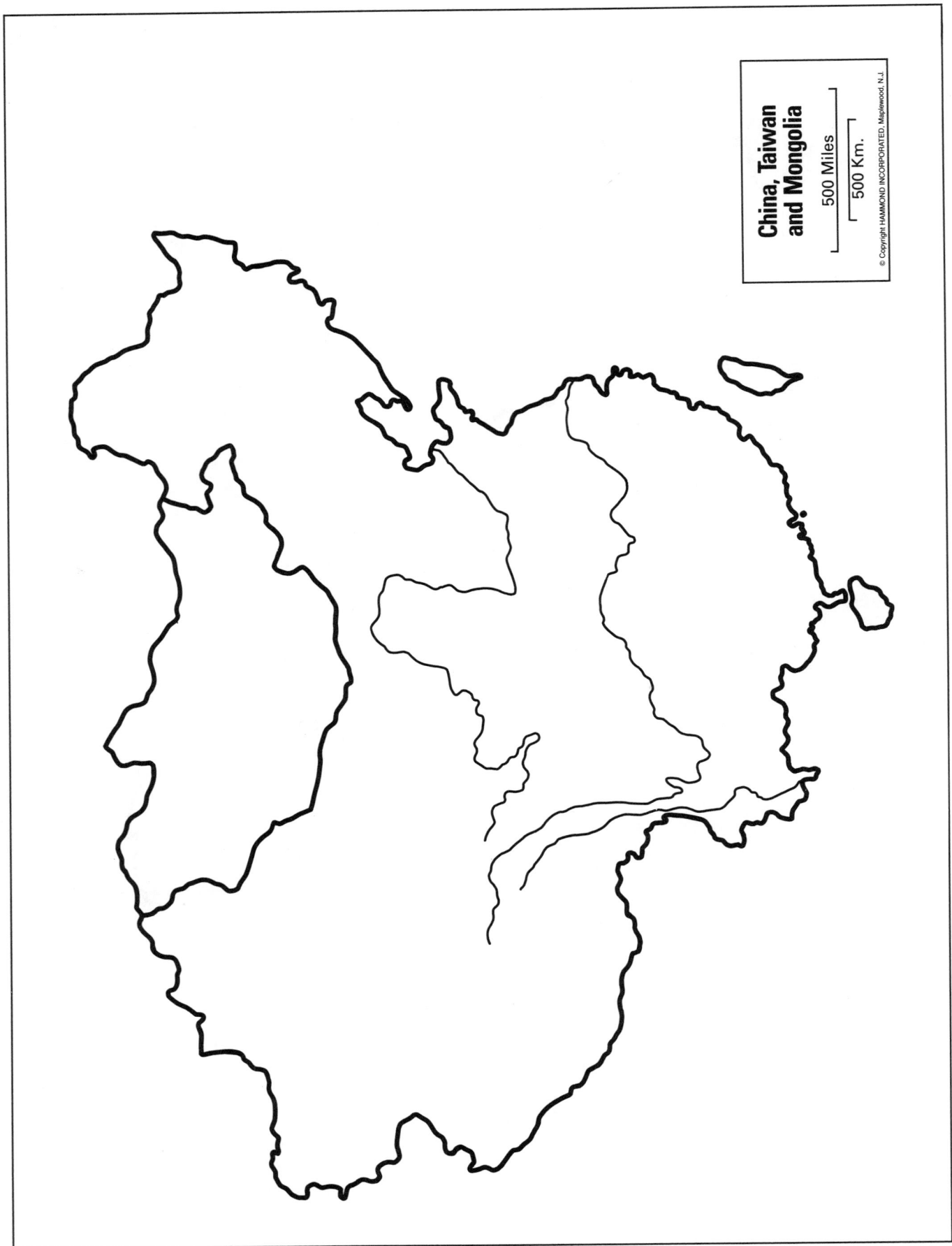

China, Taiwan and Mongolia

500 Miles

500 Km.

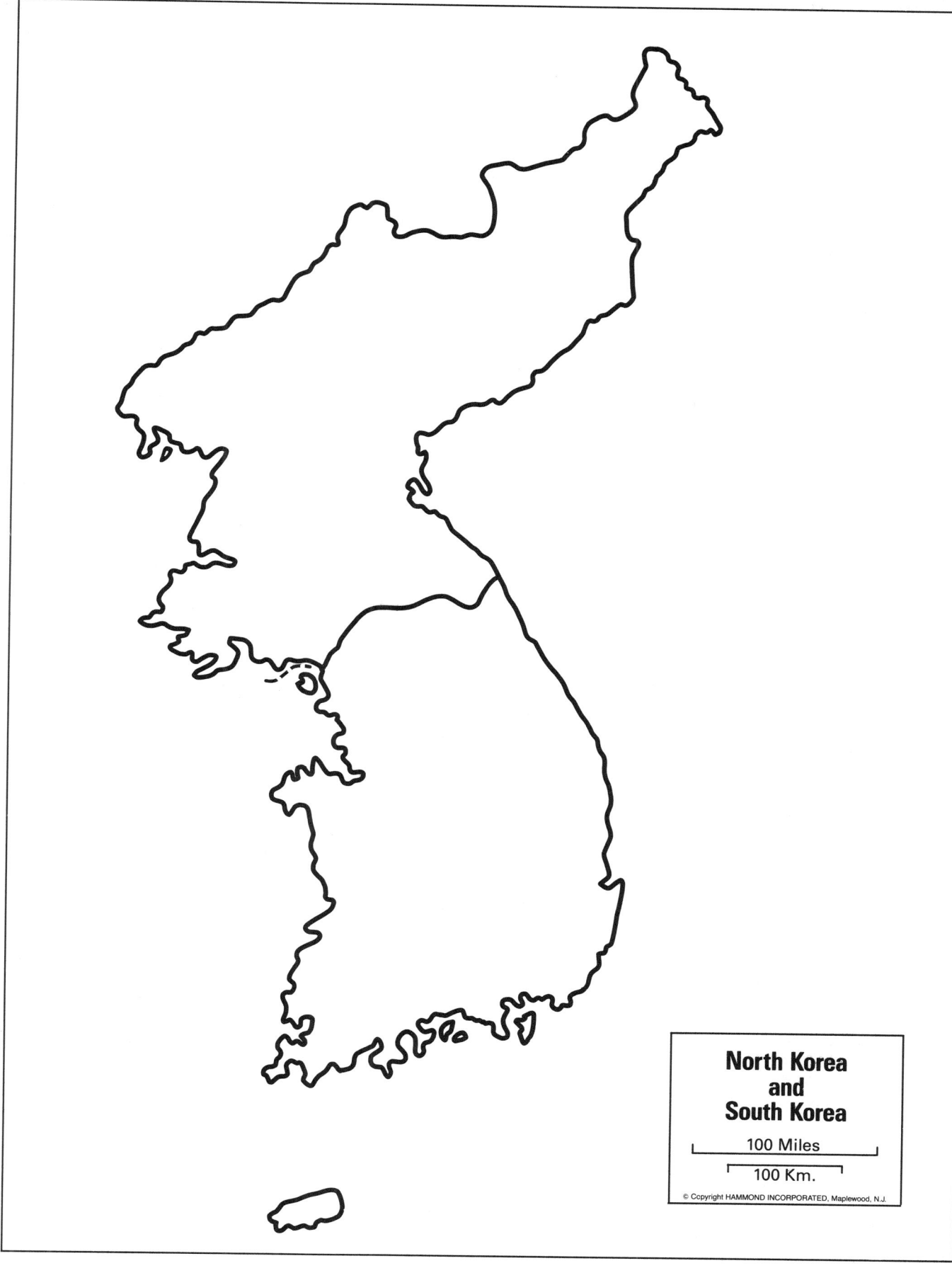

**North Korea
and
South Korea**

100 Miles

100 Km.

© Copyright HAMMOND INCORPORATED, Maplewood, N.J.

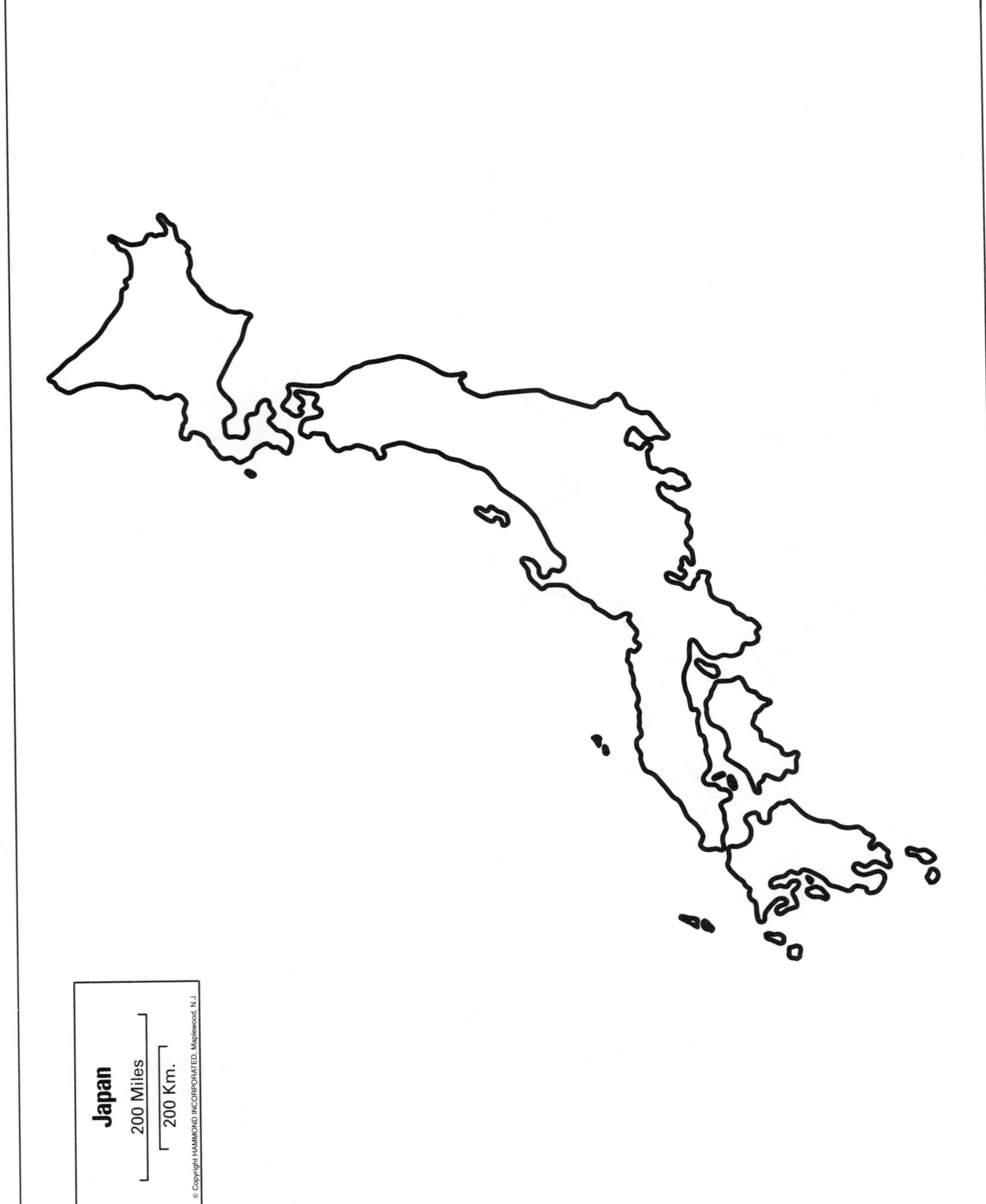

Japan

200 Miles

200 Km.

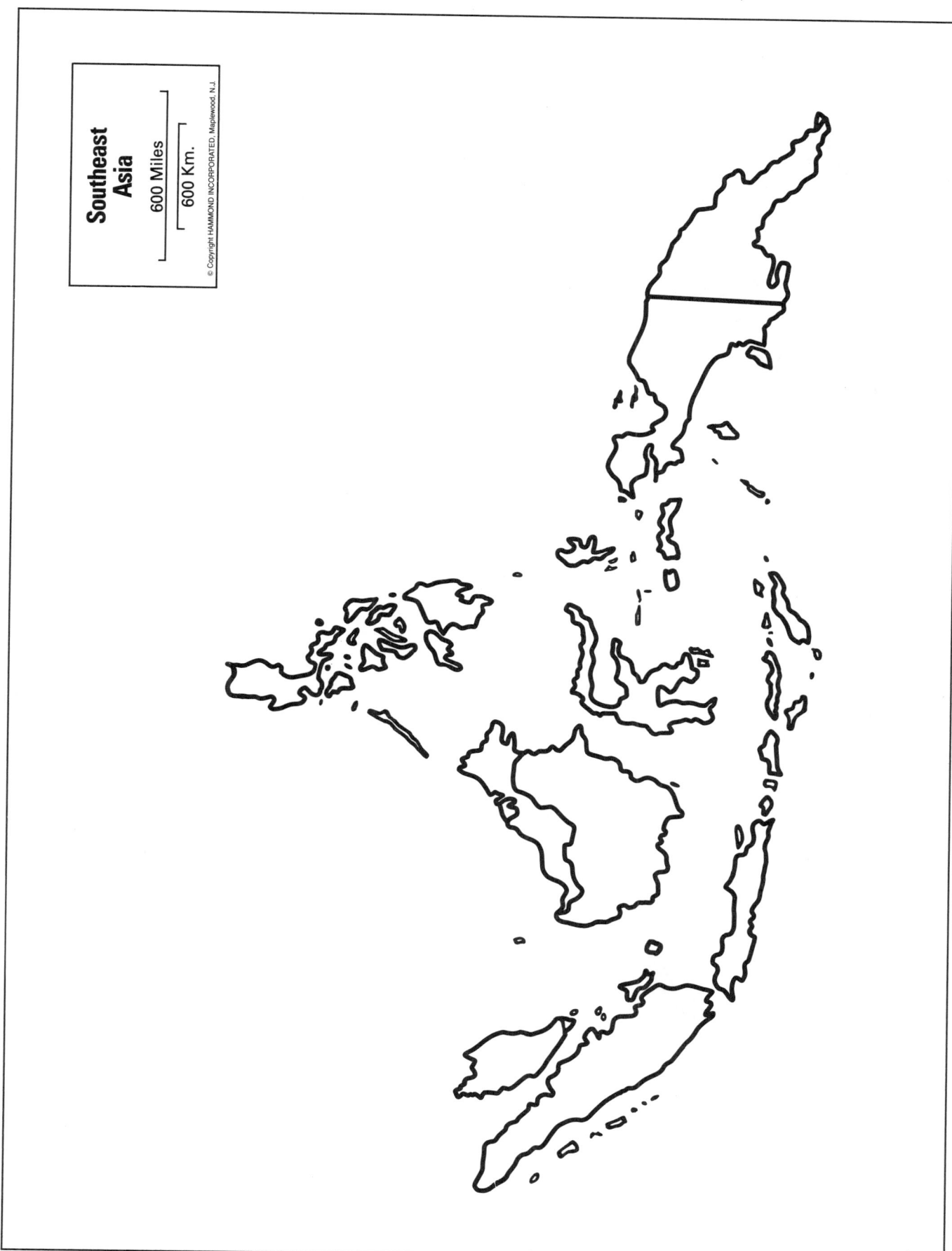

Southeast
Asia

600 Miles

600 Km.

© Copyright HAMMOND INCORPORATED, Maplewood, N.J.

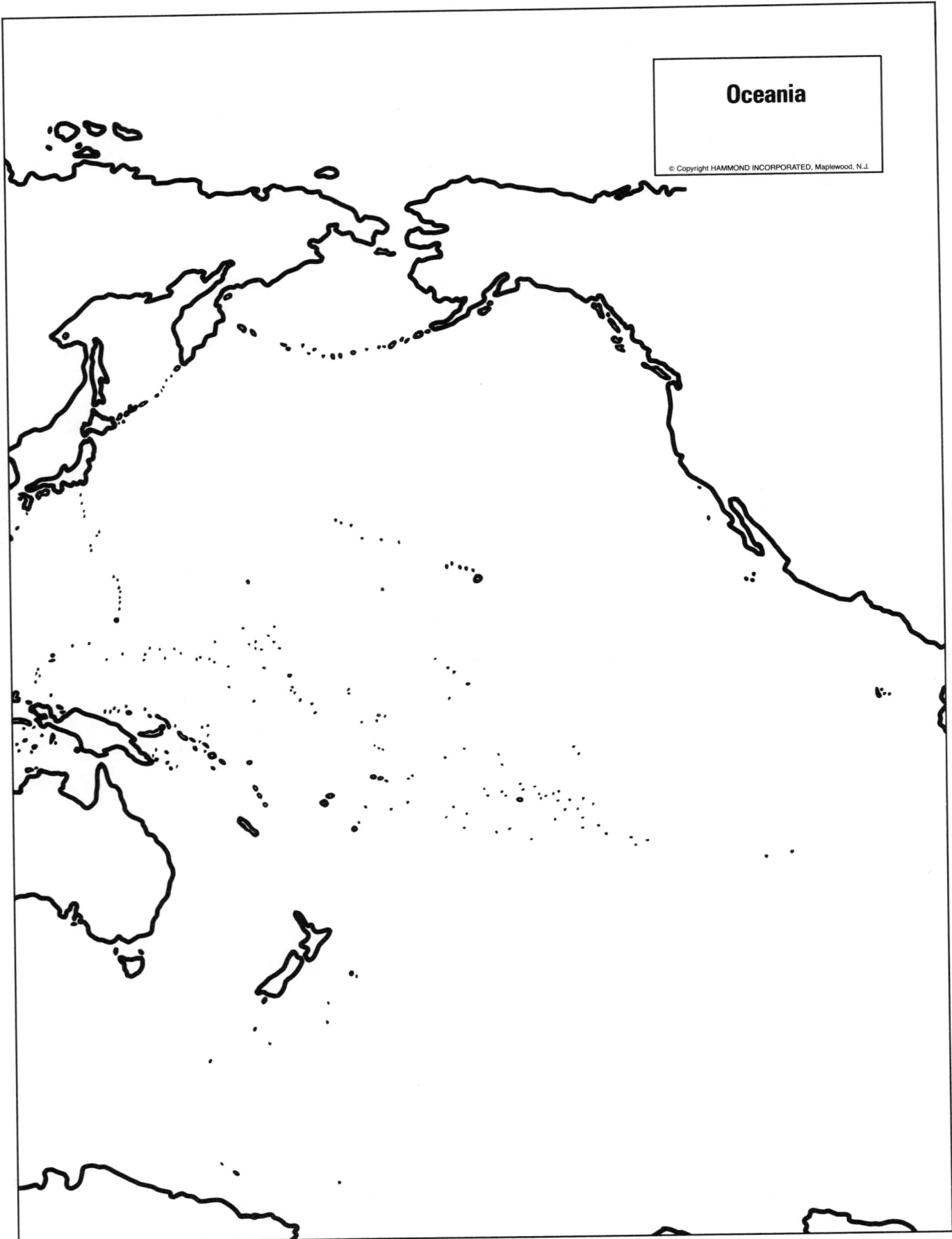

Oceania

© Copyright HAMMOND INCORPORATED, Maplewood, N.J.

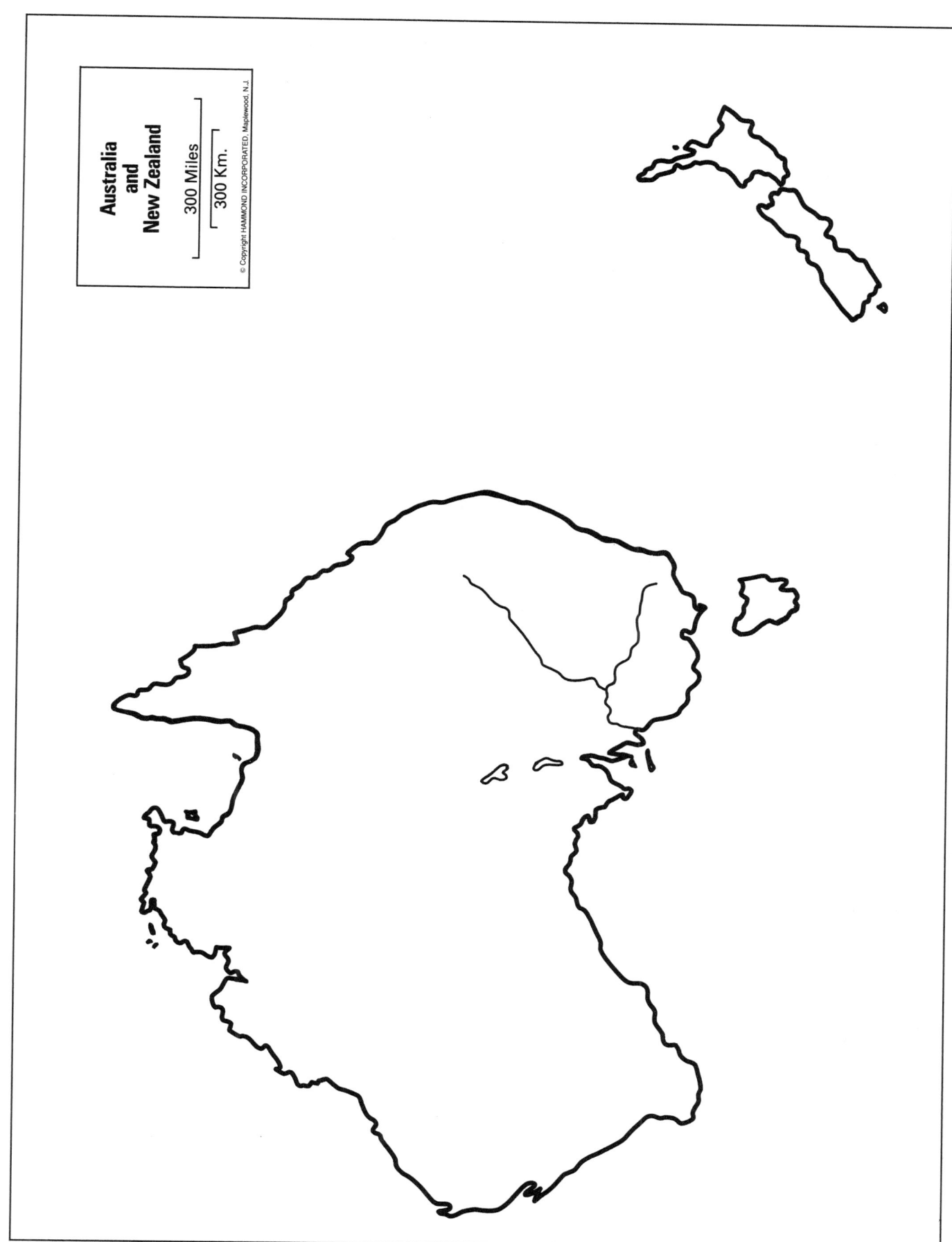

Australia
and
New Zealand

300 Miles

300 Km.

Africa

1000 Miles

1000 Km.

Western Africa

500 Miles

500 Km.

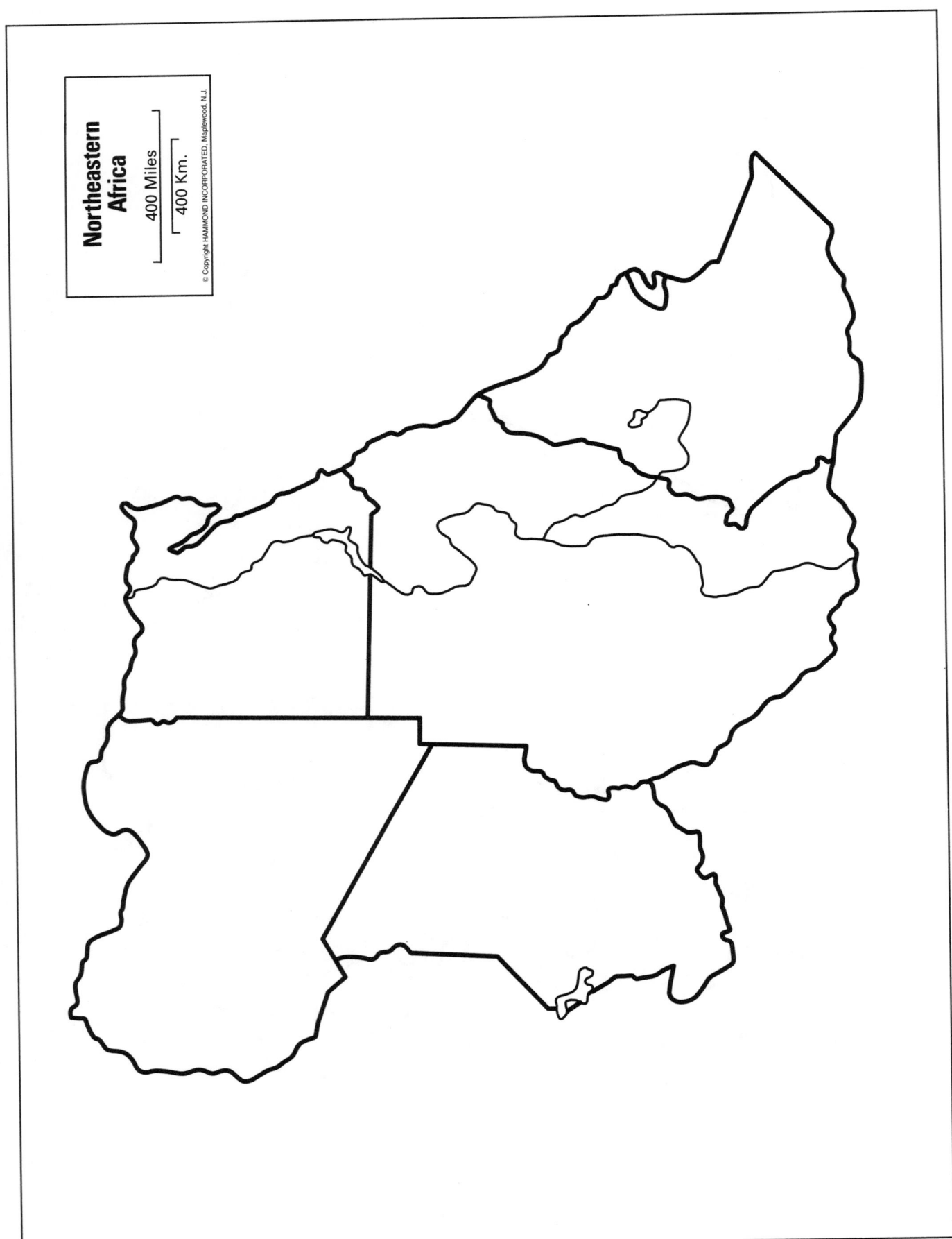

Northeastern
Africa

400 Miles

400 Km.

© Copyright HAMMOND INCORPORATED, Maplewood, N.J.

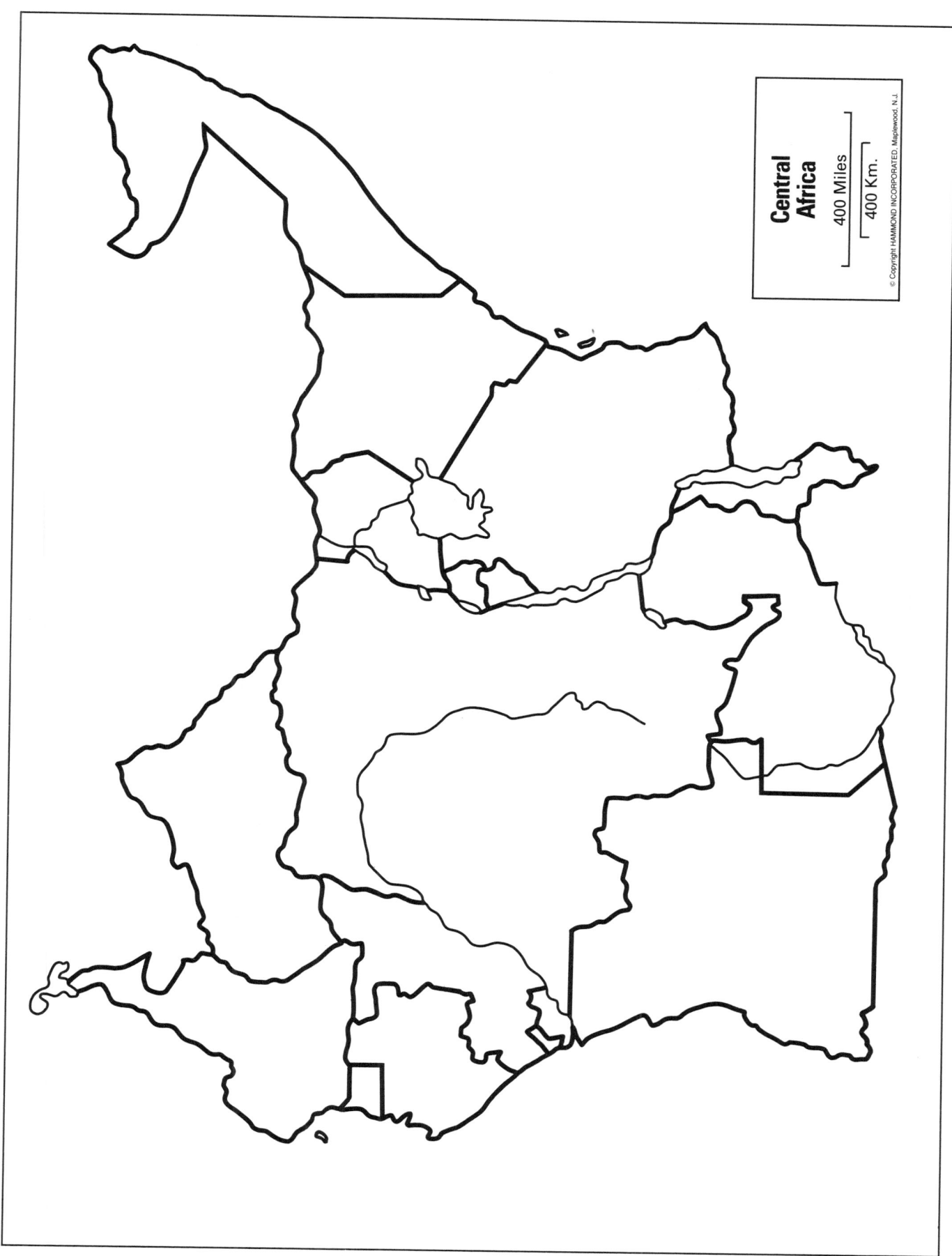

Central Africa

400 Miles

400 Km.

590

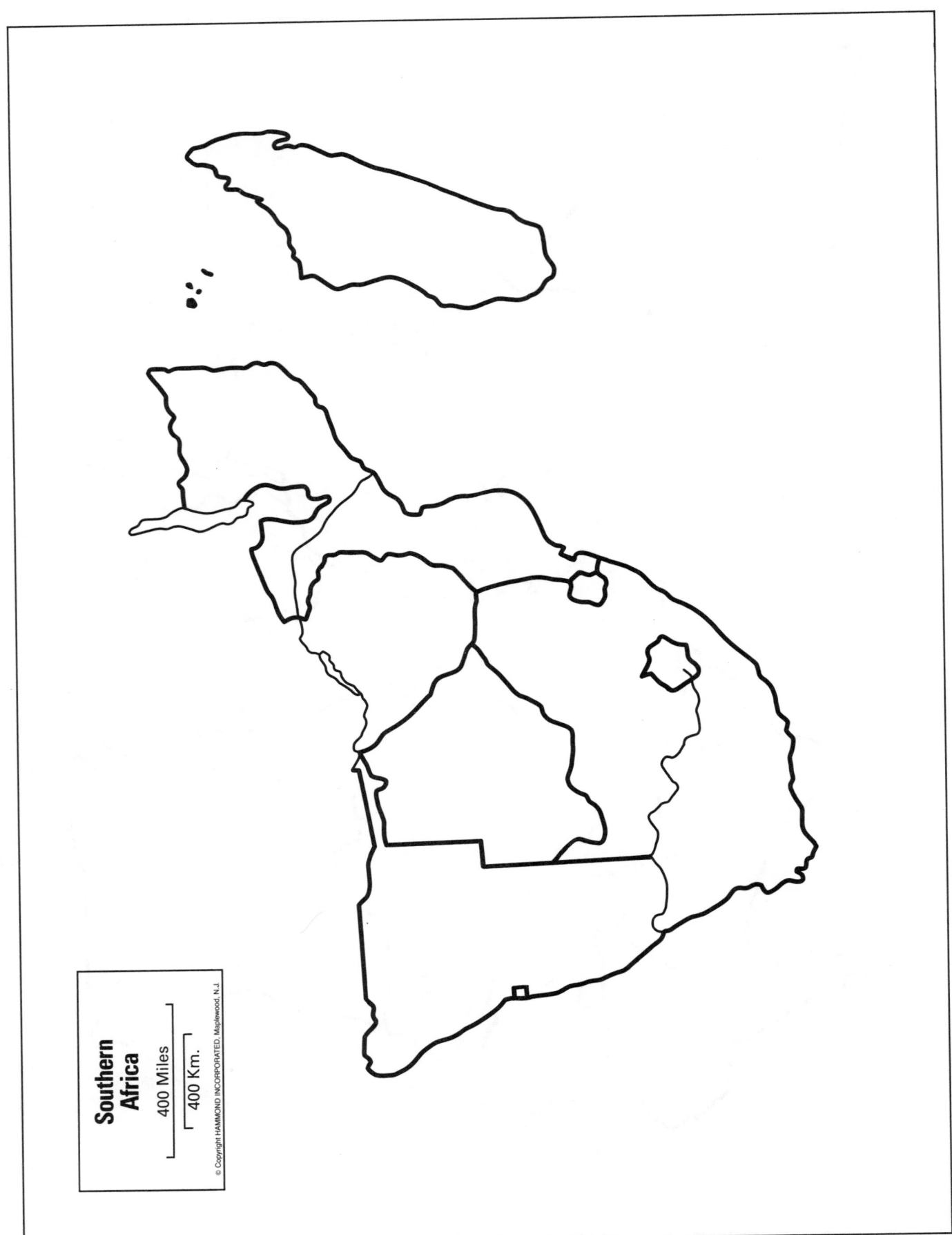

Southern
Africa

400 Miles

400 Km.

© Copyright HAMMOND INCORPORATED. Maplewood, N.J.

**South
America**

600 Miles

600 Km.

© Copyright HAMMOND INCORPORATED, Maplewood, N.J.

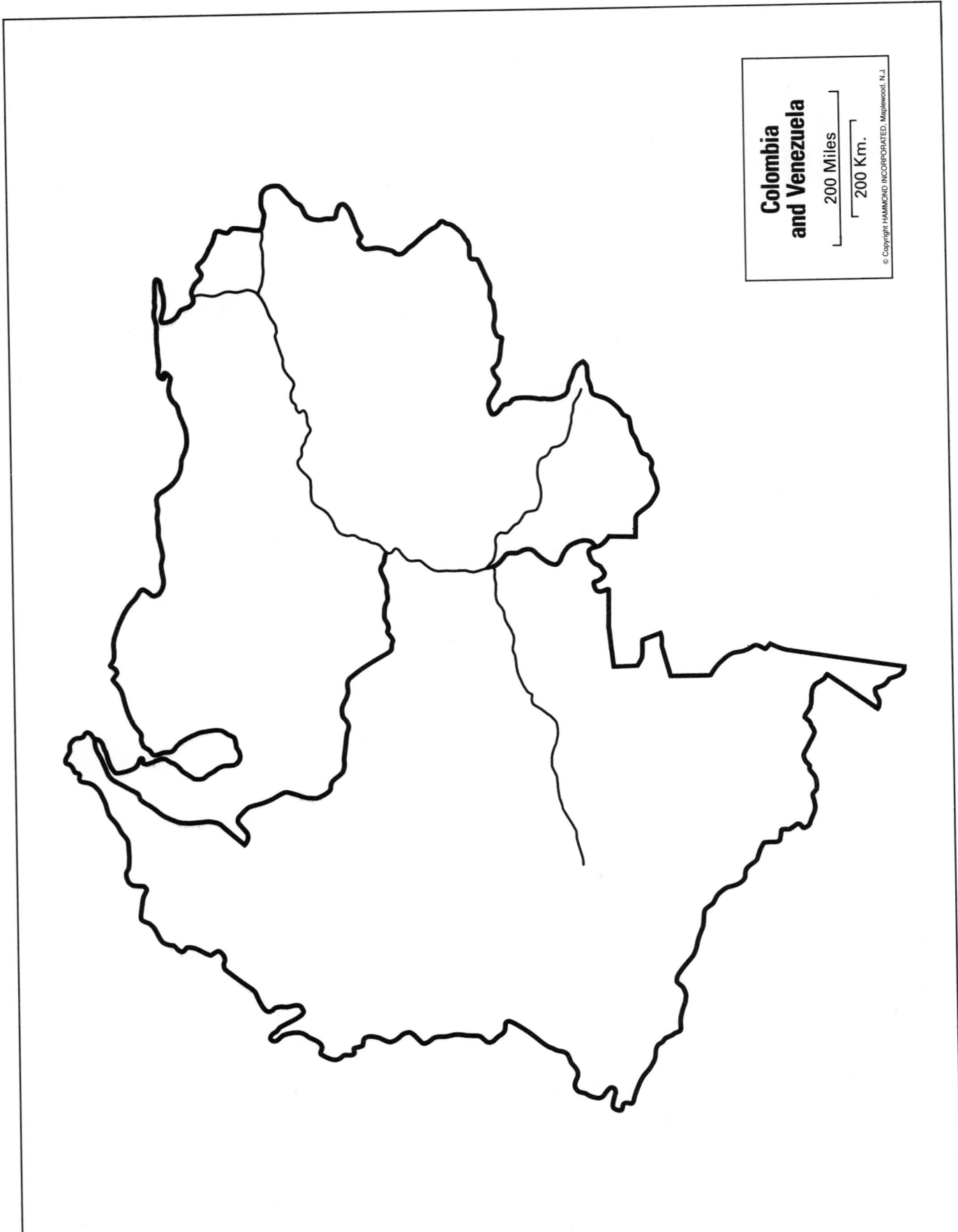

**Colombia
and Venezuela**

200 Miles

200 Km.

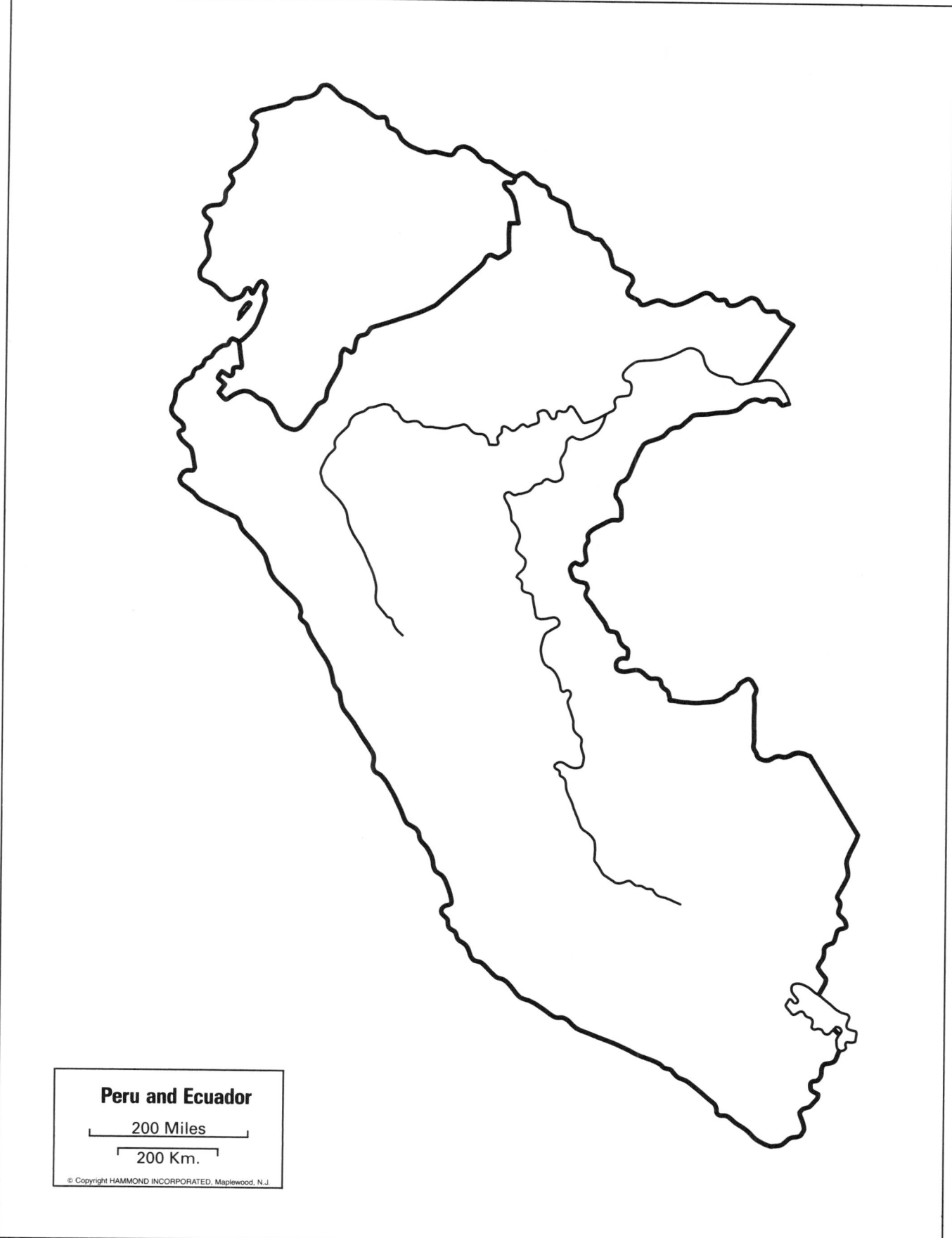

Peru and Ecuador

200 Miles

200 Km.

© Copyright HAMMOND INCORPORATED, Maplewood, N.J.

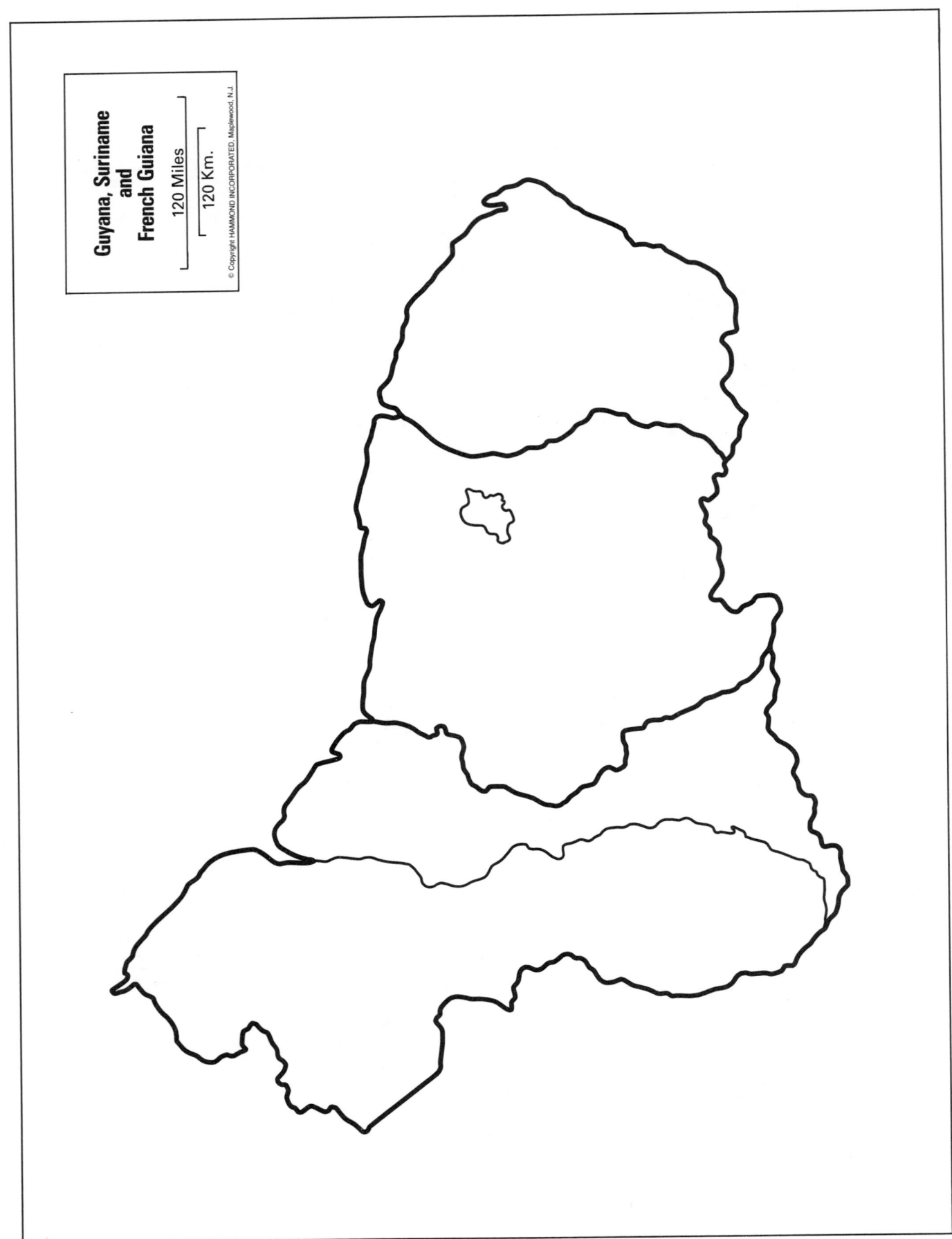

Guyana, Suriname
and
French Guiana

120 Miles

120 Km.

Brazil
and Bolivia
500 Miles
500 Km.
© Copyright HAMMOND INCORPORATED, Maplewood, N.J.

**Argentina,
Chile, Paraguay
and Uruguay**

400 Miles

400 Km.

© Copyright HAMMOND INCORPORATED, Maplewood, N.J.

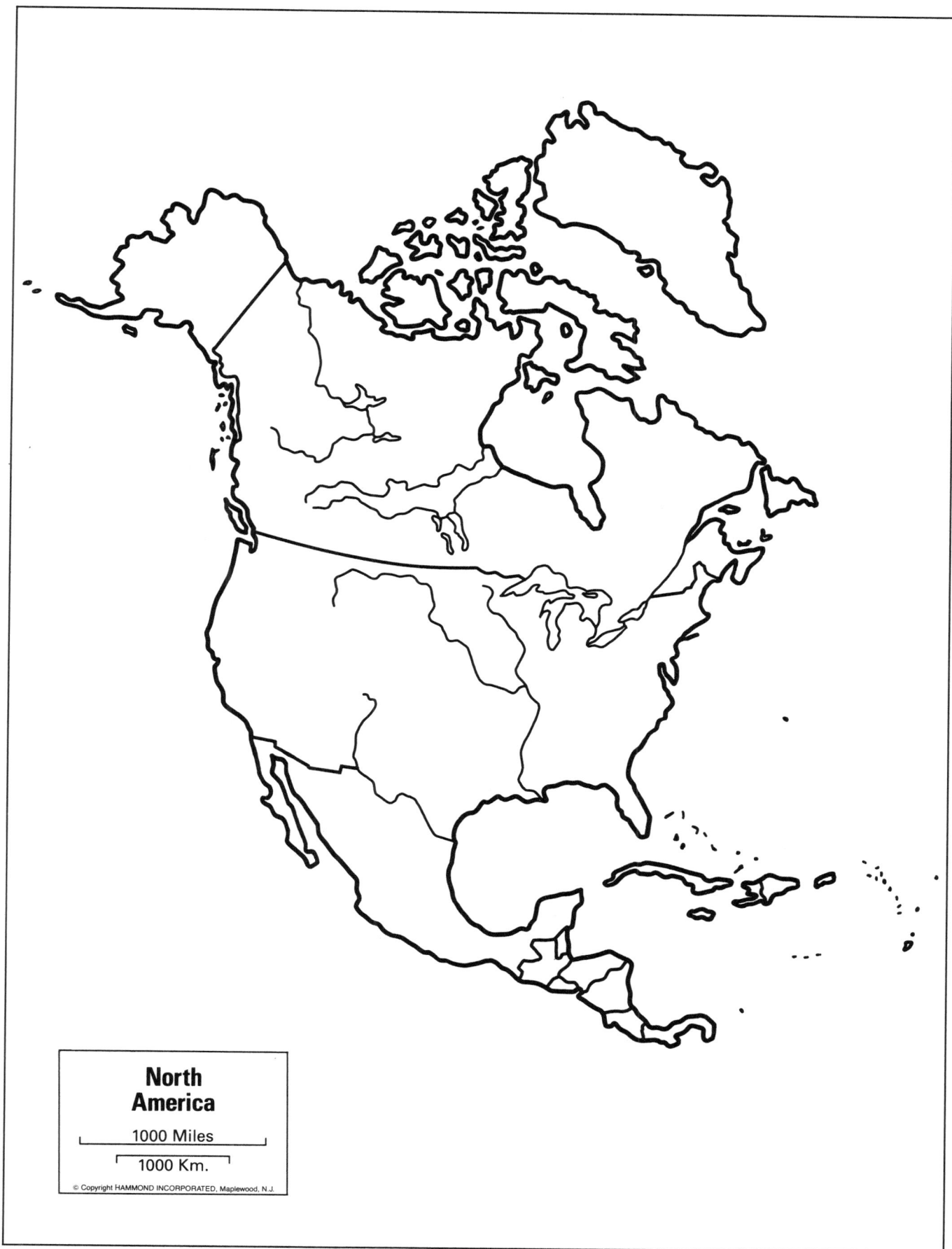

**North
America**

1000 Miles

1000 Km.

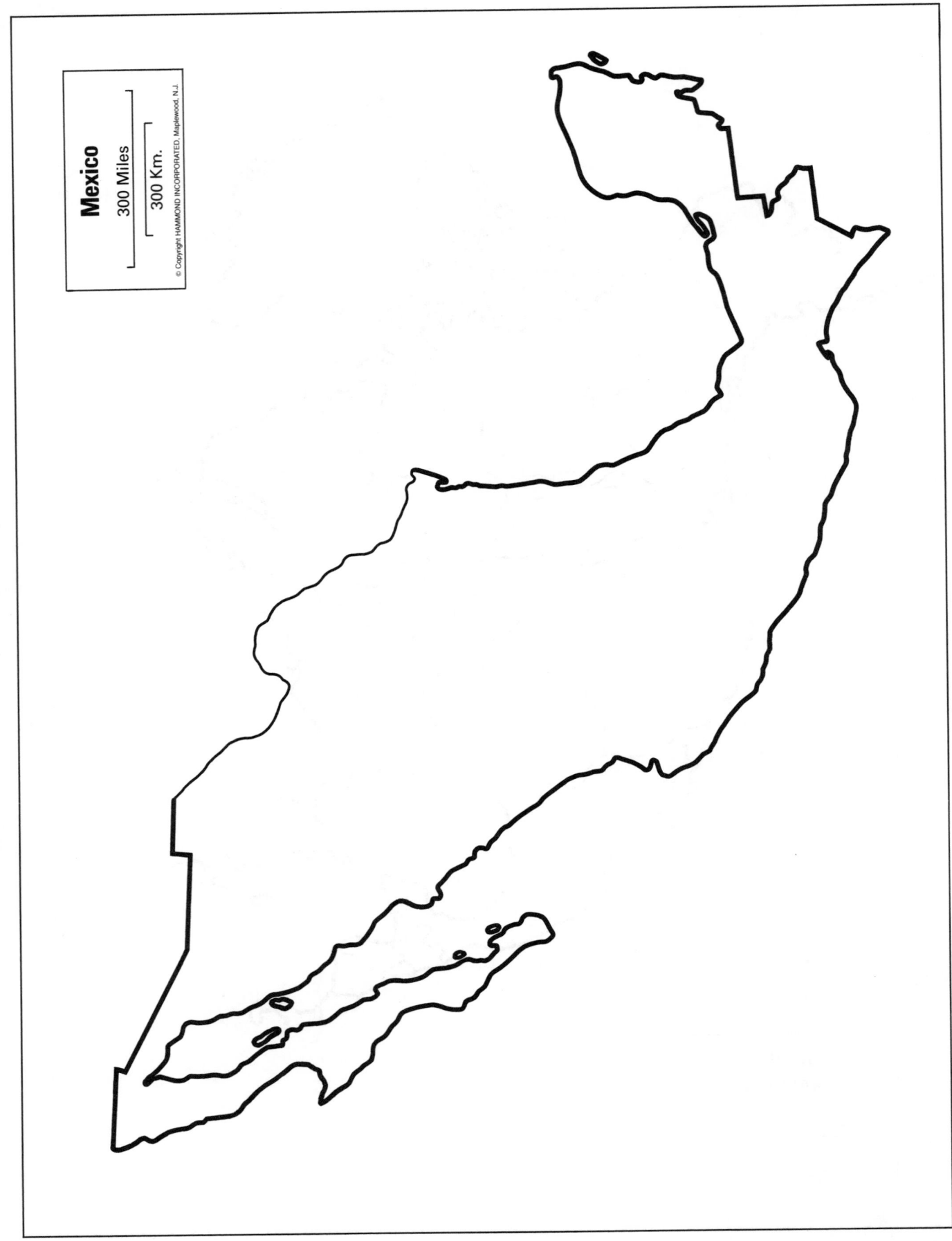

Mexico

300 Miles

300 Km.

© Copyright HAMMOND INCORPORATED, Maplewood, N.J.

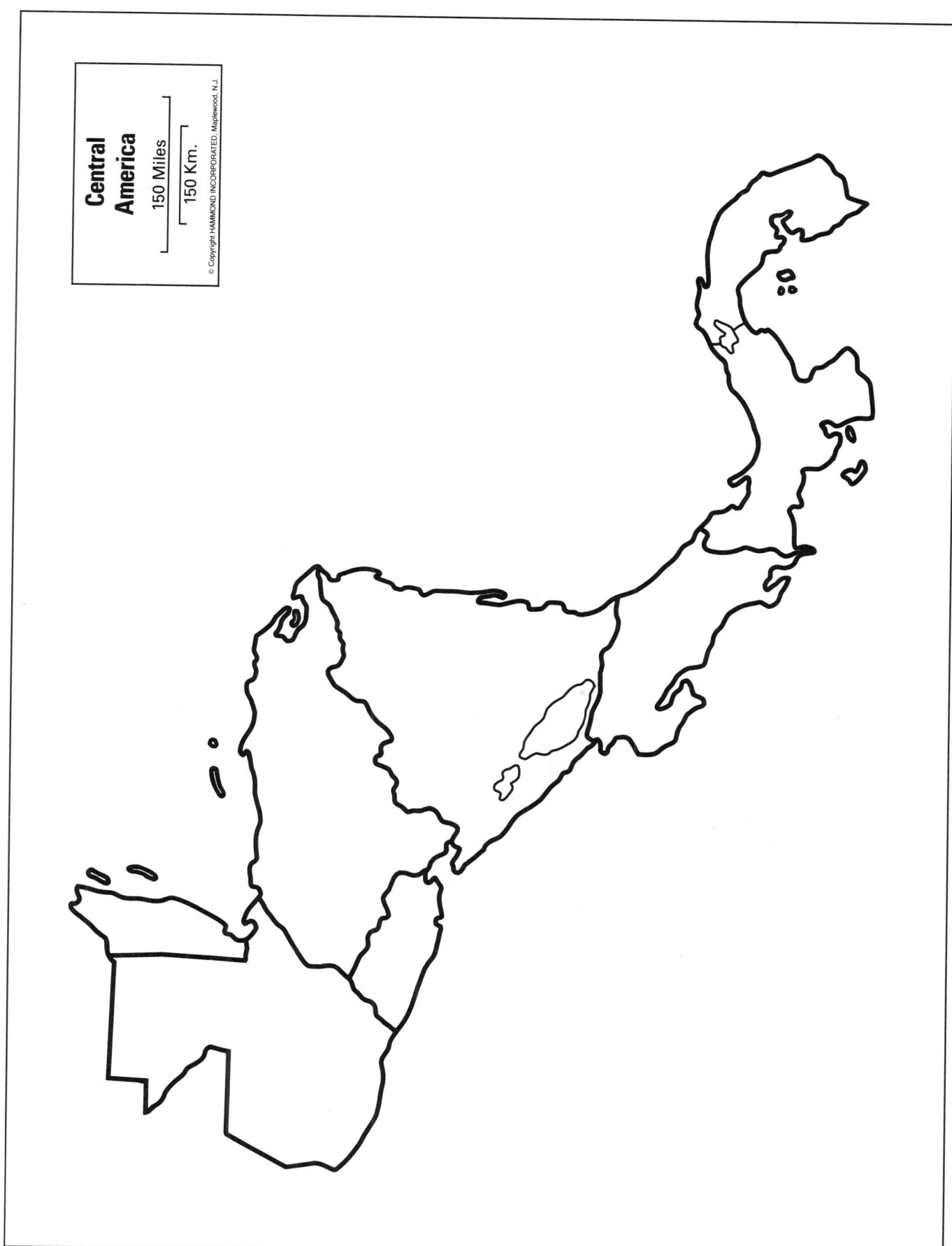

Central America

150 Miles

150 Km.

© Copyright HAMMOND INCORPORATED, Maplewood, N.J.

600

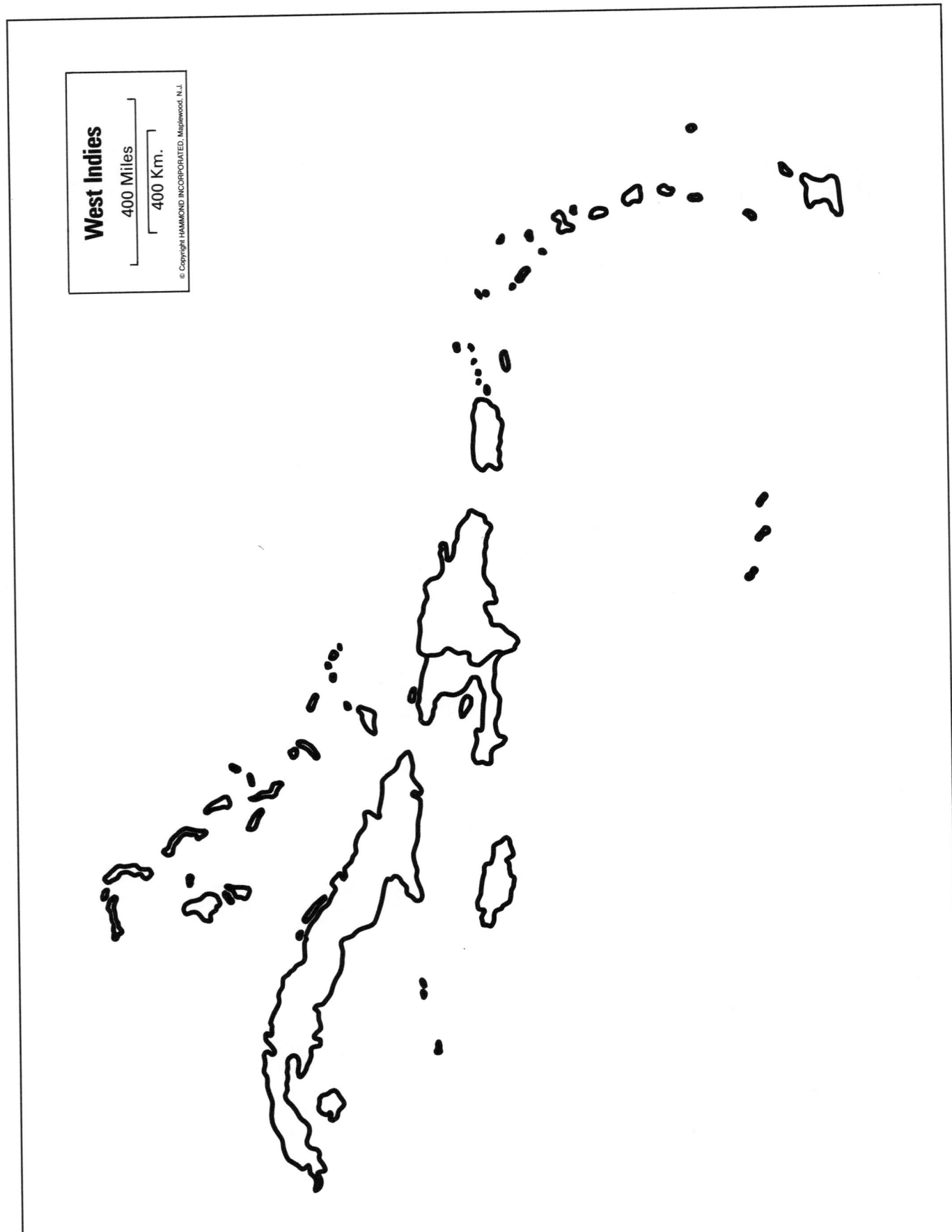

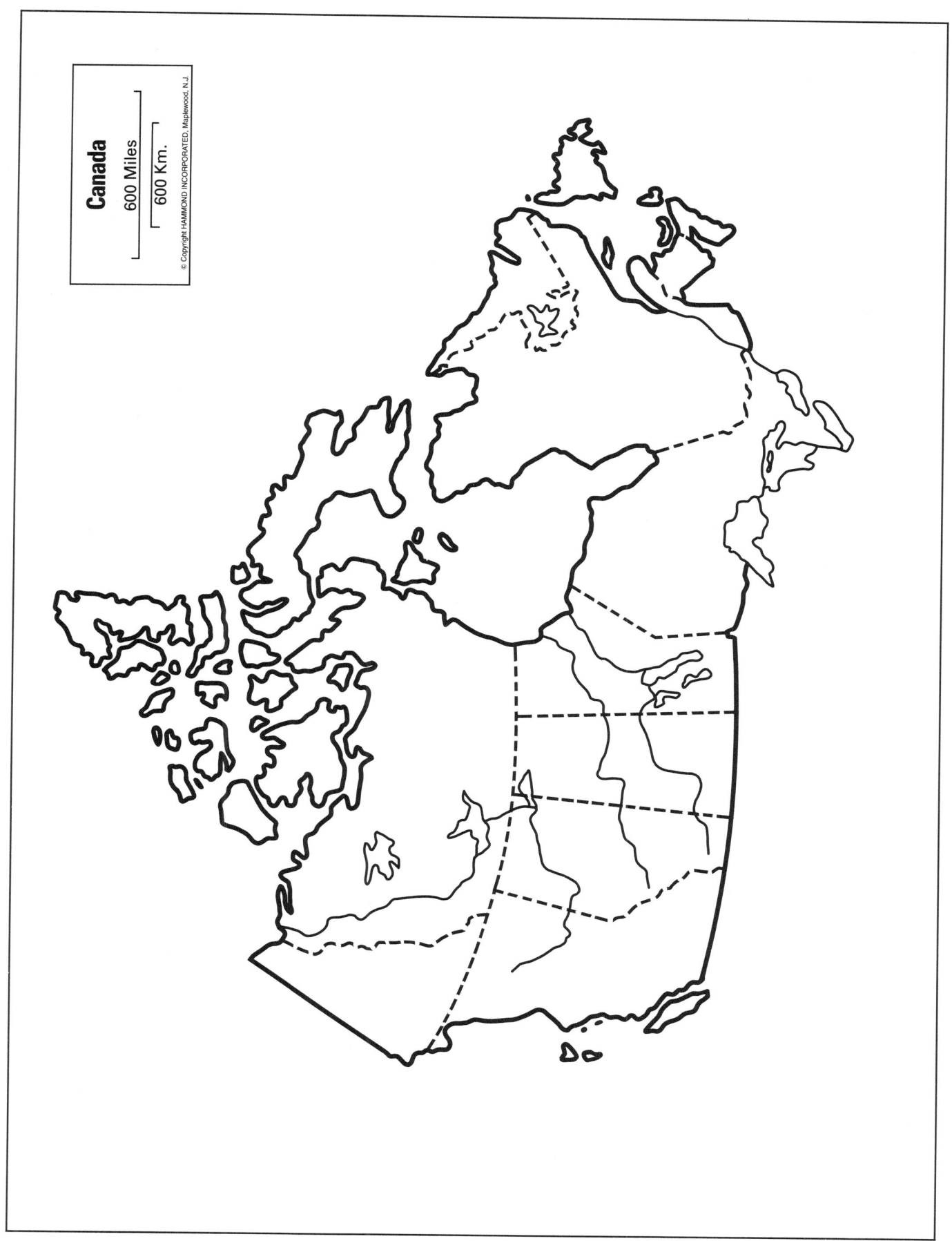

Canada

600 Miles

600 Km.

© Copyright HAMMOND INCORPORATED, Maplewood, N.J.

602

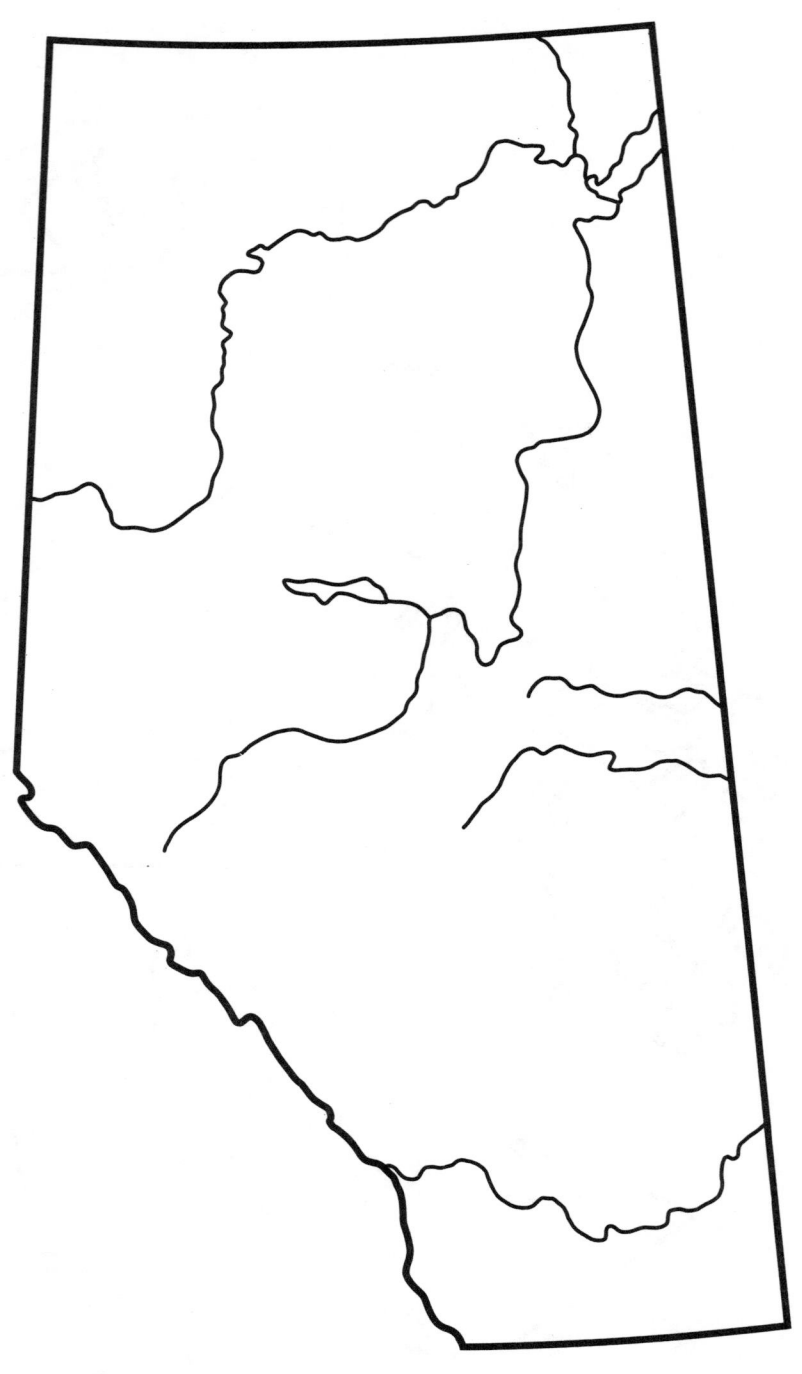

Alberta

200 Miles

200 Km.

© Copyright HAMMOND INCORPORATED, Maplewood, N.J.

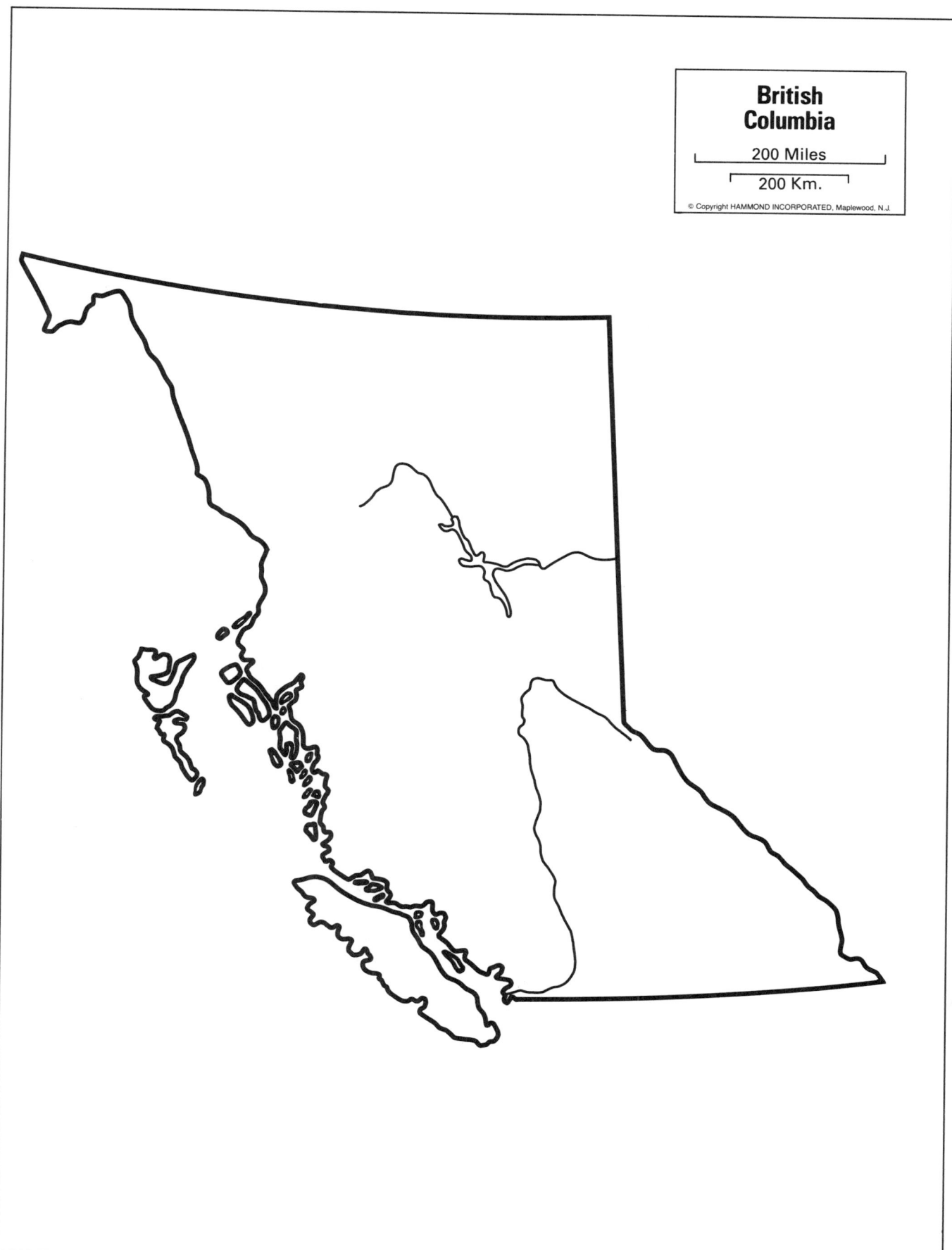

British Columbia

200 Miles

200 Km.

© Copyright HAMMOND INCORPORATED, Maplewood, N.J.

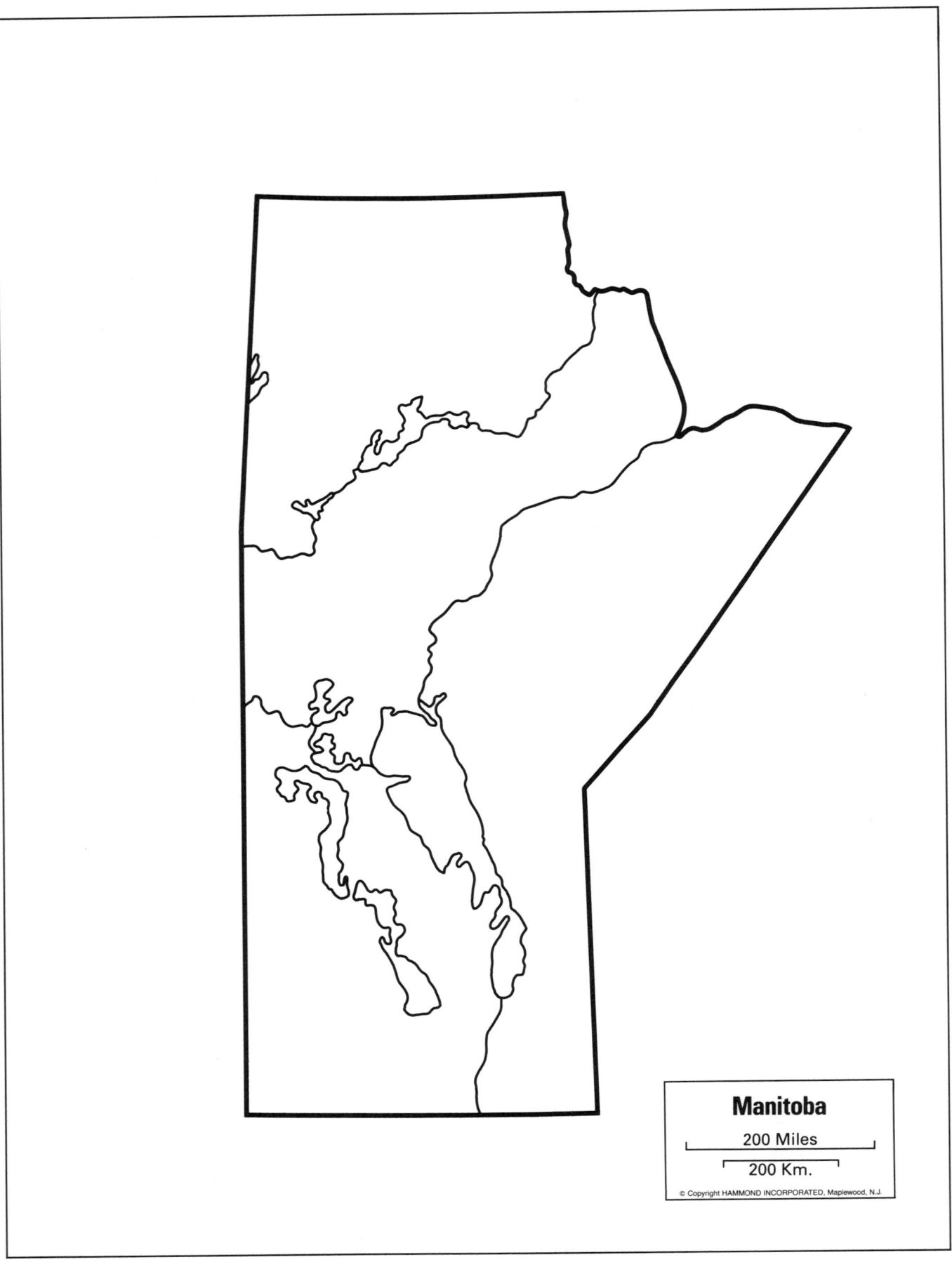

Manitoba

200 Miles

200 Km.

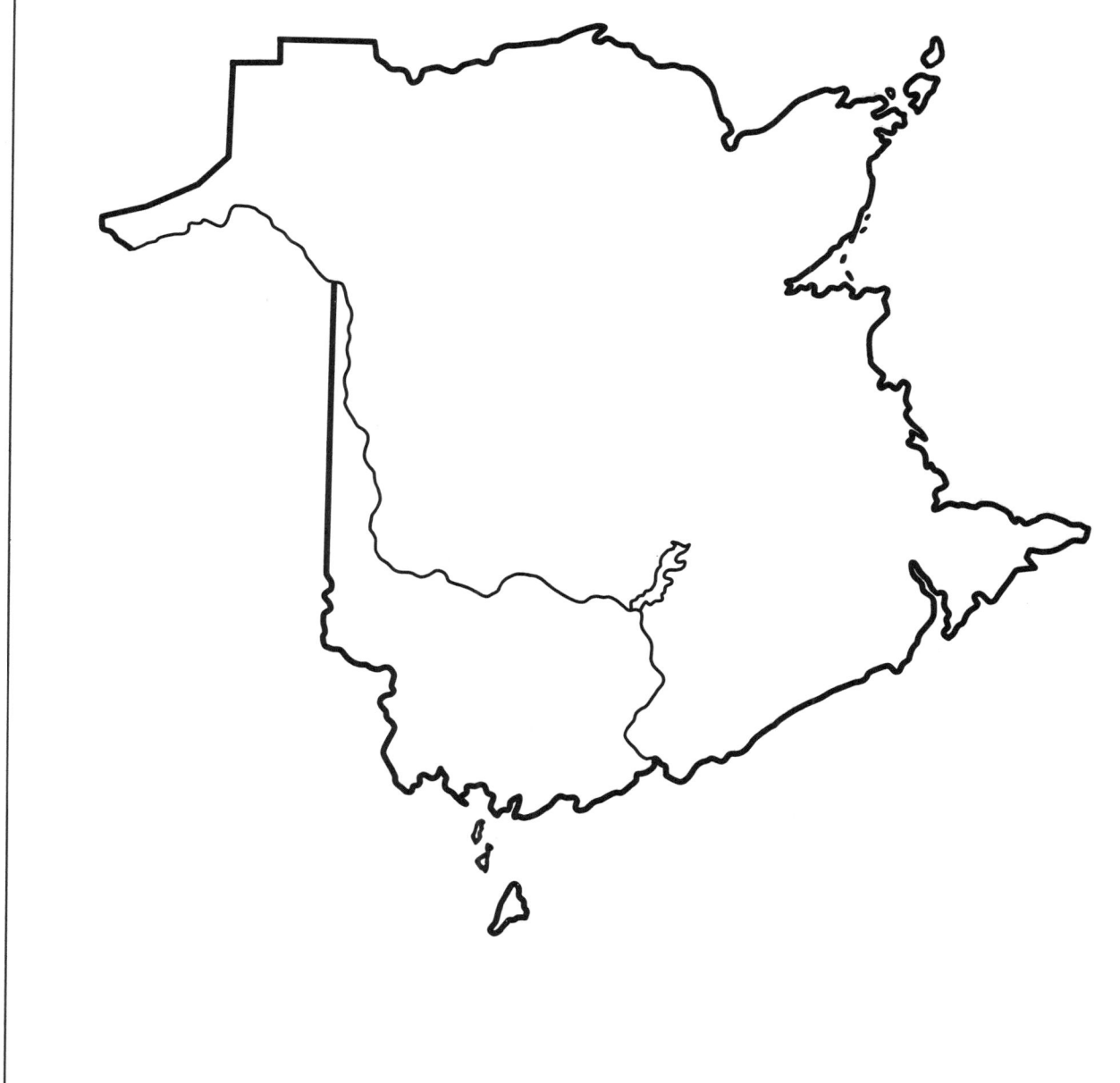

New Brunswick

60 Miles

60 Km.

© Copyright HAMMOND INCORPORATED, Maplewood, N.J.

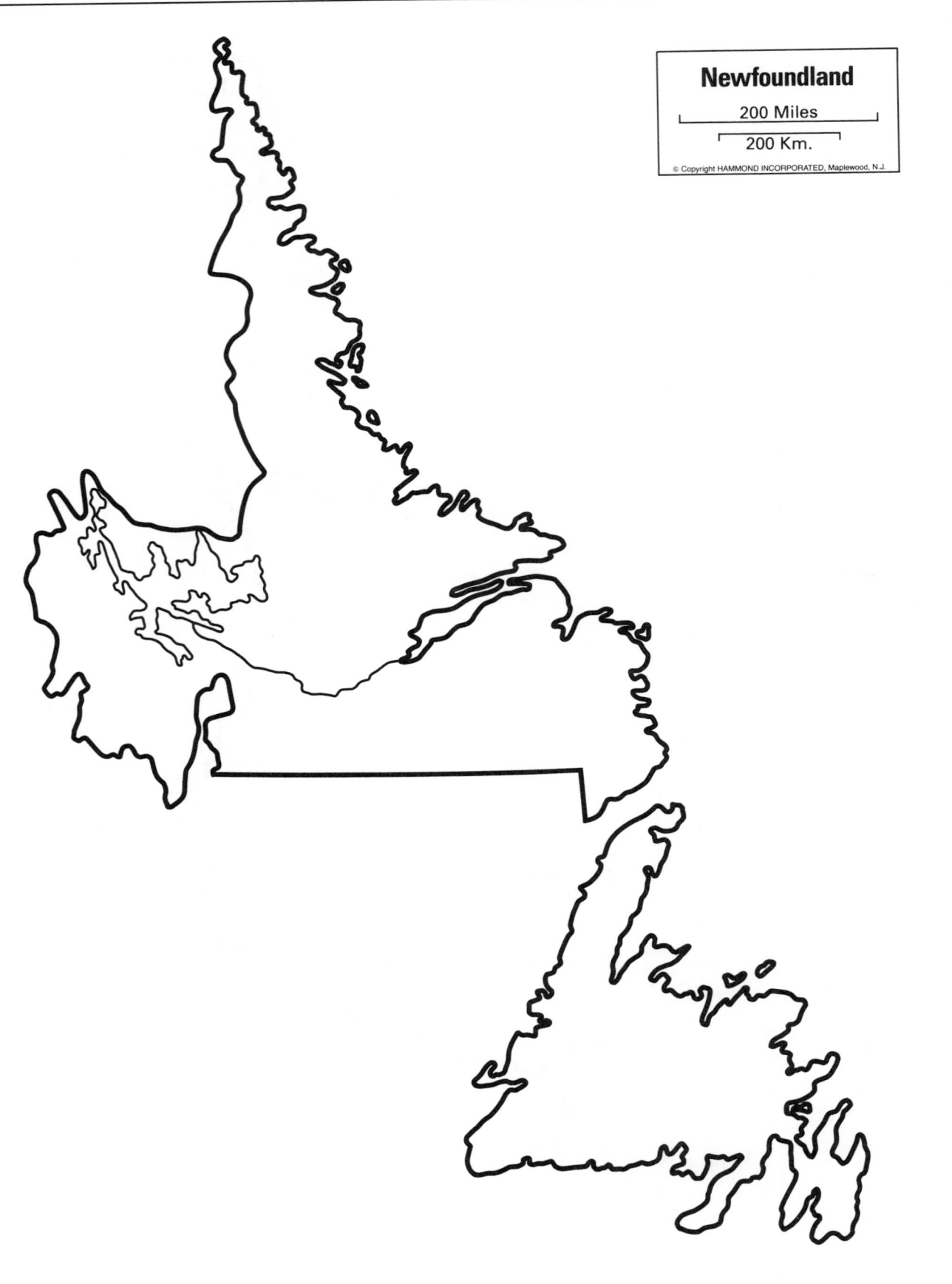

Newfoundland

200 Miles

200 Km.

© Copyright HAMMOND INCORPORATED, Maplewood, N.J.

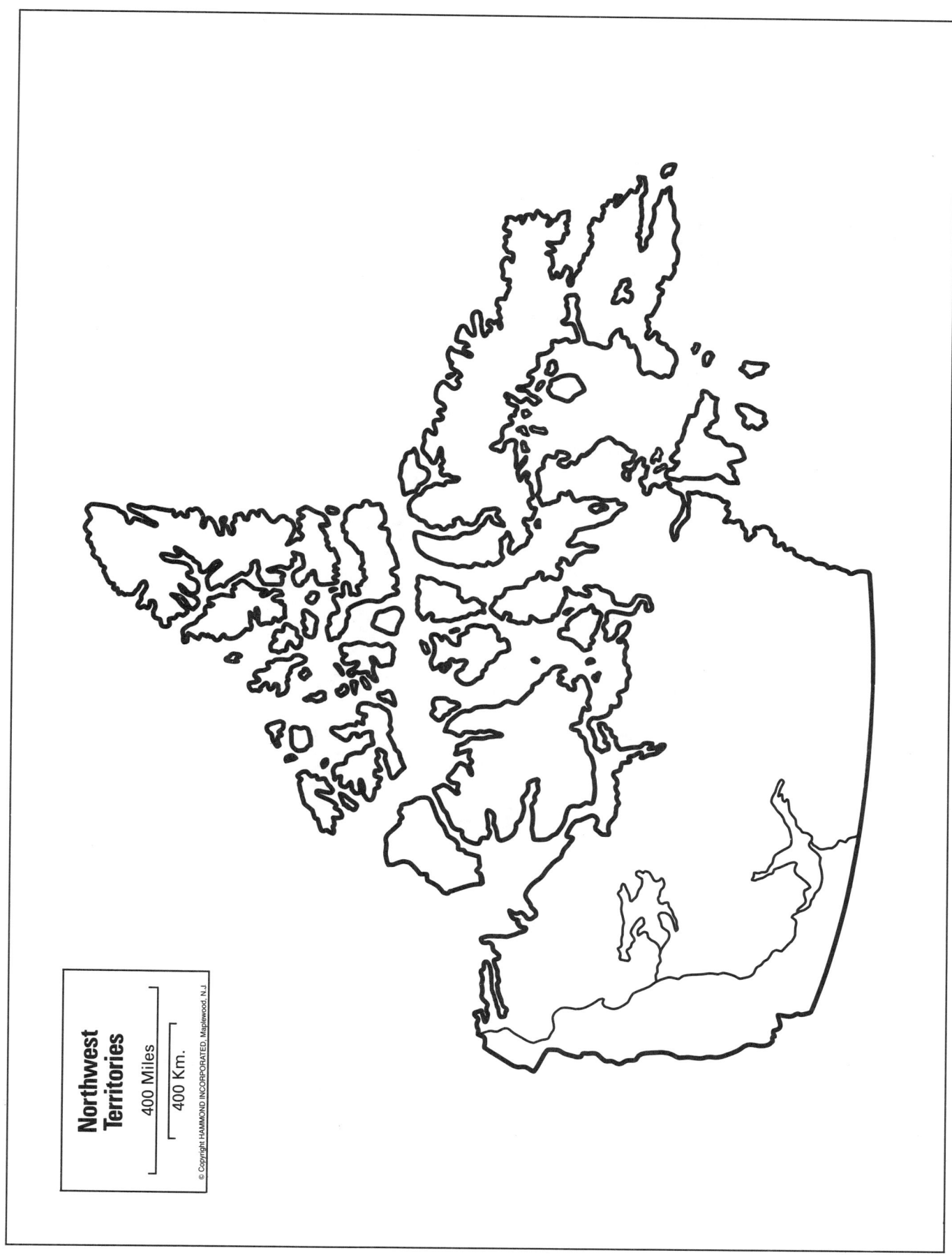

Northwest Territories

400 Miles

400 Km.

© Copyright HAMMOND INCORPORATED, Maplewood, N.J.

608

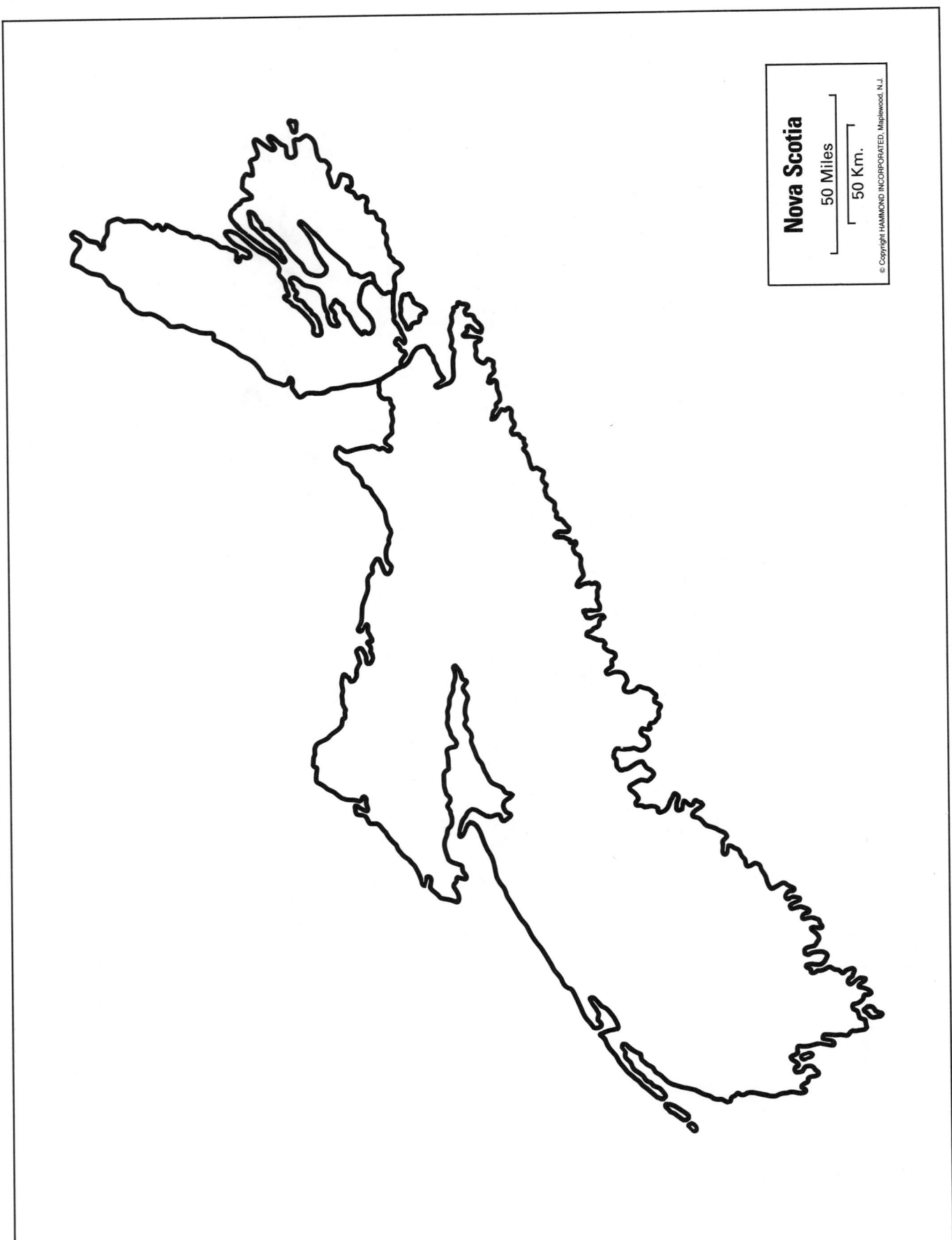

Nova Scotia

50 Miles

50 Km.

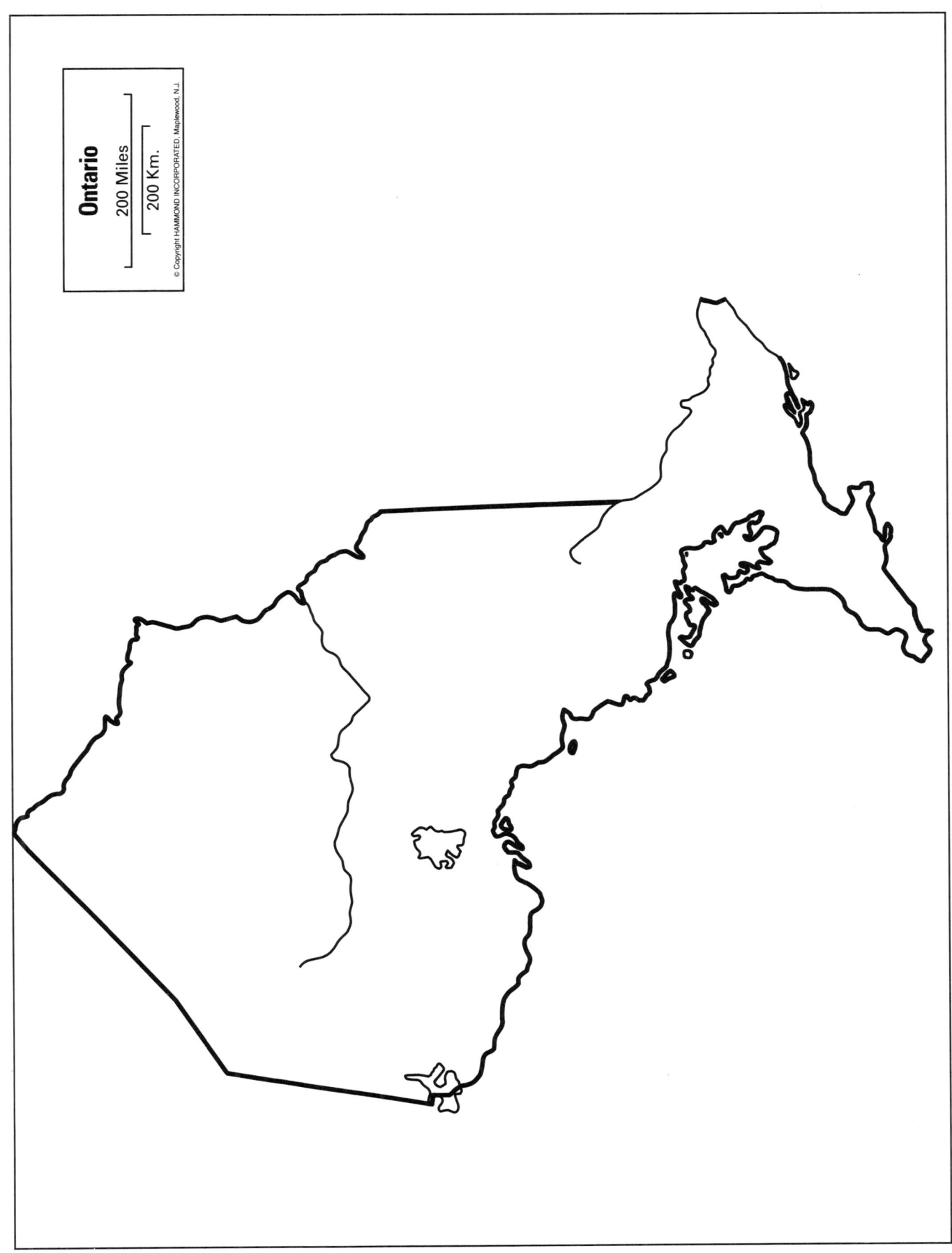

Ontario

200 Miles

200 Km.

© Copyright HAMMOND INCORPORATED, Maplewood, N.J.

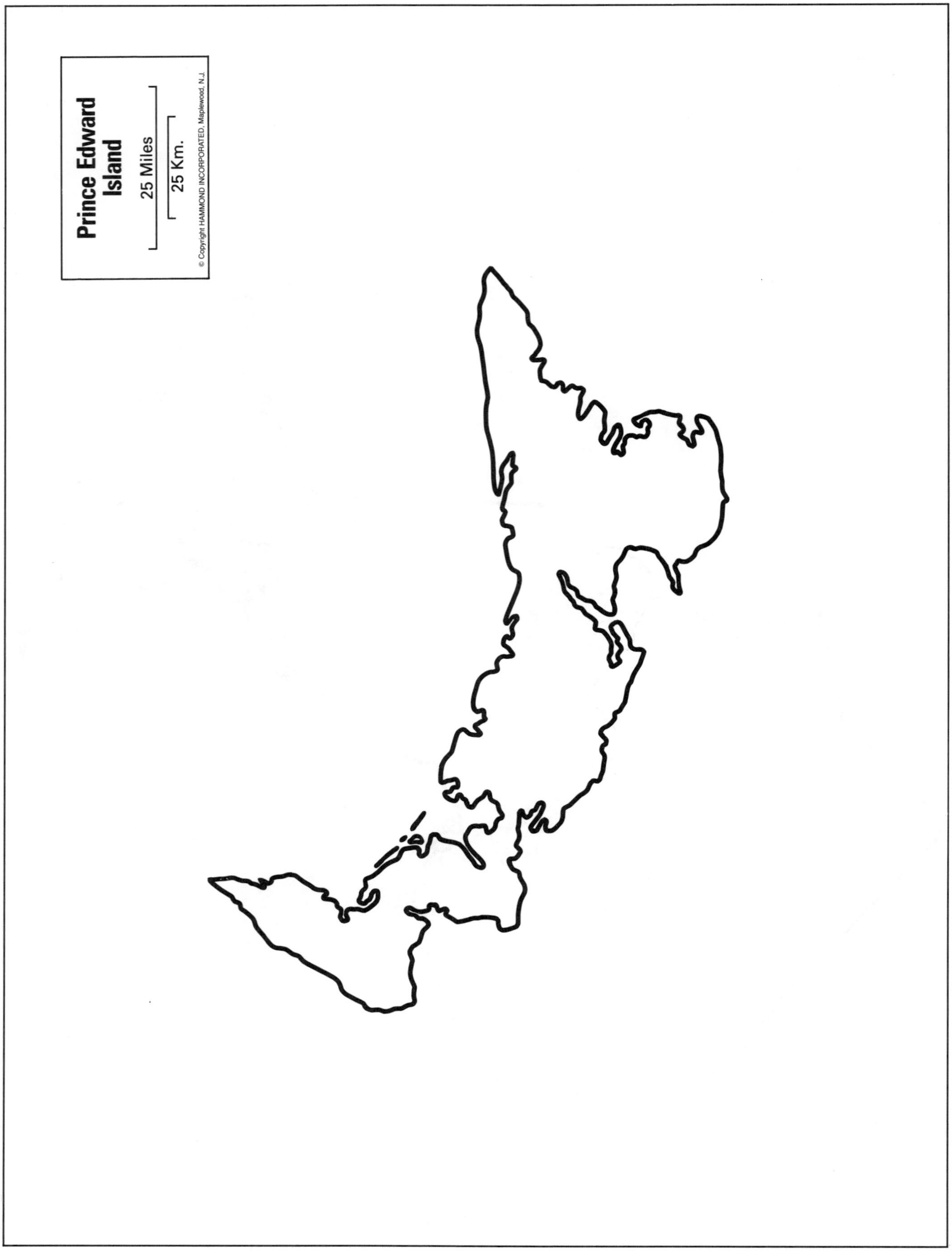

610

Prince Edward
Island

25 Miles

25 Km.

© Copyright HAMMOND INCORPORATED, Maplewood, N.J.

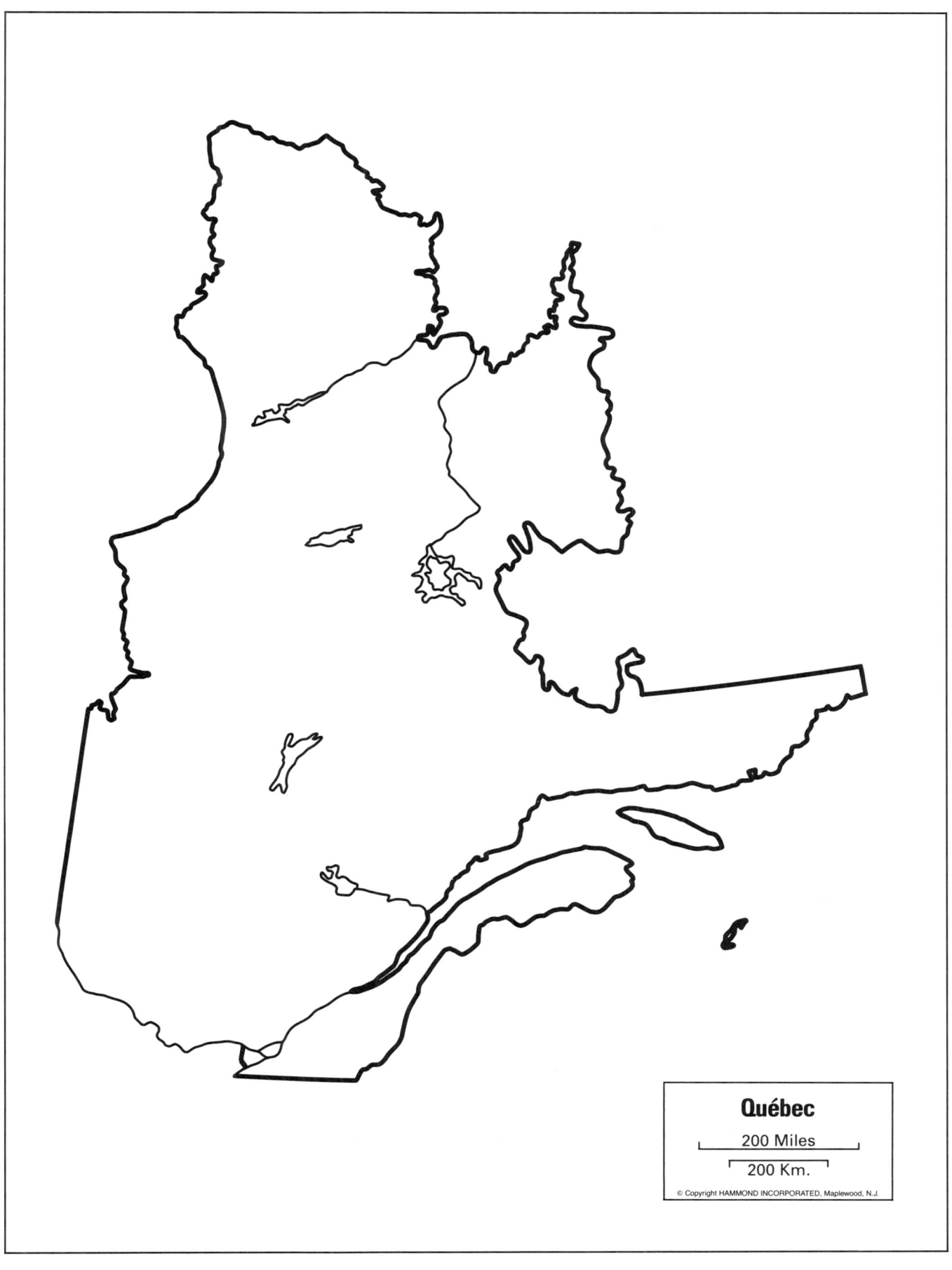

Québec

200 Miles

200 Km.

© Copyright HAMMOND INCORPORATED, Maplewood, N.J.

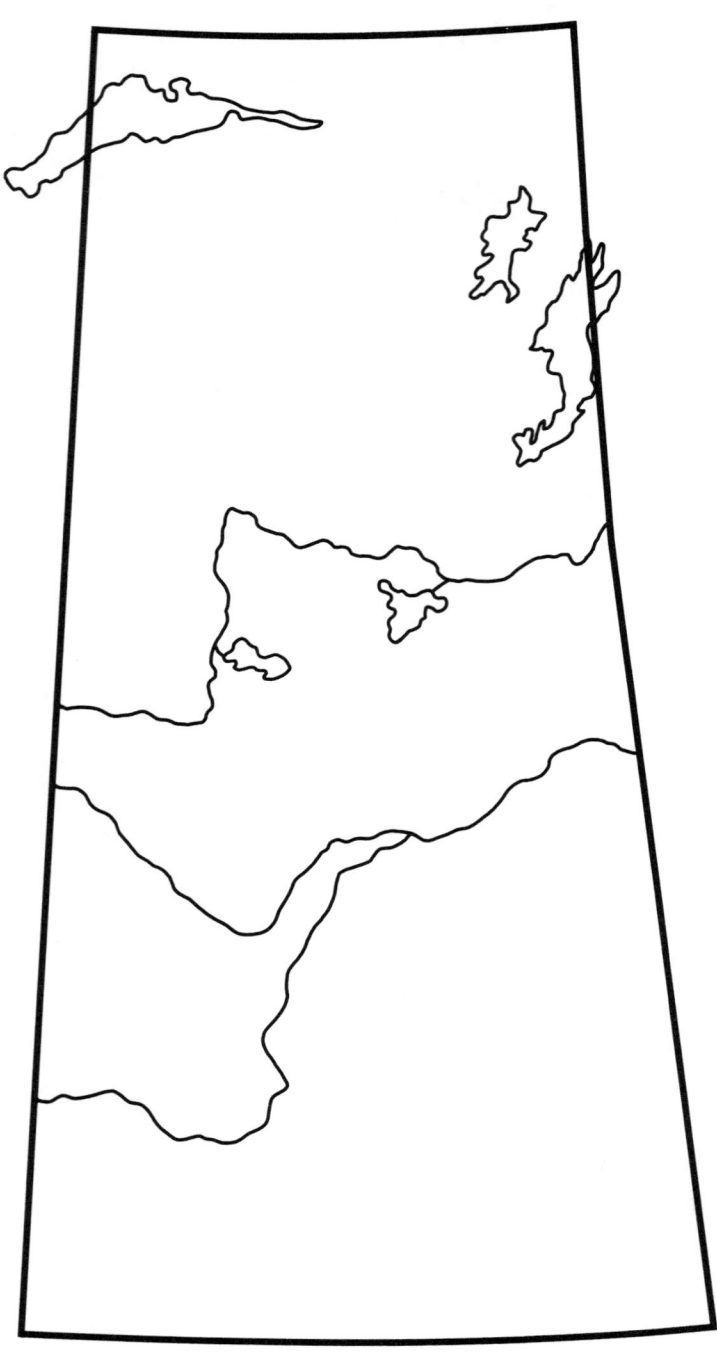

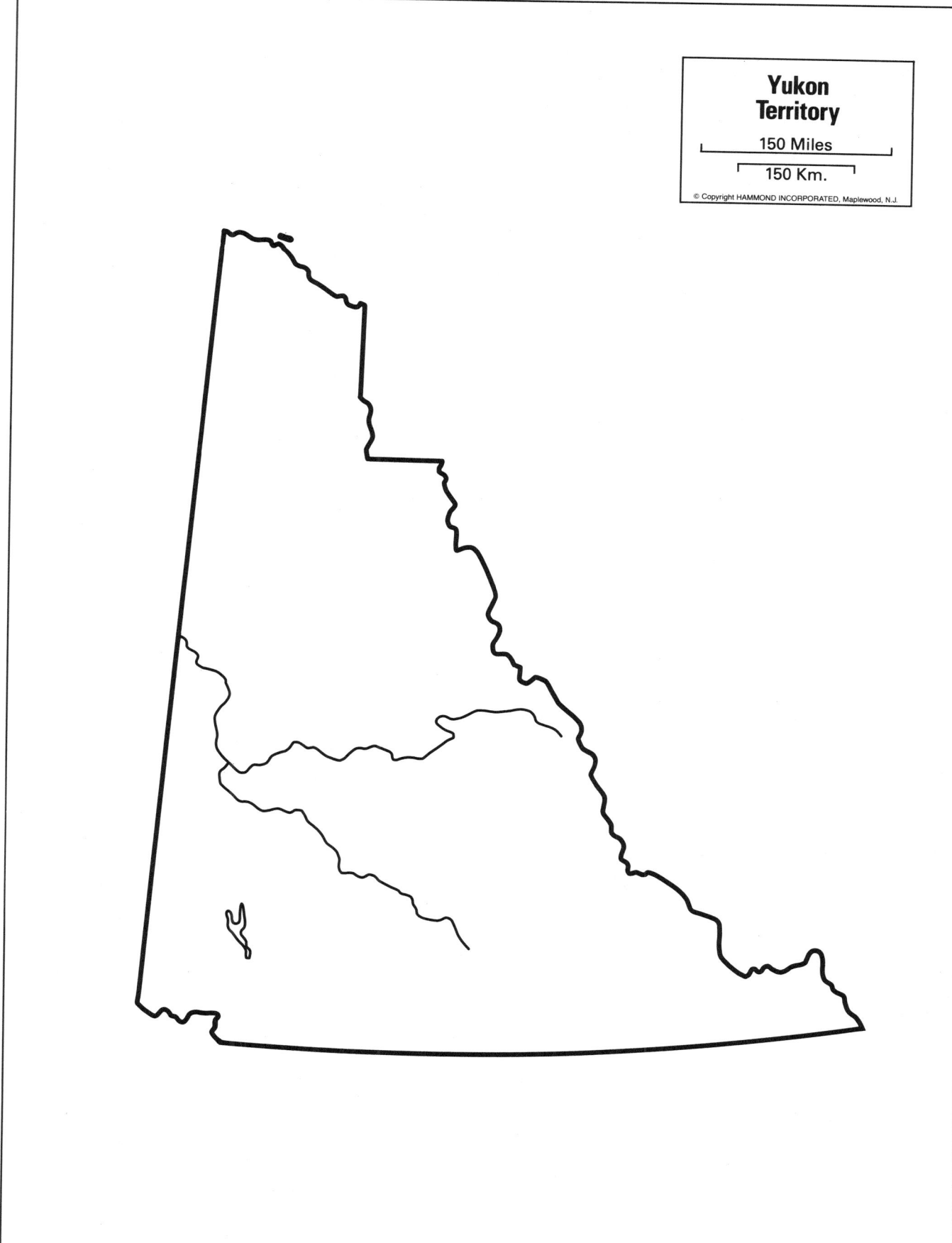

Yukon Territory

150 Miles

150 Km.

United States

400 Miles

400 Km.

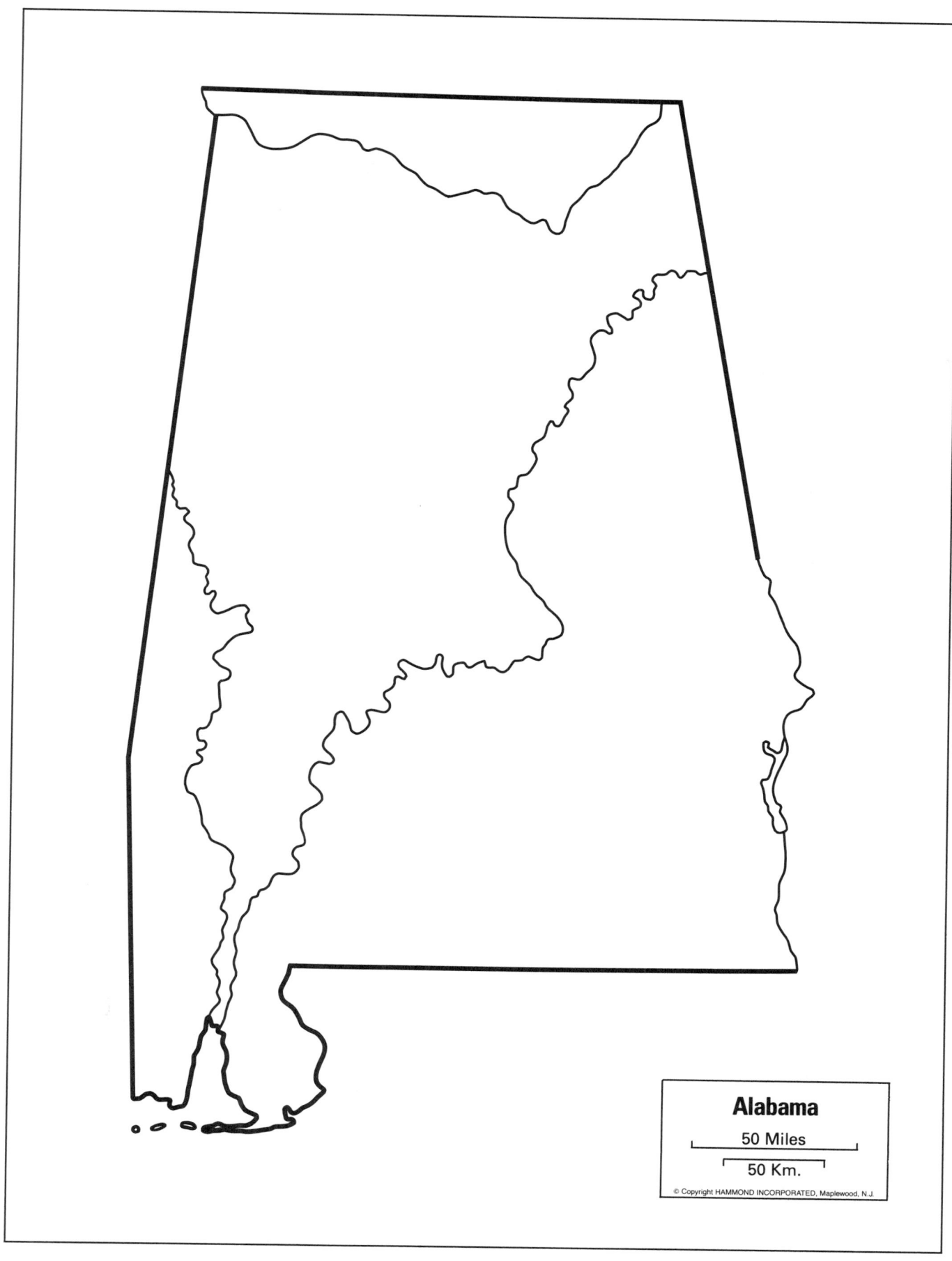

Alabama

50 Miles

50 Km.

© Copyright HAMMOND INCORPORATED, Maplewood, N.J.

616

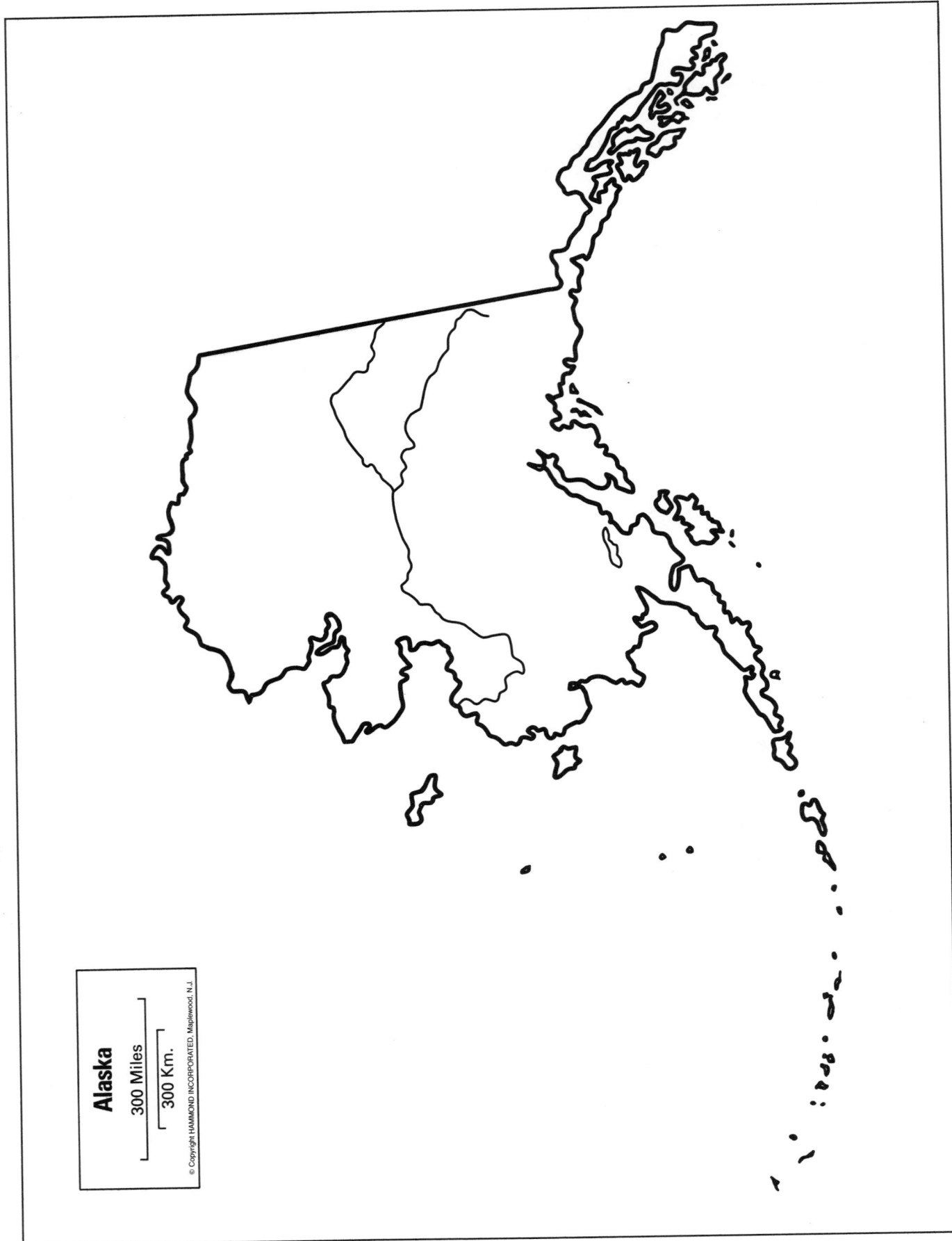

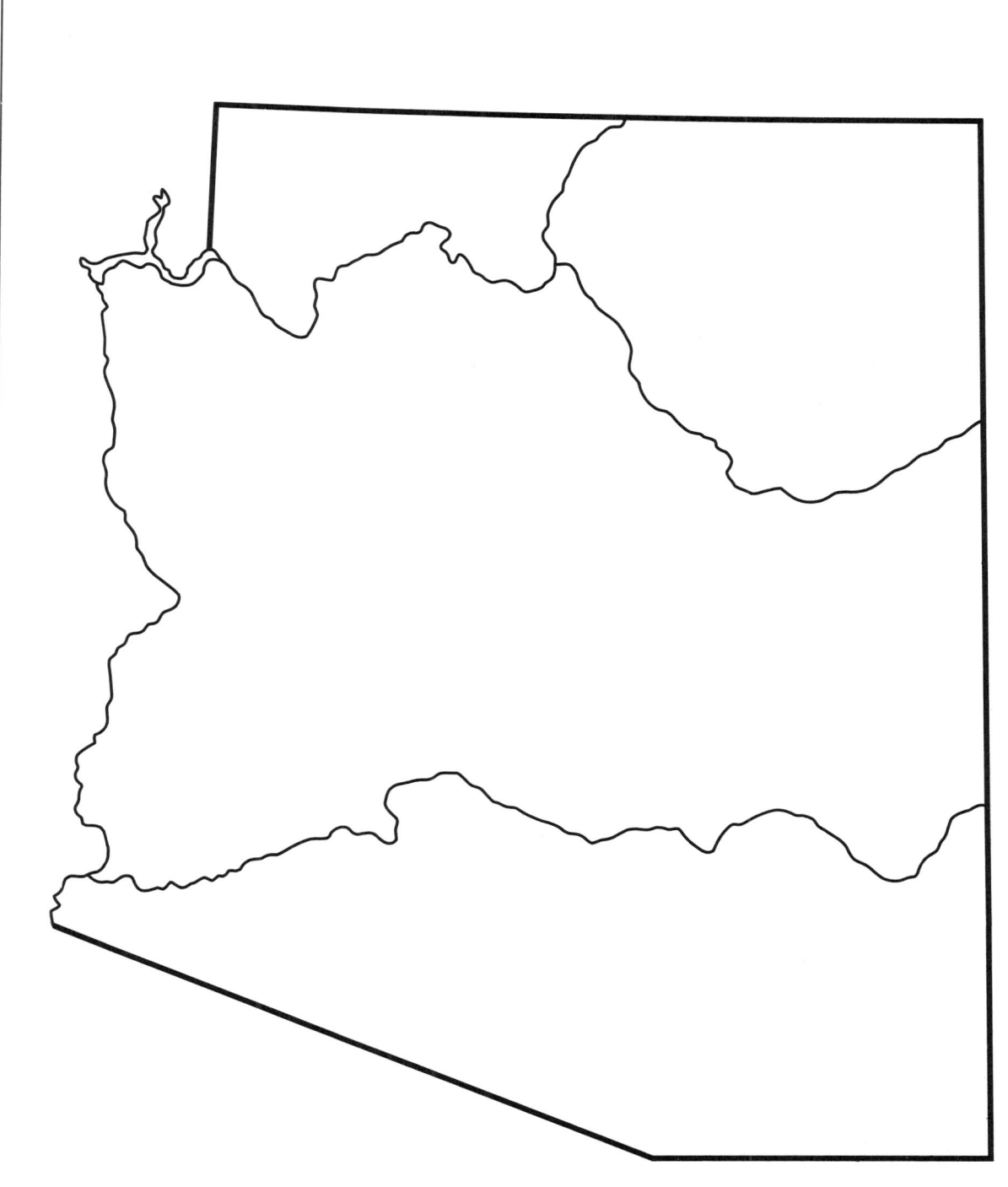

Arizona

80 Miles

80 Km.

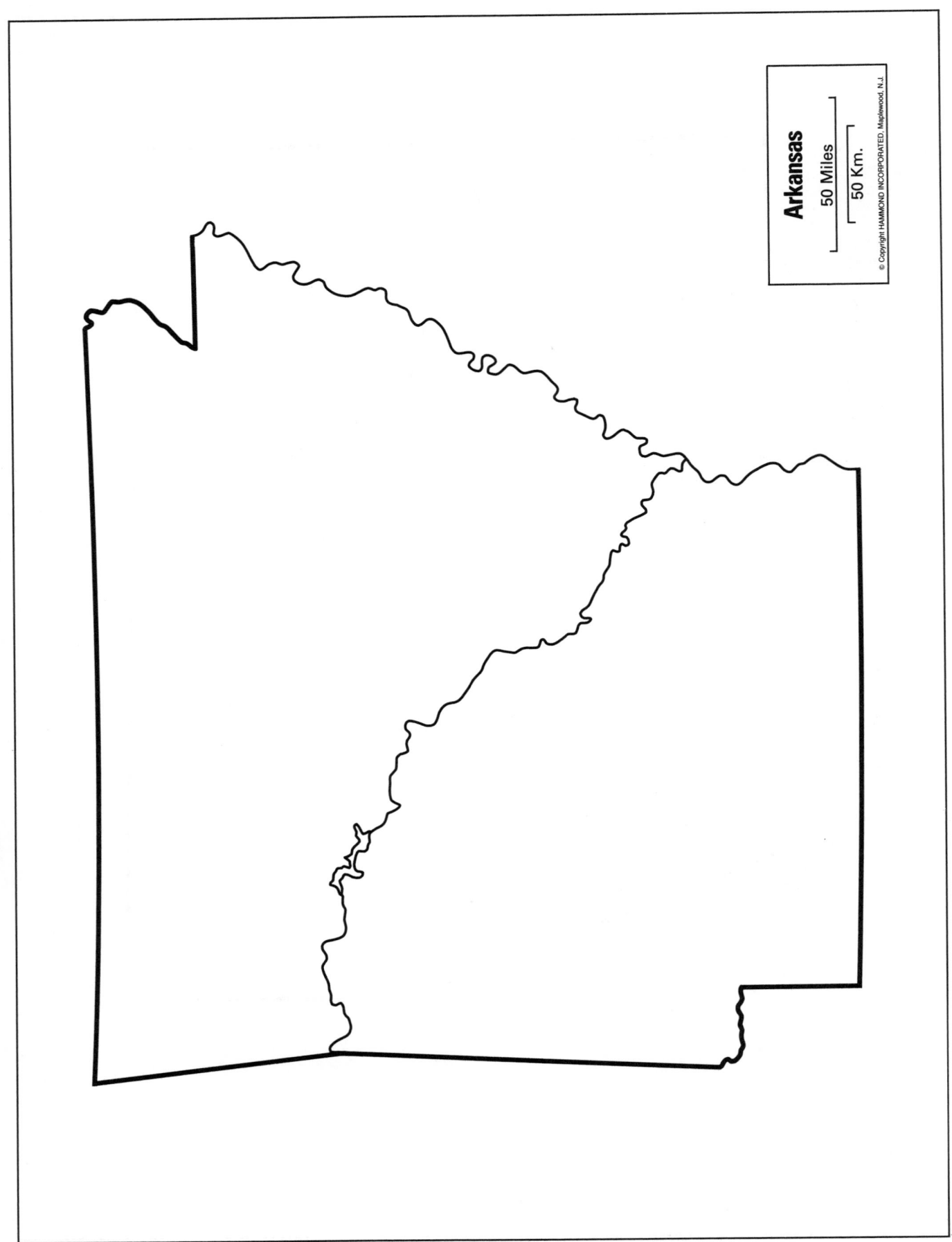

Arkansas

50 Miles

50 Km.

© Copyright HAMMOND INCORPORATED, Maplewood, N.J.

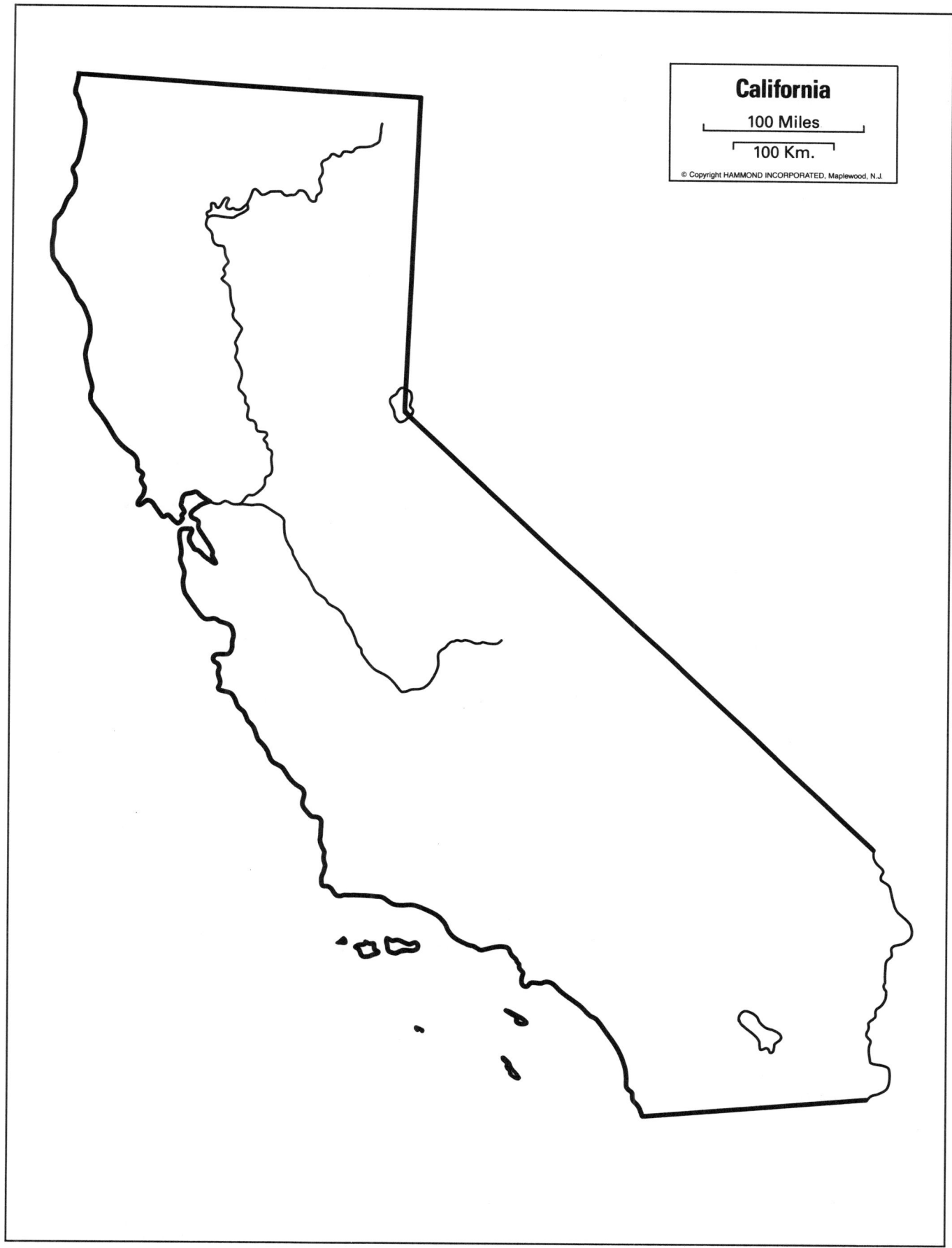

California

100 Miles

100 Km.

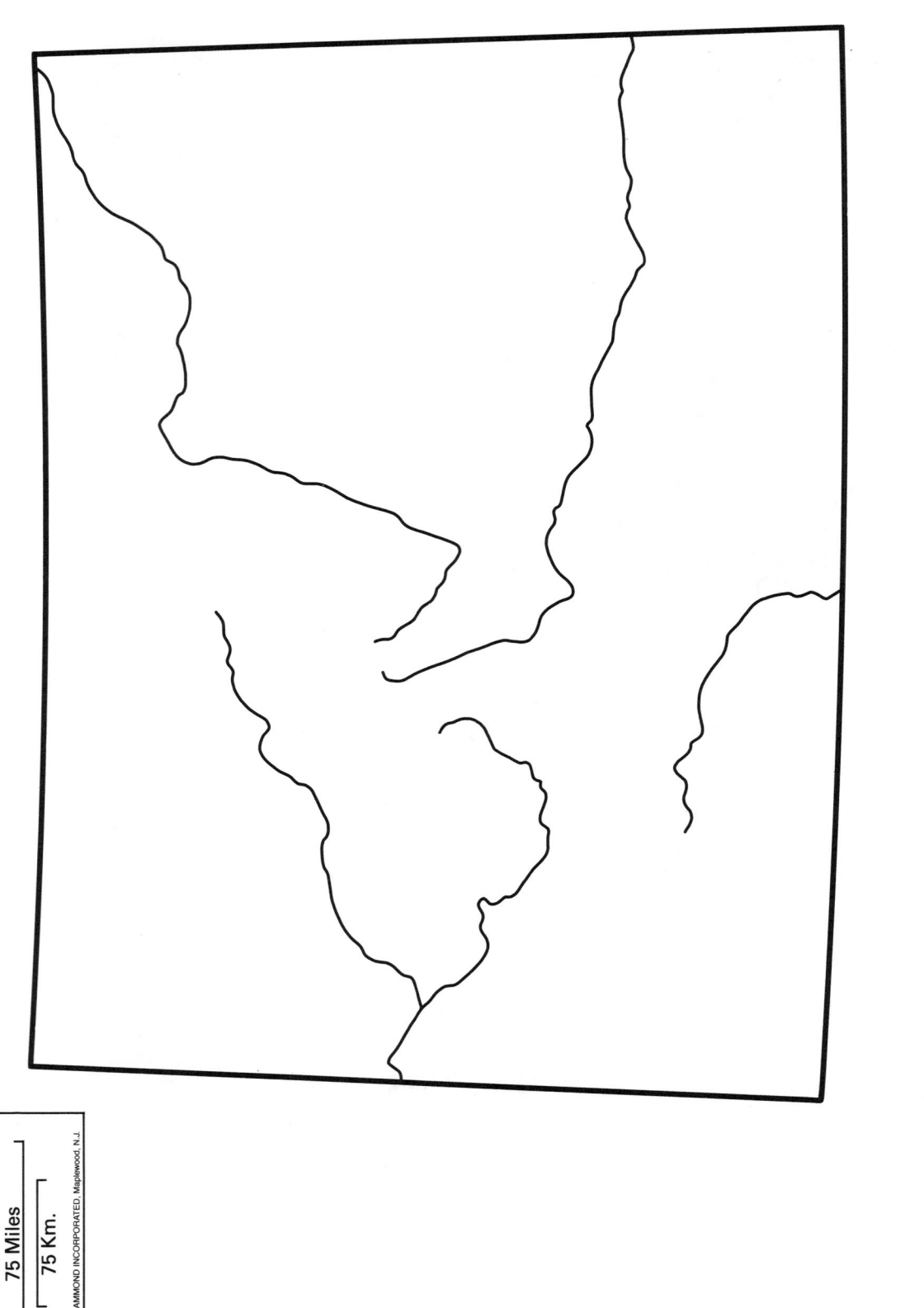

Colorado

75 Miles

75 Km.

© Copyright HAMMOND INCORPORATED, Maplewood, N.J.

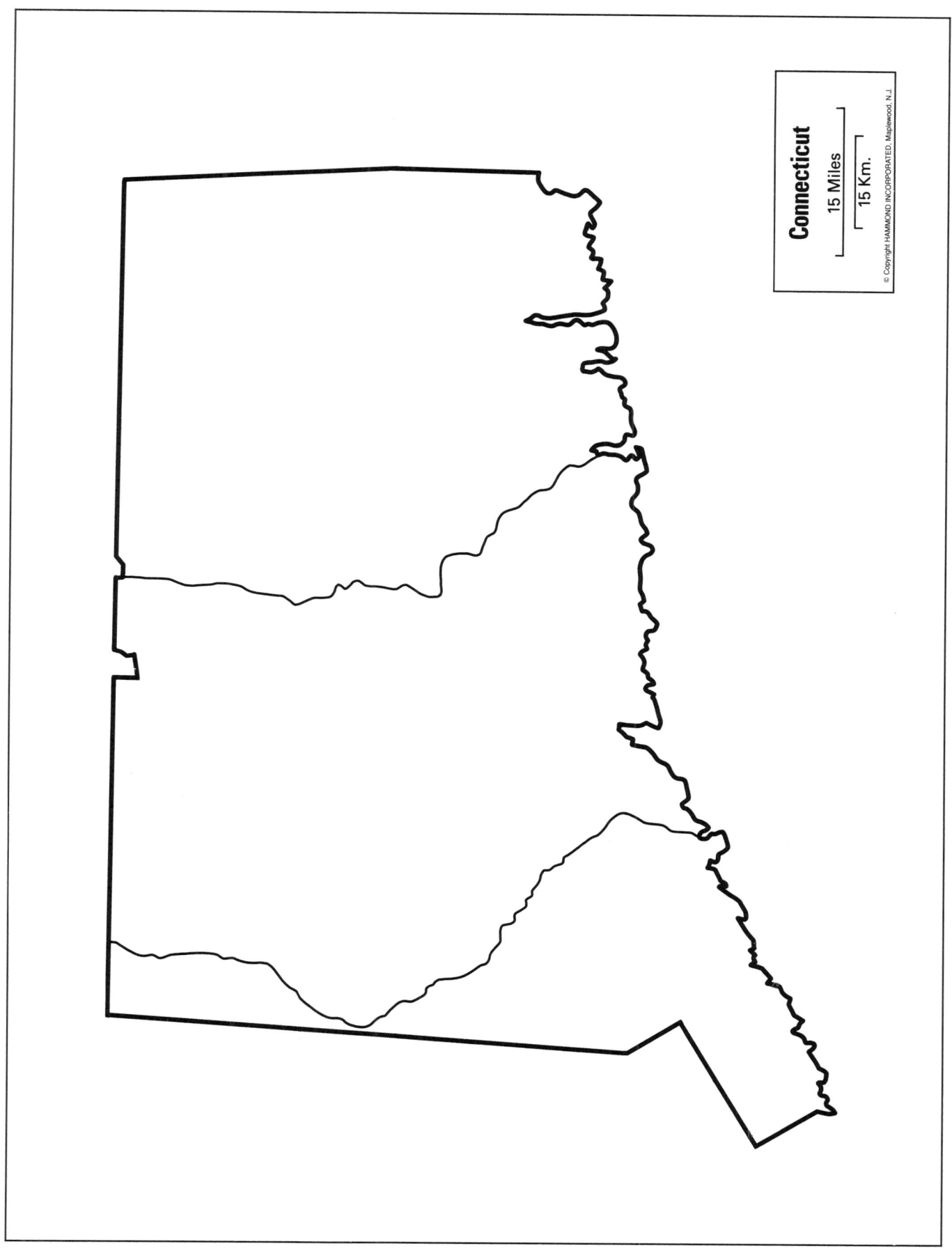

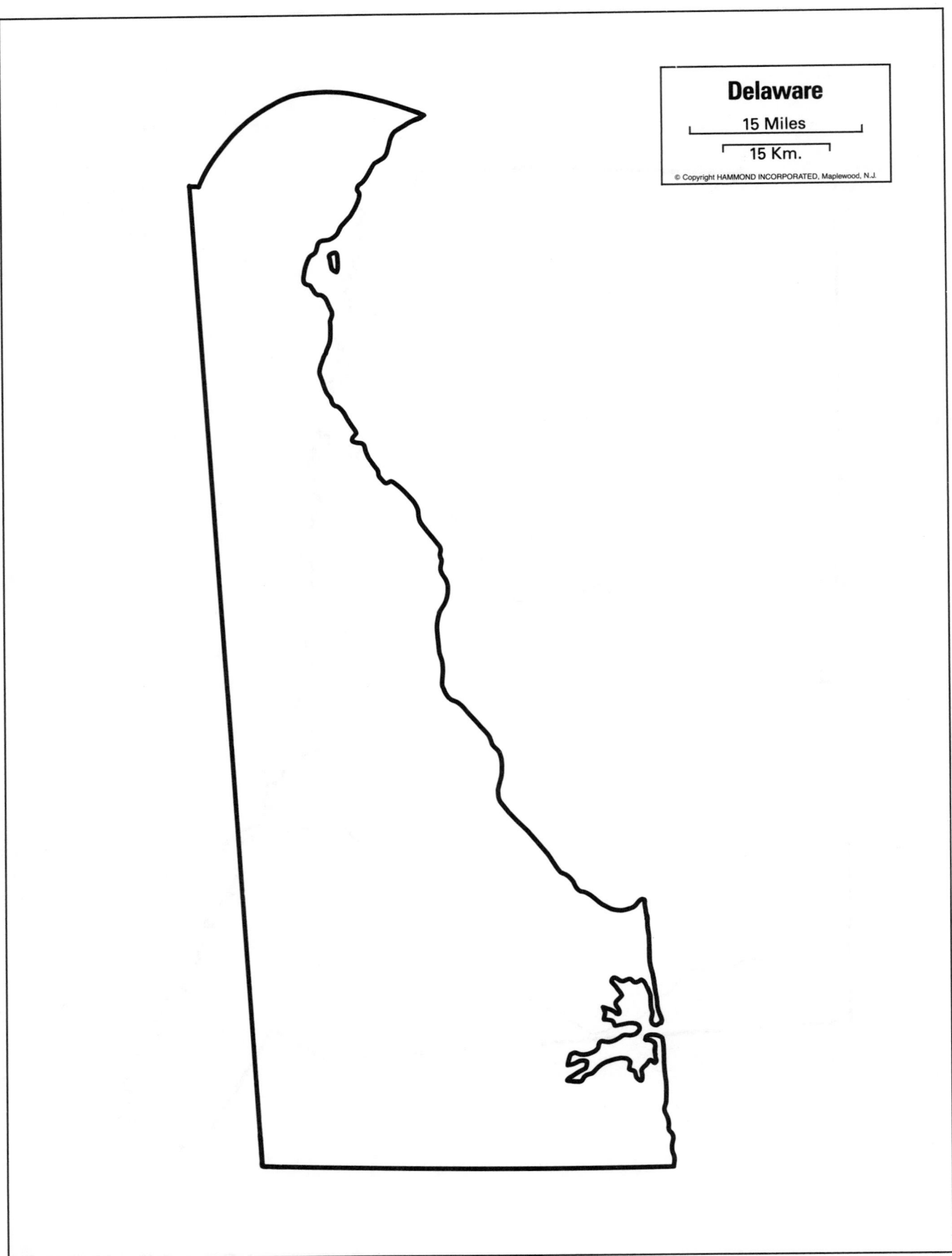

Delaware

15 Miles

15 Km.

© Copyright HAMMOND INCORPORATED, Maplewood, N.J.

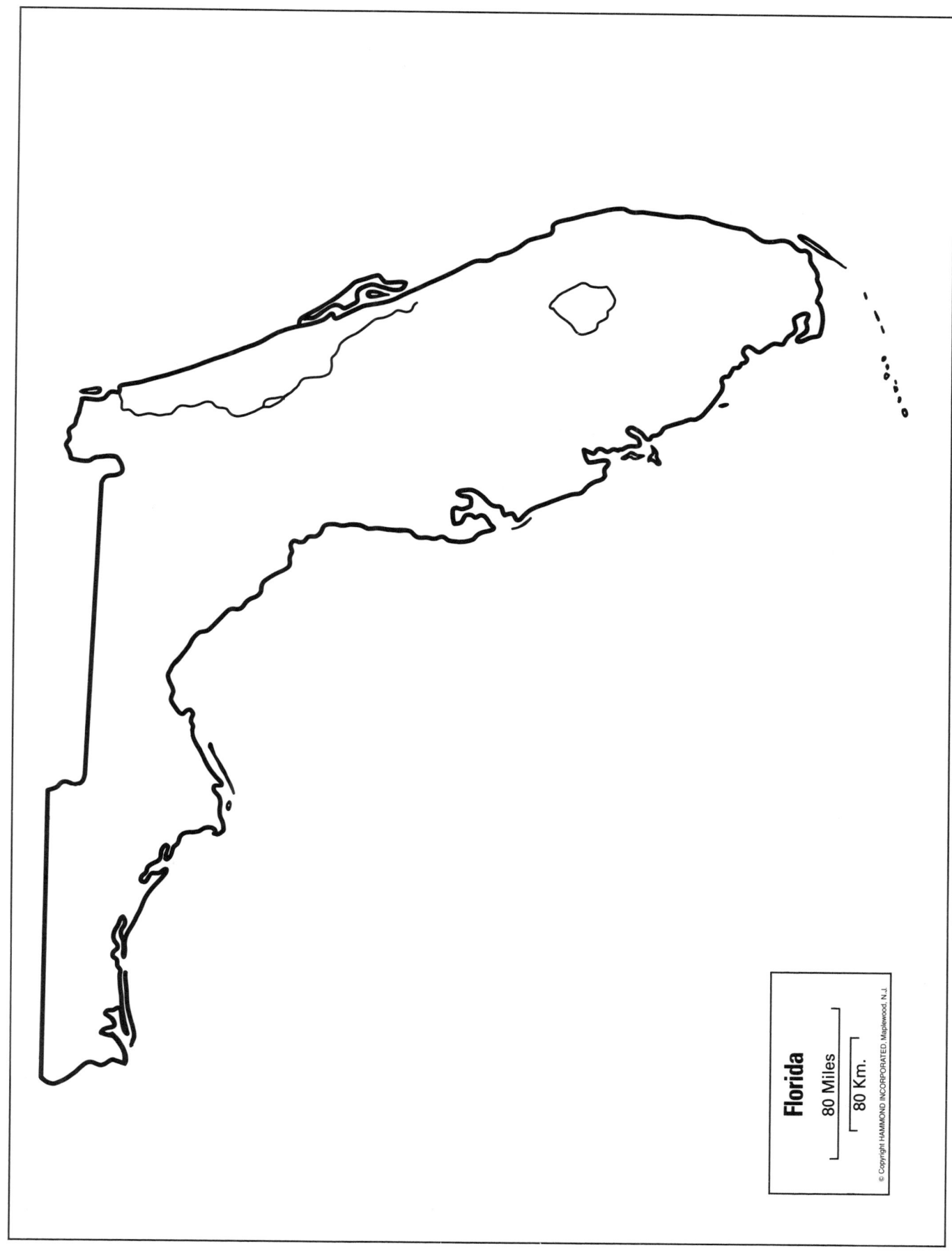

Florida

80 Miles

80 Km.

© Copyright HAMMOND INCORPORATED, Maplewood, N.J.

624

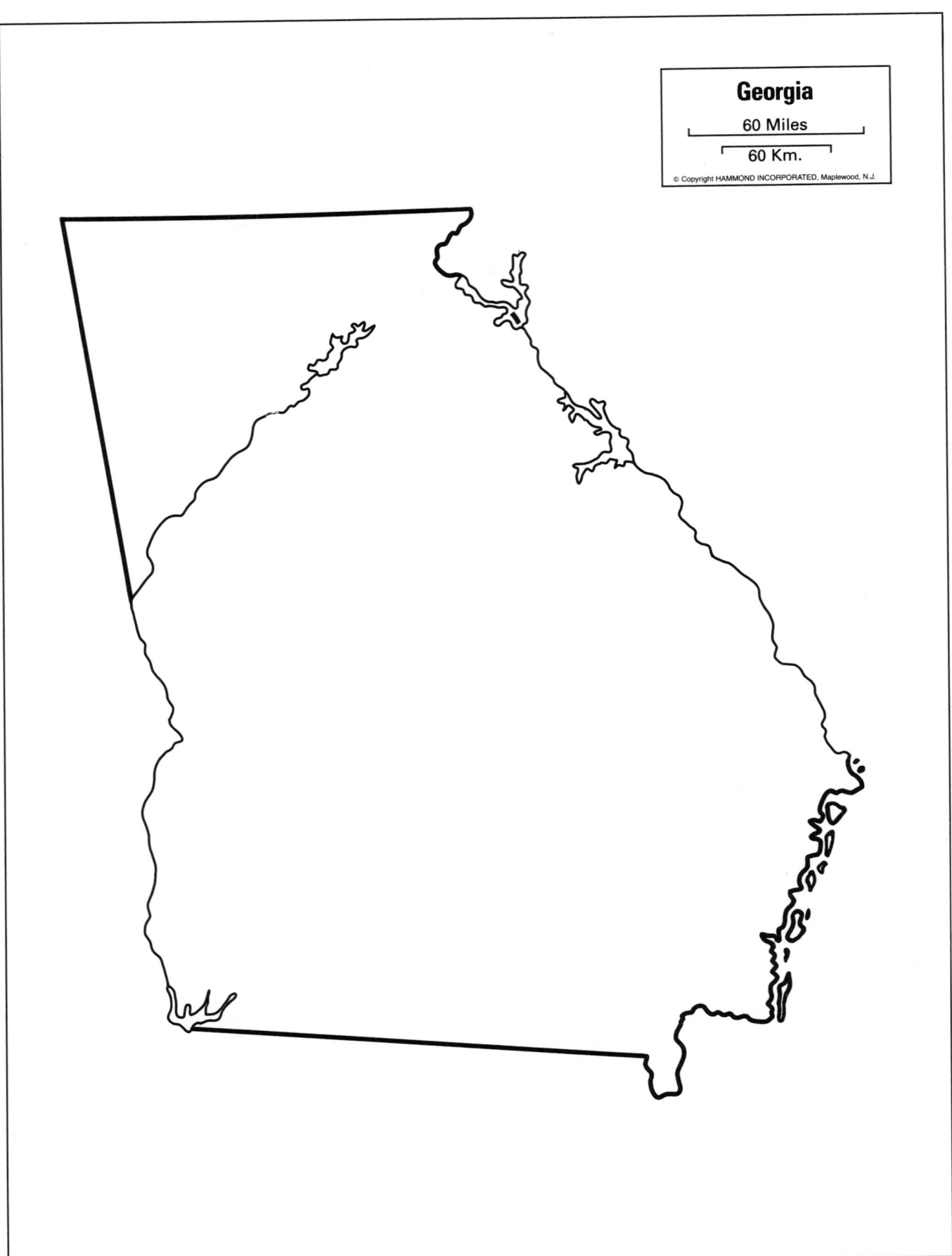

Georgia

60 Miles

60 Km.

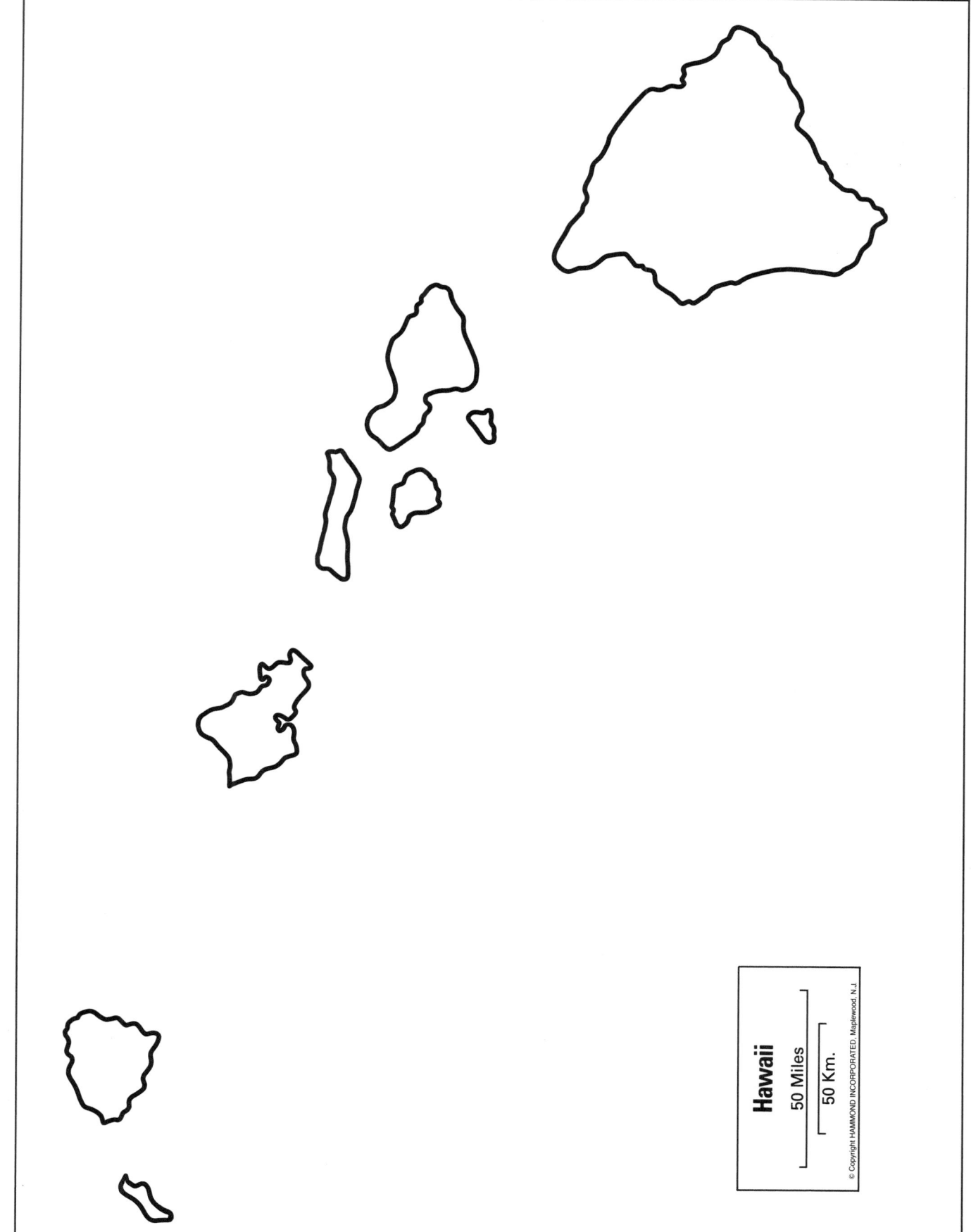

Hawaii

50 Miles

50 Km.

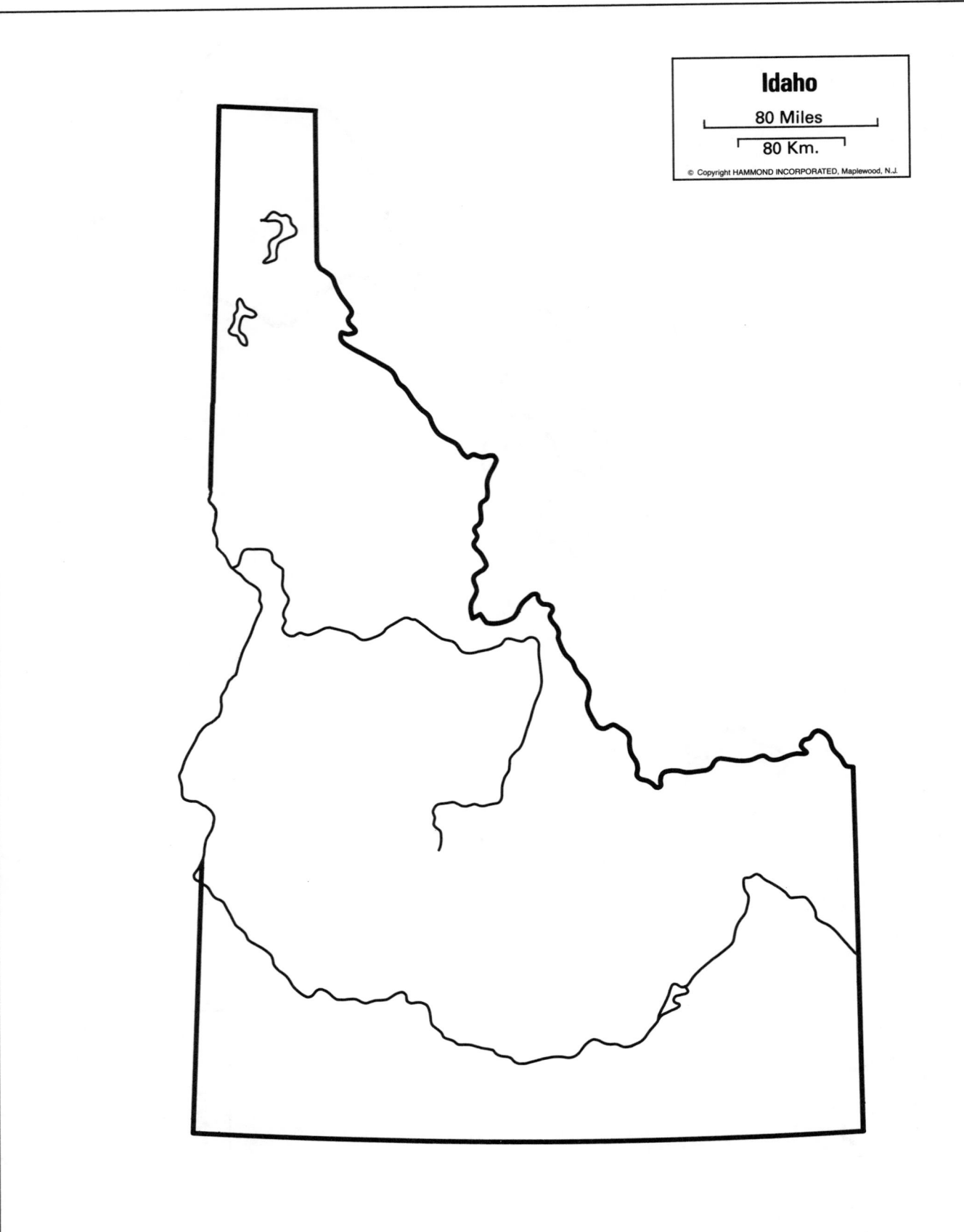

Idaho

80 Miles

80 Km.

© Copyright HAMMOND INCORPORATED, Maplewood, N.J.

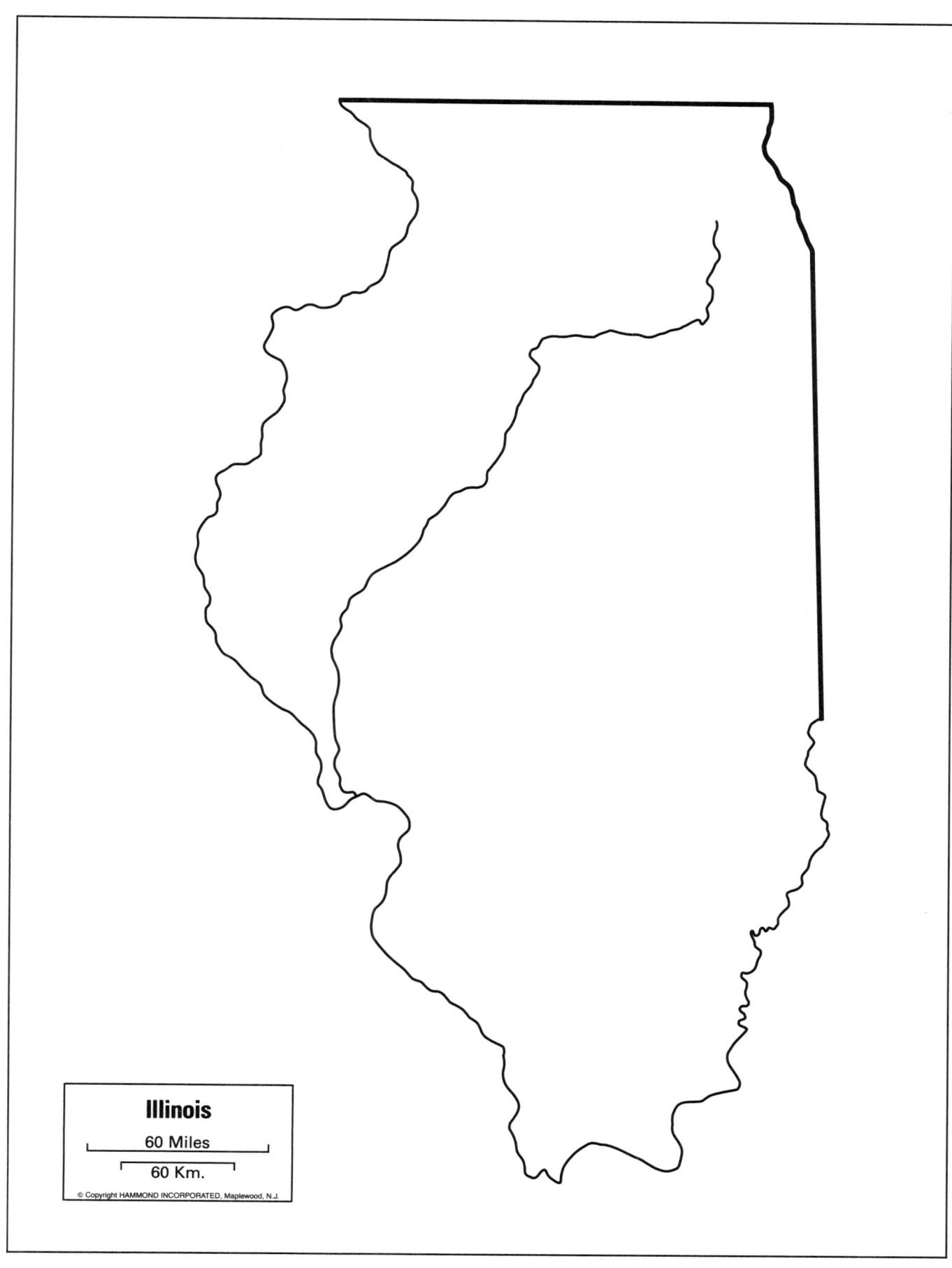

Illinois

60 Miles

60 Km.

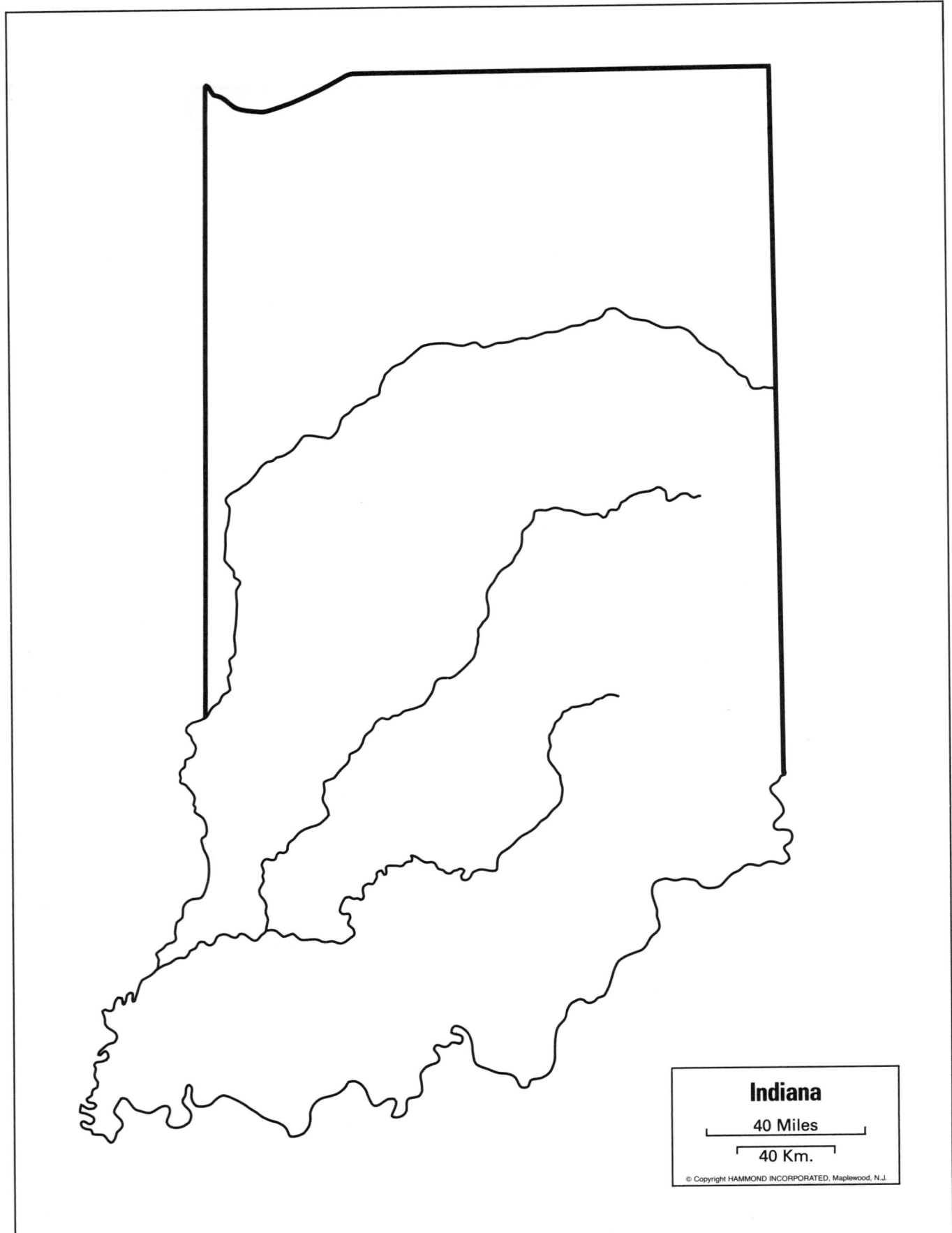

Indiana

40 Miles

40 Km.

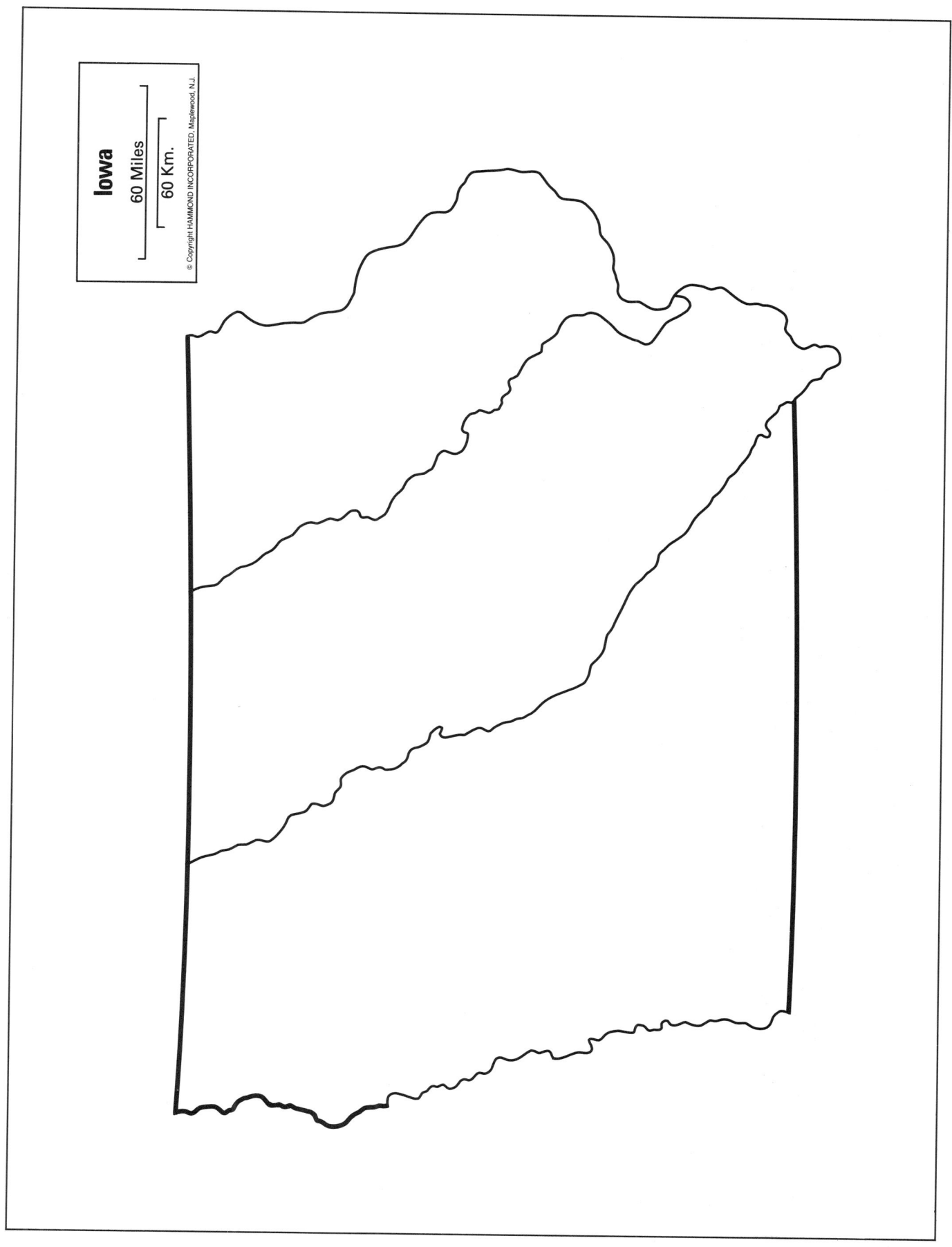

Iowa

60 Miles

60 Km.

© Copyright HAMMOND INCORPORATED, Maplewood, N.J.

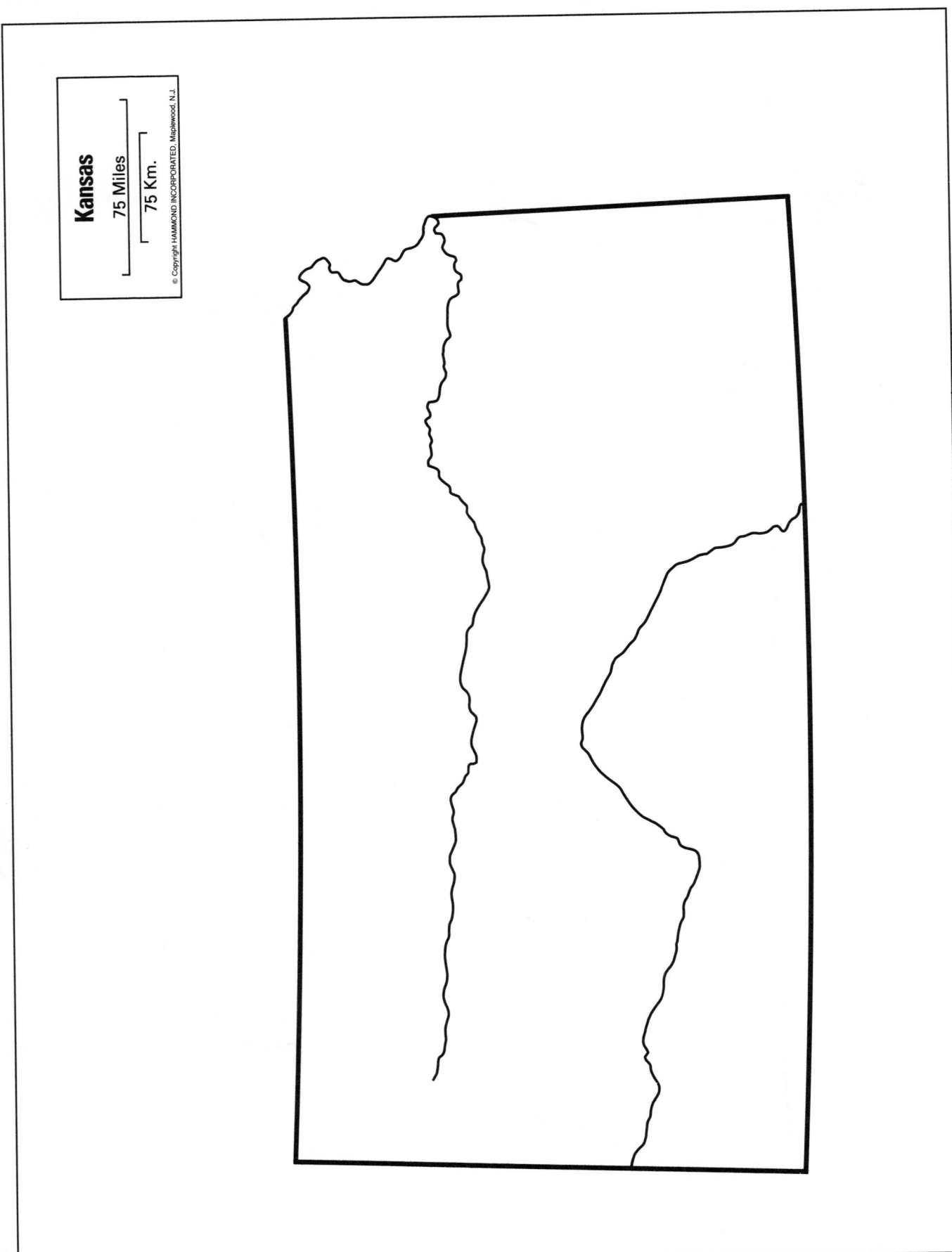

Kansas

75 Miles

75 Km.

© Copyright HAMMOND INCORPORATED, Maplewood, N.J.

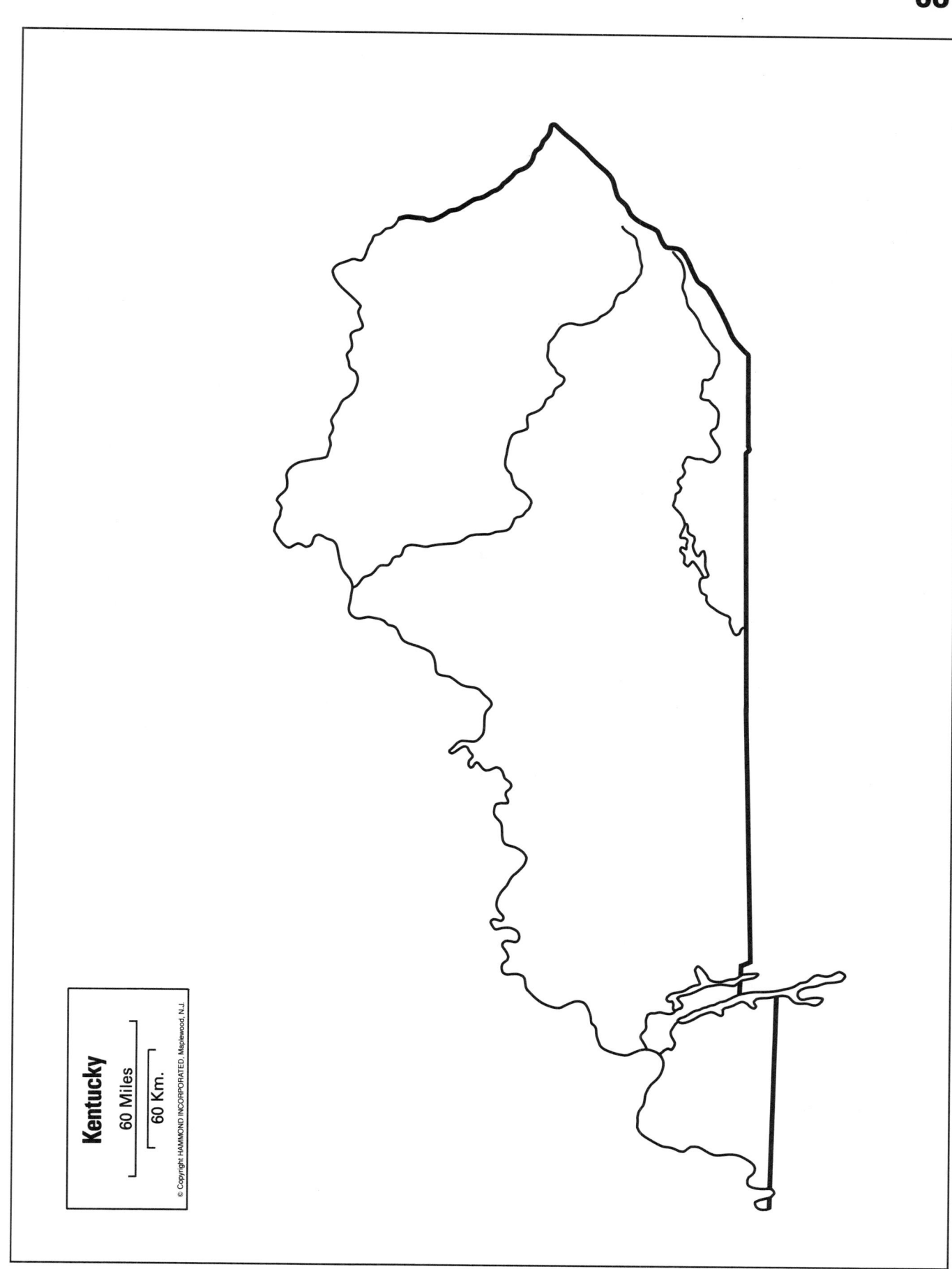

Kentucky

60 Miles

60 Km.

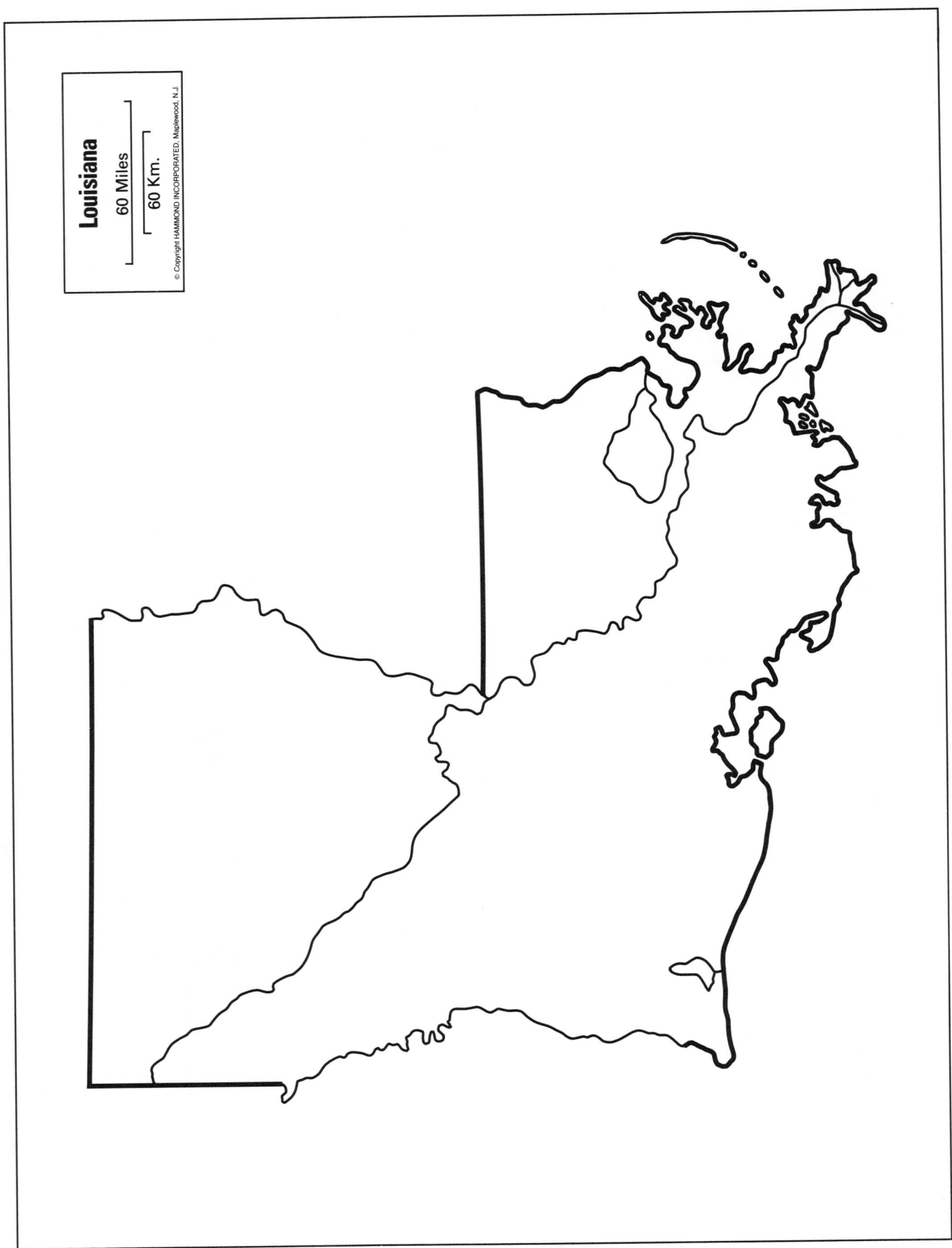

Louisiana

60 Miles

60 Km.

© Copyright HAMMOND INCORPORATED, Maplewood, N.J.

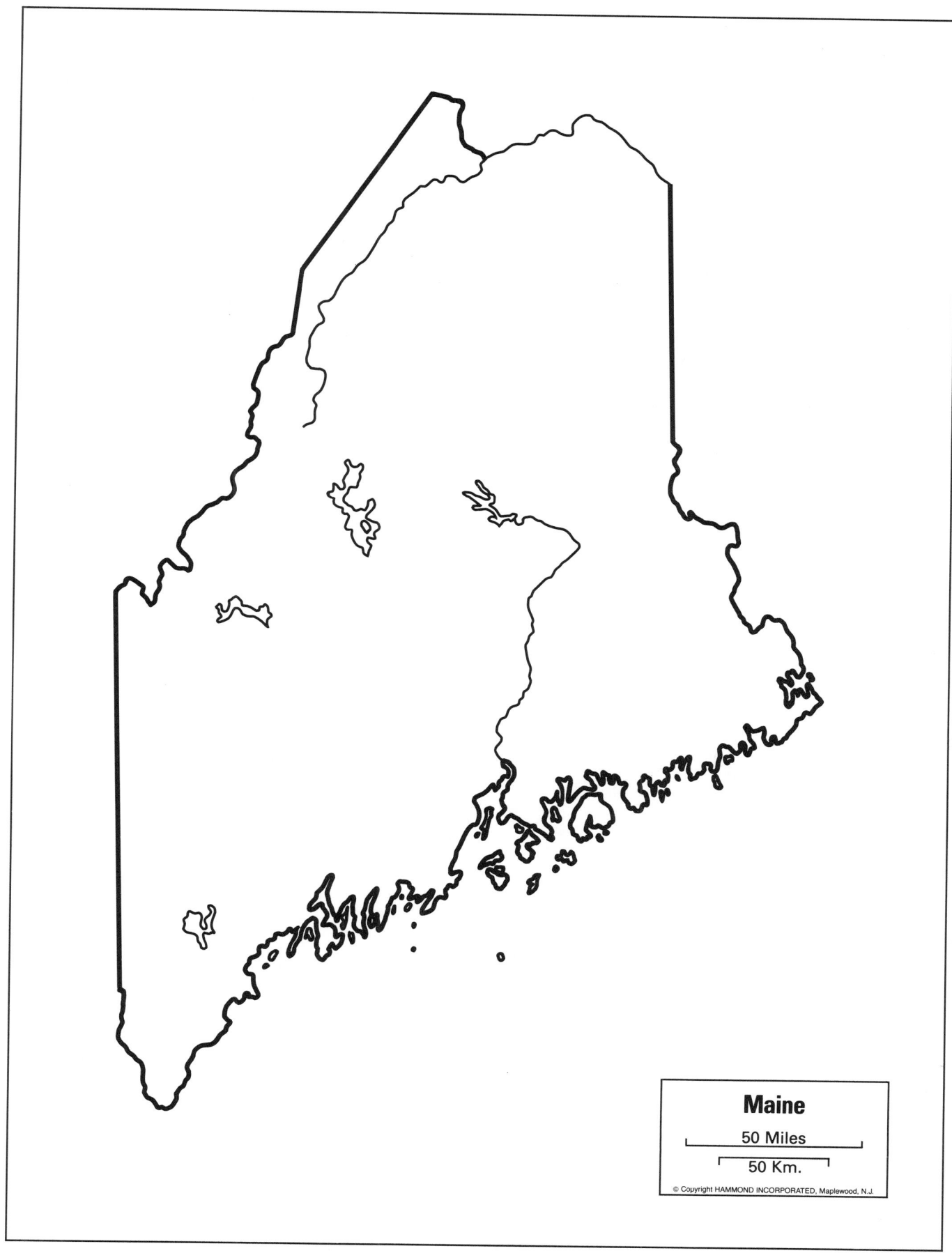

Maine

50 Miles

50 Km.

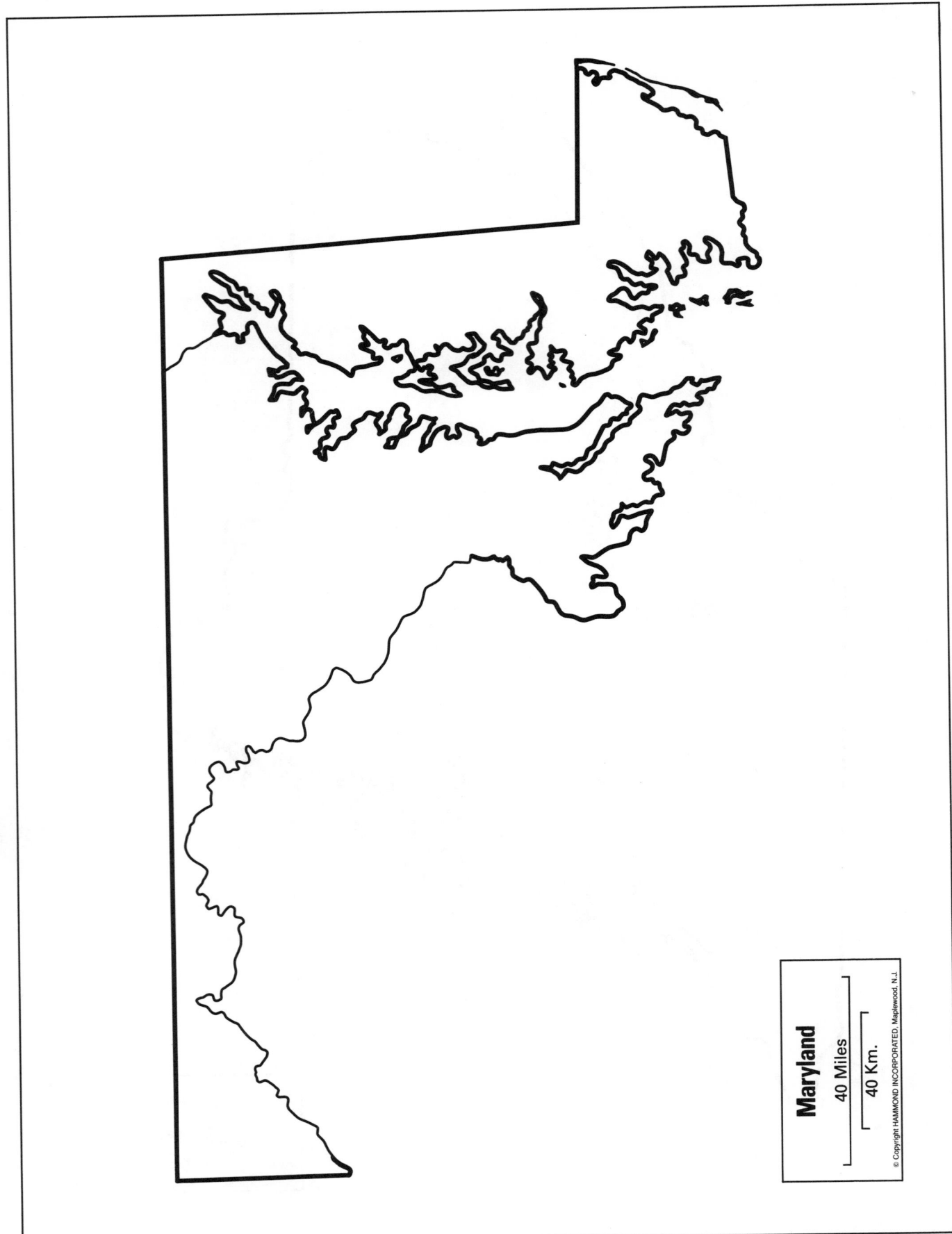

Maryland

40 Miles

40 Km.

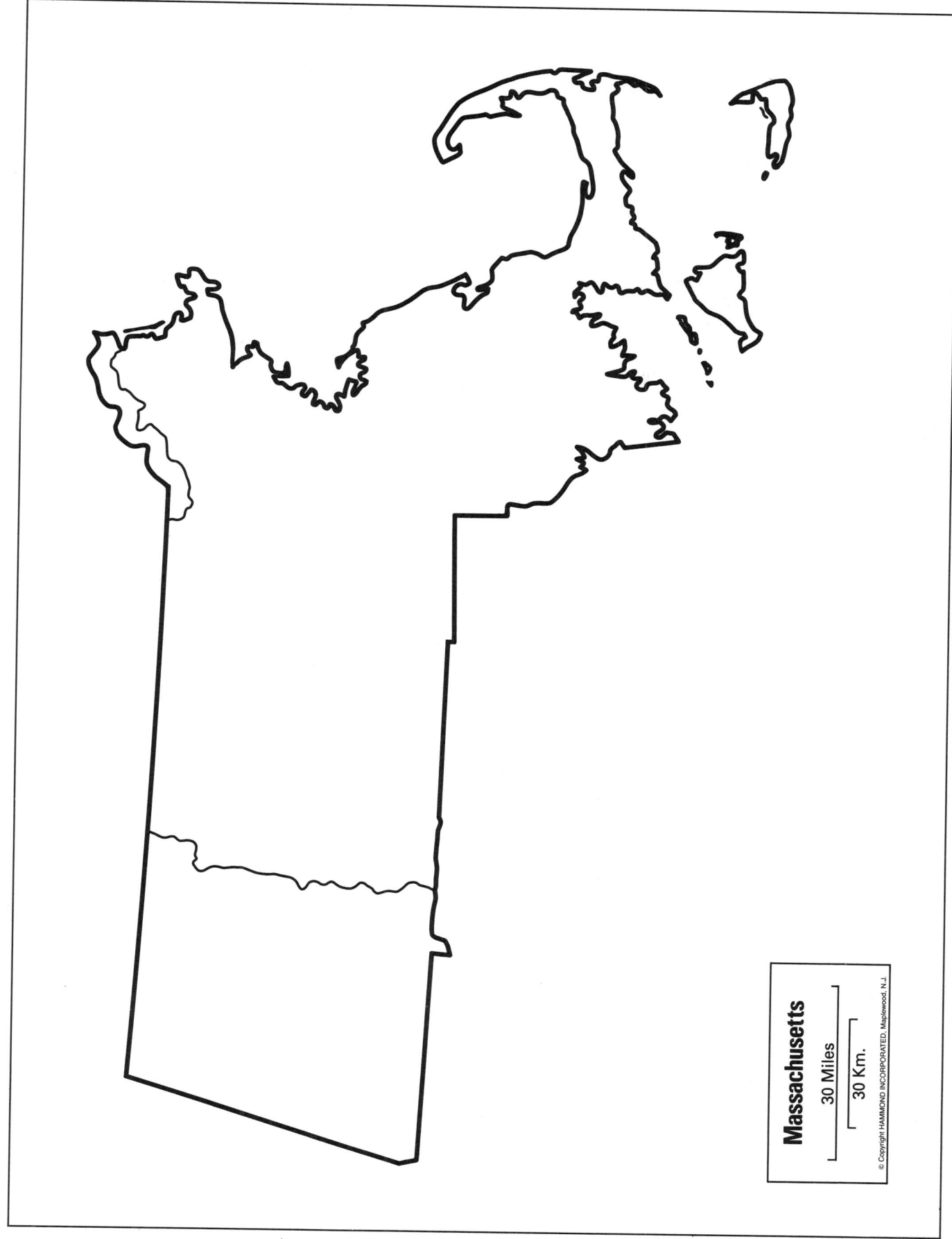

Massachusetts

30 Miles

30 Km.

Michigan

80 Miles

80 Km.

© Copyright HAMMOND INCORPORATED, Maplewood, N.J.

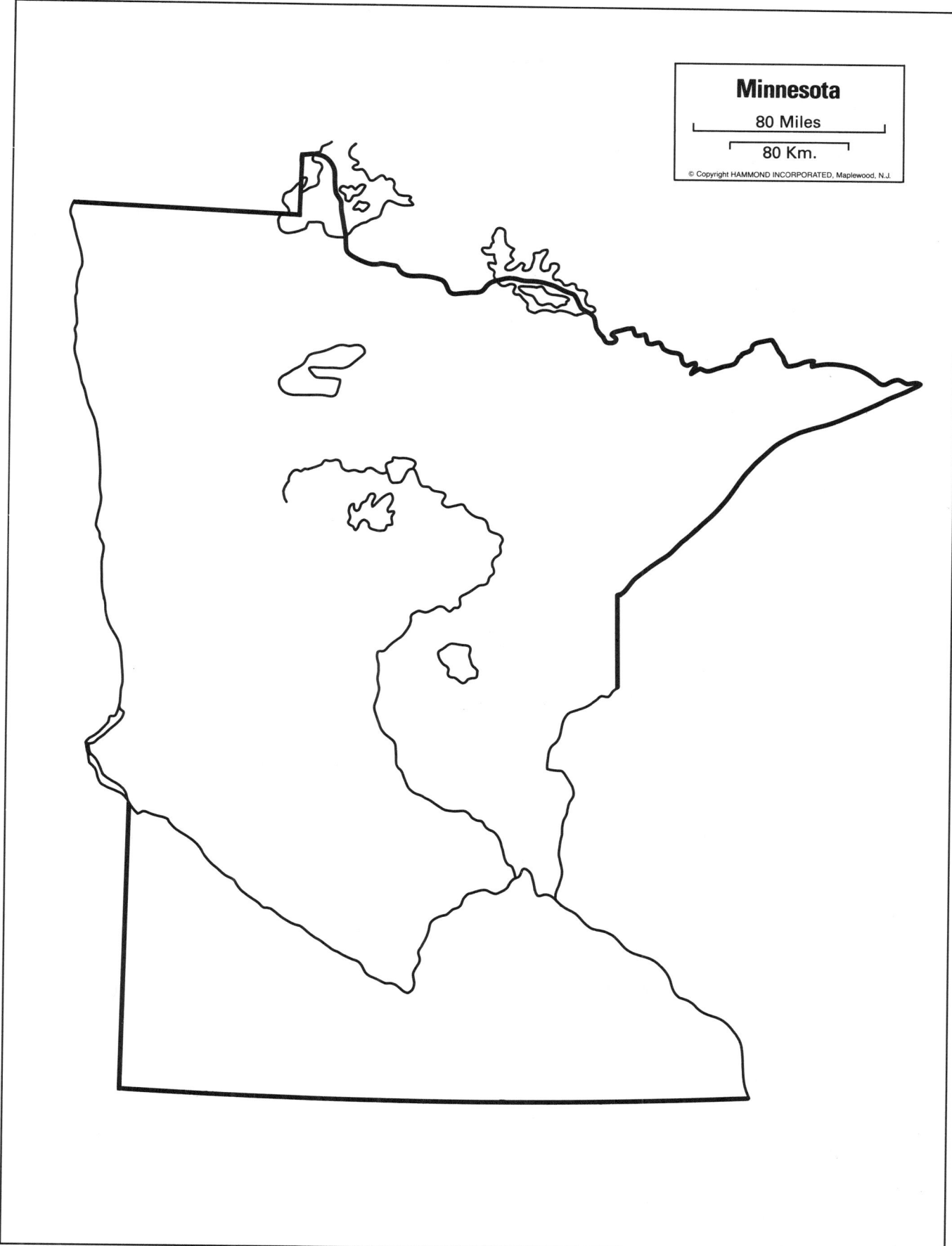

Minnesota

80 Miles

80 Km.

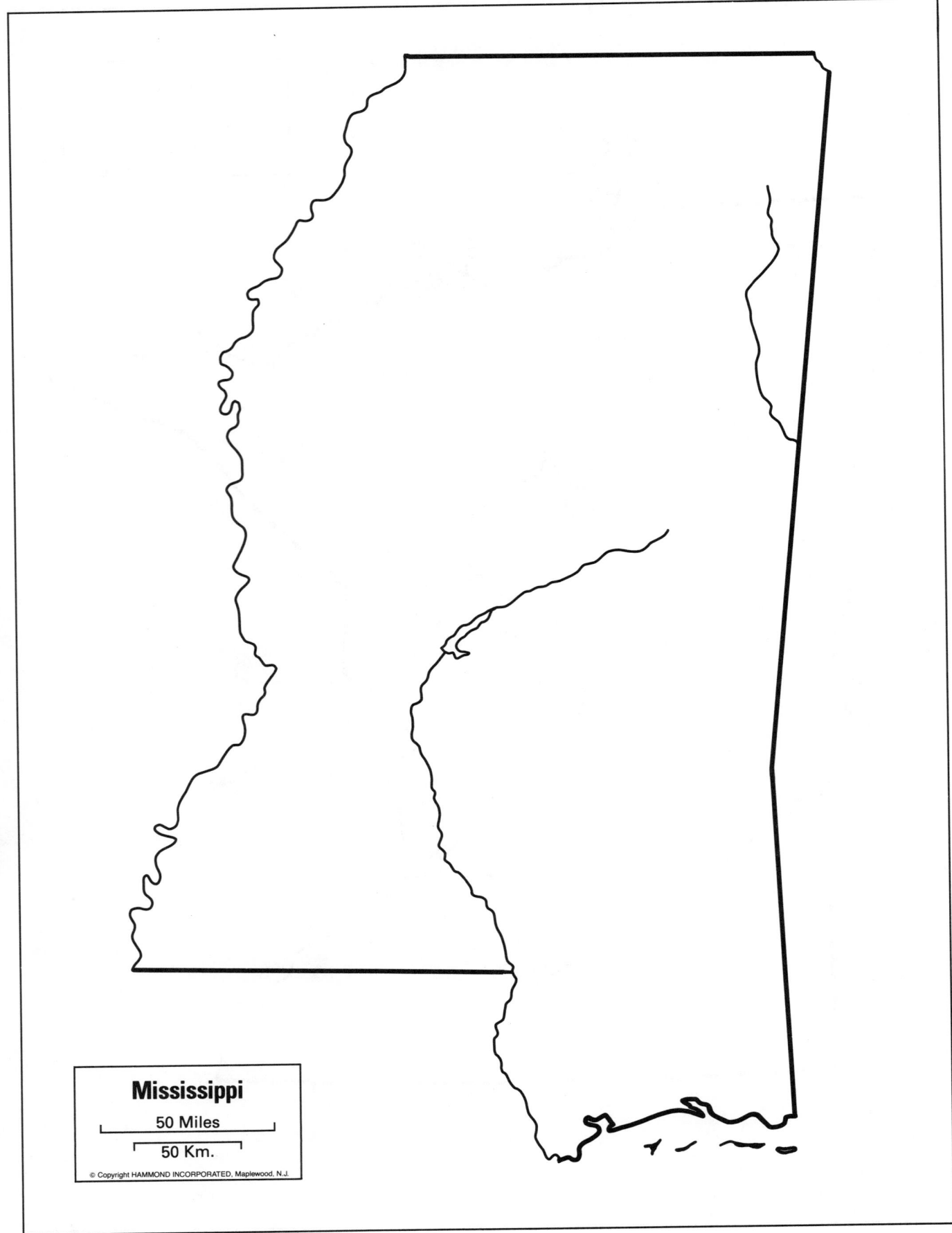

Mississippi

50 Miles

50 Km.

© Copyright HAMMOND INCORPORATED, Maplewood, N.J.

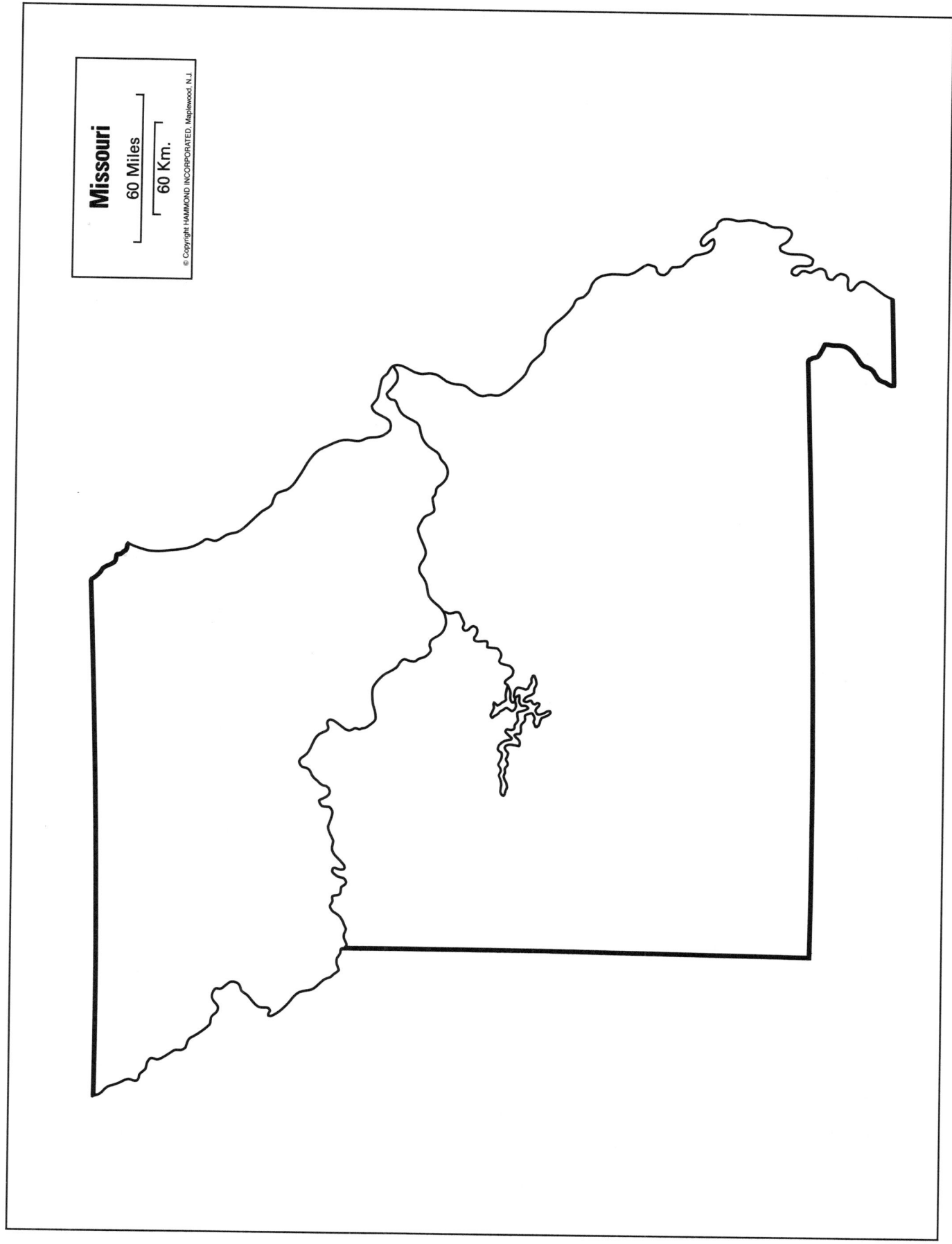

Missouri

60 Miles

60 Km.

© Copyright HAMMOND INCORPORATED, Maplewood, N.J.

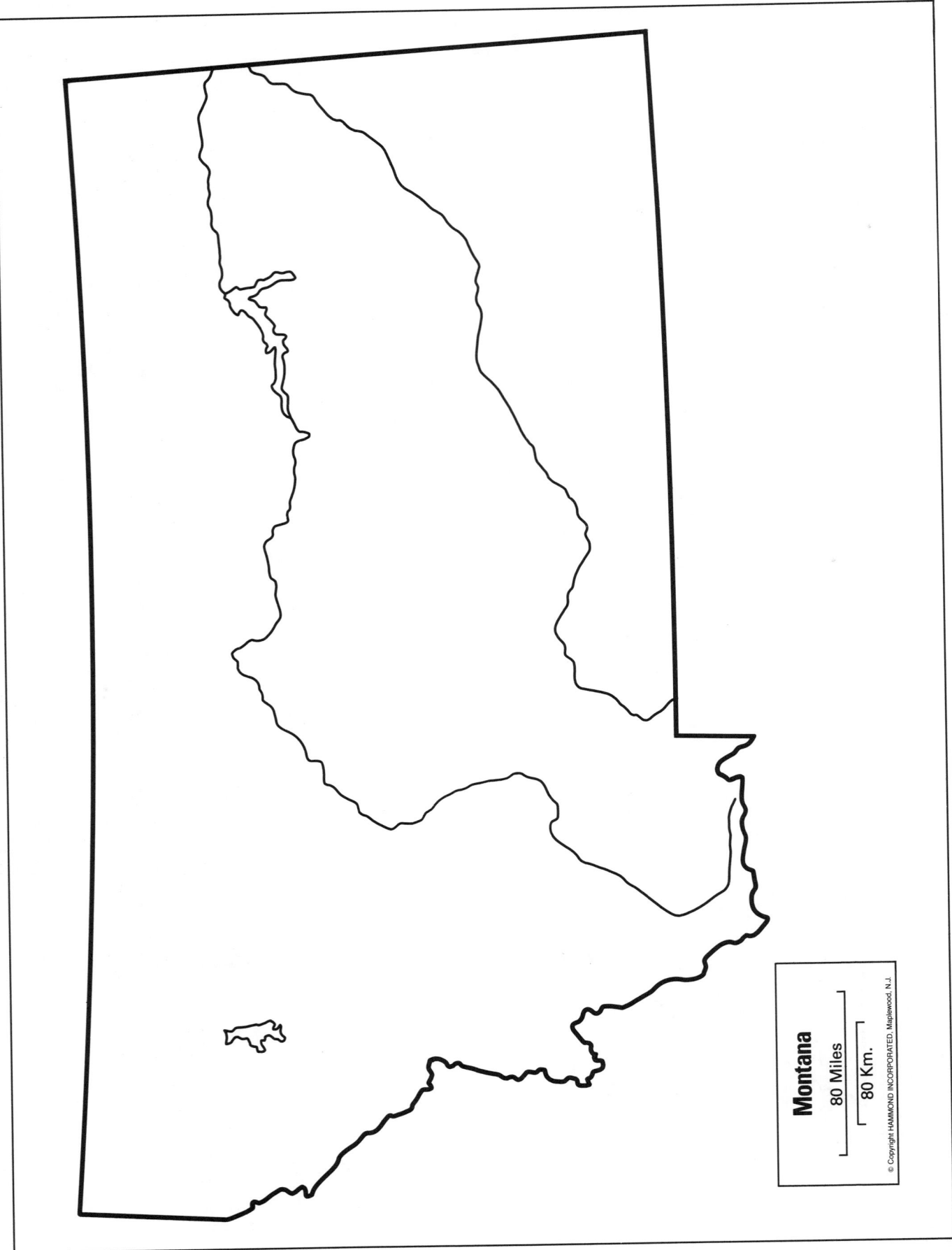

Montana

80 Miles

80 Km.

© Copyright HAMMOND INCORPORATED, Maplewood, N.J.

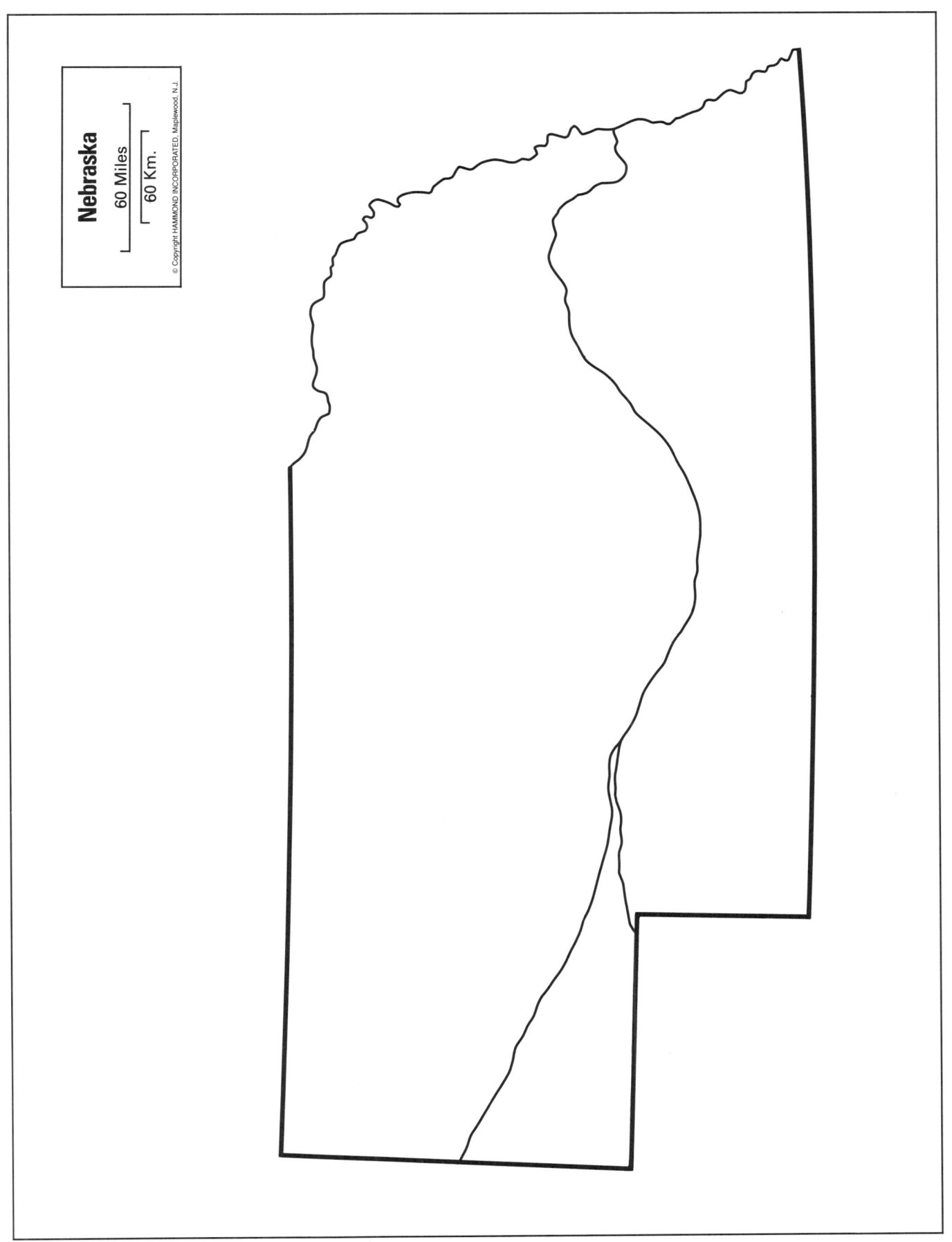

Nebraska

60 Miles

60 Km.

© Copyright HAMMOND INCORPORATED, Maplewood, N.J.

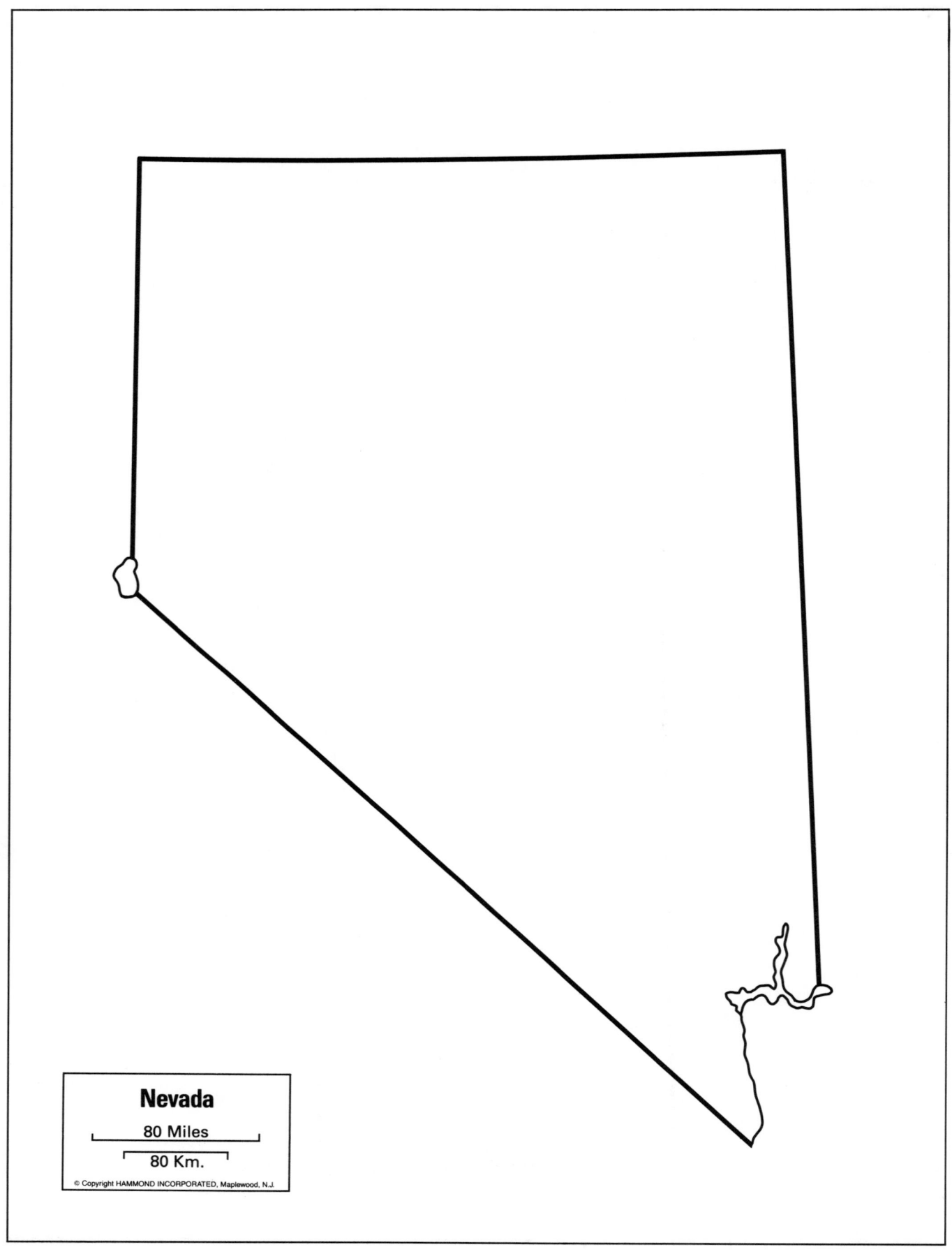

Nevada

80 Miles

80 Km.

© Copyright HAMMOND INCORPORATED, Maplewood, N.J.

New Hampshire

25 Miles

25 Km.

© Copyright HAMMOND INCORPORATED, Maplewood, N.J.

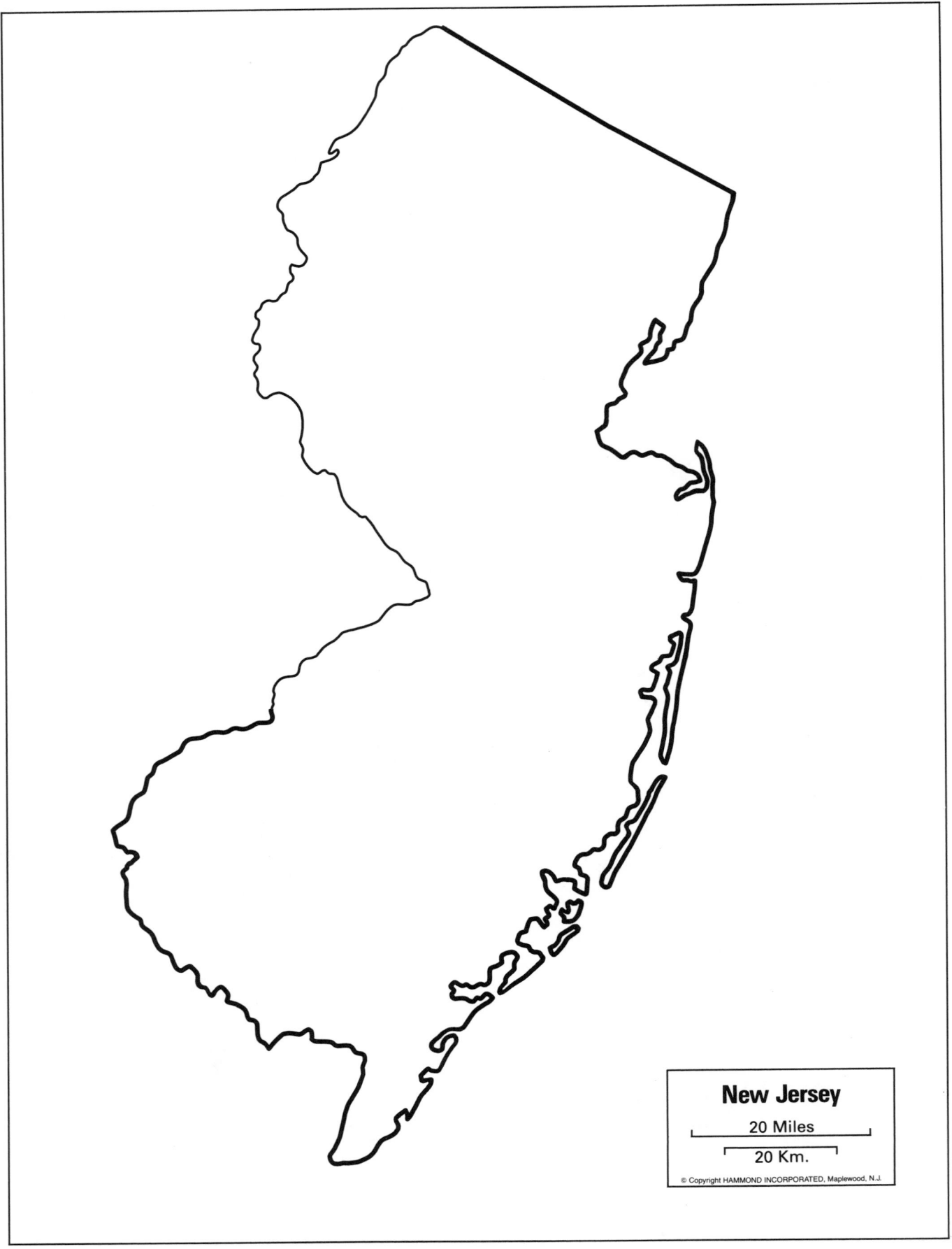

New Jersey

20 Miles

20 Km.

© Copyright HAMMOND INCORPORATED, Maplewood, N.J.

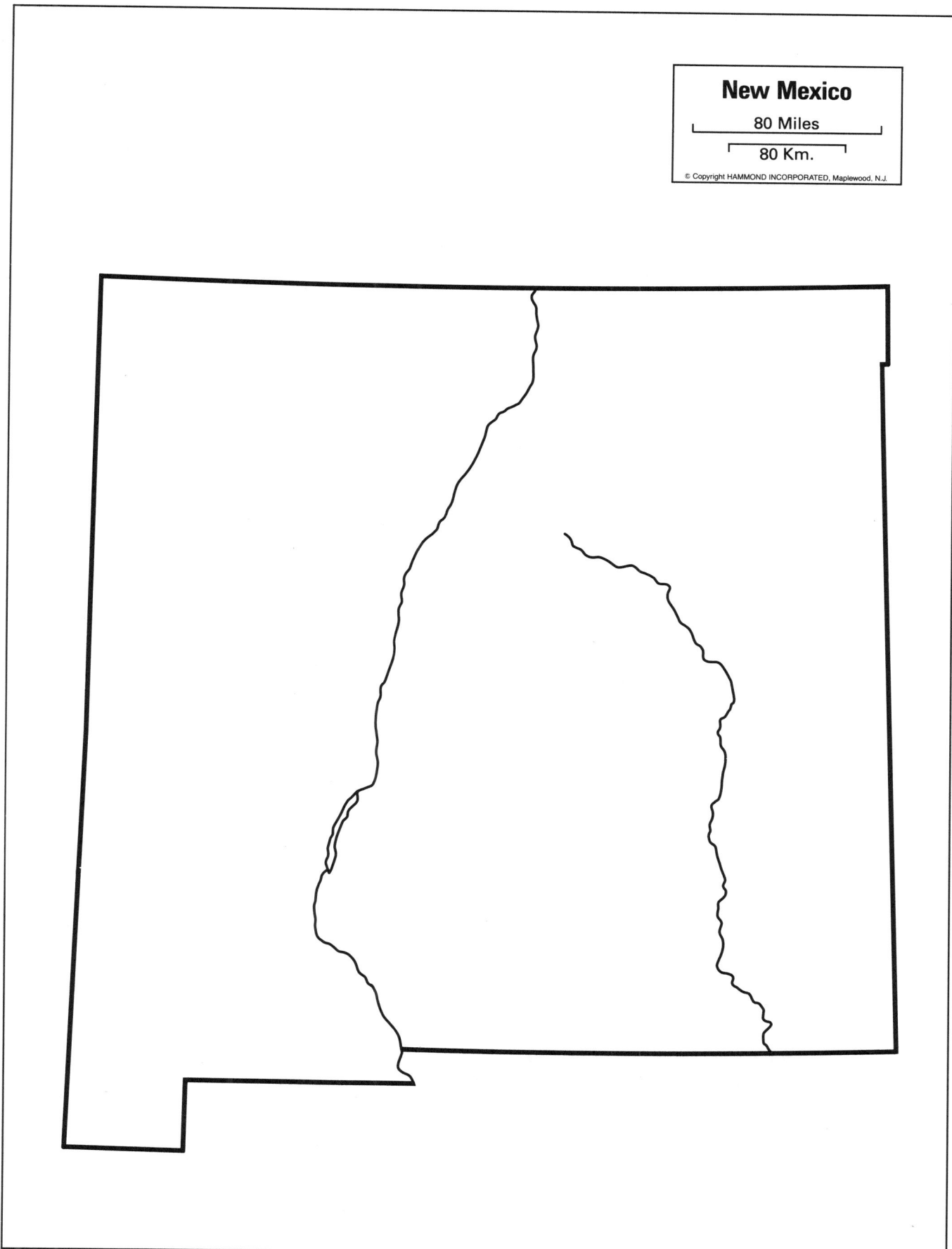
New Mexico
80 Miles
80 Km.
© Copyright HAMMOND INCORPORATED, Maplewood, N.J.

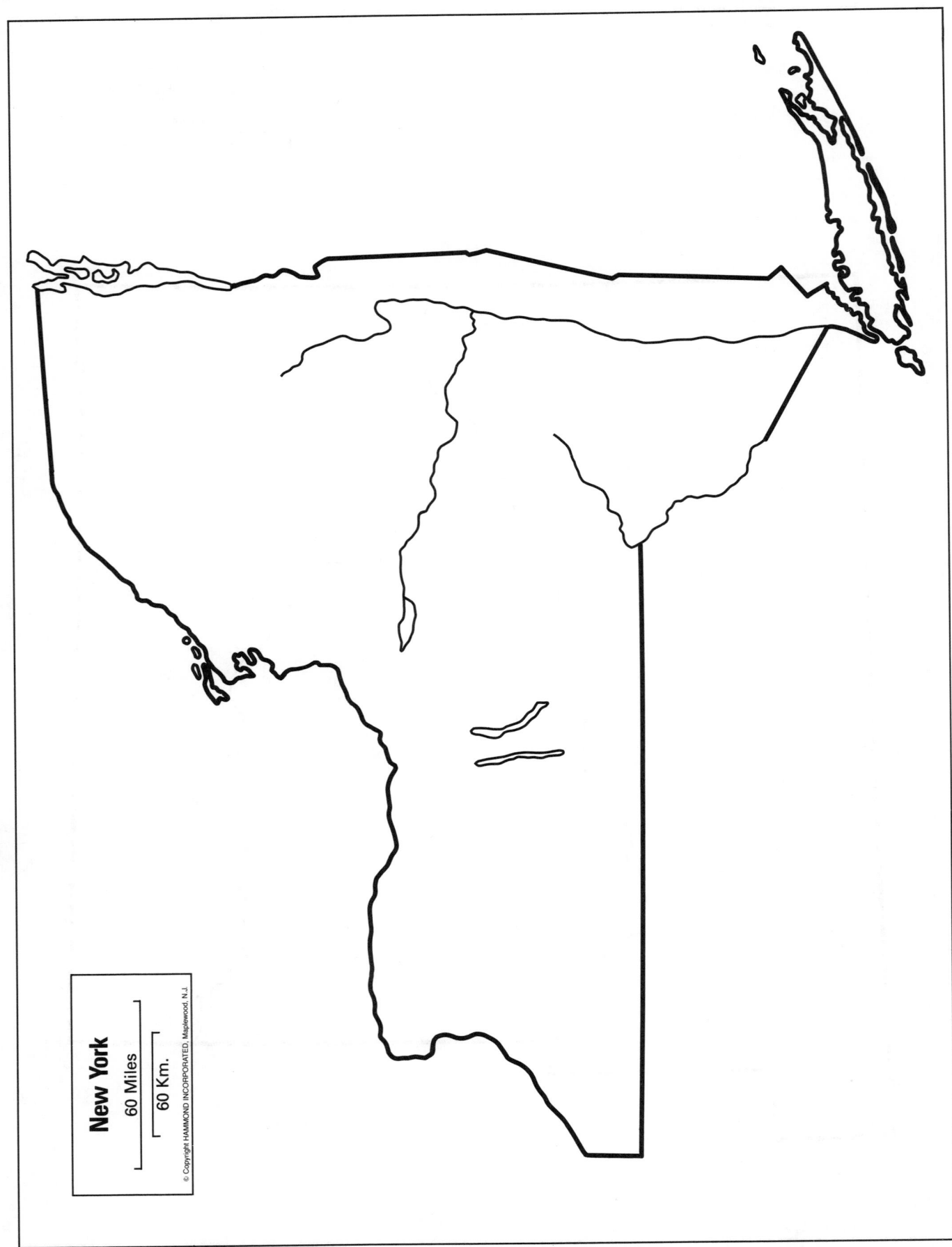

New York

60 Miles

60 Km.

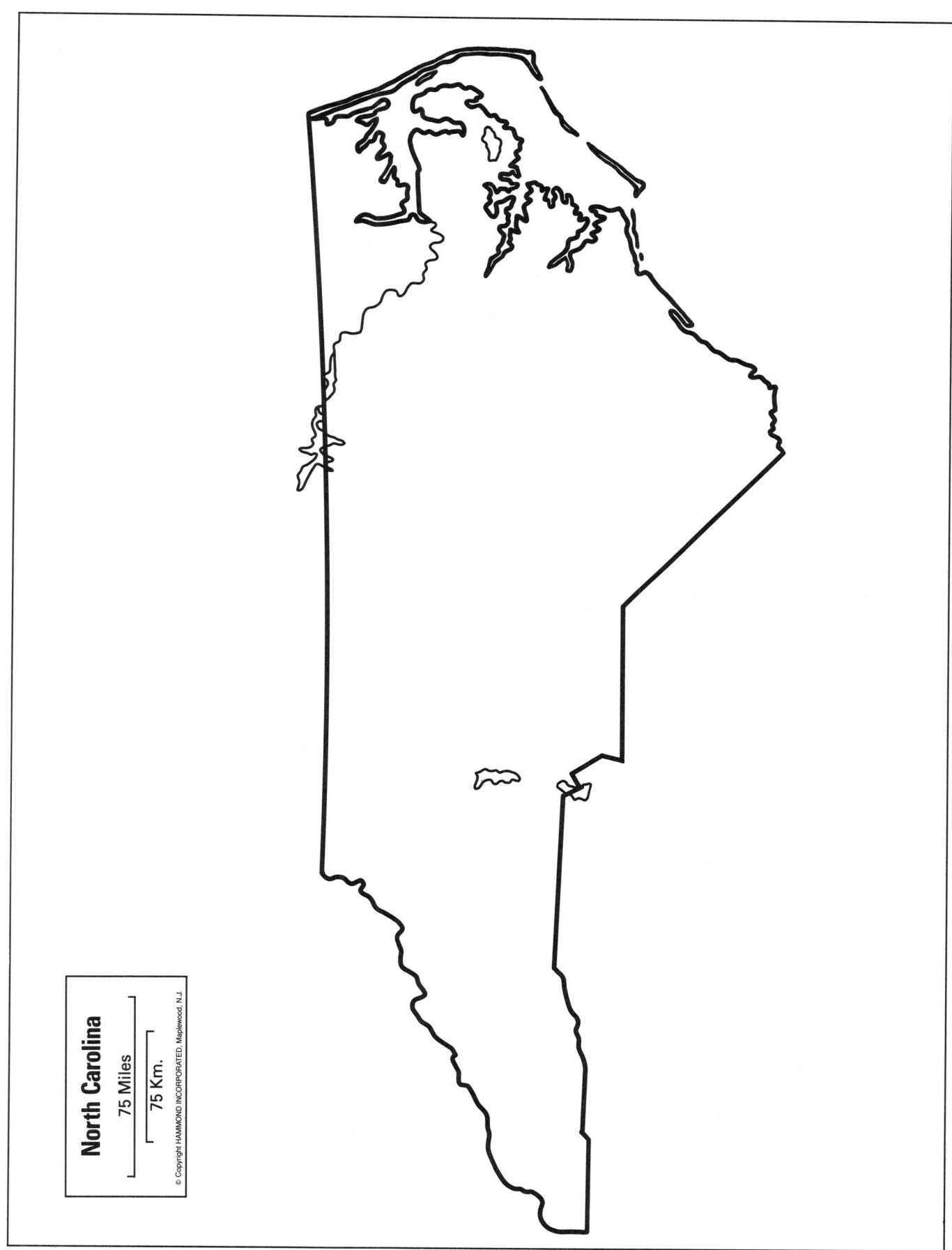

North Carolina

75 Miles

75 Km.

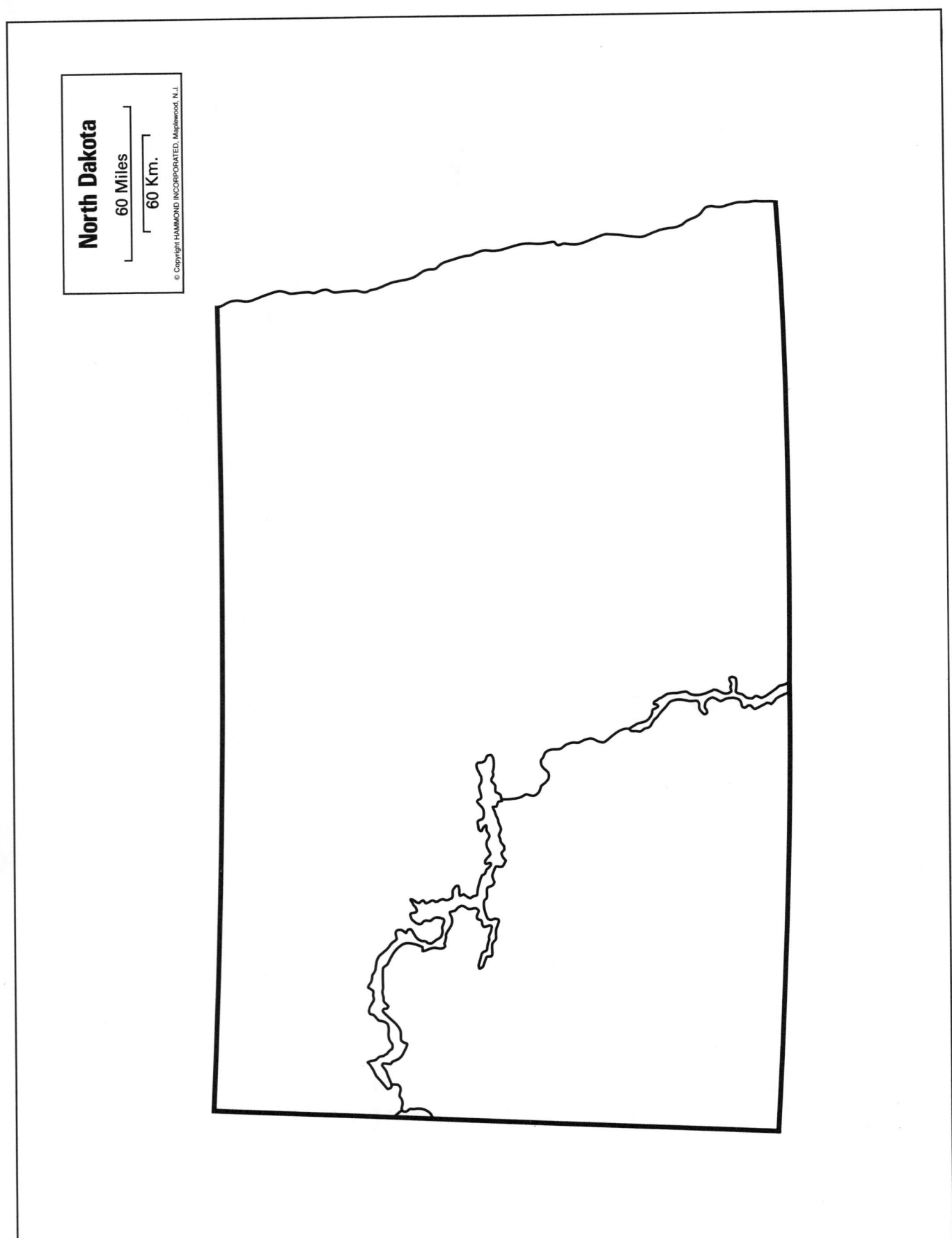

North Dakota

60 Miles

60 Km.

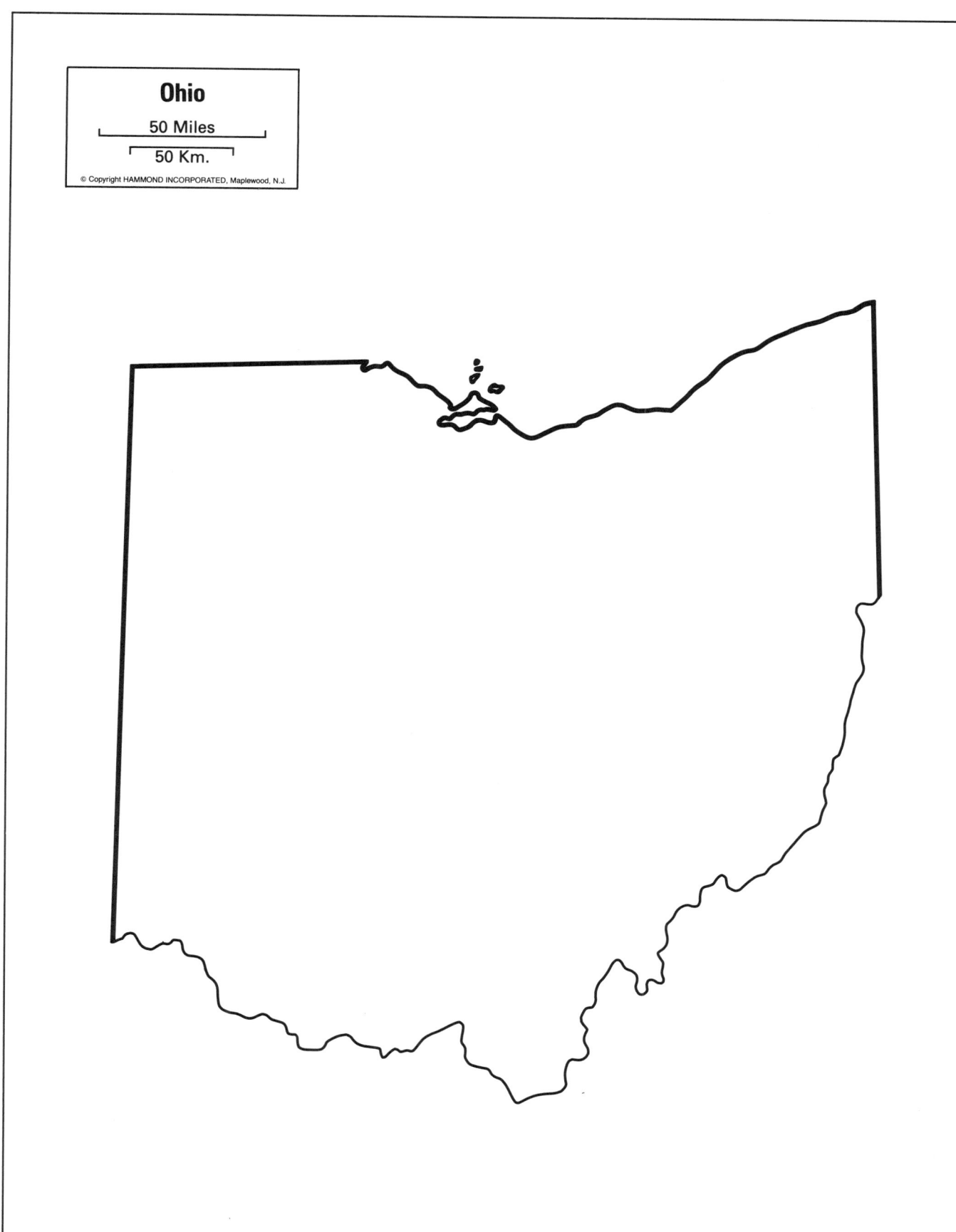

Ohio

50 Miles

50 Km.

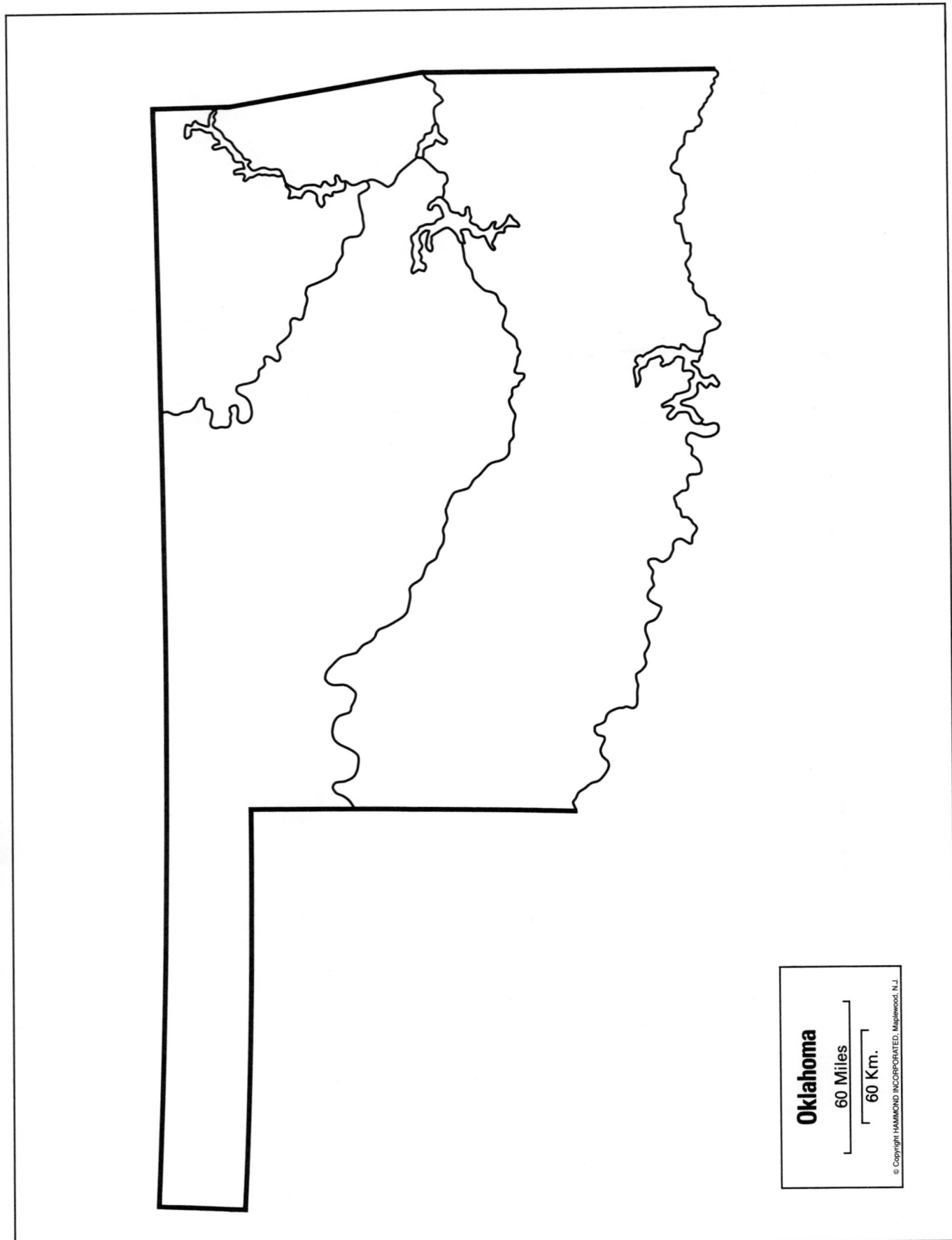

Oklahoma

60 Miles

60 Km.

© Copyright HAMMOND INCORPORATED, Maplewood, N.J.

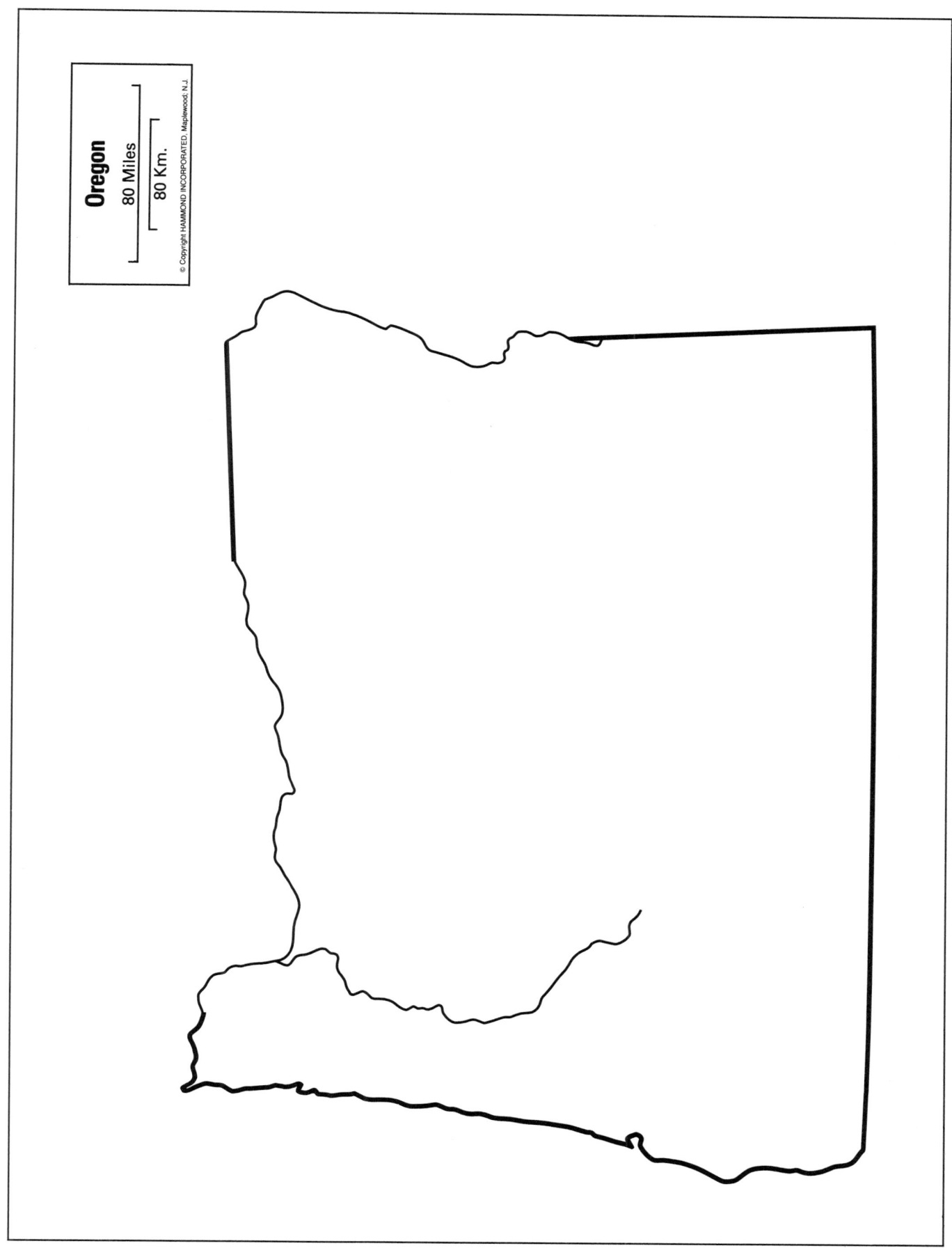

Oregon

80 Miles

80 Km.

© Copyright HAMMOND INCORPORATED, Maplewood, N.J.

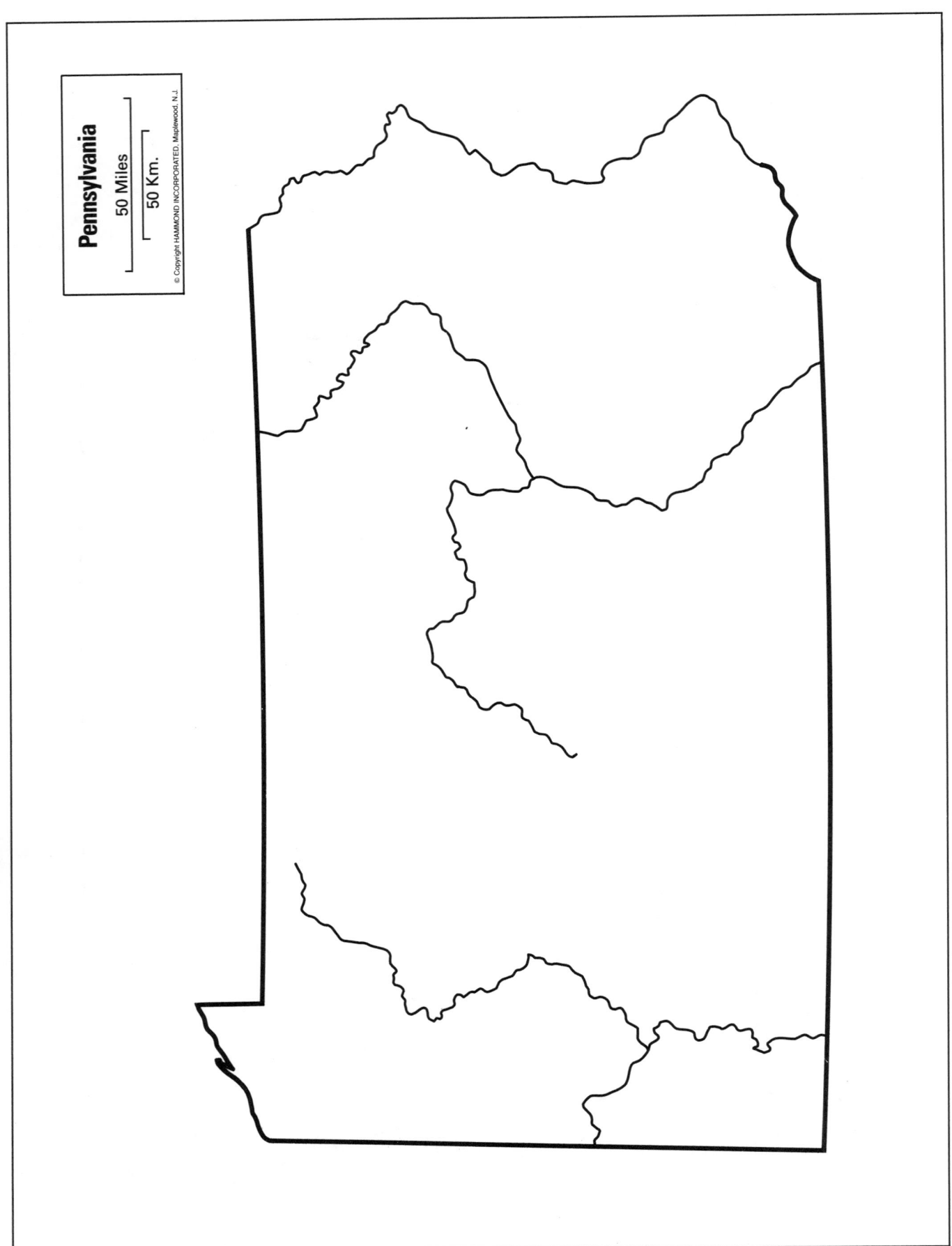

Pennsylvania

50 Miles

50 Km.

© Copyright HAMMOND INCORPORATED, Maplewood, N.J.

Rhode Island
15 Miles
15 Km.
© Copyright HAMMOND INCORPORATED, Maplewood, N.J.

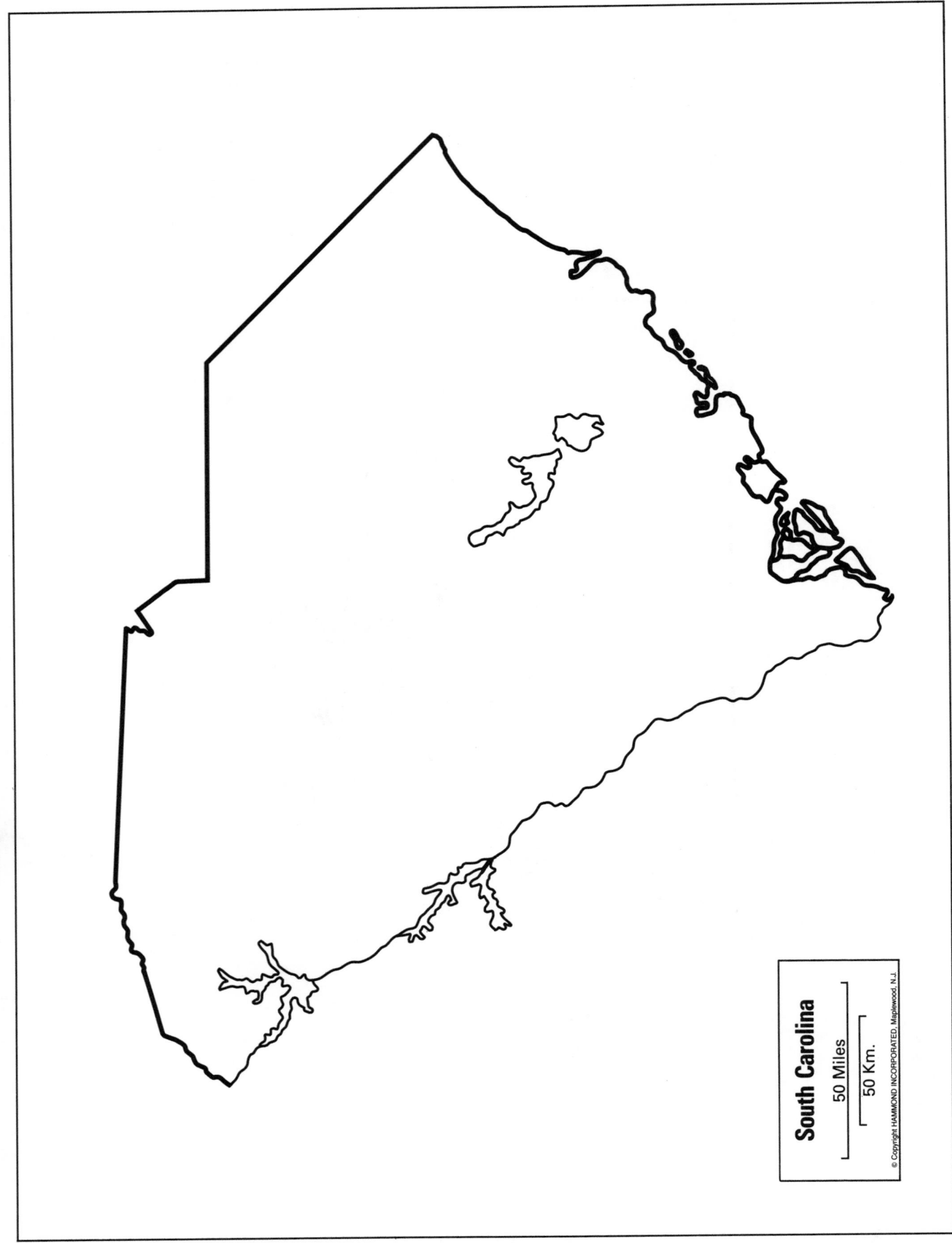

South Carolina

50 Miles

50 Km.

© Copyright HAMMOND INCORPORATED, Maplewood, N.J.

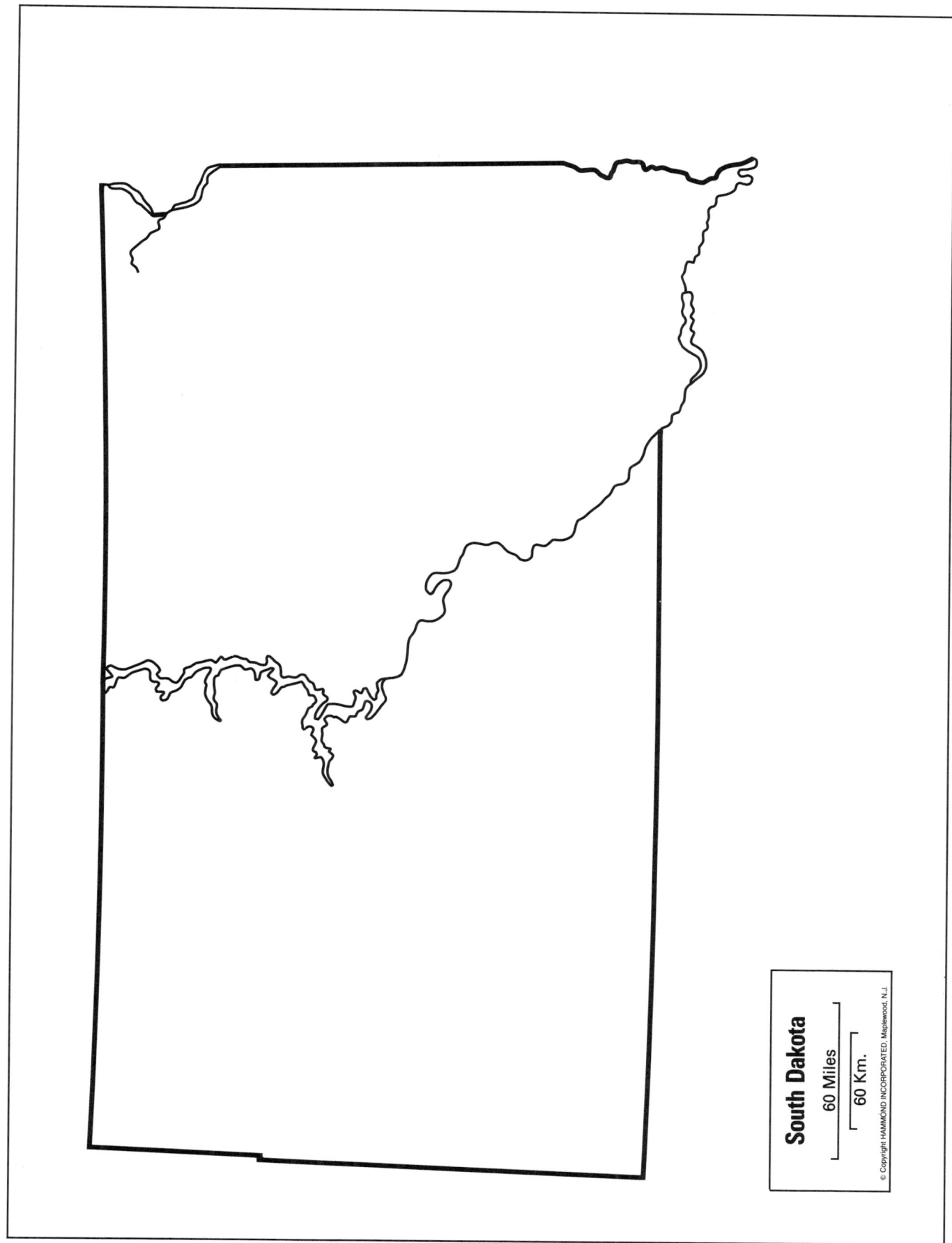

South Dakota

60 Miles

60 Km.

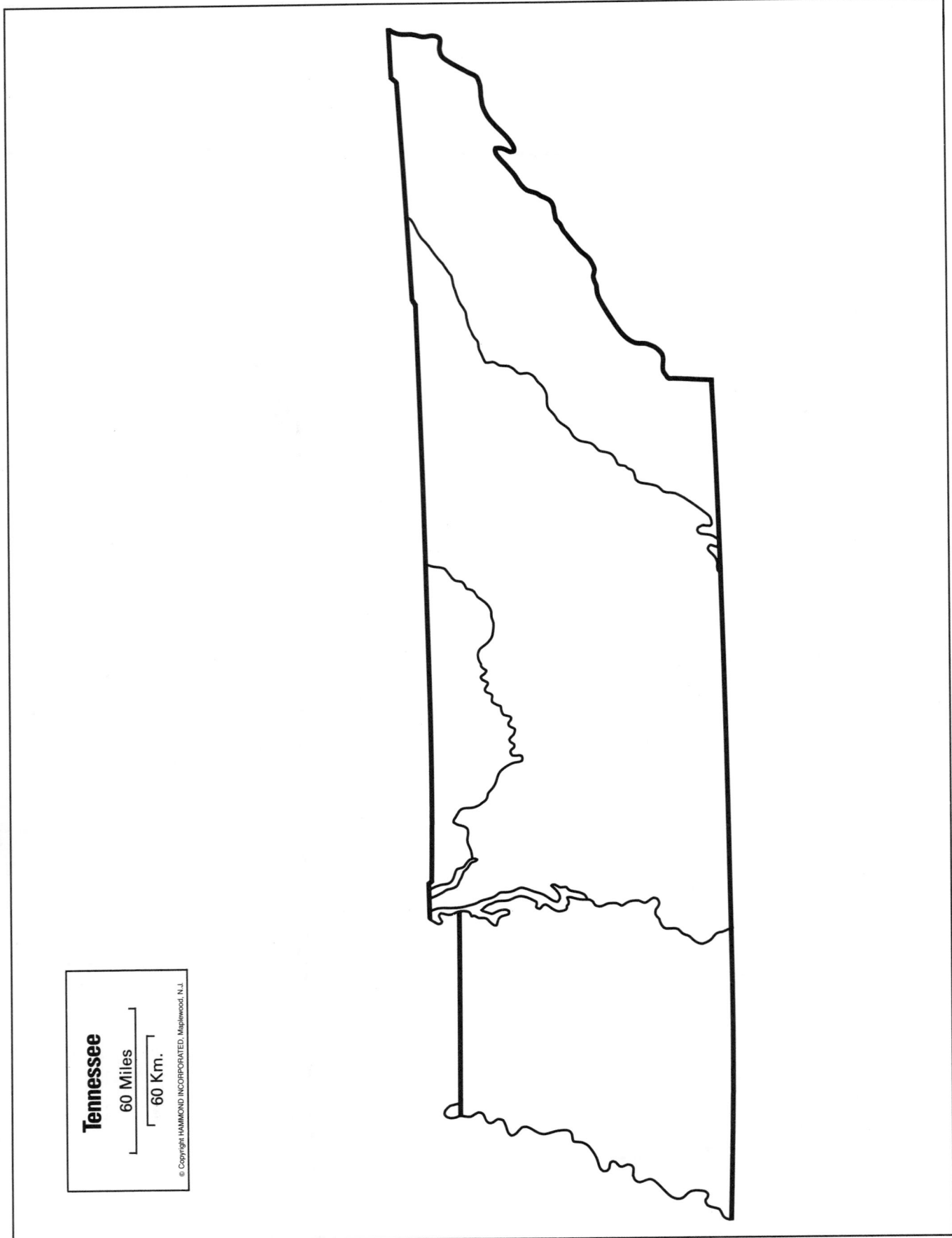

Tennessee

60 Miles

60 Km.

© Copyright HAMMOND INCORPORATED, Maplewood, N.J.

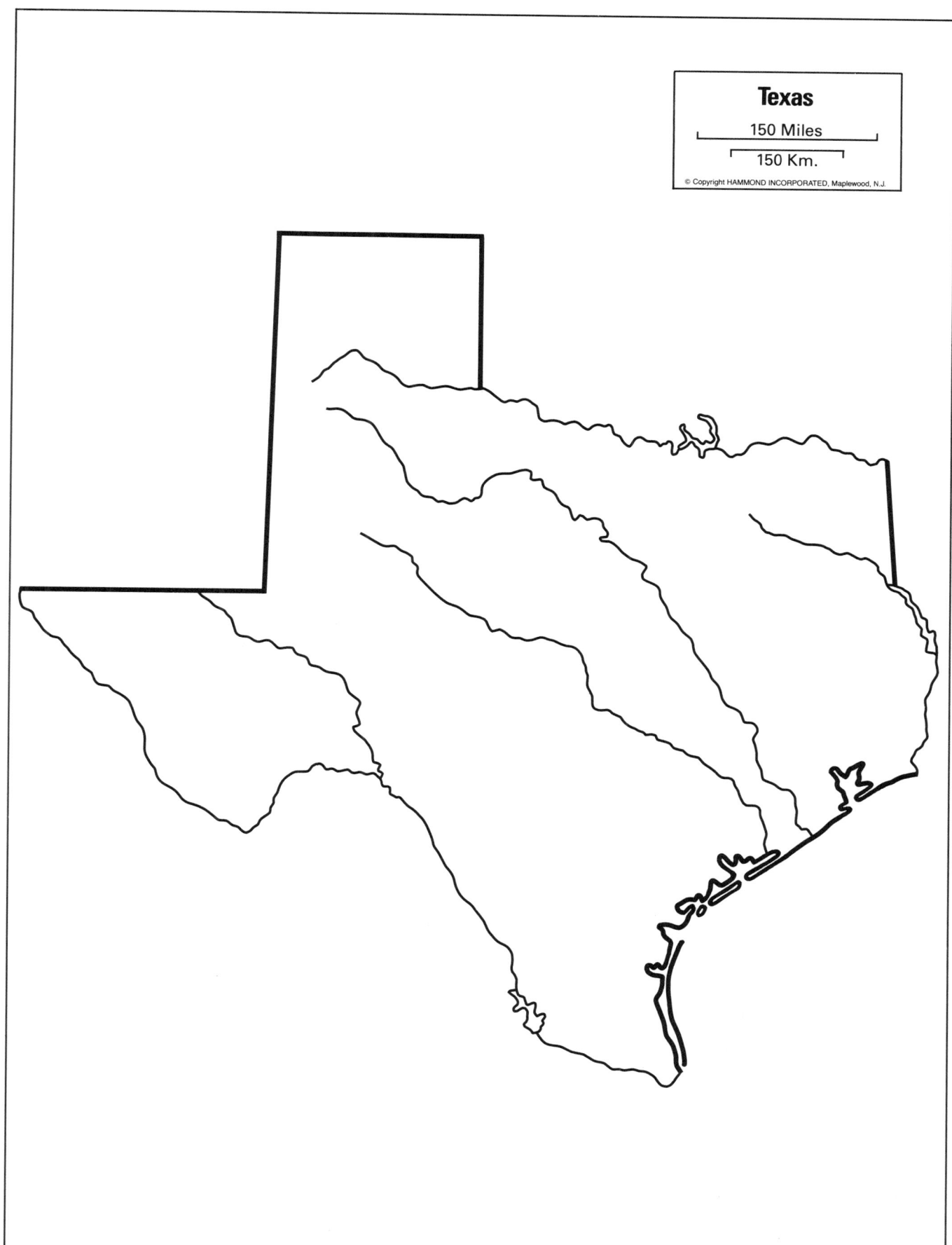

Texas

150 Miles

150 Km.

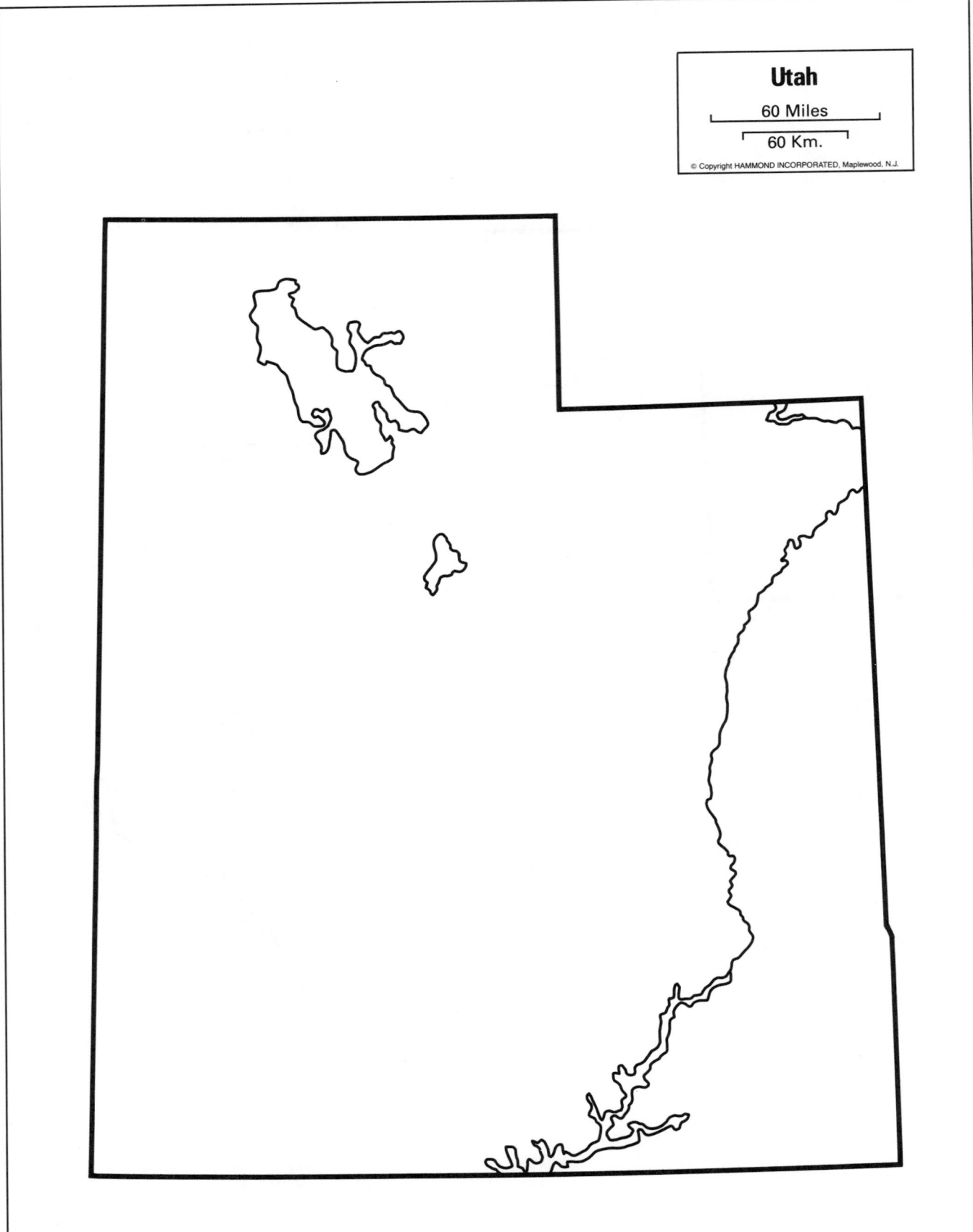

Utah

60 Miles

60 Km.

Vermont

25 Miles

25 Km.

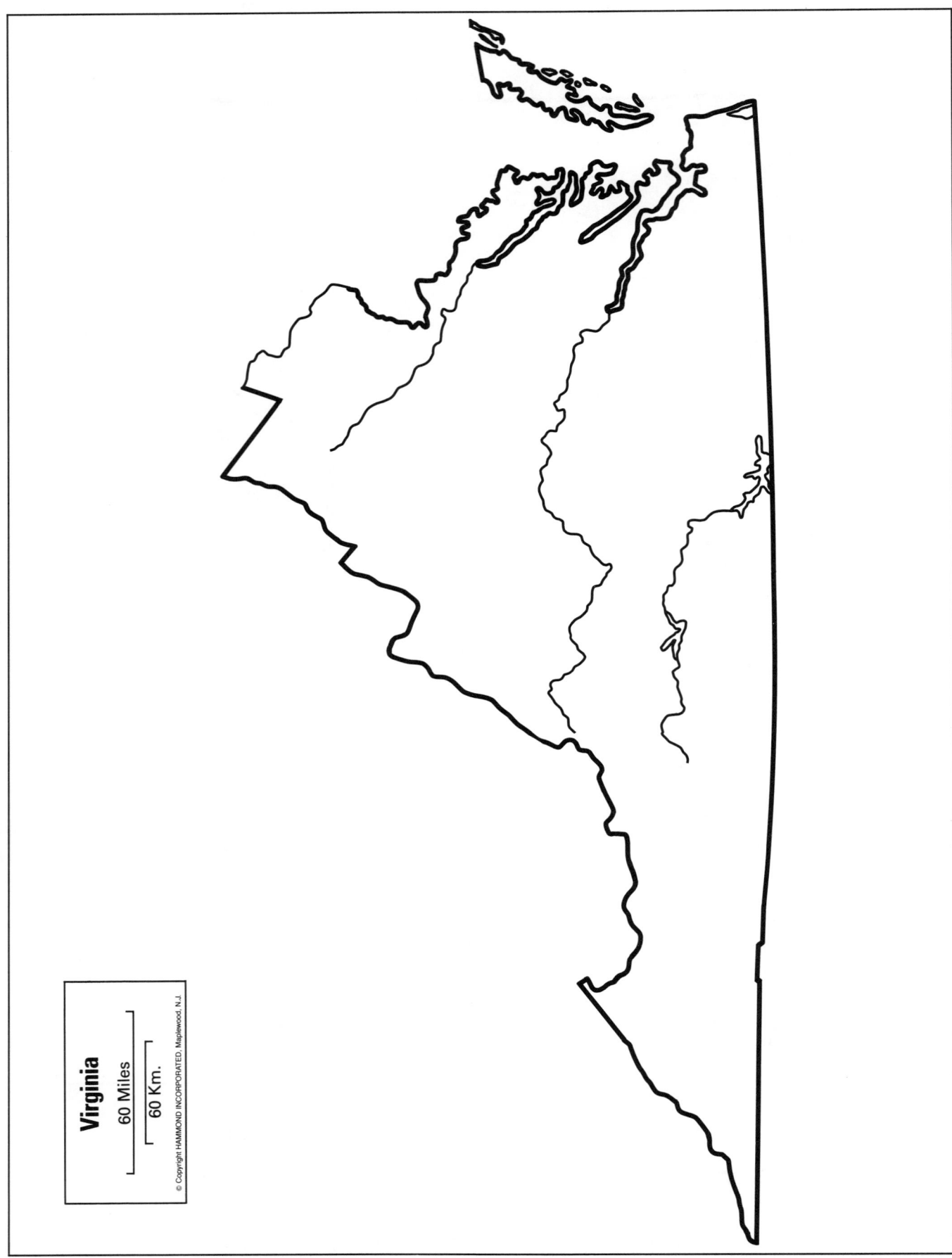

Virginia

60 Miles

60 Km.

© Copyright HAMMOND INCORPORATED, Maplewood, N.J.

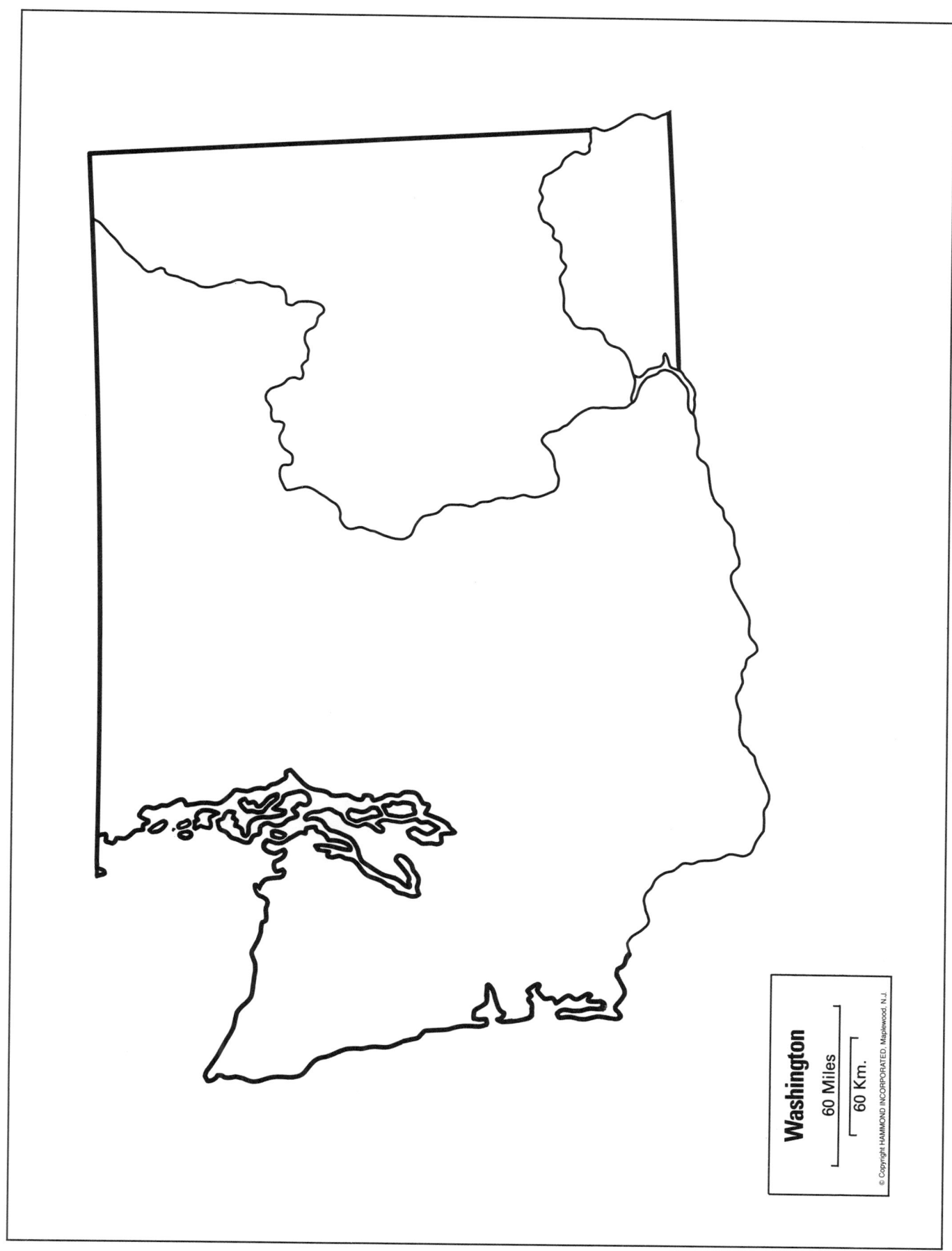

Washington

60 Miles

60 Km.

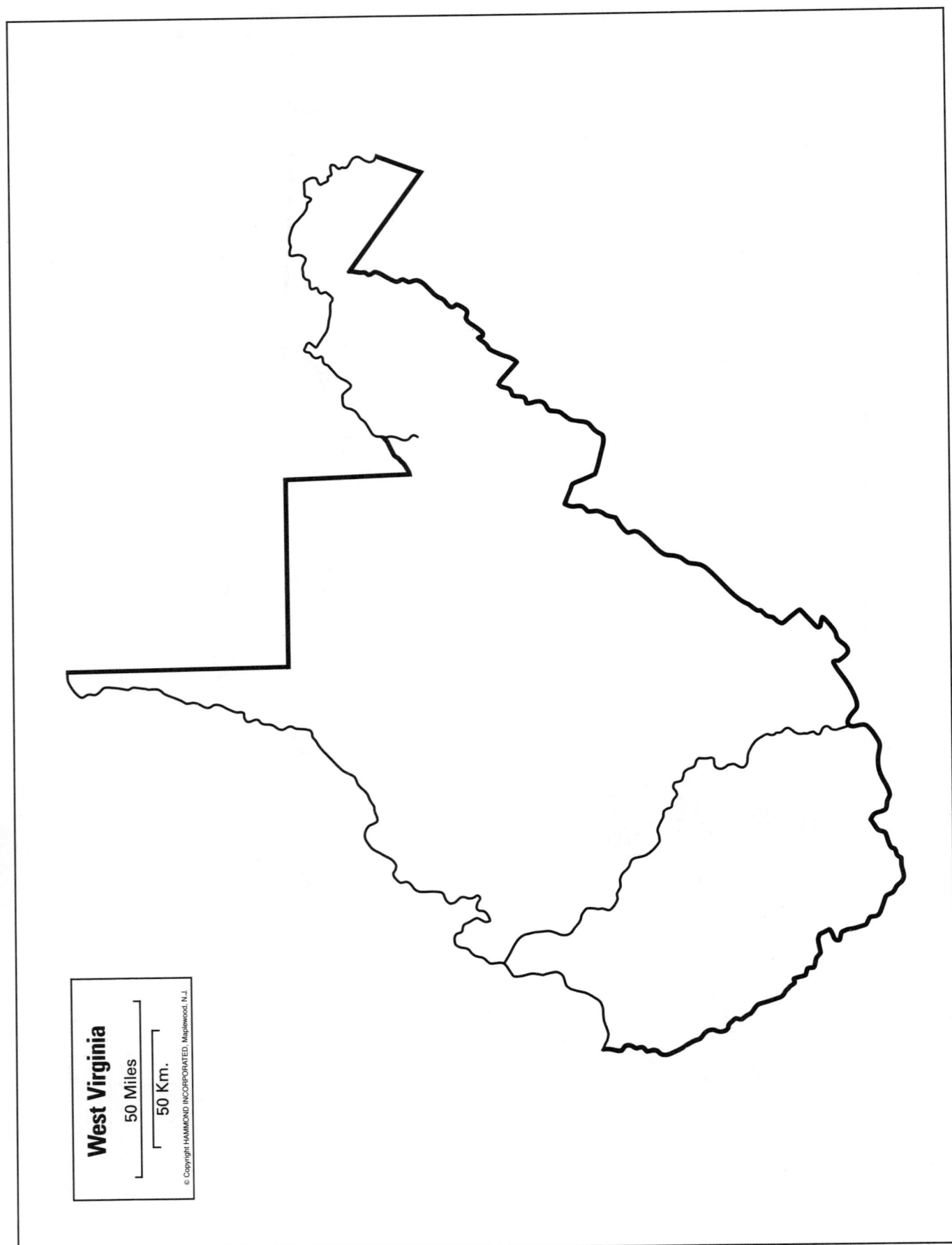

West Virginia

50 Miles

50 Km.

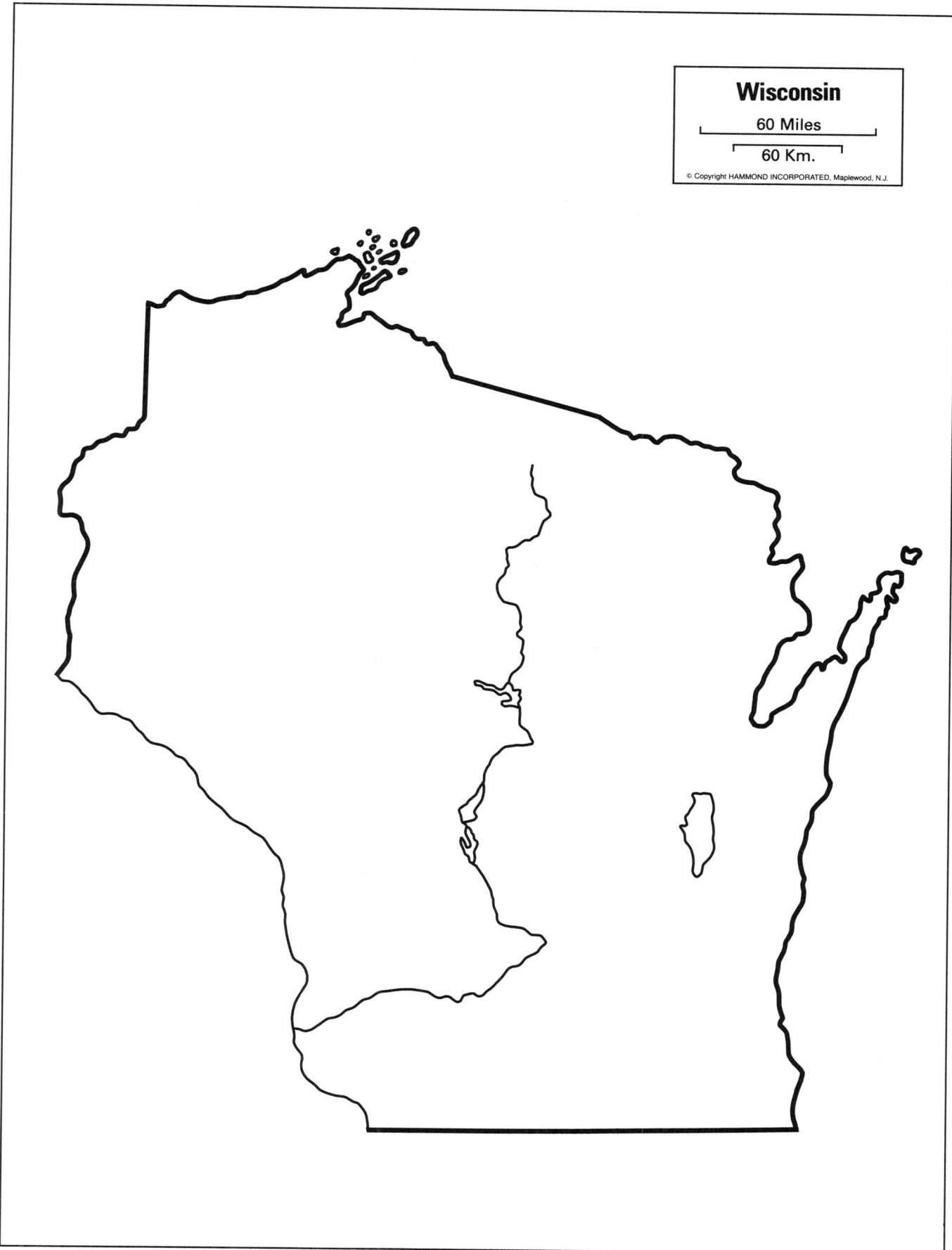

Wisconsin

60 Miles

60 Km.

664

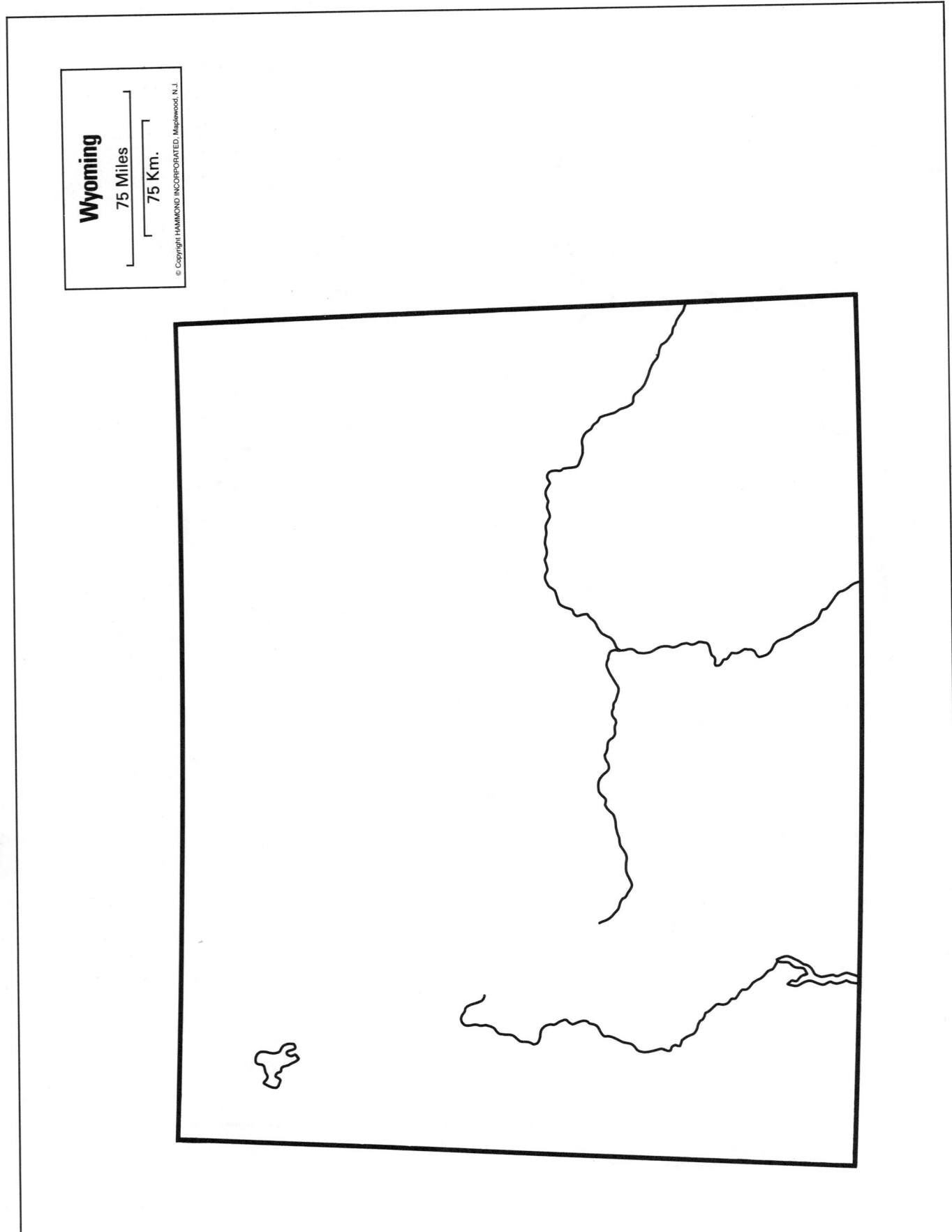

Wyoming

75 Miles

75 Km.

How to Study

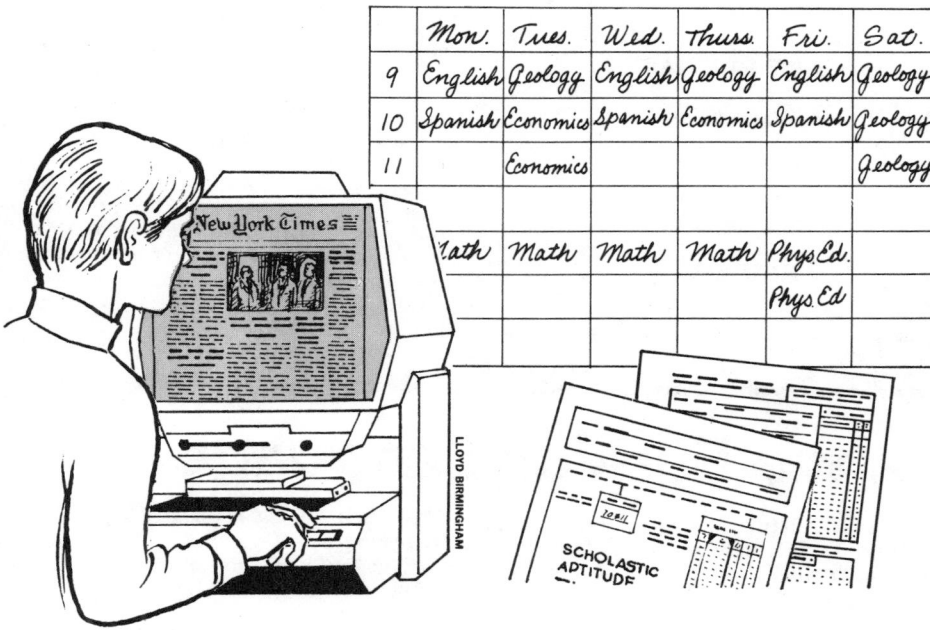

	Mon.	Tues.	Wed.	Thurs.	Fri.	Sat.
9	English	Geology	English	Geology	English	Geology
10	Spanish	Economics	Spanish	Economics	Spanish	Geology
11		Economics				Geology
	Math	Math	Math	Math	Phys.Ed.	
					Phys.Ed	

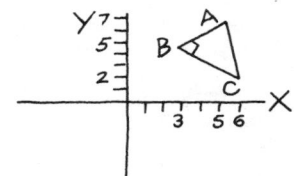

College study demands good work habits. Course loads are heavy, and competition is keen. The bulk of the responsibility for learning rests on your shoulders. You cannot depend on your teachers to review materials you are supposed to cover on your own. Unless you study efficiently, you will be swamped with work and worry by the time your first college Christmas vacation arrives.

To be a good student, you do not have to be outstandingly intelligent, but you must know how to use your time efficiently. Nothing is more important, yet many students never learn how to use their time.

Combining a successful academic career with important extracurricular activities requires planning. No scientist plunges into research without careful planning. No successful executive takes any action without careful planning. The student without a plan for daily activities lives from one study crisis to the next and learns far less than can be learned. You have surely heard that the first year of college is the most difficult, that the dropout rate is highest of all the four years. The principal reason is that entering freshmen do not plan their study time properly and have no awareness of how to prepare for a test.

Very few people have ever scored highly on a test without preparing for it. In addition to class preparation and reading during the course of the semester, most individuals need to do some form of concentrated study immediately prior to an exam. This does not mean cramming, that is, trying to force months of undigested material into your head in the last days before a test. This does mean giving a sharp edge to your systematic preparation through selective study and practice focused directly on the coming test.

This approach is also important for getting high marks on standardized tests. It is generally agreed that there are ways to prepare for all of these tests that can help the student taking them do considerably better. The cumulative nature of the material covered in the major standardized tests in the United States makes careful preparation especially crucial. You will test better if you study well. Good study habits enable you to absorb and retain much more information. Even if you have done poorly in the past, you can develop your abilities with the proper application, planning, and practice. In addition, proper preparation is the best antidote for the test anxiety that many students suffer from.

This volume is designed to develop your studying, writing, and test-taking skills. It begins with specific techniques for effective study in foreign languages, mathematics, science, and the social sciences. The "How to Write a Top-Notch Exam" section brings together all those techniques for the final step: testing. It shows you exactly how to prepare for tests in all your courses, write good papers, and get higher marks on exams.

The final section gives specific advice for preparing for each area of the SAT, ACT, GRE, GED, and College Board Achievement Tests in mathematics, English, U.S. history, and world history, as well as the College Board Advanced Placement Tests in English literature, calculus, U.S. history, biology, and chemistry. The section provides 69 pages of sample practice problems from these same tests, with answers and explanations of how to arrive at the answers.

This volume is intended for students who make good grades but want to do better as well as for students who make poor grades but want to improve. So if you really want to improve, apply the information you read here. You soon will be able to realize your full potential as a student, enjoy your college years more fully, and come away with a far better education.

IMPROVING STUDY SKILLS

Constant scrambling to keep up, worry about whether you are learning effectively, the desperation of being swamped by assignments—all are harmful to your work and to your peace of mind.

You can avoid these pitfalls and enjoy college more by being prepared with better study habits. Good study habits can be developed with practice and perseverance.

Important within every discipline are the common principles of study: careful identification of what is to be learned, frequent review, self-recita-

- • BE PREPARED
- • FOCUS
- • PRACTICE
- • PERSEVERE
- • REVIEW

tion, and self-testing. Other, more specific, methods are useful for particular college courses. Understanding the differences and potential difficulties of each individual subject places you a step ahead and provides extra time you can use to gain thorough mastery of the material.

Read this section carefully and put its suggestions to work. It is important to develop your study skills early on. Knowing *how* to study and prepare for tests is essential to your journey toward a successful and enjoyable college career.

How to Learn a Foreign Language

Despite the fact that almost every college freshman has already had two or more years' experience in foreign language study, no single area of college work is subject to more haphazard, ineffective, and wasteful study techniques. In fact, it can be said that foreign language study is too often characterized by a complete absence of study techniques. The typical student treats language courses as a necessary nuisance to be disposed of as quickly as possible. The opportunity to really learn a foreign language seldom seems to enter into the picture. The results are useful to no one. Most of our college students can do little more than translate a bit of another language. A few years after college, even this skill disappears.

Yet ability in languages is needed if you want to go on to graduate studies. Business is becoming more international in character than ever. Opportunities abroad are increasing. Travel overseas is becoming almost commonplace. While colleges have for years required work in foreign languages, today more than ever before, the requirement becomes meaningful.

One result of the interest in languages is that high schools and colleges are increasing their language offerings. We are growing accustomed to seeing Russian added to courses of study. But if you want to appreciate the range of languages studied in a university, read this list taken from a recent Bulletin of the School of General Studies, Columbia Uni-

versity: Albanian, Arabic, Armenian, Azeri-Turkic, Bengali, Bulgarian, Chinese, Czech, Estonian, Finnish, French, Georgian, German, Greek, Hebrew, Hindi, Hungarian, Irish, Italian, Japanese, Kalmyk-Mongolian, Kazan-Turkic, Korean, Latin, Lithuanian, Persian, Polish, Portuguese, Provençal, Romanian, Russian, Serbocroatian, Slovak, Spanish, Swedish, Tibetan, Turkish, Ukrainian, Urdu, Uyghur, Uzbek, Yiddish.

Language study has its own special problems and techniques. The following pages are designed to help you learn languages effectively and make your top marks while doing it.

The first thing you will notice in our discussion of foreign language study techniques is the emphasis on repetition. If you have not studied a language in high school, you will find out soon enough that learning the vocabulary and grammar of a language is mainly an exercise of your memory. It is through the *principle of overlearning* that we make our memories work for us. Simply expressed, overlearning makes use of meaningful repetition beyond the point of initial understanding. Thus, when you encounter new words and new rules, repeat them fifteen times; not until you merely understand them but until they have become stamped on your memory.

In the following sections on homework, classroom work, translation, and examinations you will find that the more often you expose yourself to new material, the better you will learn it.

The will to learn a foreign language. Regardless of how important languages are and how much influence your knowledge of them will have upon your career, if you do not *want* to learn a foreign language, you are going to be miserable in college language courses. Maybe you have already found out how unhappy Latin or German can make the unwilling student.

No one can convince you that you want to learn a language if you do not. Countless essays can list all the reasons for studying French. Popular magazines can supply all the charming anecdotes anyone would ever want to read about "three words of Polish and how they saved a man's life." The virtue of being able to say *please* and *thank you* in all the languages of the world can be repeated a thousand times. Yet, somehow or other, the taste for speaking or writing a language cannot be taught. You either have it right now or you do not.

Children take to languages because they like sound, because they enjoy learning. Indeed, children can even be talked into wanting to learn a new language. But you cannot. What are you going to do about it? You must do something, because here are some requirements typical of those you will meet in American colleges:

- • Two years of a modern foreign language
- • Three years of a classical language and two years of a modern foreign language

- Candidates for a degree must demonstrate speaking knowledge of at least one modern language other than their own
- Students must be able to read and translate the scientific literature of at least one language other than their own

The only thing that will help you master these demands is true interest. For those who do not naturally like languages, there is one ray of hope. *Success breeds interest; interest returns success.*

If you can experience some success in your study of languages, you will discover interest you have not experienced before. The French proverb, *rien ne réussit comme le succès,* cannot be denied. Nothing succeeds like success.

If you have had persistent lack of interest in languages and have failed to do as well in them as you should, the best thing you can do for yourself right now is to *find out just how to study a language for maximum results and make a fresh start toward proficiency.* The fact is that language study has all the fascination of science and social studies, and the thrill of being able to converse in another language is unique.

Let us now lay our plans for successful study. In most of the discussion that follows, French is the language used for illustration. The choice of French is for the author's convenience; you are not being advised to choose French as your language.

How to do your homework.

Learning languages is more an exercise of memory than is any other subject you will study in college. While there is system in foreign grammar and spelling that enables you to think many things out, in order to become truly proficient in a language, your memory must serve you well. In reading, speaking, or writing a language, you must be able instantly to call the right expression to your mind. Although this does not sound easy, you will find it within your power if you work intelligently toward mastery.

Memory depends on

- *Selecting* what you want to remember,
- *Organizing* the material to be learned in a form that lends itself to easy learning,
- *Spacing* your learning effort.

Your foreign language textbooks help you in all three respects: selecting, organizing, and spacing. They *select* for you short, varied exercises, each designed to teach you one specific fact, bit of information, or principle. They *organize* the material in a general way, but you will have to organize it further so that it is in the form easiest for you to learn. Finally, the textbooks *space* the learning effort for you if you keep up with your assignments. An assignment in a history textbook, by contrast, demands that you select the material to be learned, organize it completely on your own, and space the learning effort yourself.

There are four steps involved in doing your homework in a manner guaranteed to produce results:

1. Read through the pages assigned.
2. Learn new vocabulary.
3. Study grammar section.
4. Practice and review.

Let us discuss each one in turn and find the best procedures for accomplishing them.

Step 1: Read through the pages assigned. The emphasis is upon the word *read.* Read the new vocabulary and its meanings, read the grammatical principles exactly as stated, read the English sentences you are going to translate later on, read the French sentences in French, and read whatever other review sections appear.

If you are doing your work in your own room, where you cannot disturb others, *read the lesson aloud.* Trying to sound out the French words will help you become accustomed to their sounds. Reading the rest of the lesson aloud will force you to pronounce every word. The few minutes you spend in this way previews your next class session. It is customary for many language teachers to give written and oral quizzes almost daily. You can expect any part of the lesson to form the subject matter of the quiz.

There are many advantages in reading through your lesson in this manner. For one thing, many of the items in a lesson are quite easy to learn. There are cognate words—words of two or more languages that derive from the same language, including one you know well—that are learned immediately upon recognition. There are rules of grammar that appear so logical you are able to grasp them at once. There are idiomatic constructions that stick in one reading.

In this reading, then, you are finding out which parts of the lesson are going to make the greatest problems for you. When you come to the thorough studying of the lesson, you will know what will have to be emphasized and what will take little time. The repetition from one part of the lesson to another actually gives you several exposures to the same material, and so you learn just by reading alone.

Step 2: Learn new vocabulary. What is the best way to learn vocabulary? Regardless of whether your primary objective is to read, speak, or write a language,

> read new vocabulary
> speak new vocabulary, and
> write new vocabulary.

- Read the first new word aloud *five* times.
- Look away from your text and say the word *five* times, pronouncing it as well as you can.
- Read the English equivalent, *but do not say it.*
- Write the new word *five* times. The first time on an index card, the others on any sheet of paper. This paper will be discarded at the end of the lesson, but the card will be saved for later review. When you write a *noun,* always include the definite article so that you will learn the gender of the noun at the same time. When you write an *adjective,* give both masculine and feminine forms.
- Repeat the process for every word in the list. After you have finished, you will have *one card for each word.*
  WARNING: As you say each French word, do not say its English equivalent. Your object is not to learn the words French men and women have for English words. You want to learn French.
- After you have finished the last word in the list, go back to each word card. On its reverse side, write a short sentence *in French* using the word on the face. If you are studying the first lesson in an elementary French text, you will have trouble finding enough words to make a sentence. Try. Look at the other words in the lesson for what you need. The object of writing this sentence is to help you learn a new word without having to think of its English equivalent. Avoiding English will help you establish the habit of thinking in French, which is essential for mastery.

The extra time you take in learning your first words of French in this way

USE CARDS—*with a new word on one side and a sentence using that word on the other—to help study foreign language vocabulary. Do not include a translation of the word.*

le chapeau

Le chapeau de mon frère est noir.

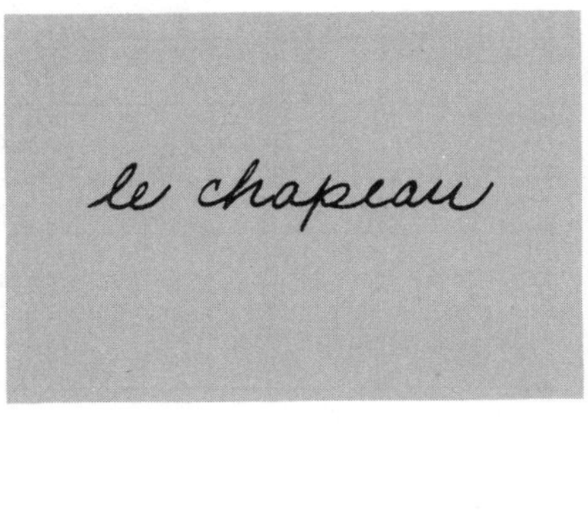

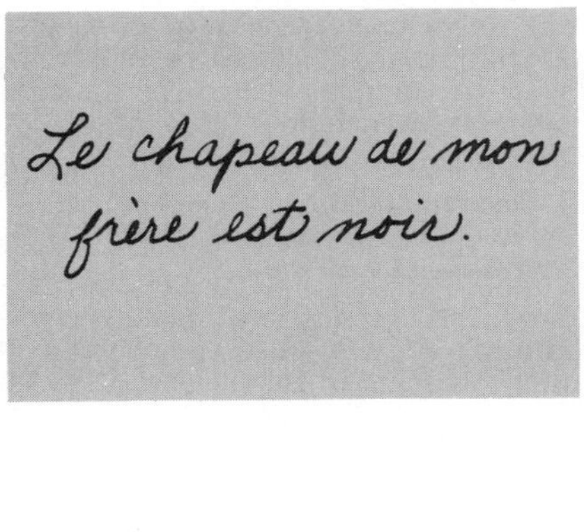

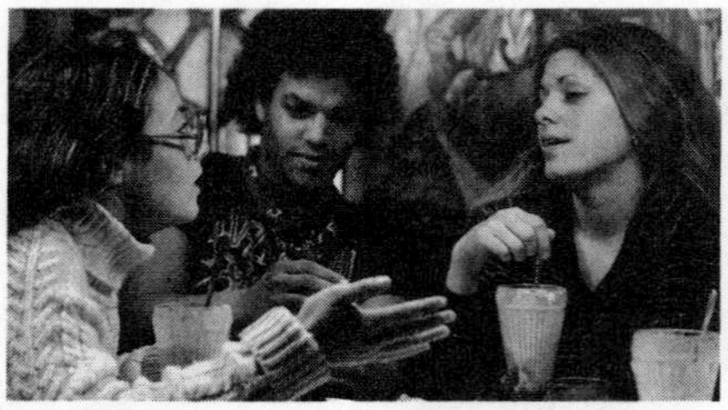

CHATS *with other students are best conducted in the foreign language you are studying.*

will pay off. Until French pronunciation no longer gives you trouble, you will find it helpful to mark the pronunciation of a new word on the face of its card. This can be done either in phonetics, if you can handle this useful tool, or in the English alphabet. *Il* = eel, *elle* = ell, *moi* = mwah. By listening carefully in class as your teacher explains and demonstrates correct pronunciation, you will soon be able to omit pronunciation entries on your cards.

Your biggest barrier to good pronunciation of a foreign language is the self-consciousness that hits most of us when we tackle something new and strange. The sounds of French are not difficult if you are willing to pitch in and sound silly for a while until you catch on. When your teacher enunciates a new word, say the word to yourself. This will help fasten the new sound to the word itself. Every time you use the word from then on, you will hear it also until you become fluent.

Why all these techniques to avoid writing English words? You are steering clear of the greatest pitfall to mastery of a foreign language: the easiest and most damaging thing for you to do when you are approaching a new language is to learn it as a translation. Of course translating is easier, faster, more immediately satisfying than any other technique. Who cannot learn *je* = I, *tu* = you, *il* = he, *elle* = she, by merely repeating the list over and over again? Countless thousands of American students have done this, have passed their French courses, and *have not learned French.* Every time they have to think of a pronoun, they run through the list they have learned until the right word pops out. Can you picture them conducting a conversation in this matter? They have learned French words and their English equivalents, but not how to put the words together with other words.

Contrast that kind of rote learning with the manner in which the same students learned their first *sentences* in French:

"Bonjour, monsieur. Comment allez-vous?"

"Très bien, merci, et vous?"

From the first day in almost every beginning French class, teachers drill their students in this greeting. No at-

tempt is made to translate word by word. There is no bothering with English. And every student learns these French sentences.

Everything you study in French should be studied the same way. Study French, not new foreign synonyms for English words.

The sooner you are able to write sentences, the sooner you will be using all of your language ability. Even if some of your sentences sound childish to you, they are sentences and they have

meaning. And you will not need to translate them when you study them, for you will know what they mean as soon as you see them in studying. Every time you go over them, you will be *reading a foreign language.* What is more, you will be reading something you have *written.* When you can say the sentence aloud without looking at your card, you will be *speaking* the language. And reading, writing, and speaking are the key to vocabulary building.

ESSENTIAL TERMS FOR UNDERSTANDING GRAMMAR

You may not know the terms of grammar as well as you should. But your language teachers will expect you to know them thoroughly. Do you know the *parts of speech?*

Parts of Speech

	DEFINITION	EXAMPLE
noun	name of a person, place, thing, or idea	John, New Jersey, ball, democracy
article	used before nouns to limit their application	a, an, the
pronoun	word used in place of a noun	he, them, it
verb	word or words used to express an action, condition, or state	eat, go, grieve
adjective	word used to describe or limit meaning of a noun or word used as noun	happy, funny, sad, hopeful
adverb	word used to modify verb, adjective, or other adverb	happily, quickly
preposition	word used to show relationship between word in a sentence and a noun or word used as a noun	between, into, among
conjunction	word or words used to connect other words or groups of words	and, either . . . or, because, so
interjection	word or words used to express emotion, but having no grammatical relationship with the other words in a sentence	oh! golly! hurrah!

There are several dozen terms that are used in describing the functions of words within sentences. While some of them are not used widely in English, there are at least *ten* you will have to know in foreign language study.

Additional Grammatical Terms

	DEFINITION	EXAMPLE
active voice	verb is in active voice when its subject performs act	I *hit* the ball.
antecedent	word or expression to which a pronoun refers	I know the *man* who is going by.
auxiliary verb	verb that assists other verbs in forming their tenses, voices, and moods	It *was* heard no more. I *ought* to go home.
complement	word or phrase used to complete the meaning of a verb	He was called *Corky.* The dinner was *delicious.*
intransitive verb	verb that does not require an object to convey meaning	Annie *swims* beautifully. The tide *was running.*
number	changes in nouns, pronouns, and verb to designate singular or plural	boy, boys he, they, eats, eat
object	*direct*—noun completing sense of transitive verb	Dick lifted the *cat.*
	indirect—noun indirectly affected by sense of verb	Johnny sent a gift to his *mother.*
passive voice	verb is in passive voice when its subject is acted on	The choice *was made* by me.
person	changes of verbs and pronouns to indicate speaker, person spoken to, person spoken of	I do. You go. He fights.
transitive verb	verb that requires object to convey meaning	We *found* gold. We *got* what we wanted.

How many of these terms do you already know? If you do not know them all, *learn them now,* before you meet them in your foreign language study. By learning these terms now, you remove one obstacle to successful study.

Sets of vocabulary cards have been published for the foreign language student. By putting down a few dollars, the student obtains some hundreds of drill cards all made up and ready to study. Impressed by the fact that a lot of the work has already been done, the student uses the printed cards in preference to working up his or her own.

These cards have limited value. For one thing, the words you will meet in them may not be the same ones your teacher wants you to learn. For another, and this a more important, *the work of making your vocabulary cards is part of the vocabulary building process.* You meet the words, you write them, you think of a sentence and write it down. These several exposures to each word add up to a great deal of the effort you will have to put out anyway, and as you work on your cards, you are exposing yourself to the new words in the various ways you will want to practice them. Reading a card someone else has printed robs you of valuable learning time.

If your vocabulary is going to grow, you must work at it, and the first time you meet an unfamiliar word you want to learn is the best time to learn it. When you put off learning the new vocabulary in a lesson you are doing, you make succeeding lessons that much harder. Unfortunately, you also make yourself more and more reluctant to go at vocabulary intelligently, because the number of words you must learn increases rapidly with the passing weeks of a semester.

Step 3: Study grammar section. Grammar is not an end in itself for the college student. While the scholar finds satisfaction in exploring the *system* of a language, you want to learn the *language.* Grammar is only a tool to that end, necessary though often troublesome.

The modern language teacher asks students to communicate first and then learn grammar. As communication gets under way, grammar is introduced when needed. Your textbooks follow the same practice. You learn some words. You learn to read them, write them, and speak them. Only when you can communicate to some extent is it time to learn the rules that govern language.

To learn grammar first is surely to put the cart before the horse, but grammar must be learned eventually if you are to master a second language as quickly as possible.

The grammar section in every lesson in your textbook will state, explain, and illustrate one or more principles of grammar. Your job is to incorporate that rule into your thinking in the language. The strategy is to *understand* the principle, *memorize* its exact meaning, and *put it into practice* in the language you are studying.

Here is how to do it. First make sure you understand the terms it employs. In studying grammar, you will be learning abstractions that can be applied throughout all the years of study you will undertake, all the conversations you will have, all the books you will read, and all the letters and translations you will write.

When you understand what each term in a grammar lesson means, read each rule aloud five times.

Now put the book aside and recite the rule aloud correctly from memory five times. Do so many recitations seem excessive? Repetition is essential if you are going to make each rule part of you. Once it is part of you, it will be unnecessary to think of it again. If you do not make it part of you, it will always be necessary to think about the form of what you want to express instead of thinking of the substance.

For some students, it is advisable to write out the more difficult rules of grammar. While the object of studying rules of grammar certainly is not to be able to quote them from memory, some students find rules easier to learn by writing rather than speaking them. If you find it helpful to write out rules, try putting them in your own words to test your understanding. You can remember better when you express a rule in your own words.

Step 4: Practice and review. The practice exercises provided in a lesson are at least as important as the vocabulary and rules of grammar presented. If you use practice exercises properly, you reinforce the points made in the lessons.

- **Read illustrative material aloud five times** and get the point of every example supplied.

    As you repeat the phrases and sentences your text supplies to show you how to use the rules of grammar being taught, see how the examples illustrate those rules. *Never work through an illustration of a principle without thinking of what it shows.*

- **Write your own illustrations and read them aloud.** Besides teaching you a rule, your own example one day will be useful in compositions you write, when you find that idiomatic and grammatically correct expression comes easily to you.

- **Study review exercises.** Students generally fail to grasp the significance of the review exercises they do as part of each lesson. The function of the review exercise is to take you back and forth systematically across everything you have studied commencing with the beginning of a semester. Knowing that your classroom time is limited, the textbook writer makes sure that you get enough practice time in the language by forcing you to review.

- **Review the day's new vocabulary.** As the final part of each day's homework, go over once more the words you met in that lesson. The best way of accomplishing this is to use your vocabulary cards.

Look at the face of each card, say the word aloud, and then try to recall the sentence that is on the back of the card. If you can, you surely know the word. Do *not* think of its English meaning. By working only with your cards, you avoid contact with English and develop the habit of thinking in the foreign language.

As you look at each card, you are testing yourself to see how much you have learned. When you find that you know a word, mark the face of the card with a *check.* If you do not know the word, study the back of your card to refresh your memory, but do not mark the card. Go through all the cards for the day in this way.

As the days go by, you will be accumulating a large store of cards. *Review each card daily.* When you have checked a card three times, signifying that you have recognized its meaning on three separate occasions, put that card in an inactive alphabetical file. Keep that file on your desk. It is your glossary of terms you will meet again and again during your French studies. It will also serve as review material before tests. In time you will know some of the words so well that there will be no need for keeping cards on them. Eliminate them to keep your file within practical bounds.

The cards that do not have their quota of three checks are your active file. *They go with you wherever you go.* Keep them in your pocket, not hidden away in your briefcase. They are to be used whenever you have a spare moment on a bus, waiting for a class, just before you go to sleep at night. In addition, establish one time of the day for regular review. Some students find that they learn new words best if they study them just before breakfast. Others like to study before they go to language class. Find out when you learn them best and study them at the same time each day.

Whenever you do your studying, do not neglect vocabulary. It is easy to learn a few words a day, difficult to learn a week's backlog at one sitting.

We have seen how to attack your daily work in languages. The four steps in doing a lesson effectively will help you make top grades if you follow them. Now let us go on to further discussion of effective language study.

The art of translation. The most common expression in reviews of translated novels and plays is, "The work suffers in translation." This is understandable. Not only must a language be translated, but history, culture, and manners as well. In light of the trouble even professional translators have in preserving the flavor of an original text, the student might protest that as a beginner he or she cannot be expected to do well. Your teachers understand the problems inherent in translating. Yet even when you are translating for the first time, you must be concerned with the quality of your effort.

The most obvious requirement of a good translation is that it preserve the meaning of the original. A further requirement, and in this you cannot expect to be proficient for a long time, is that it preserve the *literary qualities* of the original.

The best example of how not to translate a French sentence comes happily in the satiric song, *La Plume de Ma Tante.* The song is based on the opening sentence in the typical old-fashioned French primer, in which everyday words are combined in sentences that unfortunately are not everyday. As difficult as it is to conceive of anyone ever uttering this particular sentence, many thousands, if not hundreds of thousands, of students learned French through studying it and others like it:

> La plume de ma tante est
> sur le bureau de mon oncle.

The songwriter has translated this ineptly as:

> The pen of my aunt is
> on the bureau of my uncle.

What mistakes have been made in this translation? For one, the French word order has been taken over into English, so we automatically do not have an English sentence. The second is in the translation of *bureau.* We do have bureaus in English, but the French *bureau* means *desk.* The primer translated correctly for us, but the song has a little fun at the expense of those who teach French through such quaint sentences.

The word order of any language you study is different from ours. If you expect this, you will not be upset when you encounter it. There is no special logic in the word order of any language; there is only custom. Take the manner in which we address letters in this country. We give first the name of the person who is going to receive the letter, then his house number and street, and finally his city and state. What is the first information the post office needs in sorting mail? Surely not the name of the recipient. Europeans do a lot better by giving the state and town before the street address. But they list the name of the recipient first too.

Don't fall into the trap of using convenient but incorrect cognates. *Plume* in French is not *plume* in English. And *on parle français* means *French is spoken,* not *one speaks French.*

Translate meanings, not words. Read through material you are going to translate to get the flavor and intent of the original. Then read through the opening sentence once more before translating it.

Do the same for the second sentence and all the rest. Students make the mistake of translating each word as they come to it. Keeping the unbroken thought unit of the sentence in front of you as you work will ensure that you come up with a translation of thoughts.

Observe the tone of the material to be translated so that you can capture it in your translation. Don't put the King's English in the mouth of a person who obviously would not use it.

As you acquire knowledge of vocabulary and sentence structure, you will find that translating from one language to another is an enjoyable art.

Making the most of class time.

If you want to progress rapidly in language, make your time in class an integral part of your effort. You will have practice in vocabulary, explanations of points of grammar, review of your textbook. It is not necessary to make more than an occasional note in the French class. Rather you must consider class time as a help in learning material already covered in your study.

One of the main functions of your class sessions will be to help you acquire an "ear for French." The practice you get merely by listening to your teacher is invaluable. Pay attention to exactly how each sound is made and how words are grouped. When you recite in class—and later when you are practicing alone—imitate your teacher's speech as closely as possible. There is no reason why you must sound like an American in Paris when you attempt to speak French. But if you are very self-conscious about how you sound, that is exactly what will happen.

There is always the possibility of buying French records to develop a good accent, but they are not necessary. Records are excellent if you attempt to study a language on your own. As long as you are studying the language with a teacher who speaks well, you might just as well forget records. They are not as good practice as the classroom, where you have the opportunity to have your own speech criticized. Going to French movies is good for your speech after you have made some progress in the language, but movies are not a substitute for class practice.

French movies serve a more important function for you. They can become a link between you and the culture you explore when you undertake study of the French language. Reading a French newspaper can also help in this way. The most important activity of all for the serious student of French is to join La Maison Française or whatever other French club meets on your campus. Almost every modern language department on a campus will organize

FOREIGN LANGUAGE *magazines can be a big help in learning a new language.*

a club for its students to help them in their studies by providing an opportunity for conversation in the language. Coffee hours, lectures, and discussions are scheduled that can do much to help you progress rapidly.

Examinations.

Prepare for tests by reviewing all the study materials you have—your vocabulary cards, the review exercises in your textbook, the rules of grammar you have studied. Check over any returned quizzes. Look especially at the mistakes you have made to be certain that you will not make the same mistakes again.

Many language tests have an oral section, in which your teacher dictates a selection you have not seen before. Your job is to write it perfectly. It will test how well you have studied the spelling of vocabulary. As your teacher dictates, he or she will read through the entire selection first and then go back over it phrase by phrase at a pace slow enough for you to take dictation. During the first reading, concentrate on understanding what the teacher is saying. During the second reading, listen without writing until the teacher comes to the end of a phrase, and then put it down correctly. When the dictation is over, read it for meaning.

The written language examination is perhaps the easiest kind of test for the student in the sense that he or she can predict almost exactly what will appear on it. In keeping up with your day-to-day work, you are taking the final examination over and over again. The sentences you translate in every lesson appear in almost the same form on tests. This is far different from other courses, such as the social sciences, in which the subject matter ranges far and wide. The student has to spend a good deal of time in selecting the points of emphasis to concentrate on for examinations. Another advantage of the foreign language test is that it tests only your ability in the specific subject. In other tests, your ability in English composition is put to the test almost as much as your knowledge of subject matter. Your ability to reason is also on trial. Thus, language test preparation is not as difficult as preparation for other tests you will take.

When a test paper is returned to you, check it carefully to find out where you have missed your mark. Relearn the points you missed. Where mistakes are due to carelessness, you may want to write the corrected version of the answer a few times in order to get rid of the tendency to make the same mistake again.

The study of classical languages.

Because so few students select Latin or Greek these days, no mention has been made up until now of the differences between studying modern and classical languages.

Both can be studied in the same manner up to a certain point. The vocabulary and grammar can be tackled in the same way, but the grammar of the classical languages is more complex than that of most modern languages. Parsing a Latin sentence—figuring out how a sentence is put together—can approach the complexity of solving a difficult problem in mathematics.

The marked difference is in the orientation of the teaching of the two groups of languages. Practically no attempt is made when teaching Latin, for example, to help the student speak the language. The focus of attention is upon reading the great classical literature. The progress of the student is from Caesar to Cicero and on to Vergil and Ovid. Thus, translation becomes the principal activity of the students

once they get on their feet in grammar.

Students sometimes use translations in studying classical texts, but they must be used with care. Word-for-word translations, called trots or ponies, can save time in a difficult translation, but they do not teach the grammatical interrelationships of a sentence. By all means, take advantage of the trot, but don't make the mistake of trying to memorize it. You will have no trot with you in class, so you must work through all your lines anyway.

The main thing to keep in mind as you approach a foreign language is that *repetition* is your greatest study aid in this field. The mastery of a foreign language is largely an exercise of the memory, and the best way to make your memory work for you is to repeat the material over and over again.

How to Study Mathematics

You will probably have at least one year of college mathematics. If you are like many other students, it will be the greatest single obstacle standing between you and the bachelor's degree.

Why do so many students find mathematics difficult? It is hard to say. Yet somewhere along the line, probably at the point where arithmetic leaves off and algebra begins, a great many otherwise capable students lose their taste for the subject. Undoubtedly much of the difficulty comes from poor reading and listening habits. Also to blame is the student's inexperience in the kind of thinking required for mathematics. Mere counting skill is replaced by abstract reasoning of the highest order. The final explanation that comes to mind is that students approaching college mathematics find it strangely impractical in the sense that the problems considered are totally detached from their experience.

Yet the inherent interest of mathematics cannot be denied, and the need for mathematics is greater than ever before. Astronomy, engineering, chemistry, physics—all science and technology use mathematics, but it finds a place outside these fields as well. Economics, psychology, sociology, and demography use mathematical techniques. Today, computers speed their work and make available solutions of problems that never before could have been tackled. These computers require the attendance of trained mathematicians. Business uses the machines in making forecasts of needs, production, and sales. It can easily be seen that mathematics is no ivory-tower subject.

You will find that once you get into college math, both the theory and application are far more difficult and complicated than anything you met in

high school. The learning techniques that worked for arithmetic and elementary algebra will not be much help to you when you come up against calculus and analytic geometry. The material that follows will show you, first, how to understand and commit to memory the theoretical aspect of college math, and, second, how to apply these theories intelligently in your homework, classroom work, and examinations.

Are you sure of your fundamentals?

Mathematics is certainly one field in which it is unwise to run before you have learned to walk. Never mind the stories about Albert

Einstein's youthful difficulties with arithmetic. If your arithmetic and algebra are weak, you cannot hope to do well in higher mathematics. Take this brief test devised to find out whether you are as strong as you should be.

Accuracy is most important, but time yourself to see whether you complete the test in a reasonable amount of time.

You should have used no more than ten or twelve minutes for this test without making a single mistake. If you took longer, or if you were uncertain about how to handle some parts of the test, now is the time to brush up on your fundamentals. If you still have your high school mathematics texts, use them. If you do not, or if you feel that you would profit from a good re-

MATH TEST

Add		(a) 369	(b) 6412	(c) 6	(d) 1
		856	7359	3	9
		492	1165	7	5
		771	4920	2	6
		182	8863	5	7
				9	2
				3	4
				1	3
				4	8
				5	6
				9	7
				8	8

Multiply	(e) 68.417	(f) 21,986	(g) 34.972	(h) 8268
	386.4	7.26	.0651	1.025

Divide	(i) $26.509\overline{)193.621736}$	(j) $.0163\overline{)62.94082}$

Find the square root   (k) 4199.04

Multiply   (l) $(x - 3)(x - 3) =$

(a) 2670 (b) 28,719 (c) 62 (d) 66 (e) 26,436.3288 (f) 159,618.36 (g) 2276.6772 (h) 8474.7
(i) 7.304 (j) 3861.4 (k) 64.8 (l) $x^2 - 6x + 9$

view and explanation of all the mathematics you have studied until now, consult Haym Kruglak and John T. Moore, *Basic Mathematics with Applications to Science and Technology.* You will find explanations there of the principles and computational techniques of *arithmetic, algebra, geometry, trigonometry,* and other basic mathematical subjects. The book has the added feature of being arranged as a self-study text, with problems worked out for you and additional problems provided for self-test. Answers to all the problems are provided in the book, so you can get immediate feedback on your progress. As you review your basic skills, remember that it is important to increase *speed* as well as *accuracy.*

Do you know how to read mathematics?

Have you seen students rocking back and forth in their seats trying to memorize a formula? They are committing it to memory as though it were a mysterious rite that will help them to a place among the chosen. Ask them what the formula means, and they are speechless.

It is a rare test that will ask you only to supply a formula. Formulas are methods for solving problems. Mathematics tests ask you to read a problem and work it through to an answer. While it is undeniable that you must know the proper formula to apply, indeed have it right at your fingertips, you must also understand it and be able to apply it. Thus it is not enough merely to memorize every formula you encounter in your studies. You must make certain of its meaning and know how to put it to work.

For example, it is all very well to know that "the area of the square erected on the hypotenuse of a right triangle equals the sum of the squares erected on the other two sides." It is also good to know this fact as $a^2 = b^2 + c^2$. But do you know how to use this equation? Can you picture it in your mind? Can you draw it? Can you take a square root? In short, can you apply the Pythagorean theorem to a typical problem, such as:

> Find the length of the hypotenuse of a right triangle whose other sides are 6 and 8 inches long.

If you have only memorized a formula but have neglected to learn how to use it, you have not *really read* the theorem. And precise reading is 90 per cent of the battle in mathematics. Understanding a discussion in a mathematics text and being able to reproduce it after you have finished reading are the results of precise reading.

How to do your math homework.

The next few pages will show you a surefire technique for doing your mathematics homework.

As you will see, the technique is simply a way of reading mathematics. This approach to the subject may be an eye-opener for you.

Step 1: Read the introduction. Read the introductory section of the assignment to identify and understand the principle it teaches.

Some students try to do homework problems without bothering to read the introductory section of the assignment. They do this to save time. But does it work? As they attempt to solve each problem, they go back and forth between it and the sample problem the author solved for them. This kind of learning, in which the student in essence tries to deduce principles himself instead of relying on the author, is wasteful. First of all, it is hit or miss. And the misses often go uncaught. Secondly, the drill work that is built into the lesson is lost by the student because he is not aware of what is being drilled until well into the lesson *if at all.*

You know by now that learning mathematics is a cumulative process. If you have not mastered what went before, you will always have difficulty. Let us take as an example the *point-slope form* of an equation which you should encounter about half-way through your first semester in college mathematics. You will not be able to do this lesson if you have failed to understand the equation for the slope of a line, which is one of the first things you learn in analytic geometry.

Here is an explanation of the point-slope form from *Analytic Geometry,* by John Wesley Young, Tomlinson Fort, and Frank Millett Morgan. It is a textbook for freshman mathematics:

> In the last chapter we stated that a very important problem of analytic geometry is to learn how to plot a curve when its equation is given. A second important problem is, given a curve, to find its equation with respect to a given set of coordinate axes. We shall now consider the simplest case of this problem, namely, where the given curve is a straight line.
>
> Let the given line pass through a fixed point P_1 (x_1, y_1) and have a given slope of m. Since the line has a slope we know it is not parallel to the y-axis. Let P (x, y) be a variable point on the given line. Then, equating slopes, we have
>
> $$\frac{y - y_1}{x - x_1} = m \text{ or}$$
>
> (I) $\quad y - y_1 = m (x - x_1).$
>
> This equation is satisfied by the coordinates of every point on the line and by no other points, since the ratio $\frac{y - y_1}{x - x_1}$ formed for a point (x,y) not on the line does not equal m.
>
> Equation (I) is called the *point-slope equation* of a straight line. It enables us to write the equation of the line passing through any given point and having any given slope.

ALWAYS READ *introductory or explanatory information.*

Have you identified and understood the definition being taught? Do you understand the steps taken to arrive at the point-slope form? Can you repeat them without consulting the text? If the answers to all three questions are *yes,* then you have read precisely. If not, then you must go back and read again. This time, in reading, try this method:

1. Make certain you understand the meaning of every word in the discussion.
2. Visualize every step along the way. If you can see the action portrayed in the sentences, then you understand them.
3. If you find a particular sentence difficult to comprehend, repeat the discussion up to that point. When you are sure you know it well, try the difficult sentence again.

You will be able to see from this brief excerpt how the textbook authors have tried to teach carefully what they want the student to learn. How foolish to skip this introduction and try to do homework problems directly!

Exactly what have the authors done for you? They have provided a definition and justification for a concept that will be useful as you proceed further into the subject. To memorize the definition without understanding the reasoning behind it is very difficult. The term *point-slope form* must become second nature to you. And so must every other concept the book introduces. Page after page, lesson after lesson, you will find information introduced along with reasoning to support it. You must not try to skim the information and skip the reasoning. It is far easier to learn facts when you understand them than when you accept them blindly.

The next help you receive in the typical lesson is in the form of sample exercises.

Step 2: Do the sample exercises. Sample exercises are an integral part of the lesson to be studied. How you use these exercises will determine how well you understand the principles being taught and whether you will be able to work problems based on those principles. Thus, these samples are the pivot around which the entire lesson turns. As you use them, one part of your mind is on the text you just finished reading, and one part of your mind is saying, "Now this is the way I will be doing things shortly, so I had better pay attention."

- *Read* each step carefully.
- *Understand* every term used.
- *Follow* the reasoning behind each manipulation.
- *Solve the problem all over again on your own.*

Inspect the sample exercise that follows the discussion of *point-slope form* in Young, Fort, and Morgan. See whether the example adds to your understanding.

> *Example.* Find the equation of the straight line passing through $(1, -2)$ and having a slope of -3.
> Solution: $x_1 = 1$, $y_1 = -2$, $m = -3$.
> Substituting in $y - y_1 = m(x - x_1)$,
> we have $\qquad y + 2 = -3(x - 1)$
> or $\qquad 3x + y - 1 = 0$

It is a good idea to reserve a section of your loose-leaf notebook for working through the sample problems that your author gives you. As you do them, be sure to include in your proof every step that you require, even though the author has left some out. Writing out the steps in a problem in this way is far better than merely reading through what the author has written. It guarantees that you are working along with the author. If you are to *learn* as effectively as possible and *remember* as long as necessary, that understanding is vital. If, as you work, you also think of the *why* and the *how,* your learning will be that much better.

The mathematics work sheets that accumulate in your notebook will be a handy review for you before examinations. If you work your sample problems on one side of the sheet only, then the blank sides can well be used for taking notes in class. If you are careful to take class notes on the sides opposite your homework for the same material, then your mathematics review material will be complete and well organized for study.

In your notebook or on index cards, you should keep a list of terms that you have come across in your studies so that you can drill yourself on them until you have mastered them.

Step 3: Recite the principle you have learned. Once you have completed the sample problems in the lesson, repeat from memory the principle they illustrate. Do this either in your own words or the words of the textbook if you can. Be sure that you understand exactly what the words mean if you use the exact words of the textbook.

If you cannot repeat the principle, go back to the opening section of the lesson and read it through again. Only when you feel you know what it means should you go on. Indeed, unless you know what it has said, you cannot go on, because in the last section of the lesson you will have to demonstrate your understanding. Incidentally, in class you probably will be asked to re-

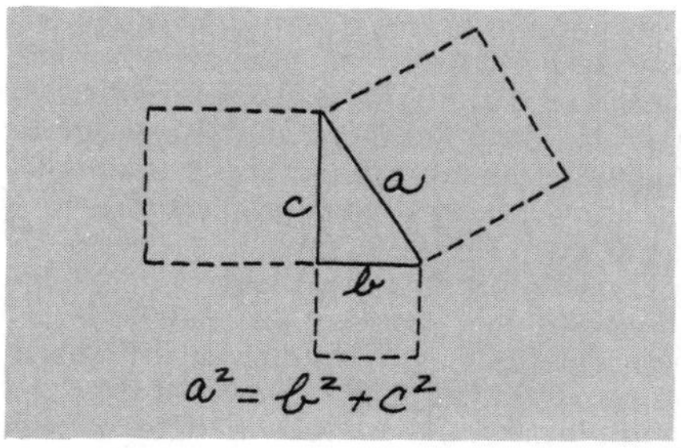

DRAWING A DIAGRAM *can often help solve a mathematics problem.*

cite the principle anyway. You may as well make certain you can recite creditably before going to class.

To test your alertness now, try to recall the expression the above lesson in analytic geometry has been trying to teach you. Think for a moment. What does it mean? Can you give the form of the equation that expresses it?

Further helps with homework.

Homework problems are your tests of how well you have learned, your rehearsals for tests you will take one day, and your guarantee of *overlearning.* And the extent of your overlearning will determine *how long you remember.* Even if you feel you understand a principle on first reading, working an assortment of problems is beneficial. With their help, you retard the inevitable forgetting that begins to operate just as soon as we learn something. With their help, you learn to apply principles in all the ways you will be expected to use them. Homework problems are powerful aids to effective learning.

Students are tempted to use sample exercises as matrixes—forms in which to insert numbers—for the homework problems they have to solve. It seems so simple to save time by merely substituting numbers in the sample problems that textbooks have already worked out for you. Doing your homework in this way is a sure way to miss the entire point of doing homework. As a number-substituter, you can find solutions to problems all day long without learning a thing!

Mathematics textbooks are not written by newcomers to the art of teaching. The textbooks you will use are the result of years of careful observation of students and their needs. The tendency of students to borrow freely from sample solutions is well known. Thus your textbooks will make an effort to frustrate mere substitution. Problems will be inverted, and the kinds of answers required will be different from one problem to the next; in short, you will not find meaningless guesswork very satisfactory.

As you approach each problem in an assignment, *see it as an example of a principle being taught.* Then (1) you will understand the proper approach

to the problem, and (2) you will help yourself drive the principle home at the same time.

Use drawings freely to help in solving problems. If you have ever seen a mathematician at work, you know that he or she can hardly think without a piece of chalk or a pencil in hand. The mathematician always seems to want to draw a curve or diagram to help his or her thoughts.

Wherever possible, do the same. A drawing will often make clear an otherwise difficult formula or definition. In solving a problem, a drawing will help you find the direction you need. What is more, drawings will help you remember.

Here is an exercise from another part of the same textbook we have been using for our discussion in this section. Perhaps you cannot do the work described, but you can surely follow the discussion. Read the problem carefully to see what is asked. What would your procedure be if you were asked to solve this problem?

> Find the slopes of the sides of the triangle with vertices $(5, 7)$, $(6, 2)$, $(3, 5)$ and prove the triangle is a right triangle.

There are actually four problems within this problem. Did you find them? The terms employed in the problem must be understood—slope, triangle, vertices, locations of points $(5, 7)$ etc., right triangle. Do you know them all? If you do not, you cannot go on without help.

Now diagram the problem. You will see how the problem suddenly comes to life. You can see that you need to find the slopes of AB, AC, and BC. After you have determined the slopes, you can go on to prove that this triangle is a right triangle. Do you see how the drawing helped?

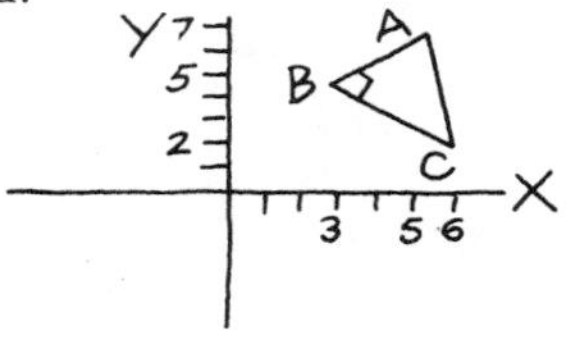

See how effective a drawing is in this problem taken from page 5 of *Calculus* by Lyman M. Kells.

> Consider a block (see Figure 1) moving on a straight smooth track *AB* inclined $18'6'$ to the horizontal. If the block passes point *A* with a speed up the incline of 100 ft./sec. and reaches a point distance s from A in t seconds, then $s = 100t - 5t^2$ approximately.

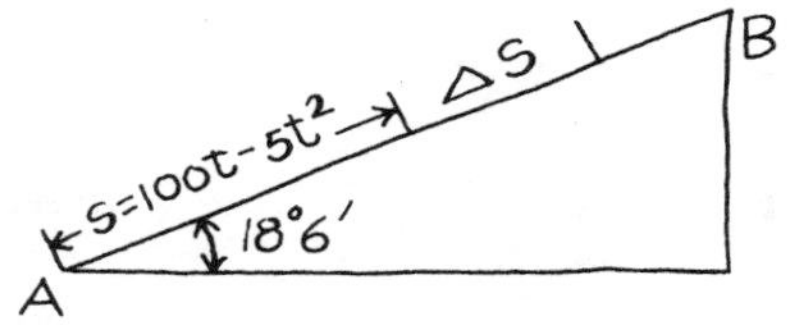

With the description of the problem just beginning, the author has given us a drawing that will help the student understand the problem.

When you are working a problem, draw it so you can understand it as you go along. Pretty pictures are not necessary; the crudest kind of picture will do as long as it is *big enough to read easily* and as long as you *label clearly and correctly.*

High school *algebra* can be learned easily by most students because its concepts are not much different from arithmetic. You may have resorted to representing algebraic symbols by real objects to help yourself visualize a difficult problem, but by and large you felt little need for this practice. In *geometry* you surely used drawings as study helps. If you acquired the habit then, you know how helpful it is. Practice it whenever you can in college mathematics. It will save time, improve the quality of your learning, and help you remember.

Do homework under test conditions. Unfamiliar situations are apt to give us difficulties. Looking ahead to a test without knowing what sort of questions we will be asked, how much time we will have for answering, or how long it will take us to write the answers, can be uncomfortable. The tension that builds up inside us because of the strangeness of the situation can harm the quality of our work.

In one sense, homework problems are a test: you have read a statement and discussion of an idea or principle. You have worked through sample problems that further clarify the points being made. When you get to the assigned problems, you are ready to see how much you have learned. If you do these problems in the spirit of a test, they become the best possible preparation for the tests your teachers will give you.

Simulate test conditions. When you are ready to do your problems, set a time limit and do your best to observe it. If you cannot get through your work on time, you are either working too

A TIME LIMIT *on homework can help simulate test conditions.*

LLOYD BIRMINGHAM

slowly or you have been too harsh with yourself in deciding the amount of time you should have. If you feel that you are working fast enough, ask your teacher how long he or she thinks you should have to work at your problems. Find out how much work is expected from you on an actual test.

While you can expect your homework assignments to vary in difficulty and so take varying amounts of time to complete, you should try to turn out more and more work in a given time. You will want to have time to check your computations during a test, so be sure to allow time for checking your homework tests, too. Careless errors reduce test grades.

Inspect the questions you are going to answer to make certain you know exactly what each word means. Make sure you do not overlook important words in the questions. Missing a single word can delay your understanding of a question and even set you off on the wrong track.

As you work, make certain that you use enough paper and write clearly enough so that you will be able to read your computations over easily.

If, when you read a question, you come up with a complete blank, *stop and think.* Just where does the difficulty lie? Perhaps your author has deliberately worded the question so that it looks totally different from the other problems you have been working. Read it through again and again until it becomes clear. Use drawings to see whether they can help in getting you started. If you have tried your best and cannot come up with the solution, leave that question and go on with the next problem. After you have worked that one or the one after it, you will usually find that you have discovered the approach needed for the problem that has given you trouble.

It is not uncommon for students to draw a blank on a question or two during a mathematics test. The worst thing they can do during the test is to sit there hopelessly. As time begins to slip away, they become more and more frantic. Not only do they fail to answer the one difficult question, they do not even attempt to answer later questions they may well be able to complete.

The opportunity in mathematics to rehearse for a test is not available in most other subjects. In such courses as literature and history, for example, you will not have the chance to write essays as rehearsal for examination.

Take care in computing. If you are going to make the highest grades you are capable of, you will have to be precise in computing the answers to homework and test problems. To develop the careful attitude you need during a test, work your homework problems with the same degree of care that you will want to display when you are taking a test.

The first consideration in working a problem is to make sure you are

headed in the right direction before you begin to work. Just what are you after in a problem? Have you been asked to supply an equation? Supply it. The measurement of an angle? A line? A velocity? The location of a point?

What units will your answer be expressed in? Will you have a choice of degree of accuracy, such as is possible with decimals and degrees? Will you have to reduce fractions?

All this is well understood by students, of course, but in the heat of a test or their desire to get through homework problems as fast as possible, they frequently go astray.

One technique of which students are not always aware is that of predicting the range of possible answers to a problem before they set to work. If you can estimate in advance the reasonable upper and lower limits to the answer to a problem, you safeguard against having to work right through to the end of a problem before you know you have gone completely haywire. Careful reading of a problem will usually tell you what you need for a prediction. Drawing the problem in the form of a sketch or graph can also help. Measurement of an angle, a line, an area, or a volume lends itself to this technique. In a rate or speed problem, you usually have to resolve two extremes to find an answer. It is easy to see that the result must fall somewhere between the extremes. Have you ever watched a mathematics teacher go at a problem on the blackboard? He does not plunge right in. The few moments he spends inspecting the problem are devoted to estimating the range of answers. You will learn techniques for doing this in every mathematics course you take. Practice them until they are habitual.

Once you have begun to work on the problem, take care to *perform each step accurately.* If you do not, despite the fact that you have looked ahead in the problem and know where you are supposed to be heading, you will come up with an answer that will force you to retrace your steps completely.

In studying arithmetic, you were taught to check *addition* by adding the column of figures upward instead of down, *subtraction* by adding, *division* by multiplying, and *multiplication* by dividing. In *elementary algebra,* you checked your reasoning by substituting values found in the equation you started with. This is still good practice for arithmetic and algebra where the problems you encounter lend themselves to such methods.

College mathematics does not often give you the same opportunity to check your work so easily. The solution to a typical problem requires many steps of many different kinds. Thus, checking an entire problem is an arduous task for which you do not always have the time. There are two ways to overcome this. One is to become as proficient as you can at the basic computational skills so that you can rely on your ability. The other is to *check each step in a solution as you go.* There are definite check points you can look at to find the most frequent causes of errors.

Observe the restrictions of the *signs* associated with the values you are manipulating. Did you remember to change a negative value to positive when you moved it from one side of an equation to the other? Did you treat exponents properly in adding, subtracting, multiplying, and dividing values? There is plenty of room for careless error there.

Did you double check every *reading* you made in a table? Use a ruler for taking numbers from a table. Read first from column and row headings to your value; then read from your value to columns and rows.

Care in computation will minimize errors and save time.

Repeat rules and principles from memory. While you may think it impossible to memorize exactly the textbook formulations of all the principles you will encounter in a semester's work in mathematics, it is entirely possible to memorize them in your own words. And you will find it beneficial to do so. After you have completed a lesson—discussion, sample problems, and homework problems—go back to the *principle* you have learned and try to commit it to memory.

If you have done your work properly until that point, the chances are excellent that you will already know the principle by heart in your own terms. And that is the best way to know it, because that is the way you will always think of it anyway. But test your memory before you leave your homework. If you find that you cannot get anywhere near stating the principle, you have not been focusing your attention on what the lesson was trying to do for you.

If you have difficulty in committing a rule to memory, try these four simple techniques:

- *Read* the rule silently to understand every term in it,
- *Draw* a picture of what it represents or *write* a sample equation to show you understand,
- *Read* the definition aloud several times,
- *Write* the definition on a card so that you can drill it whenever you have time.

Here is another use of the index card. The definitions, principles, and rules must be learned just as much as the meanings of new vocabulary in a foreign language. If you have especial trouble in memorizing a principle of mathematics, consulting a pack of cards regularly throughout a semester will help you. The procedure is much the same as that used for vocabulary development. Look at the opening words of a principle or rule and try to give the rest from memory. Look at a term whose meaning you want to learn and see whether you can define it. The

$$Variance = \frac{\sigma^2}{n}$$

$$Standard\ Deviation = \frac{\sigma}{\sqrt{n}}$$

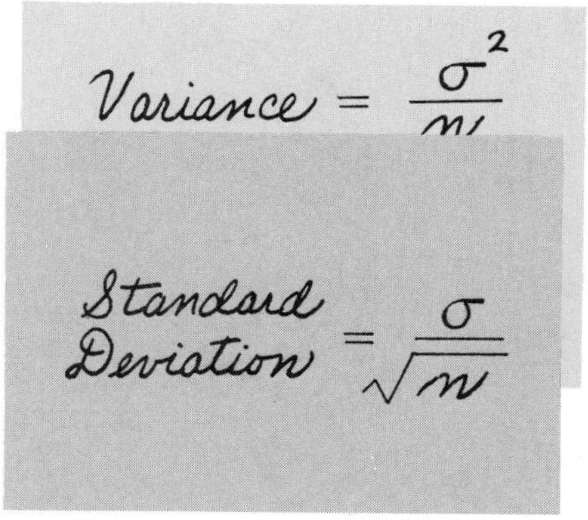

USE INDEX CARDS *to drill yourself on principles or rules.*

definition on the back of the card will serve as a reminder when you cannot remember the correct definition. Use a system of check marks to retire cards from your active study file. Your inactive file can be consulted before tests to make sure you remember all you should.

All these techniques will help you memorize. The principle is the employment of as many senses as possible in learning. By following the above suggestions, you help understanding and memory by seeing, hearing, and touching the material to be learned.

Students are sometimes scornful of the help provided by writing out a statement they must learn. But what better way to prepare for a written test than by writing out what you must learn!

Another point must be made before leaving the subject of memorizing mathematical principles. In the case of extremely difficult concepts, students —even advanced students—no matter how hard they work, sometimes are not able to understand a principle they have to use. In this case, the student has no alternative but to memorize *verbatim* and seek understanding elsewhere. Perhaps it will come from a teacher, perhaps from working through the problems he or she will encounter while doing homework. You can expect this dilemma to arise just as often in studying physics as in mathematics. This is understandable. Do not panic when you just cannot learn something the first time you try it. The technique of memorizing may help you over it.

Always have one foot in the past. Because mathematics is a building subject with a foundation upon which are placed successive layers of knowledge, each process and principle you learn must be kept firmly in place while you are learning others. Overlearning, to retard forgetting, is especially important in mathematics because you have so much to remember through a semester. To keep everything constantly fresh in mind, work back regularly over every topic covered during a semester.

You may find that your teacher will give you a short test at the conclusion of each unit in a term's work, but that is not always so. Even if your teacher does test you regularly, do not think

you have seen the last of a particular subject when you have been tested on it once. There are mid-semesters and finals to think about. Besides, you will have to know the content of each mathematics course you take in the courses you take afterwards.

In keeping up on material that accumulates during a course, you can use returned test papers. They will show you where you are weakest and they will also show you the kinds of problems you can expect on final examinations. Another technique is to go back to the sample problems you have worked in your loose-leaf notebook. You can also go to the problems in your textbook that your teacher did not give as homework assignments. Finally, there are other textbooks available in your college library that will give you further review.

Whatever technique you adopt for review of past topics in a mathematics course, be sure that you keep up with your review schedule. Make review a part of your calendar. It will eliminate last-minute cramming.

Work hardest at the most difficult problems. If you come up against a difficult concept in a mathematics course, don't give up on it. Memorizing the concept even without understanding it has already been mentioned as one help. You know that you can ask your teacher for help. Other students can help you too, although you have to make sure that you get the right information. A student who has already taken the course you are taking can frequently be an excellent tutor because he or she has gone through the same difficulties you are experiencing.

Perhaps the best way to overcome a difficulty by yourself is to consult another textbook. The words of another author may show you the light when your own textbook cannot.

Once you have understood the concept that gave you trouble, take plenty of time to fasten that new understanding in your mind. Do all the homework problems you have been assigned and do other problems as well. You can get these other problems from your textbook and from the other textbooks you have consulted. Review the work more frequently than is your practice. When you finally have the knowledge securely, you can abandon the all-out effort just described.

You may say that you have enough trouble getting through your regular homework without digging up extra work for yourself. But your regular homework was not enough to teach you the work. Somewhere along the line—sometimes dangerously close to the end of a term—you will have to make the additional effort necessary to master every topic assigned. You may as well undertake it as soon as you discover the deficiency. If you put it off, you will make learning advanced topics that much more difficult. Putting off needed study is a trap for the unwary.

Making the most of class time. If you have ever wrestled for hours with a mathematics problem and then gone to class where your teacher resolved your problems in a matter of moments, you appreciate the tremendous importance of classroom work in mathematics. In fact, the ease with which you frequently get to the heart of a troublesome concept by listening to a teacher can be dangerous. The student in trouble in mathematics is sorely tempted to rely completely on class discussion instead of trying to work things out independently.

Homework helps you remember what you learn in class. It also teaches you to think in mathematics.

Yet you can get much from your teacher and you must be ready to get as much as possible. The extent to which you will learn in the classroom will depend on how well you do your independent work. These rules for good listening apply completely to the subject of mathematics:

1. Do your homework before coming to class so that you will understand the discussion and be able to ask questions about anything that troubles you. A student who is unprepared sometimes does not know enough to ask a question or is too embarrassed to reveal his or her ignorance.

CONCENTRATING *on what your teacher is saying is more important than taking copious notes.*

2. When your teacher goes over material you have already learned, use the opportunity for overlearning. Pay strict attention to the teacher, thinking with him or her and trying to work one step ahead.

3. If your teacher presents a problem on the blackboard, do not struggle to copy it into your notes if one like it is already in your textbook or loose-leaf notebook. Think with your teacher as he or she works.

4. Focus your attention on the principle being taught and on the method of computation. What your teacher is working through for you is what you will have to do one day on a test.

5. If your teacher works ahead of your assigned problems, concentrate on the material being taught. The help the teacher gives you will come in handy when you sit down later to study that material in your textbook. Do not bother with taking notes. Mathematics problems are worked too rapidly for you to learn very much from frantic note-taking.

6. Whatever notes you do take ought to be written in the same section of your notebook in which you write your solutions of sample problems. If you write the problems on one side of the sheet only, you can use the opposite side for classroom notes.

One final reminder: In all your work in mathematics, develop the habit of verbalizing equations so that they have meaning for you, and learn the exact meaning of every symbol you encounter. Learning mathematics is not unlike learning a foreign language. It is not enough for you just to pronounce it. You have to know what it means if you are going to use it properly.

How to Study Science

Whether in lecture hall, library, classroom, or laboratory, poor science students exhibit one common trait: They are so taken up with detail that they do not grasp the central principle of a unit of study. Because they bog down in detail, they cannot hope to do well in their courses. You will be shown how to go about your science studies so you can make your best grades.

Surely the brightest academic star in the minds of the people of our country today is science. Never before have military success, economic strength, national health, and agricultural output so depended on it. The lion's share of student scholarship aid goes to science students. The competition among businesses for each year's crop of college graduates is keenest for science majors. Foundations and the government support scientific research at a level far beyond that of the social sciences and the arts. All the communications media leap eagerly on news of every scientific advance.

If science comes easily to you, look carefully at these fields—anatomy, astronomy, biochemistry, biology, botany, chemistry, geology, meteorology, microbiology, physics, zoology. These are some of the science offerings awaiting you in college.

If science has been less than a joy, you probably wonder how many courses will be required and how to get through them painlessly.

Whether or not your major interest lies in science, you will surely take one or more years of science. And whether or not you ever make direct use of science, you will profit greatly from your training if you go about it correctly. Nothing is more important than learning the scientific method of either forming a theory from the facts or testing a hypothesis with the facts.

The study problems you will face in science are much like those in other courses. You must read and listen effectively, prepare for and write examinations. The principles of study are the same: careful identification of what is to be learned, frequent review, recitation to oneself, and testing.

This chapter shows you how to develop the vocabulary you will need to listen and read effectively, how to do a reading assignment, and how to learn from a science lecture. Finally, you will find special techniques for getting your best grades in science:

1. How to attack a problem that has you stumped;
2. How to adapt your studying to special situations;

3. How to identify and remove stumbling blocks to effective study;
4. How to profit from a science demonstration; and
5. How to apportion time strategically before an examination.

Build your science vocabulary. If you are going to read and listen with maximum effectiveness in the sciences, you will have to pay special attention to vocabulary building.

Read this paragraph from an elementary geology textbook. How many of its words are familiar to you?

Geology is a very broad science and therefore has a number of subdivisions, each of which emphasizes certain phases of the subject. One branch of the study (cosmology) treats of the early history of the earth and the relation of the earth to other heavenly bodies in the Universe, such as the sun, the other planets, and other stars; another (petrology) is devoted to the study of the character and origin of all types of rock; still another (structural geology) deals with the arrangement or the structural relations of rocks and particularly with their relations to each other. Other branches are concerned with the forces and movements (dynamic geology) that have affected the rocks and the results of these movements and with the various land forms (geomorphology) or contour of the surface of the earth and the origin of the mountains, valleys, and plains. A biological branch (paleontology) is the study of the remains of ancient life that are found in the rocks and the evidences of the gradual development of that life throughout the known eras of geologic time. It is closely related to a study of the history of the earth (historical geology) as shown by its rocks and particularly the record of events that is revealed in the rocks. An economic branch (economic geology) treats of the occurrence, origin, and distribution of the materials of the earth that are valuable to man. It includes the study of deposits of the metals, coal, petroleum, and many other substances.

Did you find that the names of the subdivisions of geology were unfamiliar: cosmology, petrology, structural geology, dynamic geology, geomorphology, paleontology, historical geology, economic geology?

If some of these words *are* familiar to you, unless you have studied geology before, you may know them in a sense other than the one intended here. Cosmology, for example, is used in philosophy. Just because most English words have multiple meanings, don't be fooled into thinking you understand a scientific term when all you may know of the term is a nonscientific definition.

Another pitfall must be avoided. The word *petrology* resembles *petroleum*, and you might think that petrology deals with oil rather than the much broader "study of the character and origin of all types of rocks," as your geology textbook defines it.

So we see that almost at once—from *an elementary textbook*—your reading in geology meets the challenge of new vocabulary that must be understood and committed to memory if you are to be able to read with real understanding. And *each page* in such a book may introduce additional words you have never before encountered.

How would you get along in biology if you did not learn new words as you came to them? Here is an excerpt from an elementary textbook in biology.

The bryophyta in their morphological features occupy a position intermediate between the green thallophytes and the pteridophytes. Although undoubtedly derived from green algae, there is no evidence that they bridge the gap between these primitive forms and vascular plants and it seems best to conclude that they represent a side line of development which has not been ancestral to any higher types. The group consists of forms commonly known as mosses and liverworts, or anthocerotes, often placed with the liverworts. About 23,000 species of bryophytes are known, all of which are of relatively small size in comparison with other land plants, rarely exceeding a decimeter in length. They are essentially land plants and, for the most part, are restricted to moist and shaded situations, requiring an abundance of water for reproduction and successful growth. A few are aquatic, and this aquatic habit is thought to have been acquired secondarily and not to be primitive. A very few have adopted what appears to be a xerophytic habit, living in the shallow crevices of rocks, where they are exposed to extreme temperatures and drying winds. Such forms, however, grow only during wet weather and are remarkable for their ability to withstand long periods of drought. Although abundantly represented among the plants that make up the flora of the forests, ravines, and the north slopes of uplands in temperate regions, bryophytes seldom become a conspicuous part of the vegetation. Acid bogs of the north temperate regions, including certain types of tundra of the far north, may consist largely of bryophyte species. In tropical forests also, especially at high altitudes, bryophytes may make up a considerable part of the vegetation and often include epiphytic species which hang in festoons from the trees and shrubs. Although significant because of the role that they play in plant succession, bryophytes have in general very little economic importance. Within recent years, however, a number of the species of the genus *Sphagnum,* the peat mosses, have been used as a garden mulch, as a material to increase the water-retaining property of certain poor types of soil, and as a means of maintaining the relatively high soil acidity required by certain decorative and otherwise economically important plants.

The authors of the textbook assume you know the meanings of some fancy words: bryophyte, morphological, thallophytes, pteridophytes, vascular, liverworts, hornworts, anthocerotes, xerophytic, tundra, and epiphytic. Indeed you must know them, for they are representative of the vocabulary of the sciences. Note that this selection was taken from a late section of the textbook, so you would probably have met all these words at least once before. But if you had not made the necessary effort to learn and remember their meanings when you met them for the first time, you would have a lot of dictionary-thumbing to do just to read one paragraph.

The best way to learn any new vocabulary is to use index cards in the same way you might use them to study foreign language vocabulary and mathematical principles. The authors of science textbooks generally define specialized words when they use them for the first time, so you are spared the difficulty of looking all of them up. You can use the sentences you find the words in as examples for your cards.

CREATE YOUR OWN FLASH CARDS *to help you learn new scientific vocabulary. On one side place the new word; on the other side put a definition and a sentence using the new word.*

tundra

undulating treeless plain of northern arctic region
——————
Acid bogs of the north temperate regions including certain types of tundra of the far north may consist largely of bryophyte species

---

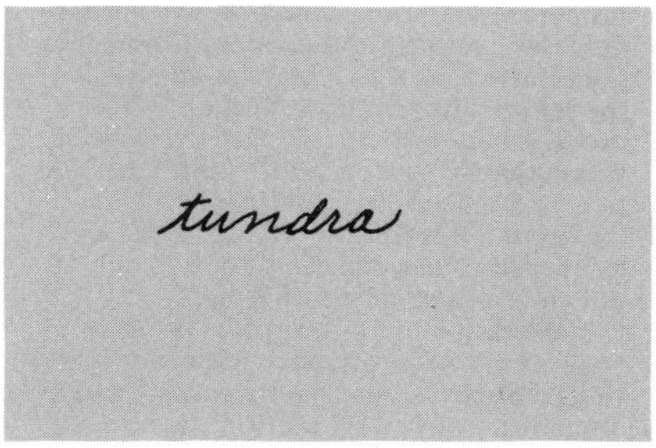

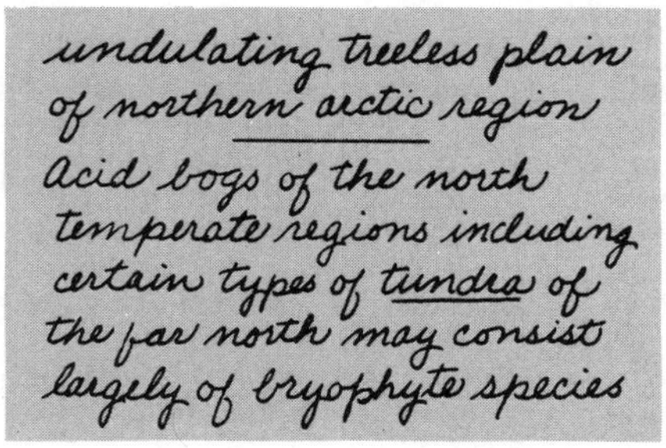

BUILDING SCIENCE VOCABULARY

Many teachers and writers emphasize the value of learning common Latin and Greek *roots* and *affixes* as an aid in learning English vocabulary. Perhaps their point would be better taken if more students had studied classical languages in high school. If Latin and Greek can help you anywhere, however, it is in studying the vocabulary of the sciences—particularly biology.

Bryophyte, thallophyte, pteridophyte, xerophyte, and epiphyte obviously share a common ancestor. It is the Greek word *phyton,* a plant.

Your desk dictionary will show

bryon, moss

thallos, young shoot

pteris, fern

xeros, dry

epi, upon

so that we move quite easily to

bryophyte, any of the mosses or liverworts

thallophyte, any of a phylum of shootlike plant forms (e.g., fungi, lichens)

pteridophyte, any of a phylum of plants which includes the fern

xerophyte, a drought-resistant plant

epiphyte, a plant which grows upon other plants, but is not parasitic, deriving the moisture for its development chiefly from the air (e.g., moss).

Exercise extreme caution in guessing the definitions of words containing parts you recognize! In the list just given, a student can easily confuse *pteris,* fern, with *pteron,* meaning feather or wing, which the student may know from the word *pterodactyl.*

Knowledge of roots and affixes gives no more than a clue to meaning. It is not a substitute for a dictionary or textbook definition combined with systematic study of the meaning and use of a scientific term.

It is important to get to work right away and stay with the job. You will meet so many new words in each chapter of a textbook that if you do not learn them as soon as you come to them, you will find yourself completely bogged down in difficult terminology after a semester has been under way just a short time.

The special demands of science readings.

If there is one kind of study in which you must not even think about *speed* of reading, it is your first reading for a science course. You will not be burdened with vast amounts of reading, as you sometimes are in social science courses. Each reading assignment may run no more than several pages. Obviously the emphasis is upon *quality* of reading.

The ideas and information in a science textbook come thick and fast. If you are going to read well, you will have to keep three things in mind:

1. Determine what is to be learned.
2. Read for understanding.
3. Master it so that it becomes part of you.

Let us take each of these steps through typical reading assignments in a geology textbook.

I. Determining what is to be learned.

Read very carefully the first section of the assignment. Your purpose is to find out whether the author uses that section to forecast what he is going to do in the chapter or part of one that you are going to read. If you are told what he is going to cover, then you have your *outline of the chapter* right in front of yourself. You know the main questions that are going to be dealt with, and you can easily set up your notebook. If you see that the writer does not habitually forecast the scope of a chapter in the early part of the book, the chances are that he will not do so in the remaining chapters. But find out. Some students do not wake up to the organization of a book until they have read more than half of it.

The opening section of a chapter has other purposes as well. Frequently it provides background knowledge that will be essential for understanding the rest of the chapter. It may give the central thought of the entire chapter. The most frequent use, of course, is to present the first of a series of ideas that make up the entire chapter.

Whatever the use to which an author puts chapter openings, learn to recognize it so that you can get right to work.

Read the last section of the assignment to see whether it summarizes the highlights of the chapter. In one form, this can be a *restatement* of what has been covered thoroughly in the chapter itself. As often as not, a chapter can end in a *series of questions and problems* designed to test your understanding and recollection of what has been covered. If the opening paragraphs of a chapter do not outline the chapter, and

the headings of the individual sections are unsatisfactory, then the closing section of the chapter may do the job for you. If the help is in the form of questions, you should read them in advance to see whether they can be the precious outline that will be so useful to you in your reading. However a textbook outlines its chapters, recognize the outline and use it.

Let us put into action the principle of determining what is to be learned. We will use the geology textbook we used earlier. Let us examine a section less than 15 pages in length and amply illustrated to see what we can learn—in two minutes—of the job that faces us in reading that chapter. If you can use your imagination, it is not necessary for you to have a copy of the book in front of you now. A quick look shows that the chapter is divided into sections, the first untitled, the rest titled. Let us first examine the role of the opening section.

> *Chapter 5:* ATMOSPHERE,
> WEATHER,
> AND CLIMATE

The atmosphere is the blanket of air that covers the rocks and the waters of the earth. Its mass is less than a millionth part of that of the earth, but its activities and influences are far-reaching. Its presence is necessary to sustain the varied life of the earth, and it acts as a blanket to equalize the temperatures of the earth's surface. It serves as a medium for the transfer of water that is evaporated from lands and seas and that is precipitated as rain upon the earth, wearing away the rocks and transporting them to the seas. It is one of the chief agents of weathering.

The weather of any one place is the temporary state of its atmospheric conditions—its temperature, air pressure, wind, cloudiness, and precipitation. Its climate is the composite of the weather over a long period of time. Climate is described in terms of mean annual temperature, temperature variations, humidity, amount and seasonal distribution of precipitation, storms, and winds. Meteorology (the study of the atmosphere) and climatology are separate branches of earth science, and so a detailed treatment of them is beyond the scope of this text, but some consideration of the atmosphere, of weather, and of climate is essential to an understanding and appreciation of the effects of the atmosphere upon geologic processes. Just as soils and vegetation are determined largely by climate, so geologic processes, especially the weathering of minerals and rocks and the erosion of the land, differ greatly from place to place in different climates.

What has this section done for us? Essentially, the chapter title has been expanded by showing us what the three terms, atmosphere, weather, and climate, *mean* and how they are *important* in studying geology. If you had not before now made the connection between geology and these terms, you should be aware now of why they must be considered in geology.

Have the authors outlined the chapter yet? No. So we go on to the second step, inspecting section headings:

Composition of the Air.
Changes with Altitude.
Atmospheric Stratification.
The Aurora Borealis, or Northern Lights.
Sources of Heat.
Weight of the Air.
Distribution of Air Pressures.
Movements of the Atmosphere.
Cyclonic Storms.
Moisture of the Air.

Here are the *ten main topics* of the chapter. As you inspect them, you can imagine the examination questions that a teacher can ask. They might be:

What are the sources of the earth's heat?
How does air pressure vary with altitude?
How does the moisture of the air
affect the weathering of rock?

Of course, many more come to mind. From the very beginning, as you read a chapter, think ahead to what you are expected to learn from it, to the examination questions that can be based on it. The more actively you think along these lines, the sharper your grasp of what you read, the longer your memory of it.

Inspection of the final section of the chapter reveals only that it is devoted to a bibliography that you will not find useful in the ordinary course of events. Should you want to read further on the topics of the chapter; should you have a term paper to write; should the chapter as written require further explanation before you understand it, then this bibliography is your guide. As far as immediate usefulness is concerned, you find nothing for you in the bibliography. You are ready to proceed to the second step in your reading of the chapter at hand.

2. Reading for understanding.

The first section heading in the chapter was "Composition of the Air." Write the section heading in your notebook. Put the notebook aside. You are ready to

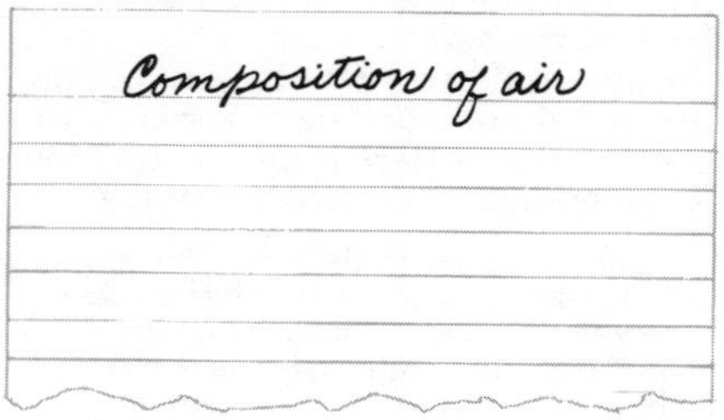

Composition of air

read. What will you read *for*? To find the "composition of the air." All the way through this section, keep in mind that this is what you are after. When you have finished reading the section, you will be able to give a general answer to the question from memory: "What is the composition of the air?" Your mind and memory are ready.

Dry air is a mechanical mixture of gases consisting of about 78 percent nitrogen, 21 percent oxygen, and 0.94 percent argon by volume. Additional constituents include carbon dioxide, hydrogen, and ozone in minute amounts and, locally, certain volatile organic substances, sulfurous gases, chlorine, etc., from volcanoes and other sources. Water vapor also is an important part of the air, probably averaging about 1.2 percent of the total volume. Its abundance varies according to the temperature; it forms about 2.63 percent at the equator, 0.92 percent at Lat. 50°N., and 0.22 percent at Lat. 70°N. Fine earthy matter, smoke, soot, pollen, spores, bacteria, volcanic dust, meteoric dust, etc., may be spread as impurities through a considerable part of the atmosphere, sufficiently at times to darken the sun and reduce visibility. The obvious evidence of the presence of dust in the atmosphere is in the occurrence of the red colors at dawn and twilight. Dust particles have an important function in that certain types of particles serve as nuclei, or centers, around which water vapor condenses to produce cloud particles.

Question: What is air composed of? *In your notebook:*

> *Composition of air*
> *gases, water vapor, fine*
> *earthy matter*

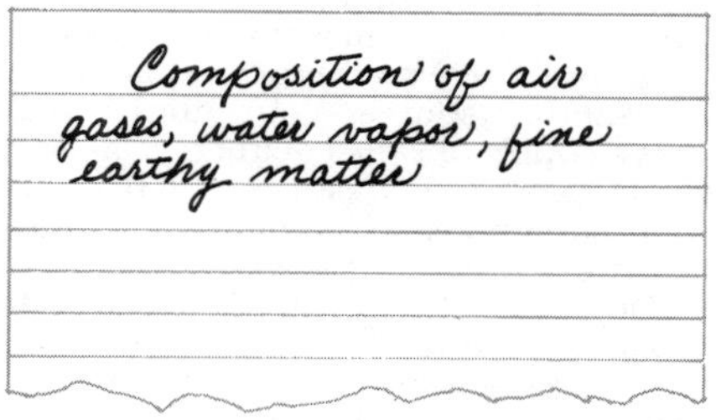

Can you go further from memory? Try to give the important details your textbook introduced to describe the three constituents. *Make your memory work.*

> *gases - primarily nitrogen (78%)*
> *oxygen (21%)*
> *argon (0.94%)*
> *water vapor - averages more than 1%*
> *of total volume, presence*
> *varies directly with*
> *temperature*
> *fine earthy matter - smoke, soot,*
> *pollens, dust serves as*
> *nuclei for water vapor*
> *that condenses to produce*
> *cloud particles*

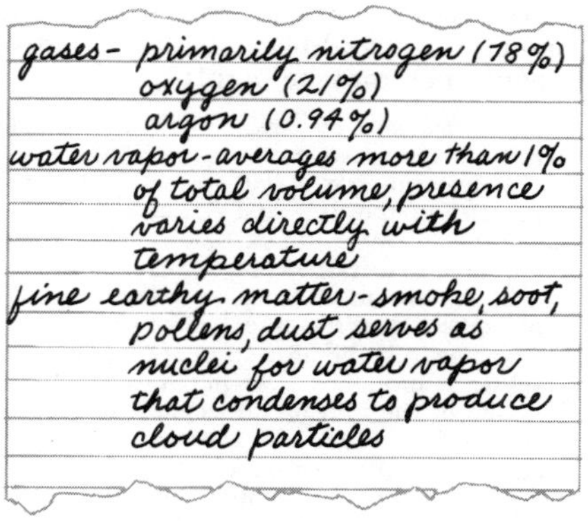

Quite enough. Were you able to do most of this without looking back?

Of course, you have not completed your study of this section. You may have done well in the notes you just wrote, but will you remember the information, a week, a month, three months from now? That degree of learning will come about only through careful review.

But if you were able to read the section *once* and remember enough to write the notes supplied above, then you have made a good start. You are ready to go on to the remaining sections of the chapter. Let's read one more section for another look at how the technique works. Remember that you must read to find the main idea of the section. It is called "Changes with

Altitude"; be ready, therefore, to answer the question: "What is the effect of changes in altitude upon the composition of the air?"

The air extends to great elevations above the land. Mountain climbers have reached elevations of more than 29,000 feet on Mount Everest, and observers in balloons and airplanes have reached elevations of more than 17 miles. Rockets carrying meteorological instruments have reached elevations of approximately 250 miles; meteors, white-hot from friction with the atmosphere, have been observed about 125 miles high; and auroral discharges are seen 375 miles aboveground.

Because the air is heated chiefly at the bottom, the temperature of the air decreases upward about 1°F. for every 300 feet of difference of vertical elevation to altitudes of 6 to 8 miles, above which a zone of nearly constant temperature (about −67°F.) is reached. Differences in altitude account for the pronounced differences in temperature and corresponding differences in climate, in vegetation, and in habitability of places having the same latitude. A change in altitude of 1 mile in general is about equal to a change in latitude of 800 miles.

The dust and other earthy material in the air are confined essentially to the lower layers of the atmosphere. As one ascends into the air, the smoke and coarser dust are left behind. The water vapor becomes less and less, until at 6 or 7 miles above sea level in the middle latitudes it is so cold that practically no moisture can remain in the air. Consequently no ordinary clouds exist. This altitude marks the lower limits of the *stratosphere,* a region of cold, clear, thin, dry air where there is a nearly constant temperature of about −67°F.

About one-half the mass of the atmosphere occurs in the lower 18,000 feet. Thus at an elevation of about 3½ miles one is above more than half of the atmosphere. *Explorer II,* a United States Army balloon, reached an altitude of 72,395 feet, or 13.71 miles, above sea level. It was above 96 percent of the mass of the atmosphere.

Question: What is the relationship between altitude and air? *In your notebook:*

> *Changes with Altitude*
> 1. *air exists far above earth*
> 2. *as you go up - temperature,*
>   *earthy material and*
>   *water vapor decrease.*
> 3. *air thins rapidly with*
>   *altitude*

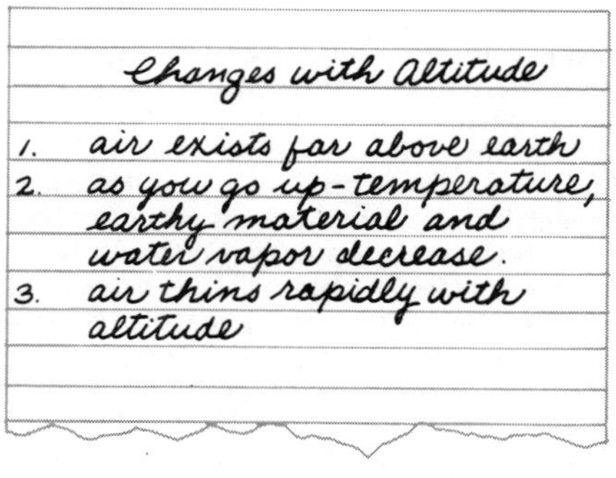

You will want more specific information than this in your notes. How much can you give from memory? When you have exhausted your recollection, go back to your textbook to pick up the remaining notes and check your memory on the details you remember.

Now your notes might look like these:

> 1. *Air exists far above earth*
>
> | | |
> |---|---|
> | *375 mi* | *Auroral discharges* |
> | *250 mi* | *rockets* |
> | *125 mi* | *meteors* |
> | *17 mi* | *mountain climbers* |
>
> EARTH
> 2. *As you go up*
> a. *temp. decreases about 1°*
>   *every 300 feet up to 6-8 miles*
> b. *6-8 miles on up - 67°F prevails*
> c. *earthy materials and water*
>   *vapor decrease*
> 3. *Air thins rapidly as you go up*
> a. *beginning of atmosphere (6-7 mi.)*
>   *air is cold, clear, thin, dry*
> b. *about ½ mass of atmosphere*
>   *occurs in lower 18,000 feet*
> c. *balloon 13.71 miles up is above*
>   *96% of atmosphere*

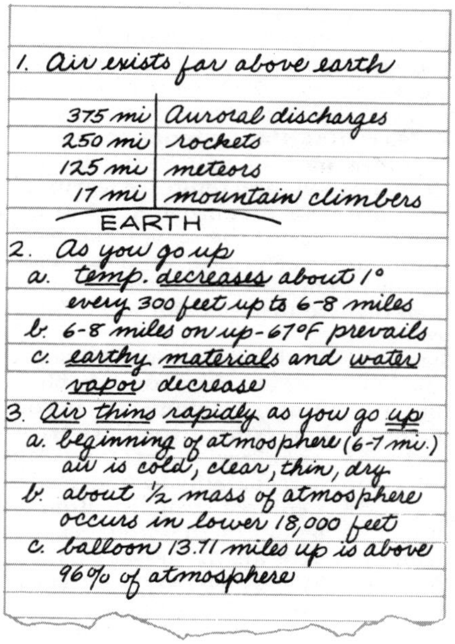

Now you have the gist of the section, and you are ready to go on. But if you were not able to give at least the three general statements (air exists far above earth, etc.), then you have not read well enough. You need to work at strengthening your reading ability.

The temptation is strong for students to sit with pen in hand, spearing each fact as they come to it in their reading. This stenographic procedure is not suitable for a college student. It teaches you almost nothing. It gives you a substitute textbook. From the start of your reading of an assignment, you must emphasize, "What do I understand of what I am reading?" "What can I remember of what I am reading?" "How much can I give back of what I am reading if someone were to stop me and ask me to recite?"

And when you finish a section of your reading, you must ask yourself the questions your teachers will ask you. Only when you have answered these questions in your notebook *from memory* can you feel that you really are reading properly. While this attitude toward reading for study purposes can be applied to other kinds of reading as well as to science, there are certain characteristics of textbooks in other areas of study that require some additional discussion.

When you are satisfied that you have recorded all the material you need for effective study and review, you are ready to go on to the next section of the assignment.

After you have completed the assignment, you are ready to enter the final phase of the study process. Think of what you have accomplished thus far. First, you subdivided a reading assignment into its component parts and arranged them for efficient study. Then, one by one, you read each part, extracting the important information well enough so that as you completed each section, you were able to recite the gist of what you had read in the form of written notes. This combination of finding information and comprehending it well enough to recite it is an important step toward top grades.

3. Mastering the material so that it becomes part of you.
Periodic review and recitation reinforce learning. They are your organized effort to retard forgetting. If the review and recitation are performed in a manner closely resembling your final examination, then you cannot fail to perform well.

Step 1: Review. Read through the notes you have written after you complete the entire reading assignment. Can you understand everything you have written? Are your abbreviations clear? Can you improve readability by underscoring, using colored pencils, Roman numerals, letters of the alphabet, indentation? Are all the notes correct? Perhaps you misunderstood an early part of the chapter that further reading corrected for you. Has some of the material become so obvious to you that you should not waste space and study time on it? Is there unnecessary repetition? Have you omitted anything?

Step 2: Recitation. Looking only at the section headings in your notes, recite what you can recall of the notes themselves. When you falter in a section—and you surely will, for you have worked hard through the reading and are no longer as alert and fresh as when you began to work—look back at the notes.

Never leave your notes until you can pretty nearly recite them from memory. You may be quizzed on that material on the next morning. You may have to recite part of the material in class. Your understanding of the next day's lecture hinges on how well you know what you have been assigned to read.

Step 3: Periodic recitation. Once each week throughout the semester, go over the material in your notes. At first, look only at section headings and try to recite the material under them. Read your notes over again only to check your recitation or to fill in information you cannot recall. As time goes by, the chapter titles themselves will suffice to recall all the notes to you.

This is quite different from the usual practice of students and it is far superior. What most students do is to read and reread all their notes many times. Periodic recitation in the manner described not only forces you to go over the material many times, but also shows you whether you are learning as you go. You will be tested sooner or later on whether you can *recite* the material, not on whether you have read it. Prepare yourself directly—by reciting.

As a term goes by, you will find that you know certain material so well that you will not have to keep on going over it. Don't waste your time on it. But be certain that you really know the material well before you leave off studying

it. Go back to it for a final recitation just before tests.

Proper study of chemistry and physics entails some of the work described in "How to Study Mathematics." You will find, as you take up the sciences in college, that textbooks in chemistry and physics usually provide exercises and problems at the ends of chapters. You will be required to do most of these problems as part of your assignments. Thus they become a part of your review, a built-in guarantee of overlearning. Do them in the same way prescribed for homework problems in mathematics.

In writing your notes on readings in chemistry and physics, you will find that you do not need to write nearly as many notes as you will have to take in descriptive sciences, such as biology and geology. A chapter in a physics or chemistry text is broken down into a series of principles and techniques followed by proofs and illustrations. If you learn the principle, and understand and work through the proofs and illustrations, your notes will be brief. The important function of note-taking will be obscured if you substitute laborious copying in a notebook for real effort at understanding.

The notes you take on principles will be extremely valuable if you follow the procedure suggested for your notes in mathematics. Write only when you have understood. Write from memory as much as possible. This recitation marks a real step forward in mastery of your material. When you have completed a chapter, follow the same procedures for systematic review and recitation that were developed in the first portion of this chapter.

How to attack a problem that has you stumped.
In the section on mathematics, you were told that you should devote the lion's share of your study time to the parts of a course you find most difficult. This is true in physics and the other sciences as well. In studying science, you can expect to come up against concepts that seem to be just too much for you to cope with.

It is important that you do not give up prematurely on a topic just because it is difficult. Study as best you can, trying all the techniques given for difficult mathematics problems. Use drawings freely. Read problems carefully for clues you may have overlooked. Go on to your next problem, because it may make the needed mental connection for solving the problem giving you trouble. Check your computations and reasoning. A silly slip may have thrown you off. Recite a difficult concept over and over again. Think back to preceding work. By building up once more to the concept that stumps you, the trouble may disappear.

Don't make the mistake, however, of staying up half the night on a home-

work difficulty. An hour of study while you are fresh is worth ten when you are exhausted.

Often, in the morning after a frustrating session with a difficult problem, you will find that you are able to go back at the topic and lick it quickly. What has happened is that you have assimilated the parts of the problem you understand well so that—with the freshness of the next day—you have the mental resources to overcome the trouble of the preceeding night. But this does not mean that going to sleep on a difficult problem will automatically solve it the next morning. If you have already worked hard with the material, the various parts of a problem will fall into their proper places when your mind is rested.

If the trouble confronting you concerns a concept that just does not seem to make sense—and you inevitably will find some—try reading an explanation in another source. Your library will have copies of other textbooks, as will your campus bookstore and the second-hand bookstores that thrive in almost every campus town.

Don't run off to another source after a single reading. Go over the material two or three times before you give up. Then the change in writing style, the possibility of a different explanation, a happy choice of example, or a good illustration may do the trick.

Here are two discussions of a subject covered in most first-year physics courses. Neither discussion is superior to the other. They are different from one another, and because they are different, they may be helpful.

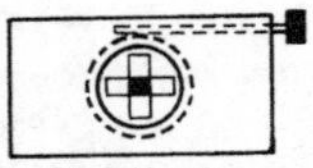

Polarization by crystals. If we have two pieces of tourmaline crystal (cut parallel to the axis and about 1 mm. thick) mounted in a framework (Fig. 1), we may rotate

FIG. 1. Mounting for rotating a tourmaline crystal.

one crystal over the other by means of the worm gear. If the projection apparatus is set up as in Figure 2, we may project the image of the tourmaline crystals on the screen. When their axes are parallel, considerable light will be transmitted; but when one crystal is rotated, the transmitted light through the center will gradually decrease. When the crystals are at right angles ("crossed"), the light through the center is extinguished.

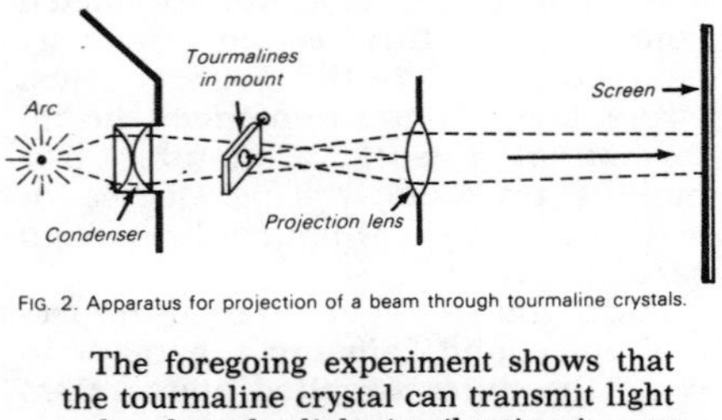

FIG. 2. Apparatus for projection of a beam through tourmaline crystals.

The foregoing experiment shows that the tourmaline crystal can transmit light only when the light is vibrating in one plane. We can visualize this fact by a crude mechanical model. Suppose we set up transverse waves in a rubber tube. If the tube is vibrating up and down, we may erect two grids of vertical slats without interfering with the vibratory motion of the tube. But if we turn one of the grids at right angles to the other as in Figure 3, no transverse vibrations can pass through the second grid. These grids represent the tourmaline crystals.

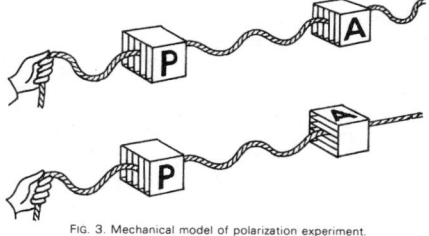

FIG. 3. Mechanical model of polarization experiment.

The experiment with the tourmaline crystals leads one to suppose that light is a transverse rather than a longitudinal vibration since a grid would not stop longitudinal vibrations. The light which strikes the crystal is vibrating in a plane at right angles to the beam, or line, of propagation, but in all directions. After it has passed through the crystal, it is vibrating in only one direction and thus is said to be *plane polarized.*

Now here is the same topic discussed in another textbook:

Polarization of Light. — The wave character of light is demonstrated by the phenomena of interference and diffraction; the transverse wave nature of light is revealed by *polarization.* This phenomenon can be illustrated by a simple test using two thin plates of a mineral called *tourmaline,* the plates having been cut from the crystal in a particular manner. A beam of light is passed through one of the plates and, except for a slight tinting due to the color of the tourmaline, remains unchanged in appearance. It has, however, been profoundly altered, as a test with the second plate placed in the path will show. When the plates are parallel the light passes through both, but when one is turned the amount of light transmitted becomes less, and when they are at right angles the light is almost entirely quenched, and the overlapping region appears dark.

A somewhat similar effect can be pictured for a mechanical wave by supposing transverse vibrations in all directions to be set up in a rope stretched horizontally. When the rope is unobstructed the waves will travel freely along its entire length, but if the test is repeated with the rope passed through a vertical slit, the horizontal components of the vibrations will be prevented from traveling beyond the slit and only the vertical components will be transmitted. A second slit will produce no further change if it is vertical also, but if it is turned to the horizonal all vibrations beyond will be quenched.

The significance of the test with the tourmaline plates will be considered by the aid of Fig. 1. Light is regarded as a wave in which the vibrations are transverse; that is, in planes at right angles to the line of propagation. For natural light,

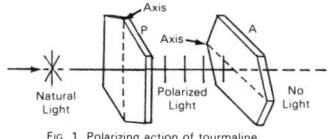

FIG. 1. Polarizing action of tourmaline.

it is supposed that in these planes, the vibrations occur in all directions, a few of which are represented by the radial lines

on the incident ray in the figure. Tourmaline transmits only vibrations or their components which are parallel to the crystal axis. Thus, in the light transmitted by the first plate, *P,* the vibrations are restricted to a single plane, as represented by the short dashes in the figure. This light is said to be plane polarized. The second plate, *A,* when crossed with the first as shown, extinguishes the light because the vibrations incident upon it have no components along the direction in which it is capable of transmitting. Plate *P* is used to polarize the light and is called the *polarizer,* and the plate *A* is used to analyze the polarization and is called the *analyzer.*

It is believed that light waves, like radio waves, are due to magnetic and electric fields which continually build up and collapse, and which are at right angles to each other. In specifying the plane of vibration of a light wave, the plane of the electric field is meant.

The term polarization implies a lack of symmetry around the axis of propagation. The fact that a light wave can be polarized is taken as evidence that the wave is transverse, as a longitudinal wave appears to be inherently symmetrical with respect to its direction of travel.

As you can see, both of these authors try to describe polarization by means of a comparison. One student may find the analogy of a rubber tube more vivid, while another student may understand polarization through the rope analogy. If you find that you cannot come to grips with the presentation of an idea in one science textbook, try going to another. It may be that you will want regularly to consult two versions of every topic you study. In the interests of saving time, you probably will prefer to use the second text as your ace in the hole.

Sometimes, students will use the same technique in another way. If they find that they are having undue difficulty in grasping the science lectures they attend, they will try to sit in on other lectures on the same topics given by a different teacher. This can often be arranged on a large campus.

How to adapt your studying to special situations.

In some science courses, you will find that the textbook seems to be the core of the work. Everything you need to know is in it, and the lectures apparently serve the purpose only of making clear what you have already covered in the text. To many students, it is disappointing to find that the lecturer follows the text so closely that while the course is exceptionally easy, lectures are so unexciting that they would just as soon stay away from them. Your first task in such lectures is to listen carefully as the lecturer reviews the content of the course. Hold your note-taking to a minimum by reading carefully in your textbook before attending lectures. If you take your reading notes along with you to the lectures, you can spend your time reviewing them with the lecturer and thus save yourself a good deal of review time.

On the other hand, you will often find yourself in a course in which the lecturer seems to be teaching a course entirely different from the one the textbook writer had in mind. This kind of course is much harder for the student who is interested only in making high grades. For the student who is eager to understand various points of view, who wants to go as deeply as possible into a subject, who wants to broaden his outlook, the organization of this course is tailor-made. He has the opportunity to roam far beyond the limits set by a single textbook.

In such a course, you must concentrate your primary learning effort on the lecture itself. The notes you take must be far closer to complete than in the other type of course. Your study time must favor your lecture notes.

At the same time, do not neglect the problems assigned in your textbook. They are still rehearsals for the problems you will have to solve one day on an examination.

When a course concentrates upon lectures in the manner described, it is often useful to discuss with a friend a lecture you have just heard. The purpose of such a brief review is to make sure you have understood exactly what was going on and also to give yourself an opportunity to recite the material just covered.

In many courses, your instructor will issue a course syllabus, which can be helpful in many ways. First of all, the syllabus will usually contain all the reading assignments and all the test and report dates for the semester so that class time will not have to be spent on such announcements. In addition, you will find a list of lecture topics and often a brief outline of the lectures themselves.

You can expect to find no more than a list of the subtopics of each lecture. Yet they are useful in that they direct your attention toward what is to be covered in each hour. You can write the headings supplied by these notes into your notebook in preparation for the lecture. With the format of the lecture before you, your job is to listen and comprehend what is said under each of the headings. The syllabus topics also become review material for you, since you have a list of all the topics that have been covered in the semester. What you must know about these topics is, of course, the substance of the lectures themselves.

How to identify and remove stumbling blocks.

A deficient background in mathematics may cause difficulty in chemistry or physics—particularly physics. Unless you can handle algebra fairly well, you will be poor at manipulating the equations you encounter in the sciences. Students who cannot understand calculus will find physical concepts tough to manage. So college advisors often will steer students away from physics if they are poor in math.

There is another possible source of trouble that may hold you back in science. A special requisite of chemistry and physics is that you understand principles in the order in which they are taught. If you miss one link in the chain, you may not be able to understand fully what follows. Thus if you suddenly find that a formerly easy science has become impossibly tough, make certain that you have not misunderstood material that went before. Check through all the chapter titles in your textbook to see whether you can find any gaps in your knowledge.

It is because of this building nature of the sciences—each principle resting on one before—that we have stressed careful preparation of every assignment in a course.

How to profit from a science demonstration. One feature of the typical science lecture that often proves a pitfall for the student is the *demonstration.* Because of the elaborate preparations that are made for the demonstration, because of the essentially theatrical nature of the presentation, some students seem to feel that their role at the demonstration is to sit back and enjoy it. Yet you must get more from the demonstration than the spectacle alone.

By definition, a demonstration is intended to make clear for you a principle or theory that your lecturer wants to drive home. No matter how complete your notes on a demonstration may be, they will be useless to you if you have failed to understand the theory being illustrated.

What kind of notes should be taken of a demonstration? Your primary job of note-taking is to make a clear diagram of the experimental set-up, labeling every item correctly. You will probably find that you can use symbols to represent the various kinds of apparatus. If you want to do this, try to copy the standard symbols used in the diagrams in your textbooks.

As you watch, make the mental connections between the events you are watching and the theory they are illustrating. Every step in the demonstration is understood to be "in relation to" the principle. As you study your lecture notes, each time you come to that diagram, think of how you would explain what you saw.

How to apportion time strategically before an examination. When you are ready to review for an important test in science—midterm or final—do not forget to go over the material of the entire period covered by the examination. Inspect your quiz grades and quiz papers to see where your strengths and weaknesses lie. For example, if you are preparing for a final in a physics course in which your midterm examination grade was a *C,* you probably ought to divide your study time to give the first half of the term's work two-thirds of your effort, the final half only a third.

The reason is that review of the first half will improve your understanding of the second half. Putting greater emphasis on the second half will mean you are wasting time. Your mastery of the later work is only as good as your understanding of what went before. If your work during the first half of a term has been satisfactory, change the ratio back to two-thirds on the second half, one-third on the first.

How to Study the Social Sciences

Perhaps the biggest surprise for a college freshman is the discovery of the social sciences. Before coming to college, the student took courses in *social studies,* or something similar under a different name. He or she studied *geography,* but that was years before. Surely that freshman had some *history* and has heard of *psychology*—who has not? But when he or she gets to college, lo and behold! there are courses called *anthropology, government, economics, political science,* and *sociology.* And strangely, on the typical campus, more students major in the social sciences than in biology, chemistry, and physics combined, even though before leaving high school, most of them would not have been able to name, much less define, more than a few of the many subjects in the social sciences. As a bare minimum, most colleges require two years' work in the social sciences.

You surely understand the scope of *history* and *geography,* but do you understand what is involved in the other social sciences?

Anthropology studies man's physical characteristics, where he is found, his races, his adaptation to his environment, his primitive culture.

Economics studies production, distribution, and consumption of goods and services. It is concerned with the organization of management and labor, and how they are interrelated.

Political science studies forms of political administration; political theory, and political institutions.

Psychology studies the mind in all its operations.

Sociology studies the institutions and functions of human groups.

The social sciences are founded upon principles and theories just as the sciences are. They pursue fact wherever possible in support of these principles and theories. They investigate and predict. A great deal of your study time will be spent learning evidence for what has been established. This is the easiest part of your job, for it resembles most closely the kind of study you are used to from high school days. College study of the social sciences, however, goes beyond memorizing facts. The theories are far more important. In fact, you may often have more difficulty in understanding the principles of social sciences than in remembering the material.

Special problems. First, you will have the same problem you have whenever you enter a new area of study: the vocabulary will be strange for you. To make your life just a little bit tougher, the vocabulary of social science has a difficulty all its own—you will find that some new words you meet are used only by a single author in a field. Or a single word may be used to mean different things to different authors. And so you will have to learn words and definitions that you will find only in the writings of a single author!

Secondly, you may find that reading the social science classics presents certain special difficulties besides vocabulary. In science readings in most colleges, the student does not go to the original articles and notebooks of the scientists responsible for a particular observation or theory. Rather, he reads textbooks written by men and women who are primarily teachers as well as scientists. They interpret and clarify for the student. In the social sciences, this is often not the case.

The student may have a textbook that he or she can use as a guide to material that is being studied, but the student also has original sources to read. And these are often more difficult than the textbooks themselves. This problem is so important that it is given a great deal of attention later on in this section, where you are shown how to deal with social science readings in sources other than textbooks.

One point must be made now about how to cope with the presentation of social science theory in original sources. If you find yourself experiencing heavy weather in trying to get through a particular author, turn to an interpretive article or book on that author. Once you have seen what others have to say about a particular theory, you will find that you can profit more from the original source itself. Finding a book or article on any of the great social scientists presents no problems. Your first stop would be a suitable encyclopedia, such as the *Encyclopedia of Social Sciences* or the *Encyclopedia Britannica*. The *Reader's Guide to Periodical Literature* will help you find current sources, and the card catalog in your college library will also be valuable. Two hours of reading about a particular theory will often save you far more than that amount of time when you return to the original works.

As you read social science theory, you should learn to associate theory with the scholar who originated it. This association will help you understand references made by your teachers and by authors you will read. It is a good idea, however, to go one step beyond this. Repeat the process you used for learning rules of grammar; restate every theory you must learn in your own words. The best way to do this is to find an example with which you can always associate the theory.

Reading a social science textbook.

When you read a social science text you will, of course, bear in mind the principles of good reading. You will look at the beginning and the end of the chapter for an outline of the material that the author intends to cover. In addition to this, you will often find questions at the ends of chapters.

Here, for example, are the questions that appear at the end of Chapter 12, "Determinants of Length of Life," in *Population Problems* by Paul H. Landis (American Book Company).

1. What is meant by the "life span"? What possible factors have a bearing on its length?
2. Why is length of life a suitable subject for the sociologist as well as for the biologist?
3. What factor is primarily responsible for greater length of life?
4. Compare the average length of life of peoples of selected nations. Do you attribute the differences primarily to differences in biological characteristics of peoples or to differences in culture?
5. On what basis do insurance companies predict the length of life of a population or of a particular individual or group?
6. What are the principal factors of environment that tend to terminate the potential life span prematurely? Discuss them briefly.
7. How might a better system of medical organization increase the average length of life?
8. Can the average length of life be raised in the future to the extent that it was during recent decades? Defend your answer.
9. Comment on the social importance of increased longevity.

If you inspect these questions before reading the chapter on which they are based, you will know just what to look for.

Let us examine a typical chapter from a social science textbook to see how you will work through it in your studying.

Your first objective is to determine what is to be learned from the chapter assigned. Keep that in mind as you read the *opening section* of John Frederick Dashiell's *Fundamentals of General Psychology*. Psychology was selected for this discussion because of the widespread student interest in this subject. Any of the other social sciences could have been used just as easily.

Chapter IX: SENSORY FUNCTIONS
Sensitivity in General

The Importance of Studying Sensory Phenomena. There can be no expression without impression, no response without stimulation. A man does nothing, is not active, in any manner involving the effectors studied in the last chapter, unless in some way he is being influenced by energy changes occurring inside or outside of him which play upon his receptors—provided we except a few cases of smooth muscle and gland excitation by hormones. The student interested in the phenomena of human nature and in their prediction and control must have some definite knowledge as to how men are sensitive to influences: to what kind of forces or influences they are sensitive; at what degree of intensity; and at what places on or in the body the influences must be applied. Many are the practical questions that turn upon such facts. What are the most effective colors for switch lights and street-crossing signals? Can all men see them equally well? What is the best form of illumination for a factory? How fine a difference can the average pilot detect in the directions of the motions of his airplane when it is enveloped in clouds? Do different pilots vary much in this regard, and can such variations be measured and tested? How good an "ear" and what kind of "ear" must one have to become a successful violinist? What are the essentials of a good musical tone? Just what is the nature of the differences of tones which proceed from various string, wood-wind, and brass instruments? In what way does the rolling of a ship excite nausea? When one is learning to operate a typewriter, what controls the speed and accuracy of the strokes? Why is the touch method of typing recommended? In learning to hold a billiard cue or a fencing foil precisely right, what receptors are involved? To put all this in a nutshell: no attempt systematically to understand the hows and whys of human behavior can be at all successful unless consideration be given to the *paramount rôle of stimulation in the initiating and in the controlling of behavior.*

A second reason for the study of human sensitivity presents itself as soon as we recognize the other centuries-old motive for psychological study—the analysis of one's own personal and private conscious experience. It is a fact that the great majority of thoroughgoing inquiries into the nature of consciousness have been highly analytical in character, and have discovered as the basis of consciousness sensations of one sort or another. One's awareness of an object perceived or of an event imagined or dreamed, the feelings of his emotional responses, and even the processes of thinking as he is conscious of them—all are held to be reducible to the primordial sensory experiences of particular colors,

tastes, sounds, pressures, strains, and the like. This analysis of one's consciousness, while for the most part exceedingly difficult for the untrained, is well typified by some fairly easy and common analyses attempted by the average man. He may, for example, examine the experience he calls the taste produced by his lemonade to determine whether it has sour-ness enough or sweet-ness enough, or he may examine the taste of his breakfast cereal to see whether the sweet-ness and the salt-ness of the taste are properly balanced. To summarize: any systematic study of psychology from the introspective point of approach must recognize *the central importance of sensations* (that is, the individual's awareness occasioned by stimulations) *in the analysis of consciousness.*

In keeping with the aims of this book as announced in the first chapter, we shall, for the most part, approach the sensory processes in the objective rather than the subjective manner, though supplementing the former with the latter at a few points. Putting it more simply: our primary inquiry will be to see how our hypothetical subject reacts to the various forms of stimulation which we bring to bear upon him and what differences in his actions are explainable by the changes of stimulation; but we shall now and then amplify this account by asking him, "How does it 'feel' or appear?"

A more general reason for including sensitivity in our survey of psychology lies in the fact that this division of psychology has probably been more thoroughly worked out in its details than any other; and it would be an unfair introduction to the field if we did not give the reader some acquaintance with some of these details.

In these four paragraphs, you encountered the words *sensory, phenomena, effectors, receptors, hormones, analytical, primordial, introspective, objective, subjective, hypothetical,* and *amplify.* Learn the words you do not know to read this psychology textbook effectively.

From a quick reading of this opening section, you can see the *general plan* of the entire assignment. In a few moments, you will examine the *section headings* and *illustrations* of the chapter, and then read the *last section* of the chapter to see whether there is further help available in identifying what is to be learned. The brief section you have just read gives you insight into the importance of the chapter. Because not more than a minute or two will be needed to make a few notes on this topic, make them now.

1. in understanding behavior of others

    a. what are men sensitive to?
    b. how sensitive are they?
    c. where in the body are they sensitive?

2. in understanding our behavior

    a. perceiving objects
    b. imagining and dreaming
    c. thinking

Now you have read and understood this introductory section and can see the general scheme and importance of this chapter. Quick inspection shows that the author gives you two kinds of headings within the chapter, one more general than the other.

The main headings in the chapter:

Cutaneous Sensitivity
Gustatory Sensitivity
Olfactory Sensitivity
Kinesthetic Sensitivity
Static Sensitivity
Organic Sensitivity
Auditory Sensitivity
Visual Sensitivity
Some Quantitative Problems
A Concluding View of Receptive Processes

These ten topics are the structure of the remainder of the chapter. As a result of a few minutes' effort, you understand that the chapter will study one by one the various senses and types of sensitivity of humans. You will keep in mind as you read these sections that *the study of sensory phenomena helps us understand the behavior of people.*

As you get into each of these discussions, you will find it subdivided further. "Cutaneous Sensitivity," for example, is broken down into "Stimuli and Receptors," and "Some Special Phenomena." It will probably be best for you to plan on taking notes under all the subheadings, but how much you will write will depend on the importance of each individual section.

Knowing the purpose and the general structure of the reading assignment, go on now to the last section to see what it can tell you about the body of the chapter. The title, "A Concluding View of Receptive Processes," seems to promise general insights that can be valuable for understanding the rest of the chapter. (If you are alert, the four opening words of this section should be a signal to you in your reading.)

Let us now summarize the roles played by the different classes of receptors in the life economy in the light of the preliminary descriptions and analyses of human and animal behavior we have set forth in earlier chapters. The primary sources of human and of subhuman behavior are to be found in the metabolic processes occurring within the body and especially in the inadequate relations of external conditions to these processes. the *interoceptors* are the sensitive organs most directly implicated here. Next, the organism when it gets into action proceeds to make some changes in its environment. In this the *exteroceptors* act the part of advance guards through which the specific characters of the surroundings play upon the body and modify the directions of movements. Further refinement of the movements is secured through the co-ordinations made possible by the *proprioceptors.*

A simple illustration lies at hand in the behavior of a hungry child. The empty stomach sets up interoceptive impulses which initiate motion and locomotion: the child goes after food. The direction in which he goes is determined by the smell or by the sight of cookies or apples, the sight of doorways, and by other exteroceptive stimulations. The maintaining of his

NEWSPAPERS *and journals can be a source of supplementary information.*

general bodily positions, and the effective reaching for and taking hold of and eating of a cooky or an apple, depend upon his proprioceptive organizations.

Coupled with a dictionary definition of the three key terms (interoceptors, exteroceptors, proprioceptors), the illustration of the child gives good insight into the concepts discussed. When you go on to read the body of the chapter, you will see how important these three terms are.

Now let us go on to study the effective use of other kinds of social science readings.

Reading other materials in social science.

You will often have to read materials other than textbooks. This is because textbooks in many courses have so grand a scope that they cannot go deeply enough into all aspects of the subject they are covering. Another reason for assigning readings in sources other than textbooks is to teach you how to "look for yourself." By going to original documents, treatises by experts, and other specialized sources, you learn the tools of scholarship. Being able to locate and evaluate information is essential in your advanced college courses, and valuable all through life.

Reading in such sources sometimes causes great difficulty for the student who is accustomed to the style and format of textbooks. Besides being tailored to meet the time requirements of a college semester, the typical college textbook is written to accommodate the level of knowledge and ability of students in most colleges. The additional readings you will have to master in the social sciences are not subject to the same restrictions.

Let us examine two works, one a *history textbook* and the other a *history,* to find out how they compare in depth and difficulty. The topic is the emergence of the C.I.O. (Congress of Industrial Organizations) as a factor in the American labor movement. See first how a textbook, *The American Nation,* by John D. Hicks, covers this event.

One result of the labor turmoil that characterized these years of change and experiment was the division of organized labor itself into two competing camps. The American Federation of Labor, led since 1924 by William Green, adhered consistently to the Gompers policy of cooperating with capital as long as wages and working conditions remained satisfactory. With the capitalistic system as such it refused to quarrel, provided only that labor obtained a reasonable reward for the work it was called upon to do. Furthermore, the A.F. of L. still set much store by the crafts union type of organization, and opposed with vigor all attempts to organize all the workers in a given industry, regardless of their skills or lack of skills. The Federation, so its critics complained, had lost touch with the problems of the ordinary worker. After the destruction of the NRA in 1935, John L. Lewis, militant head of the United Mine Workers, took the lead in the formation of a Committee for Industrial Organization, the purpose of which was to promote the unionization of industries as units, and not in accordance with specified trades or skills. In this endeavor he was officially opposed by the A.F. of L., but, with the support of his own and several other powerful unions, he sent organizers into many of the great mass-production industries, such as automobiles, steel, textiles, rubber, aluminum, plate-glass, and furniture. Unmindful of LaFollette's warnings as to the hazards of Communist infiltration, Lewis, to make haste, accepted the assistance of numerous Communist sympathizers. The effectiveness of their work was immediately apparent, but the presence of Communists and "fellow-travelers" in high places was to plague the C.I.O. for many years to come. In most instances the C.I.O. plan of organization seemed to meet a long-felt need; old unions took on new life, and new unions were founded as needed. For cooperating with Lewis in this work ten unions were suspended in 1936 by the A.F. of L., and as a result, the C.I.O. assumed a permanent character that its prime movers had not first intended. Claiming to represent a membership of nearly four million workers as against the five million of the A.F. of L., the C.I.O. changed its name in November, 1938, to the Congress of Industrial Organizations, adopted a constitution after the A.F. of L. model, and elected Lewis as its first president.

What have you learned from this short piece, all there is in Hicks on this split of the two unions? Contrast it, for example, with the treatment in *The Coming of the New Deal* by Arthur M. Schlesinger, Jr. Schlesinger devotes an entire chapter to what he calls "Emergence of the CIO." The total number of words in that chapter is approximately 4500. By comparison, the Hicks treatment looks skimpy.

Schlesinger's book is more than 600 pages long, devoted to the events of but two years in American history. The Hicks work, on the other hand, recounts the "History of the United States from 1865 to the Present," and it runs only one hundred pages longer. How many pages would there be in Schlesinger's book if it covered all the material covered by Hicks with the amount of detail exemplified by the chapter on the CIO?

It is possible to make the contrast between a *history textbook* and a *history* even more dramatic by comparing a few sentences in Hicks's volume with the treatment by Schlesinger of the same matters. On the presence of Communists in the C.I.O., Hicks wrote:

> . . . Unmindful of LaFollette's warning as to the hazards of Communist infiltration, Lewis, to make haste, accepted the assistance of numerous Communist sympathizers. The effectiveness of their work was immediately apparent, but the presence of Communists and "fellow-travelers" in high places was to plague the C.I.O. for many years to come.

This is what Schlesinger had to say on the same topic. Remember that your purpose in reading this is to see the rich possibilities of history beyond the brief sketch that a textbook can give.

> If he [Lewis] had few ideas, he had a burning vision—the vision of a mass workers' movement, bringing "industrial democracy" to the nation by giving labor its deserved stature in American society. And the very intensity of this vision introduced a new militancy into the life of labor. "The time has passed in America," said Lewis, "when the workers can be either clubbed, gassed, or shot down with impunity. I solemnly warn the leaders of industry that labor will not tolerate such policies or tactics." His old-fashioned militancy opened the way for new ideas and ideologues—Socialists or ex-Socialists like Hillman and Dubinsky, or like the young Reuther brothers, struggling to build a union in Detroit; Trotskyites, Lovestoneites, Stalinists. With the tolerance of a man indifferent to ideas, Lewis welcomed them all, confident that he could turn the zeal of each to his own purposes. Needing manpower for the battles of steel and rubber, he even suspended his old hatred of Communism. "Industry should not complain if we allow Communism in our organization," he observed. "Industry employs them." "Never refuse to work with anybody," he told the Newspaper Guild, "who's willing to work with you." He went so far as to declare an agnosticism about the Soviet Union. "To determine what is actually taking place in Russia is quite impossible—at least for me," he told Selden Rodman with unwonted modesty, adding, "I think we will solve our own difficulties in our own way." Lee Pressman left his government job and became Lewis's counsel in the CIO. Communists went into the field as CIO organizers. When someone expostulated to Lewis about the Communist influx, he is said to have replied, "Who gets the bird, the dog or the hunter?"
>
> The CIO had a spirit of its own, however, diverging both from the Communists and from Lewis. Unlike the Communists, the CIO militants wanted a free and democratic America; unlike Lewis, they wanted a new America. But for the moment all united in their adherence to the Lewis gospel: "Let the workers organize. Let the toiler assemble. Let their crystallized voice proclaim their injustices and demand their privileges. Let all thoughtful citizens sustain them, for the future of labor is the future of America."

So we see how two sentences in a *history textbook* become two paragraphs in a *history*. While both serve their purpose, you can see that the textbook view of things is not enough for the proper study of history.

Did you notice that the authors of the two books in question had different attitudes toward what they were observing? Which was the more sympathetic toward Lewis? You will find such disagreement many times in your reading. One of the things you will learn from consulting a variety of sources in your social science studies is how to detect an author's point of view.

You will find a box on this page with a list of the steps to follow when reading a book. These techniques apply to the reading of an entire book, but often, in your courses, you will want only to read a single chapter of a given book. Even if this is the case, it is a good idea to look at the preface of the book so that you will be able to associate the name of the author with the ideas represented. Then turn to the chapter that concerns you at the moment. Inspect it in detail for its plan.

Even when books are not arranged in a helpful manner, there still are ways in which you can get to the heart of an assignment before you actually begin to read. Let us have a look at a book with fewer obvious helps than the books just discussed: *The Challenge of Man's Future* by Harrison Brown.

Subtitled *An Inquiry Concerning the Condition of Man During the Years That Lie Ahead,* this book deals one by one with the factors necessary for humanity's survival on earth in the years to come. Against the population growth pattern, Brown plots our needs for food and energy, and our chances for satisfying these needs. This is a provocative book that calls for thought and action by each of us to promote the necessary concern of government to meet "the challenge of man's future." Let us assume that in one of your social science courses you have been assigned the reading of the chapter entitled "Food."

First you would examine the entire book briefly. There is a *preface* of but a few pages that can be read quite easily. Beginning in the third page, which is the next to last, you read:

> . . . the present position of machine civilization is a very precarious position. . . . Whether or not it survives depends upon whether or not man is able to recognize the problems that have been created, anticipate the problems that will confront him in the future, and devise solutions that can be embraced by society as a whole. . . . In the light of what we know of the nature of man, it would appear that the possibilities of solution are remote. . . .
>
> I believe man has the power, the intelligence, and the imagination to extricate himself from the serious predicament that now confronts him. The necessary first step toward wise action in the future is to obtain an understanding of the problems that exist. This in turn necessitates an understanding of the relationships between man, his natural environment, and his technology. I hope that this study will in some measure contribute to that understanding.

The preface has given you an understanding of the scope of the book and the author's thesis that the world is in trouble but can get out of it if we try hard. There are *an index, a list of suggested readings, chapter titles,* and *numbered sections within the chapters,* but that is the limit of the help the reader receives in peering into the heart of the work before actually beginning to read. There are no handy section headings that we have come to depend on in our reading for study purposes. This book is typical of many in its arrangement, and you will have to learn to study such a book if you want to get on in the social sciences.

Don't think that you must begin with the first word in the chapter and plow on through to the end. A quick check of the chapter organization will do much for you. Let us turn now to the chapter "Food" to see how this works. It begins:

> All living things require energy if they are to survive. Most animals, including man, obtain their energy by ingesting other living things and burning their organic matter with oxygen:
>
> Organic matter + oxygen →
>   carbon dioxide + energy
>
> In the case of higher animals, such as man, organic matter is eaten, oxygen is taken in through the lungs, the oxygen reacts with organic matter in the body, carbon dioxide is expelled, and the energy is used by the body for various activities. . . .

Since the opening paragraph moves so deliberately to make a point, it would appear that our chapter summary must lie elsewhere—if one exists at all. After

---

THREE STEPS IN READING A BOOK

Whether you have an easy or hard time in reading will depend upon how you go about it.

Step 1 Inspect preface, foreword, table of contents, index, and whatever other keys are provided to the plan of the book.

Step 2 Read first chapter carefully to find scope, importance of book, relationship of work to other works, and to become familiar with style of writing.

Step 3 Read chapter by chapter:
inspect chapter to determine goals for reading,
read to find out just what is said,
write notes from memory to show that you have really understood and are ready to learn, going back only to check your accuracy in remembering or to pick up additional detail.

all, what you have read thus far is certainly not an original thought. Now turn to the *first sentences of the first few paragraphs* to see what you can learn in this way:

1. All living things require energy if they are to survive.
2. A man lying in bed and performing no external work requires a certain minimum energy intake.
3. A man who weighs 125 pounds and who is engaged in moderate activity requires about 2,600 calories per day, while a man weighing 200 pounds requires 3,700 calories per day.
4. The main sources of food energy are carbohydrates, the most important of which are starches (the main constituents of potatoes and cereals) and sugar.
5. A second important source of energy is fat, which provides about twice as much energy per pound as do carbohydrates.
6. We know from experience, however, that a person who consumes a diet consisting only of carbohydrates or fats will soon perish.
7. Protein is the principal constituent of the cells which make up the human body, and a liberal supply is needed in food throughout life for growth and repair.

The author apparently uses the first sentence of a paragraph as a topic sentence. By reading the seven sentences just quoted, you have a recognizable and unified development, do you not? This knowledge will help you a great deal as you read through the entire book.

It is evident by now that the first section of the chapter is designed to give you a picture of the life-sustaining requirements of human beings. It would be easy to sketch in a heading for the first section of your notes: *Man's Food Requirements.*

Let us go on to the end of the chapter to see what we can find there in a few moments. We will read only the opening sentence of each of the last eight paragraphs:

1. In the half of the world that is badly undernourished, an increase in food production of approximately 50 percent is necessary if people are to have adequate nutrition.
2. Such increases are clearly possible in principle.
3. Thus we see that when we consider population limitation solely on the basis of potential food supply, enormous increases of numbers of human beings are possible in principle.
4. However, it must be emphasized that an enormous food-production potential is no guarantee against starvation.
5. In the undernourished half of the world, most people are farmers barely able to produce sufficient food for their own needs.
6. At the present time there is insufficient food production to provide adequate nourishment for the people of the world, and the population is rising quite rapidly.
7. The underdeveloped areas are in the position, however, of being unable to provide new capital at the necessary rate.
8. Thus far we have seen that increased food production in the world requires increased industrialization.

This brief look at the end of the chapter has disclosed a clear outline of the food production problem. Increased food production is necessary and possible; the potential to provide it is not the whole story; parts of the world are already suffering badly; the world's population is exploding; areas that must develop food resources don't have the financial capacity to do so; increased food production demands industrialization, which in turn will require greater development of natural resources (the apparent subject of the next chapter, entitled "Energy").

So the heart of the chapter is summarized in the last eight paragraphs. Do you see that you have the entire chapter at your fingertips? Your task now is to fill in the details of the argument.

Take one further look at the chapter just to convince yourself of the tremendous possibilities inherent in inspecting a chapter before plunging into it. The chapter has nine numbered sections, and we know that Harrison Brown makes the first sentences of his paragraphs count for a great deal. The opening sentences of his sections should be particularly revealing for you as reader:

1. All living things require energy if they are to survive.
2. Since World War II the average American has consumed annually about 250 quarts of milk, 360 eggs, 170 pounds of meat, poultry, and fish, 190 pounds of grain, 130 pounds of potatoes, 65 pounds of fats and oils (including butter), 120 pounds of citrus fruits and tomatoes, 360 pounds of other vegetables and fruits, 110 pounds of sugar, 20 pounds of beans, peas, and nuts, and 20 pounds of chocolate, coffee, and tea.
3. The total land area of the world amounts to about 36 billion acres.
4. For the entire time during which man has existed on the earth he has competed with other animals for food.
5. The land areas of the world provide man with his food, but they provide him, in addition, with a multiplicity of products which enable him to clothe and shelter himself and to produce a variety of goods which increase the comfort of his daily life.
6. The food production of the world can be increased in a variety of ways.
7. Low crop yields can result from any one of a number of causes.
8. Plants can be limited in their growth rates by a variety of factors.
9. In the half of the world that is badly undernourished, an increase in food production of approximately 50 percent is necessary if the people are to have adequate nutrition.

So you see that the opening sentence of each of the sections of the chapter tells you a good deal of what the section contains. Knowing the point of each topic as you come to it makes the reading of each section meaningful. Surely the few minutes spent in getting the feel of a chapter will help you study.

This method of taking your bearings before actually reading applies as well to magazine or journal articles. Once you have sifted them to identify what you want to know, apply the study techniques you have already learned.

How to Write a Top-Notch Exam Paper

Examinations are the payoff! Every college student must take them—usually several sets of them each year. No matter how good your recitations, reports, and term papers are, your college record will be unsatisfactory if you do not learn to do well on your examinations.

Main types of examinations.

There are four main types of examinations: essay, brief essay, quick-scoring, and oral. Let's take a quick look at each:

1. An *essay* test is a test in depth, demanding thorough exploration of a limited number of broad topics. You are asked to recall information, differentiate between what is important and what is not, perceive relationships between ideas, and then write a well-organized, clearly expressed paper that shows the results of your thought. Your ability as a writer is almost as important as your knowledge of subject matter.
2. The *brief-essay* test is designed to cover a greater number of topics than can be included on an essay test. Your answers in the brief-essay test are a paragraph or two in length, discussing specific topics without relating them to one another, in contrast to the essay test, in which each answer is many paragraphs long and thoroughly integrated. Your ability to write a good paragraph is on display in the brief-essay test, but you do not have the responsibility of developing a complete theme.
3. The *quick-scoring* test is composed of the familiar true-false,

	Mon.	Tues.	Wed.	Thurs.	Fri.	Sat.
9	English	Geology	English	Geology	English	Geology
10	Spanish	Economics	Spanish	Economics	Spanish	Geology
11		Economics				Geology
12						
1	Math	Math	Math	Math	Phys.Ed.	
2					Phys.Ed	
3						

	Mon.	Tues.	Wed.	Thurs.	Fri.	Sat.
2	Spanish	Economics	Spanish	Economics	Spanish	Geology
3	Spanish	Economics	Spanish	Economics	Spanish	Geology
4	Geology	English	Geology	Math	Geology	Economics
5	Geology	English	Geology	Math	Geology	Economics
7	Math	Spanish	Math	English	Math	
8	Math	Spanish	Math	English	Math	
9	Math	Spanish	Math	English	Math	

THE SAMPLE SCHEDULE (left) *is followed throughout the term; the final exam study schedule* (right) *suggests the concentrated effort the student follows in the final weeks of the term.*

multiple choice, matching, and identification types of questions. The widest range of subject matter can be covered in a quick-scoring test, and no demands are made on your ability as a writer.

4. The *oral* test can be of several types. It can last anywhere up to several hours. The setting can range from an informal conversation with one teacher while both of you are seated in easy chairs to the ordeal of standing before a panel of teachers. You can be subjected to a series of brief questions on a wide selection of topics. You can be given a few broad questions that you are expected to explore fully.

Final review strategy.

Good habits of study, good reading and writing, careful lecture and laboratory work—all these qualities result in good test performance. You have formed, or are on your way to forming, the habit of regular and purposeful study. You read and look and listen carefully for the main ideas your teachers will ask for on tests. Above all, you periodically review all the material of each course you are taking. The week does not pass without your going back over notes to recite the heart of what you have been studying. *Each session of this kind is a miniature review for examinations.*

There remains only the need to work out effective procedures for getting all you can from your study and review *during the final weeks of a semester.*

The way to begin is to *survey your final review requirements in every course you are taking.* One month before final examinations, set time aside for taking stock in each course of

1. What you know well,
2. What you should know better,
3. What you do not know at all.

This means going through your notes, your laboratory manuals, and your textbooks that you have not outlined in your notes.

To show how this is done, let us use a sample program. In your *freshman composition,* you have been writing themes all semester long, and the

chances are that you will have a final impromptu theme instead of a test, so you will not have to study for it. If an *English usage* test is scheduled, you may have some reviewing to do. The bulk of your reviewing will be done for your courses in *economics, geology, mathematics,* and *Spanish.*

Take stock of every topic covered in each of these courses. As you discover a topic you do not feel strong in, make an entry in your notebook for that topic, including where you will find the material to be studied, and how long a period you will need for studying it.

In *economics,* for example, you may have:

	Economics	
topic	source	time
Federal Reserve System	text book pp 81-96 lecture notes pp 28-32	3 hours
operation of commodity markets	textbook pp 103-121 lecture notes pp 91-98	3 hours
. . .	. . .	. . .
total time needed		. . . hours

Do this for each of your courses. When you have, you are ready for the next step in the process.

Create a new study schedule for the final weeks of the semester. Adapt the work schedule you have been using during the semester to fit in additional hours where they will do the most good. Some of the additional time you will need is found by adding hours to your work schedule and by foregoing some of your social life for the weeks remaining in the semester. If you have been working well all through the semester, you probably have found yourself using fewer study hours than you had originally scheduled.

If you start your final review early enough, you will find that there is time enough to do right by all the topics you know need attention. *One month before the end of a semester is the best time.* If you wait until time gets short,

your review schedule will be dangerously crowded. The groundwork is laid in your day-to-day homework and reading assignments. You cannot prepare adequately for a test in a few days if you have neglected to study all semester long. This cannot be overemphasized. The final review is just the last in your program of periodic reviews and recitations for each course.

Final review procedure.

By the end of a semester you will have refined the organization of your notebook so that:

1. All related information on a given topic that you have gathered from various sources—lectures, reading, discussions—now appears in the same section of your notebook.
2. A good deal of material has been taken out of your notes. Now you have progressed sufficiently so that elementary information and skills are second nature to you.
3. Misconceptions, ambiguities, and redundancies have been edited during your day-to-day review. What is left is the hard core that you need for your tests.
4. The sectioning of your notes—the arrangement of topics under appropriate titles—now reflects the larger topics that have emerged as the semester went on.

Thus, the bulk of your notes has been reduced, and your study materials are in proper focus. You can now put the finishing touches on your understanding of the material.

- If you are preparing for an *essay test,* spend your time outlining essays you must be prepared to write.
- If you are preparing for a *brief-essay test,* spend your time identifying all possible subjects for such essays and preparing brief notes for the paragraphs you will write in answering the questions.
- If you are preparing for a *quick-scoring test,* read all the material you can be quizzed on, identifying the questions that can be asked.
- If you are preparing for an *oral test,* you will spend your time

thinking through all your topics and what you might want to say about them.

Preparing for an essay test.

If your notes have been well taken and carefully studied, then any essay test you face can demand nothing more from you than you should demand from yourself as you study. That is why you have been told to go through the exercise of periodic review and recitation so often during a semester. Each session of study is your rehearsal for the real thing.

When a teacher prepares an essay test, do you think he or she looks with a fine-tooth comb for the least important, the most minute jots of information with which to plague you? Certainly not. *The material that receives greatest emphasis during a semester is the subject matter of an essay test.* In preparing for an essay test, then, your first important job is to *select the major themes* that will be the most logical candidates for questioning. In an essay test, you will have to answer three or four major questions during a two- to three-hour period. Your teacher may give you a choice among five or more questions from which you will select the ones you can answer best. The most sensible review procedure for you to follow is to *make up questions based on the outstanding areas of the course and then outline your answers.*

You know what is most important in each course you take, so this procedure is not difficult.

For example, if you are taking a course on the history of the American labor movement, you might expect a question such as:

Compare and contrast the practices and philosophies of the A.F. of L. and C.I.O. in the period immediately following the creation of the C.I.O.

Do you recall the discussion of the philosophy of John L. Lewis quoted on pages 684–685?

In any of several social science courses, you might read Harrison Brown's book cited on pages 684-685. A reasonable question based on this reading might be:

Discuss the problem of food production and the world population explosion.

Of course, these are not the only questions that can be developed on the topics mentioned. Scholars in these areas would be able to do far better than the above sample questions. They would ask that the information be related to other sources that had been assigned during the semester. They would always go beyond asking you merely to report on what you have read; they would ask you to think deeply. As you go over the major topics in a course, you must bear in mind that comparisons and contrasts must be drawn, conclusions attempted, and hypotheses

devised. As you come to the end of a course, the major topics of the course should be fairly obvious to you. In preparing for tests, put yourself in the place of the teacher and ask what questions *you* would write if you were conducting an examination.

This point must be reemphasized: it is not enough merely to identify the topics you will be tested on. You must go on to *actually writing possible examination questions,* for this process will lead you to the next step—*thinking through and outlining possible answers.*

As you do this, you are not merely working toward top test grades. You are also working in the most direct way possible toward *effective use of knowledge.* And your ability to *use* knowledge is just as important as the knowledge itself. If you can list the ten most important areas of a term's work (and ten is an arbitrary number—there may be more, there may be fewer), you are reviewing and perfecting your grasp of the entire subject. By going on to the next step—writing questions and outlining suitable answers—you are demonstrating and perfecting your ability to handle the material. Proper preparation for an essay test may teach you more than all the lectures you have attended in a course. Outlining answers to all conceivable important questions for an examination is also an excellent aid in learning how to organize your thoughts and express them well.

Here are two guides to use in outlining during review:

1. For every essay question, adopt a position and stick to it.

"Man's survival on this planet is possible only if. . . ."
"The fundamental difference between the philosophies and practices of the A.F. of L. and the C.I.O. was. . . ."

Either of these sentences, if completed, takes a position that must be maintained throughout your essay if you are to end up with a unified, effective discussion.

2. Gather supporting evidence and memorize key facts. THIS IS ESSENTIAL. One claim or generalization piled upon another proves nothing. Facts, facts, facts. Be as specific as you can.

Read these two sentences in response to the first question:

"Man needs a certain minimum daily food intake."
"A man weighing 165 pounds requires as many as 4500 calories a day if he is engaged in heavy physical labor."

Which of these sentences has greater impact?

Keep these guides in mind as you prepare your outlines before a test. As you go over the broad organization of your notes in a course, you should be developing and strengthening your point of view concerning the major problems of the course. Having a point

of view and being able to express it clearly and succinctly will help you in every question of a test.

Preparing for a brief-essay test.

Teachers are leaning more and more toward tests that demand answers in the form of brief essays, usually no more than a paragraph or two in length. These paragraphs leave no room for evasion and padding. You must come right to the point, answer the question with the material it asks for, and then stop writing at once so that you have time for the rest of the test. Because you must express yourself crisply and pointedly in the brief essay, this type of test is quite difficult for many students.

Review for the brief-essay test is just as extensive as for the essay test. You must survey all you have studied, to find areas of weakness needing special attention. Your review is divided into two phases: (1) you must "spot" typical subjects for brief essay questions, and (2) you must think through good answers to each question you find and decide on a topic sentence that will set the tone of your response.

As you become accustomed to taking brief-essay tests, you will find yourself continually looking for questions while you study during a semester. You may spot some during lectures. It is good practice to use the left-hand pages in your lecture notes for special items that require attention. As a lecture proceeds, you may feel that something the lecturer has just said could easily become a brief essay topic. Make an appropriate entry on that left-hand page. When you are doing your reading for your courses, you will come across material in the same way. Again, an entry in your notebook will help you when the time comes for final examination review. In class discussion, the same technique will come in handy. Your skill at recognizing possible questions and automatically recording your impressions will help you greatly.

If you follow this practice steadily throughout a semester, you will find yourself with a first-class collection of brief essay subjects that you can review just before examinations. Whatever subjects you miss during the semester will be found in your final review.

What constitutes suitable material for a brief essay? If you think of the space limitations of the brief essay, then you will be guided in selecting topics properly. In *history,* for example, identifying some historical figure or event lends itself to the brief essay. In *sociology, anthropology,* and *psychology,* there are terms and ideas to be defined and illustrated. In *literature,* a question on the meaning and importance of a school of writers could be treated in brief-essay form. In a science such as *biology,* a description of a process or anatomical feature could be answered in a brief essay.

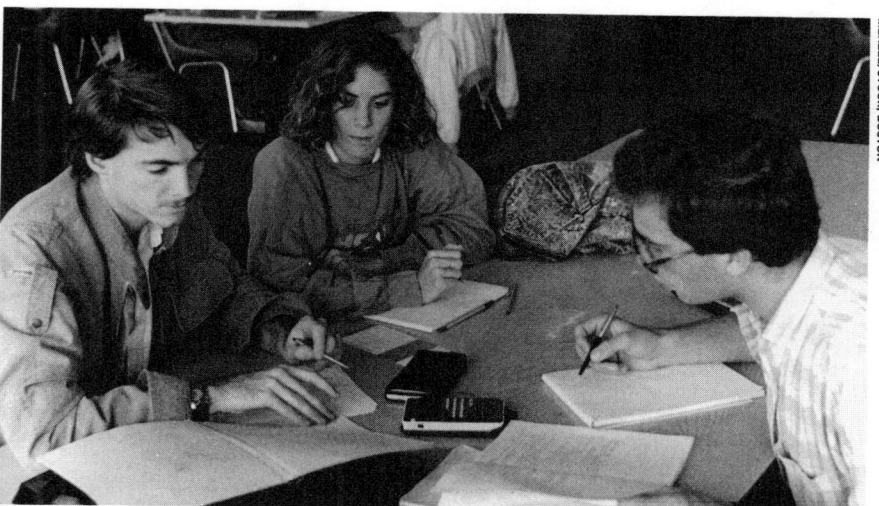

MENZEL/STOCK, BOSTON

GROUP STUDY *is particularly effective when all the participants are equally serious, equally intent on success, and equally well prepared.*

How about reviewing with others?

Many students like to study with their friends before a big test. If a study group is organized successfully and managed intelligently, it can serve a worthwhile purpose. But no student should think that group study is designed to replace individual work. Rather it should serve only as a check on the subject matter to show whether an important section of a course has been overlooked for one reason or another. In addition, it should be a means of learning how much the student really does understand of every topic in a course.

The general rules for organizing a study group are these:

1. The group should be composed of no more than five students who work well together.
2. There should be a brief planning session to agree on the purposes of the group and a plan of procedure. This meeting should be no later than three weeks before a final examination, and everyone should leave the planning meeting with a definite assignment to review intensively that segment of the course in which he or she will later lead discussion.

3. At the next meeting, a few days later, each member should appear with an outline of the material for which he or she is responsible. Copies of these notes should be distributed and gone over with the others.
4. Devote two or three more meetings to quizzing one another on the various topics of the course. Each student should prepare questions that may appear on the test, and the entire group should work together discussing reasonable answers.

Under these conditions, such group effort can be worthwhile. Experience will tell you whether you can benefit from working in this way and will influence your decision about whether or not to participate in further ventures of this kind.

The jitters and what to do about them.

There is all too much talk about the fear students have of impending examinations. The best attitude toward tests is one of *healthy respect.* To be sure, no student can be entirely happy or confident about an oncoming test.

- If you are superbly prepared for a test, you may wonder whether you will do as well as you expect.
- If you are half-prepared, you wonder whether your instructor will be so uncooperative as to ask only about that half of the course you have not studied thoroughly.
- If you are not prepared at all, you wonder whether there is any chance whatsoever of passing.

When you come right down to it, there are probably two causes for the pre-examination jitters. One of them is lack of proper preparation and the other is psychological inability to perform on examinations. It is beyond the scope of this book to deal with the latter cause, but the first is by far the most frequent. If you follow the study procedures described here, you will enter your examinations with confidence and with the assurance that you know all the material about which you will be tested. There are very few cases of pre-examination jitters among students who do have the confidence that comes from being prepared.

One final word on tests.

In many courses you will take in college, you will have more than one major examination during a semester. You may have a second test at mid-semester or perhaps even more. These tests will usually run for only 1 hour, the duration of regular class meetings.

What has been said about preparing for final examinations applies here, too. But there is one feature of these tests that is different from most final examinations. You have the opportunity to see your paper after the teacher has read and evaluated it. You may even be able to review it in class.

A returned test paper can provide valuable help in preparing you for the other tests you will take during that semester and throughout the rest of your college career. If you examine the paper carefully to see the kind of errors you have made, you may be able to avoid similar errors in the future.

For example, you may find that you have misunderstood some of the semester's work, or you have understood the work but failed to convey your thinking properly. Perhaps you have overemphasized details and given scant attention to important ideas. You may have organized your answers badly. You may have read the test questions badly. You may have prepared on the wrong topics. Whatever the mistakes you have made, take proper steps to avoid the same errors in the future.

By the same token, you must look carefully at those parts of the test you did best. What were the characteristics of certain answers you gave that made them outstanding? If you can discover the pattern of those answers, you may learn something significant about your grasp of the subject and about how to write a top-notch examination paper.

A GOOD STORY . . . WHETHER TRUE OR NOT

Every campus has its legend concerning the student who managed to pass a course without being able to answer a single question on the final examination. Don't try to become a legend.

Years ago, a student wrote his American literature teacher the following letter in lieu of an examination paper:

Dear Prof:

I can't answer any of the wonderful questions you have devised, and it pains me because I know how hard you must have worked putting them together. Now I know that I cannot pass your course without passing the final examination, but Ruthie doesn't know that. And Ruthie means a lot to me. Let me tell you about Ruthie.

The letter continued in a glowing mood about the glories of this paragon of young womanhood, about how she expected so much of the poor student, about how he did not want to fail her. The legend has it that the student received an A for Ruthie's sake, but there is some doubt as to whether the story has any basis in fact.

THE TACTICS OF TAKING AN EXAMINATION

If you want to avoid trouble and get the best grades possible with your knowledge and skill, get right to work when you sit down. Have a definite routine to follow from the moment you take your seat in the examination room.

GET SET FOR THE TEST

Have nothing with you except the materials you will need for taking the test. To carry notes or a textbook into an examination, unless you are specifically authorized to do so, is a serious error. Not because they are temptations, but because you will feel impelled to study them until just before the test gets under way.

Don't worry yourself by finding things you have not learned. Relax and follow directions. If you miss a single instruction your teacher gives because you are boning up in a last-ditch effort, you will lose much more than you gain.

Examine your test papers. Do you have all the question-and-answer sheets you will need? Write your name and other identifying information wherever needed. There is no point in wasting the time allotted to the test itself on these housekeeping tasks.

GET RIGHT DOWN TO WORK

ON AN ESSAY TEST:

1. **Read all the questions through quickly** to select those you will answer—if you have a choice. *If you find ambiguity in the language of the questions, ask your teacher for help at once.*

2. **Underscore the key words** in each question you are going to answer: *describe, compare, identify the main elements,* etc. Your essays will be organized in accordance with these words.

3. **Set up a time budget.** In the case of a test in which there are four questions of equal weight (this information will be supplied on the question sheet) and you have two hours in all, take about 25 minutes for outlining and writing each essay. Reserve the final 20 minutes for all-important editing. Guard against getting all wound up in one question you particularly like and forgetting about the others until there is insufficient time left for answering them. If the test questions are of unequal weight, budget your time appropriately. It is common to hear students exclaim midway through a test that they had "just noticed that all the questions were weighted differently." The time to find this out and to plan your work is before the test begins.

4. **Think.** Here the distinction first arises between outstanding students and those who will merely get by. Can you now demonstrate to your teacher that you have thought carefully about the problems in front of you by writing maturely and persuasively? As ideas come to mind, you are working on the next step in the process.

5. **Outline briefly the answers to all the questions you are going to work on.** Don't bother with detail, but think of the broad ideas of the essay you will write. Check with your teacher as to what ways of outlining are permissible. You may be able to use the first pages of your examination booklet, the back of your examination booklet, or a separate sheet of paper.

   Outline all the essays before you begin writing the first one. Students sometimes write themselves out on the first few questions of a test and then draw a blank on the last questions because they have become fatigued.

6. **Choose first the essay you feel you can do best, and get to work**—with one eye on your watch. It is far better to work ahead of the time schedule you set up than to immediately fall behind it by tackling the most difficult question on the test for you. Besides, you will not feel as good after working hard on a tough question as you will if you can get off to a flying start.

   Remember the importance of setting the tone of your response by stating your attitude on each question at the start. Then hit hard with facts and more facts. Nothing can give greater strength to an answer.

   One good essay on the first question you select will build your confidence for the entire test. After you have done this essay, choose the next one you feel most like doing, and so on until you have finished.

7. **Read through your outline** before you undertake an essay. Add to it any important ideas you will want to develop under the main headings you set up at the start. You may want to reorganize the outline. Do so with numbers and arrows. Don't waste time making your outline look beautiful.

8. **Remember that you are being judged on how well you write as well as on how much you know.** The student who wanders along in an essay, citing a fact here and a fact there in unconvincing manner, cannot hope to do well on a test. The most important idea to keep in mind as you outline an essay and as you actually write it is that *you are answering a specific question.* If your essay fails in this—no matter how brilliant the information and style—it is not satisfactory. A good way to work is to imagine that you are being asked a question in class and that your teacher and classmates are listening to your words and criticizing your effort. Write for them.

9. **Edit your work** for clarity, completeness, accuracy, mechanics of style, and appearance. You may find that you can increase the effectiveness of your writing by underscoring important ideas and by using Roman numerals to make divisions clear. Don't undertake any substantial rewriting unless you are blessed with a good deal of extra time—an unlikely occurrence. Your answers should represent your best writing. Whatever corrections you add should not make your work difficult to read.

ON A BRIEF ESSAY TEST:

1. **Budget your time.** This means, first of all, finding out how many questions you must answer. Then, on the basis of how the test questions are scored, set up goals for your work during the test. A question worth ten points should be given twice the time you allot to a question worth five points. Going beyond the kind of answer expected cannot give you more points than are allotted to the question, but it can rob you of time needed to complete the test.

   Don't forget that you must leave time for editing your answers. While you work at your answers, check the time frequently in order to keep to your schedule.

2. **Underscore the key words in each question** in your first reading of all the test questions before undertaking to answer any of them. As in the essay test, the key word or words of a question will help you organize your answer.

3. **Read again the questions you cannot answer readily.** A second reading may trigger the recollection you need. As you read, think of the meaning of the question, taking special note of the important words in the question. Even if you cannot recall what you need to know, this second reading will help plant the question in your mind. Later in the test, while you are working on some other question, the answer to the troublesome question may come to mind. When this happens, make a quick note of the thought that has come to you.

4. **Read once more the first question you are going to answer, and get to work.** Answer each question as directly as you can. A good aid in writing an effective brief essay is to say to yourself, "If I were permitted only a one-sentence answer to this question, what would that sentence be?" From the first sentence on, you must give your teacher the feeling that he or she is reading the work of someone who knows the subject matter. Above all, do not deliberately answer wide of the mark. You will get no credit for answering a question that has not been asked.

5. **Review all your answers** for clarity and accuracy. If you write poorly, your grades will suffer no matter how good the content of your answers.

   (Read again the discussion on page 698 of how to write an essay test answer—particularly in regard to writing and editing. What is said there applies here as well.)

ON A QUICK-SCORING TEST:

1. **Estimate how far along in the test you should be** after half an hour, an hour, etc. Write that estimate in the margin of your answer sheet, where you can see it during the test. Don't forget to include time for checking your paper.

2. **Make certain that you know the symbols that are to be used in writing your answers** before you begin to work. Why get halfway through a test before you discover that you are not following directions in regard to the form of your answers?

3. **Answer at once every question you can answer easily,** after reading carefully for comprehension. Where in the course did the material come up? What are the implications of the question? Knowing the background of the question will help you decide the best answer to it.

4. **Skip any question you are not sure of** after one careful reading, but *star that question* so that when you come back to the question sheet for the second go-around you will be certain not to miss it.

5. **When you have gone through the entire test once, check back** to see whether you have overlooked any pages of the test. Because they are concentrating so hard on their work, students frequently overlook an entire page of questions.

6. **See how much time you have left** and then go through the test questions once more at a pace that will give you at least one more chance at each unanswered question. By now, some of them can be answered easily, but others will demand a great amount of time. Obey the instructions of your teacher in regard to guessing. It is foolhardy to guess wildly if you are subject to heavy penalties.

7. **Read quickly the entire test** in the remaining time to *make sure you have not mismarked questions whose answers you know.* This is particularly important in machine-marked tests. It is quite common for students to mismark an entire column by failing to align question and answer sheets properly.

   If you come across any questions whose answers you want to change, make certain that your reasons for doing so are overwhelmingly correct. *Don't begin guessing wildly because of panic late in a test. You take a real risk of ruining correct answers.*

ON AN ORAL TEST:

1. **Be yourself.** Your examiners realize that the situation puts you under a strain, and will make allowances for that.

2. **Before attempting an answer, try to establish in your mind the exact direction you want your response to take.** You may be asked for definitions that can be given in one sentence.

   More likely, your questions will demand answers that resemble brief or even full-length essays. Be guided by the key words in the questions, and then come quickly to the point in the first sentence of your answer. *If you find that you have gone part of the way through a discussion and realize that you are on the wrong track, do not hesitate to ask for permission to start again.* If your second answer is correct, you will not lose credit for the false start.

3. **Observe the standards of good speech.** The language of your spoken answers will count as heavily as that of your written answers on an essay test.

4. **Think.** The emphasis in most oral examinations is on finding out how clearly you think. Try to reason carefully. A foolish stab at an answer is not what the examiners are after.

BREAKS *before exams help relieve tension and get you ready to do your best work. Once an exam begins, focus on the task at hand.*

MAJOR STANDARDIZED EXAMINATIONS

In many countries around the world, tests are used as the chief means of determining who can be considered for admission to certain types of schools. In Japan or the United Kingdom, for example, the scores on such tests often permanently determine the social and financial position of a person. Consequently, in those countries, much of education is directed toward passing such tests.

The United States does not have a rigid system of national tests. Instead, several tests sponsored by nonprofit boards are widely used for specific purposes. The nonprofit testing agencies that develop the tests are for the most part the creation of associations of colleges and universities, school systems, and educational associations. These boards and agencies are the American Council on Education, the College Entrance Examination Board, the American College Testing Program, and Educational Testing Service. They are

If you are planning to apply to a college or university, find out which tests you must take and what your scores will be used for. Different schools have different rules.

not specifically set up by or sanctioned by the federal government. With the exception of the Tests of General Educational Development (GED—discussed later), there is no such thing as a passing score on these tests, in sharp contrast with national testing programs abroad. Furthermore, except for the GED, a high score does not ensure acceptance at a particular school. At the same time, a low score does not always result in rejection.

Despite the apparent looseness of the American system, many students work hard to obtain high scores on such tests. These scores are often combined with school grades, personal inter-

views, essays, and recommendations from teachers to determine whether a college or university will admit a student; to select the courses in which a student will be placed; or to grant college course credit for courses not taken at the college level. Some colleges and universities require that students take specific tests; others accept and use the results of various examinations selected by the student who is applying to the school; and a few schools pay no attention to some tests while accepting others.

While the standard tests differ in many ways, for the most part they have several common characteristics.

The largest part of each test consists of a number of questions or problems, which test makers call *items*. Most items are designed so that there are four or five different possible responses. Such responses are called *foils*. One and only one foil is the correct choice, while the other foils are *distracters*. An item with these characteristics is a *multiple-choice item*, although some specific kinds of multiple-choice items go by other names as well.

The main reason for the popularity of multiple-choice items is that they are easy to grade, or *score*. Most tests use a separate score sheet to record the correct choice. Machines have been developed that can identify the position of pencil marks on such score sheets. Since machine scoring is faster and more accurate than hand scoring, it is the method of choice. Sometimes, however, parts of tests, such as essay questions, must be scored by experienced teachers trained to use scoring guidelines provided by the test maker.

Nearly all items are *pretested;* that is, the items are administered as a test to groups of students similar to the students who will take the actual test. Although all items are prepared by curriculum and testing specialists, the pretest is needed to eliminate ambiguous items and to make sure that there is a suitable range of items from easy to difficult. Pretest results are often used to arrange items so that easier ones are placed near the beginning of the test.

The following sections provide detailed descriptions of important individual tests, tips on how to take the tests, and items similar to those that appear on the actual tests. Each sample item is accompanied by a brief discussion of how to select the correct choice.

GOVERNMENT-SPONSORED NATIONAL TESTS *are not used in the United States, but many tests developed by independent organizations are used nationally for specific purposes.*

USING THE ANSWER SHEET

The typical answer sheet for a standardized test, with several different sections and lots of little circles to fill in, can sometimes seem a little daunting. However, there are really only two main sections to an answer sheet. One is reserved for personal information and the other for answers to questions.

Your Name:
(Print)   Last   First   Middle
Signature: Date: /   /
Home Address:
(Print)   Number and Street
   City   State   Zip Code

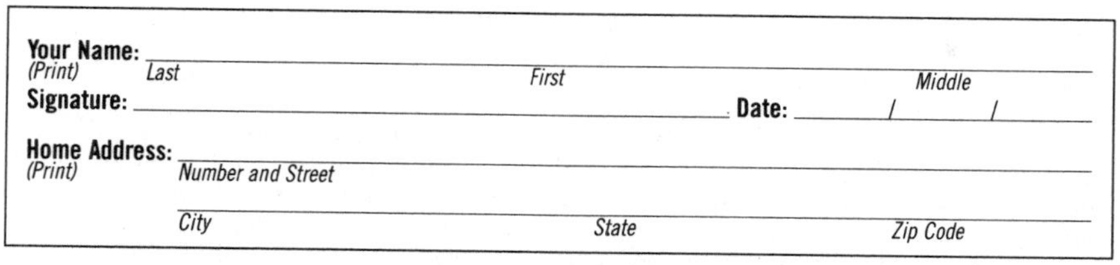

You will be asked to print certain information on the form, usually your full name and address, Social Security number, and date of birth. Some of the spaces provided ask you to spell out the information by filling in the corresponding circles. For instance, if your birthday is April 8, 1974, you must fill in the circle next to "Apr.," next to "0" and "8" for the day, and next to "7" and "4" for the year.

First 5 letters of Last Name	Date of Birth (Month, Day, Year)	Social Security Number or ID Number

Sex: ○ Female ○ Male

Test Code   **Registration Number**

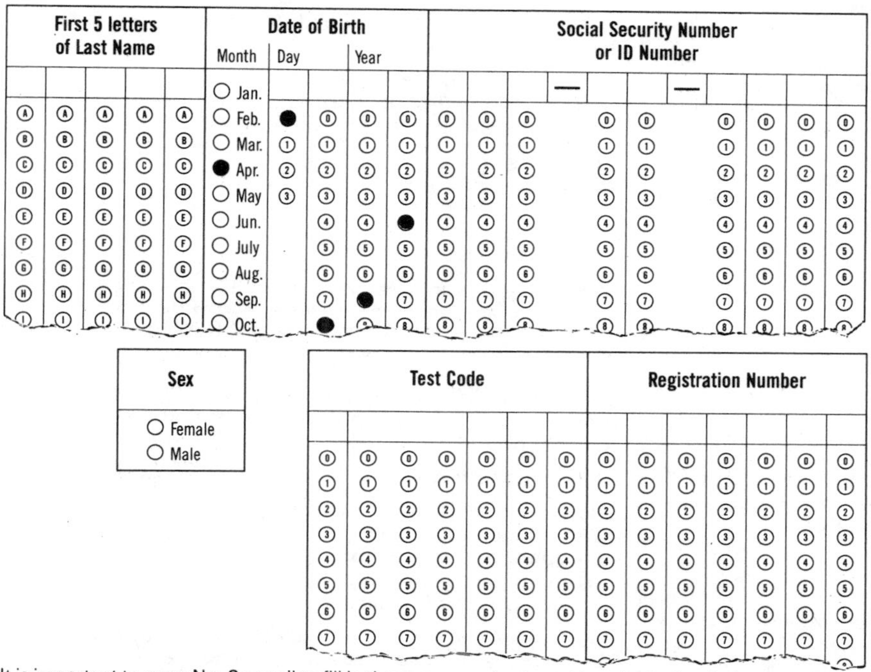

It is important to use a No. 2 pencil to fill in these answer sheets and to color in the circles completely. The answer sheets are scored by computer scanners; if you do not use a No. 2 pencil, or if a circle is only partially filled, the computer may misread the answer and score it incorrectly.

In the part of the form where you answer test questions, you will find circles with letters in them that correspond to answer choices in your test booklet. Some tests letter their answers A through E on each question, others use A through E and F through J on alternate questions. Always check the problem number against the test booklet; it is easy to put the answer in the wrong space.

Part 1 (questions 1–45, answer bubbles A B C D E / F G H I J)

Part 2 (questions 1–45, answer bubbles A B C D / F G H I)

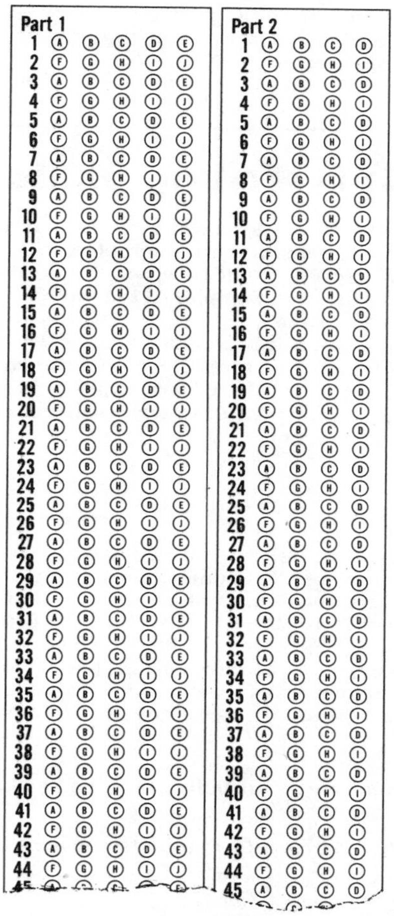

The GED

The Tests of General Educational Development, known familiarly as the GED, are also called the high-school equivalency test. Anyone who is not a high-school student or graduate can take the GED if he or she meets certain simple requirements of states, territories, or provinces for age, time out of school, and resident status. All U.S. states, the District of Columbia, Puerto Rico, eight U.S. territories or possessions, and provinces and territories of Canada, except Quebec and Ontario, accept the GED. There are slight differences from place to place on what is considered a passing score.

A person who passes the test receives an official document that is equivalent to a high-school diploma. Colleges and businesses accept a passing score on the GED as the equivalent of a high-school diploma. Passing the GED is often vital in obtaining a job or being considered for promotion.

A person who has not attended or completed high school still has many opportunities to learn the basic skills in a variety of ways. Reading books, magazines, or newspapers regularly, watching the news or educational programs on television, developing skills in mathematics on the job, conversing with friends and relatives, and many other activities can provide an educational background similar to that obtained in high school. The main purposes of the GED, successfully accomplished since 1942, are to prove that individuals learn from the experiences of everyday life and to reward those who have done so. Millions of people have received equivalency certificates. Nearly three-quarters of a million people take the test in any year. About 400,000 each year earn their equivalency certificates.

The skills tested on the GED are the ones that most people recognize as basic: reading, writing, mathematics, science, and social studies. There are multiple-choice items on interpreting popular and classical literature as well as the other arts; sentence structure, word usage, spelling, punctuation, and capitalization; arithmetic, algebra, and geometry; life and physical sciences; and history, economics, political science, geography, human behavior and social interaction. Additionally, each person taking the test must write about a topic that most people would be expected to know something about (the *essay* section).

More of the test is devoted to frequently used skills than to higher-level skills; for example, half of the mathematics test is devoted to arithmetic, and half of the literature and arts test concerns popular literature. Items are designed to test important ideas and thinking skills, not to search out obscure facts.

States and Canadian provinces differ on how the test is to be taken. The entire group of individual tests, called the *battery,* takes a full day to complete, with 7 hours 35 minutes allowed for actual test taking; but many of the over

3000 GED test centers allow persons to take parts of the test on separate days.

Further information about the GED and the locations of test centers can be obtained from any one of many different sources: the guidance department in a local high school or the school district office; adult education centers; state or provincial education departments or ministries; or

The GED Testing Service
American Council on Education
One Dupont Circle N.W.
Washington, DC 20036
Telephone: (202)939-9490

GED Writing Skills Test

The writing skills test is in two parts, a set of 55 multiple-choice items you must complete in 75 minutes, and an essay on a specific topic of general interest you are given 45 minutes to write. Samples of the mutiple-choice items are given on this page.

The multiple-choice items deal with common errors in sentence structure, usage, and punctuation. The errors are included in short paragraphs with numbered sentences. Some sentences are correct as written, but most contain a single error.

Directions: Choose the one best answer to each item.

(1) Virtually everyone have a favorite way to read a newspaper. (2) Some people prefer to read the first few pages and skimming the rest of the paper. (3) Others begin with the sports section. (4) After finding out the latest happenings in the world of sports. (5) They turn to the rest of the news or to a feature section. (6) Whichever way one reads a newspaper, they are our most popular daily source of news and entertainment.

Sentence 1: Virtually everyone have a favorite way to read a newspaper.

What correction should be made in this sentence?

(1) replace everyone with everybody
(2) change have to has
(3) change a favorite to their favorite
(4) change newspaper to Newspaper
(5) no correction is necessary

Choice (2) is correct. The pronoun everyone is singular and therefore takes the singular verb has. The pronoun their (choice 3) suggests that everyone is plural. Everyone and everybody (choice 1) have the same meaning. The word newspaper (choice 4) is a common noun and should begin with a small (lower-case) letter.

Sentence 2: Some people prefer to read the first few pages and skimming the rest of the paper.

What correction should be made in this sentence?

(1) change prefer to preferred
(2) insert a comma after read
(3) change skimming to skim
(4) change some to most
(5) no correction is necessary

Similar ideas should be expressed in similar form within a sentence. Thus, "people prefer to read the first few pages and skim" (choice 3) is correct. Notice that the sentence could also have been written correctly as "Some people prefer reading the first few pages and then skimming the rest," but that was not one of the choices given.

Sentences 4 and 5: After finding out the latest happenings in the world of sports. They turn to the rest of the news or to a feature section.

Which of the following is the best way to write the underlined portion of these sentences? If you think the original is the best way, choose option (1).

(1) sports. They
(2) sports and they
(3) sports. they
(4) sports; they
(5) sports, they

Choice (5) is correct. Sentence 4 is incomplete. By combining it with sentence 5, you have one complete sentence. It consists of two clauses, which must be separated by a comma. Choice (4) is incorrect because the first clause is a dependent clause and so cannot be followed by a semicolon.

Sentence 6: Whichever way one reads a newspaper, they are our most popular daily source of news and entertainment.

What correction should be made in this sentence?

(1) change whichever to which
(2) change one to you
(3) change source to sources
(4) change they are to it is
(5) no correction is necessary

The pronoun they is plural. Its antecedent is singular, newspaper. Therefore, the pronoun must also be singular—it, not they—and we would write it is rather than they are (choice 4). Choice 2 is wrong: It would read you reads.

(1) When writing a letter of complaint, remember that a direct and courteous letter will most likely receive prompt attention. (2) State your specific problem. (3) And suggest how you would like to see it rectified.

(4) Your letter shouldn't imply that a company has deliberately tried to cheat you. (5) A fine company will often honor reasonable letters of complaint.

Sentences 2 and 3: State your specific problem. And suggest how you would like to see it rectified.

Which of the following is the best way to write the underlined portion of these two sentences?

(1) problem. And suggest
(2) problem or suggest
(3) problem and suggest
(4) problem; and suggest
(5) problem suggest

Choice (3) is correct. It uses and to connect independent clauses having the same subject, you (understood). Most teachers will not accept a sentence beginning with And (choice 1). Choice (2) changes the meaning. Choice (4) uses a semicolon followed by and, which is avoided in punctuating short independent clauses. Choice (5) leads to a run-on sentence.

Sentence 4: Your letter shouldn't imply that a company has deliberately tried to cheat you.

What correction should be made in this sentence?

(1) change <u>has</u> to <u>have</u>
(2) change <u>Your</u> to <u>One's</u>
(3) change <u>should'nt</u> to <u>shouldn't</u>
(4) change <u>you.</u> to <u>you!</u>
(5) no correction is necessary

Choice (3) is correct. In a contraction, an apostrophe is used in place of a missing letter. In <u>shouldn't</u> the apostrophe replaces the missing <u>o</u> in <u>not</u>. Choice (1) uses a plural verb, <u>have</u>, with a singular noun, <u>company</u>. Choice (2) mistakenly mixes the pronoun <u>one</u> with the pronoun <u>you</u> at the end of the sentence. Choice (4) adds an unnecessary exclamation point and does not correct the misspelling of <u>should'nt</u>.

Sentence 5: A fine company will often honor reasonable letters of complaint.

If you rewrote sentence 5 to make it begin with <u>Reasonable letters of complaint</u>, the next words should be

(1) are often honored
(2) is often honored
(3) were often honored
(4) often become honored
(5) gets honored often

Choice (1) is correct. The plural verb <u>are</u> agrees with the plural subject <u>letters</u>. In choices (2) and (5), the verbs <u>are</u> singular. Choice (3) uses a past verb in a paragraph that is in the present tense. Choice (4) is incorrect because <u>become honored</u> is an awkward expression in this sentence.

GED Social Studies

<u>Directions:</u> Choose the <u>one best answer</u> to each item.

The following questions are based on the map of the United States and on the reading selections that follow.

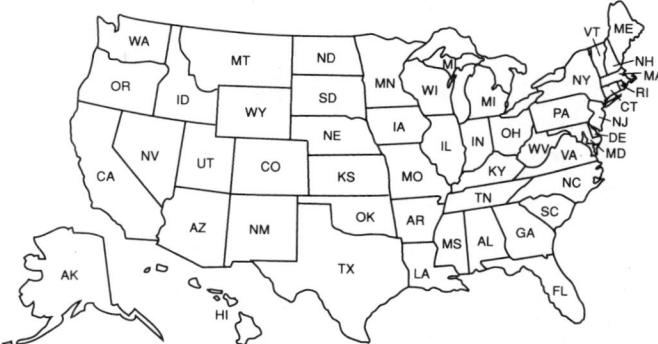

States had become a principal form of government in the United States even before it gained its independence from England. How to preserve the power of the states and yet develop a single new country was one of the main issues that confronted the new country in writing its constitution. A compromise was finally reached by the writers of the U.S. Constitution by basing the number of representatives in the House on population while keeping the number of senators at two for each state. In addition, at first the senators were to be elected by state legislatures.

As the nation grew, so did the number of states. Sometimes, new states were carved from the original 13 states, as in 1820 when Maine voted to separate from Massachusetts. Just as today there are two nations of North Korea and South Korea as a result of World War II, we have the two states of Virginia and West Virginia as a result of the American Civil War, also called the War Between the States. The states had to decide whether to stay within the Union or to leave. For states in the Deep South or the Northeast, the choice was easy. Border states, from Maryland through Virginia, Kentucky, Tennessee, and Missouri, found themselves caught in the middle.

Which one of the following states was not one of the original 13 states?

(1) Georgia
(2) Virginia
(3) Maine
(4) Rhode Island
(5) Delaware

Choices (1), (2), (4), and (5)—Georgia, Virginia, Rhode Island, and Delaware—were among the 13 British colonies that became states. Maine was not a separate colony but was part of the Massachusetts Bay Colony and did not become a state in its own right until 1820. The correct answer is choice (3).

Of the 50 states, California has the largest population, with over 23 million people. Alaska has the smallest population, with just a little over 400,000 people.

In which part of the United States government do both California and Alaska have the same number of elected representatives?

(1) their state legislatures
(2) the United Nations
(3) the U.S. Senate
(4) the U.S. House of Representatives
(5) the U.S. Department of Agriculture

The key to this question is "the United States government." This eliminates choices (1) and (2). State legislatures and the United Nations are not part of the government of the United States. California has more representatives there than does Alaska, so choice (4) is wrong. The Department of Agriculture has no elected representatives, so choice (5) is wrong. The correct choice is (3). Under the U.S. Constitution, each state has equal representation in the Senate, regardless of population.

After the end of the Second World War, three countries were divided into Communist and non-Communist parts. Which country is still divided today?

(1) Germany
(2) Korea
(3) Poland
(4) Vietnam
(5) Switzerland

Choices (3) and (5) can be eliminated at once. Poland and Switzerland were not divided. Vietnam, choice (4), was reunited as a Communist state after the United States withdrew from it in 1975. Germany, choice (1), formerly divided into West Germany and East Germany, was reunited as a capitalist state in 1990, when the occupying countries agreed to leave Germany. The correct choice is (2), since only Korea has yet to reunite its two parts, South Korea and North Korea.

Which so-called Southern border states remained with the Union during the Civil War?

(1) Tennessee and Kentucky
(2) Virginia and North Carolina
(3) Alabama and Mississippi
(4) Pennsylvania and Ohio
(5) Florida and Georgia

The border, of course, is that between the North and the South, and two important clues to this question are the words "Southern" and "border." In choices (2), (3), and (5), one or both of the states are Southern but they do not touch the border between Northern and Southern states. Choice (4) is wrong because Pennsylvania and Ohio are Northern states. The correct choice is (1). Your map shows that Kentucky borders on Illinois, Indiana, and Ohio. It also shows that Tennessee borders on Missouri.

Easier multiple-choice items are often scattered through the test. You can go through the test more than once, marking items to come back to in the test booklet.

Directions: Read the following passage and answer the question that appears after it.

In most of tropical South America, rain forests are being cleared for the creation of new crop and grazing land that yield food for a growing population. Many people criticize policies that let this happen. Rain forests absorb carbon dioxide that could contribute to global warming, and they produce oxygen that almost all animals require. Rain forests contain a host of species found nowhere else on Earth, as well as some of the last people living as they did in the Stone Age. Finally, conversion of rain forests to agriculture fosters the loss of soil, either to the forces of erosion or to a form of hardening that endangers tropical soils.

Each of the answers below is an unhappy result of the destruction of South America's tropical rain forests EXCEPT:

(1) loss of oxygen-producing plants
(2) loss of potentially valuable animal and plant species
(3) creation of new crop and grazing land
(4) soil erosion
(5) displacement of people living there

This question demands careful reading. The key word is EXCEPT, which asks you to find the answer that is not unhappy, that is, not always the same as happy. Choices (1), (2), (4), and (5) are unhappy results of deforestation. The correct answer, choice (3), may or may not be a happy result. While it has dangerous effects on soil, it feeds populations—at least for a while.

GED Interpreting Literature and the Arts

This section of the GED asks questions about the kinds of things a person reads, so it might be called a reading comprehension test. In a real GED test, each sample of writing, called a *passage,* is followed by more than one question. Here, to give you experience with the different types of passages used, each passage is followed by a single question.

SITEMAN/STOCK, BOSTON

GRANT/PHOTO RESEARCHERS

VISUALLY IMPAIRED STUDENTS *can take the high school equivalency test using the same means by which they normally study. Both audiotape and Braille versions are available.*

As a method of preserving food, canning is both simple and inexpensive. There is little danger as long as canners follow basic guidelines. For example, they should use glass jars with specially prepared lids. The jars must have no cracks or chips. Both jars and lids must be clean when the food is placed in the jars and covered. In the easiest canning method, the filled jars are boiled for at least 15 minutes to sterilize the contents. As the jars cool, a vacuum seal forms.

The danger in home canning probably occurs when

(1) food is not properly sterilized
(2) glass jars are used
(3) a vacuum seal forms
(4) filled jars are boiled for 15 minutes or more
(5) jars and lids are clean

This question asks about information that is not directly given in the passage. The first step is to find the key word danger in the passage. It appears in the second sentence. Then the passage goes on to describe how to can food safely. You can rule out choices (2), (3), (4), and (5) because these choices list parts of the safe canning process. Only choice (1) refers to something that could be unsafe.

> Fog creeps,
> Slow, soundless.
> It oozes, it seeps
> Along river beds
> And road beds.
> Like a dream,
> Fog drifts into sleep.

In this poem, fog is compared to

(1) a river bed
(2) a road bed
(3) a dream
(4) sleep
(5) all of these

In a comparison, two things are said to be alike. In this poem, the word like is actually used in the sixth line, so choice (3) is correct. If like is not used, look for other clues. For example, the poem might have said "As quiet as a dream / Fog drifts into sleep," or "Fog is a dream / That drifts into sleep." In both cases, fog is still being compared to a dream.

People have always made up the words of every language ever spoken. While no one knows exactly who made up all the words that have existed at one time or another, we usually know who created the words introduced in the recent past. Some of these words come from older words or from people's names. For example, telephone is Greek for "far sound" and poinsettia comes from the name of the U.S. minister to Mexico, James R. Poinsett, who introduced the flower to the United States. The best recent words work with no definition. In one of James Thurber's books, for example, a character announces that he will slit you from your "guggle to your zatch." While it is not clear exactly where either the guggle or zatch is, one gets the point. Dr. Seuss has added grinch to our vocabulary.

This passage implies that people make up new words

(1) because they are tired of the old words
(2) because new words express ideas more clearly than old words
(3) because new words can be more fun than old words
(4) by accident while they are trying to say something else
(5) as a way of keeping the meaning secret

Although the passage mentions a word created to describe a new device, the telephone, and one that named a flower for which there was no English name previously, poinsettia, the main focus is on words that people made up to be amusing. Thus, the correct choice is (3), "because new words can be more fun than old words." Choice (2) would suggest that the new words are clearer than the old ones, but the passage suggests that it is not clear what such words as guggle and zatch mean. Choice (5) suggests that new words are used as a sort of a code, which can be true, but is not true of the words cited in the passage. Neither Choice (1) nor choice (4) is suggested by anything in the passage.

Here it is . . .
. . . the all-new COOKIE SENSATIONS!
Sweet, crunchy, satisfying—
Everything you've always wanted in a cookie,
(5)   and more . . .
. . . they're HEALTHY, too.
No cholesterol!
Lower fat content than similar cookies!
Only natural fruit sweeteners used! *
(10) Delicious crunchy texture comes from nuts,
wheat germ, and rolled oats.
Be the first to try COOKIE SENSATIONS!
*(other sweeteners used in chocolate chips
and other added flavors)

For sweeteners, COOKIE SENSATIONS uses

(1) only natural sweeteners
(2) only chocolate chips
(3) only those in added flavors
(4) all of these
(5) nothing at all

This question asks for a specific detail, so you should look for information about just that detail. In this case, the information can be found in two places in the advertisement. Choices (1), (2), and (3) are all included as sweeteners, so choice (4) is the best answer.

GED Science

<u>Directions:</u> Choose the <u>one best answer</u> to each item. The items below refer to the following article.

If you were to travel to Colorado, you might visit Cliff Palace, a natural shelf carved into a high sandstone cliff. This rocky ledge was the home of Native American Pueblos hundreds of years ago. Sandstone, a sedimentary rock made mostly of the mineral quartz, varies in color from golden yellow to red to brown. Impurities or other minerals give the sandstone its color. Unlike igneous rock, such as granite, sedimentary rock forms in layers. When sedimentary rock wears away, or erodes, it splits along these layers. Because of the way sandstone erodes, the Pueblos were able to use loose pieces of sandstone as blocks to make walls within the rocky ledge, forming many rooms that can still be seen today.

The golden yellow color of Cliff Palace shows that it is made of what type of rock?

(1) granite
(2) quartz
(3) sandstone
(4) sedimentary
(5) igneous

Choice (3) is correct. The first sentence states that Cliff Palace is made of sandstone. Choice (2) is incorrect because, although sandstone is mostly quartz, quartz is a mineral and not a rock. Although sandstone is a sedimentary rock, choice (4) is incorrect because the question specifies the golden yellow color of the rock. Choice (5) is incorrect, since the only mention of igneous rock in the passage comes in classifying granite as igneous.

The property of sandstone that enabled the Pueblos to make use of it for shelter is that sandstone

(1) forms and erodes in layers.
(2) is made of quartz, which has many other uses.
(3) has many impurities.
(4) can be yellow, red, or brown.
(5) is less likely to erode than granite.

Choice (1) is correct. The eroding sandstone formed the blocks used to build Cliff Palace. Although quartz might have had other uses, choice (2) does not explain that it helped the Pueblos build the dwelling. Choices (3) and (4) are true, but they have nothing to do with the question. Choice (5) is incorrect. Sandstone is more likely to erode than granite.

What is the principal difference between sandstone and granite?

(1) Both contain quartz.
(2) Sandstone is a sedimentary rock, and granite is an igneous rock.
(3) Both rocks are found in Cliff Palace.
(4) Sandstone and granite both form in layers.
(5) Sandstone and granite have a variety of colors.

Choice (2) is correct. The passage clearly makes this distinction between the two types of rock. Although both contain quartz (choice 1), and may vary in color (choice 5), these are similarities, not differences. Choice (3) is incorrect. It is not mentioned that granite is found in Cliff Palace. Even if it were found there, this answer would not answer the question. Choice (4) also is not correct as a statement and does not establish a difference between the rocks.

GED Mathematics

Unlike other tests in the GED battery, the mathematics test does not require the student to read paragraphs. Instead, short word problems are given that focus on practical situations and require simple algebra or basic geometry to find the solutions. Formulas you need are given to you. Here are the formulas that you will need for the items below.

AREA (A) of a rectangle $A = lw$; where l = length,
                                                w = width

simple interest (i) $i = prt$; where p = principal,
                                                r = rate,
                                                t = time

In some actual GED test questions, you are given too little information. If there is too little information to solve the problem, the correct choice is "Not enough information given." No questions of this type are included with the following samples. Some questions in the sample may give you too much information, and your job will be to deal only with the information you actually need. GED testing centers do not allow candidates to use calculators during a test.

<u>Directions:</u> Choose the <u>one best answer</u> for each problem.

Last year, the Watsons paid $600 a month in rent. This year, they will pay $640 a month. By what percent did their rent increase?

(1) $6\frac{2}{3}$
(2) 14
(3) 40
(4) $93\frac{3}{4}$
(5) 140

To find a percent of increase, find the amount of increase. Then write a fraction for the amount of increase over the original amount.

$$\begin{array}{r} \$640 \\ -600 \\ \hline 40 \end{array}$$ Fraction of increase: $40/600$

Change the fraction to a decimal and then to a percent. Express the remainder of the decimal beyond the hundredths place as a fraction.

$$600\overline{)\begin{array}{l} 0.06\,4/6 = 6\frac{2}{3}\% \quad \text{The correct choice is (1).} \\ 40.00 \\ 36.00 \\ \hline 4.00 \end{array}}$$

Ron made and sold salad dressing at a county fair. He spent $55 on ingredients and $33 on bottles. He sold 50 bottles of Special Hot Dressing at $3 a bottle and 60 bottles of Super Cool Dressing for $2 a bottle. What was his profit?

(1) $88
(2) $182
(3) $215
(4) $270
(5) $358

To find the amount of profit, subtract expenses from total income. To find Ron's income, multiply $3 × 50 and $2 × 60 and add the results.

$3 × 50 = $150
$2 × 60 = 120
         $270 Total Income

Ron's expenses were the cost of ingredients and bottles.

$55 + $33 = $88 Total Expenses
$270 − $88 = $182 Profit The correct choice is (2).

Find the amount of simple interest on a loan of $4000 at 11% annual interest for 6 months.

(1) $110
(2) $220
(3) $440
(4) $446
(5) $2640

Simple interest is found by the formula $i = p \times r \times t$, where p is the principal, r is the rate, and t is the time in years. In this problem, the principal is $4000, the rate is 0.11, and the time is $6/12$ or $1/2$.

$$i = 4000 \times 0.11 \times 1/2.$$
$$= 440 \times 1/2$$
$$= \$220 \qquad \text{The correct choice is (2).}$$

The square root of 39 is between which of the following pairs or numbers?

(1) 3.9 and 4.9
(2) 4 and 5
(3) 5 and 6
(4) 6 and 7
(5) 38 and 40

One way to solve this is to square some of the numbers. 3.9 and 4.9 are close to 4 and 5, but harder to square, so start with 4 and 5.

$$4^2 = 16 \qquad\qquad 5^2 = 25$$

Both of these squares are less than 39, so the square root has to be greater than 5. The largest number among the choices that is easy to square is 7.

$$7^2 = 49$$

Since 49 is greater than 39, $\sqrt{39}$ must be less than 7. Try 6.

$$6^2 = 36$$

Because 39 is between $6^2 = 36$ and $7^2 = 49$, $\sqrt{39}$ must be between 6 and 7. The correct choice is (4).

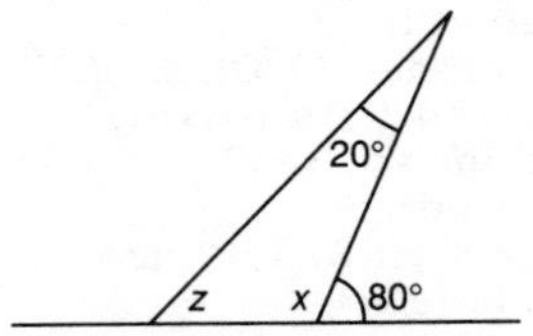

In the triangle above, what is the measure of z?

(1) 20°
(2) 30°
(3) 40°
(4) 50°
(5) 60°

The angle outside this triangle is supplementary to the angle labeled x. So $x = 180° − 80° = 100°$. The sum of the angles in a triangle is always 180°. The sum of two of the angles of the triangle is $100° + 20° = 120°$. Therefore, $z = 180° − 120° = 60°$. The correct choice is (5).

A room is 15 feet wide, 24 feet long, and 9 feet high. How many square yards of carpeting are needed to cover the floor?

(1) 40
(2) 45
(3) 120
(4) 360
(5) 1080

This problem has more information than you need. You do not need to know how high the room is in order to find the area of the floor. The area of the floor is found by multiplying length × width.

$$A = 15 \times 24$$
$$= 360 \text{ square feet}$$

The unit is important. The problem asks for the area in square yards. There are 3 feet in one yard, so there are 9 square feet in one square yard.

$$360 ÷ 9 = 40 \text{ The correct choice is (1).}$$

If $x + 3y = 20$ and $x = 2y$, then $x =$

(1) 2
(2) 3
(3) 4
(4) 8
(5) 10

Substitute for x in the first equation so that you can find the value of y. Then use the value of y to find x.

$$x + 3y = 20$$
$$2y + 3y = 20$$
$$5y = 20$$
$$y = 4$$
$$x = 2y$$
$$x = 2(4) = 8$$

The correct choice is (4).

Scholastic Aptitude Tests (SATs)

The Scholastic Aptitude Tests (SATs) of the College Board, prepared by Educational Testing Service, are well known. Average scores on these tests, or on sections of the tests, are widely viewed as indicative of the quality of education and of the student. This is because great numbers of high school juniors and seniors take the tests each year, and many of the best colleges require students to take the SATs before they will be considered for admission.

The basic idea of the SAT is that by measuring certain verbal and mathe-matical skills, one can predict how well most students will do in college. It is clear that skills not tested by the SAT, such as creativity and hard work, are also factors in college success, but the verbal and mathematical skills are thought to be a testable foundation for other skills.

Preparation for the test. An ideal aptitude test would measure what students are capable of accomplishing, not what they have learned. The SAT tries to do this, but most people—including the people who administer the SAT—agree that it has not completely achieved this goal. Since the SAT does not measure inborn capacities, it is possible to improve scores on the SAT by preparing for the test. Certainly, study of vocabulary and practice with mathematical reasoning have been shown to help. Also, everyone agrees that familiarity with the kinds of questions asked on the SAT improves scores. There remains considerable disagreement between the test developers and those who help students prepare for the tests about how much SAT scores can be improved for individual students.

Educational Testing Service, which prepares the SAT, thinks that practice with sample tests should be enough to prepare students for the test. They recommend that you briefly review a sample test for an hour or so, get the materials together that you will need for taking the test (see below), relax, and get a good night's sleep. However, many students go through weeks or months of special training in how to handle the kinds of items that appear on the SAT. Educational Testing Service studies show that such courses on the average raise scores only 10 to 25 points per section, which is not much out of 800 possible points per section.

Thus, sample items and sample test directions such as those that follow can be used to develop the familiarity that Educational Testing Service believes is the basic preparation for the test. Most teachers would also recommend regular vocabulary practice for several months preceding the verbal test. Courses in high school algebra and geometry help prepare for the mathematics sections. Educational Testing Service recommends that students who plan to take the test read widely and take rich and demanding academic courses. These actions will certainly help most students not only to increase scores on the test, but also to succeed in college once they get there.

Nature of the test. The verbal and mathematical tests are both scored separately.

The verbal section consists of four types of multiple-choice items:
1. Twenty-five items in which the student is given a test word and five choices of other words, one of which has the *opposite meaning* of the test word.
2. Twenty items in which the student is presented with a pair of words and five choices of other pairs. In one of the choices, the two words have the *same relationship* to each other as do the given pair.
3. Fifteen items in which the student is given a sentence with two words missing and five choices of pairs of words that could be inserted. The correct choice will produce a sentence that makes good sense.
4. Twenty-five items based on reading several paragraphs (a *passage*) from literature, science, social studies, or other subjects. The items are intended to determine how well the test taker understands the passage.

Each item is either a question with five choices for the answer, or the first part of a sentence with five choices of ways to complete the sentence.

In addition to the regular verbal section, the SATs contain an additional

Test of Standard Written English (TSWE). The TSWE has an entirely different purpose from that of the SAT. Schools use the TSWE to place students they accept in the correct freshman English class. Essentially, there are two types of items in the TSWE:

1. Twenty-five items in which the student is given a sentence with four parts underlined and an underlined statement that says "No error." The requirement is to identify the underlined part of the sentence that contains an error, or to indicate that there is no error in the sentence.

2. Twenty-five items in which the student is given a sentence with one part underlined, followed by five choices of replacements for the underlined part. The correct choice, which may be to replace the underlined part with exactly the same text, will produce a good sentence, while all the other four choices will have flaws.

In the mathematics section, there are two types of items, but the exact number of items of each type can vary. The total number of items is 60, and the total time allotted is one hour. The test is given in two half hour sections of 25 items and 35 items, because about half the items in the second set are of a type that is thought to be answered more quickly than standard multiple-choice items. Thus, there are about 41 to 43 standard multiple-choice items and 17 to 19 items of the special type, called quantitative comparison questions.

Quantitative comparison items are based on deciding whether one of two quantities is greater than, less than, or equal to the other quantity. In some cases there is not enough information to tell. Thus, these items, unlike all other SAT items, have only four choices, the fourth being "not enough information." The separate score sheet used with the SAT allows for five choices, labeled A, B, C, D, and E. If you mark the E choice for a quantitative comparison item, that item will not be scored; that is, it will neither be counted for you nor against you.

Although the actual test that will be scored contains two verbal sections, two mathematics sections, and the TSWE, the test that is taken contains six sections. The sixth section is used by the Educational Testing Service, but is not included in your score. Some of

the items in the sixth section are previously tested items that are used to ensure that the scores on this test will be comparable to scores on earlier tests. Other items are newly written and destined for use on future tests. This section, called the equating section, may be either verbal, mathematical, or TSWE.

The sections do not come in the same order from test to test. Since you cannot tell which is the equating section, you will need to answer all sections as if they were included in your score.

Tips for improving your scores. All items score the same amount, so you should answer the easy questions first. Where possible, the SAT helps you do this by starting sections with the easy questions. Thus, the easiest analogy items or quantitative comparison items, for example, are first. When items in the verbal section relate to a reading passage, it is not possible to arrange the items from easy to hard. In sections other than reading comprehension, if you find that the items are getting too difficult in one group, move on to the beginning of the next group.

Guessing is not a good idea, because small deductions are made for incorrect responses (except for the E response on quantitative comparison items). If you can eliminate one or two choices as definitely wrong, however, you will do better in guessing among the rest. In other words, you will score higher if you do not answer any item for which you have no clue, and you will most likely score higher if you guess when you think you know but are not sure or when you can surely eliminate some of the choices as definitely incorrect.

Make sure all your responses are marked on the separate answer sheet. Anything written on the test booklet itself will not be scored. This also means that you may use the test booklet as a scratch sheet, and you may mark those items you wish to return to later.

Further information about the SAT may be obtained from your high school guidance office, or from:
College Board ATP
CN 6200
Princeton, NJ 08541-6200

GET A GOOD NIGHT'S SLEEP *and eat a good meal before your test. It is important to be well rested and properly nourished.*

SAT Verbal Sections

Antonyms. Antonym items (opposites) are one of the four types of questions used in the verbal section. Although there are 25 items in all, they generally appear in groups of 10 or 15, which are then given in a single section of the test along with other verbal items. Thus, in the verbal part, there will be two *mixed* sections, which may include antonyms, analogies, sentence completion, and reading comprehension.

(A)

(B)

(C)

(D)

(E)

Sometimes it helps to visualize the antonym questions on the SAT. A barn is usually a large structure ("as big as a barn"). The opposite would be a small building, such as the dollhouse shown as choice B.

<u>Directions:</u> Each question below consists of a word in capital letters that is followed by five lettered words or phrases. Choose the word or phrase that is most nearly <u>opposite</u> in meaning to the word in capital letters. Since some of the questions require you to distinguish fine shades of meaning, consider all choices before deciding which one is best.

TACITURN: (A) rowdy   (B) outgoing   (C) aggressive   (D) belligerent   (E) loquacious

Taciturn is used to describe a person who is "habitually silent." An antonym for *taciturn* would be *talkative,* or a word that carries the same meaning. Choices (A), (B), (C), and (D) all suggest types of active behavior. Only *loquacious,* meaning "talkative," is a true antonym for *taciturn.* The correct choice is (E).

WAX: (A) subdue   (B) wane   (C) enhance   (D) eliminate   (E) vex

Although wax is a substance produced by bees or various substances like beeswax, the choices are all verbs, not nouns. Still, the verb *wax* that means "to treat or rub with wax" does not appear to work either. You must think of a totally different meaning for the verb *wax,* in this case, the verb that means "to grow in size or luminosity." This meaning is most familiar when it is applied to the moon, which <u>waxes</u> as it appears to grow larger and brighter. When it appears to diminish in size and brightness, the moon <u>wanes.</u> Thus the correct choice is (B).

POLYMORPHIC: (A) verbal   (B) careless   (C) uniform   (D) intelligent   (E) defined

Here the student with a sound understanding of prefixes and roots has a distinct advantage. Prefixes and roots clearly reveal the meaning of the vocabulary word and its antonym. *Polymorphic,* from *poly-* for "many" and *morph* for "shape" or "form," means "having many forms." The antonym is (C) *uniform,* from *uni-* for "one" and *form* for "shape" or "form." Knowing prefixes and roots often brings dividends. This time such knowledge is a bonanza.

SERPENTINE: (A) narrow   (B) subjective   (C) parochial   (D) straight   (E) apelike

Picture a serpent, or snake, to help you remember that *serpentine* means "winding" or "twisting." Choices (B) and (C) have little to do with the opposite of this meaning. Choice (E) is aimed at the student who looks for gimmicks—here, an animal name as part of the word. Choice (A) may look good at a glance, but something can surely be narrow and serpentine at the same time. Thus, there is only one antonym for *serpentine.* (D) is the correct choice.

ADJACENT: (A) remote   (B) triangular   (C) congruent   (D) sloping   (E) indistinguishable

If you vaguely remember that adjacent angles are studied in geometry, you may be attracted to choices (B), (C), or (D), since they are all terms used in that subject. If you remember just what adjacent angles are, however, you will recall that they are two angles that are next to each other in a specific way. The geometric meaning reflects the general meaning for *adjacent* of "near" or "close." Thus, the opposite is a word that means "far away." The correct choice is (A), *remote.*

INTERMITTENT: (A) rhapsodic   (B) constant   (C) relenting   (D) exasperating   (E) durable

Intermittent means "starting, stopping, and starting again," as in "intermittent rain showers." If you are familiar with prefixes, you can piece together a hint to the definition from *inter-* for "between." (The Latin root *mittere* means "send.") Choices (A) and (D) thus are clearly not antonyms for *intermittent.* Choice (C) refers to part of an intermittent occurrence. Choice (E) is tempting, but it suggests longevity rather than regularity. The best choice is (B).

PEDESTRIAN: (A) shameless (B) convincing (C) stimulating (D) active (E) driven

The common meaning of *pedestrian* is "one who walks." If choice (E) were *driver*, it might be thought of as a poor antonym for *pedestrian*. Look closely: All the choices are adjectives. Therefore, you must consider the less familiar adjective meaning of *pedestrian*: "ordinary" or "dull." Thus, the antonym for the adjective *pedestrian* is *stimulating*, choice (C).

IMPROMPTU: (A) rehearsed (B) thorough (C) whimsical (D) cautious (E) official

Impromptu means "made or done without preparation"; "done on the spur of the moment." Choice (C) is closer to being a synonym than an antonym. Choices (B), (D), and (E) all suggest deliberate actions, but choice (A) supplies the most precise antonym, since the word means "previously practiced."

LABYRINTHINE: (A) herculean (B) dangerous (C) uncomplicated (D) current (E) winding

You may recall that in Greek myth the Minotaur lived in a complex maze called the Labyrinth. Thus, *labyrinthine* means "complicated" or "intricate." Choices (B) and (D) can easily be rejected. Choice (E) is a word associated with a labyrinth—more nearly a synonym than an antonym. Choice (A) may snare the hasty reader who notices that it, like *labyrinthine*, is based on Greek myth. The correct antonym for *labyrinthine* is choice (C).

AFFLUENCE: (A) hardship (B) poverty (C) intolerance (D) strength (E) reluctance

The meaning of *affluence* is "wealth," which is unrelated to choices (C), (D), and (E). Choice (A), *hardship*, could easily be associated with a lack of wealth. *Poverty* is a better antonym for *affluence*, so the correct answer is choice (B).

AGORAPHOBIA: (A) hydrophobia (B) nyctophobia (C) acrophobia (D) claustrophobia (E) xenophobia

It is a good idea to learn the names of the various types of deep-seated fears, or phobias. They often appear in test items. *Agoraphobia* is "an abnormal fear of open places." Choices to eliminate include (A), which literally is "fear of water," a symptom of the disease rabies; (B), which means "fear of the dark"; (C), which means "fear of heights"; and (E), which means "fear of strangers." Choice (D), *claustrophobia*, or "fear of enclosed places," is the appropriate antonym for *agoraphobia*.

DISCRIMINATE: (A) compare (B) confuse (C) apply (D) abuse (E) accept

The verb *discriminate* is often used in a negative sense in connection with racial prejudice, but *discriminate* has a positive side as well. Essentially, *discriminate* means "to see differences; to be able to distinguish." Choice (C) is unrelated. Choice (A) has a meaning similar to that of *discriminate*. Choices (D) and (E) refer to the negative sense of *discriminate* in a manner of speaking, but not to the basic meaning of *discriminate*. Choice (B) is correct, because one who is unable to see differences will not be able to distinguish them.

LETHAL: (A) harmless (B) pleasant (C) urgently needed (D) comfortable (E) inviting

You probably have heard such expressions as "lethal weapon" and "lethal dose." *Lethal* means "deadly." Although choices (B), (D), and (E) do not suggest anything causing death, they are not the opposite of deadly. The correct choice is *harmless*, (A).

SYNTHETIC: (A) original (B) genuine (C) duplicate (D) causing pain (E) proper

Synthetic means the same as *artificial*, describing something produced by humans. The word *natural* comes to mind as the opposite, but *natural* is not among the choices. Because many things that are synthetic are viewed as imitations of natural substances, *synthetic* has acquired a secondary meaning of "fake." Looking for the opposite of "fake" among the choices leads to *genuine*, choice (B).

APPROPRIATE: (A) relinquish (B) punish (C) attract (D) seize (E) conquer

Although *appropriate* is most often used as an adjective meaning "suitable" or "proper," all the choices here are verbs. This should not cause trouble, since the verb *appropriate* means "take possession of." Choice (B) is not related to this meaning in any way. Choices (C), (D), and (E) are actions one might employ to take possession of something or someone. The correct choice is (A), *relinquish*, which means "surrender" and is the opposite of "take possession."

CHIDE: (a) endear (B) admonish (C) whisper (D) embrace (E) praise

To chide is "to scold" or "to express disapproval." Since *admonish* is a synonym for *chide*, you can immediately reject choice (B). Choice (C) seems possible, but one can scold in a whisper. While choices (A) and (D) suggest opposite feelings to the meaning of *chide*, their basic meaning is not opposite. Since when you praise someone, you express approval, which is the opposite of disapproval, the correct answer is *praise*, choice (E).

NOVICE: (A) veteran (B) candidate (C) leader (D) foreigner (E) teacher

A novice is a beginner at something. Therefore, someone who has been around for some time and has a lot of experience would be the opposite of a novice. That definition does not fit a candidate (choice B) or a foreigner (choice D). While it might be true of a leader or a teacher, (choices C and E), it is not necessarily true that either a leader or teacher has been leading or teaching for a long time. A veteran, however, is "a person of long experience," so the best choice is (A).

VANITY: (A) precision (B) ignorance (C) lack of desire (D) unselfishness (E) humility

Vanity means "excessive pride." The antonym for *vanity* would describe a person with little or no pride. Clearly, choices (A), (B), and (C) have nothing to do with this meaning, so the correct answer is either choice (D) or (E). Choice (D) is attractive, but a person can be unselfish and vain at the same time. A humble person cannot be proud, so the correct answer is *humility*, choice (E).

CONTEST: (A) consider (B) invoke (C) support (D) individualize (E) take issue

There are at least two meanings for *contest*. Put the accent on the first syllable, and you have a noun. Accent the second syllable, and *contest* is a verb. Since the choices are all verbs, the latter is intended. As a verb, *contest* means "dispute" or "challenge." Choice (E) is synonymous with this definition, so it is wrong. Although *consider*, *invoke*, and *individualize* all have positive senses, they do not guarantee the opposite of "dispute" or "challenge." Since *support* does make that guarantee, the correct choice is (C).

MEAN: (A) qualified (B) industrious (C) relevant (D) superior (E) aimless

Mean can be a noun, a verb, or an adjective, but since all the choices are adjectives, you can begin by considering *mean* as an adjective. Although most people today use *mean* as an adjective to describe someone who is cruel, *mean* also can be defined as "inferior" or "shabby." Since this is the opposite of *superior*, the antonym intended is choice (D).

INALIENABLE: (A) transferable (B) derivable (C) given by others (D) exploited (E) foreign

The word inalienable is most familiar from the U.S. Declaration of Independence, in which an archaic form, "certain unalienable Rights," is often misquoted as "certain inalienable rights." In either case, the prefix in- or un- warns that the opposite is alienable, but that word is not listed. The presence of the root alien suggests that foreign might be the correct choice, but "not foreign rights" does not make sense in the Declaration. Neither do choices (B) or (D). While Choice (C) makes sense by itself—"certain rights not given by others," the full passage refers to the rights having been given by the Creator, which results in a contradiction. The correct choice is (A). Inalienable rights are those that cannot be transferred to others.

Analogies. The second type of item used in the SAT verbal section is called an *analogy,* since it involves a correspondence in some respect between things that are not alike except for that respect. All SAT analogies are correspondences between word pairs. Analogies are more difficult than antonyms because in them you must first select the specific meanings of both words in the pair.

In the first example below, for instance, the pair is NYLON:FABRIC. *Nylon* can mean a fiber, a plastic, a kind of cloth made from the fiber, or a kind of stocking. *Fabric* also has multiple meanings, including "any material construction" and "cloth made by knitting, weaving, or felting." To determine which pair of meanings is the one intended, you begin by looking for pairs of meaning that show some relationship, such as "fiber":"cloth" or "kind of cloth":"kind of cloth." Then you need to look at the five choices in the same way to find the correct one.

LLOYD BIRMINGHAM

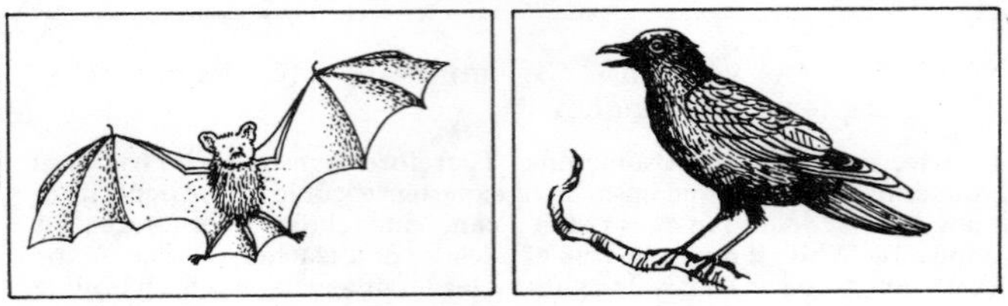

(A)

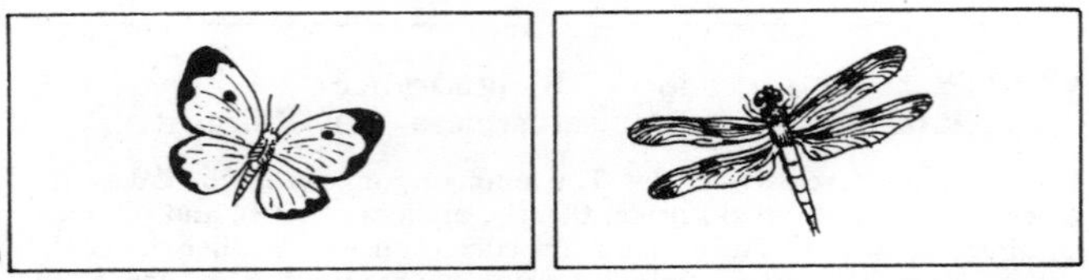

(B)

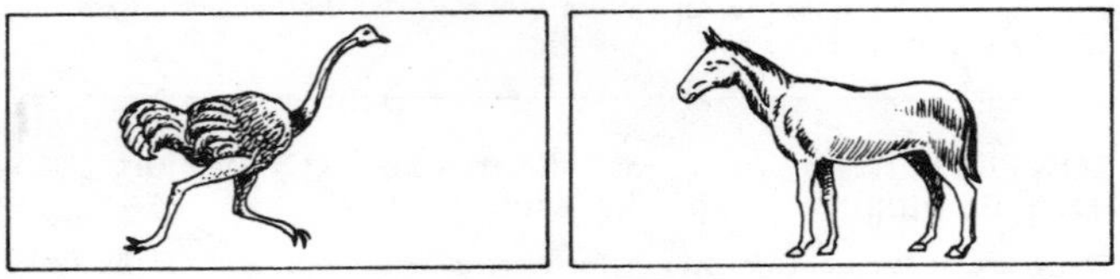

(C)

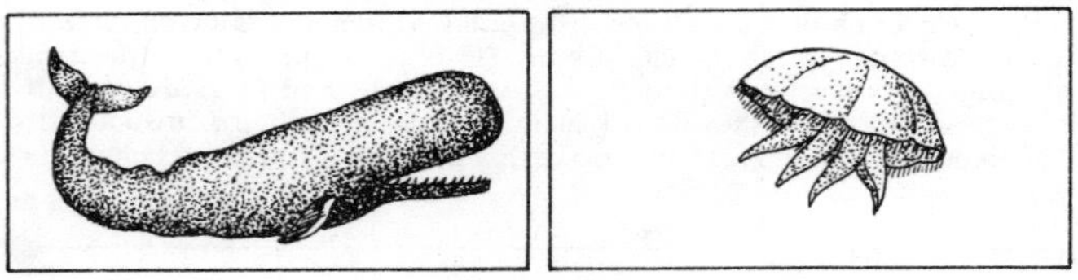

(D)

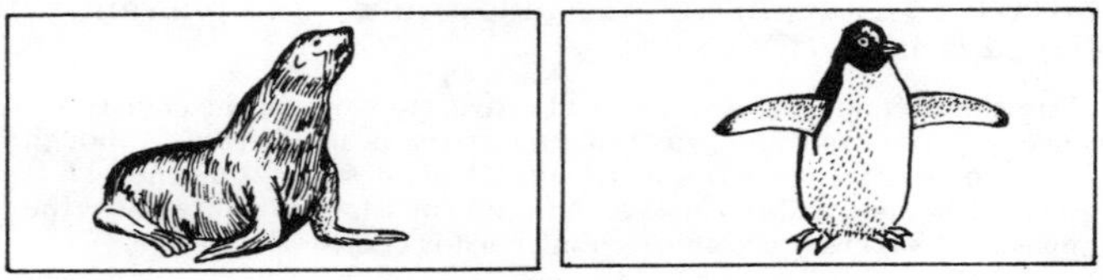

(E)

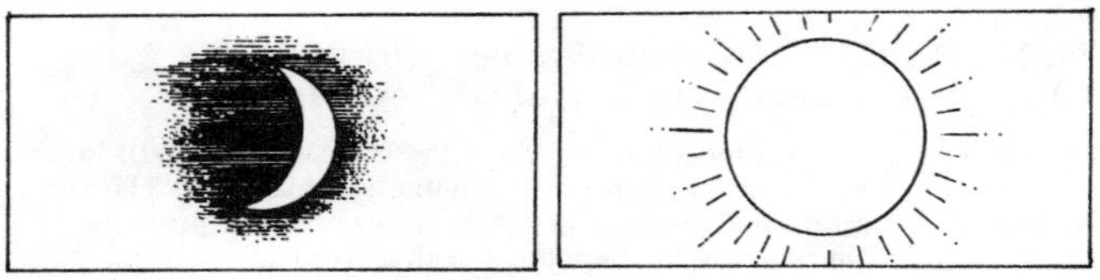

As with antonym items, it can be helpful in answering analogy questions to visualize the problem. The analogy here is bat::crow. For this problem it is important to remember that a bat is a mammal and a crow is a bird. Therefore the answer is D, seal::penguin.

NYLON : FABRIC :: (A) sweater : wool
(B) notebook : paper (C) statue : marble
(D) oxygen : air (E) carrot : vegetable

A good way to find the correct choice in analogy items is to put the relationship of a word pair into a sentence. For example, the relationship "kind of fiber:fabric" can be expressed as "<u>Nylon</u> is a kind of <u>fabric.</u>" Then find another pair of words related in the same way by testing them in the same sentence. For example, "A sweater is a kind of wool"; "a notebook is a kind of paper"; "a statue is a kind of marble"; "oxygen is a kind of air"; and "a carrot is a kind of vegetable." The only one that works is choice (E), carrot:vegetable. If you started with "Some <u>fabrics</u> are made from <u>nylon,</u>" the test sentences for the other suggested choices would then become "some wool is made of sweaters"; "some paper is made of notebooks"; "some marble is made of statues"; "some air is made of oxygen"; and "some vegetables are made of carrots." The only candidate in that group is "Some air is made from oxygen," but that has to be rejected because air is a mixture of gases. The only acceptable choice, then, still is (E).

CLUB : GOLF :: (A) racket : tennis (B) pitcher : baseball
(C) strike : bowling (D) track : racing
(E) touchdown : football

Although a person may belong to a <u>golf</u> club, none of the choices concerns an association or membership. Thus, <u>club</u> in this analogy refers to the device used to hit the ball in the game of golf. Your sentence has to be as specific as possible to work here. A sentence such as "A <u>club</u> is used in <u>golf</u>" does not discriminate among the choices. A sentence such as "A <u>club</u> is used to hit the ball in the game of <u>golf</u>" precisely indicates that choice (A), *racket:tennis,* is correct.

VETERINARIAN : ANIMALS :: (A) doctor : medicine
(B) pediatrician : children (C) surgeon : hospital
(D) psychiatrist : schizophrenia (E) dermatologist : skin

The only meaning that makes sense here is "A <u>veterinarian</u> is a doctor who treats <u>animals,</u>" which easily eliminates choices (A) and (C), but leaves the other three as possibilities. You need to make the original relationship more specific, such as "A <u>veterinarian</u> is a doctor who treats diseases of <u>animals.</u>" The more specific sentence rules out choices (D) and (E) and leaves (B) as the correct choice.

CHAPTER : NOVEL :: (A) student : auditorium
(B) story : word (C) song : medley (D) crowd : outcry
(E) artist : painting

State the relationship as, "A <u>chapter</u> is part of a <u>novel.</u>" Similarly, a <u>song</u> is part of a <u>medley.</u> Although a <u>word</u> is part of a <u>story,</u> choice (B) reverses that order, and a story is not a part of a word. Only choice (C) exactly expresses the perceived relationship.

ASTRONOMER : TELESCOPE :: (A) teacher : blackboard
(B) dentist : tooth (C) soldier : canteen
(D) doctor : stethoscope (E) singer : voice

It is always important to get a specific relationship. If you say "An <u>astronomer</u> uses a <u>telescope,</u>" you haven't eliminated any choices. If you say "An <u>astronomer</u> uses a <u>telescope</u> to gather information," you have limited your choices. Looking over the available choices, you can spot (D), and think "A doctor uses a stethoscope to gather information." None of the other choices works in that way, so choice (D) is correct.

BOXER : RING :: (A) dancer : music (B) actor : stage
(C) golfer : tee (D) skater : skates (E) comedian : jokes

The given relationship is "A <u>boxer</u> performs in a <u>ring.</u>" The only choice with the same relationship is (B), "An actor performs on a stage." Although one statement uses *in* and the other uses *on,* this small discrepancy would be important only if it were needed to help decide among choices that are close. Since the relationship is between a performer and the place where the performance occurs, choice (B) is correct.

BEAVER : LODGE :: (A) snake : grass (B) cow : farm (C) fish : ocean (D) insect : garden (E) hornet : nest

You need to choose between "A beaver lives in a lodge" and "A beaver builds a lodge." The first sentence does not make any discrimination among choices available. The second sentence has the same relationship as choice (E), *hornet:nest,* but the other choices do not. Snakes do not build grass, cows do not build farms, and so forth. Choice (E) is correct.

COIN : PAYMENT :: (A) stamp : letter (B) umbrella : protection (C) shoe : leather (D) camera : picture (E) purse : money

A coin can be used as a form of payment. Although it is easy to see that each pair describes a close relationship, only "An umbrella is a form of protection" makes sense and has the same relation, that of performing a function, as coin does to payment. Choice (B) is correct.

BEE : SWARM :: (A) salmon : fish (B) dog : puppy (C) bear : carnivore (D) bison : herd (E) cat : feline

One possibility for the relationship between bee and swarm would be that between an animal and a form of motion. The choices do not support that relationship. Another relationship between bee and swarm is that a group of bees is called a swarm. Since a bison is part of a herd, choice (D) is correct.

GULLIBLE : FOOLED :: (A) inquisitive : questioned (B) mysterious : understood (C) argumentative : ignored (D) dependable : admired (E) sensitive : offended

A gullible person is easily fooled. While someone who is inquisitive can be questioned, someone who is mysterious can sometimes be understood, someone who is argumentative can be ignored, and someone who is dependable is admired, these relationships are not always true. The only pair that surely has this relationship is *sensitive:offended,* for one definition of *sensitive* is "easily offended." The correct choice is (E).

ZEPHYR : WIND :: (A) flakes : snow (B) ice : hail (C) drizzle : rain (D) warmth : sun (E) shade : cloud

A zephyr is a "gentle breeze." Thus, its relationship to wind is that it is a kind of wind that is not very strong. A shade is not a kind of cloud (choice E). The pairs *flakes:snow, drizzle:rain,* and *warmth:sun* are plausible candidates; but flakes make up a heavy snow as well as the few flakes that constitute a weak snow; and, while warmth might be a mild form of the sun's heat, it is not a form of the sun itself. A drizzle is a small amount of light rain, just as a zephyr is a small amount of light wind. Thus, the only correct choice is (C).

STORY : RESOLUTION :: (A) treaty : peace (B) train : caboose (C) piano : key (D) confession : sentence (E) cabin : log

The connection between story and resolution is that the end of a story is its resolution. (While there might be a story about someone's resolution, this sort of connection is not inevitable. In looking for the correct choice in an analogy item, it is important to look for connections that always happen, not those that might happen. Then to discriminate among the possible choices, pay attention to details.) It is tempting to think that peace follows a treaty, choice (A), or a sentence usually follows a confession, choice (D), but unlike the resolution of a story, which is part of the story, the peace and the sentence are not part of the things they follow. Similarly, although a key can be part of a piano, choice (C), or a log may be part of a cabin, choice (E), neither one is the final part. Only *train:caboose* shows a relationship in which the caboose is the final part of the train, so the correct choice is (B).

MALNUTRITION : FOOD :: (A) pneumonia : bacteria (B) atrophy : exercise (C) headache : pain (D) virus : stomach (E) depression : grief

The relationship "Malnutrition is caused by inadequate food" is very precise, and there are no alternatives in meaning involved. None of the other relationships is exactly the same, but one cause of atrophy (of muscles) is inadequate exercise. Because the other pairs can easily be ruled out, the correct choice is (B), *atrophy:exercise.*

DEER : DOE :: (A) sheep : ewe (B) cat : kitten (C) buck : stag (D) bull : cow (E) horse : stallion

A doe is a female deer. If you also know that a ewe is a female sheep, then you will recognize it immediately as the correct choice. In that case you can move on to the next item to save time, although if you feel you are not going to have a problem with time, you might want to examine the other choices to see if there could be some sort of trick. Also, if you are unsure of what a ewe is, you may have to go carefully through the other choices to eliminate them: A kitten is a baby cat; a stag is a buck; a cow is female, but it is a bovine animal, not a bull; and a stallion is a male horse. Since a doe is a female deer, the only possibility is choice (A), *sheep:ewe.*

ANGUISH : SORROW :: (A) friendliness : friendship (B) ecstasy : happiness (C) carelessness : clumsiness (D) revenge : revolution (E) adviser : consultant

Although anguish and sorrow are close synonyms, anguish is an intense form of psychic pain, while sorrow is a generalized sadness. In this case, pure synonyms such as choices (A), (C), (D), and (E) would therefore be incorrect. Choice (B), in contrast, has the same relationship as *anguish:sorrow.* Ecstasy is an intense form of joy, and happiness is a generalized feeling. Further, one would expect both anguish and ecstasy to be short-lived, while both sorrow and happiness can pervade a person's life for long periods of time. Choice (B) is correct.

QUARRY : LION :: (A) range : buffalo (B) mine : gold (C) kitten : cat (D) gravel : chicken (E) prey : falcon

The word quarry has several meanings, both as a noun and a verb. In relation to lion, however, it makes sense only when it refers to the animals that the lion hunts and eats. While a *buffalo* eats the grass on the *range,* choice (A), it does not hunt or consume the range itself. One meaning of quarry suggests the word *mine,* but that is not the meaning in this analogy. Thus, choice (B) is wrong. Similarly, a lion is a kind of *cat,* but a cat's relation to its *kitten* is far different from that of a lion to its quarry, making choice (C) wrong. *Gravel* also suggests another meaning of quarry, but even though a chicken does consume some *gravel,* it cannot be said to hunt it, making choice (D) wrong. Choice (E), *prey:falcon,* is an exact match. Just as a lion hunts its quarry, a *falcon* hunts its *prey.*

CLOAK : DAGGER :: (A) spy : counterspy (B) paper : gift (C) pin : dress (D) cover : book (E) stamp : letter

While the expression "cloak-and-dagger" refers to spying, the relationship between a cloak and a dagger is not the same as the antagonistic relationship between a *spy* and a *counterspy,* choice (A). Similarly, although you could put a dagger through a cloak and a pin through a dress, the order is reversed in choice (C). A *cover* is part of a *book,* choice (D), but a cloak is not a part of a dagger. A *stamp* can be attached to a *letter,* choice (E), but a dagger could only be wrapped in or concealed by a cloak. The correct choice is (B), since a gift can be wrapped in *paper,* just as a dagger can be wrapped in a cloak.

BLACK : GRAY :: (A) white : bright (B) noise : sound (C) sun : planet (D) mountain : hill (E) pink : red

In essence, gray is a diminution or a less intense form of black, but *bright* is more intense than *white,* so choice (A) is not correct. *Noise* is not necessarily more or less intense (loud) than other sounds—just more annoying—so choice (B) is wrong. The *sun* is different from a *planet* in a basic way, since it is undergoing thermonuclear reactions that produce vast amounts of energy, so choice (C) is wrong. While *pink* can be a watered-down *red,* the relationship is in the other direction from that of black:gray, making choice (E) wrong. The correct choice is (D), since a *hill* is the same thing as a *mountain,* only less so, just as *gray* is the same thing as *black,* only less so.

A good tip: Remember that many words have different meanings when they are used as different parts of speech.

Sentence completion. The third form of item in the verbal section of the SAT involves sentence completion by filling in blanks. Like the antonym and analogy items, sentence-completion items are intended to evaluate vocabulary and logical thinking. In many ways the sentence-completion items are also a test of ability to read and comprehend, since a clear understanding of an entire sentence—and often its implied context—is needed for many of the items.

Directions: Each sentence below has one or two blanks, each blank indicating that something has been omitted. Beneath the sentence are five lettered words or sets of words. Choose the word or set of words that best fits the meaning of the sentence as a whole.

The candidate's inability to gain the support of any major newspaper resulted in a feeling of --- among her opponents.

(A) rejection   (B) disappointment   (C) optimism
(D) hostility   (E) urgency

Even before looking at the choices on an item like this, you should think about how the candidate's opponents would feel, based on the first part of the sentence. Would they be encouraged if the newspapers did not support their rivals? Would they be depressed? Since lack of newspaper support is said to give the opponents a better chance to win the election, look for a word among the choices that expresses a feeling representative of this. Choice (C), optimism, fits such a feeling, while the others do not.

Although aluminum is a competitive material in the marketplace, its presence is --- in the recycling of steel.

(A) destructive   (B) unnoticed   (C) overshadowed
(D) stabilized   (E) beneficial

The word *although* suggest that the effect of aluminum on the recycling of steel somehow stands in contrast to the competition between the two metals. Since the first part of the sentence sets up this contrast, the second part of the sentence must show the other side of the relationship. As a competitive material, aluminum is in some way harmful to steel, so the contrasting word, and correct choice, is beneficial, choice (E).

After restlessly listening to what Eddie called his parents' old-fashioned music, he was --- finally to have a chance to play some of the more --- tunes.

(A) relieved . . current
(B) resigned . . childish
(C) delighted . . unfamiliar
(D) reluctant . . sprightly
(E) willing . . popular

If Eddie has been "restlessly listening" to something, one would assume he would be glad to hear something completely different. Choices (B) and (D) begin with words that suggest something that Eddie also does not want to do, so neither is correct. Choice (E) begins with a word that, while not as negative as those that start choices (B) and (D), suggests that Eddie is going along somewhat reluctantly with listening to the more popular tunes. While choice (C) starts with a positive note in delighted, the unfamiliar does not seem to fit the rest of the sentence. Only choice (A), in which Eddie is relieved to play current tunes, correctly reflects the expectation of how Eddie might feel after listening to his parents' music.

Although the food was --- prepared, the meal was a --- culinary experience.

(A) hastily . . crude
(B) painstakingly . . memorable
(C) eagerly . . fascinating
(D) exquisitely . . disappointing
(E) lavishly . . delightful

Once again the word *although* suggests that there should be a contrast between the two clauses in the sentence. The way the meal turned out was not consistent with the way the food was prepared. Therefore, you should look for words that are opposites or near opposites. The words in choice (D) come closest to being opposites and, when inserted into the sentence, make a logical statement.

During a blackout, most people are forced to substitute --- plans for their usual life-styles.

(A) common   (B) interesting   (C) drastic
(D) alternative   (E) whimsical

The word *substitute* suggests that the plans during a blackout will be different from those when there is no blackout. The choices common, interesting, drastic, and whimsical fail to suggest this difference. The correct choice is alternative, choice (D).

The 1980 United States Olympic hockey team --- the world by defeating the highly favored and --- unbeatable Soviet team.

(A) amused . . probably
(B) stunned . . seemingly
(C) angered . . absolutely
(D) explored . . evidently
(E) represented . . hardly

By looking at the second word in each pair, you can use the fact that the Soviet team was soundly beaten to eliminate choices (A), (C), and (D). Choice (E) does not make sense, since the United States team would be unlikely to represent the world, and hardly is a peculiar modifier for *unbeatable*. Choice (B) makes sense because, although the Soviet team was seemingly unbeatable, it was in fact beaten, and this is the kind of event that could have stunned the world.

Her dream of becoming the first female baseball player on the team was --- by an insensitive coaching staff.

(A) fulfilled   (B) acknowledged   (C) encouraged
(D) revolutionized   (E) thwarted

An insensitive coaching staff would not be interested in fulfilling, choice (A); encouraging, choice (C); revolutionizing, choice (D); or even acknowledging, choice (B), her dream. An insensitive staff would most likely thwart the dream. The choice that completes the logic of the sentence is (E).

Criticism does not --- but --- his determination, driving him to elevate his efforts to new heights.

(A) encourage . . augments
(B) produce . . involves
(C) impede . . enhances
(D) lessen . . ridicules
(E) invoke . . overlooks

The signal word *but* suggests that you are looking for two words with opposite meanings. Therefore, you can eliminate choices (A), (B), and (D). The second word of the missing pair should show a positive effect on his determination. Based on this, you can now eliminate choice (E). Test the words for choice (C) in the sentence. They work, so choice (C) is correct.

Because of his need for ---, he agrees to make public appearances only when he is assured of a supportive audience.

(A) attention   (B) competition   (C) approval
(D) involvement   (E) diversity

Think of the needs of a person who would make public appearance only when assured of a supportive audience. This should suggest that you can eliminate choices (B), (D), and (E). In addition, a need for attention, choice (A), would not cause him to limit his public appearances. Since he will appear only before a supportive audience, he needs approval, choice (C).

With his team trailing by a point in the final seconds of the game, Kevin lunged for the ball, scooped it up, and flung it --- toward the hoop.

(A) willingly   (B) desperately   (C) crazily
(D) peculiarly   (E) mercilessly

Every clue in this sentence points to a desperate situation, so choice (B) is the correct choice. A check of the other choices shows that none makes sense in the sentence no matter what Kevin was feeling at the time.

An outstanding baseball player in his day, Slugger was --- as he helplessly watched his talent --- over the years.

(A) outraged . . evolve
(B) enthusiastic . . surge
(C) undecided . . ridiculed
(D) devastated . . diminish
(E) flattered . . imitated

This sentence suggests that the first blank must be filled by a word with strong negative feelings, which eliminates all choices but (A) and (D). While it makes no sense that Slugger would be outraged to see his skills evolve—a positive conclusion should not make a person angry—he would be devastated to watch the skills diminish. Choice (D) is correct.

Most people growing up in the 1960's failed to realize that the baseball cards they should have --- would some day be valuable collector's items.

(A) hoarded   (B) discarded   (C) shared   (D) abused
(E) inspected

From the sentence it is apparent that baseball cards worth little in the 1960's can be sold to collectors today for large sums. If people knew that this situation would arrive more than a quarter of a century later, they would have wanted to save the cards. Choice (A), hoarded, is the correct answer.

Donna insisted that no amount of --- would deter her from her goal of attending college.

(A) encouragement   (B) intensity   (C) longevity
(D) endurance   (E) adversity

After substituting each of the five word choices in the sentence, you find that the only word that clearly suggests a potential deterrent for Donna is choice (E), adversity.

Most people thought of the young lawyer as arrogant, since she --- to --- to even the slightest error in judgment.

(A) decided . . conform
(B) refused . . admit
(C) confessed . . adjust
(D) returned . . adhere
(E) feared . . react

Here, the correct word pair will complete a statement to illustrate the definition of *arrogant*. Since arrogance involves a pretension of superiority, first-word choices confessed (C) and feared (E) can be eliminated. Of the remaining word pairs, only choice (B) is consistent with the definition of *arrogant*.

In an attempt to increase public ---, some advertisers suggest that their products are --- by doctors.

(A) confidence . . recommended
(B) indignation . . treated
(C) apathy . . endorsed
(D) awareness . . misused
(E) skepticism . . rejected

Since it is illogical to assume that advertisers would want to increase public indignation, apathy, or skepticism directed at their products, you can eliminate choices (B), (C), and (E). The word pair for choice (D), when inserted in the sentence, also produces an illogical statement. Choice (A) makes the only logical statement within the context of the sentence.

He considers himself an original thinker, never allowing the findings of others to --- his judgment.

(A) support   (B) contradict   (C) influence
(D) reinforce   (E) reflect

Anyone who considers himself an original thinker probably would not care whether the findings of others support, contradict, reinforce, or reflect his judgment. His status as an original thinker would be threatened, however, if he allowed the findings of others to influence his judgment. Therefore, the best choice is (C).

Our guide made no effort to be --- as he rushed us through the museum, rattling off information while --- our questions.

(A) diplomatic . . honoring
(B) courteous . . ignoring
(C) informative . . inviting
(D) flippant . . dismissing
(E) impatient . . distorting

As this sentence is phrased, the first word of the pair must describe what the museum guide "made no effort to be." You can easily reject choices (D) and (E). Choice (C) is debatable since he did give information, though it was rattled off. Based on the guide's actions, you can assume that he did not invite questions. You can now eliminate choices (A) and (C). Only choice (B) completes a logical sentence.

When the first mailboxes were erected in Paris, in 1653, messengers --- for their --- put mice in the boxes to destroy the mail.

(A) thrilled . . future
(B) thankful . . pets
(C) searching . . homes
(D) fearful . . livelihoods
(E) collecting . . hobbies

Consider the effect the first mailboxes must have had on the lives of people who delivered messages for a living. This new development would not have caused them to be thrilled or thankful. The best choice is (D), fearful . . livelihoods.

Even though the enemy troops --- at his border, the young ruler --- to change his policies.

(A) frolicked . .began
(B) fought . .continued
(C) gathered . .refused
(D) debated . .elected
(E) retreated . .declined

Even though, like *although,* suggests that there will be a contrast between the two clauses in the sentence. Furthermore, while troops might be expected to fight, gather, or retreat, one does not expect them to frolic or debate. Also, choices (A) and (D) do not supply the desired contrast. Choice (E) is unsuitable, since if the enemy troops are retreating, it seems reasonable that the ruler would continue the policies that caused the retreat. A similar situation prevails with choice (B). The correct choice is (C): Even though the enemy troops gathered at his border, the young ruler refused to change his policies.

The most --- outcome of Alfred's action was that his company would soon --- as its financial situation deteriorated.

(A) unexpected . .falter
(B) damaging . .prosper
(C) important . .complain
(D) incredible . .repeat
(E) likely . .fold

In this sentence the key word is the last one: *deteriorated.* Once you accept the premise that the company is now in increasing financial trouble, you can reject choice (B), especially since prospering would not be damaging. Looking at choice (A), one would expect that a company in financial trouble would falter, so that would not be unexpected. For choice (C), it is difficult to see how a company's complaining would be important. Choice (D) does not make any sense. The correct choice is (E). It is likely that a company with a deteriorating financial condition will fold.

As she walked into the woods, Maria observed the --- pattern made by the animal tracks in the snow.

(A) unyielding   (B) disgusting   (C) intricate
(D) definitive   (E) eclectic

In this case, the main point being tested can be said to be that of the size of one's vocabulary. Unyielding, disgusting, definitive, and eclectic are not words one would use to describe a pattern of tracks. But the tracks of animals that overlap in various ways can be said to be intricate. Thus, (C) is the correct choice.

Reading comprehension. The remaining verbal section of the SAT tests ability to understand what is read. Unlike the other SAT items, these items are all based on several paragraphs of text (a *passage*) that are like passages from a novel, short story, biography, personal essay, informative essay, or argumentative essay. Each passage is designed to provide all information required to answer correctly the items that follow it.

Directions: Each passage below is followed by questions based on its content. Answer all questions following a passage on the basis of what is <u>stated</u> or <u>implied</u> in that passage.

Dandelion is what we named the woodchuck that makes its home under our garage. (It's easy to guess his major food passion!) He's a fine specimen, too. His thick, glossy fur shades from light brown on his belly to deep red-brown along his spine. Both back feet and front feet are black, with strong claws for digging burrows and defending himself. His ears are small, round, and close to his head. His eyes are large, and his nose is black. We assume Dandelion is a male, since we've seen no offspring.

It's characteristic of a marmot to sit upright on its rear legs, and Dandelion does that after every few bites during his frequent meals. Marmots are described as lazy and slow-moving. He is both. In the morning sunlight he is a rug flung across the stones, feet spread wide, and eyes closed. As summer wears on, he grows fatter and fatter, preparing for his winter's sleep. We don't know if we'll see this groundhog on February 2, but probably we won't, since the snow will still be deep then.

Dandelion is quite a charming animal. He will continue to be charming—and welcome—as long as he doesn't raid the garden. So far, he hasn't. As other squirrels do, Dandelion likes seeds, grass, and nuts. He is especially fond of popcorn, when he can get it.

Based on this passage, names for this kind of animal include

(A) dandelion, marmot, lazybones, squirrel
(B) woodchuck, dandelion, groundhog, animal
(C) woodchuck, marmot, groundhog, squirrel
(D) specimen, rug, groundhog, squirrel
(E) dandelion, specimen, lazybones, popcorn

The first sentence clearly states that "we named" this particular animal Dandelion, so that's a proper name and can be eliminated, making choices (A), (B), and (E) incorrect. Choice (D) includes <u>specimen</u>, which may refer to any representative of a kind of thing or animal. Choice (C) includes only names for this type of animal.

It can be inferred that a woodchuck's favorite food is

(A) dandelions
(B) popcorn
(C) seeds
(D) nuts
(E) grass

The clues to the correct answer appear in the first two sentences. Choice (A) is correct. While all the foods mentioned are foods that a woodchuck eats, only dandelions are specifically referred to as "his major food passion." The woodchuck loves popcorn, too, but that's apparently not a regular item in his diet, since he eats it "when he can get it."

The sentence "He has a short, rather broad tail" would best be placed

(A) in paragraph one because paragraph one contains mostly short sentences
(B) in paragraph one because paragraph one gives Dandelion's physical description
(C) in paragraph two because paragraph two contains many longer, more complex sentences
(D) in paragraph two because paragraph two is about Dandelion's behavior
(E) in paragraph three because paragraph three is about human reactions to Dandelion

Each answer includes a reason for making the choice. The determining factor is not likely to be sentence length, so choices (A) and (C) can be eliminated. Also, paragraph one has long sentences as well as short ones. If you evaluate the content of the sentence, it's clearly part of a physical description of the animal. Most of the physical description is in paragraph one, so choice (B) is the best answer.

The actual meaning of "he is a rug flung across the stones" in the second paragraph is that the animal

(A) lacks normal strength
(B) has fur that would make a nice rug
(C) finds the hard stones uncomfortable
(D) is relaxed and limp as he sleeps in the sun
(E) is furry and very warm, like many rugs

The actual meaning of the description is not the same as the literal meaning of the words. To determine what the author is saying, look at the context of the description. The woodchuck is lazy and slow-moving, he is in the morning sunlight, his feet are spread wide, and his eyes are closed. You can conclude that he is probably warm and that he is asleep. Therefore, choice (D) is the best one.

The best title for this passage would be

(A) "A Woodchuck's Favorite Foods"
(B) "Animals That Hibernate"
(C) "One Fine Woodchuck"
(D) "Ground Squirrels of All Kinds"
(E) "Marmots Around the World"

To determine the correct answer, review each paragraph to see if each title covers it well. Choice (A) does not cover paragraphs one and two. Choices (B) and (D) can be eliminated because no other hibernating animals or ground squirrels are mentioned in the passage. Choice (E) also refers to more than the passage contains (no other marmots are mentioned in the passage). Only choice (C) includes all the information in the passage but no more than that.

Nearly 2000 years ago, the Roman Empire included much of the island now known as Great Britain. Julius Caesar invaded Britain in 55 B.C. and defeated its ruler. His heir, the emperor Augustus, negotiated a settlement with the British leaders under which they would pay taxes but keep their independence. This treaty, settled in 27 B.C., lasted only until 43 A.D., when the emperor Claudius invaded and conquered the southern part of the island we call England. By 83 A.D., the entire island group was ruled by the Romans. It was known as the province of Britannia.

But Britannia was a long way from Rome, and it was not easy for the Romans to maintain their rule without a great deal of fighting. In 122 A.D., the emperor Hadrian visited his province with the intention of settling matters. He ordered the army to build a wall across the island between what today are England and Scotland. The wall separated the "civilized" Romans and the northern "barbarians."

Hadrian's Wall, as we call it, is 80 miles long. It varies in thickness from 8 to 10 feet and averages 15 feet in height. At each Roman mile a milecastle was built, an enclosed structure with gates, barracks, and a cooking area. Each milecastle was about 60 feet square. Evenly spaced between each pair of milecastles, two turrets were built into the wall. A turret was 20 feet square and had stairs leading up from the ground level. In addition, two ditches ran along Hadrian's Wall, one to the north and the other to the south.

(1) Contrary to long-held belief, Hadrian's Wall was probably not intended primarily as part of a defense system in time of war. (2) Many Roman soldiers married local women and had families in Britannia. (3) Instead, the wall most likely marked a political and economic boundary. (4) Smugglers trying to avoid paying taxes, travelers who wanted to avoid being seen, and others who had reason to keep their movements quiet were the probable targets for the wall's guardians.

According to the passage, for a long time people believed that Hadrian's Wall was intended to be primarily

(A) a political boundary
(B) a military defense
(C) an economic defense
(D) all of these
(E) both (A) and (C)

The sentence numbered (1) in the last paragraph of the passage begins "Contrary to long-held belief." This implies that a clause following that phrase and including the word *not* will include an idea that people believed for a long time: "Hadrian's Wall was probably *not* intended primarily as part of a defense system. . . ." In other words, for a long time people believed that Hadrian's Wall was primarily a military defense. Although the passage implies that the belief was incorrect, the item does not ask what the primary purpose of the wall was. It asks what people believed it was for a long period of time. Choices (A) and (C) or both—choice (E)—reflect present-day thinking. Choice (B) is correct.

It can be inferred from the passage that soldiers lived

(A) on top of the wall
(B) in the milecastles
(C) in the turrets
(D) behind the wall
(E) in the nearby towns

The word *inferred* tells you that the needed information is not directly given in the passage. However, everything you need is given. In paragraph three, each milecastle is described as having "gates, barracks, and a cooking area." Barracks are living quarters for soldiers, so the inclusion of a cooking area makes it likely that soldiers lived in the milecastles, which is choice (B). The other choices may be possible but are less likely.

It was not easy for the Romans to maintain their rule over Great Britain because

(A) Hadrian's Wall was 80 miles long
(B) many smugglers traveled between north and south
(C) Rome is a long way from Great Britain
(D) the Romans thought Britain was populated by uncivilized people and was not worth fighting for
(E) the Roman soldiers were unwilling to fight

To find the answer, look for the phrase "maintain their rule" or something similar. (In this case, it's the exact wording, but it may not be exact in other items.) You can eliminate choice (E) right away, since nothing is ever said about the fighting quality of Roman soldiers. Choices (A), (B), and (D) are all mentioned in the passage, but are not given as reasons for difficulty in maintaining Rome's rule. The correct choice is (C).

The sentence that does not belong in the last paragraph of the passage is

(A) sentence (1)
(B) sentence (2)
(C) sentence (3)
(D) sentence (4)
(E) all the sentences belong in the last paragraph

This question requires that you understand the main idea of the paragraph. Then you must decide if all the sentences are about the main idea, which is choice (E), or if one sentence does not belong. In this case, the correct answer is choice (B); the soldiers' families have little or nothing to do with why Hadrian's Wall was built.

According to the passage, the Roman ruler who conquered Great Britain was

(A) Julius Caesar
(B) Augustus
(C) Claudius
(D) Hadrian
(E) the passage does not specify

The correct answer is choice (E). Julius Caesar, choice (A), invaded Britain, while Augustus, choice (B), negotiated a treaty with the British rulers. Claudius, who is choice (C), conquered only the southern part. The remaining choice, (D), is Hadrian, who did not conquer any of England; he built the wall.

HAND-HELD CALCULATORS, *like the ones being used by many students in this large class, are not as yet allowed to be used in major standardized examinations. It is anticipated that this rule will be changed in the next few years.*

GRACE/STOCK, BOSTON

Although they lived far from other people, the rest of the world still intruded from time to time. Sometimes they heard a horse clattering past on the distant road; another time a gunshot brought their heads up sharply. Once they stumbled on an abandoned building deep in the woods. Its roof was open to the sky and the window holes gaped darkly. The door hung at a slight slant on its hinges. They left without saying a word. Long association made speech unnecessary most of the time. In this instance, both knew there was nothing here for them and did not even look to see if they were of the same mind. The old house made them uncomfortable, as if it might somehow be theirs. Their lives did not include the concept of neglect or abandonment: It wasn't they who had been neglected or abandoned, but instead they had neglected and abandoned the world. So they rejected this visible sign of humans once present but now gone, choosing to continue instead in the solitary, speechless patterns developed over long years.

This passage is about

(A) one character
(B) two characters
(C) three characters
(D) many characters
(E) no characters

This is a straightforward question about a detail. In order to choose the answer, you must look for clues to number. The words "they" and "them" indicate more than one character, so you can eliminate choices (A) and (E). The word "both" indicates that choice (B) is correct.

It appears that the setting for this passage is

(A) a wooded area
(B) a ghost town
(C) a desert
(D) a small town
(E) a beach near an ocean

This is a question about a detail, but it requires an inference to answer it. The clues are "the distant road" and "deep in the woods." These clues make choice (A) the best answer, although we are not certain the others are wrong.

To the characters, it seemed that the house they found symbolized their

(A) frustration, anger, and guilt toward each other
(B) happiness and fulfillment in their lives
(C) loneliness and longing for the company of other people
(D) need to find a place to live and be happy
(E) rejection of others and acceptance of solitude

To answer this question, look for key words such as "symbol," "represent," "sign," or "signal" with respect to the house. You can eliminate choice (B), because the house made them uncomfortable. There is no indication of the emotions mentioned in choices (A) or (C) anywhere in the passage. Choice (D) might be possible, but the word "rejected" in the last sentence indicates that choice (E) is the better of the two.

It can be inferred that the characters in the passage

(A) cannot speak to each other
(B) do not want company or any change in their lives
(C) abandoned and neglected the house in the woods
(D) are frightened by horses and guns
(E) are superstitious about old, abandoned buildings

This inference question asks for an evaluation of the overall effect of the passage rather than a conclusion about a specific part of the passage. The mood of the passage is set by the descriptive words and the actions of the characters. It is clear that the characters could speak if they wished ("speech unnecessary"), so choice (A) can be eliminated. The house was abandoned and neglected before they "stumbled" on it. Since that word suggests that they had not known it was there, we can eliminate choice (C). They may be frightened of guns, but they don't seem to be alarmed by horses, and their motives for leaving the house seem to have nothing to do with superstition. With choices (D) and (E) eliminated, choice (B) is left.

According to the passage, the characters are living where they are

(A) by their own choice
(B) because they have been exiled
(C) because they have nowhere else to go
(D) as a punishment
(E) temporarily, until they find a better place

The information to answer the question is given in the passage, although it may not be given in exactly the words used in the question. The best choice is (A) because the passage directly states that "they had neglected and abandoned the world . . . choosing to continue instead. . . ." All the other choices might be possible, but they are not supported by the choice of words in the passage.

SAT Mathematics Sections

Standard multiple-choice mathematics. The mathematical sections of the SAT contain approximately equal numbers of arithmetic, algebra, and geometry items. Most of the geometry is fairly simple, but a few questions are based on ideas not usually encountered until students take a high school geometry course.

Although the SAT mathematics sections reflect content through two years of high school mathematics (algebra and geometry), the more experience with high school mathematics one has, the easier the items will seem. As a student takes second-year algebra or more advanced courses, the contents of the earlier courses frequently are used as tools. When this happens, learning becomes much deeper and more an integral part of the student's overall knowledge of the subject.

Directions: In this section, solve each problem, using any available space on the page for scratch work. Then decide which is the best of the choices given.

Denise sold pottery at the outdoor market on two Saturdays. On the first Saturday, she earned \$120. On the second Saturday, she earned \$160. What percent increase were her second Saturday's earnings over her first Saturday's earnings?

(A) 20%   (B) 25%   (C) $33\frac{1}{3}$%   (D) 40%   (E) 75%

To find the percent increase, find the amount of the increase. Then write a fraction for the amount of increase over the original earnings. Finally, change the fraction to a percent.

$$\$160 - \$120 = \$40$$

$$\frac{\$40}{\$120} = \frac{1}{3} = 33\frac{1}{3}\%$$

The correct choice is (C).

George scored 80, 78, 85, and 86 on his social studies quizzes. He would like to have an average of 85 after his next quiz. What score must he get?

(A) 85   (B) 90   (C) 91   (D) 96   (E) 100

The average is found by adding all the scores and dividing by the number of scores. If George wants to get an average of 85, he must have all five scores add up to 5 × 85, or 425. The total of his first four scores is 329. Subtracting 329 from 425 = 96. The correct choice is (D).

If $12 \cdot 12 \cdot 12 = 6 \cdot 6 \cdot Q$, then $Q =$

(A) 6   (B) 12   (C) 36   (D) 48   (E) 72

There are several ways to approach this problem. You might multiply 12 by 12 by 12 and divide by 6 times 6. You would save a lot of time by simply comparing both sides of the equation and determining the missing factors.

$$12 \cdot 12 \cdot 12 = 6 \cdot 6 \cdot Q$$
$$6(2) \cdot 6(2) \cdot 6(2) = 6 \cdot 6 \cdot Q$$

The factors on the left that are missing from the right are 2, 2, and 6(2). So Q must equal the product of 2, 2, and 12. The correct choice is (D).

Louise borrowed $2000 for 6 months at 8% simple annual interest. She must repay the loan in full with interest at the end of 6 months. How much will she have to pay then?

(A) $2008   (B) $2080   (C) $2160   (D) $2320
(E) $4000

To find out how much she must repay, first find the interest. Use the formula $i = p \times r \times t$, where p is the principal, r is the rate, and t is the time in years.

$$i = \$2000 \times 0.08 \times \frac{6}{12} = 160 \times \frac{1}{2} = 80$$

The total to be repaid is the principal plus interest: $2000 + $80. The correct choice is (B).

A number is divisible by 4 if its last two digits are divisible by 4. Only one of the following is divisible by 12. Which number is divisible by 12?

(A) 32,013   (B) 31,248   (C) 30,020   (D) 36,028
(E) 36,114

If a number is divisible by 12, it must be divisible by 4 and by 3. If it is divisible by 3, the sum of its digits is divisible by 3. These two divisibility tests, for 4 and for 3, can be used to determine which of the numbers is divisible by 12. This is much faster than dividing each of the numbers by 12. Using the divisibility test for 4, we can eliminate (A) and (E). The sums of the digits for (B), (C), and (D) are 18, 5, and 19 respectively. Therefore, the correct choice is (B).

If $\frac{12}{x} = 3$ and $\frac{y}{4} = 2$, then $\frac{5 + x}{y + 4} =$

(A) $\frac{5}{8}$ (B) $\frac{5}{4}$ (C) $\frac{1}{2}$ (D) $\frac{9}{4}$ (E) $\frac{3}{4}$

First, solve for each variable. Then substitute their values in the expression on the right and simplify it.

$$\frac{12}{x} = 3 \qquad \frac{y}{4} = 2$$
$$x = 4 \qquad y = 8$$
$$\frac{5 + x}{y + 4} = \frac{5 + 4}{8 + 4}$$
$$= \frac{9}{12} = \frac{3}{4}$$

The correct choice is (E).

The sum of two consecutive even integers is 30. Which of the following is the larger number in the pair?

(A) 14   (B) 15   (C) 16   (D) 18   (E) 20

Solve this problem by letting n = the smaller even number and $n + 2$ the larger even number.

$$n + n + 2 = 30$$
$$2n + 2 = 30$$
$$2n = 28$$
$$n = 14$$
$$n + 2 = 16$$

The correct choice is (C).

Find the average of $2x + 5$ and $6x - 1$.

(A) $3x + 2$ (B) $4x + 4$ (C) $4x + 3$ (D) $8x + 4$
(E) $4x + 2$

To find the average of two algebraic expressions, add the expressions and divide by 2. Then simplify the expression.

$$\frac{2x + 5 + 6x - 1}{2} = \frac{2x + 6x + 5 - 1}{2} = \frac{8x + 4}{2}$$
$$= \frac{4(2x + 1)}{2}$$
$$= 2(2x + 1) = 4x + 2$$

The correct choice is (E).

If x and y are positive integers such that $x^2 + y^2 = 20$ and $x > y$, then $x - y =$

(A) 1   (B) 2   (C) 3   (D) 4   (E) 6

This problem requires some reasoning. Since x and y are positive integers, x^2 and y^2 are both perfect squares. Perfect squares less than 20 are 1, 4, 9, and 16. The two perfect squares that add to 20 are 4 and 16. Since $x > y$, $x^2 = 16$, $x = 4$; $y^2 = 4$, $y = 2$ and $x - y = 4 - 2 = 2$. The correct choice is (B).

If the operation # is defined for all positive x and y by

$$x \# y = \frac{2xy}{x + y},$$

which of the following is true for positive x, y, and z?
I. $x \# x = x$
II. $x \# y = y \# x$
III. $x \# (y \# z) = (x \# y) \# z$

(A) I only   (B) I and II only   (C) I and III only
(D) II and III only   (E) I, II, and III

This is a newly defined operation. Apply the operation correctly.
I $x \# x = \frac{2x(x)}{x + x} = \frac{2x(x)}{2x} = x$
I is true.

II $x \# y = \frac{2xy}{x + y}$; $y \# x = \frac{2yx}{y + x}$

II is true because of the commutative properties for multiplication and addition.
III This expression is more complicated. Instead of working it out algebraically, substitute any three values of x, y, and z. Let $x = 2$, $y = 3$ and $z = 4$:

$$x \# (y \# z) = 2 \# (3 \# 4)$$
$$= 2 \# \frac{(2 \cdot 3 \cdot 4)}{3 + 4}$$
$$= 2 \# \frac{24}{7} = \frac{(2 \cdot 2 \cdot \frac{24}{7})}{2 + \frac{24}{7}} = \frac{\frac{96}{7}}{\frac{38}{7}} = \frac{96}{38}$$
$$(x \# y) \# z = (2 \# 3) \# 4$$
$$= \frac{2 \cdot 2 \cdot 3}{2 + 3} \# 4$$
$$= \frac{12}{5} \# 4$$
$$= \frac{2 \cdot \frac{12}{5} \cdot 4}{\frac{12}{5} + 4} = \frac{\frac{96}{5}}{\frac{32}{5}} = \frac{96}{32}$$

Since the results are different, III is not true. The correct choice is (B).

If 50% of x is 25% of y, then y is what percent of x?

(A) $12\frac{1}{2}\%$ (B) 25%   (C) 50%   (D) 75%   (E) 200%

The best way to have a clear picture of the problem is to write an algebraic expression for it.

$$0.5x = 0.25y$$

To find what percent y is of x, solve the equation for $\frac{y}{x}$.

$$\frac{0.5x}{0.25} = y \qquad \frac{0.5}{0.25} = \frac{y}{x} \qquad 2 = \frac{y}{x}$$

Change 2 to a percent. The correct choice is (E).

Find the value of x if $2x^2 - 7x = 4$.

(A) $-\frac{1}{2}$ or 4   (B) $\frac{1}{2}$ or 4   (C) $-\frac{1}{2}$ or -4 (D) -1 or 4
(E) -1 or -4

Many quadratic equations can be solved by factoring. First, rewrite the equation so that one side equals 0. Factor the expression on the other side. Let both factors equal 0 and solve for x.
$$2x^2 - 7x - 4 = 0$$
$$(2x + 1)(x - 4) = 0$$
$$2x + 1 = 0 \quad x - 4 = 0$$
$$2x = -1 \qquad x = 4$$
$$x = -\frac{1}{2}$$
The correct choice is (A).

Simplify the expression $\dfrac{12x^4\, yz^5}{3x^6\, z^4}$

(A) $15x^{10}\, z^9$ (B) $9x^2\, yz$ (C) $4x^2\, yz$ (D) $\dfrac{4yz}{x^2}$

(E) $\dfrac{4x^2\, y}{z}$

Use the laws of exponents to simplify this expression. Consider each part of the expression separately.

$$\frac{12x^4\, yz^5}{3x^6\, z^4} = \frac{12 \cdot x^4 \cdot y \cdot z^5}{3\, x^6\, z^4} = \frac{4yz}{x^2}$$

The correct choice is (D).

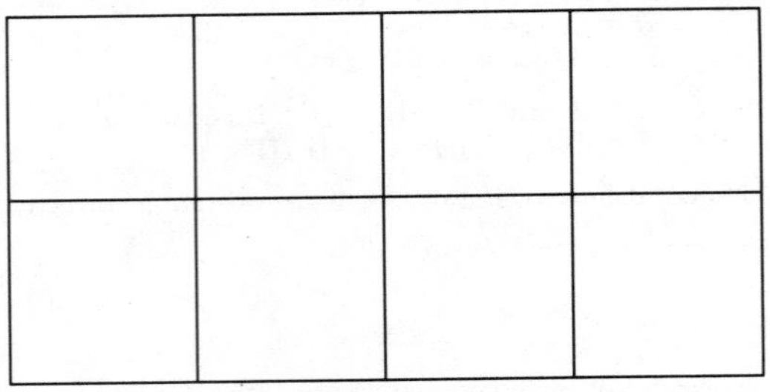

The figure above is a rectangle divided into eight equal squares. If the perimeter of the rectangle is 3, what is the perimeter of one of the squares?

(A) $\frac{3}{11}$ (B) $\frac{1}{4}$ (C) $\frac{3}{8}$ (D) 1   (E) 4

The perimeter of the rectangle is the sum of all the line segments around the rectangle. There are twelve segments in all in the perimeter. Since the figure is composed of squares, all the line segments are congruent. Therefore, the measure of each line segment in the figure is 3 divided by 12, or ¼. The perimeter of one square is 4(¼). The correct choice is (D).

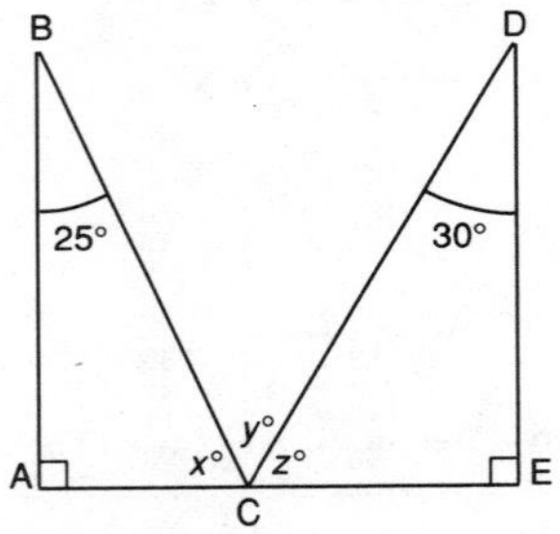

In the figure above, AE is a line segment. What is the measure of y?

(A) 55°   (B) 60°   (C) 65°   (D) 125°   (E) 180°

There are two right triangles. In each, you are given the measure of one acute angle. In order to find x and z, use the fact that the acute angles in a right triangle are complements. Then $y = 180 - (x + z)$, since the three angles form a straight angle.

$x = 90 - 25 = 65; z = 90 - 30 = 60$
$y = 180 - (65 + 60)$
$y = 180 - 125$
$y = 55$

The correct choice is (A).

Circle O has a diameter of 4. Circle P has a radius of 3. What is the ratio of the area of circle O to the area of circle P?

(A) 4 to 3   (B) 2 to 3   (C) 3 to 4   (D) 16 to 9
(E) 4 to 9

The formula for the area of a circle is $A = \pi r^2$. The area of circle O is $2^2\pi$. The area of circle P is $3^2\pi$. The ratio of their areas is 4π to 9π or 4 to 9. The answer is (E).

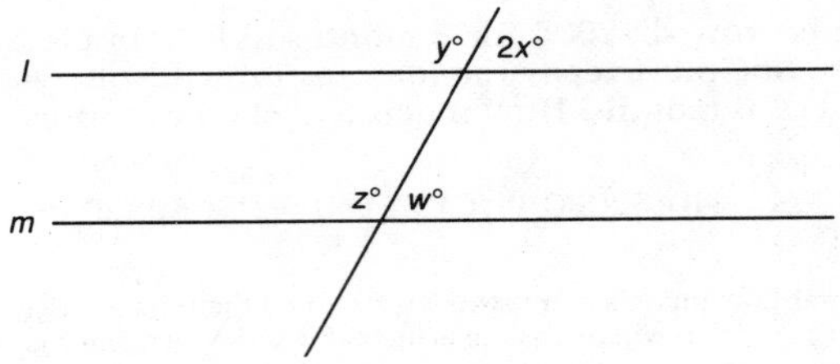

In the figure above, lines l and m are parallel. Which of the following must equal $180 - x$?

(A) $x + y$ (B) $x + z$ (C) $y + z$ (D) $y + w$
(E) $z + w$

Since the lines are parallel, $2x$ and z are equal, y and w are equal, and $2x$ is supplementary to y and w. This gives us a few equations that involve 180 and x:

$180 - 2x = y$ and $180 - 2x = w$
$180 - x - x = y$ $180 - x - x = w$
$180 - x = y + x$ $180 - x = w + x$

Therefore, the correct choice is (A), since $180 - x = y + x = x + y$.

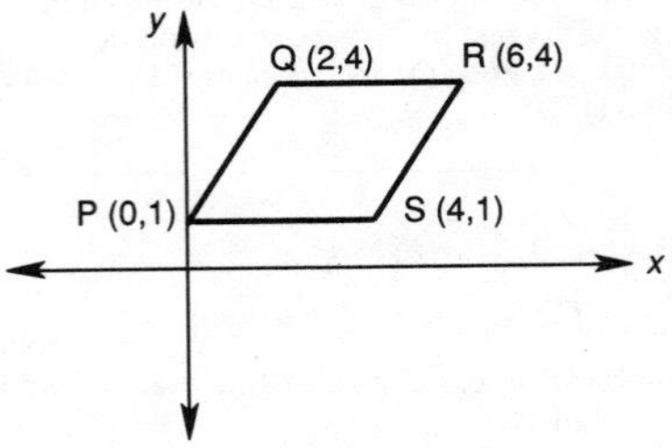

In the figure above, what is the area of parallelogram $PQRS$?

(A) 4   (B) 8   (C) 12   (D) 16
(E) It cannot be determined from the information given.

The formula for the area of a parallelogram is $A = bh$, where b is the base and h is the height. The height is the measure of a perpendicular from one vertex to the base. If PS is the base, the height can be measured by the distance parallel to the y-axis.

$A = bh$
$A = 4(3) = 12$

The correct choice is (C).

The graph of the equation $y = 2x - 3$ can be described as

(A) a circle with its center at $(2, 3)$
(B) a line that goes through the points $(0, -3)$ and $(\frac{3}{2}, 0)$
(C) a circle that has a radius of 3 and a center at $(0, 2)$
(D) a line parallel to the x-axis
(E) an angle with its vertex at $(2, -3)$

Since this is an equation that has only the first power of both x and y, it must be a line, which eliminates choices (A), (C), and (D). The slope-intercept form of a line is $y = mx + b$, where m is the slope and b is the y intercept. For the given equation, the slope would be 2 and the y intercept would be -3, which eliminates choice (D)—where the slope is 0—and strongly implies choice (B). Checking both points in the equation confirms this choice.

Test of Standard Written English (TSWE)

Although the Test of Standard Written English is not a part of the SAT score, it is an important part of the test battery, since many colleges and universities use scores on it for placement in freshman English. There are two types of items. We have labeled these "error location" and "sentence correction." In the error-location items that follow, you need only have a good feeling for *bad* English—at least, what is considered bad in standard written English, the kind that most college instructors require to be used in anything except fiction and poetry.

Error location items

Directions: The following sentences contain problems in grammar, usage, diction (choice of words), and idioms.
   Some sentences are correct.
   No sentence contains more than one error.
   You will find that the error, if there is one, is underlined and lettered. Assume that elements of the sentence that are not underlined are correct and cannot be changed. In choosing answers, follow the requirements of standard written English.
   If there is an error, select the <u>one underlined part</u> that must be changed to make the sentence correct.

The older generation <u>maintain</u> that modern athletes are
                     A
not <u>so</u> proficient <u>as those</u> <u>who</u> performed long ago.
    B   C   D
<u>No error.</u>
  E

The subject of the sentence, *generation,* includes many people, but it refers to a single group. Therefore, *generation* requires a singular verb—*maintains,* not *maintain.* Choice (A) should read, "The older generation <u>maintains</u> that . . ."

In a <u>current</u> TV commercial, the manufacturer <u>insists</u> that
       A   B
Brand X is <u>clearly</u> the <u>gentlest</u> of the two soaps. <u>No error.</u>
            C   D   E

When a sentence compares two things, you must use the comparative or *-er* form (*gentler*) rather than the superlative or *-est* form (*gentlest*). Choice (D) should read, ". . . the <u>gentler</u> of the two soaps."

If the food <u>you ordered</u> smells <u>badly,</u> ask the waiter to
             A   B
return <u>it</u> to the kitchen and <u>bring you</u> a new portion.
       C   D
<u>No error.</u>
  E

Linking verbs, like *smells,* do not express a mental or physical action. They help to make a statement by connecting the subject (noun or pronoun) with a word (adjective) that describes it. Here, the subject *food* must be described by the adjective *bad,* not the adverb *badly.* Choice (B) should read, "If the food you ordered smells <u>bad</u> . . ."

William Henry Harrison <u>died</u> of pneumonia just thirty
                        A
days after he <u>took</u> the <u>oath of office</u> <u>as the ninth</u> president
               B   C   D
of the United States. <u>No error.</u>
                         E

When an action in the past has taken place before another action in the past, the past perfect tense *had taken* is used, not the past tense *took.* Choice (B) should read, ". . . just thirty days after he <u>had taken</u> the . . ."

<u>By the time</u> we <u>arrived</u> at the ski resort, twelve inches <u>of</u>
  A   B   C
new snow had <u>all ready</u> fallen. <u>No error.</u>
              D   E

This sentence contains an example of words often confused. *All ready* means "completely ready; all prepared." *Already* means "previously." Since the sentence suggests that the new snow had fallen before the time of arrival, choice (D) should read, ". . . new snow had <u>already</u> fallen."

After <u>all these</u> years, I still <u>remember</u> Jenny, a sweet little
       A   B
<u>freckle-faced</u> girl, <u>who</u> I met at the World's Fair. <u>No error.</u>
  C   D   E

In this sentence, you must decide whether to use *who* or *whom.* If one of these pronouns is the subject of the verb, use *who;* if it is the object of the verb, use *whom.* Here, the pronoun is the object of the verb *met.* To see this more clearly, try substituting a more familiar pronoun: "I met she" (subject of verb) or "I met her" (object of verb). Choice (D) should read, ". . . girl, <u>whom</u> I met . . ."

Most literary critics <u>agree</u> that <u>the author's</u> latest novel is
                       A   B
<u>nowhere near</u> as insightful <u>as her</u> earlier works. <u>No error.</u>
  C   D   E

The expression *nowhere near* is a poor English substitute for the correct form *not nearly.* Choice (C) should read, ". . . latest novel is <u>not nearly</u> as insightful . . ."

Ms. Thomas, <u>as well as</u> several other <u>committee members,</u>
              A   B
<u>work</u> from four to six hours <u>each day</u> to raise money for
  C   D
charity. <u>No error.</u>
           E

A verb must agree in number with its subject (singular—singular; plural—plural). The number of the subject ("Ms. Thomas") is not changed by a phrase following the subject ("as well as several other committee members"). Since the subject is singular, it calls for the singular verb *works,* not *work.* Choice (C) should read, "Ms. Thomas . . . <u>works</u> . . ."

<u>Although</u> the penguin is a bird that <u>cannot fly,</u> <u>it is able to</u>
  A   B   C
swim <u>quick</u> underwater. <u>No error.</u>
      D   E

The verb *swim* must be modified by an adverb—*quickly,* not the adjective *quick.* (Remember that most adverbs end in *ly.*) Choice (D) should read, ". . . swim <u>quickly</u> underwater."

After a few months, <u>Karen realized</u> she <u>would not have</u>
                      A   B
enough time <u>for</u> playing the violin, practicing karate, and
             C
<u>to campaign</u> for office. <u>No error.</u>
  D   E

Related ideas must be expressed in similar form within a sentence. Match nouns with nouns, verbs with verbs, adjectives with adjectives, and so on. Here the sentence uses gerunds to express the first two related ideas, *playing* and *practicing.* Therefore, the third related idea must also be expressed with a gerund, not an infinitive. Choice (D) should read, ". . . and <u>campaigning</u> for office."

The homework assignment <u>was to</u> <u>match up</u> the <u>words</u> in
                          A   B   C
column one <u>with the definitions</u> in column two. <u>No error.</u>
             D   E

This sentence is unnecessarily wordy. No preposition is needed after the word *match.* Choice (B) should read ". . . <u>match</u> the words . . ."

The teacher told Jason to <u>bring</u> the letter
                          A

to the <u>principal</u> and to <u>return</u> with a reply
       B   C

<u>as soon as possible.</u> <u>No error.</u>
        D   E

Bring and *take* have slightly different meanings. *Bring* indicates motion toward the speaker (for example, <u>bring</u> it to me). *Take* indicates motion away from the speaker (for example, <u>take</u> it to him). Since the sentence indicates action away from the speaker, choice (A) should read, "The teacher told Jason to <u>take</u> the letter to the principal . . ."

After Mr. Roberts and Mr. Williams <u>escorted</u> their wives
                                    A

<u>to the party,</u> <u>they</u> soon began <u>to argue.</u> <u>No error.</u>
       B   C   D   E

This sentence includes an ambiguous pronoun reference. It is unclear who "began to argue." The pronoun *they* could refer to Mr. Roberts and Mr. Williams or to their wives. Replace the confusing pronoun. Choice (C) should read, ". . . <u>the two men</u> soon began to argue" or ". . . <u>the two women</u> soon began to argue."

We were <u>interested and</u> <u>prepared for</u> the news <u>of the</u> latest
           A   B   C

<u>developments</u> in the Middle East. <u>No error.</u>
     D   E

The words *interested* and *prepared* should both be followed by prepositions to introduce the object *news*. Thus, "prepared <u>for</u>" is correct, but *interested* must also be followed by a preposition. Choice (A) should read, "We were interested <u>in</u> and prepared for . . ."

If the Petersons had <u>began</u> <u>their</u> fishing trip
                       A   B

a week earlier, they would not <u>have had</u> to worry about
     C   D

the holiday traffic. <u>No error.</u>
                        E

The past tense of *begin* is *began*. However, the past perfect tense is used here ("had _____"). The past perfect tense of *begin* is *had begun*. Choice (A) should read, "If the Petersons had <u>begun</u> . . ."

David <u>was flattered</u> to learn that teachers <u>in the</u> Art
          A   B

Department compared <u>his</u> drawings <u>with Picasso.</u>
                       C   D

<u>No error.</u>
    E

As it is written, the sentence omits words necessary to make the meaning clear. David's drawings are not being compared with Picasso, but with Picasso's drawings. Choice (D) should read, ". . . with <u>those of</u> Picasso."

A vocabulary <u>notebook</u> or vocabulary <u>flashcards</u>
                A   B

is essential <u>for review</u> <u>when studying</u> for a standardized
                 C   D

test. <u>No error.</u>
          E

When a singular noun *notebook* and a plural noun *flashcards* are joined by *or,* the verb agrees with the nearer noun. Since the nearer noun, *flashcards,* is plural, the verb must also be plural, *are,* not *is*. Choice (C) should read, "A vocabulary notebook or vocabulary flashcards <u>are</u> essential . . ."

<u>Long after</u> the tornado <u>had passed,</u> the small village
      A   B

<u>continued to</u> suffer from <u>it's</u> effects. <u>No error.</u>
      C   D   E

The only time *it's* takes an apostrophe is as a contraction for *it* and *is*. The possessive adjective *its* modifies the noun *effects*. Choice (D) should read, ". . . suffer from <u>its</u> effects."

Sentence revision items.

The other items on the Test of Standard Written English require the student to improve poorly written sentences where necessary. Obviously, this is more difficult than locating errors and not correcting them. For both parts of this test, however, the best preparation is wide reading of correctly written English, which helps to develop an eye for what is correct. While the explanations that follow the items often use grammatical terms, most items depend largely upon having a good eye. You do not need to know the grammatical terms if you have a good grasp of standard written English.

Directions: In each of the following sentences, some part or all of the sentence is underlined. Below each sentence you will find five ways of phrasing the underlined part. Select the answer that produces the most effective sentence, one that is clear and exact, without awkwardness or ambiguity. In choosing answers, follow the requirements of standard written English. Choose the answer that best expresses the meaning of the original sentence.

Answer (A) is always the same as the underlined part. Choose answer (A) if you think the original sentence needs no revision.

Nitrogen is part of your body <u>and makes up</u> 97 percent of the air you breathe.

(A) and makes up
(B) but makes up
(C) which makes up
(D) having made up
(E) although it makes up

The conjunction *and* is used to connect relatively equal parts of a sentence. Choices (B) and (E) suggest that the two parts of the sentence present contrasting ideas. In choice (C), the pronoun *which* is ambiguous. Choice (D) suggests a causal relationship between the two ideas presented in the sentence. Choice (A) is correct.

George Washington was a big <u>man, he stood</u> 6 feet, 2 inches tall and weighed a muscular 200 pounds.

(A) man, he stood
(B) man; he stood
(C) man, with him standing
(D) man in height; he stood
(E) man by standing

Choice (A) is incorrect because even with a comma, this is a run-on sentence. Choices (C) and (D) are unnecessarily wordy. Choice (E) incorrectly suggests a causal relationship between the two major clauses. Choice (B) is correct because the semicolon is properly used to separate main clauses that are not joined by a coordinating conjunction.

Meredith jumped to her feet <u>whenever she heard the telephone ring.</u>

(A) whenever she heard the telephone ring
(B) whenever she heard that the telephone rang
(C) although she heard the telephone ring
(D) at the time she hears the telephone ring
(E) hearing the telephone ring

Choices (B), (C), and (E) change the meaning of the sentence. Choice (E) has the additional problem of creating an unclear reference by omitting the pronoun "she." Choice (D) is wordy and improperly shifts to the present tense. Choice (A) is correct.

Each item scores the same amount, so you should answer easy questions first. Wild guessing is not a good idea.

The young actress <u>refused accepting constructive criticism or to grant spontaneous interviews.</u>

(A) refused accepting constructive criticism or to grant spontaneous interviews
(B) refused to accept constructive criticism or granting spontaneous interviews
(C) refusing to accept constructive criticism or to grant spontaneous interviews
(D) refused the acceptance of constructive criticism or to grant spontaneous interviews
(E) refused to accept constructive criticism or to grant spontaneous interviews

Choices (A), (B), and (D) are incorrect because they lack parallel structure. The two related parts of the sentence should use the same verb form (either "to accept" and "to grant" or "accepting" and "granting"). Choice (C) doesn't complete the thought of the sentence. Only choice (E) uses parallel structure correctly in a complete sentence.

<u>At first, telephone numbers were resisted by people who were customers of the telephone company as a threat to their individuality.</u>

(A) At first, telephone numbers were resisted by people who were customers of the telephone company as a threat to their individuality.
(B) At first, telephone numbers threatened the individuality of resisting customers.
(C) At first, telephone numbers were resisted by customers as a threat to their individuality.
(D) A threatened telephone company resisted giving phone numbers to its first customers.
(E) The first telephone company threatened its customers with individual phone numbers.

Choice (A) is wordy. Choices (B), (D), and (E) change the meaning of the original sentence. Choice (C) is correct because it expresses the meaning of the original sentence concisely and clearly.

<u>When the Dean of Admissions reviewed Sam's college application,</u> he noticed that Sam had neglected to sign his name.

(A) When the Dean of Admissions reviewed Sam's college application
(B) After the Dean of Admissions had reviewed Sam's college application
(C) When the Dean of Admissions reviews Sam's college application
(D) When a review of Sam's college application was made by the Dean of Admissions
(E) The Dean of Admissions, having reviewed Sam's college application

Choice (B) changes the meaning of the original sentence. Choice (C) shifts to the present tense. Choice (D) uses the passive voice to create an awkward construction. Choice (E) results in an awkward construction when combined with the rest of the sentence. Choice (A) is correct.

The heart, along with thousands of miles of veins and arteries, <u>supply vital oxygen to all parts</u> of the body.

(A) supply vital oxygen to all parts
(B) supplies vital oxygen to all parts
(C) supplies oxygen to all vital parts
(D) supplies much needed vital oxygen to all parts
(E) has supplied vital oxygen to all parts

Choice (A) is incorrect because the subject *(heart)* requires a singular verb. The relationship between the subject and its verb *(supplies)* is not changed by an intervening phrase. Choice (C) is incorrect because it changes the meaning of the original sentence. Choice (E) also changes its meaning by introducing a new tense. Choice (D) is redundant—*much needed vital.* Choice (B) is correct.

<u>Having read the newspaper accounts of inner turmoil, war seemed inevitable.</u>

(A) Having read the newspaper accounts of inner turmoil, war seemed inevitable.
(B) Newspaper accounts of inner turmoil having been read, war seemed inevitable.
(C) While reading the newspaper accounts of inner turmoil, we felt that war was inevitable.
(D) We felt that war was inevitable, having read the newspaper accounts of inner turmoil.
(E) Having read the newspaper accounts of inner turmoil, we felt that war was inevitable.

Choice (C) changes the meaning of the original sentence. Choices (A), (B), and (D) are incorrect because each contains a dangling participle. The subject of the sentence, *we,* must be modified by the participle construction, as it does in (E), the correct choice.

<u>Herbert Hoover was the first president to have a phone installed on his desk and he was the 31st president of the United States.</u>

(A) Herbert Hoover was the first president to have a phone installed on his desk and he was the 31st president of the United States.
(B) Herbert Hoover was the first president to have a phone installed on his desk, he was the 31st president of the United States.
(C) Herbert Hoover, the 31st president of the United States, was the first president to have a phone installed on his desk.
(D) Since he was the 31st president of the United States, Herbert Hoover was the first to have a phone installed on his desk.
(E) Herbert Hoover was the 31st president of the United States to have a phone installed on his desk.

Choice (A) is incorrect because it gives equal importance to both main clauses. Choice (B) is a run-on sentence. Choices (D) and (E) change the meaning of the original sentence. Choice (C) is correct because it emphasizes the main idea of the sentence, while including other information between commas that act to set off part of the sentence in the way that dashes or parentheses do.

Quantitative Comparison

Because the quantitative-comparison items are unlike almost any other exercises in mathematics, it is important to get some experience with them before taking the test. The directions below describe their nature in detail. Remember to study the directions.

These items, like all SAT items, are answered by marking the correct choices on a separate answer sheet. All SAT answer sheets have five choices on the sheet that can be marked, but quantitative-comparison items provide only four choices. Therefore, if you mark the fifth choice, (E), you will get no credit. It will be as if you had skipped the item. It is always important to make sure that the answer you mark on the sheet is the one you intend. The machine scorer pays no attention to anything except what is on the answer sheet.

Probably these items have the most important directions with which to become familiar with all types of test items, since the type is so rare in nontesting situations. Make sure that you understand the directions, including the three notes at the end.

If you mark the E choice for a quantitative comparison item, that item will not be scored.

CLOSE ATTENTION *to test instructions without a feeling of panic will enable you to do your best.*

Directions: Each of the following questions consists of two quantities, one in Column A and one in Column B. You are to compare the two quantities and answer

A   if the quantity in Column A is greater;
B   if the quantity in Column B is greater;
C   if the two quantities are equal;
D   if the relationship cannot be determined from the information given.

Notes: 1. In certain questions, information concerning one or both of the quantities to be compared is centered above the two columns.
2. In a given question, a symbol that appears in both columns represents the same thing in Column A as it does in Column B.
3. Letters such as x, n, and k stand for real numbers.

Column A	Column B

$$a = -\frac{1}{3}$$
$$b = \frac{1}{5}$$

$$\frac{b}{a} \qquad\qquad \frac{a}{b}$$

Substitute the given values for a and b in each expression. Simplify the expressions and compare.

$$\frac{b}{a} = \frac{1/5}{-1/3} \qquad\qquad \frac{a}{b} = \frac{-1/3}{1/5}$$

$$= \frac{1}{5} \div \frac{1}{3} \qquad\qquad = -\frac{1}{3} \div \frac{1}{5}$$

$$= \frac{1}{5} \cdot -3 = -\frac{3}{5} \qquad = -\frac{1}{3} \cdot 5 = -\frac{5}{3} = -1\frac{2}{3}$$

The correct choice is (A) since $-\frac{3}{5} > -1\frac{2}{3}$.

$$\frac{2}{3} - \frac{1}{6} \qquad\qquad\qquad \frac{7}{18}$$

Evaluate the expression in Column A and compare it with the expression in Column B.

$$\frac{2}{3} - \frac{1}{6} = \frac{4}{6} - \frac{1}{6}$$

$$= \frac{3}{6} \text{ or } \frac{1}{2} \qquad \frac{1}{2} > \frac{7}{18}$$

The answer is (A).

Column A	Column B

x is an integer less than 0.

$$3x \qquad\qquad \frac{x}{x} + x$$

One approach is to make a table of values for x and look for a pattern in the values of the two given expressions.

x	-1	-2	-3	-4
$3x$	-3	-6	-9	-12
$\frac{x}{x} + x$	0	-1	-2	-3

From the table, you can see that the expression in Column B is always greater than the expression in Column A, and that relationship will continue to be true for all values of x that are less than 0. The correct choice is (B).

$$S = \{0, 2, 4, 6, 8\}$$
$$T = \{2, 4, 6, 8\}$$

A number that is a member of S but not of T.

A number that is a member of both S and T.

The only number that is a member of S but not of T is 0. The numbers that are members of both sets are 2, 4, 6, and 8. Any of the numbers described in Column B are greater than the number described in Column A. The choice is (B).

$$3.14 \qquad\qquad\qquad \pi$$

While 3.14 is a useful, often used approximation for π, it does not equal π. π is an irrational number with an infinite number of decimal places that begins 3.14159 . . . . The correct choice is (B).

A die with the numbers 1 through 6 on each of its faces is to be rolled.

The probability of obtaining an odd number.

The probability of obtaining a number that is three or less.

There are six possible outcomes of this experiment that are all equally likely. Three of the possibilities are odd. Three of the possibilities are three or less. Therefore, the probabilities of the two events described in Columns A and B are equal. The correct choice is (C).

$$x \qquad\qquad\qquad -x^3$$

For this type of problem, it is important to consider the range of values of x. Think of the two graphs:

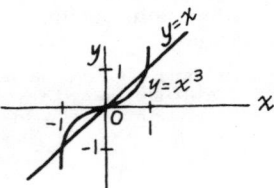

If x is a positive number greater than 1, Column B's expression will be greater than Column A's. If x is less than -1, Column A's expression will be greater than Column B's. Between -1 and 1, the situation changes from $x^3 > x$ to $x < x^3$ at 0. For $x = 0, 1$, or -1, the two expressions are equal. Therefore, the correct choice is (D).

$$x = 500$$
$$y = 499$$
$$(x + y)(x - y) \qquad\qquad 1000$$

Although the given values of x and y are large, the problem can be solved mentally. The sum of x and y is 999; the difference between x and y is 1. Therefore, $(x + y)(x - y) = 999 \times 1 = 999$. The correct choice is (B).

Column A   Column B

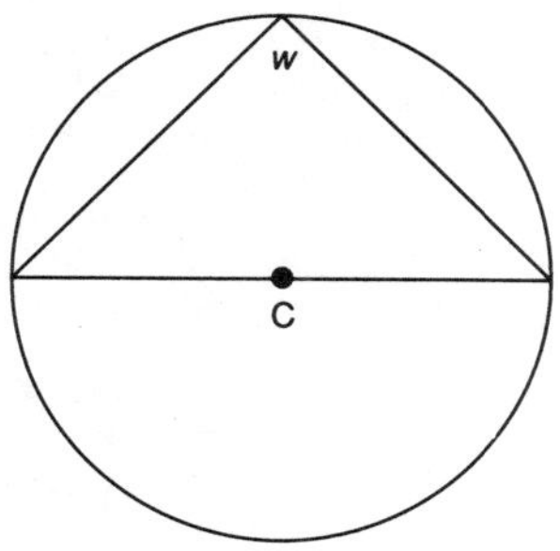

C is the center of
the circle; $w > 0$.

90° w

w is the measure of an angle inscribed in a semicircle. Its measure is half the measure of its arc of 180°, which is 90°. Therefore, the correct choice is (C).

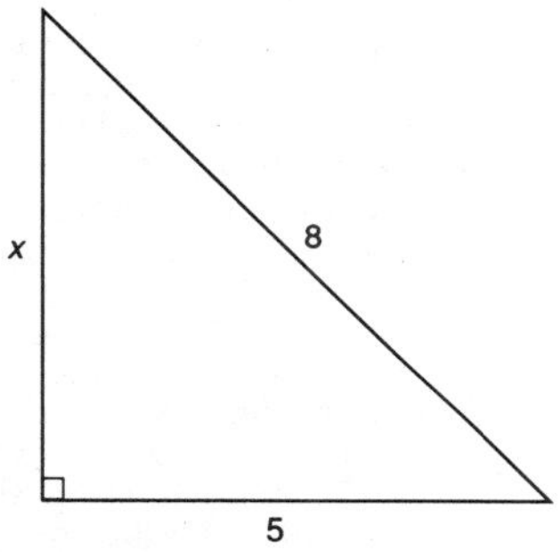

x $\sqrt{39}$

In a right triangle, the Pythagorean relationship states that
$a^2 + b^2 = c^2$ Substitute the values given in the drawing.

$x^2 + 5^2 = 8^2$
$x^2 + 25 = 64$
$x^2 = 39$
$x = \sqrt{39}$ The correct choice is (C).

Column A   Column B

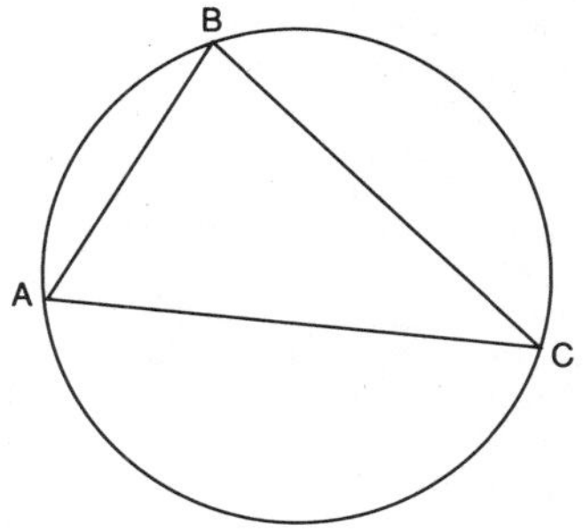

The diameter of the circle is 1.
A, B, and C are on the circumference.

The perimeter of   3
triangle ABC.

If the diameter is 1, then the largest possible value of AC is 1. The measures of AB and BC must each be less than 1, since if $AC = 1$, $\angle B = 90°$, and AC is the hypotenuse of a right triangle. Therefore, the perimeter of ABC must be less than 3. The correct choice is (B).

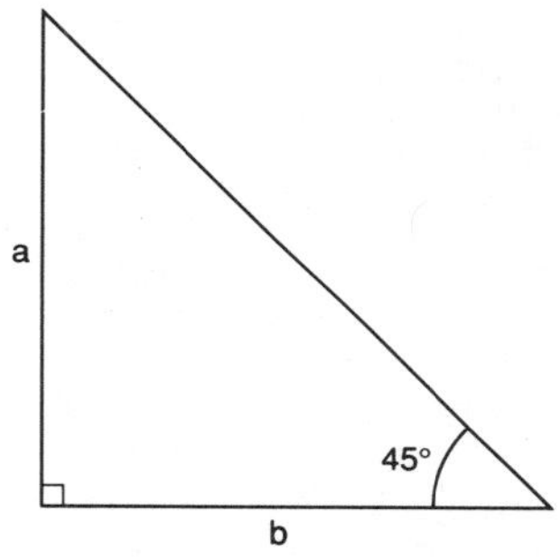

a b

Since the figure is a right triangle, the angle opposite b measures 90° − 45° = 45°. Since the two acute angles are equal, the triangle is isosceles. The correct choice is (C).

The ACT Assessment

The American College Testing (ACT) program has many of the same purposes as the SAT and its embedded Test of Standard Written English. Both batteries of tests are used to help institutions of higher learning predict the academic success of their applicants, and both are used for placement of entering students in appropriate classes. Some colleges prefer one or the other, but many will accept either. Some situations require taking both; for example, you may want to seek a scholarship that requires an ACT assessment even though the school you plan to attend requires an SAT.

There are significant differences in the two sets of tests. While the SAT tests only verbal and mathematical *aptitudes*, ACT tests academic *achievement* in four areas: English,

mathematics, reading, and science reasoning. The fundamental idea behind ACT is that measuring the specific skills and knowledge expected from juniors in secondary school is the best way to predict how the same students will fare in developing further skills and knowledge in college. ACT items are based on the objectives that state education departments have developed for grades seven to twelve, nationally used textbooks for those grades, and the expert opinions of educators working with students in those grades.

Since ACT measures academic achievement, most of the items involve applying knowledge and reasoning skills to specific situations. Often the items are designed to combine knowledge and skills from several different parts of the curriculum.

Nature of ACT. All of the items on ACT are multiple choice, with four choices for each item. Alternating items have the choices indicated as A, B, C, D and F, G, H, J; this helps prevent mistakes caused by marking a choice on the wrong line on the separate answer sheet.

Because there are only four choices and because incorrect choices are not penalized, *guessing is a good strategy.* You should try to answer every question even when you have no idea what the answer is. Four items answered randomly are likely to increase your score, but four items skipped will not. Obviously, guessing is an even better strategy when you can eliminate one or more of the choices.

The four different subject areas are separated into four tests, administered consecutively. Time allowed for each test ranges from 35 to 60 minutes, for a total test time of 2 hours 55 minutes. The longest amount of time is spent on mathematics.

Except for mathematics items, ACT items relate to short, connected sequences of sentences that are called *passages*. The passages are representative of material one might read in a textbook, an essay, or—in part of the reading test—a novel or short story. The passages are expected to be interesting reading for a junior in secondary school.

For the reading test, the passages are taken from published sources, but the English and science reasoning tests use passages especially designed for ACT. Although the English test assesses skills that must be learned outside the passage—such as punctuation and grammar—in general, the information needed to find correct choices is in the passage. In the reading test, the passages are chosen from four subject areas: prose fiction, humanities, social studies, and natural sciences. Equal emphasis is put on each area.

The mathematics test covers the content of academic-track mathematics for junior high school and secondary school. Academic students in most schools would be expected to complete courses in this part of mathematics by the end of grade eleven. The emphasis is heavier on the mathematics of the early grades, especially elementary algebra, than on the higher grades, with less than 10 percent of the test devoted to trigonometry.

Timing of ACT. Most students take ACT in the second semester of their junior year of high school. At this point, students probably have completed all the courses needed for ACT if they have been on an academic track. Those students who have not taken all the appropriate courses will have time to take the courses they need in their senior year. Thus, they can readily make up for any deficiencies they have and retake the test before their college applications are all in. ACT is offered during the early summer and in fall as well as in spring.

Preparation and test-taking rules. In general, the preparation for ACT is the same as that for the SAT (see above). You will need some sort of photo identification or else a valid, signed physical description from a school counselor or officer as well as an admission ticket. You are also responsible for bringing your own No. 2 pencils. Bring three pencils if you normally do not break pencil points while working. If you know that you press hard on a pencil, bring more. A wristwatch is helpful and ought to be part of your equipment. Don't try to bring one with a calculator on it. Calculators are not allowed by ACT in any form. Also, if your watch has an alarm, do not set it to time the tests. This is forbidden. Only your pencils, your watch, your identification, and your admission ticket can accompany you to this test. Books and scratch paper are forbidden. If you need scratch paper, write on your test booklet. Put your answers on the answer sheet, but do not use it as scratch paper.

The battery of tests is always given starting at 8:00 A.M. If you are late, you cannot take the test. Also, keep in mind that you cannot leave the room once the test begins, except for a short break after the first two tests. If you have to leave before completion of the test battery, you are allowed to try again at the next test date. If you cannot take that test, you need to register again and start all over.

As for long-term preparation, you might want to spend most of your time reviewing subjects you have not taken for a while. The idea is to overcome any forgetting factor. Remember: This is a test of academic *achievement*. If you took biology as a freshman and are taking ACT as a junior, it may be more useful to review biology than physics, which you are taking now. Even more important, work on any subjects that you have never studied. For example, if you did not take geometry in school, you probably will need some help in that subject. However, it is more useful to recognize long before you plan to take ACT that you will need some understanding of geometry and should take the course when it is offered.

Strategy. Answer as many items as possible, but do not answer without thinking about them. In theory, a person answering all items at random would get a score of 9 (out of a possible 36). The average for college-bound students is 20 to 21, depending on the year when the test is given. The score is reported separately for each main area— with a top score of 36 in each—and also for seven subtests—with a top score of 18 for each.

ACT does not give you a lot of time to answer each question, so you can improve your scores by answering the easy questions quickly. Because of the way ACT is structured—based on passages for the most part and on various mathematical disciplines—the easy questions are NOT mostly at the beginning. So you should plan from the start to run through each test in the battery *twice*.

For additional information about ACT, inquire at your high school guidance office, or write:

American College Testing Program
P.O. Box 168
Iowa City, Iowa 52243

SUCCESS IN A MATH TEST *requires careful attention to diagrams. Even when there is no diagram, you will find it helpful to make a sketch for the problem in your test booklet.*

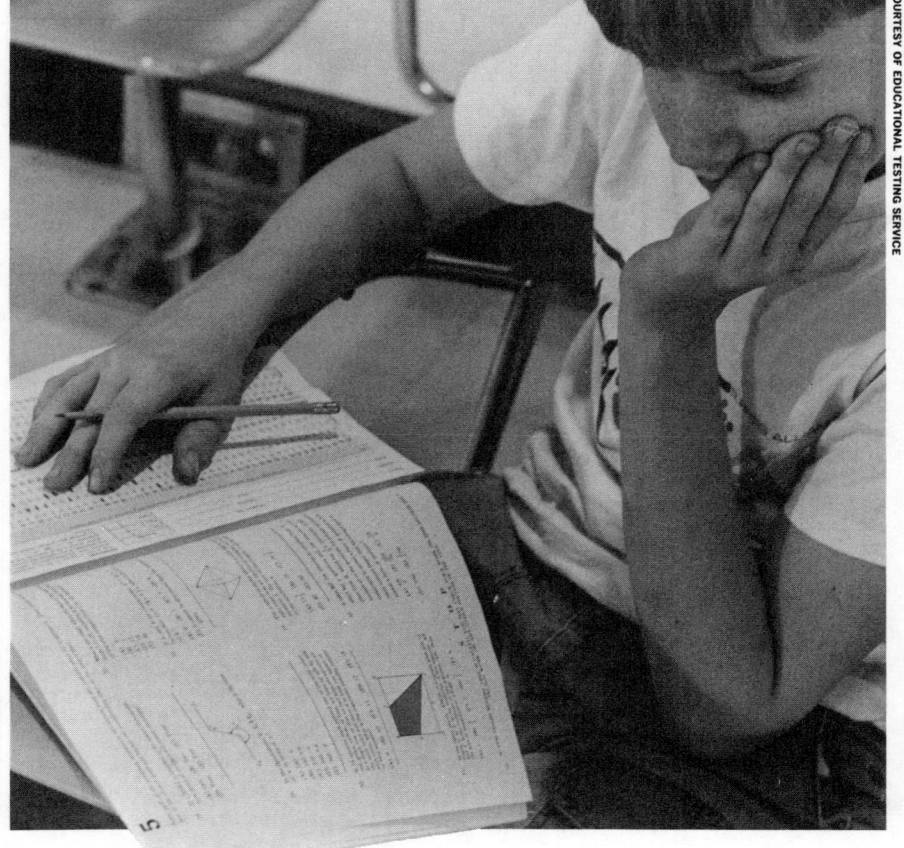

COURTESY OF EDUCATIONAL TESTING SERVICE

English Test

The ACT English Test contains 75 items that must be completed in 45 minutes. This would suggest a speed of 36 seconds per item, but that speed does not take into account that you need time for reading the passages. To complete the entire test, therefore, you should average about 30 seconds for each item. While the sample given below is based on a single passage, the actual test uses five different passages that are in five different writing styles.

This test is scored both as a whole and in two subsections, one based on Usage/Mechanics, which contains 40 items, and another based on Rhetorical Skills, which contains the remaining 35 items. Usage/Mechanics refers to such skills as choosing the word that is correct for standard written English, punctuation, capitalization, and sentence structure. Rhetorical Skills reflects the ability to write clearly and persuasively. Approximately equal numbers of the Rhetorical Skills items are devoted to writing strategy, organization of ideas, and writing style.

Although you should read the whole passage through before answering any of the items, as you answer the items you also should return to the passage frequently, particularly to the underlined portions. It is helpful to reread the portion of the passage with what you think to be the correct answer substituted for the original wording.

<u>Directions:</u> In the passage that follows, certain words and phrases are underlined and numbered. In the right-hand column you will find alternatives for each underlined part. You are to choose the one that best expresses the idea, makes the statement appropriate for standard written English, or is worded most consistently with the style and tone of the passage as a whole. If you think the original version is best, choose "NO CHANGE."

You will also find questions about a section of the passage or about the passage as a whole. These questions do not refer to an underlined portion of the passage, but rather are identified by a number or numbers in a box.

Read the passage through once before you begin to answer the questions that accompany it. You cannot determine most answers without reading several sentences beyond the question. Be sure that you have read far enough ahead each time you choose an alternative.

PREPARATION FOR COLLEGE ENTRANCE EXAMINATIONS *is often made available during regular classes. Informal study sessions with other students are also helpful.*

Once upon a time, many people thought no one should read science fiction stories. Parents didn't want children to read "escapist" magazines. Such far-fetched adventure stories were <u>not literature they</u> were not fit for
1
young minds to read.

Of course, much science fiction *is* poorly written. Many stories have shallow plots, stereotyped characters, and <u>not interestingly written</u>. But are
2
all westerns well written and interesting? Consider mystery stories, spy <u>novels, just</u>
3
plain mainstream novels. How many of them could be called <u>"great literature?"</u>
4

1. A. NO CHANGE
   B. not. Literature they
   C. not literature but they
   D. not literature; they

D. is correct. Choice A. is wrong because two related thoughts are expressed and they must be separated. Choice B. puts a period at the wrong place. In Choice C. the conjunction *but* results in nonsense.

2. F. NO CHANGE
   G. uninteresting writing
   H. not interesting written
   J. are written uninterestingly

G. is correct because it sets up a parallel construction (modifier and noun) with the other descriptions. Choice H. is ungrammatical. Choice J. is wrong because it results in a construction that is not parallel.

3. A. NO CHANGE
   B. novels. Just
   C. novels just
   D. novels, and just

D. is correct. Choices A. and C. are wrong because each word is part of a different item in a list, and items must be separated. Choice B. creates a sentence fragment.

4. F. NO CHANGE
   G. "great literature"?
   H. "great literature?
   J. "great literature."?

G. is correct. When quotation marks fall at the end of a sentence, the punctuation mark that ends the sentence usually goes inside the quotation marks. The exceptions are question marks and exclamation points that punctuate the sentences they are in, rather than the quotations.

continued

The truth is that most books are not great literature. They are amusing or interesting or frightening <u>but not thought provoking</u>. This is neither <u>more but not less</u> true of science fiction than of other types of stories and novels.

Certainly, in the past, some science fiction magazines featured <u>stories and tales</u> about "bug-eyed monsters" and "invasions from Mars." These events are unlikely. But "being swept off your feet by a handsome millionaire" is hardly more likely. Few people have "<u>single-handedly stopping</u> an illegal arms sale."

Open a modern science fiction <u>novel. You're</u> likely to find a story about how people act and react in new situations. These new situations just happen to be on another planet or on a space ship or in the future, instead of taking place on Earth right now. Often the plot of a science fiction story would work equally well in another kind of novel.

[1] Furthermore, science fiction <u>helps stretches</u> the imagination. [2] Both writers and readers get a chance to try out some far-fetched ideas. [3] Most of <u>these</u> will never become reality. [4] But television, submarines, and computers are among the things that first made <u>they're public appearances</u> in science fiction stories. [13]

5. A. NO CHANGE
   B. and not thought provoking
   C. but thought provoking
   D. or not thought provoking

A. is correct. All the other choices make non-sense out of the sentence.

6. F. NO CHANGE
   G. more and less
   H. more nor less
   J. more or less

H. is correct. Choices F. and G. do not make sense with *neither*. Although choice J. makes sense, *or* is the wrong word to use with *neither* (either/or, neither/nor).

7. A. NO CHANGE
   B. stories, and tales
   C. stories
   D. stories and, tales

C. is correct because *stories* and *tales* have the same meaning, so only one of them is needed. Adding a comma just adds another problem.

8. F. NO CHANGE
   G. single-handedly stop
   H. single-handed stopped
   J. single-handedly stopped

J. is correct. Choices F. and G. result in wrong verb tenses (*have stopping* and *have stop*). In both choices H. and J., *stopped* is correct, but choice H. uses the wrong modifier (an adjective instead of an adverb).

9. A. NO CHANGE
   B. novel. Your
   C. novel, you're
   D. novel you're

A. is correct. Choice B. uses *your*, a possessive adjective, instead of *you're*, a contraction of *you are*. Choices C. and D. incorrectly combine the two sentences.

10. F. NO CHANGE
    G. stretches
    H. help stretch
    J. helps, stretches

G. is correct. Only one verb is needed, so choice F. is wrong. In choice H., both verbs are plural instead of singular. Adding a comma in choice J. only adds another mistake.

11. The antecedent of the pronoun *these* is:
    A. science fiction writers
    B. science fiction readers
    C. televisions
    D. far-fetched ideas

D. is correct. Put each of the suggested antecedents into the sentence after *these* to see how it fits. (*Most of these ideas* is the only one that makes sense when it's added.)

12. F. NO CHANGE
    G. there public appearances
    H. their public appearances
    J. public appearance

H. is correct. Choice F. uses *they're* instead of *their*, a possessive adjective. Choice G. uses an adverb (*there*) in place of *their*. Choice J. would have been correct if the subject of the subordinate clause (*that*) did not have a plural antecedent (*things*), making *that* plural. For this reason, *appearances* is correct.

13. In order to maintain the flow of ideas, sentence [3] should be:
    A. put after sentence [1]
    B. kept where it is now
    C. put after sentence [4]
    D. removed entirely

B. is correct. Sentence [3] provides a good transition from the idea in sentence [2] to the idea in sentence [4]. If sentence [3] came after sentence [1] or after sentence [4], the ideas would be confusing. If it were removed, the ideas in sentences [2] and [4] would not be connected very well.

continued

Is science fiction "escapist"

reading? Perhaps it is. Yet everyone

needs to <u>escape, at times, isn't</u> that
                              14
what travel advertisements offer?

"Get away to a magic island!" or

"Escape to paradise!" are familiar

themes. <u>Well I</u> don't need to travel to
        15
magic islands or paradise. I can

escape to my favorite distant planet

or an entirely <u>new place. Depending</u>
                          16
on whether I want something

familiar or something new. <u>Its</u> the
                            17
best vacation I can <u>find, then</u> I can go
                      18
out into space myself to see what

wonderful things actually exist there.

---

14. F. NO CHANGE
  G. escape at times, isn't
  H. escape, at times isn't
  J. escape at times. Isn't

J. is correct. The two ideas need to be in separate sentences. All the other choices simply move unneeded commas into different places without making the thought clear.

---

15. A. NO CHANGE
  B. Well, I
  C. Well. I
  D. Well; I

B. is correct. In this sentence, *well* is an interjection that must be set off by a comma. It is not, however, emphatic enough to be set off in a clause or sentence of its own.

---

16. F. NO CHANGE
  G. new place depending
  H. new place, depending
  J. new, place depending

H. is correct. If it is not changed, then *Depending* is the first word of a sentence fragment. Choice G. is wrong because the dependent clause should be set off from the main clause. In choice J., the comma is in the wrong place.

---

17. A. NO CHANGE
  B. It's
  C. its
  D. it's

B. is correct. Choice A. leaves a possessive adjective *(Its)* where a contraction of *it is* should be. Notice that both choices C. and D. start the sentence with small letters.

---

18. F. NO CHANGE
  G. find. Then
  H. find, when
  J. find until

J. is correct. The word *then* doesn't make sense in the sentence, nor does the word *when*. The word *until* continues the idea already expressed in the sentence.

Mathematics Test

The mathematics test provides 60 minutes for 60 items. It emphasizes reasoning about numbers, not memorizing formulas or computation. In addition to the score for the entire test, scores are also reported for three subtests: Pre-Algebra/Elementary Algebra has 24 items, while Intermediate Algebra/Coordinate Geometry and Plane Geometry/Trigonometry have 18 items each. More specifically, pre-algebra is 20 percent of the test, elementary algebra is 20 percent, intermediate algebra and coordinate geometry together are 30 percent, plane geometry is 23 percent, and trigonometry is just 7 percent.

Although you have one minute for each item, you should try to complete the items in less than a minute to give time to review and recheck your work. ACT test makers advise solving the problem, not eliminating answers by working backward; but sometimes it is fairly easy to eliminate some or all of the incorrect choices. Checking is especially important no matter how you arrive at your answers. Check each answer in the original item and be sure your answers are reasonable. Test items are not written about people who weigh thousands of pounds or about distances between towns of less than a mile.

Many items require several steps to complete, and distractors—incorrect answers—are often based on completing only a few of those steps. Thus, it is especially important to make sure you have gone through all the steps called for.

<u>Directions:</u> Solve each problem and choose the correct answer. Do not linger over problems that take too much time. Solve as many as you can; then return to the others in the time you have left for this test.

<u>Note:</u> Unless otherwise stated, all of the following should be assumed.
1. Illustrative figures are NOT necessarily drawn to scale.
2. Geometric figures lie in a plane.
3. The word *line* indicates a straight line.
4. The word *average* indicates an arithmetic mean.

The value of $[9 - (6 - 11)] + [(14 - 3) - (3 - 6)]$ is:

  A. -10
  B. -6
  C. 12
  D. 18
  E. 28

With this type of exercise, it is important to work carefully. There are parentheses inside brackets. Work in the innermost parentheses first. Be careful to record the correct signs.

$$[9 - (6 - 11)] + [(14 - 3) - (3 - 6)] = [9 - (-5)] + [11 - (-3)]$$
$$= [9 + 5] + [11 + 3]$$
$$= 14 + 14$$
$$= 28$$

The correct choice is E.

During his last four basketball games, Peter scored 28, 24, 31, and 36 points. Peter wants to have an average of 30 points after his next game. How many points must he score in the fifth game?

  F. 28
  G. 29
  H. 30
  J. 31
  K. 32

The correct choice is J. To obtain an average of 30 over five games, Peter must score a total of 5×30, or 150 points in all. He has already scored 119 points $(28 + 24 + 31 + 36)$. $150 - 119 = 31$.

The area of a square with a side x is 3. What is the area of a square with side $2x$?

  F. $2\sqrt{3}$
  G. 6
  H. 12
  J. 18
  K. 36

If the area of a square with side x is 3, you know that $x^2 = 3$. The area of a square with side $2x$ is $(2x)^2 = 4x^2$. If $x^2 = 3$, $4x^2 = 4 \times 3 = 12$. The correct choice is H.

If $2(x + 4) = 12$, find $x - 3$.

A. -2
B. -1
C. 1
D. 2
E. none of these

It is important to read the whole question. You not only must solve for x, but you are asked to find the value of $x - 3$.
$$2(x + 4) = 12$$
$$2x + 8 = 12$$
$$2x + 8 - 8 = 12 - 8$$
$$2x = 4$$
$$\frac{2x}{2} = \frac{4}{2}$$
$$x = 2$$
$$\text{If } x = 2, x - 3 = 2 - 3 = -1.$$
The correct choice is B.

How much more is $\frac{1}{2}$ of $\frac{5}{6}$ than $\frac{5}{6}$ of $\frac{1}{2}$?

A. $\frac{5}{6}$
B. $\frac{1}{2}$
C. $\frac{1}{3}$
D. $\frac{1}{12}$
E. 0

While you can get the correct choice by computing
$$\frac{1}{2} \times \frac{5}{6} - \frac{5}{6} \times \frac{1}{2},$$
a little reasoning will save you some time. Since the order of the factors does not affect the product, $\frac{1}{2}$ times $\frac{5}{6}$ and $\frac{5}{6}$ times $\frac{1}{2}$ will have the same product. Therefore, their difference is 0. The correct choice is E.

If $2^{n+2} = 16$, then n equals

F. 0
G. 1
H. 2
J. 4
K. 6

The correct choice is H. To solve equations with exponents, it is important to remember that each side of the equation must have the same base.
$$2^{n+2} = 16 \qquad 2^{n+2} = 2^4$$
$$n + 2 = 4$$
$$n = 2$$

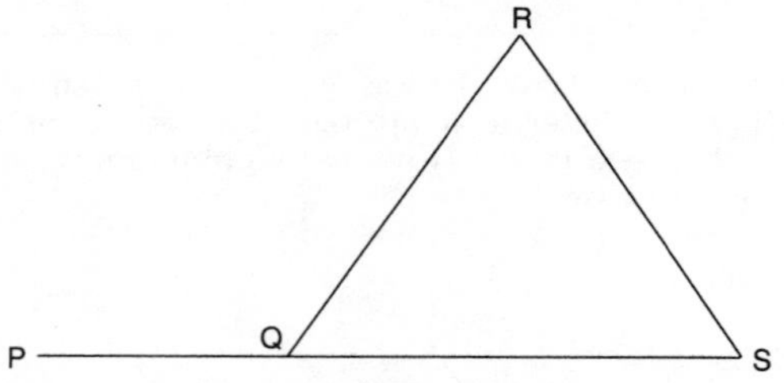

In triangle RQS, $QR = RS$. QS is a segment of PS. Angle RQP measures 125°. Find the number of degrees in angle R.

A. 45
B. 55
C. 70
D. 110
E. 125

Since $QR = RS$, angle $RQS =$ angle RSQ. Angle RQP and angle RQS form a straight angle, so the sum of their measures is 180.
$$180 - 125 = 55$$
$$\text{angle } RQS + \text{angle } RSQ + \text{angle } R = 180$$
$$55 + 55 + \text{angle } R = 180$$
$$110 + \text{angle } R = 180$$
$$\text{angle } R = 180 - 110 = 70.$$
The correct choice is C.

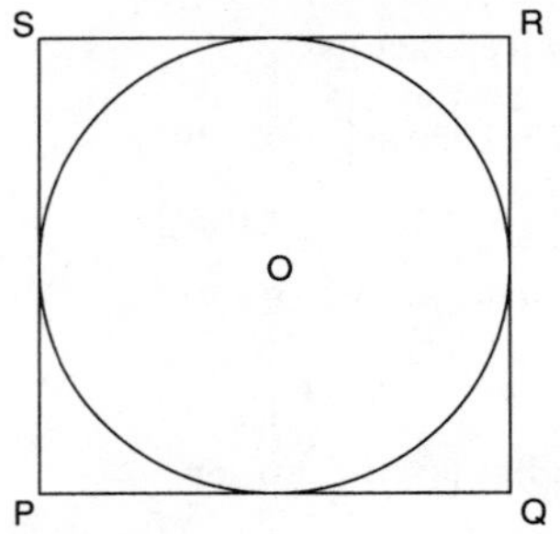

The area of square $PQRS$ is 64 square inches. Find the area of circle O.

F. 16π
G. 32π
H. 64π
J. $32\pi^2$
K. $64\pi^2$

The circle is inscribed in the square. The diameter of the circle has the same length as the side of the square. Find the diameter first. The diameter is the same length as one side of the square, which we will designate as s. Since $s^2 = 64$, $s = 8$. Therefore, the diameter of O is 8. The area of a circle is found using the formula $A = \pi r^2$, where r is the radius. The radius of the circle is half the diameter, or 4.
$$A = \pi r^2$$
$$A = \pi \cdot 4^2$$
$$= 16\pi$$
The correct choice is F.

Two trains leave Bay City at noon. One travels due east at 60 mph. The other travels due north at 80 mph. How many miles apart are the trains at 2 P.M.?

A. 100 mi.
B. 140 mi.
C. 200 mi.
D. 240 mi.
E. 340 mi.

Draw a diagram. In two hours, one train covers 120 miles and the other 160 miles. Their paths and a line connecting their new positions form a right triangle.

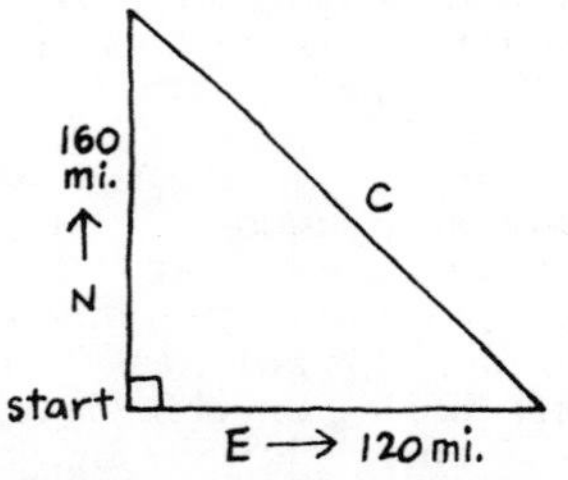

You could compute the hypotenuse, but there is an easier way. Since all the choices are whole numbers, the sides of the right triangle must be proportional to one of the common right triangles with all integral sides, such as a 3-4-5 right triangle or a 5-12-13 right triangle. Note that $120 = 3(40)$; $160 = 4(40)$. The distance between them, c, must therefore be $5(40) = 200$. The correct choice is C.

What number added to 70% of itself is equal to 136?

A. 76
B. 80
C. 96
D. 106
E. 206

It is useful to write and solve an equation for this problem.
$$\text{Let } x = \text{the number}$$
$$x + 0.70x = 136$$
$$1.7x = 136$$
$$x = \frac{136}{1.7}$$
$$x = 80$$
The correct choice is B.

The Clark family spent \$92,000 to build a house. Of this cost, 12% was for plumbing and heating, 4% for electrical wiring, and 8% for kitchen appliances. How much money was spent on other items?

F. \$76,000
G. \$22,080
H. \$69,920
J. \$24,000
K. \$84,200

The other items amount to 100% − 12% − 4% − 8%, or 76%, of the total. 76% of \$92,000 = \$69,920. The correct choice is H.

Since 76% is very close to 75%, you might estimate $\frac{3}{4}$ of 92,000 to find the correct choice:
$$\frac{3}{4} \times 92{,}000 = 3 \times 23{,}000 = 69{,}000.$$
The only choice close to this number is H.

If $(x - y)^2 = 60$ and $xy = 20$, find $x^2 + y^2$.

F. −40
G. 40
H. 80
J. 100
K. 140

Begin by squaring $x - y$:
$$(x - y)^2 = (x - y)(x - y)$$
$$= x^2 - 2xy + y^2$$
$$= x^2 + y^2 - 2xy$$
We know the value of $(x - y)^2$ and of xy.
$$60 = x^2 + y^2 - 2(20)$$
$$60 + 2(20) = x^2 + y^2$$
$$60 + 40 = x^2 + y^2$$
$$100 = x^2 + y^2$$
The correct choice is J.

If the angles of a triangle are in the ratio 1:2:3, the triangle is

F. acute
G. isosceles
H. right
J. equilateral
K. obtuse

Write an equation using the fact that the sum of the angles of a triangle is 180°. The angles of the triangles can be represented by x, $2x$, and $3x$.
$$x + 2x + 3x = 180$$
$$6x = 180$$
$$x = 30$$
If $x = 30$, $2x = 60$ and $3x = 90$. So the angles of the triangle measure 30°, 60°, and 90°. The correct choice is H.

A town council wants to form a subcommittee of three members to investigate a way of improving the recreation facilities of the town. There are six members of the council. In how many different ways can the subcommittee be formed?

A. 2
B. 3
C. 6
D. 20
E. 120

The order in which council members are named to the subcommittee does not matter. Here, you need to find out how many combinations of three can be made from a total of six. Remember that the number of combinations of n items taken r at a time is $n!/(r!(n − r)!)$, where the sign ! means to take the factorial.
$$\frac{6!}{3! \times 3!} = \frac{6 \times 5 \times 4 \times 3 \times 2 \times 1}{(3 \times 2 \times 1)(3 \times 2 \times 1)} = 5 \times 4 = 20.$$
The correct choice is D.

Reading Test

The ACT Reading Test contains 40 items that are to be answered in 35 minutes, which gives the average time per item as 52.5 seconds, but that does not allow time for reading the four passages. If you are keeping track of your time, you should try to complete each passage and set of associated items in about 8 minutes. That schedule allows you 3 minutes at the end for looking over your choices.

The four passages are equal in weight and encompass social studies, natural sciences, prose fiction (literature), and arts or humanities (art, music, philosophy, theater, architecture, or dance). The test is also scored for two subtests: Social Studies/Science and Arts/Literature.

Remember that you can return to the passage as often as needed to answer the questions.

Reading a passage is not unlike studying a complex picture. By quickly going through the passage or briefly looking at the picture, you will be able to get the main idea—in this case that a crime has been committed. A second run-through or closer study will reveal the details. The details of interest in an ACT passage have items referring to them. If the items are all about street signs, you do not need to worry about what the crime was. If the items are about the crime, you should ignore the street signs. In addition to observing the details, you may need to draw inferences. For example, an item might require deciding what specific crime has been committed, or who the victim was. While there are easily found clues to identify such information from the picture, the information is not shown explicitly.

DRUSKIS/PHOTO RESEARCHERS

ITEMS BASED ON PASSAGES *are common. Learn to look for clues in titles, paragraph structure, and footnotes.*

Directions: There are four passages in this test. Each passage is followed by several questions. After reading a passage, choose the best answer to each question. You may refer to the passages as often as necessary.

Passage I

Only a few hundred years ago, most of the people in the world could neither read nor write. Furthermore, they had no need for these skills. Each family raised much of its own food and hunted animals for meat. Money earned
5 by family members was used to buy items for which the family's homemade or homegrown goods could not be traded. Only people who did not have to earn a living had the time or the need to learn to read and write.

There were always exceptions to this. Sometimes par-
10 ents saw that reading and writing were keys to better jobs or social advancement, so they insisted that their children learn. Some individuals have such a thirst for knowledge that they will learn in spite of all obstacles.

Within the past few hundred years, there has been a
15 change in educational opportunities. The modern world demands basic reading and writing skills, especially in the industrialized nations. As developing nations progress beyond mere subsistence for most of their populations, these nations also create a situation in which
20 all citizens must have basic skills in order to function productively.

Think about it. If you walk into a supermarket and cannot read the labels, what can you buy? Cereal boxes have cartoon characters or other fanciful pictures on them; if
25 you cannot read the names, would you know the boxes contain cereals? Your child is ill and the doctor tells you what medicine to get for her. If you can't read, can you find and use the medicine you are told to buy? Think about all the things you do easily and quickly that require
30 reading.

In spite of this emphasis on reading, in spite of our culture's assumption that everyone can read, there are millions of people in the United States who cannot read well enough to function effectively. Without including
35 the rest of the world, if 250 million people live in the United States, then at least 3 million people are adult nonreaders. This is a conservative estimate; the actual number is probably much higher.

The nonreaders are not children in school—they are
40 parents and grandparents. It is an appalling statistic for a nation as wealthy as the United States. Perhaps the most appalling thing, though, is that the adult nonreader is a person who is ashamed to admit his or her illiteracy. Fear of ridicule and loss of a job often keep the people who
45 need help most from asking for it.

Always go through each test at least twice— once to answer as many easy questions as possible, the other times to deal with more difficult items.

According to the passage, the assumption that everyone can read and write is

A. based on conditions from long ago.
B. true only in industrialized nations.
C. not true even in the United States.
D. true everywhere in the modern world.

The correct answer is C. In the paragraph beginning on line 29, the author says that "there are millions of people in the United States who cannot read well enough to function effectively." A. is incorrect because most people long ago could neither read nor write. B. is incorrect because in the United States, one of the industrialized nations, millions of people cannot read well. D. is absurd.

In the past, people who could not read or write were uneducated because they

F. didn't have time or money for learning.
G. were unable to learn.
H. didn't want to learn to read and write.
J. were ashamed and afraid of asking for help.

F. is correct. This question requires you to infer the answer from clues given in the first paragraph. Answers G. and H. are not supported by any statement in the passage. J. refers to the last line of the passage, which is about people in today's world.

One example in the passage of a place where reading skills are essential is in

A. a developing nation.
B. a family.
C. a church.
D. a supermarket.

The answer is D. The question asks for a *place mentioned in the passage,* so A. and B. are wrong. Choice C. is wrong because churches are not mentioned in the passage.

The most likely change in educational opportunities today, compared with the past, is that

F. more adults need education than in the past.
G. education takes less time today.
H. education is more widely available.
J. fewer people need to be educated.

The question deals with "change in educational opportunities." H. is the only choice that addresses opportunity. Since the other choices do not, they are incorrect.

The figure of 3 million nonreaders includes

A. nonreading children only.
B. nonreading adults only.
C. both nonreading children and nonreading adults.
D. only people living in developing nations.

The answer is B. It can be found in the sentence beginning on line 32. A. and C. are incorrect because children are specifically excluded in line 36. D. is incorrect because the information given refers to the U.S. population.

The second paragraph of this passage implies that
F. people who cannot read are not interested in knowledge.
G. a few people learn to read despite societal obstacles.
H. people who cannot read should blame their parents.
J. no parents make their children learn to read for altruistic reasons.

Although the stem of this item asks what the passage implies, you should not read more into something than it suggests. The context is still a few hundred years ago. At that time there were obstacles to learning to read, but some people learned anyway for reasons stated in the passage, so the correct choice is G. Because of the obstacles, no judgment was made on the people who failed to learn to read, so neither choice F. or choice H. is correct. Although the passage specified other reasons than altruism for parents making their children learn, it did not rule out that possibility, so choice J. is also wrong.

Passage II

"A permit? Just to put in a new water heater?" Yes, you may need a permit for that, and for many other things as well. Many communities now require plumbing permits for nearly all plumbing work, whether new or replace-
5 ment. If a pipe is moved or replaced, if a fixture is added or moved, or if a building is attached to an existing city sewer system, a permit is probably needed.

Some people grumble, saying that government is getting too involved in people's lives. Well, maybe it is. But
10 think about some of the horror stories you've heard about badly done work that causes damage to someone's home and possessions. Permits can't prevent broken pipes or fixtures. But if issuing permits and inspecting the work can help minimize damage, isn't the inconvenience
15 worth it?

Think about that water heater again. A water heater seems like a simple enough device. Why should someone need a permit to replace a failed water heater? Water heaters keep water at a high temperature, in many cases
20 above 140 degrees. As long as you control the use of the water, it's fine to have it that hot. But suppose something breaks. Water at that temperature can badly hurt someone nearby unless it can be channeled away from living areas.

25 Furthermore, water heaters must be installed carefully. If they're installed improperly, they can explode and hurt or even kill home owners and their families. Issuing permits won't prevent all problems, but they may prevent some.

30 Other plumbing fixtures aren't as dangerous, of course, but badly installed pipes or fixtures can cause a lot of annoying and expensive damage. External work, such as providing septic tanks and leach fields, needs to be done properly, or tanks and fields will fail quickly and cost a
35 great deal more than necessary. Even a hookup to an existing sewer system can be a problem if it's not done correctly.

The author of this passage feels that government

F. is too involved in people's lives.
G. is not involved enough in people's lives.
H. is protecting people by requiring some permits.
J. should not allow individuals to have plumbing businesses.

H. is the correct answer. This question requires you to make an inference to find the answer. The last sentence in the second paragraph gives the clue to choosing the correct answer. F. is what the author says many people think, while G. and J. have no basis in the passage at all.

According to the passage, plumbing permits may prevent

A. water heaters from exploding.
B. fixtures from breaking down.
C. government from getting too involved in our lives.
D. some problems caused by badly done work.

The correct answer is D. The sentence beginning on line 12 contradicts answers A. and B. C. is incorrect because it states that plumbing permits may encourage, not prevent, excessive government interference.

One reason for issuing plumbing permits that is NOT given in the passage is

F. to protect the consumer.
G. to ensure that work is done properly.
H. to help prevent damage or injury.
J. to generate income for a community.

The answer is J. All the other answers can be found in the passage, although the passage may not use exactly the same words as the answers do.

The first paragraph leads one to believe that a permit is needed if

A. a new sink is installed.
B. a broken pipe is replaced with a same kind of pipe.
C. a new water heater is correctly installed.
D. any of A., B., or C. is undertaken.

The answer is D. since the first paragraph specifies both B. and C.: pipe replacement requires a permit, as does a new water heater. While A. is not specified, it is strongly implied.

Plumbing permits for external work help protect people against

F. problems with bathroom plumbing.
G. premature failure of septic tanks and leach fields.
H. problems with town-owned treatment plants.
J. injury from failure of water heaters.

G. is the correct answer, which can be found in the sentence starting on line 30. Answers F. and J. are both internal plumbing problems, and H. is not discussed.

Passage III

They hop, they gnaw, they have long ears and large eyes, and they love carrots and apples and seeds. But they are not rodents at all, although most people think they are. Rabbits are lagomorphs. They do have some
5 similarities to rodents, such as the need to gnaw in order to keep their teeth from growing too long.

What's the attraction of rabbits? Well, they are cute. Their big eyes and round shape appeal to humans' protective instincts. Rabbit fur is soft and warm, ideal for winter
10 wear for humans as well as for rabbits. Many people also think rabbit is delicious to eat. Rabbit meat is certainly nutritious, although it is not a complete protein and humans cannot live on rabbit alone. Still, eaten with beans or rice, rabbit provides all the nutrients you need with
15 less fat and cholesterol than present in other meats.

It goes without saying that many people are uncomfortable with the idea of eating rabbits because, they say, rabbits are so cute and helpless and furry. They may also like rabbit fur better when it's on the rabbit than on a
20 person. How about angora wool, then? It's soft and fine and warm, and the rabbit is not hurt at all by the collection process. It does take a great deal of wool to make any garment, so angora rabbit wool is expensive, but somehow that seems to make it more attractive rather than
25 less.

As pets, rabbits are great. They can be housebroken as cats are, and rabbits are quiet. Their major drawback as house pets is their need to gnaw. Rabbit food is made to be hard to satisfy the animal's need to use its teeth, but the
30 instinct is always there. House rabbits have been known to bite through electric wires and take mouthfuls of wooden furniture.

Don't keep your rabbit too warm. Remember that the animal's fur is effective as an insulator. Temperatures
35 that humans find comfortable for bare skin are much too hot for that furry little body. Rabbits also need to be dry and protected against drafts. An all-metal wire cage is a good home: It makes the rabbit feel safe, the rabbit cannot eat its home, the cage is easy to keep clean, and the
40 owner can check on the rabbit easily and quickly.

According to the article, rabbits are

A. pests that humans want to get rid of.
B. an excellent food source for humans.
C. cute but not useful in any way.
D. useful as food, as pets, and for fur and wool.

The answer is D. Clues to this answer appear throughout the passage. A. is incorrect because nothing in the passage supports this statement. B. is incorrect because rabbit meat is not a complete protein. C. is incorrect because rabbits are useful.

From the tone of the passage, it can be inferred that the author

F. likes rabbits very much.
G. thinks rabbits do not make good pets.
H. neither likes nor dislikes rabbits.
J. dislikes rabbits.

F. is the correct answer. Again, the answer is supported by clues throughout the passage. G. is directly contradicted by the first sentence on line 25. H. and J. are both inferences that are not supported by clues in the passage.

The difference between lagomorphs and rodents is

A. lagomorphs gnaw but rodents do not.
B. both lagomorphs and rodents gnaw.
C. rabbits are lagomorphs.
D. not given in the passage.

D. is correct. The passage says only that lagomorphs are not rodents, not how they are different. . . is directly contradicted by information in the passage. B. is not a difference but a similarity. C. is true but does not state a difference.

It can be inferred from the passage that rabbits may die if they are

F. kept warm and bathed once a week.
G. kept cool, dry, and out of drafts.
H. housed in all-metal wire cages.
J. raised for their wool.

The answer is F. This is a somewhat tricky question because it asks you for the opposite of what the passage states. G. and H. state what the passage says rabbits need. J. is directly contradicted in the information given in the sentence beginning on line 20.

According to the passage, some people do not like to eat rabbit because

A. rabbit meat tastes awful.
B. rabbit meat isn't nutritious.
C. they think rabbits are cute.
D. rabbits aren't rodents at all.

The answer is C. A. is an opinion not stated in the passage. B. is incorrect, according to the passage. D. is true but has nothing to do with why people do or don't eat rabbit.

Passage IV

In South America, on a grassy plain between the Amazon and Tocantins rivers, lie the remains of an ancient civilization. Great mounds rising above the floor of the floodplain are covered by ruined dwellings. The mounds
5 themselves, usually oval, rise about 20 feet above the forest floor, above the level of seasonal flooding. The tallest one rises about 65 feet. These mounds are not simply piles of earth; most of them are at least 10 acres in area, and the largest mound known covers more than 50 acres.
10 With 30 or 40 ancient people living in each of 8 to 12 houses, there would have been 200 to 400 people living on an average mound. Larger mounds could have housed 1,000 residents. Many mounds were built separate from nearby mounds, but there were also clusters of mounds.
15 Such a cluster might have housed 10,000 or more people. Thus, the total population of the area may have been more than 100,000 people.
These indigenous South Americans maintained a highly developed civilization for more than a thousand
20 years. The people raised and stored food. They produced beautiful, carefully modeled pottery decorated with many colors and formed into a variety of shapes for many uses. They used precious and semiprecious stones as ornaments and made stone tools of all kinds. The people
25 traded with each other and with people of other cultures from distant parts of South America.

We have not been able thus far to discover why this ancient civilization vanished. It had disappeared by 1300 A.D., long before European explorers arrived in South
30 America. As one would expect, by the time the Europeans arrived, other civilizations had spread across the territory once held by the Mound Builders. These later civilizations owed much in their art, tools, and other cultural artifacts to their predecessors.

According to the passage, most mounds were built

F. after the Europeans arrived.
G. to house one or two families.
H. large enough for hundreds of people.
J. for people to farm, not as living quarters.

H. is correct. The passage clearly states that an average mound would have had 200 to 400 people living on it. Since this civilization disappeared before the Europeans arrived, F. can be ruled out. G. is a possible answer, but it is contradicted by information in the passage. J. is not discussed anywhere in the passage.

The civilization discussed in the passage was mostly located

A. in the Andes Mountains.
B. in the Amazon River floodplain.
C. in the jungles near the Amazon River.
D. along the South American coastline.

The correct answer is B. Again, the passage clearly states that the mounds were built on the floodplain between the Amazon and Tocantins rivers. The Andes Mountains and the South American coastline, mentioned in A. and D., are never discussed in the passage. C. is plausible, but the passage supports B. more closely.

It can be inferred that the mounds were built in order to

F. protect the inhabitants from floods.
G. provide a defense against animals and invaders.
H. create better farmland for people.
J. keep people busy, since most people had no jobs.

F. is the answer, and the clue to choosing F. is found at the end of the sentence beginning on line 3. G. may also be true, but nowhere in the passage is there any clue to support this. H. is incorrect since people lived in houses on the mounds and nothing is said about where they farmed. J. is not supported in any way by the information in the passage.

Based on information in the passage, it is fair to say that an ancient civilization can be described as highly developed if it

A. supported more than 10,000 people.
B. lasted more than a thousand years.
C. built mounds at least 20 feet high and 10 acres in size.
D. created artifacts that are beautiful as well as useful.

The correct answer is D. All the statements here are true with respect to the Mound Builders, but only D. is relevant to cultural development. The clue to this is found in paragraph 3. By inference, the correct answer must also be applicable to other highly developed cultures. Again, only D. is generally applicable to other cultures.

According to the passage, the Mound Builders' civilization disappeared because

F. the Europeans arrived.
G. other civilizations invaded their territories.
H. of diseases and crime.
J. of factors not yet discovered by us.

J. is the correct answer. The last paragraph of the passage states specifically that there is no indication of why the civilization disappeared. F. cannot be true, since the Europeans arrived after the Mound Builders disappeared. G. and H. may be true, but there is no way to know at this time.

Science Reasoning Test

The ACT Science Reasoning Test is also a 40-item, 35-minute test with passages, but there are seven passages instead of the four in the Reading Test. You have only about 35 to 40 seconds to answer the items, leaving a couple of minutes to read each passage. Although you can take an average of 5 minutes for each passage and associated items, it would be better to take a bit more than 4 minutes to allow 3 to 7 minutes for review of your answers. In the example below, only two passages are given.

The contents of the passages include biology, chemistry, physics, astronomy, and geology and other earth sciences. There are three types of items: 38 percent are data representation (graph and table reading); 45 percent require research summaries (how were the experiments described designed and what did they mean?); and 17 percent are based on conflicting viewpoints within the passage. No subtest scores are reported.

The approach to these items is essentially the same as that for the Reading Test, although you may need to pay more attention to the details in the passages.

Directions: There are two passages in this test. Each passage is followed by several questions. After reading a passage, choose the best answer to each question. You may refer to the passages as often as necessary.

Passage I

Some scientists are experimenting with marine organisms harvested from the ocean and think that these sea-dwelling creatures may someday provide a source for new drugs. In the blue-green waters of the Caribbean Sea,
5 marine biologists dive along the coral reefs for samples of algae and marine invertebrates such as sponges and mollusks. Back aboard the research ship, cells taken from each organism are ground up and mixed with alcohol. The cell extracts then are placed in separate culture
10 dishes containing viruses and bacteria, the microorganisms that cause many diseases. Surprisingly, some of the algae and sponge extracts show that they can inhibit the growth of these microorganisms. Other marine invertebrates show the ability to stop the growth of cancer cells
15 in a laboratory dish. When a marine organism shows potential for use as a drug, it is taken to other laboratories, where further testing is done. There, some algae have shown the ability to stimulate the immune systems of test animals to fight disease more effectively. However, it will
20 take more time and research to isolate the active agent from each extract and to convert it into a drug that people can take. Once that is done, the new drug will have to undergo extensive testing. Despite the time involved in the development process, there is great potential for ob-
25 taining drugs from the sea.

According to the passage, which organisms show potential as a source of useful drugs?

A. algae and viruses
B. sponges and bacteria
C. coral and marine vertebrates
D. algae and marine invertebrates

D. is correct. In the second sentence of the passage, the author states that samples of algae and marine invertebrates such as sponges and mollusks were taken as samples. Although algae are mentioned in choice A. and sponges are mentioned in choice B., each is paired with an incorrect answer; microorganisms are mentioned later in the passage as disease-causing organisms. Choice C. is incorrect because no mention is made of marine vertebrates.

Which statement best describes the scientific research reported in the passage?

F. Scientists have been testing drugs that are derived from the extracts of marine organisms.
G. Marine scientists dive throughout the Caribbean to get samples of algae, sponges, and mollusks that are in danger of extinction.
H. Using extracts, scientists test the ability of marine organisms to inhibit the growth of disease-causing organisms.
J. Marine invertebrates are grown in laboratories and tested for their ability to inhibit the growth of disease-causing organisms.

H. is correct. The author says that extracts, and not drugs, are used in tests, so F. is incorrect. No mention is made that the marine organisms being tested are endangered, nor are they grown in laboratories, making choices G. and J. incorrect.

Which organisms do scientists classify in the same kingdom?

A. sponges and mollusks
B. bacteria and viruses
C. algae and sponges
D. algae and bacteria

A. is correct. Sponges and mollusks are both in the animal kingdom. The passage describes sponges and mollusks as examples of invertebrates, animals without backbones. Bacteria are classified as monerans; algae are plantlike protists; and viruses are not classified in any kingdom. Thus B., C., and D. are incorrect.

The immune system of an animal

F. fights disease.
G. inhibits the animal's growth.
H. kills all bacterial cells.
J. is usually stimulated by algae.

F. is correct. The immune system may inhibit bacterial growth, but not the growth of the animal itself, so G. is incorrect. The immune system may kill some harmful bacteria, but not all bacteria, especially helpful bacteria in the intestinal tract. For this reason, H. is incorrect. Only the immune systems of animals being tested under laboratory conditions were found to be stimulated by some algae, so J. is incorrect.

A group of cells ground up and mixed with alcohol is referred to in this passage as

A. an invertebrate.
B. an extract.
C. a microorganism.
D. a drug.

B. is correct. In the third sentence of the passage, the author describes how an extract is made. All other choices are wrong.

From this passage, what can you infer about the process of producing a safe, useful drug?

F. It is a simple procedure that can be done easily.
G. With scientific cooperation, a drug can be produced immediately after its source is discovered.
H. Producing a drug involves much time and research.
J. No inference from the passage can be made.

H. is correct. Although no precise time is established in the passage, it can be inferred that collecting the organisms, isolating the active agent, and producing and testing a drug takes a good deal of time. Certainly, the procedure is not simple (choice F.), a drug cannot be produced immediately after finding its source (choice G.), and H. supplies a valid inference (choice J.).

Because there are only four choices and because incorrect choices are not penalized, guessing is a good strategy.

You may be able to improve your score on the ACT by preparing for the test.

Passage II

Lasers have become part of our everyday life and have many uses. These concentrated beams of light are used in scanners at supermarket checkouts. Carbon dioxide lasers produce the intense heat needed to weld airplane and
5 automobile parts. Argon gas lasers are used to perform the delicate task of repairing a retina during eye surgery. Still another kind of laser is bounced off satellites in order to measure tiny changes in Earth's crust, enabling geologists to determine the probability of an earthquake.
10 A laser has three basic parts. Each laser has a lasing medium, a substance that will emit light when it is properly stimulated. The lasing medium can be a solid, liquid, or gas. Secondly, a laser has a pump, something that can provide the laser with energy. The third component is a
15 mirror or other device used to control the direction of the laser beam.

The laser gets its name from the first letters of the five main words that describe how it works: *l*ight *a*mplification by *s*timulated *e*mission of *r*adiation. Before the laser
20 is turned on, the electrons of the lasing medium are in a low-energy, unexcited state. When the pump is turned on, it emits radiation—light energy—which stimulates some of the unexcited electrons, causing them to jump to a higher energy state. The excited state is not a stable one,
25 so the electrons soon drop back to the low-energy state. As they do, they release energy in the form of light. Because the electrons are stimulated by light of a particular color or wavelength, they emit light of the same wavelength as the light that stimulated them. The light emissions from
30 many electrons join together to amplify the light and form a laser beam.

According to the passage, the three parts of a laser are

A. a lasing medium, a pump, and a mirror.
B. a solid, a liquid, and a gas.
C. stimulation, emission, and radiation.
D. light, amplification, and stimulation.

A. is correct, as shown in the second paragraph. B. is incorrect; the lasing medium may consist of any of these states of matter, but these are not *parts* of a laser. C. and D. offer several of the terms that describe how a laser works, but they are not *parts* of a laser.

Which statement best describes laser light?

F. It is radiation of the same wavelength.
G. It is a beam of stimulated electrons.
H. It is made of a solid, liquid, or gas.
J. It is a single stimulated emission of radiation.

F. is correct. Laser light is of the same wavelength. G. is incorrect. The beam is not made of electrons, but rather is formed by the radiation emitted from electrons. H. describes the lasing medium, not the light. Laser light is made from many emissions, so J. is incorrect.

Electrons emit radiation

A. when they jump to a higher energy state.
B. when they return to a low-energy state from a high-energy state.
C. only when they are stimulated by a different wavelength.
D. when the pump is turned off.

B. is correct. In the third paragraph, the author states that an excited electron emits light or radiation when it leaves the unstable high-energy state and returns to the low-energy state. Electrons do not emit radiation when they jump to a higher energy state, so A. is incorrect. C. is incorrect because electrons emit radiation of the same wavelength as the stimulating radiation. The laser beam is formed while the electrons are stimulated by the pump, so D. is incorrect.

Eye surgery can be performed, and airplane parts can be welded. These functions

F. use the same laser technology.
G. are the most important applications of lasers.
H. require lasers that produce the same wavelength.
J. use different types of gas lasers.

J. is correct. In the first paragraph, the author states that argon gas lasers are used in eye surgery and carbon dioxide lasers are used in welding. Carbon dioxide and argon are gases. The two applications do not use the same laser technology, nor do they operate at the same wavelength, because the lasing media differ. These facts make choices F. and H. incorrect. No indication of the relative importance of laser technologies is given in the passage, so choice G. is incorrect.

Visible radiation made of all the same wavelength would appear to your eye as

A. an intense beam of red light.
B. a flash of white light.
C. light of one color.
D. all the colors of the visible spectrum.

C. is correct. The wavelength of radiation determines its color as suggested in the third paragraph. The wavelength is not specified, so the answer cannot be red light, making choice A. incorrect. Both white light (B.) and all the colors of the visible spectrum (D.) consist of light of many different wavelengths.

When laser light is amplified, it is

F. strengthened.
G. pointed in one direction.
H. reduced to a lower energy state.
J. made unstable.

F. is correct. Many emissions at the same wavelength strengthen the beam. The direction of the light is controlled by the mirror, so G. is incorrect. Electrons jump from an unstable high-energy state to a lower energy state and emit radiation. This fact makes H. and J. incorrect.

The College Board Achievement Tests

Developed by Educational Testing Service, test makers for the SATs, and based on ideas similar to those behind ACT, the College Board Achievement Tests form the third leg of the college admissions tripod. Like the SAT and ACT, the Achievement Tests are required by some colleges and universities but are optional for many others. A college often will require one to three specific tests of the 14 one-hour assessments—15 if you count two versions of the English Composition Test separately. No institution requires that a student take all 14, and with good reason, as they include two levels of mathematics and five foreign languages. Typical requirements include English Composition, one foreign language, one of the two history tests, or Mathematics Level 1. Some colleges or universities recommend, but do not require, one or more tests. Most students who want to attend such institutions take the recommendation seriously—and take the tests.

A student hoping to attend a particular college should find out which achievement tests are required while there is still time to take courses to prepare for the tests. Since the achievement tests are based on knowledge of a particular subject, course work in that subject is essential—except for English Composition, which is based on correct use of the language. For example, studying German would not help a student get into a school that requires the French Achievement Test for entrance. More typically, most schools do not specify which language achievement test will be required. Thus, any student planning to apply to a college that requires a language test is well advised to take an extra year or two of one of the tested languages in secondary school.

One fee allows you to take one, two, or three of the tests at a single session.

Tests offered. The 15 tests offered in 14 subjects form five larger groups: English, Foreign Languages, Social Studies, Mathematics, and Sciences. The tests cover what is essentially the content of the academic track in secondary school.

Specifically, the tests are as follows:

English

English Composition, Version I: entirely multiple choice; it covers written and spoken English, but not knowledge of the basis of English grammar or the history of the language. Described further on page 729.

English Composition, Version II: a multiple-choice portion similar to that of Version I, but two-thirds as long, and an essay on a specified topic. Described further on page 729.

Literature: a test of the student's ability to read and analyze specific passages from poetry, fiction, drama, and literary nonfiction. It does not deal with the history of literature and does not require the student to answer items about well-known works except for those based on specific passages from works that are given to the student to read. Generally, there are six to eight passages and about 60 items based on the passages. One hour is allotted to complete the test, so you need to average less than a minute per item, considering that time will be consumed in reading the passages.

More than half the items come from English literature; 35 to 45 percent of the items come from American literature; and no more than 10 percent come from other sources. You are expected to be familiar with the vocabulary that is commonly used in literary criticism, terms such as *stanza, allegory, meter,* or *speaker.*

Items are divided equally among the literature of the Renaissance and 17th century; the literature of the 18th and 19th centuries; and 20th-century literature. About 10 percent of the test is based on drama, with the remainder based equally on prose and poetry.

Foreign Languages

The French, German, and Spanish tests are alike in that they use multiple-choice items to test grammar by examining sentence and paragraph structure, specific vocabulary, and reading. They do not test listening comprehension, free writing, or speaking.

The Hebrew test is similar to the French,

A student hoping to attend a particular college should find out which Achievement Tests are required while the student still has time to take courses to prepare for the test.

German, and Spanish tests, except that it does not test vocabulary separately. **The Latin test** is 65 percent translation and reading comprehension, 30 percent grammar and syntax, and 5 percent derivatives. *Derivatives* refer to items that test the student's ability to recognize the Latin word that is the basis of a specific English word, which is presented in context. Like the other foreign language tests, all items are of the multiple-choice type.

Social studies

American History and Social Studies: a multiple-choice test concerned mainly with the history of the United States from pre-Columbian times to the present. In addition, from 10 to 12 percent of the items are devoted to the methods, concepts, and generalizations of the social sciences. More information about this test is on page 734.

European History and World Cultures: multiple-choice items, with at least half of them on European history and close to half about the remainder of the world, excluding the United States and Canada. About half the items concern the period since 1750 A.D., and half deal with earlier times. A small percentage of the items cut across time or space considerations. There is somewhat more emphasis on cultural history than one would expect from a standard political and diplomatic history. Additional information about this test is on page 736.

Mathematics

Mathematics Level I: essentially a test of the standard sequence that is the typical academic student's mathematics curriculum in secondary school—algebra I, geometry, algebra II with trigonometry. It also includes at least 12 percent of items that are often outside that core curriculum—for example, logic and number theory. Half the test is devoted to algebra and plane geometry. Depending on specific courses of instruction, approximately half the test is based on material usually studied in the freshman and sophomore years. Further information about this test is on page 731.

Mathematics Level II: excludes items dealing with plane geometry and most of first-year algebra to concentrate on the mathematics that is more typical of the junior and senior years of secondary school. However, many students today take first-year algebra in eighth grade, which allows them to take other mathematics courses a year earlier. A

student who has taken second-year algebra as a sophomore and another mathematics course as a junior could take the Level II test at the end of the junior year, but a student who is a year behind that schedule would do better to wait until the senior year.

Some of the specific topics covered in Mathematics Level II are coordinate geometry, solid geometry, trigonometry for angles of all sizes (not just the angles in right triangles), elementary functions, and vectors.

Sciences

Biology Test: multiple-choice items that are 50 percent recall, 30 percent application, and 20 percent interpretation of high school biology. While many students today take a second biology course, the topics considered are those of a typical high school introductory course generally taken in ninth or tenth grade. The content of such an introductory course varies greatly, however, so this test tries to make sure that most students will be familiar with the majority of the content on the test.

Chemistry Test: like the Biology Test, based on the single introductory course offered in secondary school. It is about 30 percent recall, 55 percent application, and 15 percent interpretation. In addition to the usual multiple-choice items that have a single answer, the Chemistry Test sometimes includes multiple-choice items that require a combination of choices for the correct answer. These items are structured so that each combination is considered one choice. Other types of items that occur regularly in the Chemistry Test are *classification questions* and *relationship analysis questions,* but like the combination items mentioned above, such items are put into a form that is essentially the same as a five-choice completion item.

Physics Test: based on the introductory course, its 75 items are 20 to 33 percent recall, 40 to 53 percent application, and 20 to 33 percent interpretation. Looked at another way, the items are approximately apportioned as follows: 40 percent about mechanics, 20 percent about electricity and magnetism, 20 percent about optics and waves, 10 percent about thermodynamics, and 10 percent about particle and nuclear physics and Einstein's theories. Like the Chemistry Test, the Physics Test contains both standard multiple-choice items and classification items that are a slightly different form of multiple-choice item.

Timing for taking the tests.

Achievement tests are offered five times each school year: November, December, January, May, and June.

If a college requires one or more achievement tests for admission, you should plan take the tests in your junior year of secondary school or no later than January of your senior year. November or December tests are the most common. These require registering for the tests in September or October, so you need to have a clear idea as you enter school in the fall of the year in which you will take the tests of what you are going to do.

Some students prefer to apply for early action or early decision college admission programs. Early action means that your application must get in sooner than the applications of other students and that the college will notify you of its decision in December instead of in April. For early decision, you also must respond to the college early. For early action, you can wait until after April college acceptances and rejections have been received before you must take action. Early decision is chosen most often by students who have a strong preference for one or two institutions and who feel that they have a good chance to get into their schools of choice.

For either early action or early decision, the achievement tests must be taken earlier—by June of the junior year at the latest.

A few tests are not offered during every session. In December, Version II of the English Composition Test is offered, while Version I is available on the other four test dates. European History and World Cultures, German, Hebrew, and Latin are given only in December and June.

What to bring to the tests.
You will need an admission ticket, positive identification, and two No. 2 pencils. Make sure the pencils have erasers, since you may change your mind about some answers, especially if you have time to check your work. Do not bring calculators, books, or anything else that might be interpreted as an aid in doing the test.

Test-taking tips.
The following tips apply to all the College Board Achievement Tests. Specific information for individual tests beyond that given above appears before each of the four sample tests that follow.

The Achievement Tests are graded like the SAT, so the same general rules apply. Do not guess unless you can eliminate at least one of the choices; you will have a small amount deducted from your score for each wrong guess. On the other hand, if you can eliminate one or more of the choices—or think you know the answer but are not quite sure—guessing or going with the suspected choice is a good strategy.

Usually, easier items of any one type are placed near the beginning of that type of item. Note that this does not apply to items based on reading passages or groups of items based on a diagram. Those items often cannot be arranged from easy to difficult. For sets of items not based on a passage or diagram, if you are going through a set of

one type and find that you do not know the correct choice for several in a row, skip ahead to the next type of exercise. You may want to mark in your test booklet any items skipped in this way so they will be easy to find later. A good scheme would be to indicate the skipped items with a check mark that can easily be altered to a sort of X with another mark when you have completed the item. In that way you can go through the test several times and mark off each item as you answer it.

When you get to the end of the test, return to the harder items and do as many of them as you can. This strategy will maximize your score by making certain you have answered all the items that are easy for you. Remember: You get the same score for a correct choice on an easy item as you get for a difficult one. Most students who get good scores on the Achievement Tests do omit some items.

As with all tests that use answer sheets and are machine scored, make certain that the only marks on your answer sheet are the marks that indicate what you think the correct choices are. (Of course, you will also supply your name or other required data to identify the answer sheet.) If the machine sees extra marks, it may not give you credit for some items that you have answered correctly. If an item has only four choices, the answer sheet will still provide room for five, since answer sheets are designed for use with various types of tests. If you accidentally mark the last, or (E), choice on the answer sheet when the item has only four choices, and you really meant to mark the last of the item choices, (D), the answer will not count. So be careful.

Since only the answer sheet is scored, you can write anything you like in your

test booklet. The most useful things to write, of course, are calculations for mathematics items, other notes, such as underlining parts of a passage, and indications that you need to return to a particular item.

Tests included here.
This section presents tips on four of the most popular tests, along with sample items and explanations of how to approach the items. The four tests are *English Composition, Version I; Mathematics, Level I; American History and Social Studies;* and *European History and World Cultures.* Many of the tips for test taking apply to the other tests as well.

Scoring on the Achievement Tests.
The basic scoring system is the same as that used for the SAT. The lowest possible score is 200, while the highest possible score is 800. There is a margin of error of about ±30 points in the score, so two students of equal ability and knowledge could score 570 and 630 on the same test.

You are allowed to take the tests more than once, so if you have a serious cold or are otherwise handicapped when you take the test the first time, you may want to try again. Scores will not necessarily go up, however, and both scores will be reported to colleges and universities. In addition, different schools may have different rules. Some look at the most recent score, others look for the higher score, and some even take an average.

Scores are sent not only to the schools you designate, but also to you and to your secondary school guidance department.

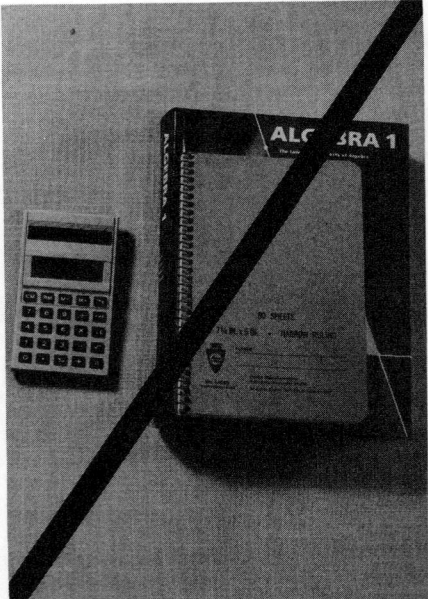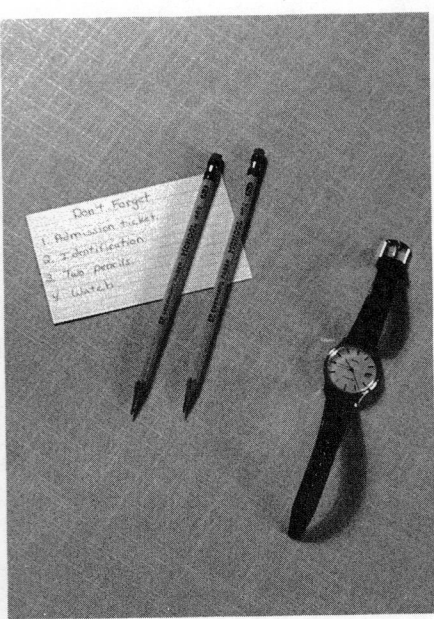

ADMISSION TO THE ACHIEVEMENT TESTS *requires a ticket and positive identification, such as a driver's license. You will also need two No. 2 pencils. A watch is helpful, but calculators, books, and notebooks are forbidden.*

English Composition Achievement Test

Unlike all the other College Board Achievement Tests, the English Composition Test measures skills that are learned more outside the classroom than in it. It is concerned with five main challenges that confront writers: being consistent in such matters as subject-verb agreement and parallelism; expressing ideas logically, including correct use of words that signal subordination and comparison; being clear and precise in diction, and avoiding wording that is ambiguous or vague; following the conventions of writing with regard to case, verb forms, negatives, and so forth; and recognizing correct sentences. Two of the three types of items resemble those in the SAT Test of Standard Written English (TSWE), although items in the English Composition Achievement Test are generally more difficult than those in the TSWE. Nevertheless, you can get additional practice for this test by working the TSWE items that are supplied on pages 711–713. The third type of item involves a specific change in one part of a given sentence; the test taker is to make any additional changes in the sentence that may be required. The third type is not included in Version II, the version that contains an essay. In Version I all items are given in standard multiple-choice format.

In Version I there are 90 items to be answered in one hour, so you need to average 40 seconds an item just to complete the test. In Version II there are only 60 multiple-choice items to be accomplished in 40 minutes, which works out to the same 40 seconds per item. The Version II essay has 20 minutes allotted, so the total test time remains one hour.

The essay is on a single specified topic that changes from test to test. Each year two different topics are used, one on the Saturday test in December and the other on the Sunday test in December. Topics are chosen to be general enough that anyone can be expected to have an opinion on the topic. For example, the topic used on December 7 in 1985 was "The more things change, the more they stay the same." Each essay is read by two different readers shortly after the test is given, and the total score of the two readers is then added. Since each reader can score the essay from one to six, the total possible scores range from two for a very poor essay to twelve for an excellent one. If the two readers score the essay more than two points apart, however, a third reader is called in to reconcile the discrepancy. The third reader's score will have to be within two points of one of the first two readers, so there will be two scores that are two points or less apart to be added to form the reported score. The score is then weighted so that it represents one-third of the total, while the multiple-choice items are the remaining two-thirds.

Directions: The following sentences contain problems in grammar, usage, diction (choice of words), and idiom.
  Some sentences are correct.
  No sentence contains more than one error.
You will find that the error, if there is one, is underlined and lettered. Assume that all other elements of the sentence are correct and cannot be changed. In choosing answers, follow the requirements of standard written English.
If there is an error, select the one underlined part that must be changed in order to make the sentence correct.
If there is no error, choice E is correct.

A minor disagreement <u>between</u> good friends may
                          A
<u>eventually develop</u> into a <u>real</u> serious and <u>irreconcilable</u>
        B   C   D
difference of opinion. <u>No error</u>.
                            E

The adjective *serious* must be modified by an adverb—*really*, not the adjective *real*. (Remember that adverbs modify adjectives, verbs, and other adverbs.) Choice (C) should read "a <u>really</u> serious . . ."

Jenny <u>forgot</u> to pick up her package <u>although</u> the post
       A   B
office <u>sent</u> her three notices <u>during</u> the past week.
       C   D
<u>No error</u>.
 E

When two actions have taken place in the past, the past perfect tense is used to indicate the earlier of the two actions. Choice (C) should read ". . . the post office <u>had sent</u> her . . ."

When <u>discussing</u> the accomplishments of Babe Ruth and
       A
Henry Aaron, baseball fans <u>seldom agree</u> on who <u>was</u> the
                             B   C
<u>best</u> of the two. <u>No error</u>.
 D   E

When a sentence compares two persons or things, you must use the comparative degree (better) rather than the superlative degree (best). Since two people are being compared, Choice (D) should read ". . . the <u>better</u> of the two."

Mrs. Jennings was startled <u>to learn</u> <u>that</u> her dinner
                            A   B
<u>was ruined</u> <u>while talking</u> on the phone. <u>No error</u>.
 C   D   E

This sentence contains a dangling elliptical clause. More simply stated, something was left out, making the sentence appear to suggest one thing while meaning another. As it is written, the sentence seems to say that the dinner was talking on the phone. You must make clear that Mrs. Jennings was doing the talking. Choice (D) should read ". . . while <u>she was talking</u> on the phone."

The liver, one of the <u>body's</u> <u>most complex</u> organs,
                       A   B
<u>function</u> as the <u>main</u> food-processing center. <u>No error</u>.
 C   D   E

A verb must agree with its subject, regardless of any intervening phrase. The subject of this sentence, *liver,* is singular, and therefore takes a singular verb, *functions.* Choice (C) should read, "The liver, one of the body's most complex organs, <u>functions</u> . . ."

The judge told the jury that the trial <u>could have come</u> to a
                                         A
<u>speedier</u> conclusion if they <u>would have studied</u> the
 B   C
transcripts <u>more thoroughly</u>. <u>No error</u>.
             D   E

This sentence contains an "if" clause (". . . if they would have studied . . .") as part of a contrary-to-fact past tense sentence. Therefore, the verb *had studied,* not *would have studied,* is required. Choice (C) should read ". . . if they <u>had studied</u> . . ."

<u>Each</u> teacher <u>and</u> guidance counselor <u>were</u> expected to
 A   B   C
report to school early to make final preparations for
<u>the arrival</u> of the students. <u>No error</u>.
 D   E

When singular subjects are joined by *and*, they generally take a plural verb. However, when preceded by each, the subjects are treated as a singular and require a singular verb. Choice (C) should read, "Each teacher and guidance counselor <u>was</u> . . ."

You get the same score for a correct choice on an easy item as on a difficult one.

Directions: In each of the following sentences, some part of the sentence or the entire sentence is underlined. Beneath each sentence you will find five ways of phrasing the underlined part. The first of these repeats the original; the other four are different. If you think the original is the best of the alternatives, choose answer A; otherwise choose one of the others. Select the best version.

By working after school and on weekends, his income increased dramatically.

(A) By working after school and on weekends, his income increased dramatically.
(B) His income increased dramatically by working after school and on weekends.
(C) His income, by working after school and on weekends, increased dramatically.
(D) His income after school and on weekends increased dramatically.
(E) By working after school and on weekends, he increased his income dramatically.

Choice (A) is incorrect because the position of the gerund phrase seems to suggest that his income was doing the working. The same is true for choices (B) and (C). Choice (D) changes the intended meaning of the original sentence. Choice (E) is correct because inserting the word *he* makes clear who worked "after school and on weekends."

William Roentgen called his invention x-rays because at first he did not understand what they were, and "x" is a scientific symbol for the unknown.

(A) because at first he did not understand
(B) without understanding
(C) although at first he did not understand
(D) and at first he did not understand
(E) which he did not understand at first

Choice (A) is correct. The word *because* shows the causal relationship between the two parts of the sentence. None of the other choices indicates a causal relationship. Choices (D) and (E) create awkward constructions.

After reviewing the evidence, the jury had no choice but to imply that the defendant was guilty.

(A) had no choice but to imply that the defendant was guilty
(B) had chosen to imply that the defendant was guilty
(C) had no choice but to infer that the defendant was guilty
(D) chose to infer that the defendant was guilty
(E) was guilty of implying that the defendant had no choice

Choice (A) is incorrect because it uses *imply* instead of *infer*. These words are often confused. *Imply* means "suggest"; *infer* means "come to a conclusion." Choice (B) is wrong for the same reason. Choices (D) and (E) change the intended meaning of the sentence. Choice (C) is the correct answer.

Although it looks very much like a garden cucumber, the sea cucumber is actually an aquatic animal.

(A) Although it looks very much like a garden cucumber, the sea cucumber is actually an aquatic animal.
(B) Because it looks very much like a garden cucumber, the sea cucumber is actually an aquatic animal.
(C) The sea cucumber looks very much like an aquatic animal but is actually a garden cucumber.
(D) The sea cucumber looks very much like a garden cucumber, which is actually an aquatic animal.
(E) The sea cucumber looks very much like a garden cucumber, so it is really an aquatic animal.

Choice (A) is correct. The word *although* suggests that the sentence will present contrasting ideas. Choice (B) changes the meaning of the original sentence by suggesting a ludicrous causal relationship. Choices (C), (D), and (E) drastically change the meaning of the original sentence.

Our neighbor's dog kept us awake as it either barked or was whining all night.

(A) barked or was whining all night
(B) was barking or whined all night
(C) barked or whined all night
(D) was barking all night or whining
(E) barks or whines all night

Choices (A) and (B) are incorrect because of faulty parallelism. The two related parts of the sentence must use the same verb form. Choice (D) is an awkward attempt at parallelism. Choice (E) is an example of parallel structure, but has incorrectly introduced verbs in the present tense. Only choice (C) uses parallelism correctly to express the meaning of the original sentence.

Directions: Each of the following sentences is to be rephrased according to the directions that follow it. You should make only those changes that the directions require. Keep the meaning of the revised sentence as close to the meaning of the original sentence as the directions for that sentence allow.

The patient's lower back pain was relieved by the doctor's performance of physical therapy.

Begin with The doctor

(A) performance of
(B) performed
(C) while performing
(D) performs
(E) has performed

To answer this type of question, follow the directions given and construct a new sentence. Then choose a word or phrase among the choices supplied that is contained within your sentence. In this case the sentence that best keeps the meaning of the original sentence is "The doctor performed physical therapy to relieve the patient's lower back pain." Therefore (B) is correct. None of the sentences that could be constructed to contain the other choices comes as close in meaning and tense.

The octopus is classified as a mollusk; however, it has no hard shell to protect its body.

Change however to although

(A) never having had
(B) body. The octopus
(C) mollusk. Although
(D) mollusk; although
(E) body, the octopus

Choice (E) is correct: "Although it has no hard shell to protect its body, the octopus is classified as a mollusk." The sentence could also have been constructed as "The octopus is classified as a mollusk, although it has no hard shell to protect its body." However, none of the choices fit this sentence. The use of either (B) or (C) results in an incomplete sentence. Choice (D) uses a semicolon incorrectly. Choice (A) leads to a very awkward construction.

The ancient Greeks awarded victorious athletes with crowns made of laurel leaves.

Begin with Victorious.

(A) have awarded
(B) were awarded
(C) awards for athletes
(D) were awarding
(E) awarded

"Victorious athletes in ancient Greece were awarded crowns made of laurel leaves." This is a passive construction in which the subject *athletes* receives the action of the verb *were awarded*, maintaining the original meaning. Choice (B) is correct. Choices (A), (D), and (E) are written in the active voice (subject performs the action) and therefore change the meaning of the original sentence. Any construction containing (C) would also change the meaning of the sentence.

Sara Delano Roosevelt was the first woman to see her son inaugurated for a second term as president of the United States. She was the mother of Franklin D. Roosevelt.

Combine these two sentences into one, beginning with <u>Sara Delano</u>.

(A) Roosevelt, and therefore was
(B) Roosevelt, as the first woman
(C) Roosevelt, being the mother
(D) Roosevelt, the mother of
(E) Roosevelt, and she was

For this item, you should observe that the first sentence contains the main idea, while the second sentence is merely an identification of Sara Delano Roosevelt. "Sara Delano Roosevelt, the mother of Franklin D. Roosevelt, was the first woman to see her son inaugurated for a second term as president of the United States." This sentence includes the original second sentence as an appositive phrase, and this is a good way to identify the subject. Choice (D) is correct. Choice (A) makes no sense, and choice (C) is unnecessarily wordy. Choice (B) reverses the importance of the two original sentences. Choice (E) gives undeserved equal emphasis to both sentence parts.

The jury determined that it was the plaintiff, not the defendant, who committed the crime.

Change <u>who committed</u> to <u>committed</u>.

(A) determined who was the plaintiff
(B) determined that the plaintiff
(C) determined it was not the plaintiff
(D) determined not the plaintiff
(E) determined the committed plaintiff

Choice (B) is correct. Removing the pronoun *who* makes *committed* the principal verb in the dependent clause beginning with *that*. Therefore, the new sentence becomes "The jury determined that the plaintiff committed the crime, not the defendant." The other choices do not result in sentences that retain the meaning of the original sentence.

Mathematics Achievement Test

The 50 items in Mathematics Level 1 are to be completed in an hour, so you have one minute and twelve seconds on the average for each one—although it is generally better to try to average one item a minute and thus leave ten minutes for checking all your answers.

The Level 1 test is approximately 30 percent algebra, 20 percent plane geometry, 12 percent coordinate geometry (graphing), 12 percent fractions, 12 percent miscellaneous topics such as logic and number theory, 8 percent trigonometry, and 6 percent solid geometry. Care is taken not to tie the mathematical symbolism to any one textbook or course of study. Most of the items are standard multiple-choice items, carrying letters to identify the choices, but some are modified items. That is, while the items still provide five choices, some of them permit choices that may combine two or more different answers. In that case, the combinations are identified by Roman numerals.

As in all mathematics tests, it is important to pay attention to what is being asked before trying to solve the problem. Drawing a figure can often help. Since the test booklets are not scored, you can draw anything you wish in the booklet. It is important to keep the answer sheet clean except for your identification and the marks you write for the correct choices.

If you are going through a set of items of one type and find that you do not know the correct choice for several in a row, skip ahead to the next type of exercise.

<u>Directions:</u> For each of the following problems, decide which is the best of the choices given.

<u>Notes:</u> (1) Figures that accompany problems in this test are intended to provide information useful in solving the problems. They are drawn as accurately as possible EXCEPT when it is stated in a specific problem that the figure is not drawn to scale. All figures lie in a plane unless otherwise indicated.

(2) Unless otherwise specified, the domain of a function f is assumed to be the set of all real numbers x for which $f(x)$ is a real number.

If $ab + a = 12$ and $b + 1 = 3$, then $a =$

(A) 36   (B) 15   (C) 9   (D) 4   (E) 2

Notice that the first expression can be factored: $ab + a = 12$
$$a(b + 1) = 12$$

Substitute 3 for $b + 1$: $a(3) = 12$
$$a = 4$$
The correct answer is (D).

The solution of the pair of equations
$$jx + ky = 1$$
$$kx + jy = 4$$
is $x = -1$, $y = 2$. What are the values of j and k?

(A) $j = 3$,   (B) $j = 2$,   (C) $j = 1$,   (D) $j = 2$,
   $k = 2$ $k = 3$ $k = 1$ $k = -2$

(E) $j = -1$
   $k = 1$

Substituting the given solutions results in a new system of equations in variables j and k.

$$j(-1) + k(2) = 1 \qquad -j + 2k = 1$$
$$k(-1) + j(2) = 4 \qquad -k + 2j = 4$$

Solve for j and k by adding 2 times the first equation to the second, which eliminates j.

$$-2j + 4k = 2$$
$$\underline{2j - k = 4}$$
$$3k = 6,$$
$$k = 2$$
$$-(2) + 2j = 4$$
$$2j = 6$$
$$j = 3$$

The correct choice is (A).

How many integers are in the solution set of $|3x + 1| > 2$?

(A) None   (B) One   (C) Two   (D) Three
(E) Infinitely many

To solve an absolute value inequality, remember that absolute value is a measure of distance along the number line. This sentence states that the distance from some point is greater than 2 units, a description that would fit infinitely many points. You can also tackle this problem algebraically. If the absolute value of $3x + 1$ is greater than 2, then the expression itself must be either greater than 2 or less than -2. This enables you to rewrite the sentence as two separate inequalities:

$$3x + 1 < -2 \qquad 3x + 1 > 2$$
$$3x < -3 \qquad 3x > 1$$
$$x < -1 \qquad x > \tfrac{1}{3}$$

Again, there are infinitely many integers that fit these conditions. The correct choice is (E).

If the points $A(-1, 1)$, $B(2, 4)$, and $C(5, 1)$ are connected to form triangle ABC with sides AB, BC, and CA, the area of the triangle will be:

(A) 2   (B) 6   (C) 9   (D) 12   (E) 40

Sketch the points on a grid. To find the area of a triangle, use the formula $A = \frac{1}{2}bh$. AC is convenient to use as the base; its length is 6. The height from B to the base is 3.

$$A = \frac{1(6)(3)}{2} = 9$$

The correct answer is (C).

If a and b are even integers, which of the following must be an odd integer?

$$\text{I } \frac{ab}{2} \qquad \text{II } ab + 1 \qquad \text{III } \frac{ab + 1}{2}$$

(A) I only   (B) II only   (C) I and II only
(D) II and III only   (E) I, II, and III

This problem requires some careful reasoning. The product of any two even integers is an even integer. The expression in I will always be even, since both a and b have a factor of 2. Dividing out one factor of 2 will leave at least one other, which makes the quotient even. The expression in II will always be odd. The product, ab, is even. Adding 1 to any even number will produce an odd number. The expression in III will certainly never be even, since an odd number is being divided by 2. However, it will not always be an odd number since it may very well not be an integer at all. Therefore, the correct answer is (B).

If x is not equal to 0, then $(4^{4x})(2^{3x}) =$

(A) 8^{7x} (B) 4^{7x} (C) 2^{11x} (D) 2^{12x} (E) 8^{12x}

Expressions with exponents can be combined only if they have the same base. Since $4 = 2^2$, begin by rewriting the first factor of the expression:
$$(2^{2 \cdot 4x})(2^{3x}) = (2^{8x})(2^{3x})$$
Then use the laws for exponents:
$$(2^{8x})(2^{3x}) = 2^{8x + 3x}$$
$$= 2^{11x}$$
The correct answer is (C).

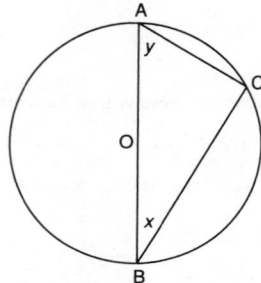

AB is a diameter of circle O. What is the measure of angle y if $x = 30°$?

(A) 30°   (B) 45°   (C) 50°   (D) 60°   (E) 90°

Since angle C is inscribed in a semicircle, it measures 90°. Therefore, ABC is a right triangle and angles x and y are complementary. $y = 90° - 30° = 60°$. The correct answer is (D).

What is the area of a triangle whose sides measure 5, 5, and 8?

(A) 10   (B) 12   (C) 20   (D) 24   (E) 40

Begin by making a drawing.

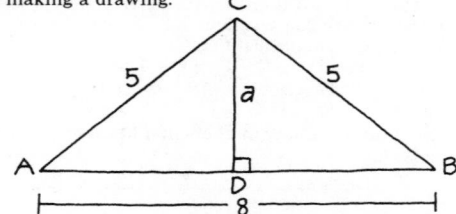

To find the area of a triangle, you need to know the base and the altitude. The altitude is perpendicular to the base. This triangle is isosceles, so the altitude bisects the base, making $AD = DB = 4$. Use the Pythagorean theorem to find the altitude.
$$a^2 + 4^2 = 5^2$$
$$a^2 + 16 = 25$$
$$a^2 = 9$$
$$a = 3$$
To find the area of the triangle, use the equation $A = \frac{1}{2}ba$, where A is the area, b is the base, and a is the altitude. The area is $\frac{1(3)(8)}{2} = 12$. The correct choice is (B).

Lines l, m, and n are parallel. Which labeled angles are equal?

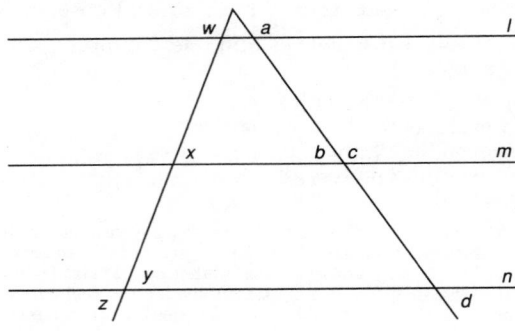

(A) x, y, and z
(B) w, x, and y
(C) w, a, and c
(D) a, b, and c
(E) b, d, and z

Three parallel lines are cut by two different transversals. It may help to mark the figure, indicating which angles are necessarily equal. Two kinds of angles formed when a transversal crosses parallel lines are equal: alternating angles (such as w and x) and corresponding angles (such as a and c). There are four different angle measures here, marked as 1, 2, 3, and 4.

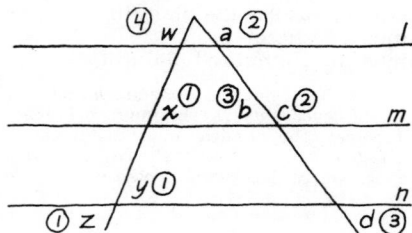

The correct answer is (A).

One side of a cube measures $x + 2$. What is the surface area of the cube?

(A) $6x + 12$ (B) $x^2 + 4x + 4$ (C) $6x^2 + 4$
(D) $4x^2 + 16x + 16$ (E) $6x^2 + 24x + 24$

A cube is a solid figure with 6 congruent faces. Each face is a square. The surface area is 6 times the area of one of these squares.
area of one square: $(x + 2)^2 = x^2 + 4x + 4$
area of 6 squares: $6(x^2 + 4x + 4) = 6x^2 + 24x + 24$
The correct answer is (E).

If a line contains the points $(-2, 1)$ and $(3, 6)$, then its x-intercept is

(A) -3 (B) 0   (C) 1   (D) 3   (E) 4

To find the x-intercept, find the equation of the line. The x-intercept is the value of x when $y = 0$ in that equation. Use the slope-intercept equation. First find the slope, m.
$$\text{Slope } m = \frac{y_2 - y_1}{x_2 - x_1}$$
$$= \frac{6 - 1}{3 - (-2)}$$
$$= \frac{5}{5} = 1$$
Substitute the slope into the slope-intercept equation $y = mx + b$, where $m = 1$ and b is the y-intercept.
$$y = x + b$$
Choose one point, say $(3, 6)$, for (x, y). So, $x = 3$ and $y = 6$, and the equation becomes
$$6 = 3 + b$$
$$3 = b$$
The equation of the line is $y = x + 3$.
Substituting 0 for y, $0 = x + 3$, or $-3 = x$.
The correct choice is (A).

Which of the following is the equation of a line that is perpendicular to the line with equation $3x + y = 7$?

(A) $3x - y = 7$ (B) $3y - x = 4$
(C) $3y + x = 7$ (D) $3x - 3y = 5$
(E) $3x + y = -2$

Two lines are perpendicular if their slopes are negative reciprocals. The slope of the given line is found by using the form $y = mx + b$. $3x + y = 7$ can be rewritten as $y = -3x + 7$, so the slope is -3. The negative reciprocal of -3 is $\frac{1}{3}$. Any equation that can be rewritten as $y = \frac{1}{3}x + b$ will yield a line that is perpendicular to the given line.

$$y = \frac{1}{3}x + b$$
$$3y = x + 3b$$
$$3y - x = 3b$$

The only equation that matches this form is (B).

In the right triangle below,

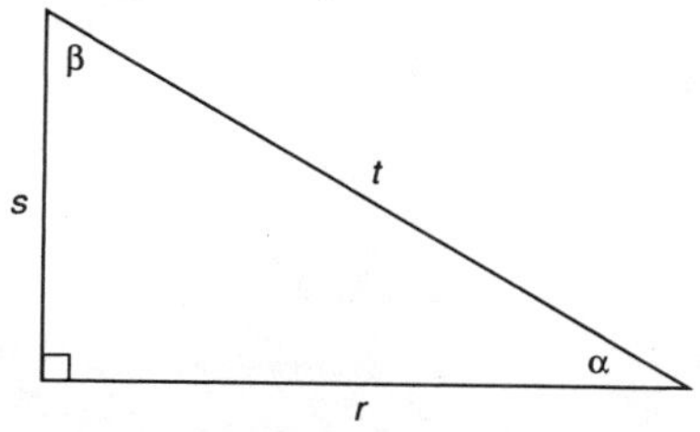

cosine α is equal to which of the following?

I $\sin \beta$ II $\dfrac{r}{t}$ III $\dfrac{s}{t}$

(A) I only   (B) II only   (C) III only   (D) I and II
(E) I and III

The cosine of an angle is the ratio of its adjacent side to its hypotenuse. In this drawing, the side adjacent to α is r and the hypotenuse is t. It is also true that the cosine of an angle is equal to the sine of its complement. So $\cos \alpha = \sin \beta$. Therefore, the correct answer is (D).

If θ is an acute angle and $\sin \theta = \dfrac{3}{5}$, then $\tan \theta =$

(A) $\dfrac{2}{5}$ (B) $\dfrac{4}{5}$ (C) $\dfrac{5}{3}$ (D) $\dfrac{3}{4}$ (E) $\dfrac{4}{3}$

The sine of an angle is the ratio of its opposite side to its hypotenuse.

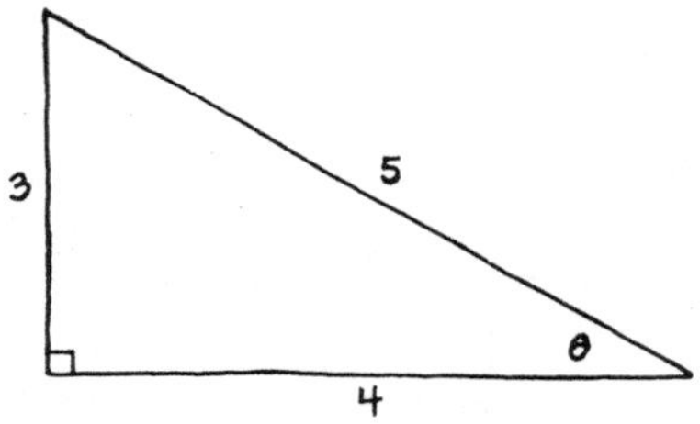

The sketch labels the corresponding parts of the right triangle for θ. The adjacent side is 4, since this is a 3-4-5 right triangle. The tangent is the ratio of the opposite side to the adjacent side. The correct choice is (D).

If $f(x) = \dfrac{x + 2}{x}$ and $g(x) = \dfrac{x^2}{2}$, then $f(g(4)) =$

(A) $1\dfrac{1}{8}$ (B) $1\dfrac{1}{4}$ (C) $2\dfrac{1}{2}$ (D) 8 (E) 12

To find the value of function f of function g, first find the value of $g(4)$. Then use that value for x in $f(x)$.

$$g(4) = \frac{4^2}{2} \qquad g(4) = 8$$
$$f(8) = \frac{8 + 2}{8} = \frac{10}{8} = 1\frac{1}{4}$$

The correct answer is (B).

If $f(x) = 2x - 3$ and $g(x) = 3x - 5$, for what value of a will $f(a) = g(a)$?

(A) -8 (B) 0 (C) 2 (D) 3 (E) 8

To find out which value of a gives the same result for function f and function g, solve this equation:

$$2a - 3 = 3a - 5$$
$$-3 + 5 = 3a - 2a$$
$$2 = a$$

The correct choice is (C).

If an operation $*$ is defined for all real numbers x and y by the equation $x * y = 2x - xy$, then $3 * (-1) =$

(A) 9 (B) 7 (C) 2 (D) 3 (E) 0

Substitute 3 for x and -1 for y.

$$2(3) - (3)(-1) = 6 - (-3) = 6 + 3 = 9$$

The correct choice is (A).

"If p, then q" is a true statement under which of the following conditions?

    I p is true and q is true
    II p is true and q is false
    III p is false and q is true
    IV p is false and q is false

(A) I only   (B) I and II   (C) I and III   (D) I and IV
(E) I, III, and IV

Think of the truth table for "if p, then q." It may help to use some common-language example such as, "If it is raining, then I will go to the movies."

$$p = \text{It is raining}$$
$$q = \text{I will go to the movies}$$

In the table, T means "true" and F means "false." So the first line of the table means that each part and the combined statement are true.

If p, then q	p	q
T	T	T
F	T	F
T	F	T
T	F	F

The logical statement "If p, then q" is true except in the case where p is true and q is false. So, the correct choice is (E).

In the figure below, a cone is inscribed in a cylinder. If the volume of the cylinder is 90π, what is the volume of the cone?

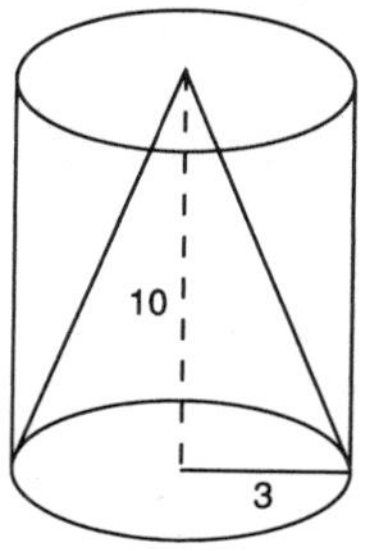

(A) 90π (B) 45π (C) 30π (D) $30\pi^2$ (E) 45

The volume of a cylinder is 3 times the volume of a cone with the same base and height, so the easy way to solve this is to think $\frac{1}{3}$ of 90π is 30π; the correct choice is (C). You could also—but using up more time—calculate the volume of the cone from the formula $V = \frac{1}{3}Bh$, where B is the base of the cone and h is the height.

If you need scratch paper, write on your test booklet. Do not write on the answer sheet.

American History and Social Studies Achievement Test

In this test you have one hour to answer 95 items, so you have to be quick—you have less than 40 seconds average for each item. To allow yourself time for checking your choices at the end, you should try to maintain a pace of 17 items every ten minutes.

The test can be viewed two ways—by the approach to history or by the time period covered. By approach, from 30 to 34 percent is devoted to political history, 16 to 20 percent to social history, 16 to 18 percent to economic history, 11 to 15 percent to foreign policy of the United States, 10 to 12 percent to methods and generalizations about history, and 8 to 10 percent to intellectual or cultural history. By time periods covered, approximately 18 percent of the test deals with the period before the Constitution (going back to pre-Columbian times), 35 percent is from the inauguration of George Washington to the start of the Spanish-American War, another 35 percent is from 1899 to the present, and 12 percent is not chronological.

Most of the material is covered in elementary or secondary school American history courses, but it also may be dealt with in government, civics, economics, or problems of democracy courses. The best preparation is a solid secondary school American history course, but taking some of the other courses mentioned might help somewhat. While you are required to recall basic information about American history, little emphasis is placed on specific dates or details. Instead, you will need to have a good grasp of the main events in American history.

Directions: Each of the questions or incomplete statements below is followed by five suggested answers or completions. Select the one that is best in each case.

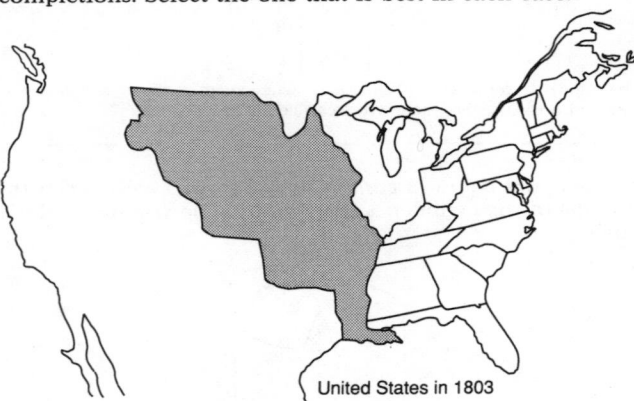

United States in 1803

In 1803 the United States bought the territory shown on the map for $15 million. This land acquisition came to be known as

(A) The Gadsden Purchase
(B) 54-40 or Fight
(C) Seward's Folly
(D) The Louisiana Purchase
(E) The Northwest Passage

There are two clues in the stem of this item: the map itself and the date of the land acquisition. In 1803 Thomas Jefferson was president. Jefferson sent Lewis and Clark off to explore the newly acquired territory of Louisiana. The Gadsden Purchase came much later, shortly before the Civil War (it was intimately involved in the issues that led to the war). "54-40 or Fight" was a slogan for Americans who wanted to expand into western Canada. Seward's Folly was another major land purchase, but it was Alaska and it came much later than 1803. The Northwest Passage, which is a sea route to the Pacific from the Atlantic north of North America, might be confused with the Northwest Territories, a large part of the land bought in the Louisiana Purchase, but it is certainly not the same. The correct choice is (D).

During the Civil War, Northern Democrats opposed to the war effort were known as

(A) Butternuts
(B) Carpetbaggers
(C) Copperheads
(D) Know Nothings
(E) Sons of Liberty

All the terms refer to people who believed in or did something. To find the correct choice, we need only look at terms from the Civil War years. The Sons of Liberty date from the American Revolution, long before the Civil War, thus eliminating choice (E). Carpetbaggers were Northerners who went South after the Civil War to take jobs under Reconstruction governments, so choice (B) is not correct. Choices (A) and (C) are both from the Civil War. Butternuts were soldiers or supporters of the Confederacy. Copperheads were Northern Democrats who opposed the war, making choice (C) the correct one.

THE BETTMANN ARCHIVE

The land forces shown above included a future president as second in command. They played an important part in a war that was, however, won largely at sea, a war that resulted in control of several large islands by the winner of the war. This war is best known as

(A) the Hawaiian War
(B) the Spanish-American War
(C) the Pacific Theater
(D) the Bay of Pigs
(E) the Russo-Japanese War

There are a number of clues in the stem. The picture shows soldiers dressed as a casual expeditionary force around the turn of the century. Therefore, the future U.S. president could not be Lincoln (who served in the Blackhawk War) or any other 19th-century president. The lack of standard uniforms suggests that neither world war, in each of which future presidents served (e.g., Truman, Eisenhower, Kennedy), could be involved. Large islands that have been controlled by another nation include the Hawaiian Islands, which were annexed at about the right time, but no war was involved. The Pacific Theater refers to the part of World War II fought against the Japanese in the Pacific Ocean; this resulted in short-term control of the large islands of Japan, but it does not match the time frame of the photograph. The Russo-Japanese War occurred at about the right time, but these troops are gathered around an American flag. In any case, the Japanese won that war and did not acquire additional whole islands (although they were awarded half the large island of Sakhalin). The Bay of Pigs was a battle in Cuba that troops supported by the United States lost, so no islands were acquired. The correct choice, therefore, must be (B), the Spanish-American War. The troops pictured are the Rough Riders, whose second in command was Teddy Roosevelt. They fought in Cuba, but it was the U.S. Navy that won control of Cuba, Puerto Rico, and the Philippines. The words control of in the stem are an additional clue, since the islands were not incorporated into the United States. Cuba became independent after the war, but the United States ran Cuba's foreign policy and stationed troops there (troops remain there to this day). The Philippines were controlled by the United States until after World War II, and Puerto Rico remains a commonwealth of the United States.

The Abscam Scandal involved

(A) Republicans breaking into Democratic Party files
(B) a breach of national security during the Vietnam War
(C) FBI undercover efforts to identify corrupt public officials
(D) sending illicitly raised funds to the Nicaraguan contras
(E) illegal leasing of U.S. oil reserves to a corporation in return for bribes

If you know recent history, you may recall the names associated with incorrect choices such as "Watergate" for choice (A), "Pentagon Papers" for choice (B), "Iran-Contra" for choice (D), and "Teapot Dome" for choice (E). The correct choice is (C); Abscam (Arab Scam) was an FBI operation intended to find corrupt public officials.

The *CSS Alabama*

(A) was sunk at Pearl Harbor
(B) is a major tourist attraction in Mobile Bay
(C) was sunk off the coast of France
(D) was an ironclad ship in the Confederate Navy
(E) played a major role in the Barbary Coast wars

Knowing that the *CSS Alabama* was a Confederate Navy raider during the Civil War, choice (E) is quickly eliminated since the Barbary Coast troubles took place decades before the Civil War. Likewise, choice (A) is out since the Pearl Harbor attack took place in 1941. Choice (D) is a possibility except that the *Alabama* was not an ironclad. Choice (B) might be believable except for the fact that the *Alabama* was sunk by the U.S. Navy off the French coast. Choice (C) is correct.

CULVER PICTURES

The importance of ships like the one shown above in American history is that they brought

(A) the pilgrims to New England
(B) European immigrants to Ellis Island
(C) Columbus and other early explorers to the New World
(D) Leif Ericson and the Vikings to the coast of North America
(E) the United States to a position as the second largest international trader

It is easy to reject choice (B), since the great waves of European immigrants came by steamship, not by sailing ship. Also, the ship pictured does not resemble the simple "dragon ships" of the Vikings (choice D). While both the Spanish galleons (choice C) and ships like the *Mayflower* (choice A) were full-rigged sailing ships, these early ships were short and stubby, not long and sleek like the U.S. clipper ship pictured. These speedy sailboats traded all over the world and put the United States just behind Great Britain in international trade during the 1840's and 1850's. After the Civil War, however, various advances by other nations resulted in the loss of the dominant position of the clippers. The correct choice is (E).

Aaron Burr was

(A) vice president during Jefferson's two terms
(B) tried and convicted of treason
(C) tied with Jefferson in the election of 1800
(D) Alexander Hamilton's brother-in-law
(E) elected governor of New York in 1804

Aaron Burr is one of the most colorful figures of the postcolonial period. He was a New Yorker, a vice president, tried for treason, and involved with Alexander Hamilton, giving each of the choices a veneer of truth. Although Burr was vice president, he served only during Jefferson's first term, making choice (A) incorrect. His involvement with Hamilton was not through family but through a feud that ended with Burr killing Hamilton in a duel. Thus, choice (D) is out. Burr ran for governor but lost—just in case choice (E) looks attractive. The correct answer is choice (C). Burr tied with Jefferson in the electoral college in 1800, whereupon the House of Representatives chose Jefferson as president and Burr as vice president.

The word "Okay" (or OK) probably derives from

(A) all correct
(B) a musical by George Gershwin
(C) a World War II military code
(D) a Martin Van Buren campaign organization
(E) a boxing term

This calls for a bit of knowledge of the presidential campaign of 1840. This said, we can eliminate the incorrect choices. Gershwin wrote a musical entitled *Oh, Kay!* in 1926, which eliminates choice (B). World War II came long after 1836, so eliminate (C). Choice (E) is a test writer's bit of fun since the boxing term is "KO." This leaves us with two possibilities. Choice (A) is the meaning OK has come to have and seems to have come from a misinterpretation of the word's correct origin. The correct answer is (D). Martin Van Buren (who lost his bid for reelection) lived near Albany, New York, in a house called Old Kinderhook. The initials O.K. became a secret name for the Democratic clubs in New York. The opposition Whigs somehow never figured this out and invented the meaning "oll korrect," attributing the misspelling to former President Jackson.

The American Colonization Society was concerned with

(A) *Mayflower* descendants' genealogies
(B) encouraging Americans to settle Mexican Texas
(C) transporting freed American slaves to Africa
(D) teaching English to Filipinos after the Spanish-American War
(E) encouraging revolutions against Spain and Portugal in South America

All of the choices seem plausible. The society was supported mainly by Southern slaveholders who sought to resettle freed slaves in Africa. Although very few slaves were sent back, the result was the founding of the West African republic of Liberia. The correct choice is (C).

Andrew Jackson's wife Rachel

(A) gave the first Easter egg roll on the White House lawn
(B) served ice cream for the first time at the White House
(C) was an important champion of the American Indian
(D) gave boisterous receptions in the Blue Room
(E) died before Jackson's first inauguration

The correct choice is (E). Rachel Jackson died in December, 1828, before her husband's inauguration. This eliminates choices (A), (B), and (D), since she never lived in the White House. Remembering Andrew Jackson's campaigns against Native Americans, it is not only highly unlikely that Mrs. Jackson would have been one of their champions, it is untrue.

Luther Burbank was a

(A) horticulturalist
(B) cosmetologist
(C) mortician
(D) evangelist
(E) cinematographer

The correct choice is (A). Luther Burbank developed over 800 new plant varieties, including the commercially valuable Idaho potato.

FELGER/GRANT HEILMAN

This strange shape is made of raised earth and is 1348 feet long if measured along the curves. It was most likely made by

(A) Native Americans in the Midwest or Southern United States
(B) early settlers as a defense against Native Americans
(C) Native Americans of the Four Corners region or the American desert
(D) unknown visitors to the desert near Nazca, Peru
(E) Native Americans of the northwest coast of the United States

The easiest choice to reject is (D), for this is a test of American history, so Peru could not be involved. In any case, the large, fanciful figures in the Nazca region are made by scraping away the top layer of the desert soil, not by building large mounds. Also, choice (B) makes no sense, since most of the mound could easily be walked around—it is only about a tenth of a mile long. Therefore, it must be one of the three choices that involve Native Americans. The early inhabitants of the Four Corners region and American desert built large communal pueblos and round kivas, but no mounds. The Northwest is noted for totem poles. The Mound Builders were pre-Columbian Native Americans of the Midwest and South, so the correct choice is (A). In fact, the illustration shows Serpent Mound, in Ohio.

The Society of the Cincinnati comprises

(A) Ohio businessmen
(B) American Indian tribal chieftains
(C) descendants of Revolutionary War officers
(D) retired Roman legionnaires
(E) Midwestern farmers

Choice (C) is correct. The society was founded by officers who fought in the American Revolution, and it was named for the Roman general Cincinnatus. George Washington was its first president general. Membership is restricted to the oldest male descendants in direct or collateral lines. The city of Cincinnati, Ohio, was named after the society.

The Articles of Confederation refer to

(A) the first Constitution of the United States
(B) the secession of the Southern states
(C) the merging of Southern and Northern Baptist conventions
(D) the unification of the AFL-CIO
(E) fund-raising rules for umbrella organizations such as United Fund and Community Chest

If you recall that the Southern states formed the Confederate States of America, choice (B) is tempting although it is wrong. And just as wrong are choices (C), (D), and (E). The correct one is (A). The Articles defined the United States government from 1781 to 1789, when the present Constitution was adopted.

The Trail of Tears refers to

(A) the Lewis and Clark expedition
(B) the Wilkes expedition to Antarctica
(C) Commodore Perry's entry into Tokyo Bay
(D) pre-Union-Pacific route to California
(E) forced removal of American Indians to the Oklahoma Territory

Although the name might, with some stretching at times, apply to all the choices, (E) is the correct one. Thousands of displaced people died during the winter of 1838 when the Indians were forced to move to Oklahoma.

The Hartford Convention of 1815 resulted in

(A) attempted secession by New England states
(B) successful conclusion of the War of 1812
(C) industrial expansion in the Northeast
(D) the end of the Federalist Party
(E) adoption of a states' rights platform by the Federalist Party

Although some leaders of the convention had the secession of New England in mind, it did not happen, so choice (A) is not right. The War of 1812 ended after the convention, eliminating (B). Despite their protestations, the war did not harm manufacturing in New England, and the convention certainly had no effect on it. Thus, (C) is incorrect too. Although the convention had much to do with states' rights, the Federalist Party did not adopt a platform as the convention was not, in theory, a party meeting. Choice (E) is, therefore, ruled out. The unintended result of the Hartford Convention was the attachment of a stigma of unpatriotism to the Federalist Party in the aftermath of the War of 1812. From this the party, which by then was a regional party, never recovered. (D) is the correct choice.

European History and Cultures Achievement Test

Like the American History Achievement Test, this has 95 standard multiple-choice items to be answered during a one-hour period. It is designed to measure achievement in understanding the development of Western and non-Western cultures, as well as knowledge of the techniques and basic concepts of the social studies.

More specifically, this test devotes about 58 to 62 percent of its items to Europe, 9 to 11 percent to the Middle East, 7 to 9 percent to eastern Asia, 6 to 8 percent to Africa, 4 to 6 percent each to South Asia and Latin America, and 3 to 5 percent to global issues. Chronologically, approximately 46 to 50 percent of the items concern the period since 1750 A.D., 16 to 20 percent the period between 1450 and 1750, and 10 to 15 percent each the period from 750 to 1450 and the period before 750; 6 to 10 percent of the items are cross-chronological.

There is more emphasis on items that have visual clues in this test than in other Achievement Tests. In particular, you should be prepared for maps, cartoons, artifacts, buildings, and other illustrations as the main part of the stem.

Directions. Each of the questions or incomplete statements below is followed by five suggested answers or completions. Select the one that is best in each case.

Peter the Great brought each of the following changes to Russia EXCEPT

(A) mercantilist policies
(B) freedom for the serfs
(C) a new capital city
(D) an army modeled on western military traditions
(E) an expanding central government

(B) is the correct answer. Choices (A), (C), (D), and (E) describe changes wrought by Peter during his reign (1682–1725). The serfs, however, did not obtain their freedom until 1861.

The people who made this painting on a rock wall were

(A) of a type called the Neanderthals
(B) people much like ourselves who lived near the end of the last Ice Age
(C) Australian aborigines
(D) modern artists living in Paris in the early 20th century
(E) people who lived in a large cave near Peking (now Beijing), China

Choices (A) and (E) refer to human ancestors or relatives that are not known to have any art at all. Although this is a part of a cave painting, so-called Peking man, who lived in caves, was of a species called *Homo erectus* that made only very primitive tools such as hand axes. Australian aborigines made and continue to make many paintings on rocks, but their paintings are not as representational as those shown here. Modern artists may have been influenced somewhat by these paintings, but they are not known to paint on rock walls of caves. The correct choice is (B). The Cro-Magnons were physically the same as modern humans. Toward the end of the last Ice Age, some 11,000 years ago, they created many paintings and some sculptures in the caves of northern Spain and southern France.

"His Majesty's Government view with favor the establishment in Palestine of a national home for the Jewish people, and will use their best endeavors to facilitate the achievement of this object. . . ." These words come from

(A) Wilson's Fourteen Points
(B) the Balfour Declaration
(C) the Constitution of Israel
(D) the Entente Cordiale
(E) the Camp David accords

The correct answer is (B), the Balfour Declaration, which stated Britain's support for a Jewish state. Wilson's Fourteen Points (A) did not deal specifically with a Jewish state although they did include the idea of national self-determination. Although Britain did administer Palestine, it is unlikely that the Israeli Constitution would mention the British government, so (C) is incorrect. (D) was an agreement between Britain and France in 1904, and (E) refers to agreements between Israel, Egypt, and the United States in 1978.

One of the few democracies in Africa is the government of

(A) Qatar
(B) Suriname
(C) Libya
(D) Tonga
(E) Botswana

The correct choice is Botswana, (E), which is a parliamentary democracy. Qatar, (A), is a kingdom on the Arabian peninsula. Suriname, (B), in South America, currently has a military government. Libya, (C), is in Africa, but has long been controlled by the dictator Muammar al-Qaddafi. Tonga, (D), although a democracy, is in the South Pacific.

Athens won a decisive victory over Persia during the Persian War at

(A) Philippi
(B) Tours
(C) Marathon
(D) Issus
(E) Zama

The correct choice is (C), Marathon. Choice (A), Philippi, was the city in Macedonia where Marc Antony and Octavian defeated the murderers of Caesar. At Tours, (B), Charles Martel defeated the Muslims. At Issus, (D), Alexander the Great defeated the Persians, and at Zama, (E), the Romans defeated Hannibal.

Western Europe during the ninth to twelfth centuries was characterized by

(A) the breakdown of feudalism
(B) the rise of capitalism
(C) the ravages of the Black Plague
(D) the flourishing of Romanesque architecture
(E) the development of strong nation-states

The correct choice is (D). This period was the high point of feudalism, so (A) is incorrect. Choice (B), the rise of capitalism, did not begin until later and (C), the Black Plague, did not ravage Europe until the 14th century. Choice (E), the development of strong nation-states, came with the decline of feudalism.

This cartoon shows

(A) riots created by publication of Adam Smith's *Wealth of Nations*
(B) agitation over the planting of corn from the New World in fields that had been planted with wheat
(C) abolitionists in the United States during the 1840's and 1850's
(D) an organized effort in England to repeal laws forbidding the import of cheap grain
(E) the Glorious Revolution

The main clues are the posters that say "Anti-cornlaw League." The Corn Laws were laws designed to protect British agricultural and landowning interests by setting a floor on the price at which grains such as wheat (all such grains are called *corn* in England) could be imported. They were abolished in 1846 as a result of a concerted, well-organized campaign against them. They had nothing to do with the grain that Americans call *corn,* choice (B). The time period is right for the American abolitionists, but the posters are wrong. The Glorious Revolution occurred about 150 years earlier and saw the replacement of King James II with William and Mary (see following item). Adam Smith's 18th-century book advocating, among other things, free trade caused no riots upon publication. The correct choice is (D).

THE GRANGER COLLECTION

The region marked on this map was all under the dominion of one ruler at this point in history. What does this region represent?

(A) the Roman Empire
(B) the Ottoman Empire
(C) the empire of Charlemagne
(D) the Spanish Empire
(E) the empire of Peter the Great

Both the Roman Empire and the Ottoman Empire included regions to the east of the boundary of the area marked on this map, so it could not be choices (A) or (B). The Spanish Empire was largely in the New World, not in Europe. Peter the Great's empire was Russia. Therefore, the correct choice is (C), the empire of Charlemagne. In a sense this is a trick question, because the Holy Roman Empire of about a hundred years later had similar boundaries, but the Holy Roman Empire was not among the choices.

THE BETTMANN ARCHIVE

This card represents membership in an organization that is remembered as

(A) the Wobblies
(B) the First International
(C) the Paris Commune
(D) the Comintern
(E) the A.F.L.-C.I.O.

A major clue is the signature of Karl Marx as the corresponding secretary for Germany. Marx was one of the founders of the First International, so choice (B) is correct. The Wobblies (choice A) were the International Workers of the World, a rival organization to the A.F.L. (American Federation of Labor) early in the 20th century. The Paris Commune (choice C) of 1871 was also too late for this card, and in any case was not an international organization, although it had members of the International Working Men's Association active in the commune. The Third International, or Comintern (choice D), was created shortly after the Communist revolution in Russia as a partly disguised arm of the new Soviet Union. The A.F.L.-C.I.O. (choice E) is the parent organization of labor unions in the United States today and was founded much later than the 19th century.

The superiority of the longbow over mounted knights protected by armor was demonstrated at

(A) Crécy
(B) Blenheim
(C) Trafalgar
(D) Actium
(E) the Marne

The correct choice is (A), Crécy, where an important battle was fought in 1346, when knighthood was in flower. Blenheim, (B), and Trafalgar, (C), were both fought after the development of gunpowder, which had made the longbow obsolete. Actium, (D), occurred in 31 B.C. before the longbow was invented, and the Marne, (E), was one of the opening battles of World War I.

The most important result of England's Glorious Revolution in 1688 was

(A) a victory for Protestantism
(B) the expulsion of James II
(C) the supremacy of parliamentary government
(D) universal manhood suffrage
(E) the establishment of cabinet government

The Glorious Revolution did mark a victory for Protestantism (A) by the expulsion of Catholic King James II (B). However, the most important result was that the supremacy of parliamentary government (C) was secure in England. Choices (D), universal manhood suffrage, and (E), cabinet government, would come later.

One man who rose to rule a nation as a consequence of the revolutions of 1848 was

(A) Metternich
(B) Napoleon III
(C) Garibaldi
(D) Castlereagh
(E) Louis Philippe

It was Napoleon III, (B), who became the ruler of France. Choice (A), Metternich, the Austrian leader, was overthrown in the revolution and a similar fate befell the French king Louis Philippe, (E). Choice (C), Garibaldi, fought in the Revolution of 1848 in Italy but did not rise to rule a nation, nor did Castlereagh, (D).

As emperor, Augustus did each of the following, EXCEPT

(A) preserve the old republican forms
(B) extend Roman roads in the empire
(C) build magnificent buildings in Rome
(D) reduce piracy at sea
(E) plot the death of Julius Caesar

Augustus smoothed the transition from republic to empire by preserving the old republican forms (A). He also improved the Roman world (B), brought peace to it (D), and beautified the capital (C). Not only did Julius Caesar die before Augustus became emperor, but Augustus—then known as Octavian—was neither in Rome at the time nor one of the plotters. Thus, choice (E) is correct.

After British India was partitioned into India and Pakistan, their two governments were initially led by

(A) Mountbatten and Gandhi
(B) Nehru and Jinnah
(C) Zia and Singh
(D) Sukarno and Magsaysay
(E) Nkrumah and Marcos

The correct choice is (B). Nehru and Jinnah were directly involved in the establishment of India and Pakistan and became the first to head the new governments. Lord Mountbatten (A) was the last British viceroy of India, while Gandhi was a spiritual leader but never head of the Indian government. Sukarno and Magsaysay (D) and Nkrumah and Marcos (E) were leaders of other nations. Zia and Singh (C) are recent leaders of Pakistan and India.

After World War II, which of the following did <u>NOT</u> occur in France's overseas empire?

(A) war in Algeria
(B) fall of Dien Bien Phu
(C) independence for the Ivory Coast
(D) the Fashoda affair
(E) independence of Guinea

War in Algeria (A) occurred during the 1950's, while France lost Dien Bien Phu (B) in Vietnam in 1954. After World War II, France granted independence to all the nations in its African empire, which included the Ivory Coast (C) in 1960 and Guinea (E) in 1958. However, the Fashoda affair (D) occurred in 1898, when France and Britain confronted each other in an area of the Sudan claimed by both countries.

The immediate cause of the Franco-Prussian War in 1870 was

(A) the Ems dispatch
(B) the fall of Bismarck
(C) French defeat in Mexico
(D) the Dreyfus affair
(E) the Zimmerman telegram

The correct choice is (A). Since the dispatch was published by Bismarck to precipitate war, (B) is clearly incorrect. The French defeat in Mexico (C) may have induced France to regain its lost prestige by going to war with Prussia, but it was not the immediate cause of the conflict. The Dreyfus affair (D) did not occur in France until the 1890's, more than 20 years after the war; and the Zimmermann telegram (E) was sent during World War I.

Prepare to use visual clues if you are going to take history achievement tests. Practice studying pictures, cartoons, and maps from your textbooks.

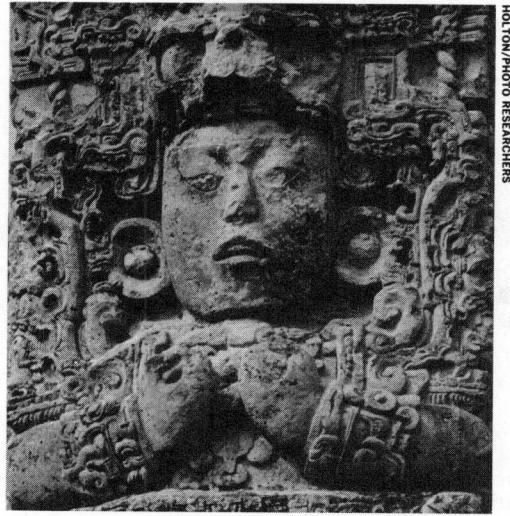

HOLTON/PHOTO RESEARCHERS

Of the following hypotheses about the stone bas-relief shown above, which is most likely to be valid?

(A) It was taken from an ancient Egyptian tomb
(B) It is from a New England tombstone
(C) It is a fine example of stone carvings found in Central America
(D) It is the work of a cubist artist—Pablo Picasso, for example
(E) It is a representation of one of the kings of Babylon.

Although (B), (C), (D), and (E) deal with stone carvings, typical Egyptian art, as in (A), is usually painted or rounded sculpture, so (A) is unlikely. New England tombstones, if they featured drawings cut in stone at all, generally had recognizable Christian religious symbols, such as angels. This makes (B) unlikely. The ornate style of this engraving is incompatible with the very plain style of bas-reliefs from Mesopotamia, which rules out (E). The general style of this carving is basically that of the Central American Maya. Thus, choice (C) is correct. Although (D) might be possible—a modern artist could, for example, copy the art of a non-Western civilization—no work of modern art has used the Mayan style as its basis.

The Advanced Placement Tests

The College Board not only sponsors the SAT and the 14 Achievement Tests, it also offers more than 16 tests that can be taken by secondary school students for college credit. These tests, known as the Advanced Placement Tests, cover most of the freshman courses commonly offered in college. Among the most popular tests are those on literature, calculus, American history, biology, and chemistry, which are covered in this volume. Other tests include such typical freshman courses as art, physics, mechanics, computer science, European history, and foreign languages.

The achievement tests are rigorous. For example, only 2 percent of high school seniors attempt the Advanced Placement Examination for calculus. Each complete test usually takes three hours. Most students have little hope of passing one of these tests without having taken a course in high school that is designed to replace a college course. Such courses are usually designated

with the letters *AP,* as in "AP calculus" or "AP biology." The more technical a subject is, the less likely it is that a student can pass the AP test without a specific course. Thus, it is possible to pass the AP test in literature, or American history, with only the ordinary secondary school courses, while it is nearly impossible to pass AP tests in calculus or chemistry without taking a course designed for this purpose.

Different schools require different scores for college credit. Scores are granted on a five-point scale:

5 extremely well qualified
4 well qualified
3 qualified
2 possibly qualified
1 no recommendation

Almost all schools accept a score of 4 or 5 for college credit; however, many schools also accept a score of 3. Check with the school you plan to attend to find out what score will be acceptable for college credit. Some of the tests are so difficult that you can get a score of 5

by correctly answering only half the items in them.

Typically, an Advanced Placement Test consists of two parts: a multiple-choice part and a part devoted to free writing of some kind, such as an essay. The multiple-choice section of the AP examinations is scored like the other College Board multiple-choice examinations in that wrong answers are penalized by small deductions. Thus, unless you can eliminate some of the choices, you should not guess. If, however, you think you know what the correct choice is or if you are sure that one or more of the choices are not correct, you will gain points in the long run by guessing.

In addition to the Advanced Placement Examinations, the College Board also publishes and administers the College-Level Entrance Examination, or CLEP. Some schools will give college credit for good scores on CLEP. For the most part, however, CLEP is used by adults who have been out of high

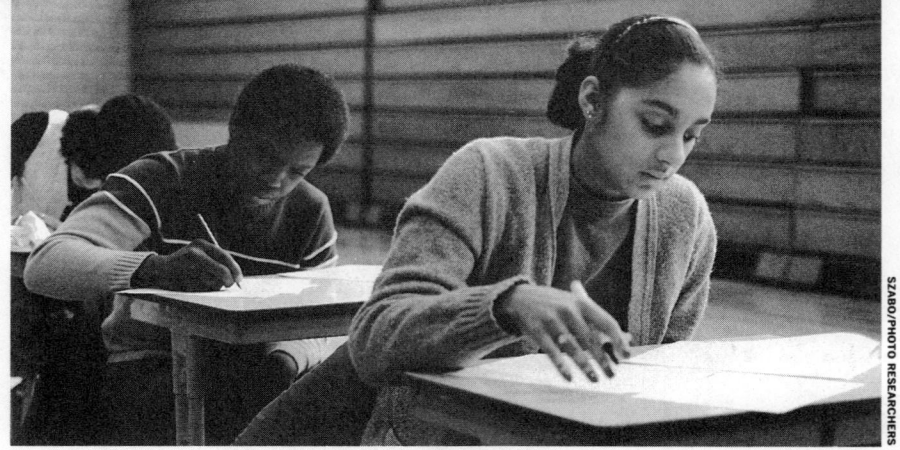

THE ADVANCED PLACEMENT TEST *is one of the few standardized exams that may require you to write an essay. Come prepared with a pen as well as two pencils.*

the actual test for which the students are preparing may come before the end of the school year. Some courses, such as American history or advanced biology (a course after the typical freshman course), may be offered in the junior year of high school. It is generally more effective to take the test in the same year as you take the course, so you may want to take some AP exams as a junior. For example, about three-quarters of all American history tests are taken by juniors in high school rather than by seniors.

Note that one difference between a strict multiple-choice test and a test that combines multiple choice with essays or free responses is that you may need to write part of the time in ink. When there is an essay section in a test, you may be required to bring your own pen. If so, make sure you bring at least two pens. You are also, of course, required to bring No. 2 (medium soft) pencils, preferably with erasers.

school for some years and decide that they wish to enter college. Thus, CLEP is not usually a rep acement for an AP examination, but in some circumstances it may be. If you are interested in substituting CLEP for an AP exam, you should first make sure that the

school you plan to attend will accept it.

In general, the Advanced Placement Examinations are given in mid-May. Depending on the region of the country, school may be nearly over or still have a month to run. An AP course in high school generally recognizes that

Advanced Placement Test of English Literature and Composition

This test is one of two that students can take as an Advanced Placement Examination in English. The other test, Language and Composition, is briefly discussed and sampled at the end of the following practice test. The following sample items are similar to those in the AP exam labeled Literature and Composition.

Multiple-choice items. The actual test consists of 55 to 65 multiple-choice items and two or three essays. The samples that follow represent the multiple-choice portion of the examination. For these items you will need to analyze at least one poem and several prose passages, which can come from works of fiction or from essays. Since you are allowed 75 minutes for the multiple-choice portion of the examination, considering the time you need to read the passages, you should average approximately one minute per item to complete the test. A little faster pace is even better, as it gives you time to review your choices. To facilitate this review, circle correct choices in your booklet and mark the score sheet.

The passages are often difficult to read. You should take advantage of every help offered when analyzing a passage before starting on the items. Pay attention to footnotes in which difficult or obscure words or references are explained. If there is a title, start by reading it, as it can help you focus on the main idea. If there is no title, try to find or formulate the main idea yourself. Make sure you understand each sentence before reading the next one. You are allowed to write in the book; it often helps to underline or circle important sentences or words.

The penalty for wrong answers discourages guessing. If you can eliminate at least two of the choices, however, the probability of guessing the correct choice among the remaining three choices is high enough to make guessing a good strategy.

The multiple-choice portion of the test will count for 40 percent of the entire score for the test. You will need to get at least half of the multiple-choice items correct to score a 3 for the complete test, the score that most schools accept as passing.

Essays. The essay topics are general statements about literature or life that must be discussed in the context of specific works supplied by the test or chosen by the student. A poem or prose passage may be provided; the student then will be asked to discuss some specific aspect of it. Another essay question may provide a theme and a list of works or authors from which you are to pick two to indicate how the theme is presented in literature. Sometimes you are allowed to select your own works to illustrate the theme; however, in that case, you are expected to select literary works, not merely popular ones.

At least one essay will be based on analysis of a poem, which will be supplied. You will also be asked to analyze the poem in a specific way. For example, you may be asked to break the poem down into elements, analyze comparisons and contrasts in the poem, explain how the poet uses various tonal elements, or discuss the emotional or poetic structure of the poem. Often the essay topic is quite specific, such as "How do the opening line and the last line summarize the poem in different ways?" or "Which figure of speech does the poet use to symbolize loss?" In such cases, it is important to remember that you are writing an *essay,* not simply supplying an answer to a question. While the essay may be short—250 words is acceptable if the words are the right ones—it must provide a detailed analysis of the way that the poem expresses the idea suggested in the question.

With all the essay items it is important to
1. Be sure you have a clear idea of what the topic is;
2. Use works with which you are familiar, even if you think that some work suggested would fit the topic better but you are only partly familiar with it;
3. Write a thesis statement that summarizes the main idea or ideas that will be in the essay—do this *before* starting the essay;
4. Plan your order of attack with main points and supporting points arranged in a logical fashion—an outline is the most useful way to do this;
5. Be sure to cite specific evidence from literature for every point you are making—don't just offer your opinion; and
6. Carefully read your essay after you have written it to be absolutely sure you have addressed the topic asked for in the examination.

You will have 105 minutes to write the two or three essays, which count for 60 percent of your total score. Each essay, however, has its own time limit—typically 30 to 60 minutes, depending on how many essays there are and the expected length of an essay.

Sample multiple-choice items

<u>Directions</u>: Read each poem or prose passage carefully and answer the accompanying questions.

The first eight questions refer to the following poem.

THE RIVER OF LIFE
Thomas Campbell (1774–1844)

The more we live, more brief appear
    Our life's succeeding stages:
A day to childhood seems a year,
    And years like passing ages.

The gladsome current of our youth,
    Ere passion yet disorders,
Steals lingering like a river smooth
    Along its grassy borders.

But as the care-worn cheeks grow wan,
    And sorrow's shafts fly thicker,
Ye stars, that measure life to man,
    Why seem your courses quicker?

When joys have lost their bloom and breath
    And life itself is vapid,
Why, as we reach the Falls of Death,
    Feel we its tide more rapid?

It may be strange—yet who would change
    Time's course to slower speeding,
When one by one our friends have gone
    And left our bosoms bleeding?

Heaven gives our years of fading strength
    Indemnifying fleetness;
And those of youth, a seeming length,
    Proportion'd to their sweetness.

"The River of Life" should be classified as a(n)

(A) sonnet
(B) elegy
(C) lyric
(D) ballad
(E) epic

The correct choice is (C) <u>lyric</u>. A lyric poem is a reflective work with a regular rhyme scheme and meter. It reveals a poet's feelings about a subject. A <u>sonnet</u> is a 14-line poem, an <u>elegy</u> is a poem of lamentation, a <u>ballad</u> tells a <u>story</u> in verse, and an <u>epic</u> is a long narrative poem that gives an account of a hero or heroine.

The last two lines in the third stanza exemplify the technique of

(A) hyperbole
(B) irony
(C) synecdoche
(D) metonymy
(E) apostrophe

The correct choice is (E) <u>apostrophe</u>. An apostrophe is a direct address (usually as a digression) to someone not present, or to a personified object or idea. In this poem, Campbell digresses briefly to speak directly to "Ye stars." The remaining choices name other literary techniques: <u>hyperbole</u> uses exaggeration for emphasis, <u>irony</u> offers a contrast between actual and suggested meaning, <u>synecdoche</u> uses a part to represent an entire object or idea, and <u>metonymy</u> substitutes a related word for an entire object or idea.

"Sorrow's shafts" (stanza three, line 2) is a metaphor for

(A) old age
(B) death
(C) river
(D) pain
(E) life

Choice (D) <u>pain</u> is correct. The line "And sorrow's shafts fly thicker" refers to the pain of sorrow. This pain is metaphorically compared to the pain inflicted by a "shaft," or spear.

Water imagery is used to symbolize the flow of time for the elderly in stanza

(A) one
(B) two
(C) three
(D) four
(E) six

The correct answer is (D) <u>four</u>. The last line of this stanza asks why the elderly "Feel . . . its tide more rapid?" Notice that the last line in stanza three mentions "courses," but this word refers to the "stars" addressed in the previous line. Notice also that stanza two speaks of "a river smooth," but the stanza is not about elderly people, and the question was specifically about the elderly.

The poem shifts its focus to the seemingly more rapid passages of time in stanza

(A) two
(B) three
(C) four
(D) five
(E) six

The correct choice is (B) <u>three</u>. After a brief mention of the overall theme, the first two stanzas dwell on the apparent slowness of time in our youth. Stanza three shifts the focus with the signal word "But" and focuses entirely on elderly people's perception of time. It is they whose "courses [seem] quicker."

This poem is about each of the following EXCEPT

(A) bereavement
(B) reflection
(C) acceptance
(D) repression
(E) changes

The correct choice is (D) <u>repression</u>. The poet neither represses his feelings nor alludes to <u>repression</u>. <u>Bereavement</u> is suggested in stanza five, lines 3 and 4; <u>reflection</u> is exhibited as the poet thinks back to the days of his youth. (In a larger sense, this is a poem of reflection.) The poet shows total <u>acceptance</u> of the apparent <u>changes</u> in the flow of time as one grows older.

The theme of this poem is that the passage of time

(A) is fair only to the young
(B) is unfair to everyone
(C) is more fair as we grow older
(D) is unfair to the old
(E) is fair to people of all ages

The correct choice is (E) <u>is fair to people of all ages</u>. The poet speaks of time moving slowly—"lingering like a river smooth" etc. when we are young, and moving quickly as we grow older—"its tide more rapid" etc. The poem suggests throughout that this is as it should be. The theme of fairness in time's varying rate of movement is summarized in the final stanza.

"The River of Life" can be classified as a poem in the style of

(A) the Romantic movement
(B) the modernist movement
(C) the transcendentalists
(D) the Elizabethans
(E) the Cavaliers

While all of the five groups of poets frequently wrote lyric poetry, it is fairly easy to eliminate the modernists (B), the Elizabethans (D), and the Cavaliers (E), since the language and diction is not modern and does not reflect the 16th or 17th centuries. The dates for Thomas Campbell—a poet vastly popular in his time whose reputation has declined considerably since—suggest either the early Romantic movement or the very early transcendentalist movements. If you recall that Campbell was a Scot, you will know the correct choice is (A), since all the transcendentalists were Americans. Another way to eliminate choice (C) is to recall that most transcendental poetry was heavily influenced by Buddhism and Hinduism, whose central ideas are contrary to the central idea of "The River of Life."

The next seven questions refer to the following passage.

From "The Coketown Population," *Hard Times*, by *Charles Dickens (1812–1870)*

It was a town of red brick, or of brick that would have been red if the smoke and ashes had allowed it; but as matters stood it was a town of unnatural red and black like the painted face of a savage. It was a town of machin-
5   ery and tall chimneys, out of which interminable serpents of smoke trailed themselves forever and ever, and never got uncoiled. It had a black canal in it, and a river that ran purple with ill-smelling dye, and vast piles of buildings full of windows where there was a rattling and a trem-
10 bling all day long, and where the piston of the steam-engine worked monotonously up and down like the head of an elephant in a state of melancholy madness. It contained several large streets all very like one another, and many small streets still more like one another, inhabited
15 by people equally like one another, who all went in and out at the same hours, with the same sound upon the same pavements, to do the same work, and to whom every day was the same as yesterday and tomorrow, and every year the counterpart of the last and the next . . .
20   You saw nothing in Coketown but what was severely workful. If the members of a religious persuasion built a chapel there—as the members of eighteen religious persuasions had done—they made it a pious warehouse of red brick, with sometimes (but this is only in highly orna-
25 mental examples) a bell in a birdcage on the top of it. The solitary exception was the New Church; a stuccoed edifice with a square steeple over the door, terminating in four short pinnacles like florid wooden legs. All the public inscriptions in the town were painted alike, in severe
30 characters of black and white. The jail might have been the infirmary, the infirmary might have been the jail, the townhall might have been either, or both, or anything else, for anything that appeared to the contrary in the graces of their construction.

The style of writing employed in this selection is an example of

(A) humanism
(B) naturalism
(C) impressionism
(D) romanticism
(E) transcendentalism

Choice (B) naturalism is correct. Naturalism is often used synonymously with realism, depicting life as the author sees it. However, naturalism tends to focus on the negative, even repulsive, aspects of reality. Humanism takes an optimistic view of human potential; impressionism emphasizes immediate aspects of life without careful examination; romanticism depicts idealized characters and events; and transcendentalism is a more philosophical form of romanticism.

"It was a town of machinery and tall chimneys, out of which interminable serpents of smoke trailed themselves forever and ever, and never got uncoiled." This sentence (lines 4–7) means each of the following EXCEPT

(A) the town was being strangled by the effects of industrialization
(B) the town was taking on a monstrous appearance
(C) the town was reverting to primitive customs
(D) the town's plight appeared endless
(E) smoke from the chimneys reminded one of coiled serpents

The correct choice is (C), the town was reverting to primitive customs. The Industrial Revolution, with all its negative manifestations, still represented the most advanced technology of the time.

The description of "the piston of the steam-engine" (lines 10–12) is an example of

(A) paradox
(B) metaphor
(C) irony
(D) simile
(E) personification

The correct answer is (D), simile. Simile is a comparison between two unlike objects, using the word "like" or "as" as part of the comparison. A metaphor makes a similar comparison without using the word "like" or "as"; both irony and paradox suggest contradictions. Personification, choice (E), appears attractive, but this figurative device gives human qualities to objects, animals, ideas, or natural occurrences. Furthermore, it attributes these qualities directly, without employing "like" or "as."

An example of the defilement of nature can be found in the

(A) pavement
(B) red bricks
(C) bird cage
(D) river
(E) public inscriptions

Choice (D), river, is correct. While all of the choices refer to negative features of the town, only the "river that ran purple with ill-smelling dye" (lines 7–8) exemplifies a violation or desecration of nature.

The author suggests that the inhabitants of the town

(A) took pride in their work
(B) lacked creativity
(C) were master builders
(D) experienced the comforts of life
(E) spoke very little

The correct choice is (B), lacked creativity. The last sentence of the first paragraph describes a town inhabited by a robotic breed of people for whom the sameness of their lives appears to be their greatest source of comfort.

Dickens implies that any visitor to Coketown would likely

(A) be repulsed
(B) find a job
(C) lose his way
(D) improve its image
(E) recognize each feature

Choice (C), lose his way, is correct. The passage strongly suggests that a visitor would have great difficulty distinguishing between the various streets and buildings. The visitor might be repulsed (choice A), but this would depend more on the individual's background and expectations than on the features of this industrialized town. The passage emphasizes sameness and regimentation of the town rather than its repulsiveness.

The words "pious warehouse" (line 23) are used

(A) reverently
(B) ironically
(C) inadvertently
(D) optimistically
(E) ambiguously

Choice (B), ironically, is correct. The implied criticism here is that a building that should be a "pious" house of worship is, in reality, a replica of the other "red brick" structures in the town. While the word "pious" suggests reverence (choice A), this interpretation is immediately denied by the juxtaposition of "warehouse."

If you think you know what the correct choice is or are sure that one or more of the choices are not correct, you will gain points in the long run by guessing.

Advanced Placement Test of Language and Composition

This test is the other of the two AP English tests. The fundamental structure and grading are the same for Language and Composition as for Literature and Composition, except that there is no poetry in Language and Composition and there is more emphasis on analyzing grammar and language usage.

Of the two or three essays for the Language and Composition test, at least one will involve analysis of a prose passage supplied with the test.

Grading and time allotments are the same as for the Literature and Composition test (see page 740.)

Multiple-choice items

Directions: Read each prose passage carefully and answer the accompanying questions.

The questions are based on the following passage.

It is a proverbial fact that dreams melt away in the morning. They can, of course, be remembered; for we only know dreams from our memory of them after we are awake. But we very often have a feeling that we have only
5   remembered a dream in part and that there was more of it during the night; we can observe, too, how the recollection of a dream, which was still lively in the morning, will melt away, except for a few small fragments, in the course of the day; we often know we have dreamt, with-
10   out knowing *what* we have dreamt; and we are so familiar with the fact of dreams being liable to be forgotten, that we see no absurdity in the possibility of someone having had a dream in the night and of his not being aware in the morning either of what he has dreamt or
15   even of the fact that he has dreamt at all. On the other hand, it sometimes happens that dreams show an extraordinary persistence in the memory. I have analyzed dreams in my patients which occurred twenty-five and more years earlier; and I can remember a dream of my
20   own separated by at least thirty-seven years from today and yet as fresh as ever in my memory. All of this is very remarkable and not immediately intelligible.

Sigmund Freud: from *The Interpretation of Dreams.*

This passage can best be defined as

(A) narration
(B) exposition
(C) description
(D) argumentation
(E) didacticism

Choice (B), exposition, is correct. Exposition is a form of writing in which the author attempts to explain a subject. Other forms of writing may enter into exposition. For example, a writer may describe a person, a setting, or an event to illustrate a point of view. In this passage, description, as well as narration and argumentation are subdued—the overall approach being to communicate information. A didactic writer projects his or her opinion in a preachy or moralizing tone, often to the extent that style overshadows subject matter. This is clearly not evident here.

The word "melt" in line 8 is used

(A) ironically
(B) literally
(C) metaphorically
(D) symbolically
(E) pedantically

Choice (C), metaphorically, is correct. A metaphor is an implied comparison between two dissimilar objects. Here, the author implies a comparison between the dwindling recollection (or melting) of dreams and a solid, but transient, object (like a chunk of ice) that diminishes "except for a few small fragments, in the course of the day."

The subject of the verb "will melt" in lines 7–8 is

(A) we
(B) recollection
(C) dream
(D) lively
(E) morning

The correct choice is (B), recollection. Choice (A), we, is the subject of the entire independent clause between the two semicolons and has "can observe" as its verb. Choice (C), dream, may appear at first to be a good candidate, but dream is the object of a preposition, which makes it ineligible to be a subject. Choice (D), lively, is an adjective (despite the -ly suffix that makes it seem to be an adverb) and so cannot be a subject. Choice (E), morning, like dream, is the object of a preposition.

The last sentence of the passage implies that the writer

(A) is more impressed with his own dreams than with the dreams of others
(B) finds the concept of dreams extremely confusing
(C) would like to encourage the readers to suggest their opinions on the subject of dreams
(D) is going to present a more detailed explanation in the pages that follow
(E) is extremely proud of the fact that he is able to recall a thirty-seven-year-old dream

The correct choice is (D), is going to present a more detailed explanation in the pages that follow. By referring to the remarkable nature of dream recall and saying that this phenomenon is not immediately intelligible, he suggests that it will become intelligible as one reads on. The writer is obviously knowledgeable in his subject, eliminating choice (B). He refers to his own and his patients' recollections of dreams to illustrate the longevity of certain dreams, thus eliminating choices (A) and (E). There is no suggestion that the author seeks to elicit the dreams of his readers (C).

A person is most likely to remember a dream

(A) during the night
(B) after many years
(C) during the course of a day
(D) immediately on awakening
(E) after it is analyzed

The correct choice is (D), immediately on awakening. The author says in lines 6–9, "the recollection of a dream, which was still lively in the morning, will melt away . . . in the course of the day." Although he speaks of dreams that show "an extraordinary persistence in the memory" (lines 16–17), these are suggested as being exceptional.

The author refers to his own dream to illustrate a kind of

(A) partiality
(B) selfishness
(C) arrogance
(D) irony
(E) sophistication

The correct answer is (D), irony. After establishing the ephemeral nature of dreams, he introduces the seemingly contradictory nature of a personal dream that has not faded in nearly four decades. His purpose is not to separate his experience from those of others, but to use his experience to suggest the remarkable potential for the occasional longevity of dreams.

According to this passage, most people, on hearing that someone is unable to recall a dream, would probably

(A) tend to think the person was hiding the truth
(B) try to help the person remember his/her dream
(C) be unable to understand the problem
(D) empathize through personal experience
(E) consider the person to be ignorant

The correct answer is (D), empathize through personal experience. The author suggests in lines 10–15 that we would empathize with this common experience: ". . . and we are so familiar with the fact of dreams being liable to be forgotten, that we see no absurdity in the possibility of someone having had a dream in the night and of his not being aware in the morning either of what he has dreamt, or even of the fact that he has dreamt at all."

Advanced Placement Calculus

There are two different Advanced Placement Examinations in calculus. Calculus AB represents a course in elementary functions with emphasis on intuitive understanding of differentiation and integration. Calculus BC is more rigorous and represents more closely a two-semester freshman college course. Items that would be included only in the more rigorous examination are marked **[BC]** in the material that follows.

Scoring on the two sections of this examination differs. Section 1 is a standard multiple-choice test, and there is a penalty for random guesses. Section 2 consists of free-response items—the student must write answers. Well-reasoned answers that are correct will get more credit than correct answers that are not so elegant. Each section counts for exactly half the total score.

The entire test takes three hours. Generally, half or slightly more than half the time is spent on Section 1.

Section 1
Choose the correct answer.

$$\int_1^3 x^{-2}\, dx =$$

(A) $-\dfrac{4}{3}$ (B) $\dfrac{4}{3}$ (C) $-\dfrac{2}{3}$ (D) $\dfrac{2}{3}$ (E) $\dfrac{1}{6}$

This item asks for the value of a definite integral. For a function $f(x)$—in this case $f(x) = x^{-2}$—the definite integral can be found by first finding the antiderivative of $f(x)$, usually indicated by $F(x)$—in this case, $F(x) = -x^{-1} + C = \frac{-1}{x} + C$. The constant C for the antiderivative drops out when evaluating a definite integral. The formula for a definite integral is

$$\int_a^b f(x)\, dx = F(x)\Big|_a^b = F(b) - F(a)$$

Then, for $F(x) = \dfrac{-1}{x}$

$$\frac{-1}{x}\Big|_a^b = \frac{-1}{3} - \left(\frac{-1}{1}\right) = -\frac{1}{3} + 1 = \frac{2}{3}$$

The correct choice is (D).

$$\int_1^7 \frac{1}{x+1}\, dx =$$

(A) $\ln 8$ (B) $\ln 2$ (C) $2 \ln 2$ (D) $3 \ln 2$ (E) $\ln 6$

Again the problem is to evaluate a definite integral. You need to remember the correct antiderivative for $\frac{1}{x+1}$.

$$\int_1^7 \frac{1}{x+1}\, dx = \ln [x+1]\Big|_1^7$$

There are a number of formulas for derivatives and antiderivatives in calculus. You need to memorize the basic ones for this test. You will not be given formulas on the test.

$$\ln [7+1] - \ln [1+1] = \ln 8 - \ln 2$$

While this answer is correct, it is not one of the choices given. Note that $\ln 8$ is the same as $\ln 2^3 = 3 \ln 2$.

$$3 \ln 2 - \ln 2 = 2 \ln 2$$

The correct choice is (C).

If $y = \dfrac{2}{x^3 - 3}$, then $\dfrac{dy}{dx} =$

(A) $\dfrac{2}{(x^3 - 3)^2}$ (B) $\dfrac{-6x^2}{(x^3 - 3)^2}$ (C) $\dfrac{6x^2}{(x^3 - 3)^2}$

(D) $-6x^2$ (E) 0

You need to remember the rule for the derivative of a quotient. If the quotient is $\frac{u}{v}$, the numerator of the derivative is the difference of the expression in the denominator times the derivative of the numerator minus the expression in the numerator times the derivative of the denominator, or $v \cdot \frac{du}{dx} - u \cdot \frac{dv}{dx}$, while the denominator is the square of the denominator, or v^2. Thus, when $u = 2$ and $v = x^3 - 3$, then $\frac{dy}{dx} = \frac{(x^3 - 3)(0) - 2(3x^2)}{(x^3 - 3)^2}$, or $\frac{-6x^2}{(x^3 - 3)^2}$. The correct choice is (B).

If $f(x) = (3x + 2)^3$, then the third derivative of $f(x)$ at $x = 1$ is

(A) 18 (B) 0 (C) 270 (D) 162 (E) 54

To find the third derivative, you need to find the derivative of the function, which will be another function, generally designated as $f'(x)$. Then find the derivative of that function, $f''(x)$, which is called the second derivative. The third derivative, $f'''(x)$, is the derivative of the second derivative.

$$f'(x) = 3(3x + 2)^2(3) = 9(3x + 2)^2$$
$$f''(x) = 18(3x + 2)^1(3) = 54(3x + 2)$$
$$f'''(x) = 54(3x + 2)^0(3) = 162$$

Notice that the third derivative is a constant. The qualification "at $x = 1$" was not needed for the correct choice, (D), but was inserted so that various incorrect choices could be evaluated.

Note that you should expect the nth derivative of a polynomial function of degree n to be a constant. In this item, you would still have to take the three derivatives to determine which constant, but knowing that the answer should be a constant might help to avoid some of the possible incorrect choices.

If $\dfrac{dy}{dx} = \sin 3x$, then $y =$

(A) $3 \cos 3x + C$ (B) $\cos 3x + C$ (C) $\dfrac{1}{3} \sin 3x$

(D) $\dfrac{1}{3} \cos 3x$ (E) $-\dfrac{1}{3} \cos 3x + C$

For this item you are given the derivative and asked to find the antiderivative, which is essentially the same as the indefinite integral. It is easy to eliminate choices (C) and (D), since they do not have a constant of integration. All indefinite integrals have such a constant. Now take the derivatives of the other three choices to see which one works. To select among the three remaining choices, begin by noticing that $u = 3x$ is a function of x and $\cos 3x$ is a function of u. In other words, the chain rule applies:

$$\frac{dy}{dx} = \frac{dy}{du}\frac{du}{dx}$$

so $\frac{d}{dx} \cos 3x = -3 \sin 3x$. The factor for $\cos 3x$ varies in the three choices from 3 to $\frac{1}{3}$ to $-\frac{1}{3}$. If you look at the three as multiplied by $-3 \sin x$, the only one that gives you $\sin 3x$ by itself is $-\frac{1}{3}$. Therefore, the correct choice is (E), since $-\frac{1}{3}(-3 \sin 3x) = \sin 3x$. In other words, $\frac{d}{dx}(-\frac{1}{3} \cos 3x + C) = \sin 3x$.

$$\lim_{x \to \infty} \frac{2x^3}{100x - x^3} =$$

(A) 0 (B) -2 (C) $-\infty$ (D) 2 (E) ∞

One usually finds limits of complicated expressions by using various tricks that have been developed over the years. For the limit of a rational expression, the trick is to divide both the numerator and the denominator by the highest power of the variable—in this case, by x^3. The result is that you can find the limit of an equivalent expression that is much easier to find than the limit for the original expression:

$$\lim_{x \to \infty} \frac{2}{100/x^3 - 1} = \frac{2}{-1} = -2$$

The correct choice is (B).

If $x^3 + xy + y^2 = 0$, then in terms of x and y, $\dfrac{dy}{dx} =$

(A) $\dfrac{3x^2 + y}{x + 2y}$ (B) $\dfrac{-3x^2 - y}{3}$ (C) $\dfrac{3x^2 + y}{3}$

(D) $\dfrac{x + 2y}{3x^2 + y}$ (E) $\dfrac{-3x^2 - y}{x + 2y}$

Since you are given an equation that is in terms of both x and y instead of a function of x, implicit differentiation is involved. Instead of solving for y, which is difficult because of the presence of both the xy and y^2 terms, differentiate the given equation with regard to x. In this case, keep in mind that xy is a product and follows that rule, while y^2 has the basic form u^n. The first form of the derivative is

$$3x^2 + x \cdot \frac{dy}{dx} + y(1) + 2y \cdot \frac{dy}{dx} = 0, \text{ or}$$
$$x \cdot \frac{dy}{dx} + 2y \cdot \frac{dy}{dx} = -3x^2 - y$$
$$(x + 2y)\frac{dy}{dx} = -3x^2 - y$$
$$\frac{dy}{dx} = \frac{-3x^2 + y}{x + 2y}$$

The correct choice is (A).

$$\int_0^1 (e^x + e^{-x})dx =$$

(A) 0   (B) $\dfrac{e^2 + 1}{e}$ (C) $\dfrac{e^2 - 1}{e}$ (D) $\dfrac{1}{e^2}$ (E) 1

To begin with, you need to know that the derivative of e^x is the same function, e^x, but if u is some function of x, then the derivative with respect to x of e^u is

$$y' = \frac{du}{dx}$$

Applying this rule to the definite integral gives

$$\int_0^1 (e^x + e^{-x})\,dx = [e^x - e^{-x}]\Big|_0^1, \text{ so } F(b) - F(a) \text{ is}$$

$$(e^1 - \frac{1}{e^1}) - (e^0 - \frac{1}{e^0}) = \frac{e^2 - 1}{e} - (1 - 1) = \frac{e^2 - 1}{e}$$

The correct choice is (C).

[BC] Describe the curve given by the parametric equations

$$x = 2\cos t, \ y = 3\sin t$$

(A) a circle centered at the origin with the radius 6
(B) an ellipse centered at the origin with a major axis of 6 and a minor axis of 4
(C) a hyperbola centered at the origin with vertices at $(-3, 0)$ and $(0, 3)$
(D) a parabola with a vertex at the origin
(E) a sinusoidal curve with a period of 2π and an amplitude of 3

You can eliminate some possibilities by plotting the easiest points, the points for which $t = 0$ and $t = \frac{\pi}{2}$. For $t = 0$, $(x, y) = (2, 0)$; while for $t = \frac{\pi}{2}$, $(x, y) = (0, 3)$. This eliminates choice (A) because a circle centered at the origin could not go through both $(2, 0)$ and $(0, 3)$. Choice (D) is also eliminated on the same grounds. The other choices, however, could conceivably include the two points. By finding other points, you could continue to narrow the choices down until you had just one. There is a better strategy, however.

In general, to find the graph of parametric equations without plotting a lot of points, find the Cartesian or rectangular equation that has the same graph. Often this will be an easily recognized equation in Cartesian coordinates.

When parametric equations include both the sine and cosine, it generally helps to start with the trigonometric identity.

$$\sin^2 t + \cos^2 t = 1$$

The given parametric equations can be rewritten as

$$\cos t = \tfrac{x}{2}, \ \sin t = \tfrac{y}{3}$$

When you substitute these values into the trigonometric identity, you get
$$\tfrac{x^2}{2^2} + \tfrac{y^2}{3^2} = 1$$

This should be immediately recognizable as the equation of an ellipse centered at the origin with vertices at $(2, 0)$, $(-2, 0)$, $(0, 3)$, and $(0, -3)$. Note that two of these points are the ones found earlier by looking at easily calculated values of the parametric equations. Since this ellipse also has a major axis of 6 and a minor axis of 4, the correct choice is (B).

If $y = 2\sin x \cos x$, then $dy/dx =$

(A) $2\sec^2 x$ (B) $2\cos x$ (C) $2\cos 2x$ (D) $\cos 2x$
(E) 1

There are two ways to approach this problem. The easier way depends on recognizing that $2\sin x \cos x$ is one side of the trigonometric identity for the sine of a double angle: $\sin 2x = 2\sin x \cos x$. Thus, instead of differentiating the product $2\sin x \cos x$, you can differentiate the easier composite function $\sin 2x$.

$$y = \sin 2x$$
$$dy/dx = \cos 2x(2) = 2\cos 2x,$$

so the correct choice is (C).

If you fail to recognize the double-angle formula, you can use the rule for differentiating a product.

$$y = 2(\sin x \cos x)$$
$$dy/dx = 2[\sin x \,(-\sin x) + \cos x \cos x]$$
$$= 2(\cos^2 x - \sin^2 x)$$

This is correct, but the answer in this form is not shown among the choices. You *still* have to remember a double-angle formula from trigonometry:

$$\cos 2x = \cos^2 x - \sin^2 x$$

Therefore, $dy/dx = 2\cos 2x$, choice (C).

If $f(x) = x^2 - 2x^3$ is defined for all real numbers x, then if there is a relative maximum of the function, it is at $x =$

(A) 0   (B) $-\dfrac{1}{3}$ (C) $\dfrac{1}{6}$ (D) $\dfrac{1}{3}$
(E) there is no relative maximum

A relative maximum occurs in a region where a graph that has been increasing reaches its local high point and begins to descend. At the top of its path, so long as the path is continuous and smooth, the slope (or first derivative) will be 0. A slope can also be 0, however, at a point of inflection, where the graph levels off and then continues rising or falling, whichever way it is moving before the point of inflection. Thus, there are two things to look for in solving this problem: (1) places where the derivative is 0 and (2) the change in sign of the derivative at those places. Finally, examine the second derivative to make sure that the apparent relative maximum is not a point of inflection.

First-derivative (f') test: $f'(x) = 2x - 6x^2$
Set f' equal to 0 and solve: $0 = 2x - 6x^2$
$$0 = 2x(1 - 3x)$$
$$0 = 2x \ or \ 0 = 1 - 3x$$
$$x = 0 \ or \ x = \tfrac{1}{3}$$
Number-line test:
The function f' changes sign when $f' = 0$, so it separates the real number line into three intervals: the interval of the line to the left of 0, the interval between 0 and $\frac{1}{3}$, and the interval to the right of $\frac{1}{3}$. By examining the behavior of f' for sample values in those intervals, you can tell how the function behaves for the whole interval. You only need to know the sign of f' at the sample value, not the value itself. Easy values to compute would be for $f'(-1)$, $f'(0.1)$, and $f'(1)$.

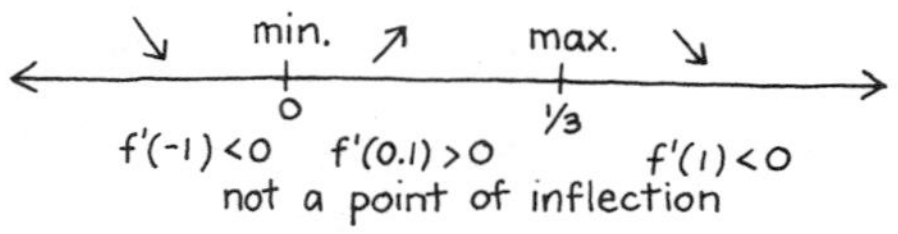

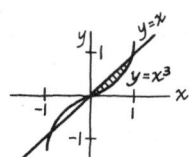

Second-derivative (f'') test:
A point of inflection occurs when the second derivative changes sign, which for a smooth curve can happen only when the second derivative is 0. Find the second derivative. Set it equal to 0, and solve.
$$f''(x) = 2 - 12x$$
$$0 = 2 - 12x$$
$$12x = 2$$
$$x = \tfrac{1}{6}$$
The only point of inflection is where $x = \frac{1}{6}$.
Therefore, the correct choice is (D), $x = \frac{1}{3}$.

The area bounded by $y = x^3$ and $y = x$ on the domain $[0, 1]$ is

(A) $\dfrac{1}{2}$ (B) $\dfrac{1}{8}$ (C) $\dfrac{1}{16}$ (D) $\dfrac{1}{4}$ (E) $\dfrac{3}{4}$

The area under a single curve is the definite integral for the given domain, but this problem involves the area between two curves. If you designate the function for the upper curve as f_u and the function for the lower curve as f_l, then the area above the interval $[a, b]$ is

$$\int_a^b (f_u - f_l)\,dx$$

You may want to sketch the two graphs on the same grid to see which is the upper curve and which is the lower. Since the upper curve in this region is the graph of $y = x$, it is f_u in the definite integral.

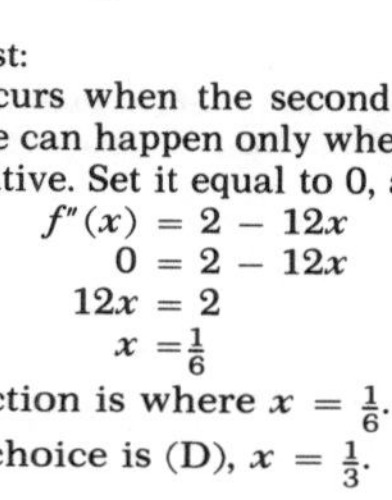

$$\int_0^1 (x - x^3)\,dx = \frac{x^2}{2} - \frac{x^4}{4}\Big|_0^1$$
$$= [\frac{1}{2} - \frac{1}{4}] = \frac{1}{4}$$

The correct choice is (D), $\frac{1}{4}$.

If $y = 2x^3 - x^2$, then the slope of the tangent line at the inflection point is

(A) $\dfrac{1}{3}$　(B) $-\dfrac{1}{6}$　(C) $\dfrac{1}{6}$　(D) $-\dfrac{1}{3}$　(E) 0

The second derivative is 0 at points of inflection, while the first derivative gives the slope of the curve at any point. Therefore, first find the second derivative and then find the value that makes it equal to 0. Use that value and the first derivative to find the slope.

$$y = 2x^3 - x^2$$
$$y' = 6x^2 - 2x$$
$$y'' = 12x - 2$$

Set y'' equal to 0.

$$12x - 2 = 0$$
$$12x = 2$$
$$x = \tfrac{1}{6}$$

Now evaluate y' for $x = \tfrac{1}{6}$.

$$y' = 6x^2 - 2x$$
$$y'(\tfrac{1}{6}) = 6(\tfrac{1}{6})^2 - 2(\tfrac{1}{6})$$
$$= \tfrac{1}{6} - \tfrac{2}{6}$$
$$= -\tfrac{1}{6}$$

The correct choice is (B).

[BC] Find the interval of convergence of the series

$$\sum_{n=1}^{\infty} \frac{x^n}{n}$$

(A) $-1 \le x < 1$　(B) $x \le -1 \text{ or } x \ge 1$

(C) $-1 \le x \le 1$　(D) $-1 < x < 1$　(E) $-1 < x \le 1$

First of all you should recognize that x^n/n is a power series. A power series either converges at 0 and diverges everywhere else (not one of the choices), converges absolutely everywhere (not one of the choices), or converges in an interval of the form $|x| < c$, where c is some real number, and possibly at c and $-c$ as well. This theorem about power series means that you can reject choice (B) immediately, since it is of the form $|x| \ge c$. (A), (C), (D), and (E) are all still possible. To choose among them, you need to check the series for $x = -1$ and $x = 1$. For $x = -1$, the series becomes

$$-1 + \tfrac{1}{2} - \tfrac{1}{3} + \tfrac{1}{4} - \cdots$$

or

$$-(1 - \tfrac{1}{2} + \tfrac{1}{3} - \tfrac{1}{4} + \ldots)$$

This is a well-known series that you should recognize as converging; or use Leibnitz's theorem to show that it converges. For $x = 1$, the series becomes

$$1 + \tfrac{1}{2} + \tfrac{1}{3} + \tfrac{1}{4} + \cdots$$

a series well-known as divergent. Therefore, the correct choice is (A), $-1 \le x < 1$.

[BC] A particle moves in two dimensions according to a path defined by the equations

$$x = 2 \cosh 3t \times y = 2 \sinh 3t$$

where t represents time. What is the acceleration of the particle at time t?

First note that the position of any particle at all times can be expressed by the vector

$$R = ix + jy$$

where i and j are the unit vectors for two dimensions. By substituting for x and y, one gets

$$R = i(2 \cosh 3t) + j (2 \sinh 3t).$$

Differentiating the position vector once with respect to time gives the velocity vector v.

$$v = i(6 \sinh 3t) + j (6 \cosh 3t)$$

Differentiating with respect to time again gives the acceleration.

$$a = i(18 \cosh 3t) + j(18 \sinh 3t)$$
$$= 9[i(2 \cosh 3t) + j(2 \sinh 3t)]$$
$$= 9R$$

Therefore the acceleration vector is nine times the position vector.

Section 2

Find the area bounded by the curve $y = x^3 - 5x^2 + 2x + 8$ and the lines $x = 1$, $x = 3$, and the x axis.

This is a case in which a graph or a sketch of a graph is almost essential. To make the sketch, first evaluate $y = x^3 - 5x^2 + 2x + 8$ for $x = 1$ and $x = 3$.

$$1^3 - 5(1^2) + 2(1) + 8 = 1 - 5 + 2 + 8 = 6$$
$$3^3 - 5(3^2) + 2(3) + 8 = 27 - 45 + 6 + 8 = -4$$

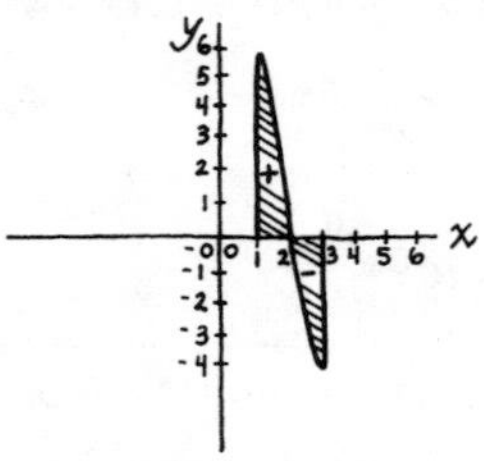

To find the intervals on which you should evaluate the definite integral, you need to know where the graph of $y = x^3 - 5x^2 + 2x + 8$ crosses the x-axis. Use your test-taking skills here. It is unlikely that the test maker would ask for a value here that is not an integer, and the only integer between 1 and 3 is 2. See whether 2 is a zero of $y = x^3 - 5x^2 + 2x + 8$.

$$2^3 - 5(2^2) + 2(2) + 8 = 8 - 20 + 4 + 8 = 0$$

It is, so the interval for the upper region is $[1, 2]$, and the interval for the lower region is $[2, 3]$. Note that the definite interval for a region below the x-axis will be negative. To get the total area of the figure described, you need to use the absolute value of the region below the axis. In other words, if you define

$$\int_1^2 (x^3 - 5x^2 + 2x + 8)\, dx = A_1$$

and

$$\int_2^3 (x^3 - 5x^2 + 2x + 8)\, dx = A_2$$

then

$$A_{total} = A_1 + |A_2|$$

With this in mind, you can proceed to compute the definite integrals, taking great care with the arithmetic, which involves fractions.

$$A_{total} = \tfrac{37}{12} + \left| -\tfrac{29}{12} \right| = \tfrac{66}{12} = \tfrac{11}{2}$$

Find the volume generated when the area bounded by $y = x^3$, $y = 8$, and $x = 0$ is rotated about the x-axis.

As in the last item, a sketch is helpful. First make a sketch of the indicated area.

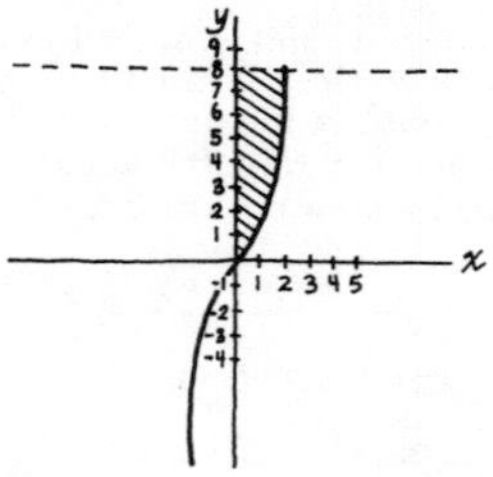

Now picture that figure rotated about the x-axis. Except for the origin, there will be a hole in the solid of revolution. This indicates that you will need to use the method of evaluating the volume that is variously called the "washer," "ring," or "shell" method. If R is the radius of the outside of the "washer" formed when a typical slice of the region is graphed and r is the radius of the hole, then

$$\pi \int (R^2 - r^2)\, dx$$

is the required volume, since the area of each entire washer is πR^2 and the area of each hole is πr^2. In this case $R = 8$ and $r = y = x^3$.

$$\pi \int_0^2 (8^2 - [x^3]^2)\, dx$$

$$\pi \int_0^2 (64 - x^6)\, dx \quad = \left[64x - \frac{x^7}{7}\right]\Big|_0^2 \cdot \pi$$
$$= ([128 - \tfrac{128}{7}] - [0])(\pi)$$
$$= (\tfrac{896}{7} - \tfrac{128}{7})\pi = \tfrac{768\pi}{7}$$

For the function $f(x) = 5 - 6x^2 - 2x^3$ defined on the interval $-3 \leq x \leq 1$, find (a) the maximum points; (b) the minimum points; (c) any points of inflection; (d) any intervals of upward concavity; then (e) graph the function over the given interval.

First, find both the first and second derivatives.
$$f(x) = 5 - 6x^2 - 2x^3$$
$$f'(x) = -12x - 6x^2$$
$$f''(x) = -12 - 12x$$

Then set each derivative equal to 0 to find the x coordinates of the maxima, minima, and points of inflection.
$$f'(x) = -12x - 6x^2 = 0$$
$$-6x(2 + x) = 0$$
$$-6x = 0 \text{ or } 2 + x = 0$$
$$x = 0 \text{ or } x = -2$$

This means that the tangent is horizontal at $x = 0$ and -2, but it does not tell you whether the points on the curve are maxima, minima, or points of inflection.
$$f''(x) = -12 - 12x = 0$$
$$-12x = 12$$
$$x = -1$$

This implies that the curve has a point of inflection at $x = -1$, and furthermore that the two points located by setting the first derivative equal to 0 must be either maxima or minima. Check the second derivative at each of the values for x. At $x = 0$, $-12 - 12x$ is negative, which implies that the point on the curve is a relative maximum. Similarly, at $x = -2$, $-12 - 12x$ is positive, so the point on the curve is a relative minimum.

These are not all the relative maxima and minima that must be identified, since relative maxima and minima also occur at the ends of the domain, that is at $x = -3$ and $x = 1$. You now have almost all the information needed to answer the five parts of the item. You still need to locate the actual points, not just the x values for the points. The easiest way to do this is to use synthetic division.

	-2	-6	0	5
-3	-2	0	0	5
-2	-1	-2	4	-3
-1	-2	-4	4	1
0	-2	-6	0	5
1	-2	-8	-8	-3

Finally, remember that the interval of upward concavity will be the region for which the second derivative is negative. Since the second derivative is 0 at $x = -1$ and negative at $x = 0$, it must be negative for all values of x to the right of -1.

Putting all this information together, you can answer:
(a) the maximum points are $(-3, 5)$ and $(0, 5)$
(b) the minimum points are $(-2, -3)$ and $(1, -3)$
(c) the point of inflection is $(-1, 1)$
(d) the graph is concave upward for $-3 < x < -1$
(e)

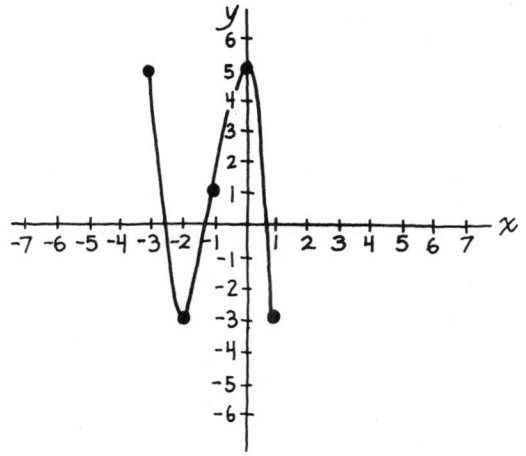

Given $f(x) = \dfrac{x^2}{x^2 - 1}$

(a) give the equation(s) of the vertical asymptote(s)
(b) give the equation of the horizontal asymptote
(c) locate the relative maximum point or points
(d) sketch the graph

Note that this is a rational function (the ratio of two polynomials). Vertical asymptotes will occur when the function is undefined. For rational functions, this will occur when the denominator is 0. Solve $x^2 - 1 = 0$ to find when this will occur: $x = \pm 1$ is the solution to that equation, so the function will be undefined if $x = 1$ or -1.
(a) The equations of the vertical asymptotes are $x = 1$ and $x = -1$. For rational functions, horizontal asymptotes can be found by comparing the degrees of the polynomials and the ratio of the coefficients of the highest degree terms, but a more general rule is that the limit of a function as x goes to infinity, if such a limit exists, is a horizontal asymptote.
$$\lim_{x \to \infty} \frac{x^2}{x^2 - 1}$$

Often, a good way to find the limit of a rational function is to divide both numerator and denominator by the highest power of the denominator, which does not change the limit's value.
$$\lim_{x \to \infty} \frac{1}{1 - \dfrac{1}{x^2}} = 1$$

(b) The horizontal asymptote is $y = 1$. To find the relative maximum point(s), you usually find the value(s) for which the first derivative is 0. Then examine the second derivative. For rational functions in which you know the asymptotes, there is an easier way. The two vertical asymptotes separate the graph into three strips. Within each of these strips, the function will have the same sign. You can examine the values at suitable points in each of the three strips to find the sign of the function.

For $x < -1$, use -2: $f(-2) = \frac{(-2)^2}{(-2)^2 - 1} = \frac{4}{3}$, so the function is positive in this strip.

For $-1 < x < 1$, use 0: $f(0) = \frac{0^2}{0^2 - 1} = 0$, which does not tell what we need to know. Try some other number, such as ½: $f(½) = \frac{(½)^2}{(½)^2 - 1} = -\frac{1}{3}$. Thus, the function is negative in the interval except for the point $(0, 0)$, which is a relative maximum.

For $x > 1$, use 2: $f(2) = \frac{2^2}{2^2 - 1} = \frac{4}{3}$, so the function is positive in this interval.
(c) The three tests above imply that the only relative maximum is at the origin. This is made clearer when you sketch the graph.

To sketch the graph, return to the behavior of the function in the three strips defined by the vertical asymptotes. In the left-most strip, there are two asymptotes—one vertical and one horizontal—that the graph must approach, and the graph is all above the x axis (which implies in this case that it is above the horizontal asymptote at $y = 1$). The same is true of the right-most strip. The only places that the graph can go is to approach each asymptote "at infinity."

Meanwhile, between the vertical asymptotes, the graph is entirely negative except for its relative maximum at $(0,0)$. This part of the graph must also approach both asymptotes, approaching each asymptote at "negative infinity."

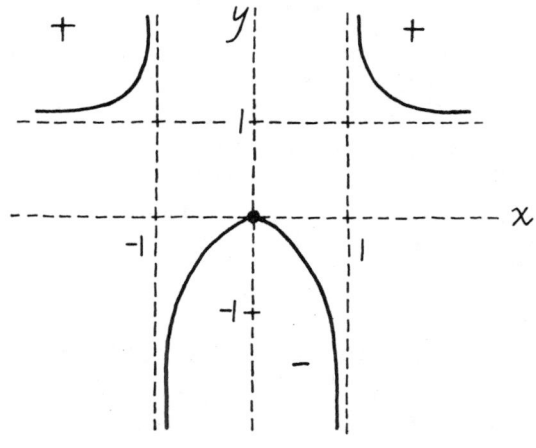

American History Advanced Placement Examination

The American History Advanced Placement Examination is scored on the same five-point system as the other Advanced Placement Tests. It consists of three types of items: standard multiple-choice items and two different kinds of essay questions. One of the two types of essay items is termed the Document Based Essay Question (DBQ) and, as might be expected from the title, it consists of an essay question about several related documents from American history that are supplied to the student. In the standard essay section, you are given a list of five essay topics from which you choose one to discuss. The scores are weighted so that the two essay types are worth the same and the scores on two essays taken together are worth as much as the score on the multiple-choice items. In other words, 50 percent of your score will come from the multiple-choice items and 25 percent from each of the two types of essay.

Content covered. Reflecting the content of the typical college course, the AP exam places more emphasis on the history of the United States as a nation than on the events that led up to adoption of the Constitution in 1789. Furthermore, since the test is administered before many schools have concluded their course, and since most American history courses are chronological, less emphasis is placed on the period after World War II. This is especially true of the essay questions.

Six periods or features of American history are especially emphasized in the test:

the Revolution and the Constitution
the Jacksonian era
the Civil War and Reconstruction
the Populist and Progressive movements
the Great Depression and the New Deal
America as a great power after World War II

About a third of the items in both the multiple-choice and the essay sections are concerned with what might be termed American politics, while another third are concerned with social and economic change. The remaining third includes items that range through diplomacy, foreign policy, and cultural change.

Multiple-choice items. There are 100 items in this section of the test, and you are given 75 minutes to answer them, which translates into 45 seconds an item. About 16 or 17 of the items are usually concerned with the period before the Constitution, about 50 items deal with the period from the Constitution until the start of World War I, and the remaining 33 items or so date from World War I to the present.

As is typical in a College Board examination, answers are made on a separate score sheet, so you can and probably should write in the examination booklet. For example, you can skip difficult questions in a first run-through, but mark them in order to find them again later. For any given student, the difficulty of some of the items will vary, so you should not assume that items are arranged from easiest to most difficult.

Also, a fourth of a point is deducted for wrong answers, so do not guess at random. If you can eliminate one or two choices or have a feeling that one particular answer is correct, you will do better statistically by answering the item.

The Document Based Essay Question (DBQ). Although this essay is based on documents supplied to you along with the test, note that you are also supposed to bring your own knowledge of material outside of the documents to the essay. You are given the documents, which may include maps, graphs, or other artwork as well as printed material;

the DBQ itself; and five choices of standard essay questions. For 15 minutes you are expected to study the documents and all six of the questions. During that time you can make notes on what you plan to do. Then you have 40 minutes to write the DBQ essay.

In the essay itself, you need to use the documents, but do not rely on them completely. Summaries of the documents get poor grades. Lengthy quotations slow you down and are not needed. Your job is to weave together a connected essay that uses both what is in the documents and information about American history that is not in the documents.

The standard essay. You should choose the topic you will write on during the initial 15-minute period. If you have time, make a short outline of the essay during that period as well, although reading the documents carefully can take much of the quarter hour. Otherwise, make a brief outline when you begin the 50-minute period of time allotted for writing the standard essay.

Both the DBQ and the standard essay are written in booklets of lined 8½ × 11 paper that are supplied by the administrators of the test. The booklets have the number assigned to each of the essay items printed on the back. You are to circle the number of the topic you chose.

Because five different questions are provided, they usually cover items that deal with different periods from American history.

In this volume we do not provide samples of either type of essay item. You may want to order from

College Board Publications Office
Advanced Placement Program CN6670
Princeton, New Jersey 08541-6670

the following booklet: *Advanced Placement Course Description: History (American History, European History)*—one booklet for the two examinations. This contains additional useful material on both the multiple-choice items and the essay questions.

Multiple-choice items

Directions: Each of the questions or incomplete statements below is followed by five suggested answers or completions. Select the one that is best in each case.

The Harding administration is, unfortunately, known best for the Teapot Dome scandal. The Teapot Dome was

(A) the cover of a teapot into which bribe money was placed
(B) a derogatory reference to the well-bred Eastern Republicans who uncovered the scandal
(C) a reference to the Capitol's dome, under which lobbyists were able to influence the Congress
(D) an oil reserve in Wyoming leased to an oil company in return for payments to the secretary of the Interior
(E) the old symbol of the Republican Party

Even if you don't know the answer, you can come close to it by eliminating incorrect choices. Choice (B) is unlikely since Harding was a Republican and members of a party, wherever they are from, are usually not eager to publicize their own wrongdoing. Choice (C) can be ruled out, since lobbyists have influenced legislators since long before and long after Harding's time. Also, congressional scandals do not attach themselves to the executive branch. Choice (E) is a bit of nonsense thrown in for the fun of it; the elephant has long been the party's symbol. Choices (A) and (D) are harder to deal with. In all likelihood, if bribe money had been left in a teapot, it would be called the Teapot scandal, not the Teapot Dome scandal. The correct choice is (D). It was the lease of this Wyoming oil reserve that blew the lid off everything.

Make sure you know what you need to bring to the test. AP essays must be written in ink, so you may need two pens as well as a supply of No. 2 pencils.

The President of the United States is elected

(A) by a direct vote of the people
(B) by the House of Representatives
(C) from the Democratic or Republican party
(D) only after a televised debate
(E) by electors chosen by the people of each state

Each of the choices contains an aspect of truth. However, only one is correct: choice (E). Under our system, the President is elected by electors from each state. Choice (A) is wrong because in voting for President, we actually vote for electors pledged to vote for that candidate—the vote is not directly for the candidate. While it is true that when the electors deadlock or there is no majority for one candidate, the House of Representatives makes the choice, this is not the usual way the President is elected. Choice (B) is therefore wrong. Choice (D) is wrong because no debate, televised or not, is required before an election. It may be on its way to becoming a custom, but it is perfectly possible to have the election without a debate. And there was no TV when we started.

The Articles of Confederation failed to give Congress power over taxation and trade because

(A) the Congress was meant only to be symbolic
(B) the states did not want to give up sovereignty by granting powers they refused to recognize in the British Parliament
(C) no money was needed, since congressmen were unpaid
(D) each state's constitution required it to support the national government and eliminate trade barriers
(E) the Articles could be easily changed if the need arose

This question calls for knowledge of the American colonial period and its immediate aftermath. The Congress, despite its frequent weakness, was not meant to be symbolic, so choice (A) is out. There is some truth to choice (C), since congressmen served without pay. But the question asks about taxation and trade and even if the assertion of choice (C) were true, it would not answer the whole question. Choice (D) can be eliminated because state constitutions did not concern themselves with national government. Finally, while the Articles of Confederation could be changed, doing so was not easy—unanimous consent of the states was needed, and that eliminates choice (E). Choice (B) is the correct one. Parliament's powers over trade and taxation were among the reasons the American colonies fought to be free of England. In the early postcolonial period, the colonial experience seemed a good reason to deny these powers to the national government.

President Tyler is best remembered for

(A) the admission of Texas as a state
(B) the beginning of the Civil War
(C) changing from one political party to another
(D) saying "I would rather be right than be President"
(E) the end of slavery

Remembering that President Tyler was in office before the Civil War eliminates choices (B) and (E). Choice (C) is tricky. Tyler did change parties while in office but it is not what he is best remembered for. As for choice (D), it was Henry Clay who said this and he never did become President. During the years before the Civil War, a number of states joined the Union, and Tyler pushed strongly for the admission of Texas. Thus, the correct choice is (A).

As a result of World War II, the United States remained as an occupying power in which European country until 1990?

(A) Poland
(B) England
(C) Albania
(D) Italy
(E) Germany

Choices (A), (B), and (C) were not enemy states, and one does not occupy the "good guys." Italy, choice (D), actually fought on the Allied side in the end and thus escaped any occupation. The correct choice is (E). Until the reunification of Germany in 1990 with the approval of the four World War II Allies (U.S., France, England, and the Soviet Union), the United States, along with England, France, and the Soviet Union, occupied the wartime German capital of Berlin.

The triangular building shown in the photograph is

(A) an example of typical work by Frank Lloyd Wright
(B) an early example of a skyscraper
(C) a Tudor-revival building from the early 20th century
(D) an innovative building by I.M. Pei
(E) an 18th-century building preserved in a city setting

The Flatiron Building, shown in the photograph, is a well-known early skyscraper in New York, so the correct choice is (B). Although Frank Lloyd Wright, choice (A), designed a skyscraper that was never built, his typical work includes many private homes and several public buildings using patterned concrete or cantilevered sections. Tudor-revival, choice (C), is marked by a combination of wood and stucco or rock that is called half-timbered and is generally used for private residences. I.M. Pei, choice (D), is noted for his use of glass-wall construction; a typical skyscraper of his design would be the John Hancock Tower in Boston, which is covered with reflective glass. Since it is apparent that this building has more than ten stories, it could not be an 18th-century building, choice (E). Buildings with ten or more floors were not put up until after the invention of safe elevators in 1852, half a century after the end of the 18th century.

All of the following states gained at least part of their territory as a result of the Louisiana Purchase EXCEPT

(A) Montana
(B) Iowa
(C) Mississippi
(D) Missouri
(E) Arkansas

The key to answering this question is to remember that the Mississippi River formed the western border of the United States prior to the Louisiana Purchase. The correct answer is, therefore, (C). The state of Mississippi is east of the river.

The Great Plains is also known as America's

(A) Vacationland
(B) Milkbucket
(C) Breadbasket
(D) Sunbelt
(E) Hunter's Paradise

The key to answering this question is knowing that the main industry in this area of North America is agriculture. The main crops of the Great Plains are wheat, corn, and soybeans. From the first of these comes the nickname shown in choice (C), the correct choice. As for the other choices, (A) is found on Maine's automobile license plates; (B) seemed to be a good foil to breadbasket; (D) refers to the economically growing Southern tier of states; and (E) may have been true once, but the vast bison herds are long gone.

The five permanent members of the United Nations Security Council are

(A) Britain, France, Germany, United States, Soviet Union
(B) Britain, France, United States, Soviet Union, China
(C) Britain, France, United States, Soviet Union, Japan
(D) Britain, France, United States, Soviet Union, Switzerland
(E) Britain, France, United States, Soviet Union, Canada

To answer this question quickly, remember that the United Nations was created by the victorious allies from World War II. Each of these nations was given a permanent seat on the Security Council. If you do not remember which these were, it is possible to eliminate all but the correct choice. Both choices (A) and (C) include one of the losing Axis powers, Germany and Japan. Despite their current prominence in world affairs, these countries are not permanent members of the Security Council. Choice (D) includes Switzerland, which was neutral during the war and is not now a UN member. While Canada, choice (E), played an important role in the war, it was not one of the five principal Allies and does not have a permanent seat on the Security Council. Choice (B) is correct.

Woodrow Wilson's Fourteen Points

(A) were intended to form the basis for peace negotiations after World War I
(B) set the terms for peace with Mexico
(C) were adopted as the Democratic Party platform in 1912
(D) were written initially as anti-German propaganda
(E) proposed the establishment of the United Nations

The Fourteen Points had nothing to do with the Mexican troubles or the election of 1912 and were formulated after those two events, eliminating choices (B) and (C). Wilson was vitally interested in establishing a permanent international organization so (E) might be possible. However, it was the League of Nations, the UN's predecessor, that one of the Fourteen Points anticipated. There's a thread of truth to (D) since there was a propaganda aspect to the statement of principles. But it was not their sole purpose, and Wilson believed in them strongly. The correct choice is (A).

One United States President has been impeached:

(A) James K. Polk
(B) William Henry Harrison
(C) Grover Cleveland
(D) Andrew Johnson
(E) Richard M. Nixon

This question requires you to know what "impeached" means, since being impeached and being removed from office are not the same. It helps to know the Civil War period, since the correct choice is (D). Andrew Johnson, Lincoln's successor, was impeached by the House of Representatives. The Senate, by one vote, found in the President's favor and Johnson was not removed from office. Choice (E) may fool some people. President Nixon voluntarily resigned from office before the House of Representatives could vote on impeachment charges.

Which of the following is NOT TRUE about the Cuban missile crisis?

(A) The Soviet Union attempted to change the balance of world power.
(B) Premier Khrushchev underestimated President Kennedy.
(C) The Soviet Union gained international prestige by placing missiles in Cuba.
(D) The resolution of the crisis was a contributing factor in Khrushchev's removal from power two years later.
(E) The United States was prepared to invade Cuba.

In order to find the right answer, it is necessary to know what was true about the missile crisis. Because Khrushchev underestimated President Kennedy, he took the chance of altering the balance of power by placing missiles in Cuba. Had the Soviet Union not removed the weapons, the United States was prepared to invade. It is believed that the resulting loss of face contributed to the removal of the Soviet premier two years later. Choices (A), (B), (D), and (E) are, therefore, true. Since the question asks which statement is NOT true, the correct choice is (C).

Among the last invading foreign troops to leave the Soviet Union at the end of World War I were those of

(A) Switzerland
(B) Germany
(C) Austria
(D) the United States
(E) Yugoslavia

Knowledge of history and the process of elimination will help you make the right choice. Switzerland was neutral and had no troops involved in the war, ruling out choice (A). Yugoslavia did not exist as a country until after the war, eliminating choice (E). Choices (B) and (C) are traps for the unwary. The Allied powers and the Soviet Union fought against Germany and Austria. However, the Soviet Union made a separate, and early, peace with Germany and Austria. The correct answer is (D). Along with its other allies (Britain, France, and Japan), the United States sent troops to Siberia supposedly to help 15,000 Czech prisoners rejoin the fight against Germany. By the time U.S. soldiers arrived, the Czechs were free and there were no Germans or Austrians around. Allied troops wound up fighting against the Bolsheviks, who made up the legitimate Soviet government, which was not a declared enemy.

Advanced Placement Biology

As with most of the Advanced Placement Examinations, AP biology consists of two parts. Part one consists of 120 multiple-choice items. Surprisingly, part two is not free response —questions with no answer choices supplied—as in AP calculus; instead, it consists of four essay questions, more in the manner of AP English. Scoring for the test is on the same five-point scale as other Advanced Placement Tests.

Multiple-choice items. Ninety minutes are allowed for the 120 multiple-choice items, so you have 45 seconds for each item. As usual on College Board tests, there is a penalty for wrong answers, so guessing should be limited to those items for which you can eliminate one or two of the choices or for which you think you know the correct choice but are not sure.

There have been many spectacular advances in biology in the past few years, so the content of this test changes more rapidly than the content of a literature, history, or calculus test. It is important to be as familiar as possible with the content of a current introductory biology textbook at the college level.

The multiple-choice items fall into four main categories: objective questions of fact; questions of judgment; questions requiring interpretation of data; and questions requiring computation. Although the objective questions are often the easiest, they are not grouped at the beginning. Instead, easier items are scattered through the test as breathers. The easy items count as much as any, so you may find it useful to proceed rapidly through the test once, marking items that are skipped, and then return for a second, or even a third, round.

Essay questions. The second section of the test, consisting of four mandatory essay questions, also takes 90 minutes. The essay questions are thought by the test maker to be about equal in difficulty, so it is suggested that you allow 22 minutes for each one.

Although these are called essay questions, they do not have to be essays that can be thought of as making a case for a particular thesis. For example, the essay question might ask what are the endocrine glands, the function of each, the hormones they produce, their location in the body, and the methods by which they are controlled. In that case, the essay can best be written by making a careful summary of the main facts required in a sensible order. The people who grade the essays assign points to the facts that could be included in answering each question, so it is important to support your answer with as many facts as possible. For example, if an item asks about means of reproduction, you ought to include specific types, ranging from budding and cell division to sexual reproduction, preferably with several variations on sexual reproduction, supporting each one by giving the reproductive habits of a particular species.

Sample items similar to those on the multiple-choice section of the test follow.

Sample multiple-choice items

<u>Directions:</u> Each of the questions or incomplete statements in this section is followed by five suggested answers or completions. Select the ONE that is BEST in each case.

A polypeptide chain is likely to form which of the following organic molecules?

(A) monosaccharide
(B) disaccharide
(C) polysaccharide
(D) protein
(E) nucleic acid

Choice (D) is correct. Polypeptides are chains of amino acids joined together. A chain of approximately 75 amino acids or more constitutes a protein. Monosaccharides, disaccharides, and polysaccharides are carbohydrates. Nucleic acids are polymers of nucleotide chains.

The two organelles most associated with the energy needs of a cell are

(A) chloroplasts and mitochondria
(B) Golgi apparatus and vacuoles
(C) endoplasmic reticulum and ribosomes
(D) cell nucleus and nucleolus
(E) chromosomes and chromatin

Choice (A) is correct. Chloroplasts are the sites of photosynthesis, and mitochondria are the sites of cellular respiration. These two processes are associated with converting energy into a form useful to the cell. Organelles in choice (B) are for storage and transport; choice (C), for protein synthesis; choice (D), for control of cell activities and reproduction; and choice (E), for reproduction.

Which process is described by the following equation?

$$38 \text{ ADP} + 38\text{P} \quad\quad 38 \text{ ATP}$$

$$C_6H_{12}O_6 + 6O_2 \rightarrow 6CO_2 + 6H_2O$$

(A) photosynthesis
(B) deamination
(C) anaerobic respiration
(D) aerobic respiration
(E) hydrolysis

Choice (D) is correct. During aerobic respiration, glucose combines with oxygen to yield stored energy in the form of ATP molecules; carbon dioxide and water are produced as waste products. Anaerobic respiration does not require oxygen; photosynthesis is basically this equation in reverse. Deamination is the removal of nitrogen, and hydrolysis is the splitting of water molecules.

Which process is most likely to be important during an immune response to disease?

(A) phagocytosis
(B) erythroblastosis
(C) transduction
(D) oogenesis
(E) photophosphorylation

Choice (A) correctly identifies the process of white blood cells engulfing bacteria. Choice (B) is the attack of Rh negative cells on Rh positive cells. Choice (C) is the transfer of DNA. Choice (D) is the formation of egg cells, and choice (E) is ATP production that uses energy.

The chrysanthemum is a plant that generally flowers in the autumn. Which statement best describes why?

(A) The flowering of a chrysanthemum depends on the loss of chlorophyll and the appearance of other pigments in the fall.
(B) The flowering of a chrysanthemum depends on the decrease in the amount of carbohydrates transported through the phloem from the leaves.
(C) The chrysanthemum flowers when the photoperiod is shorter than a critical length.
(D) The chrysanthemum flowers when the photoperiod is longer than a critical length.
(E) The flowering of a chrysanthemum does not depend on the photoperiod.

Choice (C) is correct. The decrease in the amount of daylight during the autumn shortens the photoperiod and stimulates the chrysanthemum to flower. The changes in photosynthesis or transport brought on by the change of season are not the factors that stimulate flowering.

Which blood vessel is likely to carry blood with the highest proportion of deoxygenated hemoglobin?

(A) right pulmonary vein
(B) left pulmonary vein
(C) aorta
(D) inferior vena cava
(E) internal carotid artery

Choice (D) is correct. The inferior vena cava leads to the heart, transporting blood that has already delivered oxygen to cells in the lower portion of the body, so the blood is substantially deoxygenated. The pulmonary veins are rich in oxygenated blood because they enter the heart directly from the lungs. Both the aorta and the internal carotid, the artery that leads to the brain, contain a high proportion of oxygenated blood.

All chordates are characterized by

(A) a ventral nerve cord and embryological gill slits
(B) a bony vertebral column and closed circulatory system
(C) an endoskeleton made of bone and cartilage
(D) internal fertilization and development within the placenta
(E) a dorsal nerve cord and embryological gill slits

Choice (E) is correct. Chordates have a dorsal rather than ventral nerve cord, making choice (A) incorrect. Although all vertebrates are chordates, there are some invertebrate chordates that lack a vertebral column and bony skeleton, so choices (B) and (C) are incorrect. Only vertebrate mammals have the characteristics described in choice (D).

Which statement best describes the alternation of generations found in moss reproduction?

(A) The 2N spores from the spore capsule germinate into the gametophyte protonema. After fertilization, the 1N sporophyte generation is produced.
(B) The 1N spores develop into a spore-bearing protonema.
(C) The gametophyte generation grows inside the archegonium of the sporophyte.
(D) Spores germinate to produce the sporophyte generation. After egg cells are fertilized by sperm cells, the gametophyte generation is produced.
(E) Spores germinate to produce the gametophyte generation. After egg cells are fertilized by sperm cells, the sporophyte generation is produced.

Choice (E) is correct. The spores released from a moss spore capsule are 1N and develop into the protonema or gametophyte generation. The gametophyte may develop either egg or sperm cells, and after the two unite, a 2N sporophyte develops inside the archegonium of the gametophyte. Eventually the sporophyte develops a spore capsule containing 1N spores, and the cycle is repeated. Choice (A) has the 1N and 2N generations reversed. Choice (B) is incomplete and misses the 2N part of the cycle. Choice (C) is incomplete, since it does not mention both generations. Choice (D) has the gametophyte and sporophyte generation reversed.

When pea plants that have yellow, round seeds are crossed with other pea plants that have yellow, round seeds, a small number of the offspring have green, wrinkled seeds. The results show that

(A) the cross is an example of hybridization of two traits
(B) all the alleles inherited by the offspring are homozygous
(C) both parents were dihybrids
(D) the cross is an example of sex-linked inheritance
(E) the cross is an example of codominance

Choice (C) is correct. The parents are hybrids for the traits of seed color and texture; that is, they show the dominant traits of yellow, round seeds and carry the recessive traits for green, wrinkled seeds. Choice (A) is incorrect; the parent generation consists of two hybrids. Choice (B) is incorrect; the parents are heterozygous for the two traits. There is no evidence that these traits are either sex-linked or codominant (choices D and E); both traits are inherited in a dominant-recessive pattern.

The best description of adaptive radiation is

(A) an increase in the number of species adapted to different ways of life in an environment
(B) adaptation of a species to equatorial climates
(C) a reduction in the natural selection of a species
(D) an evolutionary pathway that leads to mass extinction
(E) allopatric speciation due to geographic isolation

Choice (A) most correctly defines adaptive radiation. The term has little to do with a specific climate as choice (B) suggests. Choice (C) is incorrect because natural selection does play a role in the evolution of a species. Adaptive radiation may sometimes but not always prevent rather than produce mass extinction, so choice (D) is incorrect. Speciation may occur during adaptive radiation, but as a result of adaptation to different niches within an environment rather than geographic isolation, making choice (E) incorrect.

Identify the biome characterized by trees such as pine and spruce, which have no understory.

(A) tropical rain forest
(B) temperate deciduous forest
(C) taiga
(D) tundra
(E) savanna

Choice (C) is the correct answer; the taiga is the northern belt of coniferous forest. The rain forest contains many hundreds of tree species and a lush understory, so choice (A) is incorrect. The deciduous forest (choice B) contains hardwoods, not conifers such as pine and spruce. The tundra (choice D) has only stunted trees, and the savanna (choice E) is the tropical grassland of Africa.

The animal phylum characterized by a body consisting of a coelom divided by septa and locomotion by paired setae is

(A) Platyhelminthes
(B) Annelida
(C) Arthropoda
(D) Mollusca
(E) Echinodermata

Choice (B) correctly identifies the phylum in which the segmented worms are classified. They have a segmented body cavity or coelom and move with bristles or setae. Platyhelminthes (choice A) are the flatworms. Arthropoda (choice C) are invertebrates with jointed legs. Mollusks and spiny-skinned invertebrates (choices D and E) do not have the characteristics described.

Easier AP multiple-choice items are often scattered through the test. You can go through the test more than once, marking items to come back to in the test booklet.

Advanced Placement Chemistry

This test includes three sections. The multiple-choice section carries 45 percent of the grade; the free-response section, about 20 percent; and the essay section, about the remaining 35 percent of the grade.

Multiple-choice section. Most commonly there are 75 items and 90 minutes allowed to answer them. In other years there are 85 items and 115 minutes allowed. While the 75-item test allows 1 minute 12 seconds per item and the 85-item test allows about 1 minute 17 seconds per item, it is best to pace yourself at a minute per item in either test to afford time for checking your work. The reason for the slightly longer time per item on the 85-item test is that it includes chemical equations, which for the 75-item test are left to the free-response section.

The usual College Board penalty of a quarter point for a wrong answer is used, so guessing should be limited to items for which you can eliminate choices or for which you suspect you know the answer but are not certain.

Easy items are scattered through the test. Plan to go through more than once and mark skipped items along the way.

The items cover the following topics:
> Atomic structure and periodicity
> Chemical bonds
> Stoichiometry
> Phases of matter
> Reaction kinetics
> Equilibrium
> Thermodynamics
> Electrochemistry

Note that a copy of the periodic table of the elements is made available to students taking the Advanced Placement Chemistry exam. Except for this, you are on your own.

Free-response problems. There are three free-response items. One is mandatory, but you may choose either one of the other two. A free-response item is one that does not supply choices, but which generally has a specific answer rather than requiring an essay on a topic. You have 90 minutes for this section and the essay section that follows when the total time on the multiple-choice section is 75 minutes. You have 75 minutes for the two sections when the multiple-choice section is allotted 115 minutes. Your goal should be to spend no more than 20 to 25 minutes on each free-response item and leave the rest for the essays.

While the topics covered are the same as the list for the multiple-choice items, the mandatory item is always on the subject of equilibrium. The other two items can cover any of the remaining seven content areas, but they will be on two different areas. Thus, in a typical year, you may have to answer one item on acid-base equilibrium but can choose either an item on electrochemistry or on stoichiometry. Each item is worth the same amount. After the multiple-choice samples given below, you will find items of the type that occur on the free-response section.

Each free-response item typically has three or four subitems. Of those, the first two are fairly standard questions of the kind that should have been practiced previously in your course work. The remaining subitem or subitems are generally more difficult and require deeper insights.

To get full credit for an item, you need to show the work you have done in getting the answer. Do not merely write the answer, even if you arrive at it intuitively. Also, you can get partial credit for correct steps that eventually lead to a wrong answer. If you do reach a wrong answer in one part and have to use it again in another part, you will not be penalized if the second part is done in a way that would have produced the correct answer if incorrect work had not been used.

Essays. You are given five essay topics from which to choose three. Typically, the topics are in the fields from the list given above that were not used in the three free-response items. Since you should have about 40 minutes left from your combined time for this section and the free-response section, you will want to spend from 10 to 15 minutes per question. Nothing will be gained by writing essays on more than three topics. The first three essays you write will be graded, and the remaining two will be ignored.

Like the free-response questions, the essay question is usually given in several parts. This is not like writing an essay about literature or history. Although you will need to explain procedures and discuss the theory of chemical reactions, there generally are right answers to all parts of the essay items. We do not supply sample essays in this volume.

Sample multiple-choice items

<u>Directions</u> Select and answer from the five choices given.

Which of the following samples contains the largest number of atoms?

(A) 10.0 g of Cl_2
(B) 10.0 g of H_2O
(C) 10.0 g of C_6H_6
(D) 10.0 g of CCl_4
(E) Each sample contains the same number of atoms.

The correct answer is (B). Reasoning alone will not give the answer to this question. It is necessary to compare the number of moles of atoms in each sample. Therefore, the correct answer requires finding the molar mass of each compound by using atomic weights from the periodic table, calculating the number of moles in each sample, and finding the number of moles of atoms. The calculation for choice (B) is shown below.

Molar mass of $H_2O = [2 \times (1 \frac{g}{H} \text{ atom})] + 16 \frac{g}{O}$ atom

$$= 18 \frac{g}{1} \text{ mol } H_2O$$

$$\left(\frac{1 \text{ mol } H_2O}{18 \text{ g } H_2O}\right) (10 \text{ g } H_2O) \left(\frac{3 \text{ mol atoms}}{1 \text{ mol } H_2O}\right) = 1.6 \text{ mol atoms}$$

The other answers, found in the same manner, are (A) 0.28 mol atoms, (C) 1.5 mol atoms, and (D) 0.32 mol atoms

---

The atomic numbers of four elements are listed below. Which of these elements has two *s* electrons and one *p* electron in its valence shell?

(A) 3
(B) 13
(C) 23
(D) 33
(E) 43

The correct answer is (B). Elements with two *s* and one *p* valence electrons, or a total of three valence electrons, are in Group IIIA (also called Group 13) of the periodic table. The quickest way to find the answer is to consult the periodic table and locate the element with one of the given atomic numbers that falls in Group IIIA. It is aluminum, which has the atomic number 13.

Atoms of A have a high electronegativity and high electron affinity. Atoms of B have a low electronegativity and low electron affinity. What kind of bond forms between A and B?

(A) coordinate covalent bond
(B) covalent bond
(C) hydrogen bond
(D) ionic bond
(E) metallic bond

The correct answer is choice (D). Ionic bonds form between metals of low electronegativity and low electron affinity, such as Na^+ or Ca^{2+}, and nonmetals of high electronegativity and high electron affinity, such as F^- or O^{2-}.

Because of hydrolysis, solutions of most salts are acidic or basic. Which of the following salts will give a basic solution?

(A) KBr
(B) NH_4Cl
(C) $NaC_2H_3O_2$
(D) $CuSO_4$
(E) $KHCO_3$

The correct answers are (C) and (E). To answer this question requires remembering that the acidity or basicity of a solution is not affected by the cations of alkali metals or alkaline earth metals, or by the anions of strong acids. Also, you must know that hydrolysis of other cations gives acidic solutions, and hydrolysis of other anions gives basic solutions. Compounds (A), (B), and (D) can be eliminated because HBr, HCl, and H_2SO_4 are strong acids, and their anions do not hydrolyze. Compounds (C) and (E) will both give basic solutions because they contain the anions of weak acids combined with cations that do not affect acidity or basicity.

Which one of the following mixtures will be a buffer solution?

(A) 50.0 mL of 0.10 M NaOH
   + 50.0 mL of 0.20 M $HC_2H_3O_2$

(B) 50.0 mL of 0.10 M KOH + 50.0 mL of 0.20 M HCl

(C) 50.0 mL of 0.10 M NH_4OH + 50.0 mL of 0.20 M HCl

(D) 50.0 mL of 0.10 M NaCl
   + 50.0 mL of 0.20 M $HC_2H_3O_2$

(E) 50.0 mL of 0.10 M HNO_3
   + 50.0 mL of 0.01 M $NaNO_3$

The correct answer is choice (A). This question requires knowing what a buffer is, knowing which are strong and weak acids, and also some careful analysis because the answer is not as obvious as it seems. A buffer solution, one that resists changes in pH when small amounts of acid or base are added, contains equal molar amounts of a weak acid and a salt of that acid. You might immediately settle on choice (E) as the right answer because it is the only mixture that contains equal molar amounts of an acid and a salt, but this would be wrong because HNO_3 is a strong acid. Choices (B) and (C) can also be eliminated because the solutions contain strong, not weak, acids. This leaves (A) and (D). Choice (D) cannot be a buffer because it contains a weak acid, but no salt of that acid. To verify that choice (A) is correct, you must see that half the acetic acid ($HC_2H_3O_2$) will react with the NaOH to give a solution of equal molar amounts of acetic acid and its salt, sodium acetate.

The reaction below is first order in A_2 and second order in B.

$$A_2 + 2B \rightarrow 2AB$$

Which equation represents the rate of this reaction?

(A) $-\frac{\Delta[B]}{\Delta t} = -\frac{1}{2}\frac{\Delta[A_2]}{\Delta t} = k\,[AB]^2$

(B) $-\frac{1}{2}\frac{\Delta[B]}{\Delta t} = -\frac{\Delta[A_2]}{\Delta t} = k[B]^2[A_2]$

(C) $-\frac{1}{2}\frac{\Delta[AB]}{\Delta t} = +\frac{\Delta[A_2]}{\Delta t} = k[B]^2[A_2]$

(D) $+\frac{1}{2}\frac{\Delta[AB]}{\Delta t} = -\frac{\Delta[B]}{\Delta t} = k[A_2]^2\,[B]$

The correct answer is choice (B). Answering this question requires remembering the meaning of first and second order, and remembering how to write the concentration changes of reactants and products with time. First, checking the rate law part of the expression, which must be $k[B]^2[A_2]$ because the reaction is second order in B and first order in A_2, shows that choices (A) and (D) can be eliminated. Next, choice (C) can be eliminated because it has a + sign for $\Delta[A_2]/\Delta t$—since A_2 is a reactant, its concentration must decrease with time (− sign) not increase (+ sign). This leaves choice (B) as the correct answer. To check, note that it has minus signs for both reactant concentrations and a half factor to account for the two molecules of B.

Sample free-response items

What is the volume at standard temperature and pressure of a gas that occupies 16.5 L at 350°C and 0.275 atm?

In this gas law problem, the quantity of gas is constant, the initial volume is known, and the initial and final temperature and pressure are known, since at standard temperature and pressure, T = 273 K and P = 1.00 atm.

$P_1 = 0.275$ atm $V_1 = 16.5$ L $T_1 = 350 + 273 = 623$ K
$P_2 = 1.00$ atm $V_2 = ?$ $T_2 = 273$ K

Since volume decreases with increasing pressure and also decreases with decreasing temperature, V_2 is

$$V_2 = V_1\left(\frac{P_1}{P_2}\right)\left(\frac{T_2}{T_1}\right) = (16.5 \text{ L})\left(\frac{0.275 \text{ atm}}{1.00 \text{ atm}}\right)\left(\frac{273 \text{ K}}{623 \text{ K}}\right)$$
$$= 1.99 \text{ L}$$

Given the following equations

$\frac{1}{2}N_2 + \frac{1}{2}O_2 \rightarrow NO$ $\Delta H° = 91$ kJ

$2NO_2 \rightarrow 2NO + O_2$ $\Delta H° = 114$ kJ

find $\Delta H°$ for the reaction

$\frac{1}{2}N2 + O_2 \rightarrow NO_2$

The equations given must be manipulated so that their sum gives the desired equation and its $\Delta H°$ value. You must know the relationships between how equations are written and their $\Delta H°$ values. Since $\frac{1}{2}N_2$ is a reactant and NO is a product, the first equation need not be reversed. Since NO_2 is a product, the second equation must be reversed.

$\frac{1}{2}N_2 + \frac{1}{2}O_2 \rightarrow NO$ $\Delta H° = 91$ kJ
$2NO + O_2 \rightarrow 2NO2$ $\Delta H° = -114$ kJ

To eliminate the unwanted intermediate NO and to give the desired equation, the second equation must be divided by 2.

$\frac{1}{2}(2NO + O_2 \rightarrow 2NO_2)$ $\Delta H° = \frac{1}{2}(-114$ kJ$)$

which gives

$NO + \frac{1}{2}O_2 \rightarrow NO_2$ $\Delta H° = -57$ kJ

The desired equation, therefore, is found as follows:

$\frac{1}{2}N_2 + \frac{1}{2}O_2 \rightarrow NO$ $\Delta H° = 91$ kJ
$NO + \frac{1}{2}O_2 \rightarrow NO_2$ $\Delta H° = -57$ kJ
_____
$\frac{1}{2}N_2 + \frac{1}{2}O_2 \rightarrow NO_2$ $\Delta H° = 34$ kJ

Write a net ionic equation for the reaction of an excess of hydrochloric acid with calcium carbonate.

To answer this question, you must know that solid $CaCO_3$ reacts with HCl to form $CaCl_2$ and carbonic acid, H_2CO_3, which immediately decomposes to H_2O and CO_2. Then you must know which reactants and products are solids, gases, or liquids and remember that the formulas of these compounds are written in full. You must also know which are soluble ionic compounds. Write them as ions in solution, and drop any spectator ions. Here, $CaCO_3$ is a solid, $CaCl_2$ is a soluble ionic compound, CO_2 is a gas, H_2O is a liquid, and the Cl^- ions are spectator ions.

$2H^+ + 2Cl^- + CaCO_3 \rightarrow Ca^{2+} + 2Cl^- + CO_2 + H_2O$
$2H^+ + CaCO_3 \rightarrow Ca^{2+} + CO_2 + H_2O$

When ethane, C_2H_6, is burned completely, it combines with oxygen to give carbon dioxide and water. How many grams of water can be formed from 5.00 g of ethane and 5.00 g of oxygen?

Any question involving quantities of reactants or products is a stoichiometry problem, and the balanced equation is needed:

$$2C_2H_6 + 7O_2 \rightarrow 4CO_2 + 6H_2O$$

Since the quantities of both reactants are given, this is a limiting reactant problem. Before grams of water as a product can be found, it is necessary to determine which is the limiting reactant by calculating the grams of one reactant required by the other:

$$5.00 \text{ g } O_2 \left(\frac{1 \text{ mol } O_2}{32.0 \text{ g } O_2}\right)\left(\frac{2 \text{ mol } C_2H_6}{7 \text{ mol } O_2}\right)\left(\frac{30 \text{ g } C_2H_6}{1 \text{ mol } C_2H_6}\right)$$
$$= 1.34 \text{ g } C_2H_6$$

Since 5.00 g of oxygen only require 1.34 g of ethane, the oxygen is in excess and ethane is the limiting reactant. Therefore, the 5.00 g of ethane is used to calculate the grams of water formed:

$$5.00 \text{ g } C_2H_6 \left(\frac{1 \text{ mol } C_2H_6}{30.0 \text{ g } C_2H_6}\right)\left(\frac{6 \text{ mol } H_2O}{2 \text{ mol } C_2H_6}\right)\left(\frac{18.0 \text{ g } H_2O}{1 \text{ mol } H_2O}\right)$$
$$= 9.00 \text{ g } H_2O$$

The K_{sp} of silver sulfate is 1.5×10^{-15} at 25°C. Calculate the molarity of a saturated silver sulfate solution at this temperature.

The answer to this question must be calculated from the K_{sp} expression for silver sulfate. To write this expression you must know the formula for silver sulfate and write the equation for its equilibrium with water so you can choose the exponents for the concentrations:

$Ag_2SO_4 \longleftrightarrow 2Ag^+ + SO_4{}^{2-}$ $K_{sp} = [Ag^+]^2[SO_4{}^{2-}] = 1.5 \times 10^{-15}$

To calculate the answer, let x equal the desired molarity. Taking into account both the number of ions formed and the exponents in the K_{sp} expression gives

$$K_{sp} = [Ag^+]^2[SO_4{}^{2-}] = 1.5 \times 10^{-15}$$
$$(2x)^2(x) = 1.5 \times 10^{-15}$$
$$4x^3 = 1.5 \times 10^{-15}$$
$$x = 1.1 \times 10^{-5}$$

The net ionic equation below is balanced. Which reactant is the oxidizing agent?

$$5BiO_3{}^- + 2Mn^+ + 14H^+ \rightarrow 5Bi^{3+} + 2MnO_4{}^- + 7H_2O$$

In a redox reaction, the oxidizing agent undergoes reduction, which is a decrease in oxidation state. Two quick ways to answer this question are to know that $BiO_3{}^-$ is an oxidizing agent or to recognize that Mn^+ must increase in oxidation state in forming $MnO_4{}^-$, meaning $BiO_3{}^-$ is the oxidizing agent. Otherwise, the answer can be figured out from changes in oxidation state. Both Bi and Mn change oxidation states. In $BiO_3{}^-$, based on an oxidation number of -2 for oxygen, and knowing that the sum of the oxidation numbers must equal the charge on the ion, the oxidation number of bismuth is $+5$:

For O in $BiO_3{}^-$: oxidation number $-2 \times 3 = -6$
For Bi in $BiO_3{}^-$:   oxidation number $= \frac{+5}{-1}$

The oxidation number of Bi in Bi^{3+} is $+3$ (equal to the charge). Bismuth, therefore, undergoes an oxidation number change of $+5 \rightarrow +3$. Since this is reduction, $BiO_3{}^-$ is the oxidizing agent.

The Graduate Record Examination

In many ways the Graduate Record Examination (GRE) is the SAT of graduate school. The GRE is developed by Educational Testing Service—the same organization that develops the SAT. It consists of a verbal and a mathematics section, although not exactly in the same format as the SAT. The GRE is mostly a multiple-choice test with five choices for each item. Familiar item types from the SATs include sentence completions, analogies, antonyms, reading comprehension, and quantitative comparisons. Items all count the same and are arranged, where possible, from easier to harder. Like the SAT, the GRE contains one section that is not used in scoring but is inserted to aid in making future tests. The idea is to test aptitude for graduate school, not achievement during previous schooling. Scores are reported on a scale from 200 to 800, with separate scores on the two different parts of the examination. The GRE is used by prestigious institutions—graduate schools, not undergraduate colleges and undergraduate schools of universities—as one of the main tools in deciding who will and who will not be admitted.

There are significant differences between the GRE and the SAT and other exams. First of all, the items in the

GRE are more difficult. Secondly, there is no penalty for wrong choices. The SAT and many other examinations prepared by Educational Testing Service discourage guessing by deducting a quarter of a point for wrong answers. The GRE does not do this. You should guess and try to answer every item even if you have no idea what the correct choice is. Thirdly, the GRE has three types of questions that are not featured, except incidentally, in the SAT. These are the data-interpretation items in mathematics and the two types of analytical items—analytical and logical reasoning. These special types of items are discussed in the material that fol-

lows just before examples of the types are presented.

Structure of the GRE. The test battery consists of seven sections, of which one is the experimental section that is not included in the scoring. Two of the scored sections test verbal ability; two test quantitative (mathematical) ability; and two test analytical (logical) ability. The order of the sections varies from year to year.

Scheduling for the GRE. Normally, the GRE is given on a Saturday

morning in February, April, October, or December, along with other tests required for specific graduate courses. The other tests are scheduled for the afternoon. There is also a GRE scheduled in June, at which time there is no other test scheduled. Persons who have religious reasons for not taking tests on Saturdays can take the tests on Mondays during the same five months.

Timing. The entire examination takes two and a half hours of actual testing time, but various instructions also take some time, so the test experience will take closer to three hours.

Sample Verbal Items for the GRE

Four types of questions are used in the verbal sections of the GRE, all familiar from the SAT. The items are given in two separate sections, each of which contains all four of the basic types—sentence completion, analogy, reading comprehension, and antonyms, generally in that order. Each of the two sections contains 38 items, for a total of 76 verbal items. Thirty minutes are allowed for each section, so you need to average about 47 seconds an item to complete the section; if you maintain an average of 45 seconds an item, however, you will have only a minute and a half to look over the section at the end.

Sentence completion items
Directions: Each sentence below has one or two blanks, each blank indicating that something has been omitted. Beneath the sentence are five lettered words or sets of words. Choose the word or set of words for each blank that best fits the meaning of the sentence as a whole.

Insomnia can be characterized by difficulty in falling asleep, -------- awakening after falling asleep, or awakening early and not being able to fall back asleep.

(A) precarious   (B) nonchalant   (C) mandatory
(D) beneficial   (E) intermittent

The concept of this sentence is that insomnia is a condition that interferes with sleep in three ways. Choices (B) and (D) are easily eliminated since they suggest that insomnia might be other than an unpleasant experience. Furthermore, there is no suggestion that the awakening is precarious, choice (A). It is also not mandatory, choice (C), since the insomniac is not awakening on command and the awakening is not required. Only choice (E), intermittent, is consistent with the rest of the sentence.

Having been subjected to the -------- of a totalitarian government, she embraced the prospect of a -------- regime.

(A) nuances . . tyrannical
(B) jubilation . . benevolent
(C) encumbrances . . democratic
(D) anarchism . . revolutionary
(E) inflexibility . . despotic

The context clue "subjected" tells you that the first word will complete a negative reaction to "totalitarian." The second word must offer a form of government clearly alternative to the totalitarian form. Choice (A) fails on both counts, while choice (B) misses the first criterion and choice (E) does not fulfill the second. Choice (D) has to be rejected because anarchism is not properly descriptive of totalitarian government. Only choice (C), encumbrances . . democratic, fulfills both requirements.

The ancient Romans developed a -------- banking system to accommodate their -------- trade network, which extended throughout Europe, Asia, and Africa.

(A) personal . . restricted
(B) sophisticated . . vast
(C) scrupulous . . flamboyant
(D) comprehensive . . insignificant
(E) mediocre . . convoluted

The sentence strongly suggests positive words for both blanks, which rules out choices (C) and (E). In addition, the ideal second word should relate to the final clause, "which extended throughout Europe, Asia, and Africa." This requirement rules out choices (A) and (D). The correct choice is (B), sophisticated . . vast.

The long-awaited peace treaty was a --------; -------- resumed just twenty-four hours after an agreement had been reached.

(A) blessing . . negotiations
(B) travesty . . hostilities
(C) subterfuge . . harmony
(D) panacea . . ennui
(E) convenience . . enmity

Once this sentence is correctly completed, the second clause should illustrate the concept of the first clause. This does not occur for choices (A), (C), (D), or (E). The virtually immediate resumption of hostilities clearly illustrates why the treaty was a travesty. The correct answer is choice (B), travesty . . hostilities.

Analogies
Directions: In each of the following questions, a related pair of words or phrases is followed by five lettered pairs of words or phrases. Select the lettered pair that best expresses a relationship similar to that expressed in the original pair.

HORTICULTURIST : NURSERY::
(A) scientist : laboratory   (B) physician : stethoscope
(C) meteorologist : clouds   (D) ornithologist : habitat
(E) pathologist : disease

Test sentences are helpful in answering analogy questions. Make up a sentence to express the relationship between the two words: A horticulturist works in a nursery. While all the other word pairs are clearly related, only choice (A) expresses the same relationship as the original pair: A scientist works in a laboratory.

Bring four No. 2 pencils and a watch to the test.

RAMSHACKLE : HOVEL::   (A) vast : horizon
(B) luxurious : palace   (C) secluded : cottage
(D) cryptic : message   (E) inaccessible : slum

To eliminate all but one choice, make up a test sentence that is as specific as possible: Ramshackle describes a dwelling place called a hovel. Choice (C) looks inviting, but a cottage need not be secluded. Choices (A) and (D) have nothing to do with places to live. Choice (E) is incorrect because slums are not always inaccessible. The answer is (B), luxurious : palace: Luxurious describes a dwelling place called a palace.

DULCET : CACOPHONOUS::   (A) erudite : inept
(B) cantankerous : magnanimous
(C) susceptible : impervious   (D) negligent : lax
(E) canny : grim

Dulcet and cacophonous are antonyms. Choice (A) comes close, but a person may be erudite (learned, scholarly) and inept (without skill). One may also be cantankerous and magnanimous; and canny and grim. Thus, choices (B) and (E) can be eliminated. Choice (D) offers two synonyms, not two antonyms. However, one cannot be susceptible (having little resistance) and impervious (impenetrable) at the same time. The correct choice is (C).

KNIGHT : MAIL::   (A) lord : serf   (B) turtle : shell
(C) letter : stamp   (D) table : leg
(E) computer : modem

At first one thinks of a letter or message when one sees the word mail, but that does not go with knight. When a common interpretation does not complete a logical analogy, look for its secondary meaning. Here, mail means a kind of armor. Now the relationship is clear: A knight is protected by his mail. Similarly, a turtle is protected by its shell. Choice (B) is correct. The other choices do not offer the idea of protection.

Reading comprehension

Directions: The passage is followed by questions based on its content. After reading the passage, choose the best answer to each question. Answer all questions following the passage on the basis of what is stated or implied in the passage.

There are many unresolved questions about early human populations in the various regions of the world.

First of all, anthropologists are trying to sort out who was human and who wasn't quite human. Most remains of modern humans date from after 40,000 years ago, but there is increasing fossil evidence that almost-modern humans lived in Africa perhaps as long as 100,000 years ago. In Europe and the Near East, however, the main population about 60,000 years ago was either a related species or subspecies, depending on which anthropologist you ask, called the Neanderthals.

It is less clear what sort of folk were living in Southeast Asia at that time, but some of them clearly were early travelers. The evidence for this was found by Richard G. Roberts and coworkers, who discovered a number of human artifacts in northern Australia that are about 50,000 years old. The team believes that the tools and paints establish that humans reached Australia from Southeast Asia about 60,000 years ago.

Which humans reached the Americas and when they reached the Americas are less certain than what happened in Australia. The establishment theory is that Asians crossed a land bridge to Alaska from Siberia 12,000 years ago, bringing with them a culture we call Clovis. Other theories range from ones suggesting that people crossed the same land bridge a few thousand years earlier to theories suggesting that people arrived almost as early as people are thought to have reached Australia. Some of the most radical scientists think that early humans arrived by some other route, for example, across the Pacific or Atlantic oceans.

The passage provides an answer to which of the following questions?

(A) How long ago was the western hemisphere peopled?
(B) Are the Neanderthals the same species as modern humans?
(C) By what signs can anthropologists recognize the Clovis culture?
(D) On what continent did modern humans originate?
(E) How long ago did humans live in Australia?

The last paragraph clearly states that the date for peopling the Americas is not resolved, so choice (A) is not correct. The parenthetical remark in the last sentence of the second paragraph—depending on which anthropologist you ask—suggests that scientists have different interpretations of whether or not Neanderthals were the same species as modern humans, so choice (B) is also unresolved. Although the Clovis culture is mentioned in the last paragraph, its characteristics are not, ruling out choice (C). While the suggestion that modern humans may go back as much as 100,000 years in Africa tends to imply an African origin, it does not actually eliminate the possibility of an Asian or even a European origin, which means choice (D) is not correct. The correct choice, (E), is the only question for which the passage cites evidence offering an answer to the question.

Based upon the passage, which theory of the peopling of the Americas is believed by a large number of anthropologists who hold important posts in universities or other institutions?

(A) Siberian people walked to Alaska from Asia about 12,000 years ago.
(B) Asians reached the Americas by crossing the Pacific Ocean in boats.
(C) Australians reached the Americas 50,000 to 60,000 years ago.
(D) Asians crossed a land bridge into North America somewhere between 12,000 and 50,000 years ago.
(E) Modern humans may have evolved in the Americas about 100,000 years ago.

The passage refers to "the establishment theory," which would be the theory held by "a large number of anthropologists who hold important posts in universities or other institutions." This theory is the one described in choice (A), so this is the correct choice. The theory in choice (B), on the other hand, is labeled as radical, while that in choice (D) is simply among the "other theories." There is no evidence in the passage that anyone believes the theories expressed in choices (C) and (E).

Antonyms

Directions: Each question below consists of a word printed in capital letters followed by five lettered words or phrases. Choose the lettered word or phrase that is most nearly opposite in meaning to the word in capital letters. Since some of the questions require you to distinguish fine shades of meaning, be sure to consider all the choices before deciding which one is best.

TUMID:
(A) titanic
(B) assertive
(C) deflated
(D) immaculate
(E) placid

Literally, tumid means "swollen." It may refer to actual physical swelling or to swollen, bombastic language. Either way, the best antonym is choice (C), deflated. Notice that the hasty test taker might misread the vocabulary word as "timid." In haste, the test taker would rise to the bait and incorrectly select choice (B), assertive.

**There is no penalty for incorrect answers
so you should answer every item,
whether or not you have any idea
what the correct choice should be.**

HALCYON:
(A) distant
(B) complex
(C) minuscule
(D) tumultuous
(E) familiar

Halcyon means "calm, peaceful." If you are not familiar with this definition, think of where you might have heard the word before. An expression such as "halcyon days of yore" should come to mind. Context reference should lead you to its connotation as something pleasant. Choice (D), tumultuous (violent; full of disturbance), has the opposite connotation, so you have sufficient reason to select choice (D). The other choices are not antonyms of halcyon.

DERELICT:
(A) sympathetic
(B) regal
(C) supportive
(D) gracious
(E) conscientious

At first glance, the noun derelict brings to mind a homeless person. However, the choices are all adjectives. As an adjective, derelict could mean "negligent" or "abandoned." There is no antonym for "abandoned" among the choices; therefore, concentrate on "negligent." Again, a familiar phrase can be a help: "derelict in his duties." The opposite of that would be "conscientious about his duties." Choice (E), conscientious, is correct. The other choices are not antonyms of "negligent."

BELLICOSE:
(A) conciliatory
(B) garrulous
(C) muffled
(D) genuine
(E) obtuse

Suppose you are not sure of the definition of bellicose. You should be familiar with the root word belli-. You have seen it in words such as "belligerent" and "rebellious," so you can conclude that words with this root generally refer to some form of violence. Indeed, belli- derives from the Latin bellum, meaning war. Bellicose means "eager to fight; warlike." Therefore, you are looking for a gentle, even pacifistic word among the choices. The best answer is choice (A), conciliatory. The other choices are not antonyms of bellicose.

LOQUACIOUS:
(A) sympathetic
(B) salient
(C) comprehensive
(D) sane
(E) mute

Loquacious means "talkative." Therefore, its antonym would have to mean "not talkative" or "silent." If you reasoned this out correctly and chose (B), salient, you neglected to read the choices carefully. "Salient" and "silent" are alike in appearance, but they are not antonyms, nor are choices (A), (C), or (D) antonyms of loquacious. The correct answer is choice (E), mute.

CURE:
(A) conjure
(B) intensity
(C) reciprocate
(D) allow to spoil
(E) reduce effectiveness

A wise test taker looks at this vocabulary word and realizes that this question will not be as easy as it appears. The people who write antonym questions for the GRE would never choose the obvious meaning for a word as common as cure. You should always be suspicious of apparently easy words. A less often used meaning for the verb cure is "to preserve" by salting, smoking, or aging or by some other chemical or physical process. The opposite of cure, then, is choice (D), allow to spoil. The other choices are not antonyms of cure.

Mathematics Sections

There are two mathematics sections in each GRE, each one with 30 items to be answered in half an hour. Each section contains three types of items: quantitative comparison, standard multiple-choice items, which are referred to as "discrete quantitative questions," and data interpretation.

Quantitative comparison. The quantitative comparison questions test the ability to reason quickly and accurately about the relative sizes of two quantities or to perceive that not enough information is provided to make such a decision. Half the mathematics items in each of the two 30-item mathematics sections are based on quantitative comparison.

Since there are only four choices for the quantitative comparison items, as opposed to five choices for other items on the test, and since all items count the same and no points are taken off for wrong guesses, guessing on every quantitative comparison item is particularly rewarding. Be sure you do not leave any of these items unanswered.

Also, since you will have less reading to do and have only four choices, you should move faster through these items than through the later mathematics items. Aim for 30 seconds an item here, which will allow you a minute and a half for each of the other items. Even if you take 10 minutes to complete these items (40 seconds an item), it will still leave you with 20 minutes, or 80 seconds an item, for the remaining, generally more difficult, items.

Directions: The following questions consist of two quantities, one in Column A and one in Column B. You are to compare the two quantities and choose

(A) whether the quantity in Column A is greater;
(B) whether the quantity in Column B is greater;
(C) whether the two quantities are equal;
(D) whether the relationship cannot be determined from the information given.

Note: Since there are only four choices, NEVER MARK (E).

Common Information: In a question, information concerning one or both of the quantities to be compared is centered under the two columns. A symbol that appears in both columns represents the same thing in Column A as it does in Column B.

Column A	Column B
	$x < y$	
x^2	y^2

Watch out. This is not as easy as it looks. Consider different values for x and y. If x and y are both greater than zero, then certainly $y^2 > x^2$. However, if $x < 0$, but has a greater absolute value than y, $x^2 > y^2$. For example, if $x = -6$ and $y = 3$, $x < y$, but $x^2 > y^2$. Therefore, the relationship between x^2 and y^2 cannot be determined. The correct choice is (D).

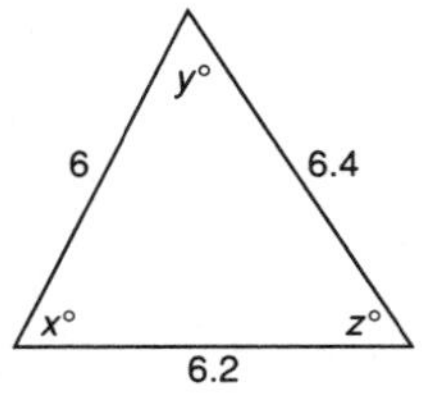

x y

In a triangle, the angles compare as their opposite sides compare. The sides are very close in measure and the angles appear to be equal. However, the angle labeled x is opposite the side labeled 6.4, which is greater than the side labeled 6.2 that is opposite the angle labeled y. Therefore, the correct answer is (A).

Column A	Column B
$(-12)^6$	$(-12)^7$

An even power of a negative number is always positive. An odd power of a negative number is always negative. A negative number is always less than a positive number. Therefore, without actually computing the value of either expression, you know that $(-12)^6 > (-12)^7$. The correct answer is (A).

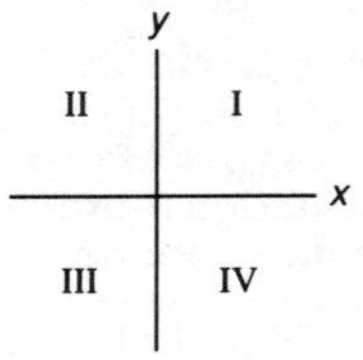

A point (x, y) in Region II.

x	y

Any point in the second quadrant will have a negative x and a positive y. Since a positive is always greater than a negative, $y > x$. The answer is (B).

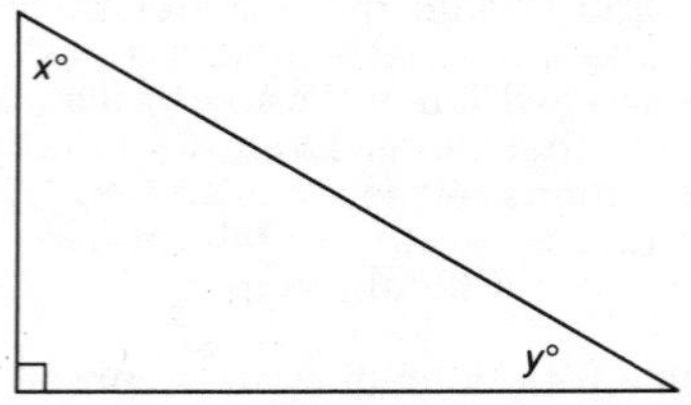

$x + y$	$90°$

Since the two acute angles of a right triangle are complementary, the sum of x and y must be 90°. The correct answer is (C).

$\dfrac{x^2 + 5x - 14}{x - 2}$	$x + 7$

The expression in Column A is undefined for $x = 2$. For all other x, the expression in Column A and the expression in Column B are equivalent, since $x^2 + 5x - 14 = (x + 7)(x - 2)$. The correct answer is (D).

Discrete quantitative (standard multiple choice).
Each question contains all information needed for answering it except for the basic mathematical knowledge assumed to be common to the backgrounds of examinees. About 10 of the 30 items in each section are of this type. Typically, after all of the quantitative comparison items, there will be five discrete quantitative items, five data interpretation items, and five discrete quantitative items. In this set of samples, however, the data interpretation sample items come at the end.

Directions: Each of the following questions has five answer choices. For each of these questions, select the best of the answer choices given.

Steve takes 3 hours to travel from New City to Beauville on his moped. Dan can make the same trip in 2 hours traveling 10 kilometers per hour faster. How far is it from New City to Beauville?

(A) 20 kilometers (B) 30 kilometers (C) 60 kilometers
(D) 80 kilometers (E) 100 kilometers

Both people covered the same distance. Using the formula $d = rt$, and letting r = Steve's rate, you get this equation: $3r = 2(r + 10)$, where $r + 10$ is the expression for Dan's rate. Solving the equation yields $r = 20$ kilometers per hour. It took Steve 3 hours at 20 kilometers per hour to cover the distance between the cities. The distance must be 60 kilometers. The correct answer is (C).

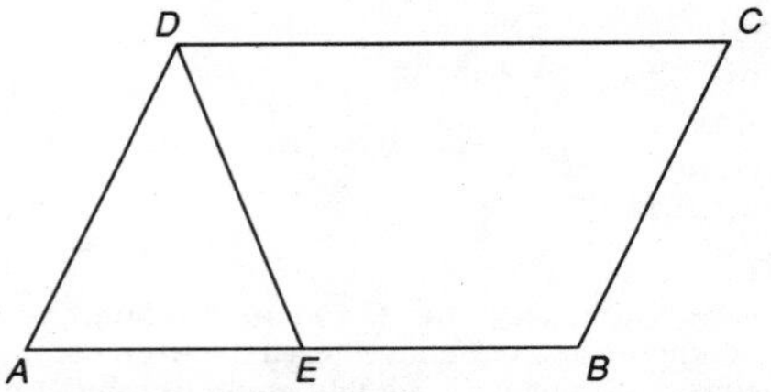

The area of parallelogram $ABCD$ is 204 cm^2. If $AE = EB$, what is the area of triangle ADE?

(A) 20.5 cm^2 (B) 51 cm^2 (C) 68 cm^2 (D) 102 cm^2
(E) 204 cm^2

Since $AE = EB$, the base of the triangle is half of the base of the parallelogram. The height of the triangle is the same as the height of the parallelogram. You are given the area of the parallelogram, so you know that $bh = 204$. The area of a triangle is one half the base times the height. So the area of triangle ADE is $\frac{1}{2}(\frac{1}{2}bh)$ or $\frac{1}{4}bh$. The area of ADE is one-fourth the area of $ABCD$. The correct choice is (B).

A building company needs $24,000,000 for work on a special project. The partners can contribute half of the money needed. An investment firm will supply 35% of the total. How much money is still needed for the project?

(A) $1,800,000 (B) $3,600,000 (C) $7,800,000
(D) $15,600,000 (E) $20,400,000

The company was able to raise half (or 50%) from partners and 35% from an investment firm. Therefore, it raised 85% in all. 15% of the total is still required; 15% of $24,000,000 is $3,600,000. Without computing, you could determine that 15% is halfway between 10% and 20%. 10% of $24,000.000 is $2,400,000 and 20% of $24,000,000 is $4,800.000. The only choice that is between these two amounts is (B). Thus, there are two ways to arrive at the correct answer.

The average of a, b, and c is 14. If $d = 10$, what is the average of a, b, c, and d?

(A) 4 (B) 8 (C) 12 (D) 13 (E) $16\frac{1}{2}$

If the average of a, b, and c is 14, then $a + b + c = 3(14)$, or 42. The sum of $a + b + c + d = 42 + 10$, or 52. Divide this sum by 4 to get the average, 13. The correct answer is (D).

Two angles are supplementary. The measure of one angle is 30° more than twice the other. What is the measure of the smaller angle?

(A) 30° (B) 50° (C) 75° (D) 130° (E) 150°

If two angles are supplementary, their sum is 180°. Let a represent the smaller angle. Then $2a + 30$ is the measure of the larger angle.
$$a + (2a + 30) = 180$$
$$3a + 30 = 180$$
$$3a = 150$$
$$a = 50$$
The correct answer is (B).

A customer service representative told a customer to deduct 10% from her bill because she received the wrong color chair. The woman paid $144 for the chair. What was its original price?

(A) $129.60 (B) $154 (C) $158.40 (D) $160
(E) $288

The payment of $144 represents $x - 0.1x$, or $0.9x$, where x is the original price of the chair.
$$\text{Solve } 0.9x = 144$$
$$x = \frac{144}{0.9}$$
$$x = 160$$
The correct answer is (D).

Data interpretation. These are also standard multiple-choice items with five choices. They are treated differently by the GRE only because they represent a slightly different set of mathematics skills than are tested in other parts of the test.

For each of these sections, there are several—usually five—items that all refer to a graph or to a table or to a pair of graphs or tables. Because much of the material is visual, especially when graphs are involved, it is best to try get the answer by inspecting the graph instead of computing. Often an item involving a table can also be solved in this way. Just make sure that you are reading the graph or table correctly. Sometimes it helps to use the edge of your answer sheet as a straightedge to avoid misreading. In any mathematics test, always stop to think whether or not your choice makes sense.

Directions: Each of the following questions has five answer choices. For each of these questions, select the best of the answer choices given.

The next three questions refer to the following graph.

CLIMATE IN FIVE LARGE CITIES

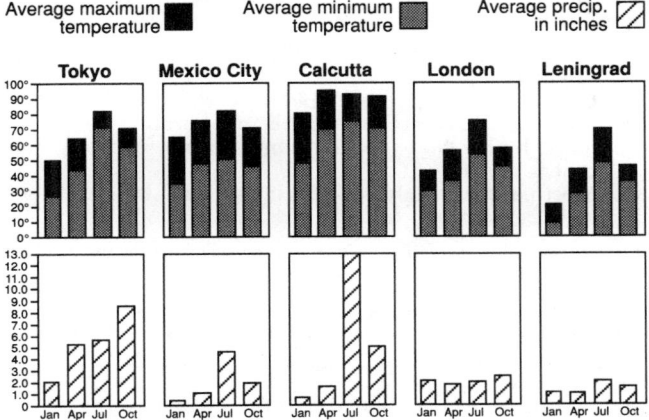

In which of the five cities is the climate most nearly constant all year round?

(A) Tokyo (B) Mexico City (C) Calcutta (D) London
(E) Leningrad

To answer this item, you need to consider both temperature and precipitation. Also, you should look at the average maximum and minimum temperatures. It helps to make a chart of the ranges of the three averages mentioned. The range is the difference between the highest month and lowest month. Use approximations, since you cannot read exact numbers from a graph.

	Ranges		
	Max. temp.	Min. temp.	Precip.
Choice (A): Tokyo	35	40	7
Choice (B): Mexico City	10	10	4
Choice (C): Calcutta	10	25	12
Choice (D): London	30	20	0.5
Choice (E): Leningrad	50	45	1.5

Choice (C), Calcutta, and choice (B), Mexico City, tie for the smallest range of average maximum temperatures, while Mexico City has the smallest range of average minimum temperatures, and choice (D), London, has the smallest range of average precipitation. Thus, you can eliminate choices (A) and (E). Choice (C), Calcutta, has a relatively high range of average minimum temperatures and the highest range of average precipitation, so it can also be eliminated, leaving Mexico City and London. Choosing between them is not easy, since Mexico City has the more constant temperatures and London has quite constant rainfall. You need to use another measure to differentiate between them. Or, if you are pressed for time, you might do well at this point to choose either one and go on to the next question. If you have time, you can calculate the standard deviations for the measurements, but if the time is not available while taking the test, even without standard deviations, you can conclude from looking at the graphs that while London has constant rain and Mexico City has a relatively constant temperature, the weather overall is more constant in Mexico City than in London. (Actually taking the standard deviations backs up this impression.) The correct choice is (B), Mexico City.

Which city is likely to have the highest annual rainfall?

(A) Tokyo (B) Mexico City (C) Calcutta (D) London
(E) Leningrad

Since you are only presented with the average rainfall for four months of each year, you have to assume that the averages are representative of each of the four seasons. Therefore, the city that has the highest sum for the four averages would be the one with the highest annual total as well. The totals for the five cities are approximately: Tokyo, about 20 inches; Mexico City, less than 10 inches; Calcutta, about 20 inches; London, less than 10 inches; and Leningrad, about 5 inches. The correct answer, therefore, lies between choice (A), Tokyo, and choice (C), Calcutta. Closer examination—you can measure by marking off the edge of a folded-over sheet of the test booklet, for example—will show that while Tokyo is just over 20 inches in total, Calcutta is just under 20 inches. Therefore the correct choice is (A), Tokyo.

Which of the five cities has almost exactly the same weather in early spring and early fall?

(A) Tokyo (B) Mexico City (C) Calcutta (D) London
(E) Leningrad

In the northern hemisphere, spring officially starts near the end of March and fall starts near the end of September. Therefore, you need only look at the three measures for April and October. (If one of the cities were in the southern hemisphere, the months would still be April and October, even though spring and fall are reversed, with fall starting in March and spring in October.) It is easy to eliminate Tokyo, choice (A), and Calcutta, choice (C), because of wide disparities in rainfall. Of the remaining three choices, London, choice (D), and Leningrad, choice (E), appear closer than Mexico City, choice (B). The difference in maximum temperatures in London is very small, while the difference in minimum temperatures appears to be slightly less than 5°. Similarly, Leningrad has no difference in maximum temperature and slightly more than 5° difference in minimum temperature. The difference in precipitation for London appears to be about half an inch. For Leningrad, the difference is a little less than an inch. Thus, while the difference in temperatures would seem to be a near tie, Leningrad has the greater difference in rainfall, so the correct choice appears to be (E), Leningrad.

Analytical Ability

The remaining two sections of the scored sections of the GRE test analytical ability. Each section has 25 items separated into analytical reasoning items, which are puzzles, and logical reasoning items, which test the ability to analyze arguments. There are 30 minutes for each of the two sections, so you have a little more than a minute for each item.

Analytical reasoning. About three-fourths of the test of analytical ability is devoted to these puzzle-based items. All the items are alike in that they are based on a complex set of relationships that must be unraveled to answer correctly the items that follow. None of the items is a trick puzzle that requires a flash of insight to solve. Although the situations are described as puzzles, most of them are realistic rather than fanciful.

A logical approach is essential in solving this kind of item. First of all, make sure you really understand the complex situation that will be the basis of the items that follow. It helps to make diagrams or notes in symbolic form. If you know standard logical symbols, use them. If you are unfamiliar with these symbols or uncertain about them, use English equivalents such as "if . . . then," "and," and "or." Remember that you can write in the test booklet, so you can underline or otherwise mark up the statement of the relationships. If you can, organize all this information in some sort of list, table, map, or diagram.

For the individual items, it is generally easier to work by elimination than by trying to find the single correct choice first. If you cannot eliminate all the items, but succeed in eliminating a few, guess. There is no penalty for a bad guess, but the reward for a good one is a full point added to your score.

Directions: The following group of questions is based on a passage or a set of conditions. In answering some of the questions, it may be useful to draw a rough diagram. For each question, select the best answer choice given.

At a neighborhood block party, seven of the neighbors enter a race around the block. By profession they are a baker, a lawyer, a butcher, a police officer, a doctor, a reporter, and a fire chief. Their names, not necessarily in the same order, are Black, White, Brown, Rose, Redd, Bluette, and Tanner. When the race was over, the following statements could be made:

Rose finished immediately after Tanner and immediately before White.
The police officer finished third, the doctor finished fifth, and the lawyer finished sixth.
Bluette finished two places behind Dr. Black.
The reporter finished just before the fire chief.
The butcher's name is Brown.

The winner of the race was

(A) Rose   (B) the butcher   (C) the fire chief
(D) Tanner   (E) Redd

You could start by eliminating as many choices as possible. Choice (A), Rose, finished after Tanner; and choice (C), the fire chief, finished after the reporter. Both (A) and (C) can be eliminated. When you read the passage originally, however, you should have made a diagram of the places people finished based on the information that you were given. Such a diagram might initially look like this:

first		
second		
third	police officer	
fourth		
fifth	doctor =	Black
sixth	lawyer	
seventh		Bluette

The seventh place is found when you note that Bluette finished two places behind Dr. Black. Now you can use the fact that the reporter finished just before the fire chief to fill in the top two places, since they are the only two consecutive places that are open.

first	reporter	
second	fire chief	
third	police officer	
fourth		
fifth	doctor =	Black
sixth	lawyer	
seventh		Bluette

At this point you know that the reporter finished first, but that is not one of the choices. You have to identify the reporter. You know that one sequence is Tanner, Rose, White, which can only be the same as *first, second, third* or the same as *second, third, fourth*. However, the butcher's name is Brown, which has to fit into the *fourth* slot. So now you have

first	reporter =	Tanner
second	fire fighter =	Rose
third	police officer =	White
fourth	butcher =	Brown
fifth	doctor =	Black
sixth	lawyer	
seventh		Bluette

The correct choice is (D), Tanner.

The runner who immediately preceded Bluette is

(A) the police officer   (B) Brown   (C) the baker
(D) Redd   (E) the fire chief

The diagram makes it easy to eliminate choices (A), (B), and (C), which are already given. You can complete the diagram by adding in the only profession and name not previously used.

first	reporter =	Tanner
second	fire fighter =	Rose
third	police officer =	White
fourth	butcher =	Brown
fifth	doctor =	Black
sixth	lawyer =	Redd
seventh	baker =	Bluette

The correct choice is (D), Redd.

Logical reasoning. The logical reasoning items are like the analytical reasoning items in that they involve a lot of information, but the information is generally related to a complex situation, and not much unlikely information is presented. The example of the race given above is typical of a problem with unlikely information. In real life, you would know the names, professions, and order of finish, and would not have to puzzle it out. The logical reasoning items are based on the kind of information that a person actually encounters in real life.

The main strategy here is to be careful about exactly what is stated in the passage and to avoid common fallacies, such as reasoning from conclusion to premise.

Directions: Each question is based on a passage or set of questions. In answering some of the questions, it may be useful to draw a rough diagram. For each question, select the best answer given.

It is important for America's continued progress that students be taught science in high school. Therefore, students need to have experience in science courses based on hands-on experience in laboratories.

Which of the following, if true, most weakens the argument above?

(A) Only people with good laboratory skills can become scientists.
(B) Only good scientists are able to work in laboratories.
(C) Some scientists are not skilled in laboratory work.
(D) Some high schools teach science more effectively than others
(E) Most people who have good laboratory skills are also good scientists.

Choices (A) and (E) actually reinforce the argument, instead of weakening it. Choices (B) and (D) neither reinforce nor weaken the argument. By elimination, then, the correct choice should be (C). According to that choice, since not all scientists are skilled in laboratory work, it may not be useful to give laboratory training to everyone who wants to learn science.

It has sometimes been noted that the farther Herman Melville's novels and stories took him from the sea, the less successful they were. Certainly, his greatest work, *Moby-Dick,* takes place almost entirely at sea, as do *Redburn* and *White-Jacket,* both of which were popular when first published. His first two novels, *Typee* and *Omoo,* are set on islands and the main characters are sailors. Among his short stories, *Billy Budd,* a shipboard story, stands out, although the highly influential *Bartleby, the Scrivener* is set in an office. Among his later novels, *The Confidence Man,* set on a Mississippi riverboat, and *Pierre,* entirely land-based, were not successful with the public, although they are popular with intellectuals today. *Pierre,* especially, is either loved or hated.

Which of the following is NOT consistent with the passage above?

(A) Melville always wrote about life at sea.
(B) Melville's first two novels were unpopular when they were published.
(C) *Redburn* and *White-Jacket* were written before *Moby-Dick.*
(D) *Moby-Dick* was written after *The Confidence Man* and *Pierre.*
(E) Melville's work became popular only after his death.

Your job here is to examine each statement to see whether it is consistent with the passage. Whether the statement is true or not is not what is being asked. For example, you may know that choice (C) is actually true, while choice (D) is false in reality. The item does not ask about reality, but only about the passage. Therefore, you cannot eliminate (D) because it is false. Indeed, there is nothing in the passage to say for sure when *Moby-Dick* was written, so (D) is consistent with the passage. Similarly (B) and (E) are contradictory, but not inconsistent with the passage. The correct choice is (A), "Melville always wrote about life at sea," since *Pierre* is land-based and *Bartleby, the Scrivener* is set in an office.

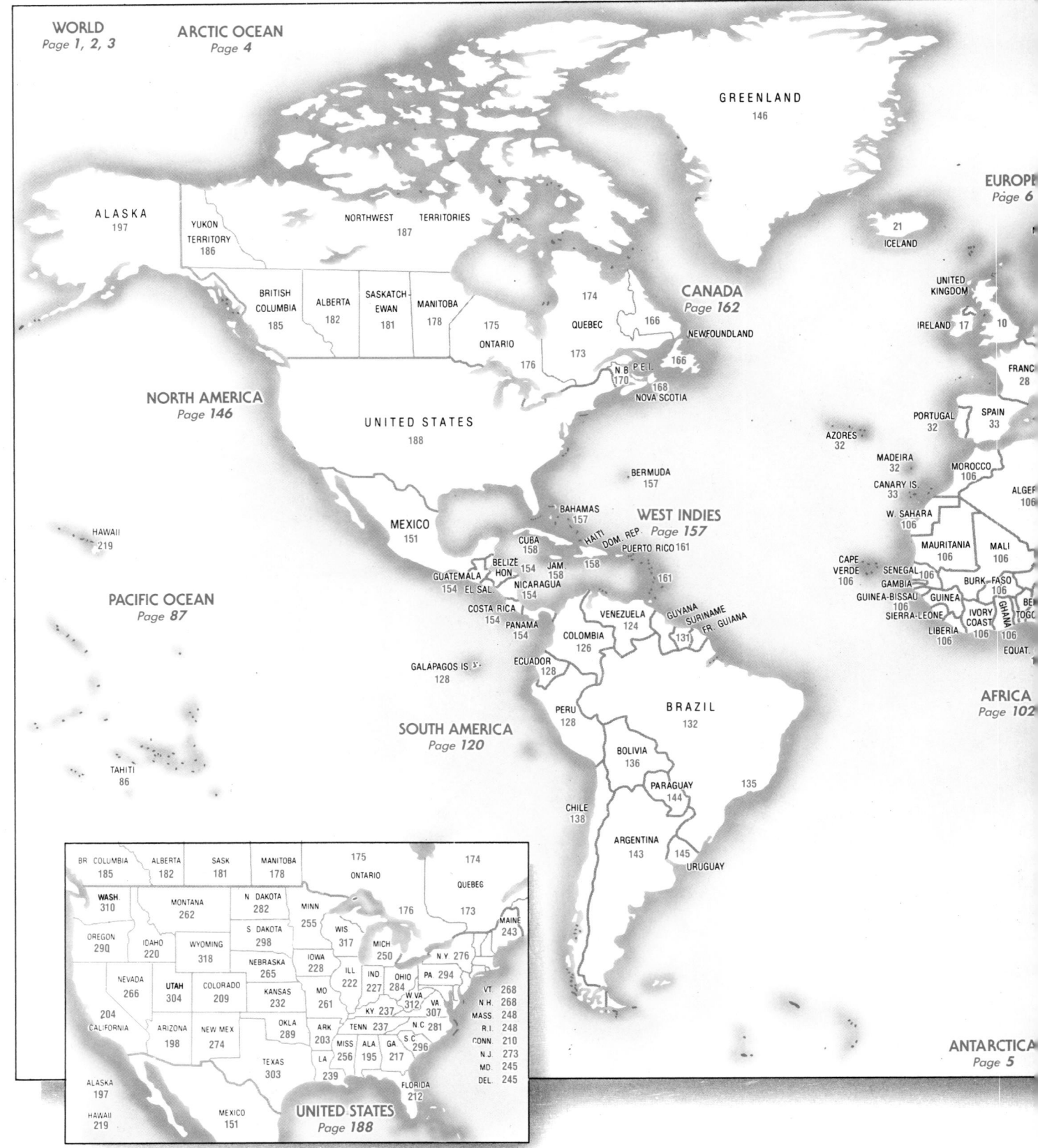
WORLD
Page 1, 2, 3
ARCTIC OCEAN
Page 4
GREENLAND
146
EUROPE
Page 6
ALASKA
197
YUKON TERRITORY
186
NORTHWEST TERRITORIES
187
21
ICELAND
BRITISH COLUMBIA
185
ALBERTA
182
SASKATCH-EWAN
181
MANITOBA
178
174
CANADA
Page 162
UNITED KINGDOM
175
ONTARIO
QUEBEC
166
IRELAND 17
10
NEWFOUNDLAND
173
176
N.B. 170
P.E.I.
166
168
NOVA SCOTIA
FRANCE
28
NORTH AMERICA
Page 146
UNITED STATES
188
PORTUGAL
32
SPAIN
33
AZORES
32
MADEIRA
32
BERMUDA
157
MOROCCO
106
CANARY IS.
33
ALGERIA
106
BAHAMAS
157
WEST INDIES
Page 157
W. SAHARA
106
HAWAII
219
MEXICO
151
HAITI
DOM. REP.
PUERTO RICO 161
CUBA
158
MAURITANIA
106
MALI
106
BELIZE
HON.
154
JAM.
158
158
CAPE VERDE
106
SENEGAL
106
GAMBIA
GUATEMALA
154
EL SAL.
NICARAGUA
154
161
BURK.-FASO
106
PACIFIC OCEAN
Page 87
GUINEA-BISSAU
GUINEA
106
SIERRA-LEONE
COSTA RICA
154
VENEZUELA
124
GUYANA
SURINAME
FR. GUIANA
131
IVORY COAST
106
GHANA
TOGO
PANAMA
154
COLOMBIA
126
LIBERIA
106
106
EQUAT.
GALAPAGOS IS.
128
ECUADOR
128
AFRICA
Page 102
PERU
128
BRAZIL
132
SOUTH AMERICA
Page 120
BOLIVIA
136
TAHITI
86
PARAGUAY
144
135
CHILE
138
ARGENTINA
143
145
URUGUAY
ANTARCTICA
Page 5
BR. COLUMBIA
185
ALBERTA
182
SASK
181
MANITOBA
178
175
ONTARIO
174
QUEBEC
WASH.
310
MONTANA
262
N. DAKOTA
282
MINN
255
176
173
MAINE
243
OREGON
290
IDAHO
220
WYOMING
318
S. DAKOTA
298
WIS
317
MICH
250
N.Y. 276
NEBRASKA
265
IOWA
228
ILL
222
IND
227
OHIO
284
PA. 294
NEVADA
266
UTAH
304
COLORADO
209
KANSAS
232
MO
261
W. VA
312
VA
307
VT. 268
N.H. 268
MASS. 248
R.I. 248
CONN. 210
N.J. 273
MD. 245
DEL. 245
204
CALIFORNIA
KY 237
ARIZONA
198
NEW MEX
274
OKLA
289
ARK
203
TENN 237
N.C. 281
S.C. 296
MISS
256
ALA
195
GA
217
TEXAS
303
LA
239
ALASKA
197
FLORIDA
212
HAWAII
219
MEXICO
151
UNITED STATES
Page 188

PAGE LOCATION KEY TO ATLAS MAPS